FUZZ ACID AND FLOWERS REVISITED

A COMPREHENSIVE GUIDE TO AMERICAN GARAGE PSYCHEDELIC AND HIPPIE ROCK (1964 - 1975)

(INCLUDES RARITY/SOUGHT-AFTER SCALE AND COMPILATIONS LISTING)

BY VERNON JOYNSON

SPECIAL THANKS TO IVOR TRUEMAN, CLARK FAVILLE AND MAX WALLER

This book is dedicated to fans and collectors of psychedelia, sixties garage and hippie rock everywhere and to my wife Seonaid and children Jasmine and Jake.

First published in Great Britain in 2004 by Borderline Productions.
This book is sold subject to the condition that it shall not be lent, resold, hired out or otherwise circulated in any form of binding or cover than it is published in.

ALL RIGHTS RESERVED. ALL CONTENTS COPYRIGHT © 2004.   ISBN 1 899855 14 9

Printed by Bell and Bain Ltd, 303 Burnfield Road, Thornliebank, Glasgow, G46 7UQ, Scotland.
Front cover painting by Andrew Linsell.

FUZZ ACID AND FLOWERS REVISITED

A GUIDE TO AMERICAN GARAGE, PSYCHEDELIC AND HIPPIE ROCK (1964-1975).

CONTENTS

FOREWORD	Page v
INTRODUCTION	Page vii
A-Z OF AMERICAN GARAGE, PSYCHEDELIC AND HIPPIE-ROCK BANDS	Page 1
Colour illustrations	(i) - (xii)
COMPILATIONS	Page 1091
REISSUE LABEL LISTINGS	Page 1099

AUTHOR'S NOTE

I have tried to ensure that this book is as accurate as possible, but some of the entries are incomplete and there are bound to be some errors. A book of this type is never really finished! I'd like to hear from anyone who is able to supply information that is missing in my book, correct errors or add additional entries. If you can do any of these please contact me care of:

fuzz@borderlinebooks.com

Vernon Joynson, September 2004.

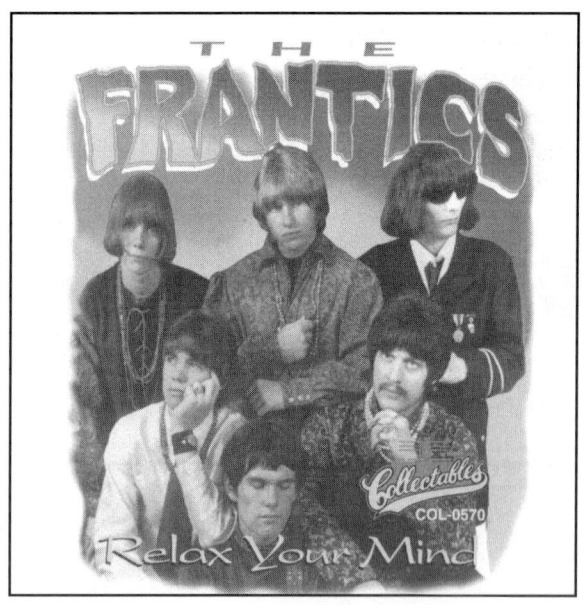

THE FRANTICS - Relax Your Mind CD.

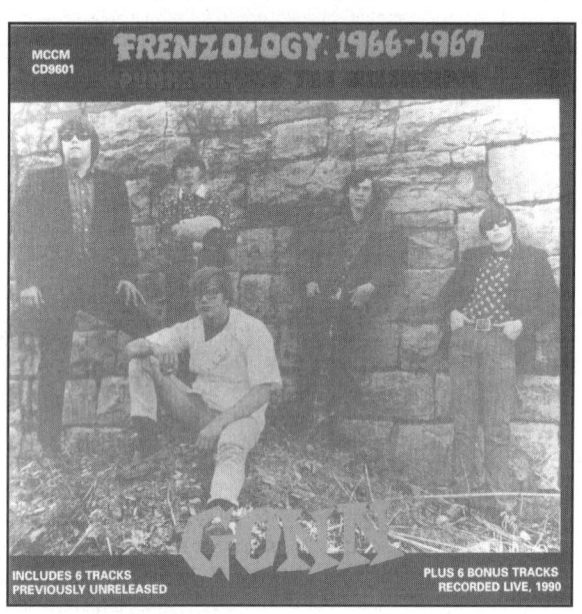

QUEEN'S NECTARINE MACHINE - Band Pic.

GONN - Frenzology 1966-1967 CD.

THE SANCTIONS/JIM AND THE LORDS - Then Came The Electric Prunes LP.

THE BEACON STREET UNION - State Of The Union Box Set.

JANIS JOPLIN - In Concert LP.

Foreword

This book is a complete rewrite of 'Fuzz Acid and Flowers'. It incorporates much of the additional information, which readers of that book have sent in, both to me and to the web site. So the book is essentially an update of 'Fuzz...', which itself followed my earlier publications 'The Flashback' and 'The Acid Trip'.

What you now have in your hands is the most detailed study of American garage, psychedelic, hippie-rock and flower-pop bands of the sixties and early seventies ever published.

The Purposes of This Book are:-

- To provide a comprehensive guide (including detailed discographies) to American garage, psychedelic, hippie-rock and flower-pop bands of the sixties and early seventies.

- To bring to your attention some of the recordings by lesser known bands of these genre. Biographies have been written about some of the better known artists and bands in this book. Consult these for more detailed histories of them.

- Countless bands sprang up in America in this era and it would be an impossible task to document them all (you can see the length of this book anyway). The ones I've included are those I consider merit an entry. Doubtless there will be many omissions. I've tried to ensure that the book is as accurate as possible but not all the information is easily verified. If you spot errors or feel strongly about omissions please email:- c/o fuzz@borderlinebooks.com, with the details.

How To Use This Book

All bands appear in alphabetical order. 'The' has been ignored as the first word of a band's name. Individual artists have been alphabetised under surnames, e.g. Tim Buckley appears in the 'B's.

Some entries are very brief, where bands or artists just released one 45 or appeared on a compilation, but for more prolific acts expect to see the following:-

Personnel Listings

Personnel are listed alphabetically by surname. Where more than one-line up occurs, these are indicated by the A-Z characters.

Personnel:

Name:	Instruments:	Line-up:
MEMBER1	gtr, vcls	A
MEMBER2	bs	AB
MEMBER3	drms, vcls	A
MEMBER4	keyb'ds	A
MEMBER5	gtr, vcls	B
MEMBER6	perc	B

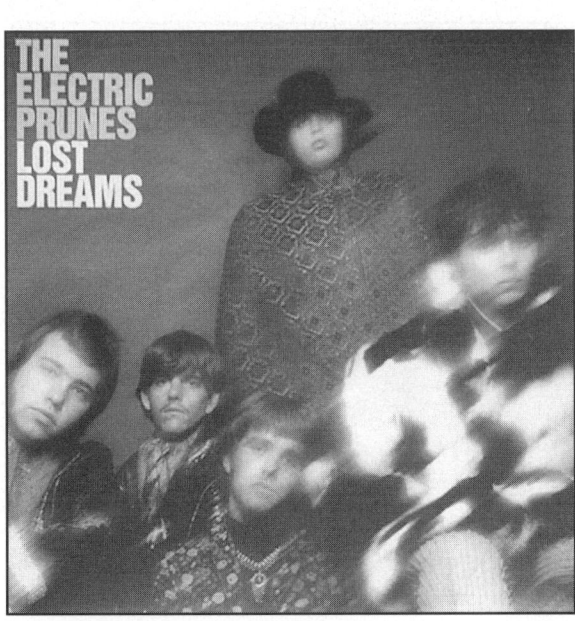

THE ELECTRIC PRUNES - Lost Dreams LP.

Album Discographies

Where more than one has been released, they are listed in order of release. Line entries are as follows:-

ALBUMS:

No/Line-up *	Name	U.S. label & Cat No	Year + R
1(A)	ALIOTTA HAYNES JEREMIAH	(Ampex 10119)	1970 - -
2(B)	LAKE SHORE DRIVE	(Big Foot 714)	c1971 - SC
3(C)	SLIPPIN AWAY	(Little Foot 711)	c1972 - -

NB: * Where albums are known to have been reissued or pirated, this is indicated. + And highest chart placing where applicable. R Rarity scale rating, where applicable.

EP Discographies (where applicable)

Where more than one has been released, they are listed in order of release, in the same format as above.

45 Discographies

Also listed in order of release. Line-up information is not supplied, but otherwise the same information is supplied as for album releases. 'c' before the year of release = circa or approximate and appears where the year of release is not known for sure.

Assorted Information About The Band Or Artist

In the text, the name(s) of other bands or artists who are featured in this book appears in bold to facilitate easy cross-reference. Where bands have tracks which are also included on compilations these are also identified in italics as for all but the most ardent collector they will be the only means of accessing the song. A list of all compilation albums referred to, along with label details, catalogue numbers and (where known) year of release, appears in the compilation section of this book. Some of these compilations had very limited pressings and are also rare now.

CD Releases

Many albums referred to in this book have now been repackaged on CD and this is often referred to in passing beneath the album discographies, where known. It has proved impossible to keep abreast of the flood of these reissues so the information is not comprehensive. Many CD compilations have been released in recent years and those known to the author are included in the compilation section of the book.

A Rarity / Sought-After Scale

Those albums and EPs that are rare and sought-after (obviously there are some rare records that nobody wants) have been given a rating to the right of the year of release. Obviously too, lots of the albums and some of the EPs mentioned can be obtained in their country of origin relatively easily. The scale below can only give a rough banding guide to value and is provided for guidance only. It is based on prices in dollars on the world market: -

-	Relatively easy to find	Less than $25
SC	Scarce	$25 -$50
R1	Rare	$50 - $100
R2	Very Rare	$100 - $250
R3	Extremely Rare	$250 - $500
R4	Ultra Rare	$500 - $1,000
R5	Seldom offered for sale but very sought-after	$1,000 - $1,500
R6	Only a handful exist and they are very sought-after	$1,500 +

PLEASE NOTE: - Any guide to the value of records is highly subjective. Any value will depend on the condition of the vinyl & sleeve, the local geographic scarcity, and the retail 'chain' (i.e. dealers will have a mark-up - they will probably offer less when buying an album than selling it). The value will also vary with time, and may go up or down. Ultimately the price at which you buy or sell any record is an individual decision, and Borderline Productions, its owners, employees and related companies cannot accept responsibility for the accuracy of this guide, or for any economic loss that may be encountered with regard to the use of this material.

Many thanks to Clark Faville for preparing this rarity scale and assessing the rarity of all sixties and seventies albums in this book. The rarity rating is to the far right of the line containing data on each album.

Credits

Several collectors have contributed in some way to this book. Particular thanks go to fellow U.K. collector Max 'Myndblown' Waller, who in addition to writing several entries, has contributed much other data. Philippe Collignon sent me several tapes (as did Tim Holden). Jeff Jarema supplied information and some illustrations. Marcel Koopman also wrote some entries. I'd also like to thank Ivor Trueman (typesetting and art work), Hugh MacLean (data), John Platt (illustrations), Ron Simpson (data), Mike Warth (data), Neal Skok (data), Bruno Thors (data), Richard Allen (data), Don Adams (data and tapes), Clark Faville who has supplied entries on numerous rare US private pressings and minor label albums, as well as providing us with the many illustrations, Mike Markesich and Andre (of Smilin' Ears magazine), Steve Allen, Costas Arvanitis, Diane Beach, Gary Behymer, Chris L. Boardman, Rieuwert Buitenga, Greg Byers, John J. Casbarian, Brian Church, Bob Cole, Jerry Corbitt, Joshua Cortopassi, Elania Dale, Dan Demainkow, D.F. Devlin, Bill Evans, David A. Finney, Mark Garland, Stephen Geer, Lolos George, George Gell, George Guilmet, Steve Gwatkin, I, Hitomi, Hoddyman, Rabbi Mark Hurvitz, Yuri Ikeda, John M. Johnson, Nick Karathanasis, David Keith, Duane King, Nancy Kinney, Jim Klahr, Benjamin Knepper, Lonnie Knight, Nick Kontogouris, Marcel Koopman, Ernie LeBeau, Leonard J. Los, Michael Lloyd, Patrik Lundbore, Hugh MacLean, Roger Maglio, Craig Malek, Peter Malick, Mike Marksesich, Ron Matelic, Mike McKay, Gary Mollica, Al Muehike, A. Mullin, Richard Norris, Richard Olsen, Brian Phillips, Malcolm Pittuck, Ken Pritchard, Steve Quinzi, Lee Rand, Mark Reed, Paul Rieger, Preston J. Ritter, Andrew Rogers, Thomas Rubino, Mark Scheuren, Bruce Shay, Don Smith, Dowald Smith, Fred Sokolow, Peter Tanz, Danny Teleport, Joroen Tenkink, Wayne Vlaky, Bill Von Hagen, and Richard Zvonar.

The following have also sent in significant numbers of e-mails containing data: Alec Palao, Andrew Brown, Aram Heller, Barry Margolis, Bob Embrey, Brent Hosier, Clark Faville, Darryl F. Riffero, Dr. Simon Trent D.S.U., Ed Worcester, Erik Lindgren, Gary Myers, George Gell, Jason Odd, Jeff Lemlich, Joe Foster, Kip Brown, Kurt Sampsel, Lloyd Peasley, Marcel Koopman, Matt Moses, Max Waller, Mike Dugo, Mike Markesich, Nick Warburton, Roger Maglio, Scott Blackerby, Stephane Rebeschini and Susie Martin-Rott. Constraints of space prevent a full list of e-mail contributors appearing here.

Where people have contributed entries to the book their full name has been credited in abbreviated form at the end of the text e.g. Max Waller (MW), Clark Faville (CF).

Disclaimer

Borderline Productions, its owners, employees or related companies are not responsible for the accuracy of the content, or for the correctness of values in a changing market, or for any economic loss which may be encountered with regard to the use of this material.

BOBBY FULLER and THE FANATICS.

THE NEW BREED - Want Ad Reader LP.

QUESTION MARK and THE MYSTERIANS - 96 Tears CD.

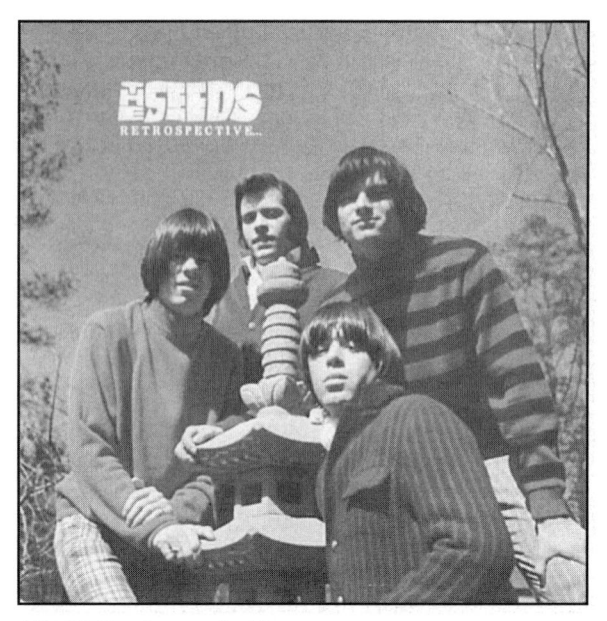

THE SEEDS - Retrospective LP.

INTRODUCTION

The mid-sixties garage band phenomena, which attracted so little attention at the time, has generated far more interest retrospectively. After the excitement of the first wave of rock'n'roll music of the late fifties, the early sixties were a relatively unexciting era in American music. On the West Coast, in particular, there was a plethora of surf-orientated instrumental bands, whose music was still rooted in rock'n'roll and who produced some memorable guitar runs, but for the most part the scene was dominated by dance bands and balladeers. Enter Beatlemania and the British Invasion sound, as it became known, and things rapidly changed. The music of The Beatles and their other European contemporaries derived from American rhythm and blues and rock'n'roll to which was added enthusiasm and a fresh interpretation of these musical styles. Yet Beatlemania, Merseybeat, the British Invasion (whatever you want to call it) was more than just another new musical style ... with their hair styles, fashion and opinions, these bands heralded a new youth culture.

All over America thousands of teenagers started rock'n'roll bands, which were initially influenced by the British Invasion sound, which itself had its roots in American rock'n'roll. Most of these bands were full of average teenagers who could only manage a few chords on a guitar but they transformed thousands of kids into weekend stars among their peers. The better ones got to play at local fraternity parties, dances, shopping centres ... anywhere the opportunity allowed really ... the really good ones made it to bigger venues ... the lucky ones got to cut a record (often a one-off recording deal was the prize for winners of local 'Battle Of The Band' competitions, which were a regular feature at weekend dances in most American towns and cities in this era), the more enterprising ones raised enough bucks themselves to have a record pressed. A minority of these got played on the local radio station and those that caught on became local hits maybe ... the big national labels were always searching for exciting new talent and, as you'll notice when you delve into the meat of this book, some of these local releases were picked up by major labels for national distribution. This offered the opportunity of a hit record, indeed a few of these discs became million-sellers. The 45 discographies in this book show the highest placing in Billboard's Hot 100 of all discs listed (and the equivalent placing for all albums listed in Billboard's Top 200 Album Charts for that matter) so you can see the discs and artists that really won through to, (so far as most garage bands are concerned) stardom. Sadly, most discs and the artists who created them remained in total obscurity.

The term garage band referred to the space where many of these bands rehearsed and to a musical phenomenon. In fact, the music they played was very varied but more than anything else the timely invention of the fuzztone box in the mid-sixties helped mould this sound. In its purest form, this was a crudely-recorded, raw (even savage), primal three-chord sound, thrashed out on Vox guitars and cheesy Farfisa organs laced with lots of fuzz and snarling vocals. Lyrically, they tended to deal with the problems of teenage life - social restrictions and uncooperative parents and girlfriends (for the American garage band was almost exclusively a male phenomenon as rock'n'roll had been before it). 1965 and 1966 were the prime years of the 'garage' band.

TIMOTHY LEARY - THE PSYCHEDELIC EXPERIENCE LP.

Around the Spring of 1966 marijuana and LSD were introduced to the college and high school campuses, by 1967 they were in widespread use among America's youth. When these naive teenage bands began experimenting with psychedelic drugs the result was sometimes very interesting leading to some of the most demented recordings ever made - the chords became more discordant, the basic rock'n'roll rhythms were broken down and the lyrics started to deal with peoples dreams or more often their nightmares. 1967 and 1968 were the prime years of 'garage psych' as it became known, but the term has been widely abused and misused, particularly by dealers who apply it as widely as they can in the hope of raking in extra cash for records, which are not 'psychedelic' at all. Hopefully, some of these have been exposed in this book, which also guides you to those bands who were the real McCoy... bands like **The Calico Wall** who on *Flight Reaction* sought to recreate the paranoia of someone sitting in an airplane prior to take off and fearing that it would crash; **The Bees**, who related a nightmare in their *Voices Green and Purple*, which was one of many records which recounted vivid descriptions of colours associated by acid-inspired dreams; **The William Penn V**, who hallucinated a guru and wrote a song about it; **The Bohemian Vendetta**, who sang of 'skies paved with marshmallow love' on their *Paradox City* or **Cosmic Rock Show**'s *Psiship* with lyrics like, 'Ride it to the moon/Psychedelic space ship/I got the feeling it'll be another bum trip!'... there were countless others. Of course only some garage bands experimented with psychedelia, thousands of them were content to stick more closely to their more basic primal thrash.

As those of you who read my earlier books ('The Acid Trip' and 'The Flashback') know not only garage bands experimented with psychedelia, psychedelic music grew out of other influences as diverse as folk, the

THE CHOCOLATE WATCHBAND - Forty Four LP.

PEBBLES Vol. 3 Compilation LP.

LOVE - Elektra Masters LP.

COUNTRY JOE - Country Joe Sings Resist (Rag Baby EP).

blues, beat and rock'n'roll. The term 'psychedelic' really relates to human perception and experience whilst under the influence of psychedelic drugs. It is sometimes equated with 'mind expanding' yet it arguably means something more because new wave music was mind-expanding without being psychedelic. It's tended to be applied to music that is mystical, drug induced or designed to recreate the (psychedelic) drug experience. In its most literal form psychedelia is basically "trippy", uses distortion, minor keys (generally) particularly minor 7ths and relates to consciousness (mind) expansion as derived from the drug culture of the sixties. Psychedelia brought electricity, mysticism and hitherto unknown musical freedom to rock and pop. A whole new range of instruments - sitars, theremins, wind chimes and other electronic devices were introduced to rock and pop music for the first time.

This new radicalism was not solely confined to the music, a new youth culture was born with its own ideology and audience characterised by the hippie. Hippie audiences and music were very different from the 'garage' or 'garage psych' scenes. Many of the emerging psychedelic rock groups like **The Doors**, **Jefferson Airplane** and **Country Joe and The Fish** strove to push back the musical frontiers and preoccupation with three-minute pop songs was soon surrendered in favour of experimentation and improvisation, as audiences sought after even more 'far out' sounds. The 'hippie' culture had its own underground press and rock journals like 'Rolling Stone' and 'Mother Magazine'. In their dress hippies sought to re-create the visions of beauty and vividness of colour associated with the LSD experience. They wore kaftans, beads, bells and flowery shirts. 'Head shops' sprang up in centres like San Francisco, New York and elsewhere throughout the States selling joss sticks, pipes, books about hallucinogenic drugs and various other forms of psychedelic paraphernalia. 'Flower power' as it became known represented the commercial side of psychedelia in the same way that the 'flower-pop' acts included in this book represented the commercial arm of psychedelic music. Indeed, whilst the underground groups whose lyrics were often ladened with drug references for the benefit of turned-on kids were liable to have their records banned from the airwaves: the 'flower-pop' acts like **The Mamas and Papas**, **Lovin' Spoonful**, **Turtles** etc. whose lyrics talked of peace, love and flowers, often sold records in large quantities achieving sustained commercial success, as you'll see when you browse through the book. It was these bands who took psychedelia (albeit in diluted form) beyond its essentially elitist audiences to the masses, which is why they are included here.

The new psychedelic culture encompassed all related art forms. The light shows, psychedelic posters and record sleeves all represented a further attempt to recreate the LSD experience. The light shows initially developed in the San Francisco area with names as exotic as the groups they served (e.g. North American Ibex Alchemical Company, Garden Of Delights, Head Lights, Pacific Grass and Electric). They usually consisted of film slides and liquids on a transparent dish through which the light was projected onto a wall. The dishes were movable, enabling artists to make the swirling colours move in time with the rhythms of the music. Strobe lighting (on-and-off flashing light giving the impression of stopping motion) was first widely used in this era.

Equally derivative of the San Francisco music scene was the growing art of rock posters - essentially an attempt to translate the vivid impressions of an acid trip onto paper. These were usually vivid in their use of colours and concepts. Eventually San Francisco's Art Museum mounted an exhibition of posters, 'The Joint Show' and their designers - Rick Griffin, Wes Wilson, George Hunter, Alton Kelly, Stanley Mouse, Victor Moscoso etc - became nationally known art figures. George Hunter and Michael Hunter (of **The Charlatans**) designed one of the very earliest posters to advertise their residency at the Red Dog Saloon, Virginia City in Nevada. When the 'Acid Tests', a series of free-form events, were organised by **Ken Kesey** and His Merry Pranksters in 1965, artist Norman Hartweg designed a poster to advertise them. Alton Kelley (a member of The Family Dog collective) produced the first three handbills and helped with the posters for the three dances held late in 1965 at the Longshoremen's Hall, San Francisco. **Jefferson Airplane**, **The Charlatans**, **The Marbles** and **The Great Society** played at the first on 16 October, **The Lovin' Spoonful** and **Charlatans** played at the second on 24 October and **The Mothers (Of Invention)** and **Charlatans** appeared at the third on 6 November. By 1966 these rock posters had become prolific. Between February 1966 - November 1968 at least 147 posters were produced in the numbered landmark series to promote San Francisco - based concerts mostly at the Avalon Ballroom and the Fillmore Auditorium. After the Family Dog ceased to stage rock shows at the Avalon, the new production company (Soundproof's) first event was a **Grateful Dead** dance accompanied by Rick Griffin's 'Aoxomoxoa' poster. The band later used Griffin's title and art for their third album sleeve. Rock promoter Bill Graham also used posters to promote his early Mime Troupe Shows and Benefits and the concerts staged at the Fillmore between 1966-71. A series of handbills were also produced to promote concerts at

THE NAZZ.

The Matrix (originally created by **Jefferson Airplane**'s Marty Balin) between 1965-66. Indeed by 1966 most concert halls in America were using rock posters to promote their shows. Posters were also produced for the Trips Festival, a mixed media event, which was the culmination of the 'acid tests', as **Kesey** called them, and was held at Longshoreman's Hall in San Francisco between 21-23 January 1966. This, more than any other event, marked the inauguration of 'acid rock' as a musical phenomena. Although **The Grateful Dead** starred at The Trips Festival, it was more than just a rock event - all kinds of avant-garde artists working in various media took part. In short, it was an attempt to stimulate the LSD experience with the drug available for those who wanted to try it. Further Trip Festivals were held elsewhere in America, but before long LSD was made illegal and people were forced to be more discreet with its use.

Another landmark in the history of the hippie culture was the Human Be-In held on 14 January 1967 in Golden Gate Park, San Francisco. 20,000 people gathered there on that sunny January day. Three of the city's top groups played there - **Jefferson Airplane**, **Grateful Dead** and **Quicksilver Messenger Service** and **Jefferson Airplane** wrote a song, *Saturday Afternoon*, to commemorate the event. Stanley Mouse, Alton Kelley and Rick Griffin were among those who designed posters for this event, which heralded the 1967 'Summer Of Love' in which people from all over America and beyond converged on San Francisco to create a new way of life which challenged the nation's prevailing social values. The 'Be-In' inspired 'The Monterey Rock Festival' held later that year in the resort area 150 miles downcoast from San Francisco.

Although overshadowed by San Francisco in the early psychedelic era, Los Angeles (which had always been a major recording centre) and Southern California generally was a vibrant music centre in the mid and late sixties. In the early sixties it had been the recording base of the surf/hot rod music and groups like The Beach Boys, Jan and Dean and a plethora of lesser known ones. By 1965 it became the centre of the emerging folk-rock music. The main influences on this type of music had been Bob Dylan (who I've not covered in this book as so much has already been written about him) and protest singers like **Barry McGuire**. Groups like **The Byrds**, **Buffalo Springfield** and later Crosby, Stills, Nash and Young put folk material to a rock format, playing music characterised by acoustic guitar (at first) and fresh, melodic harmonies. Some of them later experimented with psychedelia, but generally their music was more commercially orientated than their San Francisco counterparts.

The second distinguishable strand to emerge from Los Angeles in this era was the music of the heavy rock and rock/blues bands. Of these, the most interesting were probably two bands signed to Jac Holzman's Elektra label - **The Doors** and **Love**. **The Doors**, in both name and music were clearly influenced by LSD. Yet their brand of 'acid' rock was different from that of their San Francisco contemporaries. They took the acid experience less literally, their lyrics tended to centre around leader Jim Morrison's obsessions with the newconsciousness and their struggle against social repression, for example *Break On Through (To The Other Side)* rather than urge their audience to turn onto LSD and love one another. Morrison was well-read, his lyrics were often poetical and concerned with his obsessions

GRATEFUL DEAD - Axomoxoa LP.

with freedom, which resulted from his reading the works of various existentialist writers. These factors made **The Doors** something of an anachronism among the acid bands and also rather special. Indeed, they were the most controversial and commercially successful of the West Coast underground bands. **Love**, started out as a folk-rock act but their experimentation with drugs led them in a rather different direction to that of their contemporaries. At their best, they attained the melodic musical harmonies associated with the finest L.A. folk-rock bands and yet the surrealism and nihilism of their lyrics set them apart, though they do bear some comparison with **The Doors**.

Los Angeles too boasted a number of influential music venues, mostly in the vicinity of the Sunset Strip. The most popular was the Whisky-a-Go-Go, which soon became not only an important venue for the San Francisco bands, but also a springboard for many of L.A.'s own acts like **The Doors**, **Love** and **The Byrds**. Other significant venues were The Troubador, the Shrine Auditorium, The Kaleidoscope, the Ash Grove, Ciro's (where **The Byrds** were frequent performers), Pandora's Box and the Sea Witch. Strangely, Los Angeles was never a great centre for rock posters. The Pinnacle concert production company was the first significant concert and production company to put on rock concerts and dances in Los Angeles, mostly at the Shrine Auditorium. The posters designed by local artist John Van Hamersveld for these events are now legendary works. Los Angeles also had a prolific garage band scene. Many of the biggest and best garage bands like **The Seeds**, **The Standells**, **Music Machine**, **Sons Of Adam**, came from the city and countless more roared out of its surrounding suburbs. As you turn the pages of this book and read about the recordings

JOHN KAY (Steppenwolf).

NEIGHB'RHOOD CHILDR'N.

CROME SYRCUS.

of bands like **The Avengers**, **The Grains Of Sand**, **The Lyrics**, **The Starfires**, **Limey and The Yanks**, and **The Human Expression** you can imagine how exciting the city's music scene in the later half of the sixties must have been.

San Diego, although the third largest metropolis in California, failed to develop its own musical style and was mostly influenced by Los Angeles to its North, but its major venues were frequently visited by top bands. Its most significant venues were The Hippodrome (managed by Trans Love Airwaves Productions), which had a San Franciscan, Rebecca Galdeano, as its poster artist and modelled itself on that city's Avalon Ballroom and The Community Concourse.

Elsewhere in the States psychedelic rock venues were mushrooming. A group of students at the University of Texas in Austin set up the Vulcan Gas Company, the State's first psychedelic dance hall. Many of the State's top bands played there (**The Conqueroo** and **Shiva's Headband** played at the grand opening on 27 and 28 October 1967) and a local artist, **Gilbert Shelton**, designed several posters for the venue.

Texas is best remembered for tough garage punkers in this era - bands like **Larry and The Bluenotes**, **S.J. and The Crossroads**, **The Bourbons** and hundreds more. Another Texas speciality was garage psych, not only did it produce some relatively well known demented geniuses like Roky Erickson and the **13th Floor Elevators** and **The Moving Sidewalks**, it also produced countless more obscure acts like **The Mind's Eye**, **The Outcasts**, **The Remaining Few**, **Stereo Shoestring** and **Thursdays Children**, whose discs are now sought-after and highly-valued by collectors.

Chicago was less closely associated with psychedelia, being the home of the urban blues, but it produced acts like **The Paul Butterfield Blues Band**, **The Buckinghams**, **Cryan' Shames** and **The American Breed**, as well as some seminal garage bands like **The Shadows Of Knight**, **The Del-vetts**, **The Knaves**, **The Rovin' Kind** and **Saturdays Children**. It also had several notable dance halls, like the Kinetic Playground (where much of the Concert Art was produced by Mark T. Behrens) and the Aragon Ballroom.

Detroit and its suburbs produced one of the most vibrant and unique local garage band scenes in America in this era. The opening of The Hideout Club in May 1964 and the associated record company proved a catalyst for several promising garage acts fronted by **The Fugitives** (who later evolved into **SRC**) and **The Underdogs** and as more clubs like the Crows Nest, the Hullabaloos, the Pumpkin and the Birmingham-Bloomfield Teen Center, opened up the number of bands proliferated further - **The Tidal Waves**, **The Yorkshires**, **The Unrelated Segments**, the Anglophile-influenced

TANGERINE ZOO - Gig Flyer.

Human Beinz. By 1967, the smaller clubs had been over-shadowed by the Grande Ballroom, which boasted its own poster artist Gary Grimshaw (and later Carl Lundgren) whose psychedelic handbills were a match for any poster designed by San Francisco's own artists. All the city's top bands - **MC5**, **The Rationals**, **The Woolies**, **SRC**, **The Frost** (formerly **The Bossmen**) played there and a second wave of local groups like **The Amboy Dukes**, Psychedelic **Stooges**, **Third Power**, **Frijid Pink**, **Teegarden and Van Winkle** emerged too. By then, the city was very much associated with the heavy rock genre.

The Pacific Northwest, from the late fifties onwards had been the home of some of the finest instrumental combos in the land, bands like **The Wailers**, The Ventures and **The Frantics**. What characterised them from the 'also rans' of the era was their very strong, powerful, upfront rhythm section. The music of the Northwest was raw, aggressive and powerful and the phenomenal commercial success of acts like **Paul Revere and The Raiders** and **The Kingsmen** encouraged other local garage bands to seek the same without compromising any of their grungy sound. Among its major venues were Seattle's Eagles Auditorium, the Aqua Theatre and the Seattle Ballroom and Portland's Crystal Ballroom, Memorial Coliseum and Beaver Hall. Seattle also had well-established regional labels like Jerden, Etiquette and Seafair - Bolo that gave emerging young groups access to good studios and experienced producers. Indeed Jerden had various subsidiaries like Burdette, Panorama and Piccadilly and recorded countless garage bands in this era. These well established regional labels also had good access to major labels and national distribution channels as well as influence over regional radio stations meaning that local hits could relatively easily become regional hits, which could then be leased to one of the majors and become a national hit. All of these factors are thought to have contributed to the generally good quality of Northwest recordings in this era. The prime Northwest garage band was **The Sonics**, who exuded a surly demeanour and created one of the rawest, toughest garage sounds. People as diverse as The Kinks, Bruce Springsteen and The Sex Pistols have acknowledged **The Sonics**' influence on their own music. The Northwest produced several other garage bands of note such as **The Bootmen**, **The Brigade**, **The Live Five**, **The Night Walkers**, **Mr. Lucky and The Gamblers** and **The Wilde Knights** as well as psychedelic acts like **Cotton Mouth**, **The Crome Syrcus**, **The Daily Flash**, **The Floating Bridge**, **The New Tweedy Bros!** and **The Lollipop Shoppe**.

Boston had a thriving garage scene, featuring bands like **The Remains**, **The Barbarians**, and **Teddy and The Pandas**, but more exciting was the emergence in 1968 of the so called 'Bosstown Sound', which featured outfits like **Ultimate Spinach**, **The Beacon Street Union**, **Freeborne**, **Phluph** and **Earth Opera**. The city's own psychedelic scene soon sprouted

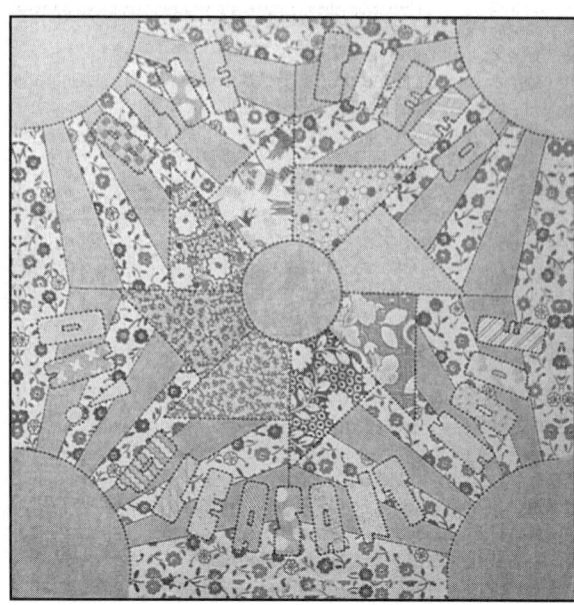

BLUE CHEER - Oh! Pleasant Hope LP.

QUICKSILVER MESSENGER SERVICE - Just For Love LP.

from small clubs into larger psychedelic dancehalls like the Boston Tea Party, the Ark, the Crosstown Bus, Club 47 and the Psychedelic Supermarket.

Minneapolis was a sort of mecca for much of the Midwest producing some first rate psychedelic bands like **C.A. Quintet, Calico Wall**, **The Litter** and **The Electras** as well as more commercially successful acts like **The Trashmen**.

There's only been space to mention a few of the major cities here but throughout America most towns and cities had their own garage bands and psychedelic scenes in this era. Some of the finest records of this genre came from the Midwest States and places like Colorado as you'll see as you browse through this book. Not all the bands in this book were garage or psychedelic bands, many were more loosely associated with the hippie movement and the music they played was more grounded in folk and the blues. The flower-pop and bubblegum bands represented the more commercial side of psychedelia and garage music. Ah yes, bubblegum - the basic beat of bubblegum records like *Simon Says*, *Gimme Gimme Good Lovin'*, *1,2,3, Red Light*, *Quick Joey Small* and *Yummy, Yummy, Yummy* was the basic sound of rock and roll and had close links with the garage band sound, the difference being that infantile lyrics were substituted for the usual rage, aggression and snarling vocals. So that's why the main bubblegum acts are included here, too.

We've mentioned the music, the fashion, the new art forms associated with the hippie culture, but the movement was more than just that - it was advocating a new lifestyle in a rapidly changing country. As the sixties evolved American society became very volatile indeed. Certain key events like the assassination of President J.F. Kennedy, the growth of the Free Speech Movement, the freedom marches in Mississippi and the draft and the country's entrenchment in the Vietnam War sparked off a challenge and defiance towards the American establishment among the Nation's youth. The hippie culture was very much a part of this mood. The word hippie was first used in a San Francisco Examiner article in September 1965 about a coffeehouse called The Blue Union in the heart of the Haight Ashbury area of San Francisco and the clients who patronised it. The movement's close association with psychedelia was cemented by **Ken Kesey** and The Merry Pranksters' activities in organising the Acid Tests and Trips Festival. It even had its guru, **Dr. Timothy Leary** (a Havard psychologist), who announced in September 1966 that he was forming a psychedelic religion, The League for Spiritual Discovery. He called a formal press conference at the New York Advertising Club and called on Americans to "turn on, tune in and drop out".

At its most extreme, the hippie life-style would involve dropping-out of conventional society and discarding one's material possessions to live off the land in communes. Obviously, this represented a reaction against the growing materialism, violence and impersonality of Western Society (i.e. many rock songs of this era were imploring audiences to love their neighbours because they were their brothers) and the related pressures of urban life (i.e. 'let's quit the city and get back to the land') was also a regular theme in lyrics of this era. As one might expect given the experimentation and improvisation of its music the hippie life-style was essentially individualistic with its emphasis on meditation and doing 'ones own thing' as a means to self-fulfilment and realisation. On a more superficial level, long hair was a manifestation of both this new-found freedom and an act of defiance against the standards of conventional society.

By 1969 the hippie movement was dead, discredited in the violence of the Altamont Rock Festival, and almost all its dreams remained unfulfilled, but sociologically and musically these were very exciting times. What follows is an encyclopaedic guide to the garage, psychedelic, hippie-rock and related music which came out of America in the sixties and early seventies.

Vernon Joynson.

THEZE VISITORS.

IRON BUTTERFLY - Ball CD.

IT'S A BEAUTIFUL DAY - Choice Quality Stuff LP.

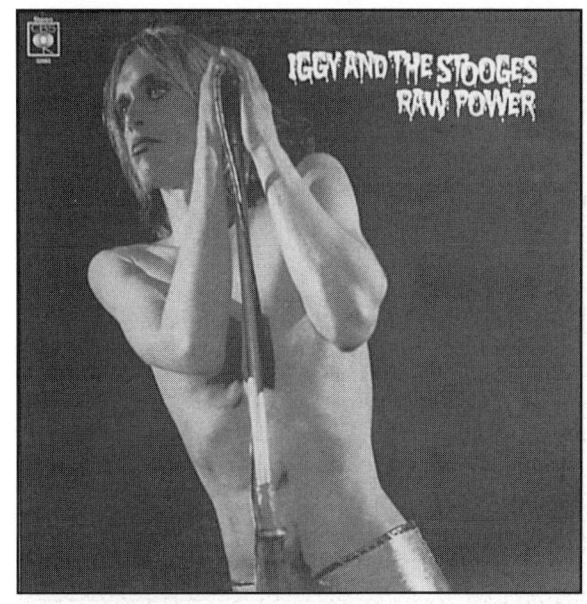

IGGY and THE STOOGES - Raw Power LP.

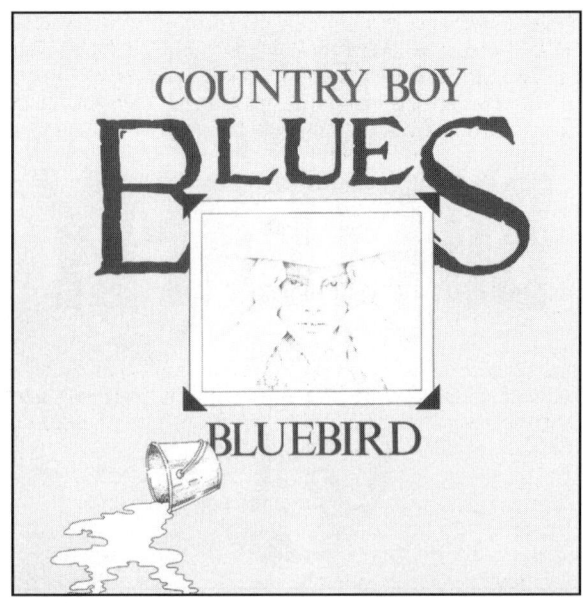

BLUEBIRD - Country Boy Blues LP.

BLUES MAGOOS - Basic LP.

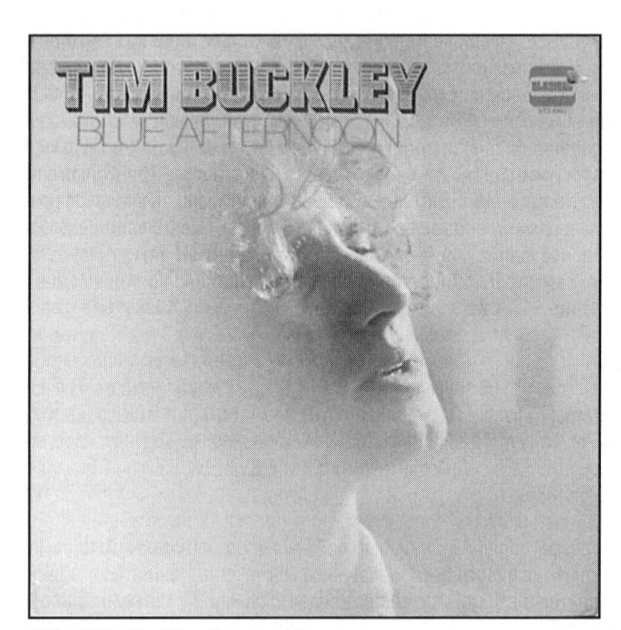

JANIS JOPLIN - Pearl LP.

TIM BUCKLEY - Blue Afternoon LP.

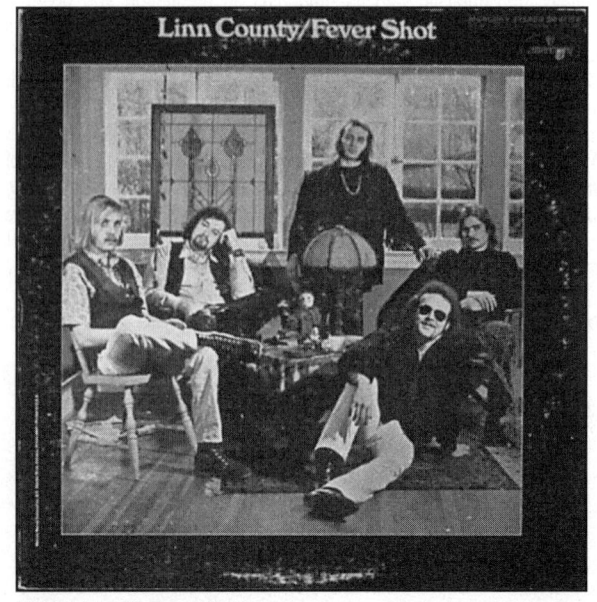

THE SUNSHINE COMPANY - Happy Is LP.

LINN COUNTY - Fever Shot LP.

A.B. SKHY - A.B. Skhy LP.

Aardvark

| 45: | Wish I Could Tell You / |
| | Change For Ever | (Zoological Gardens 8606) c1968 |

Wisconsin and Illinois are both claimed as home turf. Whatever, *Wish...* is a haunting melodic garage-ballad with echoey vocals, keening guitar and moody Hammond vibes. Flip over for another good example of the garage-ballad genre, full of yearning with a reflective piano solo. One for late night unwinding. (MW)

Aardvark

45:    Salty Dog / The Kiss That Touches Me   (Bullet 800) 196?

A subsidiary label of JEMKL (outta Miami & Nashville) may hint at possible locations for this band. *Salty Dog* blasts off with some discordant distorto-fuzz, and later features liberal doses of wah-wah. It is essentially an uptempo late sixties rocker with a driving beat, like *Emerge*-period **Litter** but with less bite. *Kiss* is a soul-tinged last-dance ballad. (MW)

Aardvarks

Personnel incl: DARRELL DINGLER   A

45s:	I'm Higher Than I'm Down/That's Your Way	(Vark 2058) 1966
	I Don't Believe/I Don't Need You	(Fenton 2090) 1966
	Let's Move Together/Cherie, Can't You Tell	(Forte 2021) 1968
	Let's Move Together/	
	Cherie, Can't You Tell	(Talpa 68101) 1968

Erroneously thought to be a Chicago band, this act was in fact from Muskegon, Michigan. They were formed in late '64 under the name The Hitch Hikers, but later pulled the "Aardvarks" moniker from the first page of the dictionary.

Released on their own Vark label *I'm Higher Than I'm Down* despite the title wasn't a "drug" song. The flip, *That's Your Way*, is another fine number full of jangly guitar. The Vark release was recorded / produced and pressed by Fenton Records from Grand Rapids, Michigan, for whom they also recorded their second 45. The 'A' side to this, *I Don't Believe*, is a reasonable punker.

The *Let's Move Together* single was originally released on Forte, but was later re-issued by the band's ex-manager, after he had left town with a bunch of their money.

The band also recorded two unreleased songs: *I Can't Explain* which is a moody guitar and organ original and *People Of This Land* a sparse protest tune with lonesome sounding harmonica.

Compilation appearances include: *I Can't Explain* on *Project Blue, Vol. 5* (LP); *I Don't Believe* on *Destination Frantic!* (CD); *I'm Higher Than I'm Down* on *Michigan Mayhem Vol. 1* (CD), *Pebbles, Vol. 11* (LP) and *Sixties Archive Vol. 7 - Michigan Punk* (CD); and *That's Your Way* on *Sixties Rebellion, Vol. 6* (LP & CD). (VJ/MW/KBn/MM)

Aardvarks

| 45: | Subconscious Train Of Thought/ | |
| | Unicorn Man | (Arch ARA 1303) 1968 |

A rare and little-known late sixties fuzz guitar monster, produced by **Steve Cropper** at his studio in Tennessee, although the band was based in Florrisant, Missouri. *Subconscious Train Of Thought* can be heard on *A Lethal Dose Of Hard Psych* (CD). (CF/MW)

Aardvarks

45:    Josephine / Reminiscing   (Bell 1059) 1965

A different, Minneapolis, outfit who included Dave Waggoner later of **South 40** and **Crow**. (MW)

Aargons

45:    Do The Dog / Spiked   (Casino 1012) 196?

Do The Dog - a dirty-dancing frat-punker circa 1965 from Topeka, Kansas - has been taken out for a walk on *Monsters Of The Midwest, Vol. 2* and Tom Tourville's CD compilation *Midwest Garage Band Series - Kansas*. Woof! (MW)

Aaron

ALBUM: 1   MUSIC BY AARON   (Private Pressing) 1974 R1

From Virginia, a four-piece band with guitar and organ interplay and a melodic hard psych material. Only 500 copies pressed, housed in a homemade textured cover. (SR)

Abandoned

45:    Come On Mary/Around And Around (The Abandoned 4867) 1966

This four piece frat rock band from Chicago formed in 1964 as The Satin Flames when they were all eleven year olds. *Come On Mary*, a simple frat rock raver was recorded in March 1966, at the Stereo Sonic Recording studios in Chicago and released on their own label. The flip, *Around And Around* was a cover of the Chuck Berry classic.

Compilation appearances include: *Around And Around* and *Come On Mary* on *Sixties Rebellion, Vol. 9* (LP & CD); and *Come On Mary* on *Back From The Grave, Vol. 6* (LP). (VJ)

Abbreviations

45:    True Fine Lovin'/?   (N/K) 1965

The work of a very obscure Rocky Mount, South Carolina band. The 'A' side can be heard on *Tobacco-A-Go-Go, Vol. 2* (LP). (VJ)

John Howard Abdnor and The Involvement

Personnel:	JOHN HOWARD ABDNOR	ld vcls, gtr	A
	J. HARRIS		A
	EDDIE LIVELY	gtr	A
	JAMES		A
	RONNIE		A

ALBUM: 1(A)   INTRO TO CHANGE   (Abnak ABST-2072) 1969 -

From Fort Worth, Texas, a rock group led by **John Abdnor**, formerly in **Jon and Robin**. As it was recorded in 1969, this short album (21 minutes) contains lots of horn arrangements, but the tracks are generally rather dynamic and benefit from the friendly vocals of **Abdnor**, in a R&B style. The album ends with the longest track, *Relaxation* culminating with a nuclear explosion while the singers keep on singing "Relaxation, you need relaxation"...

Ed Lively, their guitar player, was previously in **The Mods** and **Whistler, Chaucer, Detroit and Greenhill**. He would later play with Freddie King and record some good albums of Texas blues. (SR)

Abdo-Men

45:   The Only Bad Thing About Her /
      All Alone Am I   (Arcola UA-407-41259) 196?

Two low-key strummed Beatlesque pop numbers by a cleverly named group from Duluth, Minnesota. A crude and sparse sound from Arcola Recording of St.Paul, gives the impression of dating from 1964 although a much later date has been suggested. Both sides were penned by R. Redosevich. (MW)

Abel

Personnel: CHARLES BOLDS   bs   A
            TOM CATALANO   drms   A
            LARRY CHIESA   vcls, trumpet   A
            ABEL SANCHEZ   gtr, vcls   A
            DAVID SPEDIACCI   sax, vcls   A

ALBUM: 1(A)   PLEASE WORLD   (Fantasy) 1971 -

From San Francisco, an average horn-rock group with some latin influences and competent guitar work, previously known as The Prophets. Tom Catalano would later create his own label, TomCat, and work with Nancy Sevins, the vocalist for **Sweetwater**. (SR)

A.B. Skhy

Personnel: TERRY ANDERSON   drms, vcls   A
            DENNIS GEYER   gtr, vcls   AB
            JIM MARCOTTE   bs   AB
            HOWARD WALES   keyb'ds   A
            JAMES CURLEY COOKE   gtr, vcls   B
            RICK JAEGER   perc   B
            (RUSSELL DaSHIELL   gtr   A)
            (JIM LIBAN   hrmnca   A)
            (OTIS HALE   flute   A)
            (DAVE ROBERTS   horn arrangements A)
            (ELVIN BISHOP   gtr   B)
            (WALLY ROSE   piano   B)
            (BEN SIDRAN   harpsichord   B)

ALBUMS: 1(A) A.B. SKHY   (MGM SE 4628) 1969
        2(B) RAMBLIN' ON   (MGM SE 4676) 1970
                                                      HCP
45:   Camel Back / Just What I Need (PS) (MGM 14086) 1969 100

Originally known as New Blues, they were basically an electric blues band with horns and some jazz influences. From Milwaukee, Wisconsin they relocated to San Francisco where they became a popular live attraction at venues like the Fillmore and Avalon in the late sixties. Produced by Richard Delvy (**Chamber Brothers**, Challengers), their first album contains a mix of original songs and covers (*You Upset Me Baby* and Keith Jarrett's *It's Love Baby*, *24 Hours A Day*) and is still very nice to hear. The 45 cuts are from this album.

Terry Andersen and Howard Wales then left, the latter to play with **Harvey Mandel**, **Jerry Garcia** and the **Grateful Dead**. They were replaced by Rick Jaeger and James Curley Cooke (ex-**The Versitones** and **The Steve Miller Band**).

Still in the same style, their second album was recorded in March 1970 and produced by **Kim Fowley** and Michael Lloyd. Cooke had obviously became their leader, writing most of their original material. The covers this time were Fats Domino's *I'm Walkin*, Doc Pomus's *My Baby Quit Me* and a version of *Groovin'*. The excellent and long track *Gazebo* was clearly jazz oriented and dedicated to **Gabor Szabo**. The band also started work for a third album which was never completed.

Upon their demise, **Cooke** went on to Cat And The Fiddle and also played with Boz Scaggs and Ben Sidran. After some years out of the music scene, he came in 1980 back with a decent solo album *Gingerman* (First American). Rick Jaeger joined **Crowfoot** and became a session man.

A CD, *A.B. Skhy, Featuring Howard Wales* (One Way 30011) has recently been issued. (VJ/MW/SR)

The Abstracts

Personnel: HENRI MARIO DONDINI   organ   A
            TONY PELUSO   vcls, gtr   A
            MICHAEL THATCHER   drms   A
            PIERRE ARMAND VIGEANT   bs   A

ALBUM: 1(A)   THE ABSTRACTS   (Atco Pompeii SD 6002) 1968 -

45:   Smell Of Incense / See The Birdies   (Atco Pompeii 66679) 1968

The Abstracts were formed by Peluso and Dondini, both from Los Angeles and Pierre Vigeant (from Montreal) whilst they were in high school. They discovered Thatcher (from Dallas) in a 'Battle Of The Drums Contest' in L.A. County and asked him to join their group. Their album was recorded for the small Pompeii label at Sound City Studios in Fort Worth, Texas, produced by Darrell Glenn and David Anderson and engineered by J. "T-Bone" Burnett. It was rather patchy on the whole but with a few highlights and ranged from soft to heavy, sometimes psychy, pop. The 45 catches two of their better efforts: a lightweight cover of the **West Coast Pop Art Experimental Band**'s psych-pop nugget (also covered by **Southwest FOB**, **Pawnbrokers** and nineties Norwegian folk-psychers Smell Of Incense); *See The Birdies* is a slab of **Vanilla-Fudge**-essenced heavy acid-pop.

Apart from the material written by Peluso, the album also contains a cover of Gerschwin's *Summertime* and *Any Old Time*, a **Pat and Lolly Vegas** song. *Smell Of Incense* on the album was credited to Peluso, not to the **WCPAEB**! On the 45 however, the song is credited correctly to **Markley**-Morgan.

In 1971 Peluso was in Instant Joy, the backing group of **Mark Lindsay** (ex-**Paul Revere and The Raiders**) and then went on to play with the Carpenters and Seals and Croft. (MW/SR/EW)

A.B. SKHY - Ramblin' On LP.

Abstract Sound

45s:	Your Gonna Break My Heart/		
	Judge Him If You Can	(CBM no #)	1966
	Blacked Out Mind/I'm Trying	(Gray Sounds GS 006)	1967
	Blacked Out Mind/I'm Trying	(Sound Of Soul SOS 1002)	1967

Despite the Gray Sound label address of Brooklyn, New York, this group was from Springfield, New Jersey. *Blacked Out Mind* is an interesting, if uninspiring keyboard-heavy punker that is not in the least psychedelic despite its title. The flip unashamedly rips off the backing keyboard track from *96 Tears* and is again a little pedestrian.

Their 1966 punker *You're Gonna Break My Heart* was misspelt *Your...* on the label, which also credited the group as **Abstrack Sound**. The flip is an excellent understated protest song.

Compilation appearances have included: *Blacked Out Mind* on *Basementsville! U.S.A.* (LP); *I'm Trying* on *Bad Vibrations, Vol. 1* (LP) and *Prisoners Of The Beat* (LP); and *You're Gonna Break My Heart* on *Psychotic Reactions* (LP). (MW/MM)

The Accents

Personnel:	SKIP DAKLIN	bs	A
	TOM GROENE (aka TOM NYSTROM)	drms, vcls	A
	BILL MILLER	keyb'ds	A
	KEN SANDS	gtr, vcls	A

45s:	Howlin' For My Baby/		
	Wherever There's A Will	(Bangar 605)	1964
	Wherever There's A Will/		
	Howlin' For My Baby	(Garrett 4008)	1964
	You Don't Love Me/Searchin'	(Bangar 629)	1964
	Searchin'/You Don't Love Me	(Garrett)	1964
	Why/Road Runner	(Bangar 648)	1964
	Why/Road Runner	(Garrett 4014)	1965
	Wherever There's A Will/Louisiana Man	(Twin Town 707)	1965
	Muffin Man/Someone To Love	(Twin Town 711)	1965
	No One Heard You Cry/Your Time Has Come	(Bear 1977)	1966

These punkers were based in Minneapolis, Minnesota and also appeared on the compilation, *The Big Hits Of Mid-America, Vol. 1* (Garrett 20l/Soma 1245) in 1964, with *Howlin' For My Baby*, *Searchin'*, *Wherever There's A Will* and *Why*. In 1965, they appeared on the Bud-Jet compilation series with *Muffin Man* on *Top Teen Bands Vol. 1*, *Louisiana Man* on *Top Teen Bands Vol. 2* and *Road Runner* on *Top Teen Bands Vol. 3*.

Why was a Lonnie Mack composition.

More recent compilation appearances have included: *Howlin' For My Baby* and *Why* on *The Big Hits Of Mid-America - The Soma Records Story* (LP); *You Don't Love Me* on *Garagelands Vol. 2* (CD); and *Why* on *Sixties Rebellion, Vol. 9* (LP & CD). (VJ/MW/BMr)

The Accents

Personnel:	VIC BUNDY	keyb'ds	AB
	PAT JERNS	drms	AB
	GEORGE PALMERTON	bs	A
	RON PETERSON	vcls	A
	LAURIE VITT	sax	AB
	BILL CAPP	vcls	B
	DOUG LING	bs	B
	KATHI McDONALD	vcls	

45s:	Sticky/Linda Lou	(Jerden 728)	1964
	All Of My Life/I Want Your Love	(Panorama 10)	1965

A different act also from the Seattle area in the Pacific Northwest. They evolved out of a Bellingham **Wailers**-styled act called The Night People, led by Reginald Shannon (bs), with Gary Hill (ld gtr), Laurie Vitt (sax) and some other musicians from Seattle. Laurie Vitt was recruited at short notice, after their original sax player had quit:- "I played with them for about three months, but the band was starting to fall apart, mostly because the keyboard player and drummer were driving up from Seattle. At the same time, Ron Peterson from **The Frantics** had entered Western and their band too fell apart. We hired Ron to take Gary Hill's place - I liked Gary, but he and Shannon had a major falling out and, if you can believe it, Shannon owned the PA system so the band stuck with the PA. We continued to use The Night People name but it was clear that Reginald had to go. We also picked up Vic Bundy and Pat Jerns when the keyboard player and drummer dropped out, all within the space of a month. The Night People had become pretty well known in the Northern part of the state so we had lots of bookings. Ron Peterson couldn't get along with Reginald either and before long we started thinking that it was time for him to go. Ron contacted George Palmerton about replacing Reginald and he agreed. So, in a major falling out, with threats by Reginald about lawsuits, we threw him out and got George. As it turned out, George was great, not only as a bass player, but as a singer. We changed our name to The Frantics, mainly to keep Reginald off our backs - and he was fuming to say the least. He claimed that he owned The Night People name. We then decided to record *Linda Lou* but Ron was worried that we might face legal problems if we did a record under the name Frantics. So we changed our name to **Ron Peterson and the Accents**".

"We then did the *Linda Lou* record with *Sampan* (written by Bundy) as the flip side. The voice introducing us on that record is Pat O'Day from KJR Radio Station in Seattle. It was this group, Ron Peterson and the Accents, who first tried out Kathi at a small grange hall in Mt. Vernon. Kathi was 13 at the time and she blew us away. I might add that Vic Bundy was either 13 or 14 and I was 18. As time went on, Kathi sang with us more and more and we started paying her $10 per night. At some point George Palmerton quit (he was driving up from Seattle), but on very good terms - we regretting seeing him go, and we replaced him with Doug Ling. Doug was an animal and a mediocre musician so it was clear that he wouldn't last. Ron Peterson decided to quit soon after and he also left on good terms. In the meantime Ron had coerced me into singing, which of course scared me to death. He was basically priming us to continue without him and it turned out that I wasn't too terrible. Then we hired Bill Capp who not only was a decent guitar player, but a good singer. We kept the name **The Accents** for a while but added "Bellingham" to it and did the *Bacon Fat* record which got some local air time but that was about it. One of our booking agents suggested **The Bellingham Accents** part arguing that it made us sound British."

Linda Lou has also resurfaced on the cassette only compilation *History Of Northwest Rock Vol.7*.

Laurie Vitt is now Curator of Reptiles and Professor of Zoology at Sam Noble Oklahoma Museum of Natural History! (MW/LV)

The Accents

45:	Friendly Stranger/People Are Funny	(Gazzari 90391)	196?

Previously thought to have been the San Diego **Accents**, this 45 was by another bunch, so who were they? The label is from Hollywood, California, and the song credits are Paolucci-Tutalo and Paolucci-Tutalo-Fallon respectively. Answers on an email please!

The Accents

45s:	Birds In My Tree / She Cried	(Planet 82468)	1968
	Slow Down / Go Now	(Freeform 203)	1970

Aram Heller's New England bible 'Till The Stroke Of Dawn' informs us that they hailed from Rhode Island and that the top side on the Planet 45 is a **Strawberry Alarm Clock** cover. (MW/AH/MM)

The Accents (featuring Sandi)

Personnel:	DON BECK	sax	A
	TONY JOHNSON	drms	AB
	GABE LAPANO	vcls, keyb'ds	AB
	DON LOVAS	gtr	AB
	FRANK MANNIX	bs	AB
	DOUG MYERS	sax	B
	SANDRA 'SANDI' ROUSE	vcls	B

			HCP
45s:	Better Watch Out Boy/Tell Me	(Commerce C 5012) 1964	-
	Better Watch Out Boy/Tell Me	(Challenge 59254) 1964	133
	I've Got Better Things To Do/		
	Then He Starts To Cry	(Charter CR 1017) 196?	-
	What Do You Want To Do/		
	I Really Love You	(Liberty 55813) 1965	-
	On The Run/He's The One	(Karate 529) 196?	-

This San Diego-based group was previously known as **The Accents**, who played live concerts but made no recordings (line-up 'A'). **The Accents** held open auditions for a female vocalist and were so knocked out by Sandi Rouse that they gave her top billing! Their first 45 was a huge local hit (Los Angeles - San Diego) and the group was immediately picked up by Challenge records who re-released their 45 with national distribution and that Summer it made the charts in markets all across the country. Their subsequent singles met with similar success, but the group broke up when Myers was drafted. Mannix and Johnson later formed a group with David and Rick Randle called **The Brain Police** who eventually made an incredible album in 1968, after Johnson and Mannix had moved on. Johnson later became a sought-after live and session drummer, playing with Mary Wells, Junior Walker, Commander Cody, Maria Muldaur, **Hoyt Axton** and others. **Sandi and The Accents** were the most popular group in San Diego in 1964 - 1966, and staged a thirty year reunion concert there in 1996 that was a sold-out, standing-room only event. Their sound was R&B and soul-based pop rock. (CF)

The Aces

A band who have three cuts on *Thee Unheard Of*, a compilation of Michigan acetates. *Train's Late* - an Elvis-style ballad, a really raw version of Bo Diddley's *Who Do You Love*, and a great garage ballad *I Can Hear The Rain Drops* with rainstorm effects and a big nod to the Cascades. The trouble is that the latter track is really *I Can Hear Raindrops* by **The Noblemen 4**. The other "**Aces**" tracks are also thought to be different artists. It turns out that many of the 'acetates' on *Thee Unheard Of* are actually modern forgeries manufactured by a fraudster who took the tracks from obscure sixties 45s to exploit the compiler's interests.

Who Do You Love has also subsequently appeared on *Sixties Archives Vol. 7 - Michigan Punk* (CD). (VJ/MW/MM)

Aces Combo

Personnel:	HOWARD CAYWOOD	drms	A
	MICHAEL EARNHARDT	bs	A
	TIM ERVIN	ld gtr	A
	JOHNNY NANCE	gtr	A
	JOHNNY YARBROUGH	gtr	A

ALBUM: 1(A) INTRODUCING (Justice 134) c1967 R2

NB: (1) reissued on CD (Collectables CD 0605) 1995.

THE ACES COMBO - Introducing CD.

A schoolboy quintet, all 14 or 15 according to the reproduced liner notes, trot through some favourite covers - surf/instrumental (*Wipe Out*, *Apache*), ballads (*Under The Boardwalk*, *My Girl*), frat/dance (*Shake A Tail Feather*, *The Monkey Time*) and pop/beat (*Pied Piper*, *This Boy*). Kudos to Collectables for reissuing these extremely rare and expensive albums. Curiosity is satisfied without selling the family china, though the general sound of these lesser known Justice albums is the pre-fuzz 1964/1965 period and of more interest to fans of beat/pop/frat than the "class of '66" clan. (MW)

Acme Thunder

Personnel incl:	MITCH ALIOTTA	gtr, bs, vcls	A
	TED ALIOTTA	bs, vcls	A
	JOHN JEREMIAH	keyb'ds, vcls	A
	HARVEY MANDEL	gtr	A
	BOB PARISIO	drms, vcls	A

ALBUM: 1(A) LET'S ALL GET NAKED (Rox Records ROX 69) 1975 SC

From Illinois, **Acme Thunder** was founded by **Harvey Mandel** and four members of **Aliotta Haynes Jeremiah**. A bluesy hard-rock biker album, the result is far from being interesting. (SR/NK)

The Acoustics

45: My Rights/I Want Your Love (Canaltown 254) 196?

This mid-sixties combo, who operated out of Palmyra in New York State, recorded a catchy folk-punk song, *My Rights*, about the plight of the high school kid penned in by parents, teachers et el. It's captured in all its splendour on *Pebbles, Vol. 16* (LP). (VJ/MM/MW)

Acrobat

| Personnel incl: | BILL JONES | gtr | A |

ALBUM: 1(A) ACROBAT (TMI 1004) 1972 -

45: α Better Than Today/Better Than Today (TMI 75-0108) 1972

NB: α promo only.

A rural prog-rock group with delicate vocal harmonies and acoustic/electric instruments. They were probably from the Memphis Area, where TMI, owned by **Steve Cropper**, was based and who also released albums by **Edgewood** and **Watchpocket**. (SR)

Action Unlimited

45: Thinking To Myself / My Heart Cries Out (Parkway P-115) 1966

A bouncy melodic male-harmony popper (think of an upbeat **Association**) backed by a haunting dreamlike ballad with harmonies and oscillating psychedelic effects. Both sides were composed by a C. Trisko. The group personnel is unknown and may have just been another anonymous Los Angeles sessioneer aggregation. Historical significance and interest is assured by the production wizardry of **Curt Boettcher**, that would be given greater exposure with **Millennium** and **Sagittarius**.

You can also find the excellent 'B' side on the 1998 Arf! Arf! CD comp *No No No*, subtitled *28 Moody Somber and Tragic '60s Garage Rock Sagas*. (MW)

The Actioneers

45: No One Wants Me/It's You (Shane 57) 1966

A sixties garage band from Texas (most probably Houston). Their 45 is rather primitive with both sides featuring pounding drum work, sloppy tambourine and guitars low in the mix - great stuff!

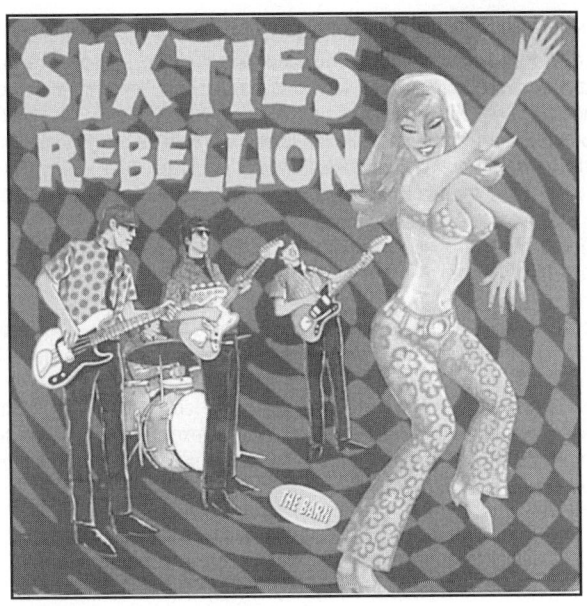

Sixties Rebellion Vol. 2 (Comp LP) including The Actioneers.

Compilation appearances have included: *It's You* and *No One Wants Me* on *Sixties Rebellion, Vol's 1 & 2* (CD) and *Sixties Rebellion, Vol. 2* (LP); and *No One Wants Me* on *Teenage Shutdown, Vol. 8* (LP & CD). (VJ)

Act Of Creation

Personnel incl:	?? SAMPSON	A
	ERIC SAMPSON	A
	KEN WHITMAN	A

45:   I've Just Seen You/Yesterday Noontime   (Capitol 5973) 1967

The above is an interesting and as yet uncompiled 45 by a Plymouth, Massachusetts band. It must be said that both sides are nearer to pop than psych/garage: the 'A' side seems on the verge of breaking into a fuzzy freakout but never does, the 'B' side is pop a lá **Merry Go Round** but with some psychedelic effects added.

The Sampson brothers would later form **The Buzzards** who issued a decent heavy garage 45. (MW)

Act III

45:   Made For You / M.F.Y.   (Kookaburra 501) c1966

Breezy harmonious pop with baroque flourishes from an unknown outfit who also released this track as by the **Travel Agency**. The flip is a different, almost instrumental, mix of the 'A' side. Thought to be Californian, but perhaps confused with the Viva band - is there an Aussie connection here? (MW)

Adam

Personnel:	JIMMY FITZSIMMONS	A
	DONALD HENNY	A
	ADAM MILLER	A
	EDWARD SCHNUG	A

45:   Eve / Where Has My Little Girl Gone   (Mala 547) 1966

Eve is a strange and chaotic psych-punker that is hard to describe. Beginning with a fabulous instrumental passage which kicks into *Eight Miles High* mode, it evolves into an off-the-wall punker with fuzz guitar, keening backing vocals and screams that give it a nightmarish aura. The avalanche of guitars returns at intervals and the whole affair concludes abruptly in an odd anti-climax. Check it out on *Incredible Sound Show Stories Vol.7* and *A Lethal Dose Of Hard Psych*.

The flip is just as bizarre in that it's a straight harmony-vocal ballad.

Possibly just a NYC studio aggregation, Henny, Miller and Schnug turned up again in 1967 as the **Balloon Farm**. (MW/MM)

Anthony Adams

ALBUM: 1   AN EYE IN EACH HEAD   (Harlequin HR1 1001) 1973 SC

A very strange sci-fi concept album about the history of man told by the flies who inherit the Earth after mankind has disappeared! The songs include *The Age Of Stone*, *The Day I Lost Control Of My Body*, *Journey Of Eternity* and *The Age Of Uniglobe (The Fourth Scroll)*. The album was recorded with all sorts of instruments (various keyboards, guitar, strings, horns). (SR)

Addis and Crofut

Personnel:	STEPHEN ADDIS	A
	BILL CROFUT	A

ALBUMS:	1(A)	SUCH VERY INTERESTING PEOPLE	(Verve) 1963 -
	2(A)	ADDIS AND CROFUT	(Columbia) c1966 SC
	3(A)	EASTERN FERRIS WHEEL	(Columbia) c1968 SC
	4(A)	LIVE CONCERT RECORDING	(Private Pressing) c1967 SC?

NB: (4) was issued in a plain white sleeve.

From the East Coast, a folk duo whose Columbia albums reputedly contain some good acid folk tracks with Eastern influences. They released at least ten albums on various labels, including some private pressings. (SR/RMh)

The Advancement

Personnel:	COLIN BAILEY	drms, perc	A
	LYNN BLESSING	vibes, hrmnca, organ	A
	JOHN DE ROSE	classical gtr	A
	HAL GORDON	conga, drms, perc	A
	A.A. JOHNSON	gtr	A
	LOU KABOK	bs	A
	RICHARD THOMPSON	organ, harpsichord	A

ALBUM: 1(A)   THE ADVANCEMENT   (Philips PHS 600-328) 1969 SC

A sixties Hollywood outfit whose album is one of those strange late sixties barrier-breaking experimental efforts trying to fuse different musical genres. **Orient Express**, **Autosalvage** and **John Berberian** are other similar projects which spring to mind. This particular one is an attempt to fuse jazz with folk, rock and acid. Interesting but its success is debatable.

Lynn Blessing also released a solo album in 1969, *Sunset Painter* and Lou Kabok went on to play with **Gabor Szabo**. (MW)

Advantes

45:   Done It Again /
      Feel A Whole Lot Better   (Tripper 60611) 1966

A crude jangley garage-ballad also featured on the 'desperate garage punkers' compilation *I Can Hear Raindrops*, backed by a cover of a **Byrds**' classic. Check it out there unless you've $100 plus for an original. It's been speculated (but not proven) that the band came from Pennsylvania. (MW/MM)

Adventurers

45s:	Baby Baby My Heart / Lover Doll	(Reading R-602) 1966
	Jane Doesn't Live Here Anymore / Cheryl's Theme	(Reading R-603) 1966

From Catasauqua, Pennsylvania. Invasion, beat and earlier teenbeat influences give the first 45 a charming 1964 sound - so won't appeal to the class of '66.

You can also find *Baby, Baby, My Heart* on *Bad Vibrations, Vol. 3*. (MW)

AFTER ALL - After All LP.

Aerial Landscape

45s:	Proposition 13 / Are You Sleeping	(RCA Victor 47-9432) 1967
	Coming Of Goodbye/ Both Sides Now	(RCA Victor 47-9520) 1968

Proposition 13 is driving orchestrated female-vocal folk-pop with trumpet flourishes, that'd appeal to flower children or fans of **Bob Lind**. The flip is an extremely soppy male-led harmony-pop ballad. (MW)

Aerosmith

Personnel:	TOM HAMILTON	bs	A
	JOEY KRAMER	drms	A
	JOE PERRY	gtr, vcls	A
	STEVE TYLER	vcls	A
	BRAD WHITFORD	gtr	A

				HCP
ALBUMS:	1(A)	AEROSMITH	(Columbia 32005) 1973	166 -
(up to	2(A)	GET YOUR WINGS	(Columbia 32847) 1974	74 -
1975)	3(A)	TOYS IN THE ATTIC	(Columbia 33479) 1975	11 -

NB: (1) reissued as *Aerosmith Featuring Dream On* 1976, HCP # 21. There have been a number of compilations *Big Ones And Young Lust: The Anthology*, *Greatest Hits* and *Classics Live 1 & 2*. The most recent *O'Yeah! Ultimate Aerosmith Hits* (Columbia 508477 2) is a 2-CD set and the only compilation to include all their hits from their Geffen and Columbia years.

			HCP
45s:	α	Dream On/Somebody	(Columbia 45894) 1973 59
(up to		Same Old Song And Dance/	
1975)		Pandora's Box	(Columbia 46029) 1974 -
		Spaced/Train Kept A Rollin'	(Columbia 10034) 1974 -
		S.O.S. (Too Bad)/Lord Of The Thighs	(Columbia 10105) 1974 -
		Sweet Emotion/Uncle Salty	(Columbia 10155) 1975 36
	β	Walk This Way/Round And Round	(Columbia 10206) 1975 -
		Toys In The Attic/You See Me Crying	(Columbia 10253) 1975 -

NB: α reissued (Columbia 10278) 1976, HCP #6. β reissued (Columbia 10449) 1977, with *Uncle Salty* on 'B' side, HCP #10.

Aerosmith formed in Boston, Massachusetts during the early seventies. Tyler, from New York city, was a veteran of **Chain Reaction** and The Strangeurs. He met Perry at an ice cream parlour where Perry worked during the Summer while both were vacationing in Sunapee, New Hampshire. Perry invited Tyler to sit in with his group **The Jam Band**. After shifting through several line-ups, the above members moved to Boston and built up a local following.

The band signed to Columbia in 1972 after Clive Davis saw them at Max's Kansas City. According to legend, Jerry Wexler from Atlantic also spotted the band that night, but declined to make an offer as he thought they weren't ready to record. The self-titled debut album attracted moderate interest at first, as the band toured as an opener for The Mahavishnu Orchestra, The Kinks, Mott The Hoople and Sha Na Na. Initially, **Aerosmith** were slagged off in the press as a third-rate Rolling Stones clone. By 1975, though, the Jack Douglas produced third album *Toys In The Attic* found the band really gelling; it became such a success that the band's debut single *Dream On* was reissued and hit the US Top Ten, and the debut album, retitled *Aerosmith featuring Dream On* also recharted and climbed to US No. 21.

Although outside the scope of this book, 1977 saw **Aerosmith**'s commercial and artistic peak with *Rocks*. Following that album came a long downward slide due to excessive drug use, where both musical quality and record sales suffered. After some personnel changes in the eighties, however, the original quintet reunited and detoxed, became even more commercially successful making one of the most suprising and dramatic comebacks in rock history. (JPs)

Aesop and The Fables

Personnel incl:	DAVID BURT?	A
	ORYSIA LUBINSJI ?	A
	PIERRE 'PETE' OUELETTE gtr	A

45:	Grass/You'll Be My Pride	(Panorama 29) 1966

From the Pacific Northwest, this outfit included Pierre Oulette, who had earlier played with **Don & The Goodtimes** and **Paul Revere & The Raiders**. The other personnel listed above may be incorrect. (VJ/MW/DR)

Aesop's Fables

Personnel:	RONNY ALTERVILLE	bs, gtr, vcls	A
	SONNY BOTTARI	vcls, perc	A
	ROBERT DI MONDA	flute	A
	JOE FRATICELLI	sax	A
	FRANK KREPALA	gtr	A
	LOUIS MONTARULI	trumpet, trombone	A
	JOHN SCADUTO	drms, ld vcls	A
	BARRY TAYLOR	keyb'ds, vcls	A

ALBUM:	1(A)	IN DUE TIME	(Cadet Concept LPS-323) 1969 -

		HCP
45s:	Hidin' My Love/I've Got Troubles	(Atco 6453) 1966 -
	Girl, I've Got News For You/Yes, I'm Back	(Atco 6508) 1967 -
	Take A Step/What's A Man To Do	(Atco 6523) 1967 -
	Slow And Easy/The Truth	(Atco 6565) 1968 -
	I'm Gonna Make You Love Me/	
	They Go Out And Get It	(Cadet Concept 7005) 1969 123
	Temptation 'Bout To Get Me/	
	What is Love?	(Cadet Concept 7011) 1969 -
	What Is Love?/And When It's Over	(Cadet Concept 7016) 1969 -

Possibly a contentious inclusion for this Hampstead, Long Island group. Though we can't comment on their other releases, their *What Is Love* 45 contains most characteristics associated with the "Long Island sound". *And When It's Over* is very different from **The Vagrants'** rampantly heavy version of **Bert Sommer**'s pop melodrama, starting with an encouraging dreamy intro but then replacing the guitar lines with brass and orchestra.

The album was recorded at Syncron Sound Studios, Wallingford, Connecticut and produced by Bob Gallo and Louis Cofredo, who were also the producers of **Sum Pear** (also with John Scaduto on drums). It should please fans of Chicago and other horn rock groups, but is for too heavily orchestrated and full of brass arrangements to be of real interest to fans of psychedelia. All their material was original, bar the **Bert Sommer** cover. (VJ/MW/MM/SR)

A Euphonious Wail

Personnel:	DOUG HOFFMAN	drms, vcls	A
	BART LIBBY	keyb'ds	A
	SUSANNE REY	vcls	A

	STEVE TRACEY	gtr, vcls	A
	GARY VIOLETTI	bs, vcls	A

ALBUM: 1(A)   A EUPHONIOUS WAIL   (Kapp KS 3668) 1973 SC

Heavily influenced by San Francisco bands (**Big Brother and the Holding Company** and **Jefferson Airplane** quickly come to mind), the Santa Rosa, California-based **A Euphonious Wail** sound more '68' than '73.

Built around the talents of drummer Doug Hoffman, keyboardist Bart Libby, singer Suzanne Rey, singer/guitarist Steve Tracy and bassist Gary Violetti, the band's self-titled 1973 debut teamed them with producer Brian Ingoldsby, although Lowell Levinger (of **Youngbloods** fame) reportedly also helped out. It does have a couple of momemts, but for the most part the album is surprisingly lame and uninspired. Lead vocalists Rey and Tracy have decent, if unexceptional voices (though Rey tends to screach in the higher registers). Taken individually guitar and keyboard propelled rockers such as *Pony*, *We've Got the Chance*, *When I Start To Live* and *F#* aren't bad, but stretched over an entire album, there simply isn't much to stand out, and the songwriting is average. The band were even less successful when they tried slowing things down - check out the lame ballads *Did You Ever* and *I Want To Be A Star*. Needless to say, the album vanished without a trace.

The Michael Hawes cover drawing is interesting, depending on how you look at, you can see something completely abstract, or possibly obscene. (SB/VJ)

Jeff Afdem and Springfield Flute

See **Springfield Rifle**.

Affection Collection

Personnel:	DON CHRISTENSON	keyb'ds, vcls	A
	TIM COMEAU	drms	A
	MIKE DOGGETT	ld gtr	A
	ROY HASSELL	bs	A
	HAL ROWBERRY	vcls	A

ALBUM: 1(A)   THE AFFECTION COLLECTION   (Evolution 2007) 1969 -

45s:	In Apple Blossom Time /		
	Time Rests Heavy On My Hands	(Maudz 001)	1967
	In Apple Blossom Time /		
	Time Rests Heavy On My Hands	(United Artists 50268)	1968
	Plastic Flowers / Feelin' So Good	(Maudz 003)	1968
	Girl / I'll Be There	(Maudz 004)	1968
	Girl / I'll Be There	(Evolution 1004)	1969
	Watch Her Walk / I Don't Mind	(Evolution 1013)	1969
	Feelin' Fine / Can't Put Her Down	(Maudz 1000)	1970

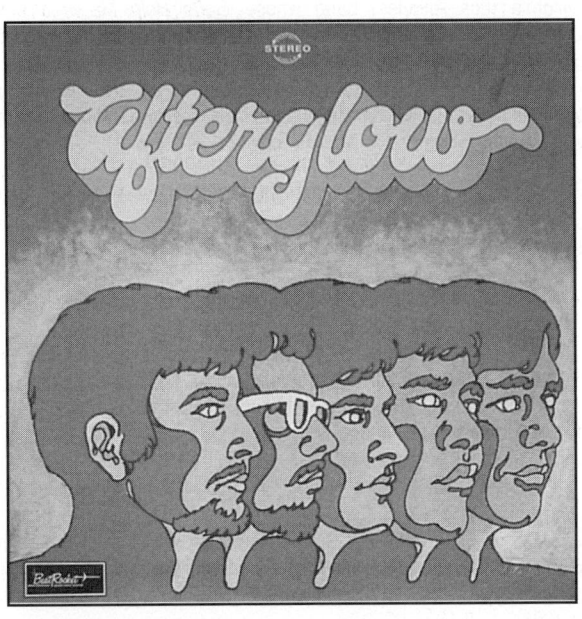

AFTERGLOW - Afterglow LP.

The Maudz label was run by Norman Petty and based in Clovis, New Mexico, where the band recorded. It has not been confirmed yet that the band hailed from there. Their original compositions were filed with Petty's publishing company Dundee Music. Billboard reported that they were signed to Evolution in February 1969.

Hassell was a co-writer of both sides of the 45 by Sledgehammer - *I'll Stop Pretending / Someone's Here A Watchin'* (Maudz 45-005), September 1969 - perhaps he was a member of that group?

Their album, which features tracks like *Watch Her Walk*, *Time Rests Heavy On My Hands* and *The Collector*, is mellow pop-psych.

Compilation appearances have so far included: *Time Rests Heavy On My Hands* on *Killer Cuts*. (MW/JI/SR)

A 440

Personnel incl:	IAN HOFFMAN	drms	A
	CARLOS LUEVANO	gtr	A
	CRAIG MEACHAM	bs	A
	TED NEELEY	vcls	A
	MICHAEL RAPP	keyb'ds	A
	YVONNE WERSON	vcls	A
	ROCK ROMANO	gtr	

ALBUM: 1(A)   ULYSEES - THE GREEK SUITE (dbl)
                (20th Century Fox TCF 1101) 1978 -

45s:	It's Just Your Mind/Torture	(Soma 103) 1967
	When I Get Out/So Watch Out	(Cinema 006) 1967
	Instructions! Please Do Not Open Before Christmas/	
	Santa Claus Is Comin' Yeah	(Cinema 008) 1967

This Houston band was best known for *Torture*, a driving psychedelic punk track with raw vocals, powerful drumming and rich organ work, which Rock Romano co-wrote with Messrs Clark and Sartie.

Formerly a guitarist with **The Six Pents** and later with **The Fun and Games Commission**, Romano played on the Soma 45 but was not a regular member of this outfit.

The band operated on and off during the seventies and eighties recording an album in 1978 but line-up data is hard to come by. The band's sole album was a rather forgettable effort entitled *Ulysses, The Greek Suite*. Released for 20th Century Fox, the resulting 23-track, double album set was clearly intended as a concept piece built on ancient Greek mythology. Written and arranged by keyboardist Michael Rapp, musically the set showcased the talents of singers **Ted Neeley** and Yvonne Iverson. **Neeley** wasn't half bad, displaying a nifty gruff voice that was well suited for more mainstream rock (the MOR Ambrosia-styled *Ithaca*). Recalling Yvonne Elliman, Iverson wasn't as impressive, though it didn't matter since her performances were scattered far and wide. Exemplified by material such as the instrumental *Greetings From Olympus*, *Ulysses Theme* and *Island Of The Lotus Eaters* the collection was heavy on pomposity, complete with spoken word narratives and over-the-top ELP-styled synthesizers and keyboards. Hardly something to get excited about, though it would have made for dandy background music when you were studying the Classics.

Ted Neely also had a solo career.

Compilation appearances include: *Narathelia Glows In The Dark* and *When I Get Out*, two unreleased tracks from 1967, on *Houston Post - Nowsounds Groove-In* (LP); *Torture* on *Acid Visions* (LP), *Acid Visions - The Complete Collection Vol. 1* (CD) and *Mindrocker, Vol. 4* (LP). (VJ/MW/CF/SB)

After All

Personnel:	MARK ELLERBEE	drms	A
	ALAN GOLD	keyb'ds	A
	BILL MOON	bs, vcls	A
	CHARLES SHORT	gtr	A

ALBUM: 1(A)   AFTER ALL   (Athena 6006) 1970 R1

NB: (1) also released in Australia on Interfusion. Reissued on CD (Gear Fab GF-161) 2000 and vinyl (Gear Fab GF 420LP).

AGAPE - Victims Of Tradition LP.

The album, which is easy to find, is organ-dominated progressive rock with a psychedelic taint and a clear classical influence. The group comprised members from various bands in Tallahassee, Florida. They got together with lyricist Linda Hargrove (later a Nashville songwriter) to create a concept album, to "emulate the new styles of the era; acid-rock, classical rock, surrealism in lyrics and complexity of form". A one-off project, all returned to their individual careers as soon as it was finished in 1969. (VJ/RM/MW)

Afterglow

Personnel:	LARRY ALEXANDER	drms	A
	RON GEORGE	bs	A
	GENE RESLER	vcls	A
	ROGER SWANSON	organ	A
	TONY TECUMSEH	gtr	A

ALBUM: 1(A) AFTERGLOW (MTA 5010) 1968 R2

NB: (1) reissued on CD (Sundazed SC 6074) 1995 and on vinyl (Beat Rocket BR 127) 2001.

From Chico, California, this band was originally known as The Medallions. Their album, which was produced by Larry Goldberg and Leo Kulka (aka Leo De Gar Kulka, a regular at Golden Gate studios, in San Francisco), consists of soft pop with a tinny organ backing and memorable tunes. Some of the tracks such as *Susie's Gone*, *It's A Wonder*, and *Afternoon* are extremely psychedelic and Side One is much the stronger of the two.

Something of a cross between **Country Joe and The Fish** and British North American Act, their album is certainly worth investigation and has been reissued on CD by Sundazed, with four previously unissued tracks - alternate versions of *Susie's Gone*, *Chasing Rainbows*, *Afternoon* and *Morning*. These are looser and less rigid alternate backing tracks.

Compilation appearances include: *Morning* on *Psychedelic Crown Jewels, Vol. 1* (CD); *Susie's Gone* on *Beyond The Calico Wall* (LP & CD) and *Pebbles, Vol. 2 (ESD)* (CD); and both *Morning* and *Susie's Gone* on *Crystalize Your Mind* (CD). (VJ)

Aftermath

Personnel:	MIKE DAVIS	bs	A
	DANNY DEMIANKOW	ld gtr	A
	SCOTT GIUS	gtr	A
	BRAD GOODMAN	drms	A
	GARY LA PRELL	vcls	A

Formed in North Hollywood in early 1966 after Danny and Gary met in Continuation School (a sort of halfway house for social misfits). They decided to form a band and got together in earnest with the rest of the guys. They got to play gigs at places like Pandora's Box, the Hullabaloo and It's Boss and were auditioned for a record deal at A&M but lost out to the **Merry Go Round**. Their increasing indulgence in psychedelics and brushes with the law were their downfall, the final straw coming when Danny was arrested backstage at one gig and thrown into Juvenile Hall for three months. Although they didn't make it onto vinyl at the time a tape of them playing three songs back in the Summer of 1966 survived and their very loose version of Van Morrison's *Gloria* found its way onto *Highs In The Mid Sixties, Vol. 20*. Danny now lives in Oregon and plays with The Miracle Workers. Scott plays in Top 40 bands in Venice (not far from LA). Brad lives in Hawaii - he's now a born again Christian and plays in Top 40 bands; Gary is a construction worker in Simi Valley (outside LA) and Mike, well he kinda vanished and the others haven't heard of him for several years. (VJ)

Agape

Personnel:	FRED CABAN	gtr, vcls	A
	MIKE JUNGKMAN	drms, organ	A
	JOHN PECKHART	bs	A
	RON TURNER	manager	A

ALBUMS: 1(A) GOSPEL HARD ROCK (Mark MRS 2170) 1971 R2
2(A) VICTIMS OF TRADITION (Renrut Records AGAPE 101) 1972 R3

NB: (1) and (2) have been issued on CD by Agape Communications (AC001 and AC002 respectively).

Yep! Perhaps it could only happen in America. This California outfit (from Azusa) are preaching the gospel using a hard rock format and musically it's pretty good too. Fred Caban was the brain behind the project - he wrote the lyrics, music and supplies the vocals on all the tracks. The opening cut on the first album *Blind* is pretty bluesy, there's plenty of fuzz on tracks like *Trust* and a good echoed guitar on *Freedom*. The magnum opus is the final track, *Rejoice*, which deals with the end of the world and the coming of Christ. Imaginative, maybe even psychedelic, this track in particular is well worth a listen. Their second album is more laid back than the first but both are equally sought-after.

There's also a CD release by Hidden Vision entitled *The Problem Is Sin: Live And Unreleased* which was supposed to be their third album in 1973. The CD contains 70 minutes of music. (VJ)

The Agents

45: Gotta Help Me/Calling An Angel (Rally 504) 1965

A California (Los Angeles) band whose *Gotta Help Me* is a Mersey-influenced record with a guitar riff very similar to one in The Searchers' *When You Walk In The Room*.

Compilation appearances include: *Gotta Help Me* on *The Cicadelic 60's, Vol. 4* (CD) and *Highs In The Mid Sixties, Vol. 20* (LP). (VJ)

The Age Of Reason

Personnel:	ANDY ADAMS	fuzz bass	A
	KENNY DALE	gtr	A
	LARRY RUSSELL	drums	A
	SID SHERES	ld gtr	A
	ALAN TURNER	ld vcls	A

45: (Your Love Is Like A) Magnet/
I'm A Free Man (Ascot 2230) 1967

A teen garage quintet from the Bronx, New York. Their sole 45 became a sought-after item many years later after *Magnet*, a brooding punk-popper, was included on the 1983 compilation LP *Ear-Piercing Punk* (reissued on CD in 1996).

Larry Russell recalls: "Our original name was The Loose Ends but, when we recorded Magnet on 9/8/66, our manager decided to change our name (that night) because there had been another band with the same name that had a record deal before us."

"On that day we recorded 4 songs, the other two besides the single were (It's A) Dirty Shame, which was going to be our follow-up single, and Pride, written by our producer and which, in our opinion, sucked. I have copies of all of those recordings."

Their 45 did well enough to make the national charts and the band found themselves opening for top division acts like The Four Tops, Drifters, **Box Tops** and **Young Rascals**. However the big push from the label did not materialise and the follow-up never happened. The band called it a day in the Spring of 1968. Thirty-five years on *Dirty Shame* has finally been unveiled, on *Psychedelic States: New York Vol. 1* (CD). It's a catchy swinger that harks back to upfront 1964-era Merseybeat shouters, punctuated with "yeah"s aplenty.

Larry Russell was 16 when the record was cut. He went on to tour with Billy Joel, Gary U.S. Bonds, Mary Travers, and Robert Gordon. In the late nineties he was the percussionist for superstar Bryan Adams. (MW/MM/JLh/LR)

The Age Of Reason

See **Reason**.

Aggregation

Personnel:	LE WAYNE BRAUN	ld gtr, vcls	A
	DALE BURT	piano, organ, vcls	A
	BAYARD GREGORY	drums, timpani, bongos, tambourine, toilet, vcls	A
	RICHARD JONES	gtr, vcls	A
	LEO POTTS	flute, clarinet, sax, recorder, kazoo, vcls	A
	BILL SISSEOV	bs, trombone, vcls	A
	LEMOYNE TAYLOR	flute, clarinet, sax, slide whistle, vcls	A

ALBUM: 1(A) MIND ODYSSEY (LHI 12008) 1967 R3

NB: (1) counterfeited on vinyl (Thorns S-12008) 2000.

Y45: Sunshine Superman/Maharishi (LHI 1209) 1968

The album sounds like a studio project. It's atmospheric, psychedelic mood music and includes some mellow instrumentals with Eastern moves, flute passages and dreamy arrangements. Ideal music to unwind by. At times it's reminiscent of **The Electric Prunes** *Mass In F Minor* period, especially on *White Light*, with its cathedral choir sound. On the down-side there's some brassy arrangements that creep in too often and concocted lyrics and vocals which are occasionally rather lame. *The City Of Toys And Games* is sorta swing-era melody pop update - the toilet flush at the end eloquently sums it up. *Life's Light* makes amends though. It commands pretty high prices but musically has limited appeal.

Recording on Lee Hazlewood's LHI label probably places this as a Los Angeles-based project. (MW)

Don Agrati

ALBUM:	1	HOMEGROWN	(Elektra EKS-75057) 1973 -

45s:	α	I'll Have To Say Goodbye/Oh Oh	(Checker) 1963
	β	Summertime Game/ Little People	(Orange Empire OE 91647/8) c1964
	α	It's Better This Way / One Good Turn Deserves Another	(Capitol 5362) 1965
	α	Don't Let It Happen/Out	(Challenge 59328) 1966
	α	Children Of St. Monica / Good Man To Have Around The House	(Canterbury 501) 1967
	α	Impressions With Yvonne / Leaving It Up To You	(Canterbury 507) 1967
		One Man Woman / Story	(Elektra 45846) 1973
		Blood Stream / Two Bit Afternoon	(Elektra 45860) 1973

NB: α by Don Grady. β by Don Grady with the **Palace Guard**.

Born **Don Agrati**, but better known as Don Grady, this California musician, singer, songwriter and producer, had previously been the popular star of the U.S. TV show 'My Three Sons' and during the mid-sixties toured the country doing telethons. In 1964, he recorded a single with the **Palace Guard** and in 1967 was behind the **Yellow Balloon** project.

His solo 45s are now quite rare and sought-after. In 1973, he recorded a solo album under his real name. Co-produced by **Agrati** and Marlin Greene, *Homegrown* may interest fans of California sunny rock pop. (SR)

Aim

Personnel:	LOREN NEWKIRK	keyb'ds	A
	PATRICK O'CONNOR	bs	A
	MICHAEL OVERLY	ld gtr, vcls	A
	WARREN 'BUGGS' PEMBERTON	drms	A
	(ALAN ESTES		A)
	(DAVID SHERR	oboe	A)

ALBUM: 1(A) AIM FOR THE HIGHEST (Blue Thumb BTS 64) 1973 SC

A short-lived Californian group, **Aim** was formed by three members of **Christopher Cloud** : Overly, O'Connor and Pemberton plus Loren Newkirk, a good keyboard player who often worked with Chris Darrow. Their album rarely turns up.

Warren "Buggs" (or Bugs) Pemberton was English and had previously been with Jackie Lomax in the Undertakers and also played on several of his solo albums.

Their album was one of the last to be issued on the Blue Thumb label. (SR/VJ/BK)

Air

Personnel:	TOM COPPOLA	keyb'ds	A
	GOOGIE	keyb'ds, vcls	A
	MARK ROSENHAGEN	drms	A
	JOHN SIEGLER	bs	A

ALBUM: 1(A) AIR (Embryo SD 733) 1971 -

A jazzier label-mate to **Floating Opera** with a similar cover. (VJ/BK)

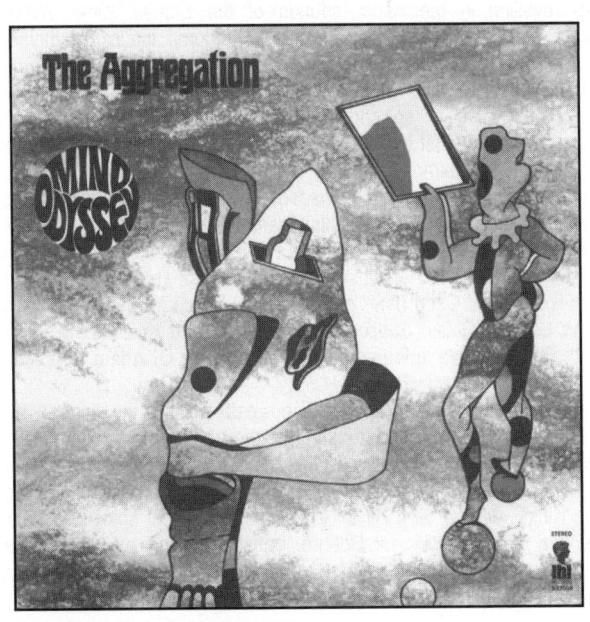

The Aggregation - Mind Odyssey LP.

A.J.

Personnel:	TOM ARNOLD	drms	A
	LANCE GESSLER	bs	A
	ANDREW J. GOULARD	gtr	A

ALBUM: 1(A) LAST SONG FIRST SIDE   (Black Walnut) 197? SC

A privately pressed album of rural/hard rock recorded live on 31st October 1973. No date or local area is designated, but 1974 would be a best guess on the year of release. (VJ)

Akers, Lee, and The Electric Generation

ALBUM: 1 HEAVY, HEAVY, HEAVY   (Crown CST 600) 1969 SC

On the same budget exploito label as the **(Electric) Firebirds / 31 Flavors** comes another anonymous assortment. Though the title might encourage hopes of more proto-grunge, 'heavy' this is NOT. The vocalist sounds like a gruffer version of Creedence Clearwater Revival's John Fogerty, and the bulk of the material is in similar bluesy rock'n'boogie territory. The rest is country-rock and big ballads with piano to the fore. (MW)

Steve Akin

45s: Baby You're A Habit I Gotta Break /
 Take Your Time   (Ash A-2001) 1969
 It's Heavy / I'm Trippin' Alone   (Ash A-2002) 1970

A solo artist from Houston, Texas. The second 45 comes across like a pot-smokin' cowboy - trippy lyrics with a stoned folkie vibe over laid-back guitar rock. Very cool. It has subsequently resurfaced on the vinyl compilation *I'm Trippin' Alone*, and also appears on *Psychedelic Experience, Vol. 3* (CD). (MW)

Alamo

Personnel:	LARRY DAVIS	bs	A
	LARRY RASPBERRY	vcls, gtr	A
	RICHARD ROSEBROUGH	drms	A
	KEN WOODLEY	keyb'ds, vcls	A

ALBUM: 1(A) ALAMO   (Atlantic SD 8279) 1970 -
NB: (1) reissued on CD (Black Rose BR 138).

45s: Been Some Changes / All New People   (Atlantic 2795) 1971
 Get The Feeling / Question Raised   (Atlantic 2816) 1971

ALAMO - Alamo CD.

Formed by four Memphis musicians, **Alamo** released a decent hard rock album. Larry Raspberry was previously in **The Gentrys** and would later form the Highsteppers. Richard Rosebrough went on to play with the **Hot Dogs** and Big Star, whilst Ken Woodley later played with **Don Nix** and would team up again with Rosebrough on the first solo albums by Alex Chilton. (SR/MW)

Jim Alan

ALBUM: 1 TALES OF THE SONGSMITH   (Circle) c1974 R2?

From Wisconsin, a mystic folk musician in the same style as **Gwydion**. The cover shows him standing in a forest with headband, robe, long beard, pentacle and guitar! (SR)

The Alarm Clocks

Personnel:	BRUCE BOEHM	ld gtr	AB
	MIKE PIERCE	bs, vcls	ABCD
	BILL SCHWARK	drms	ABCD
	FRANK RECSIK	vcls	BCD
	BOB KALAMASZ	gtr	CD
	RICK CAON	gtr	D

NB: line-ups 'B' and 'C' as The Purple Haze, line-up 'D' as The Looking Glass.

ALBUM: 1(A) YEAH!   (Norton ED-285) 2000 -

45: No Reason To Complain/Yeah!   (Awake No. 107) 1966

In 1983 Tim Warren unleashed *Back From The Grave, Vol. 1* on a moribund world and awoke both a new and an older generation to some of the rawest, crudest sonic assaults from the mid-sixties. Amongst his first selection was both sides of a killer garage-punk 45 with superbly snotty Jaggeresque vocals, by this little known group from Ohio. Cover versions by eighties garage bands followed: *Yeah* by Thee Fourgiven (on the *Battle Of The Garages Vol. III* comp, 1984) and Italy's Sick Rose (*The Exploding Underground* comp, 1988); *No Reason To Complain* by The Lyres (*Lyres Lyres* LP, 1986) and Mystic Eyes (*Our Time To Leave* LP, 1988). With further compilation appearances of *No Reason To Complain* on the *Acid Dreams Epitaph* CD and *Acid Dreams - The Complete 3 LP Set*, and both tracks also appearing on *Garage Kings* (Dble LP), this rare 45 became a holy grail for garage collectors.

So who were these guys? A brief synopsis of the comprehensive history unveiled on the Norton release follows: - Parma, a suburb of Cleveland, Ohio, in 1964; Bruce Boehm got bitten by the Beatle bug, picked up a guitar and formed The Perceptions with drummer Tim Douglas and bassist Jeff Suveges. In 1965 he left for a steady gig with another Parma group, **The Night People**. Nearby neighbour Mike Pierce persuaded him to start a group revelling in the wilder sounds of the Stones, Kinks, Who and Animals. With Bill Schwark on drums, the moptop trio called themselves **The Alarm Clocks**. Once they began to get local gigs Boehm quit **The Night People**. In Spring 1966 they recorded their 45 at a small Cleveland studio, SIR - 200 or so copies of the 45 eventually arrived on their personally chosen label in August 1966. They returned to SIR soon after to record gig-gettin' demos featuring raw'n'savage covers of *Louie Louie*, *Money*, *It's All Over Now*, *Bald-Headed Woman*, *I'm Alright*, *She's About A Mover*, and *Route 66*. When vocalist Frank Recsik joined in the Summer of '67 they became known as The Purple Haze. At the end of the year Boehm quit and was replaced again by Bob Kalamasz (his successor in The Perceptions). Rick Caon (later of **The Choir**) joined for the last incarnation, as The Looking Glass. Subsequently Schwark and Kalamasz would team up with Bill Constable in the embryonic **Damnation Of Adam Blessing**.

Norton's fine twelve-track retrospective *Yeah!* gathers the original 45 and the aforementioned 1966 demos, plus three basement recordings from 1965 by The Perceptions - *Wipe Out*, *I'm A Fool* and *Tree Stump Theme*. The latter was a tribute to local heroes The Tree Stumps whose rendition of the Kinks' *All Day And All Of The Night* at a local shindig in February 1965 was the inspiration for Boehm, transforming his musical aspirations and setting him on the route that wound up as The Alarm Clocks (oof!). (MW)

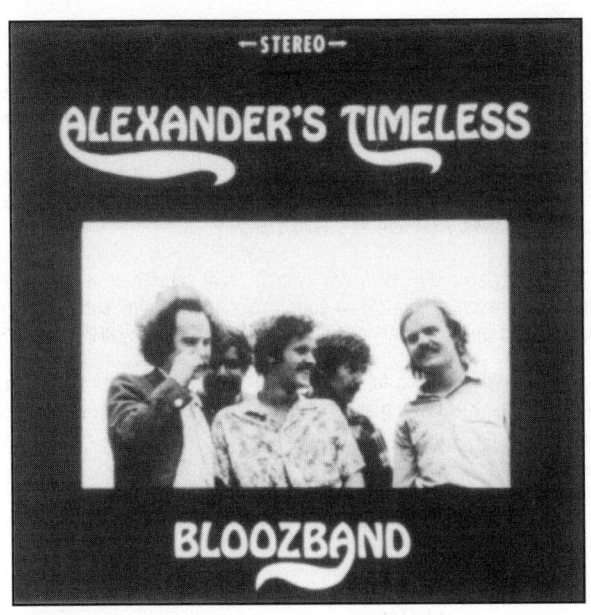

ALEXANDER'S TIMELESS BLOOZBAND - Self Titled LP.

Dick and Anne Albin

| Personnel incl: | ANNE ALBIN | vcls, banjo, autoharp dulcimer, jawharp | A |
| | DICK ALBIN | vcls, gtr, dulcimer mandolin | A |

ALBUMS: 1( ) MAHATMA GANDHI SPAT HERE (Phonygraph ADA 1) 1973 -
2( ) !QUE ASCO! (Phonygraph ADA 2) 1974 -
3( ) REDROSE, GREEN BRIARS AND MILK WHITE STEEDS (Phonygraph ADA 3) 1975 -
4( ) NO COMMERCIAL APPEAL (Phonygraph ADA 5) 1976? -

All albums feature traditional American folk music and quirky originals by this husband and wife hippie duo from Kentucky. Though no longer a couple, both are still actively making music. In particular, Anne McFie, as she now is known, has become a successful (predominately country) songwriter and nationally known UFO researcher. (HS/SR)

Albino Gorilla

ALBUM: 1 DETROIT 1984 (Kama Sutra KSBS 2028) 1970 -

Housed in a strange sleeve with a perforated silhouette of an albino gorilla, comes this album of psych soul, with various covers: *Going To A Go Go*, **Blues Project**'s *Wake Me Shake Me*, and at least two tracks from their main influence, the Temptations: *Psychedelic Shack* and *Cloud Nine*. (SR)

Aldermen

45: House Of Wax / ? (Sir Graham 102) c1966

An excellent fuzz garage-punker from Los Angeles' East Side, that can be appreciated at last on the *Rampart Records EP* along with **Cannibal & The Headhunters** and the **Atlantics** (Dionysus/Bacchus BA05, 1995). Originally compiled on the 1969 double-album *East Side Revue* (Rampart 3303), the track was written by Chick Carlton, who had performed as Chick Carlton & The Majestics before turning to writing for other local acts including the **Sunday Funnies** and the Enchantments. (MW)

Gordon Alexander

ALBUM: 1 GORDON'S BUSTER (Columbia CS 9693) 1968 SC

A Californian singer whose sole album was produced by **Curt Boettcher** and released at the same time as the **Millennium** *Begin* album. It contains the wonderfully titled *A Bunch Of Us Were Sitting Around A Candle In San Francisco Getting Stoned And I Hope You're There Next Time* plus *Windy Wednesday*, *Thinking In Indian* or *Topanga*. Some dealers compare it to **Skip Spence**'s *Oar*, but we haven't heard it yet. (SR)

Alexander Rabbit

Personnel:	CHARLES BRODOWICZ	gtr, keyb'ds	A
	LEN DEMSKI	bs	A
	ALAN FOWLER	drms	A
	CHRIS HOLMES (DUKE WILLIAMS)	gtr, keyb'ds	A
	STEVE SHIER	vcls	A

ALBUM: 1(A) THE HUNCHBACK OF NOTRE DAME (THE BELLS WERE MY FRIENDS) (Mercury SR 61291) 1970 -

This band was based in New Jersey and was previously known as **The Galaxies IV**, and their most popular live song was a version of the Spanish classic *Malaguenia*.

Their album has been sadly neglected and is an excellent melodic psych/progressive cross-over item, with some similarities to **Gandalf**. Recorded in New York's Associated Recording Studios, the album was co-produced by Irving Spice and Max Ellen (the eccentric Jerry Samuels (aka **Napoleon XIV**) engineering). In spite of the goofy title, the collection of original material (a rote cover of Otis Redding's *I've Been Loving You Too Long* being the one exception), was diverse and surprisingly engaging. While the extended title track bogged down in Procol Harum-meets-Tolkien art-rock mysticism (not a pretty combination), elsewhere the band displayed considerable versatility, capably polishing off nifty rockers (the scorching *Goin' Down*), **Association**-styled ballads (*My Woman*) and decent pop-rock (*Faraway Man*). While it wasn't the year's most consistent release, the fact it was so diverse was part of its charm. Well worth looking for and you can still find the LP at a decent price.

Credits on the album are limited to song-writing, and as Alan Fowler left the group just prior to the album photo shoot he is not pictured on the back sleeve.

Their guitar player, Chris Holmes, later went on to form **Duke Williams and The Extremes** together with drummer Hank Ransom, from the Philadephia group **Elizabeth** and T.J. Tindall of the **Edison Electric Band**. They released at least two albums. Alan Fowler went on to Pickins who released an album on the Ariola America in 1978. The album was produced by T.J. Tindall with guest appearances by TJ and Chris Holmes (a.k.a. Duke Williams). Fowler is now running his new publishing company "River Towne Music". Duke Williams currently plays in The Paul Plumeri Blues Band. (VJ/FHy/SB/SR/RMh)

Alexander's Rock Time Band

45: Number One Hippie On The Village Scene/ The Travel Song (J&T 2022) 1967

This 45 was by **The Coachmen**. They later became **Professor Morrison's Lollipop**. See the **Coachmen** entry for further details.

Alexander's Timeless Bloozband

Personnel:	CHARLES LAMONT	A
	C. LOCKHART	A
	L. MARKS	A

ALBUMS: 1(A) ALEXANDER'S TIMELESS BLOOZBAND (Smack 1001) 1967 R2
2(A) FOR SALE (Uni 73021) 1968 SC

45s: α Love So Strong / Horn Song (Matamat 101) 1967
Maybe Baby / Maybe Baby (Kapp K 967) 1967

NB: α also released on Uni (55044) 1967. They probably released other 45s.

A bluesy outfit with some psychedelic influence. Charles Lamont also released a solo album in 1969, *A Legend In His Own Time* (Uni 73076),

A FISTFUL OF FUZZ (Comp CD) including The Aliens.

which consists of melodic psych/pop with orchestrations. All the songs were written by Lamont and it features a version of *Love So Strong* which can also be found on the **Alexander's Timeless Bloozband** *For Sale* album. Both albums were produced by Tony Cary, but Lamont's solo effort cannot be recommended.

The second 45 was a cover of the Buddy Holly/Norman Petty classic. (VJ/CF/SR)

The Alibi

45: Sunshine/Oh She Was A Beautiful Woman (Dody DO 335) 1968

Thought to be from New England, this flower-pop 45 may be of interest. Seen described as 'trippy pop-psych' - *Sunshine* is uplifting harmonious pop, with maybe just a psychy tinge. The flip is also pleasant pop with interesting time changes and warbling keyboards. Produced by Dody Sinclair, both sides were composed by Mike Christy and arranged by Tony Mazza, Dave Rossi and Mike Christy. (MW)

Alien City

ALBUM: 1 ALIEN CITY (Dog Star Productions) c1974 SC

A strange album about extra-terrestrial visitors, recorded by a hippie group from the Seattle area, with male/female vocals, trippy lyrics and rather loose songs. (SR)

Alien Nation

ALBUM: 1 EAT THE DAY (Private Pressing) 1970 SC

A hippie-folk group with good vocals. (SR)

The Aliens

Personnel:	NICKY BONIS	organ	A
	DOUG COWARD	bs	A
	JOHN DAVIS	ld gtr	A
	CONRAD DEDACATORIA	drms	A
	STEVE GREEN	gtr	A
	GAYLE "POONEIL" HOLLOWMAN	vcls	A
	ROBBIE HOUSE	vcls	A
	BILL SECHMAN	vcls	A

45s:	Come Fly With Me / Season Of The Witch	(Son Of A Witch 1801) c1968
	Love Someone / Tobacco Road	(Telastar 1401) c1968

An octet from Norfolk, Virginia who were strongly influenced by the "San Francisco sound", especially **Jefferson Airplane**. *Love Someone*, an uptempo pop-rocker with **Airplane**-style vocals and heavy acidic guitar, is featured on *Aliens, Psychos And Wild Things* (CD).

The first 45 *Come Fly With Me* was a local hit. Their arrangement of Donovan's *Season of The Witch* adds a nightmarish atmosphere and more heavily fuzzed guitar - it lies in wait on *A Fistful Of Fuzz*. (BHr/ST/MW)

Aliotta Haynes

Personnel incl:	MITCH ALIOTTA	gtr, bs, vcls	A
	TED ALIOTTA	bs, vcls	A
	SKIP HAYNES	bs, gtr, vcls	A

ALBUM: 1(A) MUSIC (Ampex 10108) 1970 -

From Illinois, a psychedelic rock group with songs like *Rockefeller's Blues* and *Uppers And Downers*. After this album they met John Jeremiah and became the imaginatively named **Aliotta Haynes Jeremiah**.

Mitch Aliotta previously played with **Rotary Connection**. (SR)

Aliotta Haynes Jeremiah

Personnel:	MITCH ALIOTTA	gtr, bs, vcls	ABC
	TED ALIOTTA	bs, vcls	A CD
	SKIP HAYNES	bs, gtr, vcls	ABC
	JOHN JEREMIAH	keyb'ds, vcls	ABC
	RON ZETA	drms	A
	BOB PARISIO	drms, vcls	B
	DENNY SEIWELL	drms	

ALBUMS:	1(A)	ALIOTTA HAYNES JEREMIAH	(Ampex 10119) 1970 -
	2(B)	LAKE SHORE DRIVE	(Big Foot 714) c1971 SC
	3(C)	SLIPPIN AWAY	(Little Foot 711) c1972 -

Based in Chicago, this group recorded three albums which still have to attract attention from collectors. In 1975, they teamed up with **Harvey Mandel** and became **Acme Thunder**.

Their occasional drummer, Denny Seiwell, went on to play with Paul McCartney in the Wings and became a session man. In 1970, John Jeremiah also played organ on *Message To The Young*, one of the "psychedelized" albums by Howlin' Wolf. (SR)

Alive 'n' Kickin'

Personnel:	VITO ALBANO	drms	A
	PEPE CARDONA	vcls	A
	JOHN PARISIO	gtr	A
	BRUCE SUDANO	keyb'ds	A
	SANDY TODLER	vcls	A
	THOMAS WILSON	bs	A

ALBUM: 1(A) ALIVE 'N' KICKIN' (Roulette SR-45052) 1970 129 - HCP

45s:	Tighter, Tighter/Sunday Morning	(Roulette 7078) 1970 7
	Just Let It Come/ ?	(Roulette) 1970 69

As a New York City based sextet, **Alive 'n Kickin'** started their careers playing the city's club circuit. Their initial break came when they attracted the attention of **Tommy James** of Shondells fame. Impressed by the band he offered to help them record a song he'd recently written. In true indian giver form, before they could record *Crystal Blue Persuasion* **James** withdrew the offer (**James and the Shondells** releasing it themselves). Redeeming himself, in its place **James** offered the band another track titled *Tighter And Tighter*.

Feeling that the song was overly commercial, the band was initially reluctant to record the track. They ultimately relented recording it as a single for Roulette (**James**' label). With the song generating considerable attention, Roulette Records rushed the band into the studio to record a supporting album. Produced by **James** and Bob King, the *Alive 'n Kickin'* proved a minor surprise. Anyone hearing *Tighter And Tighter* (let along looking at the fun-in-the-sun album cover), would have justifiably concluded these guys were little more than a top-40 pop band. Wrong conclusion. Powered by Todler's tough voice (her bluesy delivery occasionally bore a startling resemblance to **Joplin** - check out *Kentucky Fire*), the set of largely original material rocked with impressive energy. While it may not have made for the year's most original set, tracks such as *Junction Creek* and *Mississippi Mud* saw the group displaying a penchant for above average blues-rock.

In 1976, Cardona, Albano and Wilson briefly reformed the band and began playing New York clubs doing top 40 covers. Sudano reappeared as a member of Brooklyn Dreams and married disco diva Donna Summers.

Tommy James and Bob King also produced **Neon**. (SR/SB)

Davie Allan and The Arrows

Personnel:
DAVIE ALLAN	ld gtr		AB
LARRY BROWN	drms		A
PAUL JOHNSON	gtr		A
STEVE PUGH	bs		A
TONY ALLWINE	gtr		B
DREW BENNETT	bs		B
DON MANNING	drms		B

NB: **Davie Allan** has confirmed that Paul Johnson wasn't really in the band but was grabbed to fill out a publicity shot. Both he and Steve Pugh did play on two released tracks however: *Dance The Freddie* (the flip to *Moondawg '65*)and *I'm Looking Over A Four Leaf Clover"* (the flip to *Baby Ruth*).

HCP

ALBUMS:
1( ) APACHE '65 (Tower (D)T-5002) 1965 - SC
2( ) THE WILD ANGELS (Soundtrack) (Tower (D)T-5043) 1966 17 SC
3( ) THE WILD ANGELS VOL. 2 (Soundtrack) (Tower (D)T-5056) 1967 94 SC
4( ) DEVIL'S ANGELS (Soundtrack) (Tower (D)T-5074) 1967 165 SC
5( ) BLUES THEME (Tower (D)T-5078) 1967 - R1
6( ) MONDO HOLLYWOOD (Soundtrack) (Tower (D)T-5083) 1968 - -
7( ) CYCLEDELIC SOUNDS (Tower (D)T-5094) 1968 - SC
8( ) THE HELLCATS (Soundtrack) (Tower ST-5124) 1968 - SC
9( ) WILD RACERS (Soundtrack) (Sidewalk ST-5914) 1969 - SC

NB: (2) reissued on CD.

SONGS WE TAUGHT THE FUZZTONES (Comp CD) including Davie Allan.

HCP

45s:
α War Path / Beyond The Blue (Cude 101) 1963 -
α War Path / Beyond The Blue (Marc 107) 1963 -
Apache '65 / Blue Guitar (Sidewalk 1) 1964 -
Apache '65 / Blue Guitar (Tower 116) 1965 64
Moondawg '65 / Dance The Freddie (Tower 133) 1965 -
Baby Ruth/
I'm Looking Over A Four Leaf Clover (Tower 142) 1965 -
Space Hop / Granny Goose (Tower 158) 1965 -
Theme From The Wild Angels / U.F.O. (Tower 267) 1966 99
Blues Theme/Bongo Party (Tower 295) 1967 37
χ Angel With A Devil's Heart / I'm Leavin' ( ) 1967 -
Devil's Angels / Cody's Theme (Tower 341) 1967 -
Blue Rides Again / Cycle-Delic (Tower 381) 1967 97
Shape Of Things To Come /
Wild In The Streets (Tower 446) 1968 -
α It's The Little Things You Do/You And Me (MGM 14299) 1971 -
α Head Over Heels / Here It Comes (MGM 14374) 1972 -
β Dawn Of The 7th Cavalry /
Little Big Horn (MGM 14432) 1972 -
β Dawn At Wounded Knee / Little Big Horn (MGM 14432) 1972 -
α Pleasure Girl / And Evil Did Too (MGM 14560) 1973 -
β Apache '73 / Run Of The Arrow (MGM 14650) 1973 -
α White Man Beware/
Where Do We Go From Here (Aoa 113) 1976 -
Stoked On Surf / Outer Surf (What 12-601) 1982 -
Stoked On Christmas / Flashback (Macola MRC-0901) 1984 -
Chopper / Open Throttle (In The Red ITR 0381) 1995 -
The Born Losers Theme / The Glory Stompers ( ) 19?? -

NB: α as Davie Allan. β as The Arrows. χ unreleased. There are also two rare French EPs with picture sleeves: *Apache '65/Blue Guitar/Red Roses For A Blue Lady/Indian River* (Capitol EAP 60000) 1965 and *Theme From The Wild Angels/Rockin' Angel/Blues Theme/Bongo Party* (Capitol EAP 405043) 1967.

A mid to late sixties instrumental band from Hollywood, California. They specialised in doing a lot of soundtracks and there may have been a connection with **Max Frost and The Troopers**. In September 1967, *Blues Theme*, taken from the *The Wild Angels* film soundtrack reached No 37 in the U.S. charts.

Larry Brown later played with **The Moon** and Tony Allwine (aka Wayne Allwine) took up the long-standing role as the third official voice for "Mickey Mouse"!

In the nineties **Davie Allan** made at least two further albums: *Fuzz Fest* (Total Energy NER 3016) 1998, and *Loud Loose And Savage* (Dionysus ID123368), 1999. Still an amazing guitar player, with his trademark, a rich sustaining fuzz tone sound. He was inspired particularly by Duane Eddy, The Ventures' Nokie Edwards and Henry Mancini, whose songs are nearly the only covers he includes in his recent live and recorded work.

Compilation appearances have so far included: *Blues Theme*, *Cycle-Delic* and *Mind Transferral* on *Angel Dust - Music For Movie Bikers* (LP); *Moonfire* on *Mondo Hollywood* (LP); *Blues Theme* on *Battle Of The Bands* (CD), *Nuggets Box* (4-CD) and *Songs We Taught The Fuzztones* (Dble LP & Dble CD); and *Glory Stompers* on *The Glory Stompers* (LP). (MW/CMn/VJ/JR/SR)

Beau Allen

45s:
α My Time / See Her Honey (Instr) (Allen Records 1001) 1968
α I Hope You're Proud /
Dreamin' (PS) (Allen Records 1008) 1968
β Stand By Me/That's All I Want (Allen) 1968
Part Of Me /
What A Love Can Do (HFA International 1012) 1968
Fallen Angel / Pusher Man (HFA International #1013) 1968
My Time / Waiting For Me (HFA International #1014) 1969
My Time / Waiting For Me (Scepter 12247) 1969
Give Me Your Love /
What A Love Can Do (HFA International #1016/#1012) 1970
Georgia Ground /
Fallen Angel (HFA Internatioanl #1016/#1013) 1970

NB: α as **Bo Allen**. β as **Bo and The Weevils**

A Vidalia, Georgia artist who recorded as **Beau Allen**, Bo Allen and Bo And The Weevils. A borderline inclusion - his material covers a wide variety of styles taking in early sixties sounding ballads, cabaret/club sounds, teen-beat, through straight pop and rock. His choice and most relevant cuts have been compiled - *I Hope You're Proud* on on *Psychedelic States: Georgia Vol. 1* (CD) and *Kicks & Chicks* (which mentions that he also put out a "Best of, 8 track") and *Give Me Your Love* - a good garagey-pop number which sounds more like 1966 than 1970 - on *The Garage Zone Vol. 1* and *The Garage Zone Box Set*. Of possible interest is *Georgia Ground*, a fine pop-rocker with flowing lead, use of wah-wah and a tinge of country. (MW/SR)

Chris Allen and The Good-Timers

| 45: | My Imagination / Sorry 'Bout That | (New World) 1967 |

A little known band from Indiana. Their cool fuzz-punker *My Imagination* has also been included on *Garage Punk Unknowns, Vol. 8*, whilst the flip also appears on *Hang It Out To Dry*. (VJ/MW)

Steve Allen and The Gentle Players

ALBUM: 1 STEVE ALLEN AND THE GENTLE PLAYERS
(Dunhill DS50021) 1967 SC

NB: (1) also released in Canada.

A jazzy flower power pop album, with "groovy" songs like *Here Comes Sgt. Pepper*, *So Nice*, *San Francisco (Be Sure to Wear Some Flowers In Your Hair)*, *Something Stupid*, *Groovin'*, *Flowers And Love*, *59th Street Song* and *Flower Revolution*. It was recorded with the help of **Gabor Szabo** and **Hal Blaine**. (SR)

Alley Cats

| 45: | Cut Loose / Big Pigalle | (Verna 501) 1965 |

These Alley Cats were from Houston, Texas. They also recorded as the Terrible Teens, London Teens and **Bad Habits** - their bad habit being that they couldn't stick with one name. (MW)

Alley Cats

| 45: | I Should Have Stayed At Home Tonight/ Lily Of The West | (Epic 9778) 1965 |

Produced and written/co-written by Ted Varnick, this 45 is swingin' beat-pop with a hint of country and plenty of attitude and swagger. Ted Varnick was based in The Bronx, New York and had a hand in the 45 by **The Descendents**, who were from Yonkers. It seems likely that **The Alley Cats** were from NYC too. (MW/MM)

The Alliance

| 45: | (I'm Not Your) Steppin' Stone/ Somewhere They Can't Find Me | (Americana 1003) 196? |

A cool fuzzy cover of **Boyce and Hart**'s, *Steppin' Stone* and a competent stab at Simon & Garfunkel's classic on the other side. From Ruston, Louisiana, both tracks have also resurfaced on *Sixties Rebellion, Vol. 14* (LP & CD). (VJ)

Allies

| 45s: | I'll Sell My Soul / Burning Flask | (Valiant V-748) 1966 |
| | I Would Love You / Sound Of Children | (Reprise 0674) 1968 |

A Los Angeles area outfit. *I'll Sell My Soul* is a superb moody folk-punker, whilst the flip, *Burning Flask* is very **Byrdsy** with delightful harmonies and a swaying beat. Recommended for **Byrds**-spotters and **Dovers** fans everywhere. It has yet to be established whether the Reprise 45 is by the same group.

Compilation appearances have so far included: *I'll Sell My Soul* on *Punk Classics, Vol. 3* (7" EP), *Punk Classics* (CD), *Sixties Rebellion, Vol. 14* (LP & CD) and *Acid and Flowers* (CD). (MW)

Keith Allison

ALBUM: 1 IN ACTION (Columbia CL-2641) 1966 SC

45s:	I Ain't Blamin' You/?	(CBS 43619) 1966
	Action, Action, Action/?	(CBS 43900) 1966
	Birds Of A Feather/?	(CBS 44853) 1969
	Everybody/?	(CBS 45115) 1970

Keith Allison was the star of the popular TV Show 'Where The Action Is'. His album *In Action* was produced by Gary Usher and contains garage songs recorded with **Paul Revere and The Raiders**, who were regulars on his TV show.

Allison also recorded with **Dennis Ezba** and **The Unknowns**, before joining the '**Raiders** in the seventies. (SR)

Duane and Greg Allman

| Personnel incl: | DUANE ALLMAN | gtr | A |
| | GREG ALLMAN | vcls, keyb'ds | A |

ALBUM: 1(A) DUANE AND GREG ALLMAN (Bold 33-301) 1970 SC

NB: (1) released in two different sleeves designs: a color gatefold and a black and white one.

| 45: | α Morning Dew/I'll Change For You | (Bold 200) 1971 |

NB: α double sided promos on red vinyl exist.

An album issued to cash in the **Allman Brothers Band** success. It's composed of tracks recorded after the demise of **Hourglass**, when both brothers had returned to Florida.

The best tracks are an excellent cover of *Morning Dew* and *I'll Change For You*. Curiously, some tracks have a very poor sound and are in fact other versions of **Hourglass** tracks with new titles and composers (*Come Down And Get Me* credited to Ray Gerald is in fact *Down In Texas* by Eddie Hinton).

The recordings were made originally as demos with the backing by **31st Of February**, who the brothers were jamming with at the time. The band are not credited however, because they contracted to Vanguard by the time the album appeared.

Bold was a small Florida label from Hialeah, run by Steve Alaimo. (SR/NK)

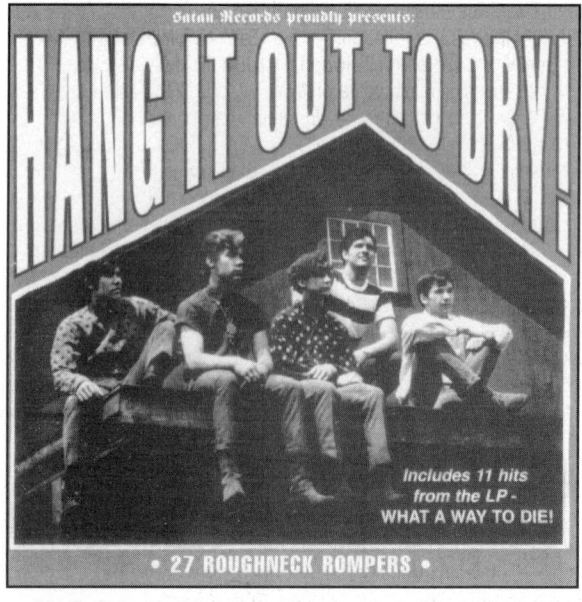

HANG IT OUT TO DRY (Comp CD) including Chis Allen and The Goodtimers.

ALL OF THUS - All Of Thus LP.

Allman Brothers Band

Personnel:	DUANE ALLMAN	ld gtr	ABC
	GREGG ALLMAN	organ, ld vcls	ABC
	DICKY BETTS	ld gtr	ABC
	JAI JOHANNY JOHANSON	drms	ABC
	BERRY OAKLEY	bs	ABC
	BUTCH TRUCKS	drms, perc	ABC
	THOM DOUCETTE	hrmnca	B

HCP

ALBUMS: 1(A)	THE ALLMAN BROTHERS BAND		
(up to		(Atco SD33-308)	1969 188 -
1972) 2(B)	IDLEWILD SOUTH	(Atco SD33-342)	1970 38 -
3(B)	LIVE AT FILLMORE EAST (dble)		
		(Capricorn 2802)	1971 13 -
4(C)	EAT A PEACH	(Capricorn 2CP0102)	1972 4 -

NB: All these albums have been reissued on vinyl and CD. (3) issued in Quad with alternate recordings (Capricorn CX4-0131) 1974, this is in the R1 category.

HCP

45s:	Black Hearted Woman/		
(up to	Every Hungry Woman	(Capricorn 8003)	1971 -
1972)	Leave My Blues At Home/Revival	(Capricorn 8011)	1971 92
	Whipping Post/Midnight Rider	(Capricorn 8014)	1971 -

After **Hourglass**, Duane and Gregg Allman teamed up in 1969 with Butch Trucks of the **Thirty-first of February**, Berry Oakley and Dick Betts (from **Second Coming**) and Jay Johanny Johanson. **The Allman Brothers Band** was essentially a blues-rock fusion act with some country and even classical influences. Fired by Duane Allman's inventive lead and slide guitar work, and supported by their two drummers (an idea probably inspired by the **Grateful Dead**), the group soon became very popular, especially in the South (they were established near Macon, Georgia).

Their first album was released in 1969 and recorded in New York by Adrian Barber. It contains five Gregg Allman originals plus a Muddy Waters cover and *Don't Wan't You No More* by Spencer Davis. The inside of the gatefold sleeve shows the group naked, sitting in a river.

Reinforced by Thom Doucette, a bluesy harmonica player, *Idlewild South* was recorded in Macon, Miami and New York and produced by Tom Dowd and Joel Dorn. All their material was original, except a version of Willie Dixon's *Hoochie Coochie Man*.

Their third album, the double *Live At Fillmore East*, is one of the greatest live sets ever and was recorded in New York in 1971. With only seven cuts, two of them over 19 minutes, there are no wasted notes and no useless jams. It helped secure the **Allman Brothers Band** reputation as a hot live act second only perhaps to the **Grateful Dead**.

The follow-up, *Eat A Peach* was also a double album, partly recorded live. It is notable for the 34 minute jam of Donovan's *First There Is A Mountain*, which takes up two sides of the album. The inside gatefold is a psychedelic drawing with magic mushrooms and various hallucinations.

Duane Allman died in 1971 and Berry Oakley in 1972, both in motorcycle accidents in the same Georgia area. The group's subsequent releases are more Southern Rock and country-oriented and are out of scope of this book. (SR)

Allman Joys

Personnel:	MIKE ALEXANDER	bs	A
	DUANE ALLMAN	ld gtr	A
	GREGG ALLMAN	organ, gtr, ld vcls	A
	BILL CONNELL (CONNEL)	drums	A
	(TOMMY AMATO	drms	A)
	(RALPH BALLINGER	bs	A)
	(BOBBY DENNIS	gtr	A)
	(JACK JACKSON	gtr	A)
	(RONNIE WILKINS	piano	A)

ALBUM: 1(A) EARLY ALLMAN   (DIAL DL 6005) 1973 SC

NB: (1) also sometimes seen as *The Allman Joys*. (1) also issued in France (Mercury) 197?.

45: α Spoonful /You Deserve Each Other   (Dial 4046) 1966

NB: α 'B' side is non-LP.

Duane Allman was born in 1946 and grew up in Nashville with his brother Gregg. In 1958 the Allmans moved South to Daytona Beach, Florida. They formed several groups (the Y-Teens, the House Rockers) and finally the **Allman Joys**. In 1966, **John D.Loudermilk**, the songwriter (*Tobacco Road*) heard them playing live in a small Nashville club, the Briar Patch, and decided to take them into the studio to cut some sides. One of these, a psychedelic version of Willie Dixon's *Spoonful*, was released locally as a single on Buddy Killen's Dial label and sold well locally. They returned to the studio to record more tunes but the album was shelved when the band toured the South for several months and broke up upon the formation of **Hourglass**. It was eventually released in 1973 to cash in the **Allman Brothers** success...

The album has clear blues and R&B influences which permeate these early efforts, especially in Gregg's strong emotive vocals, but some of this material has a garageey edge to it, most notably on Gregg's own compositions; - *Gotta Get Away*, a spirited fuzzy thumper; *You'll Learn Someday* - a wistful jangley folk-rocker ala **Beau Brummels**; *Doctor Fone Bone* - a raucous rocker sounding like an early **Golliwogs/Creedence**. Their version of *Spoonful* is more uptempo than usual and features some hot fuzz runs from Duane.

The personnel listed without parenthesis is the four-man line-up that gigged as the **Allman Joys** and who recorded the Dial 45. The additional "members" shown appeared on studio recordings, Ronnie Wilkins, for example, was a session player who co-wrote tons of songs with John Hurley and others... just check out the *Gentry Time* album by **The Gentrys** for five Wilkins songs on one album alone!

Brian Connell later played with **The Rubberband**. (MW/SR/JLh)

The All Night Workers

Personnel incl: LLOYD BASKIN   A

45: Why Don't You Smile?/
     Don't Put All Your Eggs In One Basket (Round Sound 1) 1965

Both tracks on this 45 were written by a pre-**Velvet Underground** Lou Reed and John Cale together with a guy called Vance and another called Terry Phillips. Phillips had been an early collaborator with Phil Spector, and was at this time in charge of Pickwick, who occasionally put out singles like this and *The Ostrich* by the Reed's The Primitives. Phillips also worked with the **Hobbits** and several other New York groups.

It may be that **The All Night Workers** were college mates of Lou Reed, and for certain the band had a large following from Fall 1966 through to Spring 1967 at Syracuse University, where they used to perform with a black soul-singer as **Otis and The All Night Workers**. It has also been suggested that some members of **The Blues Magoos** were in this act. Most of them moved to New York and formed **The Albert** who released LPs on Perception. Lloyd Baskin was later in **Seatrain**.

Why Don't You Smile? is a very appealing song, great vocals (rather soulful) and lots of commercial appeal. It was later covered by the U.K. Downliners Sect, but you can hear the original on *Mayhem & Psychosis, Vol. 1* (LP) and *Mayhem & Psychosis, Vol. 1* (CD). (VJ/MW/MKk/JFr/CWs/SR)

All Of Thus

Personnel:	DON CORBIT	gtr, bs	A
	BARRY DALGLEISH	drms	A
	JERRY HEUKENSFELD	organ, piano	A
	JOHN JOHNSTON	gtr, piano, organ	A

ALBUM: 1(A)   ALL OF THUS   (Century 27916) 1966 R3

NB: (1) reissued on Rockadelic (RRLP 11.5) 1994 SC.

A late sixties garage rarity, which was reissued by Rockadelic in 1994. There are a few competent cover versions (Roger McGuinn's *Bells Of Rhymney*, Stevie Winwood's *Keep On Running*, and Bacharach & David's *Walk On By*), and lots of originals penned by John Johnston. These range from good organ driven garage punkers like *Last Night* and *Bye Bye Baby* to catchy garage ballads like *Kind Of A Dream, Just A Little* and *Artificial Lies*, which seem to be their speciality. A New York band. (MW/VJ)

All Saved Freak Band

Personnel incl:	DAVE BECKER	gtr
	MIKE BURKEY	bs
	ED DURKIS	gtr
	TOM ERITANO	drms
	ROB GALBRAITH	vcls
	LARRY HILL	piano, vcls
	TIM HILL	perc
	PHIL KEAGGY	gtr
	CAROL KING	organ, vcls
	MORGAN KING	bs
	JOE MARKKO	gtr, vcls
	RANDY MARKKO	bs
	KIM MASSMANN	violin, gtr, vcls
	PAM MASSMANN	cello, gtr, vcls
	NORRIS McCLURE	gtr, vcls
	THOMAS MILLER	vcls
	GLENN SCHWARTZ	gtr, vcls
	DANA VANDERNIC	drms

ALBUMS: 1( )   MY POOR GENERATION
  (Rock The World Enterprises Records NR 7825) 1973 R2
2( )   FOR CHRISTIANS, ELVES AND LOVERS
  (Rock The World Enterprises Records LP ASFB 1001) 1976 SC
3( )   BRAINWASHED   (Rock The World NR 5974) 1976 SC

NB: (1) reissued on vinyl 1976 (R2) and CD (Hidden Vision) 199?. There's also *Sower War Again* LH 818 8) 1981, a collection of non-LP recordings 1971-6; and a limited edition 50 copy CD *Anthology 1973-81*.

The **All Saved Freak Band** evolved from an outfit called Preacher And The Witness Band. Formed by Larry Hill and Joe Markko, they played a mix of gospel, Christian rock, heavy blues and psychedelic folk with female vocals. Their albums are sought-after by some collectors now.

Two early members Miller and Randy Markko were killed in a car crash in 1971. It was at this time that the band members moved from Kent State to a five acre farm in Orwell, Ohio.

ALL SAVED FREAK BAND - My Poor Generation CD.

Glenn Schwartz was previously in The Pilgrims in 1964, **The James Gang** and **Pacific, Gas and Electric**. He later spent some time in a mental institution, when Phil Keaggy filed in on guitar.

In the early nineties Larry Hill, Laura Markko, and Pam and Kim Massmann were still living on the farm. Glenn Schwartz still gigs regularly and is recognised as a guitar legend in Cleveland and often preaches in an evangelical style during his shows. (SR/RMh)

All That The Name Implies

Personnel:	ALLAN BREE	gtr, vcls, hrmnca	A
	NICK FEVA	12-string gtr, vcls	A
	ROY JIMINEZ	vcls	A
	MELINDA PARKES	vcls	A
	MARLENE RYAN	vcls	A
	(EMILE LATIMOR	congas	A)

ALBUM: 1(A)   ALL THAT THE NAME IMPLIES   (ORO ORO-4) 1968 R1

45s: Black Tuesday/So Am I   (Oro 45-2) 1968
  Liar/August Pine   (Oro 45-3) 1968

This five-piece folkie collective, augmented by Emile Latimor on congas, produced an album and two 45s on this little known ESP subsidiary. The album rarely turns up - actually, its existence wasn't even suspected until it popped up on a list in 2000. The 45s are less elusive - only *Black Tuesday* is a non-LP track, though others are alternate versions.

Their sound is mellowed-out and distinct - gruff male vocals intertwine with sweet female and male harmonies over laid-back strumming and congas, with occasional flute or tambourine. Religious references and a 'back to the woods' vibe push this into the flower-children/hippie zone of the folk spectrum. (MW)

Tandyn Almer

45:   Degeneration Gap/
  Snippin' The Silver Chord   (Warner Bros. 7446) c1969

A California songwriter, pianist and producer, **Tandyn Almer** was in the first line-up of the **Association** and wrote *Along Came Mary* as well as *Message Of Our Love*, both with the assistance of **Curt Boettcher**. He also penned *Musty Dusty* for **Sagittarius**.

Between 1966 and 1970 he produced several harmony pop and soft psychedelic acts like the **Paper Fortress** and **Dennis Olivieri**. He is also reputedly credited for the invention of a sophisticated "bong waterpipe"!

His only single is sadly not very interesting. (SR)

Alphabetical Order

Personnel incl: MIKE CROSBY
FRED DAVIDSON
BOB LAMAR
BOB McDANIEL
RICHARD PERRYMAN

45s:	Under My Thumb/My Little Red Book	(Lemco LEM 4402) 1967
	All Over The World/ Miss Blue Eyes	(Rising Sons RS 45-710) 1968
	All Over The World/ Gonna Fight The War	(Soul Boulevard 1002) 1968

From Louisville, Kentucky, their first 45 is quite sought-after. Both sides are keyboard-led garage with moody and soul-infected vocals. *Under My Thumb* is a decent jerker with sinuous reedy runs, marred only by falsetto 'bah bah bah' backing vocals. *My Little Red Book* is a pretty competent stab at **Love**'s classic, and has subsequently resurfaced on *Sixties Rebellion, Vol. 8* (LP & CD). Sadly, by their second release they'd turned to a more pop/club sound. (MW)

Al's Untouchables

Personnel:	BILL ALLEY	bs	A
	RON HAMAD	vcls, gtr	A
	AL HUNTZINGER	drms	A
	BOB KEITH	keyb'ds	A
	MEL WIDENER	ld gtr	A
	RON BRESLER	drms	B
	DICKIE DOUGLAS	gtr	B
	TOMMY HANKINS	bs	B
	BRUCE NUNEMAKER	gtr	B

45s:	α	Church Key/Danny Boy	(Hunt 450) 1964
	β	Come On Baby/Stick Around	(Hunt 1140) 1966

NB: α as **Al & The Untouchables**. β as **Al's Untouchables**.

Actually a Johnny And The Hurricanes-style instrumental band from Iowa City, Iowa, but both sides of their *Come On Baby* 45 feature screaming garage-punk. Al Huntzinger played on the first 45, and was manager of the second line-up. He was also later in **The Untouchables**.

Their story is told on an excellent 1992 EP (MCCM 9102), which compiles both 45s. Other compilation appearances include:- *Come On Baby* and *Stick Around* on *Boulders, Vol. 4* (LP); and *Come On Baby* on *Teenage Shutdown, Vol. 4* (LP & CD). (VJ/MW)

Randy Alvey and The Green Fuz

Personnel:	RANDY ALVEY	vcls	A
	LES DALE	ld gtr	A
	R.E. HOUCHENS	bs	A
	JIMMY MERCER	gtr	A
	MIKE PEARCE	drms	A

45:	Green Fuz/There Is A Land	(Big Tex 445) 196?

This punk band hailed from Bridgeport in North Texas, just Northwest of Fort Worth and were for a while a popular local attraction in the area. Randy was just 15 when this single was made. Mastered on a portable reel to reel cassette and recorded in a rock constructed cafe after hours, which probably explains the echoey sound, it's hardly surprising the production sounds so crude. Only 500 copies were pressed at the time, but today, *Green Fuz* has become something of a cult classic. The flip was a ballad credited to R.E. Houchens. Minus Les Dale the band recorded again as Natchez.

More recently, *Green Fuzz* has been covered by The Cramps, the Miracle Workers, Germany's Beatitudes, the Seclusions and by Dino Sorbello's Laughing Sky on their *Free Inside* CD retitled as *Here We Come*.

Compilation appearances have so far included: *Green Fuz* on *Pebbles, Vol. 2* (LP), *Pebbles Vol. 2* (CD), *The Essential Pebbles Collection, Vol. 1* (Dble CD), *Pebbles Box* (5-LP), *Best of Pebbles, Vol. 1* (LP & CD), *Pebbles, Vol. 3* (ESD) (CD); *Great Pebbles* (CD), *Trash Box* (5-CD), *Acid Dreams Epitaph* (CD) and *Acid Dreams - The Complete 3 LP Set* (3-LP). (VJ/MW/GR)

Alzo

Personnel:	JOHN BAL	bs	A
	BOB DOROUGH	keyb'ds, perc	A
	ALZO FRONTE	gtr, vcls	AB
	BILL GOODWIN	drms	A
	STUART SCHARF	gtr	A

ALBUMS:	1(A)	ALZO	(Ampex A10130) 1971 -
	2(B)	ALZO	(Bell 6079) 1972 -

45s:	You're Gone / That's Alright	(Ampex 11052) 1971
	You've Gone / Don't Ask Me Why	(Bell 45247) 1972
	Looks Like Rain / ?	(Bell 45288) 1972

Produced and arranged by Bob Dorough (an acolyte of **Tom Rapp**), a folk rock singer/songwriter from New York, typical of the early seventies and very mellow.

Alzo Fronte had earlier been part half of the duo **Alzo and Udine**. (SR)

Alzo and Udine

ALBUM:	1	C'MON AND JOIN US	(Mercury SR 61214) c1969 -

45s:	Sitting In The Park / So Down	(Steed) 1968
	I Can't Believe It / Lead You Down That Road	(Mercury 72872) 1968
	C'mon And Join Us / Define	(Mercury 72895) 1968
	Rain/ ?	(Mercury 72933) 1969
	Hot Time In The City / All Of My Lovin'	(Mercury 72962) 1969

An obscure hippie duo with original material. **Alzo Fronte** later had a solo career. (SR)

The Amberjacks

45:	Hey Eriq! / Blue Jaunte	(Migliore CR 727661/2) 1966

Also known as Terrozoid and The Amberjacks, this outfit were from Baldwin, Long Island. Another 45 may exist featuring a track *Put You Down*.

PEBBLES Vol. 2 (Comp LP) includes Randy Alvey and The Green Fuz.

Compilation appearances have included:- *Blue Jaunt* on *Teenage Shutdown, Vol. 6* (LP & CD); and *Hey Eriq!* on *Psychedelic Unknowns, Vol. 4* (LP & CD), *Back From The Grave, Vol. 8* (CD) and *Back From The Grave, Vol. 8* (Dble LP). (MW/MM)

Ambertones

45s:		Charlena / Bandido	(GNP Crescendo 329) 1963
		Chocolate Covered Ants/One Summer Night	(Dottie 1129) 1965
	α	I Need Someone / If I Do	(Dottie 1130) 1965
		Clap Your Hands / Cruise	(Rayjack 1001) 1965
		Clap Your Hands / Cruise	(Newman 601) 1966
		I Can Only Give You Everything / I Only Have Eyes For You	(Rayjack 1002) 1966
		I Can Only Give You Everything / I Only Have Eyes For You	(Treasure Chest 001) 1966

NB: α was repressed on a pale blue label circa 1969, the original is on a dark blue label. Two further 45s may be by the same band:- *99% / You Don't Know Like I Know* (White Whale 242) 1967 and *A Million Tears / Little Bit Of Lovin'* (White Whale 302) 1969.

Los Angeles' East Side has its own very special and vibrant scene, drawing on a plethora of musical styles from its wide ethnicity. In the sixties there was a wave of mainly Hispanic bands which peaked after the British Invasion hit. Adopting rock'n'roll, pop, beat and garage sounds and flavouring them with their own musical heritage produced some fascinating and compelling results. These found an outlet on local labels like Linda, Faro, Rampart, Whittier and Chattahoochie which have been revisited in recent years by reissues, compilations and retrospectives. First division proponents of the 'East Side Sound' include **Thee Midniters**, **Cannibal & The Head Hunters** (*Land of 1,000 Dances*), and **The Premiers** (*Farmer John*). The lesser knowns now available on reissues and compilations include the **East Side Kids**, **Romancers** (aka **Smoke Rings**), Atlantics, Jaguars, Enchantments, **Sunday Funnies**, Blendells ... and the **Ambertones**, who can be heard on Rampart's 1969 double-LP compilation *East Side Revue* (*I Need Someone, I Only Have Eyes For You*) and *East Side Revue, Vol. 1* (*I Need Someone*).

Clap Your Hands is worth checking out - a fine frat-garage raver.

Recent compilations of this genre include the Dionysus/Bacchus CD *The East Side Sound* and its same-name vinyl counterpart on Telstar. Their cover of the Troggs' *I Can Only Give You Everything* can also be found on *Boulders, Vol. 4* (LP) and *Garage Punk Unknowns, Vol. 7* (LP). *If I Do* is on *Basementsville! U.S.A.*. (MW/MM)

The Amboy Dukes

Personnel:	JOHN DRAKE	vcls	AB
	STEVE FARMER	gtr	AB
	RICK LOBER	piano, organ	A
	TED NUGENT	gtr	ABCD
	DAVE PALMER	drms	ABCD
	BILL WHITE	bs	A
	GREG ARAMA	bs	BCD
	ANDY SOLOMAN	keyb'ds	BC

				HCP
ALBUMS:	1(A)	1ST ALBUM	(Mainstream 6104) 1968	183 SC
(up to	2(A)	JOURNEY TO THE CENTER OF THE MIND		
1972)			(Mainstream 6112) 1968	74 SC
	3(C)	MIGRATION	(Mainstream 6118) 1968	- -
	4(-)	THE BEST OF THE ORIGINAL AMBOY DUKES		
			(Mainstream 6125) 1969	- -
	5(D)	SURVIVAL OF THE FITTEST		
			(Polydor 24-4035) 1970	129 -
	6(D)	MARRIAGE ON THE ROCKS/ROCK BOTTOM		
			(Polydor 6073) 1970	191 -

			HCP
45s:		Baby Please Don't Go/ Psalms of Aftermath	(Mainstream 676) 1968 106
	α	Journey To The Center Of The Mind/ Mississippi Murderer	(Mainstream 684) 1968 16
		Scottish Tea/ You Talk Sunshine, I Breathe Fire	(Mainstream 693) 1968 114
	α	Good Natured Emma/Prodigal Man	(Mainstream 700) 1969 -
		For His Namesake/Loaded For Bear	(Mainstream 704) 1969 -
		Flight Of The Birds/?	(Mainstream 711) 1969 -

NB: α also released in France with a PS (Vogue INT 80140) and (London 69024).

AMBOY DUKES - First LP.

This Detroit-based group are of particular interest as their leader, Ted Nugent, later attained rock stardom. **The Amboy Dukes** attracted national attention when the title track of their second album became a U.S. Top Twenty hit. Nugent's frenzied guitar playing also made them a prime 'live' attraction, and the number that usually closed their shows, Them's U.K. hit *Baby Please Don't Go* included on their first album is also featured on *Nuggets*. A typical punk garage band, **The 'Dukes** should, by rights, have faded back into obscurity post-1969. But Nugent's persistence kept them on the road and the band, having gone through various personnel changes, was still putting out largely tasteless albums into the seventies. A compilation *The Best of The Amboy Dukes* (Mainstream 6125) was also issued in the seventies, but the best compilation of their material is the double LP *Journeys And Migrations* (Mainstream) in 1974. Another compilation of their material was *Dr Slingshot* (Mainstream MRL 414) in 1974.

Steve Arama went on to form **Ursa Major** with **Dick Wagner** from **Frost**.

Original guitarist, Steve Farmer, has also recently been collaborating with neo-psych/acid-goth band **Babylonian Tiles**, co-writing and playing on their *Shadows On The Wall* 45 (Saint Thomas STP 0056) 1998. Babylonian Tiles have also covered another **Amboy Dukes**' track: *Saint Philips Friend* (STP 0043) 1997.

Compilation appearances have included:- *Baby Please Don't Go* on *Nuggets - Original Artyfacts From The First Psychedelic Era 1965-1968* (Dble LP); *Journey To The Center Of The Mind* on *Michigan Rocks* (LP), *Nuggets* (CD), *Best of '60s Psychedelic Rock* (CD) and *Nuggets, Vol. 1* (LP); *Baby Please Don't Go* and *Journey To The Center Of The Mind* on *Nuggets Box* (4-CD); and *You Talk Sunshine, I Breathe Fire* on *Michigan Brand Nuggets* (LP) and *Michigan Nuggets* (CD). (VJ/SR)

America Is Hard To Find

Personnel:	DANIEL BERRIGAN	vcls	A
	JOHN HOSTETTER		A
	ALLAN SORVALL		A
	DAVID TURNER		A

ALBUM:	1(A)	AMERICA IS HARD TO FIND	
			(Multi Trax ZB-176/7) 1971 SC

A local New York release. Berrigan handles Side One on his own, with poetry and (mostly) oratory concerning his subversive behaviour and subsequent jail time. Side two will be of more interest to readers, it being a garagey rock mass; rather like a poor man's version of **The Electric Prunes**' *Mass In F Minor*. (CF/SR)

American Beetles

Personnel:	BILL ANDE	ld gtr	A
	TOM CONDRA	gtr	A
	DAVE HIERONYMUS	drms	A
	JIM TOLLIVER	bs	A

45s:	Don't Be Unkind / You Did It To Me	(Roulette 4550) 1964
	School Days / Hey Hey Girl	(Roulette 4559) 1964
	She's Mine / Theme Of The American Beetles	(BYP 1001) 1964
	It's My Last Night In Town /	
α	You're Getting To Me	(BYP 101/2) 1964
β	I Wish You Everything / Say You Do	(Yorey 1001) 1965

NB: α also issued on Mammoth (102). β also issued in Canada on Barry (3307).

Miami's answer to the Beatles? This outfit had already been going since the late fifties as the Ardells and the new moniker was not a bad idea to catch the latest musical craze in 1964. Unfortunately they chose a tough act to be compared to and none of their numerous 45s resulted in major success. So it was time for a rethink and another name change to - the **The Razor's Edge**.

Compilation appearances have included: *Hey, Hey Girl* on *Searching For Love* (LP). (MW)

American Blues

Personnel:	FRANK BEARD	A
	DOUG DAVIS	A
	DUSTY HILL	A
	ROCKY HILL	A

ALBUMS:	1(A)	AMERICAN BLUES IS HERE	(Karma 1001) 1968 R3
	2(A)	AMERICAN BLUES DO THEIR THING	(Uni 73004) 1969 R2

NB: (2) reissued by See For Miles (SEE 99) 1987, (1) and (2) have also been reissued on one CD (Afterglow) 199?.

45:	If I Were A Carpenter / All I Saw Was You	(Karma 101) 1969

NB: Album versions, although 'A' side is edited.

One of the better known Dallas bands of this era **American Blues** were originally known as **The Warlocks** and also an important stepping stone for Dusty Hill and Frank Beard before they went on to join ZZ Top. Their first album was produced by **Scotty McKay** and recorded at Robin Hood

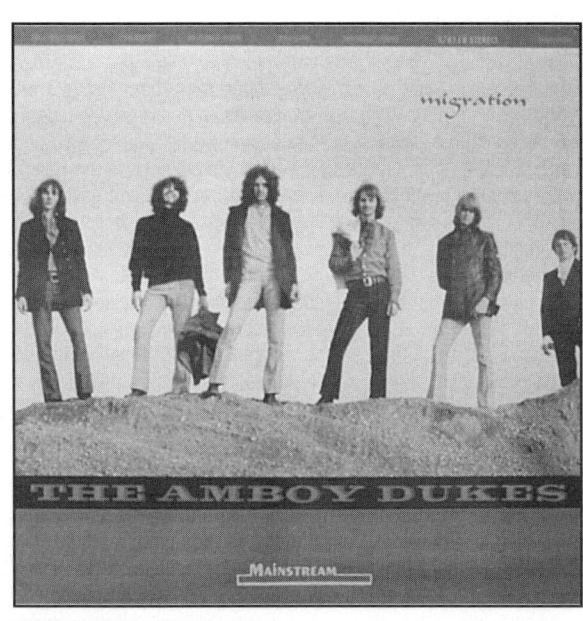

AMBOY DUKES - Migration LP.

AMERICA IS HARD TO FIND - America Is Hard To Find LP.

Brian's studio in Tyler, Texas. Side one is predominantly psychedelic and a 45 from it was issued the following year. Side two was in more of a heavy rock style. It did well enough to attract the interest of EMI subsidiary UNI who signed the band. The result was *Do Their Thing*, which was basically a blues rock album with some psychedelic trappings. It did have its moments and *You Were So Close To Me*, *Softly To The Sun*, *Just Plain Jane* and *Dreams* are the better tracks. However, the sales were poor and UNI quietly dropped the band.

There was a second band of this name who released one 45, *Say So/Your Love Is True* (Amy 997) during the 1960s.

Compilation appearances have so far included *If I Were A Carpenter* and *All I Saw Was You* on *A Journey To Tyme, Vol. 1* (LP) and *If I Were A Carpenter* on *Reverberation IV* (CD). (VJ)

American Blues Exchange

Personnel:	ROGER BRIGGS	gtr	A
	ROY DUDLEY	vcls, hmnca, tamb	A
	PETER HARTMAN	bs	A
	DAN MIXTER	gtr, recorder, harmony	A
	DALE REED	perc, harmony	A

ALBUM:	1(A)	AMERICAN BLUES EXCHANGE BLUEPRINTS	(Tayles TLS 1) 1969 R4

NB: (1) reissued on Heyoka (Hey 204) 1985 and on CD (Flash 55). Reissued officially on CD by Gear Fab (GF-120) 1998, with extra material not included on the bootlegs.

This band consisted of students at Trinity College in Hartford, and they mainly played a college parties and dances in the Connecticut / Massachusetts areas between 1968 and 1970. Aside from *Burlington Letter*, a sensitive 'acid' guitar ballad, their album is broadly-speaking a collection of late sixties bluesy numbers, with some great laid-back dual guitar leads. Don't let the "blues" in the band name put you off, however, as there's a Cream/Blind Faith influence on tracks like *The Taker* and *Ode To The Lost Legs Of John Bean*, and it's an album that will also appeal to fans of laid-back West Coast rock, as well as the blues.

Recorded at the Gallery studio in East Hartford, Connecticut, the album had an original pressing of 1,000 although only 400 were sold - the remainder being given away or binned over the ensuing years.

After the band split and went their separate ways, all continued to pursue their musical hobby, and now reside in the Connecticut / Massachusetts area, except for Dale Reed who moved out to L.A. Indeed Roger Briggs still records and releases limited edition cassette tapes for friends and interested people to this day!

AMERICAN BLUES - Is Here LP.

Compilation appearances have included: *Age Child* on Gear Fab's *Psychedelic Sampler* (CD). (VJw/thankstoRBs)

The American Breed

Personnel:	AL CINER	gtr	A
	CHUCK COLBERT	bs	A
	LEE GRAZIANO	drms	A
	GARY LOIZZO	vcls, gtr	A
	KEVIN MURPHY	keyb'ds	A

			HCP
ALBUMS: 1(A)	AMERICAN BREED	(Acta (Dot) 38002) 1967	- -
2(A)	AMERICAN BREED II 'Bend Me Shape Me'		
		(Acta (Dot) 38003) 1968	99 -
3(A)	PUMPKIN POWDER SCARLET AND GREEN		
		(Acta (Dot) 38006) 1968	- -
4(A)	LONELY SIDE OF THE CITY	(Acta (Dot) 38008) 1968	- -

			HCP
45s:	I Don't Think You Know Me/		
	Give Two Young Lovers A Chance	(Acta 802) 1967	-
	Step Out Of Your Mind/Same Old Thing	(Acta 804) 1967	24
	Don't Forget About Me/Short Skirts	(Acta 808) 1967	107
	Bend Me, Shape Me/Mindrocker	(Acta 811) 1967	5
	Green Light/Don't It Make You Cry	(Acta 821) 1968	39
	Ready, Willing And Able/		
	Take Me If You Want Me	(Acta 824) 1968	84
	Any Way That You Want Me/Master of Fate	(Acta 827) 1968	88
	Keep The Faith/Private Zoo	(Acta 830) 1969	-
	Hunky Funky/Enter The Master	(Acta 833) 1969	107
	Room At The Top/Walls	(Acta 836) 1969	-
	Cool It (We're Not Alone)/The Brain	(Acta 837) 1969	-
	Can't Make It Without You/		
	When I'm With You	(Paramount 0040) 1971	-

This outfit formed in Chicago in 1966 and were originally known as **Gary and The Night Lites** and **The Light Nites**. They began life as a kinda top 40 frat band releasing three 45s as **Gary and The Night Lites** and one as **The Light Nites**. When they signed to Acta they changed name to **The American Breed**. They continued the brief relationship they had with Bill Traut at Dunwich (as **The Light Nites**) and he became their producer for their first few Acta singles. They are most remembered for a soul-influenced pop sound best represented by *Bend Me, Shape Me*, which was by some way their biggest hit, but I've included them here on the strength of their earlier psych pop hit, *Step Out Of Your Mind* and *Green Light*, which was in a similar vein. Like many Chicago bands of this era they had quite a brassy sound. Although they were primarily a singles band their second album did make it to No 99 in the U.S. Album Charts. After several personnel changes the group evolved into Ask Rufus (who were later known as simply Rufus). Gary Loizzo was also involved in an outfit called Jamestown Massacre in the late sixties and early seventies.

Their compilation appearances to date have included:- *Bend Me, Shape Me* on *Nuggets Vol. 5* (LP); *Step Out Of Your Mind* on *Nuggets, Vol. 11* (LP); an otherwise unreleased recording of *What Now My Love?* from July 1967 on the *Early Chicago* (LP) compilation; *Partridge Weiners Radio Spot* and *Temperature's Rising Radio Spot* on *Oh Yeah! The Best Of Dunwich Records* (CD); *The Alone Phone* Radio Spot and the previously unreleased *It's Getting Harder* on *If You're Ready - The Best Of Dunwich... Vol. 2* (CD).

In 1995, Varese Vintage issued a 17-track compilation *Bend Me Shape Me* which also contains an interview with Gary Loizzo. (VJ)

American Dream

Personnel incl:	ROB CARLSON	ld vcls, gtr	AB
	DAVID NOYES ROBERTS	bs	A
	ALAN SILVERMAN	ld gtr	AB
	PAUL PAYTON		B

45:	Love Is A Beautiful Thing/		
	Jug Band Music	(Bovi RM 45027/8) c1967	

Despite the sweet harmonious vocals on the above 45, this Providence, Rhode Island group sound more like **The Vagrants** than **The Young Rascals** with some wonderfully vicious and heavy fuzz. Their **Lovin' Spoonful** cover is more true to the original and, therefore, something of a disappointment by comparison.

About 1,000 copies of their single were sold, mostly locally. Their line-up was renewed and in 1969 Paul Payton joined them. They changed their name to Benefit Street but only recorded demos, which remain unreleased. Rob Carlson would later form **Carlson and Gailmor**, who released an album on Polydor in 1971. (MW/SR/PPn)

American Dream

Personnel:	MICKEY BROOK	drms	A
	DON FERRIS	bs, vcls	A
	NICKY INDELICATO	gtr, vcls	A
	NICK JAMESON	ld gtr, piano, vcls	A
	DON LEE VAN WINKLE	gtr, vcls	A

			HCP
ALBUM: 1(A)	THE AMERICAN DREAM	(Ampex A 10101) 1970	194 SC

45:	Good News / I Ain't Searchin'	(Ampex 11001) 1970

AMERICAN BLUES - Do Their Thing LP.

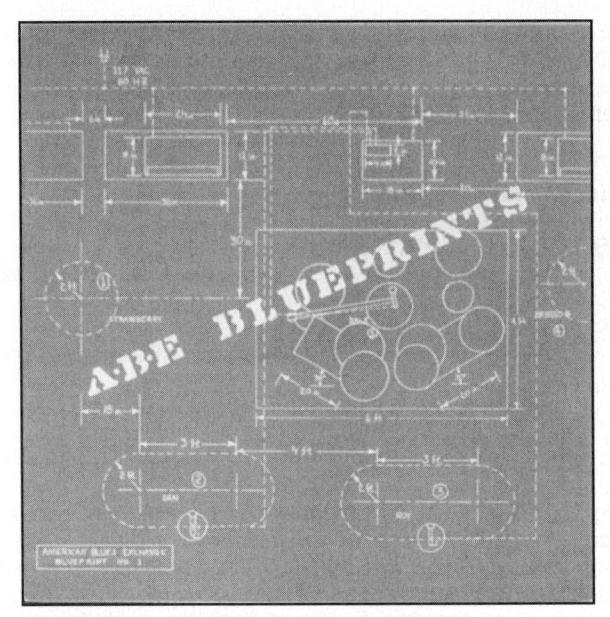

AMERICAN BLUES EXCHANGE - A.B.E. Blueprints LP.

From Philadelphia. It is a pretty good debut album of heavy rock with three guitars, but what makes it stand out is the superb production job by Todd Rundgren, who also engineered the recording. It spent two weeks in the lower reaches of the Top 200, peaking at No. 194.

Nick Jameson would later join Foghat and **Paul Butterfield**. He also released a solo album in 1977 on Bearsville. (MW/THd/SR)

American Eagle

Personnel:	GREG BECK	gtr, vcls	A
	GENE HUBBARD	keyb'ds, vcls	A
	ROBERT LOWERY	ld vcls	A
	FRED ZEUFELDT	drms, vcls	A

ALBUM:	1(A)	AMERICAN EAGLE	(Decca DL 75258) 1970 SC

45s:	Family / Gospel	(Decca 32788) 1971
	On The Rack /	
	Ballad Of A Well-Known Gun	(Decca 32833) 1971

Previously known as the **Surprise Package** (with Mike Rogers instead of Gene Hubbard) these guys lineage stretches way back through numerous Pacific Northwest bands including the **Viceroys**, **Galaxies** and **Rock Collection**. They appear to have been based in California by this time. The album is predominantly straight-ahead riff-heavy rock with soulful vocals. The **Vanilla Fudge** style rework of the Moody Blues' *Nights In White Satin* drives that particular comparison home. (MW)

The American Eagles

Personnel incl:	CHUCK LEAVELL	keyb'ds	A
	JOHN BUCK WILKIN	gtr, vcls	A
	JOHN WYKER	gtr, vcls	A

45:	Me And Bobby McGee/Nashville Sun	(Liberty 56125) 1969

A short-lived Nashville group formed by **Wilkin** after the end of **Ronny and The Daytonas**. Both tracks would also be released on his solo album. Leavell would later play with the **Allman Brothers Band**, Sea Level and the Rolling Stones. John Wyker had a big hit with *Sailcat* in 1972 and kept on producing Southern rock and soul acts. (SR)

American Express

45:	You're Going to be the One/You And Me	(Teen Town 111) 1969

Pop with horns, on the same label as **The Sidewalk Skipper Band**. (SR)

The American Four

Personnel incl:	JOHN ECHOLS	ld gtr	A
	ARTHUR LEE	vcls, gtr	A

45:	Lucy Baines/Soul Food	(Selma 2001) 1964

This was a short-lived 1964 Los Angeles band of Lee's which recorded just the one rather commercial 45, with *Lucy Baines* being the better track. The band soon evolved into The Grassroots and later still into the seminal **Love**.

Compilation appearances have so far included: *Lucy Baines* and *Soul Food* on *A Journey To Tyme, Vol. 5* (LP); and *Lucy Baines* on *Magic Carpet Ride* (LP) and *California Acid Folk* (LP). (VJ)

American Legend

45:	Back In The U.S.S.R. / Sunshine Morning	(D.J. 101) 1969

From Mason City, Iowa. A good hard-rockin' Beatles cover backed by a light poppy number with way too many bah-bah-bah's. (MW)

American Revolution

Personnel:	RICHARD BARCELONA	gtr, vcls	A
	DANIEL DERDA	drms	A
	EBBIE HADDAD	keyb'ds, vcls	A
	JOHN KEITH	bs, vcls	A

ALBUM:	1(A)	AMERICAN REVOLUTION	
			(Flick-Disc FLS 45,002) 1968 SC

NB: (1) promo copies issued in mono with sticker.

45:	Cold Wisconsin Nights /	
	Come On And Get It	(Flick Disc 902) 1968

A late sixties Hollywood hippie type rock band. Barcelona and Keith later played in **Edge**, who issued an album in 1970. The *American Revolution* album, produced by Harley Hatcher, is quite heavily orchestrated with pleasant vocal harmonies, particularly on *In The Late Afternoon*, *Rainbow In The Rain* and *Love Has Got Me Down*. Some of the songs have a psychedelic taint, but it's predominantly rather good psych-pop.

Producer Harley Hatcher, was an exploitation film composer, member of Mike Curb's gang and as an army buddy of Elvis he sang in ad-hoc groups with the King. (VJ/JFr/DJe)

ERIC ANDERSEN - 'Bout Changes 'N' Things Take 2 LP.

American Standard

Personnel incl: KEVIN FALVEY? A

45:	Every Day /	
	Just About Dead	(Magnet Productions MAG 301) 1969

Both sides of the sole 45 by this Rhode Island band were composed by Kevin Falvey. *Every Day* is a low-key dirge with pseudo-classical keyboard moves - a bit of a downer, man. The flip is altogether better - a pumping hard rocker with wah-wah, spirited keyboards and fluid lead. (MW)

The American Way

45: Lady Dressed In Black/? Sho-Boat 105 1968

A stately ballad with psychy touches, *Lady Dressed In Black* graces *Fuzz, Flaykes And Shakes Vol. 4* (LP & CD), which suggests Oklahoma or Kansas as their likely homeground. Mississippi has also been suggested. (MW)

American Zoo

Personnel:
- B. BOTTRELL A
- DAVE DANIELI A
- BILL HAWKINS A
- J. MARTZ A

45s:	Mr Brotherhood/Magdalena	(Reena 1026) 1967
	What Am I ?/Back Street Thoughts	(Reena 1030) 1967

This band recorded at least two 45s for this Hollywood-based label in late 1967. *Mr Brotherhood* was poppy psychedelia with trippy lyrics and sound effects. It was released in two quite different versions - one with organ to the fore and an extra verse and the other was an abridged version with guitar more to the fore and the 'trippy effects'.

Compilation appearances have included: *Mr. Brotherhood* (full version) on *High All The Time, Vol. 2* (LP); and *Mr. Brotherhood* (abridged version) on *Psychedelic Unknowns, Vol. 11* (CD) and *Slowly Growing Insane* (CD). (VJ)

Peter Anders

ALBUM:	1	PETER ANDERS	(Family Production FPS 2705) 1972 -

45:	Sunrise Highway/Baby, Baby	(Buddah BDA-3) 1967

Born Peter Andreoli, **Peter Anders** is best known for his work with Vini Poncia in **The Tradewinds**, **The Innocence**, **Anders and Poncia** and Map City productions.

ERIC ANDERSON - More Hits From Tin Can Alley LP.

Recorded in Los Angeles, his solo album is typical of the singer/songwriter style, with some good songs but also several fillers. Its main interest is maybe the participation of several noted musicians like Hamilton Wesley Watt (**Euphoria**) and **Mike Deasy**. (SR)

Anders and Poncia

ALBUM:	1	THE ANDERS AND PONCIA ALBUM	
			(Warner Bros. WS 1778) 1970 -

45s:	So It Goes/	
	Virgin To The Nite	(Kama Sutra Records KA240) 1967
	Take His Love/	
	I'm Beginning To Touch You	(Warner Bros. 7271) 1969
	Lucky/Make A Change	
	(To Something Better)	(Warner Bros. 7294) 1970

Originally based on the East Coast, Vini Poncia and **Peter Anders** are better known for their records as **The Tradewinds** or **The Innocence**, but they also recorded several records as **Anders and Poncia**. After a 45 in 1967, they moved to Los Angeles and recorded their album with Californian sessionmen and production by Richard Perry. It's mainly folk-rock and pop-oriented, the highlight being a decent version of Leiber/Stoller's *Smoky Joe's Cafe* with great slide guitar by Ry Cooder.

After 1972, **Anders** went solo while Poncia became friends with Ringo Starr and had a successful songwriter and production career. (SR)

Eric Andersen

HCP

ALBUMS:	1	TODAY IS THE HIGHWAY	(Vanguard 79157) 1965 - -
(up to	2	'BOUT CHANGES AND THINGS	
1972)			(Vanguard 792206) 1966 - -
	3	'BOUT CHANGES AND THINGS, TAKE 2	
			(Vanguard 79236) 1967 - -
	4	MORE HITS FROM TIN CAN ALLEY	
			(Vanguard VSD 79271) 1968 - -
	5	A COUNTRY DREAM	(Vanguard VSD-6540) 1968 - -
	6	AVALANCHE	(Warner Bros. WS 1748) 1970 - -
	7	ERIC ANDERSEN	(Warner Bros. WS 1806) 1970 - -
	8	THE BEST OF	(Vanguard VSD 7/8) 1971 - -
	9	BLUE RIVER	(Columbia 31062) 1972 169 -

NB: Mono pressings of the Vanguard albums also exist. (1) and (2) also released in the U.K. by Fontana. Most of the Vanguard albums have been reissued in the seventies.

Of Norwegian origin, **Eric Andersen** was one of the best Greenwich Village folksingers and poet/songwriters during 1963/64, but his career has always been undermined by bad luck, poor judgement and mismanagement. After two good folk albums, his response to Dylan going electric was to re-record his best album with a rhythm section, hence the *Take Two* in the title.

His next effort, *More Hits From Tin Can Alley*, was ruined by the florid production of Al Gorgoni and features the usual New York musicians : **Al Kooper**, Hugh McCracken, Herb Lovelle, Bob Rafkin, Bobby Gregg, Paul Harris, Paul Griffin, plus some tasteful guitar parts of Amos Garrett. It contains one outstanding fast track, *'Mary Sunshine* with McCracken (or **Kooper**?) doing a fantastic **Bloomfield** impersonation on electric guitar.

Following the collapse of the original folk scene, he pursued one fad after another, turning country and western for *Country Dream* and using Sgt Pepper-like orchestration for his Warner albums, which sold poorly. In 1972 he moved to Columbia and released one of his best albums, *Blue River*. Unfortunately the master tapes for the follow-up albums were lost and **Andersen** reappeared only in 1975, as a singer/songwriter in the James Taylor mould. He kept on recording for Arista and eventually returned to Norway.

In 1991 and 1994 he recorded two sympathetic albums with Rick Danko (The Band) and Jonas Fjeld. His songs have also been sung by other groups including: *Violets Of Dawn* by the **Robbs** and the **Blues Project** and *Think About It* by **Len Novy**. He is sometimes credited as Eric Anderson. (SR)

101 Strings - Astro Sounds From Beyond The Year 2000 LP.

Al Anderson

Personnel:	DONN ADAMS	trombone	A
	TERRY ADAMS	piano	A
	AL ANDERSON	vcls, gtr, electric piano	A
	AL LEPAK	bs	A
	JEFF POTTER	harp	A
	TOM STALEY	drms	A

ALBUM: 1 AL ANDERSON (Vanguard VSD 79324) 1972 -

NB: (1) there was also a quadraphonic issue (VSQ 40018). Reissued on CD in 1998.

HCP

45s:	We'll Make Love/Just Want To Have You Back Again	(Vanguard 35168) 1972	101
	Ain't No Woman Finer Lookin'/ You're Just Laughin Inside	(Vanguard) 1972	-

The former leader of **The Wildweeds**, **Al Anderson** joined **NRBQ** in 1971 and shortly after released a solo album with Jeff Potter from **Clean Living**, (**Anderson** had guested on their second album) plus Tom Staley, Donn and Terry Adams from his new group. Produced by Maynard Solomon and engineered by Jeff Zaraya, it offers a good humoured mix of country blues, folk and R&B numbers, all penned by **Anderson** except for a cover of Hank Williams' *Honky Tonkin'*.

The two 45s are from the album. **Al Anderson** later released further albums during the seventies and eighties. (SR)

David Anderson

Personnel:	DAVID ANDERSON	vcls	A
	(CALVIN ARLINE	bs	A)
	(SUDIE CALLAWAY	backing vcls	A)
	(TOMMY GOODWIN	piano, organ	A)
	(EMIL HANDKE	drms	A)
	(STANLEY KIMBALL	gtr	A)
	(LAVERNA MOORE	backing vcls	A)
	(JULIAN SPARKS	trumpet	A)
	(SONNY THROCKMORTON	backing vcls	A)

ALBUM: 1(A) CHILDREN OF THE MIST (King KS 1120) 1969 ?

Produced by Darrell Glenn and **David Anderson**, this little known album was recorded in Macon and Nashville. It's a folk-rock affair with some pop, country and psych influences. **Anderson** had a good voice, in the same syle as **Don Nix** and several of the tracks are interesting, notably for the guitar parts, whilst others are spoilt by the production. Two songs were penned by Texas guitarist **John Nitzinger** and eight by the mysterious Houston and Hardy. The only cover is the title track, a **Buzz Clifford** composition. Not a masterpiece, but it may interest some curious readers. (SR)

The Anglo-Americans

45:	The Music Never Stops/ Are You Ready For This?	(Chattahoochee 605) 1966

A solid pop-thumper that comes with ringing guitars and a nod to The Beach Boys. The flip is full of 'hip' lyrics and a take on Bob Dylan circa 1965 lyric and sound-wise. Tongue-in-cheek folk-rock. (MW)

Anglo-Saxon

45:	Ruby/You Better Leave Me Alone	(Lucky Eleven) 1967
	Ruby/You Better Leave Me Alone	(Tower 401) 1968

The 'A' side was a pop hit for the **First Edition** (as *Ruby (Don't Take Your Love To Town)*) but this unknown group presumably from Michigan recorded a good sneering punky version with Dylan-like vocals and Animals style organ arrangement. The song was penned by country star Mel Tillis. The flip was a decent Jimmy Reed rip-off.

Their sole 45, it was picked up for national release by Tower, early in 1968. (SR/GGc)

The Angry Men

45:	Come With Me (To Another World)/ Love Is Gone	(Torch T-1001/2) 1967

Soft and restrained 'garage-ballads' from Rochester, New York, sounding anything but angry and coming on more like a lounge-bar band. (MW/MM)

Animated Egg

ALBUM: 1 ANIMATED EGG (Alshire SF-5104) 1967 R1

The Burbank, California-based Alshire label was best known for its cheapo international music (eg. *The Sounds Of Spain*, *The Tijuana Sound*, *Hawaiian Paradise*) and 101 String MOR collections. In pursuit of profit rather than content, 1967 saw the label shell out some cash to have anonymous studio musicians write and record a series of psych-oriented instrumentals. Slapping a pseudo-trippy cover on the results (ignore the dazed long haired teens pictured on the cover since they certainly had nothing to do with the set), the cleverly titled *The Animated Egg* proved surprising accomplished. With little at stake, the anonymous band (no performing or writing credits are provided), roared through an all-instrumental set; material such as *A Love Built On Sand*, *I Said, She Said, Ah Cid* and *Sock It My Way* are heavy on fuzz, feedback and swirling organ. Elsewhere, *Sippin' An Trippin'* offered up a nifty slice of **Byrds**-styled jangle rock, while *Tomorrow* was a blatant rip off of The Spencer Davis Group's *Gimme Some Lovin'*.

To make it even more complicated, Alshire recycled some of the material (and other stuff apparently recorded at the same sessions) credited to 101 Strings - *Astro Sounds From Beyond The Year 2000*, with a wonderful cheesy cover, and as Bebe Bardon and 101 Strings - *The Sounds Of Love*.

Some of the album's better cuts have recently resurfaced on compilations. You'll find *I Said, She Said, AhCid* on *Relics, Vol. 2* (LP) and *Relics Vol's 1 & 2* (CD); whilst *Sock It My Way* has turned up on *Turds On A Bum Ride, Vol. 1* (Dble LP) and *Turds On A Bum Ride Vol. 1 & 2* (Dble CD). Both tracks also appear on *Lycergic Soap* (LP).

The *Everything You Always...* CD also includes three cuts, credited under the **Astro Sounds...** moniker: *Flameout*, *Barner X-69* and the delightfully titled *A Disappointing Love Affair With A Desensitized Robot*. (VJ/CF/SB)

ANONYMOUS - Inside The Shadow LP.

Anonymous

Personnel:	RON MATELIC	vcls, gtr	A
	JOHN MEDVESCEK	drms	A
	MARSHA ROLLINGS	vcls	A
	GLENN WEAVER	vcls, gtr, bs	A

ALBUM: 1(A) INSIDE THE SHADOW
(A Major Label AMLS 1002) 1976 R4

NB: (1) came in a blue and white cover, black and white label, with insert. 500 copies were pressed. *Anonymous* (A Major Label AMLS 1002) 1981 R2, was a repressing of the *Inside The Shadow* album - this time untitled, with a slightly modified cover (black and white cover, red and white label, no insert). (1) reissued by OR (OR 015) 1996, in a limited edition of 375.

Hailed from Indianapolis, Indiana, but recorded on a label based in Milwaukee, Wisconsin, by **Jim Spencer**. This is a superb album of melodic guitar driven rock which blends exquisitely with Marsha's vocals on tracks like *J Rider*, *Up To You*, *Pick Up And Run* and *Baby Come Risin'*, which is probably the album's finest moment. If you like ringing guitar work and harmonic vocals, this album is for you. They've been likened to **Jefferson Airplane**!

Ron Matelic and John Medvescek had earlier played for **Sir Winston and The Commons**. The **Anonymous** album has been reissued by OR records, early in 1997, along with another album *No Longer Anonymous* recorded by Ron, John and Marsha circa 1979, under the name **J. Rider**. This was later reissued by OR records as a limited edition of 375 in 1996 (OR 016).

There was another band called **Anonymous** who had a cut on the *Let Them Eat Jellybeans* (Faulty Records) 1981 compilation. The style of music is reputedly something like The Residents. (VJ/CF)

The Answer

Personnel incl:	TODD ANDERSON	vcls	A
	MICHAEL FRIEDMAN	bs	A
	MIKE SIMPSON	gtr	A
	BOB SHUMAKER	drms	A
	CHIP WRIGHT	gtr	A
	MARK BATTERMAN	keyb'ds	B

45: Why You Smile/I'll Be In (White Whale 225) 1965

A little known garage band from Berkeley, California. Mark Batterman joined the band in late '66 from **Haymarket Riot** (formerly The Livin' End), whilst Anderson and Friedman formed **The Drongos** after **The Answer** split in 1966.

The catchy 'A' side has resurfaced on *Sixties Rebellion, Vol. 3* (LP & CD), the 'B' side on *Highs In The Mid-Sixties, Vol. 1* (LP) and *Teenage Shutdown, Vol. 9* (LP & CD). (MW)

Anthem

Personnel:	BARTHOLOMEW	gtr, vcls	A
	BOBBY HAYE	drms, vcls	A
	GREGG HOLLISTER	bs, vcls	A

ALBUM: 1(A) ANTHEM (Buddah BDS-5071) 1970 -

Signed by Buddah the trio's self-titled 1970 album teamed them with producer Stan Vincent. Musically *Anthem* offered up a fairly entertaining mix of commercial pop (the title track) and slightly more experimental numbers (the extended *Misty Morns*). While it wasn't one of the year's most original offerings, all three members (guitarist Bartholomew, bassist Gregg Hollister and drummer Bobby Howe), were gifted with decent voices and on tracks such as *Florida* and *Queen* they displayed a knack for crafting some pretty harmonies. One of the three had a voice that sounded uncannily like **The Monkees'** Michael Nesmith.

Gregg Hollister later played with Rockspur (DJM, 1978). (SR/SB)

Anthrax

See the **Formerly Anthrax** entry.

Ant Trip Ceremony

Personnel:	STEVE DeTRAY	ld gtr	A
	GEORGE GALT	gtr, vcls, hrmnca, bs	AB
	ROGER GOODMAN	vcls	AB
	GARY ROSEN	bs, gtr, vcls	AB
	MARK STEIN	ld gtr, flte, bs	AB
	JEFF WILLIAMS	drms	AB

ALBUM: 1(A/B) 24 HOURS (C.R.C. 2129) 1968 R4

NB: (1) reissued on Resurrection (R1). The vinyl reissue is exact and indistinguishable from the original except for the fact that it's on dark blue vinyl and must be held to a bright light to check. If you can't see colour through it, it's probably an original. (1) reissued on CD by Anthology (Ant 2311) 1995, with a newly designed cover. (1) reissued legitimately on CD by Collectables (Col-CD-0717) 1999 but with a different running order.

Steve Detray, a student at Oberlin College in Ohio, took a break in 1966 and early 1967 to spend time in Logan, Utah with his brother. While out there, he formed a band which he named **Ant Trip Ceremony** after a suggestion from a local English professor who had seen the term in a novel. The phrase was a description of modern human society and Detray thought it an appropriate name for his band. Before he returned to Oberlin for the 1967/8 academic year, Steve disbanded the band but retained the name when he formed a new electric rock band at Oberlin. Gary Rosen, George Galt, and Mark Stein had been playing together in a blues band. Stein was a flute major at Oberlin, Roger Goodman was also a student, and the only non-college member was the drummer, Steve Williams, a 16-year-old local kid who had some jazz-drumming experience.

The band mainly played gigs at Oberlin and were noted for long improvisatory jams. Their album was recorded in two sessions, the first in February 1968 and the second some months later. Steve Detray was only present for the first session as he left the College in the Spring of 1968. Technical faults affected the recording: the KLH deck used for playback had a faulty right speaker and the mixdown was affected as a result with vocals sounding further back in the mix than originally intended. The producer, David Crosby, was a fellow-student at Oberlin and contrary to legend is *not* the **David Crosby** of **The Byrds**/CSN&Y fame. Only 300 copies of the album were pressed and sold around campus.

A blend of folk, blues, jazz and Eastern psychedelia, the album is at its best on the more meditative pieces like *Pale Shades Of Gray* with it's eerily beautiful snakecharmer melody and *What's The Matter Now* which is based on on a reflective "Goodbye Pork Pie-Hat" riff. *Four In The Morning* and

Riverdawn are also in this lullingly insistent vein whilst *Elaborations* is a lengthy raga-ish instrumental with some very effective flute. Some of the covers like *Get Out Of My Life Woman* and **Eric Andersen**'s *Violets Of Dawn* are no more than adequate, but their version of *Hey Joe* is much more exciting.

The band disbanded as the members left college. Steve, George, Gary, and Jeff still perform while Roger is retired from teaching college. Steve Williams later played with such greats as Clark Terry, Al Hall and Herb Lovette, whilst Rosen was a Bluesbander prior to his conversion to folk music. Goodman came from England originally. (LP/VJ/CF)

Aorta

Personnel:	JIM DONLINGER	gtr, vcls	AB
	BILLY HERMAN	vcls, drms	A
	BOBBY JONES	bs, vcls	A
	JIM NYEHOLT	keyb'ds	AB
	MIKE BEEN	bs, gtr, vcls	B
	TOM DONLINGER	drms, perc	B

			HCP
ALBUMS:	1(A) AORTA	(Columbia 9785) 1969	168 -
	2 AORTA 2	(Happy Tiger 1010) 1970	- SC

NB: (1) also released in France: (CBS S7-63690) 1969. (1) reissued on CD by Buy Or Die.

45s:	Shapes Of Things To Come/Strange	(Atlantic 2545) 1968
	Strange/Ode To Missy Mtfzspkik	(Columbia 44870) 1969
	Sand Castles/Willie Jean	(Happy Tiger 567) 1970

These two albums of acid psychedelia are highly rated by some. Their first album is consistently good throughout and is certainly recommended. A wide range of material is held together by tight playing and some fine guitar/organ interplay. Unfortunately, the second album pales by comparison and is largely uninspired with no real highlights.

The band came from Chicago and during the mid-sixties were a popular Top 40's lounge group, going by the name of **The Exceptions**. After a couple of years of regurgitating the latest hits, they were getting bored and were looking for room to explore their musical talents, when producer Bill Traut (of Dunwich Records) approached them with an offer to record an album of original material. All of the group with the exception of Pete Cetera lept at the chance, and with the bass slot now filled by Bobby Jones, they renamed themselves as **Aorta**.

Curiously their first album was released the same month as three other Chicago acts signed to Columbia **Illinois Speed Press**, **The Flock**, and Chicago (who incidentally included Pete Cetera). This was a marketing ploy to push a "Chicago" scene and all four albums entered the Billboard Top 200, with **Aorta**'s peaking at around 168 and remaining in the chart for a respectable six weeks. Incidentally, the basic tracks and vocal tracks for the first album were recorded at Great Lakes Recording studio in Sparta, Michigan, with one track *Sprinkle Road To Cork Street* referring to two roads in Kalamazoo, Michigan.

Been and the Donlinger brothers had all formerly played in **The Rotary Connection**, another Chicago act, and Been and Jim Dolinger were later in Lovecraft. Nyeholt also played with **The Rotary Connection** during a brief period between the two albums, and Billy Herman went on to play for **New Colony Six**. Michael Been later played with **Moby Grape** members Jerry Miller / **Bob Mosley** in Fine Wine, and is still active on the music scene.

Tom Donlinger later played drums on several Van Morrison albums. His brother dropped their last name (which they had already shortened from Dondelinger) and recorded as James Vincent, playing in a Christian jazz/fusion style.

Aorta were also the creative force behind **Coven**'s first album. Once again it was Bill Traut who got them all together, but Jim Donlinger wrote most of the songs, arranged them, played guitar and sang backup. Jim Nyeholt also played keyboards. They were very coy in the liner notes, but Mike Been and Tom Donlinger are named (as "Practici").

The compilation *Psychedelic Dream* features three tracks from their first album:- *What's In My Mind's Eye*, a beautiful piece of orchestrated pop-psych; *Sleep Tight*, a rather disjointed song which wasn't one of their finest moments but ended with some pleasant keyboards and *Catalyptic*, a cover of a **Colours** song, which is another keyboard dominated number with some occasionally scintillating guitar. The latter track has often puzzled collectors, as it fits neatly into the 'concept' of *Aorta*, but is pre-dated by the **Colours** version. In fact, Bill Traut had received a demo of the track, and suggested it to **Aorta** for their album, but other than that there's no direct link between the groups.

Anyone interested in digging into **Aorta**'s roots may be interested in the Collectables CD *The Quill Records Story: The Best of Chicago Garage Bands*, which includes two **Exceptions** singles: *As Far As I Can See* and *Business As Usual*.

Also recommended is the 45 version of *Strange*, which includes different guitar and can be found on *U-Spaces: Psychedelic Archaeology, Vol. 1* (CDR). (VJ/BSw/SR/MPr/SMu/JNy)

Apes of Wrath

ALBUM:	1 APES OF WRATH	(Private Pressing) c1972 R1

Released by the band on their own label in a limited pressing of 500, the album includes a cover of Donovan's *Hey Gyp*, the very heavy *3 Billion Blind Mice*, and *The Apes Of Wrath*, *Mankinds Lies*, *Old Joe* and *Hypnotize The Masses*, with lots of fuzz guitar and guitar leads. (SR)

The Apocalypse

45s:	We Have Lost The Way / Do You Remember	(Apocalypse A-002) c1966
	God Is My Home / Summer Brings Rain	(Apocalypse # Unkn) 196?

Described as "gospel garage", from Grand Rapids, Michigan. *We Have Lost The Way* doesn't preach - it's upbeat folkie-rock. The lilting folk-ballad on the flip is more obvious in its religious message, as is the label's motto - "and ye shall sing praises unto Him". (MW)

Apokolips

45:	High Strung Woman / All Shook Up	(Varmint 45-110) 1972

On a Silvis, Illinois label and described as "70s garage" - in reality it's fifties rock'n'roll transplanted to the seventies by a hard rockin' local outfit. The top side is a boogie-rocker with harp and is backed by the Elvis rocker with a Jerry Lee impersonator on piano. Good rockin' - yeah, garage? - no way, Jose. (MW)

ANT TRIP CEREMONY - 24 Hours LP.

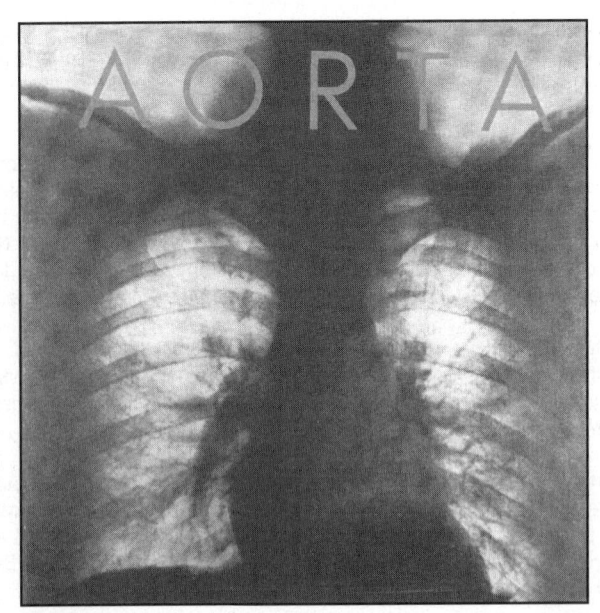

AORTA - Aorta CD.

The Apolloes

Personnel incl?: JIM YOUMANS   A

45s:			
	Hey / Laugh In My Face	(Apolloe No #)	1965
	Summertime Blues / Gone	(Soupa 001)	1966
	Summertime Blues / Slow Down	(Look 001)	1966/7
α	Summertime Blues / Slow Down	(White Cliffs 262)	1966/7
β	Chained And Bound / ?	(SAC 1001-1/2)	1967

NB: α and β as The Swingin' Apolloes. β may have been issued as a one-sided 45 only.

A mystery outfit from Atlanta, Georgia who went under the name of The Swingin' Apolloes on their later 45s. Jim Youmans may have been a member. In 1967 he produced a 45 by The Younger Brothers and **The Apolloes** were used for the recording sessions. *Laugh In My Face* was written by Wayne White, leader of local heroes **The Famen** (of *Crackin' Up* fame). It's a dynamic Searchers inspired folk-punker punctuated with guitar and keyboard flourishes over slick drum rolls. *Hey* is a solid thumper, composed by Jim Youmans. He also produced *Chained And Bound* - composed by Chester, Lane and Freeman. Clues aplenty but no confirmation of band personnel yet.

Chained And Bound is a dreamy psychedelic gem: bitter-sweet vocals glide over a shifting swirl of echoing and backward guitars, *Too-Much-To-Dream* bassline and sympathetic cymbals. Lovelorn lyrics, with unsettling depressive imagery, enhance its fragile charm. Experience it on *Psychedelic Crown Jewels, Vol. 3* (CD) which also features both sides of their debut.

You can also find *Slow Down* on *Mayhem & Psychosis, Vol. 2* (CD) and *Laugh In My Face* on *Psychedelic States: Georgia Vol. 1* (CD). (MW/RM)

The Apollos

Personnel:	DAVE HARNEY	gtr	ABCD
	DON HARNEY	gtr	ABCD
	JIM PRICE	bs	ABCD
	JAN SYLVESTER	drms	A
	WAYNE GROVES	drms	B
	JON PARISI	gtr	B
	TOMMY VORHAUER	vcls	BC
	WAYNE GOUBILEE	drms	CD
	DWIGHT JAMES	keyb'ds	CD
	DOUG COLLIS	vcls	D

45s:		
That's The Breaks/Country Boy	(Delta MUM 183)	1965
Target Love/It's A Monster	(Montgomery 0011/2)	1966

A garage band from the Falls Church area of Virginia, whose 45s were characterised by fizzling, speedy guitar work and catchy Farfisa organ. *That's The Breaks*, *Target Love* and *It's A Monster* are all superb examples of the garage fuzz genre. They might have got more recognition if they'd signed for a major label, but they were turned down by MGM and are best remembered now for their two 45s.

Prior to their first 45 the band recorded a demo EP at Edgewood Recording Studios in Washington, DC - the prize for winning a local battle of the bands. Two covers - the Beach Boys' *Dance Dance Dance* and the Videl's *Mr.Lonely* - were joined by debut versions of *That's The Breaks* and the instrumental *Country Boy*.

Compilation appearances have so far included: *Target Love*, *It's A Monster* and *That's The Breaks* on *Pebbles, Vol. 13* (LP); *That's The Breaks* and *Target Love* on *The Finest Hours of U.S. '60s Punk* and *Sixties Archive, Vol. 5* (CD); *That's The Breaks* on *Signed, D.C.* (LP); and *Dirty Water* and *I'm Crying* on *Green Crystal Ties, Vol. 8* (CD). For completists, however, the best source for their recordings is *Washington D.C. Garage Band Greats!*, which features a previously unreleased alternate version of *That's The Breaks*, the original releases of *Target Love* and *It's A Monster* and four previously unreleased, if interior, live recordings:- *Little Latin Lupe Lu*, *Good Lovin'*, *Time What Let Me* and *Green Onions*. (VJ/MW/BE)

Apollo's Apaches

Personnel incl:	MALLOW	A
	MALLOW	A
	O'CONNOR	A

45s:			
	Cry Me A Lie / Why Tolerate	(Anybody's 6088)	1966
	Boss - Be Good To Me / Cry Me A Lie	(Barra-Donna 29)	1967
α	Now That You've Gone / Why I	(Barra-Donna RJM/DJM)	1968

NB: α as The Beautiful Apollo. They also recorded a fourth 45 on Barra-Donna in 1968.

A Garfield Ridge, Chicago band whose first two 45s are well worth investigating. Two further 45s were released on Barra-Donna, one as The Beautiful Apollo. This marked a departure to a harmony-pop style - *Now...* is catchy and midtempo, *Why I* is more frantic and reminiscent of the Isley's Shout.

Compilation appearances have included:- *Cry Me A Lie* on *Psychedelic Unknowns, Vol. 4* (LP & CD) and *Teenage Shutdown, Vol. 15* (LP & CD); *Why Tolerate* on *Garage Punk Unknowns, Vol. 8* (Dble LP); *Boss - Be Good To Me* and is on *Let's Dig 'Em Up, Vol. 3*; and *Be Good To Me* on the *Yeah Yeah Yeah* CD. The latter was recorded at the debut 45 sessions but not released at the time as a reworked version appeared on their next release. (MW/MM)

The Apostles

Personnel:	CRAIG BETCHER	drms, vcls	ABCDEF
	JIM LaBRESH	gtr	ABCDEF
	RICH SMITH	ld gtr	ABCDEF
	LARRY WEAVER	bs	AB
	JEFF LYMAN	bs	CDEF
	GEORGE DOSE	organ	D
	TY TRUEX	keyb'ds	E
	TIM TUPPER	organ	EF
	STAN RUD	gtr	F

45:	Help Me Find A Way/	
	Unchain My Heart	(Welhaven 125935) 1967

Also known as **Thee Apostles**, this outfit from Rochester, Minnesota, underwent several line-up changes. In mid-1966 they won a local Battle Of The Bands competition at Olmsted County Fair and with it a recording contract with Welhaven Records. After scraping their first effort, a cover of Marsha And The Vandellas' *Heat Wave* and an original composition, *Naughty Girl*, because they didn't think they were good enough, they returned to the studio in late 1966 to record the above 45. The 'A' side was a classic garage effort with pounding drums, strong lead guitar and raw lead vocals. The flip was a soulful rendition of the Ray Charles hit, which was also covered by many other garage bands e.g. **Starfires**, **Undertakers**. The 45 has become rare and sought-after.

In the Spring of 1967 the band turned psychedelic, touring the Midwest quite extensively as a psychedelic roadshow and changing name to Stormy Monday. Under this name they continued with various line-ups until 1973. (VJ/MW)

The Apostles

ALBUMS: 1 ON CRUSADE   ('No Label') 1964 R2
         2 AN HOUR OF PRAYER WITH   ('No Label') 1965 R2

NB: (1) and (2) were pressed by Ace Recording.

This was a prep-punk group from Philips Academy, Massachusetts, who recorded two albums. A cover of The Kinks' *You Really Got Me*, from their second album, later resurfaced on *Garage Punk Unknowns, Vol. 7* (LP). The albums are now very expensive to acquire. (MW)

The Apostles

45: I'm A Lucky Guy/Tomorrow   (WGW 18702) 1967

From South Plainfield, New Jersey this was their sole release. *I'm A Lucky Guy* later resurfaced on *Open Up Yer Door, Vol. 2* (LP). (MM/MW)

The Apostles

45: Tired Of Waiting / Stranded In The Jungle   (A2 401) 1967

A Kinks cover and a fuzzy frat-garage number with a novelty vibe is the sole 45 left by these **Apostles**. The A-Squared label from Ann Arbor, Michigan was run by Jeep Holland and put out some cool 45s by **The Rationals**, **MC5**, **SRC** and **Thyme**.

Stranded In The Jungle has been re-aired on *Basementsville! U.S.A.* (LP). (MW)

Apothecary

ALBUM: 1 APOTHECARY   (Paramount PAS 6071) 1973 -

A five-piece band with decent guitar work and Beatlesque harmonies. (SR)

Appaloosa

Personnel incl: ROBIN BATTEAU   violin, vcls   A
                 JOHN PARKER
                 CROMPTON   ld vcls   A
                 DAVID REISER   A
                 GENO ROSOU   A
                 (AL KOOPER   keyb'ds, harpsichord,
                                  gtr   A)

                                                          HCP
ALBUM: 1(A) APPALOOSA   (Columbia CS 9819) 1969 178 -

A forgotten baroque rock group, produced by **Al Kooper** who also played on it. Their eleven songs were originals penned by their young leader John Parker Crompton. The album spent four weeks in the Top 200, peaking at No. 128.

Robin Batteau became a session man and also recorded some solo albums. (SR/VJ)

Apparition

45: Apparition/Astral Spirit   (Nebula NBS 1 / 10971) 1974

This terrific 45 couples the mid-tempo organ dominated *Apparition* with *Astral Spirit*, a suitably slow-motion piece, with plenty of cosmic atmospherics and pretty stupid lyrics. Altogether very dark and very amateurish. Both songs credit Scott Campbell and Arthur Sokoluk, and the single was produced by Campbell. Although issued in 1974, there is a lyric sheet (featuring a nice silhouetted graveyard) which identifies the publishing date as 1971.

The band were from Piscataway, New Jersey. (SPr/MW)

Apperson Jackrabbit

Personnel incl?: STEVE CURTIS   A
                  MIKE SIMMONS   A

45: That's Why/Shadows Falling   (Calmis 45-001) 1967

Understated garage-punkers - the top side features nifty pickin' and reeks of ATTITUDE. The uptempo flip is unusual for the inclusion of piano but makes up latterly with some tasty guitar runs. Both sides were composed by Simmons & Curtis. It's unclear who these guys were, but they were apparently from somewhere in California.

Compilation appearances have so far included: *That's Why* on *Fuzz, Flaykes, And Shakes, Vol. 4 - Experiment In Color* (LP & CD). (MW)

The Apple Corps

45: You'll Never Know/Don't Leave Me   (Subtown ST-601/2) 1969

A dire ballad backed by a tasty garage-punker from Old Saybrook, Connecticut. (MW/MM)

The Apple-Glass Cyndrom

Personnel: BILL AGUIRRI   vcls   A
            JOHNNY MULHAIR   keyb'ds   A
            SCOTT REBTOY   bs   A
            DALE SILLS   drums   A
            JON WILLIAMS   ld gtr   A

45: α Someday/Going Wrong   (Column 691) 1969

NB: α reissued by Sundazed (S 134) on gold wax and with a picture sleeve.

From Clovis, New Mexico. The 'A' side is in the Pink Floyd vein while the 'B' side is poppier. Both tracks have also resurfaced on *Sixties Rebellion, Vol. 15* (LP & CD) and you can also find *Someday* on the *Psychedelic Experience* CD. (MW)

Sixties Rebellion Vol. 15 (Comp CD) including The Apple-Glass Cyndrom.

The Applepie Motherhood Band

Personnel:	RICHARD BARNABY	bs, vcls	AB
	JACK BRUNO	drms, vcls	AB
	JOE CASTAGNO	gtr, vcls	A
	TED DEMOS	gtr, vcls	AB
	JEF LABES	keyb'ds, vcls	AB
	ADAM MYERS	hrmnca, vcls	B
	BRUCE PAINE	vcls	B
	MICHAEL SORAFINE	gtr, vcls	B

ALBUMS:	1(A)	APPLE PIE MOTHERHOOD BAND	(Atlantic 8189) 1968 -
	2(B)	APPLE PIE	(Atlantic 8233) 1969 -

45:	Long Live Apple Pie/Flight Path	(Atlantic 2477) 1968

From Boston, this act evolved out of a garage band called C.C. And The Chasers. Richard Barnaby recalls: "As C.C. and the Chasers, we were a garage band. Jack was only thirteen at the time and we rehearsed in the basement of a friend, Tom Harrington in Arlington Mass, since none of our parents would have it! We covered **The Byrds**, and had a few originals, and when psychedelics hit, they hit us as well. We moved from Boston and lived in Greenwich Village from 1965-1969 and were the house band at the Bitter End Cafe. There we backed up a number of the groups of the day including **First Edition** (with Kenny Rogers), Neil Diamond, Linda Rondstadt and **The Stone Poneys**, Jerry Jef Walker, Joni Mitchell, etc. Having signed to Atlantic we moved into the psychedelic venues such as Electric Circus, Cafe Au Go Go, and The Ark. With our second album we lived and played in Vermont, and toured the East Coast, and Mid-West from Toronto to Miami. We also toured both as a "B" group (supporting other groups like **Chambers Brothers**, **Mamas and Papas**, **Jefferson Airplane**, **Butterfield Blues Band**) and in our own right."

A good rock outfit whose albums deserve CD reissue. You can check out two of their cuts, *Born Under A Bad Sign* and *Gypsy* on *The Best Of Bosstown Sound* (CD).

The band were also known as **The Sacred Mushroom** for a while, when they first relocated to New York, but adopted the **Applepie Motherhood Band** moniker after a sarcastic retort stuck. Richard: "Our manager, Marvin Laganoff got us a record deal with Atlantic, but they didn't like the **Sacred Mushroom** name because it was "too druggy". I remember Ted Demos (lead guitar) saying "Well how about the 'Applepie Motherhood Band' then" in *total* sarcasm, and it just stuck... all you had to do was look at us to know it was a joke."

After the band split up, Jef Labes went on to the **Colwell-Winfield Blues Band**, Van Morrison, Bonnie Raitt, **Jesse Colin Young**, and is now teaching music in elementary school in Marin County, California, which he describes as "...the most rewarding work I've ever done". He's also writing satirical musicals including "Di Di Diana", a satire exploring "Who killed Diana?"; Jack Bruno played with **Second Coming** a Jacksonville Florida act and contempories of **Allman Bros Band**; then with Ted Demos he formed Shakey Legs Blues Band, before becoming Tina Turner's drummer for the past fifteen years. Bruce Paine went on to the lead role as "Claude" in the San Francisco based musical "Hair" for several years, whilst Michael Sorafine also took the second male lead in the same production; Ted Demos went on to become one of L.A.'s finest Art directors and set designers for film, T.V. and commercials and both he and Bruce Paine still perform together from time to time. (VJ/RBy)

Appletree Theatre

Personnel:	JOHN BOYLAN		A
	TERRY BOYLAN		A
	(LARRY CORYELL	gtr	A)
	(ERIC GALE	gtr	A)
	(HERB LOVELLE	vcls	A)
	(CHUCK RAINEY	bs	A)

ALBUM:	1(A)	PLAYBACK	(Verve Forecast 3042) 1968 SC

NB: (1) also issued in the U.K. (Polydor 2353.051).

45s:	Hightower Square/	
	Who Do You Think I Am	(Verve Forecast KF 5071) 1967
	Lotus Flower/	
	What A Way To Go	(Verve Forecast KF 5082) 1968

A studio project spotlighting the talents of brothers John and **Terry Boylan** (with support from guitarist Larry Coryell and various L.A. sessions players), **The Appletree Theatre** survived long enough to release one of the year's more interesting collections.

Co-produced by the brothers (Pete Spargo serving as executive producer), 1968's *Playback* offered up a rather weird concept piece (admittedly the plotline was largely lost on us). Written by the brothers, the collection contains a bizarre collage of interlaced vocal narratives, sound effects, song fragments, balanced by an occasional pop piece (*Hightower Square*, the bouncy *Brother Speed* and the trippy *You're The Biggest Thing In My Life*). One personal favourite is the backward tape instrumental *Lotus Flower*. There was no doubt the Boylans' were talented. Anyone doubting this statement need merely check out the collision of musical genres compressed into *The Sorry State Of Staying Awake* - country and western, blue-eyed soul; they even find time to make mention of LSD! On the other hand, the album was simply too experimental for the normal listener - no matter how strung out they may have been. Hard to adequately describe, imagine **The Association** having overdosed on bad acid and you might get a rough feel for the set...

John Boylan, who wrote *Brother Speed*, was also a member of **Hamilton Streetcar**, and they too recorded the track.

After this project, which was a little ahead of its time, **Terry Boylan** later made three solo albums in 1969, 1977 and 1980 and John went into management and later became a producer, with Linda Ronstadt and **Russ Giguere** (who covered his *Brother Speed*) among his credits. (VJ/SR/KSI/SB)

Arbors

Personnel:	EDWARD FARRAN
	FRED FARRAN
	SCOTT HERRICK
	TOM HERRICK

HCP

ALBUMS:	1	A SYMPHONY FOR SUSAN	(Date 3003) 1967 144 -
	2	ARBORS FEATURING I CAN'T QUIT HER	
			(Date TES 4017) 1968 - -

HCP

45s:	Anybody Here For Love/	
	Girl With The Heather Green Eyes	(Mercury 72456) 1965 -
α	A Symphony For Susan/Love Is The Light	(Date 1529) 1966 51
	Dreamer Girl/Just Let It Happen	(Date 1546) 1967 -
	Graduation Day/	
	I Win, The Whole Wide World	(Date 1561) 1967 59

THE BEST OF THE BOSSTOWN SOUND (Comp CD) including The Applepie Motherhood Band.

	Love For All Seasons/With You Girl	(Date 1570) 1967 -
β	Valley Of The Dolls/You Are The Music	(Date 1581) 1967 -
χ	The Letter/Most Of All	(Date 1638) 1969 20
δ	I Can't Quit Her/Lovin' Tonight	(Date 1645) 1969 67
ε	Motet Overature/Touch Me	(Date 1651) 1969 -
	Julie, I Tried/Okolona River Bottom Band	(Date 1672) 1970 -

NB: α also issued in the UK (CBS 202410) 1966. β also issued in the UK (CBS 3221) 1968. χ also issued in the UK (CBS 4137) 1969. δ also issued in the UK (CBS 4379) 1969. ε also issued in the UK (CBS 4640) 1969.

The Arbors were essentially a soft pop rock group with vocal harmonies, their material being partly based on re-arranged covers of current hits. They formed at the University of Michigan in Ann Arbor Their second album consists of psych soft-rock a lá **Association**, with a cover of **Al Kooper**'s tune and some baroque arrangements.

Four of their 45s charted. Their biggest and arguably best hit was a great arrangement/production of *The Letter*. (SR/GM/JW/VJ)

Arbuckle

ALBUM: 1 ARBUCKLE (Musicor MS 3???) c1971 -

A hippie-rock group with smooth harmonies. (SR)

Archie Whitewater

Personnel:
JIM ABBOTT	drms	A
BOB BERKOWITZ	keyb'ds	A
SAM BURTIS	trombone	A
TRAVIS JENKINS	sax, flute, vcls	A
FRED JOHNSON	ld vcls	A
PETER LaBARBERA	vibes	A
PAUL METZKE	gtr	A
LYN SHEFFIELD	sax, vibes	A
TONY VECE	bs	A

ALBUM: 1(A) ARCHIE WHITEWATER (Cadet Concept LPS 329) 1970 -

From New York, this album consists of a mix of psychedelia, horn-rock and jazz housed in a strange "Statue of Liberty" cover. Peter LaBarbera was a noted session man, also working with Loudon Wainwright and Marc Klingman. (SR)

Arch Of Triumph

Personnel:
T. ARENA	ld gtr	A
JIMMY McMAINS	ld vcls, keyb'ds, gtr	A
S. McMAINS	bs	A
?? ??	drms	A

ALBUMS: 1 THE STORY OF BAXTER WILLIAMS (CBS 7 63458) c1968 ?
2 title unknown (Date) 1970 ?

NB: (1) French release as 'Les Irresistibles'.

45s: α My Year Is A Day / She And I (Date 2-1618) 1968
(US) β Sunshine And You / Lands Of Shadow (Date 2-1634) 1969

NB: α and β also released in the UK on CBS 3330 and 3600 respectively, but as by "The Beloved Ones".

45s: α My Year Is A Day/ She And I (CBS 3330) 1968
(French) Dreams Of Dolls/The Fire (CBS 3913) 196?
Why Try Too Hard/ Things In Between (CBS 4222) 196?
Peace Of Love/My Love Is With Me Today (CBS 5100) 196?

NB: French releases as Les Irresistibles. α reissued Arabella 101488).

This Los Angeles band relocated to France in the mid-sixties where they met with some success as Les Irresistibles, releasing several 45s and an album. On their return to the US they adopted a new moniker with a distinctly French connection - Arch Of Triumph (as in L'Arc De Triomphe) but were concurrently known as the Beloved Ones, and under this name their 45s were released in the UK.

The French liner notes of the *My Year...* 45 mention that Jimmy and S. McMains were twins, born 7.9.1951 in Washington DC and T. Arena was born 8.4.1951 in Canton, Ohio. Their unknown drummer, who was NOT William Sheller, was born 5.28.1951 in Bethesda, Maryland. William Sheller was more a musical director/songwriter than a real member of the group. The single was produced by John Naikce.

Both US 45s deliver orchestrated flower-pop with a melodramatic flair and harmonious vocals. Pick of the crop is the enchantingly wistful *Lands Of Shadow* which graces the *Justavibration* and *Psychedelic Voyage Vol. 2* compilations (credited to 'Beloved Ones'). *My Year Is A Day* can be found on the worthy pop-psych compilation *Collecting Peppermint Clouds*, which must be given credit for unravelling the band's different identities and history. The compiler also mentions that they released a 1970 LP on Date in the US, whose details remain elusive.

Frenchman William Sheller appears to have been their musical director; he shared some songwriting credits, co-writing *My Year...* with T.Arena. He became a well-known solo singer in France and remains active in music 30-odd years on. (MW//SR/PM)

The Argyles

Personnel:
STEVE ANDERSON		A
LOUIS CABAZA	keyb'ds, bs	A
CHRIS HOLZHAUS	gtr	A
STEVE PERRON	vcls	A
BENNY TREIBER		A
ANDY ZSUCH	drms	A

45s: White Lightnin'/Farmer John (Pic One 136) 1966
Still In Love With You Baby/
Turn On Your Love Light (Jox 055) 1966

An historically interesting mid-'60s band which formed in 1961 and operated out of San Antonio, Texas. **The Argyles** later became **The Mind's Eye** and **The Children**. Promotional copies of their second 45 appeared on red vinyl, whilst their debut is wild'n'raucous waxing offering a different slant on *Farmer John* with one word changed - "I'm in love with your MOTHER"! An ode to the brewing of moonshine, *White Lightnin'* is a catchy fuzz-rocker with a novelty flavour. (VJ/MW/AB)

Arica

ALBUM: 1 HEAVEN (Just Sunshine JSS-1) 1973 SC

Probably from New York, an obscure hippie group influenced by Eastern music and spirituality. Their album was recorded with various instruments: sitar, tablas, congas, flute, electric guitar and gongs. For fans of the **Sufi Choir** or **Om Shanti**. (SR)

Ariel

45: I Love You / It Feels Like I'm Crying (Brent 7060) 1966

A San Francisco outfit, supposedly ex-**Banshees** of *They Prefer Blondes* fame. Adopting **Beau Brummels**-style vocals, the top side is a soft pop-ballad, but it's the upbeat garage-pop on the flip that's the choice cut. (MW)

Ark

45: Poverty Train/Daily Reminder (MGM K 13789) 1967

A stunningly powerful 45. Both sides have appeared on *Incredible Sound Show Stories, Vol. 8* (LP), where *Daily Reminder* is compared favourably to **Clear Light** - baroque touches, vocals effects, time changes and a superb guitar break - an unsung nugget. *Poverty Train* is no slouch either, a slow burner with Animals influences and tour-de-force vocals. A stunningly powerful 45 from an outfit whose origins remain unconfirmed. (MW)

The Ark

Personnel:	MICHAEL KNUST	gtr	A
	JERRY LIGHTFOOT	bs	A
	STEVE WEBB	drms	A

A short-lived Texas group formed in 1969 by Michael Knust from **Fever Tree**. They are supposed to have cut an album for Polygram but it was never released. (SR)

The Arkay IV

ALBUM: 1 FOR INTERNAL USE ONLY   (Marion 22595) 1968 R4

NB: (1) Reissued as *The Mod Sound Of The Arkay IV* (Cicadelic CICLP 1003) 1988 and on CD with The Outcasts *Meet The Outcasts* album as *Battle Of The Bands* (Collectables COL-CD-0519).

45s:	Surprise Love/Another Way	(Marion 17811/2) 1966
	Down From #9/When I Was Younger	(Marion 18805/6) 1967
	Demotion/I'll Keep On Trying	(Marion 21667/8) 1968

From Erie, Pennsylvania, they issued three 45s and an album (Marion 22595) between 1966-68. Their album has been reissued as *The Mod Sounds Of...* by Cicadelic (CICLP 1003) 1988, and also on CD by Collectables as *Battle Of The Bands*. This CD combines **The Arkay IV**'s album and **The Outcasts** *Meet The Outcasts!* It contains 26 tracks including previously unreleased demos.

Another album exists from 1976 that was apparently put together from tapes recorded in the first half of the seventies. As scary as that might sound initially, this record has a decidely retro feel and is worthy of investigation. Shown as by **The Weigaltown Elemental Band**, *Don't Hurt Yourself* (Old Ridge Records W 761) is in the R1 category.

The band reformed in the eighties and released a 45 *Feelin' Good Tonight / Every Morning* (American Artists A 4857) 1985. There's also a CD available entitled *When We Was Younger*.

Compilation appearances have so far included: *Demotion* and *Valley Of Conneaut Creek* on *Green Crystal Ties, Vol. 6* (CD). (VJ/MW/CF)

Armageddon

Personnel:	MARK CREAMER	gtr, vcls	A
	ROBERT LEDGER	bs	A
	JAMES PARKER	gtr, vcls	A
	JOHN STARK	drms, vcls	A
	(SKIP BATTYN	bs	A)

ALBUM: 1(A) ARMAGEDDON   (Amos AAS 7008) 1969 -

A Los Angeles band, although Mark Creamer, Jim Parker and John Stark were earlier members of the Texan outfit **Kitchen Cinq**. They did not release any 45s on this label but the album is now a very minor collectable. They sound influenced by Cream on a couple of tracks and also covered *Tales Of Brave Ulysses*. The album, which was produced by Tom Thacker, also contains a weird cover of *The Magic Song (Bibbidi Bobbidi Boo)*, from Disney's "Cinderella".

Robert Ledger went on to play in **Simon Stokes' Nighthawks**, whilst James Parker and John Stark also played on Them's U.S.-only album *In Reality*. Marc Creamer played for his wife (Laura Creamer)'s band, **Eve**, on their *Take It And Smile* album, (LHI 3100) 1970 (also produced by Tom Thacker and featuring Ry Cooder, James Burton, **Hal Blaine** and Sneaky Pete). Finally, **Skip Battyn** played in **The Evergreen Blueshoes** and would later join **The Byrds**. (VJ/SR)

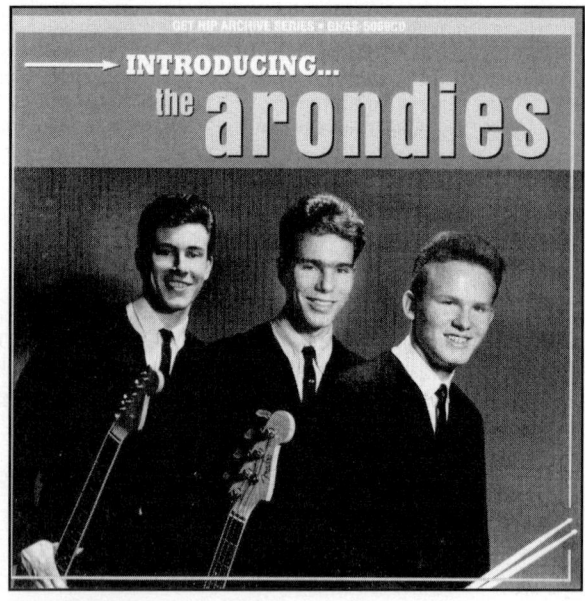

THE ARONDIES - Introducing CD.

Arnold Bean

Personnel:	GARY BURNETTE	A
	TODD CHRISTIANSON	A
	MIKE GUTHERIE	A
	HERB GUTHERIE	A

ALBUM: 1(A) COSMIC BEAN   (SSS International SSS-21) 1970 -

45: α SPECIAL BONUS SINGLE! (PS)
                   (SSS International AAA-PB-1) 1971

NB: α on blue wax, is a label sampler of LP tracks by **Arnold Bean** (selected cut is *Fortune And Fame*), **Benninghoff** and **H.Y. Sledge**.

Arnold Bean formed in Germany in 1964 then pulled up roots in the late sixties to head for the States. (SR/MW)

The Arondies

Personnel:	JIM PAVLACK	gtr, vcls	A
	GARY PITTMAN	bs, vcls	A
	BILL SCULLY	drms, vcls	A

ALBUM: 1 INTRODUCING ... THE ARONDIES
                   (Get Hip GHAS-5069) 1999 -

NB: (1) also issued on CD with same catalogue number.

45s:	α	69 / All My Love	(Sherry 198/9) 1965
		One Dead Chicken/Keep On Going	(Astra 1005) 1966/67
	β	Class Of '69 / All My Love	(Sherry 198/9) 1969
	χ	Class Of '69 / All My Love	(Astro 1014) 1969

NB: β and χ are a reissue of α. β coloured vinyl.

A Pittsburgh, Pennsylvania band. *69* is a very simplistic and largely instrumental song, which was later reissued in 1969, when someone figured they could make some money by re-dedicating it to the class of '69. More recently the track can be heard on *Burghers, Vol. 1* (LP & CD), and Get Hip's retrospective album collects the first two 45s and nine unreleased tracks from masters and acetates, all recorded in 1964 and 1965. A healthy mix of instrumentals, garage ballads, folk-rockers and proto-punkers are on offer that stand up well against local rivals the (pre-**Swamp Rats**) **Fantastic Dee-Jays**. Vinyl fans will also be interested in a 7" reissue of *69* with a previously unreleased cut *El Rondie* on the flip, (Get Hip GHAS 69) 1998.

After **The Arondies** split, Bill Scully went on to play in a group with Herb Marshall (ex-Splendors/Isley Brothers), whilst Jim Pavlack and Gary Pittman headed for Detroit and session work for Motown and Stax. Pavlack and

Pittman recruited drummer Jack O'Neill from The Oncomers, and played with Billy Sharay as Soul Congress, with whom they had a nationwide hit with *Do It* in 1971.

Other compilation appearances include: *Bull Fight Song* on *Terry Lee Show WMCK* (LP). (MW/BSj)

Arrangement

45s:	You / Mr. Tripper	(Scepter 12229) 1968
	The Child Of The Times / River Road	(Scepter 12258) 1969
	We've Got A World To Build/Chautauqua	(Scepter 12289) 1970

Dreamy harmony pop with occasional psychy effects for flower-pop fans. On their first 45 *You* is an **Association**-like ballad, whilst *Mr.Tripper* is upbeat midtempo pop nearer to the **Turtles**. Another apparently different **Arrangement** from Jackson Michigan put out a 'soul-garage 45 *Midnight Trip / Mean ...* on Small Town (103) circa 1970. (MW)

Arrogance

Personnel:	DON DIXON	bs, perc, vcls, gtr, strings	AB
	JIMMY GLASGOW		A
	MIKE GREER	gtr	A
	ROBERT KIRKLAND		A
	MARTY STOUT	keyb'ds	AB
	SCOTT DAVIDSON	drms, perc	B
	ROBERT KIRKLAND	gtr, perc, vcls	B
	(DON BROOKS	hrmnca	B)
	(LARRY PACKER		B)
	(ALLEN SANDFORD	strings	B)
	(ERIC WEISSBERG	banjo	B)

ALBUM:	1(B)	RUMOURS	(Vanguard VSD 9369) 1976

(Selective)

45s:	An Estimation/Black Death	(Crescent City CCSS 1091) 1969
	Open Wide/Lady Luck And Luxury	(Vanguard 35193) 197?
	Final Nickel/?	(Vanguard 35196) 197?

From Greensboro, this lot went on to become one of Central North Carolina's most prolific bands in the 1970s and also recorded as **Greer**. *Black Death* tended towards hard rock a lá Black Sabbath - a sign of the times in 1969 - but it had great vocals. You'll find it on *Tobacco A-Go-Go, Vol. 1* (LP). Don Dixon went on to become a nationally known producer, playing a part in the 'Athens scene' producing both R.E.M. and Mitch Easter's *Let's Active*.

Their 1976 album is reputedly pleasant, with *Open Wide* being the stand-out track. (VJ/MW/SR/PPn)

ARS NOVA - Ars Nova LP.

The Arrogants

45:	Golden Stairs/	
	Look For Tomorrow	(Living Legend LL-101/2) 1965

A very obscure 45 from Hollywood, California which features a sultry and simple Beatlesque ballad. The mid-tempo flip is the stronger with its ringing and reverbed guitars more in a Searchers/**Beau Brummels** vein, and both exude a tentative charm. Any impact is more in its historical significance as the first release on **Kim Fowley**'s modestly named Living Legend label and as the vehicle for two songs by budding writers Michael Lloyd and James Greenspoon. Lloyd arranged this and **Fowley** produced - was this their first recorded collaboration? Michael Lloyd would of course go on to achieve cult and legendary status as the whizz-kid behind the **West Coast Pop Art Experimental Band** and as a writer, arranger and producer (often in cahoots with **Fowley**) of so much more that is documented through-out this book - e.g. **A.B.Skhy**, **American Revolution**, **Fire Escape**, **Grains Of Sand**, Laughing Wind, **Rubber Band**, **St. John Green**, and **The Smoke** (on Capitol/Sidewalk). He also worked in partnership with Mike Curb and went on to become the youthful vice-president of MGM records. He continues to produce and command considerable respect to this day. The recent retrospective on the early days of **WCPAEB** (*Volume One* on Sundazed) features an interview with Michael that mentions the period but not this group - apparently he was also playing with a band called the Rogues around the time which featured Shaun and Danny Harris prior to the formation of **WCPAEB**.

So, we have to ask, who actually were **The Arrogants**? (MW)

Ars Nova

Personnel:	MAURY BAKER	perc, keyb'ds	A
	WYATT DAY	gtr, keyb'ds, vcls	AB
	BILL FOLWELL	trumpet, bs	A
	GIOVANNI PAPALIA	gtr	A
	JON PIERSON	trombone, vcls	AB
	JONATHAN RASKIN	bs, gtr, vcls	A
	WARREN BERNHARDT	keyb'ds	B
	JOE HUNT	drms	B
	ART KOENIG	bs	B
	JIMMY OWENS	trumpet	B

ALBUMS:	1(A)	ARS NOVA	(Elektra EKS-74020) 1968
	2(B)	SUNSHINE AND SHADOWS	(Atlantic SD 8221) 1969

NB: (2) has been reissued on CD by Repertoire (REP 4377-WY) 1993.

45s:	Fields Of People/	
	March Of The Mad Duke's Circus	(Elektra 45631) 1967
	Pavane For My Lady/Zarathustra	(Elektra ?) 1968
	Sunshine And Shadows/Walk On The Sand	(Atlantic 2625) 1969

In a sometimes almost desperate search to elevate the standard of rock, many groups shared the desire to marry their music with classical compositions. **Ars Nova** succeed better than most in making a convincing attempt, since their brand of cross-over incorporates not only baroque instrumentation in a psychedelic environment, but also baroque composition techniques such as fugas, chorales and pavanes, often scored for brass and guitar. On their first album, produced by Paul Rothchild and Arthur Gorson, they also write lovely tunes and the whole album does, surprisingly enough, not become as pretentious as it could have been, the name of the band notwithstanding. Two of the tracks even get covered (*Fields Of People* by The Move and *I Wrapped Her In Ribbons* by Galliard, both U.K. bands!). Other highlights include *March Of The Mad Duke's Circus*, with vaguely renaissance-like harmonies and *General Clover Ends A War*, a bitter and driven satire on military affairs. Most tracks were penned by Wyatt Day, sometimes helped by Jon Pierson. Greg Copeland, a young songwriter also working with Steve Noonan and Jackson Browne, wrote the lyrics of four songs.

The formation changed after the first album and among the departing members, Maury Baker went on to play on **Tim Buckley**'s *Starsailor*, **Janis Joplin**'s *Kosmic Blues* and Augie Meyer's *Head Music* albums. Bill Folwell guested on the second **Insect Trust** album and Jonathan Raskin appeared on **Tom Rush**'s *Circle Game*.

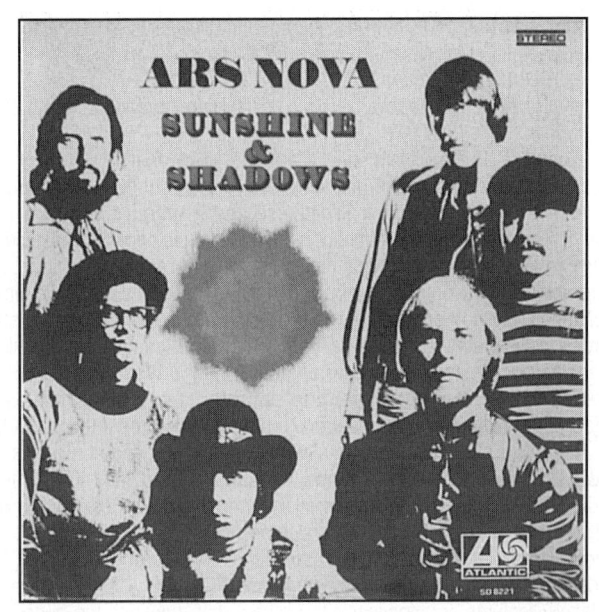

ARS NOVA - Sunshine And Shadows LP.

Their second effort in a completely revised line-up still finds them in good form regarding the playing, but they seemed to have lost their interest in the subtle art of their first. Some unusual harmonies are still to be found, but nevertheless more in a conventional rock frame.

After **Ars Nova**, Raskin, Day, Hunt, Owens and Pierson, formed a short lived studio group called **Terminal Barbershop**, together with Eric Weisberg, Joe Farrell and Dick Hurwitz. They released a mediocre album, *Hairstyles*, in 1969. Jon Pierson became a studio musician and played with Lou Reed.

Snap up the first album when you come across it. Compilation appearances have so far included:- *March Of The Mad Duke's Circus* on *Elektrock The Sixties* (4-LP); *I Wrapped Her In Ribbons* on *Kings Of Pop Music Vol. 2* (LP); and *And How Am I To Know* on *Hallucinations, Psychedelic Underground* (LP). (MK/SR/NK)

Art Collection

Personnel incl: RAY COLUMBUS   vcls   A

EP: 1 RAY COLUMBUS & THE ART COLLECTION (Distortions DR 1016) 1994

NB: (1) contains four tracks from 1967 including *Kick Me*.

45s:			
α	She's A Mod / The Cruel Sea	(Philips 40251)	1965
α	Where Have You Been?/She's Back Again	(Phillips 40326)	1965
β	Kick Me / She's A Mod	(Colstar 1001)	1967
	We Want A Beat / I Need You	(Colstar 1002)	1967
	I Would Rather Blow A Bagpipe / In The Morning Of Today	(Colstar 1003)	1967
	Till We Kissed / Tonight Is The Time (PS)	(Colstar 1004)	1968
	I Go To School/Morning	(Sundazed S 119)	1996

NB: α as Ray Columbus and The Invaders. β as Ray Columbus and The Art Collection.

This transcendent San Mateo, California, combo uncannily clones that heart-stopping Who's *Sell Out* sound. The band was led by vocalist Ray Columbus (Invaders) who later formed **Powder**. Columbus was originally from New Zealand.

The second 45, *Where Have You Been?* is a big beat orchestrated ballad, backed by a cool crunchy garage number similar to the other **Art Collection** sounds.

You can also find *Kick Me* on *Off The Wall, Vol. 1* (LP).

You can read more about him in the "Dreams Fantasies and Nightmares" book. (VJ/MW/SBn)

Arthur (Arthur Lee Harper)

ALBUMS:	1	DREAMS AND IMAGES	(LHI 12,000) 1968 R1
	2	LOVE IS THE REVOLUTION	(Nocturne NRS-905) 1969 R3

NB: (2) released as by **Arthur Lee Harper with Second Coming**. (2) reissued in 1998 (Synton T 9806).

The first album, recorded in November 1967, is a soft wistful folk LP by a Californian solo folkie, **Arthur Lee Harper**. Imaginative dealers may call this 'dreamlike psych' but they're only dreaming of how much they can boost its price! He did not release any 45s for Lee Hazelwood's label, but later released a privately pressed album under his real name. This is reputedly better and rockier. (VJ/MW)

Art of Lovin

Personnel:	PAUL APPLEBAUM	ld gtr	A
	JOHNNY LANK	bs	A
	BARRY TATELMAN	sax	A
	GAIL WINNICK	vcls	A
	SANDY WINSLOW	perc	A

ALBUM: 1(A)   ART OF LOVIN'   (Mainstream S/6113) 1968 R2

NB: (1) counterfeited on CD 1997. Also counterfeited as a 2-on-1 CD with the **Velvet Night** album.

45: You've Got The Power/Good Times   (Mainstream 687) 1968

A Massachussefts outfit whose album is full of interesting and quite imaginative pop/folk-rock, obscure enough to have been reissued. Apart from a cover of **Tim Hardin**'s *Hang On To A Dream*, all the songs were penned by Paul Applebaum. It's certainly worth hearing. (VJ)

David Arvedon

ALBUM: 1   IN SEARCH OF THE MOST UNFORGETTABLE TREE WE EVER MET (1969-1974)   (Arf! Arf! AA-053/4) 1995 -

Take **David Arvedon**, a bona fide sixties New England legend, add seasoned studio cats, and inflict a severe case of lyrical weirdness, aardvarks, and quality songwriting in the league of Lucia Pamela and **The Shaggs**. The double CD compilation, which includes his limited edition album, 8-track, both 45s and extra unreleased material is about as contorted and convoluted as homegrown music gets. **David Arvedon** was with Psycho's Psychopaths aka the **Psychopaths** in the sixties.

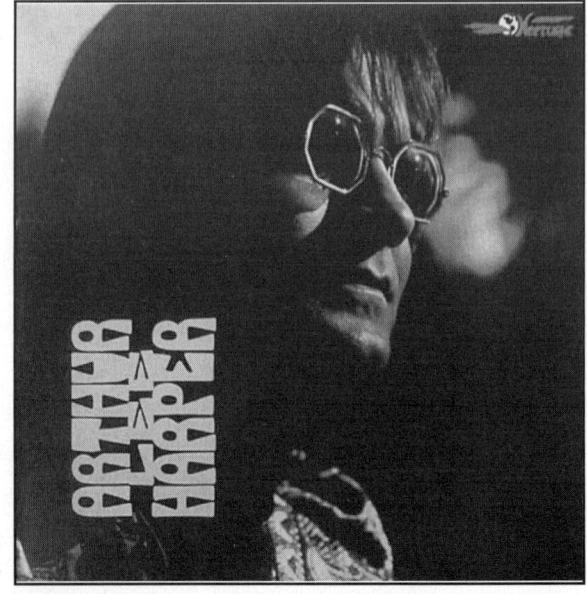

ARTHUR LEE HARPER - Love Is The Revolution LP.

You can also find a previously unreleased cut *Buckets Of Water* on the strange *Only In America* CD compilation.

The Ascendors

45:	I Won't Be Home/?	(Lee) 1966

From the Hornell, New York area. The 'A' side has resurfaced on *Back From The Grave, Vol. 8* (Dble LP) and the track was also covered in 1997 by the Others (a nouveau Italian garage-psych band) on their 10" *So Far Out* under the title *Won't Be Home*. (VJ/MW)

The Ascots

45:	Who Will It Be? / So Good	(Frat no #) 1966

This band came from Pontiac, Michigan, where they were a frequent live attraction in local teen clubs between 1964 and August 1966 when their lead guitarist and drummer quit for college. *So Good* is a raw recording with rockabilly-style guitar, but the label name says it all.

Compilation coverage has so far included:- *So Good* on *Back From The Grave, Vol. 6* (LP), *Punk Classics, Vol. 2* (7" EP) and *Michigan Mayhem Vol. 1* CD; *Who Will It Be?* on *Teenage Shutdown, Vol. 8* (LP & CD). (VJ/MW/MM)

The Ascots

Personnel incl:	RICK DESILETS	vcls		A
45s:	Monkey See - Monkey Do/You Can't Do That		(Super 102) 1965	
	Midnight Hour / Midnight Hour Part 2		(Super 103) 196?	
	Sookie Sookie / Put Your Arms Around Me		(Super 104) 196?	
α	I Need You / Knock On Wood		(Super 105) 106?	

NB: α only 200 copies pressed.

A Rhode Island outfit who leant towards R&B and soulful sounds. Much of their output is described as "soul-garage". Their debut showcases a chunky beat number with a fratty sound, backed by a forceful slowed-down version of the Beatles song.

Rick Desilets would release a solo 45, which is not recommended by Aram Heller in his New England bible 'Til The Stroke Of Dawn'. Aram also reveals that members of the Ascots would later form **The Deviled Ham**. (MW)

The Ascots

Personnel incl?:	M. BORDEN		A
	R. BORDEN		A
45s:	Summer Days / ?	(Blue Fin) 1966	
	I Won't Cry / Wonder Of It All	(Blue Fin BL-Fl-101) c1966	

From the Anaheim area of Los Angeles on the same label as **Deepest Blue**. This unknown group's upbeat folk-rock-jangler *Summer Days* shines on *Fuzz, Flaykes And Shakes Vol. 3* (LP & CD). (MW)

The Ashes

Personnel:	AL BRACKETT	bs	A
	JOHN MERRILL	gtr	A
	PAT TAYLOR	vcls	A
	JIM VORGHT	drms	A
ALBUM:	1(A) THE ASHES	(Vault 125) 1966 R1	
45s:	Is There Anything I Can Do?/ Every Little Prayer	(Vault 924) 1966	
	Dark On You Now/Roses Gone	(Vault 936) 1967	
	Homeward Bound/Sleeping Serenade	(Vault 973) 1971	

ART OF LOVIN' - Art Of Lovin' CD.

The above line-up is that featured on the album. This Los Angeles band's original drummer was, of course, Spencer Dryden, before he joined **Jefferson Airplane**. The remaining members, aside from Taylor, later teamed up with Bill Wolff, Lance Feat and Sandi Robinson to become **The Peanut Butter Conspiracy**.

The Ashes also have four tracks (both sides of their first two singles) on the 1967 Vault compilation, *West Coast Love-In* (LP). *Every Little Prayer*, *Is There Anything I Can Do?*, *Dark On You Now* and *Roses Gone* are all characterised by the distinctive melodies that typified so many mid-sixties English bands like The Fortunes. They feature Sandi Robinson rather than Pat Taylor on vocals. Their album is well worth a spin. A very hippyish sixties album with nice lead vocals. (VJ)

Jan Ashton

One time vocalist-drummer with **The Vejtables** (she sang lead on their local hit *I Still Love You* and their cover of **Tom Paxton**'s *Last Thing On My Mind*), she recorded an electro-folk track *Cold Dreary Morning*, which was a good platform for her vocal talents but remained unreleased until its inclusion on *Nuggets, Vol. 7* (LP), after leaving **The Vejtables** and prior to joining **The Mojo Men**.

Both unreleased 1967 tracks *Cold Dreary Morning* and *About My Tears* have been re-aired on the CD compilation *Someone To Love* (CD), part of Alec Palao and Big Beat's utterly essential *Nuggets From The Golden State* series. (VJ/MW)

A Small World

45s:	Wheel Of Fortune / Joni Joni	(Pacific Challenger 140) c1968
	I See You / The Life You Lead	(Mira 250) 1968

Los Angeles area releases by an unknown outfit , whose *Wheel Of Fortune* is appealing mid-tempo melodic garagey-pop with some fuzz buried low in the mix, **Turtles**' style 'ba-ba-baaa's, but with upfront brassy outbursts. *Joni* is much better - a galloping fuzz-popper without the brass. It's not certain that the Mira 45 is by the same group. (MW)

Assemblage

Personnel:	STUART AVERY	vcls	A
	PAUL KINGERY	gtr, vcls	A
	JOHN ORLICH	drms	A
	ROBIN ROBBINS	keyb'ds	A
	WALLY STAHL	bs, vcls	A
ALBUM:	1(A) THE ASSEMBLAGE ALBUM		
		(Westbound WB 2004) 1972 -	

45s: Satisfaction/Black And White   (Westbound 177) 1971
      Shotgun/?   (Westbound) 1971

On the same label as **Teegarden and Van Winkle** and **Funkadelic**, a Detroit hippie band heavily inspired by the Rolling Stones (they cover *Satisfaction*) with fuzz guitar, organ and female background vocals.

The band started in 1967 as Stuart Avery Assemblage and Wally Stahl had previously played in The Jagged Edge. (SR/NK)

Associated Soul Group

ALBUM: 1 TOP HITS OF TODAY   (Contessa CON 15012) 1968 -

This album is one of the more celebrated and rated examples of a subgenre which tends to go under the banner of 'exploito', which has gained interest and become more collectable in the last few years. Whilst covering many styles of music and moving into 'exotica' territory, we're only concerned here with trying to unravel those that exploited the psychedelic, garage or flower-power genres.

What is 'exploitio' - briefly it's the cash-in on the latest musical wave at minimal cost. Both the music and artists are exploited by covering or reworking (and often retitling) current hits in the latest styles. Songwriting and artist credits or identity rarely appear because the artists were just a bunch of session musicians. Occasionally a real group would be hired on the cheap who couldn't (and at the time wouldn't have wanted to) reveal their true identity (not unlike Elton John's early career as a hired hand on all those U.K. 'Top Of The Pops' albums). The music is frequently reused and recycled appearing on different albums, labels, with new arrangements and often a new title. Mike Curb of Sidewalk was already having great success in recycling music and groups - his 'house-band' were **Davie Allan & The Arrows** who went under many assumed names. This was very effective in cutting down on studio and artist costs, to provide cheap music for the masses and still make big bucks.

THE LABELS: generally found on budget labels like Contessa, Crown, Alshire, Wing, Wyncote, Custom, Design (equivalents in the U.K. would include Music For Pleasure, Starline and Marble Arch, and Europa on the continent).

SLEEVES/ARTWORK: It's with psychedelia that most tried to cash in. Sleeve designs tend to be in two camps: splashes and swirls of colour in paisley or oil-slide style accompanied by San Francisco poster-sytle lettering, or a semi-clad leggy chick surrounded by records (as in this case). Even the LP artwork got recycled too - in the case of this LP the same design was used on a **Firebirds** album.

MUSIC: The music ranges from totally naff to quite awesome: fuzz-psych extravaganzas, covering Hendrix or just trying to sound like him; fuzzy jazz-lounge instrumentals or instrumental reworkings (and renames) of recent hits; awful MOR pop or loungey ballad muzak. Unfortunately these extremes can be experienced on just one platter making the notion that it was one 'artist' unrealistic. Very few of these LPs don't have at least a couple of barfers.

FAKE GROUPS: This is where confusion really starts - Some albums give the impression that it's a bona-fide group via a picture or sleeve notes but the same music may turn up elswhere under a different artist name and sometimes track name, e.g. **Animated Egg**. Also rumoured to be a bogus group is the **Purple Fox** - *Tribute To Jimi Hendrix* album.

NON-GROUPS: Most of these are session musicians but even then one album will not be by one group of sessioneers - given the reappearance of the same tracks on other albums and the different syles and sounds - the name is most likely just a convenient and colourful handle for a collection of material. Examples: **Associated Soul Group**, Projection Company, Rasput & Sepoy Mutiny, **T. Swift & The Electric Bag, Underground**. Most of these 'names' had just the one release - one exception is the conglomeration known as **101 Strings**.

BONA-FIDE GROUPS: the **Firebirds** are thought to have been a genuine gorup. Another example is the Chimps, who recorded the rather good *Monkey Business* album on Wyncote (two Monkees covers and some good garage sounds) - they would later be known as the **(Thomas A.) Edison Electric Band**.

ASSOCIATION - Birthday CD.

These LPs throw other outfits into question - the Projection Company LP features three covers of **Id** *Inner Sounds* LP tracks - *Wild Times, Don't Think Twice* and *Boil The Kettle*. The first two turn up on the **Associated Soul Group** album and are exactly the same tracks. Whilst not the same as on the **Id**'s album, they sound close enough to question whether the bunch who recorded as the **Id** were behind some of the material on these two albums.

So what about the **Associated Soul Group** album itself? In the main it's above-par: five tracks recycled on the Projection Company album; covers include a great version of *Are You Experienced* (**T.Swift & The Electric Bag** do this too), an awful *Up Up And Away* (5th Dimension), *Macarthur Park* (Jim Webb/Richard Harris) and two Simon & Garfunkel numbers with rehashed (i.e. misheard) lyrics - *Sound Of Silence* and *Scarborough Fair*. Other tracks sound remarkably like the **Animated Egg** to add to the confusion.

Any further information or unravelling of this tangled skein will be most welcome!! (MW)

The Association

Not a garage or psychedelic band as such, this Los Angeles band largely falls outside the remit of this book. If you were one of the lucky people who purchased *'An American Rock History: Vol. 1 - California, The Golden State'* you can read all about them in there. They did, however, manage one foray into psychedelia, a rather strange record *Pandora's Golden Heebie Geebies*, named after Pandora's Box, the infamous Sunset Strip nightclub. You'll find it on *Nuggets Vol. 5* (LP). (VJ)

The Assortment

45: First I Look At The Purse/
     Bless Our Hippy Home   (Sound Spot 2224) 1967

This lot hailed from the Lansing area, around Central Southern Michigan. The 'A' side is a pretty good cover of a Contours song, the flip's rather an unusual Farfisa-laden song with classic lyrics and effective folk-punk vocals. It's resurfaced on *Highs In The Mid-Sixties, Vol. 19* (LP). (VJ)

The Astral Projection

45: Rosa-Lynn/Our Love Is A Rainbow   (Maverick 711) 1970

Sole 45 from a Duncanville, Texas outfit. Despite the vocalist's occasional Elvis pretensions, this mid-tempo garage-ballad has an infectious guitar refrain. *Our Love* is more rocky but with some solid fuzz. *Rosa-Lynn* was written by a guy from Carbondale, Pennsylvania, who now says that the 45 was not supposed to be released.

Rosa Lynn can also be found on *Acid Dreams Vol. 2* (LP). (MW/MM)

Astral Projection

Personnel:
JAY BERLINER	class. gtr		A
LOR CRANE	perc		A
AL GORGONI	gtr		A
JOSEPH MACHO Jr.	bs		A
HUGH McCRACKEN	gtr		A
FRANK OWENS	piano		A
BUDDY SALTZMAN	drms		A

ALBUM: 1(A) THE ASTRAL SCENE (Metromedia ?) 1968 R1

NB: (1) reissued on CD (Gear Fab GF-153) 2000 and vinyl (Gear Fab GF-206).

A NYC studio project. In addition to the personnel above there's string, horn and woodwind sections - in the former is Harry Lookofsky, father of the **Left Banke**'s Michael Brown (Lookofsky). Al Gorgoni was previously one half of Just Us, with Chip Taylor. **Hugh McCracken** had fronted his own outfit the Funatics, and became an in-demand session player.

If orchestrated concept hippie-flower-pop is your bag (man), this should appeal. Garageniks, on the other hand, should steer clear. (MW/SR)

Astronauts

Personnel:
BOB DEMMON	gtr, bs	ABCDEF
BRAD LEECH	drms	A
STORMY PATTERSON	bs	ABC
RICHARD OTIS FIFIELD	vcls, gtr	BCDEFG
JIM GALLAGHER	drms	BCDE
DICK SELLARS	gtr	B
DENNIS LINDSEY	gtr	CD
MARK BRETZ	gtr	EFG
RON JENKINS	drms	F
ROBERT CARL MCLERIAN	bs	G H
TONY MURILLO		G H
PETER M. WYANT		G H

HCP

ALBUMS:
1(C) SURFIN' WITH THE ASTRONAUTS (RCA Victor LSP-2760) 1963 61 SC
2(C) ROCKIN' WITH THE ASTRONAUTS (RCA Victor PRM-183 MONO) 1964 - SC
3(C) EVERYTHING IS A-OK (RCA Victor LSP-2782) 1964 100 SC
4(C) COMPETITION COUPE (RCA Victor LSP-2858) 1964 123 SC
5(C) THE ASTRONAUTS ORBIT KAMPUS (AOK) (RCA Victor LSP-2903) 1964 - SC
6(C) GO...GO...GO!!! (RCA Victor LSP-3307) 1965 - SC
7(C) FOR YOU FROM US (RCA Victor LSP-3359) 1965 - SC
8(C) DOWN THE LINE (RCA Victor LSP-3454) 1965 - SC
9(D) TRAVELIN' MEN (RCA Victor LSP-3733) 1967 - SC

NB: (6) & (7) have been reissued on one CD by Collectables (COL-2709) 1997. (8) & (9) reissued on one CD by Collectables (COL-2710) 1997.

EPs:
1 SURFIN' WITH THE ASTRONAUTS (RCA Victor SPC-1128 MONO) 1963
2 BEAT! ASTRONAUTS! ROCK! (RCA Victor SPC-1203 MONO) 1963
3 WURLITZER DISCOTHEQUE MUSIC (RCA Wurlitzer WLP5-100 MONO) 1964

HCP

45s:
Come Along Baby/Trying To Get To You (Palladium 610) 1962 -
α ?Geneva Twist / Take 17 (Jan Ell 459) 1962 -
α ?Blues Beat / Ski Lift (Vanruss 1000) 196? -
α ?Ridge Route / Blast Off (Luney 100) 196? -
Baja / Kuk (RCA Victor 47-8194) 1963 94
Hot Doggin' / Everyone But Me (RCA Victor 47-8224) 1963 -
Competition Coupe / Surf Party (RCA Victor 47-8298) 1964 124
Go Fight For Her /
Swim Little Mermaid (RCA Victor 47-8364) 1964 -
Theme from 'Ride The Wild Surf' /
Around & Around (RCA Victor 47-8419) 1964 -
Can't You See I Do / I'm A Fool (RCA Victor 47-8463) 1964 -
Almost Grown / My Sin Is Pride (RCA Victor 47-8499) 1965 -
Tomorrow's Gonna Be Another Day /
Razzamatazz (RCA Victor 47-8545) 1965 -
It Doesn't Matter Anymore /
The La La La Song (RCA Victor 47-8628) 1965 -
Main Street / In My Car (RCA Victor 47-8885) 1966 -
Better Things / I Know You Rider (RCA Victor 47-9109) 1966 -
β Sally Go 'Round The Roses /
Pay The Price (RCA Victor 47-9227) 1967 -

NB: α not confirmed as by this **Astronauts**. β as **Sunshine Ward**

For garage/psych purists with raised eyebrows at this entry, scoff ye not. Boulder's famous **Astronauts** may tend to be regarded as just an instrumental or surf group, but this is being grossly unfair, and I've been as guilty as many in that regard until recently. Yes, they did do instrumentals but vocals were predominant in their later material. What's more this talented bunch embraced beat, Invasion, and folk-rock styles to keep pace with the rapidly changing sounds of the times. Interested now? Read on.

Kicking off as the Stormtroopers in 1959 (lineup 'A') they changed their name to **Astronauts** on releasing their first 45. On winning a contract with RCA they spent much of their time based in Los Angeles to record, lap up the surf and sunshine vibes and appear in some surf movies. *Baja* was a sizable hit and set them fair with RCA - resulting in nine LPs and a large handful of 45s in just four years. When the bubble finally burst and their name and sound seemed to be a fading star at the onset of the psychedelic era, they changed their name to Sunshine Ward in an attempt to revive their fortunes. It didn't work, RCA lost interest and original mainstay Bob Demmon departed. The others tried one last relaunch after more personnel shuffles, firstly as **Sunshine Ward** and then after one final name change as **Hardwater**.

Collectables has recently reissued their LPs on 2-for-1 ('twofer') CDs and the pair above might interest readers of this book. For those into the original vinyl and still to be convinced, try the *Travelin' Men* album (which includes covers of *I Know You Rider*, *Midnight Hour*, and the **Beau Brummels**' *Laugh Laugh*) or the more obviously Merseybeat influenced *Down The Line* LP (the Big O's title track, *Down Home Girl*, *Walking The Dog*, *Sweet Little Rock And Roller*, *Memphis Tennessee*). The obvious weakness with their last two LPs is that there are no group originals at all, unlike their earlier releases. So, although they may have adapted to playing these styles, writing them was a different proposition. However, it would be unkind to brand them a 'covers band'.

Appearances - on beat/garage/psych compilations - have been restricted to their rare debut *Come Along Baby* on *Highs In The Mid-Sixties, Vol. 18* (LP); *Tomorrow's Gonna Be Another Day* on *Let's Dig 'Em Up, Vol. 2 - The Count Game* (LP) and *Let's Dig 'Em Up, Vol. 1* (CD); *Baby, Please Don't Go* on *Out Of Sight* (LP); and both *Can't You See I Do* and *My Sin Is My Pride* on *Prisoners Of The Beat* (LP). (MW)

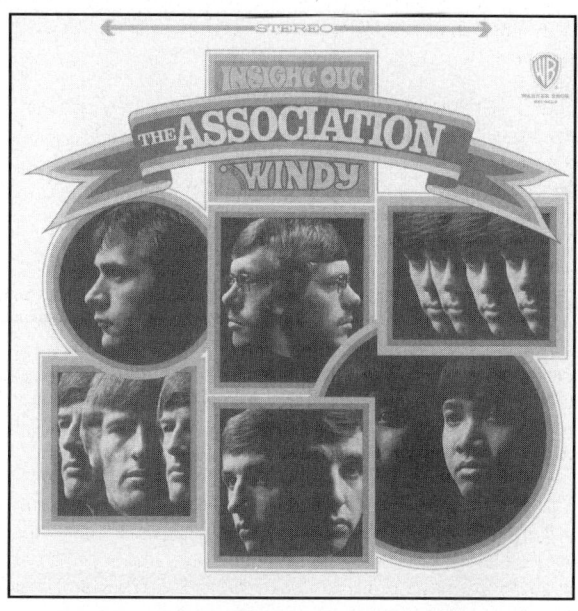

ASSOCIATION - Insight Out CD.

Asylum

Personnel:	DAN DINKINS	gtr, vcls	A
	BOB KING	bs	A
	ELAINE LaZIZZA	keyb'ds, vcls	A
	KEN WARD	drms, vcls	A
	BUDDY WILLIAMSON	keyb'ds	A

ALBUM: 1(A) FIRST AND LAST   (No label NR 3217) 197? R2

Can you imagine a more perfect name for a band based at a military academy in Virginia in the early seventies?

Elaine's vocal ability impresses in a Karen Carpenter kind of way, although it will disappoint most readers to learn that a substantial amount of the music on this album also walks this path. The opening cut *I Want You Everyday* is the hardest rocking and it's unfortunate that more of the band's repertoire doesn't match it.

To answer the obvious question: no it's not a co-ed military academy, Elaine was the daughter of a Captain at the facility.

This album is held in high regard by collectors of the genre, although the merits of such pursuits have not been calculated by the majority. Proceed with caution! (CF)

The Asylum Choir

Personnel:	MARC BENNO	vcls, drms	A
	LEON RUSSELL	vcls, gtr, keyb'ds	A

ALBUMS:	1	LOOK INSIDE THE ASYLUM CHOIR	(Smash 67107) 1968 -
	2	THE ASYLUM CHOIR II	(Shelter 8910) 1971 -

NB: (1) reissued in 1971 (Smash SRS-67107, group photo cover), (2) also issued in Holland (Philips 6369107) 1971. (2) reissued in 1974 (Shelter 2120), 1976 (Shelter 52010) and 1979 (MCA 684).

45s:	Soul Food/Welcome To Hollywood	(Smash 2188) 1968
	Indian Style/Icicle Star Tree	(Smash 2204) 1969
	Straight Brother/Tryin' To Stay Alive	(Shelter 7313) 1971

A Los Angeles-based venture, which for **Russell** and Benno represented a largely unsuccessful journey into psychedelia. After a first single as **Le Cirque**, their debut album was released. This sold badly, partly because the cover featured a toilet roll, but mainly because the music was quite patchy. A mix of pop, R&B and psychedelia, with arrangements (especially on the second side). Smash later reissued it with a group cover. Benno and **Russell** wrote all the songs, with the assistance of Greg Dempsey (**Daughters Of Albion**), Bill Boatman, **Jerry Riopelle** and the mysterious Markham and Wilson, who may have played on the backing group.

THE ASTRAL PROJECTION - The Astral Scene LP.

ASYLUM - First And Last LP.

Although the second album was recorded in April 1969, Mercury did not release it on their Smash subsidiary and **Russell** bought the tapes to release it on his own Shelter label two years later. It's bluesier than the debut and contains some good songs (notably an anti-Vietnam song *Ballad To A Brother*).

Russell and Benno's involvement is the main reason why collectors seek out these albums.

Born in 1947 in Dallas, Benno would later play with **The Doors** (on *L.A. Woman*), Rita Coolidge and Rick Roberts. He also released three excellent albums on A&M between 1970 and 1972, recorded with Ry Cooder, Jesse Ed Davis and Clarence White. Afterwards he disappeared only to return in 1979 with *Lost In Austin* (with Eric Clapton). In the nineties, he has recorded two good texas blues albums. (VJ/SR)

Atlantics

Personnel incl:	CARMEN	vcls	A
	JIMMY	vcls	A

45s:	Let Me Call You Sweetheart / Home On The Range	(Rampart 614) 1964
	Beaver Shot / Fine, Fine, Fine	(Rampart 643) 1965
	Sloop Dance / Sonny & Cher	(Rampart 647) 1965
α	When I Look Into My Life / ?	(Ramrod) 196?

NB: α may be by a different group.

Part of Los Angeles' East Side scene, this was a group Mexican Americans out of El Monte. They have been well compiled: - *Beaver Shot* (written by Max Uballez of the **Romancers/Smoke Rings**) and *Sloop Dance* feature on *The East Side Sound, Vol. 1* (CD); *Beaver Shot* and *Fine Fine Fine* on *Rampart Records EP* (7"); *Beaver Shot* on *The East Side Sound, Vol. 1* (LP); *Sonny And Cher* on *The East Side Sound Vol. 2* (LP); *Home On The Range* on *The West Coast East Side Sound, Vol. 2* (CD); *Sloop Dance* on *The West Coast East Side Sound, Vol. 3* (CD); *Beaver Shot* on *The West Coast East Side Sound, Vol. 4* (CD); and finally *Sloop Dance* is also on 1969's double-album compilation *East Side Revue* and *East Side Revue, Vol. 1* (LP).

An album *Live At The Nite Lite* (Hashish) c1970, was probably recorded by a different **Atlantics**, but has been described as "lounge act with wah wah guitar and a pretty little vocalist with a big voice". (MW/SR)

Atlantis Philharmonic

Personnel:	ROYCE GIBSON	perc, vcls	A
	JOE DI FAZIO	keyb'ds, bs, vcls	A

ALBUM: 1(A) ATLANTIS PHILHARMONIC   (Dharma 802) 1974 SC

NB: (1) reissued on CD (Lasers Edge LE 1005).

On the same label as **Ken Little**, a progressive duo whose album is highly-rated by some collectors. It is good progressive rock with classical and psychedelic influences. The music in places is spacey and dreamy. (SR/CG)

Atlee

Personnel:	DON FRANCISCO	drms, vcls	A
	BRUCE SCHAFFER	keyb'ds, vcls	A
	MICHAEL STEVENS	gtr, vcls	A
	ATLEE YEAGER	ld vcls, bs	A

ALBUM: 1(A) FLYING AHEAD (ABC Dunhill DS 50084) 1970 SC

45: Rip You Up / Will We get Together (ABC Dunhill D-4254) 1970

Produced by Joel Sill, **Atlee** were a good hard-rock quartet from California. All the tracks on their sole album were penned by **Yeager** and demonstrate the band's skill and their sense of humour: *Jesus People*, *Dirty Sheets*, *Dirty Old Man* and *Let's Make Love* are just some highlights of a very consistent album. Still working with Michael Stevens, **Atlee Yeager** would go on to issue another album on Chelsea in 1973.

Yeager also played bass on **Damon**'s album whilst Stevens and Francisco went on to **Highway Robbery**. (MW/CF/SR)

Attila

Personnel:	BILLY JOEL	keyb'ds, vcls	A
	JON SMALL	drms	A

ALBUM: 1(A) ATTILA (Epic BN 30030) 1970 SC

After **The Hassles**, Billy Joel and Jon Small formed **Attila**, a keyboards/drums duo a la **Lee Michaels**. Joel was then playing a distorted Hammond B-3 and the forceful percussions help to create some strange sounds, very very far from *Honesty*! The record was a total flop but is now beginning to attract the attention of some collectors. (SR)

Attila and The Huns

Personnel incl:	BARRY BERDAL	bs	A
	DOUG DEUEL	gtr	A
	MIKE PEACE (PEASE)	ld gtr	AB
	WALTER STANIEC	drms	A
	RICH LeGAULT	drms	B
	DENNIS LEWAN	bs	B
	BENNY WISNIEWSKI	gtr	B
	BARB SPENCE	vcls	

45s:	Cheryl / The Lonely Huns	(Sara 6511) 1965
	Hula Shake / Hurry Back	(Magic Touch 2009) 1967
	Walking In The Vineyards /	
α	Here's Where I Get Off	(Magic Touch 2070) 1969
	The Vineyards Of My Time /	
	Here's Where I Get Off	(Magic Touch 2071) 1969

NB: α credited to The Huns Of Time.

Initially based in Thorp, Wisconsin this soulful combo was assembled in 1964. In 1967 they got a contract on Lenny LacCour's Magic label almost by accident. They'd been contacted by an agency in Milwaukee after finishing second in a Battle Of The Bands in Wausau. They got lost and ended up at the studios of Dave Kennedy, who passed them onto Lenny laCour who liked what he heard, signed them, and would later come up with a new name for them - **The Filet Of Soul**.

Their poppiest confection, *The Vineyards Of My Time*, can also be found on *Every Groovy Day* (LP). (MW/TT/GM)

Atwood Electric Iceman

45: Michoacan/Bossier City (UNI 55216) 1970

This song co-written by **Kim Fowley** and A. Allen was also recorded by Doug Sahm for the "Cisco Pike" soundtrack.

This obscure single was produced by Tom Ayres for Banker's Musical Industries. (SR)

Debbie Au

ALBUM: 1 DON'T BE AFRAID (Trilogy Arts) 1971

A Christian soft-rock singer, her orchestrated album is rare but not recommended. (SR)

August

Personnel:	JOHN BETZ	bs, vcls	A
	RICH KNICKERBOCKER	gtr, kazoo, vcls	A
	LARRY SPURRIER	drms, bs, vcls	A

ALBUM: 1(A) AUGUST (The Nise Sound A-31/2) 1968 R5/R6

NB: (1) only 200 copies pressed originally. Reissued on heavy duty vinyl (Shadoks 014) 2000.

A trio of fresh-faced youths, said to be from New Jersey (though the album seems to have been recorded in Philadelphia). It is extremely rare - asking prices in the region of $2500 accompanied by descriptions like "garage folk-rock" have generated interest and finally a reissue to satisfy curiosity.

Even the above description is somewhat optimistic and if you're expecting an undiscovered garage monster you'll be disappointed. This is muted lo-fi pop - from moody to perky - permeated by a coy charm evoked by vulnerable vocals and hesitant harmonies. The good-timey vibe of **The Lovin' Spoonful** is much in evidence (they cover *Full Measure*) and some Anglophile whimsy, via the Beatles' *Eleanor Rigby*.

The album was recorded, after-hours, in a restaurant. (MW/CF)

Aum

Personnel:	WAYNE CEBALLOS	hmnca, vcls, gtr, keyb'ds	A
	LARRY MARTIN	drms, vcls	A
	KEN NEWELL	bs, vcls	A

NB: Later members included Reese Martin, Boots Houston, Sean Silverman and Steve Bowman.

AUGUST - August LP.

AUM - Resurrection LP.

ALBUMS: 1(A) BLUESVIBES (Sire 97007) 1969 SC
2(A) RESURRECTION (Fillmore 30002) 1969 -

NB: (1) also issued in France (Sire SHK 8401) 1969. (2) was also issued in France (CBS S 63911) 1970.

45s: Bye Bye Baby/Resurrection (Fillmore 7000) 1970
Aum/Little Brown Hen (Fillmore 7001) 1970

Led by singer/multi-instrumentalist Wayne Ceballos, the little know **Aum** stand as also-rans in the lexicon of sixties San Francisco bands. With drummer Larry Martin and bassist Ken Newell rounding out the trio, the group's initial reputation stemmed from their jam-oriented concerts.

Initially signed by the London-affiliated Sire label, as one would expect from the title, the group's 1969's *Bluesvibes* found them working in a distinctively blues-vein. Reflecting the band's live act, the Richard Gottherer produced debut featured a series of seven extended jams, (the shortest song clocking in at four minutes). With Ceballos writing the majority of the material, in spite of period excesses (e.g. aimless soloing), originals such as *Mississippi Mud* and *Chilli Woman* weren't half bad. Moreover, Ceballos proved a decent singer, injecting considerable energy into his performances. Among the few short-comings, the band's ponderous cover of John Loudermilk's *Tobacco Road* would've been suitable for **Vanilla Fudge**.

One of the first acts to be signed to Bill Graham's Fillmore label, 1969's *Resurrection* teamed the band with producer David Rubinson. As one might have guessed from the album title (let alone the back cover which showed three crosses), their sophomore effort found the band pursuing a pseudo-religious agenda. In spite of occasionally clunky lyrics and an irritating degree of echo, Ceballos-penned material such as *God Is Back In Town*, the ballad *Only I Know* and *Today And Tomorrow* wasn't too bad. Boasting a nifty Ceballos guitar solo, the stately title track is the stand-out cut. Elsewhere, the driving *Bye Bye Baby* and *Little Brown Hen* recall **Quicksilver Messenger Service**. Certainly not likely to get top-40 airplay, but San Francisco certainly turned out worse sounding bands. Commercially the band did nothing; the trio calling it quits shortly thereafter.

In 1975, Larry Martin would play with **Charlie Musselwhite**. (VJ/SR/GM/SB)

Aura

Personnel:	SAM ALESSI	organ, piano, vibes	A
	GEORGE BARR	trumpet, vcls	A
	FRED ENTESARI	sax	A
	ANDY FOERTSCH	trombone	A
	DENNIS HORAN	drms	A
	AL LATHAN	vcls, perc	A
	JERRY SMITH	bs, vcls	A
	BILL WAIDNER	gtr	A

ALBUM: 1(A) AURA (Mercury SRMI 620) 1971 -

A powerful horn-jazz-rock outfit from Los Angeles. The stand-out cut on the album is *Life Is Free* on Side Two. Chuck Greenberg (flute, sax) and Terry Quaye (congas) also guested on the album. (VJ)

The Aussies

45: Slippin' And Slidin'/Oo Poo Pah Doo (Take Five 631-9) 196?

An obscure sixties combo from Arizona. (VJ)

Autosalvage

Personnel:	SKIP BOONE	bs, piano	A
	DARIUS DAVENPORT	vcls, keyb'ds, drms, gtr, bs, perc	A
	THOMAS DONAHER	vcls, gtr	A
	RICK TURNER	gtr, banjo	A

ALBUM: 1(A) AUTOSALVAGE (RCA Victor LSP 3940) 1968 R1

NB: (1) reissued on vinyl by Edsel in 1988 (ED 286). (1) also counterfeited on CD and later reissued officially (Acadia ACA 8011) 2001.

45: Parahighway/Rampant Generalities (RCA 9506) 1968

Formed in 1966 by bluegrass fanatic Thomas Donaher and multi-instrumentalist Darius Davenport, **Autosalvage** was one of the mid-sixties more impressive jug band outfits. Boasting an exceptionally talented line-up, including ex-Ian and Sylvia sideman Rick Turner and bassist Skip Boone (brother of the **Lovin' Spoonful**'s Steve Boone), the band's sound melded authentic jug band moves with rock instrumentation, a sense of enthusiasm and a willingness to expanded into progressive and out of the ordinary directions.

Reportedly dscovered by **Frank Zappa** while on a visit to New York, with **Zappa**'s support the group was signed by RCA Victor. Their album, *Autosalvage* offered up one of 1968's odder musical hybrids. Exemplified by original material such as *Land Of Their Dreams*, *Burglar Song* and *Rampant Generalities* the collection featured a weird mixture of **Byrds**-styled country rock (*Rampart Generalities*), blues-rock (*Good Morning Blues*), psychedelia (*Auto Salvage*) and outright pretense. What made the set truly maddening was the fact that while all four members were undeniably talented, they seldom brought those talents together. Among the few tracks worth hearing more than once were the nifty title effort and the single *Parahighway/Rampart Generalities*. Not to sound too damning, the band's willingness to try new things makes it oddly endearing, if not particularly commercial, or memorable. Unfortunately, it all came to little avail since the band called it quits shortly thereafter.

AUTOSALVAGE - Autosalvage LP.

Boone and Davenport subsequently reappeared supporting the short-lived **Bear** and then as sessions players, including Terence Boylan's 1969 solo album. Rick Turner went on to work with **Jerry Corbitt** and **Jeffrey Cain**. He later became a well-known guitar builder/repairer (notably for Ry Cooder).

Compilation appearances include: *Land Of Their Dreams* on *Psychedelic Frequencies* (CD). (VJ/SR/SB)

Autumn People

Personnel:	STEVE BARAZZA	drms	A
	LARRY CLARK	gtr	A
	DANNY POFF	keyb'ds	A
	CLIFF SPIEGEL	bs	A

ALBUM: 1(A) AUTUMN PEOPLE   (Soundtech 3020) 1976 R2

This album by an obscure Arizonan band has generated some interest from collectors. A hippie progressive album it features some weaving organ work and superb guitar leads. (VJ)

The Avant Garde

Personnel incl: CHUCK WOOLERY   A

HCP
45s:	Yellow Beads/Honey And Gall	(Columbia 4-44388) 1967 -
	Naturally Stoned/Honey And Gall	(Columbia 4-44590) 1968 40
	Fly With Me/ Revelations Revelations	(Columbia 4-44701) 1968 130

This band is best known for *Naturally Stoned* which hit the Billboard chart at No. 40. and is best described as orchestrated 'psychedelic pop' (the lyrics may be psychedelic but the music is pop) with the backing sounding like a James Bond-type movie theme. It is the flip side which has been compiled however: *Honey and Gall* resurfacing on *Psychedelic Unknowns Vol. 8* (LP & CD) and being an unusual and captivating hippie-psychedelic effort.

Yellow Beads is also dreamy acoustic hippie-pop in their unique style. The final 45 reverts to more standard orchestrated pop format effort on *Fly With Me* but is rescued by the electrified folk-pop flip.

All their material was composed by B. Fowler or C. Woolery, who it turns out is none other than Chuck Woolery, who would later become one of America's top game show hosts-- he was the original emcee of "Wheel of Fortune" before adding his brand of smarminess to the matchmaking "Love Connection". (MW/DDv/TTi)

The Avengers

Personnel:	GERRY BLAKE	keyb'ds	A
	HENRY GONZALES		ABC
	JIM ROBESKY		ABC
	DUGAN TURNER	drms	A
	LOUIS WEISBERG	ld gtr	ABC
	GARY BERNARD	drms	B
	MIKE HUESTIS	drms	C

45s:	You Can't Hurt Me Any More/When It's Over	(F-G 104) 1965
	Be A Caveman/Broken Hearts Ahead	(Starburst 125) 1965
	Shipwrecked/I Told You So	(Starburst 128) 1966
	It's Hard To Hide/Open Your Eyes	(Current 109) 1966
	Strange Faces / Softly As I Leave You	(American 101) 1967

This garage outfit from Bakersfield, California but were part of the Los Angeles club scene. Their finest moments were probably *Be A Caveman*, a slice of three chord arrogance and *Open Your Eyes*, a fine song with superb instrumentation and catchy folk-rock vocals. *Shipwrecked* is a Farfisa-led song with fine throaty vocals, and *You Can't Hurt Me Any More* has a rockin' beat with a neat choppy solo. *It's Hard To Hide*, is a jaunty folkish rocker, with a neat reverb effect on the organ - in stark contrast to the primitive beat displayed on *Be A Caveman*. A band well worth checking out, especially for that second single.

The Avengers were managed by Bakersfield KAFY DJ Mike Lunky, and Ken Johnson also wrote *I Can Read Between The Lines*, the flip to Gary Lewis and The Playboys 1966 hit *Green Grass*. After **The Avengers** disbanded, Ken Johnson returned to the Bakersfield music scene and became involved in Gary Paxton's Bakersfield International studio crowd as a session player and songwriter.

Through Paxton and with fellow Bakersfield performer and songwriter Dennis Payne, they recorded a series of albums for Al Sherman's Alshire International label in the late 1960's as the **California Poppy Pickers**. Paxton leased various other recording projects to Alshire, which may have involved Johnson.

Dugan Turner later played with **The Donnybrooks**, while Blake and Huestis formed the **United Sons Of America**.

As one might expect, **The Avengers**' material has been heavily compiled including: *Be A Caveman* on *Highs In The Mid-Sixties, Vol. 1* (LP), *Boulders, Vol. 1* (LP), *Best of Pebbles, Vol. 1* (LP & CD), *Pebbles, Vol. 2* (CD) and *Pebbles, Vol. 3 (ESD)* (CD); *Open Your Eyes* on *Acid Dreams Epitaph* (CD), *Acid Dreams - The Complete 3 LP Set* (3-LP), *Folk Rock E.P.* (7") and *Ya Gotta Have... Moxie, Vol. 1* (Dble CD); *Open Up Your Eyes* and *It's Hard To Hide* on *Highs In The Mid-Sixties, Vol. 20* (LP); *It's Hard To Hide* on *Pebbles Vol. 8* (CD); *Shipwrecked* on *Garage Punk Unknowns, Vol. 3* (LP); and *I Told You So* on *Garage Punk Unknowns, Vol. 1* (LP). (VJ/MW/RLs/JO/MDow/DTu)

The Avengers

45s:	Reflection/Irresistable You	(Kama 780) 1967
α	Lavender Blue/ Tossin And Turnin	(Kama 781) 196?

NB: α as Danny Bowens and The Avengers.

From Syracuse, New York State. The first 45, *Reflection*, is decent garage but their second features an old R&B ballad with a garage-soul flip and isn't recommended.

You can also find *Reflection* on *Echoes In Time, Vol. 2* (LP), *Echoes In Time Vol's 1 & 2* (CD) and *I'm Trippin' Alone* (LP). (VJ/BPn)

The Avengers

45s:	The Kiss I Never had / Your Picture	(Van Dyk VD-1611/2) 196?
	Crying All Alone / No Wonder	(Mr. Genius 402) 196?

Both 45s are thought to emanate from a Philadelphia area band in the mid-to-late sixties. The Van Dyk 45 is awful pre-beat pop with keening female-male vocals and should be avoided. *Crying All Alone* is a big beat ballad with brass BUT done with garage style and sentiments plus a great fuzz and brass solo - definitely different and a pleasant surprise (though probably not for purists). The flip is a brassy pop ballad.

Compilation appearances have included: *No Wonder* and *Crying' All Alone* on *Searching For Love* (LP). (MW)

The Avengers

Personnel:	LEE BAKER	gtr	A
	JIM DICKINSON	12-string gtr	A
	BILL DONATI	drms	A
	JOE GASTON	bs	A
	BOBBY LAWSON	vcls	A
	JOE LEE	gtr, vcls	A
	TERRY MANNING	organ, vcls	A

45s:	Batman Theme/Batarang	(Ardent 106) 1966
	Batman's Theme / Back Side Blues	(MGM 13465) 1966

DAVID AXELROD - Song Of Innocence CD.

From Memphis, these **Avengers** recorded *Batarang* in 1966, an excellent bluesy instrumental cut with great guitar leads and organ. Cashing in on the Batman craze, these masked marauders turned out to be none other **Lawson and Four More** augmented by **Jim Dickinson** and Lee Baker. This 45 appeared between their two **Lawson and Four More** releases on Ardent.

Lee Baker would later be in **Moloch**, **Jim Dickinson** was previously in the **Jesters** and would have a very prolific career, notably with Ry Cooder.

It has still to be confirmed whether the MGM 45 has any connection to this outfit at all - it may just have been another caped crusader cash-in by a same-name outfit ("Holy confounding coincidences, Batman").

Batarang has subsequently been compiled on *It Came From Memphis* (Upstart 022) 1995. (SR/MW/RHI)

Avlons

45: Mad Man's Fate / Come Back Little Girl   (Pyramid 6-6877) 1966

An obscure outfit from North Carolina, whose *Mad Man's Fate* comes on like the Animals doing a moody soul ballad - eminently listenable but unlikely to appear on a garage compilation. The less interesting flip (in my opinion), a low-key garage affair with neat harp, appears on *Lost Generation, Vol. 1* (LP). (MW)

The Awakening

ALBUM: 1 GOD COME DOWN
(Christos Records CS-1001) 1974 R1?

A Christian group, their album tried to portray the life of Jesus Christ in song. It's rather patchy and ranges from folk-rock to hard-rock, from acoustic tunes with flute to songs with dreamy echoed vocals and fuzz guitar. The group consists of four guys and four gals, only identified by their first names: Eve, Marilyn, Flip, Davy, Wayne, Cindy, Doug and Sam. The labels and sleeve of this obscure album have no track listing and no indication of the origin of this group. (SR)

A Warm Puppy

45: Around A Fountain/Colorful Love   (Bullet 4512) 1968

Max Waller drew my attention to this 45 which has not yet figured on any compilations. The 'A' side is an airy psychedelic effort, the flip a heavily-Vanilla Fudge inspired slice of bombast with a psychedelic edge. (VJ)

David Axelrod

ALBUMS:	1	SONG OF INNOCENCE	(Capitol ST-2982) 1968 R1
(up to	2	SONGS OF EXPERIENCE	(Capitol) 1969 SC
1976)	3	EARTH ROT	(Capitol SKAO 456) 1970 -
	4	MESSIAH	(RCA LSP-4636) 1972 -
	5	THE AUCTION	(Decca DL 7355) 1972 -
	6	HEAVY AXE	(Fantasy F 9456) 1974 -
	7	SERIOUSLY DEEP	(Polydor PD 6050) 1975 -

NB: (1) reissued on Capitol in the mid-seventies with different sleeve.

45:    Leading Citizen (Pt. 1)/(Pt. 2)   (Decca 33009) 1972

David Axelrod was a producer, arranger and songwriter, who is now mostly remembered for his work with the **Electric Prunes**' *Mass In F Minor* and *Release Of An Oath*. He formed **Pride** in 1970 and he also released several solo albums which may interest some readers looking for a mix of psychedelia with neo-classical arrangements. (SR/NK)

Axis Brotherhood

45:    Return/Signed D.C.   (Woody 101) 196?

From New Mexico. Their competant cover version of **Love**'s *Signed D.C.* can also be heard on *Sixties Rebellion, Vol. 8* (LP & CD), *New Mexico Punk From The Sixties* (LP) and *Sixties Archive, Vol. 4*. (VJ)

Hoyt Axton

ALBUMS:	1	MY GRIFFIN IS GONE	(CBS 33103) 1969 -
(selective)	2	JOY TO THE WORLD	(Capitol ST-788) 1971 -

Hoyt Axton began his career in the sixties as a songwriter for the Kingston Trio and his songs have been covered by Ringo Starr, Three Dog Night and many other popular acts. He was also an actor and a country singer. A multi-faceted talent, he also wrote two excellent songs dealing with the subject of drugs which were popularized by **Steppenwolf**: *The Pusher* and *Snow Blind Friend* (the latter also covered by **Tim Williams**). His song *Never Been To Spain* was covered by **Morning**.

Several of his albums may be of interest to some readers, notably *Joy To The World*, with a fantastic hard-blues version of *The Pusher* (with Chris Darrow on electric fiddle) and *California Women*. His 1969 album *My Griffin Is Gone* was also considered "a psychedelic relic" by Rolling Stone.

Hoyt Axton worked with **Arlo Guthrie** in the early seventies but sadly died in 1999.

Compilation appearances include: *The Pusher* on *First Vibration* (LP). (SR/EH)

DAVID AXELROD - Songs Of Experience CD.

The Aya Singers

Personnel incl: STEVE BORTH   A

ALBUM: 1   THE GREAT CONTROVERSY
(His Word HW-108 AYA) c1974 -

From Richardson, Texas, a Christian folk-rock group with male/female vocals, guitars and flute. (SR)

Azitis

Personnel: DONALD LOWER   bs   A
             STEVE NELSON   perc   A
             DENNIS SULLIVAN   organ, piano   A
             MICHAEL WELCH   gtr, flte   A

ALBUM: 1(A)   HELP   (Elco SC EC 5555) 1971 R4

NB: (1) counterfeited on vinyl as a limited, numbered edition of 300 copies (ELCO102), 1997. Also counterfeited on CD and reissued officially on CD by the band themselves.

45:      From This Place/Hope To Save   (Elco 1/2) 1971

Hailing from Citrus Heights, near Sacramento, California, this outfit's now ultra-rare and sought-after album is similar in mould to **Agape** with religious lyrics, but not quite as good. Musically, this is a keyboard dominated progressive which also has some good guitar moments and melodic vocals. All the songs are penned by the band with *The Prophet*, *From This Place* and *Judgement Day* among the album's finer moments.

The band had previously been known as **Help**, but changed their name to **Azitis** following a conflict with the Decca band **Help**. After the Decca group broke up, they reverted to their original moniker to record a further 45. (VJ/CF/MW)

Aztecs

ALBUM: 1   LIVE AT THE AD-LIB CLUB OF LONDON
(World Artists) 1964 SC

A rave-up live-set by a little-known group. Their album has a photo of the Beatles in a corner of the front cover, quoting them as saying "The Best Club We've Ever Been In"! (SR)

Aztex

45:      I Said More/The Little Streets In My Town   (Staff 194) 1967

Hailed from Gary, Indiana where they had started life in 1963 as The Valuables, a Beatles/Everly Brothers covers band. In late 1966, having developed a harsher persona, they recruited the lead singer/guitarist from The Squires, another popular Gary band, and recorded the above 45. Just 100 copies were pressed for friends and family. *I Said Move* is a pretty powerful rocker, whilst the flip is an uptempo effort with jangly folk-punk guitar and tambourine.

Compilation appearances have so far included: *I Said Move* on *Back From The Grave, Vol. 4* (LP) and *Back From The Grave, Vol. 2* (CD); and *The Little Streets In My Town* on *Back From The Grave, Vol. 5* (LP). (VJ)

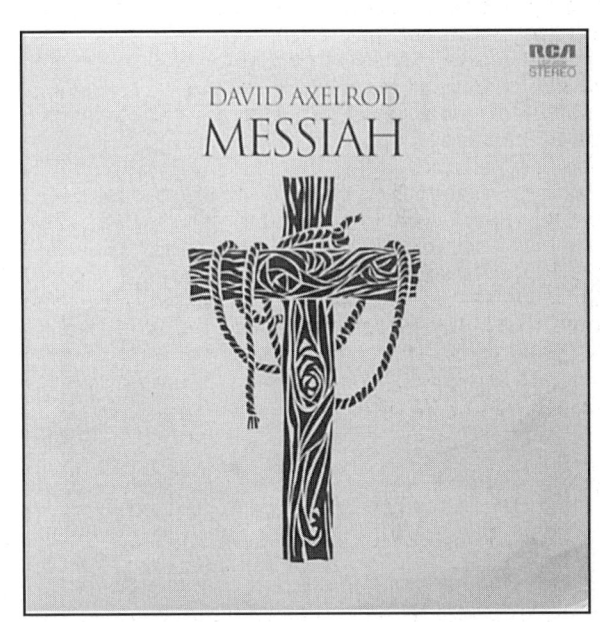

DAVID AXELROD - Messiah LP.

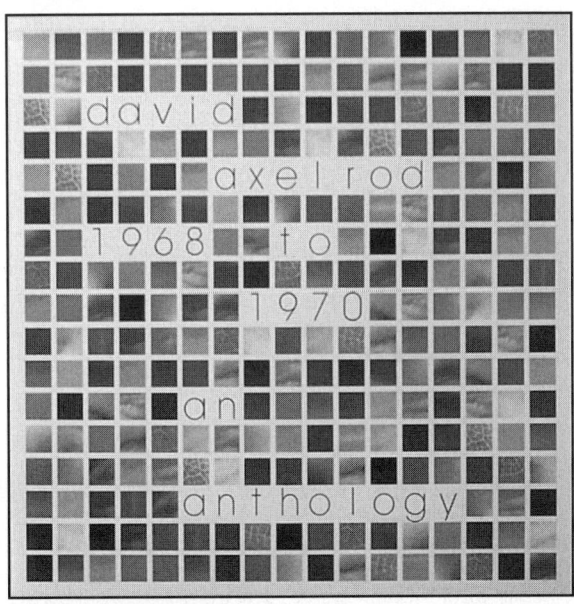

DAVID AXELROD - Earth Rot LP.

DAVID AXELROD - Anthology LP.

DAVID AXELROD - Heavy Axe CD.

AZITIS - Help LP.

AZITIS - Help 45 PS.

THE AMBOY DUKES - Journey To The Center Of The Mind CD.

J RIDER (ANONYMOUS) - No Longer Anonymous LP.

DAVID ARVEDON - In Search of The Most Unforgettable Tree... CD.

THE BACHS.

The Bachs

Personnel:	BLAKE ALLISON	bs, ld vcls	A
	JOHN BABICZ	drms, perc	A
	MIKE DeHAVEN	gtr	A
	JOHN 'BEN' HARRISON	ld gtr	A
	JOHN PETERMAN	gtr, ld vcls	A

ALBUM: 1(A) OUT OF THE BACHS (Roto Records # unkn) 1968 R6

NB: (1) reissued on the Del Val label in 1992, and later pirated on CD and vinyl (Flash 43) 1997.

This is a highly collectable garage-psych classic from Chicago, indeed only 100 copies were ever pressed so original copies inevitably change hands for megabucks. Some of the finest garage cuts include *You're Mine*, *Free Fall* and *Minister To A Mind Diseased*, whilst *My Independence Day* and the superb *Tables Of Grass Fields* are more psychedelic. Just 350 copies of the first reissue were pressed so this album is destined to remain rare, although the more recent 'Flash' reissue will help collectors find copies in the short term. Essential. Just dig that distorted fuzz guitar on *Minister To A Mind Diseased*. All twelve cuts are original Allison-Peterman compositions.

The band formed in the Winter of 1965 and stayed together for about three years. John Babicz:- "John Harrison and I are from Lake Forest, the others from Lake Bluff, just up the road. Harrison and Mike DeHaven had played in a high school group The Appollos."

After they split, John Babicz joined the army, where he spent the next 22 years. He and John Harrison now live in Tucson and still play golf together. Mike DeHaven is in Illinois and Allison Blake and John Peterman in Massachusetts.

I'm A Little Boy and *Tables Of Grass Fields*, from *Out Of The Bachs*, have also resurfaced on *A Trip On The Magic Flying Machine*. (VJ/JBz)

Bachs Lunch

45: Will You Love Me Tomorrow / You Go On (Tomorrow T-911) 1967

Carole King is written large across this East Coast girl group 45. It's her label, her production and on the top Side one of her classics - reworked in a slow, deliberate and dramatic style with forlorn female vocals. *You Go On* is even stronger - a brooding baroque beat-ballad written by Rick Philp and Dave Palmer of **The Myddle Class** (credited as "Philip Palmer"), which lends weight to a rumour that the group was heavily involved with and played on this 45. (MW)

The Backdoor Men

Personnel incl:	FRED HOSTETTER	gtr	A
	STEVE KREIDER	vcls, hrmnca	A
	DEAN TAGGART	drms	A

45: Evil/Corinna, Corinna (Fujimo) 196?

This garage band operated out of Goshen, Indiana. *Evil* had quite a bluesy influence a la Yardbirds, whilst the flip was, by comparison, a pretty lame cover of the Ray Peterson hit.

Compilation appearances have included:- *Evil* on *Hoosier Hotshots* (LP) and *Mayhem & Psychosis, Vol. 2* (CD). (VJ)

Backdoor Society

Personnel incl: RICHARD PASH A

45: I'm The Kind / I'm Getting Better (Shoremen 1900) 1966

NB: 'B' side credited to Richard Pash and The Backdoor Society

The sole 45 by this Avon Lake, Ohio group is rare and easily commands 3-figure asking prices. *I'm The Kind*, accessible again on *Highs In The Mid-Sixties, Vol. 21*, is a pretty good effort and the lyrics "I'm gonna make it now, just like I said would, I'll be big someday" reflected the optimism of the times. (VJ/MW/GGI)

Backgrounds

45: Day Breaks At Dawn/ Oh Baby Please Take Me (Cenco 110) 1967

An unknown Californian band with just one known and keenly-sought 45. Kickin' off with a **'Prunes**-like howl, *Day Breaks At Dawn* is a sizzlin' fuzz-punker with awesome guitar-work. An intense, raw but powerful vocalist cranks ups the testosterone levels. Quite simply - stunning.

Get to hear it on *Fuzz, Flaykes, And Shakes, Vol. 2* (LP & CD) or *Let's Dig 'Em Up, Vol. 3* (LP). (MW)

The Backseat

45: Where Is Mary/Like You Do (Linda 125) 1967

From East L.A. comes this dreamy harmony-drenched ballad coupled with uptempo pop. Produced by Larry Tamblyn of **The Standells**, *Like You Do* is also on the 1969 double album compilation *East Side Revue* (Rampart 3303). (MW)

The Bad Boys

Personnel:	DEMETRI CALLAS	gtr	A
	DANNY CONWAY	drums	A
	GARY R. ST. CLAIR	gtr, bs	A

45: Love/Black Olives (Paula 254) 1966

THE BACHS - Out Of The Bachs LP.

This band were based around Frederick in Maryland, NOT Louisiana as has been assumed due to their 45 on the Paula label. Previously known as Billy Joe & The Continentals, they split with Billy Joe Ash in mid-65 and the trio carried on as **The Bad Boys**, touring widely. In 1968 they came to the attention of Columbia Records and changed name to **Flavor** (not to be confused with the psychedelic New York outfit of that name) and recorded three 45s for Columbia.

This 45 is a classic - *Love* is a wicked catchy fuzz-punker that has been compiled on *All Cops In Delerium* (aka *Good Roots*) (LP), *Louisiana Punk Vol. 2* (LP), *Sixties Archives Vol. 3* (CD) and *Mindrocker Vol. 13*. Written by Gary St.Clair it was covered in 1967 by the **Corners Four**. The uncompiled flip is a glorious mid-slow fuzzy instrumental with a blueish tinge, keyboard and bass solos, and exploito-movie / club-a-go-go vibes that would fit right onto the **Animated Egg** album. (MW/BE)

The Badd Boys

45s:	Never Going Back To Georgia/	
	River Deep Mountain High	(Epic 10119) 1967
	Folks In A Hurry/I Told You So	(Epic 10165) 1967

Good enough to get signed by a major label, Mike Markesich tells us that from checking the copyright/publishing, this band were actually from the U.K., rather than the U.S.

Compilation appearances have included: *I Told You So* on *Of Hopes And Dreams & Tombstones* (LP) and *Psychedelic Unknowns, Vol. 7* (LP & CD); *Never Going Back To Georgia* on *Boulders, Vol. 4* (LP), *Searching For Love* (LP) and *Ya Gotta Have... Moxie, Vol. 1* (Dble CD). (MW/MM)

The Bad Habits

Personnel:	JERRY BEACH	ld gtr	A
	DANNY HARRELSON	piano, organ	A
	PORTER JORDAN	gtr, bs	A
	BILL "SCOTTY" SCOT	drms	A

| 45: | Hook Nose And Wooden Leg / | |
| | Don't Take My Love Away | (Scepter 12126) 1966 |

A Houston pop outfit who were also known as the **Alley Cats**, London Teens, and Terrible Teens. Their Huey P. Meaux produced 45 couples male harmony-pop that has a novelty feel (screeching vocals ala Pipkin's *Gimme Dat Ding*) with a half-decent rockin' popper. The latter has a frantic guitar break but suffers from twittering female backing vocals.

Bill Scott: "We recorded the song at Robin Hood Bryan's Studios in Tyler Texas. The group consisted of Danny Harrelson, Jerry Beach, Porter Jordon, and myself on drums and the screeching vocals you mentioned. At 59 years old now I am certain that I can no longer hit those notes."

"Porter Jordon wrote the lyrics to *Hook Nose* and I wrote the lyrics to *Don't Take Your Love Away* and did the vocals on the record. The girl singers were hired singers from Tyler Texas. The use of the other group names you mention was the way you did things in those days. You came out with several different names on several different records at the same time, hoping one would hit the charts. *Hook Nose* came out when Lloyd Thaxton pantomimed it on his nationwide television show."

"Prior to starting the **Bad Habits**, I had been playing on the road in the Bob Luman Show with three guys named Dean Mathis (bs), Mark Mathis (piano) and Billy Sandford (ld gtr). On a trip to Nashville to cut a session for Luman, we were introduced to Wesley Rose (publisher Acuff-Rose Publishing Company). At a dinner with John D Loudermilt and others, Wesley Rose suggested we cut a demo tape and send it for him to listen to. We had been playing with a new version of *Bye-Bye Love* by the Everly Brothers with the high singing parts performed by Larry Henley. We made the tape at my home in Shreveport and sent it to Wesley. Wesley liked it and set up a recording session for Dean, Mark and Larry and used session musicians to record John D Loudermilt's new song, *Bread And Butter*. The success of *Bread And Butter* broke up our group, so I started the **Bad Habits** with a new manager, Jack Rhodes (Writer - *Silver Threads and Golden Needles*), Rhodes Publishing Company in Mineola Texas. Jack recorded us at Robin Hood Bryans in Tyler Texas. Then Jack and I turned the tape over to Huey Meaux and he got us released on Scepter. We started enjoying success with *Hook Nose* and some of the other songs were hitting around the country on independent labels. The whole thing fell through when Huey Meaux was arrested on a morals charge and that was that. I had us booked as the warm-up band for the Rolling Stones in Sacramento, California, and two of the wives of the guys refused to let them go. So that was the end of that."

Jerry Beach is still playing in Shreveport. We don't know where the rest of the guys are. (MW/BSt)

The Bad Habits

| 45s: | Bad Wind/Images: The City | (Paula 307) 1972 |
| | Touch The Sun/Louie, Louie | (Paula 374) c197? |

Recorded in Shreveport, the second single by this obscure Northern Louisiana band (probably different from the other **Bad Habits**) offers a good garage psych song with keyboards on *Touch The Sun* (written by Jack Russell and Ron Difulio) and a fuzzed out version of the garage classic.

On the first 45, whilst the 'A' side is a nicely orchestrated pop opus, the meat is to be found on the flip. It begins with heavy fuzz before turning into the same kind of music as on the 'A' side. Quite unexpectedly, though, a middle piece with stark and discordant trumpets and a quirky guitar solo comes forth, hovering on the verge of avant-garde and lifting the whole effort some rungs up on the ladder. (SR/MK)

The Bad Roads

Personnel:	BUZ CLARK	ld vcls	A
	KENNY COOLEY	tamb	A
	TERRY GREEN	ld gtr	A
	MIKE HICKS	bs	A
	DANNY KIMBALL	drms	A
	BRIANT SMITH	gtr	A

| EP: | 1 | THE BAD ROADS | (Sundazed SEP 143) 1999 |

45s:	Too Bad/Blue Girl	(JIN 210) 1967
	Till The End Of The Day /	
	Don't Look Back	(Raintyre 1000) 1967

From Lake Charles, Louisiana this outfit evolved out of the Shadows and the Avengers. Their first 45 with its sneering vocals and fuzztone guitar defines classic mid-sixties American punk.

Several members went on to the Lemon Blue.

THE BAD SEEDS and ZAKARY THAKS - A Texas Battle Of The Bands CD.

The Sundazed EP brings together both 45s in a neat pic sleeve annotated by Jud Cost and Brown Paper Sack's Andrew Brown and with reminiscences from Danny Kimball and Briant Smith.

In the eighties *Bad Girl* has been covered by the Miracle Workers on the *Moxie's Revenge* LP and *Too Bad* by the Morlochs on their *Uglier Than You'll Ever Be* CD.

Compilation appearances have so far included: *Blue Girl* and *Too Bad* on *Pebbles, Vol. 9* (LP); *Too Bad, Til The End Of The Day* and *Blue Girl* on *Louisiana Punk Groups From The Sixties, Vol. 2* (LP) and *Sixties Archive Vol. 3*; *Blue Girl* on *Mindrocker, Vol. 4* (LP) and *We Have Come For Your Children* (Cass); and *Blue Girl* and *Too Bad* on *Acid Visions* (LP) and *Acid Visions - The Complete Collection Vol. 1* (3-CD). Strangely, both *Acid Visions* compilations miscredit *Too Bad* as *Outside Looking In* by 'The Unknowns'. (VJ/MW)

The Bad Seeds

Personnel:	BOBBY DONAHO	drms	A
	HENRY EDGEINGTON	bs	A
	ROD PRINCE	gtr, vcls	A
	MIKE TAYLOR	gtr, vcls	A

ALBUM: 1(A) THE J-BECK STORY PART 1: BAD SEEDS
(Eva 12034) 1983

NB: (1) also issued on CD, together with the equivalent **Zakary Thaks** album as *A Texas Battle Of The Bands*, Collectables (COL-CD-0652) 1995.

45s:	Taste Of The Same / I'm A King Bee	(J-Beck 1002) 1965
	Zilch Pt.1 / Pt.2	(J-Beck 1003) 1965
	All Night Long / Sick And Tired	(J-Beck 1005) 1966

This Corpus Christi outfit was discovered by Carl Becker, who ran the J-Beck / Cee-Be record label, playing at the Surf Club. They had formed in 1964 - Taylor had previously fronted an outfit called The Four Winds and Prince and Donaho had played together in The Titans. For a while they were *the* Corpus Christi act. Their first 45, a punkish Stones-inspired number, attracted some local interest. They followed it up with a double-sided instrumental and the 'A' side of their third and final effort was a version of the **13th Floor Elevators**' *Tried To Hide*, which had not been released at the time. They also appeared as the back-up band on the 'B' side of the 1966 45 *Down The Road I Go* by Tony Joe and The Mojos.

Rod Prince later played in the New Seeds and **Bubble Puppy**.

Eva/Collectables' posthumous release features their three 45s, two other J-Beck 45s Mike Taylor recorded under the name **Michael** after **The Bad Seeds** split and two previously unreleased cuts: *Checkerboard* and *Arkansas*. Other compilation appearances include:- *All Night Long* on *Off The Wall, Vol. 1* (LP); *A Taste Of The Same* on *Son Of The Gathering Of The Tribe* (LP); and both *A Taste Of The Same* and *I'm A King Bee* on *Green Crystal Ties Vol. 1* (CD); (VJ/MW/SR/MM)

The Bad Seeds

45:	King Of The Soap Box/He's Lying	(Columbia 4-43670) 1966

From Erlanger, Kentucky. This outfit's sole known 45 is full-blown jingle-jangle ala-Byrds-via-Dylan on the 'A' side, which can be heard on *Mindrocker, Vol. 7* (LP). The flip is equally jangley but is more in the Searchers / **Beau Brummels** mould. (MW/MM)

The Bag

Personnel:	JOE DI MARZO	A
	AL ESPOSITO	A
	DAN MAHONY	A
	JAY SAVINO	A

ALBUM: 1(A) REAL   (Decca DL-75057) 1968/9 -

45s:	Nobody's Child/Nickels 'n' Dimes	(Decca 32279) 1968
	Down And Out/Up In The Morning	(Decca 32409) 1968

BAGATELLE - 11pm Saturday LP.

	I Want You By My Side/	
	Red Purple And Blue	(Decca 32463) 1969

A 'psychedelic soul' group, thought to be based in New York City. **Jimmy Curtiss** produced their album and co-wrote two songs for it.

Of the 45 cuts: *Nickels 'n' Dimes* has an acid flavour thanks to some good fuzz; the rest delve into funky, brassy or orchestrated soul-rock. (VJ/MW/SR)

Bagatelle

Personnel:	WILLIE ALEXANDER	vcls, piano, perc	A
	DAVID "TURK" BYNOE	bs	A
	MARK GOULD	trumpet	A
	FRED GRIFFITH	vcls	A
	LEE MASON	drms	A
	MARSHALL O'CONNELL	gtr	A
	STEVE SHRELL	sax, flute	A
	DAVID REDTOP THOMAS	vcls	A
	RODNEY YOUNG	vcls	A

ALBUM: 1(A) 11 PM SATURDAY   (ABC ABCS-646) 1968 -

45: Such A Fuss About Sunday/What Can I Do   (ABC ?) 1968

An integrated soul/rock group whose album was produced by **Tom Wilson**. Notable for featuring Willie "Loco" Alexander and Lee Mason (both ex-**Lost**), it may interest the fans of psyche/soul a la **Chamber Brothers**, although it's not as good.

Compilation appearances include: *Back On The Farm* on *Tom's Touch*, a compilation of **Tom Wilson** productions; *Everybody Knows* and *Back On The Farm* on *The Best Of Bosstown Sound* (Dble CD); and *Everybody Knows* on *Family Circle - Family Tree* (CD). (SR)

Kali Bahlu

ALBUM: 1 COSMIC REMEMBERANCE
(World Pacific WPS 21875) 1967 SC

45:	Lonely Teardrops/	
	The Yogi Tripper	(Terra Records DM 1001/2) 196?

NB: Canadian release.

Cosmic droning sitar, fronted by shrill spoken vocals that soon start to irritate. This is a rambling cosmic hippie journey of philosophy into whimsical fantasy, so garage-niks should keep well clear. Four meandering tracks - *Cosmic Rememberance, A Game Called Who Am I, How Can I*

Tell My Guru, and *A Cosmic Telephone Call From The Angel Liesle And The Buddha* eloquently describe where this is coming from. Mellow meditation music or cosmic twaddle?

The 45, presumably released prior to the album and perhaps better than any of her subsequent work, was released on a Victoria, British Columbia record label, suggesting that Bahlu may have been Canadian.

Kali Bahlu may also have been in **Lite Storm**. (MW/MMs)

Baker Street Irregulars

45:	I'm A Man Part 1 / Part 2	(Largo 5002) c1966

From Lancaster, Pennsylvania, their extended version of Bo Diddley's classic song really is very impressive indeed - some superb guitar work and lots of sound effects. Well worth a listen it has been compiled on *Pebbles, Vol. 14* (LP) and *The Essential Pebbles Collection, Vol. 2* (Dble CD). (VJ/MW)

Baldwin and Leps

Personnel:	MICHAEL BALDWIN	vcls, violin	A
	LEPS	gtr	A

ALBUM:	1(A) BALDWIN AND LEPS	(Vanguard VSD 6567) 1971	-

NB: (1) reissued on CD and LP (Vanguard VMD 6567) 2001.

A unusual duo violin/guitar outfit who released this rarely seen album in 1971. It's notable for the side-long *Calamandatine Brown* with his five parts (*Hannah*, *Headin' West*, *Spirit*, *The Dealer* and *Bella Donna*). The lyrics are interesting, tackling subjects such as drugs dealing, people going to Canada to run from the draft, prostitution, teenagers leaving New York for California etc. The music has some haunting moments.

Recorded in New York, the album was produced by Lor Crane and all their material written by Michael Baldwin. (SR)

The Balladeers

45s:	Words I Want To Hear/High Flying Bird	(Cori CR 31001) 1965
	Used To Be/	
	Goin' Out Of My Head	(Seven Seas 201, 215/6) 1967

From Framingham, Maine. Their Cori 45 contains a cool harmony beat-ballad that could only come from New England, backed with an okay version of *High Flying Bird*. Unfortunately their Seven Seas 45 contains club / cabaret-type male-female harmony vocal pop and is best avoided. (MW/MM)

BALDWIN AND LEPS - Baldwin And Leps LP.

Ballin' Jack

Personnel:	JIM COILE	horns	A
	RONNIE HAMMON	drms	A
	TIM MCFARLAND	piano	A
	LUTHER RABB	bs, vcls	A
	GLENN THOMAS	gtr	A
	JIM WALTERS	gtr, trumpet	A
	BILLY McPHERSON	sax	

HCP

ALBUMS:	1(A) BALLIN' JACK	(CBS 30344) 1971	180 -
	2(A) BUZZARD LUCK	(CBS 31468) 1972	- -
	3(-) SPECIAL PRIDE	(Mercury 1672) 1973	- -
	4(-) LIVE AND IN COLOR	(Mercury 1700) 1974	- -

HCP

45s:	Super Highway/Only A Tear	(CBS 45312) 1971 93
	Found A Child/Never Let 'Em Say	(CBS 45348) 1971 -
	Hold On/Ballin' The Jack	(CBS 45464) 1971 -
	I'm The One You Need/Playin' The Game	(CBS 45698) 1972 -
	Thunder/Try To Relax	(Mercury 73401) 1973 -
	Sunday Morning/This Song	(Mercury 73429) 1974 -

Originating from Seattle, **Ballin' Jack** was an early seventies rock group with brass. Luther Rabb and Jim Walters began recording together in 1965 with **Emergency Exit**, and Rabb had also a brief spell with **Calliope**. Billy McPherson was fomerly with The Regents, who started out in Tacoma-Lakewood, Washington.

Their track *Found A Child* was compiled on the Columbia catalogue sampler *Different Strokes*. (SR/RMh)

The Balloon Corps

45s:	Up In Smoke/Perfect Vision	(Bell 796) 1969
	Muddy Water/Make It Right	(Dunhill 4219) 1969

Previously known as **The Underground Balloon Corps** and **The Snaps**, from Pennsylvania, they had veered towards a rockin' sound ala **Creedence Clearwater Revival** by the Dunhill 45. (MW)

The Balloon Farm

Personnel:	MIKE APPEL	A
	DON HENNY	A
	JAY SAKS	A
	ED SCHNUG	A

HCP

45s:	α	A Question Of Temperature/	
		Hurtin' For Your Love	(Laurie 3405) 1967 37
		Farmer Brown/Hurry Up Sundown	(Laurie 3445) 1968 -

NB: α Some copies with mispressed label as *A Question Of Tempature*.

An East Coast band who were probably based in New York (although Florida has also been mooted as their home). *A Question Of Temperature*, an excellent psychedelic punk effort, has been heavily compiled and is well worth checking out. It was also a minor hit.

Some of the above mentioned personnel later reappeared in **The Huck Finn**.

Compilation appearances include: *A Question Of Temperature* on *Mindrocker, Vol. 3* (LP), *Nuggets Box* (4-CD), *Nuggets, Vol. 1* (LP), *Acid Dreams - The Complete 3 LP Set* (3-LP), *Acid Dreams Testament* (CD), *Acid Dreams, Vol. 1* (LP), *20 Great Hits Of The 60's* (LP), *Battle Of The Bands* (CD), *Boulders, Vol. 4* (LP), *Glimpses, Vol's 1 & 2* (CD) and *Glimpses, Vol. 1* (LP); Finally, *Hurtin' For Your Love* appears on *Turds On A Bum Ride Vol. 6* (CD). (VJ/MW/TJH/EW)

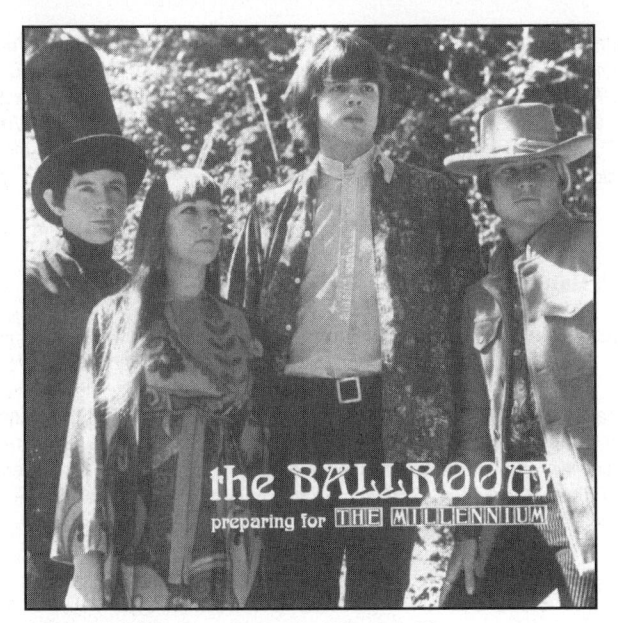

THE BALLROOM - Preparing For The Millennium CD.

Ballroom

Personnel:	JIM BELL	vcls, oboe	A
	CURT BOETTCHER	vcls, gtr	A
	MICHELE O'MALLEY	vcls	A
	SANDY SALISBURY	vcls, gtr	A
	(RON EDGAR	drms	A)
	(LEE MALLORY	vcls, gtr	A)

NB: Ancillary personnel also included a large slice of the "Wrecking Crew" with **Mike Deasy**, Ben Benay, Butch Parker, Mike Henderson, Jerry Scheff, Jim Horn, Jim Troxell, and Toxie French.

ALBUM: 1(A) PREPARING FOR THE MILLENNIUM
(Rev-Ola CREV 058 CD) 1998

45: Spinning, Spinning, Spinning/
Baby Please Don't Go   (Warner Brothers 7027) 1967

At long last **Curt Boettcher** has started to achieve deserved recognition. His **Millennium** and **Sagittarius** exploits are reasonably documented and have seen reissues over the last decade. But his earlier projects and one-offs as creator, arranger and producer have remained legend only amongst a handful of specialist collectors. Now thankfully, Rev-Ola has started a series that should see his star shine again. **The Ballroom** CD kicks off with twenty-two tracks that document his post-**Goldebriars** period, centered around **Ballroom** and Summers Children, and includes demos that were to mature with **Millennium** and **Sagittarius**. It's a treasure trove for lovers of creative dream-pop and the soft underbelly of psychedelia, complete with a fascinating and informative booklet by Dawn Eden.

Ballroom's sole 45 is one of the many highlights of the CD. *Spinning* is much akin to the rather twee and harmony-drenched styles of **Sagittarius** and **Millennium**, but *Baby Please Don't Go* is not to be missed, his amazing interpretation is totally different to the usual garage-punk ravers that had gone before - a psychedelic rain-dance that eventually reels off into chaotic effects - wow!

An article on Curt by Kingsley Abbott appeared in Record Collector no. 229 (September 1998).

Baby Please Don't Go has also surfaced on *Incredible Sound Show Stories, Vol. 8* (LP) and *A Heavy Dose Of Lyte Psych* (CD). (MW/JFr/DE)

Bamboo

Personnel:	WILL DONICHT	vcsl, bs, gtr, tack piano	A
	DANIEL LEE HALL	vcls, organ, piano, rocksichord, gtr, tack piano	A
	BRENDEN HARKIN	maracas, arranger	A
	PETER HODGSON	bs	A
	KEN JENKINS	accoustic bs	A
	SANFORD KONIKOFF	drms	A
	DAVE RAY	vcls, gtr, bottleneck, leslie gtr, hrmnca	A
	RED RHODES	steel gtr	A

ALBUM: 1(A) BAMBOO   (Elektra EKS-74048) 1969 -

A California group led by Dave Ray, who was previously part of the blues/folk trio Koerner, Ray and Glover. Produced by Allan Emig and recorded on the Feather River in Keddle, California, their only album contains a mix of folk, blues, rock and country highlighted by four excellent tracks: *Girl Of The Seasons, Blak Bati Chari Blooz, Sok Mi Toot Tru Luv*, all with inventive organ and guitar parts and *Keep What Makes You Feel Nice*, a progressive blues a la **Butterfield Blues Band**. All their material was original and the use of strange instruments (rocksichord, Leslie guitar, tack piano) provide some unusual effects. As usual with Elektra, the sound quality is excellent.

Dave Ray later released solo albums and Sanford "Sandy" Konikoff, who had previously played with Gentle Soul, became a session drummer, notably working with **Leon Russell**, **Grinder's Switch** and Ben Sidran. Brendan Harkin later played in **Papa Nebo**, Free Beer and Starz. (SR)

The Ban

Personnel:	RANDY GUZMAN (aka RANDY GORDON)	drms, vcls	A
	TONY McGUIRE	gtr, vcls	A
	OLIVER McKINNEY	keyb'ds, vcls	A
	FRANK STRAIGHT	bs	A

45: Bye-Bye/Now That I'm Hoping   (Brent 7049) 1965

From Lompoc, California, this bunch evolved into **Now**, when Tony McGuire was drafted and David Zandonatti came aboard. They subsequently relocated to San Francisco, hooked up with producer Matthew Katz and became **Tripsichord Music Box**!!

Compilation appearances include: *Bye Bye* on *Boulders, Vol. 4* (LP).

Banana and The Bunch

Personnel:	EARTHQUAKE ANDERSON	hrmnca	A
	JOE BAUER	drms	A
	MICHAEL KANE	bs	A
	LOWELL "BANANA" LEVINGER	vcls, gtr, bs, piano	A
	STEVE SWALLOW	bs	A

ALBUM: 1(A) MID-MOUNTAIN RANCH
(Raccoon 13 / Warner BS 2626) 1972 -

45s: Vanderbilt's Lament/Vanderbilt's
Lament (mono)   (Raccoon 10 / Warner WB 7621) 1972
Back In The USA/
Back In The USA (mono) (Raccoon 11 / Warner WB 7626) 1972

An excellent addition to **The Youngbloods** discography. The only solo album of Lowell "Banana" Levinger, backed by the other **Youngbloods** (sans **Jesse Colin Young**) and the renown jazz bass player Steve Swallow. The album contains a mix of rock, folk, bluegrass and more experimental tracks. The singles are from the album. In 1973, Levinger took part in the production of the **A Euphonious Wail** album and then apparently vanished from the music scene.

Banana was also in charge of **The Youngbloods**' record label, Raccoon, and as such produced the albums of **Michael Hurley**, High Country, **Joe Bauer** and Kenny Gill. After taking part in the production of the **A Euphonious Wail** LP in 1973, he vanished from the music scene. He can however be found playing on *Here Goes Nothin'* (1987), by Zero, a Bay Area group featuring John Cipollina, Steve Kimock and Martin Fierro.

The singles are from the album. (SR)

BANCHEE - Banchee/Thinkin 2-on-1 CD.

Banchee

Personnel:	PETER ALONGI	ld gtr, vcls	AB
	JOSE MIGUEL DEJESUS	gtr, vcls	AB
	VICTOR WILLIAM DIGILIO	drms	AB
	MICHAEL GREGORY MARINO	bs, vcls	AB
	JOHNNY PACHECO	perc	A
	FERNANDO LUIS ROMAN	perc, vcls	B

ALBUMS:	1(A)	BANCHEE	(Atlantic 8240) 1969 SC
	2(A)	THINKIN'	(Polydor 24 4066) 1971 SC

NB: (1) and (2) reissued on one CD (Lizard LR 0713-2) 2001.

45: I Just Don't Know / Train Of Life (Atlantic 2708) 1970

This band, along with **Sir Lord Baltimore**, **Yesterday's Children** et al were among the East Coast's premier heavy blasters of the post-psychedelic era. Check out *I Just Don't Know* and *Evolmia* from their amazing first album on Atlantic. The second album has longer, less structured cuts with seemingly endless guitar soloing... nevertheless, both are recommended.

The first album was produced by **Warren Schatz** and Stephen Schlaks.

Compilation appearances have included: *I Just Don't Know* on *Psychedelic Frequencies* (CD). (CF/MW)

The Bandits

Personnel:	GREG BIGSBY	ld gtr	A D
	STEVE HEARD	vcls, keyb'ds	AB
	DAVE HENDRICKS	sax, vcls, gtr	ABCD
	BOB PERRY	vcls, ld gtr	AB
	JOHN SIMPSON	drms	AB
	TOM DEETS	ld gtr	B
	DAVE JOHNSON	ld gtr	C
	RUSS KAMMERER	drms	CD
	SCOTT STRONG	bs	CD

45s:	Tell Me/Little Sally Walker	(Jerden 773) 1965
	Queen Jane / I Remember The Girl	(Panorama 34) 1966

From Mercer Island, Washington. In mid-1967, they became **The Chicago Express**, with the line-up: Dave Hendricks (vcls), Greg Bigsby (ld gtr, vcls), David Baroh (gtr, vcls), Scott Strong (bs) and Russ Kammerer (drms). At the end of the year, **Chicago Express** splintered again with Dave Baroh switching to bass, and Russ Kammerer joining with John Soltero to form a power trio called **The Punch**. In March of 1968 Pat Gossan was added on keyboards, but **The Punch** split in August '68 with David Baroh (and later John Soltero) going on to **Bluebird**. Russ Kammerer went on to **The Locomotive** and Pat Gossan joined the **Floating Bridge**.

Compilation appearances have included: *Little Sally Walker* on *Northwest Battle Of The Bands, Vol. 1 - Flash And Crash* (LP & CD), *Northwest Battle Of The Bands, Vol. 1* (CD), *Battle Of The Bands, Vol. 1* (LP), *History Of Northwest Rock, Vol. 2* (CD) and *The History Of Northwest Rock, Vol. 4* (LP); *Queen Jane* on *History Of Northwest Rock, Vol. 5*; and *Tell Me* on *History Of Northwest Rock, Vol. 6*. (MW/DR/DB)

The Bandits

45s:	Highway 65 / Come On Pretty Girl	(Twin Town TT 701) 1965
	All I Want To Do / Buzzy	(Studio City SC 1031) 1965

A band from Minneapolis who also recorded as **Jesse J. And The Bandits** and **King Krusher And The Turkeynecks**. Two further 1965 tracks *Downtown* and *The Krusher*, appeared on sixties Minneapolis sampler on *Top Teen Bands, Vol. 3* and this latter track has reappeared on *Sixties Rebellion, Vol. 12* (LP & CD). (MW)

The Bandits

Personnel incl:	CHARLES O'KELLY	vcls	A

45: A Woman / What Did I Say (Perfection No. 507) c1967

This unknown Georgia band backed singer Charles O'Kelly on their sole 45 on the Perfection label, based in Marietta.

The dirgey *A Woman* is compiled on *Psychedelic States: Georgia Vol. 1* (CD). (MW)

Band Of Wynand

45: Day-Time Nite-Time / What Am I To Do (Gemini G-501) 1967

Day-Time.. is a cool jangley swirly folk-punker with sultry **Byrds'** harmonies that has been included on the excellent *Fuzz Flaykes & Shakes Vol. 1* (LP & CD), whose liners give their location as Los Angeles.

The 45 was originally released as by the **F.B.I. (Four Boys Incorporated)** with identical titles, label and number. Perhaps they were 'encouraged' to change their name by some bureau heavies?! (MW/CF)

The Band Without A Name

Personnel incl:	RICHARD FAITH	keyb'ds	A
	MARK GROSECLOSE	drms	A
	EDDIE HADDAD		A
	DAVID MARKS	ld gtr	A

45s:	Turn On Your Lovelight/Perfect Girl	(Tower 246) 1966
	Theme From Thunder Alley/Time After Time	(Sidewalk 913) 1967

The Band Without A Name were managed by Casey Kasem and they played at two clubs on the Sunset Strip as the house band during 1965-66. David Marks had previously played with The Beach Boys and both he and Eddie Haddad were in Dave and The Marksmen, until they broke up in 1965. Marks then formed **The Band Without A Name**, with Mark Groseclose (Affectionately known as 'Goosegrease' by their fans). Mark was a great drummer, and had played live with the Beach Boys for a month in 1962 when Dennis hurt his hand. Mark had also drummed for The Survivors, a short-lived side project of Brian Wilson who released one single, *Pamela Jean*, and did session work for The Honeys.

They ended up backing Sonny and Cher (who were still Caesar and Cleo at the time), played with **Bobby Fuller** and also with the post-Spector Teddy Bears.

Their first 45, *Turn On Your Lovelight* received some airplay on KRLA and the band got to open for acts like **Thee Midniters** and Monte and The Crystals, as well as playing 'The Teenage Fair' in 1965 and '66.

Their second 45 came from the "Thunder Alley" soundtrack and was thought to have possibly been **Davie Allan and The Arrows** in disguise. However Davie Allan, Mark Groseclose and David Marks don't remember doing the track, so it could just as easily be the work of another band/session musicians and issued as **The Band Without A Name** by their record company.

The real **Band Without A Name** did cut a version of Fats Domino's *Whole Lotta Lovin'*, a song called *Tavelin'* that we assume was an original and a cover of *I'm Blue* without vocals. None of these have were released.

The band are thought to have been from the San Fernando Valley or Hawthorne area.

David Marks later played with **The Moon** and also did session work for **Buzz Clifford**, The Full Treatment, Danny Brooks, **Delany and Bonnie** amongst many others. (BCr/SR/EG)

Nikhil Banerjee

ALBUM: 1 RAGAS FOR MEDITATION (Capitol ST-10518) 1969 SC

A rare sitar raga psychedelic album with two side long cuts: *Raga Hemant* and *Raga Bhatiyar*. (SR)

Bang

Personnel:	TONY D'IORIO	drms	A
	FRANK FERRARA	bs, vcls	ABC
	FRANK GLICKEN	gtr, vcls	ABC
	DURIS MAXWELL	drms	B
	JEFFREY CHEEN	perc	B
	(BRUCE GARY	drms	BC)

ALBUMS:	1(A)	BANG	(Capitol ST-11015) 1972
	2(B)	MOTHER/BOW TO THE KING	(Capitol ST-11110) 1972
	3(C)	BANG MUSIC	(Capitol ST-11190) 1973

NB: (1) reissued on CD (Lizard Records LR 0707-2) 2001. (2) reissued on CD.

45s:		Future Shock/Questions	(Capitol 3304) 1972
		Keep On/Red Man	(Capitol 3386) 1972
	α	Idealist Realist/No Sugar Tonight	(Capitol 3474) 1972
		Love Sonnet/Must Be Love	(Capitol 3622) 1973
	β	Feels Nice/Slow Down	(Capitol 3816) 1974

NB: α released in France with PS (Capitol 2C 006-81339). β double sided promo version also exists.

BANG - Mother/Bow To The King CD.

Straight forward seventies rock and roll, formed by Tony D'Iorio, this band were thought to be from Florida, but this is not the case. They did in fact come from Pennsylvania, but played in Florida quite a lot. Some of this confusion is no doubt because there was a Florida act called the Bangles (also known as the Bangs) that by 1971 was calling itself Sun Country.

Produced by Jeffrey Cheen and John Palladino, recorded in Miami and L.A, their second album is a kind of concept album, with distinct "Mother" and "Bow To The King" sides, label presentation and cover art. All the material was written by Cheen, Ferrara and D'Iorio (who had then chosen to leave the group but continued to write lyrics for them) with the exception of a cover of Randy Bachman's *No Sugar Tonight*. Four of its eight tracks were featured on singles and the album is rather good, full of energetic songs. (RBc/SR/JLh/MW)

BANGOR FLYING CIRCUS - Bangor Flying Circus CD.

Bangor Flying Circus

Personnel:	ALAN DE CARLO	gtr, vcls	A
	MIKE TEZGA	drms	A
	DAVID WOLINSKI	bs, keyb'ds	A

HCP

ALBUMS:	1(A)	BANGOR FLYING CIRCUS		
		(Dunhill DS-50069) 1969	190	-
	2(-)	PREPARED IN PEACE	(Capitol ST-11147) 1973	- -
	3(-)	LAST LAUGH	(Capitol ST-11240) 1973	- -

NB: (1) also released in the U.K. (Stateside SSL 5022) in 1970, reissued on CD by One Way (22119). (2) also released in the U.K. (Harvest SHSP 4010). (2) and (3) were released as Flying Circus.

45s:	Come On People/Change In Our Lives	(Dunhill 4226) 1969
	Mama Don't You Know/Someday I'll Find	(Dunhill 4323) 1970

Originally formed in Chicago by ex-**H.P. Lovecraft** drummer Mike Tezga, who later formed Lovecraft. Their album, which got to no. 190 in the U.S. album charts, contained some good organ and guitar work and there's a case for its inclusion here. They relocated to L.A. and later evolved into Flying Circus recording two more albums. Upon their demise, in 1970, Wolinski and De Carlo formed Madura.

Compilation appearances have included: *Come On People* on *Undersound Uppersoul* (LP). (VJ)

The Banned

Personnel incl:	BILL AUBEL	A
	DAN AUBEL	A
	BERT ??	A

45s:	My Life Is My Own /	
	Nothing Matters But You	(Fontana 6004) 1967
	It Could't Happen Here (stereo)/	
	(mono) (PS)	(Fontana 6016) 1967
	Annie Went To Ohio /	
	Goodbye, Groovy, Goodbye	(Fontana 6021) 1967

A New Jersey quartet, who played in a pop rock style. The had a good live reputation, and performed The Beatles' *Sgt. Pepper* album live, within weeks of the albums release. (SR/DG)

The Banshees

Personnel:	FRANK BUCARO	vcls	AB
	TOM LITO	drms	AB
	RICK NADOLINI	bs	A
	JACK SMEAD	ld gtr	AB
	RON ROUSE	ld gtr	AB
	PETE SHELDON	bs	B

45:	Project Blue / Free	(Dunwich 129) 1966

A Chicago band, whose *Project Blue* was a head-banging assault on the senses with some superb guitar riffs and is considered one of the city's classic recordings. If you hear it - you'll know why. The band were also known as The Fugitives and later The Prophets, whilst Pete Sheldon had earlier played in the U.K. group Tornados.

Smead now runs a New York bar, Rouse became a lumberjack, Bucaro became a priest and Lito relocated to Texas. *Project Blue* was also covered by **The Endd** who operated out of La Porte, Indiana.

Compilation appearances have so far included: *Project Blue* on *Mindrocker, Vol. 2* (LP), *Pebbles, Vol. 9* (LP), *The Dunwich Records Story* (LP) and *Oh Yeah! The Best Of Dunwich Records* (CD). (VJ)

Banshees

45s:	They Prefer Blondes / Take A Ride With Me	(Solo 1) 1965
	Never Said I Loved You / So Hard To Bear	(Solo 2) 1965

Formed at Mills High School in Burlingame, in the South Bay area of San Francisco as an instrumental combo called The Black Knights in 1962. Later in 1964 vocals were added and they changed name to **The Banshees**. *They Prefer Blondes*, is a sort of wailing **Kingsmen**-style punk song. In 1967 they changed their name again to **Ariel**.

Compilation appearances have included:- *They Prefer Blondes* on *Boulders, Vol. 4* (LP), *Back From The Grave, Vol. 2* (LP) and *Garage Kings* (Dble LP); and *Take A Ride With Me* on *Teenage Shutdown, Vol. 11* (LP & CD). (VJ/MW/AP)

Bantams

ALBUM:	1	BEWARE	(Warner Bros. W-1625) 1966 SC

45s:	Follow Me /	
	Meet Me Tonight, Little Girl	(Warner Bros. 5695) 1965
	Good Lovin' Girl/ I'm So Lucky	(Warner Bros. 5868) 1966

Housed in a neat cartoon style cover, a trio of pre-teen kids aimed at the kids market, with covers of *Susie-Q*, *Please, Please Me*, *Sheila*, *Do You Love Me*, *Over You*, *Ticket To Ride* and *Twist And Shout*. (SR)

Dave Banyase and Sum Guys

45:	Just A Little Bit /	
	Open The Door To Your Heart	(Solid Rock W-003/4) 1967

Some guys from the Detroit suburbs chose two popular R'n'B numbers, by Roscoe Gordon and Darrell Banks respectively, for their sole platter. Both have a loose'n'live feel - but club sounds rather than garage. *Just A Little Bit* (also covered by the Zombies, **Tommy Burk and The Counts** and Aussie acts Tony Worsley and The Blue Jays, Chosen Few and Purple Hearts) is the stronger thanks to some neat guitar solos. (MW)

Barbara

ALBUM:	1	SINGS FOR LIFE	(Lazarus) 1973 -

A rare and quite odd Christian folk singer, her album came in a black and white cover with gothic lettering. (SR)

Barbara and Ernie

ALBUM:	1	PRELUDE TO	(Cotillion SD 9044) 1971 -

A rather weird but interesting duo. Barbara was a pretty young black woman, while Ernie was a white male in his forties (and looking extremely tired on the front cover !). A soft psych/jazz hybrid, their album contains several interesting tracks, notably a long and spacey cover of the **Airplane**'s *Somebody To Love* and *Listen With Your Heart* with sitar. (SR)

The Barbarians

Personnel:	BRUCE BENSON	gtr	A
	JERRY CAUSI	bs	A
	JEFF MORRIS	gtr	A
	VICTOR MOULTON	drms, vcls	A

ALBUM:	1(A)	THE BARBARIANS	(Laurie LLP 2033) 1965 R2

NB: (1) reissued (Rhino RHLP 1008) 1979, and later on CD by Bomp/Voxx. (1) reissued on CD as *Are You A Boy Or Are You A Girl?* with both sides of their debut 45 (Sundazed SC 6153) 2000. Another CD reissue on One Way (17965), is retitled *Are You A Boy Or Are You A Girl?* and contains *Moulty* as a bonus track. There is also a compilation (Line OLLP 5067).

HCP

45s:	You've Got To Understand/Hey Little Bird	(Joy 290) 1964 -
	Are You A Boy Or Are You A Girl?/	
	Take It Or Leave It	(Laurie 3308) 1965 55
	What The New Breed Say/Susie Q	(Laurie 3321) 1965 102
	Moulty/I'll Keep On Seeing You	(Laurie 3326) 1966 90

NB: There's also an extremely rare French EP with PS: *Are You A Boy Or Are You A Girl?/What The New Breed Say/Susie Q/I've Got A Woman* (Vogue INT 18027) 1966.

From Provincetown, Massachusetts, this punk band who were once regulars on 'Shindig', are best known for their 1965 single *Are You A Boy Or Are You A Girl?* and *Moulty*, the story of how their drummer lost his hand (in a fireworks accident when he was 14)!

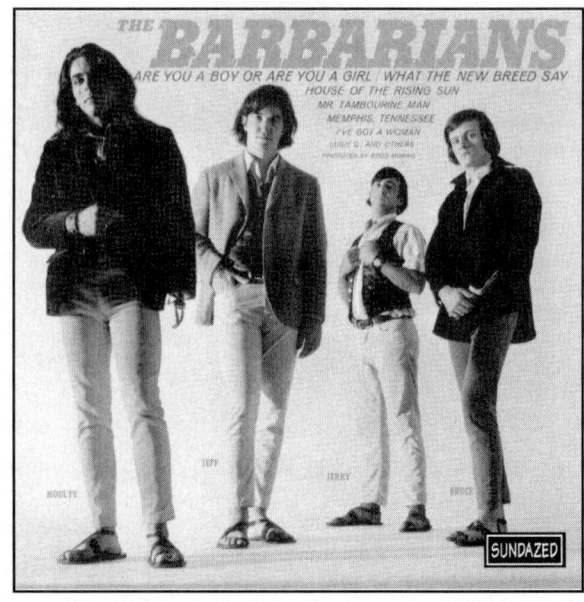

THE BARBARIANS - Are You A Boy Or Are You A Girl? CD.

After they split up, remaining members Bernie Fieldings, Jerry Causi and Bruce Benson went to San Francisco in 1967 and formed **Black Pearl**. Moulty went into the cleaning business in Abington, Massachusetts as the Moulton Cleaning Co. In 1995, he reformed the band as **Moulty and the Barbarians** with his sons, Tory and Eric, and twins Ken and Karl Olson.

Compilation coverage has so far included: *Are You A Boy Or Are You A Girl* and *Moulty* on *Nuggets Box* (4-CD); *Hey Little Bird* on *New England Teen Scene* (CD), *New England Teen Scene, Vol. 2* (LP), *Trash Box* (5-CD) and *Best of Pebbles, Vol. 1* (LP & CD); *Moulty* on *Nuggets* (Dble LP); *Are You A Boy Or Are You A Girl* on *Nuggets, Vol. 1* (LP), *Even More Nuggets* (CD), *We Have Come For Your Children* (Cass) and *20 Great Hits Of The 60's* (LP); and *You've Got To Understand* on *Follow That Munster, Vol. 1* (LP) and *Hide & Seek Again* (LP). (VJ/LP/SR)

Barber Green

45:	Life / Gliding Ride	(F-Empire GRS 1106)	1968

On a very obscure label out of Eugene, Oregon, **Barber Green** was the work of five teens from Brownsville, who were managed by Jack Richardson. The band took their name from a road paving machine (a' la **Buffalo Springfield**) and mostly played local dances, with one show in Eugene.

The 'A' side to their 45, *Life*, is pleasant acoustic folk-pop. The flip, *Gliding Ride*, kicks off innocuously enough but one is suddenly woken by a brief fuzzy outburst before a return to the sparse'n'simple theme. The next verse ends with another burst, then an all-too-short bridge where the guitarist is allowed his head, and a denouement wrapped in some fine lead. So it ends, with potential unfulfilled - this could have been so good if only they'd let rip.

Compilation appearances have so far included: *Gliding Ride* on *Psychedelic Experience Vol. 4* (CD). (MW/MM/GGI)

Barbie

ALBUM:	1	JOURNEY TO JESUS	(Private pressing) 1971 -
	2	SINGS FOR LIFE	(Private pressing) 1973 -

A female Christian folk singer/songwriter and guitar player. Her two albums are highly-rated by some dealers. (SR)

The Bar Boys

Personnel:	TOMMY ARNOLD	keyb'ds	A
	GREG LYNN	bs	A
	EDDIE ROSS	drms	A
	DAVID YATES	drms	A

45:	Hit The Road Jack / That's The Sound Of My Heart	(Lyar 101) 1968

The Bar Boys formed in Paragould, Arkansas in 1967. Their version of *Hit The Road Jack* starts in unpromising fashion with a brassy intro but it improves as the vocalist warms to his task, finally erupting into a great fuzzy guitar break immediately followed by a brief flute interlude. The flip is classy booming keyboard-led pop with a crisp Motown-influenced swing in the rhythm section.

Ron Hall's book, 'Playing For A Piece Of The Door', provides the personnel above and reveals that the 45 was recorded at Sonic studios in Memphis, TN. (MW)

The Bards

45:	Alibis/Thanks A Lot	(Emcee 013) 1966

Not to be confused with the better known Pacific Northwest outfit, this Fort Worth band was rumoured to have issued three 45s in all during the mid-sixties. *Alibis* is unexceptional but you'll find it on *Flashback, Vol. 5* (LP), *Gathering Of The Tribe* (LP), *Highs In The Mid Sixties, Vol. 13* (LP), *Teenage Shutdown, Vol. 10* (LP & CD) and *Texas Flashback, Vol. 5* (LP).

They evolved out of **Johnny Diamond & The Royal Five**. (VJ/MW)

The Bards

Personnel:	MIKE BALZOTTI	keyb'ds, vcls	ABCD
	JOHN DRANEY	ld vcls	A
	BOB GALLOWAY	drms, vcls	ABCDE
	MARDI SHERIDAN	ld gtr, vcls	AB D
	CHUCK WARREN	bs, vcls	ABCDE
	'APPLE ANDY'	gtr	C
	MARK CHELSON	vcls, sax	C
	CORDELL COBERT?		F
	BOB GALLLOWAY		F

ALBUMS:	1(A)	THE BARDS - FIRST AMERICAN	
		(Piccadilly 3419)	1980 SC
	2(D)	RESURRECT THE MOSES LAKE RECORDINGS	
		(Gear Fab GF-183)	2002

NB: (1) is a 10-track selection comprising seven 45 cuts and three unreleased tracks, issued without the band's knowledge. (2) is a CD reissue of an unreleased 1968 LP.

45s:	α	The Owl and The Pussycat/Light Of Love	(Piccadilly 224) 1966
	β	My Generation/Jabberwocky	(Panorama 52) 1967
		The Jabberwocky/My Generation	(Piccadilly 232) 1967
		Never Too Much Love/Light Of Love	(Piccadilly 242) 1967
		Never Too Much Love/Jabberwocky	(Capitol 2041) 1967
		The Owl and The Pussycat/ The Light Of Love	(Capitol 2148) 1968
	χ	Oobleck / Moses	(Together T-113) 1969
		Goodtime Charlie's Got The Blues/Tunesmith	(Jerden 907) 1969
		Goodtime Charlie's Got The Blues/Tunesmith	(Parrot 337) 1969
	δ	Jubilation/Our Love	(Parrot 344) 1969
		Walla Walla/Day By Day	(Parrot 351) 1970
		I Want You/Freedom Catcher	(Burdette 103) 1971

NB: α was originally scheduled for release as Panorama 46 but was never released. β Not released. χ as **Moses Lake**. δ as "The Bards featuring Bob Galloway".

Operated out of Moses Lake, Washington between 1961-69. They evolved out of a school teen combo called The Fabulous Continentals, who were a late fifties and early sixties covers outfit. They took their new name, **The Bards** from Roget's Thesaurus - the word 'Bard' meaning 'a travelling English minstrel, poet ...' they were a travelling group of musicians and the reference to England clinched it because they wanted to sound like The Beatles. They even became a foursome when John Draney, their lead vocalist, left to join the army.

Their big break came when *Never Too Much Love*, an original arrangement of an old Curtis Mayfield tune, made it to No 67 nationally in the Cash Box Top 100, although it seems not to have figured in the Billboard charts. It created the opportunity for them to tour with big name acts like **The Turtles**, The Dave Clark Five and **Paul Revere and The Raiders**. During 1967 Mardi Sheridan left the band for a while to head for San Francisco and was temporarily replaced by virtuoso guitarists known as Apple Andy and Mark Chelson, who joined from **George Washington and the Cherry Bombs**. When Sheridan returned they headed for L.A. to find a producer.

In Hollywood they met **Curt Boettcher** and Keith Olsen and in 1969 under their production recorded an unreleased album, although this resulted in the break-up of the band. After its completion **Curt Boettcher** wanted to go back to the Northwest to sing with the band which delighted Mike and Mardi but not Bob and Chuck who wanted to get back on their old gig circuit and preserve their autonomy. So the split came when Mike and Mardi left and ultimately headed to L.A. to pursue writing and recording careers, although Bob and Chuck regrouped and carried on with the name for a while. For their **Boettcher**/Olsen period, they renamed themselves **Moses Lake** and a 45 was released under that moniker on Together Records.

In 2002 Gear Fab released the **Moses Lake** album. It's a pot-pourri of late sixties sounds, from bouncy pop to acidic rock, with an underground vibe - decidededly ambitious and uncommercial. Not the usual dreamy, harmony pop associated with **Boettcher** although his influence is clear in the harmonies and multi-layered arrangements. It comprises seven tracks including the Together 45 pairing and *The Creation*, a religious seven-movement mini-rock-opera.

In the late seventies and early eighties Jerry Dennon released the *History Of Northwest Rock* series on the Great Northwest label, plus a slew of retrospective LPs on the First American and Piccadilly labels. Many of the latter are hard to find, amongst them the **Bards**' retrospective, of which band members were unaware. Ten tracks were selected: seven 45 cuts (*My Generation, The Owl And The Pussycat, Light Of Love, Never Too Much Love, The Jabberwocky, Goodtime Charlie's Got The Blues* and *Tunesmith*) and three unreleased tracks (*By The Time I Get to Phoenix, I Kissed Her Feet*, and *Be Happy*).

Michael Balzotti later played in a duo with Seattle singer/songwriter Michael Langdon called The Michaels. Mardi Sheridan now works in advertsing; Chuck Warren manages an irrigation company in Moses Lake; Bob Galloway raises show horses and Mike Balzotti owns a real estate company in Seattle.

Compilation appearances have so far included: *Freedom Catcher* on *The History Of Northwest Rock, Vol. 3* (CD); *Light Of Love* on *Northwest Battle Of The Bands, Vol. 1 - Flash And Crash* (LP); *Light Of Love* and *The Owl and The Pussycat* on *Northwest Battle Of The Bands, Vol. 1 - Flash And Crash* (CD); *My Generation* on *Battle Of The Bands, Vol. 2* (LP), *Northwest Battle Of The Bands, Vol. 2 - Knock You Flat!* (LP & CD), *Northwest Battle Of The Bands, Vol. 2* (CD) and *The History Of Northwest Rock, Vol. 3* (LP); *The Owl and The Pussycat* on *Northwest Battle Of The Bands, Vol. 1* (CD), *Battle Of The Bands, Vol. 1* (LP), *History Of Northwest Rock, Vol. 2* (CD), *The History Of Northwest Rock, Vol. 2* (LP); *Never Too Much Love* and *Tunesmith* on *The History Of Northwest Rock, Vol. 1* (LP); and *Goodtime Charley's Got The Blues* on *History Of Northwest Rock, Vol. 6* (cass). (VJ/MW)

The Bare Facts

Personnel incl: BILL WILLIAMS — A

45s:	Bad Part Of Town/Georgiana	(Jubilee 45-5544) 1966
	The Only Thing / To Think	(Josie 978) 1967

From Portsmouth, Ohio. *Bad Part Of Town*, which shouldn't be confused with **The Seeds** song of the same name, is superb - great vocals and a superb guitar break.

Bill Williams would later graduate to **Southwest F.O.B.**, Seals & Crofts and Toto!

Compilation appearances have so far included: *Bad Part Of Town* on *Mayhem & Psychosis, Vol. 2* (LP), *Mayhem & Psychosis, Vol. 1* (CD) and *Psychedelic Microdots Of The Sixties, Vol. 3* (CD); and both *Bad Part Of Town* and *Georgiana* on *The Finest Hours of U.S. '60s Punk* (LP) and *Sixties Archive Vol. 5* (CD). (VJ/MW)

THE FINEST HOURS OF US 60's PUNK (Comp LP) including The Bare Facts.

The Barking Spyders

45: I Want Your Love / Hard World — (Audio Precision 45001) 1966

NB: Sometimes seen listed as "#4201" which is it's RCA matrix no.

Despite the label name, precision was AWOL the day they laid down *I Want Your Love*. So out-of-sync that it's been compiled on *Pebbles, Vol. 11* (LP), *Teenage Shutdown, Vol. 4* (LP & CD) and *Psychedelic Crown Jewels Vol. 3* (CD), hailed as 'low fi' and 'inept genius', and elevated to the status of garage classic! Where are these guys now?

From a Dallas, Texas. (MW/MM)

Barnaby Bye

ALBUMS:	1	ROOM TO GROW	(Atlantic SD 7273) 1973 -
	2	TOUCH	(Atlantic SD 18104) 1974 -

45s:	I Think I'm Gonna Like It/Dreamer	(Atlantic 2984) 1973
	Blonde/Take Me With You	(Atlantic 3244) 1974
	Can't Live This Way/	
	Happy Was The Day We Met	(Atlantic 3266) 1974

An obscure rock group. Housed in a repulsive sleeve, their first album ends with a great cover of The Beatles' *She's Leaving Home*. (SR)

Steve Baron Quartet

Personnel:	STEVE BARON	vcls, acoustic gtr	A
	BILL DAVIDSON	electric gtr	A
	JEF LOWELL	bs, vcls	A
	TOM WINER	piano, organ	A
	(HERB LOVELLE	drms	A)
	(BILL LA VORGNA	drms	A)

ALBUM: 1(A) THE MOTHER OF US ALL
(Tetragrammaton T-123) 1969 -

Despite his name, the **Steve Baron Quartet** didn't just play jazz but an intriguing mix of rock and folk, with strong jazz influences prevalent especially on the guitar parts. The '**Quartet** were formed in 1967 in New York by **Steve Baron** who had earlier participated in the Greenwich Village folk revival of the early sixties. Helped by session drummers, they released only one album in 1969, for the small Californian label Tetragrammaton. (This label also released **Joshua Fox**, **Ivory** and **Quatrain** and was partly owned by Bill Cosby). Produced by Mike Berniker and arranged by Manny Albam, the best tracks are *Bertha Was The Mother Of Us All*, *Don't You Hate The Feeling* and the eleven minute *Shadow Man*. These are extremely gentle, intimate and sensitive songs set to uncommon accompaniments. The fragile nature of the music may offend rock fanatics, but makes great late night fodder. Some of the other tracks, however, suffer from the addition of strings.

Curiously Pete Townshend penned the enthusiastic liner notes "all the sounds spontaneously and simultanously imploding and exploding. Just like nature! The Quartet make Natural Music. Jai Baba!"

In 1970, Bill Davidson joined **Gas Mask** for *Their First Album* (and last!). (SR/MK)

The Barons

45: Come To Me/Only The Young — (Monocle 001) 1967

This garage band hailed from San Antonio in Texas and the 'A' side of their sole 45 contains some good organ and guitar work although the vocals could be more upfront. The flip was an instrumental. *Come To Me* was later included on *Flashback, Vol. 1* (LP), *Texas Flashbacks, Vol. 1* (LP & CD) and *Texas Flashback (The Best Of)* (CD). (VJ)

TEXAS FLASHBACKS Vol. 3 (Comp CD) including The Barons.

The Barons

Personnel:
DON BABB	A
CURLY BENTON	A
RONNIE MARCOTT	A
JOHN NITZINGER	A

45s:
You're Gonna Get Hurt/I'll Never Be Happy	(Torch 102) 1965
Live And Die/Don't Look Back	(Torch 103) 1965
Don't Burn It/I Hope I Please You	(Brownfield 1035) 196?

A different act which formed at Haltom High School in Fort Worth, also in Texas. All three 45s were written by **John Nitzinger** who later formed his own band in the seventies and then went on to play for Alice Cooper in the early eighties. The 'A' side of their second 45, *Live And Die* was a good folk-rocker, but their best effort was *Don't Burn It*, an anti-draft folk protest song. Benton also went on briefly to play in **Nitzinger**'s band but sadly died young of cancer.

Compilation appearances have so far included: *Don't Burn It* on *Flashback, Vol. 3* (LP), *Texas Flashback, Vol. 3* (LP & CD) and *Highs In The Mid Sixties, Vol. 13 - Texas Part Three* (LP); *I'll Never Be Happy* on *Class Of '66!* (LP); and *Live And Die* on *Texas Punk, Vol. 9* (LP) and *Acid Visions - Complete Collection, Vol. 3* (3-CD). (VJ)

The Barons

Personnel:
DAVID BORDERKIRCHER	ld vcls	A
DEE EBERSBACK	drums, vcls	A
DANNY FREEMAN	keyb'ds, gtr, vcls	A
JIM KATT	gtr, vcls	A
GLEN NORMAN	bs	A

45s:
| Drawbridge / Lovin' Man | (Tener T1011) 1967 |
| Reach For The Sky / Colors Of Love | (Tener T1021) 1967/8 |

From Orlando, Florida this band lasted through many personnel changes, after the original line-up detailed above, right up to 1977 - quite a feat. *Drawbridge* is a cool power-punker with a killer fuzz riff throughout, right up with the likes of **The Del-Vetts**' *Last Time Around*. *Lovin' Man* harks back to a 1964-5 R&B-influenced U.K. beat style. *Reach For The Sky* is a cool **Raiders**' like fuzzed pop-punker.

Compilation appearances include: *Drawbridge* on *Yeah Yeah Yeah* (CD) and *Psychedelic Crown Jewels Vol.2* (CD & Dble LP); *Drawbridge* and *Lovin' Man* on *Sixties Rebellion, Vol. 5*; *You Must Believe Me* on the sought-after *Bee Jay Demo, Vol. 2* 1967 LP (Tener 1014); *Colors Of Love* on the equally rare *Bee Jay Video Soundtrack* LP (also issued as Tener 1014, in 1968); *More Today Than Yesterday* and *Spinning Wheel* on *Bee Jay Sampler, Vol. 1* (LP); both *Vehicle* and *25 Or 6 To 4* on *Bee Jay Sampler* (LP); and *Reach For The Sky* on *Psychedelic States - Florida Vol. 2* (CD). (MW/RM)

The Barons

ALBUMS:
| 1 THE BARONS | (Solar 101) 1970 R1 |
| 2 BY REQUEST | (Solar 10?) c1971 R1 |

45s:
| Mellow Moonlight/Strung Out On You | (Solar 506) c1970 |
| Wounds Of Love/Put Me In Jail | (Solar 513) c1970 |

Another **Barons**, from Corpus Christ, Texas. Their two albums feature covers of Moody Blues, Sonny Boy Williamson, Isaac Hayes, **Creedence**, **Buffalo Springfield** and Ten Years After as well as more mellow tracks. (SR)

Baron Thomas and The Blue Crystals

45s:
| α Be Bop A Lula / Hey Baby | (Courier 116) 1965 |
| Tension/We'll Be Thru For Ever | (Courier 8150) 1966 |

NB: α as **The Blue Crystals**.

From Bowling Green, Ohio. *Tension* is a typically crude garage punk recording - not a bad effort, though. You'll also find it on *Highs In The Mid-Sixties, Vol. 21* (LP) whilst their rendition of *Be Bop A Lula* has also appeared on *Garage Punk Unknowns, Vol. 1* (LP). (MW/GGI)

The Baroque Brothers

45:
| So Glad Was I/Baroque Au Go Go | (Back Beat 562) 1966 |

The Beatles meet **The Byrds** in *So Glad Was I* with some George Harrison chords for good measure. Similar sonic territory to **The Coastliners**, this outfit hailed from Houston, Texas. The flip is a 'live' club instrumental work-out with sax. (MW)

Baroque Monthly

Personnel:
SANDY EDELSTEIN		A
JIM KELLY	keyb'ds	A
DAN MASYS	ld vcls, ld gtr	A
JON RICKLEY	drums	A
DAVE SAMPSON	bs	A

45:
| I'll Be Lonely / You Are Your Only Mystery | (Ironbeat HR 1167) 1968 |

A latter-day one-off moniker for **The Jaguars** of Columbus, Ohio, who formed around 1964 whilst students at the Bexley and Eastmoor high schools. *You Are Your Only Mystery*, which Dan Masys says was influenced by the Beatles' *Eleanor Rigby* and the **Left Banke**'s *Walk Away Renee*, is a soft-baroque-rock charmer with horns and piano and a vaguely hippie aura - but don't let that put you off, it's highly rated by many. Save a fortune and judge for yourself by checking it out on *Psychedelic Crown Jewels Vol. 2* (CD & Dble LP).

Prior to this **The Jaguars** had a 45 that made it to the acetate stage in 1964/5, *Two Can Play / The Day You're Mine*. The former is also on *Psychedelic Crown Jewels Vol. 2*. Ironbeat was a subsidiary of Mus-I-Col, whose legacy is to be explored in two volumes by Get Hip shortly.

In '99 Dan Masys is Associate Clinical Professor of Medicine in California, Sampson is an engineer for Lockheed Martin, Kelly a gymnastics teacher in New Jersey, Rickley lives in Indiana and Edelstein's whereabouts are unknown. (MW/GGI/RM)

The Baroques

Personnel:
RICK BIENIEWSKI	bs	A
JAY BORKENHAGEN	gtr, keyb'ds, vcls	A
JACQUES HUTCHINSON	gtr	A
DEAN NIMMER	drms	A

ALBUM:
| 1(A) BAROQUES | (Chess 1516) Jun. 1967 R1 |

NB: There are also two retrospective compilations. *The Baroques* (Baroque Records DRP-9005) 198? on vinyl and *Purple Day* (Distortions no #) 1996 on CD.

THE BAROQUES - Baroques LP.

45s:	Mary Jane / Iowa, A Girl's Name	(Chess 2001) 1967
	I Will Not Touch/Remember	(Baroque 4553/4) 1968

The Baroques came from Milwaukee, Wisconsin and were one of the first psychedelic bands in the area. Their original album *Baroques* is excellent and also includes their best track, *Musical Tribute To The Oscar Weiner Wagon*. This, starts slowly, culminating in a kaleidoscopic interplay of guitar and drums. A consistently high standard is also maintained throughout almost all the album with *Rose Colored Glasses*, *In Silver Light* and *Purple Day* featuring fine guitar interplay which captures the band at its best.

Originally known as The Complete Unknowns they dressed in baroque costumes and always played with a white pot-bellied stove on stage which contained the controls for their light show. After the first album Chess wanted them to record material like *Chippie, The Hippie From Mississippi* which the band refused to do. They were subsequently released from their Chess contract and released their own 45 *I Will Not Touch You* in April, 1968. The band split some six months later.

Wayne Will, an original member, was drafted in August 1966. Jay stayed in music business, Jacques is now a communications professor at University of Colorado, Dean an art professor at Massachusetts College of Art and Rich is a travelling salesman.

Anyone interested in finding out more should take their pick between two retrospective compilations. The vinyl *The Baroques* put out by the band on their own label, contains some of their finer tracks from their original album (*Mary Jane*, *Musical Tribute To The Oscar Weiner Wagon*, *Iowa, A Girls Name* and *Bicycle*), otherwise the material is all new. *Sunflowers* and *At The Garden Gate*, both from February 1968, are more in a progressive vein with lots of extended instrumentation. Still, quite interesting though. The CD, *Purple Day* covers similar ground with rarities and "best of" material alike.

Not surprisingly their material has also been heavily compiled. You can find *Mary Jane* on *Psychedelic Crown Jewels, Vol. 1* (CD & Dble LP); *Musical Tribute To The Oscar Weiner Wagon* on *Mindrocker, Vol. 6* (LP); *I Will Not Touch You* and *Remember*, on *Glimpses, Vol. 2* (LP) and *Glimpses, Vol. 1 & 2* (CD); *I Will Not Touch You* on *Gone, Vol. 1*; *Nothing Left To Do But Cry* on *Highs In The Mid-Sixties, Vol. 15* (LP); *Iowa, A Girl's Name* on *Turds On A Bum Ride, Vol. 2* (Dble LP) and *Turds On A Bum Ride Vol.'s 1 & 2* (CD); and finally, *Remember* on the vinyl version of *The Psychedelic Experience, Vol. 1* (LP). (VJ/MW/LP)

The Barracuda

Personnel incl:	PETE SANDO	vcls	A

HCP

45s:	α	Dance Of St. Francis / Lady Fingers (PS)	(RCA 9660) 1969 113
		Julie (The Song I Sing Is To You)/ Sleeping Out The Storm	(RCA 9743) 1969

NB: α also issued in Germany with a different picture sleeve - the musicians shown are 'bogus' i.e. didn't play on the 45.

A New York City area group whose material was written and/or produced by Alan Gordon and Gary Bonner of **Magicians**' fame and **Turtle's** hit songwriters. Interesting late sixties pop, rather than garage or psychedelia, it's worth a spin.

Pete Sando, who sang on the first 45, was also guitarist in **Gandalf**.

Compilation appearances have included: *The Dance Of St. Francis* on *Glimpses, Vol. 2* (LP), *Glimpses, Vol's 1 & 2* (CD), *Garagelands Vol. 2* (CD) and *Bring Flowers To U.S.* (LP). (VJ/MW/PS)

The Barracudas

Personnel:	BUTCH EARNHARDT	sax, organ	A
	CHRIS LAYNE	gtr	A
	MIKE PARKER	ld gtr	A
	SAM SHAW	bs	A
	DONNIE THURSTON	drms	A

ALBUM: 1(A) A PLANE VIEW OF THE BARRACUDAS
(Justice 143) 1967 R2

NB: (1) reissued on CD (Collectables COL-CD-0606) 1995.

45s:	I Can't Believe/20-75	(Cuda no #) 1966
	Days Of A Quiet Sun/Apple Pie	(Satori 507) 1969

Highland Springs just to the East of Richmond, Virginia, (not Winston-Salem in North Carolina as was stated on the *Tobacco-A-Go-Go* compilation) was this band's home. They formed in late 1964 as a six-piece but soon solidified into the five-piece listed above in early 1965. Donnie Thurston's dad became their manager and they took part in various 'Battle Of The Bands' during 1965. Their first 45 in 1966 comprised an unimpressive folk-rocker on the 'A' side and an instrumental cover on the flip. They put it out on their own Cuda label. The same session also produced *I'll Never Fall Again*, their best original, and a bizarre medley of *Gloria, Baby Please Don't Go*, which remains unreleased.

In 1967, they recorded an album for Justice Records of Winston-Salem, North Carolina. Besides two originals:- *I Can't Believe* and *I'll Never Fall Again*, the album comprised sloppy teenage versions of *Blue Feeling*, *Feel A Whole Lot Better*, *Not Fade Away*, *I Call Your Name*, *Shotgun* and *I'm A Man*, which were so faithfully rendered and devoid of fuzz that they sound more U.K. than U.S.. Clearly The Rolling Stones were their inspiration. One of the better tracks was *I'm A Lover Not A Fighter*, a frat-rocker from the Kinks' second album but *Shotgun*, in particular, was a pityful attempt at exploiting sixties soul music. Nevertheless the album sold over 700 copies and the band became popular on the college frat-rock circuit.

THE BARRACUDA - Dance At St. Francis (German 45 PS).

By 1968 they had progressed into a **Hendrix**/Cream-type heavy jam sound, but suprisingly their final 45 in 1969 was a folk-rocker. They quit in late 1969. Their album is now quite a big collectors' item but it's really overrated.

Compilation appearances include: *I Can't Believe* on *Project Blue, Vol. 3* (LP); *Not Fade Away* on *Tobacco A-Go-Go, Vol. 1* (LP) and *I'm A Man* on *Tobacco A-Go-Go, Vol. 2* (LP); (VJ/MW)

The Barracudas

Personnel:	TERRY FONTANILLE	ld gtr	A
	ALEX HAAS	drums	A
	JOHN HAAS	vcls	A
	TOMMY McNABB	bs	A

45:	Baby Get Lost/Honest I Do	(Zundak 101) 1965

From Bunkie, Louisiana and originally known as the Pickles, their story is revealed in Andrew Brown's 'Brown Paper Sack #1', thanks to Mark Prellberg. Their screamin' raver was unleashed on the world in April 1965 and graces *Back From The Grave, Vol. 6* (LP), coming on like a younger and speeded-up version of the Pretty Things. The flip was a slower Stones-style effort.

They disbanded in 1967 with John and Tommy forming **Nobody's Children** - no known releases and not to be confused with at least half-a-dozen same name outfits. John Haas was tempted away to lend his vocal talents to **Jimmy & The Offbeats**, who then renamed themselves as **John Eric & The Isosceles Popsicles** who recorded *I'm Not Nice* on the USA label. (AB/MPg/MW/KBn)

The Barracudas

45:	What I Want You To Say/	
	When You Told Me Goodbye	(Downey 138) 1965

Another **Barracudas**, most likely from the Los Angeles area. The groups name is spelled 'Baracudas' on the record label. *What I Want You To Say*, along with the unissued tracks, *The Reason Why*, *These Ironic Days* and *I Can't Believe You're Really Mine*, can also be found on the top-drawer garage punk compilation *Scarey Business* (CD).

The Barracudas

Personnel incl:	MIKE AKIN	keyb'ds	A
	TOMMY GASS	vcls	AB
	ROBIE ROBICHAUD	bs	AB
	BOB ROLSKY	drums	AB
	PAT STOREY	ld gtr	A
	RICK HAZELTINE	ld gtr	B
	TERRY SIDELINKER	keyb'ds	B

45s:	Realize / It's High Time	(Flare 200,848/9) 1966
	No Matter What You Do /	
	Wait For Tomorrow	(Critique 1075627) 1967
	No Matter What You Do /	
	Wait For Tomorrow	(Smash S-2181) 1968

Yet another **Barracudas**, this time from Bangor, Maine. Their first single was released locally, whilst *No Matter What You Do* was in the vein of **The Buckinghams**.

Robbie Robichaud went on to do solo work for Noel Paul Stookey (of Peter, Paul & Mary fame)!

Compilation appearances have included:- *Wait For Tomorrow* on *Psychedelic Experience, Vol. 4* (CD); and *It's High Time* on *It's Finkin' Time!* (LP) and *Yeah Yeah Yeah* (CD). (LRd/MW/MM/TS)

GREEN CRYSTAL TIES Vol. 2 (Comp CD) including The Basement Wall.

Tom Barsanti and The Invaders

45:	You Can't Sit Down/For Your Precious Love	(Delta 2134) 1966

This 45 was issued on a New Mexico label, and has an earlier frat-rock feel. (VJ)

Bartel

Personnel:	JOHN BARTEL	keyb'ds, vcls	A
	ABE BLASINGAME	drms	A
	LARRY O'BRIEN	gtr	A
	LOU STELLUTE	reeds	A

ALBUMS:	1	JOHN BARTEL	(Perception) 1969 -
	2	THE JOHN BARTEL THING	(Capitol ST 274) 1969 -

45:	Summer In The City/ On The Road	(Perception) 1969

NB: also released in France with PS (America AM 17034).

This little known New York group released two albums combining rock, blue-eyed soul and some free jazz influences. After a first album released on **Jimmy Curtiss**' label, they were signed to Capitol.

Their cover of **The Lovin' Spoonful**'s *Summer In The City* was so changed that it's impossible to recognize the original song! (SR)

The Basement Wall

Personnel:	TERRY BOURDIER	bs	A
	BARRIE EDGAR	drms, vcls	A
	RICHARD LIPSCOMB	ld gtr, vcls	A
	GEORGE RATZLAFF	keyb'ds, vcls	A

ALBUM:	1(A)	THE BASEMENT WALL	(Senate) 1963

NB: There's also a retrospective compilation *The Incredible Sound Of...* (Cicadelic 992) 1985, which has been reissued on CD (Collectables COL-CD-0524), together with **The New Breed**'s *Want Ad Reader*.

45:	Never Existed/Taste Of A Kiss	(Senate 2109) 1968

This fairly atypical garage punk band hailed from Baton Rouge, the State Capital and petrochemical industry centre in Louisiana. Perhaps they played in Texas a lot because they certainly seem to have been connected with the Lone Star State. *Texas Punk, Vol. 8* (LP) and *Acid Visions - Complete Collection, Vol. 3* (3-CD) captures a live recording of the band at the Act III in 1967. It's pretty raw stuff as they work their way through versions of *Louie Louie*, *We Ain't Got Nothing Yet*, *Hungry*, *Double Shot Of My Baby's Love*, *Like A Rolling Stone* and *The Basement Exit*.

Never Existed, their stab at immortality, can be heard on *Relics, Vol. 1* (LP), *Relics Vol's 1 & 2* (CD) and *Boulders, Vol. 10* (LP). *The Cicadelic 60's, Vol. 4* (LP) also contains an alternate take of the song. Ronnie Weiss (**Mouse And The Traps**) was on hand in the studio to wield lead guitar on this master-piece.

George Ratzlaff went on to form **Pot Liquor**, who recorded three albums of respectable blues-rock for Janus between 1970-73.

The retrospective on Cicadelic/Collectables may be a reissue of their original album on Senate, if indeed it was ever officially released. Many collectors are very dubious of its existence. Also of interest is *Vol. 2/There Goes The Neighbourhood* (COL-CD-0541), which contains 18 tracks, mainly covers of classic mid-sixties tunes.

Other compilation appearances have included:- *Everything, I'm Not That Slow, Never Existed* on *The Cicadelic 60's, Vol. 2* (CD); *Never Existed* and *You* on *Green Crystal Ties Vol. 2* (CD); and both *Louie Louie* and *We Ain't Got Nothing Yet* on *Green Crystal Ties Vol. 7* (CD). (VJ/MW/JRe)

Robbie Basho

ALBUMS:
1. THE SEAL OF THE BLUE LOTUS (Takoma C-1005) 1965 -
2. THE GRAIL AND THE LOTUS (Takoma C-1007) 1966 -
3. BASHO SINGS (Takoma C-1012) 1967 -
4. THE FALCONER'S ARM, VOL. 1 (Takoma C-1017) 1967 SC
5. THE FALCONER'S ARM, VOL. 2 (Takoma C-1018) 1968 -
6. VENUS IN CANCER (Blue Thumb BTS-10) 1969 -
7. SONG OF THE STALLION (Takoma C-1031) 1970 -
8. ZARTHUS (Vanguard VSD 79339) 1972 -
9. THE VOICE OF THE EAGLE (Vanguard VSD 79???) 1972 -

NB: (4) also released in the UK (Sonet) 1969. Later albums include: *Visions Of The Country* (Windham Steel 1005) 1979, and *Art Of The Acoustic Steel Guitar* (Windham Steel 1010) 1980.

Discovered by **John Fahey** who signed him to his Takoma label, **Robbie Basho** was a singer and acoustic guitar player combining his folk and country roots with Native American, Arabic, Persian and Indian music. His work can be compared to **Sandy Bull** or **Peter Walker** and may also interest fans of **Kaleidoscope** or **John Berberian**, even if it's more meditative than the latter. His records are quite sought after now, especially *Zarthus* with its raga *Llord Of The Blue Rose*. (SR/NK)

Basic Things

Personnel incl: HERMANN BENNETT vcls A

45: Ninety-Nine And A Half/ You'll Still Dreaming (Purple Can 101) 196?

Operating around Port Arthur in Texas, this act recorded just one 45 at Jones Studios in Houston. The 'A' side was an organ driven punker, the flip a pleasant slow song. (VJ)

The Baskerville Hounds

Personnel:
- WILLIAM EMERY — vcls, bs — A
- MICHAEL MACRON — drms, vcls — A
- LAWRENCE MEESE — vcls, ld gtr — A
- DANTE ROSSI — vcls, gtr — A
- JACK TOPPER — piano, organ, vcls — A

ALBUM: 1(A) FEATURING SPACE ROCK PART 2 (Dot DLP 25823) 1967

NB: **The Baskerville Hounds** have recently released a new CD, *Look At Us Now*, ( ) April 2000. This contains new versions of *Hurtin' Kind*, *Mine Forever*, and *Space Rock* as well as ten new original songs.

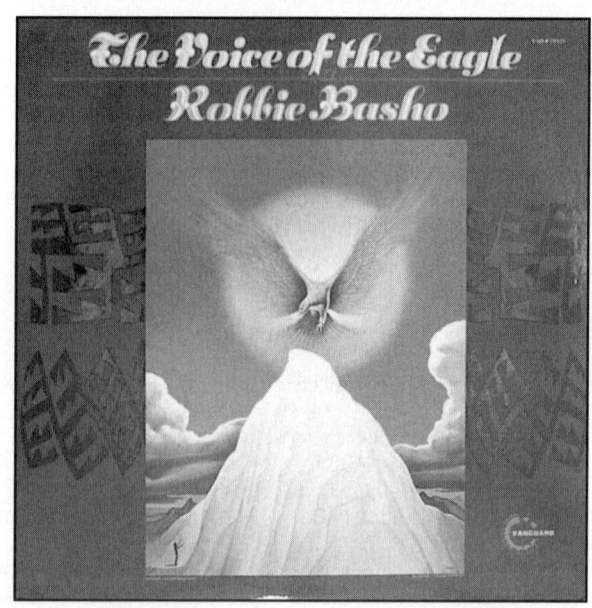

ROBBIE BASHO - The Voice Of The Eagle LP.

HCP

45s:
- α The Hurtin' Kind/Mine Forever (Tema 817) 1965 -
- β Debbie/Although I Was To Blame (Tema 125) 1965 -
- δ Space Rock Part 1 /Part 2 (Tema 128) 1965 -
- Christmas Is Here/Make Me Your Man (Tema 131) 1965 -
- All You Had To Do Was Ask / Who Does She Love (Tema 132) 1966 -
- Space Rock Part 1 /Part 2 (Tema 128) 1967 -
- Space Rock Part 1 /Part 2 (Dot 17004) 1967 -
- Debbie/Jackie's Theme (Dot 17017) 1967 -
- Baby Am I Losing?/Never On Sunday (Dot 17037) 1967 -
- Caroline/Last Night On The Back Porch (Buddah 17) 1967 -
- Hold Me/Here I Come Miami (Tema no #) 1969 -
- Hold Me/Here I Come Miami (Avco Embassy 4504) 1969 88
- χ The Hurtin' Kind/Mine Forever (Mar no #) 19?? -
- Route 66 / Hold Me (Bowie 12268) 1981/2 -

NB: α released as **The Tulu Babies**. β initially released as **The Tulu Babies** and subsequently as **The Baskerville Hounds**. χ is a bootleg of α, miscredited as **The Talula Babies**. δ reissued 1967 prior to being leased to Dot.

A Cleveland, Ohio, band, originally known as **The Tulu Babies**. The inclusion of their first 45 on Eva's *Florida Punk From The '60s*, where it states that they weren't a Florida band in the liner notes, has nonetheless caused much confusion. The title of the flip to their first 45, as **The Baskerville Hounds** served only to add to this. *Hold Me*, incidentally, was the P.J. Proby song. It gave them their only hit peaking at No. 88. Neither a garage or a psychedelic outfit as such, **The Tulu Babies/Baskerville Hounds** dabbled in both at times. *The Hurtin' Kind* was probably their finest moment and later resurfaced on *Everywhere Interferences* (LP). *Space Rock Part 2* which also got a further airing on *Pride Of Cleveland Past* (LP) is an organ-driven instrumental. By no means outstanding it is probably the pick of the crop on a disappointing album which includes reasonable covers of *Penny Lane*, *Never On Sunday* and *I'm A Believer* and some rather average originals. Apparently they were also known for not being the best looking bunch around.

Recently **The Baskerville Hounds** have released a new CD, *Look At Us Now*, which contains new versions of *Hurtin' Kind*, *Mine Forever*, and *Space Rock* as well as ten new original songs. The band are also resuming live performances.

Other compilation appearances include: *I Can Take It* on *Let's Dig 'Em Up, Vol. 1* (CD). (MW/GGl/VJ)

Bassetts

45: A Little Love From You / So Bad (Mercury 72624) 1966

Whether this was a real New York City group or the **Changin' Times** under a pseudonym is open to conjecture.

Artie Kornfeld produced this 45 and with Steve Duboff, the other half of the **Changin' Times**, composed the top side. It's a fuzzy pop ditty, unfortunately in that terribly twee waltzing 'vaudeville' style, with inevitable kazoo. The flip is great '64-style Merseybeat. (MW)

The Bassmen

45:	Last Laugh/Come Home	(Gallantry 745)	1965

Hailing from Tucson, Arizona, they were also known as **Bobby and The Bassmen**. *Last Laugh* can also be found on *Boulders, Vol. 5* (LP), *The Tucson Sound 1960-68 - Think Of The Good Times* (LP) and *Ya Gotta Have... Moxie, Vol. 1* (Dble CD). (MW)

The Bassmen

45:	I Need You/Leigh Anne	(Vaughn Ltd VA-101)	1966

A different act from Alabama. You can also find *I Need You* on *Garage Zone, Vol. 2* (LP), *The Garage Zone Box Set* (4-LP), *A Journey To Tyme, Vol. 4* (LP) and *Ya Gotta Have... Moxie, Vol. 1* (Dble CD). (KBn/MW)

Bastille

45:	Trying To Be Free/The Music Ship	(Bastille 30299/30300)	1973

From New Bedford, Massachusetts, featuring wah-wah and heavy keyboard vibes. (MW)

Gil Bateman

45s:	Wicked Love/Goodnight Irene	(Panorama 12)	1965
	Sneakin' Up On You/ Daddy Walked In Darkness	(Jerden 779)	1965
	(Alt flip) One Eyed Cat/ Daddy Walked In Darkness	(Jerden 779)	1965
	How To Do It/Wicked Love	(Piccadilly 227)	1966
	The Night Before/How To Do It	(Piccadilly 249)	1967

Max Waller drew my attention to this little known but ubiquitous Pacific Northwest artist who also turned his talents to production (**Bards**, **Ceptors** amongst others). *Daddy Walked* is a fine reworking of *House Of The Rising Sun* with strong vocals and guitar. Much of his other material is garagey pop with a hard edge.

THE BASKERVILLE HOUNDS - Featuring Space Rock Part 2 LP.

Compilation appearances have so far included: *Daddy Walked In Darkness* on *Mindblowing Encounters Of The Purple Kind* (LP), *Northwest Battle Of The Bands, Vol. 2 - Knock You Flat!* (LP & CD) and *Northwest Battle Of The Bands, Vol. 2* (CD); and *Wicked Love* on *Bad Vibrations, Vol. 1* (LP & CD). (VJ)

The Bats

45:	Nothing At All/Big Bright Eyes	(HBR 445)	1965

An obscure outfit offer this evocative folk-rock 45, with some Moody Blues type vocal 'ooos' on the tragic 'A' side, that graces Moxie's *Folk Rock E.P.* (7"), whilst *Big Bright Eyes* is a more upbeat strummed affair. This act may have just been a studio aggregation, featuring **Danny Hutton** (and possibly Larry Goldberg). **Hutton** issued several solo 45s (including what may be a different version of *Big Bright Eyes* on HBR 453), before joining **Cory Wells and The Enemys**. He and Cory would later team up with Chuck Negron to become Three Dog Night.

Incidentally, the brooding *Nothing At All* was covered by the **Love Exchange** on their eponymous album in 1967. (VJ/MW)

Battalion Tweed

45:	But It's Alright / Last Time	(Mr.G. 810)	1968

A Connecticut band, who dug **The Young Rascals**, tackle J.J. Jackson's popular soul-popper *But It's Alright* (also covered by Them, **The Red Dogs**, **Morning Reign** and **Canoise**). This is a lively rendition with swirling keyboards, a little fuzz, and latterly brassy fanfares.

The flip is not a Stones' cover but a pulsating keyboard-led club dance instrumental with background vocal taunts and a great fuzz break. It ain't garage, rather a blood brother to that fave-rave of "Northern soul" circles - *Footsee* by the Chosen Few. (MW)

Skip Battin

Personnel:	SKIP BATTIN	bs, vcls, gtr	A
	JOHN GUERIN	drms	A
	SPANKY McFARLANE	backing vcl	A
	ROGER McGUINN	12-string gtr	A
	BILLY MUNDI	drms	A
	CLARENCE WHITE	gtr, mandolin, dobro	A

ALBUM:	1(A)	SKIP BATTIN	(Sign Post SP 8408)	1972 -

45s:	The Ballad Of Dick Clark/same (mono)	(Signpost 7001)	1973

NB: double-sided promo copy.

Singer, bassist and songwriter, **Skip Battin** (or Battyn) began his long career in the fifties in the pop duo Skip and Flip (Flip was Gary Paxton). A long time friend of **Kim Fowley**, in 1969 he formed the **Evergreen Blueshoes** and played with both **Armageddon** and Gene Vincent. In 1970, he joined the **Byrds** in time for their *Untitled* album. He also played on **Zevon**'s *Wanted Dead Or Alive* album.

His 1972 album is essentially country pop but may interest some readers as all the songs were co-written by **Battin** and **Fowley** and the backing group comprised two **Byrds** (McGuinn and White), one ex-**Mothers** and **Rhinoceros** member (Billy Mundi) plus Spanky McFarlane from Spanky and Our Gang. Some tracks (*Undercover Man*, *Cobras*, *Captain Video*, *Four Legs Are Better Than Two*) are interesting if you appreciate **Battin**'s nasal voice.

Battin later joined the New Riders Of The Purple Sage and the Flying Burritos Brothers and kept on recording with various country-rock formations in the seventies and eighties. He released a second solo album, *Navigator* (Appaloosa) in 1981. (SR/HS)

Joe Bauer

Personnel:
EARTHQUAKE ANDERSON	hrmnca	A
BANANA	gtr, piano	AB
JOE BAUER	drms	AB
JACK GREGG	bs	A
MICHAEL KANE	bs	AB
STEVE SWALLOW	bs	A
KENNY GILL	piano	B
BILL MITCHELL	tenor	B

ALBUMS:
1(A) MOONSET (Raccoon 3 / Warner WS 1901) 1971 –
2(B) CRAB TUNES / NOGGINS (Raccoon 8 / Warner WS 1914) 1971 –

Two albums by **The Youngbloods** drummer: noises, improvisations, folk and blues. Not an easy listening experience! (SR)

Baxter

Personnel:
DOUG ARIOLA	gtr, vcls	A
STEVE BELGRADE	gtr, vcls	A
LAWRENCE DI NATALE	drms	A
STEVE KIRSHENBAUM	keyb'ds	A
EDWIN PERRY	bs, vcls	A

ALBUM: 1(A) BAXTER (Paramount PAS 6050) 1973 SC

A prog rock album with guitar and organ interplay. (SR)

Baxter's Chat

45: Don't Come Around Today/? (Pearce 5812) 1967

Hailing from Southeast Kansas this outfit travelled to Cavern Studios in Independence Missouri to record this 45, a pleasing organ-dominated pop 45. There's also rumoured to have been a second fuzz drenched 45, but I don't have details of this.

Don't Come Around Today can also be found on *Monsters Of The Midwest, Vol. 3* (LP). (MW)

Bay Ridge

Personnel:
JOSEPH "JOEY" CARBONE	ld vcls, bs	A
ROBERT "RED" GAMBALE	organ	A
HUGO "AUGIE" PEROTTI	gtr, vcls	A
PETER PINTO	drms	A
RICHARD "RITCHIE" ZITO	ld gtr, vcls	A

45s: Back Track/
I Can't Get Her Out Of My Mind (Atlantic 2431) 1967
Without You/I Will Wait (Atlantic 2520) 1968

From Bay Ridge in Brooklyn, New York, this quintet were originally known as The Chosen Few. Both 45s have a garagey feel but also lean more towards **Vanilla Fudge**-styled R&B/soul-tinged vocals and keyboards. On the plus side there is some strong guitar work and good use of fuzz on *Without Her* and *I Can't Get Her Out Of My Mind* is reasonable garagey-pop. Their best effort however is *I Will Wait* - a good garagey workout and a song that actually is "One Chord", which the group modulates up to a higher key at the end.

Joey Carbone became music director for the long-running TV talent show 'Star Search'; in 2002 he produces and composes for popular Japanese singers. Ritchie Zito would play guitar for Elton John before becoming a very successful producer for the likes of Cher, Heart, Cheap Trick, Bad English and Eddie Money; he was named No. 1 American producer in Billboard magazine in 1990.

I Can't Get Her Out Of Mind has turned up again on *Psychedelic States: New York, Vol. 1* (CD). (MW/MM/VJ)

The Baytovens

Personnel:
CARL DEPOLO	A
JON GREEN	A
RICHARD GREEN	A
DWIGHT PITCAITHLEY	A

45s: α My House / Luv Look Away (Leander) 1966
Waiting For You / Such A Fool (PS) (Belfast 67-1001) 1967

NB: α not released.

A cleverly named bunch from San Leandro, California... *Waiting For You* is a pleasant pop song whose chord progression features an open or suspended chord where the ears would expect a full major. The flip side, *Such A Fool* is a **Beau Brummels** derived gem with a mesmerizing guitar figure and a plaintive spine-tingling chorus. The perfect song of lost love when the fog rolls in over Frisco's moody landscape. It's got an old-style almost gold-rush aura about it.

All four cuts by the band are/were to appear on a forthcoming volume in the *Nuggets From The Golden State* series on Big Beat. (SH/MW)

B.B. and The Oscars

45s: 1,2,3 Red Light/Hold Me Tight (Guilford 101) 1967
The House That Jack Built/Hush (Guilford 102) c1967

A garage group with sax and guitar, both 45s are so-so cover versions with their first being an instrumental produced by B. Buchman. The Baltimore based Guilford label also released a 45 by **Gross National Product**. (SR/JV)

B.C. and The Caveman

45: As Long As I'm Around/? (Stone Age 814P-0001) 196?

A Michigan band whose rather mundane *As Long As I'm Around* can be heard on *Michigan Mixture, Vol. 2* (LP) and *Let 'Em Have It! Vol. 1* (CD). (VJ)

The BC's

45: Oh Yeow!/Comin' On Home (Ruff 1015) 1966

Hailing from West Texas they reworked **The Shadow Of Knight**'s *Oh Yeah* Texas punk style. You can hear the result on *Texas Punk, Vol. 9* (LP) and *Acid Visions - Complete Collection, Vol. 3* (3-CD). (VJ)

Paul Wayne Beach

ALBUM: 1 ON DOWN THE ROAD (Private pressing) 1972 R1

A rare album, in a folky/country rock vein, highly praised by some dealers specialized in private pressings. (SR)

Beach Bums

Personnel incl:
BOB SEGER	vcls	A
DOUG BROWN		A

45: Ballad Of The Yellow Beret/
Florida Time (Are You Kidding Me Records 1010) 1966

The first single released by **Bob Seger**, in March 1966. **The Beach Bums** were in fact the Omens and the song was a parody of Sgt Barry Adler's *Ballad Of The Green Beret*. It was a hit in Michigan but when Sadler complained the 45 was withdrawn.

Compilation appearances have included: *Ballad Of The Yellow Baret* on *Michigan Brand Nuggets* (LP), *Michigan Nuggets* (CD) and *Best of Hideout Records* (CD). (SR)

The Beachcombers

Personnel:	DAVE ANDERSON	bs	A
	TERRY BIGGS	ld gtr	A
	STAN FOREMAN	electric piano	A
	PAUL LOVE	gtr	A
	DAVE REED	sax, vcls	A
	JIM WYNANS	drms	A

CD:	1( )	THE LEGENDARY BEACHCOMBERS LIVE IN THE GREAT NORTHWEST	( ) 1997

45s:	Purple Peanuts / Chinese Bagpiper	(Jerden 719) 1963
	Tossin' And Turnin' / The Wheeley	(Jerden 734) 1964
	All To Pieces / The Wheeley	(Panorama 11) 1965

Formed in 1961 in Aberdeen, Washington (home of Kurt Cobain) they played the entire Northwest region until 1968. They did shows with **The Wailers**, **Sonics**, **Viceroys**, **Bootmen**, etc and played all the great dance halls including Parkers, Pearls, Target Ballroom, etc.

The Beachcombers recorded for Jerden Records, home of the **Kingsmen**, Dave Lewis, Ian Whitcomb, and others. The band had several instrumentals that received big airplay on Northwest radio. In 1989 the original members of the band got together again to play for their high school class reunion. They had so much fun that they decided to play a limited number of dates each year. Currently billed as "The Legendary Beachcombers", the band plays about ten dates a year... car shows, class reunions, corporate functions, country club sixties nites. etc. In 1997, the band released a live CD titled "The Legendary Beachcombers Live in the Great Northwest".

Compilation appearances include: *Farmer John* and *The Wheeley* on *History Of Northwest Rock, Vol. 2* (CD) and *The Wheeley* on *History Of Northwest Rock, Vol. 5* (Cass).

Thanks to Stan Foreman for pointing out we'd missed this bunch!

The Beach Niks

45s:	Like Stoned/Good Things	(MMC 007) 1965
	Last Night I Cried/It Was A Nightmare	(MMC 008) 1965
	Last Night I Cried/It Was A Nightmare	(Sea Mist 1001) 1965

A well respected punk outfit from Newell, a very small town in Western Iowa. You can check out *Last Night I Cried* on the cassette compilation, *Monsters Of The Midwest, Vol. 1*. (VJ)

The Beach Nuts

HCP

45:	Out In The Sun (Hey-O)/Someday Soon	(Bang 504) 1965 106

This 45 is thought to be the work of **The Strangeloves** under yet another pseudonym and it narrowly missed the Top 100. (TTi/VJ)

The Beachnuts

Personnel:	HAROLD HENRY	bs	A
	MIKE JOHNSON	gtr	AB
	CARL STEVENS	ld vcls, organ	A
	TOM STREW	drms, vcls	AB
	BILL WALLS	ld gtr	AB
	MIKE GARCIA	organ	B

45s:	α	Babba Diddy Baby / I'm Angry Baby	(Remus 5000) 1965
		Professional Loving Man/ What's Gone Wrong	(Tiki 68-21/22) 1968

NB: α released as by The Heart Attacks.

THE BEACON STREET UNION - The Eyes Of... LP.

Formed in 1962 this Virginia Beach bunch started out playing surf music. In 1965 they released their debut 45 as The Heart Attacks although they continued to be known as **The Beachnuts**. Mike Johnson got his draft papers at the end of 1965. On his return in late 1967 the group reformed and lasted till the end of the decade, releasing one more 45 in 1968.

Babba Diddy Baby, an infectious frat-stomp with what sounds like steel drums, was first compiled on *Boulders, Vol. 10* (LP) in the eighties and makes a welcome re-appearance on *Aliens, Psychos And Wild Things* (CD) - a professional comp of the Tidewater sixties scene. The CD includes an unreleased, slightly extended version of *What's Gone Wrong* (under the original master-tape title of *What Makes You Think*) - cool '68 pop-rock with neat tempo changes and spiralling guitar solos. The other side of the Tiki platter is catchy frat-pop with a soulful swagger.

Babba Diddy Baby can also be found on *Ya Gotta Have Moxie, Vol. 2* (Dble CD). (BHr/ST/MW)

The Beacon Street Union

Personnel:	ROBERT RHODES	keyb'ds, brass	A
	PAUL TARTACHNY	gtr, vcls	A
	WAYNE ULAKY	bs, vcls	A
	RICHARD WEISSBERG	drms	A
	JOHN LINCOLN WRIGHT	vcls, perc	A

HCP

ALBUMS:	1(A)	THE EYES OF THE BEACON STREET UNION	(MGM SE 4517) 1968 75 -
	2(A)	THE CLOWN DIED IN MARVIN GARDENS	(MGM SE 4568) 1968 173 -

NB: (2) also issued in France (MGM) 1969. Both albums have been reissued on one CD (Head 3497) 1997 but with an edited version of *Baby Please Don't Go*. More recently See For Miles have reissued both albums on one CD (SEECD 495) 1998, this time with the full sixteen minute *Baby Please Don't Go* but with a track omitted from the first album. (1) reissued on LP (Akarma AK 157) 2001. (2) reissued on LP (Akarma AK 164). (1) and (2) reissued on CD, together with the **Eagle** album as a 3-CD Box set *State Of The Union* (Akarma AK 157/3).

45s:	South End Incident (I'm Afraid) / Speed kills	(MGM K 13865) 1967
	Blue Suede Shoes/ Four Hundred And Five	(MGM K 13935) 24th 1968
	Mayola/May I Light Your Cigarette?	(MGM K 14012) 1968
	Lord Why Is It So Hard / Can't Find My Fingers	(RTP 10011/2) 1969

This group, part of the 'Bosstown Sound', were energetically promoted in 1968. Their debut album, though often pretentious, was a mini-psychedelic masterpiece. The material, a mixture of acid rock, blues, and ballads, was usually original and often interesting. The album is recommended it you are able to obtain a copy. Their second effort continued in a similar vein, but contained the orchestrated *Clown's Overture* and *Angus Of Aberdeen*. Also of note on the album were a sixteen minute version of *Baby Please Don't Go*, a most unusual track entitled *May I Light Your Cigarette?* and a version of the Carl Perkin's classic *Blue Suede Shoes*. The back cover of this album pictures the band walking on top of a cloud and their strange music was undoubtedly largely drug-induced. Either or both albums are well worth checking out and both met with some commercial success.

Wright, Ulaky and Rhodes all played for **Eagle**, who issued an album for Janus Records. Then in 1977, John Lincoln Wright released a country music album titled *Takin' Old Route One*. Wright has pursued a career as a country singer and remains a popular entertainer today in the New England area.

Compilation appearances have included: *Four-O-Five* on *Garagelands Vol. 2* (CD). (VJ/SPr/MW/SR)

BEACON STREET UNION - The Clown Died In Marvin Gardens.

Bead Game

Personnel:	R. GASS	keyb'ds	A
	JIM HODDER	drms, perc, ld vcls	A
	LASSIE SACHS	bs	A
	JOHN SHELDON	ld gtr	A
	K. WESTLAND HAAG	gtr, vcls	A

ALBUM: 1(A) WELCOME (Avco Embassy 33009) 1970 R1

NB: There's also (A) *Baptism* (American Sound AS 1004) 1996, Ltd to 900 copies.

45: Sweet Medusa/Country Girls (Avco Embassy 4539) 1970

From Boston, their debut album's stand out cuts are the opening track *Punchin Judy*, *Mora* and *Country Girl* a very pleasant slow number. All the cuts on the album were written by the band and some contain pretty good fuzztone guitar.

The band also appeared in a so-so suburban melodrama, *The People Next Door*, performing the amazing theme song and one other number. Rather than hunt down this scarce film, fans are recommended to hunt down the soundtrack album on Avco Embassy. The whole band were apparently also part of Freedom Express who released *Easy Ridin'* (Mercury) 1970, a horn-rock album notable for fine guitar and organ work.

Baptism was apparently recorded at Natural Sound in Mayward, Massachusetts in 1970, before they signed to Avco-Embassy and it has a very laid-back vibe. While occasionally a bit rough, none of the eleven tracks comes anywhere close to psych. Material such as *Water Boy*, *20 Dollars Bill* and *Mr. Sorry* are mainstream pop-rock. Elsewhere, tracks such as *Steamballin'* and *What A Day* opted for a mild country-rock flavor. It's a nice, but forgettable collection. John Sheldon recalls: "I was the last person to work on that project, doing final mixes in 1971. We couldn't find a label who would release it, so as far as I know, the master tapes were simply left at the studio."

Jim Hodder went on to play with Steely Dan on their first two albums. Prior to **Bead Game**, John Sheldon was Van Morisson's Guitarist for the Spring and Summer of 1968. John: "We rehearsed in the basement of my house, and he was writing a lot there and in my back yard. Currently, I am a composer and song writer. My song *September Grass* is coming out on James Taylor's new CD - end of this summer." (VJ/SB/MMs/JSN)

David Beal

Personnel:	DAVID BEAL	A
	MARK BEAL	A
	WAYNE HAMILTON	A
	TOM LEMAY	A
	KAREN THARP	A

ALBUM: 1(A) LET HIM SHINE (Worship Renewal Ministries 257) c1974 -

From Houston, Texas, a Christian folk rock singer with acoustic and electric instruments and all original tunes. The album was housed in a rather nice grey cover with religious drawings. (SR)

Beans

ALBUM: 1 BEANS (Avalanche 9200) 1972 -

An obscure hippie-rock album with some weird tracks. (SR)

Bear

Personnel:	ERIC KAZ	keyb'ds, vcls	A
	STEVE SOLES	vcls	A
	ARTIE TRAUM	gtr, vcls	A
	(SKIP BOONE	bs	A)
	(DARIUS DAVENPORT	drms	A)

ALBUM: 1(A) GREETINGS CHILDREN OF PARADISE (Verve Folkways 3059) 1969 -

45: Don't Say A Word/Greetings (Verve Folkways 5096) 1968

Bear were part of Boston's music scene in the late sixties. Originally known as Children Of Paradise, they also recorded the theme music for an early Brian De Palma film 'Greetings', with Robert De Niro... Hence their album title! The album is worth investigating. Two of its better tracks include, *What*

BEAD GAME - Baptism LP.

BEAR - Greetings Children Of Paradise LP.

Difference?, a laid back, jazzy number and *It's Getting Very Cold Outside*. The group was helped out by Steve Soles and Darius Davenport from **Autosalvage**.

Eric Kaz played in **The Blues Magoos** during 1969 and 1970, and in Mud Acres (during 1972) with Artie Traum. All three members became session musicians during the seventies. (VJ/NK)

The Bearcuts

ALBUM: 1 BEATLEMANIA (Somerset) 1964 SC

Supposedly "recorded in London, England", **The Bearcuts** were supposed to "swing in Beatlemania" with the usual covers of the Fab Four: *I Want To Hold Your Hand*, *Love Me Do*, *Please Please Me* and *She Loves You* plus some original material like *Liverpool Stomp* and *Your Barber Is A Beatle Too*. Another attempt to cash in on the English Invasion. (SR)

Paul Bearer and The Hearsemen

Personnel incl:	PAUL BEARER		A
	ED WESTBY		A

45: Route 66/I've Been Thinking (Riverton 105) 1966

From Albany, Oregon. *I've Been Thinking* has been exhumed on *Teenage Shutdown, Vol. 10* (LP & CD). (VJ/MW/DR/MM)

The Bear Fax

45s:	I Wanna Do It (Marry You)/	
	Love Is A Beautiful Thing	(Fuzz 901) 196?
	Out Of Our Tree/Turn Over	(Fuzz 4141) 196?

A mid-sixties punk outfit from Texas. Their best known song is *Out Of Our Tree*, a brash punk rocker, by virtue of its inclusion on *Flashback, Vol. 4* (LP), *Texas Flashbacks, Vol. 4* (LP) and *Texas Flashback (The Best Of)* (CD). (VJ)

Bear Mountain Band

ALBUM: 1 ONE MORE DAY (Predator) c1975 R3

A loud hard-rock/heavy psych group with lots of fuzz guitar and gritty vocals. This private pressing is now extremely rare and expensive. The problem is that there's only one very good track (*One More Day*) plus many very average ones. Another proof that "very rare" doesn't always mean "very good"! (SR)

Beast

Personnel:	LARRY FERRIS	drms	AB
	GERRY FIKE	keyb'ds	AB
	MIKE KEARNS	woodwind	AB
	KENNY PASSARELLI	bs, hrmnca	A
	DAVID RAINES	vcls	AB
	DOMINICK TODERO	trumpet	A
	ROBERT YEAZEL	gtr, vcls	AB
	ROGER BRYANT	bs	B

				HCP
ALBUMS:	1(A)	BEAST	(Cotillion 9012) 1969	195 -
	2(B)	HIGHER & HIGHER	(Evolution 2017) 1970	- -

45: Communication/Move Mountain (Evolution 1028) 1970

Based in Denver, Colorado, this outfit played Eastern-influenced, mainly instrumental music. Their first album, *Beast*, is the more melodic and mellow of the two, with sophisticated arrangements dominated by the flute and trumpet. A couple of songs have soul influences. The best tracks are: the hypnotic *Floating* and *When We Rise*, which features some good guitar work. Their second album is more diverse with no trumpet. The material ranges from good-time music (two short tracks) to heavy rock (*Move Mountain*). There are also melodic and jazzy moments and the highlights are *Communication* and *I Am*.

Bob Yeazel had previously been with the Denver group **The Super Band** and during a short stint in Los Angeles had played on the third **West Coast Pop Art Experimental Band** album.

Their albums were recorded at Norman Petty's studios in Clovis, New Mexico.

Bob Yeazel and Larry Ferris went on to play in **Sugarloaf**. Kenny Passarelli would later play with Joe Walsh's Barnstormer, Tommy Bolin, Steven Stills, Elton John, Hall and Oates, etc. (VJ/MW/HS)

BEAST - Beast LP.

Beaten Path

45: Doctor Stone/Never Never (Jubilee 5556) 1966

A punk band from Brooklyn, NY. *Doctor Stone* is on *Boulders, Vol. 4* (LP) and a stereo version appears on *Psychedelic Microdots Of The Sixties, Vol. 3* (CD). (VJ/MW)

Beatin' Path

Personnel:	RUDY BENTZ	bs	A
	CRAIG FORESTO	gtr	A

	RON MALINOWSKI	keyb'ds	A
	RON MASLER	drums	A
	STEVE MUSSER	ld vcls	A

45: Original Nothing People/I Waited So Long   (Fontana 1583) 1967

NB: reissued by Get Hip (GHAS-15) 1998, with a picture sleeve.

From Reading, Pennsylvania, this outfit started life as **The Starlites** with two 45s on Barclay and later became **Soul Generation**, who had a 45 on Dater, before changing name again to **Beatin' Path**. Their finest moment, *Original Nothing People*, with its rich organ backing and catchy punk sound can also be heard on *Boulders, Vol. 1* (LP), *Mayhem & Psychosis, Vol. 1* (LP), *Mayhem & Psychosis, Vol. 1* (CD) and *Ya Gotta Have... Moxie, Vol. 1* (Dble CD). (VJ/MW)

The Beatle-ettes

45: Only Seventeen/Now We're Together   (Jubilee 5472) 1964

A one-off recording venture for this optimistically-named all girl garage band. New York was their home and their garage response to the Beatles invasion *Only Seventeen* can be heard on *Girls In The Garage, Vol. 1* (LP & CD). It was produced by the legendary Shadow Morton (aka **Shadow Mann**). (VJ)

Beat of The Earth

Personnel:		
	MORGAN CHAPMAN	A
	RON COLLINS	A
	KAREN DARBY	A
	JR NICHOLS	A
	PHIL PEARLMAN	AB
	BILL PHILLIPS	A
	SHERRY PHILLIPS	A
	JOE SIDORE	AB
	WENDELL KEESEE III	B
	RICK MANDELBAUM	B
	TONI SARTORIO	B
	BILL YOUNGER	B

ALBUMS:				
1(A)	THE BEAT OF THE EARTH	(Radish AS 0001)	1967	R3
2(B)	THE ELECTRONIC HOLE	(Radish AS 0002)	1970	R3
3(A)	OUR STANDARD THREE MINUTE TUNE	(Radish AS 0001½)	1994	R1

NB: (1) had a pressing of 500. (2) was for demo use only and had a pressing of about 150 copies. (3) had a pressing of 500 and is a collection of unreleased recordings from 1967 - not a reissue of (1) as often advertised.

Beat Of The Earth was assembled by Phil Pearlman, who had earlier released a surf/hot rod 45 *Chrome Reversed Rails* (shown as by Phil and The Flakes, on the Fink label). One of the earliest known electric experimental bands, **The Beat Of The Earth** sound very similar to their East-coast counterparts **The Velvet Underground** on albums (1) and (3) listed above. These two records were recorded live in the studio during the Summer of 1967 and consist of long, unstructured jams using a myriad of acoustic and electric instruments. This early incarnation of the band is the one most familiar to collectors and copies of the first album have been changing hands for hundred of dollars since the mid-eighties. The music the band produced during this period is not for everybody (compare to the long tracks on the first two **Velvet Underground** albums), but their debut remains an unusual and rare item of significance from the California rock scene.

During 1968-9 the line-up of the band was in constant flux and **Beat Of The Earth** made no known "proper" recordings, but Pearlman continued to add to his own collection of demos using local studios in off-hours via his friendship with the engineer Joe Sidore. At the end of 1969, Pearlman assembled *The Electronic Hole* strictly for personal use - specifically, to draft musicians for his new band. Several names are listed on the sleeve but I believe this is actually very close to being a Phil Pearlman solo project. The album is entirely different stylistically from the earlier one in that it abandons the freeform improvisational approach in favour of

BEAT OF THE EARTH - The Electronic Hole LP.

'compositions' including a wild cover of **Zappa**'s *Trouble Comin' Every Day*. None of the tracks are given titles on the album which complicates singling any out for commentary, but there are real highlights and the raw, unpolished feel only serves to make it utterly magical. Pearlman plays sitar on one track to great effect, and another has the thickest wall of fuzz guitars imaginable - an effect he created by running his Fender amplifier into the amp circuit of a child's chord organ ("sounded great for about two weeks, then it blew up!"). There are few albums I known of that have such an eclectic yet appealing sound.

Had the story ended here it would have been a real tragedy, as Pearlman's finest hour was yet to come. Six years later (with who knows what in between), recording commenced on the majestic **Relatively Clean Rivers** album with an entirely new band and musical vision. (CF/SR)

The Beaubiens

45: Time Passed/A Man Who's Lost   (Malibu 67001) 1967

The work of an obscure Michigan band. Lotsa fuzz guitar and good vocals. *Times Passed* later resurfaced on *Michigan Mayhem Vol. 1* (CD) and *Highs In The Mid Sixties, Vol. 19* (LP). (VJ)

Beau Brummels

Personnel:			
	RON ELLIOTT	gtr, vcls	ABCDE
	RON MEAGHER	bs	ABCD
	DECLAN MULLIGAN	gtr, vcls	A
	JOHN PETERSEN	drms	ABC
	SAL VALENTINO	vcls	ABCDE
	DON IRVING	gtr, vcls	C

				HCP
ALBUMS: 1(A)	INTRODUCING	(Autumn (S)LP 103)	1965	24 -
(up to 2(B)	VOLUME 2	(Autumn (S)LP 104)	1965	- -
1968) 3(C)	BEAU BRUMMELS 66	(Warner Brothers W(S) 1644)	1966	- -
4(D)	TRIANGLE	(Warner Brothers W(S) 1692)	1967	197
5(A/B)	THE BEST OF THE BEAU BRUMMELS	(Vault (S)LP 114)	1967	- -
6(E)	BRADLEY'S BARN	(Warner Brothers WS 1760)	1968	- -
7(A/B)	VOLUME 44	(Vault SLP 121)	1968	- -

NB: (1) also released in France as *Laugh, Laugh* (Vogue INT 4006) 1966. (7) Previously unreleased tracks and mixes from their Autumn albums. 1973 saw the release of *The Beau Brummels Sing* (Post 6000) while *Original Hits* (JAS 5000) was issued in 1975 (both contain material from their Autumn days). Rhino have (re-)issued three albums so far: *The Best Of The Beau Brummels* (RNLP-101) 1981, *Introducing* (RNLP-102) 1982 and *From The Vaults* (RNLP-104) 1982. The German reissue label Line have reissued *Introducing* (OLLP 5108) 1981, *Volume 2* (OLLP

5113) 1982 and *Good Time Music* (OLLP 5275) 1982. (4) was reissued on CD in 1996. (1) and (2) have also been reissued on CD by Sundazed (SC 6039 and SC 6040) in 1995 with many extra tracks. (1) was also released in the U.K. (Pye NPL 28062) in 1965, (6) was released in the U.K. (Edsel ED 151) in 1985 and there's also *Autumn In San Francisco* (Edsel ED 141), which was released in 1985. 1994 saw the release of a 26 track rarities double CD, *Autumn Of Their Years* (Big Beat CDWIKD 127), which contained 16 previously unreleased tracks and demos. 1996 saw the release of *San Fran Sessions* (Sundazed SC 11033) 1996, a 60-track 3-CD box set with demos, alternate versions, cuts from the never-released third Autumn album and lots more. There are also two later vinyl issues *North Beach Legends* (Sundazed LP 5088) 2001 and *Gentle Wandering Ways* (Sundazed LP 5089) 2001. There's also a bootleg: *Beau Brummels* (Flying Horse FC 001) recorded live at the Roxy on 31st May 1975 by Valentino/Elliott/Petersen/Mullican, with poor sound quality.

				HCP
45s:	α	Laugh, Laugh/Still In Love With You Baby	(Autumn 8) 1964	15
(up to	β	Just A Little/They'll Make You Cry	(Autumn 10) 1965	8
1969)	χ	You Tell Me Why/I Want You	(Autumn 16) 1965	38
	δ	Don't Talk To Strangers/In Good Time	(Autumn 20) 1965	52
	ε	Good Time Music/Sad Little Girl	(Autumn 24) 1965	97
		One Too Many Mornings/She Reigned	(Warner Brothers 5813) 1966	95
		Here We Are Again/Fine With Me	(Warner Brothers 5848) 1966	-
		Don't Make Promises/Two Days 'Till Tomorrow	(Warner Brothers 7014) 1967	-
		Magic Hollow/Lower Level	(Warner Brothers 7079) 1967	-
		Lift Me/Are You Happy	(Warner Brothers 7204) 1968	-
		Long Walk Down To Misery/I'm A Sleeper	(Warner Brothers 7218) 1968	-
		Cherokee Girl/Deep Water	(Warner Brothers 7260) 1969	-

NB: Also released in the U.K. were α (Pye 7N 25293) 1965, β (Pye 7N 25306) 1965, χ (Pye 7N 25318) 1965 and δ (Pye 7N 25333) 1965. ε was planned (Pye 7N 25342) but cancelled. There are also three rare French EPs with PS (Vogue INT 18002), (Vogue INT 18010) and (Warner WB 112).

While they only had two big hits, **The Beau Brummels** were one of the most important and underrated American groups of the sixties. They were the first U.S. unit of any sort to successfully respond to the British Invasion. They were arguably the first folk-rock group, even predating **The Byrds**, and also anticipated some key elements of the San Francisco psychedelic sound with their soaring harmonies and exuberant melodies. Before their demise, they were also among the first bands to record country-rock in the late sixties.

The key axis of the band was formed by guitarist/songwriter **Ron Elliott**, who penned most of the **Brummels**' moody and melodious material, and singer **Sal Valentino**, owner of one of the finest voices in mid-sixties rock. Spotted by local DJ Tom Donahue in a club in San Mateo (just South of San Francisco), the group were signed to Donahue's small San Francisco-based label Autumn Records in 1964. With Sly Stewart (later **Sly Stone**) in the producer's chair, they made the Top 20 right off the bat with

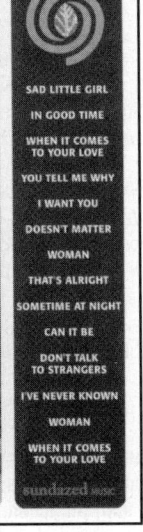

BEAU BRUMMELS - Volume 2 CD.

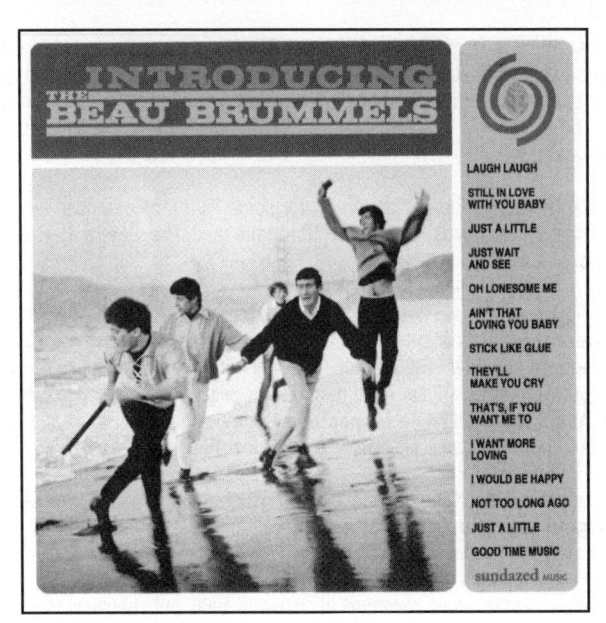

BEAU BRUMMELS - Introducing CD.

Laugh, Laugh. The melancholy, minor-key original sounded so much like the British bands inundating the airwaves that many listeners initially mistook the **Brummels** for an English act. The follow-up single, *Just A Little*, was another excellent, melancholy number that became their biggest hit, making the Top Ten.

The Beau Brummels made a couple of fine albums in 1965, dominated by strong original material and featuring the band's ringing guitars and multi-part, mournful harmonies. The best of their early work is nearly as fine as **The Byrds**' first recordings, yet the band were losing ground commercially, partially because Autumn, being such a small label, lacked promotional muscle. *You Tell Me Why* was their only other Top 40 hit, though *Sad Little Girl* and **The Byrds** knockoff *Don't Talk To Strangers* were excellent singles. The band also shuffled personnel a few times, and **Ron Elliott** was unable to stay on the road because of diabetes. Autumn was sold in 1966 to Warners, who made the dumb move of forcing the band to record an entire album of Top 40 covers - ignoring the fact that original material was one of **Brummels**' primary fortes.

Regrouping as a trio, the group recorded the critically acclaimed, more experimental album *Triangle*, in 1967. Their last Warners LP, *Bradley's Barn*, found the group branching into country-rock, a year or so before it became fashionable. The **Beau Brummels** did reform for an unimpressive reunion album in 1975, and although **Ron Elliott** and **Sal Valentino** continued to make music and work on various low-profile projects of their own, they've never made records on par with the **Brummels**' vintage work.

Ron Elliott later played in **Joyous Noise (Musical Ensemble)**

Compilation appearances have so far included: *Laugh, Laugh* on *Nuggets Box* (4-CD); *Laugh, Laugh* and *Just A Little* on *Nuggets* (CD) and *Nuggets, Vol. 7* (LP); *Magic Hollow* on *Psychedelic Visions* (CD); *Laugh, Laugh*, *Stick Like Glue*, *If You Want Me To*, *Don't Talk To Strangers*, *Sad Little Girl* and *Still In Love With You Baby* on *San Francisco Roots* (LP); *When It Comes To Your Love* on *Sundazed Sampler, Vol. 2* (CD); *The Jerk* and *Sad Little Girl* on *The Autumn Records Story* (LP).

This entry has been compiled with a great help from Richie Unterberger. (RU/MW/SR)

The Beauchemins

Personnel:	NANCY BURBA	vcls	A
	PAM FUNKHOUSER	vcls, tamb	A
	LEE KRISKE	vcls, gtr	A
	PAUL MARSHALL	vcls, gtr, hrmnca	A
	VERNE WILLIS	vcls, banjo	A

45s:		My Lovin' Baby / Shenandoah	(Mustang 3015) 1965
	α	What Have They Done With The Rain / A Field Of Yellow Daisies	(Scarlet 502) 1966

NB: α as by The Tree Toppers.

A Los Angeles vocal folk-rock group. Their debut presented *My Lovin' Baby*, a protest song of sorts in **Byrdsian** 12-string-jangle mode. The lyrics were essentially a draftee's love-letter to his girl, explaining his reluctance to go off to fight his government's fight in Vietnam ("they have called on me to go and die").

The band managed to get on the bill for some high profile shows, including opening for **The Byrds**, **Love**, **The Standells**, and **The Seeds** at The Trip, It's Boss, and Whisky A-Go-Go.

Upon discovering that there was a band called the Bo-Shay Men, Bob Keane changed their name to The Tree Toppers for the next single, released in January 1966. The melodious harmony-popper *A Field Of Yellow Daisies* has a lush, multi-harmonious peace-love vibe reminiscent of **The Association** and **The Mamas and Papas**. Amazingly, the band didn't find out about the name change, until after the 45 was pressed!

On both 45s, Bob Keane brought in his usual group of great L.A. session players to assist the band on the folk-rock 'A' sides, although the 'B' sides were recorded by the band alone.

Two more tracks were recorded in January 1966 but, because the band had changed their sound considerably, *Good Enough For Me* and *What Have They Done* were not released.

Original **Beauchemins** songwriter/lead vocalist Paul Marshall later joined **The Strawberry Alarm Clock**, circa '69, around the time of their final UNI album, *Good Morning Starshine*. He also appeared during a party scene in Russ Meyers' 'Beyond The Valley Of The Dolls' (he can seen singing his self-penned *Girl From The City*). (MW/BTs)

The Beau Denturies

Personnel incl: BURNHAM A
HARRIMAN A

45: Straight Home/Don't Quit Now (Encore 1001) 1966

Akron, Ohio was home to this mob. Over an incessant fuzztone riff the singer tells of a lousy date... how he watched an awful movie and ended up taking home a girl that was 'downright ugly'! Quite a little gem that later turned up on *Highs In The Mid-Sixties, Vol. 21* (LP) and on *Riot City!* (LP).

They were later known as **The Zoo** / **Yellow Pages**. (MW)

The Beau Gentry

An obscure band, probably from the Chicago area. The previously unissued track *Black Cat Blues* was included on *If You're Ready - The Best Of Dunwich Records Vol. 2* (CD). (VJ)

THE BEAUCHEMINS.

The Beau Phenom

45: Call Off Life/Peyote Peyote Lowding (Co-op 520) 1969

Strange titles and a pretty strange psychy 45 from New Haven, Connecticut. *Call Off Life* is an anti-Nam protest dirge with the odd gun effect and military-style drumming. The flip is even weirder - a slowed-down take of the *Shake Rattle And Roll* melody with nonsensical lyrics. (MW)

Beauregarde

Personnel: BEAUREGARDE vcls AB
OMAR BOSE organ B
DAVE KOLPEL bs B
JAY LUNDELL drms B
ALLEN ROBINSON congo, sax B
GREG SAGE ld gtr B

ALBUM: 1(B) BEAUREGARDE (F-Empire SP 7104) 1971 R1

NB: (1) counterfeited on vinyl circa 1987 and on CD (GRC 010) 2000.

45: Testify/I (NWI 2758) 19??

NB: Some copies with PS.

Beauregarde, a professional wrestler that toured the USA in the late sixties and early seventies, recorded the album at Sound Productions in Portland with young area musicians. The personnel on the 45 (which is pre-album) is unknown, but it is not the same crew that recorded the album. Greg Sage and Dave Kolpel later figured prominently in The Wipers, another Oregon band. The album is crude bluesy rock with **Beauregarde**'s heavy-handed, occasionally humorous vocals to the fore. Sage himself is said to be producing a CD reissue of this rare local album. (CF)

Beauregarde

45: Mama Never Taught Me How To Jelly Roll/
Popcorn Popper (International Artists 123) 1968

A different unknown group, most likely based in Texas. The 45 was produced by Dave Carroll. (VJ/NK)

The Beautiful Apollo

See **Apollo's Apaches**.

Beautiful Daze

45s: City Jungle Parts 1 / 2 (RPR R-101) 1967
City Jungle Parts 1 / 2 (Spread City 101) 196?
α City Jungle Part 1 / City Jungle Part 2 (Alpha 618) 1968

NB: α as **More Beautiful Daze**.

This amazin' 45 was recorded on Hollywood-based labels although the band were originally from the Pacific Northwest. Full of feedback, it culminates into a psychedelic haze. You'll find both sides of the 45 on *Acid Dreams, Vol. 1* (LP), *Acid Trip From The Psychedelic Sixties* (LP), *High All The Time, Vol. 1* (LP) and *Sixties Archive Vol. 8* (CD); Part 2 on *Psychedelic Unknowns, Vol. 6* (LP & CD) and *Everything You Always Wanted To Know...* (CD); and Part 1 on *Acid Trip From The Psychedelic Sixties.*, *Psychedelic Unknowns, Vol. 4* (LP & CD), *Pebbles Vol. 3* (CD) and *Great Pebbles* (CD). (VJ/MW)

The Beaux Jens

45: She Was Mine/Trouble Baby (Sound Of The Screen 2162) 1967

Formed at high school in Grand Ledge, a small town about 15 miles West of Lansing (Michigan's State Capital), in March 1966, they soon became a local teen attraction. The above 45 was the quartet's sole stab for stardom. It was recorded at the Great Lakes / Fenton studios in Sparta, Michigan

BEAUREGARDE - Beauregarde CD.

and released by The Screen, a local teen club, on its own label (a Fenton subsidiary). *She Was Mine* is a good organ-led mid-sixties punker on which the band sing about their 'little girl with lovely blue eyes'. You'll find it on *Acid Dreams Epitaph* (CD), *Acid Dreams - The Complete 3 LP Set* (3-LP), *Back From The Grave, Vol. 6* (LP), *Boulders, Vol. 3* (LP) and *Let 'Em Have It! Vol. 1* (CD). (VJ/MW/KBn)

Beaver and Krause

Personnel: PAUL BEAVER — keyb'ds, sound effects — A
BERNIE KRAUSE — keyb'ds, sound effects — A
various sessionmen — various — A

ALBUMS:
1(A) RAGNAROCK ELECTRONIC FUNK (Limelight 86069) 1969 -
2(A) IN A WILD SANCTUARY (Warner Bros. WS 1850) 1970 -
3(A) GANDHARVA (Warner Bros. WS 1909) 1970 -
4(A) ALL GOOD MEN (Warner BS 2624) 1972 -
5(A) A GUIDE TO ELECTRONIC MUSIC (Comp) (Nonesuch K 73018) 1975 -

NB: (2) and (3) were reissued on one CD (Warner Archives 9 45663-2) 1994.

Among the first American masters of synthesizers and electronic music, **Beaver and Krause** are credited on countless records between 1965 and 1975: **Doors**, **Byrds**, Neil Young, Beach Boys as well as several soundtracks including "Rosemary's Baby", "Candy", "Performance" etc.

They also recorded four albums of synthesizers, moogs, flutes, tablas, guitars and various sound effects (live voices, birds, monkeys, sea...), creating a kind of "musical trip", a little like Don Robertson's albums.

Gandharva, which is probably their best album, also features **Mike Bloomfield**, Ronnie Montrose, Howard Roberts and Gerry Mulligan.

Paul Beaver died in 1975. Bernie Krause has also released an entire album of songs called *Fish Wrap* on which ALL the sounds are sampled animal or fish sounds, as a Nature Conservancy fundraiser. (SR)

Beaver and The Trappers

Personnel incl: RICHARD CORRELL ? — A
JERRY MATHERS — A

45: In Misery/Happiness Is Havin' (White Cliffs 236) 1966

From Los Angeles, this band were formed by Jerry Mathers, the actor who played 'Beaver' on the TV series "Leave It to Beaver" in the late fifties. Richard Correll who played "Richard" in 'Leave It To Beaver' may also have been in the band. The flip side has turned up on *Boulders, Vol. 10* (LP) and *Hipsville 29 B.C.* (LP). (VJ/AB/CVr/MW)

The Beaver Patrol

45: ESP/Just Like A Lady (Columbia 4-44139) 1967

A very obscure band from Hollywood, Florida produced by Richard Gottehrer. They reworked The Pretty Things *LSD* as *ESP*, slowing it down in the process. A fine psychedelic punk number with some infectious fuzztone guitar playing, it is their only known recording and you'll also find it on *Pebbles, Vol. 11* (LP), *E.S.P.* on *Boulders, Vol. 4* (LP) and *Ya Gotta Have... Moxie, Vol. 1* (Dble CD).

The same *ESP* song was later recorded by **Big Brother featuring Ernie Joseph** and an earlier in a faster punkier version by **Rain**. (VJ/MW/LP)

Joe Beck

Personnel: JOE BECK — gtr, bs, vcls, piano — A
(RANDY BRECKER — trumpet — A)
DONALD MCDONALD — drms, perc — A
(DON PAYNE — bs — A)
(DANNY WHITTEN — gtr, vcls — A)

ALBUM: 1(A) NATURE BOY (Verve Forecast FTS-3081) 1969 SC

An attempt at mixing psych, rock and jazz with some classical influences. **Joe Beck** was a very gifted guitar player who composed, arranged, conducted and produced this album in 1969. Six of the nine tracks are over five minutes long and give **Beck** the opportunity to show his remarkable guitar skills, obviously influenced by **Hendrix**.

The best moments are probably *No More Blues*, *Rapid Disintegration Of A Chamber Orchestra*, *Ain't No Use In Talkin* and the title track (written by Eden Ahbez). The guitar, bass and drums parts are constantly good but some arrangements may sound a bit dated now.

Danny Whitten (**Rockets**, Crazy Horse) plays on two tracks including his own *Let Me Go*. Donald McDonald had earlier been in **Jeremy and The Satyrs**.

Joe Beck also issued several jazz albums in the late seventies. (SR/CF)

Beckett Quintet

45s: Baby Blue/No Correspondence (Gemcor 5003) 1965
Baby Blue/No Correspondence (A&M 782) 1965

The work of an L.A. outfit, this 45 was 'directed' by Capitol (and Beach Boys) studio legend Nick Venet. Despite being picked up by A&M the 45

BEAVER & KRAUSE - Gandharva CD.

sank without trace. You'll find both sides on *A Journey To Tyme, Vol. 1* (LP) and the flip, which featured some great reverb, can also be heard on *Pebbles, Vol. 9* (LP), *Pebbles Vol. 8* (CD), *Garagelands, Vol. 1* (LP), *Garagelands, Vol. 1 & 2* (CD), *The Essential Pebbles Collection, Vol. 1* (Dble CD) and for some reason on Eva's *Swamp Rats vs. Unrelated Segments* (LP) compilation. The 'A' side was a nice folk-rock version of Dylan's *Baby Blue*. (VJ/EW)

Billy Joe Becoat

ALBUM: 1 LET'S TALK FOR A WHILE (Fantasy) 1970 -

Following **Richie Havens**' success, several labels signed black folk-rock singers and **Billy Joe Becoat** was Fantasy's attempt. Housed in a stunning yellow, orange and red 'flames' cover with a peace sign in the middle, his album contains ten self-penned songs, with a voice somewhere between **Tim Buckley** and **Havens**. (SR)

Jack Bedient and The Chessmen

Personnel:			
	JACK BEDIENT	vcls, gtr	AB
	BILL BRITT	bs, vcls	AB
	JEWELL HENDRICKS	drms	AB
	KEVIN WOODS	vcls, gtr	AB
	WALTER HANNA	keyb'ds	B

ALBUMS:
1 LIVE AT HARVEYS   (Fantasy 3365) 1965 SC
2 WHERE DID SHE GO   (Satori 1001) 1967 R1
3 JACK BEDIENT   (Executive Productions) c1969 -
4 SONGS YOU REQUESTED   (Chessmen) 19?? -
5 IN CONCERT   (Chessmen) 19?? -
6 TWO SIDES OF JACK BEDIENT (Trophy) 19?? -

45s:
The Mystic One/Question   (Era 3050) 1961
Silver Haired Daddy/Pretty One   (Trophy 1001) 1964
Dream Boy (Count Your Dreams)/
Drummer Boy (Please Play Us A Song)   (Palomar 2212) 1965
See The Little Girl/Here I Am   (Fantasy 595) 1965
See The Little Girl/
Looking For A Good Love   (Fantasy 595) 1965
Double Whammy/I Want You To Know   (Fantasy 598) 1965
Glimmer Sunshine/Where Did She Go   (Rev 104/5 - 66) 1966
I Could Have Loved You So Well/
Love Workshop   (Columbia 4-44302) 1967
Pretty One/See That Girl   (Columbia 4-44481) 1968
The Pleasures Of You/It's Over   (Columbia 4-44565) 1968
My Prayer/Independence Day   (Columbia 4-44671) 1968
I've Been Loving You/
I Could Never Lose My Love For You (Executive Prod. 21) 1969
Beautiful (Takes A Trip) /
Release Me   (Executive Productions 21) 1969

Originally formed in Wenatchee, Washington, this outfit relocated to Nevada, where they spent most of their time as a showband and regular attraction in Reno and Las Vegas. Over their long history this band changes with the times covering early sixties sounds, garage, folk-rock, protest, ballads. If they could be said to have a sound it's of a pop-group with strong vocals, harmonies and melodramatic arrangements. Their latest material would've suited Gene Pitney or the Walker Brothers! Garage collectors need look no further than the compilations:- *Highs In The Mid-Sixties, Vol. 7* (LP) features *Double Whammy* and *I Want To Know*; *Highs In The Mid-Sixties, Vol. 14* (LP) gives an airing to *Rapunzel*, a track from their reputedly excellent third album; and *Glimmer, Glimmer* from their third album on Satori has resurfaced on *Let's Dig 'Em Up, Vol. 2* (LP) and *Let's Dig 'Em Up, Vol. 1* (CD).

Walter Hanna recalls: "I became the first additional member, as organist for the Chessmen in the mid-sixties, rounding out the group to five members. This followed their first Washington state to central California club successes with the original members: Jack - barely able to play rhythm guitar - a fantastic voice, as the centerpiece; Bill Britt on steady 6-string bass, backing vocals and some lead, plus comedy; Kevin Woods on fair lead, good rhythm guitar, backing vocals, plus comedy; and Jewel Hendricks on drums, at the time I joined."

HIGHS IN THE MID-SIXTIES Vol. 14 (Comp LP) includes Jack Bedient and The Chessmen.

"I was playing a Wurlitzer electric piano with a small home-style Lowrey organ at a pizza parlor in Belmont, California, near S.F. This was a local group doing fifties-sixties Top 40, R&B, with new Beach Boys surf music, Buffalo Springfield, Ray Charles, etc. The Chessmen "discovered" me playing there while they were checking out the local scene, ready to start an engagement at a nearby Redwood City club. We exchanged numbers; they told me to come see them, pretty much offered me a job 'on the spot'. I followed up, went to see them play: with steady good-paying work lined up and a repeat offer, I joined up. I think the hurried addition of an organist was their manager's suggestion with upcoming better bookings in Nevada hotels."

"As it turned out, this was the beginning of **Jack Bedient and The Chessmen**'s first real big-money success, mainly in Nevada, changing gradually from a dance-club band into more of a 'Vegas show group' act which worked great at first, as the local radio station picked up on the song singles. As I joined and went to Nevada with them, 'instant local stardom' continued for nearly two years. This was unfortunately followed by a slow decline, neglecting new songs and funny bits. So, poor and intermittent bookings into the wrong venues that didn't fit the band which was now part-dance, part-show, some Jack Bedient standards that went over well - but no longer really good at just one thing. It was a tired performance, singing the same not-too danceable, but not-too listenable songs, repeating the same copycat comedy bits, most of which were picked up watching the singing duo, Gaylord and Holiday. They worked for years after their two 45 hits in the fifties ("at the shomakers shop... shoes that kept her feet a dancing, a dancing, all the livelong day..." another I can't recall - something with a clock?). These two guys were wise - since they couldn't survive on the strength of two old singles that weren't dance songs, but novelties, they got funny, learned newer songs they could sing to a sit-down audience, continally updated music and comedy, paid writers for funny bits to add to their show, and remained a viable name act for years, easily bookable for big bucks on the Nevada casino and nationwide big hotel circuits."

"As the Chessmen had become more popular, Jack, with our Reno manager Bob Dee's urging, was trying to 'secretly' slip away and become a single big-name artist, like Roy Orbison, Jimmy Rogers, Andy Williams, etc. They made a fair effort to keep this a secret (duh - lots of resentment) and keep the band intact in the meantime, in case his solo career didn't work out well. I didn't follow his career after I left, but think he finally fizzled out, though he had some local popularity here and there. Reliable gossip I heard years later said he was working as a solo act with his guitar at Harold's club in Reno hotel in one of their in-house bars."

"But back to better days: I became a member; Bob Dee had the Chessmen lined up with good Nevada bookings: the Golden Hotel in Reno, the Silver Nugget nearby in Carson City, and Harvey's Hotel and Casino just up the hill at Lake Tahoe. We soon were headlining at the Golden Hotel (later to become Harrah's Club), soon with around-the-block audience lines to see us. Jack and The Chessmen moved from the backstage bar at Harvey's, Lake Tahoe, to opening act status for Sarah Vaughn, then Rowan and

Martin, later appearing with them at the Riviera in Vegas. During the Reno/Carson/Tahoe era, we had four No. 1 "Top-40" hits on the local Reno radio station, one of which reached No. 16 in Sacramento. This was around the time of the Beatles vs Rolling Stones English invasion, Animals, Yardbirds - for most American groups, pre-psychedelia."

"The drug scene in Nevada consisted of the casino pit bosses making easily available a steady supply of Dexamil Spansules, a great, 'tiny-time-pill' combination of the 'upper' Dexadrine and 'downer' Miltown (Mother's Little Helper) which kept you wide awake without being 'wired' for 12-24 hours. If you weren't near a 'cool' casino, the constant stream of truckers through everywhere always had something 'speedy' on hand. A user could stay up for days, gambling, drinking, 'making out', etc. My fun-filled, idiotic, but surprising, 'speed-run' record was five days without sleep (plus three differerent groupies in 24 hours - oh the shame). This event ended when the noise and shaking of my car woke me up in time to survive, as I ran straight off a curve of the main highway between Reno and Carson city into the sagebrush of the Nevada desert."

"The Chessmen's popularity was not able to break out of the local area, though we did follow **Question Mark and The Mysterians** into a popular Sacramento night club booking on one occasion, and recorded a few more singles and an album while I was a member. I wrote the song, *Drummer Boy (Please Play Us A Song)* on one side of a 45 we released that got some airplay, and *Waltz Tune* on another record, possibly *Live At Harvey's*, that we recorded during a Lake Tahoe engagment. One interesting note: The original four Top-40 Reno hits were on Fantasy Records, a small, unknown studio in San Francisco - before they signed **Creedence Clearwater Revival**, who already had their own local following! Prior to **Creedence**, one of the few one-hit artists Fantasy had was Vince Giraldi of *Cast Your Fate To The Wind*."

"The 'Long Decline': Time passed quickly and popularity faded. Following a dreary dinner plus music/entertainment booking at a dead Bakersfield eatery, Bob Dee actually booked us into the Playboy Club (I keep thinking the "Tiger-A-Go-Go" disco?) at the S.F. airport. Jack had grown gradually worse at playing guitar and singing in rhythm with the band after a couple of classy bookings when part of the show was Jack Bedient backed by the house orchestra - his dream come true. Jack's attitude towards 'his' musicians reflected this - we got 'no respect', especially drummer Jewel and I, and later Jewel's replacement. With Bob Dee and Jack's maneuvering to get him in the solo limelight, 'The Chessmen' were cut to a trio of Jack with Bill and Kevin - drummer and keyboard as sidemen with a cut in pay! As front-men Bill and Kevin might potentially have survived if Jack's solo career didn't go big-time. I think Jack had a 'Plan B' similar to Gaylord and Holiday's "Vegas show group" setup. They got the big money, a couple of regulars got a reasonable 'retainer' rate of pay; otherwise local union musicians were hired as needed, and paid scale."

"So, Jewel, the original drummer was relegated to sideman status with a cut in pay, and so was I, just before we did the *Live At Harvey's* album. Jewel quit soon after, moved to L.A. and went to work for his girlfriend's brother, the guy who had just designed, patented, and begun to manufacture the original helicopter camera mounts used in almost every big action movie on the big screen for years. Jewel was replaced by Art - can't recall the last name - and I stayed as a sideman for a while, needing the money, which was still pretty good, and enjoying the life-style. It's an old story in music 'show-biz' - one person in a successful group is willing to dump the others, despite their hard work on the way up. That's a different situation than being in a dead-end band moving from one subsistence gig to another. And, it's a different situation from a long-term success combination deciding to call it quits and go their own ways - some then on to personal star status. Jack had the voice, absolutely beautiful - but, lacking strong musicianship, he needed musicians with him that knew his weaknesses and could compensate."

"As The Chessmen began to slip little by little nearing a couple of years of local stardom, he developed an arrogant, 'it's a privilege to play for me' attitude. The Playboy Club (Tiger-a-Go-Go?) turned into the last straw for me. About four nights into the gig, we were playing *Black Is Black, I Want My Baby Back*, with the cool turn-around beat the Four Tops made famous. Jack lost the beat and was playing and singing a beat behind, then turned around and yelled at me and Art something like, 'get with it!', loud enough for the customers to hear. The new drummer and I had already had a couple of arguments with him on previous gigs about this. On the break, I called him aside with the drummer in tow, and told him he had to stop pulling this stunt. Jack said something like, 'If you don't like it, why don't you quit?' Coincidence made it payday and next day off! I came and got my gear while Art was getting his. Art took off; I headed for Los Angeles into a long career of fun garage and original bands, a few 'almost-made-it' big rock 'n' roll bands, and many better-to-forget traveling club bands, always with Hollywood as home base."

"Except for the great studio and concert tour drummer, Richard Crooks, who I played with in our high school rock'n roll band, The Rhythm Rockers, (Gilroy, California, class of '60!), the best group talent I played with and closest I came to fame was with a four-member group, Unicorn, based in L.A. It was probably 1971 through '72 when we had a run of popularity playing the local beach cities and Hawaii. We were a three-part harmony C.S.N. and similar cover group: me on keybass - imitation Ray Manzarek - Hammond organ with Hohner electric piano on top - Leslie plus Sunn bass amps, tenor vocals and some lead; Danny on drums; Pamela on soprano vocals (plus good tambourine); and - just beginning to write originals - our lead guitarist, Cecelio Rodriguez from Santa Barbara, playing a Les Paul (Junior?) without a pick into a Marshall, singing most lead vocals. We had about a two year run, did really well at the Coral Reef Hotel in Hawaii, in a huge Red Noodle restaurant with an all-night cabaret license, big dance floor and stage. We played the 'Festival of the Sun' concert in Diamond Head Crater, an all-day event with **Santana** headlining, and **Quicksilver Messenger Service**, a few other well-known groups and some lesser-known Hawaiian rock bands. When Unicorn broke up, I stayed in L.A., Pam went home to Washington state. Cecelio? He went to Hawaii to get together with his new friend, Henry Kapono - Cecelio and Kapono, 'ya know..." (MW/DR/GB/WH)

Bedforde Set

Personnel:	NORMAN BULL	bs	A
	LEWIS MILLER	organ	A
	STEVE SCHEIN	drums	A
	WILLIAM SINGER	ld gtr	A

45:	Girl, Go Run Away/		
	A World Through A Tear	(RCA 47-9068)	1967

From Rockville and Silver Spring, Maryland. Another one-off venture by a rather talented rock quartet judging by the sound of this 45. The 'A' side is a powerful garage-rock rendition with hard drivin' organ and some ripping electric guitar. You can also find it on *Mindrocker, Vol. 9* (LP) and *Fuzz, Flaykes, And Shakes, Vol. 3* (LP & CD). (VJ/MW/MM/BE)

Bedlam Four

Personnel:	BOB DERRICKSON	ld gtr	A
	GREG HUPPERT	keyb'ds	A
	DICK POGUE	drms	A
	JACK TAYLOR	bs	A

BEDLAM FOUR - No One Left To Love (45 PS).

45s:	Hydrogen Atom/Watch It Baby	(Armanda A 001) 1967
	No One Left To Love/	
	Psychedelic Mantra	(Caped Crusader CC 73) 1991

Came out of Minneapolis, Minnesota and are best known for the bizarre and completely 'over the top' *Hydrogen Atom*. They were previously known as **The Echomen**. Back in 1967 they also had a cut on *Money Music*, a compilation of some of the best Minnesota sixties bands which had a very limited pressing. The *Hydrogen Atom* 45 is also very sought-after and expensive.

The Caped Crusader release is a fabulous package featuring pictures and information on the band plus two previously unreleased tracks. *No One Left To Love* is a garage raver and *Psychedelic Mantra* consists of almost five minutes of fuzzy Eastern psychedelia. This is a must-have for any collection of garage/psychedelic rock.

You can also find *Hydrogen Atom* on *Sixties Rebellion, Vol. 11* (LP & CD), *Changes* (LP), *The Magic Cube* (Flexi & CD), *Pebbles, Vol. 2 (ESD)* (CD), *Mayhem & Psychosis, Vol. 3* (LP) and *Mayhem & Psychosis, Vol. 2* (CD). (VJ)

The Bed of Roses

Personnel:	F. DASH		A
	J. LIGHT		A

45s:	I Don't Believe You / Hate	(Deltron 813) 1966
	Quiet! / I Gotta Fight	(Tea 2577) 1968

Bay City, Michigan, was home to this band. Their debut, on Saginaw's Deltron label, featured a competent version of one of Dylan's less well known songs backed by an acid-tainted instrumental.

In 1967 they went the way of many other bands and headed for San Francisco. By early '68 they were back home, recording their follow-up in an upstairs room of a local record shop. *Quiet!* isn't - it's a raucous jerky rocker with a nifty fuzz break and outro - it was composed by F. Dash; the flip, composed by J. Light, is another riff-heavy rocker with larynx-wrenching vocals ala **Blue Cheer**.

Compilation appearances have included: *Hate* on *Highs In The Mid-Sixties, Vol. 6* (LP); and *Quiet!* on *Psychedelic Crown Jewels Vol. 3* (CD). (VJ/KBn/MW/MM)

Bedpost Oracle

Personnel incl:	ROBERT M. DAVITT	A
	TED GULICK	A

FUZZ FLAYKES, & SHAKES Vol. 1 (CD) includes Bedpost Oracle.

45s:	The Break Of Dawn/Love Isn't Dead	(Corby CR 230) 1970
	Somebody To Love/Chest Fever	(Oracle 29002) 1971

A psychedelic outfit worth investigating. Both 45s were on California labels and the band are thought to have been from Los Angeles, possibly Pomona. The cover of **Jefferson Airplane**'s *Somebody To Love* was good.

Compilation coverage has included:- *Somebody To Love*, *Chest Fever* and *Love Isn't Dead* on *Brain Shadows, Vol. 1* (LP & CD); and *The Break Of Dawn* on *Fuzz Flaykes & Shakes Vol. 1* (LP & CD).

The Break Of Dawn, has also been covered by the Wicked Ones in 1991. (VJ/MW)

Beech-Nuts

45:	My Iconoclastic Life/Nature's Company	(Showcase 6602) 1967

My Iconoclastic Life has lots of mouth harp and really classic growling punk vocals and really maladjusted lyrics like "My life is nil, I just take pills, sit for hours watching the flowers, I'm so alone I scream and moan without you". You can check it out on *What A Way To Die* (LP), *Hang It Out To Dry* (CD) or *I Was A Teenage Caveman* (LP). Apparently, the band who came from Brooklyn, NY, were committed to a mental institution en bloc after the record's release.

Rumours of Lou Reed's involvement with this act are incorrect. (VJ/MW/MM)

The Beeds

45s:	Run To Her/You Don't Have To	(Team 519) 1968
	Love Hurts/You're Wrong	(Buddah 210) 1971

Almost certainly a studio project for the Team label, a sub-division of Buddah. *Run To Her* is a classic of its genre - an uptempo melodic rock song, with Merseybeat harmonies, chiming guitars and reedy organ. It can be found on *Mindrocker, Vol. 8* (LP).

Produced by Jim Calvert and Norman Marsano, the later 45 on Buddah in 1971 was written by Buddy Vidal, Steve Couto and Ritchie Mann and may of course be by an entirely different outfit. (VJ/SR)

The Beefeaters

Personnel:	GENE CLARK	vcls	A
	MIKE CLARKE	drms	A
	DAVE CROSBY	gtr, vcls	A
	CHRIS HILLMAN	bs, vcls	A
	ROGER McGUINN	gtr, vcls	A

45:	Please Let Me Love You/Don't Be Long	(Elektra 45013) 1964

L.A.-based, Clark, McGuinn and **Crosby** had previously played with another L.A. band, The Jet Set and Chris Hillman had been with The Hillmen. In addition to the 45, both sides on which can be heard on *Elektrock The Sixties* (4-LP), they recorded a four track EP and then evolved into **The Byrds**. (VJ)

The Beefeaters

45:	Don't Hurt Me/Change My Mind	(N/K) 1966

From Dallas, the 'A' side to this band's 45 is influenced by the **13th Floor Elevators**, whilst the flip is notable for its 12-string Rickenbacker guitar.

Both sides can also be found on *Acid Visions - Complete Collection, Vol. 2* (3-CD), *Texas Punk: 1966, Vol. 1* (LP) and *Green Crystal Ties Vol. 3* (CD). (VJ)

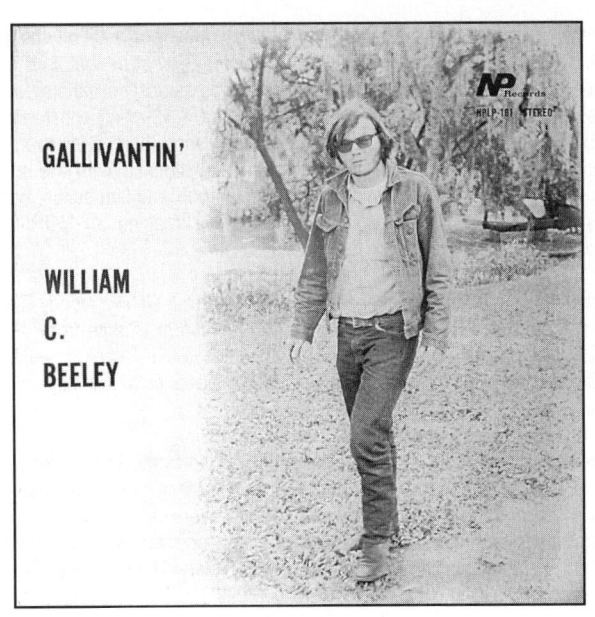

WILLIAM C. BEELEY - Gallivantin' LP.

William C. Beeley

ALBUM: 1 GALLIVANTIN' (North Park Records NPLP-101) 196? R4

A fine local Texas folk album, very simple and unencumbered, just acoustic guitar and **Beeley**'s confident, purposeful vocal. He is effectively portrayed as a rambler on the cover; three evocative B&W photos of him in rough travelling clothes, unshaven, hair too long, you can almost see the cops escorting him to the county line! The highlight of the album is a 10'00" version of **Buffy Sainte Marie**'s *Little Wheel Spin And Spin/Codine* medley that is just remarkably dark and creepy. Not for all, but a major landmark for collectors of the genre that the likes of Bob Dylan, Davy Graham and **Perry Leopold** occupy. (CF)

Beep Beep and The Roadrunners

45s:	True Love Knows/Shiftin' Gears	(Vincent 222) 1965
	Watermelon Man/Don't Run	(Vincent ?) 1966
	Watermelon Man/Don't Run	(Audio Dynamics 152) 1966

Formed in Worcester, an industrial metropolis and college town in Massachusetts, in 1962. They set out as an instrumental surfin' quintet doing covers of The Ventures and other surfing hits. By 1963 they had adapted to the British invasion by adding vocals and by the time of their first 45 they were a popular local attraction. The 'A' side, which was a typical teen beat effort, can be heard on *Back From The Grave, Vol. 7* (LP) and the flip a pounding surf-instrumental resurfaced on *Strummin' Mental, Vol. 5*. In 1966 they hired an organ player and became a seven-piece recording their second 45, which was in an Animals soulish vein. There was also a third 45, which I don't have details of, in 1969 and it wasn't until 1973, after 11 years together that they finally downed their instruments. The *Watermelon Man* 45 may actually have only been released on Audio Dynamics. (VJ)

The Bees

Personnel:	GEORGE CALDWELL	vcls	A
	PETER FERST	gtr	A
	RON REYNOLDS		A
	CARY SLAVIN	drms	A
	JOHN YORK	bs	A
	ROBERT ZINNER?		A

45s:	Leave Me Be/		
	She's An Artist (She Belongs To Me)	(Mirwood 5003) 1965	
	Forget Me Girl/Baby Let Me Follow You Down	(Mira 210) 1966	

A San Francisco outfit who'll appeal to fans of garagey folk-rock. Their first 45 is in this vein with Robert Zinner's (not the Zombies') *Leave Me Be*, compiled on Moxie's *Folk Rock E.P.* (7") and *Ya Gotta Have Moxie, Vol. 1* (Dble CD). It's backed by Bob Dylan's *She Belongs To Me*. The second 45 also features a Dylan cover on the 'B' side. The top side, *Forget Me Girl*, graces *Highs In The Mid-Sixties, Vol. 20* (LP).

After the band split in early-to-mid '66 Caldwell and Zinner teamed up with guitarist Richard Fortunato, fresh ex-**Vejtable** and former **Preacher**, in the **W.C. Fields Memorial Electric String Band**, later known as **ESB**. Cary Slavin went on to play with **The Factory** and John York went on to join **The Byrds** in 1968 and have a prolific career as a session musician. A friend of **Kaleidoscope**'s Chris Darrow, he is featured on several of his solos albums and finally released a solo album, *The Claremont Dragon* in 1999. (VJ/MW/SR)

The Bees

45:	Voices Green And Purple/ Trip To New Orleans (PS)	(Liverpool LIV 62225) 1966

From La Verne near Los Angeles, California and often confused with San Francisco's **Bees**, this band are often cited as a classic example of the influence of LSD on a teenage rock band. They produced the remarkable *Voices Green And Purple* with lyrics that recount a bum LSD trip culminating in echoes screaming over a demented 'Riot On Sunset Strip' beat.

A garage-psych classic, it was first compiled on *Pebbles, Vol. 3* (LP) and has since appeared on *Pebbles Vol. 3* (CD), *Pebbles, Vol. 2 (ESD)* (CD), *Best of Pebbles, Vol. 1* (LP & CD), *Great Pebbles* (CD), *Nuggets Box* (4-CD), *Trash Box* (5-CD) and *Songs We Taught The Fuzztones* (LP & CD), who covered it in 1984 on their *Leave Your Mind At Home* LP. The flip, a more routine folk-blues number a-la Rolling Stones, can be heard on *Highs In The Mid-Sixties Vol. 2* (LP) and *Teenage Shutdown, Vol. 9* (LP & CD). (VJ/MW/MM)

Bees

45s:	Shy Boy / Jadoo	(Bees 3622) 1966
	Shy Boy / Where Is My Baby	(Sunville 495) 1966

This particular swarm of **Bees** buzzed around Ft. Myers, Florida. (MW)

Beethoven Four

45:	Oh Pretty Baby / I'm Leaving Today	(Don-Lee 0003) 196?

Oh Pretty Baby is on Eva's *Sixties Archive Vol. 7 - Michigan Punk* (CD) which implies that they may have hailed from Michigan. (MW)

Beethoven 4

Personnel:	HAYWARD FOWLER	bs	A
	JOEY HALL	ld gtr	A
	BOBBY HILL	keyb'ds	A
	DUANE LOVETT	drms	A
	DONNIE SMITH	gtr	A
	LARRY BUTLER		
	LARRY McBRAYER		

45s:	Don't Call On Me / Hairy Dog	(Tag 4000/1) 1966
	Sets My Soul On Fire / Miserlou	(Talos 11-1313) 1968
	She Don't Care / Look All Around	(Talos 11 # unkn) 1970

Joey Hall and Donnie Smith first formed as The Pyramids in Tifton, Georgia with Duane Lovett on drums and Joey's brother Jimmy on bass. When the latter was drafted Hayward Fowler came in as a replacement and they became the **Beethoven 4**, although they'd expanded to a quintet with Bobby Hill on keyboard (and so were sometimes known as The Beethovens).

Sets My Soul On Fire can be found on *Garage Punk Unknowns, Vol. 8* (LP) and *Psychedelic States: Georgia Vol. 1* (CD). It's a rowdy reedy fuzz-punker that sounds more like 1966 than from the Summer of 1968.

The band lasted into the seventies going through several personnel changes. They held a 30 year reunion and in 2002 there were plans for a reunion LP to be recorded at the 82 Studio in Tifton, owned by Joey Hall. (MW)

Beethoven's Fifth

45: Come Down/The Last Thing On My Mind   (MGM 13746) 1967

This was the work of a very obscure outfit. The 'A' side, a timeless pop-punk ballad, can be found on *Pebbles, Vol. 9* (LP). (VJ)

Beethoven Soul

Personnel: OTIS HALE   woodwind   A
            ANDREA KOURATOU   strings   A
            JOHN LAMBERT   bs   A
            DICK LEWIS   keyb'ds   A
            BILL POWELL   gtr   A

ALBUM: 1(A) BEETHOVEN SOUL   (Dot DLP-25821) 1967 -

45: Good Time Gal/Walls Are High   (Dot 17031) 1967

Los Angeles was home to this mid-sixties band whose soft-rock album with female vocals is now a minor collectable. Lambert, Lewis and Hale all went on to play together in **Pollution**, a late sixties L.A.-based rock band with jazz undertones. (SR)

BEETHOVEN SOUL - Beethoven Soul LP.

The Bel-Aires

45: Ya Ha Be Be/If You Love Me   (Discoteque 1004) 1967

Hailed from Grand Rapids in Western Michigan where they'd all been pals at Wyoming High School, Their rather undistinguished organ punker, *Ya Ha Be Be* can be heard on *Back From The Grave, Vol. 1* (LP) and *Garage Kings* (Dble LP). (VJ/MW/KBn)

Vincent Bell

ALBUMS: 1 THE BIG SIXTEEN   (Musicor MM2047) c1965 -
         2 POP GOES THE ELECTRIC SITAR
                                        (Decca DL 74938) 1967 -

Beware of opportunist '(exploito) psych' tags, they are way off the mark here. The sleevenotes to *Pop Goes The Electric Sitar* state that **Bell** was a virtuoso, a musician's musician amongst professional guitarists, and a consultant for Danelectro, with whom he created a 12-string christened the "Bellzouki" and the Coral Electric Sitar showcased here. However, little virtuosity is on display - this is an instrumental album where the electric sitar simply plays the melody line of well-known pop and film songs, backed by a full orchestra and oooo'ing female choir - imagine an MOR/muzak version of Lord Sitar.

Tracks that suffer this treatment include *Goin' Out Of My Head*, *Eleanor Rigby*, *You Don't Have To Say You Love Me*, *More* (theme from 'Mondo Cane') and *Lara's Theme* from 'Dr. Zhivago'. Ravi Shankar would be horrified, I suspect, to hear what could only be a curio for fans of sitar music.

Vincent "Vinnie" Bell was an active session man from the New York area and is featured on guitar or sitar on hundreds of albums. He was often used by **Alan Lorber** for his projects. In the seventies, **Bell** would release several albums of instrumental covers of hits or soundtracks. One 1968 gig in NYC included playing with The Portraits (Gary Myers' band) on their 'Schaffer Beer' commercial. (MW/SR/GM)

The Belles

45s: La Bamba/Sleep Walk   (Tiara 703) 1965
      Melvin/Come Back   (Tiara 100) 1966

Miami, Florida was home to this all girl garage band. After a rather lame debut disc they took the tune to Van Morrison's *Gloria* and converted it into *Melvin* - their tribute to Melvin Bucci, lead singer of **The Vandals**. It's become something of a girl punk classic. The flip, is similarly a rather thrashy garage number.

Compilation appearances have so far included: *Melvin* on *Riot City!* (LP), *Vile Vinyl, Vol. 1* (LP), *Vile Vinyl* (CD), *Garage Punk Unknowns, Vol. 4* (LP) and *Pebbles, Vol. 1 (ESD)* (CD); *Come Back* on *Girls In The Garage, Vol. 1* (LP); and both *Melvin* and *Come Back* on *Girls In The Garage, Vol. 1* (CD). (VJ)

Denny Belline and The Rich Kids

Personnel incl: DENNY BELLINE   A
                 RICHARD SUPA   A

ALBUM: 1(A) DENNY BELLINE AND THE RICH KIDS
                                    (RCA Victor LSP-3655) 1966 -

45s: Money Isn't Everything/Summer Girl (RCA Victor 8883) 1966
      Outside The City/Grey City Day   (RCA Victor 9041) 1966

A Long Island New York combo fronted by Perry Como's nephew! Definitely not a garage outfit but they did produce some decent covers in the style of **Young Rascals/Vagrants**. Previously known as Denny Belline & the Dwellers, Denny went solo and the Rich Kids renamed themselves **Man**, which resulted in Swansea's Man being known as Manpower stateside for a couple of years. Related 45s are set out below, but see separate entry for **Man**:-

Denny Belline & Dwellers:
45s: It Happens That Way/
      Little Lonely Girl   (RCA Victor 8665) 1965

Denny Belline solo:
45s: Living Without You/Forget About Me (Columbia 45123) 1970
      Rosemary Blue/?   (RCA JH-10171) 1975

Compilation appearances have included: *Money Isn't Everything* on *Boulders, Vol. 5* (LP) and *Gone, Vol. 2* (LP). (VJ)

The Bellingham Accents

Personnel: VIC BUNDY   keyb'ds   A
            BILL CAPP   gtr   A
            PAT JERNS   drms   A

DOUG LING	bs	A
LAURIE VITT	sax, vcls	A
KATHI McDONALD	vcls	A

45: Bacon Fat/Sampan (Jerden 746) 1965

NB: 'B' side recorded whilst the band were still known as **The Accents**

From Bellingham, Washington, this act had earlier recorded two 45's as **The Accents** with Ron Peterson. Laurie Vitt:- "Kathi McDonald started with us when she was 13 and we were still **The Accents**. Eventually Ron Peterson quit and was replaced by Bill Capp and we picked up Doug Ling on Bass and changed the name to **The Bellingham Accents**."

After a change of drummer and bass players they became **(Kathi McDonald and) The Unusuals**.

Laurie Vitt is now Curator of Reptiles and Professor of Zoology at Sam Noble Oklahoma Museum of Natural History.

The Bells of Rhymey

45: She'll Be Back/The Wicked Old Witch (Dicto 1003) 1965

A Michigan band and probably a studio group. *She'll Be Back* was written by **Dick Wagner** and had an immediate appeal and some snarling fuzz guitar. Although a potential hit it never enjoyed any commercial success and all it's remembered for now is its appearance on *Highs In The Mid-Sixties, Vol. 19* (LP) and *Killer Cuts* (LP). They also have a simple and previously unreleased little ditty called *Rich Man's Woman* included on *Thee Unheard Of* (LP) compilation. (VJ)

The Beloved Ones

See **Arch Of Triumph**.

The Beloved Ones

See **The Dearly Beloved** entry.

Toby Ben

| Personnel incl: | TOBY BEN | vcls | A |

ALBUM: 1(A) WAKE UP TO THE SUNSHINE
(Venture VTS-4003) 1968 -

45: Married Woman/I Don't Want You (Columbia 43898) c1966

NB: as Toby Ben Blues Band.

An obscure California singer, in a breezy pop-psych vein combining various styles on songs like *You Know My Mind*, *Draft Call*, *Chicago Trane Blues*, *Don't Lie To Me Baby* and *Peace, Wake Up To The Sunshine*.

Venture was a small Beverly Hills label which also released the first **Southwind** album. Their records were distributed by MGM. (SR)

The Benders

Personnel incl:	PAUL BARRY	drms	A
	GERRY CAIN	gtr	A
	GENO JANSEN	bs	A
	TOM NOFFKE	gtr	A

45: Can't Tame Me/Got Me Down (Big Sound 815N3006) 1966

This quartet were students at Stout University in Marinette, Wisconsin on the Michigan border and some distance East of Wausau, where the Big Sound label was based.

JOHN BERBERIAN - Music Of The Middle East LP.

Can't Tame Me has appealing vocals and a frantic beat and there's lots of fuzz guitar work. It's featured on *The Midwest Vs. The Rest* (LP), *Back From The Grave, Vol. 8* (Dble LP) and *Back From The Grave, Vol. 8* (CD).

Gerry Cain later turned up in The Why Four who cut the punker *Hard Life*. Paul Barry returned to Milwaukee and formed oldies-band Barry's Truckers in 1970. He ran his own studio and started the Lulu label to promote local talent. (VJ/KBn/GM/MW)

The Bends

45: If It's All The Same To You (Rebel 103) 196?

This one track was the sole vinyl output by this Pennsylvania band. It appeared as the 'B' side of an easy-listening tune by a guy called Smokey. There's some fine organ and it races along very nicely. You can check it out on *Back From The Grave, Vol. 7* (LP) or *Pennsylvania Unknowns* (LP). (VJ)

Bengali Bauls

Personnel:	HARE KRISHNA DAS	dotara	A
	JIBAN DAS	tabla	A
	LUXMAN DAS	khrmack	A
	PURNA DAS	khrmack, kartaljulie	A
	SUDHANANDA DAS	harmonium, kartaljulie	A

ALBUM: 1(A) BENGALI BAULS AT BIG PINK
(Buddha BDS-5050) 1970 -

Coming from Calcutta, India, the **Bengali Bauls** were a group of street musicians who arrived in the USA in 1967. They played the Fillmore with the **Byrds** and the New York Town Hall with the **Butterfield Blues Band** and were invited by Albert Grossman, Bob Dylan's manager, to stay at the Band's house, Big Pink, near Woodstock.

Garth Hudson of the Band recorded and produced their album in December 1967, which was then shelved and eventually released in 1970 on Buddah. The music is "India's Soul Music" with vocals and should appeal to the tabla fans. The album is also a curiosity for collectors of The Band. Purna and Luxman Das also appeared with Bob Dylan on the front sleeve of his *John Wesley Harding* album. The **Bengali Bauls** returned to Calcutta in 1969. (SR)

Tim Bennett

ALBUM: 1 CIRCLES (Private pressing) 1975 SC?

A melodic folk-rock singer and guitarist with a backing group. Some songs suffer a bit from rich arrangements. (SR)

Benninghoff

Personnel:	DAVID ADKINS	drms, gtr, organ	A
	JOHN RAINEY ADKINS	gtr, special effects	A
	R.J. BENNINGHOFF	piano, organ, rocksichord	A
	DON HUTCHINSON	clarinet, sax	A
	ROXANNE HUTCHINSON	flute, sax	A
	KENT PHILLIPS	bs, gtr	A
	LARRY SHELL	gtr, piano	A

ALBUMS:	1	BEETHOVEN BITTERSWEET		
		(SSS International SSS-15)	1971	-
	2(A)	CHURCH BACH (SSS International SSS-17)	1971	-

NB: According to Osborne's Rockin Records there's another LP, title unknown, on the Plantation label. It also lists the artist as Benninghoff's Bad Rock Blues Band but both SSS LPs are credited to **Benninghoff**.

| EP: | 1 | FREE! Special Bonus Single! (PS) | (SSS-PB-1) 1971 |

NB: (1) is a promo EP on blue wax that showcases tracks from LPs (1) and (2) plus a track apiece from LPs by **Arnold Bean** and **H.Y. Sledge**.

R.J. Benninghoff was previously with **The Berkeley Kites**, who'd released at least four poppy 45s between '67 and '69 on Minaret (a divisional label of SSS).

The promo EP 45 proclaims "With a degree in education and a major in medieval history, **Benninghoff** plays almost all instruments, sings and composes. His music skills exhibit a delightfull (their spelling) fusion of the past and present for universal acceptance by contemporary listeners." Harumph... what you get is literally 'baroque' rock, i.e. covers of classical works on harpsichord in a rock setting.

Church Bach, for example, reworks Bach classics with some good wild fuzz guitar but, alas, a lame harpsichord. (SR/MW)

Jay Bentley and The Jet Set

| 45s: | Watusi '64 / I'll Get You | (GNP Crescendo 332) 1964 |
| | Come On-On /Everybody's Got A Dancin Partner But Me | (GNP Crescendo 347) 1965 |

NB: All four tracks were also compiled on a French EP (Vogue 18006) 1965.

This band, possibly from the Los Angeles area, married beat sounds to a US dance-club vibe to produce some great party poppers. *Watusi '64* gets the toes tappin', *Come On-On* gets every limb a-shakin'. Both flips switch down several gears to last-dance territory. The 45s were produced by Buzz Cason and Tommy Allsup.

The involvement of Buzz Cason indicates a possible Nashville connection. (MW)

JOHN BERBERIAN - Middle Eastern Rock LP.

Bentleys

| 45: | Now It's Gone / Night Time In The City | (Devlet 443/4) 1966 |

Previously thought to be from Allentown, Mike Kuzmin's Pennsylvania. discography 'Sounds From The Woods' reveals that they were from Stroudsberg, Pennsylvania and were previously known as the Devils, releasing one fratty 45 in 1964 - *The Devil Dance / Just Like That* (Devlet 393).

Now It's Gone is a dynamic teen pop-punker brimming with commercial potential - echoes of Merseybeat, a soupcon of the Big O in the lead vocals, cool harmonies, topped off with rattlin' tambourine, restrained fuzz and a great stop-start outro.

This classy nugget can be found on *Pennsylvania Unknowns* (LP), *The Night Is So Dark* (LP) and *The Cicadelic 60's, Vol. 4* (CD). (MW)

Terry Ber

| ALBUM: | 1 | THROUGH THE EYES OF TERRY BER |
| | | (World Pacific WPS 31???) c1967 - |

Housed in a psychedelic cover, a poetic singer/songwriter hippie chick. Interesting but the album suffers a little from overproduction. (SR)

John Berberian

Personnel:	SOUREN BARONIAN	clarinet, bongos, sax, zills	ABCD
	JOHN BERBERIAN	oud	ABCD
	JACK CHALIKAN	canun	A
	STEVE PUMILIAN	finger cymbals, def, dumbeg, tambourine	ABCD
	JAMES SHAHRIGAN	bs	A
	BOB TASHJIAN	vcls, dumbeg, perc	ABCD
	JOHN VALENTINE	gtr	AB
	JOHN YALENEZIAN	dumbeg	A
	CHET AMSTERDAM	bs	BCD
	EMIN GUNDUZ	canun	B
	HACHIG KAZARIAN	clarinet	B
	ROSKO	vcls	C
	JOE BECK	"amplified rock gtr & fuzz"!	D
	ED BRANDON	gtr	D
	BILL LA VORGNA	drms	D

ALBUMS:	1(A)	IMPRESSIONS EAST	(Mainstream S/6023) 1964 SC
	2(A)	OUD ARTISTRY	(Mainstream S/6047) c1965 SC
	3(B)	MUSIC OF THE MIDDLE EAST	(Roulette # unkn) 1966 ?
	4(C)	MUSIC AND GIBRAN	(Verve Forecast FTS-3044) 1968 SC
	5(D)	MIDDLE EASTERN ROCK	(Verve Forecast FTS-3073) 1969 R1
	6(A)	OUD ARTISTRY	(Mainstream 802) (Dble) 196/7? R1
	7( )	ECHOES OF ARMENIA	(Olympia) c1972 SC
	8( )	THE DANCE ALBUM	(Olympia) c1973 SC

NB: (3) is by The John Berberian Ensemble and was reissued in Italy in 2001 on 180-gram vinyl and CD (Universal UV 023). (4) is by ROSKO (a DJ from WNEW-FM) with The John Berberian Ensemble. (5) is by "John Berberian and the Rock East Ensemble", later reissued on LP. (6) is a repackage of (1) and (2). It has been reissued itself in 2000 as a limited edition box-set.

Middle East ethnicity from New York City, more than two decades before the rather hyped "World Music" movement. **John Berberian**, an accomplished oud player and a student in Business Studies at Columbia University in the mid-sixties, gathered around him a troop of skilled musicians to perform the music of his forefathers.

With a foundation of traditional music from Turkey, Armenia, Greece, Arabia and North Africa, they created a captivating blend of exotic rhythms, melodies and improvisations on the first two albums, transporting the listener to bustling bazaars and scorched sands.

JOHN BERBERIAN - Ode To An Oud (LP Box Set).

Oud Artistry is an album of infinite beauty and one of the best fusion album's ever made. Every track is a winner. The music radiates warmth, spirituality and tension, while blending Arabian, Armenian and Turkish material with ease and grace. Most strongly recommended!

The pricey and much-sought *Music Of The Middle East* ups the swing'n'swirl factor with some frantic whirling-dervish workouts. The flamenco-like flourishes in *Oud Solo* are irresistible. A truly uplifting selection that has thankfully been reissued.

Music And Gibran is a collaboration with Rosko, a DJ at WNEW-FM. Subtitled 'A Contemporary Interpretation Of The Author Of "The Prophet" ', this is a predominantly-spoken mystical journey through the works of Kahlil Gibran, a Lebanese poet who died in 1931. One of Gibran's books, The Broken Wings, was made into a film at the time of the LP and won an award at the Sorrento Film Festival.

Middle East Rock is **Berberian**'s most accessible album for the curious. Here he fuses Middle Eastern vibes with Western rock to produce some fascinating results - check out *The Oud And The Fuzz* on *Turds On A Bum Ride, Vol. 2* (Dble LP) or *Turds On A Bum Ride Vol. 5* (CD).

John Berberian should appeal to all who enjoy the exotic strains of **Kaleidoscope** and **Orient Express**.

Berberian kept on recording in the early seventies. His subsequent albums (at least two on Olympia) are in the traditional Eastern/Armenian/Turkish folk vein. (VJ/MW/MK/SR/MG)

Rob Berge Band

ALBUM: 1 POPCORN   (Private Pressing) 1974 SC ?

From Wisconsin, a breezy rural folk singer/songwriter with electric and acoustic guitars, piano, drums, pedal steel and banjo. The album is housed in a homemade B&W cover. (SR)

The Berkley Five

Personnel: RON GIBSON   ld gtr   A
            STEVE JONES   bs   A
            BILLY KELLOGG   drms   A
            DAVE PARSON   gtr   A
            PAT RILEY   ld vcls   A

45: You're Gonna Cry/In The Midnight Hour   (Boss BOS 004) 1966

A garage band from Umatilla in Lake County, Florida. *You're Gonna Cry* starts off as a plaintive mid-tempo garage tune which explodes into a frantic screeching finale. It has resurfaced on *Sixties Rebellion, Vol. 4* (LP & CD) and *Psychedelic States: Florida Vol. 1*. (VJ/MW/JLh)

Berkeley Kites

Personnel incl: R.J. BENNINGHOFF?   A

45s: Hang-Up City / Let's Get Together   (Minaret 123) 1967/8
   α   Hang-Up City / Mary-Go-Round   (Minaret 132) 1968
   α   Alice In Wonderland /
         What Goes Up Must Come Down   (Minaret 140) 1969
         Willow Run /
         Let Me Treat You Like A Woman   (Minaret 145) 1969

NB: α also issued in the U.K. by Polydor (56742 and 56770 in 1968/9 respectively).

A pop group who flirted with toytown pop-psych and *Pet-Sounds*-inspired harmony sunshine-pop. *Alice In Wonderland* is in *Rubble* territory and has a cool vibe, with flute, muted brass, and fuzz chords low in the mix. The flip has better fuzzwork but this is subjugated by awful brasswork that includes a really naff 'big top' refrain. The *Mary Go Round* 45 is tame bouncy harmony-pop with brass, whilst their final 45 is another fluffy pop-psych offering with *Willow Run* being the stronger cut.

Both *Alice In Wonderland* and *Willow Run* 45s were produced by Finlay Duncan.

R.J. Benninghoff wrote their material. He went solo and, as **Benninghoff**, released two LPs on SSS in 1971 - *Beethoven Bittersweet* (SSS-15) and *Church Bach* (SSS-17). Literally 'baroque-rock', these reworked classical pieces by Beethoven and Bach via harpsichord doodlings in a rock setting.

Minaret was one of the numerous labels managed by Shelby Singleton, the man behind SSS, Amazon, Plantation and Double Bayou.

There is speculation that the band were based in Florida. (SPr/MW/SR)

The Bermuda Jam

Personnel: GLEN MELLO   A
            PAUL MUGGLETON   A
            ANDY NEWMARK   drms   A
            JAMES O'CONNOR   A

ALBUM: 1(A) BERMUDA JAM   (Dynovoice 31907) 1969 -

One track, *Good Trip Lollipop - An Antihystahymn*, has resurfaced on *Turds On A Bum Ride, Vol. 2* (Dble LP) and *Turds On A Bum Ride Vol. 1 & 2* (Dble CD). It's from the above mentioned album and very psychedelic. They are thought to have come from California and Andy Newmark was later in **Sly and The Family Stone**. The album is a schizophrenic affair - one side comprises interesting, if gimmicky psych, the other uninteresting soul. (VJ)

Bermuda Triangle

ALBUM: 1 BERMUDA TRIANGLE
                                    (Winter Solstice SR-3338) c1973 R2

A mellow psych act with spacey female vocals. (SR)

The Berries

45: I've Been Looking/Baby, That's All   (IGL 133) 1967

From Des Moines, Iowa, they were originally known as The Coachmen, but changed their name after learning about the Lincoln, Nebraska **Coachmen**. *Baby That's All* is an irresistibly melodic fresh'n'breezy pop-harmony number. The flip, a Hollies cover laced with ringing twelve-string hook-lines.

Compilation coverage has included:- *Baby, That's All* on *Monsters Of The Midwest, Vol. 4* (LP); *I've Been Looking* and *Baby, That's All* on *The IGL Rock Story: Part Two (1967 - 68)* (CD) and *The Best of IGL Folk Rock* (LP). The band also have two numbers, an earlier version of *I've Been Looking* and *That Boy*, under their earlier Coachmen moniker on the *IGL Dance Jamboree '66* (Dble CD). (MW/LP)

The Berries

45:	What In The World /		
	Baby, Let Me Follow You Down	(Delaware 5010)	1966

A rare 45 by a Chicago area outfit who chose to cover local heroes **The Vectors** and Bob Dylan. Both feature neat harmonica and great harmonies reminiscent of **Saturday's Children** or **The Cryan' Shames**.

What In The World is on *Pebbles Vol. 7* (CD) and *Class Of '66!* (LP); *Baby...* graces *The Essential Pebbles Collection, Vol. 2* (Dble CD). (MW)

The Berrys

Personnel:	MIKE ABRAHAM	bs	A
	FRANK COONS	organ	A
	JOE CORAZZI	gtr	A
	JIMMY FRANCHINI	vcls	A
	SONNY JOHNSON	drms	A

45s:	Midnight Hour/Sand And Sea	(Lavette LA 5011/12)	1966
	Midnight Hour/Sand And Sea	(Challenge 59358)	1967

Formerly known as **The Viscount V**, this youthful outfit were part of a vibrant garage and soul scene in Albuquerque, New Mexico. Originally issued on **Lindy Blaskey**'s Lavette label, their legacy comprises a lightweight cover of *Midnight Hour* backed by a mournful garagey ballad. (MW/MDo)

Berwick Players

Personnel incl:	JOHN ARMSTRONG?	A
	MIKE NORRIS?	A

45s:	I Found Out About You / Images	(Look 5008)	1968
	Love You Every Way / Hah Le Rama La	(Look 5014)	1968/9
	Days Of Melancholy / Way Back Home	(Look 5021)	c1969

Catchy late-sixties harmony-pop, featuring neat wah-wah on *Days Of Melancholy*, on Nashville's Look label. (MW)

The Best

ALBUM:	1	WE GOTTA GET OUTA THIS PLACE/BEST OF THE BEST	(Recorded Publications Co. 96) 1966 R4

NB: (1) had a limited edition reissue in 1996.

This split album on a Camden, New Jersey, label, saw a limited reissue in 1996. It features one side each by **The Best/The Gents**, two unknown local combos, who run through a bevy of typical garage covers in a 'prep rock' style. Very basic stuff - no fuzz, no off-the-wall ravers - just honest and workmanlike attempts that may sometimes sound flat and far from inspiring. But then that's what is so appealing about this genre and why serious collectors will pay a fortune for an original.

One track from the album *You Meant Nothing To Me* can also be found on *Oil Stains, Vol. 2* (LP). (MW)

Best Of Friends

Personnel incl:	RICH DEE	A
	DOUG SHAFFER	A
	DAVE WESLEY	A

45s:	You Ought To See My Love Today /		
	Feel Pink	(Laurie 3432)	1968
	Melodies / All The World Is Mine	(Laurie 3450)	1968

Both their 45s feature summery pop with strong harmonies. (MW)

Karen Beth

ALBUMS:	1	THE JOYS OF LIFE	(Decca DL 75148)	1967 -
	2	HARVEST	(Decca)	1970
	3	NEW MOON RISING	(Buddah)	1975

45:	Hard Luck Mama/?	(Decca 32816)	c1968

The first two albums contain some dark and introspective moody folk songs with beautiful female vocals, somewhere between **Karen Dalton** and the English singer Bridget St. John. The second album combines electric and acoustic guitars and the third was recorded with John Hall (ex-**Kangaroo**), and Harvey Brooks and is more country-rock oriented. (SR/NK)

Bethlehem

ALBUM:	1	BETHLEHEM	(Maranatha)	c1974 -

An obscure Christian rock album. (SR)

Bethlehem Asylum

Personnel:	CHARLES DECHANT	sax, flute, vcls	A
	CHRISTIAN GANDHI	piano, trombone, alto flute	A
	DANNY FINLEY	ld gtr, vcls	A
	BUDDY HELM	drms, perc	A
	JIM NEIMAN	bs, vcls	A

ALBUMS:	1(A)	COMMIT YOURSELF	(Ampex 10106)	1970 -
	2(A)	BETHLEHEM ASYLUM	(Ampex 10124)	1971 -

45s:	Child Of The Mountain/Talkin' 'Bout Love	(Ampex 11009)	1970
	Child Of The Mountain/Talkin' 'Bout Love	(Ampex 11020)	1970
	Ring My Bell/?	(Ampex 11041)	1971

This band's two albums are worth a listen with the first album being the better of the two. It contains lots of jazzy instrumentation and the better tracks are *Sea Rider* (which has lots of good piano work), *Sailboat Ride* (which features some nice sax and flute) and *Earth* (which also has some good flute pieces and jazzy piano). The final cut *It's About* starts with some rather discordant guitar work. The first 45 was taken from this album but consisted of the two most commercial but least interesting tracks. There's more of a country influence on the second album, particularly to the vocals - a good example of this would be *Ring My Bell*, which was also issued as a single. Also of note are *Blind Man's Buff*, which is quite bluesy and has some good flute pieces and *Tales From The Citadel* for its spacey intro. which soon gives way to the sort of jazzy instrumentation that characterises both albums.

They originated from the Clearwater/Tampa area in Florida although they toured extensively all around the South and had a good live reputation and were often double-billed with **The Allman Brothers**.

Buddy Helm (ex-**Those Five**) went on to play briefly with **Frank Zappa** and then **Tim Buckley**. Charles Dechant later played with the Hall and Oates band, with whom he has spent the last 15 or more years. The guitarist/vocalist Danny Finley went on to the Kinky Friedman and the Texas Jewboys band and co-wrote many songs over several albums. Christian Ghandi has been missing many years, any info would be appreciated and Jim Neiman is now deceased. (VJ/PLn)

The Bethlehem Exit

Personnel incl:	PETER SALTZBACH	gtr	A
	WILKIE		A

| 45: | Walk Me Out/Blues Concerning My Girl | (Jabberwock 110) 1966 |

This 45 which is sought-after by collectors was the work of a San Francisco-based band which operated between 1966 and 1970. From Walnut Creek, an East Bay Suburb, at least one member, Peter Saltzbach, was later in the New Delhi River Band, a 7-piece San Francisco outfit whose break-up resulted in the formation of two new groups, New Riders Of The Purple Sage and Shango. Chicago blues was the inspiration for *Walk Me Out*, a mutation of what was originally a Jimmy Reed song.

Compilation coverage has included *Blues Concerning My Girl* on *Pebbles, Vol. 21* (LP), *Pebbles Box* (5-LP) and *Trash Box* (5-CD); and both *Walk Me Out* and *Blues Concerning My Girl* on *California Halloween*. (VJ/MW)

Better Half

Personnel incl:	BOB KROPKOWSKI	keyb'ds	A
	BUDDY NOVAK	drms	A
	TOMMY THOMPSON	bs	A/B
	BENNY WESTERFIELD	gtr	A
	BILL WHITNEY	bs	A/B
	DOUG LEWIS	gtr	C

| 45: | Good Lovin / City Song | (Chatim 1777/8) c1969 |

Late sixties/early seventies soul-infused pop-rock seen described as 'garage'. Well it ain't - *Good Lovin* is funky rock though it isn't the James Brown song.

The band formed in Baltimore in 1969; it's not recalled whether the original bassist was Whitney or Thompson. Westerfield left in 1970 and was replaced by Doug Lewis, former leader of another Baltimore group, **The Peppermint Rainbow**, who had split after some success in 1968-9 with at least five 45s and an LP on Decca. (MW/JV)

Better Half-Dozen

Personnel:	JOHN D'ANTONI	bs	AB
	TED GENTER	keyb'ds	A
	MIKE MANGIAPANE	ld gtr	AB
	ED McNAMARA	gtr	AB
	RICHARD MOORE	drms	AB
	STEVE SKLAMBA	ld vcls	AB
	GRANCO MEIER	keyb'ds	B

| 45: | I'm Gonna Leave You/ I Could Have Loved Her | (U-Doe 105) 1966 |

This outfit came together in New Orleans in 1965 as The Forces Of Evil, a name which didn't endear them in some quarters, so they became The Avantis... only to switch name again to the Better Half-Dozen in the Summer of '66 when U-Doe label boss Frank Uddo took an interest.

It's a typical punk 45 with lots of organ. The top side is definitely the stronger of the two with a pulsating beat throughout. Both sides can be heard on EVA's *Louisiana Punk From The Sixties* (LP) and *Sixties Archive Vol. 3* (CD).

A second 45 was recorded but not released. Sklamba departed in mid-'67 and the band continued on into '68 as The Better Half. (VJ/AB/MW)

Better Sweet

Personnel incl:	JOHN COMISKY	vcls	A
	TRAVIS WAMMACK	ld gtr	A
	RITA ?	drms	A

| 45: | I Can't Do It By Myself/Like The Flowers | (M.O.C. 667) 1967 |

The top side of this 45 is gruff R'n'B-infused pop, rather like early **Wildweeds**. It's the Comisky-composed flip, *Like The Flowers*, that's the attraction here - a catchy garage-pop effort.

BETTY - Handful LP.

Producer (and 'A' side composer) Argel Reynolds recalls that the group featured singer John Comisky and a girl drummer called Rita. They were from New Jersey but were going to college in McKenzie, Tennessee. They cut the record at Royal in Memphis with Travis Wammack guesting on lead guitar. It was their sole release. Comisky would return to New Jersey.

About the same time that Reynolds was producing this band, he went to England and Germany and wrote and cut two sides with a UK band called The Fleets, which became the first release on the Hip label in 1966. Apparently the girlfriends of the band didn't want them to come over to the US to promote it so the record died. No UK release can be traced.... resulting in confusion amongst collectors over the band's origins ever since.

Compilation appearances include: *Like The Flowers* on *Glimpses, Vol. 2* (LP), *Glimpses, Vol's 1 & 2* (CD), *Bad Vibrations, Vol. 3* (LP) and *Turds On A Bum Ride Vol. 3* (CD). (MW/RHI)

Betty

Personnel:	ANTHON DAVIS	vcls, gtr	A
	TOM JORDAN	keyb'ds	A
	KERRY KANBARA	bs	A
	MIKE McMAHON	vcls, gtr	A
	AL RODRIGUEZ	drms	A

| ALBUM: | 1(A) | HANDFUL | (Thin Man Records AFP 703) 1971 R5 |

NB: (1) reissued on vinyl (Shadoks 019) 2000.

Hideously rare hard-rocker from Los Angeles, California. Try to imagine **Dragonfly** merging with **Canned Heat** and you'll be close. As only 200 copies were pressed and sold by the band at gigs, this record is very rare! If you like crude, powerful heavy rock, this one is not to be missed... and if you don't, then you can be content in the knowledge that the band members unanimously give it the "thumbs down" 30 years later!

Handful is actually the second album the band recorded - their first remains unheard. (CF)

Alex Bevan

Personnel:	TOM BAKER	drms	A
	ALEX BEVAN	gtr, vcls	A
	ROLLY BROWN	gtr	A
	JIM NICE	bs	A

| ALBUMS: | 1(A) | NO TRUTH TO TELL | (Big Tree BT 2006) 1970 - |
| | 2( ) | ALEX BEVAN | (Fiddlers Wind FD-1001) 1976 - |

From Clevelend, a decent mix of breezy folk and psychedelia that went totally unnoticed at the time. The second album contains three cuts with a full band and electric lead guitar, whilst the others are mostly acoustic guitar: *Rainbow, Silver Wings, Shadowdancer, Streamline, Skinny*. (SR)

B.F. Trike

Personnel:	ALAN JONES	bs, vcls	A
	MIKE McGUYER	gtr, vcls	A
	BOBBY STREHL	drms, vcls	A

ALBUM: 1(A) B.F. TRIKE (Rockadelic RRLP 1.5) 1989 R1

NB: (1) recorded 1971 but unissued originally. Rockadelic issue comes with insert. Also issued on CD (Rockadelic no#) 1997, and pirated on vinyl in Europe, 2000.

Originally known as **Hickory Wind** with the same line-up, this trio went to Nashville early in 1971 and laid down tracks for a proposed RCA album. It didn't happen. Eventually Rockadelic issued it - you'll need deep pockets for the limited vinyl version which disappeared all too quickly, so get the CD if this genre is to your tastes.

Musically it's quite varied but right 'in' with the heavy rock/psych school of the time. Launched by the fuzz-psych rework of *Time And Changes* it continues with some brisk and catchy rockers, characterised by excellent not-too-heavy drumming that swings rather than just being solid or pedestrian. Fluid fuzzed leads (the outstanding *Lovely Lady*), the odd lighter moment (*Sunshine*), and an irresistible cool boogie-rocker *Six O'Clock Sleeper*, absolutely tailor-made for Z.Z.Top, provide contrast and demonstrate their versatility. With perhaps the exception of the sentiments in *Be Free*, it has stood the test of time remarkably well and Mike McGuyer is totally justified in standing proudly by it. A shame on you, RCA! Heartily recommended. (MW)

Bhagavad Gita

45: Long Hair Soulful/
Long Hair Soulful (Instr.) (Philips 40485) 1967

This strange 45 came with a picture sleeve and an explanation of the subject matter - a painting by Paul Klee. Stoned psych; one side features cool vocals with hip oblique lyrics, the other is an instrumental version. Arranged by Roger Karshner, with Chuck Mangione, I guess this is 'art-rock'. He continued this theme as **National Gallery**, presumably with the same nameless Cleveland musicians. You'll also find the instrumental on *Beyond The Calico Wall* (CD). (MW)

Bhagavan Das and Amazing Grace

ALBUM: 1 SWAHA (dbl) (Private Pressing) 1974 R1

Deeply influenced by Eastern religions, this New York hippie group released a double album with sitar, tablas, tamboura, guitar and slide guitar in 1974, with songs like *Mountain Sita Ram, Dancing In My Heart, Ring Song, Just Can't Keep From Crying* and *Jesus Gonna Make Up My Dyin' Bed*. The records came in a colorful blue/red/orange gatefold sleeve with inserts. (SR)

Bhang

45: Black Eyed Peas / Mellow Day (Monster 0003) 196/7?

Late sixties/early seventies hard bluesy rock backed by a mellow meandering workout, penned by Messrs Namowicz and Wood. From Michigan (Detroit or Lansing area) on the same label as **Magic** and Plain Brown Wrapper. (MW)

Big Brother and the Holding Company

Personnel:	PETE ALBIN	bs, gtr	ABCDEFG H I
	SAM HOUSTEN		
	ANDREWS	ld gtr	ABCDEFG H I
	DAVE ESKERSON	gtr	A

B.F. TRIKE - B.F. Trike... CD.

	CHUCK JONES	drms	AB
	JAMES GURLEY	ld gtr	BCDEF I
	DAVE GETZ	drms	CDEFG H I
	JANIS JOPLIN	vcls	D
	DAVE NELSON	ld gtr	E
	TED ASHBURTON	piano	F
	MIKE FINNEGAN	organ	F
	NICK GRAVENITES	vcls	F G H
	MIKE PRENDERGAST	gtr	F
	DAVE SHALLOCK	ld gtr	G H
	KATHY McDONALD	vcls	H I
	JOHN DAWSON	gtr	

HCP

ALBUMS:	1(D)	BIG BROTHER	(Mainstream 6099) 1967 60 SC
(up to	2(D)	CHEAP THRILLS	(Columbia CBS PC 9700) 1968 1 -
1972)	3(G)	BE A BROTHER	(Columbia CBS PC 30222) 1970 134 -
	4(C/H)	HOW HARD IT IS	(Columbia CBS KC 30738) 1971 157 -

NB: (1) also issued in mono (R1). (1) reissued by Mainstream and Columbia in 1968. (1) issued by Fontana and London in the UK. (1) issued as (Vogue CLVXMA 165) and (London 195011) in France. (2) also issued in mono (R2). (2) and (3) issued by CBS in UK. (2),(3) and (4) issued in France on (CBS S7 63392), (CBS S 64118) and (CBS S 64317). *Cheaper Thrills* was originally issued as *Live* by Rhino on album in 1984. With the addition of the previously unissued *Hall Of The Mountain King* (from April 1967), it's now available on CD (Acadia ACA 8001) 2000. (3) reissued on CD (Acadia ACA 8026) 2002. (4) reissued on CD (Acadia ACA 8028) 2002. *Live In San Francisco, 1966*, which was originally issued on vinyl in 1983, is now available on CD (Varese Sarabande 302 066 344 2) 2002, but with only fair to good sound quality is for completists only.

Janis Joplin Solo: HCP
ALBUMS:	1	I GOT DEM OL' KOZMIC BLUES	
			(Columbia CBS 9913) 1968 5 -
	2	PEARL	(Columbia 30322) 1970 1 -
	3	IN CONCERT	(Columbia 31160) 1971 4 -
	4	GREATEST HITS	(Columbia 32168) 1973 37 -
	5	JANIS	(Columbia 33345) 1974 54 -
	6	FAREWELL SONG	(Columbia PC 37569) 1981 104 -

NB: (4) reissued on CD (Columbia CK 65869) 1999. Her fans will also be interested in *Box Of Pearls: The Janis Joplin Collection* (5-CD box set) (Columbia CSK 65937) 1999.

HCP

45s:	Blindman/All Is Loneliness	(Mainstream 657) 1967 110
	Down On Me/Call On Me	(Mainstream 662) 1967 43
	Bye Bye Baby/Intruder	(Mainstream 666) 1967 118
	Women Is Losers/	
	Light Is Faster Than Sound	(Mainstream 675) 1967
	Coo Coo/The Last Time	(Mainstream 678) 1967 84
	Piece Of My Heart/Turtle Blues	(Columbia 44626) 1968 12
α	Kosmic Blues/Little Girl Blue	(Columbia 45023) 1969 41

α	Try (Just A Little Bit Harder)/ One Good Man	(Columbia 45080)	1969 103
α	Maybe/Wake Me, Lord	(Columbia 45128)	1969 110
α	Me And Bobby McGee/Half Moon	(Columbia 45314)	1970 1
α	Cry Baby/Mercedes Benz	(Columbia 45379)	1970 42
α	Get It While You Can/Move Over	(Columbia 45433)	1970 78
α	Down On Me/Bye, Bye Baby	(Columbia 45630)	1970 91
	Keep On/Home On The Strange	(Columbia 45284)	1971 -
	Nu Boogaloo Jam/Black Widow Spider	(Columbia 45502)	1971 -

NB: α as by Janis Joplin.

The mercurial figure in this group was undoubtedly singer Janis Joplin, born in Port Arthur, Texas in 1943. She was very much out of place in this quiet Texan community, considered 'way out' by her school mates because she dressed differently and held different values and, therefore, grew up as rather a loner. Until now, neither she nor her family had exhibited any musical talent, but at the age of seventeen she discovered the blues, idolizing the songs of Leadbelly and Bessy Smith. She sang locally as a blues singer in Austin, Texas before dropping out of college and heading for San Francisco with Chet Helms, one of her few friends at the time. Janis arrived in Frisco at the beginning of the whole flower-power era - acid was becoming a big thing and underground clubs were beginning to open up all over the city. Chet Helms was organising the first hippy dances at the Avalon in San Francisco. One of the early groups trying to establish themselves were **Big Brother and the Holding Company**, who had begun gigging in the basement to 1090 Page Street. They were originally known as The Blue Yard Hill and also nearly called themselves Tom Swift and His Electric Grandmother. Helms became their manager, but the group felt they needed another singer. Realising Janis' potential Helms had sent Travis Rivers, a friend of his, to Texas to fetch her. He was just in time for she was about to join the **13th Floor Elevators**. **Big Brother** was born....

In their early days they gigged regularly around the underground clubs alongside **The Jefferson Airplane**, **The Grateful Dead** and the many other exponents of the San Francisco Sound. Joplin's talent as the vocalist was immense. Her raucous gutbucket vocals complemented the strength of the band's electric music. Her roots were in the blues and she was at her best singing bluesy numbers which caused many to think she was the greatest female white blues singer. On stage, too, she was a powerful spectacle - appearing to be wild and working herself into a frenzy.

Undoubtedly, **Big Brother** was one of the most popular San Francisco groups at this time. Inevitably, they were soon offered a recording contract, first by Mainstream, a small Chicago label. They recorded an album which the record company did not release until after their appearance at the Monterey Festival in 1967. Prior to this festival the band was practically unknown outside of San Francisco. The festival launched them nation-wide and Janis demolished the hippies with her screaming, mourning bluesy voice and her sexual act - she became a star overnight.

Mainstream then released their debut album *Big Brother and The Holding Company*. However, the band, feeling they had improved vastly since

BIG BROTHER AND THE HOLDING COMPANY - Big Brother (UK) LP..

BIG BROTHER AND THE HOLDING COMPANY - Cheap Thrills CD.

recording it, fought vainly to block it. The opening track *Bye Bye Baby* demonstrated the raucousness of Joplin's amazing voice. In another track *Light Is Faster Than Sound* she blends effectively with the group's other vocalists. *Call On Me* was an equally effective slower number. However, some of the material on the album was comparatively weaker. For example, *Women Is Losers* once again featured Joplin's vocal gymnastics but over a rather unimaginative *I'm A Man* style guitar riff. Tracks like *Blindman* where other group members took the vocal lead were understandably inferior. On the final track *All Is Loneliness*, a strange sounding affair, the group come nearest to achieving **Airplane**-like harmonies. Very early pressings off the album have only 10 tracks. Later editions feature two later tracks *Coo Coo* and *The Last Time*.

Their follow-up album *Cheap Thrills* was released on Columbia, who had rejected the original title 'Dope, Sex and Cheap Thrills' and a photograph chosen of the band featuring them in bed. Instrumentally, the band had improved. Opening track *Combination Of The Two* was a fine illustration of their driving rock and Joplin's gutbucket vocals. 'We're goin' knock you, rock you, sock it you now' she growled. The slower *I Need A Man To Love* and *Summertime* also saw her in fine form. *Oh Sweet Mary* opens with an acid guitar intro and once again captures the band at their more harmonious. However, the prominent tracks on the album were *Piece of My Heart* and *Ball and Chain*. The former showed the group at their best and was a hit in the U.S. and also in the UK, where the group never attained the popularity they enjoyed in their homeland. The song possessed a catchy chorus and Janis growled in the opening verse and chorus, whilst *Ball and Chain* was a longer, more bluesy number executed in a similar vein.

Joplin probably realized the instrumental limitations of the **Holding Company**, which certainly lacked subtlety. She left the band in 1968 and performed with various backing bands prior to the release of her first solo effort *I Got Dem Ol' Cosmic Blues Again*. She then found a new backing group, The Full Tilt Boogie Band (John Till (gtr), Richard Bell (piano), Brad Campbell (bs), Ken Pearson (organ) and Clark Pierson (drums). With this line-up she started recording *Pearl*. Tragically she died accidentally of a heroin overdose on 4th October 1970 in a Hollywood motel room before the album was complete. The strains and stresses of overnight stardom had taken their toll. At first she had resorted to booze, but the loneliness of her life in contrast to her stardom on stage had driven her to narcotics. The album was completed and issued after her death. Among the material was her only U.S. No. 1 *Me and Bobby McGee*. Also on the album were *Get It While You Can*, a song which described her own live-for-today approach to life and two of her own compositions *Mercedes Benz* and *Move Over*. All subsequent releases are compilations, which ironically out-number her original recordings.

Meanwhile, **Big Brother** struggled on. **Nick Gravenites** and Kathi McDonald (ex-**Unusuals**) joined up as vocalist and they recorded *Be A Brother* and *How Hard It Is*, which were inevitably inferior in quality to their material with Joplin. They finally split up in 1972. *Featuring ... JJ* was a reissue of their first album. However, that *Cheap Thrills* album is a fine example of the bluesy side of San Francisco music at that time.

In 1984 Edsel issued a compilation LP *Cheaper Thrills* (Edsel ED 135) which includes previously unissued material from a live concert at California Hill on 28th July 1966. It gives a good insight into the band's music in their early days. Different pressings of this album have been issued by Made To Last and Rhino in the US. Also in 1985 *Joseph's Coat* (Edsel ED 170) emerged.

Big Brother reformed in 1987 with all the original members, are still playing gigs today.

Columbia's 1999 *Box Of Pearls* is a beautifully packaged five-CD box set, which contains all of her solo and **Big Brother** albums and adds a number of previously unavailable recordings to each remastered disc. In addition, there's a five-track bonus disc of unreleased material from the *Cheap Thrills* sessions.

Compilation appearances have included: *Ball And Chain* on *Psychedelic Perceptions* (CD). (VJ)

Big Brother (featuring Ernie Joseph)

Personnel:			
	CORY COLT	gtr, bs, organ, vcls	AB
	STEVIE DUNWOODIE	drms, perc, vcls	A
	ERNIE JOSEPH (ERNIE OROSCO)	vcls, ld gtr, bs	AB
	RUBEN THE JET (RUBEN OROSCO)	bs, gtr, drms, sax, vcls	A
	BRIAN FAITH	drms, bs	B

ALBUMS: 1(A) CONFUSION (All American AA-5770) 1970 R3
2(B) SOUTH EAST TOUR (Akarma AK 036) 1999 -

NB: (1) counterfeited in 1989, but reissued officially by Akarma on vinyl and CD (AK 013) 1998. (2) also on CD (Akarma AK 036) 1999.

45: ESP/Brother, Where Are You (All American 5718) 1970

NB: 'B' side is non-LP, 'A' side features a different mix to LP version.

A Californian band (commune/family) who recorded their first album in Hollywood. Produced by Bill Holmes, the album is patchy. Its best tracks are the hard-rocking *ESP* and the dreamy *Wake Me Up In The Morning*. The album also includes an interesting long version of *Saint James Infirmary*.

Before **Big Brother**, **Ernie Joseph** was known as Ernie Orosco and formed several Santa Barbara outfits including **Ernie and The Emperors**, **Ernie's Funnys** and **Giant Crab**.

Like many of the All American projects recently put out by Akarma, it's not clear to what extent *South East Tour* and *An All American Emperor* (shown as by **Ernie Joseph**) were issued originally, or if they ever existed at the time at all. These may have seen test-pressing-only releases in the sixties, like **Indescribably Delicious**, but even that possibility remains unconfirmed. Half of the songs featured on *South East Tour*, are taken from the Comes Forth LP by **Giant Crab**.

The band may also be responsible for the *ESP* 45 by the group **Rain**. (VJ/MW/AP/CF/NK)

Big Foot

Personnel:			
	VIRGIL BECKHAM	bs	A
	GERRARD BELISLE	horns	A
	SPENCE EARNSHAW	drms	A
	DAVID GARLAND	keyb'ds, horns	A
	ART MUNSON	gtr	A

ALBUM: 1(A) BIG FOOT (Winro 1004) 1968 -

A late sixties/early seventies San Francisco-based rock/horn rock outfit arguably of peripheral relevance to their book, although their album is a very minor collectable. They certainly had pedigree. Art Munson had been with The Righteous Brothers, Beckhorn went on to The Ritchie Furay Band, Earnshaw to **The Wackers** and Garland later played with Bobby And The Midnights.

Dave Garland and Virgil Beckham later played on a privately released album, *Fred Field And Friends* (Maranatha HS 031) 1976, which is reputedly quite pleasant later seventies hippie-rock. (VJ)

The Big Game Hunters

45: See The Cheetah/Swingin' Shepherd Blues (UNI 55008) 1968

A psychedelic novelty single by a very obscure group, possibly from California. (SR)

The Big Inners

45: Ethmoiditus Cum Polyposis/Do You Wonder (Panorama 16) 1965

Up there with *Prognosis Stegnosis* as a mouthful of a title, this is an ode to allergies that Buddy Holly never recorded and featured, very aptly, on *The Big Itch Vol. 6*! More derivative beat on the flip. Great group name. (MW)

Big Lost Rainbow

Personnel:			
	J.P. BAILHE	bs, vcls	A
	ADAM BERENSON	piano, vcls	A
	RID PEARSON	gtr, piano, sax, vcls	A
	ROBIN PFOUTZ	cello, vcls	A
	TONY MORSE	flute, gtr, vcls	A
	OTIS READ	gtr, harp, piano, vcls	A

ALBUM: 1(A) BIG LOST RAINBOW (Private Pressing) 1973 R1

NB: (1) has been reissued officially on CD (Gear Fab GF 118) 1998 and vinyl (Akarma AK 078) 2000.

This home-produced effort was recorded at Sheffield Recording Studios in Timonium, Maryland and Dynamic Sound Studios, New Haven, Connecticut in August and September 1973. Only 200 copies were pressed which explains its rarity. Musically the album certainly isn't psychedelic or garage - most tracks are pleasant acoustic folk with lots of guitar and flutes. Of particular note is *Brothers* because it's different from the rest with lots of jazzy piano. Most of the tracks are written by Rid Pearson.

Pearson, is now a major thriller-writer and plays bass for the Rockbottom Remainders, a band made up of writers like Stephen King and Dave Barry who play music for a hobby.

Compilation appearances have included *Sail* on Gear Fab's *Psychedelic Sampler* (CD). (VJ/LP)

BIG BROTHER (featuring Ernie Joseph) - Confusion LP.

BIG LOST RAINBOW - Big Lost Rainbow LP.

Big Sir

45: Heart Teaser,Crowd Pleaser/
New Day Sunshine   (GRT 10) c1970

Possibly from California, an unknown psychedelic rock group with organ and guitar. *Heart Teaser* was co-written by Scott English. (SR)

Big Sounds

45: Whang Dang/Go Ahead And Cry   (San Dun 003/4) 1965

A garage band from Dallas, Texas. *Go Ahead And Cry* is a reasonable beat number, with a vocalist that sounds like he's smoked too many Marlboro's... Check it out on *Sixties Rebellion, Vol. 2* (LP) and *Sixties Rebellion Vol's 1 & 2* (CD). (VJ)

The Big Three

Personnel:	DENNY DOHERTY	vcls	A
	CASS ELLIOT	vcls	A
	TIM ROSE	vcls, gtr	A

ALBUMS: 1(A) BIG THREE   (FM Revolver 307) 1963 -
2(A) LIVE AT THE RECORDING STUDIO
    (FM Revolver 311) 1964 -

NB: (1) reissued in mono/stereo (Roulette R(S) 42000) 1967. There's also a retrospective CD *Featuring Mama Cass Elliot, Tim Rose & Jim Hendric* (Sequel NEMCD755) 199?.

45s: Winkin' Blinkin' And Nod/Banjo Song   (FM Revolver 3003) 1963
Come Away/Rider   (FM Revolver 9001) 1963
Winkin' Blinkin' And Nod/The Banjo Song   (Tollie 9006) 1964
Nora's Dove (Dink's Song)/
Grandfather's Clock   (Roulette 4689) 1966

A folk group, whose members Elliott and **Doherty** went on to the **Mugwumps** and later the **Mamas and Papas**. **Tim Rose** had also a subsequent solo career.

Their first 45, *The Banjo Song* was an old folk tune, that is notable **Rose**'s powerful arrangement. Later, Shocking Blue would re-use the tune, almost note for note, for their smash hit *Venus*. (SR/EW)

Billy and The Kids

45s: Say You Love Me/It's Not The Same   (Julian 104) 1966
When I See You/Do You Need Me   (Julian 109) 1967

Hailed from Wenatchee in the heart of Washington State, You'll find the 'A' side of their first 45, *Say You Love Me*, a teen punker, on *Back From The Grave, Vol. 6* (LP). *When I See You* has also appeared on *Diggin' For Gold, Vol. 7, In The USA* (LP).

Another single *Shut Down Again/Troubles Of My Own* (Decca 31951) 1966, was by a different act with a similar name: **Billy and The Kid**. (VJ/KBn/MM)

Billy Rat and The Finks

Personnel incl: WALLY SHOOP   gtr   A

45: Little Queenie/All American Boy   (IGL 122) 1967

Spirit Lake in Northern Iowa was home to this band. Their fine version of Chuck Berry's *Little Queenie* can now be heard on *Midwest vs The Rest*. Wally Shoop, who played guitar on this also had an earlier release as Wally Shoop and The Zombies on the Soma label. (VJ)

Edwin Birdsong

ALBUM: 1 DANCE OF SURVIVAL   (Bamboo) 1974? SC

From Philadelphia, a black psychedelic soul group, with lots of fuzz guitars. (SR)

The Birdwatchers

Personnel:	EDDIE MARTINEZ	drms	A
	JOEY MURCIA	ld gtr	A
	BOBBY PUCCETTI	keyb'ds	A
	JERRY SCHILLS	bs	A
	SAMMY HALL	vcls	

NB: **Sammy Hall** joined the band in 1966.

ALBUM: 1 SOUTH FLORIDA'S BIRDWATCHERS
    (Florida Rock 4001) 1980 -

NB: (1) is a retrospective compilation of various 45s.

45s: Love, Emotion, Desire / I Don't Care   (Tara 100) 1964
  Blue Suede Shoes / She Tears Me Up   (Tara 1001) 1964
  Wake Up Little Susie / She Tears Me Up   (Tara 1002) 1965
  It's A Long Way Home / It Doesn't Matter   (Marlin 1902) 1965
α   Real Appeal / While I'm Gone   (Living Legend 101) 1965
  Girl I Got News For You / Eddies Tune   (Scott 27) 1966
  Girl I Got News For You / Eddies Tune   (Mala 527) 1966
  I'm Gonna Love You Anyway /
  A Little Bit Of Lovin'   (Mala 536) 1966
  I'm Gonna Do It To You /
  I Have No Worried Mind   (Mala 548) 1966
β   Hey Schroeder / ?Can I Do It?   (Marlin # unkn) 1967
  Mary Mary (It's To You That I Belong) /
  Cry A Little Bit   (Mala 555) 1967
  Turn Around Girl / You Got It   (Scott 29) 1967
  Turn Around Girl / You Got It   (Laurie 3399) 1967
  Put A Little Sunshine In My Day /
  Then You Say Boh Bah   (Scott 30) 1967
χ   While I'm Gone / I'll Remember You   (Living Legend 110) 1967
δ   Dreamin' In The Rain /
  You Don't Need A Reason   (Victory 2000) 1968
ε   Rock Steady / Little David   (Scott 401) 1968
ε   Rock Steady / Little David   (Laurie 3480) 1968
φ   Spinning Wheel / Rhyme Tyme   (Scott 402) 1969
  Hold Onto Me / Hey Little People   (Acetate only) 1969
  Mr. Skin / Come Home Baby   (Geminix 5501) 1972

NB: α as 'Gary Stites and The Birdwatchers'. β as 'Security Blankets'. χ as 'Legendary Street Singers', 'B' side by The Gents Five. δ as 'Glass Bubble'. ε with Duane Allman as '**The New Rock Band**'. φ as 'Mousetrap'.

This long-lived group from Tampa, Florida produced mainly highly-derivative beat/pop fare, though enjoyable nonetheless. They recorded under several other assumed names, including two 45s with Duane Allman as **The New Rock Band**.

The 1980 retrospective album collects most of their 45s from 1965 to 1967 - (4, 6, 7, 8, 9, 11, 12, 13, 14 above). The version of *Mary Mary* here is a different veriosn to the 45. There's also two cuts - *Hey Schroeder* and *Can I Do It* - which the compilers imply were not released, but these could be the unconfirmed 45 No. 10 above.

Some copies of the *Mary Mary* 45 come with a paste-over label where the title is given as *It's To You That I Belong*. Ordered by a Miami radio station because of perceived marijuana connotations, this 45 variant is known as a "WQAM copy".

A Bobby Puccetti composition, *Heard You Went Away*, was recorded by the **Proctor Amusement Co.**.

Joey Murcia went on to join **Magic** whose rare album *Enclosed* has seen a reissue. **Spirit** fanatics should note the cover of *Mr. Skin* on the Geminix 45.

Sam Hall, who joined the band in 1966, was previously in **The Mor-Loks** and The Trolls. He became a Christian in the late sixties or early seventies and later toured as **Sammy Hall and The Sammy Hall Singers**. Jerry Schills was previously with Milwaukee's **Legends**.

Compilation coverage has so far included: *Mary Mary (It's To You That I Belong)* on *Marijuana Unknowns* (LP & CD) and *Psychedelic States - Florida Vol. 2* (CD); *I'm Gonna Love You Anyway* on *Garage Zone, Vol. 2* (LP), *The Garage Zone Box Set* (4-LP) and *Ya Gotta Have Moxie, Vol. 1* (Dble CD); and *Girl I Got News For You* on *Searching For Love* (LP).

Thanks to Jeff Lemlich and his excellent Florida book 'Savage Lost' for helping to flesh out the 45 discography.

Gary Stites (whom **The Birdwatchers** backed on one release) had a few hits circa 1959-61. (MW/GM/JLh/RM)

Birmingham Sunday

Personnel:	PHIL GUSTAFSON		A
	JEAN HEIM		A
	WARD JOHNS		A
	JOHN KVAM		A
	JOE LA CHEW		A
	DEBBIE PARKE	vcls	A

ALBUM: 1(A) A MESSAGE FROM BIRMINGHAM SUNDAY
(All American AA 5718) 1968 R5

NB: (1) reissued officially on vinyl and CD (Akarma AK 014) 1998.

BIRMINGHAM SUNDAY - A Message From... LP.

This was a local California album recorded by a local Nevada group in December 1967. Only three or four original copies of this record have surfaced, despite being on a "real" label, and produced by **Strawberry Alarm Clock** guru Bill Holmes. According to the band, however, a few hundred copies were pressed at the time.

On offer is a pleasant Summer-Of-Love flower-pop with occasional outbursts of acidic guitar. This should appeal to fans of the **Peanut Butter Conspiracy**.

As the master tapes were sadly not available for the reissue, it was mastered from vinyl, with a great deal of digital noise reduction employed. (CF/MW)

Birtha

Personnel:	ROSEMARY BUTLER	bs, vcls	A
	OLIVIA LIVER FAVELA	drms	A
	SHERRY HAGLER	keyb'ds	A
	SHELLY PINIZOTTO	ld gtr	A

ALBUMS: 1(A) BIRTHA (Dunhill DSX 50127) 1972 -
2(A) CAN'T STOP THE MADNESS (ABC Probe) 1973 -

NB: (1) and (2) also released in the UK (Probe SPBA 6267 and 6272 respectively). (1) also issued in France by Pathe Marconi. (2) also issued on Dunhill (DSX 50136) 1973. (1) and (2) reissued on one CD.

Like Fanny, this was an early seventies hard-rock group formed by four Californian girls, and best avoided. Rosemary Butler did session work for The Doobie Brothers and Boz Scaggs. She later joined Jackson Browne's group. (SR/CG)

Biscuit Davis

Personnel:	ROBERT ANTHOINE	drms	A
	TOM BAILEN	gtr, vcls	A
	DERRIK HOITSMA	gtr, bouzouki, violin, vcls	A
	BOB THIELE Jr.	gtr, keyb'ds, vcls	A
	TODD ZIMMERMAN	bs	A
	(and guests - nineteen of them!)		A)

ALBUM: 1(A) PLAYING ON THE MOON
(Flying Dutchman - Amsterdam AM 12014) 1973 SC

A remarkably '**Dead** - sounding group of young country - rock musicians. A very good album in the hippie-rock mould! Bob Thiele Jr produced the album which was issued on his father's Amsterdam label. Bob Thiele senior also being a well-known jazz producer. The album is housed in a nice psychedelic gatefold sleeve and contains a surprising long cover of *Gasoline Alley* (Rod Stewart / Ron Wood) plus a cover of *Another Saturday Night* (Sam Cooke). All the other tracks were composed by the group members. (CF/SR)

Bit 'A' Sweet

Personnel:	MITCH LONDON	bs, drms, vcls	A
	RUSSELL LESLIE	drms, vcls	A
	DENNIS DE RESPINO	keyb'ds, gtr, vcls	A
	JACK MIECZOWSKI	gtr, sitar, vcls	A

ALBUM: 1(A) HYPNOTIC I (ABC ABCS 640) 1968 R1

45s: Out Of Sight, Out Of Mind /
Is It On - Is It Off? (MGM 13695) 1967
2086/Second Time (ABC 11125) 1968

This band were from the Plainedge and Massapequa area of Nassau County, Long Island, New York. The sleeve is one of the best points about their album, which apart from a couple of tracks, *Travel* and *A Second Time* is not recommended, although it has some interesting sound effects and phasing. Their cover of *Out Of Sight, Out Of Mind* which is not on the

BIT A SWEET - Hypnotic I LP.

LP, is worth hearing and can be found on *Psychedelic Unknowns, Vol. 4* (LP & CD), *Sixties Choice, Vol. 2* (LP) and *The 60's Choice Collection Vol's 1 And 2* (CD). Their album track *Speak Softly* has reappeared on *Electric Psychedelic Sitar Headswirlers, Vol. 7* (CD).

Bit 'A' Sweet also appeared in the movie "Blonde On A Bum Trip" performing *Out Of Sight, Out Of Mind*, plus one other track.

Out Of Sight, Out Of Mind was written by their producer, Steve Duboff of **The Changin' Times**. (VJ/MW/KBn/MM/PP)

Bits 'n' Pieces

45: Look Out Linda/Who Could I Turn To? (Dee Gee 2005/6) c1964

Also seen listed as Antler 2005, this is pure Beatles-inspired invasion sound. Basic but catchy uptempo beat backed by a slow beat-ballad. Group origins are unknown, both sides are credited to one 'Buck Ram'. (MW/MM)

Bitter Creek

Personnel incl?: DAVID CARR   A

45: Plastic Thunder / Behind The Smiles   (Mark IV #6809) 1970

A mystery bunch thought to be from Atlanta, Georgia. Their aptly titled *Plastic Thunder* is a noisy chunk of **Blue Cheer**-inspired fuzzed acid-rock; and a resounding inclusion on *Psychedelic States: Georgia, Vol. 1* (CD). (MW)

Bittersweets

Personnel incl: PAUL BENNETT   drms   A
                 ALLAN CHITWOOD   bs   A
                 GREG FARLEY   gtr   A
                 BOB SUTKO   vcls, hrmnca A

45s: Cry Your Eyes Out / She Treats Me Bad   (Hype 1001) 1966
      She Treats Me Bad / Road To Rann   (Chari C-102) 1966
      In The Night / Another Chance   (Original Sound OS-70) 1967

Originally from Scottsdale, Arizona they enjoyed some local success. In late 1967 they added Paul "Skip" Ladd, from the Laser Beats, to their ranks and became known as **Twentieth Century Zoo**.

Compilation appearances have so far included: *Another Chance* on *Mindrocker, Vol. 13* (LP); and *She Treats Me Bad* on *Fuzz, Flaykes, And Shakes, Vol. 5* (LP & CD). (MW/MM)

The Bittersweets

45: The Hurtin' Kind/Summertime   (Tema PXT 001) 1965

An all girl garage band from Cleveland, Ohio. *The Hurtin' Kind* is a nice folk-rocker with pleasant harmonies which can be heard on *Girls In The Garage, Vol. 1* (LP & CD). The song was a hit around the Cleveland area for the **Tulu Babies** the same year (aka **The Baskerville Hounds**). (VJ)

The Bittersweett

45: She Lied /I'll Feel A
     Whole Lot Better   (Prestige Productions PP66-162) 1966

Details about this Fairfield, Alabama group remain elusive. The Jarrett/Jones/Lacey composed *She Lied* can be heard on *Psychedelic States: Alabama Vol. 1* (CD). (MW)

B.J. And The Hobson Brothers

45: To Those Wishing / Mad Sad Man   (Valor V-45-101) 196?

Rock'n'roll ballads filtered through Merseybeat and 1964/5 Invasion sounds results in an excellent 45 with strong raw vocals from 'B.J.'. Both sides were written by Dennie Hobson. Described as 'garage', which it may be in spirit, this is simply classy U.S. beat. No details on this group have come to light yet - hopefully there are more 45s too. (MW)

Anna Black

ALBUMS: 1 MEET ANNA BLACK   (Epic BN 26384) 1968 R1
         2 THINKIN' ABOUT MY MAN   (Epic BN 26444) 1969 R1

A good and long forgotten bluesy rock singer. Her first album included a spooky version of *Eleanor Rigby*, *Freedom Train* with fuzz guitar plus several other interesting tracks like *Little Annie Weed*, *The Tullys And The Tolpins* and *Gloomy Sunday*.

On her second album she was backed by James Burton on guitar and the title track was compiled on on the Epic catalogue sampler *Rockbusters* (LP). (SR)

T.J. Black

45: Gotta Turn Myself On, Babe /
     She Belongs To Me   (Jubilee 45-5516) 1965

Moody folk-rock by a Dylan-clone, who pays his dues on the flip. (MW)

Black and Blues

Personnel incl: BOB McDONALD   A
                 G. KOPKO   A

45s: Come To Me/Bye Bye Baby   (UA 50245) 1968
      Candy Castles/Midsumer Night's Dream   (Talun TUS-0715) 1969

Anderson, a town about 40 miles North East of Indianapolis in Indiana was home to this band, whose first 45 was a fine two-sided fuzz-pop single. *Bye Bye Baby* is a very appealing *Mona/Who Do You Love?* style song.

Compilation appearances have included: *Come To Me* and *Bye Bye Baby* on *The Finest Hours of U.S. '60s Punk* (LP) and *Sixties Archive, Vol. 5* (CD); and *Come To Me* on *Trash Box* (5-CD). (VJ/KBn/JY)

Blackburn and Snow

Personnel incl: JEFF BLACKBURN   gtr, vcls   A
                 SHERRI SNOW   vcls   A
                 CHICKEN HIRSCH   drms   A

BLACKBURN and SNOW - Something Good For Your Head CD.

CD:	1(A)	SOMETHING GOOD FOR YOUR HEAD	
			(Big Beat CDWIKD 189) 1999

45s:	Stranger In A Strange Land/	
	Uptown-Downtown	(Verve VK-10478) 1967
	Time/Postwar Baby	(Verve VK-10563) 1967

One of the first wave of San Francisco bands, they formed in 1966 recording these two fine 45s the following year. They were due to release an album for Verve in April 1968 but it never appeared and apparently they had cuts on an ultra rare four album *Box Set* compilation of early Californian outfits on Colgems, which would now be virtually impossible to obtain. Still, you can find *Stranger In A Strange Land* on *Sounds Of The Sixties San Francisco, Vol. 1* (LP).

Jeff Blackburn went on to play for a number of Californian outfits including Jesse Wolf and Wings (early seventies), Silver Wings (1972/73), and **Moby Grape** (in the mid- seventies). Sherri Snow played briefly with Dan Hicks And His Hot Licks (in the late sixties) and Chicken Hirsch drummed for **The Cleanliness And Godliness Skiffle Band** (late sixties) and then the seminal **Country Joe And The Fish** (during the late sixties). He later owned a 'head' shop in San Francisco.

The Big Beat retrospective CD collects 20 tracks from their 1966 period at Trident Productions, also the fertilising ground for the **Mystery Trend** and the **Chambers Brothers**. Blackburn and Snow's forte was dramatic or dreamy chiming electrified folk-rock with confident strident vocals, brimming with the bright-eyed innocence and self-belief of the hippie generation. The vocals especially epitomise the emerging "San Francisco sound"... comparisons to early **Jefferson Airplane** or Jan Ashton-period **Vejtables** are inevitable. Both Verve 45s are included and turn out to be just the tip of the iceberg; hidden gems are revealed which justify a reappraisal - *Yes Today*, *Takin' It Easy* and *Do You Realize* are quite simply stunning. With comprehensive notes from Alec Palao, this is a must for any West Coast afficionado. (VJ/SR/MW)

Black Death

45:	Rock And Roll With Ork/In Need	(Cathedral 417) 19?

The band played in Minnesota in the late sixties/early seventies and this piece of psychedelia is now sought-after by some collectors. (VJ)

J.D. Blackfoot

Personnel:	J.D. BLACKFOOT	ld vcls, gtr	ABCDE
	KENNY MAY	bs	AB
	DAN WALDRON	drms, perc	ABCD
	JEFF WHITLOCK	gtr	AB
	CRAIG FULLER	gtr	BC
	STERLING SMITH	keyb'ds	CD
	PHIL STOKES	bs	C
	TONY BAKER	keyb'ds, sax	D
	FRANK GIBSON Jr.	drms, perc	D
	BOB JACKSON	gtr	D
	BILLY KRISTIAN	bs	D
	SONNY MANAHERA	steel gtr	D
	JIMMY SLOGGET	sax	D
	MIKE WALKER	keyb'ds	D
	BILLY CARROLL	drms, backing vcls	E
	BUDD FOWLER	bs, piano, backing vcls	E
	GEORGE MOBLEY	ld gtr, acoustic gtr	E
	(JOHN DURZO	bs	D)
	(J. HUFF	violin	D)
	(SUE MOORE	vcls	D)

ALBUMS:	1(B)	THE ULTIMATE PROPHECY	
(up to			(Mercury 61288) 1970 R1/R2
1976)	2(D)	SONG OF CRAZY HORSE	(Fantasy 9468) 1974 -
	3(E)	SOUTHBOUND AND GONE	(Fantasy 9487) 1975 -

NB: (1) original copies with insert. Also issued in Canada, UK and Holland. The UK and Dutch pressings have a completely different cover and the Dutch version is gatefold. (1) Reissued on CD (Tokala 5947-2). (2) reissued on CD (Sisapa Record Co. 5945-2). (4) reissued on dble CD (Tokala). There's also a double CD compilation, *Footprints* ( ).

45s:	α	Who's Nuts Alfred?/Epitaph For A Head	(Philips 40625) 1969
(up to		I've Never Seen You/One Time Woman	(Philips 40679) 1970
1976)	χ	Wonderin' Where You Are /	
		It Don't Mean A Thing	(Peace 50944) 197?
	β	Savage/Almost Another Day	(Peace 61776) 197?
		Every Day Every Night/	
		Save This World Today	(Peace 82941) 197?
		Twilight/Dove On The Ocean	(Fantasy 741) 1975

NB: α some promo copies with picture sleeves. β 'B' side was included on *Song Of Crazy Horse* LP, dating 45 as 1974 or earlier. χ as J.D. Blackfoot with Uncle Billy.

This group was originally from Columbus, Ohio. They started out as a combination of two local groups, **The Ebb Tides** and Tree. They continued as Tree and won a recording deal from Mercury as a prize in a local band competition. The resulting 45 (which has become a collectors item due to the burning hard-rock of *Epitaph For A Head*) generated enough interest that the label optioned an album from the band.

The Ultimate Prophecy is arguably the best rock album ever from Ohio. Craig Fuller was added to the line-up just before recording and his country/folk influence dominates the music on Side One of the album. *Angel* and *We Can Try* are particularly good, the latter being one of the earliest heavy-rock-meets-country songs extant; a style that later dominated the American music scene when groups like The Eagles and Linda Ronstadt homogenised and neutered it. These tracks have edge and power, though - and should not be overlooked. Side two of the album was

J.D. BLACKFOOT - The Ultimate Prophecy CD.

J.D. BLACKFOOT - The Song Of Crazy Horse CD.

taken up with the *Ultimate Prophecy* suite, an engaging life-cycle mini-opera that plays out its theme of birth-death-reincarnation against a backdrop of some truly stunning hard-rock music. Despite its 20 minute plus running time, the whole of this side became an instant FM underground classic across the midwest and its popularity stretched into the eighties. Most of the music on this side was composed by guitarist and original Tree member Jeff Whitlock, with lyrics by **J.D. Blackfoot** and drummer Dan Waldron. The album itself has always been scarce, but it was fetching serious money even in the seventies in places like Chicago, Detroit, and St Louis where it was a late-night FM staple. It remains an essential American rock record with wide appeal, and is highly recommended.

The album credits two people who don't actually play on it - Phil Stokes on bass (the actual bass player was Kenny May - he was replaced after the recording), and Sterling Smith (ex-**Grayps**) on keyboards (also joining after the recording, there are no keyboards on the album!). The line-up with Phil and Sterling did however record some unreleased material.

In September 1970, **J.D. Blackfoot** left the group and most of the rest of the band continued to play as **Osiris**. (**Osiris** in turn would later metamorphosise into two other groups, one being the **Load**, who recorded a keyboard driven progressive rock album *Praise The Load* in '77.)

In 1972, **J.D.** and his wife went to New Zealand for a month's holiday and liked it so much they spent most of the next two years there! Indeed, his *The Song Of Crazy Horse* album was assembled largely from recordings made at Auckland's Stebbing Studio with local luminaries such as Billy Kristian and Frank Gibson. The disc won New Zealand's 'Best Album Of The Year Award' in 1974 and the original New Zealand pressing with booklet and poster are highly sought-after. The eighteen-minute title track was inspired by the Indian story of "Bury My Heart At Wounded Knee".

Back in the US, **J.D.** assembled a new group with some of the musicians from other sixties Columbus area bands like **The Four O'Clock Balloon** and **The Myrchents**. They recorded *Southbound And Gone* at Fantasy's Studios in Berkeley, California. The title cut *Southbound And Gone* was co-written by Blackfoot and Mobley, and the album also included *We Can Try*, an old Blackfoot/Fuller collaboration. Four tracks are mentioned as being taken from the obscure rock opera "Space And Mary Jane" and two songs were released as a single.

In 1982, **J.D. Blackfoot** released the double LP *Live In St. Louis* (Bison) and in 1984 an EP, *Nobody's Business/Let Her Go/Stay The Night Away/He Walks On Past* (Bison B-77), 1984.

After leaving the band Craig Fuller and Phil Stokes co-founded Pure Prairie League. Fuller was later a member of American Flyer together with Doug Yule (**Velvet Underground**), Eric Kaz (**Blue Magoos**) and Steve Katz (**Blues Project**). They released two albums for United Artists in 1975 and 1976 of average country-rock produced by George Martin. Later still, Craig Fuller became lead singer for the reformed Little Feat in the early nineties.

Blackfoot, who changed his name to Van Dervort in 1970, sold the worldwide rights to Fantasy Records some years ago, but retained exclusive rights to the New Zealand market. Currently living in Columbus, Ohio, he still makes recordings.

Compilation appearances have included: *Epitaph For A Head* on *Songs We Taught The Fuzztones* (LP & CD), *Trash Box* (5-CD) and *High All The Time, Vol. 2* (LP). (GGI/VJ/SR/CBe/CF/PSs/SS)

Black Merda

Personnel:	ANTHONY HAWKINS	gtr	A
	CHARLES HAWKINS	gtr	A
	TYRONE HYTE	drms	A
	VEESEE L. VEASEY	bs	A

ALBUMS:	1(A)	BLACK MERDA	(Chess CH 1551) 1970 R1
	2(A)	LONG BURN THE FIRE	(Janus JSX-3042) 1972 SC

NB: (1) reissued on vinyl (Funky Delicacies/Tuff City) 1996. (2) as by Mer-da

45:	Cynthy-Ruth/Reality	(Chess 2095) 1970

NB: There's also a French 45, with picture sleeve: *Prophet / Cynthy-Ruth* (Chess 169556L) 1970.

A black outfit which operated out of Mississippi but recorded in Chicago. The 1996 reissue describes the group as "folk rock funkateeers" (sic) and their music is a rather interesting combination of blues, rock and soul with loads of guitar parts clearly inspired by **Hendrix**. *Cynthy-Ruth* is the most commercial cut. Its better moments include *Over And Over*, a bluesy instrumental, *Reality*, a laid back effort with some nice bluesy guitar work and *Windsong*, a slow instrumental, very similar to Fleetwood Mac's *Albatross*. The first album was recorded in the Winter of 1970 and produced by the enigmatic "Swan". As **Blak-Mer-Da** they also produced at least one 45 by **Fuji**.

The band were latterly known as Mer-da and their 1972 album is a decent sort of psychedelic/blues, with quite strong guitar. (VJ/SR/MW/MJ)

Black Orchids

Personnel:	ROBIN TROWBRIDGE	drms	AB
	JOHN WHERLE	gtr	ABC
	ROB HAMER	bs	BC
	PAUL BENNINGTON	drms	C
	JOE STEVENS	bs	

ALBUM:	1(B/C)	THE BLACK ORCHIDS	(Private Pressing) c1972 R2

J.D. BLACKFOOT - Southbound And Gone LP.

A limited private pressing issued in a plain white sleeve, made for fans and friends of the band. The music is reputedly psychedelic with long guitar solos. The band was formed by John Wherle and Robin Trowbridge in Charleston, West Virginia in 1970 and recorded the album in John Wherle's basement studio.

Robb Trowbridge: "A friend, Jack Griffith told me that John Wherle was looking for a drummer for a two man band. I took my drums over to his house and after months of practice, and I mean months, we had **Black Orchids**. We had to perfect a type of sound because we were just a two man band. Guitar and drums. John developed a style he called subharmonics, which used a type of dreamy open string chords. Joe Stevens came along when we played the Earth Day Festival in 1970, at Kanawha State Forest with many other bands. John and I felt we could get a bigger sound with the added bass. All our songs were written by ourselves except a cover of *Yellow Cab Man* by Gun and they were all instrumentals". (SR/RTe)

Black Pearl

Personnel:	BRUCE BENSON	gtr	A
	JERRY CAUSI	drms	A
	BERNIE FIELDINGS	vcls	A
	TOMMY MOLCAHY	second ld gtr	A
	JEFF MACKAY MORRIS	ld gtr	A
	O'CONNOR	drms	A

HCP
ALBUMS: 1(A) BLACK PEARL (Atlantic SD-8220) 1969 130 -
2(A) BLACK PEARL LIVE AT THE FILLMORE
(Prophesy PRS-1001) 1970 189 -

45: Mr. Soul Satisfaction/White Devil (Atlantic 2657) 1969

When Moulty, **The Barbarians** drummer left the band, the remaining members (Fieldings, Causi and Benson) moved from Boston to San Francisco and with the addition of fellow Bostonian Jeff Morris and Molcahy and O'Connor formed **Black Pearl** in 1967.

The band's three guitar line-up created one of the first heavy psych groups, with strong R&B roots. Their first album, produced by Lee Kiefer and Richard Moore, contained nine short tracks, with titles like *Crazy Chicken*, *White Devil* and *Mr. Soul Satisfaction*. Its cover was designed by Eve Babitz.

The second album was recorded live at the Fillmore West in September 1968 and contained an eleven minute version of James Brown's *Cold Sweat*.

Bernie Fieldings also guested on **Fusion**'s *Border Town* album.

Compilation appearances include *Forget It* on *Nuggets, Vol. 6* (LP). (SR/MW)

Black River Circus

45: Love's Gonna Carry Me (Home) /
A Ritual Melody (MRC MR-1096) 1969

An unknown outfit on a Waynesboro, Virginia label. Sounds more like '66/'67 again - soulful keyboard-dominated pop ala **Young Rascals** is backed by a 'groovy' exploito-style keyboard instrumental which seems out of place on *Acid Dreams, Vol. 2* (LP). (MW)

Blackrock

45: Blackrock "Yeah, Yeah"/
Bad Cloud Overhead (Selectohits SOH008) c1969

A black psychedelic rock group. (SR)

The Black Sacks

This band originated from Houston, Texas. Two of their tracks: *The Way I Feel* and *Take Out* have subsequently resurfaced on *Acid Visions - The Complete Collection Vol. 1* (3-CD). (VJ)

The Black Sheep

Personnel:	BUDDY ('Fly Man')		A
	DEAN ('Gopher man')		A
	MARK HARMON ('Cartoon Man')		A
	JOE MASTERSON ('Monkey Man')		A
	MIKE ('Trash man')	ld gtr	A

45s:	I Told You / Baa-Baa	(Bellcor 102) 1965
	It's My Mind / Arthur	(Vision 464-440) 1966
	It's My Mind / Arthur	(Columbia 4-43666) 1966
	Feeling Down / Suzanne	(Columbia 4-43974) 1967

From La Canada, California this outfit changed their name to Trayne in 1967. *It's My Mind* is featured on Moxie's *Folk Rock E.P.* (7") and *Ya Gotta Have Moxie, Vol. 1* (Dble CD). It's a breezy uptempo folk-beat number, whilst the flip is a cool uptempo instrumental with furious strumming and harp. The fourth 45 is pleasurable too. Both 45s were produced by **Jerry Riopell**, with arrangements by Murray MacLeod, who were later behind **The Parade**. (MW/MM)

Blackstone

Personnel incl: MAX WEINBERG drms A

ALBUM: 1(A) BLACKSTONE (Epic 26294) 1971 -

A progressive, hard-rock outfit. Weinberg later played with Bruce Springsteen and Ian Hunter. (CG)

The Blackstones

45: Chicago City /
Barrel Of Dreams (AS) (Teen Tunnel TT-101) 1999

This 45 is a reissue of a recently discovered International Recording Co. acetate out of Chicago. It is thought to be a Northside band whose name was hijacked by Jeff Boyan for his pre-**Saturday's Children** outfit **Dalek/Engam: The Blackstones**. *Chicago City* is a raw adolescent party punker and is backed by an attempt at a Beatlesque ballad. (MW)

Black Swan

Personnel:	TOM BRIGHT	drms	A
	SAUL CHAIT	bs	A
	JEFF COHEN	gtr, keyb'ds	A
	MARK HANESWORTH	gtr	A
	BRUCE GOOD	ld gtr	A

Named after the Tyrone Power movie, **Black Swan** were formed out of the exodus of kids heading off to San Francisco in the late sixties. Tom Bright was one of a bunch of kids from Austin, Texas, who, fed up with red-neck aggression, dropped out of University to head West.. but when his "get rich quick" band broke up on arrival, he answered an ad and joined a couple of musicians by the name of Bruce Good and Jeff Cohen.

With the addition of Saul on bass, they secured a three month residency at a bar and moved to a farm in Sonoma, North of the Golden Gate Bridge.

Under the wing of Matthew Katz, they recorded a couple of tunes, *Lady Blonde* and *She Encircles Me* for his now legendary compilation *Fifth Pipe Dream* (LP & CD). Both are quite commercially orientated tunes, with sprinklings of brass, and harmony vocals in a **John Sebastian / Lovin' Spoonful** vein. *She Encircles Me* is particular memorable for it's waltz feel, although both songs were really at odds with the long-extended jams coming from all other corners of San Francisco at the time.

BLACK VOY ALLEY - Black Voy Alley LP.

Katz then arranged for **Black Swan** to move en-masse to Seattle, but after a month or so of playing the Encore Ballroom to "thin crowds and little cash", Tom quit and moved back to California, finding himself learning to do light shows... He recalls: "I muffed it bad at Matthew's faux-**Moby Grape**'s first appearance (made up of a number of the 17-year-old staff musicians). I accidentally threw white light on the boys before the crowd had been acclimatised to them singing familiar songs in the dark - their covers were only 60% close - and it was immediately obvious that bouncing, live-wire **Skip Spence** was NOT onstage, nor was even a single other actual **Grape**. The crowd rather effectively rebelled and stormed the box office."

As to **Black Swan**, in 1971 a 45 appeared on the UK Ember label, and an album appeared the following year, but these are by a different, probably European band. The 'A' side is sinister and slight, whilst the non-album flip is sung in the style of a Greek folk/pop song.

ALBUM: 1 BLACK SWAN (MCA/Embassy MAPS 5666) 1972 -

45: Echoes And Rainbows/Belong, Belong (Ember EMBS 303) 1971

Prior to leaving Texas, Bright also played on **Gilbert Shelton**'s sole 45, as well as playing with local notables such as Powell St. John, **Steve Miller**, Mance Lipscomb and John Lee Hooker.

Bruce Good now sells cruise ship berths out of San Francisco and Jeff Cohen lives in Mill Valley and records TV ad music. Bassist Saul Chait was last heard of selling Mazdas in Petaluma, California, whilst drummer Tom Bright went on to race motorbikes professionally and is now a print broker, industrial consultant, and political candidate in Sacramento, California. (VJ/HH/MW/TBt)

Black Voy Alley

Personnel:	MARK NOWICKI	bs, vcls	A
	SANDY PIZZO	keyb'ds, vcls	A
	CRIS SMITH	gtr, vcls	A
	JOHN WILLIAMS	drms, vcls	A

ALBUM: 1(A) BLACK VOY ALLEY (Black Voy Alley Records BVA 82172) 1972 R2

A hard partyin' Texas bunch that recorded at Audio Recorders in Phoenix. Their rare album is (sadly) made up entirely of cover songs from the era... sad because they play pretty well and an album of original material could well have been a real monster.

While this band deserves public ridicule for its disturbing fixation with Three Dog Night (three covers!), these boys rack up serious bonus points for including *Stairway To The Stars* by the (then) rather obscure Blue Oyster Cult! Add a Who tune and a couple of Deep Purple covers and the overall vibe is one of drunken teens at backyard parties in the suburbs while the parents are out of town. Plenty of bands did the same across the USA but few were this proficient - and even fewer made enough money at it to record professionally and press records. (CF)

The Black Watch

45: Left Behind/I Wish I Had The Nerve (Fenton 2508) 1967

A Cedar Springs, Michigan outfit on what is now a very collectable label. *Left Behind* can also be heard on *The Chosen Few, Vol. 2* (LP), *Chosen Few Vol's 1 & 2* (CD) and *Teenage Shutdown, Vol. 7* (LP & CD). (MM/MW)

Blackwell

Personnel:	JOHN BUNDRICK	keyb'ds	A
	RANDY DEHART	drms	A
	GLENN GIBSON	vcls	A
	JIMMY SMITH	gtr	A
	TERRY WILSON	bs	A

ALBUM: 1(A) BLACKWELL (Astro 9010) 1969 R1

HCP
45s:	Wonderful/Dirty Story	(Astro 2002/1000) 1969	89
	Almost Gifted/Outside	(Astro 1001) 1969	-
	Doin' It/ ?	(Astro 1003) 1969	-
α	Down On The Farm/Little Man	(Astro 6003) 1970	-

NB: α flip side was by Logan Smith.

A Texas rock and roll outfit, whose songs had strong vocals and some psychedelic influence. John "Rabbitt" Bundrick was later involved with The Who and one of their cuts *Outside* has resurfaced recently on both *Acid Visions - The Complete Collection Vol. 1* (3-CD) and the *'69 Love-In* (CD) compilation on Collectables. (VJ)

Blackwood Apology

Personnel:	RON BECKMAN	bs	A
	DENNIS CRASWELL	drms, vcls	A
	DENNIS LIBBY	piano, vcls	A
	DALE MENTON	gtr, vcls	A
	BRUCE PEDALTY	organ, vcls	A
	(GREG MALAND	keyb'ds	A)

ALBUM: 1(A) HOUSE OF LEATHER (Fontana SRF-67591) 1969 -

Dale Menton was involved in several Mankato and Minneapolis-based sixties bands including **The Gestures**, The Best Things and **The Madhatters**. He was the writer and architect of this rock concept album, which was recorded in Chicago, although the artists responsible for it were mostly from Minneapolis. Craswell was earlier with **The Castaways** and later played for the Chicago band **Crow**, who moved to Minnesota. Pedalty was a session man and Greg Maland one of Minnesota's best keyboard players.

Greg Maland is perhaps best remembered as Gregory Dee (of Gregory Dee and The Avanties fame). He was also in the **Castaways** with Libby and Craswell, from 1966 until 1969. (VJ/MW)

Blades of Grass

Personnel:	BRUCE AMES		A
	MARC BLACK		A
	FRANK DiCHIARA		A
	DAVE GORDON		A

ALBUM: 1(A) ARE NOT FOR SMOKING (Jubilee JGS 8007) 1968 -

NB: (1) also issued in Canada.

45s:	Happy / That's What A Boy Likes	(Jubilee 5582) 1967
	Just Another Face / Baby, You're A Real Good Friend Of Mine	(Jubilee 5590) 1967
	Help / Just Ah	(Jubilee 5605) 1967
	Charlie And Fred / You Won't Find That Girl	(Jubilee 5616) 1968
	You Turned Off The Sun / The Way You'll Never Be	(Jubilee 5622) 1968
	I Love You Alice B.Toklas / That's What A Boy Likes	(Jubilee 5635) 1968
	Love Her And Cherish Her / Pageant	(Jubilee 5662) 1969
	It Isn't Easy / My Someone	(Fine Fl-57027) 1970

The Jubilee 45s are mainly summery harmony-pop. One highlight is a cover of the Peter Sellers film title-track *I Love You Alice B.Toklas* (also recorded by **Harpers Bizarre**). **The Blades'** version is noteworthy for vocal phasing and psychy effect-laden intro and outro. *The Way You'll Never Be* is a cover of labelmates the **Fifth Estate**. For their 45 on Fine, this Rochester, NY combo turned to heavier garage-pop sounds - *It Isn't Easy* in particular features some great fuzz breaks.

Their album has an amusing title, but is may be disappointing for 'psych' fans. Twelve short tracks are included with emphasis on harmony singing which at times take on a mild psychedelic tinge. A few unexciting covers of songs like *Help!* and *Walk Away Renee* give the album an uneven quality. On the positive side there are innocent sunshine pop tracks like *Just Ah*, *Or Is It The Rain* and the best cut *Just Another Face* with its inventive orchestration and fine harmonies. Still, on the whole, this is too boyish and bland to convince.

Compilation appearances have included: *It Isn't Easy* on *Seeds Turn To Flowers Turn To Dust* (LP & CD); and *Just Another Face* on *Bring Flowers To U.S.* (LP). (SR/MW/MK)

Hal Blaine

ALBUM:	1	PSYCHEDELIC PERCUSSION	(Dunhill DS 50019) 1967 SC

Selective
45s:	Love-In (December) / Wiggy (November)	(Dunhill D-4091) 1967
	The Invaders / Secret Agent Man	(Dunhill D-4102) 1967

Hal Blaine was one of the best American drummers and can be found on literally thousands of albums recorded in the Los Angeles studios from the late fifties to the eighties. His album was an attempt to cash in the psych movement but it flopped. Recorded with **Paul Beaver** and **Emil Richards**, it features a lot of unusual instruments (Bean Bags, Buggy Whip, Celeste, Vibra-Fuzz Tone, Wobble Board, Beaver Electric Modulation Apparatus...) and tracks like *Love-In, Trippin' Out, Freaky, Wiggy, Kaleidoscope, Tune In-Turn On...*

You can also find his *Secret Agent Man* on *Penny Arcade, Dunhill Folk Rock Vol. 2*; and the instrumentals *Love-In (December)* on *Everything You Always Wanted To Know...* (CD) and *Wiggy (November)* on *Buzz Buzz Buzzzzzz Vol. 2* (CD). (SR/MW)

Lindy Blaskey and The Lavells

Personnel incl:	LINDY BLASKEY		A

45s:		Gonna Be Free / ?	(Red Feather # Unkn) 1961
	α	Wine Wine Wine/ Meet Me Tonight In Your Dreams	(Lavette LA 5001/2) 1963
		My Baby Done Left Me/ I'll Get Along Somehow	(Space SR 0003/4) 1965
		Papa Oom Mow Mow/ Would You Believe	(Space SR 0005/6) 1965
		You Ain't Tuff/Let It Be	(Space SR 0007/8) 1966
		Sweets For My Sweet/Movin' Away	(Space SR 0009/10) 1966
		You Ain't Tuff/Let It Be	(Challenge 59354) 1967
	β	Out Here In Vietnam/ What's Her Name	(Lavette LA 5005/6) 1966

NB: α as Lindy and The Lavels. β Lindy Blaskey solo effort.

Blaskey ran the Albuquerque-based Lavette label and fronted this New Mexican sixties pop outfit whose case for inclusion here is marginal. The second 45 was credited simply to Lindy And The Lavels. It all sounds rather passe now. At the time Blaskey produced or played on all the Lavette label's releases.

Compilation appearances have included:- *You Ain't Tuff* and *Le It Be* on *Mindrocker, Vol. 5* (LP), *Psychedelic Microdots Of The Sixties, Vol. 1* (CD) and *I Turned Into A Helium Balloon* (CD); *Papa Oom Mow Mow* on *The Big Itch*; and all of the **Lindy Blaskey and The Lavells** 45s (except their 1961 debut) can be found on *Chicago 60's Punk Vs. New Mexico 60's Pop - The Little Boy Blues And Lindy Blaskey And The Lavels* (LP). (VJ/MW)

The Blazers

45s:	Hula Hop Party/Vive La Campagne	(Golden Crest 552) 196?
	Beaver Patrol/Shore Break	(Acree 101) 1963
	Bangalore/Sounds of Mecca	(Acree 102) 1963
	Grasshopper/A Little Bit Of Slop	(Mundo 864) 1964
	Masked Grandma / Summer Sessions	(Dot 16623) 1964
	The Grasshopper Twist I / II	(Seaside 617) 196?
	Sit Down / ... Cried	(Singular 1003) 196?

This California (Hollywood?) band's forte was raucous guitar and sax instrumentals - e.g. *Beaver Patrol* on *Garage Punk Unknowns, Vol. 6* (LP). The 1963 *Battle Of The Beat* LP features two **Blazers** tracks - *Mag Wheels* and *Money* (the latter "with vocals"). *Strummin Mental Vol. 3* features a **Blazers** with an instrumental called *Poison* which may be this group.

A predominently instrumental/surf group, their inclusion here is thus marginal. No known connection to other **Blazers**... (VJ/MW)

The Blazers

Personnel incl:	D. HORD?	A
	H. HALTER?	A

45:	I Don't Need You/Lovin' To Do	(Brass 306) 1966

From Kansas City, Missouri. *I Don't Need You*, composed by D. Hord, is catchy garagey-beat with haunting electric piano. The Halter-composed flip is derivative saxy rockin' pop with echoes of DC5's version of Berry Gordy's *Do You Love Me*.

Compilation appearances include: *I Don't Need You* on *Monsters Of The Midwest, Vol. 1* and *Project Blue, Vol. 5* (LP). (VJ/MW)

The Blazers

45:	Graveyard / You Are My Sunshine	(Royalty no # (matrix 867L-5266)) 196?

Another **Blazers** (reportedly from Michigan) whose rare, unheard and uncompiled "garage" 45 comes with a picture insert. (MW)

Blessed End

Personnel:	KEN CARSON	bs	A
	MIKE PETRYLAK	drms	A
	STEVE QUINZI	keyb'ds	A
	JIM SHUGARTS	gtr	A
	DOUG TETI	vcls	A

ALBUM:	1(A)	MOVIN' ON	(Tns J 248) 1971 R2

NB: (1) counterfeited in 1992. Reissued officially on CD with a bonus track (Gear Fab GF-112) 1998 and on vinyl (Akarma AK 118) 2000.

This band came from Philadelphia and their album is excellent **Doors**-influenced psychedelia with similar keyboards and a vocalist who sounds like Jim Morrison. Consistently good throughout, this is recommended. All ten tracks were self-penned and arranged by the band. The

BLESSED END - Movin' On LP.

album was produced by Carl Sandell and recorded at "The New Sound" studios in Springfield, Pennsylvania. Teti's vocals are excellent and reach their peak on tracks like *Sometimes You've Got To Be Strong* and *Dead Man*. The album's finest moments include *Nightime Rider* and *Movin' On*, which both feature superb keyboard work.

Steve Quinzi adds: "Mike, Jim, Ken and myself were from Ridley Park Pa., a suburb of Philadelphia, whilst Doug was from Springfield. We are all from more or less working class backgrounds. We met in high school (Ridley High) and the band had already been together about a year when I joined in the Fall of 1970. Up until that that time they had two guitars. The other guitarist - Lenny Perchowsky - had left the band to go off to medical school. The first time we played together we hit it off both musically and personally, Mike and I became best friends and remain so to this day."

"We played at school dances, pep rallies, battle-of-the-bands, splash parties, and coffee houses around town. It was a wonderful time. As we became more familiar with each other, Jim and I began writing songs together. We got the idea to record the album when a local recording studio owner called me and asked if I'd be willing to loan him my farfisa organ (for use at a recording session) in exchange for recording time. Needless to say I accepted his offer. Over a period of about 3 months, Jim and I worked up what we felt were our ten best songs, and the band started rehearsing them. We recorded the whole album in one day (Summer '71). Like a Godsend, three very good paying gigs came up in one week, and we used the proceeds to finance the pressing of the albums. Ken designed the cover."

"Shortly after recording the album, Ken left the band to join the navy. This, as I was later to realize, was the beginning of the end for the band. The only other recording we did was a remake of *Can't Be Without Her* that we did with a sub bass player."

"Ken's replacement was Rick Swanson. Rick and Jim did not get along, so sometime later Jim left and was replaced by Ernie Fletsig. The band took on more a hard rock edge and began to play frat parties at the numerous fraternity houses in Philadelphia. We also played some cheesy clubs. Ernie suffered a mental breakdown brought on by a drug problem and had to leave the band. He was replaced by Lou Grieco who did not get along with Mike. By this time (winter '73) I was sick of what things had become and left to join a top 40 band playing nightclubs full-time. **Blessed End** was formally disbanded. A few months later Doug joined me in the new group, but a year later was fired after a bitter dispute with the other members. I never saw him again."

"I believe that Doug went to medical school. Mike became an auto mechanic. Ken and Jim worked in sheet metal fabrication at the Boeing helicopter plant in Ridley Park. Ken passed away from cancer a few years ago."

"I'm the only one who continued in music. I moved to Miami, Florida in '78, where I now do music production for advertising and corporate presentations. I am also a new age artist with two albums out (*The Pond*

and *Vanishing Rainforest*). A third *Rhythm Of The World*, on Pacific Time Records, is released in April '99 and is in an ambient-techno style. A dance remix of one of the cuts *Mirage* has also been released as a CD single."

Leading reissue label, Gear Fab have re-releasd *Movin' On* on CD.

Compilation appearances have included: *Movin' On* on Gear Fab's *Psychedelic Sampler* (CD). (VJ/CF/SQ/JSu)

Lynn Blessing

Personnel:	JOHN BECK	gtr	A
	LYNN BLESSING	vibes, hrmnca, vcls	A
	ROBERT HIRTH	gtr	A
	SNEAKY PETE KLEINOW	steel gtr	A
	WOLFGANG MELZ	bs	A
	MEL TEFORD	drms	A

ALBUM: 1(A) SUNSET PAINTER (Epic BN 26488) 1969 -

Originally from Cicero, Indiana, **Lynn Blessing** was a talented vibes and harmonica player who had previously played in **The Advancement** and **Cosmic Brotherhood**. His sole solo album is an instrumental mix of jazz, rock, folk and country, produced by the jazz flutist Paul Horn. The material contains five covers (Beatles's *Mother's Nature Son*, **Byrds**' *Child Of The Universe*, Dylan's *Country Pie*, a Judy Sill song and a surprising version of *Pinball Wizard*) plus some originals penned by **Blessing**, Hirth or Melz (*Cosmic Cowboy*, *Anacalypsis* and the only track with vocals, *Where There Is Grass*). The album begins with these words: "Just sit back, relax and take off your shoes".

The backing musicians were all part of these Hollywood sessionmen, equally at ease with jazz, psychedelia, rock or pop. John Beck also released a solo album and Wolfgang Melz went on to play with **Gabor Szabo**. (SR)

Michael Blessing

45s:	The New Recruit/	
	A Journey With Michael Blessing	(Colpix 787) 1966
	Until It's Time For You To Go/	
	What Seems To Be The Trouble Officer	(Colpix 792) 1966

Michael Blessing was in fact Mike Nesmith before he joined the **Monkees**. He was obviously searching for some direction, as these two singles manage to display four different styles! *The New Recruit* is a folk-rock novelty about a new Army recruit wishing to learn how to kill his enemies, whilst the flip is an excellent instrumental acid raga with lots of echo. On the second 45, *Until It's Time For You To Go* is an awful orchestrated ballad while the "B" side is a funny protest song a lá Dylan, complete with harmonica.

These two singles are now sought-after. (SR)

Arthur Blessitt and The Eternal Rush

Personnel:	J.P. ALLEN	bs	A
	ARTHUR BLESSIT	vcls	A
	BILL HARRIS	drms	A
	JIM McPHEETERS	vcls, gtr	A
	O.J. PETERSON	organ, vcls	A

ALBUM: 1(A) SOUL SESSION - AT HIS PLACE
(Creative Sound CSS 15308) c1969 R1

An extremely strange album, between stoned-on Jesus folk-rock and anti-drug propaganda, housed in a great psychedelic cover with a strange logo combining a cross and a peace sign, rock musicians and a portrait of Blessitt. **Arthur Blessitt**, a preacher "Minister to Sunset Strip", "tells it like it is" on two long tracks: *Soul Session* (14'23") and *White Slavery, Black Panthers And The Hell's Angels* (16'19"), O.J Peterson sings *Glory Hallelujah* and Jim McPheeters *Tell It To Jesus* and *God's Love*.

The liner notes explain that **Blessitt** has an all-night psychedelic Gospel Club at 8428 Sunset Strip in L.A., that his congregation is composed of acid heads, speed freaks, bikers, prostitutes, hippies, pushers, Black Panthers, Hell's Angels and that **Blessitt** is a preacher who cares enough to dare enter the strip joints, hippie pads, topless bars and love-ins with the message of Jesus-Christ! (SR)

Bliss

Personnel:	CORKY ALDRED	drms, vcls	A
	RUSTY MARTIN	bs	A
	BRAD REED	gtr, vcls	A

ALBUM:	1(A)	BLISS	(Canyon 7707) 197? R2

45:	Ride The Ship Of Fools/Gangster Of Love	(Canyon 34) 19??

A raw, heavy power trio from Arizona that recorded at Audio Recorders in Phoenix. The album bears no date, but sounds circa 1970 - comparable perhaps to **Wildfire**, **Banchee** or **Rock Island**. Roughly half the album is top-notch hard-rock and it seems surprising that it hasn't been reissued.

Despite having a similar catalogue numbering system, this label seems to be unrelated to the New Mexico-based Canyon Records that issued the **Xit** albums. The liner notes are written by an East Coast DJ who claims to have "watched them work this thing out for the last five years", suggesting that other recordings by this crew may exist. (VJ/CF)

BLISS - Bliss LP.

The Blokes

45:	All American Girl/Slander's Child	(Dante 2545) 1967

A very obscure 45 from the Michigan area. *All American Girl* was co-written by **Dick Wagner** (leader of **The Bossmen**). Great organ and protest lyrics - you could give it a spin on *Highs In The Mid-Sixties, Vol. 6* (LP). (VJ)

Bloodrock

Personnel:	RICK COBB	drms	AB
	ED GRUNDY	bs, vcls	ABC
	STEVE HILL	keyb'ds, vcls	ABC
	LEE PICKENS	ld gtr, vcls	A
	JIM RUTLEDGE	ld vcls	A
	NICK TAYLOR	gtr, vcls	ABC
	WARREN HAM	vcls, woodwind	BC
	RANDY REEDER	drms	C

HCP

ALBUMS:	1(A)	BLOODROCK	(Capitol ST 435) 1970 160
	2(A)	2	(Capitol ST 491) 1971 21
	3(A)	3	(Capitol ST 765) 1971 27
	4(A)	USA	(Capitol SMAS 645) 1971 88
	5(A)	LIVE (dbl)	(Capitol SVBB 11038) 1972 67
	6(B)	PASSAGE	(Capitol SW 11109) 1973 104
	7(C)	WHIRLWIND TONGUES	(Capitol EST 11259) 1973 -
	8(-)	BLOODROCK 'N' ROLL	(Capitol SM 11417) 1976 -

NB: (1), (2) and (3) were also released in the U.K. and Europe. (1) reissued on CD (Repertoire REP 4534-WY). (2) reissued on CD (Repertoire REP 4535-WY). (8) is a compilation, also released in Europe (SPR 80536).

HCP

45s:	α	Certain Kind/Certain Kind	(Capitol) 197? -
		D.O.A./Children's Heritage	(Capitol 3009) 1971 36
	α	Help Is On The Way/Short Interview	(Capitol) 197? -

NB: α promo only.

From Fort Worth, Texas, this band evolved out of **Crowd + 1** and desite quite a prolific output, met with little success. Probably their best known track is *D.O.A.* from their second album, which is a heavy organ-based threatening piece with police sirens, and is very much in the anti-war, anti-space race, anti-everything vein of the era. Another notable cut *Breach Of Lease* off their third album is intense, starting slowly and building up to an amazingly heavy climax. The live version is also particularly hot, whilst the humorous *Melvin Laid An Egg* from the debut is another musical high point.

Actually, Cobb didn't play on the debut album; Rutledge played drums on it and early on, **John Nitzinger** too was considered (somewhat) a member of the band and wrote or co-wrote many of the songs.

After the live album, Rutledge and Pickens left and Warren Ham joined as a vocalist and woodwind player for the last two albums. For their final album (*Whirlwind Tongues*), Cobb left and was replaced by drummer Randy Reeder who had previously played in **John Nitzinger**'s band and later played with a group called Alexis. Warren Ham later went on to form the Ham Brothers and released an album as such in 1977. Later still, he went on to play in former Kansas guitarist/keyboardist Kerry Livgren's Christian rock group AD for, we believe, two albums - *Time Line* and *Art Of The State*. In the eighties Warren was also in Black Rose.

Producer **Terry Knight** was involved in the first three albums after which the band did the production themselves or co-produced (Peter Granet and Ed Grundy on the last two albums; with John Palladino on USA). (CS/HH/RBc/MPo)

Blood, Sweat and Tears

Personnel:	RANDY BRECKER	trumpet	AB
	BOBBY COLOMBY	drms, vcls	AB
	JIM FIELDER	bs	AB
	DICK HALLIGAN	trombone	AB
	STEVE KATZ	gtr, vcls, flute	AB
	AL KOOPER	vcls, keyb'ds, ondioline	A
	FRED LIPSIUS	alto sax, piano	AB
	JERRY WEISS	trumpet	A
	DAVID CLAYTON-THOMAS	vcls	B
	(JOHN SIMON	keyb'ds, arrangements	A)

HCP

ALBUMS:	1(A)	CHILD IS FATHER TO THE MAN	
(up to			(Columbia CS 9619) 1968 47 -
1970)	2(B)	BLOOD, SWEAT AND TEARS	
			(Columbia PC 9720) 1969 1 -
	3(B)	THREE	(Columbia KC 30090) 1970 3 -

NB: All also released in England and Holland. Reissued on CD.

HCP

45s:	You've Made Me So Very Happy/	
(up to	Blues Part 2	(Columbia 44776) 1968 2
1970)	Spinning Wheel/More And More	(Columbia 44871) 1969 2

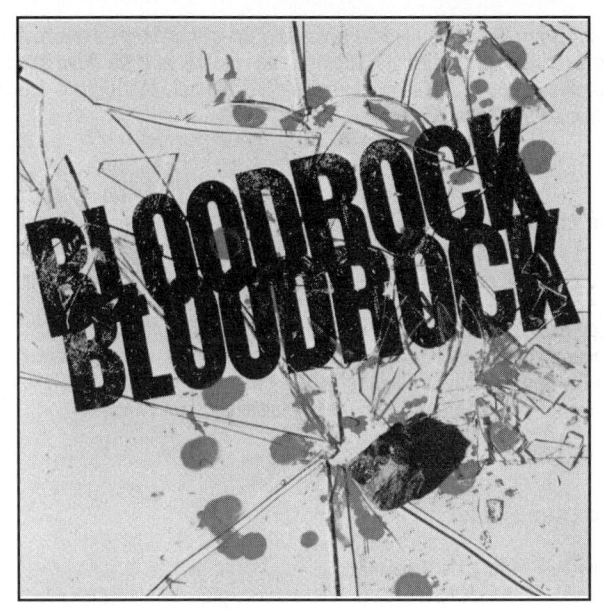

BLOODROCK - Bloodrock CD.

And When I Die/Sometimes In Winter	(Columbia 45008) 1969	2
Hi-De-Ho/The Battle	(Columbia 45204) 1969	14
Lucretia Mac Evil/Lucretia's Reprise	(Columbia 45235) 1970	29

When the **Blues Project** disintegrated in 1968, **Kooper** and Katz formed **Blood, Sweat and Tears** with Jim Fielder and several jazz musicians. Their new project was extremely ambitious and mixed rock, jazz and classical influences, with the use of various keyboards and impressive horn and string sections to produce "bigger sounds". The first album was produced by **John Simon** and benefited from an intensive promotion campaign from Columbia who launched them as an "art rock" group. Housed in an amusing cover (each musician was pictured with a look-a-like child seated on his knees), it combines songs written by **Kooper** with covers of **Tim Buckley** (*Morning Glory*), Randy Newman, Harry Nilsson (*Without Her*) and Carole King-Gerry Goffin (*So Much Love*). Steve Katz wrote the good *Meagan's Gypsy Eyes* and the album is definitely interesting, if not for everybody's taste.

The line-up changed for the next album, with **Kooper** being replaced by the Canadian shouter David Clayton-Thomas. **Blood, Sweat and Tears** then became commercially successful with hits like *Spinning Wheel* and *Lucretia McEvil* but most of the initial inventiveness had disappeared and the group became, along with Chicago, an example of these competent but lifeless groups with horns, sounding more like a big band than a rock group. (SR/VJ)

Bloody Mary

Personnel: anonymous   A

ALBUM: 1   BLOODY MARY   (Family Productions FPS 2707) 1974 R1

Solid New York area heavy rock band, **Sir Lord Baltimore** drummer / vocalist John Bradley is listed on the cover as an engineer, but may also have contributed musically to the recordings. (CF)

Mike Bloomfield

HCP

ALBUMS:
1. BLOOMFIELD/KOOPER/STILLS: SUPER SESSION (Columbia CS 9701) 1968 12 -
2. THE LIVE ADVENTURES OF MIKE BLOOMFIELD AND AL KOOPER (Columbia KGP_6) 1969 18 -
3. LIVE AT BILL GRAHAM'S FILLMORE WEST (Columbia CS 9883) 1969 - -
4. IT'S NOT KILLING ME (Columbia CS 9883) 1970 127 -

NB: There's also an album of 1964-5 material including previously unreleased material, *I'm Cutting Out* (Sundazed LP 5105) 2001.

Born in Chicago in 1943 into a wealthy family, **Mike Bloomfield** began recording in 1963 with Blues musicians: Yank Rachell, Sleepy John Estes, Big Joe Williams...

In 1965, he joined the **Paul Butterfield Blues Band** playing on their first two albums. Arguably the first American guitar hero, playing with Bob Dylan at the Newport Folk Festival and on *Highway 61 Revisited*, he also recorded two 45s with **Barry Goldberg** as **The Chicago Loop**. In 1967, he formed **The Electric Flag** and began guesting on albums of **Mother Earth**, **Moby Grape**, **Nick Gravenites**, **Janis Joplin**, **Barry Goldberg**, **Tim Davis**...

Bloomfield's solo career was first linked to the former **Blues Project** member **Al Kooper**, who he'd met during the sessions with Dylan. He then teamed up with **Nick Gravenites** for the *Live At Fillmore West* and *It's Not Killing Me*, albums, both recorded with Mark Naftalin and members of **Southern Comfort**. In 1973, **Bloomfield** recorded the bluesy *Triumvirate* with John Hammond and **Dr. John**. In 1975, after the lacklustre reunion of the **Electric Flag**, he formed the "supergroup" KGB with **Goldberg**, Ray Kennedy (ex-**Group Therapy**), Rick Grech (ex Family/Blind Faith) and the former **Vanilla Fudge** Carmine Appice. KGB was in fact a total failure.

Bloomfield went on to release several other solo albums, which fall out of the time frame of this book. He sadly died in 1981 of an accidental overdose.

As well as an artist, **Bloomfield** was also a producer, often working with **Nick Gravenites** or Norman Dayron. His credits are mainly on blues albums by the likes of Otis Rush, Sam Lay and James Cotton etc..

NB: for contractual reasons, **Mike Bloomfield** is sometimes credited as Makal Blumfeld, Fast Fingers Finkelstein, Great...

Compilation appearances have included *The 59th Street Bridge Song* on *Pop Revolution From The Underground* (LP). (SR)

The Bloomsbury People

Personnel:	PAUL DuJARDIN	bs	A
	GREG JANICK	keyb'ds	A
	DENNIS LANTING	gtr	A
	MIKE LORENZ	drms	A
	SIGMUND SNOPEK III	keyb'ds, trombone	A
	JAN WYDERKA	vcls	A

ALBUM: 1(A)   BLOOMSBURY PEOPLE   (MGM SE-4678) 1970 -

45s: α   Have You Seen Them Cry / Madeline   (Page 843K-1109) 1969
           Gingerbread Man/Witch Hellen   (MGM 14158) 1970

NB: α non LP tracks.

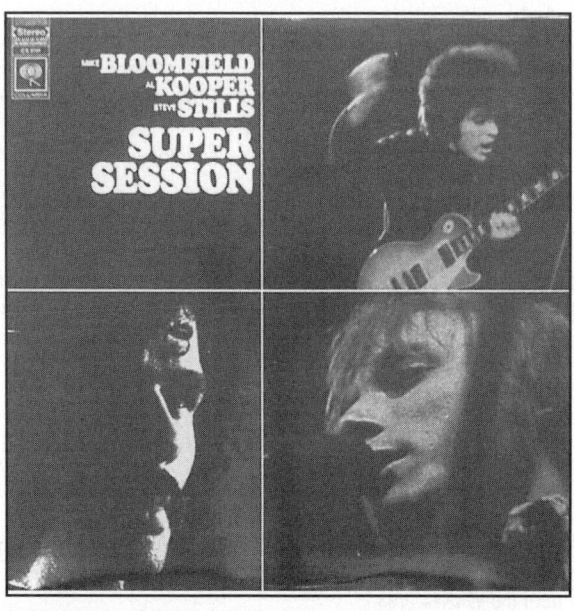

BLOOMFIELD, KOOPER, STILLS - Super Session LP.

Formed by students at the University Of Wisconsin, in Waukesha. Their debut 45 is orchestrated baroque-rock/pop with progressive moves and switches and tasty guitar flourishes. The second takes one of the more memorable LP tracks and the non-LP *Witch Hellen*, a catchy hard-rocker with fluid guitar also appears on *Psychedelic Unknowns, Vol. 5* (LP& CD).

Snopek later had his own band and then pursued a solo career. (VJ/SR/MW/CR)

The Blox

Personnel incl: R. TURNER   A

45s:	The Way I'm Gonna Be/	
	Say Those Magic Words	(Solar 235) 1967
	Hangin' Out/Everyday's Gonna Be Fun	(Solar 237) 1967

This outfit hailed from Houston in Texas. The brainchild behind them was Fred Carroll, who'd started the International Artists label but later sold the name to Lelan Rogers. Carroll produced both 45s and the band actually recorded material for International Artists although nothing was published.

Say Those Magic Words was a **Strangeloves**/Pomus-Schuman composition. *The Way I'm Gonna Be* is bouncy pop with a keyboard motif that brings to mind the Beach Boys' *California Girls*. *Hangin' Out*, an atypical sixties garage punk number with a short psychedelic interlude, can also be heard on *Flashback, Vol. 3* (LP), *Texas Flashback Vol. 3* (LP & CD), and *Highs In The Mid-Sixties, Vol. 23* (LP). (VJ/MW)

Bill Blue

ALBUMS:	1	INDIAN SUMMER BLUES	(Feather 6969-1) c1972 SC
	2	STREET PREACHER	(Feather 7001) 1975 SC

From Richmond, Virginia, a solid blues-rock singer. He kept on recording in the late seventies and released at least another album *Sings Like Thunder* in 1979 on Adelphi. (SR)

The Blue Angels

45:	Shake A Tail Feather /	
	Dance With Me Lynda	(Cap Records C-077) c1965

A Chicago garage group with good vocals, guitar and sax, produced by Stewart Productions. (SR)

Blue Ash

Personnel:	BILL BARTOLIN	vcls, gtr	AB
	DAVID EVANS	drms, vcls	A
	JIM KENDZOR	vcls	AB
	FRANK SECICH	vcls, bs	AB

ALBUMS: 1(A)	NO MORE NO LESS	(Mercury SRMI 0666) 1973 -
(selective)2(B)	FRONT PAGE NEWS	(Playboy 34918) 1978 -

A Youngstown-area Ohio band who were active from the late sixties through to the late seventies. They played a kind of Beatle-influenced melodic power-pop.

The Blue Banana

45:	Spicks And Specks/My Luv	(Kanwic Records HFCS-152) 1968

You'll find both sides of this Kansas band's 45, which originally came out in a picture sleeve, on *A Journey To Tyme, Vol. 5* (LP). They were a four piece from the Wichita area.

Their cover of the Bee Gees' *Spicks And Specks* adds resonant keyboards and a chorus of Turtlesque bah-bah-bah as a finale. *My Luv* is heavier keyboard-led pop with waspish fuzz and a great solo that buzzes around in an Easterly direction. (VJ/MW)

The Bluebeards

45:	Come On - A My House/I'm Home	(Date 2-1547) 1967

Ohio has been suggested as a likely source of this bunch. Ross Bagdasarian appears to have had a hand in this whirling dervish of a neo-Eastern pop-psych ditty. They look back to a Beatles 1964 take-off on the flip, complete with mop-top shakin' falsetto 'ooo's. (MW)

The Blue Beats

Personnel:	LANCE DRAKE	ld gtr	A
	JONATHAN LEE	gtr	A
	LOUIS MAZZA	drms	A
	PETER ROBBINS	bs	A

ALBUM:	1	BEATLE BEAT	(A.A. RECORDS 133) 1964? SC?

45s:	β	Superman/I Can't Get Close	(Beowoolf 1061) 196?
		Extra Girl/She's The One	(Allen Associates # unkn) 1966
		Extra Girl/She's The One (PS)	(Columbia 43790) 1966
	α	Born In Chicago/	
		I Can't Get Close (To Her At All)	(Columbia 4-44098) 1967

NB: Flip to α is a re-recorded version of the flip to β.

A classy Invasion-influenced outfit from Danbury, Connecticut who produced some quality 45s with commercial potential - except that they seemed to be running at least a year behind the latest sounds.

Extra Girl, a Lee-Drake composition, is chunky Invasion beat with a Beatlesque charmer on the flip, composed by Lee and Robbins. Their superb R'n'B cover of **Nick Gravenites**' *Born In Chicago* is also given a '65 Yardbirds-style treatment with reverbed harmonica and Fender wall of sound. The Lee-Drake composed flip is minor-mood Merseybeat (Searchers-style but without the 12-string jangle). Both Columbia 45s were produced by Bob Wyld and Art Polhemus, who also handled the **Blues Magoos**.

After a change of personnel and name they released one last excellent haunting pop 45 in July 1967 , as the No. 1 - *The Collector / Cracks In The Sidewalk* (Kapp K-824).

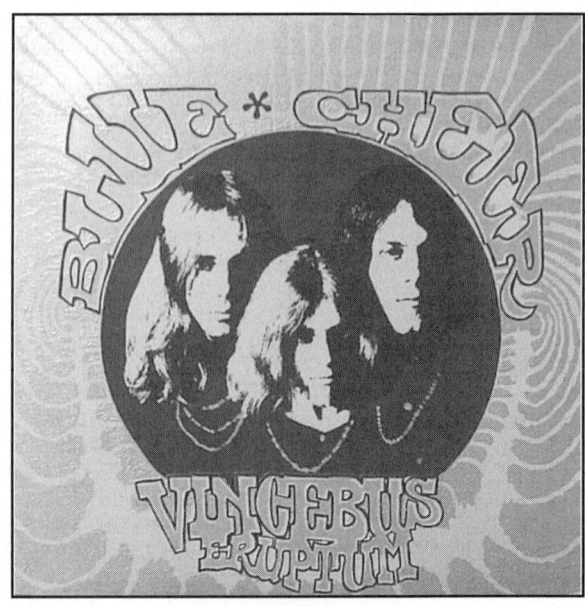

BLUE CHEER - Vincebus Eruptum LP.

BLUE CHEER - Outside Inside LP.

Then in 1968 a 45 appeared, credited to 'The All Night Workers' - *The Collector / Misery* (Mercury 72833). To these ears *The Collector* is exactly the same track as the Kapp 45 but with different (slightly weaker) lead vocals. There are no obvious connections other than writer Sonny Curtis; even the publishing house is different. The Mercury 45 was "imagineered by: Joey and Steve with Bill at Syncron '68".

Compilation appearances have included: *Extra Girl* on *New England Teen Scene, Vol. 2* (LP) and *Born In Chicago* on *Psychotic Reactions* (LP). (MW/MM)

The Bluebird

Personnel:	DAVID BAROH	vcls, gtr	AB
	PHIL KLITGAARD	drms	AB
	KEVIN MARIN	bs	AB
	FRANK "TONY" PUGEL	ld gtr	AB
	JOHN SOLTERO	ld gtr	B

NB: Line-up 'A' August '68 to February '69. Line-up 'B' Feb '69 to April '74.

ALBUM:	1	COUNTRY BOY BLUES	(Picc-A-Dilly PIC 3382) 1980 R1

45s:	Modessa/Goin' Down	(Burdette 101) 1970
	Billy Drake/I Shall Be Released	(Jerden 918) 1970

This band came from Mercer Island, Washington. *Modessa* is a **Byrdsian** folk-rock ballad reminiscent of *Chesnut Mare* and about a ship wreck. The flip is a much more rocky upfront affair, though still with good harmonies and some excellent ringing guitars. The first two 45s and six other tracks were also assembled onto the *Country Boy Blues* album. Three members of **Bluebird** reputedly recorded the Grand Theft album, on which David Baroh recalls: "We kept this a closely guarded secret for years, but with the release of the new Grand Theft CD *Hiking Into Eternity*, we decided to come clean with the truth!"

Compilation appearances have included *Modessa* and *Goin' Down* on *The History Of Northwest Rock, Vol. 3* (CD) and *Billy Drake* on *History of Northwest Rock, Vol. 5*. (MW/DR)

The Bluebird

45s:	Windy Linda/Touch	(Dilley 113) 197?
	Here I Am/From The Country	(Dilley 115) 197?

A different **Bluebird**, unconnected to the Washington mob. (VJ/MW)

The Blue Bus

Personnel:	DAN HABEN	drms	A
	GARY KOUTNIK	gtr, vcls	A
	CHRIS LARSON	vcls, gtr, bs, drms	A
	DOUG LaTANT	bs, drms	A
	MIKE LaTANT	bs, keyb'ds, drms, vcls	A
	ROMAN OLES	gtr, vcls	A

ALBUM: 1(A) YOUR MIND'S MOVING TOO FAST (Vee LC 10259) 2001

A teenage garage band who appear not to have released a 45 in their lifetime. One track, *Black Candles*, resurfaced on the Euro CD version of *The Magic Cube* in 1999, not long before the retrospective LP appeared on a German label.

Unless there's an insert missing, no historical background is provided except for a list of personnel against each track. From this it can be gleaned that they recorded these demos between 1967 and 1970 with a fluid line-up featuring several different combinations of the above in two's three's and four's. They were built around guitarist/vocalist Roman Oles, who appears on all cuts except the sole cover, **Love**'s *Signed D.C.*.

Their repertoire runs from surfy garage instrumentals through folk-punk and on to psychy-garage. I'd guess this band to be from South California: - there's a strong **Byrds** flavour in the minor-mood material and especially in the closing *Jam #1*, which could be uncharitably described as someone attempting *Eight Miles High* after a few pints too many; a nod in the direction of **The Electric Prunes** with some siren-like sustain and feedback; and the excellent *People Looking At Me* has a whiff of **Love** in the belligerent strumming and hispanic flavour. (MW)

Blue Cheer

Personnel:	DICK PETERSON	bs, vcls	ABCDEFG H I
	LEIGH STEPHENS	gtr, vcls	AB
	PAUL WHALEY	drms	ABC F H? I
	BURNS KELLOGG	keyb'ds	BCDE
	RANDY HOLDEN	gtr	C
	NORMAN MAYELL	drms, gtr	DE
	BRUCE STEPHENS	keyb'ds, bs	D
	GARY YODER	gtr, hrmnca	E
	TONY RAINIER	vcls	F
	ANDREW MacDONALD	gtr, vcls	G I?
	DAVE SALCE	drms	G
	DIETER SALLER	gtr	I

HCP

ALBUMS:	1(A)	VINCEBUS ERUPTUM	(Philips 600.264) 1968 11 -
	2(B)	OUTSIDE INSIDE	(Philips 600.278) 1968 90 -
	3(C/D)	NEW! IMPROVED! BLUE CHEER	
			(Philips 600.305) 1969 84 -
	4(D)	BLUE CHEER	(Philips 600.333) 1969 - -
	5(E)	THE ORIGINAL HUMAN BEING	
			(Philips 600.347) 1970 188 SC
	6(E)	OH PLEASANT HOPE	(Philips 600.350) 1970 - SC
	7(F)	THE BEAST IS BACK	(Megaforce MRI 1069) 1985 - -
	8(G)	BLITZKREIG OVER NUREMBERG	
			(Thunderbolt THBL091) 1990 - -
	9(H)	HIGHLIGHTS AND LOWLIVES	
			(Nibelung Records 23010-412) 1990 - -
	10(I)	DINING WITH THE SHARKS	
			(Nibelung Records 306.0010.1) 1991 - -

NB: (1) also issued in mono (R2). (1-7) reissued on CD. (8) recorded live in Germany 1988. (9) also issued on CD (23011-421). (1-4) and (6) reissued on vinyl in original sleeves and on CD in digipak by Akarma, (AK 011, AK 012, AK 016, AK 017 and AK 018 respectively) 1998. There's also a 16 track 'Best Of' CD called *Good Times Are Hard To Find*. Fans will also be interested in *Live And Unreleased '68/'74* (Captain Trip CTCD 023) 1996, which contains three tracks from the "Steve Allen" show 1968 with five unreleased cuts from Gold Star studios in 1974.

HCP

45s:	Summertime Blues/Out of Focus (PS)	(Philips 40516) 1988 14
	Just A Little Bit/Gypsy Ball	(Phillips 40541) 1968 92
	Feathers From Your Tree/Sun Cycle	(Philips 40561) 1968 -
	West Coast Child Of Sunshine/	
	When It All Gets Old	(Philips 40602) 1969 -
	All Night Long/Fortunes	(Philips 40651) 1969 -

Hello L.A., Bye Bye Birmingham/ Natural Men	(Philips 40664)	1970 -
Fool/Ain't That The Way	(Philips 40682)	1969 -
Pilot/Babaji (Twilight Raga)	(Philips 40691)	1970 -

A San Francisco-based heavy rock group who specialised in high volume rock. They were popular around the Bay Area but never caught on nationally or internationally. Their debut album is best remembered for its heavy electrified version of Eddie Cochran's *Summertime Blues*, which became a No. 14 U.S. hit in the Summer of 1968. It also contained a powerful version of *Rock Me Baby* and four other compositions all played with characteristic energy and volume. For many their second album with Paul Whaley's excellent heavy rock drumming was their best, but *Original Human Being* was their most psychedelic, particularly on songs like *Babaji*. The band operated originally between 1967-71 but reformed in 1975, 1978 and 1985. On the final occasion they recorded an album comprised of new recordings and reworks of old classics like *Summertime Blues*, *Babylon*, *Parchment Farm* and *Out Of Focus*.

Prior to **Blue Cheer**, Paul Whaley's phenomenal drumming had ventured forth with **The Oxford Circle**, whose stunning 45 pointed towards the sonic-assault territory that **Blue Cheer** would claim. Whaley's fellow pioneers included pre-**Kak** members Dehner Patten and Gary Yoder (the latter would feature in the 1970 **Blue Cheer** line-up). Whaley's circle of influence did not end there. He inspired cousin Randy Hammon to start his own garage band ventures, whose trail led to the **Savage Resurrection**. Dick Peterson had recorded a brace of 45s before **Blue Cheer** - with brother Jerri and Danny Mihm, later of the **Flamin' Groovies**, in Sacramento's **Group "B"**.

Band offshoots included **Pilot** (with Bruce and **Leigh Stephens**, Micky Waller and Martin Quittenton (ex Steamhammer)), **Silver Metre** and **Mint Tattoo**. After **Pilot**, Bruce Stephens recorded two solo albums: *Bruce Stephens* (World) 1978 and *Watch That First Step* (Strawberry) 1981.

Leigh Stephens also recorded a solo album entitled *Red Weather* (Phillips PHS 600.294) 1969 R1. It's an excellent psychedelic record in the vein of **Quicksilver** and was recorded at London's Trident studios with help of such notables as Nicky Hopkins, Kevin Westlake, Micky Waller and Eric Albrona. It also had a U.K. release (Philips SBL 7897) 1969 R2, and has recently been counterfeited on CD. **Leigh** also recorded a rare promo-only 45, *Red Weather/Saki Zwadoo* (Philips 40628) 1969, which may have been a promotional-only release and had a non-album 'B' side. He recorded a second solo album in 1971, *And A Cast Of Thousands* (Philips / Charisma CAS 1040), however, despite a cover of *Jumpin' Jack Flash* it is marred by too many background singers and horns.

The recently issued *Live And Unreleased Vol. 1* (Captain Trip CTCD 023) 1996, CD contains live recordings from 1968 and an unreleased demo from 1974 which was produced by **Kim Fowley**. In addition *Vol. 2* also contains live recordings from San Jose in 1968 and some rare studio cuts. Both CDs were issued in Japan. In 1986, Rhino issued *Louder Than God*, a best of compilation.

BLUE CHEER - New! Improved! LP.

Norman Mayell had previously played with **Sopwith Camel**.

Compilation appearances have included: *Summertime Blues* on *Nuggets, Vol. 1* (LP), *Highs Of The Sixties* and *Best Of 6O's Psychedelic Rock* (CD); *Summertime Blues* and *Out Of Focus* on *Electric Food* (LP); *Summertime Blues* and *Out Of Focus* on the bootleg compilation *California Easter*, and *The Red House* on *California New Year*. (VJ/AMe/GBs/DU/CF/CLe/SR/GW/MW)

The Blue Chips

Personnel incl:	?? LANE		A
	?? SIMON		A
	PAUL TETLEBAUM		A

45:	Where / Keep Looking For Love	(Roaring 804)	1967

A high school band from Rego Park, New York who were formed in 1964 after seeing The Beatles on the Ed Sullivan Show. Three years later they got to release their sole 45, produced by Pete Antell, who was also involved with **The Wild Ones**.

Where is a ringing, raucous stomper; it has reappeared on *Sixties Rebellion, Vol. 7* (CD & LP) and *Psychedelic States: New York, Vol. 1* (CD). (MW/MM)

The Blue Echoes

Personnel incl:	TOM COLLINS	drms	A
	ERIC GULLIKSEN	12 string gtr, bs, vcls	A
	TOM ZAGRYN	ld gtr, vcls	A

45s: α	Blue Bell Bounce/Tiger Talk	(Bristol B-101)	1963
	Roseanne/How Do I Tell Her	(BEP 103)	1964
β	Respectable / Young Blood	(BEP 104)	1964

NB: α later issued on Lawn (L-225) a subsidiary of Swan and later reissued on Lost Nite and Itzy (11). β Most copies destroyed - roughly 12 copies known to exist.

From Worcester, Massachusetts, this outfit got together at Worcester Polytechnic Institute and are notable for including pre-**Orpheus** bassist Eric Gulliksen. Their first 45, originally issued on Tom Zagryn's Bristol label, was a local hit - significant enough to be picked up by Swan. Eric recalls: "If you listen hard, you can hear Tom Collins' bass drum pedal squeaking throughout".

The group's name came from their use of home-built tape-delay echo units. Eric: "...we used the echo units on vocals and guitars. I played electric 12-string and doubled on bass guitar. Our initial 'claim to fame' was that we were playing a New York style of R&R-cum-R&B called 'shake' with a beat typified on *Tiger Talk* - nobody else in the area could play this stuff".

Local station WORC-AM, known to the industry for sniffing out future trends and hits, picked up on *Blue Bell Bounce*. It reached No. 5 on their charts and generated much label interest. The group signed with Swan who issued it on their Lawn subsidiary. "Unfortunately it was released on the day that JFK was shot and, as you may know, for several weeks no radio station played any R&R at all, so the record died".

For the second 45, the Bristol label was renamed BEP ('Blue Echo Productions'). Incidentally Tom Zagryn also produced **Squires'** *Going All The Way* 45, but sold the rights, when they signed to Atco. He also produced their earlier 45 as **The Rogues'** too.

Eric adds:- "How in the name of all of the gods of music did you ever come up with the 'Respectable' 45? When we recorded it we went to a different pressing plant than the one we had been using, to try to save money (mistake no. 1). Unfortunately this company went into bankruptcy before we received product (we'd already paid for it). We screamed and yelled and threatened lawsuit, and finally received product. However, they had rushed it so much that they had evidently applied the labels before the ink was dry; they were all smudged, print had transferred from one to another, etc. The sound wasn't too bad, but nothing to write home about. Anyway, at the end of the day, we never released this record, and destroyed most of the copies (mistake no. 2). There may be as many as a dozen copies in existence (Tom and I each have one), but there wouldn't be any more than that. The record numbers on Bristol and BEP are sequential (B-101 through B-104). B-102 was a record which Tom and I wrote and produced - *Andromeda/Swamp Rat* - by a group from Gardner, MA, named Kenny and the Night Riders. It was a good record, sold very well in Gardner, but never went anywhere else".

Gulliksen had also previously worked with a few folk groups of various names. One of these, including Jack McKenes had a Kennedy Tribute 45, *The Man* as **The College Boys**. He played concurrently with **The Blue Echoes** and Wanderers until the Fall of 1963, resigning from the latter as **The Blue Echoes**' popularity and commitments were increasing and they were about to release their debut 45.

Compilation coverage has so far included: *Tiger Talk* on *Scum Of The Earth, Vol. 1* (2nd Edition LP), *Scum Of The Earth, Vol. 2* (LP) and *Scum Of The Earth - Complete Collection* and *Blue Bell Bounce* on *Oldies I Forgot To Buy* (CD). (MW/EGn)

The Blue Feeling

Personnel:	ROSS BALDOCK	ld gtr	A
	STEVE FEUDNER	gtr	A
	TOMMY RAML	drms	A
	JACK WESTFALL	bs	A

45: Tell Her No / And My Baby's Gone (Night Owl J-6861) 1968

A local Sheboygan, Wisconsin act who made a valiant stab at the Zombies' *Tell Her No*. A difficult one to tackle given the class of the original; the lead vocalist is no Colin Blunstone and the timing is tricky... there's a couple of awkward moments. Give 'em 7 out of 10 for effort. Their upbeat Moody Blues cover (also done by **The Jynx** and **Stillroven**) is an easier task and comes off fine.

Tommy Raml was previously with **The Matadors**. (MW/GM)

Blue Mountain Eagle

Personnel:	RANDY FULLER	bs, gtr, vcls	A
	BOB "B.J." JONES	ld gtr, vcls	A
	JOEY NEWMAN	ld gtr, keyb'ds, vcls	A
	DON PONCHER	drms, vcls	A
	DAVID PRICE	gtr, vcls	A

ALBUM: 1(A) BLUE MOUNTAIN EAGLE (Atco SD 33-324) 1970 SC

NB: (1) also released in France (Atco 503 048) 1970.

45: Yellow's Dream/Marianne (Atco 6770) 1970

NB: *Marianne* is a non-LP cut.

A short-lived Californian band who came into existence in July 1969, when **Dewey Martin** left **New Buffalo**. The remaining band members were left with a recording deal struck on the strength of **Martin**'s previous connections with **Buffalo Springfield**, so all that was needed was a simple name change and to recruit a Joey Newman (ex- **Don and The Goodtimes** / **Touch**) as a replacement.

Produced by Bill Halverson and recorded in L.A. in August and December 1969, the album will interest guitar lovers. The highlight and opening track, *Love Is Here*, is a memorable guitar-driven heavy rocker and others like *Feel Like A Bandit*, *Loveless Lives* and the more mellow *Yellow's Dream* feature more good guitar work. Others exhibit more than a touch of country influence and the album becomes a bit flat in places on Side Two. All the songs were written by group members, except *Trivial Sum*, a Terry Furlong/Richard Bowen composition.

In 1970 **Blue Mountain Eagle** played on bills with **Love**, Eric Burdon and War, Pink Floyd and **Jimi Hendrix**. Fuller left in May 1970 to join **Dewey Martin's Medicine Ball** and the band split in late 1970 after Poncher left to (briefly) join **Love**.

BLUE MOUNTAIN EAGLE - Blue Mountain Eagle LP.

Randy Fuller was **Bobby Fuller**'s brother and later had his own band. David Price, Bob Jones and Don Poncher went on to work with Augie Meyer (**Sir Douglas Quintet**) for his *Western Head Music* album in 1973. Don Poncher became a successful session man, working with Bobby Whitlock, Jim Price, Chris Jagger, Joe Cocker and also Arthur Lee (on his *Vindicator* album, 1972). (VJ/SR/NW)

Blu-Erebus

| Personnel incl: | LARRY DEATHERAGE? | vcls | A |
| | BRUCE EVANS? | gtr, vcls | A |

45: Willowgreen / Plastic Year (King James 8-9255) 1968

A Mt.Airy, North Carolina group who rose from the ashes of **The Nomads** (of *Thoughts Of A Madman* fame). A highlight on *An Overdose Of Heavy Psych* CD, *Plastic Year* "features some killer fuzz/wah wah and lurking organ. From the opening chord to the final chorus, this is a prime example of four-star late sixties psychedelia. Lyrically the song tells of one heck of a screwed-up chick...". *Willowgreen* is a mellow pop song with harpsichord and wah wah guitar. This establishes a link to another **Nomads**-associated outfit, Willow Green who released a cheesy fuzzy-pop 45 composed by Evans-Deatherage - *Fields Of Peppermint / Fields Of Peppermint (Instr)* (Whiz #619) 1968/9. (MW/ELn)

Blue Ridge

Personnel:	GEOFF DANIELIK	gtr, vcls, hrmnca	A
	JOHN HAUSER	drms	A
	CLAUDE HUGEL	bs, gtr, vcls	A
	GENE WOEFEL	ld vcls	A

ALBUM: 1(A) BLUE RIDGE (No label) 1974 R2

Local New York rural/hard-rock, similar to **Headstone**. Only 100 copies were pressed, according to a band member and the album comes in a generic nature scene cover with a blank back. The album contains an abysmal rock & roll medley and the rest of the material is also rather uninspired. (CF/SR)

Blue Rose

Personnel:	TERRY FURLONG	gtr	A
	STU PERRY	drms	A
	DON PONCHER	drms	A
	DAVE THOMSON	gtr, bs	A
	JOHN URIBE	bs	A

ALBUM: 1(A)　BLUE ROSE　　　　　　　(Epic 31252) 1972 -

A melodic rock group from California. It may interest some readers as Terry Furlong was in the **Grassroots** and Don Poncher drummed for **Blue Mountain Eagle**, Augie Meyers and Arthur Lee. (SR)

Blue Sandelwood Soap

Personnel:
	DAVE BERGSLAND		A
	DAN KNUDSEN		A
	STEVE LUCK	bs	A
	HARLEY TOBERMAN		A

CD:　1(A)　LORING PARK LOVE INS　(Get Hip GHAS 5006) 1996

NB: (1) is a retrospective compilation containing all the band's existing recordings.

45:　Friends I Haven't Met Yet/
　　Love! pirT　　　　　　　(Aesop's Lable 103) 1968

Hailed from Minneapolis. Max Waller drew the 45 to my attention. The 'A' side is a mellow psychedelic ballad with a catchy instrumental refrain - keyboard dominated with brass that's not too intrusive. The flip features nonsensical psychedelic lyrics and is somewhat fragmented - a strange trip (shades of the **West Coast Pop Art Experimental Band**?).

Harley Toberman, also produced some of **T.C. Atlantic**'s material and wrote material for them under his nickname "Toby". (VJ/MW/JSz)

BLE SANDELWOOD SOAP - Loring Park Love-Ins CD.

Blue Scepter

45:　Out In The Night/Gypsy Eyes　　(Rare Earth 5040) 1972

This outfit was actually **SRC**. Their excellent *Gypsy Eyes* can be found on *Echoes In Time, Vol. 1* (LP) and *Echoes In Time, Vol's 1 & 2* (CD). (VJ)

Blues Company

Personnel:
	TOM JURECK	bs	A
	HAMILTON ROTH	drms	A
	TIM WARD	gtr, vcls	A

45s:
Experiment In Color/She's Gone	(Great Lakes 3002)	1968
Experiment In Color / She's Gone	(AMG 10108)	1968
You're Dead My Friend/I'm Comin'	(Pear 517684 2202)	1968
Love Machine/B.C. Boogie	(Pear 5l7684 2203)	1969

A late sixties outfit from Bay City, Michigan, they had earlier released a 45 *Life Has Been So Good To Us / Playthings 5X5* under the name **Ides of March**. The 45 had no label name and is extremely rare! They changed their name after hearing about Chicago's **Ides of March**.

Their first 45, *Experiment In Color*, is a killer acid-tinged freak-out with lots of wah-wah guitars, backed by *She's Gone*, with its haughty vocals and fine driving guitars. The final follow-up, *Love Machine* features a fuzzy freakout and is almost as good as the debut.

Compilation appearances have included: *Experiment in Color* on *Highs In The Mid-Sixties, Vol. 5* (LP), *Let 'Em Have It! Vol. 1* (CD) and *Fuzz, Flaykes, And Shakes, Vol. 4* (LP & CD); *Love Machine* on *Michigan Mayhem, Vol. 1* (CD); and both *Love Machine* and *She's Gone* on *Highs In The Mid-Sixties, Vol. 6* (LP).

Tim Ward later went solo recording as **Timmothy**. (VJ/KBn/CF/MW)

Blues Image

Personnel:
	MANUEL BERTEMATTI	drms, vcls	ABC
	SKIP CONTE	keyb'ds	ABC
	MALCOLM JONES	bs	ABC
	JOE LALA	perc	ABC
	MIKE PINERA	gtr, vcls	AB
	DENNIS CORRELL	vcls	B
	KENT HENRY	gtr	C

HCP

ALBUMS:
1(A)	BLUES IMAGE	(Atco SD33-300)	1969	112 -
2(B)	OPEN	(Atco SD33-317)	1970	147 -
3(C)	RED WHITE AND BLUES IMAGE	(Atco SD33-348)	1971	- -

NB: (3) also issued in France and the U.K..

EP:　1　Clean Love / Pay My Dues /
　　　　Parchman Farm　　　　　(Atco 33317) 1970

HCP

45s:
Can't You Believe In Forever / Parchman Farm	(Image 5833)	1968 -
Lay Your Sweet Love On Me / Outside Was Night	(Atco 6718)	1969 -
Ride Captain Ride / Pay My Dues	(Atco 6746)	1970 4
Gas Lamps And Clay / Running The Water	(Atco 6777)	1970 81
Rise Up / Take Me Back	(Atco 6798)	1970 -
Behind Every Man / It's The Truth	(Atco 6814)	1971 -
Ride Captain Ride /(Van Morrison) Into The Mystic (DJ Promo)	(Warner Bros. Pro 499)	1971 -
Ride Captain Ride / (Robert John) The Lion Sleeps Tonight	(Atlantic 13119)	197? -

An energetic mix of blues, rock and hard rock from Miami/Tampa, Florida. They enjoyed a Top 5 hit with *Ride Captain Ride* in 1970. Their guitarist, Mike Pinera, would leave in 1970 to join **Iron Butterfly** and later **Ramatam**. He was replaced by Kent Henry (ex-**Charity** and **Genesis**). The group presumably disbanded when Henry later joined **Steppenwolf**. Joe Lala became a studio percussion player and Manuel Bertematti would team up again with Pinera for the sole album by the New Cactus Band in 1973 on Atlantic. (SR/TI/VJ)

The Blues Magoos

Personnel:
	GEOFF DAKING	drms	A
	MIKE ESPOSITO	gtr	A
	RON GILBERT	bs	A
	RALPH SCALA	vcls, organ	A
	EMIL THIELHIEM	vcls, gtr	ABC
	RICHIE DICKON	perc	B
	ROGER EATON	bs, vcls	B
	ERIC KAZ	hrmnca, vcls, keyb'ds	BC
	JOHN LIELLO	vibes, perc	BC
	COOKER LO PRESTI	bs	C
	JOEY STEC	gtr, vcls	

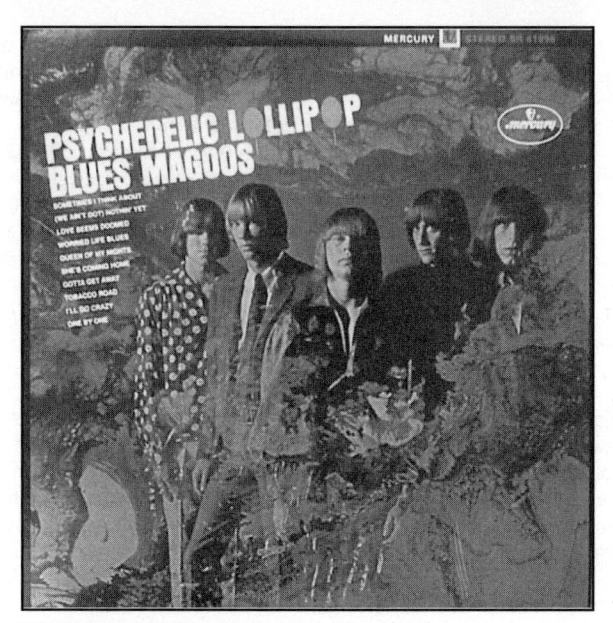

THE BLUES MAGOOS - Psychedelic Lollipop LP.

				HCP
ALBUMS:	1(A)	PSYCHEDELIC LOLLIPOP	(Mercury SR 61096) 1966	21 SC
	2(A)	ELECTRIC COMIC BOOK	(Mercury MG 21104) 1967	74 SC
	3(A)	BASIC BLUES MAGOOS	(Mercury ST 61167) 1968	- -
	4(B)	NEVER GOIN' BACK TO GEORGIA	(ABC S697) 1969	- -
	5(C)	GULF COAST BOUND	(ABC S710) 1970	- -

NB: (1) has been reissued on CD. (2) originally issued with insert.

				HCP
45s:	α	So I'm Wrong And You Are Right/ People Had No Faces	(Verve Folkways 5006) 1966	-
		Tobacco Road/ Some Times I Think About You	(Mercury 72590) 1966	-
		(We Ain't Got) Nothing Yet/ Gotta Get Away	(Mercury 72622) 1966	5
		Let Your Love Ride/Who Do You Love?	(Ganim 100) 1967	-
		Let Your Love Ride/Love Seems Doomed	(Ganim 100) 1967	-
		Pipe Dream/ There's A Chance We Can Make It	(Mercury 72660) 1967	60/81
		One By One/Dante's Inferno	(Mercury 72692) 1967	71
		I Wanna Be There/ Summer Is The Man	(Mercury 72707) 1967	133
		Life Is Just Cher O'Bowlies/ There She Goes	(Mercury 72729) 1967	-
		Jingle Bells/ Santa Claus Is Coming To Town	(Mercury 72762) 1967	-
		I Can Hear The Grass Grow/ Yellow Rose	(Mercury 72838) 1968	-
		Heartbreak Hotel/ I Can Feel It (Feelin' Time)	(ABC 11226) 1969	-
		Never Goin' Back To Georgia/ Feelin' Time (I Can Feel It)	(ABC 11250) 1969	113
		Gulf Coast Bound/Sea Breeze Express	(ABC 11 283) 1970	-

NB: α also reissued by Verve Folkways in 1967. There's also: a rare French EP with PS: (We Ain't Got) Nothing Yet/I'll Go Crazy/Love Seems Doomed/Tobacco Road (Mercury 126221) 1967; and a rare promo only EP from Brazil (We Ain't Got) Nothing Yet/Love Seems Doomed/One By One/Dante's Inferno (Mercury DC 68.000) 1968.

This group came from New York's Bronx area, were originally known as **Bloos Magoos** and gigged regularly around Greenwich Village before Mercury offered them a recording contract in 1966. Their title is misleading, for they specialised in quasi-psychedelic electrical music rather than the blues.

Their best moments are on their early albums and (We Ain't Got) Nothing Yet from their first album was a U.S. No. 5 in 1966. It also contained a fine version of **J. D. Loudermilk**'s Tobacco Road.

The second album contained a thin comic book full of all sorts of offers to turn you on whilst you played the album. Musically it was their magnum opus. The opening cut, Pipe Dream, had a good garage organ sound; There's A Chance We Can Make It featured some fine psychedelic guitar work; Life Is Just A Cher O'Bowlies had a gorgeous beginning followed by more guitar mayhem and Side One also contained a discordant, extended cover of Van Morrison's Gloria. Side two was more restrained, although Take My Love was an uptempo song with catchy organ work and the penultimate track, Rush Hour, included a storming electric guitar extravaganza.

On stage they appeared in Vidal Sassoon hairstyles and specially designed 'electric' suits. The fifth album, made with a changed personnel, marked a downward turn however, which was not arrested by subsequent studio efforts. In their final days, however, Joey Stec from **The Millenium** joined the band which coincided with a resurgence as a live attraction.

When the group disbanded, Eric Kaz went solo and recorded two lame seventies pop rock albums. In 1976, he also formed American Flyer, a country-pop group produced by George Martin, with Craig Fuller (ex-**J.D. Blackfoot** and Pure Prairie League), Steve Katz (ex-**Blues Project** and **Blood, Sweat and Tears**) and Doug Yule (ex-**Velvet Underground**). He kept on working with Fuller in Fuller/Kaz (CBS, 1978). Cooker Lo Presti went on to play with Ringo Starr.

In 1967 (We Ain't Got) Nothing Yet was covered by England's Spectres who soon became Status Quo.

Compilation appearances have so far included: (We Ain't Got) Nothin' Yet on Nuggets, Vol. 1 - The Hits (LP); Excerpts From Nuggets (CD); More Nuggets (CD); Nuggets From Nuggets (CD); Battle Of The Bands (CD); Tobacco Road on Nuggets - Original Artyfacts From The First Psychedelic Era 1965-1968 (Dble LP) and Nuggets Box (4-CD); I Can Hear The Grass Grow on Nuggets, Vol. 11 (LP); Dante's Inferno on Songs We Taught The Fuzztones (LP & CD); Jingle Bells on Turds On A Bum Ride, Vol. 1 (Dble LP); Who Do You Love on Turds On A Bum Ride, Vol. 2 (Dble LP); Jingle Bells and Who Do You Love on Turds On A Bum Ride, Vol. 1 & 2 (CD); Let Your Love Ride on Turds On A Bum Ride, Vol. 4 (CD); There She Goes and Rush Hour on Electric Food (LP); and Dante's Inferno, Jingle Bells, Let Your Love Ride, People Had No Faces, So I'm Wrong, Who Do You Love on Filling The Gap (4-LP); The band also recorded a commercial for Great Shakes which was based around the riff of We Ain't Got Nothin' Yet. It has resurfaced on Psychotic Reactions and Great Shakes Shake-Out (EP). (VJ/MW/JFr/SR/ML)

Blues Messengers

45s:	High Wednesday (I'll Stay With You) / Whadya Come Back For?	(Adonis 05/06) 1968
	Yesterday Girl / I Won't Ask For More	(Adonis 0702) 1968/9

THE BLUES MAGOOS - Electric Comic Book LP.

An obscure group with two late sixties platters on a Fort Lauderdale label - it has also been suggested that they were from Hollywood, Florida. *High Wednesday*, a strange acid-rocker with some **Iron Butterfly** moves, gets another airing on *Psychedelic States: Florida Vol. 1* (CD). (MW)

The Blues Project

Personnel:			
ROY BLUMENFELD	drms		ABCDEF
TOMMY FLANDERS	vcls		A
DANNY KALB	ld gtr		ABC EF
STEVE KATZ	gtr, vcls		ABC
AL KOOPER	org, vcls		AB
ANDY KULBERG	bs, flte		ABCD
JOHN McDUFFY	keyb'ds		C
RICHARD GREENE	violin		D
JOHN GREGORY	gtr, vcls		D
DON KRETMAR	bs, sax		DEF
DAVID COHEN	gtr, keyb'ds		F
BILL LUSSENDEN	gtr		F

HCP

ALBUMS:
- 1(A) LIVE AT THE CAFE A GO GO (Verve FT 3000) Mar. 1966 77 SC
- 2(B) PROJECTIONS (Verve FTS 3008) Nov. 1966 52 SC
- 3(B) BLUES PROJECT AT THE TOWN HALL (Verve FTS 3025) Jul. 1967 71 SC
- 4(D) PLANNED OBSOLESCENCE (Verve FTS 3046) 1968 - -
- 5(-) AL KOOPER, ROY BLUMENFELD, DANNY KALB, STEVE KATZ, ANDY KULBERG OF THE BLUES PROJECT (comp) (Verve Forecast FTS-3069) 1968 - -
- 6( ) BEST OF THE BLUES PROJECT (Verve FTS 3077) 1969 199 -
- 7(E) LAZARUS (Capitol ST 872) 1971 - -
- 8(F) BLUES PROJECT (Capitol EST 11017) 1972 - -
- 9(A) REUNION IN CENTRAL PARK (MCA 8003) 1973 - -

NB: (4) and (6) also issued in France. (3) reissued on CD in Japan. (8) reissued on vinyl (Pickwick SPC-3657) 1979. CD releases include *Reunion In Central Park* (1973), *'79 Reunion LP* and a *Best Of* CD with five extra tracks. *Anthology*, a double set containing 36 tracks, was also released on Chronicles in 1996, whilst Rhino released *The Best of The Blues Project* (R 170165) 1989, which includes an interesting **Al Kooper** interview and one unreleased version of *Wake Me, Shake Me*. Finally, there's *Bleeker Street Blues* (Goldtone GT-015) 2000, a German CD containing 13 tracks recorded live at the Matrix in San Francisco on 7th September 1966.

HCP

45s:
- Back Door Man/Violets Of Dawn (Verve Folkways 5004) 1966 -
- Catch The Wind/ I Want To Be Your Driver (Verve Folkways 5013) 1966 -
- Where There's Smoke, There's Fire/ Goin' Down Louisiana (Verve Folkways 5019) 1966 -
- α Wake Me, Shake Me/? (Verve Folkways 5028) 1966 -
- I Can't Keep From Crying Sometimes/ The Way My Baby Walks (Verve Folkways 5032) 1966 -
- No Time Like The Right Time/ Steve's Song (Verve Folkways 5040) 1967 96
- β Gentle Dreams/ Lost In The Shuffle (Verve Folkways 5063) 1967 -

NB: α unissued. β both tracks non album. There's also a rare French EP with picture sleeve: *No Time Like The Right Time/I Can't Keep From Crying Sometimes/Steve's Song/The Way My Baby Walks* (Verve 519 905), 1967.

This white blues-band simply burst onto the New York music scene between 1965 and 1966. Founder **Danny Kalb** had contributed two acoustic guitar tracks to a 1964 Elektra blues-folk compilation album *The Blues Project*. After hearing **Tim Hardin** playing electric guitar in Greenwich Village soon after he decided to form his own band to play a similar combination of jazz, blues, R&B, and rock. Roy Blumenfeld was the first to join and soon after Andy Kulberg was enlisted. Artie Traum was the fourth member in what was at first called The Danny Kalb Quartet. The band gigged extensively in Greenwich Village between April and June 1965 but Danny left to go to England for the Summer. He only returned when the possibility of a recording contract was broached but Artie Traum had left in the meantime and a new rhythm guitarist was needed. Steve Katz, previously with the **Even Dozen Jug Band**, was recruited at around the same time as **Flanders**, who'd been in the Boston-based **Trolls**, joined.

They were originally going to record for Columbia and recorded a couple of tracks (*Violets Of Dawn* and *Back Door Man*) in September/October which were later released as their first single for Verve records. The session man on piano was **Al Kooper** who was offered a permanent gig with the band. In his early days, **Al Kooper** had been a Tin Pan Alley/Brill Building production writer (*This Diamond Ring*, *Who Wears Short Shorts*, etc.) and was with Bob Dylan on *Highway 61 Revisited* and *Blonde On Blonde*, playing the organ in a way that would influence many American and English groups. **Kooper** kept on doing sessions with New York-based singers during his stay with the group.

In October 1965, the band were offered a residency at the Cafe A Go Go in Greenwich Village where they began to get a huge following. Here, their first 'live' album was recorded and highly acclaimed. The band were one of the city's main live attractions playing three concerts in Central Park in the same year. In January 1966, **Flanders** left after an argument and signed with Verve as a solo artist. The vocals were now to be shared, with Danny doing the blues numbers, Steve the folk, and Al the R&B and rock tunes. The *Live At The Au Go Go* album was released soon after with most of the material recorded after **Flanders**' departure. It sold over 20,000 copies in its first month of release.

They expanded their horizons from New York City and toured the country, eventually headlining San Francisco's newly opened Avalon Ballroom and causing a sensation (Grace Slick for example becoming thoroughly dissatisfied with her band, **The Great Society**, after witnessing the **Project** in action).

Their deliberate attempt to get a hit single with the **Rascals**-style number *Where There's Smoke There's Fire* (which Danny hated) failed and they proceeded to record the classic *Projections* album which contained great studio versions of some of their concert favorites, like the 11-minute *Two Trains Running* and the jazzy *Flute Thing* as well as folk ballads and full-pelt rock. Their next attempt at a hit, *No Time Like The Right Time* actually had some chart success but unfortunately Danny was beginning to show signs of mental collapse and Al, who was unwell also, left the band after a dispute over his wish to add horns to the band. John McDuffy joined as replacement and played with them at the Monterey Festival and on the *Lost In The Shuffle* 45 (which he wrote).

However the band had virtually disintegrated by this time and Verve released the *Live At The Town Hall* album, which was actually only partially live, many of the tracks being unused studio cuts with overdubbed fake applause. Meanwhile Danny was hospitalized after a two-week acid trip but even so the band played a final series of gigs at the Au Go Go in September 1967 (with Danny's brother Jonathan playing in his place). Immediately after, Al and Steve formed **Blood, Sweat and Tears** and Andy and Roy moved to San Francisco while waiting for Danny to recover before starting a new version of **The Blues Project**. As Danny failed to get better

THE BLUES PROJECT - Projections LP.

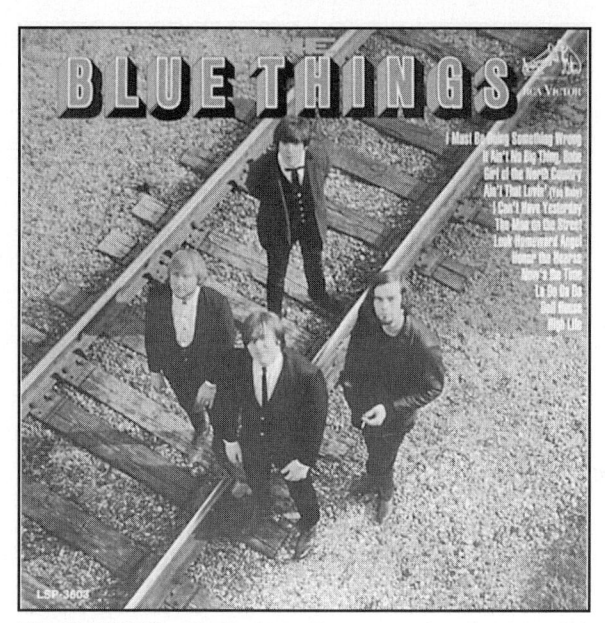

THE BLUETHINGS - The Bluethings LP.

they recruited violinist Richard Greene, guitarist John Gregory, and bassist Don Kretmar to record another album, *Planned Obsolescence*, in fulfillment of their Verve contract. The new band, however, soon took the name **Seatrain** (in fact, *Planned Obsolescence* had included one track entitled *Niart Aes Hornpipe* - "Seatrain" backwards).

1971 saw **Kalb** and Blumenfeld reviving the group with Kretmar. This trio recorded the under-rated *Lazarus* in London, under the nominal guidance of Shel Talmy (although Roy and Danny say his contribution was minimal). Following this, David Cohen (ex-**Country Joe and The Fish**), ex-member **Flanders**, and guitarist Bill Lussenden were added for the *Blues Project* album. The band eventually split in 1972, but were reunited in early 1973 for a one-off gig in Central Park which MCA recorded and released on an album.

The Blues Project are usually considered one of New York's finest bands and their first three albums (two of which capture their exciting 'live' sound) are recommended.

Tommy Flanders left the **Blues Project** at the request of Verve Records, who wanted to pursue his career as a solo artist, but dropped him after his first recording, the splendid *Moonstone* (Verve Forecast FTS-3075) 1969. After the group finally disbanded, he moved to California and left the music business to pursue a career as a male model for catalogues and later worked for an advertising agency.

In 1969, **Danny Kalb** issued an excellent blues album with another ex-**Even Dozen Jug Band** member, Stefan Grossman, *Crosscurrents* (Cotillion SD 9007) and also backed the blues singer Jimmy Witherspoon on his Bluesway albums. Of fragile health (apparently reinforced by an involuntary "chemically induced" nervous breakdown in 1967), **Kalb** did not perform for nearly two years. He stopped recording between 1973 and 1993, until the release of an acoustic blues album in France on Legend Records.

Roy Blumenfeld kept on doing sessions with Mark Spoelstra and many others. He is still recording with **Nick Gravenites** (*Don't Feed The Animals*, 1994).

Compilation appearances include *No Time Like The Right Time* on *Nuggets - Original Artyfacts From The First Psychedelic Era 1965-1968* (Dble LP), *Nuggets, Vol. 11* (LP) and *Nuggets Box* (4-CD). (VJ/SR/MW/LP)

The Blues Spectrum

ALBUM: 1 WE WERE THE BLUES SPECTRUM
(Private Pressing) 1970 R1?

Their album contains garagey blues jams with some horns. (SR)

The Blues Uv Purple

See **The Powers Uv Purple** entry.

The Bluethings

Personnel:	MIKE CHAPMAN	ld gtr	AB
	BOBBY DAY	drms	A
	RICHARD SCOTT	bs	AB
	VAL STECKLEIN	vcls, gtr	A
	LARRY BURTON	vcls	B
	RICHARD LARZALERE	drms	B

ALBUM: 1(A) THE BLUETHINGS   (RCA LSP 3603) 1966 R2

NB: (1) reissued on CD and LP. There have also been some comprehensive retrospective releases. On Vinyl, there's *The Bluethings Story Vol. 1 1964-5*, *Vol. 2 1965-6* and *Vol. 3 1966* (Cicadelic 973, 974 and 975 respectively) 1987; whilst on CD there's *The Bluethings Story Vol. 1* and *Vol. 2* (Collectables COL-CD-0518, and COL-CD-0540) 1993. Both formats contain more or less the same material, with the CDs featuring some additional material but with a couple of tracks omitted.

45s: α La Do Do Do/Just Two Days To Go (Damen Acetate no #) 1964
α Love's Made A Fool Of You/
Silver And Gold   (Damen Acetate no #) 1964
α P's And Q's/So You Say   (Damen Acetate no #) 1964
Mary Lou/Your Turn To Cry   (Ruff 1000) 1965
Pretty Thing-Oh/Just Two Years Ago   (Ruff 1002) 1965
La Do Da Da/
I Must Be Doing Something Wrong (PS)   (RCA 8692) 1965
Doll House/Man On The Street   (RCA 8860) 1966
The Orange Rooftop Of Your Mind/
One Hour Cleaners   (RCA 8998) 1966
You Can Live In Our Tree/Twist And Shout   (RCA 9203) 1967
Somebody Help Me/Yes, My Friend   (RCA 9308) 1967

NB: α as The Blue Boys.

From Hays in a sedate college town in rural West Kansas came **The Bluethings**, who were one of the best acts to come out of the Midwest in the sixties. They formed in 1964 as The Blue Boys cutting the three acetate 45s listed above, before changing names in 1965. Starting out very much in the folk-rock and Merseybeat mould, they recorded two 45s for Ruff, which led to them mistakenly being considered a Texas band. They then switched to RCA and their *La Do Da Da* was a drivin' rework of an old Dale Hawkins rocker. The follow-up *Doll House* was quite a strong folk-rock ballad later included on their first album. The late Summer of 1966 marked an important turning point in the band's career. Now influenced by the wave of psychedelia sweeping the world and the enormously influential *Revolver* album by The Beatles, their live concerts at this time were legendary and included a fair splattering of Beatles' songs. *The Orange Rooftop Of Your Mind* single exemplified their new sound and marked the zenith of their recording career. The song is about a girl caught up in the rat race, but she can't take the pace so her mind is slowly snapping. The flip concerned a psychiatrist whose only hold on sanity came from his patients. Both songs were characterised by an East Indian sound with a Middle East organ and guitars tuned and played like sitars. After the release of the 45 Val left the group, suffered a nervous breakdown and was hospitalised. He was replaced by Larry Burton and early in 1967 the band returned to the studio and cut two originals - *Caroline* and *You Took The Fight*, which can be heard on *The Bluethings Story, Vol. 3*, along with a number of covers of popular songs like *Talk, Talk*. In May 1967 they released another great psychedelic single. *You Can Live In Our Tree* - an ecological protest song, interesting for its sound effects and rhythmical diversity - which had been recorded back in September 1966 and still featured Val on vocals. The flip - a rather interesting version of The Isley Brothers' *Twist And Shout* - was by the new band. They made their final recording foray in September 1967 with a fine cover of The Spencer Davis Group's song *Somebody Help Me* backed by *Yes, My Friend*, another group original, before eventually fading away.

Their album, released at the zenith of their career in 1966 is recommended, but if you can't find this the three record series issued by Cicadelic Records in 1987 (which **Stecklein** helped compile) and it's equivalent two volume CD is more accessible. *Vol. 3* of the vinyl is essential to connoisseurs of psychedelia. It includes five previously unreleased **Stecklein** compositions from Spring 1966:- *It Ain't No Big Thing, Babe, You Can't Say We Never Tried, High Life, Now's The Time* and *Take Seven* (co-written with Mike Chapman); *The Coney Island Of Your Mind* (an early version of *Orange Rooftop* written by Val and recorded by him and Mike alone); both sides of *The Orange Rooftop* and *Tree* 45s and the later band's two originals from early '67.

The band also made a plethora of posthumous compilation appearances including: *The Orange Rooftop Of Your Mind* on *Mayhem & Psychosis, Vol. 1* (LP), *Mayhem & Psychosis, Vol. 1* (CD) and *Psychotic Moose And The Soul Searchers* (LP); *The Orange Rooftop Of Your Mind, Doll House, La Do Da Da, Twist And Shout* and *You Can Live In Our Tree* on *Mindrocker, Vol. 9* (LP); *Somebody Help Me* on *Midwest Garage Band Series - Kansas* (LP); *Your Turn To Cry* on *Monsters Of The Midwest, Vol. 3* (LP); *Ain't That Lovin' You Baby* and *Twist And Shout* on *Texas Punk Groups From The Sixties* (LP) and *Sixties Archive, Vol. 2* (CD); *Twist And Shout* on *Flashback, Vol. 2* (LP) and *Texas Flashbacks, Vol. 2* (LP); *The Orange Rooftop Of Your Mind, Pretty Thing - Oh* and *Twist And Shout* on *Monsters Of The Midwest, Vol. 1*; *You Can't Say We Never Tried* and *Pennies* on *Green Crystal Ties, Vol. 2* (CD); *Waiting For Changes* and *Hollow* on *Green Crystal Ties, Vol. 5* (CD); and *Talk, Talk* on *I Wanna Come Back From The World Of LSD* (CD).

Val Stecklein put out a folky solo LP, *Grey Life* (Dot DLP 25904) (SC) in 1968 and two 45s:- *Sounds Of Yesterday/Say It's Not Over* (Dot 17200) in 1968 and *All The Way Home/I Wonder Who I'll Be Tomorrow* (Dot 1723 1) in 1969. He also played and recorded with **Ecology** in 1970 and in 1964 had previously played in folk group The Impromtwos, who issued a private-press album titled *On Campus*.

Sadly **Val Stecklein** died in May 1993. (VJ/MW/LP)

Blue Wood

| 45: | Turn Around/Happy Jack Mine | (Jet Set JSR 45 4) 1966 |

Cool uptempo beat with some fine fret-work that accelerates considerably in the break. It's a shame that the flip's a Country and Western-styled pop novelty. The label was based in Santa Barbara, California. (MW)

Boa

Personnel:	RICHARD ALLEN	drms	A
	TED BURRIS	vcls, bs	A
	BOB MALEDON	piano, organ	A
	PAUL MANNING (aka CAPTAIN HOOK)	gtr, vcls	A
	BRIAN WALTON	organ, piano	A

ALBUM: 1(A) WRONG ROAD (Snakefield SN 001) 1971 R3

NB: (1) reissued on CD by Gear Fab (GF-113) 1998, with two bonus tracks. Also reissued on vinyl (Gear Fab/Comet GFC 419LP).

This late sixties Michigan band came from the Rochester, a small town 30 miles from Detroit. Their album was a limited edition private pressing and is now rare and sought-after. Quite a varied album, it is well worth searching out. The opening cut, *Never Come Back*, which features some fine keyboard and guitar work, sounds similar to **The Doors** and **Blessed End**. Hard-rockers, like the title track and *I Think I Been Had*, which include competent guitar work, appear alongside gentle, keyboard dominated ballads and soft rockers like *You Tell Me You Love Me, Don't Go Away* and *Angelisa*, the finest track on the album which boasts some unusual piano work.

Compilation appearances have included: *Wrong Road* on Gear Fab's *Psychedelic Sampler* (CD). (VJ)

Boa Constrictor and Natural Vine

| Personnel: | GEORGE FIGGS | all instruments | A |
| | BEN SYFU | all instruments | A |

BOA - Wrong Road LP.

ALBUM: 1(A) BOA CONSTRICTOR AND NATURAL VINE (Vanguard 65111) 1968 -

A folk duo from Baltimore with some psychedelic influence, who did not release any 45s for Vanguard. Their album was recorded with a Nagra recording machine in Searsmont, Maine and then at Apostolic Studios, New York.

Ben Syfu also played on the **Family Of Apostolic** album. (VJ/SR)

The Boards

| 45: | You're A Better Man Than I/ Please Tell Me Why | (Yardly 400) 1966 |

A British-influenced garage band who played in Dallas, Texas during the mid-sixties. *Please Tell Me Why* can be heard on *Shutdown '66* (LP). (VJ)

Bobby and I

| ALBUM: | 1 BOBBY AND I | (Imperial) c1968 SC? |

| 45s: | Catching The Time In Your Hand/ Love Is For The Sharing | (Imperial 66348) 1968 |
| | On Rose Walk/ Be Young, Be Foolish, Be Happy | (Imperial 66436) 1968 |

Probably from California, a soft pop male/female duo with some psychy overtones. (SR)

Bobby and The Dukes

| 45: | Ah, Ah, Ah/Come On Along With Me | (Philips) c1965 |

An obscure group, whose music ranges between garage and white R&B. (SR)

Bocky and The Visions

| Personnel incl: | BOCKY DEE'O (aka ROBERT DiPASQUALE) | vcls | A |

45s:	Mojo Hanna / Spirit of '64	(Redda 1501) 1964
	I Go Crazy/Good Good Lovin'	(Redda 1504) 1964
	To Be Loved/The Bounce	(Redda 15050) 1964

Mojo Hanna / Spirit of '64	(Philips 40224)	1964
I'm Pickin' Petals/I'm Not Worth It	(Philips 40242)	1964
α Listen To The Beat Of My Heart/ Give Me A Minute Of Your Time	(Philips 40279)	1965

NB: α released as by Bocky.

From Cleveland, Ohio. They are best known for *Spirit Of '64* on which they implore The Beatles to 'move over, don't be so selfish... we did the twist and sang the shout long before you ever sung it out'! Later they say 'We're the spirit of '64. This is the beginning of the Twist and Shout War!

At the end of the decade **Bocky** was to be found in **Wazoo**.

Compilation appearances have included: *The Spirit Of '64* on *Highs In The Mid Sixties, Vol. 9* (LP); and *I'm Not Worth It* on *Pride Of Cleveland Past* (LP). (VJ/MW/GGl)

Bodacious D.F.

Personnel:	MARTY BALIN	vcls	A
	DEWEY DAGREAZE (GREG DEWEY)	drms, perc, vcls	A
	CHARLIE HICKOX	keyb'ds, vcls	A
	MARK RYAN	bs, vcls	A
	VIC SMITH	gtr, vcls	A

ALBUM:	1(A)	BODACIOUS D.F.	(RCA APL1-0206) 1973 -

NB: (1) reissued (RCA AVL1-4243) 1978.

After the commercial failure of **Grootna**, Marty Balin formed **Bodacious D.F.** with the former **Grootna** members Vic Smith and Dewey Dagreaze (aka Greg Dewey, ex-**Mad River**). Their only album is an interesting West-Coast effort with excellent "acid" guitar parts and Balin vocals. Anna Rizzo (ex-**Grootna**) guests on one track: *Good Folks* and the album is co-produced by Doc Storch and Bill Wolff (of **Peanut Butter Conspiracy**, **Fusion**, **Sound Machine**...).

Mark Ryan had earlier played with **Quicksilver Messenger Service** and **Country Joe**. Vic Smith later played with Flying Island, a progressive rock group. (SR)

Bodine

Personnel:	DAVID BROOKS	keyb'ds	A
	ERIC KARL	gtr, vcls	A
	JON KELIEHOR	drms	A
	STEPHEN LALOR	gtr, vcls	A
	KERRY MAGNESS	bs	A

ALBUM:	1(A)	BODINE	(MGM SE 4652) 1969 -

45:	Easy To See/ Keep Lookin' Through My Window	(MGM 14088) 1969

Following Jon Keliehor's departure from **The Daily Flash** in June 1967, he briefly worked with an old Seattle friend and former **Kingsmen** bass player Kerry Magness in Pam Polland's band, Gentle Soul. Only a demo of one song was recorded before the project fell apart. The pair soon got picked up by Paul Rothchild who was auditioning musicians for what would become **Rhinoceros**. Also involved in the auditions was ex-**Fantastic Zoo** singer/guitarist Eric Karl. The threesome opted out of the auditions early on and met up with Lalor (who had disbanded **The Daily Flash** by this point) and David Brooks, who had met Lalor in San Francisco. The quintet decided to form a new band in early 1968 initially called Popcorn.

The group were active mainly in the Northwest and in early 1969 changed name to **Bodine**. Signed to MGM, the band recorded an album which has some fine moments. Produced by Bill Cowsill, he was obviously influenced by George Martin's work with The Beatles because the album contains some tracks that have a distinctive Beatle sound. Eric Karl was the main songwriter/singer although Magness and Lalor also contributed. Karl however, produced the strongest material. The highlights include the rockers, *Short Time Woman* and *Into My Life*. (NW)

The Bodrockers

Personnel:	MIKE BECK	bs	A
	KIBI BROWNLOW	piano	A
	LEON McNEAL		A
	RALPH SHELTON III		A
	PAUL TROUSDALE	vcls	A

45:	I've Waited For Too Long/ Born Not To Ramble	(Bolo 755) 1965

From Seattle, Washington, both sides of their 45 were written by Beck and Trousdale, who went on to play in the acclaimed **Brave New World**. (DR/MW)

The Boenzee Cryque

Personnel:	SAM BUSH	vcls	A
	GEORGE GRANTHAM	drms	A
	TERRY JONES	gtr	A
	MALCOLM MITCHELL	gtr	A
	DAN NASH	gtr	A
	JOE NEDDO	bs	A
	RUSTY YOUNG	gtr	A

45s:	The Sky Gone Gray / Still In Love With You	(Chicory 406) 1967
	The Sky Gone Gray / Still In Love With You	(Uni 55012) 1967
	You Won't Believe It's True / Watch The Time	(Uni 55022) 1967

NB: There is also a 12" acetate of *Ashbury Wednesday* from the "Psych Out" soundtrack in existence.

From Colorado, this act later migrated to Los Angeles. Their first 45 was produced by Frank Slay and was a No. 1 hit in Colorado. The 'B' side is a cover of the **Beau Brummels** song, but both songs are basically horn dominated pop.

Boenzee Cryque also have one track, *Ashbury Wednesday*, featured in the classic cult hippie film "Psych Out", and on the associated *Psych Out* soundtrack album. The track is featured in the movie where Jack Nicholson's Band "Mumblin Jim" are performing on some ballroom stage complete with oil lights a throbbin! It features an inverted *Purple Haze* riff and is a exploito-classic.

George Grantham and Rusty Young went on to form Pogo which later became **Poco**. Sam Bush was later in New Grass Revival and had a solo career. (SR/PPe/MW/BC/MDo/JRe)

Curt Boettcher

ALBUM:	1	THERE'S AN INNOCENT FACE	(Elektra EKS 75037) 1973 -

NB: (1) reissued on CD (Elektra AMCY-2830) 199? and (Sundazed SC 6184) 2002. There's also a retrospective CD: *Misty Mirage* (Poptones MC 5007CD) 2001.

45s:	Share With Me/Sometimes	(Together 117) 1969
	I Love You More Each Day/Such A Day	(Elektra 45834) 1973

An important figure of the Los Angeles scene, **Curt Boettcher** began in the early sixties with a folk group, **The Goldebriars** and then became a prolific songwriter, arranger and producer, founding **Ballroom**, **The Millenium** and **Sagittarius**; and working with **The Association**, **Lyme and Cybelle**, Your Gang, **Friar Tuck**, **Michele**, **Eternity's Children** and many many more.

His productions are generally characterized by their inventive multi-layered harmonies and imaginative arrangements. His only solo album is in the same vein and, if his sales were low, it is now beginning to be sought-after by collectors of soft psych and Californian sophisticated folk-rock with harmonies, indeed as are all the records bearing his name.

Curt Boettcher died in 1987, when still only 43.

Misty Mirage is a retrospective CD, comprising unreleased session tracks from 1969, together with demos, outtakes and radio ads. (SR)

Boffalongo

Personnel:	KEITH GINSBERG	gtr	A
	LARRY HOPPEN	bs, gtr, vcls	AB
	BASIL MATYCHAK	keyb'ds, vcls	AB
	RITCHIE	drms	AB
	DOC ROBINSON	bs, vcls	B
	WELLS KELLY	drms	B

ALBUMS:	1(A)	BOFFALONGO	(United Artists UAS 6726) 1969 -
	2(B)	BEYOND YOUR HEAD	(United Artists UAS 6770) 1970 -

NB: (2) also released in the U.K. (United Artists UAG 29130) in 1970.

45s:	Mr. Go Away/Tomorrow Not Today	(United Artists 50607) 1969
	Please Stay/Mr. Go Away	(United Artists 50656) 1970
	Dancing In The Moonlight/ Endless Question	(United Artists 50699) 1970

From the New York area. Their first album is essentially progressive rock and features some pretty good guitar work and keyboards. Their second album, however, is not as good. Both were produced by Steve and Eric Nathanson, who also worked with **Omnibus** and **Music Asylum**.

When the group disbanded, several members went on to form King Harvest and later Orleans. Keith Ginsberg played with the Blues Brothers in 1980. (VJ/SR)

Boggs Water and Sewage

Personnel:	REMINGTON CUSSEN	ld gtr	A
	JOEL "BJ" HOWELL	drms	A
	WILBUR HUNDLEY	bs	A
	DON "SWBN" LOVETT	vcls, perc	A
	BOB MOORE	gtr	A
	KEITH "TOWNIE" WINKLER	keyb'ds	A
	various	hrns	A

From Charlottesville, Virginia, **Boggs Water and Sewage** (1968-71) were a consummate cover band. WUVA radio disk jockey Lovett's smooth vocals backed by the driving rhythm section of Howell and Hundley made the band popular at fraternity parties and mixers, playing dance favorites from the great R&B, soul and beach music artists of the era. Known as Charlottesville's answer to **Chicago Transit Authority**, BW&S added several jazz-rock covers to its repertoire before disbanding in 1971 when, remarkably, the core band members graduated.

BO GRUMPUS - Before The War LP.

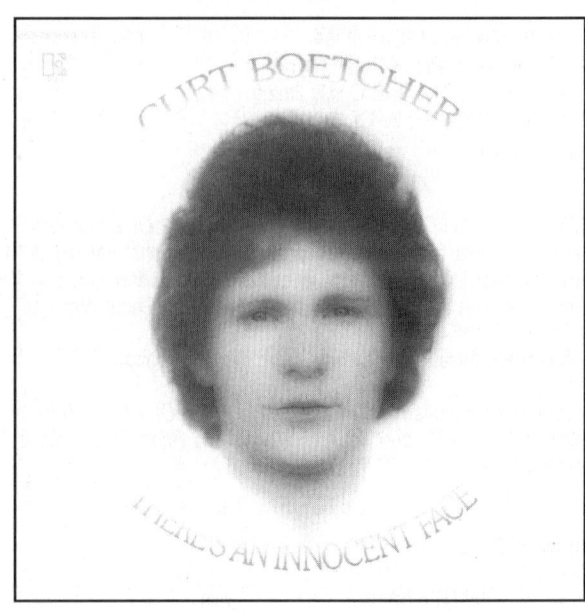

CURT BOETTCHER - There's An Innocent Face... CD.

Bo Grumpus

Personnel:	RONNIE BLAKE	drms	A
	JIM COLEGROVE	bs, gtr	A
	JOE HUTCHINSON	gtr, bs	A
	ED MOTTAU	gtr	A

ALBUM:	1(A)	BEFORE THE WAR	(Atco SD 33.245) 1968 -

EP:	1	BO GRUMPUS	(Atco EP C 4562) 1968

NB: (1) contains four cuts from their LP.

This band's album was produced by the late Felix Pappalardi and includes N.D. Smart (of **The Remains**) on drums. *Sparrow Time* and *Think Twice* have good fuzz guitar but it's predominantly a soft folk-rock LP. Mottau, Colegrove and Blake went on to form the rockier **Jolliver Arkansaw**.

Jim Colegrove was originally from Springfield, Ohio, and was co-founder of **Teddy and The Rough Riders**, a rock'n'roll outfit who made three singles and an album for Tilt/Huron/Mega City labels in the early sixties. In 1966, he was with the intriguingly named **Thee Rubber Band**, and the same year moved to New York to play with **The Hobbitts** (whether the same act as **The Hobbits**... is unknown). Later, in 1967 he switched from guitar to bass, and joined **Bo Grumpus**. Subsequently, he's recorded with **Hungry Chuck**, and **The Juke Jumpers**. Jim's story also sees him play alongside Canadian act **Ian and Sylvia**, as part of their backing group **Great Speckled Bird** (also with N.D. Smart), **Todd Rundgren**, **Paul Butterfield** and **Allen Ginsberg** amongst many others.

Ed Mottau later played with Elliot Murphy, David Peel and John Lennon on his *Walls And Bridges* and *Rock & Roll* albums. (VJ/SR)

Bohemian Vendetta

Personnel:	BRIAN COOKE	organ, vcls	A
	NICK MANZI	ld gtr	A
	CHUCK MONICA	drms	A
	VICTOR MUGLIA	bs	A
	RANDY POLLOCK	gtr	A

ALBUM:	1(A)	BOHEMIAN VENDETTA	(Mainstream S/6106) 1968 R2

NB: There's also a collection of rarities *Enough* (Distortions DR 1038) 1997.

45s:	Enough/Half The Time	(United Artists 50174) 1967
	Riddles And Fairytales/ I Wanna Touch Your Heart	(Mainstream 681) 1968

A New York City band who issued just the one album, which is now a rare collectors' item. Prior to this they'd recorded the above 45 on United Artists.

Their album contains some fine and often demented acid rock, particularly on *All Kinds Of Highs* and the superb *Paradox City*. There's also an interesting psychedelic version of *Satisfaction*, although the slowed-down cover of *The House of The Rising Sun* is a little tedious. If you're into psychedelic guitar you should enjoy this album - it's full of great guitar-work and also has good songs.

Nick Manzi had earlier played with **Faine Jade** in a band called **The Rustics** and **Bohemian Vendetta** later backed him on the classic *Introspection* album.

The classic *All Kinds Of Highs* can also be found on the top-drawer *Psychedelic Crown Jewels, Vol. 1* (Dble LP & CD), whilst the non-LP cut *Enough* has resurfaced on *Ear-Piercing Punk* (LP & CD), *The Essential Pebbles Collection, Vol. 1* (Dble CD) and *Enough* has resurfaced on *Filling The Gap* (4-LP), *Best of Pebbles, Vol. 2* (LP & CD) and *Pebbles, Vol. 1 (ESD)* (CD) compilations. Another track, *Paradox City*, which has a catchy verse and nightmarish refrain with plenty of organ and raunchy fuzz guitar, can also be heard on *Beyond The Calico Wall* (LP & CD).

Fans of the band will also want to check out Distortions' collection of rarities, acetates and non-album cuts, entitled *Enough!*. Released on both vinyl and CD, the CD contains extra material.

Nick Manzi later played with **Dust Bowl Clementine**, who had an eponymous album on Roulette (2SR-42058) 1970. (VJ/MW/SR)

Buddy Bohn

ALBUMS:			
1	BUDDY BOHN - FOLKSINGER	(Leedon LL 31000)	1963 -
2	PLACES	(Happy Tiger HTR-M-1001)	1970 -
3	A DROP IN THE OCEAN	(Capitol SMAS 878)	1972 -

NB: (1) Australian release on Festival subsidiary. (3) also issued on (EMI TPSA 7503) 1972.

45s: Follow Me/? (Columbia JZSP 114021) 1966

A folk-rock singer/troubadour who recorded three albums on three big labels in three different continents! His first album was released on the Australian Festival subsidiary, and coincided with a feature story in 'TIME' magazine, entitled "Troubadours" (Feb. 8th 1963). His second was released on the same label as **Mason Proffit**, Ecology and **Aorta**, suggesting Illinois was his base at the time.

He then moved to Deep Purple's Purple/EMI label in the UK and Capitol in the US for his third album. Produced in London by Jerry Lordan (composer of The Shadows *Apache*!), this was recorded with a full orchestral backing and contains several dreamy, drifting songs (*Picallilli Lady*, *Reflecting Butterfly* and *Curious Yellow*). One track, *Vermouth Rondo*, became an international radio hit, the royalties from which later built Buddy a beach house in Bodega Bay, California.

Buddy has made further recordings to those shown above, including five albums/CDs on the Budwick label as "Moro" (his real middle name). (SR)

The Bojax

| Personnel incl: | BOBBY HOLLIDAY | vcls | A |

45s:	Hippie Times/Go Ahead And Go	(Panther)	1967
	Fast Life/Don't Look Back	(Panther PAN 4)	1968
α	I've Enjoyed As Much Of You As I Can Stand/?	( )	1968

NB: α may have been withdrawn shortly after release.

A garage-punk band out of Greenville, South Carolina. Rudy Wyatt of **The Wyld** produced the first 45 and played on the second. Bojax singer Bobby Holliday sang on **The Wyld**'s *Know A Lot About Love*. The band stayed together until 1969, releasing a third single for which I don't have complete info. The excellent *Go Ahead And Go* has resurfaced on *Back From The Grave, Vol. 8* (CD & Dble LP).

Their debut 45 is a cool Kinks-inspired punker with a slab of attitude and samples some phrasing and melody of Dylan's *Like A Rolling Stone*. Hippie *Times* is a driving uptempo belter. *Fast Life* is a hypnotic garage-swinger stuffed with power-chords and searing leads. The flip is a too-faithful rendition of **The Remains**' *Don't Look Back* and lacks bite. *Don't Look Back* charted locally. (VJ/MW/JWs/TW/AB)

BOHEMIAN VENDETTA - Bohemian Vendetta LP.

Bold

Personnel:	MICHAEL CHMURA	keyb'ds	A
	TIMOTHY GRIFFIN	drms, perc, vcls	A
	DICK LA FRENIERE	gtr	A
	ROBERT LA PALM	gtr, vcls	A
	STEPHEN WALKER	bs, ld vcls	A

| ALBUM: | 1(A) | BOLD | (ABC ABCS 705) | 1969 - |

45s:	Gotta Get Some/Robin Hood	(Cameo 430)	1966
	The Train Kept A Rollin'/		
α	Found What I Was Looking For	(Dyno Voice 232)	1967

NB: α issued as by **Steve Walker and The Bold**. No 45s, LP or non-LP, can be traced on the ABC label.

Hailing from the Springfield area of Massachussetts the band formed out of an outfit called The Esquires and also operated under the moniker **Steve Walker and The Bold**.

The album was a Bill Szymczyk production recorded at "Hit Factory". It's a decent experimental soft-rock album with a nice blend of covers (*All I Really Want To Do*, *For What Its Worth* and *It's All Over Now Baby Blue*) given the group's own unique re-interpretation and originals. Among the better originals are *Free Fugue*, *Child Of Love*, *Words Don't Make It* and *Friendly Smile*, which has some nice organ work. Worth a listen.

Gotta Get Some with its raw vocals and driving beat is a fine punker, also featured on *Pebbles, Vol. 9* (LP), *Pebbles Vol. 10* (CD), *Pebbles, Vol. 1 (ESD)* (CD) and *Mindrocker, Vol. 11* (LP). It became a fave with The Fuzztones and duly appeared on their *Lysergic Emanations* LP - latterly compiled again on *Songs We Taught The Fuzztones* (Dble LP & Dble CD). Their superb rendition of *Train Kept A Rollin'* can be enjoyed on *Pebbles, Vol. 10* (LP) and *Pebbles, Vol. 10* (CD), preferably at full volume. It's a very loose version delivered at breakneck speed. Other groups to cover the song included **The Cynics**, Precious Few, **The Rogues**, and **The Scotty McKay Quintet**.

The Bold were an important act locally and actually quite popular. Many of their fans thought the production on the ABC album was weak, and so refused to buy it at the time. They were apparently a way better band live than any of their recordings, although very 'East Coast' in their sound. Bob La Palm and Timothy Griffin went on to found a band called **Clean Living** whose records are worth checking out if you can find copies. Tim Griffin also played drums in James Taylor's road band very briefly. (VJ/JSr/SR)

BOLDER DAMN - Mourning LP.

Bolder Damn

Personnel:	JOHN ANDERSON	vcls	AB
	BOB EATON	drms	AB
	GLENN EATON	gtr	AB
	MARC GASPARD	keyb'ds	A
	DEAN NOEL	bs	A
	RON REFFETT	bs	AB

ALBUM: 1(B) MOURNING (Hit) 1971 R4/5

NB: (1) reissued on vinyl (Rockadelic RRLP 3.5) 1991 and on CD (Rockadelic) 1998. Reissued on vinyl (Void VOID 21) 2001.

This outfit formed in Fort Lauderdale, Florida in the Summer of 1969. They played a sort of heavy rock music in the Black Sabbath/Alice Cooper vein and had a spectacular live show, opening for many 'big name' acts. The above album was recorded in just four hours and pressed in limited quantities for distribution to local fans. Just when major labels were beginning to show an interest John Anderson and Ron Reffett were drafted leading to the band's demise.

The album's recent reissues on Rockadelic/Void have brought it to a slightly wider audience because the original release is obviously ultra rare. If you're into heavy rock you'll like this. *Rock On* and *Breakthrough* have a great beat and driving guitar, whilst *Dead Meat*, which takes up most of Side Two, shows they were willing to experiment. It's very heavy, quite imaginative and espoused the revolutionary lyrics which were common from bands in this era. The final cut *BRTCD* featured some fine fuzz guitar work. (VJ)

Tiffany Bolling

ALBUM: 1 TIFFANY (Canyon LP-7708) 1969 -

A sexy blonde female pop singer with some psych influences on tracks like *Wind Of Heaven*, Strangers *See You In My Face*, *Thank God The War Is Over*, *Set The Children Free*, *Part One-Part Two* and *Love Still Remains*. (SR)

The Bompers

45: Do The Bomp/Early Bird (HBR 441) 1965

A failed attempt at launching a new dance craze. This studio group probably included **Danny Hutton** who was then signed with HBR. (SR)

Boomerang

Personnel:	JO CASMIR	bs, vcls	A
	JAMES GALLUZZI	drms	A
	RICHARD RAMERIZ	gtr	A
	MARK STEIN	keyb'ds, vcls	A

ALBUM: 1(A) BOOMERANG (RCA LSP-4577) 1971 SC

An unimaginative hard-rock group formed by Mark Stein after **Vanilla Fudge**. The group disappeared soon after the failure of their album. Ramirez later played in the hard-rock band Striker. (SR/CG)

Bondsmen

45: I See The Light/Our Time To Try (AMH 6704) 1968

From Durham, the home of Duke University in North Carolina. They won three Raleigh Battle of The Band competitions in the sixties and were perhaps Durham's best band. *Tobacco A-Go-Go, Vol. 1* features their competent cover of **The Five American's** hit and the more interesting 'B' side - which opens with a compelling drum beat followed by a very heavy guitar riff leading into a psychedelic frenzy. A promising effort, only the vocals let it down. There was a second 45, which could possibly be *Out Of Sight* / ? (Justice 1003) 196?.

Our Time To Try is also featured on *A Lethal Dose Of Hard Psych* (CD). (VJ/MW)

Bone

| Personnel incl: | MARK McHUGH | hrmnca | A |

45: It's An Easy Thing/
     Everybody's Gone Into April (Poison Ring PRR 712) 1969

Formed out of The Creations and known briefly as the Freudian Slip, this outfit was based in New Haven, Connecticut. The intriguingly titled flip is what draws most to this 45, though it is not so mindbending as hoped - nonetheless it's an infectious and melodic rocker. The 'A' side is uptempo Vaudeville-pop.

The 45 was produced by Tom Duffy.

Mark McHugh had earlier played on a 45 by **The Original Sinners**. (MW)

Bones

Personnel:	CASEY CUNNINGHAM	drms	A
	DANNY FARAGHER	bs, vcls	A
	JIMMY FARAGHER	keyb'ds, vcls, horns	A
	GREG TORNQUIST	gtr, vcls	A

ALBUM: 1(A) BONES (Signpost SP 8402) 1972 -

Previously known as the **Peppermint Trolley Co.**, these four musicians recorded an average bar rock album in 1972. (SR)

Bonne Villes

Personnel:	NELSON M. BRADSHAW	ld gtr	A
	DONALD W. CARTNER	drms	A
	CURTIS "BUZZY" COBB	sax, keyb'ds	A
	GARY HOWE	second vcls	A
	JAMES ALAN LOVETTE	ld vcls	A
	CARL F. STEELE Jr.	bs	A

ALBUM: 1(A) BRINGING IT HOME (Justice JLP 146) 1966 R2

NB: (1) reissued on CD (Collectables COL-0623) 1997.

45: Naughty Girl / ? (Pyramid 6536) 1966

Another Justice rarity is dusted off by Collectables to reveal a sextet from Salisbury, North Carolina. Not completely obscured by time in this case, since their *Naughty Girl* graced the eighties Tarheel compilation *Tobacco A Go Go, Vol.II* - a slice of garagey frat-rock punctuated throughout by honking sax. Like many of the other Justice LPs, it is predominantly covers of soul, R&B, blues and ballads (*Stand By Me*, *Monkey Time*, *My Girl*, *Midnight Hour*, *Under The Boardwalk*) in a competent but uninspiring club style with no real bite and little variation - even their cover of *96 Tears* is rather flat, although they do try to belt it with a more raucous vocal style on *Bring It On Home To Me*. Once more with this series, curiosity is satisfied but the buzz factor is absent.

Other compilation appearances include *96 Tears* on *Green Crystal Ties, Vol. 3* (CD). (MW)

Sonny Bono

Personnel:	HAROLD BATTISTE		A
	SONNY BONO	vcls	A
	MAC REBENNACK		A

ALBUM:	1(A)	INNER VIEWS	(Atco SD 33-229) 1967 -

45:	Laugh At Me/Tony	(Atco 6369) 1967
	But You're Mine/ ?	(Atco 6381) 1967

Produced, composed and "sung" by **Sonny Bono** (from Sonny and Cher), *Inner Views* was his "psychedelic" album. It has the reputation of being of the worst albums of the sixties, and in fact it's a strange listening experience: **Bono**'s voice is not exactly easy to like, the tracks are too long (*I Just Sit There* lasts 12'15") and the lyrics are "groovy" ("She started smoking pot just to keep herself from flipping but it wasn't strong enough so she graduated to tripping" from *Pammie's On A Bummer*). The musicians got so bored that they started working on their own project during the sessions, creating what would become **Dr. John, the Night Tripper**. (SR)

Bon Tempe

Personnel incl:	BOB AKERS	flute	A
	JOHN ALBRITHON	sax	A
	BILL NELSON	gtr	A

ALBUM:	1(A)	BON TEMPE	(Private Pressing) 1975 -

From Kentfield, California, a hippie quintet strongly influenced by free jazz and weird sounds. Their rare album includes tracks like *Velvet Pumpkii*, *The Moth*, *Hot Cellums*, *Niles Nood*, *Johnny Pluto* and *Lothlorien*. (SR)

Jack Bonus

ALBUM:	1(A)	JACK BONUS	(Grunt FTR-1005) 1972 -

NB: (1) also released in Germany.

Jack Bonus was a sax and flute player who can be heard on albums by **Grootna**, **Earth Opera**, **Papa John Creach**, **Tom Paxton** and the Rowan Brothers.

He was also a friend of the **Jefferson Airplane**, who let him release an album of original material on their label. Unfortunately, although he was a decent sax player, he was barely able to sing and this album is a real disaster, full of mid-tempo tracks with awful vocals. The only redeemable feature is the Bay Area musicians involved: Freddie Roulette on hawaiian steel guitar; Tom Coster (**Santana**) on organ, Lorin and Chris Rowan, Skip Olsen, Bruce Conte, Billy Wolff, Ed Bogas and Jamie Howell. (SR)

Boo Boo and Bunky

45:	This Old Town/Turn Around	(Brent 7045) 1965

An obscure California folk-rock outfit. *This Old Town* can be heard on *Open Up Yer Door, Vol. 2* (LP) and *Victims Of Circumstance, Vol. 2* (LP & CD), whilst the flip has resurfaced on the *Folk Rock E.P.* (7") and *Ya Gotta Have Moxie, Vol. 1* (Dble CD). (VJ)

Book of Changes

Personnel:	BOB BAILEY	vcls	AB
	SAUL LEWIS	keyb'ds, vcls	AB
	ROLAND OELLER	bs	AB
	ARTHUR PENTHOLLOW	drms	AB
	FRANK SMITH	gtr	AB
	JOSEPH BRACKETT	keyb'ds	B

45:	I Stole The Goodyear Blimp/	
	Suddenly I'm Desperately In Love	(Tower 337) 1967

The was the third and final phase of San Francisco's **Vejtables**. Both sides of the 45 can be heard on *What A Way To Come Down*, another CD in Big Beat's essential 'Nuggets From The Golden State' series, compiled and annotated by Alec Palao and confirming the personnel above. *I Stole The Goodyear Blimp* has also appeared on *Glimpses, Vol. 3* (LP).

Musician and writer Roland Oeller was originally from Milwaukee, WI. and released his first record in 1958 under the name of Roland Stone - *Lost Love / Moanin' Soul* (USA 1212). In the early sixties he joined The Royal Lancers shortly before they became The Apollos, who released a 45 in 1964 but are best known for backing Paul Stefan and later Danny Peil. In 1966 he relocated to San Francisco. He would have a short spell with the embryonic **Moby Grape** before leaving the music biz. (MW/GM)

Boondoggle and Balderdash

ALBUM:	1	BOONDOGGLE AND BALDERBASH	(UNI) 1971 -

An obscure hippie country-rock group with a "wild west" look: dusty old clothes, moustaches, guns and hats. (SR)

Boot

Personnel:	DAN ELIASSEN	vcls, bs	A
	BRUCE KNOX	gtr, vcls	A
	MIKE MYCZ	gtr, vcls	A
	JIM O'BROCK	drms, vcls	A

ALBUMS:	1(A)	BOOT	(Agape 2601) 1972
	2(A)	TURN THE OTHER CHEEK	(Guinness 36002) 1977

NB: (1) reissued on CD (Lizard Records LR 0706-2) 2001.

BOOT - Boot CD.

| 45: | Hey Little Girl / Liza Brown | (Agape 9008) 1972 |

Their first album is rare and came out on a Texas label 'though they hailed from New Port Richey, Florida, and had earlier recorded as **The Split Ends**. It's basically hard rock with some psychedelic guitar work. Their second album is rather mundane heavy rock. (CF/MW/SMR/JOk)

The Bootiques

| 45: | Did You Get Your Fun/Mr Man On The Moon | (Date 1513) 1966 |

A Californian sunshine pop group produced by **Curt Boettcher**. (SR)

The Bootles

| 45: | I'll Let You Hold My Hand/? | (GNP Crescendo 311) 196? |

An early all girl band. The 'A' side can also be heard on *Girls In The Garage, Vol. 2* (LP) and *Girls In The Garage, Vol. 1* (CD). (VJ)

The Bootmen

Personnel:	NEIL ANDERSON	gtr	A
	BARRY BALANTI (*)	drms	A
	BUTCH HANUKANIE	keyb'ds	A
	JOHN STONE	vcls	A
	JIM STOVER	bs	A
	DUANE McCASLIN	bs	
	FRED DICKERSON	gtr	
	MARK MARUSH	sax	
	MICHAEL MOORE	keyb'ds	

NB: 'A' = Original line-up. The rest were later members. (*) spelling may be incorrect - could be Barry Bellandi. Neil Anderson remembers the original line-up at Wilson H. S. in Tacoma as Barry Bellandi, Ron Gardner, himself and maybe Rudy Bachelor on ele. piano, and Wayne Reich on bass.

45s:	1,2,3,4/Black Widow	(Etiquette 10) 1964
	Love You All I Can/Forevermore	(Riverton 101) 1965
α	Wherever You Hide/ Ain't It The Truth, Babe	(Riverton 104) 1966

NB: α On this 45, Dave Roland (**Wailers**) played on the 'A' side and Dean Whitbeck played drums on the flip.

The Bootmen evolved out of a Puget Sound high school group called The Solitudes. They got their big break when Ron Gardner, a part-time member of **The Wailers** introduced them to the owners of Etiquette Records, Kent Morrill and Buck Ormsby, who insisted on a name change to **The Bootmen**.

They soon became a popular Northwest dancehall attraction operating out of Tacoma in Washington. Their grungy garage sound was typified by *Ain't It The Truth, Babe* a track you can check out on *Highs In The Mid-Sixties, Vol. 7* (LP), which described it as a mixture between **Mitch Ryder** and **Paul Revere and The Raiders**.

Neil Anderson later joined **The Wailers**, whilst Fred Dickerson and Duane McCaslin went on to **Cotton Mouth**. (VJ/MW)

Born Again

Personnel:	STEVE AVERY	gtr	A
	LARRY OTIS	gtr	ABC
	STUART RAMSAY	bs	AB
	BRICE SULLIVAN	vcls, piano, hrmnca	ABC
	LLOYD WICK	drms	AB
	ROD MOXIE	bs, gtr	B
	MIKE DUNCAN	keyb'ds	C
	BILLY JOHNSON	drms	C
	(MALCOLM CECIL	bs	A)
	(ROGER DOLLARHIDE	keyb'ds	A)

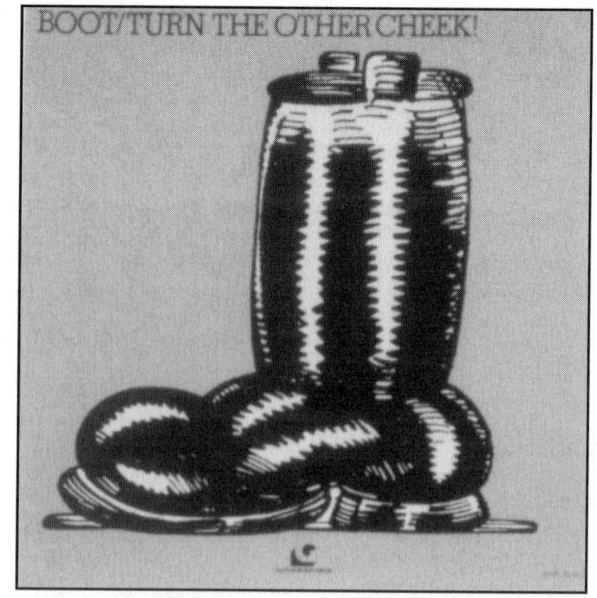

BOOT - Turn The Other Cheek LP.

| ALBUM: | 1(-) BORN AGAIN PAGAN | (Rockadelic RRLP 42) 2001 |

NB: (1) a handful were pressed on clear vinyl.

Originally from Marin County in Northern California and calling themselves **Red Mountain**, a demo tape they recorded at Sierra Sound Labs in Berkeley attracted the attention of producer Roger Dollarhide (**Randy California**'s *Kapt. Kopter And The Fabulous Twirly Birds*) who invited them to relocate to Los Angeles. In late 1969 and early 1970, several recording sessions took place at SunWest Studios in Hollywood that appear for the first time on the Rockadelic collection. In addition, guitarist Larry Otis contributed music to an original movie soundtrack in 1970, *The Velvet Vampire*, and a piece from this movie also figures on the *Born Again Pagan* collection. The album concludes with three demo tracks from 1971 by the 'C' line-up, recorded in San Francisco.

While the music produced by the various line-ups of the group varies enough in style as to defy categorisation, there are no weak moments on this album. Sullivan's snarling lead vocal technique will appeal to fans of both sixties and seventies music, and no one will find fault with Otis' remarkable command of the guitar (Dollarhide introduced Otis to Ike Turner as "the best rock guitar player in the world", and Turner apparently agreed - hiring Otis for the Ike and Tina Turner Revue in 1974).

Otis worked extensively as a session guitarist in Los Angeles beyond the timespan of this book. In 1992 he recorded an album of rock 'n' roll music with his friend Rúnar Júlíusson of Thor's Hammer (*Rúnar And Otis* (Geimsteinn Records GSK 156)), and the Icelandic label has just released a new album of his instrumental guitar works that may appeal to readers (*New Beginnings* GSCD 197). (CF)

Boruk

| ALBUM: | 1 BLACKHOLE BOOGIE | (Private Pressing) c1970 SC |

A strange poet with background music, very short tracks (twenty-five on a single album). (SR)

The Boss Five

| 45: | Please Mr President/You Cheat Too Much | (Impact 1003) 1966 |

Primitive-sounding punkers issued on Detroit's Impact label. The 'A' side, a punk, novelty number, can be heard on *Psychedelic Unknowns, Vol. 4* (LP & CD); the flip, another raw punker has resurfaced on *Highs In The Mid-Sixties, Vol. 5*, even though it's now known that the band came from Hewlett and Lynbrook, Long Island. The 45 was recorded in New York and produced by Dickie Goodman although he isn't credited on the label.

Both sides of the 45 also feature on *The Best Of Impact Records* (CD). (VJ/KBn/MW/MM)

The Bossmen

Personnel incl:	WARREN KEITH	piano, vcls	A
	LANNY ROENICKE	bs, vcls	A
	DICK WAGNER	ld gtr, vcls	A
	PETE WOODMAN	drms	A

CD: 1 THE COMPLETE BOSSMEN
(Wagner Music Group no #) 1995

45s: α Take A Look (My Friend)/It's A Shame (Soft D-121) 1964
Thanks To You/ Help Me Baby (M&L 1809) 1964/5
Here's Congratulations/Bad Girl (Dicto 1001) 1965
Wait And See/You're The Girl For Me (Dicto 1002) 1965
Wait And See/You're The Girl For Me (Lucky Eleven 227) 1966
Tina Maria/On The Road (Lucky Eleven 001) 1966
Baby Boy/You And I (Lucky Eleven 231) 1966/7

NB: α is not on the Texas 'Soft' label, and was apparently also issued on Beck 112.

This Flint, Michigan quartet are notable for including **Dick Wagner**, who would become a key character on the rock scene in Northern Michigan; a prolific writer his name turns up as writer and producer for numerous other acts - **Bells Of Rhymney**, **Cherry Slush**, **Sand**, **Terry Knight and The Pack**, and **The Wanderers** to mention just a few.

In 1967 he formed **Dick Wagner and The Frosts** with Don Hartman (guitar), Jack Smolinski (bass), and Bob Rigg (drums). They soon switched to the more snappy moniker **Frost**, released several 45s and three hard-rock LPs on Vanguard. **Wagner** went on to play with Lou Reed and in 1974 joined the revamped Alice Cooper band.

The 1995 CD collection features all the 45s above plus three of the earliest Frost tracks - *A Rainy Day*, *Sunshine*, and *Little Girl*.

Thirty-five or more years on **Dick Wagner** was still active on the Saginaw scene, inspiring a new generation of musicians. (VJ/MW)

The Bossmen

45s: Mashed Potatoes / Bad Boss Man (Score 1001) 1963
I'm Ready / Self Pity (Score 1003) 1964
Fever Of Love / Good Lookin' Woman (Busy Bee 1001) 196?
That Ticket To Ride / I Can't Help It (Busy Bee 1002) 196?
Dr. Feelgood / ? (Versa 102) 196?

NB: These 45s may not be in correct sequence and it has yet to be confirmed that (5) is by the same band.

Originally from Texas, these **Bossmen** relocated to Chicago. The Score and Busy Bee labels were owned by Lenny LaCour. He would later be involved in the Milwaukee scene, which had led to the erroneous assumption that this group hailed from there.

Some of their 45s are powerful rockers and two examples, *I'm Ready* and *Fever Of Love*, can be heard on *Highs In The Mid-Sixties, Vol. 5* (LP) and *Highs In The Mid-Sixties, Vol. 6* (LP) respectively.

Several other **Bossmen** were around in the sixties: a Colorado outfit circa 1962, with no known releases; a Missouri band with the 'soul-garage' *Gonna Lose My Mind* (Burdland 8635); and another of unknown origins with a 1964 release - *Apologies / Take It Easy* (Vim 72). (GM/MW/VJ)

The Boss Tweads

Personnel:	STANLEY BERG	keyb'ds	A
	TIM HOFSTAD	drms	A
	PAUL LARSON	bs	A
	GENE MILLER	gtr	A
	SHELLY SEVERSON	ld gtr	A

45: Goin' Away/It's Best You Go (Studio City 1056) 1966

Studio City was a Minneapolis-based label but the band themselves were from South Dakota. The 45 is very rare and sought-after and the 'A' side

I TURNED INTO A HELIUM BALLOON (Comp CD) includes The Boston Tea Party.

has had a further airing on *Root '66 - Minnesota Teen Bands (1964-1967) The Frozen Few* (LP). (VJ/MW/MDo)

The Boss Tweeds (seen sometimes as Bostweeds)

45s: Faster Pussycat! Kill! Kill!/? (Eve Productions) 196?
Little Bad News/Simple Man (Chattahoochee 689) 1965
She Belongs To Me/Lisa (Chattahoochee 701) 1966

This was a different outfit from Los Angeles who recorded at least three 45s. *Faster, Pussycat! Kill! Kill!* was the theme to Russ Meyer's film of the same name and was written by Bert Fhester. Eve Productions was Meyers' film company whilst their second and third 45s were released on Chattahoochie, which was being run by **Kim Fowley** at the time.

In the eighties, *Faster, Pussycat! Kill! Kill!* was given a new lease of life when it was covered by the Cramps. You can find the original on *Born Bad, Vol. 1*, whilst *Little Bad News* has also resurfaced on *Garage Punk Unknowns, Vol. 5* (LP). (VJ/MW/JFr)

Boston Tea Party

Personnel:	RICHARD DE PERNA	bs	A
	ROBERT DE PERNA	organ	A
	TRAVIS FIELDS	vcls	A
	DAVE NOVOGROSKI	drms	A
	MIKE STEVENS	ld gtr	A

ALBUM: 1(A) BOSTON TEA PARTY (Flick Disk 45000) 1968

NB: (1) promo copies issued in mono with sticker.

45s: Spinach/Laugh (Big Boss FW-1002) 1967
Spinach/Words (Big Boss FW-1002) 1967
Words/Spinach (Challenge 59368) 1967
Is It Love?/Don't Leave Me Alone (Fona 311) 1967
My Daze/Rose In The Night (Vogue International 101) 1967
Free Service/I'm Telling You (Flick Disk 900) 1967

Formed in 1963 this band became based in Burbank, California. People seem to have mixed views on the album, but it is not one which collectors particularly seek out. The band also had cuts on the original Soundtrack of the movie *Cycle Savages*. Their drummer, Novogroski, went on to play for **The Edge**, while Mike Stevens later fronted the highly-rated heavy-rock band **Highway Robbery**, who issued an album, *For Love Or Money* (RCA Victor LSP-4735) 1972.

Compilation appearances have included: *My Daze* on *An Overdose Of Heavy Psych* (CD); and both *Spinach* and *Words* on *I Turned Into A Helium Balloon* (CD). (VJ/MW/CF/DJe)

Bo St Runners

45:   Alladin/Johnny B. Goode   (KR 117) 1966

NB: One-sided promo copies also exist.

Unconnected to the US **Bow St Runners**, the UK Bo St. Runners, and the Missouri Bo St Runners (who recorded for Pearce). Their cover of *Alladin* was written by Artie Kornfield and Steve Duboff, two songwriters who issued their own version under the **Changin' Times** moniker.

Their version of *Alladin* is a decent mid-tempo folk-rocker with harmony vocals and electric 12-string.

The 45 was recorded in Phoenix, but the bands own location isn't yet known. (MM/JKl)

Bottle Company

45:   Barkley Square/Lives For No One   (Hideout 1230) 196?

An obscure Michigan outfit. *Lives For No One* is pretty standard garage punk, but it has been compiled on *Let 'Em Have It!, Vol. 1* (CD), *Michigan Mixture, Vol. 2* (LP) and *Best of Hideout Records* (CD). (VJ)

Botumles Pit

45:   13 Stories High/My Girl   (Psychadelic 113) 1966

This oufit hailed from San Antonio in Texas in the mid-sixties. The 45 was released as by **The Suedes**, and stickers placed over the band name as "Botumles Pit".

Compilation appearances include: *13 Stories High* on *Back From The Grave, Vol. 4* (LP); *Back From The Grave, Vol. 2* (CD); *Scum Of The Earth* (Dble CD) and *Scum Of The Earth, Vol. 2* (LP). (VJ/MT)

Bougalieu

Personnel:	LESTER FIGARSKI	bs	ABC
	BILLY GALLAGHER	gtr	ABC
	PARKER KENNEDY	ld vcls	AB
	GEORGE MILNE	drms	A

	MIKE ROTHMAN	ld gtr	ABC
	LARRY SCARANO	drms	B
	PARKER WHEELER	ld vcls	C

45s: Let's Do Wrong/When I Was A Child   (Roulette 4767) 1967
   Let's Do Wrong/When I Was A Child   (Roulette 4776) 1967

From Albany, New York, this band's 45 was issued twice, with the first issue featuring a much cleaner version of *Let's Do Wrong*. Both takes appear on *Psychedelic Microdots Of The Sixties, Vol. 3* (CD), whose liner notes reveal the above personnel and that they once opened for the **Young Rascals** at Siena College. The second version is described as a "thrashing monster of a take"...

The band also played down in Florida, where they eventually migrated, after Parker Kennedy blew his vocal chords and had been replaced by Parker Wheeler.

Other compilation appearances have included: *Let's Do Wrong* on *Boulders, Vol. 2* (LP) and *Pebbles, Vol. 1 (ESD)*. (VJ/MW/JJ)

The Bounty Hunters

45:   Somewhere/The Sun Went Away   (Romain 1010) 196?

This group operated out of Philadelphia. The 'A' side is a punk ballad with lots of farfisa organ. The flip is also an organ-led song, but a little more uptempo.

Compilation appearances include: *The Sun Went Away* on *No No No* (CD); *The Sun Went Away* and *Somewhere* on *Return Of The Young Pennsylvanians* (LP) and *Gathering Of The Tribe* (CD). (VJ)

The Bourbons

45:   A Dark Corner/Of Old Approximately
   (A Time For A Change)   (Royal Family 267) 1967

A Texas band from San Antonio were responsible for this gem. The flip is a raw garage rocker with sneering vocals.

Compilation appearances include: *A Dark Corner* and *Of Old Approximately* on *Texas Punk Groups From The Sixties* (LP) and *Sixties Archive, Vol. 6* (CD); *Dark Corner* on *Acid Dreams - The Complete 3 LP Set* (3-LP) and *Acid Dreams Testament* (CD); and *Of Old Approximately* on *Flashback, Vol. 6* (LP) and *Highs In The Mid-Sixties, Vol. 11* (LP). (VJ)

The Bourbons

Personnel incl: JIMMY GRANDMONT   drms
   AL LORUSSO

ALBUM: 1   HOUSE PARTY 1964-66   (Arf! Arf! AA-058) 1996

NB: (1) contains 28 previously unreleased cuts including tracks by the early line-ups Chevells and Vandells.

A garage band from Braintree, Massachusetts, whose finest moments and more are now captured on the above CD. Grandmont later played in **The Morning After**.

Compilation appearances include: *Little Black Egg* on *The Arf! Arf! Blitzkrieg 32 Track Sampler* (CD).

THE BOURBONS - House Party CD.

Bow Street Runners

ALBUM: 1   BOW STREET RUNNERS
   (B.T. Puppy BTPS 1026) 1970 R4

NB: (1) initially counterfeited on vinyl and then reissued on CD & LP in original cover (Sundazed SC6112) 1996.

BOW STREET RUNNERS - Bow Street Runners LP.

This is one of those interesting albums that linked the psychedelic and progressive eras. An album of imagination, variety and different moods. It's not all good - some cuts are plain bad - but others are superb. The opening track, *Electric Star*, is an exquisite slice of floating, melodic psychedelia, which occasionally lapses into dementia. *Watch* veers towards acid rock with some fine guitar licks. *Another Face* has a haunting keyboard introduction but then picks up tempo with lots of fuzz guitar. Those three tracks are the highlight. A few songs are bluesy but often contain unpredictable mood changes and the final track, *Steve's Jam*, contains lots of good fuzz guitar. This album is horrendously rare, so pick up the Sundazed reissue if you can.

Compilation coverage has so far included: *Watch* on *Psychedelic Crown Jewels, Vol. 1* (Dble LP & CD) and Gear Fab's *Psychedelic Sampler* (CD); *Electric Star* on *The Psychedelic Experience, Vol. 1* (LP); and *Another Face* on *Relics, Vol. 2* (LP) and *Relics Vol's 1 & 2* (CD). (VJ)

Boy Blues

Personnel incl:	JOHN PALMER		A

45s:	α	Living Child / Think About It Baby	(Vardan 538) 1966
		Coming Down To You/Living Child	(Frantic CR-2131/2) 1967

NB: α some copies in PS.

From Chico, California. *Coming Down To You* is a catchy number reminiscent of the 'Batman' theme with a great fuzz-lead break. John Palmer had previously played with The Boys and **The Plague**; he later moved on to Lincoln's Promise and **Savage Resurrection**.

Compilation appearances include: *Comin' Down To You* on *Psychedelic Disaster Whirl* (LP), *Ya Gotta Have Moxie, Vol. 1* (Dble CD), *Yeah Yeah Yeah* (CD) and *Boulders, Vol. 10* (LP). (VJ/MW)

Boyce and Hart

Personnel:	TOMMY BOYCE	A
	BOBBY HART	A

				HCP
ALBUMS:	1(A)	TEST PATTERNS	(A&M SP 4126) 1966	200 -
	2(A)	I WONDER WHAT SHE'S DOING TONIGHT?	(A&M SP 4143) 1967	109 -
	3(A)	IT'S ALL HAPPENING ON THE INSIDE	(A&M SP 4162) 1968	- -

			HCP
45s:	In Case The Wind Should Blow/ Simon Smith And The Amazing Dancing Bear	(A&M 826) 1966	-
	Out And About/My Little Chickadee	(A&M 858) 1967	39
	Sometimes She's A Little Girl/ Love Every Day	(A&M 874) 1967	110
	I Wonder What She's Doing Tonight/ The Ambushers	(A&M 893) 1967	8
	Goodbye Baby (I Don't Want To See You Cry)/ Where Angels Go, Trouble Follows	(A&M 919) 1968	53
	Alice Long/P.O. Box 9847	(A&M 948) 1968	27
	We're All Going To The Same Place/6 + 6	(A&M 993) 1968	123
	I'm Gonna Blow You A Kiss In The Wind/ Smilin'	(Aquarian 380) 1968	-
	Maybe Somebody Heard/ It's All Happening On The Inside	(A&M 1017) 1969	-
	L.U.V./I Wanna Be Free	(A&M 1031)	111

NB: There's also a French EP with PS: *Out And About/In The Night/Sometimes She's A Little Girl/I Should Be Going Home* (A&M EAM 1001) 1966.

This duo came from California and had both previously had solo careers. They were better known as songwriters, most notably for **The Monkees**, although they also enjoyed some chart success. *I Wonder What She's Doing Tonight*, an appealing pop song with a strong beat, can be heard on *Nuggets, Vol. 3* (LP) and *More Nuggets* (CD).

They returned in the seventies as part of Dolenz, Jones, Boyce and Hart - a kind of seventies **Monkees** doing old material much of it written by Boyce and Hart.

Tommy Boyce committed suicide in Nashville in 1995. He was just 55 years old. He had also released a solo album in 1967 entitled *A Twofold Talent* (Camden CAL/S-2202). (VJ/SR)

Terence Boylan

Personnel:	WALTER BECKER	bs, gtr	A
	TERRY BOYLAN	gtr, vcls	A
	DON FAGEN	piano, organ	A
	DARIUS DAVENPORT	drms	
	JIMMY JOHNSON	drms	
	HERB LOVELLE	drms	

ALBUM:	1(A)	ALIAS BOONA	(Verve Forecast FTS-3070) 1969	-

Released shortly after the Boylan brothers' **Appletree Theatre**, *Alias Boona* was musically totally different. Clearly a singer/songwriter project, it will probably disappoint those expecting to find a sequel to **Appletree Theatre**. All the songs were written and produced by **Boylan**, except for a cover of Dylan's *Subterranean Homesick Blues* (an obvious influence), and are a bit lacklustre, with the few electric guitar solos being interesting but very brief.

However, this album is now sought-after, mainly for the presence of Becker and Fagen who would later form Steely Dan. One of the drummers, Darius

THE BOY BLUES.

Davenport, had been in **Autosalvage**. **Terry Boylan** would release two other albums, *Terence Boylan* (1977) and *Suzi* (1980) on Elektra/Asylum. Recorded with several members of the Eagles, both were carefully produced but rather boring. (SR)

Amos Boynton and The ABC's

From Houston, Texas, and featuring Edgar and **Johnny Winter**. They were later known as **The Great Believers**. An unreleased recording, *The Ballad Of Bertha Glutz*, has resurfaced on *Acid Visions* (LP) and *Acid Visions - The Complete Collection Vol. 1* (3-CD). It is actually a different version of **The Great Believers**' *Comin Up Fast* with different lyrics, vocals and a much heavier fuzz guitar line. It was recorded in Tyler, Texas. (VJ)

The Boys

| 45: | You Deceived Me /When I Think | (Emcee 015/16) 1966 |

A garage punk combo from Fort Worth in Texas. *You Deceived Me* changes pace frequently, and is a typically catchy slice of garage - Texan style.

Compilation appearances include: *You Deceived Me* on *Flashback, Vol. 2* (LP), *Texas Flashbacks, Vol. 2* (LP & CD) and *Texas Flashback (The Best Of)* (CD); and *When I Think* on *It's A Hard Life* (LP). (VJ)

The Boys

| 45: | Sticks And Stones / Rocks in My Head | (Lowery Music NRC 511) 196? |

A Jacksonville, Florida band. When they split, members teamed up with remnants of The (Florida) Deep Six to form **Mouse and The Boys**. (MW/JLh)

The Boys From New York City

45s:	These Are The Things/Take It Or Leave It	(Laurie 3412) 1967
	Mary And John/I'm Down Girl	(Laurie 3434) 1968
	Goin' To California/A Little Bit Harder	(Laurie 3443) 1968

From Westbury on Long Island, New York, this group evolved out of **The Energy Package**. Their most worthy effort is *I'm Down Girl*, a decent pop-punker, with *Goin' To California* a close second. The rest of their Laurie output is straight pop or ballads.

You can also find *I'm Down Girl* on *Destination Frantic!* (LP & CD). (MW/MM)

Boys Next Door

Personnel:	JIM ADAMS	gtr, vcls	A
	SKEET BUSHOR	keyb'ds, vcls	A
	STEVE DRYBREAD	bs, vcls	A
	JIM KOSS	drms, vcls	A
	STEVE LESTER	ld vcls, ld gtr	A

| CD: | 1(A) THE BOYS NEXT DOOR | (Sundazed SC 11061) 1999 |

45s:	α	Central High Playmate / Cold 45	(Soma 1428) 1965
		Why Be Proud / Suddenly She Was Gone	(Soma 1439) 1965
		There Is No Greater Sin / I Could See Me Dancing With You	(Cameo 394) 1965
		Mandy / One Face In The Crowd	(Atco 6443) 1966
		The Wildest Xmas / Xmas Kiss	(Bad 1301) 1966
		The Wildest Xmas / Xmas Kiss	(Atco 6455) 1966
		Begone Girl / See The Way She's Mine	(Atco 6477) 1967

NB: α as the Four Wheels.

Not for the garage and psych clan, but sixties pop fans read on... This clean-cut quintet from Indianoplis were obviously influenced by the Beach Boys, for whom they opened on several occasions, right down to the striped shirts. Initially adopting the surf/hot-rod sound, their debut 45 was re-credited to the Four Wheels, deemed to be a more suitable handle.

Thereafter they followed their heroes (and villains?) towards California's smooth moody harmony-pop ala *Pet Sounds*, adding other influences to produce some fine mid-sixties pop pastiches: *Begone Girl* successfully takes on **The Association**; *There Is No Greater Sin* sounds like the Beach Boys covering Dylan and adds baroque flourishes; *See The Way She's Mine* adds a Midwest horn flavour to the recipe.

To their credit, whilst highly derivative, much of their material was self-penned, mainly by Koss and Lester. Of the covers:- three tracks (the final 45 and the unreleased *Lorali*) were written for them and produced by smooth balladeer Bobby Goldsboro, for whom they'd performed backing duties; *Why Be Proud* came from **The Gestures**' Dale Menten.

The CD comprises all their releases, including four tracks as the Four Wheels, radio spots, one live and several unreleased cuts. A detailed history and interview with Steve Lester by Jeff Jarema rounds off yet another quality retrospective from Sundazed.

Compilation appearances have included: *Suddenly She Was Gone* on *Bad Vibrations, Vol. 1* (LP) and *Soma Records Story, Vol. 1* (LP); and *Why Be Proud* on *Soma Records Story, Vol. 2* (LP) and *The Big Hits Of Mid-America - The Soma Records Story* (LP). (MW)

Boystown

| 45: | Hello Mr. Sun/End Of The Line | (Sotto 124) c1967 |

Another **Kim Fowley** and Michael Lloyd production, in a California psych-pop style. (SR)

The Boyz

Personnel incl:	PAUL MAHALEC		A
	BILL MILLAY	bs	A
	RICK NIELSEN		A

45s:	Never Be Lonely/Come With Me	(Destination 630) 1966
	Hard Times All Over/Never Be Lonely	(Destination 7719) 196?
	The Laugh's On Me/Charlotte	(IRC 9531) 19?
	The Laugh's On Me/Charlotte	(Kiderian 45130) 19?

A late sixties Chicago outfit whose *Come With Me* can be heard on *Highs In The Mid-Sixties, Vol. 4*. It's poorly produced but quite appealing. A 1976 album, *A Kiderian Records Sampler* contains a whole side of their music.

(This outfit was supposedly was born out of The Phaetons and from **The Boyz** went on to **Grim Reapers**, **Fuse** and eventually Cheap Trick). (VJ)

Victor Brady

Personnel:	VICTOR BRADY	steel drms, vcls	A
	MURRAY GORDON	bs	A
	PETER PSARIANOS	gtr	A
	GARY REAMS	drms	A

| ALBUM: | 1(A) BROWN RAIN | (Polydor 24-4036) 1970 SC |

| 45: | You Got Me/I've Got The Urge To Move | (MGM 13663) 1967 |

This very unusual album features a fusion between the steel drum sound with heavy progressive music. The leader, **Victor Brady**, plays wild improvisations with his instrument on self-composed rock tunes. The guitar is always present, with dense rhythm, sometimes clean, sometimes heavy and fuzzy. **Brady** sings on all tracks with his loud voice.

There are severe dissonants, fuzz solos, many steel drum pyrotechnics and an inclination towards long tracks (greatly so on the opening *Glass House*).

On the other side there is psych-pop on *Hallucinodream*, hypnotic tribal chaos on *Soul Fungi* and a kind of weird R&B combined with Asian effects on *Once Upon A Candle*. The title cut of more than 11-minutes starts with a heavy fuzz riff over a Chinese harmonic pattern, but turns out to be hard-rock askew, like a more psyched-out version of Eric Burdon with traces of **Blue Cheer**. Only the closing cut *It's A Good World* outside tramples the same ground over and over. Very uncommon and thus recommended. (PM/MK)

Bob Brady and The Con Chords

45s:	Everybody's Going To The Love In/It's Been A Long Time Between Kisses	(Chariot Records 526)	196?
	More, More, More Of Your Love/ It's A Better World	(Chariot Records CH101)	196?
	Illusion/I Love You Baby	(Chariot Records 525)	196?
	It's Love/ Love Is The Master (I'm The Slave)	(Chariot Records 527)	196?
	Tell Me Why/Goodbye Baby	(Chariot Records C100)	196?

From Baltimore, Maryland area, they had a Regional hit with *Everybody's Goin To The Lov-In*. They also played around in the Washington area a lot and were very popular there for a number of years. By the early seventies **Brady** was with a group called Energy, who released at least one 45, in 1973.

They were a little more on the soul side than many garage bands. Interested readers should be aware of his offshoot groups Pen Lucy, and **Coyote**. Both released records, most notably the eponymous *Coyote* (Chariot 500) c1972. (JPr/MW/JV)

John Braheny

ALBUM:	1	SOME KIND OF CHANGE	(Pete S 1104)	1968 SC
45s:		Grey Day / Free Fall	(Pete 703)	1968
		Long Way Home / Long Way Home	(Pete 704)	1968

NB: There is apparently another 45 featuring a different (and better) version of *Some Kind Of Change*. Details, anyone?

An appealing album by a California folkie who mixed electric and acoustic folk; it is quite varied and in many ways ahead of its time. Much of it has a country / folk vibe with some fine orchestration, but the title track is quite a heavy rock song with loads of echo and prominent use of an oscillator. The closing track *Silver Cord* is a long, trippy guitar instrumental. *Free Fall* is another trippy, droning affair which also made it onto a 45.

All songs were written by **Braheny** and also include the beautiful ballad *December Dream* which was covered by the Linda Ronstadt's **Stone Poneys** on their second album *Evergreen Vol. 2*. A version also crops up on the recent **Fred Neil** 2-CD *Many Sides Of* compilation where the song is wrongly hailed as a lost composition by that great songwriter!

Musicians on the album included Rick Cunha of **Hearts and Flowers**.

John Braheny went on to run the Los Angeles Songwriters Showcase and has written a well-known book about songwriting. (SR/GM/TF/MW)

The Brain Police

Personnel:	TONY JOHNSON	drms	A
	FRANK MANNIX	bs	A
	DAVID RANDLE	gtr	AB
	RICK RANDLE	vcls, gtr, keyb'ds, hrmnca	AB
	NORMAN LOMBARDO	vcls, bs	BC
	SID SMITH	drms	BC
	LARRY GRANT	gtr	C
	(BENNY BENNETT	perc	B)

ALBUM: 1(B) THE BRAIN POLICE (K.B. Artists WR 4767) 1968 R6

NB: (1) issued as a demo disc in a plain sleeve. Some copies included a letter of introduction from their manager dated 15th October 1968. (1) has been reissued on Rockadelic (RRLP 26) 1997. There are two different versions of the reissue. Fifty copies came on coloured vinyl with a special folder containing inserts (R2) and 600 copies were pressed on black vinyl with several inserts (R1). (1) later reissued on CD, with ten extra tracks (Shadocks Music 008).

45: World Of Wax/Smoking At Windsor Hill (Head X 2002/3) 1969

The Brain Police were one of San Diego's most popular late-sixties groups. Rick Randle had been in **The Other Four/The Man-Dells** and Tony Johnson and Frank Mannix came from **Sandi and The Accents**, two bands that had been local phenomenons. In 1967, Norman Lombardo (**The Other Four**) and Sid Smith, a local drummer who had led a group called **The Roosters** who issued a 45 on A&M Records of *Shake A Tail Feather / Rooster Walk* (A&M 746) 1964, (Sid plays drums and sings lead vocals on this!) replaced Johnson and Mannix. This was the magical line-up that recorded the demo album in 1968. Recorded on a primitive 4-track machine, the record displays a degree of talent seldom seen in a teenage band. Through a unique combination of pop songs and heavy rock (all original material, written by Rick and Norman) **The Brain Police** created a remarkable document of American rock's transitionary period between flower-power and the guitar-led heavy rock that dominated the scene in 1969. The original demo album was pressed for promo use and the copies were sent to club owners and record labels - it is impossibly rare - the Rockadelic reissue is highly recommended, providing, of course, that you can find it! The reissue included a reprint of the letter included in the original and a fistful of psychedelic posters from the groups 1967 - 1968 tenure as San Diego's top draw.

Norman and Sid left San Diego in 1969, relocating to the San Francisco Bay Area and along with Norman's old friend Larry Grant (**The Other Four/The Man-Dells**) recorded the 45, using session musicians from the 'Frisco area who remain unknown. *World Of Wax* is radically different from the version on the 1968 demo album, and, as well, the 'B' side reveals that this band had little in common with the San Diego **Brain Police**. Within the next few months, Sid accepted an offer to record and tour with Roy "Treat Her Right" Head. Rick Randle hooked up with the legendary **Framework** just as they were disintegrating, and then he and their drummer Carl Spiron played together in a two-man band (ala **Lee Michaels** / Frosty) that never recorded but played a few well - received live shows as The Rick Randle Band. Sometime in 1969, Rick journeyed up to the Bay Area to join Norman and the two formed a short-lived group called The Dry Creek Road Band who recorded an album for Grunt records (produced by Paul Kantner of **The Jefferson Airplane**!) that remains unreleased, and played live in the area, including a gig at the Fillmore West. At about this time, the pair were asked to play in The Dudes, a top-notch band being assembled to back the up and coming singer Rita Coolidge. This band also included **Spooner Oldham**, Chris Ethridge and Randy Bishop - three musicians whose list of credits would fill this entire page. Rick then joined two hard-rock outfits, Bighorn and Child, recording and touring with each, and then formed the Seattle-based Randle-Rosburg Band, which became Striker, who released a highly-rated heavy rock album (Arista 4165) in 1978.

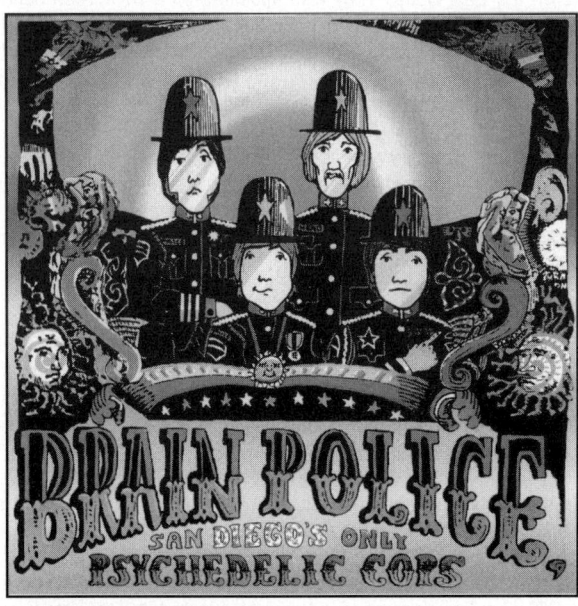

BRAIN POLICE - Brain Police CD.

The Brain Police had a most remarkable lineage for an "unknown" group - talent most exemplified by Rick Randle who is well remembered by all who came in contact with him as one of the true "naturals", a born singer / musician / performer who is ranked by many as one of the greatest the West Coast has ever produced.

You can also find *I'll Be On The Inside, If I Can* on *Love, Peace And Poetry: American Psychedelic Music* (LP & CD); and the album version of *My World Of Wax* on *The Shadoks Music Sampler* (CD). (CF/MW)

The Brain Train

Personnel:	MICHAEL NEY	drms	AB
	ROBBIE ROBISON	gtr, vcls	AB
	BOB SEALS	gtr, vcls	AB
	DALLAS TAYLOR	drms	AB
	WANDA WATKINS	vcls	A
	DOUGLAS LUBAHN	bs	B

45:	Black Roses/Me	(Titan FF-1738) 1967

The full story of this band has finally been revealed thanks to Lee Joseph's compilation *Take The Brain Train To The Third Eye* (LP & CD), annotated by Mike Stax. The theme of this recommended retrospective is the artists and releases in the hands of Bud Mathis, a boxer-turned-music-entrepreneur based on the Sunset Strip in the sixties.

Originally known as Garnerfield Sanitarium (line-up 'A') with an unusual double-drummer configuration, this local L.A. group were heard and picked up by Bud Mathis in 1966. Through him they acquired bassist Doug Lubahn but lost Wanda Watkins (who'd join another Mathis act **The Joint Effort**) and were rechristened **The Brain Train** (line-up 'B').

In late '66/early '67 they laid down *Black Roses* (written by Wolfgang Dios, a songwriter signed by Mathis) and *Me*. Mathis took these on the label trail and managed to get the group a contract with Elektra. At that point he was persuaded by Elektra to let Paul Rothchild take over as the group's manager. This triggered the band's final stage of metamorphosis into the venerated **Clear Light** - losing Robbie Robison and gaining Cliff DeYoung (vcls) and Ralph Schuckett (keyb'ds).

In September 1967 **Clear Light**'s first 45 was released - *She's Ready To Be Free / Black Roses* (Elektra 45622). Bud Mathis had retained the rights to the **Brain Train** material, and as this wasn't going to be used, he leased out the original recordings to Titan, who put out the excellent and sought-after **Brain Train** 45 the following month.

Black Roses is very similar to the finished Elektra product, where **Byrdsy**-jangle confronts Yardbirds-style-rave-ups. *Me* veers towards sheer dementia with crashing distorted guitars, demonic drumming (ala *7 And 7 Is*) and a chorus of eerie chants, reminiscent again of The Yardbirds (*Still I'm Sad*).

Both sides of the Titan 45 and an unreleased instrumental take of *Me* appear on *Take The Brain Train...* (LP & CD). Other compilation appearances include:- *Black Roses* and *Me* on *Scarey Business* (CD); *Me* on *The Chosen Few, Vol. 2* (LP), *Chosen Few Vol's 1 & 2* (CD) and *30 Seconds Before The Calico Wall* (CD). (MW/VJ)

The Brakmen

Personnel incl:	GORDON KRUSE	ld gtr, bs	A

45:	Minutes And Minutes/Movin'	(LSK WS-2391/2) 1967

From Fremont in Nebraska, this band were inducted to the Nebraska Music Hall of Fame on 9th June 2001. A second but unconfirmed 45 on LSK - *Nitey Nite* - is thought to exist.

Compilation appearances include: Both *Minutes & Minutes* and *Movin'* on *Garage Zone, Vol. 2* (LP) and *The Garage Zone Box Set* (4-LP). (VJ)

LOVE, PEACE AND POETRY: American Psychedelic Music (Comp LP) including The Brain Police.

Bram Rigg Set

Personnel:	RICHIE BEDNARZYCK	organ	A
	BOBBY SCHLOSSER (DAMON ROBEY)	ld vcls	A
	PETER NERI	ld gtr	A
	JERRY POULTON	bs	A
	BENNET SEGAL	drms	A

45:	I Can Only Give You Everything/ Take The Time, Be Yourself	(Kayden 400) 1967

NB: also released in the U.K. on Stateside (SS 2020).

Formed in Spring of 1966, with members coming from North Haven and Wallingford, Connecticut. The group got their moniker when a few of the guys spotted the name 'Bram Rigg' on a gravestone in the local cemetery, and decided to go with it. Their version of *I Can Only Give You Everything* and the original *Take The Time Be Yourself* were recorded at Syncron Studios in Wallingford. The original was credited as 'Trod nossel' an 'in-phrase' used by their manager, and later became the new name of Syncron Studios in Wallingford in 1968.

The 45 came out on a New Jersey owned and operated label, and after a few months, received regional airplay in Albany, New York State, Orlando Florida, and the Washington D.C. area. **The Bram Rigg Set** played every weekend in the state and when the single caught on elsewhere, traveled up and down the East Coast. They also appeared on a D.C. Teen bandstand show, and were set to lip-sync their 45, but before they could go on, the 45 was misplaced by the studio engineer. The band wanted to lip - sync to the **Wildweeds** *No Good To Cry* which was also popular at the time in the area, but the station manager wouldn't let them do it.

The Bram Rigg Set also appeared in the film 'A Show With A Very Long Title' which was a conceptual idea of teen bands and teen fashion that was shot in the New Haven area in 1966. **The Shags** appear in the film, while the **Bram Rigg Set** lip-sync *I Can Only Give You Everything* on the platform at the New Haven train station.

Bobby Schlosser (stage name Damon Robey) was involved with a local radio station as a DJ, and decided to quit the band in mid-1967. Local recording engineer and manager Doc Cavalier took some of the guys from the **Bram Rigg Set** and some from **The Shags** to form a 'real' musical group he dubbed **Pulse**. Subsequently **The Shags** split up in the Fall of 1967.

Compilation appearances have included: *I Can Only Give You Everything* and *Take The Time - Be Yourself* on *Psychotic Moose And The Soul Searchers* (LP); *I Can Only Give You Everything* on *Ear-Piercing Punk* (CD); *Take The Time, Be Yourself* on *Fuzz, Flaykes, And Shakes, Vol. 5* (LP & CD) and *Garage Music For Psych Heads, Vol. 1*. (VJ/MW/MM)

Brand X

45: She Lied/You Keep Coming Back For More (Sequoia 501) 1967

An obscure Californian punk band. *She Lied* can also be heard on *Boulders, Vol. 5* (LP) and *Ya Gotta Have Moxie, Vol. 1* (Dble CD). (VJ/MW)

Brand X

45: Come On Home/
Stop! In The Name Of Love (Steel Breeze STM-3786/7) 1970

Whether this is the California outfit of that name is unconfirmed. Heavy duty post-**Vanilla Fudge** with ladles of fuzz is what we're hearing here. Why they had to follow the **Vanilla Fudge** trail and fudgify motown songs is a mystery since *Come On Home* is the winner by far. (MW)

Brandywine

ALBUM: 1 AGED (Brunswick BL 754171) 1969 SC

A rock quartet with flashy guitar and strong harmonies. Their material ranged from hard-rock to mellow songs. (SR)

The Brass Button

45: Before My Time/same (mono) (Bell 876) 1969

NB: promo copy.

Although it was produced by Dale Hawkins and written by Ronnie Weiss and David Stanley (both from **Mouse and The Traps**), this single is in fact best avoided as it's a lame pop song with rich string arrangements by Al Gorgoni. (SR)

Brass Monkey

ALBUM: 1 BRASS MONKEY (Rare Earth RS-523) 1971 -

On the same label as **Lost Nation** and **Crystal Mansion**, this group released an album of heavy rock like **Vanilla Fudge**, with covers of *You Keep Me Hangin' On*, *Bang Bang*, *Proud Mary* and *All Fall Down*. (SR)

Brass Toad

45: In The Back Of My Mind/
Easy To Be Hard (Two Worlds 1071) 196?

PSYCHEDELIC EXPERIENCE (CD comp) including Brass Toad.

From Orange, Texas, end-of-decade/seventies 'psych' that is rated by some. It's a bit too gruff and serious to get one high though, with the 'A' side also having an orchestrated feel. Check it out for yourself on *Psychedelic Experience* (CD). (MW)

Brat

Personnel:	RITCHIE BRUBAKER	vcls, gtr	A
	GARY ERBE	drms	A
	ROGER FLORES	gtr	A
	SCOTT HEATH	bs	A

ALBUM: 1(A) BRAT (No label R 2826) 1972 R3

NB: (1) is a one-sided mono album issued in a plain sleeve. Only 50 copies were pressed.

This band were previously known as The Jackals and were gigging in the San Diego area at least as far back as 1968, when they opened a show headlined by **Framework** and **Kaleidoscope**. The six cuts on the **Brat** demo album include covers of *The Nazz Are Blue* and *The Kids Are Alright*, plus originals in a rural / hard-rock / Neil Young style. Brubaker still performs with his band The Roosters, the group he's been in since the late seventies... and he's known today as Ritchie Rooster. Roger Flores had previously played with **The Gnarly Beast**. (CF)

The Brave New World

Personnel:	MIKE BECK	bs	AB
	GEORGE M. GUILMET	keyb'ds, backing vcls	A
	JOHN KENNEDY	drms	A
	GUS MOLVIK	ld gtr	AB
	PAUL TROUSDALE	ld vcls	AB
	RON ADCOCK	drms	B
	MIKE WHALEN	keyb'ds	B

NB: Line-up 'A' 1966. Line-up 'B' 1967.

45s:	α	It's Tomorrow/Cried	(Panorama 51) 196?
		It's Tomorrow/Cried	(Piccadilly 225) 1966
	β	It's Tomorrow/Cried	(Epic 10123) 1967

NB: α Not released. Another pressing of β retitles *Cried* as *Don't You Know You Better Love Me*.

From Seattle, Guilmet, Kennedy and Molvik had all played at various times during 1964-5 in Mr. Clean and The Cleansers. Mr. Clean (a black vocalist, sax-player and band leader) used non-black sidemen so he could perform for both predominantly black inner-city Seattle clubs and general high school/college audiences. Mr. Clean blended traditional blues, R&B and motown with The Rolling Stones and similar material by miscellaneous American groups after the British invasion. Paul Trousdale knew members of **The Daily Flash** and **The Crome Syrcus**, two primary sources of the Seattle/San Francisco psychedelic sound. He wrote songs, mixing this genre with blues, which the three former members of Mr. Clean supported with their heavy R&B background.

Mike Beck blended both traditions. He'd played with Kennedy and Guilmet during 1963-4 in The Newports, the first Seattle group Guilmet had led. Tom Blessing of Tom Thumb And The Casuals was the sax player and sometimes lead singer in the group. The Newports played much material from the early Northwest sound. When Guilmet formed what was later to be named **Brave New World** in 1966, it was on Beck's suggestion that Trousdale should be auditioned as lead singer - they both attended the same high school, and had played together in **The Bodrockers**.

Brave New World played at the first major psychedelic rock concert in Seattle at the Eagles Auditorium in the Spring of 1967 (the Trips Festival named after its promoter Trips Lansing). They lasted as a more-or-less continuous band in various forms until 1973. By then Molvik and Guilmet had become the band's songwriters and lead vocalists. Beck was the other original member at this time.

Epic paid for a series of recording sessions of the band after *It's Tomorrow* was released, although it is uncertain whether the tapes still exist. Live tapes from 1972 definitely do, as does an early '67 astonishing rendition of

Signed D.C. recorded for Jerry Dennon. Incidentally, another version of their 45 was released on Epic 10123 with the flip-side entitled *Don't You Know You Better Love Me*, though it is the same track as *Cried*. Another song by the group, *I See*, was first published on *Battle Of The Bands, Vol. 2* (LP). They only recorded three songs in 1966. Jerry Dennon of Jerden first bought all three but then sold two to Epic, keeping *I See* for this and other Northwest collections.

Retrospective compilation appearances include: *Signed D.C.* on *Northwest Battle Of The Bands, Vol. 1* (CD); *Cried* on *Psychedelic Unknowns, Vol. 9* (CD); *It's Tomorrow* on *Boulders, Vol. 10* (LP), *History Of Northwest Rock, Vol. 5* and *Ya Gotta Have Moxie, Vol. 1* (Dble CD); *I See* on *The History Of Northwest Rock, Vol. 3* (LP); and both *It's Tomorrow* and *I See* on *The History Of Northwest Rock, Vol. 3* (CD) and *Northwest Battle Of The Bands, Vol. 2* (CD).

Gus Molvik's son is the lead singer/lead guitarist Taine Downe (Gus Molvik Jr. or 'Little Gus') of the contemporary L.A. band Faster Pussycat. (MW/DR/VJ)

The Breakers

45s:	All My Nights, All My Days/		
	Better For The Both Of Us	(Riverton 102)	1965
	All My Nights, All My Days/		
	Better For The Both Of Us	(Jerden 789)	1966

From the Pacific Northwest. *All My Nights, All My Days*, their finest moment, can be found on *Battle Of The Bands, Vol. 2* (LP) and *The History Of Northwest Rock, Vol. 3* (LP). This is actually Tacoma's **Wailers** under a pseudonym. (VJ)

The Breakers

Personnel incl: BOB GARVEY   A

45s:	Jet Stream/Beachhead	(DJB 116)	1964
	She's Bound To Put You Down/		
	Tears In The Rain	(Romco 101)	1965
	Long Green/Splivit Shuffle	(Celmor 1002)	1966/7

This band operated out of Wichita, in Southern Central Kansas, during the mid and late sixties. They started out playing surf rock and by 1966 had become an eight piece horn-rock outfit. It's really their second 45 (their garage rock phase) which may interest readers and you can cheek out *She's Bound To Put You Down* on *Garage Punk Unknowns, Vol. 5*. (VJ)

PEBBLES Vol. 16 (Comp LP) including Bobby Brelyn.

The Breakers

Personnel:	GARY JOHNS	vcls	A
	TOM KECKLER	bs	A
	MIKE LADD	ld gtr	A
	RICHARD LEWIS	gtr	A
	STEWART LEWIS	vcls	A
	EDDIE TATUM	drms	A

45:	Don't Send Me No Flowers, I Ain't Dead Yet/		
	Love Of My Life	(Amy 938)	1966

This garage/punk outfit came from Memphis Tennesse and the 'A' side of the 45, a classic 'pleading' ballad with fine fuzztone guitar, was written by Donna Weiss, a Nashville songwriter who years later won a Grammy for her composition *Bette Davis Eyes*. **The Breakers** were all high school mates aged 15-22, and their sole stab at stardom came when they caught the ear of Charlie Rich's manager, Sy Rosenburg. Stewart Lewis remembers: "He drove us to Nashville to record the song and although it only reached No. 25 in Memphis we heard that it did well in the Santa Barbara, California area. We didn't release any other records however. We just played locally and did the occasional "Battle of the Bands" contest against local bands like **The Gentrys** and The Boxtops. They won, naturally."

"After a few years of garage band fun, everyone drifted away to college, other bands, and real work. Playing in the band launched a couple of music-related careers. Tom Keckler went on to develop quite a reputation making custom-made guitars for the rich and famous and Gary Johns made a career out of music locally, ending up playing in a band with Duck Dunn and **Steve Cropper**, two noted Memphis studio musicians".

Compilation appearances have included: *Don't Send Me No Flowers (I Ain't Dead Yet)* on *Pebbles, Vol. 12* (LP), *Pebbles, Vol. 10* (CD), *Pebbles, Vol. 3 (ESD)* (CD) and *The Essential Pebbles Collection, Vol. 1* (Dble CD).

Other **Breakers** hailed from Phoenix (Arizona), Wichita (Kansas), and Tacoma (Washington)... the latter being **The Wailers** under a pseudonym. (VJ/MW/JCs)

The Breakers

45:	Say You're Mine / Once More	(Moxie MRC 103) 1964

These **Breakers** came from Phoenix, Arizona and released just one 45. (MW)

The Breakers

45s:	Jet Stream / Beach Head (instrs)	(DJB 116)	1964
	She's Bound To Put You Down /		
	Tears In The Rain	(Romco 101)	1965
	Long Green / Splivit Shuffle	(Celmor 1002)	c1967

This outfit broke out in Wichita, Kansas and released three 45s, each in the style of their time... surf, garage and horn-rock respectively. Both sides of their instrumental debut are on *Strummin' Mental, Vol. 4* and *She's Bound To Put You Down* is compiled on *Garage Punk Unknowns, Vol. 5* (LP) and the *Midwest Garage Band Series - Kansas* (CD). (MW/TT)

Bobby Brelyn

45s:	I Sit By... /Yes You Do	(Jorel S-5133/?)	1967
	Hanna/I Know I'll Cry Tomorrow	(Jorel S-5396/7)	1968
	Bits & Pieces/?	(Jorel)	196?

Brelyn (real name Bob Konecnik) was actually a late sixties Chicago-based pop artist, but *Hanna* a rather Dylanesque punk song with some good guitar has been included on *Pebbles, Vol. 16* (LP), *Pebbles, Vol. 7* (CD), *Psychedelic Unknowns, Vol. 6* (LP & CD) and *Boulders, Vol. 11* (LP). It was rather out of character, with his other releases, with *I Know I'll Cry Tomorrow* being a country and western ballad and *Bits & Pieces* being described as "fuzz with slight horns". (BM/MW/VJ)

SONGS OF FAITH AND INSPIRATION (Comp CD) includes Brew.

The Brentwoods

| 45: | Yeah, Yeah, No, No/Babe You Know | (Ovr 101) 1967 |

Although this flower-pop 45 bears all the hallmarks of L.A. the band were from West Texas. The flip side can be found on *Highs In The Mid-Sixties, Vol. 12* (LP). (VJ)

Brethren

Personnel:	TOM COSGROVE	gtr, vcls, perc	A
	MIKE GARSON	keyb'ds	A
	RICK MAROTTA	drms	A
	STU WOODS	bs, clavinette	A

| ALBUMS: | 1(A) | BRETHREN | (Tiffany TFS 0013) 1970 - |
| | 2(A) | MOMENT OF TRUTH | (Tiffany TFS 0015) 1971 - |

A New York rock group with good guitar and organ work and a rather "funky" sound on some tracks. Their second album contains original material and three covers: a long version of **Dr. John**'s *Loop Garoo*, *The Sun And The Moon* by Mark Klingman and *Freedom Blues* penned by E. Reeder. Well played, but nothing outstanding. A marginal case for inclusion.

The four members became active session men during the seventies and eighties. (SR)

Brew

Personnel:	TOMMY LOZANE	vcls	A
	MARK	drms	A
	JOHN MEKENIAN	organ, piano	A
	RONNY REYES	ld gtr, vcls	A
	ART SANCHEZ	bs, vcls	A

| ALBUM: | 1(A) | A VERY STRANGE BREW | (ABC 672) 1969 SC |

This was the work of an obscure California quintet who may have spent time in Texas too. It's rumoured that a few of them were at some point members of **Impala Syndrome**. The album, which contains some interesting guitar work, is a marginal case for inclusion here and it's yet to become a real collectable.

Members later formed Yaqui, who released one album *Yaqui* (Playboy Records) 1973, which was dedicated to Don Juan and Carlos Castaneda. Musically, it sounded similar to **Santana**.

Compilation appearances include *What Do You See In My Mind?* on *Songs Of Faith And Inspiration* (CDR & CD). (VJ/SR)

Brewer and Shipley

Personnel:	MICHAEL BREWER	vcls, gtr, piano	ABCD
	TOM SHIPLEY	vcls, gtr, bs	ABCD
	HAL BLAINE	drms	A
	RUSSELL BRIDGES (LEON RUSSELL)	organ, piano	A
	JIM GORDON	drms	A
	MILT HOLLAND	perc	A
	MIKE MELVOIN	organ	A
	JIM MESSINA	bs	A
	JOE OSBORN	bs	A
	LYLE RITZ	bs	A
	LANCE WAKELY	gtr, harp	A
	RIENOL ANDINO	congas	B
	APPLEJACK	hrmnca	B
	MICHAEL BLOOMFIELD	gtr	B
	RICHARD GREENE	fiddle	B
	ROBERT HUBERMAN	bs	B
	BOB JONES	drms	BC
	JOHN KAHN	bs, wah-wah	BCD
	IRA KAMIN	keyb'ds	B
	MARK NAFTALIN	keyb'ds	BCD
	FRED OLSON	gtr	B
	ORVILLE RED RHODES	pedal steel	B
	FRED BURTON	gtr	C
	DANNY COX	vcls	C
	JERRY GARCIA	pedal steel	C
	NICK GRAVENITES	vcls	C
	NOEL JEWKES	flute	C
	DIANE TRIBUNO	vcls	C
	BILL VITT	drms	C
	JOSE CHEPITO ARIAS	perc	D
	JOHN CIPOLLINA	gtr	D
	SPENCER DRYDEN	drms	D
	JOHN HARTMAN	drms	D
	DAVID LA FLAMME	elec. violin	D
	GLEN WALTERS	drms	D

HCP

ALBUMS:	1(A)	DOWN IN L.A.	(A&M SP 4154) 1968 - -
(up to	2(B)	WEEDS	(Kama Sutra BS 2015) 1969 - -
1971)	3(C)	TARKIO ROAD	(Kama Sutra BS 2024) 1970 34 -
	4(D)	SHAKE OFF THE DEMON	(Kama Sutra BS 2039) 1971 164 -

NB: *One Toke Over The Line* (Buddah 74465 99811 2) 2001 is a collection of their early seventies material mostly compiled from their *Weeds* and *Tarkio Road* albums.

HCP

45s:	One Toke Over The Line/	
(up to	Oh Mommy	(Kama Sutra KA 516) 1970 10
1972)	Tarkio Road/	
	Seems Like A Long Time	(Kama Sutra KA 524) 1970 55
α	Shake Off The Demon/?	(Kama Sutra KA 539) 1971 98
	Indian Summer/	
	Song From Platte River	(Radioactive Gold RD 77) 1972 -

NB: α two-sided mono/stereo promo copies exist.

From Kansas, **Brewer and Shipley** were primarily a hippie duet with strong country-rock roots. They would be beyond the scope of this book if it wasn't for their lyrics, which often deal with drugs (*One Toke Over The Line*, *Oh Mommy*, *Back To The Farm* ...), their hippie values (*People Love Each Other*, *Fifty States Of Freedom*..) and for their numerous links with the Bay Area musical scene.

The pair first met at the Blind Owl coffeehouse in Kent, Ohio, during 1964, however they didn't get togther until mid-1967. In the interim Shipley (born 1942 in Mineral Ridge, Ohio) spent some time working the Toronto folk circuit. Brewer (born 1944, Oklahoma City), meanwhile travelled to L.A. in late '65 with partner Tom Mastin and formed **Mastin & Brewer**. After Brewer's brother Keith replaced Mastin in late 1966, the Brewer brothers continued to write untill mid-1967, when Mike landed a songwriting job with Good Sam Music, an affiliation of A&M. Here he arranged for Shipley to also be recruited, and during the Summer, they began recording their debut album. This was partially recorded at **Leon Russell**'s house.

During 1967 they wrote songs individually for **The Nitty Gritty Dirt Band** and **The Poor** amongst others. **H.P. Lovecraft** also covered the collaboration *Keeper Of The Keys*, which appeared on the duo's debut album.

Their first album was produced by Allen Stanton (who also worked with **The Byrds** and **Mort Garson**) and Jerry Riopelle. *Down In L.A.* defined their style: short, well structured songs with harmonies, good lyrics and the use of excellent musicians: Russell Bridges (better known as **Leon Russell**), Lance Wakely (pre-**Joyous Noise**), Jim Messina (**Buffalo Springfield/Poco**), plus the usual L.A. sessionmen.

Brewer and Shipley then decided to move to Kansas (they would return to California only to record) and signed a new contract with Kama Sutra. Their first two albums for their new label were **Nick Gravenites**. Some of the best musicians of the San Francisco scene play on these albums, including: Richard Greene (**Seatrain**), Mark Naftalin (**Butterfield Blues Band**, **Mother Earth**, **Quicksilver**), Michael Bloomfield, Bob Jones (**We Five**, Southern Comfort), **Jerry Garcia**, John Cipollina, David La Flamme (**It's A Beautiful Day**), Spencer Dryden (**Jefferson Airplane**),...

Not surprisingly, all their albums offer some good guitar solos. However *Weeds* and *Shake Off The Demon* are probably the best. The former contains a superb elongated cover of *Witchi Tai To*, the Indian hymn penned by **Jim Pepper** (ex-**Free Spirits**), whilst *Shake Off The Demon*, with its title track, *Working On The Well* and *Natural Child* (with the electric violin of David La Flamme) being excellent.

Brewer and Shipley kept on recording for Kama Sutra and Capitol after 1972 but their albums are more conventional. (SR/NW)

Bridge

45s:	The Life Of A Day/A Beautiful Day	(Co-op 519) 1969
	Love Is There/Gotta Get Back	(Roulette R-7081) 1970

The first 45 used to be picked up fairly easily, but nowadays this New Haven, Connecticut, outfit's late mid-tempo psych ballad is quite hard to obtain. Solid-backing with moody mellotron and some burning guitar backed with a straight pop-rocker. The later 45 is dramatic mid-tempo pop-rock with some searing guitar on one side and a harp solo on the other.

Compilation appearances include: *Love Is There* on *Sixties Rebellion, Vol. 11* (LP & CD). (MW/MM)

The Bridge

ALBUM: 1 JUST FOR YOU
(Crescent City Studios #CCSS-1226) 1970 -

A six-piece mixed male/female Jesus Rock group from Greensboro, North Carolina. They issued at least one other album. (SR)

The Brigade

Personnel:	BOB ANDERSON	drms	ABC
	ERIC ANDERSON	keyb'ds	ABC
	PETER BELKNAP	vcls	ABC
	TIMMY VETTER	bs	A
	ED WALLO	gtr	ABC
	MARK HARTMAN	bs	B
	DENNIS STEINDL	bs	C

ALBUM: 1(C) LAST LAUGH   (Band N Vocal 1066) 1970 R5

NB: (1) counterfeited (Del Val) 1991, and reissued officially in a deluxe package with poster (Shadocks 011) 2000.

Formed in North Portland, Oregon during the Summer of 1966. They won the KLSN Radio Portland Teen Fair Battle Of The Bands on 9th June 1968 and received a 1954 custom purple Cadillac Hearse as a prize! By now they were a top local attraction and the same year they signed to the American Record Company and recorded a demo which received a lot of local airplay. They went on to record an album for the B&V label in 1970

THE BRIGADE - Last Laugh LP

but split up before it was released. Consequently it received little airplay and flopped. The band all went on to college or further education. Today the album is exceedingly rare and even the limited edition reissue on Rockadelic, which has been restricted to just 350 copies, seems destined to become the same before long. Musically, it consists of keyboard-dominated progressive rock and pretty uninspired progressive rock at that on Side One. The second side is much better, with some exhilarating keyboard playing on *Self-Made God* the highlight. (VJ)

The Brigands

Personnel:	JOHNNY HARTMAN	gtr, ld vcls	A
	CAESER PACIFICI	ld gtr	A
	SAM MULDAVIN	drms	A
	ELLIOT WERTHEIM	bs, vcls	A

45:	I'm A Patient Man/	
	(Would I Still Be) Her Big Man	(Epic 1001) 1966

45 Acetates:

(Would I Still Be) Her Big Man /	
My One Chance To Make It	(Belinda acetate) 196?
My Closest Living Relative /	
Five Minutes To Train Time	(Belinda Acetate) 196?

This band formed in 1965 in Forest Hills, New York. The 'B' side to their 45, *(Would I Still Be) Her Big Man*, is a song about a guy working himself into the ground to pay for his girlfriend's expensive habits. It was written and produced by Arthur and Kris Resnick of **Third Rail** fame and is pretty good, with sharp lyrics and typical garage instrumentation.

Johnny, Caesar and Elliot were students at Forest Hills High School, and Sam went to Stuyvesant High School. Johnny, Caesar, and Elliot had begun jamming together and recruited Sam to sit in on drums for a gig they had in a building basement. **The Brigands** gigged at school dances and opened at alcohol-free night clubs.

Johnny Hartman lived in the same apartment building as song writers Artie and Kris Resnick. Artie arranged for the band to record a demo and then took it from studio to studio, trying to get a deal. Epic bit the hook, and at a meeting at Johnny's house, their parents signed 5-year contracts with the label.

Patient Man was pick hit of the week on WJET in Erie Pennsylvania.

In addition to the 45, two uncredited Belinda acetates have been unearthed in the UK, featuring both tracks from the Epic 45. As a result *Her Big Man* has been compiled on *Purple Heart Surgery, Vol. 2* (LP) and *My Closest Living Relative* on *Incredible Sound Show Stories, Vol. 10* (LP). Coincidentally *Five Minutes...* is exactly the same title as a song by the Opus IV.

BRIGG - Brigg CD.

Other compilation appearances include: *(Would I Still Be) Her Big Man* on *Nuggets Box* (4-CD), *Sixties Punk Ballads Sampler* (LP), *Sixties Archive, Vol. 5* (CD), *Back From The Grave, Vol. 2* (LP) and *Garage Kings* (Dble LP). (VJ/MW/KM)

Brigg

Personnel:	RUSTY FOULKE	vcls, gtr	A
	ROB MORSE	acoustic gtr	A
	JEFF WILLOUGHBY	bs, flute, piano, vcls	A

ALBUM: 1(A) BRIGG (Susquehanna Sound Productions LP 301) 1973 R2

NB: (1) has been counterfeited on vinyl (Hablabel) 198? and counterfeited on CD (MER 32-158).

This is an album of folk-tinged psychedelic rock, from a Danville, Pennsylvania band, although some dealers have previously listed them as Canadian. Not a particularly memorable album, but quite pleasant.

After **Brigg** broke up, Rusty Foulke (who later changed his name to Galen Toye Foulke) and Jeff Willoughby formed The Hybrid Ice Company. This group later shortened the name to Hybrid Ice and lasted from 1973 until the mid-nineties, releasing two albums: *Hybrid Ice* (A Street Records LP 1211) 1982 and *No Rules* (Pilot Records PR-8809) 1987.

The *Brigg* album was actually recorded after **Brigg** had broken up and Hybrid Ice had formed; it was **Brigg**'s only album release, and there were no singles either. The three record labels used by **Brigg** and Hybrid Ice (SSP, A Street, and Pilot) were all based out of Susquehanna Sound Productions in Northumberland, Pennsylvania, where all three albums were recorded.

A Rusty Foulke song called *Magdalene* from the first Hybrid Ice album was later recorded by Boston for their *Third Stage* album. (JPu/VJ)

Bright Image

45: People In The Town/Julip Sanctuary (Amigo 114) 196?

A Philadelphia-based band. *People In The Town* features lots of fuzzy guitar and wailing vocals. It has been compiled on *Return Of The Young Pennsylvanians* (LP) and *Gathering Of The Tribe* (CD). (VJ)

George Brigman

Personnel:	JEFF BARRETT	drms	A
	GEORGE BRIGMAN	gtr, vcls, bs	A
	RON COLLIER	harp, conga	A

ALBUMS:	1(A)	JUNGLE ROT	(Solid SR001) 1975 R5
	2( )	2ND ALBUM	(Cassette only) 1977 -

NB: There's also *I Can Hear The Ants Dancin'* (Or 004) 1995, a vinyl reissue of the 1982 cassette of the same name.

45: Blowin' Smoke/Drifting (Solid SR 8417) 1977

NB: shown as by Split.

A local Maryland group. *Jungle Rot* is full of **Stooges** - like raw electric punk, superb psychedelic guitar, and is very hard to find now. More accessible and in similar vein is *Human Scrawl Vagabond* (Resonance 33-8602) 1987 - a recent Dutch release. This includes material from his obscure *I Can Hear Ants Dancing* cassette and a five-track *Silent Bones EP* (from 1985) together with six previously unreleased tracks and is full of fuzztone guitar.

I Can Hear Ants Dancin' has also been reissued on vinyl by OR records. (CF/VJ)

The Briks

Personnel:	RICHARD BORGENS	ld gtr	AB
	CECIL COTTON	vcls	A C
	LEE HARDESTY	gtr	ABC
	MIKE MARONEY	bs	ABC
	STEVE MARTIN	drms	A
	PAUL RAY	vcls	B
	CHRIS VAN DER CULT	drms	BC
	JAMIE HERNDON	ld gtr	C

45s:	I'm Losing/		
	It's Your Choice (Acetate)	(Rhodes Recording No #)	1966
	Can You See Me?/Foolish Baby	(Bismarck 1013)	1966
	Can You See Me?/Foolish Baby	(Dot 16878)	1966
	NSU/From A Small Room	(Bismarck 1020)	1967

Originally known as The Embers when they formed at Texas Tech early in 1965. They relocated to Dallas in the Summer of that year and renamed themselves **The Briks**. Their first 45, which was preceded by an acetate, sold around 5,000 copies and was a hit locally. *Foolish Baby* was a pounding punk number, later compiled on *Flashback, Vol. 5* (LP); *Texas Flashbacks, Vol. 5* (LP) and *Highs In The Mid-Sixties, Vol. 13* (LP). The 45 was leased to Dot for nation-wide distribution but did not become the big hit the band hoped for. Their progress was further interrupted when Cotton, Martin and their manager Reggie Lange were drafted in the Summer of 1966 although Cotton later rejoined the band in January 1967 when his original replacement Paul Ray left to join The Cobras. Later in 1967 a live tape was made of the band at The Northwood Country Club and this can be heard on Side Two of *Texas Punk, Vol. 8*. They also recorded a second

GEORGE BRIGMAN - Jungle Rot LP.

45, a rather weak cover of The Cream song *NSU* which flopped. Having failed to achieve success they disintegrated during 1968, but Richard Bergens later turned up on **The Truth** 45 and Cecil Cotton later moved to San Francisco where he played in The Snakes with Steve Karnavas (ex-**Chapparals**).

The Briks have been extensively covered in Cicadelic's Texas Punk series. Apart from occupying one side of *Texas Punk, Vol. 8*, they have six tracks on *Texas Punk, Vol. 7*. In addition to *Can You See Me?*, *Foolish Baby* and *N.S.U*, there are three previously unreleased tracks: the cover version of The Animals' *Baby, Let Me Take You Home* as performed by the band on the Sump 'N' Else TV Show; and *Over You*, a folk-rock melody and *Keep Down* with Paul Ray on vocals. *Texas Punk, Vol. 6 - Dallas, 1966* features *It Won't Be Wrong* and *It's Your Choice* - two previously unreleased tracks the last of which had been recorded along with *I'm Losing* early in 1966 prior to the first 45. All of the tracks included on the Cicadelic vinyl compilation series, also appear on the Collectables CD box set *Acid Visions - Complete Collection, Vol. 3* (3-CD). (VJ)

Brimstone

Personnel:
GREGG ANDREWS — vcls — A
KEN MILLER — bs, voice — A
BERNIE NAU — keyb'ds, clarinet, voice — A
JIMMY PAPATOUKAKIS — — A
CHRISTOPHER WINTRIP — gtr, voice — A

ALBUM: 1(A) PAPER WINGED DREAMS (Langco 30534) 1973 R2

NB: (1) counterfeited on vinyl (PP 1022) 1989, limited to 250 copies. (1) reissued on CD.

45: Home Cooking/Visions Of Autumn (Langco 3122/3) 1973

The album is melodic, early seventies progressive rock, with the title track probably the pick of Side One. Side two is a complex suite in five movements. Each movement, except the last is symbolic of something. The first, an instrumental composition on a childhood fantasy, symbolises the Crown of Creation. The second is symbolic of the Resurrection. It features some nice solo vocals complimented by intermingled harmonies. The third is symbolic of The Conception of Life and culminates in lots of instrumentation and percussion. The fourth is the most melodic part of the suite. Lyrics dominate the music but there's some nice guitar work and counter-pointing vocals. Given what has gone before the epilogue is a little disappointing but overall this is worth investigation. It was recorded in Youngstown, Ohio, although the band came from Cleveland. (VJ/MW/GGI)

Brimstone

45: Blowin' In The Wind/Trinket (Firebird 1800) 1969

A soulful outfit from Florida. Their 45 was produced by Arthur Aaron and Stan Schwartz (MW/GGI/SR)

The Brimstones

45: It's All Over Now But The Crying/
What Is This Life? (MGM 13653) 1966

This Dallas, Texas band, had no other recorded output. The 'A' side later resurfaced on *Pebbles, Vol. 17* (LP). It's a rather demented R&B influenced fuzz-rocker superimposed with rather emotive vocals. (VJ/MW)

The British Colonels

Played a lot around the Dallas area of Texas in the mid-sixties but never made it onto vinyl at the time. *Texas Punk, Vol. 9* (LP) and *Acid Visions - Complete Collection, Vol. 3* (3-CD) include *Come Back*, a rather inconsequential previously unreleased recording by the band. (VJ)

BRIMSTONE - Paper Winged Dreams CD.

The British Walkers

Personnel incl:
ROY BUCHANAN — gtr — A
BOBBY "THE KID" HOWARD — vcls — ABCDEFG H
MIKE KENNEDY — drms — AB
JUNIOR GIL — bs — AB
JIMMY CARTER — gtr — BCD
GARY KINGERY — drms — C
RONNIE WELBORNE — bs — C
JACK BROOKS — bs — DEFG
STEVE LACEY — drms — DEFG
TED SPELEOS — gtr — EF
JOHN HALL — bs, keyb'ds — F
TONY FALSO — — G
GEOFFREY RICHARDSON — — G
MIKE ZACK — drms — H

                                              HCP

45s: I Found You/Diddley Daddy (Try 502) 1964 -
The Girl Can't Help It/
Lonely Lover's Poem (Charger 108) 1965 -
α Watch Yourself/Bad Lightnin' (Manchester 651120) 1965 -
α The Story of My Life/
Bad Lightnin' (Manchester 651121) 1965/6 -
β Sh'mon / Sh'mon Pt.2 (Soultime 001) 1966 -
χ Shake/That Was Yesterday (Cameo 466) 1967 106

NB: α recorded by Bobby Howard with Nashville session players. β released as by Mr. Dynamite. χ recorded by Bobby Howard, Larry Kidwell and Chartbusters members.

Originally a Virginian outfit called Bobby Howard and The Hi-Boys (line-up 'A'). Bobby Howard had already established himself on the scene with **Link Wray**'s band, the␣Wraymen, and continued to record with Wray and as a solo artist.

Bitten by the Invasion bug, they changed to an Anglophile name and style and soon became a big attraction on the Washington, D.C. scene alongside **The English Setters**, **Fallen Angels**, **Chartbusters** and Telstars.

The debut 45 reflects the Liverpool influence - a Beatlesque pop ballad backed by a driving Bo Diddley beat-stomper with harmonica. It was written and produced by Roy Buchanan. *Watch Yourself*, written by Bobby Howard and **Link Wray**, looks to Bo Diddley again for the shufflin' rhythm with a nod to the Rolling Stones for moody attitude, then adds some cool slippery-smooth guitar runs - one of the class cuts on *Sixties Rebellion, Vol. 16* (LP & CD). *Bad Lightnin'*, notable for more great harmonica and raw vocals is on the *Signed, D.C.* (LP) compilation. Bob Embrey reveals in his fanzine, "D.C. Monuments", that the Manchester 45s were recorded in Nashville by Bobby Howard with session musicians.

Shake is one of the more accomplished cover versions and can be heard on *A Journey To Tyme, Vol. 4* (LP) - excellent R&B vocals, great rhythm section and an unexpected fuzz solo. The flip is an orchestrated beat ballad. Bob Embrey notes that this 45 was actually recorded in New York City by Bobby Howard with members of **The Chartbusters** and Larry Kidwell of Lawrence and The Arabians on keyboards.

Bobby Howard left soon after in 1967 and joined **The Mad Hatters** briefly before forming the Sweet, a blue-eyed soul group who put out a couple of 45s on Smash. He'd team with **Link Wray** again in the early seventies and release a solo album as Mordicai Jones.

The British Walkers strolled on through many line-ups but never recorded again and finally folded in 1969. Bobbie Howard was the only member to play on all their recordings.

Amongst a host of local heroes that passed through their ranks the most famous is original guitarist **Roy Buchanan**, already a seasoned and in-demand player at the time. He would move on through a succession of other bands (Outcasts, Fourmost, Uncalled Four) and famous artists before a solo career that came to prominence in the early seventies with the sublime instrumental *Sweet Dreams*.

Mike Zack, who replaced Steve Lacey, was from Lawrence and The Arabians and would go on to many other outfits including Wild Honey, Reasons Why, **Puzzle**, Cherry People and Nils Lofgren's band.

Jimmy Carter moved on to the **Telstars** and was reunited with Zack in Wild Honey. Steve Lacey also joined the **Telstars** and would move on to Smalltalk, **Puzzle** and Tractor.

Hall and Speleos teamed up with Boston emigres **Barbara Keith** and ex-**Remains** drummer N.D.Smart to form **Kangaroo**. John Hall would find greater success in the mid-seventies with Orleans.

Thanks to Bob Embrey and his "D.C. Monuments" fanzine (issue #2 is devoted to **The British Walkers**) for straightening out the personnel details.

For more info on the D.C. scene check out Mark Opsasnick's 'Capitol Rock' (Fort Center Books, 1996). (MW/VJ/BE)

B. Brock and The Sultans

ALBUM: 1 DO THE BEETLE (Crown) 1964 SC

Another Beatles look-alike released on a budget label, with a cover of *I Want To Hold Your Hand* and extremely imaginative song titles: *Beetle Walk*, *Do The Beetle*, *Mexican Beetle*, *Fast Beetle*, *Little Brown Beetle*... (SR)

Jaime Brockett

ALBUM: 1 REMEMBER THE WIND AND THE RAIN
(Oracle) 1969 SC

NB: (1) reissued (Capitol) 1969.

A Boston folk-rock singer. Mainly notable for one track, *Legend Of The USS Titanic*, his album was first released on Oracle and then licensed by Capitol, on the same deal as **Brother Fox and The Tar Baby**. (SR)

The Brogues

Personnel:	RICK CAMPBELL	organ, vcls	AB
	GREG ELMORE	drms	AB
	EDDIE RODRIGUES	gtr	AB
	BILL WHITTINGTON	bs	AB
	GARY GRUBB (nee DUNCAN)	vcls	B

EPs: 1(A/B) THE BROGUES (Line/Taxim 3012) 198?
2(A/B) Someday/But Now I Find/I Ain't No Miracle Worker/
Don't Shoot Me Down (Sundazed SEP 114) 1996

NB: (1) and (2) contain both their 45s.

45s: Someday/But Now I Find (Twilight 408) 1965
Someday/But Now I Find (Challenge 59311) 1965
Don't Shoot Me Down/
I Ain't No Miracle Worker (Challenge 54316) 1965

Although **The Brogues** lifespan extended a mere nine months, and their recorded output was limited to just two 45s, they are remembered some thirty years on as one of the best sixties punk bands - and as a precursor to **Quicksilver Messenger Service**.

The Brogues formed towards the end of '64, playing their first gig on News Years Eve that year and quickly gathering a following in their home town of Merced, California. It wasn't long before they cut a couple of demo tracks at a studio in Fresno, and the Hush label picked up on the stronger of them, *Someday*. (The other track, *Journey* is reputedly a poor instrumental which sounds like a TV theme tune). They were quickly signed up by Hush who prompted them to re-record the track at Coast Recorders, San Francisco for their first 45. Although *Someday* wasn't typically representative of the band's sound - being more of a folk-rocker, it's still pretty decent and the flip is more akin to their Brit-Invasion influences.

The 45 was a local hit around Bakersfield and Fresno, and they even got to play alongside bands such as the Zombies and plug the 45 on an L.A. TV show. It was also around this time that they recruited (pinched) Gary Grubb from another local group The Ratz, his vocal style fitting **The Brogues** penchance for "American music with a British accent", i.e. Brit Invasion styled R&B revved up with passion and ferocity.

Someday was licensed by major indie Challenge, and the new label took them to L.A. to record a follow-up - *Miracle Worker* being selected from a pile of demo acetates and the flip *Don't Shoot Me Down* being written by the band almost on the spot.

This epic punk 45, should have burned up the charts, but unfortunately **The Brogues** were in the hands of bigger forces... within a few weeks Eddie and Rick had received draft notices and had no option to quit. With the heart torn out of the band, auditions were held, but it was quickly realised that the magic could not be re-constructed, and they decided to disband.

Greg and Gary decided to stay in San Francisco, forming **Quicksilver Messenger Service**, whilst Bill went on to **Family Tree**, together with ex-**Ratz** member Bob Segarini.

Compilation coverage has so far included both sides of both their 45s plus the demo version of *Someday* on *The Hush Records Story*; both sides of their first 45 on *Sound Of The Sixties: San Francisco Part 2* (LP); both sides of their second 45 on *Psychedelic Microdots, Vol. 1* (CD) and *I Turned Into A Helium Balloon* (CD); *Don't Shoot Me Down* on *Garage Music For Psych Heads* and *Pebbles, Vol. 10* (LP); and *I Ain't No Miracle Worker* has resurfaced on *Mindrocker, Vol. 1* (LP), *Nuggets, Vol. 6* (LP), *Nuggets Box* (4-CD), *Trash Box* (5-CD), *Excerpts From Nuggets* (CD), *Best of Pebbles, Vol. 1* (LP & CD) and *Sundazed Sampler, Vol. 1* (CD).

PEBBLES Vol. 10 (Comp LP) including The Brogues.

For a more indepth and eloquent article on **The Brogues** see Alec Palao's write-up on Hitomi I's Trans-World '60s Punk:Cutie Morning Moon website: http://60spunk.m78.com/ (VJ/MW)

Bronin Hogman Band

ALBUM: 1 BRONIN HOGMAN BAND (Gamut) 1974 R1

From Manchester, New Hampshire, this band was formed while all eight band members were still in High School. After all the members graduated, and with one album under their belt, they became a popular act on the New England college circuit, often opening for major acts. This album is a progressive rock effort dominated by keyboards and synthesizers. This is not a psychedelic record, but it will appeal to to collectors of local progressive rock albums. (HS/SR)

Donnie Brooks

45s: Abracadabra/
I Know You As A Woman (Happy Tiger HT 526) c1969
Hush/I Know You As A Woman (Happy Tiger HT 544) c1969
My God And I/Pink Carousel (Happy Tiger HT 551) c1969
(I Wanna) Have You For Myself/
Rub-A-Dub-Dub (Happy Tiger HT 566) c1970
I'm Gonna Make You Love Me/
Pink Carousel (Happy Tiger HT 579) c1970

Donnie Brooks is now largely forgotten but released nearly 30 singles between 1959 and 1971 on various labels. Most of them are pop, but the ones released for the Happy Tiger label in the late sixties are quite interesting, in a California pop-rock vein.

Produced by Ray Ruff, the **Joe South** song, *Hush*, was arranged by Keith Olsen (ex-**Music Machine** and **Millenium**) while **Val Stoecklein** wrote the flip, arranged by Dick Hieronymus. (SR)

Terry Brooks and Strange

Personnel: TERRY BROOKS ld gtr, vcls AB
BOB GRIFFIN bs A
JOHN KOTCH keyb'ds, moog B
DONNIE CAPETTA bs B
JIM CHAPMAN drms B
(DONALD L. HALL strings A)
(DON HASTE drms A)
(BOB CARA bs B)
(BRIAN LEARY drms B)

TERRY BROOKS and STRANGE - Translucent World LP.

ALBUMS: 1(A) TRANSLUCENT WORLD
 (Outer Galaxie TW 1000) 1973 R1
2(B) RAW POWER (Outer Galaxie OG 1001) 1976 R1

NB: (1) and (2) reissued as Psycho 34 (1985) and Psycho 2 (1984) respectively. (1) and (2) reissued on CD by Akarma (AK 001 and AK004 respectively). Also of interest is *To Earth With Love* (Star People SPR 0005) 1980, reissued on CD by SPM and by Strange Records (CD001) 1995; and *High Flyer* (Star People SRP 0013) 1981. There is also a rare test pressing with one side of the *High Flyer* album pressed on both sides, 75 copies were pressed on orange vinyl and had Criteria Studios labels glued on by hand.

45s: α Jimi/Hey Mr Lonely Man (Outer Galaxie 305322) 197?
α A Thousand Miles From Nowhere/
Annihilation (Outer Galaxie 32157) 197?
α Color My World/
Queen Of The Mountain (Outer Galaxie 11229) 197?
Hay, Mr. Lonely Man/
Are You My Friend (Outer Galaxie 11520) 1974

NB: α As Strange. Later 45's as **Terry Brooks and Strange** include: *Bottom Line/Do You Believe* (Star People 0001) 1979; *Do You Believe/Bottom Line* (Star People 0002) 1979; *Disco Queen/I Promise You My Love* (PS) (Star People 0003) 1979; and *Disco Queen/What Kind Of Man* (PS) (High Frequency 4178) 1978. There was also a 12" with two different versions of *Mr. Strange*, *Mr. Strange/Mr. Strange* (12") (Florida Rock Inc. 4002) 1987, which came with a copy of a document where a certain Dr. Chisholm attests that Mr. Brooks may be a bit strange, but not mentally insane.

This heavy Florida-based seventies psychedelic rock outfit is worthy of investigation. All of the material is written (or in one case co-written), arranged, directed and produced by **Terry Brooks**, and pretty mindblowing some of it is too.

The stand out track on the first album is *Ruler Of The Universe*, which is full of psychedelic guitar and sound effects. *The Kiss Of A Butterfly* is full of fuzz guitar and *Lost* is more laid back in style.

On *Raw Power*, *Fields And Fields Of People* and *Love Me* are quite strong vocal numbers, *Are You My Friend?* and *To The Far Side Of Time* are space rock and the title track, a powerful psychedelic haze. The whole of Side Two is taken up by the 19-minute long *Life Jam*, which sounds largely improvised and not wholly successful.

The first albums are only recommended to connoisseurs of space-rock and psychedelic freakouts, but the third is really psychedelic hard-rock and *Bottom Line*, *Woman* and *Mister Strange* are all strong songs. This album should have a much wider appeal.

Compilation appearances have so far included *Ruler Of The Universe* on *Endless Journey - Phase Three* (LP) and *Endless Journey - Phase I & II* (Dble CD). (VJ/MW)

Broth

ALBUM: 1 BROTH (Mercury SR 61298) 1970 SC

NB: (1) also released in Germany (Mercury 6338 032).

This heavy progressive group thought to have come from New York with eight members (including horns and latin percussions) released an album which is now a very minor collectable. One of its cuts, *I'm A King*, was also included on Mercury's 1970 *Dimension Of Miracles* compilation. (VJ/RRf/SR)

Brother Fox and The Tar Baby

Personnel: RICHIE BARTLETT gtr A
TOM BELLIVEAU bs A
DAVE CHRISTIANSEN gtr A
BILL GARR drms, perc A
STEVE HIGH vcls, perc A
JOE SANTANGELO keyb'ds A

ALBUMS: 1(A) BROTHER FOX AND THE TAR BABY
 (Oracle 703) 1969 SC

2(A)　BROTHER FOX AND THE TAR BABY
(Capitol ST-544) 1969 -

This band also recorded as The Traits. Their album is pretty varied but a couple of tracks, *To Your Dreams* and *Mr. Sleepy*, veered towards psychedelia. Bartlett had previously been with The Profets, who didn't make it onto vinyl and **The Front Page Review**, who recorded an album for Big Mouth in 1967, which was never released. He played in The Fools in 1980. His involvement certainly places them in New England, almost certainly Boston. Both albums are identical, the first being released privately.

Tom Belliveau is the same 'Ducky' Belliveau involved with **Pugsley Munion**. (VJ)

Brotherhood

Personnel:	RON COLLINS	organ	A
	DRAKE LEVIN	gtr	A
	MICHAEL SMITH	drms	A
	PHIL VOLK	bs	A

ALBUMS: 1(A)　BROTHERHOOD　　(RCA Victor LSP-4092) 1968 -
　　　　2(-)　BROTHERHOOD BROTHERHOOD
　　　　　　　　　　　　　　　　(RCA Victor LSP-4228) 1969 -

45:　　Box Guitar/Jump Out The Window　(RCA Victor 47-9621) 1968

Formed by **Levin**, Volk and Smith after their exit from **Paul Revere and The Raiders**, and cultivating a similar pop territory. The first album contains strident pop with some heavier sounds than their predecessors but also adds some unwelcome brass and orchestration. One immediate standout is *Doin' The Right Thing (The Way)*, a dramatic, sitar-influenced power-popper straight out of the **Paul Revere and The Raiders** school. Otherwise it is fairly undistinguished pop and ballads.

They also recorded as **Friendsound**. (MW/CF)

Brotherhood

Personnel:	MICHAEL COE	flute, gtr, vcls	A
	BILL FAIRBANKS	bs, piano, gtr, vcls	A
	JEFF HANSON	ld gtr, vcls	A
	DON HOSKINS	drms	A
	JOHN HURD	keyb'ds, bs, vcls	A

ALBUM:　1(A)　STAVIA　　　　(Private Pressing) 1972 R1

From Ohio, this **Brotherhood** (unconnected to the ex-**Raiders** bunch), played an interesting mix of psych and prog-rock with some latin influences, a roaring organ, a strong guitar and an electrified flute. Only 200 copies were pressed. (SR/NK)

BLC (Brother Love Congregation)

Personnel incl:　LARRY ANDERSON
　　　　　　　　B.S. HYPENFINKLE

45s:　Bringing Me Down/
　　　She's Gonna Love That Boy　　(Kumquat 1) 1968
　　　I Don't Want To Go/
　　　What Can You Do When You're Lonely?　(Kumquat 3) 1970

A Texas band, originally known as **Brother Love Congregation**, who issued their first 45 under this name. The 'A' side can be heard on *The Cicadelic 60's, Vol. 2* (LP) and *The Cicadelic 60's, Vol. 4* (CD), whilst the 'B' side has resurfaced on *Sixties Rebellion, Vol. 2* (LP) and *Sixties Rebellion Vol's 1 & 2* (CD). They followed this with a pretty good psychedelic single *I Don't Want To Go* which later appeared on *Acid Visions Vol. 2* (LP) and *Acid Visions - The Complete Collection Vol. 1* (3-CD).

Apparently the same group may also have recorded as Jeremiah one 45:- *Jeremiah/Forever Never Comes* (Kumquat 2) around 1969. (VJ)

TERRY BROOKS and STRANGE - Raw Power LP.

Brothers

45s:　Today Is Today/With The Rain　(White Whale WW 250) 1967
　　　The Girl's Alright/ Love Story　(White Whale 255) 1967

Probably a studio group, this California act a lá **Association** released two pop 45s. These were produced by Ted Glasser and arranged by Mike Rubini for Feigin and Lasseff Production. The first offers two songs written by Vern McIntire and Dorlee, the second is slightly better, with **Warren Zevon** and Randy Newman songs.

Zevon may have played with the Brothers for a while. (SR)

Brothers

Personnel:	DANNY GUY		A
	TOM GUY		A

ALBUMS:　1(A)　RAINBOW RIDER　(Windfall KC-32178) c1970 -
　　　　　2(A)　EMERALD CITY　(Private Pressing) c1973 -

Housed in an amazing sleeve with magic mushrooms, the first album by these brothers will interest fans of mellow psych, with cuts like *Magical Man*, *The Prophet* (with sitar), *Mighty Ocean* and the title track. Windfall was a subsidiary label of Columbia.

Their second album was released on a local Tennessee label. (SR)

The Brothers and Sisters

45s:　I Call Your Name/And I Know　(Soft 979) 1966
　　　I Call Your Name/And I Know　(Tower 262) 1966

A pretty dire garage punk outfit from Texas judging by *And I Know* which can be found on *Flashback, Vol. 3* (LP), *Texas Flashbacks, Vol. 3* (LP and CD) and *Garage Punk Unknowns, Vol. 2* (LP). This was a different group from the Texas Valley's Brothers & Sisters who released *See What Tomorrow Brings* on Pharaoh (153) in 1966. (VJ)

Brothers Grim

45:　　You'll Never Be Mine/Scuzzy　(Triple Tigrrr 7) 196?

A folk-rock outfit from Los Angeles. The 'A' side includes loads of screaming girls. Not a bad effort, it can be heard on *Garage Punk Unknowns, Vol. 4* (LP). (VJ)

Bob Brown

Personnel:	BOB BROWN	vcls, gtr	AB
	JOE CLARK	piano, organ	AB
	MARSHALL HAWKINS	bass	A
	ROLAND HENDERSON	viola, violin	A
	BILL LaVORGNA	drms	A
	ORIN SMITH	gtrs	AB
	LORNA BEARD	violin	B
	RUSTY CLARK	viola	B
	EDDY GOMEZ	bs	B
	ALETA GREENE	backing vcl	B
	RICHIE HAVENS	backing vcl	B
	BILL KEITH	pedal steel	B
	ERIC OXENDINE	bs	B
	ROB WINDSOR	drms	B

ALBUMS: 1(A) THE WALL I BUILT MYSELF
　　　　　　　　　　(Stormy Forest SFS 6007) 1970 -
2(B) WILLOUGHBY'S LAMENT
　　　　　　　　　　(Stormy Forest SFS 6008) 1971 -

Produced in New York by **Richie Havens** on his own label, **Bob Brown** is a psych/folk singer influenced by **Tim Buckley**. Both albums are interesting, although very similar in style: dreamy vocals, some melancholic long tracks (*Icarus*, *Light Of Children Come*, *Seek The Sun*), with a competent backing group.

Not to be confused with **Bobby Brown**, as some dealers do! (SR)

Bobby Brown

ALBUMS: 1 THE ENLIGHTENING BEAM OF AXONDA
　　　　　　　　　　(Destiny DR 4002) 1972 R1
2 LIVE　　　(Destiny DR 4001) 1978 SC
3 PRAYERS OF A ONE MAN BAND
　　　　　　　　　　(Destiny DR 2002) 1982 SC

NB: (1) has been repressed many times! Earliest known pressing says on back cover "For additional copies, send $5.00 to...", the second pressing says a higher price, third pressing higher etc. (2) copies say "Send $6.25" on the back. (3) was his last known album. Copies say "Send $8.50" on the back.

A Sacramento, Californian multi-instrumentalist who uses a wide range of homemade instruments on these three albums. Musically, they could be described as psychedelic folk and at their better moments a mystical atmosphere is achieved. Sadly, however, on some occasions (particularly *Mambo Che Chay* on the first) **Bobby Brown** sounds extremely like Rolf Harris! They were released on his own label and the original pressings have become minor collectors items. **Bobby Brown** performed his one-man-band act extensively up and down the West Coast through the eighties and sold his records out of his van. (VJ/CF)

BOBBY BROWN - The Enlightening Beam Of Axonda LP.

Charlie Brown

Personnel:	CHARLIE BROWN	vcls	A
	BOB FERNBACH	autoharp	A
	SHERRY NOYES	accordion	A
	HARMONICA SLIM	hrmnca	A
	GENE TAMBOR	gtr, vcls	A
	MATT UMANOV	gtr	A
	PAT WINSTON	vcls	A

ALBUM: 1(A) TETON TEA PARTY　(Broadside BR 305) 1966 SC

Born Charles Edward Artman and son of a Methodist minister in Northern Iowa, **Charlie Brown** was, according to the extensive liner notes of his only album "a mystic, poet, folksinger, baker of bread, builder of tepees and prophet of The New Age Of Consciousness". After moving to California and experimentating with various religions, "often with the help of certain chemical catalysts", **Brown** adopted an identity with the Indian and chose to live in tepees and organized Indian Ceremonies, which got him arrested for possession of peyote. He also attracted the attention of the local police for building up his tepee on various sites (University of California, military bases etc.).

Housed in a superb sleeve which shows him like a kind of new Messiah (bearded, long-haired, surrounded by fire, shining cross, masks, mountains etc.), the album sadly doesn't live up to expectations. Produced by Anthony Kent and recorded in New York in 1966 with some local folk musicians, it consists of traditional folk, the best track being the long *Ballad Of Earl Durand*, the story of a man "Born too late a mountain man, he was shot down in the Tetons, by the Law's bloodthirsty band". It may interest fans of the first **Holy Modal Rounders** albums. (SR)

Doug Brown

45:　TGIF/The First Girl　(Hide Out 1008) 1966

From Ann Arbor, an obscure single by the former Omens leader and future member of **Beach Bums** and **Bob Seger and The Last Heard**.

Compilation appearances include *First Girl* on *Best Of The Hideouts* (LP). (SR)

Scott Brown and The Tempests

ALBUM:　1　TEN SPEED　(Fish Creek) 1975 SC

A rural-rock outfit from Oregon. (SR)

Brown Dust

Personnel:	PAUL CISNERES	horns	A
	CHARLES LONGORIA	bs, vcls	A
	LARRY NORAGER	gtr	A
	VINNIE PARELO	drms	A
	FRANK RAMES	vcls	A
	GEORGE STANLEY	horns	A

ALBUM: 1(A) BROWN DUST　(Family Productions) 1972 -

45:　Do You Believe In Magic?/
　　Fantasy Folk　(Family Productions 0904) 1972

A little known hippie band with good guitar work, horns and West Coast country-rock influences. They covered a **Lovin' Spoonful** song on their 45. Family Productions also released albums by **Sleepy Hollow**, **Mama Lion** and **Velvert Turner**. (SR)

Brownscombe and Kleiner

ALBUM:　1　FIND A SIMPLE LIFE　(Private Pressing) 1974 R2?

From New Jersey, a rare folk duo mixing original material (*Red Dog*, *Great Spirit*) and some traditionals. Only 300 copies were pressed. (SR)

TYMES GONE BY (Comp LP) including Brym Stonz Ltd.

Brownstone

Personnel:	MICHAEL FRASS	keyb'ds, vcls	A
	DAVID P. HOFFMAN	gtr, vcls	A
	SAMUEL F. JOHNSON	drms	A
	BARBARA LOPEZ	vcls	A
	STEVE SELBERG	bs, oboe, vcls	A
	DOUGLAS WELBAUM	ld gtr	A
	(DAVE DICKERSON		A)
	(BOB GISONNO		A)
	(TOM JUSTIN		A)
	(TOM SCOTT		A)

ALBUM: 1(A) BROWNSTONE (Playboy PB 110) 1973 -

Recorded in Los Angeles and produced by Al Schmitt, Russell Schmitt and Jerry Hudgins, this album should interest West Coast fans with its powerful female vocals and good guitar work a la **Fear Itself**. Al Schmitt, who had previously worked with the **Jefferson Airplane** and **Ivory**, managed the Pentagram label, and obviously knew what to do with the fine voice of Barbara Lopez and the fluid guitar of Doug Welbaum. The choice of material was judicious too: Free's *Be My Friend*, Ike Turner's *Too Much Woman*, *Sweet Lullaby* by Randi Jacobs and six originals co-written by the group members and Bob Gisonno.

The liner notes state that the group formed circa 1967 as Fair Befall. (SR)

Bruthers

Personnel incl: JOE DELIA   A

45:     Bad Way To Go/Bad Love   (RCA-Victor 47-8920) 1966

From Pearl River, New York. The 'A' side, a frantic punker, is something of a classic with some great organ. Check it out on *Pebbles, Vol. 8* (LP), *Pebbles, Vol. 10* (CD), *Mayhem & Psychosis, Vol. 1* (LP) or *Mayhem & Psychosis, Vol. 1* (CD). The flip has resurfaced on *The Garage Zone, Vol. 1* (LP), *The Garage Zone Box Set* (4-LP) and *Ya Gotta Have Moxie, Vol. 1* (Dble CD). (VJ/MW/MM)

Bryd(e)s

Personnel:	DAVE INMAN	bs	AB
	JOHN JAMNIK	organ	AB
	BAYARD JONES	drms	AB
	FRANKIE LAURIE	vcls, gtr	A
	JIM WESLEY	gtr	AB
	BOB STANLEY	ld gtr, vcls	B

45:     Your Lies/
        Why Did You Have To Break My Heart?   (Raynard 10038) 1965

NB: Although both sides of this 45 were written by Bob Stanley, it was recorded before he joined the band.

From Lake County, Illinois, only 500 copies of their 45 were pressed. The 'A' side, *Your Lies* is a Kinks-influenced song, notable for catchy organ and very abrupt ending.

Bob Stanley, who wrote both tracks, joined the band after his outfit, The Empires fragmented into **The Outspoken Blues**. After the 45, **The Bryds** modified their name slightly, becoming **The Brydes** and making several further recordings, none of which have been released.

After **The Brydes** split in 1967, Bob joined **The Outspoken Blues**. He also wrote *Gotta Take It Easy* for **Michael and The Messengers** and later composed the song *Take Me Back*, which was recorded by **The Flock**.

Compilation appearances have included *Why Did You Break My Heart* on *Shutdown '66* (LP) and *Your Lies* on *Back From The Grave, Vol. 6* (LP). (VJ/JS)

Bryllig and The Nymbol Swabes

45:     I'm Gonna Love You Anyway/
        Back Again   (TRX 45-T-5016) c1968

A totally obscure group, their 45 has been compared to a lightweight **Strawberry Alarm Clock** by some dealers. (SR)

The Brymers

45:     Sacrifice/I Want To Tell You   (Diplomacy 30) 196?

An obscure San Jose outfit of whom I know nothing. *Sacrifice* can be found on *Sacrifice* on *Boulders, Vol. 4* (LP) and *Garage Punk Unknowns, Vol. 2* (LP). (VJ)

The Brym-Mars

45:     Keep On Going /
        Brighter Than The Stars   (eEe REcords RI 2772B) 196?

Out of Raliegh N.C. came **The Brym-Mars**, who recorded one single for eEe (Embers Entertainment Enterprises), a label put together by The Embers, who were known for their "Shag Beach" music. (VJ)

Brym Stonz Ltd

Personnel incl:	CURTIS KIRK	A
	LESLIE ROBERTS	A
	DWAYNE SAUNDERS	A

45:     Times Gone By/You'll Be Mine   (Custom 143) 1967?

A minor league garage/psych outfit from Tyler, Texas. Max Waller tells me the 'A' side is a pedestrian ballad psychedelic only by virtue of some deeply serious but (nowadays) hilarious lyrics - "variations of oceans of lavender skies" - crimson thoughts in a green and yellow mist"! The flip is brooding mid tempo garage in a folk- rock vein with a nifty bass line.

Compilation appearances have included: *You'll Be Mine* on *Project Blue, Vol. 3* (LP) and *Tymes Gone By* on *Tymes Gone By* (LP). (VJ)

Bubba

ALBUM: 1   AND THEN CAME BUBBA   (Columbia CS-9971) 1970 -

A young folk singer-songwriter with acoustic guitar, his album contains songs like *Yellow Beads*, *The Pounding Status Quo*, *The Messenger Of Life*, *Lament-#1* and *Sociological Bind*. (SR)

BUBBLE PUPPY - A Gathering Of Promises LP.

The Bubble Gum Machine

ALBUM: 1 BUBBLE GUM MACHINE (Senate (2)1002) 1967 SC

A little unknown band. Not a bubble gum group, as they play a mix of dreamy pop and pop-psych. The band were apparently killed while on a USO tour in Vietnam. (SR/KKe)

Bubble Puppy

Personnel:	ROY COX	bs	A
	DAVID FORE	drms	A
	TODD POTTER	ld gtr	A
	ROD PRINCE	ld gtr	A
	CLAYTON PULLEY		
	TOMMY SMITH		

HCP
ALBUM: 1(A) A GATHERING OF PROMISES
(International Artists IA 10) 1969 176 R1

NB: (1) reissued on Decal (LIK 33) 1988 in the UK, and on CD by Collectables (COL-CD-0558). Also of interest is *Wheels Go Round* (One Big Guitar OBGLP 9004) 1987.

HCP
45s: Hot Smoke And Sasafrass/
Lonely (International Artists 128) 1969 14
If I Had A Reason'/
Beginning (International Artists 132) 1969 128
Days Of Our Time/
Thinkin' About Thinkin' (International Artists 136) 1969 -
What Do You See?/
Hurry Sundown (International Artists 138) 1969 -

They started rehearsing in San Antonio in 1967 using the temporary name Willowdale Handcar although prior to this Prince, Cox and Fore had played together in Corpus Christi as The New Seeds. The name **Bubble Puppy** was chosen whilst they were high on acid at a Hendrix Concert flicking over the pages of Aldous Huxley's 'Brave New World'. With their new name they headed for Austin where they played at the now legendary Vulcan Gas Company but after being signed by International Artists, they moved on to Houston. Their first 45 reached No. 14 in the U.S. charts in March 1969 and combined hard-rock with fresh vocal harmonies. It was a highly regarded single in the U.K., and was covered on 45 by both The Nite People and The Mooche in 1969. Their album, which actually reached No. 176 in the U.S. Album Charts, was similar in style and, although their three subsequent 45s never achieved the success of the first, they became International Artist's most successful act after the **13th Floor Elevators**.

During a tour with **Steppenwolf** Nick St. Nicholas convinced them to move to California which they did, signing to **Steppenwolf**'s ABC/Dunhill label.

Here they changed their name to **Demian** issuing an album in 1971. Later in 1977 they reformed as Sirius. However, the story was not over. They re-emerged in 1987 with a new album which contained new versions of their old classics as well as fresh material but which frankly showed them to be a shadow of their former selves.

Compilation appearances have so far included: *Hot Smoke And Sasafrass* on *Best Of '60s Psychedelic Rock* (CD); *Days Of Our Time* on *Kicks & Chicks - Original 1960s Acid Punk* (LP); *Beginning* on *Relics, Vol. 1* (LP) and *Relics Vol's 1 & 2* (CD); *Thinkin' About Thinkin'*, *Day Of Your Time* and *What Do You See* on *Austin Landing* (LP); *Hurry Sundown* (single mix) on *Austin Landing, Vol. 2* (LP); and *Thinkin' About Thinkin'*, *If I Had A Reason* and *What Do You See?* on *International Artists Singles Collection* (LP). (VJ)

The Buccaneers

45: You Got What I Want/Standing In The
Shadow Of Your Love (Sevens International SI-1007) 1966

From the Dallas/Fort Worth area of Texas. The 'A' side, a cover of The Sorrow's 1965 U.K. hit, can be heard on *Flashback, Vol. 5* (LP), *Texas Flashbacks, Vol. 5* (LP) and *Highs In The Mid Sixties, Vol. 11* (LP). Quite a good version, it has some interesting guitar work near the end and altered lyrics in the chorus. The flip has also resurfaced on *Sixties Rebellion, Vol. 2* (LP) and *Sixties Rebellion Vol's 1 & 2* (CD). (VJ)

The Buccaneers

45: You're Never Gonna Love Me Anymore/
I'm A Fool (Amigo 104) 1966

A different band who hailed from Philadelphia, Pennsylvania. The 'A' side, a very credible commercial punk offering with up front vocals, powerful guitars and tambourines, has resurfaced on *Pebbles, Vol. 9* (LP). The flip can be heard on *Return Of The Young Pennsylvanians* (LP) and *Gathering Of The Tribe* (CD). It's a typical garage-punker which is well worth a listen. (VJ)

Roy Buchanan

Personnel incl: ROY BUCHANAN gtr A

ALBUM: 1 BUCH AND THE SNAKE STRETCHERS
(up to (BIOYA-Blow It Out Your !@#$%) c1971 R2
1972)

NB: (1) Counterfeited in the early eighties without the burlap cover.

An excellent guitarist with a specific sound, **Roy Buchanan** had a long career, from the early sixties to the mid-eighties. He notably played with **The British Walkers** and several other bands. His solo album released as "Buch and the Snake Stretchers" is now extremely rare and sought-after. It was released in a real burlap sack, with a hand-stenciled title, and recorded with rather primitive equipment. It includes some good tracks like *The Fugitive*, *Since You've Been Gone*, *The Messiah Will Come Again*, *Johnny B. Goode*, the instrumental *Sweet Dreams* and a cover of Neil Young's *Down By The River*.

Buchanan kept on recording but, although some are really interesting, his solo albums are out of scope of this book. He died tragically in jail in the late eighties. (SR)

The Buchanan Brothers

ALBUM: 1 MEDICINE MAN (Event ES 101) 1969

45s: You Don't Know/Get Down With The People (Event 201) 1968
Don't Stop Now/You Don't Know (Event 205) 1969
Medicine Man, Pt. 1/Pt.2 (Event 3302) 1969
Son of a lovin' man/I'll Never Get Enough (Event 3305) 1969

| α | The Last Time/The Feelin' That I Get | (Event 3307) 1969 |
| | Sad Song With A Happy Soul/Rusianna | (Event 3309) 1970 |

NB: α also released by Decca in France with a PS and by Parlophone in Australia.

A six-piece pop-rock band produced by Cashman, Pistilli and West for a small label. Their only album contains a cover of the Stones' *The Last Time*. (SR)

The Buckinghams

Personnel:	NICK FORTUNE	bs	ABC
	CARL GIAMARESE	ld gtr, vcls	ABC
	DENNIS MICCOLIS	organ	A
	JON-JON POULOS	drms	AB
	DENNIS TUFANO	gtr, vcls	ABC
	MARTY GREBB	keyb'ds, horns	B
	(JIM GUERCIO	bs	)

			HCP
ALBUMS:	1(A)	KIND OF A DRAG	(USA 107) 1967 109 -
	2(B)	TIME AND CHANGES	(Columbia CS 9469) 1967 58 -
	3(B)	PORTRAITS	(Columbia CS 9598) 1968 53 -
	4(B)	IN ONE EAR AND GONE TOMORROW	
			(Columbia CS 9703) 1968 161 -
	5( )	MADE IN CHICAGO	(Columbia 33333) 1975 - -
	6( )	ROMPIN' AND STOMPIN'	(Capitol ST 440) 19?? - -
	7(A/B)	GREATEST HITS	(Columbia CS 9812) 1969 73 -

NB: (1) reissued on CD by Sundazed with bonus tracks (SC 6126) 1999. (2) and (3) reissued on one CD (Sundazed SC 11073) 1999. (4) reissued on CD (Sundazed SC 11074) 1999 with nine bonus tracks. There is also a retrospective *Made In Chicago* (Acadia ACA 8019) 2002.

		HCP
45s:	Sweets For My Sweet/	
	Beginner's Love	(Spectra-Sound 003) 1965 -
	I'll Go Crazy/Don't Want To Cry	(USA 844) 1966 112
	I Call Your Name/Makin' Up And Breakin' Up	(USA 848) 1966 -
	I've Been Wrong/Love Ain't Enough	(USA 853) 1966 -
	Kind Of A Drag/You Make Me Feel So Good	(USA 860) 1966 1
	Laudy Miss Claudy/I Call Your Name	(USA 869) 1967 41
	Summertime/Don't Want To Cry	(USA 873) 1967 -
	Don't You Care/	
	Why Don't You Love Me (PS)	(Columbia 44053) 1967 6
	Mercy, Mercy, Mercy/	
	You Are Gone (PS)	(Columbia 44182) 1967 5
	Hey Baby (They're Playing Our Song)/	
	And Our Love (PS)	(Columbia 44254) 1967 12
	Susan/Foreign Policy (PS)	(Columbia 44378) 1967 11
	Back In Love Again/	
	You Misunderstand Me (PS)	(Columbia 44533) 1968 57
	Where Did You Come From?/	
	Song Of The Breeze (PS)	(Columbia 44672) 1968 117
	This Is How Much I Love You/	
	Can't Find The Words (PS)	(Columbia 44790) 1969 -
	It's A Beautiful Day (For Loving)/	
	Difference Of Opinion (PS)	(Columbia 44923) 1969 126
	I Got A Feelin'/It Took Forever (PS)	(Columbia 45066) 1970 -

Special Juke Box Disc:
	I Got A Feelin'/It Took Forever (PS)	(Columbia 45066) 1970 -
	Interview + 'Kind Of A Drag'	(Play Me Play Back 1013) 1966 -
	Veronica/Can We...	(Red Label 71001) 1981 -

NB: There's also a French EP with PS: *Kind Of A Drag/You Make Me Feel So Good/Don't Want To Cry/I'll Go Crazy* (Columbia ESRF 1841) 1967.

Originally known as The Pulsations, The Falling Pebbles, The Centuries and later The Buckingham Fountain, this Chicago-based act came together in 1965. Their biggest early exposure was on WGN-TV's "All Time Hits" show in 1965, playing cover hits of the day. Their first 45 release was a cover of the Drifters/Searchers' hit *Sweets For My Sweet* on Spectra Sound. They were soon signed by the Chicago-based USA Records. Their first three 45s were also substantial local hits but their big 'national' break came when *Kind Of A Drag* (written by Jim Holvay of local Chicago band The Mob) climbed to the top of the U.S. Singles Charts in February 1967. This resulted in Columbia buying their contract from USA Records and Jim Guercio, who was later involved with **The Mothers Of Invention** taking over production of their recordings.

They enjoyed two further Top Ten hits with *Don't You Care* (which was again written by Holvay and fellow Mob member, Gary Beisber) and *Mercy Mercy*, which took a top twenty instrumental hit by jazz musician Cannonball Adderly earlier that year and added vocals. Their first two albums also sold quite well peaking at No's 109 and 58 respectively in the Album Charts.

Not a psychedelic or garage band as such they did release a 45, *Susan*, which was an attempted venture into psychedelia and this was their most relevant recording to this book, whilst their first album is quite garagey, and of their early 45 cuts *Don't Want To Cry* is a great fuzz raver and *I've Been Wrong Before* is a great British-inspired slice of garage-pop.

Although they fell from favour in 1968, following a drug bust, they struggled on until 1970 and their *Greatest Hits* compilation, released in the Summer of 1969, made No. 73 in the U.S. charts. Incidentally, Martin Grebe, who joined the band in 1968 had earlier played in Chicago act **The Exceptions**.

Carl Giamarese and Dennis Tufano later signed to A&M Records as a duo (recording under that name) and met with further chart success. They were one of a number of acts managed by Jon-Jon Poulos before his drug-related death on 26th March 1980. Marty Grebb also played with **Dick Campbell** and became an active session musician during the seventies.

THE BUCKINGHAMS - Portraits LP.

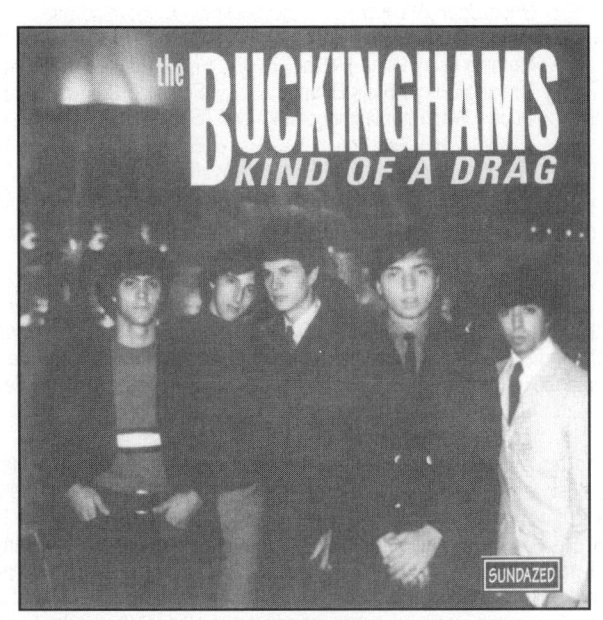

THE BUCKINGHAMS - Kind Of A Drag CD.

The Buckinghams reformed in 1980 and again in 1981 for the annual Chicago festival. In 1985/86 they released two cassettes *Sincerely Yours* and *A Matter Of Time*, and for their 30th anniversary in 1996 a live CD/cassette and video *Places In Five* was released. They have also recently released their first new album of mainly original material *Terra Firma*, available on CD.

The vinyl junkies out there may want to know that in 1966 they released a juke-box only 45 on red wax. It consisted of a track from their first album and interviews with the band and is now one of the rarest sixties recordings out of Chicago. The compilation *Psychotic Reactions* (LP) also includes their rare *I'm A Man* cut featured only on the first pressing of their debut LP (and the Sundazed CD reissue). A right roarin' rave-up it is too which is why it was replaced makes you wonder if **The Litter** had heard this.

You can also find *I've Been Wrong* on *Pebbles, Vol. 6* (CD) and *I Don't Want To Cry* (the flip side to their first 45 on USA Records) on both *Glimpses, Vol. 1* (LP) and *Glimpses, Vol's 1 & 2* (CD). (VJ/CM/BSw/SSa/SR)

Mickey Buckins and The New Breed

Personnel:			
	BILL McBRIDE	drms, vcls	AB
	MICKEY BUCKINS	vcls, gtr	AB
	TOMMY BECK	bs, vcls	AB
	ALLEN EASTERLING	keyb'ds	AB
	BENNY GOODWIN	gtr	A
	DON SRYGLEY Jr.	ld gtr, vcls	B

45s:	Silly Girl / ?	(Norala) 1966
	Seventeen Year Old Girl / Long Long Time	(South Camp 7004) 1967
	Reflections Of Charlie Brown / Big Boy Pete	(South Camp 7007) 1967

A snappy quintet who formed in 1965 in Muscle Shoals, Alabama. Their self-financed debut on Quin Ivy's Norala label got enough local success for him to sign them to the Atlantic-distributed South Camp label.

Their second 45 coupled a swingin' popper with a moody R&B ballad. The third and final 45 is their strongest, featuring an accomplished cover of UK pop-psych band Rupert's People - a stately ballad with atmospheric keyboards, heavily influenced by Procol Harum's *Whiter Shade Of Pale*. The flip tackles Harris and Terry's evergreen *Big Boy Pete* (also covered by **The Tidal Waves**, **Paul Revere**, **The Pirates**...) in frat-party style with some cool fuzz.

Thirty-seven years on, Mickey Buckins still resides in the area and remains in the business as a studio musician, songwriter and producer.

The original group minus Benny Goodwin (replaced by Don Srygley, Jr) reunited at the Muscle Shoals Bands Of The '60s Reunion concert in 1992.

TIM BUCKLEY - Tim Buckley LP.

Their renditions of *Mustang Sally* and *Silly Girl* are captured on the CD of that name (*Alabama Music Hall Of Fame 1993-01*) alongside contributions from Terry Woodford and The Mystics, The Del-Rays, The Weejuns, Mark V with Dan Penn, Hollis Dixon and The Keynotes, Bobby Denton and Travis Wammack. The CD is available through the Alabama Music Hall Of Fame website at http://www.alamhof.org

Compilation appearances include *Reflections Of Charlie Brown* on *Psychedelic States: Alabama Vol. 1* (CD). (MW)

The Buckle

Personnel incl:	SAM NEELY	gtr, vcls	A

45:	I've Got Something On My Mind/Woman	(LP1 1001) 1967

This Corpus Christi pop outfit's 45 is thought to be the first record Neely played on. He went on to achieve minor fame as a singer/songwriter in the seventies. The 'A' side, a pleasant cover of a **Left Banke** composition, can be heard on *Highs In The Mid-Sixties, Vol. 12* (LP). (VJ)

Tim Buckley

				HCP
ALBUMS:	1	TIM BUCKLEY	(Elektra EKS 74004) 1966	- SC
(up to	2	GOODBYE AND HELLO	(Elektra EKS 74028) 1967	171 -
1972)	3	HAPPY SAD	(Elektra EKS 74045) 1969	81 -
	4	BLUE AFTERNOON	(Straight STS 1060) 1969	192 SC
	5	LORCA	(Elektra EKS 74074) 1970	- -
	6	STARSAILOR	(Straight STS 1064) 1970	- SC
	7	GREETINGS FROM L.A.	(Warner Bros. BS 2631) 1972	- -

NB: (1), (3) and (6) also originally released in France (Elektra CLVLXEK 115, EKS 74045 and Straight C062 9294). (4) reissued in Greece (1985). Most of these albums have now been reissued on CD. There's also a double LP, *Dream Letters* live in London in 1968. *Honeyman: Recorded Live 1973* (Edsel EDCD 450) 1995 is a CD taken from a radio show broadcast in November 1973, after the release of the poorly-received *Sefronia* album, but which shows him to be in good form. *Live At Ultrasonic Studios* (Demon) 1995 is a nine-track CD recorded Live At Ultrasonic Studios, Long Island, New York on November 27th, 1973. *Once I Was* (Strange Fruit SFRCD 084) 1999 compiles his BBC sessions. There's a CD called *Return Of Star Sailor* comprising live performances from 1967 and 1975, which should interest collectors. *The Copenhagen Tapes* (PLR PLRCD 018) 2000 contains material from a recently-unearthed concert recording during a 1968 European tour. There's also a 2-CD collection *Morning Glory: The Tim Buckley Anthology* (Elektra/Rhino R2 76722) 2001. *The Dream Belongs To Me - Rare And Unreleased Recordings 1968/1973* (Manifesto 40706) 2001 offers more live material.

45s:	α	Grief In My Soul/Wings	(Elektra 45606) 1966
(up to		Aren't You The Girl/ Strange Street Affair Under Blue	(Elektra 45612) 1967
1972)		Once Upon A Time/ Lady Give Me Your Heart	(Elektra 45618) 1967
		Morning Glory/Once I Was	(Elektra 45623) 1967
		Morning Glory/Knight Errant	(Elektra EKSN 45018) 1967
		Once I Was/Phantasmagoria In Two	(Elektra EKSN 45023) 1967
		Wings/I Can't See You	(Elektra EKSN 45041) 1968
		Pleasant Street/Carnival Song	(Elektra EKSN 4504) 1968
		Happy Time/So Lonely	(Straight 4799) 1970

NB: α promo copies have *Wings* as the 'A' side - can anyone confirm which is A & B on stock copies?

Buckley was born in Washington D.C. on the 14th February 1947. He spent much of his early childhood in Amsterdam and New York, before his parents took him to Southern California, aged 10, and eventually settled in Anaheim.

During his mid-teens, he performed in various country bands and played folk music around Los Angeles. However, his musical taste soon grew to take in jazz and rock'n'roll, which were both to be significant for his later work. He also developed an act with poet Larry Becket (who wrote many of the lyrics for future **Buckley** songs) and bassist, Jim Fielder, who later played with **Buffalo Springfield**, **The Mothers** and **Blood, Sweat and Tears**. During this period, he was introduced to Herb Cohen, who became his manager and arranged a recording deal with Elektra for him. Holzman was apparently bowled over by his latest acquisition.

How far **Buckley**'s music was influenced by the West Coast's acid rock movement is difficult to gauge. Many of his songs sound drug induced and, of course, he sadly died on 29th June 1975 from a heroin/morphine overdose.

His debut album contained all originals, five written by **Buckley** himself and the remainder-including arguably the best material *Song Slowly Song, I Can't See You* and *Valentine Melody* - by **Buckley** and Becket. The material was folk-based, often with a melancholic tinge that **Buckley** was to develop further on later recordings. **Van Dyke Parks** played keyboards on this album too.

The release of *Goodbye and Hello* coincided with the zenith of the Haight-Ashbury peace and love movement. The title track was supposed to convey the idea of saying goodbye to bad things and hello to good things. Another fine album, aside from the superb title track, it contained an anti-war song *Man Can Find The War*, beautiful numbers like *Carnival Song* and *Phantasmagora In Two, Hallucinations* and *Morning Glory*, which became one of his best known songs. **Jerry Yester** is credited as Recording Director on the album and Jac Holzman as Production Supervisor. It peaked at No. 171 in the U.S. Album Charts.

Commercially, **Buckley** was now at the peak of his career and most of 1968 was spent touring. *Happy Sad* was released in early 1969. Around the same time he made a brief visit to England playing with The Incredible String Band at The Queen Elizabeth Hall. *Happy Sad*, which was produced by **Jerry Yester** and Zal Yanovsky (of **Lovin Spoonful** fame), was a progression on his earlier recordings. *Buzzin' Fly* is a classic number.

Strange Feelin' and *Love From Room 109* were both beautifully mellow. Unfortunately, much of Side Two is taken up by *Gypsy Woman* - a rather tedious song. In commercial terms this was to be his most successful album. It climbed to No. 81 in the U.S. charts.

Blue Afternoon, which **Buckley** produced himself, was much less commercial, and even more melancholic, than his earlier work but this should not deter readers of this book. In terms of popularity stakes though, his eagerness to explore with different musical forms left his audience behind. Among the best tracks on this are *So Lonely, Cafe*, a sensitive love song, *Blue Melody* and *The River*. It did climb to No. 192 in the U.S. Album Charts.

Lorca was recorded at the same time as *Blue Afternoon*, and produced by his manager, Herb Cohen. It's a strange, melancholic jazz-influenced album on which the title track (named after the name of famous Spanish poet Frederico Garsia Lorca) and *I Had To Talk With My Woman* were outstanding.

Starsailor was an even stranger avant-garde album. These five albums are also strongly recommended. However, having lost his audience through his

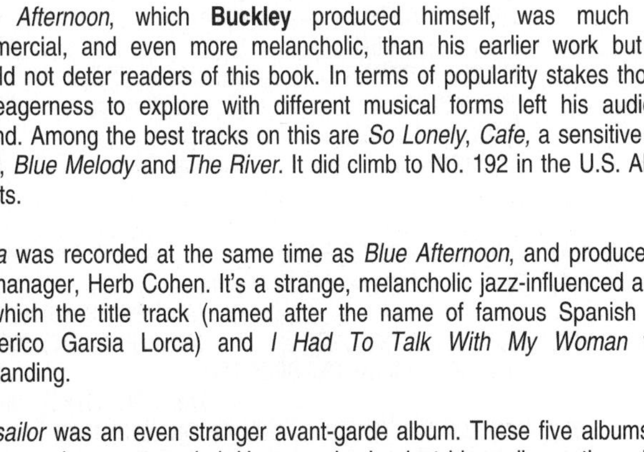

TIM BUCKLEY - Happy Sad LP.

eagerness to experiment **Buckley** became something of a recluse, spending much time with his family and doing some acting - he appeared in productions of 'Zoo Story' and 'No Exit'.

The work he did after his lay-off was more commercial, less interesting and certainly less relevant to this book, and he was definitely on a downward trend at the time of his death. However, **Buckley**'s talent cannot be denied, nor can his influence and significance for Californian rock in the late sixties. His voice was tremendous, many of his songs were beautiful and his albums sound better with time on account of their depth.

Buckley sadly died of a heroin overdose on 29th June 1975. Although he had earlier experienced both drink and drug problems, he was completely off both at the time of his death. Some sources reported that **Buckley** thought he was taking cocaine, not heroin, until it was too late. The man who owned the house where he died was convicted of involuntary manslaughter. His lay off from drugs would also have reduced his tolerance. At the time of his death **Buckley** was in debt - his sole possessions were a guitar and an amplifier!

There are two **Buckley** bootlegs around - *Happy Mad* and *Live At Starwood*, which are reputedly of excellent quality and an insight into what he was like live. He also recorded a live album which was never issued. Among his more accessible recordings are *Best Of Tim Buckley* (Rhino RNLP 11 2) and *The Late Great Tim Buckley - An Anthology* (WEA 250770-1) 1984.

Two recent CD releases have been *Dream Letter Live* London 1968, a European two CD release which came with a booklet, and *The Peel Sessions*, a mini CD of live sessions on this BBC Radio Show. *Once I Was* compiles material from his two BBC sessions - John Peel in 1968 and the 'Old Grey Whistle Test' in 1974. There's also an additional live cut *I Don't Need It To Rain*, recorded in Copenhagen in December 1968. The material from the 1968 BBC session is particularly good.

The Copenhagen Tapes contains material from a 1968 European concert. Three of the four songs featured are from his *Happy/Sad* album, the other the 21-minute *I Don't Need It To Rain* was previously available on *Live At The Troubadour 1969*.

Morning Glory: The Tim Buckley Anthology is a well compiled, exhaustive selection of his material and includes one rarity - a stripped down version of *Song To The Siren*, recorded for the **Monkees** TV show, complete with an introduction from Mickey Dolenz.

His son Jeff Buckley followed in his footsteps, releasing a number of recordings in the troubadour style, starting in 1994.

Compilation appearances have included: *Song Slowly Song* on *Kings Of Pop Music Vol. 2* (LP); *Hallucinations* on *Psychedelic Perceptions* (CD); *Aren't You The Girl, Strange Street Affair Under Blue, I Can't See You, No Man Can Find The War, Pleasant Street, Dream Letter* and *Morning Glory* on *Elektrock The Sixties* (4-LP). (VJ/EW/VZ/CG)

TIM BUCKLEY - Goodbye And Hello LP.

The Buck Rogers Movement

45s:	α	Baby Come Home/	
		Would You Believe	(21st Century 601) 1967
		Do Christmas Trees Really Grow/	
		Music To Watch Xmas Trees Grow By	(21st Century 602) 1967
		Take It From Me Girl / L.A.	(21st Century 603) 1968

NB: α later pressings had the A-side title changed to *Baby Come On*.

From Palmer, Massachusetts. *Baby Come On* (originally titled *Baby Come Home*) is the choice cut from this combo, which is a great rocker, with excellent drumming and looping bass.

Their third 45 has been described as blue-eyed soul.

Compilation appearances have included *Baby Come On* on *Relative Distance* (LP) and *Son Of Gathering Of The Tribe* (LP). (BM/MW/AH/ELn)

Bud and Kathy

45:	Hang It Out To Dry / Letter To An Angel	(Downey D-136) 1966

From the Los Angeles area, *Hang It Out To Dry* is a great smart-ass Sonny and Cher sounding rocker with sneering attitude and great riff and harmonica.

Alec Palao reports that track was written by Pat McGowen of Pat and The Californians but that the Downey vaults revealed no more info on this duo or their backing musicians.

Compilation appearances have included *Hang It Out To Dry* on *Hang It Out To Dry* (LP & CD) and *Scarey Business* (CD). (BM/MW)

The Buddahs

45:	Lost Innocence/My Dream	(Smell-Dee 101) 196?

Apparently this was Bakersfield's only 'punk' band. Their catchy *Lost Innocence* can be heard on *Pebbles, Vol. 2* (LP), *Pebbles Vol. 2* (CD), *Pebbles Vol. 9* (CD), *Pebbles Box* (5-LP) and *Trash Box* (5-CD). (VJ)

Bue-Cotts

45:	The Wrench Dance/	
	I'm Going To Come Home To You	(Aircap AP-102) 1965

A cool find issued on a Minneapolis label. *The Wrench Dance* is a nice frat party/dance number. Sadly, no group details have yet come to light. (BM/MW)

BUFFALO SPRINGFIELD - Retrospective CD.

BUFFALO SPRINGFIELD - Last Time Around LP

The Buffaloes

45:	She Wants Me/You Told Me Lies	(GMC 10000) 1966

Thought to be from NYC or New Jersey, *She Wants Me* has a cool loping garagey beat, whilst the flip is a tender soulful beat ballad. You can also find *She Wants Me* on *Psychedelic Unknowns, Vol. 9* (CD). (MW)

Buffalo Springfield

Personnel:	RITCHIE FURAY	gtr, vcls	ABC
	DEWEY MARTIN	drms	ABC
	BRUCE PALMER	bs	AB
	STEPHEN STILLS	gtr, vcls, keyb'ds	ABC
	NEIL YOUNG	gtr, vcls, hrmnca	ABC
	DOUG HASTINGS	gtr, vcls	
	JIM MESSINA	bs, vcls	

HCP

ALBUMS:	1(A)	BUFFALO SPRINGFIELD	(Atco 33200) 1967 80
	2(A)	BUFFALO SPRINGFIELD AGAIN	(Atco SD 33266) 1967 44
	3(C)	LAST TIME AROUND	(Atco SD 33256) 1969 42
	4(-)	THE BEST OF/RETROSPECTIVE	(Atco SD 33283) 1969 42
	5(-)	EXPECTING TO FLY	(Atlantic 2462012) 1970 (UK only)
	6(A)	THE BEGINNING	(Atlantic R1 K 30028) 1973 -
	7(-)	BUFFALO SPRINGFIELD dbl	(Atco SD Z 806) 1973 104

NB: (1) also issued in mono (SC). First pressings mono and stereo do not contain the hit *For What It's Worth* (SC). (2) mono promos exist (R1). (2) and (4) reissued on CD. (4), (5) and (7) are compilations. (6) is a reissue of (1). (4) was also reissued in 1972 on Atco (SD 38105). There are also two French compilations, *A Legend Vol. 1* and *Vol. 2*, (Atco 40321 and 40322 respectively) 1973.

HCP

45s:		Nowadays Clancy Can't Even Sing/	
		Go And Say Goodbye	(Atco 6428) 1966 110
		Everybody's Wrong/Burned	(Atco 6452) 1966 -
		For What It's Worth/	
		Do I Have To Come Right Out And Say It	(Atco 6459) 1967 7
		Bluebird/Mr. Soul	(Atco 6499) 1967 58
	β	Rock'n'Roll Woman/	
		A Child's Claim To Fame	(Atco 6519) 1967 44
		Expecting To Fly/Everydays	(Atco 6545) 1967 98
		Uno Mundo/Merry Go Round	(Atco 6572) 1968 105
		Special Care/Kind Women	(Atco 6602) 1968 107
		On The Way Home/Four Days Gone	(Atco 6615) 1968 82
	α	Pretty Girl Why/Questions	(Atlantic 226006) 1969

NB: α U.K. only. There's also a rare French EP: *For What It's Worth/ Burned/Everybody's Wrong/Pay The Price* (Atco 123, 1967). β also released in France with a PS (Atco 61).

This now legendary band were formed when Stephen Stills headed to Los Angeles from New York to form a new group. Having failed to form a group with **Van Dyke Parks** and been rejected for **The Monkees** because of his crooked teeth he persuaded Ritchie Furay, originally from Dayton, Ohio to join him. It was in Dayton that by chance they met Young, a Canadian from Ontario, who had backed the Au Go Go Singers, and recruited him to their ranks too. **Dewey Martin** joined at Young's insistence. He originated from Ontario too and had recorded as **Sir Raleigh & The Coupons**, been a session drummer in Nashville before prior moving to L.A. where he played for two bluegrass outfits The Dillards and M.F.Q. (**Modern Folk Quartet**).

Their debut album was stunning, full of original material written by either Stills or Young. When *For What Its Worth* became a smash hit in 1967 it was withdrawn and re-issued with the hit single replacing *Don't Scold Me*. Dealing as it did with the riots on Sunset Strip in 1966 *For What It's Worth* became something of a hippie anthem. The album included quite a few love longs, whilst *Out Of My Mind* and *Burned* previewed Young's fine guitar work. It climbed to No. 80 in the Album Charts.

Upheavals within the band led to their second album *Stampede* being shelved, although it was later available as a bootleg. The follow-up when it came was worth waiting for and contained some of their best work:- *Expecting To Fly*, Stills' *Everydays* and the ambitiously orchestrated *Broken Arrow*. Commercially this fared better than their debut peaking at No. 44 in the U.S. Album Charts.

Their first two albums are recommended but primarily conflict between Stills and Young led to their disintegration in May 1968. *Last Time Around* was a retrospective and comparatively disappointing release pieced together by Furay and Messina. It had a predominance of soft rock songs including Furay's *The Hour Of Not Quite Rain* and *Kind Woman* and the distinctive group harmonies of the first two albums were largely discarded as individual group members performed their compositions how they wished. Along with their *Best Of/Retrospective* album it was their most successful commercially, both reaching No. 42 in the Album Charts. Ironically this band who, on account of the strength of their material, vocal harmonies and superb guitar work became a legend, met with little major success at the time. Doug Hastings of **The Daily Flash** filled in for Young when Young quit the band between July and September 1967.

Young and Stills, of course, later enjoyed solo careers and played together in Crosby, Stills, Nash and Young. Messina and Furay both played in **Poco** and **Palmer** had a solo career.

Martin formed **New Buffalo Springfield** (quickly shortened to New Buffalo) before having a solo career with **Dewey Martin's Medicine Ball**

The Beatles' album *The Beatles Were Born* (Italian bootleg?) features an unreleased alternate take of **Buffalo Springield**'s *Bluebird*.

Compilation appearances have included *Broken Arrow* on *Psychedelic Frequencies* (CD) and *Flying On The Ground Is Wrong* on *First Vibration* (LP). (VJ/NW/SR)

Buff Organisation

45:	Studio "A"/Upside Down World	(Original Sound OS-80) 1968

Paul Buff (of **Music Machine**, **Mad Andy's Twist Combo**, **Friendly Torpedoes** and many more projects) is behind the dials again for this effect-laden harmony-pop-psych ditty backed by a fuzz and phase-washed instrumental. I guess he's been listening in on **Curt Boettcher**.

Upside Down World can also be savoured on *Buzz Buzz Buzzzzzz, Vol. 2* (CD).

The Buggs

ALBUM:	1	THE BEETLE BEAT	(Coronet 212) 1964 SC

Subtitled "The Original Liverpool Sound" and featuring a cover of *I Want To Hold Your Hand*, the **Buggs** (another misspelled beetle!) recorded this English Invasion influenced album. (SR)

The Bugs

Personnel incl:	DICK LEVIATHIAN	vcls		A
	ED McGEE	gtr		A
	ROSE	bs		A
45s:	α Albert Albert/Strangler In The Night		(Astor 001) 1964	
	Pretty Girl / Slide		(Astor 002) 1964	
	Pretty Girl / Slide		(Polaris 0001) 1964 ?	

NB: α with Albert De Salvo.

An English invasion influenced outfit from Marlborough, Massachusetts. They were originally know as Albert De Salvo and The Bugs and the first 45 was credited as such. Indeed *Strangler In The Night* was somewhat notorious as it was about and credited to Albert De Salvo, the Boston Strangler. The song was actually written by ghost writer James Vaughn, who got drafted three weeks after making the single. The narration for Strangler was done by Dick Leviathan, who was a well-known radio personality from New York City. The Sex Pistols of the sixties?

The Bugs have reputedly reformed, for some live performances complete with striped Bumblebee suits!

Compilation appearances have included: *Pretty Girl* on *Pebbles, Vol. 9* (LP); *Strangler In The Night* on *Psychedelic Unknowns, Vol. 6* (LP & CD); *Slide*, *Pretty Girl*, *Albert Albert*, *Strangler In The Night* and *Gonna Find Me A Girl* (previously unreleased) on *The Polaris Story* (CD); and *Slide* on *Scum Of The Earth, Vol. 1* (2nd Edition LP), *Scum Of The Earth, Vol. 2* (LP), *Scum Of The Earth* (CD); and *Back From The Grave, Vol. 7* (Dble LP). (VJ/MW/JFr)

Bulbous Creation

ALBUM:	1	YOU WON'T REMEMBER DYING	
		(Rockadelic RRLP 13.5) 1994 -	

An extremely rare and previously unreleased 1969/1970 heavy psychedelic album housed in a superb sleeve. It was recorded in the Cavern Sound Studio, Missouri. The opening cut, *End Of The Page*, has a lovely guitar intro and the other highlight is the lengthy *Let's Go To The Sea*, which features some great **Hendrix**' psychedelic guitar work. The remainder of the album comprises harder edged rock cuts, their own interpretation of *Stormy Monday* and *Hooked*, which is the best moment on the album vocally. Worth checking out. The band hailed from the Kansas/Missouri area. (VJ)

Bull

Personnel:	JERRY FRIEDMAN		A
	BARRY GORDON	ld gtr, bs, vcls	A
	ANDY MUNSON	bs	A
	(PAUL GRIFFIN	keyb'ds	A)
	(HERB LOVELLE	drms	A)
ALBUM:	1(A) THIS IS BULL	(Paramount PA-5028) 1970 SC	
45s:	Don't Cry My Lady/?	(Paramount 0063) 1970	
	Diggin' On Mrs. Jones/?	(Paramount 0144) 1972	

Produced by Jerry Friedman and Andy Munson, this is an album of loud blues-rock with liner notes by B.B. King. There's some good guitar on *Feelin' Pretty Good* and *Everybody Wanna Do*. The album was recorded with session musicians from the New York studios and some tracks feature female singers and strings. (SR)

Sandy Bull

Personnel:	SANDY BULL	gtr, oud, banjo, bs,	
		perc, vcls	ABC
	BILLY HIGGINS	drms	A
	DENNY CHARLES	hand drms	C

ALBUMS:
1(A) FANTASIAS FOR GUITAR AND BANJOS (Vanguard VSD-79119) 1963 SC
2(A) INVENTIONS FOR GUITAR, OUD... (Vanguard VSD-79191) 1965 SC
3(B) E PLURIBUS UNUM (Vanguard VSD-6513) 1968 SC
4(C) DEMOLITION DERBY (Vanguard VSD 6578) 1970 -
5(-) THE ESSENTIAL SANDY BULL (dble comp) (Vanguard ?) 1974 -

NB: (1) and (2) reissued on vinyl and CD, 2001 with the original catalogue numbers.

A student of Eric Darling (of The Weavers), **Sandy** first played folk and country music before he developed his ability of incorporating different styles of music together. His earliest recordings were with The Samplers (KAPP / 1961) and The Washington Square Singers (Continental / 1962).

A multi-instrumental virtuoso, who as early as 1963, was into Eastern music and instruments. A near prodigy on guitar and banjo, he became a student of jazz as well as Indian and Arabic music. This eclectic mix resulted in *Blend*, a 22-minute track taking up one side on his first album, *Blend II* on his second and *Electric Blend* on his third.

Ornette Coleman's drummer, Billy Higgins, backed him up on his first two albums and 'Rolling Stone' magazine once described his music as " (a) smack freak's work-outs for acid eaters".

Since **Bull** played all the instruments on most of his songs, he regularly used overdubbing at a time when studio techniques were largely underdeveloped. Unfortunately a heroin habit interrupted his progress in 1972 and it wasn't until the late eighties that he was able to make a come back.

Afflicted with lung cancer for some years, **Sandy Bull** eventually succumbed to the disease on 11th April, 2001. (SR/EH/HS)

Bullangus

Personnel:
GENO CHARLES — drms, perc — A
LARRY LA FALLE — gtr, vcls — A
DINO PAOLILLO — gtr, vcls — A
RON PICCOLO — organ, piano, vcls — A
FRANKIE PREVITE — vcls, perc, recorder — A
LENNY VENDITTI — bs — A

ALBUMS:
1(A) BULL ANGUS (Mercury SRM-1-619) 1971 SC
2( ) FREE FOR ALL (Mercury SRM-1-629) 1972 SC

45s: Run, Don't Stop/
Uncle Duggie's Fun Bus Ride (Mercury 73265) 1972
Children Of Our Dreams/Loving Till End (Mercury 73313) 1972

SANDY BULL - Fantasias For Guitar And Banjos LP.

A hard-rock outfit, whose album contained some hints of psychedelia. The first was recorded in New York. (VJ/VZ/MW)

Bulldog

Personnel:
GENE CORNISH — gtr — A
DINO DANELLI — drms — A
BILLY HOCHER — bs, vcls — A
ERIC THORNGREN — gtr — A
JOHN TURK — keyb'ds — A

HCP
ALBUMS:
1(A) BULLDOG (Decca 75370) 1972 176 -
2(A) SMASHER (Buddah 840031) 1973 - -

NB: (1) reissued on MCA.(1) and (2) also released in the UK on MCA and Buddah.

HCP
45s: Good Times Are Comin'/No (Decca 32996) 1972 44
Are You Really Happy Together/
I'm A Mad Man (MCA 40014) 1973 116
I Tip My Hat/I'm A Mad Man (MCA 40050) 1973 -

This New York group was formed by Cornish and Danelli after the end of **The Rascals**. Their music was totally different from their previous group, as they were playing a mix of hard-rock and bluesy pop. Their lead singer was almost a "screamer" (especially on their version of *Rockin' Robin*) and the two guitarists were efficient. On a completist note, the whole group backed B.J. Thomas on his album *Songs* from 1973. Clearly a "second division" act, although it may interest some readers. Their first album spent eleven weeks in the Top 200, peaking at No. 176 and they had a couple of hit singles too.

In 1978, Cornish and Danelli would release three better-avoided albums as Fotomaker on Atlantic. During the seventies, John Turk played keyboards behind various blues singers (Taj Mahal, B.B. King, C. Musselwhite). (SR)

Bump

Personnel:
ALAN GOLDMAN — gtr — A
JERRY GREENBERG — drms, vcls — A
PAUL LUPIEN — keyb'ds, vcls — A
GEORGE RUNYAN — ld vcls, bs — A

ALBUM: 1(A) BUMP (Pioneer PRSD 2150) 1970 R3

NB: (1) was repressed a few years back and has been pirated on CD. A legitimate CD reissue, on Gear Fab (GF-142) 2000, includes the first 45 as bonus tracks.

45s: Winston Built The Bridge/
Sing Into The Wind (Pioneer 2147) 1969
Got To Get You Back/State Of Affairs (Pioneer 2148) 1970

From Michigan. Original pressings of the album, which is an organ-based progressive affair somewhere between The Nice and Van der Graaf Generator, are sought-after by collectors. The opening cut, *Sing Into The Wind*, is one of the most commercial tracks, with a catchy introduction and great keyboards. *State Of Affairs* is a gentle organ-based pop song. *Daydream* has dramatic vocals but a weaker song structure. *Spider's Eyes* has a great organ intro and some fine guitar/organ interplay. The remaining material is less convincing, however, though the ten-minute finale, *Lifeline - Decisions - You Can't Even Think*, does have its moments.

You'll also find the punkier *Winston Built The Bridge* on *Gone, Vol. 1* (LP) and *Mind Blowers* (LP). (VJ)

The Bumps

Personnel:
JOHN CLEAVER — sax — ABC
BOB GREER — bs — ABC
LARRY RICHSTEIN
(aka RUBE TUBIN) — ld gtr — A
ROBERT VAN DEN AKKER — drms, ld vcls — ABC
GARY R. WALSH — keyb'ds — ABC

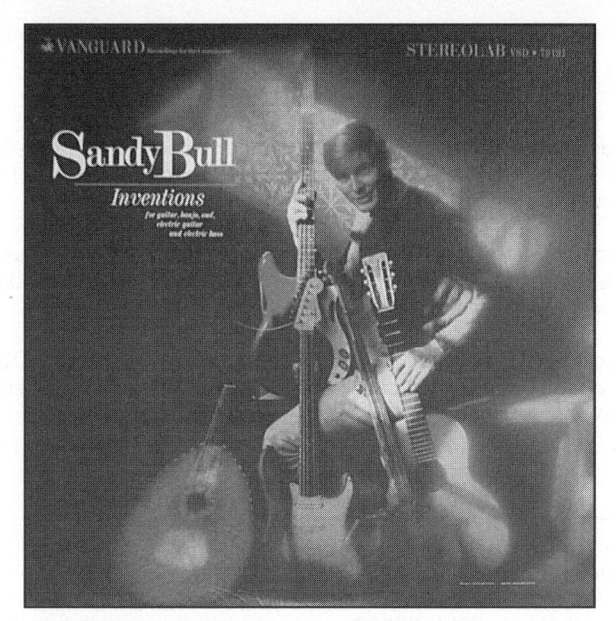

SANDY BULL - Inventions... LP.

| JOHN KNAPP | ld gtr | B |
| PAT HEWITT | ld gtr | C |

NB: Line-up 'A' 1965-67. Line-up 'B' 1968. Line-up 'C' 1969.

45s:	You Don't Love Me Anymore/		
	Can't Say I Told You So	(Sin-A-Way 301)	1966
	Baby Blue/Please Come Down	(Piccadilly 238)	1967
	Hey Girl/Wake Up, Wake Up	(Piccadilly 245)	1967
	It Wasn't Real/Hard Woman	(Piccadilly 251)	1968
	Ode To A Toad/Shining	(Walrus TMC-001/2)	1969

From Seattle, Washington, **The Bumps** started out as a **Wailers**-style R&B dance band, but by 1967 they were playing a wide range of music from punk through to folk-rock through to commercial pop. Led by drummer/vocalist Robert Van Den Akker, they were very popular in the Vancouver, B.C. area and their fourth 45 was produced by **Viceroys/Surprise Package** organist Mike Rogers.

By their fifth and very elusive final release they'd moved into heavy rock territory: *Ode To A Toad* has an underground vibe despite some brass passages and Cream-like riffs drive the hard-rocker *Shining*.

Please Come Down undoubtedly remains one of their finest moments - a dramatic garage ballad with shimmering fuzztone.

Two of their best punk style offerings have appeared on a handful of compilations including:- *Please Come Down* on *Battle Of The Bands, Vol. 2* (LP), *The History Of Northwest Rock, Vol. 3* (LP), *The History Of Northwest Rock, Vol. 3* (CD) and *Northwest Battle Of The Bands, Vol. 2* (CD); *Hey Girl* on *Highs In The Mid-Sixties, Vol. 16* (LP); and both *Hey Girl* and *Please Come Down* on *Northwest Battle Of The Bands, Vol. 2 - Knock You Flat* (LP & CD); *It Wasn't Real*, a lightweight pop affair with Latino rhythm and brass also appears on *Bring Flowers To U.S.* (LP). (MW/DR/VJ)

Bunky and Jake

Personnel:	ALAN "JAKE" JACOBS	vcls, ld gtr	AB
	ANN ROCHELLE "BUNKY" SKINNER	vcls, gtr	AB
	MIKE MATHEWS	organ	B
	DOUGLAS HAYWOOD RAUSCH	bs	B
	MICHAEL ROSA	drms	B
	(RAY BARRETTO	congas	B)
	(CHARLIE CHIN	2nd Tenor	B)
	(ERNIE HAYES	piano	B)
	(BUZZY LINHART	vibes	B)
	(FELIX PAPPALARDI	bs	B)
	(CHUCK RAINEY	bs	B)
	(PERRY ROBINSON	clarinet	B)

| ALBUMS: | 1(A) | BUNKY AND JAKE | (Mercury SR-61142) 1968 - |
| | 2(B) | LAMF | (Mercury SR-61199) 1969 - |

45s:	α	Taxicab / I'll Follow You	(Mercury 72813) 1968
		Big Boy Pete / If I Had A Dream	(Mercury 72846) 1968
		Bump In My Groove / Uncle Henry's Basement	(Mercury 72901) 1969

NB: α also released as a double-A side DJ-only promo (Mercury DJ-98).

Based in Greenwich Village, New York, Jacob's pedigree had already been established with **The Magicians**, whose dynamic amalgam of pop and punk was showcased on *Nuggets* with *An Invitation To Cry*. Their two scarce albums mix electric rock with blues and fifties harmonies and were recorded with the support of **Buzzy Linhart**.

Bunky and Jake both attended the School of Visual Arts on West 14th Street, New York and were popular with art students, performing at the Pratt Institute and the School Of Visual Arts. Ann Rochelle "Bunky" Skinner may have come from Philadelphia originally, as she has a Black Philly accent.

Allan Jacobs and Mike Rosa went on to form the underrated **Jake and The Family Jewels**, while Doug Rauch joined **Linhart** in **Music**. (SR/MW/PKr)

The Buoys

Personnel:	FRAN BROZENA	gtr, keyb'ds	A
	CHRIS HANSON	drms	A
	GERRY HLUDZIK	bs	A
	BILL KELLY	gtr, flute	A
	CARL SIRACUSE	gtr, vcls, keyb'ds	A
	BOB GRYZIEC	bs	

| ALBUM: | 1(A) | TIMOTHY | (Scepter SLP-24001 / SPS-593) 1971 - |

NB: (1) also released on Wand. Two pressings of their album exist on Scepter, the first and rarest with a plain cover with sticker, a lyric insert and poster, the second with a picture of the group on front cover.

45s:	These Days / Don't You Know It's Over	(Scepter 12254) 1969
	Timothy/It Feels Good (PS)	(Scepter 12275) 1970
	Give Up Your Guns / Prince Of Thieves	(Scepter 12318) 1971
	Bloodknot / Tell Me Heaven Is Here	(Scepter 12331) 1971
	Don't Try To Run / Dreams	(Polydor 14170) 1973
	Liza's Last Ride / Downtown Singer	(Polydor 14201) 1973
	Don't Cry Blue / Borderline	(Ransom 4904) 1975

From Forty Fort near Wilkes-Barre, Pennslyvania. This early seventies group had a controversial hit with *Timothy*, a song dealing with cannibalism!

BUMP - Bump LP.

Siracuse had been in **The Glass Prism**, a Wilkes-Barre group who'd made waves locally and released two albums on RCA; Hludzik was from a group called The Odd Power; and Gryziec had been in the Scranton group, Thee Avantis. Kelly and Hludzik would later reappear in 1980 with Dakota, a Boston-Kansas sound-alike, on one album on CBS. (SR/MW/MKn)

Wilburn Burchette

ALBUMS:
1. OCCULT CONCERT (Amos 7014) 1971 SC
2. WILBURN BURCHETTE OPENS THE SEVEN GATES OF TRANSCENDENTAL CONSCIOUSNESS (Ebos 0001) 1972 SC
3. GUITAR GRIMORE (Burchette Bros 001) 1973 SC
4. PSYCHIC MEDITATION MUSIC (Burchette Bros 002) 1974 SC
5. MUSIC OF THE GODHEAD (Burchette Bros 003) 1974 SC
6. TRANSCENDENTAL MUSIC FOR MEDITATION (Burchette Bros 004) 1976 SC
7. MIND STORM (Burchette Bros 007) 1977 SC

NB: Presumably there are more LPs (Burchette Bros 005 and 006).

These albums are now beginning to interest some collectors. **Burchette** was a guitarist and synthesizer player and these are very odd albums, of both instrumental music and electronic noodling. Proceed with caution! (VJ/CF)

Burgundy Blues

Personnel:
- BURT COMPTON — drms
- BOB LEWIS — bs — A
- BILL SABELLA — organ — A
- TIM YERO — ld gtr, vcls — A

45: I'll Get You Back Again / Nothing Without You (Argee 100) 1966

A Miami High School band who were originally known as The A-Men. Their sole 45, which did not feature drummer Compton, was produced by local enterprenuer R.G.Deeb on his Argee label. Tim Yero's *I'll Get You Back Again* is an echoey beat-punker with sinuous keyboards, chiming guitar and catchy melody. It has reappeared on *Vile Vinyl, Vol. 2* (LP), *Vile Vinyl* (CD), *Time Won't Change My Mind* and *Psychedelic States - Florida Vol. 2* (CD).

The latter reveals that Sabella would team up with Alberto DeAlmar (from **The Pods**) and former members of **The Gents Five** to form the **Leaves Of Grass**, who released one 45 on the Platinum label in 1968. Sabella and DeAlmar later relocated to Gainseville and formed Celebration. (MW/JLh)

The Burgundy Runn

45: Stop!/How Far Up Is Down (Lavette LA 5013/4) 1966

A sixties punk outfit from New Mexico. *Stop!* written by Dave Schmuck, is highly-rated and can be heard on *The Magic Cube* (Flexi & CD), *New Mexico Punk From The Sixties* (LP), *Sixties Archive, Vol. 4* (CD) and *Teenage Shutdown, Vol. 9* (LP & CD).

The Chesterfield Kings covered *Stop!* on their self-titled 1985 album.

Danny Burk and The Invaders

Personnel incl:
- DANNY BURK — ld vcls, gtr — A
- JIMMIE CRAWFORD — ld gtr — A
- EDDIE SHERIDAN — drms — A
- VAN GRAY — bs — A

45s:
- Ain't Going Nowhere/Till I'm Sure (Ara 216) 1965
- α Promise Her Anything, Give Her Me/The World (Leopard 200) 1966
- α A Bit Of Alright / Won't You Come On Home (Leopard 201) 1968
- α Every Night About Now/Tomorrow Night (Leopard 202) 1969

NB: α by **Danny Burke**.

From Memphis, Tennessee this band were active between 1964-65. Their *Ain't Going Nowhere* is a superbly venomous snarling punker in the Pretty Things style. *Till I'm Sure* is a beat ballad.

Danny Burk, who also released the three solo 45s listed above, was the younger brother of Tommy from **Tommy Burk and The Counts**. Danny now lives and works in Nashville.

Compilation appearances include *Ain't Going Nowhere* on *Hang It Out To Dry* (LP & CD) and *A History Of Garage And Frat Bands In Memphis* (CD). (MW/RHI)

Tommy Burk and The Counts

Personnel incl:
- THOMAS BOGGS — drms — A
- TOMMY BURK — ld vcls, ld gtr — A
- JOHN GREAR — vcls — A
- DAN MORELOCK — vcls — A
- STEVE O'KEEFE — vcls — A
- MIKE STOKER — bs — A
- WAYNE THOMPSON — gtr — A

NB: The above is the main personnel as there were few, if any, personnel changes over the years of 1962-1968.

45s:
- You'll Feel It Too / Counted Out (Nat 100) c1962
- α Stormy Weather/True Love's Gone (Nat 101) c1963
- Cute / Ding-A-Ling (Rich-Rose 1001) c1963
- You Took My Heart / George's Theme (Rich-Rose 1002) c1964
- She Told A Lie / You Took My Heart (Rich-Rose 1003) c1964
- Just A Little Bit / (Don't Hafta) Shop Around (Rich-Rose 711) c1965
- You Better Move On/Just A Little Bit (Atco 6340) 1965
- Without Me/Maggie's Farm (Southern Artists 2026) 1965
- Laughing Inside/Change Your Mind (B--J 101) 1965/6
- Rainy Day Lovin'/Smile (Hip H-1180/1) c1967

NB: α later released on Smash Records.

This band operated out of the Memphis, Tennessee area. Both *Stormy Weather* and *Just A Little Bit* were regional hits in the Memphis/Mid-South area and also got picked up for national release by major labels. However, when *Just A Little Bit* was taken up by Atlantic (Atco) they, inexplicably, switched it to the 'B' side and opted for a rather flat cover *You Better Move On* for the 'A' side.

Their first five 45s are doo-wop/group affairs, and *Just A Little Bit* is probably the first, which 'fits' within the remit of this book. Especially notable is *Laughing Inside*, an excellent Merseyish number with harmony vocals and chiming guitars. The flip is also good, sorta mid-tempo, a more "Yank" sounding tune replete with a 'lesliefied' guitar tone (i.e. the guitar was plugged into a leslie speaker cabinet, commonly used for hammond B-3 organs to achieve a tremoloed sound without reverb).

You can also hear *Without Me* on *A Journey To Tyme, Vol. 4* (LP).

Thomas Boggs later toured with The Box Tops and now owns several restaurants in the Memphis area. Tommy Burk became a college educator. His younger brother Danny also lead **Danny Burk and The Invaders**. (VJ/MM)

The Burlington Express

45: One Day Girl/Memories (Cavern 2207) 1967

NB: They also had 7" and 4 song EP Acetates on Damen.

Topeka in Northwest Kansas was home to this outfit, whose live shows were apparently great - full of Yardbirds, Who and Stones covers. Judging by two of the surviving tracks the EP Acetate was a medley of powerul

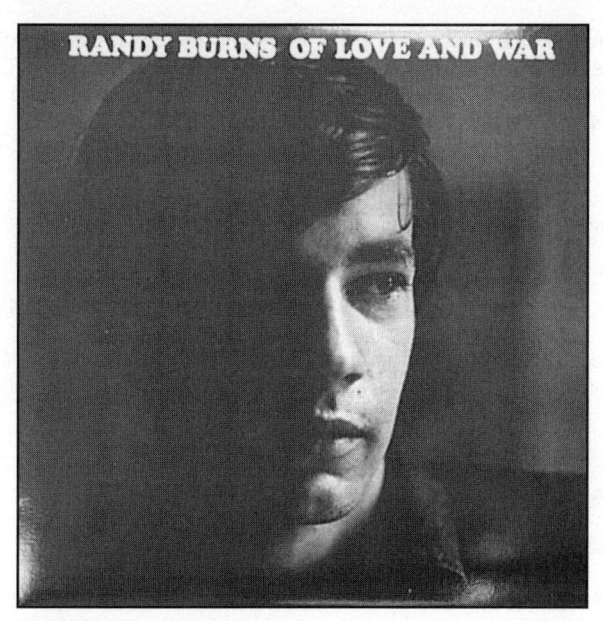

RANDY BURNS - Of Love And War LP.

fuzz-filled covers as evidenced by *Stroll On* and *I'll Feel A Whole Lot Better*.

Their Cavern 45 was produced by **Bluethings**'s guitarist Michael Chapman.

Another 45 - *A Girl/?* (Roach 39099) 196? - is believed to be by a different group, yet also rumoured to be from Kansas. Can anybody confirm this?

Compilation appearances have so far included: *One Day Girl* on *Monsters Of The Midwest, Vol. 1* (Cass), *Fuzz, Flaykes, And Shakes, Vol. 5* (LP & CD) and *Love Is A Sad Song, Vol. 1* (LP); *Memories* on *Fuzz, Flaykes, And Shakes, Vol. 3* (LP & CD); *I'll Feel A Whole Lot Better* on *Monsters Of The Midwest, Vol. 3* (LP); and *Stroll On* on *Monsters Of The Midwest, Vol. 2* (LP). (VJ/MW)

The Burlington Express

Personnel:	BILL BURLING	bs	A
	CRAIG HERON	gtr	A
	DAVE KAPPUS	drms	A
	KEN MATTSON	gtr	A
	JEFF HILGER	drms	
	MARK LILLIS	gtr	

45:	Shake/Three Time Loser	(Prod 01) 1968

Not to be confused with the Topeka group, these guys were from Eau Claire in Wisconsin. They formed in 1964 and were originally known as The Dimensions. Their sole 45, a cover of Sam Cooke's *Shake*, appeared in the Spring of 1968. They split in 1969 and Bill Burling turned up in Cross Town Traffique the following year. (MW/GM)

The Burlington Squires

Personnel:	DAVID BOLES	ld vcls	A
	DENNIS GRAYSON	keyb'ds	A
	KERRY SCHOOLFIELD	ld gtr, bs	A
	JIM SUTPHIN	ld gtr, bs	A
	STEVE TURNER	drms	A

45:	World / Back Up	(Tener 1016) 1968

Formed in 1963 when The Tide merged with The Squires, this popular Melbourne, Florida quintet toured the Southeast and made TV appearances in Southern Florida. The 'A' side to their 45, *World*, is a simmering harmonious punker with dual fuzz attacks. The flip, *Back Up* is equally excellent, with more searing fuzz and a brain-warping break, building to a great climax.

Thirty-three years later Steve Turner occupies the drum-stool behind Dolly Parton.

Compilation appearances have included: *World* on *Psychedelic States: Florida Vol. 1* (CD) and *Back Up* on *Psychedelic States: Florida Vol. 3* (CD) (MW/RM)

Abner Burnett and The Burn-Outs

Personnel incl:	ABNER BURNETT	vcls, gtr	A
	UDELL	piano	A
	JANUS WAGNER	piano	A

ALBUM:	1(A)	CRASH AND BURN	(Worpt WPA-101) 1976 SC

A weird psych/folk singer from West Texas who recorded this rare album in San Antonio. Limited to 500 copies, the highlights are the 12'20" *That's What You Get For Calling Me A Spook*, a rocking version of **Fred Neil**'s *The Other Side Of This Life*, a cover of **Steve Miller**'s *Baby's Calling Me Home* and *Call In The Buzzards*.

Abner Burnett is still active on the music scene - for more up to date info, check the following websites:- http://www.worpt.com and http://www.mp-3.com/AbnerBurnett (SR)

The Burning Bush

45:	Keep On Burning/Evil Eye	(Mercury 72657) 1967

A one off venture by this Georgia band for Mercury. *Evil Eye*, with its demented vocals and superb psychedelic guitar work is strongly recommended.

Compilation appearances have included: *Evil Eye* on *Mayhem & Psychosis, Vol. 2* (LP), *Mayhem & Psychosis, Vol. 2* (CD), *Pebbles, Vol. 2 (ESD)* (CD) and *Sixties Rebellion, Vol. 11* (LP & CD). (VJ)

Randy Burns

Personnel:	RANDY BURNS		AB
	MATT KASTNER	gtr, vcls, keyb'ds	B
	A.J. MULHERN		B
	BRUCE SAMUELS	bs	B

ALBUMS:	1( )	OF LOVE AND WAR	(ESP 1039) 1967
(up to	2( )	EVENING OF MAGICIAN	(ESP 1089) 1968
1973)	3( )	SONG FOR AN UNCERTAIN LADY	(ESP 2007) 1970
	4(B)	AND THE SKYDOG BAND	(Mercury SR 61329) 1971
	5(B)	I'M A LOVER NOT A FOOL	(Polydor PD 5039) 1972
	6(B)	STILL ON OUR FEET	(Polydor PD 5049) 1973

NB: (1-3) all reissued on CD. (1) reissued on vinyl (Get Back GETLP 1022) 2000.

45s:	Living In The Country/?	(Mercury 73198) 1971
	Hold On/?	(Polydor 14143) 1972

Another example of the ESP group of folk singers. **Burns** may not have been the best of his label-mates, but at least on his *Magician* album fuses in a little rock and comes off as a more accessible **Tim Buckley**.

His first album contains moody introspective folk, with covers of songs by **Eric Andersen**, **David Blue** and **Tom Ghent**.

He continued recording into the seventies for Mercury and Polydor with an electric back-up band, the Skydog Band, reinforced by session men like David Bromberg. (SR/MMs)

Burnside

45:	I Need No Help From You / Taking Her Hand	(United Artists 50329) 1968

Late sixties pop by an unknown group. *Taking Her Hand* is compiled on *Every Groovy Day* (LP). (MW)

BURNT SUITE - Burnt Suite LP.

Burnt Suite

Personnel:	WOODY ANDREWS	vcls, bs, claves	A
	JYM CIFALDI	drms, vcls	A
	WILLIAM 'LIZARD' FLORIAN	vcls, gtr, piano	A

ALBUM: 1(A) BURNT SUITE   (bjw Records CSS-9) 197? R2

A pretty rare local Connecticut private press. The band manage to create both pop and hard rock music with equal success, although the darker material suffers by the conspicuous absence of fuzztone. Had Lizard incorporated a Big Muff in his hardware pile, this album would be in the R5 category! *Finest Thing In Life* has a distinctly Beatlesque feel to it.

The band are thought to have come from Canton, Connecticut. (CF/VJ)

Burton and Cunico

ALBUM: 1 STRIVE, SEEK, FIND   (Paramount) 1971 -

A decent hippie folk-rock duo. (SR)

The Bush

Personnel incl: GREG ECKLER   drms   A

45s:	Got Love If You Want It/ Feeling Sad And Lonely (PS)	(Hiback 102) 1966
	Don't You Fret/To Die Alone	(Hiback 104) 1966
	Who Killed The Ice Cream Man/ I'm Wanting Her	(Hiback 110) 1966

This garage band operated in San Bernardino, California between 1965 and 1966. Their first 45 was a catchy stab at the R&B standard, *Got Love If You Want It*, whilst the flip *Feeling Sad And Lonely* includes some nice mouth harp and some effective echoed vocals and instrumentation in places.

Their second single was produced by **Kim Fowley** and the 'A' side was a cover of the Kinks song.

Greg Eckler went on to play for **Light**, and eighties surf-instrumental band Jon & The Nightriders.

Compilation appearances have so far included: *Don't You Fret* on *The Garage Zone Box Set* (4-LP), *The Garage Zone, Vol. 4* (LP) and *Ya Gotta Have Moxie, Vol. 1* (Dble CD); *To Die Alone* on *Kim Fowley - Underground Animal* (LP & CD) and *Vile Vinyl, Vol. 2* (LP); *Feeling Sad And Lonely* on *No No No* (CD), *Sixties Choice, Vol. 2* (LP) and *The 60's Choice Collection Vol's 1 And 2* (CD); *Got Love If You Want It* on *Pebbles, Vol. 8* (CD), *Scum Of The Earth, Vol. 1* (LP) and *Scum Of The Earth* (CD); and *I'm Wanting Her* on *Psychedelic Unknowns, Vol. 3* (LP & CD);   (VJ/MW/SR)

Terry Bush

45:	Do You Know What You're Doing?/ Fare Thee Well (PS)	(RCA 74-0413) 1971

An odd anti-drug song listing around thirty different kinds of drugs with a sing-along chorus! The picture sleeve also lists the dangerous drugs... (SR)

Bushes

Personnel incl: RON STOCKERT   organ   A

ALBUM: 1(A) ASSORTED SHRUBBERY   (Growth) 1968 R1

A white soul rock act with organ and some fuzz guitar, their album is rare but not recommended. They were possibly from California, as Ron Stockert later played with Three Dog Night. (SR)

The Bushmen

45s:	Baby/What I Have I'll Give To You	(Dimension 1049) 1965
	You're The One/Lonely Weekend	(Mustang 3002) 1965

Both sides of the Dimension 45 can be heard on *Mindrocker, Vol. 8* (LP). The 'A' side, by far the better of the two is a straight-ahead rocker with strong punk and British R&B influences. The flip is a **Byrds**-style folk-rocker with lots of 12-string guitar. The outfit were Californian, probably from L.A..

The Bushmen

Personnel:	ROGER POLLACK	vcls, bs	AB
	NEIL RASMUSSEN	drms	AB
	RONNIE SMITH	gtr	AB
	GENE WALKER	ld gtr	A
	JOE LO FRESO	keyb'ds	B

45: Down Home Girl / Empty Heart   (Sundazed S 138) 1998

Although no 45s were released during their tenure in the sixties, these **Bushmen** have had two unreleased covers unearthed by Sundazed. Notes from Jud Cost and recollections by Joe Lo Freso set the scene...

This particular tribe of **Bushmen** had formed as a quartet in the early sixties in Fresno, California; in 1962 they were augmented by 12-year-old keyboardist Lo Freso. In 1964 they won the KMAK Battle Of The Bands with their rendition of *Gloria*. Their prize was to be the official band of sponsor 7-Up for a year, playing fairs and shopping centres etc.. Part of the deal was that they were renamed The 7-Up Action Boys. All went fine until they asked to play as **The Bushmen** at the newly opened Rainbow Ballroom in Fresno; 7-Up vetoed this, so the band quit the sponsorship.

Nothing is revealed about what happened subsequently nor how this pair of Stones-influenced punkers came to be recorded but not released in 1965.

James Holley, later of Fresno's Coachmen (who became **The Everyday Things** and ultimately **Canterbury Fair**) was in this group at some point. Joe Lo Freso would rejoin him in 1968 in **The Canterbury Fair**. (MW)

The Busters

45: Bust Out/Astronauts   (Arlen) 1963

A frat-rock/garage group. (SR)

The Butlers

45: Shop Around/It's A Fine Time (Parkway P-148) 1967

A hand-clapping footstomper with blistering fuzz in **The Chartbusters**' vein. The flip too includes some wicked fuzz breaks and screams but also some pretty insipid male/female vocals - a hybrid at odds with itself. (MW)

Paul Butterfield's Blues Band

Personnel:
JEROME ARNOLD	bs	AB DE	
PAUL BUTTERFIELD	hrmnca, gtr, flute, vcls	ABCDEFG	
SAM LAY	drms	A	
SMOKEY SMOTHERS	ld gtr	A	
ELVIN BISHOP	ld gtr	BCD	
MIKE BLOOMFIELD	ld gtr	B	
BILLY DAVENPORT	drms	B DEF	
MARK NAFTALIN	keyb'ds	BCDE	
CHARLES DINWIDDIE	flute, mandarin, sax	C(D) G	
KEITH JOHNSON	trumpet	C	
BUGSY MAUGH	bs	C(D)	
DAVE SANBORN	sax(alto)	C	
PHIL WILSON	drms	C(D)	
BUZZY FEITEN	ld gtr	EF	
TED HARRIS	keyb'ds	FG	
ROD HICKS	bs	FG	
GEORGE DAVIDSON	drms	G	
TREVOR LAWRENCE	sax	G	
STEVE MADAIO	trumpet	G	
RALPH WALSH	ld gtr	G	
FRED BECKMEIER	bs		
DENNIS WHITTED	drms		

NB: Line-up 'D' appear as The Icebag Four along with producer John Court on their *In My Own Dream* album.

HCP

ALBUMS:
- 1(B) PAUL BUTTERFIELD BLUES BAND (Elektra EKS 7294) 1965 123 SC
- 2(B) EAST/WEST (Elektra EKS 7315) 1966 65 SC
- 3(C) RESURRECTION OF PIGBOY CRABSHAW (Elektra EKS 74015) 1968 52 -
- 4(D) IN MY OWN DREAM (Elektra EKS 74025) 1968 79 -
- 5(E) KEEP ON MOVING (Elektra EKS 74053) 1969 102 -
- 6(F) LIVE (Elektra 7E 2001) 1970 72 -
- 7(F) SOMETIMES I FEEL LIKE SMILIN' (Elektra EKS 75013) 1971 124 -
- 8(-) GOLDEN BUTTER - DOUBLE (Elektra 7E2005) 1972 136 -
- 9(A) AN OFFER YOU CAN'T REFUSE (Red Lightnin' R008) 1972 - -

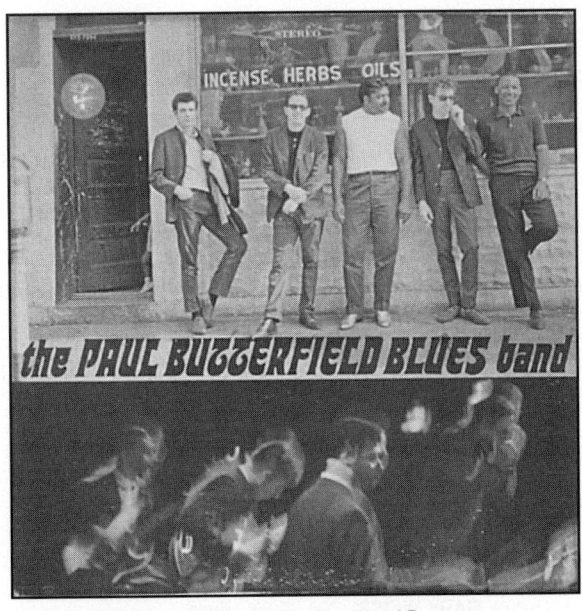

PAUL BUTTERFIELD BLUES BAND - East West LP.

NB: (1) reissued on vinyl (Sundazed LP 5095) 2001. (2) reissued on CD (Winner 447) 1996 and on vinyl (Sundazed LP 5096) 2001. (3) reissued on vinyl (Sundazed LP 5097) 2003. (4) reissued on vinyl (Sundazed LP 5098) 2003. (9) reissued in the UK 1982. There's also a compilation *The Paul Butterfield Blues Band* (Edsel ED1 50) 1985.

45s:
Come On In/ I Got A Mind To Give Up Living	(Elektra 45609)	1966
Run Out Of Time/One More Heartache	(Elektra 45620)	1967
α In My Own Dream/?	(Elektra 45643)	1968
Where Did My Baby Go/In My Own Dream	(Elektra 45658)	1969
α Love March/?	(Elektra 45692)	1970

NB: α credited to **Paul Butterfield**. There's also an extremely rare French EP with PS: *I Got My Mojo Working/Shake Your Money Maker/Born In Chicago/Mystery Train* (Vogue INT 18063).

Paul Butterfield was born on 17th December 1942 in Chicago where he later formed his racially integrated R&B band in 1964. The original line-up included Jerome Arnold and Sam Lay who had previously comprised the rhythm section of a band fronted by Howlin' Wolf, but shortly afterwards **Butterfield**'s former University of Chicago classmate Elvin Bishop joined and they signed to Elektra. **Mike Bloomfield** was brought in on slide guitar and Mark Naftalin joined on keyboards during the recording of their first album. One of their early live gigs was at the July 1965 Newport Folk Festival but it did not go down well with the folk purists among the audience. However, they impressed Bob Dylan who invited them to back him later that day in what was his very first non-acoustic set.

The band travelled to New York in January 1966 to record their self-titled debut album which comprised a hard-hitting battery of electric blues numbers. It made No. 123 in the Billboard album charts. In June the same year they contributed five tracks to *What's Shakin'*, an Elektra various artists LP which also featured **The Lovin' Spoonful**, Eric Clapton, **Tom Rush** and **Al Kooper**. *East/West* followed in December 1966. The title track, which was over 13 minutes long, included many Eastern instrumental influences. The album peaked at No. 65 in the Billboard charts. **Mike Bloomfield** departed shortly after its release to form **Electric Flag**.

1967 was a quiet year for the band but **Butterfield** did cut an EP with John Mayall that was released in the U.K. by Decca. When **Butterfield** returned with *Resurrection Of Pigboy Crabshaw* in February 1968 (Pigboy Crabshaw was Bishop's nickname) it was with a fresh rhythm section and a three piece horn section. Climbing to No. 52 in the Billboard charts this was to be **Butterfield**'s most successful album. Although it followed the usual blues format, it had a distinct soul influence. Compositions included Booker T's *Born Under A Bad Sign* which Albert King had made famous, and *One More Heartache*, a Smokey Robinson song which had been a hit for Marvin Gaye. However, many of **Butterfield**'s fans and some critics yearned for high-powered, white electric blues and regretted the band's latest soulful direction.

When *In My Own Dream* emerged later in 1968 it was also slated in some sections of the music press. The line-up was basically the same as for the previous album, although producer John Court joined forces with Buggy Maugh, Charles Dinwiddie and Phil Wilson to provide vocal harmonies as The Icebag Four and **Al Kooper** guested on organ on a couple of tracks (*Drunk Again* and *Just To Be With You*). The album was musically diverse ranging from bar-room blues, to folk blues and electric music, and was criticised as being too fragmented. However, if much of it was uneven, the title track was distinctly innovative with the Icebag Four's backing vocals lending a gospel feel to the song. It reached No. 79 in the U.S. album charts.

Elvin Bishop left in 1968 to form his own band and was replaced by Buzzy Feiton for *Keep On Moving*, a heavy album with lots of brass, which could only reach No. 102 in the U.S. album charts. The band appeared at the Woodstock festival in 1969 and one of their songs, *Love March* was included on the original *Woodstock* album.

Live recorded with a new line-up live at L.A.'s Troubadour club in 1970, and produced by Todd Rundgren, saw some upturn in their fortunes (albeit temporary) reaching No. 72. It contained a selection of material from their three previous albums, *Everything's Going To Be Alright* (also featured on the *Woodstock 2* album) and three tracks which do not appear on other **Butterfield** albums:- *The Boxer*, *Number 9* and *Get Together Again*.

By now **Butterfield** was tired of touring and he broke up the band in 1971 after a final studio album *Sometimes I Feel Like Smilin'*, which could only manage the 124 spot in the album charts. *Golden Butter Live Double*, a double retrospective compilation, peaked to No. 136 the following year. 1972 also saw the release of *An Offer You Can't Refuse* which featured his earliest recordings back in 1963 with Smokey Smothers' band in Chicago, by specialist U.K. blues label Red Lightnin'. They account for one side of the album. The other side features Walter Horton, backed by musicians like Buddy Guy. This album was reissued again in 1982. More recent still is the Edsel 1985 release which is now the most accessible guide to the music of the **Butterfield Blues Band**. 1995 also saw the release on CD of *The Original Lost Elektra Sessions* (Rhino RZ 73505), which compiled material from an abandoned 1965 first album, which is largely dominated by powerful blues covers. It contains 19 tracks in all.

Bugsy Maugh later recorded two interesting albums for Dot. **Paul Butterfield** died in the nineties.

If you're into high powered white electric blues these guys are essential for you, but if you're garage-punkers or into demented psychedelia give them a miss.

Compilation appearances have included *Morning Blues* on *Kings Of Pop Music Vol. 1* (LP); *Born In Chicago* on *Kings Of Pop Music, Vol. 2* (LP); and *East-West* on *Elektrock The Sixties* (4-LP). (VJ/SR)

Butterfingers

ALBUM: 1 BUTTERFINGERS (POT Records SLP-457) 197? R5

NB: (1) issued in plain white sleeve circa 1970. Reissued on vinyl (Little Indians 6) 1998 and on CD (Shadoks Music 004) 1999, in a newly designed cartoon sleeve.

Another mystery group with a hideously rare private press to their credit. **Butterfingers** are thought to have come from Texas, as their album is rarely sighted far from the Houston area.

Musically, this band will have wide appeal amongst readers of this book - wild psychedelic guitar on every cut, that druggy underground vibe that was so prevalent in the 'States during this era but seldom was captured on vinyl (and was never allowed on radio). The lead vocalist has an obnoxious "soulish" vocal technique that irritates, however and overall the band come across as one-dimensional.

Several collectors are quite certain that **Butterfingers** were a black group, but they sound simply hillbilly to me. Adding Texas to the equation makes the latter interpretation more likely, although still speculative.

Despite what may appear as a lukewarm review, many collectors rate this album highly, and the reissue is certainly recommended. (CF)

PAUL BUTTERFIELD BLUES BAND - In My Own Dream LP.

BUTTERFINGERS - Butterfingers LP.

Butter Rebellion

Personnel incl?:	DAN REEDER		A
	FRED ROWE		A
	MARK STRUHS		A

45: I Cannot Turn Around/Aftermath (Maudz 45-002) 1968

On the 'A' side of this 45, is a pleasant pop ditty with tuneful keyboards and some fuzz buried low - promising. The flip is a melodic mid-tempo ballad about fighting abroad, punctuated by some searing bursts of fuzz.

Butter Rebellion may have come from Florida, although an act by this name played at the 'Butte Central Prom' in Butte, Montana, in 1968. This act who are thought to have come from Boise, Idaho, had a good live reputation and included a good cover of *My Girl* in their set.

The Maudz label was one of many run by Norman Petty. Both tracks are published by his Dundee Music publishing house and it is almost certain that the tracks were recorded at his legendary Clovis, New Mexico studio, to which countless garage bands from all over the US made pilgrimages in the sixties. (MW/SWg)

Buzz and Bucky

See **Ronny and The Daytonas**.

The Buzzards

| Personnel incl: | ?? SAMPSON | | A |
| | ERIC SAMPSON | | A |

45: Courage/Burned (Alberta 12) 1969

Formed by the Sampson brothers from Plymouth, Massachusetts, who were previously active in **Act Of Creation**.

The 45 was the sole release on the Alberta label, which was owned and funded (and hyped) by Vik Armen, a DJ of WPRO Radio in Providence.

The flip to this decent heavy garage 45, *Burned*, can also be found on *High All The Time, Vol. 1* (LP). It's the better of the two tracks. (VJ/PPn)

Buzzsaw

Personnel:	RICK FENTEL	bs	A
	EDDIE WEISS	gtr	A
	GARY WEISS	drms	A

CD: 1 FROM LEMON DROPS TO ACID ROCK!
(Collectables COL-CD-0659) 1995

45:	I Live In The Springtime/		
	I Can Make You Happy	(RCI 47-8000)	1972

From Chicago, **Buzzsaw** were a short-lived acid rock trio who were formed in 1970. Eddie and Gary Weiss had earlier been in the reknowned **The Lemon Drops**, and **Watermelon**, and in fact **Buzzsaw** are best known for a version of **The Lemon Drops**' classic *I Live In The Springtime*. The liner notes to Collectables *Chicago Garage Band Greats - The Best Of Rembrandt Records 1966-1968* reveal that this was in fact the same recording as the earlier **The Lemon Drops**, but in a previously unreleased stereo mix.

Collectables CD anthology *From Lemon Drops To Acid Rock!* also compiles recordings from 1969 which fans of **The Lemon Drops** will enjoy.

Compilation coverage has so far included: *I Live In The Springtime* on *Highs In The Mid-Sixties, Vol. 4* and *Pebbles, Vol. 6* (CD); *Walking Through A Rainbow*, *I Can Make You Happy*, *Nowhere To Go* and *Roll On, Angeline* on *Chicago Garage Band Greats - The Best Of Rembrandt Records 1966-1968* (CD); *Saturn Is Just A Few Days Away* and *Death Calls* on *Green Crystal Ties, Vol. 6*. (VJ/MW/LP)

The By Fives

Personnel incl: JON WILLIAMS ld vcls A

45:	I Saw You Walking/		
	That's How Strong My Love Is	(Tomi 106)	1966

A very short-lived 1966 garage/punk group formed by Williams in Dallas, Texas. The 'A' side can be heard on *Texas Punk, Vol. 6* (LP), *Acid Visions - Complete Collection, Vol. 3* (3-CD) and *Highs In The Mid-Sixties, Vol. 11*. It's a very primitive recording. In the Summer of 1966 Jon left to form **The Word D**. (VJ)

The Byrds

Personnel:	GENE CLARK	vcls, perc	A C
	MIKE CLARKE	drms	ABCD
	DAVE CROSBY	gtr, vcls	AB
	CHRIS HILLMAN	bs, vcls	ABCDE
	ROGER MCGUINN	gtr, vcls	ABCDEFG
	KEVIN KELLY	drms	E
	GRAM PARSONS	gtr, keyb'ds, vcls	E
	GENE PARSONS	drms, vcls	F
	CLARENCE WHITE	ld gtr	F G
	JOHN YORK	bs	F
	SKIP BATTIN	bs	G

THE BYRDS - Mr. Tambourine Man LP.

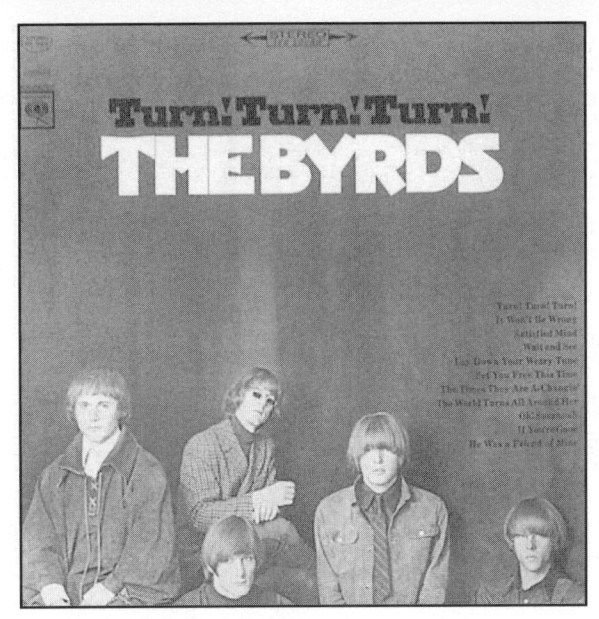

THE BYRDS - Turn! Turn! Turn! LP.

HCP

ALBUMS:	1(A)	MR TAMBOURINE MAN	(Columbia CS 9172) 1965	6 -
(up to	2(A)	TURN TURN TURN	(Columbia CS 9254) 1966	17 -
1972)	3(B)	FIFTH DIMENSION	(Columbia CS 9349) 1966	24 -
	4(B)	YOUNGER THAN YESTERDAY	(Columbia CS 9442) 1967	24 -
	5(A/B)	GREATEST HITS	(Columbia CS 5516) 1967	6 -
	6(D)	THE NOTORIOUS BYRD BROTHERS	(Columbia CS 9575) 1968	47 -
	7(E)	SWEETHEART OF THE RODEO	(Columbia CS 9670) 1968	77 -
	8(F)	DR BYRD AND MR HYDE	(Columbia CS 9755) 1969	153 -
	9(-)	PREFLYTE	(Together 1001) 1969	84 -
	10(F)	THE BALLAD OF THE EASY RIDER	(Columbia CS 9942) 1970	36 -
	11(G)	UNTITLED (dbl)	(Columbia G 30127) 1970	40 -
	12(G)	BYRDMANIA	(Columbia KC 30640) 1971	46 -
	13(G)	FARTHER ALONG	(Columbia KC 31050) 1972	152 -
	14(-)	GREATEST HITS VOLUME 2	(Columbia PC 31795) 1972	114 -

NB: (1)-(14) issued by CBS in the UK. (9) recorded in 1964, later reissued in 1972 (Columbia KC 32183) HCP 183. (4), (6) and (7) reissued as Edsel ED 227, ED262 and ED 234 (1987) respectively. **Byrds** collectors will also want *Never Before* (Murrayhill/Re-Flyte MH 70318) 1988, which compiles rare masters and remixes and comes with a booklet of photos, memories and a complete sessions file up to 1967. Most of these albums are now available on CD. Sony reissued (1), (2), (3) and (4) on CD in 1996 with many bonus tracks. (6), (7), (8) and (10) followed in 1997. Sundazed reissued (1) - (4) on vinyl (LP 5057 - 5060) with many bonus tracks in 1999. Columbia/Sundazed have also issued a two set series of rarities on vinyl *Sanctuary I* (Columbia/Sundazed LP 5061) 2000 and *Sanctuary II* (Columbia/Sundazed LP 5065) 2000. *Sanctuary III* (Columbia/Sundazed LP 5066) 2001 covers the *Ballad Of Easy Rider/Untitled* 1969/70 period. (9) reissued on vinyl (Poptones MC 5044 LP) 2001 and (Sundazed LP 5114) 2001. All their U.S. singles, both released and proposed, from the first three years of their career are assembled on the 2-LP *The Columbia Singles '65 - '67* (Columbia/Sundazed LP 5130) 2002.

HCP

45s:	Lover Of The Bayou//So You Want To Be A Rock And Roll Star		
(up to	Goin' Back/Chimes of Freedom	(Scholastic 1602)	196? -
1972)	Mr Tambourine Man/		
	I Knew I'd Want You	(Columbia 43271)	1965 1
	All I Really Want To Do/		
	Feel A Whole Lot Better	(Columbia 43332)	1965 40
	Turn Turn Turn/		
	She Don't Care About Time	(Columbia 43424)	1965 1
	Set You Free This Time/		
	It Won't Be Wrong	(Columbia 43501)	1966 63
	Eight Miles High/Why	(Columbia 43578)	1966 14
	Fifth Dimension/Captain Soul	(Columbia 43702)	1966 44
	Mr Spaceman/What's Happening?	(Columbia 43766)	1966 36
	So You Wanna Be A Rock'n'Roll Star/		

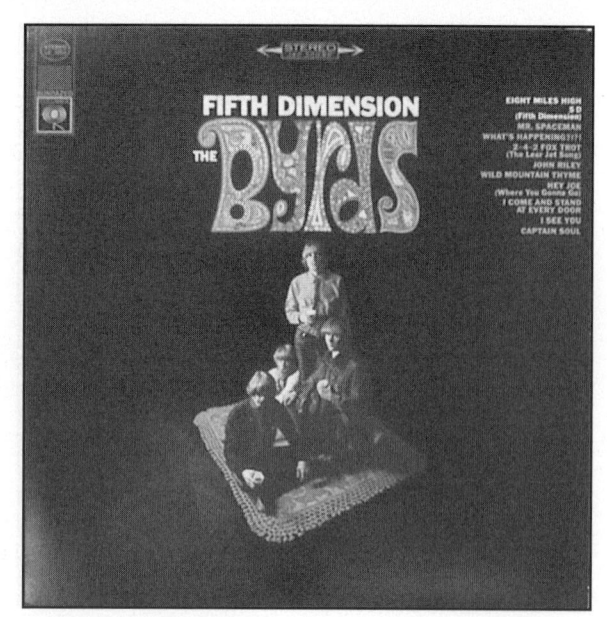

THE BYRDS - Fifth Dimension.

Everybody's Been Burned	(Columbia 43987)	1967 29
My Back Pages/Renaissance Fair	(Columbia 44054)	1967 30
Have You Seen Her Face?/ Don't Make Waves	(Columbia 44157)	1967 74
Lady Friend/Old John Robertson	(Columbia 44230)	1967 82
Goin' Back/Change Is Now	(Columbia 44362)	1967 89
You Ain't Going Nowhere/ Arfificial Energy	(Columbia 44499)	1968 74
Pretty Boy Floyd/I Am A Pilgrim	(Columbia 44643)	1968 -
Bad Night At The Whiskey/ Drug Store Truck Drivin' Man	(Columbia 44746)	1968 -
Lay Lady Lay/Old Blue	(Columbia 44868)	1969 132
Ballad Of Easy Rider/ Wasn't Born To Follow	(Columbia 44990)	1969 65
Jesus Is Just Airight/ It's All Over Now, Baby Blue	(Columbia 45071)	1970 97
Chestnut Mare/Just A Season	(Columbia 45259)	1970 121
Glory Glory/Citizen Kane	(Columbia 45440)	1971 110
America's Great National Pastime/ Further Along	(Columbia 45514)	1971 -
Jesus Is Alright/Mr Spaceman	(Columbia 45761)	1972 -

NB: There are also four French EPs and three singles, all with PS.

The Byrds spearheaded the Los Angeles folk-rock movement. Every member of the band had been involved in music from a fairly early age. Leader, James McGuinn (he changed his name to Roger in 1968) was born in Chicago, where he had backed Bobby Darin and the Limelighters among others. Guitarist, Gene Clark, from Missouri, had supported The New Christy Minstrels for a while and **Dave Crosby**, the only member who originated from L.A., had played in Les Baxters Balladeers, a group of similar ilk. Chris Hillman had been playing folk music around local coffee bars, before becoming attracted to bluegrass music, first with Scoftsville Squirrel Breakers and later with The Hillmen, a group who synthesized folk and bluegrass.

In the Summer of 1964, McGuinn, **Crosby** and Clarke began rehearsing in L.A. as a trio called The Jet Set. There they met Jim Dickson who had just produced an album for The Hillmen. When it became clear that neither The Jet Set nor The Hillmen were going to make it independently, Dickson persuaded Hillman to join the band, and drummer Mike Clarke, a friend of **Crosby**'s, was added to complete the five man line-up. Their main influences in this period were The Beatles and Dylan and in 1964 Dickson got the group a one-record-and-option deal with Elektra. They changed their name to The Beefeaters and released *Please Let Me Love You* - a Beatles influenced record which flopped.

Changing their name to **The Byrds**, they negotiated a deal with Columbia and released Dylan's *Mr Tambourine Man* as a single. In fact, of the group, only McGuinn played on the record - the remaining instrumentation was provided by **Hal Blaine**, **Leon Russell** and Larry Knetchel. The record soared to the top of the U.S. charts and also reached No. 1 in the U.K. It also marked the emergence of folk-rock as a potent musical force. Their follow-up single *All I Really Want To Do* was beaten to the top of the U.S. charts by Sonny & Cher's cover version. It reached No. 4 in Britain. Their first two albums contained some fine folk-rock compositions, too, with the title track of the second LP *Turn! Turn! Turn!* returning the group to the top of the U.S. charts and reaching No. 26 in the U.K. Arguably, their music lacked excitement, although its harmonies were close to perfection.

Their next single was a flop, but follow-up, *Eight Miles High* in the Spring of 1966 was arguably one of the earliest psychedelic recordings. It reached No. 5 in the U.K. in May 1966, and was a bigger hit in the US.

Gene Clark quit the group at this stage and **The Byrds** began to tire of the folk-rock formula which hitherto had been responsible for their success. Their next LP *Fifth Dimension* experimented with electronics. This was their first album without any Dylan songs and included numbers like the title track and *Mr. Spaceman*, which inaugurated the group's space rock phase. However, a gap was emerging between the group and their audience. This was evidenced in the failure of *Fifth Dimension* as a single and explains why the group henceforth struggled to achieve further chart success.

Their next album *Younger Than Yesterday* developed the experimentation of their previous album. It contained McGuinn's *CTA 102*, a strange spacey number, Hillman's *Have You Seen Her Face?*, *Thoughts and Words* and *Time Between* and two **Crosby** classics *Renaissance Fair* and *Everybody's Been Burned*. Perhaps the stand-out track, however, was the McGuinn-Hillman composition *So You Want To Be A Rock and Roll Star?*. Unfortunately, the album failed to achieve the recognition it deserved as it was overshadowed by The Beatles' *Sergeant Pepper* album, released around the same time.

Despite their change of direction, **Crosby** was becoming increasingly dissatisfied with the group. So much so around this time he openly gigged with **The Buffalo Springfield** when they opened **The Byrds** show. He wanted to record more political songs, and was also upset by **The Byrds**' refusal to perform one of his compositions, *Triad* (later recorded by **Jefferson Airplane** and CSN and Y). He finally left mid-way through the recordings of their pop-orientated songs like *Goin' Back* and *Wasn't Born To Follow*. However, both were gems and arguably two of the strongest in the group's repertoire. The latter was featured in the soundtrack to the film *Easy Rider*, winning the group wider acclaim. They were now beginning to develop a cult following, and attracting attention among the influential San Francisco audiences, who had previously tended to ignore them.

The arrival of Gram Parsons at this stage influenced the group's direction. Originating in Florida, he had run away from his adoptive home to Greenwich Village. Here, at the tender age of 16, he was singing protest songs. Two years later he had formed The International Submarine Band who released two obscure singles in New York before moving to Los Angeles to record what is generally regarded as the earliest country-rock album *Safe At Home*, now a collectors' item. Although he only played with the group for a short time, Parsons had an enormous influence on **The Byrds**' music. Their next album, *Sweetheart Of The Rodeo*, which also

THE BYRDS - Younger Than Yesterday LP.

THE BYRDS - Sweatheart Of The Rodeo CD.

featured Kevin Kelley who replaced Mike Clarke, inaugurated their country-rock phase. It was recorded in Nashville, Tennessee. Once again **The Byrds** had opened an enormous gulf between themselves and their audience, who were still acclimatizing themselves to the musical direction of the band's previous three albums. Retrospectively, however, the album would win acclaim as a notable early country-rock work.

But the group was now disintegrating. Parsons left, refusing to do a tour of South Africa, and then on the band's return, when McGuinn wanted the band to move away from country-rock, Hillman left to join Parsons and form The Flying Burrito Brothers. McGuinn had to form a new band with Gene Pasons (drms), Clarence White (gtr), and John York (bs). Their first album *Dr. Byrd and Mr Hyde* was weak and still dependent on the country influence. But the follow-up *The Ballad Of An Easy Rider* was an improvement. At this time they benetifted from the inclusion of some of their songs in the film *Easy Rider*.

Before the release of double-album *Untitled*, Skip Battin (previously with Skip and Flip) replaced John York on bass. The band was acquiring a good reputation as a 'live' affraction, and one of the two albums was a 'live' recording. The stand-out song on the album was *Chestnut Mare* which returned the group to the U.S. singles charts and reached No. 19 in the U.K. Also of note was the bleaker *Just A Season*.

Sadly, they failed to capitalise on the temporary upturn provided by *Untitled*. They reached their lowest ebb on the subsequent two albums and McGuinn disbanded the group. One year later he reformed the original **Byrds** who in 1973, made a disasterous album, *The Byrds*. It really was the end of the road for the band, althouh McGuinn went on to produce a number of solo albums which still displayed that distinctive **Byrds** sound.

Compilation appearances have so far included: *Mr. Tambourine Man* on *Nuggets, Vol. 10* (LP); *Eight Miles High* on *Nuggets, Vol. 9* (LP), *Psychedelic Perceptions* (CD) and *The Best Of Beat, Vol. 3* (LP); *Renaissance Fair* and *Eight Miles High* on *Psychedelic Dream: A Collection of '60s Euphoria* (Dble LP); *Eight Miles High* and *Why?* on *Sixties Years, Vol. 2 - French 60's EP Collection* (CD); *Hey Joe, My Back Pages, Mr. Tambourine Man, He Was A Friend Of Mine, So You Want To Be A Rock and Roll Star, Roll Over Beethoven* (from a Swedish radio broadcast on 29th March 1967) on *California Acid Folk* (LP); *Rennaissance Fair, Lady Friend* and *Have You Seen Her Face?* (all live) on *The California Christmas Album* (LP); and *Artificial Energy* on *First Vibration* (LP).

Recent CD releases which may interest collectors include a European release *Fly Into Passion*, which features a live New York concert in 1970; an Australian CD *Full Flyte 1965-70* (Raven), which includes some rare recordings among its 27 cuts; and *In The Beginning* (Rhino), which consists of 17 cuts from 1964.

Fans of **David Crosby** will also be interested in a couple of tracks by his first band Les Baxter Balladeers, *Willie Jean*, has resurfaced on *Turds On A Bum Ride Vol. 5* (CD) and *Turds On A Bum Ride Vol. 6* (CD) includes *Come Back Baby*. (VJ)

Byron and The Mortals

Personnel incl: BYRON KEITH DAUGHERTY   A

45:        Music/Do You Believe Me?   (X-Preshun 1/2) 1966

Recorded on a Lake Elsimore, California label, the above 45 was their sole stab for stardom. The 'A' side was a Herman's Hermits styled pop song, the flip, a good amalgam between sixties punk and R&B.

Byron went on to **The Generations** who had one single *Set Me Free / Please Help Me* (Generation Records). This 7" is basically a *Face To Face* era Kinks rip-off, but *Set Me Free* is not The Kinks song. He also played with **Muscle & Hair** and recorded a country album, *Byron Keith Daugherty* (Fantasy Records) in 1974. A couple of 'Byron Dougherty' compositions - *Vahalla* and *Love Is Blue* also appear on *Dancing Madly Backwards* by Axcraft, which was 'reissued' recently on LP and CD.

Compilation coverage has included *Do You Believe Me?* on *Pebbles, Vol. 9* (LP), *Pebbles Vol. 8* (CD), *Pebbles, Vol. 1 (ESD)* (CD) and *Teenage Shutdown, Vol. 4* (LP & CD). (VJ/MW/BPs/SRn)

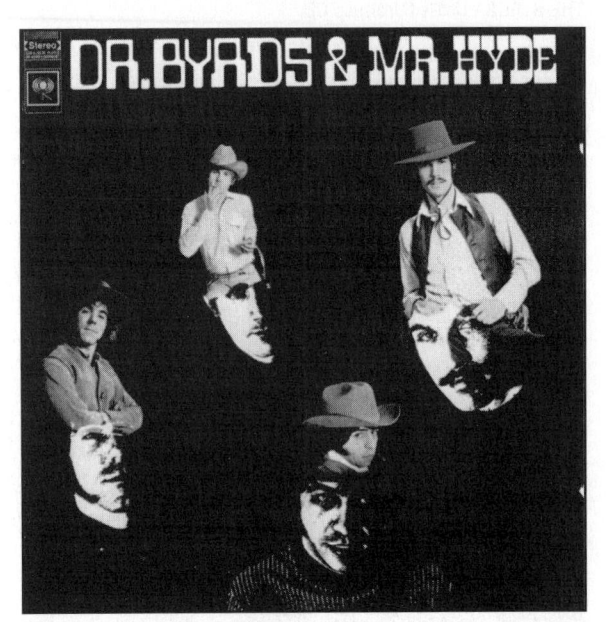

THE BYRDS - Dr. Byrd & Mr. Hyde CD.

THE BYRDS - The Ballad Of Easy Rider CD.

THE BYRDS - Untitled/Unissued CD.

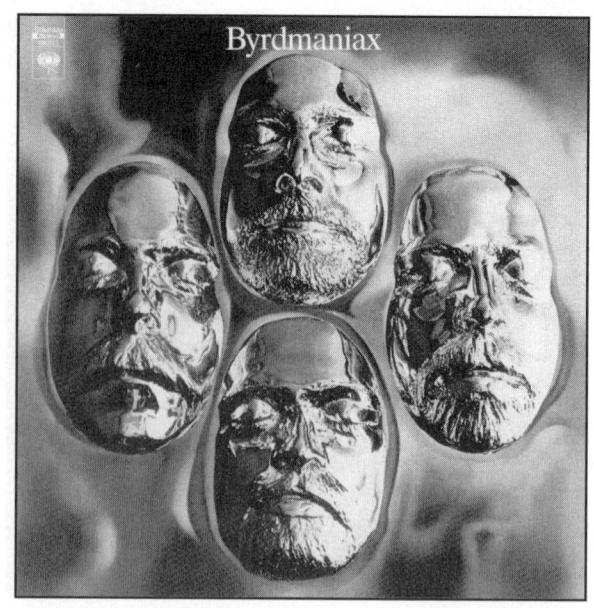

THE BYRDS - Byrdmaniax CD.

THE BYRDS - Farther Along CD.

THE BYRDS - Notorious Byrd Brothers CD.

THE BYRDS - Live At The Fillmore 1969 CD.

THE BYRDS - Never Before CD.

Caeser and his Romans

| 45: | Green Grass Makes It Better/ | |
| | Why Make A Fool Of Me | (GJM REC's Inc. GJM 505) 1966 |

Note the spelling of Caeser, since there were several similarly named outfits about. This particular combo came from Buffalo, New York, and were later known as Big Wheelie and The Hubcaps (output unknown). Both sides of their 45 are decent garage-beat with cool keyboards. *Green Grass* has a frat/party atmosphere whereas *Why* is a more interesting beat-punker. (MW)

Caesar and The Romans

45s:	Baby Love/When Will I Get Over You	(Scepter 12237)) 1969
(partial	Leavin' My Past Behind / Jailhouse Rock	(Scepter 12264) 1969
list)		

An obscure garage group, their version of The Supremes' *Baby Love* is full of fuzz guitar. (SR/MW)

Cafe Feenjohn

| ALBUM: | 1 | CAFE FEENJOHN | (Fran) 1965 SC |

An oud-led quartet recorded live in a club. It may interest fans of **John Berberian** or **Sandy Bull**. There's at least another album. (SR)

Jeffrey Cain

Personnel:	BANANA	pedal steel	A
	JOE BAUER	drms	A
	JEFFREY CAIN	gtr, vcls	AB
	JESSE COLIN YOUNG	vcls, bs	AB
	SCOT LAWRENCE	keyb'ds	A
	EDDIE OTTENSTEIN	ld gtr	AB
	RICK TURNER	bs	A
	EARTHQUAKE ANDERSON	hrmnca	B
	TOM BISCHOFF	drms	B
	DOUG TRUMBLEY	bs	B

| ALBUMS: | 1(A) | FOR YOU | (Raccoon 2/Warner WS 1880) 1970 - |
| | 2(B) | WHISPERING THUNDER | (Raccoon 12/Warner BS 2618) 1972 - |

| 45: | Tomorrow/Lonely Boy | (Altera 001) 1966 |

NB: as by Jeff Cain And The Youngbloods.

Jeffrey Cain was a close friend of **The Youngbloods**, providing songs for their albums and also for **Jerry Corbitt** debut. Not surprisingly **Cain**'s two albums were released on **The Youngbloods**' Raccoon label. The first, *For You*, with its Rick Griffin lettering, is in fact an extra **Youngbloods** LP, as the whole group are featured backing **Cain**. Rick Turner (ex-**Autosalvage**) produced this fine example of West Coast psych-folk which also contains some spoken poems.

His second album, which was produced by **Jesse Colin Young**, is equally interesting but more electric. Eddy Ottenstein shows his skills on several fast numbers like *Whispering Thunder*, *Bless My Soul* or *When I'm Thirsty*.

Both albums are recommended but are getting hard to find. (SR)

The Cake

| ALBUMS: | 1 | THE CAKE | (Decca DL 74927) 1967 - |
| | 2 | A SLICE OF CAKE | (Decca DL 75039) 1968 - |

| 45s: | I Know/You Can Have Him (PS) | (Decca 32212) 196? |
| | Fire Fly/Rainbow Wood | (Decca 32235) 1968 |

An all girl sixties pop group with some psychedelic influences. As they were managed by Greene and Stone, the producers team also in charge of **Iron Butterfly** and **Buffalo Springfield**, they were probably based in California. (SR/EW)

Caldera

Personnel incl:	JOHN ATKINS		A
	ROBERT MARGOULEFF	moog	A
	TOBY SAKS		A

| ALBUM: | 1(A) | A MOOG MASS (STABAT MATER) | (Kama Sutra) 1972 - |

NB: (1) also released in the UK.

The title of this album says everything! A strange mass recorded with the help of Robert Margouleff of **Tonto**. (SR)

Gayle Caldwell

| ALBUM: | 1 | CELEBRATION OF LIFE | (AM SP-4196) 1968 - |

A Californian singer. The best tracks are titled *Lonely Lily*, *Understanding* and *Cycles* and offer an interesting mix of soft-rock and psych. (SR)

The Calico Wall

45s:	Flight Reaction/	
	I'm A Living Sickness	(Dove Acetate no number) 196?
	Flight Reaction/Beep	(Tuttle 1107) 1967

Hailing from the suburbs of Minneapolis, they produced a single entitled *Flight Reaction* which attempted to recreate the thoughts of someone sifting in an airplane before takeoff and, fearing that the plane will crash, experiencing an attack of paranoia. An acid punk classic, it is now available to all on several compilations, and is well worth checking out.

Their original recordings are red-hot and now practically impossible to find - however be warned that *Beep* is just that - a continuous tone... A reissue 45 exists, coupling *Flight Reaction* with the equally brilliant *I'm A Living Sickness*: fuzz laden, with great sound effects and tonsil tearing vocals. This is also becoming rare and sought-after

Flight Reaction additionally appears on *Money Music*, a rare 1967 compilation of Minneapolis bands.

Retrospective compilation appearances include:- *Flight Reaction* on *Changes* (LP), *Mayhem & Psychosis, Vol. 2* (LP), *Pebbles, Vol. 3* (LP), *Pebbles, Vol. 3* (CD), *Pebbles, Vol. 2 (ESD)* (CD) and *Pebbles Box* (5-LP); *I'm A Living Sickness* on *Best of Pebbles, Vol. 1* (LP & CD), *Psychedelic Unknowns, Vol. 1* (Dble 7"), *Psychedelic Unknowns, Vol's 1 & 2* (LP), *Songs We Taught The Fuzztones* (Dble LP & Dble CD), *Acid Dreams Testament* (CD) and *Acid Dreams - The Complete 3 LP Set* (3-LP); Flight

FREE FLIGHT (Comp LP) including The Calico Wall.

Reaction and *I'm A Living Sickness* also appear on *Trash Box* (5-CD), whilst *Free Flight (Unreleased Dove Recording Studio Cuts 1964-'69)* (Dble LP & CD) includes *Flight Reaction* and *I'm A Living Sickness* plus two unreleased cuts *Look Over Yonder's Wall* and *Lotta Lovin'*; and *Beep (Excerpt)* on *Everything You Always Wanted To Know...* (CD).

I'm A Living Sickness was later covered by Green Telescope and The Fuzztones. (VJ)

Randy California

Personnel:	CHARLIE BUNDY	bs, vcls	A
	RANDY CALIFORNIA	gtr, vcls	A
	CASS STRANGE DRUMS		
	(ED CASSIDY)	drms	A
	LARRY (FUZZY) KNIGHT	bs	A
	HENRY MANCHOVITZ	drms	A
	TIM McGOVERN	drms, vcls	A
	CLIT McTORIUS (NOEL REDDING)	bs	A

ALBUM:	1(A)	KAPT. KOPTER AND THE (FABULOUS) TWIRLY BIRDS	(Epic KE 31755) 1972

(up to 1972)

NB: (1) reissued on CD with bonus tracks.

45:	Walkin' The Dog/Live For The Day	(Epic 5-10927) 1972

The first solo album by the guitarist of **Spirit** should interest fans of rock trios a lá **Hendrix**. Recorded with three different rhythm sections, one including Noel Redding (who was then recording the **Road**'s album in the same studio), it includes two covers of the Beatles (*Rain* and *Day Tripper*), one of Paul Simon (*Mother And Child Reunion*) and three songs written by **California**, *Evil*, *Downer* and *Rainbow*.

California (real name: Randy Wolfe) used a lot of pyrotechnic effects on his guitars and the result, quite loud, can be compared to the albums of **Velvert Turner** or **Peter Kaukonen**. It is rumoured than a *Kaptain Kopter, Volume II* album was recorded but then shelved when **California** reformed **Spirit**. He would later record several other solo albums, which are rarely as interesting as his first effort.

Randy California died on 2nd January 1997 after he and his son were hit by a freak wave in Hawaii. Both were sadly drowned. (SR)

California Bear

45s:	Hand My Head/Virgin Dreams	(M&H MH-101) 1969
	In My Dreams/Eulogy	(M&H MH-1543/8047) 1969

From Riverside, California, featuring one Bruce Terry. Late sixties soft-rock with the odd psychedelic touch. Only the atmospheric echoey *Eulogy* with its short but excellent guitar solo can be recommended here. (MW)

The California Poppy Pickers

Personnel:	DON LARSON	vcls, bs	A
	MIKE MESSER	vcls, gtr	A
	TOM SLIPP	drms	A
	RANDY WILCOX	vcls, gtr	A

ALBUMS:	1( )	SOUNDS OF '69	(Alshire S-5152) 1969
	2( )	HAIR / AQUARIUS	(Alshire S-5153) 1969
	3( )	TODAY'S CHART BUSTERS	(Alshire S-5163) 1969
	4(A)	HONKY TONK WOMEN	(Alshire S-5167) 1969 SC

NB: (2) also reissued on Quadraphonic (Alshire Audio-Spectrum AS-9) 1972.

This outfit was basically a studio project for Al Sherman's Alshire label, with Gary Paxton providing the musical side of the venture.

Al Sherman was the label boss of Alshire International label, which followed a simple philosophy, if you see a successful musical trend follow it. It didn't

BOBBY CALLENDER - Rainbow LP.

matter if it was rock, muzak or country as long as it sounded like the real thing without any copyright infringements. Studio groups were assembled to produce copycat albums with group projects like the Zero-Zero-Seven Band (after the John Barry Seven), The Village Men (after the folk group, the Village Stompers), Fats and the Chessmen (Fats Domino), Rusty Dean {Top #10 country hits}, Los Norte Americanos (The Tijuana Brass), **The California Poppy-Pickers** (**The Mamas and Papas** meets country-rock), The Sons of the Purple Sage (The Sons of the Pioneers), The Bakersfield Five (Buck Owens Buckaroos) and so on.

The other main force behind the record deal was Gary Paxton, who had a 1960 hit with *The Monster Mash* as the Hollywood Argyles' and worked the Hollywood music scene as an engineer, producer, session musician, writer and music publisher with his Garpax and Maverick Music companies. He was heavily involved in the surf and Hot-Rod crazes, joining other L.A. session players as 'members' of various groups. Paxton had previously worked with **Skip Battin** in the Pledges {1956-1957}, Gary and Clyde {1957}, formed his own group {1957-1958} and produced the duo Skip & Flip, most notably for their 1959 million hit version of Gary's *It Was I*.

When Gary started his own Hollywood studio in 1965 his early session players included Gib Guilbeau, Gene Parsons, Clarence White, Carl Walden (steel gtr, vcls, gtr) Jerry Scheff (bs), Bruce Oakes (gtr, vcls), Vern Gosdin and Rex Gosdin.

In 1967, Gary relocated his studio one hundred miles away to Bakersfield and built a session crew that comprised Gib Guilbeau (vcls, gtr, fiddle}, Gene Parsons (vcls, drms, hrmnca), Clarence White (dobro, ld gtr), Ben Benay (gtr, vcls), Vern Gosdin (gtr, vcls), Rex Gosdin (gtr, bs, vcls), Wayne Moore (bs, vcls), Leo Leblanc (steel gtr), Ken Johnson (vcls, bs, drms, gtr) and Dennis Payne (vcls, gtr, bs).

During the 1965-1968 period, most of the session crew had their own singles leased by Gary Paxton to various labels, the most sucessful to emerge was the Gosdin Brothers, Rex and Vern. Their work on Gene Clark's 1967 solo debut for Columbia had gone largely unobserved, but their own 1967 single *Hangin' On* on Paxton's Bakersfield International label provided them with a country top No. 10 hit and their record deal was bought out by Capitol Records.

Paxton's studio suffered further desertion in 1967 with Clarence White, Gib Gulibeau, Wayne Moore and Gene Parsons leaving to form the group Nashville West to work a club in El Monte, California. This ground breaking country-rock group lasted until mid-1968 when White and Parsons joined **The Byrds**. In fact, the core of his studio crowd were mainly country musicians and played in various club bands and even did session work for other labels.

Paxton himself recorded for his own and other labels, including Capitol Records. One of his Bakersfield International productions was **Eternity's Children**'s second album *Timeless* for Tower Records, a subsidiary label of Capitol.

In 1969, Paxton started leasing his studio masters to Al Sherman, that year alone the masters of the last few years were compiled into various albums for the Alshire label. Alshire International releases by The Bakersfield Five, Rusty Dean {in reality Gary Paxton and Gib Guilbeau supplied the vocals}, and The Modern Country Friends, were basically various songs that were cut in Gary's studio. Some were previously issued as singles, then reissued on the albums. Even Gib Guilbeau's first official Alshire release the *Cajun Country* 1969 album, was taken from 1965-1966 sessions.

The California Poppy Pickers were really Paxton's last solid project with Alshire. The studio group simply featured Ken 'Kenny' Johnson and Dennis Payne, with Bakersfield pedal steel player Leo LeBlanc added when needed. Ken Johnson appeared as the main singer and backing vocalist, he also played guitar, bass and drums. Kenny had been in the Bakersfield group **The Avengers** in the mid-sixties and wrote almost everything that came out of the Paxton Bakersfield studio, especially in the later period. Also appearing on the albums with Ken Johnson was Dennis Payne, who was another of the label's country-orientated performers, having co-written songs and played bass for Bakersfield singer Red Simpson's first two Capitol Records albums in 1966. He also played in the Buckshots and recorded Paxton produced singles for various labels during the sixties. His first single in the mid-sixties was actually issued on Al Sherman's A S label. For the **California Poppy Pickers** sessions, Johnson and Payne each recieved a flat fee of $200 for each album.

Housed in a budget sleeve, *Today's Chart Busters*, their third album was subtitled "The Big Hits From Coast to Coast" and contained some covers (notably the Beatles' *Get Back* and *Ballad Of John And Yoko*) and three instrumental tracks, with harmonica and crude fuzz guitar, written by the producer and guitarist Gary Paxton.

Apparently there was a falling out between Paxton and Sherman, for the **California Poppy Pickers** album *Honky Tonk Women*, a different studio, producer and session crew were used. **The California Poppy Pickers** were Don Larson (vocals and bass), Mike Messer (vocals, guitar), Tom Slipp on drums and Randy Wilcox on vocals. It was recorded at Wilshire Sound Studios, Hollywood in 1969, and co-produced by Phil Volk and **Drake Levin** (ex-**Paul Revere & The Raiders**). It was a one-off deal and they were in reality **Wilson McKinley**. They used the proceeds from this recording to fund the release of an original EP in 1970 on Rocking Chair Records.

Gary continued to lease material to other labels, the *Guitar Country* (1969-1970) album by Bakersfield's Big Guitars on the Bakersfield-based Jaisco label may have been credited to a 'talented new country group from L.A.', but consisted of older material with Clarence White and Dennis Payne.

Most of Paxton's informal session crew went on to work in the country music industry and still do to this day. Dennis Payne continued to write and perform, he signed to the Bakersfield-based Mosrite Records just as the company folded in 1969, he had yet to record for the label. In 1976, he moved to Nashville, where he worked with Gary Paxton and Vern Gosdin among many others as a producer and sideman. He now runs his own studio.

In 1970, Paxton was declared bankrupt and his operations were closed down, by this stage his Bakersfield holdings included a record store, a marina, rental properties, his own home and a string of publishing companies and small label deals. With his Bakersfield empire shattered, he moved to Nashville and built a career as a songwriter, continuing with recording and music publishing in the country gospel field. (JO/CF/MW/SR/DP/DLn)

Bobby Callender

ALBUMS:	1	RAINBOW	(MGM SE-4557) 1968 SC
	2	THE WAY (FIRST BOOK OF EXPERIENCE) (Dble)	(Mithra) 1971 SC
	3	LE MUSEE DE L'IMPRESSIONNISME	(Philips) c1972 R1?

NB: (1) came with lyric sheets. (1) also reissued on CD with two extra tracks by Big Beat (CDWIKD 179) 1998 (1) reissued as a dble LP (Akarma AK 128/2) 2000. (2) reissued on CD (Akarma AK 129) and as a dble LP (3 sides music, 1 side engraved with Akarma logos) (Akarma AK 129/2) 2000. (3) as **Robert Callender**, it could have been released only in Netherlands.

			HCP
45s:	Little Star/Love And Kisses	(Roulette 4471) 1963	95
	You've Really Got A Hold On Me/ I Can't Get Over You	(Coral 62517) 1967	-
	Sweet Song Of Life/ Vicissitude(Or A Day At Jaffry's)	(Coral 62528) 1967	-
	Rainbow/Symphonic Pictures	(MGM 13965) 1968	-

The first album consists of music to be seriously stoned to. Young negro-turned-mystic Bobby is joined by an orchestra and a host of other musicians including Funatics' Hugh McCracken for a trip to the local soul-serious opium-den hippie scribblings, here. Sitars and tablas abound in this artifact of an era. Find a paisley cushion, adopt lotus position and contemplate your inner self (or navel fluff!). Produced by **Alan Lorber** whose other 'in' projects included **Ultimate Spinach**.

The second album is a double, more conceptual, piece. The third is a homage to the 19th century painters and was recorded with a full orchestra, sometimes heading into progressive territory, with good electric guitar work, flutes and organ. Still with **Lorber**, **Robert Callender** also co-produced the aural documentary album by **The Groupies**.

Before **Callender** embarked on a recording career, he was a radio producer for Murray the K at New York station WINS.

Compilation appearances have included *I'm Just High On Life* on *Journey To A Higher Key, Vol. 1* (LP). (MW/LP/SR)

The Calliope

Personnel incl:	JAMES BENTLEY		A

45s:	Streets of Boston/ Awaiting (The Truth)	(Audio Seven MG 152/4) 196?
	Kaleidoscope Calliope/ Everybody's High	(Audio Seven MG 151/3) 196?

Hailing from the affluent suburb of Short Hills, one of New Jersey's more prosperous New York suburbs, their finest moment was *Streets Of Boston* which can be heard on *Attack Of The Jersey Teens* (LP). It's rather demented with a haunting spoken intro, military drums and rather menacing guitar. The second 45 was an unsuccessful attempt at a flowery psychedelic pop song which one reviewer commented sounded 'like the legendary Stardust Cowboy on drums!' The warped dynamo behind this group was James Bentley, who wrote all four songs. (VJ)

Calliope

Personnel incl:	PAUL GOLDSMITH	gtr	AB
	CLYDE HEATON	organ	A
	DANNY O'KEEFE	bs, vcls	A

BOBBY CALLENDER - The Way (First Book Of Experience) LP.

	JOHN SIMPSON	drms		AB
	LUTHER RABB	bs		B
	SCOTT STRONG	keyb'ds		B

ALBUM: 1(A) STEAMED (Buddah BDS-5023) 1968 -

45: Rainmaker's Daughter/Hello Hello (Buddah 83) 1969

From Seattle, the driving force behind this short-lived outfit was singer/songwriter Danny O'Keefe, who later had one or two Top 20 hits (including *Magdalena*). They made a bit of a splash locally, but like a lot of Seattle bands, they seemed much better live than on record. It seems that bands from Seattle during that period did not get very good support from their record companies... obviously things have changed since then! **Calliope**'s first album is now a very minor collectable, and the second may have remained unissued. The *Steamed* album includes cover versions of *Hello* (**Lee Michaels**), *California Dreamin'* (with a very good psychedelic guitar solo), *Hound Dog, Jimmy Bell* (a traditional number), *Like A Rolling Stone* (Dylan), *Nadine* (Chuck Berry) and four originals - two by Goldsmith and two by O'Keefe.

John Simpson, who was tragically killed in a plane crash in 1973, had previously played with Scott Strong in **The Bumps** and may also be the guy who played drums in **Christopher**. Prior to joining **Calliope**, Scott Strong also acted as their road manager. Paul Goldsmith and Luther Rabb had earlier been in **Emergency Exit** and Clyde Heaton in **The Dimensions**. Luther Rabb later played with **Ballin' Jack**.

Compilation appearances have included: *California Dreamin* on *Psychosis From The 13th Dimension* (CDR & CD). (CBn/DR/VJ)

Calliope

Personnel incl: J. ANDRON A

45s: Ryan 5/I'll Take It Back (Epic 10372) 1968
Friends Of Mrs Fisher / We've Made It (Shamley 44013) 1969
α Clear Mud / Wiser (Shamley 44020) 1969

NB: α also released in the U.K. (Uni UN 514) 1969.

This **Calliope** produced at least three excellent mellow folkie-rock 45s. The first, *Ryan 5*, sounds exactly like **West** (who also recorded on Epic), whilst the flip *I'll Take It Back* is mellow but uptempo San Francisco psychedelic sounds.

Both sides of their second effort, which were written by A.J.Andron and produced by Brian Ross, maintain the standard. *We've Made It* features male/female vocals, good organ, two flute solos and a short but brilliant guitar, whilst *Friends Of Mrs Fisher* has male vocals with female backing,

FUZZ FLAYKES AND SHAKES Vol. 3 (Comp CD) including The Camel Drivers.

an unusual rhythm (a little like The Beatles' *Octopus Garden*) and interesting lyrics about a man "who wants to escape from the life he's leading today".

Their final 45, *Clear Mud*, is another track of particularly high quality with strong rhythm and layered flute, Hammond and good harmonies.

You can check out *Ryan 5* on *Incredible Sound Show Stories, Vol. 8* (LP), but it's about time some of their other 45s re-materialised too! (VJ/SPr/MW/SR)

Cambridge

Garage punkers from Rochester, Michigan who have two cuts:- *I'm Coming Back* and *Lonely Lisa* on *Michigan Mixture, Vol. 2* (LP). *Lonely Lisa*, a punk ballad, sounds the stronger of the two. (VJ)

Cambridge

Personnel:	LONNY BOWERSOX	vcls, gtr		A
	CHARLES FISCHER	keyb'ds		A
	CHAS GUNTHER	vcls, gtr		A
	TOM STINE	drms		A
	DAN VOGAN	vcls, gtr, banjo, steel gtr	A

ALBUM: 1(A) SHARE A SONG (Green Dolphin 6024 N3B) 197? R2

A local Pennsylvania or Ohio band, excellent country-rock private press in a **Byrds**/Flying Burrito Brothers style. (CF)

The Camel Drivers

Personnel: TOM CURDIN A

45s: You Made A Believer Of Me / Give It A Try (Top Dog 200) 196?
The Grass Looks Greener /
I'm Gonna Make You Mine (Top Dog 201) 1968
The Grass Looks Greener /
It's Gonna Rain (Top Dog A-100) 1968
Sunday Morning 6 O'clock /
Give It A Try (Top Dog A-103) 1968
Sunday Morning 6 O'clock /
Give It A Try (Buddah BDA-61) 1968
Forgive Us/? (Top Dog A-104) c1968
Everybody's Got To Do His Own Thing/
Dont Throw Stones At My Window (Buddah BDA-85) 1969

The *Fuzz, Flaykes And Shakes Vol. 3* (LP & CD) compilation features their smooth-running garage-popper *The Grass Looks Greener*, released in two differing versions by this Olivet, Michigan band. The compilers tracked down band member Tom Curdin who revealed that the band had formed in 1963 and lasted until 1976. Their peak arrived in 1968 with *Sunday Morning 6 O'Clock*, a big local hit that was picked up by Buddah, did well across the US and in Canada. (MW/TSz/LJ)

Hamilton Camp

Personnel:	HAL BLAINE	drms	A
	HAMILTON CAMP (BOBBY CAMP)	vcls, gtr	ABC
	VAN DYKE PARKS	keyb'ds	A

ALBUMS: 1( ) AT THE GATE OF HORN (Elektra EKL 207) 1964 -
(selective) 2( ) PATHS OF VICTORY (Elektra EKS 7278) 1965 -
3(A) HERE'S TO YOU (Warner) 1967 -
4(B) WELCOME TO THE HAMILTON CAMP (Warner) 1969 -

NB: (1) as Bob Gibson and Bobby Camp. (2) as Bobby Camp.

A folk singer/songwriter, also known as Bobby Camp. He is mostly remembered for having composed the fantastic *Pride Of Man*, on his *Paths*

Of Victory album, which was later covered by **Quicksilver Messenger Service** on their first album. Although his material is generally of interest, his records often suffer from the rich arrangements provided by well-known studio musicians, like **Van Dyke Parks** or Felix Pappalardi. (SR/NK)

Dick Campbell

Personnel:	MIKE BLOOMFIELD	12 string gtr	A
	PAUL BUTTERFIELD	harp	A
	DICK CAMPBELL	vcls, gtr	A
	PETE CETERA	bs	A
	MARTY GREBB	keyb'ds, tambourine	A
	BILLY HERMAN	drms	A
	MARK NAFTALIN	organ	A
	SAM LAY	drms	A
	ARTIE SULLIVAN	tambourine, vcls	A
	JIMMY VINCENT	gtr	A
	LARRY WRICE	drms	A

ALBUM: 1(A) SINGS WHERE IT'S AT (Mercury MG 21060) 1966 -

NB: (1) a mono pressing, SR 61060, also exists.

45s:	α	She's My Girl /	(Great 4703) 1963
		Miami /	(Betty 1212) 1964
		The Blues Peddlers/ People Planners	(Mercury 72511) 1965
		Train To Hollywood / Sugar Ripe	(Cuca 6962) 1969

NB: α is not confirmed as by this artist.

Dick Campbell was a folkie/hippie character from Monroe, Wisconsin. According to Cuca's Jim Kirchstein, everyone thought he was a little odd - "(he) used to ride his bike around town, dressed like a hippy, and he had a little bag that he carried his money in". Nonetheless Kirchstein was impressed enough to take him on as an engineer and producer at Cuca, and believes he went on to work for a publishing house in Los Angeles.

In late 1966, he played guitar on the **Talismen**'s *Glitter And Gold* 45. He also produced **Easy Street**.

His album, produced by Lou Reizner, showed him to be a singer/songwriter heavily influenced by Bob Dylan. He was backed by the **Butterfield Blues Band** plus various Chicago musicians (including a young Pete Cetera, ex-**Exceptions**, later with Chicago). The album is rare and sought-after but is better avoided, the songs being weak and **Campbell**'s voice too close to Dylan's.

Dick Campbell passed away in 2002. (SR/GM/MW)

Canadian Legends

45: I'm A Believer / Just One Girl (White Cliffs 259) 1967

Not a Canadian-based outfit, nor the work of the Milwaukee, Wisconsin **The Legends** who adopted the **Canadian Legends** moniker whilst in Florida. The 45 puts amended lyrics to the **Monkees**' hit... (MW/GM)

The Canadian Rogues

Personnel:	RONNIE HAREL	vcls	A
	WILLIE METTS	ld vcls	A
	DANE STREETS	gtr	A

45s:	Have You Found Somebody New /	
	You Better Stop	(Fuller 2597) 1965
	Oop-Poop-A-Doop/Keep In Touch	(Charay 19/P-5017) 1966
	Oop-Poop-A-Doop/Keep In Touch	(Palmer 5017) 1967
	Run And Hide/	
	Love And Dreams (PIC INSERT)	(Paris Tower PT-112) 1967
	Do You Love Me?/Mickey's Monkey	(Rogue 1967) 1967

From Lakeland in Central Florida. Their best known song is *Keep In Touch*, a Pretty Things inspired number with a Diddley shuffle. First released on the Fort Worth-based Charay label in 1966, it was later picked up in 1967 by the Detroit-based Palmer label.

PSYCHEDELIC STATES - FLORIDA Vol. 1 (Comp CD) including The Canadian Rogues.

Their debut 45, charted locally on WLCY radio in August 1965, whilst their final effort from December 1967 consisted of two Motown covers.

Thirty-three years later Harel and Streets still play together in The Rogues with Carl Chambers (ex-Ron and The Starfires).

Compilation appearances have included: *Keep In Touch* on *Psychedelic States - Florida Vol. 1* (CD), *Garage Kings* (Dble LP) and *Back From The Grave, Vol. 2* (LP); and *You Better Stop* on *Garage Punk Unknowns, Vol. 8* (LP). (VJ/MW/JLh/RM)

Candle

Personnel:	DUANE BRYANT	drms	A
	JEFFREY HOOVEN	vcls, gtr, keyb'ds	A
	DOUG KRAATZ	violin, viola	A
	ANDY NARELL	keyb'ds, steel drum	A
	DON PEAKE	gtr	A
	RICHARD ROBERTS	perc	A
	JOHN SKELTON	vcls, flute	A
	ROBERT VERNE	vcls, gtr	A
	DAVEY WISON	vcls, bs	A
	L.J. WOLKEN	accordian	A

ALBUM: 1(A) CANDLE (Greene Bottle GBS 1003) 1972 -

An abundance of unusual instruments and the desire to write emotional songs make for at least some interesting listening, here, although the album is not entirely successful. Most of the blame lies with producer and label-owner Charles Greene who's production lacks clarity. This combined with a tendency for simplistic melodies, tear down a large part of the building the musicians are attempting to erect. So, despite the large possibilities which the band seem to have, not much is actually coming forth in terms of inspiring (and inspired) music. Best cut: the quiet yet passionate ballad *Sleepy Lylah*. (MK)

Jimmy C and The Chelsea Five

45: Play With Fire/Leave Me Alone (Zero 1003) 1965

This mob apparently went to high school in Dallas with **Kenny And The Kasuals**. *Leave Me Alone*, a folk-punker, is to be found on *Highs In The Mid-Sixties, Vol. 23* (LP), whilst *Play With Fire* can be found on *Killer Cuts* (LP). (VJ)

Candy Company

45:	Sugar/Stone	(ABC)	c1967

An forgotten pop group, their 45 was one of the **Curt Boettcher**'s "Our Productions" starring the usual suspects, in this case mainly Lee Mallory and **Ruthann Friedman**. (SR/JFr)

Candymen

Personnel:	DEAN DAUGHTRY	keyb'ds	A
	BILLY GILMORE	bs	A
	RODNEY JUSTO	vcls	A
	BOB NIX	drms	A
	JOHN RAINEY ADKINS	gtr	A

HCP
ALBUMS: 1(A) THE CANDYMEN (ABC ABCS 616) 1967 195 -
2(A) BRING YOUR CANDY POWER (ABC ABCS 633) 1968 - -

HCP
45s: α Georgia Pines/Movies In My Mind (ABC 10995) 1967 81
Deep In The Night/Stone Blues Man (ABC 11023) 1967 -
Sentimental Lady/Ways (ABC 11048) 1967 -
Candyman/Crowded Room (ABC 11077) 1968 -
It's Gonna Get Good In A Minute/
Go And Tell The People (ABC 11141) 1969 -
I'll Never Forget/Lonley Eyes (ABC 11175) 1969 -
Happy Tonight/Papers (Liberty 56172) 1970 -

NB: α also released in the UK (HMV POP 1612) 1967.

Originally the Webs, out of Dothan, Alabama. Two 45s were released with original vocalist Bobby Goldsboro before his departure to schmaltzy pop stardom. His replacement was Rodney Justo from Florida's Rodney & The Mystics. A psychedelic pop outfit they acted as Roy Orbison's back-up band. They did achieve a minor hit with *Georgia Pines* and their debut album also crept into the Album Charts climbing to No 195. Daughtry, Nix and Justo were all later involved in the Georgia-based Atlanta Rhythm Section.

Candymen specialized in live reproduction of complex Beatles and Beach Boys material, like *A Day In The Life* or *Good Vibrations*, and that gave them quite a following when they first appeared in New York in the Summer of 1967. Unfortunately for them, their original material and records were not up to their live shows.

Rodney Justo also recorded a 45 with **Noah's Ark**.

There was another different act, **Joe Dee & The Candymen** who had at least one album *The Twist* (Diplomat FM/S/100) 1962. (VJ/PDg/SR/JMc/MW/JLh)

Canebreak (aka Canebreak Singers)

Personnel incl:	MIKE CRESPO	A
	HENRY SHERBURNE	A

45:	Another Day /	
	I Don't Really Like You	(Montel-Michelle 969) 1966

From Baton Rouge, Louisiana. Originally a folk group, but they went electric when Henry (of **The Playgue**) sat in. 1968 saw one further 45 on Columbia as by Love-Michael. Crespo's *I Don't Really Like You* is an excellent folk-rocker covered in 1967 by fellow Louisianans the **Distortions**. (AB/MW)

Cannabis

Personnel:	LONNY GASPERINI	keyb'ds	A
	BRIAN KELLY	gtr	A
	BOB RANDELL	drms, vcls, acoustic gtr	A
	TONY RODRIGIJEZ	ld gtr	A
	KEITH TWEEDLY	vcls	A
	GARY WILKINSON	bs, vcls, acoustic gtr	A

CANNABIS - Joint Effort LP.

ALBUM: 1(A) JOINT EFFORT
(Amphion Seahorse AS 8100) 1972 R1/R2

NB: (1) reissued officially on CD by Gear Fab (GF-114) 1998.

The above album consisted of early seventies open air hippie festival rock from Lincoln, Rhode Island. Recorded at Methuen, Massachusetts the band is now far flung with original members in California (Brian Kelly), Florida (Bob Randall) and Puerto Rico (Tony Rodriguez). The remainder still live in Rhode Island.

The band had a decidedly country-rock feel and the principal song writers (Randall and Wilkinson) were influenced by artists as diverse as "The Band" and "Yes".

Compilation appearances have included *I Can't Roll* on Gear Fab's *Psychedelic Sampler* (CD). (MW)

Canned Heat

Personnel:	STUART BROTMAN	bs	A
	FRANK COOK	drms	ABC
	BOB "THE BEAR" HITE	vcls	ABCDEFG H
	HENRY "SUNFLOWER" VESTINE		ABC FG
	AL "THE OWL" WILSON	vcls, gtr, hrmnca	ABCD
	MARK ANDES	bs	B
	LARRY "THE MOLE" TAYLOR	bs	CDE
	ADOLFO "FITO" DE LA PARRA	drms	DEFG H
	HARVEY MANDEL	gtr	E G
	ANTONIO "TONY" DE LA BARREDA	bs	FG
	JOEL SCOTT HILL	gtr, vcls	G
	ED BEYER	keyb'ds	H
	RICHARD HITE	bs	H
	JAMES SHANE	gtr, vcls	H
	(JOHN LEE HOOKER	gtr, vcls	F)
	(MAC REBENNACK	keyb'ds)	
	(LITTLE RICHARD	vcls	G)
	(ELLIOT INGBER	gtr on 6)	
	(MARK NAFTALIN	keyb'ds on 6)	
	(ERNEST LANE	keyb'ds on 6)	

HCP
ALBUMS: 1(C) CANNED HEAT (Liberty LRP-3526) 1967 76 -
(up to 2(D) BOOGIE WITH CANNED HEAT
1975) (Liberty LRP-3541) 1968 16 -
3(C) VINTAGE (Janus JLS 3009) 1967 173 -

4(D)	LIVIN' THE BLUES	(Liberty LST-27200)	1968	18 -
5(D)	HALLELUJAH	(Liberty LST-7618)	1969	37 -
6(C/D)	CANNED HEAT COOKBOOK (comp)	(Liberty LST-11000)	1969	86 -
7(F)	FUTURE BLUES	(Liberty LST-11002)	1970	59 -
8(E)	'70 CONCERT, LIVE IN EUROPE	(Liberty LST-7641)	1970	133 -
9(F)	HOOKER'N'HEAT	(Liberty LST-35002)	1971	73 -
10(-)	CANNED HEAT COLLAGE (comp)	(Sunset SUS-5298)	1971	- -
11(C)	LIVE AT THE TOPANGA CORRAL	(Wand 693)	1971	- -
12(G)	HISTORICAL FIGURES AND ANCIENT HEADS	(United Artists UAS-5557)	1971	- -
13(H)	THE NEW AGE	(United Artists UA-LA049F)	1973	- -
14(-)	THE VERY BEST OF (comp)	(United Artists UA-LA431-E)	1975	- -

NB: (1) later issued on (LST-7526). (2) later issued on (LST-7541). (3) reissued on CD *Don't Forget To Boogie: Vintage Heat* (Varese Sarabande 302 066 345 2) 2002. (8) later issued on (United Artists UAS-5509). (11) recorded 1969.

HCP

45s:	Rollin' and Tumblin'/Bullfrog Blues	(Liberty 55979)	1967	115
(up to	Evil Woman/World In A Jug	(Liberty 56005)	1967	-
1973)	On The Road Again/Boogie Music	(Liberty 56038)	1968	-
	On The Road Again/Amphetamine Annie	(Liberty 56073)	1968	16
α	Going Up The Country/One Kind Favor	(Liberty 56077)	1968	11
	The Chipmunk Song/Christmas Blues	(Liberty 56079)	1968	-
	Time Was/Low Down	(Liberty 56097)	1969	67
	Poor Moon/Sic'Em Pigs	(Liberty 56127)	1969	119
	Get Off My Back/Change My Ways	(Liberty 56140)	1969	-
	Let's Work Together/I'm Her Man	(Liberty 56151)	1969	26
	Sugar Bee/Shake It And Break It	(Liberty 56170)	1970	-
α	Future Blues/Goin' Up The Country (live)	(Liberty 56180)	1970	-
	Goin' Up The Country/On The Road Again	(Liberty All Time Hits 54572)	1970	-
	Woolly Bully/My Time Ain't Long	(Liberty 56217)	1971	105
	Whiskey and Wimmen/Let's Make It	(United Artists 50779)	1971	-
	Long Way From L.A./Hill's Stomp	(United Artists 50831)	1971	-
	Rockin With The King/I Don't Care What You Tell Me	(United Artists 50892)	1972	88
	Cherokee Dance/Sneakin' Around	(United Artists 50927)	1972	-
	Rock & Roll Music/Lookin' For My Rainbow	(United Artists UA-XW197-W)	1973	-
	Harley Davidson Blues/You Can Run, But You Sure Can't Hide	(United Artists UA-XW243-W)	1973	-

NB: α not issued.

The formation of **Canned Heat** evolved in 1964 from Al Wilson, **John Fahey** and Mike Perlowin's ideas about starting an independent record company to reissue old blues records. Al "Blind Owl" Wilson (b. 1943 in Boston), was a music major at Boston University, who wrote articles on bluesmen like Robert Pete Williams and Son House, had a high-pitched voice with a unique vocal technique and played harmonica and guitar. In 1964, with the help of the blues historian Dick Waterman, Wilson had managed to track down Son House and revive his interest in playing blues, as he hadn't picked up a guitar in twenty years. Strangely enough on the same day in 1964, **John Fahey** and guitarist Bill Barth (later with **Insect Trust**) rediscovered elder bluesman Skip James in Mississippi and also brought him out of retirement. Barth and Fahey with another guitarist, Henry Vestine, promoted Skip's appearance at the 1964 Newport Folk Festival.

Mike Perlowin was another folk-blues guitarist having moved to L.A. from New York in 1961. He studied guitar at the Ash Grove's school of folk music, where one of his teachers was Clarence White, then with the Kentucky Colonels. Mike also played in a bluegrass outfit the Four Farfels with future **Stone Poney** Herb Steiner.

While Fahey, Wilson and Perlowin discussed their record label plans, Fahey remembered Bob "the Bear" Hite (b. Feb 1945, California} a record store manager and blues '78 collector, who owned a rare copy of the Library of Congress recording of Muddy Waters and it was decided to bring Bob into the group's plans.

Mike Perlowin remembers: "Bob was working at a record store at the time that was actually very close to where I was living. I called him, and he agreed to meet with the three of us. We realized that we could all play, so we decided to form a band instead. As soon as we said we wanted to play electric, **John Fahey** lost interest, so in the begining it was Bob and Al and me. We spent three days in Bob's house (he was living with his parents at the time, as was I) listening to records and making plans. We had a rehearsal in which Bob brought in a drummer named Keith Sawyer and I dragged in bassist Stu Brotman. Unfortunately for me, I was more of a folk style player (Fahey was my biggest influence at the time) and couldn't play rock very well, so I was fired and replaced by Kenny Edwards (pre-**Stone Poneys**), who was also fired and replaced by Henry Vestine, a former member of the Beaus".

The band was then thinking of calling themselves either "The Heavies" {due Bob's large size) or "The Black and Blues" but they finally chose "Canned Heat".

Mike Perlowin remembers: "Mike Bass who was sharing a place with Al and myself was talking to Steve Mann, another L.A. folk-blues guitarist who thought the band should all dress up as cops and call themselves The Heat. Bass came up with the name **Canned Heat**, after an old 1928 record, *Canned Heat Blues*, by a guy named Tommy Johnson, which was about drinking sterno to get high".

As 1964 moved into 1965, the nucleus remained Bob Hite and Al Wilson. By this stage Al had played harp on the Son House's 1965 LP *The Father Of Folk Blues* and had appeared on some **John Fahey** recordings (who gave him the Blind Owl nickname). He also guested on some sessions with **Fred Neil**.

The group was fairly informal and had basically dissolved, with Henry 'Sunflower' Vestine having left to join the **Mothers of Invention** briefly in 1965 before being sacked by **Zappa**.

In 1965 they reformed, with Stuart Brotman (bass) and new drummer Frank Cook, who had actually backed artists ranging from Chet Baker to Dobie Gray. This version also failed to take off and the group disbanded again in early 1966, the public being not interested by their traditional blues repertoire. Later that year, Wilson, Hite, Vestine and Cook rejoined with Mark Andes on bass (Brotman joined **Kaleidoscope** in 1967), and performed with a predominant boogie sound mixed into their electric blues. They performed their first show at the Ash Grove in Los Angeles and soon became the resident band of the Kaleidoscope, another L.A. club.

In early 1967 due to the efforts of their manager, Skip Taylor, they were signed to Liberty Records. In March 1967, Mark Andes left to join **Spirit** and was replaced by Larry "The Mole" Taylor (born 1942, NYC} who was an accomplished bass player in demand in the L.A. studios (notably with **The Monkees**). His brother Mel Taylor was in The Ventures.

In April 1967, they started cutting demos at RCA studios in Chicago but these songs, notably a totally different version of *On The Road Again*, remained unheard until 1994. In May they re-cut some material for their self-titled first album, issued in July but preceded by the *Rollin And*

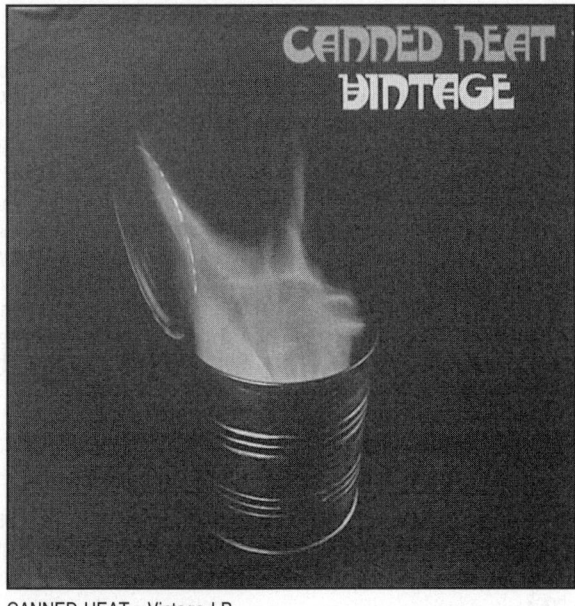

CANNED HEAT - Vintage LP.

Tumblin' single in June. Produced by Cal Carter, the album featured blues covers of material like Guitar Slim's *The Story Of My Life*, *Dust My Broom*, Sonny Boy Williamson's *Help Me*, Willie Dixon's *Evil Is Going On* and a few originals like *Bullfrog Blues*.

On 17th June, 1967, they played the Monterey Pop Festival (three tracks from their performance later appeared on the 1992 4-CD *Monterey Pop Festival* set). As with many other acts that performed at the event, it brought them a national audience and their debut album rose to No. 76 in the charts. They then began touring, but got busted in Denver for drug possession. To make bail, they received an advance from Liberty Records in exchange for their publishing rights!

Not long after, Mexican-born Adolfo "Fito" De La Parra (b. 1948, Mexico City) replaced Frank Cook on drums, after Cook had left to form **Pacific, Gas & Electric**. Tito had played in bands since 1958, in Mexico (Los Sparks, Los Hooligans, Los Juniors, Javier Batiz And The Finks) and with Los Sinners entered California illegally in 1965 where they became Los Tequilas (sic) and recorded two albums for RCA. In late 1965, they were caught by the police and sent back to Tijuana. De La Parra, who was married to an American woman, returned to California and joined Larry Barnes And the Creations, a club band from Torrance, and then **Sotweed Factor** and Bluesberry Jam (which evolved into **Pacific Gas and Electric**).

In late 1967, **Canned Heat** recorded a lot of material for their new album, but these versions of *The Hunter*, *Whiskey And Women*, *Shake Rattle And Roll*, *Mean Old World*, *Fannie Mae*, *Gotta Boogie (The World Boogie)* remained unissued until the 1994 EMI compilation CD *Uncanned*.

In January 1968, *Boogie With Canned Heat* was released. A Texas radio station picked up on one track, *On The Road Again*, and public interest led to its release as a single. It became a hit in the U.S and in Europe.

Produced by Dallas Smith, the album also featured classics like *Amphetamine Annie* (based on the death by overdose of one of Hite's friends) and *Evil Woman* (penned by Larry Weiss, who also wrote *Hi Ho Silver Lining* and *Bend Me, Shape Me*). The blues pianist Sunnyland Slim played on some tracks, but generally the album gets stuck in the boogie mode, especially with the eleven minutes of *Fried Hockey Boogie*.

Soon after that, Al Wilson, Vestine and Taylor appeared on Sunnyland Slim's album *Slim's Got His Thing Going On*. They toured Europe that year and won a faithful audience in several countries, notably in Germany.

October 1968 saw the release of *Livin' The Blues 1968*, a two album set which included the hit single *Goin' Up The Country*. The group was then totally immersed on drugs and was playing very long "psychedelic boogie" tracks, with extended improvisations. Two examples can be found on this album: *Parthenogenesis* (almost twenty minutes) and the live forty-one minute *Refried Boogie* which took up a whole LP and is rather self-indulgent. **John Fahey**, **Dr John** and John Mayall guested on the album.

In July 1969, their next album, *Hallelujah*, featured guests such as Mike Pacheco, Javier Batiz (the Mexican friend of De La Parra), Skip Diamond, Elliot Ingber (from **Fraternity Of Man**), Ernest Lane and Mark Naftalin. Most of them were just adding vocals to the proceedings. The album was a fairly tight set with several highlights: *Same All Over*, *Time Was* and *Sic'em Pigs*, but it produced no major hits.

In July, largely due to his drug abuse, Vestine left and formed Sun, that went nowhere. His replacement was the Chicago blues guitarist **Harvey Mandel**. In August 1969, **Canned Heat** appeared at the Woodstock Festival. (They were subsequently in the film and on the two albums).

With their chart success and sudden lack of new material, a compilation album soon followed, *The Canned Heat Cookbook*, in October 1969. They also appeared on the Together Records compilation *Early L.A* (1969, 2 tracks) and *Vintage Heat 1969*. Hite and Vestine also spent time compiling albums for Imperial Records 'Legendary Masters' series.

In 1969, when blues singer Wilbert Harrison reworked his *Let's Stick Together* as *Let's Work Together* (an early 1970's U.S hit), **Canned Heat** cut their version, which was issued in January 1970 in the U.K and became a hit. They concentrated on touring the U.K. and Europe and also played the Isle Of Wight Festival in 1970. *Canned Heat '70 Concert: Recorded Live In Europe* was released in Europe in June 1970 and some months later in the USA with the usual mix of blues covers (*That's All Right Mama*,

CANNED HEAT - Livin' The Blues LP.

Bring It On Home, *Let's Work Together*) and original material (*Pulling Hair Blues*, *London Blues*, *Goodbye For Now*). In August 1970, their new album was titled *Future Blues* and contained three songs already used on their live album. It's the final **Canned Heat** studio album to feature Alan Wilson. *Future Blues* was also one of their most focused efforts and the group themselves handled the production with Skip Taylor. From Alan Wilson's sadly all too fitting *My Time Ain't Long* to an heavy blues version of Arthur Crudup's *That's All Right, Mama*, the album has an experimental edge that went far beyond their usual lengthy solos. **Dr. John** appears on two tracks: *London Blues* and *Skat*, a late-1940's-style jump blues novelty. The group was so popular that Liberty appointed the making of "The Kanned Korn Komix", a 20 page comix book a lá Robert Crumb, dedicated to the crazy adventures of the Bear, the Owl, the Snake and the Raccoon. Copies of the comic were included in early pressings of the album.

In May 1970, Larry Taylor and **Harvey Mandel** left the group to join John Mayall. Henry Vestine rejoined with Antonio 'Tony' De La Barreda on bass, a friend of De La Parra. That month they cut a double album with John Lee Hooker.

The label Wand then released a live album, *Live At Topanga Corral*. It features six long and energetic tracks 'recorded in 1966 and 1967', with one original, *Bullfrog Blues*, and five covers (*I'd Rather Be The Devil*, *Dust My Broom*, *Wish You Would* etc.). It was in fact recorded at the Kaleidoscope in 1969, but the group changed the name of the location and date as they were already signed to Liberty when the recordings occurred. Al Wilson died September 3rd 1970 from an overdose and was replaced by **Joel Scott Hill** from **The Strangers**, Jerome (formed with De La Barreda) and **L.A. Getaway**. A live recording of this line-up from an August 1971 concert in Finland *Live At The Turku Rock Festival* was issued (Bear Tracks BTS 964410) 1990 on CD and double album.

Early 1972 saw the release of *Historical Figures And Ancient Heads* album, a rather patchy album. The group was obviously looking for a new direction after the death of Wilson and the tracks (which featured three different lead guitarists, Vestine and **Hill** being complemented by a returning **Mandel** on one track) range from rock tracks (*Hill's Stomp*, *Rockin With The King*, with Little Richard) to boogie (*Utah*, *Cherokee Dance*) or more melacholic tracks (*I Don't Care What You Tell Me*, by and with Charles Lloyd). The cover art was quite scary, the group being depicted as old people looked after by nurses on the front sleeve and reduced to naturalized heads surrounded by dead flowers, shells, butterflies and material used for heroin injection on the gatefold. In June 1972, De La Barreda quit, with Larry Taylor re-joining for a short spell. **Joel Scott Hill** also left the group and later joined the Flying Burrito Brothers.

In 1973 **Canned Heat** had evolved into the line-up of Henry Vestine, Fito de la Parra, Bob Hite and his brother Richard Hite (bs, tuba, gtr) replacing Larry Taylor and other new members James Shane (gtr, bs, vcs, sax) and Ed Beyer (keyb'ds, ex-**Smoke**). This version produced the *New Age* album in March 1973. From here onwards the group floundered with multiple line-up changes and recordings on small labels that fall outside the scope of this book.

"The Bear" died in 1981 from a heart attack. The surviving members, mainly led by drummer Fito de la Parra, continued touring and recording, although heavily relying on live albums. After recruiting new vocalist Walter Trout, they followed with James Thornbury, {who fronted the band from 1985 to 1995} then Robert Lucas assumed lead vocals.

They recorded as **The Canned Heat Blues Band** in 1996 for A&M, which was Vestine's last recording with the group, as he died in Paris in December 1997. A further release in 1999 *Boogie 2000* was issued on the Ruf label.

Compilation appearances have included *Amphetamine Annie* on *First Vibration* (LP) and *Smokey The Bear Song* on *Glimpses, Vol. 3* (LP). (JO/SR/CF)

Cannibal and The Headhunters

Personnel:
CANNIBAL"FRANKIE" GARCIA		A
JOE JARAMILLO		A
ROBERT JARAMILLO		A
RICHARD LOPEZ		A

ALBUMS:
1	LAND OF 1,000 DANCES	(Rampart R(M)(S)-3302) 1966 R1	
2	LAND OF 1,000 DANCES	(Date TE(M)(S)-3001) 1966 SC	

NB: (2) is a reissue of (1), also reissued on CD.

45s:
Land Of 1,000 Dances/ I'll Show You How To Love Me	(Rampart 642)	1965
Nau Ninny Nau/Here Comes Love	(Rampart 644)	1965
Follow The Music/I Need Your Loving	(Rampart 646)	1965
Out Of Sight/Please Baby Please	(Rampart 654)	c1966

East L.A. frat-rockers. This Mexican-American band started out playing at the Shrine Auditorium in L.A. in 1965 and their most famous track was *Land Of 1,000 Dances*.

Compilation appearances have included: *Land Of 1000 Dances* on *East Side Revue, Vol. 1* (LP), *East Side Revue* (Rampart 3303) (1969 Dble LP), *The East Side Sound, Vol. 1* (LP) and *Rampart Records EP* (7" EP); *Land Of 1000 Dances* and *I Need Your Loving* on *The West Coast East Side Sound, Vol. 1* (CD); *Land Of 1000 Dances* and *Nau Ninny Nau* on *The East Side Sound, Vol. 1 - 1959-1968* (CD); *Nau Ninny Nau* on *The West Coast East Side Sound, Vol. 2* (CD); *Follow The Music* and *Here Comes Love* on *The West Coast East Side Sound, Vol. 3* (CD) and *Please Baby Please* on *The West Coast East Side Sound, Vol. 4* (CD); (VJ/MW/NK)

The Cannons

Personnel:
JERRY CRATZENBERG	bs	A
MIKE KEILHOFER	gtr	AB
LEE LARSON	vcls	AB
PETE LOEB	sax	AB
MIKE TURK	drms	AB
JIM PERKINS	bs	B

45s:
Sweet Georgia Brown / Lonesome	(Fan Jr. 5504)	1966
Day To Day / Love, Little Girl	(Night Owl 1312)	1967

This Madison, Wisconsin quintet formed in 1965 and spent several years touring across Wisconsin, Illinois and Michigan. Around 1966 they thought about recording a version of the **Strangeloves**-penned *I Wanna Do It* but felt it was too suggestive. It didn't bother label-mates **Robin and The Three Hoods**, who picked it up and achieved an area hit.

Day to Day is a pleasant folk-rocker, likened to **The Beau Brummels**, and can be heard on *Highs In The Mid-Sixties, Vol. 15* (LP), which mis-credits the title as *Days Go By*. (VJ/GM/MW)

Canoise

Personnel:
BOB COATES	gtr, vcls	AB D
PAT CURTO	drms, vcls	ABCD
NEAL DUNNING	bs, vcls	A CD
DOUG SWANSON	gtr, bs, vcls	ABC
GRANT GULLICKSON	tamb, vcls	B
LARRY SUESS	gtr, keyb'ds, vcls	BCD
GARY GILBERTSON	keyb'ds	C
ROB STYER	gtr	C

NB: Line-up 'A' 1965-1966; 'B' 1967-1968; 'C' 1970-1974; 'D' 1981-now. The above formed the main line-ups who recorded - other musicians involved at various times included: DAN BURNICE, MARC WROE, WILLIE POUNDS drms (1968), DAVE BERGET, MIKE FLAHERTY bs (1968), PAULA ELSNER, LANCE GULLIKSON vcls (1970s Hawaii chapter), BOB MILES drms (1973-1974).

CDs:
1	NOW... AND THEN	(private)	1993
2	THE TRUE STORY	(private)	c1995
3	PLUGGED IN	(private)	c1996

45s:
Born In Chicago / Something I Could Do	(IGL 120)	1966
There's Something About You Baby / Oh No Not My Baby	(Sonic 141)	1967
You're No Good / Right Track	(Sonic 153)	1968
One Too Many Things / Look Inside	(Trim 1973)	1971

Canoise (pronounced CANOY) was formed in St.Cloud, Minnesota in the Fall of 1965 by four freshmen at St.Cloud College. All had previously served time with other outfits: Pat Curto in the Men From Uncle; Bob Coates in the Nightmen; Neal Dunning and Doug Swanson in the Trolls. Their first 45 was released on IGL in Summer 1966 before they expanded to a five-piece with vocalist Grant Gullickson. Shortly after that Neal was drafted and Larry Suess, from the Mort Plank IV, was brought in, necessitating Doug switching from twelve-string to bass. Two more 45s were released on IGLs Sonic label before a period of rapid personnel turnover resulted in the departure of all the original members by late 1968, the last being Bob and Grant who joined Zarathustra.

In 1970 four of the original members got together again with new member Gary Gilbertson to reform **Canoise**. Just one 45 was waxed by this line-up which was based in Hawaii for over two years before returning to tour the geographical and climatic extremes of mainland USA (from Alaska to Phoenix!). This second chapter ended in 1974. Pat went on to Tanglefoot and Maiden America, Neal joined Danny Stevens and F Troop, Larry went solo and got a degree in psychology, Grant went solo and cut two albums (*Ivory*, *Bobbidazzler*), Bob completed medical school, and Doug moved to Connecticut.

The third and latest chapter stared in 1981 with Bob, Pat, Larry and Neal reuniting as an annual event, but latterly playing all over Minnesota and marking their 25th anniversary with a guest appearance by Doug.

Recently Bob Coates has co-ordinated the release of the three private CDs which cover their entire history - *Now... And Then* concentrates on live recordings by the current line-up - eighteen tracks performed in June 1993 (predominantly covers of sixties pop, ballad, soul, R&B and rock evergreens). It also features *Something I Could Do* (first 45, 1966), two unreleased tracks (from 1967 and 1968) and *Look Inside* (from the 1971

CANNED HEAT - Live At Topanga Corral/Vintage 2-on-1 CD.

45); *The True Story* CD is a studio recording odyssey - the four 45s, two 1966 radio spots, nine unreleased tracks from the 1966-1968 period, four tracks from the current line-up (two from 1982 and two from 1995) plus a 1977 track featuring Grant and Lance Gullickson with Larry Suess and Bobbidazzler; *Plugged In* is all new recordings featuring contributions by seasoned Twin Cities musicians, including Larry Wiegand of **Crow** fame. All are available direct from Bob Coates at 6013 Porter Lane, Edina, MN 55436, USA.

As for the original 45s...... The first couples a good cover of **Nick Gravenites**' *Born In Chicago*, with solid rhythm and accomplished guitar work, and a charming harmonious midpace beat-ballad written by Doug Swanson (echoes of the Beatles and Everlys). The second covers Goffin-King and Holland-Dozier-Holland in soul-pop mode with smooth harmonies and deep-throated lead. The third contains two more covers in a pop ballad vein but again the lead vocals try to take on a Elvis/cabaret style - it doesn't really come off, despite some fuzzed guitar on *Right Track*. Of the unreleased studio tracks from this period Paul Butterfield's *Come On In* stands out - above-par R&B-infused pop with waspish fuzz and better, i.e. less affected, vocals. The fourth Hawaii-period 45 covers Dylan in a good-timey folkie-rock style with sweet male-female harmonies, a piano solo and countrified guitar licks. The flip, an original, is overtly country-rock.

This band may not appeal to garage fuzz'n'farfisa purists but is definitely for those who enjoy the accomplished Midwest pop-rock sounds of the likes of **Dee Jay and The Runaways**, **The Rumbles** and The Coachmen.

Compilation appearances include *Born In Chicago* and *Something I Could Do* on *The IGL Rock Story Part One (1965-67)* (CD) and *There Is Something About You Baby* on *Roof Garden Jamboree* (LP). (MW/BCs)

CANTERBURY FAIR - Canterbury Fair CD.

Canterbury Fair

Personnel:	CHERYL CHURCHMAN	vcls	A
	JAMES HOLLEY	drms, vcls	A
	PHILIP HOLLINGSWORTH	bs, keyb'ds, vcls	ABCDE
	JOHN HOLLINGSWORTH	keyb'ds, vcls	BCDE
	JOE LO FRESO	keyb'ds	BC
	SEAN CORSARO	drms	CD
	DAVID HOLLINGSWORTH	drms, bs	E

ALBUM:	1	CANTERBURY FAIR	(Sundazed SC 11064) 1999

45:	Song On A May Morning / Days I Love	(Koala 8081) 1968

The Hollingsworth brothers first played together in 1965 with James Holley (who also did time with **The Bushmen**) in Fresno band The Coachmen. In 1966, the addition of Steve Bryant (guitar and vocals) precipitated a name change to **Everyday Things**, though Bryant soon left. In 1967, the brothers joined **Kings Verses** in time for their trip to Los Angeles to seek success and fortune - when this didn't work out Philip returned to Fresno and formed **Canterbury Fair** with Holley again plus vocalist Cheryl Churchman.

John had remained in L.A. for the rest of 1967, attending Cal State. On his return home in early '68 he presented a wealth of newly-penned keyboard material that determined a new direction and configuration for the band - a keyboard-bass-drums format, with the addition Joe Lo Freso (also from **The Bushmen**) on Hammond.

With continuing apathy from record labels, Holley departed at the end of 1968 but not before securing Corsaro as a replacement, who in turn found them a new manager. The group relocated to San Francisco for a while, eventually returning to Fresno without Corsaro, whose place was filled by brother number three, David. They carried on until 1980 with various string players augmenting the line-up.

The CD comprises 10 tracks from their most creative period (1967 to 1969) highlighting their predominantly instrumental neo-classical or baroque flavoured recitals. *Song On A May Morning* from their rare 45 is their most commercial offering - a catchy slice of West Coast pop-psych.

Not for garage purists - this should should appeal to those who like soft-psych or the baroque tendencies of **The Left Banke** and **Ars Nova**.

Compilation appearances have also included: *Song On A May Morning* on *Son Of The Gathering Of The Tribe* (LP) and *A Journey To Tyme, Vol. 2* (LP); and *The Man* (an unreleased track from the 45 sessions in 1968 that didn't make it onto the Sundazed collection) on *Fuzz, Flaykes, And Shakes, Vol. 4* (LP & CD). (MW)

Canterbury Music Festival

ALBUM:	1	RAIN AND SHINE	(BT Puppy BTPS-1018) 1968 R2

45s:	First Spring Rain/Poor Man	(BT Puppy 541) 1968
	Super Dooper Trooper/Mister Snail	(BT Puppy 553) 1968
	Sunny Day/Mister Snail	(BT Puppy 562) 1969

A baroque and breezy pop band a lá **Left Banke** or **Association**. Their album also contains one good psych garage track. Like many other records on BT Puppy, it doesn't seem to have been properly distributed. (SR)

Canticle

Personnel:	HOWARD FULLBROOK	vcls, gtr, violin	A
	PETER LAMBERT	violin	A
	HOWARD McDERMOTT	vcls, gtr	A
	FRANK PRESS	vcls, gtr	A

45:	Like A Rolling Stone/My Mind's Eye	(Century 36685) 1970

Acoustic hippie-folkie workouts of Bob Dylan and the Small Faces, the latter notable for the use of the fiddle. The band were playing at the London Troubadour when they were approached by an American record producer called Robert Reiter. Howard Fullbrook:- "He was in London, Ontario looking for Canadian artists to record and within a week we were in London making the record. We never saw or heard anymore from him after that day in the studios. We did learn, through a friend in Canada, that the single had been released but we never received a copy of the record or even heard the final result!" (MW)

Capes of Good Hope

Personnel:	JOEL CORY		A
	MIKE HORN		A
	MIKE JACOBSEN		A
	YOGI LANDEM		A
	DICK TOOPS		A

45s:	Shades/Lady Margaret	(Round 1001) 1966
	Winter's Children/
	If My Monique Would Only Dance	(Round 1002) 1966

From Chicago. *Shades* kicks off like a certain **Bob Lind** folk-pop classic, whilst the flip is another matter:- weeping Eastern guitars, tablas, suitable stony vocals and numerous start/stops - still poppy but infused with incense. *Lady Margaret* can be found on *A Heavy Dose Of Lyte Psych* (CD). The follow-up unfortunately reverts to harmony pop, with **Left Banke** keyboard textures. (MW)

Caps

45s:	Three Little Picknicks/?	(White Star 101) 1959
	Red Headed Flea/Daddy Dean	(White Star 102) 1959

Red Headed Flea can be heard on *Garage Punk Unknowns, Vol. 6* (LP). The band hailed from Akron, Ohio. (VJ)

Captain Beefheart

Personnel:			
(up to 1972)	PAUL BLAKELEY	drms	A
	RY COODER	gtr	A
	JOHN FRENCH (DRUMBO)	drms	ABCDE
	JERRY HANDLEY	bs	AB
	DOUG MOON	gtr	A
	RUSS TITELMAN	gtr	AB
	DON VAN VLIET (CAPTAIN BEEFHEART)	vcls, harp	ABCDE
	JEFF COTTON (ANTENNAE JIMMY SEMENS)	b'neck gtr	BC
	ALEX ST CLAIRE (SNOUFFER)	gtr	B
	MARK BOSTON (ROCKETTE MORTON)	bs	CDE
	BILL HARKLEROAD (ZOOT HORN ROLLO)	gtr, flt	CDE
	VICTOR HAYDEN (THE MASCARA SNAKE)	bs, cla, vcls	C
	ELLIOT INGBER (WINGED EEL FINGERLING)	gtr	D
	ED MARIMBA (ART TRIPP)	gtr, vibes	DE
	ROY ESTRADA (OREJON)	bs	E

				HCP
ALBUMS:	1(A)	SAFE AS MILK	(Buddah BDS 5001) 1967	- SC
(up to 1972)	2(B)	STRICTLY PERSONAL	(Blue Thumb BTS1) 1968	- -
	3(C)	TROUT MASK REPLICA (dbl)	(Straight FTS 1053) 1969	- SC
	4(D)	LICK MY DECALS OFF BABY	(Straight FTS 1063) 1970	- -
	5(B)	MIRROR MAN	(Buddah 2365-002) 1971	- -
	6(D)	SPOTLIGHT KID	(Reprise RS 2050) 1972	131 -
	7(E)	CLEAR SPOT	(Reprise MS 2115) 1972	191 -

CAPTAIN BEEFHEART - Safe As Milk CD.

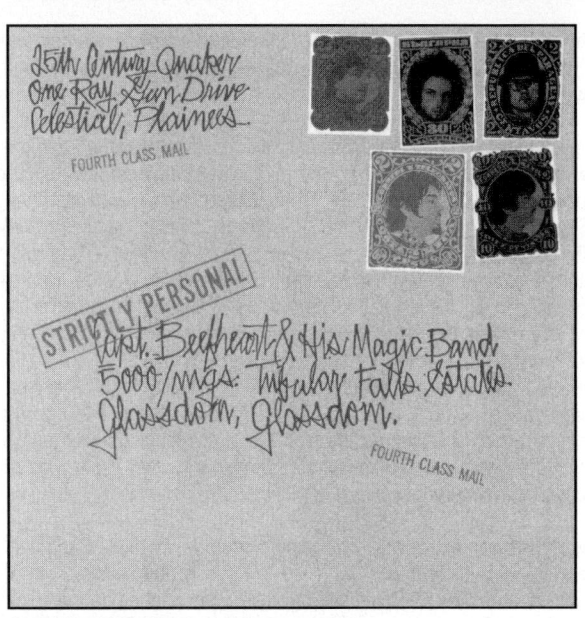

CAPTAIN BEEFHEART - Strictly Personal CD.

NB: (1) reissued several times on vinyl and CD including one as *Drop Out Boogie* (Buddah 2349-002) 1970. Of the CD reissues, (One Way OW 29088) includes nine outtakes, but the re-mastered (Buddah 7446599605-2) 1999 version is superior. (2) reissued several times on vinyl and also on CD (EMI 7243 8 29654 2 8) 1994. (3) reissued several times on vinyl and on CD (Reprise 2027-2) 1989. (4) reissued several times on vinyl and CD. (5) recorded 1967/8, this has also been reissued several times on vinyl, with the CD *The Mirror Man Sessions* (Buddha Records 7446599606-2) 1999 including five extra cuts. (6) and (7) reissued several times on vinyl and as 2-on-1 CDs. Also relevant within this time-frame are: *The Legendary A&M Sessions* (A&M AMY 226), a five track mini-album of 1965 recordings, subsequently reissued several times on vinyl and CD; and *Grow Fins* a lavish five CD set of early rare material, that is essential for **Beefheart** fans. This has also been released as two double album sets. *The Best Of Captain Beefheart And The Magic Band* (EMI 7243 5 39383 21) 2002 actually compiles material from his Virgin and Liberty years and remember that the mid-seventies were hardly **Beefheart**'s creative peak. *Magnetic Hands* (Viper CD 011) 2002 features 'live' material. The best are *Orange Claw Hammer* and *Gimme Dat Harp Boy* from a 1975 Knebworth gig and *Dali's Car* and *Beatle Bones 'N' Smokin' Stones* from a Portsmouth Guildhall gig from the same year. Some cuts are from later concerts.

45s: (selective)	Diddy Wah Diddy/ Who Do You Think You're Fooling?	(A&M 794) 1966
	Moonchild/Frying Pan	(A&M 818) 1966
	Yellow Brick Road/Abba Zaba	(Buddah DA 9) 1967
	Plastic Factory/Where There's A Woman	(Buddah DA 108) 1970
	Click Clack/ I Want To Booglerize You Baby	(Reprise 1068) 1971
	Click Clack/Glider (promo only)	(Reprise) 1972
	Too Much Time/Lo Yo-Yo Stuff	(Reprise PRO 547) 1972
	Too Much Time/ My Head Is My Only House	(Reprise 1133) 1972

Beefheart (real name Don Van Vliet) was born in Glendale, California in 1941. One wonders what the Lancaster High School, which included **Frank Zappa** and Van Vliet could have been like. After playing briefly with a band called The Blackouts, the 'mad captain' took the name **Captain Beefheart** and formed The Magic Band in 1964, which was based in Los Angeles. His first single for A&M was a version of Bo Diddley's *Diddy Wah Diddy*.

His debut album, which was rejected by A&M and eventually released by Buddah in the U.S. and Polydor in England, sounded like nothing that had been heard before. **Beefheart**'s growling and grunted vocals were most unusual, his vocal range most impressive, but some of the lyrics almost inaudible. Nonetheless, the material was of a consistent standard, with *Autumn Song*, *Zig Zag Wanderer*, *Electricity* and *Yellow Brick Road* among the stronger numbers.

Mirror Man, the next album he recorded, was rougher and not released until 1971. It is not considered one of his best.

Strictly Personal, was even less commercial, but represented a musical progression. Raw blues numbers like *Ah Feel Like Ahcid* and *Gimme Dat Harp Boy* were combined with more imaginative tracks like *Trust Us*, *On Tomorrow* and the excellent *Kandy Korn*, which features some superb intertwined guitar work, and displays **Beefheart**'s vocals at their howling and growling best. The album was apparently mixed without his supervision.

However, this line-up disintegrated after the album, St Clair left to work in a car wash and Handley joined a printing works. Then **Beefheart** by chance bumped into his old school mate **Frank Zappa**, who was busy setting up his Straight record label. With the promise of complete recording freedom **Beefheart** started work with a revised line-up on an album. The result was inevitably bizarre. Many would find *Trout Mask Replica* completely bewildering on an initial hearing. The band apparently recorded it in four hours and added the lyrics in four and a half hours without hearing the music! Most of the songs on the album are formless in the traditional sense, but far from being spontaneous, the band had rehearsed the material to the point of obsession. The album became an underground classic, regarded by many as the pinnacle of challenging music and hated by others. It was certainly atmospheric. **Beefheart**'s next album was similar but lacked the apparent spontaneity of *Trout Mask Replica*.

Following the band's return from a nationwide tour in 1971, **Beefheart** and **Zappa** fell out and **Beefheart** switched to Reprise and changed his line-up bringing in a couple of influential figures:- Elliot Ingber, formerly of **The Fraternity of Man** who became known as Winged Eel Fingerling and Artie Tripp (Ed Marimba) from **The Mothers of Invention**. The resultant album, *The Spotlight Kid*, was his first album to make any impression in the Album Charts peaking at No 131. His next, *Clear Spot*, was made without Fingerling, but with Roy Estrada on bass. Musically this was one of **Beefheart**'s best albums and it also made the album charts peaking at No 191.

Here we leave **Beefheart** - his subsequent recordings being outside the time-frame of this book. He and his band were an almost unique phenomena in the history of rock. Quite unlike anyone else, especially on those early recordings, and musically at odds with mainstream rock, these recordings are essential for connoisseurs of progressive rock.

Compilation appearances have included: *Diddy Wah Diddy* on *More Nuggets* (CD), *Nuggets Box* (4-CD), *Nuggets, Vol. 6* (LP) and *Excerpts From Nuggets* (CD); and *Electricity* on *Psychedelic Frequencies* (CD). (VJ)

Captain Darby and The Buccaneers

45:     Who Do They Watch/Lookout   (Buccaneer 100) c1966

A rare single of psych-pop with electric harpsichord, produced by Ray Allen who was also in charge of the **Chateaus**. (SR)

Captain Freak and Lunacycle Band

45:     20th Generation Sad/
        What Ever Happen To Superman   (Jamie 1397) 1968

A promising group name, but as often found, a deceiving result, as the singer is a sub-Dylan clone backed by piano and tuba! This single was produced by Jon Dorn and Howard Boggess (who cowrote the 'A' side with Lone) and arranged by Richard Rome. (SR)

Captain Groovy and His Bubblegum Army

45:     Captain Groovy and His Bubblegum Army/
        Dark Part Of My Mind Part 1   (Super K 104) 1969 128

Jerry Kasenetz and Jeff Katz, who were the masterminds behind the commercially successful late sixties bubblegum music which gave us acts like **The Ohio Express**, **The Music Explosion** and **The 1910 Fruitgum Company**, made this 45 themselves using a pseudonym. Sporting metallic fuzztone guitars and typically warbled bubblegum lyrics, you'll find it on *Boulders, Vol. 9* (LP) or *Mindrocker, Vol. 5* (LP).

An instrumental *Bubblegum March (Or Blowing Bubbles Through Rose Coloured Glasses)* appears on the *Everything You Always Wanted To Know...* (CD), and Erik Lindgren's sleeve-notes suggest that the same track

CAPTAIN BEEFHEART - Grow Fins CD Set.

also appeared as the flip to Super Cirkus' *Dong-Dong-Diki-Di-Ki-Dung* 45 (Super K 9)... whilst *Dark Part Of My Mind* also appeared on the flip to a **Crazy Elephant** 45 (Bell 763) and has been compiled on *Lycergic Soap* (LP), *Turds On A Bum Ride Vol. 1 & 2* (Dble CD) and *Turds On A Bum Ride, Vol. 1* (Dble LP). Confused? Well the explanation may be that **Captain Groovy and his Bubblegum Army** started life as a sound track to a cartoon show, which was cancelled, with some of the tracks later being recycled. (VJ/MW)

Captain Milk

Personnel incl: EDWIN HUBBARD   A

45:     Hey Jude/Impossible Dream   (Tetragrammaton T-1542) 1968

A Beatles cover, largely instrumental, by an obscure group, probably from California. **Captain Milk** was Edwin Hubbard, who also produced this 45. (SR)

Capus David

45:     Hour Of The Wolf / Dream Child   (Raydar) 1972

An obscure single, the 'A' side is a long melodic track with fuzz guitar and an intense rhythm. (SR)

C.A. Quintet

Personnel: JIMMY ERWIN   bs   A
             KEN ERWIN   trumpet   A
             RICK PATRON   drms   A
             TOM POHLING   ld gtr   A
             DOUG REYNOLDS   keyb'ds, vcls   A

ALBUMS: 1(A) TRIP THRU HELL   (Candy Floss 7764) 1969 R4/R5
         2(A) C.A. QUINTET-LIVE 1971   (Private Press) 1984

NB: (1) has been subjected to the following 'defective' reissues: as Psycho 12 (1983), a Greek pirate, and CD on Eva. All of these only include one-half of the stereo mix - missing out much of the guitar parts. Fortunately, Sundazed have reissued the album offcially, on CD with 12 bonus tracks (Sundazed SC 11021) 1995, and as a double LP with 14 bonus tracks (Sundazed LP 5037) 1995.

45s: Mickey's Monkey/I Want You To Love Me Girl   (Falcon 70) 1967
        Blow To My Soul/She's Got To Be True   (Falcon 71) 1967
        Smooth As Silk/Dr Of Philosophy   (Candy Floss 102) 1968

All three of these 45s and originals of this Minneapolis-based band's debut album are very rare and expensive collectors' items. The album, which was produced by band leader Ken Erwin, commences and concludes with the 12.30 minute long instrumental title track, which at times contains some interesting sound effects. However, the standout track is a piece of classic paranoid acid dementia *Cold Spider*,. The *Live* album is very disappointing.

They also had two cuts *Mickey's Monkey* and *Blow To My Soul* on the *Money Music* (August 100) 1967 compilation of Minneapolis bands, which had a very limited pressing and has also become very rare.

Although the album has been subject to many 'reissues', these were without the bands approval, and only included one-half of the stereo mix. The Sundazed reissue, corrects matters, and includes a number of alternate takes and previously unreleased cuts, together with sleevenotes including an interview with Ken Erwin, and studio engineer Steve Longman.

Retrospective compilation appearances include: *Dr. Of Philosophy* on *Sundazed Sampler, Vol. 2* (CD) and *Garagelands Vol. 2* (CD); and both *Cold Spider* and *Blow To My Soul* on *Changes* (LP), *Endless Journey - Phase Two* (LP) and *Endless Journey - Phase I & II* (Dble CD). (VJ/MW)

The Caravans

| 45: | This Little Old Lady/Three Musketeers | (Key-Man 101) 1966 |

A garage band from San Antone, Texas. One track, *3 Musketeers*, has resurfaced on *Hipsville, Vol. 2* (LP). The above 45 was issued as by 'Allivyn and The Caravans'.

Caravelles

Personnel:	RICK ANDERSON	bs	A
	JERRY BRECI	gtr	A
	JOHN FITZGERALD	ld vcls, hrmnca	A
	MIKE LIPMAN	ld gtr	A
	DANNY REED	keyb'ds	A
	DOUG STEINER	drms	A

45s:	Lovin' Just My Style/Self-Service	(Onacrest 502) 1966
	Lovin' Just My Style // Self Service	
	Lovin' Just My Style (instr) (PS)	
		(Dionysus/Bacchus Archives BA 1146) 2000

The Caravelles were from Phoenix, Arizona. They were managed and produced by Hadley "Who Loves You Madly" Murrell, a disc jockey at the practically all-black KCAC, Phoenix's AM soul station in the mid-sixties. For the most part, Murrell is better known for the legendary Phoenix soul acts he produced, which included The Servicemen, The New Bloods, Eddie and Ernie (who were in The New Bloods) and the Soulsetters. **The Caravelles**' flip to *Lovin' Just My Style* was a garagey cover of The New Bloods' *Self Service*, which had gotten enough local attention in Phoenix to get picked up by 20th Century-Fox for national distribution.

John Fitzgerald, **The Caravelles**' lead singer, had a reputation as "the Mick Jagger of Phoenix", and the group opened for the Dave Clark Five at Veterans Memorial Coliseum in Phoenix.

Rick Anderson was later in **The Superfine Dandelion** and The Tubes. It's unclear whether or not he played on *Lovin' Just My Style*, though. Drummer Neal Smith, who was in-between stints with The Laser Beats and Alice Cooper, joined **The Caravelles** in 1966, just before they changed their name to The Holy Grail. Contrary to rumours, Smith was not on the Onacrest record.

Their reissue 45 adds an instrumental take of *Lovin'*.. and comes in a neat picture sleeve with a band history by Dan Nowicki.

You can also hear the catchy *Lovin' Just My Style*, with its typical garage style guitar work, on *Pebbles, Vol. 8* (LP) or *Boulders, Vol. 1* (LP). Very much a case of The Kinks meet The Yardbirds. (VJ/DN)

The Cardboard Box

Personnel:	BARRY BERGER	gtr	A
	DAVE DUDAS	drms	A
	ERIC KISSINGER	bs	A
	JACK LORENZO	keyb'ds, vcls	A

| 45: | Come On Baby / Carol | (Regime M-69075) 1969 |

From Pottstown, Pennsylvania. this band were previously the Ethics who released one 45 on the Up Tight label in 1967. *Come On Baby* is on *A Lethal Dose Of Hard Psych* (CD). (ELn/MW)

Cardboard Village

| ALBUM: | 1 | SEA CHANGE | (Cardboard Village) 1969 R2 |

An almost entirely acoustic folk album with guitar, flute, bongos and male/female vocals, and some sparse electric touches. Some dealers describe it as being "Airplane-type female psych" but it's in fact more in the acid/hippie blues folk style. They came from Massachusetts. (SR)

The Cardinals

45s:	Tomato Juice/I Want You	(Cha Cha 740) 1965
	Hatchet Face/Go Go Baby	(Cha Cha 741) 1965
	Saturday Night/	
	I'm Gonna Tell On You (PS)	(Cha Cha 742) 1965
	I'm Gonna Tell On You/	
	When You're Away (PS)	(Cha Cha 748) 1966

A mid-sixties college outfit based in Muncie, Indiana. *Go Go Baby* is a rather primitive stomper, which can also be found on *Pebbles, Vol. 7* (CD). Other compilation coverage has included: *Tomato Juice* on *Open Up Yer Door! Vol. 1* (LP); *Hatchet Face* on *Hipsville, Vol. 2* (LP); and *I'm Gonna Tell On You* on *Follow That Munster, Vol. 1* (LP). (VJ/MW/KBn)

The Caretakers

45s:	Heart Of Love/Good Inside	(Rock-It 2002) 1968
	The World Outside/Summer Moments	(Rock-It 2004) 196?
	East Side Story/Epic	(Rip-Off 1001) 196?
	Hidden Steps/You Don't Have to Pretend	(Worm 1001) 196?

From the San Bernadine/Riverside area of California. You'll find *East Side Story* on *Pebbles, Vol. 9* (CD) and *Boulders, Vol. 5* (LP). Another cut, *Hidden Steps* can also be heard on *Boulders, Vol. 4* (LP). (VJ)

C.A. Quintet - Trip Thru Hell LP.

The Caretakers of Deception

45: Cuttin' Grass/X+Y=13 (Sanctus 5511/2) 1967

A psychedelic punk outfit from Los Angeles. *Cuttin' Grass* is notable for its brash vocals and some compelling guitar riffs. The flip is much mellower, with a sparse arrangement and a melody that sticks in the brain.

Compilation coverage has so far included:- *Cuttin' Grass* on *Psychedelic Disaster Whirl* (LP), *Sixties Archive, Vol. 8* (CD), *Acid Dreams - The Complete 3 LP Set* (3-LP), *Acid Dreams Testament* (CD), *Acid Dreams, Vol. 1* (LP) and *Acid Trip From The Psychedelic Sixties* (LP); and *X + Y = 13* on *Pebbles, Vol. 8* (CD), *Psychedelic Unknowns, Vol's 1 & 2* (LP), and *Psychedelic Unknowns, Vol. 2* (Dble 7"). (VJ)

Cargo

Personnel: TONY DECKER — A
DEAN WILDEN — A

ALBUM: 1(A) I SEE IT NOW (RCA LSP-4178) 1969 -

A Christian psych-rock duo from Utah, with tracks like *Cross With No Name*. Their album was recorded in California. (SR)

Cargoe

Personnel: TIM BENTON — A
BILL PHILLIPS — A
TOMMY RICHARD — A
MAX WISLEY — A

ALBUM: 1(A) CARGOE (Ardent ADS 2802) 1972 -

EP: 1 I Love You Anyway / Things We Dream Today / Heal Me (Ardent ADA-2903) 1972

45s: α Feel Allright / Wondering (Beautiful 101) 1971
α Feel Alright / Tokyo Love (Ardent ADA-2901) 1972
I Love You Anyway/ Things We Dream Today, Heal Me (Ardent 2903) 1972

NB: α feature different versions of *Feel Al(l)right*.

The band hailed from Tulsa, Oklahoma where they built a strong local folowing before relocating to Memphis to record. The first 45 was recorded at Dan Penn's Beautiful Sounds studio. A good response resulted in a contract with Ardent, the same label as Big Star. Produced by **Terry Manning**, formerly of **Lawson and Four More**, their style is also strong pop-rock with melodic hooks and great vocals (early power-pop if you will), compared to Badfinger by Ron Hall.

The four members guested on the album by **The Hot Dogs**, their label mates.

The band returned to Oklahoma in 1973 and broke up soon after. For more details of them and others on the Memphis scene (1960-1975), refer to Ron Hall's book 'Playing For A Piece Of The Door'. (SR/MW)

Carmel Covered Popcorn

45: Suzie Q/Looking For A Place (Vistone 2055) 1968

A Californian (probably L.A.) outfit's decent cover of *Suzie Q* in "West Coast" style rather than **Creedence Clearwater Revival** boogie. (MW)

Carnival of Sound

45: Don't Come Around / I Can't Remember (USA 892) 1967

A late 1967 release from a Chicago outfit, believed to be **The Trolls** undergoing an identity crisis. See the **Troll(s)** entry for further details. (MW)

PSYCHEDLIC DISASTER WHIRL (Comp LP) including The Caretakers of Deception.

Carp

Personnel: GARY BUSEY — drms, vcls — A
JOHN CROWDER — bs — A
RON GETMAN — gtr — A
GLEN MITCHELL — piano — A
(BOBBY BRUCE — fiddle — A)
(BUZZ CLIFFORD — vcls — A)
(SNEAKY PETE KLEINOW — steel gtr — A)
(DAN MOORE — vcls — A)
(GORDON SHRYOCK — vcls — A)

ALBUM: 1(A) CARP (Epic E30212) 1969 -

45s: α Save The Delta Queen/ Mammoth Mountain Blues (Epic 10632) 1969
Page 258/Pine Creek Bridge (Epic 10647) 1969

NB: α Promo copies exist with mono version of *Save The Delta Queen* on the flip.

Carp was formed in the Spring of 1966 by four Oklahoma State University students. Produced by **Dan Moore** and **Buzz Clifford** (who also both produced the **East Side Kids** album), their only album is a consistent mix of rock, blues and country with some excellent guitar parts. All the material is original, except for *The Great Kansas Hymn* (penned by Michael McGinnis) and the lyrics often have a religious feel.

Gary Busey would later become an actor and, as "Teddy Jack Eddy", played drums with another Oklahoma native, **Leon Russell**. John Crowder, Glen Mitchell and Ron Getman became session musicians and later played with Loudon Wainwright, Tony Bird, Janis Ian etc.. (SR)

Chris Carpenter

45s: This World (Is Closing In On Me)/ Waterfalls (Sidra 9006) 196?
This World (Is Closing In On Me)/ Waterfalls (Oceanside OS 100) 196?
This World (is Closing In On Me)/ Waterfalls (United Artist 50266) 1968

This Detroit gentleman first released this same 45 as by **Preston** on Sound Paterns 110. *This World (Is Closing In On Me)* is an atmospheric piece of doomy psych with orchestration, some neat effects and eerie guitar. The **Preston** version, which is a much hotter rendition with the fuzz guitar and mysterious organ much louder in the mix can be heard on *Magic Carpet Ride* (LP). *Waterfalls* is a rather strange track; a ballad with effects galore and vocals like Bobby Vee on acid! Both sides have also been compiled on *A Heavy Dose Of Lyte Psych* (CD), whilst the flip has also resurfaced on *Incredible Sound Show Stories, Vol. 8* (LP). (MW/KBn)

The Carpetbaggers

45:	Let Yourself Go/	
	Just A Friend	(Limited International 407) 196?

Another obscure one. *Vile Vinyl, Vol. 1* (LP) and *Vile Vinyl* (CD) both include *Let Yourself Go*. The group possibly hailed from Tennessee. (VJ)

Carr/Kahl

Personnel:	BOB CARR	gtr, vcls, hrmnca	A
	BILL KAHL	gtr	A
	(GLORIA HECHT	vcls	A)
	(JEF SCHROEDER	bs	A)
	(WAYNE THOMAS	flute	A)

ALBUM: 1(A) COMMUNICATION 1 (Grotesque GS 101) 1971 R1

A private pressing from Michigan. For folk fans, this is an undiscovered gem. Kahl is a terrific guitarist who sounds like he was influenced by Davy Graham, especially on the longer tracks which move into Eastern territory. Overall, the record is largely an instrumental work - Carr sings only two tracks and these sound very much like the vocal tracks on the *A Cid Symphony* album by **Fischbach and Ewing**. Hecht adds two layers of wordless voice to one short cut, making it a highlight of Side One. Side Two of the album is all instrumental, concluding with an achingly beautiful piece that was lifted from **Jefferson Airplane**'s *Surrealistic Pillow* album, *Today*. This track is quite breathtaking, especially when Thomas' flute appears and the song largely breaks contact with the **Airplane** song of the same name. The album has a nice, tasteful-yet-druggy cover design that enhances the overall package. (CF)

The Carriage Trade

45:	Wild About My Lovin'/Rag Mama	(FilmWays FW-107) c1968

Probably from California, a good **Lovin' Spoonful** soundalike, written/produced by **Dan Moore** and Don Dalton. Both men also produced the third 45 by the **Plymouth Rockers**. (SR)

Carrie Nations

Personnel incl:	LYNN CAREY	vcls	A

45:	Come With The Gentle People/	
	In The Long Run	(20th Century Fox 6721) 1970

A studio project put together for Russ Meyer's legendary "Beyond The Valley Of The Dolls" movie. In addition to the above 45, the 'band' have six cuts (*Come With The Gentle People, Look On Up At The Bottom, In The Long Run, Sweet Talkin' Candy Man, Find It* and *Once I Had A Love* on the soundtrack album *Beyond The Valley Of The Dolls* (LP).

Lynn Carey provided vocals for the project and co-wrote two of the songs with Phillips. Lynn Carey, was the former singer of **C.K. Strong** and future **Mama Lion** vocalist. (SR/SCI)

Carroll's Mood

45:	Out She Goes / No One's Waiting For Me	(AOK 1026) 196?

A punk-ballad 45 by an obscure Texan act. They later became **Sights and Sounds**.

Compilation appearances include: Both *Out She Goes* and *What You're Doing To Me* on *Green Crystal Ties, Vol. 8* (CD) and *The History Of Texas Garage Bands, Vol. 3 - The AOK Records Story* (CD); *Out She Goes* and *I Walk Alone* on *The History Of Texas Garage Bands, Vol. 4 - West Texas Rarities* (CD).

Carrot Tree

45:	Dum Dum / Circus Time	(RCA Victor 47-9877) 1970

Dum Dum is strong bubblegum. It was written by Roger Joyce and B. Barberis formerly of **New Order**, which suggests this was an East Coast (New England?) act. *Circus Time* is Anglophile pop-psych with swirling electronic effects, likely to appeal to fans of the Rubble/Circus Days compilations. (MW)

Dean Carter

45:	The Rockin' Bandit/?	(Milky Way 4) 196?
	Jailhouse Rock/Rebel Woman	(Milky Way 11) 196?

From Illinois. *Jailhouse Rock* was a classic double-sided punk 45. *Jailhouse Rock* was a cover of a 1957 rock'n'roll song by Elvis Presley.

There may have been another 45, *Run Rabbit Run* (Milky Way 8), although it's possible that this track was the flip side of *The Rockin' Bandit*. Anyone out there able to confirm details?

Compilation appearances include: *Jailhouse Rock* and *Rebel Woman* on *Ear-Piercing Punk* (LP), *Pebbles, Vol. 6* (CD); *Rebel Woman* on *The Essential Pebbles Collection, Vol. 1* (Dble CD); and *Jailhouse Rock* on *Best of Pebbles, Vol. 3* (LP & CD). (MW/TJH/MGm)

Susan Carter

Personnel:	SUSAN CARTER	vcls	A
	(RANDY BRECKER	horns	A)
	(DICK HALLIGAN	horns	A)
	(HOWARD LESHAW		A)
	(HERB LOVELLE	drms	A)
	(TERRY PLUMERI	bs	A)
	(AL PORCINO		A)
	(ELLIOT RANDALL	gtr	A)

ALBUM: 1(A) WONDERFUL DEEDS AND ADVENTURES
(Epic BN 26510) 1969 -

Subtitled "A Collection of Stirring Scenes And Moving Accidents", this album was initially prepared in Laurel Canyon by Susan and arranged by Dick Halligan of **Blood, Sweat and Tears**. Produced by Les Carter in New York and recorded in 1968/69, it was recorded with **Blood, Sweat and Tears** and several New York session men like **Elliot Randall** and Herb Lovelle.

Clearly influenced by the "art rock" scene and the attempts of groups like **Blood, Sweat and Tears** to mix rock, jazz, pop and soul, **Susan Carter** choose to sing mostly covers including the Beatles' *I'm So Tired*, **Buffalo**

CARR/KAHL - Communication 1 LP.

Springfield's *Bluebird*, Donovan's *Young Girl Blues*, Randy Newman's *Illinois*, a **James Taylor** song, two jazz compositions by Nat Adderley and Billie Holiday plus two original tracks: a medley written by Laura Nyro and the best track, the long *Jam Session: Cruising With The Blues* by the Carter couple. As Susan Carter had a good voice, the overall result has its moments, even if some of the arrangements now sound dated. (SR)

The Cartunes

| 45: | Keep The Fire Burning / Chanda | (Roulette 7011) 1968 |

This outfit from Hazelton, Pennsylvania were previously known as **Ognir and The Nite People**. (MW)

The Cascades

45s:	Flying On The Ground/Main Street	(Smash 2101) c1967
(partial	Two Sided Man/	
list)	Everyone is Blossoming (PS)	(Probe CP-453) c1968

This group from California recorded between 1962 and 1972 for various labels (Valiant, Warner Bros., Smash, RCA, Uni). They are mainly known for their early sixties pop hits with vocal harmonies, their biggest success being *Rhythm Of The Rain*. They deserve an inclusion here as, circa 1966/67, they recorded some good psychy pop singles, including the ones listed above. (SR)

Cashman Vaquero Band

| Personnel incl: | DOUG CASHMAN | | A |

| ALBUM: | 1 | TRIBUTE TO BERRY OAKLEY | |
| | | | (Private Pressing) 1975 R1 |

| 45: | Security / San Francisco Sunset | (Bridgeville) 1976 |

A rare psychedelic blues-rock album, dedicated to the late **Allman Brothers Band** bassist. Only a few hundred copies were pressed, with cuts like *San Francisco Sunset* and *There's No Tellin*. (SR)

The Castaways

Personnel:	DENNY CRASWELL	drms	ABCDE
	ROY HENSLEY	vcls	ABCDE
	LONNIE KNIGHT	gtr	A
	DICK ROBY	gtr	ABC
	BOB FOLSCHOW	gtr	BCD
	JIM DONNA	keyb'ds	CD
	TOM HUSTING	gtr	E
	DENNIS LIBBY	keyb'ds, vcls	E
	GREGORY MALAND	keyb'ds, vcls	E

NB: Lineup 'A' 1962-3, 'B' 1963, 'C' 1963-1965, 'D' 1965-1966, 'E' 1966-1969.

| CD: | 1 | LIAR, LIAR - THE BEST OF THE CASTAWAYS |
| | | (Plum 14032) 1999 |

| EP: | 1(B/C) | THE CASTAWAYS | (Soma CA-03) 1987 |

NB: (1) is a bootleg EP featuring their three Soma 45s.

HCP

45s:	Liar, Liar/Sam	(Soma 1433) 1965 12
	Liar, Liar/Sam	(Apex 76969) 1965 -
	Goodbye Babe/A Mans Gotta Be A Man	(Soma 1492) 1965 101
	Goodbye Babe/A Mans Gotta Be A Man	(Apex 76970) 1965 -
	She's A Girl In Love/	
	Why This Should Happen To Me	(Soma 1461) 1967 -
α	Liar, Liar/Surfin' Bird	(Soma 1469) 1967 -
β	I Feel So Fine/Hit The Road	(Taunah 7745) 1967 -
	I Feel So Fine/Hit The Road	(Bear 2000) 1967 -
	Walking In Different Circles/	
	Just On High	(Fontana 1615) 1968 -
	Lavendar Popcorn/What Kind Of Face	(Fontana 1626) 1968 -

NB: α a reissue 45, flip by The Trashmen. β 500 copies pressed.

Formed at the University of Minnesota in Minnesota in 1962 where they started the group largely for self-amusement and to entertain fellow students. In 1963 Lonnie Knight left to form **The Rave-Ons** and was replaced by Bob Folschow.

Liar, Liar (composed by Jim Donna and Denny Craswell) was a spectacular debut that climbed to No. 12 in the Summer of 1965. Despite several fine 45s they'd never reach those heights again.

Before their follow-up Dick Roby left to go solo. In late 1966 Bob Folschow was called up for service and Jim Donna went back to college. Replacements were found in Tom Husting and Dennis Libby (from Dudley and The Doo-Rytes) and Gregory Maland (better known as Gregory Dee of Avanties fame). This line-up lasted until the band folded in 1969, after which Craswell, Libby and Maland moved onto **Blackwood Apology**. Craswell was later in **South 40** and **Crow**. Other members are thought to have been in **Hope**.

Twas far from the end for **The Castaways**... *Liar Liar* was/is a blissfully simple pop song of under two minutes long. From the opening drum beat, keyboard strains and falsetto lead, it is instantly recognisable. The pining guitar motif, girl put-down lyrics and a break preceded by one chilling scream, add up to a great slice of sixties garage-pop.

It first appeared on album in 1966 on the Bud-Jet label *The Big Hits Of Mid-America, Vol. 2* (LP), accompanied by *Sam*. It would probably have been forgotten after the sixties but for its inclusion on Lenny Kaye's *Nuggets - Original Artyfacts From The First Psychedelic Era 1965-1968* (Dble LP) compilation in 1972. Since then it has appeared on *Wild Thing*, *We Have Come For Your Children*, *More Nuggets* (CD), *Nuggets From Nuggets* (CD), *Psychotic Reactions* (Topline label), *Soma Records Story, Vol. 2* (LP) and the *Nuggets Box* 4-CD boxset. Outside of the collector set, appreciation of it has been kept alive in films (notably 'Good Morning Vietnam'), soundtracks and on TV. Quite rightly it has come to be regarded by many as a sixties classic.

After Bob Folschow was called up for service, he played with Ed Truman (drums, ex-**Marke V**) and Lee Caplin (keyb'ds) as **The Castaways**. At the time, Bob was using the surname Bob Leroy and stationed in Fayetteville, North Carolina. This outfit played for two years, in and around Durham, Chapel Hill and points North and South, including schools, bars, public venues and a gig at Duke University.

In the late seventies Jim Donna revived his own version of **The Castaways**, which was still going strong in 2000.

In 1987 Hensley, Craswell, Roby and Folschow formed The Original Castaways with Al Olivera, on the heels of the interest generated by 'Good Morning Vietnam'.

MONEY MUSIC (Comp LP) including The Castaways.

The 22-track retrospective CD collects all their 45 tracks and adds: three unreleased '66 tracks - *Lead Me On*, *Everytime*, *Watching The Time Go By*; *Work Song* - a solo release by Dick Roby; and six tracks from the two revived **Castaways**. With detailed liners from Jim Oldsberg and input from several band members, this is a fine testament to a GREAT Midwest pop act.

Other compilation appearances include: *Liar, Liar*, *Sam* and *Goodbye Babe* on *The Big Hits Of Mid-America - The Soma Records Story* (LP); *Sam* and *Goodbye Babe* on *Soma Records Story, Vol. 1* (LP); *A Man's Gotta Be A Man* and *Why This Should Happen To Me* on *Soma Records Story, Vol. 3* (LP); *Feel So Fine* on the rare 1967 Minneapolis sampler *Money Music* and *Just On High* on *Psychedelic Experience, Vol. 2* (CD) and on *The Psychedelic Experience, Vol. 2* (LP). (VJ/MW)

The Castaways

45:	You Were Telling Lies/	
	Ain't Gonna Cheat On Me	(Tornado 1003) 1965

An obscure garage band from Lake Charles, Louisiana who would later be known as The Sound Rebellion. *You Were Telling Lies* is a primitive snarling punker, whilst the flip, *Ain't Gonna Cheat On Me* has some catchy lyrics. Both sides have resurfaced on *Sixties Rebellion, Vol. 9* (LP & CD) and *Hang It Out To Dry* (LP & CD). (MW)

Castells

Personnel incl:	CHUCK GIRARD	vcls	A

45s:	Just Walk Away/An Angel Cried	(Decca 31834) 1965
	I Thought You'd Like That/Life Goes On	(Decca 31967) 1966

Another **Castells**, this lot were produced by Gary Usher and were "rather conservative" in their tastes. Chuck Girard who was also in The Hondells, later went into Christian music. (RR/GM)

Castels

Personnel incl:	RICHARD CLEMENTS	gtr	A	
	DAVE MILLER	bs	A...	X
	DON MILLER	gtr	A...	X
	PERRY YORK	drms	A	
	JIMMY PIERCE	drms		X
	JOHN GLORIA	gtr		

45s:		Save A Chance /		
(partial		Children Who Dream	(Wildfire Record Co. W-105)	1965
list)	α	Save A Chance / Children Who Dream	(Black Gold 306)	1965
		In A Letter To Me / We Better Slow Down	(Solomon 1351)	1967
		I'd Like To Know / Rocky Ridges	(Solomon 1352)	1967/8
		I'd Like To Know / Rocky Ridges	(Laurie 3444)	1968

NB: α mis-spells group name as Castells.

A Memphis group who blended beat and folk-rock to produce some vibrant sounds. *Save A Chance* is raw upbeat Brummelesque, first issued on the local Wildfire label - this is unearthed on *Fuzz, Flaykes, And Shakes, Vol. 3 - Stay Out Of My World* (LP & CD). The jangle quota was upped on the more polished Black Gold 45 version, compiled on *Leaving It All Behind*. This is also excellent but many will still prefer the original. The flip, by the way, is a swaying Everlys-style ballad.

Save A Chance can also be found on *A History Of Garage And Frat Bands In Memphis* (CD).

Marijuana Unknowns (LP & CD) includes *Rocky Ridges*, a slow beat ballad with flute, water effects, smooth harmonies and psychy vibe. It includes the immortal line "Pass the grass and I'll keep saying something I don't mean".

The Miller brothers started out as The Seltaeb Trio but became **The Castels** in 1965. They continued under this name until 1970 by which time they were back to a trio again (line-up 'X') and became The Miller Bros.

MARIJUANA UNKNOWNS (Comp LP) including Castels.

They released an album and several 45s in the seventies. For their full story see Ron Hall's Memphis book, 'Playing For A Piece Of The Door' (Shangri-La Projects, 2001, ISBN 0-9668575-1-8). (MW/IT)

Lynn Castle with Last Friday's Fire

45s:		The Lady Barber/Rose Colored Corner	(LHI 17003) 1968
		I Can't Help The Way I Feel/	
		What Is She Thinking Of	(LHI 17007) 1968
	α	Stand And Shout/Something's Happening	(LHI 17019) 1969

NB: α Credited to Last Friday's Fire.

Produced by Lee Hazlewood on his label, this obscure group released three singles. The first one is truly interesting, with good female vocals and a fine guitar part on the 'A' side and an equally good flip, notable for its unusual break. It sounds quite a lot like **The Music Emporium**! The third 45 is in a more straight-ahead hard rock mode and is shown as by Last Friday's Fire. **Mike Condello** was involved with the band at this point. (SR/CF)

Cast of Thousands

Personnel:	BOBBY FORMAN	horns	A
	BUGS HENDERSON	ld gtr	A
	CHRIS LINGWALL	drms	A
	MIKE McCULLOUGH	bs, gtr	A
	JIM RIGBY	vcls	A
	STEVE TOBOLOUSKY	gtr, piano	A
	STEVIE RAY VAUGHN	gtr	A

45s:	α	Girl Do What You Gonna Do/	
		My Jenny Wears A Mini	(Soft 1002) 1966
		Have It Your Way/Power Vested In Me	(Soft 1002) 1967
		Long Way To Go/Carter's Grove	(Amy 11,040) 1967
		Country Gardens/The Cast's Blue	(Amy 11,056) 1967

NB: α also issued on (Tower 276).

Hailing from Dallas in Texas. Their first 45 was picked up by Tower for nationwide release and much later the 'A' side was included on *Boulders, Vol. 5* (LP). The flip to their next 45 had earlier appeared on the reverse to early versions of their first 45. Lineup (A) also had two cuts - *Red, White And Blue*, a rockabilly-influenced effort and *I Heard A Voice Last Night*, which featured some good guitar work - on the compilation *A New Hi, Dallas 1971-Part 1* (Tempo 2). Bugs Henderson played on their last two 45s on his way to **Mouse And The Traps** from The Sensors and Stevie Ray Vaughn later fronted Double Trouble.

Their third single was produced by **Don Nix** and Dale Hawkins, who also produced **Mouse And The Traps**. (VJ/MW/SR)

HIGH ALL THE TIME Vol. 2 (Comp LP) including Catfish Knight.

The Catalinas

| 45: | The Coco Cherry Mash/ Talkin' Bout You Now | (Chase Candy Co. 912/913) 1967 |

An obscure Midwest band from St Joseph, Missouri. You'll find *The Coco Cherry Mash* on *Monsters Of The Midwest, Vol. 1* (Cass) and *Mondo Frat Dance Bash A Go Go* (CD). Both sides have also resurfaced on *Drink Beer! Yell! Dance!* (LP). (VJ)

The Catamorands

| 45: | Over You/Never Say Goodbye | (D.G.M.R. 101) 196? |

Yearning beat-ballads influenced by British invasion sounds but also harking back to pre-beat 'teen pop' sounds from Nashville, Tennessee. (MW)

Catch

| ALBUM: | 1 CATCH | (Dot DLP 25956) 1969 - |

| 45s: | I'm On The Road To Memphis/Amber | (Dot 17277) 1969 |
| | Storm/City Ditty | (Dot 17304) 1969 |

A five-piece from California. All the tracks are written by M. Collings/R. White, who were also responsible for **Feather** - *Friends* on Columbia in the late sixties. Musically, it's very different; whereas **Feather** sounds like the third **Chocolate Watchband** album, *Catch* is poppier with quite a few orchestrated numbers like *The Dandelion And The Butterfly* and the 8 ½-minute *Nine Roses*. The one exception is the glorious psychedelic rocker *Crash And Burn*.

There was also another outfit of this name from Belmond, Iowa, who were previously known as The Confederacy. They recorded one side of a *Booking Agent Disc Sampler* on Sensational Sounds (5079). The flip side was by Stack. (VJ)

Catfish Knight and The Blue Express

Personnel incl: J. KNIGHT   A

| 45s: | I Can't Keep From Cryin' / Deathwise | (Verve 10607) 1968 |
| | See Saw / Web Of Trouble | (Verve 10629) 1968 |

Hidden away on the back of a solid brassy popper, is *Deathwise* - a fuzz extravaganza that kicks off like the Stones' *Paint It Black* before moving into freakout territory. The nearest comparison to these ears is **Mystic Tide**.

The second 45 is of less interest - *See Saw* is back to bland and brassy pop with a laid-back rock ballad featuring piano on the flip.

Compilation appearances have included *Deathwise* on *A Lethal Dose Of Hard Psych* (CD) and *High All The Time, Vol. 2* (LP). (MW)

Cathedral

Personnel incl: RUDY PERRONE   gtr, vcls

| ALBUM: | 1 STAINED GLASS STORIES | (Delta #unk) 197? - |

| 45: | Stain Glass Stories/? | (Headsong ?) c1972 |

A New York prog-psych group, in the same style as **Harlequin**. (SR)

Cat Mother and The All Night Newsboys

Personnel:	CHARLIE CHIN	gtr, vcls	A
	MICHAEL EQUINE	drms	ABCD
	ROY MICHAELS	bs, gtr, vcls	ABCD
	LARRY PARKER	vcls, gtr	AB
	BOB SMITH	keyb'ds, vcls	ABCD
	PAUL JOHNSON	gtr	B
	JAY UNGAR	bs	B
	STEVE DAVIDSON	perc	CD
	CHARLIE PRITCHARD	ld gtr, slide gtr	C
	CHARLIE HARCOURT	ld gtr	D

HCP

ALBUMS:	1(A)	THE STREET GIVETH AND THE STREET TAKETH AWAY	(Polydor 244001) 1969 55 -
	2(B)	ALBION DOO-WAH	(Polydor 244023) 1970 - -
	3(C)	CAT MOTHER	(Polydor 245017) 1971 -
	4(D)	LAST CHANCE DANCE	(Polydor 245042) 1973 - -

NB: (3) and (4) credited to Cat Mother.

HCP

45s:	α	Good Old R'n'Roll/ Bad News (PS)	(Polydor 14002) 1969 21
		Can You Dance To It/Marie	(Polydor 14007) 1969 115
		Last Go 'Round/I Must Be Dreaming	(Polydor 14027) 1970 -
		Relax Your Mind/The Other Side	(Polydor 14073) 1971 -
		Letter To The President/Ode To Oregon	(Polydor 14126) 1972 -
		She Came From A Different World/ Three And Me	(Polydor 14138) 1972 -

NB: α also issued in France in (PS) (Barclay 61138) 1969 and in the UK (Polydor BM 56543) 1970.

MAYHEM & PSYCHOSIS Vol. 1 (Comp LP) including The Cavemen.

A diverse band worthy of investigation, they were originally formed on the East Coast and their music had a strong blues and country-folk influence. Their first album was recorded at Electric Ladyland in New York and produced by **Jimi Hendrix**, for whom they opened at several of his concerts, including the famous L.A. Forum concert.

Like **Hendrix**, the band were under management contract with Michael Jeffery and in attempt to escape his clutches their second album was recorded at Pacific High Recording studios in San Francisco in late 1969. Hence the inclusion of some of their material on *The Pacific High Studios Christmas* album in 1970.

For the *Cat Mother* album they returned to New York and shortened their name to **Cat Mother**.

They were still together in the late seventies.

Band member Jay Ungar (ex-**Family of Apostolic**) recently achieved some level of fame recording *Ashokan Farewell*, used in the U.S. ministeries "The Civil War". Charlie Harcourt later played for U.K. band Lindisfarne. (VJ/SR/NWn)

The Cats Meow

| 45s: | Confusion/La La Lu | (Decca 31940) 1966 |
| | House Of Kicks/True True Lovin' | (Decca 32037) 1966 |

Almost certainly a studio group who had just two vinyl outings. Their first 45 *Confusion* was a beaty, guitar instrumental, but their finest moment is usually considered to have been *House of Kicks*, an appealing combination of surf-harmony falsettos and driving punk guitars. You can find it on *Pebbles, Vol. 13* (LP). (VJ)

Cavaliers

| 45: | Seven Days of Cryin'/? | (Crisis no number) 1966 |

This very promising punker was the work of a really obscure garage band from Lynwood, California. You'll find *Seven Days Of Cryin'* on *Back From The Grave, Vol. 7* (Dble LP), although it's erroneously been omitted from the track listings on the actual record. (VJ/MW)

The Cavaliers

45s:	Sea Weed/Pride	(Pharoah 137) 1965
	That Hurts/Symbol Of Sin	(Pharoah 146) 1966
	The Last Four Words/	
	Ballad Of Thee Kavaliers	(Pharoah 150) 1966
	Congregation For Anti-Flirts Inc./	
	Back To You	(Pharoah 154) 1967

This band were also known as Thee Kavaliers. Various members went on to The Playthings, Blacksmith and Translucent Umbrella.

Compilation appearances include: *Congregation For Anti-Flirts, Inc.*, *Pride* and *See Weed* on *Acid Visions - Complete Collection, Vol. 2* (3-CD) and *Texas Punk, Vol. 5* (LP); and *Congregation For Anti-Flirts, Inc.* on *The Cicadelic 60's, Vol. 2* (CD) and *The Cicadelic 60's, Vol. 4* (LP). (VJ)

Cavalry Twill

| 45: | All You Need Is Love/The Girl | (MGM K 13849) c1968 |

Starting this Beatles anthem with the intro of *Strawberry Fields* is quite a feat. This version soon develops into an uncanny combination of scorching fuzz guitar over trite Flowerpot Men-like backing, complete with multiple vocals and 'la la la's. The 'B' side (by producer Neil Levenson) is a B-film instrumental with vague Balkanesque leanings. Obscure! (MK)

Cave Dwellers

| 45: | Run Around/You Know Why | (Jim-Ko 41085) 1967 |

A Chicago-based mid-sixties garage band. You'll find *Run Around* on *Pebbles Vol. 6* (CD), *Back From The Grave, Vol. 8* (Dble LP), *Back From The Grave, Vol. 8* (CD) and *Glimpses, Vol. 4* (LP). (VJ)

Cave Dwellers

| 45: | Meditation/Night Runner | (Bay Town 003) 1968 |

A different outfit from the Bay Area in California.

Compilation appearances include *Meditation* on *Boulders, Vol. 6* (LP), *Psychedelic Experience, Vol. 2* (CD) and *Ya Gotta Have Moxie, Vol. 1* (Dble CD).

The Cavemen

45s:	Small World/	
	Whatever Will Be, Will Be	(20th Century 6643) 1966
	All About Love/Bo Diddley	(C.S.A. 18285) 1967

An obscure Rochester, New York State band whose *Small World* has resurfaced on the *Everywhere Interferences* (LP), *Sick And Tired* (LP) and *Follow That Munster, Vol. 1* (LP). (VJ/MW)

The Cavemen

Personnel:	ANDY JOHNSON	ld gtr	AB
	SERGIO ROACH	gtr, vcls	AB
	ROBERT TIFF	bs	A
	PAULI WALTERSON	drms, vcls	A
	BOB JABOUR	bs, vcls	B
	TONY REY	drms, vcls	B

| 45: | It's Trash / The Pillow Bit | (Chelle PH 148) 1966 |

Former members Pauli Walterson and Bob Jabour have produced the *Key West Psychedelic Daze Volume #1 (1965-1975)* compilation, which at last reveals the identities behind this band and two other Key West, Florida outfits - Paloma (who also featured Pauli Walterson and Tony Rey - one track from 1972) and Overseas Highway (nine tracks from 1970 to 1978 featuring comp co-producer Jim Dean). No new nuggets by **The Cavemen** however - just their moment of immortality, *It's Trash*. With its superb iron-lunged vocals, savage guitar-led instrumentation and fine use of echo it typifies all that's best about mid-sixties psychedelic punk.

The Key West compilation dangles a carrot by stating that **The Cavemen** did record an LP which only made it to the test pressing stage (ten copies, it says, also on the Chelle label). Let's hope that any nuggets thereon may be revealed in a future volume.

Jabour had earlier played in a band with Vince (Vinnie) Martell who went on to the **Pigeons** before hitting the jackpot with **Vanilla Fudge**. Rey went on to play with **Eric Andersen** and latterly a band called Guarapo. Roche was later in a Led Zeppelin cover band.

Additional info is provided by the liners on the excellent *Teenage Shutdown* series, which reveals that the band included two former Coachmen (Jabour and Rey?) and would be known latterly as the 4th Generation until they split.

Other compilation appearances include: *It's Trash* on *Mayhem & Psychosis, Vol. 1* (LP), *Mayhem & Psychosis, Vol. 1* (CD), *Off The Wall, Vol. 2* (LP), *Pebbles, Vol. 3 (ESD)* (CD), *Trash Box* (5-CD), *Teenage Shutdown, Vol. 4* (LP & CD), *Best of Pebbles, Vol. 3* (LP & CD) and *Psychedelic States: Florida Vol. 3* (CD). (MW/VJ/MM/JLh)

BACK FROM THE GRAVE Vol. 5 (Comp LP) including Centrees.

The Cavemen

Personnel incl: KARL KENNINGTON   vcls   A

45:    Summertime/No Reply   (Leaf 6670) 1967

This band came from Rockford, Illinois and recorded on a Janesville, Wisconsin label. Their 45 features a soft ballad backed by a very basic reading of the Beatles number, sounding more like 1964-era beat.

The band must have enjoyed a large local following as *Summertime* spent thirteen weeks at No. 1 in their local chart. Rick Nielson (later of Cheap Trick), also paid them complements when they became the only band to beat his **Grim Reapers** at the Sherwood Lodge 'Battle Of The Bands'.

In 1968, the band signed to Mobie Records in Chicago and changed names to **The Iron Gate**. (MW/KH)

Ceeds

45:    You Won't Do That/Too Many People   (Emlar 1001) 196?

Thought to have been a Colorado outfit. The 'A' side can be heard on *Garage Punk Unknowns, Vol. 2* (LP). (VJ)

The Cellar Dwellers

Personnel incl: FRANK BEARD   drms   A

45:    Bad Day/Call   (Steffek 1921) 1968

An historically significant Fort Worth outfit on account of being one of Beard's early bands. Previously with The Hustlers he went on to **The Warlocks** and later became drummer with megastars ZZ Top. The band were the house band at Pat Kirkwood's Cellar Club hence their name and inevitably their 45 is rare and sought-sfter. *Bad Day*, a Merseybeat influenced song, was included on *Texas Punk, Vol. 9* (LP) and *Acid Visions - Complete Collection, Vol. 3* (3-CD). (VJ)

The Cellar Dwellers

45:    Love Is A Beautiful Thing/Working Man   (Lance 111) 1967

A sixties punk outfit from the Albuquerque area of New Mexico. *Working Man* has also appeared on *The Psychedelic Sixties, Vol. 1* (LP), *Boulders, Vol. 5* (LP) and *The Cicadelic 60's, Vol. 4* (CD). Both sides of the 45 also appear on *I Wanna Come Back From The World Of LSD* (CD). (VJ)

The Cellar Dwellers

See **Mike Vetro and The Cellar Dwellers** entry for information on this Florida based act. (VJ)

The Celtics

Personnel incl: JAMES CHESHIRE   vcls   A
               WALLY GARDNER   A
               JACK WATKINS   A

45s: And She'll Cry / Jail   (Linjo 106) 1966
       Wondering Why / Man That's Gone Mad   (Coronado 133) c1966

From El Paso, Texas. *And She'll Cry* is a promising tune and moves in all the right places with a distinctly moody menacing beat that is underplayed without developing into overkill. It can be found on *Diana's Rootin' Tootin' Wild Teenage Rock 'N' Roll Party!* (LP), *Sixties Rebellion, Vol. 2* (LP) and *Sixties Rebellion, Vol's 1 & 2* (CD). *Jail* is an ode to delinquency with spoken vocals delivered in a aptly rebellious and don't-give-a-damn attitude. (VJ/MW)

The Celtics

Personnel incl: RONNIE HAMMOND   vcls   A

45s: Times With You/It's A Lonely Life   (Dante 2291) 1968
       For Your Love/Looking For You   (Dante 2295) 1968

This Georgia, Atlanta band featured lead vocalist Ronnie Hammond who eventually joined the Atlanta Rhythm Section in 1977 just before they hit the jackpot with *Imaginary Lover*.

Times With You is a pumped-up punk-popper with scorching lead breaks. It can be appreciated, belatedly, on *Sixties Rebellion, Vol. 3 - The Auditorium* (LP & CD) and *Psychedelic States: Georgia Vol. 1* (CD). (MM/MW)

Center Family

ALBUM: 1   SHANTI-DAS/SERVANT OF PEACE   (Vector) 1973 -

Another example of a community managed by an Indian guru and releasing an album to show the world how happy they were. Mostly acoustic folk with Indian instrumentation, chanting. (SR)

The Center Line

ALBUM: 1   SAYIN IT... TOGETHER   (Vanco 1008) c1970 -

From Washington State, an awful album with some spoken pieces and a 14-minute long (very long!) *Peace Medley* of Beatles' songs including *Eleanor Rigby*, *We Can Work It Out*, *Within You Without You*, *All You Need Is Love*, *Carry That Weight* and *Hey Jude*. Between pop-rock and lounge music, not recommended at all! (SR)

Central High School

ALBUMS: 1   SOUNDS OF '67   (Private Pressing) 1967 R1
           2   SOUNDS OF '68   (Private Pressing) 1968 R1

These albums came out of a real Central High School from Bridgeport, Connecticut and came with stunning psych sleeves. The music is a mix of folk with female vocals plus electric backing and garage numbers. (SR)

Central Park

45:    Flower Hill/Who Wouldn't Want To Be Loved   (Amy 11019) 1968

Produced by Wes Farrel, the manager/producer of **Elephant's Memory** and **Beacon Street Union**, this was a Beatles inspired group who apparently issued only this single. (SR)

Central Park

ALBUM: 1 CENTRAL PARK (Paramount PAS-1036) 1974 -

A forgotten folk-rock quartet with vocal harmonies and some interesting guitar parts. They are probably unrelated to the other group. (SR)

Centrees

Personnel:	BOSMA	A
	BOSMA	A
	CANTER	A
	REINHARDT	A

45: She's Good For Me/Why (Wildwood 19045/6) 1967

From the rural communities of Tipp City and New Carlisle, near Dayton, Ohio. This very young garage quartet set out as a surf outfit called The Rhythm Riders circa 1963/4. The surf influence is still evident in their garage rocker, *She's Good For Me*, which can be heard on *Back From The Grave, Vol. 5* (LP), and the flip is good too. (VJ/MW/GGI)

Centuries

45: The Fourth Dimension/? (Cleopatra 3) 196?

Garage Punk Unknowns, Vol. 6 (LP) features *The Fourth Dimension* from this New Jersey band. (VJ)

The Centuries

45s: Lonely Girl/I'd Cry For You (Rich RR-102) 1965
Don't Let It Fade Away/Just Today (Rich RR-112) 1966

A cool outfit from Oklahoma City. The first 45 starts with a yearning pre-beat style teen ballad but the flip is the reason why it is sought-after - simple but very effective beat-garage with fuzzed guitar. The later 45 sadly fails to follow up this promise, reverting to basic beat-pop ballads - with horns on the flip. (MW)

The Centurys

Personnel:	BILL BELLAMY	gtr	AB
	JIM TAYLOR	drms	AB
	TONY VOLZ	gtr	AB
	PAT WELLBERG	gtr	AB
	WINK KELSO	vcls	B

45: Whole Lotta Shakin' Goin' On /
Gandy Dancer (Mark C # unkn) 1964

Formed initially as a four-piece instrumental outfit while still at school in Alamo Heights, San Antonio, Texas. With the addition of a vocalist they moved towards the new Invasion/beat sounds and issued their own 45, featuring covers of Jerry Lee Lewis and the Ventures. They also recorded an album's worth of material which remained unreleased - although the four recently compiled tracks are supposedly from that project. They continued through to 1966 when, with the departure of Tony Volz and a name change to the **Pandas**, they put out the awesome *Walk* 45. For the band's full story check out Andrew Brown's 'Brown Paper Sack #1' zine.

Four unreleased tracks from 1964 have recently resurfaced. You'll find: *Johnny B. Goode* on *Texas Punk, Vol. 3* (LP) and *Acid Visions - Complete Collection, Vol. 2* (3-CD) and *Back From Eternity*, *New Orleans* and *City Surfin* on *Acid Visions - Complete Collection, Vol. 3* (3-CD). (AB/MW)

The Centurys

Personnel:	BILLY BEARD	ld gtr, vcls	A
	BOB KOCH	ld vcls, keyb'ds	A
	JOHN LACAVONE	bs, vcls	A
	LARRY McKINNEY	gtr, vcls	A
	BERNIE ORNER	drms, vcls	A

CEYLEIB PEOPLE - Tanyet LP.

EP: 1(A) THE RENCO DEMOS (Bona Fide BF 7001) 1984

45s: And I Cried/? (BBB-4002) 1966
Endless Search/Hard Times (Swan S-4265) 1966

This punk quintet were based in Lebanon, Pennsylvania. The *Renco Demos* EP features four tracks from 1965:-*83*, *So The Prophets Say*, *Don't Bother* and *Together To Stay*. They also recorded a version of Jerry Lee Lewis' *Whole Lot A Shakin'* in 1965.

Compilation appearances include: *Endless Search* on *Pennsylvania Unknowns* (LP); *Hard Times* and *And I Cried* on *Return Of The Young Pennsylvanians* (LP); *83* and *Hard Times* on *Teenage Shutdown, Vol. 1* (LP & CD); and *Hard Times* on *Boulders, Vol. 1* (LP) and *Ya Gotta Have Moxie, Vol. 1* (Dble CD). (VJ)

The Ceptors

45: I Can't Make It/I Need Her (Panorama 1001) 1967

Solid thumpin' Pacific Northwest sounds, produced by **Gil Bateman**, from Washington state. *I Can't Make It* - not the Small Faces track despite the Stevie Marriott vocal mannerisms - is also on *Psychedelic Crown Jewels Vol. 3* (CD) and *Northwest Battle Of The Bands, Vol. 2* (CD). (VJ/MW)

The Certain Scene

45: Welcome Back Among The Living/
So This Is Love (ERA 3200) 1968

Produced by Dick Parker and Dick Torst (who also wrote the plug side), this obscure group seems to have released only one 45. Still working under the "2-D Productions" moniker, Parker and Torst also produced **Rabbit Mackay**. (SR)

The Ceyleib People

Personnel:	RY COOTER (RY COODER)	slide gtr	A
	MIKE DEASY	gtr	A
	SEAN DEASY	drms	A
	LYBUK HYD	gtr, sitar	A
	JOE OSBORNE	bs	A
	LARRY KNECHTEL	vcls	A

ALBUM: 1(A) TANYET (Vault 117) 1968 R2

NB: (1) was also released in Germany with a different sleeve (Polydor International 623262) 1968. Reissued on CD (Drop Out Records DO CD 1991), with both mono and stereo versions on one CD.

45: Changes/Ceyladd Beyta (Vault 940) 1968

A West Coast group, most of whose personnel went on to greater achievements. Osborne, as a member of The Dillards and later as a session musician for Simon and Garfunkel among others; Knechtel as a member of Bread and session musician for Dave Mason, **Lee Michaels**, Art Garfunkel and Neil Diamond among others, and Cooder, of course, has made many significant solo albums and done session work for numerous artists. The album is an excellent collection of Indian-influenced instrumentals.

Compilation appearances have included: *Changes* on *Beyond The Calico Wall* (CD) and *Ceyladd Beyta* (rare alternate 45 mix) on *Everything You Always Wanted To Know...* (CD). (VJ/SR)

Chad & Jeremy

Personnel: JEREMY CLYDE   vcls, gtr   A
             CHAD STUART   vcls, gtr, banjo,
                                  keyboards, sitar   A

HCP

ALBUMS: 1 YESTERDAY'S GONE
                                  (World Artists 2002) 1964 22 -
         2 CHAD AND JEREMY SING FOR YOU
                                  (World Artists 2005) 1965 69 -
         3 BEFORE AND AFTER   (Columbia 9174) 1965 37 -
         4 I DON'T WANT TO LOSE YOU BABY
                                  (Columbia 9198) 1965 77 -
         5 THE BEST OF CHAD AND JEREMY
                                  (Capitol 2470) 1966 49 -
         6 MORE CHAD AND JEREMY (Capitol 2546) 1966 144 -
         7 DISTANT SHORES   (Columbia 2564) 1966 61 -
         8 OF CABBAGES AND KINGS
                                  (Columbia 2671) 1967 186 -
         9 THE ARK   (Columbia 2899) 1968 - -

NB: (1), (4), (7), (8) and (9) reissued on CD. The World Artists recordings have been compiled on a number of CD's, the best of which is *The Best Of Chad And Jeremy* (One Way 31380) which has twenty tracks including all the World Artist singles. Perhaps of more interest to psych fans however is the twenty track compilation CD *Painted Dayglow Smile* (Columbia Legacy 47719) from their Columbia years.

HCP

45s: Yesterday's Gone/Lemon Tree   (World Artists 1021) 1964 21
         A Summer Song/
         No Tears For Johnny   (World Artists 1027) 1964 7
         Willow Weep For Me/
         If She Was Mine   (World Artists 1034) 1964 15
         If I Loved You/Donna, Donna   (World Artists 1041) 1965 23
         What Do You Want With Me/
         A Very Good Year   (World Artists 1052) 1965 51
         Before And After/Fare Thee Well (Columbia 43277) 1965 17
         From A Window/My Coloring Book (World Artists 1056) 1965 97

CHAD & JEREMY - Yesterday's Gone CD

         I Don't Want To Lose You Baby/
         Pennies   (Columbia 43339) 1965 35
         September In The Rain/
         Only For The Young   (World Artists 1060) 1965 -
         I Have Dreamed/Should I?   (Columbia 43414) 1965 91
         Teenage Failure/Early Morning Rain (Columbia 43490) 1965 -
         Distant Shores/Last Night   (Columbia 43682) 1966 30
         You Are She/I Won't Cry   (Columbia 43807) 1966 87
         Rest In Peace/Family Way   (Columbia 44131) 1967 -
         Painted Dayglow Smile/Editorial (Columbia 44379) 1967 -
         Sister Marie/Rest In Peace   (Columbia 44525) 1968 -
         Paxton Quigley's Had The Course/
         You Need Feet   (Columbia 44660) 1968 -

Ex-public schoolboys Chad Stuart and Jeremy Clyde were regarded by Americans as examplars of that pinnacle of Western civilization, the Archetypal Englishman, and were hence far more popular stateside than at home - the English being less infatuated with Englishness than Americans. Realising early on that their appeal lay in the States, they moved their base of operations to Los Angeles and can be regarded as an American act for the purposes of this book.

The two met in 1962 while studying at the Central School of Speech and Drama in London and formed a duo, performing folk-based pop material. They signed with Ember Records and had a minor U.K. hit (No. 37) in late 1963 with their debut single, *Yesterday's Gone*. U.S. label World Artists picked up the U.S. rights to the duo and *Yesterday's Gone* reached No. 21 in the States in June 1964 followed three months later by their biggest hit, *A Summer Song*. *Willow Weep For Me* and *If I Loved You* (from the musical "Carousel") were also sizable hits but when World Artists failed to pay the pair any royalties, they teamed up with Allen Klein who quickly signed them to Columbia Records in March 1965. Their musical style remained the same, a softly melodic but rather cloying harmony-pop, except for a foray into Righteous Brothers-territory with *I Don't Wanna Lose You Baby* and a comedy single (*Teenage Failure*), but they were frequently on TV - not only performing their hits but also demonstrating their acting skills on Batman, the Patty Duke Show, and the Dick Van Dyke Show.

In late 1965, while on tour in the mid-West, they discovered future Chicago and **Blood, Sweat and Tears** manager James William Guercio, who was then playing in a Chicago group called the Mob. They employed him as their bassist and he wrote several songs for them including their final top-40 hit, *Distant Shores*, and later became their manager.

Wearied by the insubstantial nature of their musical output so far, the pair decided to go for something more ambitious and joined up with **Byrds** and **Sagittarius**-producer Gary Usher in 1967 for the concept album, *Of Cabbages And Kings*. The entire second side was devoted to the five-movement *Progress Suite* which told the story of man from Creation to Nuclear Holocaust. The album however is better remembered by psyche-holics for the 6'46" opening track, *Rest in Peace*, a gently satirical number inspired by Tony Richardson's film adaptation of the Evelyn Waugh novel, "The Loved One".

Their musical swansong, *The Ark* (spelt Arc on some pressings), was easily their best album with a number of highly evocative tunes like *Pipe Dream*, *Pantheistic Study For Guitar And Large Bird*, and *Transatlantic Trauma 1966*. Gary Usher spent $75,000 in making it a production tour-de-force but was sacked by Columbia for his pains when it failed to chart. The duo also wrote the music for the movie "Three In The Attic" around this time.

By this time, Jeremy had decided to devote his flagging energies to acting and the pair split up. Since then, Jeremy has become a well-known actor in England on TV and in the movies while Chad remained in the U.S. writing music for television and stage. The two reunited in 1983 for an album, *Chad Stuart & Jeremy Clyde*, and also in 1986 for an oldies tour.

Compilation appearances have included *Progress Suite Movement* on *First Vibration* (LP).

Bill Chadwick

45:    Talking To A Wall/If You Have The Time   (Dot 45-17226) 1969

Bill Chadwick was a friend and a songwriter of **The Monkees**. This rare single was produced by Mike Nesmith and Davy Jones co-wrote the flip. (SR)

CHAD & JEREMY - Ark CD.

The Chain Reaction

Personnel:	DON SOLOMAN	keyb'ds	A
	STEVE TALLARICO	vcls, hrmnca	A

45:   The Sun/When I Needed You   (Date 1538) 1966

This outfit operated out of Sunapee, New Hampshire and were orginally known as The Strangers. Influenced by The Rolling Stones, they turned professional in '64 becoming The Stranguers and then **The Chain Reaction**. A 45 for the CBS subsidiary Date met with little success, although the band were regulars on the NY circuit and even got to open for The Yardbirds.

After they eventually folded in June 1967, Tallarcio worked in the studio with the last version of **The Left Banke** before working the New York club scene with Chain in 1967-1968. He then moved back to Boston where that group split in 1969, worked with Fox Chase (1969) and William Proud (1970) before trying out for the reforming Jeff Beck Group.

Tallarico was then teamed up with **The Jam Band** by Henry Smith, a roadie and gofer not only for The Stranguers, but also the Yardbirds, The Jeff Beck Group and even Led Zeppelin. In 1970 he changed names to Steve Tyler and with the remnants of **The Jam Band** formed **Aerosmith**.

Compilation appearances have included *When I Needed You* on *Psychedelic Unknowns, Vol. 4* (LP & CD). (JO/VJ/MW/BPs)

The Chain Reaction

45:   Believe In Me /
      Bring It On Home To Me   (Audio Dynamics AD 107) 1968

This **Chain Reaction** came from Springfield, Massachussetts and this, their sole 45, was produced by Dick Booth. (MW/DBh/AH)

The Chain Reaction

45:   You'll Never Know /
      G.Y.S. (Get You Some Lovin')   ((blank) #67-764) 1967

One of several bands using this name in the mid-sixties, this bunch came from Jacksonville, Florida. Nothing more is known except that *G.Y.S.* was composed by James Alan Bartlett and it comes across as garagey frat that swings. It's been unearthed on *Psychedelic States - Florida Vol. 2* (CD).

It would appear that they couldn't decide what to christen their custom label so it bears the template " (blank) " in small type.

Other **Chain Reaction(s)** bands around in the mid-late sixties, with no links to the listed outfits (pun intended), include bands from: Connecticut, Florida, Massachussetts (2), and parts unknown (45s: *Ever Lovin' Man/You Should Have Seen Her Yesterday* (Verve 10611) 1968 and *Definitely Dixie/I've Got A Lot Of Love Left In Me* (Dial 4070) 1968). (MW/MM/JLh/RM)

Chain Reactions

45:   Life / What Am I Supposed To Do   (Francis 201,436/7) 1967

The only known waxing by a group from Old Saybrook, Connecticut. According to Aram Heller in his New England bible, 'Till The Stroke Of Dawn', the 'B' side of this 45 is "good moody garage ala The Mauve" yet it remains uncompiled. (MW)

Chakras

45:   City Boy/Agnes Vandalism   (Reprise O859) 1969

The 'A' side is agreeable pop-rock, nothing special at all. The 'B' side (also by Michael Kaplan) is better: anglophile pop-psych like a heavier Hollies with nice background choir. (MK)

Chalis

ALBUM: 1   ONE MORE CHANCE   (Ellen Abby 25389) 1975 SC

A symphonic prog group, their eleven tracks are original. The album sleeve doesn't give any indication about the group or its state of origin. (SR)

The Challengers

45:   Moon, Send My Baby/Dream   (Kix International 2263) 196?

A very young band from Wilson, a town about 40 miles due East of Raleigh in North Carolina. They are therefore unconnected to the Milwaukee, Wisconsin band **The Challengers (Of Who)**. The 'A' side has a super bluesy intro which gives way to a slightly manic uptempo punk thrash. You'll find it on *Tobacco A-Go-Go, Vol. 1* (LP). (VJ)

The Challengers

Personnel:	RICHARD DELVY	drms	A
	ART FISHER	gtr	A
	ED FOURNIER	gtr	A
	RANDY NAUERT	bs	A

ALBUM: 1   LIGHT MY FIRE WITH CLASSICAL GAS
(selective)   (GNP Crescendo GNPS 2045) 1968 -

From California, these **Challengers** began in the early sixties as a successful instrumental surf group and several of their album sleeves featured Rick Griffin drawings. They somehow managed to survive throughout the sixties and issued this album in 1968. Side One is purely instrumental and contains covers of **The Doors'** *Light My Fire*, **Steppenwolf**'s *Born To Be Wild* and Cream's *Sunshine Of Your Love* plus three pop songs. The guitar parts are competent, but the addition of strings and horns spoil it. Side Two features vocals on some original tracks and more covers, but once again with rich arrangements. Overall, a total failure. (SR)

The Challengers (Of Who)

Personnel incl:	JOHN BEASTER	drms	AB
	PAT CLARK	bs	A
	MIKE HOULIHAN	ld gtr	AB
	JOHN McCURDY	vcls	A
	KEITH PENTLER	keyb'ds	AB
	DAVID WAYNE (WAEHNER)	keyb'ds	AB
	CHRIS CONNORS	gtr	B

45s:	The Challengers Take A Ride On The Jefferson Airplane/	
	I Wanna Hold You	(Night Owl J-6794) 1967
α	It's Love/Leave Me Be	(Night Owl 1457) 1969
	Hear My Message/	
	I Wanna Hold You	(Age Of Aquarius 1500) 1970

NB: α as **The Challengers Of Who**.

This Milwaukee, Wisconsin band's first 45 features a psyched-out instrumental which is a blatant tribute to the kings of American acid rock. You'll find it on *Highs In The Mid-Sixties, Vol. 15* (LP) and *Buzz Buzz Buzzzzzz, Vol. 1* (CD).

The band was never known as The Challengers Of Who, as billed on their second 45. John Beaster told Gary Myers in his book on fifties/sixties Wisconsin bands, 'Do You Hear That Beat', that "it was just someone's dumb idea for the record".

Their cover of the Zombies' *Leave Me Be* can be heard on *Badger Beat Chronicles* (LP).

Mike Hoolihan was later in The Picture, who also included John Beaster's brother Mike on drums. (VJ/GM/MW)

David Chalmers

ALBUM:	1 PRIMEVAL ROAD	(Same Old Label) 1976 R1/R2

NB: (1) reissued on River Records with different track line-up.

From Illinois. In the **Hendrix** style, an album full of guitar excursions and decent vocals. (SR)

Chamaeleon Church

Personnel:	CHEVY CHASE	drms, keyb'ds, vcls	A
	KYLE GARRAHAN	bs, ld gtr, piano, vcls	A
	TED MYERS	gtr, vcls	A
	TONY SCHEUREN	gtr, bs, harpsichord, vcls	A

ALBUM:	1(A) CHAMAELEON CHURCH	(MGM 4574) 1968 -

NB: (1) reissued on LP and CD (Akarma AK 130) 2000.

45:	Camillia Is Changing/Your Golden Love	(MGM 13929) 1968

This sole album is full of great flower-power pop with heavenly vocals that will appeal greatly to fans of **Left Banke** and **Cryan' Shames**. Prior to **Chamaeleon Church**, Ted Myers and Kyle Garrahan had been in The

CHAMAELEON CHURCH - Chamaeleon Church LP.

Lost and after the band's demise, Myers and Scheuren went on to **Ultimate Spinach**. Kyle Garrahan too pursued a solo career, whilst Chevy Chase went on to fame and fortune with a career in films.

Apparently their album did not truly represent the bands own "sound". During the recording of the album, for example, the bass drum was given its own track but is all but missing from the final mix - Chevy was apparently "rippin' mad" when he heard the final result.... Producer **Alan Lorber** had wanted to give them an easy soft-rock feel - a phrase that didn't even exist back then, but which was somewhat akin to **Orpheus**, who had achieved some success at the time with their blend of soft psychedelia.

Ted Myers later wrote a song around '72 called *Going In Circles* which was recorded by Three Dog Night as the flip side of one of their biggest hits, *The Family Of Man*. It also was used in a movie called "X,Y & Z". Later Myers recorded an album with studio musicians, called *Glider*, a single *Your Like A Melody* and he is now is an A&R Director for Rhino Records. Tony Scheuren went on to the National Lampoon, where he appeared with Chevy in a road company of "Lemmings" (an off broadway spoof on Woodstock written by Tony Hendra). After that he was in some other road shows and appeared regularly on the Radio Hour. Scheuren is also featured on several National Lampoon albums, two of which were grammy nominated... *Missing White House Tapes* and *Goodbye Pop*.

Compilation appearances have included: *Off With The Old* and *In A Kindly Way* on *The Best Of Bosstown Sound* (CD); *Off With The Old*, *In A Kindly Way*, *Here's A Song*, *Ready Eddie? (Waltz For Debby)*, *Camillia Is Changing*, *Your Golden Love*, *Remembering's All I Can Do*, *Blueberry Pie*, *Blueberry Pie* (alt), *Tompkins Square Park* and *Spring This Year* on *Family Circle - Family Tree* (CD). (VJ/MS)

The Chambermen

45:	Louie Go Home/Midnight Hour	(Chambermen 1292) 196?

Came out of Spokane, Washington and put this out on their own label. The 'A' side, one of the most recorded Northwest songs, can be found on *Highs In The Mid-Sixties, Vol. 7* (LP). It had a catchy guitar riff and typical garage organ backing. (VJ)

The Chambers Brothers

Personnel:	GEORGE CHAMBERS	bs	AB
	JOE CHAMBERS	gtr	AB
	LESTER CHAMBERS	hmnca	AB
	WILLIE CHAMBERS	gtr	AB
	BRIAN KEENAN	drms	B

			HCP
ALBUMS:	1 PEOPLE GET READY	(Vault LP(S)-9003) 1966	- -
(up to	2 THE CHAMBER BROTHERS	(Vault LP/VS-115) 1967	- -
1971)	3 THE TIME HAS COME		
		(Columbia CL 2722/CS 9522) 1967	4 -
	4 THE CHAMBER BROTHERS SHOUT		
		(Vault VS-120) 1968	- -
	5 A NEW TIME A NEW DAY	(Columbia CS 9671) 1968	16 -
	6 LOVE, PEACE AND HAPPINESS		
		(Columbia KGP 20) 1969	58 -
	7 FEELIN' THE BLUES	(Vault VS-128) 1969	- -
	8 THE CHAMBER BROTHERS GREATEST HITS		
		(Vault VS-135) 1970	193 -
	9 A NEW GENERATION	(Columbia C-30032) 1971	145 -
	10 THE CHAMBER BROTHERS GREATEST HITS		
		(Columbia C-30871) 1971	166 -

NB: (1) was also released in the U.K. (Vocalion VA-L/SAV-L 8058) in 1966, (3) was also released in the U.K. (Direction 8-63407) in 1968, (5) was also released in the U.K. (Direction 8-63451) in 1969, (6) was also released in the U.K. (Direction 8-66228) in 1970, (7) was also released in the U.K. (Liberty LBS 83276) in 1970, (9) was also released in the U.K. (CBS 64156) in 1971, (3) and (5) were issued on a double album in 1975 (Columbia CG-33642). 1996 saw the release of *Time Has Come Today*, a CD compilation on Legacy.

| 45s:
(UK releases up to 1971) | Love Me Like The Rain/
Pretty Girls Everywhere
Call Me/Seventeen
All Strung Out Over You/Falling In Love
Up Town/Love Me Like The Rain
Time Has Come Today/Dinah
I Can't Turn You Loose/
Do Your Thing (PS)
Are You Ready/You Got The Power
To Turn Me On
People Get Ready/
No No Don't Say Goodbye
Wake Up/
Everybody Needs Someone
Have A Little Faith/
Baby Takes Care Of Business
Love Peace And Happiness/
If You Want Me To
Funky/Love Peace And Happiness
By The Hair Of My Chinny Chin Chin/
Heaven | (Vocalion VL 9267) 1966 -
(Vocalion 9276) 1966 -
(CBS 202565) 1967 -
(Direction 58-3215) 1968 126
(Direction 58-3671) 1968 11
(Direction 58-3865) 1968 37
(Direction 58-4098) 1969 113
(Direction 58-4318) 1969 -
(Columbia 44890) 1969 92
(Direction 58-4367) 1969 -
(Direction 58-4846) 1970 96
(CBS 5389) 1971 106
(CBS 7689) 1971 - |

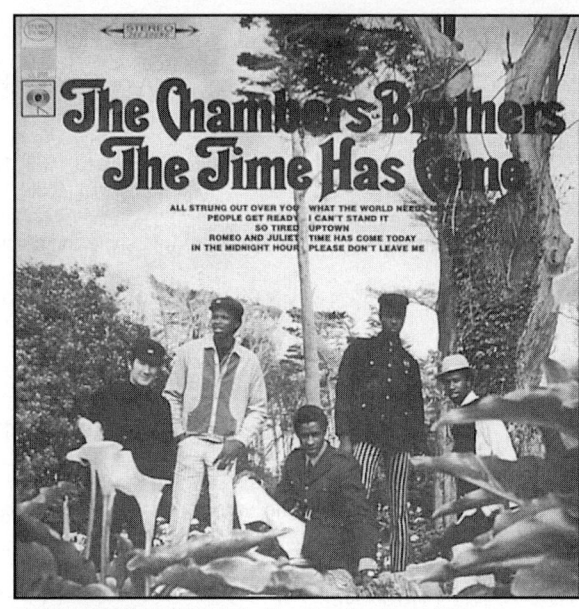

THE CHAMBERS BROTHERS - The Time Has Come LP.

This group of Mississippi-born brothers started out as gospel singers in the 1950s. Keenan joined in 1965 when they switched to a rock format. They went on to record several albums and singles enjoying five U.S. Top 100 hits. It was their biggest, *Time Has Come Today* which has most relevance to this book. It peaked at No 11 in the US. It is a good example of what might be termed 'psychedelic soul'.

Also noteworthy are the title track from *A New Time A New Day* which features shards of guitar with leslie speaker effect, over what sounds like a black power anthem. The central instrumental section of the track also features a freak-out with lots of strange sound effects and wild guitar... unique violent psychedelia!

The title track from *Love, Peace and Happiness*, reissued on CD (GNPD-2224) may also be of interest: a side-long wonder with a lengthy psychedelic instrumental section in the middle (with lot's of wah-wah and echo). This is quite a nice track, but is surrounded by a lot of mediocre, poorly recorded gospel r&b.

There's also an album from 1972, *Oh My God* (Columbia C-30871), which remained unreleased.

Compilation appearances include: *Time Has Come Today* on *Nuggets, Vol. 9* (LP), *Best of '60s Psychedelic Rock* (CD) and *Even More Nuggets* (CD); *You Got The Power* on *Pop Revolution From The Underground* (LP); *(She Don't Want To) Tie Me Down, Don't Lose Your Cool, Girl, We Love You* and *There She Goes* on *West Coast Love-In* (LP). (VJ/TA)

The Chancellors

45: On Tour/Rout 66 (D&C Records DC-22) 1966

This garage band hailed from Potsdam, New York. They cut the above punker in 1966 for a Schenectady, New York label. *On Tour* has resurfaced on *Back From The Grave, Vol. 8* (CD) and *Back From The Grave, Vol. 8* (Dble LP). (VJ/MSh)

The Chancellors

Personnel incl:	RICK GARFIELD	drms	A
	JIM OVAITT	keyb'ds	A

45s:	One In A Million / Journey	(Fenton 2066) c1967
	Dear John / 5 Minus 3	(Fenton 2072) 1967
	Places We Once Knew / Something For Sure	(Chamus 3448) 196?

Highly-touted and collectable garage-punkers from Michigan. Their instrumental Garfield-Ovaitt duet, *5 Minus 3* implies that the band was a quintet.

Compilation appearances include:- *Dear John* on *When The Time Run Out, Vol. 1* (LP & CD); *Journey* on *Project Blue, Vol. 5* (LP); and *5 Minus 3* on *Killer Cuts* (LP) and *Buzz Buzz Buzzzzzz Vol. 2* (CD). (MW)

Chancellors Ltd

45: You Be The Judge/From The Sublevels (Dene 101) 1966

From Houston in Texas. The 'A' side, which is undistinguished, can be found on the *Riot City!* (LP) compilation. So far as I know they were unrelated to The Chancellors, a sixties punk band who also cut two 45s and came from Houston. (VJ)

Kenny Chandler

45s:	Treetop/Consideration	(Bandbox 224) 1959
	Drums/The Magic Ring	(United Artists 342) 1961
	Please, Mister Mountain/ What Kind Of Love Is Yours	(United Artists 384) 1961
	Man On The Run/Leave Me If You Want To	(Laurie 3140) 1962
	It Might Have Been/Yours And Yours Alone	(Coral 62309) 1962
	I Can't Stand Tears At A Party/ I Tell Myself	(Laurie 3181) 1963
	I Don't Know Why/Happy To Be Unhappy	(Amy 890) 1963
	S.O.S. (Sweet On Susie)/Come Softly To Me	(Epic 9758) 1965
	Heart/Ain't Gonna Hurt You	(Epic 9862) 1965
	I'll Be Coming Back/Sunshine Sweetheart	(Epic 10009) 1966
	Sleep/Nickels And Dimes	(Tower 354) 1967
α	Beyond Love/Charity	(Tower 405) 1968
	I'll Be Home/Leave Me If You Want To	(Laurie 3577) 1971

NB: α Also released in the UK (Stateside SS 2110) 1968. There was also a UK 45 *Heart/Wait For Me* (Stateside SS 166) 1963.

From Harrisburg, Pennslyvania. His *S.O.S. (Sweet On Susie)* was a Top Ten Canadian hit in June 1965. Indeed it spent four weeks in the Top 10 and eight in the Top 40. He also charted in the USA with *Heart*. (VJ/GM)

Changing Colours

45s:	Girl For All Seasons/Want You By My Side	(Tower 457) 1967
α	Da-Da-Da-Da /same	(Tower 492) 1968

NB: α promo copy.

A "groovy" pop group, their first single was produced by Philip Vance and written by Jerry Vance. The second one was produced by Vance/**Curtiss**/Philips for Perceptions Productions and written by **Jimmy Curtiss**, Marcia Vance, Jim Tracy and Parks Wilson. As most of these names can also be found on **The Hobbits** albums, we assume that **Changing Colours** was a studio side project for **Jimmy Curtiss** and his associates based in New York. (SR)

The Changing Scene

ALBUM: 1 THE CHANGING SCENE (Avco Embassy) 1970

45s: Is It Really Worth It/
Sing Me Something Pretty (Fontana 1669) 1969
Sweet And Sour/? (Avco Embassy 4538) 1970

A forgotten group, a bit like the **Lovin' Spoonful**, with some weird songs. (SR)

Changing Times

45: I'm Alone/Cry (Mark VII 101 3) 1967

Operated around the Waco-Temple area of Texas in the 1960s. The flip, which has a chiming intro and pleasing vocals, appeared on *Flashback, Vol. 4* (LP) and *Texas Flashbacks, Vol. 4* (LP & CD). (VJ)

The Changing Times

Personnel:	SANDY CHARLES	AB
	RICK DAVIDSON	AB
	GARRY FORD	AB
	DALE HASTINGS	AB
	RICK LAYMON	AB
	JOE REYNOLDS	B

A different Dallas outfit who were known as The Gentlemen prior to 1966. They didn't make it onto vinyl at the time but *Texas Flashbacks Vol. 1 - Dallas* (LP) included five unreleased cuts by line-up 'B':- *She Don't Know, About Me And You, Near You Babe, Life's A Game* and *Just Look Back*. None of these have much to commend about them.

Three of the above tracks, *She Don't Know, Near You Babe* and *About Me And You* also appear on *Psychedelic Microdots Of The Sixties, Vol. 2* (CD). (VJ)

Changin' Times

Personnel:	STEVE DUBOFF	A
	ARTIE KORNFELD	A

HCP

45s: Pied Piper / Thank You Babe (Philips 40320) 1965 87
How Is The Air Up There /
Young & Innocent Girl (Philips 40341) 1966 -
I Should Have Brought Her Home /
Goin' Lovin' With You (Philips 40368) 1966 -
Aladdin /
All In The Mind Of A Young Girl (Philips 40401) 1966 -
Free Spirit (She Comes On) /
You Just Seem To Know (Bell 675) 1967 -
When The Good Sun Shines /
Show Me The Way To Go Home (Bell 711) 1968 -

This talented NYC-based songwriter duo would achieve some success but also saw this eclipsed by covers of their songs. A vibrant blend of catchy and occasionally punky folk-rock-pop, some of these titles should be familiar - Crispian St.Peters achieved a U.K. No. 5 with his version of *Pied Piper*, which was also covered by the **Human Bein(g)z**, La De Da's, and both the **Aces Combo** and Tony & The Fabulous Spades on their respective Justice albums. It was originally a minor hit for the **Changin' Times**. New Zealand's garage gods the La De Da's also covered the **Changin' Times** finest moment *How Is The Air Up There* - hear it on *Ugly Things, Vol. 3* or *Wild Things, Vol. 1*. It's a dynamic snarling garage-pop blast that would've fit right into the **Standells**' repertoire.

Artie Kornfeld went on to be one of the quartet that created and organised Woodstock - with Joel Rosenman, John Roberts and Michael Lang. Steve Duboff subsequently released a solo 45 - *In The Peaceful Valley (Woodstock '69) / Song For You* (Cotillion 44051) 1969.

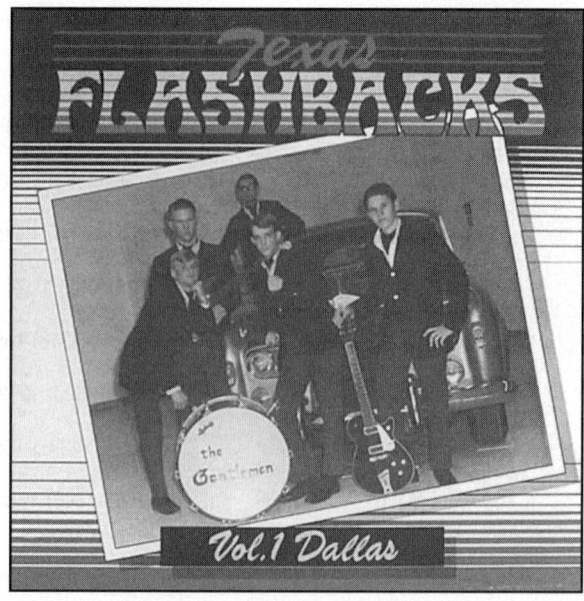

TEXAS FLASHBACKS Vol. 1 (Comp LP) including The Changing Times related Gentlemen.

Their names continue to turn up on songwriting credits and as arrangers or producers of other acts. Steve Duboff and Dave Morris composed *Out Of Sight, Out Of Mind* was covered by **The Marauders**, **Limey & the Yanks**, the **Bit 'A Sweet**, and in the eighties by the Outta Place. Artie Kornfeld production credits include 45s by the **Bassetts**, Carnival Connection, Guild Light Gauge, Tuneful Trolley and the Unclaimed (with **Milan**), **Bert Sommer**'s eponymous LP on Kama Sutra in 1971 and **Swampgas**.

Compilation appearances have included: *How Is The Air Up There* on *Open Up Yer Door, Vol. 2* (LP), *Vile Vinyl, Vol. 1* (LP) and *Vile Vinyl* (CD); *Pied Piper* on *Turds On A Bum Ride, Vol. 5* (CD); and *Thank You Baby* on *Turds On A Bum Ride, Vol. 6* (CD). (MW)

Changin' Tymes

Personnel:	BRUCE BARHAM	bs, vcls	A
	CHARLES FERRER	gtr	AB
	GLEN FRAZIER	ld gtr	AB
	LARRY MOORE	drms	AB
	BRIT WARNER	12-string, organ, vcls	AB
	WAIN BRADLEY	bs	B

45: Chicago Street Fight / Blue Music Box (M.U.M.A. Muma 1) 1968

A gloriously rare 45 on the 'Memphis Underground Music Association' label whose design incorporates the peace salute. The choice cut *Blue Music Box* - "a ferocious 1968 grinder that's reminiscent of a track off MC5's *Kick Out The Jams*" - kicks off the essential CD compilation *A Lethal Dose Of Hard Psych*.

More recently the track appeared on *A History Of Garage And Frat Bands In Memphis* (CD) compilation, whose companion book by Ron Hall gives the personnel above and tells their story ('Playing For A Piece Of The Door', published in 2001 by Shangri-La Projects). (MW/ELn)

The Changin' Tymes

Personnel incl:	R. GRAY	A
	F. KING	A

45: Bye Tyme / Just A Little (Vaughn-Ltd 752) 1966

Not to be confused with the identically-spelt (but later) outfit from Memphis, this group were from somewhere in Alabama. *Bye Tyme* is a moody but smoothly-paced jangle-rocker, whose inner pain is revealed only by some unexpected crashing fuzz chords towards the end. It merits repeated plays and can be found on *Psychedelic States: Alabama Vol. 1* (CD). (MW)

The Chants

45: Hypnotized/Elaina (B.Ware 869) 1966

A mid-sixties folk-punk band from Dallas in Texas. You can check out *Hypnotized* on *Flashback, Vol. 3* (LP), *Texas Flashbacks, Vol. 3* (LP & CD), *Highs In The Mid Sixties, Vol. 11* (LP) or *Gathering Of The Tribe* (LP) and *Elaina* has been included on *Punk Ballads Sampler* (LP). (VJ)

The Chaparrals

Personnel:	JAMIE BASSETT	bs, hmnca	ABC
	STEVE KARNAVAS	drms	ABC
	CHUCK McKAY	vcls, gtr	ABC
	WAYNE ROSSEE	ld gtr	ABC
	TOMMY CASHWELL	keyb'ds	B
	VERNON WOMACK	keyb'ds	C

This much-travelled mob formed in North Texas State University late in 1964. They journeyed to Miami and then headed to Orlando where Cashwell joined their ranks. His connections with a booking agency got them gigs throughout the South but the rest of he band were not interested in gigging in the North so they parted company with him. Returning to Dallas in 1966 and adding Womack to their line-up they recorded a number of songs which were unable to attract any record labels at the time but which have subsequently been compiled (See below). In 1968 they set off again to try their luck in California. After a spell in L.A. they split up in San Francisco. Karnavas remained there forming The Snakes with ex-**Briks** vocalist Cecil Cotton, but the rest went back to their homeland.

Compilation appearances have so far included: *So Good* on *The Cicadelic 60's, Vol. 5* (LP) and *Acid Visions - The Complete Collection, Vol. 1* (3-CD); *Get Off My Cloud, If Your Heart Were Only Wise, Move On, One More Time, Satisfaction, So Good, Wake Up, Girl* on *Texas Punk, Vol. 7* (LP); *Get Off Of My Cloud, If Your Heart Were Mine, I'll Go Crazy, Move On, One More Time, Satisfaction, So Good, Wake Up, Girl* on *Acid Visions - Complete Collection, Vol. 3* (3-CD); *I'll Go Crazy* on *Texas Punk, Vol. 9* (lp); *Blues From A Jefferson Airplane* and *Respect* on *The Cicadelic 60's, Vol. 4* (LP) and *The Cicadelic 60's, Vol. 2* (CD). (VJ)

The Chapin Brothers

Personnel incl:	HARRY CHAPIN	vcls	A

ALBUM: 1(A) CHAPIN MUSIC (Rock-Land RR 66) 1966 R1

Harry Chapin's first group, recorded with his two brothers and their father (on drums). Their *Chapin Music* was a mix of harmony pop and folk with some garage tracks. In the seventies, Harry Chapin would become a popular mainstream pop singer / songwriter and record a dozen of albums. (SR)

Betsy Chapman

ALBUM: 1 A GIFT OF LOVE (Capitol) 1970 SC?

Another obscure album on Capitol, this one was recorded by a pure-voiced female folk singer covering Ewan MacColl, **Buffy Sainte-Marie** and some Erik Satie pieces set to lyrics with some light baroque arrangements. (SR)

The Chapparals

45: Roxanne/Without You (Notsuch 003/4) 196?

NB: released as by Chaparral Trio.

A trio of brothers from Houston. They have *Roxanne*, which was released as a test pressing, included on *Houston Hallucinations* (LP) and a previously unissued cut, *I Tried So Hard* included on *Epitaph For A Legend* (Dble LP). (VJ)

The Chaps

45s:	Tell Me/Forget Me	(Paula 236) 1966
	Remember To Forget/You'll Be Back	(Paula 250) 1966
	To Kingdom Come/Wait A Minute	(Soft 1032) 1969
	Jemima Surrender/Ozark Smokehouse	(Soft 1032) 1969
	Maybe I'm Amazed/Wait A Minute	(Soft 1032) 1970
	Golden Slumbers - Carry That Weight/ Ozark Smokehouse	(Soft 1033) 1971
	Get Me Off This Plane In Time/ Little Red Wagon	(Soft 1043) 1971
	Cry, Just A Little/Ozark Smokehouse	(Demand 303) 19?
	Population Zero/Water Hole	(Madella 105) 19?

Out of the Dallas/Fort Worth area of Texas, their first 45 was in the garage genre but the rest were more rock-oriented. *Wait A Minute* has a trotting beat underpinned by a continual fuzz guitar line - only broken by the sudden intrusion of a harpsichord... unusual and quite cool - especially the freaky ending!

Compilation appearances have included: *Wait A Minute* on *Sixties Rebellion, Vol. 2 - The Barn* (LP) and *Sixties Rebellion Vol's 1 & 2* (CD); and *Tell Me* on *Sick And Tired* (LP).

Possibly connected with the following Dallas-Fort Worth record - by L.B. Gibson & **The Chaps**:-

45: Treat Her Right/Oh Boy (Charay 1003) 1969 (VJ/MW)

Chapter V

45s:	The Sun Is Green/Dolly's Magic	(Verve Folkways KF5046) 1968
	Headshrinker/Dolly's Magic	(Verve Forecast KF5067) 1968

A psych-folk act similar to **Buffalo Springfield**. (SR)

Chapter VI

45: Fear/Oracle (Original Sound OS-78) 1966

An obscure group, probably Californian. *Fear* is a good organ driven mid-tempo track with an excellent intro and male vocals, whilst *Oracle*, is also an interesting organ-driven piece. The 45 was produced by Brian Ross with the 'A' side written by Mike Payne and the flip by D.Mandish / S.Libbea and R.Helgeson.

Compilation appearances have included: *Oracle* on *U-Spaces: Psychedelic Archaeology Vol. 1* (CDR) and *Fear* on *Boulders, Vol. 6* (LP). (SR)

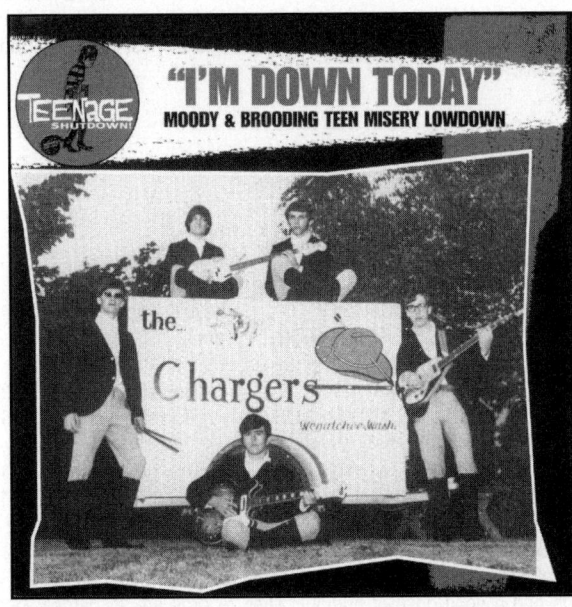

TEENAGE SHUTDOWN Vol. 6 (Comp CD) including The Chargers.

THE CHARLATANS - Alabama Bound LP.

Charade

| 45: | And You Do/Somebody's Watching You | (Epic 5-10644) 1970 |

Produced by Barry Kornfeld, **Charade** was a heavy rock group with horns and fuzz guitar. *And You Do* is a good cover of the **Sly Stone** song. (SR)

Chargers

| 45: | Taxi/I'm So Alone | (Julian 106) 1965 |

More obscurities by an obscure Wenatchee, Washington band. Compilation appearances have included: *Taxi* on *Garage Punk Unknowns, Vol. 2* (LP) and *I'm So Alone* on *Teenage Shutdown, Vol. 6* (LP & CD). (VJ)

Chariot

Personnel:
PUG BAKER	drms	A
LARRY GOULD	bs, vcls	A
MICHAEL KAPLAN	gtr, vcls	A

ALBUM: 1(A) CHARIOT (National General NG 2003) 1971 SC

Described by some as a Cream-influenced blues and hard-psych trio, others find them more progressive with cosmic flower-power sensibilities. They evolved out of a sixties band called The Knack and the above album was recorded in Hollywood. National General were owned by the National General Cinema corporation and their releases were distributed by Buddah. (VJ/SR/SBn/CF)

Charisma

Personnel:
BERNIE KORNOWICZ	bs	A
SUZI LANGLOIS	lyrics	A
TOM MAJESKI	gtr, vcls	A
BOB MOCARSKY	keyb'ds, perc	A
RITCHIE TORTORIDGE	drms	A

ALBUMS: 1(A) CHARISMA (Roulette SR 42037) 1969 -
2(A) BEASTS AND FIENDS (Roulette SR 42054) 1970 -

45s: Bizwambi/? (Roulette 7075) 1970
What It's Like/? (Roulette 7096) 1971

Produced by Bruce McGaw and Ed Vallone and recorded in New York, this group released two albums in a psych/prog style with some light jazz touches and a good dose of humour. Their records are still largely ignored and hard to find.

After a first self-titled album, *Beast And Fiends* came housed in an amusing cartoon cover. *Dirty Pigs Don't Get Far In This World*, *The Age Of Reptiles*, *The No-Tell Motel* and *Bizwambi, Ritual Dance Of The Reptiles*, all penned by Majesky and Langlois, pay witness to their unusual sources of inspiration.

Several tracks are purely instrumental, with interesting keyboards and guitar parts. (SR/MW)

Charity

Personnel:
BLOSSOMS	vcls	A
JOHN CORTINAS		A
WALT FLENNERY		A
KENT HENRY	gtr	A
JEFF OXMAN	vcls	A
JAMES PETERS		A

ALBUM: 1(A) CHARITY NOW (Uni 73061) 1969 -

A Los Angeles outfit whose main claim to fame was the inclusion of Kent Henry, previously of **Genesis** and later of **Steppenwolf**. The album, which I haven't heard, is yet to excite collectors but some felt it deserved a mention.

Walt Flennery had earlier played with **Love Exchange**. (VJ)

The Charlatans

Personnel:
MIKE FERGUSON	piano	AB
GEORGE HUNTER	vcls, harp	ABC
SAM LINDE	drms	AB
RICHARD OLSEN	bs	ABCD
MIKE WILHELM	gtr	AB D
DAN HICKS	gtr, vcls	BC
PATRICK BOGERTY	piano	C
TERRY WILSON	drms	CD
DARRYL DE VORE	keyb'ds	D
(LYNN HUGHES	guest vcls	B)

ALBUM: 1(B) CHARLATANS (Philips 600.309) 1969 R1

NB: They also recorded an unreleased album for Karma Sutra in 1966, reissued on Groucho Marx in Italy 1979 and as *Alabama Bound* by Eva in 1983. More recently (1) has been reissued on CD by One Way (31442) which also includes their first 45 for Kapp. Ace has issued *The Amazing Charlatans* (Big Beat CDWIKD 138) in 1996, a 23-track CD with four unreleased tracks, recorded with **Sly Stone** in 1965, and nine demo recordings from 1966. It also includes a commercial they did for Groom and Clean hairdressing in 1966. There is also a very limited reunion album from 1991.

THE CHARALATANS - The Charlatans LP.

THE CHARLATANS - Amazing Charlatans CD.

45s:	The Shadow Knows/32-20 (PS)	(Kapp 779) 1965
	Radio Spot (Special DJ release of them talking)/	
	Radio Spot (Special DJ release of them talking)	(Philips 34) 1969
	High Coin/When I Go Sailin' By (PS)	(Philips 40610) 1969

The Charlatans were the very first San Francisco underground rock band. Their story begins back in the Summer of 1964 when George Hunter, inspired by the Beatles, decided to form a rock band. He got together with Richard Olsen, an old college friend, and Mike Wilhelm, a folk singer who had been at school with him. Later that year, Mike Ferguson, who owned an antique shop in San Francisco and had just returned from a trip to Mexico, joined as pianist. Sam Linde was their original drummer, although he was later replaced by Dan Hicks. Hicks had known some of the group at the San Francisco State College. He had done a bit of drumming but his interest really lay in guitar and vocals. At the start the group played Chuck Berry numbers and R&B standards like *Got My Mojo Working* and *My Babe* but gradually they evolved the folk-rock repertoire for which they had become famous. Eventually the group were offered a residency at the Red Dog Saloon in Virginia City, Nevada, one of the states adjacent to California. Virginia City, once a thriving mining town, was in danger of becoming something of a ghost town when the silver ran out and its population fell from 30,000 back in the 1870s to just 450 in the 1960s. However, around the late 1960s it became a tourist haunt for people armed with cameras and interested in America's history. The manager of the Red Dog Saloon had originally wanted **The Byrds** to play there, but by then their *Mr. Tambourine Man* single had given them international popularity so he had to settle for **The Charlatans**. To mark the occasion of their first appearance Mike Ferguson designed what is generally thought to have been the first rock poster. Here **The Charlatans** acted as a magnet for the whole hippie scene. News of them soon got around and acid heads came from Reno, 'Frisco and as far afield as Seattle and Los Angeles to hear them play. The Red Dog Saloon predated any of the San Francisco venues and at the time it was the only place on the West Coast where you could hear the new music. When the group arrived at the saloon they were submitted to an unexpected audition - they did this out of their heads on acid! Apparently, The **Charlatans** had no hassle from the police - there were only a handful of them anyway and they all used to listen to the band, on one occasion even the Governor of Nevada being in the audience.

But things began to go wrong. Despite being packed almost every night, the saloon made a loss because no admission charge was levied so profits could only be made from beer and wine sales. The owner had left his 22 year old son in charge and was not pleased when he found, on returning to discover the reasons for this loss, that everyone was having a ball at his expense. To make matters worse his visit coincided with two members of the group getting busted on the way back from San Francisco with more drug supplies for the group.

Eventually the band headed back to San Francisco for good, taking with them a reputation on a par with anybody. Before long, record companies began to take an interest in them and they eventually signed with the **Lovin' Spoonful**'s label, Kama Sutra. In retrospect, they would have done better to wait for a company to offer them the sort of advance RCA had offered The **Jefferson Airplane**. The group cut a nine-track album for Kama Sutra which included the **Buffy St. Marie** song *Codine* (later recorded by many other 'Frisco bands), amazing versions of traditional songs like *Alabama Bound* and *32-20 Blues*, and the old Coasters' song *The Shadow Knows* and two songs featuring Lynne Hughes, who worked as a barmaid at the Red Dog Saloon (and later sang with **Tongue and Groove** and **Stoneground**) on vocals - *Side Track* and *I'd Rather Be The Devil*. **The Charlatans** had wanted *Codine* backed by *32-20* released as a single, but the record company got cold feet because of the mention of 'drugs' in *Codine* and cut off all contact with the band. This was disastrous for **The Charlatans** and ironic when one considers that the song was condemning drugs rather than advocating their use.

At this point, Mike Ferguson left the group to join **Tongue and Groove** with Lynne Hughes, to be replaced by Patrick Bogery, and Dan Hicks gave up the drums to concentrate on the rhythm guitar. So Terry Wilson, who had been playing with David LaFlamme and Jaime Leapold in a group called **The Orkustra** came in on the drums. But they struggled to get work and Hicks, Bogerty and Hunter left the group for good. Hicks to set up Dan Hicks and His Hot Licks. The remaining three (Wilhelm, Olsen and Wilson) recruited a keyboard player Darryl De Vore and were determined to have a final fling. They negotiated a new contract with Philips, although the resulting album was a mediocre affair. This time **The Charlatans** called it a day for good.

The tragic story of **The Charlatans**, probably one of San Francisco's most talented bands, that of a group taken for a ride by its record company, was sadly typical of this era.

THE CHARLATANS - Live Reunion 1991 LP.

Readers of this book may also want to check out a solo album *Wilhelm* (Zig Zag UA 221) released in 1976, featuring Mike Wilhelm and a host of session musicians. Many consider that Side One captures **The Charlatans**' spirit far better than their albums did.

Dan Hicks has recently toured to promote the new Hot Licks album *Beatin' The Heat*, a studio recording featuring guests Elvis Costello, Rickie Lee Jones, Brian Setzer, Tom Waits and Bette Midler. Richard Olsen still performs with his Richard Olsen Orchestra. George Hunter now runs a cabinet making shop in Sonoma county. Mike Ferguson died from complications of diabetes in the early eighties.

Two LPs from Eva *The Charlatans* (Eva 12004) and *Alabama Bound* (Eva 12017) collect their material, but the recent CD reissues from Ace and One Way are superior.

Compilation appearances have so far included: *32-20* and *The Shadow Knows* (45 versions) on *Mindrocker, Vol. 3* (LP); *Codine* (unreleased version) on *Nuggets, Vol. 7* (LP); *Codine* on *Nuggets Box* (4-CD); *No. 1* on *The Autumn Records Story* (LP) and *No. 1* and *Jack O' Diamonds* on *The California Christmas Album* (LP). (VJ)

The Charles

45:	Motorcycle/Down By The Riverside	(Calliope 138) 1966

Another very obscure act, They were Rochester, New York's answer to **Leather Boy Milan.**

Compilation appearances have included: *Motorcycle* on *Scum Of The Earth, Vol. 1* (LP), *Scum Of The Earth* (CD) and *Victims Of Circumstance, Vol. 2* (LP & CD). (VJ)

Charmer

Personnel:	TOM DELLING	drms	A
	DUANE HITCHINGS	keyb'ds, effects	A
	STEVE ROSS	vcls, gtr	A
	RON SPACER	bs	A

ALBUMS:	1(A)	YOUR PRESENCE REQUESTED	(Illusion CM 1070) 1976 R1
	2(A)	DO IT TO IT	(Illusion CM 1071) 1976 R1

A power rock group. All 10 songs on their first album are composed and produced by Steve Ross and recorded in Florida. The first track, *Psychedelic Ride*, is a raucous boogie hard rock jam and psychedelic only by title. There is a hint of psychedelia in *Mirror Of Darkness* and *Fun Of Your Lies*. *Way Home* has a good swirling guitar and a garage feelin'. In a more wild garage vein is *Zodiac Blue*.

Duane Hitchings was in **Cactus** for their *'Ot 'N' Sweaty* album, and their final album as The New Cactus Band. The first album may have been recorded in 1971. (VJ)

Charolette Wood

Friendly Indians was the last recording by **The E-Types** in 1967. It was released in 1968, on *San Francisco International Pop Festival, Vol. 1* compilation (Colstar 1005), recredited by their manager Ron Roupe to the fictional outfit **Charolette Wood.** Check out Jud Cost's full story on the *Introducing The E-Types* CD (Sundazed SC 11026). *Friendly Indians* also appears on *Son Of The Gathering Of The Tribe* (LP) and *Psychedelic Patchwork* (LP). (MW)

The Chartbusters

Personnel incl:	MITCH CORDAY	drms	A
	JOHN DUBAS	bs	A
	VINCE GIDEON	gtr	A
	VERNON SANDUSKY	gtr, vcls	A

			HCP
45s:	She's The One/ Slippin' Thru Your Fingers	(Mutual 5O2) 1964	33
	Why (Doncha Be My Girl)/Stop The Music	(Mutual 508) 1964	92
	You're Breakin' My Heart/ Can't You Hear Me Calling	(Mutual 511) 1965	-
	New Orleans/Lonely Surfer Boy	(Crusader 118) 1965	134
	Kick Wheeler/Selfish Girl	(Crusader 124) 1965	-
	One Bird In The Hand/Maybe Leavin' You/One Bird In	(Crusader 129) 1966	-
	The Hand Is Worth Two In The Bush	(Bell 652) 1966	-
	Grass Houses/Dance Dance	(Bell 683) 1967	-

Originally known as Bobby Poe & The Poe Kats, from Kansas, they moved to Washington DC at the start of the sixties. Bobby Poe dropped out of performing to handle the management side, but the remaining members carried on under the same name, backing Big Al Downing. In 1964, as a side project and in response to the wave of Invasion sounds, they cut *She's The One* with the above line-up as **The Chartbusters**, and bust 'em they did! This meant leaving the comfort of Big Al and going for it as a bona-fide sixties band. They took their chance and, having invaded the sixties invasion, stayed with it through to the end of the decade. Few genuine rock'n'roll groups from the fifties can have made the transition more successfully or lastingly.

SAN FRANCISCO INTERNATIONAL POP FESTIVAL Vol. 1 (Comp LP) including Charolette Wood.

Vernon Sandusky later became lead guitarist for Roy Clark, a guitarist, banjo and fiddle player from Virginia. *She's The One* can also be heard on *Nuggets, Vol. 4* (LP). (MW)

Chateaus

Personnel incl:	JERRY FENDER?		A
	JIM GOODMAN?		A

45:	Since You Have Gone/I'm the One	(Smash 2021) 1966

Probably from Midwest or Dakota (their publisher was Falls City Music and Near North Music), this unknown **Byrds**-ish group was produced by Ray Allen. Both sides of their 45 were penned by Jerry Fender and Jim Goodman, who we presume were band members. The 'A' side is kinda like **The Byrds** *Bells Of Rhymney* with some Dylan harmonica and the 'B' side close to a Searchers-type sound. 12-string guitar throughout. (KG/SR)

Chateaux

Personnel incl:	TOMMY BOLIN	gtr	A

45:	Reference Man Pt. 1/Pt. 2	(Eye 1000) 1968

From Vermillion, South Dakota, this band included a certain Tommy Bolin on guitar. Until around 1967 they were **The Shattoes**, formerly the Galaxies, who'd been on the scene since 1963.

Bolin would become a reknowned axe-wielder and writer. He went on to increasing prominence with **Zephyr** and Energy, before replacing Joe Walsh in **The James Gang** circa 1973. He left after a couple of LPs, released two solo LPs and had a brief stint with Deep Purple (replacing Ritchie Blackmore) until their 1976 breakup. He died young, of a heart attack, at the end of 1976.

Compilation appearances have included: *Caught Up In The Blues* on IGL's *Roof Garden Jamboree* (LP); *Reference Man Part 1* on *30 Seconds Before The Calico Wall* (CD) and *Mr. Refernce Man* on *The IGL Rock Story: Part Two (1967 - 68)* (CD). (VJ/MW)

The Chayns

Personnel incl:	CHARLIE EDDLEMAN	vcls, keyb'ds, gtr, bs	AB
	MILES WELLS	ld gtr	A
	JIM FRIZZELL	vcls, keyb'ds, bs	B
	LARRY MILLEGAN	bs	B
	JOHN STEPHENSON	vcls, drms	B

45s:	Night Time/Live With The Moon	(Chayn-Reaction 001) 1965
	Night Time/	
	Live With The Moon	(International Artists 114) 196?
	There's Something Wrong (In This Place)/	
	I See It Thru'	(International Artists 119) 196?
	Run and Hide/	
	Why Did You Hurt Me?	(Chayn-Reaction 002) 1968
	You/Let Yourself Go	(Chayn-Reaction 003) 1971

From San Antonio, Texas, this band were formed out of Paul Alien and The Baroques. Best known for their version of *Night Time* which was picked up by Lelan Rogers for release on his International Artists label, their remaining material was unexceptional.

In '67/'68 the original line-up split up. Miles Wells and Charlie Eddleman, then put together a new line-up ('B') with Jim Frizzell (ex-**The Rel-Yea's**) and other members of the band he was in at the time. This later line-up lasted until 1972, when **The Chayns** finally called it a day.

Compilation appearances have included: *Night Time* on *Epitaph For A Legend* (Dble LP); *Live With The Moon* on *Austin Landing* (LP); *Run And Hide* and *Why Did You Hurt Me* on *A Journey To Tyme, Vol. 1* (LP); *Run And Hide* on *Austin Landing, Vol. 2* (LP); *Why Did You Hurt Me* on *Boulders, Vol. 1* (LP) and *Ya Gotta Have Moxie, Vol. 1* (Dble CD). (VJ/MW/JF)

Chaz (and The Classics)

45s:	Alice (in Wonderland)/Gentle Thursday	(Picture 6981) 196?
	Cindy (I'm A Soldier Now)/	
	Dream Boat Overseas	(Picture 6995) 196?
	Girl Of The 13th Hour/	
	Stardust On You	(Picture 6999) 1966

Thought to have been based in Houston, they recorded their first two 45s under the name Chaz. The third 45, *Girl Of The 13th Hour*, a snotty punker with a tinge of psychedelia, was issued under the longer name. Check it out on *Highs In The Mid-Sixties, Vol. 11* (LP). (VJ)

The Checkmates

Personnel:	BILLY CARDEN	vcls	A
	BARON CONKLIN	gtr	A
	DAVE MACK	organ	A
	JACK McCURDY	trumpet	A
	JON MUELLER	tenor sax	A
	GEORGE OUTLAW	drms	A
	RODDY PORTER	bs	A
	SAMMY WINSTON	tenor sax	A

ALBUM:	1(A)	MEET THE CHECKMATES	(Justice 149) c1967 R2

NB: (1) reissued on CD (Collectables COL-CD-0617) 1996.

The appetite was whetted when Collectables started reissuing the much-vaunted Justice albums which are rarely seen and go for astronomical figures. Tim Warren had already made the **Tempos** waxing available again which had just lived up to expectations - with the **Barracudas**, **Invaders**, Mod and The Rockers, **Stowaways** albums in the same stable, expectations of the remaining unknown combos was probably unreasonably high. So it's not surprising to discover that they occupy soul/lounge/club territory, well away from garage/beat sounds. What's more, they perform, almost exclusively, the same covers as each other in a perfunctory style. Stick to the known Justice garage-classics and enjoy them at an affordable price. (MW)

The Checkmates

45:	Talk To Me / ?	(Champ 2009) 1967

On the Nashville label that put out 45s by the Originals, Three From Three and **Thee Saints & The Prince Of Darkness** comes a classic style punker with superbly snarled and pissed-off vocals and booming backing. No fuzz fest but probably the best cut on *Psychedelic Crown Jewels, Vol. 2* (Dble LP & CD). (MW/RM)

The Checkmates International

Personnel:	JEFFREY BRYAN	bs	A
	STEVEN BRYAN	organ	A
	RICHARD CHADWICK	drms	A
	BILLY LEE	ld vcls	A
	PAT STEPHENS	gtr, vcls	A

45:	Thinkin' About You /	
	Once Upon A Love Affair	(Thunderbolt 201,091) 1966

A quintet from Savannah, Georgia whose ages ranged from 14 to 19 released their sole 45 in late '66. *Thinkin' About You* is featured on *Hang It Out To Dry* (LP & CD), *Sixties Rebellion, Vol. 14* and *Psychedelic States: Georgia, Vol. 1* (CD). (MW)

Chelsea

Personnel:	CHRIS ARIDAS	gtr	A
	MICHAEL BENVENGA	bs, vcls	A
	MIKE BRAND	gtr	A
	PETER CRIS	drms, vcls	A
	PETER SHEPLEY	vcls	A
	(JOHN CALE	viola	A)

ALBUM:	1(A)	CHELSEA	(Decca DL 75262) 1970 R1

Produced by Lewis Merenstein, a group mainly notable for featuring Pete Cris(s) without make-up (he would later become the drummer of Kiss). Their album contains some good psych-rock tracks and John Cale (**Velvet Underground**) is credited on some of the cuts.

Their song *Hard Rock* was compiled in 1971 on *The MCA Sound Conspiracy* (MCA 734837). (SR/CF/NK)

Chelsea Beige

Personnel:	CHRIS EFTHIMIAN	drms	A
	STAFFORD L.JAMES III	drms	A
	KENNETH LEHMAN	alto sax, clarinet	A
	JOHN SCARZELLO	trumpet, fluegel horn	A
	BILLY SCHWARTZ	ld gtr	A
	ALLAN SPRINGFIELD	vcls	A

ALBUM:	1(A)	MAMA MAMA LET YOUR SWEET BIRD SING	
			(Epic Records E-30413) 1971 -

NB: (1) also released in Holland, (BN 26296).

Springfield, Efthimian, Lehman and Scarzello were previously in **The Last Ritual**. Produced by John McClure, their only album as **Chelsea Beige** is better than its predecessor but still contains (too) many horn arrangements. (SR)

Chentelles

45:	Be My Queen/Time	(Fenton 2132) 1967

This was the work of five 13 and 14 year olds from a West Michigan high school. Originally they had a girl drummer too. *Be My Queen*, a good uptempo teenbeat rocker, can be heard on *Back From The Grave, Vol. 3* (LP). The group lasted until 1968 when its members headed off to various colleges. (VJ)

Cherokee

Personnel:	DAVID DONALDSON	gtr, hrmnca	A
	GEORGE DONALDSON	gtr	A
	ROBERT DONALDSON	keyb'ds, vcls	A

ALBUM:	1	CHEROKEE	(ABC ABCS 719) 1971 -

45:	Rosianna / All The Way Home	(ABC Paramount 11295) 1970
	All The Way Home/	
	Girl, I've Got News For You	(ABC 11304) 1971

This was a later version of **The Robbs** (from Milwaukee, Wisconsin). The flip side to the 45 is a rather ordinary pop song and can be heard on *Nuggets Vol. 5* (LP).

Their album, which was recorded with the help of Chris Hillman, Gib Guilbeau and Sneaky Pete Kleinow, is of minor interest, mainly for country rock fans. (VJ/MW/SR)

The Cherokee

| 45: | I Can't Reach You/ | |
| | Willie And The Hand Jive | (Ranwood R-808) 1968 |

This 45 contains quite cool harmony covers of The Who's *I Can't Reach You* and Johnny Otis' *Willie And The Hand Jive*. One of the few rock groups to be released on this label, information on the band has so far proved illusive. (BM)

Cherry People

Personnel incl:	DAVID ALVES	drms	A
	CHRIS GRIMES	gtr	AB
	DOUG GRIMES	ld vcls	AB
	PICK KELLY	bs	A
	EDWIN "PUNKY" MEADOWS	ld gtr, vcls	AB
	ROCY ISAAC	drms	B
	JAN ZUKOWSKI	bs	B

| ALBUM: | 1(B) | CHERRY PEOPLE | (Heritage 35000) 1968 - |

NB: (1) reissued on CD.

45s:	α	And Suddenly / Imagination	(Heritage HE 801) 1968
		Gotta Get Back /	
		I'm The One Who Loves You	(Heritage HE-807) 1968
		Feelings / Mr.Hyde	(Heritage HE-810) 1969
		Light Of Love / On To Something New	(Heritage HE-815) 1969
	β	Light Of Love/same (mono)	(Heritage HE 815) c1968
		The Sea And Me / Come On Over	(Hot Corn # Unkn) 197?

NB: α some copies with picture sleeve. β is a double sided promo.

The Cherry People were a popular mellow pop group that some dealers try to describe as psychedelic. They're definitely not, on record anyway, but are remembered as one of the most commercially successful D.C. area bands of the late sixties.

The core of the band was the Grimes brothers and Meadows, who formed the Intruders in 1964 in Washington, D.C.. A year later they moved to Arlington, Virginia and became **The English Setters**, under which name they released three 45s. Come the Summer of '67 they changed their name again, to **The Cherry People**, after a trip to New York where they landed a new manager Ron Haffkine and a deal on the Heritage label.

Throughout their long history numerous other D.C. musicians came and went as their rhythm section. Prior to the LP, Alves and Kelly left. The Grimes-Meadows triumvirate was joined by drummer Rocky Isaac (formerly with The Tejuns, **The Creatures** and **The Fallen Angels**) and bassist Jan Zukowski (**Nobody's Children**).

The debut 45 covered the 'B' side of a 1967 **Left Banke** 45 - *And Suddenly*, co-written by Michael Brown and **Bert Sommer**. This can be found on the *Colossus Gold* album, a catalogue sampler released in 1970 on this short-lived label.

Their second single was produced by Ron Haffkine and Barry Oslander.

The band split in 1972 and Punky Meadows went off to form **Angel**. The Grimes brothers reformed **The Cherry People** soon after but folded again finally in 1975.

YA GOTTA HAVE... MOXIE Vol. 1 (Comp CD) including Cherry Slush.

Above are the generally-known facts but they barely scratch the surface or even give the correct impression. The band's full history is far more complex and throws their recorded output into a totally different light, thanks to label/management shenanigans. For example, the band apparently sounded nothing like their album (on which they played on just one track). To get the full low-down, check out Mark Opsasnick's 1996 book Capitol Rock (ISBN 0-9655017-0-1). (SR/MMs/MW)

Cherry Slush

Personnel:	BRIAN BENNET	keyb'ds, vcls	A
	GENE BRUCE	ld gtr	A
	MARK BURDICK	gtr, vcls	A
	DICK COUGHLIN	drms, vcls	A
	ART HAUFFEE	bs	A
	DAN PARSONS	ld vcls	A

HCP

45s:	I Cannot Stop You/	
	Don't Walk Away	(Coconut Groove 2032) 1968 -
	I Cannot Stop You/Don't Walk Away	(USA 895) 1968 119
	Day Don't Come/Gotta Take It Easy	(USA 904) 1968 -

This group was most significant for the involvement of **Dick Wagner** (a central figure in the active Michigan rock scene, who led groups like **The Bossmen** and **The Frost**). Although he wasn't a member of **Cherry Slush**, he was a close friend and helped out as a studio musician, writer, producer and arranger. Their finest moment *I Cannot Stop You* contains some good guitar hooks from **Wagner** along with some crystal clear harmonies, but over-all it's not that memorable.

The two releases of *I Cannot Stop You* feature different mixes with horns more prominent on the U.S.A. release. Dick Coughlin:- "We recorded it at Audio Sound Studios in Cleveland, Ohio and the horns were played by Dr. Don Sheets, who played four different parts. He is now a local Veteranarian."

Three 'previously unreleased' tracks on *Thee Unheard Of* compilation are by a different act entirely and include, a cover of The Beatles' *Birthday*, *Feel A Whole Lot Better* and the weaker *See Suzie Run*.

Amazingly **The Cherry Slush** are still gigging today and will shortly be releasing a CD *The Cherry Slush Looking Back*, which features all four of their sixties 45 tracks.

Compilation appearances include: *I Cannot Stop You* on *Mindrocker, Vol. 2* (LP), *The Seventh Son* (LP), *Boulders, Vol. 5* (LP), *Gone, Vol. 1* (LP) and *Ya Gotta Have Moxie, Vol. 1* (Dble CD); whilst *Don't Walk Away* is on *Love Is A Sad Song, Vol. 1* (LP). (VJ/DC)

The Chesapeake Juke Box Band

ALBUM: 1 THE CHESAPEAKE JUKE BOX BAND
(Green Bottle Records GBS 1004) 1972 -

Housed in a gimmick cover, an album with female vocals mixing commercial rock with odd tracks. (SR)

Chesmann Square

Personnel:	GARY HODGDEN		AB
	RON HOGDEN		AB
	STEVE HODGDEN		AB
	DAVE HUFFINES		A
	JIM McALLISTER		B

| 45: | Circles (Instant Party)/Try | (Lion 1002) 1969 |

These Beatles-imitators had a large local following around their home town of Kansas City, Missouri. They were originally known as The Chesmann and their sole 45 came in a picture sleeve. Their cover of Pete Townsend's *Circles* has resurfaced on the cassette compilation, *Monsters Of The Midwest, Vol. 1* and the *High All The Time, Vol. 2* (LP).

The group started in 1964 and eventually called it quits around 1973. Both Gary Hodgden and Jim McAllister later turned up in Michael Browne's post-Stories venture, the Beckies, alongside Scott Trusty. Thereafter Gary and Ron have been involved in heavy metal outfits, whilst Jim retired to studio work. (VJ)

The Chessmen

Personnel:	DOYLE BRAMHILL	drms, vcls	A
	TOMMY CARTER	bs	A
	BILLY ETHERIDGE		A
	JOHNNY PEEBLES	ld gtr, vcls	A
	SAMMY PIAZZA	drms	A
	ROBERT PATTON	ld gtr	A
	JIMMY VAUGHN	ld gtr	A

45s:	Save The Last Dance For Me/	
	Dreams And Wishes	(Bismarck 1010) 196?
	I Need You There/Sad	(Bismarck 1012) 1966
	You're Gonna Be Lonely/No More	(Bismarck 1014) 1966
	No More/	
	When You Lost Someone You Love	(Bismarck 1015) 1966

A popular mid-sixties Dallas band with a strong live reputation. They underwent frequent line-up changes but all of the above were members at some time. Although their original 45s are hard to come by many tracks have been retrospectively compiled. In particular, the 'A' side, to their second 45, *I Need You There* is a killer punk masterpiece, backed by a folk-rocker.

This outfit harboured quite a lot of talent and unsurprisingly many of them were involved in other projects later. Doyle Bramhill played with Stevie Ray Vaughn and Double Trouble, Bill Etheridge briefly replaced Larnier Greig in ZZ Top before being edged out by Dusty Hill, Sammy Piazza went on to Day Creek Road and later still to **Hot Tuna** and Jimmy Vaughn was in the Fabulous Thunderbirds.

Compilation appearances have included: *I Need You There* and *Sad* on *Texas Punk Groups From The Sixties* (LP) and *Sixties Archive, Vol. 2* (CD); *I Need You There* on *Flashback, Vol. 6* (LP), *Texas Music, Vol. 3* (CD) and *Teenage Shutdown, Vol. 10* (LP & CD); *No More* on *Highs In The Mid-Sixties, Vol. 13* (LP); *No More* and *You're Gonna Be Lonely, Texas Punk, Vol. 6* (LP) and *Acid Visions - Complete Collection, Vol. 3* (CD). (VJ)

The Chevelle V

Personnel:	JACK CHISHOLM	vcls, ld gtr	A
	TOMMY NIXON	bs	A
	TOMMY SWINDLE	organ	A
	CHARLIE TAYLOR	drms	A
	BOBBY VANNOY	gtr	A

45s:	I'm Sorry Girl/Come Back Bird	(UMI 100) 1966
	Come Back Bird/Koko Joe	(Askel 45-7) 1966
	Dangling Little Friends/	
	Stone and Steel Man (PS)	(Titan 1737) 1967

Hailing from Abilene, a sizeable town in Western Texas, this garage punk outfit has received good compilation coverage. In particular, *Come Back Bird* is a pretty fine effort, but *Dangling Little Friends* is a real gem, with a hypnotic beat and scathing lyrics.

The Titan 45 was recorded in Hollywood after the band won the 'Vox Starfinder' Battle Of The Bands in 1966.

Compilation appearances have included: *Come Back Bird* on *The Cicadelic 60's, Vol. 2* (CD), *Flashback, Vol. 2* (LP), *Texas Flashbacks, Vol. 2* (LP) and *Gone, Vol. 2* (LP); *Come Back Bird* and *I'm Sorry Girl* on *Texas Punk: 1966, Vol. 1* (LP) and *Green Crystal Ties Vol. 3* (CD); *Come Back Bird*, *I'm Sorry Girl* and *Koko Joe* on *Acid Visions - Complete Collection, Vol. 2* (CD); *Koko Joe* on *Texas Punk, Vol. 3* (LP); *Dangling Little Friends* and *Stone And Steel Man* on *Bad Vibrations, Vol. 2* (LP); *Dangling Little Friends* on *Scarey Business* (CD). (VJ)

The Chevelles

| 45: | Chevelle Stomp/Dear Sue | (Bangar Records 616) 1964 |

The "A" side of this 45 is a cool rock instrumental with good guitar licks, greasy sax, and piano. The "B" side is a ballad. In 1965 they merged with the VanDels and evolved into **Dee Jay and The Runaways**. You can also find both sides of the 45, along with *Blue Chevelle* and *Mala Boo* on the **Dee Jay and The Runaways** Arf Arf! CD *Peter Rabbit*. (SR)

The Chevrons

| Personnel incl: | MIKE NUCCIO | | A |

45s:	Love, I Love You/Dreams	(MMC 016) 1968
	Love, I Love You/Dreams	(Independence 88) 1968
	Mine Forever More/	
	In The Depth Of My Soul	(Independence 94) 1969

This outfit hailed from Omaha in Eastern Nebraska. Their final 45, *Mine Forever More* is a boy-band harmony-popper. The group evolved into a local rock band, Pilot, in the early 1970's.

Compilation appearances have included: *Dreams* and *Mine Forever More* on *Monsters Of The Midwest, Vol. 1* (Cass) and *Mine Forever More* on *Bring Flowers To U.S.* (LP). (MW)

BRING FLOWERS TO U.S. (Comp LP) including The Chevrons.

CHILD - Child CD.

Chevrons (V)

45s:	Hey Little Teaser/What Everyone Wants	(Fenton 2092) 196?
	I Lost You Today/Niat Pac Lavram	(Nook 2010) 1966

From Grand Rapids, Michigan. There's a strong rockabilly influence in the guitar work on *I Lost You Today*, which was released under the **Chevrons V** moniker. The 'B' side to this 45 featured the same song recorded backwards.

Compilation appearances have so far included: *Hey Little Teaser* and *What Everyone Wants* on *Best Of Michigan Rock Groups, Vol. 2*; *Hey Little Teaser* on *Michigan Mayhem, Vol. 1* (CD), *Michigan Mixture, Vol. 2* (LP) and *Teenage Shutdown, Vol. 8* (LP & CD) and *Niat Pac Lavram* on *Teenage Shutdown, Vol. 11* (LP & CD). (MW/KBn)

Chicago Loop

Personnel:	MIKE BLOOMFIELD	gtr	A
	BARRY GOLDBERG	organ, piano	AB
	JUDY NOVY	vcls, perc	AB
	CARMINE RIALE	bs	AB
	JOHN SIOMOS	drms	AB
	BOB SLAWSON	vcls, gtr	ABC
	JOHN SAVANNO	gtr	B
	P.J. BAILEY	drms	C
	JACKIE DANA	gtr, vcls	C
	STEPHEN WASSERMAN	bs	C

HCP

45s:	(When She Wants Good Lovin') My Baby Comes To Me/ This Must Be The Place	(Dynovoice 226) 1966 37
	Richard Corey/Cloudy	(Dynovoice 230) 1967 -
	Can't Find The Words/Saved	(Mercury 72755) 1967 -
	Technicolor Thursday/ Beginning At The End	(Mercury 72802) 1968 -

NB: (1) first pressing on a blue label with silver print. Later pressings had the same design, but were multi-coloured. In Canada (1) was released on the Bell label, with writers credits for *(When She Wants Good Lovin') My Baby Comes To Me* as J. Novy - B. Slawson - C. Riale - J. Siomos, whereas on all the Dynovoice issues the credit is Lieber - Stoller!

Originally known as Time, this band were formed by **Barry Golberg** and cut a six-track demo in 1966, on which **Mike Bloomfield** appears to have helped out. Apart from **Golberg**, Judy Novy had previously recorded an album with her older brother as Len & Judy. Bob Slawson had been in a couple of folk bands, like the Almanac Singers.

The first two 45s were produced by Bob Crewe and Al Kasha on Crewe's label and the first hit the Billboard charts at No. 37.

Barry Golberg was soon recruited by **Mike Bloomfield** for Electric Flag, but Bob Slawson put together a new **Chicago Loop** and signed a new deal with Mercury.

The band also did a *Macleans Commerial* released on the *Macleans Is What's Happening* album (Macleans MR-6555) 1966. This features tracks by Jeannie Brittan, Tommy Roe, Peter and Gordon, The Four Coins, **Mitch Ryder and The Detroit Wheels**, Marilyn Maye, The Tokens and Stan Getz/Astrud Gilberto. They are all doing a 30-second song about the wonder of Macleans toothpaste. It sounds like **Mike Bloomfield** is playing the guitar on the '**Loop**'s version of the commercial.

The Mercury 45s are brash uptempo popsters. The final effort is good pop - with - fuzz backed by a strange unsettling number with spiralling fuzz that gives it a psychy feel and a somewhat off-the-wall ending. Their first Mercury 45 is nowhere near as good.

John Siomos and Carmine Riale also played with **Mitch Ryder**. (MW/SPr/JLh/SR/RAd)

Chicago Transit Authority

Personnel:	PETER CETERA	bs, lead vcls	A
	TERRY KATH	gtr, lead vcls	A
	ROBERT LAMM	ld vcls, keyb'ds	A
	LEE LOUGHNANE	trumpet	A
	JAMES PANKOW	trombone	A
	WALTER PARAZAIDER	woodwind	A
	DANIEL SERAPHINE	drms	A

HCP

ALBUM:	1(A)	CHICAGO TRANSIT AUTHORITY	(Columbia PG 8) 1969 171 -

NB: (1) also issued in France, U.K., Germany, Holland etc and reissued on CD (Rhino/Atlantic R2 76171) 2002.

Produced and conceived by James William Guercio, a Chicago producer already responsible for **The Buckinghams**' success, **Chicago Transit Authority** were one of the first "big rock bands with horns". Their first album is really interesting, notably for *Free Form Guitar*: seven-minutes of **Hendrix**-like improvisation on guitar and *Liberation*: 15 minutes recorded live and full of great guitar mayhem courtesy of Terry Kath. *Prologue* was recorded at the famous Democratic Convention of Chicago in August 1968, during the confrontation between black militants and the police. There's also a cover of Steve Winwood's *I'm A Man*. Unfortunately, after this good debut, the group became known as Chicago and that's a totally different story, really out of the scope of this book!

Terry Kath, their talented guitarist, killed himself while playing Russian Roulette in 1977. Pete Cetera had earlier played with **The Exceptions**. (SR)

Child

Personnel:	CHICK	bs	A
	JOEY	organ, piano, chimes	A
	PAUL	ld vcls, gtr, hmnca	A
	TEDDY	ld vcls	A
	TOMMY	drms, perc	A

ALBUM:	1(A)	CHILD	(Jubilee JGS 8029) 1969 -

NB: (1) has been reissued on CD.

45:	You'll Never Walk Alone/?	(Jubilee 5673) 1969

This short-lived outfit specialised in melodramatic cover versions of popular songs of the day. The album, which was recorded at Select Sound Studios, in New York, includes slowed down versions of classics like *Hold On I'm Comin*, *You'll Never Walk Alone*, *Old Man River* and the instrumental *Exodus*. All come with lots of very heavy organ in the same mould as **Vanilla Fudge**. Certainly worth a spin. (VJ)

Childe Harold

| 45: | Brink Of Death/Anne With Love (PS) | (Limelight L-3084) 1968 |

An interesting sole waxing by this five-piece, presumably from the New York area. Produced by electronics wizard Walter (aka Wendy Carlos), the 'A' side was also written by **Bert Sommer** of **Left Banke** fame. *Brink Of Death* is a haunting lament with phasey vocals and lots of orchestration, as one would expect, plus doses of strange effects. Strangely enough the flip, though not penned by **Sommer**, sounds much more like the **Left Banke** - a kind of psychy baroque-pop.

Compilation appearances have included: *Brink Of Death* and *Anne With Love* on *Incredible Sound Show Stories, Vol. 8* (LP) and *Brink Of Death* on *A Heavy Dose Of Lyte Psych* (CD). (MW)

The Children

Personnel:	LOUIS CABAZA	keyb'ds, bs, vibes	ABC
	CHRIS HOLZHAUS	gtr	ABC
	STEPHEN PERRON	vcls	ABC
	ANDREW SZUCH Jnr	drms	A
	BENNY TRIEBER		A
	MIKE MARECHAL		B
	CASSELL WEBB	bs, vcls	C
	KENNY CORDAY		

ALBUM: 1(C) REBIRTH (Cinema 0001) 1968 R2

NB: Also released by Atco (SD-33-271) 1968 in a regular cover. The Cinema issue had a fold-out sleeve. Later issued on CD (Gear Fab GF 187) 2002.

HCP

45s:	Picture Me/Enough Of What I Need	(Laramie 666) 1967 -
	Maypole/I'll Be Your Sunshine	(Atco 6633) 1968 -
	Pills/Once More	(Cinema 025) 1970 -
	From The Very Start/Such A Fine Night	(Ode 66005) 1970 105
	Hand Of A Lady/Fire Ring	(Ode 66013) 1971 -

One of the more commercial acts to come from San Antonio, Texas in the 1960s, Perron, Cabaza, Szuch, Trieber and Holzhaus had all previously been with **The Mind's Eye**. It had been speculated that Bill Ash (ex-**The Stoics**) had been in **The Children** as a version of **The Stoics** *Enough Of What I Need* appeared on the flip of **The Children**'s first single. Chris Holzhaus has, however, told us that he played on all **The Children**'s recordings and that Bill Ash had only been an early member of **The Mind's Eye**.

Mike Marechal replaced Trieber after Trieber was killed in a drag boat accident at McQueeney Lake outside San Antonio Texas in 1968. Their second 45 was taken from their album - a collection of pleasant pop and psychedelia produced by Lelan Rodgers. There may also have been a test pressing for an LP on Ode.

Cassell Webb was later in **Saddlesore** and went on to production work and a solo career. She is now based in the UK. Perron also enjoyed a brief solo career but sadly committed suicide, whilst Holzhaus went on to **Eastwood Review**.

There's also a CD with **Thursdays Children** entitled *Stoned Sixties*. It was released on Collectables (COL-CD-0600). The Gear Fab reissue CD features 16 non-album bonus tracks from **The Children** and associated bands such as **The Argyles**, **Mind's Eye** and **Stoics**. This is highly recommended.

Compilation appearances include: *Francene* on *'69 Love-In* (CD); and *Enough Of What I Need* on *Highs In The Mid-Sixties, Vol. 23* (LP) and *Acid Visions - The Complete Collection Vol. 1* (3-CD).

The Children's cover of Ian Whitcomb's *This Sporting Life* on *Boulders, Vol. 5* and *Ya Gotta Have Moxie, Vol. 1* (Dble CD) is by a different L.A. band. (VJ/MW)

The Children of Darkness

| 45: | She's Mine/Sugar Shack A-Go-Go | (Royce 5140) 1966 |

Allegedly from 'Oblong' in Southern Illinois, this was their sole vinyl venture. The 'A' side, is a typical garage punker with great organ about an independent-minded girl whose really cool. The flip, is a sing-along party track, with brilliantly numbskull lyrics.

There's some dispute over the bands origins. Oblong is indeed located in East Illinois, due West of Robinson in Crawford County, (which borders Indiana just North of Vincennes), but its also said that the band claimed to come from here as a joke that was meant to go along with the name **The Children of Darkness** being a reference to a Casket / Coffin...

Compilation appearances include: *She's Mine* on *Back From The Grave, Vol. 2* (LP) and *Garage Kings* (Dble LP) and *Sugar Shack A Go Go* on *Pebbles Vol. 7* (CD) and *Hipsville, Vol. 2* (LP). (VJ/MW/KBn)

Children of One

Personnel:	LES GRINAGE	cello, dilruba	A
	KONRAD KAUFMAN	drms, perc	A
	BALA KRISHNA	sitar	A
	LAKSHMI	tanpura	A
	LEONARD LONERGAN	soprano sax	A
	MARCELLA MALMOLI	vcls	A
	LUCAS MASON	flute, piano	A
	PAULA MASON	vcls	A
	IRIN POELLIOT	vcls	A
	PETER SOKOLOW	bs clarinet	A
	VERA SOKOLOW	vcls	A

ALBUM: 1 CHILDREN OF ONE (Real R-101) 1970 R1

A New York band whose album of Eastern-based improvisational music features wordless female vocals. (CF)

Children Of Stone

Personnel:	DAVE CARRUTHERS	ld gtr	A
	FRANCES GORRE	vcls	A
	ERV NAGY	bs	A
	RAY NAKAMOTO	vcls, gtr	A
	TIM STOVER	organ	A
	RICK TAYLOR	drms	A

| 45: | He Is Mine/Mary, Can't You See | (Love 146/7) 1967 |

Teen folk-rock from North Highlands, California. The minor-key gem *Mary, Can't You See* can also be found on *The Sound Of Young Sacramento* (CD). (MW)

Children of The Mushroom

Personnel:	DENNIS CHRISTENSEN	drms	A
	JERRY McMILLAN	vcls, gtr, flte	A
	AL PISCIOTTA	bs	A
	JIM ROLFE	ld gtr	A
	?? ??	keyb'ds	A

| 45: | You Can't Erase A Mirror/August Mademoiselle | (Soho 101) 1968 |

This outfit came from Thousand Oaks, California with one awesome 45. The 'A' side being a psychedelic ballad, whilst the flip is also an enchanting psychedelic folk-rock track. Unsurprisingly the 45 commands a very high price tag, and has been heavily compiled.

They started off doing **Doors** type material, then turned into sort of an **Iron Butterfly** "clone". In fact, the lead singer, Jerry McMillan, was rumored to have auditioned with **Iron Butterfly**, and possibly even sang on their first album, *Heavy* (check the credits on the album - the vocals for one song are listed as "Darryl with Jerry" - could it be?). By late 1970, Jerry was also playing flute, and their material had progressed into a sort of psychedelic version of Jethro Tull.

Compilation appearances have so far included: *You Can't Erase A Mirror* on *The Magic Cube* (Flexi & CD); *August Mademoiselle* on *Pebbles, Vol. 9* (CD) and *Filling The Gap* (4-LP); *You Can't Erase A Mirror* and *August Madmoiselle* on *Psychedelic Unknowns, Vol. 11* (LP), *Slowly Growing Insane* (CD) and *The Human Expression And Other Psychedelic Groups - Your Mind Works In Reverse* (CD). (MW/BEn/VJ)

Children of The Night

45:   World Of Tears/Don't Cry Little Girl   (Bella 45-101) 1967

From Old Saybrook, Connecticut. You'll find *World Of Tears* on the *Psychedelic Disaster Whirl* (LP), which shows that the band only had rather crude recording techniques. (VJ)

The Chimes

45:   #38/Foolish Pride   (Matrix S 777) 1968

Dothan, Alabama's answer to **Dave Diamond and The Higher Elevation**. Composer Douglas Huber was a local DJ who came up with some weird alliterative lyrics, spoken **Bob Markley**-ilke, over music composed by **The Chimes**. OK, it's not quite 'out there' with **Dave Diamond**'s classic *Diamond Mine* but *#38* is quite weird'n'wonderful, with flange and tremolo effects and great harmonica.

It awaits your pleasure on *The Essential Pebbles Collection, Vol. 2* (Dble CD) and *Psychedelic Crown Jewels Vol. 3* (CD). (MW/MM)

Chin

See **King Harvest** entry.

Chips & Co

45s: Let The Winds Blow/Marbletown   (MS 191) 1965
      Every Night/You're You   (ABC Paramount 10749) 1965
      Walk Tall/Ace Of Spades   (ABC Paramount 10769) 1966

These are the work of a Connecticut band. *Let The Winds Blow* has a driving beat, reverberating guitar and typically tough-sounding punk vocals. You'll find it on *The Midwest Vs. The Rest* (LP) and *Tougher Than Stains* (LP). (VJ)

Chirco

Personnel: S.H. FOOTE   keyb'ds   A
            JOHN NAYLOR   gtr   A
            TED MACKENZIE   drms   A
            ANVIL ROTH   vcls   A
            BRUCE TAYLOR   bs   A

ALBUM: 1(A) THE VISITATION   (Crested Butte CB 701) 1972 R1

NB: (1) reissued on CD (Gear Fab GF-130) 1999 and vinyl (Akarma AK 071). Both reissues appear to have a mastering error that sounds like a skip at the beginning of *Dear Friends*.

45:   Mr. Sunshine / Golden Image (PS)   (Crested Butte 1200) 1972

Previously known as Sassafrass, this progressive rock outfit came from Westchester County, NY, although they also spent some time recording in New England. There's a lot of fuzz and vibes on their fine album, which Barry Tashian of **The Remains** helped the band record. Every track's a winner in what is for the most part a stunning blend of guitar and keyboards. The finest moment is probably the final track *Child of Peace* and there's also a cover of Barry Tashian's *Mister Sunshine*.

The album was originally issued on a local Colorado label, although the band were apparently never based there - a very curious marketing strategy!

Compilation appearances have included *33 Years* on Gear Fab's *Psychedelic Sampler* (CD). (VJ/MW/MSk/CF/NK)

CHIRCO - The Visitation LP.

The Chob

Personnel: KEITH BRADSHAW   bs   A
            ROBBIE CRNICH   keyb'ds   A
            DAVE ELLEDGE   drms   A
            DICK HANSON   vcls, gtr A
            QUINTON MILLER   ld gtr   A

45s: We're Pretty Quick/
      Ain't Gonna Eat Out My Heart Anymore (Lavette LA 5016) 1966
      I'm Not Your Steppin' Stone/Why Am I Alone?   (QQ 724) 196?

Arguably their first 45 was one of the best 45s to come out of New Mexico in the mid-sixties. They came from the Albuquerque and were also responsible for *Why Am I Alone?* credited to Choab (a euphemism for pimple!).

Compilation appearances have so far included: *We're Pretty Quick* on *Mayhem & Psychosis, Vol. 1* (LP), *Mayhem & Psychosis, Vol. 1* (CD), *The Chosen Few, Vol. 1* (LP), *Chosen Few, Vol's 1 & 2* (CD), *Songs We Taught The Fuzztones* (Dble LP & Dble CD) and *Teenage Shutdown, Vol. 4* (LP & CD); *We're Pretty Quick* and *Ain't Gonna Eat Out My Heart Anymore* on *New Mexico Punk From The Sixties* (LP) *Sixties Archive, Vol. 4* (CD); and *Why Am I Alone?* on *Punk Classics, Vol. 1* (7" EP), *Punk Classics* (CD) and *Teenage Shutdown, Vol. 3* (LP & CD). (VJ)

The Chocolate Balloon Company

45:   Gotta Get This/
      Little Girl I Love You So   (Choc-Balloon CB-1) 196?

A self-pressed effort, *Gotta Get This* can be heard on *Boulders, Vol. 5* (LP) and *Ya Gotta Have Moxie, Vol. 1* (Dble CD). (VJ)

The Chocolate Light Bulbs

45:   I'll Forgive You Girl/Poor Little Girl   (Lennan 1263) 196?

A little known garage band from California. The 'A' side has resurfaced on *Sixties Rebellion, Vol. 9* (LP & CD). (VJ)

The Chocolate Moose

45s: Take A Ride/The Chocolate Moose Theme (Spotlight 1012) 1966
      Rosie/Half-Peeled Banana   (Spotlight 1015) 1966

This punk outfit came from Dallas, Texas. (VJ)

Compilation appearances include: *Chocolate Mouse Theme* on *Mayhem & Psychosis, Vol. 2* (LP), *Mayhem & Psychosis, Vol. 1* (CD), *Boulders, Vol. 1* (LP) and *Ya Gotta Have Moxie, Vol. 1* (Dble CD); and *Take A Ride* on *Boulders, Vol. 2* (LP). (VJ)

The Chocolate Paintbox

CD: 1 IT CAME TO ME IN A DREAM
(Collectables COL-CD-0597) 1995

An early seventies rock band from Texas. The above CD has 10 tracks. Little is known or revealed on the CD liner notes. Sadly a lot of the music is also pretty anonymous and uninspiring, despite the liner description of 'acid trips' and 'psychedelia' - mellow folk/blues- rock it certainly is.

All the songs were written by R. Hillburn and D. Michael Franklin. (MW/NK)

The Chocolate Pickles

45: Hey You/? (Darn-L 451-5-10A) 1967

An obscure recording on a little known Michigan label. You'll find *Hey You*, with its fuzz and derogatory vocal style on *Highs In The Mid-Sixties, Vol. 6* (LP). (VJ)

Chocolate Telephone Pole

45: Let's Tranquilize With Color /
One By One (Jack O'Diamonds J.O.D. 1011) 1967

Such a trippy group name and 'A' side title, it may sound like it's gotta be wonderful psych but, too often, it's exploito psych or tame MOR flower-pop put out by a producer with studio musicians, eager to catch the latest trend; such is the case here.

Alex Zanetis, owner of a small Nashville label, harvested some studio musicians and issued this flowery-pop offering in late 1967. Should appeal to fans of **The Love Generation**, Fifth Dimension and **Free Design** but there's something missing - the lull in the middle is obviously where a guitar or keyboard solo was to be inserted!

This curio can be heard on *Psychedelic Crown Jewels, Vol. 3* (CD). (MW/RM)

Chocolate Tunnel

45s: Highly Successful Young Rupert White/
Ostrich People (In-Sound 403) 1967
Highly Successful Young Rupert White/
Ostrich People (Era 3185) 1967

Possibly an L.A.-based outfit. *Ostrich People* has resurfaced on the *All Cops In Delerium - Good Roots* (LP) compilation. (VJ)

Chocolate Watchband

Personnel:			
PETE CURRY	drms	A	
JO KEMLING	organ	AB	
MARK LOOMIS	gtr	ABCDE	G
DANNY PHAY	vcls / gtr	AB	G H
NED TORNEY	ld gtr	AB	G
RICH YOUNG	bs	AB	
GARY ANDRIJASEVICH	drms	BCDE	G H
DAVE AGUILAR	vcls	CD	F
BILL FLORES	bs	CDEFG	H
SEAN TOLBY	gtr	CDEFG	H
TIM ABBOTT	gtr	E	
CHRIS FINDERS	vcls	E	
MARK WHITTAKER	drms	EF	
PHIL SCOMA	ld gtr		H

NB: Danny Phay vcls (AB), gtr (GH).

ALBUMS: 1(C) NO WAY OUT (Tower 5096) 1967 R2
(up to 2(D) THE INNER MYSTIQUE (Tower 5106) 1968 R2
1972) 3(E) ONE STEP BEYOND (Tower 5153) 1969 R2

NB: (1) reissued on CD (Sundazed SC 6023) 1994 with three bonus tracks: *In The Midnight Hour* (previously unreleased), *Psychedelic Trip* (previously unreleased) and *Milk Cow Blues*. (2) reissued on CD (Sundazed SC 6024) 1994 with the 45 version of *She Weaves A Tender Trap* as a bonus cut. (3) reissued on CD (Sundazed SC 6025) 1994 with two bonus tracks from the "Riot On Sunset Strip" soundtrack: *Don't Need Your Lovin'* and *Sitting There Standing*. (1) has also been reissued as *No Way Out..., Plus* (Big Beat/Ace CDWIKD 118) 1993, which includes eight bonus tracks (including 45 cuts like *She Weaves A Tender Trap* and *Sweet Young Thing*, an alternate take of *Misty Lane* and two tracks by line-up 'B' *Don't Let The Sun Catch You Crying* and *Since You Broke My Heart*). (1) and (2) have also been reissued on one CD by Eva (with inferior sound quality) and (1) and (2) have also been reissued on vinyl, with one additional track in the case of (1). There have also been a number of compilations, including *Forty Four* (Big Beat) 198? which includes all of the material, which the band actually played on; *The Best Of The Chocolate Watch Band* (Rhino) 198?; and *Are You Gonna Be There?* (Eva 12048) 198?.

EPs: 1 Sweet Young Thing/Come On/I'm Aware/Milk Cow Blues
(Eva 2004) 198?
2 SITTING THERE STANDING (Sundazed SEP 109) 1996

NB: (1) is a bootleg. (2) Contains *Sitting There Standing*, *'Till The End Of The Day*, *Sweet Young Thing* and *Are You Gonna Be There*. *'Till The End Of The Day* and *Are You Gonna Be There* are previously unreleased instrumental backing tracks.

45s: Sweet Young Thing/Baby Blue (Uptown 740) 1966
α Blues Theme/Loose Lip Sync Ship (HBR 511) 1966
Misty Lane/She Weaves A Tender Trap (Uptown 749) 1967
Are You Gonna Be There (At The Love In)/
No Way Out (Tower 373) 1967

NB: α as **The Hogs**. In the late eighties, the bootleg label Eva also issued a promo 45, *Let's Talk About Girls/In The Past* (EVA JBR 4) 198?

This San Jose band formed in the Summer of 1965 at Foothills College in Los Altos and were discovered late the following year by Ed Cobb. Their original line-up included Pete Curry on drums, who went on to become guitarist / songwriter with The Halibuts. His time in the band was severely limited however, and after their first gig was replaced by Gary Andrijasevich. Although nothing was released by the first couple of line-ups (*), they were reputedly on par with the "classic" **Chocolate Watchband**, with Dan Phay being a particularly charismatic front-man.

The band were also friends with another act called The Topsiders who for a short while included **Skip Spence**, prior to his joining **Jefferson Airplane**. In 1965, both bands underwent a number of changes, with Phay, Torney and Kemling all leaving to join The Topsiders (who then became **The Other Side**), whilst Sean Tolby, moved from The Topsiders to **The Chocolate Watchband**. Indeed Mark Loomis (ex-Shandels) also had a brief spell with **The Other Side** after Rich Young was drafted, before he decided to reform the '**Watchband** with Gary Andrijasevich and Jo Kemling. The latter opted to stay with **The Other Side** however, and bassist, Bill Flores (ex-Shandels) and, a vocalist, biology student Dave Aguilar, were

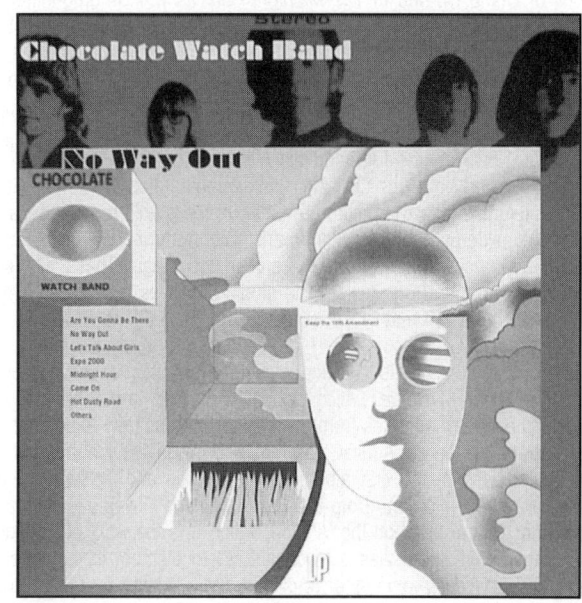

CHOCOLATE WATCHBAND - No Way Out LP.

CHOCOLATE WATCHBAND - Inner Mystique LP.

drafted in to complete **The Chocolate Watch Band**'s new line-up. Heavily influenced by British R&B outfits like The Stones and The Yardbirds, the band gigged regularly around the Bay Area supporting bands like **The Doors**, **Big Brother and The Holding Co.** and **The Mothers of Invention**.

They were signed to Tower and recorded a debut single in 1966. The 'A' side, written by Cobb, was a fine Stones' influenced number, but with an uniquely Californian interpretation. Inexplicably, Tower issued the single on its black R&B subsidiary label, Uptown, which did not, as a white group on this label, attract the airplay it deserved.

On Cobbs insistence, **The Chocolate Watch Band** returned to the studio to record a cover version of *Blues Theme*, originally performed by **Davie Allan and the Arrows**, on the soundtrack to *The Wild Angels*. However, Tower were not convinced of its commerciality, and Cobb leased the finished master to Hanna-Barbera records. It was released, under the pseudonym, **The Hogs**, as HBR 511, with *Loose Lip Sync Ship*, which culminates into a strange psychedelic piece of dementia, on the flip side. It was quite successful locally and **Davie Allan**'s version of *Blues Theme* became a Top 40 hit.

The 'A' side of their next single *Misty Lane* was more commercial and not as powerful as *Sweet Young Thing*. The flip was an uncharacteristically reflective, quieter number with a stringed and woodwind section.

1967 saw the band record two tracks *Don't Need Your Lovin'* and *Sitting Here Standing*, on the soundtrack to *Riot On Sunset Strip*. September 1967 saw the release of their debut album *No Way Out*. Essentially a collection of psychedelic punk, containing the impressive *Let's Talk About Girls*, punk versions of *Come On* and *In The Midnight Hour* as well as drug-influenced songs like *Expo 2000*, *The Dark Side Of The Mushroom*, *Gossamer Wings* and the title track. Many of the songs have an Eastern influence. It has later been revealed that the band did not play on the spacier tracks on this album, for which Cobb used session musicians. It is now known, too, that arranger Don Bennett and not Dave Aguilar sang the vocals on *Let's Talk About Girls*. However, the full band did play on *Are You Gonna Be There (At The Love In)/No Way Out* their next single lifted from the album. Aguilar's explanation for the mixed-up nature of the studio recordings is that the band considered themselves primarily live performers who "loved to challenge big-name groups and blow 'em off the stage. That's where we got our excitement and our kicks". The studio stuff was considered a mere sidelight which they left mainly in Cobb's hands.

The Eastern influence was developed further on their excellent second album, *The Inner Mystique*, which appeared in February 1968 and was actually comprised of outtakes from the first album plus new recordings that didn't feature the band. Aguilar, Loomis and Andrijasevich had all quit before the release of the first album leaving Flores and Tolby to fill their spaces with other musicians from the San Francisco Bay Blues Band. The band did not appear at all on the 'A' side, which was the work of Ed Cobb's session musicians. There was a mystical/Eastern element to instrumentals *Voyage Of The Trieste* and *Inner Mystique*, (both written by Cobb) and in their cover version of **We The People**'s *In The Past*. The band itself did play on Side Two, which included a remix of Dylan's *Baby Blue* taken from their first single, an excellent version of Ray Davies' *I'm Not Like Everybody Else* and **The Brogues**' *I Ain't No Miracle Worker*. Flores and Tolby also quit in late '67, prior to the album's release, although this was because of the problems in maintaining a stable line-up rather than any frustration with Cobb's influence over the bands recordings.

With no band to promote the release, a year passed before Ed Cobb persuaded some members to reform the band and have another go. Guitarist Danny Phay (from **The Other Side**) came back in as a replacement for Dave Aguilar, who decided not to get involved again. The band wrote all the material for the resultant *One Step Beyond* album, but aside from *I Don't Need No Doctor*, it's comparatively disappointing. They split again after this album was released in 1969 and an attempted reformation in 1970 lasted just one month.

Also of note was a short-lived act known as The Tingle Guild, who included Mark Lomis, Dan Phay, Gary Andrijasevich plus his cousin Chris Ramey. Original drummer, Pete Curry, also returned to the fold for a while, but presumably the band fizzled out...

Dave Aguilar was reported, in 1983, to be Professor of Astronomy at Colorado University and he then moved into doing research for the aerospace industry. Rich Young now gigs in the bay area with Jerry Miller of **Moby Grape** fame. Sean Tolby is now dead.

Later revelations that the band did not play on some of their album tracks perhaps diminish a little of their reputation, but they remain one of the most interesting West Coast bands and they made some fine music.

In 1999, the band reformed for a gig at the 3-day "66-99" event in San Diego on 12th June and later at the New York 'Cavestomp '99!' on Nov 5-7th alongside **The Standells**, **Monks** et al.

Compilation appearances has included: *Are You Gonna Be There (At The Love-In)?* on *Sundazed Sampler, Vol. 2* (CD), *Excerpts From Nuggets* (CD), *Nuggets, Vol. 2* (LP); *Are You Gonna Be There (At The Love-In)?* and *Sweet Young Thing* on *More Nuggets* (CD); *Are You Gonna Be There (At The Love-In)*, *Let's Talk About Girls*, *Sweet Young Thing* on *Nuggets Box* (4-CD); *Let's Talk About Girls* on *Nuggets - Original Artyfacts From The First Psychedelic Era 1965-1968* (Dble LP), *Nuggets* (CD); *Sweet Young Thing* on *Pebbles, Vol. 7* (LP), *Nuggets, Vol. 6* (LP); *No Way Out* on *Psychedelic Perceptions* (CD); *Don't Need Your Lovin'* and *Sitting There Standing* on *Riot On Sunset Strip* (LP); and *Don't Need Your Lovin'* on *Garage Music For Psych Heads*. (VJ/CKg/SR/AP/LP)

The Choir

Personnel:			
	JIM BONFANTI	drms, vcls, tamb	ABCDEFG
	WALLY BRYSON	ld gtr	ABC
	DAVE BURKE	bs	A
	DANN KLAWON	gtr, drms, hrmnca	A D F
	DAVE SMALLEY	vcls, gtr	ABCD
	JIM SKEEN	bs	BC
	KENNY MARGOLIS	keyb'ds	CDEFG
	JIM ANDERSON	ld gtr	D
	DENNY CARLETON	bs	E
	RANDY KLAWON	ld gtr	E
	PHIL GIALLOMBARDO	organ	EFG
	RICK COON	gtr	FG
	BOB McBRIDE	bs	G

ALBUM: 1(-) CHOIR PRACTICE (Sundazed LP 5009) 1993
NB: Contains *It's Cold Outside* and many previously unreleased tracks, also on CD (SC 11018) 1994, which contains 18 tracks.

EP: 1 THE CHOIR (Bomp (04-EP) 197?
HCP
45s: It's Cold Outside/I'm Going Home (Can Am 203) 1967 -
It's Cold Outside/I'm Going Home (Roulette R-4738) 1967 68
No One Here To Play With/
Don't You Feel A Little Sorry For Me (Roulette R-4760) 1967 -

	Changing My Mind/	
	When You Were With Me	(Roulette R-7005) 1967 -
	Gonna Have A Good Time Tonight/	
	So Much Love	(Intrepid 75020) 1969 -

Originally called **The Mods**, this band formed in Mentor (near Cleveland), Ohio in 1964, adopting that particular musical genre popular in Cleveland - U.K. mod-pop. The line-up revolved through many changes with members constantly coming and going. The nucleus was Wally Bryson, Jim Bonfauti and Dave Smalley (3/4 of the Raspberries). Jimmy Skeen was another member. When they recruited vocalist Eric Carmen from Cyrus Erie they became The Raspberries.

Their vinyl zenith was the classic *Its Cold Outside*, a melodic, Merseybeat-influenced pop song, which has subsequently been heavily compiled. The flip, was much more punkish.

The EP, released in the late seventies, features five unreleased tracks:- *Anyway I Can*, *Don't Change Your Mind*, *I'd Rather You Leave Me*, *Treeberry* and *I Only Did It Cause I Felt So Lonely*. The group split in 1970.

Upon **The Choir**'s demise Margolis moved immediately to Los Angeles, where he formed another ambitious group, Sanctuary, with Richard Tepp and eventually Rick Caon. Jim Bonfanti briefly considered leaving music but instead approached a post-Cyrus Erie/Quick Eric Carmen about forming a 'bar band'. Enthusiasm soon took over and the 'bar band' idea was shelved in favour of a totally English-inspired group, somewhat along the same lines as The Mods and Cyrus Erie. With the addition of Wally Bryson and a band mate of his from the group Fortega, John Alleksic, the new band settled for the name Raspberries and a reactionary (for 1970) British Invasion/Beach Boys' sound. In a bold move, they even adopted shorter, vintage Beatle-length haircuts and matching suits. By the Summer of 1972 (and with Dave Smalley added as Alleksic's replacement), The Raspberries were positioned at No. 5 nationally with the classic *Go All The Way*. Other hits followed. After three albums, Bonfanti and Smalley left the Raspberries over a long-running dispute with Carmen over image. Bryson and Carmen continued with The Raspberries for one more album, 1974's *Starting Over* (voted one of the best albums of the year by 'Rolling Stone'). Though the album yielded a sizeable hit in *Overnight Sensation* (Hit Record), the band soon ground to a halt. By 1976 Eric Carmen re-established himself as a top ten recording artist, though now in an ultra-commercial singer/songwriter mould. Bryson, who went on to record albums with Tattoo and Fotomaker in the late seventies currently plays in the Cleveland area band, Sittin' Ducks, with Dann Klawon and Kenny Margolis.

While not every ex-member of **The Choir** is still involved in music Denny Carleton currently enjoys an international cult following for the home studio pop creations he releases through his Green Light label. Randy Klawon keeps the spirit of The Mods and **The Choir** alive; he currently performs obscurities like The Pretty Things' *Come See Me* and Yardbirds' *Little Games* in a band called The Newcastle Quartet.

CHOCOLATE WATCHBAND - One Step Beyond LP.

THE CHOIR - Choir Practice CD.

Compilation appearances have included: *It's Cold Outside* on *Nuggets Box* (4-CD), *Pebbles Box* (5-CD), *Pebbles, Vol. 2* (LP), *Pebbles, Vol. 4 (ESD)* (CD), *Pride Of Cleveland Past* (LP), *Excerpts From Nuggets* (CD) and *Great Pebbles* (CD); *I'm Going Home* on *Highs In The Mid-Sixties, Vol. 9* (LP) and *Best of Pebbles, Vol. 2* (LP & CD); *I'm Going Home* and *It's Cold Outside* on *Pebbles, Vol. 2* (CD) and *Trash Box* (5-CD); *Don't You Feel A Little Sorry For Me*, *I'm Going Home*, *It's Cold Outside*, *No One Here To Play With*, *When You Were With Me* on *Psychedelic Microdots Of The Sixties, Vol. 3* (CD); and *Any Way I Can* on *Sundazed Sampler, Vol. 1* (CD).

It's Cold Outside was also later covered by The Chesterfield Kings. (VJ)

The Chosen Few

45s:	Synthetic Man/Lost Man Alive	(Liberty 55919) 1966
	Asian Chrome/Earth Above, Sky Below	(Liberty 55962) 1966/7

From Simi Valley, California. Rumours of a third 45: *I Know Your Name Girl/I Never Really Knew* (Liberty ?) 1966/7 are unsubstantiated.

Compilation appearances have included: *Asian Chrome* on *Boulders, Vol. 7* (LP) and *Ya Gotta Have Moxie, Vol. 1* (Dble CD); and *The Earth Above, The Sky Below* on *U-Spaces: Psychedelic Archaeology Vol. 1* (CDR). (VJ/MW)

The Chosen Few

Personnel:	MIKE DURE		A
	BOB SEGARINI	gtr, vcls	A
	VANN SLATTER		A

45s:	I Think It's Time/Nobody But Me	(Northbeach 1003) 1965
	I Think It's Time/Nobody But Me	(Autumn 17) 1965

A mid-sixties San Francisco-based outfit. Slatter and Dure both went on to **Family Tree** and Segarini played in several San Francisco/Californian bands including Ratz, Us, **Family Tree**, **Roxy** and **The Wackers**.

It's likely that Gary Wagner of **Parish Hall**, was connected to this outfit as he is credited as songwriter on their North Beach 45.

Compilation appearances have included: *I Think It's Time* and *Nobody But Me* on *Autumn Single Box*, *Dance With Me - The Autumn Teen Sound* (CD) and *Sound Of The Sixties: San Francisco Part 2* (LP); and *Nobody But Me* on *Mindrocker, Vol. 1* (LP). (VJ)

The Chosen Lot

Personnel incl:	ANTHONY BRAZIS		A
	RICK COGHILL	ld gtr	A

45: Time Was/If You Want To   (Sidra 9004) 1967

Both sides of this superb 45 are accomplished affairs composed by Tony Brazis. The band were previously known as **Tony and The Bandits** and hailed from Middleton, Ohio but moved to Oxford to attend college. *Time Was* is a hypnotic garagey power-popper with fuzz and Eastern influences that pushes all the right buttons. The flip is noteworthy too - a shimmering hook-laden fuzzy garage-ballad.

Rick Coghill also played with The Glass Wall.

Compilation appearances have included: *Time Was* on *Psychedelic Unknowns, Vol. 8* (LP & CD); and *Sixties Archive, Vol. 6* (CD). (MW/GGI/MM/KBn/MB)

The Chozen Ones

45: Cold Summer / How Many Times   (Frog 867-JFB-2) 1967

Believed to be from Long Island, NY, this combo's sole 45 is a decent two-sider, labelled 'soul rock' on the top side and 'folk rock' on the flip. Actually, *Cold Summer* is moody fuzz-pop - the soul flavour is in the forceful vocals and raucous yelps.

Compilation appearances have included: *Cold Summer* on *Sick And Tired* (LP); *How Many Times* on *From The New World* (LP); *Cold Summer*, *How Many Times*, *Marshmallow Cake* and *Scarlet's Not Here Yet* on *Frog Records Story, Vol. 1* (CD). (MW)

Chris and Craig

Personnel:	CHRIS DUCEY	A
	CRAIG SMITH	A

45: Isha/I Need You   (Capitol 5694) 1966

Produced by Steve Douglas, *Isha* is a noteworthy Indian/folk-rock amalgam containing something that sounds like a sitar and/or a harpsichord. Fast paced and an engaging pop song, it appears to have so far eluded compilers.

It appears that Craig Smith later recorded as **Maitreya Kali**, whose *Inca* album features some tracks written by Chris Ducey (aka **Chris Lucey**, aka **Bobby Jameson**, aka Robert Parker James). Curiously the liner notes indicate that some of the *Inca* material was recorded in 1965 by Capitol, begging the question - were **Chris and Craig** the same people as **Maitreya Kali** and **Chris Lucey**? (JMe)

Chris, Chris and Lee

ALBUM: 1 CHRIS, CHRIS AND LEE   (CC&L no#) c1968 -

A rare Christian psych-folk trio with a cover of **Tim Hardin**'s *If I Were A Carpenter* and original songs like *Flying Bird*, *Once* and *Wish You Were Here*. (SR)

Richard Christensen and Tartaglia

ALBUM: 1 MUVE   (Capitol) c1968 -

45: Fifty Six Seasons/Spires   (Capitol 1C006-80239) c1968

NB: German single with PS.

A weird poet reading/declaming his texts over a mix of soft-rock with orchestration, keyboards and some female chorus, but also with lots of heavy psych guitar on some tracks, like the weird *Spires*. If some tracks sound like Richard Harris, others may interest fans of the **Zodiac Cosmic Sounds** and similar projects.

Tartaglia also released records under his name. (SR)

Christmas Spirit

45: Christmas Is My Time Of Year/
    Will You Still Believe In Me   (White Whale 290) 1968

Christmas Spirit were in fact the **Turtles** singing two Christmas songs with Linda Ronstadt, then with the **Stone Poneys** . (SR/KG)

Christopher

Personnel:	RICHARD AVITTS	gtr	ABC
	DOUG TULL	drms	AB
	LEON RUDNICKI	bs	A
	DOUG WALDEN	vcls, bs, keyb'ds	BC
	TERENCE HAND	drms	C
	RON KRAMER	perc	C
	JOHN SIMPSON	drms	C

ALBUM: 1(B/C) CHRISTOPHER   (Metromedia MD 1024) 1970 R3

NB: (1) has also had a limited edition repressing on Amos and has been pirated on CD by Buy Or Die. Later released officially on CD (Gear Fab GF 108) 1997 and vinyl (Akarma AK 408).

This Texas outfit's psychedelic/progressive album has been increasingly attracting attention from collectors in recent years and has also had a limited repressing on vinyl and CD, including an official reissue by Gear Fab. It combines some fine fuzzy psychedelic guitar work on tracks like *Dark Road*, *In Your Time*, *Disaster* and *The Wind*, whilst *Magic Cycles* leans towards the progressive genre. Well worth tracking down.

They formed in 1968 in Houston, Texas and were originally known as United Gas. When they landed a contract with Metromedia, a name change was suggested to avoid confusion with **Pacific Gas and Electric**, although the band continued to perform as United Gas. The new name was inspired by St. Christopher and Avitts and Walden's material took on a spiritual flavour.

During the recording of the album, Doug Tull was having severe problems with drugs. He attempted suicide, was fired, and the album was completed using session musicians (line-up 'C'). Tull then formed **Josefus**; but he would eventually commit suicide.

Doug Walden was the brother of Snuffy Walden (of Stray Dog).

CHRISTOPHER - Christopher LP.

Compilation appearances have included *Queen Mary* on Gear Fab's *Psychedelic Sampler* (CD). (VJ/MW/RM/SR)

Christopher

Personnel:	GARY LUCAS	drms	A
	BILL McKEE	bs	A
	STEVE NAGLE	gtr	A
	FRANK SMOAK	ld gtr	A

ALBUM: 1(A) WHAT'CHA GONNA DO? (Chris-tee PRP 12411) 1970 R5

NB: (1) reissued on Rockadelic subsidiary (Animus Ochlus AOLP 102) 1990 and later on (Atlas 12 411 15) 1999. (1) also reissued officially on CD (Scenescof SCOFCD 1003) 1999.

This is another fine album by an entirely different band, from North Carolina. Only 100 copies were pressed originally making it an ultra-rarity, although the recent reissues on Rockadelic/Atlas will bring it to the attention of a wider audience. There's lots of good guitar work on this album, from the fuzz psych of *Holiday* (with its effective drumming) and *Modern Day Oracle* to the bluesy guitar on *Day Of Sunshine* and the title cut and the more melodic and mellow mood of *The Great Clock* and *Fugue*. Recommended. (VJ/MW)

Christopher and The Chaps

Personnel incl: MICHAEL BROWN (LOOKOFSKY)   A

45:	It's Alright Ma, I'm Only Bleeding / They Just Don't Care	(Fontana 1530) 1965

NB: also issued on (Philips 1 530) 1966.

A Bob Dylan cover is backed by a composition co-written by one M. Lookofsky, later to achieve acclaim as Michael Brown with **The Left Banke**, **Montage**, **Stories** and The Beckies.

Loofofsky had undergone classical musical training and his father, Harry, was a respected musician who owned a recording studio and gave his son much encouragement in his career as a producer and pianist. This debut effort was produced by Harry Lookofsky's World United Productions, but sank without a trace.

Check out *They Just Don't Care* on *From The New World* (LP). (MW/LP)

Christopher and The Souls

Personnel:	DEE EDWARDS	drms	A
	JAY HAUSMAN	gtr	AB
	ALLEN KIRSCH	vcls	ABC
	DAVE SMITH	ld gtr	ABC
	BRIAN VOSS	bs	A
	JERRY EBENSBERGER	bs	BC
	DAVID LOTT	drms	BC
	MURRAY SCHESINGER	gtr	C
	CHRISTOPHER VOSS	vcls	C

45:	Diamonds, Rats and Gum/ Broken Hearted Lady	(Pharaoh 151) 1966

The Souls were a McAllen, Texas band who gigged in the Texas Valley area with other area acts - including the Marauders and **Cavaliers**. In 1966 they were approached by Christopher Voss, who was the elder brother of their original bassist. Chris wanted to record two songs he'd written and they were duly waxed on the local Pharaoh label. The 45 features line-up 'C' but with Chris replacing vocalist Allen, hence the new moniker. Kudos and thanks to Andrew Brown for allowing us to fill in the details from his 'Brown Paper Sack #1' zine which divulges the histories of many Louisiana and Texas sixties bands.

Lyrically, the 'A' side was unusual with words like "I'll give you rats and five pieces of gum and then you'll know I'm not a bum!".

CHRISTOPHER - Whatcha Gonna Do? LP

Compilation appearances include: *Diamonds, Rats, And Gum* on *Texas Punk, Vol. 5* (LP) and *Acid Visions - Complete Collection, Vol. 2* (3-CD). (VJ/AB/MW)

Christopher Cloud

Personnel:	TOMME BOYCE	gtr, vcls	A
	BUGGS PEMBERTON	drms	A
	PATRICK O'CONNOR	bs	A
	MICHAEL OVERLY	lead gtr, vcls	A
	(BEN BENAY	hrmnca	A)
	(ALLAN LINDGREN	keyb'ds	A)

ALBUM: 1(A) BLOWIN' AWAY   (Chelsea BCL1-0234) 1973 -

A little known group formed by Tommy Boyce from **Boyce and Hart** in the early seventies. The cover art is rather intriguing, with a face lost in a cloud on the front sleeve and the band hidden in a thick smoke cloud on the back.

Recorded in Hollywood, most of their material was written by Boyce, who also produced the album, and Overly. The music is typical of the early seventies, with several tracks strongly influenced by the Rolling Stones (*Brand New Boogie At 10 A.M* is even dedicated to Jagger) plus some slower numbers.

The interest in this album mainly resides in the lyrics, with many name dropping phrases (about Mick Jagger, Rod Stewart, Lenny Bruce, Ralph Nader and Doris Day) and counterculture examples, especially in the long *Celebration* and in *Sandra, The Cat Lover* with:

"I'd probably want to go there
Just to smell the scent of fresh stoned air
People smokin' hash and rolling marijuana
Like it was legal
Just livin' every day,
Without a moment of waste to spare"

The album also contains two strange covers: Paul Simon's *Cecilia* (rather awful) and the old *Zip A Dee Doo Dah*.

After this album, Overly, O'Connor and Pemberton formed **Aim**. (SR)

Christopher Milk

Personnel:	THE KIDDO	bs	A
	JOHN MENDELSOHN	vcls, drms	A
	RALPH OSWALD	gtr	A
	MR. TWISTER	vcls	A
	G. WHIZZ	drms	A

ALBUM: 1(A) SOME PEOPLE WILL DRINK ANYTHING (Reprise MS-2111) 1972 -

EP: 1 CHRISTOPHER MILK (UA SP-66) 1971

45: I Want to Hold Your Hand/Speak Now Or Forever Hold Your Peace (Reprise REP-1164) 1972

A California group formed by a rock critic, **Christopher Milk** was a "comic rock" group. Their records included mostly parodies (*I Want To Hold Your Hand* sung by a Bob Dylan imitator...) and songs like *In Search of R. Crumb*, sometimes with good guitar parts. Their EP was available only by mail order. (SR)

Chrysalis

Personnel:	PAUL ALBUM	bs	A
	JAMES 'SPIDER' BARBOUR	gtr	A
	NANCY NAIRN	vcls	A
	JON SABIN	ld gtr	A
	DAHAUD SHAAR	perc	A

ALBUM: 1(A) DEFINITION (MGM E/SE-4547) 1968 -
NB: (1) reissued in 1993.

A New York band who recorded just one album. All the tracks were composed by group leader Barbour, who came originally from Canton, Ohio. Musically their album is soft, intricate psychedelia with a few more intense tracks also included. Most notable is *Dr. Roots Garden*, which has an early "Floydish" feel to it, whilst the album as a whole has a very strange sound that is exceptionally unique with beautiful clear female vocals.

It is thought that mono copies of the album were DJ only. Price guides tend to list these as worth less than stereo copies but in fact they are 20 times harder to locate!

Barbour had at least one of his later songs recorded by Martha Velez. Dahaud Elias Shaar went on to play drums with Van Morrison first appearing on his *His Band And The Street Choir* album. He is also the drummer on the live *It's Too Late To Stop Now* and *Veedon Fleece* releases. Paul Album also played with **Fear Itself**. (SR/EDMoulin/VJ/DMy)

Churchill

ALBUM: 1 CHURCHILL (Attarack AT-5003) 1970 -

45: Freedom's For The Birds / Better Not Wait 'Til Tomorrow (Attarack ATT 105) 1970

GONE Vol. 1 (Comp LP) including The Church Mice.

Co-produced by Ray Harris, Emory Gordy and Ed Cobb (**Standells**, **Zoo**), a rock trio with some blue-eyed soul influences. Most of their material was penned by **Spooner Oldham** and Cobb and as they also cover The Box Tops' *Cry Like A Baby*, they may have come from the Memphis area. Some tracks (*Doggone*) are decent but overall the result sounds rather uninspired.

The cover art is rather funny, with a dusty hand doing the peace sign. The band are of course totally unrelated to Israeli Churchills. (SR/MW)

The Churchill Administration

45: Summer / I Just Met You (Cha Cha Records C-779) c1969

A soft pop group, possibly from the Chicago area. (SR/HMa)

Churchill Downs

45: I Gotta Get Back To My Baby/ The Amazing Three (Amazing 3 SJQ-101) 1968

Obscure California outfit kick off with a catchy strummed pop-rocker then turn to heavier rock sounds, which is well worth repeated listens. Despite the intrusion of some brass (actually not too much of a distraction), there's some lowdown fuzz and distortions to be savoured. One to look out for. (MW)

The Churchkeys

45: To Angela/To Angela (Instr) (Big Sound Records 1002) 1967

From North Dakota, a horn rock/garage group with decent vocals. (SR)

The Church Mice

Personnel:	OZZIE	A
	ARMAND SCHAUBROECK	A
	BLAINE SCHAUBROECK	A
	BRUCE SCHAUBROECK	A

45: Babe We're Not Part Of Society/ College Psychology On Love (PS) (House Of Guitars L-43) 1965

Prior to this band Armand had been in an outfit called **Kack Klick**.

Armand Schaubroek spent some time in jail in the early seventies and then began a solo career with at least five albums (including the triple LP set *A Lot Of People Would Like To See Armand Schaubroek Dead*, the double *Live At The Hollywood Inn*, *Ratfucker* and *I Came To Visit But Decided To Stay*) in a style very influenced by Lou Reed. He now runs Mirror Records, home to the Chesterfield Kings, and with brother Blaine, the House of Guitars store, in Iron-dequoit, New York. He also produced **Jerry Porter**'s album.

Compilation appearances include *Babe We're Not Part Of Society* on *Gone, Vol. 1* (LP) and *Prisoners Of The Beat* (LP). (MW/SR)

Chy Guys

45: Say Mama/You'll Never Believe Me (Mobie 3422) 1965

Tom Tourville's 'Back Door Men' book places them in Rockford, Illinois but their name implies that they were probably from Chicago (Chi-town). The 'A' side has resurfaced on the *Ho-Dad Hootenanny* (LP) compilation. (VJ/GM)

The Chylds

Personnel:	JOHN BERECEK	ld gtr	A
	TIM HOGAN	gtr, keyb'ds	A
	AL TWISS	bs	A
	JOE VITALE	drums	AB
	DAVE JACKSON		B
	DENNY JACKSON		B

45s:	Hay Girl/I Want More (Lovin')	(Giant 101) 1967
	Hay Girl/I Want More (Lovin')	(Warner Bros. 7058) 1967
	Deep Inside/Psychedelic Soul	(Warner Bros. 7095) 1967
	Grey Days / No More Tears	(Ivanhoe 1801) c1969

From Canton, Ohio and previously known as **The Echos**. By the final 45 all bar Joe had been replaced by the Jackson brothers. Their finest moment is *Hay Girl*, an uptempo punker with an effective organ backing which gives way to a drum roll chorus and becomes quite psychedelic half way through before reverting back to a more usual garage punk style. Interested? Well, it's resurfaced on *Highs In The Mid-Sixties, Vol. 9* (LP), *Boulders, Vol. 1* (LP) and *Ya Gotta Have Moxie, Vol. 1* (Dble CD). Don't get too excited about the *Psychedelic Soul* 45 however - it's more soul than psych!

Joe Vitale had previously done time with **The Measles** (a group featuring Joe Walsh amongst others) and would go on to Marble Cake who didn't make it onto vinyl. In the seventies he rejoined Joe Walsh when Walsh went 'solo' after the **James Gang**. Vitale contributed vocals, keyboards, synth and flute in addition to drums, and was Walsh's main 'Barnstormer' from 1972's *Barnstorm* album through to 1978's *But Seriously Folks*. For those who groaned when Walsh joined the Eagles, this represents his peak period which of course includes the *Smoker You Drink..* album featuring the classic *Rocky Mountain Way*. During this stay Joe V. also found time to do a solo album - *Roller Coaster Weekend* (Atlantic SD 18114, 1974). (MW/GGI/VJ)

The Chymes

45:	He's Not There Anymore/	
	Quite A Reputation	(Chattahochee 715) 1966

This Los Angeles band issued at least one 45 in the mid- sixties. An all-girl band who specialised in harmony pop it seems we have Howard Kaylan (of **The Turtles**) to thank for discovering them.

Compilation appearances have included: *He's Not There Anymore* on *Girls In The Garage, Vol. 1* (LP) and *Highs In The Mid-Sixties, Vol. 2* (LP); *He's Not There Anymore* and *Quite A Reputation* on *Girls In The Garage, Vol. 1* (CD); and *Quite A Reputation* on *Girls In The Garage, Vol. 2* (LP). (VJ)

The Cicadelics

45:	We're Gonna Love This Way/	
	What Can I Do?	(Psychidelic Sound 1001) 1967

A sixties punk band from Angleton, a small town in Southeast Texas about 30 miles South of Houston, who had the Texas-based Cicadelic label named after them. Their own record label did spell psychedelic with an *i*.

Compilation appearances have included: *We're Gonna Love This Way* on *Flashback, Vol. 1* (LP), *Texas Flashbacks, Vol. 1* (LP & C&), *Texas Flashback (The Best Of)* (CD), *Acid Visions - The Complete Collection Vol. 1* (3-CD), *Austin Landing, Vol. 2* (LP) and *The Human Expression And Other Psychedelic Groups - Your Mind Works In Reverse* (CD); *We're Gonna Love This Way* and *What Can I Do?* also appear on *Texas Psychedelic Punk, Vol. 11*, an unreleased compilation for which an acetate exists. (VJ)

Don Ciccone

45:	There's Got To Be A Word/	
	Down When It's Up	(Kama Sutra 506) 1968

Produced by Stan Vincent and Mike Duckman, a rare solo 45 by the lead singer of **The Critters**. (SR)

The Cindells

| 45: | Don't Bring Me Down/McDougal Street | (Shag) 1965 |

From Cortland, New York. *Don't Bring Me Down* was a cover of The Pretty Things classic.

Compilation appearances have included *Don't Bring Me Down* on *Back From The Grave, Vol. 8* (Dble LP) and *Back From The Grave, Vol. 8* (CD). (VJ)

The Cindermen

Personnel incl:	DICK 'CINNAMON' CINDER	vcls	A

45s:	Think Of Me/I'm Happy	(Moonglow 5002) 1965
	If I Can't Love You/On Forever	(Moonglow 5005) 1965
	Don't Do It Some More/True Love	(Moonglow 5012) 1966
	Don't Knock It/I Can't Believe It	(Moonglow 5014) 1966
	I Can't See You/Stay Away	(Moonglow 5016) 1966
	Miss Connie You're A User/	
	You've Lost That Lovin' Feeling	(Moonglow 5021) 1967

From Fresno, this mob were house band for a year at L.A.'s "Cinnamon Cinder" club. *Don't Do It Some More*, a catchy number, is said to be their best effort.

Compilation appearances have included: *Don't Do It Some More* on *Pebbles, Vol. 8* (LP), *Pebbles, Vol. 8* (CD) and *Songs We Taught The Fuzztones* (Dble LP & Dble CD); *Don't Knock It* on *Boulders, Vol. 7* (LP) and *Ya Gotta Have Moxie, Vol. 1* (CD). (VJ)

The Cinders

| 45: | Good Lovin's Hard To Find/Poison Ivy | (RIC S-156) 1965 |

Rockin' beat covers by this Texas outfit, notable as an early outing for J.D. Souther. (MW/MM)

Circuit Rider

Personnel incl:	THORN OEHRIG		A

| ALBUM: | 1 | CIRCUIT RIDER | (C.R. 666) 1980 R2 |

Although not released until 1980, this album was recorded in Norwalk, Connecticut, during September/October 1971. The 1980 release suffers from poor production and sounds like it's taken from a demo tape. Still, it has its moments. *Old Time Feeling* and *How Long* have psych-folk

CIRCUS - Circus (Hemisphere) CD.

influences and, in similar vein but heavier and faster is *Just For Today*. The 'B' side is notable for the crazed, psychy experimental *Limousine Ride*, which featured a jazz-influenced guitar line. (VJ)

Circus

Personnel:	PHIL ALEXANDER	vcls, keyb'ds	A
	TOM DOBECK	drms	A
	DAN HRDLICKA	vcls, ld gtr, 12-string gtr	A
	MICK SABOL	vcls, gtr	A
	FRANK SALLE	vcls, bs	A

ALBUM: 1(A) CIRCUS (Metromedia LPS 7401) 1973 SC

45s: α Feel So Right / Jonah's Fable (Metromedia 0112) 1972
Stop, Wait And Listen/I Need Your Love (Metromedia 265) 1972

NB: α also issued in promo form with mono/stereo versions of *Feel So Right*.

A melodic rock album from Cleveland. This is one of the early examples of what became branded as 'power-pop' (strictly speaking outside of this book's remit), an early-to-mid seventies style that was particularly popular in Cleveland thanks to its premier exponents, The Raspberries. A dynamic pastiche that mixed elements of sixties mod, pop and hard rock (especially the Who, the Stones and the **Nazz**) and grafted them onto slickly-produced, hookladen and dramatic teen-pop.

Compilation appearances have included *Stop, Wait and Listen* on *Pride Of Cleveland Past* (LP). (SR/MW)

Circus

Personnel:	AL CROWE	drms	A
	RANDY GLODOWSKI	gtr, vcls	ABCDEFG
	GARY KONKOL	gtr	AB
	WAYNE KOSTROSKI	bs, vcls	ABCDEFG
	FRED OMERNIK	keyb'ds, vcls	ABCDEFG
	RAY CYR	drms, perc, congas	BCDE
	MIKE RICHSON	gtr	C
	GUNNAR ANTELL	gtr	D
	BRETT PETERSON	gtr, bobro, banjo	EF
	JIM ASH	drms	FG
	TERRY KNOLL	gtr	G

ALBUM: 1(E) CIRCUS (Hemisphere HIS-103) 1974 SC

NB: (1) reissued on CD (Gear Fab GF-162) 2000, with both 45 cuts added as bonus tracks.

45: I'm Walkin' / Bar Room Wiggy (Panda 6075-29) 1975

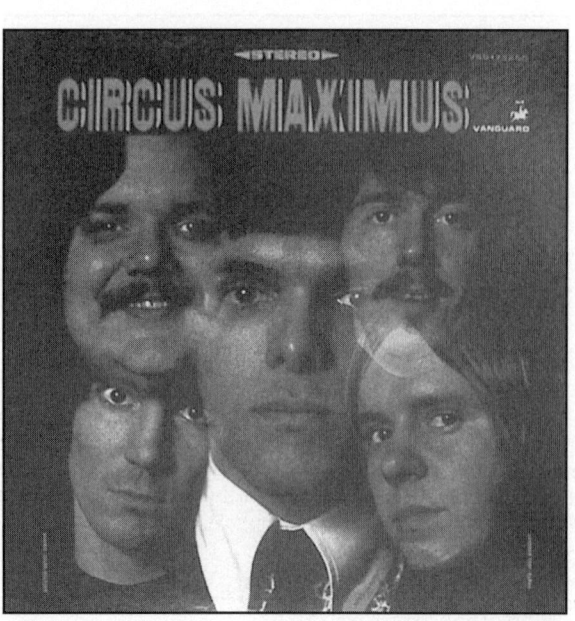

CIRCUS MAXIMUS - Circus Maximus LP.

Released on a local label based in Madison, Wisconsin, this album was produced by Corky Siegel (**Siegel Schwall Band**) and is a decent combination of heavy rock and blues with jamming guitars and keyboards. Particularly noteworthy is the 12-minute. *Old Age*.

The band formed in Stevens Point, Wisconsin in 1969 and was known as Sound Street (line-up 'A'). They toured throughout the state plying their particular brand of blues and rock. In 1970 they signed up with North Central Productions, brought in Ray Cyr on drums, changed their name to **Circus** and relocated to Madison, Wisconsin. Their touring expanded to take in the Midwest, the South and New England. In 1972 Konkol was diagnosed with a rare form of terminal cancer and had to be replaced (he died in 1973).

In 1973, after a few more personnel changes, they got to record their album which was released in 1974. They continued to tour widely, opening for the likes of Ted Nugent, B.B.King, The Raspberries, **Hot Tuna**, **John Sebastian**, Bonnie Bramlett, Firefall, Styx and the Amazing Rhythm Aces.

Their sole 45 appeared in 1975 (this is included on the CD reissue). There seemed to be no label interest in a second album and the band folded in 1976. (SR/MW)

The Circus

Personnel incl: POYNER A

45: Bad Seed (You're A Bad Seed)/
Burn Witch Burn (Offe 101) 196?

A raw punk outfit from somewhere in Texas. The 'A' side is pretty dire garage/punk and the flip's pretty raw too - the story of a guy who strangled a witch who spat in his eye before dying. Poyner wrote and produced both songs.

Compilation appearances have included: *Bad Seed (You're A Bad Seed)* on *Flashback, Vol. 3* (LP), *Texas Flashbacks, Vol. 3* (LP & CD), *Sixties Archive, Vol. 2* (CD) and *We Have Come For Your Children*; and both *Bad Seed* and *Burn Witch Burn* on *Texas Punk From The Sixties* (LP). (VJ)

The Circus

45: Games We Play/Change Of Face (Rembrandt ?) 1966

Reggie Weiss signed this Chicago act to his Rembrandt label when they were a top act for Ted and Marvin Stuart's Chicago booking agency. Despite their commercial sound his attempt to mould them into a tight pop group did not succeed in commercial terms.

Compilation coverage has included: *Games We Play* on *Chicago Garage Band Greats* (LP); and *Games We Play*, *No Reservations Necessary* and *Sands Of Mind* on *Chicago Garage Band Greats* (CD).

They may also have released a 45 for Jambee and there was a U.K. act called **Circus** who had one 45 released in the US: *Sink Or Swim / Gone Are The Songs Of Yesterday* (USA 903) 1968. (VJ/MW/SPr)

Circus Maximus

Personnel:	BOB BRUNO	ld gtr, keyb'ds, vcls	A
	DAVID SCHERSTROM	drms	A
	PETE TROUTNER	vcls, gtr, perc	A
	JERRY 'JEFF' WALKER	gtr, vcls	A
	GARY WHITE	bs	A

ALBUMS: 1(A) CIRCUS MAXIMUS (Vanguard VSD 79260) 1967 SC
2(A) NEVERLAND REVISITED
(Vanguard VSD 79274) 1968 SC

NB: (1) has been reissued on vinyl and CD. (2) reissued on vinyl. (1) and (2) reissued on a 2-on-1 CD (Vanguard/Comet VCD 79260/74).

45: Negative Dreamer Girl/Lonely Man (Vanguard 35063) 1967

Hailing from Austin, Texas, this band played a mixture of hard-rock, folk-rock and West Coast with flower-power lyrics. Their two albums are not easy to come by, but they are not expensive and recommended for their excellent guitar work. The first album contains seven Bob Bruno songs (mostly psychedelic with some jazzy touches, notably on *Wind*) and four by Jerry Jeff Walker (which are more folk-rock oriented).

At the end of 1967 they gave a unique concert at the Carnegie Hall with the New York Pro Musica, a baroque ensemble.

Their second album is equally interesting and contains songs like *Mixtures* and *Parallel* which are really nice. Neither of these albums sold well however and the group broke up.

Jerry Walker later enjoyed a long and successful solo career, as a singer and a songwriter (his *Mr. Bojangles* was covered by many artists, including the **Nitty Gritty Dirt Band** and Bob Dylan).

Compilation appearances have included: *Hello Baby*, *Neverland* and *Oops I Can Dance* on *The New Sound Of Underground* (LP); and *Rest Of My Life To Go* on *Songs Of Faith And Inspiration* (CDR & CD). (VJ/SR)

CIRCUS MAXIMUS - Neverland Revisited LP.

The Cirkit

Personnel:	SCOTT GLEMSIECK	organ	A
	DAVE GOLDMAN	bs	A
	BRUCE HAINEY	gtr	A
	RAD HANSEN	vcls	A
	JIM SHINDELL	ld gtr	A

45:	Yesterday We Laughed/I Was Wrong	(Unicorn 34941) 1967

NB: came in a purple paisley picture sleeve.

This band operated out of Michigan City in Indiana between 1966-68, although front man and author of both sides of the 45, Rad Hansen originated from the Deep South. They travelled to Universal Studios in Chicago to record this 45 and *Yesterday We Laughed*, in particular, had some fine grungy reverb guitar work.

Compilation appearances have included: *Yesterday We Laughed* on *Psychedelic Moods - Part Two* (CD); *I Was Wrong* and *Yesterday We Laughed* on *Hoosier Hotshots* (LP). (VJ/MW/KBn)

Cirkyt

45:	That's The Way Life Is/ Six Page Letter (PS)	(Jody 6703/4) 1967

The band were from New York.

Compilation appearances include: *That's The Way Life Is* on *Garage Punk Unknowns, Vol. 1* (LP). (VJ)

Le Cirque

Personnel:	MARC BENNO	A
	BILL BOATMAN	A
	LEON RUSSELL	A

45:	Land Of Oz/I'll Be Thinking Of You	(Buddah BDS-14) 1968

Two slices of Beatles influenced psychedelia, especially on *Land Of Oz*, a **Russell**/Boatman composition with its arrangements a la *Strawberry Fields*/*Lucy In The Sky*. The flip, written by Benno, is not as good.

After this commercial failure, Benno and **Russell** formed **Asylum Choir** and Bill Boatman went on to play with Taj Mahal, Don Preston and various **Leon Russell**'s projects. (SR)

Citations

Personnel:	ALAN	A
	ANTHONY	A
	BILL	A
	DOUG	A
	JAMES	A
	KEN	A
	MIKE	A
	OTHA	A
	VICTOR	A
	plus 1 unnamed	A

A 10-piece "zebra" (black'n'white) outfit from Dayton, Ohio. Their sole recorded legacy is the brassy and soulful *Good Love* (wherein James Brown meets *Good Lovin'*), composed by members A. Woodall and D. Simon. It appears on *WONE, The Dayton Scene* (Prism PR-1966), the souvenir LP of the 1966 WONE-sponsored three-day battle of the bands which features one cut each from the twelve winning acts. (MW)

City

Personnel:	JIM GORDON	drms	A
	CAROLE KING	vcls, keyb'ds	A
	DANNY KOOTCH	gtr, vcls	A
	CHARLES LARKEY	bs	A

ALBUM:	1(A)	NOW THAT EVERYTHING'S BEEN SAID	(Ode Z12-44012) 1968 SC

45:	That Old Sweet Roll (Hi-Di-Ho)/ Why Are You Leaving	(Ode ZS7 119) 1968

NB: white label promo copies exist, stock copies not verified. Both tracks are taken from the LP.

Originating from the New York scene, this decent pop-rock group is of most interest for its members solo careers:- Carole King was formerly a Brill Building songwriter with her first husband Gerry Goffin. Their melodic songs were covered by several groups, notably *Wasn't Born To Follow* by **The Byrds** and *Take A Giant Step* by Taj Mahal. As a singer/songwriter, Carole King would become extremely popular with her best seller album *Tapestry* in 1972.

Previously with **The King Bees** and **The Fugs**, Danny Kootch (or Kortchmar) went on to play with **James Taylor**, formed **Jo Mama** with Charles Larkey in 1970 and became a session musician. One of the best American drummers, Jim Gordon can be found on hundreds of records and went on to play with **Delaney and Bonnie**, **Leon Russell**, Traffic and Derek and The Dominos to name just a few.

Charles Larkey was in **The Myddle Class** and married Carole King. He would later commit suicide. (SR/KSI)

City Blues

ALBUM: 1 BLUES FOR LAWRENCE STREET (Nouveau) 1967 R3

From California, an extremely rare album of blues-psych, with interesting guitar leads. It was apparently released only as a promo on this short-lived label. (SR)

The City Limits

Personnel:	JEFF BEALS	bs	A
	DAN DENTON	sax	A
	JEFF LaBRACHE	drms	A
	KEVIN MASON	vcls	A
	ALAN PARK	gtr	A
	RIC ULSKY	keyb'ds	A

45: Stagger Le/Backyard Compost (Uptown 728) 1966

From Seattle, Washington the band's members had previously been in The Imperials, Rocky and The Riddlers and **Rocky and His Friends**. Under this name they cut a fine version of *Stagger Lee* in a straight forward rock and roll format. After their demise Jeff Beals went on to play with **The Kingsmen**, Ric Ulsky joined **The Association** and Jeff LaBrache played with **West Coast Natural Gas / Indian Puddin' and Pipe**. They had a previously unreleased version of *Tossin' and Turnin'* included on *Battle Of The Bands, Vol. 1* (LP) in 1966.

Retrospective compilation appearances have included: *Tossin' and Turnin'* on *Northwest Battle Of The Bands, Vol. 1 - Flash And Crash* (LP & CD), *Northwest Battle Of The Bands, Vol. 1* (CD) and *The History Of Northwest Rock, Vol. 4* (LP).

City Squires

Personnel:	JIM BRICKNER	A
	D.J.KOHLER	A
	D.RAND	A

| 45s: | Jenny Jenny/Russian Ho Ho | (Tema PXT-137) 1967 |
| | Is It Time / Lonely Boy | (Tema PXT-141) 1967 |

A Cleveland, Ohio pop outfit who became **The Gregorians**. *Is It Time* is cute Anglo-style pop ala Tremeloes or Marmalade. *Lonely Boy* is a soft pop ballad. (MW/GGI)

The City Zu

Personnel:	MIKE COX	bs	AB
	MIKE GARLAND	drms	AB
	CHUCK HARCUS	keyb'ds	AB
	DOUG HEATH	ld gtr	A
	BRAD MILLER	gtr	AB
	JERRY 'ZU' MATHESON	sax, ld vcls	AB
	RON FOOS	ld gtr	B
	DAVE ROLAND	drms	

45s:	Give A Little Bit/I'll Find Another	(Columbia 44342) 1967
	Eeny Meeny/Too Much, Too Soon, Too Fast	(Dot 17166) 1969
	Quick Like A Bunny/Stop Running Away	(Dot 17266) 1969

Formed in Bellevue, Washington State in 1965 as The Zu, they became **The City Zu** after local DJ, Pat O'Day suggested that "City Zu" would add a more bubble-gum appeal. They played in a gritty punky pop style not dissimilar to **Paul Revere** but with more harmony. They secured a record deal with Columbia and when the resulting 45 flopped did a further two for Dot. In fact, their 45s did garner heavy airplay, but problems with distribution meant their 45s didn't hit the stores until much later, and conseqently sold far fewer than they otherwise might.

Still, *Too Much, To Soon, Too Fast*, a punky pop number with some adventurous harmonies, can be heard on *Highs In The Mid-Sixties, Vol. 16* (LP), although the end result is a rather messy production.

Around the time of the 45s, **The City Zu** got to open for many of the big names that came to town, including The Who, Herman's Hermits, Dave Clark Five, Sonny and Cher, Yardbirds and **The Byrds**.

Dave Roland also hit the skins for **The City Zu** after **The Wailers** had split up in 1969. Foos and Heath went on to play for a later **The Sonics** line-up and in both had spells in **Paul Revere and The Raiders** (Foos 1974 - 77, Heath 1972 - 77 with both rejoining circa 1980).

The band is still going strong today although Jerry Zu is the only original member left. They are mostly to be found playing the casino circuit in Nevada, although they are still based in Seattle. (VJ/MW/SC/KCandJZu)

C.K. Strong

Personnel:	CHRISTOPHER BROOKS	bs	A
	LYNN CAREY	vcls	A
	RON GRINEL	drms	A
	JEFFERSON KEWLEY	gtr	A
	GEOFF WESTEN	gtr, organ, piano, vcls	A

ALBUM: 1(A) C.K. STRONG (Epic BN-26473) 1969 -

45: Daddy/Stormbird (Epic 10534) 1969

A loud and bluesy rock group with the screaming vocals of Lynn Carey and loads of guitar on tracks like *Stormbird*, *Baby Let Me Out*, *Mean Hearted Man* and the nine-minute *Trilogy*. The group was managed by Robert Fipztpatrick, an associate of Robert Stigwood. He would recommend their young female singer to the Hollywood composer Stu Phillips and that gave birth to the **Carrie Nations** project.

Lynn Carey would soon become better known as **Mama Lion**. The guitarist Jefferson Kewley later played with Sandi Szigeti. (SR/NK)

Clann

| Personnel incl: | TONY DIONISIO | A |

45s:	Stubborn Kind Of Fellow/	
	I've Found Somebody	(General American GAR 103) 1966
	Tall Towers/Hey Baby	(General American GAR 109) 1967

After an average first effort this Columbia, Missouri, bunch turn out the cool mid-tempo fuzzer *Tall Towers*. The flip reverts back to a much earlier British Invasion sound unfortunately. Tony Dionisio was also a member of **The Vandals**, who also had one 45 on the same label.

Compilation appearances include *Hey, Baby* on *Time Won't Change My Mind* (LP). (MW)

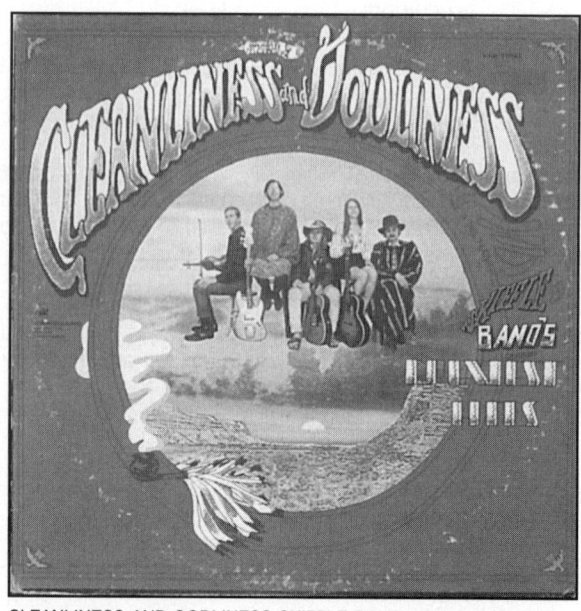

CLEANLINESS AND GODLINESS SKIFFLE BAND - Greatest Hits LP.

Clap

Personnel:	DAVE AURIT	gtr, sax, vcls	A
	SCOTT MERCIER	drms, perc	A
	JIM MORRISON	bs, vcls	A
	STEVE MORRISON	vcls, harp	A
	KEITH TILL	gtr, vcls	A

ALBUM: 1(A) HAVE YOU REACHED YET?
(Nova-Sol NSLP 1001 AB) 1971 R4

NB: (1) reissued on Phaze II (CPS 001).

This is a very rare Manhattan Beach, California album from the early seventies. The sound is reputedly closer to '66/67 punk and some collectors rate it highly. A sixth and occasional member was Les Hurst (drms). It's not *the* Jim Morrison on the album. (VJ)

Kathy Clarke

45:	My Summer Prayer / Little Girl Called Sad	(International Artists 105) 1966

A little known artist from Texas who's *Little Girl Called Sad* was included on *Girls In The Garage, Vol. 4* (LP). It was one of the earliest releases on the International Artists label in 1966, and consists of lightweight pop with some baroque strings on the 'A' side and folk-rock influences on the flip. (VJ/MK)

The Classmen

45s:	Julie/Any Old Time	(Pearce 5806) 1967
	The Yang Yang (The Heart String)/ Poor, Poor Johnny	(Pearce 5813) c1967
	His Girl / Michaelangelo	(Pearce 5826) 196?
	Graduation Goodbye /	(Pearce # unkn) 196?

Another Kansas City, Missouri outfit. You'll also find *Julie* on *Monsters Of The Midwest, Vol. 1*. The second 45 is soul-tinged, brassy, dirgeful and not recommended. This outfit should not be confused with the Detroit "Classmen" who issued 45s on J, Volkano and Impact. (VJ/MW)

Claytons

45s:	Puttin' Me On/Need Mine Too	(M 4982) 1966
	I Want You/The Claytons	(B.Racker) 196?

From Fort Wayne, Indiana. *Puttin' Me On* has resurfaced on *Boulders, Vol. 5* (LP) and *Ya Gotta Have Moxie, Vol. 1* (Dble CD). There is another 45 by possibly the same group?:-

This features a cover of the **Buffalo Springfield** classic, with female vocals and big production by Tim O'Brien. (VJ)

The Cleanliness and Godliness Skiffle Band

Personnel:	ANNE JOHNSTON	vcls, gtr, mandn, woodblocks	ABC
	PHIL MARSH	vcls, gtr	ABC
	RICHARD SAUNDERS	bs	ABC
	HANK BRADLEY	vcls, mandn, fiddle	C
	BRIAN VOORHEES	vcls, gtr, hmnca	C
	(CHICKEN HIRSCH	drms	A)

ALBUMS: 1(A) THE CLEANLINESS AND GODLINESS SKIFFLE
 BAND'S GREATEST HITS (Vanguard VSD 79285) 1968 -
 2( ) MASKED MARAUDERS (Reprise 6378) 1969 -

NB: (2) as **The Masked Marauders**.

45:	α I Can't Get No Nookie/Cow Pie	(Deity 0870) 1969

NB: α as **The Masked Marauders**.

An 'acid' influenced skiffle band, their album though weak technically, is good fun if you can obtain a copy. Their second album, under the pseudonym, **The Masked Marauders**, was an attempted imitation of Dylan, Lennon-McCanney, Harrison and Jagger. They were based in San Francisco.

NB. Hirsch, Johnston and Marsh all played at various times with Country Joe (McDonald). (VJ)

Clean Living

Personnel:	TIMOTHY GRIFFIN	drms, perc, vcls	AB
	PAUL LAMBERT	pedal steel, dobro	AB
	ROBERT "TEX" LA MOUNTAIN	gtr, vcls	AB
	ROBERT LA PALM	gtr, vcls	AB
	NORMAN SCHELL	gtr, ld vcls	AB
	FRANK SHAW	gtr, bs, vcls	AB
	ELLIOTT SHERMAN	keyb'ds	A
	JEFFREY POTTER	keyb'ds, hrmnca, perc	B
	(K.P. BURKE	hrmnca	A)
	(AL ANDERSON	gtr	B)
	(GUILLAUME "SNAKE" LA PALM	fiddle	B)
	(MIKE MANDEL	piano	B)
	(TIM PITT	gtr	B)

ALBUMS: 1(A) CLEAN LIVING (Vanguard VRS 79318) 1972 -
 2(B) MEADOWMUFFIN (Vanguard VSD 79334) 1973 -

NB: Rare quadraphonic pressings of both album exists (VSQ 40009 and VSQ 40025 respectively).

45s:	Backwoods Girl/ In Heaven There Is No Beer	(Vanguard 35162) 1972
	Jenny Regardless/Old Time Music	(Vanguard 35170) 1972
	Far North Again/Me And You	(Vanguard 35171) 1973

Bob LaPalm and Timothy Griffin were previously in **Bold** and went on to form **Clean Living** with various musicians. This group offered a good-humored mix of country, blues, rock and good time music.

Produced by Maynard Solomon, their first album is musically diverse, with three different lead singers and material covering rock (Berry's *Sweet Little Sixteen*), bar songs (*In Heaven There Is No Beer*), delicate ballads (*Charles Street*) and "religious" songs (*Jesus Is My Thing*, *Jesus Is My Subway Line*).

In 1973, Danny Weiss (**Everything is Everything**) produced *Meadowmuffin*. Norman Schell was now clearly the lead singer and the album loses in variety what it gains on direction. Being more country-oriented, it's probably less interesting than its predecessor. (SR)

Clear Blue Sky

45:	Morning Of Creation/Ugly Girl	(Romat 1005) 1967

Recorded in Greenville, a small town in Eastern North Carolina, which I believe is a leading market centre for bright leaf tobacco. *Morning Of Creation* sounds like **Jefferson Airplane** without the extra dimension that Grace Slick's vocals gave them. Despite this, the layered harmonies are quite effective and the rhythm section is quite competent. You'll find it on *Tobacco A-Go-Go, Vol. 1* (LP). (VJ)

Clear Blue Sky

Personnel:	DAN ANGOTT	organ, vcls	A
	KEITH BUCKLEY	bs, vcls	A
	JOHN ROCCO	gtr, vcls	A
	LES WARD	drms	A

Along with Mark Lepine (vcls) and Dave Lawrence (bs), Angott, Ward, and Rocco were previously in the Tryumphs who, in 1966, committed to tape at least two songs: covers of the Yardbirds *Mr. You're A Better Man Than I* and the **Byrds** *Chimes Of Freedom*. In 1968, after Lepine and Lawrence had left and Keith Buckley joined, the band switched names to **Clear Blue Sky**. Though they were popular in their home town surroundings of Northwest Detroit, they were never able to achieve widespread success. **Clear Blue Sky** never officially recorded, but tapes survive of the band's versions of *Along Comes Mary*, *Uncle Jack*, *I'm So Glad*, *Are You Happy?*, *Can't Take It* and the group original *Mr. Pebbles*, which should definitely interest many garage/psych fans.

Buckley and Angott continued to record throughout the seventies and eighties, and in December 1999 completed cover versions of a few of their favourite songs by sending tapes back and forth between Michigan and North Carolina! When not creating music, the pair stay busy by running the My First Band web site (www.myfirstband.com), a site that requests submissions from members of former sixties garage bands such as **Clear Blue Sky** and documents their histories accordingly. A book is also currently in the planning stages. (MDo/DA/KB)

CLEAR LIGHT - Clear Light LP.

Clear Light

Personnel:	CLIFF DE YOUNG	vcls	AB
	DOUGLAS LUBAHN	bs	AB
	MICHAEL NEY	drms, perc	AB
	RALPH SCHUCKETT	organ, piano, celeste	AB
	BOB SEAL	gtr, vcls	A
	DALLAS TAYLOR	drms	AB
	DANNY KORTCHMAR	ld gtr	B

HCP
ALBUM: 1(A) CLEAR LIGHT (Elektra EKS 74011) 1967 126 -

NB: (1) also issued in France and the U.K.. (1) reissued on Edsel (ED 245) 1988 and again on CD (Collectors Choice Music CCM 271-2) 2002. (1) also reissued on vinyl (Sundazed LP 5125) 2002.

45s: Black Roses/She's Ready To Be Free (Elektra EK 45622) 1967
They Who Have Nothing /
The Ballad Of Freddie And Larry (Elektra 45626) 1967
α Night Sounds Loud/? (Elektra EKSN 45027) 1968

NB: α U.K. release.

This heavy rock band from Los Angeles was a novelty at the time, possessing two drummers. Their only album was a fair debut, although the band never looked likely to break into the first division of American rock. It achieved modest commercial success peaking at No 126 in the Billboard Album Charts. Often their songs lacked distinctive melodies. This was not the case, however, with *A Child's Smile*, the shortest and one of the best tracks on the album. Another strong track *Black Roses* was issued as a 45. The non-album flip side, which is excellent, was taken from the film "The President's Analyst" which they appeared in briefly.

De Young later went solo (two albums and four 45s on MCA between 1973/5) and pursued an acting career. Seal went on to the **Peanut Butter Conspiracy**. Lubahn, who had earlier done session work for **The Doors** went on to play for an outfit called Dreams and Ney and Kortchmar later played together in The City, an early seventies trio, Dallas Taylor (ex-**Factory**) went on to fame as drummer for Crosby, Stills, Nash and Young and Danny Kortchmar was also in **King Bees**.

Sand, another track from their album, was also covered by a Mexican outfit, Los Land Jets, (in Hispanic) entitled *Mira*. The 1988 Edsel reissue of their album includes one track *She's Ready To Be Free* which was not on the original album. This 45 'B' side, which was also featured in the James Coburn cult classic 'The President's Analyst', is also included as a bonus track on the Collector's Choice Music CD reissue.

Compilation appearances include: *The Ballad Of Freddie and Larry* on *Kings Of Pop Music, Vol. 2* (LP); *Sand* on *Endless Journey - Phase Three* (LP) and *Endless Journey - Phase I & II* (Dble CD) and *Black Roses* and *Mr Blue* on *Elektrock The Sixties* (4-LP). (VJ/MW/SR)

Clefs of Lavender Hill

Personnel:	COVENTRY FAIRCHILD	vcls, gtr	ABCD
	TRAVIS FAIRCHILD	gtr, vcls	ABCD
	BILL MOSS	bs	A
	FRED MOSS	drms	A
	JOHN HAIR	drms	B
	TED NAPOLEON	drms	C
	FRANK MILONE	bs	D
	STEVE ZARICKI	drms	D

HCP
45s: First Tell Me Why/Stop! Get A Ticket (Thames 100) 1966 -
Stop! Get A Ticket/First Tell Me Why (Date 1510) 1966 80
One More Time/So I'll Try (Date 1530) 1966 114
It Won't Be Long/Play With Fire (Date 1533) 1966 -
Gimme One Good Reason/Oh Say My Love (Date 1567) 1967 -

Itinerant Vaudeville performers Joseph Ximenes and his sister Lorraine, originally from Brooklyn NY, were better known as Travis and Coventry Fairchild. Whilst in Miami in 1966 they were teamed up with the Moss brothers, from local trio **The Twilights**, to become **The Clefs Of Lavender Hill**.

A quartet of appealing Invasion-pop 45s appeared in quick succession and the impetus was carried into recording an album. Such a promising start was snuffed out however when Date chose to shelve the album. The Moss brothers departed and, although the **Clefs** soldiered on for another couple of years, nothing further was released.

After their demise former-**Montells** drummer Napoleon would encounter Milone in the power-trio Smack.

Stop! Get A Ticket was also covered by Cleveland's **Baskerville Hounds** (as **The Statesmen**).

Travis also co-wrote *No Place Or Time* for **The Echoes Of Carnaby Street**.

Compilation appearances have so far included: *Stop! Get A Ticket* on *Nuggets Box* (4-CD), *Open Up Yer Door! Vol. 1* (LP) and *Pebbles, Vol. 4* (ESD) (CD); *Stop! Get A Ticket*, *First Tell Me Why*, *So I'll Try*, *One More Time*, *It Won't Be Long*, *Play With Fire*, *Oh Say My Love* and *Gimme One Good Reason* on *Everywhere Interferences* (LP) and *One More Time* on *Psychedelic States: Florida Vol. 3* (CD). (MW/JLh/TTi)

Clee-Shays

Personnel:	?? BERKA	A
	?? BRAUSE	A
	?? JOHNSON	A
	?? KILSO	A
	?? LARRISON	A

45: Spend All My Money/Annabelle Zodd (Monex 5232) 1968

Both songs written by this Des Moines, Iowa, quintet are noteworthy. *Spend All My Money* is a catchy fuzz-rocker with call-and-response vocals.

BILL CLINT - The Crying Of A Generation LP.

Annabelle Zodd switches to a dreamy Anglophile flower-pop style with accomplished **Cryan' Shames**-like harmonies. There's also a retrospective CD of their work *The Dynamic Guitar Sounds Of....* (Sundazed SC 11049) 1999. (VJ/MW)

The Cliches

| 45: | Save It For Me/Why, Why, Why | (Wes Mar 1020) 1966 |

Minor league garagey folk-rocker and beat-punker from somewhere in Ohio. Class Of Shutdown 66.

Compilation appearances include *Why Why Why* on *Let's Dig 'Em Up, Vol. 1* (CD). (MW)

Click

| Personnel: | 'CLICK' HORNING | vcls | A |

| ALBUM: | 1 | CLICK | (ABC ABCS-677) 1969 - |

45s:	Drifters Medley/Sun Come Up	(Laurie LR-3365) 1966
	Fat Lady In The Wicker Chair/	
	Dancing Babies	(Laurie LR-3402) c1967
	Girl With A Mind / Rainmaker	(Laurie LR-3419) 1967

The singer/songwriter "Click" Horning first released three singles of orchestrated bubblegum pop, produced by Lou Stallman and arranged by Joey Scott. In 1969 he released an album which contains some decent folk rock numbers and a good psych-folk track with sitar, although most of the tracks are orchestrated and best avoided. (SR/MW)

Clicker

Personnel:	JEFF EISENBERNER	keyb'ds	A
	CHRISTINE HESS	vcls	A
	LYNN MCLAUGHLIN	vcls	A
	BOB SCHMIDTKE	gtr	A
	JEFF TRACY	drms	A
	STEVE TRACY	bs, vcls	A
	DICK WIEGEL	gtr	A

| ALBUMS: | 1(A) | CLICKER | (Hemisphere 5180) 1973 SC |
| | 2(A) | HARDE HAR HAR | (Clicker 1975) 1975 R1? |

An excellent heavy progressive group with some furious guitar solos and male/female vocals. Their albums rarely turn up. (SR)

Buzz Clifford

| ALBUM: | 1 SEE YOUR WAY CLEAR | (Dot DLP-25965) 1969 |

45s:	Swing In My Back Yard/ Bored To Tears	(Capitol 5880) 1967
(partial	On My Way/Fourteen Karat Fool	(A&M 878) 1967
list)	Children Are Crying Aloud/	
	So Good At Loving You (Baby, I Could Be)	(Dot 17329) 1969
	I Am The River/Proctor And Gunther	(Dot 17344) 1969

Buzz Clifford began his career in 1957 and had a big novelty hit in 1960 with *Baby Sittin' Boogie*. After several 45s and one album (*Baby Sittin' With Buzz*), he moved to California and began working with **Daniel Moore**.

Between 1967 and 1973, both men would play a key role in the Los Angeles Sound, as producers, songwriters and arrangers. Their production credits include the **Hamilton Streetcar**, the **East Side Kids** and **Colours**, as well as some non-California groups like **Carp** and **Head Over Heels**. **Buzz Clifford**'s songs would be recorded by several of the groups he produced plus many other pop and rock acts including **David Anderson**.

Produced by Richard Delvy, his album *See Your Way Clear* was recorded with **Daniel Moore** plus a who's who of Los Angeles and Texas musicians: Rob Edwards, Gary Montgomery and Carl Radle (**Colours**), David Marks and **Matthew Moore** (**Moon**), David Doud, Michael Doud and David Potter (**East Side Kids**), Ed Lively and Joseph "T-Bone" Burnett (**Whistler, Chaucer, Greenhill and Detroit**), Stephen Bruton, Jim Keltner and Bernie Leadon (**Hearts and Flowers**). All the tracks were written by **Clifford**, except for **Dan Moore**'s *Hollywood Joe* and Ricky Sheldon's *We'll All Get By*. The album is not excellent but has its moments.

Clifford appears to have stopped recording and producing after 1974. (SR)

Doug Clifford

| ALBUM: | 1 COSMO | (Fantasy 9411) 1972 - |

The drummer of **Creedence Clearwater Revival** recorded only one solo album, and after hearing the result, it's easy to understand why! (SR)

The Clingers

45s:	α Gonna Have A Good Time/	
	And Now You Know Me	(CBS 44766) 1969
	Round, Round, Round/Mean It	(MGM 14110) 1970

NB: α Dutch pressing with PS.

An all girl rock group. Their first single, a cover of the Easybeats' *Gonna Have A Good Time*, was produced by **Kim Fowley**. They may be related to the Clinger Sisters, who released three pop singles on Tollie in 1964. (SR)

Clinging Hysteria

Personnel:	?? ??		A
	BILL FINKY		A
	JEFF SMITH		A
	GEORGE TATEHAM		A

A Michigan outfit who ripped off The Doors' *Soul Kitchen* renaming it *The In Sound*. Their decidedly inferior version can be heard on *Michigan Mixture, Vol. 2* (LP). (VJ)

Bill Clint

Personnel:	JIM ANDERSON	drms	A
	BILL CLINT	vcls, gtr	A
	RUSSELL DAHNEKE	gtr	A
	BOB STERN	bs	A
	KENNY STOVER	keyb'ds	A

| ALBUM: | 1(A) THE CRYING OF A GENERATION | |
| | | (Joint Artists JA 332) 1975 SC |

A local Bay Area release. Some copies were issued with a poster showing the cover art and a statement from **Clint**: "I am no longer afraid to admit it - I am an insane animal", which may be true, but regrettably is not much in evidence on the album itself. **Clint** himself sounds more depressed than crazy, and actually breaks down in tears on the eleven minute *Angels Don't Need Friends*. Much of the album is acoustic folk. (CF)

The Clique

Personnel incl:
- TOMMY PENA — bs
- SID TEMPLETON — gtr, keyb'ds
- JERRY 'FUNCTION' COPE — drms
- RANDY SHAW
- DAVE
- OSCAR
- MIKE TEAQUE

ALBUM: 1( ) THE CLIQUE (SUGAR ON SUNDAY)   HCP
(White Whale WW 7126) 1969 177 -

NB: (1) reissued on CD (Varese Vintage VSD 5953) 1998 with 45 bonus tracks.

45s: HCP
- Splash 1 /Stay By Me   (Cinema 001) 1967 -
- Splash 1 /Stay By Me   (Scepter 12202) 1967 113
- Love Ain't Easy/Gofta Get Away   (Scepter 12212) 1968 -
- Superman/Shadow Of Your Love   (White Whale 312) 1969 -
- α Sugar On Sunday/Superman   (White Whale 322) 1969 22
- I'll Hold Out My Hands/Soul Mates   (White Whale 333) 1969 45
- My Darkest Hour/?   (White Whale 335) 1969 -
- Sparkle And Shine/I'm Alive   (White Whale 338) 1970 100
- Memphis/Southbound Wind   (White Whale 361) 1970 -
- β Judy Judy Judy/Judy Judy Judy   (White Whale 367) 1970 -

NB: α also issued in Argentina (Deram 1117). β Promo only.

Pena, Templeton and Cope joined this band from **The Lavender Hour** and Mike Teaque and Steve Headley from the same band were also briefly members of **The Clique**, who operated in Austin, Texas between 1966-71. They are best known for their fine cover of the **13th Floor Elevators'** *Splash 1* which was also featured on *21 KILT Goldens, Vol. 2*.

Two of their three Top 100 hits, *Sugar On Sunday* and *Sparkle And Shine*, were written by **Tommy James and The Shondells**. Most of the White Whale 45s are from the album, but they may also have recorded a non-album 45 from Laurie. Teaque was later in Just Us, who issued a 45 on Mod International, and Tiger's Claw.

REM later covered *Superman*, which was written by their album producer Gary Zekley and M. Bottler, on *Life's Rich Pageant*.

THE CLIQUE - The Clique LP.

Retrospective compilation appearances have included: *Gotta Get Away* and *Splash 1* on *Austin Landing, Vol. 2* (LP); *Splash 1* on *Endless Journey - Phase One* (LP) and *Endless Journey - Phase I & II* (Dble CD); and *I'll Hold Out My Hand* and *Sugar On Sunday* on *Happy Together - The Very Best Of White Whale Records* (CD). (VJ/ML)

The Cliques

45: So Hard/?   (Custom) 1966

Hailed from Champaign, Illinois - their 45 was recorded in nearby Urbana. You can hear the short punker with raw vocals on *Back From The Grave, Vol. 7* (LP). They appeared in a locally televised 'Battle Of The Bands' competition in 1966. (VJ)

Clockwork

Personnel:
- MIKE BUGARA — gtr, vcls — A
- MIKE DURUTTYA — horns, vcls — A
- JIM KORLESKI — vcls, keyb'ds — A
- BILL McCREA — vcls, perc — A
- JIM MILLER — hrmnca — A
- JOHN SINERI — drms — A
- DAVE SORGE — gtr — A
- GARY ZEIGLER — bs — A

ALBUM: 1(A) CLOCKWORK   (Greene Bottle 1013) c1972 -

Housed in an unipak cover, an obscure group, somewhere between Crosby Stills Nash and Young and **Blue Mountain Eagle**, with covers of Paul Simon's *Hazy Shade Of Winter*, Steve Stills' *Rock & Roll Woman* and *Hitchcock Railway*.

Greene Bottle was a subsidiary label of Paramount. (SR)

Clockwork Orange

45s:
- Sweet Little Innocent Lorraine/Help Me   (Rust 5119) 1967
- Image Of You/What Am I Without You   (Rust 5126) 1968

This New York City combo produced two interesting 45s. Whilst *Lorraine* is quaint post Sgt. Pepper 'psychedelic pop', *Help Me* is rather heavier and is rather reminiscent of early **Iron Butterfly**. *Image Of You* is disappointing soulful pop but it's the flip again that comes up trumps. Pumped up psych-pop with some wonderful licks.

Compilation coverage has so far been limited to: *What Am I Without You?* on *Mindrocker, Vol. 13* (LP) and *Help Me* on *Turds On A Bum Ride, Vol. 4* (CD). (MW)

Clockwork Orange

45: Do Me Right Now/Your Golden Touch   (Creole 1002) 1967

A different group from Paducah, Kentucky. The 45 above is an excellent garage psych two-sider. Both sides have resurfaced on *Pebbles, Vol. 12* (LP) and *Pebbles, Vol. 10* (CD). (MW)

Cloud

Personnel incl:
- GOLDTEIN — A
- HOFFMAN — A

45: Cool Jane/The Frightened Sparrow   (Audio Fidelity AF-155) 1969

NB: double-side promos also exist. Also released in France with a PS (AF 11001).

Written by Hoffman and Goldstein, a rather boring song with decent organ but poor vocals, in a prog-pop vein. The band headlined the Boston Tea Party, Jan. 5-6th, 1968 playing with **Ill Wind** and may have been based in Boston. (SR/SBn)

CLOUD - Gig Flyer.

Clouds

| 45: | Visions/Migada Bus | (Independence 82) 1967 |

This Los Angeles band also had the same 45 issued under the name **The Looking Glasses** on the Media label. **The Clouds** version can be found on *Psychedelic Unknowns, Vol. 6* (LP & CD) and you'll find **The Looking Glasses** version on *Pebbles, Vol. 11*. They're exactly the same. *Visions* is glorious mystical psychedelic punk that goes from frantic to spaced-out and back again. *Migada Bus* is a pleasant instrumental in a baroquey style with fuzzy edges. (VJ)

Cloudwalkers

| 45: | Sunglasses / Never Told Me So | (Capco 106) 1965 |

Despite the appearance of *Sunglasses* on *The Midwest Vs The Rest, Vol. 1* (LP) and *Pebbles Vol. 8* (CD), this band were actually from Brooklyn, New York.

Sunglasses was a British-influenced rave-up with lots of mouth harp. The flip is reputedly a worthwhile psych-folk outing. (MW/MM)

Clover

Personnel:
ALEX CALL	vcls, gtr	A
JOHN GIAMBOTTI	bs, gtr, vcls	A
MITCH HOWIE	drms	A
JOHN McFEE	ld gtr, pedal steel, piano, vcls	A
(ED BOGAS	fiddle, gtr, piano	A)

NB: Bruce Campbell also plays banjo on their second album.

ALBUMS: 1(A) CLOVER (Fantasy 8395) 1970 -
(up to 2(A) FOURTY NINER (Fantasy 8405) 1971 -
1972)

NB: (1) also released in France by America (30 AM 6044, 1970). (1) and (2) also released in the U.K. by United Artists.

| 45: | Shotgun/ Wade in The Water | (Fantasy ?) 1970 |

NB: also released in France with a picture sleeve (America 17016) 1970.

McFee, Call and Howie all met at Tamalpais High School and formed the Tiny Hearing Aid Company. In 1967, when they teamed up with Giambotti - formerly with the bluegrass act The Valley Boys and the Outfit, they became **Clover**. The next two years were spent giging around venues like the Avalon and the Fillmore, before John Fogerty of **Creedence Clearwater Revival** helped them to sign a contract with Fantasy.

Their first album is supposed to have been recorded without a mixing desk. It contains some excellent West Coast rock and country rock selections, notably *Wade In The Water* (a la **Mad River**), *Lizard Rock'n'Roll Band* and *Shotgun* (the only non original track).

The second album is more country rock oriented but is still interesting with *Mr. Moon*, *Chicken Butt* and *Keep On Trying*. Both albums were produced by Ed Bogas, who was the fifth member of the group and an active studio musician (also with **David and Tina Meltzer**) and soundtrack composer (notably for Ralph Bakshi's 'Fritz The Cat').

Clover drifted back into obscurity and finally, circa 1975, McFee, Call and Giambotti came to England with new members Huey Lewis, Micky Shine and Sean Hopper to launch a new career. This new line-up of **Clover** somehow managed to play with Elvis Costello on his first album, *My Aim Is True*, and even signed a new recording contract with Vertigo/Mercury which resulted on two new albums in 1976 and 1977 (*Clover* and *Unavailable*), which are totally different from their previous efforts.

A gifted guitarist, John McFee also played on several Californian recording sessions (Janey and Dennis, **Tim Davis**, **Norman Greenbaum** etc.) and joined the Doobie Brothers in 1980. Alex Call went solo and is still recording for the German label Taxim. The two later members, Huey Lewis and Sean Hopper, went on to form Huey Lewis and the News and sold some millions of records during the eighties. (VJ/SR)

Timothy Clover

ALBUM: 1 THE CAMBRIDGE CONCEPT OF TIMOTHY CLOVER - A HARVARD SQUARE AFFAIR (Tower ST 5114) 1968 -

An album of orchestrated pop-psych, recorded at Olmsted, New York, by Tea-Pot Productions (Bruce Patch and Lennie Petze) and Larry Jaspon. The front cover shows what some dealers may describe as a psychedelic collage, with portraits of Kennedy and Washington, British and American flags, indian warriors, "Tea" stickers, leaves... and bears the subtitle "The Bean Town Sound" (to be compared to the Boss Town Sound!).

Apart from the best track, the dreamy *Tear-Drop Mobile* composed by F. Gelfand and G. Katz, all the material was written by the producers, assisted on some tracks by T. Landry, S. King, L. Collins and R. Morse. A studio project, it still has to attract interest.

Bruce Patch:- "As I remember it... I had produced a single by a group called The Rondells and Lennie Petze was one of the guitar players. We became friends and started writing songs together. We then produced a **Teddy and The Pandas** album for Tower (I had produced and managed the group on a couple of Musicor releases) and then came up with the **Timothy Clover** idea to capitalize on the rash of Boston groups that were getting signed. We wrote a bunch of songs and had no artist so our friend Larry Jaspon who was a local booking agent had some bar band and the singer from that group become **Timothy Clover**. I don't think they ever did one gig under that name." (SR/JFr/BPh)

The Clue

| 45: | She's The Reason/Bad Times | (Byron 101) 196? |

From Midland, Texas, **The Clue** recorded one of the classic acid punk singles from that state, *Bad Times*, with rich organ backing.

Compilation appearances have included: *Bad Times* on *All Cops In Delerium - Good Roots* (LP), *Pebbles, Vol. 8* (LP), *Mayhem & Psychosis, Vol. 3* (LP) and *Mayhem & Psychosis, Vol. 2* (CD). (VJ)

The Coachmen

Hailed from Independence, Missouri. Their previously unreleased cut, *Too Many Reasons*, a routine garage punker, has since resurfaced on *Monsters Of The Midwest, Vol. 2* (LP). (VJ)

The Coachmen

| 45: | A Sunday Kind Of Woman/ | |
| | It Was Like A Song | (Audio House 7-128F78) 196? |

Yet another **Coachmen**. This crew were based in Lawrence, the state capital of Kansas, where they played during the mid and late sixties. (VJ)

The Coachmen

| 45: | Grapes Of Wrath/ | |
| | Summer Should Bring Happiness | (Sea-Ell 106) 1968 |

Yet another **Coachmen**, this time from Texas. The 'A' side, which can best be described as hippie psych, has resurfaced on *Sixties Rebellion, Vol. 15* (LP & CD). Both tracks also appear on *The History Of Texas Garage Bands, Vol. 1 - The Sea Ell Label Story* (CD). (VJ)

The Coachmen

Personnel:	RICK BELL	gtr, keyb'ds, vcls	A
	RED FREEMAN	gtr	A
	CRAIG PERKINS	bs	AB
	JIM REINMUTH	gtr, keyb'ds	A
	JEFF TRAVIS	ld gtr	AB
	BRUCE WATSON	drms	AB
	FRANK ELIA	gtr	B
	KELLY KOTERA	keyb'ds	B

| CD: | 1( ) | STILL ROCKIN' | ( ) 1999 |

NB: (1) contains original recordings of *Mr. Moon, Nothing At All, Linda Lu, My Generation*, and *Time Won't Change* plus fifteen new recordings, including a re-recording version of *Mr. Moon* and two new originals.

HCP

45s:	Mr. Moon/Nothing At All	(MMC 010) 1965 -
	Mr. Moon/Nothing At All	(Bear 1974) 1966 114
	Linda Lou/I'm A King Bee	(Bear 1976) 1966 -
	My Generation/No Answer	(MMC 013) 1966 -
	Tyme Won't Change/Tell Her No	(MMC 014) 1967 -
α	Number One Hippie On The Village Scene/	
	The Travel Song	(J&T 2022) 1967 -
β	You Got The Love/Lady	(White Whale 275) 1968 -
β	Angela/Duba Duba Do	(White Whale 288) 1968 -
β	Oo Poo Pah Susie/You Take It	(White Whale 293) 1969 -

NB: α as **Alexander's Rock Time Band**. β as **Profesor Morrison's Lollipop**.

Probably the best known of the outfits using this moniker, they were based in Lincoln, Nebraska and played in a cool melodic beat-rock style. A local supergroup with Jim Reinmuth and Bruce Watson having previously spent time in The Chandells and the remainder coming from The Viscounts, they would have some success over the next three years. *Mr. Moon* was a local phenomenon and sizeable hit in the Midwest which made some impression nationally, but as the decade unfolded the band changed its name to prevent becoming dated, firstly to **Alexander's Rock Time Band** and then **Professor Morrison's Lollipop** with a more straightforward pop sound.

The earlier releases are certainly worth a spin and you'll find *My Generation* on *Monsters Of The Midwest, Vol. 4* (LP), *No Answers* on *Brain Shadows, Vol. 2* (LP & CD) and *Mr. Moon* on *Searching For Love* (LP).

Incidentally, the band hosted their own local TV show "The Coachmen Show" in Omaha, where they performed their own hits and featured guest appearances by other local bands. The programme was on air for six months, with each song being pre-recorded in one take.

Bruce, Red, Jeff, Rick and Craig are planning on performing occasionally "as money and logistics allow" which, considering that the members reside in three different parts of the country, might prove difficult. Red, Jeff and Bruce all continue to write original music, as evidenced by *Stand Tall* (a real rocker!) and *Heartland* on the new CD, and they hope to release another CD in the future, dependent on sales for the *Still Rockin'* release. (MW/MDo/RFr/BWn)

SEARCHING FOR LOVE (Comp LP) includes The Coachmen.

The Coachmen

Personnel incl: WAYLAND HUEY   A

| 45: | Say You Love Me / Hush Broken Heart | (Gala # Unkn) 1964 |

From Abilene, Texas. Wayland Huey formed **The Livin' End** after **The Coachmen** split in 1964. Both sides of the 45 can also be found on Collectables **Livin' End** retrospective: *Unreleased Texas Garage Sounds* (COL 0715) 1998. (MW)

The Coachmen

| 45: | Drambuie / ? | ('No Label' 22047) 1966 |

From Penfield, New York. Their spirited ode *Drambuie* was composed by Coachmen and future Mistics member D.Leschom; it's on *Let's Dig 'Em Up, Vol. 1* (LP) and *Teenage Shutdown Vol. 12* (LP & CD).

After the band split, some members joined The Quirks. (MM/MW)

The Coachmen

Personnel:	BRIAN COSTELLO	vcls, gtr	A
	MIKE DAVIES	gtr	A
	RICK FITZPATRICK	vcls, gtr	A
	SKIP KELLY	bs	A
	PAUL KERN	drms, vcls	A

| 45: | And That's Why/Money | (Esar 107/8) 1965 |

British invasion sounds on the Esar label of Sacramento, California. Both sides can also be found on *The Sound Of Young Sacramento* (CD). (VJ)

The Coastliners

HCP

45s:	The Lonely Sea/	
	Big Mike, The Sidewalk Surfer	(Astro 109) 1965 -
	Alright/Wonderful You	(International Artists 101) 1965 -
	Alright/Wonderful You	(Back Beat 554) 1965 -
	She's My Girl/I'll Be Gone	(Back Beat 556) 1966 121
	California On My Mind/I See Me	(D.E.A.R. 1300) 1967 115

Sometimes known as the Beach Boys Of Texas this Houston-based act set out as a surfing outfit and actually recorded the first 45 on International

Artists. Their final effort was a harmony pop effort and along the way they made a few punkier recordings, including *Alright*, which was written by Ross-Vanadore, and later recorded by **The Legends**.

They were previously known as the Carrousels with one 45 (*Merseybeat/It's Funny*) on Astro 105 (1965) and latterly as the **U.S. Males**, (*Come Out Of The Rain/Open Up Your Heart* (Brittania 101) in 1968)).

Compilation appearances include: *Alright* and *I'll Be Gone* on *Texas Punk From The Sixties* (LP) and *Sixties Archive, Vol. 2* (CD); *My, My Oh My* (previously unreleased) on *Houston Post - Nowsounds Groove-In* (LP) and *My Kind Of Girl* (previously unreleased) on *Houston Hallucinations* (LP). (VJ)

The Cobblers

Personnel incl:	MIKE MEIDL	gtr	A
	BOB MISKY	drms	A
	PAT NUGENT	ld gtr	A
	RON SPANBAUER	vcls	A
	BOB WEISAPPLE	bs	A
	NICK CHRISTAS	gtr	B

45s:	Smokin' At The Half Note/ Maybe I Love You	(Studio City 1060) 1966
α	Next 21st Of May / My Baby Kicked The Bucket	(Tee Pee 45/46) 1968

NB: α as The Syndicate.

This Oshkosh, Wisconsin group travelled to Minneapolis to record their debut, which is much touted amongst collectors, yet remains uncompiled.

Soon after they changed their name to The Syndicate Of Sound only to find out about the California band who hit the charts with *Little Girl*. They shortened it to The Syndicate, still oblivious of another California combo already using that name, and released a 45 in early 1968.

Pat Nugent was later in seventies band Blue Tail Fly and Bob Misky worked with Chicago outfit Skip Arne and The Dukes. Nick Christas was thought to be doing blues gigs in San Francisco. (VJ/GM/MW)

The Cobblestones

Personnel?:	JIM JACOBS	A
	LEHMANN	A
	PEARSON	A

45s:	It Happens Every Time / I'll Hide My Head In The Sand	(Den-Ric 9421/01) 1967
	I'll Hide My Head In The Sand / It Happens Every Time	(Mobie 3424) 1967
	Flower People / Down With It	(Mobie 3425) 1967

From Bloomington, Indiana, this previously unhailed outfit made good use of fuzz and farfisa. Their repertoire ranged from garage (*I'll Hide My Head...*) to flower-pop (*Flower People*) and a fuzzy instrumental laid on a Mona-beat (*Down With It*) - these three are compiled on *Psychedelic Crown Jewels, Vol. 3* (CD). *Down With It* also appears on *Buzz Buzz Buzzzzzz, Vol. 2* (CD). (MW/MM/RM)

The Cobras

Personnel:	BOBBY HERNE	gtr	A
	GARY LEAVITT	gtr, vcls	A
	JAY LEAVITT	drms	A

45:	I Wanna Be Your Lover/Instant Heartache	(Big Beat 1002) 1966

From Smyrna Mills, Maine. This New England teen band have been well represented on recent compilations.

The Leavitt brothers were later in **Euclid** and Bobby Herne produced their album. Herne, a chicken farmer and exceptional guitar player, had previously played with the Exotics (on Coral) and DJ and The Soulbeats. He went on to produce and arrange numerous New England acts in the sixties and seventies, including the infamous album *Philosophy Of The World* by **The Shaggs**. He died suddenly in May 1998 and Aram Heller's zine 'Banjo Room Revisited #2' chronicles parts of his legacy.

Compilation appearances include: *Instant Heartache* on *New England Teen Scene, Vol. 1* (LP) and *Teenage Shutdown, Vol. 14* (LP & CD); *I Wanna Be Your Love* on *New England Teen Scene, Vol. 2* (LP), *Teenage Shutdown, Vol. 1* (LP & CD) and *I Was A Teenage Caveman* (LP); *Instant Heartache* and *I Wanna Be Your Love* on *New England Teen Scene* (CD). (VJ/MW/JC)

The Cobras

45:	If I Can't Believe Her/I'm Hurtin'	(Scoop 103) 196?

A different outfit. *If I Can't Believe Her* resurfaced on *Boulders, Vol. 5* (LP) and *Ya Gotta Have Moxie, Vol. 1* (Dble CD). Anyone out there who can fill in the gaps?

The Cobras

45:	Come On Back/Summertime	(Feature 201,264/5) 196?

Yet another **Cobras**. Anyone out there who can identify this bunch?

The Cobras

45:	Try/Good Bye	(Milky Way MW-006) 1966

This lot hailed from Danville, Illinois, and their sole effort is low-key moody garage-beat.

Compilation appearances include: *Goodbye* on *Tymes Gone By* (LP). (MW)

Dennis Coffey and Detroit Guitar Band

ALBUM:	1 EVOLUTION	(Sussex SXBS 7004) 1971

From Detroit, **Dennis Coffey** is a guitarist and producer, often associated with Mike Theodore (on **Paul Parrish**'s *Forest Of My Mind* for instance). If his prolific solo production throughout the seventies is generally in the funk style and totally out of the scope of this book, his first album may interest some readers, as it contains ten instrumental tracks (including a cover of *Whole Lotta Love*) with three guitars, a sitar and percussions. (SR)

BUZZ BUZZ BUZZZZZZ Vol. 2 (Comp CD) including The Cobblestones.

Linda Cohen

ALBUM: 1 LEDA (Poppy) 1972

During the seventies, **Linda Cohen** recorded several instrumental albums combining folk and baroque/chamber influences, sometimes with psych sounds. Her presence here is mainly due to the involvement of several former members of **Mandrake Memorial**, notably Craig Anderton who played guitar and self-invented instruments and also had a hand on the production. Mostly suited for late night listening, her records will not appeal to everybody. (SR)

Stephen Cohn

ALBUM: 1 STEPHEN COHN (Motown M 789V1) 1973 -

45: Power Is/Take It Now (Motown 1330) 1973

One of the very few white acts signed on Motown, **Cohn** was a singer songwriter a lá **James Taylor**. His album was recorded in Hollywood with studio musicians: Jim Gordon, Ben Benay (**Goldenrod**), Lincoln Mayorga, Jim Keltner, Larry Carlton, Dick Rosmini and the jazz bassist Buell Neidlinger. Some tracks use tablas, harpsichord, female choirs or flutes, but the result is clearly in the "also ran" category. (SR)

Cold Blood

Personnel:			
FRANK J. DAVIS	drms	A	
ROD ELLICOTT	bs	AB	
LARRY FIELD	gtr	A	
DANNY HULL	sax	AB	
JERRY JONUTZ	sax	AB	
LARRY JONUTZ	trumpet	AB	
RAUL MATUTE	keyb'ds	AB	
DAVID PADRON	trumpet	A	
LYDIA PENSE	vcls	AB	
SANDY McKEE	drms	B	
(MIC GILLETTE	trumpet	AB)	
(JOSE CHEPITO ARIAS	perc	B)	

HCP

ALBUMS: 1(A) COLD BLOOD (San Francisco Records SD 200) 1969 23 -
(up to 2(B) SISYPHUS (San Francisco Records SD 205) 1970 60 -
1974) 3(-) FIRST TASTE OF SIN (Reprise RS 2074) 1972 133 -
4(-) THRILLER (Reprise RS 2130) 1973 97 -
5(-) LYDIA (Warner 2806) 1974 126 -

HCP

45s: You Got Me Humming/If You Will (San Francisco 60) 1970 52
(up to I'm A Good Woman/I Wish I Knew How It
1974) Would Feel To Be Free (San Francisco 61) 1970 125
Too Many People/I Can't Stay (San Francisco 62) 1970 107
Understand/Shop Talk (San Francisco 66) 1970 -
Down To The Bone/
Valdez In The Country (Reprise 1092) 1971 -
Baby I Love You/? (Reprise 1157) 1971 -

A soul/blues group with horns who was popular on the San Francisco rock scene, playing regularly at the Fillmore. Their sound was based on the bluesy vocals of Lydia Pense.

Their first album is notable for its fine Rick Griffin artwork but the music was rather uninspired and the horn arrangements quite messy. The same can be said of their following albums, which became more and more sou-oriented. They all sold quite well.

Their first drummer, Frank Davis, also played with **Loading Zone** and shouldn't be confused with the Texan **Frank Davis** (**Travel Agency**, **Saddlesore**).

You can also find *Shop Talk* and *Too Many People* on *San Francisco Sampler - Fall 1970*. (VJ/SR)

Cold Sun

Personnel:			
TOM McGARIGLE	gtr	A	
BILL MILLER	electric autoharp	A	
HUGH PATTON	drms, chimes	A	
MIKE WAUGH	bs	A	

ALBUM: 1(A) DARK SHADOWS (Rockadelic RRLP 2.5) 1990 R1
NB: (1) Issued with an insert and colour photo of the band.

A Texas group. Contrary to popular belief, the Rockadelic release above is not a straight reissue of an acetate. An acetate *was* found with several tracks by this group (only one known copy exists, now in a private collection) and through this acetate, information leading to the group was dug up. The leader of the band was found to have several tapes of sixties material and from these tapes the *Dark Shadows* album was mastered. Most of the material on the Rockadelic album does not appear on the acetate.

This release is well worth picking up - a genuinely psychedelic item with lots of superb and, often discordant, electric autoharp and sustained fuzz guitar and lots of fresh ideas. The vocals don't always reach the same standard, but this album is recommended.

Bill Miller later played on Roky Erickson's 1981 album *The Evil One*. (CF/VJ)

COLD SUN - Dark Shadows LP.

Coldwater Army

Personnel:			
BOB GARRETT	vcls, keyb'ds	A	
BOBBY GOLDEN	gtr	A	
KENNY GOLDEN	bs	A	
RICHARD HUGHES	drms	A	
NICK JONES	trumpet, vcls	A	
DALE MILER	sax	A	
BOB SPEARMAN	keyb'ds, vcls	A	

ALBUM: 1(A) PEACE (Agape 2600) 197? SC

From Florida, a mix of psych, prog and Southern rock which may interest some. Bobby Golden and Bob Spearman went on to form Stillwater in the mid-seventies. (SR)

Cole and The Embers

45s: Hey Girl/? (Star Trek 1220) 1967
Love Won't Hurt You (possibly flip of above)/
Love Won't Hurt You (possibly flip of above) (Star Trek) 196?

A St Louis band from the late sixties. *Hey Girl* followed the simple punk format with a droning farfisa organ backing and just a hint of progressivism in the brief organ solo midway through.

Compilation appearances have included: *Hey Girl* on *Pebbles, Vol. 13* (LP) and *The Essential Pebbles Collection, Vol. 2* (Dble CD). (VJ)

Collage

Personnel:	DONNA		A
	JERRY		A
	JODIE		A
	RON		A

ALBUM: 1(A) THE COLLAGE (Smash 101) 1967 -

A nice psychedelic sleeve for a totally disappointing pop quartet. (SR)

Collective Star

ALBUM: 1 GARUDA (Private Pressing) 1974 SC

This obscure group played a mix of psychedelia with strange effects and some Middle Eastern influences. (SR)

The College Boys

Personnel:	DAVE BEABER	gtrs, vcls	A
	ERIC GULLIKSEN	12 str gtr, bs, vcls	A
	JACK McKENES	banjo, bs, vcls	A

45: The Man / Song Of The Traveller (Swan S-4166) 1963

Significant for containing pre-**Orpheus** members Jack McKenes and Eric Gulliksen, this is the group referred to in the liner notes for *The Best Of Orpheus* retrospective CD as The Wanderers. A tribute to the late JFK, the record was produced by Tom Zagryn and Eric Gulliksen, and recorded in the cellar of a fraternity house on a Webcor tape recorder. Eric recalls: "As we already had a relationship with the Swan label via **The Blue Echoes**, we trotted it down to Philadelphia and Swan jumped on it thinking they would make a bundle. However, no Kennedy records made it in the US; people (and rightly so) just didn't want to see someone make money from the tragedy of JFK's death. For many years, though, I received air play royalties (in small amounts) from the four corners of the earth".

COLOURS - Atmosphere LP.

Keith Colley

45: Enamorado /Shame, Shame, Shame (Columbia 4-44410) 1968

A Californian singer, this 45 was produced by Gary Usher. The flip was later a hit for the Magic Lanterns and is of interest here as **Curt Boettcher** sang the backing vocals. **Colley** started recording in 1959 and in the next decade released at least twelve singles for various labels. (SR)

The Colony

45: All I Want/Things On My Mind (Platter 105) 1967

The outfit came from Ventura, California and had a great constipated-sounding vocalist. *All I Want* later appeared on *Pebbles Vol. 8* (CD), *Boulders, Vol. 1* (LP) and *Highs In The Mid-Sixties, Vol. 1* (LP). (VJ/RSs)

Coloring Book

45: Smokestack Lightning/
You Make Me Feel So Good (Pacific Challenger 117/8) c1966

The cover of *Smokestack* is rather lightweight but includes some wailing harp and is laid-back rather than a bluesy rave-up. Their cover of the Zombies classic is rather insipid. (MW)

The Colors of Night

45: C-0-L-0-R-S/? (Regime 6964) 1967

C-0-L-0-R-S can be heard on *Pennsylvania Unknowns* (LP) - they hailed from Philadelphia. (VJ)

Colours

Personnel:	CHUCK BLACKWELL	drms	A
	JACK DALTON	gtr	A
	ROB EDWARDS	ld gtr	A
	GARY MONTGOMERY	piano	A
	CARL RADLE	bs	A

ALBUMS: 1(A) COLOURS (Dot 25854) 1968 -
2( ) ATMOSPHERE (Dot 25935) 1969 -

NB: (1) & (2) later reissued as double set (Paramount 81030).

HCP
45s: Brother Lou's Love Colony/Lovin' (Dot 17060) 1967 -
Love Heals/Bad Day At Black Rock, Baby (Dot 17132) 1968 106
Hyannisport Sequel/Run Away From Here (Dot 17181) 1968 -
Angie/God Please Take My Life (Dot 17280) 1969 -

English spelling for a U.S. group seems illogical enough, but the liner-notes from their first album tell us that they 'have the crystalline sharpness of the Beatles before they turned acid'. That seems a dangerous thing to postulate. The first track, though, completely lives up to these pretensions and must be reckoned among the very best attempts at an orchestrated psych sound. Easily switching from key to key and with disturbingly many time-changes, which at first sound completely innocent, this particular track conveys a sense of drama seldom equalled. Menacing harmonies and superb instrumentation underscore the sorry tale of a bored lad, who vainly tries to rob a liquor store - with a tragic outcome: *Bad Day At Black Rock, Baby* "I'm carving a gun from an old piece of wood, dip it in black paint, it looks pretty good".

Other tracks can't quite keep the standard that high, but feature several more highlights and very versatile playing, like the sitar droned *Rather Be Me*, the commune-song *Brother Lou's Love Colony* with bagpipes and later covered by Moon, and the eerie *Cataleptic*. Definitely an underestimated album. Their second album is sadly not in the same class. Without any credits to other musicians than Dalton/Montgomery, this album takes in some progressive rock, some undigested country and also has a cluttered production. Only the very last track on Side Two *You're High* comes anywhere near the former style and intensity. This album is best forgotten. The first needs rehabilitation.

From Tulsa, Radle and Blackwell were close friends of **Leon Russell**. They both guested on **Don Preston and The South**'s album and later enjoyed successful careers. Carl Radle was with **Delaney and Bonnie**, Derek and The Dominos, J.J. Cale and Eric Clapton. Chuck Blackwell played with Taj Mahal, Joe Cocker and **Leon Russell**. Rob Edwards has also previously played with **Eddie and The Showmen**.

Where Is She, a Dalton/Montgomery song, surfaced on **Harper and Rowe**'s album, whilst *Cataleptic* was also covered by **Aorta**. (MK/SR/BCr)

Columbus Circle

ALBUM: 1 ON St. JOHN'S EVE (Pharoah) 1976 -

From Glastonbury, Connnecticut, a rare album with two totally different music on either side. The first has a mix of prog and neo classical music with dissonant effects and percussions, whilst Side Two contains short songs with female vocals, wah wah guitar, organ and flute.

The group is sometimes mistakenly listed as Glastonbury. (SR)

Colwell - Winfield Blues Band

Personnel:	BILL COLWELL	gtr	A
	CHUCK PURRO	drms	A
	JACK SCHROER	alto sax, tenor sax, soprano sax	A
	CHARLES 'MOOSE' SORRENTO	vcls, piano	A
	COLIN TILTON	tenor sax, flute	A
	MIKE WINFIELD	bs	A

ALBUMS: 1(A) COLD WIND BLUES (Verve Forecast FTS-3056) 1968 -
2( ) LIVE BUST (Za-Zoo) c1970 SC

NB: (1) reissued (Akarma AK 148) 2001.

Whilst the extended version of *Dead End Street* from their debut album had a lot of exposure on the early FM stations on the U.S. East Coast at least, of more interest is the six-minute intrumental *Govinda* which is a great hindiesque groove with mallets on the drums, soprano sax and electric guitar played like a sitar... (undoubtedly they had heard the new **Butterfield Blues Band**'s *East West*). For the most part, the album consists of urban blues-rock in the Chicago style, although there's no harmonica.

Possibly from Chicago or Boston, *Cold Wind Blues* was recorded in New York and produced by Bob Bateman. It has the written endorsement of Will and Lester Chambers of the **Chambers Brothers** on the back cover...

Definitely more of a progressive blues than a psych item, the cover is standard issue record company psychsploito smoke and double exposure band/nature photo that is actually quite nice... tinted lavender even...

The group later released a rare live album before disbanding. In 1970, Tilton and Schroer were recruited by Van Morrison for his *Moondance* album and Shroer kept on working with Van the Man up until 1975. In 1972, Winfield and Tilton also worked with Martha Velez on her album *Hipnotized* and Tilton also played on solo albums by Ellen McIllwaine, the former **Fear Itself** singer. In the mid-seventies, Chuck Purro went on to play with the James Montgomery Band, a blues band from Boston, along with Peter Malick from **Listening**. (PPe/SR)

The Combenashuns

45: What'cha Gonna Do/Hey Uncle Sam (Leo 3801) 196?

A Bethlehem, Pennsylvania outfit, you'll find *Whatcha Gonna Do* on the *Pennsylvania Unknowns* (LP) compilation. *Hey! Uncle Sam* also appears on *Follow That Munster, Vol. 2* (LP). (VJ)

COMFORTABLE CHAIR - Comfortable Chair LP.

Bill Comeau

ALBUM: 1 FRAGMENTS FROM AN UNKNOWN GOSPEL (Avant-Garde) 1969 -

On this Christian label, an ambitious folk album with lyrics penned by **Bill Comeau**, described as a "poet/composer/singer/playwright/seeker/dreamer, and music composed by Carmel Signa, a "composer/teacher/free spirit/hurried and sometimes happy soul".

Bill Comeau went on to form **The Incredible Broadside Brass Bed Band**. (SR)

The Comets

Personnel:	ALAN DENNY	gtr, keyb'ds	A
	MIKE HALL	drms	A
	BUDDY HOBGOOD	ld gtr	A
	TIM PEPPER	bs	A
	MIKE RUSSELL	vcls	A
	JOE STONESTREET	sax	A

CD: 1(A) MERCY MERCY (Collectables Col-0620) 1997

NB: (1) Originally recorded for release on Justice in 1966, but not issued.

Formed in 1963 at Hill Junior High School in Winston-Salem, North Carolina, **The Comets** recorded twelve tracks for Calvin Newton's Justice Records Label in 1966. Aside from the typical cover versions, including three Chuck Berry tunes, the Rolling Stones' *The Last Time* and Wilson Pickett's *In The Midnight Hour*, the band recorded three original lightweight pop compositions: *What You've Done*, *Someday You'll See*, and *Do You Remember*. Sadly, before the fruits of their endeavours could be released the label went bankrupt.

That was thought to be the end of **The Comets** saga, but the story doesn't end there.... After Justice closed its doors in '67, the building became home to various businesses (it's now a Carpet store!). However, circa 1975 it was home to an advertising agency. Tim:- "After the break up of **The Comets**, Mike Russell, our lead singer, went on to perform with several bands. He went on the road for a while and in the process made a number of friends who like all musicians drifted in and out of the music business. One of his friends, Tom Vickers, was working in this advertising studio at the old Justice building. In the back was a great big old desk that had very deep drawers in it. No one knew how long the old thing had been there. Well, Tom had gone back to this old desk to look for a roll of double sided tape to work on a layout with. Reaching way back in the lower drawer he found two boxes of Scotch Recording Tape. Each box had one reel of 7" X1/4" recording tape in it and on the front of the boxes was a label that just said **The Comets**."

Over the next few years, the tapes languished on the shelf, until Mike Russell accidentally discovered a Collectables reissue of another Justice album. The tapes were verified by Calvin Newton and at last released by Collectables.

Today, Buddy lives in Orlando and Mike Hall in Massachusetts, but the other four remain in Winston-Salem.

Compilation appearances include *The Last Time* on *Green Crystal Ties Vol. 10* (CD). (MDo/TP)

Comfortable Chair

Personnel:			
	TAD BACZEC	ld gtr	A
	GARY DAVIS	keyb'ds	A
	WARNER DAVIS	drms	A
	GENE GARFIN	vcls, perc	A
	GREG LEROY	bs, ld gtr	A
	BERNIE SCHWARTZ	vcls	A
	BARBARA WALLACE	vcls	A

ALBUM: 1(A) COMFORTABLE CHAIR (Ode 212 44005) 1969 -

45s: Be Me/Come Soon, Some Day (Ode 109) 1969
I'll See You/Now (Ode 112) 1969

A Los Angeles band whose main claim to fame is that they were discovered by Jim Morrison. Their album was produced by Robbie Krieger and John Densmore (also of **The Doors**). It has some very pleasant moments. They sounded similar to **It's A Beautiful Day** and **Peanut Butter Conspiracy**. The group also appeared and played two songs in an exploito movie called "How to Commit Marriage", with Jackie Gleason, Bob Hope and Jane Wyman.

Bernie Schwartz was also a songwriter who began recording singles in 1963 and released an interesting album, *The Wheel* in 1969 or 1970, with Gene Garfin and **Euphoria**.

Greg Leroy later worked for Neil Young and Crazy Horse. (VJ/SR)

Comin' Generation

Personnel:			
	DENNIS BEERY	drms	A
	EDD KOLAKOWSKI	ld vcls, keyb'ds	A
	STEVE TRUXELL	bs	A
	BOB WEBB	gtr	A

45: Hey Girl / Get Out Of My Life Woman (Dupree D-1304) 1967

This outfit were from Alliance, Ohio. Bob Webb went on to the Measles and Lacewing. *Hey Girl*, from their sole 45, is on *Lost Generation, Vol. 1* (LP). (GGI/MW)

Coming Generation

Personnel:			
	ED CONNOR	gtr	A
	ROGER EDDINGTON	bs	A
	STEVE EDDINGTON	ld gtr	A
	BOB FROBISCH	keyb'ds	A
	GIRARD STEICHEN	drms	A

A quintet from Dwight, Illinois. They contributed two cuts to *A Psychedelic Six-Pack Of Sound*, a 1968 sampler album of six local Illinois bands. *Without You* is a harmonious acoustic folkie-pop ballad. *Down To The City* is much better, a catchy folk-rocker notable for its use of a siren - one of the few 'psychedelic' moments on the album.

Steve Eddington in the early - mid seventies played in **New Colony Six**, and currently plays in Heartsfield. (MW/SD)

A PSYCHEDELIC SIX-PACK OF SOUND (Comp LP) including Coming Generation.

Coming Times

45: Pork & Beans/Keep The Music Playing (Josie 954) 1966

This one 45 was the sole vinyl excursion by this obscure outfit which is thought to have come from New York or Philadelphia. Judging by the 'B' side *Keep The Music Playing*, which can be heard on *Pebbles, Vol. 12* (LP), they deserved better with this than a return to total obscurity. It's got some nice pop harmonies, but perhaps suffered from being a low cost production. (VJ)

The Common Market

45: I Love My Dog/Wings (RCA 47-9302) 1967

A melodic pop-rock single. (SR)

Common People

Personnel:			
	JOHN BARTLEY III	gtr	A
	WILLIAM FAUSTO		A
	MICHAEL McCARTHY	bs	A
	DENNY ROBINETT	gtr, vcls	A
	JERRALD ROBINETT	drms	A

ALBUM: 1(A) OF THE PEOPLE BY THE PEOPLE FOR THE PEOPLE FROM THE COMMON PEOPLE
(Capitol ST 266) 1969 R2

NB: (1) has been counterfeited on vinyl. (1) reissued on CD (Ascension ANCD 022).

This album was recorded in California and they may have been a Californian band. Mellow, soft psychedelia similar to **Gandalf** the album is recommended and increasingly attracting interest from collectors. (VJ)

Commons Ltd.

45: Roses Are Red (My Love)/
I'm Going To Change The World (MOD M-1005) 1966

Top side is mid-tempo Invasion beat (complete with 'yeah yeah's that was originally done by **The "You Know Who" Group**). The winner here is an excellent cover of The Animals' song with a superb, and all too short, fuzz break that's a highight on the *The Quill Records Story* (CD) and *Pebbles, Vol. 7* (CD). Rumour is that they hailed from Illinois. (MW)

Communicaton Aggregation

Personnel incl: BUZZ CASON   A
                 BOBBY RUSSELL   A

45:   Freakout USA/Off The Wall   (RCA Victor 47-8930) 1966

A Nashville studio aggregation featuring Bobby Russell (Bobby Russel and The Beagles). He was also involved in many of the acts on the budget Hit label (Jalopy Five, Beasts, Doodles) who covered hits of the day. *Freakout USA* has resurfaced on *Boulders, Vol. 11* (LP) and *Ya Gotta Have Moxie, Vol. 1* (Dble CD). Wacky rather than psychedelic. (VJ/MW/JLh)

Compton and Mele

Personnel incl: BURT COMPTON   A
                 STEVE MELE   A

ALBUM: 1(A) ROCK AND ROLL GENIUS   (Wizard 303) c1973 SC

From Florida, between hard-rock, psych and seventies rock, with a cover of **Nazz**' *Open My Eyes*. Only 500 copies were pressed. (SR)

Bobby Comstock and The Counts

Personnel incl: BOBBY COMSTOCK   ld vcls   A

ALBUM: 1 OUT OF SIGHT   (Ascot ALM 13026) 1966 SC?
NB: (1) also relesaed on stereo (ALS 16026)

45s: Right Hand Man/Always   (Ascot 2164) 1965
(partial   I'm A Man/I'll Make You Glad   (Ascot 2175) 1965
list)   This Magic Moment/Shotgun Sally   (Ascot 2193) 1966
              Can't Judge A Book/Out Of Sight   (Ascot 2216) 1966
         α   Annabelle Jane/Help Me Girl   (Bell 828) 1969

NB: α by Comstock Ltd.

A prolific rock singer, **Bobby Comstock** began recording in the late fifties. He recorded at least one album and twenty singles between 1959 and 1972 on various labels: Blaze, Triumph, Atlantic, Jubilee, Festival, Lawn, Ascot and Bell. His style would follow the fashion and his mid-sixties records were done with a backing group, the Counts, in a garage style a lá Yardbirds. (SR)

Conception

45: Babylon/The Game   (Perfection P-1001) 196?

You'd be excused for thinking this 45 is by two different groups. The 'A' is a cover of **Blue Cheer**'s brain-buster, suitably heavy with phasing; the 'B' is a mellow jazzy West Coast workout - a cure for *Babylon* presumably! (MW)

Concern

See **Guitar Ensemble** entry.

Concrete Rubber Band

Personnel: D. LONG   vcls, keyb'ds, gtr   A
            J. LONG   vcls, keyb'ds   A
            B. RHODES perc   A

ALBUM: 1(A) RISEN SAVIOR   (American Artists AAS 1164) 1974 R3

A Missouri label, so the band may be from there as well. A very rare and strange rock album with religious themes - male and female lead vocals, electronic embellishments, very strangely recorded. The record actually has several dropouts in the pressing, apparently the result of tape flaws. Only two or three copies are known in collections. (CF)

COMMON PEOPLE - Of The People... LP.

(Mike) Condello

Personnel: MIKE CONDELLO   gtr, keyb'ds   A
            DENNIS KENMORE   drms   A
            BILL SPOONER   gtr   A
            RAY TRAINER   bs, keyb'ds, flute   A

ALBUM: 1(A) PHASE 1   (Scepter SPS 542) 1966 SC
NB: (1) as **Condello**. Mike Condello also recorded a solo album *No Bathing In The Pond* (Takoma TAK 7116) 1984. There's also a retrospective CD, *Mike Condello - Presents Wallace And Ladmo's Greatest Hits* (Epiphany W&L 1954) 1994.

EPs: 1 BLUBBER SOUL   (Ladmo L-007-1) 1965
      2 MIKE'S MINI ALBUM   (Blitz Kpho-Tv 005) 1967
      3 MAKES A COMEBACK: (Blitz-Big 006) c1967
      4 COMMODORE CONDELLOS SALT RIVER NAVY BAND
                                         (Blitz Cheap) 1976

NB:(1) as Ladmo Trio. (2), (3) & (4) as **Commodore Condello's Salt River Navy Band**. (1) contains *Obese Man*, *Shapes Of Things*, *Michelle* and *Run For Your Life*. (2) Sgt. Pepper parody. (3) contains *Soggy Cereal*, *Sonic Boom*, *Time Machine* and three other tracks.

45s: α Rudolph The Red-Nosed Reindeer /
         Little Drummer Boy   (Ladmo 631-12) 1964
      β Let's Really Hear It (For Hub Kapp) /
         Work Work   (Take Five 631-5) 1964
      β Sigh, Cry, Almost Die / Bony Maronie   (Capitol 5215) 1964
      β Little Volks /
         What You're Doin' To Me   (Framagratz F-101) 1965
      ε I Can't Help The Way I Feel /
         What Is She Thinking Of   (LHI 17007) 1967
      ε Something's Happening /
         Stand Up And Shout!   (LHI 17019) c1967
      χ Ho, Ho, Ha Ha, Hee Hee, Ha Ha/
         Pollen's Found A Home In My Nose   (Ranco 2003) 1968
      δ Crystal Clear/See What Tomorrow Brings (Scepter 12233) 1968
      δ Goodnight/I'm So Glad It Ain't Me   (Scepter 12261) 1969
      δ Goodnight (3:58 Mono) /
         Goodnight (5:06 Stereo) Promo   (Scepter 12261) 1969

NB: α as Ladmo. β as Hub Kapp & The Wheels. χ as by 'Commodore Condello's Salt River Navy Band'. δ as **Condello**. ε as Last Friday's Fire.

Formed in Arizona but based in California, **Condello**'s *Phase One* album has some interesting moments. Their *Makes A Comeback* EP included *Soggy Cereal*, (which has become rather well-known by virtue of its inclusion on *Pebbles, Vol. 3* (LP), and *Sonic Boom*, a **Hendrix**-influenced blast (compiled on *Brain Shadows, Vol. 2* (LP & CD)). **Mike Condello** later joined Elton Duck, a L.A.-based late seventies/early eighties new wave trio, and then recorded a solo LP in 1984. Bill Spooner ended up in The Tubes and Dennis Kenmore joined Pollution, a late sixties/early seventies jazz-influenced rock band.

Condello also produced an album for **Warren S Richardson**, which may be a Bill Spooner solo project.

Much of **Condello**'s material is collected on the CD *Wallace And Ladmo's Greatest Hits*. *Brain Shadows, Vol. 2* (LP & CD) also features *The Time Machine*, a rather catchy number by **Commodore Condello's Salt River Navy Band**.

Both singles as Last Friday's Fire for Lee Hazelwood's LHI label were produced by him. As Last Friday's Fire they had also earlier backed Lynne Castle on her solo 45: *The Lady Barber / Rose Colored Corner* (LHI 17003) 1967. (VJ/MW/JH)

The Confederate Society

Personnel incl: MARK MECCIA   A

Acetate: I'm Through With You/
           Pride/Ticket To Ride/Hold On I'm Coming   (Unreleased) 1967

Came from Glen Ridge, New Jersey and true to their name often did sport confederate uniforms for their gigs. An important part of their live repertoire was a fine version of *Hey Joe*, but that never did make it onto vinyl. Indeed their sole vinyl appearance came when *Pride*, an odd mix of the **Byrds** and Merseybeat sung to standard punk lyrics, was later included on the *Attack Of The Jersey Teens* (LP) compilation. (VJ)

Seth Connors

45s: Blue Colour/Cry, Cry, Cry   (Verve Folkways 5037) 1968
       In The Naked City/
       Why Concern Yourself   (Verve Forecast 5067) 1968

A New York pop-rock singer. *In The Naked City* is rather catchy but partly ruined by the production of Rick Shorter, who wrote *Why Concern Yourself*, also recorded by **Street**. (SR)

The Conqueroo

Personnel: BOB BROWN   gtr   A
             SUPER SPADE (ED GUINN)   flute, bs A
             FAT CHARLIE (PRITCHARD)   ld gtr   A
             GERRY STORM   drms   A

MIKE CONDELLO - Presents Wallace & Ladmo's Greatest Hits CD.

ALBUM: 1(A)   FROM THE VULCAN GAS CO.   (5 Hours Back 008) 1987

45:      1 To 3/I've Got Time (PS)   (Sonobeat 103) 1968

One of Austin's best-loved bands of this era they opened their own club, The Vulcan Gas Company in 1967 and among its attractions were the **13th Floor Elevators** and many of the best black blues singers of the era. The club lasted until 1970. Their 45 appeared in a picture sleeve and featured some fine 'acid' guitar work. Indeed the band have been referred to as Austin's **Grateful Dead**. They moved to San Francisco for a while and whilst there Brown and Guinn also worked as The Angel Band. Disillusioned **The Conqueroo** split and returned to Texas. They reformed briefly in the mid-seventies.

Their retrospective album is a live recording from 1968. It features fine guitar work on *Passenger* and *Banana And The Cat* but is patchy overall so primarily for archivists. Ed Guinn and Bob Brown also cut a long demo tape about early 1967 of entirely fresh material, but this hasn't resurfaced to date. They also helped back comic artist and Austin resident **Gilbert Shelton** on his sole 45.

Bob Brown later married and subsequently divorced Julie Christenson of Divine Horseman fame.

From the eighties through the mid-nineties, Ed Guinn had a successful recording studio in Austin. He also played the part of the scared truck driver in the 'Texas Chainsaw Massacre' movie.

Compilation appearances have included *1 To 3* and *I've Got Time* on *Texas Psychedelia From The Sixties* (LP) and *Sixties Archive, Vol. 6* (CD). (VJ/SR)

The Conservatives

45:   One Too Many Mornings/
      A Little Bird Told Me So   (Tribe 8326) 1965

On the same label as the first **Sir Douglas Quintet** releases, another group produced by Huey Meaux. The 'A' side is a Bob Dylan song. (SR)

The Contents Are

45s: I Don't Know/Direction Of Mind   (ROK 6709) 1967
       Future Days/New Mexico   (ROK 6907) 1967

Hailing from Davenpoo, Iowa, this mob actually made an album although I've no details of it. Consequently their best known recording is *Direction Of Mind* by virtue of its inclusion on the compilation, *Dirty Water - The History Of Eastern Iowa Rock Volume 2* (LP). This one shows a strong **Byrds** influence. The first 45 was recorded in Minneapolis. (VJ)

The Continental Co-eds

Personnel: CAROLYN BEHR   A
             CAROL GOINS   A
             MARY JO HOFMANN   A
             NANCY HOFMANN   A
             VICKI STEINMAN   A

45:   I Don't Love You No More/Medley Of Junk   (IGL 105) 1966

This lot hold the distinction of being the only all girl band from Minnesota ever to record in the 1960s. The girls came from the Pipestone and Fulda areas down in the extreme Southwest corner of the State. They were a popular local live attraction at clubs and teen fairs in the region. The 'A' side, *I Don't Love You No More* is a fairly typical garage punk effort, whilst the flip, consists of an instrumental surf-influenced medley.

Compilation appearances include: *Let's Live For The Present* on *The Arf! Arf! Blitzkrieg 32 Track Sampler* (CD); *Ebb Tide* and *Let's Live For The Present* on *IGL Dance Jamboree '66* (CD); *I Don't Love You No More* on *The Best Of IGL Garage Rock* (LP), *Glimpses, Vol. 2* (LP), *Glimpses, Vol's*

1 & 2 (CD) and *Girls In The Garage, Vol. 2* (LP); *Medley Of Junk* on *Girls In The Garage, Vol. 1* (LP); and *I Don't Love You No More* and *Medley Of Junk* on *The IGL Rock Story: Part One (1965 - 67)* (CD) and *Girls In The Garage, Vol. 1* (CD). (VJ)

The Continental V

45s:	Wake Me Up Girl/Tell Me Why	(Radel 107)	1967
	Wake Me Up Girl/Tell Me Why	(Continental 101)	1967

The 'A' side to this Houston outfit's sole vinyl offering, *Wake Me Up Girl* is pretty trippy.

Compilation appearances include *Wake Me Up Girl* on *Flashback, Vol. 3* (LP), *Texas Flashbacks, Vol. 3* (LP & CD) and *Texas Flashback (The Best Of)* (CD). (VJ)

The Continentals

45s:	Take Me/She Wants You	(AOK 1025)	1966
	I'm Gone/Blue Moments	(Gaylo 124)	196?

From West Texas. *I'm Gone*, is a fast punk number with a tambourine solo!

Compilation appearances have included *I'm Gone* on *Riot City!* (LP), *Texas Punk From The Sixties* (LP), *Sixties Archive Vol. 2* (CD) and *Teenage Shutdown, Vol. 4* (LP & CD); *Take Me* on *The History Of Texas Garage Bands, Vol. 3* (CD) and *She Wants You* on *The History Of Texas Garage Bands, Vol. 4* (CD).

The Continentals

45:	Sick And Tired / Almost A Man	(D&C DC-20)	1966

This Messina, New York group had evolved out of The Panthers. Their Summer 1966 release appeared on the Schenectady label that put out notable 45s by **The Chancellors** and **The Oscar Five**.

Sick And Tired - a great Anglophile punker, where Kinks riffs mesh with strong raunchy vocals and cool harmonica - is a stand-out on *Sick And Tired* (LP), *Fuzz, Flaykes, And Shakes, Vol. 5* (LP & CD) and *Psychedelic States: New York Vol. 1* (CD). *Almost A Man* can be found on *The Night Is So Dark* (LP). (MW)

The Continentals

Personnel:
LARRY BOWIE	vcls, organ, gtr	A
LAVONNE MOON	vcls, drms	A
JOHN WHITLEY	vcls, bs, gtr	A
PAUL WHITLEY	vcls, ld gtr	A

45:	Continentals Jam /		
	House Of The Rising Sun	("The Continentas" 418)	1965

Pine Mountain and West Point were the hometowns of this Georgia quartet who came together in 1962. Their basement recorded debut appeared around the time they became **Soul, Inc.**; they would also be known briefly as The Buckinghams, before the Chicago act hit the charts, just prior to their split in the Summer of 1966. Larry Bowie was later in **The Rock Garden**.

The reedy rocker *Continentals Jam* can be found on *Psychedelic States: Georgia Vol. 1* (CD) along with **Soul, Inc.**'s *Ode To A Girl*. (MW/RM)

Curley Cook and The Versitones

45:	Avalanche/Long Road To Nowhere	(Norcur NR 100)	1966

One of the first records by the future **Steve Miller Band / A.B.Shky** member. The 'A' side is a good instrumental track with fine guitar, the 'B' side is a ballad written by Ricky Lee.

The Norcur label was based in Hobbs, New Mexico. (SR)

Shep Cooke

Personnel incl:
VINNIE BELL	electric sitar	A
DAVID BROMBERG		A
SHEP COOKE	gtr, vcls	ABC

ALBUMS:	1(A)	HAVE U GONE BALD INSIDE YOUR HEAD?		
			(Vanguard VSD 6256)	1969 -
	2(B)	SHEP COOKE	(WWC 001)	1976 -
	3(C)	CONCERT TOUR OF MARS	(Sierra SRS 8705)	1980 -

NB: (1) released as **Shep**.

Shep (Walter) Cooke was originally from Tucson, Arizona and had previously played with **Intruders**, who evolved into **Quinstrells** and finally became **The Dearly Beloved**. He would later tour and record with **The Stone Poneys** and **The Floating House Band**

All three solo albums are singer/songwriter efforts. The Vanguard album (credited to **Shep**) is the weakest and for the most part **Shep** sounds unsure of himself and comes across rather wimpy. The second is a local Tucson effort and is fairly difficult to find, but on this album he is much more comfortable with the material and is more confident in his playing and singing. It is a good local folk record for collectors of that genre. The third album is a more polished effort and picks up where the second left off, it also features other former members of the **Stone Poneys**. (VJ/MW/HS)

Cookin Mama

Personnel incl:
SHERRY FOX	vcls	A

ALBUM:	1(A)	NEW DAY	(Rock Bottom)	c1972 R1

NB: (1) reissued (Piccadilly) 1980.

From San Francisco, on the same label as **Ofoedian Den**, **Cookin Mama** was a rural jamming rock group with a horn section, influenced by the **Grateful Dead** and the **Sons Of Champlin**.

Both pressings of their only album are now hard to find. Sherry Fox would later be in **Oasis**. (SR)

Don Cooper

ALBUMS:	1	DON COOPER	(Roulette)	1970 -
	2	BLESS THE CHILDREN	(Roulette)	1970 -
	3	BALLAD OF C.P. JONES	(Roulette)	1971 -
	4	WHAT YOU FEEL IS HOW YOU GROW	(Roulette)	1972 -

NB: (2) also released in Germany (Vogue LDVS 17210).

From New York, a largely forgotten folk-rock singer. His second album was recorded with **Elliot Randall** on guitar, Terry Plumeri on bass and Bobby Notkoff (**Rockets**, **Heavy Balloon**). The rather unusual combination of electric fiddle, guitars and harmonica gives a interesting touch to tracks like *A New Gun*, *Tins Cans And Alleyways*, **James Taylor**'s *Something In The Way She Moves* and the title track. (SR)

Marty Cooper

ALBUM:	1	A MINUTE OF YOUR TIME	(Barnaby BR-15004)	1972 -

A largely forgotten figure of the Los Angeles scene, **Marty Cooper** was active between 1966 and 1974 as a producer (**Vanguards**, **United Fruit Co.**) and songwriter for local groups. He was often associated with Lee Hazelwood. Co-produced with Ken Mansfield (**Sand**), his only solo album is a decent mix of country-rock, folk and soft-rock, with his *View From Ward 3* previously been recorded by **Hearts and Flowers**. (SR)

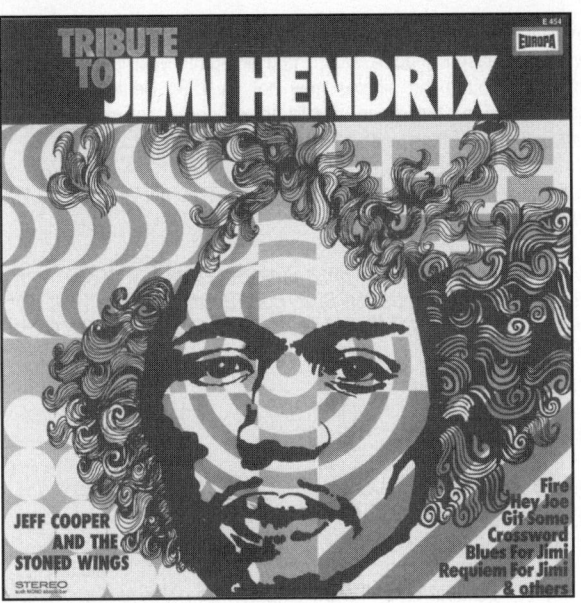

JEFF COOPER AND THE STONED WINGS - Tribute To Jimi Hendrix LP.

Ry Cooper

| 45: | 1983/The Life Game | (Musicor 1148) 1969 |

An excellent folk-rock singer with a raging voice, some organ and a great electric guitar, obviously influenced by Dylan and the protest songs a lá *Eve Of Destruction*. Contrary to what it may seem, it's totally unrelated to Ry Cooder. (SR)

Jeff Cooper and The Stoned Wings

Personnel incl: JEFF COOPER (?) A

ALBUM: 1 TRIBUTE TO JIMI HENDRIX
(Germany/Europa E 454) 197? R1

Despite only being released in Germany, this album is likely of American origin. The musicians are uncredited. The bulk of the tracks on the album were included on another mysterious non-U.S. issued record **Purple Fox**. The group sounds uncannily like The Exkursions.

Compilation appearances include *Fire* on *The Stars That Play With Dead Jimi's Dice* (LP). (CF)

Copperhead

Personnel:	JOHN CIPOLLINA	gtr	AB
	MARIO CIPOLLINA	bs	A
	NICKY HOPKINS	keyb'ds	A
	JIM MURRAY	gtr	A
	PETE SEARS	bs, keyb'ds	A
	CASEY SONOBAN	drms	A
	MARK UNOBSKY	gtr	A
	JASPER "HUTCH" HUTCHINSON	vcls, bs	B
	JIM McPHERSON	vcls, piano, bs, perc	B
	GARY PHILIPPET	vcls, gtr, organ	B
	DAVID WEBER	drms, perc	B

ALBUM: 1(B) COPPERHEAD   (CBS CS 32250) 1973 -

NB: (1) also released in the U.K. and Holland. (1) Reissued by Edsel (ED 136) with one bonus track and on CD (Acadia ACA 8005) 2001.

| 45: | Roller Derby Star/Chameleon | (CBS 4-45810) 1973 |

NB: *Chameleon* is non LP but does appear on the Edsel reissue. A double-sided promo edition also exists.

When John Cipollina left **Quicksilver Messenger Service** in 1971, he formed **Copperhead** with Jim Murray and Casey Sonoban (two members of the first **Quicksilver** line-up), his brother Mario (who later found fame with Huey Lewis and The News) and various other musicians. Their frequent rehearsals and gigs didn't allow them to get a recording contract and in 1972 Cipollina assembled a new line-up with Gary Philippet (ex-**Front Line**), Jim McPherson (ex-**Stained Glass**), David Weber and Hutch Hutchinson. A record, *Sealed For Your Protection*, was ready to be released on Just Sunshine Record but was eventually shelved. Finally *Copperhead* was issued by CBS in 1973 and is a superb example of San Francisco Sound, with seven original tracks and a new version of *Kibitzer*, already recorded by McPherson with **Stained Glass**. A must for fans of **Quicksilver** and Cipollina's guitar.

Two bootlegs with a good sound quality also exist: *Drunken Irish Setter*, recorded live on December 16th, 1972 in San Francisco (Oh Boy 1-9026, CD) and *Live 1973*, recorded for KSAN-FM (Blue Velvet FCP002, LP). Both contain tracks not present on the album.

Cipollina, McPherson and Philippet also played on one track of Kathi McDonald's *Insane Asylum* (Capitol ST-11224) 1974.

After **Copperhead**, Cipollina, Weber, McPherson and Hutchinson joined Terry and The Pirates and played with various local groups. Hutch Hutchinson became a renowned bass session player and is still active in the studios.

John Cipollina, who had been plagued with asthma for much of his life, died in 1989 of emphesema. (SR)

Copper Plated Integrated Circuit

ALBUM: 1 PLUGGED IN POP   (Command COM-945) c1969 -

An album of electronic pop done with various keyboards and early synthesizers. (SR)

Corbett and Hirsh

Personnel:	MIKE CORBETT	vcls, flute, vibes, perc	A
	JAY HIRSCH	gtr, keyb'ds, mandolin, accordion	A
	HUGH McCRACKEN	gtrs, mouth harp, sitar	A
	JOHN SIOMOS	drms	A
	(LEW HARBINGTON	french horn	A)
	(RUSSEL GEORGE	fiddles	A)
	(PAUL GRIFIN	keyb'ds	A)
	(AL ROGERS	drms	A)
	(CHRISTIE THOMPSON	keyb'ds	A)
	(ERIC WEISBERG	pedal steel gtr	A)

ALBUM: 1(A) MIKE CORBETT AND JAY HIRSCH WITH HUGH McCRACKEN   (Atco SD 33-361) 1971 -

In 1971, **Hirsch and Corbett** recorded, wrote and produced this good album which is in the same vein as their previous group, **Mr. Flood's Party**. Tracks like *Gypsy Child*, *Annie's A Wizzard*, *Fly With Me* or *Butterfly Day* all contain fine vocals and lyrics with interesting instrumentation. The album was recorded in New York.

John Siomos was previously in **Chicago Loop** and **Music**. **Hugh McCracken** was a very active musician at the time on the East Coast. (SR)

Jerry Corbitt

Personnel:	ED BOGAS	moog	A
	JERRY CORBITT	gtr, mouthharp, vcls	ABCD
	CHARLIE DANIELS	mandolin, bs, fiddle, gtr	ABCD
	GREGORY DEWEY	drms	AB
	BERNIE KRAUSE	moog	A
	RICK TURNER	bs, gtr	A
	RON MBULA WILSON		A
	JESSE COLIN YOUNG	vcls	B
	EARL GRIMSBY	bs	CD

	JEFFREY MEYER	drms	CD
	JOE ROMAN	keyb'ds	CD

ALBUMS:	1(A)	CORBITT	(Polydor 24-4003) 1969 -
	2(B)	JERRY CORBITT	(Capitol ST-771) 1970 -
	3(C)	CORBITT & DANIELS, LIVE I	(Tiger Lily 14001) 1976 -
	4(D)	CORBITT & DANIELS, LIVE II	(Tiger Lily 14002) 1976 -

Corbitt was previously in **The Youngbloods** and left them in 1968. He went on to become a producer (**Mad River**, Janey & Dennis) and a solo artist. His first album featured Rick Turner (from **Autosalvage**), Greg Dewey (from **Mad River/Country Joe**), Bernie Krause (from **Beaver & Krause**) and Charlie Daniels who also produced all his albums. (Daniels was also producing **The Youngbloods** at that time). Not surprisingly, it sounds a bit like **Corbitt**'s previous group and contains some excellent West Coast tracks like *The Kahuna Song*, *Out Of The Question* or *Banned In Boston*. Most songs were penned by **Corbitt** and **Jeffrey Cain**.

His second album is very disappointing and best avoided. **Corbitt** also figured on most of **Jesse Colin Young**'s solo albums and teamed up again with Charlie Daniels in 1976 for two good live albums of original material plus some covers (like *John Deere Tractor* written by Lawrence Hammond, ex-**Mad River**). (SR)

Corcoran Brothers

ALBUM:	1	FOR A FEW LOVIN' MINUTES	(Bard BLP 102Z) 1967 -

A fragile acoustic folk duo with breezy, dreamy vocal harmonies and introspective lyrics with acoustic guitar, bass and occasional flute (played by Jimmy Mosher). The best tracks are *These Woods Are Friendly*, *Gypsy Peace*, *East Wind* and *Walk Now In The Evening*. The album also features some spoken passages.

Rumoured to be from Maryland, their album is beginning to be sought-after by collectors of "real people" albums. (SR)

The Cords

Personnel incl:	JIM BERTLER	bs, gtr, organ, sax
	BERTIN BIEDA	
	MATHEW GAWLIK	
	EARL HYLOK	
	JAMES KENZIERSKI	
	KENNETH MACH	
	SEBASTIAN NOCINSKI	
	KEVIN SCHRODER	

45s:	Cords, Inc./Think	(Cuca JS-1512) 1970
	Ghost Power/Waiting Here For You	(Cuca JS-1513) 1970

THE CORPORATION - The Corporation CD.

From Pulaski, Wisconsin, these guys were actually Franciscan brothers. They also released a polka album that presumably includes all the above members, although the singles may not. In 1994 Bertler said, "My main purpose in starting the group was to show people that religious life wasn't all just prayer, that there was a fun side, too."

Ghost Power is a really good punk thrash instrumental. Sounds like they had a lot of fun recording this!

Cords, Inc. can be heard on *Buzz Buzz Buzzzzzz Vol. 1* (CD) with *Ghost Power* haunting the companion *Buzz Buzz Buzzzzzz Vol. 2* (CD) plus *Back From The Grave, Vol. 1* (LP) and *Garage Kings* (Dble LP). (MW/GM/VJ)

The Cords

Personnel incl:	BILLY STULL?	A
	GLEN WILBANKS?	A

45s:	Country Church / Termites	(Rakki 101) 1965
	I'll Do Just What I Want To Do/ Ain't That Love	(Atco 6687) 1969

An outfit from Amarillo, Texas whose second 45 is produced by Norman Petty and is a surpisingly excellent platter from 1969. *I'll Do Just....* is well-crafted baroque-tinged pop with good (i.e. unobtrusive) orchestration and a defiant mood.

Ain't That Love is a great fuzz-rocker featuring a brief wah-wah solo.

Compilation coverage has included *I'll Do Just...* on *Every Groovy Day*; and *Sixties Rebellion, Vol. 15* (LP & CD). (MW)

Cornbread

ALBUM:	1	CORNBREAD	(Mega 31-1003) c1970 SC

45:	Blessed Be The Name Of Charley Jones/ Payin' My Dues	(Mega 0011) 1970

Probably from Tennessee, an obscure group mixing blues rock, psych rock and country, with some heavy fuzz guitar and organ. (SR)

The Cornells

Personnel incl:	PETER LEWIS	A

ALBUM:	1(A)	BEACH BOUND	(Garex 100) 1963

The above album has been re-issued on vinyl (LP 5013) 1995 and CD (SC 6061) 1996 by Sundazed as *Surf Fever! The Best Of The Cornells* and contains three bonus tracks. Peter Lewis later played with **Moby Grape**.

Corners Four

45:	Love/It's So Right	(Philips 40448) 1967

Reputedly an Ohio outfit, *Love* is a poppier version of the track done by Louisiana's **Bad Boys**. Forget the flip. (MW)

The Cornerstone

45s:	When You Wake Me, Girl/Moving Day	(Liberty 56110) 1968 -	HCP
	Holly Go Softly/Love, Nothing More	(Liberty 56148) 1968	104
	It's Gotta Be Real/ Without Her, Father Paul	(Liberty 56179) 1969 -	

A forgotten soft-rock group, with daring lyrics on some of their songs. *Holly Go Softly* narrowly missed the Top 100 in 1970. (SR)

CORPUS - Creation A Child LP.

The Cornerstones

Personnel incl: STEPHEN ROOD   A

45s:	You Rule Me/	
	Our Love Is All Through	(Metrobeat MBR-4447) 1967
	When Will My Day Come?/	
	It's Gonna Be That Way	(Metrobeat MBR-4455) 1967

Originally out of Grand Forks, North Dakota, they went to Minneapolis hoping to make it big. Their first effort, *You Rule Me*, a garage rocker, was very successful in the Dakotas. The follow-up, *When Will My Day Come?* was less successful and they called it a day. The 'A' sides of both 45s and their frantic, previously unissued version of James and Bobby Purify's classic soul number *Shake A Tail Feather* can all be heard on *The Best Of Metrobeat! Vol. 1* (LP). (VJ)

The Coronados

45s:	My Beautiful Dream/You Fool	(Todd 1097) 1964
	Querida/Love Me With All Your Heart	(Purdy 101) 1964
	Theme From Black Orpheus/	
	Joanna's Theme	(Four Corners 115) 1965
	Johnny B. Goode/Shook Me Down	(Parliament 750) c1966

An obscure harmony pop-rock group, their surprising version of *Johnny B. Goode* was done in a soft-pop style. (SR)

Corporate Body

Personnel:	BOB JACOBS	piano	A
	PETER JAMES	vcls	A
	ROB MATHENEY	drms?	A
	WALT MESKELL	gtr	A
	RICK RICCOBONO	bs	A

ALBUM:	1(A)	PROSPECTUS '69	(MGM SE-4624) 1969 -
45s:		Soul Owner's Song/	
		Mr. Nickles And Dimes	(Music Factory MU 416) 1968
		Annabelle/Wait And See	(MGM 14045) 1969

The first 45 features very moody and serious, rambling rock with an unexpected chord progression and good guitars on the 'A' side. Unfortunately the 'B' side reveals what I fear are their true faces: half-baked soul with irritating horn interventions. There's a short middle-piece with another great guitar part, though, and even a harpsichord.

We haven't heard the MGM releases, which also include a version of *Soul Owner's Song*. (MK/RB)

The Corporation

Personnel:	KENNETH BERDOLL	bs, vcls	A
	JOHN KONDOS	gtr, keyb'ds, flute	A
	NICK KONDOS	drms, vcls	A
	PATRICK McCARTHY	keyb'ds, trombone	A
	DANIEL VINCENT PEIL	vcls	A
	GERARD JON SMITH	ld gtr, vcls	A

                                                                            HCP

ALBUMS:	1(A)	THE CORPORATION	(Capitol ST-175) 1969 197 SC
	2(A)	HASSELS IN MY MIND	(Age of Aquarius 4150) 1970 - -
	3(A)	GET ON OUR SWING	(Age of Aquarius 4250) 1970 - -

NB: (1) also released in the UK (Capitol E-ST 175, 1969) and in France (Capitol 2C062-80161); it was reissued on CD in 1995 (Repertoire REP 4539-WP). (2) and (3) were reissued on one LP, *Age of Aquarius* and on one CD (Eva EVA B 43) 1995.

45s:	Highway/I Want To Get Out Of My Grave	(Capitol 2467) 1969
	You Make Me Feel Good/	
	Sitting By The Sea	(Age Of Aquarius J-1496) 1969

Formed in Milwaukee in 1968 at Cudahy's Galaxy Club where the Kondos brothers joined up with members of an outfit called Eastern Mean Time. Some months later they were heard by Capitol reps at another club The Bastille, which the band had bought into.

With a contract for an album the band journeyed to Detroit to record at Terra Shirma studios with producer John Rhys. Released in February 1969, the album is notable for the side-long psychedelic rework of John Coltrane's *India*. All tracks on Side One were group compositions. It was successful in several regions (No. 3 in Milwaukee) but only rose to No. 197 in the national charts.

The group made more recordings but a deal for a second Capitol album fell through and this material was eventually spread across two albums released by the band on Age Of Aquarius, a Cuca custom label.

Compilation appearances include *Yes I Know* on *Sixties Archive, Vol. 8* (CD). (VJ/MW/SR/GM)

Corpus

Personnel:	JAMES CASTILLO	bs	A
	RICHARD DELEON	gtr, ld vcls	A
	WILLIAM GRATE	ld gtr, vcls	A
	FRUDY LIANES	drms	A
	GILBERT PENA, Jnr	lyrics	A

ALBUM:	1(A)	CREATION A CHILD	(Acorn 1001) 1970/1 R3

NB: (1) has been reissued on vinyl (Breeder RPR 007-3C-567) 1986 and also counterfeited on vinyl and CD. (1) later reissued on vinyl and CD (Akarma AK 113).

From Corpus Christi in Texas as their name suggests. There's some good guitar work on the album, which is essentially blues-based. The reissue is worth investigating, but don't fork out lots of bucks on the original. (VJ/SR)

Corruption, Inc

Personnel:	TOM HETZLER		A
	JIM LOGEL	vcls	A
	MIKE McCLEARY	gtr	A
	DAVE MEYERS	drms	A
	THOM WESSELS	gtr	A

45:	She's Gone/Somewhere	(Hunt 1201) 1966

Muscatine Iowa's only rock band at the time, recorded their sole 45 upstairs in a store in Iowa City. The 'A' side, with its impressive double track vocal and screeching intro, is reminiscent of **The Seeds** and can be found on the compilation, *Dirty Water - The History Of Eastern Iowa Rock Volume 2* (LP). Tom Hetzler went on to join **The Daybreakers**. (VJ/MW/SMR)

COSMIC SOUNDS - The Zodiac LP.

The Corvets

Personnel incl:	EDDIE BARKDOLL		A
	NORMAN BARKDOLL		A

45s:	You Don't Want Me/Want To Be Happy	(Soma 1425) 1964
	So Fine/Can It Be	(Re-Car 9014) 1965
α	Nobody Likes This Man/Goin' Away	(Cardinal 0075) 1966

NB: α shown as The New Corvets.

From Minneapolis, **The Corvets** brand of frat-rock was popular locally, with *You Don't want Me* and *So Fine* being local hits. The band also appeared on two rare compilations:- *Can It Be* on Bud-Jet's 1965 *Top Teen Bands, Vol. 1* and *So Fine* on *Top Teen Bands, Vol. 2*.

Two early 45s:- *Wailin' Wailin' Party / Scramble* (Soma 1164) 1960 and *Say Mama/?* (Soma) 19??, are probably by a different act.

Retrospective compilation appearances have included:- *You Don't Want Me* on *Destination Frantic!* (CD), *Big-Hits Of Mid America* (Dble CD) and *The Soma Records Story, Vol. 2* (LP). (BM/MW)

Corvettes

Personnel:	CHRIS DARROW	vcls, gtr, bs	AB
	JEFF HANNAH	vcls, gtr	A
	JOHN LONDON	drms	AB
	JOHN WARE	bs	A
	BERNIE LEADON	gtr	B

45s:	Back Home Girl/ The Lion In Your Heart	(Dot 45-17244) 1969
	Beware Of Time/Level With Your Senses	(Dot ?) 1969

Formed by Jeff Hannah and Chris Darrow when the **Nitty Gritty Dirt Band** disbanded, Darrow had earlier played in **Kaleidoscope**. The two **Corvettes** 45s were produced by Michael Nesmith, who had recently left the **Monkees**.

The Corvettes soon became Linda Ronstadt's back-up band when she left the **Stone Poneys**. She had heard about them through Nesmith, who had written the **Stone Poneys**' hit *Different Drum*. When Jeff decided to reform the **Dirt Band**, Bernie Leadon (ex-**Hearts and Flowers**) joined the band. This aggregation stayed with Linda until Bernie was asked to join the Flying Burrito Brothers, and John Ware and John London, the rhythm section, teamed up with Nesmith in his First National Band. Chris continued to play with Linda off and on for a number of years.

Musically interesting, it's a mix of West Coast and Californian country-rock with excellent guitar and vocals. (SR/CDw)

The Cosmic Brotherhood

Personnel:	HERSCH HAMEL	sitar, tambura	A
	MILT HOLLAND	tabla	A
	BILL PLUMMER	sitar, string bass	A
	RAY NEOPOLITAN	sitar	A
	JAN STEWARD	sarode, tambura	A
	(RAY ANTHONY	gtr	A)
	(LYNN BLESSING	vibes, bells	A)
	(DENNIS BUDIMER	gtr	A)
	(MIKE CRADEN	transceleste, duo vigong, American tree bells, boo bams, surrogate vithara, "which stand"(?)	A)
	(BILL GOODWIN	drms	A)
	(CAROL KAYE	fender bass	A)
	(MIKE LANG	piano, harpsichord	A)
	(MAURICE MILLER	drms	A)
	(TOM SCOTT	sax, flute, electronics	A)

ALBUM: 1(A) BILL PLUMMER AND THE COSMIC BROTHERHOOD (ABC Impulse A-9164) 1967 SC

NB: (1) as **Bill Plummer and The Cosmic Brotherhood**.

45s:	α	Journey To The East / Arc 294	(ABC Impulse 45-266) 1967
		Sunshine World/Yentra II	(A&M 1097) 1969

NB: α as **Bill Plummer and The Cosmic Brotherhood**.

Born in Boulder, Colorado in 1943, Bill Plummer moved to Los Angeles twenty years later to pursue a jazz career. Already trained on piano, string bass, trumpet, marimba and vibraharp, he added the sitar to his repertoire under the tutelage of Ravi Shankar. He played and toured with Herb and Lorraine Geller, Nancy Wilson, the Paul Horn Group, Buddy DeFranco Quartet and Pete Jolly Trio amongst others. In 1966 he toured with Tony Bennett and Buddy Miles and formed an experimental group The Jazz Corps, which included Lynn Blessing and Maurice Miller.

His love of jazz and interest in Indian music comes together on this 1967 album where jazz workouts sit alongside Eastern ragas and blend with some contemporary pop-rock influences - exotic renditions (ala Lord Sitar or Folkswingers) of Bacharch's *The Look Of Love* and **Byrds**' *Lady Friend* are enchanting rather than cheesy.

The sitar extravaganza should appeal most to psych fans of an Eastern persuasion: the trippy *Journey To The East* (with deadpan spoken vocals) has since appeared on *Journey To The East* (LP); the ten-minute *Arc 294* is a heady cacophany where exotic instruments do battle on a field of freeform jazz.

The A&M 45 switched to more accessible pop-psych sounds: *Sunshine World* is catchy and quite heavy sitar-pop; *Yentra II* is a stately sitar instrumental that starts off like **Zodiac Cosmic Sounds** then builds gradually to a heavy crescendo - most excellent.

Lynn Blessing released a solo album in 1969. (MW)

The Cosmic Camel

Personnel:	RUSS BEUTLICH	ld gtr	A
	LIZ GREEN	ld vcls	A
	SAMMY GREEN	keyb'ds	A
	WILLIAM THACKER	bs, ld vcls	A
	EDDY WASSMAN	drms	A

45:	The Suzanne Love Mirage / The King's Winetaster	(Tener 1030) 1968

The Cosmic Camel was the 1968 line-up of an evolutionary Gainesville, Florida band that changed name every year (from 1966 to 1972) as members left or transferred to other schools. Frat parties were the band's staple diet though they did gig in other cities, venturing as far as Southern Georgia.

In 1966 Beutlich and Wassman had arrived from Orlando where they'd been in Jerry and The Gents. They recruited Liz Green, from West Palm

Beach, after she held them off first place in a 1966 University of Florida talent contest. Thacker, from Clermont, was also known as DJ "Montana" on a Gainesville radio station. Manager Brian Morris, from Orlando, was another local DJ. Sammy Green was from Jacksonville.

The Suzanne Love Mirage, unearthed on *Psychedelic States - Florida, Vol. 2* (CD), is a fragmentary folk-psych opus of moods and movements with a San Francisco vibe, alternating from fuzzed dirge to cantering folk-rock. The keyboard-led lament *The King's Winetaster* is on *Psychedelic States: Florida, Vol. 3* (CD).

Just 50 copies of the 45 were pressed, to be given out at concerts. (MW/RBh/RM)

Cosmic Michael

ALBUMS:	1	COSMIC MICHAEL	(Bliss) 1969	R3
	2	AFTER AWHILE	(Bliss) 1970	R1

A solo artist whose first album was issued in New York. Its poorly produced piano/vocals - led rock music is an acquired taste. Certainly an interesting record overall but the value is difficult to justify. The second album was a local Los Angeles release made after he moved to California to catch the wave and is simply awful.

Both albums have primitive paste-on covers which are missing, more often than not. (CF/MW)

Cosmic Rock Show

45:	Psiship/Rising Sun	(Blitz 469) 196?

Hailing from Duluth, Minnesota this band recorded just one 45 which is quite sought-after. The flip, is a slowed down version of The Animal's *House Of The Rising Sun*. The 'A' side is pretty weird with lyrics like: 'Ride it To The Moon/Psychedelic Space Ship/I Got The Feeling/It'll Be Another Bum Trip'.

Compilation appearances include: *Rising Sun* on *Only In America* (CD), *Psychedelic Unknowns, Vol's 1 & 2* (LP) and *Psychedelic Unknowns, Vol. 1* (Dble 7"); and *Psiship* on *Beyond The Calico Wall* (LP & CD). (VJ)

Cosmic Sounds

Personnel incl:	CYRUS FARYAR	vcls	A
	MORT GARSON		A

ALBUM:	1	THE ZODIAC	(Elektra EKS 74009) 1967	-

NB: (1) pirated on CD (FID 32) 1997.

THE COSMIC TRAVELERS - Live! At The Spring Crater Celebration... CD.

This album was an idea of Jac Holzman, the owner of the Elektra label. Composed by **Mort Garson** and Jacques Wilson, it was produced by Alex Hassilev and released in May 1967. The album was recorded by a group of session musicians and featured **Cyrus Faryar** of the **Modern Folk Quartet** on vocals. The electronic instruments were played by **Paul Beaver**. A track is allocated to each of the twelve signs of the zodiac on the above album. Instrumentals are superimposed by narrative and the two do not always blend effectively together. An unusual and rather enjoyable album, although it's clearly not for garage or psych-pop fans. The back sleeve mentions "Must Be Played In The Dark"!

Two years later, **Garson** and Wilson would prepare a series of twelve albums dedicated to the Signs Of The Zodiac.

Compilation appearances have included: *Aries* on *Kings Of Pop Music, Vol. 2* (LP), *Elektrifying* (LP), *Turds On A Bum Ride, Vol. 1* (Dble LP) and *Turds On A Bum Ride Vol. 1 & 2* (Dble CD); and *The Moon Child* on *Hallucinations, Psychedelic Underground* (LP). (VJ/CA/MW/SR)

The Cosmic Tones

A little known garage band from Texas whose *Gonna Build Me A Woman* was included on *Garage Punk Unknowns, Vol. 8* (LP). (VJ)

The Cosmic Travelers

Personnel:	JOEL CHRISTIE	bs	A
	DRAKE LEVIN	gtr	A
	DALE LOYOLA	drms	A
	JIMMY McGHEE	gtr	A

ALBUM:	1(A)	LIVE! AT THE SPRING CRATER CELEBRATION DIAMOND HEAD, OAHU, HAWAII (Volcano CT 00004) 1972 R3/R4

NB: (1) was recorded live on 1st April 1972. Of only a handful of copies known to exist, one was found with a large poster inside. Reissued on CD unofficially (Dodo DDR 511) 2001.

A local Hawaii release by a Los Angeles group. Joel Christie is ex-**Lee Michaels Band**. **Drake Levin** had been in **Paul Revere and The Raiders**, **Brotherhood** (on RCA), **Lee Michaels Band**, **Friendsound** and **Emmit Rhodes**. Dale Loyola was previously in **Hook**. The very rare album consists of long, jamming cuts loaded with crazed fuzz guitar solos. (CF)

Cotton Mouth

Personnel:	FRED DICKERSON	ld gtr	A
	BOB JENKINS	ld vcls	A
	DUANE McCASLIN	bs	A
	DEAN WHITBECK	drms	A

45s:	Mr Fishker's Glory/Sunshine Saleslady	(Sabrina 4) 1968
α	Rivers Invitation / Hog For You Baby	(Little Piggy 109) 196?

NB: α may not have been released.

Based in Olympia, Washington, this band included Fred Dickerson and Duane McCaslin, who had earlier played in **The Bootmen**. **Cotton Mouth** were a great live act circa 1968 and *Mr. Fishker's Glory* is one of the rarest and finest slices of psychedelia to come from the Pacific Northwest. Strongly recommended with lots of fuzz guitar. (MW/DR)

Cottonwood

Personnel:	RICK ALLEN		A
	DAVID FARRELL		A
	DOUG PHILLIPS		A
	GARY ROWLES	gtr, vcls	A
	DAVID WEYER		A

ALBUM:	1(A)	CAMARADERIE	(ABC ABCS-729) 1971 -

From California, a short-lived outfit formed by the guitarist Gary Rowles after **Love** broke up. The music reflects the sleeve: bearded men running in the fields or meditating by the sea. It may sound quite naive and dated now.

Rowles would later back Flo and Eddie and in 1973 join Richard Torrance and Eureka, an interesting Californian rock group (lovers of West Coast guitars may check their two albums on Shelter). (SR)

Cottonwood South

| Personnel incl: | JACKIE DANZAT | ld vcls | A |

ALBUM: 1(A) COTTONWOOD SOUTH   (Columbia 33009) 1974 -

A forgotten group, whose album veered between Southern rock and melodic rural rock, with some good guitar parts. (SR)

The Counsellors

Personnel:	BOB CONDIT	bs, vcls	A
	DOUG FAIELLA	ld gtr, vcls	A
	MURRAY HENDRICKSON	drms, vcls	A
	PHIL ROBISON	ld vcls	A
	DENNY STITH	organ	A
	JERRY BORDEN	gtr	
	DALE STOPHER	bs	

| 45s: | Why Don't You / Love Go Round | (Ironbeat HR-1251) 1968 |
| | It Must Be Love / With Only Me | (Ironbeat # unkn) 196? |

From Columbus, Ohio. *Love Go Round* starts off hesitantly with a coy intro but gradually builds in confidence from poppy garage to a waspish fuzz solo and a memorable outro - neat, hear it on *Psychedelic Crown Jewels, Vol. 2* (Dble LP & CD). (MW/RM)

Count and The Colony

45s:	Can't You See/That's The Way	(Pa Go Go 121) 1967
	Say What You Think/Symptoms Of Love	(Pa Go Go 201) 1967
	Say What You Think/Symptoms Of Love	(SSS Int'l 711) 1967

From Flint, Michigan. *Can't You See* has resurfaced on *Gone, Vol. 2* (LP), *Glimpses, Vol. 2* (LP), *Glimpses, Vol's 1 & 2* (CD), *Sixties Archive Vol. 7* (CD) and *Teenage Shutdown, Vol. 1* (LP & CD). (VJ)

The Countdown 5 (Five)

Personnel incl:	JOHN BALZER		
	MALCOLM HAYES		
	TOMMY MURPHY		

45s:	Bamboo Hut/Shout	(Pic 1 123) 1965
	Do What You Do Well/My Own Style Of Living	(Pic 1 131) 1966
	Uncle Kirby (From Brazil)/Speculation (PS)	(Toucan TI) 1967
	Uncle Kirby (From Brazil)/Speculation	(Cinema 010) 1967
	Time To Spare/Elevator	(Toucan TCI) 1968
	Time To Spare/Elevator	(Cinema ?) 1968
	Maybe I'll Love You/ Willie And The Hand Jive	(Cinema 026) 1968
	Uncle Kirby (From Brazil)/We Are All One	(Cinema 031) 1968
α	Shaka Shaka Na Na/ Money Man	(Cobblestone 745) 1969

NB: α as **The Countdown Five**.

Hailing from Galveston in Texas this band is best-known for *Uncle Kirkby (From Brazil)* with its interesting rhythms and effective guitar playing. The 45 originally appeared in a picture sleeve.

Compilation coverage has included: *Uncle Kirkby (From Brazil)* on *Uncle Kirby (From Brazil)* on *Flashback, Vol. 1* (LP), *Texas Flashbacks, Vol. 1* (LP & CD), *Texas Flashback (The Best Of)* (CD), *'69 Love-In* (CD); *Money Man, Shaka Shaka Na Na* on *A Journey To Tyme, Vol. 3* (LP); *Speculation* on *Fuzz Flaykes & Shakes, Vol. 1* (LP & CD); *Elevator* on *Every Groovy Day* (LP); *Money Man* on *Searching For Love* (LP); *Uncle Kirby* and *Candy* on *Houston Post - Nowsounds Groove-In* (LP); and they also have three previously unreleased recordings:- *Willie And The Hand Jive* (the famous Shuggie Otis number), *Sweet Talk* and *Candy* on *Houston Hallucinations* (LP), although aside from the latter they are not on a par with the best of their released material. (VJ/MW)

The Countdowns

| Personnel incl: | LARRY BARRETT | vcls, gtr | A |

| 45s: | You Know I Do/Strange Are The Shadows | (Fiji 691) 1965 |
| | You Know I Do/Strange Are The Shadows | (Bear 1968) 1985 |

The 45 was the work of a high school band from the Iowa City suburb of Coralville, previously The Friars. Larry Barrett wrote, sang and played guitar on *You Know I Do*, an undistinguished effort which can be found on either *Dirty Water - The History Of Eastern Iowa Rock Volume 2* (LP) or on *Monsters Of The Midwest, Vol. 4* (LP). The band later changed their name to **Uncle and The Anteaters** and Barrett was also later involved in **The XL's** and **Fire and Ice**. (VJ)

The Countdowns

Personnel incl: RON GRAY

45s:	α	No More/Ajax The Tin Knight	(N-Joy NJ 1013) 1966
		Cover Of Night/?	(N-Joy NJ 1015) 1966
		Can't You See?/Cover Of Night	(N-Joy NJ 1016) 1966
		Hold Back The Sunrise/The Shake	(HBR) 196?

NB: α credited to Ron Gray and The Countdowns.

Hailing from West Monroe, Louisiana, *Cover Of Night*, was a raw, bluesy garage punk rendition. The band were originally known as Ron Gray and The Countdowns and their first 45, *No More*, was released under this name. Written by Ron Gray, it has a pretty good beat.

Compilation appearances have include: *No More* on *Louisiana Punk Groups From The Sixties, Vol. 2* (LP) and *Sixties Archive, Vol. 3* (CD); *Can't You See* on *Follow That Munster, Vol. 1* (LP); and *Cover Of Night* on *Highs In The Mid-Sixties, Vol. 22* (LP).

The Countdowns

| 45: | Skies Will Be Happy To See You/ She Works All Night | (WG 1) 1967 |

COUNT FIVE - Psychotic Reaction LP.

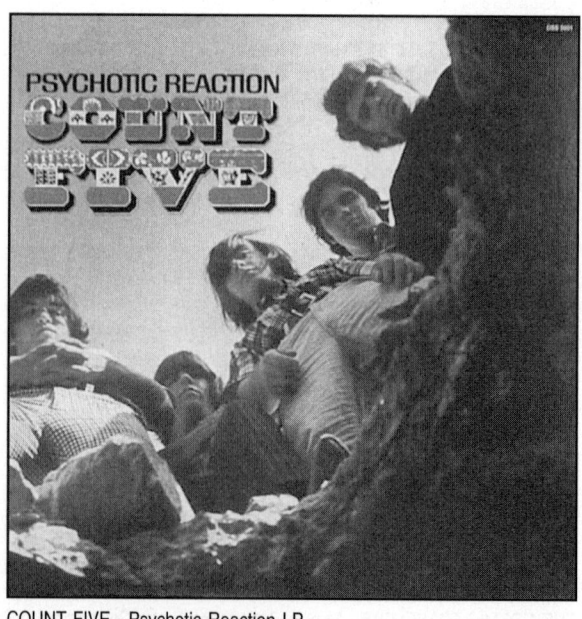

This 45 was the work of a different act from Holyoke, Massachusetts. *Skies Will Be Happy To See You* has also resurfaced on the *Gone, Vol. 2* (LP) compilation.

Other bands of this name in this era included one from the Bay Area of California who had two 45s on Link and one who had a 45 on Image. (VJ/MW/CRd)

The Count Five

Personnel:	CRAIG ATKINSON	drms	A
	SEAN BYRNE	vcls, rhythm gtr	A
	ROY CHANEY	bs	A
	KENN ELLNER	vcls, tamb, hrmnca	A
	JOHN MICHALSKI	ld gtr	A

HCP

ALBUM: 1(A) PSYCHOTIC REACTION
(Double Shot DSM 1001) 1967 122 SC

NB: (1) reissued on vinyl and CD by Performance (PERF 398) and added all the Double Shot non-album singles sides making it a total of 18 tracks. There's also a 14-track 1987 live album on CD entitled *Psychotic Reaction Live* (PERF 396).

HCP

45s:	α	Psychotic Reaction/		
		They're Gonna Get You	(Double Shot 104) 1966	5
		Peace Of Mind/The Morning After	(Double Shot 106) 1966	125
		You Must Believe Me/		
		Teeny Booper Teeny Booper	(Double Shot 110) 1967	-
		Merry-Go-Round/Contrast	(Double Shot 115) 1967	-
		Declaration Of Independence/		
		Revelation In Slow Motion	(Double Shot 125) 1968	-
		Mailman/Pretty Big Mouth	(Double Shot 141) 1969	-

NB: Some foreign 45s include:- α issued in Argentina (Fermata 3 F 0166). *Peace Of Mind / The Morning After* (Apex 77026) 1966 (Canada) and *Revelation In Slow Motion / Declaration Of Independence* (PS) (AZ SG 48) 1967 (France). There's also a rare French EP with PS: *Psychotic Reaction/They're Gonna Get You/Can't Get Your Lovin/The Morning After* (Disc AZ 1058)

This San Jose high school/student band reached the U.S. Top Ten with the title track of their only album, now a collector's item. Their album also made No 122 in the U.S. Album Charts, and the group toured the U.S. performing with the Hollies, Beach Boys, **Rascals**, **Byrds**, Dave Clark Five, Sony and Cher, **The Doors**, Them and Peter and Gordon to name but a few.

Aside from the classic *Psychotic Reaction*, their album was full of driving rock songs, of which *Double Decker Bus* was the next best. A German Line compilation *Dynamite Incidents 1983* contains some of their non-album 45's. One side plays at 33 r.p.m. and the other at 45 r.p.m. Also Edsel have released a 13-track compilation, *Psychotic Reaction* (Edsel ED 225) 1987.

Psychotic Reaction has become something of a garage standard. It was well covered at the time by the like of **Fire Escape**, **Leathercoated Minds**, **Positively 13 O'Clock** and **Underground**.

Compilation appearances include: *Psychotic Reaction* on *Nuggets - Original Artyfacts From The First Psychedelic Era 1965-1968* (Dble LP), *Nuggets Box* (4-CD), *Nuggets* (CD), *Nuggets From Nuggets* (CD), *Nuggets, Vol. 1* (LP), *Psychedelic Frequencies* (CD), *Battle Of The Bands* (CD), *Excerpts From Nuggets* (CD), *We Have Come For Your Children* (CD), *Highs Of The Sixties* (LP), *Wild Thing* (LP), *Tough Rock* (LP) and *Best Of Psychedelic Rock* (CD); *You Must Believe Me* on *Sound Of The Sixties* (Dble LP) and *Sixties Archive Vol. 1* (CD); and *Teeny Bopper, Teeny Bopper* on *Sounds Of The Sixties San Francisco, Vol. 1* (LP). (VJ/SR/ML)

Country Coalition

Personnel:	DICK BRADLEY	A
	JOHN KURTZ	A
	PEGGIE MOJE	A
	TOM RINEY	A

ALBUM: 1(A) TIME TO GET IT TOGETHER
(Bluesway/ABC BLS 6043) 1970 -

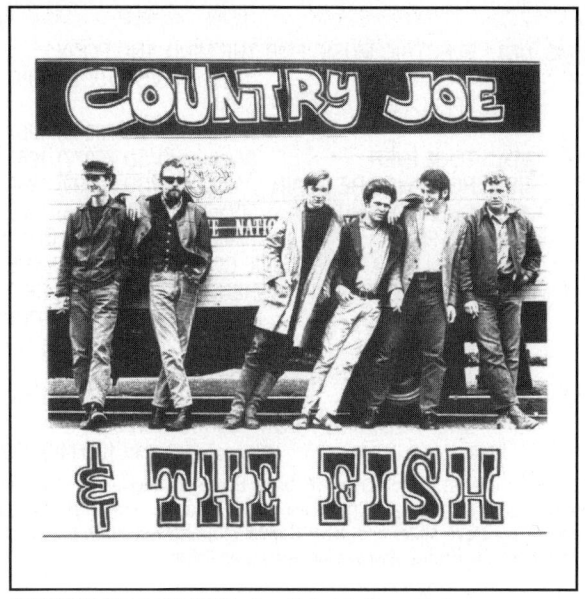

COUNTRY JOE & THE FISH - Rag Baby EP (Rag 1002).

45s:	How Do I Love You/		
	Time To Get It Together	(Bluesway 61034)	1970
α	Age Of Angels/		
	Take To The Mountains	(Bluesway/ABC 11279)	1970
α	Think About Now/Keepin' Free	(Bluesway/ABC 11286)	1970

NB: α The flip sides are non LP tracks.

Housed in several different sleeves (at least three), **Country Coalition**'s album is extremely patchy. Only its opening track, *Your One Man Band*, is really interesting, with good guitar work and vocals. The remaining songs hesitate between West Coast, pop and country pop and are best avoided. The album was produced by Bob Todd and arranged by Don McGinnis at the American Recording studios in Hollywood. Several additional musicians were used, like Mike Rubini, Louie Shelton, Joe Osborn and Kenny Loggins, who also wrote one song. The other tracks were penned by various songwriters including Carole King and Gerry Goffin, Larry Murray (**Hearts and Flowers**) and **Steve Gillette**. (SR)

Country Gentlemen

45: Saturday Night/For You (Breni 7058) 1967

A California outfit. The 'A' side, written by Bill Alessi, can be found on *Boulders, Vol. 7* (LP), *Mindrocker, Vol. 12* (LP) and *Ya Gotta Have Moxie, Vol. 1* (Dble CD). (VJ)

Country Joe and The Fish

Personnel:	MIKE BEARDSLEE	vcls	A
	COUNTRY		
	JOE MCDONALD	gtr, vcls, hmnca	ABCDEFG
	BARRY MELTON	gtr	ABCDEFG
	CARL SHRAGER	perc	AB
	BOB STEELE	bs	AB
	RICHARD SAUNDERS	bs, gtr, vcls	B
	PAUL ARMSTRONG	perc	C
	BRUCE BARTHOL	bs	CD
	DAVID COHEN	keyb'ds, vcls	CDE
	JOHN FRANCIS GUNNING	drms	C
	CHICKEN HIRSCH	drms	DE
	MARK RYAN	bs	E
	PETE ALBIN	bs, gtr	F
	DAVE GETZ	drms	F
	MARK KAPNER	keyb'ds	FG
	GREG DEWEY	drms	G
	DOUG METZNER	bs	G

ALBUMS:	1(D)	ELECTRIC MUSIC FOR THE MIND AND BODY		HCP
		(Vanguard VSD 79244)	1967	39 -
	2(D)	I-FEEL-LIKE-I'M-FIXIN'-TO-DIE		
		(Vanguard VSD 79266)	1967	67 -
	3(D)	TOGETHER (Vanguard VSD 79277)	1969	23 -
	4(E)	HERE WE ARE AGAIN (Vanguard VSD 79299)	1969	48 -
	5(-)	GREATEST HITS (Vanguard VSD 6545)	1969	74 -
	6(-)	C J FISH (Vanguard VSD 6555)	1970	111 -
	7(-)	THE LIFE AND TIMES OF COUNTRY JOE AND THE FISH FROM HAIGHT-ASHBURY TO WOODSTOCK		
		(Vanguard VSD 27/28)	1976	197 -
	8(-)	RE-UNION (Fantasy 9530)	1976	- -
	9(-)	THE EARLY YEARS (The Rag Baby EP's)		
		(Rag Baby AMR 3309)	1981	- -
	10( )	LIVE! FILLMORE WEST 1969 (Dble)		
		(Vanguard-Comet 139/140)	2000	- -

NB: Of recent interest to collectors will be a European double CD *The Vietnam Experience*. LPs (1), (2) and (7) have been reissued. (10) includes cameo appearances by **Steve Miller** and **Jerry Garcia**. (10) also issued on CD (Vanguard VCD 139) 1996, the double vinyl version listed is an Italian-only issue.

EPs:	1(A)	SONGS OF OPPOSITION (PS)	(Rag L-1001) Oct. 1965
	2(C)	COUNTRY JOE AND THE FISH (PS)	
			(Rag 1002) Jun. 1966
	3(C)	COUNTRY JOE AND THE FISH (PS)	
			(Rag 1002-RB3) 1967
	4(-)	COUNTRY JOE SINGS RESIST (PS)	(Rag L-1003) 1971

NB: (1) *The I-Feel-Like-I'm-Fixin'-To-Die Rag* plus one other track. 'B' side contains two tracks by Pete Krug. Issued in an oversize envelope jacket printed on both sides. (2) *Bass Strings* plus two other tracks. The first edition was issued in hard carboard PS with group name above and below the front sleeve photo. (3) *Bass Strings* plus two other tracks. Subsequent editions issued in hard carboard PS with group name entirely above front sleeve photo. (4) *Kiss My Ass* plus two other tracks. Joe McDonald is backed by **Grootna** on this EP. Issued in oversize envelope jacket printed on both sides. (2) and (3) are different pressings of the same EP. These EPs were issued on the LP *The Early Years* in 1981 and reissued on Decal LIK 8 (1987), One Way and Sequel (NEX CD 228) 1992. (2) features *Bass Strings*, *Thing Called Love* and *Section 43* and can also be heard, along with **The Frumious Bandersnatch**, **Mad River** and **Notes From The Underground** EPs, on one CD, *The Berkeley EPs* (Big Beat CDWIKD 153) 1995. More recently, Akarma has produced a deluxe LP-size box set containing (1), (2) and (4) in their original packaging plus seven double sided pages of sheet music, lyrics and text (Akarma 2019/3) 2001, also issued as a CD box set.

County Joe McDonald Solo: HCP

ALBUMS:	1	THINKING OF WOODY GUTHRIE (Vanguard)	1969 -
(up to	2	TONIGHT I'M SINGING JUST FOR YOU	
1972)		(Vanguard VSD 6557)	1970 -
	3	QUIET DAYS IN CLICHY (Five tracks on Soundtrack UK)	
		(Sonet SNTF 622)	1970 -
	4	HOLD ON IT'S COMIN' (Vanguard VSD 79314)	1971 -
	5	WAR WAR WAR (Vanguard VSD 79315)	1971 185
	6	INCREDIBLE LIVE! COUNTRY JOE	
		(Vanguard VSD 79316)	1972 179

Country Joe and the Fish: HCP

45s:	Not So Sweet Martha Lorraine/			
	Masked Marauder	(Vanguard 35052)	1967	95
	Janis/Janis (Instrumental)	(Vanguard 35059)	1967	-
	Who Am I?/Thursday (PS)	(Vanguard 35061)	1967	114
	Rock And Soul Music Pt1 /Pt2	(Vanguard 35068)	1967	-
	Here I Go Again/			
	You Drive Me Crazy	(Vanguard 35090)	1969	106
	Janis/			
	I-Feel-Like-I'm-Fixin'-To-Die-Rag	(Vanguard 35112)	1970	-

NB: In the U.K. only the first 45 and 'Here I Go Again/it's So Nice To Have Love' (Vanguard VA3) were issued. Other European releases included: The Fish Cheer + F.U.C.K/Rock and Soul Music (Vanguard 119023) 1969 - a French single with B&W picture of Country Joe at Woodstock with a big "F.U.C.K." written on the sleeve. The French censors were probably unable to read English! Country Joe also had a solo 45 in France: *Tiger by the Tail / Friend Lover Woman Wife* (Vanguard 119028L) 1970, which was housed in a picture sleeve showing a B&W picture of Country Joe.

Country Joe and the Fish were the wittiest, most political and most reflective of the Bay Area 'acid' rock bands. Their radicalism emanated mainly from Country Joe McDonald, who was born of leftist parents in El Monte, California in 1942. His Christian name, Joe, was apparently after Joseph Stalin. Musically, his main influences were country and he wrote his

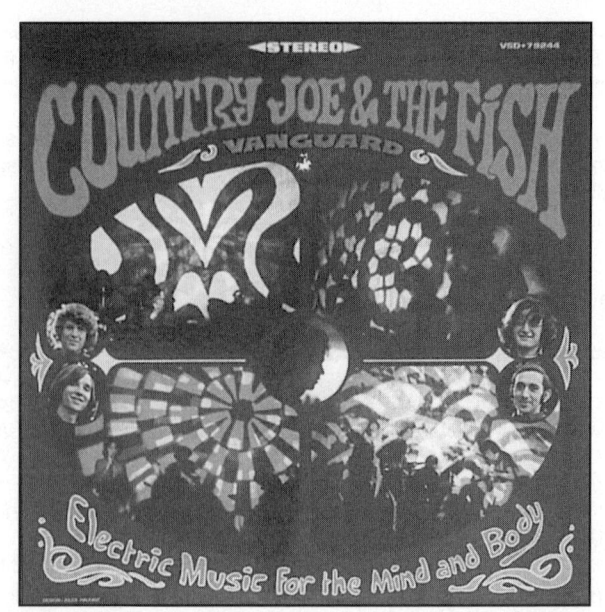

COUNTRY JOE & THE FISH - Electric Music For The Mind And Body LP.

first song *I Seen A Rocket* in support of a colleague's campaign for student presidency. In 1964 he made *The Goodbye Blues* (his first recording) with Blair Harriman. His first group was The Berkeley String Quartet. Then, with **Barry Melton** and Bruce Barthol he played in the 13-strong Instant Action Jug Band. The *Rag Baby* EPs were the first recordings credited to **Country Joe and the Fish**. They were released starting in 1965 on the Rag Baby label, Rag Baby was a left wing pamphlet magazine. The group, which was based in Berkeley, eventually developed and recorded their superb debut album *Electric Music For The Mind And Body*. Written to trip to, this was one of the classic albums of the period and contained a broad range of material. There was *Not So Sweet Martha Lorraine*, a song of social satire, drug songs like *Flying High*, *Bass Strings* and *Section 43*, a daring political skit *Superbird* and the closing love song *Grace* (presumably about Grace Slick of **The Jefferson Airplane**) was full of acid-inspired lyrics.

I Feel Like I'm Fixin' To Die was also excellent including a more polished version of its title track; *Janis*, the beautiful love song McDonald wrote at the end of his romance with Janis Joplin; *Eastern Jam*, an electric instrumental with fine guitar interplay and *Who Am I?* which captures the band in more reflective mood. Also of interest were the drug-induced *Thought Dream*, the *Bomb Song* an anti-nuke anthem and the notorious *Acid Commercial*:-

"Now if you're tired
Or a bit run down
Can't seem to get your feet off the ground
Maybe you oughta try a little bit of LSD
Only if you want to"

"Shake your head and rattle your brain
Make you act just a bit insane
Give you all the psychic energy you need
Eat flowers and kiss babies
LSD.. for you and me...."
(from *Acid Commercial*)

Country Joe left **The Fish** after this album, getting married and recording a solo album. **Barry Melton** kept the band together either as **The Fish** or The Incredible Fish and individual band members wrote their own material. The band reformed a few months later as The Country Joe and The Fish Revue. Although nowhere near as good as their first two albums *Together*, which included the results of their individual enterprise still has some fine moments notably on *An Untitled Protest*- another anti-Vietnam protest song and *The Streets Of Your Town* and *Bright Suburban Mr and Mrs Clean Machine* which were both protests against their own environment. McDonald is still credited as one of the band on the album sleeve and he appeared on some of the tracks. During 1968 these were extensive personnel changes and as a result *Here We Are Again* was disappointing.

They appeared at the Woodstock Festival on 21-24 August 1969, with a modified line-up, and performed their infamous *Fish Cheer*, but only McDonald and **Melton** now remained from their definitive line-up. They also appeared in Michael Wadleigh's full length movie of the festival in 1970. The same line-up recorded their *CJ Fish* album. After this the band disintegrated. Briefly in the mid-seventies the whole 1967 line-up reformed for a series of live gigs and the disappointing *Reunion* album.

Barry Melton later recorded an album with **Melton, Levy and The Dey Brothers**.

Country Joe and the Fish were one of the best and most interesting of the late sixties Bay Area rock bands. Their first two albums remain classics of the genre.

Compilation appearances have included: *Rock And Soul Music* on *The New Sound Of Underground* (LP); *Bass Strings* on *Nuggets, Vol. 7* (LP); *Fish Cheer* and *Rock And Soul Music* on *Pop Music Super Hebdo* (LP); *Bass Strings*, *Section 43* and *Thing Called Love* on *The Berkeley EPs* (CD); *We're The Crackers* and *All I Need* which don't seem to appear elsewhere on *Zachariah* soundtrack LP; and *Death Sound Blues* from 1968 on *The California Christmas Album* (LP). (VJ/SR/CF)

The Country Roads

ALBUM: 1 THE COUNTRY ROAD (No label) c1971 R1

From Kentucky, an unknown quartet, with a style somewhere between rock, garage, country and bar music. Their rare album contains mostly covers including: **Tommy James**' *Draggin' The Line*, **Hoyt Axton**'s *Never Been To Spain*, Dale Hawkins' *Suzy Q* and **The Doors**' *Hello I Love You*. (SR)

Country Weather

Personnel:	BILL BARON	drms	A
	DAVE CARTER	bs, vcls	A
	STEVE DERR	gtr, vcls	A
	GREG DOUGLASS	ld gtr, vcls	A

ALBUM: 1(A) LIMITED EDITION (No label) 1968/9 R6
EP: 1 DESPERATE ( ) 19??

NB: (1) Rumoured to consist of tracks recorded for a compilation on Fillmore Records which was eventually shelved, the EP's existence has not been confirmed.

This one-sided 12" album was issued in a plain sleeve. Only 50 copies were pressed and it is the rarest record from the San Francisco sixties scene. It includes *Time Is Leaving Me Behind*, a pleasant, melodic pop-folk number with good guitar moments and the superb finale *Fly To New York*, a driving number with excellent guitar work, really catch the ear. *New York City Blues* is routine blues but *Carry A Spare* features some pretty good guitar jamming.

COUNTRY JOE & THE FISH - I-Feel-Like-I'm-Fixin'-To-Die LP.

COUNTRY JOE & THE FISH - Together LP.

Greg Douglass became a well-regarded Californian musician first with Terry and The Pirates and later with **The Steve Miller Band**.

He performed his first gig in June 1964 with The Statics for a P.T.A. sponsored event. Throughout 1965 Greg was with the Vibrants, leaving them in 1966 to replace Paul White in the Virtues. By late 1967, the Virtues changed their name to **Country Weather** and played the Avalon, Fillmore and throughout Northern California and the Pacific Northwest. Their 'almost' record deal never materialized and by 1973 the band broke up.

After the split Greg and Bill Baron formed Mistress with Brian Kilcourse. Their album which was produced by Mallory Earl was again never released and by August 1974 Mistress called it quits. At this time Greg's reputation was growing. Aside from working with Terry and the Pirates, he had played on **Link Wray**'s 1973 album and performed with Van Morrison's back up band and Mario Cipollina's band Soundhole. He later worked with **Hot Tuna** on their *Yellow Fever* album and joined **The Steve Miller Band** in 1977.

He is still performing and recording today with two solo albums on the German Taxim label.

Compilation appearances have included: *Time Is Leaving Me Behind*, *New York City Blues*, *Carry A Spare* and *Fly To New York* on *California Acid Folk* (Dble LP). (CF/VJ/SR)

The Counts

Personnel:	CENTER CHARLES CASE	keyb'ds	A
	HOWARD HORNSBY	sax	A
	JIM NICHOLS	drms	A
	DAN OLASON	ld gtr	ABCDEFG
	PETE RICHES	bs	ABCDEFG
	AL SCANZON	sax	ABCDEF
	BILL OLASON	organ	BCDFG
	MIKE LEARY	drms	B
	RICH PEARSON	tpt	BCD
	PHIL CREORE	drms	C
	GEORGE O'BRIEN	drms	E
	JIM WALTERS	tpt	EF
	DAVE HUMMON	drms	FG

45s:	Turn On Song/Enchanted Sea	(Sea Crest 6003) 1964
	Doggin'/Then I Cried	(Sea Crest 6004) 1964
	Chitlins, etc/	
	Clyde, Clyde, The Cow's Outside	(Panorama 9) 1965
	Come Now/Since I Fell For You	(Panorama 33) 1966

Formed in Ballard, Washington in 1959, their personnel underwent a number of changes, and in addition to the personnel listed above, Mike Smale, Steve Lervold and Craig Parker provided keyboards in early line-ups, with Dick Gazewood also playing sax. By 1964 they had secured a record deal with Sea Crest Records. *Turn On Song* won them a lot of regional recognition and they got to play with many major acts before they evolved into Rubber Band in 1967.

In addition to their four 45s they had one cut, *Trick Bag* on the compilation *Battle Of The Bands, Vol. 1* (LP) in 1966, on which Billy Burns provided vocals. Other vocalists on their recordings include Woody Carr on *Then I Cried*.

Early member Steve Lervold later played with James Henry & The Olympics, whilst Dan Olason was last reported working as a Boeing executive and brother Bill is a dentist in Seattle.

Retrospective compilation appearances have included: *Trick Bag* on *Northwest Battle Of The Bands, Vol. 1 - Flash And Crash* (LP & CD), *Northwest Battle Of The Bands, Vol. 1* (CD), *History Of Northwest Rock, Vol. 2* (CD) and *The History Of Northwest Rock, Vol. 4* (LP). (VJ/MW/DR)

The Counts

| 45: | Night Of Misery/If I Look Back | (Wam 1006) 1965 |

A different outfit from Warren, Ohio, whose *Night Of Misery* has resurfaced on *Garage Punk Unknowns, Vol. 7* (LP). (VJ/MW/GGl)

The Counts

| 45: | Now You're Gone / Old Man River | (Teen 900) 196? |

Another Ohio **Counts**, from Cincinnati this time. The wimpy garage-ballad *Now You're Gone* is on *Love Is A Sad Song, Vol. 1* (LP) and *No No No* (CD). (MW/GGl)

The Counts IV

| 45s: | Listen To Me/Lost Love (PS) | (J.C.P. 1006) 1967 |
| | Spoonful/Where You Are | (Date 1526) 1966 |

This outfit consisted of personnel from the Seymour Johnson Air Force Base in North Carolina. They had a very Anglophile sound which is evidenced by *Listen To Me*. They then signed up to record a 45 on the nationally distributed Date label. The 'A' side *Spoonful* (which is not the often covered Howlin' Wolf classic) is a live recording, more in the 'frat rock' mould and not really a progression on their first effort.

Compilation appearances have included: *Listen To Me* on *Tobacco A-Go-Go, Vol. 1* (LP), *Scum Of The Earth, Vol. 1* (LP) and *Scum Of The Earth* (CD); and *Spoonful* on *Highs In The Mid-Sixties, Vol. 22* (LP). (VJ)

COUNTRY JOE & THE FISH - Here We Are Again LP.

The Couriers

| 45: | Feelings/Stomping Time Again | (C.V. 500) 1968 |

From the Lancaster area of Pennsylvania, this outfit started out as a soul band but became more and more rock orientated and sound very Rascal-ish on their sole 45, *Feelings*. The band finally split in 1968.

Compilation appearances have included: *Feelings* on *Crude PA, Vol. 1* (LP); and *Feelings* and *Stompin' Time Again* on *Stompin' Time Again!* (CD). (VJ)

Coven

Personnel incl:	JIM DONLINGER		A
	JINX DAWSON	vcls	AB
	MIKE "OZ" OSBOURNE	bs	AB
	STEVE ROSS	drms	AB
	ALAN ESTES	bs	B
	JOHN HOBBS	keyb'ds	B
	CHRISTOPHER NIELSEN	gtr, vcls	B
	FRANK SMITH		B
	(JIM NYEHOLT	keyb'ds	A)

ALBUMS:	1(A)	WITCHCRAFT - DESTROYS MINDS AND REAPS SOULS	(Mercury 61239) 1969 SC
	2( )	COVEN	(MGM 4801) 1971 -
	3(B)	BLOOD IN THE SNOW	(Buddah BDS 5614) 1974 -

NB: (3) also released in England (Buddah BDLH 5011).

45s:	α	I Shall Be Released/I've Come Too Far	(SGC 003) 1969
		Wicked Woman/White Witch Of Rose Hall	(Mercury 72973) 1969
		I Guess It's A Beautiful Day Today/One Tin Soldier	(MGM 14308) 1971
		One Tin Soldier/Say Goodbye, Cause You're Leavin'	(Warner Bros. 7509) 1971
		Jailhouse Rock/Nightingale	(Lion 102) 1972
		Jailhouse Rock/Nightingale	(MGM 14348) 1972
		I Think You Always Knew/One Tin Soldier	(ABC 11377) 1973
	β	I Need A Hundred Of You/Blood On The Snow	(Buddah BDS 417) 1975

NB: α may be by a different act. β UK release.

A heavy rock outfit from Indiana notable for the screaming vocals of Jinx Dawson. They released at least three albums. Produced by Bill Traut (**Aorta**, **Shadows of Knight**...), their first one attempted to mix psych-rock with Black Mass "liturgy" for generally enjoyable results and contained ten tracks including: *Black Sabbath*, *Dignitaries Of Hell*, *Pact With Lucifer*, *For Unlawful Carnal Knowledge*... The album came with a nice gatefold cover with lyrics and several pictures of the "ceremony".

The first album features members of **Aorta** and in particular Jim Donlinger wrote most of the songs, arranged them, played guitar, and sang backup. Their subsequent releases were in the same style musically, but abandoned the 'satanic' theme.

The group featured Mike "Oz" Osbourne, formerly with UK act the Magic Lanterns. He is not Ozzy Osbourne of Black Sabbath, although some dealers mention it on their lists.

One of **Coven**'s tracks *One Tin Soldier* appeared on three of their 45s and was also featured in the movie 'Billy Jack'.

Jinx Dawson was born on a Friday the 13th and actually is named Jinx on her birth certificate. (SR/RNi/MW/SMu)

Joe Covington's Fat Fandango

Personnel:	JOE E. COVINGTON	drms, vcls	A
	SENATOR PATRICK CRAIG	keyb'ds	A
	STEVIE MIDNITE	gtr	A
	JACK PRENDERGAST	bs	A

COYOTE - Coyote LP.

ALBUM: 1(A)   JOE E.COVINGTON'S FAT FANDANGO
(Grunt BLF1-0149) 1973

45:   Boris The Spider /
      I'll Do Better Next Time   (Original Sound 74) 1967

NB: as **Joey Covington**.

After a **Kim Fowley**/Michael Lloyd produced 45, **Joe Covington** played drums with Jorma Kaukonen and Jack Casady for the first live gigs of **Hot Tuna**. He eventually became the drummer of the **Jefferson Airplane** for *Bark*, but quit the group in 1973 to go solo.

His sole album was released on Grunt, the '**Airplane** label, and produced by Pat Ieraci. Musically patchy, it contains seven tracks written by **Covington** and mixes good West Coast guitar solos with loose improvisation and generally weak vocals.

Covington had earlier been in **The Fenways** and also later played on **Peter Kaukonen**'s *Black Kangaroo* and **Papa John Creach**'s first album. After 1973, he apparently retired from the music scene but can however be found drumming on **Nick Gravenites**' *Blue Star*, an album from 1980. Patrick Craig was in **West Coast Natural Gas/Indian Puddin' and Pipe** until their break up in 1971, then played with Van Morrison and **Buddy Miles** before forming the Tazmanian Devils in 1976.

Compilation appearances have included: *I'll Do Better Next Time* on *Kim Fowley - Outlaw Superman* (LP); and *Boris The Spider* on *Mindrocker, Vol. 12* (LP). (SR/CF)

The Cowboys 'n' Indians

45:   Vanilla Days and Chocolate Nights/
      Jack In The Box   (Kama Sutra 249) 1968

A psych-pop single. (SR)

The Cowsills

Personnel:	BARRY COWSILL	bs	A
	BILL COWSILL	gtr	A
	BOB COWSILL	gtr	A
	JOHN COWSILL	drums	A

45:   All I Wanta Be Is Me/And The Next Day Too   (Joda 103) 1965

The 'A' side to the above 45, *All I Wanta Be Is Me*, is quite an excellent garage record with almost sneering vocals. It has also resurfaced on *Hipsville 29 B.C.* (LP).

Former Navy man Bud Cowsill brought a couple of guitars back to Newport, Rhode Island. from Spain for his two older sons Bill and Bob (18 and 16 at the time). They taught themselves to play and were soon augmented by their younger brethren, Barry (11) and John (10). Precursors to The Osmonds brand of sibling pop, they were also managed by their father.

After the JODA 45 they had considerable success and released eight albums and numerous 45s on MGM, Philips and London between 1966 and 1971, although these fall outside the remit of this book. Bill Cowsill went solo and put out an album in 1970. Sister Susan joined the group at a later stage and released some solo 45s in the mid-seventies.

Their flower-power *The Rain, The Park, And Other Things*, is also reputedly worth a spin. (BM/MW)

Coyote

Personnel:	ROD ARMENT	keyb'ds, gtr, vcls	A
	CHUCK BEATY	gtr, vcls	A
	LIZ HEIN	flute	A
	JIM KESTLE	bs, vcls	A
	TIM LLOYD	drms	A
	RUSTY STEELE	keyb'ds, gtr, vcls	A

ALBUM: 1(A)   COYOTE   (Chariot CH-500) 197? R2

Recorded in Maryland, this mid-seventies sounding hard-edged rural rock album is worth investigation. A very high standard of musicianship is maintained throughout, and the band leaks an unusual sense of humour into their all-original material. The record has a very cool sleeve as well. (CF)

Crabby Appleton

Personnel:	FELIX "FLACO" FALCON	perc	A
	MICHAEL FENNELLY	gtr, vcls	A
	CASEY FOUTZ	keyb'ds	A
	HANK HARVEY	bs	A
	PHIL JONES	drms	A

HCP
ALBUMS: 1(A)   CRABBY APPLETON   (Elektra EKS 74067) 1970   175 -
        2(A)   ROTTEN TO THE CORE   (Elektra EKS 74106) 1971   - -

NB: (1) reissued on CD (Collectors' Choice CCM 285 2) 2002. (2) reissued on CD (Collectors' Choice CCM 286 2) 2002.

HCP
45s: α My Little Lucy/Some Madness   (Elektra) 1970 -
(selec β Go Back/Try   (Elektra 45687) 1970 36
-tive)

NB: α also released in France with a PS (Vogue/Elektra INT 80258). β also released in Australia (Astor).

Formed by Michael Fennelly after the end of **Millennium** and **Sagittarius**, **Crabby Appleton** was one of the early seventies California rock groups signed by Elektra, along with **Rhinoceros** or the **Wackers**. Their first album was produced by Don Gallucci (from **Don and The Goodtimes** and **Touch**) and enjoyed reasonable success, climbing to No. 125 in the Charts. This allowed them to release a second album on which they used some female background vocals. Their music was characterized by Fennelly's vocals (sometimes inspired by Robert Plant) and his good lead guitar work. Their songs combine hard-rock and melodic pop-rock.

Fennelly later moved to England and released two solo albums: *Lane Changer* with Rod Argent (Epic KE 32703, 1974) and *Strangers Bed* (Mercury SRM 1-1043, 1975). Felix Falcon became a session musician.

Compilation appearances have included *Go Back* on *Elektrock The Sixties* (4-LP) and it is this **Nazz**-like slice of power-pop that the band are best remembered. (SR/VJ)

The Crabs

Personnel:	JERRY DeJONG	ld gtr	A
	ROBBIE LEFF	rhythm gtr, vcls	A
	ED RUDNICK III	bs	A
	ALEC SMITH	drms	A

45: Chase Yourself/Bye Bye My Little Girl (Universal 30495) 1967

Formed in 1966 by childhood friends Alec Smith and Robbie Leff, **The Crabs** were managed by prominent Houston agent and big-band leader, Buddy Brock, who produced their only record, *Chase Yourself* b/w *Bye Bye My Little Girl* on Brock's own Universal label. Both songs were written by Leff.

Chase Yourself met with no success on Houston radio (many thought that the 'B' side should've been the A-side) but it did chart in Beaumont, Texas and Lake Charles, Louisiana where **The Crabs** also made their one and only TV appearance on a local morning show. There they lip-synched their single and promoted that night's appearance at the opening of a Lake Charles nightclub, The Cave. One embarrassing moment of the live TV show: Someone in the booth mistakenly played the opening 20 seconds of the 45 at 33rpm... no doubt the longest 20 seconds in the brief career of **The Crabs**.

Typical songs from the group's set list included those of the Yardbirds, The Beatles, Gerry and The Pacemakers, **Johnny Rivers**, **Sam The Sham and The Pharaohs**, **Paul Revere and The Raiders**, Wilson Pickett and **Roy Head** and The Traits.

After playing steadily for almost two years the group broke up when drummer Smith went off to college in El Paso and Leff moved to Los Angeles to pursue songwriting. Although Leff's music never enjoyed great success, his songs were recorded by a diverse group of artists including Nancy Sinatra, **Johnny Winter** and Alice Cooper.

Leff moved back to Houston in 1982 where he currently performs in the sixties music duet, Speedy Mancini with singer/drummer Dale Marks. Alec Smith is married with two grown children and is in the insurance business. Jerry DeJong was last heard of teaching guitar and Ed Rudnick's whereabouts are currently unknown.

Compilation appearances include: *Chase Yourself* on *Highs In The Mid-Sixties, Vol. 12* (LP) and *Acid Visions - The Complete Collection, Vol. 1* (3-CD).

The Crackerjack Society

45: Walk In The Sky/ Listen To This Side (Columbia 44434) 1966

A very obscure garage band. (SR)

The Cradle

Personnel incl: MURRAY WECHT   A

45: What A Summer/It's The Wrong Time (Jubilee 5549) 1966

A forgotten group with the flower-power *What A Summer*. The flip is more up-tempo in a British Invasion style. This single was written and produced by Murray Wecht. (SR)

The Craftsmen

ALBUM: 1 WHAT CAN WE SAY? (Zap 3009) c1967 R2

An Ohio group, between garage and the Beach Boys, with songs like *Kicks, Everyday I Have To Cry, Surfin' USA, Your Summer Dream* and *Then I Kissed Her*. Only a few hundred copies were pressed and came in a blank die-cut cover. (SR)

Joe Crane and His Rhythm Devils

Personnel:	JOE CRANE	vcls, gtr, keyb'ds	A
	JOHN REWIND	gtr	A

EP: 1 JOE CRANE AND HIS RHYTHM DEVILS (PS) (No label) 1970

A San Francisco blues-rock group fronted by **Joe Crane**. Originating from Conroe, Texas, **Crane** was a pianist, guitarist, songwriter and singer who had previously played with Texas musicians like **Roy Head**, Huey Meaux and **Johnny Winter**. He moved from Texas to California in 1967, while he was in the Coast Guard and then became the only white member of the Buzzards, an Oakland bar band. In 1970, **Crane** met the producer Jack Leahy and organised the Rhythm Devils. After the release of their rare privately pressed 33rpm EP, their line-up changed and the group became the **Hoodoo Rhythm Devils**. (SR)

Crash Coffin

ALBUM: 1 CRASH COFFIN (Mus I Col) 1974 R2

Released on the same Ohio label as **Owen-B**, **The Myrchents** and **J.H. and The Esquires**, this album was released with two different covers: the first has "Crash Coffin" hand written in blue and red, the second has a plain white cover with the label logo. Perhaps because the musicians got tired of all the handwriting! It's musically diverse, ranging from psych-folk to bluegrass, with rather naive vocals. (SR)

Crawdaddy

45s:	Shake A Hand/Moment Of Madness	(Colossus 105) 1969
	I Gotta Get To Know You/?	(Colossus 144) 1970

Another forgotten pop-rock group, produced by Jerry Ross. (SR)

Crazy Elephant

Personnel:	BOB AVERY	drms	A
	RONNIE BRETONE	bs	A
	KENNY COHEN	keyb'ds, sax, vcls	A
	HAL KING	vcls	A
	LARRY LAUFER	keyb'ds, vcls	A

ALBUM: 1( ) CRAZY ELEPHANT (Bell 6034) 1968 -

    HCP

45s:	Gimmie Gimmie Good Lovin'/ Dark Part Of My Mind	(Sphere Sound 77005) 1968
	Gimmie Gimmie Good Lovin'/ Dark Part Of My Mind	(Bell 703) 1968 12
	Sunshine, Red Wine/Pam	(Bell 804) 1969 104
	Gimmie Some More/My Baby (Honey Pie)	(Bell 817) 1969 116
	There's A Better Day A-Comin' (Na Na Na Na)/ Space Buggy	(Bell 846) 1969
	Landrover/There Ain't No Umbopo	(Bell 875) 1970 -

This bubblegum outfit was originally put together in the studio by producers Jerry Kasenetz and Jeff Katz with Robert Spencer, formerly of The Cadillacs, on vocals. The above line-up is for the touring group that was formed later. They are best remembered for *Gimmie Gimmie Good Lovin*, which had the pounding beat and immediate appeal that typified bubblegum music, but the flip is superb slice of U.S. psychedelia with a long organ introduction and haunting vocals.

Although the album includes *Gimme Gimme Good Lovin'*, the rest of the material is also different. The opening cut is a long version of *Respect*, featuring heavy organ and flute solos. Apparently the 45 group was a studio creation but the band which recorded the album was formed by New York musicians, who'd earlier recorded as **Livin End**.

Kenny Cohen had started his musical career in Florida with **The Group**, a garage band based in Cocoa Beach.

CREATION OF SUNLIGHT - Creation Of Sunlight LP.

Dark Part Of My Mind also appears to have been released as the flip to **Captain Groovy and His Bubblegum Army**'s sole 45 and can be found on *Buzz Buzz Buzzzzzz Vol. 2* (CD). Another track, *In A Castle* has resurfaced on *Psychosis From The 13th Dimension* (CDR & CD). (VJ/SR/MW/JLh)

The Crazy Teens

45:	Crazy Date/?	(Scott 19) 196?

From Tuscaloosa, Alabama, you'll also find *Crazy Date* on *Scum Of The Earth, Vol. 1* (LP) and *Scum Of The Earth* (CD). (MW)

Papa John Creach

Personnel:	JACK BONUS	sax	A
	DAVID BROWN	bs	A
	JACK CASADY	bs	AB
	JOHN CIPOLLINA	gtr	A
	JOEY COVINGTON	drms	A
	PAPA JOHN CREACH	electric violin, vcls	AB
	JERRY GARCIA	gtr	A
	PAUL KANTNER	gtr	A
	JORMA KAUKONEN	gtr	AB
	MIKE LIPSKIN	organ	A
	SKIP OLSEN	bs	A
	SAMMY PIAZZA	drms	AB
	DOUGLAS RAUCH		A
	CARLOS SANTANA	gtr	A
	PETE SEARS	bs	A
	GRACE SLICK	vcls	A
	ZULU	backing group	B

ALBUMS:	1(A)	PAPA JOHN CREACH	(Grunt FTR-1003) 1971 -
	2(B)	FILTHY	(Grunt FTR-1009) 1972 -

45:	The Janitor Drives A Cadillac/ Over The Rainbow	(Grunt 65-0501) 1971

Born in 1917, **Papa John Creach** was a black violin player who joined **Hot Tuna** in 1970 and the **Jefferson Airplane** in 1971. His first album for Grunt (the '**Airplane**' label) can interest the Bay Area fans because of the participation of the whole of '**Airplane**, plus **Jerry Garcia**, John Cipollina, Pete Sears, Carlos Santana...

Musically patchy, it contains some excellent tracks (*The Janitor Drives A Cadillac*, sung by Grace Slick and written by **Covington**; *Plunk A Little Funk, Everytime I Hear Your Name* and *String Jet Rock* with Casady, Kaukonen and Piazza in an electric formation). Alas, insipid covers of *Over The Rainbow* and *Danny Boy* reduce the global quality of this surprising album.

In 1972, **Papa John** created his own group, Zulu, and recorded his second album *Filthy* which is not as good, his main highlight being the Kaukonen composition *Walking The Tou-Tou*.

Creach later joined Jefferson Starship and kept on recording under his name during the seventies. He died in the early nineties. (SR)

Creation of Sunlight

Personnel:	RON CLARK		A
	CARL ESTRELLA		A
	JERRY GRIFFIN	keyb'ds, vcls	A
	BOB MORGAN		A
	STEVE MONTAGUE		A
	DON SAIN		A
	GARY YOUNG		A

ALBUM:	1(A)	CREATION OF SUNLIGHT	(Windi ST 1001-1002) 1968 R4

NB: (1) reissued on vinyl in 1990 and on CD (Mystic 7) 1997, ( ) 2000 and again (Void VOID 28) 2002.

45:	David/The Fun Machine	(Windi 1006) 196?

A very rare Southern California pop-psych album with dual organ, fuzz and sunshine vibes similar to **Strawberry Alarm Clock**. The band were previously known as Sunlights Seven and recorded an unreleased, acetate-only album in Hollywood: *Sunstroke*, circa 1967. Their repertoire largely comprised of early versions of songs re-recorded for the **Creation Of Sunlight** album. (VJ/SR/CF)

Creations

Personnel:	LLOYD BETTS	gtr	A
	BILL BROWN	organ	A
	GRADY BROWN	bs	A
	RAYMOND BROWN	drms	A
	DAVID JONES	ld gtr	A
	BOBBY PERRY	trumpet	A
	BOBBY SUTTON	vcls	A

EP:	1(A)	TO WHOM IT MAY CONCERN	(Norton EP-101) 2001

The Norton EP comprises four previously unissued tracks 'recorded live in the bedroom' in 1966 by this teen combo from Elizabeth City, North Carolina. Unusually for the times, all the material is original and each clocks in at over three and a half minutes. Despite the lo-fi quality, they shine through on this homemade demo.

The Animals and Yardbirds appear to be the prime influences. *Better Watch Out* is a moody punker with Burdonesque vocals and a visceral guitar solo; *I'm Mad* has a great Yardbirds-style rave-up; *Soul And Feeling* (with "it's very own sound") is a bluesy slow-burner with a rockin' middle section; finally *To Whom It May Concern* is the band's roll-call number which provides the personnel above (strangely the leader and drummer Raymond Brown is omitted from the label's personnel list). Whatever, 35 years on they've made it! (MW)

Creation's Disciples

45:	Psychedelic Retraction/ I'll Remember (RED VINYL)	(Dawn 309) 196?

From South Bronx, New York, their superb psych-punk effort *Psychedelic Retraction* can be heard on *Psychedelic Unknowns, Vol. 4* (LP & CD), *Destination Frantic!* (LP & CD) and *Ear-Piercing Punk* (CD). (VJ/MW)

Creatures Inc.

Personnel incl: ROCKY ISAAC   drms   A

45s:	Letters Of Love / All About Love	(Oxon Hill 1001) 1965
α	Stop Your Sobbing/Letters Of Love	(Jet Set 1004) 1966

NB: α as by The Creatures.

Originally from Rome, New York they relocated to Washington D.C. and picked up a couple of new members from Georgetown outfit The Tejuns en route. *Letters Of Love*, rather a nice harmony pop effort in the Zombies mould, can also be heard on *Highs In The Mid-Sixties, Vol. 22* (LP) and *Fuzz, Flaykes, And Shakes, Vol. 5* (LP & CD).

Rocky Isaac went on to play and record with **The Fallen Angels** and **The Cherry People**. (VJ/MW/BE)

Creedence Clearwater Revival

Personnel:	DOUG CLIFFORD	drms	AB
	STU COOK	bs	AB
	JOHN FOGERTY	vcl, ld gtr	AB
	TOM FOGERTY	gtr, vcls	A

HCP

ALBUMS:	1(A)	CREEDENCE CLEARWATER REVIVAL	(Fantasy 8382) 1968	52 -
(up to 1976)	2(A)	BAYOU COUNTRY	(Fantasy 8387) 1969	8 -
	3(A)	GREEN RIVER	(Fantasy 8393) 1969	1 -
	4(A)	WILLY AND THE POOR BOYS	(Fantasy 8397) 1969	3 -
	5(A)	COSMO'S FACTORY	(Fantasy 8402) 1970	1 -
	6(A)	PENDULUM	(Fantasy 8410) 1970	5 -
	7(B)	MARDI GRAS	(Fantasy 9404) 1972	12 -
	8(-)	CREEDENCE GOLD	(Fantasy 9418) 1972	15 -
	9(-)	MORE CREEDENCE GOLD	(Fantasy 9430) 1973	61 -
	10(B)	LIVE IN EUROPE	(Fantasy CCR1) 1974	143 -
	11(-)	CHRONICLE (THE 20 GREATEST HITS)	(Fantasy CCR 2) 1976	100 -

NB: All these albums have also been released in Germany, England, Italy, France and Holland. Several reissues exists on vinyl and CD. Countless compilations have also been released, without any rarities.

HCP

45s:	Suzy Q, pt. 1/Suzy Q, pt. 2	(Fantasy 616) 1968	11
	I Put A Spell On You/ Walk On The Water	(Fantasy 617) 1968	58
	Proud Mary/Born On The Bayou	(Fantasy 619) 1969	2
	Bad Moon Rising/Lodi	(Fantasy 622) 1969	2/52
	Green River/Commotion	(Fantasy 625) 1969	2/30
	Down On The Corner/Fortunate Son	(Fantasy 634) 1969	3/14
	Travelin' Band/Who'll Stop The Rain	(Fantasy 637) 1970	2
	Up Around The Bend/ Run Trough The Jungle	(Fantasy 641) 1970	4
	Lookin' Out At My Back Door/ Long As I Can See The Light	(Fantasy 645) 1970	2
	Have You Ever Seen The Rain/ Hey Tonight	(Fantasy 655) 1971	8
	Sweet Hitch Hiker/Door To Door	(Fantasy 665) 1971	6
	Someday Never Comes/ Tearin' Up The Country	(Fantasy 676) 1972	25

NB: All these singles are LP tracks and have also been released by Bellaphon on Germany with picture sleeves, by America and Fantasy in France with picture sleeves, by Fantasy in Italy with picture sleeves and by Liberty in the U.K.. Two other singles: *Bootleg/Good Golly Miss Molly* (America 17010) 1968 and *Molina/Sailor's Lament* (Fantasy 17038) 1971, were also issued in France.

When they renamed themselves with this strange name, the former **Golliwogs** were wishing to make a new start, relying on their roots: raw blues-tinged sounds from Memphis and New Orleans. Their first 45, a good cover of Dale Hawkins' *Suzy Q* reached No. 11 in the charts in October 1968. The debut album was greeted with much critical approval and sold surprisingly well, reaching No. 52 in the charts. The following albums established **Creedence** as a very popular act. The prolific songwriting skills of John Fogerty helped the group to release six albums in three years and most of the songs were a powerful mix of blues, rockabilly, rock and R&B

CREEDENCE CLEARWATER REVIVAL - Self Titled CD.

with clever lyrics, often expressing the working-class sensibility (*Fortunate Son*, *Lodi*). They were probably the only San Francisco band whose public thought they were from Louisiana or Tennessee.

In February 1971, **Tom Fogerty** had quit the band to pursue a solo career. John gave in to the demands of the rhythm section for more artistic freedom and their final album, *Mardi Gras*, was an artistic disaster, the singing and songwriting abilities of Cook and **Clifford** being really limited.

When the group broke up, **Doug Clifford** recorded a solo album *Cosmo* (Fantasy 9411) 1972, which is better avoided. **Clifford** and Cook kept on working together, first with Doug Sahm (the excellent *Groover's Paradise* was produced by **Clifford**) then with the Don Harrison Band and Russell DaShiell. Stu Cook then worked with Roky Erickson (he produced *The Evil One*) and later formed Southern Pacific, a successful country rock act with other San Francisco veterans (John McFee, Keith Knudsen).

In 1996, **Clifford** and Cook formed Creedence Clearwater Revisited and are still touring, mostly in Northern Europe.

John Fogerty first created the Blue Ridge Rangers, a country/blues/hillbilly act whose album sold quite well (it was in fact Fogerty solo playing all the instruments!) and went "really" solo in 1973, recording some singles and an excellent *John Fogerty* in 1975. Being in a long-term procedure with Fantasy to get his royalties back, he stopped recording for ten years and finally came back in 1985 with *Centerfield* which was very successful. He is still recording and touring. (SR/VJ)

Creme Soda

Personnel:	ART HICKS	drms, vcls	A
	DON JUNTUNEN	ld gtr, bs	A
	BILL TANON	gtr, bs, harp, mandolin, perc, vcls	A
	JIM WILSON	bs, keyb'ds, perc, vcls	A

ALBUM:	1(A)	TRICKY ZINGERS	(Trinity CST-11-LA) 1975 R2

NB: (1) original pressing has photo of group on cover, and had twelve tracks. Reissued (Trinity CST-12-LP) 1977. This pressing has a black & white 'title' cover and includes only nine tracks, omitting *Numero Uno*, *The Beat Song* and *Daydreamin'*.

45s:	Keep It Heavy/And That Is That	(Trinity 112) 1975
	Keep It Heavy/And That Is That	(Trinity 45121) 1975
	(I'm) Chewin' Gum/Roses All Around	(Trinity 45122) 1975

Hailed from Milwaukee, Wisconsin, where they first started playing together in 1972. Both 45s are from their album, which contains quite a range of styles. Melodic soft rock predominates as evidenced by *Give It Up*, *Tonight*, *Deep In A Dream*, *Keep It Heavy* and *Daydreamin'*; but there's also a

CREME SODA - Tricky Zingers (Orig) LP.

couple of weirder more psychedelic tracks in the early Pink Floyd mould - *Numero Uno* and *The Beat Song*; some rockabilly/punk *(I'm) Chewin' Gum* and *When The Sun Shines* and a bit of punk/blues on *That Is That*. Overall, it's worth investigating. Don Juntunen, incidentally, later played with Oklahoma.

There were rumours of another album entitled *Live Zingers*, but this is now known not to exist.

Compilation appearances have included: *Tonight* and *Keep It Heavy* on *Endless Journey - Phase Two* (LP); and *Tonight* on *Endless Journey - Phase I & II* (Dble CD). (VJ/CF)

The Crimson Bridge

ALBUM:　1　THE CRIMSON BRIDGE　　　(Myrrh MST-6503) c1973

Described on the back cover as "rock-jazz-latin-progressive-blues-acid-folk sounds", this album contains lots of lead guitar (but also some horns) and may interest some curious readers. Side one has five originals:- *Better Times*, *Comin'*, *He's Alive*, *Easy Ways*, and *Birthright*. Side two is a side long *Suite* broken into three movements *Searching In Reality*, *Experience* and *Beginning Of Joy*.

Myrrh was a Christian rok/folk label. (SR)

Gary Criss and His Crystals

Personnel incl:　GARY CRISS　　　　　　　　　　A

ALBUM:　1(A)　LIVE　　　　　　　　　　(EB) 1965 SC?

From New Jersey, a frat rock/white R&B group with sax, performing covers of *Mickeys Monkey*, *On Broadway*, *Let The Good Times Roll*, *What Now My Love*... Another example of a "live" performance recorded in the studio with fake applause.

Gary Criss alos recorded a 45 for Diamond and may also have recorded 45s for Stateside and Strand in the late fifties/early sixties. He was later drummer for **The Glass Bottle**. (SR/JosephVaccarino)

The Critters

Personnel:			
DON CICCONE	rhythm gtr, vcls	A
CHRIS DARWAY	keyb'ds, autoharp, vcls	AB
JACK DECKER	drms	AB
KENNY GORKA	bs, vcls	ABC
BOB PODSTAWSKI	sax, vcls	A
JIM RYAN	gtr, vcls	ABC
BOB SPINELLA	keyb'ds	C
PAUL GLANZ	gtr	C
JEFF PELOSI	drms	C
AL MILLER	keyb'ds	

HCP

ALBUMS:　1(A)　YOUNGER GIRL　　(Kapp KS-3485) Aug. 1966　147　-
　　　　　2(B)　TOUCH AND GO WITH THE CRITTERS
　　　　　　　　　　　　　　　　　(Project 3 PB 4001) 1968　-　-
　　　　　3(C)　THE CRITTERS　　　(Project 3 PB 4002) 1969　-　-

HCP

45s:　Georgianna/I'm Gonna Give　　(Musicor MU-1044) 1964　-
　　　I'm Telling Everyone/No One But You　(Prancer PR-6001) 1965　-
　　　Children And Flowers/He'll Make You Cry　(Kapp 727) 1965　-
　　　Younger Girl/Gone For A While　(Kapp 752) 1966　42
　　　Mr Dieingly Sad/It Just Won't Be That Way　(Kapp 769) 1966　17
　　　Bad Misunderstanding/Forever Or No More　(Kapp 793) 1966　55
　　　Marryin' Kind Of Love/New York Bound　(Kapp 805) 1967　111
　　　Don't Let The Rain Fall Down On Me/
　　　Walk Like A Man Again　(Kapp 838) 1967　39
　　　Little Girl/Dancing In The Streets　(Kapp 858) 1967　113
　　　Good Morning Sunshine/
　　　A Moment Of Being With You　(Project 3 1326) 1967　-
　　　Touch'n'Go/Younger Generation　(Project 3 1332) 1968　-
　　　Cool Sunday Morning/
　　　Lisa But Not The Same　(Project 3 1349) 1968　-
　　　I Just Want To Sit Right Here And Look At You/
　　　She Said She Loved Him　(Project 3 1363) 1969　-

NB: There are also two French EPs with PS from 1966 (Vogue Kapp KEV 13028 / 13031 respectively).

This New Jersey flower-power pop quintet first attracted attention when they recorded *Younger Girl*, a **John Sebastian** song from the first **Lovin' Spoonful** album. The 45 gave them the first of their four U.S. Top 100 hits and their first album was a delightful summery disc.

Originally called The Vibra-Tones, when they signed up to Kama Sutra Records, they were forced to record covers although the band had a large amount of original material ready. After recording the Jackie DeShannon song *Children And Flowers* for their first Kama Sutra single, the band wanted the **Don Ciccone** original, *Mr Dieingly Sad* for their second but when the label insisted on *Younger Girl*, four of the members went on strike rather than record the song. Subsequently, only Don and Kenny appeared on the single.

The record company then relented and *Mr Dieingly Sad* became their biggest hit. Soon after Don and Bob left to join the Air Force and a few months later, Jack Decker was drafted. Chris Darway then left to return to college and Jimmy Ryan and Kenny Gorka were left to carry the name with some hired musicians

CREME SODA - Tricky Zingers (1977 reissue) LP.

In late 1967 they signed to Enoch Light's Project 3 label, whose interest lay in making interesting use of cutting edge recording technology rather than music per se. They were subsequently featured on Light's "Popular Science" series of stereo/quad test albums.

Jim Ryan later worked with Carly Simon and Gumhill Road, Bob Spinella went on to **Steeplechase**, an altogether heavier outfit whose LP, *Lady Bright* is quite collectable. Kenny Gorka later became the manager of The Bitter End in New York City; **Don Ciccone** went off to write songs (for the Innocence) and later joined The Four Seasons, whilst Chris Darway became "Inventor in Residence" at Princeton University.

Their most successful 45, *Mr Dieingly Sad* can also be heard on *Nuggets, Vol. 11* (LP), whilst you can find the earlier *No One But You* on *Destination Frantic!* (CD); and *Don't Let The Rain...* on *Every Groovy Day* (LP). (MW/JFr/VJ/LP/SR/DG)

Cromagnon

| Personnel: | BRIAN ELLIOT | A |
| | AUSTIN GRASMERE | A |

ALBUM: 1(A) CROMAGNON (ESP 2001) 1969 -
NB: (1) reissued on CD by ESP as *Cave Rock*.

This duo came from Connecticut. Their album was weird, full of sound effects and improvised music. Originals are still possible to obtain relatively cheaply, although the album has also been reissued on CD. *Caledonia* was also included on an ESP sampler. It previews the rage/angst music represented well by Ministry in the late eighties. (VJ)

The Crome Syrcus

Personnel:	JOHN GARBORIT	ld gtr	A
	LEE GRAHAM	vcls, bs, flte	A
	ROD PILLOUD	drms	A
	DICK POWELL	mouth harp, keyb'ds	A
	TED SHREFFLER	keyb'ds	A

ALBUM: 1(A) LOVE CYCLE (Command RS 925) 1968 SC
NB: (1) has been counterfeited on vinyl.

45s:	White Korte Feather/Blue Morning	(Merrilyn 5303) 196?
	Lord In Black/Long Hard Road	(Piccadilly 256) 1968
	Take It Like A Man/Crystals	(Command 4111) 1968
	Take It Like A Man/Cover Up	(Command 4111) 1968
	Lord In Black/Elevator Operator	(Jerden 921) 1969

CROMAGNON - Cave Rock CD.

Originally from Seattle **The Crome Syrcus** relocated to San Francisco. The title track of their album, a 17-minute composition, commences with religious chanting superimposed upon electric organ, which later gives way to an extended psychedelic suite. *Crystals* on Side One is notable for some fine flutework, and the preceding track, *You Made A Change In Me* is a soothing gentle number. The Command 45 was taken from the album. They won a songwriting award in the Bay Area in 1969.

Compilation appearances have included: *Lord In Black* on *Psychedelic Unknowns, Vol. 3* (LP & CD), *Filling The Gap* (4-LP); *Elevator Operator* on *History Of Northwest Rock, Vol. 6*; and *Elevator Operator* and *Long Hard Road* on *The History Of Northwest Rock, Vol. 3* (CD). (VJ)

David Crosby

ALBUM: 1 IF I COULD ONLY REMEMBER MY NAME
(Atlantic SD 7203) 1970 -
NB: (1) also released in the U.K., France, and Germany.

Recorded shortly after the death of his girlfriend, Christine Gail Hinton, the first solo album by **David Crosby** contains some decent tracks but will not appeal to everyone, and many will find it boring. It's main interest today is probably the stellar backing group: four members of the **Dead** (Garcia, Lesh, **Hart** and Kreutzmann), two from **Santana** (Shrieve and Rolie), four from the '**Airplane** (Grace Slick, Kantner, Casady, Kaukonen), one from **Quicksilver** (Freiberg), plus Graham Nash, Neil Young, Joni Mitchell and Laura Allen.

The music is very laid back and as one may expect, given the personnel, contains some good guitar parts. The material was penned by **Crosby** with some help from Young, Nash, **Garcia**, Lesh and Shrieve. The strangest track is an accapella version of the French traditional *Orleans, Beaugency*.

The album was engineered by Stephen Barncard, who also worked with **Chet Nicholls** and went on to form **Oasis** (the US one!). **David Crosby** worked throughout the seventies and eighties with Graham Nash and occasionally Steve Stills and Neil Young. He also spent various periods in jail. After some severe health problems, he is now intensively touring and recording, solo or with his two groups, CPR and the reformed CSN&Y.

David Crosby was of course one of **The Byrds**. (SR)

Crosscut Saw

ALBUM: 1 MAD, BAD, AND DANGEROUS TO KNOW
(Private Pressing) 197? R1

A wild Florida acid blues-rock outfit with raw vocals and good guitar leads. (SR)

Crowd + 1

45: Don't Hold Back/Try (Capitol 2259) 196?

From Fort Worth, Texas, this outfit later became **Bloodrock**. (MPo)

The Crusade

45: Psychedelic Woman/Fade Away (Golden North 103) 196?

Psychedelic Woman, a guitar-driven garage-punker with snarling vocal, from Juneau, Alaska. Tthe flip, *Fade Away*, is a slow number with catchy guitar and sound effects.

Compilation appearances include: *Psychedelic Woman* on *Scum Of The Earth, Vol. 1* (LP), *Scum Of The Earth, Vol. 2* (LP) and *Scum Of The Earth* (CD); and *Psychedlic Woman* and *Fade Away* on *Incredible Sound Show Stories, Vol. 4*. (VJ)

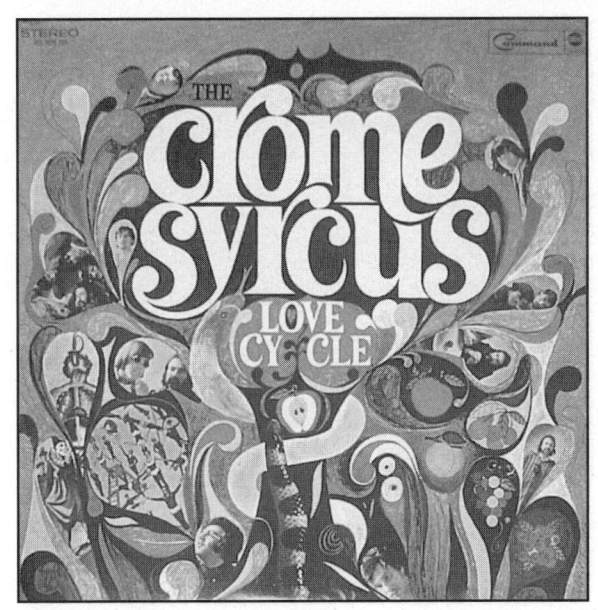

THE CROME SYRCUS - Love Cycle LP.

THE CRYAN' SHAMES - Sugar And Spice LP.

The Crusaders

ALBUM: 1 MAKE A JOYFUL NOISE WITH DRUMS AND GUITARS
(Tower ST50??) 1966

A five piece gospel-rock group. With the addition of a female singer, they later became **Love Exchange**. They are obviously totally unconnected to the funk/jazz Crusaders.

One track from the album, *God Lives* later resurfaced on the CD compilation *Songs Of Faith And Inspiration*. (SR/DJ)

The Cryan' Shames

Personnel:
DENNIS CONROY	drms		ABC
TOM DOODY (TOAD)	vcls		ABCD
JIM FAIRS	ld gtr		ABC
JIM PILSTER (J.C. HOOKE)	drms, tamb, vcls		ABCD
DAVE PURPLE (GRAPE)	bs, keyb'ds		A
GERRY STONE (STONEHENGE)	gtr		AB
LENNY KERLEY	bs, vcls		BCD
ISAAC GUILLORY	gtr, vcls		CD
DAVE CARTER	ld gtr		D
AL DAWSON	drms		D

HCP
ALBUMS: 1(A) SUGAR AND SPICE   (Columbia CP 2589) 1966 192 -
        2(C) A SCRATCH IN THE SKY
                                       (Columbia CP 2786) 1967 156 -
        3(D) SYNTHESIS   (Columbia CP 9719) 1968 184 -

NB: (1) reissued with five additional tracks - the 'A' sides of their third - seventh 45s (Decal LIK 37) 1988. There's also a Columbia Legacy eighteen track compilation entitled *Sugar And Spice (A Collection)* 1992. (1), (2) and (3) also issued on CD (Sundazed SC 6186 - SC 6188) 2002.

HCP
45s: Sugar And Spice/
      Ben Franklin's Almanac   (Destination 624) 1966 49
      I Wanna Meet You/
      We Could Be Happy   (Columbia 4-43836) 1966 85
      Mr. Unreliable/Georgia   (Columbia 4-44037) 1967 127
      It Could Be We Are In Love/
      I Was Lonely When (PS)   (Columbia 4-44191) 1967 85
      Up On The Roof/Sailing Ship   (Columbia 4-44457) 1968 85
      Young Birds Fly/Sunshine Psalm (Columbia 4-44545) 1968 99
      Greenberg, Glickstein, Charles, David Smith & Jones/
      The Warm   (Columbia 4-44638) 1968 115
      First Train To California/
      A Masters Fool   (Columbia 4-44759) 1969 -
      Rainmaker/Bits And Pieces   (Columbia 4-45027) 1969 -

Originally known as The Travelers, this Chicago-based act were clearly influenced by the British music invasion. Indeed it was their cover version of *Sugar And Spice*, which had given The Searchers a big U.K. hit back in 1963, which attracted the attention of Columbia, leading them to take over the distribution of their 45. A latter cover of Lennon-McCanney's *You're Gonna Loose That Girl*, which was probably intended as the follow-up, got lost somewhere in their switch from Destination to Columbia and only got an airing much later when Happy Tiger included it on their *Early Chicago* compilation.

After signing to Columbia they concentrated on putting out their first album which had a considerable **Byrds** influence and some good original compositions, notably Jim Fair's *Ben Franklin's Almanac*. It also contained some well done cover versions of classics like, *Hey Joe*, *If I Needed Someone*, *We Gotta Get Out Of This Place*, *We'll Meet Again* and *She Don't Care About Time*. It peaked at No. 192 in the U.S. Album Charts.

Further 45s followed:- another Jim Fair composition from their debut album, *I Wanna Meet You*, which became a minor hit, and *Georgia*, which was even less successful.

Gerry Stone was drafted and further line-up changes took place before they began work on a second album. The result was rather bland but a marked advance in terms of production and harmony. Commercially it was more successful than their first, climbing to No. 156. Meanwhile they enjoyed a minor 45 hit with *It Could Be We Are In Love* - one of their more inventive singles. Like the follow-up, *Up On The Roof*, it made the No. 85 spot.

Their third album *Synthesis* had strong material and lavish instrumentation but could only manage No 184 in the Album Charts. For this release Dave Carter had joined from the recently disbanded **Saturday's Children**.

In 1969, Carter, Kerley, and Dawson joined with members of **Aorta** to do an album of Navy public service spots under the moniker **Aorta/Cryin' Shames Ensemble**. The following year the band called it quits and Kerley formed **Possum River**.

Isaac Guillory gave it a go solo and moved to England where he recorded an album in the folky 'singer-songwriter' mould. In the nineties Jim Pilster, who got his nickname because he had a hook instead of a left hand was still singing for a re-formed **The Cryan Shames**, for which Tom Doody also makes occasional appearances.

Compilation appearances have included: *Sugar And Spice* on *Nuggets - Original Artyfacts From The First Psychedelic Era 1965-1968* (Dble LP), *Nuggets Box* (4-CD) and *Nuggets, Vol. 3* (LP); *A Journey To Tyme, Vol. 2* (LP), *Ben Franklin's Almanac* on *Pebbles Vol. 7* (CD), *Garage Music For Psych Heads* and *Destination Frantic!* (CD); and *You're Gonna Lose That Girl* on *Early Chicago* (LP). (VJ/MW/LP)

The Crystal Ball

45:	Trans-Love Airways (Fat Angel)/	
	You're A Big Girl Now	(Smash S-2092) 1967

A stoned psych one-off cover of Donovan, backed by a **Lovin' Spoonful** cover in a melodic pop vein. Produced by Roger Karshner (**Bhagavad Gita**, **National Gallery**), Richard Toops and Joel Corey (of the **Capes Of Good Hope**).

You can also find *Trans-Love Airways* on *Sixties Rebellion, Vol. 11* (LP & CD). (MW)

Crystal Circus

Personnel?:	JACK BIELAN	keyb'ds	A
	NICK DUNMAN		A
	BOB FELDMAN	vcls	A
	KAUFMAN		A
	GREG MUNFORD	vcls, keyb'ds	A
	GARY "SOLO" SOLOMON	vcls, sax, clarinet, flute	A

ALBUMS: 1(A?) THE CRYSTAL CIRCUS
(Test pressing with blank labels AA 5733) 1968

2(A?) IN RELATION TO OUR TIMES (Akarma AK 134) 2001

NB: (1) reissued as (2). (2) also issued on CD.

45:	In Relation / Merry Go Round	(All-American 3333) 1967

NB: Shown as by Strawberry Sac.

The personnel above are as credited on the Akarma album but all may not be as it seems.... a reissue of an untitled 1968 album, allocated a catalog # of All-American AA-5733-LPD, that only made it to the test-pressing stage. One copy surfaced in 2000 with a price-tag of $1500.

This group/project was in Bill Holmes' All-American stable of inter-twined groups from in and around the Santa Barbara, California area. Greg Munford had been with **Thee Sixpence** up to the point that they recorded the *Incense And Pepermints* (sic) 45 and became **The Strawberry Alarm Clock**. Crystal Circus would appear to have been his next venture. He was involved in other projects and a 45 released in '67 by The Shapes Of Sound - *Lost Weekend / Twisted Conversation* (All-American 343) - is a likely candidate, given that *Twisted Conversation* turns up on the **Crystal Circus** LP. Munford, Solomon and Bielan were certainly involved with another band on All-American, **The Indescribably Delicious**, and are credited on the **I.D.** album reissue - *Good Enough To Eat* (Akarma AK 046) 2000. Bob Feldman also pops up amongst the composer credits. HOWEVER you should refer to the **I.D.** entry to get the real facts behind the band, their "LP", and their experiences of Gary "Solo" Solomon and Bill Holmes.

If this is a bona fide album, one has to wonder why it was not released, given the success of the **Strawberry Alarm Clock**. The vocal style and arrangements on the soft-centred pop-psych numbers (*In Relation*, *Merry Go Round*, *Circus And Zoo World*) are uncannily similar. There are trippy vibes and elegant baroque gestures (*Castles*, *Twisted Conversation*) counterbalanced by harder material that harks back to the sounds of **Thee Sixpence**:- strident garage-pop with blistering guitar (*Don't Say I Didn't Warn You*), Cream-like fuzz-grunge (*The Difference Between Us*), and brass-pop bombast (*Never Again*).

Whatever the real truth behind it, this reissue unearths a fine selection of '67-'68 confectionery - recommended. (MW)

Crystal Chandelier

45s:	The Setting Of Despair/	
	It's Only You	(United Artists 50284) 1968
	Suicidal Flowers/Land Of Love	(Cobblestone 730) 1969

A psychedelic punk outfit from Providence, Rhode Island. *Suicidal Flowers* had a distinctively Eastern flavour and is well worth checking out.

CRYSTAL CIRCUS - In Relation To Our Times LP.

Compilation appearances have included: *Suicidal Flowers* on *Pebbles, Vol. 3* (LP), *Pebbles, Vol. 3* (CD), *Pebbles, Vol. 2 (ESD)* (CD), *Pebbles Box* (5-LP), *Acid Dreams - The Complete 3 LP Set* (3-LP), *Acid Dreams Epitaph* (CD), *Trash Box* (5-CD) and *Great Pebbles* (CD); and *The Setting Of Despair* on *Punk Ballads Sampler* (LP), *Sixties Archive, Vol. 5* (CD), *Son Of The Gathering Of The Tribe* (LP) and *Acid and Flowers* (CD).

The *Suicidal Flowers* track later gave name to the psychedelic necro-folk-rock band **The Suicidal Flowers** from York in the UK. (VJ/MW/ELn)

Crystal Garden

45:	Flash/Peach Fuzz Forest	(Bay Town) c1968

From Hayward, California, a good psych single with an interesting lead guitar. *Peach Fuzz Forest* later resurfaced on *Turds On A Bum Ride, Vol. 3* (CD). (SR)

Crystal Mansion

45:	If I Live/Goin To Carolina	(Colossus) 1968

An obscure folk-pop group (SR)

Crystal Palace

45:	Valley Of Peace/Padded Walls	(Eyelid EL-103) c1969

A rare and rather amateurish psych-rock group. Both songs feature the same riff. (SR)

Crystal Rain

45s:	Hey Ma Ma/Funeral At Dawn	(Vangee 904100) 1969
	You And Me/World On Fire	(Dynamic Sound 91101) 1969

This band came from Dayton, Ohio. Their first 45, *Hey Ma Ma* has quite a hypnotic quality, with well thought out fuzz, keyboard pulses and inventive drumming. Their follow up *You And Me*, is also a fine tripped-out, echo-soaked mind-blast. Check it out!

Compilation appearances have included: *Hey Ma Ma* and *You And Me* on *Sixties Rebellion, Vol. 11* (LP & CD); *Hey Ma Ma* on *A Lethal Dose Of Hard Psych* (CD); *You And Me* on *An Overdose Of Heavy Psych* (CD), *Turds On A Bum Ride, Vol. 2* (Dble LP), *Turds On A Bum Ride Vol. 1 & 2* (Dble CD), *Echoes In Time, Vol. 2* (LP) and *Echoes In Time Vol's 1 & 2* (CD); and *World On Fire* on *Turds On A Bum Ride Vol. 3* (CD). (MW/VJ))

Cucumber

| 45: | Don't Make Me Cry/Under | (Cobblestone CB 715) 1968 |

An obscure outfit which recorded just this one 45. The flip is a heavy fuzz instrumental number, whilst the top-side, also composed by a Robert Esposito, is a heavy mid-tempo fuzzy thriller.

Compilation appearances include: *Under* on *Psychedelic Unknowns, Vol. 6* (LP & CD) and *Everything You Always Wanted To Know...* (CD); and *Don't Make Me Cry* and *Under* on *Turds On A Bum Ride Vol. 3* (CD). (VJ)

Culls

| 45: | Midnight To Six Man / Walk On By | (MY 2918) 1967 |

The *Midnight To Sixty-Six* (LP) compilation revisits the **Culls**' rather conservative cover of the Pretties' classic on their sole 45. Based in Little Rock, Arkansas, the MY label seems to have had a monopoly on the area's burgeoning mid-sixties scene and released fine 45s by the likes of the **Dutch Masters**, Egyptians, **Romans** and **Spires Of Oxford**. (MW)

The Cult

| 45s: | Fire And Flood/ I Don't Know | (20th Century Fox 621) 1965 |
| | Here I Stand/You Know, You Really Hurt Me Girl | (20th Century Fox 6636) 1966 |

A mystery outfit from Riverside, Long Island. They released two moody pop-punk 45s that are proving popular now with compilers: *Fire And Flood* is on *Every Groovy Day*, *I Don't Know* is on *Leaving It All Behind*, and *Here I Stand* on *Vile Vinyl, Vol. 1* (LP) and *Vile Vinyl* (CD). (VJ/MW/MM)

Curfew

| ALBUM: | 1 LET THERE BE DARK: AND THERE WAS DARK | (United Artists UAS 6746) 1970 SC |

| 45: | Photogenic Jenny/ Wait For The Moment | (United Artists 50651) 1970 |

A faceless outfit, who get no credits or pictures on this minor-league U.A. album. However, they do produce the odd bit of vibrant heavy keyboard pop-rock with strong fuzzy guitar. *Photogenic Jenny* kicks off nicely in that vein, but the album quickly disappoints, slipping into insipid easy-pop. Whilst a couple of other tracks return to form - the Cream-inspired *Something Inside Of Me* for example, overall it's a patchy effort with no real identity.

Compilation appearances include *Photogenic Jenny* on *Songs Of Faith And Inspiration* (CDR & CD). (MW)

Current Event

ALBUMS:	1 HITS OF THE BEATLES	(Ambassador) c1967 -
	2 WHAT IS TRUTH?	(Ambassador) c1968 -
	3 HITS OF THE ROLLING STONES	(Ambassador) c1971 -

An obscure 'exploito' group. (SR)

Don Curry and The Instigators

| Personnel incl: | DON CURRY | A |

| 45: | Bony Moronie Revisited/ A Million Years Or So | (Texas Record Co 2086) 196? |

A garage band out of Waco, Texas. The 'A' side of their 45 can be found on *Punk Classics, Vol. 4* (7") and *Punk Classics* (CD). (VJ)

Jimmy Curtiss

Personnel:	JIMMY CURTISS	A
	BILLY ELMIGER	A
	JOHN TRIVERS	A
	JAN WILLIAMS	A
	HOWIE WYETH	A

| ALBUM: | 1(A) LIFE | (Perception PLP-1) 1970 - |

NB: (1) shown as by J.C.

45s:	Not For You You're What's Happening Baby	(Laurie 3312) 196?
	The Girl From The Land Of 1000 Dances/ Let's Dance Close	(Laurie 3315) 1965
α	Psychedelic Situation/ Gone But Not Forgotten	(Laurie 3383) 1967
β	For What I Am/Johnny Get Your Gun	(Perception P-2) 1970

NB: α also released in Germany (Ariola 19632). β features a non-LP track on the 'A' side.

From Bayside, Queens, NYC. This guy was involved in several different musical ventures between 1961 and 1973. Throughout he was a phenomenal songwriter. In the early days he sold songs to Bobby Darin and Ellie Greenwich. In 1963 he went into advertising but still continued writing in the evenings. He had records out on UA and Warner Brothers which aren't shown above because they fall outside the remit of this book. In 1967 he turned full-time to singing/songwriting forming an association with Ernie Maresca at Laurie Records. *Psychedelic Situation*, which really falls into the short-lived but successful bubblegum phenomenon, can be heard on *Pebbles, Vol. 16* (LP) and *Incredible Sound Show Stories, Vol. 4* (LP). He met with more success as a songwriter, most notably writing *Child Of Clay*, a hit for Jimmie Rodgers.

He later formed his own Perception label, releasing an album on it, before going into TV and commercials in 1973. His solo album is quite interesting, with various styles covering folk and pop, with some strings arrangements. Its best tracks include *You Can't Tell A Man By The Songs He Sings* for its wah wah guitar and bass work, whilst *Lack O' Testicle Blues* is about a soldier ready to be sent to Vietnam but willing to burn his draft card. His backing group, on this, Elmiger and Wyeth also released two albums as **Albert** in 1970/1.

His most interesting period was with Decca from 1967 to 1969 where he was a member of **The Hobbits**, who released one album of soft psychy sounds and another of folk plus a couple of 45s. He also produced and wrote for **The Bag** who had an album and two 45s of 'psychedelic soul' (sic).

Baubles, Vol. 1 features **The Hobbits** '*Down To Middle Earth*. (VJ/SR/MW/MMs)

Custer and The Survivors

| 45: | I Saw Her Walking/Flapjacks | (Golden State 657) 1965 |

NB: later issued on Ascot (2207) 1966.

The legend of Golden State Recorders in San Francisco has been revitalised of late, notably by Jud Cost and Alec Palao's excellent zine 'Cream Puff War' and their various collections on Big Beat's *Nuggets From The Golden State* series and Sundazed compilations.

Though most stuff was leased out to local and national labels, Leo De Gar Kulka's studio also had its own label which put out a few 45s including efforts by Poor Souls, **Gold**, **Donnybrookes**, Astros, Zorba and The Greeks, Hyde St IV and Seventh Dawn.

Custer is sadly not one of the more memorable - solid pop with horns, backed by an instrumental. (MW)

Custer's Last Band

From Florida, this band appeared on the rare 1968 *Bee Jay Video Soundtrack* sampler album (Tener 1014), with *To Love Somebody*. Their track was miscredited on the album as by 'Custer's Last Stand'. (SMR)

Customs Five

Personnel incl: S. CARTER   A

45: Let's Go In '69/Little Louie   (Task 45-108) 1965

Let's Go In '69, a good teen punk effort, can be heard on *Pebbles, Vol. 14* (LP) and *Teenage Shutdown, Vol. 11* (LP & CD). The flip, *Little Louie* also appears on *Ho-Dad Hootenanny* (LP). (VJ)

Cutty Sark

45s: Gloria/Cutty Sark Theme   (Zuma 448) 196?
      Dusty/The Night Of The Phantom   (Zuma 652) 196?

This garage band were based in Fort Worth in Texas in the mid-sixties. They also recorded the **Larry and The Blue Notes**' song, *Night Of The Phantom* as **Zuma**. (VJ)

Cyclones

45: She's No Good/Time For Me To Leave   (Lee 5467) 196?

This obscure outfit are thought to have been based somewhere in Pennsylvania - St. Marys has been suggested. *She's No Good* is a strongly Stones - influenced garage punker.

Compilation appearances have included: *She's No Good* on *Back From The Grave, Vol. 4* (LP) and *Back From The Grave, Vol. 2* (CD); and *Time For Me To Leave* on *I Can Hear Raindrops* (LP). (VJ/MW)

Cykle

Personnel:	KEN ALLEN	vcls	A
	JEFF HARDIN	gtr, vcls	A
	GRADY POPE	bs, vcls	A
	JIMMY SOSSAMON	drms, keyb'ds	A
	RALPH STEPHENS	gtr, vcls	A
	RICKEY WILSON	keyb'ds, vcls	A

ALBUM: 1(A) CYKLE   (Label 9-261) 1969 R4

NB: (1) has been bootlegged on vinyl and CD, and has also been reissued officially on CD (Gear Fab FG 106) with several bonus tracks, and on vinyl (Gear Fab LP-GF203).

45: If You Can/In Love My Friend (PS)   (Label 101) 1969

NB: both tracks from the LP, some copies with PS.

This band was from the Lumberton area of North Carolina. Sossamon had earlier been in **The Young Ones**, who issued a 45 on the Super Cool label, and another on Mu Records (shown as by **Psychic Motion**). The other members of **Cykle** were known as The Glory Cykle (with Ken Allen on drums) before Sossamon joined, first as manager and sponsor, and then as drummer, freeing Allen to concentrate on lead vocal duties. This is the line-up that recorded the highly-rated album above in early 1969. All the material was written by Sossamon and pretty imaginative stuff it is too. Many collectors place the **Cykle** album in the Top 10 of American private press sixties records and there is plenty to recommend it. The first aspect is the recording - about the best sound you will ever hear on a private press from the era. It's so good, in fact, that even the reissues sound great despite the unavailability of the master tapes. The tracks range from engaging pop (*A Little Faith*, *In Love My Friend*) to intense fuzz-punk (*Walkout Of My Mind*). The album plays like a compilation of great sixties 45 sides!

Gear Fab have reissued the album officially on CD, with many bonus tracks and this is highly recommended. Two of the best cuts - the epic *Walkout (Of My Mind)* and *It's Her* also feature on their top-drawer *Psychedelic Crown Jewels, Vol. 1* (Dble LP & CD) compilation.

Other compilation appearances include: *Walkin' Through My Mind* on Gear Fab's *Psychedelic Sampler* (CD); *If You Can* on *Tobacco A-Go-Go, Vol. 1* (LP) and *Sixties Archive Vol. 8* (CD); and *Lesson To Learn* and *Do My Thing* on *Endless Journey - Phase Three* (LP). (CF/VJ/MW)

CYKLE - Cykle LP.

Cynara

Personnel:	CAL HILL	bs	A
	LES LUMLEY	perc	A
	MICHAEL TSCHUDIN	keyb'ds	A
	JEFFREY WATSON	vcls, perc	A
	CHIP WHITE	drms	A

ALBUM: 1(A) CYNARA   (Capitol ST 547) 1970 SC

45: Cynara / Stoned Is   (Capitol 2974) 1970

Cynara is a keyboard dominated jazz-rock group that issued one album in 1970. The LP features exceptional keyboard playing from Michael Tschudin (ex-**Listening**) and fine expressive vocals from Jeffrey Watson. Almost every track features multi-tracked piano, organ, harpsichord and vibes, all played by Michael Tschudin. The album consists of five songs and one extended melodic jazz piece featuring veteran jazz drummer Elvin Jones. The songs are quite unusual, often with a Middle Eastern flavour. The multiple keyboards and percussion give them a sound not really comparable to anything else we've heard. The album was recorded in New York and produced by Ken Cooper.

There isn't a weak track on this album. Recommended.

In the late seventies, Michael White went on to play with Tom Waits and Michael Tschudin with Tim Curry. (VJ/TA/SR/MW)

The Cynics

Personnel:	PAUL CHRISTENSEN	gtr	AB
	SANDY GREGORSON	drms	AB
	RONNIE RAMBO	ld gtr	A
	BOB RODRIGUEZ	bs	A
	JOHN RODRIGUEZ	vcls	AB
	RILEY MORRIS	bs	B

45: You're A Better Man Than I/
    Train Kept A Rollin'   (Bear 001) 196?

This Fort Worth garage band formed at Paschal High School. Strongly influenced by the British invasion their sole 45 comprised two superb Yardbirds cover versions. In particular *Train Kept A Rollin'* includes lots of fuzztone and feedback. When Ronnie left the band and Bob Rodriguez was drafted to the marines another old Paschal High School mate Riley Morris came in on bass. The new line-up recorded *I'll Go*, which was written and engineered by 'T-Bone' Burnett. On the flip was a strange cover of Ray Davies' *Don't You Fret* which included lots of sound effects culminating in what was meant to be a nuclear explosion to mark the end of the band. These recordings remain unissued but an acetate does exist.

Compilation appearances have included: *You're A Better Man Than I* and *Train Kept-A-Rollin'* on *Texas Punk Groups From The Sixties* (LP) and *Sixties Archive, Vol. 2* (CD); and *Train Kept A-Rollin'* on *Flashback, Vol. 5* (LP). *You're A Better Man Than I* and *Train Kept A-Rollin* also feature on an unreleased acetate *Texas Psychedelic Punk, Vol. 11*. (VJ)

Cyrcle of Sound

| 45: | Lies/Lost | (VOL no #) c1968 |

Presumably from Texas, a single issued on the label of Augie Meyers (**Sir Douglas Quintet**). The 'A' side has been described as being garage-punk with snotty vocals, punchy guitar, and rhythmic horns, while the flip is more horn oriented. (SR)

The Cyrkle

Personnel:
DON DANNEMANN (aka 'The Sheet Metal Prince')		vcls	AB
TOM DAWES		gtr, sitar, harmonica, vcls	AB
MARTY FRIED (aka 'Troy Honda')		perc, drms	AB
EARL PICKENS		keyb'ds	A
MICHAEL LOSEKAMP		keyb'ds	B

HCP

ALBUMS:				
1(A)	RED RUBBER BALL	(Columbia CS 9344)	1966	47 -
2(B)	NEON	(Columbia GS 9432)	1967	164 -
3( )	THE MINX (Soundtrack LP)	(Flying Dutchman/Amsterdam AMS 12007)	1970	- SC

NB: (1) reissued on CD (Sundazed SC 11108) 2001. (2) reissued on CD (Sundazed SC 11109) 2001. (3) reissued on vinyl 2000 and on CD (Sundazed SC 11106) 2003.

HCP

45s:				
	Red Rubber Ball/Red Rubber Ball (Promo Issue on Red Vinyl)	(Columbia 43589)	1966	-
	Red Rubber Ball/ How Can I Leave Her (PS)	(Columbia 43589)	1966	2
	Turn-Down Day/ Big Little Woman (PS)	(Columbia 43729)	1966	16
	Please Don't Ever Leave Me/ Money To Burn	(Columbia 43871)	1966	59
α	Camaro/SS 396 (flip by **Paul Revere and the Raiders**)	(Columbia Special Products 466)	1966	
	I Wish You Could Be Here/ The Visit (She Was Here) (PS)	(Columbia 43965)	1967	70
	We Had A Good Thing Goin'/ Two Rooms	(Columbia 44108)	1967	72
	Penny Arcade/The Words	(Columbia 44224)	1967	95
	Don't Cry, No Fears, No Tears Comin' Your Way/ Red Chair Fade Away (Mislabel, track is 'Turn Of..')	(Columbia 44366)	1967	-
	Don't Cry No Fears, No Tears Comin' Your Way/ Turn Of The Century	(Columbia 44366)	1967	112
	Reading Her Paper/Friends	(Columbia 44426)	1968	-
	Where Are You Going?/ Red Chair Fade Away	(Columbia 44490)	1968	-
	It's A Lovely Game, Louise/ Squeeze Game	(Film Score 1170)	1970	-

NB: α was "created exclusively for Chevrolet dealers".

Originally known as The Rhondells, the group were formed at Lafayette College in Easton, Pennsylvania with Jim Maiella on drums. They were apparently spotted by Nat Weiss, who introduced them to Brian Epstein, who became their manager. When they changed their name to **The Cyrkle** - that name was suggested to Brian Epstein by John Lennon.

Their debut single for Columbia in 1966, *Red Rubber Ball* written by Paul Simon and Bruce Woodley (of The Seekers), was a U.S. hit. Follow-up *Turn-Down Day* 1966 also charted and the group was part of The Beatles 1966 U.S. tour. After this, Earl Pickens left the band to concentrate full-time on medical school and was replaced by Michael Losekamp on keyboards.

The interesting harmony-pop outfit was by now based in New York City and *Turn-Down Day* was a good example of their dabbling with Eastern raga/sitar sounds, as was the **Byrdsy** raga composition *The Words*. They enjoyed further minor hits including another Paul Simon and Bruce Woodley composition, *I Wish You Could Be Here* and a Neil Sedaka song *We Had A Good Thing Goin'*. They also achieved some commercial success with their albums which reached No's 47 and 164 respectively.

The *It's A Lovely Game, Louise* 45 coupled two tracks from the film 'The Minx', which are on the film soundtrack album issued on the Amsterdam label in 1970. The album features only **The Cyrkle**'s contributions (penned by Dawes and Dannemann) - dreamy or swingin' harmony-pop, mainly instrumentals with 'oooos' or 'ba-ba-bas', in a style similar to **The Association** or **Harpers Bizarre**. The film's almost-obligatory "opium-den" number, *Nicole*, is the stand out track - a hypnotic four-minute sitar and flute number which builds into a screaming raga freakout.

Another collectable oddity from this group is a 5" cardboard interview 45 from Teen Scoop magazine. On this they reveal that *Red Rubber Ball* was originally written for The Seekers and never got past the demo stage.

After their demise, Dawes and Dannemann went on to make commercials, Fried became a lawyer and Losekamp went on to play with Green Lyte Sunday. However, later in 1981, Dannemann and his wife Eileen recorded *I Did It For You/Mother and Lover* (Mother GD 2), which Eileen had written as a tribute to John Lennon.

Compilation appearances have included: *Red Rubber Ball* and *Turn Down Day* on *Nuggets, Vol. 3* (LP); *The Words* on *Psychedelic Perceptions* (CD); *Please Don't Ever Leave Me* and *We Had A Good Thing Goin'* on *Sixties Years, Vol. 2 - French 60's EP Collection* (CD); and *Red Rubber Ball* on *Even More Nuggets* (CD). (VJ/MW/EW)

CYNARA - Cynara LP

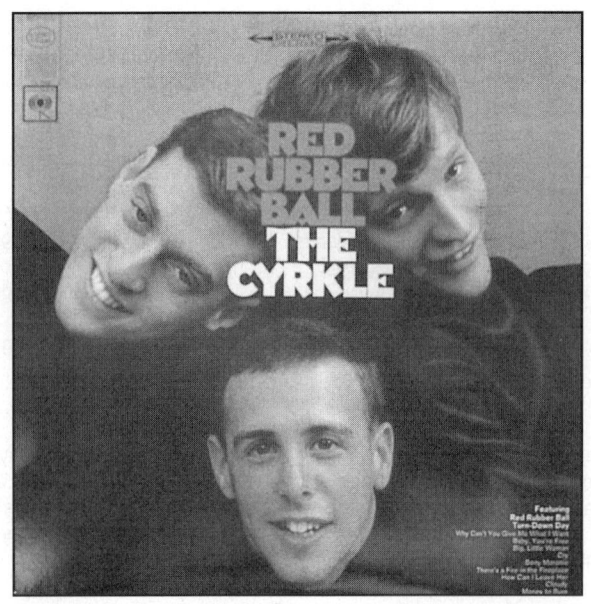

THE CYRKLE - Red Rubber Ball LP.

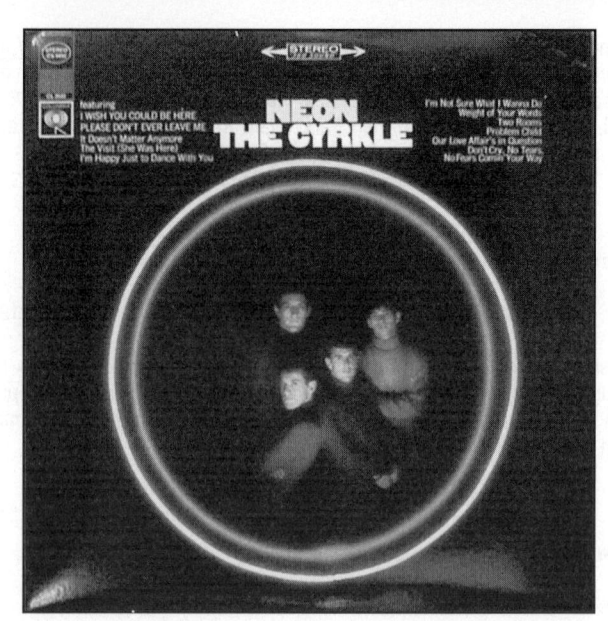

THE CYRKLE - Neon LP.

THE MINX Soundtrack LP featuring The Cyrkle.

COUNTRY JOE & THE FISH - CJ & The Fish CD.

COUNTRY JOE & THE FISH - Life And Times Of... LP.

COUNTRY JOE & THE FISH - First Three EPs LP.

Daddy Dewdrop

Personnel:	LARRY BROWN	drms	A
	TOM HENSLEY	keyb'ds	A
	BILL PERRY	bs	A
	STEVE RILLERA	gtr, vcls	A

ALBUM: 1(A) DADDY DEWDROP (Sunflower SNF 5006) 1971 SC

HCP

45s:	α	Chick A Boom/ John Jacob Jingleheimer Smith	(Sunflower 105) 1971	9
	β	Fox Huntin'/ The March Of The White Corpuscles	(Sunflower 111) 1971	-
		Chantilly Lace/Migraine Headaches	(Sunflower 119) 1972	-

NB: α also issued in the UK (Stateside SS 2187). β also issued in the UK (Stateside SS 2192).

Produced by Dick Monda and Don Sciarrotta in Torrance, California, **Daddy Dewdrop** included Tom Hensley (ex-leader of **Masters Of Deceit**) but was very probably more a studio project than a "real" group. Released on a short-lived subsidiary label of MGM, their album is musically diverse, with rock, psych, R&B and good-time music influences. The playing is quite tight, the lead singer has a powerful voice and the songs titles are often intriguing or amusing: *March Of The White Corpuscles* (a good song and the only Hensley composition), *Migraine Headaches*, *Johnny Do It Faster*, *Abracadabra Alakazam* and *Fox Huntin (On The Week End)*. Overall the album, which rarely turns up, is pleasant but of minor interest. The songs were composed by Janice Lee Gwin, Monda or Sciarrotta with the help of Kenny Rogers (the funky *Diggin' On Mrs Jones*), Paul Robin or Leonard Reid.

One of their 45s, *Chick A Boom* was featured in the 'Archies' cartoon show.

Bill Perry and Larry Brown went on to play in **Gunhill Road**, while Hensley was a sough-after session musician. (SR/RNi)

Tommy Dae

ALBUM: 1 TOMMY DAE (Hitt 7001) 1970 -

45s:		Destiny / I'm In Love	(M-Z 100) 196?
		Janie / It Was A Lie	(Goldisc G-12) 196?
	α	Twinkle Dello / Please Don't Treat Me This Way	(Glo 5227) 196?
	β	You Made Me Cry / It Was A Lie	(Hitt 101/2) 196?
		Tampico Rage / Lost Horizon	(Hitt 591/2) 196?
	χ	I'll Be Coming Home / It's Gonna Be Alright	(Hitt 6403/4) 1964
	δ	You've Got It Made / Looking For A Summertime Girl	(Hitt 6601/2) 1966
	δ	Poor Man / ?	(Hitt 6605/6) 1966
	ε	Itsy Bitsy Teenie Weenie Yellow Polka-Dot Bikini/ Summertime Girl	(Diamond D-226) 1967
	φ	I Shall Walk / It Could Be So Nice	(Hitt 7002) 1970
	γ	Just As Long As You Are Mine / It's Time We Got Together	(Hitt Prod 7201) 1972

NB: α as Tom Dae Trio, β as Tommy Dae's Tensionettes, χ as Tommy Dae and The Tensionettes, δ as High Tensions, ε as Tom Dae and The High Tensions, φ as Tom Dae Turned On, γ as Tom Dae "Love 70". Another possibly related 45 was released as by **The Cirkyt**:- *Six Page Letter / That's The Way Life Is* (PS) (Jody 6703/4) 1967

From Rockville, Connecticut, **Tom Dae** cut a large and varied selection of discs under numerous names. Aram Heller reveals in his New England bible, 'Till The Stroke Of Dawn', that Tommy's real name was Draus and that father Frank provided help and connections via his job at a big record label. Much of his material falls well outside the boundaries of our interest - the album is apparently in lounge mode - but he did dabble in garage and psych. *You Made Me Cry* is said to be a decent garage effort, *I Shall Walk* is a psychy phase-filled opus and is compiled on *A Lethal Dose Of Hard Psych* (CD) and *Exploding Plastic Inevitable, Vol. II*. The final 45 is in hard-rock mode.

Erik Lindgren notes in the *Lethal Dose* liners that the **Cirkyt** 45 is thought to be the High Tensions minus one member, though this remains unconfirmed. (MW/AH/ELn)

The Dagenites

Personnel:	JOHN BARDI	ld gtr	AB
	ROGER FALLIN	drms	AB
	BRUCE KENNETT	gtr	A
	GEOFF ROBINSON	bs	A
	JULIAN BARDI	bs	B
	JIMMY MUSGROVE	vcls	B
	JON ROWZIE	gtr	B

45s:	I Don't Want To Try It Again/ Now That Summer's Gone	(Pixie 204) 1965
	I'm Gonna Slide/ Now That Summer's Gone	(Heigh-Ho 619) 1965

Oxon Hill, Maryland was home to these garage punkers. They got together in 1964 and got a manager who also happened to manage **Link Wray**, so they played shows with **Wray** every week at the 1023 Club. Their first 45 was recorded in the Spring of 1965 at a Dayton, Ohio, studio and released on the local Pixie label. The band lasted until June 1966.

Two more tracks - *Fugitive* and *Poison Ivy* - were recorded at the NYC session that produced the second 45 but were never released.

Thanks to Bob Embrey for the personnel details (DC Monuments zine #7).

Compilation appearances have included: *I'm Gonna Slide* on *Psychedelic Unknowns, Vol. 3* (LP & CD); *I Don't Want To Try It Again* on *Back From The Grave, Vol. 8* (Dble LP), *Back From The Grave, Vol. 8* (CD) and *Highs In The Mid-Sixties, Vol. 9* (LP). (MW/VJ/KBn)

The Daggs

45:	You Don't Know Like I Know/ Tales Of Brave Ulysses	(Decade 5992) 1967/8

An obscure garage band from Illinois. The 'A' side, is a slow punker with some simple but tasty fuzz guitar. The track has resurfaced on *Sixties Rebellion, Vol. 9* (LP & CD). (VJ)

The Daily Flash

Personnel:	DON MacALLISTER	bs	ABCD
	DOUG HASTINGS	ld gtr	A
	JON KELIEHOR	drms	AB
	STEVE LALOR	gtr	ABCD

THE DAILY FLASH - I Flash Daily LP.

	CRAIG TARWATER	gtr	BCD
	TONY DEY	drms	C
	RON WOODS	drms	D

ALBUM: 1(-) I FLASH DAILY (Psycho 32) 1984 SC

NB: (1) is a compilation of 45 sides, unreleased studio demos and live tracks from 1966-67. (1) pirated on CD with two additional tracks: *Grizzly Bear* and *When I Was A Cowboy* (Flash 60) 199?.

EPs:
1. Jack Of Diamonds/Queen Jane/Green Rocky Road/ The French Girl (Moxie 1014) 1983
2. Jack Of Diamonds/The Girl From North Alberta/ Grizzly Bear/When I Was A Cowboy (Sundazed SEP 120) 1996

NB: (2) consists of previously unreleased tracks from 1966.

45s: α Queen Jane Approximately/Birdses (Parrot 305) 1966
Queen Jane Approximately/Jack Of Diamonds (Parrot 305) 1966
The French Girl/Green Rocky Road (UNI 55001) 1967

NB: α was withdrawn prior to release, so that their cover of **Dino Valente**'s *Birdses*, which Parrot found too 'twee' could be replaced with the folk-rocker *Jack Of Diamonds*.

Formed in the Summer 1965, **The Daily Flash** became Seattle's first alternative psychedelic band. The band members were from very diverse backgrounds. MacAllister had previously played with a bluegrass trio, The Willow Creek Ramblers, which he had founded. Hastings was a red hot guitarist who'd briefly played in **The Dynamics**, Keliehor was a classical percussionist and jazz drummer and Lalor, a New York folk musician who had been a member of the San Francisco folk group, The Driftwood Singers.

They were discovered performing at the Door, a downtown Seattle club, by a local record distributor, who released their first single. The 'A' side, *Queen Jane Approximately*, was a fine Bob Dylan cover, however the 45 was poorly recorded and received little promotion outside of the Northwest. It did not sell.

Buffalo Springfield's manager Charlie Greene saw the potential of the band and invited them to L.A to re-record *Queen Jane Approximately*. In the Spring of 1966, **The Daily Flash** headed for San Francisco and played at the Avalon Ballroom before heading on to Los Angeles, where they played numerous shows at the Whisky A Go Go with bands such as **The Byrds**, **Sons Of Adam** and **Love**. A second single was issued but gained insufficient airplay to launch the band nationally. After this they began to disintegrate with Hastings leaving in late May '67 for a brief spell with **Buffalo Springfield**.

Craig Tarwater (gtr), was living near Jon Keliehor at the time, and whilst with **Sons Of Adam** had gigged with 'Flash at the Whisky in '66. He was recruited, but in July, Keliehor too left to be replaced by Tony Dey. Keliehor later auditioned for 'Project Supergroup', Elektra Records attempt at forming a supergroup.

The group finally disbanded in 1968.

After **Buffalo Springfield**, Hastings auditioned for **Clear Light** but this didn't work out and he joined Keliehor in Project Supergroup. They both appeared on David Ackles's debut album, although Keliehor was subsequently dropped in favour of Billy Mundi and the band became **Rhinoceros**.

During 1968 Keliehor and Lalor put together the five-piece outfit Popcorn with ex-**Kingsmen** bass player Kerry Magness, who had failed the Project Supergroup audition. The band recorded as **Bodine** in October 1969. Keliehor also played with **Jeff Simmons** in 1969.

Lalor joined Danny O'Keefe's support band in late 1969 and Keliehor later moved to London to perform at the London School of Contemporary Dance. MacAllister played with **Barry Goldberg** and then joined Hastings in **Dr John**'s Autumn 1969 tour band. He subsequently died of a heroin overdose.

Craig Tarwater had also previously played with **The Other Half** and went on to play with **Buddy Miles** and **Frank Zappa** as well as playing on Arthur Lee's *Vindicator* album. Another ex-**Dynamics**, Ron Woods also later played with **The Buddy Miles Express**.

The Psycho/Flash retrospective, which is recommended, includes both sides of their two released 45s, three unreleased studio cuts, a live recording of Herbie Hancock's *Cantaloupe Island* (from the Eagles Auditorium, Seattle in October 1967) and an extended live recording of *Queen Jane Approximately* at the Whiskey A Go Go in November 1966. An important psychedelic folk-rock band, **The Daily Flash** deserved greater recognition.

Hastings, Lalor and Keliehor had a re-union in 1994. Steve Lalor is still active on the local Seattle music scene, whilst Craig Tarwater now lives in Walla Walla, Washington and operates a mail order business called Video School of Guitar as well as his local music store, Blue Mt. Music Inc.

Compilation appearances include: *Jack Of Diamonds* on *Psychedelic Unknowns, Vol. 9* (CD) and *Nuggets Box* (4-CD); *Green Rocky Road* on *Sounds Of The Sixties San Francisco, Vol. 1* (LP); *The French Girl* on *Baubles - Down To Middle Earth* (LP); *Jack Of Diamonds* and *Violets Of Dawn* on *Nuggets, Vol. 8* (LP). The latter track is a superb period flower-power piece. (VJ/NW/CF)

Daily News

45: Everything/Poor Mans Son (Parrot) c1967

A rock single by an obscure group. (SR)

Daisy and Arthur

45: Let's Ride Again/School Days (Dynovoice DY-911) 1968

A pop-rock duo produced and written by Bob Crewe, with some fuzz guitar on *Let's Ride*. (SR)

Daisy Chain

Personnel:	CAMILLE	vcls, keyb'ds	A
	ROSEMARY LANE	vcls, bs	A
	DEE DEE LEA	vcls, drms, flute, hrmnca	A
	SHEL LEE	vcls, gtr	A

ALBUM: 1(A) STRAIGHT OR LAME (United International 13001) 1968 R2

NB: (1) issued in both mono and 'duophonic' versions.

45: It's My World/Beach Ball (Fontana 1629) 1968

This all-girl group came from Los Angeles, although their album is on the same label as New Jersey act **Dick Watson 5**. Musically it is an extremely rare flower-power/garage affair. It is now sought-after, but the quality of the

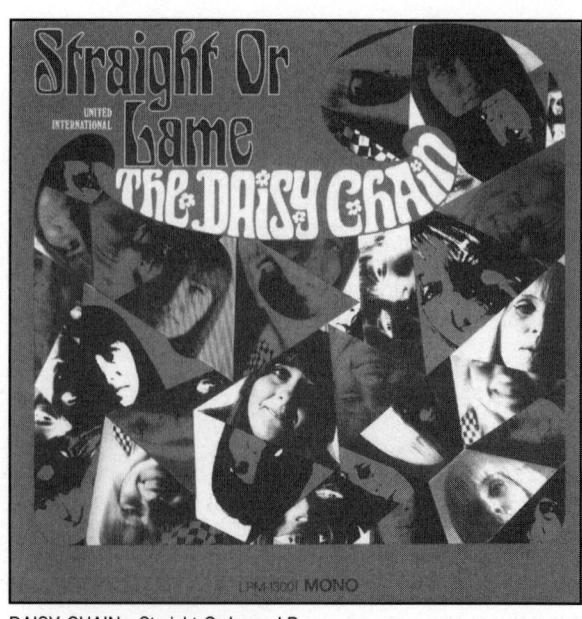

DAISY CHAIN - Straight Or Lame LP.

pressing is not for audiophile lovers. It includes tracks like *I'll Come Running*, *All Because Of Him*, *Run Spot Run*, *Got To Get You In My Arms* and *Superfluous Daisy*.

It's not confirmed whether the 45 is by the same act. (SR/MMs/CF)

Dakila

ALBUM:	1 DAKILA	(Epic) 1972 -

45s:	El Dubi/Gozola	(Epic 10913) 1972
	Searching For My Soul/El Dubi	(Epic 10942) 1973

From the Bay Area, a **Santana** soundalike: latin influences with searing guitar, strong organ and loads of percussions. Their guitarist later played in the Golden Dragon Band, whose album is rare and sought-after. (SR)

Floyd Dakil Combo

ALBUM:	1 LIVE	(Ashley 101) 1967 ?

45s:	Dance Franny Dance/	
	Look What You've Gone And Done	(Jetstar 103) 1964
	Dance Franny Dance/	
	Look What You've Gone And Done	(Guyden 2111) 1965

This Texas outfit enjoyed a regional hit with this 45. They later became the **Floyd Dakil Four**.

Recently Collectables have issued a compilation CD entitled *Dance Franny Dance*.

Compilation appearances have included: *Dance Franny Dance* on *Pebbles, Vol. 1* (LP), *Pebbles, Vol. 1* (CD), *Pebbles, Vol. 4 (ESD)* (CD), *Pebbles Box* (5-LP), *Trash Box* (5-CD) and *Texas Music, Vol. 3* (CD). (VJ)

Floyd Dakil Four

45s:	Bad Boy/Stoppin	(Earth 402) 196?
	Kitty Kitty/It Takes A Lot Of Hurt	(Earth 403) 196?
	You're The Kind Of Girl/Stronger Than Dirt	(Earth 404) 196?

Known earlier as **Floyd Dakil Combo**, this band were based in Dallas and are best known for *Bad Boy* a strong rocker. Dakil later recorded a solo 45, *Merry Christmas Baby/One Girl* (Atco Pompeii 66687).

Compilation appearances have included: *Bad Boy* on *Flashback, Vol. 1* (LP), *Texas Flashbacks, Vol. 1* (LP & CD) and *Texas Flashback (The Best Of)* (CD). The track was also included on an unreleased metal acetate *Texas Psychedelic Punk, Vol. 11*. (VJ)

Dalek/Engham: The Blackstones

Personnel:	GEOFF BRYAN	A
	DAVE KELL	A
	JERRY McGEORGE	A
	TOM OSBORNE	A

45s:	Never Feel The Pain/Could It Be Love	(Invictus 3751) 197?
	You Don't Know Better/	
	She Tells Me With Her Eyes	(Invictus 3755) 197?

Also known as **Engam: The Blackstones**. The band also included Jerry McGeorge and were basically the same band as **Saturday's Children**. Strangely enough, *You Don't Know Better*, on the **Dalek: The Blackstones**' 45, was credited to Bryan-McGeorge and to Bryan-Holder on the **Saturday's Children** Dunwich 45. Some doubt has been expressed as to whether Bun E. Carlos was in this band as McGeorge and Bryan were from Indiana and Carlos at the time was in The Paegens (probably from Rockford, Illinois). They also released a third 45 on Invictus, *Never Feel The Pain*, which had a catchy beat but suffered from indistinctive vocals.

DAMNATION OF ADAM BLESSING - Which Is The Justice... LP.

For the full lowdown on the band from Jerry McGeorge himself, check out Jeff Jarema's essential 'zine "Here 'Tis # 6" - Jerry later went on to **Shadows of Knight**, and **H.P. Lovecraft**.

The 45's listed on Invictus were recordings made in 1965 and issued in the seventies as a 'Collector Series'.

Compilation appearances have included *Never Feel The Pain* on *Pebbles Vol. 6* (CD) and *Highs In The Mid-Sixties, Vol. 4* (LP). (MW/VJ/KBn)

Karen Dalton

ALBUMS:	1 IT'S SO HARD TO TELL WHO'S GOING TO LOVE YOU	
		(Capitol) 1969 -
	2 IN MY OWN TIME	(Just Sunshine) 1972 -

Karen Dalton was part of the New York folk scene in the late sixties and a friend of **Fred Neil**. Her last recording session seems to have been her participation on *Alleged In Their Own Time*, an album by **The Holy Modal Rounders** recorded in 1973 but released only in 1975. Drug problems sadly prevented her from pursuing her career. (SR)

The Dalton Gang

Personnel:	JOHN BAZZELL	A
	AUBURN BURRELL Jr.	A
	RICHARD FOXWORTH	A
	DAVID GRIFFIN	A
	JAMES McCLURE	A

45:	Our Love /	
	Stubborn Kind Of Fellow	(Kimberly-Ann KA-127) 1967

A Jacksonville, Florida combo who hit their peak in 1967 with the release of their sole 45. Originally managed by Bill Conrad, they came under the wings of WPDQ DJ "Uncle" Dino Summerlin, who put out their 45 on his own label, named after his daughter. He ensured that it did well in the local charts (peaking at #4 in WPDQ's Super Survey in June). The band debuted on TV on Summerlin's "Shakin Up Summer" show, opening for **Joe South**. They'd also written the show's theme tune and that was released and duly charted locally in August.

By the end of the sixties they were no more. Burrell joined Dennis Yost and The Classics IV. Their memory is revived by the appearance of *Our Love*, a cover of the Ernie and Petie song, on *Psychedelic States: Florida Vol. 3* (CD). (KCs/MW)

Damnation of Adam Blessing

Personnel:	RAY BENICK	bs	AB
	ADAM BLESSING	vcls	AB
	BOB KALAMASZ	gtr, vcls	AB
	JIM QUINN	gtr, vcls, perc	AB
	BILL SCHWARK	drms	AB
	KEN CONSTABLE		B

HCP

ALBUMS:	1(A)	THE DAMNATION OF ADAM BLESSING (United Artists UAS 6738) 1969 181 SC
	2(A)	SECOND DAMNATION (United Artists UAS 6773) 1970 - -
	3(B)	WHICH IS THE JUSTICE (United Artists UAS 5533) 1971 - -

NB: (1) reissued (Akarma AK 100) 2000. (2) reissued (Akarma AK 101) 2000. (3) reissued (Akarma AK 102) 2000. (1)-(3) reissued as a 3-CD box set (Akarma AK 102/3) 2000.

HCP

45s:	Morning Dew/Cookbook	(United Artists 50609) 1969 -
	Last Train To Clarksville/Lonely	(United Artists 50666) 1970 -
	Back To The River/Driver	(United Artists 50726) 1970 102
	Fingers On A Windmill/Leaving It Up To You	(United Artists 50819) 1971 -
	Cookbook/Leaving It Up To You	(United Artists 50912) 1972 -

From Cleveland, Ohio, a good psychedelic hard-rock outfit which did achieve some modest commercial success. Their first album is excellent, with surprising covers of *Last Train To Clarksville*, *Morning Dew* and *You Don't Love Me*, plus a good original penned by William "Bill" Constable. The *Second Damnation* is also interesting, with *Back To The River*, *Money Tree* and *In The Morning*. There's already a Southern rock feel in some songs.

After three albums, they renamed themselves **Glory** and released an LP on Avalanche in 1973.

Eric Stevens, who later worked with Brownsville Station, produced their albums and Bill Schwark had previously played with **The Alarm Clocks**.

Compilation appearances have included *Eve* on *A Lethal Dose Of Hard Psych* (CD). (VJ/SR/MW)

Damon

Personnel:	RICHARD BARHAM	durbeki	A
	CHARLIE CAREY	ld gtr	A
	DAVID DEL CONTE (DAMON)	vcls, gtr	A
	LEE PASTORA	perc	A
	MIKE PASTORA	perc	A
	HELENA VLAHOS	finger cymbals	A
	ATLEY (ATLEE) YEAGER	bs, vcls	A
	CARL ZARCONE	drms	A

ALBUM:	1(A)	SONG OF A GYPSY	(Ankh A-968) 1968 R6

NB: (1) issued first in a B&W non-gatefold sleeve and then in a deluxe black gatefold sleeve with the front cover printing embossed in gold foil. The non-gatefold edition was counterfeited in Belgium in 1993, and two pirate CD's editions also exist, one on Afterglow (013). In 1998 an official CD reissue was made available by the band (Daily Bread Ministries no #), and later that year a deluxe official repress (with the original gatefold sleeve and a bonus 7" EP) was produced in a limited edition (Little Indians 3).

45s:	Song Of The Gypsy/Oh, What A Good Boy Am I	(Ankh A-1) 1968
	α Don't You Feel Me/Poor Poor Genie	(Ankh A-2) 196?

NB: α may also exist with *Poor Poor Genie* as the 'A' side.

The **Damon** recordings are amongst the most sought-after and widely-loved of the late-sixties underground scene. Simply put, they convey emotion and power in a very concise and believable way. *Song Of A Gypsy* is is an excellent psychedelic album and both gatefold/non-gatefold versions are monster rarities. There's lots of fuzz guitar and a mystical feel about tracks like *Do You* and *The Night*. *I Feel Your Love* has a sleepy, stoned atmosphere sounding rather similar to **The Deep**. Another track, *Birds Fly So High*, has 'snake charming' music, again creating a sort of Eastern mystical feel.

Based in Los Angeles, David Del Conte and Charlie Carey had already pursued careers in popular music for many years before deciding to embrace the underground rock movement. Del Conte released a considerable number of 45s; it is possible that as much as half of his discography will be found to be too early to fall within the time-frame of this book. The last recordings he made pre-**Damon** (aside from a handful of acetates never made available to the public) may be of interest to readers. As Damon Lane, he issued at least three singles on the Del Con label - these possess a unique **Byrdsy** jangle over which his trademark authoritative voice presides.

The first **Damon** single has a non-album 'B' side and a different lead vocal than the album version of the 'A' side. (It is, by all accounts, significantly rarer than the album and fortunately these tracks are included as one side of a 7" EP of bonus material with the reissue on the Little Indians label.) The record set the tone of the band's campaign which ran the course of 1968 - the message of love and self-expression coupled with an almost arrogant disregard for the establishment:

"I wake up each day about noon
I live in a rainbow-coloured room
I break every rule in the book
I don't even bother to look
I laugh at the heat, I've got bells on my feet
And oh, what a good boy am I"

The album itself is made up of (similarly) short, urgent tracks that overflow with Carey's amazing distorted leads and Del Conte's powerful, otherworldly voice. The title track opens Side One in dramatic fashion; the opening lyric "Today I feel like cryin', Today I feel like dyin'" delivered in a most convincing manner. It's obvious right away that you're listening to something very special. If there really is such a thing as psychedelic music, this is surely it.

It should be noted that the sound quality of this album is exemplary. Like the **Cykle** album, the fidelity is so good that even the bootlegs impress...

Del Conte and Carey, despite living roughly a thousand miles apart, continue to perform together and collaborated on a new album project in 1998. The resulting CD release, *Gypsy Eyes* has much to recommend it, not the least of which is the fact that it sounds like a second **Damon** album! The closing track, *The Gift*, is truly mindblowing, as good as anything on the first album.

Atley Yeager subsequently performed and recorded as **Atlee** in Southern California.

You can also find the album version of *Song Of A Gypsy* on *Love, Peace And Poetry: American Psychedelic Music* (LP & CD), but obviously, the **Damon** album is an essential purchase. (CF/VJ)

DAMON.

DAMON - Song Of A Gypsy CD.

Damon

ALBUM: 1 DAMON/FEELING ALONE (Witherspoon 30522) c1969 R1

From North Dakota, this **Damon** was a local DJ and his rare and very strange album contains mostly spoken "hip" poetry with a musical background. Some cuts, like *High On A Hill* and *Leslie's No Fool*, feature a full band with fuzz guitar, while some of the others were recorded with only harmonica and acoustic guitar. (SR)

Dennis Damon

45s:	Debbie / Satisfy You	(Campo 953) 1965
	Debbie / Shout! Bama Lama	(United Artists 984) 1966

An artist with a split personality - *Debbie* is an awful drippy teen ballad in a Bobby Vee/John Leyton style with a toe-curlingly soppy spoken passage. But flip it over and *Satisfy You* is a hard rockin' bluesy workout with raucous vocals, scintillating guitar, and hard drumming that sounds way ahead of its time - amazin'. *Debbie* was picked up for national exposure on UA and the flip was changed to a swingin' cover of Otis Redding's *Shout! Bama Lama*.

It was produced by Major Bill Smith, responsible for **Larry and The Blue Notes** amongst many other acts from the Fort Worth, Texas area - perhaps **Damon** was too. (MW)

Sterling Damon

45: Rejected/My Last Letter (International Artists 108) 1966

Damon was probably based in Houston, Texas. The 'A' side of his 45, which has a strange backing, has subsequently surfaced on *Highs In The Mid-Sixties, Vol. 23* (LP) and *International Artists Singles Collection* (LP). (VJ)

Dan and Dale

Personnel:	JOHN GILMORE		A
	DANNY KALB	gtr	A
	TOM McINTOSH	trombone	A
	JIMMY OWENS	trumpet	A
	PAT PATRICK		A
	SUN RA	keyb'ds	A

ALBUM: 1(A) THE SENSATIONAL GUITARS OF DAN AND DALE
PLAY BATMAN (Tifton) 1966 R1

NB: (1) reissued on vinyl and CD (Universe UV 016) 2001.

45: Batman Theme/ ? (PS) (Tifton) 1966

Dan and Dale were a studio group supervised by **Tom Wilson**. Their musicians included Sun Ra and his Arkestra and **Danny Kalb** (of **Blues Project** fame). Apart from *Batman* and *Robin's Theme*, all the other tracks are instrumental.

A rare and expensive curiosity, hard to find in good condition as it was originally aimed at the children's market. (SR)

Dancing, Food and Entertainment

Personnel:	TOM GLASS	bs	A
	MARK PIERCE	keyb'ds	A
	DENNIS REED	gtr	A
	NAOMI RUTH-EISENBERG	violin, vcls	A
	WAYNE THIBAULT	drms	A

An obscure psychedelic band from Berkeley, California who were founded by ex-Jazz Mice member Tom Glass. Picked up by Bill Graham's booking agency (Millard) in mid-1968, they opened for Ten Years After at the Fillmore West the weekend of November 16th, 1968 (where they replaced **Country Weather** who cancelled because of illness); played the Avalon Ballroom with **Santana** and did several gigs opening for the **Grateful Dead**. The band never got an album or single pressed, but recorded three songs at the infamous Sierra Sound Labs in Berkeley that were destined for a never-pressed EP.

Needless to say their name has been a big hindrance with regard to archival research... Thus, **Dancing, Food and Entertainment** have been largely overlooked by sixties psychedelic historians.

Naomi Ruth-Eisenberg went on to join ex-**Charlatan** Dan Hicks' band as one of the "Hot Licks". (IT/DRd)

Dan-Dees

45s:	Think About It/Take A Look At Yourself	(Jorel 108) 1968
	Dandy/Memphis	(Vest 8002) 196?

A late sixties Chicago outfit. *Think About It* features some nice fuzzy folk-rock guitar augmented by a pounding beat and thoughtful lyrics. It's also on *Pebbles, Vol. 21* (LP).

The 45 on Vest may be by a different group. (MW)

Charley D. and Milo

ALBUM: 1 CHARLEY D. AND MILO (Epic BN 26539) c1970 -

DAN and DALE - The Sensational Guitars... LP.

On this major label, a soft rural-rock and folk-rock duo that went totally unnoticed at the time. They mixed their original material with covers of Dylan and **Richard Farina**. (SR)

Danes

Personnel:	RICK BANDAS	bs	A
	BILL HUDDLESTON	gtr	A
	CHARLES JESTER	vcls	A
	W.R. LYNCH	drms	A
	JOHN REAGAN	ld gtr	A
	JERRY JACK TERRELL	vcls	A

45s:	Come On Baby / Most Of All	(Le Cam 718) c1961
	Hey Hey Baby / High On A Hill	(Smash S-1962) 1965
	To Make Me A Man / Lost Love	(Tower 247) 1966
α	Just A Dream /	(Charay 303) 196?

NB: α is unconfirmed.

From Fort Worth, Texas, several of this group's recording sessions were produced by Ray Hildebrand (aka "Paul" of Paul and Paula fame).

Bandas, Huddleston and Lynch all went on to **The Gnats**, whilst Lynch later played in Texas Valley group **Foamy Brine**. (MW/AB/JLa)

THE DANES.

Nick D'Angelo and The Farmers

Personnel incl:	NICK D'ANGELO	vcls	A

45:	Mr. Zeppelin Man/Time To Be A Woman	(Chime 109) 19??

Long Islanders **Nick D'Angelo and The Farmers** cut a demented track called *Mr. Zeppelin Man*, which has resurfaced on *Hipsville 29 B.C.* (LP), solely for their own private use. Except for the drummer, the rest of the band were all D'Angelo's brothers, and you'll be pleased to know that today Nick lends his considerable talent to the Hare Krishna movement. (VJ)

Danny and Jerry

45s:	We've Got A Groovy Thing Goin' /	
	You Must Be Fooling	(Ronn 5) 1967
	Connection / I've Got Pride	(Ronn 12) 1967
	Mo'reen / I Can't See Nobody	(Ronn 24) 1968

The Jewel family of labels (with subsidiaries Paula and Ronn) was based in Shreveport, Louisiana but it's not known whether this duo was from there.

Their second 45, *Connection* features great fuzz guitar and organ, on an otherwise average Stones cover. (BM/MW)

Danny and The Counts

Personnel incl:	ERIC HUREQUE	bs	A
	JOE HUREQUE	drms	A
	DANNY PARRA	ld vcls, gtr	A
	IRENE PORRAS	vcls	A
	KEN PRICHARD	ld gtr	A
	JAVIER VENISULA	organ	A
	JOE ??	vcls	A

45s:	For Your Love/It's All Over	(Frog Death 4) 196?
	You Need Love/Ode To The Wind	(Coronado 136) 1966

The band was formed around 1960 and maintained a popular following into the late sixties. They played Tejano music and soul in the early days later switching to a Texas garage band sound influenced by Beatles, Stones, **Bobby Fuller** etc..., but without abandoning their Tejano roots. **Danny and The Counts** recorded on the same label as **Bobby Fuller** (Coronado) did in his early years. A staple of the El Paso rock scene, they were ahead of the times in the punk evolution and showmanship played as much part in the **Count's** act as did the music...

Their second 45, *You Need Love* was typical Texas punk, but the flip was a smoother, more psychedelic track.

Compilation appearances include: *You Need Love* on *Pebbles, Vol. 5* (LP), *Pebbles, Vol. 5* (CD), *Sixties Archive, Vol. 2* (CD) and *Great Pebbles* (CD); and *You Need Love* and *Ode To The Wind* on *Texas Punk From The Sixties* (LP). (MW/VJ/KP)

Danny and The Other Guys

45:	Hard Times/ 5 for $14.50	(C.P. 101) 196?

Chicago punkers. The 'A' side can be heard on *Garage Punk Unknowns, Vol. 2* (LP). (VJ)

Danny and The Sessions

45s:	Big Boss Man/I Knew You Would	(Saligo 6501) 1965
	Grand Time and Gay Nights/Mojo	(Cobra 11 14) 196?
	My Angel Diane/Hey Babe	(Cobra 1253) 196?

From San Antonio in Texas. *Mojo* got a second airing on *Garage Punk Unknowns, Vol. 7* (LP). (VJ)

Danny's Reasons

Personnel:	LEE DAHLIN		A
	BOB GONYEA		A
	FRANK MARENOS		A
	STEVE MAURER	drms	A
	DANNY STEVENS	vcls	A
	CEDRIC VAN DEUSEN		A

45s:	Little Diane/Believe Me	(IRC 6935) 1966
	Under My Thumb/Triangles	(Carnaby 101) 1967
	With One Eye Closed/Think Of You	(Hand 9-420) 1969
	Young Emotion/Hard Old Times	(Uncle Sam 19361) 1972
	Vision Of Love/Time	(Great Hall 30297) 197?

This mob operated out of Minneapolis in Minnesota from 1965 until at least 1972. Danny Stevens was otherwise known as Danny Capri. Their early recordings were the best. You'll find their cover of Dion's *Little Diane* on *Hipsville 29 B.C.* (LP). Better still was *Triangles*, a punk screamer which has resurfaced on *Pebbles, Vol. 22* (LP), *Changes* (LP) and *The Essential Pebbles Collection, Vol. 2* (Dble CD). They also figured on the now rare compilation, *Gathering At The Depot*, which featured *With One Eye Closed* back in 1970. (VJ)

The Dantes

Personnel incl:	BARRY HAYDEN	ld vcls	A
	JOE HINTON	perc	A
	CARTER HOLLIDAY	bs	A
	LYNN WEHR	gtr	A
	DAVE WORKMAN	ld gtr	A

45s:	Can't Get Enough Of Your Love/80-96	(Jamie 1314) 1966
	Under My Thumb/Can I Get A Witness?	(Cameo 431) 1966
	Connection/Satisfied	(Main Line 1366) 196?

From Columbus, Ohio, some of their recordings were reasonable Stones covers although *Can't Get Enough Of Your Love*, is a fast moving soul-rocker. **The Dantes** performed with many top name groups such as **Jimi Hendrix**, **Byrds**, Roy Orbison, Bobby Goldsboro, **Strawberry Alarm Clock**, **The Outsiders**, Neil Diamond, Them and J. Frank Wilson to name a few.

Compilation appearances have included: *Can I Get A Witness* on *Mindrocker, Vol. 11* (LP); *80-96* on *Sick And Tired* (LP), *Everything You Always Wanted To Know...* (CD), *The Garage Zone, Vol. 4* (LP) and *The Garage Zone Box Set* (4-LP); *80-96* and *Can't Get Enough Of Your Love* on *Garage Monsters* (LP); and *Can't Get Enough Of Your Love* on *Highs In The Mid-Sixties, Vol. 9* (LP). (VJ/MW/GGl/BKr)

The Dantes

45s:	Top Down Time/How Many Times?	(Rotate 5008) 1964
	Dragon Walk/Zebra Shoot	(Courtney 713) 1964

A different act from Carnegie, Pennsylvania, their *Top Down Time* resurfaced on *Pebbles, Vol. 4* (LP) and *Pebbles Vol. 4* (CD), whilst both sides of the Courtney 45 are included on *Strummin' Mental, Vol. 4*. (MW)

The Dard

45:	I Know/Sounds Of Life	(Evolution 1005) 1970

An obscure hard-rock group produced by Norman Petty, the former producer of Buddy Holly. (SR)

The Darelycks

Personnel:	STEVE LAREAU	ld gtr	ABC
	TOM POMPONIO	bs	ABC
	JOHN TIBERIO	drms, ld vcls	ABC
	ANDY BOSSO	drms	BC
	MIKE MALCOLM	gtr	BC
	MIKE MURPHY	backing vcls	B
	JOE CALABRESE		C
	JIM GILBERT		C

45:	Bad Trip / Wait For Me	(Fine FI 111) 1966

This Rochester, New York band started out as a trio in 1965. They expanded to a seven-piece (line-up 'C'), although only those noted as line-up 'B' were featured on the 45. Tiberio had switched from drums to lead vocals by this point.

Pomponio wrote the music for *Bad Trip* and Tiberio's lyrics came together after reading about Timothy Leary's experiments with LSD in a 'Time' magazine article. The band believed this to be the first-ever psychedelic single (or ABOUT psychedelics?) - it might have been on the East Coast, but...

Regardless, it's a cool garage-punker with an affected vocal style that gives it an air of tongue-in-cheek novelty. It has remained popular with collectors and compilers alike - reappearing on *High All The Time, Vol. 1* (LP), *Sixties Rebellion Vol. 16* (LP & CD) and *Psychedelic States: New York, Vol. 1* (CD). (MW/MM)

Darius

Personnel:	BEN BENAY	ld gtr	A
	MIKE DEASY	gtr	A
	TOXEY FRENCH	drms	A
	ROBERT J. OTT (DARIUS)	vcls	A
	JERRY SCHEFF	bs	A

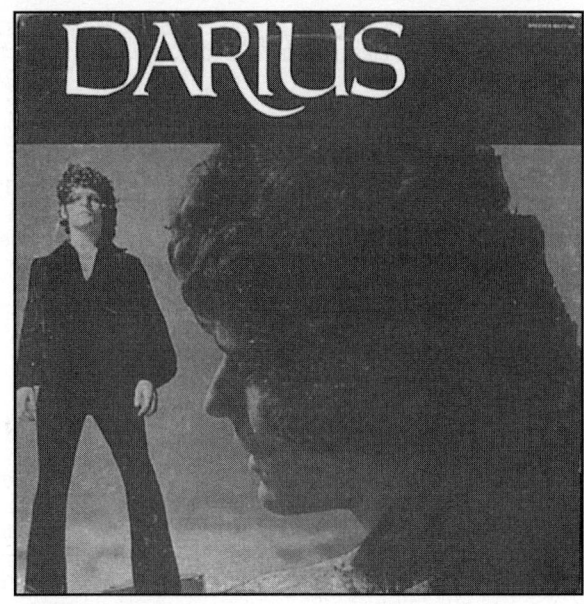

DARIUS - Darius LP.

ALBUM:	1(A) DARIUS	(Chartmaker CSG 1102) 1968 R3

NB: (1) counterfeited on vinyl (Breeder 005-C2-565) 1986 and on CD (Flashback 009) 199?. (1) reissued officially on CD with three bonus tracks (World In Sound WIS-1001) 2001.

45:	Hello Stranger/I Don't Mind	(Chartmaker 419) 1968

Darius was based in Hollywood, California and was backed by **Goldenrod** and **Mike Deasy**. The album is all originals and the music very melodic with upfront vocals and a style veering towards progressivism. Particularly stunning are *Mist-Veiled Garden* and *I Feel The Need To Carry On*. Funk and blues influences are more evident on Side two of the album.

The 45 was taken from a projected second album on Chartmaker, *Hello Stranger*, which was never released.

Producer Pat Glasser went on to work with Three Dog Night.

Darius went on to record a 45 for Metromedia as Bobby Joe Ott, *Flint River Inn*, but the company was bought out by Bell and the track sank in the changeover.

He then returned to his home town of Cleveland, Ohio and under the name of Darius James played the club circuit. In 1974, a bad automobile accident put his musical plans on hold and he spent the next six years having re-constructive surgery. In 1980, he put a band called The Earthlings together and went back to Hollywood to play the Showcase Club Circuit and despite many recordings, no deal was forthcoming.

In 1990, Darius went back to Cleveland and met Barbara McFaul aka: Honeygirl. He then concentrated his efforts on recording and producing Honeygirl, also producing/directing three music videos with her.

In 2000, he started singing/writing and recording again along with Honeygirl and The Earthlings...

You can also find *Shades Of Blue* on *Love, Peace And Poetry: American Psychedelic Music* (LP & CD). (VJ/MRz)

The Dark Horsemen

Personnel:	MACK BENTLY	A
	MACK LANE	A
	DAVE ROOF	A
	TOM ROOF	A

45:	You Lied / Girl, Stand By Me	(The Dark Horsemen 3720) 1966

A rare private-press 45, mastered in Miami, Florida. However this quartet is thought to have emanated from the Jacksonville area. *You Lied*, an uptempo punker, is to be found on *Back From The Grave, Vol. 8* (Dble LP) and *Psychedelic States: Florida Vol. 1* (CD). *Girl Stand By Me*, a sultry ballad, is on *Psychedelic States: Florida Vol. 3* (CD). (VJ/MW/JLh/RM)

The Dark Knights

| 45: | Send Her To Me/Dark Knight | (IGL 111) 1966 |

The work of a garage quintet from Storm Lake, Iowa. Both sides of the 45 have also resurfaced on *The Best of IGL Folk Rock* (LP) and *The IGL Rock Story: Part One (1965 - 67)* (CD). (VJ)

Darkseid

| 45: | Ground Zero/Land Of The Darker Sun | (Brooks RSR-6) 1973 |

Awesome heavy psychedelic fuzz-rocker on a label out of Hampton, Virginia, that could just as easily be from 1968 or 1969. Both sides are excellent. *Ground Zero* is the more upbeat with female-male vocals, tribal drumming and searing breaks. *Darker Sun* has a backing track reminiscent of Uriah Heep's *Gypsy*, some scorching leads and a doom-laden feel. Quite superb in fact, for the genre.

There's a **Darkseid**, noted in Mike Kuzmin's excellent discography on Pennsylvania ('Sounds From The Wood'), who released one 45 in 1971 on their own name label - *Space Bass/Shamokin' Woman*. Noted as a possible Pennsylvania outfit presumably due to the Shamokin' in the title - is it the same group as this lot? (MW)

Darkstarr

Personnel:	PAUL FISHER	bs	A
	JOHN MEYERS	ld vcls	A
	DAVE SESTITO	gtr, vcls	A
	JOHN SCHILLACI	drms, perc	A

| CD: | 1(A) | DARKSTARR | (Cosmicdaze 101) 19?? |

This is a very rare release, but we've no other details. (PM)

Dark Shadows

See **Cold Sun**.

Daughters Of Albion

| Personnel: | GREG DEMPSEY | vcls, gtr | A |
| | KATHY YESSE | vcls | A |

GARAZE ZONE Vol. 1 (Comp LP) including David and The Boys Next Door.

ALBUM: 1(A) DAUGHTERS OF ALBION (Fontana SRF 67586) 1968 SC

NB: (1) came with a pair of mini-posters, approx 8"x11", featuring surrealistic hippie drawings. (1) also released by Fontana in U.K. (STL5486) and Holland (887806).

A hippie psych-pop duo who were produced and arranged by **Leon Russell**. All the songs were written by Greg Dempsey (sometimes helped by Dave Luff) and some arrangements are obviously influenced by the Beatles's *Sgt. Pepper* album. Quite pleasant, but nothing essential.

Graced with a really good voice, Kathy Yesse recorded a solo album in 1974 (produced by Greg Dempsey) as Kathy Dalton, *Boogie Bands And One Night Stands*. This was also released with one different track as *Amazing*, with both titles appearing on **Frank Zappa**'s Discreet label. While the record itself is unremarkable, failing to showcase her considerable talents, it's worth noting that she was backed by Little Feat with guest appearances including **Van Dyke Parks**, Sneaky Pete, Carl Wilson, Billy Hinsche (of **Dino, Desi and Billy**) and others. (SR/MMs/EW)

Daughters of Eve

45s:	He Cried/Don't Waste My Time	(Spectra Sound 920) 1966
	Symphony Of My Soul/Help Me Baby	(USA 891) 1967
	Stand By Me/Hey Lover	(USA 1779) 1967/8
	Social Tragedy/1000 Stars	(Cadet 5600) 1968

NB: Also an unknown 45 on Destination.

One of Chicago's top late sixties all girl groups. Compilation appearances have included: *Don't Waste My Time* on *Girls In The Garage, Vol. 1* (CD), *Girls In The Garage, Vol. 2* (LP) and *Girls In The Garage, Vol. 4* (LP). (VJ)

Dave and The Customs

45s:	Ali Baba/Shortenin' Bread	(DAC 500) 1963
	The Local/You Should Be Glad	(DAC 501) 196?
	Mizerlou/Bony Morony	(DAC 502) 196?
	I Ask You Why/He Was A Friend Of Mine	(DAC 503) 1966

Decent garage-folk-rock on the last 45 shown here. From Pomona, California. *I Ask You Why* is also on *From The New World*; *Ali Baba* is also on *Diggin' Out*. (MW)

Dave and The Shadows

| Personnel incl: | DAVE KALMBACH | A |
| | DAVE NOWLEN | A |

| ALBUM: | 1(A) | TWO SIDES OF CHRISTMAS | (Fenton) 1964 ? |

45s:	Here After/Blue Down	(Check-Mate 1011) 1962
(Partial	Dancing Cheek To Cheek/At The Fair	(Check-Mate 1016) 1962
List)	Playboy/Faith 7	(Fenton 942) 1964

From Sparta, Michigan. Leader Dave Kalmbach was the owner and engineer of the Fenton label. *Playboy* was later included on the cassette compilation *Best Of Michigan Rock Groups, Vol. 1*. (MW/FU)

Dave and The Squires

| 45: | The Girl Of My Dreams/ Ferry Cross The Mersey | (Radex R 65121) 1965 |

Out of Freeport, Illinois. *The Girl Of My Dreams* is a fairly routine punk ballad which can also be heard on *Love Is A Sad Song, Vol. 1* (LP), *Punk Ballads Sampler* (LP) and *Sixties Archive, Vol. 5* (CD). (VJ)

Dave and The Stalkers

Personnel:	CALVIN COKER	ld gtr	A
	DAVE CONWAY	vcls, gtr	A
	DON CROWE	drms	A

	BILL VICKERY	bs	A
	(CAREY RICHARDS	keyb'ds	A)

45:	Please Don't Ask Me Not To Cry / How Can I Tell Everybody	(Drake CP 1013) 1965

Just 500 copies of this 45 were pressed on a custom-label 45 recorded in a basement studio in Anderson, South Carolina. **Dave and The Stalkers** were a quartet from Royston, Georgia, who were augmented by Carey Richards on keyboards for the recording session.

Considering the reported paucity of technology employed (two mics hooked up to a reel-to-reel!) the sound is surprisingly good and comes over as a cross between the Beatles and the Stones. You can judge for yourself as *How Can I Tell Everybody* features on *Psychedelic States: Georgia Vol. 1* (CD). (MW/RM)

David

ALBUM:	1	DAVID	(Mother Lode) 1973 SC

From Albuquerque, New Mexico, a hippie-rock band with a prominent horn section. Rare, but not interesting. (SR)

THE DAVID - Another Day, Another Lifetime LP.

The David

Personnel:	MARK BIRD	A
	WARREN HANSEN	A
	TIM HARRISON	A
	CHUCK SPIETH	A

ALBUM:	1(A)	ANOTHER DAY, ANOTHER LIFETIME	
			(VMC V 124) 1967 R1/R2

NB: (1) also reissued on vinyl and CD in Greece in the late eighties.

45s:	40 Miles/Bus Token	(20th Century Fox 6663) 1966
	People Saying - People Seeing/	
	40 Miles	(20th Century Fox 6675) 1967
	I'm Not Alone/Sweet December (PS)	(VMC 716) 1967

The David, who came from Los Angeles, made an interesting album which has now become a collectors' item. The title track blends Eastern, chantlike overtones with Western orchestrational motifs. Other tracks are often characterised by driving rhythms played alongside oddly spaced melody lines. Much of the material - which was all written and composed by Warren Hansen - is heavily orchestrated. Hansen also invented an instrument, which he called the Plasmatar, to provide the vibrant rasp on one track *Mirrors of Wood*, which also contains some fine fuzztone. The final track *Of Our Other Days* had considerable commercial potential with a calypso- style melody and hypnotic beat.

The second 45 includes a fabulous non-album scuzzy-sitar-punker: *People Saying, People Seeing*.

Compilation appearances have included: *40 Miles* and *I'm Not Alone* on *Pebbles, Vol. 9* (CD) and *Boulders, Vol. 6* (LP); *I'm Not Alone* and *Sweet December* on *Sixties Archive, Vol. 8* (CD) and *Acid Trip From The Psychedelic Sixties* (LP); *People Staying, People Seeing* on *Seeds Turn To Flowers Turn To Dust* (LP & CD) and *U-Spaces: Psychedelic Archaeology Vol. 1* (CDR); and *40 Miles* on *Gone, Vol. 1* (LP). (VJ/MW)

Mogan David and His Winos

ALBUM:	1	SAVAGE YOUNG WINOS	(Kosher) 1973 -

45:	Nose Job / The Big War	(Kosher KMW-1) 1971/2

From somewhere in California. *Nose Job* was originally included with an issue of 'Mad' magazine and has subsequently resurfaced on *Sixties Rebellion 12: Demented* (LP & CD) and *Mad Music* (CD). The Kosher 45 may also have been issued as by **Mogan David and The Grapes Of Wrath** who released the following:

Little Girl Gone / Hot Blood	(Cha Cha) 1971? unconfirmed
Street Baby / Party Games	(Kosher KMW-2) 1972

(MW)

David and The Boys Next Door

Personnel incl:	DAVID KERSHENBAUM	A

45s:	Land O'Love/If I Was King	(Skipper 828 R-1240) 1965
	Spring Fever/It Ain't No Use	(Del-Ray 3059) 196?

Springfield, Missouri, was home to his band. David Kershenbaum composed both sides of the Del-Ray 45. *Land O'Love* can also be found on *Drink Beer! Yell! Dance!* (LP), *The Garage Zone, Vol. 1* (LP) and *The Garage Zone Box Set* (4-LP). (VJ/MW)

David and The Giants

45s:	Ten Miles High / I'm Down So Low	(Crazy Horse 1300) 1966
	Superlove / Rolling In My Sleep	(Crazy Horse 1307) 1966
	A Letter To Josephine / Super Good Feeling	(Fame 1467) 1967
	On Bended Knees /	
	Someday (You're Gonna Be Sorry)	(Amy 983) 196?
	Don't Say No / Love 'Em And Leave 'Em	(Capitol 2893) 1970

It's not confirmed that all these 45s are by the same act, but the *Ten Miles High* and *On Bended Knees* 45s were both produced by Rick Hall at Fame studios. In particular, *Ten Miles High* is great white soul, mid-tempo with major phasing effects.

The "David" in question is rumoured to be David Hood, a Muscle Shoals musician, who among other things, played on the first Boz Scaggs LP. (BM/MW)

Dianne Davidson

ALBUMS:	1	BABY	(Janus 3031) 1971 -
	2	BACKWOODS WOMAN	(Janus 3043) 1972 -
	3	MOUNTAIN MAMA	(Janus 3048) 1972 -

NB: (2) also released in the UK (Janus 6310 209).

A "big mama" hippie country folk singer, acoustic guitarist and songwriter, **Dianne Davidson** also sang behind **Leon Russell**, J.J. Cale and Alexander Harvey. Her second album was recorded in Nashville with local musicians plus Tracy Nelson (**Mother Earth**) and the enigmatic "Laurel

Canyon" and "Honey Combs" on vocals. It contains four self-penned songs plus covers of Elton John, Cat Stevens, Alex Harvey, the classic Bryant/Boudleaux song *Rocky Top* and two John Drummond songs. She also recorded three singles for Janus and one for RCA. These records are for you if you like big voiced white female singers. (SR)

Frank Davis

45:    The Sandpiper/?   ( ) c1969

This Texas engineer, songwriter, producer and musician is now a kind of cult figure for fans of Texas psychedelic rock. As an engineer, he was an associate of Walt Andrus and worked on sessions by the **13th Floor Elevators**, **Children**, the **Fever Tree** and many other sixties productions. As a musician, he was involved in the **Travel Agency** and took part in the formation of the short-lived **Saddlesore** with **Mayo Thomson** (ex-**Red Crayola**) and Cassell Webb (ex-**Children**). It's also known that he recorded circa 1966 an album worth of songs for a concept project known as "Metamorphosis", which still remain unreleased.

He also released some singles on local labels, most of them being extremely hard to find now and credited either to **Frank Davis** or to the Frank Davis Foundation.

This **Frank Davis** should not be confused with the Bay Area drummer who recorded with **Cold Blood** and **Loading Zone**. (SR)

Jeff Davis

ALBUM: 1   DEAR JEFF   (Tap LP-0030) c1970 SC?

An acid-folk singer and guitarist, from Houston. The album was recorded at Dale Mullins Studios in Houston, produced by Dale Mullins and Randy Callaway. It contains very introspective lyrics, some with a Christian bend. Mostly acoustic, it features a bit of electric guitar on tracks like *Clouds*, *Sorrows Come Too Fast* and *Leavin' Sea*. (SR)

Tim Davis

Personnel:

JAMES CURLY COOKE	gtr	AB
TIM DAVIS	vcls, drms	AB
MIKE FINNIGAN		A
DOUG KILLMER		A
SONNY LEWIS		A
JOHN McFEE	gtr	A
HART McNEE		A
BILL MEEKER		A
STEPHEN MILLER	keyb'ds	AB
PETER MINTON	keyb'ds	A
TRACY NELSON	vcls	A
RICHARD OLSEN		A
DONNA THATCHER	vcls	A
LINDA TILLERY	vcls	A
LONNIE TURNER	bs	A
JOHN WILMETH		A
KEN ADAMANY	piano	B
MIKE BLOOMFIELD	gtr	B
JOHN KAHN	bs	B
BOZ SCAGGS	gtr	B
BEN SIDRAN	piano	B

ALBUMS: 1(A) PIPEDREAM   (Metromedia KMD 1054) 1972 -
             2(B) TAKE ME AS I AM   (Metromedia BLM 1-1075) 1972 -

Tim Davis was the drummer in the **Steve Miller Band** for their first five albums. He went solo, recording two albums for Metromedia with several California musicians: Turner, Sidran, Scaggs and Cooke (**Steve Miller Band**), Linda Tillery (**Loading Zone**), Richard Olsen (**Charlatans**), John McFee (**Clover**), Tracy Nelson (**Mother Earth**), Stephen Miller (**Linn County**)... *Take Me As I Am* is the better of the two, being in the **Steve Miller Band** mould.

Davis came from the Children's Service Society, an orphanage in Milwaukee where he was with Ken Adamany. In 1964, he formed "Tim Davis and the Chordairres" with Curley Cooke in Madison, Wisconsin, where the other local groups included Tracy Nelson and the Imitations and Steve Miller and the Ardells. In 1965, Davis, Adamany, and Cooke got together with **Miller** and Scaggs and played occasionally as the Knight Trains before **Miller** drifted South to Chicago to form the Goldberg-Miller Blues Band. The Chordairres reformed and played the affluent resort town of Lake Geneva every week for at least a year. In late 1966, **Miller**, back from Texas after the failure of his Chicago band, called from San Francisco to ask **Davis** and Cooke to join him in his new band. (SR)

Jan Davis and The Routers

45s: Time Funnel/Walkin' Back   (RCA) 1966
      α Boss Machine/Fugitive   (A&M 733) 1967

NB: α as Jan Davis.

An interesting guitarist in the same style as **Davie Allan and The Arrows**: wild instrumental rock tracks with occasional sound effects (motorbikes, barking dogs...). The first single was produced by **Davis**, the second by Jimmy King. (SR)

Dean Davis Company

ALBUM: 1   STONE COUNTRY ROAD   (Private pressing) c1974 SC

A scarce album of ethereal folk-psych with female vocals. (SR)

Tim Dawe

Personnel:

TIM DAWE (JERRY PENROD)	vcls, acoustic gtr	AB
ARNIE GOODMAN	keyb'ds	AB
CHRIS KEBECK	gtr	A
CLAUDE MATHIS	drms	A
DON PARRISH	bs	A
RALPH BENKUS	perc	B
MITCHELL HOLMAN	bs, hrmnca	B
PATRICIA PICKENS	vcls	B
JERRY ROSS	gtr	B
HAL WAGENET	ld gtr	B

ALBUMS: 1(A) PENROD   (Straight/Warner STS 1058) 1969 SC
            2(B) TIMOTHY AND MS PICKENS WITH NATURAL ACT
                               (Half Moon Bay Records HMB 01) 1976 SC

NB: (1) also released in France.

RELICS Vol 1 & 2 (Comp CD) including The Day After.

Tim Dawe, aka Jerry Penrod, was from San Diego and an early member of **Iron Butterfly**. He reappeared on the scene in 1969 with an album on **Frank Zappa**'s Straight label. *Penrod* was a superb debut, full of psychedelic folk-rock with lots of organ, harpsichord and brilliant acid guitar. Four masterpieces are included:- *Nite Train Home*, *Junkie John*, *Sometimes Alone* (with strong percussion) and *Didn't We Love*. The result stands comparison to another more well known Straight artist, **Tim Buckley**. Quite surprisingly, however, the backing group doesn't seem to have played on other albums (unless they were using pseudonyms).

Dawe then wrote songs for Rod Taylor and **It's A Beautiful Day** (*Places Of Dreams* and *Bitter Wine* on *Choice Quality Stuff/Anytime*).

In 1976, he returned with an interesting West Coast album produced by the ex-**It's A Beautiful Day** member Mitchell Holman, who also played bass on it. Another ex-**It's A Beautiful Day** member, Hal Wagenet, also played guitar, whilst Patricia Pickens was an excellent vocalist. On this album **Dawe** included versions of *Bitter Wine* and *Junkie John* together with nine new songs. It was recorded in Coos Bay, Oregon.

In 1978, he produced *A Night On The Wine Cellar* (Cabernet GWC 101), a live folk-blues album on which he sang three new songs, along with Billy Roberts and other California local artists. (SR/CF)

The Dawgs

Personnel incl:	GAYLON LATIMORE (GAYLAN LATIMER)	A
	BOB SHARP	A

45:	Shy/Won't You Cry For Me	(Pic 1119) 196?

Operated out of Texas. Beatlesque harmonies are to the fore on the Invasion beat sounds of *Shy*, whilst *Won't You Cry For Me* looks towards Jay and The Americans for a yearning teenbeat-ballad.

Latimore went on to record a 45 with Sharp under the name Bob and Gaylon before playing with **The Silverlones**, **Eastside Transfer** and **Heather Black**. After **The Silvertones** he recorded three 45s under the pseudonym **Gaylon Ladd**. (MW)

The Dawks

Personnel:	JIM	A
	TERRY LAWSON	A
	LOU	A
	MIKE	A
	STEVE	A

45:	A Good Thing / Poison Ivy	(Prism) 1966

In 1966, a three-day battle of the bands was sponsored by WONE of Dayton, Ohio to highlight the local talent. Twelve bands were selected by the judges to record at Mega-Sound studios and each had on cut on the resultant *WONE, The Dayton Scene* LP (Prism PR-1966). **The Dawks**' selection, *A Good Thing*, is driving teenbeat with a big sound and strong Mersey influence. It appeared again on their own 45 on Prism. (MW)

The Dawnbreakers

45s:	I'll Never Ask You Why / Love Me Or Let Me Be	(Trophy Int. 1503) 1966
	Alligator / The Bounce	(Trophy Int. 1504) 1966

From Kentucky, their uptempo cover of **Soul Inc.**'s frat punker, *The Alligator* has some nice fuzz guitar. You can also find it on *Sixties Rebellion, Vol. 14* (LP & CD) and *It's Finkin' Time*. The first single is mostly notable for some good organ parts.

It's not known whether **The Dawnbreakers**'s 45: *Hear Me Now/Looking For Evergreens* (Dunhill D-4095) 1967, is by the same act. (VJ/SR)

DAY BLINDNESS - Day Blindness CD.

The Day After

This outfit recorded a song called *The Graduate*, which is a soft, haunting number, but has little special to differentiate it from the crowd.

Compilation appearances have included: *The Graduate* on *Oil Stains, Vol. 2* (LP), *Relics, Vol's 1 & 2* (CD) and *Relics, Vol. 2* (LP). (VJ)

Day Blindness

Personnel:	FELIX BRIA	vcls, bs, organ	A
	DAVE MITCHELL	vcls, drms	A
	GARY PIHL	vcls, gtr	A

ALBUM:	1(A)	DAY BLINDNESS	(Studio 10 DBX 101) 1969 R1

NB: (1) counterfeited on CD (Flash 42) 1997 and reissued legitimately on CD (Gear Fab GF-184) 2002.

45:	House And A Dog/Middle Class Lament	(Studio 10 2494) 1969

The above is an unexceptional San Francisco studio album, with some competent organ work, but little else to distinguish it, save possibly the final and longest track *Holy Land* - an attempt to sound like **The Doors**', *The End*.

Gary Pihl went on to become Sammy Hagar's guitarist and in the nineties was a member of the platinum-sellers Boston. (VJ/SR)

Daybreak

ALBUM:	1	DAYBREAK	(Dome) 1974 R1

Presumably a High School Project, this album came with two posters and a lyric sheet. Musically it's a mixture of psychedelia with fuzz guitars and Christian folk-rock similar to **Holy Ghost Reception Committee**. (SR)

Daybreak

ALBUM:	1	DAYBREAK	(RPC) 1971 R3

From the New York area, an extremely rare album supposed to cross garage-psych and West Coast sounds. Any additional information welcomed. (SR)

PSYCHEDELIC MICRODOTS Vol. 1 (Comp CD) including The Daybreakers.

The Daybreakers

Personnel incl:
- TERRY BECKLEY — bs, vcls
- MIKE BRIDGES — gtr
- BUDDY BUSCH — keyb'ds
- MAX COLLINS — ld vcls, keyb'ds
- DENNY MAXWELL — gtr
- BRUCE PETERS — vcls
- PAUL THOMAS — bs

45: Psychedelic Siren/Afterthoughts (Dial 4066) 1967

Hailing from Iowa City this band underwent frequent personnel changes but featured the personnel listed above at various times. They recorded just the one 45 at the time. The 'A' side features a screeching siren intro, and backing distinguishes what was otherwise a routine psychedelic/punk single. An album of their material has subsequently been put out on Unlimited Productions Rock 'n' Roll label (RRRLP-0002). The group later became Rox in 1969, but folded in 1971. After a five year lay-off they re-emerged as Cruisin'(1976-79).

Compilation appearances have included: *Psychedelic Siren* on *Psychedelic Microdots Of The Sixties, Vol. 1* (CD), *Psychedelic Unknowns, Vol's 1 & 2* (LP), *Psychedelic Unknowns, Vol. 1* (Dble 7") and *I Turned Into A Helium Balloon* (CD). *Dirty Water - The History Of Eastern Iowa Rock Volume 2* (LP) also includes a live rendition of *Respect* from 1988. (VJ)

Days of The Week

Personnel incl:
- M. HAYNES — A
- S. MITCHELL — A

45: Home At Last / Little Latin Lupe Lu (Malcolm Z. Dirge MZD-45005) 1966

With the inclusion of *Home At Last*, a wistful folk-rocker composed by Haynes and Mitchell, on *Psychedelic States: Alabama Vol. 1* (CD) it is hoped that more info may come to light about this group from Birmingham, Alabama. (MW)

The Daytonas

See **Ronny and The Daytonas**.

Daze of The Week

45: One Night Stand/? (Piece 1003) 1966

Their sole vinyl offering, the Piece label operated out of Tacoma, Washington where the band also originated. *One Night Stand* is an aggressive garage punker with snotty vocals. Strangely enough the track also appears on Piece 1002, backed by *You Gotta Give, Baby* and credited to the Grotesque Mommies. The same group?

You can find *One Night Stand* on *Highs In The Mid-Sixties, Vol. 22* (LP). (MW/GGl)

The Deacons

Personnel:
- JOHN CHINCHILLA — drms — A
- EARL PRITCHARD — ld vcls — A
- GARY STARZECKI — bs — A
- DICK WEEKS — sax — A
- RICH YOUNGBERG — ld gtr — A

45s:
- Donna/Baldie Beat (Re-Car 9001) 1964
- The Baldie Stomp/Baldie Beat (Re-Car 9004) 1964
- Candy Man/Think It Over (Re-Car 9012) 1965
- Empty Heart/Problems About Baby (Soma 1452) 1965
- Empty Heart / Bring It On Home To Me PS (Sundazed S 140) 1998

Not a garage band at all, but a popular Minneapolis-based dance group who seemed to make songs about 'The Baldies', a sixties Minneapolis gang. Their finest moment, *Empty Heart* has recently been reissued with the bonus of an unreleased *Bring It On Home To Me* from the same sessions, and rounded off with a brief history from Minnesota mastermind Jim Oldsberg.

Compilation appearances have included: *The Baldie Stomp* on *Ho-Dad Hootenanny* (LP), *Victims Of Circumstances, Vol. 1* (LP), *Mondo Frat Dance Bash A Go Go* (CD) and *Baldy Stomp* on *Top Teen Bands, Vol.2* (LP); *Empty Heart* on *Soma Records Story, Vol. 1* (LP), *The Big Hits Of Mid-America - The Soma Records Story* (LP) and *Hipsville, Vol. 3* (LP); *Baldie Beat* on *The Big Itch* and *Top Teen Bands, Vol. 1* (LP); and *Candy Man* on *Top Teen Bands, Vol. 3* (LP). (VJ/MW)

The Dead Beats

45: Can't Go On This Way / Trust Me (Coe West 002) 1967

An obscure band who recorded their sole 45 at Robert Quimby's home studio in Deland, Florida. Daytona Beach has been suggested as their home-turf.

Compilation appearances have included: *Can't Go On This Way* on *Psychedelic States - Florida Vol. 1* (CD); *Can't Go On This Way* and *Trust Me* on *Drive-In A Go Go! Vol. 1* (CD). (MW/JLh)

The Dead Beats

45: She Don't Love Me/I'm Sure (Gray Ant 108) c1966

A rare and obscure garage single. Presumably unconnected to the Florida **Dead Beats**.

Compilation appearances have included: *She Don't Love Me* on *Teenage Shutdown, Vol. 2* (LP & CD). (SR)

Deadend

45: Just Like A Season/ I Ain't Got Nobody (Voice Of The Junkyard 24425) 197?

A hippie-rock 45 which came in a picture sleeve. The band were from Grand Forks in North Dakota, although the disc was recorded in Minneapolis. (VJ)

Deadlys

Out of Columbus, Ohio, they featured with one track *On The Road Again* on the *Hillside '66* sampler of Columbus bands. It's a raw and poorly produced version of a **Lovin' Spoonful** song, but has subsequently resurfaced on *Highs In The Mid-Sixties, Vol. 9* (LP) and *Teenage Shutdown, Vol. 11* (LP & CD). (VJ)

Ritchie Dean

45s:	α Goodbye Girl!/I'd Do Anything	(Tower 102)	1964
	Why Can't You Love Me (Like You Used To) / Now	(Tower 121)	1965
	Time (Can't Heal This Pain Of Mine) / Farewell Angelina	(Tower 183)	1965
	Old Cathedrals / It's Raining It's Pouring	(Tower 228)	1966

NB: α also released in the U.K. (Capitol CL 15374). A German language version also exists.

Based in NYC, the first 45 is mid-sixties pop-rock. It's in fact **Warren Schatz** in disguise.

Compilation appearances have included *Time* on *The Lost Generation, Vol. 2* (LP) and *Boulders, Vol. 6* (LP). (SR/MW)

Christopher Deane

45:	Angel's Last Trip/Purgatorio	(Sidewalk 906)	1966

Probably a garage-psych single. (SR)

The Dearly Beloved (Beloved Ones)

Personnel:
LARRY COX	vcls	AB
SHEP COOKE	bs	AB
TERRY LEE	gtr	AB
PETE SCHUYLER	drms	A
TOM WALKER	gtr	AB
RICK MELLINGER	drms	B
LENNY LOPES	drms	
VAL VALINTO	bs	
TOM RIPLY	vcls	

ALBUM:	1(A/B) ROUGH DIAMONDS: HISTORY OF GARAGE BAND MUSIC VOL 6 - DEARLY BELOVED	(Voxx 200.018)	1984

45s:	α Peep Peep Pop Pop/It Is Better	(Boyd 157)	1966
	Peep Peep Pop Pop/It Is Better	(Columbia 4-43797)	1966
	Wait Till Mornin'/You Ain't Gonna Do What You Did With Him To Me	(Columbia 4-43959)	1966
	Merry Go Round/Flight Thirteen	(Splitsound SSDG-5)	1967

NB: α credited to The Beloved Ones.

PEBBLES BOX SET (Comp LP Set) including The Dearly Beloved.

Forming in 1963 as **The Intruders** and later known as **The Quinstrells** they became known as **The Dearly Beloved** in late '65 and were Tucson's most popular sixties band. Shortly after their name change Dan Gates, a DJ from a local radio station KTKT came along with the tape of a song called *Peep Peep Pop Pop*. The group were not at all keen at first but eventually he persuaded them to record it at the Audio Sound Recorders Studio in Phoenix and a record deal was negotiated with the New Mexico-based Boyd label. They got the band's name wrong on the label and the 45 was released in 1966 and credited to The Beloved Ones. It was a No. 1 hit in Tucson that year and held the No. 1 position for many weeks on KTKT radio. Consequent upon its success the 45 was leased to Columbia, who at least got the band's name right. With national distribution the 45 almost made Billboard's Top 100.

Fuelled by their success, the band headed to L.A. to record an album for Columbia. They recorded twenty songs in all in just three half-day sessions! These sessions spawned their next 45. Tom Walker wrote the 'A' side, the flip was the work of **The Grodes'** leader Manny Freiser. The posthumous Voxx compilation includes some tracks from this session, but Columbia didn't promote the band or release the album. Around this time Pete Schuyler left the band and was replaced on drums by Rick Mellinger from **The Grodes**.

On a further trip to L.A. the band were spotted playing with **The Leaves** by a White Whale rep. and this led to them signing a new record contract (having sued Columbia to get out of their previous one). Larry Cox had to return to Tucson the next day to get married so they left L.A. at 3 a.m. taking turns with the driving. Eventually they all fell asleep including the driver. Inevitably they crashed and Larry Cox was killed instantly. The rest of the band sustained injuries. To make matters worse Larry's death negated their White Whale contract because it contained a clause stating that the band would have to stay intact.

The band tried to keep going but never successfully replaced Larry. The 'A' side of their final 45 was a haunting song written by Larry about death ironically shortly before his own tragic demise. The flip, a punker with a ripping bass line, was a regional hit. Vocalist Jim Perry sang on the 'A' side and Terry Lee took the vocal role on the flip. Arguably this 45 was their finest moment, and both sides can be heard on the Voxx compilation.

The band disintegrated when **Shep Cooke** left to join Linda Ronstadt's backing band, **The Stone Poneys**. Although he soon returned to Tucson to rejoin **The Dearly Beloved** he got into a motorbike accident shortly after his return and couldn't play for six weeks. This led to the final break-up.

Tom Walker and **Shep Cooke** have remained active in the music scene. Walker going on to play for Arizonia outfit Butterscotch and later composing songs used on the Chuck Wagon and The Wheels album. **Cooke** recorded as Shep in 1969 and formed **The Floating House Band** in 1970. He later made some solo albums as well as playing on albums by Jackson Browne, Tom Waits and Linda Ronstadt. Pete Schuyler joined the marines and now works in electronics, Terry Lee is a successful Tucson architect and Mellinger is an inhalation therapist. Tom and Shep still continue to gig together.

The Voxx compilation is an excellent guide to their career with full liner notes by Lee Joseph which have been summarised here. It contains all the band's better 45s and some of their unreleased recordings for Columbia.

Compilation appearances have included: *1965 KTKT Radio Promo, Flight Thirteen, Iceman (Wild About My Loving), I'm Not Coming Back, It's All Over, I've Got A Girl, Keep It Moving, Merry Go Round, Music Revolution, Peep Peep Pop Pop, Strange Feeling, Wait Till The Mornin'* and *You Ain't Gonna Do What You Did To Him To Me* on *Let's Talk About Girls!* (CD); and *Flight 13* on *Pebbles Box* (5-LP), *Acid Dreams - The Complete 3 LP Set* (3-LP), *Acid Dreams Epitaph* (CD), *The Tucson Sound 1960-68* (LP), *Trash Box* (5-CD) and *Boulders, Vol. 6* (LP). (VJ/SR)

Mike Deasy

ALBUMS:	1	LETTERS TO MY HEAD	(Capitol ST-11170)	1973 -
	2	WINGS OF AN EAGLE	(Sparrow SPR 1009)	1976 -

NB: (2) by Mike and Kathy.

45:	Beauty/Eli Wheeler	(Capitol 3518)	1973

An excellent guitarist, **Mike Deasy** was a member of the "Wrecking Crew", the group of Los Angeles musicians who recorded hundreds of sessions in the Hollywood studios during the 1965/75 period. The "Wrecking Crew" also included Ben Benay, Larry Knechtel, Jerry Scheff, Jim Horn, Joe Osborn, Jim Troxel, Toxey French as well as several other renowned players like **Hal Blaine** and **Mike Melvoin**.

His discography is extremely large and the part we present here probably represents a small proportion of what he really recorded. From what we've been able to gather, after playing in several California surf groups, **Mike Deasy** began a studio career circa 1965 and was then behind several projects like **The Flower Pot**, **The Ceyleib People**, **Friar Tuck**, **Michele and Your Gang**. He often worked with **Curt Boettcher**.

Among his session work and collaborations, we must include mention of the albums by **Mark LeVine**, **Gentle Soul**, **Tongue and Groove**, **Curt Newbury**, **Smokestack Lightning**, **Mark Spoelstra**, **Spontaneous Combustion**, **Stapleton-Morley Expression** and **Peter Anders**.

In 1969, he formed the short-lived **Gator Creek** with other L.A. musicians and kept on doing session work, but his seventies work is generally outside the scope of this book as he generally played on mainstream rock or pop acts, although the album he did with Spider has its moments.

His two solo albums from 1973 and 1976 went unnoticed. The Capitol one is a decent rock effort with some light acoustic tracks and some heavy ones. The album recorded with his wife Kathy is in a Christian country-rock vein. (SR)

The Debonaires

| 45: | Never Mistaken/Summertime | (Rite 0785) 1966 |

A Chicago-based mid-sixties garage band.

Compilation appearances have included: *Never Mistaken* on *The Chosen Few, Vol. 1* (LP), *Chosen Few, Vol's 1 & 2* (CD), *Pebbles Box* (5-LP), *Trash Box* (5-CD) and *Teenage Shutdown, Vol. 3* (LP & CD). (VJ)

The Debonairs

Instrumentalists from San Antonio in Texas. They didn't make it onto vinyl back in the 1960s but their *Lonely Is The Summer* has subsequently been compiled on *Texas Punk, Vol. 9* (LP), *Acid Visions - Complete Collection, Vol. 3* (3-CD) and *Green Crystal Ties, Vol. 3* (CD). (VJ)

Debris

Personnel:	CHARLES (POISON) IVEY	syn	A
	JOHNNY GREGG	drms, vcls	A
	OLIVER POWERS (RECTOMO)	vibraharp	A
	(RICHARD DAVIS	sax, organ	A)
	(DIRK E. ROWNTREE	perc	A)

ALBUM: 1(A) STATIC DISPOSAL (Static Disposal PIG 0000) 1976 R1
NB: (1) reissued on CD (Anopheles Records 004). (1) reissued on clear vinyl (Anopheles Records 006) 2002, limited to 1000 copies and including a previously unreleased 1975 practice recording of **The Stooges** *Real Cool Time* - a different version to that included on the earlier CD reissue.

Formed in Chickasha, Oklahoma in 1975, the band were apparently high on acid when they recorded this, so unsurprisingly the result is pretty demented psychedelia. Modulators and synthesizers, a vibraharp and more are utilised to good effect. Indeed the album is full of sound effects and echoes.

All the material is written and arranged by Ivey and Powers and many psych heads will want it in their collection. The recent CD reissue comes complete with bonus tracks and a detailed history.

Sadly Oliver Powers died of a massive brain aneuryism on June 22nd 2001. (VJ)

The Debs

| 45s incl: | Goodbye Boy/Give Him My Love | (Mercury 72458) 196? |

NB: Above info from promo copy without indication of 'A' or 'B' side.

This girl-group made two 45s for Mercury. They're sometimes thought to have come from England, since *Sloopy's Gonna Hang On*, which has resurfaced on *Girls In The Garage, Vol. 4* (LP), was issued there shortly after it came out in America, but it's pretty clear they originated somewhere on the East Coast and were probably a studio group.

Their *Goodbye Boy/Give Him My Love* 45 credits Dennis Lambert and Louis Pegues as vocal producers. *Goodbye Boy* was written by the same pair, whilst *Give Him My Love* has Donovan/Dunn credited as songwriters. (VJ/MC)

The Decades

| 45: | I'm Lovin' You/Thinking Of You | (Sully 121) 196? |

Probably the sole stab for stardom for this band, who recorded for this West Texas label, but are thought to have come from Oklahoma. (VJ)

The Decades

| 45s: | I'm Gonna Dance/On Sunset | (Lady Luck 001) 1967 |
| | I'm Gonna Dance/On Sunset | (Era 3174) 1967 |

This was a different outfit from California.

Compilation appearances have included: *I'm Gonna Dance* on *Off The Wall, Vol. 2* (LP); *On Sunset* on *Psychedelic Experience, Vol. 2* (CD), *Psychedelic Unknowns Vol. 8* (LP & CD); *I'm Gonna Dance* and *On Sunset* on *Victims Of Circumstances, Vol. 1* (LP). (VJ)

The Decades

| 45: | C'mon Pretty Baby/Strange Worlds | (Janie JL 10645/6) 1964 |

More **Decades**, this time from Akron, Ohio. This particular bunch were also known as **The Rats** but only for the *Rats Revenge* 45, immortalised on *Back From The Grave Vol's 1* and *2*. *C'mon Pretty Baby*, a rather repetitive early sixties rock'n'roller, has been compiled recently on the *Follow That Munster, Vol. 1* (LP). Its flip, *Strange Worlds*, is a pretty decent Tornadoes/Ventures type instrumental surprisingly not featured on the *Strummin' Mental* series. (MW/GGI)

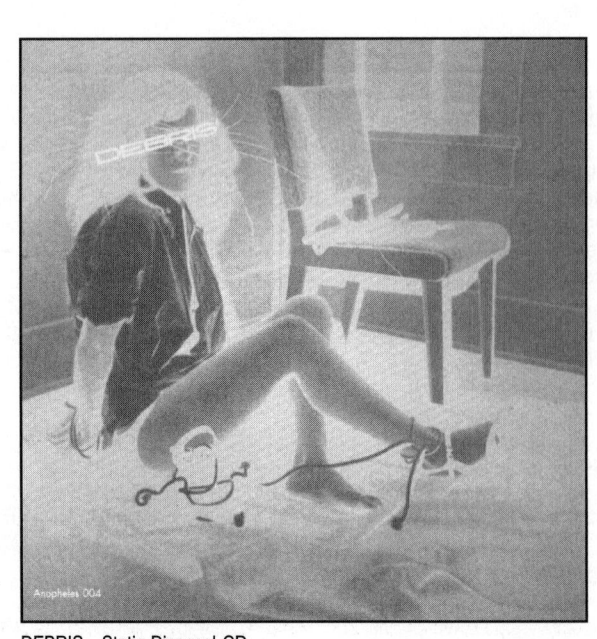

DEBRIS - Static Disposal CD.

DECEMBER'S CHILDREN - December's Children LP.

The Decades

| 45: | There Ain't No Way / | |
| | Pledging My Love | (Great Scott 1002/3) c1967 |

A horn-garage-rock 45 from yet another **Decades**. Possibly from Ohio, as the 45 is on a Cincinnati label, but not the Akron (**Rats**) bunch. (MW/GGI)

December's Children

Personnel:	BRUCE BALZER	gtr	A
	CRAIG BALZER	gtr, keyb'ds, vcls	A
	RON PAPALED	drms, perc	A
	BILL PETTI	bs, vcls	A
	ALICE POPOVIC	vcls	A

ALBUM: 1(A) DECEMBER'S CHILDREN (Mainstream 6128) 1970 R1/R2

45: Sweet Talkin' Woman/Back Road Rider (Mainstream 728) 1970
NB: "double-headed" promo copies also exist.

From Cleveland, Ohio and based around the Balzer brothers. The above album, which was recorded in Miami, is not outstanding. The band's sound was characterised by the vocal harmonies of Craig Balzer, Petti and Popovic and some competent guitar work. *Living (Way Too Fast)*, which captures Alice Popovic's vocals at their most poignant and the opener *Trilogy*, which displays the band's harmonies to best effect, are arguably the best tracks.

Bruce Balzer later played with Ambleside (also spelt Amblesyde, after a street on which the band rented a house), whilst both brothers played in Circus, an early seventies power-pop band who had an album on Metromedia, and Windfall. They later went on to form a band called 747 which was signed to Planet Records in late 1979 and had its named changed to American Noise due to some protests from Boeing or the record company.

American Noise's eponymous album (Planet P-8) 1980 topped the Charts in Cleveland and few other areas.

Craig and Bruce Balzer are now both married and run a specialty advertising firm out of Greater Cleveland, Ohio, USA.

There was also another band of this name from Chicago, which recorded 45s for Twin, Capitol, Liberty and three for World Pacific. *Backwards And Forewards / Kissin' Time* (World Pacific 77887) actually made No 123 in the charts in 1968, but this was a different outfit so far as we know, whose style was brash brassy pop with harmonies. This 45 was produced, arranged and written by Ray Whitley.

Another **December's Children**, likely Californian, released a 45 (*Somethin' Fresh/Mitch's High* produced by Jerry Riopell), on Corio later leased to Columbia - fresh faced pop a la **Monkees** with good fuzz.

Another D.C. 45 exists on the Balance label. If you can work out which one is which, well done! (VJ/MW/GGI/AJ/SR)

December's Children Ltd

45: Signed D.C./So Long Ago (Domestic Sound DS 123) 196?

A different band from Washington D.C. who recorded a fine version of Arthur Lee's classic ode to a junkie *Signed D.C.* in true ballad punk style. It's included on the *Signed, D.C.* (LP) compilation, which was named after it and on *Sixties Rebellion, Vol. 8* (LP & CD). (VJ)

The Decisions

45: Tears, Tears/Don't You Know It's Love (Topper 1013) 196?

The above was this band's sole release and one of just five releases on this label, The 'A' side is a pretty lame effort. In fact they took *Just Like Me* (The **Paul Revere and The Raiders** and **Wild Knights** classic) altered the lyrics and added a new guitar lead. If you want to hear the result it's on *Highs In The Mid-Sixties, Vol. 19* (LP). They came from Kalamazoo, Michigan. (VJ/KBn)

Declaration of Independence

| 45s: | Morning Glory Man/Letter To Ruth | (Mr. G. 804) 1967 |
| | House/Next Stop - Dead End Street | (Mr. G. 805) 1968 |

Not garage or psychedelic, but polished flower-power pop, produced by Johnny Cymbal. (MW)

Dedicated Followers

| Personnel incl: | BONNIE FRENCH | vcls | A |
| | DENNIS HULSE | | A |

A Circleville, Ohio, group who were finalists in the 1967 Paxton Theatre Battle Of The Bands (which was won by Proud Destiny). They did not get to release a 45; one track was captured for posterity on the Hillside label's *1967 Promotion* EP alongside contributions from **The Gears**, Emeralds, and **Internal Canitery Sin**. Their version of *Harlem Shuffle* is notable for its unusual folkie vibe, due to the male lead vocal being counterpointed at intervals by solo female harmonies. (DCe/MW)

The Dedications

| 45: | Midnight Gray / | |
| | A Place In The Sun | (Sounds Of Birmingham 104) 1969 |

All that is known about this group is that they were from Birmingham, Alabama. *Midnight Gray* was released in early 1969 but it sounds like it came from 1966, with hints of the Animals in the vocals and keyboard frills. Check it out on *Psychedelic States: Alabama Vol. 1* (CD). (MW)

Terry Dee and The Road Runners

45: Feel No Pain/Some Other Guy (Ventura 502) 1966

A Beatlesque ballad backed by a swaggering fifties-inspired garage-rocker from University City, Missouri.

Some copies came with labels reversed.

Compilation appearances include *Some Other Guy* on *The Essential Pebbles Collection, Vol. 1* (Dble CD). (MW)

Dee Jay and The Runaways

Personnel:			
	CHUCK COLEGROVE	gtr	A
	BOB GODFREDSON	gtr, bs, vcls	ABCD
	GARY LIND	vcls	ABCD
	JOHNNY SENN (JAY)	bs, gtr, vcls	ABC
	DENNY STOREY (DEE)	drms, vcls	ABCD
	TOM VALLIE	organ, vcls	ABCD
	DERRY KINTZI	keyb'ds	CD
	RUSTY DAVIS		
	SAM FRENCH		
	GRANT GILMORE		
	JIM GROTH		
	ROGER HUGHES		
	JIM JOHAN		
	TERRY KLEIN		
	JIM WIENER		
	ROGER WHITMORE		

CD:	1(-)	PETER RABBIT	(Arf!Arf! AA-067) 1997
			HCP

45s:	Jenny Jenny/Boney Moronie	(IGL 100) 1965 -
	Love Bug Crawl/The Pickup	(Coulee 109) 1965 -
	Peter Rabbit/Three Steps To Heaven	(IGL 103) 1966 -
	Peter Rabbit/Are You Ready?	(Smash S-2034) 1966 -
	Peter Rabbit/Three Steps To Heaven	(Smash S-2034) 1966 45
	She's A Big Girl Now/	
	He's Not Your Friend	(Smash S-2049) 1966 -
	Keep On Running/Don't You Ever	(Sonic 132) 1966 -
	Keep On Running/Don't You Ever	(Stone 45) 1967 -
	My Gal/Doesn't Matter Anymore	(Sonic 148) 1967 -
	Sunshine Morning/And I Know	(Sonic 158) 1967 -
	Love Tender, Love/	
	While You Were Sleeping	(Dee Jay 101) 1982 -

Hailing from Spirit Lake / Dickens / Estherville and Armstrong, this band played an important slice in the history of Iowa rock. Johnny Senn (Jay) was instrumental along with Cliff Plagman and Roger Blunt in setting up the IGL Studios and *Jenny Jenny* became the label's first recording. As only 100 copies were pressed it's understandably now extremely rare. *Peter Rabbit* a rather popish song was picked up by the Chicago-based Smash label and earned the band an appearance on Dick Clark's 'Where The Action Is' show as well as a place in the charts. However, when the big breakthrough never came they reverted to Sonic for three further 45s, including a cover of the Spencer Davis hit *Keep On Running*, on which they were joined by local vocalist Terry Klein.

The core of the group were former members of the **Chevelles** and the VanDels who joined forces in 1964 due to draft and other member depletion. Line-up "C" recorded *Peter Rabbit*. From 1966 John Senn 'retired' to concentrate on the IGL studio work, though he continued to be involved and record with the group. After line-up "D", personnel was very fluid to cover departures and touring. The band officially split in 1968 but IGL continued well into the seventies becoming a cult collector's label since its demise and the label has been well compiled in recent times on album and CD by Arf!Arf! and Get Hip.

These details and a comprehensive story of the band are to be found on Erik Lindgren's retrospective CD, which contains 32 tracks including four by the **Chevelles**. It confirms that the band was an adept outfit covering rockin', instrumental and frat genres in a pop vein, and ballads in an accomplished Four Seasons style. Their appeal will lie with connoisseurs of sixties midwest pop - you'll find neither fuzz nor psych here. In 1981 Storey and Senn got together to revive the name and laid down four more tracks. Two were put out on a 45, and three are featured on the CD.

Kintzi, Storey and Powell all went on to record solo 45s for IGL/Sonic along with *Peter Rabbit* song writer Tim Smith, Johnny Senn latter recorded an album for IGL with a new band, The Fortunes. The retrospective 45 release in 1982 also comes with a photo and history of the band.

Also briefly in the band was a guy called Roger Hughes, who later formed Bands Of Gold who recorded one 45, *You Won't Change Me/It's Over* (Smash 2058) in the late sixties. Prior to his spell with the band he'd produced one 45, *In A Thousand Cities/Is It Really Love?* (Sultan 1002), with a Sioux City- based project called Denny and The Dukes.

THE IGL ROCK STORY PART 1 (Comp CD) including Dee Jay and The Runaways.

Compilation appearances have included: *Don't You Ever* on *Roof Garden Jamboree* (LP); *The Gorilla* on *The Arf! Arf! Blitzkrieg 32 Track Sampler* (CD); *Jenny Jenny* and *The Gorilla* on *The Best Of IGL Garage Rock* (LP); *Jenny Jenny, The Gorilla, Peter Rabbit, She's A Big Girl Now, Boney Maronie* on *The IGL Rock Story: Part One (1965 - 67)* (CD); *Keep On Running* and *Take A Look At My Baby* on *The IGL Rock Story: Part Two (1967 - 68)* (CD). (VJ/MW/ELn)

The Deep

Personnel:		
	MARK BARKAN	A
	DAVID BROMBERG	A
	RUSTY EVANS	A
	(D. BLACKHURST	A)
	(C. BLUE	A)
	(A. GELLER	A)
	(L. POGAN	A)

ALBUM:	1(A)	PSYCHEDELIC MOODS OF THE DEEP
		(Cameo Parkway 7051) 1966 R3

N.B. (1) stereo and mono editions exist of the original pressing with the stereo version being significantly more valuable. Reissued on Cicadelic (977) 1987, and also on CD (Collectables).

This was a Philadelphia-based studio-only project. The album, which is an extremely rare and quite costly collectors' item, has until recently been shrouded in total mystery. It was produced by Mark Barkan and **Rusty Evans**. Both were also involved in **Freak Scene** whose album *Psychedelic Psoul* (CBS 9456) 1968 is virtually a second **Deep** LP. We also know that David Bromberg was involved in the project. The other personnel listed above have been deduced from songwriting credits and may also have been involved.

Their album is very strange, full of weird sound effects, haunting vocals and acid-soaked lyrics. It is based on a psychedelic-folk format. Some, such as *Color Dreams* and *Your Choice To Choose*, sound very **Seeds**-like. Others, like *Shadows On The Wall* and *Wake Up and Find Me* are haunting acid ballads.

"Wake up and find me
With dreams of liquid nights
And never ending lights"
(from *Wake Up and Find Me*).

Arguably the best two tracks are *Turned On* and *Psychedelic Moon* - which are both very odd. The album is recommended listening. Fans of the band will also be interested in a series of outtakes released on CD by Collectables, *Part 2* and *Part 3* contains alternate takes and unreleased tracks which were recorded in 1966), whilst *Part 4* (which also features tracks by **Hydro-Pyro**) and *Part 5* are now also available on CD through Collectables.

Barkan went on to a group called **Hydro Pyro**. In 1970 **Rusty** released a solo album as **Marcus**.

Compilation appearances have included: *Psychedelic Moon* on *The Psychedelic Experience, Vol. 1* (LP); *Trip #76* on *Echoes In Time, Vol. 1* (LP) and *Echoes In Time Vol's 1 & 2* (CD); *Color Dreams* on *Gathering Of The Tribe* (LP) and *Gone, Vol. 1* (LP); *Pink Ether* and *Psychedelic Moon* on *Green Crystal Ties, Vol. 9* (CD). (VJ/CF)

The Deepest Blue

Personnel:			
	ALEX "EARL" SHACKELFORD	ld vcls	A
	RUSSELL JOHNSON	ld gtr, vcls	A
	KEN ZABEL	organ	A
	RICK EDWARDS	gtr, backing vcls	A
	BRUCE LAVOIE	bs, backing vcls	A
	RUSS "SOUPY" MAURO	drms	A

45:	Pretty Little Thing/ Somebody's Girl	(Blue-Fin BL-FI-102) 1966

Fine Stones-influenced garage punkers from Pomona, California. Starting out as a surf/grease combo in the early sixties, The Doves had stabilized as the above line-up by 1965. Soupy Mauro and Ken Zabel were Pomona locals, Earl Shackelford and Bruce Lavoie hailed from Ontario, Russ Johnson was from England, and Rick Edwards was from Montclair.

Earl Shackelford recalls: "We played mostly in the teen clubs - the Oasis, Hilltop, Pace Setter, Discoteen - what's known today as The Inland Empire. And some beer bars - no-one cared the how old you were then. College fraternity parties were always the best unless some drunken jocks decided you were dead meat and you had to fight off the sweaty block heads as you tore down your equipment and threw it into your trusty band mobile. Oh yeah.. those were the days alright."

"We went out of state once to a little bar in Pocatello, Idaho. I was sick with strep throat so we played instrumentals mostly and lived on bar food for several days, (slim jims, jerky, and beer). That was our tour. We did work in Hollywood a couple of times on the Strip, but we all hated Hollywood. We played with **The Leaves** once, and **The Seeds** ... although I don't remember playing with them - Ken Zabel says we did. High Schools were a good gig except that we were banned from all of them after one gig at each, for various reasons (hee hee hee)!"

In the Summer of 1966 they released their sole 45 as **The Deepest Blue**. "Our main influences were The Stones, Animals, Them, early Moody Blues. We changed our name during the time of our recording - we thought it was more commercial."

Sadly the 45 bombed and the band split soon after, leaving a few tracks recorded for an album in the can. Tragedy struck soon after: Soupy Mauro died in a motorcycle accident; one year later Rick and three members of a band, with whom he was doing a car tour, went off the road in the middle of the night, to join Soupy.

Thereafter Earl "bummed around for several years doing what most people were doing in the late sixties, singing in coffee houses until I returned to Los Angeles and began to perform with various bands again in the early seventies, experimenting with all the jumbled forms of psych/country/ rock/acid that was affecting musicians at the time".

"Eventually I teamed up with Walter Egan, thanks to mutual friend and musician Chris Darrow of **Kaleidoscope** fame, whom I'd known for years after **The Kaleidoscope** had recorded one of my songs *I Found Out* (on the *Beacon From Mars* album). We formed a band called Wheels and played the Los Angeles circuit until Walter got a solo record contract.

"I worked with him in some capacity on most of his records. He had a top ten hit (*Magnet And Steel*) and recorded two or three of my songs for his string of albums on CBS and MCA/Backstreet labels. During this time, 1978 to be exact, I worked with James Williamson on Iggy Pop's LP *New Values* arranging and singing backup vocals. From that time on I've been involved at various levels with friends putting out CD's, playing the guitar and writing."

And what of the others? "Ken Zabel lives in Boise, and was recently playing with a bluesband, The Ramblers; Bruce Lavoie just retired from the union after having been in road construction for 30 years; Russ Johnson disappeared somewhere - Australia we believe - and hasn't been heard from since 1969."

Compilation appearances have included: *Pretty Little Thing* on *Off The Wall, Vol. 2* (LP), *Mayhem & Psychosis, Vol. 3* (LP), *Mayhem & Psychosis, Vol. 2* (CD), *Teenage Shutdown, Vol. 10* (LP & CD); *Somebody's Girl* on *Sixties Choice, Vol. 1* (LP), *The 60's Choice Collection, Vol's 1 And 2* (CD) and *Fuzz, Flaykes, And Shakes, Vol. 2* (LP & CD); *Pretty Little Thing* and *Somebody's Girl* on *Boulders, Vol. 6* (LP) and *Ya Gotta Have Moxie, Vol. 1* (Dble CD). (VJ/MW/MM/ES)

Deep Six

ALBUM:	1	THE DEEP SIX	(Liberty LRP-3475) 1966 -

NB: (1) stereo copies released on (LST 7475).

HCP

45s:	Rising Sun/Strollin' Blues	(Saw-Man 001) 1965 -
	Rising Sun/Strollin' Blues	(Liberty F-55838) 1965 122
	Things We Say / I Wanna Shout	(Liberty F-55858) 1966 -
	When Morning Breaks / Counting	(Liberty F-55882) 1966 -
	Why Say Goodbye /What Would You Wish From The Golden Fish	(Liberty F-55901) 1966 -
	Image Of A Girl / C'mon Baby	(Liberty F-55926) 1966 -

A six-piece (five men, one woman) from San Diego, California whose bag was folk-rock and harmony-pop. Their fifth Liberty 45, *What Would You Wish From The Golden Fish*, is an amazing pop-sike tune complete with fuzz guitar and hammer dulcimer, with lyrics based on the old story of the mythical fish who granted wishes. The 'A' side, *Why Say Goodbye*, is more straight forward pop, but pleasant nonetheless.

Their album combined folk, soft-rock and flower-pop and includes several covers, notably the Stones' *Paint It Black*, Neil Diamond's *Solitary Man* and *A Groovy Kind Of Love*.

One track from an earlier 45, *Rising Sun* can also be found on *Nuggets, Vol. 10* (LP) and *Bring Flowers To U.S.* (LP). (KSI/MW/SR)

Deep Six

Personnel:	LARRY DREGORS	ld gtr	A
	KEN FULLER	bs	A
	BILLY HARDEN	gtr	A
	MAURICE "MOUSE" SAMPLES	ld vcls	A
	TEDDY VAUGHN	drms	A

THE DEEP - Psychedelic Moods Of... CD.

45s:	Last Time Around / One And One	(Soft 960) 1966
α	Start From Here / I Don't Wanna Cry	(Charay 16) 1966

NB: α as 'Florida Deep Six'.

From Jacksonville, Florida, this band comprised former members of the Vikings and would evolve into Mouse and The Boys.

Last Time Around graces *Let's Dig 'Em Up* (LP), *Let's Dig 'Em Up, Vol. 1* (CD) and *Psychedelic States - Florida Vol. 2* (CD). It's a majestically simple Invasion-infused beat-punker with an edgy arrogance in the vocals and utterly cool in its restraint. (MW)

Deep Soul Cole

Personnel incl:	FRED COLE	ld vcls, bs	A
	LARRY WILIAMS	gtr	A

45s:	Poverty Shack/Rover	(Eldorado) 1964

NB: acetates only.

Poverty Shack was recorded by none other than Fred Cole, who recorded this 45 in 1963, at the age of 15, at the El Dorado studios in Los Angeles. Cole sings lead and plays bass, Larry Williams plays guitar and is the producer and The Blossoms are the back-up singers. Fred was managed at the time by Mike Tell, son of a Las Vegas newspaper owner. Mike took Fred to L.A. where he stayed for a couple of weeks with Larry Williams, met Stevie Wonder and lots of other black acts. For the cover of the record they dumped a bucket of water over Fred's head, to make him look like he had sweated his guts out. It's the very first recording by this outrageous person and it has resurfaced on *Sixties Rebellion, Vol. 9* (LP & CD). Later Cole would turn up in The Lords, **The Weeds**, **Lollipop Shoppe**, **Zipper**, King Bee, Torpedos, Rats, Desperate Edge, Western Front and, finally, Dead Moon.

Deep Water Reunion

ALBUM:	1	DEEP WATER REUNION	(Jerral 1009) c1970 -

A Minneapolis group, **Deep Water Reunion** (also known as DWR) combined folk-rock, pop and mellow psych-rock. Their rare album includes songs like *Baby Blue*, *Good Morning Starshine*, *Break My Mind*, *Steel Rail Blues* and a cover of the Beatles' *Hey Jude*. (SR)

Deerfield

Personnel:	CHARLIE BRICKLEY	bs, vcls, mandolin	A
	STEVE COLEMAN	lead pedal steel gtr, vcls	A
	JOHN GUERRY	piano, organ, bs	A
	DENNIS HANSON	drms	A
	MICHAEL HICKMAN	gtr, piano	A

ALBUM:	1(A)	NIL DESPERANDUM	(Flat Rock FRS 1) 1971 SC

NB: (1) reissued on CD (Gear Fab GF-148) 2000.

Formed in Houston, Texas in 1968, they were originally known as The Dream Machine. Their album, a mixture of country rock and psychedelia, has attracted increasing interest from collectors. It was issued with a letter (in envelope) stuck inside the cover.

Charles Bickley is now the owner of a small Austin Texas-based label named Buttermilk Records which released several vinyl albums and singles in the seventies. in fact he's stiill releasing 25 year old masters on new vinyl and CD of Texas Blues, Rock, Jazz, Cajun, and more. (CF/MW)

The Defiant 4

45:	Away From My Home/My Time Is Now	(Delta 2195) 196?

This band hailed from New Mexico. The 'A' side resurfaced on *Boulders, Vol. 10* (LP) and *Ya Gotta Have Moxie, Vol. 1* (Dble CD). (VJ)

The Defiants

45:	What I'd Say/?	(Defiant?) 1966

A different New Mexico band. (VJ)

The Defiants

Personnel:	STEVE HENSLIN	ld gtr	A
	JERRY RYER	gtr	A
	MIKE SHAW	bs	ABC
	DUANE SMITH	drms	A
	DICK NEWMAN	ld gtr	B
	LOREN WALSTAD	gtr/ld gtr	BC
	JERRY WHEELER	drms	B
	JOHN COLLINS	gtr	C
	TERRY SHAW	drms	C

NB: Line-up 'A' 1961-1962, 'B' 1963, 'C' 1963-1967.

45:	Maggie's Farm/Bye Bye Johnny	(Studio City Records) 1965

The 'A' side of this sole 45 offering from Minnesota's **Defiants** can also be found on *When The Time Run Out* (LP & CD).

The lynch pin of the band, Mike Shaw started in The Nightbeats in 1960 and played with The Embers in 1961. In 1967 Loren Walstad left the group to join **The Underbeats** and Budd Setzaphant took over lead guitar. This line-up was short-lived, however, as Terry Shaw and John Collins, were soon drafted. Before leaving for service, Terry played a short stint with The Country Ramblers.

When he came home in 1969, Terry formed The Shaw-Allen Trio with Mike Shaw and Jim Allen (rhythm guitar). This act became a popular live attraction, breaking attendance records on the ballroom circuit, and receiving an award from the Ballroom Operators Association each year until their demise in 1975. At different times the band was augmented by Duane Larson (keyboards, harmonica and trumpet) and Danny Grossnickle (lead guitar, keyboards). The band also recorded two albums: *This Side-That Side*" 1970 (as Shaw, Allen and Shaw) and *South Fork Crow River* 1972. In one form or another, the band has continued to this day as the Shaw Band.

A musical family, Mike and Terry Shaw's oldest brother, Dennis, had a band from 1958-1959 called The Chancellors and later The Rockets. Mike's three sons also have a band called the Shaw Brothers.

DEERFIELD - Nil Desperandum CD.

THE DUNWICH RECORDS STORY (Comp LP) including The Del-vetts.

The Del Counts

Personnel incl: KELLY VINCENT   A

ALBUM: 1(A) THE DEL COUNTS (Dove acetate no number) 1964/5 ?

45s:			
(up to 1972)	Let The Good Times Roll/Bird Dog	(Soma 1430)	1966
	What Is The Reason?/With Another Guy	(Soma 1465)	1967
	What Is The Reason?/With Another Guy	(Apex 77058)	1967
	Ain't Got The Time/Don't Ever Leave	(Mar-Bil 109)	1968
	Who Cares/Don't Let The Green Grass	(Hand 2173)	1972

A long standing Minneapolis band who were still rehearsing 45s as late as 1974. The album was never released.

Compilation appearances have included: *Bird Dog* on *Riot City!* (LP), *Soma Records Story, Vol. 1* (LP); *Let The Good Times Roll* on *Gamma Knee Kappa - The Best In Frat Rock* (LP); *Let The Good Times Roll* on *Soma Records Story, Vol. 3* (LP); and *With Another Guy, What Is The Reason, Bird Dog* and *Let The Good Times Roll* on *The Big Hits Of Mid-America - The Soma Records Story* (Dble CD). (VJ)

The Delights

45s:	Long Green/Find Me A Woman	(Delaware 1712) 1965
	Every Minute, Moment, Hour/ Just Out Of Reach	(Smash S-2072) 1966

Based in Chicago this band's *Long Green* was a grungy cover of **The Kingsmen**'s track.

Compilation appearances include: *Long Green* on *Highs In The Mid-Sixties Vol. 4* (LP) and *Pebbles, Vol. 6* (CD); and *Just Out Of Reach, Every Minute, Every Hour, Every Moment* on *The Quill Records Story - The Best Of Chicago Garage Bands* (CD). (VJ)

Delirium

45: Never Comin' Home/?   (Vibra 136) 1967

From Mechanicsville, New York. *Never Comin' Home* found a new home and audience on *Diggin' For Gold, Vol. 7* (LP). (MW)

Del-Rays

Personnel:	BILLY COFIELD	sax	AB
	JOHN DANIELS	drms	AB
	JIMMY RAY HUNTER	vcls	AB
	JIMMY JOHNSON	gtr	AB
	BILLY SCOTT	keyb'ds	AB
	LARRY YORK	bs	AB
	JIM CRONEY	bs	B
	JIMMY EVANS	drms	B
	LOUIE ROBERTSON	keyb'ds	B

45s:	Hot Toddy / ?	(Fame #unkn) 1962
	Night Prowl / Windy And Warm	(R and H 1002) 1964
	Dimples / Fortune Teller	(R And H 1005) 1965
	Like I Do / Fortune Teller	(Atco 6348) 1965

Formed in 1959 in Muscle Shoals, Alabama this band's style predates the British Invasion and garage waves but they're a fine example of the more rockin' sounds around in Deep South in the early-to-mid-sixties. Their debut was a brassy instrumental *Hot Toddy*. Later efforts were in an accomplished frat-pop style, notably garage-band fave *Fortune Teller* (reportedly from 1963 and re-released in 1965).

An expanded line-up reunited for the 1992 Muscle Shoals Bands Of The '60s Reunion concert. The CD of the event (Alabama Music Hall Of Fame 1993-01) captures them swingin' through *Hot Toddy, Love Potion No. 9, Fortune Teller* and *Ya-Ya*.

Fortune Teller had already reappeared on the *Lost Gems From The 60's, Vol. 1* EP and *Like I Do* is on *Searching For Love* (LP). (MW)

The Del-tinos

Personnel incl: MICHAEL "CUB" KODA   gtr   A

ALBUM: 1(A) GO! GO! GO!   (Sounds Interesting 013) 1985

45s:	Go! Go! Go!/Ramrod	(Del-Tino 100) 1963
	Nightlife/Pa Pa Ooh Mau Mau	(Sonic 1451) 1965
	Ramblin' On My Mind/ I Got My Mojo Workin'	(Del-Tino 200) 1966

From Detroit, Michigan, **The Del-tinos** were an early band of Cub Koda. The album is a collection of their goodies on noted collector Erik Lindgren's Sounds Interesting label. In 1969 Koda formed Brownsville Station whose success peaked in 1974 with *Smokin' In the Boys Room*, a massive hit which sold over two million copies. He continued to write and release solo works as well as recording and performing in numerous bands and travelling Oldies road shows. He also wrote about music, via a monthly "Vinyl Junkie" column and as co-author of the 1998 book "Blues For Dummies". Highly-regarded as a purveyor of blues and rockabilly styles, he was dubbed "America's Greatest Houserocker". On the 1st July 2000, at the age of 51, he died of complications arising from kidney dialysis.

Nightlife also got another airing on the *Gone, Vol. 2* (LP) compilation. (VJ/KBn/MW/DSd)

The Del-vetts

Personnel:	LESTER GOLDBOSS	gtr	A
	BOB GOOD	bs	A C
	JIM LAUER	ld vcls, ld gtr	ABC
	PAUL WADE	drms	AB
	JACK BURCHALL	bs	BC
	JEFF WEINSTEIN	gtr	B
	ROGER DEATHERAGE	drms, vcls	C

45s:	Little Latin Lupe Lu/Ram Charger	(Seeburg Jukebox 1018) 1965
	Last Time Around/Everytime	(Dunwich 125) 1966
	I Call My Baby STP/ That's The Way It Is (PS)	(Dunwich 142) 1966

Formed in Chicago back in 1964, playing Chuck Berry covers for kids in the well-to-do Highland Park Suburb of the city. They soon became a popular live attraction and cut a 45, produced by Bill Traut for Seeburg back in 1965, before signing to Traut's Dunwich label to record their magnum opus, *Last Time Around*. This was a superb 45 with some really rousing guitar work and great vocals. Indeed it sold very well locally and, for a while, the group all owned Corvettes.

The follow-up, *I Call My Baby STP*, became something of a hot rod anthem and is now very rare. Picture sleeve copies also included a free STP sticker!

When it didn't happen for **The Del-vetts** they changed their name to the **Pride and Joy**. Their bassist/singer, Jack Burchall, later played with Bloodrock (not the Texas one). He was later in The Jump 'n' The Saddle Band who had a U.S. hit with *The Curly Shuffle*. Jim Lauer is, reportedly, locked away in a mental institution.

Compilation appearances have included: *Last Time Around* on *Off The Wall, Vol. 1* (LP), *Mayhem & Psychosis, Vol. 2* (LP), *Mindrocker, Vol. 2* (LP), *Nuggets Box* (4-CD); *Nuggets, Vol. 2* (LP), *Sundazed Sampler, Vol. 1* (CD), *Early Chicago* (LP) and *Excerpts From Nuggets* (CD); *Ram Charger* on *Pebbles Vol. 4 - Various Hodads* (CD); *Last Time Around, Every Time, That's The Way It Is* on *The Dunwich Records Story* (LP); *Last Time Around, Everytime, I Call My Baby STP, That's The Way It Is* on *Oh Yeah! The Best Of Dunwich Records* (CD). (VJ)

Demian

Personnel:	ROY COX	bs, vcls	A
	DAVID FORE	drms	A
	ROD PRINCE	gtr, vcls	A
	TODD POTTER	gtr, vcls	A

ALBUM: 1(A) DEMIAN (ABC 5718) 1971 R1

NB: (1) has been reissued on CD by TRC (048) 1994.

45: Face The World/Love People (ABC 11297) 1971

Formed from the ashes of **Bubble Puppy** (in which all four had previously played) and signed to ABC on the advice of **Steppenwolf**'s Nick St Nicholas, they took their new name from the title of a Hermann Hesse novel and headed back to Houston after a spell in California. *Face The World* was the gem on an impressive hard-rock album. Later in 1977, Prince and Potter played together in Sirius. (VJ)

The Demons of Negativity

Personnel:	G. ANDREWMANESS	gtr	A
	URSULA DRABIK	voice	A
	RIC HADDAD	drms	A
	ARAM HELLER	bs	A
	ERIC LINDGREN	keyb'ds	A

An eighties combo whose classic slice of modern psychedelia, *Resurrection*, which appeared originally on a 1988 Boston compilation called *These Dogs Live In The Garage/The Arf! Arf! Sampler, Vol. 2*, can now be heard on *Beyond The Calico Wall* (LP & CD), a compilation which Eric Lindgren actually compiled! Modelled on Dave Diamond's sixties acid trip narrative, *The Diamond Mine*, this nugget is every bit as good. Recommended listening.

An instrumental version of *Ressurection* can also be found on *Buzz Buzz Buzzzzzz, Vol. 2* (CD). (VJ)

The Denims

Personnel:	ARNIE BELOSIC	bs, sax	A
	STEVE CURRY	ld vcls	A
	RONNIE LISOWSKI	keyb'ds	A
	PETE PUNCHOWSKI	gtr, ld vcls	A
	DOUG SUPER	ld gtr	A
	MIKE ZACCOR	drms	A

45s:	α	Ya Ya/I'm Your Man	(Columbia 4-43312) 1965
		The Adler Sock/The Adler Sock	(ADI) 1965
	β	Sad Girl/Everybody Let's Dance	(Columbia 4-43367) 1965
		Salty Dog/Salty Dog Man	(Cavort 122333) 1966
		The Ghost In Your House Is Me/	
		I Do Love You Baby	(Mercury 72572) 1966
		White Ship/Salty Dog Man	(Mercury 72613) 1967

NB: α also released in the UK (CBS 201.807). β produced by Bob Johnston, the future producer of Leonard Cohen and Dylan.

This popular New York City band came into being when singer/dancer/actor Steve Curry united with a neighbourhood band from Queens. Their debut *I'm Your Man* is a ringin' rockin' punker with a swinging beat and fluid guitar runs. Shortly after this they were asked to promote the 'Adler Sock' company, the resultant disc being given away with each purchase. Their name proved useful when they were sought out the folowing year by the Scrub Denim Jeans company to do a similar promotion for their 'Salty Dog' brand.

Also in 1966 they met **Jimi Hendrix** when he was playing with **Curtis Knight and The Squires** at The Cheetah club in Manhattan. He even played with them for some engagements at Ondine's, a club frequented at the time by The Rolling Stones prior to their national tour and where they first encountered the soon-to-be-celebrated guitarist.

By the time of their final 45, *White Ship*, they sounded like they were experimenting with LSD:-

"Let me take you on a trip,
A voyage upon a pure white ship,
Of pretty maids, set the costs
Informed me that the ship was boss,
When the waves destroyed the sea
The ship went down with all our sanity
Ride baby ride - so deep in my mind
Ride baby ride - leave reality behind
Oh No!"
(from *White Ship*)

The liner notes to *A Fistful Of Fuzz* state that, contrary to previous belief Adrian Belew was not in this band, but rather a similarly named group from Kentucky. Belew became a renowned guitar player in the seventies playing with **Frank Zappa** and in the eighties was a key member of the resurrected King Crimson, as well as releasing several solo albums.

The band split at the end of 1966 when Punchowski and Zaccor were drafted.

Compilation appearances have included: *I'm Your Man* on *Mindrocker, Vol. 7* (LP), *The Essential Pebbles Collection, Vol. 2* (Dble CD), *Psychedelic Patchwork* (LP) and *Psychedelic States: New York Vol. 1* (CD); *White Ship* on *Boulder Punk EP Box*, *Pebbles, Vol. 7* (LP), *60's Punk E.P., Vol. 1* (7"), *A Fistful Of Fuzz* (CD); *Salty Dog Man* on *Fuzz, Flaykes, And Shakes, Vol. 2* (LP & CD); and *The Adler Sock* on *Highs In The Mid-Sixties, Vol. 9* (LP). (VJ/MW/LP/SR/MM)

DEMIAN - Demian CD.

Denis and The Times

Personnel:	PARIS AIKEN	drms	A
	DEAN BURLAGE	gtr	A
	DENIS BURLAGE	vcls	A
	GUY BURLAGE	ld gtr	A
	SKIP WATTS	bs	A

45s:	Flight Patterns/Just If She's There	(Trend 1036) 1967
	Whenever You Want Me/	
	Denis Dupree From Danville	(Trend 1051) 1969

Denis and The Times were formed by the three Burlage brothers and two friends in Norfolk, Virginia. With promotional help from their father they released their debut 45 in the Fall of 1967 - and Dad should've been proud, 'cause his boys produced a classic that's revered to this day.

From the opening ringing chords to the final flourish of spacey effects, *Flight Patterns* is a wondrous piece of *8 Miles High*-inspired psychedelic folk-rock complete with freakout guitar break. Good enough indeed to have graced **The Byrds**' *Younger Than Yesterday* or *Fifth Dimension* platters. Compilers seem to agree - you'll find it on *30 Seconds Before The Calico Wall* (CD), *Sixties Rebellion, Vol. 9* (LP & CD) and *Aliens, Psychos And Wild Things* (CD). The flip ain't half bad either - check it out on *Killer Cuts* (LP) and *Ear-Piercing Punk* (CD).

Their second 45 was released in the Spring of '69. *Whenever...* is a heavy pop ballad with strident vocals and punctuated by fuzz attacks. The flip is a faithful cover of the Cryan' Shames (on their *Scratch In The Sky* album) - but with a harder edge and burnin' guitar. (VJ/MW/BHr/ST)

Denise & Co

A really obscure girl garage group about whom nothing is known. They have *Boy, What Will You Do Then*, an R&B influenced punker with cool lyrics, included on *Girls In The Garage, Vol. 1* (LP & CD). (VJ)

Depot Rains

Personnel incl:	DENNY FRY	vcls	A
	NICK HADCLIFF	drms	A
	LENNY SLOAT	gtr	A

From Muscatine, Iowa, this folk-rock outfit emerged out of two of the town's early garage bands:- **The Rogues** and The Coachmen. The *Dirty Water - The History Of Eastern Iowa Rock Volume 2* (LP) compilation features two of the fruits of a 1968 recording session at RCA's studio in Chicago:- *7-1 1 Hour (Whiskey Hollow)*, a Denny Fry folk-rocker and *I Am Lost*, another folk number written by Lenny Sloat with Lenny performing on vocals. (VJ)

Derby-Hatville

45s:	Turn Into Earth/You'll Forget Me	(Sea-Ell 102) 1967
	Scorched Sand/Instant Replay	(Sea-Ell 104) 1968

Hailed from Lubbock in West Texas and made nil impression. Their different treatment of The Yardbirds' *Turn Into Earth* can be found on *Highs In The Mid-Sixties, Vol. 12* (LP), whilst *The History Of Texas Garage Bands, Vol. 1 - The Sea Ell Label Story* (Dble CD) features four 1967 tracks - *You'll Forget Me*, *Instant Replay*, *Scorched Sand* and the unreleased *This Girl* (an early version of *Instant Replay*). (MW)

The Descendants

45:	Lela/Garden Of Eden	(MTA 112) 1966

A group of high school teens from Yonkers, New York - NOT San Francisco as previously touted. *Lela* is a frantic punker with an instantly catchy Bo Diddley shuffle-beat. It was co-written by Bronx-based producer Ted Varnick, who was also behind a fine 45 by **The Alley Cats**.

30 SECONDS BEFORE THE CALICO WALL (Comp CD) including Denis and The Times.

Compilation appearances have included: *Lela* on *Pebbles, Vol. 7* (LP), *Sounds Of The Sixties San Francisco, Vol. 1* (LP), *Bo Did It!* (LP) and *Psychedelic States: New York Vol. 1* (CD). (MW)

Destiny's Children

45:	Your First Time/The Fall Of The Queen	(Ventural 730) c1966

A Houston, Texas outfit. The flip to their sole 45, *The Fall Of The Queen*, has resurfaced on *Sixties Rebellion, Vol. 2* (LP), *Sixties Rebellion, Vol's 1 & 2* (CD) and *Teenage Shutdown, Vol. 10* (LP & CD). (VJ)

Destiny's Children

Personnel:	MARK COURTER	drms	A

45:	For Me/The Collectors	(Pyro 52) 1966

From Phoenix, Arizona, both sides of this 45 contain excellent punk, and have re-appeared on *Legend City, Vol. 1* (LP & CD), *The Garage Zone, Vol. 1* (LP), *Ya Gotta Have Moxie, Vol. 1* (Dble CD) and *The Garage Zone Box Set* (4-LP). (VJ)

Detroit

Personnel:	JOHN "THE BEE" BADANJEK	drms, vcls	A
	W.R. COOKE	bs, vcls	A
	DIRTY ED	congas, tamb	A
	STEVE "DECATOR GATOR" HUNTER	ld gtr	A
	HARRY PHILLIPS	keyb'ds	A
	MITCH RYDER	ld vcls	A
	BRETT TUGGLE	gtr	A
	(BOOT HILL	keyb'ds, hrmnca	A)
	(MARK MANKO	gtr	A)
	(JOHN SAUTER	bs	A)

ALBUM:	1(A)	DETROIT	(Paramount PAS 6010) 1971 -

NB: There's also a retrospective live album, *Get Out To Vote - Live At The Hill Auditorium 1st April 1972* (Total Energy) 1997.

45s:	It Ain't Easy/ Long Neck Goose	(Paramount PAA-0094) 1971
	Rock 'N' Roll/Box Of Old Roses	(Paramount PAA-0133) 1971
	Gimmie Shelter/	
	Oh Oh, La La La, Dee Da Doo	(Paramount PAA-0158) 1972

Produced by Bob Ezrin and recorded in Toronto, **Detroit** was a fine example of the "High Energy" bands coming out of Michigan, like **MC5**, the **Stooges** or **Frost**. Formed by **Mitch Ryder** and his stalwart drummer John Badanjek, with Phillips and Cook (both ex Catfish), Steve Hunter and Dirty Ed, their music was a powerful mix of hard-rock and rhythm and blues. Their material ranged from original cuts penned by **Ryder** and Badanjek, to covers of *Let It Rock*, Lou Reed's *Rock 'n' Roll* and Wilson Pickett's *I Found A Love*. Erzin and Steve Hunter would later work with Lou Reed and Alice Cooper.

1997 saw the release of a live show recorded in 1972 and produced by John Sinclair, the Detroit DJ associated with **MC5**.

You can also find *Rock 'n' Roll* on *Michigan Rocks, Vol. 1*. (SR)

Detroit Riots

| 45: | Pebble Stone/A Fast Way To Die | (Dearborn D-582) 1967/8 |

Minor league garage from a label named after the Southwest surburb of Detroit which had an active garage scene, highlighted by Cicadelic's *Psychedelic Sixties, Vol. 3*, which compiles the area's other garage label Wheels 4.

Compilation appearances include: *A Fast Way To Die* on *Sixties Rebellion, Vol. 16* (LP & CD). (MW)

The Detroit Wheels

Personnel incl?:	JOHN BADANJEK	drms	A
	JOE CUBERT	gtr	A
	JIM MCCARTY	gtr	A

45s:	Linda Sue Dixon/ Tally Ho	(Inferno I-5002) 1968
	Think (About The Good Times)/	
	For The Love Of A Stranger	(Inferno I-5003) 1968

Recorded after **Mitch Ryder** went solo, two interesting heavy-rock singles with wailing lead guitars. (SR)

Deuces Wild

| 45: | Hey Little One/Come Easy Go | (Deuce 101/2) 1966 |

Both sides of the Amarillo outfit's psychedelic 45 can be found on *Texas Punk, Vol. 10* (LP). The 'A' side was a haunting song and the flip made interesting use of reverb and echo. The Deuces Wild on Faro and Vault were a different outfit from California. (VJ)

DEVILED HAM - I Had Too Much To Dream Last Night LP.

Deviled Ham

| ALBUM: | 1 | I HAD TOO MUCH TO DREAM LAST NIGHT |
| | | (Super K 6003) 1968 SC |

The album, produced by Big Al Pavlow, contains many cover versions, including *Come On In* and *Alligator WIne* (which is awful), as well as a medley comprising the title track (given slower and tedious treatment compared to the original) and *Rosemary's Baby*. They were previously known as **The Ascots**, from Rhode Island, who had issued four soulish 45s on the local Super label.

Generally the album is best avoided. (VJ)

The Devilles

45s:	You've Made Up My Mind/Baby Blue	(Kerry 1109) 1966
	Ma Ma's Baby/Denise	(Kerry 1110) 1966
	Cry Baby/High Blood Pressure	(Studio City 1045) 1966

A teen rather than garage band from Duluth, Minnesota. All three discs are reputedly good and now quite sought-after. The band later became **Second Thought** and recorded three 45s on the Gloria label.

Compilation appearances have included: *You've Made Up My Mind* on *Root '66* (LP); *High Blood Pressure* on *Gamma Knee Kappa - The Best In Frat Rock* (LP) and *Mama's Baby* on *Hipsville, Vol. 3* (LP). (VJ)

Devils

See the **Bentleys** entry.

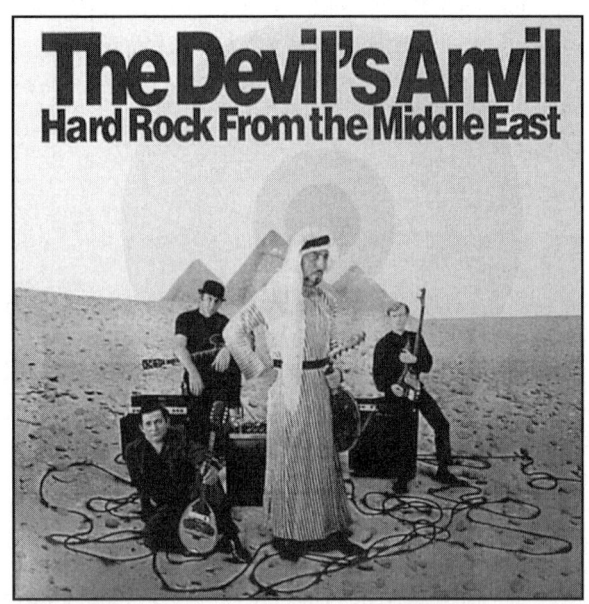

DEVIL'S ANVIL - Hard Rock From The Middle East LP.

Devil's Anvil

Personnel:	ELIEZER ADORAM	accordion	A
	KAREEM ISSAY	oud, vcls	A
	STEVE KNIGHT	gtr, bs, bouzouki	A
	JERRY SAPPIR	ld gtr, vcls	A
	(BOBBY GREGG	drms	A)
	(HERB LOVELLE	drms	A
	(MIKE MOGEL	durbeki	A)
	(FELIX PAPPALARDI	bs, gtr, tamboura, perc, vcls	A)

| ALBUM: | 1(A) | HARD ROCK FROM THE MIDDLE EAST |
| | | (Columbia CS 9464) 1967 R1 |

NB: (1) reissued on CD together with the **Freak Scene** album. Also reissued on vinyl by Fantasia in 1999 (Shaitun DVA 1031).

45:	Karkadon / Hala Laya (PS)	(Columbia 4-43817)	1966

This New York band were heavily influenced by Oriental and Greek music. Seven songs are sung in Arabic, two in Greek and one in Turkish. *Misirlou* is sung in English by Pappalardi. All of their songs were covers of traditional or popular numbers. Musically the album is in a similar vein to **Orient Express**, **Kaleidoscope** and **John Berberian**. Steve Knight and Felix Pappalardi went on to play for **Mountain**. Bobby Gregg played with Eric Anderson, John Cale and Bob Dylan among others. (VJ/MW)

Devil's Brigade

45s:	Dreaming Is/Hey Mister Man	(United Artists UA 50291)	1968
	Hey Nonna Na/Blue Plastic Spoons	(Mainstream 702)	1969

The first 45 contains harmonious orchestrated pop-psych with baroque touches, which may appeal to **Left Banke** fans. The second, which may be by a different group, consists of heavy blues-derived rock with a soulful singer and much (unsatisfactory) guitar and organ to the fore. (MW/MK)

Dialogue

ALBUM:	1 DIALOGUE	(No label) 1973	R2

NB: (1) was repressed in 1974 on Cold Studio. R2. The first pressing had no mention of Cold Studio anywhere. Both came with inserts.

This obscure psychedelic album, from Pennsylvania, is a significant collectors' item. It will mainly interest fans of rock a lá Badfinger, Beatles or early McCartney. (CF/SR)

Dave Diamond and The Higher Elevation

45:	The Diamond Mine/Crazy Bicycle	(Chicory 408)	1967

Dave Diamond was a Los Angeles disc jockey and on this 45 he was backed by the **Higher Elevation** from Greeley, Colorado. Previously known as **The Monocle**'s, *Diamond Mine* was actually a reworking of one of their earlier tracks *The Spider And The Fly*.

Diamond Mine is a classic 'weirdo' song.

In 1979, the track was also covered by The Wicked and their version can be heard on Arf! Arf!'s *Only in America* (CD).

Compilation appearances have included: *The Diamond Mine* on *Pebbles, Vol. 3* (LP), *Pebbles, Vol. 3 - The Acid Gallery* (CD), *Pebbles Box* (5-LP), *Pebbles, Vol. 2 (ESD)* (CD), *Psychedelic Unknowns, Vol. 2* (LP), *Sixties Rebellion, Vol. 12* (LP & CD) and *Trash Box* (5-CD). (VJ/MW)

Johnny Diamond and The Royal Five

45:	Thanks A Lot Baby / Pretty Little Girl	(Soft 981)	1966

From Fort Worth, Texas, they later evolved into **The Bards**.

Dickens

45:	Sho' Need Love/		
	Don't Talk About My Music	(Scepter SCE 12322)	c1969

An obscure group, possibly with future members of **NRBQ**. (SR)

Dick Rabbit

45s:	Take Me To L.A./You Come On Like A Train	(Deltron 895)	196?
	Trip/Love	(Great Lakes)	196?

A heavy rock three-piece from the Saginaw/Flint area of Michigan. The 'B' side to their first 45, *You Come On Like A Train*, is a hard rocker with some good guitar work. The 'A' side, *Take Me To L.A.*, isn't quite as heavy and has quite a commercial slant to it. On their second 45, *Love*, captures the band at their most psychedelic and demented, but *Trip* is rather disappointing by comparison.

Compilation appearances have included: *Take Me To L.A.* and *You Come On Like A Train* on *Michigan Mixture, Vol. 1* (LP); *Love* and *Trip* on *Michigan Mixture, Vol. 2* (LP); and *You Come On Like A Train* on *Sixties Archive, Vol. 6* (CD). (VJ/KBn)

Dick Watson 5

Personnel:	JIM McCARTHY		A

ALBUMS:	1(A)	BAKER STREET	(United International 1001) 19??	R1
	2( )	THE WORLD OF DICK WATSON		
			(United International) 196?	R1

NB: (2) unconfirmed.

45s:	I'd Do It Again/		
	A Married Man	(United International UI 1014)	19??
	I'll Make It Up Some Other Way/?	(United International)	1965/6

This band recorded a rare local New Jersey album. One track, *Cold Clear World*, has resurfaced on *Highs In The Mid-Sixties, Vol. 22* (LP) and *Pebbles, Vol. 3 (ESD)* (CD).

Jim McCarthy was in this band prior to forming **The Godz**, and recalls that *Baker Street* was their take on a rock'n'roll Broadway musical. (VJ/DSb)

The Different Parts

Personnel incl:	STEVE BROUSSARD	A
	RON VICE	A

45:	Why / I	(AMS AMS-001)	1967

An Abbeville, Louisiana aggregation whose sole 45 was released on manager Allen Schriefer's vanity label. *Why* is five-star moody folk-punk with a sinuous blending of jangle and fuzz; *I* is a lightweight beat ballad. Both sides reappeared on *Follow That Munster, Vol. 1* (LP) and *Why* has also resurfaced on *Psychedelic Crown Jewels, Vol. 3* (CD). (MW/RM)

Cheryl Dilcher

ALBUMS:	1 SPECIAL SONGS	(Ampex)	1971 -
	2 BUTTERFLY	(A&M SP-4394)	1973 -
	3 BLUE SAILORS	(Butterfly)	1977 -

From Allentown, Pennsylvania, a pretty hippie folk-pop singer/songwriter who began in the coffee circuit. Some of her songs were included in the

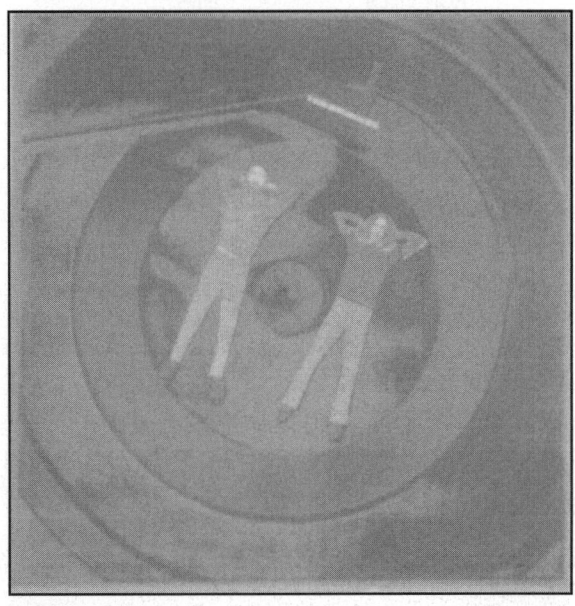

DIALOGUE - Dialogue LP.

Hippie Goddesses CD compilation but her albums on A&M and Butterfly are quite lame. (SR)

The Dimensions

Personnel:	JACK BRUNSFIELD	drms	A
	BARRE PROBST	ld gtr, vcls	A
	STEVE PURNELL	gtr, keyb'ds	A
	JIM SEBASTIAN	vcls	A
	TOM?	bs	A

ALBUM: 1(A) FROM ALL DIMENSIONS (No label 1666) 1966 R6

NB: (1) pirated on vinyl by Eva (12018) 198?. (1) reissued on CD (Collectables).

From Park Ridge, Illinois. The album is a classic of the 'prep-rock' garage genre, rather like the **Rising Storm** album, only this supposedly had a pressing of just 100 making it a mega-buck rarity. The Eva reissue has an extra track and costs a lot less! (VJ/MW)

THE DIMENSIONS - From All Dimensions LP.

The Dimensions (Five)

Personnel:	LEE DARK	ld vcls	A
	CLYDE HEATON	keyb'ds	A
	BILL HOAK	bs	A
	JOE VILLA	gtr	A
	RON VILLA	drms	A

45s:	She's Boss/Penny	(Panorama 25) 1966
	She's Boss/Penny	(HBR 477) 1966
	Baby What Do You Say/Knock You Flat	(Panorama 41) 1966

A garage outfit, from the Rainier Beach area of South Seattle and influenced by **The Viceroys**. Their finest moment, *She's Boss* was captured on *Battle Of The Bands, Vol. 1* (LP) in 1966. It's a stark garage punker, which although a regional hit, deserved to do better.

All the band members grew up / went to South Seattle schools, 'Franklin' and 'Rainier Beach' and presumably the band were either formed in High School or college. By 1967, however, **The Dimensions** had cratered and a new band formed called **Lyte**.

Clyde Heaton later played with **Calliope**. Bill Hoak became a born-again Christian and moved to Nashville for a time before settling in Knoxville. Lee Dark became a hairdresser and Joe Villa was last heard to be teaching music at Cornish College in Seattle.

Retrospective compilation appearances have included: *Penny* and *She's Boss* on *Northwest Battle Of The Bands, Vol. 1 - Flash And Crash* (CD); *Knock You Flat* on *Northwest Battle Of The Bands, Vol. 2 - Knock You Flat!* (LP & CD), *History Of Northwest Rock, Vol. 2 - The Garage Years* (CD) and *Northwest Battle Of The Bands, Vol. 2* (CD); *She's Boss* on *The History Of Northwest Rock, Vol. 2* (LP) and *Northwest Battle Of The Bands, Vol. 1* (CD); and *Penny* on *Bad Vibrations, Vol. 1* (LP & CD). (MW/DR/RCn)

The Dinks

45s:	Nina-Kocha-Nina/Penny A Tear Drop	(Sully 914) 1965
	Ugly Girl/Kocka-Mow-Mow	(Sully 925) 1966

This odd bunch originally hailed from Beloit in Kansas, but appear to have relocated to West Texas. *Nina-Kocha-Nina* and *Kocka-Mow-Mow* are both more frat-rock / 'trash' than garage with slightly demented nonsensical lyrics. The flip to the first 45, *Penny A Tear Drop* is a folk-rocker.

Compilation appearances include: *Ugly Girl* on *The Lost Generation, Vol. 2* (LP); *Kocka-Mow-Mow* on *Monsters Of The Midwest, Vol. 4* (LP) and *Midwest Garage Band Series - Kansas* (LP); *Penny A Tear Drop* on *Texas Punk, Vol. 9* (LP) and *Acid Visions - Complete Collection, Vol. 3* (3-CD); and *Nina-Kocka-Nina* on *Boulders, Vol. 6* (LP).

Dino, Desi and Billy

Personnel:	DEZI ARNAZ JR.	A
	BILL HINSCHE	A
	DINO MARTIN	A

ALBUMS:	1	I'M A FOOL	(Reprise R(S)-6176) 1965 -
(selective)	2	OUR TIMES ARE COMING	(Reprise R(S)-6194) 1966 -
	3	MEMORIES ARE MADE OF THIS	
			(Reprise R(S)-6198) 1966 -
	4	SOUVENIR	(Reprise R(S)-6224) 1966 -

			HCP
45s:	Since You Broke My Heart/We Know	(Reprise 0324) 1964	
	I'm A Fool/So Many Ways	(Reprise 0367) 1965	17
	Not The Loving Kind/		
	Chimes Of Freedom	(Reprise 0401) 1965	25
	The Rebel Kind/		
	Please Don't Fight It (PS)	(Reprise 0426) 1965	60
	Superman/I Can't Get Her Off My Mind	(Reprise 0444) 196?	94
	It's Just The Way You Are/Tie Me Down	(Reprise 0462) 1966	-
	Look Out, Girls/		
	She's So Far Out, She's In	(Reprise 0496) 1966	-
	I Hope She's There Tonight/Josephine	(Reprise 0529) 1966	-
	Pretty Flamingo/		
	If You're Thinking What I Am	(Reprise 0544) 1966	128
	Two In The Afternoon/		
	Good Luck, Best Wishes To You	(Reprise 0579) 1967	99

DIRTY FILTHY MUD - The Forest Of Black 45 PS.

Kitty Doyle/Without Hurtin' Some	(Reprise 0619)	1967 108
My, What A Shame/Inside Outside	(Reprise 0653)	1967 -
Tell Someone You Love Them/ General Outline	(Reprise 0698)	1968 92
Someday/Through Spray Colored Glasses	(UNI 55127)	1969 -
Hawley/Let's Talk It Over	(CBS 44975)	1969 -
Lady Love/A Certain Sound	(Reprise 0965)	1970 -

Dino is Dean Martin's son, Desi is Desi Arnaz' kid and Billy Hinsche played with the Beach Boys road show (his sister married Carl Wilson). Dino died in a 1987 plane crash and his younger brother Ricci has reformed the group as Ricci, Desi & Billy.

There's also an album called *The Rebel Kind! The Best Of* (Sundazed SC 11034) 1996 which was issued on CD only. It contains 20 tracks (all their single 'A' sides plus many non-album sides). They enjoyed quite a bit of chart success over the years.

Compilation appearances include *I'm A Fool* on *Even More Nuggets* (CD). (VJ/EW)

Phill Dirt and The Mound Builders

Personnel incl: TOM HECKMAN A

ALBUM: 1(A) IT'S PRETTY MUCH A PRIVATE GOOBER
(Private Pressing) 1967 SC?

This little-known group played a mix of acid folk and jug music. The band formed in Maynard, Massachusetts in the Summer of 1967 and most of its members were students at Denison University in Ohio. About 500 copies were made and most of these were sold at school. (SR/THn)

Dirty Blues Band

Personnel:			
PAT MALONE (PAT MALONEY)	keyb'ds	AB
JOHN MILLIKEN	drms	A
LES MORRISON	bs	A
ROD 'GINGERMAN' PIAZZA	vcls, hrmnca	AB
GLENN ROSS (CAMPBELL)	gtr	A
ROBERT SANDELL	gtr	A
GREGG ANDERSON	bs	B
RICK LUNETTA	gtr	B
DAVE MITER	drms	B
(JIMMY FORREST	sax	B)
(WILLIE GREEN	sax	B)
(FREDDIE HILL	trumpet	B)

ALBUMS: 1(A) DIRTY BLUES BAND (ABC-Bluesway BLS 6010) 1967 -
2 STONE DIRT (ABC-Bluesway BLS 6020) 1968 -

NB: (1) and (2) also issued in the U.K. by Stateside.

Both are traditional electric blues albums, dominated by Piazza's fiery vocals and harmonica. Piazza later formed the Southside Blues Band with George "Harmonica" Smith, who were subsequently re-named Bacon Fat by Mike Vernon of Blue Horizon. The band was based in Southern California. (CF/SR)

Dirty Filthy Mud

Personnel incl: KYLE HUNTER A

45: The Forest Of Black/
Morning Sun Flower (PS) (Worex R-2340) 1968

From Oakland, California, this band recorded their only 45 at Sierra Sound Labs in Berkeley. It was issued in a thick cardboard art sleeve like the **Frumious Bandersnatch** and **Country Joe and The Fish** EP's (which explains why it is often referred to as an "EP"!). *The Forest Of Black* is one of the most blatantly psychedelic recordings from the Bay Area sixties scene, with wild electronic effects and druggy lyrics that seem to have been inspired by **Country Joe**'s *Bass Strings*:

"I go down to the seashore to wash my brain
When I go down to the seashore to wash my brain
I never come back feelin' the same now
I never come back feelin' the same
What do I see in the sea?
What do I see in the sea?
Well, it's me lookin' deep inside of me
I said it's me lookin' deep inside of me
I said it's me... yeaaoww!
(from *The Forest of Black*)

The original 45 has become very expensive and nearly impossible to locate at any price.

Compilation appearances have included: *Forest Of Black* on *Psychedelic Experience, Vol. 2* (CD), *The Psychedelic Experience, Vol. 2* (LP), *Endless Journey - Phase Three* (LP) and *Endless Journey - Phase I & II* (CD). (CF)

Dirty John's Hot Dog Stand

Personnel:		
P.J. COLT		A
CAREY MANN JR		A
STANLEY MELILLO		A
A. MERCURIE		A
KENNY PAULSON		A

ALBUM: 1(A) RETURN FROM THE DEAD
(Amsterdam 12004) 1970 R1/R2

NB: (1) a large percentage of known copies have a poor pressing.

45: Hard Driving Man/Growing Old (Amsterdam AM 85014) 1970

Produced by Charlie Dreyer and Bobby Hern, this Boston quintet released their only album in 1970. Carey Mann (ex-**Ill Wind**) and P.J.Colt wrote four of the nine tracks (*Hard Driving Man, Growing Old, Living In A Cloud, River*). Some excellent tracks, especially *Growing Old* which contains, slowly rotating, grinding fuzz-filled psych, with an ethereal trumpet and a heart-felt solo guitar. A cover of Irving Berlin's *Blue Skies* (7'10" of guitar and thunder noises) has its moments, but alas there's also some very regrettable soul-blues crossover with horns (*Hard Driving Man*). The album comes in a great gatefold cover with a hearse, mushrooms and a forest made of musicians' heads.

According to Aram Heller's New England bible, *'Til The Stroke Of Dawn*, they came from the New England area. (MK/AH/MW/SR/CF)

DIRTY JOHN'S HOT DOG STAND - Return From The Dead LP.

Dirty Martha

Recorded at MSI Studios in Camden in the late sixties - *She's Not There* is the Zombies song with some overwrought male vocals, the flip by Murray Goodman and Terry Wade is a laid-back lounge-ballad with piano and brassy crescendos. Just a coincidence or is there some connection between this group and another New Jersey bunch called **Victoria**, given that the latter's music was published in 1971 by Dirty Martha Music Co.? (MW)

Dirty Shames

Personnel incl:	BOB LARSEN?	A
	MARTY WONS?	A

45:	I Don't Care/Makin' Love	(Impression 112) 1966

Los Angeles area punkers whose one excellent 45 has been well compiled. *Makin' Love* was also covered by **The Sloths**.

Compilation appearances have included: *I Don't Care* on *Pebbles, Vol. 8* (CD), *60's Punk E.P., Vol. 1* (7"), *Boulders Punk EP Box*, *Teenage Shutdown, Vol. 14* (LP & CD) and *Highs In The Mid-Sixties, Vol. 2* (LP); and *Makin' Love* on *Vile Vinyl, Vol. 1* (LP), *Vile Vinyl* (CD) and *Garage Punk Unknowns, Vol. 4* (LP). (VJ/MW/MM)

Dirty Shames

45s:	Coconut Grove/Walk Away	(Philips 40436) 1967
	Blow Your Mind/	
	Would You Like To Take A Ride	(Philips 40474) 1967

Two lads and a lass from Montana who delivered two platters of breezy harmony-pop and folk-rock. *Blow Your Mind* has reappeared on *I'm Trippin' Alone* (LP). *Coconut Grove* was a cover of a **Lovin' Spoonful** song. (MM/MW)

Dirty Wurds

45s:	Why/Takin' My Blues Away	(Marina 502) 1966
	Born In Chicago/Midnight Hour	(Chess 1983) 1967
	Not This One /	
	Mellow Down Easy (PS)	(Caped Crusader CC-76) 1996

This band operated from Chicago. Their screeching punk single *Why* is a 'must have'. In 1996 Mark Prellberg's Caped Crusader label released a 45 of unreleased nuggets from 1966.

Compilation appearances have included: *Why* on *Mayhem & Psychosis, Vol. 1* (LP), *Mayhem & Psychosis, Vol. 1* (CD), *Pebbles, Vol. 5* (CD), *Pebbles, Vol. 5* (LP) and *Great Pebbles* (CD). (VJ/MW)

Disciple

ALBUM:	1	COME AND SEE US AS WE ARE
		(Avco Embassy AVE 33015) 1970 SC

45:	Better Than You (Mental So) / ?	(Avco 4536) 1970

A soft psych-pop act with mixed male/female vocals, decent guitar and organ. Their album inludes a cover of The Beatles' *Got To Get You Into My Life*. (SR)

The Disciples

45:	It's Over/Respect	(Feature Records SS-9427) 196?

This killer punk 45 was recorded in Minneapolis, but the band came from Norman on the Southern perimeter of Oklahoma City, Oklahoma. (VJ)

The Disciples of Shaftesbury

45:	My Cup Is Full/	
	Times Gone By	(International Artists 109) 1966

Essentially a pop outfit from Houston, Texas judging by *Times Gone By* which can now be heard on *International Artists Singles Collection* (LP). Nonetheless, the 45 is one of the more sought-after on the label. (VJ)

Disraeli

Personnel:	AL	vcls	A
	MATHE MATHRE	vcls	A
	TOM STANGLAND	ld gtr	A
	ROGER		A
	STEVE		A
	GENO		A

45s:	What Will The New Day Bring/	
	Spinnin' Round (PS)	(Mantra 113) 1968
	Say You Love Me/	
	I've Seen Her One Time (PS)	(Mantra 114) 1969
	The Lonely One/You Can't Do That	(Mantra 115) 1969
	Tomorrow's Day/Humidity	(Mantra #?) 196?

From Astoria, Oregon. Their first 45 kicks off with a wistful folk-rocker backed by a more up-tempo soft-rocker. Their other 45s remain elusive but based on this one, worth searching out. (MW)

Distant Cousins

Personnel:	RAYMOND BLOODWORTH	A
	LARRY BROWN	A

HCP

45s:	Let It Ring/To Have And To Hold	(Dynovox 203) 1965 -
	Slipper Your Mind/Empty House	(Dynovoice 208) 1965 -
	Gently Goodbye/No More You (PS)	(Date 1501) 1966 -
	Here Today, Gone Tomorrow/	
	She Ain't Lovin' You	(Date 1514) 1966 102
	Stop Runnin' Round Baby/	
	Take This Woman Will You	(Date 1542) 1966 -
	Empty House/	
	Mr. Sebastian (Write Me A Song)	(Date 1560) 1967 -

The Big Apple's answer to Peter & Gordon? This New York duo's 45s should appeal to fans of crisp'n'classy beat, pop and folk-rock with a garagey edge. They wrote (and co-wrote, mainly with N. Nader or producer Bob Crewe) nearly all of their material. If their names seem familiar, it's because their songwriting talents were appreciated by others, including: - **Richard & The Young Lions** - the classic *Open Up Your Door*, *You Can Make It*, *Nasty*, *Lost And Found* and a cover of **Distant Cousins'** *To Have And To Hold* and **Missing Links** - *Behind Locked Doors* and *You Don't Love Me Anymore*.

She Ain't Lovin' You, which was a big hit in Ohio and made some impression nationally, has been compiled on *Boulders, Vol. 10* (LP) and *Ya Gotta Have Moxie, Vol. 1* (Dble CD). *Let It Ring* - a vibrant Beatlesque raver - also adorns *Psychotic Reactions* (LP). (MW/GGI/VJ)

The Distant Galaxy

See **Don Sebesky**.

The Distant Sounds

45:	It Reminds Me/Dreamin'	(Citation 17371/2) 1966

Cool swingin' garage-beat from Worcester, Massachusetts. The flip is a slow guitar instrumental in the Shadows' mould.

Compilation appearances have included *It Reminds Me* on *Bad Vibrations, Vol. 1* (LP). (MW)

Distortions

45s:			
	Hound Dog / Can You Tell	(Sea 100)	196?
	Take This Ring / You Know I'm On My Way	(Sea 101)	196?
	Smokestack Lightning / Hot Cha	(Sea 102)	196?
	I Ain't Gonna Eat Out My Heart Anymore / Thank ...	(Malcolm Z.Dirge 45000)	196?
	Smokestack Lightning / Behind My Wall	(Malcolm Z.Dirge 45002)	1966
	A Love That Loves You / Behind My Wall	(Smash S-2068)	1966
	I Don't Really Like You / I Found A Girl	(Casino 501)	1967
α	Let's Spend Some Time Together / Gimme Some Lovin'	(Malcolm Z.Dirge 45008)	1968

NB: α also released on Capitol (2223) 1968.

From the Southern shores of Louisiana. Embracing beat, folk-rock and garage styles but with a strong soul/R&B flavour, they're generally labelled as 'soul-garage', if that's your bag. But don't write them off if it isn't - the Casino 45 is a fine example of low-key garage-ballads. *I Don't Really Like You* in particular is in a muted Searchers/**Beau Brummels** folk-rocker style and is a cover of Baton Rouge's Canebreak (aka Canebreak Singers) who would later be known as Love-Michael, with one 45 on Columbia. (MW/MM)

The "D" Men

Personnel:	DON ASKEW	(lyrics only)	AB
	RICK ENGLER	gtr	AB
	DOUG FERRARA	bs	AB
	BILL SHUTE	gtr	AB
	WAYNE WADHAMS	keyb'ds, ld vcls	AB
	CHUCK LEGROS	ld vcls	B
	(KEVIN GAVIN	vcls	)

NB: Kevin Gavin was the band's manager, but helped out recording some of the group's vocals.

45s:	Don't You Know/No Hope For Me	(Veep V 1206) 1964
	I Just Don't Care/Mousin' Around	(Veep V 1209) 1965
	So Little Time/Every Minute Of Every Day	(Kapp 691) 1965

A Stamford, Connecticut combo originally known as The Demen. Their name was truncated by a Veep publicist who also insisted that each member have a D-name (Dwayne, Don, D'Arcy, Duke, D.Wm)...

Their debut single, a garagey beat-pop affair in the style of The Searchers, was picked as a hit by Billboard, Cashbox, and Record World, but when the parent label, UA, decided to promote Shirley Bassey's *Theme From Goldfinger* heavily instead, it failed to make the charts.

For their second effort, they got to perform *I Just Don't Care* on Hullabaloo on March 30th, 1965, but again it failed to ignite the public's interest. The flip, *Mousin' Around* was a surf-style instrumental.

Their final 45, *So Little Time* is teen pop-punk, influenced by **The Beau Brummels** with some nicely reverberating guitar chops.

Askew and Wadhams went on to become **The Fifth Estate** who released several 45s on Jubilee and one on Red Bird. You can find much of the **D-Men** and **Fifth Estate** material on the *Ding Dong: The Witch Is Back* CD retrospective.

Compilation appearances have also included *So Little Time* on *Psychedelic Unknowns, Vol. 8* (LP & CD). (MW/LP)

DMZ

45:	Somewhere In Between/ Somewhere In Between - Part 2	(MTA 135) 1967

Echoey harmony-pop with baroque flourishes, effects and some orchestration. The flip is an instrumental take and would be ideal as a soundtrack for one of those 'swinging sixties' movies. (MW)

DR. JOHN, THE NIGHT TRIPPER - Gris Gris CD.

Doctor Feelgood

Personnel:	RALPH COOPER	perc	A
	BILLY "SONNY" CORELLE	bs	A
	PAUL RIVERS	gtr	A
	DICK WINTERS	horns, vcls	A

ALBUM: 1(A) SOMETHING TO TAKE UP TIME
(Number One) 1971 R1?

From Massachusetts, a bluesy underground rock outfit, unrelated to the more well-known UK bunch, but presumably named after the same R&B standard. The album with a flute played in the early Jethro Tull style, contains originals with track titles like *Nasal Greens And Toe Jam*, *The Roach Did It* and *Smoke Dream*.

Winters, Cooper and Corelle were all in a 1963 Beverly, Massachusetts based group named the Sensations. Shortly after the group renamed themselves **Teddy and The Pandas**, Winters left the group, then Cooper. Winters and Cooper went on to form another North Shore based band named the Warlocks.

When Teddy Dewart left the **Pandas**, Paul Rivers took his place as lead guitar. Soon after being dragged into the 'Bosstown Sound' and *Basic Magnetism* album debacle by their management, the **Pandas** folded (about 1969). Corelle and Rivers joined with the by-then-defunct Warlocks players Winters and Cooper to form the jazz oriented **Doctor Feelgood**.

Dick Winters had the remarkable ability to play two horns at once in any combination of flute and/or saxophone. (SR/BW)

Dr. John, The Night Tripper

Personnel incl:	DIDIMUS	perc	ABCD
	RONNY BARRON	keyb'ds	A
	HAROLD BATTISTE	bs	AB
	BUDDY BOLDEN	flute	A
	JOHN BOUDREAUX	drms	A
	DAVE "GONCY O'LEARY"		
	DIXON	perc	AB
	SHIRLEY GOODMAN	vcls	AB
	JESSIE HILL	vcls, perc	AB
	DR JOHN	vcls, gtr, keyb'ds	ABCD
	PLAS JOHNSON	sax	A
	JOANIE JONES	vcls	AB
	TAMI LYNN	vcls	AB
	STEVE MANN	gtr	A
	ERNEST MC LEAN	gtr, mandolin	A
	BOB WEST	bs	A
	AL FRAZIER	bs	B
	CHARLIE MADUELL	sax	B

	JOHN McALLISTER	tablas, keyb'ds, transceleste	B
	ALVIN ROBINSON	gtr, vcls	BC
	RAY DRAPER		D

				HCP
ALBUMS:	1(A)	GRIS-GRIS	(Atco SD-33324) 1967	- -
(up to	2(B)	BABYLON	(Atco SD-33270) 1968	- -
1975)	3(C)	REMEDIES	(Atco SD-33316) 1969	- -
	4(D)	THE SUN, MOON AND HERBS	(Atco SD-33362) 1971	184 -
	5( )	GUMBO	(Atco SD 7006) 1972	112 -
	6( )	IN THE RIGHT PLACE	(Atco SD 7018) 1973	24 -
	7( )	DESITIVELY BONNAROO	(Atco SD 7043) 1974	105 -
	8( )	TRIUMVIRATE	(Columbia 32172) 1974	105 -
	9( )	HOLLYWOOD BE THY NAME	(United Artists UALA 552) 1975	- -

NB: (1) to (4) also released in the U.K. by Atlantic. Also reissued on CD by Atco. (1) reissued on CD (Collectors Choice CCM 01312). (8) with Michael Bloomfield and John Hammond.

			HCP
45s:	I Walk On Guilded Splinters Pt. 1/Pt. 2	(Atco 45-6607) 1968	-
(up to	Mama Roux/Jump Steady	(Atco 45-6635) 1969	-
1974)	The Patriotic Flag Waver/?	(Atco 45-6697) 1969	-
	Wash Mama Wash/Loup Garoo	(Atco 45-6755) 1970	108
	Iko Iko/Huey Smith Medley	(Atco 45-6882) 1972	71
	Wang Dang Doodle/Big Chief	(Atco 45-6898) 1972	-
	Let The Good Times Roll/Stack-A-Lee	(Atco 45-6900) 1972	-
	Right Place Wrong Time/ I Been Hoodooed	(Atco 45-6914) 1973	9
	Such A Night/Cold Cold Cold	(Atco 45-6937) 1973	42
	Let's Make A Better World/ Me, You = Loneliness	(Atco 45-6971) 1974	-
	(Everybody Wanna Get Rich) Rite Away/ Mos 'Scocious	(Atco 45-6597) 1974	92

Malcolm "Mac" Rebennack, also known as **Dr. John**, Mac Rabinac or Dr. John Creaux, is an extraordinary singer, guitar player, pianist, producer and songwriter who took a very active part in the Hollywood scene between 1965 and 1972.

Born in New Orleans in 1940, Mac Rebennack began playing professionally in the Crescent City Studios in 1954, when he was only 14 and his first album was released in 1957. Working with Specialty and Ace Records, he started songwriting and producing for local singers and in 1960 he was already President and A&R man of Ric & Ron Records, a local label. After a long stay at the Fort Worth federal prison in 1964 due to a drug bust, Mac Rebennack had to leave New Orleans for Los Angeles where he teamed up with exiled New Orleans musicians: Harold Battiste, Earl Palmer, Red Tyler, Melvin Lastie and Plas Johnson, who were at the time in demand as studio musicians.

Battiste (who was Sonny & Cher's musical director) introduced Rebennack to both **Sonny Bono** and Phil Spector as a keyboard and guitar player. After a while, he began playing piano for the **Mothers of Invention** but had to leave as **Zappa** refused to work with musicians who used drugs. (Rebennack later explained that he began taking narcotics of all kinds since he was 12 and only got 'clean' in the eighties. His career was subsequently marred by drug busts, debts, bad contracts, problem with managers etc.) He was also very active in the Los Angeles studios, playing keyboards and/or guitar, often uncredited, on recordings by **Oxford Circle**, **Iron Butterfly**, **Buffalo Springfield**, **Hourglass**, **Future**, **John Sebastian**, Sonny & Cher and dozens of other rock, psych, soul, blues and pop acts. He was also a producer for Mercury Records and their short-lived Pulsar subsidiary (where he worked with **Wayne Talbert** and produced two Graham Bond albums among many others).

In 1967, he thought up the concept of forming a musical group around the personality of Dr. John, a 19th century New Orleans root doctor and, through Harold Battiste (together with his Sonny & Cher job), managed to cut a few tunes on "free" studio time at the Gold Star Studios. Ahmet Ertegun was at first very surprised to be asked to release an album that had been recorded "on the sly", but finally agreed to release it on Atco. The album, Gris-Gris, fell right into the "hippie" groove of the time and soon became a kind of underground hit, being supported by the free form radio stations and receiving good reviews. It's quite easy to understand why when reading the lyrics of Gris Gris Gumbo Ya Ya:

"They call me Dr. John
Known as the Night Tripper
Got my satchel of gris gris in my hand
Tripping up, back down the bayou
I'm the last of the best
I'm known as a gris-gris man
Got many clients come from miles around
Running down my prescriptions
Got medicine cure all y'all's ills
Got remedies of every description"

Other tracks include Walk On Gilded Splinters and Croker Courtbullion whilst the music can best be described as "voodoo rock". The **Dr. John** live shows were also totally unusual for the California scene, Rebennack and his group using the old minstrel shows and New Orleans carnival outfits:- smoke, feathered clothes, snakes, make-up, candles, limbo sticks and burning incense. Rebennack and his group also began hanging out with Emmett Grogan's Diggers, the local Hell's Angels and were often in trouble with all sorts of authorities.

In 1968, Atlantic asked them to do a second album. Rebennack and Battiste wrote songs about the end of the world, using unusual rhythms and named it Babylon. The title track had these lyrics, just before the sound of an atomic explosion :

"No politicians, no high religions to guide you from the dark
No more love-ins, no more human be-in's will light up Griffith Park"

A true psych gem, Babylon is a strange album, with the croaking voice of **Dr. John** mixed with lots of percussion, guitars and female vocals. The final track, The Lonesome Guitar Strangler is about a character "smoking psychedelic guitar picks and strangling guitar players", every day he gets one more and the lyrics cite **Gabor Szabo**, **Jimi Hendrix**, Wes Montgomery and Ravi Shankar, with a short example of their style every time. Scary!

After that, Rebennack got busted once more, this time in St Louis, Missouri, and had to spend time in the UCLA Neuropsychiatric Center for a detox attempt. He finally escaped from there and went to Miami. In the meantime, the third **Dr. John** album, Remedies, had come out and was in fact "finished" by **Dr. John**'s new managers, Brian Stone and Charlie Greene (who also worked with **Buffalo Springfield**, **Iron Butterfly** and Sonny & Cher). The side-long Angola was about the Louisiana prison farm although the critics thought it was about the African country.

The group then went to Europe for a long and chaotic tour, with many drug and visa problems. Rebennack wanted to record a triple concept album: The Sun, Moon and Herbs and recorded it in London, with many guests including Mick Jagger, Eric Clapton and his Dominoes, Doris Troy, Graham Bond, Ray Draper and Chris Mercer. During the sessions, Stone and Greene tried unsuccessfully to sign **Dr. John** to the Blue Thumb label and somehow most of the original tapes were lost. Rebennack then signed a new management contract with Albert Grossman and finally a single album

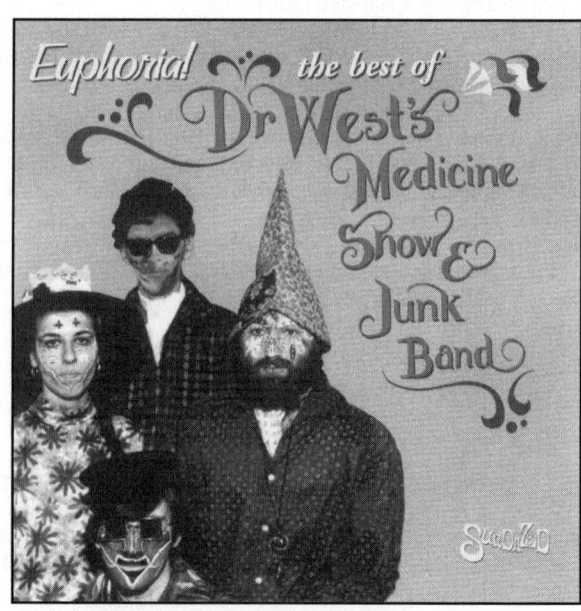

DR. WEST'S MEDICINE SHOW AND JUNK BAND - Euphoria CD.

was rescued from the project and released on Atco. Housed in a superb gatefold sleeve, the result is not surprisingly, not very convincing although it still has its moments.

After this album, Mac Rebennack and his singers worked with the Rolling Stones on *Exile On Main Street* and with The Band. He later returned to New Orleans and his following albums are out of the scope of this book (although many of them are excellent). Deeply involved with the New Orleans beliefs, Rebennack even fronted the 'Dr. John's Temple Of Voodoo', a local "church" in the early seventies.

His songs have often been covered including:- *United States Of Mind* by **Great Jones**, *Walk On Gilded Splinters* by both Humble Pie and Marsha Hunt, *Headin Closer To Home* by **Great Bear** and *Glowin'* by several different groups.

For further readying, check out "Under A Hoodoo Moon, The Life Of The Night Tripper", his very sincere memories published in 1994.

Dr. John is still recording and touring extensively. (SR)

Dr. Spec's Optical Illusion

Personnel:	MARSHALL CLYBURN	ld gtr	A
	BRYCE "PINKY" HATCHETT	bs	A
	KRIS SHERMAN	gtr, vcls	A
	SCOTT SHERMAN	drms, vcls	A
	RICK STELMA	keyb'ds	A

45:	Tryin' To Mess My Mind / She's The One	(Flambeau 103) 1967

Thanks to Andrew Brown's "Brown Paper Sack #1" for the line-up and informing us that this New Orleans band were originally known as the Illusions and would later be known as Flavor from 1969 through to about 1973. Both sides of this 45 are hard-edged punk veering towards psychedelia with confident vocals and lots of organ.

Compilation appearances have included: *Tryin' To Mess My Mind* and *She's The One* on *Louisiana Punk From The Sixties* (LP), *Sixties Archive Vol. 3* (CD) and *Teenage Shutdown, Vol. 10* (LP & CD). (AB/MW)

Dr. T. and The Undertakers

Personnel:	TONY ASCI	ld vcls, keyb'ds	A
	BOB BARBARA	gtr	A
	BOBBY JABO	ld gtr	A
	JERRY JOHNSON	drms, vcls	A
	LOUIE RODRIGUEZ	bs	A
	BOB USHERSON	bs	A

45s:	Times Have Changed / Deceased	(Epitaph 1001) 1966
	Blue Blue Feeling /Undertaker's Theme	(Target 101) 1966
	It's Easy Child / Times Have Changed	(Target 4610) 1967

From the Miami area, this band featured Bobby Jabo, who went on to **The Kollektion** and **Katmandu**. The *Undertaker's Theme*, a cool'n'cheesy club-a-go-go instrumental, is re-aired on *Psychedelic States: Florida Vol. 1* (CD). It was previously released on their debut 45 as *Deceased*, also compiled on *The Boss Instrumentals EP!* (7").

Other compilation appearances include *Times Have Changed* on *Psychedelic States: Florida Vol. 3* (CD) (MW/JLh)

Dr. West's Medicine Show and Junk Band

Personnel:	JACK CARRINGTON	junk instruments	A
	EVAN ENGBER		A
	NORMAN GREENBAUM	vcls	A
	BONNIE ZEE WALLACH		A

ALBUMS:	1(A)	THE EGGPLANT THAT ATE CHICAGO		
			(Go Go 22-17-002)	1967 -
	2(A)	NORMAN GREENBAUM	(Gregar GG-101)	1970 -

NB: (2) is a repackaging of (1) with two single tracks ("Gondoliers" and "Daddy-I-Know") but without "The Eggplant" and "Nora". (1) was also released in the U.K. (Page One POLS 017) in 1969. There's also an excellent CD retrospective, *Euphoria!! The Best Of* (Sundazed SC 11070) 1998, which contains twenty-five tracks including many previously unreleased cuts.

45s:	α	The Eggplant That Ate Chicago /		
(US)		You Can't Fight City Hall Blues	(Go Go 00100)	1966
	β	Gondoliers, Shakespeares, Overseers, Playboys And Bums /		
	χ	Daddy I Know	(Go Go 00102)	1967
	δ	You Can Fly / The Circus Left Town Today	(Go Go 00104)	1967
		Bullets La Verne / Jigsaw	(Gregar 00106)	1968

NB: α flip is non LP. β also on Gregar LP. χ and δ non LP. δ as by **Dr. West's Medicine Band.**

45s:	Gondoliers, Shakespeares, Overseers, Playboys And Bums/		
(UK)	Daddy I Know	(CBS 202658)	1967
	The Eggplant That Ate Chicago/		
	You Can't Fight City Hall Blues	(CBS 202492)	1967
	Bullets La Verne/Jigsaw	(Page One POF 061)	196?

This band had a minor hit with one of the all-time greatest novelty songs, *The Eggplant That Ate Chicago*, in 1967. Their album, produced by Tony Marer, was released by a small California company, Go-Go Record and distributed by Epic.

Anyone wishing to check their blend of Spike Jones and Bonzo Dog Band should look out for Sundazed's CD retrospective *Euphoria! The Best Of...*, which contains 25 tracks, including all their 45s and plenty of unreleased cuts... completely zany, off the wall, deliciously goofy stuff!!

Singer Norman Greenbaum hit the big time with *Spirit In The Sky* in 1970. He came from Boston originally.

Jigsaw has also resurfaced on *Exploding Plastic Inevitable* and you can also hear a radio commercial as the bonus track on *Psychedelic Unknowns, Vol. 3* (LP & CD). (VJ/MW/SR)

Dick Dodd

ALBUM:	1	FIRST EVOLUTION OF DICK DODD	
		(Tower ST-5142)	1968 -

45s:	Little Star/Lonely Weekends	(Tower 447)	1968
	Fanny/Don't Be Ashamed To Call My Name	(Tower 490)	1969
	Guilty/Requiem: 820	(Attarack 102)	c1969

These solo efforts by **The Standells**' drummer may interest readers. The album is now a minor collectable. (VJ)

The Dogs

45:	Don't Try To Help Me/Soul Step	(Treasure 007)	c1967

An obscure Philadelphia outfit whose, *Don't Try To Help Me* is a typical garage-punker which has a very catchy guitar riff.

Compilation appearances have included *Don't Try To Help Me* on *Return Of The Young Pennsylvanians* (LP), *Tougher Than Stains* (LP), *Back From The Grave, Vol. 8* (CD) and *Back From The Grave, Vol. 8* (Dble LP). (MW)

Dogwood

ALBUM:	1	AFTER THE FLOOD	(Private Pressing) c1974 R2

A rare Christian folk trio with female vocals. (SR)

Denny Doherty

ALBUM:	1	WHATCHA GONNA DO	(Dunhill DS-50096) 1971 -

Produced by Bill Szymczyk, this solo album by the former **Mamas and Papas** member, backed by **Barry McGuire**, Eric Hord, Brian Garofalo, Russ Kunkel and Buddy Emmons. It has yet to attract much attention. (SR)

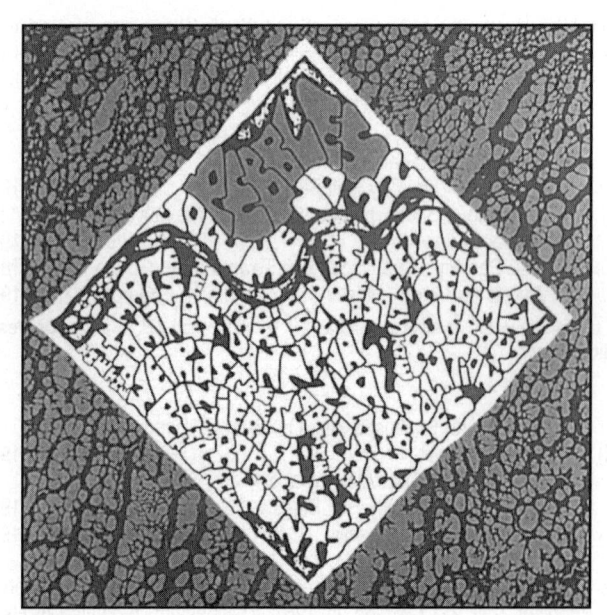

PEBBLES Vol. 22 (Comp LP) including The Dominos.

Dolphin

Personnel:	BOB BERBERICH	drms	AB
	GEORGE DALY	gtr	AB
	PAUL DOWELL	bs, vcls	A
	NILS LOFGREN	gtr	AB

45s:	Let's Get Together / Grubb's Blues	(Phoenix PH 3) 1968
α	It's Better To Know You / The last Time I Saw You	(Sire 45-SI-4107) 1969

NB: α released as **Paul Dowell and The Dolphin**.

On the demise of **The Hangmen**, Dowell Daly and Berberich approached a young and talented guitarist called Nils Lofgren. Nils was with the Crystal Mesh, who'd recorded some demos in NYC with Richard Gottehrer (**Strangeloves**) producing - Gottehrer would produce both **Dolphin** 45s too. After the second 45 Dowell split to California and the remaining trio (line-up B) became the first incarnation of Grin. They'd take the trail to L.A. themselves and the rest, as they say, is history.

Their first 45 on the short-lived Sire subsidiary (also responsible for a 45 and album by **David Santo**) features a heavyish version of the hippie anthem and a decent bluesy (first?) Lofgren original, credited to "Nils Lothgrin". He wrote both sides of the more commercial orchestrated pop-rock follow-up. Neither are outstanding but will be of great interest to his loyal legion of fans. (MW)

Dick Domane

ALBUM: 1 DICK DOMANE   (Map City) 1970 -

Probably originating from the New York area, a strange pop-rock singer who used some fuzz guitar on his songs. (SR)

Domestic Help

45s:	A Woman Owns The Biggest Part Of Man/ The Bad Seed	(Acta 805) 1965
	You're The Potter / Try To Forgive Them	(Acta 814) 1967

This group's origins remain a mystery, though L.A. is a good bet. The first 45 features a decent folk-rocker backed by a mid-tempo garage lament with disturbing lyrics and both cuts feature excellent guitar work. The second 45 is melodramatic orchestrated pop with the odd burst of unwelcome brass -a disappointment after their first release. (MW)

The Dominions

45:   Spanish Harlem/I Need Her   (Graves 1091) 1966

A mid-sixties punk outfit. The label was based in Eugene, Oregon and the band were made up of college students at the local University of Oregon. The flip, a pretty strong punker, has since resurfaced on *Highs In The Mid-Sixties, Vol. 16* (LP). (MW/GGI)

The Dominos

45:   Where Comes The Dawn / A Matter Of Fact   (Kleo 171) 196?

This outfit is though to be from Wisconsin, though there is also a Chicago area bunch with a 45 on Cha Cha and an obscure instrumental group with a 45 on Domino to confuse matters further. *A Matter Of Fact* is decidedly weird. It steals a riff from *Purple Haze* and at times disintegrates into a sort of haze of confusion. Interesting. To make matters more confusing, the same recording was released as *Dooley Vs. The Ferris Wheel* by **IRA**.

You can also find *A Matter Of Fact* on *Pebbles, Vol. 22* (LP). (MW)

Don and Jerry with The Fugitives

Personnel:	DON GRIFFIN	A
	JERRY STRICKLAND	A

45s:	α	In The Cover Of Night/I Can't Quit	(Fabor 140) 1965
	β	One Year Today/ Big Man (That Ain't Love, It Ain't Right)	(Fabor 141) 1965

NB: β by Delna Lee with **The Fugitives**. α was also issued on Action (1012).

Another mystery outfit whose *In The Cover Of Night* is a rather accessible garage punker - good vocals and an effective organ-led backing. As Fabor Robinson's label was based in Burbank, California they may have come from California, although Louisiana has also been suggested. The second 45 featured Delna Lee (a guy not a gal) and both sides were written by Don and Jerry. *One Year Today* is an early-sixties teen ballad, the flip a frantic beat number.

Another 45 as by Don And Jerry is probably the same ouftit:-

45:   Better Run And Hide/Too Much Confusion (N-Joy NJ 1018) 1966

Compilation appearances have included: *In The Cover Of The Night* on *Sixties Choice, Vol. 1* (LP) and *60's Choice Collection Vol's 1 And 2* (CD). (MW/VJ)

Don and The Agitators

45:   Going Back Home/?   (Lucky Token 109) 1964

From the label that brought us the pre-Turtles *Crossfires* first waxing, so L.A. seems the likely source of this outfit.

Compilation appearances have included: *Going Back Home* on *Boulders, Vol. 7* (LP) and *Ya Gotta Have Moxie, Vol. 1* (Dble CD). (VJ)

Don and The Goodtimes

Personnel:	DAVE CHILDS	bs	ABC
	DON GALLUCCI	keyb'ds	ABCDEFGH
	BOB HOLDEN	drms	ABCDEF
	DON McKINNEY	sax, vcls	A
	PETE OULETTE	gtr	A
	JIM VALLEY	gtr	B
	CHARLIE COE	gtr	CD
	RON OVERMAN	bs	DEFG
	JOEY NEWMANN	gtr	E

JEFF HAWKS	vcls, gtr		F G H
JOHN BORDONARO	drms		G H
BRUCE HAUSER	bs		H

```
                                                                    HCP
ALBUMS:  1(B)  WHERE THE ACTION IS     (Wand WDS 679) 1966 - -
         2(-)  GREATEST HITS           (Burdette 300)  1966 - R1
         3(F)  SO GOOD                 (Epic BN 26311) 1967 109 -
         4(-)  HARPO                   (Panorama 104)  196? - -
```

NB: (3) a mono copy also exists (Epic LN 24311). (4) shown as by Jim Valley. There's also a few compilations including:- *Goodtime Rock 'n' Roll* (Piccadilly PIC-3394) 1981; a 21-track CD *Don & the Goodtimes* (Jerden JRCD7016) 1994; and an LP retrospective *Original Northwest Sound Of...* (Beat Rocket BR 130) 2000.

```
                                                                    HCP
45s:  α  Turn On Song/Make It                   (Jerden 740)  1964 -
         Turn On/Make It                         (Wand 165)   1964 -
         Straight Sceptre/
           There's Something On Your Mind        (Wand 184)   1965 -
         Little Sally Tease/You'll Never Walk Alone (Jerden 762) 1965 -
         Little Sally Tease/Little Green Thing   (Dunhill 4008) 1965 -
         I'll Be Down Forever,'Big Big Knight    (Dunhill 4015) 1965 -
         Hey There, Mary Mae/
           Sweets For My Sweet                   (Dunhill 4022) 1966 -
         You Were A Child/I Hate To Hate You     (Piccadilly 223) 1966 -
         Blue Turns To Grey/I'm Real             (Jerden 805)  1966 -
         You Were A Child/I Hate To Hate You     (Jerden 808)  1966 -
         I Could Be So Good To You/
           And It's So Good (PS)                 (Epic S-1 01 45) 1967 56
         Happy And Me/
           If You Love Her Cherish Her And Such  (Epic 5-10199) 1967 98
         Sally! (Studio A At 6 O'Clock In The Morning)/
           Bambii                                (Epic 5-10241) 1967 -
         May My Heart Be Cast Into Stone/
           Ball Of Fire                          (Epic 5-10280) 1968 -
         Colors Of Life/You Did It Before        (Burdette 3)  1968 -
```

NB: α Not released.

Formed in Portland, Oregon in 1964 when Don Gallucci was forced to leave **The Kingsmen** because he was still in high school and unable to tour. Gallucci drafted in Bob Holden, a good friend of his, on drums and Holden brought with him Don McKinney, who had played sax with him in a band called The Imperials. With the bass and guitar slots filled by Dave Childs and (ex-**Paul Revere & The Raiders**) Pierre Oulette, **The Goodtimes** started out playing at The Chase in Portland, Oregon, but soon became a popular regional attraction. Their debut recording in 1964 was *Turn On Song*, an instrumental which featured McKinney's wailing sax and Oulette's superb guitar. It became a big regional hit. However, in 1965 Oulette left to join **Aesop and The Fables** and was replaced by Jim Valley on guitar. As well as being one of the region's finest guitarists he was a talented songwriter and his songwriting opened up new opportunities for the group. For example, he wrote *Little Sally Tease* for the band, which became a gigantic regional hit and was recorded by several national acts such as **The Standells** and **The Kingsmen**. The 45 was picked up by Dunhill and the band went to L.A. to record *Sweets For My Sweet* and *Mary Mae* with **P.F. Sloan** and Steve Berry handling the arrangements. Whilst there they appeared on several Top TV shows. Indeed L.A. became their base until their demise.

On New Years Day, 1966, they shared the bill with **Mr. Lucky and The Gamblers** at Portland's Oriental Theatre and Don and the lads were so impressed they helped get them a record deal with Jerry Dennon's Panorama label and wrote and produced a couple of songs for them.

Sweets For My Sweet went on to become a huge hit in the Northwest, but whilst they were working on a new single, *Blue Turns To Grey* Jim Valley left to join **Paul Revere and The Raiders**, with whom in late 1966 they appeared as regulars on *'Where The Action Is'*. They also signed for Epic in 1966, bringing them two national hits, *I Could Be So Good To You* and *Happy And Me* in 1967. Just when they seemed to be at the pinnacle of their career their world fell in around them - *'Where The Action Is'* was cancelled, two members quit and their next single bombed. By 1968 the band had evolved into **Touch**. John Bordonaro: "I replaced drummer, Bob Holden in the fall of 1967. Bruce Hauser, who I played with in The Gretschmen from Connecticut, also played with **Don and the Goodtimes** in 1968 when we went thru a series of names until our manager Howard Wolf, came up with the name **Touch**."

Their most successful album, in commercial terms, had been *So Good*, which rose to No 109 in the U.S. charts. Produced by Jack Nitzsche and Stu Phillips, it's very pop-oriented, with several English covers (Troggs' *With A Girl Like You*, Beatles' *Good Day Sunshine* and Spencer Davis' *Gimme Somme Lovin'*), two Nitzsche selections and four Ron Overman compositions. It hasn't aged well and sounds a bit naive now.

Newman had earlier played in **The Liberty Party**. Don McKinney went into personnel management and record production and Bob Holden became a recording engineer. Later still Gallucci became a producer/engineer for Elektra Records. Don Gallucci was last reported working in real estate, Ron Overman is a pastor in Arkansas, Jim Valley works in education with gifted children, Dave Child is a machinist, Pete Oulette works in advertising, Charlie Coe (who had joined them from **Paul Revere and The Raiders**) is in food sales, Joey Newman is a studio musician and has also recorded two gospel albums, Jeff Hawks is a hair stylist in L.A. and Bob Holden works as a recording engineer in Seattle. Interestingly, McKinney, Child and Holden are all active with Christian music in some way and Gallucci is active in the Christian ministry.

The band's material has been quite well documented on some of the regional compilations:- *Blue Turns To Grey* and *Little Sally Tease* appeared on *Battle Of The Bands, Vol. 1* (LP); *You Were Just A Child* on *Battle Of The Bands, Vol. 2* (LP); and *Lip Service*, *Tall Cool One* and *Louie, Louie* were on *The Hitmakers* (LP).

In 1994, Jerden Records issued a **Don & The Goodtimes** CD called simply *Don & the Goodtimes*. Its 21 tracks cover virtually all of their recorded output from *Money* and *Little Sally Tease* to *You Were Just A Child* and *I Could Be So Good To You*. Highly recommended.

In 2000, Sundazed turned their attention to the Northwest, specifically Jerry Dennon's sixties empire (Jerden, Piccadilly and Burdette labels). *The Original Northwest Sound Of...* compilation showcases **D&TG's** earlier (1964-1966) raucous R&B and punkier material - 16 cuts which include nearly everything on that elusive 1981 retrospective *Goodtime Rock 'n' Roll* album plus classics like *Little Sally Tease* and *I'm Real*.

Compilation appearances have included: *Little Latin Lupe Lu* on *Northwest Battle Of The Bands, Vol. 1 - Flash And Crash* (LP); *Little Latin Lupe Lu*, *Money* and *The Turn On Song* on *Northwest Battle Of The Bands, Vol. 1 - Flash And Crash* (CD); *Little Sally Tease* and *Louie, Louie* on *Northwest Battle Of The Bands, Vol. 2 - Knock You Flat!* (CD); *Blue Turns To Grey* and *Little Sally Tease* on *Northwest Battle Of The Bands, Vol. 1* (CD); *You Were A Child* and the previously unreleased *Runnin' Not Walking* on *Northwest Battle Of The Bands, Vol. 2* (CD); *Little Sally Tease* and *The Turn On Song* on *History Of Northwest Rock, Vol. 2 - The Garage Years* (CD); *You Were Just A Child* and *Little Sally Tease* on *The History Of Northwest Rock, Vol. 1* (LP); *Blue Turns To Grey* and *I Could Be So Good To You* on *The History Of Northwest Rock, Vol. 2* (LP); *The Turn On Song* on *The History Of Northwest Rock, Vol. 2* (LP); and *The Witch* on *The History Of Northwest Rock, Vol. 4* (LP). (VJ/MW/SR/BCh/JB)

DON & THE GOODTIMES - Orignal Northwest Sound Of... LP.

Donnybrookes

Personnel incl: TERRY GIFFORD
(SNEAKY O'FENNEMAN) vcls A

45: You're Gonna Cry/Time Will Tell (Golden State 608) 1966

You're Gonna Cry is also on *Pebbles, Vol. 17* (LP). It begins with a soulful blues feel and works up into a climax of blistering guitars. Superimposed on all this is Gifford's emotive style which owes a lot to Eric Burdon. Definitely one worth investigation.

The band were from Fairfield, California. In 1967, they were known as **Stone Henge**, and, in 1968, they became the **Maze** who issued the highly-rated *Armageddon* album. (VJ/MW/AP/JCa/EW)

The Donnybrooks

Personnel:	MIKE CLAUGHTON	vcls (gtr)	AB
	GREG HARRIS	gtr	A
	TOM KEENE	bs	AB
	TONY NORTON	ld gtr	AB
	DUGAN TURNER	drms	AB

45: Always Getting Hurt/I'm Going For You (Canterbury 505) 1967

From Bakersfield, California, this band formed in 1963 when Dugan Turner splintered with **The Avengers** (yes - that **Avengers**). Managed by KFAY disc jockey Mike Lundy, they played the Sunset Strip often, as well as performing with Sonny and Cher, The Beach Boys, **Lovin' Spoonful**, **Chad and Jeremy**, **Paul Revere and The Raiders**, and The Yardbirds, among others. Though the Canterbury single was their only release, they did record demos in Hollywood for Ken Handler, then with the Mattel Toy Company.

The 45 consists of harmonious folk-rock-pop ballads, with the winner being the tender Byrdsy *Always Getting Hurt*.

The Donnybrooks dissolved when some of them decided to attend college. Turner later joined a local band named Air Circus. (VJ/MDo/MW/DTu)

The Door Nobs

Personnel:	DON GREEN	gtr	A
	MIKE MANGUSO	drms	A
	FLOYD WESTFALL	vcls, ld gtr	A
	JERRY WESTFALL	vcls, bs	A

45: Hi-Fi Baby/I Need Your Lovin' Babe (Viv 10) 1965

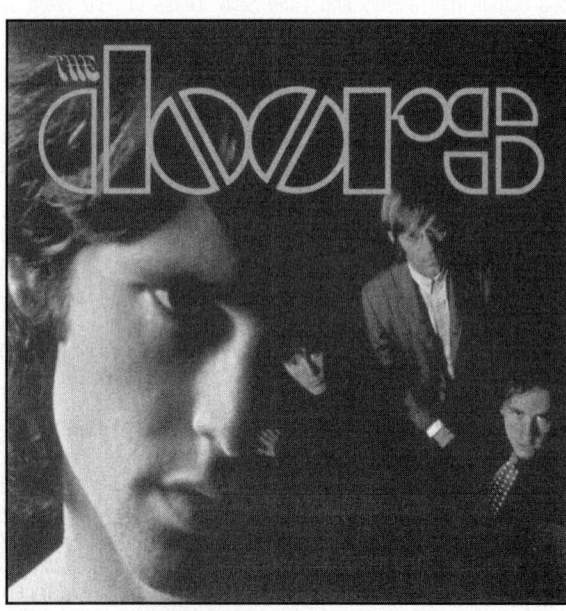

THE DOORS - The Doors CD.

From Phoenix, Arizona, **The Door Nobs** included brothers **Floyd** and **Jerry** Westfall, who as a duo would achieve regional stardom and record five singles for Presta and Double Shot between 1966 and 1967. *Hi-Fi Baby* was a big Phoenix hit in the Fall of 1965. The guitar-driven screamer is not a typical garage-rocker. In fact, it is a surf-frat-garage hybrid that blurs genres so much that years later it was included on the primarily rockabilly *Desperate Rock and Roll Vol. 4*. The Merseyish ballad *I Need Your Lovin' Babe* includes harmonica by Michael Bruce, later of **The Spiders** and **The Nazz**. **The Door Nobs** also recorded four raucous demos and three other songs at Debra Recording Studio in Phoenix that remain unreleased. *Hi-Fi Baby* originally came out with two label variations. It also can be heard on Bear Family's *Phoenix Panorama: The Viv Labels*. (DN)

The Doors

Personnel:	JOHN DENSMORE	drms	AB
	ROBBIE KRIEGER	gtr	AB
	RAY MANZAREK	keyb'ds, vcls, bs	AB
	JIM MORRISON	vcls	A

ALBUMS: (up to 1972)

					HCP
1(A)	THE DOORS	(Elektra 74007)	1967	2	-
2(A)	STRANGE DAYS	(Elektra 74014)	1968	3	-
3(A)	WAITING FOR THE SUN	(Elektra 74024)	1968	1	-
4(A)	THE SOFT PARADE	(Elektra 75005)	1969	6	-
5(A)	MORRISON HOTEL	(Elektra 75007)	1970	4	-
6(A)	ABSOLUTELY LIVE (dbl)	(Elektra 29002)	1970	8	-
7(A)	LA WOMAN	(Elektra 75011)	1971	9	-
8(A)	13	(Elektra 74079)	1971	25	-
9(B)	OTHER VOICES	(Elektra 75017)	1971	31	-
10(A)	WEIRD SCENES INSIDE THE GOLDMINE				
		(Elektra 26001)	1971	55	-
11(B)	FULL CIRCLE	(Elektra 75038)	1972	68	-

NB: Numerous posthumous releases have appeared. Of particular interest may be the 1987 release *The Doors Live at the Hollywood Bowl* (Elektra 960741-1) which captures the band on stage on 5 July 1968. Most of these albums are now available on CD. Real fans of the band may want to invest in *The Complete Studio Recordings* (7-CD box set) (Elektra 7559 62434 2). *Bright Midnight: The Doors Live In America* (Elektra/Bright Midnight Records 7559-62656-2) 2001 compiles live recordings from 1969/70. *Live In Hollywood: Highlights From The Aquarius Theatre Performances* (Bright Midnight/Elektra 7559 62733 2) 2002 captures two 1969 live concerts at the Aquarius Theatre, Los Angeles.

			HCP
45s:	Break On Through (To The Other Side)/		
	End Of The Night	(Elektra 45611) 1967	126
α	Light My Fire/Break On Through	(Philco-Ford HP 9) 1967	-
	Light My Fire/The Crystal Ship	(Elektra 45615) 1967	1
	People Are Strange/Unhappy Girl	(Elektra 45621) 1967	12
	Love Me Two Times/Moonlight Drive	(Elektra 45624) 1967	25
	The Unknown Soldier/		
	We Could Be So Good Together	(Elektra 45628) 1968	39
	Hello I Love You/Love Street	(Elektra 45635) 1968	1
	Touch Me/Wild Child	(Elektra 45646) 1968	3
	Wishful Sinful/Who Scared You	(Elektra 45656) 1969	44
	Tell All The People/Easy Ride	(Elektra 45663) 1969	57
	Runnin' Blue/Do It	(Elektra 45675) 1969	64
	You Make Me Real/Roadhouse Blues	(Elektra 45685) 1970	50
	Universal Mind/The Icewagon Flew	(Elektra 45708) 1970	
	Love Her Madly/		
	(You Need Meat) Don't Go No Further	(Elektra 45726) 1971	11
	Riders On The Storm/The Changeling	(Elektra 45738) 1971	14
	Tightrope Ride/		
	Variety Is The Spice Of Life	(Elektra 45757) 1971	71
	Ship With Sails/In The Eye Of The Sun	(Elektra 45768) 1972	-
	Get Up And Dance/Treetrunk	(Elektra 45793) 1972	-
	The Mosquito/It Slipped My Mind	(Elektra 45807) 1972	85

NB: α is a kind of precursor to the flexi disc, this was issued in the 'Hip Pocket' format 4 (10cm) series of 45s that were issued in picture envelopes.

The Doors more than any other band, broadened the appeal of 'acid rock' and carried it beyond the acid-heads and students to the wider teeny bopper audience. However, theirs was a different brand of 'acid' rock from **The Jefferson Airplane**, less psychedelic and more surreal, their lyrics were concerned with the struggle against social repression and did not romanticise about the virtues of psychedelic drugs. Their significance in the

THE DOORS - Strange Days LP.

evolution of rock is immense - to attend a Doors concert was to undergo a novel experience of rock theatre. On stage, Morrison, one of the late sixties' leading sex symbols, was electrifying. Although some say he lacked a good singing voice, he was an artist of many moods who could shout loudly and furiously or sing softly and mysteriously.

The group formed in 1965 when Morrison, son of a U.S. admiral, met Ray Manzarek whilst studying at the UCLA. Morrison was more interested in poetry than music, but claimed to hear strange songs inside his head. It was Manzarek who encouraged him to get them down on tape. Manzarek persuaded Morrison to play in his own band, **Rick and The Ravens** and later he also recruited the other group members, Robbie Krieger and John Densmore, from a group called The Psychedelic Rangers. Jim Morrison apparently chose the name **The Doors** from a line of William Blake: 'There are things that are known and things that are unknown, in between are the doors'. The inference of opening doors to new perception and discovery fitted well into the acid scene. They got their first gigs in small clubs along the Sunset Strip. The record companies showed little interest at first but eventually Elektra, then a small company who had made inroads into the rock market with another top L.A. band, **Love** offered them a contract after Arthur Lee had persuaded Jac Holzman to go to hear them. Their first single, *Break On Through* appeared to stem from Morrison's obsession with freedom which came from extensive reading of existentialist texts. At the time, however, it was widely understood to refer to a younger generation's struggle against repressive adult society. Their follow-up *Light My Fire*, an edited single, also from their first album, was a rock masterpiece and shot to No. 1 in the US. Probably the most fascinating track on the first LP, however, was *The End*, a long, semi-improvised tale of madness, patricide and incest. Their follow-up LP *Strange Days* was even more imaginative and equally bizarre, containing songs of mystery like *People Are Strange* as well as songs of rage and confusion like *When The Music's Over*.

Their reputation as a live band also grew from strength to strength. A Doors gig was not merely a rock concert but more a theatrical show. In their debut at the Fillmore West, for example, they opened the show third on the bill to **The Young Rascals** and **The Sopwith Camel**, but dominated the proceedings. In 1968 they embarked upon a successful European tour which included a memorable appearance at The Roundhouse in London. Although they were co-billed with **Jefferson Airplane**, they attracted practically all the publicity.

However, by 1969 the acid dream was fading and their third LP saw a change of direction, away from acid psychodramas towards areas of political concern - the stand out track *The Unknown Soldier* being a straight-forward political protest song. It was also issued as a single. Somewhat surprisingly, another track *Hello, I Love You* which sounded very much like The Kinks' *All Day And All Of The Night* gave them another No. 1 hit.

Meanwhile, the pressures of rock stardom were beginning to tell on Morrison, who in the height of the acid explosion had taken LSD over 250 times, but was now fast becoming an alcoholic. He arrived increasingly late for concerts and, as the band played before increasingly younger audiences, every concert bordered on utter chaos. He had been arrested in New Haven, Connecticut, in December 1967 for using obscene language and staging a riot. But following an appearance in Miami, in March of 1969, he was charged with lewd and lascivious behaviour, indecent exposure, open profanity and drunkenness, although in the subsequent court case he was found guilty of only profanity and this was the subject of an appeal at the time of his death. In the short-term, the result of his arrest on the group was catastrophic; venues were cancelled at Jacksonville, Dallas, Pittsburgh, Providence and Syracuse - indeed they were banned nearly everywhere. More ominously, perhaps, many city radio stations removed their songs from playlists. Gradually as things simmered down they got gigs again, although on Morrison's insistence they cut down on their live performances, Their two new albums of this era *Morrison Hotel* and *LA Woman* were both highly acclaimed. Gone was the rage and confusion of their 'acid' days, in its place was fine relaxed music which has proved more durable over time.

Morrison Hotel was a nice contrast of driving rockers like *Roadhouse Blues* and *You Make Me Real* and relaxed music like *The Spy* and *Indian Summer*. *Absolutely Live* contained an impressive medley opening with the much-covered *Who Do You Love* and *The Celebration Of The Lizard*. *L.A. Woman* was a rather inconsistent album but at its best contained some of the band's best music including the doomy *Riders On The Storm* and *Love Her Madly* which both brought them further singles chart success.

By now, however, Morrison was much worse for over-indulgence in life and alcohol, and quit the band to spend a few months in Paris with his wife, Pamela. He would never return to the States. Much mystery surrounds his death on 3 July 1971, which was officially attributed to a heart attack in his bath, But only his wife and the doctor who issued his death certificate saw his body, and no autopsy was conducted. The Parisians preferred to believe that he had OD'd on heroin (many of the clubs he frequented were junkie haunts). Admittedly, a bath tub is often the first place heroin victims are placed to resuscitate them, although Morrison was known to have a fear of hypodermic needles and his wife kept her own heroin habit a secret from him. It is, however, more probable that he may have snorted a lethal dose of the drug. Alternatively, there are those who believe he staged his own death to escape the pressures of public life which were clearly taking their toll. Only Pamela could have known the truth, and she outlived him by just three years, dying herself from a heroin overdose in May 1974. Essentially, of course, he followed the line of rock stars who died from self-abuse - indeed, a young death was almost inevitable from the time he attained stardom.

The remaining members continued as a trio. Their first effort *Other Voices* was not too bad, but *Full Circle* was very weak indeed suggesting they had exhausted their inspiration. Numerous posthumous releases followed and also worth investigation are two bootlegs:- *The Lizard King* recorded at The Roundhouse in 1968 and *Moonlight Drive* recorded at The Matrix, San Francisco in 1967, although both are hampered by their quality.

An American Prayer was issued on CD in 1995. A CD was issued in 1996 (Ozit) entitled *Stoned! But Articulate*. It contains a 16-minute interview with Jim Morrison.

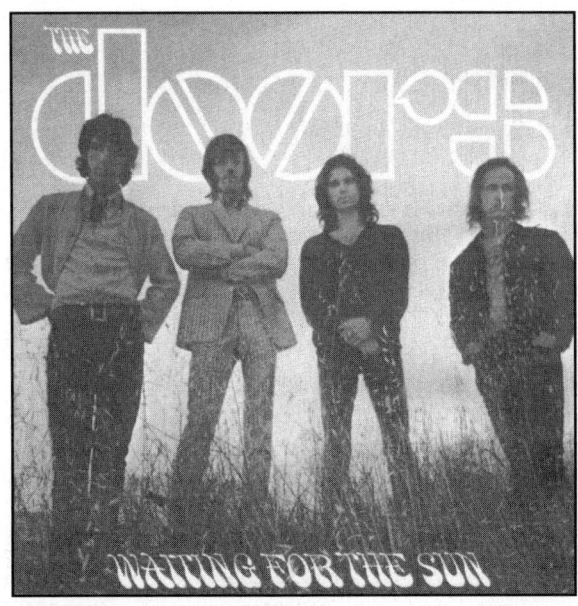

THE DOORS - Waiting For The Sun CD.

THE DOORS - Soft Parade CD.

When Manzarek left Jess Roden was pulled in on vocals and Krieger and Densmore formed The Butts Band along with Roden, Roy Davies (keyb'ds) and Philip Chen (bs).

Compilation appearances have included: *Tell All The People* and *My Wild Love* on *Kings Of Pop Music, Vol. 1* (LP); *Love Me Two Times* on *Kings Of Pop Music, Vol. 2* (LP); *Go Insane* on *Mind Blowers* (LP), *Turds On A Bum Ride Vol. 1 & 2* (Dble CD) and *Turds On A Bum Ride, Vol. 2* (LP); and *Five To One* on *Hallucinations, Psychedelic Underground* (LP).

Real fans of the band may want to invest in the 7-CD box set *The Complete Studio Recordings*. Each CD is housed in a thick card miniature replica of the original album cover. It includes an *Essential Rarities Disc*, which is basically a selection of demos and rarities culled from an earlier 1997 Elektra box set. The new set comes with a lavish 76-page colour booklet, including many photos of the group, a commentary covering each album and the complete lyrics for the studio albums.

Live In Hollywood: Highlights From The Aquarius Theatre Performances will delight diehard **Doors** fans. Highlights of this CD set of two LA 1969 gigs are typically rambling versions of *When The Music's Over* and *Light My Fire* (the latter preceded by a brief excerpt from *Celebration Of The Lizard*). The set comes with informative and lengthy sleevenotes by Danny Sugarman and **Doors**-producer Bruce Botnik and a contemporary gig review from the 'Los Angeles Times'.

The Doors are deservedly remembered as a vital band in the evolution of rock and Morrison is still regarded as one of rock's most creative figures. (VJ)

Doppler Effect

45:	God Is Alive In Argentina/ Memphis Woman (PS)	(Ego 1626) 1966

The 'A' side to this 45 is good hippie-psych with some good fuzz guitar. It has resurfaced on *Highs In The Mid-Sixties, Vol. 18* (LP), indicating that they came from Colorado although Mike Markesich, has linked them to Malibu, California.

God Is Alive In Argentina can also be found on *Psychedelic Experience, Vol. 2* (CD). (VJ/MW)

The Do's and The Don'ts

45s:	I Wonder If She Loves Me / Our Love May Not Live Again	(Red Bird 10-072) 1966
	Be Sure / Still Remember The Past	(Zorch 103) 196?
	Cherry Lane / Girl In The Corner	(Zorch 104) 1967
	The Scrogg / Loving You The Way I Do	(Zorch 105) 196?
	Woman / No One To Talk My Troubles To	(Zorch 106) 196?
	Let The Sun Shine Free / She's Walking Out Of Life	(Zorch 107) 196?
	Hot Rock & Roll To Go / Being With You Girl	(Zorch 108) 196?

This clean-cut act from Ely, just South of Cedar Rapids in Eastern Iowa, later became **Rog and The Escorts**. (VJ)

The Doughboys

Personnel:	MIKE CARUSO	bs	A
	RICHIE HEYMAN	drms	A
	WILLIE KIRCHOFER	gtr	A
	MYKE SCAVONE	ld vcls	A

45s:	Rhoda Mendelbaum/You're A Pip Mr Hip	(Bell 662) 1967
	Everybody Knows My Name/Candy Candy	(Bell 678) 1967

From Plainfield, New Jersey, they evolved out of The Ascots. *Rhoda* is reasonable orchestrated pop with baroque flourishes. The flip is a poppy piss-take of fashion victims but has a glorious freaky'n'fuzzy break and outro that come as a pleasant surprise. The Crewe/Gaudio *Everybody* borrows a couple of lines of melody and vocal style from Sonny and his *I Got You Babe* but is decent orchestrated pop nonetheless. *Candy Candy*, written by **Milan** (Leather Boy), is straight bubblegum pop.

You'll also find *Rhoda Mendelbaum* on *Psychedelic Unknowns, Vol. 8* (LP & CD).

Myke Scavone later got together with Bill Bartlett from **The Lemon Pipers** members as Ram Jam. They had a big hit in 1977 with the **Kasenatz-Katz** produced *Black Betty* which Scavone sang lead on. Richie Heyman later played with **Golgotha** and then recorded as Richard X, creating several albums of well-received power pop in the eighties.

The Doughboys have recently re-formed and are playing gigs in the New Jersey/New York area. (MW/GF)

Douglas Fir

Personnel:	TIM DOYLE	keyb'ds	AB
	RICHIE MOORE	gtr	AB
	DOUGLAS A. SNIDER	drms, ld vcls	AB
	BRUCE BYE	bs	B

ALBUM:	1	HARD HEARTSINGIN'	(Quad 5002) 1970 R1

NB: (1) reissued on CD (Gear Fab GF-149) 2000.

DOUGLAS FIR - Hard Heartsingin' LP.

45:	Smokey Joe's / Comin' Back Home	(Quad QU 104) 1970

Originally known as The Sun Trio, this Oregon outfit spent two years putting together an album's worth of material. Snider made the trip to Hollywood to do the record label rounds. Following a chance elevator encounter, he landed a deal with MGM's Quad label. Bruce Bye was added to the line-up and the band toured briefly before the label folded.

The title track is pretty powerful with strong, soul-based vocals, effective organ backing and occasionally some good guitar work too. Apart from three more mellow, laid-back numbers most of the remaining material is very rocky. There's some good keyboards too, on a couple of tracks and the vocals are powerful and appealing throughout.

Recommended. (CF/VJ/MW)

Douglas Idaho

Personnel:	VINCE MOBECK	bs	A
	DAVE MOLTZEN	ld vcls, gtr	A
	DAVE REESE	drms	A
	DAVE STINSKI	ld gtr, backing vcls	A

45:	Prince Of Darkness/ Taming The Snake	(No label S-80 778-37105) 1974

This Minneapolis, Minnesota band independently pressed this punkish 45 in the early seventies, which is now rare and sought-after by some collectors. The band took their names from the two streets, Idaho Ave and Douglas Drive where Dave Moltzen and Dave Stinski were living and were put together as a outlet for Dave Moltzen's songwriting.

Dave Moltzen and Dave Stinski had been friends since a young age and both became interested in playing music after seeing the Beatles on the 'Ed Sullivan' show as did scores of others. Their first band effort while still teenagers was called Eternal Death and although the band never went further than their basement the collaboration did produce their first song, a co-written instrumental called *Breakthrough*.

As the years went on Dave Moltzen started focusing more on songwriting and Dave Stinski, became quite an acomplished lead guitar player. The two remained good friends but lost contact temporarily in in the early seventies. Then one day Moltzen called Stinski to see if he would be interested in playing lead guitar on a song or two he had wrote. Stinski agreed and the two quicky renewed their friendship.

After teaming up with the other two players, Vince Mobeck and Dave Reese, the question of what to call this new group was asked. Many names were tossed around until finally deciding on **Douglas Idaho**. The name was taken from the streets that they lived on. Stinski lived in an apartment on Douglas Avenue with his new wife and Moltzen was still living with his parents on Idaho street. Both lived in the city of Crystal which is in Minnesota.

That year (1974) the foursome booked recording time in the best studio in Minneapolis (at the time) called 'Sound 80'. During the recording process the group wanted something special to make the song *Prince Of Darkness* sound darker and foreboding so they rented a Mellotron organ from the studio and that did just the trick. Another stumbling block they ran into was that Dave Moltzen found he just couldn't quite sing as high as he had hoped on a harmony line for *Snake River* that was higher in pitch than the main vocal. Out of desperation Dave Stinski gave it a try and hit it the note dead-on which was much to the surprise of everyone, including himself, since he had never attemped to sing before!

After the two tracks were recorded and mixed, they had 1,000 45s pressed and started distributing them themselves to local radio stations and record stores. The radio station that gave the single the most airplay was KQRS 92.5, still the biggest station in Minnesota. After a couple of weeks, the requests came flooding in and when the stations started playing the 'B'-side, *Prince Of Darkness*, things really got wild; local record stores couldn't keep them in stock, 'Sam Goody' alone bought 200 copies and sold them all within a few weeks. The boy's had finally "made it", or so they thought.

Without playing gigs or re-stocking store orders, the 45 stopped getting played on the radio after a few months and the few remaining copies were never sold. The last surge of interest came when *Snake River* was played again, right after dare-devil 'Evil Knevil' attempted to jump the Grand Canyon.

Dave Molzten moved to L.A. in '75, becoming a staff songwriter with E.H. Morris & Co. for two years. He then moved to Nashville in '78, signing with MCA music publishing. In the eighties/nineties he signed with three other publishers with 15 or so songs published, two were recorded by female country artists, but none released commercially. Dave Stinski has since recieved his degree in music and become one of Minnesota's finest jazz guitar players. Dave Reese switched over to guitar/vocals and in the mid-eighties fronted the very popular local new-wave band called Sometimes Y, which Dave Stinski occasionally filled in on lead guitar for. Vince Mobeck went on to play bass in the jazz quartet, Sara Brozzie and later on opened his own chain of ice cream parlors. (VJ/JJa/DMnandDSi)

The Dovers

Personnel:	BRUCE CLASWON	ld gtr, backing vcls	ABC
	TIMMY GRANADA	ld vcls, gtr	ABC
	ROBBIE LADEWIG	bs	ABC
	RICK MORININI	drms	A
	TONY "GOOSEY" RIVAS	sax, tamb, backing vcls	A
	RANDY BUSBY	drms	BC
	NICK HOFFMAN	gtr	C

ALBUM:	1(A/B)	WE'RE NOT JUST ANYBODY	(Misty Lane 057) 2001

NB: (1) 10" with insert.

45s:	She's Gone/What Am I Going To Do?	(Miramar 118) 1965
	I Could Be Happy/People Ask Me Why	(Miramar 121) 1965
	I Could Be Happy/People Ask Me Why	(Reprise 0439) 1965
	The Third Eye/Your Love	(Miramar 123) 1966
	She's Not Just Anybody/About Me	(Miramar 124) 1966

A Beatles-influenced combo from Santa Barbara, who started life as The Vandells. Their compilation appearances have given them a cult following making it impossible to acquire any of their 45s at realistic prices. Their first 45 consists of two folk-rock ballads, whilst the second charted locally. Shortly afterwards Rick Morinini left the band, being replaced by the drummer from **Ernie and The Emperors**, in time for *The Third Eye* - a stand-out raga piece. Their fourth and final 45 also includes some great guitar work.

Compilation appearances have included: *What Am I Going To Do* on *Nuggets Box* (4-CD); *She's Gone* and *What Am I Going To Do* on *Pebbles Vol. 2* (CD) and *Pebbles, Vol. 2* (LP); *She's Not Just Anybody* on *Pebbles, Vol. 7* (LP) and *Pebbles Vol. 8* (CD); *Your Love* on *Sixties Rebellion, Vol. 6* (LP & CD); *The Third Eye* on *Highs In The Mid-Sixties, Vol. 20* (LP) and *30 Seconds Before The Calico Wall* (CD); and *People Ask Me Why* and *I Could Be Happy* on *The Cicadelic 60's, Vol. 2* (LP).

The great news is that you can have their complete recorded output on one disc. After many years seeking out and talking to many of the band members, Mike Markesich has been able to piece together their story on this absolutely essential release.

Few modern bands have been brave enough to attempt to cover **Dovers**' songs, given the very high esteem in which they're held. So hats off to Buffalo, New York's Mystic Eyes for attempting *She's Gone* (1997 45 on Get Hip GH-188). Buy it yourself so you can judge whether they've succeeded in doing it justice. (VJ/MW/CMn)

Paul Dowell and The Dolphin

See the **Dolphin** entry.

The Down Children

45:	I Can Tell/Night Time Girl	(Philips 40441) 1967

I Can Tell can also be heard on *Return Of The Young Pennsylvanians* (LP). This seems to have been a one-off venture on a national label for the quintet. *I Can Tell* is most notable for containing a kinda guitar freak-out towards the end of the song.

Some members later went on to **The In-Sex**. (VJ)

Down From Nothing

ALBUM: 1 DOWN FROM NOTHING (Private Pressing) 1970 R3

Probably from Chicago, this band issued a rare album containing a breezy mix of psych, prog and jazz, with nice guitar, keyboards and sax interplay.

Some of his members later played in **Pound**. (SR)

Downtown Collection

45: Washington Square/Sunshine (Strobe ST 351) 1968

Flower pop-psych ditty to stop the hippie-train to California, by extolling the virtues of Washington Square and Greenwich Village. The flip would have driven them away again. Produced by 'Leather Boy' **Milan**. (MW)

The Drag Kings

45: Midnight Drag Of Paul Revere/
I'm A Lonely Boy (Wayne-way 105) 1964

A rock'n'roll influenced garage band from Waynesboro, Virginia. You'll find the 'A' side to this 45 on the *Signed, D.C.* (LP). Another 45, instrumentals this time, may be by the same band: *Nitro / Bearing Burners* (United Artists UA-676) 1963. (MW)

Dragonfly

Personnel:	B. DAVIS	A
	J. DUNCAN	A
	G. JIMERFIELD	A
	R. RUSSELL	A

ALBUM: 1(A) DRAGONFLY (Megaphone 1202) 1970 R2

NB: (1) has been reissued on vinyl by Eva.

The above album by this Colorado band is superb, full of driving rhythms and excellent psychedelic guitar. It's easy to see why copies of this collectors' item now change hands for a fair bit. My personal favourites were *I Feel It*, *Portrait Of Youth* and the spacey *Miles Away*, although it's difficult to single out tracks as such a high standard is maintained throughout.

The same outfit released an album for Megaphone under the name **Legend**, a couple of years earlier, along with an early 45 version of *Portrait Of Youth*.

Compilation coverage has included: *She Don't Care* on *Reverberation IV* (CD), *Blue Monday* on *Sixties Archive, Vol. 8* (CD) and additionally *Crazy Woman* is featured on an EP that came with the book 'Le Rock Psychedelique Vol.1' for those who want to brush up on their French. (VJ/MW)

Dragonwyck

Personnel:	JACK BOESSNECK	drms	A
	TOMMY BREHM	gtr	A
	JOHN HALL	keyb'ds	A
	MICHAEL GERCHAK	bs, vcls	A
	BILL PETTIJOHN	vcls	A

ALBUMS: 1(A)	DRAGONWYCK	(No label) 1970 R5
	2 DRAGONWYCK	(Acetate only) 197? R4
	3 FUN	(Acetate only) 197? R4

DRAGONWYCK - Rockadelic CD reissue.

NB: (1) was a demo album issued in plain white jacket. Reissued on vinyl (Rockadelic RRLP 4.5) 1992 with insert and on CD (Rockadelic) 1996. (2) reissued on vinyl in Europe, 199?. (3) issued under their new name Fun

45: Lovin' The Boys/The Music (Peckar NR 4710) 197?

NB: shown as by Dragon Wyck.

From Cleveland, Ohio their ultra-rarities are well worth seeking out for connoisseurs of psychedelia. The first album, which was only issued as a demo disc, is an effective blend of keyboards and guitar. *Fire Climbs* is the outstanding track but there are lots of other highs on this album which is well worth searching for, although even the Rockadelic reissue has become difficult to obtain.

Their next effort didn't get beyond the acetate stage. Even more keyboard-orientated than the first one with lots of synthesiser it perhaps inevitably leans more towards the progressive genre. A different version of *Fire Climbs* and the final track, *Freedom Son* are among the highlights and there's still some fine psychedelic guitar work in places. Fortunately, you can now check it out on the European reissue.

Their third venture was made under the name Fun. The opening cut, *Music* is superb, whilst on the whole this acetate is more experimental than their earlier recordings. *I Shall Stay*, for example, is quite chaotic. They went on to evolve into Moonlight Drive releasing some 45s and a mini-album with quite a lot of Doors' covers. (VJ/CF)

Dreamies

| Personnel: | BILL HOLT | various | A |

ALBUM: 1(A) AURALGRAPHIC ENTERTAINMENT
(Stone Theatre DM 68481) 1974 R2

NB: (1) has been pirated twice on vinyl and at least once on CD. Original copies came with a booklet. (1) reissued officially on CD (Gear Fab GF-146) 2000.

A very cool local Delaware private press of psychedelic-folk with sound collages weaving in and out. The cover states that it's "an incredible mental experience" and it's out there! Bill Holt's style was inspired by The Beatles and composer John Cage. The mood of the album reflects the dreams of a young man caught in the middle of the Cold War. From the trauma of President John Kennedy's assassination, through the psycho politics of the 1960's and early 1970's, acoustic guitar, Moog synthesizer, and sound effects from the period are used to paint a hauntingly surreal and beautiful musical tapestry of the times. Side One, *Program Ten*, and Side Two, *Program Eleven* deliver over fifty minutes of very personal music that many critics feel was twenty-five years ahead of its time. Rolling Stone writer David Fricke (at the time a fledgling critic writing for The Drummer in Philadelphia), called **Dreamies** "endless hours of mental entertainment".

Composer Bill Holt created **Dreamies** using a four-track recorder, an acoustic guitar and one of the original Moog synths. The album cover was modeled after a box of "Total" breakfast cereal. The recording took two years to complete and was done in Holt's home studio in Wilmington, Delaware. It was mastered at the renowned Sigma Sound in Philadelphia (the same place David Bowie recorded his memorable mid-seventies dance album). It was originally sold via direct mail through Rolling Stone magazine. Holt is currently working on *Dreamies Program 14*. (CF/VJ/BHo)

Dream Merchants

| ALBUMS: | 1 | SOUL KNIGHT | (Capitol ST 102) 1968 - |
| | 2 | STRANGE NIGHT VOYAGE | (A&M SP 4199) 1969 - |

NB: (1) and (2) issued as by The Merchants Of Dream.

| 45: | Rattler/ | |
| | I'll Be With You In Apple Blossom Time | (London 1015) 1967 |

I'm told the *Strange Night Voyage* album, a concept pop-psych offering based on the Peter Pan fairytale, was recorded in New York. The cover contains no information about the musicians - there were six - but the producers were Vincent Testa and George Shadow Morton (aka **Shadow Mann**), who also produced The Shangri-Las and later the New York Dolls. This probably means **The Dream Merchants** were not the same band as the San Francisco-based **Merchants of Dreams**. (VJ)

Dreams and Illusions

Main Personnel:	AL CHARNET	gtr	A
	HERBERT LOVELLE	drms	A
	LOUIS MAURO	bs	A
	MEL OLMAN	piano	A
	DANNY SCHLOSS	vcls, composer	A

NB: Plus a brass, string and Latin percussion section.

| ALBUM: | 1(A) | DREAMS AND ILLUSIONS | |
| | | (Verve Forecast FTS-3040) 1967 | |

One of those cross-genre explorations or just a psychedelic cash-in? Despite some occasional bursts of psychedelic guitar, this appears to be a studio-only project. Trendy, musically competent, but lacking feel or spirit and therefore ultimately unconvincing. (MW)

John Drendall - B.A. Thrower - and Friends....

Personnel:	VERN ALBAUGH	flute	A
	TOM CARUSO	gtr	A
	JOHN DRENDALL	vcls, gtr, bs	A
	DICK DUNHAM	drms, vcls	A
	ROSS MAXWELL	perc	A
	MIKE SKORY	keyb'ds	A
	JAMES SPILLANE	vcls	A
	BRAD THROWER	bs, keyb'ds, gtr, hrmnca, perc	A
	NELSON WOOD	hrmnca	A

| ALBUM: | 1(A) | PAPA NEVER LET ME SING THE BLUES..... |
| | | (Deacon Productions 4113-27) 197? R4 |

A rare and excellent blues/rural-rock item from Michigan, and probably the best album ever produced at Bryce "Uncle Dirty" Roberson's Sound Machine studio in Kalamazoo. Some terrific players contribute to this little-known record. Don't let the size of the personnel listing scare you; on a track-by-track basis, only three to five musicians appear and the results are quite stunning. *Old Man Gibbs* and *I Feel* are both dark, bluesy, and (at a stretch) even psychedelic.

This is one of only a handful of private press albums that I know of with a proudly American rural blues sound - being without any of the pervasive heavy riffing blues produced in England beginning in the late-sixties. It could be compared to Bill Homans' *Merry Airbrakes* or **Denny King**'s album on Specialty in this respect.

Drendall, Thrower, Spillane, Skory and Dunham also appear on an album shown as by Bluejohn (*Boots And Bottles*, Black River Records 544) from about the same vintage (1973?); this release is equally rare but a great deal less inspired. A further album with most of the same crew exists, but I don't have details. (CF)

The Driving Stupid

Personnel:	RICHARD EHRENBERG	gtr, vcls	A
	DWIGHT HARRIS	bs, vcls	A
	JEFF HILDT	drms, gtr, vcls	A
	ROGER KELLEY	ld gtr, vcls	A

| 45: | Horror Asparagus Stories/ | |
| | The Reality Of (Air) Fried Borsk | (KR 102 (0116)) 1966 |

NB: single sided white label promo copies numbered 116 also exist. There's also a CD compilation *Horror Asparagus Stories* (Sundazed SC 11111) 2002.

This is generally heralded as one of the acid punk classics of the sixties, with off the wall lyrics, psychotic vocals and one of the simplest guitar solos imaginable. The flip is even better with an out of key '*I'm A Man*' rhythm to lyrics like 'You stand on the table, Rugs creep up the legs, Tiny green lobsters, Throw spiders eggs'. Copies of the 45 were apparently plentiful in San Francisco, even enthralling **Big Brother and The Holding Company**, to the extent that they wrote a song *The Driving Stupid*, in tribute, but little was known about the group.

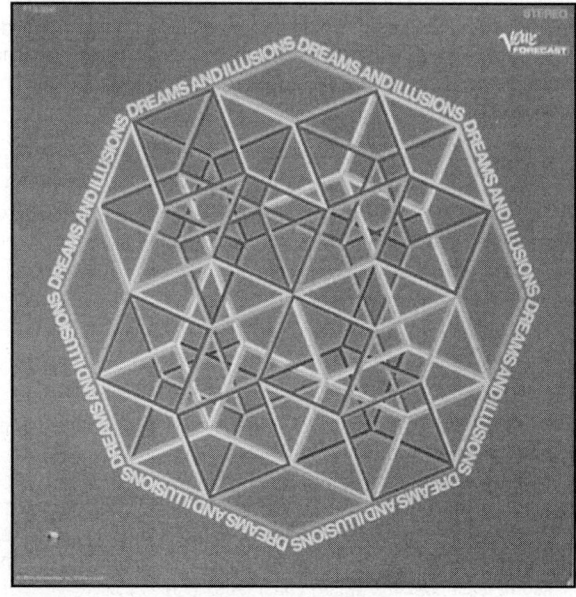

DREAMIES - Auralgraphic Entertainment LP.

DREAMS AND ILLUSIONS - Dreams And Illusions LP.

A second 45 was tantalisingly advertised in the July, 1966 issue of "The Lance". This featured a full page ad promoting **The Driving Stupid**'s next single: *My Mother Was A Big Fat Pig* b/w *Green Things Have Entered My Skin, Gladys*. Both tracks were recorded in Jerry Wilson's Nu-Mex Sound Studios in June, 1966, but the 45 doesn't appear to have been released. In fact Dick Stewart, the publisher of the original 'Lance' Newsletters in Albuquerque in the mid-'60's remembers:

"Jerry Wilson of Nu-Mex Sound ordered and paid for a full page ad in the July, 1966 issue. I don't recall ever hearing the cuts but, according to Jerry at that time, the songs were recorded and I remember him being hot on them. I'm not convinced that the 45 was released on Wilson's QQ record label. Nevertheless, I saved a handwritten letter that was given to me from one of my staff members that lends credence to the existence of the record and the possible label that issued it. It was addressed to Marshal Chess of Chess Records, Chicago, Illinois. The staff writer is unknown (although it could be Jerry himself) and there is no date on the letter; however, I did receive it sometime in late 1966." (Chess handled disribution for KR at the time.)

Dick was incidentally the founding member of **King Richard and The Knights** and also the founder of Lance Records who released 45s by **The Kreeg** and **Fe-Fi-Four Plus Two**: "I do remember the ad causing quite a stir (good and bad) as the song titles were so radically new at the time. In fact, it was the Lance Newsletter's first experience with psychedelic musical expressions although the term psychedelia had not yet found a home during the time the ad was run."

In fact, **The Driving Stupid** didn't come from Chicago or New Mexico, but were originally from New Jersey... They recorded the two demo tracks in Jerry Wilson's New Mexico studio on route to find fame and fortune in Hollywood. The band tragically existed for only one Summer and never got to perform anywhere, as band leader Roger Kelley recalls:- "We could barely play our instruments, and I taught one of the members how to play guitar on the drive to the East Coast. The best guitarist in the band was our drummer, but he had to be the drummer, because it was his drum kit. In Hollywood we hung out with Jim Morrison, Neil Young, Steve Stills and got to meet The Mothers Of Invention. We were also (probably) the first 'white' act to sign to Chess."

"Hollywood went nuts over us, and we had offers from many labels and clubs in L.A., but we were all enrolled in different colleges in the East including U.N.C., Harvard and Penn State. If we'd dropped out of school, we'd all have been drafted and sent to Vietnam, so at the end of the summmer we split up."

Most tantalising of all, is the news that **The Driving Stupid** recorded an album's worth of material, the masters of which still exist! Kelley:- "We did about eight songs in Albuquerque, and then got a record deal with Koppelman and Rubin in Hollywood. We re-recorded everything, and added four tunes for a total of twelve. The Albuquerque tapes rock harder, as it was a two-track studio, and we pretty much had to blow 'live.' Also, Koppelman and Rubin made us change lyrics on two of the songs, and they lost a bit of juice in the transformation. A lot of juice when it came to one song that made fun of postmen. Really. They were afraid we'd offend the U.S. Post Office. *Horror Asparagus Stories* was originally called *My Mother Was A Big Fat Pig*, which was also the first verse. We had to change the verse to 'My mother was a little wren'. Thankfully, nothing else was 'censored."

Compilation coverage has so far included:- *Horror Asparagus Stories* and *Reality Of Air Fried Borsk* on *Pebbles, Vol. 3* (CD), *Pebbles Box* (5-LP) and *Trash Box* (5-CD); and *The Reality Of (Air) Fried Borsk* on *Pebbles, Vol. 3* (LP) and *Pebbles, Vol. 2 (ESD)* (CD).   (VJ/MDo/DJe/RKy)

Driving Wheels

45:   One Year Ago From Today/
      She's My Only World   (Pan Am PA-4001) 1966

The 'A' side can be heard Eva's *Sixties Punk Ballads Sampler* (LP) and *Sixties Archive, Vol. 5* (CD). The vocals are good, but the production and instrumentation is rather ordinary. From San Antonio, Texas apparently, though they could also be the Louisiana outfit, Jay & the Driving Wheels who issued at least nine 45s as the Lanor label. (VJ)

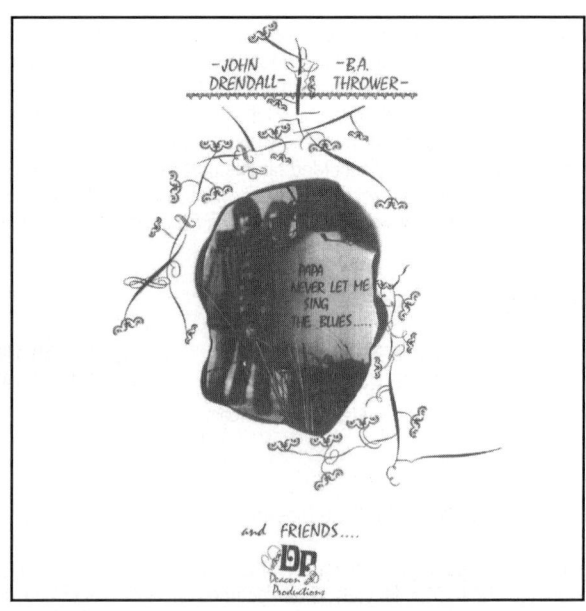

JOHN DRENDALL - B.A. THROWER & FRIENDS - Papa Never Let Me Sing The Blues LP.

Drnwyn

Personnel: DAVID W. HAAG   gtr, mandolin, syn   A
             JOHN VOLIO   acoustic gtr, vcls   A
NB: plus some assistance.

ALBUM: 1(A)   GYPSIES IN THE MIST   (Wilderland 31778) 1978 R2

A later effort by this Salem, Ohio band. There's some melodic guitar work on the title track which is the high point of an album of varied music styles. If you like good guitar work, this album, which is already quite rare, is worth seeking out. (VJ)

The Drongos

Personnel incl: TODD ANDERSON   vcls   A
                  MICHAEL FRIEDMAN   bs   A

45:   Under My Thumb/If You Want To Know   (White Whale 235) 1966

From Berkeley, California, and featuring ex-members of **The Answer**. Their Stones cover is competent but not exceptional, whilst the flip is a mid-slow ballad with reedy solo. (MW)

The Druids

45:   Doctor's Friend/
      She's Got A Secret (To Hide)   (Thunderbird 505) 1967

New York City is thought to have been the home of this band. Both sides of their 45 got a second airing on *A Journey To Tyme, Vol. 3* (LP). (VJ)

The Druids

45s: Jelly Belly/Over And Over   (Broad Covetten Haven 2001) 1965
       The Girl Can't Take A Joke /
       I Can't Leave You   (Select 743) 1965

From Hingham, Massachussetts, Aram Heller's 'Till The Stroke Of Dawn' book, also tells us that they were previously an instrumental group known as the Internationals. You'll also find *Jelly Belly* on *Garage Punk Unknowns, Vol. 6* (LP) and Erik Lindgren's *Mondo Frat Dance Bash A Go Go* (CD), whose titles dispels any doubt whatsoever about the musical content! (AH/MW)

Druids

45:	Cool, Calm And Collected /	
	Sorry's Not Enough	(MNO MNO-101) 1966

Another **Druids**, from San Jose, California. *Cool, Calm And Collected* is just that, a folk-punker in an early **Beau Brummels** mould and can be heard on *Time Won't Change My Mind* (LP) and *Fuzz, Flaykes, And Shakes, Vol. 2* (LP & CD). (MW/AP)

Druids

Personnel:	BARRY CONNOR	gtr	A
	STU MADER	drms	A
	DEAN MAXWELL	12-str gtr	A
	MARTY TORBERT	gtr	A
	JOE TOWNEND	bs	A

45s:	It's A Day /	
	A Man Should Never Cry (PS)	(Columbia 4-43450) 1965
	Puffin / Old Willow	(Columbia 4-43639) 1966

This circle of **Druids** came together in June 1965 whilst attending the University of Scranton, Pennsylvania. They put out two folk-pop 45s, of which the debut is by far the stronger. Mike Kuzmin notes in his "Sounds From The Woods" book (about the sixties Pennsylvania scene) that they'd evolved out of folk group The Ravens and toured with label-fellows **Paul Revere and The Raiders**.

Martin Torbert popped up again as writer of the **Kings Ransom**'s *Shadows Of Dawn* (it is not known if he was a member) prior to releasing a solo 45 on the same label - *Magic Girl / All Of Tomorrow* (Integra 106) 1967. (MW)

The Druids of Stonehenge

Personnel:	DAVE BUDGE	vcls	A
	CARL HAUSER	ld gtr, vcls, keyb'ds	A
	STEVE TINDALL	drms, keyb'ds	A
	BILLY TRACY	gtr	A
	TOM WORKMAN	bs	A

ALBUM:	1(A)	CREATION	(Uni 73004) 1968 R2

NB: (1) has been reissued and also issued on CD.

EP:	1	Who Do You Love/Pretty Thing/I Put A Spell On You/	
		Baby Please Don't Go/Bald Headed Woman/	
		I Who Have Nothing	(Sundazed SEP 127) 1996

NB: The first four songs of the (double) EP above were recorded in New York in 1965, the other two were recorded in Los Angeles in 1966. All six tracks are previously unreleased.

45:	A Garden Where Nothing Grows/	
	Painted Woman	(Uni 55021) 1967

This outfit came from Columbia and Syracuse Universities in New York, but relocated to Los Angeles in 1966. The band reputedly included Elliot Randall on lead vocals at one time. Randall later played with **Sea Train** prior to forming Randall's Island in 1971. However, the line up for their sole album, which was produced by Jerry Goldstein, was that shown above. It's a fairly routine rock album, which includes cover versions of Jay Hawkins' *I Put A Spell On You* and Dylan's *It's All Over Now Baby Blue*. Not really worth searching for, but it has recently had a limited repress. Their 45 was later included on the album.

The recent double 7" EP on Sundazed contains some brilliant Pretty Things-styled raucous R&B / garage - particularly the rollercoaster rendition of *Who Do You Love* and Them inspired *Baby Please Don't Go*. The EP, which is recommended, comes with detailed sleeve notes from Mike Stax and Jud Cost, which reveal how **The Druids**' played in front of their idols The Rolling Stones, whilst they were house band at the Ondine - a trendy Manhattan club. They also jammed with Eric Burdon and **Jimi Hendrix**.

The Druids Of Stonehenge also opened shows for **Moby Grape**, **The Blues Project** and **Big Brother & The Holding Company** in their time.

THE DRUIDS OF STONEHENGE - Creation LP.

Compilation appearances have included *I Put A Spell On You* on *Songs Of Faith And Inspiration* (CDR & CD); and *Six Feet Down* and *Pale Dream* on *Baubles - Down To Middle Earth* (LP). (VJ/MW)

Drydock County

Personnel:	PETER GORMANN	drms	A
	ROY KELLETT	bs	A
	RICH MANGO	gtr	A
	VINNIE MITCHELL	gtr	A
	STEPHAN	organ, piano	A

ALBUM:	1(A)	DRYDOCK COUNTY	(Mercury) c1970 -

45:	Fish Bite Better In Summertime/Same (mono)	(Mercury) c1970

This New York quintet was also known as Supa Heat and between 1967 and 1970 were the backing group of several artists produced by Wes Farrell, including **The Cowsills**, the Everly Brothers and Cashman, Pistilli & West. Farrell finally helped them to get a recording contract and their sole album contains some good psych-pop cuts:- *Together As Friends*, *Sesame Summer* (in a CSNY vein) and *Fish Bite Better In The Summertime*, as well as poor covers of **Buffalo Springfield**'s *Mr. Soul*, **Lovin Spoonful**'s *Blues In The Bottle* and the Stones' *Last Time*. This patchy album came with a small poster. (SR)

Dryewater

Personnel:	ROBERT BLAIR	bs, vcls	A
	RICHARD DRYE	ld vcls, gtr	A
	SHAYE DRYE	keyb'ds, vcls	A
	GARLAND WALKER STIDHAM	drms	A

ALBUM:	1(A)	SOUTHPAW	(J.T.B. NR 5122) 1974 R3

NB: (1) has had an official limited repress of 350 copies (Void 04).

From North California, an interesting rural hard-rock album. Occasionally the lead vocals get a bit strained and screechy, but when the band shines it has great moments. *Don't Let Her Sleep Too Long* has a confident, sinister quality to it that satisfies. (CF)

The Dry Gins

45:	She's A Drag/You're Through	(Montel-Michelle 959) 1966

The Dry Gins were from Lafayette, Louisiana, and were also known as **The Rogues**. While playing a gig in Baton Rouge, they were spotted by

DRYEWATER - Southpaw LP.

Cyril Vetter from **The Greek Fountains** who got them a recording contract with Montel-Michelle. It was Vetter who suggested they change their name to **The Dry Gins** for this 45. The band called it quits in late 1966.

Compilation appearances have included *You're Through* on *The Essential Pebbles Collection, Vol. 1* (Dble CD); and *She's A Drag* on *Back From The Grave, Vol. 8* (CD) and *Back From The Grave, Vol. 8* (Dble LP). (MW)

Duffy

45:	Come Back, Come Back/Hello There Girl	(Dial 4097)	1970

An unknown artist whose 45 was produced by Buddy Killen and probably recorded in Nashville. The 'A' side, which is full of studio gimmickry with lots of echoplex and other sound effects, can be heard on *Beyond The Calico Wall* (LP & CD) and is well worth checking out. The flip is reputedly awful - an insipid song sung through a megaphone. (VJ)

John Dugan

ALBUM:	1	JOHN DUGAN	(Black Baron)	1966

NB: (1) Limited to 100 numbered copies, cover is black matte with Xerox graphic covering 3/4 of front. Artists name and pressing # handwritten on Xerox. Mono.

From Santa Clara, California. The sound style on this album is similar to **Phil Ochs** solo acoustic work, though the lyrics are not as politically vehement and in some cases even whimsical. Production quality is very high.

Could this be the same **John Dugan** who was involved in the production of "The Texas Chainsaw Massacre"? Any help would be appreciated. (CH)

The Dukes (aka Royal Jones and The Dukes)

Personnel:	SONNY CRIPE	gtr	A
	GARY JONES	ld vcls, gtr	AB
	TOM PINKERMAN	bs	A
	DAVE REDDING	sax	A
	?? ??	drms	A
	GENE JONES	ld vcls, organ	BC
	KEITH KILMER	drms	BC
	JAY PURVIS	gtr, ld vcls	BC
	SKIP WALTERS	bs	B
	DAVE WORKMAN	sax	BC
	MIKE KISER	bs, hrmnca, vcls	C

45s:	α	I Don't Love You Anymore / Do It Now	(Fujimo 4454)	196?
		Walking The Dog / Please Come Home	(Fujimo #unkn)	196?
	β	Take Your Love /?	(Fujimo #unkn)	196?
		The First Time I Saw Her / Take You're Love	(Signet 3265)	1967

NB: One of the Fujimo 45s came in a picture sleeve and there may be more 45s on that label. α and β were released as **Royal Jones & The Dukes**. β 'B' side mispelt "Your" on label.

This was Goshen, Indiana's top band in the mid-sixties. Formed in 1963 by the Jones brothers, they underwent several personnel changes but their most stable line-ups are shown above. They recorded a few 45s for Fujimo and one for the Chicago-based Signet label, Gary Jones left the band in 1966 and was replaced by Jay Purvis who wrote *Take Your Love*, which has recently got another airing on the *Hoosier Hotshots* (LP) compilation. It's very much in the folk-garage mould and worth a listen. They later signed to Columbia who clearly wanted to turn them into a Midwest version of **Paul Revere and The Raiders** and fit them with navy uniforms and a new moniker Gene Paul Jones and The American Navy. When the band made it clear they didn't want to know, Columbia simply didn't record them and they soon were no more.

Sadly, Gary Jones died in April 1995 and Keith Kilmer on November 29th 2001. (VJ/MW/PY)

Duke Williams and The Extremes

Personnel incl:	HANK RANSOM	drms	A
	T.J. TINDALL	gtr	A

ALBUMS:	1(A)	A MONKEY IN.... IS STILL A MONKEY		
			(Capricorn CP0133)	1973 -
	2(A)	FANTASTIC FEDORA	(Capricorn CP0133)	1974 -

This rather loose aggregation of musicians was fronted by T.J. Tindall (ex-**Edison Electric Band**) and included the drummer Hank Ransom, from the Philadelphia group **Elizabeth** and the guitar player of **Alexander Rabbit**.

Their two albums range from Southern rock to white soul with horns and bar rock, and are of mediocre interest here. As with many large groups, they were probably better live.

Richie Sambora of Bon Jovi was also in this band at some point (SR/RMh)

Monte Dunn and Karen Cruz

Personnel incl:	KAREN CRUZ	vcls	A
	MONTE DUNN	gtr	A

ALBUM:	1(A)	MONTE DUNN AND KAREN CRUZ		
			(Cyclone CY 4101)	c1969 SC

45:	Baby, You Been On My Mind/ Jump In A Yellow Cab	(CBS 43765)	1966

NB: **Monte Dunn** solo.

THE DUKES.

Guitarist **Monte Dunn** was a session musician who can be found on many albums of sixties folk-rock, such as **Peter Walker**, **David Blue**, **Fred Neil** and **Buffy Sainte-Marie**. He also recorded this rare folk album with Karen Cruz which was housed in a lovely psychy cover. (SR)

Duplex

Pebbles, Vol. 16 (LP) includes a live version of *Louie, Louie* by this band at a 'Battle Of The Bands' competition in Hawaii and originally isued on *Battle Of The Bands* (LP) (Star SRM 101) 1964. It is pretty undistinguished. Most of the other participants were surf instrumentalists. (VJ)

Dust

Personnel:	KENNY AARONSON	bs, gtr, dobro	A
	MARC BELL	drms, vcls	A
	RICHIE WISE	gtr, vcls	A

ALBUMS:	1(A)	DUST	(Kama Sutra KSBS 2041) 1971 -
	2(A)	HARD ATTACK	(Kama Sutra KSBS 2059) 1972 -

NB: (1) and (2) have been reissued. First pressings of both are on a pink Kama Sutra label, (2) with gatefold sleeve.

45s:	Stone Woman/?	(Kama Sutra 534) 1971
	Love Me Hard/?	(Kama Sutra 541) 1972

A New York hard-rock trio, highly regarded by some. Marc Bell later played with Richard Hell's Voidoids and the Ramones. Kenny Aaronson went on to play with Stories, joined the Rick Derringer Band and played with several hard-rock groups including HSAS (Hagar, Schon, Aaronson, Shrieve). He also played on Blue Oyster Cult's *Club Ninja* album.

Richie Wise and Kenny Kerner (their producer and collaborator) went on to produce the first two Kiss albums. Richie also has a producer credit and photo on Savoy Brown's *Greatest Hits/Live*.

It's rumoured that **Dust** also laid down some tracks for a third album that was never finished. (SR/KS/CG)

Dust Bowl Clementine

Personnel:	BRUCE BRADT	piano, organ, vcls	A
	EDWARD EVANS	bs, gtr, vcls	A
	ANTHONY FABIANO	drms, perc, vcls	A
	CHUCK LASKOWSKI	ld vcls, 12-string gtr	A
	NICK MANZI	gtr, vcls	A
	(GEORGE CHRIST	hrmnca	A)
	(BARRY WEBER	gtr	A)

ALBUM:	1(A)	DUST BOWL CLEMENTINE	(Roulette SR-42058) 197? -

45:	Goin' Back Down To The Country/Patchin' Up	(Roulette ?) 1970

NB: also issued in France with a PS (45 VR 19 5083) 1971.

Chuck Laskowski is in fact **Faine Jade**'s real name and he also wrote most of the **Dust Bowl Clementine** material. Bruce Bradt (**Illusion**) and Nick Manzi (**Bohemian Vendetta**) had already worked with him on his *Introspection* album.

Produced by Michael Earle and recorded in Hempstead, New York, the album is clearly country-oriented, most of the songs dealing with the same subject: *Going Back Down To The Country* (the only one penned by Manzi), *Farm Song*, *Get Back Home*, *Country Man*. Some good guitar solos by Manzi help to improve the final result, but this album is more a curiosity than a masterpiece. (SR)

Dutch Masters

Personnel:	EARL DENTON	vcls	A

THE DUKES.

45s:	Burnin' Up The Wires / Way Down Feelin'	(MY 2916) 1967
	The Expectation / You're Nearby Me	(MY 2926) 1967

Assembled by MY label-owner Earl Denton in Little Rock, Arkansas, to provide backing for his vocals, the band continued without him after the debut and produced one excellent 45. *The Expectation*, a "midtempo fuzz-grinder", has subsequently resurfaced on Erik Lindgren's *A Lethal Dose Of Hard Psych* (CD) compilation, which notes that the band decked themselves out like the depiction of Dutch dudes on cigar boxes.

One member was later in **The Hombres**.

The Expectation has also been compiled on *Pebbles, Vol. 4 (ESD)* (CD). (MM/MW)

Dwight Douglas and The Jayhawkers

Personnel incl:	DWIGHT DOUGLAS	A

45:	Interstate 45/Mr. Big	(Astra 3008) 196?

From Detroit, this 45 was by **Jay Hawkers**, who had several 45s under that moniker. You can also find *Interstate 45* on *Scum Of The Earth, Vol. 1* (LP) and *Scum Of The Earth* (CD). (VJ)

The (Dynamic) Dischords

Personnel incl:	TOM RADINE	A

45s:	Age Of Caesar/I Love Life	(Mark Custom 4000) 196?
	This Girl Of Mine/Passageway To Your Heart	(IGL 150) 1968

Operated out of Oakes, a small town in the Southeast of Nonh Dakota. After recording their first 45 in Moorhead, North Dakota, they became the only band from that state to sign for the IGL label, based in Milford, Iowa. The result was a good punk 45 with *Passageway To Your Heart* especially noteworthy. Later, in 1971, they recorded a reasonable hard-rock 45. By then they were known simply as The Dischords.

Compilation appearances have so far included: *Passageway To Your Heart* on *The Midwest Vs. Canada* (LP), *The Best Of IGL Garage Rock* (LP), *Gathering Of The Tribe* (CD) and *The IGL Rock Story: Part Two (1967 - 68)* (CD). (VJ)

The Dynasty

Personnel:	FRED ANDERSON	bs	A
	DON BEETCHER	drms	A
	JACK CASPER	ld gtr	A
	MARK CASPER	gtr	A

KEN CLARK	keyb'ds	A
DAN EGNASH	keyb'ds	
MIKE POLASKI	keyb'ds	A

45s: I've Gona Shout/I'm Cryin' (Royal Court 262) 1966
Flying On The Ground Is Wrong/
Soul Kitchen (Westchester W-1156) 1968

A youthful garage quintet from Superior, Wisconsin. Their first 45 is much sought-after. *I've Gotta Shout* has also resurfaced on the compilation *The Midwest Vs. Canada* (LP) and is a bone-crunching punker with an *I'm A Man* type guitar riff. The flip is an Animals cover.

Their later release covers the **Buffalo Springfield** classic, but falls short in the vocals department. However their version of the **Doors**' *Soul Kitchen* is altogether better, quite excellent actually, with strong and raucous vocals.

In Gary Myer's book on the Badger state, 'Do You Hear That Beat', Jack Casper recalls some highlights for the band - opening for **Tommy James and The Shondells** and a show with **The Electric Prunes**.

A later line-up included Mike Polaski from local rivals The Emotionals.

Jack Casper went on to several other outfits, including a 14-year stint with Vegas. (VJ/MW/GM)

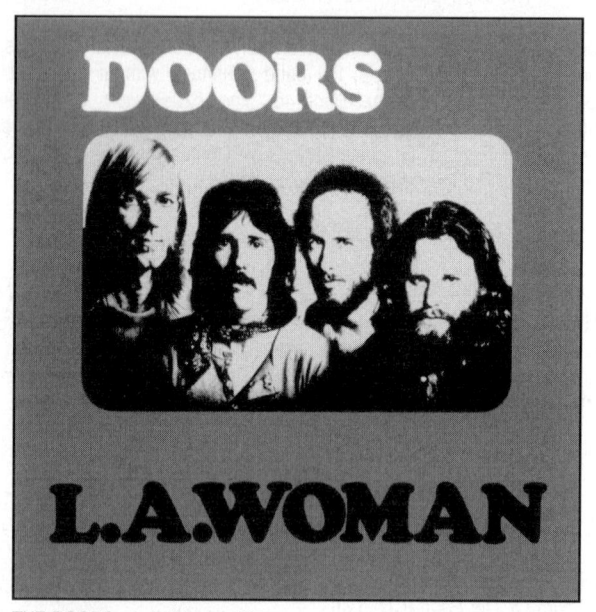

THE DOORS - Morrison Hotel CD.

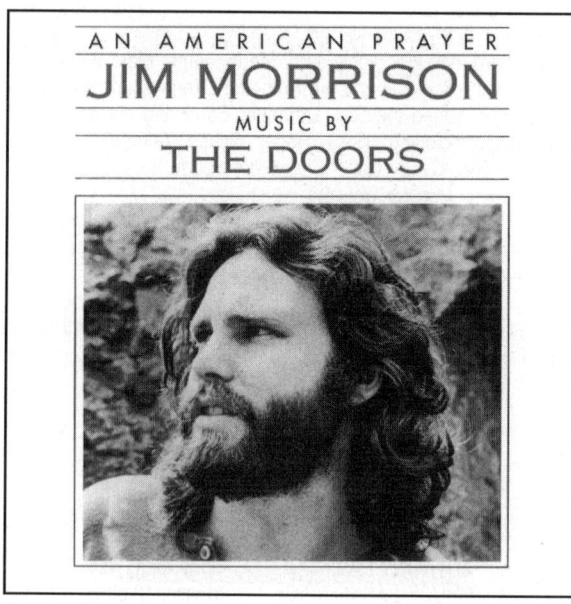

THE DOORS - L.A. Woman CD.

THE DOORS - An American Prayer CD.

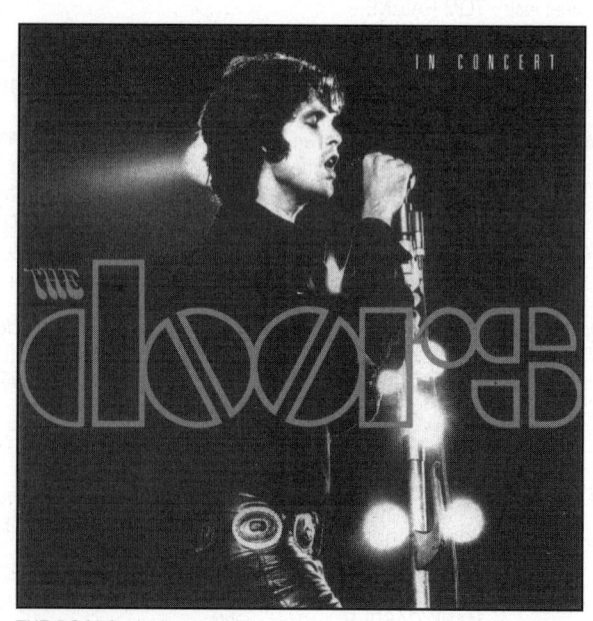

THE DOORS - In Concert CD.

THE DRUIDS OF STONEHENGE - Sundazed PS EP.

Eagle

Personnel:	ROBERT RHODES	keyb'ds, horns	A
	WAYNE ULAKY	bs	A
	JOHN WRIGHT	vcls	A

ALBUM: 1(A) COME UNDER NANCY'S TENT
(Janus JLS 3011) 1970 SC

NB: (1) also released in France (Stateside C 062 92118) 1970. (1) reissued on vinyl as by "Beacon Street Union As Eagle" (Akarma AK 173). (1) reissued on CD, together with both **Beacon Street Union** albums as a 3-CD box set *State Of The Union* (Akarma AK 157/3).

45s: Kickin' It Back To You/
Come In, It's All For Free   (Janus 113) 1970
Brown Hair/Working Man   (Janus 135) 1970

Previously known as **The Beacon Street Union**, the album, which has some nice guitar pieces, is quite good.

Lead singer John Lincoln Wright went on to become a leading country music star in Boston during the seventies, releasing at least three records: *John Lincoln Wright And The Sour Mash Boys* EP (John Lincoln Wright 92745) (his first with the group, very rare limited pressing); *Nothin' But The Rain/Pull Away From Your Man* (Esca ER00101); and *The Red Sox Song (A Day In Fenway Park)/same* (Canobie Shores CS 45100) 1976.

The *The Best Of Bosstown Sound* (Dble CD) compilation includes *Come In It's For Free*, *Kickin' It Back* and *Separated*. (VJ/SBn)

Earthen Vessel

Personnel:	DAVE CAUDILL	gtr, vcls	A
	KEN FITCH	vcls, keyb'ds	A
	ED JOHNSON	drms	A
	SHARON KEEL	vcls, keyb'ds	A
	JOHN SPRUNGER	bs, vcls	A

ALBUM: 1(A) HARD ROCK - EVERLASTING LIFE
(NRS 2587) 1971 R5

NB: (1) reissued officially on CD by Gear Fab (GF-127) 1999 and on vinyl (Akarma AK 098) 2000.

45: Life Everlasting/You Can   (NRS 591) 1971

A Lansing, Michigan band, although their rare album is on a Tennessee label. The 45 cuts are on the album. The group played hard-rock with male and female vocals (overtly religious lyrics) punctuated by loud fuzz guitar.

Compilation appearances include *Life Everlasting* on Gear Fab's *Psychedelic Sampler* (CD). (CF)

EARTHEN VESSEL - Hard Rock Everlasting Life LP.

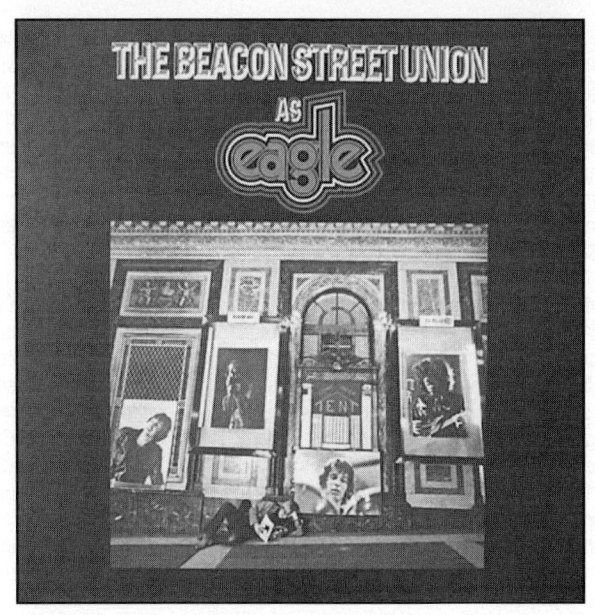

EAGLE - Come Under Nancy's Tent (Reissue) LP.

Earth Island

Personnel:	BRUCE DOSHIER	A
	BILL LISKA	A
	NICHOLAS RUSH	A
	RICHARD VANDERWOERDT	A

ALBUM: 1(A) WE MUST SURVIVE   (Philips PHS 600.340) 1969 -

45: Doomsday Afternoon/?   (Philips DJP 62 40673) 1969
NB: promo copy.

A soft-rock album which is pleasant enough and similar in style to **Strawberry Alarm Clock** with the theme of conservation running throughout. Eight of the cuts were penned by the band. The album was produced by **Kim Fowley**, who co-wrote the final two tracks, a pair of pretty awful 'green anthems' with **Skip Battin**. (VJ/RV)

Earth Opera

Personnel:	PAUL DILLON	drms, vcls, perc, gtr	AB
	DAVID GRISMAN	mandolin, piano, sax, vcls	AB
	JOHN NAGY	bs, cello	AB
	PETER ROWAN	gtr, sax, vcls	AB
	BILL STEVENSON	vibes, keyb'ds	A
	(BILL MUNDI	drms	A)
	(WARREN SMITH	drms	A)
	(JACK BONUS	sax	B)
	(HERB BUSHLER	double bs	B)
	(JOHN CALE	viola	B)
	(DAVE HOROWITZ	keyb'ds	B)
	(RICHARD GRANDO	sax, bass recorder	B)
	(BILL KEITH	pedal steel gtr	B)

HCP
ALBUMS: 1(A) EARTH OPERA   (Elektra EKS-74016) 1968 - -
2(B) THE GREAT AMERICAN EAGLE TRAGEDY
(Elektra EKS-74038) 1969 181 SC

NB: (1) and (2) also released in France (Vogue/Elektra EKS74016 and CLVLXEK 354 respectively). (2) reissued (Edsel ED215) 1987. (1) reissued on CD (Wounded Bird WOU 4016). (2) reissued on CD (Wounded Bird WOU 4038).

HCP
45s: American Eagle Tragedy/
When You Were Full Of Wonder   (Elektra 45636) 1968 -
Home To You/Alfie Finney   (Elektra 45650) 1969 97

Another of the Boston wave of rock groups, **Earth Opera** certainly possessed talent. However, they arrived on the scene a little too late to make a sustained impact.

The origins of the group lay in the rich Boston folk scene in the early sixties with the first experiences of Rowan and Grisman. A gifted songwriter, singer, mandolin and guitar player, Peter Rowan began playing in the early sixties doing bluegrass and string band music with Bill Monroe and the Bluegrass Boys and the Mother Bay State Entertainers. A master of mandolin, David Grisman had similar roots and played with Siegel, Grisman, Rose and Lewinger. Some recordings of these early Rowan and Grisman bands can be found on *The String Band Project* (Elektra EKS-7292) 1965.

Earth Opera was formed at the end of 1967 by Rowan and Grisman and their first album was housed in a strange gatefold sleeve with pictures probably taken inside an Indian temple. All the songs were credited to Rowan (*Time And Again* being co-written with Grisman) and the use of vibes, harpsichord or mandocello help creating a gloomy atmosphere on songs like *Death By Fire* or *As It Is Before*. The following year *The Great American Eagle Tragedy* pursued a similar direction. Bill Halverson had left but the four remaining members were helped by various guests, including **Velvet Underground**'s John Cale on viola, **Jim Kweskin Jug Band**'s Bill Keith and **Jefferson Airplane**'s friend Jack Bonus. Once again the sleeve was notable, this time with a collage combining a skull with the American Eagle symbol.

Both albums were produced by Peter Siegel, formerly with **The Even Dozen Jug Band** and Siegel, Grisman, Rose and Lewinger.

Commercially unsuccessful, **Earth Opera** broke up in 1969. Grisman and Rowan went to California and joined two bluegrass outfits: Muleskinner with Clarence White of the **Byrds** and Old And In The Way with **Jerry Garcia** (Grisman also played on **The Grateful Dead**'s *American Beauty*).

Peter Rowan would later join **Seatrain** and form the Rowan Brothers with his brothers Chris and Lorin. He also released several solo albums mixing rock, bluegrass and country. In the mid-seventies, David Grisman formed the David Grisman Quintet and spearheaded the Dawg Music movement, mixing bluegrass and jazz. Both are still recording.

John Nagy became a studio musician and also played with **Michael Hurley**.

You can also find *Home To You* and *The Red Sox Are Winning* (from their first album) on the compilation *Elektrock The Sixties* (4-LP), *Close Your Eyes And Shut The Door* on the Elektra compilation *Elektrifying*; *The American Eagle Tragedy* on *Hallucinations, Psychedelic Underground* (LP) and *Home Of The Brave* on *Kings Of Pop Music Vol. 2* (LP). Retrospective compilation appearances have included *The American Eagle Tragedy* and *The Red Sox Are Winning* on *The Best Of Bosstown Sound* (Dble CD). (SR/VJ)

Eastern Alliance

Personnel incl:	TIMOTHY GAY		A
	BILL WRINN		A

45:	Love Fades Away/		
	Please Don't Say You're Sorry	(Wriga 124-12)	1966

From New Haven, Connecticut, this band formed at high school around 1965. *Love Fades Away* features some nice mellow, laid back guitar work.

Bill Wrinn later recorded a solo 45, *The Devil Take New Orleans* (Poison Ring) 1969/70.

You can also find *Love Fades Away* on *Relative Distance* (LP); *Sixties Punk Ballads Sampler* (LP) and *Sixties Archive, Vol. 5* (CD). (MM/VJ)

Eastfield Meadows

Personnel:	JOHN BIERER	A
	DAVID CARPENTER	A
	WAYNE GRAJADA	A
	TONY HARRIS	A
	DWIGHT PAYNE	A
	JAMES WHITTEMORE	A

ALBUM:	1(A)	EASTFIELD MEADOWS	(VMC VS 133) 1968 -

EARTH OPERA - Earth Opera CD.

45:	Friend of Unequal Parallel/	
	Love All Men Can Share	(VMC V-745) 1968

From California, a nice mix of psych-rock, country and vocal harmonies. The album is quite sought-after by collectors. Their single was produced by Vic Briggs (Animals). Tony Harris was also a producer for the label VMC and worked with **Morning Sun** and **Pacific Ocean**. (SR)

The East Side Kids

Personnel:	DAVID DOUD	gtr	A
	MIKE DOUD	bs	A
	JOE MADRID	vcls	A
	DAVE POTTER	?	A

ALBUM:	1(A)	TIGER AND THE LAMB	(Uni 73032) 1968 -

45s:	Subway Train/Sunday Stranger	(Philips 40295) 1965
	Might Mist Blue/Chocolate Matzos	(Warner Bros. 5821) 1966
	Little Bird/I Listen To The Wise Man	(Valhalla 672) 1967
α	Close Your Mind /	
	Take A Look In The Mirror	(Orange Empire OE-500) 1967
	Taking The Time/Is My Love Strong?	(UNI 55105) 1969

NB: α both sides non-LP, written by **Bernie Schwartz**.

Although obviously connected with Texas because Dave Potter joined them from **Endle St. Cloud** and went on to Potter St. Cloud, they were from Los Angeles' East Side. The album, which is largely mainstream pop aside from a psychedelic interpretation of *Dancing In The Street*, is really one to avoid. Some tracks were written by H. Wesley Watt (of **Euphoria**) who also migrated between Texas and California. Two, *Pigeon Of LA* and *I See I Am* were written by **Buzz Clifford** of **Hamilton Streetcar**.

They were also the backing group for Jimmy Greenspoon before he joined **Kim Fowley** and Michael Lloyd and later Three Dog Night.

Written by Greenspoon for Kim Fowley Music and produced by Larry Tamblyn of **The Standells**, *Listen To The Wise Man* is compiled on *East Side Revue* and *The West Coast East Side Sound, Vol. 4* (CD), whilst *Close Your Mind* also appears on the *Psychedelic Experience, Vol. 2* (CD).

Their album was produced by **Dan Moore** and **Buzz Clifford** and in 1969/70, the Doud brothers and Dave Potter played on their solo albums. (VJ/MW/SR/KSI)

(Gaylon Ladd & the) Eastside Transfer

Personnel incl:	GAYLON LATIMORE (LADD)		A

45:	Repulsive Situation/My Life, My Love	(Pacemaker 257) 1966

This fuzz-punk 45 is generally considered **Latimer**'s best recording. Hear it on *Highs In The Mid-Sixties Vol. 23*. Prior to forming the band in Waco, he cut three solo 45s. He went on to play in **Heather Black**. (VJ)

Eastwood Review

Personnel:	RICKY HERNANDEZ	keyb'ds	A
	CHRIS HOLZHAUS	gtr	A
	LAURENT PERRON	drms	A
	MARIUS PERRON	bs	A

CD:	1(A)	RIDE DOWN TO HOUSTON		
			(Collectables COL-CD 0582)	1994

From San Antonio, Texas, the line-up included two distant cousins of the late Steve Perron (of **Mind's Eye** and **Children**) and Chris Holzhaus (of **The Argyles**, **Mind's Eye** and **Children**. Recorded in Houston at Andrus Recording Studios 1969-1970, Roy Ames was unable to get any interest outside the locals - slow and moody blues-rock wasn't the flavour of the industry then, it seems. So it languished until now - if Cream, Johnny Winter or early Fleetwood Mac appeal to you, this is worth a listen.

Chris Holzhaus, incidentally, later played guitar with Roky Erikson on his *Live At The Ritz* album. He still plays regularly around the San Antonio bar scene. Marius Perron (Bubba) is now a recording engineer and also teaches recording classes around San Antonio. An internet search inquiry under "marius perron" will bring up a string of hits regarding credits on the albums he has been involved with. He has been very involved with Michael Morales who made a local noise a few years ago. His brother Laurent Perron is not involved in music anymore and works a regular job. Ricky Hernandez still performs on the side as a freelance player with several local acts in the bar scene. (MW/MLI)

Easy Chair

Personnel incl:	PHIL KIRBY		A
	PETER LARSON	gtr	A
	ALBERT MALOSKY		A
	JEFFREY SIMMONS	gtr	A
	CRAIG KARP		B
	JIM THOMPSON		B

ALBUM:	1(A)	THE EASY CHAIR	(Vanco) 1968 R4

NB: This was a local Washington State one-sided demo album issued in a plain cover.

45:	Somebody Help Me/Hobo	(Sea-West 45-107) 1971

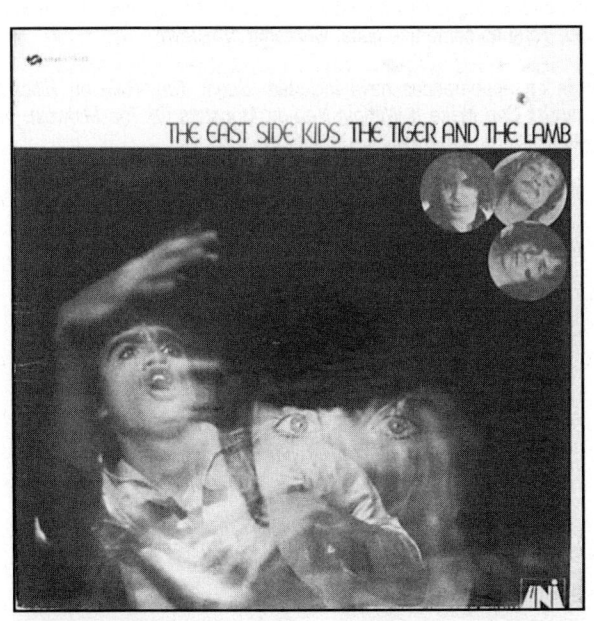

THE EAST SIDE KIDS - Tiger And The Lamb LP.

Of the three tracks on their rare one-sided album, two are long, bluesy jamming cuts that never actually go anywhere and one is an amazing Eastern/heavy psych cut. **Jeff Simmons** and other members of this band were previously managed by Matthew Katz as Indian Puddin' and Pipe, but although they were the first band to use the name, they were not the people responsible for **Indian Puddin' & Pipe**'s known recordings... that outfit was **West Coast Natural Gas**, who inherited the name when the original band split with Katz and became **Easy Chair**. Curiously, **West Coast Natural Gas** shared the bill once with the original Indian Puddin' and Pipe in Seattle.

Their 45 is markedly less interesting, with horns. The 'B' side is instrumental.

Simmons released two solo albums on the Straight label in 1969.

Ex-**Jack Eely & The Courtmen** member Bill Truitt was also in a later line-up of **Easy Chair**. (CF/DR)

Easy Steam

ALBUM:	1	TO BE ALIVE	(Conglomerate) 1976 SC

NB: (1) issued with a silkscreened sleeve or a plain white cover.

From Minnesota, a prog-rock outfit with flute and guitar interplay. (SR)

Easy Street

Personnel:	JERRY ADAMS	bs	A
	GENE BELL	drms	A
	LARRY BLACK	keyb'ds	ABC
	PHIL HOLZBAUER	gtr	ABC
	RON BUCHEK	drms	B
	JERRY STEFANI	bs	BC
	NELS CHRISTIANSEN	drms, perc	C

45s:	α	Girl Don't Leave Me / Alright	(Feature RPS-105) 1966
		Peter Pan / Boom-Bah	(Cine Vista 1003) 1968
	β	Do You Hear The Magic Music/	
		Walking In The Clouds	(Cine Vista 1004) 1969

NB: α as **The Madadors**. β later issued on Paramount (0007), 1969.

This group was from East Troy and Palmyra, Wisconsin. They formed in the early sixties as The Mad Madadors but didn't make their wax debut until 1966 as **The Madadors**. The following year they became **Easy Street**.

Returning from an Alaskan tour with **The Rascals**, they got some label interest from Cine Vista, run by **Dick Campbell**, who took them to Chicago to record. Their second 45 as **Easy Street** was picked up by Paramount and did well in North Wisconsin and Kansas City, but the national label failed to keep up with the demand.

When Buchek had to leave for a tour of duty, his seat was filled by Christiansen from The Playboys.

The band didn't last much longer. Buchek went into the construction business; Holzbauer was with oldies band Solid Gold in the seventies and Black emigrated to Denmark. (MW/MM/GM)

Sally Eaton

ALBUM:	1	FAREWELL AMERICAN TOUR	
			(Paramount PAS 5021) 1971 -

A surprising record. The ugly front sleeve makes you want to put the album back where you found it, and the first four tracks, which are boring, just confirm this impression. But with *Flower In The Air*, a raga with oriental percussion, you begin to get hooked and Side Two is really good, culminating with the seven-minutes of *Maybe My Love For You*. Swirling organ, nice guitars, and **Sally Eaton**'s voice.

The record was produced by George Brackman, Nat Shapiro and Harold Wheeler and all the songs were written by **Sally Eaton** and Brackman. (SR)

The Ebb Tides

Personnel:	BOB BENEVIDES	ld gtr	AB
	BOBBY ROBIDOUX	organ	AB
	CHARLIE ROBIDOUX	vcls	AB
	DONALD SMITH	drms	AB
	TONY TAVEIRA	bs	AB
	RAY ??		A

45:	My Baby's Gone/Sumertime	(Arco 107) 1966

An early incarnation of **Tangerine Zoo**, from Fall River, Massachusetts. Taveira had formed The Rogues (the name taken from the street gang in "West Side Story") in 1963, but joined forces with Don Smith in 1965 to form The Batmen. Once The Batmen were able to acquire the services of talented guitarist Bob Benevides, who was returning from the service, the band changed names to the **Ebb Tides** in order to accommodate the new sound.

Taveira, Benevides and Smith decided to drop the Robidoux brothers from the band when they learned that Wayne Gagnon - who had previously played with Benevides in the Rockin' Teens - had become available (he, too, was in the service). They would then add organist Ron Medieros from the Knight Riders, and briefly change their name to the Flower Pot. The band would later sign with Mainstream Records, where they finally settled on the name **Tangerine Zoo**.

The Ebb Tides lone single was recorded at ARCO Records in New Bedford, Massachusetts.

Tony Taveira later formed a seventies disco outfit with his brothers called Tavares.

You can also find *My Baby's Gone* on *Sixties Rebellion, Vol. 4* (LP & CD). (VJ/MM/MDo/TTa/BBs)

Ebb-Tides

Personnel:	DONALD KYRE	gtr, vcls	A
	DAN WALDRON	drms, vcls	AB
	MIKE WHEELER	ld gtr, vcls	AB
	MIKE WHITED	bs, vcls	AB
	BENNY VANDERVORT ('Benny Van')	gtr, vcls	B

45s:	Little Women / What'd I Say	(Clark 238) 1965
	Seance / Spirits Ride The Wind	(Jar 820J-106) 1967

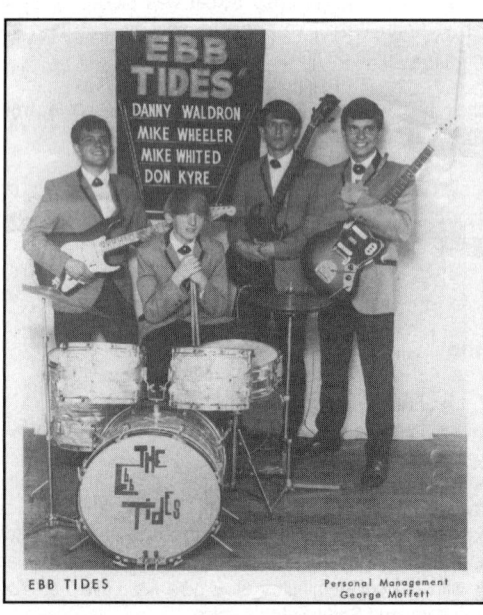

THE EBB TIDES (Ohio 1964)

The Ebb Tides were formed in Columbus, Ohio, in early 1963 by three 14-year-old high school friends, along with a local 10-year-old drummer. Promotion by a local DJ enabled the band to have their name aired frequently on local rock station WCOL in exchange for playing station-sponsored sock-hops.

In 1964, while playing at a secluded off-midway show at the Ohio State Fair, the band was heard by a talent scout from WTVN, a local NBC affiliate, and was asked to play that night at the station's pavilion. Crowd reaction was so favourable the band was contracted to perform nightly for the remainder of the fair. This engagement lead to multiple appearances on the local TV show 'Dance Party'. One of these appearances caught the interest of a regional music promoter.

Hired by Moffett Productions in 1965, the band signed to do an eleven state, three Canadian province, tour with the variety show 'Shindig All-Star Review'. The cast consisted of from 11 to 17 personnel including vocalists, Go-Go girls and a popular dance team. The band backed headliners such as Bobby Sherman, Del Shannon, Joann Castle and the Mills brothers. They also opened for **The New Colony Six**, **Terry Knight and The Pack** and **The Byrds**.

The Ebb Tides' first 45 was *Little Women*, penned by Kyre and Whited, which had a driving *Money* type of beat. The 'B' side was a cover of Ray Charles' *What I'd Say*. This 45 was recorded in Nashville in 1965.

In 1966 Don Kyre introduced the band to Ben Vandervort. An insurance salesman from D.C. in Ohio visiting relatives, Ben couldn't play a musical instrument but had a good "rock-a-billy" voice and a talent for writing lyrics. After a few guitar lessons, Ben was a band member, playing, singing and writing songs under the stage name of "Benny Van".

The second 45 is a spirited affair, literally. *Seance* is a jaunty keyboard dominated punk-pop-novelty, with ghostly 'wooooos' and tongue planted firmly in cheek. *Spirits Ride The Wind* features spoken poetic lyrics over a mellow psychy backdrop of gently cascading guitar and soft hand-drums. Benny Van would take this group on a spiritual odyssey to higher musical planes in the course of which he and they metamorphosed into **J.D. Blackfoot**.

Compilation appearances have included *Seance* on *Boulders, Vol. 6* (LP), *Ya Gotta Have Moxie, Vol. 2* (Dble CD); and rather strangely, for an Ohio outfit, on *Michigan Mayhem Vol. 1* (CD). (GGI/MW/MWd)

Barry Ebling and The Invaders

Personnel incl:	BARRY EBLING	vcls
	GARY VANDEVER	gtr, vcls

45:	I Can Make It Without You/Sunny Day Rain	(Norman 581) 1967

Came from Granite City, Illinois and were originally known as The Invaders. When Barry Ebling joined his father took over as manager. *I Can Make It Without You* has some fine guitar work from Vandever.

Compilation appearances have included: *Sunny Day Rain* on *Killer Cuts* (LP); and *I Can Make It Without You* on *Monsters Of The Midwest, Vol. 3* (LP). (VJ)

THE EBB TIDES (Ohio 1965)

THE EBB TIDES (Ohio 1966)

The Eccentrics

45:     Baby I Need You/She's Ugly   (Shane 60) 1966

Another obscure garage band from Texas. *Baby I Need You* features a compulsive rhythm guitar and is quite a superb slice of garage. The flip is a slower ballad in The Animals vein, with typical "girl put-down" lyrics.

Both sides have also resurfaced on the excellent *Sixties Rebellion, Vol. 3* (LP & CD). (VJ)

Eccentrics

45:     Podunk Holler / Weathermaster   (Fresh FR 32) 1965

Podunk Holler is a 5-star fuzz'n'farfisa punker with all the ingredients of the so-called "class of '66" - driving rhythm, raucous vocals, screams, stunning break and attitude aplenty. Amazing that this has evaded the compilers. Produced by Jeff Hagen and Kearney Barton with a label address in Sequim, Washington state. The flip is an instrumental. (MW/AB)

The Echo(es)

Personnel incl:	KENNY AHERN	ld gtr	A
	DON FEDELE	keyb'ds	A
	DONNY GOODSON	drms	A
	BILL KERTI	bs	A
	WAYNE MAGLEY	gtr	A

45s:	Every Second Of The Day/Wild Mother	(Art 198) 1966
α	Don't Know Why/Young People	(Rebound 001) 1967
α	Cheatin' Girl/Shadows	(Argee 103) 1968

NB: α released as by The Echo.

From Miami, Florida this band also issued a 45 as **The Echoes Of Carnaby Street**. After their first 45 above as **The Echoes**, they were credited as **The Echo**. *Every Second Of The Day* is on *Garage Punk Unknowns, Vol. 7* (LP). *Shadows*, a piece of fragmented psych, is on *Psychedelic States: Florida Vol. 1* (CD), which reveals that a different version made it onto a Universal Recording demo disc with a different flip (credited to **The Echoes**). (MW/JLh/RM)

The Echoes of Carnaby Street

Personnel incl:	KENNY AHERN	ld gtr	A
	DON FEDELE	keyb'ds	A
	DONNY GOODSON	drms	A
	BILL KERTI	bs	A
	WAYNE MAGLEY	gtr	A

45s: No Place Or Time/Baby Doesn't Know   (Thames E-105) 1966

From Miami, Florida, this quintet were also known as The Echoes and latterly The Echo. *No Place Or Time* was co-written by Travis "Fairchild" Ximenes of **The Clefs Of Lavender Hill**. It's a great effort - an upbeat choppy harmony popper that metamorphoses midsong into a mini acid guitar work-out. Initially compiled (erroneously) on Eva's *Louisiana Punk From The Sixties* (LP) (reissued on CD as *Sixties Archive, Vol. 3*), it has been restored to full glory on *Psychedelic States: Florida Vol. 1* (CD). The flip has some outstanding guitar-work too - check it out on *Sixties Choice, Vol. 2* (LP) or *60's Choice, Vol's 1 And 2* (CD).

Ahern and Goodson were both ex-members of **The Invaders**. (VJ/MW/JLh/RM)

The Echomen

Personnel:	RICK BARN	drms	A
	BOB DERRICKSON	ld gtr	ABC
	GREG HUPPERT	keyb'ds	A
	GARY ORLINE	gtr	A
	RANDY RYMER	bs	A
	EMMIT CASE	drms	B
	BOB RASMUSSEN	keyb'ds	BC
	JACK TAYLOR	bs	BC
	RICHARD (DICK) POGUE	drms	C

NB: line-up 'A' 1964. Line-up 'B' 1966. Line-up 'C' 1966.

45s:	Long Green/Chocolate Chip	(Fox 1) 1966
	Watch It Baby/Blue Blue Feeling	(Le Jac 3006) 1966

From Minneapolis, Minnesota, this band is most notable for later evolving into the now legendary **Bedlam Four**. Their version of *Long Green* got a further airing on *Hipsville, Vol. 3* (LP). Richard 'Dick' Pogue came in shortly before they evolved into the **Bedlam Four** and also wrote *Watch It Baby*. (VJ/MW)

Echos

Personnel:	JOHN BERECEK	ld gtr	A
	TIM HOGAN	gtr, keyb'ds	A
	AL TWISS	bs	A
	JOE VITALE	drms	A

45:     Around And Around /
        You Make Me Feel Good   (Dupree 101) 196?

An unheard and uncompiled 45 to-date, but the titles (presumably covers of Chuck Berry and the Zombies) sound encouraging. What's more interesting about this Canton, Ohio, outfit is that after this 45 they changed their name to **The Chylds**, of *Hay Girl* fame. Joe Vitale later did time with **The Measles** and Marble Cake. In the seventies, he raised his profile higher as Joe Walsh's main "Barnstormer" from 1972 to 1978, and released a solo album in 1974 - *Roller Coaster Weekend* (Atlantic SD 18114). (GGI/MW)

Eclectic Mouse

Personnel:	JOE N. CORRAL	flute	A
	BARRY DOWNS	trumpet	A
	TIM DOWNS	drms	A
	KRISTEN ENGSTRAND	piano, organ	A
	RICK FELIX	tuba	A
	STEVE FORMAN	perc	A
	BILLY GONZALES	trumpet	A
	BEN HARVEY	trombone	A
	DENNIS LYNDE	gtr	A
	JERRY MANFREDI	bs	A
	JOHN RENNER	tenor sax	A
	ERNIE SANTOS	alto sax	A
	JOHN SMART	french horn	A

ALBUM: 1(A) EVERYTHING I'VE GOT   (Capitol SKAO 395) 1969 -

45:   Everything I Got Belongs To You/
      Where Do The Hounds Go?   (Capitol 2706) 1969

Nicely packaged to look like an EMI or Harvest import (just so we knew it was sophisticated) this concept album is basically the vision of one individual... Steve Forman. Subtitled "Suite for voice, wind ensemble, percussion and electric instruments" it fits into an odd catagory of big band music that was at the same time ambitious and experimental in all the best ways one could be at the end of the sixties. A very interesting record, not always rock or psych - there are no fuzz guitars (well maybe once) and sometimes there are effects on the vocals. Lyrically it is "deep", stylistically eclectic. Kind of like Lionel Bart directing a Three Dog Night / Grand Wazoo collaboration with Gary Usher producing. There are no song titles, just six movements.

A quote from the inner sleeve notes: "Musicians are challenging the long accepted borders separating popular and intellectual music, expanding the musical vocabulary on both sides. The styles are blending and the stereotypes are disappearing. Today's competent American musician must be as familiar with Eric Clapton and **Sly Stone** as with Beethoven and Bartok, Miles Davis and Oliver Nelson, Jim Webb or Buck Owens. Past predjudices within the industry are becoming myths...". It was recorded in Arizona.

The flip to their 45, *Everything I Got Belongs to You*, compiled on *U Spaces: Psychedelic Archaology Vol. 3* (CDR) has been described as a very rare, very strange psychedelic horn freakout!

The album was written, arranged and conducted by Steve Forman, with assistant conductor, Jim Bastin and vocals by Harry Anglum (Drummer with Cornerstone) and Jack Wilkerson. (BC/TBo/PPe/VZ)

Ecology

Personnel incl: JERRY COLE   A
                 RAY RUFF   A
                 VAL STOECKLEIN   A

ALBUM: 1(A) ENVIRONMENT/EVOLUTION
                                       (Happy Tiger HT 1008) 1970 -

Occasionally psychy but mainly a melodic folk-country-rock concept album recorded at Gold Star in Hollywood. Featuring **Val Stoecklein**, ex-**Bluethings**, and Texas artist-turned producer Ray Ruff.

Compilation appearances have included *Black Mark On The Sea* on *Psychosis From The 13th Dimension* (CDR & CD). (MW)

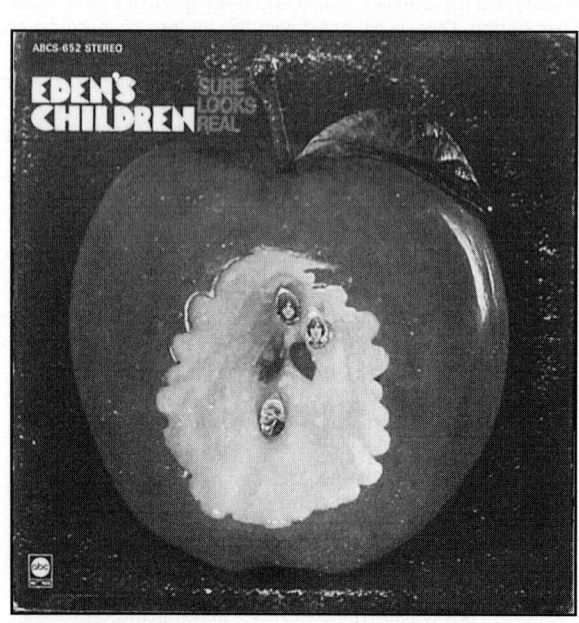

EDEN'S CHILDREN - Sure Looks Real LP.

Eddie and The Showmen

Personnel incl: EDDIE BERTRAND   gtr   A
                 ROBBIE EDWARDS   gtr   A

45s: Toes On The Nose/Border Town   (Liberty 55566) 1963
      Squad Car/Scratch   (Liberty 55608) 1963
      Movin'/Mr Rebel   (Liberty 55659) 1964
      Far Away Places/Lanky Bones   (Liberty 55695) 1964
      We Are The Young/Young And Lonely   (Liberty 55720) 1964

A California combo, Eddie was considered somewhat of a superstar locally and together with Dave and The Marksmen they did a tour of every city in California in 1964 and had several local hits in the Los Angeles, South Bay and Orange County areas. They folded after Eddie Bertrand joined the army in 1965 and Robbie Edwards was later in **Colours**.

Squad Car can also be heard on *Garage Punk Unknowns, Vol. 6* (LP). (VJ/BCr)

Eden's Children

Personnel: LARRY KILEY   bs   A
            RICHARD 'SHAM' SCHAMACK gtr, vcls   A
            JIMMY STURMAN   drms   A

                                                  HCP
ALBUMS: 1(A) EDEN'S CHILDREN   (ABC ABCS 624) 1968 196 R1
        2(A) SURE LOOKS REAL   (ABC ABCS 652) 1968 - SC

NB: (2) has been reissued. (1) and (2) have also been pirated on one CD (Head 3797) 1997.

45:   Goodbye Girl/Just Let Go   (ABC Paramount 11053) 1968

A power trio from Boston whose influences varied from hard to soft rock and from jazz to Eastern music. Their first LP included some virtuoso guitar especially on *Just Let Go* and *Don't Tell Me* and is better than their second, which was patchy but interesting in places.

Compilation appearances have included *Goodbye Girl* and *Just Let Go* on *The Best Of Bosstown Sound* (Dble CD). (VJ)

The Edge

Personnel: RICHARD BARCELLONA   ld gtr, vcls   A
            JOHN KEITH   bs, gtr, keyb'ds A
            GALLEN MURPHY   bs, gtr, vcls   A
            DAVID NOVOGROSKI   drms, vcls   A

ALBUM: 1(A) EDGE   (Nose NRS 48003) 1970 R1

45s: Seen Through The Eyes/Something New (Enith 101 1) 1969
      Sing Your Song/Ribbon And Bow   (Nose NRS 14007) 1971

Barcellona and Keith had earlier played together in **American Revolution** and Novogroski had been with **Boston Tea Party** making it likely that this was a Hollywood band although it is frequently reported as a San Francisco band. They may have also recorded 45s for Stonehenge Records. The album is not very good at all.

Compilation appearances have included: *Seen Through The Eyes* on *Pebbles, Vol. 9* (CD) and *Pebbles, Vol. 7* (LP); and *A New Breed Of Man* on *Songs Of Faith And Inspiration* (CDR & CD). (VJ/EW)

Edge of Darkness

45:   So Many Years/Mean Town   (Jamie 1363) 1968

Formed in Oswego, New York, they hooked up with management from Utica NY, which got them gigs throughout New York state and Eastern Pennsylvania. They also recorded several original tracks in Philadelphia, but a promised album was never released.

Mean Town can also be found on *Ya Gotta Have Moxie, Vol. 2* (Dble CD) and *Boulders, Vol. 6* (LP). (VJ/MM)

Edge of Freedom

ALBUM: 1 A FOLK ROCK SERVICE FOR THE SABBATH
(Covenant) c1968 -

Housed in a monochrome blue cover, an unusual folk-rock album recorded for the Jewish Service! A pressing on Bell may also exist. (SR)

Jim Edger and The Roadrunners

Personnel incl: JIM EDGER   A

ALBUM: 1(A) DIGGIN' THE '80s   (Ditch Witch 1001) 1980 -

45s:		
Little Pig/Rains (as by'Road Runners')	(Commerce 560)	1963
Little Pig/Rains	(Chan 111)	1963
Hey Little Girl/Apartment No. 9	(Hama 1002)	1963/4
Treasure Of Love/Funny How I Feel	(DJ B 117)	1964
New Girl In Town/What Is One To Do	(Bismarck 1011)	1966
Wait A Little Longer/Tennessee Stud	(Scepter 12147)	1966
You Can't Lie To A Liar/The Place	(Discovery 1001)	1967
Artificial Army/ Cheat On Your Neighbor (PS)	(Atco Pompeii 66684)	1968
Who Do You Turn To/Lots Of Time	(Ditch Witch 1001)	1968

Originally from Oklahoma City, but they spent a lot of time in Dallas and may have relocated there in 1966 for a while. A long-lived rock band, neither garage nor psychedelic - *The Place*, which later resurfaced on *Psychedelic Unknowns, Vol. 6* (LP & CD), is untypical of their output. (VJ)

Edgewood

Personnel:	DAVID BEAVER	keyb'ds, vcls	A
	DAVID MAYO	keyb'ds, gtr, vcls	A
	STEVE SPEAR	bs	A
	JIM TABUTTON	gtr	A
	PAT TAYLOR	gtr, vcls	A
	JOEL WILLIAMS	drms	A

ALBUM: 1(A) SHIP OF LABOR   (TMI Z 30971) 1969 -

A Memphis group, produced by Jimmy Johnson. Beaver, Tarbutton and Spear were all members of **The Gentrys** at different periods. This album is interesting, mixing the **Gentrys**' sound with elaborated keyboards parts. It comes in a stunning sleeve showing chained slave hands on the front and chained feet on the back. (SR)

Edison Electric Band

Personnel:	FREEBO	gtr, bs	A
	MARK JORDAN	keyb'ds, gtr	A
	RIP STOCK	vcls, drms	A
	T.J. TINDALL	gtr, vcls	A
	(NORMAN PRIDE	congas	A)
	(MICHAEL ZIEGLER	gtr	A)

ALBUM: 1(A) BLESS YOU, DR. WOODWARD
(Cotillion SD 9022) 1970 -

NB: (1) also released in France (Atlantic 650194) 1970.

45: Ship Of The Future/West Wind   (Cotillion 44071) 1970

Formerly **Thomas A. Edison Electric Band**, and originating in Pennsylvania, their album is an amalgam of jazz, rock, blues and soul influences.

The all too short instrumental *Lebanese Packhorse* is rather pleasant.

BOB EDMUND - I See No Colors LP.

Three quarters of the group are credited on Bonnie Raitt's second album. T.J. Tindall went on to form **Duke Williams and The Extremes** in 1973, while the bass and tuba player Freebo kept on working with Bonnie Raitt and played with several white blues and soul acts throughout the seventies and eighties, like the Bluesbusters (one album in 1983). (VJ/SB)

Bob Edmund

Personnel incl: BOB EDMUND   vcls   A

ALBUM: 1(A) I SEE NO COLORS   (Rabo SSJ-1163) 1970 R4

An extremely rare local folk-rock album from a New York artist. The original cover design was rejected by the printer as it portrayed Bob's photo superimposed upon an upside-down American flag; thereby "desecrating" it. Bob re-designed the sleeve and added a note about censorship. The record is quite powerful in a style reminiscent of Dylan's *Blonde On Blonde*. It has yet to see a reissue and Bob has several bonus tracks in his archives for the project. (CF)

Jonathan Edwards

45: Emma/Sunshine   (Capricorn 45-8021) 1971

A strangely moving ballad about a lost love adorns the 'A' side, very melancholic and introvert. For fans of "downer-folk" quite attractive. The 'B' side is average folk-rock. (MK)

George Edwards and Friends

45: Norwegian Wood/Never Mind I'm Freezing   (Dunwich 117) 1966

Ex-folk troubadour who cut a solo 45 for Dunwich and a raw cover of Bob Dylan's *Quit Your Low Down Ways*, that remained unreleased until its inclusion on Happy Tiger's *Early Chicago* (LP) compilation in 1971. He was working as in-house session vocalist with Dunwich before he joined **H.P. Lovecraft** in February 1967.

Retrospective compilation appearances have included: *Quit Your Low Down Ways* on *The Dunwich Records Story* (LP) and *If You're Ready - The Best Of Dunwich... Vol. 2* (CD). (VJ)

Jack Eely and The Courtmen

Personnel:	CHARLIE COE	bs	A
	JACK EELY	gtr, ld vcls	A
	LEON ETTINGER	bs	A
	MICHAEL "MONK" McGRATH	drms	A
	BILL TRUITT	keyb'ds	A

45s:	David's Mood/Louie Louie '66	(Bang 520) 1966
	Louie Go Home/Ride Ride Baby	(Bang 534) 1966

Jack Eely actually founded **The Kingsmen** and sang vocals on their classic *Louie Louie*, before leaving shortly after. After a spell with a group called **The Squires** he formed **The Courtmen**. Their *Louie, Louie '66*, is a pretty straight-forward rehash of **The Kingsmen**'s classic.

Bill Truitt went on to **Easy Chair** in 1971, whilst Charlie Coe played with **Paul Revere & The Raiders** and Michael McGrath was later with **Emergency Exit**.

Compilation appearances include *Louie, Louie '66* on *Highs In The Mid Sixties, Vol. 7* (LP). (VJ/MW/DR)

18th Century Concepts

ALBUM: 1   IN THE 20TH CENTURY BAG   (Sidewalk ST-5900) 1968 -

Produced by Mike Curb on his label, an instrumental 'exploito' project, with hits of the day (*Can't Hurry Love, Eleanor Rigby, Have You Seen Your Mother Baby?, If I Were A Carpenter*) played in the 18th century style with harpsichord, oboe... Contrary to some dealers' descriptions, it's not psych at all, just really awful. Some may find it amusing. (SR)

The Eight Feet

45:	Bobby's Come A Long, Long Way/	
	What Am I Without You	(Columbia 43505) 1966

A jangly folk-rock group, both songs were written by **Al Kooper**. (SR)

The Eighth Day

ALBUM: 1   ON THE EIGHTH DAY   (Kapp 1967) 19?? -

A flower-pop album with male/female vocals, influenced by the **Mamas and Papas**. It contains some decent tracks like *It Takes The Rain (To Make The Flowers Grow)* or *Brandy (Doesn't Live Here Anymore)*. (SR)

8th Wonders (Of The World)

45:	Must Have Your Love/Summer Dreamin'	(Uptite #002) c1967

Orchestrated psychedelic-pop melodrama by an unknown outfit on an obscure New York City label. Despite minor brass intrusions, this should appeal to Anglophile Rubble-ites - the outro guarantees a re-appraisal of first listen. The flip fails to live up to the promise - pretty straight. (MW)

DAMIN EIH, A.L.K. and BROTHER CLARK - Never Mind LP.

Damin Eih, A.L.K. and Brother Clark

Personnel:	BROTHER CLARK		
	(CLARK DIRCZ)	bs, gtr, piano, Chinese chimes	A
	DAMIN EIH	gtrs, ld vcls, synth, piano	A
	A.L.K. (A.L. KATZNER)	perc, piano, vcls, gtr	A

ALBUM:	1(A)	NEVER MIND	(Demelot NS-7310) 1974 R4

NB: (1) came with insert. (1) pirated circa 1990.

45:	Party Hats And Olive Spats/Tourniquet	(Demelot NS-7402) 1974

NB: It's rumoured that only 50 copies of this white label single exist.

According to the very cryptic liner notes on the back cover of this extremely rare private pressing, these three musicians had been playing together for seven years by the time of this album's release in 1974. Created in Minneapolis on instruments "borrowed or otherwise appropriated", this talented trio weave pieces of music into songs using both seamless and jarring segues through the course of each side.

"We all came along to see each other
To hope we could make progress like brothers
We didn't realise it could be a bother
Although our thoughts were running together like water..."
(from *Marching Together*)

"Growing older than we need to
Singing songs of being children all our lives
Throwing trees at knives
Lie down in your head, take off your eyes..."
(from *Take Off Your Eyes*)

A quantity of these albums turned up in 1985 but quickly vanished into collections. Following the release of the bootleg, demand and value has skyrocketed for the album. I haven't heard the bootleg, but the original pressing has the dynamics of a stereo demonstration record. This is not a record for garage fans, but one that will appeal to collectors of progressive, folk, psychedelic and electronic music.

By the way - the liner notes also state that Damin Eih rhymes with "flamin' tree". (VJ/SR/CF)

Elastic Prism

45s:	Time Change/In The Garden	(Kustom 101) 1968
	Red, Purple & Blue /	
	The Longer Nights Of Summer	(Jana 6969) 1969
	Going Down / Let One Hurt Do	(Jana 6970) 1970

Psychedelic Moods - Part Two (LP & CD) and *Psychedelic Experience, Vol. 3* (CD) give this Houston band's *In The Garden* an airing. Musically it leans toward heavier psychedelia in the **Iron Butterfly** and **Vanilla Fudge** tradition, but was secluded on the 'B' side of a **Third Rail** style pop ditty. (VJ/MW)

The Elastik Band

Personnel:	DAVID CORTOPASSI	A
	RUSSELL KERGER	A
	RUSTY KURIG	A
	VINCE SILVERA	A
	SCOTT WILLIAMS	A

12" acetate:		
	Rose Come Lately//Easy Come, Easy Go	
	Wouldn't You Dare/Boxkite/Taste Of Love	(UNI) 196?

45s:		Got A Better Reason Now/Mixed Emotions	(DCA DM 1033) 1967
	α	Paper Mache/Spazz	(Atco 6537) 1967
	β	I Would Still Love You/In A Family Tree	(Kapp 965) 1968
	χ	Tunesmith/In A Family Tree	(Kapp 968) 1969

NB: α trivia fans will note that *Papier Maché* was misspelt on the Atco label... the typo was corrected on the U.K. (Stateside SS 2056) release on the 45, but the EMI subsidiary misspelt the band name as **The Elastick Band** instead. β promo copies came with white label, stock copies black. χ white label radio station promo 45 also exists with *Tunesmith* on both sides.

A band they all love to hate? Reknowned for the utterly tasteless and politically incorrect, *Spazz*, their frantic punker has overshadowed their other 'pop' 45s, and probably from the band's point of view given a skewed perspective of what they were 'about'. Still a compulsive riff, with lyrics sung within an almost (modern-day) Rap style, a bluesy mid-break and a **Electric Prunes** style arrangement, are hard to ignore.

Amazingly, the *Spazz* 45 was also scheduled for release in the U.K. on EMI subsiduary Stateside, and demo copies were pressed, credited to **The Elastick Band**. Even stranger is that *Spazz* was played exactly once (almost) in Australia on Sydney radio station 2UW as a request.. about one minute into the track the DJ lifted the needle and apologised to the audience.. "I think we've heard about enough of that, I don't know what they're getting at and I don't care what they're getting at, but I find it offensive and I'm sure a lot of other people do too...."

Originally known as **This Side Up**, they recorded a 45 for Century in 1966, before a slight personnel shuffle resulted in the new moniker **The Elastik Band**.

Given the reaction to *Spazz*, it's understandable that many people are disappointed with their other three 45s, which are in a straightforward pop-ballad vein. The final 45, *Tunesmith* was a Jimmy Webb composition and was advertised in Billboard. **The Elastik Band**'s version was actually an attempt to beat another group's rendition which was then shooting up the charts somewhere in Oregon or Washington. They recorded it as a "cover record" for KAPP who flew them in from Arizona and within three days Universal recorded, pressed and distributed 45s of their cut. As a result, stations refused to play either record cause they didn't know which was the cover!

David Cortopassi later went on to play in Dangerfield, who recorded further 45s for Kapp and then he played with Rodan. Rodan also featured Scott Page on horns, who went on to play with Supertramp and Pink Floyd. Rodan's manager loved them so much he put out a 12" LP for them gratis! Acetates for this exist which contain five medium-tempo pop tracks:- *Rose Come Lately*, *Easy Come, Easy Go*, *Wouldn't You Dare*, *Boxkite* and *Taste Of Love*. It was recorded at the point the band changed names to Dangerfield.

If you haven't heard *Spazz*, and garage is your bag... then you're missing possibly one of the most tasteless records ever. Check it out on *Pebbles, Vol. 1* (LP), *Pebbles, Vol. 1* (CD), *Nuggets, Vol. 2* (LP) and *Nuggets Box* (4-CD). (IT/JCi/TA/JRe/MW/BM/VJ)

El Campo Jades

ALBUM: 1   THE 13th SONG   (Golden Eagle) 1966 SC

A Texan frat-garage rock album with good organ. (SR)

Billy Elder

45:   Poor Old Organ Grinder/
       Don't Take The Night Away   (Pathway 101) 19??

NB: also released as Pleasure (Tower 506) Sep. 1969.

This 45 features Sgt.Peppery pop backed by a haunting and heavily echoed 'baroque-psych' ballad. The latter can be heard by lucky owners of the *Growing Slowly Insane* (CD) and *Psychedelic Unknowns Vol. 11*, under its alternate personality **Pleasure**. (MW)

Elderberry Jak

Personnel incl:			
JOE CERISANO	ld vcls		A
DAVE COOMBS	bs, vcls		A
JOE HARTMAN	drms, vcls		A
TOM NICHOLAS	ld gtr, vcls		A

ALBUM: 1(A) LONG OVERDUE   (Electric Fox EF-LP-555) 1970 R1

NB: (1) reissued on CD (Gear Fab GF-178) 2001. (1) also appeared as *Eldeberry Jak* (Forest AW-14019) 1977. This edition, with misspelled band name, was mastered from vinyl and is probably unauthorised.

45:   Vance's Blues / Vance's Blues   (Electric Fox 2000) c1970

A "coal-patch" quartet from the Morgantown region of West Virginia. A couple of the members had been in an earlier outfit, J.B. and The Bonnevilles. Their album has been described as 'psychedelic' but this can only be by opportunistic dealers. That is a disservice to collectors and the band - they put together a varied collection of rural rock. Mined from a rich seam of folk it switches from driving electric rock with funky riffs or snakin' leads to reflective soft-rock with excellent acoustic guitars. It merits investigation ... BUT psychedelic it isn't.

The 1977 vinyl pressing as *Eldeberry Jak* gets no mention in the Gear Fab CD liners and may be a pirate. Whilst this features the same music, it is mastered from vinyl and credits a different line-up with Dave Coombs (bs, vcls), Mike Snyder and Tom Steele. The Tennesse-based Album World company (note AW prefix above) released highly dubious "reissues" of both **Elderberry Jak** and **Hillow Hammet**, two non-Texas groups produced by Lelan Rogers. On both albums, the band name was misspelled, the cover art changed and both were dubbed from vinyl!

Group leader Dave Coombs died in 1999.

Joe Cerisano was later in Silver Condor, then a studio musician before carving out a solo career and touring with the Trans Siberia Orchestra. (MW/CF/DHs)

The Elders

Personnel:			
JERRY BEHRING	bs		A
ROD BUDLINGY	gtr		A
RON SKINNER	drums		A
PAT SMITH	keyb'ds		A

ALBUM: 1   LOOKING FOR THE ANSWER
                                      (Audio Fidelity 6247) 1971 R1

NB: (1) also released in Italy (Audio Fidelity) 1971.

45:   Looking For The Answer /
       It's Too Late To Change   (Audio Fidelity 170) 1970/71

From Dayton, Ohio, and originally known as **Jerry and The Others**, they became **The Elders** in 1970. Their album blends driving guitar and organ with late flower power songs, it was housed in an amazing silver "skull" cover. (GGI/MW/SR)

The Electras

Personnel:			
BILL BULINSKI	gtr		AB
EARL BULINSKI	bs		ABC
JERRY FINK	drms		ABC
GARY OMERZA	keyb'ds		ABC
TIM ELFVING	vcls		BC
HARVEY KORKKI	gtr		C

45s:			
	Memories Of You/'Bout My Love/	(Scotty 6510/1)	1965
	(Just A Little) Soul Searchin'/		
	This Weeks Children	(Scotty 6607/6613)	1965
	Dirty Ol' Man/Courage To Cry	(Scotty 6619/6621)	1966
	'Bout My Love/		
	Memories... (Can Make You Happy)	(Scotty 11A/12B)	1966
α	Dirty Ol' Man/You Love	(Scotty 6620/1)	1966
β	Dirty Ol' Man/This Week's Children	(Date 2-1550)	1966
	Action Woman/Pregnant Pig	(Scotty 6720)	1967
	I'm Not Talkin'/Pregnant Pig	(Scotty 6720)	1967

NB: α 'B' side as **Twas Brillig**. β released as by **Twas Brillig**.

This garage-punk outfit was formed in Ely, Minnesota in 1962, although the line-up didn't stabilize until the Fall of 1964. All of their recordings are now hot property - their best know *Dirty Ol' Man* was written and produced by Warren Kendrick, **The Litter**'s producer. This is a superb example of mid-sixties punk with excellent snotty vocals and chainsaw guitar and became a local hit selling 5,500 copies.

Bill Bulinski was drafted in July 1966 and so didn't play on *Dirty Ol' Man* and Kendrick soon after helped the band get a deal with Columbia Records, of which Date Records was a subsidiary. Because somebody else had already copyrighted the name 'Electras', Kendrick changed their name to **Twas Brillig** and the nationwide-distributed Date single was released under this name. Shortly after, Tim Elfving was drafted which resulted in Columbia not renewing their option and the group broke up after another single. Bulinski was released from service in April 1968 and the band reformed as The Chapman Street Blues Band and then Hard Rain. They disbanded in 1969.

The Litter's *Litter - Rare Tracks* (LP) (which should really be called *The Best Of The Rest Of Warren Kendrick*) features many non-**Litter** tracks including the **Electras/Twas Brillig** tracks *Dirty Ol' Man*, *You Love*, *This Week's Children* and *Soul Searching*. The later is even stronger than **The Litter**'s version and considering that **The Litter** covered other tracks that **The Electras** had done first these guys must get justifiably pissed off when people say they're **The Litter**. Let's hope this finally puts the record straight and that **The Electras** receive due credit.

There's also an album on Get Hip (GHAS 5066), which was released in 1993, entitled *Electras vs. Scotsmen/Victors*. It contains tracks from 1965 to 1968 by Warren Kendrick's earliest project **The Scotsmen** and the pre-**Litter** **Victors**. Get Hip has also recently issued a 7": *Soul Searchin/Action Woman* (GHAS 67) on coloured vinyl. For those who prefer CDs, Erik Lindgren has put together *The Scotty Story* (CD) which includes all the album tracks plus some unreleased goodies (*Action Woman*, *'Bout My Love*, *Courage To Cry*, *Dirty Old Man*, *I'm Not Talkin'*, *Pregnant Pig*, *Soul Searchin'*, *Summertime*, *This Week's Children*, *Won't Take No For An Answer* and *Your Love*). Recommended.

Dirty Ol' Man was also compiled on the rare 1967 sampler *Money Music*.

Other compilation appearances have included: *Dirty Ol' Man* on *Mayhem & Psychosis, Vol. 1* (LP); *I'm Not Talkin'* on *The Midwest Vs. The Rest* (LP); *Action Woman* on *Open Up Yer Door! Vol. 1* (LP), *The Arf! Arf! Blitzkrieg 32 Track Sampler* (Dble CD), *Songs We Taught The Fuzztones* (LP & CD) and *Best of Pebbles, Vol. 1* (LP & CD); *'Bout My Love* on *Pebbles, Vol. 21* (LP); and both *Soul Searchin'* and *This Week's Children* on *Glimpses, Vol. 4* (LP). (VJ/MW/LP)

Electras

ALBUM: 1 THE ELECTRAS (No label ELT-201) 1962 R1

Not to be confused with the Minnesota bunch, this private press album was the work of a prep-rock band from St. Pauls Academy in Concord, New Hampshire. (MW)

The Electrical Banana

Personnel:	MICHAEL IOLI	drms	A
	PREBEN JESSEN	organ	A
	DEAN KOHLER	vcls, gtr	A
	JON SUGDEN	bs	A

45s: There She Goes Again / She's Gone (Custom acetate) 1967

NB: just 10 copies with customized labels were pressed, credited to "The Banana".

This short-lived venture came together in Vietnam whilst **Dean Kohler** (formerly of **The Satellites** out of Portsmouth, Virginia) was doing his service for Uncle Sam. Despite its rarity both sides have been preserved on *Aliens, Psychos And Wild Things* (CD) which reveals that the band adopted the Banana theme from the **Velvet Underground** album, playing in banana uniforms around the region's service clubs.

A cover of Lou Reed's *There She Goes Again* is backed by a **Kohler** original - two pleasant jangley folk-rockers recorded live (and "on tour") in an army tent. Ten copies were pressed up with individualized custom labels and distributed to all involved. **Dean Kohler** would be back in the studio again on his safe return to Portsmouth at the end of the year. (BHr/ST/MW)

The Electric Company

Personnel:	DICK FLETCHER	vcls, gtr	A
	JOHN GLAZIER	gtr	A
	DANA MORGAN	bs	A
	CRAIG PARKER	organ	A
	DICK SIDMAN	drms	A

45: Scarey Business/You Remind Me Of Her (Titan FF-1735) 1966

Previously thought to be from Los Angeles, **The Electric Company** are now known to have formed at Menlo College on the San Francisco Peninsula, and were originally known as Lothar and The Hand People (no relation to the Colorado band of the same name). They are notorious not only for the outstanding 45, but also the fact that Morgan was the original bass player of the (pre-**Grateful Dead**) Warlocks, before Phil Lesh took his place.

The 'A' side, *Scarey Business*, is a superb R&B/punker whilst the flip is more in the folk-punk genre. Both are featured on the top-drawer garage punk compilation *Scarey Business* (CD), along with two equally superb unissued cuts *You're Wrong* and *See Me Some Time*.

Other compilation appearances have included *Scarey Business* on *Psychedelic Experience, Vol. 3* (CD), *Trash Box* (5-CD) and *Best of Pebbles, Vol. 3* (LP & CD); and *Scarey Business* and *You Remind Me Of Her* on *60's Punk E.P., Vol. 4* (7") and *Moxie Punk EP* (7" Box Set). (MW)

Electric Firebirds

See **The Firebirds**.

The Electric Flag

Personnel:	MIKE BLOOMFIELD	gtr	AB
	HARVEY BROOKS	bs	A
	MARCUS DOUBLEDAY	trumpet	A
	BARRY GOLDBERG	organ	AB
	NICK GRAVENITES	vcls	AB
	BUDDY MILES	drms	AB
	HERBIE RICH	gtr	A
	PETE STRAZZA	sax	A
	ROGER TROY	bs	B

THE ELECTRIC FLAG - The Trip (Soundtrack) LP.

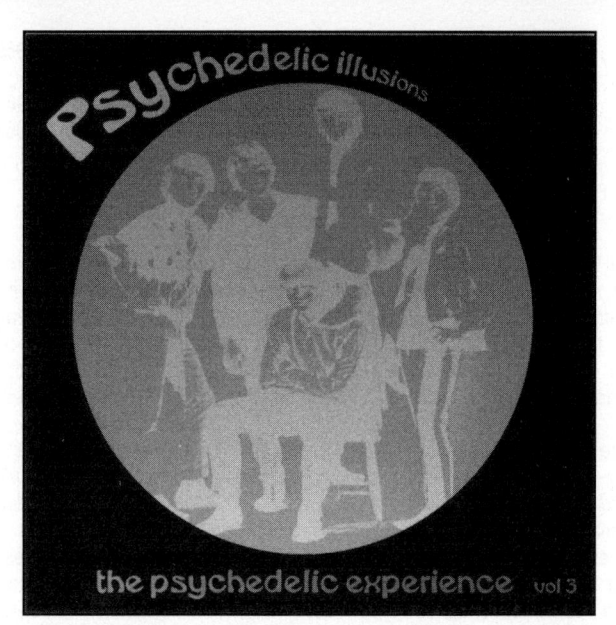

THE PSYCHEDELIC EXPERIENCE Vol. 3 (Comp CD) including The Electric Company.

HCP

ALBUMS:
1(A) THE TRIP (Soundtrack) (Sidewalk T/ST 5908) 1967 - SC
2(A) A LONG TIME COMIN' (Columbia CS 9597) 1968 31 -
3(A) ELECTRIC FLAG (Columbia CS 9714) 1969 76 -
4(A) THE BEST OF (Columbia C 30422) 1971 - -
5(B) THE BAND KEPT PLAYING (Atlantic SD 18112) 1974 - -

NB: (2) also released in the U.K. and France (CBS 62394) in 1968, (3) also released in the U.K. and France (CBS 63462) in 1969. (4) also released in France, CBS 63976. (5) also released in the U.K. (Atlantic K 50090) in 1974. (1) has been reissued on CD.

45s:
Peter's Trip/Green And Gold (Sidewalk 929) 1967
Groovin' Is Easy/Over Lovin' You (PS) (Columbia 44307) 1968
Sunny/Soul Searchin' (Columbia 44765) 1969
Sweet Soul Music/Every Now And Then (Atlantic 3222) 1975
Doctor Oh Doctor/The Band Kept Playing (Atlantic 3237) 1975

This short-lived but successful band certainly deserve a mention. They were formed in 1967 by **Mike Bloomfield** after he'd left **The Butterfield Blues Band** and were full of talent, particularly black soul drummer **Buddy Miles**, who'd done session work with Otis Redding and Wilson Pickett, Chicago singer-composer **Nick Gravenites** and keyboardist Goldberg, who'd previously played with **Steve Miller**. They played a combination of soul and Chicago blues which was flavoured with a taint of psychedelia and liberal use of flashy electronics, which were ideally suited to the times. They were also one of the first bands to use a brass section. Their first break was an extremely well received performance at the Monterey Festival in 1967. To some degree their appearance in the Peter Fonda/Roger Corman movie 'The Trip' consolidated their growing reputation. Collectors of psychedelia may be interested in this largely instrumental album, which included tracks like *Joint Passing* and *Psych Soap*, which were evocative of the growing psychedelic culture. The *Peter's Trip* 45 was also taken from the album.

Their first album proper, *A Long Time Comin'*, was basically blues-rock with an occasional hint of psychedelia. It got to No. 31 in the U.S. album charts and was certainly stronger than their next effort, *The Electric Flag*, which despite climbing to no. 76, failed to mask the internal turmoil that hard drug abuse and internal stresses had created and which led to their disintegration in 1969. They did reunite in a studio project with Mama Cass shortly after, which was completed then shelved.

In 1974 the band made a reunion album with Roger Troy replacing Harvey Brooks on bass; but the sparkle had deserted their music and the end result was patchy and can't be recommended.

After their split in 1969 **Buddy Miles** went on to form **The Buddy Miles Express**, **Barry Goldberg** made several solo albums and **Nick Gravenites** worked for **Big Brother and The Holding Company**. In 1975 Bloomfield and Goldberg were instrumental in forming KGB, one of the most disastrous supergroups ever.

A compilation CD, *Old Glory*, was issued on the Rock Artifacts label in 1995. It contains 17 tracks, among them five of which are previously unreleased. Also issued on CD in 1995: *The Best Of An American Music Band*, a 60-minute CD on One Way which contains previously unreleased alternate takes, demos and live tracks from the Monterey festival. It's available on Columbia Legacy (CK 57629) in the UK. There's also a 1983 album, *Groovin' Is Easy* (Thunderbolt), which contains previously unreleased live material.

Compilation appearances include: *Soul Searchin'* on *Pop Revolution From The Underground* (LP). (VJ)

Electric Hair

Personnel incl: ROBERT BYRNE vcls, gtr, keyb'ds A

ALBUM: 1(A) ELECTRIC HAIR (Evolution 2013) 1971 -

Recorded in Brentwood, Tennessee, this album merged the songs of the famous "First Tribal Love Rock" musical with "groovy" electronic sounds. Robert Byrne produced it and was also in charge of the "electronic realizations". The result may interest fans of psych 'exploitation' albums and collectors of period sleeves.

During the seventies, Byrne worked with Southern rock and soul acts (Delbert McClinton, Pete Carr etc.). (SR)

Electric Junkyard

Personnel: CAPLAN? A
TRUNZ? A

ALBUM: 1( ) THE ELECTRIC JUNKYARD (RCA LSP-4158) 1969 -

From New York and arranged by Frank Hunter, this was an instrumental group covering two tracks from 'Hair' plus some original tunes with promising titles: *Smoke Coming Out Of Your Ears*, *Freeway*, *The Joint*, *Annie's Place*, and *Roundtrip*. The instrumentation used is comprised of electrified horns, guitars, fuzz bass, drums and electric piano and their message is "Dig It!".

The result is as strange as the sleeve (a bearded bare-chested man with a red wig and muddy shoes sitting in a bin): messy horns-laden tracks with, from place to place, occasional excellent guitar solos for a mix of rock, psych and horn-pop. (SR)

Electric Love

45: This Seat Is Saved/
Gotta Get Back To My Baby (Charay 47) 196?

Both sides of this 45, written by one Dave Smith, appear on *The Fort Worth Teen Scene - The Major Bill Tapes Vol. 2* (LP) so we know they were based in Fort Worth in the mid-sixties. With its partly spoken lyrics the 'A' side differed from the usual punk offering. It was also included on *Flashback, Vol. 5* (LP) and *Texas Flashbacks, Vol. 5* (LP). (VJ)

Electric Piano Playground

ALBUM: 1 PSYCHEDELIC SEEDS (Bell) 1967 -

45: Flower Song/Good Vibrations (Bell 695) 1967

A short-lived, possibly studio-only outfit. The album consists of covers of popular sixties songs done in a psychedelic style, although it's also been suggested that *Psychedelic Seeds* is a "Children's" record - whether of the "Flower" variety is open to question! (VJ)

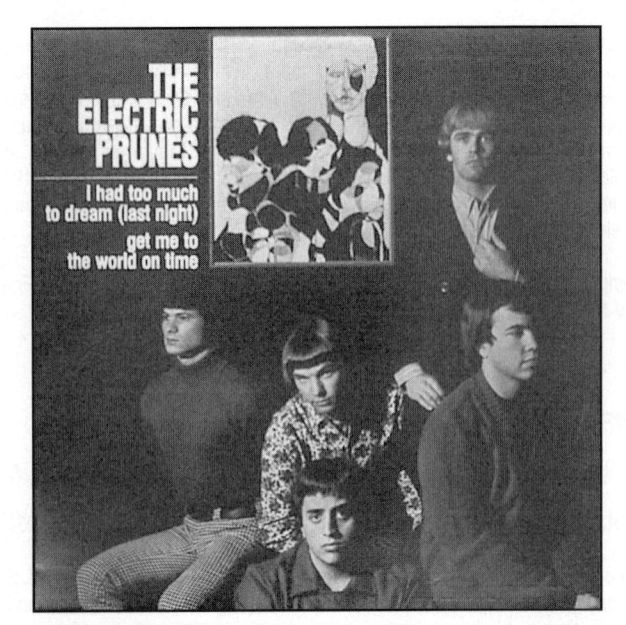

THE ELECTRIC PRUNES - Electric Prunes... LP.

The Electric Prunes

Personnel:			
	JIM LOWE	vcls, gtr, auto harp, perc	ABC
	PRESTON RITTER	drms, perc	A
	'WEASEL' SPAGNOLA	vcls, gtr	AB
	MARK TULIN	bs, keyb'ds	ABC
	KEN WILLIAMS	gtr	ABC
	MIKE WEAKLEY ("QUINT")	drms	BC
	MIKE GANNON	gtr	C
	JOHN HERREN	keyb'ds	D
	MARK KINCAID	gtr, vcls	D
	RON MORGAN	gtr	D
	BRETT WADE	bs, vcls, flute	D
	RICHARD WHETSTONE	drms, gtr, vcls	D

HCP

ALBUMS:
1(A) ELECTRIC PRUNES (I HAD TOO MUCH TO DREAM LAST NIGHT) (Reprise RLP 6248) 1967 113 SC
2(A/B) UNDERGROUND (Reprise RLP 6262) 1967 172 SC
3(C) MASS IN F MINOR (Reprise RLP 6275) 1967 135 -
4(C) RELEASE OF AN OATH (Reprise RLP 6316) 1968 - -
5(D) JUST GOOD OLD ROCK AND ROLL (Reprise RSLP 6347) 1968 - -

NB: (1) and (2) reissued on one CD (Head 3397) 1997. (1) and (2) have also been issued individually on pirate CD's with inferior quality live tracks, from the Stockholm '67 show. (3) and (4) also released in France (Vogue/Reprise CRV 6078 and CRV 6099 respectively) 1968. (3) Later reissued by Midi. (3) also reissued on CD. (4) & (5) issued on one CD. There have also been a number of worthwhile retrospective releases. *Long Days Flight* (Edsel ED 179) 1986, is a 'best of', later reissued on CD; *Stockholm '67* (Heartbeat (CD)HB67) 1997, is an official reissue of a live performance from Swedish Radio, released on vinyl and CD; *The Sanctions/Jim And The Lords: The Came The Electric Prunes* (Heartbeat (CD)HB65) 2000 is an official reissue of pre-Electric Prunes material; *Lost Dreams* (Heartbeat (CD)HB68) 2001 is a superb compilation including many rare tracks and *The Singles* (Gone Beat EP CD 77013) 1995 is a pirate CD containing 18 singles tracks.

45s:
Ain't It Hard/Little Olive (Reprise 0473) 1966
I Had Too Much To Dream (Last Night)/Luvin' (Reprise 0532) 1966 11
Get Me To The World On Time/Are You Lovin' Me More (But Enjoying It Less) (Reprise 0564) 1967 27
Dr Do Good/Hideaway (Reprise 0594) 1967 128
The Great Banana Hoax/Wind-Up Toys (Reprise 0607) 1967 -
α Sanctus/Credo (Reprise PRO 277) 1967 -
β Everybody Knows You're Not In Love/You Never Had It Better (Reprise 0652) 1968 -
I Had Too Much To Dream Last Night/Get Me To The World On Time (double A re-release) (Reprise 0704) 1968 -
α Help Us/The Adoration (Reprise PRO 305) 1968 -
α Shadows (one-sided promo) (Reprise PRO 287) 1968 -
β Hey Mr President/Flowing Smoothly (Reprise 0756) 1969 -
α Sell/Violent Rose (Reprise 0833) 1969 -
α Finders, Keepers, Losers, Weepers/
α Love Grows (Reprise 0858) 1969 -
Vox Wah-Wah Ad (Thomas 08-0001 32-0) 1966/1967 -

NB: α Promo only releases. β also released in France with PS. There are also two rare French EPs with picture sleeves.

The Electric Prunes originated from the San Fernando Valley, a suburb of Los Angeles, although many bio's mistakenly claim that they came from Seattle, since *I Had Too Much Too Dream (Last Night)* first broke in Seattle and then Boston. In fact their very first live concert to promote the record was in Seattle, and according to their drummer Preston Ritter, a DJ there started the mis-information, by claiming that the band were from that area.

More commercially successful and classier than the average punk bands, they experimented with different types of music. Their first single *Ain't It Hard* was a brash punk number written by Roger and Terrye Tillson, members of folk-rock duo, **Gypsy Trips**. It was not a hit and was not issued in the U.K. but, along with the flip side, *Little Olive* and both sides of their next single (*I Had Too Much To Dream Last Night/Luvin*), it appeared on a French EP (Reprise RVEP 60098) which is the rarest '**Prunes** item. Their debut album provided two U.S. hit singles: *I Had Too Much To Dream (Last Night)* and *Get Me To The World On Time*. Both also attracted airplay in the U.K. reaching Nos 49 and 42 respectively. The former, starts with a freaky fuzz- box intro - the brain child of their producer, Dave Hassinger. The lyrics and their sound were tailor-made for the druggy days of 1967. *Get Me To The World On Time* was a driving, urgent rocker, superimposed on top of a culminating whistle sound. Also on the album and the B side to their second single, was *Are You Lovin' Me More (But Enjoying It Less)* which used echo-drumming techniques to good effect. Some of the other numbers like *Onie* and *Train For Tomorrow*, were a little more laid back, but still featured acid guitar work. The album peaked at No 113 in the charts.

The second album, which was not issued in the UK, developed their psychedelic experience further. Recorded for the most part by line-up (A), drummer Preston Ritter recalls that he was given the choice between credited on the cover or being given royalties... In fact his replacement, Quint, only played on five tracks, *Children of Rain*, *Antique Doll*, *I, Capt. Glory* and *Long Day's Flight*. Despite the line-up changes, the album is more consistent than their debut with fine acid guitar work and effective drumming. Sadly, however, it failed to maintain their stream of hits. Of particular note are the psychedelic rockers *The Great Banana Hoax*, *Long Day's Flight* (both unsuccessful singles), - the latter a U.K.-only issue, *Children of Rain* and strange, more subtle tracks like *Wind-up Toys*, *Antique Doll* and *I Happen To Love You*. This was a fine album, and it is a pity the group didn't pursue this direction further. It made No 172 in the U.S. charts. Also of note around this time is a non-album single *Everybody Knows You're Not In Love/You've Never Had It Better*. This was also issued in the U.K. and in France. The B side is a fine dance number with a great psychedelic intro.

THE ELECTRIC PRUNES - Underground LP.

THE ELECTRIC PRUNES - Mass In F Minor LP.

Another recording of note from 1968 is a second French EP (Reprise RVEP 601 10) consisting of *Long Days Flight*, *Dr. Do Good*, *The Great Banana Hoax*, and *Captain Glory*.

Towards the end of 1967 the band embarked on a European Tour, and for many years a short poor quality tape circulated of a recording from Swedish Radio. Intrigued by the performance, '**Prunes** fan Simon Edwards spent years tracking down the master-tapes and clearing the rights to the material. In 1997 his efforts were rewarded with the release of *Stockholm '67* in a lavish gatefold sleeve, with a booklet of Gered Mankowitz photographs and tour reminicences from '**Prunes**' James Lowe and Mark Tulin. The album, which was also released on CD, is on a par with the excellent **H.P. Lovecraft** and **Shadows of Knight** live albums that have recently resurfaced and captures the band in full flight - It also includes about 45 minutes of material, approximately 20 minutes more than was originally broadcast.

Their next album *Mass In F Minor* was backed by an additional orchestra of studio musicians and as the group's identity started to be swamped by Hassinger and **Axelrod**'s grandiose concepts, members of the original outfit started to drop out of the project. Canadian band The Collectors, then based in L.A. and whose two album's were also produced by Hassinger, were brought in to plug the gaps. *Mass...* is regarded as one of the first rock operas, a mix of gregorian music and psychedelic pop with vocals in Latin, which was written, arranged and conducted by **David Axelrod** - a neoclassical musician. The opening track *Kyrie Eleison* is widely known and backed the acid trip in the cemetery scene of *Easy Rider*. The album climbed to No 135 and was re-released by Midi in 1974. They made a further album in a similar vein that may have also included members of The Collectors, before breaking up, although Dave Hassinger later attempted an unsuccessful comeback with the album, *Good Old Rock And Roll*, which contained none of the band's original members. Recent interviews of some original members, notably in *Record Collector* and Jeff Jarema's *Here 'Tis #8*, reveal that they were unaware of subsequent machinations by Hassinger so it seems unlikely that the whole truth of the post-*Mass* period will ever fully emerge.

The *Shadows* promo is horrendously rare. *Shadows* was also included in a little-known movie 'The Name Of The Game Is Kill'. It sounds like the song was originally intended for **The Doors**. A 'Record Collector' article also revealed that different mixes of their 45s were made for the European and American markets. 'For England, they felt that the music ought to be a little more up, peppier. So we would put the material on the capstan and make the songs faster', James Lowe told journalist Mark Paytress.

In July 2000 Heartbeat have released *Then Came The Electric Prunes* which unearths pre-**Prunes** Audiodisc acetates recorded chez Russ Bottomley - twelve tracks from 27th March 1965 by the Sanctions (Jim Lowe, Ken Williams, Mark Tulin and Mike Weakley) and four tracks from 29th September 1965 by Jim And The Lords (with Dave Hargrave added to the previous line-up). The Sanctions' sound is of a garage band with surf roots performing popular covers including *Long Tall Sally*, *Money*, *Moon Dog*, *Love Potion Number Nine*, *What'd I Say*, *Jack The Ripper* and of course *Louie Louie*. With the Jim and The Lords tracks - *Little Olive*, *I'm Free*, *I'm Down* and *Too Many People* - the surf influences are replaced by raw harmonica and a raucous punk style similar to Stones and **Seeds**. A folk-rock lilt on *I'm Free* marks another development since the March sessions. The sound quality is surprisingly good considering the source. With previously unseen photos this is a must-have for any **Prunes** fan.

In 2001, the retrospective *Lost Dreams* CD/Dble album compilation appeared. Produced by Jim Lowe, it contains their debut 45, the Vox wah-wah ad, a selection of the strongest tracks from the first two albums (many in unreleased studio 4-track form) plus three never-released tracks: the mythical *Shadows*, a demo of the Hollies' *I've Got A Way Of My Own* and *World Of Darkness*. The superb double-album package comes in a gatefold adorned with numerous band photos and a coloured insert sheet depicting 45 labels and picture sleeves from around the world.

The Electric Prunes were undoubtedly pioneers in experimentation with psychedelic and quasi-religious music. They certainly made some fine singles and had they not been overshadowed by San Francisco's own psychedelic sound may well have achieved wider recognition. Their first two albums, both reissued a few years ago, or alternatively the Edsel compilation are highly recommended.

Compilation appearances have included: *Long Day's Flight* on *Garage Music For Psych Heads Vol. 1*; *Get Me To The World On Time* and *I Had Too Much To Dream (Last Night)* on *Nuggets Box* (4-CD); *Everybody Knows You're Not In Love* on *Nuggets, Vol. 5* (LP); *I Had Too Much To Dream (Last Night)* on *Nuggets From Nuggets* (CD), *Nuggets - Original Artyfacts From The First Psychedelic Era 1965-1968* (Dble LP), *Nuggets, Vol. 1* (LP) and *Excerpts From Nuggets* (CD); *Get Me To The World On Time* on *Nuggets, Vol. 6* (LP) and *Psychedelic Perceptions* (CD); *Vox Wha-Wha Peddle Advert* on *Pebbles, Vol. 2* (CD), *Pebbles Box* (5-LP), *Psychotic Reactions* (LP), *Great Pebbles* (CD) and *Trash Box* (5-CD); *Ain't It Hard* on *Sound Of The Sixties* (Dble LP) and *Sixties Archive, Vol. 1* (CD); *Hey Mr. President* on *Turds On A Bum Ride, Vol. 1 & 2* (Dble CD); *Hey Mr. President* and *Mojo Walkin'* (sic - *Mojo Workin'* from Stockholm '67) on *Turds On A Bum Ride, Vol. 2* (Dble LP); and *You Never Had It Better* on *Everywhere Chainsaw Sound* (LP).

In 2002, the original line-up are recording and performing once again. (VJ/MW/SR)

The Electric Screwdriver

ALBUM: 1 WORKING THE ELECTRIC SCREWDRIVER
(Spar) c1970 SC

On the same label as the **Now Generation**, another album of exploito covers. (SR)

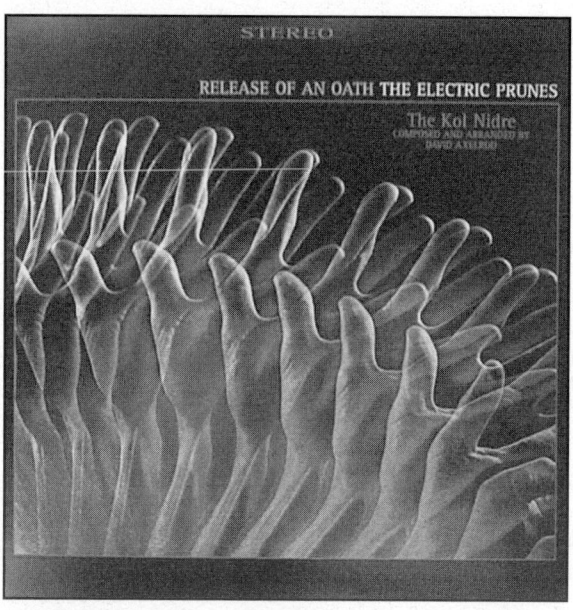

THE ELECTRIC PRUNES - Release Of An Oath LP.

Electric Toilet

ALBUM: 1 IN THE HANDS OF KARMA (Nasco 9004) 1970 R3

NB: (1) reissued on vinyl (Psycho 8) 1983 and on CD (Golden Classics Rebirth GRC 007) 1996. Later counterfeited on vinyl.

45: In The Hands Of Karma / Revelations (Nasco ET) c1970

NB: may have been promo only.

From Memphis, Tennessee, Dave Hall was a guitarist in this band, which split up when two of its members were killed in a car crash in July 1970. The album is over-rated, although the reissue is probably worth purchasing if only for the inter-whirling organ and guitar and the resultant psychedelic haze on its best track, *Within Your State Of Mind*. (VJ)

Electric Tomorrow

45: Sugar Cube/The Electric Tomorrow (World Pacific 77860) 1966

A psychedelic cash-in instrumental for uneventful trips in elevators. *Sugar Cube* has subsequently popped up on *Buzz Buzz Buzzzzzz Vol. 1* (CD), whilst *Electric Tomorrow* is on *Buzz Buzz Buzzzzzz Vol. 2* (CD). (MW)

Electric Train

Personnel incl: BILL BOWEN drms A
                 GARY PHILIPPET vcls A

45: Try Harder/Through Winter And Sunshine (Moxie M-106) p1984

The one-sided Moxie 45 was a reissue of a rare acetate and is thought to be this Marin County, California band. Former **Pullice**-man Philippet was later in the **Front Line** and **Freedom Highway**. Bowen too was later in the **Front Line** and joined another Marin outfit, the **Sons Of Champlin**, at the end of 1966.

Compilation appearances have included *Try Harder* and *Thru Winter And Sunshine* on *Ya Gotta Have Moxie, Vol. 2* (Dble CD). (MW/AP)

Electrified People

45: Electrified People/
     One Thousand Dimension In Blue (Red Lite) c1970

Two psych instrumentals full of guitars with reverb.

Compilation appearances have included: *Electrified People* on *Buzz Buzz Buzzzzzz, Vol. 1* (CD) and *One Thousand Dimension In Blue* on *Buzz Buzz Buzzzzzz, Vol. 2* (CD). (SR)

The Electro Magnetic Flowerseed

Personnel incl?: DOUG HENRY A

45: We Know / The Land Beyond (Marco 90109) c1966

Possibly from Southern Carolina, a flower-power group with a rather memorable name! (SR)

The Electronic Concept Orchestra

ALBUM: 1 MOOG GROOVES (Limelight LS-86070) 1969

45: Aquarius / Grazing In The Grass (Limelight 3090) 1969

NB: as The Electronic Concept.

THE ELECTRIC TOILET - In The Hands Of Karma LP.

Recorded with moog synthesizer, drums and guitar, its cover claims that it's "The First Album Of Electronic Rock". It includes mostly covers of current hits (*Atlantis*, *Hey Jude*, *Penny Lane*, *Feelin' Alright*). This studio project included one member of **Aorta** and came in a "groovy" cover showing a girl with headphones surrounded by flowers, a sign peace, a Beatles poster and various electronic devices. (SR)

Elephant

Personnel incl: GEOFF LEVIN gtr A
                 DICK GLASS vcls, gtr A

ALBUMS: 1(A) ELEPHANT (Capitol SMAS 11154) 1973 SC
        2(A) THE ELEPHANT (Moonwatcher 20001) 1974 SC

NB: (2) was reissued on Big Tree.

A melodic West-Coast group with superb guitar parts. Formerly with **People**, Geoff Levin was also the guitarist of Jimmy Spheeris, a Californian hippie balladeer. (SR)

Elephant's Memory

Personnel: RICHARD "CHESTER"
            AYERS gtr A
            STAN BRONSTEIN vcls, sax ABCD
            RICK FRANK drms, vcls ABCD
            MICHAL SHAPIRO vcls A
            RICHARD SUSSMAN piano, organ A
            JOHN WARD bs, gtr, drms AB
            MYRON YULES bs, trombone AB
            DAVID COHEN gtr, vcls, keyb'ds B
            GUY PERITORE (*) gtr, vcls B
            MIKE ROSE gtr B
            WAYNE TEX GABRIEL gtr C
            ADAM IPPOLITO keyb'ds, vcls C
            GARY VAN SCYOC bs, vcls CD
            CHRIS ROBISON keyb'ds D
            JOHN SACHS gtr D
            (JOHN LENNON vcls, piano C)
            (YOKO ONO vcls C)

NB: (*) misspelled on the album as 'Peratori'.

HCP
ALBUMS: 1(A) ELEPHANT MEMORY (Buddah BDS-5033) 1969 2001 -
        2(A) SONGS FROM MIDNIGHT COWBOY
                                (Buddah BDS-5038) 1970 - -
        3(B) TAKE IT TO THE STREETS
                                (Metromedia MD-1035) 1971 - -
        4(C) ELEPHANT'S MEMORY (Apple SMAS 3389) 1972 - -

	5(D) ANGELS FOREVER	(Polydor 2383 260) 1974	- -

HCP

45s:	Keep Free pt. 1/pt. 2	(Buddha ?) 1968	-
α	Crossroads Of The Stepping Stones/ Jungle Gym	(Buddah 98) 1969	120
β	Mongoose/ I Couldn't Dream	(Metromedia MM 182) 1970	50
χ	Skyscraper Commando/ Power	(Metromedia MM 210) 1970	-

NB: α also released in Germany with a PS (Buddah 201050). β also released in France with a PS (CBS 5207). χ 'A' side is a non-LP cut.

Originating from New York, **Elephant Memory** was formed in 1967 by Bronstein and Frank, who were both playing the strip joint circuit. They soon became known for their outrageous performances, with light shows, destruction of sculptures and weird outfits. After recruiting a young Israeli singer, Michal Shapiro, they were signed to the Wes Farrell Organization, a powerful management and production company. Their first album was released in February 1969 and has a flashing sleeve, the group members being pictured nude, covered with paints, in front of an elephant. An interesting record, mixing psych, dreamy ballads, jazz and hard-rock, two of the songs, *Old Man Willow* and *Jungle Gym At The Zoo* appeared on the soundtrack to 'Midnight Cowboy'. It spent two weeks at No. 200 in the Charts.

With the success of this film, Buddah released *Songs From Midnight Cowboy*, which was basically a reissue of the first album with new versions of *Everybody's Talkin'* and *Theme From Midnight Cowboy*.

Michal Shapiro, Richard Sussman and Chester Ayers then left with Richard Sussman joining **Grootna**. A new line-up was put together and the next album, produced by Ted Cooper, *Take It To The Streets* was totally different to their debut. **Elephant's Memory** were now playing a very effective hard-rock, obviously inspired by the Detroit groups of the era. Tracks like *Power*, *Piece Now*, *Damn* and *Mongoose* are powerful and *Mongoose* became a hit. Incidentally Rick Frank is credited as "Reek Havoc" on the sleeve.

Following this album, the line-up changed again and the band backed John Lennon and Yoko Ono on *Some Time In New York City* and *Approximately Infinite Universe*. Their fourth album was naturally issued on Apple and has a good reputation.

In 1973, they backed Chuck Berry on his *Bio* album and then released a final record in 1974, produced at the Rockfield Studios in Wales by Steve Smith.

Stan Bronstein launched a jazz-rock career, Rick Frank formed various local bands, but died in the nineties. Adam Ippolito went on to play with soul and funk groups and Wayne Tex Gabriel joined **Mitch Ryder**. Adrian Peritore (aka Guy Peritore) later formed Beede Oms with David Cohen and went on to play with The Motels amongst others. (VJ/SR)

The Elftone

45:	Louisiana Teardrops/ Beat The Clock	(World Pacific 77912) 1968	

Produced by **Kim Fowley** and arranged by Michael Lloyd, so what more do you want? The result is a fine blend of psych, marching rock and menace on the 'A' side. The flip starts like the **Left Banke**, although simultaneously saccharine and inept. The ramshackle accompaniment and the badly tuned guitar on this track produce something like America's answer to the Bonzo Dog Band. (SR/MK)

The Elite

Personnel:	BOB BARNES	bs	A
	ROGER BROWNLEE	vcls, gtr	A
	EDDIE DEATON	ld gtr	A
	BRUCE LAIR	drms	A

45s:	One Potato/Two Potato	(Charay 17)	1966
	My Confusion/I'll Come To You	(Charay 31)	1967
	Bye Bye Baby/All I Want Is You	(Charay 56)	1967

Formed by three seventeen year olds from Paschal High School in Fort Worth. Brownlee was a weekend addition. They won many Battle Of The Bands competitions and were the house band at Fort Worth's Teen-a-Go-Go for a while. Their first 45 was an instrumental.

Barnes and Deaton later joined a flower-power outfit, **Those Guys**, with Bob Barnes later going on to the **Yellow Payges**.

Compilation coverage has included: *My Confusion* on *Acid Dreams - The Complete 3 LP Set* (3-LP), *Acid Dreams Epitaph* (CD) and *Back From The Grave, Vol. 1* (LP). (VJ)

The Elite U.F.O.

45:	Now Who's Good Enough/Tarantula	(M.A.I.) 1966	

From Stanton, Kentucky. The 'A' side uses the riff from *Louie Go Home* while the 'B' side is a Mexican-flavoured instrumental.

Compilation appearances include *Now Who's Good Enough* on *Back From The Grave, Vol. 8* (CD) and *Back From The Grave, Vol. 8* (Dble LP). (VJ/MM)

Elizabeth

Personnel:	STEVE BRUNO	organ, bs	A
	JIM DAHME	gtr, flte, vcls	A
	BOB PATTERSON	gtr, vcls	A
	HANK RANSOME	drms	A
	STEVE WEINGART	ld gtr, harp, organ, vcls	A

ALBUM:	1(A) ELIZABETH	(Vanguard VSD 6501) 1968	SC

NB: (1) reissued on vinyl and CD by Vanguard/Comet (VSD 6501) in Italy, 2000 as part of the label's 50 year celebration. The vinyl is a 180gm release in heavy duty sleeve.

45:	Mary Anne/ The World's For Free (PS)	(Vanguard 35070) 1968	

This is a fairly standard late sixties rock album with a few highlights such as the fuzz guitar extravaganza on *You Should Be More Careful*, the rather haunting *Alarm Rings Five* and the final track *When All Else Fails*, which is more interesting than most of what has preceded it. Originally from Philadelphia they moved to New York, where they recorded their album. Earlier, drummer Stewkie Antoni, who later played with **The Nazz**, had played with them and Hank Ransome later played for **Good God** and **Duke Williams and The Extremes**.

Compilation appearances include *Not That Kind Of Guy* on *The New Sound Of Underground* (LP). (VJ/SR/MW)

ELIZABETH - Elizabeth LP.

Ellie Pop

Personnel incl: R. DUNN A
S. DUNN A

ALBUM: 1(A) ELLIE POP (Mainstream S6115) 1968 R1/R2

45: Seven North Frederick/Can't Be Love (Mainstream 686) 1968

A light 'n' fresh psychedelic-folk-pop band with quite an Anglophile sound. The album is reasonable, but nothing has yet been uncovered about the band or their location.

Can't Be Love can also be found on *Pepperisms Around The Globe* (CD & LP). (VJ/CF)

Steve Elliot

Personnel incl: STEVE ELLIOT A

ALBUM: 1(A) DEMO (No label SE 1000) 1969 R2

This was a band not a solo artist. The album is a rare local New York folk release in a cool, handmade cover - with guitars, piano, sax and flute. (CF)

Ron Elliott

Personnel:
RY COODER	gtr	A
DENNIS DRAGON	drms	A
RON ELLIOTT	gtr, vcls	A
CHRIS ETHRIDGE	bs	A
PAUL HUMPHREY	drms	A
DAN LEVITT	gtr	A
MARC McCLURE	gtr, vcl	A
LYLE RITZ	bs	A
LEON RUSSELL	brass arr.	A
BUD SHANK	flute	A
SAL VALENTINO	tamb	A

ALBUM: 1(A) THE CANDLESTICKMAKER
(Warner Bros. WS 1833) 1970 -

NB: (1) reissued on CD in Germany by Line (LECD 9.00944 O) 1990.

A must-have for **Beau Brummels** fans, the only solo album of **Ron Elliott** is a excellent follow-up to *Triangle* and *Bradley's Barn*. The side-long *The Candlestickmaker Suite* with its 14' 53" minutes of magnificence, is the most impressive track, but *All Time Green*, *To The City, To The Sea* and *Deep River Runs Blue* are interesting too.

ELYSIAN FIELD - Elysian Field CD.

Recorded at Sunwest Studios in Hollywood, all the songs were composed and produced by **Elliott**, sometime helped by Gary Downey, the co-producer.

Levitt and McClure were previously in **Levitt and McClure** whose only album was produced by **Elliott**. In 1971, McClure and Dragon formed **Joyous Noise** with some help from **Elliott**. **Ron Elliott** was later a member of Pan and Giants and reformed the **Beau Brummels** in 1975. (SR)

Ellis and Lynch

ALBUM: 1 GENTLE RAIN, PROMISE OF A NEW REBIRTH
(RA R16) 1976 -

A delicate and rather mellow female folk group with light psychy touches and Christian lyrics. Fragile harmonies, acoustic guitar, flute, piano and Arp string ensemble, for late night listening. (SR)

Elmer City Rambling Dogs

Personnel:
MIKE MASCIARELLI	drms	A
JAMES ROWLAND	ld gtr, jew's harp, hrmnca	A
RICHIE VER-L	keyb'ds	A
(BUTCH WALKER	gtr	A)
TEENY WAR	ld vcls, german slide whistle	A

ALBUM: 1(A) JAM IT (Dog Dirt DD1) 1975 SC

A local Pennsylvania, bluesy bar band. Their album is sometimes given a psychedelic tag, which is misleading as it is, essentially, **Grateful Dead** influenced hillbilly rock. All the songs were recorded between January and August 1975 by Tony Pappa at MSI Recording Studio, Pennsauken, New Jersey or by Frank Virtue, Virtue Recording Studio, Philadelphia. Produced by the group and Eddie Harris, it contains mostly original material with very crude lyrics (*Spitball King*, *Hot Prison Love*, *The Prowler*...) and an almost X-rated drawing on the front cover. (SR/CF)

The Elopers

45: Music To Smoke Bananas By/
Peak Beat (RLW 1267(1286/7)) 1967

Came out of Colorado and the above psyched-out instrumental from September 1967 can also be heard on *Highs In The Mid-Sixties, Vol. 18* (LP) and *Psychedelic Experience, Vol. 2* (CD). It's nothing special though. (VJ)

The Elusives

45: Won't Find Better Than Me / Lost Love (Philips 40379) 1966

According to Mike Kuzmin's 'Sounds From The Woods' Pa. book this act came from Northampton, Pennsylvania and were originally known as the Corvairs. They also later recorded as **The Scott Bedford Four**. (MW)

Elysian Field

Personnel:
FRANK BUGBEE	gtr, vcls	AB
MARVIN MAXWELL	drms	ABCDE
JIM SETTLE	bs, vcls	A CDE
GARY JOHNSON	bs, vcls	BC
DENNIS LEDFORD	gtr/bs	CD
MARK MICELI	gtr	CD
DENNY LILE	bs, gtr	DE
RUDY HELM	bs	E

CD: 1(-) ELYSIAN FIELD (Gear Fab GF-140) 1999

NB: (1) also released as a double LP (Akarma AK 124/2).

45s: Kind Of A Man / Alone On Your Doorstep (Imperial 66318) 1968
24 Hours Of Loneliness /
Strange Changes (Imperial 66387) 1969

In 1968 Bugbee, Settle and Maxwell broke away from Louisville's premier garage band **Soul, Inc.** to pursue a more pop-oriented style. The resultant brace of 45s on Imperial showed a strong tendency to the orchestrated pop sounds of the Classics IV - no surprise since they too were produced by the Buie/Cobb team.

After the first 45 Settle was replaced for a while by **The Oxfords'** Gary Johnson. The band wanted to move to an aggressive hard-rock style, but Imperial were having none of it, rejecting the band's own material and presenting them with more Buie/Cobb songs. The band relented for the second 45 but persisted with their chosen direction. Imperial baulked and terminated the contract. The group carried on until 1971 but nothing more was released.

Interest in their material was renewed after band members responded to the **Soul, Inc.** entry and were put in touch with Gear Fab. Two CD volumes documenting **Soul, Inc.** are now accompanied by a CD dedicated to **Elysian Field**. It comprises the 45 sides but, of more interest here, a baker's dozen of unreleased tracks that are a revelation - excellent hard-rock with scintillating guitar. The cuts vary from Cream-inspired riff-heavy bombardments to crisp vibrant rockers with occasional folk and country influences. Recommended. (MW/NK)

The Embermen Five

CD: 1 FIRE IN THEIR HEARTS (Break-A-Way BREAK 006) 2002
NB: (1) also on vinyl.

45s: Fire In My Heart /
Without Your Love (Studio City SC 1053) 1966
That's Why I Need You /
Someone To Hold (Studio City SC 1062) 1967
α Baby I'm Forgettin' You /
My Love For You Won't Die (Studio City No #) 1967
Did You Have To Be So Cruel /
Tomorrow Never Comes (PS) (Century 30851) 1968

NB: α Matrix no 7-8088.

Although this band recorded in Minneapolis, they were from Minot, North Dakota, and were a popular local draw in their home state. *Fire In My Heart* in particular, is frat-ish pop given a spirited performance.

The Break-A-Way compilation collects both sides of their four 45s and five lo-fi live tracks (although the vinyl version excludes their versions of *Gloria* and Roy Head's *Treat Her Right*). They come across as a standard garage band.

According to Tom Tourville's "Musical Winds Of The Northern Plains" the group moved into the country-rock field first as The Contagious (w/Jerry Tanner) then Pierson Lake in the seventies. (BM/MW/VJ)

The Embers

Personnel incl: JACKIE GORE vcls A

ALBUM: 1(A) BURN YOU A NEW ONE (EEE Records 1069) 1967 R1

45s: I'm Gonna Do Beautiful Things For You/
You Are So Beautiful (EEE 1004) c1968
Beach Music Medley/Cheaters Never Win (EEE 201) c1967

A Raleigh, North Carolina, white rock act sounding a lot like **The Young Rascals** (they cover *Groovin*). They released at least two other albums.

Some of their records were produced by H. David Henson. (SR)

SIXTIES REBELLION Vol. 9 (Comp CD) including The Emblems.

The Emblems

45: We're Gonna Love/Lumberjack Jack (Lamia 1547) 196?

An obscure band from Indiana. The 'A' side was written by Don Basore, from **Sir Winston and The Commons**, who also recorded it.

Compilation appearances include: *We're Gonna Love* on *Sixties Rebellion, Vol. 9* (LP & CD) and *Sixties Archive Vol. 7 - Michigan Punk* (CD). (VJ)

The Emblems

Personnel incl: ROY STRAIGIS A

45: (It Would Still Be A) Cruel World /
Whenever I'm Feeling Low (Cameo C-293) 1963

A cooing teen ballad backed by dynamic Mersey-inspired beat. This Philadelphia act were a studio-only group, according to Mike Kuzmin's 'Sounds From The Woods' Pennslyvania discography. They were later known as the **Liverpools** and released two Beatlemania cash-in albums in 1964 on Wyncote, the first of which includes *Whenever I'm Feeling Low*. (MW)

The Emergency Exit

Personnel: PAUL GOLDSMITH ld gtr ABC
BILL LEYRITZ drms A
LUTHER RABB bs ABC
JIM WALTERS gtr ABC
MIKE McGRATH drms B
AL MALOSKY drms C

45s: Maybe Too Late/Why Girl? (Ru-Ro 412) 1966
Maybe Too Late/Why Girl? (Emergency Exit) 1966
Maybe Too Late/Why Girl? (Dunhill 4060) 1966
It's Too Late Baby/
You've Been Changing Your Mind (Dunhill 4082) 1967

Formed in Seattle, Washington in the Spring of 1965. Goldsmith, Rabb and Walters had all previously played with The Nightsounds, whilst McGrath had been with **Jack Eely & The Courtmen**. They played beat-influenced music and before long became a local live attraction. Their debut 45 was eventually picked up by Dunhill and shows the band had achieved a good garage sound. In their heyday during 1967 they appeared with The Beach Boys at the Seattle Center Coliseum and at the Oregon State Fair with **B.J. Thomas and The Triumphs**.

Al Malosky joined the band from **The Liberty Party** but when Jim Walters was drafted **Emergency Exit** broke up, late in 1967. Malosky later played in **Easy Chair**.

Walters and Rabb later both played together in **Ballin' Jack**. Goldsmith also went on to several bands including Soldier and **Calliope**, in which Rabb also had a spell.

Compilation appearances include *Why Girl* (previously unreleased version recorded for Jerry Dennon in 1966) on *Northwest Battle Of The Bands, Vol. 1* (CD); and *Why Girl* (45 version) on *Boulders, Vol. 8* (LP) and *Ya Gotta Have Moxie, Vol. 2* (Dble CD). (VJ)

Emerson's Old Timey Custard-Suckin' Band

Personnel:
HOWARD LAMDEN	gtr, autoharp, vcls	A
NEIL RICKLEN	mandolin, fiddle, gtr, vcls	A
ARNOLD SELL	banjo, vcls	A
ALAN SINGER	bs	A

ALBUM: 1(A) EMERSON'S OLD TIMEY CUSTARD-SUCKIN' BAND (ESP 2006) 1970 -

This amusing band name was used by an acoustic folk-blues quartet in the style of **Michael Hurley** or **Homegas**. Their original songs were combined with covers of blues standards (*Sittin On Top Of The World* and *You Don't Miss Your Water*), Jesse Winchester's *Brand New Tennessee Waltz* and Johnny Cash's *I Still Miss Someone.*

A good album which still has to attract much attention, like several other ESP releases. (SR)

Tim Emery

ALBUM: 1 ALIAS REDD GARRETT (Ros Sound) 1973 R1

A moody psych singer with fuzz guitar, his album is extremely rare. (SR)

Emotions

45: Sometimes / Why Must It Be (Century 24742) 1966

A snappy cover of the Zombies' *Sometimes* by this obscure St.Petersburg, Florida, group graces *Psychedelic States - Florida Vol. 2* (CD). Member(s) were later in Duckbutter. (MW/JLh/RM)

(Original) Emotions

45s: You're A Better Man Than I / Are You Real? (Johnson J-746) 196?
α You're A Better Man Than I / Colour My World (South Park 10000) 1970/1

NB: α is a Canadian release, as **Original Emotions**.

Probably from about 1968, *Better Man* differs from other covers - it's pretty competent but instead of the usual Yardbirds-type rave up in the 'break', here we get some keyboard workout followed by a short drum solo - hmm. *Are You Real?* is like '68 'psych-pop', orchestrated unfortunately but the use of echoes and phasing plus some good wah-wah guitar lifts it out of the dross. (MW)

The Emperor's

45s: Searchin' Round The World / A Fool For You I've Been (Wickwire 13003) 1964
Blue Day/Laughin' Linda (PS) (Wickwire 13007) 196?
You Make Me Feel Good / Heat Wave (2+2 102) 196?
I Want My Woman / And Then (Sabra 5555) 1965

From San Bernardino, California it's not 100% confirmed that the Wickwire/2+2 group is the same as that which recorded for Sabra, but it is likely. Lelan Rodgers who produced the classic but politically incorrect *I Want My Woman* 45, was working in L.A. at the time as an independent record producer. Bill Hughes wrote both songs of the Sabra single.

Compilation appearances have included *I Want My Woman* on *Pebbles, Vol. 1* (CD), *60's Punk E.P., Vol. 1* (7"), *Boulders Punk EP Box Set*, *I Was A Teenage Caveman* (LP) and *Epitaph For A Legend* (Dble LP); *And Then* on *Austin Landing, Vol. 2* (LP); *Laughin' Linda* on *Grab This And Dance!!!* (LP); and *Blue Day* on *I Can Hear Raindrops* (LP). (MW/MM)

The Emporium

ALBUM: 1 I'M SO GLAD - IN CONCERT (Peace no #) c1970 SC

From Iowa, a large Christian group (four girls, four guys) who play harmony folk with jangling guitars and some rock songs. Their album contains mostly covers, like *Aquarius*, *For What It's Worth* and *Get Together* but they also penned the long trippy *Jesus, Jesus*, one of the tracks with fuzz guitar. (SR)

Enchanters 4

45s: I Don't Know/Like Tuff ( ) 196?
Lost You/Route 66 (Mal 1019) 196?

This garage band came from Oak Park, Illinois. Their first 45, *I Don't Know* is a mid-tempo mersey sound, while the flip is a guitar instrumental... *Lost You* has resurfaced on *Garage Punk Unknowns, Vol. 7* (LP). (MM/VJ)

The End

45: Not Fade Away/Memorandum (Cha Cha 746) 1966

Came out of Chicago. *Not Fade Away* has resurfaced on *Garage Punk Unknowns, Vol. 1* (LP). You can also find the flip on *Pebbles, Vol. 6* (CD). (VJ)

The End

45: Bad Night/ Make Our Love Come Through (Insegrievious CR 31007) c1967

Aram Heller's 'Till The Stroke Of Dawn' tells us that this bunch hailed from Philips Academy, Andover, Massachusetts, well-spring of the 'prep-rock' genre and many of its best proponents (**Rising Storm** of course). That prep-rock aura oozes through. The 'A' side is epitomises the New England garage sound and the flip is a competent beat-ballad. (MW)

I WAS A TEENAGE CAVEMAN (Comp LP) including The Emperor's.

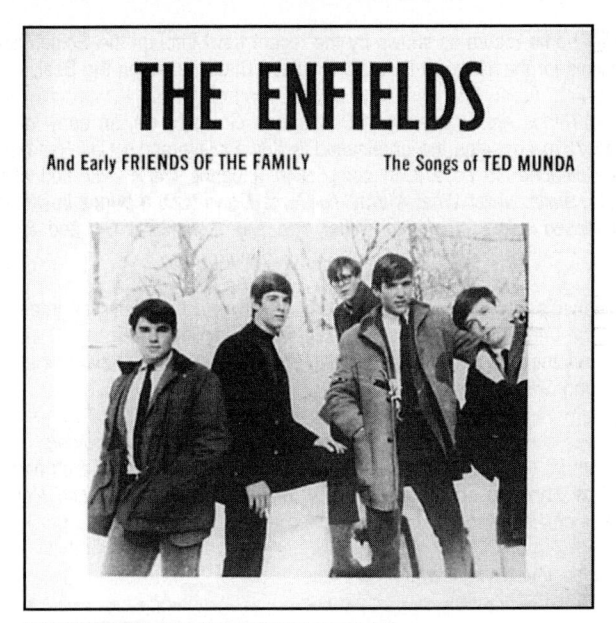

THE ENFIELDS - The Songs Of Ted Munda LP.

The Endd

Personnel incl:	LARRY ANDERSON	bs	A
	RUSS SANDERS	ld vcls	A

45s:	So Sad/Emancipation	(Seascape SS-500) 1965
	Out Of My Hands/Project Blue	(Seascape SS-501) 1966
	Gonna Send You Back To Mother/ Don't It Make You Feel Like Crying	(Seascape SS-503) 196?
	Come On In To My World/ This Is Really The Zoo Plus Two	(Seascape SS-504) 1967

Hailing from La Porte, Indiana, they originally used just one 'd' and their first folk-rock 45 was issued using that spelling. By contrast the follow-up is a primitive garage punker. The flip is a cover of **The Banshees** composition.

The 'A' side to their final effort was a heavy West Coast influenced number with fine guitar and drumming. The flip is a short acoustic guitar dominated instrumental. Mike Markesich tells us that the Seascape 502 release was by a different band.

Compilation appearances have included: *Come On Into My Mind* on *Mayhem & Psychosis, Vol. 2* (CD) and *Pebbles, Vol. 9* (LP); *Project Blue* on *Project Blue, Vol. 2 - Psychedelights 1966-70* (LP); *Out Of My Hands* on *Pebbles, Vol. 1 (ESD)* (CD), *Best of Pebbles, Vol. 2* (LP & CD); *This Is Really The Zoo Plus Two* on *Everything You Always Wanted To Know...* (CD); and *Come On Into My World* on *Hoosier Hotshots* (LP). (VJ)

The Endless

Personnel:	MIKE LYONS		A
	JACK McATEE	ld gtr	A
	PAT McATEE	bs, ld vcls	A
	CHUCK MOORMAN	keyb'ds	A
	MIKE O'BRIEN	drums	A

45:	Prevailing Darkness/Tomorrow's Song	(Cardinal 521) 1966

From Springfield, Ohio. The 'A' side, *Prevailing Darkness*, is very much in the garage punk mould and comes with snarling vocals and farfisa organ. The flip, *Tomorrow's Song*, is more sensitive - a Zombies influenced composition with chiming guitars. Apart from their sole 45, five unreleased tracks exist which include alternate versions of the 45 tracks. These are to be featured on a forthcoming CD set *The Mus-I-Col Story* on Get Hip.

Compilation appearances have included *Prevailing Darkness* on *Vile Vinyl, Vol. 2* (LP) and *Vile Vinyl* (CD); and *Prevailing Darkness* and *Tomorrow's Song* on *Highs In The Mid-Sixties, Vol. 21* (LP). (GGl/MW/VJ)

The Enemys

45:	Hey Joe!/My Dues Have Been Paid	(MGM 13525) 1966

Produced by Danny Hutton, an obscure Californian act doing a another version of this classic song, this time arranged by Cory Wells and M.Lustom.

Wells and Hutton would later form **Three Dog Night**.

Compilation appearances include *Hey Joe* on *Garagelands, Vol. 2* (LP). (SR)

The Energy Package

45:	This Is The 12th Night/ See That I Come Home	(Laurie 3392) 1967

From Westbury, NY, a town on Long Island, this act were a popular draw in the top Manhattan discotheques. Several members of this group reformed shortly after **The Energy Package**'s demise and renamed themselves **The Boys From New York City**.

NB: Any info taggin' these groups as Massachusetts-based is erroneous...

Compilation appearances have included: *See That I Come Home* on *Mindrocker, Vol. 10* (LP); and *This Is The Twelfth Night* on *Of Hopes And Dreams & Tombstones* (LP) and *Psychedelic Unknowns, Vol. 7* (LP & CD). (MM/MW)

The Enfields

Personnel:	GORDON BERL	drms	ABC
	JOHN BERNARD	gtr	ABC
	BILL GALLERY	bs	AB
	MAC MORGAN	vcls	A
	TED MUNDA	gtr	ABC
	ROBIN EATON	vcls	BC
	JOHN RHOADS	bs	C

ALBUMS:	1( )	THE SONGS OF TED MUNDA	(Distortions DB 1003) 1991
	2( )	THE ENFIELDS AND THE FRIENDS OF THE FAMILY	(Get Hip GHAS 5000) 199?

45s:	The Eyes Of The World/ The Eyes Of The World	(Richie RI-669) 1965/6
	She Already Has Somebody/ I'm For Things You Do	(Richie RI-670) 1966
	You Don't Have Very Far/Face To Face	(Richie RI-671) 1966
	Twelve Months Coming/Time Card	(Richie RI-675) 1967

This outfit formed in Wilmington, Delaware around 1964. Ted Munda and Gordon Berl had earlier played in an outfit called The Playboys with a third guy called Rick. Bernard Gallery and Eaton had previously played in a quartet named The Touchstones with a fourth guy called Charles Jenner, which played mostly surf music. With the British invasion so strong at the time they opted for a British name to reflect the sound they were striving for. There was after all a town in England called Enfield, the Royal Enfield motorcycle and a British rifle named the Enfield. They got their first break in late 1965 when they were taken under the wings of Vince Rago, who managed several local Delaware bands in the fifties and sixties. The group agreed to make a record and at Vince Rago's suggestion the same song was put on both sides so that dee-jays would know which side to play. *Eyes Of The World* created quite a lot of interest locally with its Beatle-like harmonies and some nice minor chord guitar work. The follow- up, *She Already Has Somebody*, was more polished, a minor-key folk rocker with some fine guitar work from John Bernard, and already **The Enfields** had become Wilmington's top band. *You Don't Have Very Far* was a quieter, reflective ballad but the flip, *Face To Face* was one of their finest moments with a compelling "Taxman" riff.

Bill Gallery left the band shortly after the third single. He was replaced by John Rhoads from The Wrecking Crew - another local band that included

Jeff Daking, who later joined **The Blues Magoos**. In early 1967 they travelled to the Virtue Recording Studios in Philadelphia to record cuts for a possible album. *Twelve Months Coming, Time Card* and four other songs were recorded for the album. The tape ended up costing quite a bit of money and Vince Rago decided not to buy it. The studio's owner overdubbed it with a different vocalist and sold it to Capitol records, where it remains today. Rago, meanwhile, took the band to an inferior studio in New Jersey, where less good versions of *Twelve Months Coming* and *Time Card* were recorded and released on a 45 by Rago without the band's consent. **The Enfields** decided to call it a day in disgust and the record flopped. Ted Munda, who had written all the band's songs, formed a new outfit **The Friends Of The Family** with John Rhoads and two members of another local band, The Tuds.

The Distortions retrospective album collects all **The Enfields** and most of **The Friends Of The Family** tracks together and provides an excellent insight into this obscure outfit who produced some magical moments that deserve wider recognition. Get Hip have also released a simliar CD retrospective, which also includes previously unreleased material.

Compilation appearances have included *She Already Has Somebody* and *I'm For Things You Do* on *A Journey To Tyme, Vol. 1* (LP); and *She Already Has Somebody* on *What A Way To Die* (LP). (VJ)

Butch Engle and The Styx

Personnel:	BUTCH ENGLE	vcls	ABC
	RICH MORRISON	drms	BC
	MIKE PARDEE	organ	B
	HARRY 'HAPPINESS' SMITH	bs	BC
	BOB ZAMNORA	ld gtr	BC
	LARRY GERUGHTY	keyb'ds	C

ALBUM: 1 NO MATTER WHAT YOU SAY - THE BEST OF (Beat Rocket BR 106) 2000

NB: (1) is a retrospective LP, also issued on CD (BRCD 106) 2000 with three extra tracks (1 alternate and 2 demo versions of tracks on the LP).

45s:	You Know All I Want / Tell Me Please	(Mea 4505) 1964
	I Like Her / Going Home	(Loma 2065) 1967
	Hey I'm Lost / Puppetmaster	(Onyx 2200) 1967

From Mill Valley in Marin County California, this five-piece evolved out of The Showmen who cut one rousing 45 on a tiny label based in Sausalito. As **Butch Engle and The Styx** they enjoyed the patronage of **The Beau Brummels**' Ron Elliot who produced and wrote/co-wrote nearly all of their subsequent recordings at Leo De Gar Kulka's Golden State Recorders. Occasionally he sat in on guitar too. Despite the undoubted calibre of this band (who beat off all opposition at the April 1966 Band Bash at the Cow Palace in San Francisco) and their material, just a few of their recordings made it onto record as shown by the recent trawl through the Golden State archives for the 'Nuggest From The Golden State' series on Big Beat.

Good Things Are Happening (CD) features *Going Home*, an early version of *Hey I'm Lost* plus the unreleased *If You Believe* and *I Call Her Name*; the *Someone To Love* (CD) compilation unearths *I'm A Fool* and *Smile, Smile, Smile*; whilst *What A Way To Come Down* (CD) includes three more unreleased cuts - *No Matter What You Say*, *Left Hand Girl* and *She Is Love*.

Sundazed's *No Matter What You Say* retrospective harvests all three 45s plus the unreleased tracks on the Big Beat compilations. Their CD version adds another version of *Smile, Smile, Smile* and demo versions of *Help I'm Lost* and *She Is Love*.

Previous compilation appearances include *Going Home* on *Boulders, Vol. 7* (LP) and *I Like Her* on *Boulders, Vol. 10* (LP). Both sides of their final 45 as **The Styx** are on *Sounds Of The Sixties: SFO Part Two* and *Hey I'm Lost* is on *Pebbles, Vol. 17*.

See also **The Styx**. (MW/AP)

The Englishmen

Personnel:	WARREN DANIELS	bs, vcls	A
	TOMMY HOWARD	gtr	A
	TOMMY MEDLIN	keyb'ds	A
	RONNIE WHEELER	drms	A
	JOHN WORKMAN	vcls, gtr	A

ALBUM: 1(A) SUMMER IS HERE (Justice 155) c1967 R2

NB: (1) reissued on Collectables (COL-CD-0609) 1995.

Apart from their own composition, *Summer Is Here*, we have a snappy-suited clubbie band, plodding through instrumentals, R&B, teen ballads, easy, Latin and beat covers. Even their attempt at *96 Tears* is fairly routine and flat. As with **The Checkmates**, best to stick to the known Justice classics and avoid disappointment.

Compilation appearances include *96 Tears* and *Summer Is Here* on *Green Crystal Ties, Vol. 10* (CD). (MW)

The English Muffins

Personnel:	WILLIAM CRAUN	drms	A
	MARC FARLEY	bs, vcls	A
	DANNY LEGGE	gtr	A
	ED "SHRED" SCHROEDER	ld gtr, vcls	A
	LARRY TRAITOR	vcls	A

45: Leave Or Stay/It's My Pride (Gama 702) 1966

A quintet who were at college in Bridgewater, Virginia but have tended to be regarded as a Washington, DC band. This was reinforced by the inclusion of their fuzz-fest *Leave Or Stay* on the *Signed, D.C.* (LP) compilation.

By 1967 they'd been rechristened as **The Seventh Seal** and journeyed forth to Winston-Salem, North Carolina to record what turned out to be an unreleased album for the Justice label. It was eventually released as a limited edition in 1999 - *Reflections* (Justice JLP-0).

The English Muffins on B.T. Puppy was another outfit - an all-girl group - which puts a totally different complexion on the name! (MW)

The English Setters

Personnel incl:	DAVID ALVES	
	LARRY GRAY	
	CHRIS GRIMES	
	DAVE GRIMES	
	PUNKY MEADOWS	gtr

BUTCH ENGLE & THE STYX - No Matter What You Say LP.

45s:	Tragedy/If She's All Right	(Glad Hamp 2029) 1966
	It Shouldn't Happen To A Dog/ Someday You'll See	(Glad Hamp 2033) 1966
	Wake Up/She's In Love	(Jubilee 5560) 1967

Formed in Washington D.C., but relocated to Arlington, Virginia, this band offered a pretty average garage fayre although the second 45 is decent folk-rock pop.

In 1968, Meadows and the Grimes Brothers formed the **Cherry People** and later their frontman, Punky Meadows went on to form **Angel**, who recorded for Casablanca, toured with Kiss, and also appeared in the Jodie Foster film "Foxes".

Compilation appearances have included: *Tragedy* on *A Journey To Tyme, Vol. 4* (LP) and *Garage Punk Unknowns, Vol. 7* (LP); *It Shouldn't Happen To A Dog* on *Garage Punk Unknowns, Vol. 2* (LP); and *Someday You'll See* on *Garage Punk Unknowns, Vol. 4* (LP). (VJ/MW/DSh/SR)

John English III

Personnel incl:	JOHN ENGLISH	ld vcls	AB
	JAMES 'ZEKE' CAMARILLO	bs	B
	RUDY GARZA	piano, hrmnca	B
	STEVE LAGANA	drms	B
	HAL TENNANT	ld gtr, hrmnca	B

45s:	I Need You Near /?	(Sabra # unkn) 196?
α	Moanin' / Just Don't Complain	(Moonglow M-5011) 1966

NB: α as John English III and The Lemondrops.

Formerly with **The Preachers**, this L.A.-based singer *Moanin'* 45 was actually recorded by **The Preachers** just before they split up. With no band to promote it, Moonglow decided to issue it as John English III and The Lemondrops. Another moniker used was John English III and The Carnaby Commoners, but no releases have yet come to light.

Both sides of the *Moanin'* 45 are compiled, along with the three **Preachers** singles on the 2-CD set (also available on vinyl) *Moanin'* (Bacchus Archives CD BA 1181) 2002.

Boulders, Vol. 7 (LP) includes *I Need You Near*. *Just Don't Complain*, co-composed with **The Preachers**' Rudy Garza, is on *Fuzz, Flaykes, And Shakes, Vol. 2* (LP & CD). (MW/VJ)

Enoch Smoky

Personnel:	DICKIE DOUGLAS	gtr	A

45:	It's Cruel / Roll Over Beethoven	(Pumpkin Seed 83-4010) 197?

Based in Iowa City, this band was formed in 1969 by guitarist Dickie Douglas and their popularity kept them going until 1976. Douglas had previously been with the Legends, **Al's Untouchables** and St.John and The Heads. After the latter outfit had relocated to Los Angeles the other members - Phil Jones, Felix Falcon and Casey Foutz - teamed up with **Crabby Appleton**, leaving Douglas to return alone to Iowa.

It's Cruel can be heard on *A Lethal Dose Of Hard Psych* (CD). (ELn/MW)

Entourage Music and Theatre Ensemble

Personnel:	JOE CLARK		AB
	RUSTI CLARK		AB
	MICHAEL SMITH		AB
	WALL MATTHEWS		B

ALBUMS:	1(A)	ENTOURAGE	(Folkways) 197?	?
	2(B)	THE NEPTUNE COLLECTION	(Folkways) 197?	?

A strange acid-folk troupe. Both albums were recorded and released in the early seventies on Folkways Records. The musicians on the first album are also featured on both **Bob Brown** albums (produced by **Richie Havens**).

THE ENGLISHMEN - Summer Is Here CD.

Wall Matthews later released an album with Biff Rose - *Hamburger Blues* (Sweet Jane) 1973/74, and Rusti Clark also played on a late seventies album by Wall Matthews - *The Dance In Your Eye* (Philo/Fretless).

Sadly, Joe and Rusti are both now deceased. (SR/WM)

The Epics

45:	Give Me A Chance/Louis Come Home	(Zen 202) 1965

An L.A. band - one of the few to record a variation on *Louie, Louie*. Indeed *Louis Come Home* with its superb growling vocals was one of the finest versions to come out of L.A. You'll also find it on *Highs In The Mid-Sixties, Vol. 1*. They were unconnected to any other Epics so far as is known. (VJ)

The Epics

45:	White Collar House/She Believed In Me	(Dolphin 3821) 1966

From Columbus, Ohio, this bands 45 also has a rare picture sleeve which shows the band wearing long hair wigs. Expect to pay $100+ for an original 45, $250+ with the picture sleeve!! *White Collar House* can be also heard on *Highs In The Mid-Sixties, Vol. 21* (LP). It's a pretty standard garage punker. (VJ/MW/GGl)

The Epics

Personnel incl:	BOB WINKELMAN	gtr	A

45:	Homesick/Humpty Dumpty	(Love 670312) 1967

A good trashy garage punker from Walnut Creek, California. The asking price for this 45 in 1997 was $300, probably due to the fact that this was Bob Winkelman's outfit prior to him joining **Frumious Bandersnatch**.

Compilation appearances have included: *Homesick* on *Fuzz, Flaykes, And Shakes, Vol. 4* (LP & CD) and *Humpty Dumpty* on *Garage Punk Unknowns, Vol. 8* (LP). (MW)

The Epics

Personnel:	RANDY DAVIS	bs	A
	JACK KIRECKI	ld gtr	A
	STEVE SLIGER	drms	A
	ALAN TROUTMAN	gtr	A

45:	Cruel World / I'll Be Glad	(Fuller 2680) 1965

The sole platter by this quartet from Clearwater and Tarpon Springs, Florida can fetch three figures, 35+ years on. If you wanna know why, their Merseybeat style ballad *Cruel World* can be heard again on *Psychedelic States - Florida Vol. 2* (CD). (MW/JLh/RM)

Epic Splendor

Personnel:	VIC CANONE	ld gtr	A
	EDDIE GARGUILO	drms	A
	LARRY JACK	bs	A
	PAUL MASARTI	ld vcls	A
	CHARLIE ??	organ	A

45s:	A Little Rain Must Fall/		
	Cowboys And Indians	(Hot Biscuit 1450)	1967
	It Could Be Wonderful/		
	She's High On Life	(Hot Biscuit 1452)	1968

Larry Jack, had previously played in **Little Bits of Sound** and it was through their 45 that **Epic Splendor** came about. Issued on Roulette, **Little Bits of Sound**'s 45 *What Life's About/Girls Who Paint Designs* 45 was a product of Koppelman & Rubin Associates Chardon Music, Inc. A member of that company, James Foley, approached Larry with a demo by Richard Fishbaugh of *A Little Rain Must Fall*, a moderate piano ballad. He asked Larry to put a band together to record the song and so he left **Little Bits of Sound** and joined a local group The Entire Thing, who included Masarti, Canone and Garguilo. The Entire Thing's original organ player was replaced by Charlie ???.

Hot Biscuit was a Capitol subsidiary and **Epic Splendor** (a name the record company came up with) was its first release.

Their first 45 was recorded in New York and produced by John Boylan, who went on to work with Linda Ronstadt and The Eagles, among others. It was arranged by Trade Martin, who also went on to bigger things. *A Little Rain Must Fall* was a great pop tune notable for Paul Masarti's vocal but has a very produced feel, with horn section throughout. Boylan and his brother Terence (who wrote *Shake It*, an Ian Matthews semi-hit) wrote the flip side, *Cowboy's And Indians*.

The band were promoted heavily, appearing on the 'Upbeat' show out of Philadelphia and 'Zacherley's Music' show in New York. They also had some success in the Northeast. *A Little Rain Must Fall* made the Top 30 in New York as a Pick Hit on WMCA, in the week of December 6th. 1967. They also toured with **The Stone Ponies** as well as **The Lemon Pipers**, **Blues Magoos** and **Vagrants**.

The follow up single *It Could Be Wonderful* was a cover of the UK Smoke act, from their *It's Smoke Time* LP, but **Epic Splendor**'s version was released to a mediocre reception. The group was then dropped by Capitol and drifted into the ranks of one hit wonders.

NEX MEXICO PUNK FROM THE SIXTIES (Comp LP) includes Era Of Sound.

Larry Jack latter became a successful chiropractor in Sacramento, California. (RJ)

The Epicureans

Personnel:	TOM BROCKMAN	drms	AB
	JERRY CLARK	gtr, sax	ABCD
	PHIL MESSERLI	keyb'ds	AB
	STEVE MURPHY	ld gtr, vcls	ABCDE
	WAYNE WOLTERS	bs	BC
	TIM MESSERLI	keyb'ds	CDE
	DENNIS THATE	drms	C
	DICK DUSEK	drms	DE
	JOHN GOOSSEN	gtr	E

45s:	Baby Be Mine/I Don't Know Why I Cry	(IGL 113)	1966
	Break Out And Run/Blue Side Of Lonely	(UA 551)	1969

This band hailed from Fairmont, Minnesota and they had in Steve Murphy one of the state's finest guitarists. Jerry Clark had previously been the leader of another local garage band, The Corvairs and Murphy had fronted The Pacers, who were also a local garage act. Through the latter part of 1965 and into early 1966 they competed in several local 'Battle Of The Band' type events. One of their contest wins enabled them to use some recording time at the IGL Studios in Milford, Iowa. Initially four tracks were recorded - *Pain Is Evil*, *Somewhere, Someplace, Sometime*, *My Baby Went Away* and *P W Blues*. They didn't get beyond acetate form but the band returned shortly after to record a 45, which remains sought-after by collectors today in part due to Steve Murphy's fine vocal performance. The second 45 was more in the hard rock genre. In 1971 the band became known as **Highway**.

I Don't Know Why I Cry can be heard on *The IGL Rock Story: Part One (1965 - 67)* (CD) and *The Best of IGL Folk Rock* (LP). Two of their unreleased 1966 tracks - *Pain Is Evil* and *Baby Be Mine* are also included on *IGL Dance Jamboree '66* (Dble CD). (VJ/MW)

Epitome

Personnel ?:	J. FORIENZA	A
	S. GENTILE	A
	BILLY HOCHER	A
	M. LEVA	A

45s:	I Need You/Flower Power	(Mona-Lee 219)	1967
	I Can't Face Myself / Sleep	(Kama Sutra KA-265)	1969

On their debut 45, this suburban New York City band chose to cover **The Other Half**'s *I Need You* - a slower bluesy workout with swelling keyboards that doesn't quite jell. The Billy Hocher composed flip is better than the title may suggest - bouncy pop with raw-throated vocals.

Hocher next came up with *Sleep*, uptempo power-pop with pizzicato picking and a baroque-tinted lilt. On *I Can't Face Myself* he shares credits with those listed above - other members of the band perhaps? This is a slow bluesy power-ballad with brassy outbursts.

Is this the same Billy Hocher who played bass and sang in **Bulldog**, the post-**Rascals** group formed by Gene Cornish and Dino Danelli? (MW/MM/SR)

Era of Sound

Personnel incl:	MICHAEL NARANJO	A
	REYNALDO NARANJO	A

45:	Girl In The Mini Skirt/Stay With Me	(Delta R 2255)	1967

From Espanola, New Mexico, members included native American brothers Michael and Reynaldo Naranjo. The 'A' side of their 45 is a rather catchy blast coming with a strong chorus sandwiched between the buzz of fuzztone guitars.

PSYCHEDELIC UNKNOWNS Vol. 9 (Comp CD) includes Erik and The Smoke Ponies.

Compilation appearances have included: *Girl In The Mini Skirt* on *King Richard And The Knights - Precision! - (Plus Other 60's Albuquerque Groups)* (CD), *New Mexico Punk From The Sixties* (LP), *Sixties Archive, Vol. 4* (CD), *60's Punk E.P., Vol. 1* (7"), *Garagelands, Vol. 1 & 2* (CD) and *Garagelands, Vol. 2* (LP). (VJ/MM)

Wendy Erdman

ALBUM: 1   ERDMAN   (Audio Fidelity) 1970 SC

A strange and overemotive folk singer. Her album was housed in an odd sleeve. (SR)

Eric

ALBUM: 1   ERIC   (C.E.I.) 197? R2

An inter-racial quartet named **Eric**, not a solo album, from Ohio. On offer is weak pop-rock by a semi-inept band. (CF)

Mark Eric

ALBUM: 1   A MIDSUMMER'S DAY DREAM
                                                  (Revue RS7210) 1969 R1

45s: Night Of The Lions/Don't Cry Over Me   (Revue R 11052) 1969
California Home/
Where Do The Girls Of The Summer Go   (Revue R 11064) 1970

Produced by Norman Gregg and H. Ratner, a soft psych album with orchestrations in the mould of **Sagittarius** or the Beach Boys's *Pet Sounds*. It's beginning to attract some collectors. Revue was an UNI/MCA subsidiary.

Both 45s were taken from the album.

His real name was Mark Eric Malmborg and he worked as an actor in Hollywood for several years in commercials. He made several appearances on The Partridge Family and other shows. He later spent much time playing on cruise liners! More recently, he has started making a few live performances in LA. (SR/JG)

Eric and The Norsemen

Personnel:	FOREST CLOUD	bs	A
	ROGER JOHNSON	vcls, rhythm gtr	AB
	MIKE WILLMAN	vcls, ld gtr	AB
	JIM KOCHER	drums	AB
	FRANK BERRIER	bs	B
	MITCH??	kyb'ds	B

ALBUM: 1   ERIC AND THE NORSEMEN
                              (Studio House acetate) 1967 R3

NB: (1) acetate only.

45:    Get It On/Scotch And Soda   (Chrome 45-103) 1967

This 45 was the work of a garage/frat-rock quartet from Lawrence in Kansas. The 'A' side, *Get It On* is a **Paul Revere And The Raiders** cover with some droning slide guitar and distorted orchestration.

Some Super 8mm home movie footage of the band, filmed between 1965-1968, backed by an acetate of the band's unreleased album is also known to be circulating amongst collectors. The album, like the single, is standard frat-rock fare, bringing to mind the Justice albums and features performances of, among others, *Little Latin Lupe Lu*, *Money*, *Turn On Your Lovelight*, *Little Red Riding Hood*, and *Double Shot Of My Baby's Love*.

Compilation appearances have included: *Get It On* on *Midwest Garage Band Series - Kansas* (CD), *The Garage Zone, Vol. 1* (LP) and *The Garage Zone Box Set* (4-LP); and *Norsemen's Theme* (from their unreleased album) on *Let's Dig 'Em Up, Vol. 2* (LP). (MDo/MW/MM)

Erik

ALBUM: 1   LOOK WHERE I AM   (Vanguard VRS-9267) 1968 SC

A psychedelic folk singer whose album is now beginning to attract collectors. (SR)

Erik and The Smoke Ponies

Personnel:	RICHARD KLASKO	A
	GIACONI	A

45:    I'll Give You More/
From Where I'm Standing   (Kama Sutra KA 227) 1967

From Hempstead on Long Island, New York. The 'A' side of their sole vinyl epitaph is a fuzzy punky pop effort. Both sides were written by Richard Klasko, helped by Giaconi for the unfortunately very forgettable 'B' side and produced by Klasko, Hy Mizrahi and John Linde. Linde also produced **Group Image** and the **New York Rock & Roll Ensemble**.

Compilation appearances include *I'll Give You More* on *Psychedelic Unknowns, Vol. 9* (CD) and *Victims Of Circumstance, Vol. 2* (CD). (VJ/SR/MW)

Ernie and The Emperors

Personnel incl: ERNIE (JOSEPH) OROSCO   A

45:    Meet Me At The Corner/
Got A Lot I Want To Say   (Reprise 0414) 1965

Merseybeat style pop and slightly fuzzy folk-punk from the California outfit who became **Ernie's Funnys** and later **Giant Crab**. The drummer of this particular incarnation went on to **The Dovers**.

Ernie Orosco was later known as **Ernie Joseph**, who formed **Big Brother** and released a solo album. (MW/CMn/AP)

Ernie's Funny's

Personnel incl: ERNIE OROSCO   A

45:    Thru' The Fields/Shimmey Like Kate   (Yardbird 8004) 1967

Formerly **Ernie and The Emperors** and pre-**Giant Crab**. Average pop-beat put out on the **Starfires**' label.

After **Giant Crab**, Ernie Orosco was better known as **Ernie Joseph** and formed **Big Brother** as well as releasing a solo album. (MW/AP)

ESB

Personnel:	PATRICK BURKE		A
	GEORGE CALDWELL		A
	RICHARD FORTUNATO		A
	STEVE LAGANA		A
	ROBERT ZINNER		A

45:	Mushroom People/Let Me Touch You	(In Arts IA 102) 1967

The above fivesome are credited on both sides of this 45, so it seems fair to assume they comprised the band. The 'A' side is weird and strangely fragmented and has surfaced on *An Overdose Of Heavy Psych* (CD) and *High All The Time, Vol. 2* (LP). *Let Me Touch You* is a stately Eastern-infused psychedelic ballad. In Arts was a Californian label.

Burke, Lagana and Fortunato went on to form **Fields**, a late sixties power-trio with slightly less chemical influences. **Fields** were Los Angeles based.

Richard Fortunato had earlier made some recordings with post-**Vejtables** personnel in 1966 and was also with **The Preachers** of *Who Do You Love* fame.

It appears that **ESB** was formerly **W.C. Fields Electric String Band** which latterly included George Caldwell of **The Bees**. (MW)

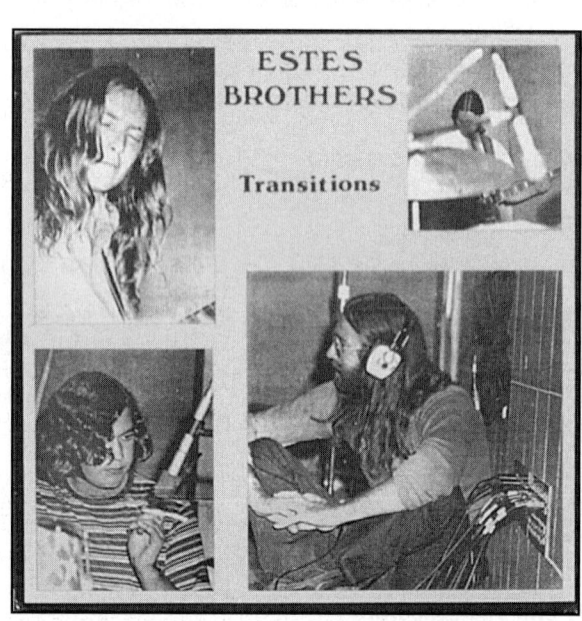

ESTES BROTHERS - Transitions LP.

The Escapades

Personnel:	RON GORDEN	keyb'ds	A
	BENNY KISNER	gtr	A
	TOMMY MINGA	vcls	A
	DALE ROURKE	bs	A
	RONNIE WILLIAMSON	drms	A

45s:	I Tell No Lies/She's The Kind	(Arbet 1010/1) 1966
	I Tell No Lies/She's The Kind	(XL 356) 1966
	Mad Mad Mad/I Try So Hard	(Verve VK 10415) 1966

A quintet from Memphis, Tennessee formed by Minga, previously with the Jesters. Their debut proved popular enough for them to embark on a tour of the South and they attracted the attention of Verve. Unfortunately the follow-up failed to build on the initial success and they returned to Memphis, breaking up the following year due to the draft. Gorden would join the reformed Bar-Kays, then went on to work for Stax for whom he designed album sleeves. He was nominated for a Grammy for Isaac Hayes' *Black Moses*.

One of the best garage punkers outta Memphis, compilation appearances have included:- *I Try So Hard* on *Killer Cuts* (LP); *I Tell No Lies* on *Pebbles, Vol. 5* (CD), *Pebbles, Vol. 5* (LP) and *A History Of Garage And Frat Bands In Memphis* (CD); *She's The Kind* on *Sixties Rebellion, Vol's 1 & 2* (CD) and *Sixties Rebellion, Vol. 1* (LP); and *Mad Mad Mad* on *Son Of The Gathering Of The Tribe* (LP), *Ya Gotta Have Moxie, Vol. 2* (Dble CD) and *Boulders, Vol. 7* (LP). (MW/RHI)

The Escorts

Personnel incl:	ROGER BOOTH	vcls	A

45:	Heart Of Mine/	
	The Twelfth Of Never	(Fredlo Records 6416) 1964

From Davenport, Iowa, an upbeat pop-rock/garage single. *Heart Of Mine* was written by Booth. (SR)

The Escorts

ALBUM:	1	BRING DOWN THE HOUSE	(Teo) 1966 R1

A Virginian garage/frat band. Their album, which was recorded live, consists of standards such as *Louie Louie, Gloria, The Last Time* and *Shout* etc.

Compilation appearances include *The Last Time* on *Oil Stains* (LP). (SR)

Esko Affair

45s:	Morning Dull Fires/Salt & Pepper	(Mercury 72887) 1969
	On Broadway/	
	On A Summer's Day With You	(Mercury 72934) 1969

From Philadelphia and formed by two brothers surnamed Esko, who'd previously been in the Liberation News Service. Touted as 'psych', which it is not, the second 45s covers *Broadway* in a heavy **Fudge**-like style with some good acidic guitar, but is orchestrated and a little brassy - on the whole above-par. The flip is a tender pop ballad with orchestra again and woodwind more to the fore.

Compilation appearances have included: *Morning Dull Fires* on *Of Hopes And Dreams & Tombstones* (LP) and *Psychedelic Unknowns, Vol. 7* (LP & CD). (MW/VJ)

Esperanza Encantanda

ALBUM:	1	ESPERANZA ENCATANDA	(Certron CS-7016) 1970 R1?

A chicano trio with female vocals sung in English and Spanish, combining folk-rock and psychy rock with organ and fuzz guitar. They did a good rendition of the Stones' *Gimme Shelter*. (SR)

The Esquires

Personnel:	TERRY HALL	A
	WES HORNE	A
	CHUCK SNELLING	A
	DICK THORNBERRY	A

45s:	Loneliness Is Mine/Come On, Come On	(Texan 103) 1966
	Loneliness Is Mine/Come On, Come On	(Glenvalley 103) 1966
	Time Don't Mean So Much/Summertime	(Glenvalley 104) 1966
	These Are The Tender Years/	
	Judgement Day	(Glenvalley 105) 1966
	These Are The Tender Years/	
	Come On, Come On	(Glenvalley 105) 1966

From Irving, Texas in the mid-sixties, although they played mainly around Dallas and Fort Worth. *Come On, Come On*, a rock'n'roller, was their best known song. All of the Glenvalley releases appeared in the same picture sleeve.

A whole side of *Texas Punk: 1966, Vol. 2* (LP) and a chunk of *Acid Visions - Complete Collection, Vol. 2* (3-CD) is given over to unreleased tracks, mixes and outtakes by the band.

Compilation appearances have included: *Time Don't Mean So Much* on *Punk Classics, Vol. 4* (7"); *Come On, Come On Come On, Come On (Reprise) Judgement Day Loneliness Is Mine These Are Tender Years Time Don't Mean So Much* on *Texas Punk: 1966, Vol. 2* (LP) and *Acid Visions - Complete Collection, Vol. 2* (3-CD); *Come On, Come On* on *Texas Flashbacks, Vol. 1* (LP & CD), *Flashback, Vol. 1* (LP) and *Teenage Shutdown, Vol. 1* (LP & CD); *Judgment Day, These Are The Tender Years* on *Green Crystal Ties, Vol. 2* (CD); and *Judgement Day* on *Highs In The Mid-Sixties, Vol. 11* (LP) and *I Was A Teenage Caveman* (LP). (VJ)

The Esquires

| 45s: | She's My Woman/Misfortune | (Dot 16954) 1966 |
| | Summer Nights/Settle Down | (Scratch SI-1234/5) 1967 |

Unconnected to the better known Texan band, this mob were from Springfield, Missouri. *She's My Woman* can also be found on *Monsters Of The Midwest, Vol. 2* (LP). It has some effective organ which blends nicely with the vocals but is hampered by lame guitar work. The Scratch 45 kicks off with a light summery popster with brass but the flip is SO much better. Understated garage-pop oozing with charm and a keening guitar break that ends way too soon - check it out on *Mindblowing Encounters Of The Purple Kind* (LP). (VJ/MW)

The Esquires

Personnel incl:	JOHN EYMAN	bs	A
	RICHARD EYMAN	ld gtr	A
	MICHAEL FRANFBURGER	gtr	A
	JOD GODFREY	drms	A

| 45: | Heartaches Stay The Night/Heat | (CFP CPR2) 1966 |

Bartow in Florida was home to this quartet. Recorded in 1965, their sole 45 was released in 1966 on the Fuller subsidiary CFP. The 'A' side, *Heartaches..* is a despairing garage ballad, telling the tale of a boy who's been dumped by girl; his pain is echoed by keening vocals accompanied by whimpers wrung out on guitar. The flip is an instrumental.

Compilation appearances have included: *Heartaches Stay The Night* and *Heat* on *Sixties Archive, Vol. 4* (CD) and *Florida Punk Groups From The Sixties* (LP); *Heartaches Stay The Night* on *Psychedelic States - Florida Vol. 2* (CD). (VJ/MW/JLh/MM)

The Esquires

| 45: | Sadies Way/Big Thing | (Alley 650A-1023) 1965 |

Yet another **Esquires** from Jonesboro', Arkansas this time. The 'A' side to this late '65 effort can be heard on *Hipsville, Vol. 2* (LP) or *A Journey To Tyme, Vol. 2* (LP). (VJ)

The Esquires

| 45: | Shake A Tail Feather/Down The Track | (Salem SR-003) 1965 |

This **Esquires** was from Springfield, Massachusetts and were late known as (Steve Walker &) **The Bold**. (MW)

The Essentials

Personnel:	S. STAY	drms	A
	J. WHEELER	ld gtr	A
	J. WHEELER	bs	A
	S. WHEELER	gtr	A

| 45: | Sunshine Baby/Freedom | (Kandy 82042) 1968 |

Sunshine baby is trite pop but *Freedom* is altogether more worthwhile - strident pop-rock with lashings of wah-wah. A 'Vibra Sound' pressing, this quartet is believed to have been based in New York.

Freedom is revisited on *Psychedelic States: New York Vol. 1* (CD). (MW)

The Estes Brothers

Personnel:	JOE ESTES	drms, vcls	A
	JOHN ESTES	ld gtr	A
	BILL MARREN	piano, vcls	A
	DON SMITH	bs	A

| ALBUM: | 1(A) TRANSITIONS | (Edcom ED-71-01-LPS) 1971 R4 |

NB: (1) reissued on Rockadelic (RRLP 17) 1994.

| 45: | Tomorrow's Sunlight / Yesterday's Blues | (Estbro # unkn) 1971 |

Thought to be from Amherst or Lorain Ohio, this outfit's over-hyped album ranges from ballads to harder rock. It does feature some good guitar jams on tracks like *Gary's Thought*. Good, but not worth the hefty price-tag - pick up the reissue instead! Bill Marren was formerly in **The Unknown Kind**, who were based in Amherst. (GGI/MW/VJ)

E.T.C.

| ALBUM: | 1 E.T.C. IS THE NAME OF THE BAND | (Windi) c1975 SC |

On the same label as **Merkin** and **Creation Of Sunlight**, but issued a few years later, this album went totally unnoticed. Some dealers describe as "cool loungy rock" or "excellent Westcoast vibe". Any additional information welcomed. (SR)

Eternity's Children

Personnel:	BRUCE BLACKMAN	keyb'ds	A
	JERRY BOUNDS	gtr	A
	LINDA LAWLEY	vcls	ABC
	CHARLIE ROSS	bs	ABC
	JOHNNY WALKER	gtr	A
	ROY WHITAKER	drms	AB
	MIKE McCLAIN	keyb'ds	BC

| ALBUMS: | 1(A/B) ETERNITY'S CHILDREN | (Tower 5123) 1968 SC |
| | 2(C) TIMELESS | (Tower 5144) 1968 R1 |

NB: There's also a retrospective CD *Eternity's Children* (Revola CREV062CD) 1999.

ETERNITY'S CHILDREN - Eternity's Children CD.

HCP

45s:	Rumors/Wait And See	(A&M 866) 1967 -
	Mrs Bluebird/Little Boy	(Tower 416) 1968 69
	Sunshine Among Us/Rupert White	(Tower 439) 1968 117
	Till I Hear From You/I Wanna Be With You	(Tower 449) 1968 -
α	Sidewalks Of The Ghetto/Look Away	(Tower 476) 1969 -
β	A Railroad Trestle In California/	
	My Happiness Day (some PS)	(Tower 477) 1969 -
	Blue Horizon/Lifetime Day	(Tower 498) 1969 -
χ	Laughing Girl/Little Boy	(Tower 499) 1969 -
	Alone Again / From You Unto Us	(Liberty 56162) 1970 -

NB: α flipside was by **Charles Ross III**. β credited to **Charles Ross E. III**, although the 'B' side is just a different mix of an **Eternity's Children** album cut. χ credited to **Charles Ross III**.

Originally The Phantoms (minus Lawley) they'd formed in Cleveland, Mississippi. After relocating to Biloxi, they recruited Linda Lawley and changed their name to **Eternity's Children**. With aspirations to become an L.A. pop-psych band, they honed their skills on the New Orleans circuit (playing as Charlie Rich's backing band?), before venturing to L.A. to record. Their main claim to fame was *Mrs. Bluebird*, a minor hit, which was produced by **Millennium**'s **Curt Boettcher** and Keith Olsen. By the time their first album was released however, Bounds, Walker and Blackman had left, with the latter replaced by Texan McClain (ex-**Neurotic Sheep**).

Overall their eponymous debut album is a top album for **Boettcher** fans, and features songs by **Boettcher** plus other **Millennium** members - including *Flowers*, a Michael Fennelly composition dropped from **Millennium**'s *Begin* album. Curiously, the "cover" of **Sagittarius**' *You know I've Found A Way* is the exact same track as the demo logged at the publishers and may not even feature **Eternity's Children** at all!

Their second album was produced by Gary Paxton in Bakersfield, with compositions by Clarence White, Gene Parsons, Ben Benay and Gary & Jan Paxton. Sounding like a tougher Fifth Dimension, with a European tinge, akin perhaps to **Glitterhouse**'s performance on the "Barbarella" soundtrack. A couple of the tracks, *Blue Horizon* and *Sidewalks Of The Ghetto* were cut with **Spooner Oldham** and Chips Moman - presumably in Memphis.

In 1969, the 45 releases get a little confusing, with consecutive Tower catalogue numbers mixing tracks credited to **Charles Ross III**, with **Eternity's Children** cuts. This begs the question, whether this parallel release was a marketing ploy, to push **Charles Ross III** on the back of the more familiar group name. In addition, their final 45 includes an unreleased **Curt Boettcher** tune on the 'B' side, which may even date back to their first album sessions.

Blackman went on to form Starbuck and later Korona.

The band also recorded a further album which wasn't released at the time. This has recently been discovered by Gear Fab and is due to be reissued together with other bonus material from '65 - '67, sometime in the near future. Alternatively, there is a Revola CD which comprises 25 tracks, covering both albums and assorted 45s from 1967-1970. This comes with a detailed history by Dawn Eden.

Compilation appearances have included *Flowers* and *You Know I'll Find A Way* on *Bring Flowers To U.S.* (LP). (VJ/MW/JFr/MM/JG)

The Ethics

45:	(A Whole Lot Of) Confusion/	
	Out Of My Mind	(Dynamic Sound 2001) 1966

From Milwaukee, Wisconsin. On December 30th 1965 they took part with a dozen local acts in the Milwaukee Sentinel Rock'n'Roll Revue. On the lo-fi album that captured the event (Century 23214) 1966 they can be heard performing *Down The Road Apiece*. In late '66/early '67 they changed their name to **Invasion**.

You can also find *(A Whole Lot Of) Confusion* on *Midnight To Sixty-Six* (LP), *Ya Gotta Have Moxie, Vol. 2* (Dble CD) and *Boulders, Vol. 6* (LP). (VJ/MW/AB)

The Ethics

45:	She's A Deceiver/It's OK	(Graves 1099) 196?

This band came from the Pacific Northwest. You'll find *It's OK* on *Psychedelic Unknowns, Vol. 5* (LP & CD). (VJ)

The Ethix

Personnel incl:	GARY DOOS	drms	A
	JIM FLANNERY	gtr	A
	CORK MARCHESCHI	bs	A

45s:	Blue Canary / Need Your Love	(D & A 6601) 1965
	Skopull / It's Time	(D & A 6602) 1966
α	?? / ??	(D & A #unkn) 1965/6
	Bad Trip/Skins	(Mary Jane NA 102) 1967

NB: α backing Rudy Grau - titles unknown.

Cork Marcheschi, later the creative force behind **Fifty Foot Hose**, grew up in the Bay Area and developed a taste for both R&B and avant-garde music - Edgar Varese was an early influence. After finishing high-school in 1963, he formed a garage band called the Hide-A-Ways with guitarist Jim Flannery (Marcheschi played bass). The band soon changed name to **The Ethix** and played constantly around the Bay Area between 1964-66. They recorded the notoriously atonal *Bad Trip* single in the bathroom of Cork's mother's house but the band ended in early 1967 when they played Las Vegas where two of the members were found to be under-age.

The band were based in San Mateo, California.

The recent Big Beat CD reissue of the **Fifty Foot Hose** *Cauldron* album also features two takes of *Bad Trip* - the 33rpm and the 45rpm versions. Both are still way out there somewhere. Subscribers to Ptolemaic Terrascope #23 also got to hear an 'unreleased acetate version' of *Bad Trip* on the accompanying free EP. *Bad Trip* and *Skins* also appear on the bootleg compilation *California Halloween* (LP). (VJ/MW/LP/AP/CF)

E-Types

Personnel incl:	DANNY MONIGOLD	bs	A
	REGGIE SHAFFER		A
	BOB WENCE		A
	CRAIG WILLIAMS		
	RANDY BARLOW		
	LARRY HOSFORD		

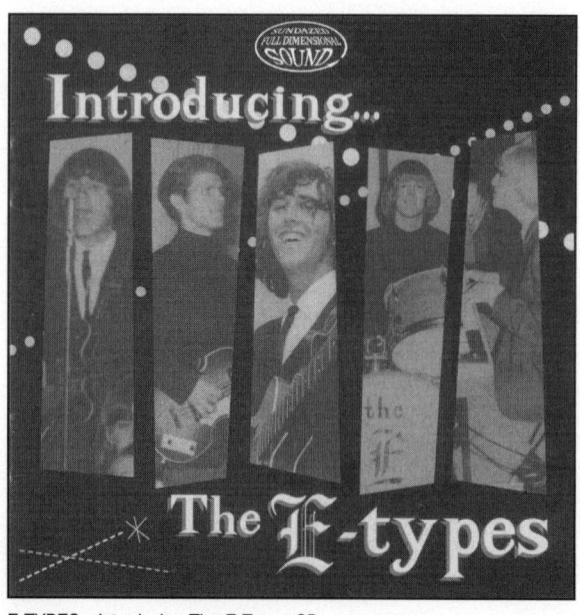

E-TYPES - Introducing The E-Types CD.

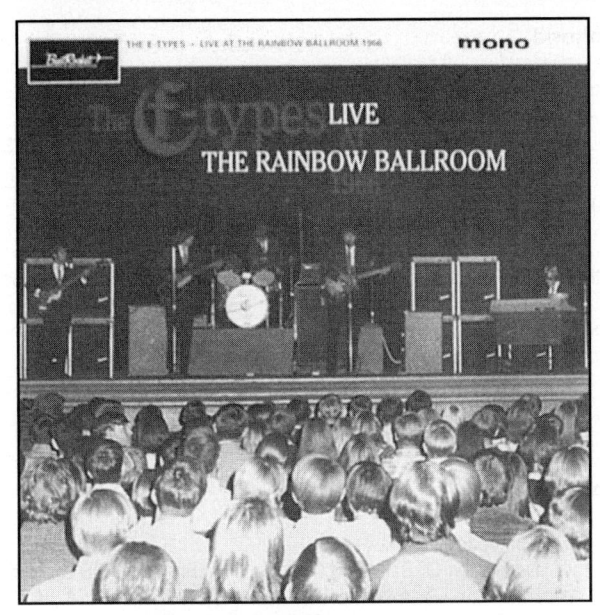

E-Types - Live At The Rainbow Ballroom LP.

ALBUMS: 1 INTRODUCING THE E-TYPES (CD)
                              (Sundazed SC 11026) 1996
         2 LIVE! AT THE RAINBOW BALLROOM IN '66 (LP)
                              (Beat Rocket BR 103) 2001

45s: α I Can't Do It/Long Before (PS)   (Link-I) 1966
      α I Can't Do It/Long Before (PS)   (Dot 16864) 1966
         She Moves Me/
         Love Of The Loved   (Sunburst SBM 45-001) 1966
         Put The Clock Back On The Wall/
         4th Street   (Tower 325) 1967
         Big City/Back To Me   (Uptown 754) 1967

NB: α feature the same picture sleeve, except for the record label logo.

From Salinas, a farming community fifty miles South of San Jose, this garage band were formed in 1966 and were regulars at local Battle Of The Bands competitions. Spurred on by Don Shepard, who conducted band rehearsals in his garage, and helped provide the band with instruments and song arrangements, they soon developed a good reputation on the San Jose scene.

When their first 45 was picked up by Dot for national distribution they attracted the attention of Ed Cobb, a L.A. producer who was already handling **The Chocolate Watch Band** and **The Standells**. Consequently he produced the Sunburst 45 - the flip was an unreleased Beatles composition. Their magnum opus, however, was *Put The Clock Back On The Wall* (a Bonner-Gordon composition). Despite the LSD inspired lyrics it was the product of an all night amphetamine session.

The Sundazed CD retrospective is a 22-track compilation which contains all of their singles plus previously unreleased tracks. Most of their 45s also appeared on Eva's 1984 compilation *The E-Types versus The Mystic Tide* (Eva 12037). Fans will also want to check out the *Live!* retrospective album, recorded at Fresno's Rainbow Ballroom in 1966, which includes their *I Can't Do It* alongside covers of Yardbirds / Who / Beatles and Dylan standards.

When the group folded in 1967, their manager recredited their last recording *Friendly Indians* to fictional outfit **Charolette Wood**, which was released the following year on the *San Francisco International Pop Festival* compilation.

In 1998, three of the original members, Bob Wence, Danny Monigold and Reggie Shaffer regrouped releasing an independent CD of new and Beatles-cover songs! You can contact them at P.O. Box 808, Moss Landing, CA 95039, to see if they still have a copies. It's reputedly well worth tracking down.

Retrospective compilation appearances included: *Put The Clock Back On The Wall* on *Nuggets Box* (4-CD), *Even More Nuggets* (CD) and *Nuggets Vol. 4* (LP); and *She Moves Me* on *Sounds Of The Sixties San Francisco, Vol. 1* (LP); (VJ/MW/DK/MM)

Euclid

Personnel: GARY LEAVITT   vcls, gtr   A
            JAY LEAVITT   drms   A
            RALPH MAZZOTA   vcls, gtr   A
            HARRY PURINO   gtr   A
            ?? ??   bs   A

ALBUM: 1(A) HEAVY EQUIPMENT
                    (Flying Dutchman - Amsterdam AMS 12005) 1970 R2

This Maine - based group contained the Leavitt brothers who had previously led the **Cobras** and Ralph Mazzota from **Lazy Smoke**. Pedigree aside, this is a powerful and inventive psychedelic heavy rock album(!) that stands on its own as a great work. With its backwards bits and oddly-effected vocals, the album, which was produced by Bobby Hearne, stands with one foot in the 1960s and one in the 1970s - leaning into the tracks with a heavy - handed metallic attitude. The album is recommended but has not been reissued yet, so it may be difficult to obtain. Gary Leavitt was killed in 1975, which effectively ended the band - a popular live attraction in the Northeast through 1974. Jay Leavitt still performs with his group Bluesberry Jam in the Maine area. (CF)

Euphoria

Personnel incl: TOM PACHECO   gtr, vcls   A

ALBUM: 1(A) EUPHORIA   (Heritage HTS 35-005) 1969 -

45:   You Must Forget (Part 1)/(Part 2)   (Heritage 831) 1971

A lightweight flower-power vocal group of two boys and two girls from Texas, although they seem to have spent time in California, too. Pacheco was later in Pacheco and Alexander. (VJ)

Euphoria

Personnel incl: DOUG DELAIN   A
                 WILLIAM LINCOLN   vcls   AB
                 HAMILTON WESLEY WATT gtr   AB

ALBUM: 1(B) A GIFT FROM EUPHORIA   (Capitol SKAO 363) 1969 R3

NB: (1) also issued in Canada on Capitol, 1970. Reissued on CD (See For Miles SEECD 465) 1995.

45:   Hungry Women/No Me Tomorrow   (Mainstream 655) 1967

Originally from California, where they had earlier recorded with **Word**, they

EUCLID - Heavy Equipment LP.

EUPHORIA - A Gift From LP

travelled to Houston around 1967 and settled there recording their superb 45 (the flip in particular is an unnerving haunting number). Both tracks later appeared on the compilation *A Pot Of Flowers* (LP). During their stay in Houston they also recorded four unreleased songs:- *Pick It Up*, *In Time*, *Walking The Dog* and *Oh Dear, You Look Like A Dog*. These are as psychedelic and good as their recorded output.

Apparently this demo impressed executives at Capitol Records, who subsequently invested a fortune recording an album in Hollywood, Nashville and London. Produced by the band and Nick Venet, *A Gift From Euphoria* is a magnificent record. The precise direction of the band is difficult to categorise, but country-rock merging with LSD will give you some idea. It has a creepy thread running through it, a foreboding darkness that is embodied most explicitly in the final track *World*:

"World, you've let me down again
I'll tell them just how bad you've been
I'll run away 'cause you don't care
And find another world somewhere
Now as I leave, I'd like to say
World, I hope we meet again someday"

Watt's guitar is noteworthy throughout the record and he explores different tones from song to song, from gentle acoustic (*Sunshine Woman*) to massive walls of distortion (*Did You Get The Letter*, *Suicide On The Hillside*, *Sunday Morning After Tea*). Sadly, Capitol seemed to be at a loss as to how to market the finished album and it barely made it past the promo stage. Indeed, it's nearly impossible to locate without the large round hole in the corner of the cover that Capitol used to designate promotional copies during the period.

Watt played guitar on a number of albums as a hired gun, most notably **Lee Michaels**' *Carnival Of Life*, where he is front and centre in the mix, blasting away. Most collectors agree this is **Michaels**' best album and Watt's fiery guitar is the primary reason. He also wrote some material for the L.A.-based **East Side Kids** and he and Lincoln wrote for, co-produced and played on **Bernie Schwartz**' solo album circa 1969/70.

A self-titled Finnish album by Finjarn and Jensen (Columbia 7E 062-37059) from 1970 includes two **Euphoria** songs, *Lady Bedford* and *Did You Get The Letter* retitled as *Windsor Bedford* and *Sorry Girl, But Now I Know Things Will Be Much Better Now You've Gone* (the latter being part of *Did You Get The Letter*'s lyric). The songwriting credits too have been changed to Finjarn and Jensen!

Doug Delain who played on the early **Euphoria** recordings, was involved with **Love** and **The Doors**. He apparently left the band in 1967, later had a sex change operation and is now known as Angela Douglas.

Retrospective compilation appearances have included: *Hungry Women* and *No Me Tomorrow* on *Mindrocker, Vol. 10* (Dble LP); *Mindrocker, Vol. 10* (LP); and *Oh Dear, You Look Like A Dog*, *Pick It Up*, *In Time* and *Walking The Dog* on *Houston Hallucinations* (LP). (VJ/MW/CF)

Euphoria

| Personnel incl: | D. WALLOCH | ld gtr | A |

ALBUM: 1 LOST IN TRANCE (Rainbow 1003) 1973 R3

NB: (1) had a limited reissue in 1990 on Rainbow (8993-1) and also on CD (AD-CD 5004).

Another **Euphoria**, this time from Milwaukee, Wisconsin. This is a heavy rock album with lots of fine guitar work, particularly on the title track, *Lost In Trance*, the most psychedelic cut, and *Enchanted*. All the songs on the album were written by lead guitarist D. Walloch.

This rare album is worth seeking out. (VJ/MW)

Euphoria

45: Somebody Listen/
Dedication Of Sally And Cher (Band Box BB 393) 1969?

Yet another **Euphoria**, from a Denver label this time. Later sixties hippie-protest-rock that doesn't really pick up until the instrumental break - a keyboard solo followed by some fine distorted guitar. The vocalist keeps saying 'Somebody Listen' but he does go on a bit - the track clocks in at 4:00. The flip is good, but a rambling affair too. (MW)

The Euphoria's Id

Personnel:	JIMMY DROWN	gtr	A
	TERRY DROWN	bs	A
	SKIP SMITH	drms	A
	JAY SNEIDER	keyb'ds	A

45s: α Morning Dew/
I Just Don't Understand You Baby (Cinema 108/9) 1965
Hey Joe/Deception's Ice (Eadit 201,366) 1967

NB: α as **The Id**

An obscure Saco, Maine band who recorded a unique version of *Hey Joe* which is truly notable for a superb raga-rock guitar break. The flip side, *Deception's Ice*, features more snappy guitar work.

The band story started back in 1963 with the Electrons, onto the Nomads, then the Id. The **Euphoria's Id** moniker was used just to avoid confusion with other Id's around at the time. After the band split some members went on to other outfits - the Fate and the Blend.

One spin-off is a solo 45 by Jimmy Drown as Jonathan Cloud - *Jonathan Cloud / Stop And Think* (Vigor VI 701) 1971- both sides of which are pleasant upbeat pop. Some ex-members of the Telstars may have been helping out on this too.

The ex-**Euphoria's Id** band **Fate** (featuring Skip Smith and Jay Snyder) recorded a demo album in the late sixties that was reissued (in part) by Rockadelic and Shadoks Music as *Sgt. Death*. See the **Fate** entry for further details.

Compilation appearances have included: *Deception's Ice*, *Hey Joe*, *I Just Don't Understand You, Baby* and *Morning Dew* on *New England Teen Scene* (CD); *Deception's Ice* on *New England Teen Scene, Vol. 3* (LP); and *Hey Joe* on *Pebbles, Vol. 22* (LP). (MW)

Rusty Evans

Personnel incl:	RUSTY EVANS	vcls, gtr	A
	GENE MITCHELL	gtr	A
	OLLIE PHILLIPS	bs	A
	BEN RIFKIN	banjo	A

ALBUMS: 1(A) SONGS OF OUR LAND
(partial   (Treasure Productions TLP 864) 1964 ?
list)   2( ) RAILROAD SONGS
               (Treasure Productions TLP ???) 1964 ?

	3( )	LIVE AT GERDE'S FOLK CITY	
		(Treasure Productions TLP ???)	1965 ?

45s:	Midnight Special/?	(Brunswick)	1958
	Talkin' From Your Heart/		
	The Night I Crashed Your Party	(HIP)	1959
	1983/The Life Game	(Musicor)	1965

Marcus Uzilevsky a.k.a **Rusty Evans**, grew up in Brooklyn. In the late fifties he released two rockabilly 45s and appeared on American Bandstand. Rusty:- "I was shaped quite a bit by my Tin Pan Alley experiences with Phil Spector writing some songs for me. By 1962 I'd drifted to the folk music cafes of the Village, where I jammed with **Fred Neil** and **Dino Valenti**."

Over the next three years he recorded four folk albums on Treasure Productions. Rusty:- "In 1962 when I sang at the Cafe Rafio on Bleeker Street, Bob Dylan would often come in and sit in with me playing piano and harmonica. Because of the hullabaloo I created with uptempo 'rock your socks off' songs, **David Crosby** (who performed quiet acoustic traditional folk ballads) preferred not to go after me..." In 1965 Rusty was in L.A. for a while, where he made one more 45. Back in New York, he formed **The Deep** and recorded the *Psychedelic Moods* album in August 1966 in just two days. It came out three months later.

At the same time, Rusty met Teddy Randazzo and together they started Eastern Productions. The first bands they signed were Facts Of Life and **Third Bardo** for whom Rusty co-wrote the classic *I'm Five Years Ahead Of My Time*. His next project was **Freak Scene** (who consisted of three members of **The Deep** plus David Bromberg). Their album *Psychedelic Psoul* sold more than 50,000 copies. Rusty:- "The ideas for the psychedelic recordings that I wrote, produced and performed on were the product of a non-drug related, indescribable shift in my consciousness. Definitely transformative. By the time I came to California I had experimented with psychedelic drugs, LSD, etc. but my non drug related epiphany experience, still remains a mystery to this day."

After its release, Rusty moved to L.A and worked for the 'Take Six' label, producing several recordings including **The Nervous Breakdown**'s *I Dig Your Mind*. Rusty: "The song which brought me to the attention of the record company was *Here We Are*. Definitely a 'summer of love' lyric, it didn't see the light of day, other than the demo on *Psychedelic Moods, Part 5: The Marcus Demos*."

"In L.A. I reconnected with many of the folkies from Greenwich Village, who'd moved to L.A. and become rock stars - Steven Stills, Peter Tork, **David Crosby** and some of the lesser known musicians such as **Tim Hardin** and **Richie Havens**."

"When I arrived in San Francisco in 1967 the Haight was buzzing. It seemed like the word had been turned inside out. Love was the theme and creativity with no commercial intent was happening." Rusty became involved with the production of Matthew Katz' *Fifth Pipe Dream* compilation, working with **It's A Beautiful Day**, **West Coast Natural Gas**, **Tripsichord Music Box** and **Black Swan**. Rusty: "Working with Matthew Katz of San Francisco Sound was like a Fellini movie..."

He stayed at the Bay Area and in 1969 he released **Marcus** LP on Kinetic, and a folk album, *Life's Railway To Heaven* (Folkways FTS 32440), in 1979. More recently he has also released two unique CD's of world music/ambient recordings under the pseudonym "Uzca". *Slice Of Light* and *Gypsy Dreams*, featuring Rusty singing in his scat/spirit language.

The renewed interest in his *Five Years Ahead Of My Time*, has also spurred Rusty to re-record it along with a new composition called *Chaos*. Both feature great guitar by his son Danny, but haven't been released. (NK/RE)

EUPHORIA - Lost In Trance CD.

Eve

Personnel incl:	LAURA CREAMER	A
	(HAL BLAINE	A)
	(JAMES BURTON	A)
	(RY COODER	A)
	(MARK CREAMER	A)
	(SNEAKY PETE	A)

ALBUM:	1(A)	TAKE IT AND SMILE	(LHI 3100) 1970 -

45s:	Anyone Who Had A Heart/Dusty Roads	(LHI 25) 1969
	Take It And Smile/You Go Your Way	(Bell 914) 1970

This female trio was previously known as Honey, Ltd and their album may interest fans of female soft hippie pop-rock with harmonies. The song selection is quite good, with songs written by **Fred Neil**, **James Taylor**, the Bee Gees, Burt Bacharach, Bob Dylan and Glenn Frey and the recording sessions included several ace L.A. musicians.

Laura Creamer was the wife of Mark Creamer, of **Armaggedon**. (SR)

Even Dozen Jug Band

Personnel incl:	MARIA D'AMATO	vcls, violin	A
	FRANK GOODKIN	banjo	A
	DAVE GRISMAN	mandolin	A
	STEFAN GROSSMAN	gtr, banjo, vcls	A
	BOB GURLAND	vcls, trumpet	A
	PETE JACOBSON	banjo, gtr	A
	STEVE KATZ	washboard, vcls	A
	DANNY LAUFFER	jug	A
	JOSHUA RIFKIN	piano	A
	JOHN SEBASTIAN	gtr, vcls	A
	PETER K. SIEGEL	gtr, banjo, vcls	A
	FRED WEISZ	fiddle	A
	(PEGGY HAINES	jug	A)

ALBUM:	1(A)	EVEN DOZEN JUG BAND	(Elektra EKS-7246) 19?? -

A seminal jug band from Cambridge, Massachusetts, although success totally eluded them. **John Sebastian** would later form the **Lovin' Spoonful**, Steve Katz the **Blues Project** and Maria d'Amato played with the **Jim Kweskin Jug Band** and become better known as Maria Muldaur. Peter Siegel became a producer and later worked with **Earth Opera**. Today Stefan Grossman is still renowned as a master and teacher of acoustic folk and blues guitar. He also recorded an excellent album *Bluescurrent* with **Blues Project**'s **Danny Kalb** in 1969. (SR/JNa/JRi)

Keith Everett

Personnel incl:	KEITH GRAVENHORST	A

45s:	Don't You Know/Conscientious Objector	(Tmp-Ting 118) 1967
	She's The One Who Loved You /	
	Lookin' So Fine	(Tmp-Ting TMP-121) 1967/8
	The Chant / Light Bulb	(Mercury 72854) 1968

These 45s are almost certainly the work of Keith Gravenhorst, who produced the first 45 and gets writer credits for both tracks on the first and third releases.

Don't You Know, a mid-tempo teen-angst ballad, was quite a big hit in Chicago. It's the 'B' side which may grab your attention however, with it's outrageous right-wing, pro-war stance, it is amusingly silly.

The Mercury 45 is a Dunwich production and the label bears its logo, regarded by many as a hallmark of quality. (SR/BM/MW)

Ever-Green Blues

Personnel:	RICK BARRIO	gtr	A
	TOM BRAY	trumpet	A
	MANNY ESPARZA	vcls	A
	STEVE LAWRENCE	organ	A
	SAM LOMBARDO	drms	A
	J. E. MOSWEYN	bs	A
	KEN WALTHER	trombone	A

ALBUMS: 1(A) 7 DO 11 (Mercury SR-61157) 1968 -
2( ) COMIN' ON (ABC ABCS 669) 1969 -

45s: Midnight Confessions/
That's My Baby (Yes) (PS) (Mercury 72756) 1967
Laura (Keep Hangin' On)/
Yesterday's Coming (Mercury 72780) 1968
Feelin' Your Love/Three's A Crowd (Mercury 72826) 1968
Funky Woman/Don't Mess Up My Mind (ABC 11198) 1969
Girl, I Got Wise/The Moon Is High (ABC 11216) 1969

The first 45 appeared with a picture sleeve and both tracks are included on their first album, as is their second 45. On the sleeve-notes they are referred to as an L.A. group and their album is recorded there, although their fan club was based in Surfside, Florida. Steve Lawrence went on to play with **Buddy Miles** in the mid-seventies and Tom Bray was with Crazy Horse in the late seventies. The better tracks on their album are the cover versions of *Midnight Confessions* and *Gimme Some Loving*.

Three's A Crowd has also resurfaced on *Boulders, Vol. 6* (LP) and *Ya Gotta Have Moxie, Vol. 2* (Dble CD). (VJ)

The Evergreen Blueshoes

Personnel:	SKIP BATTYN	bs, vcls	A
	KEN KLEIST	keyb'ds	A
	LANNY MATHIJSSEN	gtr	A
	CHESTER McCRACKEN	drms	A
	AL ROSENBERG	gtr	A

ALBUM: 1(A) THE BALLAD OF EVERGREEN BLUESHOES
(Amos 7002) 1969 -

NB: (1) also released in the UK.

45: Johnny B. Goode/Walking Down The Line (Amos 115) 1969

A typical hippie outfit with its gatefold sleeve showing eight naked people dancing in the grass while a kind of fat Pan is playing flute. Produced and arranged by Mike Post, most songs were written by the group members. *The Everblue Express* was composed by **Battyn** and the ubiquitous **Kim Fowley** and *The Raven* is an adaptation of Edgar Allan Poe.

Lots of organ, good guitars and a strong rhythm section. **Battyn** was previously in Skip and Flip and would later join **The Byrds** and the Flying Burritos Brothers. He also played on **Armaggedon**'s album and several **Kim Fowley** productions. Chester "Chet" McCracken would become the drummer of **Help** and the Doobie Brothers.

Compilation appearances include *Silver Shadows* on *Kim Fowley - Outlaw Superman* (LP & CD). (SR)

EVERYDAY THINGS - Everyday Things 10" EP.

Everpresent Fullness

Personnel:	TOM CARVEY	gtr, ld vcls	A
	TERRY HAND	drms	A
	PAUL JOHNSON	ld gtr	A
	STEVE PUGH	bs	A
	JACK RYAN	electric autoharp, hrmnca, trumpet, washboard, vcls	A

ALBUM: 1(A) EVERPRESENT FULLNESS (White Whale 7132) 1970 -

45s: Wild About My Lovin'/Fine And Dandy (White Whale 233) 1966
Wild About My Lovin'/Doin' A Number (White Whale 233) 1966
Darlin' You Can Count On Me/Yeah! (White Whale 248) 1966

A Los Angeles based act who were together between 1965 and 1966. They shared the stage at various concerts with, amongst others, **Jefferson Airplane**, **The Turtles**, **Buffalo Springfield**, **Sir Douglas Quintet** and **Love**.

One of many bands who had trouble with the record company executives of the time, their best material is said to have remained unrecorded. Their album was recorded in 1966, but White Whale cut off funding before it was completed and only released it four years later to fulfill their contractual obligation to the band. A disappointing mix of pop and country-rock with some ragtime influences, it is now rare but not particularly recommended. The best moments are probably the **Lovin' Spoonful** cover, *Wild About My Lovin'* and *The Way She Is*, written by **Warren Zevon**, who was then their stablemate on White Whale, as part of the duo **Lyme and Cybelle**.

Doin' A Number is a fast moving R&B/rock instrumental, which can be heard on *Mindrocker, Vol. 3* (LP). Some of their 45s are not on the album. *Wild About My Lovin'* can also be found on *Happy Together - The Very Best Of White Whale Records* (CD). (VJ/SR)

Everyday Things

Personnel:	STEVE BRYANT	ld gtr, ld vcls	A
	JAMES HOLLEY	drms	A
	JOHN HOLLINGSWORTH	gtr, keyb'ds	A
	PHILIP HOLLINGSWORTH	bs	A

10" EP: 1 EVERYDAY THINGS (Sundazed SEP 10-161) 2000

The EP presents six unreleased tracks recorded in 1966 by this Fresno, California quartet with recollections from Philip Hollingsworth. Forceful covers of *I Ain't No Miracle Worker*, *Mister You're A Better Man Than I*, *The House Of The Rising Sun*, *Pushin' Too Hard* and *Outcast* are joined by one original - *Song On A May Morning*.

In 1965, the Hollingsworth brothers formed a high school band The Coachmen with Holley. The following year they got together again, adding guitarist Bryant from nearby Merced. **Everyday Things** became their handle and in late 1966 they laid down these tracks, but split after just a few months.

In 1967, the brothers joined Fresno fellows **Kings Verses** in Los Angeles. On their return home they called upon Holley again and, as **Canterbury Fair**, released a 45 featuring a reworked *Song On A May Morning*. (MW)

Everyman

Personnel:	PAUL PENFIELD		A

45:	It's A Pushbutton World/ Eternal Youth	(Main Line ML-1362) 1966

A novelty-psych 'A' side - acoustic folk-pop with choruses made up of sound effect collages. The flip is an anti-protest protest song. An oddly charming 45 from Cleveland, Paul may have been one of the cast of the Banana Splits kiddies' TV show in the U.S. (this may have been shown in the U.K. too). So, hands up anyone brave enough to confirm this! If this were the case it would explain the novelty aspect and vocal style of *Pushbutton World*, but the war noises probably precluded it being broadcast to a young audience.

Chuck Mangione and Roger Karshner wrote and produced - their names appear behind many other Cleveland acts/projects -e.g. **Bhagavad Gita**, **National Gallery**. Roger was a regional rep for Capitol during the mid-sixties, covering Ohio, Virginia and Pennsylvania, and was manager of Cleveland's **Outsiders**. (GGI/MW)

Every Mother's Son

Personnel:	CHRISTOPHER AUGUSTINE	drms	A
	DENNIS LARDEN	vcls, gtr	A
	LARRY LARDEN	gtr, vcls	A
	SCHUYLER LARSEN	bs	A
	BRUCE MILNER	keyb'ds	A

HCP

ALBUMS:	1(A)	EVERY MOTHER'S SON	(MGM SE 4471) 1967 117 -
	2(A)	BACK	(MGM SE 44504) 1968 - -

HCP

45s: (selective)	Come On Down To My Boat/ I Believe In You	(MGM KGC 191) 1967 6
	Pony With The Golden Mane/ Dolls In The Clock	(MGM 13844) 1968 93

DESTINATION FRANTIC (Comp CD) including Evil.

The MGM answer to the **Monkees**. Produced and managed by Wes Farrell (who also produced **Beacon Street Union** and **Elephant's Memory**), they released two albums of lightweight pop-rock with vocal harmonies and occasional efficient organ. The first spent eleven weeks in the Charts, climbing to No. 117.

Come On Down To My Boat was a re-working of **The Rare Breed**'s second 45.

Dennis Larden would later work with Rick Nelson and the Stone Canyon Band. (SR/SNs/VJ)

Everything Is Everything

Personnel incl:	CHIP BAKER	vcls, gtr	A
	CHRIS HILLS	vcls, ld gtr, drms	AB
	JIM PEPPER	vcls, flute	A
	LEE REINOEHL	organ, trumpet	A
	JOHN WALLER	drms	A
	JIM ZITRO	drms	A

ALBUMS:	1(A)	EVERYTHING IS EVERYTHING	(Vanguard VSD-6512) 1969 -
	2(B)	COMIN' OUTTA THE GHETTO	(Embryo SD 734) 1970 -

NB: (2) as **Chris Hills' Everything Is Everything**.

HCP

45s:	Witchi Tai To/ Ooh Baby	(Vanguard Apostolic VRS-35082) 1968 69
	You Don't Need No Music/Ya Hay Ho	(Vanguard 35097) 1969 -

A short-lived outfit alledgedly from New York City whose first 45 actually made it to No. 69 in the U.S. Billboard Top 100. Danny Weiss produced the single, whilst Chris Hills was previously in **Free Spirits** alongside **Jim Pepper**, the writer of *Witchi Tai To*.

Their music consisted of pure jazz-rock, with a slight psychedelic taint.

Danny Weiss went on to become a producer on the East Coast, working with **Clean Living** and **Jim Pepper**, to name a few. He shouldn't however be confused with Danny Weis, the former **Iron Butterfly** / **Rhinoceros** member.

After their first album, the group split and Chris Hill kept on recording with a new line-up. The second album was much more jazz-orientated. (VJ/SR/VZ)

Evil

Personnel:	JEFF ALLEN	drms	A
	JOHN DALTON	gtr	A
	JOHN DOYLE	vcls	A
	MIKE HUGHES	bs	A
	STAN KINCHEN	ld gtr	A

ALBUM:	1	EVIL / THE MONTELLS	(Corduroy CORD 027) 1997

NB: (1) is a split album with **The Montells**.

45s:	Always Running Around/ Whatcha Gonna Do About It	(Living Legend 108) 1966
	Always Running Around/ Whatcha Gonna Do About It	(Capitol 2038) 1966
	I'm Movin' On/You Can't Make Me	(Norton 826) 1999

A talented Miami, Florida punk band worthy of investigation. Drummer Jeff Allen had earlier played with **The Montells / H.M. Subjects** and made frequent trips to England, where he picked up the latest releases. Subsequently **Evil** used to cover tunes by The Pretty Things, Fairies, Move, Downliner's Sect, etc. before most of their counterparts had heard of them.

The two versions of the 45 have different edits of the 'B' side with a wild guitar solo edited-out from the later Capitol release.

After **Evil** split, Jeff Alan and John Doyle carried on for a while under the bizarre moniker **Fruit Eating Chicken** and **Drek** with **Montells** members' George Walden and Danny Murphy. John Doyle quit shortly afterwards, being replaced by Frank Milone (who had played in a later line-up of **Evil**), and they changed name again to **Smack**.

Jeff Allen led an **Evil** reformation in 1994-95 and also played with U.K. combo **Flea**.

Evil and **The Montells** have recently been the subject of a vinyl retrospective album entitled *You Can't Make Me*. The **Evil** tracks include: *I'm Movin' On, I Know I'll Die, Always Runnin' Around* and two versions of *Whatcha Gonna Do About It*.

Compilation appearances include: *Always Runnin' Around* on *Sixties Choice, Vol. 1* (LP), *60's Choice Collection, Vol's 1 And 2* (CD) and *Destination Frantic!* (LP); *Whatcha Gonna Do 'Bout It* on *Scum Of The Earth* (CD), *Scum Of The Earth, Vol. 1* (LP second Edition) and *Scum Of The Earth, Vol. 2* (LP); and both *Always Running Around* and *Whatcha Gonna Do About It* on *Boulders, Vol. 3* (LP). (MW)

Evil Encorporated

Personnel:	FRANK DUNLAP	A
	DOUG GENT	A
	BOB JAMES	A
	EDDIE MICHEAL	A

NB: Eddie Micheal misspelt "Michael" on 45 label.

| 45s: | Hey You/The Point Is | (Scene SR 101) 1967 |
| | Baby It's You/All I Really Want To Do | (Scene SR 102) 1968 |

From Oak Hill, Scarbo and Fayetteville, West Virginia. The second 45 is an undistinguished garage ballad with lots of 'sha-la-la's', backed by a decent **Byrds** cover.

Compilation appearances have included: *Hey You* and *The Point Is* on *Highs In The Mid-Sixties, Vol. 22* (LP) and *The Essential Pebbles Collection, Vol. 2* (Dble CD); *The Point Is* on *Punk Classics, Vol. 1* (7"), *Sixties Choice, Vol. 1* (LP) and *60's Choice Vol's 1 And 2* (CD); and *All I Really Wanna Do* on *From The New World* (LP). (VJ/MW/MM)

The Evil I

| Personnel incl: | GEOFFREY McCABE | A |

| 45: | Love Conquers All/ | |
| | I Can't Live Without You | (Bridge Society 25-66) 1966 |

NB: reissued in 1992 (Frog FR-02) as a limited edition of 300.

The band came from Lingleston, Pennsylvania and their forte was moody garage-psych with a **Doors** flavour vocally, especially on *Love Conquers All* which is memorable more for the fluid meanderings of its keening lead. The flip is a more shambolic affair with growling fuzz and a not-quite-great solo.

Compilation appearances have included *Love Conquers All* on *Psychedelic Unknowns, Vol's 1 & 2* (LP) and *Psychedelic Unknowns, Vol. 1* (7"). (MW)

The Excels

Personnel:	ROGER BENNETT	ld gtr	A
	DANNY GOODE	bs	AB
	JAMES GOODE	gtr	AB
	GIB HARRIS	drms	AB
	RON VERMILLION	ld gtr	B

| 45s: | Let's Dance/Walking The Dog | (Gibson 210) 1965 |
| | Merchant Of Love/The First Kiss | (Gibson) 1965 |

Formed in McKinney, Texas in 1963 taking Chuck Berry as their inspiration. 1,000 copies of their first 45 were pressed and sold exclusively at Gibson

PSYCHEDELIC UNKNOWNS Vol's 1 & 2 (Comp LP) includes The Evil I.

Discount Centers. The 'A' side, *Let's Dance* is a fast rock 'n' roller that gets underway with a drum roll. The 'A' side of their next 45, *Merchant Of Love* was a ballad and the flip a raucous instrumental.

Bennett was eventually drafted, so Vermillion, a trained jazz musician came in to replace him on lead guitar during 1967. This new line-up soon fell apart and not even a change of name to The Shags in their final days could prevent this.

Compilation appearance include *Let's Dance* on *Texas Flashback (The Best Of)* (CD), *Texas Flashbacks, Vol. 1* (LP & CD) and *Flashback, Vol. 1* (LP). (VJ)

The Ex-cels

| 45: | Like A Dream/Sorrow And Pain | (Coral 62482) 1966 |

From Gloversville, New York, this seems to have been a one-off venture for Coral. The 'A' side has a shuffle rhythm and a great but short guitar break. It has also resurfaced on *Sixties Rebellion, Vol's 1 & 2* (CD) and *Sixties Rebellion, Vol. 1* (LP) - which lists them as Californian... and *A Journey To Tyme, Vol. 4* (LP). (MW/MM)

Excentrics

| 45: | Hold Me Tight(I Feel So Fine Inside)/ | |
| | What Can I Do What Can I Say | (Glo Lite GL-97) 1965 |

Invasion sounds are to the fore on this Memphis label 45, where Merseybeat meets Kinks riffs. Both sides are compiled on *Bad Vibrations, Vol. 2* (LP) and the B side is also on *Prisoners Of The Beat* (LP). (MW)

The Exception(s)

Personnel incl:	PETER CETERA
	KAL DAVID
	JAMES VINCENT DONLINGER
	MARTY GREBB/GREBE
	BILLY HERMAN
	JAMES NYEHOLT

| EP: | 1 A ROCK & ROLL MASS EP | (Flair 810) 1966 |

NB: (1) features six different rock songs with words taken from various religious prayers. The best song (relevant to this book) is *Glory To God*, a garagey-sounding tune written to the words of the Christian prayer, which features Cetera on lead vocal. It was issued in a colour cardboard picture sleeve featuring a live shot of the band.

45s:	Searchin' / Day Dreamin' Of You	(Tollie 9007) 1964
	Come On Home / Dancin' Danny	(Tollie 9043) 1965
	Down By The Ocean / Pancho's Villa	(Cameo 378) 1965
	As Far As I Can See / Girl From New York City	(Quill 114) 1966
α	As Far As I Can See / Girl From New York City	(Capitol 5982) 1967
α	Business As Usual / My Mind Goes Traveling	(Capitol 2046) 1967
α	You Don't Know Like I Know / You Always Hurt Me	(Capitol 2120) 1968

NB: α as **The Exception**.

This outfit merits an entry, since members would go onto better-known outfits. In particular: Kal David - **Rovin' Kind**, **Illinois Speed Press**, **H.P. Lovecraft** and **Fabulous Rhinestones**; Marty Grebe - **Buckinghams** and **Fabulous Rhinestones**; Pete Cetera - Chicago; Billy Herman - **Aorta** and **New Colony Six**; James Donlinger - **Aorta**; and James Nyeholt - **Aorta**. Musically **The Exceptions** material is outside the style confines of this book, being in a soulful or slick lounge-band mould.

They were latterly known as **The Exception** on the Capitol 45s, before the main body of the band decided on a change of style and identity to become **Aorta**. *As Far As I Can See* and *Business As Usual* are featured on the CD compilation *The Quill Records Story*. (MW/MM)

Exchequers

| 45: | Is There Some Girl/Greensleeves | (Boom C45-115) 1965 |

NB: issued on green vinyl.

La Crosse, in the far West of Wisconsin, was home to this folk-rock outfit, whose *Is There Some Girl* was the usual blend of 12-string guitars and melodic harmonies. You'll find it on *The Cicadelic 60's, Vol. 2* (LP) and on *Leaving It All Behind*. (VJ/MW)

The Executioners

Personnel:	ANDY GLISTA	bs	A
	TERRY GRIMM	drms	A
	DICK STRONEY	keyb'ds	A
	ED WASACZ	ld gtr	A
	RICHARD YEAGER	sax, vcls	A
	ROGER LEWIS	gtr	

45s:	α	The Guillotine/I Was Wrong	(Sunburst 108) 196?
		Don't Put Me On /The Noose	(Action 500) 1965
		Dead End (Pt. 1)/(Pt. 2)	(Action 502) 1965
		I Want The Rain (Pt. 1)/(Pt. 2) (instr)	(Swan 4259) 1966

NB: α later issued on Itzy (4).

An Youngstown, Ohio-based outfit which started off as a frat-house sax instrumental band and later turned "punk". Their first 45 is pretty cool, with each verse punctuated by the sound of a blade slamming down, and their second, *Don't Put Me On* was a typical punk song with a good beat.

The Action label was run by the band's drummer, but later in 1965 they signed to the nationally distributed Swan label. The result, *I Want The Rain*, was another punk effort with no mean commercial appeal. Sadly, it made little impression at the time. Roger Lewis was briefly a guitarist in this group and would team up with Dick Stroney again in the Poppy.

Compilation coverage has included: *Don't Put Me On* on *The Midwest Vs. The Rest* (LP); *I Want The Rain* on *Sixties Choice, Vol. 1* (LP), *60's Choice Collection, Vol's 1 And 2* (CD) and *Everything You Always Wanted To Know...* (CD). (GGI/MW/MMy)

The Executioners

| 45: | You Won't Find Me/Haunting My Mind | (Vermillion 269) 196? |

A different band from Accokeck in Maryland whose Vermillion 45 can be found on *Scum Of The Earth* (CD) and *Scum Of The Earth, Vol. 2* (LP). (VJ)

The Execitives

Personnel:	ROBERT FOURNIER	A
	TOM FOURNIER	A
	TOM GALLUCCI	A
	RONNIE HART	A
	CHUCK LOBODY	A
	DON PATILLO	A
	JEFF PRATT	A
	ART SMALLEY	A

| ALBUM: | 1(A) | GOIN' PLACES | (Executive Records 301) 1970 |

A group playing lounge pop and rock with the usual covers of seventies hits: *Aquarius, Something, Everybody's Talkin'*... recorded with a horn section, mellophone and organ. Don't believe some dealers' descriptions, it's certainly not psych! (SR)

The Exkursions

Personnel:	MIKE JOHNSON	gtr, vcls	AB
	FYL JONNZEN	drms	AB
	LEON WILSON	gtr, vcls	B

| ALBUM: | 1(B) | THE EXKURSIONS | (no label #811G-2984) 1971 R1 |

NB: (1) reissued on CD (Hidden Visions AC-025) 1998.

A Christian rock band who formed in Chicago in 1968. The album is predominantly in a heavy bluesy style with many **Hendrix**-inspired moments and some fleeting jazz influences, occasionally enhanced by good use of fuzz.

For all its overtly religious themes and lyrics however, it doesn't come across as spiritually uplifting or inspiring and could have done with some lighter 'n' brighter shades. If interested check out the *Holy Fuzz* compilation first. It contains two of the better album tracks - *Dry Ground* and the heavily-fuzzed *It's Been Set Down*. (MW)

The Exotics

Personnel:	CHRIS BROWN	drms	A
	ANDY MICHLIN	keyb'ds	A
	LAURRY MICHLIN	keyb'ds	A
	ROBERT PRICE	vcls	A

THE EXKURSIONS - The Exkursions CD.

	BLAIR SMITH	ld gtr, vcls	A
	TOM SPALDING	gtr	A
	GEOFF WEST	bs	A

ACETATE: 1 THE EXOTICS (Boyd Recording) 1967 R3

NB: (1) one-sided LP acetate containing the six songs issued on the last three 45s listed below.

45s:	α	I Said 'Hey Little Girl'/	
		I Want Your Good Loving Bad	(Nonsuch 817-93) Early 60s
		Hey Little Girl/Madge's Blues	(Polly 100) 196?
		Morning Sun/Fire Engine Red	(Monument 984) 1966
		Come With Me/Hymn To Her	(Tad 2410) 1967
		Queen Of Shadows/I Was Alone	(Tad 6701) 1967

NB: α issued as Robert Price & The Exotics.

Hailing from Dallas in the second half of the sixties, this band have been well covered in subsequent compilations (see below). Musically **The Exotics** played strong melodies in a folk-rock vein with occasional psychedelic touches - well worth a listen.

Guitarist Blair Smith was also responsible for the lead guitar work on **Scotty McKay**'s version of *Train Kept A Rollin*' - which is often miscredited to one Jimmy Page!

Come With Me was later covered by The Chesterfield Kings on their *Here Are The Chesterfield Kings* LP.

Compilation appearances have included: *Come With Me*, *I Was Alone*, *Morning Sun* and *Queen Of Shadows* on *The Psychedelic Sixties, Vol. 1* (LP); *Alone Again*, *Come With Me*, *Come With Me To Chevrolet*, *Fire Engine Red*, *Hymn To Her*, *I Was Alone*, *Morning Sun* and *Queen Of Shadows* on *Texas Punk, Vol. 4* (LP) and *Acid Visions - Complete Collection, Vol. 2* (3-CD); *I Was Alone* and *Queen Of Shadows* on *Flashback, Vol. 4* (LP), *Texas Flashbacks, Vol. 4* (LP & CD) and *Green Crystal Ties, Vol. 4* (CD); *Come With Me* on *Flashback, Vol. 5* (LP) and *Texas Flashbacks, Vol. 5* (LP); and *Come With Me*, *Fire Engine Red*, *Hymn To Her*, *I Was Alone* (3 versions), *Morning Sun* (two versions), *Queen Of Shadows*, *Radio Ad for Mitchell's Department Store* and *Radio Ad for Bill McKay Chevrolet* on *The Thingies Have Arrived!!* (CD). (MW/VJ/CF)

The Experimental Blues Band

45: Fifty Miles Back/Opus # 1 (Counterpart 2601/2) 1967

A sought-after item on this interesting Ohio label, the 'A' side of which has been described as wild fuzz garage with screams, whilst the flip is a mid-slow brooding folk rocker. The band came from Cinncinati, Ohio. (MW/MM)

ACID VISIONS THE COMPLETE COLLECTION Vol. 2 (Comp CD) including The Exotics.

The Express

Personnel:	DON ANDERSON		A
	REX CAUGHROM	keyb'ds	A
	SONNY LEDET?		A
	DENNIS MAXWELL		A

45: You Gotta Understand/Long Green (Piccadilly 226) 1966

Originally from Oklahoma City in 1962, where they were known as The Juveniles, they relocated to Portland, Oregon in 1964. Operating now as **The Express** they played there until 1969 and recorded this one mini classic. The 'A' side, is a kinda grungy R&B effort, whilst the flip, is a pretty credible version of one of **The Kingsmen**s' classic songs.

Compilation appearances have included: *Wastin' My Time* (a previously unissued fuzz pounder) on *Northwest Battle Of The Bands, Vol. 1* (CD); *You Gotta Understand* on *Highs In The Mid-Sixties, Vol. 16* (LP) and *Northwest Battle Of The Bands, Vol. 2* (CD); and *Long Green* on *Highs In The Mid Sixties, Vol. 7* (LP). (MW/DR)

Denny Ezba

45s:	α	Sunny Side of My Life/The Last Man	(Quanta Q-271) 19??
	α	Mary Diane/Brighter Tomorrows	(Renner RR-213) 19??
	α	Mister Blue/Bald Headed Lena	(Jox 061) 1967
	α	I Want To Love/Cleo's Back	(Jox 064) 1967
	β	I'm A Back Door Man/Susie Buffalo	(Jox 068) 1968
	χ	Santa Fe/Dimples	(Dome 1238) 1968
		Raining In My Heart/Cindy	(Tear Drop 3072) 1968/9
		Queen Mary/It's A Cryin' Shame	(Tear Drop 3225) 1969
	δ	Queen Mary/It's A Cryin' Shame	(Jamie 1377) 1969

NB: α as **Denny Ezba and The B.F.B.A.**. β as **Denny Ezba and The Goldens**. χ to δ as **Denny Ezba's Gold**.

A durable Texan musician who fronted a number of punk outfits in the late sixties. The first of these **Denny Ezba and the B.F.B.A.** were responsible for the first four 45s. The fifth was credited to **Denny Ezba and The Goldens**, who by the time of the last four had become known as **Denny Ezba's Gold**. These punk combos included at various times Mike Nesmith (later of **The Monkees**), M. Forney, Augie Meyer and Harvey Kagen (who achieved some success with the **Sir Douglas Quintet**), **Keith Allison** (who went on to **Paul Revere And The Raiders**) and Mike O'Dowd (later of Augie Meyer's Western Head Band). As for **Ezba**, he later embarked on a solo career recording an album *Greatest Hits of 4,000 Years Ago* (Texas Re-cord ?) during the 1980s.

Sadly, he passed away early in March 2000.

Compilation appearances include: *Dimples* on *Brain Shadows, Vol. 2* (LP & CD). (VJ/MW)

BRAIN SHADOWS Vol. 2 (Comp CD) including Denny Ezba.

The F.a.b. Company

ALBUM: 1 TAKE TIME (Pax 7001) c1970 -

From Denver, an obscure pop-psych trio which may interest fans of **Free Design** and similar groups using male/female harmonies. The best tracks are perhaps *Life Is Just A Puff Of Dreams*, *Child In Years* and *The Breath Of Winter*. (SR)

The Fab Four

45s:	Now You Cry/Got To Get Her Back	(Brass 311) 1964
	Now You Cry/Got To Get Her Back	(Coral 62479) 1964
	Welcome Me Home/Oop Shoobee Doop	(Melic 4114) 196?
	Happy/Who Could It Be	(Brass 314) 1966
	I'm Always Doing Something Wrong/ Young Blood	(Brass 316) 1966
	River Days/Got A Feeling In My Body	(Pearce 5842) 196?

A Kansas City, Missouri band. Previously known as the Fabulous Four they would later change their name to Kansas City - either way one was left in no doubt as to where "they were coming from" or where they were from!

Compilation appearances include: *I'm Always Doing Something Wrong* on *Teenage Shutdown, Vol. 9* (LP & CD); and both *Happy* and *I'm Always Doing Something Wrong* on *Monsters Of The Midwest, Vol. 1* (Cass). (VJ/MW)

The Fabs

Personnel incl:
?? CAMMARACK — A
?? CLARK — A
BOB ELLIS — drms — A

45: That's The Bag I'm In/
Dinah Wants Religion (Cotton Ball 1005) 1966

NB: reissued in 1984 by Torchlite Records.

Formed in 1966, the liner notes to *Back From The Grave* state that they originated from Fullerton, California, and that they wound up on the Texas Cotton Ball label via a business associate of their drummers mom. Whatever the story, their sole stab for stardom was a pretty good 45.

Bob Ellis later propelled the mighty **Stack**. Sadly, Ellis passed away in January 1999.

Compilation appearances have included: *That's The Bag I'm In* on *Songs We Taught The Fuzztones* (Dble LP & Dble CD), *Back From The Grave, Vol. 1* (LP) and *Garage Kings* (Dble LP); and *Dinah Wants Religion* on *Acid Dreams - The Complete 3 LP Set* (3-LP), on *Acid Dreams Epitaph* (CD), *Back From The Grave, Vol. 4* (LP), *Back From The Grave, Vol. 2* (CD) and *Flashback, Vol. 6* (LP). (MW/CF/SR)

BACK FROM THE GRAVE Vol. 4 (Comp LP) including The Fabs.

The Fabulous Apostles

45: Dark Horse Blues/
You Don't Know Like I Know (Shana 097) 1968

This outfit originated from Wichita, Kansas. Recorded in L.A. at the home studio of boy genius Michael Lloyd, **Kim Fowley** is thought to have been lurking somewhere here too... The 'A' side of their 45 is written by **WCPAEB**'s Shaun Harris and Michael Lloyd. The 'B' side is presumably the Hayes/Porter ditty favourite with soulful garage bands (Mauds, **Pied Pipers** etc). *Dark Horse Blues* can also be heard on *Glimpses, Vol. 4* (LP) and the *Midwest Garage Band Series - Kansas* (CD). (VJ/MW/JFr)

The Fabulous Depressions

Personnel:			
JIM DAUER	bs		ABCD
PHIL GROEBNER	ld gtr		ABCD
PETER KITZBERGER	organ		ABCD
JOHN TRETAULT	drms		A
GREG DEBERRY	drms		B
TIM LINDSAY	ld vcls		BC
JOHN GINKEL	drms		CD
RANDY EVANS	ld vcls		D

45: I Can't Tell You/One By One (Mead 123167) 1967

Formed in 1964, these wonderful chaps were from New Ulm, Minnesota. They'd earlier used various names like Wholly Moses, Brain Police, Manic Depression and Great Depression. Their first drummer was an 11-year old. John Tretault came in on drums, although in 1966 he left and was replaced by Greg DeBerry from Iowa. Around the same time they recruited Tim Lindsay, a talented singer, who got them lots of work around Minnesota and Northern Iowa.

After a short while Greg DeBerry was forced to leave the band when his father's business required him to be transferred out of town and John Ginkel who'd previously played with another local band, **The Shags**, was welcomed into the fold (he was Peter Kitzberger's next door neighbour). Shortly after Tom Lindsay departed to join The Royal Emperors (an Owatonna, Minnesota band) and a new vocalist Randy Evans, from the Lake Crystal area, was recruited in his place. His vocal range was well suited to the 'harder' rock and roll and blues the band was now playing. This line-up (D) recorded the band's sole 45.

The 'A' side, which later resurfaced on *Root '66* (LP), was a song of teenage love with a scorching fuzz guitar break by Phil Groebner. The flip was a good cover of a **Blues Magoos**' tune. (VJ)

Fabulous Pack

45s: α Harlem Shuffle/I've Got News For You (Lucky Eleven 003) 1967
Wide Trackin'/
Does It Matter To You Girl? (Lucky Eleven 007) 1968

NB: α issued as by The Pack.

From Detroit, Michigan, this is **Terry Knight & the Pack** minus Terry, who decided he'd make more money for less effort as their manager.

Compilation appearances include: *Wide Trackin'* on *Mindrocker, Vol. 11* (LP). (VJ)

The Fabulous Pharaohs

Personnel:			
FRED DAWSON	sax, keyb'ds		A
AUBREY FISHER	ld gtr		A
BILL RYLANDER	bs		A
EDDIE STEVENSON	drms, ld vcls		A

45s incl: Church Key/Route 66 (3-Star 2668) 196?
Hold Me Tight/
Sometimes I Think About (Reprize 36-22-36) 1967
Talkin' Bout You/Sometimes (Reprize 38-22-38) c1967

This outfit was part of Delaware's contribution to the garage-rock scene. Their first 45, *Church Key*, a grungy rocker about the evils of alcohol, is a blues tune with a fifties rock 'n' roll influence.

Both their Reprize 45s are in high demand amongst collectors on the rare occasions that copies surface.

The cornerstone members of the band, Fred Dawson and Eddie Stevenson, later recorded an album as **Mouzakis** and gigged as Capone. Fred recalls: "Aubrey quit the band early on, got married and has been a postman ever since. Bill moved to Florida to play in some club bands and I understand he is now in Atlanta doing sound for the Atlanta Symphony Orchestra."

Compilation appearances have included: *Hold Me Tight* on *Psychedelic Unknowns, Vol. 6* (LP & CD); and *Church Key* on *Garage Punk Unknowns, Vol. 4* (LP). (VJ/MW/FD)

The Fabulous Prophets

45: Gertrude/? (Combo 1000) 196?

From Nashville, Tennessee, they were also known as Larry Herman & the Fabulous Prophets.

Compilation appearances include: *Gertrude* on *Scum Of The Earth* (CD) and *Scum Of The Earth, Vol. 1* (LP). (VJ)

The Fabulous Wunz

45: If I Cry / Please (Pyramid Records no #) c1966

From Charlotte, North Carolina, a good garage-pop group. They may have released some other 45s. (SR)

Facedancers

ALBUM: 1 FACEDANCERS (Paramount PAS 6039) 1972 SC

An underrated progressive rock outfit, strongly influenced by the British prog groups (such as Yes, King Crimson or Camel), with long tracks, complex time changes, fuz guitar and swirling keyboards. (SR)

FAINE JADE - It Ain't True LP.

Faces In The Crowd

45: Clouds Of Doubt / Lonely Beach (Del-Nita 60941) 1966

Clouds Of Doubt has resurfaced on *Hipsville, Vol. 2* (LP) and the band hailed from Cleveland, Ohio. (VJ/MW/GGl)

The Factory

Personnel:	LOWELL GEORGE	ld gtr	AB
	MARTIN KIBBEE	bs	AB
	WARREN KLEIN	gtr	A
	CARY SLAVIN	drms	A
	DALLAS TAYLOR	drms	A
	RITCHIE HAYWARD	drms	B
	(EARL PALMER	drms	B)
	(EMIL RICHARDS	perc	B)
	(FRANK ZAPPA	vcls, piano	B)

ALBUM: 1(A) LIGHTNING-ROD MAN
(Bizarre/Straight R2 71563) 1993

NB: (1) is a CD retrospective, issued as **Lowell George and The Factory**, and manufactured and marketed by Rhino. Also released in Europe by Edsel (EDCD 377) 1993.

45s: When I Was An Apple/
Smile, Let Your Life Begin (UNI 55005) 1967
α No Place I'd Rather Be (UNI 55027) 1967

NB: α with **Emil Richards**.

A Los Angeles band. Line-up 'B' recorded a three track demo on the 18th August 1966, two tracks from which appeared on the first UNI 45, with the third, *Candy Cane Madness* finally appearing on Demon's *Microdelia* CD comp. Their second 45 is a rework of a Gene Vincent composition which they turned into a late sixties punker by adding a screaming fuzztone guitar. Both of their 45s were produced by ex-Teddy Bear Marshall Lieb and he also cut four or five additional tracks at the time.

The band's main significance was that Kibbee, Klein, Hayward and Taylor later played with **Fraternity Of Man**, while the late Lowell George played with **The Mothers of Invention** and achieved greater fame as an original member of Little Feat with Hayward. Dallas Taylor was also one of the two original drummers with the revered **Clear Light** and would later occupy a very successful seat behind Crosby, Stills, Nash (& Young).

Frank Zappa also cut some tracks with **The Factory** at Original Sound studios in 1966, and financed / produced / played on several more between 1967 - 1969. None were released at the time, but two have recently been released on the *Lightning Rod Man* CD by Rhino (*Lightning Rod Man* and *The Loved One*). The retrospective also contains another thirteen tracks including a live version of *Candy Cane Madness*, two post-Factory cuts: *Framed'* and *Juliet*; and studio versions of *Lost* (great garage pop), *Slow Down, Smile, Let Your Life Begin, Sleep Tonight, No Place I'd Rather Be, Hey Girl, Changes, Crack In Your Door, Teenage Nervous Breakdown* and *Candy Cane Madness*.

An interesting aside on **The Factory** is that they appeared in two '60's sitcoms: "F-Troop" (as The Bedbugs in a starring role) and "Gomer Pyle" (performing as a bar band... where both *Lost* and *Candy Cane Madness* can be clearly heard in the background).

Other compilation coverage has also included: *No Place I'd Rather Be* and *Smile, Let Your Life Begin* on *California Acid Folk* (LP); and *The Loved One* on *Psychedelic Frequencies* (CD). (VJ/MW/JFr/MDo/SR)

The Factory

45: High Blood Pressure/Lovely Path (USA 922) 1969

From Chicago. Their late sixties rock version of *High Blood Pressure* was originally done by sixties frat outfit Huey "Piano" Smith & The Clowns and can also be heard on *Pebbles, Vol. 7* (CD) and *Mindrocker, Vol. 2* (LP).

According to the *Pebbles* sleevenotes, this outfit consisted of ex-members of **The Ides of March** and **Little Boy Blues**. (VJ/MW)

Facts of Life

Personnel incl: BRUCE KLAUBER   drms   A

45:       I've Seen Darker Nights/All In Good Time   (Frana 59) 1967

From Bala-Cynwyd, which is a suburb of Philadelphia in Pennsylvania, this outfit formed in 1966 when a group of ninth formers came together at Bala-Cynwyd Junior High School. *I've Seen Darker Nights* is a pretty typical sixties garage record with up-front organ, lots of fuzz and some adventurous drumming for the times. The flip, however, is bereft of fuzz and is a very doleful garage-ballad (sniff). Both sides of the 45 were written by Yampolsky - another member of the band, perhaps?

Bruce Klauber went on to become one of Philadelphia's top jazz drummers.

Compilation appearances include: *All In Good Time* on *Class Of '66!* (LP); and *I've Seen Darker Nights* on *Crude PA, Vol. 1* (LP). (MW/VJ)

Faine Jade

ALBUM: 1   INTROSPECTION - A FAINE JADE RECITAL
                                        (RSVP ES 8002) 1968 R3

NB: (1) was reissued on Psycho (13) in 1983. More recently the album has been released on CD with four bonus tracks, plus the 'missing' *Piano Interlude* which was recorded for the album, but left off at the time it was originally released (Sandiland SL 8002) 1993 and (Big Beat CDWIKD 141) 1995. Also of interest is *It Ain't True* (Distortions 1007) 1992.

EP: 1   FAINE JADE   (Distortions DB 1009) 1992

NB: (1) contains *December's Children* from the *It Ain't True* retrospective, plus *You're All I Gotta Do*, *Crazy World* and *Widow Woman*, *Willow Woman*.

45s: α   Can't Get You Out Of My Heart/
          Look At Me   (Ye Old King 1000) 1966
          Love On A Candy Apple Day/
          It Ain't True   (Providence 420) 1966
          Doctor Paul/Introspection   (RSVP 1130) 1967

NB: α as The Rustics, limited to 100 copies, this now fetches in excess of $100. Also of interest is *Doctor Paul / Don't Hassle Me Part 2* (PS) (Distortions DB-1013) 1993, which contains two previously unreleased demos from 1967.

Faine Jade was an East Coast solo artist based around Boston. The album contains two outstanding tracks *People Games Play* - complete with sounds of the jungle - and the subtle *Cold Winter Sun Symphony In D Major*. The remainder of the album is experimental, but not outstanding (though some regard it as an absolute classic). It is, however, quite a significant collectable.

It Ain't True is a limited edition release of previously unreleased demos and acetates. Side one consisting of **Faine Jade**'s earlier outfit **The Rustics**, which led to him and Nick Manzi being signed up as staff writers for Laurie Records in 1966. **The Rustics** did issue one single on their own label, which also appears on the Distortions album, but towards the end of the year Nick Manzi left to join **Bohemian Vendetta**. **Faine** then signed a solo deal with Laurie subsidiary, Providence, which resulted in the *Love On A Candy Apple Day* 45 with his brother Jeff Jade on drums and founding **Illusion** member Bruce Bradt on organ. The 'B' side, *It Ain't True*, is an excellent psychedelic number.

In late 1967, **Faine** recorded demo versions of *Cold Winter Sun* and *I Lived Tomorrow Yesterday*, backed by the **Bohemian Vendetta**, which led to the deal with New York independent label for the *Introspection* album. The band also backed him on the album, along with Bruce Brandt and Randy Skrha (who filled in for Jeff Jade - who was in Vietnam at the time). Bruce also co-wrote two of the songs on the album. The recent CD reissue, includes a linking piano section *Piano Interlude* omitted by the record company at the time because of its uncommercial nature, as well as three album demos and a nineties tribute to John Lennon.

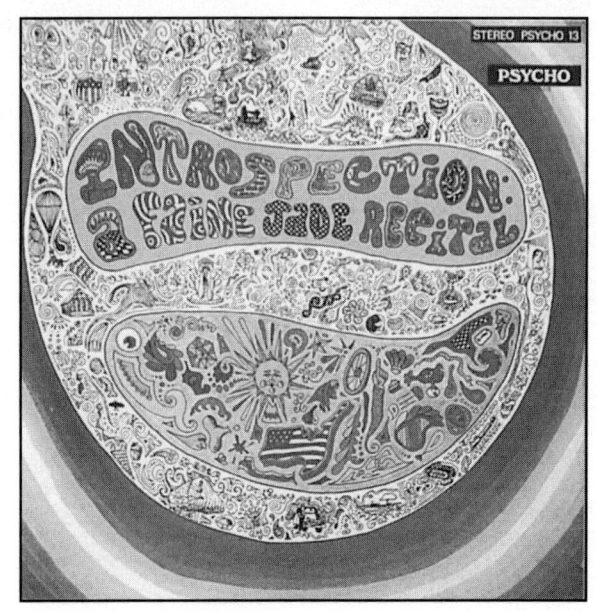

FAINE JADE - Introspection LP.

Where *Introspection* captures the arguably naive atmosphere of 1967, and naked openness that the use of psychedelics represented, Vietnam polarised political opinion, which **Faine** articulated on a 1969 recording *USA Now* before moving to Florida and working with the pre-**Allmans** outfit **Second Coming**. Later he rejoined Nick Manzi and Bruce Brandt as **Dust Bowl Clementine** who released one album, *Patchin' Up* (Roulette 1970), and opened a studio in Long Island.

Faine recently had a local hit with *Mario Taxes*, a song about the state of affairs in New York.

Compilation appearances have included: *It Ain't True* on *Mayhem & Psychosis, Vol. 1* (LP), *Mindrocker, Vol. 5* (LP), *Pebbles, Vol. 8* (LP), *Sixties Archive, Vol. 8* (CD), *A Journey To Tyme, Vol. 2* (LP), *Acid Dreams, Vol. 1* (LP) and *Acid Trip From The Psychedelic Sixties* (LP); *The Ballad Of The Bad Guys* on *Psychedelic Crown Jewels, Vol. 1* (Dble LP & CD); and both *Cold Winter Sun* and *People Games Play* on *Endless Journey - Phase Two* (LP) and *Endless Journey - Phase I & II* (Dble CD). (VJ/IT/MW)

The Fairviews

45s: Ya Gotta Be Real Good, Baby/Twinkee Lee   (Spin It 120) 1964
          Cry Over Mary Lou/Little One   (Spin It 121) c1965
          Nightmares/Little Baby Of Mine   (Spin It 122) c1965
          Windy City/Big Joke   (Spin It 123) 1966
     α   A New Direction/Discomboober   (Spin It 124) 1966

NB: α as Fairviews with The 5th Dimensions.

The *Windy City* 45 features decent mid-tempo garagey-beat that sounds more like 1965, with its early **Byrds** and British Invasion influences. A garage band from Burbank, California. They were managed by Sunset Strip enterpreneur Bud Mathis, whose retrospective compilation *Take The Brain Train To The Third Eye* (LP & CD), includes *A New Direction*, plus an unreleased version of *Discomboober* featuring Bud Mathis on vocals.

Nightmares can also be heard on *Boulders, Vol. 8* (LP). (MW/MM)

The Falconaires

ALBUM: 1   SNAKE CREEK DIVERSION PROJECT
                                        (Private Pressing) c1969 ?

An Air Force garage band with covers of *Hey Jude*, *We Gotta Get Out Of This Place*, *Big Mama Cass* etc. **Mark Lindsay** of **Paul Revere and The Raiders** wrote the liner notes. (SR)

FALLEN ANGELS - Fallen Angels LP.

Falcons

45:	There's A Tear/I Gotta See Her	(Strafford 6504)	1966

I Gotta See Her gained belated appreciation and reputation via its inclusion on the five-star compilation *Psychotic Moose And The Soul Searchers* (LP). A great Kinks-type riffin' punker with fuzz and atmospheric harmonica, totally at odds with the insipid Merseybeat flavoured lounge-ballad on the 'A' side. Now both can be experienced on *You Ain't Gonna Bring Me Down To My Knees* (CD). According to the CD leaflet, the band actually hailed from Upstate New York and would be known later as the Franklin Brothers, after they'd recorded two further unreleased tracks in 1969, also featured on the CD - *Rape The Wind* and *When Mother Nature Was A Girl*. (MW)

Fallen Angels

Personnel:
JACK BRYANT — vcls, bs — ABCDE
HOWARD DANCHIK — keyb'ds, flte — ABCD
WALLY COOK — ld gtr — ABCDE
NED DAVIS — drms — A
JACK LAURITSEN — gtr, sitar, vibes — ABCDE
ROCKY ISAAC — drms — B
RICHARD KUMER — drms — C
JOHN "THUMPER" MOLLOY — drms — D
KEVIN ARMSTRONG — bs — E
TOM MANSELL — drms — E
LARRY WILLIS — keyb'ds, B-3 — E

ALBUMS:
1(C) FALLEN ANGELS (Roulette SR 25358) 1968 SC
2(D) IT'S A LONG WAY DOWN (Roulette SR 42011) 1968 R3
3(B) RAIN OF FIRE (Wild Child! 05852) 1998

45s:
Everytime I Fall In Love/I Have Found (Laurie 3343) 1966
Have You Ever Lost A Love?/
A Little Love From You Will Do (Laurie 3369) 1966
Room At The Top/
Your Friends Here In Dunderville (Roulette 4770) 1967
Hello Girl/Most Children (Roulette 4785) 1967
α Room At The Top / Most Childen Do (PS) (Philco HP-23) c1968
β Everything Would Be Fine/
Hid And Found (Sun Dream 704) 1974

NB: α is a 'Hip Pocket' 45 - a 4" flexi in a pic envelope, a series issued by Philco. β was recorded in 1969 but released posthumously on manager Tom Traynor's local label.

Operating out of Washington D.C. this band was formed in 1965 when Wally Cook and Ned Davis of the Young Rabbits teamed up with Jack Bryant and Charlie Jones. Initially called the Disciples, then the Uncalled Four, they eventually settled on the **Fallen Angels**. Drummer Rocky Isaac was also a member at one point (he was formerly with the Tejuns, the Creatures, and later **Cherry People**) but his place was eventually taken by Richard Kumer from the **The Mad Hatters** by the advent of the first album. Lauritsen had also replaced Charlie Jones by then and Danchik had been added to make it a quintet.... Their first album has a nice paisley cover and consists of competent rock with some pleasant psychedelic interludes. The second album carried on from where the first had ended. Three tracks in particular - *One Of The Few Ones Left, Something New You Can Hide In* and *I'll Drive You From My Mind* - stand out, being full of melodic guitar work, climbing keyboards and sensitive vocals.

The band split in 1969 but in 1974 a retrospective 45 was released on their manager's own-label 45. This has an acoustic mellow rock sound until some mean guitar kicks in, and is notable for affected 'vibrato' vocals. The flip is dull by comparison and full of la-la-la-la-la's.

Both original albums are worth searching for and the second has been repressed. You can also find twelve album tracks on each of the Collectables CDs *Roulette Masters, Part 1* and *Part 2*.

In 1998, **The Fallen Angels** returned with a new CD *Rain Of Fire*. *Every Time I Fall In Love* and *Everything Would Be Fine* are updated and accompanied by eleven new tunes (all bar one by Jack Bryant). Purists who expect a time-warp back to their garage and psych sounds of 1967/8 will be disappointed; but for those without such unrealistic preconceptions, this is accomplished and mature rock with blues, folk and country influences (just the odd spot of rust in the vocals department).

Compilation coverage has included: *Have You Ever Lost A Love?* on *Mindrocker, Vol. 10* (Dble LP) whilst their decent cover of Arthur Lee's *Signed D.C.* resurfaced on *Psychedelic Moods - Part Two* (LP & CD).

For a comprehensive lowdown on the band check out issue #9 of Jeff Jarema's excellent Here 'Tis fanzine. (MW/VJ)

Fallen Angels

Personnel:
CHRIS BANDLER — A
JAY KERR — A
DAVE STEVENSON — A
RICHARD ZIPPLE — A

45:	Bad Woman/Pimples And Braces	(Eceip 1003/4)	1970

A different bunch who were formed at Syracuse University in Syracuse New York in 1965. *Bad Woman* was recorded in 1966 but not presssed until **Ron Wray** put it out on Eceip (Piece backwards) in the early seventies. *Bad Woman* remains a classic example of U.S. garage punk influenced by both British and U.S. success stories.

Compilation appearances include: *Bad Woman* on *Off The Wall, Vol. 2* (LP), *Pebbles, Vol. 1 (ESD)* (CD), *Songs We Taught The Fuzztones* (Dble LP & Dble CD), *Trash Box* (5-CD), *Teenage Shutdown, Vol. 4 - I'm A No-Count* (LP & CD), *Best of Pebbles, Vol. 2* (LP & CD) and *I Was A Teenage Caveman* (LP). (FB/MW)

The Famen (Faman)

Personnel incl: WAYNE WHITE — A

45s:
(Again) I Want To Be Your Fool /
If You Want Me (Delta Ltd.) 1965
Crackin' Up / Time Is Slipping Away (X-Pose) 1965
Sixteen Wheels / Don't Want Nobody (World Wide) 1965
α Hurry / Crackin' Up (X-Pose ASR 4022) 1966

NB: α as **Faman**.

The Famen from Atlanta, Georgia was not a usual teen garage combo; it was actually a wild rock'n'roller from Mississippi called Wayne White, based in Atlanta in the mid-sixties. In his search for fame'n'fortune (hence the moniker) he was adept at absorbing the latest sounds and using local talent, releasing four 45s in a productive twelve-month blitz in 1965-6.

Not all were in the garage genre; those that were have been compiled. His crackin' version of Bo Diddley's *Crackin' Up* (also tackled by **The Gants**) appears on *Sixties Rebellion, Vol. 1* (LP) and *Sixties Rebellion, Vol's 1 & 2* (CD). *Hurry* can be heard on *Psychedelic Experience, Vol. 4* (CD) and *Psychedelic States: Georgia Vol. 1* (CD) whose liners recount his exploits after Mike Markesich tracked him down in the nineties.

White wrote much of his material and even lent one of his compositions, *Laugh In My Face*, to **The (Swingin') Apolloes** for their debut 45, joining them on keyboards - that track is featured on *Psychedelic Crown Jewels, Vol. 3*. He then switched to a new identity, Shack Jones. By the early seventies he was doing studio work and was at the controls for Lynyrd Skynyrd's 1973 debut album. Come the eighties he was back on stage again. (MW/MM)

Family

45s:	Face The Autumn (one sided promo)	(USA 886) 1967
	Face The Autumn/So Much To Remember	(USA 886) 1967
	San Francisco Waits/Without You	(USA 894) 1968

This group of studio musicians was put together in Chicago by USA records staff producer Bobby Whiteside. *San Francisco Waits*, a flower-pop single, which successfully captures the California sunshine in its chorus, can also be heard on *Mindrocker, Vol. 2* (LP). (VJ)

Family

45:	I Wanna Do It/A Song	(Teen Town 119) 1968

A different Wisconsin band who recorded a version of **The Strangeloves'** *I Wanna Do It* in 1968. Several garage bands recorded this and **Family**'s version, which can be heard on *Highs In The Mid-Sixties, Vol. 15* (LP), is unexceptional. (VJ)

Family of Apostolic

Personnel:	BOB BERKOWITZ	piano, organ	A
	JERRY BURNHAM	bs, drms, vcls, wind	A
	LYNDON HARDY	vcls	A
	PETER SMITH	bs, oud	A
	DEIRDRE TOWNLEY	vcls	A
	GILMA TOWNLEY	drms	A
	JOHN TOWNLEY	gtr	A
	JAY UNGAR	violin, mandolin, vcls	A
	and many friends.		A

ALBUM:	1(A)	FAMILY OF APOSTOLIC (dbl)	(Vanguard 79301) 1968 -

45s:	α	Saigon Girls/Water Music	(Vanguard Apostolic 35081) 1968
	β	Just Another Day/ Did You Leave Your Heart Behind?	(Vanguard 35122) 1969

FALLEN ANGELS - It's A Long Way Down LP.

NB: α Some copies in picture sleeve, on which the artists name appears to be 'The Spirit Of Khe Sahn', although the label still credits **The Family...**, other copies shown as by John Townley and The Apostolic Family. β is non-LP.

A New York band, sometimes acoustic, at others they sounded rather like **The Fugs**. Two of the weirder album cuts, *Saigon Girls* and *Water Music* were also released on 45.

Apart from *Saigon Girls* (a Bonner/Gordon song), all their material was original and penned by the Townleys, Jay Ungar or Bob Berkowitz. Some were in fact rearranged traditional folk songs (notably *Fiddler A Dram*, also recorded by **The Youngbloods**).

John Townley founded the Apostolic studios in New York and had earlier played guitar with Gordon and Bonner in **The Magicians**. He was managing his Apostolic studio when he signed a distribution deal with Vanguard for the productions of his label, Apostolic (artists included **Far Cry**, **Boa Constrictor** and **Everything Is Everything**). He was later involved in **Gospel** and, in 1979, released an solo album in England *John Townley* (Harvest ST 12007).

Jay Ungar later joined **Cat Mother** and was active on the folk scene. (VJ/MW/SR)

Family Tree

Personnel:	NEWMAN DAVIS	drms	A
	MIKE OLSEN (LEE MICHAELS)	keyb'ds	A
	BOB SEGARINI	gtr, vcls, keyb'ds	ABCD
	BILL WHITTINGTON	bs, gtr	ABC
	MIKE DURE	gtr	BCD
	VAN SLATTER	drms	BCD
	BILL 'KOOTCH' TROACHIM	bs, vcls	CD
	JIM DECOCQ	keyb'ds	D

ALBUM:	1(D)	MISS BUTTERS	(RCA LSP 3955) 1968 -

45s:	Prince Of Dreams/Live Your Own Life	(Mira 228) 1967
	Do You Have The Time?/Keepin' A Secret	(RCA 9184) 1967
	Slippin' Thru My Fingers/Miss Butters	(RCA 9565) 1968
	He Spins Around/She Had To Fly	(RCA 9671) 1968
	Terry Tommy/Electric Kangaroo	(Paula 329) 1970

Segarini and Whittington formed this band when **The Brogues** dissolved in late 1965. They based themselves in San Francisco. In the Summer of 1966 they signed for Mira issuing the above 45. The 'A' side was a folk-rocker notable for strong vocals and a prominent harp. The flip side merged folk-rock and Merseyrock. A further seven tracks were also recorded for Mira to put out on an album which never materialised. (The tracks were *Good Day*, *May I Ride With You*, *He Doesn't Come Around*, *Up In The Air*, *Beggar*, *She Reads Magazines* and *Observations*.) After this Mira release, which was a minor hit in Northern California, the group were offered a recording contract by RCA and made the above concept album which was rather ahead of its time and Beatlesque in influence. The *Miss Butters* 45 was taken from the album, the others were non-album. As neither the album nor the singles sold, RCA dropped the band in 1969. Segarini and DeCocq later formed **Roxy**. Olsen pursued a solo career as **Lee Michaels** and Segarini and Kootch were later in **The Wackers**. Segarini also recorded a series of solo albums in the late seventies.

Compilation appearances have included *Prince Of Dreams* and *Live Your Own Life* on *Mindrocker, Vol. 8* (LP). (VJ)

The Fanatics

Personnel incl:	NEAL FORD	A
	LARNIER GREGG	A

45:	I Will Not Be Lonely/Be Mine	(Gina 1118) 1965

Formed in Houston, Texas, in 1965 out of The Ramadas when they were still in their mid-teens. Neal Ford wrote both songs. The 'A' side, *I Will Not Be Lonely* was a powerful punker. After the 45 the band became known as **Neal Ford And The Fanatics**.

Compilation appearances include: *I Can't Believe* and *I Will Not Be Lonely* on *Acid Visions - The Complete Collection Vol. 1* (3-CD) and *Acid Visions, Vol. 2*; and *I Will Not Be Lonely* on *Mayhem & Psychosis Vol. 3* (LP), *Mayhem & Psychosis Vol. 2* (CD), *Flashback, Vol. 5* (LP), *Texas Flashbacks Vol. 5* (LP) and *Highs In The Mid-Sixties, Vol. 13*. *I Can't Believe* was a previously unreleased cut from 1966. (VJ)

Fancy

Personnel:	CHRIS BERNARDONI	vcls	A
	VIC BERNARDONI	drms, vcls	A
	BOB ORSI	hrmnca, vcls	A
	PAUL OSSOLA	bs	A
	ALPHONSE RANAUDO	piano, organ, vcls	A
	DOUG SHLINK	gtr	A
	(PETE LEVIN	dtrings	A)

ALBUM: 1(A) MEETING YOU HERE (Poison Ring PRR 2238) 1971 SC

45s: All My Best (Sweet Mary)/
Goin' Down To The Sea (Poison Ring PR-716) 1971

From Connecticut, produced by Thomas "Doc" Cavalier, **Fancy** was formed by Chris Bernardoni and her brother (both ex-**Wrongh Black Bag**) and Paul Ossola from **The New Fugitives**. Their rare hard-rock album offers several good tracks (like *Black Snake*) with screaming female vocals and blistering fuzz lead guitar.

Vic Bernardoni, Ossola and Levin also played with the **Incredible Broadside Brass Bed Band** whose album was also recorded on Poison Ring.

Chris Bernardoni would later perform as Christine Ohlman and kept on recording with Orsi, Ossola and Cavalier in the Scratch Band (one album for Big Sound in 1977, also released in Germany and England) and the Yankees (the *High 'N' Inside* album released in 1978 by Big Sound in the US and by London in England). She still performs today, playing R&B and rootsy rock. (SR)

The Fantastic Dee Jays

Personnel:	TOM JUNECKO	drms	A
	DICK NEWTON	gtr, vcls	AB
	DENNY NICHOLSON	gtr, vcls	AB
	BOB HOCKO	drms, vcls	B

ALBUM: 1(B) THE FANTASTIC DEE-JAYS (Stone 4003) 1966 R2

NB: Reissued in 1996 on Millenia (FDJ 96) as *Fantastic Dee-Jays: 30th Anniversary Reissue* and also on Eva (12028) in 1983.

45s: Apache/This Love Of Ours (Sherry 309) 1965
Love Is Tuff/Two Tymes Two (Fleetwood 1096) 1965
You're The One/Two Tymes Two (Red Fox 102) 1965
Fight Fire/Get Away Girl (Tri Power 421) 1966
Love Is So Tuff/Just A Boy (Stone 044) 1968
α Fight Fire /
Get Away Girl / T&C Lancers (PS) (Get Hip GHAS-1) 1995
β Shy Girl / Two Tymes Two (PS) (Get Hip GHAS-10) 1997

NB: α and β reissue 45s in picture sleeves, α in blue wax.

Originally known as The Larks, this McKeesport, Pennsylvania band began to smoulder with some sparse beat offerings culminating in the gloriously noisy *Fight Fire*. Both sides of this fine 45 can also be heard on *Hipsville 29 B.C.* (LP) and *Love Is Tuff* resurfaced on *Burghers, Vol. 1* (LP & CD). *Fight Fire* pointed the way to the next step - the legendary **Swamp Rats**, the epitomy of great garage music.

An unreleased 1966 track *Shy Girl* has also turned up on the Pittsburgh radio-show comp *Terry Lee Show WMCK* (LP). This is one of many unreleased recordings which are known to include alternate and acoustic versions of above singles and album cuts, plus many early WMCK recordings. In all, there are 17 unreleased tracks. (MW/BSy)

FAPARDOKLY - Fapardokly CD.

Fantastic Zoo

Personnel incl:	DON CAMERON	A
	ERIK KARL	A

45s: Midnight Snack/
This Calls For A Celebration (Double Shot 105) 1966
Light Show/Silent Movies (Double Shot 109) 1967

Don Cameron and Erik Karl were the creative force behind this band which originated from Colorado and were originally known as **The Fogcutters**. They became known as **Fantastic Zoo** when the original band broke up and Cameron and Karl moved to Los Angeles in 1966, where they cut a debut single *Midnight Snack* in October of that year. Their lead singer's distinctive voice and bizarre lyrics stand them aside from typical psychedelic bands of the era.

Their best song was the excellent *Light Show* (the only psychedelic record I know of dealing with one of psychedelia's best known attributes), released in January 1967. This can be heard on *Psychedelic Experience* (CD), *Mindrocker, Vol. 6* (LP) and *Highs In The Mid-Sixties, Vol. 3*. It is an excellent example of well-crafted, laid back, subtle psychedelia.

Mindrocker, Vol. 8 (LP) features *This Calls For A Celebration*, which was in a similar mode to, though not as good as, *Light Show*. (VJ)

Fantasy

Personnel:	J. DeMEO Jr.	A
	G. KIMPLE	A
	LYDIA MILLER	A
	D. ROBBINS	A
	M. RUSSO	A

ALBUM: 1(A) FANTASY (Liberty LST-7643) 1970 HCP 194 -

45s: α I Got The Fever/Painted Horse (Imperial 66394) 1969
Understand/Stoned Cowboy (Liberty 56190) 1970

NB: α also issued in France with a picure sleeve (Liberty 2C006-90647) 1968.

From Miami, Florida, this band's first album is well worth a listen if you're into the 'West Coast sound' format, though they're closer sound-wise to **Big Brother** than **Jefferson Airplane**.

A strident female lead vocalist called Lydia belting it out and sounding not unlike her namesake - Lydia Pense - of **Cold Blood**. Some searing guitar and quite a hard-rockin' style with more blues rather than folk influences. Their album sold quite well, spending three weeks in the Top 200 with a best position of No. 194.

Stoned Cowboy, an instrumental, received considerable airplay in Miami / Detroit at the time and was on heavy rotation on KIMN-AM in Denver.

They were later known as **Year One** and their first 45 was non-album. (MW/SR/RBc/CBt/VJ)

Fantasy

ALBUM: 1 SMOKE 'EM IF YOU GOT' EM (Fantasy 79-478) c1973 ?

A local rock group from Tulsa, Oklahoma. Their album was a private pressing and contains songs like *Store Bought Girl*, *Bound And Gagged* and *Manipulation*. (SR)

Fanz

Personnel:
DUFFY JACKSON	drms	A
LITTLE KENNY	perc	A
CHARLES MICHAEL	gtr	A
MICHAEL PINERA	vcls	A
DANNY RAY	keyb'ds	A

ALBUM: 1(A) THE GRAND ILLUSION (Illusion CM 1045) c1976-79 R1

From Miami, a rare album mixing psychedlia and Southern rock. Mike Pinera was the former **Iron Butterfly** member.

The Illusion label didn't last long and is rumored to have been a tax scam label, the records being given away or destroyed after production. Other Illusion acts include **Hopney** and **Sage**. Strictly speaking, their releases which were made between 1976-79, are outside this books time-frame. (SR/CF)

Fapardokly

Personnel:
BILL DODD	ld gtr	A
MERRELL FANKHAUSER	gtr	A
DICK LEE	drms	A
JOHN OLIVER	bs	A

ALBUM: 1(A) FAPARDOKLY (UIP 2250) 1968 R2

NB: (1) Reissued in 1983 (Psycho 5), 1987 (5 Hours Back Tock 003) and on CD (Sundazed SC 6059) 1995.

The above album was issued in February 1968, but consists of recordings made between 1964-67, during which time the band played in Lancaster, California. It includes material released on 45s with Fankhauser's previous band, **The Exiles**, which by the time of the album's release was patchy and rather dated. The remainder of the album consists of folk-rock and soft psychedelia. Examples of the latter are the mysterious *Gone To Pot* and *No Retreat*. The **Fapardokly** album remains extremely sought-after.

The recent Sundazed CD includes three previously unreleased tracks *The War*, *Yes I Love You* and *Run Baby Run*.

Compilation appearances include: *Supermarket* on *Sundazed Sampler, Vol. 2* (CD); *Gone To Pot* and *No Retreat* on *Echoes In Time, Vol. 1* (LP & CD); and *Gone To Pot* on *We Have Come For Your Children*. (VJ/CF)

Far Cry

Personnel:
SEAN HUTCHINSON	bs	A
LARRY LUDDECKE	keyb'ds	A
DICK MARTIN	sax, perc	A
VICTOR McGILL	drms, perc	A
PAUL LENART	gtr	A
DAVID PERRY	gtr, vcls	A
JERE WHITTING	vcls, hrmnca	A

ALBUM: 1(A) FAR CRY (Vanguard Apostolic VSD 6510) 1968 SC

NB: (1) reissued on vinyl.

45: Shapes/Hellhound (Vanguard 35085) 1968

NB: both tracks taken from their album.

From Boston, this was a heavy psychedelic outfit with free jazz influences. Except for the classic blues track *Sweet Little Angel*, all the songs on their album were penned by the group and sung in a very rasping voice by Jere Whiting.

The album was produced by Danny Weiss (**Everything Is Everything**) and recorded in New York. It's one of the few records issued on Vanguard Apostolic, the label managed by John Townley (from **Family Of Apostolic**).

Paul Lenart went on to play with another Bostonian, **Peter Ivers**. (VJ/SR)

FAR CRY - Far Cry LP.

Fargo

Personnel:
TONY DECKER	A
DEAN WILDEN	A

ALBUM: 1(A) I SEE IT NOW (RCA Victor LSP 4178) 1969 -

FARGO - I See It Now LP.

This romantic-sounding late sixties pop offering with the occasional nod and a wink towards more vaguely psychedelic tendencies is worth a passing mention. They hailed from Salt Lake City, Utah. (VJ/NK)

FARM - Innermost Limits Of Pure Fun LP.

Fargo

45: Robins, Robins/Sunny Day Blue (Capitol 2149) 1968

This 45 could possibly be by a different band of the same name.

Richard Farina

Personnel:	RICHARD FARINA	vcls, ftr, dulcimer	ABC
	MIMI FARINA	gtr, autoharp	BC
	BRUCE LANGHORNE	gtr, tambourine	BC
	RUSS SAVAKUS	bs	BC
	CHARLES SMALL	piano, celeste	BC
	JOHN HAMMOND	hrmnca	C
	FELIX PAPPALARDI	bs	C
	ALVIN ROGERS	drms	C

ALBUMS:	1(A)	SINGER SONGWRITER PROJECT		
			(Elektra EKS-7299) 1965	-
	2(B)	CELEBRATIONS FOR A GREY DAY		
			(Vanguard VSD-79174) 1965	-
	3(C)	REFLECTIONS IN A CRYSTAL MIND		
			(Vanguard VSD-79204) 1965	-
	4(-)	MEMORIES	(Vanguard VSD-79263) 1968	-
	5(-)	LONG TIME COMING, LONG TIME GONE		
			(EMR Ent / Random House) 1969	R1
	6(B/C)	THE BEST OF MIMI AND RICHARD FARINA		
			(Vanguard VSD 21/22) 1971	-
	7	WITH ERIC VON SCHMIDT, ETHAN SIGNER AND		
		OCCASIONALLY BLIND BOY GRUNT	(Folklore) c1974	-

NB: (1) stereo pressing, also exists on mono (EKS-299). (2) and (3) as Richard and Mimi Farina. (5) is a radio show type album with music, interviews and readings in a plain cover. (6) is a reissue of (2) and (3) on a double album. (7) is a UK release with early sixties tracks (Blind Boy Grunt is in fact Bob Dylan).

45: Reno Nevada/One Way Ticket (Vanguard ?) 1965

Of Irish and Cuban heritage, Richard "Dick" Farina was caught up in the I.R.A. movement and arrested at the age of 16. At 18 he was finally deported from Ireland to the U.S.A. for his activities, attended Cornell and was dismissed after leading a demonstration. He began singing in the Greenwich Village folk circuit and briefly married **Carolyn Hester**. He returned to Europe as an actor, street singer and play writer and finally met and married Mimi, Joan Baez's sister, in 1963 in Paris.

Both returned to the U.S.A. and Richard became a published writer for various magazines and newspapers, a poet and a songwriter. His song *Birmingham Sunday* was sung by Joan Baez at the 1964 Newport festival and he got offered a contract with Elektra to appear on their 1965 *Singer Songwriter Project* along with David "Blue" Cohen, Patrick Sky and Bruce

Murdoch. The resulting record contains three **Farina** songs: *House Un-American Blues Activity Dream* (later covered by Ian Matthews), *Birmingham Sunday* and *Bold Marauder* (covered by John Kay of **Steppenwolf**).

He then formed a duo with his wife and they recorded two excellent albums, predominantly folk with nice poetic lyrics, and some oriental influences (especially on *Reflections*). The use of a rock rhythm section is very effective on several tracks. *Miles* is dedicated to Miles Davis and the superb *Reno, Nevada* was later covered by **Turnquist Remedy** and Ian Matthews. *Pack Up Your Sorrows* became a folk classic and some dozens of versions exist. Both albums are recommended.

The long liner notes of these well-received albums thank "Assorted Algerian herbs for the head", **Leary** for his Quick-Trip manual, **Paul Butterfield** and Bob Dylan.

Farina also wrote a novel, "Been Down So Long It Looks Like Up To Me", which is now considered a classic of the transitional period between beatniks and hippies.

After this very promising start, **Richard Farina** unfortunately died in a motorcycle accident in 1966.

Mimi Farina kept on singing in the folk and folk/rock circuit, recording some albums with Tom Jans in the seventies. Sadly, she died in 2001. (SR/EH)

Farm

Personnel:	DENNY AABERG	vcls, gtr	A
	DENNIS DRAGON	drms	A
	DOUG DRAGON	keyb'ds	A
	ERNIE KNAPP	gtr	A
	PHILL PRITCHARD	bs, gtr, vcls	A
	(ED CARTER		A)
	(JACK CONRAD		A)
	(DARYL DRAGON	keyb'ds	A)
	(ROGER HEATH		A)
	(ADRIEN MILLER		A)

ALBUMS:	1(A)	THE INNERMOST LIMITS OF PURE FUN		
			(Rebel Records DG-270-S 2222) 197?	R3
	2(A)	THE INNERMOST LIMITS OF PURE FUN		
			(No label Dendra 2001/2002 - S 2222/2223) 197?	R3
	3(A)	FARM - SERIES TWO	(No label F-2001) 197?	R2

NB: (1) and (2) feature the same material. (1) is an Australian release, and may be the first of the two original editions. On the Rebel pressing, the song *The Eater* is shown as *V 12 Cadillac*, but the actual audio program is the same on both. The US pressing has a B&W printed front cover with a photo of the band and text, the back is blank. The label has a crude swirl design. Of the three issues of this material, this photo cover US version has the best sound quality. (3) appears to be a reissue of

FARM - The Innermost Limits Of Pure Fun LP.

FARM - Series Two LP

(1). The cover has only "Farm" rubberstamped in the centre. The label lists the same thirteen tracks that appear on the US edition (2), but the record plays only twelve, deleting *Crumple Car*. There is no mention of *The Innermost Limits Of Pure Fun* on this edition at all, but the assumption that it is a later release is based on the "Series Two" title on the label.

The Innermost Limits Of Pure Fun was a landmark in cinematography when it was released in 1970. Filmed mostly on a kneeboard in the water by George Greenough, it provided audiences intimate, in-the-curl views previously only seen by surfers, as well as glimpses of the nomadic lifestyle. It was filmed in Australia and the USA in the late sixties. Greenough commisioned Dennis Dragon to score the movie and he gathered an impressive collection of players, not the least of which were his brothers **The Dragons**. There are a number of albums with the Dragon brothers involvement (including the compilations *A Sea For Yourself* and *Corky Carroll And Friends*), but it is this movie soundtrack that collectors consider their artistic pinnacle.

Album (1) listed above contains 50 minutes of original music by **Farm** that encompasses rock, blues, R&B, and even Eastern music that is all quite unique and will appeal to readers of this book. The movie itself, which is recommended, features roughly 30 minutes of music not included on the album. It can be located through any of several video distribution companies on the web.

As most readers will already be aware, Daryl Dragon later was The Captain alongside his wife Toni Tennille. Dennis Dragon's career extended through the seventies as a session player, through the eighties with The Surf Punks, and he is still active today in the California music scene, producing television programs that focus on local bands. He also played in another rural rock outfit, the **Joyous Noise (Musical Ensemble)**.

Another album shown as by **Farm** and involving the Dragon brothers is believed to exist, but so far none is known in the hands of collectors. (CF/MW)

Farm

Personnel:	JIM ELWYN	A
	STEVE EVANCHIK	A
	GARY GORDON	A
	ROGER GREENWALD	A
	DEL HERBERT	A
	MIKE YOUNG	A

ALBUM: 1(A) FARM (Crusade Enterprises LPS-465) c1971 R3

NB: (1) reissued as a 10" LP (Akarma AK2012) 2000.

Recorded at Golden Voice Recording Studios in South Pekin, Illinois and released on a small record label from Flora, Illinois, this **Farm** released a very obscure and rare album of heavy garage-psych with fuzz guitars,

congas, mouth harp, organ, bottleneck and timbales. The album contains five tracks including *Jungle Song*, *Let That Boy Boogie* and *Sunshine In My Window*. They thank a certain George Leeman as their friend and spiritual guide. (SR)

The Farm Band

Personnel:	DAVID CHALMERS	drms	A
	LOUISE DOTZLER	vcls	A
	THOMAS DOTZLER	vcls, keyb'ds, sax	A
	WALTER RABIDEAU	gtr, vcls	A
	MICHAEL SULLENS	bs	A
	JOSEPH	gtr, hrmnca, vcls	A
	STEPHEN	perc	A

ALBUMS:
1. THE FARM BAND (Mantra 777) 1972 R1
2. UP IN YOUR THING (Farm Records EE 1776) 1973 -
3. ON THE RIM OF THE NASHVILLE BASIN (Farm Records 1001) 1976 -
4. COMMUNION (Farm Records 1013) 1977 -

NB: (2) as Stephen and The Farm Band.

45: Everything's Gonna Be All Right/ Keep It In Mind (PS) (Farm Records FB 202) 197?

These records are the work of a Tennessee rural and vegetarian community directed by Stephen, their guru. The first album contains two albums with inner sleeves and a giant poster. Their music was somewhat inspired by the **Grateful Dead**: long bluesy jams with good guitar solos, flute and violin (several tracks last more than eight minutes). The lyrics are very religious and quite naff (*Loving You*, *Being Here With You*, *I Believe It*). The second album came with another poster explaining how their community in Summertown worked (no smoking, no alcohol, free concerts and pastoral activities). It's musically very similar to their first album. With their third, their music became more influenced by the Southern Rock like the **Allman Brothers**. *On The Rim Of The Nashville Basin* was recorded in the famous Muscle Shoals studios by Steve Melton and the country soul singer George Soule. Its psychedelic sleeve mentions its "Southern Country Boogie" style. Their fourth album was more of the same, always with the excellent guitar of Walter Rabideau.

Contrary to some beliefs, **The Farm** was totally unconnected to **Frantic**. (SR/MMs)

The Faros

Personnel:	STEVE BERG	gtr, keyb'ds	A
	GREG DAILY	ld gtr	A B
	DAN MEREDITH	drms	A B
	CHRIS WYMAN	bs	A B

FARM - Farm (Illinois) LP.

	BILL "WILBUR" VANDENBURGT	keyb'ds	B

45: I'm Cryin'/I'm Calling You Back   (Target T45-103/104) 1966

From Neenah, Wisconsin, their finest moment is this half decent berserk cover of the Animals' hit. It figures on *Highs In The Mid-Sixties, Vol. 10* (LP) and the flip is on *Badger Beat Chronicles* (LP).

Members were involved in other Target/Tee Pee groups and productions. Daily was a studio musican for the 45 by **Lord Beverly Moss and The Mossmen**.

"Wilbur" Vandenburgt was in a studio-only aggregation The 13th Hour who had a 45 the previous month - *All Right And About Time / Badger Beat* (Target 10/11). He would produce the **Love Society**'s *Do You Wanna Dance* on Tee Pee but when it took off and gained a national release on Scepter, the 'produced by Wilbur' credit magically became 'produced by Al Posniak' (the label owner). "That's always been a bit of a sore spot with me" he told Gary Myers in the Badger State bible, 'Did You Hear That Beat'. (BM/MW/GM)

Farquahr

Personnel:	DOUG "BARNSWALLOW FARQUAHR" LAPHAM	vcls, ld gtr	A
	BOB "HUMMINGBIRD FARQUAHR" MCGOWAN	banjo, gtr, mandolin, autoharp	A
	DENNIS "CONDOR FARQUAHR" MCGOWAN	gtr, vcls	A
	FRANK "FLAMINGO FARQUAHR" MCGOWAN	ld vcls	A

ALBUMS:	1	FABULOUS FARQUAHR	(Verve Forecast FTS-3053) 1968 -
	2	FARQUAHR	(Elektra EKS 74083) 1970 -

45: My Island / Teddy Bear Days   (Verve Forecast KF5085) 1968

From Boston, after their debut album, the four **Farquahr** "brothers": Barnswallow, Hummingbird, Condor and Flamingo, moved to Elektra in 1970. Produced by Jerry Ragovoy and recorded in New York, *Farquahr* is a deceptive and overproduced album, the only decent tracks being the **Lovin' Spoonful** like *Dear John Deere* and *Babe In The Woods* on Side Two.

The backing group was made of local session men: Eric Weissberg, Gary Chester, Joe Mack and Lou Mauro. (SR/NK)

Pat Farrell and The Believers

Personnel:	PAT FARRELL (PAT HENRY SICKAFUS)	bs	A
	KEITH FISTER	drms	A
	RUSSELL HIX	gtr	A
	KEITH VAN ETTEN	gtr	A

CD:	1	PAT FARREL & THE BELIEVERS	(Arf! Arf! AA-072) 1998

45s:	α	Gotta Find Her/War Boy	(Kingston 1967) 1967
		War Baby/Gotta Find Her	(Diamond 236) 1968
		All My Love/Bad Woman	(Diamond 239) 1968

NB: α credited to **Razor's Edge**.

Around 1965, Hamburg Pennsylvania's **The Triumphs** were looking for a new bassist and Pat got the job - it helped that he could sing too. They were already well established with two 45s released on Barclay in 1964 and had several other recordings that stayed in the can but are now available - see their entry. They kept this name for a couple of years until it came to the release of *War Boy*, whereupon they became the **Razor's Edge**, to avoid confusion with other Triumphs. After the release of a 45 on Kingston, it turned out that another group was using that moniker so a further name change was in order.

Bad Woman, featured on *Pennsylvania Unknowns* and *Destination Frantic!* (CD), is a superb tough pop-punker with a wicked bass line and scorching guitar. Unfortunately the 'A' side is a cover of a sloppy ballad and Pat's macho-man vocals tended toward Tom Jones here! *Gotta Find Her* on *Psychedelic Unknowns, Vol. 3* and *Sixties Rebellion, Vol's 1 & 2* (CD) is a bouncy pop number with some fine drifting organ and dreamy vocals, whilst the unreleased demo *Brand New Baby* on *Crude PA.* is again more pop than garage - being dominated by warbling keyboards.

The band eventually called it a day in 1969, Hix and Van Etten going on to Pepper Mill, a cover band. Fister had already left to join the Air Force and his replacement Joey Goheen joined the Police force (obvious choices for rock drummers?!). Pat moved into the country music field.

The CD retrospective contains seventeen tracks (ten unreleased plus two unreleased Pat Farrell solo efforts) from 1966 through 1968. I've taken the liberty of using Erik Lindgren's liner notes to confirm and extract the skeletal facts and do this band's entry justice. This CD is one of a 'set' of four 1998 releases that explore the sixties music of Eastern Pennsylvania - the other being a **Flowerz** CD (*Fltye*) and two volumes of *Eastern Pa. Rock* which cover other acts on Barclay and its associated labels.

Compilation appearances include: *Gotta Find Her* on *Psychedelic Unknowns, Vol. 3* (LP & CD), *Sixties Rebellion Vol's 1 & 2* (CD) and *Sixties Rebellion, Vol. 2* (LP); *Bad Woman* on *Pebbles, Vol. 4 (ESD)* (CD), *Pennsylvania Unknowns* (LP), *Trash Box* (5-CD), *Best of Pebbles, Vol. 3* (LP & CD), *Crude PA, Vol. 1* (LP), *Destination Frantic!* (LP & CD); and both *Gotta Find Her* and *Bad Woman* on *Eastern Pa Rock Part Two (1966-'69)* (CD). (ELn/MW)

Cyrus Faryar

Personnel incl:	MIKE BOTTS	drms	A
	CRAIG DOERGE	piano	A
	CYRUS FARYAR	vcls, glass hrmnca, gtr	AB
	BRIAN GAROFALO	bs	A
	ALEX HASSILEV	electronic score, backing vcl	A
	PAUL McCANDLESS	oboe	A
	GLEN MOORE	bs	A
	DICK ROSMINI	gtr	A
	RALPH TOWNER	gtr, mellophone	A
	COLIN WALCOTT	perc	AB
	(DAVID CROSBY	backing vcl	A)
	(MAMA CASS ELLIOT	backing vcl	A)
	(BOB GIBSON	gtr, backing vcl	A)

ALBUMS:	1(A)	CYRUS	(Elektra 74105) 1971 -
	2(B)	ISLANDS	(Elektra ?) 1973 -

PAT FARRELL and THE BELIEVERS - Self Titled CD.

The former **Modern Folk Quintet** member and voice of **Zodiac Cosmic Sounds** recorded these solo albums in 1971 and 1973. *Cyrus* was recorded in Los Angeles with the help of the members of the jazz group Oregon, **David Crosby**, Cass Elliot and various sessionmen. It's mainly composed of introspective folk-rock with some oriental influences and very religious lyrics (*Softly Through The Darkness*, *New Beginnings*, *Kingdom*). *Springtime Bouquet* is an electronic score composed by Alex Hassilev. Recorded in 1973, *Islands* is presumably in the same style.

Faryar can also be found on recordings by **Fred Neil**, Mama Cass and the **Stone Poneys** and he sung one track for the soundtrack of "Last Summer" produced by John Simon. He even produced some albums by the **Firesign Theater**. In the early seventies, **Faryar** moved to Hawaii where he produced some local groups like Country Comfort. (SR)

Fat

Personnel:	WILLIAM BENJAMIN	drms, vcls	A
	MICHAEL BENSON	gtr, vcls	ABCD
	GUY DeVITO	bs, vcls	ABC
	JAMES KAMINSKI	gtr, vcls	A
	PETER NEWLAND	vcls, hrmnca, flute, synth	ABCD
	CHRISTOPHER NEWLAND	gtr, vcls	BC
	WILLIAM PERRY	drms, perc	BC
	EDUARDO VATES	perc	B
	MARK KISLUS	drms	D
	JOE RUDOLPH	bs	D
	RON HURST	drms	
	(FELIX PAPPALARDI	organ, backing vcls	C)

ALBUMS:	1(A)	FAT	(RCA LSP 4368) 1970 R1
	2(B)	FOOTLOOSE	(Dream Merchant OU 812) 1976 SC
	3(C)	PAST DUE	(Atlantic) 1978 -

NB: (1) also issued in the UK (RCA LSA 3009) 1970. (3) unreleased at the time, this finally was issued on CD in 1995 (Dream Merchant OU 813).

45s:	Over The Hill / The Shape I'm In	(RCA Victor 47-9913) 1970
	Still Water/Jump Town Girl	(RCA 74-0408) 1970
α	Livin' Like An Outlaw / When Will I Meet You?	(Dream Merchant DM 101) 1982

NB: α early copies came in a fold-open PS, later copies in a plain white sleeve.

This Western Massachusetts band was formed in the late-sixties from a close-knit circle of friends: Peter and Christopher Newland are brothers, and Jim Kaminsky and Guy De Vito are cousins. The RCA album is quite accomplished for a first effort; Peter Newland's intelligent lyrics and gravelly voice are complemented perfectly by the lead guitars of Jim Kaminsky and Michael Benson. After the first album was released the band toured briefly as the opening act for the Allman Brothers Band. A second album was planned but the band was dropped by RCA after a drug-bust. The second RCA 45 features two songs that were slated for the second RCA album.

More recording sessions were done, but they were unable to secure another record deal. Jim Kaminsky quit the band in 1974; he would later lead his own bands in Massachusetts, Texas and France. Kaminsky also recorded an unreleased album with **Steppenwolf**; and current **Steppenwolf** drummer Ron Hirst also played with **Fat** in their later days. Drummer William Benjamin would also drop out, but would later surface with The Elevators (Arista/1980) and would continue to play in bands with Jim Kaminsky.

Christopher Newland and William Perry joined the band and are featured on the 1976 *Footloose* album that the band issued themselves. This second album shows the band in a slightly less introspective, harder rocking mode, but the end result is an album that is superior to many major label efforts. This line-up without Eduardo Vates, recorded another unreleased album for Atlantic Records in 1978. That album was produced by Felix Pappa;ardi who also played organ and contributed backing vocals to it.

Over the years **Fat** toured with and shared the stage with the likes of Grand Funk Railroad, Little Richard, Delaney and Bonnie, **Johnny Winter**, Robin Trower and many others. But eventually, most of the band had had enough and went their separate ways. Peter Newland and Michael Benson carried on with other rhythm sections, and they issued one final 45 in 1982. The "A" side, *Livin' Like An Outlaw* is a great rock 'n' roll screamer recorded in 1981; the "B" side was recorded in 1976 by the *Footloose* line-up and showcases Peter Newland's introspective songwriting talents.

Shortly thereafter **Fat** folded. Peter became a solo act, then moved to Nashville where he is a songwriter; he released a solo CD in 1999. Christopher Newland later recorded with Yuseef Lateef and is now a jazz musician living in England. Jim Kaminski currently leads his own band in the Pioneer Valley area of Massachusetts, he released a solo CD in 1998. And Mark Kislus continues to perform and record with local bands, most recently with Linee Perroncel.

Fat were too intelligent for their own good; the depth of Peter's lyrics, the musical abilities of the band and the economy of the arrangements were beyond the mental grasp of the average pot-head and too subtle for the masses. **Fat** is the quintessential band that "should have made it, but didn't".

The unreleased Atlantic album, *Past Due*, was finally released on CD in an edition of 1,000 in 1995. In this 1978 recording it seems like the band is trying too hard (maybe they figured it was their last chance?) resulting in more of a bar band sound. But it is still **Fat** and it is a worthy effort. (HS/CF/MW/SR)

Fat City

Personnel:	EVERETT BARKSDALE	bs	A
	HOWARD COLLINS	gtr	A
	BILL DANOFF	vcls, gtr	AB
	TAFFY NIVERT	vcls	AB
	JIM PARKER	gtr	AB
	(BERNARD PURDIE	drms	A)

ALBUMS:	1(A)	REINCARNATION	(ABC/Probe CPLP 4508) 1969
	2(B)	WELCOME TO THE FAT CITY	(Paramount PAS 5???) 1970

Produced by the blues guitarist Dick Weissmann and led by Bill Danoff, **Fat City** released two psychedelic folk albums of minor interest. The first album contains cuts like *Prince Of Peace*, *Easter Island*, *Holly Would* or the title track. With a renewed line-up, still reinforced by several session men (including Eric Weissberg and Richard Greene), the second album is reputedly in the same style. Bill Danoff would later marry Taffy Nivert and together they founded the Starland Vocal Band which released five albums during the seventies on RCA and Windsong.

Everett Barksdale also played with **Frummox**. (SR)

Fate

Personnel:	STEVE DORE	gtr	A
	SKIP SMITH	drms	A
	JAY SNEIDER (SNYDER)	keyb'ds, vcls	A
	ART WEBSTER	bs	A
	FRANK YOUNGBLOOD	vcls	A

ALBUM:	1(A)	SAMALENA CORPORATION PRESENTS FATE
		(Samalena) 1969 R6

NB: (1) two-sided demo album issued in plain jacket. Song titles are typed on stickers that were affixed to the record labels by hand. Reissued as *Sgt. Death* on vinyl (Rockadelic RRLP-37) 1999 and on CD (Shadoks Music 017) 2000. Both reissues have a different running order to the original and one track has been omitted.

Jay Sneider's first band The Electrons came together in Saco, Maine in 1963. They soon changed their name to The Id and would release two 45s that have become highly prized by collector's, the second as **Euphoria's Id** to differentiate them from several other Ids around at that time. Around 1967 Sneider (now Snyder) and drummer Skip Smith formed **Fate**.

The album was recorded in 1968 under the guidance of Thomas Jefferson Kaye at Studio 3 in New York, where Billy Joel's **Hassles** would record their debut album. Demos were sent out and the popular DJ Roscoe (also

FATE - Sgt. Death CD.

the voice on an album by **John Berberian**) started playing it. It would be picked up by a couple more NYC stations, yet the only record label to show any interest was Musicor. Still the band's production company (Elephant 5) chose to pass on the offer, nothing further happened and a disillusioned band went their separate ways.

Such a shame; this is an accomplished opus and so evocative of its time. The mood is reflective, often sombre, but also confrontational (as in the overtly anti-Vietnam title track). Stylistically it varies from baroque-rock with psychedelic flashes to hard melodic rock, and a strong hint of **The Doors** on the more introspective cuts. The latter comparison used to irritate Jay Snyder but the setting, key and timbre of Frank Youngblood's vocals makes this unavoidable. *Sexual Fantasy #8* is an immediate stand-out; it has a pealing George Harrison-like guitar motif that'll haunt you for months. Elsewhere they take on the blues and Bo Diddley in a hard-rock setting with searing guitar.

Jay Snyder recounts his musical odyssey and the stories behind his songs in revealing detail on both CD and album. A very welcome and recommended release. Incidentally, the opening track on the original demo album, *Prelude*, was omitted from the reissues as it was not recorded by **Fate**, instead being put together by their producer.

An article in Billboard magazine in October 1968 reported that "Fate's demonstration discs are being played on three radio stations in New York", but the only original copy so far to turn up has a mastering date of February 1969 etched in the vinyl trail-off. It could be that there were different demo discs in circulation at different times. (MW/CF)

Father Pat Berkery

ALBUM: 1 PRAYERS FOR A NOONDAY CHURCH
                                            (Glasgow 1500) 1969 R1

A spoken word religious album of some note, on which local Illinois band **Spur** provide the musical backdrop. (CF)

The Fatimas

45:     Sand Storm/Hoochy Coo   (Original Sound 72) 1967

A great single with female vocals, the 'B' side is an instrumental version of the 'A' side with sandstorm sound effects added! Both tracks were written by Petagno / Grovers / Hudson.

Compilation appearances have included: *Hoochy Coo* on *The Magic Cube* (CD), *Girls In The Garage, Vol. 2* (CD) and *Girls In The Garage, Vol. 6* (LP); *Sandstorm* on *Psychedelic Unknowns Vol. 8* (LP & CD) and *Teen Beat, Vol. 4* (CD). (SR)

Fat Water

Personnel:	BORIS ??	bs, vcls	A
	EVE ??	keyb'ds	A
	LANCE ??	gtr, vcls	A
	PETE ??	drms, vcls	A
	VICKI ??	vcls	A

ALBUM: 1(A) FAT WATER   (MGM SE 4660) 1969 -

45:     Santa Anna Speed Queen /
        Amalynda Guinevere   (MGM 14101) 1969

From Chicago, a mix of psychedelia and heavy rock, with good organ and guitars plus the powerful voice of their singer, who was probably influenced by Janis Joplin.

This outfit reportedly evolved out of **The One Eyed Jacks** from Champaign, Illinois. (SR/MW/NK)

Faun

Personnel:	DON BANDUCCI		A
	LYNN CHATWIN	vcls	A
	ROYAL MARTIN		A
	GEORGE TICKNER	gtr	A
	JAMES TRUMBO	vcls, keyb'ds	A
	ROSS VALORY	bs	A

ALBUM: 1(A) FAUN   (GreGar GG 70000) 1968 SC

NB: (1) also released in Italy with a different sleeve (Muriel) 1970.

45s: I Asked My Mother/
        Better Dig What You Find   (Gregar 7000) 1968
        Son Of A Literate Man/
        Yes I'm Really Lonely   (Gregar 7001) 1968

A San Francisco band, which strangely enough is not mentioned in Gleason's excellent book on 'The Jefferson Airplane and the San Francisco Sound'. Indeed some of the personnel may have come from Northern California. Valory and Tickner had both previously played with **Frumious Bandersnatch** and Valory later went on to play with **The Steve Miller Band** and Journey. Trumbo had previously been a solo artist and returned to this pursuit after **Faun**'s demise. The case for **Faun**'s inclusion here is marginal, as the album largely consists of odd parlour music! It is now a minor collectable. (VJ/SR)

Didi Favreau

ALBUM: 1 DIDI, REBIRTH OF WONDER   (RSVP 8004) 1968 R2?

FATHER PAT BERKERY - Prayers For A Noonday Church LP.

FEATHER DA GAMBA - Like It Or Get Bent LP.

On the same label as **Faine Jade** and therefore possibly from New York, an extremely rare album of female acid folk-rock with flute, cello and free form sounds. Some compare it to **Erica Pomerance**. (SR)

Fax

Personnel:	GREG FRITSCH	ld gtr	A
	GREG HASKELL	drms	A
	STEVE NOFFKE	bs	A
	MIKE PALMER		A

45s:	I Can Only Give You Everything/ Her Love	(Transaction 701) 1966
	Just Walkin' In The Rain/ Not Too Long Ago	(Trans-action 702) 1966
α	I'll Go Crazy/ If I Needed Someone (PS)	(Trans-action 704) 1967

NB: α as **The Lost & Founds**.

A four-piece teen garage combo from La Crosse, Wisconsin often linked with label-mates **The Ladds**. Both were billed for the *La Crosse Rock Reunion '91* show with other fifties and sixties local acts including **Marauders**, **Unchained Mynds**, Molly McGuires, **Satisfactions**, **Johnny & the Shy Guys**, and Dave Kennedy & The Ambassadors.

Alex Campbell later played with **The Ladds**.

Their raunchy, rather primitive version of *I Can Only Give You Everything* has been compiled on *Brain Shadows, Vol. 2* (LP & CD). (MW/JB)

F.B.I. (Four Boys Incorporated)

45:	Day-Time Nite-Time / What Am I To Do	(Gemini G-501) 1967

This was the original moniker used by whoever recorded this 45. It was later credited to **Band Of Wynand**. (VJ/MW)

Fear Itself

Personnel:	PAUL ALBUM	bs	A
	BILL McCORD	drms	A
	ELLEN McILWAINE	gtr, keyb'ds, vcls	A
	CHRIS ZALOOM	ld gtr	A

ALBUM:	1(A)	FEAR ITSELF	(Dot DLP 25942) 1969 SC

NB: (1) later reissued by Paramount, also released in France with a different sleeve (Dot 2C062 90484).

45:	The Letter / Born Under A Bad Sign	(Dot 17278) 1969

NB: There was also a French 45 with PS: *Mossy Dream /?* (Pathe 2C006-90648) 1969.

A late sixties San Francisco outfit, whose album is full of fuzz-blues material sounding rather like a psychedelic Groundhogs. Its more psychedelic tracks included *Underground River* and *For Suki*. Only two covers are present, a bluesy version of *The Letter* and *Born Under A Bad Sign*, both were chosen for their 45. The album is now a very minor collectors' item and was produced by **Tom Wilson**.

McIlwaine produced many solo albums in the seventies when she spent much of her time in Canada. Paul Album was also in **Chrysalis**. (VJ/SR)

The Fearsome Five

45:	It's All Right/?	(Fearsome 101) 196?

An obscure garage band, the 'A' side has resurfaced on *Hipsville, Vol. 2* (LP).

Feather

Personnel:	M. COLLINGS	A
	D. GREER	A
	R. WHITE	A
	STEVE WOODWARD	A

ALBUM:	1(A)	FRIENDS	(Columbia KC-30137) 1970 -

45s:	Kiss Of Fire / Mocassin	(Viva 635) 1969
	Friends / Salli	(White Whale 353) 1970
	Fifth Stone / No Time For Sorrow	(Columbia 4-45231) 1970
	Choo Choo Nairobi / Down The Wire	(Columbia 4-45405) 1971

They were probably from L.A. where the album was recorded. Musically we're talking typical mainstream U.S. rock, pleasant and all originals. Collings and White were also responsible for **Catch**.

Compilation appearances include *Friends* on *Happy Together - The Very Best Of White Whale Records* (CD). (VJ)

Feather Da Gamba

Personnel:	SAM CALDWELL	cello, timbales	A
	ROY CAUGHEY	vcls, drms	A
	PARKER DAVIS	vcls, bs	A
	MICHAEL DEAN	recorder, acc. gtr, perc, vcls	A
	G.S. MURRAY	organ	A
	MICHAEL YATES	gtr, vcls	A
	(ROBERT EHRHARDT	organ	A)
	(STEVE MOORE	organ, perc, vcls	A)

ALBUM:	1(A)	LIKE IT OR GET BENT	(No label DG 7743) 1971 R3

NB: (1) issued in thick white cover with front and rear paste-on slicks. Reissued on vinyl (Void 24) 2000.

A privately pressed record from Louisiana with reverb-drenched sixties style pop tracks as well as the early seventies mellow rock type stuff one would expect. *Albertson's Sunway* and *The Constant And Steady Lampman* are particularly intriguing and have a sound similar to the better tracks on the **Rubber Memory** album (minus the fuzz guitar) which, probably not coincidentally, is from the same swamp. *Surprise* concerns the joys of being a parent:

"Look at the little dear, sleeping away
He has had such a busy day
Ripping and tearing and biting away..."

...a lyric which is punctuated by a loud solo - but not a guitar; a baby screaming! (CF/SR)

The Feathers

45: Tryin' To Get To You/My Baby's Soul Good (Team 518) 1968

Another **Kasenetz-Katz** production, written by Couto, Mancini and Calitri. Their 45 is quite interesting, with fuzz and organ. Team was a short-lived label which also released the **Shadows Of Knight**'s *Shake* and **The Beeds**. (SR)

Federal Duck

Personnel:	TIMMY ACKERMAN	drms, perc	A
	JACK BOWERS	gtr	A
	TONY SHAFTEL	vcls, bs	A
	GEORGE STAVIS	gtr, vcls	A
	BOB STERN	bs, vcls	A
	KEN STOVER	keyb'ds, tuba	A
	HUCK WHITE	gtr, french horn	A

ALBUM: 1(A) FEDERAL DUCK (Musicor MS 3162) 1968 SC

The album, which was recorded in New York, contains a few good tracks including the mellow psychedelia of *Tomorrow Waits For Today* and *Peace In My Mind*. The outstanding track, however, is *Bird* with strong out-there vocals and a jazzy piano solo.

In 1969, **George Stavis** and Timmy Ackerman recorded an album for Vanguard. In 1970 Stavis, Ackerman, Stern and Bowers formed a new band **Oganookie** in Santa Cruz, California with Bruce Frye. **Oganookie** released a great country psych album in 1973, and about half the members backed up Bruce Frye in 1974 on a local Santa Cruz compilation album. (VJ/DMo)

Feebeez

45: Walk Away/Season Comes (Strange R 2216) 1966

The group came from Albuquerque, New Mexico and some copies of the 45 included a poster.

Compilation appearances have included: *Walk Away* and *Season Comes* on *Diana's Rootin' Tootin' Wild Teenage Rock 'N' Roll Party!* (LP); and *Walk Away* on *Girls In The Garage, Vol. 4* (LP). (MW)

The Feelies

Personnel:	RICK FONDELL	bs	A
	BILL HOLLAND	keyb'ds	A
	GORDY "FLASH" KJELLBERG	ld gtr	A
	SHAKEY ROE	drms	A

45s:	Louie, Louie/Warm Women	(Jerden 904) 1968
	Happy/Look At Me	(Jerden 910) 1969

Kingsmen imitators from the Pacific Northwest. Kjellberg had earlier played with **The Liberty Party**.

Compilation appearances include: *Louie, Louie* on *The History Of Northwest Rock, Vol. 3* (CD). (DR/MW/VJ)

Fe-Fi Four Plus 2

Personnel:	DANNY HOULIHAN	vcls	A
	ERNIE GONZE	bs	A
	EDDIE JAMES	gtr	A
	MIKE LAYDEN	ld gtr	A
	EDDIE ROYBAL	drms	A
	VIC ROYBAL	organ	A

FELT - Felt CD.

EP:	1	I Wanna Come Back (From The World Of LSD)/ Double Crossin' Girl/Who's Been Driving My Little Yellow Taxi Cab/Paper Place (Lance/Bacchus) 2000

NB: (1) last two songs by **Lincoln St. Exit**.

45s:	I Wanna Come Back (From The World Of LSD)/ Double Crossin' Girl	(Lance 101) 1967
	Mr Sweet Stuff/Pick Up Your Head	(Odex DR 1042) 196?

Wow, what a name! This was perhaps the best acid-punk outfit to record out of New Mexico. Danny Houlihan wrote *I Wanna Come Back*. The band have been well represented on retrospective compilations and more recently, *I Wanna Come Back...* has been covered by the likes of the Undertakers (1985 LP *The Greatest Stories Ever Told*), Nik Turner's Inner City Unit and the Mad Violets (1986 LP *World Of...*).

Dick Stewart, who ran Lance Records as well as being the main-man behind **King Richard and The Knights** has recently confirmed that Tom Bee was not a member of this band.

Compilation appearances have included: *Double Crossin' Girl* and *I Wanna Come Back (From The World Of LSD)* on *New Mexico Punk From The Sixties* (LP), *Sixties Archive Vol. 4* (CD) and *I Wanna Come Back From The World Of LSD* (CD); *I Wanna Come Back (From The World Of LSD)* on *Pebbles Vol. 5* (CD), *Pebbles Box* (5-LP), *Trash Box* (5-CD), *Pebbles, Vol. 5* (LP) and *Great Pebbles* (CD); *Mr. Sweet Stuff* on *A Journey To Tyme, Vol. 2* (LP); *Double Crossin' Girl* on *Boulders, Vol. 10* (LP); and *Pick Up Your Head* on *Everywhere Chainsaw Sound* (LP). (VJ/MW/MDo)

The Felicity

Personnel:	MIKE BOWDEN	bs	A
	RICHARD BOWDEN	gtr	A
	JIM ED NORMAN	keyb'ds	A
	DON HENLEY	drms	A

45s:	Hurtin'/Try It	(Wilson 101) 1967
	Hurtin'/Try It	(Regency 974 - Canadian release) 1967

Formed in Texarkana, Texas in 1964 they are more significant for their later achievements than this 45. All four became **Shiloh** in 1969. The Bowden brothers later played in Linda Ronstadt's band and various L.A. country-rock outfits. Henley who was in two earlier bands, The Four Speeds and The Speed, also played for Ronstadt and ended up in The Eagles, whose string arranger was Jim Ed Norman. *Hurtin'* can be heard on *Boulders, Vol. 8* (LP) and *Mindrocker, Vol. 6* (LP). It was also covered by Dewayne and The Beldettas and their rendition can be found on *Boulders, Vol. 7*. (MW)

Felt

Personnel:	ALLAN DALRYMPLE	keyb'ds	A
	TOMMY GILSTRAP	bs	A
	MYKE JACKSON	gtr	A
	STAN LEE	gtr	A
	MIKE NEEL	drms	A

ALBUM: 1(A) FELT (Nasco 9006) 1971 R3

NB: (1) counterfeited on vinyl and reissued legitimately on vinyl and CD (Akarma AK 127) 2000.

Felt came from Alabama. Their album, which is full of good guitar work and fine vocals, has become a very rare collectors' item. The band's leader, Myke Jackson, also made a solo album.

Destination is also featured on *Journey To The East* (LP). (VJ/CF/MW)

The Feminine Complex

Personnel incl:	MINDY DALTON	vcls, gtr	A
	JUDY GRIFFITH	vcls, perc	A

ALBUM: 1(A) LIVIN' LOVE (Athena 6001) 1969 R1

NB: (1) reissued on CD (Teen Beat) and vinyl (Gear Fab GF 207).

45s:
I've Been Working On You /
Six O'clock In The Morning (Athena 5003) 1968
Forgetting / I Won't Run (Athena 5006) c1968
Run That Thru Your Mind /
Are You Lonesome Like Me (Athena 5008) c1969

From Nashville, Tennessee, the **Feminine Complex** was an all girl rock quartet. Their album combines garage-rock and pop ballads. It's worth noting that the liner notes were penned by **John Buck Wilkin**, the leader of **Ronny and The Daytonas**.

Mindy Dalton later had a 45 as **Mindy and The Complex**.

The album is beginning to attract collectors, but is quite easy to find. The recent CD reissue adds several bonus tracks.

One of the album tracks, *Hide and Seek*, has also resurfaced on *Project Blue, Vol. 2 - Psychedelights 1966-70* (LP). (SR/MW/CF)

Fenner, Leland & O'Brien

Personnel:	RICH FENNER	gtr, drms, vcls	A
	JIM LELAND	ld gtr, "piano (RIP)"	A
	WICK O'BRIEN	keyb'ds, organ, bs, vcls	A

ALBUM: 1(A) SOMEWHERE SOMEDAY SOMEHOW (RPC AZM 70402) 1969 R3

NB: (1) has been reissued on vinyl (no label or #) 2001, in a newly designed paste-on sleeve, but with three less tracks than the original.

Original copies of this album are extremely rare (reportedly only 250 copies were pressed).

This was a folk trio, sometimes compared to **D.R. Hooker** or **Arthur Lee Harper**. From the opening fuzzy folk-rocker *Uncle America* they trip gently into the realms of acoustic folk and dreamy folk-psych with swirling keyboards. Very mellow and melodious. (SR/MW/CF)

The Fentons

An obscure Michigan combo who have a previously unreleased cut on *Thee Unheard Of* (LP) compilation. *Need Me Like I Need You* is a pretty typical garage punker with rather a catchy guitar riff. (VJ)

The Fenways

Personnel incl: JOEY COVINGTON
SONNY DINUNZIO
JOHNNY YORK

45s: α Will You Please Be Mine / Goodbye My Love (Kiski 2057) c1962
Moonlight Was Made For Lovers /
I'm In The Mood For Love (Joey 6202) 1962 / 63
Nothing To Offer You/
The #1 Song In The Country (Ricky 106) 1964
β Nothing To Offer You/Humpty Dumpty (Bevmar 401) 1964
χ Be Careful Little Girl (vcls)/
Be Careful Little Girl (instr.) (Bevmar 402) 1964
Walk/Whip And Jerk (Imperial 66082) 1964
Walk/Whip And Jerk (Stone 4560) 196?
Hard Road Ahead/The Fight (Blue Cat 116) 1965
δ You're The One / Some Words (Blue Star 229) 1965
ε Will You Or Won't You/True Lovers (Co & Ce 231) 1965
I'm A Mover/Satisfied (Co & Ce 233) 1966
Love Me For Myself/Satisfied (Co & Ce 237) 1966
I Move Around/A Go-Go (Co & Ce 241) 1966
I'm Your Toy/There For Pammy (Co & Ce 243) 1967

NB: α released as **Tawny Sims with The Fenways**. β also issued on Chess (1901) 1964. χ also issued on Roulette (4573) 1964. δ released as **Vogues with The Fenways** and also released on Co & Ce (229) 1965. ε released as **Four Chaps**. There may be another 45, *Never Thought I'd See The Day / ?*, which may itself have been reissued on Stone (48).

Pittsburgh in Pennsylvania was home to this band. **Joey Covington** was a member for part of '66 - '67, before he moved to California and fame and fortune with **Jefferson Airplane**. He's known to have played on at least one of their 45s, *I'm A Mover*, and may have played on another. Sonny Di Nunzio went on to **Racket Squad** and then Sebastian.

Compilation appearances have included: *Walk* and *Be Careful Little Girl* on *Terry Lee Show WMCK* (LP); and *Be Careful Little Girl* on *Burghers, Vol. 1* (LP & CD). (VJ/MW/DMr/TCx)

Fenwyck (featuring Jerry Raye)

Personnel:	KEITH KNIGHTER		AB
	PAT MAROSHEK		AB
	PAT ROBINSON	ld vcls, gtr	AB
	JERRY RAYE	ld vcls	B

ALBUM: 1(B) THE MANY SIDES OF JERRY RAYE FEATURING
FENWYCK (De Ville LP-1 01) 1967 R2

NB: (1) red vinyl. (1) has been repressed.

THE FEMININE COMPLEX - Livin' Love LP.

45s:	I'm Spinning/Mindrocker	(Challenge 59369)	1967
	Iye/I Wanna Die	(Progressive Sounds of America 103)	1967

Jerry Raye solo:
45:	The Simple Things Of Life/		
	She Just Kept Coming Around	(Perspective 6005)	196?

Jerry Raye and The New Trend:
45s:	The Devil Is A Woman / I Cry	(Deville 201)	1966
	Pray For Me / I'll Wait (Red Vinyl)	(Deville 202)	1966
	Mr.Kicks / ?	(Deville #unkn)(203 or 204?)	1966

Jerry Raye and Fenwyck:
45s:	I'm Spinning / Mindrocker	(Deville 206)	1967
	State Of Mind / Away	(Deville 207)	1967
α	Mindrocker/		
α	State Of Mind (Blue or yellow Vinyl)	(DeVille 207)	196?
	I Cry/?	(DeVille 207)	196?
	I Wanna Die / Iye	(Deville 208)	1967

NB: α details dubious, anyone able to confirm?

A whole compilation series was named after this band's fine pop-rock 45 *Mindrocker* which typified the times of 1967. Formed in 1963, by Pat Robinson, in Arcadia, San Gabriel Valley, California, the band existed for four years, before Bristol, Rhode Islander Jerry Raye came on board and they certainly possessed some talent. Pat Robinson was quite a talented songwriter and Raye possessed an appealing vocal style. However, their album suffers from variable material with *Mindrocker*, *State Of Mind* and *I'm Spinning* (the last two both penned by Robinson) among its better moments. Much of Side Two is very lightweight pop and overall it can't be recommended.

The original album is rare and pricey and was booted a few years back on black vinyl in a black-and-white sleeve (original sleeves are black-white-purple). The album should be considered as by two different outfits: **Fenwyck**'s psychy folk-rock side vs. Jerry's Raye's teen crooning side (sounding like a second division Conway Twitty). Certainly Jerry Raye's sound was out-of-date then.

Pat Robinson tells us:- "I wrote the songs *I Wanna Die*, *Iye*, *State Of Mind*, *Away*, *I'm Spinning* etc. and originally **Fenwyck** was produced by Jerry Fuller (*Travelin' Man* Rick Nelson) and legendary producer Bob Keane (Sam Cooke, Richie Valens, **Bobby Fuller Four** etc)."

"We were signed to 4-Star Productions... Challenge Records by president Joe Johnson and Dave Burgess (and Elery Hern) who thought we were a vocal group... like The Vogues, because we had previously sung our songs to Joe Johnson with just 12-string guitar. The first session was booked at American Studios (with Richie Podolor and Bill Cooper) and side men were there because the label didn't know that we played instruments... When the session started, Glen stayed on, but the rest of the session players were sent home. Jimmy Haskell did all of the string arrangements."

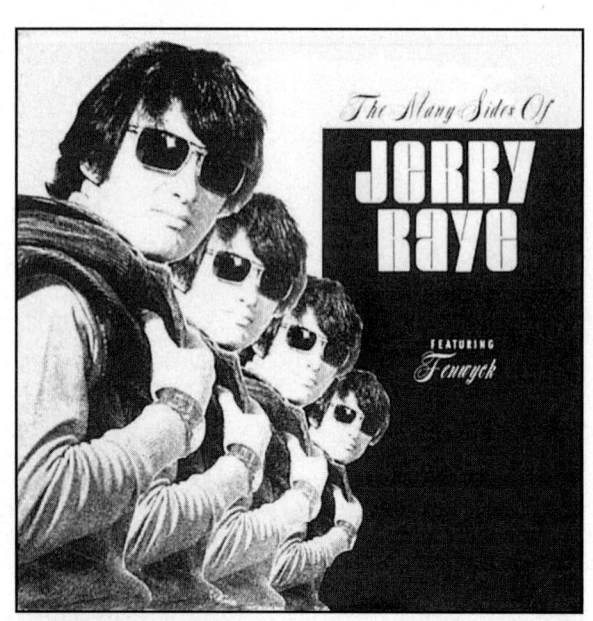

FENWYCK - The Many Sides Of... LP.

"The songs recorded here including *Mindrocker* were recorded at American Studios and Goldstar Recording Studio with legendary Stan Ross and Dave Gold engineering... in the late sixties. I sang lead and played lead guitar, but then Jerry Raye put his vocal over my vocal track and it was released as Jerry Raye featuring Fenwyck.... but we were actually a self contained band for years before meeting up with Jerry Raye."

Fenwyck then evolved into Back Pocket in 1968-69 and recorded several albums, featuring Pat Maroshek and Pat Robinson, on Allied records (Bob Keane's Del Fi Record label with a new name..). They also record at the legendary Gold Star Recording Studio with Stan Ross and Dave Gold. Back Pocket's line-up was fairly fluid, however, with frequent changes in bass and rhythm guitar players... and live they toured as a 3-4 piece band with full three-part harmonies and a power pop edge to their sound.

Back Pocket also released an album, *Buzzard Bait* (Joyce Records) 1976/4?. Pat Robinson wrote all 12 songs on this album and their first 45 from it, *Come On In*. Robinson and Maroshek where then joined by Gib Guilbeau, John Beland, Thad Maxwell for recordings at Amigo Recording Studio in North Hollywood. In 1977, the band changed names to Patrick Stagger, signing to Warner Bros./Curb and then finally to Hard Choir who recorded on Asylum Electra.

Robinson went on to produce and co-write with Gene Clark (**The Byrds** founding member) for over fifteen years and formed the group CRY (Clark, Robinson, York) in 1984 with Nicky Hopkins on keyboards and John York (**Sir Douglas Quintet**, **The Byrds** etc.). Robinson also penned *Civilized Man* and *Don't Drink The Water* for Joe Cocker, *You Got Away With Love* for Percy Sledge, *No Promise No Guarantee* for Laura Branigan and *Ain't It Just Like Love* for Glen Campbell and Billy Burnette... along with many covers by Moon Martin, Dwight Twilley, Rocky Burnette, Frankie Miller and Bette Midler.

Fenwyck compilation appearances have included: *Mindrocker* on *Mindrocker, Vol. 1* (LP), *Nuggets Box* (4-CD), *The Garage Zone, Vol. 4* (LP), *The Garage Zone Box Set* (4-LP); *Mindrocker* (Remix, unreleased version) on *Psychedelic Microdots Of The Sixties, Vol. 1* (CD); *Iye* on *Pebbles Vol. 9* (CD); *Away* (alternate version) on *Brain Shadows, Vol. 2* (LP & CD); and *I'm Spinning* (stereo), *Mindrocker* (stereo), *State Of Mind* (stereo), *Away*, *I Wanna Die* and *Iye* on *I Turned Into A Helium Balloon* (CD). (VJ/MW/PR)

Ferguson Tractor

45:	12 O'Clock High/Desperation Blues	(MTA)	1968?

An acid-garage rock rarity. *12 O'clock High* can also be found on *Echoes In Time, Vol. 1* (LP) and *Echoes In Time, Vol's 1 & 2* (CD). (SR)

Feris Wheel

45:	The Best Part Of Breaking Up (Is Making Up)/		
	Woman	(Magenda 5653)	c1967

Lower division Michigan garage-pop notable for being on the same label as Meatloaf's first waxing when he was a member of **Popcorn Blizzard** and that's all. To be fair, although the 'A' side is dire, their Zombies' cover ain't half bad. Check it out on *Bad Vibrations, Vol. 2* (LP). (MW)

Lawrence Ferlinghetti

Personnel:	JEFFERY CHIN	gtr, sitar	A
	LAWRENCE FERLINGHETTI	voice	A

ALBUM: 1(A) FERLINGHETTI (aka TYRANNUS NIX)
(Fantasy 7014) 1969 -

Ferlinghetti was a San Francisco poet, who owned the 'City Lights' bookshop. On Side One, **Ferlinghetti** is accompanied by either the sitar or guitar on three tracks: *Assasination Raga*, *Big Sur Sutra* and *Moscow In The Wilderness*. The whole of Side Two is taken up by one track *Tyrannus Nix* - a narrative attack on ex-President Nixon, before his dramatic fall from grace. An unusual, but tedious album. (VJ/SR)

FEVER TREE - Fever Tree LP.

The Ferraris

Personnel:	BILL FORD	gtr	A
	JIM GRANT	gtr	A
	BOB KUHLMANN	keyb'ds	A
	SAM NOTTLEMAN	drms	A
	CHUCK RODGERS	gtr	A

45: Can't Explain/I'm Not Talkin' (Welhaven 1001) 1966

Hailed from Winona in South-east Minnesota. This 45 was their sole vinyl offering and is becoming sought-after. *I'm Not Talkin'* was a Yardbirds' song also copied by **The Electras**. The 'A' side was a straight copy of The Who's classic hit.

They underwent several line-up changes over the years. Originally formed in 1963 as The Westcotts, they were also known at various times as The Farrarez, The Ferraries, The Fabulous Ferraris and finally The North Country Band. In 1968 they opened for The Yardbirds on their tour throughout the Mid-West, and also played with The Flying Burrito Brothers, among others.

Jim Grant later went on to a solo career, becoming one of Southern Minnesota/Wisconsin border's foremost acoustic rock artists. His debut CD *Not The Only World*, from 1995, was nominated for a Minnesota Music Award.

Compilation appearances have included *I'm Not Talkin'* on *Psychedelic Patchwork* (LP) and *When The Time Run Out, Vol. 1* (LP & CD). (VJ)

The Ferris Wheel

45: Come Baby Back/Cherrie-42533 (Randolph 004) 1966

Hailed from the small Indiana town of Winchester and just put out this one 45. The 'A' side, a typical garage-punker, later got another airing on the *Hoosier Hotshots* (LP) compilation. The flip was more pop-orientated. (VJ)

Fever Johnny

45: Zombie/
Wonderful World Of The Heart (RCA Victor 47-9071) 1967

Good fuzz-pop novelty with deep echoey Zombified vocals. The flip is an awful orchestrated Gene Pitney type ballad. There's also a 45, which maybe has no connection at all, by a similarly-named 'Mad John Fever' *Breath & Thunder / One World Lost To Another* (Century 44090) 197? whose topside is prog-rock with jazzy guitar interludes between the heavier riffin' moments. The flip is jazzy rock with pizzicato guitar and brass soloing to the fore. 'Mad John Fever' went on to become 'Starcastle'. (MW/SA)

Fever Tree

Personnel:	DENNIS KELLER	vcls	AB
	MICHAEL KNUST	ld gtr	ABC
	ROB LANDES	keyb'ds, woodwind	A
	JOHN TUTTLE	drms	A
	E.E. WOLFE III	bs	AB
	GRANT JOHNSON	keyb'ds	B
	KEVIN KELLY	drms	B
	KENNETH BLANCHETTE	bs	C
	PAT BRENNAN	vcls, keyb'ds	C
	ROBBIE PARRISH	drms	C
	JOHN CLARRY	drms	

HCP

ALBUMS:
1(A) FEVER TREE (UNI 73024) 1968 156 -
2(A) ANOTHER TIME, ANOTHER PLACE (UNI 73040) 1969 83 -
3(A) CREATION (UNI 73067) 1969 97 -
4(B) FOR SALE (Ampex A 10113) 1970 - -
5(C) LIVE AT LAKE CHARLES 1978 (Shroom SP 98004) 1998 - -

NB: (1) was reissued in 1973 as MCA 551. (1) and (2) issued on one CD by See for Miles (SEECD 364) 1993. (3) and (4) reissued on one CD. (5) reissued on CD. There's also two compilations:- *San Francisco Girls - The Best Of* (LP) (See For Miles SEE 71) 1986 and *San Francisco Girls: The Best of Fever Tree* (CD) (ERA)1992.

EPs:
1( ) Radio Spots Promo - (Five Tracks) (UNI 10) 19?
2(C) Fever Tree Return (PS) (Buttermilk 711X4779-102) 1978/9

NB: (2) contains: *Mam Hang Around, Nowadays Clancy Can't Even Sing, Rhythm Fix* and *You Don't See Me*.

HCP

45s:
Hey Mister/I Can Beat Your Drum (Mainstream 661) 1967 -
Girl, Oh Girl (Don't Push Me)/
Steve Lenore (Mainstream 665) 1967 -
α San Francisco Girls (Return Of The Native)/
San Francisco Girls (Return Of The Native) (UNI 55060) 1968 -
San Francisco Girls (Return Of The Native)/
Come With Me (Rainsong) (UNI 55095) 1968 91
Love Makes The Sun Rise/
Filigree And Shadow (UNI 55146) 1969 -
Clancy (Nowadays Clancy Can't Even Sing)/
The Sun Also Rises (UNI 55172) 1969 -
Catcher In The Rye/What Time Did You Say
It Is In Salt Lake City? (UNI 55202) 1969 -
α I Am (UNI 55228) 1970 -
I Am/Grand Candy Young Sweet (UNI 55228) 1970 -
α She Comes In Colors (Ampex 11013) 1970 -
She Comes In Colors/
You're Not The Same Baby (Ampex 11 01 3) 1970 -
α I Put A Spell On You (Ampex 11028) 1970 -
I Put A Spell On You/
Hey Joe, Where You Gonna Go (Ampex 11 028) 1970 -

NB: α double-sided promo.

Originally known as Bostwick Vine, they formed in Houston in 1966 and quickly became known as **Fever Tree**. Michael Knust had earlier been a solo artist. Like many other Texan bands of this era they spent time in San Francisco and many actually believed them to be Californians. This was partly due to their Top 100 U.S. hit *San Francisco Girls*, which reached No. 91.

Their first album was excellent, and reached No. 156 in the charts, but then decline set in. The remaining three each had moments of merit, particularly the second and third which got to No.'s 83 and 97 respectively in the charts. However the last album was released during a period when the group was breaking up and appears to have been completed using session musicians. The liner notes to the ERA CD suggest that many of the tracks were outtakes from earlier albums.

Michael Knust reformed the band in 1978, recording a four-track EP *Fever Tree Return* and the *Live At Lake Charles 1978* CD, which was released in

1998. The group style is best described as "Fever Tree gets funky" and neither release is recommended.

Kevin Kelly joined the band from **The Byrds** and went on to play in Jesse, Wolf and Wings, Clarry and Blanchette were both earlier in **The Sherwoods**.

San Francisco Girls remains the best guide to their material.

Compilation appearances have included: *Hey Mister* and *I Can Beat Your Drum* on *Mindrocker, Vol. 12* (LP); *San Francisco Girls (Return Of The Native)* on *Nuggets, Vol. 11* (LP) and *21 KILT Goldens, Vol. 2*; *Love Makes The Sun Rise* on *Psychedelic Perceptions* (CD); *Man Who Paints The Pictures* on *Turds On A Bum Ride, Vol. 1 & 2* (Dble CD), *Turds On A Bum Ride, Vol. 2* (Dble LP) and *Baubles* (LP); *I Can Beat Your Drum* on *Victims Of Circumstances, Vol. 1* (LP) and *Victims Of Circumstance, Vol. 2* (CD); *Hey Joe* on *Boulders, Vol. 8* (LP); *Girl Don't Push Me* and *Radio Commercial Alt. Take* on *Houston Post - Nowsounds Groove-In* (LP); and two radio adverts for the *Living Eye* club and *Now Sound* on *Houston Hallucinations* taken from the Radio Spots 'EP'. They also appeared on the soundtrack to *Angels Die Hard*. (VJ/JRe/JMe)

The Few

45s:	Why?/How Much Longer	(Skokie 451) 196?
	Escape/?	(Maestro 4977/4978) 1967

This Skokie, Illinois, outfit were big fans of The Animals. They split in mid '67 a few months after their second 45 was recorded to go to college. *Escape*, is a raunchy garage punker with a catchy guitar and upfront organ.

Compilation appearances include: *Why Oh Why* on *Teenage Shutdown, Vol. 8 - She'll Hurt You In The End* (LP & CD); and *Escape* on *Back From The Grave, Vol. 5* (LP) and *Back From The Grave, Vol. 2* (CD). (VJ)

The Fewdle Lords

45s:	Farewell To Today And Tomorrow / I Know	(Tiara MP-900) 1968

A mystery group thought to hail from Miami or Fort Lauderdale, Florida. The stately baroque-harmony-pop *Farewell...* has been unearthed by Jeff Lemlich on *Psychedelic States: Florida Vol. 1* (CD). The flip also gets an airing on *Psychedelic States: Florida Vol. 3* (CD). (MW)

Fields

Personnel:	PATRICK BURKE	bs	A
	RICHARD FORTUNATO	gtr	A
	STEVE LAGANA	drms	A

ALBUM:	1(A)	FIELDS	(UNI 73050) 1969 SC

45:	Bide My Time/Take You Home	(UNI 55106) 1969

A Los Angeles outfit, these three were previously known as ESB. The album, which is heavy rock with some psychedelic influence, was produced by ex-**Merry-Go-Rounder** Bill Rinehart, **ESB** may previously have been **W.C. Fields Memorial Electric Band**. (Electric String Band ESB. Get it?). (VJ)

W.C. Fields Memorial Electric String Band

Personnel?:	PATRICK BURKE	A
	GEORGE CALDWELL	A
	RICHARD FORTUNATO	A
	STEVE LAGANA	A
	ZINNER	A

45s:	Hippy Elevator Operator/Don't Lose The Girl	(HBR 507) 1966
	I'm Not Your Steppin' Stone/Round World	(Mercury 72578) 1966

FIELDS - Fields LP.

This Los Angeles band are thought to have recorded the first version of *I'm Not Your Stepping Stone*. However, perhaps their most successful number was *Hippy Elevator Operator*, which demonstrated the band's commercial aspirations and underground pretensions. Also worthy of note - *Don't Lose The Girl* is a simmering mid-slow punker with strong moody vocals probably from Richard Fortunato (based on the fabulous April'66 **Vejtables** sessions that finally saw light of day on the *Good Things Are Happening* CD). With snarling guitar and a mean break, this oozes class throughout. *Round World* has a lighter feel with orchestrated backing and softer harmonies but retains a cool folk-rock-pop aura with some sharp guitar mixed low.

A later recruit to the band was George Caldwell from **The Bees**.

Shorten the name to Electric String Band, then **ESB** and you have an outfit featuring a Caldwell, George ex-**Bees** Caldwell (+Zinner, Patrick Burke, Steve Lagana and Richard Fortunato). And when **ESB** became a three piece they became **Fields**.

Compilation appearances have included: *I'm Not Your Stepping Stone* on *Highs In The Mid-Sixties Vol. 2* (LP) and *Pebbles Vol. 9* (CD); and *Hippy Elevator Operator* on *Boulders, Vol. 3* (LP). (VJ/MW)

Fifth Avenue Band

Personnel:	KENNY ALTMAN	ld gtr, bs	A
	JERRY BURNHAM	bs, flute	A
	PETER GALLWAY	ld vcls, gtr	A
	PETE HEYWOOD	drms	A
	JON LIND	ld vcls	A
	MURRAY WEINSTOCK	keyb'ds	A

ALBUM:	1(A)	FIFTH AVENUE BAND	(Reprise RS 6369) 1969 -

NB: (1) also released in France (Vogue/Reprise 6369). (1) reissued on CD in Japan (WPCR-1870).

45:	One Way Or the Other/Fast Freight	(Reprise 0884) 1969

Produced by the two **Lovin' Spoonful** members Jerry Yester and Zal Yanovsky, this urban folk-rock group should appeal to fans of **Lovin' Spoonful**.

The cover of their album featured a black and white photo of the group in front of Delmonicos Restaurant in New York. The band were regulars in Greenwich Village during the late sixties.

Peter Gallway later formed the short-lived **Ohio Knox** and Kenny Altman became the bass player of another '**Spoonful**, **John Sebastian**. Gallway has recently released a solo album, *Redemption* (Gadfly 255). (VJ/SR/FH)

Fifth Avenue Buses

ALBUM: 1 TRIP TO GOTHAM CITY (Movietone/ABC) 1967 ?

An exploito album full of ring modulators, fuzz guitar, flute and xylophones and nonsense female vocals on tracks "inspired" by Batman, the best cuts being *Fantastic Voyage* and *Catwoman*. (SR)

The Fifth Estate

Personnel:
DON ASKEW	wordsmith		AB
RICK ENGLER	gtr		AB
KEN EVANS	gtr		AB
DOUG FERRARA	bs		AB
CHUCK LEGROS	vcls		A
BILL SHUTE	gtr, hrmnca		AB
WAYNE WADHAMS	keyb'ds		AB

ALBUM: 1(B) DING DONG! THE WITCH IS DEAD
(Jubilee JGM(S) 8005) 1967 -

NB: There's also a retrospective CD, *Ding Dong: The Witch Is Back!* ('64-'69) (Boston Skyline BSD 116) 1995.

HCP
45s: Love Is All A Game/Like I Love You (Red Bird 10064) 1966 -
α Ding Dong! The Witch Is Dead/
The Rub-a-dub (Jubilee 5573) 1967 11
The Goofin' Song/Lost Generation (Jubilee 5588) 1967 -
Heigh Ho!/It's Waiting There For You (Jubilee 5595) 1967 -
Morning Morning/Tomorrow Is My Turn (Jubilee 5607) 1968 -
Do Drop Inn/That's Love (Jubilee 5617) 1968 -
Coney Island Sally/Tomorrow Is My Turn (Jubilee 5627) 1968 -

NB: α Also released in France.

The *Ding Dong: The Witch Is Back!* is a superb CD package documenting the life and evolution of the above group, from their 1964 formation in Stamford, Connecticut as the **Demen** (line-up 'A'), their Invasion garage-beat stance as the **D-Men**, to the addition of solo vocalist Chuck Legros and a change of name and direction to **The Fifth Estate**. Comprising 28 tracks, including many demos and unreleased versions, plus a hefty 30+ page booklet - good value for money, especially if you don't have the **D-Men** 45s. Much of their later material is pretty weak pop, though.

Love Is All A Game, their debut single, came out on the imminently defunct Red Bird Records and despite being an infectious and tuneful Searchers-style number, failed to chart. Meanwhile, the songwriting team of Wadhams/Askew were also pitching songs at a number of British artists including Peter and Gordon, Cilla Black, and Freddie and The Dreamers. All of them passed but some lesser-known American acts like The Highwaymen, the Brothers Four, and Reparata and the Delrons did record their songs. They also wrote and recorded a number of advertising jingles and continually played New York's nightclub scene.

In late 1966, Chuck Legros left after walking off stage in a pique just before the band managed to interest Jubilee Records in a demo of a tune taken from "The Wizard Of Oz". The song, done in response to a dare, was arranged around a Bouree by the 17th century composer, Michael Praetorius, and made No. 11 on the US charts on June 15th 1967. It was also the title track of their album. The "B" side written by W. Wadhams and Don Askew, is decent bubblegum pop. The remainder of their Jubilee album contains tracks like *No. 1 Hippie On The Village Scene* and covers of *I'm A Believer* and *Midnight Hour*.

The follow-up single was in the good-time vein of **The Lovin' Spoonful**, but failed to repeat the success of its predecessor. In August and September 1967, the band toured as part of a package with Gene Pitney, **The Happenings**, **The Music Explosion**, **The Buckinghams**, and The Easybeats. After the tour, most of the band members decided to return to college, mainly to avoid the draft, but still found time to record occasionally. *Heigh Ho* was an attempt to cash in on *Ding Dong*'s success and was arranged around a Bach tune. Their label pressed them to record bubblegum material in keeping with the Spring 1968 trend. The group was unenthusiastic and Jubilee hired studio musicians to record an ersatz Fifth Estate single *Parade Of The Wooden Soldiers*. When the label went bankrupt shortly after, the group broke up also. Wadhams now teaches record production at Berklee College of Music in Boston. (MW/SR/LP)

Fifth Flight

Personnel: anonymous A

ALBUM: 1 INTO SMOKE TREE VILLAGE (Century 39398) 197? R1

An obscure early seventies private album of cover songs, the highlight of which is a version of Neil Young's *Sugar Mountain* with massive fuzz guitar. Overall, the album is pretty inept and is not recommended. The stock Century "mill" cover makes another appearance on this album. I think this group was from California. (CF)

Fifth Generation

45: Purple Haze/Caroline (IGL 155) 1968

Carroll, a small town in Western Iowa, was home to this obscure band. These guys could play though - check out their fine version of **Hendrix**'s *Purple Haze* on *The Midwest Vs. The Rest* (LP) or *The Best Of IGL Garage Rock* (LP) and *The IGL Rock Story: Part Two (1967 - 68)* (CD). (VJ/MW)

Fifth Generation

45: If I See Her/You Lied To Me (Fone Booth 1001) 196?

A different band, from Westfield, Massachussetts, whose *If I See Her* can be heard on *New England Teen Scene, Vol. 2* (LP) and *New England Teen Scene* (CD). (VJ)

Fifth Order

Personnel incl:
BILLY CARROLL	vcls		
T. HAY			
JEFF JOHNSON	bs		
H. LOVDAL			A
J. SENDER			A

45s: Goin' Too Far/Walkin' Away (Counterpart 2571) 1966
Goin' Too Far/Walkin' Away (Diamond D-212) 1966*
A Thousand Devils (Are Chasin' Me)/
Today (I Got A Letter) (Counterpart 2595) 1967
A Thousand Devils (Are Chasin' Me)/
Today (I Got A Letter) (Laurie 3404) 1967

FIFTH FLIGHT - Into Smoke Tree Village LP.

This Columbus, Ohio band played a form of folk-rock with a strong Merseybeat influence. This is typified by *Today (I Got A Letter)* and *Walkin' Away*. However, their *Goin' Too Far* was much punkier.

Compilation appearances have included *Today (I Got A Letter)* on *Mindrocker, Vol. 3* (LP); (VJ/MW/BKr)

The Fifth Union

Personnel:	RAY BRODENDORF	bs, vcls	A
	TED KIETA	drms, vcls	A
	STEVE MICHAELS	gtr	A
	BOB OCASIO	gtr	A

45: Love Is The Key To Peace/? ( ) 1967

A Chicago-based band. During the Summer of 1967, a chance meeting with Neil Young in a local guitar shop led to a tour of the midwest opening for **Buffalo Springfield**. Ted Kieta later switched to bass and with his brother Mike, led the Florida-based band Imagine. Proving that lightning does strike twice, a chance meeting with John Lennon resulted in Imagine being the first band to appear on Lennon's Light Horse Records label (George Harrison had Dark Horse Records), issuing two singles and two albums (1975-1981). (CF)

FIFTY FOOT HOSE - Cauldron LP.

Fifty Foot Hose

Personnel:	DAVID BLOSSOM	gtr, piano, thumb piano	ABCD
	NANCY BLOSSOM	vcls	ABCD
	GARY DOOS	drms	A
	LARRY EVANS	gtr, vcls	ABCD
	CORK MARCHESCHI	(bs), various electronic effects	ABCD
	KEN CAMPAGNA	drms	B
	TERRY HANSLEY	bs	BCD
	DOUG ?	drms	C
	KIM KIMSEY	drms, perc	D

ALBUM: 1(D) CAULDRON (Limelight 86062) 1969 R1

NB: (1) has been reissued on CD as *Cauldron... Plus* (Big Beat CDWIKD158) 1996, with bonus tracks and also on CD in the U.S. (Weasel Disc 744213 1945 3) 1994. There's also a live CD taken from a 1995 performance *Live And Unreleased* (Captain Trip CTCD 052), 1997 and a 1999 studio CD *Sing Like Scaffold* (Weasel Disc WD 19456). On vinyl, there was also a limited album of previously unreleased material dating from '66/'67 called *Ingredients* (Del Val 010) 1997.

45: Red The Sign Post (alt take)/ If Not This Time (alt take) (PS) (Get Hip GH-50) 1990

Cork Marcheschi, the creative force behind **Fifty Foot Hose**, grew up in the Bay Area and developed a taste for both R&B and avant-garde music - Edgar Varese was an early influence. After finishing high-school in 1963, he formed a garage band called the Hide-A-Ways with guitarist Jim Flannery (Marcheschi played bass). The band soon changed name to **The Ethix** and played constantly around the Bay Area between 1964-66. They recorded the notoriously atonal *Bad Trip* single in the bathroom of Cork's mother's house, but the band ended in early 1967 when they played Las Vegas where two of the members were found to be under-age.

Cork's interest in avant-garde music prompted him to build his very own musical "instrument" with two audio generators, two theremins, and various other sonic-distortion devices - a bit like the one Simeon used in the **Silver Apples**. He teamed with guitarist and fellow experimental music-enthusiast David Blossom who brought in his wife, Nancy, as vocalist. A second guitarist, Larry Evans, was added and former **Ethix**-member, Gary Doos, played drums to complete the original line-up of **Fifty Foot Hose**. Doos soon left and a couple of other drummers were tried before settling on Kim Kimsey for good. Meanwhile Cork gave up bass to devote himself to the electronics and Terry Hansley was brought in to take up bass duties.

Early on, the band played a lot of gigs, but mostly perplexed audiences with their uncompromisingly experimental approach. They recorded a demo, four tracks of which are included on the Big Beat CD and hawked it around the record companies. Limelight Records, an experimental label subsidiary of Mercury, signed the band and they recorded their album in early 1968 with Dan Healy, who also worked with **Human Expression** and later extensively with the **Grateful Dead**, as producer.

Although *Cauldron* went unnoticed at the time, partly because it didn't fit into any neat "psychedelic" mould, it has certainly stood the test of time and utilises just about every music-making electronic device then available. Audio generators, echodette, squeaky box, siren, ringing oscillator circuits, theremin - the list is almost endless. Nancy Blossom also has a beautifully clear voice which begs comparison with Dorothy Moskowitz, the vocalist with another pioneering electronic band, **The United States of America**.

Sadly, after the album disappeared without trace, several members left to join the production of the musical "Hair" (just to get a regular paycheck) and the band effectively folded.

No original 45s were issued under the **Fifty Foot Hose** moniker, but the recent release of original alternate takes of the strongest album tracks is a welcome addition and worth seeking out. The recent Big Beat CD reissue of the *Cauldron* album also features two takes of *Bad Trip* - the 33rpm and the 45rpm versions. Both are still way out there somewhere. Finally, subscribers to Ptolemaic Terrascope #23 also got to hear an 'unreleased acetate version' of *Bad Trip* on the accompanying free EP.

Kimsey later played with the **Hoodoo Rhythm Devils**, whilst Cork became a teacher and later a well-known sculptor. David Blossom was a studio engineer in San Francisco in the seventies and his name is found on many records from the era.

In the late seventies and eighties *Cauldron* influenced a number of experimental outfits - including Pere Ubu, Throbbing Gristle, and Chrome. Continuing interest in the band led to a "re-union" live album, from 1995, which appeared on the Japanese, Captain Trip label. Although only Cork Marcheschi is the only original member, *Live... and Unreleased* is rather successful, with spirited performances of *If Not This Time*, *Red The Signpost* plus six other tracks. A studio album *Sing Like Scaffold* followed in 1999 and there was also a rarities compilation *Ingredients* on vinyl in 1997.

You can also find *Red The Sign Post* on *Psychedelic Crown Jewels, Vol. 1* (Dble LP & CD) and both *Bad Trip* and *Skins* (as **The Ethix**) on *California Halloween*. (VJ/MW/LP/AP/CF)

Filet of Soul

Personnel:	RICH LEGAULT	drms	A
	DENNY LEWAN	bs	A
	MIKE PEARCE	vcls, ld gtr	A
	BEN WIESNIEWSKI	gtr	A

ALBUM: 1(A) FREEDOM (Monoquid Squid ST 4857) 1970 SC

45s:	Sweet Lovin' / Do Your Own Thing	(Dynamic 1002) 1969
α	Proud Mary / (Get Out, Get Out) We Want Peace	(Magic Touch 2078) 1969
	Moving To The Country / But I'll Try	(Zap 002) 1970

NB: α as Mike Peace and The Filet Of Soul.

As Filet Of Sound
ALBUMS:	1	LIVE	(Filet Of Sound 771) 1975
	2	PRIME CUTS	(Filet Of Sound 001) 1977
EP:	1	RAG PICKIN' MAN + 3	(Zap EP 003) 1970

As Filet Of Sound
45:	Oh Loretta / Now And Forever	(Filet Of Sound 4503) 1977

Initially based in Thorp, Wisconsin this soulful combo started in 1964 as **Attila and The Huns**. In 1967, they were signed to Lenny LaCour's Magic label and released a few 45s, before LaCour suggested a name change to **The Filet Of Soul**.

After some touring, they resettled in Chicago, where they recorded their album. By then they were heavily into **Hendrix**-style guitar work and reportedly it contains a few flashes of brilliance, although the remainder is poppy or gospel influenced.

Another Filet Of Soul was on Mercury in the early seventies which presumably forced them to alter their name to The Filet Of Sound, which saw them through to the eighties. (VJ/GM/MW)

The Final Solution

Personnel:	JOHN CHANCE	drms	A
	ERNIE FOSSELIUS	gtr	AB
	BOB KNICKERBOCKER	bs	AB
	JOHN YAGER	gtr	AB
	JERRY SLICK	drms	B

This San Francisco-based band was founded by Ernie Fosselius (who came from Berkeley) and Bob Knickerbocker (from Sunnyvale) who met in 1963, although the band proper started when the other two members joined in the Summer of 1965. They coined their name late that year, not realising what it could mean to a Jew. Although the band were a part of the early San Francisco music revolution, partly through their own volition they weren't in the big league. They tried to look different (dressing from top to bottom in black) and sound different. They auditioned for Mainstream but never made it onto vinyl because Bob Shad never liked them or their sound. Late in 1966 Bob Chance lost interest in the band and Jerry Slick (Grace's husband) came in as a replacement in November following the break-up of **The Great Society**. This, briefly, gave the band new impetus, but they never really capitalised on it and fell apart in 1967. Ernie Fosselius went on to enjoy a career in film-making and Bob Knickerbocker is now dead.

Pebbles, Vol. 22 (LP), *Pebbles Box* (5-LP) and *Trash Box* (5-CD) all include *So Long Goodbye*, a hitherto unreleased song by the band. It's a raw-sounding rather trippy jam that typified the San Francisco sound between 1966-67. Those who subscribed to the first issue of Jud Cost & Alec Palao's quality zine "Cream Puff War" also received a one-sided red flexi 45 which featured an unreleased track, *Bleeding Roses*, from 1966. (VJ/MW)

Finchley Boys

Personnel:	GEORGE FABER	vcls, harp	A
	GARRET OOSTDYK	gtr	A
	J. MICHAEL POWERS	drms, perc	A
	TABE	bs	A

ALBUM:	1(A)	EVERLASTING TRIBUTES	(Golden Throat 200-19) 1972 R2

NB: (1) reissued plus session material as *Practice Sessions* (Eva 12033) 1984, also reissued on CD with three bonus cuts.

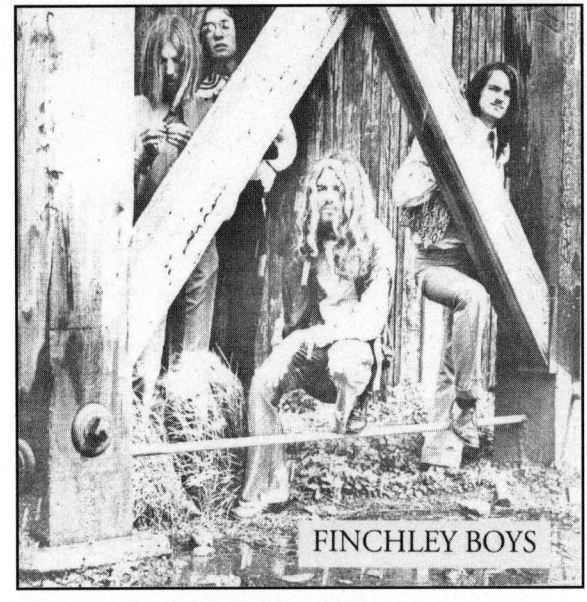

FINCHLEY BOYS - Everlasting Tribute CD.

Hailing from Champaign, Illinois, where they formed in January 1963, the band recorded the material for their album in Chicago during 1968 and 1969, although it was not released until 1972. They do not appear to have released any 45s at all. *Practice Sessions* is a reissue of their album but with five additional tracks. The best cuts on the album are their reinterpretation of Ray Davies' *I'm Not Like Everybody Else* and the superb *It All Ends*. Most of their material is very bluesy, as one might expect for a Chicago band of this era and to appreciate their music you'll need to be a fan of the blues.

Compilation appearances have included: *Outcast* on *Reverberation IV* (CD); *I'm Not Like Everybody Else* on *Endless Journey - Phase One* (LP); *It All Ends* on *Endless Journey - Phase Two* (LP); and both *I'm Not Like Everybody Else* and *It All Ends* on *Endless Journey - Phase I & II* (Dble CD). (VJ)

Finders Keepers

45:	Raggedy Ann/Lavender Blue	(Challenge 59338) 1967

Produced and written by Jerry Fuller and engineered by Bruce Botnick, an unknown Californian act, reputedly in the harmony-pop vein. Fuller also worked with **Don and The Goodtimes** and later produced the Butts Band, the group formed by Krieger and Densmore after the demise of **The Doors** (whose records were all engineered by Botnick). (SR)

Pete Fine

Personnel:	PETE FINE	gtr, vcls, perc, organ	A
	SAM HARDESTY	vcls, perc	A
	(RHINA CUEVES	flute	A)
	(MONTE FARBER	bs	A)
	(MIKE KIMMEL	drms	A)
	(ROB LEON	piano, timpani	A)

NB: Plus a seven-piece string section and two French Horn players.

ALBUM:	1(A)	ON A DAY OF CRYSTALINE THOUGHT	(No label) 1974 R4/R5

NB: (1) issued in plain cover with front and rear paste-on slicks, with insert. Info on LP labels is rubberstamped, and here the title is *On A Day Of Crystalline Thought*. Reissued on vinyl (Shadoks Music 003) 1998 and CD (Shadoks Music 003) 1999.

Totally different from his earlier band **The Flow**, **Pete Fine** changed direction completely after relocating to Arizona and the results were no less stunning. Classical and rock themes merge, as do electric and accoustic guitars, and male and female vocals. All the material was written by **Fine**. It's a difficult record to describe as nothing really sounds like it! The

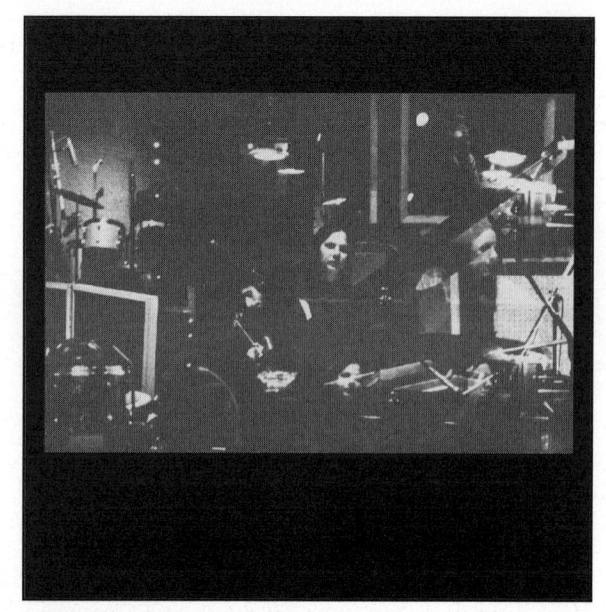

PETE FINE - On A Day Of Crystalline Thought LP.

recordings were made in New York where the core band were joined by area musicians, including **The Flow** bassist Monte Farber. Some material written by **Fine** for **The Flow** reappears here in a different light and is no less effective. Obviously, this album is recommended but as only 100 copies were pressed, obtaining an original is a difficult and expensive proposition at this point. The original pressing was not audiophile quality, either - the Shadoks reissue has better sound than any original I've heard. Certainly not for most garage fans, however.

Fine's next project was Northstar, a progressive hard-rock outfit (1975-76) that left behind an hour of studio recordings which will see release soon. Imagine **The Flow** with a female vocalist... (CF)

The Finestuff

45:     Big Brother/I Want You   (Ra-Sel 7105) 1967

A Philadelphia area band whose driving garage-rocker *Big Brother* can be found on *Killer Cuts!* (LP). The flip is a heavier affair with great guitar and a blues-rock vibe. (MW/SR)

Fine Wine

Personnel:	MICHAEL BEEN	gtr, vcls	A
	JOHN CRAVIOTTO	drms, vcls	A
	JERRY MILLER	ld gtr, vcls	A
	BOB MOSLEY	bs, vcls	A

ALBUM: 1(A) FINE WINE   (Polydor 2310 438) 1976 SC

NB: (1) German pressing.

Bob Mosley and Jerry Miller were two founding members of **Moby Grape**. After the group disbanded for the second time, they kept on working together in the California bar circuit and were joined by John Craviotto, a session drummer, and Michael Been. They managed to get a recording contract with Polydor but, for some reason, their sole album was released only in Germany. It's actually quite good, with the excellent guitar of Miller supported by a strong rhythm section. Produced by Michael O'Connor, the music is a mix of mid-seventies West Coast rock with electric blues. All the tracks were written by the group members and includes a new version of **Moby Grape**'s *8.05*. Michael Been later became the leader of The Call and had a solo career.

Mosley and Miller would keep on working on various line-ups of **Moby Grape**. (SR)

Fink Muncx IX

45:     Coffee, Tea, Or Me / ?   (Prism 1907) 1964

A Cincinnati, Ohio, outfit made up of four instrumentalists and five singers - the 45 was released purely as a fund-raiser. Basically a joke band, they did actually play live a couple of times. Lap it up on *Garage Punk Unknowns, Vol. 1* (LP) (where the band are miscredited as **Fink Muncx 4**).

The title *Coffee, Tea, Or Me* originates from a sexually explicit autobiography by a couple of airline stewardesses - whence the question "Coffee, Tea, or Me?". (GGI/MW/VJ)

Emmett Finley

ALBUM: 1 EMMETT FINLEY   (Poison Ring PRR 22??) c1972 -

Another release by this Connecticut label (also responsible for **Fancy** and **Pulse**), this one is a moody organ/guitar rural-psych album. (SR)

Mike Finnegan and The Surfs

Personnel incl: MIKE FINNEGAN   keyb'ds, vcls   A

45:     Bread and Water/Help Me Somebody   (R&S 101) 1966
NB: reissued on (Parkway 113) 1966.

An obscure single by the future leader of **The Serfs**. In the mid-late seventies **Finnigan** had a solo career with further albums and 45s on Warner Bros and Columbia.

He was also played with **Jerry Hahn**. (SR/NK)

Finnigan and Wood

Personnel:	RAY BAGBY	drms	A
	DON CLAREY	drms	A
	MIKE FINNIGAN	keyb'ds, vcls	A
	DAVE GATES	bs	A
	RAY LOECKLIE	sax	A
	JERRY WOOD	vcls, gtr	A

ALBUM: 1(A) CRAZED HIPSTERS   (Blue Thumb BTS 35) 1972 -

A good blues and heavy-rock outfit, with rough vocals and strong instrumental parts (guitar, organ, sax and harp). Mike Finnigan (or Finnegan) was previously the leader of **The Serfs** and Ray Loecklie would later play with **Mike Bloomfield** and **Jesse Colin Young**.

From Wichita, Kansas. (SR/NK)

FIREBIRDS - Light My Fire LP.

THE 31 FLAVORS - Hair LP.

Finnegan's Wake

45s: Situation Sad/Walking The Dog   (Disques Cote X-13/14) c1966
      Stay With Me Baby / You Blew It   (Val 1015) c1967

An obscure Pittsburgh, Philadelphia, outfit. Their choice cut is a strong fuzz-popper *Situation Sad*. The song is actually a cover of Michel Polnareff's *No No No No No (La Poupee Qui Fait Non)* whose success in continental Europe resulted in both a U.S. and U.K. release in 1966 (Kapp 786 and Vogue VRS 7012) and is one highlight on his *French Rock-Blues* album.

Compilation appearances include: *Situation Sad* on *Psychedelic Experience, Vol. 3* (CD); and *No No No No No (La Poupee Qui Fait Non)* aka *Situation Sad* on *Psychedelic Patchwork* (LP). (MW)

Finnicum

45: Come On Over/On The Road Again   (Ruff 1011) 1966

This West Texas band was managed by Ray Rut but isn't one of his better known bands. Nonetheless the 'A' side is a great this bubbling rocker - lots of fuzz, feedback and harp. The flip was a hard-rock version of a Dylan song.

Compilation appearances include: *Come On Over* on *Texas Flashback (The Best Of)* (CD), *Texas Flashbacks, Vol. 1* (LP & CD) and *Flashback, Vol. 1* (LP). (VJ)

Fire

Personnel: P. GLANZ?   A
            ROGERS?   A
            TAPLIN?   A
            WHITE?   A

ALBUM: 1(A) FIRE   (ABC ABCS-661) 1968

An obscure quartet whose album was produced by **Tom Wilson** and is reputedly a mix of psych and soul-rock similar to **The Rascals**. Two tracks, *One More Heartache* and *I Thought You Were A Lover*, were compiled on *Tom's Touch*, an album dedicated to **Tom Wilson** productions. Both songs are well-structured, with good organ and guitar parts. (SR)

Fire and Ice

Personnel: ANDY BAILEY   organ   A
            LARRY BARRETT   vcls, gtr   A
            JOE McCLEAN   bs, vcls   A
            LES THEDE   drms   A

McClean and Thede put this Iowa act together when **The XL's** were ripped apart by the draft. The *Dirty Water* (LP) compilation includes a McClean composition called *Person To Person* which contains some good instrumental breaks. The above line-up disintegrated in 1969, although Andy Bailey (who still plays in Iowa bands today) was involved in later line-ups. Les Thede deputised for The Daybreakers'/Rox's drummer in 1970 when he was incapacitated through illness. (VJ)

Fire and Ice Ltd.

ALBUM: 1 THE HAPPENING   (Capitol T 2577) 1966 SC

Chaotic off-the-wall instrumentals accompanied by shouted exhortations, or rambling spoken nonsense, characterize this strange trip. An early attempt at a free-form freakout - whether it works depends primarily on one's state of mind at the time. Definitely do not listen to it sober, however, as it just sounds vacuous.

There was a **Fire and Ice** who provided backing music to Capitol's notorious *LSD* documentary album (the one which tells the tale of Brian's 34th LSD trip amongst other things)... (MW/JFr)

Firebirds/The 31 Flavors (Electric Firebirds)

ALBUMS: 1 LIGHT MY FIRE   (Crown CST 589) 1969 R2
         2 DANCE PARTY TIME   (Crown CST-618) 1969 -
         3 HAIR   (Crown CST 592) 1969 -

NB: (1) was counterfeited in 1991. (2) as **Electric Firebirds**. (3) as **31 Flavours**.

An intriguing mystery outfit whose albums have become sought-after for their over-top heavy psych-blues-rock mayhem that owes much to **Hendrix**, **Iron Butterfly** and **Blue Cheer**'s *Vincebus Eruptum*. The best place to start is Erik Lindgren's superb 1997 CD compilation, *An Overdose Of Heavy Psych* which contains six primordial chunks.

The *Dance Party Time* album is lighter instrumental fare that sounds just like **The Animated Egg** but without the fuzz. Some tracks have a haunting quality because they've been recycled: *Out Of Town* is *Dark* by **The Animated Egg**; and *Doors Time* turns out to be a pedestrian version of the backing track to **The Id**'s *Boil The Kettle Mother*.

The **Associated Soul Group** Contessa album below is listed purely as conjecture in the hope that someone may establish a connection other than that it shares the same cover as the **Electric Firebirds** and is on another exploitation California label.

Possibly connected:

ALBUM: 1 TOP HITS OF TODAY (Contessa CON 15012) 1968 (MW)

The Fire Escape

ALBUM: 1 PSYCHOTIC REACTION (GNP Crescendo 2034) 1967 SC

NB: (1) reissued on CD with **The Seeds**' *Raw And Alive* LP. (1) also reissued on vinyl by GNP Crescendo. (1) has also been reissued on CD as *Psychotic Reaction Plus Ten* (King KICP 2167) 1991

45: Love Special Delivery/Blood Beat   (GNP Crescendo 384) 1967

NB: There's also a rare French EP with PS : *Love Special Delivery/Talk Talk/96 Tears/Trip Maker* (Vogue INT 18117) 1967.

The Fire Escape was actually a group of studio musicians, one of many put together by **Kim Fowley**. Their sole album, produced by Hank Levine, included competent versions of such punk classics as *96 Tears, Talk, Talk, The Trip* and, of course, the title track *Psychotic Reaction* which the record company misspelt on the album cover!

All the songs on the album were written by Hank Levine and Larry Goldberg, making it almost certainly some relation to the other phantom

FIRE ESCAPE - Psychotic Reaction LP.

group **The Mesmerizing Eye**. The remaining members are unknown, but the band were from Hollywood.

It is rumoured, but not proved that Sky Saxon and **Kim Fowley** played on the album. Like so many bands of this ilk, their demise was as fast as their rise. **Fire Escape** have one song, *Love Special Delivery*, on *Mindrocker, Vol. 1* (LP). Their version of **Fowley**'s *The Trip* (also covered by **Godfrey**) appears on the *Microdelia* CD comp.

Both 45 cuts were on their album. (VJ/MW/SR)

Firesign Theatre

Personnel:	PHIL AUSTIN	A
	PETER BERGMAN	A
	DAVID OSSMAN	A
	PHIL PROCTOR	A

HCP

ALBUMS:	1(A)	WAITING FOR THE ELECTRICIAN		
(up to			(Columbia 9518)	1968 - -
1972)	2(A)	HOW CAN YOU BE IN TWO PLACES AT ONCE WHEN YOU'RE NOWHERE AT ALL (Columbia 9884)		1970 195 -
	3(A)	DON'T CRUSH THAT DWARF HAND ME THE PLYERS		
			(Columbia 30102)	1970 106 -
	4(A)	I THINK WE'RE ALL BOZOS ON THIS BUS		
			(Columbia 30737)	1971 50 -

Although their records are worth investigating, their best work in this period is considered to have been for TV and for their free-form radio show, "Dear Friends". Primarily a comedy act, **Firesign Theatre** owed much of their early success to the 'acid-rock' period with their lyrics exploiting the way many American kids were spending their time getting stoned to well-crafted rock albums. Their repertoire extended well beyond 'acid' humour, mixing in both poignant political comment and slapstick comedy - for example their debut album dedicated one side to a series of sketches dealing with the fate of the American Indian.

Firesign Theatre also had a side-line as session men, with Gary Usher using them as 'Atmosphere' on many of his productions including

Throughout the seventies and eighties **Firesign Theatre** continued to issue a plethora of albums, whilst both Austin and Ossman recorded solo comedy albums. They've also recently recorded a video, whilst Phil Proctor and David Ossman have also worked on a film with Canadian documentarian Ron Mann called "GRASS - the social and legislative history of Marijuana....". (VJ/BPs/JFr/MPr)

1st Century

45: Looking Down/Dancing Girl (Capitol 2135) 1968

Scintillating and irresistibly catchy sitar-pop-psychedelia backed by a stoned mid-tempo groovy effort which adds a flute to the exotic instrumentation. Both tracks were penned by Sam The Sham guitarist Ray Stinett and were produced by Don Nix, so this bnd was likely from Tennessee. Both sides can also be heard on *Incredible Sound Show Stories, Vol. 8* (LP). (MW/CF)

First Chips

Personnel:	VYTO BELESKA	A
	GARY GREENBERG	A
	GENE LYNCH	A
	DENNY MURRAY	A
	DARICK NAVA	A
	ARVY TUMOSA	A
	ED WESTPHAL	A
	TED ZDANEK	A

ALBUM: 1(A) VOLUME ONE (Clay Pigeon CPP SFCV1) 1972 R2

NB: This album was subtitled *A Collection Of Early Recordings From Clay Pigeon Productions*. It has been counterfeited.

A rare Illinois local blues-rock, folk-rock item. Much of it sounds amateurish and the recording quality is poor. Most of the material was recorded between 1970 - 72. There is one rather interesting instrumental track with sound effects dating from December 1964. Otherwise on offer is experimental but disjointed blues-rock, best exemplified on the opening cut *Stoneball* and the 8'31" *Mind and Soul*, recorded live at Tinley Park High School. Other material is more acoustic-based. (VJ)

First Crow To The Moon

Personnel:	ALAN AVICK	ld gtr	A
	STUART GOLD	gtr	A
	EDDIE GREENBERG	bs	A
	ALLEN MILLER	drms	A
	JERRY MILLSTEIN	ld vcls, organ, piano	A

45: Spend Your Life With Me/
The Sun Lights Up The Shadows (Roulette 4774) 1967

Hailed from Brooklyn, New York. They were originally known as Back Door Men when they cut one 45 backing Alaina Shore, *Wrong Number/Shades Of Yesterday* on Satellite (not the Stax-related label). As **First Crow To The Moon**, they were signed to Roulette on the recommendation of Doc Pomus. They were also sometimes known as The Bootleggers. The sleevenotes to *Psychedelic Microdots Of The Sixties, Vol. 3* (CD), which includes both sides of the Roulette 45 and the previously unreleased *We Walk The Rain* (all three songs were written by Jerry Millstein), suggest that

FIRST FRIDAY - First Friday LP.

ERNIE FISCHBACK and CHARLES EWING - A Cid Symphony LP.

their name was the product of a typographical error at Roulette - their correct name was actually First Crew To The Moon, which would make more sense. All three songs are an exciting blend of punk and psychedelia.

The 45 was not really promoted at all by Roulette, who were busy pushing the latest **Tommy James** record (*I Think We're Alone Now*). Jeff Jarema interviewed the band's drummer, Allen Miller, who sang vocals on *The Sun Lights Up The Shadows Of Your Mind*. According to Miller, the band opened for **The Vagrants** and **The Lovin' Spoonful** but never The **Velvet Underground** (as previously reported). Also, Chris Stein (later of The Stilletos, Magic Tramps and Blondie) was never in this band, he was just a friend who hung around with them and was at many rehearsals. It had previously been thought that Stein was in the band, which broke up in January 1968 when Alan Avick died of leukaemia.

Compilation appearances have included: *The Sun Lights Up The Shadows* on *Magic Carpet Ride* (LP), *Of Hopes And Dreams & Tombstones* (LP) and *Psychedelic Unknowns, Vol. 7* (LP & CD); *Spend Your Life* on *Psychedelic Unknowns, Vol's 1 & 2* (LP), *Psychedelic Unknowns, Vol. 2* (7") and *Sundazed Sampler, Vol. 1* (CD); and *The Sun Lights Up The Shadows*, *Spend Your Life* and *We Walk The Rain* on *Psychedelic Microdots Of The Sixties, Vol. 3* (CD). (VJ)

First Friday

Personnel:	BOB EWAN	vcls	A
	JOHN PRENDERGAST	bs, sax, keyb'ds	A
	JIM STYNES	drms	A
	ANDY WALLACE	keyb'ds, vcls, gtr	A
	NORM ZELLER	gtr	A

ALBUM: 1(A) FIRST FRIDAY
(selective)   (Webster's Last Word WLW-S-2895) 1970 R3

First Friday comprised of students from the University of Notre Dame, South Bend, Indiana. Their album, is outstanding, with inspired playing and very tight ensemble perfrmances throughout. The lead guitar solos are particularly stunning; they could be described as ferocious in their delivery even though the songs themselves are not particularly hard-edged.

The album was recorded "live" at Golden Voice Sound Studios in Pekin, Illinois in late September 1969 and appeared in local shops in January 1970. (CF/TTn)

The First Four

45s:	Hurt Me To My Soul/		
	That's Where Your Love Has Gone	(Strata 108)	1965
	Empty Heart/One And Only Man	(Claridge 306)	1966

A garage band from Philadelphia. Their version of the Rolling Stones *Empty Heart* has resurfaced on *What A Way To Die* (LP) and *Hang It Out To Dry* (CD), whilst *One And Only Man* is on *Follow That Munster, Vol. 2* (LP). (VJ)

1st National Band

45:	The Trip Down/	
	When Once It Was Good	(Monument 45-1031) 1967

The top side has the encouraging title but is pretty tame harmony-pop and, though it has some psychedelic effects, it disappoints. However, turn it over and mellow-psych lovers are in for a treat - an entrancing mid-slow psych ballad infused with backward guitars, effects and smell of incense.

When Once It Was Good also appears on the *Acid and Flowers* (CD). (MW)

First Revelation

Personnel:	DANNY	gtr, vcls	A
	LINDA	keyb'ds, vcls	A

ALBUMS:	1	THIS SIDE OF ETERNITY	(Revelation) 1973 R1
	2	UPON THIS ROCK	(Revelation) 1975 SC

NB: There's also a vinyl compilation *First Revelation Of Danny And Lynda* (World In Sound RFR 001), limited to 500 copies.

From New York, a Christian rock group with heavy guitar and moog. They were previously known as **Danny and Linda**. (SR)

Ernie Fischbach and Charles Ewing

Personnel:	CHARLES EWING	gtr	A
	DEBORAH CLEALL		
	FISCHBACH	tamboura	A
	ERNEST FISCHBACH	dulcimer, sarod, gtr	A
	DAVID GOINES	vcls	A
	TOM HARRIS		A
	DUSTIN MARK MILLER	vcls, producer	A

ALBUM: 1(A) A CID SYMPHONY   (No label) 1967 R3

NB: (1) Originally issued as a three album set on coloured vinyl. The three discs had individual catalogue numbers: yellow vinyl #7-121/7-123, purple vinyl #7-122/7-124, and green vinyl #7-125/7-126. These were in separate printed inner sleeves on which photos of the group appear and were shrink-wrapped together. The front cover was a cardboard slick that was mostly pink; some of these were mounted to heavy posterboard, had their corners rounded and had a gold cord attached through a hole at the top for hanging. The back cover was a cardboard slick that featured a photo of an Afghan turban cap, often described as "the mandala cover". Some copies also included concert flyers. All of these items were contained in an open-top polyethylene bag. (1) reissued as a double CD (Gear Fab GF-135) 1999 and as a 3-LP box set (Akarma AK 090/3) 2000.

This unusual and decidedly uncommercial private press triple album was produced at the University Of California by Berkeley graduate Miller, who had earlier produced other records in support of the Free Speech Movement on campus. **Fischbach and Ewing** had been playing together while students at California State University - Long Beach, but came up to Berkeley to play and study music at the Ali Akbar College Of Music. The album was recorded at Fantasy Studios in Berkeley in 1967 and 1,000 copies were pressed that year. The band played frequently, usually at colleges, but also appeared at the Monterey Pop Festival, and The Human Be - In in Golden Gate Park. Their repertoire of acoustic material covered blues, flamenco guitar improvisations, Hindustani ragas, even American Indian chants. Miller added some spoken word segments to the record, and Goines is heard singing over the sound of a printing press on one track. While *A Cid Symphony* is not a widely appreciated record, it is acknowledged as a significant Bay Area collectable from the heyday of California's political and psychedelic era. (CF)

WILD MAN FISCHER - An Evening With... LP.

Wild Man Fischer

ALBUM: 1 AN EVENING WITH WILD MAN FISCHER (dbl)
                                              (Bizarre Reprise RS 6332) 1969 SC

NB: (1) also released in England (Reprise RSLP 6332).

45:     Circles/ Merry Go Round   (Bizarre 0781) 1969

Larry "Wild Man" Fischer was a Los Angeles street singer when **Frank Zappa** discovered him and decided to release and produce a double album of his "songs" on his Bizarre label.

The usual **Zappa** graphic designer, Cal Schenkel conceived the strange gatefold sleeve and the liner notes explain that "His mother had him committed to a mental institution twice".

Most of the material was recorded "live in the street in front of the Whisky A Go Go and The Hamburger Hamlet on Sunset Strip", with occasional percussion added by Art Tripp. The album was divided on four parts: "The Basic Fischer" with *Merry Go Round* and *The Madness And Ecstasy* (a recitative by **Kim Fowley**, Rodney Bingenheimer and the **GTO's**), "Larry's Songs": fifteen vocal tracks with unusual titles and really tormented vocals (*Which Way Did The Freak Go, Think Of Me When Your Clothes Are Off, I'm Working For The Federal Bureau Of Narcotics*), "Some Historical Notes " with *The Taster* (later covered by **Kane's Cousins** and the *Rocket Rock* and "In Conclusion" with *Circles* (subtitled "Larry's first psychedelic hit").

Taster and *Circles* were accompanied by over dubs provided by **Zappa** and some of the Mothers (Jimmy Carl Black and Roy Estrada). A real curiosity!

Wild Man Fischer recorded some other albums for Rhino between 1978 and 1984. (SR)

Fish 'N' Chips

45:     Four Times Faster/
        The Whole Thing Is Getting Out Of Hand   (Joy 45K-297) 1965

Excellent up-tempo pop-beat with harpsichord and a fuzz-enhanced chorus, from New England. (MW)

The 5

Personnel: CURTIS ARCENEAUX   trombone   A
            LARRY CIKO   keyb'ds   A
            ROBERT FACIANE   ld gtr   A
            RICHARD MAINEGRA   gtr   A
            BILL SUCKOW   drms   A

45:     I'm No Good/I've Lost My Girl   (JB 106) 1965

Formed Mobile, Alabama in 1964 as the Rebels, this quintet changed their name to **The 5** for the release of their 45. This was adjusted later to The Phyve.

I'm No Good is a dramatic **Beau Brummels**-like song with ringing chords and good harmonies. It can be found on *Highs In The Mid-Sixties, Vol. 22* (LP) and *Psychedelic States: Alabama Vol. 1* (CD). (VJ/MW)

The Five

45:     She Doesn't Love Me Anymore/
        I Don't Care If It Rains All Night   (Britain 100) 196?

I Don't Care If It Rains All Night, by this unknown primitive garage band, has resurfaced on *Sixties Rebellion, Vol. 2* (LP) and *Sixties Rebellion, Vol's 1 & 2* (CD). The vocalist sounds like he's about twelve and the rest of the band sound like they were similar in age... (VJ)

The Five Americans

Personnel: JOHN DURRILL   drms, keyb'ds   A
            NORMAN EZELL   bs, gtr   A
            JIM GRANT   gtr, bs   AB
            MIKE RABON   ld gtr, vcls   AB
            JIMMY WRIGHT   vcls, drms   AB
            KENNY GOLDSMITH   keyb'ds   B
            BOBBY RAMBO   gtr   B

                                                      HCP
ALBUMS: 1(A) I SEE THE LIGHT   (HBR HCP 9503) 1966 136 SC
        2(A) WESTERN UNION   (Abnak ABLP 2067) 1967 121 -
        3(A) PROGRESSIONS   (Abnak ABLP 2069) 1967 - -
        4(B) NOW AND THEN   (Abnak ABST 2071) 1969 - -

NB: (1) reissued on CD (Sundazed SC 6018) 1994, with bonus tracks. There's also two compilations: *Western Union* (Eva 12050) 1985; and *Western Union / The Best Of* (Sundazed SC 11004) 1989 featuring 20 tracks from 1964 to 1969, many in original unedited form and/or stereo mixes.

                                                      HCP
45s: α It's You Girl/I'm Gonna Leave Ya   (Jestar 104) 1964 -
      α I'm Feeling O.K./Slippin' And Slidin' (Jetstar 105) 1964 -
      α Love Love Love/Show Me   (ABC 10686) 1965 -
      α Say That You Love Me/Without You   (Abnak 106) 1965 -
         I See The Light/The Outcast   (Abnak 106) 1965 -
         I See The Light/The Outcast   (HBR 454) 1965 26
         EVOL Not Love/Don't Blame Me   (HBR 468) 1966 52
         Good Times'/The Losing Game   (HBR 483) 1966 -
         Reality/Sympathy   (Abnak 114) 1967 -
         If I Could/Now That It's Over   (Abnak 116) 1967 -
         Western Union/Now That It's Over   (Abnak 118) 1967 5
         Sound Of Love/Sympathy   (Abnak 120) 1967 36
      β 'Western Union/Sound Of Love   (Hip Pocket 10) 1967 -
         Zip Code/Sweet Bird Of Youth   (Abnak 123) 1967 36
         Stop Light/Tell Ann I Love Her'   (Abnak 125) 1967 132
         7.30 Guided Tour/See-Saw-Man   (Abnak 126) 1968 96
         No Communication'/Rain Maker   (Abnak 128) 1968 -
         Lovin' Is Livin"/Con Man   (Abnak 131) 1968 -
      χ Generation Gap/The Source'   (Abnak 132) 1968 -
      δ Virginia Girl/Call On Me'   (Abnak 134) 1969 133
         Ignert Woman/Scrooge   (Abnak 137) 1969 -
      δ I See The Light '69/Red Cape   (Abnak 139) 1969 -
         She's Too Good To Me/Molly Black   (Abnak 142) 1969 -

NB: α contain non-LP tracks. δ released as **Michael Rabon** and **The Five Americans**. β four-inch flexi-disc enclosed in a picture envelope. χ also released in France with a PS. There are also three rare French EPs with PS (Vogue INT 18087, Stateside FSE 102 and 107).

This pleasant pop-rock outfit formed in Dallas in 1964 and proceeded to enjoy a prolific recording output until they disbanded in 1970. **Mike Rabon**, Norman Ezell and John Durrill formed a successful song-writing trio and most of the band's songs were self-penned. *Western Union*, produced by Dale Hawkins, captures them at their best and includes their three main hits:- *I See The Light*, *Western Union* and *Sound Of Love*, along with covers of Steve Winwood's *Gimme Some Lovin*, Screaming Jay Hawkins, *I Put A Spell On You* and Roger Miller's *Husbands And Wives*. *Western Union* and *Sound Of Love* both received a fair degree of airplay in the U.K. where the former was covered by The Searchers, but neither charted.

Group members Jim Grant, John Durnill and Jimmy Wright, along with Bobby Rambo and Jim Glaves (from a group called The Crowd) were the backing musicians on the album *Elastic Event* (Abnak ABST-2070) 1967 by the Dallas pop-rock duo **Jon and Robin**. **The Five Americans** drummer went on to marry Javonne Braga aka "Robin" in the seventies after **Jon and Robin** and **The Five Americans** had broken up.

The Five Americans have also featured on a number of compilations. *Gimme Some Lovin'* featured on a radio station EP from 1967 or 1968, 'WLAV Memory Pack Vol.1', alongside *Cherish* by **The Association**, *Think Twice* by **The Pedestrians** and *Hey Joe* by **The Soulbenders**. More recently you'll find: - *I See The Light* on *Mayhem & Psychosis, Vol. 3* (LP), *Nuggets Box* (4-CD), *Nuggets* (CD), *Nuggets, Vol. 1* (LP), *Sound Of The Sixties* (Dble LP), *Sixties Archive, Vol. 1* (CD) and *Sundazed Sampler, Vol. 2* (CD); *Western Union* on *More Nuggets* (CD), *Sundazed Sampler, Vol. 1* (CD); and *Slippin' And Slidin'* on *Pebbles, Vol. 10* (LP) and *Teenage Shutdown, Vol. 1* (LP & CD);

Jimmy Wright stayed with **Mike Rabon** in the seventies outfit, **Mike Rabon and Choctaw**.

The band also had three EPs issued in France:- *I See The Light* and three other tracks (Stateside Vogue 18087); *Western Union/Now That Its Over/If I Could/Reality* (Stateside 103) which appeared in a picture sleeve and *Sound Of Love + 3* (Stateside 1007). (VJ/MW/TTi/SR)

Five Bucks

45s:	No Use In Tryin' / Now You're Mine	(Afton 1701) 1966
	I'll Walk Alone / So Wrong	(Omnibus 1001) 1966

"Class of '66" at the University Of Michigan (UOM) in Ann Arbor. Students who'd been in bands in their hometowns of Waukesha, Wisconsin. and Glencoe, Illinois. joined forces at UOM, releasing two cool 45s that year. Both fetch considerably more than five bucks 37 years on.

No Use In Tryin' is on *Open Up Yer Door, Vol. 2* (LP) and *I'll Walk Alone*, featuring excellent fuzz and organ work, is on *Psychedelic Crown Jewels Vol. 3* (CD). (MW/MM)

Five By Five (5X5)

Personnel:	LARRY ANDREW	gtr, vcls	A
	DOUG GREEN	drms	A
	BILL MERRITT	gtr	A
	TIM MILAM	organ, vcls	A
	RONNIE PLANTS	ld vcls, gtr	A

ALBUM:	1(A)	NEXT EXIT	(Paula LPS 2202) 1968 SC

HCP
45s:	Shake A Tail Feather/Tell Me What To Do	(Paula 261) 1967 -
	Harlem Shuffle/	
	You Really Got A Hold On Me	(Paula 283) 1967 -
	Fire/Hang Up	(Paula 302) 1968 52
	Ain't Gonna Be Your Fool No More/	
	She Digs My Love	(Paula 311) 1968 -
	Apple Cider/Fruitstand Man	(Paula 319) 1970 133
	Ain't Gonna Be Your Fool No More/	
	Too Much Tomorrow	(Paula 322) 1970 -
	15 Going On 20/Penthouse Pauper	(Paula 326) 1970 -
	Good Connection/Never	(Paula 328) 1970 -

This garage band used lots of fuzz in many of their songs. The album is now a minor collectors' item and they also enjoyed a U.S. hit when *Fire* (which was written by **Jimi Hendrix**) climbed to No 52 in 1968. Produced by Gene Kent, *Next Exit* features various covers: *Hush* (**Joe South**), *She Digs My Move* (Doug Sahm), *Soul Man* (the Sam and Dave song), *Shake*

THE FIVE AMERICANS - I See The Light CD.

A Tail Feather, *Share Your Love*... Two songs were written by Eddie Hinton and Jimmy Johnson, who are both credited as arranger or engineer and would later take an active part in the famous Muscle Shoals Studios.

Nine of their singles tracks are non-album (*Tell Me What To Do*, *Harlem Shuffle*, *You Really Got A Hold On Me*, *Hang Up*, *Apple Cider*, *15 Going On 20*, *Penthouse Pauper*, *Good Connection* and *Never*).

The inclusion of *Apple Cider* on *Austin Landing, Vol. 2* (LP), suggests that they hailed from Texas, but *Turds On A Bum Ride, Vol. 5* (CD) also features the track, and claims they came from Louisiana... whilst the more reliable *Sixties Rebellion, Vol. 8* (LP & CD) includes their fine version of **Love**'s *7 And 7 Is* (from their album) and locates the band as Oklahoma... Mike Markesich has however since established that they were from Magnolia, Arkansas. *Apple Cider* by the way is a catchy punker with some great wavering male vocals, and neat keyboard motif.

Other compilation appearances have included: *Hang Up* on *Turds On A Bum Ride, Vol. 3* (CD) and *Bad Vibrations, Vol. 3* (LP); and *You Really Got A Hold On Me* and *Soul Man* on *Born On The Bayou* (LP). (MW/SR/VJ)

Five Canadians

Personnel:	BOBBY FLORES	bs	A
	BILL KAITNER	drms	A
	RAUL PINA	gtr	A
	LOUIE SIEDLECKI	ld gtr, vcls	A
	BRUCE SVOBODA	keyb'ds	A

45s:	α	I'm Gonna Love You / Goodnight	(Flo-Pin 101) 1966
	β	Writing On The Wall / Goodnight	(Domar 1120) 1966
	χ	House Of The Rising Sun / Never Alone	(Domar 1121) 1966
	δ	Don't Tell me / Writing On The Wall	(Domar 1123) 1967

NB: α as by **The Hangman**. β also released on Stone (701) in Canada 1966. χ also released on Stone (704) in Canada 1967. δ reissued on a limited edition Canadian 45 with a Pic Sleeve - (Leaf DOMAR CDN-1001) 1997.

Andrew Brown's *Brown Paper Sack #1* 'zine is to be commended for finally unravelling the myths and presenting the full and fascinating story of this group (amongst many others, so go grab a copy).

In brief, **The Hangmen** were a quintet from around San Antonio,Texas. Following their self-promoted debut on their own label (which misprinted their name as 'The Hangman'), they came to the attention of a local self-styled promoter 'Colonel' Paul Beckingham (as in Colonel Tom Parker or Major Bill Smith). He imposed a new name on them based on the logic that non-local groups were more exotic and got more air-play - along the same lines I guess as US bands adopting British names, even accents, in the wake of the British Invasion. So, the **Five Canadians** were born and the band were publicised as invaders from North of the border (Toronto).

No wonder there has been so much confusion and debate ever since. At the time the hype only achieved limited success and despite out-of-state forays the band would remain a local phenomenon. Bobby Flores moved on to **The Infinite Staircase** and later solo 45s. Bruce Svoboda released a psychedelic 45 as **Grapple** - *Ethereal Genesis/Snail* (Rush 1394) - in 1969.

Despite the confusion and doubts perpetuated as to their origins, what is not in doubt is the testosterone drive of their music whose climax is *Writing On The Wall*. It is rightfully regarded as a classic of the garage genre and no collection is complete without it. The article mentions that it impressed others at the time - it was covered by the XL's (from St.Louis). But it is with the *Pebbles* generation that appreciation has matured and this song has now been covered by the likes of Germany's Broken Jug on their *Grand Junction* EP, girl-garage queens the Brood, and the Nines.

Compilation appearances include: *Writing On The Wall* on *Pebbles, Vol. 5* (CD), *Pebbles Box* (5-LP), *Pebbles, Vol. 5* (LP), *Trash Box* (5-CD), *Great Pebbles* (CD) and *I Was A Teenage Caveman* (LP); *Never Alone* on *60's Punk E.P., Vol. 1* (7"), *Texas Flashbacks, Vol. 5* (LP), *Flashback, Vol. 5* (LP); and both *Don't Tell Me* and *Goodnight* on *Sixties Rebellion Vol's 1 & 2* (CD) and *Sixties Rebellion, Vol. 1* (LP). (AB/MW)

The 5c Stamp

45: Gotta' Go Now / Jesse Jane   (Prestige Productions PP68-271) 1968

This group have been tracked down to the small town of Eastaboga in Alabama. The Crow-Holmes composed *Gotta' Go Now* has been unearthed for *Psychedelic States: Alabama Vol. 1* (CD). (MW)

The Five Empressions / The Five Emprees

Personnel:
TONY CATANIA	ld gtr	A
DON COOK	ld vcls	A
MIKE DE ROSE	drms	A
RON PELKEY	ld gtr	A
BILL SCHUENEMAN	keyb'ds, bs	A

ALBUMS: 1(A) THE FIVE EMPREES   (Freeport FRS-3001) 1965
2(A) LITTLE MISS SAD   (Freeport FRS-4001) 1966

NB: (1) and (2) are the same album, with different covers.

                                                                                       HCP
45s: Little Miss Sad/Nobody Cares   (Gold Standard 262) 196? -
Little Miss Sad/Hey Lover   (Freeport 1001) 1965 74
Hey Baby/Why   (Freeport 1002) 1965 -
Little Miss Happiness/
OverThe Mountain   (Freeport 1007) 1966 -
Johnny B. Goode/Hey Lover   (Freeport 1010) 1966 -
Shake/I'm In Love   (GMA 9859) 196? -
Hey Diddle Diddle/Gone From My Mind   (Smash 2065) 1966 -

From Benton Harbor, Michigan this act were picked up by Freeport records in Northern Illinois and had a minor hit with *Little Miss Sad*. More commonly known as **The Five Emprees**, they had quite a prolific output and both their albums are now minor collectables.

Founder member Ron Pelkey recalls: "We had been known as the Impressions for a few years, not knowing there was another group by that name. When we released our first record as **The Five Empressions** , The Impressions filed an injunction against us and our record company changed our name to **The Five Emprees** without consulting us. We did not like the sound of *Little Miss Sad*, but it turned out to be #2 on WLS in Chicago behind *Yesterday* by the Beatles. Making *Hey Lover* the flip side was a mistake, however, as it was probably the best recording we ever made and would have been a good follow-up."

The band recorded *Little Miss Sad*, which was given to them by their DJ-Manager Bob Richards, plus several other songs at Universal Studios in Chicago. It was written by Dick and Don Addressi, who also wrote several songs for **The Association** and the track looked like it might break nationally, Bob:- "But there were promotional blunders as well. Irv Garmissa

A JOURNEY TO TYME Vol. 4 (Comp LP) including The Five Emprees.

(our Agent and Freeport label owner) did not spend $2000 to have the song promoted nationally as he thought that it was going to be #1 in Chicago and then would take off on its own. If he had spent the money it would have gotten the song played in all markets, but as it was, #76 on Billboard was as far up the charts as I ever saw it."

"We all had a great time playing tho'. We performed with some big names including The Animals, **The Outsiders**, Neil Diamond, The Vogues, Bobby Vee, **The Lovin' Spoonful**, **Paul Revere and the Raiders** and most of the other big names of the day. If fame had come later we would have known better what to do with it. As it was, we were not ready to climb the ladder."

Don Cook and Bill Schueneman later married Ron Pelkey's sisters, making three-fifths of the band brother-in-law's! It is consequently easy for the group to stay in touch and with the exception of Mike De Rose, they still perform today at the occasional benefit gig and all are accomplished musicians. Don Cook and Tony Catania still live in Benton Harbor, Michigan, Bill Schueneman in Woodstock, Georgia, Mike DeRose in Santa Barbara, Calif., and Ron Pelkey in Alpharetta, Georgia.

Little Miss Sad can also be found on *A Journey To Tyme, Vol. 4* (LP). (MW)

Five Hungry Men

45: Bustin' Rocks/We Belong Together   (Melmar 122) 1967

This outfit came from Andalusia, Pennsylvania, but their sole 45 isn't very memorable. You'll find the 'A' side on *Pebbles, Vol. 13* (LP), *Vile Vinyl* (CD) and *Vile Vinyl, Vol. 2* (LP), though the latter compilation erroneously lists it as being the 'B' side. (MW)

Five More

45: Avalanche/I'm No Good   (Tandy 205) 196?

A mid-sixties garage punk outfit from Tucson, Arizona.

Compilation appearances have included: *I'm No Good* on *Garage Punk Unknowns, Vol. 2* (LP); and *Avalanche* on *Garage Punk Unknowns, Vol. 6* (LP). (VJ)

Five of a Kind

45: Never Again/
I Don't Want To Find Another Girl   (Vandan no #) 1965

The 45 was this Fort Worth ouffit's sole stab for stardom. The 'A' side, *Never Again* is a folk-punk anthem.

Compilation appearances include: *I Don't Want To Find Another Girl* on *Love Is A Sad Song, Vol. 1* (LP); and *Never Again* on *Highs In The Mid-Sixties, Vol. 11* (LP). (VJ)

Five of Us

Personnel incl:	PAUL CANELLA	A
	GEORGE 'TAGO' MARYVILLE	A
	ALEX VALDEZ	A

45:	α	Why Oh Why/Pretty Baby	(Keeson 125) 1965
		Hey You/I Don't Believe	(Platt) 1966
		Hey You/Need Me Like I Need You	(Current 110) 1966

NB: α With Tommy Gardner.

Previously known as The Impressions and The Temptations, they were one of Maryville's Tucson sixties outfits. *Hey You* was a cover of **The Guilloteens** track. Prior to this band Maryville was with The Showmen and when they spit he joined The Poppies, but they did not record. His final outfit was Whatever's Left. The band also recorded a 1966 acetate: *Let Me Explain / I Lied*.

Canella and Valdez would later work with **The Yellow Balloon**.

Compilation appearances have included: *Hey You* on *Boulders, Vol. 8* (LP) and *Ya Gotta Have Moxie, Vol. 2* (Dble CD); *Need Me Like I Need You* and *Let Me Explain* on *The Tucson Sound 1960-1968* (LP). (VJ/MW)

The Five # Grin

Personnel:	DAVE DORAN	vcls, gtr	A
	WILLIE KELLOGG	drms	A
	MIKE LAWSON	vcls, gtr	A
	MALCOLM McCASSY	vcls, bs	A

Pronounced "The Five Pound Grin", this short-lived San Diego band also went by the name The Survivors, and recorded a demo at White Whale Studios in Santa Ana in 1968. One of the tracks they laid down, *Never Hurt Again* resurfaced on *Brain Shadows, Vol. 2* (LP & CD). At least five songs were recorded at this session, which were cut to acetate and shopped to local Los Angeles record labels.

While *Never Hurt Again* may be the best of the surviving cuts, it is only marginally so. **The Five # Grin** boasted finely-crafted layered vocals that bear more than a passing resemblance to **Moby Grape**, as well as Doran's jaw-dropping guitar leads. In retrospect, it seems quite astonishing that they weren't picked up by a major label on the strength of this recording, despite its lack of polish.

Four tracks from this demo were re-worked a few weeks later by the same line-up, and this time they were issued as two singles credited to **Pale Fire**. By 1970, the band included Kathy "K.T." Taylor on vocals and were known as Pride and Joy.

Dave Doran had previously led several line-ups of the popular San Diego band The Voxmen. Willie Kellogg was a member of **Joel Scott Hill**'s bands, as well as **The Time Machine**. Lawson was later a member of The Docker Hill Boys, who recorded an album for Columbia Records in 1973 which remains unissued. (CF)

Sonny Flaharty and The Mark V

Personnel:	SUSAN DARBY	vcls	A
	JOHN HOLLINGER ("JASON STARBUCK III")	gtr	ABCD
	MIKE LOSENCAMP ("MIKE LOVELACE")	piano, organ	ABC
	N.D. SMART ("SEBASTIAN SMART")	drms	AB
	JIM WYATT ("FARNSWORTH WYATT")	bs	ABCD
	SONNY FLAHARTY ("PAUL WESLEY WELLINGTON")	vcls	BCD
	DOUG PORTER	drms	CD
	SKIP SHAMAN	organ	D

ALBUM: 1 SONNY FLAHARTY AND THE MARK FIVE
(Bacchus Archives BA 1151) 2001

NB: (1) issued on vinyl and CD.

45s:	α	Can't Buy My Soul / When I Close My Eyes	(Warner Bros. 7009) 1967
		Hey Conductor/ You Bring These Tears To Me	(Counterpart 2591/2) 1967
		Hey Conductor/ You Bring These Tears To Me	(Philips 40479) 1967

NB: α as by Marque V.

From Dayton, Ohio, in the late sixties and early seventies **Sonny Flaharty** released several 45s on local labels in the era. He started out playing rockabilly and continued rockin' for several years. His groups included The Sonny Flaharty Application, the Young Americans, the Mark V and later the Grey Imprint.

The Mark V were originally a Dayton, Ohio act known as The Rich Kids, fronted by a beautiful vocalist Susan Darby. They'd already changed their name to The Mark V when Darby got a solo contract with ABC and departed. They teamed with the city's respected rocker **Sonny Flaharty** but initally did not want to be associated with "old time rock and roll" so they adopted Anglo/Canadian sounding pseudonyms: - Flaharty became Paul Wesley Wellington, Mike Losencamp became Mike Lovelace, John Hollinger - Jason Starbuck III whilst Smart and Wyatt just changed their christian names to Sebastian and Farnsworth respectively.

N.D. Smart (whose father managed the band) was an in-demand drummer and was making frequent trips to New York; Doug Porter who'd played with **Flaharty** in the Young Americans would sit in for him. N.D. Smart eventually left the group (we encounter him next in **The Remains**) and Porter joined permanently. Around this time Losecamp departed for **The Cyrkle** and was replaced by Skip Shaman.

Hey Conductor, which was written by **Sonny Flaharty**, showcases his vocal talents and features some good organ work. The track was recorded in 1966 at Sambo Studios in Louisville, Kentucky, but shelved for nine months by Counterpart. Douglas Porter: "We were approached by Carl Maduri of Warner Brothers to record, but since we had signed a 'deal' with Shad O'Shay of Counterpart, we had to use the name 'Marque V' on our Warner Bros. release: *Can't Buy My Soul/When I Close My Eyes*"

Sonny Flaharty: "Nothing happened with those and Counterpart Records of Cincinnati, Ohio released *Hey Conductor*. We had picks in every major trade mag and were picked up by Phillips. In the first week we had a regional breakout, but then the record was banned for 'the most flagrant psychedelic lyric ever written...', and we lost it all in the U.S., England and most of Europe."

"I left the group and, with the Application (real band name Sonny Flaharty and Outrage) worked the circuit New York, Chicago, Dallas, L.A., San Francisco and all points in between. After a few months home I picked up an eleven piece horn band in the early seventies that was Sonny Flaharty and the Grey Imprint. We re-recorded *Hey Conductor* for Counterpart / Fraternity but the label lost its nerve before the release (while we were on the road) and added a train horn to the start, hoping to make someone think the song was about trains I guess. Anyhow it crashed and burned abruptly."

In 2001, Dionysus/Bacchus Archives released a retrospective of the band from 1963 to 1967 - a lively selection that encompasses rock'n'roll, frat, beat and fuzzed-out garage-rock. It includes a few Young Americans songs including the *Coconut Stomp I/II* 45, the Marque V 45, Mark V's *Hey Conductor*, and several unreleased originals recorded around that time.

You can also find *Hey Conductor* on *The Essential Pebbles Collection, Vol. 2* (Dble CD) and *Pebbles, Vol. 14* (LP).

Some of his other 45s are listed below:-

Sonny Flaharty and The Young Americans:
45:    Coconut Stomp I/II   (PAQ 21) 1963

Sonny Flaharty Application:
45s: The Marble Orchard/Reflections   (Philips 40532) 1968
    I'm Not The Man /
    Brave Little Boy   (Counterpart C-2651/2) 1969
    Ma Belle Made/Wrong Side Of The Road   (Fraternity 3366) 19?
  α Odyssey / Husbands Of Young Wives   (Counterpart 2654) 1969

NB: α is said to be a very strange 45, with MOR vocal, psych guitars and lyrics.

45s: Heartbreak Station / Don't Talk About Love   (Epic 9394) 1960
    Mystery Of Love / Teenage War Chain   (Huron 22004) c1961

Grey Imprint:
45:    Hey Conductor (Diff Vers.) /
    It's Over   (Counterpart 3748) 197?

(VJ/MW/MC/MDo/SF/DPr)

The Flamin' Groovies

Personnel:
GEORGE ALEXANDER	bs		A
CYRIL JORDAN	gtr, vcls		A
ROY LONEY	vcls, gtr		A
TIM LYNCH	gtr		A
DANNY MIHM	drms		A

ALBUM: 1(A) SNEAKERS   (Snazz R-2371) 1968 R1/R2

Rare first 10" album by this well-known San Francisco rock and roll group, *Sneakers* is more of a psych-pop/blues effort and due to its great tracks (like *Golden Clouds*) and its rarity, it should be included in this book. (CF)

Tommy Flanders

Personnel:
MICHAEL BOTTS		A
TOMMY FLANDERS	vcls	A
BRUCE LANGHORN		A
DENNIS McCARTHY		A
DICK ROSMINI	gtr	A
JERRY SCHEFF	bs	A

ALBUM: 1(A) MOONSTONE   (Verve Forecast KF 5076) 1969 -

NB: (1) catalogue number may be erroneous.

45s: Friday Night City/Reputation   (Verve 5064) 1967

THE FLAMIN' GROOVIES - Sneakers 10" LP.

    The Moonstone/
    Between Purple and Blue (PS)   (Verve Forecast FTS-3075) 1968
    Between Purple And Blue/
    First Time, Last Time   (MGM 14143) 1970

Musically, this solo project by **Blues Project** member **Tommy Flanders** is similar to **Tim Buckley**'s early albums. It's best tracks *The Moonstone*, *Blue Water Blue*, *Boston Girls*, and *Sleepin'* are melancholic folk with excellent vocals and jazz / West Coast influences. (SR/EW)

Flash and The Casuals/Flash and The Board Of Directors

Personnel:
CHARLES FIENBERG	vcls	A
DAVID FLEISHMAN	vcls	AB
BUDDY FOWLER	gtr	A
DAVID FRIENER	gtr	AB
GARY HOFFMAN	bs	A
JOHN McNULTY	drms	A
TERRY PAHN	vcls	A
TED GARRETSON	trumpet	B
STEVE HOLT	drms	B
MIKE STOKER	bs	B
MARK TIDWELL	gtr	B
NEWELL TUGGLE	sax	B

NB: Line-up 'A': Flash and The Casuals. 'B': Flash and The Board Of Directors.

45s:
α	Bridget / I Promise To Remember	(Block 1001)	1963
α	Midnight Hour / Uptight, Tonight	(Block Records 485)	1964
α	Bridget / Say You Love Me	(Block 1010)	1965
β	I Pray For Rain /		
	When The Love Light Is Shinin'	(Mala 586)	1968
β	Busy Signal / Love Ain't Easy	(Mala 594)	1968
β	Goodbye Debra Lewis / A World Of Hurt	(Mala 12028)	1968

NB: α as Flash and The Casuals. β as Flash and The Board Of Directors.

A Memphis group playing wild rock with loud guitars and lots of crash cymbal. Mike Stoker had been in **(Tommy Burk and) The Counts** and Mark Tidwell was from **Joe Frank and The Knights**. *Uptight Tonight* was written by **Jim Dickinson** (**Jesters**, **Avengers**) and has been compiled on *It Came From Memphis* (Upstart 022) 1995 and *A History Of Garage & Frat Bands In Memphis* (CD).

As Flash and The Board Of Directors, David Fleishman would later record some regional white soul/pop hits under the guidance of Chips Moman.

You can read their full story in Ron Hall's book on the Memphis scene (1960-1975) - 'Playing For A Piece Of The Door' (Shangri-La Projects, ISBN 0-9668575-1-8) 2001. (SR/BM/MW)

Flat Earth Society

Personnel:
PAUL CARTER	bs, vcls	A
RICK DOYLE	ld gtr, vcls	A
PHIL DUBUQUE	gtr, vcls, recorder	A
CURT GIRARD	drms	A
JACK KERIVAN	keyb'ds, vcls	A

ALBUM: 1(A) WALEECO   (Fleetwood FCLP 3027) 1968 R3

NB: (1) reissued on CD together with The Lost Kids *Space Kids* on Arf! Arf! (AA 042-2). The latter being a sci-fi audio fairy tale with incidental music. Also earlier reissued as a separate CD and on vinyl (Psycho 17) 1983. Later counterfeited on vinyl 2001.

From Lynn, just North of Boston, **Flat Earth Society** were notable for their crispy, clear vocal sound. In early 1968 they were approached by the Boston advertising firm Quinn and Johnson to make an album and a jingle for the manufacturer of the 'Waleeco' candy bar - the F. B. Washburn Candy Company. That year every 'Waleeco' bar carried a coupon advertising the **Flat Earth's Society**'s album *Waleeco* for $1.50 and six 'Waleeco' bar wrappers.

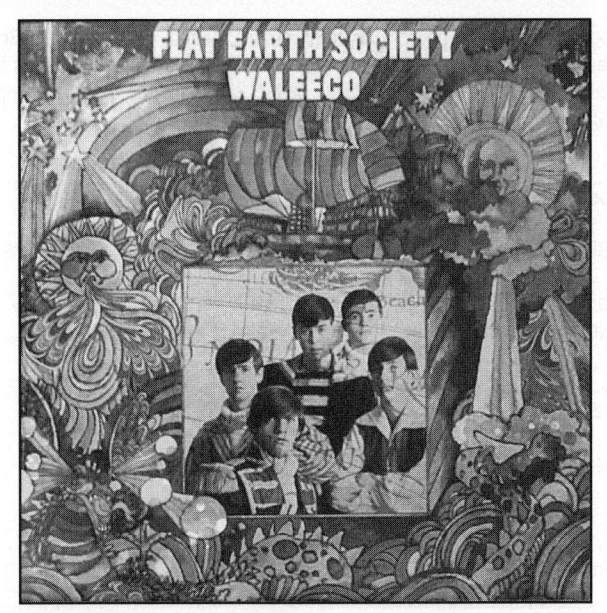

FLAT EARTH SOCIETY - Waleeco LP.

Recorded at Fleetwood Recording Studio in Revere, most of the material was written by Kerivan, the only non-original being a slow melodic version of *Midnight Hour*. The album covers quite a wide rock spectrum with goodtime (*I'm So Happy*), folk (*When You're There* and *The Prelude For Town Monk*), hard-rock (*Four & Twenty Miles* and *Shadows*), as well as psychedelia, but each track has the band's own style about it. Aside from *Feelin' Much Better*, the best tracks are arguably on the second side of the album. *Dark Street Downtown* has some haunting vocals superimposed upon swirling piano. *Portrait In Grey* is a haunting piano-oriented instrumental and *Satori*, a very strange psychedelic instrumental. The reissue is worth purchasing, although it's probably imprudent to fork out for the original should you come across a copy.

The band made a few appearances after making the album but broke up soon after.

In 1974, Fleetwood disposed of the remaining boxes of the album into the dumpster but luckily the mastertapes survived to be revived by Arf! Arf! who reissued the album in 1993 on CD in the original stereo mix (the vinyl originals had been mixed down to mono).

Paul Carter was active in the Boston music scene until the late eighties, Phil Dubuque later moved to England for a while but is now back in Boston, and Jack Kerivan became senior director of professional services at NEC. One member was also later in Copperfield.

Compilation appearances have so far included: *Feelin' Much Better* on *Psychedelic Crown Jewels, Vol. 1* (Dble LP & CD), *Endless Journey - Phase Two* (LP) and *Endless Journey - Phase I & II* (Dble CD); and *Four and Twenty Miles* on *The Arf! Arf! Blitzkrieg 32 Track Sampler* (Dble CD). (VJ/MW/LP)

Flavor

Personnel:	DEMETRI CALLAS	gtr	A
	DANNY CONWAY	drms	A
	GARY ST.CLAIR	bs, gtr	A

45s:	Sally Had A Party / Shop Around	(Columbia 4-44521) 1968
	Hearteaser / Yea I'm Hip	(Columbia 4-44673) 1968
	Coming On Home / Dancing In the Streets	(Columbia 4-44881) 1969

From around the Frederick, Maryland and Washington DC area, this trio originally came together behind Billy Joe Ash, and were known collectively as Billy Joe & The Continentals. When they parted company with their front-man in mid-65 they carried on as a trio under the name **The Bad Boys**, releasing one classy garage-punk 45 on Paula. Their named was changed again to **Flavor** after gaining a contract with Columbia, but an expected album never materialized due to the lack of chart success with their three 45s. Tim O'Brien was their producer at Columbia, not a group member, as previously suggested. Gary St.Clair released an eponymous solo album on Paramount in 1972, with O'Brien as producer again. Recently the pair have also been producing and directing the group "All For One".

There was also an album by **Flavor** called *In Good Taste* (Ju-Par 6-1002) 1977, but this is probably a different outfit. (MW)

Floating Bridge

Personnel:	RICK DANGEL	ld gtr	A
	JOE JOHANSEN	ld gtr	A
	JOE JOHNSON	bs	A
	MICHAEL MARINELLI	drms	A
	PAT GOSSAN	keyb'ds	B

ALBUM: 1(A) FLOATING BRIDGE (Vault 124) 1969 R1

NB: (1) also issued in the UK (Liberty LBS 83271) 1969, also reissued on CD (Repertoire REP 4723-WY) 1998.

| 45s: | α | Brought Up Wrong/Watch Your Step | (Vault 947) 1968 |
| | | Don't Mean A Thing/Mr Jaybird | (Vault 953) 1969 |

NB: α also released on Japan on dark red translucent vinyl with a picture sleeve (Liberty/Toshiba LR-2589).

This Seattle outfit included Dangel from **The Wailers**, who'd also played in **The Time Machine** and **The Rooks** with Joe Johnson. Their album is guitar oriented and largely blues-based. It lacks consistency, but their medley of *Eight Miles High/Paint It Black* shows them at their most inventive. One of their best tracks, *Don't Mean A Thing*, only appears on the UK pressing, plus Liberty's compilation album *Son Of Gutbucket*. More recently the track has appeared on *Nuggets, Vol. 8* (LP).

The album features elongated versions of both tracks from the first 45.

Johansen later went on to play with Little Bill and the Blue Notes. (VJ/TWg/SR/TJH/MW/CF)

The Floating House Band

Personnel:	KIT ALDERSON	vcls, autoharp, keyb'ds, gtr	A
	SHEP COOKE	vcls, bs, ld gtr	A
	BOBBY KIMMEL	vcls, gtr	A
	(PAT CLOUD	banjo	A)
	(RICK EPPING	hrmnca	A)
	(ANDY GOLD	drms	A)
	(DENNIS WOOD	perc	A

ALBUM: 1(A) THE FLOATING HOUSE BAND LP (Takoma Records c1029) 1971 SC

Released on **John Fahey**'s label, this Californian group was formed by Bobby Kimmel (ex-**Stone Poneys**) and **Shep Cooke** (**Dearly Beloved**). Their very quiet and relaxed album, mostly acoustic, illustrates the "back to the country" movement. One track is aptly titled *Shep's Goin To The Country* and the lyrics contain references to **Mark LeVine**, one of the first musicians to be concerned with this topic. Kimmel and **Cooke** wrote all the material, except covers of Paul Siebel's *Any Day Woman* and Wendy Waldman's *Livin' Like There's No Tomorrow*. Housed in a fine black and white sleeve conceived by Cooke, the record was recorded in Hollywood, produced by the band and Chuck Plotkin. Jim Hobson (**Morning**)) engineered some tracks. (SR)

The Floating Opera

Personnel:	ARTIE ALINIKOFF	drms	A
	CAROL LEES	keyb'ds	A
	GARY MUNCE	bs	A
	JOHN NEMEROVSKI	piano	A
	STEVE WELKOM	gtr	A

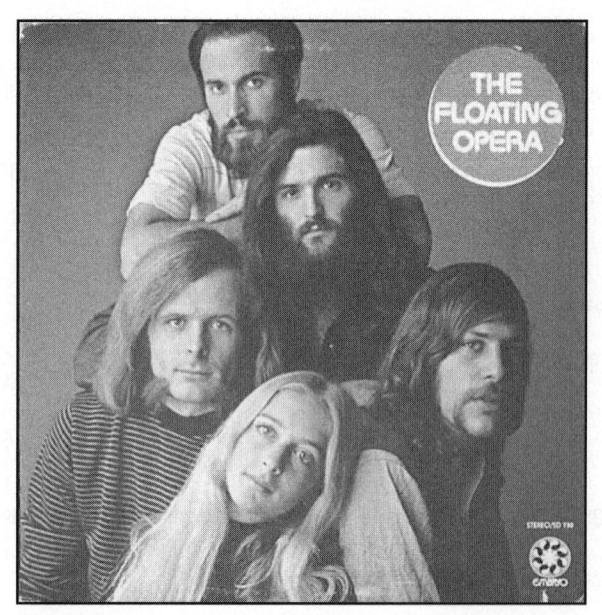

THE FLOATING OPEAR - The Floating Opera LP.

ALBUM: 1(A) THE FLOATING OPERA (Embryo SD 730) 1971 -

45: The Vision / Song Of The Suicides (Embryo 511) 197?

A hit and miss progressive album surprisingly produced by soulster **Herbie Mann**. The best track is the opener, *Song Of The Suicides*, which features some great guitar work sadly lacking elsewhere on the album, which is mostly rather ordinary. The sleeve-notes give a brief biography of the members who formed the band in Ann Arbor, Michigan. (VJ)

The Flock

Personnel incl:	RICK CANOFF	sax	A
	JERRY GOODMAN	violin	A
	RON KARPMAN	drms	A
	FRED GLICKSTEIN	gtr	A
	JERRY SMITH	bs, vcls	A

HCP
ALBUMS: 1(A)	THE FLOCK	(Columbia 9911) 1969	48 -
(up to 2(A)	DINOSAUR SWAMPS	(Columbia 30007) 1971	96 -
1971)			

NB: (1) and (2) also released in France (CBS 63733) and the U.K. (CBS S 64055). Both album were reissued as *Flock* in Holland (CBS 67278) 1972.

An ambitious mix of jazz, blues, prog and rock, with horns and the electric violin of Jerry Goodman, who would later join Mahavishnu Orchestra. They benefited from an intense promotion from CBS who tried to launch them with Blood, Sweat & Tears, **Aorta** and Chicago. Their records may sound dated now, but they sold quite well at the time and both albums made the Top 100.

Big Bird was compiled on the CBS sampler *Different Strokes* in 1971 and you can also find *Magical Wings* on *Early Chicago* (LP).

Flock reformed with a new line-up in 1975 and finally disappeared after an awful album (*Inside Out*, Mercury). (SR)

Flood

Personnel:	GEORGE CABANTING	gtr	A
	BILLY CARROLL	drms, congas	A
	FRED COVINO	bs, gtr	A
	JOHN T. MAGAZINO	vcls, conga, tamb	A

ALBUM: 1(A) THE RISE OF FLOOD (Maple # unknown) 1970 R2/R3

NB: (1) reissued as a limited edition in 1996 with no label name, also reissued on CD (Flash 64) 1998.

Long-lost seventies psych-rock from an act based in New York. Some bluesy workouts with a funky feel on occasion and rock'n'riffy numbers with great moments of intense fuzz guitar soloing, but really rather a disappointment. (VJ)

Floss

ALBUM: 1 CRUISIN (SilverCrest) 1976 R3

A rare (and late) garage-psych group covering classics. Reputedly only 100 copies were made and therefore it's now really expensive. (SR)

The Flow

Personnel:	MONTE FARBER	bs, vcls	A
	PETE FINE	gtr, vcls, synth	A
	STEVE STARER	drms	A

| ALBUMS: 1(A) | THE FLOW'S GREATEST HITS | (No label) 1972 | R5 |
| 2(A) | THE FLOW'S GREATEST HITS | (No label) 197? | R6 |

NB: (1) one-sided album limited to 100 copies. (2) two-sided version, although this was issued in the sleeve for the one-sided album and therfore only lists the songs for Side One, again only 100 copies were pressed. The 13-track version was later counterfeited in Europe on vinyl and CD as *The Flow*. (1) later reissued officially as *The Flow's Greatest Hits* (SHADOKS LP 005) 2001, in a numbered limited edition (450) of the full 13-track LP with a bonus 45 - *Things We Said Today / Bagdad Express* and poster.

From New York, this trio was responsible for one (and a half) of the most sought-after private pressings of the early seventies. The music of **The Flow** is intensely heavy but still indebted to melody. The songs are full of ideas and largely avoid the pitfalls of the usual blues-based/trio format. *It Swallowed The Sun* is about the heaviest blast of rock ever to open a record, but ten minutes later the band is gently breathing through *Meditations* and then into Bach's *Toccata In D Minor*. **The Flow** were only three, but there are no weak points to be found in their musical integrity. The original album cover is pretty mindblowing as well. About the only fault to be mentioned is the recording quality - it sounds like the music was recorded live in a big room and the vocals overdubbed later. It's not a disaster by any means, though - and the Shadoks reissue (which has considerably better sound than the bootlegs) is recommended.

Pete Fine obviously used **Flow** as a catalyst for ideas, and themes from this period turned up in all the recordings he made throughout the seventies. **The Flow** disbanded when he relocated to Arizona. He put together a new and entirely different kind of band there, and in 1974 made a solo album that holds a similarly mind-blowing status among record collectors.

Monte Farber went on to become an author. (VJ/CF/MW)

The Flower Children

| 45s: | Mini-Skirt Blues/Marching Lovers | (Castil 101) 1968 |
| | Mini-Skirt Blues/Marching Lovers | (Allied 101) 1968 |

A Los Angeles band who came up with the raunchy garage R&B style offering *Mini-Skirt Blues* in early 1968, which has an effective drum and organ intro.

Compilation appearances include: *I Can Feel It* on *The Essential Pebbles Collection, Vol. 2* (Dble CD); and *Mini-Skirt Blues* on *Highs In The Mid-Sixties Vol. 3* (LP). (VJ)

Flower of Purple

| Personnel incl?: | DOROTHY ANDREW | A |
| | RICH CLARK | A |

45: Luv's So Free/
     Luv's So Free (instr.) (RC Enterprise M650) 1967

A snaking lead underpins this mid-tempo West Coast rocker with male-female vocals by an obscure L.A. area outfit. (MW)

The Flower Pot

Personnel: MIKE DEASY   A

45s: Mr Zig Zag Man/Black Mojo   (Vault 935) 1967
      Wanting Ain't Gettin'/Gentle People   (Vault 937) 1967

This was **Deasy** operating under a pseudonym in L.A. Freaky harmony flower-pop is the groove here - with the sitar-infused *Black Mojo* being the choice cut on the first 45. *Wantin' Ain't Gettin'* is catchy stoned sitar-pop that the **Association** covered on their *Insight Out* album. Mike's other projects included **Ceyleib People**, Your Gang, **Friar Tuck**. (VJ/MW)

The Flower Power

Personnel incl: SANDI CRAIG
                 CRAIG FERGUSON
                 JOE ROLISON

45s: You Make Me Fly/Sunshine Day   (Tune-Kel 608) 1968
     α Mississippi Delta/Bye Bye Baby   (Tune-Kel 611) 1968
        Trivialities/Mt. Olympus   (Tune-Kel 612) 1968
        Don't Burn My Wings/
        Sailing Around The Sun   (Tune-Kel 613) 1969
        Stop! Check It/Orange Skies   (Tune-Kel 614) 1969

NB: α released as by **Sandi Craig & the Flower Power**.

This lot sound every bit like a San Francisco outfit but were actually from Gulfport, Mississippi. After a mellow debut 45, their second 45, released as **Sandi Craig & The Flower Power** features a decent bluesy cover of Bobby Gentry's *Mississippi Delta* with strong vocals and some searing guitar bursts.

The flip to their third 45, *Mt. Olympus*, is a smouldering slice of psych that erupts at the end with unrestrained manic feedback. In contrast, their final 45 features a laid back, almost lounge-styled, rendition of **Love**'s *Orange Skies*.

Sandi later had some success as a country singer, appearing on a Tennessee Ernie Ford TV special filmed in the USSR, of all places. By then, she was performing under a different last name.

Compilation appearances have included: *You Make Me Fly* on *Psychedelic Experience* (CD), *The Psychedelic Experience, Vol. 1* (LP) and *Garagelands, Vol. 2* (LP); *You Make Me Fly* and *Sunshine Day* on *Acid Dreams, Vol. 3* (LP); *Sunshine Day* on *Psychedelic Archives, Vol. 6*; *Orange Skies* on *Sixties Rebellion, Vol. 8* (LP & CD); *Trivialities* on *Brain Shadows, Vol. 2* (LP & CD); and *Mt. Olympus* on *Beyond The Calico Wall* (LP & CD). (VJ/MW/CRe)

Flower Power

Personnel incl: MICHAEL MELBY   gtr, vcls   AB
                 LARRY PEARL   bs, vcls, hrmnca   AB
                 STEVE PUGLIESIE keyb'ds, gtr, vcls   AB
                 JOHNNY SHERMAN   drms   A
                 JOHN COX   drms   B

45: I Can Feel It / Stop   (Tener T1010) 1967

Formed in early 1967 in Brevard County, Florida, this quartet blossomed briefly with one superb fuzz-punkadelic 45, and an otherwise unavailable cover of the Hollies' *Hard Year* on the rare double-album *Bee Jay Demo Vol. II* (Tener 1014). Cox replaced Sherman in late '67. The band went into limbo shortly after, when Larry Pearl moved to Houston to take up a post with NASA. He quickly discovered a vibrant scene there and encouraged the other three to join him ... and so they did, on January 2nd 1968, for a gig at the University Of Houston. This secondary flowering lasted only until July, when the gigs started to dry up.

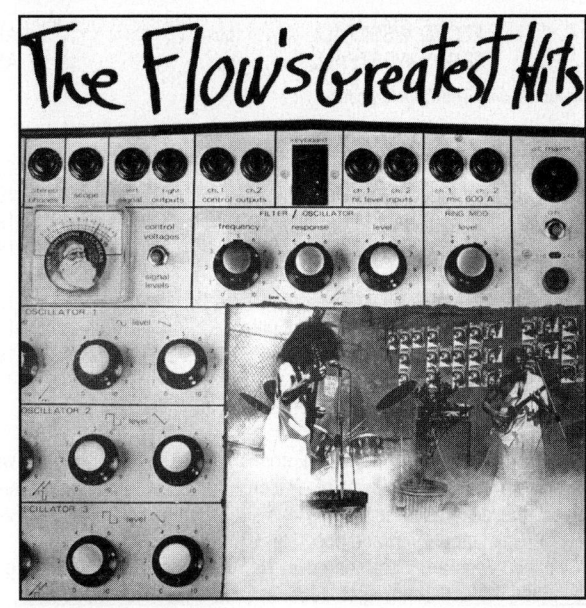

THE FLOW - Greatest Hits LP.

I Can Feel It is one of the highlights on *A Lethal Dose Of Hard Psych* (CD) and *Psychedelic States: Florida Vol. 1*, whose liners tell the group's full story. (MW/RM)

Flowers, Fruits and Pretty Things

45: Take Me Away/Wanting You   (G E P 101) 1968

Not the usual heavy psych associated with late sixties Michigan obscurities, this Saginaw outfit turn out two delicate garage ballads full of weeping guitars and yearning vocals. If this is your bag, check out *Wanting You* on *Incredible Sound Show Stories, Vol. 8* (LP) or *Take Me Away* on *Fuzz, Flaykes, And Shakes, Vol. 2* (LP & CD). (MW)

Flowerz

Personnel: MIKE LEECE   ld gtr   A
            JIM LEINBACH   drms   A
            BILL SHEFFER   keyb'ds   A
            LARRY SKILLMAN   bs gtr   A
            JEFF STOUT   vcls   A
            BARRY TUCCI   gtr   A

CD: 1(A) FLYTE   (Arf! Arf! AA-071) 1998

45s: I Need Love Now/My Sad Story   (Kingston 1967) 196?
      Flyte/Talken About Love   (Kingston 19683/19684) 196?

From Reading, Pennsylvania. Previously known as the Marauders, they became the **Flowerz** when Stout was added and Tucci replaced Danny Bausher. Now you can read their whole story and enjoy their sounds on Erik Lindgren's CD - issued as part of a quartet on the region, with **Pat Farrell & The Believers** and two volumes of *Eastern Pa. Rock* making up the set. This CD features twenty-two tracks recorded especially by the band as a 'backing soundtrack' over which they would play or sync at a live performance in Reading on February 16th 1968.

Compilation appearances have included: *I Need Love Now* on *Pennsylvania Unknowns* (LP); *Flyte* and *Talkin' About Love* on *Return Of The Young Pennsylvanians* (LP) and *Gathering Of The Tribe* (CD); and *Flyte, I Need Love Now, My Sad Story* and *Talkin' About Love* on *Eastern Pa Rock Part Two (1966-'69)* (CD). (VJ/MW)

Floyd and Jerry

Personnel: GRIER COOK   gtr   A
            JOHNNY GUTHRIE   drms   A
            KEN MULHOLLAND   organ   A

FLOYD WESTFALL	gtr		AB
JERRY WESTFALL	bs		AB

NB: Line-up 'A' with The Counterpoints.

45s:			
	Believe In Things/Girl	(Presta 1003)	1966
	Summer Kisses/Why Do You	(Presta 1006)	1966
	Dusty/If You Want Me	(Presta 1013)	1966
	Love Me Girl/This Ol' Wreck	(Double Shot 114)	1967
	Chik-A, Chik-A (I Think You're Lost)/ I'm Not Afraid	(Double Shot 124)	1967
α	Worst of Luck/Turn Out the Lights	(Presta 1020)	1968
β	It's So Easy/Northridge South	(Westfall 1002)	1981

NB: α Floyd Westfall solo. β as Floyd and Jerry Westfall.

Brothers **Floyd and Jerry** (Westfall), formerly of **The Door Nobs**, were huge stars in their hometown of Phoenix, Arizona. With their family harmonies, the act was essentially a mid-sixties mod update of the Everly Brothers. Their jangly garage-pop classic *Believe In Things* on the Phoenix-based Presta imprint soared to No. 1 on local Top 40 radio giant KRIZ's "Boss 50" chart in April 1966 but failed to click nationally. The flipside, *Girl*, was a holdover from the **Door Nobs**' repertoire that would be of equal interest to connoisseurs of Beatleseque garage. The cheery *Summer Kisses* was another regional smash in Summer '66 and *Dusty*, which was given the full-blown brass pop treatment, nearly broke big at the end of the year. **Floyd and Jerry** were signed to Double Shot and recorded *The Airplane Song* as their expected debut for the Los Angeles label. Their version was canned after **The Royal Guardsmen** released their take of the same song first. The Beatle-influenced *Love Me Girl* was released instead, followed by the minimalist proto-bubblegum of *Chik-A, Chik-A (I Think You're Lost)* at the end of the year. **Floyd and Jerry** wrote most of their own material, and also provided *Make Up Your Mind* for The Choice, another local Phoenix garage band. Their first two 45s were with The Counterpoints, and they were later backed at live shows by The Smyle. The duo even appeared in a zero-budget youth exploitation film titled 'Without Getting', which referred to the way that kids graduated from college "without getting" an education. An album was recorded but shelved after Jerry was drafted and the act went bust. Floyd Westfall released one solo single with little success. By the early 1980s, **Floyd and Jerry** were working the Phoenix-Scottsdale lounge circuit and released a "comeback" single on their own label. The group may be too pop for fuzz-punk extremists, but any of their finely crafted sixties singles would appeal to those listeners who appreciate the catchier, harmonic side of the garage experience. Think Beatles, Everlys and **Monkees**, not **Association**. (DN)

Fluff

| ALBUM: | 1 | FLUFF | (Roulette SR 3011) | 1971 - |

An average rock group, with nice harmonies, whose only album came in a superb psychedelic cover. (SR)

FLYING KARPET - Flying Karpet LP.

Fly-Bi-Nites

Personnel:	DOUG FREEDMAN	drms	ABC
	BOBBY LEVINSON	gtr	ABC
	GREG PRESMANES	vcls	ABC
	BOB WADE	ld gtr	ABC
	?? ??	bs	AB
	STEVE SHERWOOD	keyb'ds	BC
	TOMMY DEANE	bs	C

| 45: | Come On Up/Found Love | (Tiffany 564) 1967 |

Greg Presmanes formed his first high school band The Echoes in Atlanta, Georgia. Drummer Doug Freedman was the other stable member; others came and went until Presmanes secured the services of his cousin Bob Levinson, who renamed the group **The Fly By Nights**.

They recorded their sole 45 in the Summer of 1967. Just 300 copies were pressed with the band's name spelt "Fly-Bi-Nites". The top side is a fine cover of **The Young Rascals**' *Come On Up*, with a danceable beat and great guitar break. The nugget here, however, is the fabulous original *Found Love*, a dramatic pop-punker with hypnotic keyboards, dynamic bursts of guitar and dreamy vocals.

Presmanes recounts the band's story in *Psychedelic States: Georgia Vol. 1* liner notes. He left them in the Spring of 1969; the band continued, changed their name to **The Solid Soul** and shifted into funky R&B territory. They released a 45 on the local Lovett label which was picked up by the Capitol subsidiary 123.

Compilation appearances have included: *Come On Up* on *Sixties Rebellion Vol's 1 & 2* (CD) and *Sixties Rebellion, Vol. 2* (LP); and *Found Love* on *Highs In The Mid Sixties, Vol. 8* (LP) and *Psychedelic States: Georgia Vol. 1* (CD). (VJ/MW/RM)

Flying Circus

Personnel incl:	BILL BERRY	vcls	A
	JOHN HAAPALA	bs	A
	KEVIN "KID" HAAPALA	gtr	A
	JIM GRANDJEAN	gtr	A
	DON PERKINS	drms	A
	BOB McFEE	gtr	

45s:	I'm Going/Midnight Highway	(MTA 117) 1967
	Green Eyes Green World/ Got To Learn To Love	(MTA 130) 1967
	Pony Rider/Bety June (PS)	(Rock Bottom WRS 670) 1970

Decent West Coast garagey sounds, from this Marin County, California outfit, who recorded at San Francisco's Golden State Recorders. Both sides of the second 45 feature good guitar work and were produced by the ubiquitous Hank Levine and Larry Goldberg (**Afterglow**, **Neighb'rood Childr'n**, **Other Half**). The third came in a beautiful picture sleeve.

Of their other tracks, *I'm Going* is more in a garage vein and *Got To Learn To Love* is catchy pop-beat.

Another 45, *Hayride/Early Morning* (GNP Crescendo 426) 1969, was by an Australian band of the same name, with a cover of a Barclay James Harvest tune.

Compilation appearances have included: *Green Eyes Green World* on *Psychedelic Unknowns, Vol. 9* (CD); *I'm Going* on *Sixties Rebellion, Vol's 1 & 2* (CD), *Sixties Rebellion, Vol. 1* (LP), *Brain Shadows, Vol. 1* (LP & CD); *Green Eyes Green World/I'm Going Midnight Highway* on *Crystalize Your Mind* (CD); *Bety June* on *Yee-Haw! The Other Side Of Country* (LP & CD). (MW/CF/SR)

The Flying Giraffe

| 45: | Bring Back Howdy Doody/Let's Get To Gettin' | (Bell 801) c1968 |

Another **Kasenetz and Katz** production, and of course another bubblegum pop group with a name as "nice" as the **Crazy Elephant**. (SR)

FOLKSWINGERS - Raga Rock LP.

Flying Karpet

Personnel:	CHRIS	bs	A
	FRANK	gtr	A
	PAUL	keyb'ds	A
	PEPE	drms	A
	TONY	vcls, hrmnca	A

ALBUM: 1(A) THE FLYING KARPET   (Mexico/Son-Art D 179) 1968 R4

NB: (1) reissued as a limited edition of 300 (Iguana 159) 1997. Also counterfeited on CD.

Housed in a great psychedelic cover, this album consists largely of weakish cover songs including standards such as *White Rabbit, San Francisco Nights* and *My Back Pages*. Recorded by a group of mainly American draft-dodgers in Mexico, the album is on a par with a "psychedelic" **PJ Orion & The Magnates**. (CF)

The Flys

45s:	Reality Composition No. 1 /?	(Myskatonic 100) 1966
	Be What You Is/The Way Things Are	(Myskatonic 101) 1966

Hailed from McLean, Virginia. Their finest moment sounds like *Reality Composition No 1*, a real Stones-influenced garage classic with superb vocals and typical girl-put-down lyrics. By comparison *Be What You Is* sounds rather mundane.

Compilation appearances include: *Be What You Is* on *Psychedelic Unknowns, Vol. 6* (LP & CD) and *Signed, D.C.* (LP); and *Reality Composition No. 1* on *Highs In The Mid-Sixties, Vol. 22* (LP). (VJ)

Foamy Brine

Personnel incl: W.R. ("DUB") LYNCH   A

45s:	Tell Her / Ever Changing	(Brine 101) 1967
	The Change Is Made/About You	(ARV International 5017) 1969

This Texas Valley group included Dub Lynch who had previously been in **The Danes** and **The Gnats**. *Tell Her* is an accomplished garage power-popper that lopes effortlessly along. (MW/AB)

Fogcutters

Personnel incl: DON CAMERON
ERIK KARL

45s:	Cry Cry Cry/You Say	(Carthay 777) 1965
	Cry Cry Cry/You Say	(Liberty 55793) 1965
	Casting My Spell/	
	I Want Your Love Again	(Charter CR 1217) 1965
	It's My World/That's Where I'll Be	(Charter CR 1218) 1965

An excellent beat/pop combo originally from Colorado who may have moved to California (Charter is a small California label that also featured the likes of The Cascades) before splitting. Mainstays and songwriters Cameron and Karl would stay in the golden state and produce two wonderful 45s as the **Fantastic Zoo**.

This earlier work ranges from Beatlesque pop to **Beau Brummels** style *(Cry Cry Cry)* and ballads not dissimilar to the aforementioned Cascades. (MW)

The Foggy Notions

Personnel incl:	PETER HOY		A
	SUE KOFF		A
	KAPLAN	bs	A
	MAZIQUE		A

45:	Need A Little Lovin'/	
	Take Me Back And Hold Me	(Ginny 904) 1966

A Chicago garage band who were together for some time but just recorded the one 45. The 'A' side, *Need A Little Lovin'* is a powerful slow-paced punker with an unusual drum roll near the end. The flip, *Take Me Back And Hold Me* has some bluesy piano and lots of mouth organ.

Compilation appearances have included: *Need A Little Lovin'* on *Pebbles, Vol. 10* (LP), *Pebbles, Vol. 6* (CD) and *The Essential Pebbles Collection, Vol. 1* (Dble CD); and *Take Me Back And Hold Me* on *Highs In The Mid-Sixties Vol. 4* (LP) and *Pebbles, Vol. 7* (CD). (VJ/MW)

Foley and Kavanaugh

ALBUM: 1 Ways To Get Through   (Merlin) 1973 R1/R2

A double album of dreamy folk-psych with an introspective feel and fuzz guitar interplay. (SR)

Folkswingers

Personnel:	GLEN CAMPBELL	12-string gtr	A
	DOUG DILLARD	banjo	A
	RODNEY DILLARD	gtr	A
	TUT TAYLOR	dobro	A
	DEAN WEBB	bs	A
	HAL BLAINE	drms	B
	DENNIS BUDIMIR	12-string gtr	B
	HERB ELLIS	gtr	B
	LARRY KNECHTEL	keyb'ds	B
	BILL PITTMAN	bs	B
	HARIHAR RAO	sitar	B
	LYLE RITZ	fender bs	B
	HOWARD ROBERTS	gtr	B
	TOMMY TEDESCO	gtr	B

ALBUMS:	1(A)	12 STRING GUITAR!		
			(World-Pacific Records WP-1812)	1964 SC
	2(A)	12 STRING GUITAR! VOL. 2		
			(World-Pacific Records WP-1814)	1964 SC
	3(B)	RAGA ROCK	(World Pacific WP-1846)	1966 SC

45s:	Black Mountain Rag / This Train	(World Pacific 391) 1963
	12 String Special / Amor A Todos	(World Pacific 396) 1963
α	Don't Think Twice / Freight Train	(World Pacific 410) 1964
	Norwegian Wood / Raga Rock	(World Pacific 77831) 1966

NB: α as 'Bud Shank & The Folkswingers'.

The third album *Raga Rock* unashamedly cashed in on the success of Ravi Shankar and the emerging use of the sitar in Western pop-rock (Beatles, Stones, **Byrds**), offering up instrumental versions of the latest cool hit sounds, many with fuzzed guitar, and all topped off with that exotic sound. The more obvious and successful choices for such treatment are here - *Paint It Black*, a regular on later "exploito" albums of exotic-psych, *Eight Miles High* and *Shapes Of Things*. Also tackled (with varying success) are *Norwegian Wood*, **The Association**'s *Along Comes Mary*, **Outsiders**' *Time Won't Let Me*, *Kicks*, *Hey Joe*, *Homeward Bound* and **The Turtles**' *Grim Reaper Of Love*. Their own *Raga Rock* is the finale - although it starts off rather pedestrian, it's soon spiralling off into *Eight Miles High* territory, but comes back to earth way too soon.

The two 1964 albums were produced by Jim Dickson. He asked Dillards members Doug and Rodney together with Dean Webb to help him on his instrumental project, rounding it out with session guitarist Glen Campbell and Nashville based dobroist Tut Taylor, who was in L.A. to work on his own solo instrumental albums in '64.

Jim Dickson called the group **The Folkswingers** and they recorded folk and bluegrass songs to cash-in on the current trends. Basically they kept the name for the 1966 album and tried to tackle another musical trend. It's interesting to note that World Pacific actually put out a Ravi Shankar sitar album in 1965.

Jim Dickson not only went on to produce the **Byrds**, Flying Burrito Brothers and Country Gazette, but in 1964 alone, produced World Pacific sessions for The Kentucky Colonels, The Dillards (including a live album and tracks with drummer **Dewey Martin** later of **Buffalo Springfield**), sessions for the Hillmen {Chris Hillman's pre-**Byrds** Bluegrass group}, as well as the embryonic **Byrds** in their original and Jet Set/ Beefeaters formations.

A couple of the names on the *Raga Rock* release should also strike a chord - Larry Knechtel (later of Bread) and **Hal Blaine** were part of the elite corps of L.A. session musicians known as The Wrecking Crew. (MW/JO)

The Fonograf Four

45:   Don't Throw Stones/You're Not Foolin' Me   (Recettsic 69) 196?

Don't Throw Stones, by this New England garage band, has a pulsing and a rather repetitive organ 'hook', gentle beat and almost spoken vocal...

Compilation appearances include: *Don't Throw Stones* on *Sixties Rebellion, Vol's 1 & 2* (CD) and *Sixties Rebellion, Vol. 2* (LP). (VJ)

Food

Personnel:	TED ASHFORD	keyb'ds	A
	ERICK SCOTT FILIPOWITZ	bs	A
	BARRY MRAZ	drms	A
	STEVE WHITE	vcls	A
	BILL WUKOVICH	gtr	A

ALBUM: 1(A)   FOREVER IS A DREAM   (Capitol ST 304) 1969 R2

NB: (1) reissued on CD (Ascension ANCD021) 2000.

A Chicago act whose album of soft psychedelia is heavily orchestrated in places. A couple of tracks from the album were used in a porno B-movie,'The Babysitters'. A very pleasant and melodic album which maintains a high standard throughout, with the title cut and *Here We Go Again* among its finer moments. They didn't release any 45s. (VJ/MW)

The Footprints

45s: Never Say Die/Mama Rand's   (Capitol 2052) 1967
Just Lazy / You Got A Ticket To A Mobile   (Capitol 2215) 1968

From Island Park, Woodmere, New York. Their first 45 features two decent garagey beat-pop numbers that sound a bit dated by 1967, despite being punctuated by some clear ringing guitar spots and steaming organ. *Mama Rand's* was a popular live number, named after the club where they played. The second 45 is lame. (MW/MM)

Delvin Ford

ALBUM: 1   ANTI-BLUES   (Light LS-5566) c1971 SC

From Waco, Texas, a dark folk pop christian singer/songwriter with songs like *Rhetorical Question*, *Compassion*, *Awake, Sleeping Giant* and *Such Is The Day*. (SR)

Jim Ford

Personnel:	JIM FORD	vcls, gtr	A
	PAT VEGAS	bs	A
	LOLLY VEGAS	gtr	A

ALBUM: 1(A)   HARLAN COUNTY   (Sundown JHS-1002) 1969

NB: (1) reissued on CD (Edsel EDCD 519) 1997.

45:   Harlan County/Changing Colours   (Sundown SD-115) 1969

Originally from New Orleans, **Jim Ford** moved to California in 1967 and met **Pat and Lolly Vegas**. Together they wrote P.J. Proby's hit, *Niky Hoeky* and managed to get a record deal with Sundown, a small subsidiary of White Whale.

Released in 1969, *Harlan County*, his only album, is a very consistent mix of pop, country and rhythm and blues with some tracks totally relevant to this book: a fuzz-drenched version of Willie Dixon's *Spoonful*, *Dr. Handy's Dandy Candy* with his drugs-related lyrics and *I'm Gonna Make Her Love Me*. The other tracks are more pop or country oriented but **Ford**'s vocals and lyrics are constantly outstanding. The sleeve looks like a wrapped parcel, complete with stamps and rope, and credits as special assistants "red wine, white wine and little sleep"!

In 1971, **Jim Ford** went to London to record a second album. After some sessions with Brinsley Schwartz and the Grease Band, the project collapsed and the tapes disappeared.

Back in the U.S.A, he wrote some songs in 1972 for Bobby Womack and later worked with **Sly Stone** but, apart from that, little has been heard from him ever since. (SR)

Neal Ford and The Fanatics

Personnel:	"BABY" JOHN CRAVEY	drms	A
	NEAL FORD	vcls	A
	LANIER GREIG	keyb'ds	A

FOOD - Forever Is A Dream CD.

NEAL FORD & THE FANATICS - Neal Ford & The Fanatics LP.

	ROB "DUB" JOHNSON	bs	A
	"BIG" JOHN PEERLESS	gtr	A

ALBUM: 1(A) NEAL FORD AND THE FANATICS
(Hickory LPS 141) 1968 SC

45s:	δ	I Will Not Be Lonely/Be Mine	(Gina 1118) 1965
	α	Bitter Bells/Don't Tie Me Down	(Tantara 1101) 1966
	α	All I Have To Do Is Dream/Searchin'	(Tantara 1107) 1966
	α	I Will If You Want To/ Woman Who Turns Away	(Tantara 1107) 1966
	β	Shame On You/Gonna Be My Girl	(Hickory 1433) 1967
	α	Wait For Me/(I've Got A) Brand New Girl	(Hickory 1450) 1967
	χ	Get Together With Me/Rain	(Hickory 1468) 1967
	γ	I Have Thoughts For You/ That Girl Of Mine	(Hickory 1490) 1967
	α	Little World Girl/Movin' Along	(Hickory 1500) 1968
	α	Mary Wanna Marry Me/The Jones	(Hickory 1506) 1968
	α	I'll Put My Boots On Backwards/Buttercup	(Hickory 1516) 1968
	α	The Very First Time/	
	ε	That Time Of Year (Valentine)	(Pablo 7013) 196?
	φ	You Made Me A Man/ I've Got A Mind To Find Me A Woman	(ABC 11 184) 1969

NB: α, φ, β-A Side, χ-B Side, non-LP. δ as **The Fanatics**. ε as Neal Ford Solo. φ as Neal Ford Factory. γ also released in France with a PS.

Neal Ford was a prolific Houston-based artist. He formed **The Fanatics** in 1965 out of an earlier band **The Ramadas**, who had several 45s in their own right. Most of **The Ramadas** output pre-dates this book, but *Life Is So Tough* a powerful punker from 1965 is worth checking out.

They were still in their mid-teens, when they changed their name to **Neal Ford and The Fanatics** and they went on to produce a string of 45s, both punk and ballads, most of which were not on their album.

When the outfit disintegrated - Larnier Greig went on briefly to **The Moving Sidewalks** and the first ZZ Top line-up - **Ford** cut a solo 45 and then formed a new outfit, The Neal Ford Factory. He later played with **The Sound Investment** and Rick Mensik and was last reported running a Nashville-based talent agency.

Two more essential 45 reissues of awesome unreleased 1966 material have been issued by Caped Crusader: *Good Men / For You* (CC-74) and *Woman / I Can't Go On* (CC-75) both in 1995.

Compilation appearances have included: *I Can't Believe* (a previously unreleased cut from 1966) and *I Will Not Be Lonely* on *Acid Visions - The Complete Collection Vol. 1* (3-CD) and *Acid Visions, Vol. 2*; *I Will Not Be Lonely* on *Mayhem & Psychosis Vol. 3* (LP), *Mayhem & Psychosis Vol. 2* (CD), *Flashback, Vol. 5* (LP), *Texas Flashbacks, Vol. 5* (LP) and *Highs In The Mid-Sixties, Vol. 13*; *Shame On You* on *The Essential Pebbles Collection, Vol. 2* (Dble CD); *Life Is So Tough* on *Acid Visions - The Complete Collection Vol. 1* (3-CD) and *Acid Visions* (LP); *Mary Wanna Marry Me* on *U-Spaces: Psychedelic Archaeology Vol. 1* (CDR); *She Is All There Is* (previously unreleased) on *Houston Post - Nowsounds Groove-In* (LP); and *Bitter Bells* on *Highs In The Mid-Sixties, Vol. 17* (LP). (VJ/MW/SR)

Ford Theatre

Personnel:	JAMES ALTIERI	bs	A
	(WALLY MAGEE	strings	A)
	JOHN MAZZARELLI	keyb'ds, vcls	A
	HARRY PALMER	gtr	A
	JOEY SCOTT	vcls	A
	ROBERT TAMAGNI	drms	A
	ARTHUR 'BUTCH' WEBSTER	gtr	A

ALBUMS:	1(A)	TRILOGY FOR THE MASSES	(ABC ABCS 658) 1968 -
	2(A)	TIME CHANGES	(ABC ABCS 681) 1969 -

45s:	From A Back Door Window/ Theme For The Masses	(ABC 11118) 1968
	Time Changes/Wake Up In The Morning	(ABC 11192) 1969
	I've Got The Fever/Jefferson Airplane	(ABC 11227) 1969

Ford Theatre is the place where Abraham Lincoln was assassinated and the liner notes explain that "the six musicians chose this name because it corresponds to what they are trying to create - a vision of America in all its present chaos and agony".

The group were probably from Milford, Massachusetts, given that their first album gives a credit to 'the population' of that town. Produced by Bob Thiele (**Eden's Children**, **Free Spirits**), Harry Palmer and Fred Cenedella, *Trilogy For The Masses* is excellent in parts, particularly the nine-minute *101 Harrison Street*. All the tracks were written by Harry Palmer and Wally Magee (who also led the string quartet present on some tracks).

It's a pity that their follow-up, 'a musical concept' album, was not as interesting.

The 'B' side to their third 45, *Jefferson Airplane* has recently been compiled on the excellent *Acid and Flowers* (CD) and *Incredible Sound Show Stories, Vol. 7* (LP).

Harry Palmer also played on *Smooth As Raw Silk* by **Silk**, another ABC production. (SR/VJ)

The Foremost Authority

See **The Fourmost Authority**.

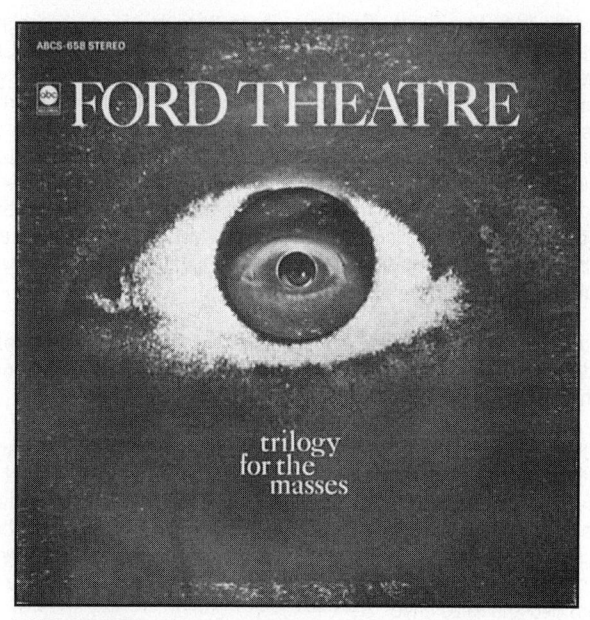

FORD THEATRE - Trilogy For The Masses LP.

FORD THEATRE - Time Changes LP.

Forgotten Times

| 45: | Little Black Egg/Won't You Be With Me | (Night Owl 678) 1967 |

A cover of **The Nightcrawlers**' hit *Little Black Egg* by an outfit from Quad Cities, Iowa. (VJ)

Formerly Anthrax

Personnel:	RICK CUTLER	drms	AB
	JACK JACOBSEN	keyb'ds	AB
	JERRY McCANN	gtr, vcls, bs, flute, hrmnca, perc	AB
	(MARTY LANHAM	banjo	A)

| ALBUMS: | 1(A) | SHOW OF HANDS | (Elektra EKS 74084) 1971 - |
| | 2(B) | LIVE AT THE NEW ORLEANS HOUSE | (Elektra no #) 1971 R2 |

NB: (2) Acetate only, issued to band members.

| 45s: | α | Stanley's Theme / These Things I Know | (Elektra 45725) 1971 |
| | β | No Words Between Us (mono)/(stereo) | (Elektra) 1971 |

NB: α double-sided promo copies also exist: *Stanley's Theme* (mono 2'38")/(stereo 3'08"). β promo only - no stock copies known to exist.

Originally from San Diego, California, these three musicians had played together in 1967 in an outfit called The National Debt. When Jerry McCann left to lead **Framework**, Cutler and Jacobsen became Anthrax, playing gigs up and down the coast as an instrumental duo. They were 'discovered' by Russ Miller of Elektra and Lonnie Mack at one such concert, and the duo recorded an album for the label in 1969, produced by Lonnie Mack. Label president Jac Holzman deemed the instrumental progressive album devoid of commercial potential and refused to release it. He suggested the band find a vocalist and Cutler and Jacobsen asked McCann to join them; after playing demos for Jac Holzman he was signed up and that was the end of **Framework**.

During the course of 1970, the trio rehearsed and recorded several times at Elektra, leaving behind a number of unissued tracks before settling on a finished album master sequence.

Elektra were also not happy with the band name and insisted on a change. The band did, grudgingly, but only to **Formerly Anthrax** (!). The label did manage to get their own back - on the album sleeve "Formerly Anthrax" appeared in brackets and smaller print below the title and it had been assumed by almost everyone since that the band was called *Show Of Hands*, and were formerly known as Anthrax. So you'll invariably find the album filed and listed under 'S'.

Whatever, this is an excellent album but in no way is it garage or psych - rather a smorgasbord of late sixties jazz-infused rock with progressive tendencies, by three talented musicians.

It opens with the Focus-soundalike *No Words Between Us* (non-lyrics with swelling keyboards and busy Bruford-esque drumming) and this feat is repeated at end of the side with the stand-out instrumental *I Want To Fly*, where velvety, Akkerman-like guitar soars over waves of reedy glissandos. (Coincidentally Akkerman's pre-Focus band Brainbox had been on Elektra in the US). Moods and instrumentation shift from cool to a soulful intensity across the ten tracks and their choice of covers showcases the variety of influences - Van Morrison's *Moondance* is jazzed up and works well; the **Jimi Hendrix** medley *May This Be Love/One Rainy Wish* is plaintive and subdued; their choice of **Richie Haven**'s *No Opportunity Necessary, No Experience Needed* will draw obvious comparisons to the Yes version recorded the same year (on their *Time And A Word* LP).

McCann provided the group with a versatile vocalist and flautist; more colours for their palette. He also supplied two compositions, *Like A Child* and *These Things I Know*, unreleased **Framework** recordings that can be compared to the Elektra album versions via the **Framework** retrospective. (Incidentally, both the unreleased session tapes and the live acetate also include several other **Framework** songs.)

Other highlights include: the bossa nova rhythms of *Stanley's Theme*; the banjo instrumental *Mount Olympus Breakdown* which starts to sound like Jimmy Page's *White Summer* and as the pace picks up and bongos join in, it seems to turn into a sitar, momentarily - a strange effect; the apt finale *Toy Piano* which builds to a climax of swooping guitar and heavy, ELP-like grandeur. Recommended to any proggie or fan of late sixties left-field rock; this album used to be seen regularly in cut-out/bargain bins and should not be difficult or expensive to acquire. Frankly, we don't know why; the only thing against it would appear to be the drab child-like paintings of the band members across the gatefold's exterior.

Days before recording was to due begin on a second studio album, Cutler was badly injured in a bike accident. **Framework** drummer Carl Spiron sat in to fulfill the band's scheduled live appearances but momentum was lost on the recording front and Elektra dropped the band.

Cutler and Jacobsen both stayed active in the music business in the San Francisco area, Cutler mainly as a session drummer although he was with Tommy Tutone's band for some time; Jacobsen played with a number of Bay Area bands through the seventies - nineties including Van Morrison, Swamp Dogg, Donald Kinsey, Norton Buffalo and Huey Lewis and The News. Jacobsen has also worked extensively in the field of equipment design and manufacturing, notably with Acoustic, Gauss and Cerwin-Vega as well as his own company RAM (Redwood Audio Manufacturing), a company that designed and built stage equipment for Foreigner, Gamma, Night Ranger and The Starship, among others. McCann is still active in San Diego as a performer and guitar teacher, and released both a cassette *Unframed* and a CD *Blue Plate Special* in 1997. The band reunited in 2000 and are currently recording a demo at Jacobsen's home studio, although now they are ironically calling themselves Show Of Hands. (MW/CF/SR)

Forsaken

| 45: | She's Alright/Babe | (MTA 106) c1966 |

An interesting 45 on the same label as Maze and many other unusual releases. The 'A' side, *She's Alright* is a poppy, catchy number with occasionally cool guitar work and lyrics defending a girl with a bad reputation. The flip is less interesting. Both tunes were written and produced by Ted Varnick. (KSI)

The Fort Mudge Memorial Dump

Personnel:	DAVE AMARAL	A
	RICHARD CLERICI	A
	JAMES DEPTULA	A
	DAN KEADY	A
	CAROLINE STRATTON	A

| ALBUM: | 1(A) | FORT MUDGE MEMORIAL DUMP | (Mercury 61256) 1970 SC/R1 |

NB: (1) has been reissued.

The above album by this Boston band contains some good tracks. All the material was written by the band. *Mr. Man* and *Crystal Forms* both portray Stratton's vocals favourably and include some good guitar work. Others, such as *Actions Of A Man* and *What Good Is Spring?* find Caroline and the band in a mellower mood. Another track *Know Today* is an instrumental, although the record cover includes lyrics for it. However, overall the album does not maintain the standard set in its opening cuts.

The album was produced by Michael Tschudin of **Listening/Cynara**. (VJ/CF)

The Fortune Seekers

| 45: | Why I Cry/Break Loose | (Trident 9966) 1966 |

Reportedly a California band. *Why I Cry* can be found on *Punk Classics* (CD), *Punk Classics, Vol. 1* (7") and *Teenage Shutdown, Vol. 9* (LP & CD). (MW)

Fortune Teller

ALBUM: 1 INNER CITY SCREAM (RMT) 1978 R2

From Baltimore, a crude album of fuzz/grunge psych by an obscure group. It was recorded in 1968 but not released before 1978. (SR)

The 49th Blue Streak

45: Foxy Lady/Fire (mbm Productions 1947) c1969

Released circa 1969 on a Crowley, Louisiana label. This band do two **Jimi Hendrix** covers, both of which are accomplished and with a high fuzz quotient. (MW/SR)

Forty Second Street Auxiliary Choir

45: You Ask Why/Springtime Feeling (Thunder 834) 1967

A rare 45 between flower-pop and folk-rock. The A side was penned by Roger Durham. (SR)

The Forum

Personnel incl: PHIL CAMPOS A
RENE NOLE A
RISELLE VAINE A

FORMERLY ANTHRAX - Show Of Hands LP.

ALBUM: 1(A) THE FORUM (Mira MLPS-3014) 1967 SC

45s: The River Is Wide Pt.1 / Pt.2 (Penthouse 504) 1966
The River Is Wide / I Fall In Love (Mira 232) 1966
The River Is Wide / A Girl Without A Boy (Mira 232) 1966
Trip On Me / It's Sunday (Mira 243) 1967
Girl Without A Boy /
Go Try To Put Out The Sun (Mira 248) 1967

On the same label as **The Leaves**, a California mixed male-female pop group with orchestrated backing. They had a big hit with *The River Is Wide*. Later efforts included *Trip On Me*, groovy flower-pop for the "beautiful people" and parents who thought they were hip.

Produced by Les Baxter in Los Angeles, with the help of session men, their album contains songs like *Girl Without A Boy*, *Trip On Me*, *It's Sunday*, *We Can Make It*, *Look The Other Way*, *The Time Is Now*, *World Of Illusion* and their 1966 hit, *The River Is Wide*.

They should appeal to fans of The Fifth Dimension and **Love Generation**. (SR/MW)

Forum Quorum

Personnel: BRIAN ALBANO drms A
ROGER CALLEO vcls, flute, keyb'ds A
BOBBY CASTALDO bs A
SAL PALAZZOLO vcls, gtr A
STURG PARDALIS vcls, gtr, bouzouki A

ALBUM: 1(A) THE FORUM QUORUM (Decca DL 75030) 1968 -

45s: Your Turn To Cry/No More Tears (Decca 32340) 1968
Just The Same/Misery (Decca 32425) 1968

A Greco-Italian American quintet from Astoria, New York. Some intriguing pop-psych with a punky edge, though occasionally straying into **Young Rascals** or **Vanilla Fudge** blue-eyed soul territory. Still, there are some nice touches of Middle Eastern promise that lift them out of the ordinary. The album can still be found fairly easily and cheaply. The 45 tracks all feature on the album. (MW)

The Forums

Personnel: DALE A
JIM DOSSETT A
GEORGE A
ERICH MEYER A
RALPH A

45: Bring It On Back /I ... (title incomplete) (Prism 1940) 1966

A white-clad teen quartet from Dayton, Ohio. In 1966 they entered the three-day Daytonian battle of the bands and, as one of the twelve winning acts, got to record a track for the souvenir album *WONE, The Dayton Scene*. Their contribution is *Bring It On Back*, a keening pop ballad that would grace their sole 45. It's been compared to the Four Seasons due to the falsetto lead, though its piercing quality sounds more like eighties castrato Jimmy Somerville. (MW)

Forvus (featuring Brooke Chamberlain)

45: Now That Summer Is Here/
It's Nothing New (Tampa Bay BC-1110) 1966

Harmony-vocal pop from Florida that would be most undistinguished, were it not for the **Rovin' Flames** providing the backing, as well as one 'Harvey Swadnungle'. (MW)

The Foul Dogs

ALBUM: 1 THE FOUL DOGS NO. 1 (Rhythm Sound 481) 1966 R3

NB: (1) reissued in the early-mid eighties on Resurrection (CX 1296) and more recently by Distortions.

A Concord, New Hampshire group whose album comprised typical local R&B/prep rock. One cut, *I'm A Man*, also appears on *Oil Stains* (LP). The album sounds very Stones-influenced, but had a couple of self-penned numbers. (VJ)

The Fountain of Youth

45s:	(Angie, Love Me) Make The Hurt Go Away/ Livin' Too Fast	(Colgems 1020) 1967
	Take A Giant Step/ Don't Blame Me (For Trying)	(Colgems 1024) 1968
	Sunshine On A Cold Morning/ Day Don't Come	(Colgems 1032) 1968
	Liza Jane/Witness People	(Colgems 5033) 1969

This band played in Fredericksburg, Texas between 1966-69 and were originally known as The Crossfires. Their early 45s were slick, well-crafted pop songs - *Day Don't Come* was also covered by Michigan's **Cherry Slush**. The most relevant song to this book was *Witness People*, a superb slice of heavy psychedelia, which was out of character from the rest of their output. Another track, *Sunshine...* features quite outstanding sixties pop and could easily be mistaken for **Emitt Rhodes** and the **Merry-Go-Round**. Their slower dramatic version of **The Monkees**' hit *Take A Giant Step* is also excellent.

Details of the Crossfires 45 are:

45: Who'll Be The One/Making Love Is Fun (Tower 278) 1966

Compilation appearances have included: *Witness People* on *Mayhem & Psychosis, Vol. 3* (LP), *Mayhem & Psychosis, Vol. 2* (CD), *Sixties Rebellion, Vol. 15* (LP & CD); *Don't Blame Me (For Trying)* on *Boulders, Vol. 8* (LP), *Ya Gotta Have Moxie, Vol. 2* (Dble CD), *Garagelands, Vol. 1* (LP) and *Garagelands, Vol. 1 & 2* (CD); *Take A Giant Step* on *From The New World* (LP); and *Day Don't Come* on *Bring Flowers To U.S.* (LP). (MW/VJ)

The Fountain of Youth

45: Hard Woman/Thing Of The Past (Sur-Speed 223) 196?

Recorded on a Nashville label, this 45 is probably the work of a different band. *Hard Woman* is a really raw, nasty punk song which you'll find on *Pebbles, Vol. 11* (LP) and *Boulders, Vol. 8* (LP). (VJ)

Four Fifths

| 45s: | If You Still Want Me/ Have You Ever Loved A Girl | (Columbia 4-43913) 1966 |
| | She'll Hurt You In The End / Life Goes Movin' On | (Associated Recording Studios) 1966 |

Teenage Shutdown, Vol. 8 (LP & CD) has scooped the unreleased *She'll Hurt You In The End* and revealed that this was a bunch of teenagers from Manhattan, who were still attending school. They'll be best remembered for the sublime **Byrds**-influenced folk-punker *If You Still Want Me*, compiled on *Pebbles, Vol. 7* (LP), *Pebbles, Vol. 4 (ESD)* (CD) and *The Essential Pebbles Collection, Vol. 2* (Dble CD).

Other Four Fifths with no known connections to the above include: a "doo-wop" 45 from 1962/3 - *After Graduation/Come On Girl* (Hudson 8101) and another outfit who cover *Talkin' Bout You* (Rage 0101, 196?). (MW/MM/PH)

TEENAGE SHUTDOWN Vol. 8 (Comp CD) including Four Fifths.

The Four Gents

45: Soul Sister/I've Been Trying (HBR 509) 1966 133 HCP

Not the Pacific Northwest outfit on Nite Owl, this bunch were from the Detroit area.

Soul Sister, a minor hit, can also be found on *S.V.R. Rock Hits Of The Sixties* (LP & CD). (VJ)

Four In The Morning

| 45: | Yesterday/LSD | (Cross Road 7002) 196? |
| | Draft Dodger Rag/? | (Cross Road 7001) 196? |

An obscure Pacific Northwest band. (VJ)

The Four Letter Words

Personnel:	DAVID DIX	drms, perc	ABC
	PHIL HUMBERG	bs, vcls	ABC
	HERB PINO	ld vcls, gtr	ABC
	HOYT TAYLOR	keyb'ds	A
	HUGHIE THOMASSON	ld gtr, vcls	ABC
	BILL MANN	gtr	B
	HOBIE O'BRIEN	gtr	C

45: The Quadruple Feature In Cinemascope And Color At The Drive In Movie Tonight/ Goodbye (Paris Tower 107) 1966/1967

Previously known as **The Rogues**, this bands 45 was written by a disc jockey at WLCY radio in Tampa. 5,000 copies of this 45 were pressed, of which approx 2,000 were sold. In 1967, the band evolved into **The Outlaws**, who later achieved fame and fortune in the mid-late seventies with hits such as *Ghost Rider* and *Green Grass And High Tides*. (IT/SMR)

4 Making Do

45: The Simple Life/? (Wells Desert 2275) 1965

This promising Los Angeles-based girl group sing about the pleasures of living in L.A. in *The Simple Life*, a simple folk ballad with melodic vocals. *Highs In The Mid-Sixties, Vol. 1* introduced the song to a wider audience. (VJ)

Four More

Personnel:
	MIKE BURROWS	drms	A
	CHUCK CARTER	ld gtr	A
	JERRY CHANDLER	ld vcls, gtr	A
	KENNY CHANDLER	bs	A

45:   Don't Give Up Hope/Problem Child   (Fairchild 1001) 1966

This raw punk 45 was the work of a band from Corpus Christi, Texas. Aged between 14 - 17, most went to King High School in Corpus Christi, and their manager/roadie/friend Dennis Fairchild put out the 45 on his "Fairchild" label.

In their time they played regularly at places in and around Corpus, including the Naval Air station at Kingsville, and The Stork Club as well as local TV and a couple of "Battle Of The Bands" contests. They also got to support Charlie Rich!

In 1967, they changed their name to The Chosen Ones, recruiting older brother Jim Chandler on lead vocals, with Jerry and Kenny switching to harmony back-up. As such they issued a further 45, *The World's Dark Side/Bald-Headed Lena* (Gulfside) 196?. The flip was also recorded by **The Lovin' Spoonful**. In the seventies they also played as The Chandler Bros, in and around Houston.

Today Mike Burrows still lives in Corpus, Jerry and Kenny reside in the Houston area and Jim has moved to California.

Problem Child, which was written by 15-year old Kenny and 17-year old Jerry Chandler, can also be found on *Highs In The Mid-Sixties, Vol. 11* (LP). (VJ)

The Fourmost Authority

45s: α Dance Dance /
          Left Hand Lawyer   (GNP Crescendo GNP-386) 1967
       β Childhood Friends/Woe Is Me   (GNP Crescendo GNP-403) 1968
       χ Go For What You Know /
          I Can't Get By   (GNP Crescendo GNP-416) 1968

NB: α seen as **The Fourmost Authority**.... χ seen as **The Foremost Authority**... and β seen as both variants! α also had a promo release with a longer version of *Dance, Dance*.

Probably from Los Angeles, this bands 45s appeared under a mix of **Fourmost/Foremost** banners. *Dance, Dance*, appeared in a longer form on promo copies, with the R&B-ish fade out being removed from later stock copies. Described by some as good uptempo rock with neat guitar solo and crisp vocals, their other material is mostly tame pop. (BM/MW)

The Four O'Clock Balloon

Personnel:
	ROGER ALTON	ld gtr	A
	PAT JENNINGS	bs	A
	JEFF ROBINSON	gtr	A
	WAYNE SHEPPARD	keyb'ds	A
	JACK WHITE	drms	A
	HAZEL WIGGET		
	(later SHEPPARD, married Wayne)	vcls	A

ALBUM: 1 NORTHLAND'S BATTLE OF THE BANDS
                    (MAGNA 71014, 2-LP) 1967 R3

NB: (1) Various Artists comp, features six tracks by **The Four O'Clock Balloon**.

45:   Two Heads/Dark Cobble Street   (Magna 71152) 1967

From Columbus, Ohio, all except Roger Alton were students at Ohio State University. As worthy winners of the third annual battle of the bands held at the local Northland's Shopping Center in 1967 they were rewarded with a whole side of the double-album that captured the event. Six tracks - *Somebody To Love, Motherly Love, Strawberry Fields Forever, Plastic Fantastic Lover, (Who Are The) Brain Police* and *Wake Me Shake Me*. Not yer usual bunch of covers, they clearly wore their influences on their sleeves (or over their kaftans). All are performed with confidence and verve, and they were certainly (two) heads above the competition judging from the rest of the album.

Second place went to the Dubonnets, third the Trolls, fourth the Thirteenth Dilemma and fifth the Lapse Of Tyme. Other groups on the album are: Tonebenders (a girl group, doing *Little Black Egg*), Verdics, Brass Tax, Restless Knights, Kings English, Rubber Band, Lo-Brows, St.John's Mod, Unchosen, Sound Of Us, and **The Lorey's** from nearby Sparta with *Don't You Care*. Unfortunately there's no track listing to know exactly who does what and the unfortunate Nazar Blues and Vi-Counts who also took part didn't make it onto the album.

After such evident promise by **Four O'Clock Balloon** the resultant 45 is a bit disappointing but judge for yourselves - their cover of **Jefferson Airplane**'s *Two Heads* is on *Glimpses, Vol. 4* (LP) and *Brain Shadows, Vol. 1* (LP & CD), whilst the flip is on *Highs In The Mid-Sixties, Vol. 21* (LP). (MW/GGI/VJ)

The Four of Us

Personnel incl:
	JEFF ALBORELL	bs	A
	PAUL KELCOURSE	gtr	A

45s: You're Gonna Be Mine/Batman   (Hideout 1003) 1965
      You're Gonna Be Mine/Freefall   (Hideout 1003) 1965
      I Feel A Whole Lot Better/
      I Can't Live Without Your Love   (Hideout 1012) 1965

A folk-rock outfit from the Detroit suburb of Grosse Pointe in Michigan. They seem to have had some connection to **The Fugitives** 'cause *You're Gonna Be Mine*, considered by many to be their finest moment, appeared under both names. For their second 45 Gene Clark's *I Feel A Whole Lot Better* was given similar treatment. The Hideout was a Detroit teen club started by Dave Leone and Ed 'Punch' Andrews in May 1964 and the following year Leone started the Hideout Record Company, which like the club, thrived for a short while.

The rare compilation album *Best Of The Hideouts* contains *Baby Blue, I Feel A Whole Lot Better* and *I Can't Live Without Your Love*. *Baby Blue*, is a competent enough version of the much-covered Dylan song. The vocals and 12-string guitar give it good treatment. The album, which has been reissued also features tracks by other Hideout regulars **The Underdogs** (4), **Yorkshires** (2), **Pleasure Seekers**, **Henchman** and **Doug Brown**.

Paul Kelcourse also played in **The Fugitives**, and along with Jeff Alborell played in The Heavy Metal Kids, with Glenn Frey (ex-**Mushrooms**)

Retrospective compilation appearances have included: *You're Gonna Be Mine* on *Psychedelic Unknowns, Vol. 3* (LP & CD); *I Feel A Whole Lot Better* on *A Journey To Tyme, Vol. 2* (LP) and *Highs In The Mid-Sixties, Vol. 6* (LP); *You're Gonna Be Mine* on *Best of Hideout Records* (CD); and *Baby Blue* on *Highs In The Mid-Sixties Vol. 5* (LP). (MW)

The IV Pack

45:   Whatzit?/?   (Hippie 2019) 196?

Came out of Danville, Virginia and their *Whatzit?* was a sort of variation on **The Count Five**'s *Psychotic Reaction*. Pretty good it is too and half way through the chorus gives way to a cosmic guitar freakout. Check it out on the *Signed, D.C.* (LP) or *Teenage Shutdown, Vol. 8* (LP & CD). (MW)

Four Real

ALBUM: 1 CONTENTMENT   (Private Pressing) c1972 ?

A Christian rock group with tracks like *Og For A Thousand Tongues To Sing*. (SR)

KIM FOWLEY - Born To Be Wild CD.

4 Score

| 45: | Mini-Skirt / ? | (Blackjack 110) 1967 |

A salacious punker dedicated to man's most popular female fashion and other turn-ons. Check out this lechers' classic on *Sick And Tired* with its exhortations of 'M - I - N - I', creepy keyboards and fuzz.

The band are thought to originate from the New York area. (MW)

The 4th Amendment

| 45: | Always Blue/Whiskey Man | (Constitution 5109) 1968 |

From Atlanta, Georgia, this garage band's *Always Blue* bears an unashamed resemblance to Sky Saxon and **The Seed's** *Pushin' Too Hard*. The flip, is in a similar vein.

Compilation appearances have included: *Always Blue* on *Pebbles, Vol. 17* (LP), *Psychedelic Unknowns, Vol. 6* (LP & CD), *Follow That Munster, Vol. 2* (LP), *The Garage Zone, Vol. 1* (LP) and *The Garage Zone Box Set* (4-LP); *Always Blue* and *Whiskey Man* on *Sixties Rebellion, Vol. 12* (LP). (VJ/MW)

Fourth Cekcion

Personnel:	LOUIE BROUSSARD	drms	A
	RICHARD CANTU	woodwind	A
	GREG ISAACS	keyb'ds	A
	STEWART ROJO	ld gtr	A
	MIKE ST CLAIR	bs	A

| ALBUM: | 1(A) | FOURTH CEKCION | (Solar 110) 1970 SC |

NB: (1) also issued on White Whale.

A little known Texan outfit whose album has become a collectors' item. Cantu later played for Richard Torrence. Probably their finest moment, *Find Yourself Another Way* is compiled on *Journey To The East* (LP). (VJ/MW)

Fourth Dimension

Personnel incl?:	?? CORBETT	A
	?? HERSHKOWITZ	A
	?? TOSCANO	A

| 45s: | Rainy Day/Land Of Make Believe | (Columbia 43778) 1966 |
| | You're My Unhappiness/Mister Blair | (Columbia 43931) 1966 |

A forgotten pop-rock group, their songs were written by Hershkowitz, Corbett and Toscano, arranged by Art Butler and produced by Dave Rubinson (**Moby Grape**, Taj Mahal). Corbett and Toscano would later front the interesting **Mr. Flood's Party**. (SR)

Fourth Way

| Personnel incl: | JOHN WILMETH | bs | A |

| 45s: | The Far Side Of Your Moon/Pink Cloud | (Soul City 765) 1968 |
| | Bucklehuggin' / Clouds | (Capitol 2619) 1969 |

A suitable track for the 'Barbarella' movie, the groovy 'A' side on their first 45 is pleasant Eastern keyboard doodling and Telstar spacey effects topped by little-girl vocals similar to *Hole In My Shoe*. Fairly far out. The flip by contrast is a stupid but amusing nursery-rhyme song with inane whistling. Undoubtedly a studio effort, songs are credited to R. Graves and Steve Venet. Steve was a Screen Gems writer and Nick Venet's brother - he wrote many songs for "Red Bird" girl groups and also composed the classic *Tomorrow's Gonna Be Another Day*.

John Wilmeth later played with **Southern Comfort**.

Compilation appearances include: *The Far Side Of Your Mind* on *A Heavy Dose Of Lyte Psych* (CD), *Incredible Sound Show Stories, Vol. 8* (LP) and *I'm Trippin' Alone* (LP). (MW/JFr/SR)

The Four Wheels

Personnel:	JIM ADAMS	A
	SKEET BUSHOR	A
	STEVE DRYBREAD	A
	JIM KOSS	A
	STEVE LESTER	A

| 45: | Central High Playmate/Cold 45 | (Soma 1428) 1965 |

This Indianapolis-based band later became The Boys Next Door, who released a 45 for Soma, one for Cameo, one for Bud and three for Atco in the mid-sixties. *Hipsville, Vol. 3* features the 'A' side of their 45.

In 2000, a master tape resurfaced with *Suddenly She Was Gone* released later by The Boys Next Door plus four unreleased tracks: the poppish *Always Together*, two garage-rockers *A Girl Named Mary* and *I Got Wild* and a mid-tempo pop-rock song, *You Cheated, You Lied*.

Compilation appearances have included: *Cold 45* on *Hipsville, Vol. 3* (LP) and *Soma Records Story, Vol. 1* (LP); and *Central High Playmate* on *Soma Records Story, Vol. 2* (LP). (VJ/MW/SR)

Kim Fowley

Personnel:	KIM FOWLEY	vcls, keyb'ds, perc	ABCDEF
	MIKE ALLSUP	gtr	C
	BEN BENAY	harp, gtr	C
	MARS BONFIRE	gtr	CD
	JIMMY GREENSPOON	keyb'ds	C
	EDDIE HOH	drms	C
	ORVILLE RED RHODES	steel gtr	C
	CARMEN RIALE	bs	C
	JOE SCHRMIE	bs	C
	WAYNE TALBERT	keyb'ds	C
	JOE TORRES	perc	C
	MICHAEL LLOYD	keyb'ds	D
	WARREN ZEVON	gtr	D

HCP

ALBUMS:	1(A)	LOVE IS ALIVE AND WELL	(Tower DT 5080) 1967 - SC
(up to	2(A)	THE INCREDIBLE KIM FOWLEY	
1974)		(Original Sound OSR-LPS-8877) 1967 - -
	3(A)	BORN TO BE WILD	(Imperial 12413) 1968 - -

4	(C)	OUTRAGEOUS	(Imperial 12423)	1968	198 SC
5	(D)	GOOD CLEAN FUN	(Imperial 12443)	1969	- -
6	(E)	IN THE UNDERGROUND	(Not issued)	1968	- -
7	( )	OUTLAW SUPERMAN	(RCA)	1971	- -
8	(F)	I'M BAD	(Capitol ST 11075)	1972	- -
9	( )	INTERNATIONAL HEROES	(Capitol ST 11159)	1973	- -
10	( )	AUTOMATIC	(Capitol 11248)	1974	- -

NB: (2), (6) and (7) not released. (3) and (4) have been reissued on one CD by Rev-Ola in 1995. (8) also issued in Germany (Capitol 81208) 1972. (9) also issued in Germany (Capitol 81385) 1973

45s: (up to 1973)

	American Dream/The Statue	(Mira 209)	1965
	The Trip/Big Sur	(Corby 216)	1965
	Mr. Responsibility/My Foolish Heart	(Living Legend 721)	1965
	Underground Lady/Pop Art '66	(Living Legend 725)	1966
α	Lights/Something New And Different	(Loma 2064)	1966
	Love Is Alive And Well/Reincarnation	(Tower 342)	1967
	Don't Be Cruel/Strangers From The Sky	(Reprise 0569)	1967
β	Fluffy Turkeys / Young America-Saturday Night	(Original Sound OS-81)	1967
χ	Born To Make You Cry/Thunder Road	(Original Sound 98)	196?
	Born To Be Wild/Space Odyssey	(Imperial 66326)	1968
	Wildfire/Bubblegum	(Imperial 66349)	1969
	The Sky Is On Fire/Citizen Kane	(RCA 74 0511)	1971
	Forbidden Love/I'm Bad	(Capitol 3403)	1972
δ	International Heroes/ESP Reader	(Capitol 3534)	1973
	Born Dancer/Something New	(Capitol 3662)	1973

NB: α also released in the U.K. (Parlophone R 5521) and (CBS 202338). β Promo copy labels state "from the LP The Incredible Kim Fowley, OSR-LPS-8877" but this was probably not released. Of special note : the dead wax has the following writings : "Rodney Underground DS Canyon Put On" and "Wait til you hear the album, photos by Ed, Art Needs Love". χ release not confirmed, although there appears to have been a UK issue (Action ACT 4606) 1972, the tracks are also compiled on the retrospective LP *Living In The Streets*. δ also issued in the UK (Capitol CL 15743) 1973. There's also a rare French EP with PS: *The Trip/Beautiful People/The Underground Lady/Curiosity* (Vogue INT 18086)(estimatd value: $150) and a French single with PS: *They're Coming To Take Me Away/You Get More For Your Money On The Flip Side* (CBS 2243).

Son of Hollywood actor Doug Fowley the multi-talented **Fowley** - singer, producer and composer - was born in Los Angeles in 1942. He got into the music business as an assistant to Marty Melcher (Terry's Dad) who ran a music publishing company. He was pals with The Cadets and other black vocal groups of the time and was a sometime member of his school-band The Sleepwalkers (notable for including at various times Bruce Johnston, Sandy Nelson, Phil Spector and various others). Among the groups **Fowley** wrote for and produced were The Jayhawks, B. Bumble and The Stingers, The Innocents and The Hollywood Argyles. In the early sixties, he was involved with The Rivingtons and **Paul Revere and the Raiders**, but it was novelty scams like *Ally Oop* and *Nutrocker* which became worldwide hits and set his career pattern.

He also ran Chattahoochie records for a time, roping other Hollywood chancers like David Gates in - **The Murmaids**, Kathy Young, and various Chicano bands like **Thee Midniters** to make up their roster. He then became a press officer for Motown and for various Brit bands inc. The Yardbirds (incidentally, **WCPAEB** came together at the end of tour party **Fowley** threw for The Yardbirds at **Bob Markley**'s house).

He moved to England for a couple of years in 1965, first working with P.J. Proby as publicist and tour manager, and then with Andrew Loog Oldham on various projects, as well as producing lots of records. Two of his 45 cuts from the period, *Pop Art '66* and *Lights*, were collaborations with Mark Wirtz, while the backing on *Don't Be Cruel* contains most of Fleetwood Mac plus sundry cronies.. Eventually however, EMI compelled **Fowley** and Wirtz to go out and find some bands and stop messing about at Abbey Road. They returned first with the Inbetweens, then later with Pink Floyd, Tomorrow, and The Soft Machine. The first two were signed, and **Fowley** took the Softs to Polydor for one 45 and a bunch of unreleased tracks. **Fowley** also discovered and named Family, cutting a one-off single for Liberty. Somewhere inbetween all this he also found time to work with Cat Stevens, The Rockin' Berries, Dave Mason and Jim Capaldi.

Upon his return to America he worked on the first **Mothers Of Invention** album and in 1967 he also formed a home for bands which was used by Sparrow, Jim Morrison, and **Rose Garden**.

Undeniably, **Fowley** had a talent for novelty songs and uncomplicated teenage anthems. An example of the former was *The Trip*, which was very popular around L.A. in 1966 and was covered by **Godfrey** and **Thee Midniters**, amongst others. In the eighties, this would be a favourite track amongst the "garage" freaks.

His first album *Love Is Alive And Well* features **The West Coast Pop Art Experimental Band** (as does the non-album 45 cut *Strangers From The Sky*) and was co-produced by **Michael Lloyd**. His second, *Born To Be Wild* contains groovy organ instrumentals; *Outrageous* is experimental hard psych and *Good Clean Fun* features Lloyd, Mars Bonfire, **Skip Battin**, **Warren Zevon**, and Rodney Bingenheimer. The latter album turns into a contract breaking farrago halfway through, as his signings to Liberty / Imperial, **Zevon** and **Johnny Winter**, were both dropped whilst it was being recorded. When **Winter** became a big star in the U.S. only a couple of months later, it was too much to bear.

He continued to record albums throughout the seventies, but in the eighties confined his activities more to songwriting, publishing and talent spotting. In the late nineties, however he's been getting more recognition from current acts, played his first gigs since 1968, including sell-out shows in London, and performed a song cycle with narration *The Ghosts Of Scotland* for BBC Radio Scotland. He's also made some bizarre dance records which have actually made the club charts - ably assisted by Joe Foster, Norman Blake, Steve New, Roni Size, William Orbit and various members of the Fall, BMX Bandits etc. One particular offshoot of all this was a strange version of **Millennium**'s *Prelude*, whilst a remix of *Animal Man* from *Outrageous* was a stand-out track on a recent Bentley Rhythm Ace project for Ministry of Sound.

Anyone interested in investigating **Kim Fowley**'s unique work should check out *Mondo Hollywood, Vol. 1* (Rev-Ola CREV036CD) 1995, a compilation CD which contains tracks from the sixties, including many of his more bizarre offerings like *The Trip* and *Gypsy Canyon*.

An earlier retrospective, *Living In The Streets* (Sonet SNTF 755) 1977, is also of interest - as it includes the Chattahoochee 45 by **Jimmy Jukebox**, the Original Sound 45 by **King Lizard**, and **Fowley**'s *Born To Make You Cry* 45. It also includes a 1974 45, recorded by **Fowley** as **Lance Romance** and four more tracks, *Summertime Frog*, *Love Bomb*, *Living In The Streets* and *Sex Dope And Violence*.

Compilation appearances have included: *Astrology* on *Kim Fowley - Underground Animal* (LP & CD); *The Trip* on *Pebbles, Vol. 1* (LP), *Pebbles, Vol. 1* (CD), *Nuggets Box* (4-CD), *Sound Of The Sixties* (Dble LP), *Sixties Archive, Vol. 1* (CD), *Excerpts From Nuggets* (CD) and *Great Pebbles* (CD); *They're Coming To Take Me Away, Ha-Haaa!* on *Napoleon Complex* (CD); *Young America Saturday Night* on *Only In America* (CD); *Animal Man* on *Turds On A Bum Ride, Vol. 1 & 2* (Dble CD) and *Turds On A Bum Ride, Vol. 2* (Dble LP); *The Trip* and *Underground Lady* on *Pebbles Box* (5-LP) and *Trash Box* (5-CD); *Strangers From The Sky* on *U-Spaces: Psychedelic Archaeology Vol. 1* (CDR); and *The Canyon People* on *Highs In The Mid-Sixties, Vol. 3* (LP) - The latter captures him explaining to CBS

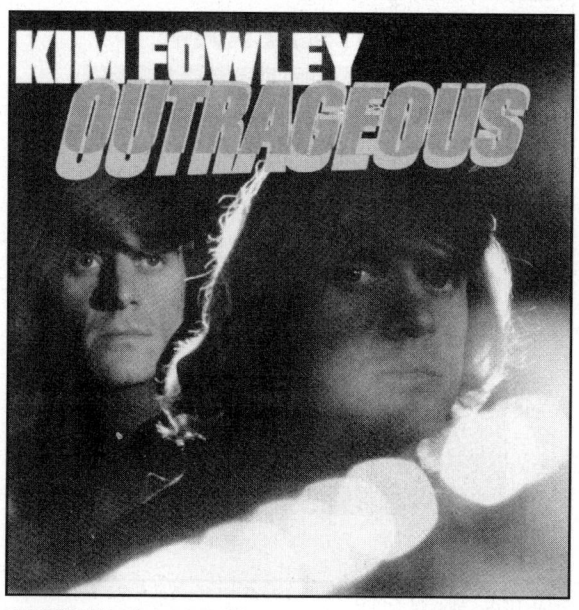

KIM FOWLEY - Outrageous CD.

news cameras, in the Summer of 1967, how 'the canyon people' had replaced the 'flower children' as America's hope for the future! (VJ/MW/JFr/SR/WHn/LA)

Lance Fox and The Bloodhounds

Personnel incl: LANCE FOX   A

45: That's Your Problem/You Got Love   (Bang 523) 1966

Both sides of this 45 have resurfaced on *Mindrocker, Vol. 13* (LP). The outfit was based in New York City. (VJ)

Fox and The Huntah's

Personnel incl: MIKE DAVIS   A
TOM FOX   A

45: Funny Kinda Day /
Love Minus Zero/No Limit   (Malcolm Z.Dirge 45004) 1966

Little has come to light about this Alabama group. Possibly from the Birmingham area, their 45 was engineered by Ed Boutwell and presumably recorded at Boutwell Studios, where the **Rockin' Rebellions** also recorded.

The Fox-Davis composition *Funny Kinda Day* can be heard again on *Psychedelic States: Alabama Vol. 1* (CD). It's a dreamy beat-ballad for the ladies and saunters along with some crisp percussive fills. Their faithful Bob Dylan cover on the flip is a little pedestrian and doesn't compare favourably with **The Leaves** version. (MW)

Fraction

Personnel: JIM BEACH   vcls   A
VIC HEMME   bs   A
BOB MEINEL   gtr   A
CURT SWANSON   perc   A
DON SWANSON   gtr   A

ALBUM: 1(A) MOON BLOOD   (Angelus 571) 1971 R5

NB: (1) was originally limited to 400 copies but has been counterfeited/reissued several times, including a limited reproduction duplicating the original "Blood Red" see-through mylar sleeve. It has also been counterfeited on CD a couple of times, including a re-press by Anthology (ANT 24.11) 199?.

45: Sanc-Divided/?   (Angelus WR 5005) 1971

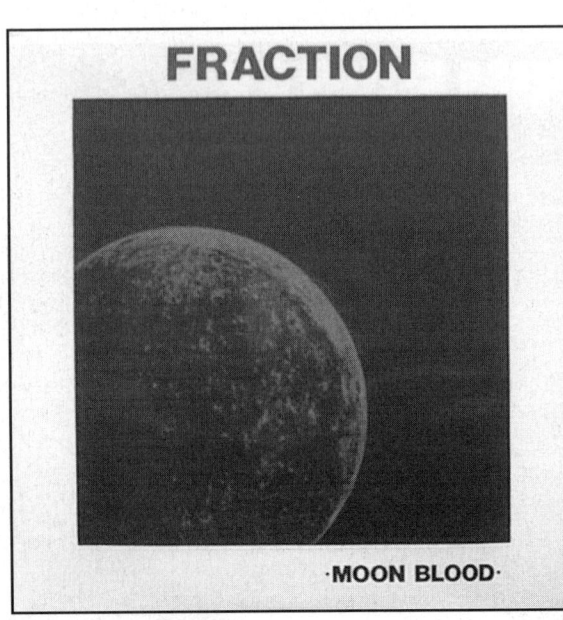

FRACTION - Moonblood LP.

This album has some good guitar and Jim Beach's vocals are reminiscent of **Doors**, although he was singing on Sunset Strip long before Jim Morrison took to the stage. *Sanc-Divided*, which was also included on the album, can be heard on the *Valley Of The Son Of The Gathering Of The Tribe* (LP) compilation.

Jim Beach had earlier sung with **Fever Tree**, although he did not record with the band. **Fraction** also recorded two further albums, which remain unreleased.

The *Filling The Gap* compilation incorrectly states that they were previously known as Stonegarden and had issued at least one 45 on Angelus entitled *Oceans Inside Me* - this is now known to be the work of a completely different outfit. (VJ/JBh)

Framework

Personnel: DREW GALLAHAR   bs, vcls   A
CLIFF LENZ   keyb'ds   A
JERRY McCANN   gtr, vcls   ABC
DANNY ORLINO   gtr   A
CARL SPIRON   drms   ABC
TERRY FANN   bs, vcls   BC
RICK RANDLE   gtr, keyb'ds, vcls   C

ALBUM: 1(A/B) SKELETON (dbl)   (Rockadelic RRLP 31/32) 2000

NB: (1) is a double album with one LP of studio cuts and rehearsal material and one live LP. It comes with extensive liner notes and several inserts and it's a limited pressing of 600 black vinyl and 100 coloured vinyl copies. (1) also issued on CD with two bonus tracks (Shadoks Music 020) 2001.

45s: α Iron Door/Funny Kind Of Sunshine   (KB Artists) 1968
I'm Gonna Move/The Direction   (Harvey Swartz HS-0001) 1969

NB: α acetate-only, issued to band members.

A legendary San Diego underground band who recorded the amazing *The Direction* 45 in 1968. Just 500 copies were pressed and as recorded here, they sound remarkably like **Frumious Bandersnatch** despite never having heard of their Bay Area counterparts! The 45 has a very clean sound as the band used small amps in the studio, but live in the sixties they cranked through over-driven stacks and their concerts are the stuff of legend. *The Direction* is a tremendous trippy dirge, with Cream-like vocals and drumming, and introspective lyrics:

"Love is something you can't feel
But hate leaves scars that never heal
I can feel the harm that's been done
Please correct me if I'm wrong
But peace has been absent for too long
I can feel the harm that's been done"
(from *The Direction*.)

McCann and Spiron had played together in **The Orfuns**, a punk band that split in 1965 when McCann ran into trouble with the law. A handful of acetates of this band survive and will see release soon.

Framework was formed in 1967 as an all-original rock group by a local production company (KB Artists) that also represented **The Brain Police**. Their first recording was made at Sunset Sound in Los Angeles and is the only known recording of line-up 'A'. In August 1968, Fann replaced Gallahar and shortly after the band stripped down to a trio. The second 45 showed a dramatic change stylistically, all connections to pop being abandoned.

At this point **Framework** became a top live draw in San Diego, playing blues-based hard-rock similar to Cream. In late 1969, Rick Randle joined the band from **The Brain Police**.

Framework folded on New Year's Eve 1970, when McCann accepted an offer to join Anthrax, who then recorded an album for Elektra as **Formerly Anthrax**. They'd gained not just a talented guitarist but, as a bonus, a flautist and versatile vocalist, who took up lead vocal duties on their accomplished jazz-prog-rock album. He wrote too and brought two compositions from the **Framework** repertoire (and featured on the Rockadelic/Shadoks retrospective) - *Like A Child* and *These Things I Know*.

FRANTIC - Conception CD.

The Rockadelic album collects all extant recordings of the band - both 45s, a rehearsal from January 1969, live concert material from late 1969 and a demo that McCann recorded at Elektra.

Jerry McCann continues to play and record in San Diego, releasing both a cassette *Unframed* and a CD *Blue Plate Special* in 1997. (CF/SR/MW)

Francisco

ALBUM:　1　COSMIC BEAM EXPERIENCE　(Cosmic Beam) 1976 SC

Housed in a colour "cosmic" cover, this obscure California psychedelic album is now a minor collector's item. Predating the New Age movement it combines electric, electronic and acoustic instruments, chorus and tranc-inducing sounds. (SR/VJ)

Joe Frank and The Knights

Personnel incl:　JOE FRANK

45s:	Five Elephants In A Volkswagen /		
	Twistin' Mississippi	(El Jay 100463)	1963
	Can't Find A Way/Won't You Come Home	(Block 510)	1966
	Can't Find A Way/Won't You Come Home	(ABC 10782)	1966

From Leland, Mississippi and featuring **Joe Frank** who, as one of the smooth popsters Hamilton, Joe Frank And Reynolds, hit the bigtime in 1975 with *Fallin' In Love*. *Can't Find A Way* found its way onto *Pennsylvania Unknowns* (LP) (which has caused much confusion as to their origins) and also *Victims Of Circumstance, Vol. 2* (LP & CD). (MW/JJe)

The Alan Franklin Explosion

Personnel incl:	ALAN FRANKLIN	gtr, vcls	AB
	(DAVE DIX	drms	B)
	(BUZZY MEEKINS	bs	B)
	(CHRIS RUSSELL	ld gtr	B)

ALBUMS:	1(A)	COME HOME BABY	(Aladin Records) 1968 -
	2(B)	BLUES CLIMAX	(Horne) 1970 R1
45:		Bye Bye Baby / Piece Of Your Love	(Horne 888-4) 1970

A marginal case for inclusion here. Musically a hard rock/blues act from Florida, with pretty wild vocals. The whole of Side Two of the second album is taken up with *Climax*, an 18-minute 10 second drivin' instrumental hard-rock rendition, which on the best scenario is reminiscent of the long instrumental jams of the San Francisco Ballrooms and at the worst monotonous.

Alan Franklin was a songwriter who recruited musicians on a session basis to record his material. His second album features Tampa musicians, David Dix and Buzzy Meekins (see **The Outlaws** entry), plus Chris Russell. The album was recorded in Orlando. (VJ/SMR)

Frantic Freddie and His Reflections

ALBUM:　1　MUSIC POWER　　　(Rice R-2828) c1968 SC

From Pennsylvania, **Frantic Freddie** was a locally famous DJ. Backed by the garage band The Moors, he performs mostly blue-eyed garage soul covers plus a humorous cut called *Day In The Life Of A Teenager*. The vocals are reputedly rather weak but the album contains some good guitar parts.

Compilation appearances include *You Told A Lie* on *Victims Of Circumstance, Vol. 2* (CD). (SR)

(The) Frantic(s)

Personnel:	MAX BYFUGLIN	vcls	A
	DAVID DAY	bs	A
	DENNIS DEVLIN	gtr	A
	JIM HAAS	keyb'ds	A
	PHIL HEAD	drms	A
	KIM SHERMAN	gtr	A

NB: Line-up 'A' shown above, was actually a later line-up of the band, and not that which recorded the *Route '66* 45.

ALBUM:　1　CONCEPTION　　(Lizard Records 20103) 1971 SC

NB: (1) has been reissued. (1) also issued on CD by SPM/World Wide Records (SPM-WWR-CD-0049) 1993 and booelegged on CD as (Flash 31). Also of interest is *Relax Your Mind* (Collectables COL-CD-0570) 1994, a CD only issue of 1968 recordings.

45s:	La Do Da Da/Route 66	(Sunco 1008) 1966
	Midnight To Six Man/Shady Sam	(Lizard 21002) 1969/70

We are informed that this group hailed from Billings, Montana, originally, though they toured all over the country. In 1968 they relocated to Santa Fe, New Mexico, then moved onto Colorado Springs before making L.A. their final base in 1969, removing the final 'S' from their name and recording the *Conception* album. All told they lasted from 1965 to 1971 and just 1,000 copies of their first 45 were pressed back in 1966.

The *Conception* album has been likened to early **MC5**, but the *Relax Your Mind* CD of an unreleased 1968 album, is more overtly psychedelic and is one of Collectables' more worthwhile reissues. It was recorded at Norman Petty's studio in Clovis, New Mexico.

When the band broke up in 1971, three members went on to form an outfit called The Cows, who recorded an unreleased album, *Hunchbacks From Outer Space*. It had been thought that **Frantic** had become an act known as **Farm Band**, however **Frantic** member Dennis Devlin, says this is false... commenting "I suppose one shouldn't discount the possibility that there may have been more than one band in the USA calling themselves **Frantic**; there were certainly several "The Frantics" as you know. Another theory springs to mind as to why they may have been connected to us. It was common practice in the Midwest during the late sixties for unscrupulous promoters to book unknown local bands into venues as touring English bands, as it was thought at the time that all musicians with long hair looked alike. When we were playing Midwestern gigs there was a bogus "Them" playing the same circuit. Most people wouldn't have known the difference. I assume these bands were encouraged to work up a few songs by whatever group they were pretending to be and hope for the best. What this is leading to is that after **Frantic** broke up, we heard rumours of a bogus **Frantic** playing back in the Midwest, apparently having learned our album. I know none of the original **Frantics** were involved, but perhaps the Farm Band started off as a bogus **Frantic**? It would be interesting to hear from a Farm Band member."

Compilation appearances have included: *Route 66* on *Punk Classics* (CD) and *Punk Classics, Vol. 5* (7"); and both *Relax Your Mind* and *Just For A While* on *Green Crystal Ties, Vol. 6* (CD). (MW/DD)

Fraternity of Man

Personnel:	RICHARD HAYWARD	drms, vcls	A
	ELLIOT INGBER	ld gtr	A
	MARTIN KIBBEE	bs	A
	WARREN KLEIN	gtr	A
	LARRY WAGNER	vcls, gtr	A

ALBUMS:	1(A)	FRATERNITY OF MAN	(ABC ABCS 647) 1968	-
	2(A)	GET IT ON	(Dot 25955) 1969	SC

NB: (1) and (2) reissued on CD by Edsel (EDCD 437 and EDCD 438 respectively) in 1995.

				HCP
45:	Don't Bogart Me/Wispy Paisley Skies		(ABC 11106) 1968	133

This Los Angeles band grew out of **Factory** of which Kibbee, Hayward and Klein were members. They are probably best known for *Don't Bogart Me*, which appeared on the soundtrack to counter-culture epic "Easy Rider".

Produced by **Tom Wilson** (**Mothers**, **Ill Wind**, **Velvet Underground**, **Harumi** etc), their albums are musically quite diverse and raw, but worth investigation. With its superb sleeve, *Fraternity Of Man* contains a cover of **Frank Zappa**'s *Oh No I Don't Believe It*, all the other tracks being group compositions. *In The Morning* is particularly notable for its lyrics ("High in the morning, high in the afternoon, high in the evening...") whilst *Candy Striped Loin's Tails* features good use of sitar, guitars and percussion.

Their second album, *Get It On* is equally as good. Once again the group composed most of the songs (including *Too High To Eat*), except for three covers (Sonny Boy Williamson's *Don't Start Me Talkin'*, *Cat's Squirrel* (also recorded by Cream) and *Trick Bag* penned by P. Weedon).

Ingber had previously played with **The Mothers Of Invention** and later became Winged Eel Fingerling with **Captain Beefheart**. Hayward later played in Little Feat (Lowell George had guested on a couple of **The Fraternity of Man**'s album tracks), and **Kim Fowley** also guested on the first album. Warren Klein later worked with **Kim Fowley** on his *I'm Bad* release.

In The Morning and *Plastic Rat* also appear on a rare compilation of **Tom Wilson**'s productions, *Tom's Touch*, released by ABC in 1969.

Retrospective compilation appearances include: *Don't Bogart Me* and *Fherinst* on *Then And Now, Vol. 1* (CD); and *Bikini Baby* on *Then And Now, Vol. 2* (CD). (VJ/SR/JFr)

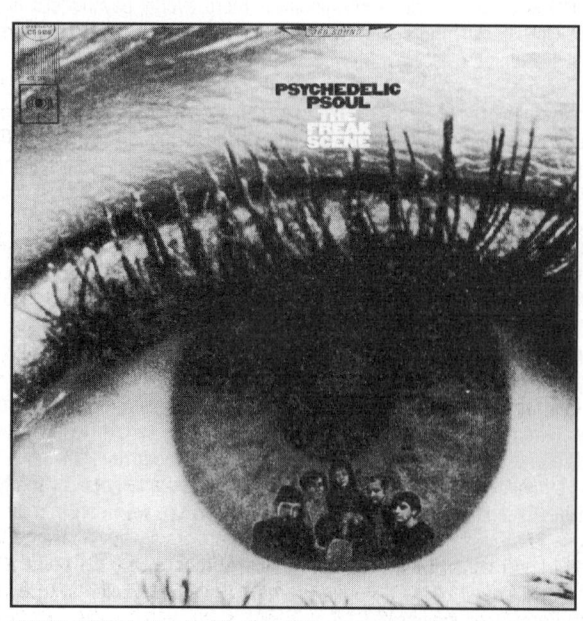

FREAK SCENE - Psychedelic Psoul CD.

Freak Scene

Personnel incl:	RUSTY EVANS	A

ALBUM:	1	PSYCHEDELIC PSOUL	(Columbia 9356) 1967 R2

NB: (1) has been counterfeited on vinyl in 1989 and also twice on CD including (Head 2896) 1997. The album has also been reissued officially on CD together with **Devil's Anvil**'s album

45:	A Million Grains Of Sand/ Behind The Mind	(Columbia 44056) 1967

The album is virtually a second **Deep** one and almost identical in style. *A Million Grains Of Sand* and *My Rainbow Life* are two of its better tracks. Some of the other material can arguably described as rubbish, or brilliant. It's now a minor collectors' item and has been reissued several times. *My Rainbow Life* was also done by **Third Bardo** and it has therefore been surmised that they were yet another of **Rusty Evans**' 'projects'. This was not the case as you'll read later in the **Third Bardo** entry. *Filling The Gap* includes a different version of *A Million Grains of Sand* that **Rusty** recorded at a later date as **Marcus**.

Compilation appearances include *A Million Grains Of Sand* on *Psychosis From The 13th Dimension* (CDR & CD). (VJ)

Fred

Personnel:	JOE DeCHRISTOPHER	gtr	AB
	BO FOX	drms	A
	KEN PRICE	keyb'ds	AB
	MIKE ROBISON	bs, gtr, vcls	AB
	DAVID ROSE	keyb'ds, violin, gtr, vcls	AB
	GARY ROSENBERG	lyrics, perc	A
	PETER EGGERS	drms, piano	B

ALBUM:	1(A/B)	FRED	(World In Sound RFR-007) 2001

NB: (1) also issued on CD (World In Sound WIS-1003) 2001.

45:	A Love Song/Salvation Lady	(Arpeggio 1057) 1971

The **Fred** album encapsulates the band's 1971-1973 period. Gathering together the 45 and seven unreleased tracks, Joe DeChristopher recounts the history of the band within the lavish heavy-duty gatefold. A brief precis:-

DeChristopher had met Price in 1967 at Bucknell University in Lewisburg, Pennslyvania and joined Price's band, Still At Large. Over the next three years the band picked up other students and evolved into **Fred**. Classmate Gary Rosenberg was the band's No. 1 fan, a college radio DJ and sometime poet - he occasionally performed with them on stage and

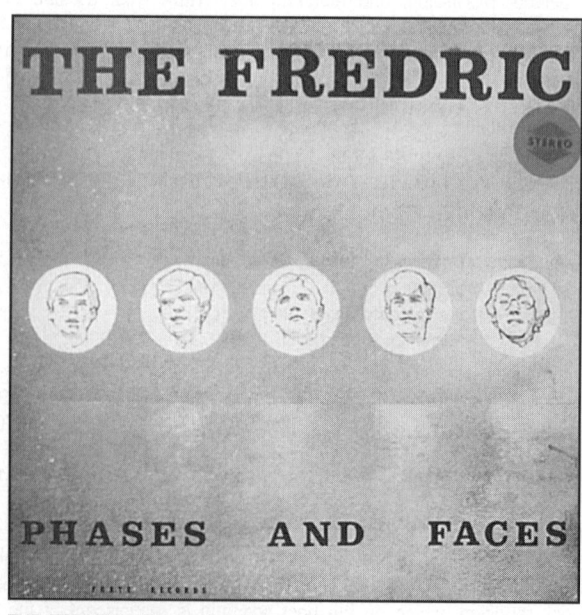

THE FREDRIC - Phases And Faces LP.

became their lyricist. He was also their guide to other sounds around, introducing them to the likes of Procol Harum, Jethro Tull, Frank Zappa and The Mahavishnu Orchestra, whose songs they would cover.

In 1970, the band graduated (or left) BU and moved into a couple of farms near Lewisburg. They continued to perform at local clubs and schools. The first recordings, which make up the bulk of the album, were done the following year and their debut 45 was released. In 1973 occasional member Peter Eggers joined the band permanently and marked the end of their formative chapter, with the departure of Gary Rosenberg. The liners announce that later recordings are forthcoming.

There's some fine fuzz solos and acidic leads with occasional wah-wah but despite being tagged as psychedelia elsewhere, there's a strong aura of mellowed, slightly trippy, pastoral rock that's coming from folk roots and gently drifting off in a prog/hippie direction. The violin adds to the non-urban vibe but is more like Curved Air than Mahavishnu.

A Love Song previously appeared on the 1982 compilation *Pennsylvania Unknowns* (LP).

There may be a further 45 on the Arpeggio label which includes a track called *Killing Confusion*, but its existence remains unconfirmed. (MW)

The Fredric

Personnel:	RON BERA	keyb'ds, trumpet, horn	A
	BOB GEIS	gtr	A
	DAVE IDEMA	drms, clawes, bongos	A
	JOE McCARGAR	vcls, perc	A
	STEVE THRALL	gtr, melodica, sitar, olivefte	A

| ALBUM: | 1(A) | PHASES AND FACES | (Forte 80461) 1968 R4 |

NB: (1) has been repressed and issued on CD with bonus tracks (Arf! Arf! AA 061) 1996.

| 45s: | 5 O'Clock Traffic/Red Pier | (Evolution 1001) 1968 |
| | 5 O'Clock Traffic/Red Pier | (Forte 3001) 1968 |

Pleasant minor league soft pop-rock with some psychy moments. From Grand Rapids, Michigan, this outfit would evolve into **Rock Garden** (who cut one 45 - *Johnny's Music Machine/Love Is A Good Foundation* on (Capitol 2806) 1970) then Garden (*The Winds Of South Chicago/The First Day Of My Life* (Capitol 2919) 1970). Both these 45s are best avoided.

Lead vocalist Joe McCargar and guitarist Bob Geis were high school mates playing in a local band. When their existing drummer and guitarist quit, shortly before a gig, they drafted in Steve Thrall, with whom they immediately struck up an accord. In the days that followed, David Idema - a family friend - and Ron Bera were added and the band began to rehearse extensively.

They soon caught the eye of a booking agent, who got them a support slot for U.K. duo **Harper and Rowe**, who were doing a U.S. promotional tour. **Harper and Rowe**, didn't want to be upstaged by a local support, so the band changed their name to **The Fredric** on their way to the first gig in Fredric, Michigan. They soon developed a good local reputation, and opened shows for **The Box Tops**, **Tommy James and The Shondells**, and **Yellow Balloon**, amongst others.

The oft-hyped-as-a psych-megabuck-rarity album has seen a boot reissue, but even better is the Arf! Arf! CD reissue, which includes the non-album *Five O'Clock Traffic* plus three cuts recorded for an aborted second album.

It should be said that, while the album may not blow your mind, the music is of a consistently high quality throughout.

Compilation appearances have included: *Federal Reserve Bank Blues* on *The Arf! Arf! Blitzkrieg 32 Track Sampler* (Dble CD); *Five O'Clock Traffic* on *Echoes In Time, Vol's 1 & 2* (CD), *Echoes In Time, Vol. 2* (LP), *Filling The Gap* (4-LP) and *Gathering Of The Tribe* (CD). (MW)

FREEBORNE - Peak Impressions LP.

The Free

| 45s: | (A Day Of Decision) For Lost Soul Blue/ What Makes You? | (Marquee 448) 1968 |
| | (A Day Of Decision) For Lost Soul Blue/ What Makes You? | (Atco 6662) 1969 |

This was the work of an obscure and too short-lived Michigan band. The 'A' side, *(A Day Of Decision) For Lost Soul Blue* is a superb venture into psychedelia with lots of fuzz, wah-wah and bizarre lyrics. After the ultra heavy topside the flip could only be a lighter affair - bright midfast handclappin' pop-rock with some finger-pickin' good guitar.

Compilation appearances have included: *(A Day Of Decision) For Lost Soul Blue* on *Sixties Rebellion, Vol. 15* (LP & CD), *Sixties Archive, Vol. 6* (CD), *All Cops In Delerium - Good Roots* (LP) and *Psychotic Moose And The Soul Searchers* (LP). (VJ/MW)

Free Agency

| 45: | Found My Way Back Home/? | (TFA 101) c1971 |

A Mormon psych-pop 45 with male/female vocals, keyboards and hand drums. It was pressed on white vinyl. (SR)

Freeborne

Personnel:	NICK CARSTOIU	gtr, keyb'ds, vcls, recorder, cello	A
	DAVE CODD	recorder, harp, perc, vcls, bs	A
	LEW LIPSON	drms, perc	A
	BOB MARGOLIN	ld gtr	A
	MIKE SPIROS	keyb'ds, chimes, trumpet, perc	A

| ALBUM: | 1(A) | PEAK IMPRESSIONS | (Monitor MPS 607) 1967 R2 |

NB: (1) has been counterfeited at least twice on vinyl in the eighties and nineties. It has also issued on CD by Afterglow in 1995, but with one track either edited or missing. More recently the album has been reissued again on CD by Distortions (DR 1041) 1998, this time with three bonus cuts!

| 45: | Land of Diana/Images | (Monitor 45-1806) 1967 |

A Boston group whose sole album, recorded at CBS Studios in New York, is excellent - full of the acid imagery which typified the Bosstown sound in 1968. Almost every track is of interest. For example *Land Of Diana* has a compelling organ intro, *Visions Of My Own* some fine woodwind instrumentation and *Inside People* unusual fuzztone vocals and pleasing keyboards.

In 1997, an alternate 45 mono mix of *Land of Diana* surfaced on Erik Lindgren's excellent *A Heavy Dose Of Lyte Psych* (CD), and in 1998, Distortions reissued *Peak Impressions* on CD together with three bonus cuts: the mono 45 version of *Images*, an alternate stereo mix of *Land Of Diana*, and *Incidental Music* - twenty-odd seconds worth of spacey keyboard noodlings.

In the mid-'70s, Bob Margolin became a member of Muddy Waters' band and he later played with the Johnny Winter Group. He is still touring and recording Chicago Blues albums. Nick Carstoiu too remains active in the music scene.

In 1978, Mike Spiros released, as "Mic Spiros and the ITMB (Incredible Two Man Band)", a rare album of atmospheric prog-rock based on keyboards and synthesizers. (VJ/MW/SR/JRe)

Free Design

Personnel:	BRUCE DEDRICK	vcls	A
	CHRIS DENDRICK	vcls, piano	A
	ELLEN DENDRICK	vcls	A
	SANDY DENDRICK	vcls	A

ALBUMS:	1	KITES ARE FUN	(Project 3 PR 5019SD) 1967 -
	2	YOU COULD BE BORN AGAIN	
			(Project 3 PR 5031SD) 1968 -
	3	HEAVEN / EARTH	(Project 3 PR 5037SD) 1969 -
	4	ONE BY ONE	(Project 3 PR 5061 SD) c1970 SC
	5	THERE IS A SONG	(Ambrotype) 1972 SC

NB: There's also a Spanish compilation, *Umbrellas* (Siesta 104) 1999, and a UK compilation CD *Best Of* (Cherry Red CDMRED 194).

45s:	Kites Are Fun / Proper Ornaments	(Project 3 1324) 1967
	You Be You And I'll Be Me / Never ...	(Project 3 1331) 1968
	Eleanor Rigby / Make The Madness Stop	(Project 3 1345) 1968
	A Leaf Has Veins / You Could Be Born Again	(Project 3 1350) 196?
	Where Do I Go / Girls Alone	(Project 3 1356) 196?
	Dorian Benediction / Summertime	(Project 3 1358) 196?
	If I Were A Carpenter / Now Is The Time	(Project 3 1360) 196?
	2002: A Hit Song / Hurry Sundown	(Project 3 1366) 1969
	Butterflies Are Free / ?	(Project 3 1370) 196?
	Bubbles / I'm A Yogi	(Project 3 1375) 196?
	Tomorrow Is The First Day Of The Rest Of My Life / Kije's Ouija	(Project 3 1383) 196?
	Don't Cry Baby / Time And Love	(Project 3 1387) 196?
	Felt So Good / You Are My Sunshine	(Project 3 1393) 196?
	Friendly Man / Stay Off Of Your Frown	(Project 3 1404) 196?
	Friends (Thank You All) / Going Back	(Project 3 1415) 196?

A sophisticated pop-psych/soft-rock group with harmony vocals led by Chris Dendrick. **Free Design** released several albums on Command/Project3 and were based in New York state. Their records may interest fans of groups like **Neon Philharmonic** and are more and more sought-after.

Chris Dendrick became an active session musician and arranger. (SR/MW)

Freedom Express

Personnel:	ZIP COCHENOUR	drms	A
	MIKE HYRCZYK	gtr, bs	A
	DAVE MILOVAC	electric piano, bs	A
	PAUL MILOVAC	gtr	A

ALBUM: 1(A) BRINGS FRESH AIR (Fresh Start FSR-1) 1975 SC

A rural-style rock album recorded at Asterik Recording Studio, Pittsburgh, Pennsylvania. It was produced by the group and Gino Manetta. Aside from the rather inane country song that opens the album, there are some fine tracks. *No Sugar* is a trashy hard-rocker with fuzz guitar, and *He's A Mercenary Soldier* is a cool acoustic rock track reminiscent of Jethro Tull. (VJ/CF)

Freedom Five

45: We Aren't Free/To Save My Soul (SRI 5527) 196?

A late sixties garage band from Oak Park, Illinois, whose 45 is highly-rated. (VJ)

Freedom Highway

Personnel:	ANDY BLAKE	gtr	A
	GEOFF EVANS	tambourine	A
	GENE GARCIA	gtr, vcls	A
	DAVE HARRIS	bs	A
	RICHARD "RICHI RAY" HARRIS	gtr, vcls	ABCDE
	CHUCK HODGE	drms	A
	KURT EICHSTAEDT	drms	B
	SCOTT INGLIS	bs, vcls	BCD
	MIKE LAMB	gtr, vcls	B
	HOWIE LAZZARINI	organ, vcls	B
	BRUCE BRYMER	drms, vcls	CDE
	GARY PHILIPPET	gtr, vcls	DE
	DAVID SCHALLOCK	bs, vcls	E

NB: Line-up 'A' initially known as City Lights, then **Freedom Highway** 1965. Line-up 'B' 1966. Line-up 'C' 1967-8. Line-up 'D' 1968. Line-up 'E' 1969-70.

ALBUM: 1(C/E) MADE IN '68 (RD Records RD 9) 2001

This act used to play at the Avalon Ballroom and outdoor San Francisco shows. Led by guitarist, singer and songwriter Richard Harris, later known as "Richi Ray". They never put out a record, but they were a great live act and over their four year life-span played with **Buffalo Springfield**, **The Doors**, **Grateful Dead**, **Quicksilver**, **Big Brother and the Holding Co.**, **Jefferson Airplane** etc.

Their retrospective album features studio recordings of two incarnations. The earliest material consists of three terrific tracks that sound like **Moby Grape** circa their debut album. The stunning *Be My Friend* has the same infectious energy as the **'Grape**'s *Omaha* and is the stand-out cut on offer here. More than half of the album was recorded in 1969 and is in a slightly more rural-rock style but still exhibiting plenty of energy and ideas. An insert is included with memoirs of two group members and an abundance of general information.

FREEDOM EXPRESS - Brings Fresh Air LP.

FREEDOM HIGHWAY.

Brymer and Schallock were both previously with **The Pullice**. Philippet had fronted The Mystics during the pre-British Invasion era that also featured Larry Otis (**Red Mountain**, **Born Again**) for a short time. He was also with **Electric Train** and **Front Line** and, after leaving **Freedom Highway**, he went on to **Copperhead**, Earthquake and The Greg Kihn band as well as playing on Kathi McDonald's album *Insane Asylum*. Schallock went on to **Big Brother**, The Sons (neé **Sons of Champlin**), and David Bromberg's band. Brymer played with the Marin-based Ducks (with an album on the Just Sunshine label, unconnected to the Santa Cruz-based band assembled by Neil Young), and played with **Barry Melton**. He is still active on the Bay Area music scene. Richi Ray Harris went on teach at Sonoma State University then took a role in the Broadway stage show "Beatlemania".

Thanks to Mike Somavilla for the use of his liner notes to *Made In '68* for this entry. (TO/CF)

Freedom of Choice

45:   Doctor Tom/Fat Man   (Wand WND-11223) 1970

Turn-of-decade fuzzy psych-rock, led by female vocals, that's both catchy and nicely brain-tingling. It should have been a massive hit but, of course, the best stuff never was. The flip is competent too, tho' lacking the fuzz 'n' effects. Nothing known about the group. (MW)

The Free For All

45:   Blue Monday/Show Me The Way   (Challenge 59339) 1966

It has been revealed at long last that this was actually Nova Scotia's **Great Scots** under a pseudonym, though they did spend plenty of time South of the U.S./Canadian border, recording in New York and later Los Angeles. Their story is revealed on two recent Sundazed releases - *The Great Lost Great Scots Album* (Sundazed SC 5052, 1997) and *Arrive!* (Beat Rocket BR 101, 1998). See their entry in the Canadian section of *Dreams Fantasies And Nightmares*.

The 'A' side was a big beat number. The flip, is an undeniably commercial pop-punk song (co-written by Keith Colley, a familiar L.A. writer, and produced by Richard Delvy, another significant figure in the L.A. scene at that time).

Compilation appearances include: *Show Me The Way* on *Psychedelic Microdots Of The Sixties, Vol. 1* (CD), *I Turned Into A Helium Balloon* (CD) and *Pebbles, Vol. 9* (LP). (MW)

Shane Freeman

45:   Blowin' My Mind/
      Killer   (Electric Ice/Stutz Records no #) c1969

Recorded and mixed at After Dark Studios (maybe based in Indiana), an obscure rock single with promising song titles. (SR)

Freeman Sound

Personnel: RAY ESCOTT   vcls   A
             L. J. FORTIER   drms   A
             JOHN HARROW   ld gtr   A
             BUSTER McCARTHY   bs   A
             KURT SUNDERMAN   gtr   A

45:   Singing My Own Song/Sixteen Tons (PS)   (Starshine 7059) 1970

A hard rockin' Cortland, Ohio, band on the same label as **Morly Grey** and Biggy Rat. Comes in a "1970 Limited Collector Edition" picture sleeve (way ahead of the times there) which also optimistically announces 'release of record to be limited to 10,000 Annually Worldwide'. The searing guitar on the 'B' side certainly merits that.

L.J. informs us that originals came out on red labels. Those on pink labels are a later pressing. The picture sleeves copies (with pink label records) were put out in the nineties by the band's "manager" Floyd Philips to enhance their collectability. (MW)

Freeport

Personnel: CRAIG HOLT   gtr, vcls   A
             ROGER LEWIS   gtr, vcls   A
             KEVIN RALEIGH   keyb'ds, vcls A
             DENNIS STADNEY   bs   A
             BILL STALLING   drms, vcls   A

ALBUM: 1(A)   FREEPORT   (Mainstream 6130) 1970 R1

45s: I Need Your Lovin/
       I Need Your Lovin (mono)   (Mainstream 730) 1970
       Now That She's Gone/
       (Don't Let Me Be) Misunderstood   (Mainstream 732) 1970

One of the last rock releases on Mainstream, it's both disappointing and directionless. Some tracks are rock-oriented (the uninteresting cover of The Animals' (*Don't Let Me) Misunderstood*), some are dreamy ballads with flute and delicate piano, whilst others are pop (their cover of Eric Carmen's *I Need Your Lovin*), all have some female vocal harmonies.

In the early eighties, Kevin Raleigh resurfaced with the Michael Stanley Band, a FM rock group. (SR)

Free Reign

ALBUMS: 1   FREE REIGN   (Private Pressing) c1973 R1
          2   ANTONYMOUS   (Bridges) c1974 -

A Kentucky band playing a mix of prog and psych-rock. Their first album was recorded live and is extremely rare. (SR)

Free Spirits

Personnel: COLUMBUS "CHIP" BAKER   gtr   A
             LARRY CORYELL   gtr, vcls, sitar A
             CHRIS HILLS   bs   A
             BOBBY MOSES   drms   A
             JIM PEPPER   sax   A

ALBUM: 1(A)   OUT OF SIGHT AND SOUND   (ABC ABC-S 593) 1967 -

Produced by Bob Thiele, **Free Spirits** were a group of talented young jazz musicians trying to do an "electric rock" album with original material. There are some really nice tracks and instrumental parts (*Angels Can't Be True*, *I'm Gonna Be Free* with its sitar, *Cosmic Daddy Dancer* with an excellent guitar...) but the vocals are generally too weak and most songs are not strong enough.

Bob Thiele was later more successful in introducing jazz musicians to rock with **Eden's Children**.

Larry Coryell had a very prolific career. **Jim Pepper** also released some solo LPs and wrote *Witchi Tai To* which was covered by **Everything is Everything**, **Harpers' Bizarre** and **Brewer and Shipley**.

Pepper died in the nineties. (SR)

Free Thinkers

Personnel incl: FRANK RONDELL   A

45s:	She's Hurt/You Were Born For Me	(Mala 517) 1965
	Why Why, Why/She's Hurt	(Mala 532) 1966

Originally from Toronto, Canada, this "project" was executed in New York. The flip to the first 45, a very solid punk-pop sound with a heavy bass, written by Wes Farrel and Doc Pomus, can be heard on *Pebbles, Vol. 12* (LP). Unfortunately *She's Hurt* is a pre-Beatles type ballad whilst *Why, Why, Why* is a mournful harmony ballad brightened only by a few bars of squealing guitar. (VJ)

The Freeways

45: I Need Love/?   (Hi Back) 1966

An unknown garage group with a good guitar break. (SR)

Freight Train

ALBUM: 1 JUST THE BEGINNING   (Fly By Nite) 1971 SC

From Philadelphia, a heavy blues-rock outfit inspired by British groups like Chicken Shack or the Groundhogs. (SR)

French Lick

ALBUM: 1 GLIDER   (Private Pressing) 1976 R1

A guitar-driven progressive outfit. The few known copies have a paste-on cover and an insert. (SR)

Fresh Air

ALBUM: 1 A BREATH OF FRESH AIR
                       (Amaret ST 5003) 1969 SC

The rarest release on Amaret (a label mainly known for the albums by **Crow**), it's a good mix of pop and hard-psych, with heavy guitar and organ. (SR)

Fresh Blueberry Pancake

Personnel:	JOHN BEHRENS	gtr, vcls	A
	TONY IMPAVIDO	bs, ld vcls	A
	GEOFF RYDELL	drms	A

ALBUM: 1(A) HEAVY   (No label B.P. 1/2) 1970 R6

NB: (1) demo album issued in plain sleeve with title sticker on shrinkwrap. Reissued in 2001, in newly-designed sleeve on heavy duty blue vinyl in a numbered limited edition of 450 (Shadoks 022).

This band was from Pittsburgh, Pennsylvania. They formed in 1968 and by 1970 they were performing primarily original material which necessitated the recording of the demo album. Only 54 copies were pressed, and they were used for promotion... it's now rather difficult to locate!

FRESH BLUEBERRY PANCAKE - Heavy LP.

It ranges from post-**Hendrix**/**Blue Cheer** brain-numbingly heavy acid-rock (watch out for the opener, *Hassles*), through bluesy moods, lighter jazzy touches, to jangley almost-folk-rock restraint. The lyrics occasionally head in a religious direction but are not preachy; the overall feel is more one of "Old Crow" than "Old Testament".

Fresh Blueberry Pancake shortened their name to Pancake before calling it quits in 1972. Having still got the master tapes, they are currently working on a CD reissue themselves.

Compilation appearances have included *Bad Boy Turns Good* on *Yee-Haw! The Other Side Of Country* (LP & CD). (CF/MW)

Friar Tuck

Personnel:	BEN BENAY	gtr	A
	CURT BOETTCHER	vcls	A
	MIKE DEASY (Friar Tuck)	gtr	A
	TOXIE FRENCH (TOXEY FRENCH)	vibes	A
	MIKE HENDERSON	organ	A
	BUTCH PARKER	piano	A
	SANDY SALISBURY	vcls	A
	JERRY SCHEFF	bs	A
	JIM TROXEL	drms	A

ALBUM: 1(A) FRIAR TUCK AND HIS PSYCHEDELIC GUITAR
                       (Dot/Mercury/MGZ 1111/SR 61111) 1967 SC

45: Alley-Oop/Sweet Pea   (Mercury 72684) 1967

This album was produced by **Curt Boettcher** and was a studio-only project. **Mike Deasy** was 'Friar Tuck' and is so depicted on the cover. A survivor from the instrumental and surf scenes he'd be involved in many other Los Angeles studio projects and outfits, often with **Curt Boettcher** and others of this particular clique of seasoned session musicians. These include **Flower Pot**, **Ceyleib People**, Your Gang and **Gator Creek**. Not one of **Boettcher**'s greatest, the album does nonetheless include vocal tracks from the pre-**Sagittarius** and **Millennium** outfit **Ballroom**.

Scheff, Benay and French also recorded as **Goldenrod**. (VJ/MW/JFr)

Friedles

Personnel:	HERMAN FRIED	gtr	A
	MIKE FRIED	gtr	A
	MILT FRIED	vcls	A
	SIMON FRIED	bs	A

45s:	The Joke's On You/?	(Not Released) 196?
α	I Lost Her/I'm So Glad	(Scope 4818) 1965
	I Lost Her/I'm So Glad	(Hanna H 1001) 1965

She Can Go/Don't Tell Me What To Do	(Bat B 1004)	196?
When Love/Love The Way You Loved Me	(Not Released)	1968

NB: α released as by The Fried Brothers.

Penns Grove, in the Southwestern tip of New Jersey, was home to this band of four brothers. They started off with a pretty primitive punk sound typified by *I Lost Her* and *Don't Tell Me What To Do*, but in mid-career were also influenced by bands like The Zombies and Searchers as evidenced on *She Can Go*. By 1968, they were experimenting with psychedelia. Sadly *When Love* was not released at the time but it's full of whining vocals and psyched-out guitar. Alas! Despite experimenting with a horn section and female back-up vocalists they vanished back into obscurity but you can hear their finer moments:. *I Lost Her, She Can Go, Don't Tell Me What To Do* and *When Love* on the *Attack Of The Jersey Teens* (LP) compilation. (VJ)

Ruthann Friedman

ALBUM:	1 CONSTANT COMPANION	(Reprise RS-6363) 1969 ?
45s:	Birdie's Blues/Halfway There	(A&M 908) 1968
	Carry On/People	(Reprise 0941) 1970

A fragile Californian folk singer, perhaps best known for writing **The Assocation**'s *Windy*. Her record will interest some readers, as it features **Peter Kaukonen** on one track. (SR/MMs)

Friend and Lover

Personnel:	JIM POST (FRIEND)	vcls, gtr	A
	CATHY POST (LOVER)	vcls	A

ALBUM:	1(A) REACH OUT OF THE DARKNESS	
		(Verve Forecast FTS 3055) 1968 -

45s:	Zig Zag/If Love Is In Your Heart	(Verve/Forecast 5091) 196?

NB: also released in France with a picture sleeve. There was also a German 45 with picture sleve: *Reach Out Of The Darkness/Time On Your Side* (Verve Forecast 518006) 1968

A husband and wife pop duo whose only album was produced by **Joe South** and Buddy Buie and recorded in Atlanta. It's mainly notable for the pop raga *Room To Let* with its sitar.

Jim Post, who wrote all the songs, would later record some singer/songwriter albums in a James Taylor mould. (SR/MMr)

The Friendly Torpedos

Personnel:	SEAN BONNIWELL	A
	PAUL BUFF	A
	BRIAN ROSS	A

45:	Nothin's Too Good For My Car /	
	So Long Ago	(Original Sound OS-95) 1970

This was a Los Angeles-based studio only product of Sean Bonniwell and Paul Buff, the studio whizz behind the **Music Machine**'s recordings. For Bonniwell completists only, it is very disappointing compared to his previous output: the 'A' is inane pop whilst the flip is country-style pop! Paul Buff would issue a similarly odd 45 as **Mad Andy's Twist Combo** on the same label. (MW)

Friendship

Personnel:	DAVE HOFFMAN	A
	MIKE GILSON	A
	KIT GROVE	A
	DUANE LANGNESS	A

ALBUM:	1(A) THE FRIENDSHIP ALBUM	(Friendship FR 3/4) c1973 ?

When Dave Hoffman and Mike Gilson left **The Unbelievable Uglies** in 1973 they formed **Friendship**. A very talented group with exceptional vocals and strong, solid musicianship, their album was recorded in their own studio in the Fargo-Moorhead area (on the Minnesota / North Dakota border). It consists soley of cover versions of older hits.

The band had a very good local following in the few years they were together, playing mostly cover arrangements of Beach Boys and Beatles songs. (VJ)

Friends of The Family

Personnel:	JIMMY CRAWFORD	drms	AB
	TED MUNDA	ld vcls, gtr	AB
	JOHN RHOADES	bs	A
	WAYNE WATSON	ld gtr	AB
	RAY ANDREWS	bs, vcls	B
	LINZEE LEE	keyb'ds, vcls	B

ALBUMS:	1(A/B) THE SONGS OF TED MUNDA	
		(Distortions DB 1003) 1991
	2(A/B) THE ENFIELDS AND THE FRIENDS OF THE FAMILY	
		(Get Hip GHAS 5000) 1993

NB: (2) duplicates some of the same material as (1).

45:	Can't Go Home/How You Gonna Keep Your	
	Little Girl Home	(Smash S-2144) 1968

Upon the demise of **The Enfields** (a Wilmington, Delaware outfit), Ted Munda quickly formed another band with John Rhoades and two former members of another local band The Turfs, Wayne Watson and Jimmy Crawford. In May 1967, they entered the Virtue Recording Studios in Philadelphia to record a six song demo, which several labels (including Kama Sutra) expressed an interest in but none would actually release. The tracks - *Time Music, Wallace, He Plays With Frogs, Funny Flowers, Blue Boat Makes Me Sad, Jello Lights* and *Bambi's March* - can now all be heard on the Distortions/Get Hip retrospectives. They perfectly showcase Munda's fine songwriting and breathtaking Zombies-style vocals.

John Rhoades left the band in the late Summer of '67, being replaced by Linzee Lee and Ray Andrews, and a further five original songs (*You See I've Got This Cold, Last Beach Crusade, Hot Apple Betty, Together* and *Sing A Song*) were recorded in July '68. These tunes were arguably Munda's finest work, with a Beatles/**Left Banke** feel, and can be found on the Get Hip CD retrospective. They were all passed over at the time, however, in favour of the two tracks *Can't Go Home* and *How You Gonna Keep Your Little Girl Home*, which were penned by Cameo Parkway staff writer Neil Brian. In fact, the band were only allowed to sing on these two cuts, with hired session musicians playing all the instruments. Subsequently, the band fell out with label owner/producer Joe Renzetti, and went their own way... they didn't record again, but did get to open for The Who and Pink Floyd at the Philadelphia Music Festival in late 1968, shortly before they split.

Ted Munda went on to play with Hotspur, who released an album on Columbia in 1974, and later in the eighties, an outfit called State Of Heart. He has also written some children's books.

Both the Get Hip/Distortions retrospectives come with detailed liner notes from Dave Brown, from which this entry has largely been taken. (VJ/MW)

Friendsound

Personnel:	RON COLLINS	organ	A
	CHRIS ETHERIDGE	bs	A
	JIM GORDON	drms	A
	DRAKE LEVIN	gtr	A
	MIKE SMITH	drms	A
	PHIL VOLK	bs	A

ALBUM:	1(A) JOYRIDE	(RCA Victor LSP-4114) 1969 SC

NB: (1) has been counterfeited.

A strange, haunting album of acid-inspired experimental weirdness, which is worth seeking out and is becoming a minor collectors' item.

Drake Levin, Mike Smith and Phil Volk were all ex-**Paul Revere And The Raiders** and together with Ron Collins also recorded as **Brotherhood**. (JTk/VJ)

Frijid Pink

Personnel:	TOM BEAUDRY	bs	A
	KELLY GREEN	ld vcls	A
	RICH STEVERS	drms, tympani	AB
	GARY THOMPSON	gtr	A
	TOM HARRIS		B
	JOHN WEARING	ld vcls	B
	CRAIG WEBB	ld gtr	B
	LARRY ZELANKA	piano, organ	B

HCP

ALBUMS:	1(A)	FRIJID PINK	(Parrot 71033) 1970	11	-
	2(A)	FRIJID PINK DEFROSTED	(Parrot 71041) 1970	149	-
	3(B)	EARTH OMEN	(Lion LN-1004) 1972	-	-
	4(B)	ALL PINK INSIDE	(Fantasy 9464) 1975	-	-

NB: (1) and 2 also issued in France (Deram SML-R 1062 and 1077 respectively). All albums have been reissued on CD. (1) with two extra tracks (Repertoire REP 4156-WZ), (2) with four bonus cuts (Repertoire REP 4172-WZ) and (3) with two non-album 45 cuts from 1972 (Repertoire REP 4465-WY). (2) also released in Colombia with a different cover (London) 19??. There's also a German compilation, *In The Beginning* (Teldec) 1973.

HCP

45s:	Tell Me Why/Cryin'Shame	(Parrot 334) 1969	-
	Drivin' Blues/God Gave Me You	(Parrot 340) 1969	-
α	House Of The Rising Sun/Drivin' Blues	(Parrot 341) 1969	7
α	Sing A Song For Freedom/End Of The Line	(Parrot 349) 1970	55
	Heartbreak Hotel/Bye Bye Blues	(Parrot 352) 1970	72
	Music For The People/Sloony	(Parrot 355) 1971	-
α	Shortly Kline/We're Gonna Be There	(Parrot 358) 1971	-
	I Love Her/Lost Son	(Parrot 360) 1972	-
	Earth Omen / Lazy Day	(Lion 115) 1972	-
	Go Now / Lazy Day	(Lion 136) 1972	-
	Big Betty / Shady Lady	(Lion 158) 1973	-

NB: α also issued with picture sleeves in France (Deram 17044, DM 309, DM 336 respectively) 1970. There was also a German picture sleeve 45: *Rainbow Rider / Earth Omen* (MGM 2006130) 1973.

From Detroit, Michigan this act were another fine example of the local hard rock and blues scene. Although they actually enjoyed three top 100 hits in the US, by far their finest moment was their highly original rock arrangement of *House Of The Rising Sun* (a traditional popularised by Dylan and The Animals), also notable for some superb guitar work.

Produced by Michael Valvano, their debut album also sold well, peaking at No. 11 in the Charts. Apart from *House Of The Rising Sun* and *Cryin' Shame* (written by Valvano), all their material was written by Beaudry and Thompson. Recorded in New York and entirely composed of original tracks penned and produced by the group, the second album also met with some commercial success, climbing to No 149. Both albums combine hard-rock and blues and are enjoyable if you like this style.

The group then broke up and Rick Stevers assembled a new line-up with Craig Webb (ex-**Lost Nation**) on guitar. Recorded in Toronto, the third album, *Earth Omen*, was produced by Vinnie Testa and Clyde Stevers and is heavier in style, with keyboards and some harder guitar work. Some ballads were also now included on here and are not their most interesting aspect. Lion Records was a subsidiary of MGM.

A fourth and final album was released on Fantasy in 1975, with an unknown line-up and style.

Compilation appearances include *House Of The Rising Sun* on *Michigan Rocks, Vol. 2* (LP). (VJ/MW/SR)

Froggie Beaver

Personnel:	RICK BROWN	drms, vcls, perc	A
	JOHN FISCHER	vcls, gtr	A
	ED STASZKO	keyb'ds, vcls	A
	JOHN TROIA	ld vcls	A

ALBUM: 1(A) FROM THE POND   (Froggie Beaver DSI 7310) 1973 SC

NB: (1) reissued on CD by Gear Fab (GF-13) 1999, with five bonus tracks - the two 45 cuts, plus three unreleased tracks from 1973.

45: Nothing For Me Here/Movin' On   (Million 34) 1972

The band originated from Omaha, Nebraska. Melodic, progressive rock, rather than psychedelic or garage, they are a marginal case for inclusion here. The album has become a minor collectable. (VJ)

Frolk Haven

Personnel:	CHARLES OSTMAN	gtr, bs, cla, vcls	A
	BAILEY PENDERGRASS	vcls	A
	STUART COPELAND	drms	A

ALBUM: 1(A) AT THE APEX OF HIGH   (LRS RF-6032) 197? R2

NB: (1) reissued in 1996.

As many of you will have noticed from the personnel details above this Berkeley, Ca., outfit contained Stuart Copeland (before he joined Curved Air/The Police). Inevitably, then, some collectors seek it out. It's a very experimental, but for the most part tedious progressive, with some psychedelic sound effects in places. (VJ)

Ethan Frome and Then Some

45: Pretty Thing/Always Leaving, Always Gone   (Happy Tiger 569) c1969

An obscure pop-rock group, their single was produced by Dean Christopher and offers covers of songs written Jeff Barry/Ellie Greenwich and Dick Monda. *Pretty Thing* is a delicately orchestrated song, a bit in the style of **The Left Banke**. The flip is more in a country-pop vein. (SR)

Front Line

Personnel incl:	BILL BOWEN	drms	A
	GARY PHILIPPET	keyb'ds	A

FRIENDSOUND - Joyride LP.

45s:	I Don't Care/Got Love	(York 9000) 1966
	Saigon Girl/Three Day Pass	(Titan 2001) 1967

From Marin County, this band were once known as The Turtles until The Crossfires took their name. The 'A' side of the 45 has some nice pipey organ.

Philippet had previously played with **Pullice** and **Electric Train** and was later in **Freedom Highway** and **Copperhead**. Bill Bowen too had been in **Electric Train** and joined the **Sons Of Champlin** in late 1966.

Compilation appearances include: *Got Love* on *Mayhem & Psychosis, Vol. 1* (LP), *Mayhem & Psychosis, Vol. 1* (CD), *Psychedelic Unknowns, Vol's 1 & 2* (LP) and *Psychedelic Unknowns, Vol. 2* (7"). (VJ/MW/AP/SR)

Front Office

45:	Girl/Wow	(Mijji 3007) 1967

Probably from California (San Jose) since the 45 was issued on the same label as the **Venus Flytrap** 45.

Compilation appearances include: *Wow* on *Psychedelic Unknowns, Vol. 6* (LP & CD) and *Everything You Always Wanted To Know...* (CD).

The Front Page News

Personnel:	SAM ROUTH	A
	GARY SMITH	A
	DAVID WADLEY	A

45:	Thoughts/You Better Behave	(Dial 4052) 1967

Came out of Fort Worth, Texas with *Thoughts* - one of the State's best fuzz guitar songs. You can find it on the *The Magic Cube* (Flexi & CD), *Psychedelic Unknowns, Vol. 4* (LP & CD), *The Cicadelic 60's, Vol. 4* (CD) or *Gone, Vol. 1* (LP) compilations. More recently, it has reappeared on Big Beat's *I Turned Into A Helium Balloon* (CD). Unlike some previous comps, these are bona-fide 100% legit, so they get access to the master tapes which are used wherever possible. This can throw up the odd anomaly and here's a good 'un. Has anyone else spotted that the CD version of *Thoughts* sounds a little different, like SLOWER? The original 45 track is 2:45 and, yes, the CD track is several seconds longer. Having retimed both and played 45 & CD simultaneously, I can only surmise that the original 45 was mastered at the incorrect speed and that the transfer for the CD was done at the correct speed, since the CD version actually sounds RIGHT - though it does take some getting used to. File this useless info alongside **Mad River**'s first album mis-master, for conversation stoppin' trivia....

A master remix version of *Thoughts*, plus *You Better Behave*, appear on Collectables' *Human Expression & Other Groups: Your Mind Works In Reverse* CD, whose liner notes reveal the personnel above and inform us that the band were actually the New Imperials from Tulsa, Oklahoma. The name change came about after recording the single in Fort Worth with producer Edwin Greines (who'd worked with the **Penthouse 5**).

You Better Behave is also now available on *Tymes Gone By* (LP). (MW/VJ)

The Front Page Review

Personnel:	RICHARD BARTLETT	gtr	A
	THOMAS BELLIVEAU	bs	A
	STEVE CATALDO	vcls, gtr	A
	DAVID CHRISTIANSEN	gtr	A
	JOSEPH SANTANGELO	piano, organ	A
	DAVID WEBER	drms	A

CD:	1(A) MYSTIC SOLDIERS	(Big Beat CDWIKD 166) 1996

Based in Boston, they initially played covers around the Boston clubs until songwriter Steve Cataldo joined the group in late 1967. Signed to MGM Records, they recorded an album in April/May 1968, produced by **Alan**

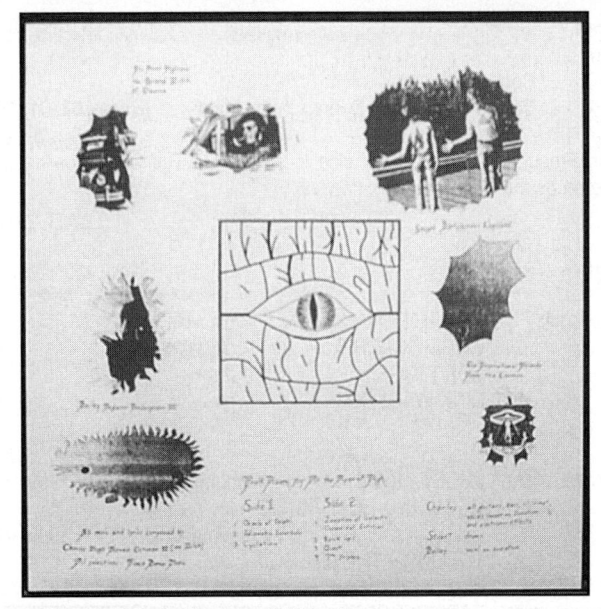

FROLK HAVEN - At The Apex Of High LP.

Lorber, who was responsible for Bosstown Sound Productions. Its release was delayed by the numerous releases of the other MGM Bosstown acts; and when the band broke up before the album's imminent release, the label decided not to proceed without a functioning band to support it. It was finally released (on CD) in 1996.

The album is less psychedelic than some of the other Bosstown releases i.e **Ultimate Spinach**, **Beacon Street Union** and is more like early prog - similar in some ways to Detroit's **SRC**. *Prophecies/Morning Blue* opens with the sounds of children playing, over which elegiac voices intone predictions of nuclear holocaust. After a gradual acceleration, the music suddenly lurches at the point of climax into a heavily syncopated, frenetic jazz piano solo in 5/4 time. *Prism Fawn* has an imperious organ/guitar riff and a driving beat. *One Eyed Minor* is a jaunty piece in a folkdance rhythm and *Feels Like Love* is a nondescript rocker, but *Silver Children* has a pleasant relaxed groove and *Valley Of Eyes* is another intense apocalyptic piece with flanged drums and bluesy 1968-style fuzz guitar. *Without You* is a dull proto-70s soft-rocker and *For The Best Offer* ends the album in a tone of enigmatic whimsy. Overall an enjoyable addendum to the Bosstown canon.

Cataldo later recorded as **St. Steven**, whilst Bartlett was in **Brother Fox And The Tar Baby**. Later still, Cataldo formed the punk band Nervous Eaters and played guitar on some Willie Alexander recordings. Essentially the band played good soft-psych.

The bonus cuts on the reissue of the **One St Stephen** album are actually by **Front Page Review**.

Compilation appearances have included: *Prohecies / Morning Blue, Silver Children* and *Valley Of Eyes* on *The Best Of Bosstown Sound* (Dble CD); and *Inside The Coloured Heaven* and *Moon In Blue* (miscredited as **St. Steven**) on *Filling The Gap* (4-LP). (VJ/LP)

Front Porch

45s:	Shake, Rattle And Roll/Song To St. Agnes	(Jubilee 5700) 1970
	Under The Boardwalk/?	(Jubilee 5717) 1971
	Wonderful Summer / Under The Boardwalk	(Jubilee 5720) 1971

A weird folk-rock group, their first 45 features an unusual arrangement of the R&R classic and has a creepy garage pop flip. (SR/BM/MW)

The Fronts

Reportedly from San Angelo, Texas.

Compilation appearances have included:- *Catch A Thief* and *Slash and Drip* on *Acid Visions - Complete Collection, Vol. 2* (3-CD); *Catch A Thief* and *The Haul* on *Green Crystal Ties, Vol. 8* (CD); and *The Haul* on *The Cicadelic '60s, Vol. 2* (CD).

Frost

45: Cool Jerk/
Behind The Closed Doors Of Her Mind   (Radex 68301) 1968

From Freeport, Illinois. The 'A' side is a cover of The Capitols song (also covered by the U.K. Creation). (MW/VJ)

Frost

Personnel:	DON HARTMAN	gtr, vcls	A
	GORDY GARRIS	bs, vcls	A
	BOB RIGGS	drms	A
	DICK WAGNER	gtr, vcls	A

				HCP
ALBUMS:	1(A)	FROST MUSIC	(Vanguard VSD-6520) 1969	168 -
	2(A)	ROCK AND ROLL MUSIC	(Vanguard VSD - 6541) 1969	148 -
	3(A)	THROUGH THE EYES OF LOVE	(Vanguard VSD - 6556) 1970	197 -
	4(A)	EARLY FROST	(Vanguard VSD-79392) 1978	- -

NB: (1), (2) and (3) have been reissued on CD. (4) is a reissue of (1).

			HCP
45s:	α	Bad Girl/A Rainy Day	(Date 1577) 1968 -
		Mystery Man/Sand In The Shadows	(Vanguard 35089) 1969 -
		Linda/Sweet Lady Love	(Vanguard 35099) 1969 -
		Donny's Blues/Rock And Roll Music	(Vanguard 35101) 1969 -
	β	Rock And Roll Music/Donny's Blues	(Vanguard 35111) 1969 105
		A Long Way From Home/Black As Night	(Vanguard 35115) 1970 -

NB: α credited to **Dick Wagner and The Frost**. β also issued in France with picture sleeve (Vanguard 119017) 1969.

A Michigan-based rock outfit whose recorded output may be of some passing interest to readers. They were originally called **Dick Wagner & The Frost** under which name they released the 45 on Date and **Dick Wagner** had earlier led the Flint-based **Bossmen**.

Whilst **Frost** enjoyed Top 100 hit singles, their albums all sold reasonably well too.

Dick Wagner later went on to **Ursa Major**.

Compilation appearances have included: *Rock & Roll Music* on *Michigan Rocks* (LP); and both *Black As Night* and *Rock & Roll Music* on *Pop Music Super Hebdo* (LP). (VJ/MW/TB)

Max Frost and The Troopers

ALBUM:	1	SHAPE OF THINGS TO COME	(Tower ST 4147) 1968 -

			HCP
45s:		Stomper's Ride/There Is A Party Going On	(Sidewalk 938) 1968 -
		Shape Of Things To Come/Free Lovin'	(Tower 419) 1968 22
		52%/Max Frost Theme	(Tower 452) 1968 123
	α	Sittin' In Circles/Paxton Quigley's Had The Course (PS)	(Tower 478) 1969 -

NB: α 'B' side is by **Chad & Jeremy**.

This 'group' were actually **Davie Allan and The Arrows**, or at least the tracks on the *Shapes Of Things* album are the more punky psychedelic cuts from all the soundtracks **Davie Allan and The Arrows** made like *Wild On The Streets*, which contained *52%* and *Shape Of Things To Come*. As these albums were released on Tower many consider that there is almost certainly a connection with **The Chocolate Watch Band**, especially as we know the latter didn't play on all their studio cuts.

The movie 'Wild In The Streets' starred Chris Jones as Max Frost and the California band **Davie Allan and The Arrows** appeared in the film as the backing band. The band had also earlier appeared in the film 'Three In The Attic', which featured their *Sittin' In Circles* 45, and the flip by **Chad & Jeremy**.

Confusingly, it is also claimed that the ubiquitous Michael Lloyd (of **The Smoke** etc.) had some involvement with **Max Frost and The Troopers**, and that **The Smoke** may have been responsible for some of the recordings.

Compilation appearances include: *Lonely Man* on *Lycergic Soap* (LP), *Sixties Archive, Vol. 8* (CD), *Turds On A Bum Ride, Vol. 1 & 2* (Dble CD) and *Turds On A Bum Ride, Vol. 2* (Dble LP); (VJ/MW/JFr)

Thomas and Richard Frost

Personnel incl:	RICHARD FROST	A
	THOMAS FROST (TOM MARTIN)	A

ALBUM:	1(A)	THOMAS AND RICHARD FROST	(UNI 73124) 1972 -

NB: There's also a previously unreleased sixteen-track CD from 1969/70, *Visualize* (Revola CRREV-4) 2002. This was originally scheduled for release (Imperial LP-12450), but shelved after mastering.

45s:	She's Got Love/The Word Is Love	(Imperial 66405) 1969
	With Me, My Love/Gotta Find A New Place To Stay	(Imperial 66426) 1969
	Fairy Tale Affair/Hello Stranger	(Imperial 66451) 1970
	Open Up Your Heart/Where Did Yesterday Go?	(Liberty 56191) 1970
	Got To Find The Light/?	(Uni 55320) 1972

From San Mateo on the San Francisco Peninsula, Rich and Tom Martin had been performing together since the beginning of the decade, starting with instrumental surf and greasy R&B in the Impressions; jangly folk-rock with The Newcastle Five; the fuzz-tinged garage-rock of **The Art Collection**, and last but not least, the thundering mod sound of **Powder**.

When **Powder** failed to ignite the American public, the pair began work as an Anglophile influenced pop duo, and were signed to Imperial. Their first 45, *She's Got Love* scrapped into the Billboard charts and an album of lush orchestrated pop was recorded, but then shelved when their follow-up 45s bombed.

In 1971, Rich and Tom signed a new deal with Uni and finally got an album, eponymously-titled and singer/songwriter-orientated, released the following year.

Their unreleased album, *Visualize*, finally saw light of day in 2002. Typical of the slightly-psych big production L.A. pop of its period, it includes their first four 45s, detailed liners by Alec Palao and reminiscences by Richard

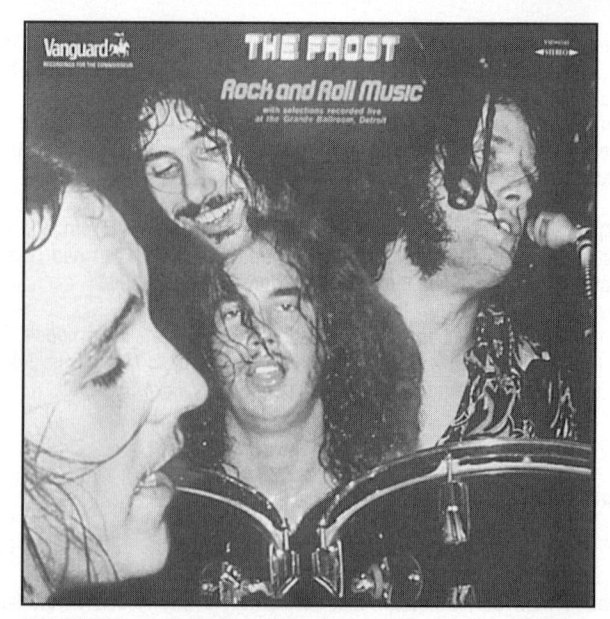

THE FROST - Rock And Roll Music LP.

Frost. The material, which has stood the test of time well, is imbued with the zeitgeist of Los Angeles in its last throes of pop innocence. The Martins heart-on-their-sleeve Anglophilic sensibility is less derivative then remarkably refreshing, with superbly recorded arrangements that any late sixties pop fan will cherish. Uncomplicated, fun, yet eminently memorable. Tony Macauley would be proud. (SR/JFr/AP)

Frumious Bandersnatch

Personnel:			
	DAVID DENNY	ld gtr, vcls	A CDEF
	BRIAN HOUGH	bs	AB
	JACK KING	drms, vcls	ABCDEF
	GEORGE TICKNER	gtr	AB
	KAJA DORIA	vcls	B
	BRET WILMOT	ld gtr	B
	ROSS VALORY	bs, vcls	C
	JIMMY WARNER	ld gtr, vcls	CD
	BOB WINKELMAN	gtr, vcls, (bs)	CDEF
	JACK NOTESTEIN	bs, vcls	DE

CD: 1 A YOUNG MAN'S SONG (Big Beat CDWIKD 169) 1996

EP: 1(C) FRUMIOUS BANDERSNATCH (Muggles Gramophone Works FB-A/B) 1968

NB: (1) originals are either on red or purple vinyl in hard cardboard PS. Counterfeited in the early eighties on black vinyl in paper PS.

From Lafayette, California, **Frumious Bandersnatch** came into existence when All Night Flight (line-up 'A' above) decided to change their name, and chose **Frumious Bandersnatch** from Lewis Carroll's "Jabberwocky" poem. The band's lynchpin, Jack King, had previously played with Shades Blue Ltd. and Denny had also been a surf act called The Breakers.

Line-up 'B' recorded just two tracks, *Now That You're Gone* plus an early version of *Cheshire* in October 1967. Neither was released at the time, but both have subsequently been included on *A Young Man's Song* CD retrospective. The band broke up at the end of the year when all their equipment was stolen; but after a short hiatus they reformed as line-up 'C', with Bob Winkelman joining from **The Epics** while Warner and Valory were recruited from The Good Timers.

This line-up recorded their classic EP which looked all set to make it big by the Summer of 1968. This contained three tracks: *Hearts To Cry*, *Misty Cloudy* and *Cheshire*. On the first of these, Warner, Winkelman and Denny put together some of the finest acid guitar playing to come out of San Francisco, but the bands' drug and alcohol-fueled manager Jim Nixon effectively killed their chances of getting a major label deal with his obnoxious behaviour (the group apparently had plenty of offers).

After Valory left to join **Faun** in late 1968, the band gradually lost impetus and finally broke up in late 1969; Tickner later joined Valory in **Faun** and both were later founder-members of Journey. Winkelman, Denny, King and Valory all later played at some time in **The Steve Miller Band**.

In 1995 Big Beat reissued their seminal EP as part of the CD, *The Berkeley EPs*, along with the June 1966 effort by **Country Joe and The Fish**, **The Mad River** and **Notes From The Underground** EPs. The following year they put together a passionate but unpolished collection of **Frumious Bandersnatch** rarities including live recordings, studio-outtakes etc, which with its 73-minute running time is definitely worth investigating.

Hearts To Cry from their EP can also be heard on *Endless Journey - Phase Three* (LP) and *Endless Journey - Phase I & II* (Dble CD). (VJ/LP)

Frummox

Personnel:			
	KENNY ALTMAN	bs	A
	EVERETT BARKSDALE	bs	A
	OMAR CLAY	drms	A
	STEVEN FROMHOLZ	gtr, vcls	A
	BOB JAMES	perc	A
	ERIC WEISSBERG	gtr, fiddle	A

ALBUM: 1(A) HERE TO THERE (Probe CPLP-4511) 1969 -

A Texas country folk-rock group with some psychedelic influences. Tracks like *Song For Stephen Stills*, *Texas Trilogy* and *Kansas Legend* may interest some readers. Their leader, Steve Fromholz, later released several solo albums between 1976 and 1979.

Among the musicians, Everett Barksdale also played with **Fat City**, Kenny Altman was in the **Fifth Avenue Band** and Eric Weissberg was a well-known studio guitarist. (SR)

Frut (of The Loom)

Personnel:			
	CRUNCHY CRYSTALS	gtr	A
	JOHN KOZMO	bs	A
	PANAMA RED	vcls	A
	SNIDELY WHIPLASH	drms	A

ALBUMS: 1( ) KEEP ON TRUCKIN' (Trash 1001) 1971 -
2(A) SPOILED ROTTEN (Westbound WB 2008) 1972 -

NB: (1) and (2) as **Frut**. (1) also released on Westbound (WB 2005).

45: α One Hand In Darkness/A Little Bit Of Bach (Loom 101) 1967
Prison Of Love/
Send Me Down (Westbound Records W 189) 1971

NB: α As **Frut Of The Loom**.

From Detroit, Michigan this outfit shortened their name to Frut and had two albums in the early seventies. Personnel on the last album was Panama Red (vcls), Crunchy Crystals (gtr), John Kozmo (bs) and Snidely Whiplash (drms)!!

Compilation appearances include: *One Hand In Darkness* on *Echoes In Time, Vol's 1 & 2* (CD) and *Echoes In Time, Vol. 2* (LP). (VJ/SR/CG)

The Fugitives

45s: Louie, Go Home/
You Know She's A Woman (Alamo Audio 108) 1966
'Till The End Of The Day/
Ferry Gross The Mersey (Roun Sound 69,70) 1967

A British-influenced garage band based in San Antonio, Texas. The 'A' side of their first 45 is pretty good, and the flip is a slow organ lead sloucher.

This lot were unconnected to the Houston band of the same name who included Sid Templeton and Steve Headley (later of **The Lavender Hour** and briefly **The Clique**) but did not record. There was also a garage band called The Fugitives in Austin in 1964-5 which didn't make it onto vinyl.

FRUMIOUS BANDERSNATCH - Frumious Bandersnatch PS EP.

They included Roky Erickson (later of **The Spades** and the **13th Floor Elevators**) and George Kinney (later of Chelsea and **The Golden Dawn**).

Compilation appearances have included: *You Know She's A Woman* on *Sixties Rebellion Vol's 1 & 2* (CD) and *Sixties Rebellion, Vol. 1* (LP); *Louie Go Home* on *Texas Punk, Vol. 9* (LP) and *Acid Visions - Complete Collection, Vol. 3* (3-CD). (VJ)

The Fugitives

Personnel incl:
JOHN BOYLES — vcls, bs — AB
ELMER CLAWSON (E.J.) — — AB
RETT NICHOLS — gtr — A
GARY QUACKENBUSH — gtr — AB
GLEN QUACKENBUSH — keyb'ds — AB
PAUL KELCOURSE — gtr — B

ALBUM: 1(A) THE FUGITIVES AT DAVE'S HIDEOUT
(Hideout 1001) 1965 R3

45s:
A Fugitive (vcl)/A Fugitive (instr) (D-Town 1031) 1965
On Trial/Let's Get On With It (D-Town 1044) 1965
You Can't Make Me Lonely/
I Don't Wanna Talk (Westchester 1002) 1965

The Hideout was a Detroit teen club and record company run by Dave Leone and Ed 'Punch' Andrews. **The Fugitives** (who were originally known as The Tremolos) and came from Birmingham (a relatively affluent Detroit suburb) were the first band they discovered. They appeared playing songs like *Louie, Louie* on the opening night of the Hideout and were also the first band to be recorded on the associated Hideout record label, although they did have earlier recordings on the local D-Town label, which are hopelessly rare. Their album, which was recorded in a basement and then re-recorded to include fake applause and audience approval, was a mixture of cover versions like *Louie, Louie* and *Love Potion No. 9* and originals like *Friday At The Hideout*. Just 500 copies were pressed and consequently they now change hands for a lot of money. Back then, copies were sold at the club for $3 each. The core of the band evolved into the Scot Richard Case and **SRC**.

Said Goodbye plus both sides of the Westchester 45 were also featured on an impossibly rare 1965 compilation *Friday At The Cage A Go Go - Long Hot Summer* (LP) which has been reissued as *Long Hot Summer*.

John Boyles is now a software designer in Waltham, Massachussetts.

Retrospective compilation appearances have included *Said Goodbye* on *Oil Stains* (LP); and *On Trial* on *Glimpses, Vol. 3* (LP). (VJ/MW/PK)

The Fugitives

45: You Can't Blame That On Me/
I'll Hang Around (Fenton 2075) 196?

This was the work of a teen outfit from West Michigan. The 'A' side, *You Can't Blame That On Me* is a typical teenbeat recording with muffled background screams and 'Wipeout' drumming.

Compilation appearances have included: *I'll Hang Around* on *The Best Of Michigan Rock Groups, Vol. 1.* and *The Lost Generation, Vol. 2* (LP); and *You Can't Blame That On Me* on *Back From The Grave, Vol. 3* (LP) and *Back From The Grave, Vol. 2* (CD). (VJ)

The Fugitives

Personnel:
BUSTER BYARD — drms — A
RICHARD DONLAVEY — ld vcls — A
JOE RUSSELL — keyb'ds — A
MICK RUSSELL — ld gtr — A
JIMMY SICKAL — bs — A
TOMMY SICKAL — gtr — A

THE FUGITIVES - On The Run With... LP.

ALBUM: 1(A) ON THE RUN WITH THE FUGITIVES (Justice 141) 19?
NB: (1) reissued on CD by Collectables (COL-CD-0613) 1996.

Yet more **Fugitives**. This was a rare garage album by an outfit from Richmond, Virginia, originally issued on the collectable 'Justice' label. Comprising four originals and eight covers - including *Turn On Your Love Light, Tossing And Turning, You Can't Catch Me, Ebb Tide* and *Get Out Of My Life Woman* - it's one of the better Justice offerings.

Compilation appearances have included: *On The Run* and *You Can't Catch Me* on *Green Crystal Ties, Vol. 7* (CD); and *On The Run* on *Hipsville, Vol. 2* (LP). (MW)

The Fugitives

Personnel:
EVAN CHARMATZ — A
RAY CHARMATZ — A
PHIL FELICIOTTO — A
TOM JOHANSON — A

45s:
Mean Woman/I'll Be A Man (Columbia 4-43261) 1965
Your Girl's A Woman/She Believes In Me (Mala 533) 1966

Mindrocker, Vol. 7 (LP) captures this group's finest moment *Mean Woman* - melodic swinging beat with ringing guitars that nod more towards The Ventures than **The Byrds**. It's a shame their other material veered towards harmony-pop/Four Seasons sounds.

Johanson hailed from New London, Connecticut; the other three from Manhattan. **The Fugitives** may have also spent some time in Florida. (MW/MDo)

The Fugitives

45: I Miss You Girl/This Is It (Clevetown CTXP-128) 1965

Good garage-beat by an outfit from Warren, Pennsylvania, according to Mike Kuzmin's 'Sounds From The Woods'. (MW)

The Fugitives

45s:
α Cry Me A River / ?Too Easy? (New Talent NT 101) 1966
Meggie / I've Gotta Go (New Talent NT 103) 1966
Easy Come, Easy Go / Wind Of Love (Midnight 101) 1969

NB: α 'B' side title unconfirmed.

Possibly from Monticello, Georgia, this is a different **Fugitives** to the pre-**Mach V** group (out of Savannah, GA.). This group released three 45s of which the most garagey track, *Meggie* (written by Tony McMichael and Rita Vest) is to be found on *Psychedelic States: Georgia Vol. 1* (CD), whose liners mention that the crude debut *Cry Me A River* "isn't bad" and that the final 45 had moved off into soul territory. (MW/RM)

The Fugitives (Bill Allan and)

Personnel incl: BILL ALLAN   A

45:     Come On And Clap/You're The Kind Of Girl   (Trend 101) 1966

Also known as **Bill Allan and The Fugitives**, they came from Madison, Wisconsin and only made this one 45. The 'A' side, *Come On And Clap*, is a frantic if poorly produced rocker and can be heard on *Highs In The Mid-Sixties, Vol. 15* (LP) and *Mondo Frat Dance Bash A Go Go* (CD). (VJ)

The Fugs

Personnel:		
AL FOWLER	flute	A
TULI KUPFERBERG	vcls, perc	ABCDEFG H I J KL
ED SANDERS	vcls	ABCDEFG H I J KL
SZABO	flute	A
PETE STAMPFEL	fiddle, hrmnca, vcls	B
KEN WEAVER	drms, perc	BCDEFG H I J KL
STEVE WEBER	gtr, vcls	BCD
JOHN ANDERSON	bs, vcls	BCDEF
VINNY LEARY	gtr, vcls	BCDEFG H
LEE CRABTREE	keyb'ds, flute	DEFG H
PETE KEARNEY	gtr, vcls	EFG H
JON KALB	gtr	F
STEFAN GROSSMAN	gtr	G
ALAN 'JAKE' JACOBS	gtr, vcls	H
DANNY KOOTCH (KORTCHMAR)	gtr, violin	I J
CHARLES LARKEY	bs	I J K
KEN PINE	gtr, vcls	I J KL
BOB MASON	drms	J K
CARL LYNCH	gtr	K
DAN HAMBURG	gtr	L
JIM PEPPER	flte	L
BILL WOLF	bs, vcls	L

ALBUMS:				HCP
(up to	1(B/C)	THE VILLAGE FUGS	(Broadside 304) 1965	142 R2
1975)	2(B/C)	THE FUGS FIRST ALBUM	(ESP-Disk 1018) 1966	- -
	3(E)	THE FUGS	(ESP-Disk 1028) 1966	95 SC
	4(E)	VIRGIN FUGS	(ESP-Disk 1038) 1966	- SC
	5(I)	TENDERNESS JUNCTION	(Reprise R(S)-6280) 1968	- SC
	6(J)	IT CRAWLED INTO MY HAND, HONEST (Reprise RS-6305) 1968		167 SC
	7(L)	BELLE OF AVENUE A	(Reprise RS-6359) 1969	- SC
	8(K)	GOLDEN FILTH	(Reprise RS-6396) 1970	- -

NB: (2) is a reissue of (1) although two versions exist, one having two different tracks. (2), (3) and (4) also released in France (ESP 538 114, 538115 and 538116 respectively) 1968. (4) came with a "Fugs Sur-Prize Package" with stickers, flip book, poster. (4) also released in France (Vogue/Reprise CRV 6083) 1968. (8) is a live set from the Fillmore East recorded in 1968. (2) reissued on CD (Fantasy FCD 9668) and again in 1995 with eleven bonus tracks (Big Beat WIKCD 119). (2) reissued on CD and Double LP (Abraxas) 1999. (3) reissued on CD (Fantasy FCD 9669) and again (Fugs CDWIKD 121) with five bonus tracks. (1) - (3) reissued on Base in Italy. (5) reissued on Edsel (XED 181) 1986, and (6) on (ED 217) 1987. Also of interest are the French (compilation?) *Fugs 4*, *Rounders Score* (Vogue/Reprise CRV 6095) 1969; the reunion *Star Piece* (dble LP/CD), (B/I/J/L) *Live From The '60s* (Fugs CDWIKD 125), the reunions *No More Slavery* (Fugs CDWIKD 145), and *Refuse To Be Burnt Out - Live In The '80s* (New Rose 56) 1985 (LP) and (Fugs CDWIKD 139) (CD), *The Real Woodstock Festival* Dble CD (CDWIK2 160) and *The Folkways Sessions*.

45s:	Frenzy/I Want to Know	(ESP 4507) 1966
α	Kill For Peace/Morning Morning	(ESP 4508) 1966
	Crystal Liason/?	( ) 19??

NB: α may not have been issued.

Named after a Norman Mailer-coined sexual euphemism, **The Fugs** were easily the most lyrically outrageous band of their era with songs explicitly documenting sex, drugs, and radical politics and were formed in New York in late 1964 as a vehicle for the satirical talents of two beat poets, **Ed Sanders** and **Tuli Kupferberg**.

Sanders, a veteran of the Civil Rights Marches, ran the Peace Eye Bookstore in NYC and published an arts magazine called 'Fuck You' which inexplicably failed to attain popular acceptance, while **Kupferberg** was another Civil Rights stalwart who'd already achieved a certain hip status when celebrated in **Allen Ginsberg**'s "Howl" for jumping off the Brooklyn Bridge and surviving.

An early line-up with two "amphetamine" flautists soon gave way to a more settled group which included Steve Weber and Peter Stampfel of the similarly anarchic **Holy Modal Rounders**. Texan Ken Weaver was added first on congas and later, when resources permitted, on a full drum-kit. Their first album was the result of two sessions in the Spring and late Summer of 1965: defiantly unprofessional but full of spirit and energy, it included musical adaptations of poems by Blake and Swinburne alongside satirical numbers like *I Couldn't Get High*, *Boobs A Lot* (a paean to cheerleaders' breasts), and *Slum Goddess*.

Meanwhile, the band's live performances were achieving notoriety for such stunts as tossing spaghetti at the audience, as well as their high obscenity content. Stampfel had left in the Summer of 1965 and was replaced by Vinny Leary who brought a more pronounced rock 'n' roll perspective to the original folky musical foundation. John Anderson, a student from Yale, was added on bass around this time.

After recording the first album, **The Fugs** embarked on a six-week tour across the U.S, adding keyboardist Lee Crabtree (who'd been first employed as **Fugs** chauffeur) to the line-up. The tour went surprisingly well, although one concert was terminated prematurely when college officials pulled the plug during a LSD-generated 45-minute rendition of *River Of Shit*.

Steve Weber left soon after and was replaced by Pete Kearney while **Sanders** was beset by obscenity charges arising from publication of his arts magazine, 'Fuck You'. It took eighteen months of court appearances to beat the charge. The band signed with ESP Disk and recorded their second album in the first two months of 1966. A more rock-oriented effort than their debut, it's considered by many to be their best and includes the anthemic satire *Kill For Peace* and the lengthy and atmospheric *Virgin Forest*. *Group Grope* celebrated free love complete with orgasmic noises while *Coming Down* detailed the downside of drugs. The album also contained two pretty ballads, *Morning Morning* and *I Want To Know*. Remarkably it made the album charts - surely the most outrageous album to have done so at that date.

Under investigation by the FBI (whose documents repeatedly referred to the band as "The Fags"), the NYC DA's office, and the Postal Service, the **Fugs** were at the same time having trouble with their record company.

THE FUGS - The Fugs First Album LP.

They were also making changes to their line-up: three lead guitarists (Jon Kalb, Stefan Grossman, and Jake Jacobs (pre-**Bunky and Jake**)) came and went and bassist John Anderson was drafted despite **The Fugs**' valiant efforts to have him exempted as mentally unfit for service.

A third album, *Virgin Fugs* (composed of outtakes from the second album sessions) took the shock quotient to even higher levels with songs like *Coca-Cola Douche*, *New Amphetamine Shriek* and *The Ten Commandments* (memorably attributed to **Kupferberg**/God). Also notable are such gems as *We're The Fugs*, *Hallucination Horrors*, *CIA Man* and *I Saw The Best Minds Of My Generation Rot* which was written by Beat Poet **Allen Ginsberg**. The lyrics to *We're The Fugs* are atypical of the taboo subjects they set out to deal with.

"We Hate War
We Love Sex
Twos or threes
Four or Fives
LSD A dimethylatr"
(from *We're The Fugs*)

More vintage **Fugs** lyrics can be heard on *Hallucination Horrors*:-

"Benzedrine
Mescaline
Pot and LSD
I Need Aquamorphine
Hallucination Horrors is what I've got
Hallucination Horrors is what I've got"
(from *Hallucination Horrors*)

The band, dissatisfied with their ESP contract (they were only receiving a royalty rate of 3%), signed with Atlantic Records in late 1966. They were promised complete recording freedom and completed an album using top Atlantic sessionmen like Bernard Purdie and Chuck Rainey but for some reason the Atlantic contract was abruptly terminated in June 1967 and the album was never released. At this time the band were well on the way to fame and fortune with **Sanders** appearing on the cover of Life magazine but the problems with Atlantic robbed the band of a great deal of momentum; in **Sanders** words, "we lost a year and that really screwed us up".

They quickly signed with Reprise and were promised a no censorship deal by label head Mo Ostin and this time the deal was honoured. Most of the ESP band had left by this time because **Sanders** was insisting on a level of professionalism they were unwilling to provide. The core trio of **Sanders**, **Kupferberg**, and Weaver enlisted a team of crack players - Ken Pine and Danny Kootch on guitars and Charles Larkey on bass. Their first Reprise album, *Tenderness Junction*, reprised much of the material from the lost Atlantic album and included the lengthy *Aphrodite Mass*, a musical adaptation of Mathew Arnold's *Dover Beach*, the celebratory *Turn On, Tune In, Drop Out*, as well as the usual obscenities (*Wet Dream*). The ubiquitous **Allen Ginsberg** also popped in to chant *Hare Krishna* but the album is best known for documenting **The Fugs**' attempt to exorcize the Evil Spirits from the Pentagon on October 21, 1967. It was, as **Sanders** admits, a failure because the Vietnam War went on for another seven years but at least the "Out Demons, Out!" chant later provided the Edgar Broughton Band with their best-known number.

Sanders and **Kupferberg** attended the Chicago demonstrations in August 1968 and their support of the Yippies was reflected in the songs *Chicago* and *Yodelling Yippie*, which appeared on *The Belle Of Avenue A* album. A second drummer, Bob Mason, had been added for their next Reprise album, *It Crawled Into My Hand, Honest* which was probably their best effort since *The Fugs*. Full of parodies of various musical styles - country, gospel, jazz, classical, Broadway musicals, etc - it resurrected the notorious *River Of Shit* as *Wide Wide River* and contained a Gregorian chant *Marijuana* intoning the various names of the drug as well as more songs about sex (*Grope Need*).

However **Sanders** was rapidly tiring of the whole affair, which had started as fun but had become a full-time business operation - he was working ten to fifteen hours a day just to keep things on an even keel and drinking too much - and he simply didn't want to become a "beatnik business person". After recording a country-flavoured and slightly tired-sounding final studio album, **The Fugs** played their last concert in Hersey, Pennsylvania in March, 1969 and quietly disbanded. **Sanders** soon after covered the Manson trial for Esquire magazine and wrote a book about Manson called "The Family" while **Kupferberg** formed a satirical theatrical group called the Revolting Theatre. **Sanders** recorded two country-parody albums, *Sander's Truckstop* (1970) and *Beer Cans On The Moon* (1973) while **Kupferberg** had released a solo spoken-word album *No Deposit, No Return* in 1967.

In 1984, **Sanders** and **Kupferberg** reformed **The Fugs** without Ken Weaver and recorded a number of albums, *Refuse To Be Burnt Out* (1985), *No More Slavery* (1986), *Star Peace* (1987), and *The Real Woodstock Festival* (1995).

Lee Crabtree died in the early seventies and Pete Kearney is also deceased; Steve Weber and Pete Stampfel are still playing; Danny Kootch played with Carole King and Don Henley; Charles Larkey also played with King and married (and later divorced) her; and John Anderson became a lawyer. (LP/VJ)

Fuji

45s:			
	Mary, Don't Take Me On No Bad Trips Pt.1/Pt.2	(Cadet 5652)	1969
	Revelations Pt.1/Pt.2	(Cadet 5665)	1970
	I'd Rather Be A Blind Man/Save A Little	(Cadet 5677)	1970

Released on a subsidiary label of Chess, a black psych-soul outfit. Their second 45, with a superb and long guitar solo, was produced by **Blak-Mer-Da**. (SR)

Bobby Fuller Four

Personnel:	BOBBY FULLER	gtr, vcls	ABC
	RANDY FULLER	bs	ABC
	LARRY THOMPSON	drms	A
	BILLY WEBB	gtr	A
	DEWAYNE QUIRICO	drms	B
	JIM REESE	gtr	BC
	DALTON POWELL	drms	C

HCP

ALBUMS: 1(B) KRLA KING OF THE WHEELS
(Mustang M(S) 900) 1965 - R2
2(C) I FOUGHT THE LAW (Mustang M(S) 901) 1966 144 R1

NB: (2) has been reissued by Line. (1) and (2) were issued on one CD by Del-Fi (DFCD 956). Besides these two albums there are many posthumous releases: *Memorial Album* (President PTL PTL 1003) 1967, *The Best Of* (Rhino RNDF-201) 1982, *The Bobby Fuller Tapes* (Rhino RNLP-047) 1984, *The Bobby Fuller Tapes, Vol. 2* (Voxx LP-100) 1985, *Live At PJs* (Del-Fi DFCD 13142) and *Shakedown! The Texas Tapes Revisited* (2 CD set on Del-Fi, 1996, recorded between 1961 and 1964). Eva have also issued two albums: *I Fought The Law* (Eva 12032) and *Live Again* (Eva 12046) 198?.

THE FUGS - It Crawled Into My Hand Honest LP.

BOBBY FULLER FOUR.

EPs:	1	Love's Made A Fool Of You/I Fought The Law/ Don't You Ever Let Me Know	(London 10179) 1966
	2	Wine Wine Wine / Baby I Don't Care / Not Fade Away / Pretty Girls Everywhere (PS)	(Eva 2003) 198?

NB: (1) is a rare French-only EP with PS, estimated value $300.

				HCP
45s:	α	You're In Love/Guess We'll Fall In Love	(Yucca 140) 1961	-
	α	Gently My Love/My Heart Jumped	(Yucca 144) 1962	-
	α	Nervous Breakdown/Not Fade Away	(Eastwood) 1962	-
	α	King Of The Beach/Wine, Wine, Wine	(Exeter 122) 1964	-
	α	I Fought The Law/She's My Girl	(Exeter 124) 1964	-
	β	Fool Of Love/Shakedown	(Exeter 126) 1964	-
		Stringer/Saturday Night	(Todd 1090) 1964	-
	β	Those Memories Of You/ Our Favourite Martian	(Donna 1403) 1964	-
	χ	Wolfman/Thunder Reef	(Mustang 3003) 1965	-
		Take My Word/She's My Girl	(Mustang 3004) 1965	-
		Let Her Dance/ Another Sad And Lonely Night	(Mustang 3006) 1965	-
		Never To Be Forgotten/You Kiss Me	(Mustang 3011) 1965	-
		Let Her Dance/ Another Sad And Lonely Night	(Mustang 3012) 1965	-
		Let Her Dance/ Another Sad And Lonely Night	(Liberty 55817) 1965	-
	δ	I Fought The Law/Little Annie Lou	(Mustang 3014) 1966	9
	δ	Love's Made A Fool Of You/ Don't You Ever Let Me Know	(Mustang 3016) 1966	26
		The Magic Touch/My True Love	(Mustang 3020) 196?	-

NB: α by Bobby Fuller. β credited to Bobby Fuller and The Fanatics. χ credited to The Shindigs. δ also released in the U.K. (London HLU 10030 and 10041). In the eighties Eva also released a bootleg 45: I Fought The Law / Shangai'd (Eva Jukebox 2) 198?.

With his blatant reverence for Buddy Holly, fellow Texan **Bobby Fuller** (born October 22nd, 1942) was a bit of an anomaly in the mid-sixties. With his Stratocaster guitar and brash, full sound, at his best **Fuller** sounded like Holly might have had he survived into the sixties. Cracking the Top 30 in 1966 with a cover of Holly's *Love's Made A Fool Of You*, and then the Top Ten with *I Fought The Law* (written by one-time Cricket Sonny Curtis and featuring future **Moby Grape** guitarist Jerry Miller), **Fuller** had just become a star when he died in mysterious circumstances in a parked car in Hollywood (the police thought it was a suicide, just about everyone who knew him disagreed). **Fuller**'s relatively short period of national stardom actually crowned a good half-dozen years of recording, during which he released many outstanding tracks. After a few local singles in his hometown of El Paso in the early sixties, he moved to California with his combo in 1964, and briefly had aspirations of playing surf music before hooking up with producer Bob Keene. In the short time he recorded for Mustang in 1965 and 1966, he waxed quite a few fine tracks (most self-penned) besides his hits, including *Let Her Dance*, *Another Sad And Lonely Night*, *My True Love*, *Never To Be Forgotten*, *Fool Of Love*, and *The Magic Touch*. Rocking, tuneful and infectiously joyous, they showed **Fuller** to be a worthy inheritor of early rock 'n' roll and rockabilly traditions without sounding self-consciously revivalist. While it's hard to imagine **Fuller** maintaining his success in the era of psychedelia, he no doubt would have gone on to produce interesting work.

A talented and prolific songwriter and a studio whiz who drew from Eddie Cochran and (though only slightly) the full guitar sound of the British Invasion as well as Buddy Holly, he recorded a great deal of unreleased studio and live material that was issued in the 1980s, when the depth of his loss began to be appreciated more widely.

Billy Webb and Larry Thompson later formed **The Rooks**, whilst Bobby's brother Randy later joined **Blue Mountain Eagle** and **Dewey Martin's Medicine Show**.

In 2001, Randy Fuller, Billy Webb, John Mueller, Larry Knechtel, Jim Thompson and Larry Thompson are preparing to release a new CD soon as The Bobby Fuller Drive.

Compilation coverage has included: *Let Her Dance* on *Nuggets, Vol. 3* (LP), *Texas Music, Vol. 3* (CD); *Wine, Wine, Wine* on *Pebbles, Vol. 2* (LP), *Pebbles, Vol. 2* (CD); and *I Fought The Law* on *Pebbles Box* (5-LP), *Trash Box* (5-CD) and *I Fought The Law* on *Battle Of The Bands* (CD). (VJ/JL/SR/LTn)

Fumin' Humins

45:	Relative Distance/Queen	(Angry Music Co. FH-2-67) 1967

This group was comprised of students at Tabor Academy in Marion, Massachusetts, and according to Erik Lindgren's excellent sleeve notes for his *An Overdose Of Heavy Psych* comp, was limited to 500 copies. *Relative Distance* features some great guitar and gave the title to Aram Heller's excellent New England nuggets *Relative Distance* (LP). It has also been compiled on *An Overdose Of Heavy Psych* (CD), but the flip, which features pleasant folk-rock, remains uncompiled. (MW)

Fun and Games (Commission)

Personnel:	JOHN T. BONNO	bs	A
	CARSON GRAHAM	drms	AB
	D.J. GREER	piano, gtr, vcls	A
	PAUL GUILLET	ld gtr	AB
	SAM IRWIN	vcls, tamb	AB
	ROCK ROMANO	gtr, vcls	AB
	JOE DUGAN	keyb'ds	B
	JOE ROMANO	bs, vcls	B

ALBUM:	1(A/B)	ELEPHANT CANDY	(UNI 73042) 1968 SC

				HCP
45s:	α	Today-Tomorrow/ Someone Must Have Lied (To You)	(Mainstream 671) 1967	-

FUN and GAMES - Elephant Candy LP.

	It Must Have Been The Wind/Holding Me Back	(Cinema) 196? -	
β	Elephant Candy	(UNI 55086) 1968 -	
	Elephant Candy/The Way She Smiles	(UNI 55086) 1968 -	
	The Grooviest Girl In The World/ It Must Have Been The Wind	(UNI 55098) 1968 78	
	We/Gotta Say Goodbye	(UNI 55128) 1969 -	

NB: α as **The Fun And Games Commission**. β promo only.

From Texas, this band evolved out of **The Six Pents**. Bobby Shad of Mainstream signed them, with two 45s as **Sixpentz**, but when they discovered the similarly named **Sixpence**, changed names again to **The Fun And Games Commission** and their first 45 was released under this name. They played mostly well-crafted pop in the **Millennium/Sagittarius** mould, with production duties being handled by Gary Zekeley of Jan and Dean and **Yellow Balloon** fame.

The Grooviest Girl In The World climbed to No 78 in the U.S. Top 100 and the band lasted until the late sixties/early seventies.

Joe Romano had also played with **A 440** and most of the band were also involved with **Mayo Thompson** (of **Red Crayola** fame).

John Bonno and D. J. Greer retired from the band just before they signed with Uni records. Sam Irwin later formed Phoenix and now has the band Duck Soup out of Austin Texas. Rock Romano went on to form Doctor Rockit and the Sisters of Mercy. He and the Sisters split and he continued to front Doctor Rockit. He also played guitar and bass with The Sheetrockers and even played bass with Duck Soup for a while. He now has a recording studio in Houston. Carson Graham played drums for several other groups and Paul Guillet retired from the professional music scene. Joe Romano went on to write and record songs, including several children's songs for Sesame Street. He now performs with Susan Elliott as Mood Indigo in and around the Houston area. Joe Dugan also played with several other groups.

An early version of *It Must Have Been The Wind* (from the Cinema 45), with great vocals and some scorching guitar work, can be heard on the *Psychotic Reactions* (LP) compilation. (VJ/MW/JFr)

Funkadelic

Personnel:			
	GEORGE CLINTON	vcls	ABCD
	RAYMOND DAVIS	vcls	AB
	CLARENCE 'FUZZY' HASKINS	vcls	AB
	EDDIE HAZEL	gtr	AB
	TAWL ROSS	gtr	A
	BILLY NELSON	bs	A
	TIKI FULTON	drms	AB
	MICKEY ATKINS	organ	A
	BERNIE WORRELL	organ	ABCD
	GARY SHIDER	gtr	BCD

FUNKADELIC - Free Your Mind CD.

FUNKADELIC - Maggot Brain CD.

WILLIAM 'BOOTSY' COLLINS	bs	C	
CATFISH COLLINS	gtr	CD	
FRANK 'KASH' WADDY	drms	CD	
FRED WESLEY	horns	CD	
MACEO PARKER	horns	CD	

HCP

ALBUMS:	1(A)	FUNKADELIC	(Westbound 2000) 1970 126 SC
(up to	2(A)	FREE YOUR MIND AND YOUR ASS WILL FOLLOW	
1975)			(Westbound 2001) 1971 92 SC
	3(B)	MAGGOT BRAIN	(Westbound 2007) 1971 108 SC
	4(C)	AMERICA EATS ITS YOUNG	
			(Westbound 2020) 1972 123 - -
	5(C)	COSMIC SLOP	(Westbound 2020) 1972 - -
	6(D)	STANDING ON THE VERGE OF GETTING IT ON	
			(Westbound 1001) 1974 - -
	7(D)	FUNKADELIC'S GREATEST HITS	
			(Westbound 1004) 1975 - -
	8(D)	LET'S TAKE IT TO THE STAGE	
			(Westbound 215) 1975 - -

NB: (3) First pressing in Unipak sleeve. All titles have been reissued on vinyl and CD.

HCP

45s:	Music For My Mother/Same (instr.)	(Westbound 148) 1969 -
(up to	I'll Bet You/Open Your Eyes	(Westbound 150) 1970 63
1975)	I Got A Thing, You Got A Thing, Everybody's Got A Thing/	
	Fish, Chips, And Sweat	(Westbound 158) 1970 80
	I Wanna Know If It's Good For You/	
	(instr.)	(Westbound 167) 1970 81
	You And Your Folks, Me And Mine/	
	Funky Dollar Bill	(Westbound 175) 1971 91
	Can You Get To That/	
	Back In Our Minds	(Westbound 185) 1971 93
	I Miss My Baby/	
	Baby I Owe You Something Good	(Westbound 197) 1972 -
	Hit It And Quit It/A Whole Lot Of B.S.	(Westbound 198) 1972 -
	Loose Booty/A Joyful Process	(Westbound 205) 1973 -
	Cosmic Slop/You Don't Like The Effects,	
	Don't Produce The Cause	(Westbound 218) 1973 -
	(Standing) On The Verge Of Getting It On/	
	Jimmy's Got A Little Bit Of Bitch In Him	(Westbound 224) 1974 -
	Red Hot Mama/Vital Juices	(Westbound 5000) 1975 -
	Better By The Pound/	
	Stuffs And Things	(Westbound 5014) 1975 99

Born in 1941 in North Carolina, George Clinton formed a doo-wop group, the Parliements, in the mid-fifties. After several line-up changes the Parliements had to wait until 1967 before they charted for the first time with the soul single *(I Just Wanna) Testify*. In 1968, Clinton formed **Funkadelic** and signed with Westbound, a new label created in Detroit by Armen Boladian (they also released several **Teegarden and Van Winkle** albums).

Funkadelic (for "Funk" and "Psychedelic") tried, rather successfully, to merge soul, funk, rock and psych and will interest fans of **Sly And The Family Stone** and **Hendrix** (a major influence on their guitarist, Eddie Hazel). In a slightly different style, another black group, **The Temptations**, tried to do the same with their *Psychedelic Shack* period.

Funkadelic kept on recording for Warner Bros. during the seventies and early eighties. Their albums were generally housed in highly coloured sleeves and the musicians were among the first to wear exuberant science fiction outfits, with strange boots, glasses, feathers etc.. A very prolific musician but also an advised businessman, George Clinton managed to sign during the same core of musicians to different labels and therefore also formed **Parliament**(Invictus and Casablanca), the Brides Of Funkenstein (Atlantic), the Parlets, Bootsy Collins Rubber Band (Warner Bros.) and the Horny Horns.

It should be noted that this George Clinton musn't be confused with the Californian white keyboard player who formed **Timber**, was an active sessionman and today composes soundtracks. It's also worth mentioning that the group backed Ruth Copeland on her album *I Am What I Am* (Invictus) 1971. (SR)

Jesse Furlough

45:   Insect Gladiator/?   (Radiant Records 6604) c1968

From Las Vegas, a hippie singer with strange lyrics, but the music is unfortunately old-fashioned teen-rock (SR/HMa)

The Furniture

45:   Keep On Running/I Love It Baby   (Stature 1105) 1968

From Galesburg, Illinois. A good cover of The Spencer Davis hit by a Chicago band. The flip side later resurfaced on *Psychedelic Unknowns, Vol. 7* (LP & CD), *Pebbles Vol. 6* (CD) and *Of Hopes And Dreams & Tombstones* (LP). (VJ/MW)

Furniture Store

ALBUM: 1   NORTHERN FRONT PRESENT...   (Kader) 1975 R1

An acid rural-folk group. The copies came with two inserts (SR)

Fuse

Personnel:	CHIP GREENMAN	drms	A
	CRAIG MYERS	ld gtr	A
	RICK NIELSEN	keyb'ds, gtr	A
	TOM PETERSON	bs	A
	JOE SUNDBERG	vcls	A

ALBUM: 1(A)   FUSE   (Epic 26502) 1969 -

NB: (1) has been pirated as an exact duplicate. Also reissued officially on CD and LP (Sony Rewind 55018-2 and 55018-1 respectively) 2002.

45:   Cruisin' For Burgers/Hound Dog   (Epic 10514) 1968

From Rockford, Illinois. The lineage of this band is reported to stretch back via certain members (Rick Nielsen is frequently mentioned) to the Phaetons, via the Boyz, and possibly the Huns. The band was actually called **The Grim Reapers** but changed their name to **Fuse** upon signing to Epic. Peterson and Nielson were also in Sick Man Of Europe and **Nazz**. Bassist Tom Peterson and Rick Nielson went on to play with Cheap Trick. This album is pretty heavy.

The 45 is non-LP and is much rarer than the album. (VJ/MW/CF)

Fusion

Personnel:	HARVEY LANE	reeds	A
	RICK LUTHER	keyb'ds	A
	GARY MARKER	bs	A
	RICHARD MATZKIN	drms	A
	BILL WOLFF	gtr	A

ALBUM: 1(A)   BORDER TOWN   (Atco 33-295) 1969 -

45:   Another Man / News Of Salena   (Atco 6715) 1969

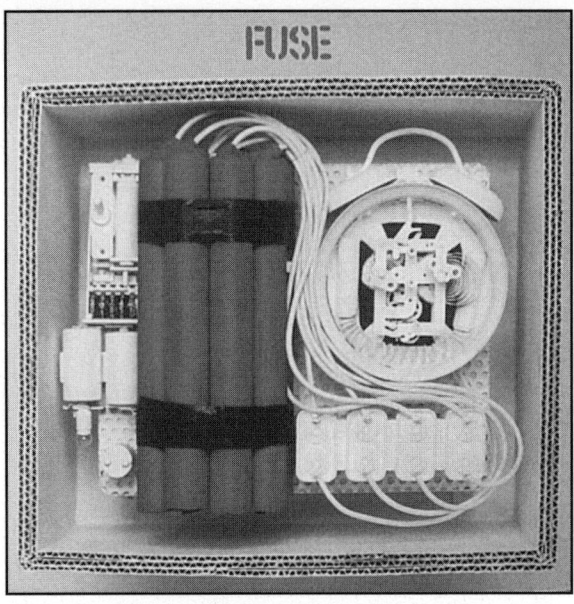

FUSE - Fuse LP.

Unusually for a sixties album, the sleeve notes to this album give a lengthy history of the members of the group. In doing so they fill in many of the missing pieces of the Los Angeles music scene jigsaw. Bill Wolff had been in **Sound Machine**, The Psychedelic Rangers (an early **Doors** incarnation) and the **Peanut Butter Conspiracy**, whilst Gary Marker had been in the **Rising Sons** with Ry Cooder and also **Sound Machine**.

Marker, Lane, Matzkin, Luther and Ry Cooder were also briefly in a band called 'The Jazz Folk', but when this group broke up Marker, Lane and Luther formed a group 'The New World Jazz Company' with future **Spirit** members Ed Cassidy, John Locke and **Randy California**. When the latter three went off to form **Spirit**, Kevin Kelly was brought in on drums to form the first version of **Fusion** but he quickly left to join the **Byrds** and Richard Matzkin was brought back in to finally form the group that recorded the above album, *Border Town*.

The record consists mainly of fairly ordinary blues-rock with a lot of tasty slide guitar. Side two sees the group exploring some new areas with some jazz and country influences. The highlight of the album is the extended closing instrumental track *Erebus* which has a strong jazz-rock feel. (TA/MW)

Future Shock

45:   It's Too Late/Riding High   (Mainstream 726) 1970

By the time of this 45 Mainstream wasn't the label it used to be and it shows on the pedestrian 'A' side, which apart from an acceptable short guitar solo is something like proto glam-rock without glamour. The flip is even worse: a lame orchestra plus band version of *Watermelon Man*, although there are no credits to state this fact on the record. Theft and boring, quite a combination! (MK)

FLOATING BRIDGE - Floating Bridge CD.

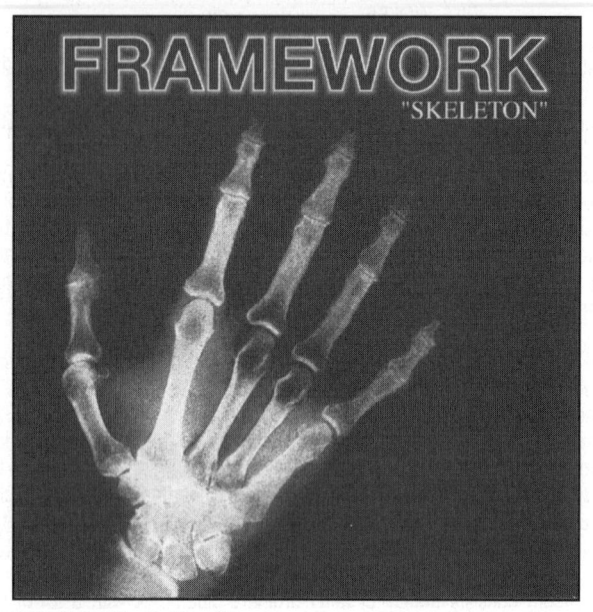

FLOOD - The Rise Of... LP.

FRAMEWORK - Skeleton LP.

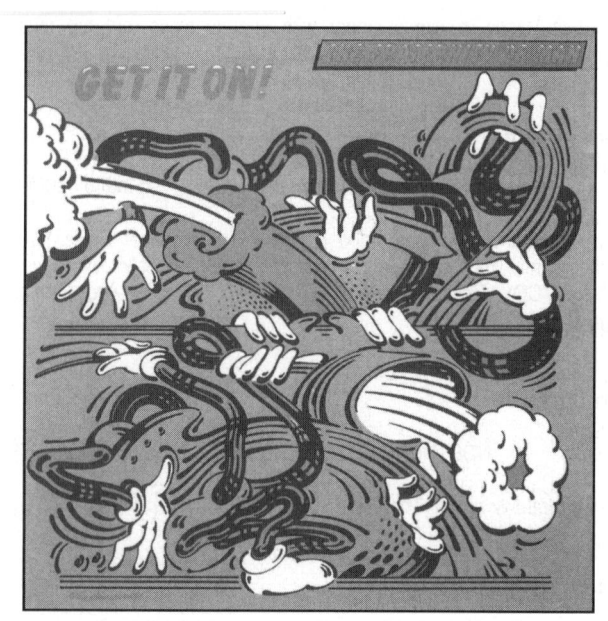

FRATERNITY OF MAN - Get It On CD.

FREE DESIGN - Best Of CD.

FRIJID PINK - Defrosted LP.

Gables

ALBUM: 1 SNAKE DANCE (Fleetwood) 196? R1

This obscure mid-sixties garage album is now a minor collectors' item. (VJ)

Gabriel Gladstar

Personnel: MICHAEL GWINN   vcls, gtr   A
            PHILLIP MORGAN vcls, gtr   A
            JIM ZEIGER   vcls, perc, flute A

ALBUM: 1(A) A GARDEN SONG (Canada/Flying Guitar no #) 1973 R1

NB: (1) reissued in the U.S. (Flying Guitar) 1981 in a black and white picture cover (R1).

This acoustic trio was based in Laguna Beach, California, in its formative years, but moved to Washington state in the early seventies and issued the first press there. They eventually returned to Laguna Beach and reissued the album in a newly - designed sleeve. The album is consistently good throughout, in a laid - back acoustic folk style, and is recommended to fans of the genre. It was originally issued in a colour "peacock" sleeve. (CF)

Galabooches

45: I'll Never Work It Out/She Doesn't Care (Staff 188) 196?

Came out of Gary, Indiana and were fronted by a 16 year old singer. The 'A' side of their Stones-influenced teen-rock 45 can be heard on *Garage Punk Unknowns, Vol. 4* (LP), but it's nothing special. (VJ)

Galactus

Personnel incl: BOB HOCKO   A

ALBUM: 1 COSMIC FORCE FIELD (Airship) 1971 SC

This group was a later incarnation of **The Swamp Rats** and is in no way psychedelic. Hard/heavy Stones-influenced rock that suffers by comparison to their garage stuff - Not recommended - for completists only. (VJ)

The Galaxies

Personnel: MARK EUGANS   sax, keyb'ds,
                              bassoon   ABCD
            BOB KOCH   ld gtr   ABCD
            RON (BOB) LOWERY vcls   ABCD
            CHUCK NAUBERT   bs   ABC
            RON RUSTAD   sax   ABCD
            BILL SLYTER   drms   A
            PHIL HANSON   drms   BCD
            STEWART TURNER   gtr   CD
            JIM STANSTEAD   bs   D

CD: 1(-) MAKING MONEY AND SURFIN' BACK TO SCHOOL
        (Collectables COL-CD-0593) 199?

45s: My Tattle Tale/Love Has Its Way   (Guaranteed 216) 1960
     My Blue Heaven/Tremble   (Dot 16212) 1961
     Shaken/Tacoma   (Seafair 110) 1961
     Stompin' Willie/Doin' The Seaside   (Etiquette 4) 1964
     I'm A Worker/Make Love To Me Baby   (Etiquette 17) 1965
     On The Beach/She Said I Do   (Etiquette 20) 1965
     I Am Yours/I Who Have Nothing   (Etiquette 25) 1966
     She Said I Do/Along Comes The Man   (Panorama 54) 1967

Formed in Tacoma, Washington, their early recordings are irrelevant to this book but when they signed to Etiquette, their career began to take off. With the onset of the psychedelic era, they became the first Northwest band to use an automatic lighting system. They also played outside the Northwest adding a string section to their recording of *I Who Have Nothing* in L.A. In search of a new image they changed their name to **Rock Collection** in 1967.

They have three cuts (*Rudolph, Please Come Home For Christmas* and *Christmas Eve*) on the 1965 compilation album *Merry Christmas*, which was reissued in 1985. *I'm A Worker* and *She Said I Do* also appeared on the 1966 compilation *The Northwest Rock Collection, Vol. 1* (LP).

Retrospective compilation appearances have included: *Along Comes The Man* on *Psychedelic Unknowns, Vol. 9* (CD), *History Of Northwest Rock, Vol. 2* (CD) and *Northwest Battle Of The Bands, Vol. 2* (CD); and *On The Beach* on *Follow That Munster, Vol. 1* (LP). (VJ/MW)

TURDS ON A BUM RIDE Vol's 1 & 2 (Comp CD) including The Galaxies IV.

The Galaxies IV

Personnel: CHARLES BRODOWICZ keyb'ds, vcls AB
            LEN DEMSKI   bs, vcls   AB
            ALAN FOWLER   drms   AB
            CHRIS HOLMES
            (DUKE WILLIAMS)   gtr, vcls   AB
            STEVE SHIER   ld vcls   B

NB: T.J. Tindall, was also an early member of this band - he later resurfaced in **Edison Electric Band**.

45s: Let Me Hear You Say Yeah/
     Till Then You'll Cry   (Veep V 1211) 1966
     Don't Let Love Look Back/?   (Mohawk) 1966/7
     Piccadilly Circus/I'm Goin' For Myself (Mohawk 169) 1966
     Piccadilly Circus/
     Don't Lose Your Mind   (RCA Victor 47-9235) 1967

This Trenton, New Jersey group's best known song is the brilliant fuzz punk raver *Don't Lose Your Mind*, but *Piccadilly Circus* is also an excellent fuzz instrumental and the Veep 45 is a decent beat effort and was probably also issued on Mohawk.

The band formed in 1964 at Blessed Sacrament Grammar School and gave over 80 performances at the 1964-5 New York World's Fair. They went on to win the worlds largest 'Battle Of The Bands' at Lambertville Music Circus and were featured in the New York Times and Readers Digest magazine.

Now at College, they added a lead vocalist, Steve Shier, and changed names briefly to Galaxie V and then **Alexander Rabbit**.

Compilation appearances have included: *Don't Lose Your Mind* on *Mayhem & Psychosis, Vol. 1* (LP), *Mayhem & Psychosis, Vol. 1* (CD), *Turds On A Bum Ride Vol. 1 & 2* (Dble CD), *Turds On A Bum Ride, Vol. 2* (Dble LP),

Glimpses, Vol's 1 & 2 (CD) and Glimpses, Vol. 2 (LP); Piccadilly Circus (from the Mohawk 45) on Buzz Buzz Buzzzzzz Vol. 1 (CD); Piccadilly Circus also appears on Pebbles, Vol. 11 (LP), but is incorrectly billed as Don't Lose Your Mind.

NB: The sleeve notes to Turds On A Bum Ride suggest that this band came from Los Angeles, but this is incorrect. (VJ/MW/RMh)

Galaxy

Personnel incl:	FRENZI FABBRI	gtr	A
	SPACE MAMA GEIGER	keyb'ds	A
	PEPPER LEONARDI	bs	A
	MISS GUNNER POWELL	drms	A

ALBUM: 1(A) DAY WITHOUT THE SUN
(Sky Queen SQR 1677) 1977 R2

NB: (1) had a limited repress in 1989. Later reissued issued on vinyl and CD (Akarma AK 008) 1998, with two bonus cuts.

This heavy progressive rock album is an important item among collectors, (though some would say it's overrated hype!). The band were almost certainly from Jacksonville, Florida.

An double album/single CD of unreleased material recorded between 1979-84, Very First Stone (Akarma AK 085(/6)) 1999, is by comparison dreadful. (VJ)

Galaxy Generation

ALBUM: 1 HAIR (Design) c1969 -

Another cheesy exploito album. (SR)

Gallery

Personnel:	JIM GOLD	ld vcls, gtr	AB
	DENNIS KOVARIK	bs, vcls	AB
	DANNY BRUCATO	drms	B
	FRED DiCENSO	gtr, vcls	B
	CAL FREEMAN	steel gtr	B

HCP
ALBUMS: 1(A) NICE TO BE WITH YOU (Sussex SXBS 7017) 1972 75 -
2(B) FEATURING JIM GOLD (Sussex SXBS 7026) 1973 - -

HCP
45s: Nice To Be With You/Ginger Haired Man (Sussex 232) 1972 4
I Believe In Music/Someone (Sussex 239) 1972 22
Big City Miss Ruth Ann/Lover's Hideaway (Sussex 248) 1973 23
River Boat Captain/Rest In Peace (Sussex 255) 197? -
Lady Luck/Maybe Baby (Sussex 259) 197? -
Love Every Little Thing About You/Friends (Sussex 512) 197? -

A soft-rock group from Detroit, produced by Mike Theodore and **Dennis Coffey**. Their debut album spent fifteen weeks in the Top 200, climbing to No. 75 and the title cut was a Top 5 single. Cal Freeman went on to play with Leo Kottke and released some instrumental albums. Jim Gold went solo and released albums on Tabu Records. (SR/TTi/NK/VJ)

Gallery Production

45: Do I Have To Come Right Out And Say It/
All Your Love (Esar 155/6) 1967

Two note-perfect covers of **Buffalo Springfield** and Bluesbreakers' tunes from a Sacramento outfit. Do I Have To Come Right Out And Say It also features on The Sound Of Young Sacramento (CD). (VJ)

Gallows

Personnel incl:	DON ACHELPOHL		A
	DENNIS CHAMBERLAIN		A
	RICHARD CHAMBERLAIN	gtr	A
	BRUCE KETTLITZ	vcls	A

45s: Slow Death / Come To The Party (It 2307) 1965
Remember Mary /
Too Many Fish In The Sea (Maintain IT-2315) 1967

This band ruled in Keokuk, Iowa until the advent of the **Gonn**. In fact **Gonn**'s Craig Moore had previously been a **Gallows**' fan, then their roadie and promoter, before forming his own bands - The Pagans then **Gonn**.

Compilation appearances have included:- Come To The Party on Drink Beer! Yell! Dance! (LP); Too Many Fish In The Sea on Basementsville! U.S.A. (LP); and Remember Mary on Leaving It All Behind (LP). (MM/MW)

The Gamble Folk

ALBUM: 1 THINKING WITH THE GAMBLE FOLK
(Creative Sound) c1973 -

A Christian folk-rock trio formed by two brothers and their sister. (SR)

Game

ALBUMS: 1( ) GAME (Faithful Virtue FVS 2003) 1969 SC
2( ) LONG HOT SUMMER (Evolution 3008) 1971 SC

NB: (1) also released on (Evolution 2021) 1970

45s: Stop, Look, Listen/Fat Mama (Faithful Virtue 7005) 1969
Julie/When Love Begins To Look
Like You (Commonwealth United 3009) 1970
Fat Mama/Girl Next Door (Evolution 1042) 1971
Two Songs For The Senorita/? (Evolution 1053) 1971

Game's two albums rarely turn up. In 1974, George Terry would join the Eric Clapton Band as second guitarist and also play with Steve Stills, while Scott Kirkpatrick would later be in Firefall and the McGuinn/Hillman/Clark Band. (SR/EW)

Gamma Goochee

Personnel incl:	EDDIE KEATING	bs, vcls	A
	SCOTT KIRKPATRICK	drms	A
	LES LUHRING	keyb'ds	A
	GEORGE TERRY	gtr	A

GALAXY - Day Without The Sun LP.

GANDALF - Gandalf LP.

| EP: | 1 | The Gamma Goochee + I'm Gonna Buy Me A Dog | (Colpix 8007 M) 1966 |

NB: French EP with picture sleeve, the other side is **Nooney Rickett** with *Bye Bye Baby/Maybe The Last Time*.

A bubble-gum crowd-pleaser, recorded with fake applause. *I'm Gonna Buy Me A Dog* was written by **Boyce and Hart** while *The Gamma Goochee* was penned by Mangiagli.

Compilation appearances include *The Gamma Goochie* on *It's Finkin' Time!* (LP). (SR)

Gandalf

Personnel:	DAVY BAUER	drms	A
	FRANK HUBACH	keyb'ds	A
	BOB MULLER	bs	A
	PETE SANDO	gtr	A

| ALBUM: | 1(A) | GANDALF | (Capitol ST 121) 1968 R3 |

NB: (1) has been counterfeited at least twice on vinyl as well as being reissued officially on CD (See For Miles SEE CD 326) in 1991. More recently it has been reissued on CD (Sundazed SC 6152) 2002 with new photos and liner notes by Mike Stax.

| 45: | Golden Earrings/Never Too Far | (Capitol P-2400) 1968 |

The above-mentioned album is excellent, but unfortunately originals are rare. The opening cut *Golden Earrings* (a 1948 hit for Bing Crosby!) is a beautiful relaxing number which culminates in a spacey climax. The album also contains sensitive covers of **Tim Hardin** compositions including *Hang On To A Dream*, a lovely version of *Nature Boy* and some strange instrumentation in *Can You Travel In The Dark Alone*, which is easily the best of Peter Sando's two originals on the album. There's also an ethereal and delicate cover of Harry Belafonte's 1957 recording *Scarlet Ribbons*. The album is a superb piece of laid back pop-psychedelia with some progressive influences as one might expect given the year of its release. It was produced by Koppelman and Rubin, who are best known for their production work for **The Lovin' Spoonful** and **The Sopwith Camel**.

Until recently next to nothing was known about the group apart from their line-up, but as the **Gandalf** album was originally issued on the "Rainbow" Capitol label, this dates it as 1968 because Capitol didn't switch to the "Light Green" label until 1969.

In fact Pete Sando tells us that **Gandalf** had their roots in Thunderbirds, an outfit formed by Bob Muller, which were based in Greenwood Lake, New York. They soon transformed into The Rahgoos and went on to play the bar circuit in Greenwood Lake, N.Y., the Jersey Shore, and various New York City clubs and coffee houses, such as The Phone Booth, Murray The K's World, Electric Circus and legendary Night Owl Cafe, in Greenwich Village.

They met songwriters Gary Bonner and Alan Gordon (of **Magicians** fame), one night at The Night Owl, who in turn introduced them to Koppelman and Rubin. Suitably impressed by The Rahgoos, and their rather unique approach, they arranged for the Columbia deal, under the new moniker **Gandalf** and ushered them in to Brooks Aurthur's Century Sound studios in New York.

Shortly after the album's release **Gandalf** guitarist Pete Sando sang on **The Barracuda** 45 *The Dance At St. Francis*, which was written and produced by Gary Bonner/Alan Gordon and charted, when it was originally released in 1969.

In the seventies and eighties, Sando played with various New York and L.A. bands, recording an unreleased album in 1981 entitled *Sandcastles*. He's recently finished a new singer-songwriter CD, *Creatures Of Habit* and co-written three tunes for a movie called "Time Served".

A CD of rare and unreleased **Gandalf** material is currently being thought about.....

Compilation appearances have included: *Golden Earrings* on *Psychedelic Frequencies* (CD); and *Can You Travel In The Dark Alone* on *Rock A Delics* (LP).

The Sundaze **Gandalf** reissue on CD is highly recommended to fans of U.S. psychedelia. (VJ/MW)

Gandalf The Grey

| Personnel incl: | CHRIS WILSON | gtr, vcls | A |

| ALBUM: | 1 | THE GREY WIZARD AM I | (GWR GWR-007) 1972 R3 |

NB: (1) counterfeited (Heyoka HEY 207) 1986.

Recorded in New York, this is guitar orientated rock with harmonious vocals and both a psychedelic and folksy taint although it lacks variety of mood. The reissue is recommended.

Chris Wilson also made some pre-album 45s, which although sought-after, are inferior to the album. (VJ)

The Gang of Saints

Personnel incl?:	STEVE BEALL		A
	MICKEY BURNS		A

GANDALF THE GREY - The Grey Wizard Am I LP.

45:   Yes, It's Too Bad / This Feeling   (PKB'S 000) 1966

Recorded in Miami, this band hailed from Adel, Georgia. *Psychedelic Crown Jewels Vol. 2* (Dble LP & CD) and *Psychedelic States: Georgia Vol. 1* (CD) showcase *Yes, It's Too Bad* - a garage ballad with outstanding bass and a delicious cascading lead motif. (MW/RM)

The Gants

Personnel:	JOHNNY FREEMAN	vcls, gtr	A C
	SID HERRING	vcls, gtr	ABC
	VINCE MONTGOMERY	bs	ABC
	DON WOOD	drms	ABC
	JOHNNY SANDERS	gtr	B

ALBUMS:	1(B)	ROADRUNNER	(Liberty LRP - 3432) 1965 SC
	2(B)	GANTS GALORE	(Liberty LRP - 3455) 1966 SC
	3(B)	GANTS AGAIN	(Liberty LRP - 3473) 1966 SC

NB: There's also three compilations: *The Gants* (LP) (Bam-Caruso KIRI 067) 1988; *Roadrunner! The Best Of The Gants* (Sundazed SC 11078) 2000; and *I Wonder* (Bam Caruso/RPM RPM BC 202) 2000.

HCP

45s:	Roadrunner/My Baby Don't Care	(Statue 605) 1965 -
	What's Happening/ Careless Hands (By The Niteliters)	(Statue 608) 1965 -
	Roadrunner/My Baby Don't Care	(TOP 5002) 1965 -
	Roadrunner/My Baby Don't Care	(Liberty 55829) 1965 46
	Little Boy Sad/ (You Can't Blow) Smoke Rings	(Liberty 55853) 1966 -
	Crackin' Up/Dr. Feelgood	(Liberty 55884) 1966 -
	I Want Your Lovin'/Spoonful Of Sugar	(Liberty 55903) 1966 -
	Greener Days/I Wonder	(Liberty 55940) 1967 -
	Drifters Sunrise/Just A Good Show	(Liberty 55965) 1967 -
α	Another Chance/Ain't Too Proud To Beg	(Statue 7006) 1969 -

NB: α Released as Sid Herring and The Gants.

Greenwood in Mississippi was home to this band which came together in 1963. At the time of line-up "A" they were actually known as The Kingsmen. They called themselves **The Gants** when Johnny Sanders replaced Johnny Freeman on guitar. The name was taken from a local shirt manufacturer! In their early days, they sounded much like The Beatles and by chance The Animals' manager Mike Jeffries spotted them playing in Mississippi and booked them as a support act for an Animals tour.

Before long they were in Alabama's Muscle Shoals studio recording their own arrangement of Bo Diddley's *Roadrunner*. It was very popular locally and after release on a couple of local labels it was picked up by Liberty and this national distribution took it to No. 46 in the national charts. An album followed and was made up from material recorded at the same session. It was a mixture of punk covers like *Gloria* and *House of The Rising Sun* and Sid Herring compositions like the melodic *My Baby Don't Care* and *Six Days In May* which underscored Herring's songwriting skills.

A Johnny Burnette composition was chosen for their second 45 but it failed to return them to the charts. The third 45 took two of the better tracks from their *Gants Galore* album which had been recorded in Los Angeles earlier that year. Compared to their first effort this was disappointing. No Herring compositions were included and the whole album consisted of cover versions, including **The Standell's** *Dirty Water*, The Yardbirds' *Shapes Of Things* and Eddie Cochran's *Summertime Blues* and *C'mon Everybody*.

In 1966, they were taken to Nashville, Tennessee, where they recorded a new 45 *I Want Your Lovin'*, a fresh-sounding record with a taint of country and western influence, although The Beatles influence was still very evident. The third (and final) album was also recorded at the same time. This contained fine covers of **Paul Revere**'s *Hungry* and **The Rascals**' *You Better Run* and some more fine Herring compositions, particularly *I Wonder*, a fine Beatlesque song. When neither the single or album made much impression they returned to Los Angeles and assisted by David Gates they recorded *Greener Days*, a good harmony-pop song, which had some regional success but failed to break through nationally.

After one further harmony-pop 45 in April 1967, Johnny Sanders quit and Johnny Freeman returned to replace him, but by the end of the year the whole band had largely collapsed. Only "largely", however, as some gigs were booked in the first half of 1969 through a Memphis Talent Agency and **The Gants** went on the road with Alston Meeks (ex-**Reets**) and Johnny Jennings taking over Johnny Sanders' guitar parts. In 1971, Herring and Wood formed **Watchpocket**. Sid Herring continued to record spasmodically and even released an album *All American Dream* in 1982.

Much of **The Gants** best material is collected on the three retrospective compilations (although Bam Caruso's early vinyl compilation omits both sides of the corkin' *Smoke Rings* 45); but you'll also find:- *I Wonder* on *Nuggets Box* (4-CD), *Pebbles, Vol. 8* (LP); *Smoke Rings* on *Let's Dig 'Em Up, Vol. 2* (LP) and *Trash Box* (5-CD); *Roadrunner* on *Garage Monsters* (LP) and *Battle Of The Bands* (CD); *Just A Good Show* on *It's Only A Passing Phase*; and both *Another Chance* and *What's Your Name* on *Garagelands Vol. 2* (CD).

Johnny Freeman is still active in the local music scene, playing together with Johnny Jennings in a band called Curb Service, where **Gants**' songs form a part of their set. Sid Herring now resides in Nashville.

Come the new millennium and it's all happening again for **The Gants**. Not only are there two decent (if overlapping) CD compilations, but **The Gants** are back in action, a headliner act for the three day Cavestomp extravaganza, also featuring the **Blues Magoos** and Troggs. (VJ/MW)

Jerry Garcia

HCP

ALBUMS:	1	GARCIA	(Warner Bros. WS 2582) 1972 35 -
(up to	2	COMPLIMENTS OF	(Round 59301) 1974 -
1974)			

NB: (2) reissued on CD (Grateful Dead GDCD 4011).

45:   The Wheel/Deal   (Warner 16146) 1972

NB: French release with PS.

"Uncle Jerry" was the co-leader of the **Grateful Dead** and a kind of musical guru for the Bay Area groups. Apart from his prolific work with the **Dead**, he also released several solo albums with various members of the **Dead** plus Bill Vitt and John Kahn, Ben Benay and even Larry Carlton. They will be of interest to "Deadheads", but are probably best avoided if you don't appreciate the **Dead**'s particular style.

As if recording with the **Dead** and solo wasn't enough, **Garcia** can also be found guesting on albums by **Jefferson Airplane** (*Volunteers* and *Early Flight*), **It's A Beautiful Day** (*Marrying Maiden*), **Link Wray**, **Papa John Creach**, **Tom Fogerty** and **Merle Saunders**. He also contributed *Love Scene* to the *Zabriski Point* soundtrack album;

Jerry Garcia died on the 9th August, 1995. (SR)

THE GANTS - I Wonder CD.

Jerry Garcia and Howard Wales

Personnel:	MARTIN FIERRO	sax	A
	JERRY GARCIA	gtr, vcls	A
	JOHN KAHN	bs	A
	BILL VITT	drms	A
	HOWARD WALES	keyb'ds	A
	(CURLEY COOKE	gtr	A)
	(MIKE MARINELLI	drms	A)

ALBUM: 1(A) HOOTEROLL ? (Douglas 30859) 1972 -

NB: (1) has been reissued on CD.

The **Grateful Dead** leader teamed up with his usual jamming rhythm section (Vitt/Kahn) and Howard Wales, the former **A.B.Shky** keyboard player for a mix of psych, jazz and blues. Curley Cooke (**Steve Miller Band**, **A.B. Skhy**) and Martin Fierro (**Sir Douglas Quintet**) guested on some tracks. Mostly recommended for Dead-heads. Wales would also play on some **Grateful Dead** albums. (SR)

Garden Club

45: Little Girl Lost-and-Found/I Must Love Her (A&M 848) 1967

A lovely flower-pop single with touches of psychedelia. (MMs)

Kossie Gardner

ALBUM: 1 PIPES OF BLUE (Dot DLP-25940) 1969 SC?

A rare album of heavy-psych played with keyboards. It includes two covers of **Hendrix** (*Foxy Lady* and *Fire*), one Cream song (*Sunshine Of Your Love*) and **Steppenwolf**'s *Magic Carpet Ride*. **Kossie Gardner** was a studio musician. (SR)

Jason Garfield

45: A Picture Of Lilli / Where Did I Lose My Way (Kef 4445) 1970

A good, crisp original composition, based on The Who's *Pictures Of Lily* with very similar lyrics, but totally different melody and arrangement. Good, crisp pop.

No clues yet as to this acts location. Another act on this label, Morningstar, are also unlocated. (BM/MW)

JERRY GARCIA - Compliments Of... CD.

Gale Garnett

Personnel incl:	GALE GARNETT	vcls	A
	EARL PALMER	drms	A
	VAN DYKE PARKS	keyb'ds	A

ALBUM: 1(A) SINGS ABOUT FLYING RAINBOWS AND LOVE
(selective) AND OTHER GROOVY THINGS (RCA LPM-3747) 1967 -

An album of Californian pop with good female vocals. **Gale Garnett** released several other solo albums and singles (even including some sung in French or Italian for the European market) and later formed **Gentle Reign**. (SR)

Kyle Garrahan

45: I Shall Be Released/Shame (Janus 109) c1969

A one-off solo 45 by **Kyle Garrahan**, who had earlier played in Boston's **Lost**. (MW)

Mort Garson

ALBUMS: 1 THE WOZARD OF IZ, AN ELECTRONIC ODYSSEY
(selective) (A&M SP 4156) 1970 -
2 SIGNS OF THE ZODIAC - ARIES (A&M SP 4211) 1970 -
3 SIGNS OF THE ZODIAC - LEO (A&M SP 4215) 1970 -
4 SIGNS OF THE ZODIAC - SAGITTARIUS
(A&M SP 4219) 1970 -
5 MOTHER EARTH'S PLANTASIA
(Homewood Productions H 101) c1973 -

45s: The Wozard Of Iz/Zi Fo Drazow Eht (A&M 962) 1970

Along with **Beaver and Krause**, **Mort Garson** was one of the first specialists of electronic sounds and early synthesizers to be active on the "pop" market. Between 1959 and 1980, he has released a large number of albums and singles under different names. Be aware that he also arranged and produced several easy listening and pop records during the early sixties! His better known project is the **Zodiac Cosmic Sounds** and he also recorded as **Lucifer**. Among the records released under his name, the *Wozard Of Iz* from 1970 is a strange electronic version of "Wizard Of Oz" with weird lyrics. The album was produced by Bernie Krause and the partner of Lee Hazelwood, **Suzie Jane Hokum**, was Dorothy. Not recommended for young kids! After that came a serie of twelve albums "dramatically narrated with electronic music accompaniment". There should have been one for every zodiac sign, but it's unsure if the twelve were actually recorded and released. The ones who are known to exist are Aries, Leo and Sagittarius. Housed in very colored sleeves, they were produced by Allen Stanton (**Brewer and Shipley**, **Byrds**), with scripts written by Jacques Wilson and electronic musical score composed and realized by **Garson**. The narrators included **Nancy Priddy**, Joh Erwin and Michael Bell. Overall it's in the same style as the **Zodiac Cosmic Sounds** but with more spoken passages. Circa 1973, **Garson** recorded *Plantasia*, an album of music to help the green plants to grow... He would later be seen like a "New Age" pioneer.

For **Mort Garson** completists, there's also an old 45: *Gas Light Village/Drum Tango* (Todd 1050) 1959, yes '59 as by 'Mort Garson and His Orchestra', as well as several other singles on MGM, Landa, Joy and Coral! It's certainly different! (SR/VJ/CA/MW)

The Gas Company

Personnel:	MIKE CLOTHER	organ	A
	BARRY CURTIS	gtr, vcls	AB
	NED NELTNER	gtr, vcls	AB
	BOB RNEBER	bs, vcls	A
	TONY WINSLOW	drms	AB
	STEVE FRIEDSON	organ	B
	JIM KENFIELD	bs	B

45: See/Couldn' Make Up My Mind (Debtone 800) 1968

This band was formed in Spokane, Washington by Ned Neltner, (formerly of **The Mark 5**) after he completed a period of military service. Curtis had previously played with **The Kingsmen** and Kenfield with **The Rock-N-Souls**. They soon relocated to Seattle and played at all the top clubs like The Happening. They toured nationally with **The Box Tops** whose managers handled their business affairs and arranged for them to record the above 45 at Ardent Studios in Memphis, Tennessee under the production of **Don Nix**. It was a big hit in the Northwest. Epic bought the material from the Ardent sessions for an album, which was never released and the band were also involved in a multimedia event with the Seattle Opera, which toured the state's schools.

The band really fell apart soon after Ned Neltner departed, dissatisfied with their art rock direction, to write songs for **The Wailers** with Buck Ormsby. He later produced **Locksley Hall**'s album and was last reported playing for JR Cadillac, a Puget Sound group. Barry Curtis plays with the reformed **Kingsmen** and Mike Clother has his own band. (VJ)

Gas Mask

Personnel:	RAY BROOKS	bs	A
	BILL DAVIDSON	electric gtr	A
	RICHARD GRANDO	wind instruments	A
	DAVID GROSS	wind instruments	A
	NICK OLIVA	keyb'ds	A
	BOBBY OSBOURNE	vcls	A
	JIMMY STRASSBURG	drms	A

ALBUM: 1(A) THEIR FIRST ALBUM (Tonsil T-4001) 1970 -

NB: (1) originally released with gatefold cover. (1) also released in France (Tonsil T 4001) 1971.

Signed to the small New York Tonsil label, the band's 1970 debut *Their First Album* teamed them with producer Teo Macero. Musically the comparison with **Blood, Sweat and Tears** simply couldn't be missed. Backed by a **BS&T**-styled horn section (Richard Grando, David Gross and Enrico Raja), singer Bobby Osborne's growl sounds little more than a David Clayton-Thomas wannabe. With Olivia responsible for the majority of the material (Gross contributing two selections), tracks such as *If You Just Think of Me*, *Light The Road* and *Just Like That* weren't bad (particularly if you liked early **BS&T**). On the other hand, why bother when the original was readily available? Sales proved non-existent; certainly not helped by a dumb name and one of the year's ugliest album covers.

Bill Davidson was previously with the **Steve Baron Quartet**. Grando also played with a latter era **Earth Opera**. (SR/SB)

Gass Co.

45s:	Come On Up/First I Look At The Purse	(PRO P 400-62/3) 1967
(selective)	Walk On By / Walk In The Sun	(Goodway 100) 1967
	Tomorrow /	
	Walk In The sun (diff.version)	(M.W. Lads 2867) 1967
	Girls That I Know Of /	
	Second Chance	(M.W. Lads 3407-1) c1967
	Sundays / What A Feelin'	(M.W. Lads MWL-4966) 196?

The first 45 listed contains soulful garage covers by a Philadelphia outfit who would become The Bubble. Their version of *First* is most excellent indeed. They also did some commercials for *M.W. Lads* that can be sampled on *Crude PA, Vol. 2* (LP) and the last 45 listed contains gentle orchestrated folkie-flower pop. *Sundays* features some very mellow use of wah-wah. Still, a long way from the Pro 45. Were composers J.Stumpo, D.Stumpo and R.Steinbronn group members? (MW)

The Gas Station

45: One Way Street/Wild Honey (Happy Tiger 582) 1970

The above 45 was this Chicago-based outfit's sole stab for stardom. (VJ)

The Gators

ALBUM: 1 IN CONCERT (Bulletin 27982) c1968 R1?

A Tennessee garage/frat-rock quartet (guitar/bass/drums/keyboards) doing covers of *My Babe*, *Down In The Boondocks*, *Can't Help Myself* and *Shotgun*. (SR)

The Gauchos

Personnel incl:	JIM DOVAL	ld vcls	A

ALBUM: 1 THE GAUCHOS (ABC ABC-506) 1965 -

45: I Know You're Fooling Around/
Uptown Caballero (ABC 10637) 1965

A Californian garage/frat-rock band. Their album was recorded live in a Fresno nightclub, 'The Party' and is mainly comprised of covers of *La Bamba*, *Money*, *Pretty Woman*, *Little Latin Lupe Lu*, *Out Of Sight*, *I'm A Man*...

Compilation appearances include *Mama Keep Your Big Mouth Shut* on *Bad Vibrations, Vol. 1* (LP & CD). (SR)

Jonna Gault and Her Symphonopop Scene

ALBUM: 1 WATCH ME (RCA LSP-4081) 1967 SC?

A scarce album of baroque pop with covers of the Beach Boys' *Good Vibrations*, the Beatles' *Eleanor Rigby* and original songs such as *The Pink Life* and *Wonder Why, I Guess?*. **Joanna Gault** also recorded two singles for RCA, one for Reprise and two for Map between 1965 and 1968. (SR)

The Gaunga Dyns

Personnel:	BEAU BREMER	ld vcls	A
	ROB CARTER	bs	A
	BRIAN COLLINS	keyb'ds	A
	RICKY HALL	drums	A
	MIKE KING	ld gtr	A
	NEALE LUNDGREN	ld vcls	A
	STEVE STAPLES	gtr	A

45s:	Rebecca Rodifer/Stick With Her	(Busy-B Zap 2) 1967
	Clouds Don't Shine/No One Cares	(Busy-B Zap 4) 1967

An interesting sounding band who came out of Louisiana. *Rebecca Rodifer* veers towards psychedelia and boasts a catchy guitar riff and a rather Eastern-influence. This is evident again on *No One Cares*, a punkier song which has a fine Eastern riff alongside a typical punk style beat.

The above line-up came together in New Orleans in late 1965 when Carter and Collins, the remnants of the original **Gaunga Dyns**, merged with another West bank outfit, The Twilights. Read their full story in "Brown Paper Sack #1", which also reveals how they came to cover the Glass Kans' *Stick With Her* on their first 45.

Compilation appearances have included: *No Ones Cares* and *Stick With Her* on *Louisiana Punk Groups From The Sixties, Vol. 2* (LP) and *Sixties Archive, Vol. 3* (CD); and both *Rebecca Rodifer* and *No Ones Cares* on *Highs In The Mid-Sixties, Vol. 8* (LP). (AB/MW)

The Gears

Personnel incl:	BOB ALWOOD	A
	JOE DANIELS	A
	DAN PETERSON	A

45s:	Feel Right / Explanantion	(Hillside 1001) 1968
	Come Back To Me /	
	Sooner Or Later	(Counterpart C-2639/40) 1968

From Columbus, Ohio. The Hillside 45 is simple and winsome Beatlesque garage-pop, and harks back to 1965. The Counterpart 45 is more with the times, and kicks off with waspish guitar but ruined by subsequent brass. The catchy pop flip has a fluid guitar solo but is spoilt as well by pointless brass tootlings. Their earliest compilation appearance is on the *Hillside '66* album where they cover **The Outsiders'** *Time Won't Let Me*. The following year Hillside put out a *Hillside '67* EP and here are **The Gears** again, this time with a rather good garage-ballad *We're Through*. No, they didn't make it onto Hillside's *1968 Promotion* 7", just in case anyone was wondering.

It's way past time that these sought-after local scene Hillside releases, and the Northlands *3rd Annual Battle Of The Bands* (featuring the **Four O'Clock Balloon** and more Columbus acts), got wider appreciation by being reissued. (MW)

Arthur Gee

Personnel:			
	BILL ALEXANDER	synth, keyb'ds, celeste	AB
	BOB ALLISON	vcls	A
	CLYDE ALEXANDER	vcls	A
	MARCUS DAMERT	gtr, celeste, perc, vcls	AB
	ARTHUR GEE	vcl, accoustic gtr, jaw harp, mouth harp	AB
	DOUG GUNN	drms	A
	RICHARD HATHAWAY	bs, drms, vcls	AB
	DONNIE KRYNOVICH	vcls	A
	DON RIGGS	drms, vcl	AB
	STEVE VAN GELDER	violin, vcl, gtr, piano	AB
	SNAZZ WALL	pedal steel gtr	A
	DAVE WILLIAMS	recorder, horns	A
	REX WILLIAMS	vcls	AB
	(PAUL BEAVER	moog	B)

| ALBUMS: | 1(A) | ARTHUR GEE | (Tumbleweed TWS 101) 1971 - |
| | 2(B) | CITY COWBOY | (Tumbleweed TWS 107) 1972 - |

NB: (1) issued with a songbook.

From Colorado, a noteworthy singer/songwriter who released two albums mixing dreamy ballads, psych, prog and country. The first one is especially good and came housed in a superb gatefold sleeve with a songbook. The lyrics are quite mystic and not always easy to understand. With a tight yet loose band backing him, **Gee** starts out on his troubled journey with conviction and musical intelligence from the very first note. Rural elements are strongly present, though never intrusive and always stylish. The production is simple and clear and the songs are mostly fairly persuasive, while **Gee**'s voice is a fine and emotional vehicle, again without anything pushy about it. The rocking *Waterweight* is quite good with its lovely flute and expert arrangement, as is the opening *Dimensions*, a sombre and introspective song. The very esoteric *Confessions* with mellotron and an eerie wavering sound could easily pass for what seems to be called "downer-folk" nowadays. Not very spectacular, but a worthwhile effort nonetheless.

The second is more on the country side but contains some nice moments too (notably on *High House* and *Re-Affirmation*).

Both albums were produced by Marcus Damerst. (SR/MK)

Joey Gee and The Come-Ons

Personnel incl:			
	RICKEY BATES	drms	A
	JOEY GEE (JOE GIANNUNZIO)	vcls, hrmnca	ABC
	BILLY MORRISON	bs	A
	CRAIG SORENSEN	gtr	A
	DON ??	gtr	BC
	MIKE ??	ld gtr	BC
	PAUL ??	drms	BC
	TOM ??	bs	B
	VAUGH RYAN	bs	C

NB: Line-up 'A' as **Joey Gee and The Bluetones**, 'B'-'C' as **Joey Gee and The Come-Ons**.

| 45s: | α | Don't You Just Know It / Little Searcher | (Sara J-6451) 1964 |
| | | She's Mean/You Know' Til The End of Time | (Sara J-6599) 1965 |

NB: α as **Joey Gee with The Bluetones**.

Joey Gee formed his first band The Bluetones (line-up 'A') in Iron Mountain, Michigan. He left them to attend broadcasting school at Career Academy in Milwaukee, Wisconsin and assembled the Come-Ons (line-ups 'B' and 'C') for the duration of his stay. They released two eagerly-sought 45s and got to open for the likes of **The Turtles**.

She's Mean is really a R&B-surf style workout and *You Know' Til The End Of Time* is raw proto-punk.

On his return to Michigan he continued to perform for a few years before carving out a career in radio. He relocated to Seattle in the early seventies and has worked for several stations under the name of Joe Cooper.

Compilation appearances have included: *She's Mean* on *Highs In The Mid-Sixties, Vol. 10* (LP); and *You Know - 'Til The End Of Time* on *Highs In The Mid-Sixties, Vol. 15* (LP).

Another 45 by Joey Gee (*Don't Blow Your Cool*/*It's More Than I Deserve* (ABC 10781) 1966) is by a different artist. (VJ/MW/GM)

The Geers

| 45: | I Need You / Please Don't Break My Heart | (SSS International 760) 1967 |

A different and unknown outfit. *I Need You* is sinuous pop-garage with a bit o'soul and a melody that you think you've heard before (echoes of *Get Ready*, for one). The flip is also derivative but with a soulful Animals-cum-Merseybeat style. (MW)

The Gee Tee's

| 45: | Put You Down/Dog | (Perfection Rock S.S.566) 1966? |

From Rockmart, Georgia, this act recorded their sole 45 in Smyrna (an Atlanta suburb) and sold copies at their local gigs. To secure an original 45 you would've needed to put up (or down) around $400 in 1997.

Compilation appearances have included: *Dog* on *Teenage Shutdown, Vol. 8* (LP & CD); *Put You Down* on *Garage Punk Unknowns, Vol. 8* (LP); and both *Dog* and *Put You Down* on *Glimpses, Vol. 4* (LP). (MW/SNs)

SIXTIES ARCHIVES Vol. 3 (Comp CD) includes The Gaunga Dyns.

General Elektrik

| 45: | Take A Step/Miami F-L-A | (Decca 32688) 1968 |

Produced by Dave Blume (**Carolyn Hester Coalition**), a rare 45 with some fuzz guitar. (SR)

The Generation Gap

Personnel:
- DANA BRINDLE — drms — A
- CRAIG HAWKINGS — vcls — A
- RICK HAWKINGS — gtr — A
- RICHARD HELD — organ — A
- JIM SEAGRAVES — ld gtr — A
- PAT SEMINARA — bs — A

| EP: | 1 | Small Things / Plastic Faces / Losing Every Trace | (Century 34184) 1968 |

| 45s: | Movin' On Strong / Trumpets | (Trip Universal 12) 1969 |
| | Letter From Seattle / Ball | (Trip Universal 19) 1969 |

A six-piece from West Palm Beach, Florida. *Plastic Faces*, from their debut 3-track EP 45, can be heard on *Psychedelic States: Florida Vol. 3* (CD). It's heavyish psych-tinted garage. For their subsequent releases they moved into funkier rock territory. (JLh/MW)

The Generation Gap

| ALBUM: | 1 | UP, UP AND AWAY | (Custom) c1968 SC |

An interesting 'exploito' garage album, with alternate versions of songs from the **Animated Egg** album. (SR)

The Generations

Personnel:
- EDWARD CHRISTIAN — rhythm gtr, vcls — A
- BILLY ELLIS — tenor sax — A
- JERRY EMORY — bs, vcls — A
- JOHN GALIFAKIS — drms — A
- MIKE HINSON — ld gtr, vcls — A
- GARY JACOBS — keyb'ds — A
- TOMMY PARSONS — vcls — A

| ALBUM: | 1(A) | MEET THE GENERATIONS COMBO | (Justice 158) 1967 R2 |

NB: (1) reissued on CD (Collectables COL-0614) 1996.

Although the orginal 1967 liner notes refer to the band as **The Generations**, the Collectables reissue lists the title as *Meet The Generations Combo*. Yet another reissue of a Justice Records album, this one is in more of a soul vein and includes cover versions of *Hold On, I'm Coming*, *Night Train*, *I Got You*, but also includes attempts at the more conventional pop fare of Gerry and The Pacemakers' *Don't Let The Sun Catch You Crying* and the **Left Banke**'s *Walk Away Renee*. (MDo)

Genesis

Personnel:
- SCOTT ASHLEY — — A
- ROGER HUYCKE — drms — A
- RAY KENNEDY — gtr — A
- DARYL MANINEN — ld gtr — A

| 45: | Window Of Sand/Would You Like To | (Ripcord 004) 1967 |

This was a later incarnation of Portland, Oregon's **Wilde Knights** who would also be called American Cheese, Fury's and **King Biscuit Entertainers** during their long and convoluted history. This is fully untangled on the **Wilde Knights**' collection album *Beaver Patrol* (Voxx VXS 200.026). You'll find *Window Of Sand* thereon. (VJ)

GENESIS - In The Beginning CD.

Genesis

Personnel:
- KENT HENRY — gtr — A
- BOB METKE — drms — A
- FRED RIVERA — bs — A
- JACK TTANNA — gtr — A
- SUE RICHMAN — vcls — A

| ALBUM: | 1(A) | IN THE BEGINNING | (Mercury SR 61175) 1968 SC/R1 |

NB: (1) has been reissued on CD (Black Rose BR 137) 2001.

| 45s: | Angeline/Suzanne | (Mercury 72806) 1968 |
| | Gloomy Sunday/What's It All About | (Mercury 72869) 1968 |

A short-lived late sixties Los Angeles band. Kent Henry went on to play for **Charity** and later for **Steppenwolf**. Fred Rivera and Sue Richman went on to play for Delaney Bramlett and The Thieves respectively. The album is worth obtaining.

Jack Ttanna had previously played with **The Sons Of Adam**, when he was known as Joe Kooken. (VJ)

Genesis with Maryann Farra

| 45: | Society's Child/One Day Boy | (Rare Bird R-5000) 1970 |

A female-led keyboard rock cover of Janis Ian's song by an unknown outfit. (MW)

Geneva Convention

| 45: | Something Beautiful / Call My Name | (Beverly Hills 45-9340) 1970 |

Produced by Bill Traut for Dunwich Productions, the 'A' side written by A.Tucker and K.Wakefield, is pop with strong bass parts and horns. The flip written by K.Chovan and J.Zdanowicz is good pop-rock similar to **Paul Revere and Raiders** (but without the guitars), and again features strong bass parts. (SR)

The Gentlemen

| 45s: | It's A Cry'n Shame/You Can't Be True | (Vandan no#) 1966 |
| | Come On (If You Can)/Only Me | (Cameo 419) 1966 |

The first 45 was certainly the work of a Fort Worth garage punk band. One of the band was later in The Werewolves, another Texan outfit. Despite the inclusion of *Come On (If You Can)* on *Highs In The Mid-Sixties, Vol. 17 - Texas Part. 4* (LP) the label makes it more likely that this was the work of a Michigan band of the same name. The cut can also be found on *Boulders, Vol. 2* (LP).

It's A Cryin' Shame can also be found on *Pebbles, Vol. 5* (CD), *The Essential Pebbles Collection, Vol. 1* (Dble CD), *Pebbles Box* (5-LP), *Pebbles, Vol. 5* (LP), *Pebbles, Vol. 1 (ESD)* (CD), *Trash Box* (5-CD) and *I Was A Teenage Caveman* (LP). (VJ/MW)

The Gentlemen Wild

Personnel:			
	CRAIG CATHEY	vcls, keyb'ds	AB
	PAGE MCCALLUM	keyb'ds	A
	DAVID VERMILYA	drms	A
	BILL WHITCOMB	bs	AB
	JAY ZILKA	ld gtr	AB
	BOB HART	drms	B
	STEVE JOSLIN	keyb'ds	B
	DAVE COOKSON	drms	
	JOHN CROWE	drms	
	JOHN PHELPS	gtr	

45: You Gotta Leave/
I Believe (Northwest International NWI 2694) 1967

Hailing from Portland, Oregon, where they formed in 1965, this band's music was an amalgam of early Northwest rock and punk. When Bob Hart joined in 1966, his father Ross took over their management and soon their fortunes prospered. They won the Oregon Battle of The Bands in May 1967, made some local and national TV appearances, became the house band at "Tork Club", a teen nightclub in Portland and opened for many big sixties acts. Their sole 45, which was very punkish in style became a big regional hit both in the Northwest and on the West Coast. When they finally disbanded in April 1969, Cathey and Vermilya went on to play with River.

Compilation appearances have included *You Gotta Leave* on *Sixties Choice, Vol. 2* (LP), *60's Choice Collection, Vol's 1 And 2* (CD), *Ya Gotta Have Moxie, Vol. 2* (Dble CD), *Highs In The Mid-Sixties, Vol. 16* (LP) and *Boulders, Vol. 3* (LP); Back in 1967, *Nowhere Man* also appeared on *Battle Of The Bands* (LP). (VJ)

Gentle Reign

Personnel:			
	MICHAEL ARAGON	drms	A
	GALE GARNETT	vcls	A
	TONY HILL	keyb'ds	A
	BRUCE HORIUCHI	ld gtr	A
	(BOB FISCHER	bs	A)
	(BOB INGRAM	gtr	A)
	(DICK ROSMINI	gtr	A)

GENTLE REIGN - An Audience With The King Of Wands LP.

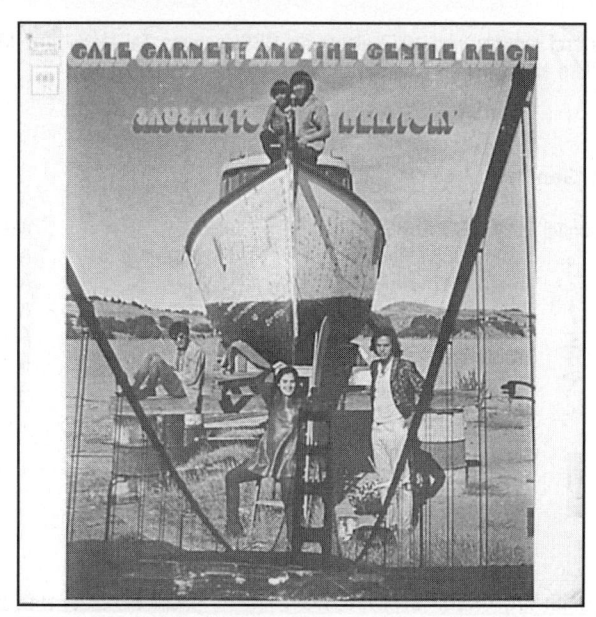

GENTLE REIGN - Sausalito Heliport LP.

ALBUMS:
1( ) GENTLE REIGN (Vanguard) 1968 -
2( ) AN AUDIENCE WITH THE KING OF WANDS (Columbia 9625) 1969 -
3(A) SAUSALITO HELIPORT (Columbia 9760) 1969 -

45: Breaking Through/Fall In Love Again (Columbia 44479) 1968

Gale Garnett had earlier made three solo albums for RCA in the early sixties. A New Zealander by birth, she came to the USA in 1951 and worked as an actress from 1957. She appeared on many TV shows including Hawaiian Eye and Bonanza. The albums are not sought-after by collectors, but pleasant and relaxing. The second includes a good version of *Dolphins*. (VJ)

Gentle Soul

Personnel:			
	TONY COHAN	tabla	A
	RY COODER	gtr	A
	MIKE DEASY	gtr	A
	PAUL HORN	flute	A
	LARRY KNECHTEL	keyb'ds	A
	SANDY KONIKOFF	drms	A
	GAYLE LEVANT	harp	A
	TED MICHEL	cello	A
	VAN DYKE PARKS	harpsichord	A
	BILL PLUMMER	bs	A
	PAMELA POLLAND	vcls	A
	RICH STANLEY	vcls	A
	RILEY WILDFLOWER	gtr	A

ALBUM: 1(A) GENTLE SOUL (Epic BN26374) 1968 R2

45s: Tell Me Love / You Move Me (PS) (Columbia 4-43952) 1967
Our National Anthem/Song for Three (Columbia 4-44152) 1968

Produced by Terry Melcher, this album is a nice example of Californian psychy soft-rock. The instrumentation (harpsichord, tabla, flute, slide guitar) provides an interesting background for the voices and songs of Pamela Polland and Rich Stanley. Among the best tracks are *Through A Dream*, *Young Man Blue* and the instrumental *Overture*. *Young Man Blue* can also be found on *Rockbusters*, a 1969 radio promo album. The 45s are not from the album.

Pamela Polland was also known as a songwriter (her *Tulsa County* was recorded by **The Byrds** and **The Rising Sons**). She formed **Gentle Soul** with Rick Stanley in 1966 as a duo and over the three years they were together, various musicians were part of the group, including Jackson Browne, Sandy Konikoff and Riley Wildflower.

After the group split, she sang with Joe Cocker for the *Mad Dogs And Englishmen* tour and album. Then she moved to Hawaii where she still lives and records. Her 1972 album for CBS features Taj Mahal and Marc McClure and is interesting. (SR)

The Gentrys

Personnel incl:
BRUCE BOWLES	vcls		AB
BOBBY FISHER	tenor sax		A
JIMMY HART	ld vcls		ABC
JIMMY JOHNSON	trumpet		A
PAT NEAL	bs		AB
LARRY RASPBERRY	ld vcls		A
LARRY WALL	drms		AB
LARRY BUTLER	keyb'ds		B
DAVID BEAVER	keyb'ds		C
MIKE GARDNER	drms		C
STEVE SPEER	bs		C
JIMMY TARBUTTON	ld gtr		C

HCP
ALBUMS:
1(A)	KEEP ON DANCING	(MGM SE-4336)	1965	99 -
2(A)	GENTRY TIME	(MGM SE-4346)	1966	- -
3( )	THE GENTRYS	(MGM GAS-127)	1970	- -
4(C)	THE GENTRYS	(Sun 117)	1970	- -

NB: (4) is a CD reissue of (1) plus *Spread It On Thick* and *Everyday I Have To Cry*. There's also a CD compilation: *Keep On Dancing* (Collectables COL-CD-5622) 1995.

HCP
45s:
Little Drops Of Water/Sometimes	(Youngstown 600)	1965 -
Keep On Dancing/Make Up Your Mind	(Youngstown 601)	1965 -
Keep On Dancing/Make Up Your Mind	(MGM 13379)	1965 4
Spread It On Thick/Brown Paper Sack	(MGM 13432)	1965 50
Everyday I Have To Cry/Don't Let It Be	(MGM 13495)	1966 77
A Woman Of The World/ There Are Two Sides To Every Story	(MGM 13561)	1966 112
You Make Me Feel Good/ There's A Love	(MGM 13690)	1967 130
I Can See/90 Pound Weakling	(MGM 13749)	1967 -
I Can't Go Back To Denver/ You Better Come Home	(Bell 720)	1968 132
Midnight Train/You Tell Me You Care	(Bell 753)	1968 -
Keep On Dancing/ Woman Of The World	(Golden Circle # unknown)	1968 -
Why Should I Cry/I Need Love	(Sun 1108)	1969 61
Cinnamon Girl/I Just Got The News	(Sun 1114)	1970 52
He'll Never Love You/ I Hate To See You Go	(Sun 1118)	1970 116
Goddess Of Love/Friends	(Sun 1120)	1970 119
Wild World/Sunshine	(Sun 1122)	1971 97
God Save Our Country/Love You All My Life	(Sun 1126)	1971 -
Changin'/ Let Me Put This Ring On Your Finger	(Capitol 3459)	1972 -
Little Gold Band/All Hung Up On You	(Stax 0223)	1974 -
High Flyer/Little Gold Band	(Stax 0242)	1974 -

NB: Some of the Sun 45s were issued on colored wax. There's also a rare French EP with PS: *Keep On Dancing/Brown Paper Sack/Hang On Sloopy/Everybody* (MGM 63628) 1966.

The Gentrys formed in Memphis, Tennessee in 1963 as a seven-man band. Their debut album *Keep On Dancing* just made the Top 100 and the title cut climbed to No 4. This was their only big hit, but they enjoyed several other minor ones. They featured Larry Raspberry as their lead singer. Their early keyboardist Rick Allen later joined **The Box Tops**.

They disbanded in 1966, but original member Jimmy Hart reformed the band in 1969 for the album on Sun, which also generated three further Top 100 hits. The album is good hard turn-of-the-decade rock that is worth a listen if you're into that particular bag. Hart was now the lead singer.

Larry Raspberry, who wasn't in the reformed line-up, joined **Alamo**, who recorded an album on Atco in 1971. **Alamo** included Richard Rosebrough who worked in the Ardent Studios, later joined Alex Chilton's band and went on to work with him in Big Star. Later still, Raspberry formed The Highsteppers.

Jimmy Hart is currently a wrestling manager known as the Mouth Of The South.

Their cover of the Zombies' *You Make Me Feel Good* is on *Garagelands, Vol. 1* (LP) and *Garagelands, Vol. 1 & 2* (CD). You can also find *Keep On Dancing* on *Battle Of The Bands* (CD). (MW/VJ/HM/SR)

Gentrys

45: Wild / Moments (Kato 0074) 1965

From Burlingame, California.

Compilation appearances include: *Wild* on *Wild! Wild!! Wild!!!* (LP) and *Back From The Grave, Vol. 7* (Dble LP). (MW/AP)

The Gents

45: I Wonder Why/Moonlight Sonata (Normandy NRS 91067) 1967

This Utah band's claim-to-fame is that in 1967 they were the number one band in the USA. After regional and state rounds, a final National Battle Of The Bands was staged in Braintree, Massachusetts which was recorded live for posterity and made available on the triple-album set *Battle Of The Bands - Ridge Arena* on the Normandy label (rumoured to exist in other forms).

First place went to Utah's **Gents**, who got an encore which was also captured. Their tracks on the triple-album set are: *You Can't Sit Down*, *Moonlite Sonata*, *Six O'Clock*, *Roll Over Beethoven*, *Come On Down To My Boat* and *Things We Said Today*. The ultimate prize was to record for the mighty Normandy label which they duly did, presenting two very different sounds from their repertoire - so different that it might be thought to be a mispress, with a **101 Strings** type ensemble on the flip of an excellent garage-punker.

Second place in the finals went to Action Brass and third to Tony's Tigers - they have two tracks preserved apiece.

Retrospective compilation coverage has so far included: *I Wonder Why* on *Destination Frantic!* (LP & CD). (MW)

The Gents

ALBUM: 1 WE GOTTA GET OUTA THIS PLACE/BEST OF THE BEST (Recorded Publications Co. 96) 1966 R4

NB: (1) had a limited edition reissue in 1996.

THE GENTS - We Gotta Get Outa This Place LP

| 45: | If You Don't Come Back/I'll Cry | (Duane 1046) 1966 |

From Bermuda, although the label Duane has New Jersey connections and the split album is on a Camden, New Jersey, label. It features one side each by **The Gents/The Best**, two unknown combos, who run through a bevy of typical garage covers in a 'prep-rock' style. Very basic stuff - no fuzz, no off-the-wall ravers - just honest and workmanlike attempts that may sometimes sound flat and far from inspiring. But then that's what is so appealing about this genre and why serious collectors will pay a fortune for an original.

Compilation appearances have included: *If You Don't Come Back* on *Pebbles, Vol. 4 (ESD)* (CD), *Teenage Shutdown, Vol. 4* (LP & CD), *The Chosen Few, Vol. 1* (LP), *Chosen Few Vol's 1 & 2* (CD) and *I Was A Teenage Caveman* (LP). (MW)

The Gents Five

Personnel incl:	RONNIE CHASSNER	vcls	A
	JERRY COHN	gtr	A
	CHRIS ??		A
	DAVE ??		A
	STEVE ??		A

45s:	A Wave Awaits / Straight Shooter	(March 7734) 1967
	I'll Remember You / While I'm Gone	(Living Legend 110) 1967

NB: (2) 'B' side credited to The Legendary Street Singers.

Out of Northwest Dade, Florida. Cohn and Chassner were later in **The Leaves Of Grass**. (MW/JLh)

Geoffrey

| ALBUM: | 1 | GEOFFREY | (Concert Arts CA 7506) 1972 R1 |

NB: (1) reissued on (Psychedelic Archives PALP 1004) 1996 as a limited edition of 290.

A very rare folky singer-songwriter album from 1972. For singer-songwriter rather than psychedelic enthusiasts. **Geoffrey** is Geoffrey de Mers who wrote seven of the eight tracks himself and co-wrote the other - *A Tale Of The Banshee* - with Erin McFadden. He also handled the production and played acoustic guitar. Pleasant but nothing special, although some dealers compare him to **Tim Buckley** or **Athur Lee Harper**.

He was based in Virginia. (VJ/SR)

Jimmy George

45:	It Was Fun While It Lasted/	
	Ain't It Something	(Viva 633) 1968

NB: promo copies have *Super Heavy* listed on flip, but this is the same recording as stock copies.

It Was Fun... is a great mid-tempo tune with neat fuzz guitar. The 45 is from late 1968, but nothing is known about the band. We can only speculate that this might be an L.A. area act. (BM/MW)

The Georgetown Medical Band

Personnel:	RICK COBB		A
	CHUCK GREENWOOD		A
	GARY P. NUNN	keyb'ds	A
	JOHNNY RICHARDSON	gtr	A

Based in Austin, Texas in the late sixties. Richardson had previously been in **The Wig** and was later in Plum Nelly, two other Austin outfits. Indeed, *The Wig Live At The Jade Room* (Texas Archive Recordings TAR-3) 1983 includes two studio practice cover versions of *Light My Fire* and *Hey Joe* by the band, who didn't make it onto vinyl at the time. (VJ)

GEOFFREY - Geoffrey LP.

The Georgia Prophets

| ALBUM: | 1 | FEVER | (Custom) c1970 ? |

45s:	For The First Time/	
	Loving You Is Killing Me	(Double Shot 138) 1969
	California/Music With Soul	(Capricorn 8006) 1970
	Don't You Think It's Time/	
	Nobody Loves Me Like You Do	(Capricorn 8009) 1970

This obscure group first released a single produced by Tommy Witcher and Roy Smith and arranged by the session musician Emory Gordy Jr, with vocals by "Billy and Barbara" on the 'A' side, the flip being a Bobby Bloom pop song.

Their album is in the 'exploito' style, with covers of Traffic's *Feelin Alright* and Neil Young's *Down By The River*. (SR)

Geronimo Black

Personnel:	JIMMY CARL BLACK	drms, vcls	A
	ANDY CAHAN	keyb'ds, drms, vcls	A
	TJAY CONTRELLI	sax, flute, vcls	A
	BUNK GARDNER	piano, sax, flute	A
	TOM LEAVEY	bs, hrmnca	A
	DENNY WALLEY	gtr, vcls	A

ALBUMS:	1(A)	GERONIMO BLACK	(Uni UNI 73132) 1972 -
	2(A)	WELCOME BACK	(Helios HR 440-5) c1980 -

Jimmy Carl Black and Bunk Gardner were previously in the **Mothers of Invention**, Tjay Contrelli was in **Love** circa *Da Capo* and Denny Walley was a member of Big Mouth.

Their first album was produced by Keith Olsen (the former **Music Machine/Millennium** member) and should particularly interest the **Zappa** and **Captain Beefheart** fans. Musically it mixes blues (*Low Ridin' Man*), instrumental tracks (*Siesta, Quaker's Earthquake*) and rock tracks (*Other Man, L.A. County Jail 59, Let Us Live*); its high point being *An American National Anthem* written by Black about the Indian killings ("Indian Land is stolen, 52 million dead, each one's head is scalped by a trick taught by white man hunters coming over the land"). The lyrics and musicianship are both really strong. Buzz Gardner, **Murray Roman** and a small string section also played on this underrated album.

Geronimo Black reformed in 1980 to record *Welcome Back* on the small Helios label, with new versions of *Low Ridin' Man*, *Other Man* and *An American National Anthem* plus four new songs and covers of *Hoochie Coochie Man* and *Lovesick Blues* with the help of other ex-**Mothers of Invention**: Ray Collins, Don Preston and Buzz Gardner. (SR)

The Gestures

Personnel:
GUS DEWEY	gtr, vcls	A
TOM KLUGHERZ	bs	A
DALE MENTON	gtr, vcls	A
BRUCE WATERSTON	drms	A

ALBUM: 1(A) MEET THE GESTURES (Sundazed LP 5021) 1996

NB: Coloured vinyl issue of unreleased album from 1965 which contains both their singles and a lot of previously unreleased tracks. Also on CD (SC 6079) 1996.

45s:
		HCP
Run Run Run/Seems To Me	(Soma 1417) 1964	44
Don't Mess Around/Candlelight	(Soma 1426) 1965	-
Run Run Run/Seems To Me	(Apex 76939) 1965	-
Don't Mess Around/Candlelight	(Apex 76953) 1965	-

Operated out of Mankato, Minnesota, but they were an important part of the Minneapolis sixties scene. They were originally known as The Jesters but altered the spelling when they discovered there was another band of the same name. *Run Run Run*, a bouncy pop tune, actually made the Billboard Charts. The song was also recorded by **The Castaways** and like them **The Gestures** were quite influenced by the British invasion sound. All four of their tracks can be heard on the 1965 compilation *The Big Hits Of Mid-America, Vol. 2* which also came out on the Soma label. Dale Menton, who fronted the band, was in several other Minnesota bands including The Best Things, **The Madhatters**, The Seraphic Street Sound and Buckwheat.

In 1996, Sundazed released *Meet The Gestures*, which contains all their single cuts, plus loads of unreleased material. The additional unreleased tracks confirm a strong British invasion beat era influence on the band. There are three more Dale Menten originals - two versions of *I'm Not Mad*, an instrumental *Savage World* and *Stand By Me*, a gentle beat ballad. The remainder of the material comprises cover versions, which injected enough of their own style and flavour to make them good sixties recordings:- *Things We Said Today* (two versions) (Beatles), *She Cried* (Jay and The Americans), *Don't Let The Sun Catch You Crying* (Gerry and The Pacemakers), *Can I Get A Witness* (Marvin Gaye), *Long Tell Texan* (Coasters) and *Hi-Heel Sneakers* (Tommy Tucker). It seems these were recorded very soon after the release of their second 45 in the hope of releasing an album which didn't happen until Sundazed stepped in!

Retrospective compilation appearances have included: *Run, Run, Run* on *Nuggets Box* (4-CD) and *Pebbles, Vol. 9* (LP); *Don't Mess Around* on *Sixties Rebellion, Vol. 7* (LP & CD); *I'm Not Mad* on *Soma Records Story, Vol. 1* (LP); *Candlelight* and *It Seems To Me* on *Soma Records Story, Vol. 2* (LP); *Don't Mess Around* and *Run, Run, Run* on *Soma Records Story, Vol. 3* (LP); *Run, Run, Run*, *Don't Mess Around* and *Candlelight* on *The Big Hits Of Mid-America - The Soma Records Story* (Dble CD); *It Seems To Me* on *Changes* (LP) and *Garage Dreams Revisited* (7"). (VJ)

Geyda

45: Third Side / ? (L.B.J. 242) 196?

A hard rock quartet from Michigan whose *Third Side* frankly sounds rather a mess. Still, you can hear it on *Michigan Mixture, Vol. 2* (LP). (VJ)

Tom Ghent

Personnel:
THE BLOSSOMS	backing vcls	A
AL CASEY	gtr, dobro	A
MIKE DEASY	gtr, special effects	A
REX HECTRE	backing vcls	A
JIM HORN	flute	A
TOM GHENT	gtr, vcls	AB
JIMMY JOYCE SINGERS	backing vcls	A
LARRY KNECHTEL	piano, organ	A
JOE OSBORN		A
EARL PALMER	perc	A

ALBUMS:
1(A)	TOM GHENT	(Tetragrammaton T-113) 1969	-
2(B)	YANKEE REBEL'S SON	(Kapp) 1970	-

THE GESTURES - Meet The Gestures LP.

The first album is an orchestrated folk-rock album that some 'deaf' dealers tend to present as psychedelic, probably because the liner notes talks about cosmic consciousness and that Ghent's publishing company was Peyotl Music. Produced by Jill Gibson, all the songs were penned by **Ghent**, who had a rather pleasant voice but no particular skills. The album is rather monotonous and better avoided.

The rarer second is presumably better. (SR)

The Ghosters

Personnel:
GUY BERLEY	gtr	A
VIRGIL CALENDER	bs	A
DON JOBE	vcls	A
MIKE LEWIS	drms	A
LANCE NELSON	keyb'ds	A

45s:
	Give It A Try/Gone	(Ghost G101) 1969
α	Traveling Light/Come Cry For Me	(?) c1969

NB: α as Don Jobe and The Ghosters

An ex-garage band from the Benton Harbor, Michigan area. (SR)

Giant Crab

Personnel:
DENNIS FRICIA	drms, horns	A
KENNY FRICIA	keyb'ds, horns, vibes	A
ERNIE OROSCO	vcls, gtr	A
RAY OROSCO	bs, keyb'ds	A
RUBEN OROSCO	bs, drms, sax	A

ALBUMS:
1(A)	A GIANT CRAB COMES FORTH	(Uni 73037) 1968	-
2( )	COOL IT HELIOS	(Uni 73057) 1969	-

45s:
Listen Girl/Summer Breezes	(Corby CR-216) 1967
Day By Day (It Happens)/Kind Of Funny	(Corby CR 217) 1967
I Started With A Kiss/The Answer Is No	(Corby CR-221) 1967
Hi Ho Silver Lining/Hot Line Conversation	(Uni 55094) 1968
Believe It Or Not/Lydia Purple	(Uni 55103) 1968
Cool It/Intensity My Soul	(Uni 55134) 1969
ESP/Hot Line Conversation	(Uni 55155) 1969

From Santa Barbara California, this band evolved out of **Ernie's Funnys**. Their albums are now very minor collectors' items, and their material patchy. For example, *Listen Girl* is excellently warped pop-punk, in a UK-freakbeat style, busy with effects, but its flip side, *Summer Breezes*, is bitterly disappointing acoustic harmony dross. Their cover of *Hi Ho Silver Lining* is also a letdown - a lightweight over-arranged pop affair - yet *Hot*

Line Conversation is a heavy, screeching fuzz-rocker. Their cover of *ESP* is more excellent hard-rock with phasing.

Ernie Orosco went on to form **Big Brother** and released a solo album, as **Ernie Joseph**. (VJ/MW/CMn/AP)

Giant Jellybean Copout

45:	Awake In A Dream/Look At The Girls	(Poppy 504) 1968

Sometimes the more weird'n'wonderful named the outfit, the less weird'n'wonderful the music. The label gives it away - the 'A' is a very good version of a **Critters**' song. So good that it probably is **The Critters** given that Jim Ryan who wrote it also produces this version. The flip is mellow Beach Boys-a-la-Pet-Sounds fare. Nothing to freak out about. (MW)

The Giant Sunflower

Personnel incl:	TERRY CLEMENTS	ld gtr	A
	RICK DEY	bs, gtr	A
	VAL GARAY	gtr	A
	EDDIE HOH	drms	A
	PATTI PHILLIPS	gtr, hrmnca	A

			HCP
45s:	More Sunshine/February Sunshine	(Take Six 1000) 1967 -	
	February Sunshine/Big Apple	(Ode 102) 1967	106
	What's So Good About Goodbye/ Mark Twain	(Ode 104) 1967	116

A Los Angeles band whose *February Sunshine*, now included on *Highs In The Mid-Sixties, Vol. 3*, typified the commercialism of flower-power pop in this era. The record was produced by Lou Adler and its professionalism and chord changes suggests it could be **The Mamas and Papas** recording under a pseudonym. It narrowly missed the Top 100.

The band formed in January 1967. (VJ/MW/RuJ)

Gideon

45:	Oh! Sweet Love/Keep It Up	(Harbour/Buddah 308) 1968

Another bubblegum pop single, written and produced by J. Levine and A. Resnick, the members of the **Third Rail** also in charge of many **Kasenetz Katz** hits. (SR)

The Gigolos

45:	She's My Baby (Part 1)/(Part 2)	(Power 259-945) 1981

Supposedly an obscure Los Angeles band, this 45 actually dates from 1981. A "fools-gold-nugget" in the vein of **Katz Kradle**, **Huntsmen** and **Wolfmen**, *She's My Baby* has nonetheless been compiled on *Pebbles Vol. 8* (CD) and *Highs In The Mid-Sixties, Vol. 20* (LP). It's a pounding rocker! (MW/MM)

Russ Giguere

Personnel:	JULES ALEXANDER	gtr, bs	A
	DON BECK	gtr	A
	BEN BENAY	gtr, bs, hrmnca	A
	JOHN BOYLAN	gtr	A
	CHRIS ETHRIDGE	bs	A
	RUSS GIGUERE	vcls, gtr, perc	A
	JUDY HENSKE	vcls	A
	JIM KELTNER	drms	A
	LARRY KNECHTEL	bs, keyb'ds	A
	RUSS KUNKEL	drms	A
	BERNIE LEADON	gtr	A
	SPOONER OLDHAM	piano	A
	HERB PEDERSEN	vcls, banjo	A
	EMIL RICHARDS	perc	A
	LYLE RITZ	bs	A
	JUDEE SILL	gtr	A
	BOBBY WOMACK	gtr	A
	JERRY YESTER	vcls	A

ALBUM:	1(A)	HEXAGRAM 16	(Warner Bros. WS 1910) 1971 -

The only solo album of **Russ Giguere** is much better than most of his previous work with the **Association**.

Hexagram 16 was co-produced by **Giguere** and John Boylan, who also contributed a song he'd earlier recorded with **Appletree Theatre**. The album is a good mix of California pop and folk with some brilliant guitar parts, the most notable songs being *In New Germany*, *Brother Speed* and the ambitiously orchestrated *Pegasus*. (SR)

Jimmy Gilbert

45:	Believe What I Say/ So Together We'll Live	(Darn-L 853-D-5264) 196?

An obscure Michigan-based outfit. Both sides of this disc can be heard on *Highs In The Mid-Sixties, Vol. 6* (LP). The 'A' side is a good pop-punk song with quite a lot of fuzz. The flip is more poppy. (VJ)

HIGHS IN THE MID-SIXTIES Vol. 9 (Comp LP) including The Gillian Row.

The Gillian Row

Personnel:	DAVE	A
	JOE	A
	LARRY	A
	TOM	A

A hairy punk quartet whose raw version of Them's *Gloria* is one of the choice cuts on the rare 1966 LP, *WONE, The Dayton Scene*. This features one cut each from a dozen Daytonian acts, selected from the WONE sponsored three-day battle of the bands.

Their image matches the sound - not prepared to pose well-dressed or in matching kit in front of a curtain or plain backdrop, these rebels with the Pretty Things look are pictured crouching in a dingy brick-and-plaster corner of a garage or cellar.

Regrettably **The Gillian Row** didn't graduate to releasing their own 45s, like **Jerry and The Others** (who provide the other choice cut on the WONE LP), **The Dawks** and **The X-cellents**. Still, you can hear their two minute twenty-four second legacy on *Highs In The Mid-Sixties, Vol. 9* (LP). (MW)

Gin Gillette

| 45: | She'll Never Let Him Go/ Train To Satanville | (Musikon 102) 196? |

This 45 was issued on a Hollywood label.

Compilation appearances include: *Train To Satanville* on *Scum Of The Earth* (CD) and *Scum Of The Earth, Vol. 1* (LP). (VJ)

Ginger

Personnel incl:	BOB EDWARDS	vcls	A
	GARY GIMMESTAD		A
	LARRY MOE		A
	CRAIG SWANSON	bs	A
	MARC TAYLOR		A

| ALBUM: | 1(A) | GINGER | (Cheap Swank) 1973 R2 |

From Minnesota, this album was released by the group after the death of Bob Edwards, their lead singer. Side One contains poorly recorded live and studio cuts recorded with Edwards, whilst Side Two consists of songs written in his memory. Musically it's rural psych-rock, organ driven, with an undermixed lead guitar and trippy effects, and vocals by a brother of Edwards. It came in a plain white cover with three inserts. (SR)

Ginger Valley

| 45: | Country Life/Ginger | (International Artists IA-142) 1969 |

NB: promo copies in translucent green vinyl.

Probably from Texas, a rural-rock group influenced by **The Byrds** (jangly guitar and harmonies), with some fuzz on *Country Life*. One of the last records released by this famous label.

Compilation appearances have included *Country Life* and *Ginger* on *International Artists Singles Collection* (LP). (SR)

Allen Ginsberg

| ALBUM: | 1 | WILLIAM BLAKE: SONGS OF INNOCENCE AND EXPERIENCE | (Verve Forecast FRS-3083) 1969 SC |

| 45: | Free John Now!/ A Counterculture Prayer For John | (Rainbow 22191) 1971 |

NB: 'A' side by **Up**.

The famous beat poet and activist recorded an album of William Blake's poems set to music. He also recorded a single to support John Sinclair (**MC5**) and worked with **The Fugs**.

Several other poets also made records or worked with groups, most notably Brautigan, who worked with **Mad River** and **Laurence Ferlinghetti**. (SR)

The Girls

45s:	My Love/My Baby	(Capitol 5528) 1965
	Chico's Girl/Dumb Song	(Capitol 5675) 1965
	Way Way Out/ Modesty Blaise	(20th Century Fox 6651) 1966

An all-girl outfit as their name suggests, they were in fact four sisters by the name of Sandoval from L.A..

Compilation appearances include: *Chico's Girl* on *Girls In The Garage, Vol. 1* (CD) and *Girls In The Garage, Vol. 2* (LP); and *My Baby* on *Girls In The Garage, Vol. 4* (LP). (VJ)

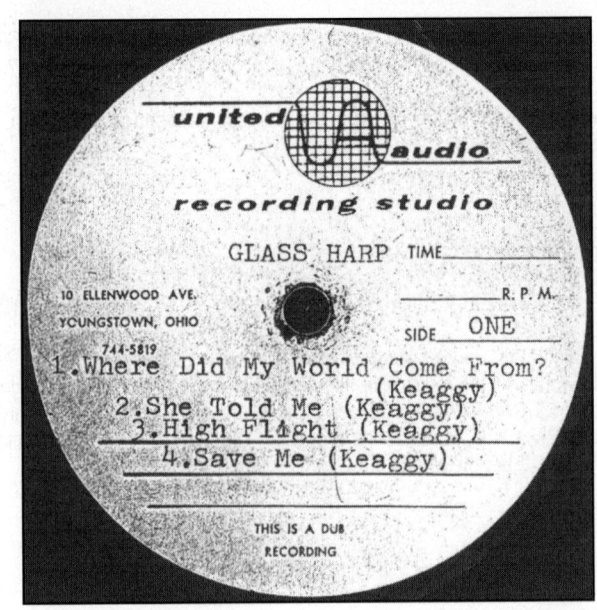

GLASS HARP Acetate Label.

Glad

Personnel:	RON FLOGEL	gtr, vcls	A
	GEORGE HULLIN	drms, vcls	A
	TOM PHILLIPS	gtr, piano, vcls	A
	TIM SCHMIDT	bs, vcls	A

| ALBUM: | 1(A) | FEELIN' GLAD | (ABC ABCS-655) 1968 SC |

45s:	See What You Mean/Bedtime Story	(Equinox 70004) 1968
	A New Tomorrow/Pickin' Up The Pieces	(Equinox 70006) 1968
	Johnny's Silver Ride/Love Needs The World	(ABC 11163) 1969
	Let's Play Make Believe/No Ma, It Can't Be	(ABC 11199) 1969

Originally formed when four sophomores at Encina High School in Sacramento, California formed a surf instrumental group called The Contenders in 1963. They were also known as Tim, Tom and Ron and The New Mind. By 1965 they had changed name again to **The New Breed** and achieved some commercial success locally. When Los Angeles producer Terry Melcher (Doris Day's son) signed them to his Equinox label, he changed their name again to the hippier-sounding **Glad**. They recorded two psychedelic 45s for Equinox, and two for ABC. Produced by Eirik Wangberg, the album is in a flower-power pop/soft-rock vein with lots of harmonies and orchestration. It's sought-after by some collectors but is in fact quite bland. Schmidt went on to play for **Poco** and later The Eagles.

Unhappy with the style imposed by Melcher, the other three formed another country-influenced outfit, **Redwing**, who recorded five albums for Fantasy during the 1970s.

Compilation appearances include *Shapes Of Things To Come* on *Songs Of Faith And Inspiration* (CDR & CD). (VJ/SR)

Gladstone

Personnel:	RANDY FOUTS	keyb'ds, roxichord	AB
	DOUG RHONE	vcls, gtrs, sitar	AB
	RON TUTT	drms	AB
	JERRY SCHEFF	bs	AB
	H.L.VOELKER	vcls	AB
	(ROBIN HOOD BRIANS	vcls	AB)
	(LYNN GROOM	vcls, mellotron	AB)
	(MICHAEL RABON	gtr, vcls	A)
	(TOM RUSSELL	vcls	B)
	(BOBBY TUTTLE	steel gtr	B)

ALBUMS:	1(A)	GLADSTONE	( ) 1972 -
	2(B)	LOOKIN' FOR A SMILE	(ABC ABCX-778) 1973 -

NB: (1) also released in the UK (Probe SPBA 6264).

			HCP
45:	A Piece Of Paper/?	(ABC 11327) 1972	45

From Tyler, Texas, a rock group fronted by Rhone (ex-**Mouse and The Traps**) and Voelker (ex-**Rio Grande**). Their two albums were produced by Robin Hood Brians and Randy Fouts.

Their two albums feature ex-members of several Texas groups: **Five Americans**, **Rio Grande**, **Michael Rabon and Choctaw**... plus the ubiquitous session men Ron Tutt and Jerry Scheff.

Musically, they were very close to **Brewer and Shipley**, **Burton and Cunico** and numerous early seventies groups with vocal harmonies, combining electric and acoustic guitars with hippie values. (SR)

Gladstone

Personnel incl:	AL GRAHAM		A
45:	What A Day/Upsome	(A&M 1061)	1968

Produced by **Lee Michaels**, an interesting 45 written by Al Graham, with Hammond organ and guitar. (SR)

The Glass Bottle

Personnel incl:	GARY CRISS	vcls, drms	A
	DENNIS DEES	vcls	A
	CAROL DENMARK	vcls	A

ALBUM:	1(A)	THE GLASS BOTTLE	(Avco Embassy AVE 33012) 1970 -

			HCP
45s:	Love For Living/?	(Avco AVE 4527) 1970	109
	I Ain't Got Time Anymore/		
	Things	(Avco Embassy AVE 4575) 1970	-

Although sometimes seen described as soft-psych or hippie-rock, the album by **The Glass Bottle** (a sextet with two female singers) is in fact a tedious vocal pop effort with a material comprised of covers and songs from soundtracks. Only one track, *Red River Sal* deserves to be heard as it has a surprising heavy rock feel with some good electric guitar work. Their album was produced by Bill Ramal and Dickie Goodman.

The 'B' side to their 45, *Things*, was a Bobby Darin cover. Gary Criss was ex-**Gary Criss and His Crystals**.

On the same label as **Liquid Smoke** or **Bead Game**. (SR/RHn/JosephVaccarino)

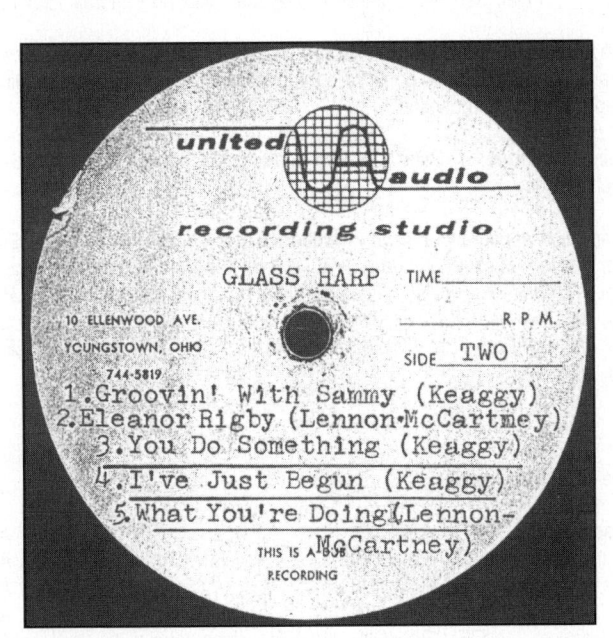

THE GLASS HARP - Acetate Label.

The Glass Candle

45:	Light The Glass Candle/	
	Keep Right On Living	(Target T 1004) 1969

Fuzz overload on the top side, whilst the flip is an excellent frenetic garage pop-rocker. Sadly the sole 45 by this Milwaukee, Wisconsin outfit.

Compilation appearances have included *Light The Glass Candle* on *30 Seconds Before The Calico Wall* (CD); and *Keep Right On Living* on *Fuzz, Flaykes, And Shakes, Vol. 5* (LP & CD). (MW/GM)

Glass Family

Personnel:	DAVID CAPILOUTO	bs, keyb'ds	A
	GARY GREEN	drms, perc	A
	RALPH PARRETT	gtr	A

ALBUM:	1(A)	ELECTRIC BAND	(Warner Bros. 1776) 1968 -

45s:	Teenage Rebellion/?	(Sidewalk 920) 1967
	Agorn/Guess I'll Let You Go	(Warner Bros. 7262) 1969
	Guess I'll Let You Go/	
	David's Rap (promo only)	(Warner Bros. PRO. 309) 1969

Produced by Richard Podolor (**Steppenwolf**, **Jamul**), a California outfit whose album is pleasant soft L.A. flower-power with several good psychedelic cuts, including *Agorn (Elements Of Complex Variables)*. Their material was written by Ralph Parrett, except for *Agorn* and *I Want To See My Baby*, which he co-wrote with Green and Capilouto.

The flip to Sidewalk 920 is unknown, it may only have been issued as a double 'A' side. *Teenage Rebellion* is good fuzzy pop.

They also had one track on the 1967 compilation *Freakout U.S.A.!*.

Retrospective compilation appearances have included: *Guess I'll Let You Go* on *Psychedelic Unknowns, Vol. 11* (LP) and *Slowly Growing Insane* (CD); *Agorn (Elements Of Complex Variables)* on *Psychedelic Visions* (CD); *I'm Losing It* on *Filling The Gap* (4-LP); and *House Of Glass* meanwhile is included on the EP accompanying the French book "Le Rock Psychedelique Vol.1". (VJ/SR)

The Glass Harp

Personnel:	JOHN S. FERRA	drms, vcls, gtr	AB
	PHIL KEAGGY	gtr, vcls	AB
	STEVE MARKULIN	bs	A
	DAN PECCHIO	bs, vcls	B

			HCP
ALBUMS:	1(B)	GLASS HARP	(Decca DL-75261) 1971 - -
	2(B)	SYNERGY	(Decca DL-75306) 1971 192
	3(B)	IT MAKES ME GLAD	(Decca DL-75358) 1972 - -

NB: (1) reissued in 1977 (MCA 293). All three albums have been issued on CD by Line.

Acetates:	1(A)	I've Just Begun/Where Did My World Come From/She Told Me	(United Audio Recorders) 196?
	2(A)	THE GLASS HARP	(United Audio Recorders) 19?? R4

NB: (1) and (2) Only 10 copies made. (2) tracks consist of *Where Did My World Come From?*, *She Told Me*, *High Flight*, *Save Me*, *Groovin' With Sammy*, *Eleanor Rigby* (Beatles), *You Do Something*, *I've Just Begun* and *What You're Doing* (Beatles).

45s:	α	ARBY'S EP (Swing Over)	( ) 1969
		Where Did My World Come From/	
		She Told Me	(United Audio) 1969
		Childrens' Fantasy/Village Queen	(Decca 32830) 1971
		The Answer/Just Always	(Decca 32915) 1972
		La De La/David and Goliath	(Decca 32995) 1972

NB: α This was a promo only 45 EP for Arby's (yes, the roast beef people). Arby's started out in Youngstown, and the EP contains four different versions of the same song *Swing Over*, an instrumental. **Glass Harp** did one cut and the remaining three were done by three other groups in different styles (jazz, etc.). The EP came with a sleeve with a crude drawing of a cow.

These albums, which are in a progressive/psychedelic style with lots of heavy guitar, are beginning to interest some collectors. The outfit formed in Youngstown, Ohio, in the late sixties and were among the State's prime flag bearers of the British invasion.

They recorded a 45 for United Audio and an unreleased acetate-album before going on to sign for Decca. Only ten copies of the acetate were made, which contained both sides of the United Audio 45 plus *I've Just Begun*, a typical slice of Zombies' - influenced pop and six other tracks. One copy of the acetate was sent to Apple Records in the hope of getting a contract, but it was rejected. The bass player on these United Audio recordings was Steve Markulin, a cousin of Joe "Ting" Markulin, **The Human Beinz** rhythm guitarist. Dann Pecchio joined later and he is featured on all the Decca recordings.

Phil Keaggy had earlier played in **The Squires**, Volume IV and **New Hudson Exit**.

Both tracks on their first 45 *Where Did My World Come From/She Told Me* were written by Phil Keaggy, who also produced several records for Ohio area garage bands and later achieved success in the Christian music movement.

One track from the United Audio acetate, *I've Just Begun* has subsequently re-surfaced on *Pebbles, Vol. 21* (LP). (VJ/MMy/GGl/MW/BWd)

Glass Menagerie

Personnel:	BRIAN GODULA	bs	A
	BOB QOUIVECT	gtr	A
	MIKE SHRIEVE	drms	A
	DAVE WILKE	gtr	A

45:	End Of The Line/Troubled Mind	(Revolve 208) 1968

A San Francisco outfit who formed in 1967 but fell apart the following year. Mike Shrieve, of course, later went on to play for **Santana** and Godula later joined Together, a 1969 San Francisco band which did not record.

There was at least one other act using the **Glass Menagerie** moniker, and their track *Mad Threads* can be found on *Off The Wall, Vol. 2* (LP). Could this be the same **Glass Menagerie** which came from Boston, and featured a pre-**Velvet Underground** Doug Yule. Answers on a £50 note please! (VJ/JFr)

The Glass Onion

ALBUM:	1	THE GLASS ONION	(Atlantic) 1969 -

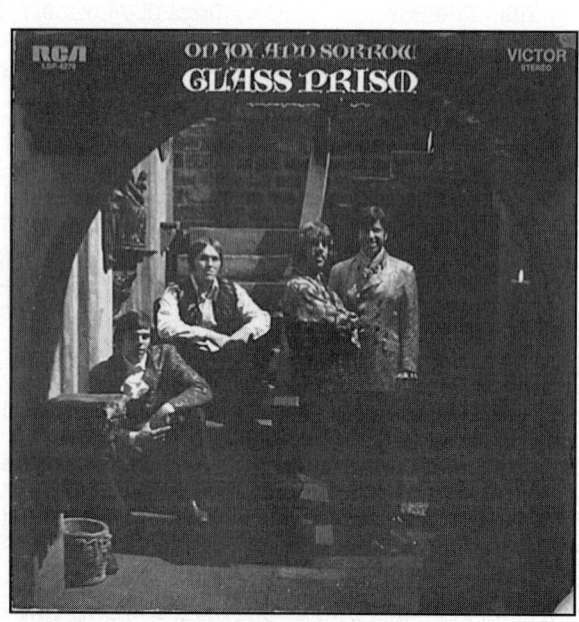

GLASS PRISM - On Joy And Sorrow LP.

A studio project directed by the famous producer Arif Mardin and recorded at Muscle Shoals Studios. This album is a melting pot of psych, jazz, funk and R&B with strings, choir, prominent drumming... Their name was taken from the Beatles' song that they also cover on the album. A curiosity. (SR)

The Glass Opening

45s:	My Head Is Heavy/I'm Your Prey	(New Wodd 001) 196?
	α	All Those Lies/Virgin Of Time	(Dondee 12563) 1970

NB: α flip side was by The Major Six.

I've seen this band variously reported as coming from Minneapolis and Kentucky. An all-girl outfit, their first 45 was rather folkish punk. *I'm Your Prey* has also resurfaced on *Girls In The Garage, Vol. 1* (LP). (VJ)

The Glass Prism

Personnel:	AUGGIE CHRISTIANO	bs	A
	RICK RICHARDS	drms	A
	CARL SIRACUSE	keyb'ds	A
	TOM VERANO	gtr	A

ALBUMS:	1(A)	POE THROUGH THE GLASS PRISM
			(RCA LSP 4201) 1969 -
	2(A)	ON JOY AND SORROW	(RCA LSP 4270) 1970 -

45:	The Raven/El Dorado	(RCA Victor 74-0205) 1969

Their first album is an attempt to set poems by Edgar Allan Poe to a rock format. Although they don't really pull it off the music isn't bad on cuts like *The Raven*. Much more relevant is the second album, which features some great guitar work, especially on *Extention 68*. Both albums are available quite cheaply. The band were mostly Italian Americans who came from the Scranton/Wilkes-Barre area of Pennsylvania. They were previously known as El Caminos and also made recordings under that name.

Tom and Rick later formed a power trio called Shenandoah with bassist Lou Cossa. Later still Cossa and Carl Siracuse joined 'one-hit' wonder band **The Buoys**, the nucleus of which then became Dakota. (VJ/TTi/CKk)

Glass Sun

Personnel:	BOB CASS	A
	MIKE CASS	A
	BRUCE ROLL	A
	RICK ROLL	A
	DAN SILLS	A

45s:	Silence Of The Morning/Oh Sandy	(Sound Pattems 139) 1968/9
	I Can See The Light/Stick Over Me	(Sound Patterns 150) 196?

A Michigan trio. Their first 45, *Silence Of The Morning* is a stunning slice of guitar-driven psychedelic punk which is well worth checking out. The flip is disappointing in comparison.

Their second 45, *I Can See The Light*, is a heavy slab of bad-trip psych-grunge.

Compilation appearances have included: *Silence Of The Morning* and *Stick Over Me* on *Michigan Mixture, Vol. 1* (LP); *Silence In The Morning* on *Sixties Archive Vol. 6* (CD), *Incredible Sound Show Stories, Vol.1* (LP & CD), *An Overdose Of Heavy Psych* (CD) and *Trash Box* (5-CD); and *I Can See The Light* on *Fuzz Flaykes & Shakes Vol. 1 - 60 Miles High* (LP & CD). (VJ/MW)

The Glitterhouse

Personnel:	HANK ABERLE	vcls	A
	MICHAEL GAYLE	vcls	A
	AL LAX		A
	MOOGY KLINGMAN	keyb'ds	A
	JOEL "BISHOP" O'BRIEN	drms, perc	A

THE GLITTERHOUSE - Color Blind LP.

ALBUM: 1(A) COLOR BLIND (DynoVoice 31905) 1968 -

45s: I Lost Me A Friend/Tinkerbell's Mind (DynoVoice 925) 1968
Barbarella/Love Drags Me Down (DynoVoice 927) 1968

Probably a studio project of the producer/arranger Bob Crewe in collaboration with Michael Gayle rather than a real group. The Philadelphia/New York-based Bob Crewe is best known for his productions with Frankie Valli's Four Seasons, whose pop-psych concept album, *The Genuine Imitation Life Gazette* is similar in sound to **The Glitterhouse**. Possibly some of the same musicians were used.

Michael Gayle wrote all the songs on their album and by far the best cuts are on Side One. *Tinkerbell's Mind*, *Princes Of The Gingerland* and *Child Of Darkness (Journey Of A Child Traveller)* are all symphonic psych-pop in a Procol Harum vein and are worth seeking out. Also of note is *Happy To Have You Here Again*, which has a good-time feel with some chirpy keyboards and nice harmonies.

The Glitterhouse, along with Bob Crewe and Charles Fox provided the music to the film "Barbarella", and are included on the soundtrack album on Dynovoice (DY 31908). (VJ/CA/MW/SB)

Glory

Personnel:	CHUCK CONWAY	drms	A
	RONALD GARNER	organ	A
	HAL HAWLEY	bs	A
	TED HAWLEY	ld gtr, keyb'ds	A
	LINDEN HUDSON	vcls	A
	RICHARD JONES	organ	A

ALBUM: 1(A) A MEAT MUSIC SAMPLER
(Texas Revolution TRR 69) 1969 R2

NB: (1) has had a limited repressing. (1) reissued on LP and CD (Akarma AK 114) 2000. There's also a mini-album CD release of tracks recorded by Linden Hudson and friends from 1974-2001: *The Lost Songs (A Meat Music Sequel)* (Akarma AK 920) 2001.

45s: Holy Roller/Climbin' The Walls (Advanced Promo 189249) 1972
But I'm Tired/
Sunshine Floods All Over Me (Skratchy 451) 1975

The album was a studio project masterminded by Linden Hudson at Walt Andrus' studio in Houston. Hudson produced, engineered and sang on it. Despite being a lighthearted exercise, it does contain some good music:- bluesy jams with guitar, harmonica and organ. Only six tracks in all, including the long *Spin Me A Rag*, *Slow Rock'n'Roll* and *Studio Blues Jam*. The liner notes written by "Jack Smack" stand out: "Meat Music is the next best thing to sex, as a matter of fact, one could say that they are one-in-the-same. When Meat music and sex are combined... well, it's swell.

In this sampler album, Glory has combined meat music with neat music and even some sweet music (...) This bit of wax will, perhaps, give you some idea about where America's Glory truly lies (or is it lays)".

Hudson and friends returned in 1972 to record the non-album *Holy Roller* 45. The later 1975 45 was an acoustic effort involving Van Wilkes and at least one former member of **Homer**. (VJ/SR)

Glory

Personnel:	RAY BENICK	bs	A
	BILL CONSTABLE	ld vcls	A
	KEN CONSTABLE	ld vcls	A
	BOB KALAMASZ	gtr, vcls	A
	JIM QUINN	gtr, vcls, perc	A
	BILL SCHWARK	drms	A
	(PHIL GIALLOMBARDO	keyb'ds	A)

ALBUM: 1(A) GLORY (Avalanche AV-LA148-F) 1973 -

From Cleveland and previously known as **Damnation Of Adam Blessing**, Glory released an album which will interest guitar lovers. Produced by Jim Quinn, one of their guitarists, it offers nine good tracks of hard-rock with good vocals, all the songs being penned by the group (*Hot Momma*, *Nightmare*, *Dawn*, *Sunny Days*...).

Avalanche was a subsidiary of United Artists. (SR)

Glory

Personnel:	JACK BUTLER	bs, gtr, vcls	AB DEFG H JKL
(up to	BOB FRIEDMAN	drms	A
1975)	JERRY RANEY	gtr, vcls	ABCDEFG H I JKL
	CHUCK SURFACE	keyb'ds	AB G
	RITCHIE KING	gtr, vcls	B
	JACK PINNEY	drms	BCDE H I JKL
	MIKE BERNEATHY	gtr	CD H
	MIKE MILLSAP	vcls, perc	CDE
	GREG WILLIS	bs, vcls	C I JKL
	JEFF JONES	gtr	E
	BRUCE MORSE	drms	FG I
	BENNY BENNETT	perc	G
	DARRYL DeLOACH	vcls	H
	ALLAN GREENE	steel gtr	H
	STEVE ARENZ	steel gtr	I
	BOBBY BALES	vcls, perc	I K
	PAUL NICHOLS	drms, perc	L

NB: Line-up 'A' - Thee Dark Ages, 1966. 'B' - Funky Buckwheat, 1967. 'C' - Blues Messenger, 1968. 'D' - 1968-9. 'E' - 1970-1. 'F' - 1971. 'G' - 1971-2. 'H' - Pig, 1972. 'I' - 1972-3. 'J' - The Buzzards, 1973. 'K' - 1973-5. 'L' - Third Planet Band, 1975.

GLORY - A Meat Music Sampler LP.

ALBUMS: 1(K) GLORY (Dragon) c1973 R3
2(E) ON THE AIR (Rockadelic RRLP 40) 2001

NB: (1) metal acetate LP, recorded live in the studio, no cover known. (2) live concert broadcast, 28th June 1970.

45s: α It Really Doesn't Matter ( ) c1970
High School Letter/Peaches (Speemo GSJ-1/2) 1973
β Standing On My Feet/You And I (Dragon JGM 101) 1974
β Love's Tide/
I Gave You Everything I Had (Dragon JGM 102) 1974

NB: α metal acetate, one song only. β shown as by George St. John and The Glory Band.

Glory was probably San Diego's longest-lived underground rock band, lasting from the late sixties until the early eighties when Raney formed The Beat Farmers (who themselves issued nine records!).

Raney and Pinney had previously played together in **The Roosters**, the house band at San Diego's Cinnamon Cinder club. Pinney, Willis, Morse and DeLoach were all ex-**Iron Butterfly** alumni, and Bennett had recorded with **The Brain Police**.

The recent Rockadelic album contains a live concert by the band from 1970 which was broadcast on San Diego's underground radio station KPRI, and here the band are revealed to be purveyors of a dark but energetic blues-rock style. Another release is planned, collecting material from several line-ups of the band and including some of their seventies vinyl output, which is all extremely rare. (CF)

Glory Rhodes

Personnel incl: J. LAVIOLETTE
KENNY LYLES ld vcls
G. NOBILE
S. SERIO
FRANKIE SPENCER ld gtr

45s: I'm Gonna Change The World /
Stay Out Of My Way (U-Doe 101) 1966
Gonna Be Somebody / Not That Kind Of Guy (U-Doe 102) 1966
One Track Mind / Run For Your Life (White Cliffs 251) c1967
Old Laces / She's A Big Girl Now (Atco 6559) 1968
Can We Go To The City / I'm So Happy (Atco 6626) 1968

From New Orleans, and initially Invasion inspired, they chose to cover the Animals' anthem of sixties youth on their excellent debut - both sides of which feature on *A Journey To Tyme, Vol. 5* (LP). By the time of the Atco 45 their edge and aggression had been dulled to an ok but uninspiring club/pop sound with strings and brass. According to Andrew Brown's "Brown Paper Sack #1" they'd last into the early seventies. (AB/MW/JRe/PB)

GLORY - On The Air LP.

THE GNATS.

The Gnarly Beast

Personnel: LEONARD ASHER bs AB
(up to DAVID BRAVENS gtr, vcls A
1971) ROGER FLORES gtr A
DENNIS GRAHAM drms, vcls A
RICK RANDLE gtr, keyb'ds, vcls A
AMADO SANTOS gtr, vcls ABCD
ROGER NEMOUR gtr, bs BCD
JIM SULLIVAN drms BCD
TERY FANN bs, vcls C

NB: Line-ups:- 'A' - 1966/67. 'B' - 1968/69. 'C' - 1969/70. 'D' - 1970/71 (aka 'The Beast').

Acetate: Cheatin' (Hollywood Central Recorders no#) 1968

NB: one-sided 8" metal acetate, one song only.

This long-lived San Diego, California band went through a number of personnel changes and included several notable musicians... Rick Randle (**Man-Dells**, **The Other Four**, **The Brain Police**); Roger Flores (**Brat**); Terry Fann (**Framework**). They also changed styles with the passing years. Line-up 'A' was a **Buffalo Springfield/Byrds**-type of band, characterised by Bravens' 12-string guitar. Line-up 'B' that recorded *Cheatin'* was a gritty blues-based rock band, and the 'C' and 'D' line-ups were loud heavy-rock (described to me as cross between The Who and Black Sabbath!). While the band recorded several times, the tapes have yet to surface, and it is possible that Amado Santos may have the band's audio archive. He was last thought to be in Houston, Texas, but his current whereabouts are unknown.

In 1972, the band became Madame Beast (with the addition of female vocalist Leslie Lyons) and toured the USA extensively after signing with a booking agency. They continued (with various personnel changes) until 1975.

The band also made a single circa 1968 that was issued under the name Mixed Grill, but details have yet to come to light. (CF)

Gnats

Personnel: RICK BANDAS bs A
BILL HUDDLESTON ld gtr A
JAY LANGHAMMER vcls A
W.R. LYNCH drms A

45: That's All Right / The Girl (Emcee 014) 1966

When Bandas, Huddleston and Lynch left **The Danes** after several years together, they formed **The Gnats** with vocalist Jay Langhammer. Although having a rather short lifespan (just five months - November 1965 to March 1966), **The Gnats** got to play with the Yardbirds (December, 1965 in Fort Worth, Texas) and in the March, 1966 at the KBOX Spring Spectacular in Dallas with **The Byrds** and **Mitch Ryder and the Detroit Wheels**. The group disbanded when Langhammer joined the Air Force. Lynch later played with **Foamy Brine**. (MW/AB/JLa)

GODZ - Contact High With LP.

G.N.P.

See **Gross National Productions**.

Go-Betweens

| 45: | Knock Knock/Have Her For My Own | (Cheer 1011) 1965 |

An obscure New York City band. Some members are rumoured to have gone on to **The Shades**.

Compilation appearances include *Have You For My Own* on *Open Up Yer Door, Vol. 2* (LP) and *Teenage Shutdown, Vol. 5* (LP & CD).

Godfrey

45s: The Trip/
Come On, Come On (as by Godfrey's Group) (Cee Jam 3) 1965
Let's Take A Trip/
The Trip (as by Godfrey & Friends) (Cee Jam # 3) 1965
Down Whittier Blvd./
Down Whittier Blvd. (instr) (Whittier 505) 1967

An L.A. disc jockey who did a cover of **Kim Fowley**'s *The Trip*, which can be heard on *Pebbles, Vol. 3* (CD), *Pebbles Box* (5-LP), *Pebbles, Vol. 3* (LP), *Pebbles, Vol. 2 (ESD)* (CD), *Sixties Rebellion, Vol. 12* (LP & CD), *Acid Dreams - The Complete 3 LP Set* (3-LP), *Acid Dreams Epitaph* (CD) and *Trash Box* (5-CD). (VJ)

God Squad

Personnel: ALAN WENDELL JACKSON A
SUSAN WEST A
LINDA WILMOTH A

ALBUM: 1(A) GOD SQUAD'S GREATEST HITS, VOL. 1
(Private Pressing 305319) c1970 SC

Recorded by students of the University of Kentucky, a Christian album mixing folk-rock, spirituals, acapella songs and some light psychy touches. The title of their only album is quite amusing, as we are still waiting for the volume 2! (SR)

God Unlimited

ALBUM: 1 RIDE ON (G.I.A.) 1970 -

A folky Christian group with choral vocals, haunting at times, and some good electric guitar, especially on the long title track. (SR)

The Godz

Personnel: JAY DILLON organ, piano, autoharp, psaltery A
LARRY KESSLER gtr, viola, violin, vcls A
JIM McCARTHY gtr, hrmnca, vcls A
PAUL THORNTON drms, autoharp, vcls A

ALBUMS: 1(A) CONTACT HIGH WITH THE GODZ (ESP 1037) 1967 -
2(A) GODZ 2 (ESP 1047) 1968 -
3(A) THE THIRD TESTAMENT (ESP 1077) 1969 -
4(A) GODZUNHEIT (ESP 2017) 1970 -

NB: (1) also issued on Fontana in Holland and (2) on Fontana in the UK. (1), (2) and (3) have all been reissued on CD by ESP.

45s: Lay In The Sun/I Want A Word With You (ESP 4503) 1966
Travelin' Salesman/Wiffenpoof Song (ESP 4548) 1967

A New York-based avant-garde rock group whose albums have not aged well but do deserve a mention here. From the same label as **The Fugs**, their recorded output (I've avoided using the word music) was even more anarchic. It tended to consist of wailing unmelodic vocals, avant-garde solos and various background noises. Their second album does include two more structured tracks, *Radar Eyes* and *Soon The Moon*, but *Squeek* probably epitomises best the sound they were striving to achieve. Overall, their third album is a slightly more structured and successful psychedelic venture, which makes more effective use of sound effects than their second effort. It also contains a few folky numbers like *Walking Guitar Blues* and *Neet Street*. Their fourth and final album was more in the mainstream rock mould but better produced. Certainly, the first three albums are for fans of highly experimental avant-garde rock only.

Jim McCarthy (ex-**Dick Watson 5**) also recorded a solo album, *Alien* (ESP-3003) 1973, on which Paul Thornton plays maraccas. The session musicians included **Left Banke** members Steve Martin and George Cameron. It's pretty typical singer/songwriter stuff with *Word Of Honour* the stand-out track.

In the nineties German label Zyx reissued the entire ESP catalogue on CD, including *Godz Bless California*, which comprised unreleased material and outtakes from 1970-74.

Compilation appearances include *Radar Eyes* on *Songs We Taught The Fuzztones* (Dble LP & Dble CD). (VJ/DSb)

Gold

Personnel: JOE BAJZA gtr A
RON CABRAL perc A
RICHARD COCO vcls A
ROY GARCIA drms A

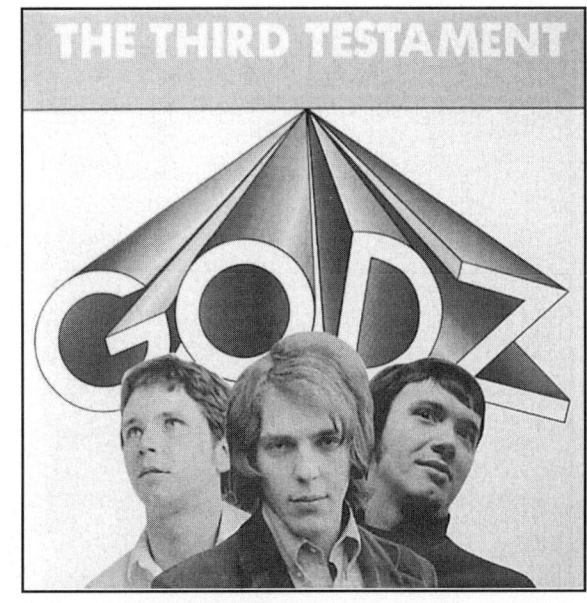

GODZ - The Third Testament LP.

	LOUIE GORSAU	drms	A
	CHICO MONCADA	bs	A
	SEBASTIAN NICHOLSON	congas	A
	ED SCOTT	gtr	A
	ROBIN SINCLAIR	vcls	A

ALBUM: 1(A) NO PARKING   (Rockadelic RRLP 20) 1995

45:   No Parking / Summer Time   (Golden State 501) 1969

From San Francisco, their 45 was part-produced by **Country Joe** in late 1969 at Leo De Gar Kulka's Golden State Recorders, whose legacy has been explored by Big Beat in the *Nuggets From The Golden State* series. *No Parking* and a previously unreleased effort *I Saw You* can be found on the Big Beat's *What A Way To Come Down* (CD) compilation. The band also recorded an album, which remained unreleased until Rockadelic came to the rescue in 1995. Side one is best: *No Parking* and *Righteous Road* are high energy rock; *Conquistadore* has some **Santana**-influenced percussion and *Summer Dresses* is essentially hippie-pop; but the stand-out track is the laid back *High On Love*, which has some lovely melodic guitar. Side two is less impressionable.

The band were managed by Ron Cabral along with his brother Dennis from 1968 to 1973. They broke up after playing San Francisco shows at both the Fillmore and Winterland with groups such as: **Big Brother and the Holding Company**, **Hot Tuna**, Ten Years After, **Malo**, and **Mike Bloomfield**. They also recorded and appeared with **Country Joe McDonald**.

Sebastian Nicholson and Richard Coco are now sadly deceased.

Lookout for a CD retrospective on World Of Sound.

Other compilation appearances include *Favours From The Sun* on *World Of Acid* (LP). (VJ/MW)

Barry Goldberg

Personnel:	BARRY GOLDBERG	organ, piano, vcls	ABCDEFG
	HARVEY MANDEL	gtr	ABCDE
	CHARLES MUSSELWHITE	hrmnca	ABCD
	RON RUBY	bs	AB
	MAURICE McKINLEY	drms	B
	DUANE ALLMAN	gtr	C
	ART GREAT	bs	C
	(MIKE BLOOMFIELD)	gtr, hrns	C E
	EDDIE HINTON	gtr	C
	EDDIE HOH	drms	CDE
	DAVID HOOD	bs	C
	DON McALLISTER	bs	CD

	BOBBY GREGG	drms	D
	BOB GREENSPAN	vcls	E

ALBUMS:
- 1(A) BLOWING MY MIND   (Epic 26199) 1966 -
- 2(B) BARRY GOLDBERG REUNION   (Buddah BDS-5012) 1968 -
- 3(C) TWO JEWS BLUES   (Buddah BDS-5029) 1969 -
- 4(D) STREETMAN   (Buddah BDS-5051) 1970 -
- 5(E) BARRY GOLDBERG AND FRIENDS (Record Man CR5016) 1970 ?
- 6(-) BLAST FROM MY PAST (comp) (Buddah BDS-5081) 1974 -
- 7(F) BARRY GOLBERG   (Atco 7040) 1974 -
- 8(G) BARRY GOLDBERG AND FRIENDS RECORDING LIVE (BUDDAH 5684) 1976 -

NB: (3) was also released in France and in England (Buddah 203 020). (6) was released in the U.K. by Polydor (2318 938) in 1974.

HCP

45s: Blowing My Mind/Think   (Epic 5-10007) 1966 -
       Ronny Siegel From Avenue L/
       Carry On   (Verve Forecast KF 5045) 1968 -
       Hole In My Pocket/Sittin In Circles   (Buddah BDA-59) 1968 103

Originally from Chicago, **Barry Goldberg** is a singer, songwriter, producer and pianist who was very active between 1965 and 1976 on the Chicago and San Francisco scenes, generally playing a combination of electric blues with soul and rock.

In 1966, after the **Goldberg-Miller Blues Band**, he released his first solo album, produced by Billy Sherrill and then formed the **Chicago Loop** with **Mike Bloomfield** who would soon move to California.

In 1967, **Goldberg** was asked to join the **Electric Flag** by **Bloomfield** and **Gravenites**. Shortly afterwards, he signed a long-term contract with Buddah Records and recorded four albums for the label, the best of which is *Two Jews Blues* containing songs like *Jimi The Fox* (dedicated to **Hendrix**), *Spirit Of Trane* (for Coltrane) and *Blues For Barry And*, with excellent guitar parts by **Bloomfield**, **Harvey Mandel**, Duane Allman and Eddie Hinton.

In 1972 he joined **Neil Merryweather** for the *Ivar Avenue Reunion* album and kept on working constantly with **Bloomfield** on his solo albums, the reformed **Electric Flag** and the creation of KGB. **Goldberg** was also a producer, notably for **Mother Earth**, David Blue, James Cotton and **The Rockets**. (SR)

Goldberg-Miller Blues Band

Personnel incl:	BARRY GOLDBERG	organ	A
	STEVE MILLER	vcls, gtr	A

45s: α The Mother Song/More Soul Than Soulful (Epic 9865) 1965
         Whole Lotta Shakin Goin On/Ginger Man   (Epic 10033) 1966

NB: α there was also a rare blue wax, promo only version in PS.

Formed in Chicago in 1965 by **Steve Miller** and **Barry Goldberg**, the band was first called the World War Three Blues Band before renaming itself as the **Goldberg-Miller Blues Band**. They broke up when **Steve Miller** moved to San Francisco in 1966. Their singles are extremely rare. (SR/EW)

Goldebriars

Personnel incl:	DOTTIE HOLMBERG	vcls	A
	SHERI HOLMBERG	vcls	A
	KURT BOETCHER	gtr	A
	RON NEILSON	banjo	A
	RON EDGAR	drms	

ALBUMS:
- 1(A) GOLDEBRIARS   (Epic BN 26087) 1964 -
- 1( ) STRAIGHT AHEAD   (Epic BN 26114) 1964 -

NB: (1) also issued in mono (LN 24087).

GOLD - No Parking LP.

45s:	Pretty Girls And Rolling Stones/Shenandoah	(Epic 9673)	1964
	Castle On The Corner/		
	I've Got To Love Somebody	(Epic 9719)	1964
	I'm Gonna Marry You/June Bride Baby	(Epic 9806)	1965

NB: There was also a UK 45 *Sea Of Tears/I've Got To Love Somebody* (Columbia DB 7384) 1964.

This teenage folk act from California is notable for including a young **Kurt Boetcher**, prior to his involvement with the legendary **Ballroom**, **Millennium**, **Sagittarius** etc.

The band also had links with **The Music Machine**. Ron Edgar drummed with **The Goldebriars**, Keith Olsen later married Sheri Holmberg and the **Goldebriars**' tour manager Sean Bonniwell later borrowed their 'all in black' image for **The Music Machine**. (AGo/JFr/MW)

Lottie Golden

ALBUMS:	1	MOTORCYCLES	(Atlantic)	1969 -
	2	LOTTIE GOLDEN	(GRT)	1970 -

A hippie singer, some of her songs were compiled on the *Hippie Goddesses* CD. (SR)

The Golden Catalinas

Personnel incl:	BOB DIX	bs	A
	JIM KELLY	drms	A
	AL POSNIAK	gtr	A
	HARRY WHEELOCK	ld gtr	A
	JUDY LEE (REETHS)	vcls	
	ROGER LOOS	sax	
	DENNY NOIE	gtr	
	PETE SORCE	vcls	

45s:	α	War Party/Crazy Twistin' Baby	(Cuca 1094)	1962
	α	Hey Little Girl/Forever And A Day (PS)	(Mundo 1000)	1963
	α	By My Window/Wo Wo	(Sara 6392)	1963
	β	It Ain't A Big Thing/Dee Dee	(Knight 100)	1965
		Come To Me/Yakety Sax	(Knight 101)	1966
		Varsity Club Song/		
		Can Your Monkey Do The Dog	(Target 101/2)	1966
		Dee Dee/Mojo Workin'	(Tee Pee 117/8)	1967
	χ	Dee Dee/Mojo Workin'	(Mean Mountain 1422)	1982

NB: α as The Catalinas, β as Denny Noie and The Catalinas. χ is a reissue 45.

Hailed from La Crosse in Southwest Wisconsin. They were originally known as The Catalinas, recording an instrumental for Cuca in 1962 and a three more 45s before adding the 'Golden' to their name in 1965.

With the new name came a change of image - gold suits, gold shoes and bleached hair. *Varsity Club Song*, a raw garage punker with classic nasal vocals and organ beat, paid homage to one of La Crosse's top teen clubs in the mid-sixties. A rather messy production though.

Drummer Jim Kelly had previously played with The Phaetons. Alan Posniak left the band in 1966 and formed Target Productions, which would be home to the Target and Tee Pee labels. Pete Sorce joined the band for the Dee Dee 45. He started performing in 1948, aged 10, and had been recording solo and with backing groups (incl. The Driftwoods) since 1959. He would also work with The Pharaohs, Good Intentions and Big Apple.

Compilation appearances include *Can Your Monkey Do The Dog* on *Tougher Than Stains* (LP); and *Varsity Club Song* on *Back From The Grave, Vol. 6* (LP). (VJ/GM/MW)

Golden Dawn

Personnel:	JIMMY BIRD	gtr	A
	BILL HALLMARK	bs	A
	GEORGE KINNEY	vcls	A
	TOM RAMSEY	gtr	A
	BOBBY RECTOR	drms	A

GOLDEN DAWN - Power Plant LP.

ALBUM:	1(A)	A POWER PLANT	(International Artists 4)	1967 R1

NB: (1) has had a limited repressing in 1979 and issued on CD by Fan Club (NRCD 4126) and Eva (B26) in 1992. Reissued on vinyl (Get Back GET 539) 1999.

Taking their name from the esoteric teachings and philosophy of the Hermetic Tradition, this band was formed in Austin in 1967. **The 13th Floor Elevators** got them a recording contract with International Artists. Indeed, George Kinney and Roky Erickson had grown up together in South Austin, attended the same school and played together in The Fugitives, a garage band from 1964/65. Kinney also played in Chelsea from late 1965 to late 1966 joining **The Golden Dawn** at the invitation of some high school friends when Chelsea fell apart.

The album is one of the best on the label with fine psychedelic instrumentation and thought provoking lyrics. Sadly, International Artists failed to promote it and the band fell apart when Kinney, determined to have nothing more to do with them, headed for California. Together with George Banks (who did the artwork for the album) Kinney later published Roky Erickson's book "Openers" whilst Roky was in Rusk State Hospital and the book helped to win his release. One cut from the album, *Starvation*, was later issued on an EP by Radarscope (RAD 88) 1978 in the U.K. along with cuts by the **13th Floor Elevators**, **The Red Krayola** and **The Lost and Found**. Copies were given away at **Red Krayola**'s 1978 reunion gig at London's Hope and Anchor pub.

Bill Hallmark went on to sing & play guitar for **Rubayyat** along with the **13th Floor Elevators'** Danny Galindo.

Compilation appearances include: *My Time* on *Endless Journey - Phase Three* (LP) and *Endless Journey - Phase I & II* (Dble CD). (VJ)

Goldenrod

Personnel:	BEN BENAY	gtr	A
	TOXEY FRENCH	drms	A
	JERRY SCHEFF	bs	A

ALBUM:	1(A)	GOLDENROD	(Chartmaker CS 91101)	1967/'68 R3

NB: (1) counterfeited on vinyl (Heyoka HEY 205) 1985 and CD 1997.

From Los Angeles, **Goldenrod** were part of the "Our Productions" crew, along with **Mike Deasy**, **Lee Mallory** and **Curt Boettcher**. As part of this talented group of people, they contributed to numerous albums and sessions in addition to those released as **Goldenrod**. Some of these included Tommy Roe, **Darius** and backing the **Association** on their first two albums. Much of this session work was done on a "conveyor belt" system; with all the instrumental tracks being cut at Gary Paxton's studio, and vocals for the more well-known acts cut at Columbia.

All three had earlier played with **Ballroom** with **Boettcher** and together with **Mallory**, they formed the basis of the original line-up of **Millennium**. Scheff contributed *Dandelion Wine* to the **Millennium** repertoire, but all three left when it looked like **Millennium** would turn into a 'proper' band rather than a studio project. **Goldenrod** are also thought to have backed **Lee Mallory** live.

The **Goldenrod** album contains four elongated tracks consisting of extended and improvised jamming with mystical titles, such as *Karmic Dream Sequences* and *Descent Of The Cyclopeans*. The former was written by **Curt Boettcher** and **Lee Mallory**, and was later also recorded by **Millennium**.

Apparently the group first met while they were recruited to back The Fifth Dimension and they all went on to become top L.A. session men; Scheff also went on to back Elvis Presley and Benay appeared in Fun Zone in the seventies. (VJ/MW/JFr)

Golden Throat

ALBUM: 1   GOLDEN THROAT   (Trim) 197? SC

From Hawaii, a rock group with Hammond B-3 organ and female vocals. The album came in a fine cover with mushrooms. (SR)

Goldrush

45:   Somebody's Turning On The People/
      Feelin' Glad   (ABC/Dunhill D-4174) c1969

Produced by Equinox Production, the company run by Terry Melcher, **Goldrush** seems to have been a short-lived flower-pop group, probably from California. *Somebody's Turning On The People* was penned by George Alexander while the flip was a cover of a **Glad** song, another group who were produced by Equinox. (SR)

The Goldtones

ALBUM: 1   LIVE AT THE TEENBEAT CLUB
                                    (La Brea LS-8011) c1965 -
NB: (1) mono and stereo pressings exist.

A frat-rock cover band who recorded on the same label as **The Starfires**. It's rumoured that Randy Seol played with this group before joining the **Strawberry Alarm Clock**, but this remains pure speculation. (SR)

GOLDENROD - Goldenrod CD.

Golgotha

Personnel: RICHARD X. HEYMAN   drms   A
            MICHAEL JANNONE   sax, perc   A
            BETSY LEE   vcls   A
            MICHAEL MELESURGO   perc   A
            B.C. SCOFIELD   gtr, vcls, bs   A

ALBUM: 1(A) OLD SEEDS BOOTLEG   (No label) 1974 R3

Very home-made local New Jersey private press with blank labels. Interesting amalgam of Little Feat (at their most laid-back) and **Grateful Dead**'s early seventies sound. Most of the tracks are guitar-led and tend to get heavy. It was issued in a plain sleeve with front cover slick glued on. (CF)

Goliath

ALBUM: 1   HOT ROCK AND THUNDER   (Bridges) 1977 -
NB: (1) Also issued on Tomorrow Records.

From Kentucky, a hard-rock act heavily influenced by Deep Purple. Their album is housed in a fantasy cover. (SR)

Goliath

Personnel: TED BARBELLA   organ   A
            NORM CONRAD   bs   A
            JERRY GILBERT   drms   A
            DENNIS JASON   gtr   A
            STEVE JASON   vcls   A
            (TOM AHRENS   special effects,
                                    3rd part harmony A)

ALBUM: 1(A) GOLIATH   (ABC ABCS-702) 1969

45s: Come With Me (To My World)/Crossroads (ABC 11235) 1969
       Yesterday's Children/
       If Johnny Comes Marching Home   (ABC 11267) 1969

Produced by Mann, Segall and Lowe and recorded at Sigma Sound studios in Philadelphia, the sole album of this forgotten group was strongly influenced by **Vanilla Fudge**, with long organ parts, various percussions, a deep voiced singer and slow motion covers of the Beatles' *Eleanor Rigby*, Bert Berns' *Are You Lonely For Me Baby*, Otis Redding's *Loving You Too Long* and Curtis Mayfield's *Man's Temptation*. The other songs were written by Barbella and Steve D'Amico, Rusty Richards and Eddie Ray. The result is not very convincing and the album went unnoticed. (SR)

Golliwogs

Personnel: DOUG CLIFFORD   drms   A
            STU COOK   bs   A
            JOHN FOGERTY   vcls, gtr   A
            TOM FOGERTY   gtr, vcls, hrmnca A

ALBUM: 1(A) THE GOLLIWOGS: PRE-CREEDENCE
                                         (Fantasy 9474) 1975 SC

45s: Don't Tell Me No Lies/Little Girl   (Fantasy 590) 1965
       Where You Been/You Came Walking   (Fantasy 597) 1965
       You Can't Be True/You Got Nothin' On Me (Fantasy 599) 1965
       Brown-Eyed Girl/You Better Be Careful   (Scorpio 404) 1966
       Fight Fire/Fragile Child   (Scorpio 405) 1966
       Walking On The Water/You Better Get It   (Scorpio 408) 1967
       Porterville/Call It Pretending   (Scorpio 412) 1967

When **Tommy and The Blue Velvets** signed with Fantasy, they became **The Golliwogs**, much to the group's embarrassment. The seven singles on Fantasy and its affiliated Scorpio label show their evolution, from a Beatles influenced group led by **Tom Fogerty** (born 9th November 1941) vocals and guitar to a rock, country and R&B act totally dominated by his younger brother John (Born 28th May 1945). A gifted singer, songwriter and guitarist, John soon relegated his brother to rhythm guitar.

GOLGOTHA - Old Seeds Bootleg LP.

The singles are rare but can be found on **The Golliwogs** compilation album released in 1975. Alternatively, compilation appearances have so far included: *Brown-Eyed Girl* on *Mayhem & Psychosis, Vol. 3* (LP) and *Mayhem & Psychosis, Vol. 2* (CD); *Fight Fire* on *Nuggets Box* (4-CD); *Brown-Eyed Girl*, *Call It Pretending*, *Fragile Child*, *Fight Fire*, *Walking On Water*, *You Better Be Careful* and *You Better Get It Before It Gets You* on *The Scorpio Records Story* (CD).

On Christmas Eve 1967, **The Golliwogs** rechristened themselves **Creedence Clearwater Revival**. (SR)

Gollum

45: Desert Heat/Prayer Of Despair (Kiderian KRP 45120 LA) 1974

Thought to be from Chicago, this 45 contains some amazing brutal mid-seventies hard-rock/psych. The flip side is mastered at 33 rpm and lasts over 6 minutes.

No names on the record, apart from "Mullog" - **Gollum** backwards. (MKy/CF)

Gonn

Personnel:			
BRENT COLVIN	drms	A	
GERRY GABLE	keyb'ds	ABC	F
REX GARRETT	gtr	AB	F
CRAIG MOORE	bs	ABCDEF	
GARY STEPP	gtr	A D	
LARRY La MASTER	gtr	B	F
DAVE JOHNSON(*)	drms	BCDEF	
JERRY HEATH	gtr	C	
SLINK RAND	ld gtr	C	
DANA GEORGES	ld gtr	D	
ALFRED BOYER	gtr	DE	
JERRY ISON	ld gtr	E	

ALBUMS:
1(A) ROUGH DIAMONDS: THE HISTORY OF GARAGE BAND MUSIC, VOL 9: GONN (Voxx 200.029) 1985
2(-) FRENZOLOGY 1966-1967 (CD) (MCCM CD 9601) 1996
3(F) GONN WITH THE WIND (LP/CD) (MCCM) 1998
4(-) LOUDEST BAND IN TOWN (LP) (Beat Rocket BR 108) 2000

45s:
α Blackout of Gretely/Pain In My Heart (Emir 9217) 1966
α Come With Me (To The Stars)/ You're Looking Fine (Merry Jaine IT-2316) 1967
β The Prophecy / Cry To Me (PS) (MCCM 6696-1) 1996
χ Pretty Girl / Head In The Clouds (PS) (MCCM 6696-2) 1996
δ Fellow Slave/The Wind (PS) (MCCM) 2000

NB: α reissued by MCCM with PS. β limited edition of 1000, first 200 on pink wax. χ limited edition of 1000, first 200 on blue wax. δ contains LP version and Live in Turin, Italy, Feb '97, orange swirl vinyl with PS.

Based in Keokuk, Iowa they emerged out of the ashes of The Pagans, a garage covers band, of which Moore, Gabel and La Master had been members. They were a controversial 'live' act and won backing from Bill Egan after he'd seen them playing a show in Burlington and wanted them to back him on a 45. The deal was, they'd back him on two songs if he'd pay for them to record two of their own. So they backed him on Eddie Cochran's *C'mon Everybody* and *Kansas City*, which never got a release, whilst their two songs were issued on the Emir label. Late in 1966 they entered a basement studio in Quincy, Illinois, to record a tape of cover versions for a guy in Florida who'd promised to get them lots of gigs down there. Fortunately, Craig Moore kept a copy of it and many of the songs can now be heard on their retrospective *Rough Diamonds* and *Frenzology* albums, because they never heard any more of the tape they sent to Florida.

1967 saw some personnel changes with Colvin and Stepp leaving to be replaced by La Master and Johnson. This line-up returned to Quincy to record another self-penned Garrett-Moore composition (the flip was a Kinks cover) which they released on their own Merry Jaine Records. Further convoluted line-ups took place in 1968.

When the split came, Gabel formed an eight piece called Mother Hooker's Blues Band and Moore and Johnson formed a blues trio, Trinity.

The Voxx album, or the later *Frenzology* retrospectives are highly recommended, containing their fuzz-punker *Blackout Of Gretely*, the keyboard-led *Come With Me (To The Stars)*, an unreleased 45 *Doin' Me In* and a number of spirited cover versions.

Craig Moore now runs a collectors label MCCM, which has put out reissue/retrospective 45s on artists including **Al's Untouchables** and **The Intruders**. Other releases include a solo double album from 1989 *Agonnagain* (coloured vinyl 500 pressed), a 1994 7" EP *Sun Session* with Jim McCarty of The Yardbirds (recorded at Sun, Memphis, 1992) with a cover of Yardbirds' *Evil Hearted You*, and a new 7" *Fine Surprise/Gonna Come For You* from an upcoming album that also features Jim McCarty, Chris Dreja and The Creation's Eddie Phillips.

As for **The Gonn**, they have continued to be held in high regard and this has led to them reforming and releasing new material in addition to being actively involved in compiling their original sixties material. The two 30th Anniversary Reunion 45s, released on Craig Moore's own MCCM imprint, reveal more about the band's recent activities. First off they reunited in 1990 for a festival held in Keokuk. Then, when Craig was assembling the *Frenzology* compilation in 1996 he got in touch with all the other members for their contributions to the project. The rekindled enthusiasm resulted in a full-blown reunion to celebrate their 30th anniversary with new recordings plus some live gigs in the U.S. and Europe.

It is to their credit that the new recordings on the 45s recapture much of their sixties spirit and sound, and will NOT dilute their reputation. The new LP, *Gonn With The Wind* is out now in multi-coloured vinyl and limited to 500 numbered copies.

Compilation appearances to date have included: *Blackout Of Gretely* on *Nuggets Box* (4-CD), *Pebbles, Vol. 1* (CD), *Pebbles, Vol. 3 (ESD)* (CD), *Best of Pebbles, Vol. 1* (LP & CD), *Chosen Few Vol's 1 & 2* (CD) and *The Chosen Few, Vol. 1* (LP); *Doin' Me In* on *Pebbles, Vol. 10* (CD), *The Essential Pebbles Collection, Vol. 1* (Dble CD), *Pebbles Box* (5-LP), *Trash Box* (5-CD); and *Signed D.C.* on *Sixties Rebellion, Vol. 8* (LP & CD). (VJ/MW/CMe)

The Go-Nuts

Personnel incl?: P. FALLON A
V. VIRZERO A

45: Flower / Be Mine (Demo-Disc A 333) 1967

An obscure group from Brooklyn, New York whose sole release elicits comparisons to **The Seeds**. *Flower* has bloomed again on *Psychedelic States: New York Vol. 1* (CD). (MW/MM)

THE GOOD DOG BANNED - The Good Dog Band LP.

Good and Plenty

| Personnel: | DOUGLAS GOOD | vcls | A |
| | GINNY PLENTY | vcls | A |

ALBUM: 1(A) THE WORLD OF GOOD AND PLENTY (Senate S-21001) 1967

Clearly a studio project, but one that's only moderately orchestrated, it contains a few really good songs and two fine singers and so produces some excellent slices of baroque pop. There's plenty of tinny organ, harpsichord and celeste and all the tracks were written by the producers Wes Farrrell and Tony Romeo. Luckily they can both write a catchy tune and also know how to arrange them to provide a sound full of appealing innocence. Some of the songs have small unexpected twists, that modestly creep under the skin and *Children Dreamin'* is particularly fine. Certainly this is one of a myriad records in soft-psych style sung by a male/female duo, but it is also one of the better ones of the era. The album also came in a great cover. (MK/VJ)

Good Cheer

Personnel:	JOHNNY CADICK	gtr, vcls	A
	CHUCK MANKER	bs, vcls	A
	VAL MUYLLE	organ, vcls	A
	J.R. (BOB) SANDERS	drms, vcls	A

ALBUM: 1(A) TIME FOR GOOD CHEER (ORS) c1972 R2

A rare private pressing released by an Indiana rock group. The self-penned 'A' side is dazzlin', covering the full range of garage/psych to "sure you ain't a brother" soul. The 'B' side is loaded with uninspired covers (*Cherish, Games People Play, I Believe In Music*). (SR/TCx)

Good Dog Banned

Personnel:	TIM CAINE (aka CAIN)	sax, gtr	A
	LEE MARKS	drms, flute	A
	CHRIS MILLER	gtr, sax	A
	DOUG MORTENSON	gtr, steel gtr	A
	DWIGHT WOLF	bs	A

ALBUM: 1(A) THE GOOD DOG BANNED (No label DM 1001) 197? R2
NB: (1) reissued officially on CD (Gear Fab GF-125) 1999.

Rare private press album from Northern California circa 1973. Only 200 copies were made, and the album came in a plain cover with front and rear paste-on slicks. Caine was formerly with **Sons of Champlin**. One of the hardest Bay Area records of the era to locate, the group plays proficient rural-rock that sounds influenced by the early seventies **Grateful Dead**.

Compilation appearances include *Rollin' Into Salyer* on Gear Fab's *Psychedelic Sampler* (CD). (CF)

Good Earth

45: Stone Free/Still Beside Me (SWAC 903S-1001) 1968

A competent, if uninspiring **Hendrix** cover in a hard slightly psychy vein. The flip is softer rock but good. The band are thought to have hailed from Michigan, but this is unconfirmed. (MW)

Good Earth

45s:	How Deep Is The Ocean?/Louise	(Dynovoice 907) 1966
	A Funny Thing Happened/ I Can See A Light	(Dynovoice 924) 1966
	There's More Than One Road To Philadelphia/ Must I Really Go Through This	(Dynovoice 929) 1967

Produced by Bob Crewe on the same label as **The Chicago Loop**, these three flower-pop singles were probably the result of long studio sessions, with pretentious arrangements and massive choral harmonies. You'll either like or hate it. (SR)

Goodees

Personnel:	KAY EVANS	A
	SANDRA JACKSON	A
	JUDY WILLIAMS	A

ALBUM: 1(A) CANDY COATED GOODIES (HIP HIS-7002) 1968

45s:	For A Little While / Would You, Could You Condition Red /	(Hip 109) 1967
	Didn't Know Love Was So Good	(Hip 8005) 1968
	Jilted / Love Is Here	(Hip 8010) 1969
	Goodies / He's A Rebel	(Hip 8016) 1969

A soft-rock girl trio from Memphis on the same rock subsidiary of Stax as **Paris Pilot**, **Southwest FOB** and **Knowbody Else**. The material on their album ranges from soft-rock to pop and psych with an elaborate studio production. Their story is told in Ron Hall's book on the Memphis scene (1960-1975) - 'Playing For A Piece Of The Door', (published in 2001 by Shangri-La Projects, ISBN 0-9668575-1-8). (SR/MW)

Good Feelins

45s:	I'm Captured/End Of A Love	(Rock-It 1007) 1967
	I'm Captured/End Of A Love	(Liberty 55981) 1967
	I'm Lost/Shattered	(Rock-It 2000) 1967

A mid-sixties San Bernardino, California punk band.

Compilation appearances have included: *Shattered* on *Boulders, Vol. 3* (LP), *Gone, Vol. 1* (LP), *Pebbles Vol. 9* (CD), *The Essential Pebbles Collection, Vol. 1* (Dble CD); and *I'm Captured* on *Vile Vinyl, Vol. 2* (LP) and *Vile Vinyl* (CD). (VJ/MW)

The Good Idea

Personnel:	BOB BLANK	vcls, sax	A
	RICK Lia BRAATEN	drms, vcl	A
	DAVE LINDER	gtr, vcl	A
	JOHN MIESEN	keyb'ds	A

45: Inside, Outside/Patterns In Life (Good Idea no #) c1968

This Christian rock/garage band came from St. Paul, about 100 miles Northwest of Minneapolis in Minnesota and operated between 1968-69. Their 45 is good and becoming hard to find and features keyboard-bass parts similar to **The Doors**.

In addition to the 45, they also recorded a track called *12:25*.

After **The Good Idea** split in 1969, Rick Lia Braaten and John Miesen formed a trio with Bill Hallquist called Final Assembly. Bill:- "I had operated lights for **The Good Idea** briefly, and had earlier played in The Transgressors and The Other Guys with Rick Lia Braaten. In '69 we began work on what was to be another concept piece like *12:25 (Christmas Story)*, called *Summertime Children* with me on lead vocal. Bob Blank offered to re-join if he could bring in bass player Terry Tilley and we became **Thundertree**".

"John Miesen shopped the **Good Idea** track *12:25* around to labels and landed a contract with Roulette. We used *12:25* as one side and completed another side with the real **Thundertree** band."

Compilation coverage has included *Inside, Outside* on *Bad Vibrations, Vol. 2* (LP). (VJ/BHa)

Good News

Personnel incl: BOB OLDENBURG   A

ALBUM: 1(A) GOOD NEWS   (Broadman Records 452-091) 1967 SC

Recorded by members of the Glorieta Baptist Assembly in Glorieta, New Mexico, an album of Christian folk and folk-rock with eighteen original songs written by Bob Oldenburg. Some dealers describe it as "folk psych" but we have serious doubts about the "psych" tag. (SR)

Good News

ALBUM: 1 GOOD NEWS   (Columbia CS9941) c1969 -

45: Open The Gates/
     Speakin' The Unknown Tongue   (Columbia 45129) c1969

A soft folk psych duo, with acoustic guitar and cello. (SR)

The Good Rats

Personnel: JOE FRANCO   drms   A
            JOHN 'THE CAT' GATTO gtr   A
            LENNY KOE   bs   A
            MICKY MARCHELLO   gtr, vcls   A
            PEPPI MARCHELLO   vcls   A

ALBUM: 1(A) THE GOOD RATS   (Kapp 3580) 1968 SC

NB: (1) also released in France (Vogue CLVXK 347) 1968.

THE GOOD, THE BAD and THE UGLY - Self Titled LP.

45: For The Sake Of Everyone/Gotta Get Back   (Kapp ?) 1968

NB: also released in France with a picture sleeve showing a big rat (Vogue/Kapp KV 538) 1968.

A Long Island Italian-American band led by the Marchello brothers. Their first album was produced by Ron Hoffkins and Barry Osslander but flopped. **The Good Rats** persevered, returning in 1974 with *Tasty* on Warner and enjoyed some success at the end of the seventies. Their singer, Peppi Marchello, was notable for his raunchy timbre.

Compilation appearances include *The Hobo* on *Turds On A Bum Ride, Vol. 3* (CD). (SR/CG)

The Good, The Bad and The Ugly

Personnel: BUBBA GOODE   vcls, gtr, bs, drms   A
            JOE PIPPS   ld vcls, bs, gtr, keyb'ds,
                           drms   A
            KENNY YETMAN   drms   A

ALBUM: 1(A) THE GOOD, THE BAD AND THE UGLY
                               (Mercury SR 61253) 1970 SC

This bunch were previously known as The Next Exit, and came from Beaumont and Port Arthur, Texas. Their sole album was produced by Huey P. Meaux and is a heavy R&B rootsy rocker, which continues where the **American Blues**' second album left off. Despite the occasional 'psych' tag by opportunistic dealers, this is definitely for those deeply into blues-rock similar to Johnny Winter, who also hailed from Beaumont and with whom they'd jammed. (MW)

Goodthunder

Personnel: WAYNE COOK   keyb'ds   A
            JOHN DESAUTELS   drms   A
            DAVID HANSON   gtr, vcls   A
            JAMES CALHOUN LINDSAY vcls, perc   A
            BILL RHODES   bs   A

ALBUM: 1(A) GOODTHUNDER   (Elektra EKS-75041) 1972 -

Recorded in Los Angeles, this is a decent album of hard-psych with some prog influences and good organ and guitar parts. Nothing exceptional but quite pleasant and masterfully produced by Paul Rothchild (**Doors**, **Love**, **Buckley**, **Joplin** etc.).

Wayne Cook went on to play in a reformation of **Steppenwolf** and become a session musician. Some members later appeared in L.A. Jets and 1994. (SR/NK)

The Goodtime Music Company

Personnel: DAVE BLUNT   organ   A
            BRAD BUTLER   vcls   A
            BRUCE BUTLER   ld gtr, bs   A
            KENNY COLVINE gtr, bs   A
            ROBERT TAYLOR drms   A

45: Aristocrat/
     Passionate Love   (Bill Rase studio acetate no #) 1967

Raw teen-punk sounds from Sacramento, recorded at Bill Rase's legendary studio. Both sides can be found on *The Sound Of Young Sacramento* (CD).

Goose Creek Symphony

Personnel: DAVE BIRKELL   bs   A
            RITCHIE HART   ld vcls, gtr   A
            BOB HENKE III   gtr, piano, organ, vcls   A
            PAUL HOWARD   gtr, dobro, vcls   A
            MIKE McFADDEN   gtr   A
            (ED BLACK   gtr   A)
            (BUDDY WHEELER   A)

ALBUM: 1(A) GOOSE CREEK SYMPHONY (Capitol SM 444) 1970 -

Formed by Mike McFadden after **Superfine Dandelion** broke up, **Goose Creek Symphony** was a rural-rock group with strong country influences. Recorded in Arizona and produced by Kelly Gordon and Tim Ramsey, their first album is worth obtaining for *Talk About Goose Creek*, eight minutes of guitar duels, with the participation of Ed Black, another ex-**Superfine Dandelion**.

Led by Charles Gearheart, their subsequent albums are too country-rock oriented to be included here. (SR)

Gordian Knot

Personnel:	PAT KINCADE	gtr	A
	DULIN LANCASTER	drms	A
	J. D. LOBUE	keyb'ds	A
	LELAND RUSSELL	bs, vcls	A
	JIM WEATHERLY	gtr, vcls	A

ALBUM: 1(A) TONE (Verve V(6) 60562) 1968 -

45s: If Only I Could Cry/Year Of The Sun (Verve 10595) 1968
Broken Down Ole Merry-Go-Round/
We Must Be Doing Something Right (Verve 10612) 1968

A short-lived San Francisco-based outfit whose album was essentially harmony/pop-rock, certainly not one for garage fans. Jim Weatherly later would become a soft country singer, releasing several albums for Buddha circa 1974/5. (VJ/SR)

Jimmy Gordon

45s: Buzzzzzz / Somethin' Else (Challenge 59194) 1963
Test Pattern / 1980 (Challenge 59355) 1967

Buzzzzzz inspired the title of Arf! Arf!'s instrumental CD compilation series, and justifiably features *Buzzzzzz* on *Buzz Buzz Buzzzzzz, Vol. 1* (CD). *Test Pattern* from his 1967 45 is on the companion *Buzz Buzz Buzzzzzz, Vol. 2* (CD).

Jimmy Gordon also was behind **Peter Pan and The Good Fairies**.

Gord's Horde

Personnel:	GORDY GILLMAN	gtr	AB
	DAN NORDALL	organ, gtr, sax	A
	TOM PRICE	drms	AB
	DALE SMITH	bs, sax	AB
	PHIL VAN GOETHEN	organ	AB
	CLIFF FELLOWS	gtr, organ	B

45: I Don't Care / Please Tell Me (Hodag 0540) 1966

Erupting out of Rhinelander, a small town in Northeast Wisconsin, *I Don't Care* is a fine folk-punker with lots of minor chords. Enjoy it on *Highs In The Mid-Sixties, Vol. 15* (LP).

Both sides of their sole release were penned by Dan Nordall just prior to his departure. Replaced by Cliff Fellows, the band became "T.H.E. Horde".

Highlights of their tenure included opening for **The Kingsmen** in Stevens Point and for **The Turtles** in Ashland, recalled leader Gordy Gillman in 'Do You Hear That Beat' (the book on fifties and sixties Wisconsin acts). Gillman became a fireman. (VJ/MW/GM)

The Gospel

45: Redeemer /
I Won't Be Sad Again (Vanguard Apostolic VRS 35084) 1969

Both sides of this hippie-folk 45 were written and produced by John Townley of **Magicians**, **Family Of Apostolic**, and Apostolic Studio fame. The 'A' side is a harmony-folk ballad with an Eastern/psychy vibe, like a spaced-out Steeleye Span. The flip is in a more trad folk-country vein, with banjo and fiddle. (MW)

Gospel Oak

Personnel:	KERRY GAINES	drms	A
	CLIFF HALL	piano, organ	A
	GORDON HUNTLEY	pedal steel gtr	A
	MATTHEW KELLY	hrmnca, gtr	A
	BOB LEGATE	gtr, vels	A
	JOHN RAPP	bs	A

ALBUM: 1(A) GOSPEL OAK (Kapp KS 3635) 1970 SC

NB: (1) also issued on Uni (UNLS 113) in 1970.

45: O. K. Sam/Go Talk To Rachel (Kapp 2115) 1970

A marginal case for inclusion since this album is basically hippie-influenced country-rock. Pleasant enough with some good guitar moments but in no way exceptional. It has yet to create much interest among collectors. Two of the best tracks were also issued on the above 45. Other memorable songs are *Recollections Of Jessica* and *St. Anne's Pretension*.

OK Sam was later 'borrowed' and recorded as *Important Exportin' Man* by the New Riders Of The Purple Sage on their *Panama Red* album. Tim Hovey (co-author of same) had been a major child movie star of the 1950's. Tragically he recently commited suicide.

John Rapp later died of a drug overdose, Gordon Huntley was later a member of Elton John's band and Matthew Kelly is a current member of Ratdog (**Bob Weir**'s **Grateful Dead** carry-overs). He has also played on many of the **Dead**'s projects over the years. Finally, Bob Legate became a successful real estate broker and currently plays with the Grateful Living. (VJ)

Gossip

45: No One's Standing In Your Way/
Whispering Wind (Gossip ARA 102268) 1968

Phoenix, Arizona's answer to **Jefferson Airplane**? Well, not quite, but pleasant West Coasty hippie folk-psych-rock with the then obligatory female vocalist. (MW)

Gove

ALBUM: 1 HEAVY COWBOY (TRX LPS-1002) 1971 -

45s: Death Letter Blues/Sunday Morning Early (TRX 45-T-5024) 1971
Silver City Bound/Looking Out My Window (TRX 5029) 1971
That's The Way/In The Morning (TRX 5031) 1971
I've Been Thinking Of You Lately/Carry On (UNI 55335) 1972
α Goin' To The Country/Mobile Blue (UNI 55354) 1972

NB: α by Scrivenor and Gove.

Probably from Texas, this album has been described as "a weird mix of country rock and psych, sorta like **Darius** meets **Euphoria** (the Capitol one)". The songs include *In The Morning (When You Dream)*, *Death Letter Blues* and *Morning Dew*.

TRX was a division of Hickory Records in Nashville. (SR/MGm/EMy)

Symon Grace and Tuesday Blues

45: You Won't Get Me Workin'/
Out Of Sight (Main Line ML 1364) 1967

NB: also released on Round (1004) 1967.

Powerful pumping fuzz-garage with soulful intonations. Sadly, the flip is very soulful and brassy. From Erie, Pennsylvania.

Compilation appearances include *You Won't Get Me Workin'* on *The Garage Zone, Vol. 4* (LP) and *The Garage Zone Box Set* (4-LP). (MW)

Graced Lightning

Personnel:	JOAN BURNSTEIN	keyb'ds, mandolin	A
	GEORGE EDWARD	drms, perc	A
	GARY GAND	gtr, bs	A
	CHRIS HERMAN	gtr, bs	A

ALBUM: 1(A) THE GRACED LIGHTNING SIDE   (No label) 1975 R2

A local Illinois one-sided album issued in a plain cover with front and rear paste-ons. Its three tracks are hard progressive rock instrumentals with great guitar. (CF)

The Graduates

45: Seventh Generation Breakthrough /
If Ever I Get Out Of This Mess I'm In   (Rising Sons 712) 1968

A blue-eyed soul group. (SR)

Don Grady

See **Don Agrati** entry.

Graffiti

Personnel:	STEVE BENDEROTH	keyb'ds	A
	JOHN ST. JOHN	gtr	A
	TONY TAYLOR	vcls	A
	RICHIE BLAKIN	drms	A
	GEORGE STRUNZ	gtr	A

ALBUM: 1(A) GRAFFITI   (ABC ABCS 663) 1968 SC

NB: (1) reissued on CD (LSD ET 5005) 1998.

45s: He's Got The Knack/Love In Spite   (ABC 11123) 1968
Do You Feel Sorry?/Girl On Fire   (ABC 11182) 1969

NB: *He's Got The Knack* and *Do You Feel Sorry?* are non-LP.

Produced by Bob Thiele (**Ford Theatre**, **Eden's Children** etc.), Eddie Kramer and Jay Senter, their album is a mix of light and heavy rock with some occasionally excellent guitar solos, leaning more towards progressive than acid or psych. Strunz and Benderoth, sometimes helped by St. John and Taylor, wrote all the songs, except *Ugly Mascara* penned by Ronald Hovanecz.

The band were based in Greenwich Village, having relocated from Washington DC when they were known as The Button, (which was the final incarnation of **The Hangmen**). The Button line-up included drummer Bob Berberich who returned to DC, teamed up with two other ex-**Hangmen** and Nils Lofgren to form **(Paul Dowell and) The Dolphin** and later Grin.

Drummer Richard Blakin, may possibly be the same guy listed as an engineer on Chicago's sixth album, from 1973.

The CD reissue includes the non-album *He's Got The Knack*. The track, which can also be found on *Turds On A Bum Ride, Vol. 3* (CD) and *World Of Acid* (LP), is a fast 'n' fuzzy mainly instrumental post-**Vanilla Fudge** rocker. The 45's flip *Love In Spite* is also pretty good heavy stuff too. (VJ/MW/SR/BE/SteveMulcahy)

A Grain of Sand

ALBUM: 1 MUSIC FOR THE STRUGGLE BY ASIANS IN AMERICA
(selective)   (Paredon) 1973 SC

A hard strummin' electrical/acoustic folk trio, obviously influenced by **Jefferson Airplane** at times. Housed in a thick cover with a book, a yellow vinyl pressing. (SR)

Grains of Sand

Personnel incl:	DOUG MARK	gtr, vcls	A
	GUY FINLEY	drms	B
	JIMMY GREENSPOON	keyb'ds, vcls	B
	MICHAEL LLOYD	bs, ld vcls	B
	SEAN McLEOD	gtr	B

45s: That's When Happiness Began/
She Needs Me   (Valiant 736) 1965
Going Away Baby/
Golden Apples Of The Sun   (Genesis 101) 1966
Nice Girl/Drop Down Sometime   (Philips 40469) 1967

This band operated out of Los Angeles, and according to the *Pebbles* liner notes the original line-up met whilst in the Navy.

Their first 45, *That's When Happiness Began*, was an Addrisi brothers composition. The song was also recorded by The Montanas and their version can be heard on *Garage Punk Unknowns, Vol. 5*. Doug Mark, who played and sang on this 45, later went on to **The Sunshine Company**.

Their second 45 was produced by **Kim Fowley** and Michael Lloyd, with the 'A' side, *Going Away Baby*, being written by Michael Lloyd and Sean McLeod. It is a catchy uptempo rocker. The flip, *Golden Apples Of The Sun*, was written by Michael Lloyd and **Kim Fowley** and is much more psychedelic, featuring some fine guitar work and culminating in a haze of confusion.

Their third and final 45, a pleasant soft pop effort, suffers by comparison to their first two releases. It's also known that the band recorded further material, with Michael Lloyd producing, which has yet to be released.

Michael Lloyd was also in **The Smoke**, **Rubber Band**, and **West Coast Pop Art Experimental Band**. He became one of America's top record producers. Jimmy Greenspoon went on to become a founding member of Three Dog Night.

Compilation appearances have included: *Going Away Baby* and *Golden Apples Of The Sun* on *Kim Fowley - Outlaw Superman* (LP & CD); *She Needs Me* on *Midnight To Sixty-Six* (LP), *Off The Wall, Vol. 1* (LP), *Pebbles, Vol. 8* (CD), *Son Of The Gathering Of The Tribe* (LP); *Going Away Baby* on *Pebbles, Vol. 1* (CD), *The Essential Pebbles Collection, Vol. 1* (Dble CD), *Pebbles Box* (5-LP), *Pebbles, Vol. 1* (LP), *Trash Box* (5-CD), *Great Pebbles* (CD) and *I Was A Teenage Caveman* (LP); *Goin' Away Baby* and *She Needs Me* on *Pebbles, Vol. 4 (ESD)* (CD); *That's When Happiness Began* on *What A Way To Die* (LP), *Highs In The Mid-Sixties Vol. 1* (LP) and *Hang It Out To Dry* (CD); and *Golden Apples Of The Sun* on *Highs In The Mid-Sixties Vol. 3* (LP). (VJ/MW/JFr)

GRAFFITI - Graffiti LP.

Grains of Sand

45:	Passing Thru'The Night/The Castaway of Capt. Haze	(American Music Makers 008) 1967

This 45 was the work of a Pittsburgh, Pennsylvania band, who had recorded earlier as **The Grand Prees**. Produced by Lou Guarino, both songs are Beatles-influenced and were written by Bob Wyler, who was probably a member of the group.

Compilation appearances have included: *The Castaway Of Capt. Haze* and *Passing Through The Night* on *Burghers, Vol. 1* (LP & CD); and *Passing Through The Night* on *Gone, Vol. 1* (LP). (MW/SR)

The Grains of Sand

Personnel incl: JERRY WOOD   A

45:	I've Got It Bad/I Wonder Why	(Swank 154) 196?

A different outfit from the better known Los Angeles and Pittsburgh bands, this mob came from Oklahoma City, where they played in the second half of the 1960s, recording this one good punk 45. (VJ)

Grand Larceny

45:	Jumpin' Jack Flash/Since I Fell For You	(Galaxy 1003) 196?

A Stones' cover from an Iowa-based garage outfit. (VJ)

Grandma's Rockers

Personnel:	JAMIE FARNUM	drms	A
	BRIAN HAAS	bs	A
	DAVE LANGE	organ	A
	JIM MAROUSIS	gtr	A
	LARRY WILLIAMS	ld gtr	A

ALBUM: 1(A)   HOME MADE APPLE PIE AND YANKEE INGENUITY
                                                       (Fredlo 6727) 1967 R5

NB: (1) reissued on Del-Val in 1993 (SC).

Just five hundred copies of this rare garage-style album were made. A private release by high school kids, it was funded by their parents and mostly given away to friends and family. Musically it's a mixture of covers of **Music Machine** and **Country Joe and The Fish** songs with standards like *Louie, Louie* and some originals too. The band hailed from Iowa and like many of these albums it's pretty disappointing musically.

Their version of *Talk Talk* has also resurfaced on *Oil Stains, Vol. 2* (LP). (VJ/MW/SB)

GRANDMA'S ROCKERS - Home Made Apple Pie LP.

Grand Prees

45:	No Time To Lose/This Lovely Day	(Scotty GQP 825) 196?

Average organ punkers from Pittsburgh on the Scotty label, though not the famed Warren Kendrick one. They later recorded as **Grains Of Sand**. (MW)

Grand Prees

45:	Heartbreak Hotel/Four Strong Winds	(Go Go 101) 1964

This **Grand Prees** probably came from Florida / Alabama. (MW)

Grand Theft

Personnel:	JIM BECKETT	drms	A
	PAUL DE BURGIS	vcls, gtr	A
	STEPHEN "BOBO" ROSS	bs	A

ALBUM: 1(A)   GRAND THEFT   (Private Pressing) 1972 R1

NB: (1) reissued on CD with six bonus tracks (Epilogue EP-1004) 1996.

From Washington, an hysterical hard-rock outfit with manic vocals, screaming guitar leads and a strong Led Zeppelin influence. The known copies are in a plain white cover. (SR)

Granfalloon

See the **Laser Pace** entry.

Granicus

Personnel:	WAYNE ANDERSON	ld gtr	A
	JOE BATTAGLIA	drms	A
	DALE BEDFORD	bs	A
	WOODY LEFFEL	vcls, ac. gtr, gtr	A
	AL PINELL	gtr	A

ALBUM: 1(A)   GRANICUS   (RCA Victor AFL 1-0321) 1973 SC

NB: (1) reissued on CD (Free Records 9702).

An obscure hard-rock group from Ohio, which may interest some collectors. In 1975, their drummer produced a flexi-disc by Pandora (Evatone), another hard-rock outfit. (SR/VJ)

Grant's Blueboys

45:	If I Were A Carpenter/ Love Is Such A Game	(Garland GR-2014) 1969

Salem, Oregon's answer to **Blue Cheer**? The 'A' side to this 45 contains an awesome version of **Tim Hardin**'s classic with some savage outbursts of fuzz and distortion. The flip is a comparatively mellow affair but still pretty wicked.

Compilation appearances include: *If I Were A Carpenter* on *High All The Time, Vol. 2* (LP). (MW)

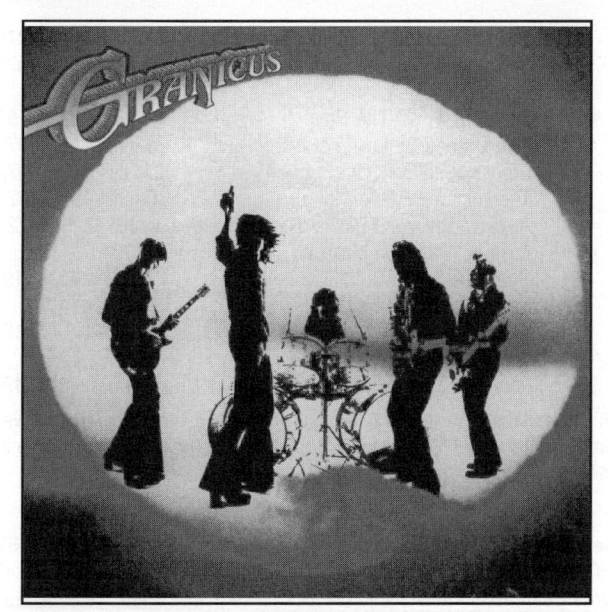

GRANICUS - Granicus CD.

Grapes Of Rath

ALBUM: 1 GLORY (Tarus) 196? R4

A very rare mix of garage fuzz and organ pop from a Pennsylvanian band, which was recorded circa 1968/69.

Compilation appearances include *On The Brink* on *Songs Of Faith And Inspiration* (CDR & CD).

The Grapes of Wrath

Personnel: STEVE (SKELTON) KELLY drms A
            WILLIAM "SONNY" LYLE   bs   A
            HUEY P. MEADOWS   gtr   A
            KENNY WAYNE   ld vcl, gtr A

45: Time Seems To Fly/Baby Come On Home (Koper) 1966

Based in Texarkana, Texas, this band were actually **Kenny Wayne** and his band **The Starchiefs**. The 45 was recorded at Buddy Knox/Ray Ruff's Checkmate studio in Amarillo, Texas in June 1965, but not released until October '66, and then under a different name due to the band changing drummers.

The 45 was recorded while **The Starchiefs** (aka **The Grapes Of Wrath**) were touring West Texas / South-western Oklahoma and the South-west parts of New Mexico on their first trip away from their usual North East Texas / South Eastern Arkansas / South East Oklahoma territory. The 45s 'B' side also featured a black session player on keyboards who used to be booked out as bogus "Booker T" and "Dave Baby Cortez" by Ray Ruff and **Grapes Of Wrath** executive producer Charlie Johnson. Both sides also featured two uncredited female vocalists, who appear on many of Ray Ruff's and Buddy Knox's recordings.

The Koper label was based in Houma, Louisiana.

Wayne was later with **Kenny Wayne And The Kamotions**. (VJ/MW)

The Grapes of Wrath

45: Cauz It Was Her/For Every Year (Vita V-006) 196?

San Pedro, California's **Grapes Of Wrath**'s derivative punker has now been immortalised on *Garage Punk Unknowns, Vol. 7* (LP). There was also a **Grapes Of Wrath** in Wisconsin who had a cut (*Flower Lady*) on sixties compilation *Badger A Go Go*. (MW)

The Grapes of Wrath

Personnel: BRENT BURNS   gtr, vcls   A
            JOHN HESTERMAN   organ, drms, gtr, bs, vcls   A
            MIKE WHITEHURST   ld gtr, vcls   A
            STEVE WHITEHURST drms, gtr, keyb'ds, vcls   A
            STUART WOOD   bs, vcls   A
            BRIAN BLACK   keyb'ds, vcls
            TERRY MERRITT   vcls
            TERRY MITCHELL   gtr, drms, vcls
            BILL MUMFORD   vcls
            GERALD TIETZ   bs
            GREG VANN   bs, vcls
            LANCE WOLF   gtr, vcls

CD: 1 GRAPES OF WRATH (Gear Fab GF-126) 1999

45: If Anyone Should Ask/Not A Man (Storm 2245) 1967

From Phoenix, Arizona this outfit lasted from 1964 thru 1973 and still get together on an annual basis. They released just one 45 and recorded at least a dozen other tracks, which are gathered together on the Gear Fab CD. The excellent power-punk-popper *Have A Good Time On Me*, from 1967, can be heard on *Psychedelic Crown Jewels, Vol. 2* (Dble LP & CD). (MW/RM)

The Grass

45: I'm Getting Tired/Y'love (Goldust 45-5016) 1966

The 'A' side, *I'm Getting Tired* is a catchy garage number written by D. Finn and L. McIntyre. The flip, composed by D. Finn, is a garage waltz (!) proclaiming various female attributes. The label is from University Park, a few miles Northwest of El Paso.

Compilation appearances include: *I'm Getting Tired* on *New Mexico Punk From The Sixties* (LP) and *Sixties Archive, Vol. 4* (CD); and both *I'm Getting Tired* and *Y'love* on *The Goldust Records Story (1965 - 1969)* (CD). (VJ/MW)

Grasshoppers

Personnel incl: BENNY ORZECHOWSKI (AKA BENNY ORR) A

45s: α Mod Socks/Twin Beat   (Sunburst 104) 1965
        Pink Champaign (And Red Roses)/?   (Sunburst 105) 196?

NB: α thought to also have been licensed to Warner Bros.

A cool garage band from Cleveland. *Mod Socks*, which was a sizeable radio hit in Cleveland, is a neat garagey update of *Short Shorts* (by the

THE GRAPES OF WRATH - Grapes Of Wrath CD.

Royal Teens). It sounds better than you might think. The flip, *Twin Beat*, is an upbeat instrumental.

You can also find *Pink Champaign* on *Pride Of Cleveland Past* (LP).

Benny Orzechowski (AKA Benny Orr), later formed the Cars! (KSI)

The Grass Roots

Personnel:
	BILL FULTON	vcls	A
	CREED BRATTON	ld gtr	B
	RICK COONCE	drms	BC
	WARREN ENTNER	vcls, gtr, keyb'ds	BCD
	ROB GRILL	ld vcls, bs	BCDE
	TERRY FURLONG	ld gtr	CD
	DENNY PROVISOR	keyb'ds	C E
	REED KAILING	ld gtr	D
	JOEL LARSON	drms	DE
	VIRGIL WEBBER	keyb'ds	D
	REGGIE KNIGHTON	gtr, vcls	E

ALBUMS: (up to 1975)

			HCP
1	WHERE WERE YOU WHEN I NEEDED YOU	(Dunhill D(S) 50011) 1966	- SC
2	LET'S LIVE FOR TODAY	(Dunhill D(S) 50020) 1967	75 -
3	FEELINGS	(Dunhill D(S) 50027) 1968	- -
4	GOLDEN GRASS (Comp.)	(Dunhill DS 50047) 1968	25 -
5	LOVIN' THINGS	(Dunhill DS 50052) 1969	73 -
6	LEAVING IT ALL BEHIND	(Dunhill DS 50067) 1969	36 -
7	MORE GOLDEN GRASS (Comp.)	(Dunhill DS 50087) 1970	152 -
8	TEMPTATION EYES	(Dunhill) 1970	- -
9	THEIR 16 GREATEST HITS	(Dunhill DSX 50107) 1971	58 -
10	MOVE ALONG	(Dunhill DSX 50112) 1972	86 -
11	A LOT OF MILEAGE	(Dunhill DSX 50137) 1973	- -
12(E)	GRASS ROOTS	(Haven ST-9204) 1975	- -

NB: (4) and (6) were also released in the U.K. and in France by Stateside. The following compilations were released: *The ABC Collection* (ABC AC-30003) 1976, *Powers Of The Night* (MCA 5331) 1982, *Greatest Hits, Vol. 1* and *Vol. 2* (MCA) 1987, *Anthology 1965-1975* (Rhino) 1991 and *All-Time Greatest Hits* (MCA) 1996. (1) was reissued in 1995 (Varese Vintage) with 6 bonus tracks.

45s:

		HCP
Mr. Jones (The Ballad Of A Thin Man)/ You're A Lonely Girl	(Dunhill 4013) 1965	121
Where Were You When I Needed You/ These Are Bad Times	(Dunhill 4029) 1966	28
Only When You're Lonely/ This Is What I Was Made For	(Dunhill 4043) 1966	96
Look Out, Girl/Tip Of My Tongue	(Dunhill 4053) 1967	-
Let's Live For Today/Depressed Feeling	(Dunhill 4084) 1967	8
Things I Should Have Said/ Tip Of My Tongue	(Dunhill 4094) 1967	23
Wake Up, Wake Up/No Exit	(Dunhill 4105) 1967	68
A Melody For You/Hey Friend	(Dunhill 4122) 1968	123
Feelings/Here's Where You Belong	(Dunhill 4129) 1968	-
Midnight Confessions/ Who Will You Be Tomorrow	(Dunhill 4144) 1968	5
Bella Linda/Hot Bright Lights	(Dunhill 4162) 1969	28
All Good Things Come To An End/ Melody For You	(Dunhill) 1969	-
Lovin' Things/ You and Love Are All The Same	(Dunhill 4180) 1969	49
The River Is Wide/ (You Gotta) Live For Love	(Dunhill 4187) 1969	31
Who Will You Be Tomorrow/ Midnight Confessions	(Dunhill) 1969	-
I'd Wait A Million Years/ Fly Me To Havana	(Dunhill 4198) 1969	15
Heaven Knows/Don't Remind Me	(Dunhill 4217) 1969	24
Walking Through The Country/ Truck Drivin' Man	(Dunhill 4227) 1970	44
Baby, Hold On/Get It Together	(Dunhill 4237) 1970	35
Come On and Say It/ Something's Comin' Over Me	(Dunhill 4249) 1970	61
Temptation Eyes/Keepin' Me Down	(Dunhill 4263) 1970	15
Sooner Or Later/ I Can't Turn Off The Rain	(Dunhill 4279) 1971	9
Two Divided By Love/Let It Go	(Dunhill 4289) 1971	16
Glory Bound/Only One	(Dunhill 4302) 1972	34
The Runaway/Move Along	(Dunhill 4316) 1972	39
Anyway The Wind Blows/Monday Love	(Dunhill 4325) 1972	107
Love Is What You Make It/ Someone To Love	(Dunhill 4335) 1973	-
Look But Don't Touch/ Where There's Smoke There's Fire	(Dunhill 4345) 1973	-
We Can't Dance To Your Music/ Look But Don't Touch	(Dunhill 4371) 1973	-

NB: There's also a rare French EP with PS: *Where Were You When I Needed You/These Are Bad Times/Ballad Of A Thin Man/You're A Lonely Girl* (RCA 8906) 1966.

The Grass Roots was originated by the writer/producer team of **P.F. Sloan** and Steve Barri as a pseudonym under which they would release a body of **Byrds**/**Beau Brummels**-style folk-rock. **Sloan** and Barri were contracted songwriters for Trousdale Music, the publishing arm of Dunhill Records, which wanted to cash in on the folk-rock boom of 1965. Dunhill asked **Sloan** and Barri to come up with this material and a group alias under which they would release it. The resulting **Grass Roots** debut song, *Where Were You When I Needed You*, sung by **Sloan**, was sent to a Los Angeles radio station, which began playing it. The problem was, there was no **Grass Roots**. The next step was to recruit a band that could become **The Grass Roots**. **Sloan** found a San Francisco group called The Bedouins that seemed promising on the basis of their lead singer, Bill Fulton. Fulton recorded a new vocal over the backing tracks laid down for the **P.F. Sloan** version of the song. The Bedouins were, at first, content to put their future in the hands of **Sloan** and Barri as producers. However, the rest of the group were offended when Fulton was told to record their debut single, a cover of Bob Dylan's *The Ballad Of A Thin Man*, backed by studio musicians. When that single, released in October of 1965, became only a modest hit, The Bedouins - except for their drummer, Joel Larson - departed for San Francisco, to re-form as The Unquenchable Thirst. **Sloan** and Barri continued to record and released *Where Were You When I Needed You*. The album never charted.

Amid the machinations behind *Where Were You When I Needed You*, no "real" **Grass Roots** band existed in 1966. A possible solution came along when a Los Angeles band called The 13th Floor submitted a demo tape to Dunhill. This group, consisting of Warren Entner, Creed Bratton, Rob Grill, and Rick Coonce, were recruited and put in the hands of **Sloan** and Barri. The first track cut by the new **Grass Roots** in the Spring of 1967 was *Let's Live For Today*, a new version of a song that had been an Italian hit, in a lighter, more up-tempo version, for a U.K. band called The Rokes. *Let's Live For Today* was an achingly beautiful, dramatic, and serious single and it shot into the Top 10 upon its release in the Summer of 1967. An accompanying album, *Let's Live For Today*, only reached number 75. The

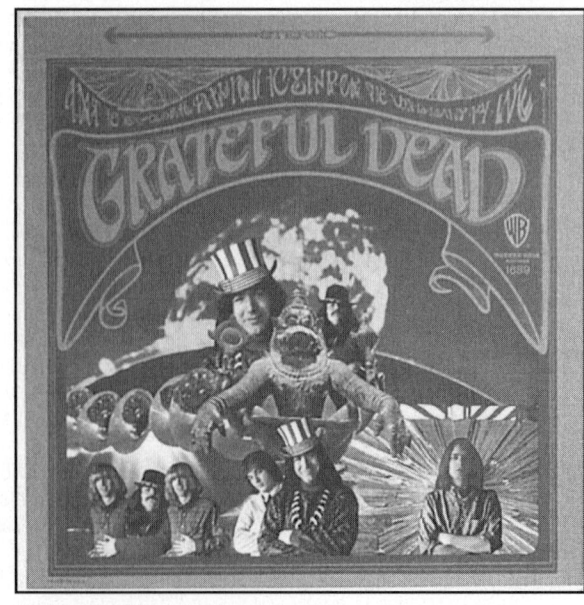

GRATEFUL DEAD - The Grateful Dead LP.

group began spreading its wings in the studio with their next album, *Feelings*, recorded late in 1967, which emphasised the band's material over **Sloan** and Barri's. This was intended as their own statement of who they were, but it lacked the commercial appeal of anything on *Let's Live For Today*, sold poorly and never yielded any hit singles. Eleven months went by before the group had another chart entry, and during that period, **Sloan** and Barri's partnership broke up, with **Sloan** departing for New York and an attempt at a performing career of his own. The band even considered splitting up as all of this was happening. **The Grass Roots**' return to the charts (with Barri producing), however, was a triumphant one - in the late Fall of 1968, *Midnight Confessions* reached number 5 on the charts and earned a gold record. *Midnight Confessions* showed the strong influence of motown and R&B.

In April 1969, Creed Bratton left the band, to be replaced by Denny Provisor (ex-**Hook**) and Terry Furlong. Now a quintet, they went on cutting records without breaking stride, enjoying a string of Top 40 hits that ran into the early seventies, peaking with *Temptation Eyes* at number 15 in the Summer of 1971. Coonce and Provisor left at the end of 1971, to be replaced by Reed Kailing, Virgil Webber, and Joel Larson - of the original Bedouins/**Grass Roots** outfit. They arrived just in time to take advantage of the number 16 success of *Two Divided By Love*, which was the last of the **Grass Roots**' big hits. **The Grass Roots** soldiered on for a few more years, reaching the Top 40 a couple of times in 1972, but their commercial success slowly slipped away during 1973. They kept working for a few more years, but called it quits in 1975.

Compilation appearances have included: *Where Were You When I Needed You* on *Nuggets, Vol. 5* (LP); *Only When You're Lonely* on *Nuggets, Vol. 10* (LP); *Let's Live For Today* on *Nuggets, Vol. 11* (LP); *Mr. Jones (Ballad Of A Thin Man)* on *Nuggets, Vol. 6* (LP); *Feelings* on *Nuggets, Vol. 9* (LP); *Let's Live For Today* and *You're A Lonely Girl* on *Penny Arcade, Dunhill Folk Rock, Vol. 2* (LP); *You're A Lonely Girl* on *Turds On A Bum Ride, Vol. 4* (CD); *Get It Together* and *I'm Living For You Girl* on *Undersound Uppersoul* (LP); *Let's Live For Today* and *Only When You're Lonely* on *Even More Nuggets* (CD); *Is It Any Wonder, Out Of Touch, Things I Should Have Said, Wake Up Wake Up* (1967) on *Dunhill Folk Rock 1*. (MW/SR)

The Grateful Dead

Personnel:	JERRY GARCIA	gtr, vcls	ABCDE
(up to	BILL KREUTZMANN	drms	ABCDE
1972)	PHIL LESH	bs	ABCDE
	RON 'PIGPEN' McKERNAN	harp, piano	ABCDE
	BOB WEIR	gtr	ABCDE
	TOM CONSTANTEN	keyb'ds	B
	MICKEY HART	perc	BC
	ROBERT HUNTER	lyrics	BCDE
	DONNA GODCHAUX	vcls	E
	KEITH GODCHAUX	keyb'ds	E
	(MERLE SAUNDERS	keyb'ds	D)

				HCP
ALBUMS:	1(A)	THE GRATEFUL DEAD	(Warner Bros. 1689) 1967	73 -
(up to	2(B)	ANTHEM OF THE SUN	(Warner Bros. 1749) 1968	87 -
1972)	3(B)	AOXOMOXOA	(Warner Bros. 1790) 1969	73 -
	4(B)	LIVE/DEAD	(Warner Bros. 1830) 1970	64 -
	5(B)	WORKINGMAN'S DEAD	(Warner Bros. 1869) 1970	27 -
	6(C)	AMERICAN BEAUTY	(Warner Bros. 1893) 1970	30 -
	7(A)	VINTAGE DEAD	(Sunflower 5001) 1970	127 -
	8(A)	HISTORIC DEAD	(Sunflower 5004) 1971	154 -
	9(D)	THE GRATEFUL DEAD	(Warner Bros. 1935) 1971	25 -
	10(E)	EUROPE '72	(Warner Bros. 3 x 2662) 1972	24 -

NB: (1) to (6) also released in France by Vogue/Warner. Recent releases which may interest collectors include *Freshly Dead*, a limited edition double live LP from 1966 when they were known as The Warlocks; *Garcia's Gang*, a limited edition 2-LP set from 1971 and *Seastones*, an ultra-rare and weird LP of electronics involving Phil Lesh which has recently had a limited reissue. *Steppin' Out With The Grateful Dead, England 1972* (Grateful Dead/Arista GDCD 4084) 2002 is a 4-CD box set of seven shows from their 1972 England tour. This is essential for deadheads.

			HCP
45s:	α	Don't Ease Me In/Stealin'	(Scorpio 201) 1966 -
(up to		The Golden Road (To Unlimited Devotion)/	
1972)		Cream Puff War	(Warner Bros. 7016) 1967 -
		Born Cross-Eyed/Dark Star (PS)	(Warner Bros. 7186) 1968 -

GRATEFUL DEAD - Anthem Of The Sun LP.

Dupree's Diamond Blues/ Cosmic Charlie	(Warner Bros. 7324) 1969 -
Uncle John's Band/ New Speedway Boogie	(Warner Bros. 7410) 1970 69
Truckin'/Ripple	(Warner Bros. 7464) 1970 64
Johnny B. Goode/ So Fine (by Elvin Bishop)	(Warner Bros. 7627) 1972 -
Sugar Magnolia/Mr. Charlie	(Warner Bros. 7667) 1972 91

NB: α counterfeited in the early 1980s. The original pressing has thinner vinyl than the fake, and "commercial recorders, inc" appears mechanically stamped in the trail-off.

Along with **Jefferson Airplane**, The '**Dead** were the other foremost San Francisco underground group.

Jerry Garcia's first guitar was electric and his idol was Chuck Berry. He met Robert Hunter, their non-performing songwriter, at San Mateo Junior College, forming a blue-grass group with him called The Wildwood Boys. Earlier, **Garcia** had met **Bob Weir** and Ron McKernan (nicknamed Pigpen) while playing on the coffee house circuit in the Bay Area. Pigpen and Bill Kreutzmann, who **Garcia** had also met when working in a music shop, were forming a rock group called The Zodiacs. The Wildwood Boys changed their name to The Hart Valley Drifters and starred at the 1963 Monterey folk festival. **Garcia**'s next group, Mother McCree's Uptown Jug Champions included Pigpen, Dawson and **Bob Weir**, they later changed their name first to The Asphalt Jungle Boys and then to The Warlocks. Kreutzmann replaced Dawson as the group's drummer and Phil Lesh was invited to play bass. This format played in Bill Graham's benefit concert for the Mime Troupe at the Fillmore.

The Warlocks had thus come from diverse musical backgrounds. Phil Lesh had a classical background, (violin and trumpet), Pigpen's father had been an R&B player and Bill Kreutzmann had been a jazz drummer. **Garcia**, himself, had played mainly bluegrass. The Warlock's early music was rooted in the blues, but under the influence of acid (legal in California until 1966) their music became less conventional. They became the house band for Ken Kesey's Merry Pranksters and the Acid Freaks associated with them. This period is well-documented in Tom Wolfe's book "The Electric Kool Aid Acid Test". A bootleg does exist of The Warlocks' music, which was apparently recorded in Los Angeles in May 1965. The strange times in which The Warlocks operated suggested the need for a 'trippier' name and, after browsing through a dictionary one day, the band came up with **The Grateful Dead**. Their association with the Merry Pranksters soon diminished following Kesey's drug bust trial, conviction and his flight to Mexico. They soon became an important force in the new exciting San Francisco music scene.

The Grateful Dead played their first gig at Magoo's Pizza Parlour in June 1965. Soon they were playing all over town - the Matrix, the Avalon, the Fillmore - at all the major dance venues. They were, of course, the key attraction at Ken Kesey's Fair Day Trips Festival held at the Longshoreman's Hall in January 1966. Despite the outrageous dress, the

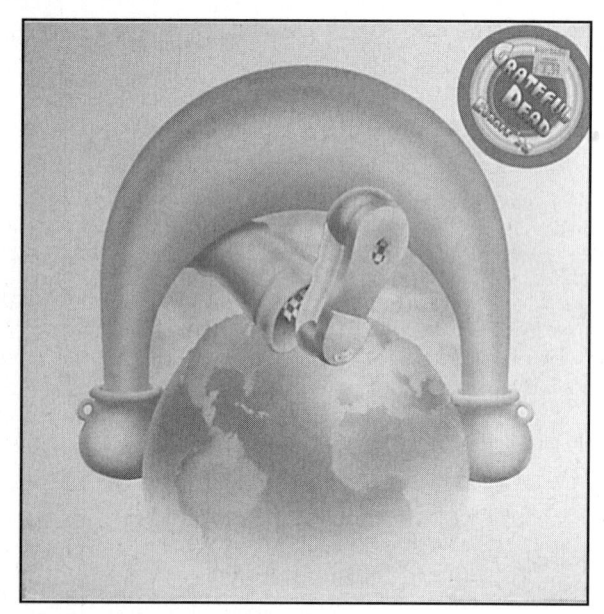

THE GRATEFUL DEAD - Europe 72 LP.

drugs and the light shows, the success of this festival was really due to the music. **The Dead** were now playing the long, trip-orientated instrumental sets for which they became renown. Such events helped their development as a community group, often playing around the city for free. Their first recording *Don't Ease Me In* was issued in 1966, by a subsidiary label of Fantasy Records. Apparently unexceptional, copies are now rare and change hands for large sums. In the early seventies, two albums - *Vintage Dead* (Sunflower 5001) 1970 and *Historic Dead* (Sunflower 5004) 1971, which were issued by Polydor in the U.K. - were released and contained material from this era in the group's history. They contain the band's interpretations of numbers such as *Dancing In The Street*, *Good Morning Little Schoolgirl* and *In The Midnight Hour*.

The publicity that events on the U.S. West Coast were attracting led to a race among the major record companies to sign up all of the major West Coast bands. **The Dead** signed for Warner Brothers - in many ways an odd choice and, in retrospect, probably the wrong one for the band. Their first album was disappointing, both in comparison with their live shows and with the early offerings of their counterparts like **The Jefferson Airplane**, **Country Joe and the Fish** and **The Steve Miller Band**. Its strongest track, *The Golden Road (To Unlimited Devotion)* was coupled with *Cream Puff War* on an US-only single (WB 7016) in 1967. This is now rare. The album, which had been recorded in three days, sold badly and to make matters worse LSD was made illegal in California and the group was inevitably busted. The band was getting into debt too but Lenny, father of **Mickey Hart**, who had recently joined the group as its percussionist, now became its manager. Later in 1970 they would have to file an embezzlement charge against Lenny Hart and replace him with John MacIntyre.

Two more psychedelic albums followed - *Anthem Of The Sun* and *Aoxomoxoa*. The first typified the long instrumentally-orientated pieces they had been playing at the Acid Tests. *Born Cross Eyed* was taken from the album, backed with a non-album track, *Dark Star* and issued as a single (WB 7186), which is also very rare. In America it was issued with a picture sleeve, although this was not a feature of U.K. copies. The picture sleeve version is now particularly sought-after by **Grateful Dead** collectors.

Aoxomoxoa is particularly memorable for its cover. A disjointed album overall, it does contain some interesting experiments in psychedelia, such as *Rosemary* and a few quite strong tracks such as *St. Stephen, Mountains Of The Moon*, and *Dupree's Diamond Blues*. Evidently, **The Dead** were unhappy with both albums, and Phil Lesh remixed and re-edited both in the early seventies.

Once again, commercially and in comparison with the offerings of their West Coast counterparts, both *Anthem Of The Sun* and *Aoxomoxoa* were disappointing.

Almost inevitably recording success eluded them until they issued *Live Dead*, a double album, in 1970. This showed them at their best, performing long, predominantly instrumental, improvised songs and included the legendary *Dark Star*, as well as *St. Stephen* and *Death Don't Have No Mercy*.

Eventually in 1970 they came up with two successful studio albums. The first, *Workingman's Dead* contained a number of short, well-constructed acoustic country-rock songs such as *Uncle John's Band* (also issued as a single), *Black Peter* and *Casey Jones*. The latter having a very catchy chorus:-

"Driving that train
High on cocaine
Casey Jones you'd better watch your speed
Trouble ahead, trouble behind
And you know that notion just caught my mind......."
(from *Casey Jones*)

The follow-up *American Beauty* also contained a number of tight songs, including a love song *Sugar Magnolia* and the autobiographical *Truckin*, which recounted the events of a year in which they had been busted again (this time in New Orleans) and had sacked their manager. They had also played their first European date at a festival near Newcastle-Under-Lyme in England. These three were the best of their early albums. Prior to *American Beauty*, Constanten, who was into scientology, left the band to concentrate on his studies. The following year a second 'live' double album was issued. Warner Brothers vetoed its original name *Skullfuck* and it became called simply *Grateful Dead*. This became their first album to go gold.

As a 'live' band they were now at the pinnacle of their achievement and in May/June of 1972 toured Europe again and issued a triple 'live' album as a record of its finer moments. They played at the Bickershaw Festival outside a depressing mining town in the North of England. By the end of the first day the audience were wallowing in mud and thoroughly miserable. Yet, gradually **The Dead**'s music won them over and before long the audience was on its feet ecstatic.

The early seventies also saw the departure of **Mickey Hart**, perhaps embarrassed by his father's misappropriation of their finances. However, *Europe 72*, which was not one of their stronger live albums, did feature two new members, Keith Godchaux (keyb'ds) and Donna Godchaux (vcls), on record for the first time.

Upon their return to the States, disaster struck. Pigpen, who had been living on a diet of little more than booze and berries had developed a serious liver disease and accompanied them on the '72 tour against doctor's advice. On 8th March 1973 he died of a stomach haemorrhage. Pigpen had been a key band member, but the group survived this blow and went on to record numerous albums throughout the seventies and into the nineties, until sadly, **Jerry Garcia** died on the 9th August, 1995.

Jerry Garcia, **Bob Weir**, Robert Hunter and **Mickey Hart** all made solo albums during the seventies. Keith and Donna Godchaux also made an unsuccessful album in 1975, whilst, earlier in the same year, Phil Lesh combined with Ned Lagin to make the *Seastones* album. Keith Godchaux was killed in a car crash in the late seventies.

The Dead have certainly proved a durable outfit. Their 'laid-back' music lacked the urgency of **The Airplane**, but was sufficiently unique to secure a

THE GRATEFUL DEAD - Live Dead CD.

THE GRATEFUL DEAD - American Beauty CD.

strong cult following. The secret of their success appears to have been their ability to adapt to the changing times and, in September/October 1981 they were in England playing three nights to packed audiences at London's Rainbow Theatre. Of the numerous compilations of their material, *Skeletons From The Closet* originally issued by Warner Bros in 1979 and reissued on Thunderbolt (THBL 01 8) in 1987, is a good introduction to their music from the early years.

More difficult to find but also of interest to 'deadheads' will be *California Christmas*, which features a version of *Turn On Your Lovelight* with Janis Joplin. *California Easter* has two tracks with them joining The Beach Boys(!) - *Riot In Cell Block Number 9* and *Searchin'*; two numbers (including *Hoochie Koochie Man* from 1963) performed by Pigpen and Pete Albin and two numbers by Jerry and Sarah Garcia, also from around 1963. *California New Year* includes *Uncle John's Band*.

You can also find a version of *Dark Star* on the *Zabriski Point* soundtrack. (VJ)

Graven Image

| 45: | I Would But I Could/Take A Bite Of Life | (V.O.L. 134) 1967 |

This 45 was a minor San Antonio outfit's sole stab at immortality - the 'A' side is an Augie Meyer penned dirge but the flip, *Take A Bite Of Life*, is good uptempo garage with a Diddleyesque beat.

Compilation appearances include: *Take A Bite Of Life* on *Mindblowing Encounters Of The Purple Kind* (LP), *Teenage Shutdown, Vol. 14* (LP & CD) and *Fuzz, Flaykes, And Shakes, Vol. 2* (LP & CD). (MW)

Nick Gravenites

Personnel:	DINO ANDINO	conga	A
	MIKE BLOOMFIELD	gtr, vcls	AB
	JOHN CIPOLLINA	gtr	A
	SNOOKY FLOWERS	baritone sax	A
	NICK GRAVENITES	vcls, gtr	AB
	NOEL JEWKES	tenor sax	A
	BOB JONES	drms	A
	JOHN KAHN	bs	AB
	IRA KAMIN	organ	A
	MARK NAFTALIN	keyb'ds	A
	GERALD OSHITA	baritone sax	A
	JOHN WILMETH	trumpet	A
	PAUL BUTTERFIELD	vcls, hrmnca	B
	MARIA MULDAUR	vcls	B
	CHRISTOPHER PARKER	drms	B
	ANNIE SAMPSON	vcls	B
	MERL SAUNDERS	keyb'ds	B

| ALBUMS: | 1(A) | MY LABORS | (Columbia CS 9899) 1970 SC |
| | 2(B) | STEELYARD BLUES | (Warner BS 2662) 1972 - |

| 45: | Theme from (Drive Again)/ | |
| | My Bag (The Oysters) | (Warner WB 7637) 1972 |

Originally from Chicago, **Nick Gravenites** moved to San Francisco and became a central figure in the Bay Area scene. Songwriter, singer, guitar player and producer, **Gravenites** is sometimes credited as Nick The Greek or Nicky Gravy. He was (and still is) a multi-talented man. Primarily known for penning *Born In Chicago* and *East-West* for the **Paul Butterfield Blues Band** on their first two albums (1965/66), he became a close friend of **Mike Bloomfield** and naturally became the lead singer of the **Electric Flag** when it was formed.

During the same period, he began working with **Quicksilver Messenger Service**, providing some of their songs (*All Night Worker*, on *Live In San Jose* and *Joseph's Coat* on *Shady Grove*) as well as producing their first album. After the demise of the **Electric Flag**, **Gravenites** became the lead singer of **Big Brother and The Holding Company** when Joplin left. He produced their underrated *Be A Brother* album as well as writing several songs for it. He also made a guest appearance on his own *Buried Alive In The Blues* on **Big Brother and The Holding Company**'s final album *How Hard It Is*.

Gravenites first solo album from 1969, *My Labors*, was partly recorded live. It was a commercial failure, largely due to a horrid cover, but still really deserves to be heard if you like electric West Coast blues. **Mike Bloomfield**'s solos are truly remarkable on the live tracks and John Cipollina is one of the "anonymous friends" playing on the studio cuts. The album was produced by Elliot Mazer.

In 1972, *Steelyard Blues* was in fact the soundtrack of a Jane Fonda/Donald Sutherland movie and contains only original bluesy tracks which were mostly written by **Gravenites** and Bloomfield. (**Gravenites** also produced the album). Two tracks from the album were also released as a 45.

Nick Gravenites production credits also include **Brewer and Shipley**, Chet McNicholls, Southern Comfort and several blues albums (Sam Lay, Otis Rush).

In the seventies, **Gravenites** kept on working with Bloomfield until he died. In the eighties, he formed the Gravenites/Cipollina Band (also known as Thunder and Lightning) and still performs, produces and records to this day. His current group, Animal Mind, features Roy Blumenfeld (ex-**Blues Project**). (SR)

Jesse Graves

| ALBUM: | 1 | JESSE GRAVES | (Gazebo) 1972 SC? |

From Philadelphia, a rare album of bluesy folk on a local label. (SR)

Graveyard 5

45s:	The Marble Orchard/	
	Untitled(Graveyard Five Theme)	(Stanco 102) 1968
	The Sure Way/?	(Dental Records) 196?

From Kelseyville/Cobb in Northern California. *Pebbles, Vol. 16* (LP) features both sides of the first 45, which is ridiculousy rare. The second 45 and its full details remain even more elusive. *Marble Orchard* begins with a heartbeat, has a mystical quality and good acid guitar - with better production it could have been a real classic. The flip is a fine reverb-fuzz instrumental. (VJ/MW/AP)

The Gravity Adjusters Expansion Band

| ALBUM: | 1 | ONE | (Nocturne) 1973 R1 |

From Los Angeles, a rare and strange album of avant-garde and experimental music, released in a cool black and white psych cover. (SR)

The Grayps

Personnel:	MIKE BAUMANN	drms	ABC
	CHARLIE CESNER	vcls	ABC
	BUD DILLAHUNT	vcls, gtr, 12-str gtr	ABC
	DON KETTELER	bs	ABC
	ED MIKUSA	vcls	ABC
	TOM RAMSEYER	gtr	A
	MIKE MEYER	gtr	B
	STERLING SMITH	organ, piano	C

45: Leader Of The Band /You Came Up With The Sun (Cobblestone Records CB 711) 196?

The Grayps started in 1965 out of Whetstone High School in Columbus Ohio, with members of The New Liberty Singers, and The Sceptors. Mike Meyer left in September 1966, with Sterling Smith joining from **The Lowbrows**.

Strong vocals gave the band a good "folk-rock" quality. The band wrote a number of songs, but only one was released as as a single, *Leader Of The Band* on a Buddah Records subsidiary.

The Grayps won the 1966 Northland Battle of the Bands in Columbus Ohio and in 1967 they backed up Sonny and Cher for four grandstand shows at the Ohio State Fair. They also opened for a number of concerts in central Ohio, including The Beach Boys (twice), **The McCoys**, **The Byrds**, Bobby Goldsboro, and **Paul Revere and The Raiders**.

The band played a number of college dates in the late sixties, and was infused with more ambitious original music with the addition of Jon Townley on guitar, and Bill Grey on vocals in 1969. Dan Lawson also played sax and sang with the band in 1969, and would later surface in the band, **Osiris**.

The Grayps re-formed in the early seventies and enjoyed some success in the studio, releasing *She Said She Gave Me Applause* which got some airplay and an appearance on Cleveland television.

Sterling Smith later played with **J.D. Blackfoot**, **Osiris** and **The Load**. (VJ/SGgSmith)

The Gray Things

45: Charity/Lovers Melody (Laurie 3367) 1966

The 'A' side of this late sixties release, which seems to have been their sole recording venture for Laurie, can be heard on *Mindrocker, Vol. 3* (LP) or *Psychedelic Unknowns, Vol. 5* (LP & CD). Seething vocals and tidy harmonies supplant a novel garage styled keyboard backing. Thought to be from New York though Florida has also been suggested. (VJ/MW)

GREAT SOCIETY - Conspicuous Only In It's Absence LP.

Great Bear

Personnel:	MICHAEL BOBAK	keyb'ds, vcls	A
	JOHN GONSKA	gtr	A
	BOB GRYZIEC	bs	A
	PAUL METZGER	drms, perc, vcls	A

ALBUM: 1(A) GREAT BEAR (Scepter SPS 585) 1971 -

Not a well-known album, but a pleasant collection of psychy keyboard-dominated MOR rock of which *Cinderella* is probably the finest moment. Another highlight is their hard-rock cover of Chuck Berry's *Almost Grown*. The songwriting on the album isn't bad but the lead singer, Michael Bobak, has an annoying vibrato similar to Erik Brann's warblings on the two mid-seventies **Iron Butterfly** reunion albums for MCA.

One track was composed by Joseph Longeria who also recorded as **Joseph**.

This act should **not** be confused with the outfit that graces the *Strangers In A Strange Land* compilation, who in fact hailed from Delhi, India.... The Indian act won a place on one of two Simla Beat compilations, funded by an Indian Tobacco company. The best tracks from these were subsequently recompiled as *Strangers From A Strange Land*, and mistakenly sold by dealers as a U.S. compilation. (VJ/RBn)

The Great Believers

Personnel:	AMOS BOYNTON	drms	A
	DAVE RUSSELL	bs	A
	EDGAR WINTER	keyb'ds	A
	JOHNNY WINTER	gtr, vcls	A

45: Comin' Up Fast (Part 1)/(Part 2) (Cascade 365) 196?

Originally known as **Amos Boynton and The ABCs** this Houston-based quartet was an early outing for the Winter Brothers who had previously played together in Black Plague. The band also recorded another **Johnny Winter** composition, *Easy Lovin' Girl*, backing **Roy Head**.

Compilation appearances include: *Comin' Up Fast (Part 1)* on *Mindrocker, Vol. 4* (LP) and *Acid Visions* (LP); and *Comin' Up Fast (Part 1)* and *Easy Lovin' Girl* on *Acid Visions - The Complete Collection Vol. 1* (3-CD). (VJ)

The Great Imposters

45: Who Do You Love?/ I Wanna Be Your Driver (PS) (Dads 6-6602) 1966

This rock foursome came from Omaha, Nebraska and their powerful rendition of Bo Diddley's classic *Who Do You Love?* can be found on *Monsters Of The Midwest, Vol. 3* (LP). The original 45 came in a picture sleeve which captured the band in full splendour with pegged Italian pants and greased hair. The were previously known as Larry Ray & The Red Tops and were still going in the 1980s. (VJ)

Great Jones

Personnel:	BILLY CADIEUX	gtr	A
	(MERRY CLAYTON	vcls	A)
	(VANETTA FIELDS	vcls	A)
	(JEFF GUTCHEON	keyb'ds	A)
	(CLYDIE KING	vcls	A)
	GARY KILLARUS	drms	A
	DAVID TOLMIE	bs	A

ALBUM: 1(A) ALL BOWED DOWN (Tonsil 4002) 1970 -

45: I'll Keep It With Mine/My Lovin' Woman (Tonsil T-0001) 1971

NB: non LP tracks.

The sleevenotes to this album tell us: 'Great Jones is an odd combination; a jazz-loving guitarist; a blues-freaking drummer; and an ex-folk singing bassist.' Well, the end result is a funk-blues album with at least three decent tracks. The first is opener *Cripple Creek*, with its bouncy bass notes and sharply accentuating drum beats. Superimposed on this are Cadieux's catchy acoustic guitar riffs. The second is the title cut, a funky piano-driven number. Also of note is *I Ain't Got Long*, on which Cadieux contributes some delicate blues guitar which blends well with Tolmie's gutsy vocals. An average album, overall, though. The 45 cuts are non-album.

Their material includes two covers (**Dr. John**'s *United States of Mind*, Sleepy John Estes' *Leaving Trunk*...) plus several good originals penned by Cadieux and Gutcheon. The album was produced by Joe Zagarino and Neville Gerson and recorded in Boston. (VJ/SR)

The Great Metropolitan Steam Band

ALBUM: 1 GREAT METROPOLITAN STEAM BAND
                                                (Decca 75143) 1969 -

NB: (1) also released in the UK (Decca MUPS 403).

45: Blues Ain't Nothin'/
     I Want A Big Butter And Egg Man   (Decca 32590) 1969

A hard group to classify, as their album combines hippie-rock, old-time jazz, folk, pop... (SR)

The Great Society

Personnel: BARD DU PONT   bs   A
            DAVID MINOR   gtr   AB
            DARBY SLICK   ld gtr   AB
            GRACE SLICK   vcls, piano   AB
            JERRY SLICK   drms   AB
            PETER VAN DE GIDER   bs   B

                                                           HCP
ALBUMS: 1(B) CONSPICUOUS ONLY IN ITS ABSENCE
                              (Columbia/CBS 9624) 1968 166 -
        2(B) HOW IT WAS   (Columbia/CBS 9702) 1968 - -
        3(B) SOMEBODY TO LOVE (Harmony 30391) 1971 - -
        4(B) COLLECTOR'S ITEM (Columbia/CBS 30459) 1971 - -

NB: (3) is a reissue of (1). (4) is a reissue of (1) and (2). Also of interest is *Live At The Matrix*, a double LP set; and *Born To Be Burned* (Sundazed SC 11027) 1996, a CD compilation of previously unreleased tracks, plus both sides of their first single.

45s: Someone To Love/Free Advice   (North Beach 1001) 1965
     Sally Go Round The Roses/
     Didn't Think So   (Columbia 44583) 1966

One of the very first San Francisco underground groups. **The Great Society** played at the first dance organised by The Family Dog at The Longshoreman's Hall in 1965. Thereafter, they gigged regularly at the Fillmore, the Avalon, the Matrix and Mother's. The nucleus of the group were Grace, with her unique vocals, her husband Darby and his brother Jerry. They recorded a single for Tom Donahue's North Beach label *Someone To Love*. The first album recorded live at the Matrix is of particular interest in that it contained an early version of Darby's *Somebody To Love* and Grace's *White Rabbit*, which **The Jefferson Airplane** were later to transform into nationwide hits. However, the record company held back its release until after the group had split and Grace had become famous. In addition to *White Rabbit*, Grace also wrote three other songs on the album *Didn't Think So*, *Often As I May* and *Father Bruce* (a tribute to Lenny Bruce). However, the group never made it nationally and when the nucleus of the band resolved to set off for India to learn sitar music Grace was snapped up by **The Airplane** who then really began to develop. Her husband Jerry joined another San Francisco band, **The Final Solution**.

They also had two cuts, *Free Advice* and *Somebody To Love* on the 1968 compilation *San Francisco Roots*.

Peter Van Gelder later played with **Saddhu Brand**.

Big Beat's *Nuggets From The Golden State* CD series has dug up many **Great Society** gems from the vaults - the *Someone To Love* CD has no less than 7 tracks from an October 1965 audition session plus the first 45 coupling and three unreleased 1966 goodies (*Born To Be Burned*, *Daydream Nightmare Love*, *Double Tryptamine Superautomatic Everlovin' Man*, *Father Bruce*, *Free Advice*, *Girl*, *Heads Up*, *Right To Me*, *Someone To Love*, *That's How It Is*, *Where* and *You Can't Cry*). My free advice is get it, and hear the cries of the San Francisco Sound being born.

Other retrospective compilation appearances have included:- *Free Advice* and *Somebody To Love* on *Nuggets, Vol. 7* (LP) and *The Autumn Records Story* (LP); *White Rabbit* on *Psychedelic Dream* (Dble LP); and *Somebody To Love* on *Psychedelic Visions* (CD) and *Microdelia* (CD). (VJ/MW)

The Great Society

45s: She's Got It On Her Mind/Second Day (Dana Lynn 70611) 1967
     She's Got It On Her Mind /
     Second Day   (Counterpart 2613/4) 1967

If garage-folk-rock is your bag, here are two superb examples of the genre on an obscure 45 from Cincinnati, Ohio. Absolute bliss. (MW)

Great White Cane

Personnel: JOHN CLEVELAND HUGHES   keyb'ds   AB
            BOB DOUGHTY   trumpet   AB
            DENNY GERRARD   bs, vcls   AB
            RICK JAMES   vcls   A
            IAN KOJIMA   sax   AB
            SONNY NICHOLAS   gtr, vcls   AB
            ED ROTH   keyb'ds   AB
            NORMAN WELLBANKS   drms   AB

ALBUM: 1 GREAT WHITE CANE   (Lion LN1005) 1972 -

American Rick James formed this band in early 1972 from the ashes of Heaven and Earth (Gerrard and Roth were also members). Thanks to his contacts in Los Angeles - Neil Young, Steve Stills (and **Bruce Palmer**), he managed to win a recording contract with MGM's subsidiary Lion Records.

The band recorded an album in Los Angeles in mid-'72 and then toured with B.B. King (playing around 15-20 state capitals). However, the group was beset with problems from the outset. The album, due to be released two weeks before each concert in the state capitals, was delayed because MGM faced a law suit from RCA. Apparently James had sold the rights (to some of the tracks) to RCA when Heaven and Earth recorded them the previous year. The album was released later in the year, by which point the band had effectively folded.

James, who left the band after a date at Massey Hall in Toronto, later formed a new group called The Stone City Band. The others meanwhile completed the tour without him. Gerrard subsequently joined Mainline's

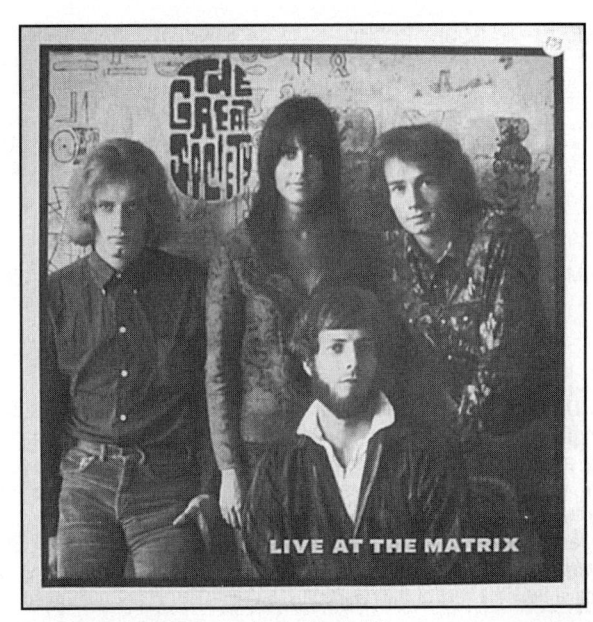

THE GREAT SOCIETY - Live At The Matrix LP.

Bump 'N' Grind Revue tour. Hughes subsequently worked with David Bendeth, Wellbanks played with Shooter and Kojima sessioned for The Stampeders and later played with Chris De Burgh. (NW)

The Greek Fountains

Personnel:	D. CHESON	A
	D. COHEN	A
	T. MICHELI	A
	C. VETTER	A

45s:	Well Alright/That's The Way I Am	(Bofuz BF-1104) 1965
	Howlin' For My Darling/Go Back Home	(Bofuz BF-1110) 1965
	Blue Jean/Countin' The Steps	(Philips 40355) 1966
	I'm A Boy/She Does It	(Pacemaker 250) 1966
	I Can't Get Away/	
	An Experimented Terror	(Montel-Michelle 976) 1966/7
	Buy You A Chevrolet/	
	What Is Right	(Montel-Michelle 983) 1966/7

From Louisiana, this band are best known for upbeat rock recordings like *Blue Jean*, *Buy You A Chevrolet* and *Well Alright*. The *Beyond The Calico Wall* (LP & CD) compilation features their *An Experimented Terror* - a completely wacky recording more in the vein of **Red Krayola** at their most experimental. This could well have been recorded on acid. By contrast, their *I'm A Boy* is a pretty straight cover of The Who hit. They later changed their name to **The Greek Fountain River Front Band**.

Other compilation coverage has included their cover of Willie Dixon's *Howlin For My Baby (The Bo-Hog Song)* on *Teenage Shutdown, Vol. 14 - Howlin' For My Darlin'* (LP & CD). (VJ)

The Greek Fountain River Front Band

Personnel:	D.CHESON	A
	D.COHEN	A
	T. MICHELI	A
	C. VETTER	A

ALBUM:	1(A)	TAKES REQUESTS	(Montel - Michelle 110) 1967/8 SC

45:	High Heeled Sneakers/	
	Warm Daddy's Choice	(Cyclin 0001) 1967/8

This was a later version of **The Greek Fountains**. The album is now rare and sought-after. (VJ)

Green

Personnel:	BOBBY BLOOD	horns	A
	GARY CASEBEER	vcls, horns, drms	AB
	WILSON FISHER	vcls, gtr, hrmnca, bs	AB
	RICHARD GARDZINA	sax, piano	AB
	JOHN MARTIN	gtr, keyb'ds, vcls	AB
	JAMES NEEL	vcls, drms	A
	JAY PRUITT	piano, trumpet	B
	(KATHY KELSEY PRUITT	cello	B)

ALBUMS:	1(A)	GREEN	(Atco SD 33-282) 1969 -
	2(B)	TO HELP SOMEBODY	(Atco SD 33-366) 1971 -

45:	Big Dipper/All My Bells	(Atco 6833) 1971

From Dallas, Texas. Their first album, from 1969 sounds a bit like **Buffalo Springfield** with horns and good lead guitar work. It's beginning to attract some attention. Two years later, a renewed line-up recorded a second album, which is considerably weaker. Most tracks were recorded live in the studio and are more like loose jams with stolen riffs and intrusive horns than real songs. The few good cuts are on the Side One: *All My Bells*, *Teenage Women* and *Can You See Me*, which are more elaborated and attractive than the rest of their material.

In 1974, Jay Pruitt worked with B.W Stevenson and in 1978 with Jules and The Polar Bear. John Martin is not the musician who began with **Southwind**. (SR)

Green Apples Dirty

45:	To The Max/Girl I Miss You So	(Mid-Evyl M 101) 196?

Mildly garagey, a melodic rocker and a ballad, spoilt by the vocalist who sounds like he wants to be a country and western singer on *Max* and Roy Orbison on the flip. From somewhere in Michigan. (MW)

Norman Greenbaum

Personnel:	JOHN COPPOLA		A
	RUSSEL DaSHIELL	gtr	ABC
	NORMAN GREENBAUM	vcls	ABC
	DOUG KILLMER	bs	AB
	NORMAN MAYELL	drms	ABC
	DAN PATIRIS		A
	CHUCK PETERSON		A
	ROBBIE ROBINSON		A
	BILL SABATINI		A
	STOVALL SISTERS	backing vcls	AB
	WILLIAM TRUCKAWAY	keyb'ds, moog	AB
	STEVE BUSFIELD		B
	BILL DOUGLAS	acc. bs	BC
	LYNN ELDER	hurdy gurdy	B
	DAN HICKS	washboard	B
	JOHN McFEE	steel gtr	B
	BILL MEEKER	drms	B
	DAN PAIK	mandolin	B
	SQUIRE	jug	B
	JERRY YESTER	chamberlain	B
	KENNY BURT	banjo	C
	JOHN CASEY	dobro	C
	RY COODER	mandolin, gtr	C
	HENRY DILTZ	glockenspiel	C
	CYRUS FARYAR	gtr	C
	MARK NAFTALIN	accordian	C
	RICHARD OLSEN	clarinet	C
	FRITZ RICHMOND	bs	C

HCP

ALBUMS:	1(A)	SPIRIT IN THE SKY	(Reprise RS 6365) 1969 23 -
	2(B)	BACK HOME AGAIN	(Reprise RS 6422) 1970 - -
	3(C)	PETALUMA	(Reprise MS 2084) 1972 - -

TEENAGE SHUTDOWN Vol. 14 (Comp CD) including The Greek Fountains.

GREENWOOD, CURLEE AND CLYDE - Onetime, Oneplace LP

45s:	Spirit In The Sky/Milk Cow	(Reprise RA 0885) 1969 (Germany)
	Spirit In The Sky/	
	Tars Of India	(Reprise RV 20237) 1970 (France)
	I.J FOXX/Rhode Island Red	(Reprise RV 20255) 1969 (France)
	Canned Ham/Junior Cadillac	(Reprise RV 20245) 1970 (France)
	California Earthquake/	
	Rhode Island Red	(Reprise 14085) 1970 (France)

NB: *California Earthquake* is non-LP.

Originally from Boston, **Norman Greenbaum** was first known as the leader of **Dr. West's Medicine Show and Junk Band**. He went solo and moved to San Francisco where he hit the big time with *Spirit In The Sky* in 1969. His three albums were produced by Erik Jacobsen (**Lovin Spoonful, Sopwith Camel, Tim Hardin**) and deserve to be heard: friendly vocals, well-structured songs with good lyrics, great guitar parts (courtesy of Russel DaShiell, who later played with **Crowfoot** and the Don Harrison Band) and solid rhythm section for a mix of "good time music", jug band style and West Coast vibes, quite reminiscent of the **Youngbloods** production. *California Earthquake*, one of his best tracks, was only released as a single and announces the "Big One" with a devastating fuzz guitar solo and good lyrics ("My advice to you is to keep your feet off the ground. As long as you're flying, you won't tumble down"). Among his usual back-up group, Norman Mayell and **William "Truckaway" Sievers** were both former members of **The Sopwith Camel**. Several guests played on his albums: two **Charlatans** (Dan Hicks and Richard Olsen), Mark Naftalin (**Butterfield Blues Band/Mother Earth**), Ry Cooder, **Cyrus Faryar** (**Modern Folk Quartet, Zodiac Cosmic Sounds**), Jerry Yester... His last album, *Petaluma*, in 1972, has a great sleeve with an eight-page leaflet (with cartoons, kids, chicken, sheeps, goats and pig pictures!) and clearly announces that **Greenbaum** had decided to settle in Petaluma to pursue his life on the farm with his family (*Grade A Barn, The Day The Well Went Dry, Dairy Queen...*). The album is more acoustic than the two other ones.

Spirit In The Sky has been reissued and covered many times, including a U.K. hit for Dr. & The Medics, but **Greenbaum** apparently left the music business for good. (SR)

Green Beans

45s:	Friction/Superstition	(Mercury 72504) 1965
α	Knock On My Door/Who Needs You	(Tower 237) 1966

NB: α issued in a picture sleeve, with the band looking like a greaser club band, but with green hair!

From the Los Angeles area. *Friction* was later given an R&B make-over by Australia's Missing Links, and their cover version is well worth searchin' out. The original is much more in a laid-back, pop vein. Another track *Who Needs You* is more uptempo, sounding like a case of **The Monkees** meet the garage.

You can find *Friction* and *Who Needs You* on *Pebbles, Vol. 8* (CD), whilst *Who Needs You* also appears on *Highs In The Mid-Sixties, Vol. 20* (LP). (VJ/MW)

The Green Giants

45:	You're Going To Lose That Girl/	
	Pity Me	(Round & Round RR-4501) 1966

A rough cover of the Beatles and a garagey beat-ballad from Omaha, Nebraska. (MM/MW)

Green Lyte Sunday

Personnel incl:	FLY BARLOW		A
	SUSAN DARBY	vcls	A
	JASON HOLLINGER		A
	RICK KALB		A
	MICHAEL LOSEKAMP		A
	JAMES WYATT		A

ALBUM:	1(A)	GREEN LYTE SUNDAY	(RCA) 1970 -

45s:	She's My Lover/Lenore	(King 6178) 1969
	Chelsea Morning/Emmie	(RCA 74-0365) 1970

Although some dealers tend to tag this album as "breezy pop psych", it's only a mediocre pop album with female vocals and covers of Joni Mitchell and Laura Nyro. It was produced by Peter Shelton. (SR)

Green Slime

45:	The Green Slime/Far Beyond The Stars	(MGM 14052) 1969

Green Slime, was used in a sixties movie of the same name. You can also find it on *Songs We Taught The Fuzztones* (LP & CD) and *A Fistful Of Fuzz* (CD). (VJ)

Greenwood, Curlee and Clyde

Personnel:	JOHN CURLEE	vcls, hrmnca, trumpet	A
	DAVE CUSHING	drms	A
	RICHARD GREENWOOD	vcls, sitar, gtr, violin	A
	CHIP HARDING	gtr	A
	REID McLEAN	flute	A
	TONY PAUL	perc	A
	JEFF SCHROEDER	bs	A
	CLYDE THOMPSON	vcls, keyb'ds, gtr	A

ALBUM:	1(A)	ONE TIME ONE PLACE	(No label GC-72105) 1972 R2

This local Minnesota electric folk album contained a couple of great Eastern - influenced tracks. The privately pressed release included an insert with lyrics and photos. (CF)

Greer

Personnel:	DON DIXON	vcls, bs	A
	JIMMY GLASGOW	drms	A
	MICHAEL GREER	gtr, keyb'ds, vcls	A
	ROBERT KIRKLAND	vcls, gtr	A
	WESLEY "BOBBY" LOCKE	drms	A
	DAVID NIBLOCK	bs	A
	MARTY STOUT	piano	A

ALBUM:	1(A)	BETWEEN TWO WORLDS	(Sugarbush 109) 1973 R3

An excellent guitar/organ led progressive hard-rock album by the musicians from **Arrogance**, from North Carolina. The long track *Nights Of Dreams* with its dreamy, atmospheric quality and treated vocals will appeal to psych fans... this track and *Send Me Back*, were recorded in Spring 1971, the remainder (*Long Ago And Not So Far Away, Limey Ladies...*) in Spring 1973, all at Reflection Studios in Charlotte. The album was produced by Roger Branch, Dixon and Kirkland. (CF/SR)

The Gregorians

Personnel incl:	JIM BRICKNER		A
	GREG BURNETT		A

45:	Dialated Eyes/Like A Man	(ABC Paramount 11225) 1969

From Cleveland, Ohio, they were formerly called **The City Squires**. Apart from pulsating keyboard effects that means it's often tagged as 'psych', *Dialated Eyes* is a provocative folkie protest-rock song that targets the sins visited by drink-addicted parents on their offspring:-

"Drunken father beats his son for sipping at his beer,
Will this hypocritical society we fear,
Come to pass,
To pass...
another ice-cube for their glass,
And his mother with the dialated eyes."

A sobering cut, recently compiled on *U-Spaces: Psychedelic Archaeology Vol. 1* (CDR) and *Fuzz Flaykes & Shakes Vol. 1* (LP & CD). The flip is brassy pop-rock with a religious slant. (MW/GGI)

Dale Gregory and The Shouters

45:	Did Ya Need To Know/I Remember	(B-Sharp 271) 1965

Hailed from Sioux Falls, South Dakota with this garage rock 45. They later became **Those Of Us**.

Compilation appearances have included: *Did Ya Need To Know* on *Root '66* (LP) and *Teenage Shutdown, Vol. 4* (LP); *Did Ya Need To Know, I Remember, My Flash On You, Summer Time* and *Suzie Q* on *Rock 'N' Roll Project - A History Of Rock In Sioux Falls 1965-1967* (CD). (VJ)

The Gremlins

Personnel incl:	KARL GEBHARDT (aka KARL X BLUE)	A

45:	Treat Her Right / No Surf	(Liverpool) 1965

From the Chicago area, Karl Gebhardt (Kal-X-Blue) went on to play in **Something Wild**.

The Gremlins

45s:	Wait/Everybody Needs A Love	(No label 8430) 196?
	Corrections/	
	We've Found A Love (PS)	(D & H Productions 90872) 1969

From Elkhart, Indiana, this band played in the '93 Reunion Jam Show with **The Dukes**, **Tikis**, etc.

Wait can also be found on *Teenage Shutdown, Vol. 2* (LP & CD). (PY)

The Grey Stokes

45:	The Legend of Tarzan/?	(Tri Con 2290) 196?

From the District of Columbia, this punk outfit's primitive recording of *The Legend of Tarzan* can be heard on the *Signed, D.C.* (LP) compilation. Its simplicity is rather appealing. (VJ)

Griffin

Personnel:	BRUCE BENTLEY	gtr	A
	JERRY BROWN	drms	A
	VINCE MORTON	keyb'ds	A

ALBUM:	1(A)	THE WORLD'S FILLED WITH LOVE	
			(ABC ABCS 634) 1968 -

45:	Murder In The Cathedral/	
	World's Filled With Love	(ABC 11064) 1968

A flower-power good-time outfit. *Magic Carpet Ride*, not the **Steppenwolf** song, is one of the few highlights on their album, which is a very minor collectable. (VJ)

Griffin

Personnel:	M. BRADY	bs, vcls	A
	G. DUCKWORTH	gtr, vcls	A
	G. GREEN	drms, vcls	A
	(JOHN D'ANDREA	flute	A)
	(JACK ARNOLD	perc	A)
	(GEORGE CLINTON	keyb'ds	A)
	(CECIL HUNT	perc	A)

ALBUM:	1(A)	GRIFFIN	(Romar RM-2001) 1972 -
			HCP

45s:	Calling You/In The Darkness	(Romar 701) 1971 -
	In Spite Of What Is Going On/	
	Music's Calling Me	(Romar 704) 1971 -
	Mississippi Lady/	
	Whatever Happens, Happens	(Romar 707) 1972 114
	Everybody/Light At The End Of The World	(Romar 709) 1972 -

Another **Griffin**, whose only album was released on the small Romar label and produced by John D'Andrea and Bob Marcucci. Recorded in Los Angeles, it include covers of Neil Young's *Down By The River* and Noah's *World Band*.

Duckworth was a competent guitarist but the group obviously doesn't have a precise style and navigates between blues-rock, Doobie Bros. style, to funk, psych and pop with strings and the album is clearly over-produced.

In Spite Of What's Going On is the strongest track but overall, the album is better avoided. One of their 45s, *Mississippi Lady*, made some impression nationally. George Clinton, who played the keyboards, is not the **Parliament/Funkadelic** leader but a California musician who led **Timber** and is present on countless records. (SR/VJ)

The Grifs

45s:	Catch A Ride/In My Life	(AMG 1002) 196?
	Catch A Ride/in My Life	(5-D 007) 196?
	Northbound/Keep Dreamin'	(Palmer 5025) 1968

These 45s were this obscure Michigan band's only stabs for stardom. *Catch A Ride* is by far the poppier of the two, whilst *Keep Dreamin'*, is a really snarlin' throaty, punk screamer.

Compilation appearances have included: *Catch A Ride* on *Michigan Mayhem, Vol. 1* (CD) and *Psychedelic Unknowns, Vol. 5* (LP & CD); and *Keep Dreamin'* on *Back From The Grave, Vol. 7* (Dble LP). (VJ)

The Grim Reaper

Personnel:	JERRY ARNOLD	organ	A
	GLEN HOBART	bs	A
	CHUCK KAYNOR	gtr	A
	ALEX KINSEL	ld vcls	A
	GENE KIRBY	ld gtr	A
	CHESTER SLIMP	drms	A

| 45: | Run And Hide/Not For The Living | (Love 101) 1967 |

NB: limited to 100 copies!

This band played the North side of San Antonio, Texas, from '65 to '70. Described as "the most solid slop rock, freaked out band on the North side", the 'A' side to their rare 45 was a cover of **The Uniques** whilst the flip featured an original.

In their time, they gigged with The Ziltches, Strawbery Alphabet, The Chains, The Ones and The Shackles.

Alex Kinsel and Jerry Arnold are both now sadly deceased. (MW)

Grim Reapers

Personnel:	CHIP GREENMAN	drms	A
	CRAIG MYERS	gtr	A
	RICK NIELSEN	gtr, keyb'ds	A
	TOM PETERSON	bs	A
	JOE SUNDBERG	vcls	A

| 45: | Hound Dog / Cruisin' For Burgers (PS) | (Smack 15) 1967/8 |

A Rockford, Illinois, quintet who were picked up by Epic in 1968. The label rechristened the band **Fuse** and re-released the Smack 45. Their eponymous album followed in January 1969 and sank without trace. **Fuse** was extinguished the following year.

Nielsen and Peterson tried again a few years later and would achieve success, acclaim and prolonged cult status with their power-pop outfit Cheap Trick. (MW)

The Grim Reapers

| 45: | Two Souls/Joanne | (Chalon 1003) 1966 |

A mid-sixties garage band from Los Angeles.

Compilation appearances have included: *Two Souls* on *Garagelands, Vol. 1* (LP) and *Highs In The Mid-Sixties, Vol. 2* (LP); *Joanne* on *Garagelands, Vol. 2* (LP); and both *Joanne* and *Two Souls* on *Garagelands, Vol. 1 & 2* (CD). (VJ)

Grinderswitch

Personnel:	ERNEST CORALLO	gtr, mandolin, vcls	A
	GARLAND JEFFREYS	ld vcls, acoustic gtr	A
	SANFORD KONIKOFF	drms	A
	BOB PIAZZA	bs	A
	STAN SZELEST	pieno, organ, hrmnca, vcls	A
	(RICHARD DAVIS	bs	A)

| ALBUM: | 1(A) | GRINDERSWITCH | (Vanguard) 1970 - |

NB: (1) reissued on CD in France (Fnac/Vanguard 662090) 1992.

| 45: | And Don't Be Late/Way Down Deep | (Vanguard 35104) 1970 |

Produced by Lewis Merenstein (Van Morrison, **Chelsea** etc.), **Grinderswitch** was fronted by the New Yorker Garland Jeffreys, who recruited some experienced musicians to back him up: Sanford Konikoff (**Gentle Soul**, **Bamboo**, **Delaney and Bonnie**...), Stan Szelest (Ronnie Hawkins, Lonnie Mack), Bob Piazza (**Ten Wheel Drive**) plus Richard Davis, one of the best bass players on the New York scene.

Their only album is influenced greatly by The Band and several tracks (like *Father, The Son And The Holy Ghost* or *Dear Jolly Jack*) really sound like outtakes from *Music From Big Pink*. Overall the album is decent but not original enough to retain attention, Jeffrey's vocal style still owing too much to Mick Jagger.

In 1973, Garland Jeffreys would start a rather successful solo career and gain a small following in Europe, particularly in France. He's still occasionally recording. (SR)

The Grodeck Whipperjenny

Personnel:	MARY ELLEN BELL	vcls	A
	JIMMY MADISON	drms	A
	DAVE MATTHEWS	piano, organ, trb	A
	MICHAEL MOORE	bs	A
	KENNY POOLE	gtr, vcls	A

| ALBUMS: | 1(A) | GRODECK WHIPPERJENNY | (People PS-3000) 1970 R2 |
| | 2( ) | SECRET SECOND ALBUM | (Le Fumme Angelo no #) 1997 |

NB: (1) was recently reissued on vinyl.

Recorded in Cincinnati, Ohio, this album was co-produced by Dave Matthews and Ron Lenhoff and was released on James Brown's People label. It's a superb psychedelic/progressive effort which is full of imagination and fresh ideas. Every track is excellent in its own right making it difficult to identify highlights, but *Conclusions* is a superb instrumental and *Evidence For The Existance Of The Unconscious* has fine keyboards and makes interesting use of echoed vocals and discordant guitars.

Grodeck Whipperjenny also appeared as the backing band on James Brown's *Sho Is Funky Down Here* album recorded at or right around the same time. They also backed Brown on a non-album 45 recorded at the same session which included the first version of *Talkin Loud and Sayin Nothin*. This 45 was later withdrawn.

The *Secret Second Album* is an Italian limited edition (of 300) reissue of James Brown's *Sho Is Funky Down Here* album under a different name. (VJ/MMn/MW/GSr/PW)

The Grodes (Tongues of Truth/Spring Fever)

Personnel:	MANNY FREISER	vcls, gtr	ABCD
	RICK LUST	keyb'ds	ABC
	RICH COTA ROBIES	bs	ABCD
	DALE SMITH	ld gtr, vcls	ABCD
	JOHN WHITE	drms	A
	RICH MELLINGER	drms	BCD
	KEITH CRAIG	trombone, keyb'ds	CD
	PATTI McCARRON		

| ALBUM: | 1(A-D) | ROUGH DIAMONDS: HISTORY OF GARAGE BAND MUSIC VOL 2 THE GRODES/ TONGUES OF TRUTH | (Voxx 200.010) 1984 |

THE GRODECK WHIPPERJENNY - Grodeck Whipperjenny LP.

45s:	Uh Huh Girl/I Won't Be There	(Tri-M 1001) 1965
	Cry A Little Longer/	
	She's Got What It Takes	(Tri-M 1002) 1966
	Love Is A Sad Song/I've Lost My Way	(Rally 505) 1966
α	Let's Talk About Girls/	
	You Can't Come Back	(Current 112) 1966
	What They Say About Love/	
	Have Your Cake And Eat It Too	(Impression 114) 1967
	Give Me Some Time/	
	Give Me Some Time (instru.)	(Splitsound SSDG 4) 1967
β	Sand/Give Me Some Time	(Splitsound SSDG 8) 1968

NB: α As Tounges Of Truth. β As Spring Fever.

Originally known at The Hustlers this band changed their name to **The Grodes** one drunken night in Phoenix in 1965. They were one of Tucsons's finest in the mid-to-late sixties. Their first two 45s were issued on a record label which their leader Manny Freiser formed with L.A. promotion man Mike Borchetta and a friend of his, actor Cass Martin. So they called it Tri-M (Manny, Mike, Martin) records. The first 45 climbed to 32 on the local KTKT chart and from hereon KTKT DJ Don Gates became their manager, producer and mentor.

Love Is A Sad Song, a pop ballad, recorded at Audio Recorders, Phoenix, was their biggest chart and sales success. Released in May 1966 it reached No 5 in the KTKT charts. However, **The Grodes** fell out with Don Gates when he announced that their version of *Let's Talk About Girls* which was actually written by Manny was by The Tongues Of Truth without consulting them about this change of name. They sacked him and the 45 reached No 37 in the KTKT charts.

Keith Craig came in on trombone for *(It's True) What They Say About Love* and later replaced Lust on keyboards, but this particular 45 made little impression. *Give Me Some Time* was their big production number, recorded over a period of three or four months - it was a Top Ten hit in Tucson. Their final 45 was recorded under the name *Spring Fever* with the band undecided whether to move to L.A. to advance their career or remain in Tucson. Around this time Patti McCarron, a girl singer, joined the band and she and Freiser left the band to head for L.A. in August 1968 where Patti signed for Liberty and released a 45 *Love Theme From Romeo And Juliet*. Manny signed to United Artists issuing a 45 *On To LA / I Went To California* (Barnaby ZS7 2044) which was recorded in 1969 but not released until 1971.

In August 1970, Patti and Manny married. They also formed the duet Fire and Rain, recording an album for Mercury in 1973 and a single, *Hello Stranger* which reached No 100 in Billboard in May 1973. They also recorded a version of *Born Free* for MGM and an album for 20th Century which was never properly promoted.

The Voxx compilation contains all their 45s except the instrumental version of *Give Me Some Time* and also has excellent liner notes on **The Grodes'** history written by Manny Freiser which this article is based on. It also includes a previously unreleased version of *I Won't Be There* which Manny had recorded in L.A. in 1964 with a different band which included Gary Paxton (gtr) and Mike Friedman (drms). It was produced by Jerry Kasenetz, who later produced a number of successful bubblegum acts such as **Ohio Express** and **1910 Fruitgum Company**.

Dale Smith became the successful owner of a Tucson Construction Company, Rich Cota Robies now works as a credit executive with a San Diego hospital, Rick Lust went in the U.S. Air Force later becoming a commercial pilot and Keith Craig is a carpenter in Tucson. Manny Freiser's *Let's Talk About Girls* was later covered and made famous by **The Chocolate Watchband**.

Cry A Little Longer was also covered by Yard Trauma on their *Music and Must've Been Something I Took Last Night* albums.

Compilation appearances have included: *Love Is A Sad Song* on *Love Is A Sad Song, Vol. 1* (LP); *Let's Talk About Girls* on *Pebbles, Vol. 1* (ESD) (CD) and *Best of Pebbles, Vol. 2* (LP & CD); *Cry A Little Longer* on *Pebbles Box* (5-LP), *Acid Dreams - The Complete 3 LP Set* (3-LP), *Acid Dreams Epitaph* (CD); *Let's Talk About Girls* and *Cry A Little Longer* on *Trash Box* (5-CD); *Alone In This World*, *Cry A Little Longer*, *Give Me Some Time*, *I Won't Be There*, *Let's Talk About Girls*, *Love Is A Sad Song*, *Sand*, *She's Got What It Takes*, *This Is Goodbye*, *Uh Huh, Girl*, *What They Say About Love* and *You Can't Come Back* on *Let's Talk About Girls!* (CD). (VJ)

The Groop

This obscure garage band recorded an acetate at The A&T Studios in Toledo, Ohio. One track, whose title has been suggested as *Alright*, has resurfaced on *Back From The Grave, Vol. 8* (Dble LP) and *Back From The Grave, Vol. 8* (CD). (VJ)

Grootna

Personnel:	JACK BONUS	sax	A
	KELLY BRYAN	bs	A
	SLIM CHANCE	gtr, vcls	A
	DEWEY DAGREAZE	drms, vcls	A
	ANNA RIZZO	vcls, ld finger	A
	VIC SMITH	gtr, vcls	A
	RICHARD SUSSMAN	piano	A

| ALBUM: | 1(A) | GROOTNA | (CBS C 31033) 1971 - |

45s:	Full Time Woman/Is It All Over	(Columbia 45461) 1971
	Waitin' For My Ship/	
	That's What You Get	(Columbia 45538) 1972

Grootna was the first group Marty Balin produced after he'd left **Jefferson Airplane**. The result was an excellent West Coast album, with strong instrumental parts and good vocals. Unfortunately, it was a total commercial failure.

Dewey Dagreaze was Greg Dewey, the former **Mad River** drummer. Greg Dewey, Vic Smith and Richard Sussman had all also played with **Country Joe McDonald**. Sussman had previously been in **Elephant's Memory**.

Slim Chance, whose real name is Austin deLone, later played with Eggs Over Easy, The Moonlighters, Commander Cody, Elvis Costello, The Fabulous Thunderbirds and many others.

Jack Bonus continued on as a producer and issued his own album on Grunt. Anna Rizzo, previously with Sky Blue, would later play and record with **Michael Bloomfield**, **Country Joe McDonald** and Kingfish. Kelly Bryan later played with Oasis and Jesse Colin Young. (SR/HS)

The Groovie Goolies

| 45: | First Annual, Semi-Formal, Combination/ | |
| | Save Your Good Lovin' For Me | (RCA 74-0383) 1969 |

A bubblegum pop single. (SR)

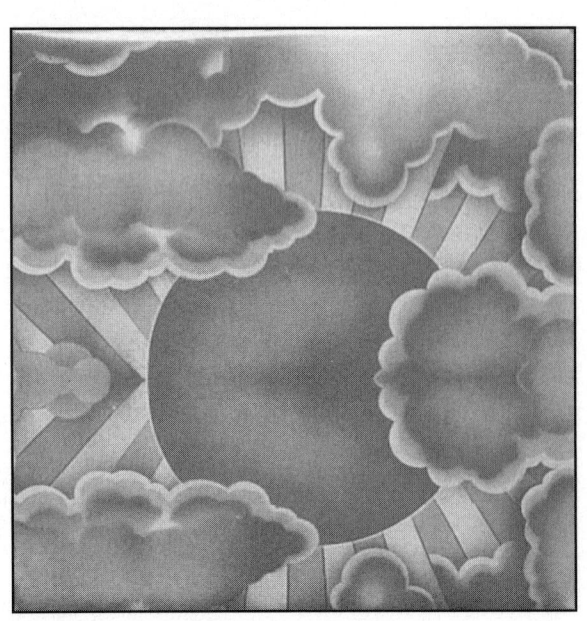

ACID DREAMS COLLECTION (Comp LP) including The Grodes.

WORLD OF ACID (Comp LP) including Groundspeed.

Gross National Product

Personnel:	JAY BARKER	bs	AB
	NICK BARKER	keyb'ds	AB
	TICE GRIFFIN	gtr	AB
	CALVIN HOOD	drms	A
	BOB ZORDICH	drms	B

45s:	Cover Girl/That's What I'll Do Now	(Guilford 103) 1968
	Cover Girl/That's What I'll Do Now	(Parrot 103) 1969
	Alice McCrea/Hey, Pop Musician	(A&M 1151) 1970

On the Baltimore-based Guilford label, this band came from the Annapolis/Severna Park area of central Maryland. They were managed by Plato Theopolis, a Baltimore area producer, who also managed the Koffee Beans. Their song *Cover Girl* was initially pitched to the cosmetic company without success and later picked up Parrot. In 1970 the group released a further 45 but split soon after.

Tice Griffin is still playing as a solo guitarist in California. (SR/ JosephVaccarino)

Gross National Productions

ALBUM: 1   P FLAPS AND LOW BLOWS
(Metromedia KMD 1053) 1972 -

Produced by Shadow Morton (aka **Shadow Mann**) and John Linde, this weird good time rock group came from the New York Area. Their only album features eleven tracks with interesting guitar interludes. (SR)

Groundspeed

45:    In A Dream/L-12-East   (Decca 32344) 1968

From Cambridge, Massachusetts. This is a wonderful progressive/ psychedelic 45. Very Anglophile, it'll appeal more to fans of the U.K. *Rubble* series than, say, *Pebbles* acolytes.

Compilation appearances have included *In A Dream* on *Relative Distance* (LP) and *World Of Acid* (LP); and *L-12 East* on *U-Spaces: Psychedelic Archaeology Vol. 1* (CDR). (MW)

The Group

45:    Why Does My Head Go Boom?/
       514 Bathtub   (Freak SS-9240-01) 1967

This slice of psychedelia was the work on an Eastern Iowa band. They travelled to Iowa City to record it.

Compilation appearances include: *Why Does My Head Go Boom?* on *The Midwest Vs. The Rest* (LP) and *Psychedelic Experience, Vol. 4* (CD). (VJ)

The Group

Personnel incl: R. SHARP   A

45:    Yesterday Is Today/Tell Me Why   (Shore Bird 1013) 1968

Came out of Oklahoma City with just this one 45 which features some nice fuzz guitar. (VJ)

Group

EP: 1   But Now It's Too Late/In Crowd/Comin' Home Baby/
       Dancing in the Streets   (Fleetwood FL 4577) 196?

Yet another **Group**, these folks put together this endearingly discordant four song EP in Massachusetts. They boasted an impressive horn section and one track has excellent flute work. (MMs)

The Group

Personnel:	STEVE BLAND	keyb'ds	AB
	RONNIE CABLE	ld gtr	AB
	BOBBY CALDWELL	drms	A
	KENNY COHEN	bs	AB
	JIMMY RUDOLPH	drms	B

45:    Land Of Lakes / Just In Case   (Troupe 5467) 1967

Also known as "The Fantastic Group", this quartet were based in Cocoa Beach, Florida. They included Bobby Caldwell who featured in several other outfits - Nightwalkers, GoMads and **Noah's Ark**.

Land Of Lakes is an atmospheric punker; a bedrock of muted reverbed-fuzz and menacing bass line, dark lead vocals, lit up at intervals by piercing shards of guitar. Check it out on *Psychedelic States: Florida Vol.3* and crank it up.

Cohen re-emerged in **Crazy Elephant**, who had an international hit with *Gimme, Gimme, Good Lovin'* in 1968/9. (MW/JLh/RTr/RE)

The Group

45:    Baby, It's You/
       Can't Get Enough Of Your Love   (Warner Bros. WB 5240) 1967

A Californian studio single produced by Gary Zekley of **Yellow Balloon** which sounds very similar to his other records. (SR)

Group Axis

45:    Not Fade Away/Smokestack Lightning   (Atco 6642) 1969

Originally from West Texas, this band were based in L.A. The 'A' side of this 45 became the title of Doug Hanner's superb Texas music magazine and has recently been compiled on *Incredible Sound Show Stories, Vol. 8* (LP). (VJ)

Group "B"

Personnel:	DAVE DAMRELL		A
	ROGER HILLE		AB
	JIM KING		A
	JACK MAY		AB
	DANNY MIHM	drms	B
	DICKIE PETERSON		B
	JERRI PETERSON		B

45s:	Stop Calling Me/She's Gone	(Scorpio 402) 1965/6
	I Know Your Name Girl/I Never Really Knew	(Scorpio 406) 1966

Looking back, Fantasy's Scorpio label managed to pick up quite a few of the "about to happen" bands on the San Francisco scene - notably **The Grateful Dead** and pre-**Creedence Clearwater Revival Golliwogs**. Amongst the 'also-rans' we find this Davis, California outfit whose inclusion is more for historical than musical reasons. Dave Damrell went on to **Kak**. Drummer Danny Mihm also played for Andrew Staples and for The Whistling Shrimp Blues Band before being persuaded by Cyril Jordan to join the **Flamin' Groovies**. Dick Peterson would of course go on to team up with **Oxford Circle**'s Paul Whaley plus **Leigh Stephens** to become brainblasters **Blue Cheer**.

All four of the bands 45 cuts also appear on Big Beats' *The Scorpio Records Story*; although a different, fluteless version of *I Never Really Knew* is included rather than that which appears on the 45. (MW)

Groupies

Personnel incl: BOBBY CORTEZ
PETE HENDLEMAN
GORDON McLAREN
RONNIE PETERS

45: Primitive/I'm A Hog For You (Atco 6393) 1965

This punk quintet came from New York and held a residency at Manhattan's Scene Club for a while. The 'A' side, *Primitive* is a superb Stones-influenced number, slow in tempo but incredibly intense.

Compilation appearances have included: *Primitive* on *Nuggets Box* (4-CD), *Pebbles, Vol. 10* (LP), *Pebbles, Vol. 3 (ESD)* (CD), *Best of Pebbles, Vol. 1* (LP & CD) and *Born Bad (Songs The Cramps Taught Us)*; *I'm A Hog For You* on *Pebbles Box* (5-LP) *Trash Box* (5-CD), *Teenage Shutdown, Vol. 1* (LP & CD) and *Ear-Piercing Punk* (LP); and both *I'm A Hog For You* and *Primitive* on *Ear-Piercing Punk* (CD). (VJ)

The Groupies

ALBUM: 1 THE GROUPIES (Earth Records ELPS-1000) 1969 -

Subtitled "The girls heard on this record report their actual life experiences, feelings and opinions within the pop music scene", this album is a documentary about the groupies, produced by **Alan Lorber**, the man behind the Boss-Town sound (**Chameleon Church**, **Puff**, **Ultimate Spinach**) and **Robert "Bobby" Callender**. It doesn't contain music, only spoken vocals with some sound effects and came with an insert which is interesting for its glossary, with the definitions of "stoned", "out of it", "plaster casters" plus many other "in" or crude expressions. (SR)

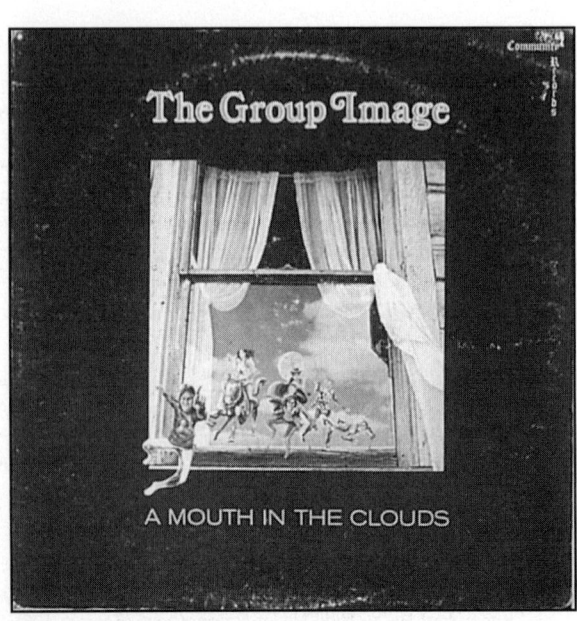

THE GROUP IMAGE - A Mouth In The Clouds... LP.

GROUP THERAPY - People Get Ready For Group Therapy LP.

The Group Image

Personnel: SHEILA DARLA A
BLACK DOUG A
DR HOK A
FREDDY KNUCKLES A
WILLIAM GUY MERRILL A
PROFESSOR LEON LUTHER RIX A

ALBUM: 1(A) A MOUTH IN THE CLOUDS ASKS: WHAT TIME ARE U? (Community A-101) 1968 SC

NB: (1) two different back cover designs exist.

45: Hiya/? (Community 3200) 1968

A hippie outfit from New Jersey. *Hiya*, a shorter version of an album track can be heard on *Pebbles, Vol. 14* (LP). The high pitched, often manic vocals, make this song at least rather a novelty. At times it recalls **Tim Buckley** in his prime. *Hiya* is the outstanding track on an inconsistent album which has its moments. There is also some fine guitar work on *Moonlight Dip* and *Aunt Ida* and on *Banana Split*, which is quite trippy in places. Definitely worth a listen.

The album was produced by Vinny Testa, Shadow Morton (aka **Shadow Mann**) and John Linde and recorded in New York. All the tracks were penned by the group.

Leon Luther Rix went on to play with **Buzzy Linhart**. (VJ/SR)

Group Inc.

45s: Like A Woman/Just Call Me Up (Staff BP-177) 1966
Like A Woman/Just Call Me Up (Freeport 1008) 1966

This Gary, Indiana outfit embraced the late '64-to-'65 Invasion and Merseybeat sounds for their sole 45, but were a little late to catch that wave. Despite this it was picked up by the Freeport label, best known for its releases by the **Five Emprees**.

Compilation appearances include: *Just Call Me Up* on *Midnight To Sixty-Six* (LP); *Like A Woman* on *Pebbles Vol. 6 - Chicago 1* (CD) and *Highs In The Mid-Sixties Vol. 4* (LP). (VJ/MW)

Group Therapy

Personnel: TOMMY BURNS vcls A
ART DEL GUDICO gtr, bs A
JERRY GUIDA organ A
RAY KENNEDY vcls A
MICHAEL LAMONT drms A

ALBUMS: 1( ) PEOPLE GET READY FOR GROUP THERAPY
                                            (RCA LSP-3976) 1968 -
         2( ) 37 MINUTES OF GROUP THERAPY
                                            (Philips PHS 600303) 1969 -

NB: There was also a UK album, *You're In Need Of Group Therapy* (Philips SBL 7883) 1969.

45s: People Get Ready/Who'll Be Next   (RCA Victor 9527) 1968
    α   Can't Stop Lovin' You Baby/I Must Go   (Philips 40598) 1969

NB: α also issued in the UK (Philips BF 1792) 1969.

A late sixties outfit. Unfortunately much of their material is of **The Vanilla Fudge** school - heavy soulful sludge. A typical example of this would be their cover of Ike and Tina Turner's *River Deep.... Mountain High* on their second album. The formula occasionally worked well, particularly on *Can't Stop Lovin' You Baby*, also from their second album. Collectors are beginning to show some interest in their albums but I wouldn't recommend them.

In 1975, Ray Kennedy formed KGB with **Mike Bloomfield** and **Barry Goldberg**. After this failed, he became a session background singer and released a decent solo album in 1980 *Ray Kennedy* (CBS).

The **Group Therapy** moniker was used by at least four bands in the sixties. (VJ)

Growing Concern

Personnel: PETE GUERINO   gtr, vcls   A
            MARY GARSTKI   vcls   A
            BONNIE MacDONALD vcls   A
            DAN PASSAGLIA   keyb'ds, vcls A
            JOHN PEDLEY   bs   A
            RALPH TOMS   gtr   A
            RALPH WILLIAMS   drms   A

ALBUM: 1(A) THE GROWING CONCERN
                                            (Mainstream S/6108) 1968 R2

NB: (1) was repressed in 1989 and is also available on CD (Golden Classics Rebirth GRC 003) 1996.

45: Tomorrow Has Been Cancelled/
     A Boy I Once Knew Well   (Mainstream 685) 1968

The above psychedelic rock album is one of the better Mainstream issues. Side one opens with *Hard Hard Year*, full of pleasant vocal harmonies and melodic guitar work. *Edge Of Time* is an uptempo number with great guitar work. *Tomorrow Has Been Cancelled* and *A Boy I Once Knew Well* both feature harmonised vocals and some great guitar. Side two relies more on covers. There's some great guitar playing in their version of *Mister You're A Better Man Than I* and in *Other Side Of Life* and they've an individual interpretation of Steve Still's *Sit Down I Think I Love You*.

An EP accompanying "Le Rock Psychedelique Vol.1" book also features *What Kind Of Life*. (VJ/MW)

GROUP THERAPY - You're In Need Of... LP.

GROWING CONCERN - Growing Concern LP.

Peter Grudzien

ALBUM: 1 THE UNICORN   (P.G. 101) 1974 R3

NB: (1) issued on CD (Parallel World) with six bonus tracks.

The album is a very rare and unusual psychedelic-folk album. **Grudzien** came from New York and some collectors rate his album, which incorporated bits of stolen classical, blue-grass and electronic experiments, very highly indeed. It has recently been reissued on CD by the Parallel World label with six bonus tracks.

Grump

45: Heartbreak Hotel/Ill Give You Love   (Magic Carpet) c1970

A rare single of heavy-psych with wah-wah and demented vocals. *Heartbreak Hotel*, the old Elvis hit, was also covered by **Frijid Pink**. (SR)

The Gs

45: Cause She's My Girl/
     There's A Time   (Young Generation 108) 1966

An average punk band from Denton in Texas judging by the flip of this 45, which can be found on *Texas Punk, Vol. 9* (LP), *Garage Punk Unknowns, Vol. 4* (LP) and *Acid Visions - Complete Collection, Vol. 3* (3-CD). (VJ)

G.T.O's (Girls Together Outrageously)

Personnel: JEFF BECK   gtr   A
            JIMMY CARL BLACK   drms   A
            MISS CHRISTINE   vcls   A
            MISS CINDERELLA   vcls   A
            CRAIG DOERGE   keyb'ds   A
            ROY ESTRADA   bs   A
            NICKY HOPKINS   keyb'ds   A
            MISS MERCY   vcls   A
            MISS PAMELA   vcls   A
            DON PRESTON   synth   A
            MISS SANDRA   vcls   A
            ROD STEWART   vcls   A

| IAN UNDERWOOD | keyb'ds | A |
| FRANK ZAPPA | tamb | A |

ALBUM: 1(A) PERMANENT DAMAGE   (Straight 1059) 1969 R2

NB: (1) also issued (Reprise RS-6390) 1970.

45:   Circular Circulation/Mercy's Tune   (Straight STS 104) 1969

The **GTO's** were formerly known as the Laurel Canyon Ballet Company. These five girls were signed to Straight after the label owner, **Frank Zappa** hired Miss Christine as a baby sitter and heard her songs. **Zappa** produced most of the album and invited some Mothers Of Invention to form the backing group: Jimmy Carl Black, Don Preston, Roy Estrada, Lowell George (who wrote and produced several tracks), Ian Underwood, Jeff Beck, Rod Stewart and Nicky Hopkins also appear in places.

The songs are notably dealing with the groupies phenomenon and the original pressing came with a booklet "The Groupie Papers" . The **GTO's** also appeared on one track on the **Wild Man Fischer** album and on the inner gatefold of Three Dog Night's *Suitable For Framing*.

A long-time girlfriend of Alice Cooper, Miss Christine died of an heroin overdose in 1972. Miss Pamela married Michael Des Barres, the singer of the English group Silverhead, and later wrote several books about her various experiences.

Compilation appearances include *Love On An 11-Year Old Level* on *Girls In The Garage, Vol. 4* (LP). (SR/VZ)

The Guerillas

45:   Don't Ever Change / Lonely   (Donna 1406) 1966

An unknown group, who appeared on Del-Fi's doorstep in Los Angeles at the beginning of '66, recorded one single and disappeared. As the topside they chose to cover *Don't Ever Change* from the Kinks' (BTs/MW)

Isaac Guillory

ALBUM: 1 ISAAC GUILLORY   (Atlantic K40521) 1973 -

NB: (1) UK release.

45:   Sidewalks Of America/Steamboat   (Atlantic 10442) 1973

NB: UK release.

After the **Cryan' Shames**, **Isaac Guillory** went solo and moved to England, where he recorded a decent folk-rock album with the help of Sam Gopal on tablas and members of Hookfoot. He also recorded with the folk-rock group Prelude. **Guillory** would later form Pacific Eardrum, a jazzy prog/soul group with British and American musicians. (SR)

The Guilloteens

Personnel:	JOE DAVIS	drms	AB
	LADDIE HUTCHERSON	bs, gtr, vcls	AB
	LOUIS PAUL Jnr.	gtr, keyb'ds, vcls	A
	BUDDY DeLANEY	bs	B
	JIM VINSON	gtr	B

45s incl: I Don't Believe (Call On Me)/Hey You   (HBR 446) 1965
For My Own/Don't Let The Rain Get You Down (HBR 451) 1965
I Sit And Cry/Crying All Over My Time   (HBR 486) 1966
Wild Child/You Think You're Happy   (Columbia 4-43852) 1966
I Love That Girl/
Dear Mrs Applebee(PS)   (Columbia 4-44089) 1967
α   I Love That Girl / Girl   (De-Shane) 19??

NB: α Buddy DeLaney solo 45 (with The Candy Soupe).

Elvis Presley once cited this Memphis-based act as his favourite local band which instantly led to a deal with the HBR label. They recorded quite extensively during 1965-66 and toured widely but success eluded them and plans for an album were scrapped.

Most of their self-penned material certainly appealed to their fellow garage bands if not the record buying public - **Five Of Us**' version of *Hey You* can be heard on *Boulders, Vol.8*; **The Moonrakers**' cover of *I Don't Believe* on *Highs In The Mid-Sixties, Vol. 18*. Unfortunately the later material was not penned by the band and degenerated into bland pop, *Crying All Over My Time* for example is a rather wimpy sounding garage effort. Of their material worthy of note - *I Don't Believe* is a decent jangly folk-rock ditty; *For My Own* is **Byrdsy** garage-pop; *I Sit And Cry* is excellent tough garage-beat similar to **The Gants**.

Louis, who left the band after *For My Own* recalls:-"We were working with Phil Spector when our manager signed us with HBR... I grew up with Elvis, he used to call me 'Highschool'. We hung out on the movie set with him when we weren't working. He was a wonderful person, we had a lot of fun, I miss him. **The Guilloteens** were his favorite band at that time and he used to come to the Red Velvet Lounge to hear us play. He had a place there in the corner where he could sit unnoticed."

Hey You was also covered in 1981 by Jonny Sevin (*Sounds Of Now* eighties compilation).

Laddie Hutcherson still lives and performs in Memphis. After quitting the band in 1968 he played in several groups before going solo.

Louis Paul performed locally in clubs fronting his own band then returned to L.A. in 1970. He appeared on recordings by 3 Dog Night, **Blues Image** and

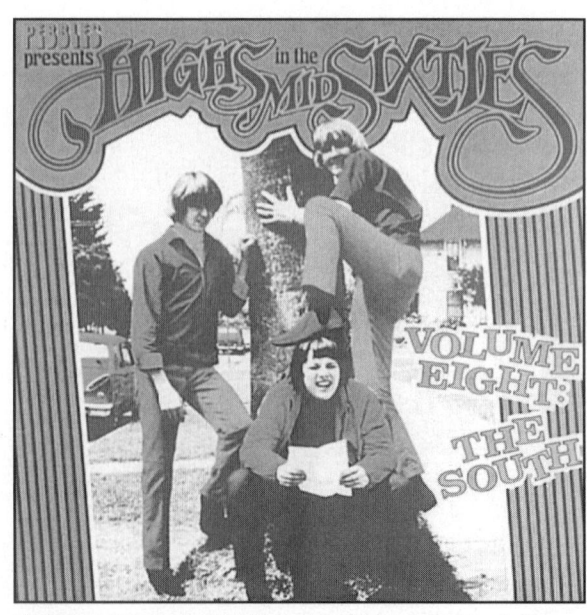

PETER GRUDZIEN - The Unicorn LP.

HIGHS IN THE MID-SIXTIES Vol. 8 (Comp LP) including The Guilloteens.

Bobby Hebb. From 1970 to 1977 he released at least nine solo 45s and put out an eponymous album on the Enterprise label in 1972.

Paul's replacement Buddy DeLaney later released a solo 45 where he claimed writer credits for both sides, even though **The Guilloteens'** *I Love That Girl* was originally co-credited to him and Joe Davis. The flip, *Girl*, is a rework of another **Guilloteens'** song, Laddie Hutcherson's *Hey You!*.

For a more detailed history and solo discography of this respected and fondly-remembered band, seek out a copy of Ron Hall's book on the Memphis scene (from 1960 to 1975) 'Playing For A Piece Of The Door', published in 2001 by Shangri-La Projects (ISBN 0-9668575-1-8).

Compilation coverage has included:- *For My Own* on *Leaving It All Behind* (LP); *Wild Child* on *Mind Blowers* (LP); *Hey You* on *Diana's Rootin' Tootin' Wild Teenage Rock 'N' Roll Party!* (LP) and *Everywhere Chainsaw Sound* (LP). (VJ/MW/JLh)

Guise

Personnel incl:	GREG HOELTZEL		A
	MIKE KRENSKI		A
	MITCHELL		A
	RAY SCHULTE		A
	WHARTON		A

HCP

45s:	Long Haired Music/		
	When You're Sorry	(Musicland USA 20011)	1967 123
	Half A Man/Chumpy McGee	(Musicland USA 20015)	1967 -
	Time/News	(Musicland USA 11 4)	1967 -
	Girl, Make Up Your Mind/		
	Nothing Else But Love	(Atco 6599)	1968 -

An obscure St. Louis, Missouri outfit, who evolved out of **Bob Kuban and The In-Men**. Their *Time/News* 45 is interesting to psych-pop collectors - *Time* is similar to Brit-pop-psych with **Turtles** harmonies whilst *News* has a tougher edge with some gruff guitar and a pulsating beat. Unfortunately the Atco 45 saw them drift towards the **Blood, Sweat and Tears** school of soul-rock.

Ray Schulte was an early member of this band, though we don't know whether he played on any of the 45s. He was of course later the leader of the excellent late-sixties combo **Touch**.

Time has resurfaced on *Incredible Sound Show Stories, Vol. 8* (LP) whilst *News* has also been compiled on *Brain Shadows, Vol. 2* (LP & CD). (MW/JGd)

Guitar Ensemble

Personnel incl:	MARY KAY JOHNSON	vcls	AB
	BOB RIVAS		AB
	ELOY MONTOYA		B

ALBUMS:	1(A)	HAVE FAITH	(No label)	c1970 -
	2(A)	YOU-N-YOU	(Guitar Ensemble LPS-812)	1971 -
	3(B)	AMERICA, WHERE ARE YOU?		
			(No label CLP-813)	1973 -

NB: (3) by Concern.

From New Mexico, a Christian folk-rock group with acoustic guitars, stunning "angelic" female vocals, organ, bass and percussion. Their first album is more folk-rock than the second, which has some psych influences. Both albums share two songs, *Have Faith* and *This Is A Man*.

In 1973, as Concern, with a new line-up and featuring electric guitar, they released a rare third album with some new versions of their old songs. (SR/KSt)

Guitar Factory

Personnel:	JOSPEH CINDERELLA	bs	A
	CARMINE D'AMICO	gtr	A
	CHRIS D'AMICO	gtr	A
	BHEN LANZARONE	keyb'ds	A
	STEVE LITTLE	drms	A
	LES PERLMAN	drms	A

ALBUM:	1(A)	PLAYS MUSIC FROM JESUS CHRIST SUPERSTAR
		(Metromedia MD 1050) 1970 -

An instrumental exploito album with some good guitar parts using fuzz or wah-wah effects, quite dated now. (SR)

Gulliver

Personnel:	DARYL HALL	keyb'ds, vcls	A
	JIM HELMER	drms	A
	TIM MOORE	gtr, vcls	A
	TOM SELLERS	bs, keyb'ds	A

ALBUM:	1(A)	GULLIVER	(Elektra EKS-74070)	1969 -

NB: (1) also issued in the UK (Elektra 2410 006) 1969.

45s:	α	Every Day's A Lonely Day/Angelina	(Elektra 45689)	1969
		A Truly Good Song/		
		Every Day's A Lonely Day	(Elektra 45698)	1970

NB: α also released in Australia by Astor.

From Philadelphia, this obscure group is mainly notable for being the first group of Daryl Hall, who later found fame and fortune with Hall and Oates. Tim Moore became a successful songwriter, background vocalist and also had a solo (and rather mellow) career with five albums between 1974 and 1979. Sellers and Helmer both became session musicians, with Helmer playing with the late Laura Nyro.

The photo on their album was taken at Bryn Mawr College, Philadelphia, which may possibly have been their stomping ground.

Compilation appearances have included *Christine* on *Elektrock The Sixties* (4-LP). (SR/AC)

Gunhill Road

Personnel:	STEVE GOLDRICH	keyb'ds, bcking vcls	AB
	GLEN(N) LEOPOLD	gtr, vcls	AB
	GIL ROMAN	gtr, vcls	AB
	(TOM WYNDER	drms	A)
	(LARRY BROWN	drms	B)
	(DENNYS LEPRI	gtr	B)
	(GENE LORENZO	keyb'ds	B)
	(BILL PERRY	bs	B)

ALBUMS:	1(A)	FIRST STOP	(Mercury SR 61341)	c1970/1 -
	2(B)	GUNHILL ROAD	(Kama Sutra KSBS 2061)	1972 -

NB: (1) issued as by 'Gun Hill Road'.

45s:	Back When My Hair Was Short/		
	We Can't Ride The Rollercoaster	(Kama Sutra 569)	1973
	Sailing/Ford, De Soto, Cadillac	(Kama Sutra 582)	1973?
	She Made A Man Out Of Me/?	(Kama Sutra 591)	1974

A little-known rock group from the New York Area. Although basically a trio, they were assisted on their second album by a number of session guests including Bill Perry and Larry Brown (ex-**Daddy Dewdrop**), Paul Cotton and George Grantham (Poco), Kenny Rogers, Andy Newmark, Reinie Press...

Their hit single, *Back When My Hair Was Short* is a great song.

Most of their material was written by Glenn Leopold and the band were managed by Paul Colby, the owner of the legendary nightclub 'The Bitter End' in Greenwich Village, New York City. (SR/GM/BGk)

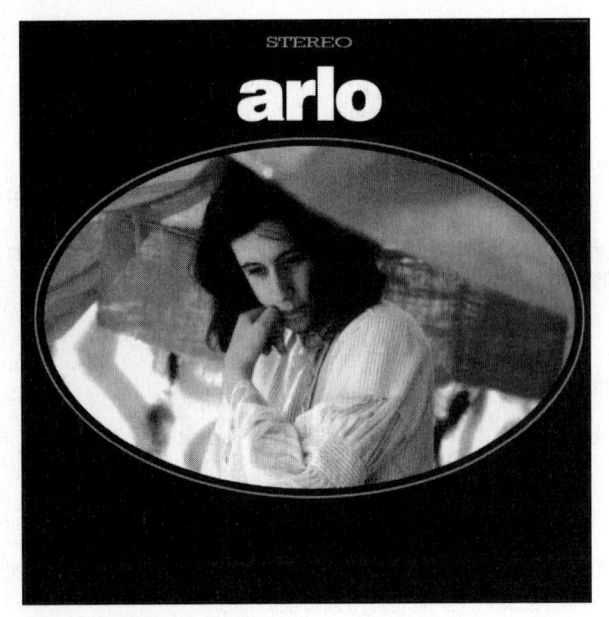

ARLO GUTHRIE - Arlo CD.

Guns and Butter

Personnel:	PAUL COHEN	gtr	A
	PETER COHEN	bs	A
	LENNY FEDERER	violin, viola	A
	JEFF LYONS	vcls, gtr	A
	RICHARD PLOSS	flute, sax	A
	PETER TUCKER	drms	A

ALBUM: 1(A) GUNS AND BUTTER (Cotillion SD 9901) 1972 -

A very marginal case for inclusion because this is an underrated progressive as opposed to garage or psychedelic album. An unusual combination of instruments works well with all tracks interesting and a couple particularly good - all were penned by the group. A predominantly Jewish line-up with a hint of traditional Jewish music in their sound. Closely followed by Lloyd Grossman, who co-produced the album and wrote the sleeve-notes.

The band came from Boston. (VJ/NK)

Sandy Gurley and The San Francisco Bridge

ALBUM: 1 SANDY GURLEY (Tower ST 51??) 1968 SC

A San Francisco hippie singer in the Janis Joplin style, with a competent back-up group using fuzz guitar. Another Goldberg / Kulka production, like **Afterglow**, **Maze** and **Mesmerizing Eye**, it contains some good cuts like *Mind Pucker* and a cover of *Can't Buy Me Love* which is very similar to the **Neighb'rhood Childr'n** version. (SR)

The Gurus

Personnel incl:	PANKIN	A
	N. SCHNEIDER	A
	J. TALBOT	A

ALBUM: 1 THE GURUS ARE HERE! (United Artists UAS 6563) 1967 ?

NB: (1) was advertised but does not appear to have been released.

45s: Blue Snow Night/Come Girl (PS) (United Artists 50089) 1966
      It Just Won't Be That Way/Everybody's Got To
      Be Alone Sometime (United Artists 50140) 1967

A mid-sixties outfit who have been variously reported as coming from New York and Los Angeles. Both sides of the first 45 are Eastern-influenced, the vocals are rather reminiscent of **Kaleidoscope**. The second 45 is rather more poppy - the 'A' side is a cover of a **Critters**' song.

Erik Lindgren's liner notes for *A Heavy Dose Of Lyte Psych* (which includes *It Just Won't Be That Way*), says that the band consisted of five music majors from the New York area, who recorded several tracks for the above album, but that United Artists pulled the plug, after the second 45 stiffed.

It's way past time someone issued this album on the strength of the 45s alone.

Other compilation appearances have included: *Everybody's Got To Be Alone Sometime* on *Mindblowing Encounters Of The Purple Kind* (LP); and *Come Girl* on *A Trip On The Magic Flying Machine*. (MW)

Margo Guryan

ALBUM: 1 TAKE A PICTURE (Bell) 1968

NB: (1) reissued on CD in Japan (Trattoria) 199?

45: Spanky And Our Gang/Sunday Mornin (Mala 12002) 1968
     Take A Picture/What Can I Give You? (Mala 12020) 1968

A soft-psych singer who wrote *Sunday Mornin*, a hit for **Spanky and Our Gang**. The non-album 'A' side was a "thank you" for recording her song. (SR/DRr)

Arlo Guthrie

				HCP
ALBUMS:	1	ALICE'S RESTAURANT	(Reprise 6267) 1967	17 -
(up to	2	ARLO	(Reprise 6299) 1968	107 -
1969)	3	RUNNING DOWN THE ROAD	(Reprise RS6346) 1969	54 -

NB: These albums were also released in the U.K. and France. (1) has been reissued several times. (2) reissued on CD (Koch KOCCD 7948).

			HCP
45s:	Motorcycle Song/Now And Then	(Reprise 0644) 1967	-
	Motorcycle Song, pt 1/pt 2	(Reprise 0793) 1968	-
	Coming In To Los Angeles/		
	Alice's Rock & Roll Restaurant	(Reprise 0877) 1969	-
	Alice's Rock & Roll Restaurant/?	(Reprise 0877) 1969	97
	Gabriel's Mother's Hiway/		
	Ballad #16 Blues	(Reprise 0951) 1970	-
	Ballad Of Tricky Fred/Shackles & Chains	(Reprise 0994) 1971	-
	The City Of New Orleans/		
	Days Are Short	(Reprise 1103) 1972	18

Son of the legendary Woodie Guthrie, Arlo appeared in 1967 with *Alice's Restaurant Massacree*, an eighteen-minute underground hit. His first album was well received, climbing to No. 17 in the Charts and a movie was later made out of the song themes. His following effort *Arlo* was live and is not recommended, although it also climbed to No. 107. **Guthrie** then teamed up with Lenny Waronker and **Van Dyke Parks** and *Running Down The Road* was recorded with two **Byrds** (Clarence White and Gene Parsons), Ry Cooder, Jim Gordon, James Burton, Jerry Scheff, John Pilla and Chris Ethridge. Essentially folk and country-rock oriented, it contains two songs of interest: the dope-smuggling anthem *Coming In To Los Angeles* and the strange title track with its chiming guitars recorded with lots of echo. Again, sales were quite good, reaching No. 54.

Arlo Guthrie performed at Woodstock and a live version of *Coming In To Los Angeles* can be found on the 'Woodstock' film and soundtrack. Still working with Cooder, Clarence White and various folk and country-rock musicians, his other albums are out of the scope of this book. (SR/VJ)

Dennis Guy

Personnel:	EMPERADOR ATON	drms	A
	RANDALL ATON	bs	A
	DENNIS GUY	vcls	A
	THOMAS GUY	gtr	A
	JAMES JEFFERS	gtr	A
	JOHN MILLIKEN	drms	A

ALBUM: 1   DENNIS GUY   (Daybreak DR2008) 1972 -

Although some some imaginative (or deaf) dealers describe it as "folk/psych", this album is in fact closer to the first few albums by Don McLean. **Dennis Guy** was a rather mellow singer/songwriter who added some very light jazz touches to his material. The best tracks are *Say You'll Be With Me* and *Hypersensitive Jester*. (SR)

Guys Who Come Up From Downstairs

45:    Growth/Nothing We Can Do   (Disc-Guys 6836) 1968

You'll find *Growth* on *Hipsville 29 B.C.* (LP) and *Ear-Piercing Punk* (CD). Blatant stuff from Cedar Rapids, Iowa. (VJ)

Gwydion

ALBUM: 1(A) SINGS SONGS FOR THE OLD RELIGION
                                    (Nemeton) 1975 R2

NB: (1) reissued in the U.K. on Psychedelic Archives in 1995 and also reissued on CD, together with his 1981 album *The Faerie Shaman* as *The Music Of Gwydion* 1998.

An Oakland, California, act whose acid-folk album, on which **Gwydion** is backed by the Wicca Blues Band, is notable for an outstanding cover photo and one great track called *Sungod*. Not that expensive to obtain in the U.S.A., it seems to have been considered a mega-rarity in Europe, which resulted in its reissue.

The late Gwydion Pennderwen, is best known for his activist role in the neo-Pagan community. Pennderwen was a friend/disciple of the late Victor Anderson. Anderson was known as a high priest in the Pagan community; a proponent, of the Feri tradition of witchcraft. **Gwydion** actually considered himself a Druid and was a member of a latter day Druid sect the New and Reformed Order of the Golden Down.

So what about the guy's music? Interestingly, at least one dealer has compared it to The Incredible String Band, but this stuff is simply too weird for such a comparison. If you've ever spent an evening in an Irish bar, you've probably heard stuff that's similar to much of 1975's *Gwydion Sings: Songs for the Old Religion*. Exemplified by largely acoustic material such as *Return Of The King*, *Harvest Dance* and *Can Ceridwen* it was clear that **Gwydion** and his associates (listed as The California Wicca Blues Band), had a keen interest in English and Irish folk music. Propelled by **Gywdion**'s decent voice (he sounds like he'd spent a great deal of time hanging around Irish bars), the album's fifteen tracks are full of Celtic imagery and mysticism (tales of kings, damsels in distress, fairies, witches, etc.). Those themes were apparently in keeping with **Gwydion**'s Pagan beliefs; the songs intended to honor Pagan days of worship, as well as reflections on seasonal rounds and love songs to Pagan Gods and Goddesses. Actually, the best track was the atypical *The Sungod*. Written by Dana Corby (damn if she didn't sound like prime era Grace Slick), and backed by one of the few electric arrangements, the song sported a weird pseudo-**Jefferson Airplane** vibe. Great song! It's certainly different and has generated a cult following (guess there are lots of European Pagan's with high incomes), willing to pay some big bucks for an original copy.

Shortly after his first album was released, **Gwydion** visited Wales and Ireland. While in Ireland he had a strange premonition that left him so shaken, that upon returning to his native California, he quit his job, basically moving into seclusion on his Mendocino Country farm. He spent the next four years in virtual seclusion, but starting in 1980 began making occasional concert appearances at various Pagan events and working in support of a reforestation project - Forever Forests.

In 1982 **Gwydion** recorded his sophomore album. Supported by the Sheila na Gig Pipes and Drums, *The Fairy Shaman* the set was far more traditional than the debut. Once again, the set was largely made up of acoustic folk material; most of it reflections of his Pagan beliefs . While the sound quality was better than the debut, it still left something to be desired. Unfortunately, shortly after the album was released, the 36 year old **Gwydion** was killed in a car accident. (VJ/CF/SB)

GWYDION - Songs For The Old Religion LP.

Gye Whiz

ALBUM: 1   I'LL BE ALRIGHT   (S.Y.M.A.) 1971 R3

An acid folk-rock singer from California sometimes compared to **Perry Leopold**. (SR)

The Gypsies

45:    Look For The One That Loves You/
       Oh Girl   (Caprice 607V-8442) 1965

This punk 45 was the work of 15 year olds from Bryan Adams High School in Dallas. The flip is a forgettable sort of dance record. Caprice was a subsidiary label of Vandan.

Compilation appearances include *Oh Girl!* on *Acid Visions - Complete Collection, Vol. 3* (3-CD) and *Texas Punk, Vol. 9* (LP). (VJ)

Gypsy

Personnel:	JAY EPSTEIN	drms	A
	JAMES C. JOHNSON	vcls, gtr	AB
	DONI LARSON	bs	A
	ENRICO ROSENBAUM	vcls, gtr, perc	AB
	JAMES 'OWL' WALSH	vcls, keyb'ds, perc	AB
	RANDY GATES	vcls	B
	BILL LORDAN	drms	B

HCP
ALBUMS:	1(A)	GYPSY (dbl)	(Metromedia M2 1031) 1970	44 -
	2( )	IN THE GARDEN	(Metromedia KMD 1044) 1971	173 -
	3(B)	ANTITHESIS	(RCA VICTOR LSP-4775) 1972	- -
	4( )	UNLOCK THE GATE	(RCA VICTOR APL1-0093) 1973	- -
	5( )	AMERICAN GYPSY	(Chess 60034) 1975	- -
	6( )	THE JAMES WALSH GYPSY BAND		
			(RCA VICTOR AFL1-2914) 1979	- -

NB: (5) as by **American Gypsy**, (6) as by **The James Walsh Gypsy Band**.

HCP
45s:	Dead And Gone/Here In My Loneliness	(Cognito 008) 196?/7? -
	Gypsy Queen Part II /	
	Dead And Gone	(Metromedia 202) 1970 62
	As Far As You Can See /	
	Here In The Garden	(Metromedia 228) 1971
	Day After Day / Lean On Me	(RCA Victor 74-0862) 1972
	Don't Bother Me /	
	Make Peace With Jesus	(RCA Victor 74-0933) 1973
	Need You Baby / Precious One	(RCA Victor APB0-0036) 1973 -

	Don't Stop For Nothin' / Magic In My Life	(Dore 907) 1975 -
α	Cuz It's You, Girl / Bring Yourself Around	(RCA Victor 11403) 1978 71
α	Love Is For The Best In Us / Don't Look Back	(RCA Victor 11480) 1979 -

NB: α as by **The James Walsh Gypsy Band**.

This long-lived outfit evolved out of Minneapolis' **Underbeats**, who'd been wowing them in the Midwest since the early sixties. Given the prodigious output under their various monikers, latterly as **American Gypsy** and **The James Walsh Gypsy Band**, they must have enjoyed much success but have retained a relatively low profile in collectors' circles since, apart from entries in Tom Tourville's ground-breaking 'Minnesota Rocked' discography. They may have relocated to California at some point, since their early album's were recorded there. The first double album is full of originals, which are psychedelic in mood with West Coast jazz-rock influences and some Southern rock tinges. One of the second album's highlights is *Another Way*, an Eastern-influenced jam which sounds not unlike early **Santana** - it's featured on the *Journey To The East* (LP) compilation.

The third album is more mainstream and not as good. It does consist entirely of originals, the better tracks being *Facing Time*, *Young Gypsy*, *Antithesis* and *Money*. Enrico Rosenbaum was the chief creative force behind **Gypsy** and sadly later committed suicide. James Walsh led several reformations in later years, and now works in a recording studio in Minneapolis doing independent production projects. Bill Lordan went on to work with **Sly and The Family Stone**, and later had a long-lasting relationship with Robin Trower, touring and recording with Trower for many years. (MW/VJ/RKg/BCy)

Gypsy Boots

Personnel: GYPSY BOOTS   A

ALBUM: 1(A) UNPREDICTABLE   (Sidewalk) 1967 -

45:     We're Havin' A Love In/I Feel So Fine   (Sidewalk 919) 1967

Rather than a group, this L.A. artist was the well-known Sunset Strip loony and 'Nature Boy', a (slightly) younger friend of Eden Ahbez and 'star' of 'Mondo Hollywood'.... He also made an album on Sidewalk and featured as a resident loony-about-Hollywood, living rough by the Hollywood Sign with the other Nature Boys. **Boots** was also a regular guest on Steve Allan's TV show, Steve used to make it a point to have local eccentrics on and one show featured **Frank Zappa** playing music on a bicycle frame way before he was famous. **Boots** was on his show a lot from the fifties onward.

At one time he lived in a tree in Topanga park...

Nowadays **Boots** spends much time promoting a health bar and generally healthy vegetarian diet.... with the enthusiastic support of Kirk and Michael Douglas, no less! (SR/JFr)

Gypsy Trips

Personnel: ROGER TILLISON   A
             TERRYE TILLISON   A

45:     Rock'n'Roll Gypsies/Ain't It Hard   (World Pacific 77809) 1965

Originally from Oklahoma but based in Los Angeles, the flip to this folk duo's 45 was covered by **The Electric Prunes** on their first 45. It has since been covered by Vancouver's Fiends on their 1992 *Zombie A Go Go* EP, and by Tim Gassen's Purple Merkins on the *Dig It* EP. *Rock 'n' Roll Gypsies* was also covered by **Hearts and Flowers**, on BOTH their Capitol albums and latterly compiled on *Nuggets, Vol. 10*. Teaming up with old friend and another Oklahoma emigre, **Leon Russell** - who now was working for the "Viva" label and adding J.J. Cale and you get **The Leathercoated Minds**' album.

In 1970, Roger Tillison made one good album, *Roger Tillison's Album* (Atco SD-355), strongly influenced by The Band And Dylan.

You can also find *Ain't It Hard* on *Pebbles, Vol. 9* (CD) and *Highs In The Mid-Sixties, Vol. 1* (LP). (MW/SR)

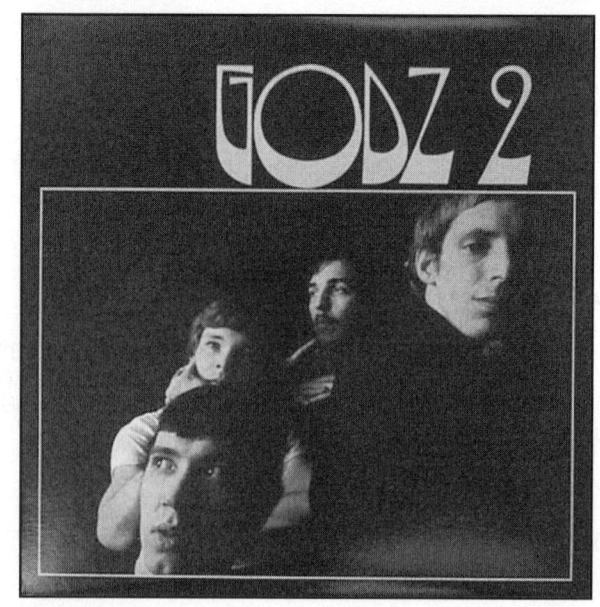

GODZ - Godz 2 LP.

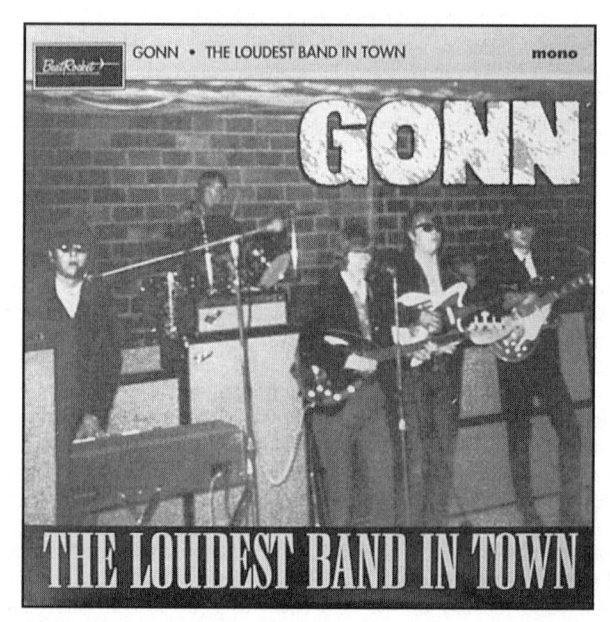

GONN - The Loudest Band In Town LP.

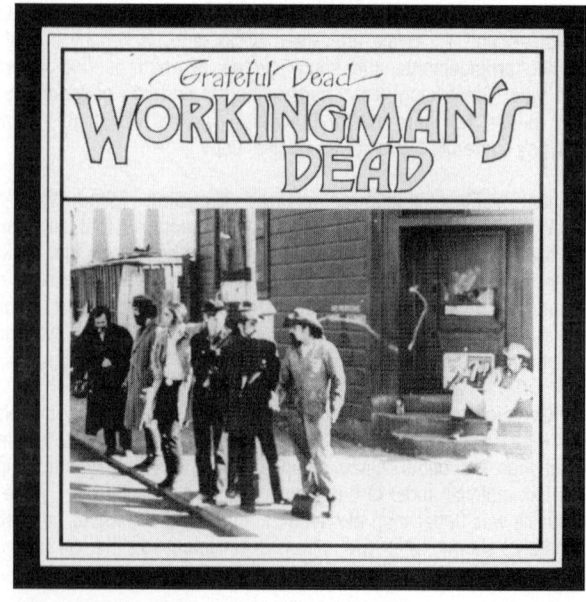

THE GRATEFUL DEAD - Workingman's Dead CD.

Bruce Haack

ALBUM: 1 THE ELECTRIC LUCIFER (Columbia) 1969 SC

NB: (1) reissued on vinyl, 2000.

An album of early electronic rock recorded with home made synthesizers, for fans of **Beaver and Krause** or **Tonto's Expanding Head Band**. *The Electric Lucifer* is not the same album as **Mort Garson**'s *Lucifer*, although it's in the same style.

Born in a mining camp in the Canadian Rockies, **Bruce Haack** went to the University of Alberta where he majored in psychology and began playing piano on a semi-professional base. He later moved to New York, wrote ballet music, Broadway and Off Broadway music, pop songs for Teresa Brewer, hundreds of commercials and invented the "dermi tron," an electronic device which allows the human body to be played as a musical device by means of skin contact...

In the late sixties, **Haack** built and played his own electronic instruments and that led him to record *The Electric Lucifer*, an album highly-regarded by some, with its hymn-like songs with human or synthetic voices alternating with dense electronic soundscapes.

Since the seventies, **Haack** has kept on recording all kinds of music, most of them beyond the scope of this book. He is seen as a pioneer of electronica. In 2000, he released *Electric Lucifer, Book 2* (QDK Media CD 037) with recordings made between 1979 and 2000. (SR)

BRUCE HAACK - The Electric Lucifer LP.

Hackamore Brick

Personnel:	ROBBIE BIEGE		A
	TOMMY MOONLIG		A
	CHICK NEWMAN		A
	BOB ROMAN		A

ALBUM: 1(A) ONE KISS LEADS TO ANOTHER (Kama Sutra 2025) 1971 -

45: Searchin'/Radio (Kama Sutra 521) 1971

Brooklyn in New York was home to this early seventies band who had a decidedly sixties sound. One reviewer described their live sound as 'like an early sixties psychedelic band'. *Nuggets, Vol. 5* (LP) features *Got A Gal Named Wilma*, a melodic number off their album which features some nice laid back guitar work. A band worth investigating and sadly too short-lived. (VJ)

Hackers

45: Keep On Running, Girl / Angel Love (J J's Jewel Wear .003) 1967

From the home of the FAME studios - Florence Alabama Music Enterprises. A decent folk-punker, *Keep On Running, Girl* can be found on *Fuzz, Flaykes, And Shakes, Vol. 2* (LP & CD). (MW)

Rosemary Haddad

ALBUM: 1 COMING HOME (No label) 1975 ?

From New Jersey, a hippie-folk singer with acoustic guitars, flute and percussion. Her album came housed in a psychy cover. (SR)

Jerry Hahn Brotherhood

Personnel:	CLYDE GRAVES	bs	A
	MEL GRAVES		A
	JERRY HAHN	gtr, vcls	A
	GEORGE MARSH	drms	A
	(MIKE FINNIGAN	keyb'ds, vcls	A)
	(MERLE SAUNDERS	keyb'ds	A)

ALBUMS: 1( ) ARA-BE-IN (Changes LP-7001) 1967 -
2(A) JERRY HAHN BROTHERHOOD (Columbia CS 1044) 1970 -

45: Captain Bobby Stout/Thursday Thing (Columbia 45195) 1970

A forgotten group fronted by a good guitarist, possibly from California. The first album came housed in a nice psychedelic art cover and was recorded in Berkeley. It contains tracks like *Ragahantar*, *Dippin' Snuff*, *In The Breeze* and *Ara-Be-In*. Ranging from psych-rock to jazz, their album was recorded with the help of **Mike Finnigan** and **Merle Saunders**. (SR)

Haircuts

Personnel incl: ROY STRAIGIS A

45: She Loves You / Love Me Do (Cameo Parkway 899) 1964

Mike Kuzmin's 'Sounds From The Woods' notes that this was a studio aggregation based in Philadelphia. They'd already released one 45 in 1963 as **The Emblems** and when Beatlemania took hold in 1964 they leapt on the bandwagon, releasing two albums on Wyncote as **The Liverpools**. (MW)

Hal and The Prophets

45: Shame Shame Shame/She's Doing Fine (Scepter 1287) 1964

This must be one of the best versions of the Jimmy Reed classic. Drivin' beat and some real mean but cool lead licks, like some early Jimmy Page. Shame on them for putting such an awful ballad on the flip. (MW)

Half Pint and The Fifths

45: Orphan Boy/Living On Borrowed Time (Orlyn 6018) 1966

A Chicago garage band. *Back From The Grave, Vol. 7* (Dble LP) features *Orphan Boy*, a bluesy song on which the Chicago influence is evident, whilst the flip can be found on *Tougher Than Stains* (LP). (VJ/MW)

Half Tribe

Personnel:	J.M. GAROUTRE	ld gtr	A
	JOHN HAWKINS	bs	A
	NICK HILTON	vcls	A
	DICK SAMMIS	drms	A
	DICK ZACHER	gtr	A

ALBUM: 1(A) ONLY STARTIN' (No label) 1965 R2

NB: (1) reissued on Resurrection (CX 1386) 1984.

From the Reading, Pennsylvania area this outfit, also known as the 'Half Tribe of Manasseh' or just 'The Tribe' left just one gloriously rare vinyl artifact - (no 45s traced) - of decent garage music featuring mainly covers - *Money*, *Empty Heart*, *Malagueña*, *Summertime*, etc. Shortly after this the band would disintegrate - Hawkins and Sammis going on to form **The Other Half** whose album is equally rare. (MW)

Sonny Hall

45:	The Battle Of The Moon/ Poor Planet Earth	(International Artists 131)	1969

This was a one-off venture on the Houston-based label. The flip, something of a novelty item, resurfaced on *Epitaph For A Legend* (Dble LP).

The Hallmarks

45:	Girl Of My Dreams/ Soul Shakin' Psychedelic Sally	(Smash S 2115)	1967

A bubblegum outfit, from Ocean Port, New Jersey, who combined well crafted harmonies with a garage-style rhythm section. They started off with a much rawer garage sound as evidenced by a previously unreleased 1966 acetate *I Know Why*. This is actually an earlier version of *Soul Shakin'*... and under this title has been covered by nineties garageniks the Mummies - whose live version is on *Follow That Munster, Vol. 2*.

Compilation appearances have included: *Soul Shakin' Psychedelic Sally* on *A Journey To Tyme, Vol. 2* (LP); and *I Know Why* on *Back From The Grave, Vol. 4* (LP) and *Back From The Grave, Vol. 2* (CD). (MW)

Sammy Hall Singers

Personnel incl: SAMMY HALL vcls A

ALBUM: 1(A) WHAT'S IT ALL ABOUT (Christian Folk) c1970 ?

An extremely strange album of Christian artists with an anti-drugs and alcohol message. One side is comprised of rather trippy folk songs with fuzz guitars, while the other is more in the country and western genre with steel guitar. The album is worth getting for its rather scary cover, which features a spoon full of cooked up heroin, a bottle of Jack Daniels and various assorted products.

Sammy Hall had previously played in the Florida garage bands **The Mor-Loks**, The Trolls and **The Birdwatchers**. (SR)

The Hamilton Face Band

Personnel:	ALAN COOPER	bs, vcls, trumpet	A
	LENNY LAKS	vcls, trumpet, bs, sax	A
	STEVE MARGOSHES	piano, trombone	A
	RUTH ROMANOFF	drms	A
	RONNIE SELDIN	gtr, bs	A
	(AMOS BLACK	wah wah pedal	A)

ALBUMS:	1( )	KABBALAT SHABBAT		
			(Temple Judea TJU-1001)	1968 SC
	2(A)	THE HAMILTON FACE BAND		
			(Philips PHS 600.308)	1969 -
	3(A)	AIN'T GOT NO TIME	(Bell 6042)	1970 -

NB: (1) private press.

45:	Banana Song / High Why And Die Company	(Philips 40603)	1969

THE HALF TRIBE - Only Startin' LP.

The Hamilton Face Band's first album *Kabbalat Shabbat*, was a private pressing from 1968. It consists of a sabbath service composed by Steven Margoshes, featuring Cantor Robert Bloch and Kirsten Sorteberg on vocals, plus Rabbi Sanford Lowe presiding over the services. It was released by Temple Judea in Valley Stream, New York.

Produced by Anne Tansey and housed in a nice sleeve, their second album is a good mix of jazz, blues and psych. All the tracks are group compositions but with some assistance of Paul Wolfe, who was credited as their lyrics writer. The best cuts are *High Why And Die Company*, *Speed Song* and *Slippery Sweet* but the whole album is worth a listen.

Before the third album, Ruth Romanoff married Ian Underwood from **The Mothers Of Invention** and was credited as Ruth Underwood. Produced by Johanan Vigoda, all the tracks were once again composed by Margoshes, Seldin and Laks, but the result is not as interesting, although *United States Atomic Energy Control Plant*, *Ghost Of A Highway Child* and a new version of *High Why And Die Company* are worth a listen.

When the group broke up, Ruth Underwood went on to play with the **Mothers (Of Invention)** and became an important element of **Frank Zappa**'s group in the early seventies. Steve Margoshes became a songwriter, notably in 1972 for the country-pop duet Hod and Marc. (VJ/MW/SR/MMs)

Hamilton Peach

45:	With The Girl That You Love/ One Way Ticket Down	(CEI CE-131)	1967

A melodic minor-mood ballad backed by a keyboard dominated instrumental. The CEI label moved from Toledo, Ohio, to Maryland in 1966 and returned in late '68, so it's likely that the band was from that area. (MW/GGI)

Hamilton Streetcar

Personnel:	JOHN BOYLAN	A
	BUZZ CLIFFORD	A
	RALPH PLUMMER	A

ALBUM: 1(A) HAMILTON STREETCAR (Dot DLP 25939) 1969 -

45s:	Invisible People/Flash	(LH1 17016)	1968
	Confusion/Your Own Comedown	(LH1 1206)	1968
	Silver Wings/I See I Am	(Dot 17253)	1969
	Brother Speed/Wasn't It You?	(Dot 17279)	1969
	Honey And Wine/Now I Taste The Tears	(Dot 17306)	1969

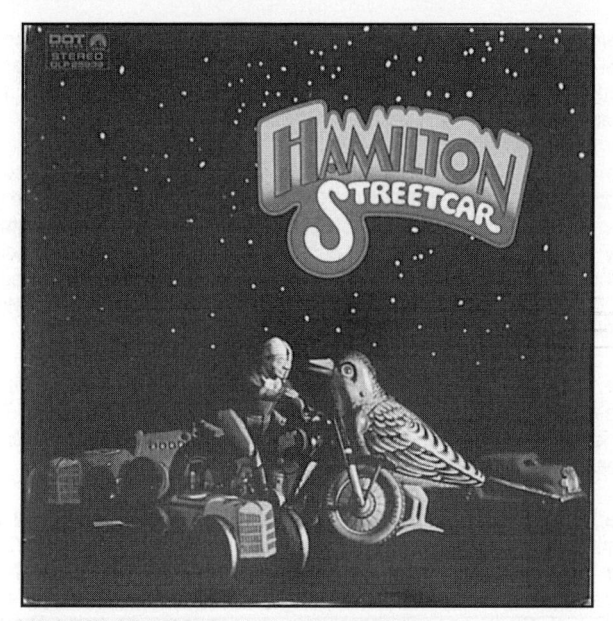

HAMILTON STREETCAR - Hamilton Streetcar LP.

This Los Angeles band's finest moment was the non-album *Invisible People*. It has a catchy organ intro, vocals of some commercial potential and some fine fuzztone guitar work. It's 'B' side, *Flash*, is more laid back.

Their album, is viewed by some as orchestral mainstream pop and rather disappointing by comparison. Others, however, think it is absolutely incredible... It features original tunes along with covers by the likes of **Lee Michaels** (*Streetcar*) and **Tim Buckley** (*Pleasant Street*). One track, written by **Buzz Clifford**, *I See I Am*, was also recorded by **The East Side Kids** on their *Tiger And The Lamb* (LP), which **Clifford** produced and contributed his song *Pigeon Of LA*. Another of **Clifford**'s songs from the album, *Now I Taste The Tears* was covered by **Beacon Street Union** on their *Clown Died In Marvin Gardens* album. A third, *Brother Speed*, written by John Boylan, was also recorded by **Appletree Theatre**, of whom Boylan was also a member. All the Dot singles are taken from the album.

Buzz Clifford also recorded a solo version of *I See I Am* on his second solo album.

John Boylan went into management and later became a producer, with Linda Ronstadt and **Russ Giguere** (who covered his *Brother Speed*) among his credits.

Invisible People was also covered by The Slickee Boys in 1983.

Compilation appearances have included: *Flash* on *Psychedelic Unknowns, Vol. 11* (LP) and *Slowly Growing Insane* (CD); *Silver Wings* on *Turds On A Bum Ride, Vol. 1 & 2* (Dble CD) and *Turds On A Bum Ride, Vol. 2* (Dble LP); and *Invisible People* on *Highs In The Mid-Sixties, Vol. 3* (LP). (VJ/KSI)

Hamlet

ALBUM: 1 HAMLET (Capitol) 1973 -

45s: I Should Have Known/Just A Touch (Capitol 3543) 1973
Lazy Summer/Little You Say (Capitol 3603) 1973
I Feel Like Smiling/Voodoo Man (Capitol 3716) 1973

An anglophile rock group so greatly influenced by the Beatles that they adopted English accents! (SR)

Hammer

Personnel:	JOHN GUERIN	drms	A
	NORMAN LANDSBERG	keyb'ds	A
	RITCHIE McBRIDE	bs	A
	JACK O'BRIEN	ld gtr	A
	JOHN DE ROBERTS	vcls	A

ALBUM: 1(A) HAMMER (San Francisco SD 203) 1970 -
NB: (1) also released in France on Atlantic.

A second generation San Francisco band whose debut album was superb. Two tracks from it (*Tuane* and *Charity Taylor*) can also be found on *San Francisco Sampler - Fall 1970*. The band also recorded a second album which was never released.

Guerin was a session artist who also had spells with **The Byrds** and Muleskinner. (VJ/SR)

Hammerhead

45: Summer Nite/Jewels (GNP Crescendo GNP-499) c1969

A hard-rock single co-written and produced by **Kim Fowley**. (SR)

Paul Hampton

ALBUM: 1 REST HOME FOR CHILDREN (Crested Butte) 1973 -

On the same label as **Chirco**, an odd singer-songwriter. Already an experienced singer and actor when he recorded this album, **Hampton** began recording in 1959 and released over twenty 45s on various labels. One of them, *Two Hour Honeymoon/Creams* (Dot) circa 1963, was a maudlin yet strangely effective rumination after a car crash where he talks to his girlfriend as he knows he's dying, set over a sleazy jazz track. (SR/PPn)

Hampton Grease Band

Personnel:	JERRY FIELDS	perc, vcls	A
	BRUCE HAMPTON	vcls, trumpet	A
	MIKE HOLBROOK	bs	A
	HAROLD KELLING	gtr, vcls	A
	GLENN PHILLIPS	gtr, sax	A

ALBUM: 1(A) MUSIC TO EAT (dbl) (Columbia G 30555) 1971 -
NB: (1) has been reissued on CD.

From Atlanta, this is a totally demented album which should appeal to fans of weird psychedelic groups. **The Hampton Grease Band** somehow managed to sign a contract with Columbia and released *Music To Eat*, a double album which seems to have had one of the worst sales in the Columbia history. It was "produced" by the group with David Baker and

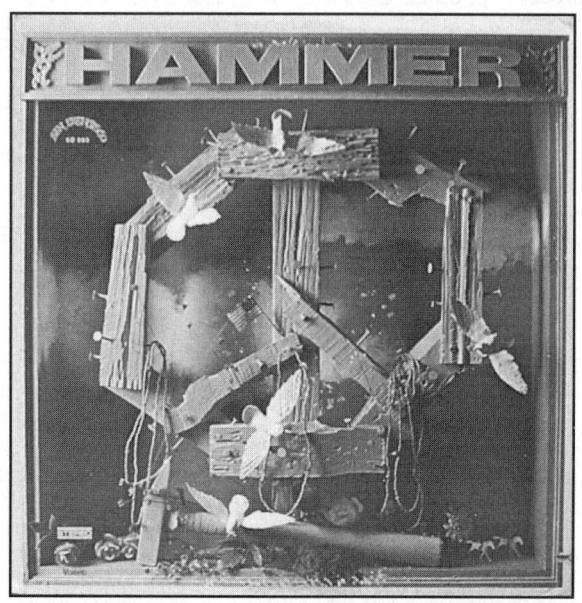

HAMMER - Hammer LP.

contains only seven long tracks: *Halifax*, *Mario*, *Six*, *Evans*, *Lowton*, *Hey Old Lady* and *Hendon*. Hampton screams, whispers, sings, a la **Captain Beefheart** or **Far Cry**, while Kelling and Phillips explore various styles of guitar, from jazz, blues and rock to oriental music and freak out experiences. The lyrics are really weird, even including the reading of the label of a paint tin. The gatefold sleeve is strange too and mentions that "the people pictured here have complete control of the North American Continent at this very second"!

Ptolemaic Terrascope magazine would later release two live tracks by the band on one of their free 45s.

Glenn Phillips went on to release several solo albums on his SnowStar label (Caroline/Virgin released some of them in England) and to play with the improvisation specialist Henry Kaiser, who often quotes him as a strong influence. The "Colonel" Bruce Hampton also had a fragmented solo career and is apparently still performing and recording. (SR)

A Handful

45: Dying Daffodil Incident/? (LHI) c1968

An obscure and weird garage group, on Lee Hazlewood label. (SR)

Gayle Haness

Personnel incl: ABIGALE HANESS vcls A

45: Johnny Ander/Love Love Go Away (Bang 535) 1966

Singer Abigale Haness recorded this 45 as **Gayle Hanness** in 1966. The 'A' side has reappeared on *Girls In The Garage, Vol. 2* (CD) and *Girls In The Garage, Vol. 7* (LP) (miscredited to Gale Haness); it's an excellent Jeff Barry production, very dramatic (in a Shangri-Las kind of way) about a teenaged boy who joins some hippies, smokes dope, then dies!

Abigale later resurfaced in **Jo Mama**. (JLh)

Lynn Haney

ALBUM: 1 REBIRTH (Tribute) c1972 SC?

A female folk-rock singer with some psychy influences, her album came housed in a black and white sleeve. (SR)

Hangmen

Personnel: BOB BERBERICH drms ABC
            GEORGE DALY gtr ABC
            TOM GUERNSEY gtr ABC
            JOE TRIPPLET vcls A
            DAVE OTTLEY vcls B
            MIKE WEST bs A
            PAUL DOWELL bs BC
            TONY TAYLOR vcls C

ALBUM: 1(C) BITTERSWEET (Monument SLP 18077) 1966 -

NB: (1) also issued in France on Monument.

45s: What A Girl Can't Do/
     The Girl Who Faded Away (Monument 910) 1965
     Faces/Bad Goodbye (Monument 951) 1966
     Dream Baby/Let It Be Me (Monument 983) 1966

One of Washington D.C.'s most popular and successful sixties bands, their story began with an act called **The Reekers** who were formed by guitarist Tom Guernsey in 1964. Following the release of their debut 45 - *Don't Call Me Flyface / Grindin'* (Ru-Jac 13) in early 1965, Bob Berberich was recruited on drums and **The Reekers** laid down early versions of *What A Girl Can't Do* and *The Girl Who Faded Away*. No 45 resulted.

After more personnel changes the band re-emerged as the **Hangmen** in April 1965, with vocalist Dave Ottley - a British ex-pat working as a hairdresser in DC. The band re-recorded the **Reekers**' tracks for their first 45 and *What A Girl Can't Do* is a classy girl-put-down belter.

The 45 was a local hit, and an in-store appearance at the Giant Record Shop in Falls Church, nearly caused a riot. Billboard magazine reported the near riot in Feb '66, when 400 teenagers gathered to hear **The Hangmen** play at the store, with a further 1,500 packed outside the shop. The police had to disperse the crowd after 15 minutes, with traffic being disrupted in the street. The shops owner told Billboard he'd sold 2,500 copies of *What A Girl Can't Do*.

The follow-up, the stunning *Faces*, is also a five-star mean'n'moody fuzz-rocker with Who power chords and obtuse lyrics - PLAY LOUD. This 45 featured new bassist Paul Dowell and Ottley moved on soon after its release to be replaced by Tony Taylor (ex-Roaches).

The third 45 was a taster for the album that appeared at the turn of the year. *Bittersweet* includes rather lame reworkings of *What A Girl Can't Do* and *Faces* and for fans of the first two garage-punk 45s it may be a disappointment. It's good, but not that good, despite a five-minute-plus version of *Gloria*, and will appeal more to pop fans with tracks like the dreamy version of the Everly Brothers' *Let It Be Me*.

By the Summer of '67 the band's direction shifted to psychedelia and their name changed to The Button. Daly and Dowell had been replaced by guitarist George Strunz and Alan Fowler, former bassist of the Mad Hatters. Founder Tom Guernsey left soon after and The Button relocated to Greenwich Village where they evolved into **Graffiti**.

When Berberich left The Button, he returned to DC. There he reunited with Dowell and Daly to form **(Paul Dowell and) The Dolphin**. Their line-up was completed by a young and talented guitarist called Nils Lofgren. Berberich also sat in with **Puzzle** for a while when their drummer was injured in a car accident.

In 1968, Tom Guernsey produced a 45 by **The Piece Kor**. He was also reunited with **Reekers** vocalist Joe Triplett, writing and producing a 45 for **The Omegas**. In the seventies he returned to performing with brother John in the band Claude Jones. Dave Ottley returned to the U.K. and is now a hairdresser in Barnet, London.

You can read all about the **Hangmen** in Bob Embrey's zine 'DC Monuments', issue #11. More recently, the band have been planning a reunion gig - probably in Washington DC in April/May 2002....

Compilation appearances have included: *What A Girl Can't Do* and *Faces* (45 version) on *Psychotic Moose And The Soul Searchers* (LP); *What A Girl Can't Do* on *Pebbles, Vol. 1 (ESD)* (CD) and *Signed, D.C.* (LP); *Faces* (45 version) on *Sixties Choice, Vol. 1* (LP) and *60's Choice Collection, Vol's 1 And 2* (CD); and *The Girl Who Faded Away* (acetate) on *Garage Dreams Revisited, Vol. 1* (7"). (VJ/MW/RuJ/BE/DO)

THE HANGMEN.

Hangmen of Fairfield County

45: Stacey/I Don't Want You Around (High Castle HC 401) 1966

A Fairfield, Connecticut outfit. *Stacey* can also be heard on *Hipsville 29 B.C.* (LP). (VJ)

Ha'Pennys

ALBUM: 1 LOVE IS NOT THE SAME (Fersch FL 1110) 1966 R2/R3

NB: (1) reissued on Resurrection in 1985.

A prep-punk outfit from Philips Academy, Andover, Massachusetts. The album is pretty low key beat in style, comprising mostly British invasion covers (e.g. *Day Tripper, Get Off Of My Cloud, Heart Full Of Sound, We Gotta Get Out Of This Place, You're A Better Man Than I*) with one original, the title folk-rock cut. Like all the prep rock albums, it's very rare. (VJ)

The Happy Dragon-Band

Personnel:			
	JOHN (BEE) BADANJEK	drms	A
	TOM CARSON	vcls	A
	DENNIS CRANER	bs	A
	MIKE de MARTINO	keyb'ds	A
	JOHN FRAGA	bs	A
	CECILY LONERGAN	vcls	A
	GARY MEISNER	gtr	A
	MIKE ORZEL	tamb	A
	CLEM RICCOBONO	vcls	A
	RALPH SARAFINO	drms	A
	SCOTT STRAWBRIDGE	gtr	A
	BRIAN WHITE	gtr	A

ALBUM: 1(A) THE HAPPY DRAGON-BAND
(Fiddlers Music Company) 1978 R2

NB: (1) has been repressed.

This is possibly a future collectors' item, certainly an unusual one. A guy called Tommy Court was the brainchild behind the band. He wrote and produced all the songs. There's lots of synthesizer on the album. The better tracks are *Positive People*, which consists of lots of electronic acrobatics; *In Flight*, an exercise in cosmic electronics; *A Long Time* and *Inside The Pyramid*, both notable for electronic sound effects and, finally, *3-D Free*, which stars with a kind of electronic freakout and carries on in a similar mould pretty much throughout with some vocals at the end.

The group came from Michigan and were related to **Phantom**. (VJ/CF)

The Happy Feeling

ALBUM: 1 THE HAPPY FEELING
(Avco Embassy AVE 330??) 1970 -

NB: (1) also released in the UK.

A flower-power pop group. (SR)

Harbinger Complex

Personnel incl:			
	GARY CLARK	bs	
	JIM HOCKSTAFF	lead vcl	
	BOB HOYLE	ld gtr	
	JIM REDDING	drms	
	RON ROTARIUS	gtr	A

45s:		
	Sometimes I Wonder/ Tomorrow's Soul Sound	(Amber 8999) 1966
	I Think I'm Down/My Dear And Kind Sir	(Brent 7056) 1966

HA'PENNYS - Love Is Not The Same LP.

From Fremont, California, originally, this San Jose band operated between 1966-67 producing two singles and appearing on Mainstream's 1967 *A Pot Of Flowers* compilation. Four tracks were included on the compilation *I Think I'm Down* and *My Dear And Kind Sir*, which had earlier been issued as a 45 on Brent and *When You Know You're In Love* and *Time To Kill*.

Compilation appearances have included: *I Think I'm Down, My Dear And Kind Sir, Time To Kill* and *When You Know You're In Love* on *Mindrocker, Vol. 10* (Dble LP); *I Think I'm Down* on *Nuggets Box* (4-CD) and *Nuggets, Vol. 12* (LP); and both *I Think I'm Down* and *My Dear Kind Sir* on *Sound Of The Sixties: San Francisco Part 2* (LP). (VJ/MW/BTr)

Tim Hardin

Personnel:			
	GARY BURTON	vibes	A
	BOB BUSHNELL	bs	A
	TIM HARDIN	vcls, gtr, piano	ABCDE
	PHIL KRAUSS	vibes	A
	EARL PALMER	drms	A
	BUDDY SALTZMANN	drms	A
	JOHN SEBASTIAN	hrmnca	A
	WALTER YOST	bs	A
	WARREN BERNHARDT	keyb'ds	DE
	EDDIE GOMEZ	bs	D
	DANIEL HANKIN	gtr	D
	DONALD MacDONALD	drms	DE
	MIKE MAINIERI	vibes	D
	BUZZ	celeste	E
	MONTE DUNN	gtr	E
	GARY KLEIN	keyb'ds	E
	PHILIPE	conga	E

HCP

ALBUMS:			
1(A)	TIM HARDIN I	(Verve Forecast FTS-3004) 1966	- -
2(B)	TIM HARDIN II	(Verve Forecast FTS-3022) 1967	- -
3(C)	THIS IS TIM HARDIN	(Atco SD33-210) 1967	- -
4(D)	LIVE IN CONCERT	(Verve Forecast FTS-3049) 1968	- -
5(D)	TIM HARDIN 4	(Verve Forecast FTS-3064) 1969	- -
6(F)	SUITE FOR SUSAN MOORE AND DAMIAN	(Columbia CS9787) 1970	129 -
7(-)	THE BEST OF TIM HARDIN	(Verve Forecast FTS-3078) 1970	189 -
8(-)	BIRD ON A WIRE	(Columbia 30551) 1970	- -

NB: (1) and (2) repackaged as double album in 1974. (1) and (2) have also been reissued on one CD (Repertoire IMS 7030). (3) reissued on Edsel (1989) and again on CD (Atlantic 7567 80780 2) 2000. (5) has been reissued on CD by Polygram in 1996 with three extra tracks. There have also been a couple of compilations: *Hang On To A Dream - The Verve Recordings* (Verve) 1995 and *Simple Songs Of Freedom: The Collection* which is a double CD set with forty-seven tracks, fifteen of which are previously unreleased (Columbia/Legacy 485108-2) 1996. *Person To Person - The Essential Classic Hardin, 1963 - 1980* (Raven RVCD 104) is an

Australian compilation that provides a good overview for anyone seeking an introduction to his career.

45s:	Hang On To A Dream/		
	It'll Never Happen Again	(Verve Forecast KF-5008)	196? -
	Misty Roses/		
	Don't Make Promises	(Verve Forecast KF-5017)	1966 -
	Misty Roses/		
	Hang On To A Dream	(Verve Forecast KF-5031)	1966 -
	Green Rocky Road/		
	Never Too Far	(Verve Forecast KF-5042)	1967 -
	Black Sheep Boy/Misty Roses	(Verve Forecast KF-5048)	1967 -
	Tribute To Hank Williams/		
	You Upset The Grace Of Living	(Verve Forecast KF-5059)	196? -
	Lady Came From Baltimore/		
	Don't Make Promises	(Verve Forecast PB 3078)	1968 -
	Reason To Believe/		
	Smugglin' Man	(Verve Forecast KF-5097)	1968 -
	Simple Song Of Freedom/		
	Question Of Birth	(Columbia 44920)	1969 50
	Reason To Believe/Smugglin'	(Verve Forecast KF-5116)	1971 -

NB: There was also a French 45 *Smuglin' Man/Misty Roses* (Verve Forecast 518909) 1968 and one Dutch 45 *Do The Do / Sweet Lady* (CBS 1016) 1972. All the 45 cuts feature on his albums. There's also a French EP with PS: *If I Were A Carpenter/Hang On To A Dream/It'll Never Happen Again/Don't Make Promises* (Verve Folkways 519 902) 1967.

In many ways rather a sad figure, **Hardin** was influential on many other performers throughout the era, although commercial success proved elusive. Born in Eugene, Oregon on 13th September 1940 and an ancestor of the notorious outlaw John Wesley Harding, he was discharged from the U.S. marines in 1961 and then embraced the early sixties Boston folk movement, singing in an emotive style that was more jazz and blues-based than folky.

Although he never achieved the kind of success he deserved, the strength of his songwriting is indisputable: *If I Were A Carpenter* was covered by Bobby Darin, and was a chart hit for Johnny Cash and The Four Tops. The song was also covered by **American Blues**, Shaggs, The Small Faces, **Electronic Rubayyat**, **Velvet Night**, **Grant's Blueboys**, **Leon Russell** and Look. Another **Hardin** composition *Reason To Believe* was also covered by Rod Stewart, Hearts & Flowers, **Scott McKenzie** and **The Critters**; *Danville Dame* was recorded by the **Blues Project** and *Yellow Cab* by **Buzzy Linhardt**.

Hardin himself had a minor U.K. hit in January 1967 with *Hang On To A Dream*. This too was covered by many bands during the psychedelic era including: **Art of Lovin'**, **Gandalf**, The Nice and **The Alan Lorber Orchestra**. It is somewhat ironic then that **Hardin**'s only U.S. hit *Simple Song Of Freedom* was not self-penned - it was written by Bobby Darin.

Although released in 1967, the Atco album contains his first recordings from 1963/64: ten folk-blues tracks; some originals (including one co-penned with Steve Weber from the **Holy Modal Rounders**), a cover of **Fred Neil**'s *Blues On The Ceiling* and some traditional songs: *Cocaine Bill*, *House Of The Rising Sun* and *Stagger Lee*.

Signed to Verve Forecast in 1966, his first real album was produced by Erik Jacobsen and used various jazz musicians plus **John Sebastian** from the **Lovin' Spoonful** (another Jacobsen production). The most well-known tracks are *Misty Roses* and *Reason To Believe* but all the tracks are equally impressive.

The back-up group on *Tim Hardin 2* is uncredited and the album, produced by Koppelman and Rubin, contains *If I Were A Carpenter*, *Lady Came From Baltimore* as well as *You Upset The Grace Of Living When You Lie*.

Live In Concert and *4* were both recorded live at Town Hall in New York in April 1968 and use MacDonald, Bernhardt and Gomez, (three members of **Jeremy and the Satyrs**). Jacobsen again produced. Both records are good and contain mainly songs from the Atco and Verve studio albums.

Hardin then moved to Columbia for what is probably his most intimate album. *Suite For Susan Moore And Damion - We Are - One, One, All In One* is a concept album dedicated to his wife, Susan Moore (already pictured while pregnant on *Tim Hardin 2* sleeve) and their son Damion. Produced by Gary Klein, its ten songs are divided into four sections:

TIM HARDIN - 1+2 CD.

'Implication I', 'II', 'III' and 'End Of Implication' and the result must be heard for his inventive songwriting.

In 1974, **Hardin** moved to Britain and signed to GM to produce what would be his last album: *Nine*. Although he intended to live permanently in the U.K. at first, he returned to America where he lived in comparative obscurity until his death on 29th December 1980, from a drug overdose. Among his last projects was an attempt to start a duo with **Tim Rose**, which sadly came to nothing. His final recording session from December 1980 was issued on album as *Unforgiven* (San Francisco Sound SFS 10810) 1981.

Compilation coverage has so far included: MGMs late sixties label-taster *The Core Of Rock* which features two of his classic originals *If I Were A Carpenter* and *Reason To Believe*. *Reading Festival 1973* captures his performance of *Hang Onto A Dream* and *Person To Person* from that festival and you can also find some 1980 performances of *Judge And Jury* and *Unforgiven* on Matthew Katz's *Then And Now, Vol. 1* (CD). *Then And Now, Vol. 2* (CD) also includes *Luna Cariba* and *Secret* from the same performances. (VJ/MW/SR/CF)

The Hardtimes

Personnel:	LARRY BYROM	bs, gtr	A
	LEE KIEFER	vcls, harp	A
	BOB MORRIS	bs	A
	BILL RICHARDSON	ld gtr	A
	RUDY ROMERO	gtr	A
	PAUL WHEATBREAD	drms	A

ALBUM: 1(A) BLEW MIND (World Pacific WPS 21867) 1968 -

NB: (1) also issued in Argentina (Trova WP-1867).

HCP

45s:	α	There'll Be A Time/		
		You're Bound To Cry	(World Pacific 77816)	1966 -
	α	Come To Your Window/		
		That's All I'll Do	(World Pacific 77826)	1966 -
		Fortune Teller/Goodbye	(World Pacific 77851)	1966 97
	β	Sad, Sad, Sunshine/They Said No	(World Pacific 77864)	1967 -
		Colours/Blew Mind	(World Pacific 77873)	1967 -

NB: α non LP. β flip is non LP.

A San Diego pop-punk band which later relocated to Los Angeles. They released several 45s and were regulars on Dick Clark's TV Show 'Where The Action Is'. Of their 45s, *There'll Be A Time*, *You're Bound To Cry*, *Come To Your Window*, *That's All I'll Do* and *They Said No* were non-LP.

Kiefer went on to do production work, Romero to a solo career, Wheatbread drummed for **Gary Puckett And The Union Gap** and

Richardson and Byrom joined **T.I.M.E.**. Byrom later played for **Steppenwolf**. Between them there's also a 45 by **New Phoenix** from 1968 (*Give To Me Your Love/Thanks on World* Pacific (77884)) - both songs credited to Rudy Romero and sounding just like the **Hardtimes** - possibly it is or maybe Romero's next venture.

Compilation appearances include: *They Said No* on *The Lost Generation, Vol. 2* (LP). (VJ/MW/ML)

Hard Times

| Personnel incl: | ROBY BENNETT | ld gtr | A |

| 45: | Can't Wait'Till Friday/ Old Wine, New Bottle | (Gray Ant 107) 1966 |

A different Washington D.C. outfit whose *Can't Wait 'Till Friday* has resurfaced on *Garage Punk Unknowns, Vol. 2* (LP).

Lead guitarist Roby Bennett is now a neurosurgeon. (VJ)

Hard Times

| Personnel incl: | MICHAEL GUNNELS | A |
| | RONALD PARR | A |

| 45: | You Couldn't Love Me / Losing You | (Ultimate 1) 1966 |

A Birmingham, Alabama, group who released their sole 45 in 1966 after winning a local Battle Of The Bands. They travelled all the way to Frankford Wayne Recording Labs in Philadelphia to record the follow-up. There exists an acetate, *Why / No Name* (Frankford/Wayne Studios no #). At that point the band changed their name because San Diego's **Hard Times** had gained national exposure via ABC-TV'S 'Where The Action Is'.

Produced by **Terry Knight** (of **The Pack**) both tracks appeared under the band's new identity, **The Rites Of Spring** - *Why / Comin' On Back To Me* (Cameo Parkway 109) - in October 1966. *No Name* had become *Comin' On Back To Me* with the addition of vocals. (JLh/MW)

Hardwater

Personnel:	RICHARD OTIS FIFIELD	A
	ROBERT CARL McLERRAN	A
	TONY MURILLO	A
	PETER M. WYANT	A

| ALBUM: | 1(A) | HARDWATER | (Capitol ST 2954) 1968 R1 |

| 45s: | City Sidewalks/Not So Hard | (Capitol 2230) 1968 |
| | Plate Of My Fare/ Good Old Friends | (Capitol Records 2373) 1969 |

Rich Fifield joined **The Astronauts** in 1963 and was their last original member when the group disbanded in 1967. Fifield plus the last line-up (Murillo, McLerran, Wyant and Bretz) went on to record one 45 as **Sunshine Ward**. When Bretz left they became **Hardwater**.

Produced by **David Axelrod**, their album is pleasant hard/soft West Coasty rock and folk-rock sounds with Crosby, Stills and Nash-like three part harmonies. Whilst neither psych, garage nor hippie-rock it still merits a mention here for its laid-back feel and some fluid guitar-work. All tracks are group originals except *City Sidewalks*, *Sanctuary* and *Good Ole Friends*, which were written by Carter-Gilbert (John and Tim), creative source behind Denver's **Rainy Daze**. *Good Luck* is in fact a rip-off of the Beatles' *Taxman*.

Coincidentally the very same Carter-Gilbert tracks appear on the **Yankee Dollar** album. Is there another connection between these two outfits?

Peter Wyant would later play with **David Axelrod** on his solo albums.

Compilation appearances include: *Sanctuary* on *Rock A Delics* (LP). (MW/AGI/SR)

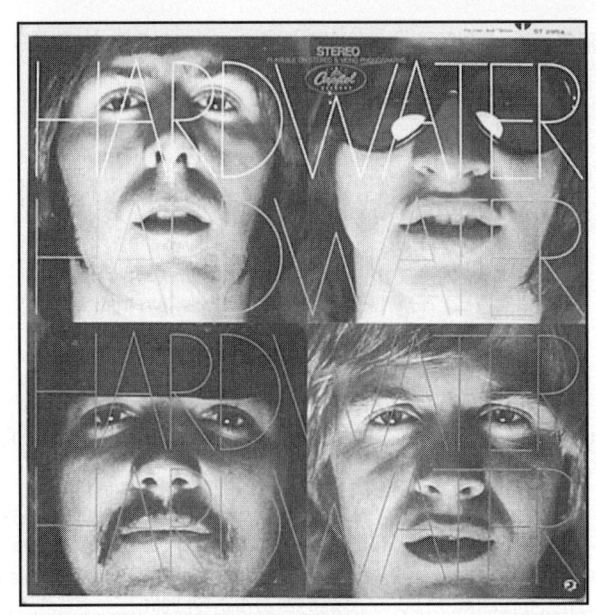

HARDWATER - Hardwater LP.

Bob Hardy

Personnel:	ROGER DUMAS	synth	A
	BOB HARDY	vcls, gtr	A
	DAVE RIFKIN	gtr	A
	CLARK YOST		A

| ALBUM: | 1(A) | DREAMER OF SONGS | (Citsatnaf #S80-1341) 1976 ? |

Recorded at Sound 80 Studios, St. Paul, Minnesota, comes this album of psych-tinged folk-rock songs, mostly originals penned by Hardy (*Dreamer Of Songs*, *Wake Up Sunshine* and *The Storm*). The label, Citsatnaf, is "fantastic" written backwards! (SR)

Harlequin

| 45: | Trees/What's Your Pleasure | (Headsong no #) c1972 |

A prog-psych group from Long Island, they released only this rare single, in the same style as **Cathedral** (both groups played the same circuit). (SR)

Ray Harlowe and Gyp Fox

| Personnel incl: | RAY HARLOWE | A |

| ALBUM: | 1(A) | FIRST RAYS | (Water Wheel WR-711) 1978 - |

The above album is now a significant collectors' item. Please note: if you're expecting sixties psychedelia, forget this - if you're into obscure rock with lots of different influences including COUNTRY(!), then "you got it". Batches of this private press have been 'unearthed' in the last few years and dealers have hyped this one to death - you have been warned!! (VJ/MW)

Harper and Rowe

| Personnel: | HARPER | vcls | A |
| | ROWE | vcls | A |

| ALBUM: | 1(A) | HARPER AND ROWE | (World Pacific WPS-21882) 1967 - |

A psych-pop duet, nothing is known about them and their backing group. Their only album was produced by Ed Ver Schure and Ralph Murphy (who also wrote eight of the twelve tracks) and they were managed by William McEuen (who also managed **Nitty Gritty Dirt Band**, **Sunshine Company** and **Hourglass**). The album is quite patchy and contains folk-pop (*Hello Sleepy Sidewalks*), rock (*Love Machine*, penned by Gordon and Griffin), and orchestrated pop (*Here Comes Yesterday Again*). One of the best tracks is *The Dweller*, with flute and guitars, composed by Marcellino and Larson. It is beginning to interest some collectors. (SR)

Harper's Bizarre

Personnel:	EDDIE JAMES	gtr	A
	JOHN PETERSEN	drms, vcls	A
	DICK SCOPPETONE	ld vcls, gtr, bs	A
	TED TEMPLEMAN	ld vcls, gtr, trumpet, drms	A
	DICK YOUNT	bs, vcls	A

HCP

ALBUMS:	1(A)	FEELIN' GROOVY	(Warner Bros. WS 1693) 1967	108 -
	2(A)	ANYTHING GOES	(Warner Bros. WS 1716) 1967	76 -
	3(A)	THE SECRET LIFE OF HARPER'S BIZARRE	(Warner Bros. WS 1739) 1968	- -
	4(A)	HARPER'S BIZARRE 4	(Warner Bros. WS 1784) 1969	- -

NB: Several compilations also exist, including *Best Of* (Warner Brothers K 56044) 1974. (1) - (4) reissued on CD (Sundazed SC 6176-6179) 2001.

HCP

45s:	Anything Goes/ Chattanooga Choo Choo	(Warner Bros. 1790) 1967 -
	59th St Bridge Song (Feelin Groovy)/ Come To The Sunshine	(Warner Bros.) 1967 -
	59th Street Bridge Song (Feelin' Groovy)/ Lost My Love Today	(Warner Bros. WB 5890) 1967 13
	Come To The Sunshine/ The Debutante's Ball	(Warner Bros. 7028) 1967 37
	Anything Goes/Malibu U	(Warner Bros. 7063) 1967 43
	Hey, You In The Crowd/ Chattanooga Choo Choo	(Warner Bros. 7090) 1967 -
	Cotton Candy Sandman/Virginia City	(Warner Bros. 7172) 1968 -
	Both Sides Now/Small Talk	(Warner Bros. 7200) 1968 123
	Battle Of New Orleans/ Green Apple Trees	(Warner Bros. 7223) 1968 95
	I Love You Alice B.Toklas/ Look To The Rainbow	(Warner Bros. 7238) 1969 -
	Knock On Wood/Witchi Tai To	(Warner Bros. 7296) 1969 -
	Soft Sounding Music/ All Through The night	(Warner Bros.) 1969 -
	Anything Goes/Virginia City	(Warner Bros. 7388) 1970 -
	Poly High/Soft Soundin' Music	(Warner Bros. 7377) 1970 -
	If We Ever Needed The Lord Before/ Mad	(Warner Bros. 7399) 1970 -
	Knock On Wood/Poly High	(Warner Bros. 7647) 1972 -
	59th Street Bridge Song (Feelin' Groovy)//Anything Goes Chattanooga Choo Choo	(Warner Bros. K 16305) 1973 -

NB: There was also a French single with a picture sleeve *Chattanooga Choo Choo*/*Hey, You In The Crowd* (Warner WV5087) 1968. (12) also released in France with a picture sleeve (Warner WV 5125) 1969. There's also a rare French EP with PS: *The 59th Street Bridge Song*/*Simon Smith*/*Come To The Sunshine*/*Debutant's Ball* (Warner WEP 1454) 1967. Reissue 45s have included: *59th Street Bridge Song (Feelin' Groovy)*/*Anything Goes* (Old Gold OG 9094) 1982.

Originating from a San Francisco surf band called the Tikis, **Harper's Bizarre** moved to Los Angeles to capitalize on the folk-rock boom. Their sound was called "California Sunshine Rock" by Lilian Roxon and it's basically a mix of folk and soft-rock with vocal harmonies. Their debut album was produced by **Leon Russell** and is a classic of its genre. On the next album, they had their biggest hit with a cover of Simon and Garfunkel's *59th St. Bridge Song (Feelin Groovy)* and also did some revivals of oldies from Cole Porter and Glen Miller, with the help of **Van Dyke Parks**.

For *The Secret Life*, they were joined by **Van Dyke Parks**, **Ron Elliot**, (**Beau Brummels**) and Randy Newman. Despite its psych sleeve, the album hasn't aged well.

On *4*, their last album produced by Lenny Waronker, their sound had hardened a bit with Ry Cooder on guitar and it contained covers of *Witchi Tai To* (**Jim Pepper**), *Blackbird* (Beatles) and *Hard To Handle* (Otis Redding) mixed with original material (notably *Soft Sounding Music*, with Cooder on bottleneck). *I Love You Alice B.Toklas* was the theme song for a Paul Mazurski movie starring Peter Sellers.

Ted Templeman went on to become the producer on **Captain Beefheart**'s *Clear Spot*, as well as for the Doobie Brothers, Little Feat and Van Halen. John Peterson also drummed with the **Beau Brummels**. (VJ/SR/MMs)

Joe Harriott Double Quintet

Personnel incl:	JOE HARRIOTT	sax	AB
	JOHN MAYER		A

ALBUMS:	1(A)	INDO-JAZZ SUITE	(Atlantic SD 1465) 1966 SC
(selective)	2(B)	INDO-JAZZ FUSIONS	(Atlantic SD 1482) 1967 SC

NB: (1) also released in France.

Born in Jamaica in 1928, **Joe Harriott** was a black jazzman, sax player and composer, who began his career in England. He got interested in Indian music and rhythms and moved to the USA in the sixties. After some albums on Jazzland and Capitol, he signed a contract with Atlantic to produce two superb examples of "West Meets East" collaborations, with their combination of indian instruments (tabla, sitar, tamboura) with jazz rhythms. These albums will interest fans of **Bill Plummer's Cosmic Brotherhood** or **Gabor Szabo**.

Harriott died of cancer in 1973. (SR)

Tony Harris

45s:	Honey / Scorpio	(Dee Gee 3002) 1965
	Super Man/How Much Do I Love You	(Dee Gee 3014) 1966

Another obscure act, the first 45 has been described as a 'fast rock'n'roll / mid-sixties Dylan-ish' affair', but it's really *Super Man* which grabs the attention. A cool hero-worship ode to 'Superman' with good vocals and guitars.

Another 45 credited to Tony Harris and The Woodies: *Poor Boy / Go Go Little Scrambler* (Triumph 60) 1964, could possibly be by the same guy. (BM/MW)

The Harrison

Personnel:	CHARLIE	A
	DAN	A
	FRANK	A
	JERRY	A
	LARRY	A

This Dayton, Ohio, quintet entered the WONE-sponsored three-day battle of the bands in 1966 and came out as one of twelve winners who got to record one cut each at Mega-Sound Studios for the souvenir album *WONE, The Dayton Scene* (Prism PR-1966).

They chose to cover the obscure Invasion-infused *I Know That I Love You* by Indiana outfit The Rick Z Combo. Perhaps **The Harrisons** were at the Dayton gig in 1965 where that act had opened for **The Strangeloves**. Shortly after that Rick Z (better known as Rick Zehringer, later Derringer) signed with the **Strangeloves**' label Bang and hit the charts as **The McCoys**. (MW)

Kent Harrison Boyles

ALBUM:	1	KENT HARRISON BOYLES	(Private pressing) 1972 R2

From Maryland, an album of psych/"real people" folk. It seems that only 500 copies were pressed. (SR)

Mickey Hart

| ALBUM: | 1 | ROLLING THUNDER | (Warner BS 2635) 1972 190 - | HCP |

NB: (1) also released in France (Warner 46 182) 1972. Later reissued on Edsel ED (1987) and on CD (Grateful Dead CD) 198?.

The first solo album by the **Grateful Dead** drummer may also interest Bay Area fans. Backed by John Cipollina and David Freiberg (**Quicksilver**), Grace Slick and Paul Kantner (**Jefferson Airplane**), Terry Haggerty and Bill Champlin (**Sons Of Champlin**), Stephen Stills and Sam Andrew (**Big Brother**), Barry Melton (**Country Joe**), the Tower Of Power Horn section, Zakir Husin (**Shanti**) and Alla Rakha, and, of course, **Jerry Garcia**, Bill Weir and Phil Lesh from the '**Dead**. **Mickey Hart** offers a mix of Indian invocations, rain sequences, **Dead**-like songs and loose improvisations with oustanding guitars and drums. The result has its moments (*Deep, Wide, Frequent, Pump Song, Gran'ma's Cookies...*). It made some impression in the Album Chart, too, climbing to No. 190 during a four week stay.

Robert Hunter, Peter Monk and **Bob Weir** helped **Hart** helped write some of the material and this album is housed in a splendid Mouse and Kelley sleeve.

Still with the **Dead**, **Mickey Hart** went on to release several albums of percussions and worked on soundtracks including work for 'Apocalypse Now'. (SR/VJ)

Harumi

| ALBUM: | 1 | HARUMI (dbl) | (Verve Forecast FT-3030-2) 1968 SC |
| 45: | | First Impressions/ Talk About It | (Verve Forecast KF 5086) 1968 |

Produced by **Tom Wilson**, this Japanese gentlemen put out a strange double album. The first two sides are fairly poppy but the last two sides each comprise one track - *Twice Told Tales Of The Pomegranate Forest* and *Samurai Memories* - where we get into heavily introverted mystical Eastern hippie rambling. A period piece, you'll either hate it or be wafted away by it. The 45 was culled from the album. (MW/SR)

Tom Harvey

| 45: | It Happens/ If You Loved Me | (International Artists IA-102) 1966 |

On this 45, **Harvey** sounds like an American incarnation of Engelbert Humperdinck interpreting (self-penned) country standards, but with the vocals out of key and with insipid pedal steel playing. A long way to the '**Elevators**, indeed. (MK)

Jimmy Haskell

| Personnel incl: | JIMMY HASKELL | | A |
| | JOE WALSH | gtr | A |

| ALBUM: | 1 | CALIFORNIA 99 | (ABC) 1971 - |

Jimmy Haskell is mostly remembered for his prolific career as an arranger and producer in the Hollywood studios. Housed in a fold out cover with a map of the USA, this extremely strange concept album is about life in California after the "big one", with the Great Plains turned into a "Marijuana and Insect Corridor" and the Florida region as a desert. This album was recorded with the usual musicians working with Bill Szymczyk, including notably Joe Walsh on guitar. (SR)

The Hassles

Personnel:	HOWARD BLAUVELT	bs	A
	JOHN DISEK	vcls	A
	BILLY JOEL	keyb'ds, vcls	A
	RICHARD McKENNER	ld gtr	A
	JONATHAN SMALL	drms	A

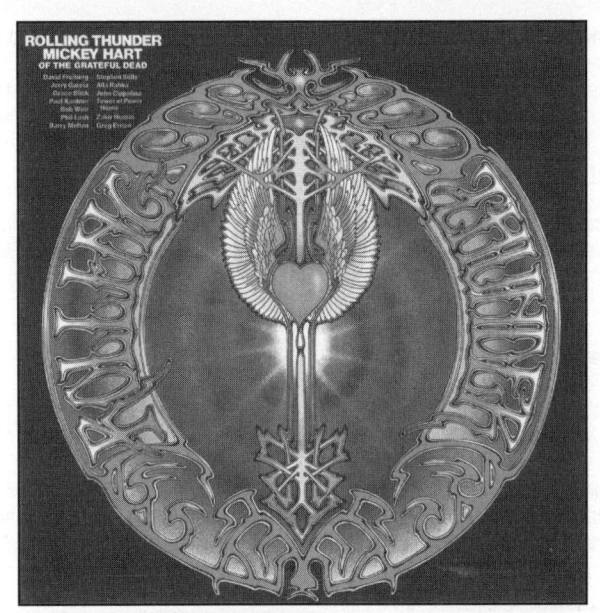

MICKEY HART - Rolling Thunder CD.

| ALBUMS: | 1(A) | HASSLES | (United Artists UAS 6631) 1967 - |
| | 2(A) | HOUR OF THE WOLF | (United Artists UAS 6699) 1969 - |

NB: There's also an album of dubious origin, *The Tough Boy* (Koala KOA-14536) 198? credited to Billy Joel and The Hassels.

45s:	You've Got Me Hummin'/ I'm Thinking	(United Artists 50215) 1967 112
	Every Step I Take (Every Move I Make)/ I Hear Voices	(United Artists 50258) 1967
	4 O'Clock In The Morning/ Let Me Bring You To The Sunshine	(United Artists 50450) 1968
	Night After Day/Country Boy	(United Artists 50513) 1969
	Great Balls Of Fire/ Travelling Bag	(United Artists 50586) 1969

NB: There's also one Italian 45 with a nice PS: *The Every Step I Take/Fever* (United Artists UA 3155) 1968.

A typical Long Island (New York) bar band, comparable to **The Young Rascals** and **Illusion**. Musically we're talking blue-eyed soul, heavy on the organ and on the second album they're trying to be psychedelic.

In 1970, Small and Billy Joel went on to form **Attila**, a totally unsuccessful duo who released one album on Epic (Epic 30030). Billy Joel, of course, went on to fame and fortune as a solo artist and Howard Blauvelt, who died in 1993, ended up in Ram Jam.

Their debut 45, *You've Got Me Hummin'* charted at No. 112, also making the Cashbox and Record World Top 100s.

A third album of dubious origin, credited to Billy Joel and The Hassels (sic) was released during the eighties and contains tracks like *Holy Moses*, *E.A.R.*, *Rabbitt*, *Extra Extra*, *Enough Is Enough* and *Crossing The Door*.

Compilation appearances include *Night After Day* on *In The Beginning* (LP). (VJ/TTi/SR)

Harley Hatcher

Harley Hatcher was an exploitation film composer and member of Mike Curb's gang. As an army buddy of Elvis he sang in ad-hoc groups with the King.

His *The Chase Is On* can be found on *Angel Dust - Music For Movie Bikers* (LP).

Hatcher also produced the **American Revolution** album.

Jeanne Hatfield

45s:	My Babe/?	(Pharaoh) 196?
	Busy Signal/?	(ARV International 5014) 196?

From McAllen, Texas.

Compilation appearances include: *My Babe* on *Acid Visions - Complete Collection, Vol. 2* (3-CD), *Texas Punk, Vol. 5* (LP) and *The Heart Beats And Other Texas Girls Of The 60s* (CD). (VJ)

The Hatfields

45s:	Yes I Do/When She Returns	(Cha Cha 754) 1966
	Kid from Cinncy/Lost In This World	(Cha Cha 790) 1967

Originally from Frankfort, Indiana, where they were known in 1965 as Sherlock and the Homelies, they migrated up to Chicago and changed their name. They specialised in pounding punkers as is evidenced by *Yes I Do* and *Kid From Cinncy*.

Their second 45 has been seen fetching $400+ thirty years later!

Compilation appearances have included: *The Kid From Cinncy* on *Back From The Grave, Vol. 5* (LP); and *Yes I Do* on *Back From The Grave, Vol. 2* (LP) and *Garage Kings* (Dble LP). (VJ/MW/MM)

Richie Havens

HCP

ALBUMS:	1	MIXED BAG	(Verve Forecast FTS-3006) 1967	182 -
(up to 1972)	2	SOMETHING ELSE AGAIN	(Verve Forecast FTS-3034) 1968	184 -
	3	RICHIE HAVENS RECORD	(Douglas 779) 1968	- -
	4	ELECTRIC HAVENS	(Douglas 780) 1968	192 -
	5	RICHARD P.HAVENS 1983	(Verve Forecast FTS-3047) 1969	80 -
	6	STONEHENGE	(Stormy Forest 6001) 1970	155 -
	7	ALARM CLOCK	(Stormy Forest 6005) 1971	29 -
	8	THE GREAT BLIND DEGREE	(Stormy Forest 6016) 1972	126 -

NB: (1) (2) and (5) were also released in France and the U.K. by Verve. (7) released in France (DiscAZ STEC LP 86) 1971. (6), (7) and (8) released in the U.K. by Polydor. (3) and (4) released in the U.K. by Transatalantic. There's also a CD compilation *Resum, The Best of* (Rhino R2711187) 1993.

45:	No Opportunity Necessary, No Experience Needed/	
	Three Days Eternity	(Verve Forecast) 1968

HAYMARKET RIOT - Live '67 LP.

One of the very few black progressive folk singers, **Richie Havens** wore beads, had a guru 'look' and was one of the first musicians to use an electric sitar. Born in Brooklyn in 1941, **Havens** began singing in the fifties, taught himself guitar and started playing the Greenwich Village coffee house circuit in 1962. He finally got a recording contract in 1967 and his Verve Forecast albums were recorded with an array of musicians including: members of **Jeremy and The Satyrs** (the whole group plays on *Something Else Again*), Harvey Brooks, Felix Pappalardi, Bruce Langhorne, Eric Weissberg, Stephen Stills and Skip Prokop. His rough voice was quite unusual at the time and he chose songs by Dylan, Lighfoot or Tuli Kupferberg (**Fugs**) to display its full range.

His records sold very well and **Havens** was invited to perform at Woodstock (*Freedom* can be found on the movie and soundtrack album). He was also able to launch his own label, Stormy Forest, on which he released his albums, plus those of **Bob Brown** and the Canadian folk trio Montreal. The two albums on Douglas contain early recordings, with overdubbed electric backing on *Electric Havens* and are not recommended.

Richie Havens kept on recording during the seventies and early eighties, but he was unable to revitalise his formula. His records always sounded too similar and he slowly vanished from the musical scene.

In the nineties, the U.K. psychedelic outfit Praise Space Electric covered *Freedom* on their *2 Leaving Demons* album. (SR)

Havenstock River Band

ALBUM:	1	HAVENSTOCK RIVER BAND (Im'press IMPS-1615) 1972 -

An obscure boogie-rock album housed in a gatefold cover. (SR)

Haymarket Riot

Personnel:	JIM DOE	gtr, vcls	A
	DENNIS MORALES	drms, vcls	A
	RON SHANKLETON	ld gtr	A
	?? ??	bs	A

45:	Leaving/A Sunny Day Song	(CLB 691) 1969

This **Haymarket Riot** came from Monroe, Michigan. They formed in the mid-sixties and were originally known as The Avengers (didn't every town have one?), changing their name to **Haymarket Riot** in late 1967 and breaking up shortly after the record was issued in 1969. Jim Doe wrote *Leaving* whilst Dennis Morales wrote *Sunny Day Song*.

Leaving has subsequently been featured on *A Lethal Dose Of Hard Psych* (CD), where it's stated that this is the **Haymarket Riot** who issued the 45 on Coconut Groove - can anyone else confirm this? (SG/MW)

Haymarket Riot

45:	Trip On Out/Something Else	(Riot 101) 1968

A psychedelic six-piece from Enid, Oklahoma, who cut one excellent 45. The 'A' side has resurfaced on many compilations (see below). Both sides of the 45 are also listed on *Pebbles, Vol. 6* (CD), but only *Trip On Out* is included on the actual disc. The Pebbles liner notes, state that the 45 was recorded in Chicago, which is incorrect - it was recorded on a trip to Oklahoma City...

For the full low-down on the band seek out a copy of 'Lost & Found # 4' fanzine.

Compilation appearances include: *Trip On Out* on *Pebbles, Vol. 6* (CD), *The Psychedelic Experience, Vol. 1* (LP), *The Arf! Arf! Blitzkrieg 32 Track Sampler* (Dble CD), *30 Seconds Before The Calico Wall* (CD) and *Follow That Munster, Vol. 2* (LP). (VJ/MW)

HAYMARKET SQUARE - Magic Lantern LP.

Haymarket Riot

Personnel:	STEVE BARSOTTI	bs	ABC
	MARK BATTERMAN	vcls, gtr	AB
	DAVE CARPENDER	gtr	ABC
	STEVE NELSON	drms	ABC
	PETE BARSOTTI	vcls	BC
	SCOTT DONALDSON		C

ALBUM: 1(C) LIVE '67 (RD Records RD 7) 2000

A Berkeley High band who initially operated as The Livin' End (line-up 'A') on the Berkeley, California scene. With the arrival of Pete Barsotti, in Spring '66, they became **The Haymarket Riot**. Scott Donaldson joined from The **Plague** (Richmond's legendary punk quartet) to replace Batterman, who left to join **The Answer** at the end of 1966.

Thrashy Who and Yardbirds-inspired punkers stretched into hard-but-fluid psychedelic-blues jams over the next year. They were captured for posterity in full flight at a gig in the social hall of the First Unitarian Church of Kensington (or FUCK for short!) on December 1st 1967, where they performed five numbers comparable to a rawer **Quicksilver Messenger Service** or **Grateful Dead**, who would have been sending similar vibrations back across the bay from The Fillmore.

Around the time of this recording they changed their name, for the last time, to Lazarus. They would last until the end of 1969. Steve Nelson joined local rivals Purple Earthquake, with whom they'd often shared bills. Dave Carpender would play lead guitar for several years with Greg Kihn.

Nothing was released during their lifetime under any of their names. The limited edition album comes in a heavy laminated gatefold, fronted by the colourful psychedelic artwork of the band's drumhead. It contains a detailed band history by Alec Palao, from which the pertinent facts above have been extracted. (MW/CF)

Haymarket Riot (Calvin James and)

45: Footsteps/Find This Woman (Stature 1104) 1967

Released by 'Calvin James and Haymarket Riot' - Calvin James is rumoured to be Jim Johnson of Minneapolis stalwarts **The Underbeats**.

Many other **Haymarket Riots** are known to have existed. In addition to the entries listed here there was also a seventies Ohio outfit. (MW)

Haymarket Square

Personnel:	ROBERT HOMA	bs	A
	JOHN KOWALSKI	drms	A
	GLORIA LAMBERT	vcls	A
	MARK SWENSON	gtr	A

ALBUM: 1(A) MAGIC LANTERN (Chaparral CRM 201) 1968 R5

NB: (1) counterfeited on Osmose (1125) 1987 and in 1996 as a ltd edition of 400 (The Sacred Temple Of The Golden Icon STG 2001) 1996. Also counterfeited on CD (LSD 007) 1996. (1) reissued officially on CD (Gear Fab GF-176) 2001 and vinyl (Gear Fab Comet GFC-417) 2001.

This Chicago band's album is notable for some catchy drumming and Lambert's powerful vocals. The music on the album was used to accompany the original Baron and Bailey Light Circus at the Museum of Contemporary Art in Chicago. Despite its reissue, original copies remain sought-after. One cut from the album, *Amapola* appears on *Psychedelic Patchwork* (LP). It's well worth seeking out a copy of the reissue.

The band did not release any 45s.

The 1996 reissue (on CD & LP) has been digitally cleaned, but even better is the official CD release on Gear Fab with the story of the band told by John Kowalski. (VJ/MW)

Haystacks Balboa

Personnel:	MARK BABANI		A
	MARK HARRISON MAYO		A
	LLOYD LANDESMAN		A
	MARK POLOTT	bs	A
	BRUCE SCOTT		A

ALBUM: 1(A) HAYSTACKS BALBOA (Polydor 24-4032) 1970 SC

NB: (1) reissued on CD (Audio Archives AACD 024).

Real heavy dudes with some grungey vocals, a mean attitude and some wicked guitar - above-par hard-rock. Although outside the musical thrust of this book, they're worth a mention especially as a couple of tracks on their album were written by Larry West, formerly of the legendary **Vagrants** and younger brother of guitar colossus, Leslie '**Mountain**' West.

Their album was produced by Shadow Morton, aka **Shadow Mann**.

Mayo and Polott still play together in an outfit called "Blue Lagoon". (MW/SR)

The Hazards

45: Hey Joe/Will You Be My Girl (Groove 502) 1966

Came out of Richmond, Virginia, with a pretty decent rendition of *Hey Joe* which can be heard on *Highs In The Mid-Sixties, Vol. 8* (LP) or *Signed, D.C.* (LP). (VJ)

The Hazards

45: Tinted Green/
Hey Little Girl (C'mon Let's Live) (Unicorn no #) 196?

These **Hazards** came from Berlin Center near Youngstown, Ohio.

Compilation appearances have included: *Hey Little Girl* on *Project Blue, Vol. 3* (LP); and *Tinted Green* on *Highs In The Mid-Sixties, Vol. 21* (LP). (GGI/MW)

H.B. and The Checkmates

45: Louise, Louise/Summertime (Lavender 1936) 1965

Hailed from Springfield, Oregon. The 'A' side *Louise, Louise* is basically *Louie Louie*, but they transposed the song into one about a girl and had the gall to claim the credit! The result, which was recorded live at the Cascade Teen Club, has not stood the test of time well.

Compilation appearances include: *Louise, Louise* on *Ya Gotta Have Moxie, Vol. 2* (Dble CD), *Boulders, Vol. 11* (LP) and *Highs In The Mid Sixties, Vol. 7* (LP). (VJ/MW)

Roy Head (and The Traits)

				HCP
ALBUM:	1	ROY HEAD AND THE TRAITS	(TNT TLP-101) 1965	- SC
(up to	2	TREAT ME RIGHT	(Scepter SS-532) 1965	122 SC
1973)	3	SOME PEOPLE	(Dunhill DS-50080) 1970	- -
	4	DISMAL PRISONER	(TMI 1000) 1972	- -

			HCP
45s:	One More Time / Don't Be Blue	(TNT 194) c1965	-
(up to	Pain /Teen-Age Letter	(Back Beat 543) 1965	-
1973)	Treat Her Right / So Long, My Love	(Back Beat 546) 1965	2
	Apple Of My Eye / I Pass The Day	(Back Beat 555) 1965	32
	Just A Little Bit / Treat Me Right	(Scepter 12116) 1965	39
	Won't Be Blue / One More Time	(Scepter 12117) 1965	-
	Get Back (Part 1) / Get Back (Part 2)	(Scepter 12124) 1966	88
	One More Time / Convicted	(Scepter 12138) 1966	-
	My Babe / Pain	(Back Beat 560) 1966	99
	Driving Wheel / Wigglin' And Gigglin'	(Back Beat 563) 1966	110
	To Make A Big Man Cry / Don't Cry No More	(Back Beat 571) 1966	95
	You're (Almost) Tuff / Tush Hog (Instr)	(Back Beat 576) 1967	-
	A Good Man Is Hard To Find /Nobody But Me (Tells My Eagle When To Fly)	(Back Beat 582) 1967	-
	Turn Out The Lights / Broadway Walk	(Mercury 72799) 1968	-
	Ain't Goin' Down Right / Lovin' Man On Your Hands	(Mercury 72848) 1968	-
	I'm Not A Fool Anymore / Mama Mama	(Dunhill 4240) 1970	-
	Puff Of Smoke / Lord Take A Bow	(TMI 9000) 1972	96
	Bit By Bit / Wait Till I Arrive	(TMI 9010) 1973	-
	Rock And Roll Mood/You Got The Power	(TMI 75-0103) 1973	-
	Why Don't We Go Somewhere And Love / Smell-A-Women	(TMI 75-0106) 1973	-
	Carol / Clyde O'Riley	(TMI 75-0113) c1973	-

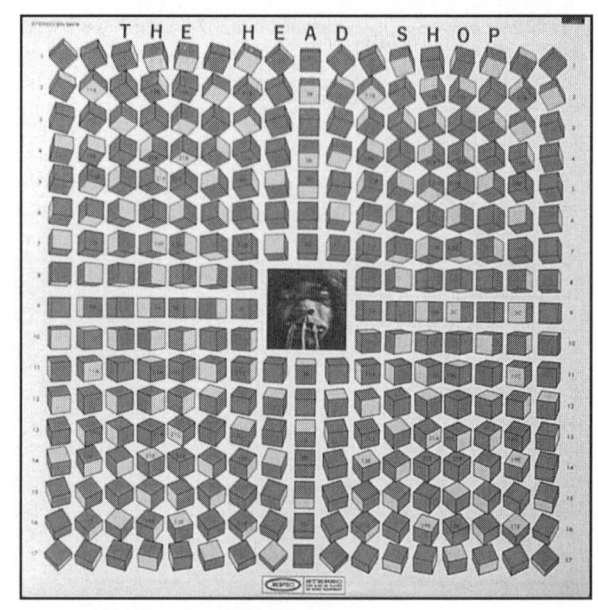

The Traits:		
45s:	Little Mama / Linda Lou	(Renner 221) 1962
	Little Mama / Linda Lou	(Ascot 2108) 1962
	Woe Woe / Got My Mojo Working	(Renner 229) 1962
	Gotta Keep My Cool / Too Good To Be True	(Garrison 3007) 1966
	Gotta Keep My Cool / Too Good To Be True	(Pacemaker 254) 1966
	Harlem Shuffle / Somewhere	(Universal 30494) 1966
	Harlem Shuffle / Somewhere	(Scepter 12169) 1966
	Parchman Farm / Tramp	(Universal 30496) 1966

From San Marcos, Texas originally, **Roy Head** relocated to Houston in 1964. His forte is soulful brassy pop-rock and he would be outside the boundaries of this book but for *You're (Almost) Tuff*, a great fuzz-rocker where Bo Diddley encounters **Count Five**'s *Psychotic Reaction*. Many of his sixties releases were recorded with the Traits and are so credited.

Roy Head scored a U.S. no. 2 hit in 1965 with *Treat Her Right*.

He also recorded *Easy Lovin' Girl* (a **Johnny Winter** composition) with **The Great Believers**.

The *Dismal Prisoner* album contains covers of Van Morrison and John Lee Hooker tracks.

Compilation appearances have included: *Easy Lovin' Girl* on *Acid Visions - The Complete Collection, Vol. 1* (3-CD) and *Acid Visions* (LP); *You're (Almost) Tuff* and *Tush Hog* on *Austin Landing, Vol. 2* (LP); *Treat Her Right* on *Texas Music, Vol. 3* (CD); and both *Driving Wheel* and *Wigglin' And Gigglin'* on *The Best Of Beat, Vol. 3* (LP). (VJ/SR/MW/AB)

Head and The Hares

45:	I Won't Come Back/ One Against The World	(H&H 200,891) 1966

THE HEAD SHOP - The Head Shop LP.

You can also hear *Won't Come Back* on *New England Teen Scene, Vol. 1* (LP). (MW)

The Headhunters

45:	Times We Shared/Think What You've Done	(Fenton 2518) 196?

Times We Shared has resurfaced on *Best Of Michigan Rock Groups, Vol. 2*. They also have a previously unreleased cut *I Need Your Love* on *Thee Unheard Of* (LP) compilation taken from one of the two versions of this track only available on Buff one-sided acetates. It's nothing to get excited about. (VJ)

Head Lyters

45:	I Need You/You'd Better Come Home	(Wand 199) 1965

A one-off venture by a New York outfit. The flip side, which mixes chords from *Twist And Shout* and *La Bamba* in a humorous way, can also be heard on *Mindrocker, Vol. 8* (LP).

There's also a 45 by a Headlyters on Phalanx (1010/1011) *Girl Down The Street/Shop Around* issued around 1965 or 1966. Phalanx is a Michigan label - so it may be the same outfit. The 'A' side, (VJ/MW)

Head Over Heels

Personnel:	JOHN BREDEAU	drms	A
	PAUL FRANK	gtr, vcls	A
	MICHAEL URSO	bs, vcls	A

ALBUM:	1(A)	HEAD OVER HEELS	(Capitol ST-797) 1971 R1

A Michigan power trio whose album is powerful and inventive - one of the best hard-rock albums on the label. Showcasing a line up consisting of drummer John Bredeau, singer/guitarst Paul Frank and singer/bassist Michael Urso, the band only managed to release one instantly obscure album, but what an LP! Produced by **Dan Moore** and **Buzz Clifford**, 1971's *Head Over Heels* is simply great. Loud, tough, yet surprisingly accessible, material such as *Road Runner* and *In My Woman* showcased the trio's knack for melodic, but crunching guitar rock. Frank and Urso had attractive voices and as we said before, they sure could generate some sound. Among the few missteps were some out of kilter harmony vocals (*Question*) and the bland power ballad *Children Of The Mist* (which was almost redeemed by Frank's nice guitar solo). Elsewhere, recorded at Detroit's Eastowne, an extended cover of Willie Dixon's *Red Rooster* and the Franks-penned *Circles* were in-concert efforts that aptly showcased the band's impressive live chops.

Frank and Urso subsequently reappeared with the band **Fresh Start**. Urso was also a late-inning member of Detroit's Rare Earth (along with the **Scorpion** guitarist Ray Monette), playing on several of their albums in the mid-seventies. (VJ/MW/SB/CF)

The Heads

Personnel:	ANGELO BUONOME	drms, perc	A
	TOMMY FRATERRIGO	vcls, bs	A
	LOU SANTILLI	ld gtr, vcls	A
	BOB (B.T) TUCALLO	keyb'ds/vcls	A

ALBUM:	1(A)	HEADS UP	(Liberty LST-7581) 1968 -

45s:	Are You Lonely For Me, Baby/You	(Liberty 56025) 1968

An obscure quartet with organ and fuzz guitar, with songs like *The Land Of Stoned Soul*, *Seeing Mr. Spouth*, *Digging Your Hease* and an awful cover of *Day Tripper*. Clearly a period piece. (SR/MMs/NK)

The Head Shop

Personnel:	DANNY	A
	DREW	A
	GEOFF	A
	JESSE	A
	JOE	A

ALBUM:	1(A)	THE HEAD SHOP	(Epic BN 26476) 1968 R1

NB: (1) has been reissued on CD.

The above is a most unusual and underrated album which was produced and arranged by **Milan**. Side one, aside from an interesting version of *Sunny*, is notable for the intros to all its songs, whilst Side Two is memorable for the invigorating *Prophecy* and the cosmic ending to the final track *Infinity*. Original copies of the album are not easy to find, as it's now a minor collectors' item, but the album is recommended.

The band, who are thought to have come from the New York / New York City area, do not appear to have released any 45s.

Compilation appearances have included: *Heaven Here We Come* on *Psychedelic Dream* (Dble LP); *Prophecy* on *Psychedelic Visions* (CD); and *Head Shop* on *Sixties Archive, Vol. 8* (CD). (VJ/MW)

Headstone

Personnel:	BARRY APPLEGATE	A
	DAVID APPLEGATE	A
	TOM APPLEGATE	A
	BRUCE FLYNN	A

ALBUM:	1(A)	STILL LOOKING	(Starr SLP 1056) 1974 R2

NB: (1) carefully counterfeited in the late 1980s and in the nineties on CD.

45s:	α	What People Say/Carry Me On	(Rome RF-4127) 19?
		Buying Time/Snake Dance	(Rome) 19?

NB: α released as by **The Headstones**.

From Ohio, this is predominantly a hard-rock album with some soft passages and psychedelic overtones. It is well worth investigating for its good guitar work and vocals. The album is sought-after among collectors and even the counterfeit is now hard to find, although Gear Fab are currently working on a legitimate CD release, so watch this space!

The two 45s feature non-album tracks.

Compilation appearances have included: *What People Say*, *Carry Me On* and *Buying Time* on *Filling The Gap* (4-LP). (VJ/MW)

The Headstones

Personnel:	MIKE FLORENCE	keyb'ds	AB
	WINSTON LOGAN	drms, vcls	A
	GLEN VAN LANDINGHAM	ld gtr	AB
	PAUL VEALE	gtr, vcls	AB
	DAVE WILLIAMS	vcls, bs	AB
	MIKE ROGERS	drms	B

CD:	1(A/B)	TWENTYFOUR HOURS (EVERYDAY)	
		(Collectables COL-CD 0700) 1997	

NB: (1) is a retrospective CD, which collects together all four **Headstones** tracks and then explores the released, live and unreleased legacy of related groups: **Seompi**, Remaining Few, **Oxford Circus**, and **Watermusic**.

45s:	Wish You Were Mine/24 Hours (Everyday)	(Pharaoh 147) 1966
	Bad Day Blues/My Kind Of Girl	(Pharaoh 152) 1966

Probably the strongest act to record on the Pharaoh label, which was based in McAllen, Texas. Their first 45 was a local hit, combining the Beatlesque *Wish You Were Mine* with *24 Hours (Everyday)* a pounding punk song with lots of fuzz, organ and fine vocals. Their follow-up did even better staying at No. 1 for two weeks running in McAllen.

A recommended and worthy CD retrospective *The Headstones: 24 (Everyday)* collects all four tracks and then explores the released, live and unreleased legacy of the related groups featuring the two leading lights in **The Headstones** - Dave Williams (**Seompi**, Remaining Few - n.b. not to be confused with the other Texas bands by this name) and Winston Logan (**Oxford Circus**, **Watermusic**). Spanning garage, psych, heavy and straight-ahead rock styles, the material ranges in sound and musical quality from average to very good.

Their material has also been compiled heavily including: *Bad Day Blues* on *The Psychedelic Sixties, Vol. 1* (LP) and *Gathering Of The Tribe* (LP); *Wish She Were Mine*, *24 Hours (Everyday)*, *Bad Day Blues* and *My Kind Of Girl* on *Acid Visions - Complete Collection, Vol. 2* (3-CD) and *Texas Punk, Vol. 5* (LP); *Wish She Were Mine* and *24 Hours (Everyday)* on *Texas Flashbacks, Vol. 1* (LP & CD) and *Flashback, Vol. 1* (LP); and both *24 Hours (Everyday)* and *Bad Day Blues* on *Green Crystal Ties, Vol. 8* (CD). (VJ/MW)

The Heard

Personnel incl:	DON MAU	A

45:	Poppies/Where Has My Summer Gone?	(Orlyn 652) 1965

This 45 was the work of a Chicago garage band, who at some point included Don Mau (ex-**Vectors**). (VJ/MW)

HEADSTONE - Still Looking CD.

HEARTS AND FLOWERS - Now Is The Time For... LP.

The Heard

| 45: | You're Gonna Miss Me/Exit 9 | (One Way 0001) 1967 |

An interesting band from Longview, Texas who covered the **13th Floor Elevators** hit. *Exit 9* is rather unusual too.

Compilation appearances have included: *You're Gonna Miss Me* on *Songs We Taught The Fuzztones* (Dble LP & Dble CD), *Texas Flashback (The Best Of)* (CD). (VJ/MW)

The Heard

| 45: | Stop It Baby/Laugh With The Wind | (Audition 6107) 1966 |

A different outfit from the Texas one. This time from Rochester, New York, The 'A' side, is a Kinks-inspired cruncher, which was later covered by The Marshmallow Overcoat on their first album *The Inner Groove*. This **Heard** was previously known as The Belvederes.

Compilation appearances include: *Stop It Baby* on *Pebbles, Vol. 7* (LP) and *Teenage Shutdown, Vol. 4* (LP & CD). (VJ)

Lindy Hearne

Personnel incl:	DeGARNO	vcls	A
	LINDY HEARNE	vcls	A
	KEY	vcls	A

| ALBUM: | 1(A) | LINDY HEARNE | (Private Pressing) 1975 SC |

A Christian folk and rock singer, her album is full of delicate vocals with acoustic and electric guitar. (SR)

The Hearsemen

| 45: | Christy-Ann/I Get That Feeling | (Wheel's 4 3619) 1968 |

This outfit operated out of the Detroit suburbs.

Compilation appearances include: *Christy Anne* and *I Get That Feeling* on *The Cicadelic 60's, Vol. 1* (CD), *The Cicadelic 60's, Vol. 3* (LP) and *The History Of Michigan Garage Bands In The 60's* (CD). (VJ/MW)

Heart

| ALBUM: | 1 | HEART | (Natural Resources) 1972 - |

An obscure male duet, on the same rock-oriented Motown subsidiary as **Road** and **Two Friends**. They are totally unrelated to the late seventies group formed by the Wilson sisters. (SR)

The Heart Attacks

See **The Beachnuts** entry.

The Heartbeats

| 45: | Cryin' Inside/Choo Choo Train | (The Head Beats 2605) 1968 |

The 'A' side of this 45, an organ punker by a girl group from Lubbock, Texas, was a Ronnie Weiss composition. According to Roy Ames, they made two 45s at Robinhood Brians' studio in Tyler, and won first prize in Dick Clark's 'Battle Of The Bands' contest the same year (1968). The girls were due to receive $10,000 in prizes, a recording contract with ABC, and nationwide tour, however, as they were aged between 12-15 they were too young to go on the road unchaperoned and their mother/manager Mrs. Jeannie Saunders nixed the whole idea.

Compilation appearances have included: *Choo Choo Train* and *Crying Inside* on *Acid Visions - The Complete Collection, Vol. 1* (3-CD); *Choo Choo Train*, *Crying Inside*, *Little Latin Lupe Lu* and *Poor Side Of Town* on *Girls Of Texas '60s* (LP & CD); *Crying Inside* on *Girls In The Garage, Vol. 3* (LP); *Choo Choo Train*, *Crying Inside*, *Everywhere*, *Little Latin Lupe Lu*, *Satisfied* and *Poor Side Of Town* on *The Heart Beats And Other Texas Girls Of The 60s* (CD). (MW)

Hearts and Flowers

Personnel:	RICK CUNHA	vcls	A
	DAVE DAWSON	gtr, vcls	ABC
	LARRY MURRAY	gtr, vcls	ABC
	TERRY PAUL		B
	DAN WOODY		B
	BERNIE LEADON	gtr	C

| ALBUMS: | 1(A) | NOW IS THE TIME FOR HEARTS AND FLOWERS (Capitol ST-2762) 1967 SC |
| | 2(C) | OF HORSES, KIDS AND FORGOTTEN WOMEN (Capitol ST-2868) 1968 R1 |

NB: (1) and (2) reissued by Bam Caruso in 1986.

45s:	Please/The View From Ward 3	(Capitol P-5897) 1967
	She Sang Hymns Out Of Tune/Tin Angel	(Capitol P-2167) 1968
	Road To Nowhere/Rock And Roll Gypsies	(Capitol P-5829) 19??

An excellent and still underrated group from Los Angeles, **Hearts and Flowers** produced two albums mixing folk-rock with Californian harmonies and country-folk.

Born in Weycross, Georgia, Larry Murray moved to Los Angeles in the late fifties and joined the Scottsville Squirrel Barkers, one of the several Bluegrass groups playing the Southern California circuit. The personnel of the Barkers fluctuated and included future **Byrd** Chris Hillman, Kenny Wertz and Bernie Leadon. The group disbanded in 1962 after releasing an album for the Crown label, *Bluegrass Favorites*, which is now extremely rare.

Murray temporarily retired from the music scene, became a TV actor and worked at the Troubadour Club in L.A.. In 1965 he met a folk-rock duo formed of David Dawson and Rick Cunha and they started working together and playing live without a drummer. They secured a deal with Capitol and their first album was released in June 1967. Masterfully produced by Nick Venet (**Fred Neil**, **Stone Poneys**, **Euphoria** and **Mad River**), *Now Is The Time For Hearts And Flowers* is a real gem. The choice of material is outstanding, with excellent covers of **Tim Hardin**'s *Reason To Believe*, **Hoyt Axton**'s *10,000 Sunsets*, Carole King's *Road To Nowhere* and Donovan's *Try For The Sun*, plus two songs of contemporary groups: *Please*, the **Kaleidoscope** song and *Rock And Roll Gypsies* by **Gypsy Trips**. Their original songs were penned by Murray, Cunha and Marty Cooper. The vocals are brilliant and Venet added some good production tricks, with some effects, violin and electric bass.

HEATHER BLACK - Heather Black LP.

The sales were unfortunately extremely poor and Capitol decided to give them a push: two new members, Terry Paul and Dan Woody, were drafted to reinforce their live impact and a promotion campaign began at the end of 1967; with limited results.

Murray and Dawson started working on their second album. Cunha, Paul and Woody left and Bernie Leadon arrived. *Of Horses, Kids and Forgotten Woman* was released in July 1968 and got the same results as the first album: critical acclaim but low sales. It notably contains *She Sang Hymns Out Of Tune*, a song originally recorded (but not released) by Jesse Lee Kincaid with the **Rising Sons**.

Due to their lack of success, the group disbanded and their records sank into obscurity before being rediscovered in the mid-eighties by Bam Caruso.

Larry Murray went on to record a good country folk-rock album, *Sweet Country Suite* (Verve Forecast FTS 3090) 1969, with backing by Swampwater, **Paul Parrish**, JD Souther and two **Nitty Gritty** members, Fadden and McEuen. He also worked with Kris Kristofferson and Jessi Colter in the early seventies. Rick Cunha would later work with Linda Ronstadt, have a career as a songwriter and sesion man and also released two decent country-rock albums: *Cunha Songs* (GRC GA 5004) 1973, with Dave Dawson and *Moving Pictures* (CBS) 1977.

Compilation appearances include: *Rock 'N' Roll Gypsies* on *Nuggets, Vol. 10* (LP) and *Rock A Delics* (LP). (SR/GGc)

The Heathens

Personnel incl: MIKE DELLARIO   vcls   A

45:   The Other Way Around/Problems   (Vibra 104) 1967

This Schenectady New York-based quintet's 45 was recorded in a garage named Vibra Studios early in 1967. The result was a cool punk 45.

Compilation appearances include: *The Other Way Around* on *Off The Wall, Vol. 1* (LP) and *Back From The Grave, Vol. 7* (Dble LP); and *Problems* on *Open Up Yer Door! Vol. 1* (LP), *Sixties Choice, Vol. 1* (LP), *60's Choice Collection, Vol's 1 And 2* (CD) and *Teenage Shutdown, Vol. 10* (LP & CD). (VJ)

Heather Black

Personnel incl: TOMMY CHRISTIAN   A
                  CARL FRIEND (?)   A
                  GAYLON LATIMORE (GAYLAN LATIMER)   A
                  HARRY O. WETSELL (?)   A

ALBUMS: 1   HEATHER BLACK   (Double Bayou DB 2000) 196? SC
          2   LIVE (dbl)   (American Playboy 1001) 196? R1

45s: There/Circles   (American Playboy 1977) 196?
       Cajun Blues/Harris County Jail (American Playboy 1992) 196?
       She's My Woman/
       Walkin' Back To Waco   (American Playboy 1005) 1970
   α   Look Around Son   (Double Bayou 2) 1970
   α   Master Nichols   (Double Bayou 4) 1970

NB: α promo only.

This outfit was most significant as a later outing for Gaylon Latimore who had earlier had a solo career as **Gaylon Ladd** and also played in **The Dawgs**, **The Silvertones** and **Eastside Transfer**.

Produced by Huey P. Meaux, the "Crazy Cajun", the Double Bayou album is really patchy: two excellent tracks, notably *Bill The Black Militant* with a fantastic guitar part and unusual lyrics, but also, alas, several insipid ballads and one of the worst songs you can imagine : *Last Words* on which Gaylon Latimore speaks to his recently deceased girlfriend. Brrrr! All the songs were written by Latimore and Christian.

Of the two Double Bayou singles, only *Look Around Son*, an awful ballad, can be found on the album.

The band later evolved into Christopher Cross. (MW/VJ/SR/NL)

Heaven

ALBUM: 1   HEAVEN   (W/W) 1970 R3

A rare Nebraska blues - rock album with horns. It has a very underground feel and came in a cool cover. (CF)

Heaven and Earth

ALBUM: 1   REFUGE   (Ovation OVQD-1428) 1972 -

NB: (1) Quadrophonic copies also exist.

A mellow psych female duo with haunting harmonies, acoustic and electric guitars, echoplex, and some strings, on songs like *Feel The Spirit*, *Sixty Years On*, *To A Flame*, *Voice In The Wind*, *A Light Is Shining* and the title track plus more. (SR)

Heavy Balloon

Personnel: FRED ADAMS   A
             JENNY DEAN   A
             MALLORY EARLE   A
             KIRBY HELMUTH   A
             WOLF JAMES   A
             MICHAEL JASON   A

HEAVEN AND EARTH - Refuge LP.

NED LIBEN		A
LORI		A
MIGHTY BABY		A
TERRY NOEL		A
BOBBY NOTHOFF		A
CHRISTIAN OSBORNE		A
PETER THE PIANO PLAYER		A
T. N. PICKOSKE		A
MIKE RATTI		A
BOB RIZZO		A
SENORITA ROSETTS		A
SKYDRAGON		A
T. O. TUPCAT		A
DAVID TYLES		A

ALBUM: 1(A) 16 TON, 32,000 LB. HEAVY BALLOON
(Elephant V Records EVS-104) 1969 R1

NB: (1) counterfeited on CD (Lyrical Sound Device LSD AZ 5001).

A New York band, their album is overrated. Musically it's rather slow, pedestrian blues, rather than psychedelic. They do not appear to have released any 45s. Among the musicians included were Bobby Notkoff (also in **Rockets** and Crazy Horse) and Chris Osborne (who played with David Peel and Yoko Ono).

They also have one cut, *Barnyard Blues* on *Magic Carpet Ride* (LP), *Sixties Archive, Vol. 8* (CD) and *Lycergic Soap* (LP) compilations. (VJ/MW)

Heavy Cruiser

Personnel incl:	NEIL MERRYWEATHER	bs, vcls	A

ALBUMS: 1 HEAVY CRUISER (Family Productions FPS 2706) 1972 -
2 LUCKY DOG (Family Productions FPS 2713) 1973 -

45: Louie, Louie/Outlaw (Family Productions 0909) 1972

Directed by **Neil Merryweather**, **Heavy Cruiser** was a short-lived heavy blues outfit formed by the musicians of **Mama Lion**, without Lynn Carey fronting, although she co-write four songs on the first album and sang backing vocals. Rather monotonous, but not completely bad.

They were based in Los Angeles, California. (SR/CF)

Heavy Feather

Personnel:	TOM CASEY	bs, gtr, perc	A
	RONNIE FOLK	keyb'ds, gtr	A
	DAVE SHADER	vibes, gtr, perc	A
	JOHN WILSON	drms, gtr	A

HEAVY BALLOON - 16 Ton, 32,000 L.B. Heavy Balloon CD.

ALBUM: 1(A) SOFT HARD AND HEAVY
(Ace Of Hearts LP-0226) 1972 -

NB: (1) only released as a white label DJ copy.

45: Brand New Day/
So Long, Farewell, Goodbye (Ace Of Hearts 0453) 1972

The Ace of Hearts label was based in Nashville, Tennessee and all the songs on this album were written and arranged by the four band members. The title pretty much gives the game away and most of the tracks are dreamy organ fuzz-soft-psych with a progressive edge. Apart from the progressive instrumentation and jamming much of the album sounds like harmony folk rock from 1969. However a few of the tracks venture into heavy rock. The song-writing is consistently good and there is excellent guitar/keyboard throughout. (CP)

The Heirs

Personnel:	JOHN ODGERS	drms	A
	BUZZ SILER	vcls, gtr	A
	RICK SILER	bs	A
	MIKE SPENCER	organ	A

45: You Better Slow Down/Do You Want Me (Panorama 39) 1966

Enrolled at the University of Oregon in Eugene, the band had an earlier release (as The Critters) on their own Design label, which was a small local hit on KGRL and led amongst other things to their opening for The Beach Boys. This brought them to Jerry Dennon's attention. By late 1967, the group had again changed their name - and this time their image - to become the bizarrely futuristic X-25, with a further 45 on Portland imprint NWI.

Big Beat's *Northwest Battle Of The Bands, Vol. 1* (CD) features an unissued demo *I'm Fast*, while *Vol. 2* includes *You Better Slow Down*. (NW)

Helgeson/Scranton Band

Personnel:	TOM HELGESON	vcls, gtr	A
	LAIRD SCRANTON	vcls, gtr	A

ALBUM: 1(A) THE HELGESON/SCRANTON/BLACK BOOTLEG
(No label RL 5071) 1971 R2

NB: (1) one-sided demo album in plain cover.

A seldom-sighted local Oregon private press of intriguing folk sounds. (CF)

THE HELGESON/SCRANTON BLACK BOOTLEG label.

HELP - Help LP.

The Hellers

ALBUM:	1	SINGERS, TALKERS, PLAYERS, SWINGERS AND DOERS	(Command) 1969 SC

45:	It's Seventy-Four In San Francisco/ Mist Of Time	(Command 4121) 1969

A strange album with a mix of soft psych, moog tracks, sound effects, odd narration and children's voices. It is now sought-after by collectors of unusual items. (SR)

Harry Hellings and The Radials

Personnel incl:	HARRY HELLINGS		A

45:	Tale Of A Crystal Ship/ Wake Up Sweet Mary	(Highland 1190) 1967

A one-off venture. The 'A' side is Californian psychedelic folk, very much in the style of **The Deep**. Check it out on the *Magic Carpet Ride* (LP) and the boot of boots *Lycergic Soap* (LP). (VJ/MW)

The Hello People

Personnel incl:	COUNTRY	ld vcls, gtr, bs	A
	GOODFELLOW	ld vcls, gtr, bs	A
	MUCH MORE	keyb'ds	A
	SMOOTHIE	ld vcls, bs, organ, sax	A
	THUMP THUMP		
	(N.D. SMART)	drms, hrmnca	A
	WRY ONE	sax, flute, tambourine	A

ALBUMS: 1(A)	THE HELLO PEOPLE	(Philips PHS 600.265) 1968 -
(up to 2(A)	FUSION	(Philips PHS 600.276) 1968 -
1968)		
		HCP

45s:	α	Let's Go Hide In The Forest/ Disparity Waterfront Blues	(Philips 40481) 1967 -
		A Stranger At Her Door/ Paisley Teddy Bear	(Philips 40522) 1968 -
		(As I Went Down To) Jerusalem/ It's A Monday Kind Of Tuesday	(Philips 40531) 1968 123
		If I Should Sing Too Softly/ Pray For Rain	(Philips 40572) 1968 -
		Anthem/Jelly Jam	(Philips 40585) 1969 -

NB: All 45s are LP cuts except α.

A mysterious six-piece band, who used to play frequently at 'La Cave' club in Cleveland, performing in mime makeup and actually performing mime onstage between their songs. N.D. Smart, who was working with **Kangaroo** at the time, caught their act and ended up drumming for them on their first two albums, both of which are underrated gems.

The first album is full of catchy, appealing songs like *It's A Monday Kind Of Tuesday* and none of the songs are credited. With the second, their music has evolved and offered a superb mix of rock, folk, blues and jazz, with a good flute player. The lyrics are more concerned, like *Anthem*:

"They say I was born in the land of the free
But the home of the briefcase is all I see
With fine houses and highways we covered the land
But freedom's a fable if the conscience is banned"

"So I'm going to prison for what I believe
I'm going to prison so I can be free
I've got something I'll die for
What else can they do
I've got something to live for
What about you?"

The same themes are present in *How Does It Feel To Be Free*, *I Ride To Nowhere* and *Dream Of Tomorrow*. This time the songs are credited to P. Weston, W.S. Tongue, L. Tasse, M. Sagarese, R. Sedita and G. Geddes, so we can assume they are the musicians hiding under the masks. Both albums were produced by Lou Futterman who went on to work with Ted Nugent.

In 1969, N.D. Smart stopped working with the band, but he resumed in 1972 with Robert Sedita, George Geddes and Lawrence Tasse. This version of **The Hello People** also did some live work with Todd Rundgren who had used Smart on some of his early albums, including *Runt*. A couple of years later two further **Hello People** albums surfaced on ABC/Dunhill, both with Smart and both produced by Rundgren.

It has also been rumored that Danny Douma was also part of this enigmatic group, but his name doesn't appear on the 1968 Philips albums. Danny Douma later became the leader of the (Big) Wha-Koo (three albums on ABC and Epic between 1976-79) and also recorded a solo album *Night Eyes* (Asylum) in 1979 with Eric Clapton and Fleetwood Mac.

The Hello People also appeared on the The Smothers Brothers Comedy Hour and The Tonight Show with Johnny Carson.

Compilation appearances include *(As I Went Down To) Jerusalem* and *Mr. Truth Evading, Masquerading Man* on *Electric Food* (LP). (VJ/SR/JO)

Help

Personnel:	CHET McCRACKEN	drms, perc, vcls	A
	JACK MERRILL	gtr, keyb'ds, vcls	A
	ROB ROCHAN	bs, vcls	A

ALBUMS: 1(A)	HELP	(Decca DL 75257) 1971 -
2(A)	SECOND COMING	(Decca DL 75304) 1972 SC

NB: (1) counterfeited on CD (Hamster Music HMP 010). (1) and (2) reissued on one CD (Free Records FR 2008).

45s:	Keep In Touch/Runaway	(Decca 32783) 1971
	Good Time Music/Hold On Child	(Decca 32879) 1971

A hard-rocking Christian band, which included drummer McCracken who had earlier played with **The Evergreen Blueshoes** and who later ended up with The Doobie Brothers. The band were from California.

Second Coming is an album for heavy rock fans. The outstanding track is *Do You Understand The Words?* for its superb psychedelic guitar work and McCracken's heavy rock drumming. The remainder of the album, which contains all original compositions, is not up to that standard but contains some quite good heavy-rock numbers, particularly, *All Day, Good Time Music* and *Hold On Child* on Side One. Surprisingly, they did not attain much commercial success and both their albums are now minor collectors' items.

Compilation appearances have included: *Do You Understand The Words* on *Endless Journey - Phase Two* (LP) and *Endless Journey - Phase I & II* (Dble CD). (VJ)

Help

Personnel:	DONALD LOWER	bs	A
	STEVE NELSON	perc	A
	DENNIS SULLIVAN	piano	A
	MICHAEL WELCH	flute	A

45s:	Life Worth Living/		
	Questions Why (PS)	(Capitol Custom 3704/3705)	1970
α	Make That Change/Always Flowing	(No label H-7-75)	1975

NB: α As The Hagio Enigma Limpidity Paradisical Band.

Basing themselves in Citrus Heights, California (near Sacramento) this group changed their name to **Azitis**, due to a conflict with the Decca band **Help** and released their album on Elco and a single featuring two cuts from the album. When the Decca group broke up they took the **Help** name back with its new, more specific definition.

Questions Why, a reasonable rocker with some good guitar work, has also resurfaced on *Relics, Vol. 2* (LP) and *Relics Vol's 1 & 2* (CD). (CF)

David Hemmings

Personnel:	JIMMY BOND	arranger	A
	DAVID HEMMINGS	vcls	A
	CHRIS HILLMAN	bs	A
	ROGER MCGUINN	gtr	A
	LEON RUSSELL	arranger	A

ALBUM:	1(A)	HAPPENS	(MGM SE 4490) 1968 -

David Hemmings is the famous sixties English actor who starred in "Blow Up". The inclusion of this obscure album here may be surprising, but is justifiable due to the quality of the tracks. It was produced in California by Jim Dickson and **Leon Russell** and engineered by Jim Messina (**Buffalo Springfield**).

There's an unreleased Gene Clark song (*Back Street Mirror*), a cover of **Tim Hardin**'s *Reason To Believe*, some arranged ballads, but also, and mainly, four really strange psychedelic ragas co-written by Roger McGuinn and Chris Hillman of **The Byrds**: *Talkin L.A.*, *Good King James*, *Anathea* and the 6'30" *War's Mistery*. On all these tracks, the 12-string guitar of McGuinn sounds like a sitar and the Indian percussions (tamboura, tablas...) add to the weirdness of the lyrics. (SR)

The Henchmen

45:	Please Tell Me/Livin'	(Punch 1009) 1965

Punch was a sub-division of the seminal Detroit-based Hideout label. The 'A' side of the Punch 45, was quite melodic but the flip, is a good guitar-blasting rocker.

Compilation appearances include: *Livin'* on *Back From The Grave, Vol. 5* (LP); and *Please Tell Me* on *Best Of The Hideouts* (LP) and *Best of Hideout Records* (CD). (VJ)

Hendrickson Road House

Personnel incl:	SUE AKINS	vcls	A

ALBUM:	1	HENDRICKSON ROAD HOUSE	(Two:Dot) 1970 R2/R3

A completely unknown album in the style of **Yankee Dollar**, released on the same label as The Ninth Amendment. (SR)

Jimi Hendrix

Although this brilliant psychedelic blues guitarist was born in Seattle, given that he was based in the U.K. for most of his career, his life and times are documented in the 'The Tapestry Of Delights'.

'**Experience** drummer, Mitch Mitchell, later played with **Ramatam** and bassist Boel Redding with Fat Mattress and **Road**. (VJ)

Henry Tree

Personnel:	CARMEN CASTALDI	drms	A
	LEROY MARKISH	ld gtr, vcls	A
	CHARLES MCLAUGHLIN	bs	A

ALBUM:	1(A)	ELECTRIC HOLY MAN	(Mainstream S/6129) 1968 SC

45:	Penfield Town/?	(Mainstream MRC 729) 1970

NB: double-sided promo copies exist, stock issue not confirmed.

From Cleveland, Ohio. Their album veers towards the progressive, with a country influence on a couple of tracks. The long title track in particular has an unnerving intro and features some good guitar work. Another highlight is quite an impressive cover of Traffic's *Dear Mr. Fantasy*. Overall, an album which is worth investigating. (VJ/GGI/MW/SR)

John Herald

ALBUM:	1	JOHN HERALD	(Paramount) c1971 -

An obscure hippie folk-rock singer. He would later work with David Bromberg and Bonnie Raitt. (SR)

The Herd

45:	Things Won't Change/The Sun Has Gone	(Octupus 257) 196?

An obscure Washington D.C. band, whose *Things Won't Change* has resurfaced on *Signed, D.C.* (LP). It's quite a strong song with effective vocals and some good fuzz guitar. I've also seen them quoted as a Chicago band, and *Things Won't Change* also resurfaced on *Michigan Mixture, Vol. 2* (LP). So, who knows? (VJ/MW)

The Herde

45:	Mister You're A Better Man Than I/?	(Cinema 6900) 196?

This Yardbirds' cover has resurfaced on the *Ear-Piercing Punk* (LP) compilation. (VJ)

Here Comes Everybody

Personnel:	CHRIS A. BURNS	A
	HANK HAWLEY	A
	JIM JACKSON	A
	GEFF JUNG	A
	VERNON JAMES SCHUBEL	A

ALBUM:	1	HERE COMES EVERYBODY	(CAB Records 101) 1974 SC

Recorded at Stilwater Sound Studio, Stillwater, Oklahoma, comes this strange concept album with a handmade cover. Six tracks on the Side One (*My Own Controls, Roy Roberts Intro, Young Roy Roberts, You Have Been Abusing Me, Yeah, Yeah, Yeah* and *Make A Buck*) and *L'opera: Johnny Got His Ray Gun*, a side long cut on Side Two, with crazy drumming and weird vocals about aliens and ray guns! (SR)

The Hermon Knights

See **The Knights** entry.

Danny Hernandez and The Ones

Personnel:	DANNY HERNANDEZ	gtr, vcls	A
	RONNIE HERNANDEZ	drms, vcls	A
	GARY MELVIN	bs	A
	JIM PITCHFORD	organ, vcls	A
	TOM TAYLOR	gtr, vcls	A

ALBUM: 1(A) BACK HOME AT THE BREWERY
(Spirit Records 964 S-2003) 1973 R2

From East Lansing, Michigan; a live album recorded as a benefit for NORML! The band tends to prefer sweaty soulish/latin cover tunes (*Them Changes*, *Dance To The Music*, *I Wanna Take You Higher*), which is typical of the era (August 1972) although the lead guitar solos are bountiful and completely insane! All things considered, a pretty cool record that will send chills down the spine of any guitar fanatic. Rather tragic cover art, though...

The album was co-produced by Bob Baldori of **The Woolies**.

Leader Danny Hernandez passed away in 2000. (CF)

Heroes

45: I Can Only Give You Everything/
Say It With A Smile (M-Gee 001) 196?

Better known bands like **The Iguanas**, **The Little Boy Blues**, **The MC5** and The Ambertones also covered *I Can Only Give You Everything*. This obscure San Jose oufifit's version later resurfaced on the *Everywhere Chainsaw Sound* (LP). (VJ)

Carolyn Hester Coalition

Personnel:	DAVE BLUME	bs, keyb'ds, melodica	AB
	SKEETER CAMERA	drms, flute	AB
	CAROLYN HESTER	vcls, gtr	AB
	JERRY KELLER	bcking vcl	A
	STEVE WOLFE	gtr, perc	AB
	DAVE MAUNEY	vibes, bs	B

ALBUMS: 1(A) CAROLYN HESTER COALITION
(Metromedia MD 1001) 1968 R1
2(B) MAGAZINE (Metromedia MD 1022) 1969 R1

45: Big City Streets/Magic Man (Metromedia MM 120) 1969

From the East Coast, **Carolyn Hester** began her career in the early sixties as a traditional folk singer and was married briefly to **Richard Farina**. Around 1968, she formed the **Carolyn Hester Coalition**, who recorded two albums for Metromedia.

Both albums were produced by Dave Blume and recorded in New York. The first is fuzzed up folk/psych/rock, like a female folk/singer/songwriter meets **Ill Wind**. The best offering is the opening cut *Magic Man* which is mindblowing fuzz psych at its best. It is hard to find weak tracks on this album. The sound is typified by an excellent laid-back fuzz guitar and political lyrics like in *Half The World* ("...Half of the world is starving, half of the world is overfed...!"). Other songs include *Be Your Baby*, the much recorded hippie anthem *Let's Get Together*, *Journey* and *Buddha (Was Her Best Man)* plus more. Recommended for folk/psych fans. The entire group without Carolyn also showed up as backing band in **Twinn Connexion**.

The rarer second album, *Magazine*, is another fine example of electric folk-rock with hippie values (the back cover shows the group doing peace signs beside Army tanks), which again should interest fans of **Ill Wind** and **Jefferson Airplane**. **Hester**'s crystal clear voice is backed by good musicians and the songs reflect the period: *Beadmaker*, *Plant the Crops In The Garden* (about the generation gap), *Just Follow Me* (described as "a simple formula for entering a world of new and enlightening experiences"), *Calico Sky*, etc. The album also contains ususual versions of *Sittin On The Dock Of The Bay*, *St. James Infirmary* and *Swing Low Sweet Chariot*. It is now a minor collector's item.

Carolyn Hester later returned to a more traditional singer/songwriter career.

Compilation appearances have included: *Rise Like Phoenix* on *Psychosis From The 13th Dimension* (CDR & CD). (SR/CP/MMs)

H.E.W.

ALBUM: 1 H.E.W. (Jam 101) c1972 ?

From Houston, a local rural melodic rock, a bit easygoing. Their album came with an insert. (SR)

Hex

45: You Cry And I'll Laugh/Doubt (Reissue.) (Hexx HY-101) 1995

From a 1967 unreleased acetate, superb heavy-psych by an obscure, belatedly appreciated combo. (MW)

Hickory Hollow

Personnel incl:	BUTLER	A
	CAMERON	A
	A. CHARMATZ	A
	FRANK GORDON	A

45: Never Happen/Home (Musitron M-107) 19?

A California combo whose *Never Happen* is a jaunty number with decent harmonies and a catchy guitar refrain. (MW)

Hickory Wind

Personnel incl:	ALAN JONES	bs, vcls	A
	MIKE McGUYER	gtr, vcls	A
	SONNY PRENTICE	vcls, gtr, bs, harp	A
	BOBBY STREHL	drms	A

ALBUM: 1(A) HICKORY WIND (Gigantic 1104) 1969 R4

Just 100 copies of this album were pressed originally making it extremely rare. The band came from Indiana and all except Prentice went on to play in **B.F. Trike**. Their album is full of variety wth the most psychedelic track

HICKORY WIND - Hickory Wind LP.

being *Time And Changes*. This has great vocals plus lots of fuzz and was later re-recorded by **B.F. Trike**. *Mr Man* is rather unusual, employing spoken lyrics over a piano/keyboard backing; *Father Come With Me* is a successful blend of droning keyboards and vocals and there are also a couple of laid-back melodic numbers in *I Don't Believe* and *Judy*, which open and close the album. Get to hear the album if you can but don't pay a fortune for a copy.

Mister Man has also resurfaced on *Love, Peace And Poetry, Vol. 1* (LP & CD).

This group is unrelated to another Hickory Wind, a country-folk group who released an album *Crossing Devil's Bridge* (Flying Fish) 1978. (VJ/MW/SR/NK)

The Hides

Personnel incl: JOHN MARSIGLIO   A

45: Don't Be Difficult/
When I See The One I Love   (Scotty no #) 1966

Formed in early 1965 in Pittsburgh, Pennsylvania, out of the ashes of The Ban-lans and The Runaways, two local bands. They recorded four tunes in Gateway studios in 1966 and paid Scotty to press two up. *Don't Be Difficult*, which was quite a punchy punker also be found on *Back From The Grave, Vol. 7* (Dble LP), *Pennsylvania Unknowns* (LP) and *Burghers, Vol. 1* (LP & CD). (VJ/MW)

The Hi-Fi's

45: I'm A Box (Mum-Mum-Mum) /
No Two Ways   (United Artists 50160) c1967

An obscure pop-rock group. (SR)

Gary Higgins

Personnel:	DAVE BEAUJON	bs	A
	JAKE BELL	gtr, vcls	A
	TERRY FENTON	organ, piano	A
	GARY HIGGINS	vcls	A
	PAUL TIERNEY	flute, mandolin, vcls	A
	MAUREEN WELLS	cello, vcls	A

ALBUM: 1 RED HASH   (Nufusmoon WMI 3673) 1973 R1

NB: (1) reissued on CD.

Connecticut electric folk/rock of a very high standard - it even approaches **Mu** territory at times on tracks like *Thicker Than A Smokey*, *Telegraph Towers* and *I Can't Sleep At Night*. Produced by **Higgins** and Chico Carillo, the album came with a lyric sheet. (CF/SR)

Higher Elevation

45s:	α	Diamond Mine/Crazy Bicycle	(Chicory 408) 1967
		Here Comes Sunshine/Thoughts Of Lila	(Liberty 56016) 1968
		Country Club Affair/Summer Skies	(Liberty 56035) 1968
		Odyssey/Highway 101	(Liberty 56094) 1969

NB: α released as by **Dave Diamond** and **The Higher Elevation**.

A Colorado outfit who backed **Dave Diamond** on his famed *Diamond Mine* featured on *Pebbles, Vol. 3*. **The Higher Elevation** evolved out of Greeley's **Monocles** and released three further 45s in their own right, mostly garage-pop with the spaced-out *Odyssey* probably the highpoint.

Compilation appearances have included: *Odyssey* on *Psychedelic Experience, Vol. 2* (CD) and *The Psychedelic Experience, Vol. 2* (LP). The lightweight *Here Comes Sunshine* can also be found on the summer-pop compilation *Bring Flowers To U.S.* (LP). (MW)

The Highlifes

45: Choose Me Over Him/No One To Tell Her   (Pit 403) 1966

This band came from Waxahachie in Texas. So far as I know the 45 above was their sole stab for stardom, although the band also recorded a version of Little Richard's *Lucille* in 1966 and another unreleased track, *Cloak And Dagger*.

Compilation appearances have included: *No One To Tell Her* and *Lucille* on *Texas Punk: 1966, Vol. 1* (LP) and *Acid Visions - Complete Collection, Vol. 2* (3-CD); and *Cloak And Dagger* on *The Cicadelic 60's, Vol. 4* (LP) and *The Cicadelic 60's, Vol. 2 - Never Existed!* (CD). (VJ/MW)

High Numbers

45: I'm A Man/High Heel Sneakers -
Mojo Working (medley)   (Ocean 8855-0594) 196?

This was recorded in an airplane locker at Chicago's O'Hare International Airport. The 4 1/2 minute cover of *I'm A Man* is pretty powerful with lots of mouth organ. Check it out on *Garage Punk Unknowns, Vol. 3* (LP). (VJ)

GARY HIGGINS - Red Hash CD.

HIGH TREASON - High Treason CD.

The High Spirits

Personnel:	RICK ANTHONY (aka BOB COHEN)	gtr	A
	RICK BECKET (aka FRANK PROUT)	bs	A
	OWEN HUSNEY	ld gtr	A
	JAY LUTTIO	keyb'ds	A
	CLIFF STONE (aka CLIFF SIEGEL)	vcls	A

45s:	Love Light/Tossin' And Turnin'	(Soma 1436) 1965
	Love Light/Tossin' And Turnin'	(Apex 76972) 1965
	I Believe/Bright Lights, Big City	(Soma 1446) 1966

A quintet who operated out of Minneapolis in the mid-sixties. Their final 45 is a hot garage recording which will interest readers.

Both sides of the first 45 were originally collected together with other twin-cities nuggets on the *The Big Hits Of Mid-America, Vol. 2* (LP).

When the band split, Owen Husney was the only member to continue in the music biz as promoter and manager, most notably for Prince! **High Spirits** also recently staged a local mini-reunion.

Retrospective compilation appearances have included: *I Believe* on *Root '66* (LP); *Tossin' and Turnin'* on *Soma Records Story, Vol. 1* (LP); *Bright Lights, Big City* and *I Believe* on *Soma Records Story, Vol. 2* (LP) and *A Journey To Tyme, Vol. 3* (LP); *(Turn On Your) Love Light* on *Soma Records Story, Vol. 3* (LP); *Bright Lights, Big City*, *I Believe*, *(Turn On Your) Love Light* and *Tossin' and Turnin'* on *The Big Hits Of Mid-America - The Soma Records Story* (Dble CD). (VJ/MW/JKw)

High Treason

Personnel:	BOBBY BLUMENTHAL	perc	A
	JOE CLEARY	vcls	A
	SAM GOODMAN	gtr	A
	EDGAR KOSHATKA	keyb'ds	A
	TERRY MORRISSEY	bs	A
	MARCIE RAUER	vcls	A

ALBUM: 1(A) HIGH TREASON (Abbott ABS-1209) 1970 R1

NB: (1) reissued on CD and vinyl (Gear Fab GF-165) 2001.

Recorded in New York, this album consists of five Edgar Koshatka originals and a pretty woeful cover of Bob Dylan's *Subterranean Homesick Blues*. It was produced by Howard Massler. Although the material is rather weak, there's nothing wrong with the playing - lots of extended jams with some good guitar and organ interplay. The very short jazzy instrumental *Circadian Rhythm* isn't marred by the rather messy production which undermines the rest of the album.

The band came from Philadelphia. (VJ/MW)

Highway

Personnel:	ERIC BANNISTER	bs, vcls	A
	DAN CAMMARATA	drms, vcls	A
	STEVE MURPHY	gtr, vcls	A

ALBUM: 1 HIGHWAY (No label # 584 N 11) 1975 R4

NB: (1) had a limited vinyl reissue of 300 copies in 1996. (1) reissued on CD by the band with four previously unreleased tracks.

A psychedelic hard-rock trio from Mankato, Minnesota. The album consists of long tight songs with great vocals and extended, flowing guitar leads on the better tracks - *Look Away*, *Meadow* and *Tomorrow*. Some of the other tracks are rather more nondescript. Their album originally had a pressing of 500 and Steve Murphy had earlier played with Minnesota's **The Epicureans**. Murphy incidentally is held in high esteem, nay reverential awe, by Midwest aficionados. (CF/VJ/MW)

Highway Robbery

Personnel:	DON FRANCISCO	ld vcls, drms	A
	JOHN LIVINGSTON TUNISON IV	bs, vcls	A
	MICHAEL STEVENS	gtr, vcls	A

ALBUM: 1(A) FOR LOVE OR MONEY (RCA LSP 4735) 1972 SC

NB: (1) also released in Peru by RCA. (1) reissued on CD.

45: Mystery Rider/All I Need (To Have Is You) (RCA 74-0782) 1972

One of the best major-label heavy-rock albums of the era, produced by Bill Halverson (**Blue Mountain Eagle**, CS&N, Freddie King). The liner notes proclaim that "the group dedicates itself to the emission of the highest levels of energy rock". Their brilliant guitarist, Michael Stevens, composed the eight tracks (*Lazy Woman*, *Promotion Man*, *Fifteen*...) while Francisco sang and drummed.

Stevens was previously with **The Boston Tea Party**, and also played on **Atlee Yeager**'s solo albums. Due to his work with **Yeager** and the "Child Of A Gypsy Commune" mention in the liner notes, some people (mainly record dealers) think he was **Damon**, but that's not the case at all. A New York native, previously in **Crowfoot** and **Atlee**, Francisco was an active musician, drummer and singer. In 1973, he was with Ron Elliott (**Beau Brummels**) in **Pan** and, in 1977, formed The Big Wha-Koo (three albums on Epic and ABC). He has an extensive recording history lasting into the 1980s. He must not be confused with another Don Francisco, a Christian singer/songwriter who released some albums during the seventies on NewPax, a label managed by Gary Paxton. (CF/SR)

HIGHWAY - Highway LP.

Kenneth Higney

ALBUM: 1 ATTIC DEMONSTRATION (Kebrutney KBH-516) 1976 SC

NB: (1) had a limited reissue in 1985.

45: I Wanna Be The King / Funky Kinky (Kebrutney) 197?

Originally from Manhattan, psychedelic-folk poet **Kenneth Higney** was based in Bayonne, New Jersey around the time of his album's release. Just 500 copies were pressed and the album is characterised by a stoned vocal style with acoustic backing and lots of effects. Some tracks like *Rock Star* also veer into heavy territory with its solid backbeat and fearsome distorted guitar. The atonal style of singing tends to be irritating, concealing what little melody there might be. An album you'll either love or hate!

Both sides of his post *Attic Demonstration* 45, were also featured on a CD, *Single 'N' Independent* which **Higney** put together on Kebrutney in 1994. The CD is a compilation of local unsigned acts. (MW)

Diane Hildebrand

ALBUM: 1 EARLY MORNING BLUES AND GREENS
(Elektra EKS-74031) 1968 -

An obscure hippie-folk singer, her album contains tracks like *The Reincarnation Of Emmalina Stearns* or *Given Time*. Probably one of the rarest Elektra releases. (SR)

Bunker Hill

45s: Hide And Go Seek Pt 1/Pt 2 (Mala 451) 1962 33
Red Riding Hood And The Wolf/Nobody Knows (Mala 457) 1962
The Girl Can't Dance/
You Can't Make Me Doubt My Baby (Mala 464) 1963 -

From Washington D.C., this guy was really a black gospel singer who in 1963 approached **Link Wray** for help with a wild rock'n'roll song. Wray got The Raymen in to back him and the result was *The Girl Can't Dance*, a frantic rocker with Hill's hollering vocals. You'll also find it on *Back From The Grave, Vol. 4* (LP). (VJ/MW)

Joel Scott Hill

Personnel:
JOHNNY CALLARD drms A
JOEL SCOTT HILL gtr, vcls ABCDEFG H I J K L M N O P Q R S TUV
HAROLD KIRBY gtr, bs, vcls AB D FG I J K L
RONNIE LYNCH sax, piano, vcls AB D
JIMMY MARINO drms B
GENE LAMAR gtr, vcls (C) FG
WILLIE KELLOGG drms D F I J K Q
BILL CARROLL drms G
EDDIE HOH drms L
JOHN BARBATA M N O R S T U V
BOB MOSLEY bs, vcls M N
JOANIE LYMAN vcls N
LEE MICHAELS keyb'ds, vcls O V
BOB BROWN bs, vcls P
TOMMY KENDALL drms, vcls P
BOB DESNOYERS bs, vcls Q
ART GIESSER gtr, organ, vcls Q
TONY DE LA BARREDA bs R
CHRIS ETHRIDGE bs, vcls S T U V
BYRON BERLINE fiddle V
MIKE T. LAWSON pedal steel V
GENE PARSONS banjo V
ERIC WHITE bs V
(ANDY GIORDINO bs C)
(SANDY NELSON drms C)
(THE BLACKBERRIES vcls E U)
(HAL BLAINE drms E)
(MERRY CLAYTON vcls E)
(CAROL KAYE bs E H)
(CLYDIE KING E U)
(LARRY KNECHTAL organ E U)
(LEON RUSSELL piano E H U)
(JESSIE PRICE drms H)
(DRAKE LEVIN T)
(SIDNEY GEORGE sax U)
(BOOKER T. JONES organ UV)
(SNEAKY PETE KLEINOW steel gtr U)
(SPOONER OLDHAM piano U)
(BOBBYE HALL PORTER conga U)
(MAC REBENNACK piano U)
(JOHN SEBASTIAN hrmnca U)
(CLARENCE WHITE gtr U)
(PRISCILLA COOLIDGE vcls V)
(RITA COOLIDGE vcls V)

NB: Line-ups: 'A' initially The Rebels, then The Strangers (Mk. I, 1958-59). 'B' The Strangers (Mk. II, 1959-60). 'C' temporary Strangers recording line-up. 'D' The Strangers (Mk. III, 1960-63). 'E' temporary Joel Hill recording line-up (late 1962). 'F' The Strangers (Mk. IV, 1963-64). 'G' temporary Los Angeles gigging line-up (1963). 'H' temporary Joel Hill recording line-up (1963). 'I' The Strangers (Mk. V, 1963). 'J' The Invaders (1964). 'K' The Joel Scott Hill Trio (Mk. I, late 1964). 'L' The Joel Scott Hill Trio (Mk. II, 1965). 'M' Joel Scott Hill Trio (Mk. III, 1966). 'N' Joel Scott Hill Trio unreleased demo (1966). 'O' Joel Scott Hill Trio (Mk. IV, 1966). 'P' The Grin (1968). 'Q' The Friendly Grin (Fall 1968). 'R' Jerome (Mk. I, 1969). 'S' Jerome (Mk. II, 1969-70). 'T' Jerome unreleased demo (early 1970). 'U' Jerome (& Friends, *L.A. Getaway* LP, Jan-Aug 1970). 'V' The Docker Hill Boys unreleased LP for Columbia (1973).

ALBUM: 1(U) L.A. GETAWAY (Atco SD 33-357) 1971 -

NB: (1) a promotional-only mono white label edition exists. Both mono and stereo promo copies were issued with a folder insert. Also issued in the UK (Atlantic 40310) 1971 and the album has been reissued on CD in Japan (Atco-East West AMCY-2763) 1998. The name of the band that recorded this album, 'Jerome', does not appear on the cover or labels.

45s: α Caterpillar Crawl/Rockin' Rebel (Titan FF 1701) 1959
β A Lost Soul/Hill Stomp (Titan FF 1702) 1959
α Young Maggie/Boogie Man (Titan FF 1704) 1960
χ Dance Of The Ants/Navajo (Titan FF 1711) 1960
δ Little Lover/I Thought It Over (Trans American 519) 1961
ε Secret Love/I Ran (Monogram) 1963
ε Monkey Business/Hannibal's Hundred (Monogram) 1963
φ Look Out/Sticks And Stones (Monogram) 1964

NB: α β χ - shown as by The Strangers. β two versions of this single were recorded, one has 'narration' on the 'A' side, one does not. All known vinyl copies are without narration, but the alternate version is thought to exist on vinyl as well. χ

JOEL SCOTT HILL & THE STRANGERS.

withdrawn shortly after release. α β χ were all compiled on the CD-only compilation *Rare West Coast Surf Instrumentals* (Ace CDCHD 806) 2001. δ shown as by Joel Hill and The Strangers. ε shown as by Joel Hill. φ shown as by The Invaders with Joel Hill.

Joel Scott Hill spent most of his boyhood in Texas, moving to San Diego with his family during the 1940s. He was a member of at least two bands that pre-date this book; The Rhythm Runners, and The Ramblers, a group that featured Junior Madeo, San Diego's first "rock" guitarslinger. Madeo had a profound influence on **Hill**, and all of his subsequent musical endeavours became vehicles for electric guitar improvisation, which was a rather provocative concept at the time (fully five years before the British invasion). **Hill**'s own band focused largely on instrumental rock and blues, and they initially called themselves The Rebels. As this almost immediately became a problem in confusion with Duane Eddy's band, they changed their name to **The Strangers** when they signed to Titan Records in Los Angeles in 1959. Several of their early 45s charted in Southern California; the most successful being *Caterpillar Crawl*. During the first part of the 1960s, **Hill** also contributed to recordings as a session guitarist; in particular on hits by Kathy Young and The Innocents and Chris Montez.

Hill was a prominent and respected figure on the California rock scene for many years; one of, if not the first West Coast guitar hero and it became quite a badge of honor to be chosen as a member of his live band or to record with him. A quick check of his extensive (but only partial) personnel list reveals connections to scores of important rock bands, which was not an accident. He could be compared, perhaps to **Frank Zappa** in this respect. **Hill** performed and recorded steadily until two incidents (namely, a gunshot wound to the leg and a broken hand in a bar fight) forced him to retreat from the public eye and recuperate. He returned to form slowly, by all accounts - but it is widely acknowledged that his best work followed his convalescence.

L.A. Getaway was recorded over several months in 1970 with yet another very impressive line-up of pros guesting. A fine West Coast album with great vocals and bluesy guitars, it was not the success it should have been. **Hill** replaced Al Wilson in **Canned Heat** before *L.A. Getaway* was released, a move that certainly didn't endear him to Atlantic Records. The album sounds, thirty years later, like a California version of Derek and The Dominos - a more optimistic record but with that same relaxed, confident flow. It's worth seeking out. As it was clear that the band proper that recorded *L.A. Getaway* ('Jerome') was no more and therefore would not be touring in support of the album, Atlantic released it with no band name on it at all!

Joel Hill's tenure with **Canned Heat** encompassed only one studio album, *Historical Figures And Ancient Heads* (United Artists UAS 5557) 1972, which includes a dazzling remake of his 1959 45 'B' side *Hill's Stomp*. Infinitely more impressive, though, is the 1990 German-only double album *Live At The Turku Rock Festival*, recorded in concert in Finland in August 1971. This is probably the best example extant of the **Joel Hill** line-up of **Canned Heat**; he sings lead on a couple of tracks and the stereo mix separates his guitar from Vestine's by placing the two wide left and right.

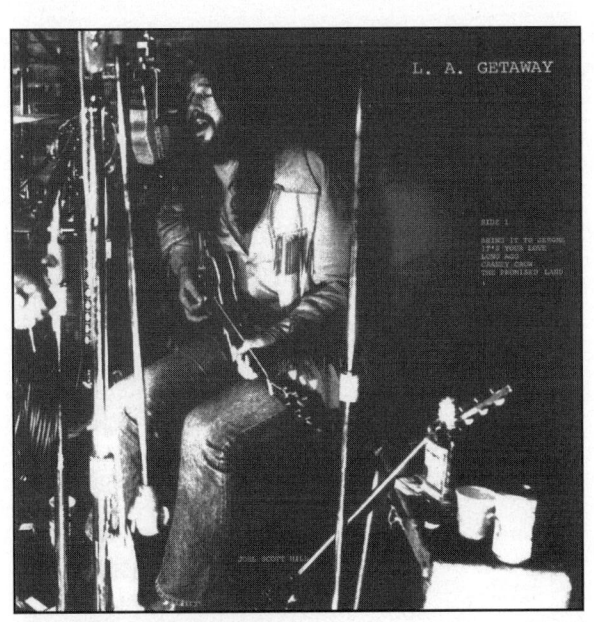

JOEL SCOTT HILL - L.A. Getaway LP.

HILLOW HAMMET - Hillow Hammet CD.

He also appears on the France-only *Memphis Heat* album, wherein **Canned Heat** back bluesman Memphis Slim. While this album did not show up in stores until 1975, it was recorded in 1971 (Barclay 80607). There's also *Gates On The Heat*, an album recorded with Clarence 'Gatemouth' Brown in the same series (Barclay 806030) 1975 which very likely includes **Hill**, but his participation is unconfirmed.

Hill's next project was a country-rock studio band called The Docker Hill Boys. It was his intention to assemble an album with this collection of studio pros, and although a considerable amount of energy was apparently invested in creating a follow-up to *L.A. Getaway*, a finished album was never released by Columbia. While The Docker Hill Boys project never came to fruition, it did convince **Hill** to pursue country-rock, which he accomplished by joining The Flying Burrito Brothers. He appears on several albums and toured internationally with the group.

Although **Hill** has been in a self-imposed retirement for some years, he has very recently been assemblying a new band for an album project. some heavy players have already offered their services; Booker T., Chris Ethridge and Willie Kellogg... it's hoped that **Bob Mosely** will contribute his considerable mojo as vocalist! (CF)

Thomas Hill

ALBUM: 1 INGREDIENTS (Mercury SR 611??) 1968 -

A poetic folksinger with some light orchestrations and strange lyrics. (SR)

Hillow Hammet

Personnel:	RONNIE BARCLEY	gtr	A
	CHUCK BENNETT	vcls, bs, keyb'ds	A
	G.C. COLEMAN	drms	A
	MIKE PREVITY	perc	A
	JACK REGISTER	bs	A
	STEVE SPENCER	organ, piano, electric piano	A
	PETE WILLIAMS	gtr	A

ALBUM: 1(A) HAMMER (House Of Fox HOF-LP-2) 1970 R2

NB: (1) also issued as white label promo labeled 'mono' although it plays stereo and commands no additional value. Counterfeited as *Hillow Hammit* (L&BJ) 1978 R2 in a newly designed cover and minus one cut (*Funky Junky*). (1) reissued on CD (Dodo Records DDR 510) 2001.

This album was produced by Lelan Rogers (of the International Artists label) and recorded in Memphis, Tennessee. The origins of the band have been the subject for speculation over the years. It was suggested that they were from Oklahoma, then Mark Opsasnich's book 'Capitol Rock' (a fine tome on the Washington D.C. scene) mooted that they were possibly from that region and included D.C. guitarist Pete "Peaches" Williams. Well, from the personnel and reproduced album sleeve notes on the Dodo reissue, the latter appears to be borne out. The notes were written by a Charlie Brown (DJ for WOL radio in Washington) who reports that he first encountered the band recording demos at a studio in Silver Springs, Maryland. He says he also suggested to their manager that they be called The D.C. Sanitation Department (?!).

OK, that's sorted..... what about the music? Reputedly it's a "good hard-rock album with lots of acid guitar". It turns out to be decent hard-rock with occasional meandering leads, Hendrixisms and outbursts of wah-wah... but what hits you in the face is the gritty soulful vocals and a tough funky edge. Regrettably, the album closes with a 7 minute version of *Oh Happy Day*, the negro spiritual. That aside, there is certainly much to recommend here.

The bootleg repress on L&BJ is a very curious item. First of all, the band name is misspelled, a track is missing and the sound quality is miserable. It's yet another product of the Tennessee 'Album World' company that also did a hack reissue of another of Lelan Rogers' non-Texas productions, **Elderberry Jak**, as well as titles by The Yardbirds, **Jefferson Airplane** and a host of Johnny Kitchen-related records. (CF/MW/PW)

Him

| 45: | It's A Man Down There/4 A.M. | (Tear Drop 3074) 196? |

This 45 was the work of Doug Sahm of the **Sir Douglas Quintet** and The Doug Sahm Band recording under a pseudonym. Huey P. Meaux produced the 'A' side.

Compilation appearances include *It's A Man Down There* on *Texas Punk From The Sixties* (LP). (VJ)

The Hinge

| 45: | Come On Up/The Idols Of Your Mind | (Tee Pee 75/76) 1968 |

This 45 features a decent cover of the **Young Rascals**' number with some great fuzz guitar. Although released on the Tee Pee label, efforts to track this band down in the Appleton area, and wider Wisconsin, have drawn a blank - so the band may just have been passing through.

Compilation appearances have included: *Idols Of Your Mind* on *Psychedelic Experience, Vol. 3* (CD); and *Come On Up* on *Highs In The Mid-Sixties, Vol. 10* (LP). (VJ/MW/GM)

The Hinge

| 45: | Now Let Me Love You / I'll Pretend | (Highland 1194) 1968 |

A pleasant jangley harmony-popper from Los Angeles with **Association**-style backing vocals is backed by a jerky popper that would've been catchy had it not kept chopping and changing pace. (MW)

The Hippies

| 45: | Wooly Bully/Boys And Girls | (Cha Cha 768) 1966 |

A cover of **Sam The Sham**'s *Wooly Bully* by a Chicago combo. The 45 may also have been released with an alternative 'B' side *Someday You're Gonna Wake Up*. (VJ)

Hip Sound

| 45: | Far Out/Too Much | (Limelight L-3082) 1968 |

A couple of electronic psychedelic excursions - instrumentals bustin' with synthesizer, oscillator and thingumeebob effects, like someone fiddling with **Fifty Foot Hose**'s equipment in the studio whilst they were taking a break. (MW)

His Majesty's Coachmen

| 45: | I Don't Want To See You / Where Are You Bound | (Gemini G-1004) 1967 |

A mystery group from the Los Angeles area on the same label as **Band Of Wynand**. *I Don't Want...* is a resounding mix of cool vocals and **Byrds**y jingle-jangle and has another outing on *Fuzz, Flaykes And Shakes, Vol. 4* (LP & CD). (MW)

The Hitch-Hikers

| 45s: | You're The One/Whispering Waves | (Hitch-Hiker 1000) 1964 |
| | Someday Baby/Make Me Feel Good | (Phalanx 1000/1) 1965/6 |

From Ann Arbor, Michigan. This act were one of the area's more popular garage acts and later changed names to **The Thyme**. (MW)

The Hitch Hikers

| 45s: | Beaver Shot/? | (HH) 1967 |
| | Stay Away/ ? | (HH) 1967 |

A garage band from Indiana. (SR)

H.M.S. Bounty

Personnel:	BILL DODD	gtr	A
	MERRELL FANKHAUSER	gtr, vcls	A
	JACK JORDAN	bs	A
	LARRY MEYERS	perc	A

| ALBUM: | 1(A) | THINGS | (Shamley SS 701) 1968 R2 |

NB: (1) reissued on Time Stood Still (TSSLP2) 1985, and CD (Afterglow 015) 1995. Sundazed have also reissued the album on CD with extra tracks (SC 6094) 1997.

| 45s: | Things/Rich Man's Fable | (Shamley 44006) 1968 |
| | I'm Flying Home/ Girl (I'm Waiting For You) | (Shamley 44008) 1969 |

H.M.S. BOUNTY - Things CD.

This brief Fankhauser project was based in Los Angeles in 1968, after he and Dodd had earlier played with **Fapardokly**. In their time, **H.M.S. Bounty** often opened for **Canned Heat**, **Electric Flag** and the **Paul Butterfield Blues Band**. They split in early 1969 when Meyers and Dodd left.

This album, which was reissued in 1985 by Cherry Red's subsidiary Time Stood Still, is a melodic amalgam of both folk and acid-rock. The latter being represented by the paranoid *Lost In The City* and *Drivin' Sideways (On A One Way Street)* with the vocalist recounting a bad trip, and mystical numbers like *Madame Silky* and *A Visit WIth Ashiya*. The album is full of hooks, harmonies and sound effects that were typical of the period. The Time Stood Still re-issue includes an additional track, *I'm Flying Home* - the 'B' side from a 1969 45.

Fankhauser went on to form **Mu**, who also included Jeff Cotton, formerly of **Captain Beefheart**.

Fankhauser was one of the more interesting rock figures to emerge from Los Angeles in the sixties. Moving to the West Coast from his birthplace of Louisville, Kentucky, he played with surfing outfits like The Sentinels and The Impacts (with Jack Jordan) and later with (Merrell and) The Exiles, prior to forming **Fapardokly**. **Mu** spent much of their time in Maui, Hawaii and were a pretty weird bunch. Fankhauser has also cut solo albums in 1976, 1983, and 1985, which are well worth investigation.

Fankhauser suffered a heart attack following a concert appearance in Pismo Beach, California in 1987 and for a while it was touch and go, but he did fully recover.

Compilation appearances have included: *Things (Goin' Round In My Mind)* and *A Visit With Ashiya* on *Baubles - Down To Middle Earth* (LP). (VJ)

H.M. Subjects

Personnel:	JEFF ALLEN	drms	A
	GEORGE HALL	bs	A
	DANNY MURPHY	vcls, bs, gtr, perc	A
	CARTER RAGSDALE	vcls	A
	GEORGE WALDEN	ld gtr	A
	JOHN WEATHERFORD	gtr	A

45s:	Don't Bring Me Down Pt 1/Pt 2	(Saint 1001) 1966
	Don't Put Me Down (censored)/	
	Don't Put Me Down (uncensored)	(Blue Saint 1001) 1966

NB: Both 45s contain the same music.

This band were previously known as **The Montells**, who were responsible for *You Can't Make Me*, one of the finest primal R'n'B 45s, matching (if not out-doing) any early Pretty Things recording. From Miami, Florida, this 45 under the **H.M. Subjects** moniker, includes two versions of The Pretties' classic, which was censored for the line '... When I LAID her on the ground'. The uncensored version can also be found on the *Psychotic Moose And The Soul Searchers* (LP) compilation or you can check out the censored version on *All Cops In Delerium - Good Roots* (LP).

The recent retrospective album *The Montells / The Evil* (Corduroy CORD 027, Australia 1997) contains all released plus some unreleased material, and so includes both versions of *Don't Bring me Down*. Highly recommended.

Jeff Allen also later played in **Evil**. (MW/VJ)

Hobbits

Personnel:	JIMMY CURTISS	A
	GINI EASTWOOD	A
	HEATHER HEWITT	A
	TONY LUIZZA	A
	ZOK RUSSO	A

ALBUMS:	1( )	DOWN TO MIDDLE EARTH	(Decca DL 74920) 1967 -
	2(A)	MEN AND DOORS-THE HOBBITS COMMUNICATE	
			(Decca 75009) 1968 -
	3( )	BACK FROM MIDDLE EARTH	
			(Perception PLP 10) 1971 R3

HOBBITS - Men And Doors - The Hobbits Communicate LP.

45s:	Daffodil Days/Sunny Day Girl	(Decca 32226) 1967
	Pretty Young Thing/Strawberry Children	(Decca 32270) 1968

A New York City band whose music was essentially straight-forward sixties pop. Produced and arranged by Terry Philips, Jerry Vance and **Jimmy Curtiss**, their records stated that it was "vocals with instrumental accompaniment". They took their name from the JRR Tolkien stories but in fact never tried to incorporate them into their songs.

The first album is mainly notable for his pseudo "hip" liner notes ("Ain't in to know one bag I can ride the yellow submarine if I want to Hey, you know the inside to trip?) and the effects on the good opening track, *Down To Middle Earth*. Several songs have promising titles *Let Me Run My Fingers Through Your Mind*, *Out Of My Mind*) but are rather deceptive. No personnel or songwriters were credited.

On *Men And Doors*, two female singers were added and the main characteristic is the constant use of a flamenco guitar played by Marius. Penned by **Curtiss**, Terry Philips and Marcia Hillman, the songs are a bit more elaborated, notably *The Journey* (co-written by Howie Sell) and *Strawberry Children*.

The third album was released on **Jimmy Curtiss**' label, Perception.

Gini Eastwood was a studio singer and later worked with B.J. Thomas.

Compilation appearances have included: *Strawberry Children* on *Acid and Flowers* (CD); and *Down To Middle Earth* on *Baubles* (LP). (VJ/MW/SR)

The Hobbits

45:	Frodo Lives /Jolly Good Fellow	(ZAR 25) c1968

Produced by C. Aragon, D. Moore and Robyn, a California vocal pop act with harmonies, totally unconnected with the other **Hobbits**. *Frodo Lives* was written by by M. Fellows and M. Rogers for Talisman Music and the flip by by C. Aragon and D. Moore for Adobe Music.

D. Moore may be **Daniel Moore**. (SR)

Hog Heaven

Personnel:	EDDIE GRAY	gtr	A
	PETER LUCIA	drms, vcls	A
	RON ROSMAN	keyb'ds, vcls	A
	MIKE VALE	vcls, bs	A

ALBUM:	1(A)	HOG HEAVEN	(Roulette 42057) 1971

NB: (1) also released in France, (Roulette SRV 56041).

45s:	Theme From A Thought/?	(Roulette 7091) 1970
	Happy/Prayer	(Roulette 7101) 1971
	If It Feels Good/?	(Roulette 7106) 1971

The Shondells became **Hog Heaven** when they split with **Tommy James**. The album has yet to attract collectors. (SR/NK)

The Hogs

45:	Blues Theme/Loose Lip Sync Ship	(HBR 511) 1966

Loose Lip Sync Ship, was actually recorded by **The Chocolate Watch Band**, using **The Hogs** as a pseudonym for contract reasons. It's a catchy, but by no means outstanding, largely instrumental song which ends in complete mayhem. A novelty.

The German **Frank Zappa** fanzine/4-volume book "The Torchum Never Stops" maintains that - just maybe - the great man himself plays guitar on *Loose Lip Sync Ship*.

Compilation appearances have included: *Loose Lip Sync Ship* on *Pebbles, Vol. 3* (CD), *Pebbles Box* (5-LP), *Pebbles, Vol. 3* (LP), *Pebbles, Vol. 2 (ESD)* (CD); *Trash Box* (5-CD) and *Great Pebbles* (CD); and *Blues Theme* on *Angel Dust - Music For Movie Bikers* (LP). Both sides of the 45 also appear on the **Chocolate Watch Band** *Forty Four* retrospective collection. (VJ/MW)

Hokus Pokus

Personnel:	BILLY CIOFFI		A
	DAN GORMAN		A
	JON HYDE		A
	MICHAEL MONARCH	gtr	A
	SCOTT THURSTON	keyb'ds	A

ALBUM:	1(A)	HOKUS POKUS	(Romar RM 2002) 1972 -

A Californian hard-rock outfit, on the same small label **Griffin**. Scott Thurston had previously been in **The Stooges** and Michael Monarch was ex-**Steppenwolf**. (SR/NK)

Randy Holden

Personnel:	CHRIS LOCKHEAD	drms	A
	RANDY HOLDEN	gtr, bs, vcls	A

ALBUM:	1	POPULATION II	(Hobbit 5002) 1969 R3

NB: (1) reissued on vinyl (Line LLP 5211 AS) 1985. Also counterfeited on CD with three bonus tracks. On vinyl, this album has also been counterfeited twice in the eighties and once in the nineties. All counterfeit versions have some degree of surface noise. Also of interest is *Early Works '64 - '66* (Captain Trip) 1997 CD.

Chris Lockheed of **Kak** helped ex-**Blue Cheer** guitarist **Randy Holden** on the above album, which is an extension of the proto-metal direction he explored on Side Two of the third **Blue Cheer** album, *New! Improved!*. Probably because **Holden** plays all the music himself, the album sounds rather one-dimensional and sparse. It certainly isn't the best record that he's played on, but it's by far the rarest, and is still highly sought-after. The stories which have circulated for years about it being withdrawn from the market immediately after release, are probably accurate. It is still held in high regard by collectors of primitive heavy-rock and copies were changing hands for hundreds of dollars over twenty years ago.

Holden had earlier played with The Fender IV, **Sons Of Adam**, **The Other Half** and **Blue Cheer**. His early works have been compiled on the CD, *Randy Holden Early Works '64-'66: The Fender IV, Sons Of Adam* (Captain Trip Records) 1997. It includes both of **The Sons Of Adams**' 45s for Decca plus three previously unreleased cuts, *Without Love, I Told You Once Before* and *You Make Me Feel Good*. It also includes the two 45s for Imperial by The Fender IV plus two previously unreleased tracks, *Highway Surfer* and *Little Ollie*.

You can also find **Randy Holden**'s *Guitar Song* on *Reverberation IV* (CD). (CF/VJ)

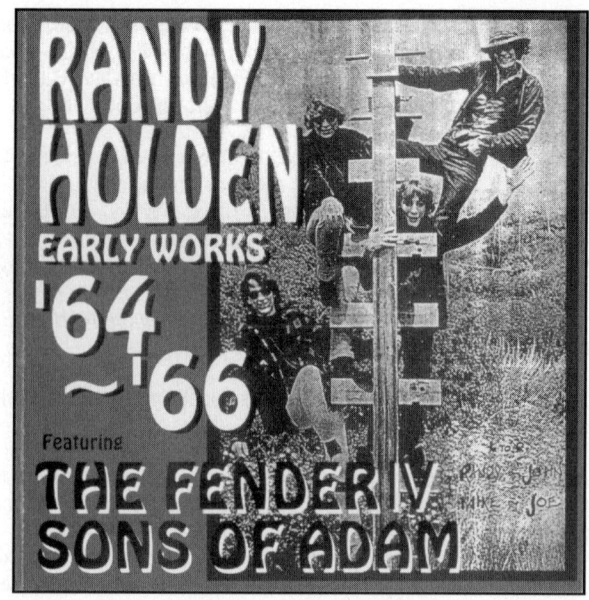

RANDY HOLDEN - Early Works CD.

Danny Holien

Personnel:	DANNY HOLIEN	gtr, vcls	A
	GaGa	drms, piano, vcls	A
	PETER JUKOFF	flute, sax	A
	STEPHEN SWENSON	bs, vcls	A

ALBUM:	1(A)	DANNY HOLIEN	(Tumbleweed TWS-102) 1971 -

Danny Holien was previously the leader of **The Shades** and **Midwest** and his only solo album may interest some curious readers. Recorded in L.A. in August 1971 for a short-lived label by Bill Szymczyk (Joe Walsh, Eagles, Silk...), it came housed in a luxuous die-cut jacket with a 16-page songbook. The lyrics talk about ecology, urban loneliness and Eastern religions and the music is mainly comprised of melodic ballads (*Colorado, Satsanga, Red Wing*), mixed with some good rock tracks similar to **James Gang** (*Lino The Wino, Wella Wella Isabella*).

The same year, **Holien**, GaGa and Steve Swenson also played on the solo album of Dewey Terry, *Chief* (Tumbleweed TWS-104). (SR)

Randy Holland

ALBUM:	1	CAT MIND	(Mother 1050) 1972 SC

Recorded on a New Brunswick, New Jersey label and recorded in Bound Brook NJ, this album is beginning to attract some attention from collectors. No band members are listed except for writing credits (R. Holland, B Bishop, L. Alpaugh).

The album as a whole has a very melancholy feel alternating between mellow, acoustic cuts like *Colours Of Sad* and *Make Me Flowers* to folk-rock cuts like *Cat Mind* and the killer *Indian Blues* with raw vocals and acidy guitar. (SR/DG)

Hollins and Starr

Personnel:	CHUCK HOLLINS	vcls, gtr, piano	A
	DAVE STARR	flute, recorder	A

ALBUM:	1(A)	SIDEWALKS TALKING	(Ovation OVQD 1407) 1971 SC

This gentle soft-rock album spans many diverse influences from pop-psych, mystical mellow passages, some quasi-classical touches and some delightful ethereal flute, trance-like vocals and fuzz guitar. Also helping out on the album are Bobby Christian (perc), Pat Ferrara (gtr), Ross Salamoni (drms), Ron Steele (gtr) and Bob Surga (bs). A few other session musicians assist on individual tracks. The highlight is the opening cut, *Talking To Myself*, but there is much to appreciate on this largely undiscovered gem. (VJ)

Rex Holman

ALBUM: 1 HERE IN THE LAND OF VICTORY
(Pentagram P-1001) 1970 SC

Probably from California. *Here In The Land Of Victory* is a very good folk-psych album, similar to the better tracks on the Brent Titcomb album, and sounding a lot like **Tim Buckley** in parts. **Holman** has a mid-range quavery voice and the songs are all very fragile, floating acoustic type of songs, with sitar, tablas and other exotic instrumentation scattered liberally throughout. The production credits "Schmitt-Douglas", and the album was recorded at Dimension Sounds, which may have been an L.A. Studio. The album cover is a very psychedelic montage featuring **Holman** superimposed over scenes of down and out street people. Not as overwhelmingly gorgeous as the **JK & Co** cover, but similar.

Holman also wrote *Bizarrek Kind* covered by **Vision Of Sunshine**. (SR/ESn)

Jake Holmes

Personnel:
JAKE HOLMES	vcls, gtr, piano	AB
TED IRWIN	gtr	AB
RICK RANDALL	gtr	A
DAVID BRIGGS	piano	B
KENNY BUTTREY	drms	B
WELDON MYRICK	pedal steel	B

HCP

ALBUMS:
1(A) THE ABOVE GROUND SOUND OF JAKE HOLMES
(Tower ST5079) 1967 - SC
2( ) LETTER TO KATHERINE DECEMBER
(Tower ST 5127) 1968 - SC
3(B) JAKE HOLMES (Polydor 24-4007) 1969 - -
4(-) SO CLOSE, SO VERY FAR TO GO
(Polydor 24-4034) 1970 135 -

45s: Genuine Imitation Life/
Hard To Keep My Mind On You (Tower 392) 1967
So Close/Django And Friends (Polydor PD 214041) 1970

Jake Holmes released his first album in 1967. It's an extraordinary psychedelic folk-rock masterpiece, then described as "a songwriter, three guitars and a mirror". The guitars of Holmes, Ted Irwin and Rick Randle (not the **Brain Police** guy) are the only backing of **Holmes**' voice and the ten short tracks are oustanding, especially the original version of *Dazed And Confused*, which was later literally stolen by Led Zeppelin.

This album was produced by Maximillian Productions and **Holmes** wrote on the back sleeve liner notes "Rick has two extra eyes. He can't word what he sees, but I hear what he sees when he plays".

HOLLINS AND STARR - Sideways Talking LP.

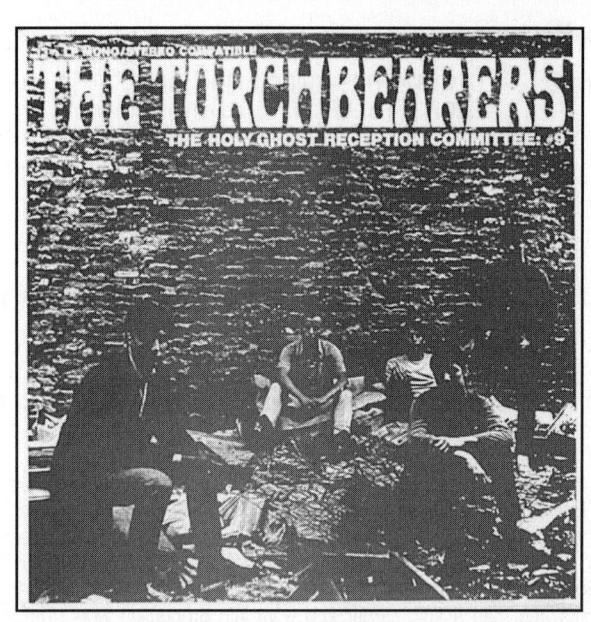

THE HOLY GHOST RECEPTION COMMITTEE No. 9 - The Torchbearers LP.

The following albums are more folky or country and not as interesting. His fourth, *So Close, So Very Far To Go* was the most successful commercially, climbing to No. 135 during its six week chart sojourn.

Ted Irwin would later play with Elliot Murphy, Roy Buchanan and various country singers.

Compilation appearances have included: *Dazed And Confused* on *Nuggets, Vol. 10* (LP); and *Leaves Never Break* on *Psychedelic Unknowns, Vol. 11* (LP) and *Slowly Growing Insane* (CD). (SR/VJ)

Holocaust

45: Savage Affection/Tutti Frutti (Red Robb 2025) 196?

An appropriately named late sixties Chicago act judging by the 'A' side, a frantic all action rocker which climaxes in vocal dementia and lots of fuzz.

Compilation appearances include: *Savage Affection* on *Mayhem & Psychosis, Vol. 1* (LP), *Mayhem & Psychosis, Vol. 1* (CD) and *Pebbles, Vol. 2 (ESD)* (CD). (VJ)

The Holy Ghost Reception Committee No. 9

Personnel:
DENNIS BLAIR	gtr	AB
RICH ESPOSITO	gtr	A
LARRY JOHNSEN	bs, gtr	AB
BOB KEARNEY	gtr	AB
MARK PULEO	gtr, mouth harp	AB

ALBUMS:
1(A) SONGS FOR LITURGICAL WORSHIP
(Paulist P-04425) 1968 R2
2(B) THE TORCHBEARERS (Paulist P-04426) 1969 R2

NB: (2) has had a limited reissue of 500 copies in 1997. There's also a CD compilation *Collected Works* (Hallucinations HCD 03) 2001.

The members of this group were all students at Regis High School in New York City. Their albums have a strong Christian theme. Indeed they were put out by the Paulist Press, a wing of the Missionary Society of St. Paul the Apostle in the state of New York. Their first album was essentially poppy, but the second one may interest readers. The lyrics were full of religious propaganda but a few of the tracks like *Magnificat 70* are instrumentally interesting. The title cut is an interesting folk-rocker and *Know They're You* is quite garagey. Overall, though, not recommended.

Dennis Blair also played in Justice who also featured Tom Viola. Dennis later became a stand-up comedian. (VJ/NK/RB)

Holy Mackerel

Personnel:
CYNTHIA FITZPATRICK	flute, vcls		ABC
GEORGE HILLER Jnr	ld gtr, bs, dobro, organ		ABC
PAUL WILLIAMS	vcls, piano		ABC
MENTOR WILLIAMS	gtr		BC
MICHAEL RAY CANNON	drms		C
JERRY SCHEFF	bs		C

ALBUM: 1(C) HOLY MACKEREL (Reprise 6311) 1968 -

45s:
I Just Haven't Got What It Takes/
Love For Everyone (Reprise 0681) 1968
Bitter Honey/To Put Up With You (Reprise 0768) 1968
Lady In Waiting/Scorpio Red (Reprise 0797) 1968

This was a short-lived Los Angeles group. Scheff had previously played with Ballroom, **Goldenrod** and **Millennium** as well as session work. He later played for TCB (an outfit comprised of some of L.A.'s top session men). Paul Williams, who'd previously auditioned unsuccessfully for **The Monkees**, went on to a prolific solo career in the 1970s and Mentor Williams, too, had a solo career and went into production work. The **Holy Mackerel** album, which paid some homage to the psychedelic music culture of the late sixties, is now a very minor collectable. (VJ)

The Holy Modal Rounders

Personnel:
PETER STAMPFEL	vcls, banjo, fiddle	A
STEVE WEBER	vcls, gtr	A

ALBUMS:
1(A) THE HOLY MODAL ROUNDERS (Prestige 14031) 1964 SC
2(A) THE HOLY MODAL ROUNDERS 2 (Prestige 7401) 1964 SC
3(A) INDIAN WAR WHOOP (ESP 1068) 1967 SC
4(A) THE MORAY EELS EAT THE HOLY MODAL ROUNDERS (Elektra 74026) 1968 SC
5(A) GOOD TASTE IS TIMELESS (Metromedia MD 1039) 1971 SC
6(A) ALLEGED IN THEIR OWN TIME (Rounder 3004) 1975 -
7(A) LAST ROUND (Adelphi AD 1030) 1978 -
8(A) PETER STAMPFEL AND STEVE WEBER: THE ORIGINAL HOLY MODAL ROUNDERS (Rounder) 1978 -

NB: (1) and (2) have been reissued. (1) and (2) reissued on one CD (Big Beat CDWIKD 176). (3) has also been issued on CD by ESP. (4) reissued on vinyl (Sundazed LP 5126) 2002. A related album *Have Moicy* (Rounder 3010) 1975, will also be of interest - credited to Michael Hurley with The Unholy Modal Rounders and Jeffrey Fredericks and The Clamtones. In 1999, Stampfel and Weber put together a reunion album with bassist Dave Reisch, *Too Much Fun* (Rounder CD 3163) 1999.

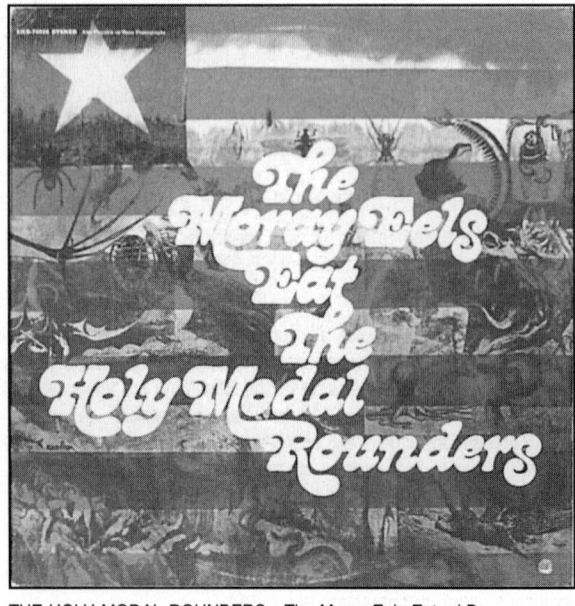

THE HOLY MODAL ROUNDERS - The Moray Eels Eat... LP

THE HOLY MODAL ROUNDERS - Indian War Whoop LP.

HCP

45: Boobs A Lot/
Love Is The Closest Thing (Metromedia 223) 1971 103

The Holy Modal Rounders were in essence Steve Weber and Peter Stampfel. Born in Philadelphia in 1942 and raised in Bucks County, Pennsylvania, Weber's unique guitar style was an important aspect of their sound. Stampfel was born in Wauwautosa, Wisconsin in 1938. Prior to the **Rounders**, he had played fiddle in numerous other musical aggregations - such as MacGrundys Old Timey Wool Thumpers, The Strict Temperence String of Lower Delancey Street and The Temperal Worth High Steppers. In October 1962, whilst in New York, Stampfel played with **Tiny Tim** and **Phil Ochs** at a Greenwich Village Club called The Third Side. Stampfel and Weber met in New York in March 1963 and they started to gig as a duo at places like The Cafe Flamenco and The Playhouse Theatre under a series of bizarre names like the Total Quintessence Stomach Pumpers before choosing **The Holy Modal Rounders**. Their gigs were crazy and interesting. Their music, which included some original material, was a diverse collection of traditional and ethnic styles. They chose to record for Prestige in preference to Vanguard or Elektra (who were also interested) because Prestige's producer Paul Rothchild smoked dope!

Their first two albums for Prestige, which were later reissued by Fantasy, were a fine collection of their material at that time. The first, for example, included their own interpretations of traditional songs like *Give The Fiddler A Dram* and *Cuckoo*; innovative covers of *Blues In A Bottle* (originally recorded by Prince Albert Hunt's Texas Ramblers in the 1930's), and Charlie Poole's and The North Carolina's Ramblers' *Hesitation Blues* as well as Weber's rehash of *Mr. Bass Mann*, rewritten as *Mr. Spaceman*. Stampfel and Weber also appeared on the first **Fugs** albums - they knew **Ed Sanders** from Greenwich Village. Stampfel also contributed to many local magazines and fanzines throughout his career.

However, in 1967, Stampfel put together a new band The Moray Eels which included Shepard, Tyler and Antonia (a long time friend of his). Sam Shepard was arguably one of America's best post-war playwrites and was also a film star, appearing in The Right Stuff and Jessica, for example. He also wrote the screenplay for Zabriskie Point. Later in the same year, Stampfel also united with Weber to record *Indian War Whoop*. It's a weird acid-folk album with no gaps between tracks and is not that good. Tyler did not play on this album and Lee Grabtree came in on keyboards.

Their 1968 album was made for Elektra in Los Angeles and included Californian bassist, John Wesley Annis. This, too, was a bit of a disaster and poorly produced. Indeed it took them a while to secure another recording contract, although eventually they wound up with Metromedia in 1971. The result *Good Taste Is Timeless* was a bit bland, although it had a few good cuts like *Spring of '65* and *Boobs A Lot*. It was disastrously re-mixed in New York by a group of stoned hippies who had not noticed that one of their speakers was malfunctioning. Metromedia went bust and further line-up changes were made.

The line-up for their 1975 album was Stampfel, Weber, Robin Remailly, Luke Faust (ex-**Insect Trust**), Richard Tyler, Dave Reich and **Karen**

Dalton. This album, which contained good material and was well-produced, is recommended. In fact the album had been recorded two years earlier, but its release was delayed.

In the period that followed Stampfel formed The Hoochie Koochie Dream Band and then, in late 1974, The Unholy Modal Rounders, who together with **Michael Hurley** and friends recorded the *Have Moicy* album, which was one of their better efforts and superior to *Last Round*, which was actually recorded in 1976.

1978 brought forth a Stampfel-Weber acoustic reunion album, which is more in the style of their first two Prestige albums, whilst 1999's *Too Much Fun* included Dave Reich. Stampfel and Weber still gig occasionally, mainly in NYC.

The Holy Modal Rounders were one of rock's most diverse and experimental bands.

Bird Song from their fourth album has subsequently resurfaced on *Elektrock The Sixties* (4-LP). It was originally featured in the cult movie *Easy Rider* and appeared on the soundtrack album. Other compilation appearances include: *Werewolf* on *Hallucinations, Psychedelic Underground* (LP).

Karen Dalton who played on their *Alleged In Their Own Time* album also released two solo albums in the late sixties/early seventies. (VJ/YI/KMy)

Holy Moses

Personnel:	BILL BATSON	keyb'ds, vcls	A
	MARTY DAVID	bs, sax, vcls	A
	CHRISTOPHER PARKER	drms	A
	TEDDY SPELIES (TED SPELEOS)	gtr, vcls	A

ALBUM: 1(A) HOLY MOSES!   (RCA LSP 4523) 1971 -

45: A Cowboy's Dream / Agadaga Dooley   (RCA 74-0496) 1970

Produced by Kim King of **Lothar and The Hand People**, their album contains some really good tracks with guitar, organ, etc. Both sides of their 45 also appear on the album.

Teddy Speleos had earlier played with **Kangaroo**, whilst Bill Batson was later the leader of eighties new wave outfit Hypstrz. Marty David was also a session man, playing with Jackie Lomax, Van Morrison, etc. (SR)

The Hombres

Personnel:	B.B. CUNNINGHAM	A
	JOHNNY WILL HUNTER	A
	JERRY LEE MASTERS	A
	GARY WAYNE MOEWEN	A

HCP

ALBUMS: 1(A) LET IT OUT (LET IT ALL HANG OUT)
                    (Verve Forecast 3036) 1967 180 SC
        2( ) THE HOMBRES   (Verve-Forecast FTS-3068) 1969 - ?

NB: (2) was not released, although some copies do exist.

HCP

45s: Let It Out (Let It All Hang Out)/
      Go, Girl, Go,   (Verve Folkways 5058) 1967 12
      It's A Gas/Am I High?   (Verve Folkways 5076) 1967 113
      The Prodigal/Mau, Mau, Mau   (Verve Folkways 5083) 1968 -
      Pumpkin Man/
      Take My Overwhelming Love   (Verve Folkways 5093) 1968 -
      If This Ain't Loving You Baby /
      You Made Me What I Am   (Sun 1104) 1969 -

This short-lived quartet came from Memphis, Tennessee. All but Masters were members of **Ronny and The Daytonas'** touring band. They had a highly individualistic sound and are best known for *Let It Out (Let It All Hang Out)* which made No. 12 in the U.S. charts in the Autumn of 1967.

The unreleased album from 1969 contains the tracks *Let It Out, It's A Gas, I'm High* and *Man Man Man*, plus a cover version of *Gloria* which turns into *Eight Miles High* before reverting back to *Gloria* again. All of these tracks also feature on their debut album, but it's not known if they are the same or different versions.

Hunter later died in 1976. Cunningham's brother, Bill, was a member of **The Box Tops**.

Compilation appearances have included: *Let It Out (Let It All Hang Out)* on *Nuggets Box* (4-CD), *Nuggets, Vol. 12* (LP) and *Excerpts From Nuggets* (CD). A later seventies reworking of the track also appears on a compilation called *Psychotic Reactions - Early American Rock Groups* (Topline TOP 153) 1986. (VJ/MW/MRo)

Homegas

Personnel:	PETER ACEVES	vcls, gtr, rack harp	A
	JIM BARDEN	hand harp	A
	RICHARD BLAUSTEIN	fiddle	A
	DAVE BROCK	hand harp	A
	JOHN HYSLOP	bs	A
	NEIL ROSENBERG	mandolin, banjo	A
	DAVE SATTERFIELD	vcls	A

ALBUM: 1(A) HOMEGAS   (Takoma C1026) 1970 -

Produced by **John Fahey** on his label, the only output of this rural community is well worth obtaining if you can find a copy. Led by Peter Aceves, it's an excellent example of folk-blues with good vocals and strong instrumental parts. The songs are all original and some are really outstanding, notably *Bumblebee, Bulldozer Blues* and *Maine*. The liner notes mention that two other (unknown) groups used to play with **Homegas**: Greazy Green and Stoney Lonesome before their house was destroyed by fire.

They came from Bloomington, Indiana. (SR/Bernella"Nell"Levin)

Homer

Personnel:	PHIL BEPKO	vcls	A
	GENE COLEMAN	drms	A
	FRANK COY	vcls	A
	HOWARD GLOOR	ld gtr, stgtr	A
	GALEN NILES	ld gtr	A

ALBUM: 1(A) HOMER
                    (Universal Recording Artist URA 101) 1970 R2/R3

NB: (1) reissued on Breeder (RPR 008-3C-568) 1986 also counterfeited on CD.

THE HOMBRES - Let It Out LP.

HOMER.

45s:	I Never Cared For You/	
	Dandelion Wine	(Universal Recording Artists 123-6/7) 1969
	Texas Lights/	
	On The Wall	(Universal Recording Artists 123-8/9) 1970
	Dandelion Wine/	
	Sunrise	(Universal Recording Artists 123-10/11) 1970

This band recorded in Houston although they originated from San Antonio in Texas. Musically they ranged from psychedelia to more progressive rock. Their first 45 was a strange rework of Willie Nelson's *I Never Cared For You* on the 'A' side. The third, particularly *Sunrise*, marked the pinnacle of their achievements in the arena of psychedelic rock. Their album is more rural-rock than psychedelic but it features some fine guitar work and is recommended. Christopher Cross, who achieved considerable success as a solo artist in the early eighties, had some involvement with their album and rumour has it that Van Wilkes played on their 45s.

Galen Niles was earlier a member of **The Outcasts** and played on their final scorching 45, *1523 Blair*. He also played as session musician on *Still In Love With You Baby* (**The Argyles**) and *Help I'm Lost* (**The Mind's Eye**).

Compilation coverage has included: *Dandelion Wine* and *Sunrise* on *Acid Visions - The Complete Collection, Vol. 1* (3-CD), *Acid Visions, Vol. 2* (LP) and *Filling The Gap* (4-LP). (VJ/MW)

The Honey Jug

Personnel:	JIM DICKINSON	keyb'ds	A
	BILL DONATI	drms	A
	JOE GASTON	bs	A
	RON JORDAN	vcls	AB
	JOE LEE	gtr	A
	TOMMY DUNCAN	keyb'ds	B
	FRED PROUTY	drms	B
	JOE SAVAGE	bs	B
	FRANK WATTS	gtr	B

45s:	Warm City Baby/Honey Say So	(HIP H-106) 1967
	For Your Love/In 1583 We...	(HIP H-110) c1968
	Warm City Baby / Honey Say So	(Hip 8018) 1969

This was initially a studio-only project in Memphis, comprising Ron Jordan (ex-Ronnie and The Devilles), the ubiquitous Jim Dickinson, plus three former members of **Lawson and Four More** (Lee, Gaston and Donati). *Warm City Baby*, a **Lovin' Spoonful** cover, is pleasantly laid-back mid-tempo pop with a trumpet solo, backed by folkie-pop. As it started to garner airplay and sales, a group was hastily assembled to perform live (line-up 'B').

They lasted long enough only to do a few gigs and record the follow-up.

For their full story seek out a copy of Ron Hall's book on the Memphis scene (from 1960 to 1975) 'Playing For A Piece Of The Door', published in 2001 by Shangri-La Projects (ISBN 0-9668575-1-8). (MW)

Honk

Personnel:	CRAIG BUHLER	sax	A
	BETH FITCHET	gtr, vcls	A
	TRIS IMBODEN	drms	A
	RICHARD STEKOL	gtr, vcls	A
	DON WHALEY	bs, vcls	A
	STEVE WOOD	keyb'ds, vcls	A

ALBUMS:	1	FIVE SUMMER STORIES, THE SOUNDTRACK	
			(Granite Music) 1972 -
	2	HONK	(20th Century 406) 1972 -
	3	HONK	(Epic 33094) 1974 -

NB: (1) also released in Australia (Image ILP-721).

45s:	Don't Take Anything/Love Machine	(Amaret 123) 1970
	Pipeline Sequence/	
	Made My Statement	(20th Century 2007) 1972
	Another Light/	
	I Wanna Do For You	(20th Century 2029) 1972
	Dog At Your Dog/Hesitation	(Epic 5056) 1974

A communal group from the hills of Laguna Beach, California. Their first album was specially written to be the soundtrack of a surf movie 'Five Summer Stories', whose poster was designed by Rick Griffin. The music is a mix of psych-rock, surf music and seventies rock, with some good tracks. The other albums are more in a mainstream California rock style. When the group disbanded, their leader and main songwriter, Richard Stekol, formed the Funky Kings with Jack Tempchin, Jules Shear and Greg Leisz. They recorded one album for Arista in 1976. The rest of the group went on to back Bert Jansch on his 1975 album *Santa Barbara Honeymoon*. In 1976, Whaley and Imboden formed La Seine (one album on Arista) with Mark Creamer (ex-**Armaggedon**). Later, Steve Wood and Tris Imboden backed Kenny Loggins and became session men. (SR)

The Hoodoo Rhythm Devils

Personnel:	ROGER CLARK	drms	A
	JOE CRANE	vcls	A
	DEXTER PLATES	bs	A
	JOHN REWIND	gtr	A
	GLENN WALTERS	drms, vcls	A

ALBUMS:	1(A)	RACK JOBBERS RULE	(Capitol ST-842) 1971 SC
(up to	2(A)	WHAT THE KIDS WANT	(Blue Thumb BTS 57) 1973 -
1973)			

NB: (2) also released by Vogue in France.

EP:	1(A)	HOODOO RHYTHM DEVILS (PS)	(No label) c1971

HOMER - Homer LP.

D.R. HOOKER - The Truth LP.

From San Francisco and previously known as **Joe Crane and The Rhythm Devils**, they became the **Hoodoo Rhythm Devils** after Glenn Walters (**Mystic Number National Bank**) joined them. Their first album is quite good and contains *Black Cadillac*, *Black Widow*, *Snake Doctor* and *Hoodoo Beat*. On the second, they were reinforced by Martin Fierro (from **Sir Douglas Quintet** and **Mother Earth**) and Chester Crill (aka Max Buda, from **Kaleidoscope**).

The band also released an EP with a hard picture sleeve. This is undated but is clearly an early release in their discography.

They released several other albums during the seventies, but went increasingly mellow and country-pop oriented.

In 1980, Joe Crane died of leukemia aged just thirty-four. (SR/CF)

The Hook

Personnel:	BOBBY ARLIN	gtr	AB
	CRAIG BOYD	drms	A
	BUDDY SKLAR	bs	AB
	DALE LOYOLA	drms	B
	DENNY PROVISOR	organ	B

ALBUMS:	1(A)	WILL GRAB YOU	(Uni 73023) 1968 -
	2(B)	HOOKED	(Uni 73038) 1968 -

45s:	Son Of Fantasy/Plug Your Head In	(Uni 55057) 1968
	Love Theme In E Major/Homes	(Uni 55077) 1968
	In The Beginning/Show You The Way	(Uni 55149) 1969

A Los Angeles band formed by Bobby Arlin after he quit **The Leaves**. The first album is hard-rock with psychedelic undertones, the second is the more structured of the two - both are worth investigating, and now minor collectors' items.

Provisor had earlier been a solo artist and later went on to play with **The Grassroots**. Lee "Buddy" Sklar became a renowned session man and played with Jackson Browne, James Taylor and many others. Bobby Arlin later reappeared in 1973 with **Wonderlick** and Loyola turned up on the rare **Cosmic Travelers** album in 1972.

Compilation appearances include: *In The Beginning* on *Psychedelic Perceptions* (CD). (VJ/MW/SR)

D.R. Hooker Band

Personnel:	D.R. HOOKER	vcls, gtr	AB
	TOM KOBELA	dobro	A
	KEN LOVELETT	vibes, perc	A
	NICK OLIVA	keyb'ds	A
	VINCENT PASTERNAK	gtr	A
	ART RYERSON	piano, vcls	A
	RICK SANDERS	synth	A
	GEORGE SHECK	bs	A
	HAYWOOD SHECK	drms	A
	STEVE MALKAN	bs	B
	BERT McDEVITT	drms, vcls	B
	BOB REARDON	keyb'ds, vcls	B
	CARROLL YANNI	ld gtr	B

ALBUMS:	1(A)	THE TRUTH	(No label XLP 1029) 1972 R5
	2(B)	ARMAGEDDON	(On Records 40725) 1979 R2
	3(-)	RAIN ON THE MOON	(No label) 1987

NB: (1) originally issued with fold-open lyric insert. Reissued (Del-Val DV 008) 1993 and again (Subliminal Sounds SUBLP 14). (1) reissued on CD (Subliminal Sounds SUBCD 15). (2) was recorded early in 1974. Original pressing has thick sleeve, later counterfeited in Europe circa 1990. (3) was a cassette only, private release.

For some, **D.R. Hooker**'s debut album is one of the real 'treasures' of the early seventies private press scene. Pretty much devoid of commercial aspirations, it's particularly notable for its heavier cuts like *I'm Leaving You* and the druggy *The Bible*. The album closes with a message played backwards: "Life is a mystery of course it's true. Look for the answer, recorded clues".

Armageddon, which did not appear until 1979, was recorded with an entirely different line-up in 1974. There are great moments on this album, although it lacks the intimacy of their debut. **Hooker**'s voice has an unpolished quality that seems somewhat awkward when his band moves into progressive rock territory on this second album. The debut is a more convincing work.

D.R. Hooker was based in Connecticut.

Compilation appearances include: *Forge Your Own Chains* on *Son Of The Gathering Of The Tribe* (LP). (CF)

Hootch

Personnel:	HENRY ERKELENZ	A
	THOMAS S. HENRY	A
	DOUG LEMIRANDE	A
	BOB MALONEY	A
	LAURA SCHAEFER	A

ALBUM:	1(A)	HOOTCH	(Pro-Gress PRS 4844) 1974 R3

NB: (1) some copies had a handmade silkscreen cover, the others a plain white one. Reissued in 1994 on Rollocks (Rollock 1001) - limited to 400 copies.

HOOTCH - Hootch LP.

From Wisconsin, this band's sole album is a very rare and mostly instrumental piece. Competent and at times quite experimental but nothing to get really excited about. (VJ/SR)

The Hooterville Trolley

Personnel:	DOUG BORTHWICK	drms	A
	BILL CHREIST	organ	A
	DON KINNEY	bs	A
	MARTIN NASSIF	ld gtr	A

45s:	No Silver Bird/The Warmth Of Love	(Lynette 551) 1968
	Signs/?	( ) 1968

From Albuquerque, New Mexico, both their 45s were recorded in Clovis, N.M. in the same studio as used by Buddy Holly. *No Silver Bird* is a great trippy song with its swirling sound effects and great lyrics:-

"Go and get ready to fly
Lock all the doors as if to hide
Don't worry about faces inside
Just come with me and hide!"

The 45 lists an address in Mississippi, which has led to speculation about the bands true location. The 45 was produced by Tom Bee who was responsible for nuggets like *I Wanna Come Back (From The World Of LSD)* by another New Mexico outfit **Fe Fi Four Plus 2** and who later played/produced **Xit**. Tom Bee was based in Laguna-Acoma Pueblo, N.M. at the time.

The same track also appeared on the **Magic Sand**'s album on Uni under a different title *Get Ready To Fly*.

The band formed at junior high school circa 1962-63. Don Kinney:- "Martin had a Silvertone guitar and I had a Fender duo-sonic. We found a drummer in our junior high school, Doug Borthwick who was truly exceptional. A guy down the street, Charlie Pineda, was a on his way to being a classical pianist and we snagged him to play electric piano, but he had a strong family and was persuaded not to get to involved. I started to play bass because we needed one and I thought Martin could do a better job on guitar, particularly with the lead parts."

"In the early years we called ourselves The Court Jesters and played at a lot of teen clubs, street dances etc., practicing in my garage and Doug's cellar. The first song we worked on was *Dream* by The Everly Bros, but we progressed onto *G.T.O.* by **Ronny and The Daytonas**, *Hang On Sloopy*, *Louie-Louie*... I'm sure you know the progression..."

"The name change to **Hooterville** Trolley came about as a round-about word play with *Tunerville Trolley*, by **The Electric Prunes**. At the time we were doing covers of The Yardbirds, Cream, **Hendrix**, **CCR** and **Buffalo Springfield**. We would improvise on tracks like *Season Of The Witch* "Super Session" style, *Toad* "Cream" style and *Summertime Blues* "Blue Cheer" style, and we got to open for **Buffalo Springfield**, Eric Burdon and The Animals, **Youngbloods**, Three Dog Night plus a couple more. The band also toured the Southwest into Colorado and Oklahoma."

"We met Tommy Bee aka. Tom Benevidez through our first manager Chris Arlith. Tommy was working with the **Lincoln St. Exit** and pushing the Native American aspect to sell them. He also managed another good band led by Mike Flemming but I can't remember their name... (*)"

"The song *No Silver Bird* (written by Ernie Phillips - a teacher at the time) was not really our style. It was recorded at Norman Petty Studios, Clovis N.M. early one morning. Martin sang and used a fuzz-tone on his telecaster. Bill played his Farfisa keyboard, Doug played a studio set of drums and I played the only bass line I could make fit, a slowed down Kinks' *You Really Got Me*. Norman Petty had just bought a string machine and was itchin' to try it out. With that quality of production work, just imagine if we had a tune with substance."

"Over a four year span, we also had two vocalists, Mike Melloy and Larry Leyba. Bill Chriest took over keyboards in 1967 and we also added a rhythm guitarist, Wayne Gallio, who played a Gretsch 'Country Gentleman' guitar."

"Doug, Martin and I continued to perform as a three piece for a few years as 'Trolley', having dropped the corny 'Hooterville' because the 'Green Acres' T.V. show was set in Hooterville. As the three-piece we started doing acid-rock stuff, complete with light show."

"Wayne Gallio, died in a car wreck in a snowstorm on Route '66. He was a truly wonderful person. Doug Borthwick too died in a motorcycle wreck and Larry Leyba is also no longer with us. Bill Chriest, (pronounced 'crist') nowadays builds homes in and around New Mexico. Charlie Pineda, our early pianist is living in Santa Fe, N.M. working in a computer consulting business. Martin Nassif, sadly developed M.S. about 10 years ago and is physically incapacitated. Mike Melloy I think moved away and I have cheerfully survived. Life today is Good - I still play guitar 2-3 times weekly."

Compilation appearances include: *No Silver Bird* on *Lycergic Soap* (LP), *Magic Carpet Ride* (LP), *Sixties Rebellion, Vol. 15* (LP & CD) and *Beyond The Calico Wall* (LP). The track was also covered by The Creation (not the UK bunch) on a 45 released on the Centurion label, which later resurfaced on the *Brainshadows, Vol. 1* compilation.

NB: (*) Could be **Rabbit Mackay and The Somis Rhythm Band**. (MW/CF/DKy)

Hoover

ALBUM:	1 HOOVER	(Epic 26537) 1970 -

A good loner folk singer. (SR/NK)

Hope

Personnel incl:	DAN FERNELIUS	
	JOHN TUTTLE	castrato vcls (!)

45:	Greenhouse/	
	Of Times You Can See	(Peace Records 9445-2859) 1970

This 45 was the work of a hippie-style quintet from Minneapolis and now interests some collectors. The flip can be found on the *Changes* compilation of Minnesota bands, along with a track called *One Man*. This latter track turns out to be by a different **Hope**, from Wisconsin. Both sides of the 45 also appear on Arf! Arf!'s essential CD *The Scotty Story*. *Of Times..* is particularly poignant and dramatic - not one for the depressed. (VJ/MW)

Hope

Personnel:	JEFF COZY	drms, vcls	A
	JAMES C. CROEGAERT	vcls, piano	A
	DAVID A. KLUG	vcls, bs	A
	WAYNE C. McKIBBIN	vcls, gtr	A
	BOYD R. SIBLEY	vcls, organ	A

PATRICK HOPNEY - Cosmic Rockout LP.

ALBUM:	1 HOPE	(A&M SP 4329) 1972 R1
45s:	Where Do You Want To Go / One Man	(Coulee 134) c1970
	Where Do You Want To Go / Little Things	(A&M 1355) 1972

A different group from Lacrosse, Wisconsin, they evolved out of the Jesters III. *One Man* was written by organist Boyd Sibley, and the track appears on their 1972 album, which was recorded in Toronto, Canada under the supervision of Jack Richardson (best known for his productions (Nimbus 9) with The Guess Who). Many other musicians, including bassist Russ Savakus assisted on the album.

You can also hear *One Man* on the *Changes* compilation of Minnesota bands, miscredited as an unreleased track by the Minneapolis **Hope**. (VJ/MW)

Patrick Hopney

Personnel:	PETER BROWN	drms	A
	PATRICK HOPNEY	ld gtr, vcls	AB
	STEVEN MYERS	bs, backing vcls	AB
	RONALD "ROCKY" BROOKS	drms	B
	CATMAN KEYS	keyb'ds	B
	RICHARD AULIE ROSS	bs	B
	KINGPIN	ld gtr, backing vcls	B

ALBUMS:	1(A)	ENDS AND MEANS	(Illusion CM 1032) 1977 R2
	2(A)	PERILS OF LOVE	(Illusion CM 1033) 1977 R2
	3(B)	COSMIC ROCKOUT	(Illusion CM 1034) 1977 R3

NB: (3) reissued on CD (Dodo DDR 513) 2001.

Recorded in Florida, **Patrick Hopney** was the stage name for Patrick Hearns of Newburgh, NY's **Sapians**. After **Hopney** relocated to Florida, he recorded these three albums, which are characterised by excellent guitar work and are now rare and sought-after.

The first two albums consist entirely of cover versions, while the third features some original material. The third album was produced by Mike Pinera (ex-**Fanz/Blues Image/Iron Butterfly/Ramatam**). Not really psychedelic, but Side One is excellent (especially *Long Ago And Far Away*"), whilst Side Two is rather lame.

Before these albums Pat worked for a number of years as a half of a duo, Hopney & Phineas (Dali), who released at least one 45 called *Acapulco Gold*. (SR/KMn/EDMoulin/SMy)

Hoppi and The Beau Heems

Personnel incl?: J. McCULLOUGH
HOWARD SYMONS

45s:	So Hard/I Missed My Cloud	(Laurie 3411) 1967
	When I Get Home/So Hard	(Laurie 3439) 1968

A short-lived Tampa, Florida act. Catchy no-frills pop-punk is their style with strong, sometimes raucous, vocals. The non-comp *So Hard* is light keyboard-driven pop-beat.

Compilation appearances have included: *I Missed My Cloud* on *Mindrocker Vol. 12* (LP), *Glimpses, Vol. 2* (LP) *Glimpses, Vol's 1 & 2* (CD); and *When I Get Home* on *Psychedelic Unknowns, Vol. 8* (LP & CD). (VJ/MW)

Paul Horn

ALBUMS: (selective)	1	COSMIC CONSCIOUSNESS - IN KASHMIR	(World Pacific) 1967 -
	2	INSIDE	(Epic XSB 139721) 1971 -

Born in New York in 1930, **Paul Horn** is primarily a jazz flutist and sax player. After graduating from the Manhattan School Of Music, he moved to California in the late fifties where he worked with Chico Hamilton and did a lot of studio sessions. In the mid-sixties, like several other californian jazz musicians (**Charles Lloyd**, **Gabor Szabo**, **Bill Plummer**), he discovered Indian music and civilization and began recording albums with sitars, tambouras and tablas. His albums should interest fans of groups like **The Cosmic Brotherhood** or Oregon, mixing sitar sounds with jazz and meditative music.

Paul Horn also played with **Gentle Soul** and **Lynn Blessing** (he produced his only album) and recorded with Ravi Shankar. (SR)

Click Horning

ALBUM:	1 CLICK	(ABC ABCS-677) 1968 ?

An album full of slow and spooky tunes like *Girl On My Mind*, *For Judith*, *My Precious* and *Theme Too*. The stand-out track is the sitar tinged *Many Times Jimbo*. (SR)

Horses

Personnel:	CHRIS HEROLD	drms	A
	DON JOHNSON		A
	MATT KELLY	vcls, gtr, hrmnca	A
	DAVE TORBERT	bs, vcls	A
	SCOTT QUIGLEY		A

ALBUM:	1(A) HORSES	(White Whale WW7121) 1969 R2
45s:	Class Of '69/Country Boy	(White Whale 301) 1969
	Freight Train/Freight Train (mono)	(White Whale 320) 1969

The Carter-Gilbert team, John and Tim, who were also responsible for the **Rainy Daze**, and later as songwriters covered by the likes of **Strawberry Alarm Clock**, **Hardwater** and **Yankee Dollar**, produced and wrote ten of the eleven tracks on this fine West Coast album.

Class Of '69 is a raucous rocker, *Asia Minor* and *Wind* have good guitar parts, some other tracks are more country-rock oriented.

The 45s were taken from the album, which is very rare now.

Matt Kelly, who was a talented harmonica and guitar player, later joined **Gospel Oak** in 1970 and then guested on several **Grateful Dead** albums after 1973. In 1975, back with Herold and Torbert, they formed Kingfish with **Bob Weir** (**Grateful Dead**), who included some **Horses** songs (*Asia Minor*, *Overnight Bag*) on their first albums. Kelly also released a solo album *A Wing And A Prayer* (Relix) 1985 and another in 2000. Dave Torbert sadly died in 1982. (MW/SR/TSh)

Bill Horwitz

Personnel:	STECK HECKER	french horn	A
	BILL HORWITZ	piano, bs, gtr	A
	RICK LEAB	drms	A

ALBUM:	1(A) LIES, LIES	(ESP) 1974 -

Produced by David Butler, **Horwitz** was a political folksinger inspired by Dylan, with songs about hippies and similar topics. (SR)

Hosanna

Personnel:	DALE ANDERSON	gtr, vcls	A
	DOUGLAS DeGRAFF	drms, vcls	A
	JOHN ERICKSON	ld vcls, perc	A
	JIM SEILER	gtr, piano, vcls	A
	JOE SEILER	bs, vcls	A

ALBUM:	1(A) IN THE MORNING	(Diversified Media) c1972 ?

"Produced by The Holy Spirit" (!), a Christian folk-rock album with some psychy touches. Their songs were adapted from various psalms. (SR)

Hot Coffee

45: Cheatin' On Me/Some Day You Will Die (Plamie P-1024) c1967

An obscure outfit on a Salinas, California label. A moody pedestrian garage 'A' side with a subdued fuzzy break and real pissed-off guy lyrics. The flip is more lively but keyboard dominated with no cool guitar break. (MW)

The Hot Dogs

Personnel:
GREG REDING	piano, gtr, vcls	A
BILL RENNIE	ld vcls, bs	A
(JACK HOLDER	gtr, keyb'ds	A)
(ROBERT JOHNSON	gtr	A)
(TERRY MANNING	ld gtr	A)
(FRED PROUTY	drms	A)
(STEVE SMITH	gtr, keyb'ds	A)

ALBUM: 1(A) SAY WHAT YOU MEAN (Ardent ADS 2805) 1972

45: Another Smile/Way To Get To You (Ardent ADA 2905) 1973

A rock duet from Memphis, their album was produced and co-written by **Terry Manning**, who also played the lead guitar parts. The musicians of **Cargoe** provided some background vocals. Their music ranged between rock similar to **James Gang**, melodic pop-rock and prog-rock, with guitar and keyboards interlaced, but the overall result is far from being memorable.

The 'A' side to their 45 is dreamily acoustic and lazy, including a reasonable cello arrangement. On the flip the melody is much better and a guitar solo is substituted for the cellos.

Jack Holder and Greg Reding would later play with **Black Oak Arkansas**. (SR/MK)

Hot Dog Stand

45: C'mon Summer's Happening/Zilch (Mala 12014) 1968

This seems to have been a one-off venture. *Zilch* is as a loose bluesy jam, with some fiery 'acid' rock style guitar - which has subsequently resurfaced on *Relics, Vol. 1* (LP), *Relics, Vol's 1 & 2* (CD) and *Buzz Buzz Buzzzzzz, Vol. 1* (CD). (VJ)

Hot Poop

Personnel incl: THOMAS BURKE A

ALBUM: 1 DOES THEIR OWN STUFF! (Hot Poop HPS 3072) 1972 R2

A California outfit and definitely wacky'n'weird. Imagine an album of instrumentals varying from cheesy organ fuzzouts, frat-rock to rinky-dink rock 'n' roll Jerry Lee Lewis style. Now top'em off with a truly demented vocalist who sounds more like a crazy cartoon character (Bugs Bunny crossed with a psychotic sheep!). Goofy-rock we'll have to call it - with tracks like *Wing Wang, Dance To The War, I Always Play With My Food* and *Screamin'* and rarely intelligible lyrics. On the psychedelic fringe, though it's more brain-scrambling than mind-expanding! (MW)

Hot Soup

ALBUM: 1 HOT SOUP - OPENERS (Rama Rama Records) 1969 -

45: You Took Me By Surprise/ Gettin' In My Way Again (Rama Rama 7775) 1969

An obscure album, housed in a great psychy cover although the music is in the nightclub style. Depending on the sources, the band was from Los Angeles or New York. (VJ/SR)

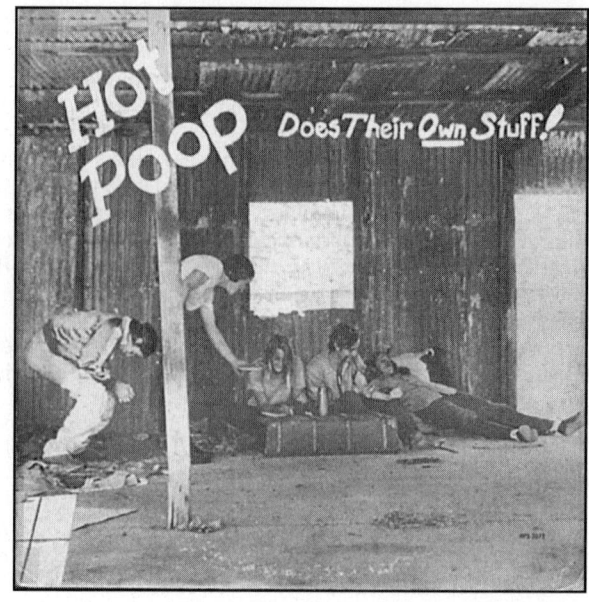

HOT POOP - Does Their Own Stuff! LP

Hound Dog Clowns

Personnel incl: KIM FOWLEY A

45s: Super Fox/ Wicked Witch (Living legend LL 1984) c1968
Super Fox/ Wicked Witch (UNI 55047) 1968

Another example of **Fowley**'s work as songwriter/singer/producer, which first appeared on his Living Legend label. How many groups has he created??

This 45 has become collectable in funk, rather than garage, circles. (SR/JLh)

Hourglass

Personnel:
DUANE ALLMAN	ld gtr, electric sitar	AB
GREGG ALLMAN	vcls, gtr, keyb'ds	AB
PAUL HORNSBY	keyb'ds, gtr, vcls	AB
MABRON McKINNEY	bs	A
(MIKE MELVOIN	keyb'ds	A)
(MAC REBENNACK	keyb'ds	A)
JOHNNY SANDLIN	drms, gtr	AB
JESSE WILLIARD CARR	bs, vcls	B

ALBUMS: 1(A) THE HOURGLASS (Liberty LRP 3536/LST-7536) 1967 -
2(B) POWER OF LOVE (Liberty LST-7555) 1968 -
3(-) THE HOURGLASS (United Artists UA-LA013-G2) 1973 -

NB:(1) and (2) have both been reissued on CD by EMI in 1992 with respectively six and seven bonus tracks. (3) is a reissue of (1) and (2) as a double album. (3) also issued on CD (BGO BGOCD 536) 2002.

45s:
Nothing But Tears/Heartbeat (PS)	(Liberty 56002)	1967
Power Of Love/I Still Want Your Love	(Liberty 56029)	1968
D.I.V.O.R.C.E/Changing Of The Guard	(Liberty 56053)	1968
She Is My Woman/Going Nowhere	(Liberty 56065)	1968
Now Is The Time/She Is My Woman	(Liberty 56072)	1968
I've Been Trying/Silently	(Liberty 56090)	1969

In the beginning of 1967, Gregg and Duane Allman, then with the **Allman Joys**, gigged at a Pensacola club. The other resident band was the Five Minutes whose members included Sandlin, McKinney and Hornsby. These five musicians shared a love for hard-rocking English acts (mainly 'Stones and Yardbirds) and for R&B. They relocated to Decatur, Alabama and, after trying out different names, settled on the Allman-Act.

Their break came when Bill McEuen, manager of the **Nitty Gritty Dirt Band**, caught their show in St. Louis and persuaded them to move to Los Angeles. Producer Dallas Smith signed them to Liberty Records, the label who had also taken two of McEuen's other clients: **Nitty Gritty Dirt Band** and the **Sunshine Company**. Since there were already several groups with almost similar names, the Allman-Act became the **Hourglass**.

The five men then realized that the fledgling Liberty label wanted to use session musicians and songwriters' songs instead of the relying on the band's talent alone. They tried to fight the process but won only a few concessions. The resulting album is, unsurprisingly, not really convincing and contains mainly pleasant pop-rock songs, the exceptions being the more electric tracks: *Got To Get Away* (the only Gregg original, already recorded with the **Allman Joys**), Jackson Browne's *Cast Off All My Fears* and Ed Cobb's *Heartbeat*. Duane Allman's guitar can be heard from time to time only. The album and the singles were a total commercial failure and McKinney left to be replaced by another former Five Minutes alumnus, Jesse Williard (Pete) Carr.

The group then demanded artistic freedom from Liberty and **Hourglass** were allowed to choose its own material, and Dallas Smith remained as their producer. Released in March 1968, *Power Of Love*, their second album, was a vast improvement on its predecessor, being much bluesier, with seven Gregg Allman songs, a Solomon Burke song, two Eddie Hinton/Marlin Greene tracks (*Down in Texas* and *Home For The Summer*), one Penn/**Oldham** cover (the title track) and a really weird instrumental version of Beatles' *Norwegian Wood*, beginning with Duane's electric sitar before degenerating into a kind of raga rock. The sales were low once again.

Hourglass were then playing live a lot, being booked every month at the Whisky A Go-Go and sometimes at the Fillmore West, including three nights with **Buffalo Springfield**, indeed Neil Young and Steve Stills wrote the enthusiastic liner notes for *Power Of Love*. They developed a strong reputation as a solid driving blues-rock outfit, but they were really unhappy with their records. With $500 from a gig, they finally rented Rick Hall's Studio in Muscle Shoals and cut some tracks on their own in April 1968 (one of these tunes *BB King Medley* is included on *Duane Allman Anthology*). The group returned to California with their tapes but Al Bennett at Liberty vetoed their release. They played some Southern gigs and eventually just drifted apart.

Gregg was then forced to finish out the contract with Liberty and had to record, using session musicians, a pop-oriented solo album which was shelved (the recorded tracks are the bonus on the CD reissues).

After this unsuccessful Los Angeles period, all the musicians would return to the Alabama / Georgia / Florida area, where they were instrumental in the creation of Southern Rock in the early seventies. Duane would first go to the Fame, Muscle Shoals and Criteria Studios to do sessions with soul and rock acts before forming the **Allman Brothers Band** with Gregg in 1969. He also was in Derek and the Dominos with Eric Clapton. One of the best slide guitar players ever, he sadly died in 1971 in a motorcycle accident. His brother is still touring with a new version of the **Allman Brothers Band**.

Johnny Sandlin, Paul Hornsby and Pete Carr are credited as producers, session players or group members with countless bands (Charlie Daniels, Wet Willie, Marshall Tucker, Sailcat, Cowboy etc.).

Compilation appearances include *I Can Stand Alone* on *In The Beginning* (LP). (SR/DS)

Household Sponge

Personnel incl:	PROSSEDA	A
	SBORDONE	A
	SIANO	A

45: Scars/Second Best   (Murbo 1017) 1967

A 45 whose acquisition would inevitably be disappointing given the choking descriptions and asking prices by specialist dealers over the years - especially when having finally obtained a copy both sides turn up on Strange Things' *Garagelands, Vol. 2* (LP) not long after!! Nevertheless this obscure New York City combo turn in two fine moody poppy psych-punkers; the 'A' side is slightly marred by some chirping female backing vocals, but the 'B' side makes up for that with a hypnotic beat and some fine yet understated distorted fuzz.

You can also find *Scars* on *Garagelands, Vol. 1 & 2* (CD). (MW)

GARAGELANDS Vol's 1 & 2 (Comp CD) including Household Sponge.

The House of Commons

45:    Till Tomorrow/Love Is A Funny Thing   (Wheel's 4 3609) 1965

From the Garden City suburbs of Detroit.

Compilation appearances have included: *Love Is A Funny Thing* and *Till Tomorrow* on *The Cicadelic 60's, Vol. 1* (CD); *Till Tomorrow* on *The Cicadelic 60's, Vol. 3* (LP); *As I'm Walking*, *Here I Am* (two versions), *It Comes And It Goes*, *Love Is A Funny Thing*, *No Regrets*, *Sally Put The Whammy*, *Summertime*, *Till Tomorrow* and *Why I Worry About You* on *The History Of Michigan Garage Bands In The 60's* (3-CD). (VJ/MW)

Houston

ALBUM: 1   HOUSTON   (SSS) 1970 -

Another obscure rock outfit on Shelby Singleton's label. This one is rather mediocre. (SR)

Houston Fearless

Personnel:	HARLEY BAKER	A
	BILL COMBEST	A
	JOE KRASOMIL	A
	BOB WALL	A

ALBUM: 1(A)   HOUSTON FEARLESS   (Imperial 12421) 1969 -

Presumably this outfit was from Houston. Their album consists of average late sixties heavyish rock and shouldn't be of much interest to readers. (VJ)

Howl The Good

ALBUM: 1   HOWL THE GOOD   (Rare Earth 537L) 1972 -

An obscure rock group on the same Motown subsidiary label as **Power of Zeus** or **Lost Nation**. Produced by Gary Wright (Spooky Tooth) who also donated two songs, on offer is undistinguished early seventies rock. (SR)

H.P. Lovecraft

Personnel:	GEORGE EDWARDS	gtr, bs, vcls	ABCD
	DAVID MICHAELS	keyb'ds, vcls	ABCD
	TONY CAVALLARI	ld gtr	BCD
	TOM SKIDMORE	bs	B
	MICHAEL TEGZA	drms	BCD
	JERRY McGEORGE	bs	C
	JEFF BOYAN	bs, vcls	D

	(FRANK BARTOLI)	bs	A)
	(KAL DAVID)	gtr	A)
	(FRED PAPPALARDO)	drms	A)

ALBUMS:	1(C)	HP LOVECRAFT I	(Philips 600252) 1967 SC
	2(D)	HP LOVEGRAFT II	(Philips 600279) 1968 SC

NB: (1) was later reissued as *This Is H.P Lovecraft*. (1) and (2) were reissued on one CD (Britonic BRTACD 010) 1997. Also relevant are:- (C/D) *At The Mountains Of Madness* (dbl) (Edsel DED 256) 1988, a compilation of their first two LPs plus their first single; (D) *Live May 11 1968* (Sundazed LP 5004) 1991, also issued on CD (Sundazed SC 11008) 1993 and (Edsel DIAB 8035) 2000.

(related albums by Lovecraft:)

ALBUMS:	1	VALLEY OF THE MOON	(Reprise 6419) 1969 -
	2	WE LOVE YOU WHOEVER YOU ARE	(Mercury SRMI 1031) 1975 -

45s:	Anyway That You Want Me/	
	It's All Over For You	(Philips 40464) 1967
	Wayfaring Stranger/Time Machine (PS)	(Philips 40491) 1967
	White Ship (Part 1)/White Ship (Part 2)	(Philips 40506) 1967
	Keeper Of The Keys/	
	Blue Jack Of Diamonds	(Philips 40578) 1968
α	We Can Have It Altogether/	
	Will I Know When My Time Comes?	(Reprise 0996) 1971
	I Feel Better/Flight	(Mercury 73698) 1975
	Ain't Gettin' None/We Love You	(Mercury 73707) 1975

NB: α released by Lovecraft.

George Edwards, an ex-folk troubadour who had cut a solo 45 for Dunwich, *Norwegian Wood/Never Mind, I'm Freezing*, and a raw cover of Bob Dylan's *Quit Your Low Down Ways*, that remained unreleased until its inclusion on Happy Tiger's *Early Chicago* (LP) compilation in 1971, was working as in-house session vocalist with Dunwich when this Chicago-based outfit was first assembled. Aside from David Michaels, the other three members of the band were borrowed from another Chicago outfit, **The Rovin' Kind**. The name **H.P. Lovecraft** was appropriated from the deceased fantasy horror writer. This initial line-up (February 1967) was responsible for the first 45, although the flip side was a George Edwards solo outtake from the previous year. The group came together as a stable entity in the Spring of 1967 (line-up B), although Tom Skidmore soon made way for Jerry McGeorge, who'd previously played with **The Shadows Of Knight** and **Dalek/Engham: The Blackstones**. (Joe Kelly, also of **The Shadows Of Knight**, was briefly in the band when Tony Cavallari, was absent for a while in late 1967).

The vocal combination of the folkie **Edwards** and Michaels, a classically-trained singer, gave the band a unique and distinctive vocal sound effectively supplemented by Michael's powerful keyboard-playing. Their debut album is one of great variety. The stand-out track was *The White Ship* and this is the song with which the group are most usually associated. Making use of a 1811 ship's bell, sombre harmonies, reeds, feedback and some baroque harpsichord pieces, it conjured up a hallucinogenic atmosphere ideally suited to the times. Also of note were an excellent upbeat version of **Dino Valente**'s hippie anthem *Let's Get Together*, which preceded **The Youngblood's** hit by over a year; *That's The Bag I'm In*, which had its roots in the garage; *Wayfaring Stranger*, a folk-based number and the dopey, sleepy number, *I've Been Wrong Before*, which gave a clear indication of the direction they would follow on their second album.

In the Spring of 1968 they relocated to Marin County in Northern California, having already briefly toured the West Coast. They became a frequent attraction at the nearby San Francisco ballrooms playing alongside most of the top Bay Area bands. Jerry McGeorge wanted to stay in Chicago and was replaced by Jeff Boyan, previously with Hezekiah and before that **Saturday's Children**. Not only was Boyan a talented guitarist, he possessed a distinctive lead voice, too.

Later that year the group moved on again to Los Angeles where they recorded a second album which contained many fine moments. The sleepiness of the tracks like *Spin, Spin, Spin, Electrallentando* and *Mobius Trip* was reminiscent of the second side of the first **It's A Beautiful Day** album. There was a fine version of *High Flying Bird*, a song recorded by many West Coast groups; *At The Mountains Of Madness*, which captured the group's vocal harmonies at their finest, and *Blue Jack Of Diamonds*, which had an unusual chiming intro. This is reputedly the first major label album where all those involved in the recording were high on acid!

H.P. Lovecraft effectively dissolved in 1969. Their first 45 got a further airing on the *Electric Food* (LP) compilation a couple of years later. A new line-up of Edwards, Tegza, Marty Grebb (ex-**Buckinghams** and **Exceptions**), Michael Been (ex-**Troys**) and Jim Dolinger (ex-**Aorta** and **Exceptions**) signed with Reprise in 1970 calling themselves Lovecraft. Edwards departed before they recorded a rockier album and 45 the following year and soon Lovecraft were no more. Tegza later joined **Bangor Flying Circus**, but he reformed Lovecraft with an entirely new line-up in 1975 and a disappointing further album and two 45s were released which attracted little attention.

Those first two **H.P. Lovecraft** albums remain rather special and Edsel's 1988 release compiles both along with additional tracks. Similarly, the live release, from a concert at San Francisco's Fillmore in May 1968, captures the band in their prime.

Retrospective compilation appearances have included: *Ban Roll Deodorant On Radio Spot* on *Oh Yeah! The Best Of Dunwich Records* (CD) and *If You're Ready - The Best Of Dunwich... Vol. 2* (CD); and *I've Been Wrong Before* on *Sundazed Sampler, Vol. 1* (CD). (VJ)

HP Lovecraft - Live CD.

The H.T. Three (H.T.3)

Personnel:	MYRON GOODMAN	drms	A
	HARLEY "TOBY" TOBERMAN	keyb'ds	AB
	HAL WITZMAN	gtr	AB
	RICK HOLTAN	bs	B
	KENNY HUSTON	drms	B

CD:	1(A/B)	THE H.T.3	(Dionysus/Bacchus Archives BA 1153) 2001

45:		Cool Breeze / Sing La La	(Aesop's Label 6045) 1965

In 1964, in the St.Louis Park suburb of Minneapolis, pianist Toberman started his own group and determined to perform his own songs rather than cover standards and current hits. In early 1965, they recorded the instrumental *Cool Breeze*, which was aimed specifically at radio stations to play in their top-of-the-hour pre-news slot. It garnered good play on local stations and by the Summer had picked up interest in Los Angeles. Toberman came unstuck when his partner blew the money he'd given him to press up 1,000 copies for the West Coast distributor. When he finally got copies out to L.A. the interest and impetus had been lost.

That incident signalled the start of the end for the group although the group returned to the studio in the Fall of '65. Both sessions are unearthed on the CD. Not standard garage fare by any means, it's an odd blend of instrumental and frat-rock sounds that will not appeal to fuzz'n'farfisa purists.

HUMAN BEINZ / MAMMALS - Split LP.

Toberman's next outlet, strangely not mentioned on this CD, was the equally off-beat **Blue Sandelwood Soap**.

Cool Breeze reappeared in 1967 on the rare Minneapolis compilation album, *Money Music*. (MW)

The Huck Finn

| Personnel: | MICHAEL APPEL | A |
| | DONALD HENNY | A |

| 45: | Two Of A Kind / We'll Catch The Sun | (Kapp K-958) 1968 |

A NYC outfit who were previously known as the **Balloon Farm**, some of whose members had previously been in **Adam**. *Two Of A Kind* is a catchy fuzz-popper with a hint of bubblegum.

Compilation appearances include *Two Of A Kind* on *Turds On A Bum Ride, Vol. 3* (CD). (MW)

Huckleberry Mudflap

45s:	Goodnight Mrs. Kollendoffer (Wherever You Are) / Blue Surf	(Line 5 1001) c1969
	Blue Surf/ Goodnight, Mrs. Kollendoffer (Wherever You Are)	(Scepter SCE 12245) 1969
	Eyes Of Blue/What A Day	(Line 5 L-5002) c1969

A great name for this Wilson, North Carolina, outfit. Soft-rock is the predominant style and the third 45 label depicts the front and rear view of a very hairy hippie's head, just so you know where they were coming from. *What A Day* is very much in that mellow genre and is the best cut by far.

The label on the debut 45 lacks the hippie head and the titles were flipped when it was picked up by Scepter. (MW/JLh)

Human Beings

45s:	Because I Love Her/ Ain't That Lovin' You Baby	(Warner Bros. 5622) 1965
	I Can't Tell/An Inside Look	(Impact 1001) 1965
	You're Bad News/Ling Ting Tong	(Impact 1006) 1966
	I Can't Tell/Yessir, That's My Baby	(Impact 1022) 1967

Not to be confused with Ohio's **Human Beinz**, this outfit were from Detroit. Their second 45, was recorded in Tucson, Arizona where the band were based briefly.

You're Bad News, is a mid-tempo punker with some fine guitar work.

Compilation appearances have included: *Because I Love Her* on *Michigan Nuggets* (CD) and *Michigan Brand Nuggets* (LP); *You're Bad News* on *Pebbles, Vol. 7* (LP); *An Inside Look* on *The Tucson Sound 1960-68* (LP) and *Garage Punk Unknowns, Vol. 5* (LP); *Ain't That Lovin' You, Baby* on *Teenage Shutdown, Vol. 1* (LP & CD); and *An Inside Look, I Can't Tell, Ling Ting Tong, Yes Sir, That's My Baby* and *You're Bad News* on *The Best Of Impact Records* (CD). (VJ/MW)

The Human Beinz

Personnel:	RICHARD BELLEY	ld gtr	A
	JOE 'TING' MARKULIN	gtrs	A
	MEL PACHUTA	bs	A
	MIKE TATMAN	drms	A

HCP

ALBUMS:	1	HUMAN BEINZ / MAMMALS	(Gateway GLP 3012) 1967 - SC
	2(A)	NOBODY BUT ME	(Capitol ST 2906) 1968 65 SC
	3(A)	EVOLUTION	(Capitol ST 2926) 1968 - SC
	4( )	LIVE IN JAPAN 1968	(Capitol 8737) 1968 - R3

NB: (1) reissued on LP and CD (Get Back GET 535) 1999. (2) reissued on CD (See For Miles See CD 327) 1991, with the mono mix, and (Collectables) with the stereo mix. (3) reissued on Decal (LIK 5) 1987, counterfeited on CD and reissued officially on CD (Ascension ANCD 030). (4) is a rare Japanese-only release, subsequently reissued on CD (Cosmic Mind HB 001 CD), and on vinyl as *Hold On Baby* (HB 001).

HCP

45s:	The Times They Are A Changing/Gloria	(Gateway 828) 1966 -
	Pied Piper/My Generation	(Gateway 838) 1967 -
α	My Generation/Evil Hearted You	(Elysian 82OF 8687) 1966 -
α	Hey Joe/Spider Man	(Elysian 3376) 1967 -
β	Nobody But Me/Sueño	(Capitol 5990) 1967 8
	Turn On Your Lovelight/ It's Fun To Be Clean	(Capitol 2119) 1968 80
	Every Time Woman/The Face	(Capitol 2198) 1968 -
	I've Got To Keep On Pushing/ This Little Girl Of Mine	(Capitol 2431) 1968 -

NB: α as by the **Human Beingz**. β also released in France with a PS (Capitol CLF 5990).

Human Beinz came from Youngstown, Ohio, and were originally known as **The Human Beingz**. The split Gateway album, with The Mammals, included four cuts by them, which display their British invasion influences - but as with their Gateway 45s, this early material is now virtually disowned by the band.

Under the guidance of their producer Alex "Lez" De Azevedo, they developed into a fine psychedelic pop group with a sense of humour. Their

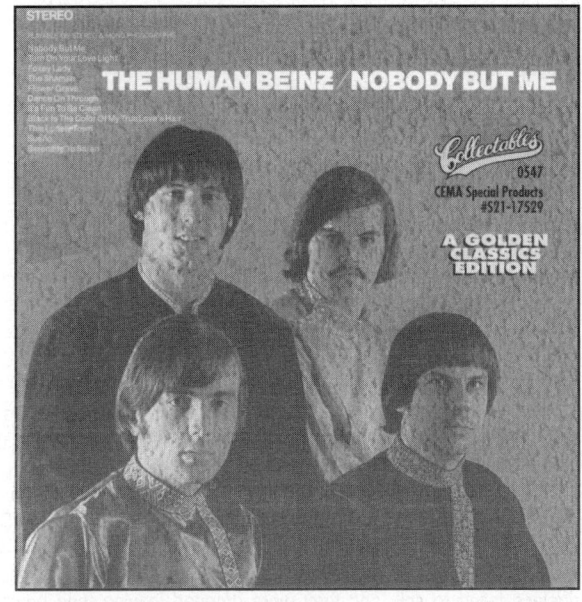

THE HUMAN BEINZ - Nobody But Me CD.

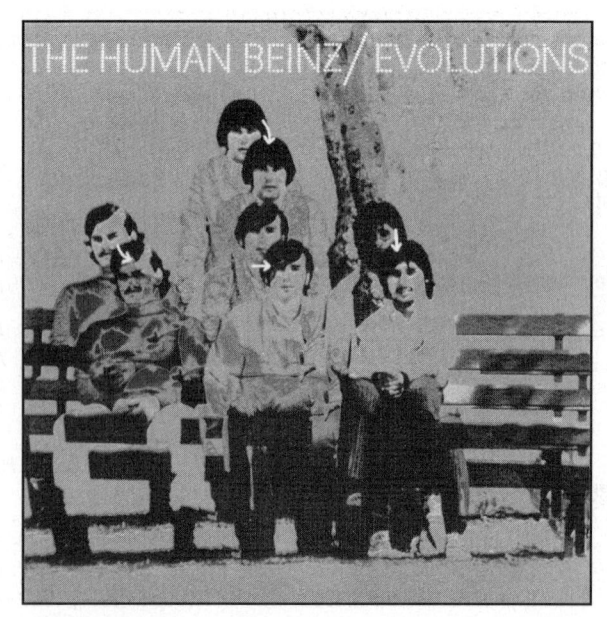

THE HUMAN BEINZ - Evolutions LP.

second album contained one of the all-time punk classics, *Nobody But Me* and the third too is recommended - consisting of anglophile pop, weird psychedelic ballads and some great psychedelia - inconsistent in places but good overall. The third album also contained a seven-minute guitar freakout *April 15th*, which was arguably their finest moment.

They also cut a very rare live album in Japan, which is probably mainly of interest to completists. It has recently been reissued together with six bonus "rare studio outtakes"; five of which turn out to be from their Gateway album plus *Evil Hearted You*, from their debut 45. A welcome release nonetheless. The CD version includes also includes their last Capitol 45.

Somewhat temptingly, a couple of full live sets from 1967 still exist and are said to show the band at their best, with a mixture of Stones / **Byrds** covers and the usual dance standards of the time.

Nobody But Me remains one of the best recordings of this period and their second and third albums are worth checking out.

Dick Belley later had a spell in **The (Pied) Pipers**.

Compilation appearances have included: *Nobody But Me* on *Nuggets Box* (4-CD), *Nuggets From Nuggets* (CD), *Nuggets, Vol. 1* (LP) and *Frat Rock! The Greatest Rock 'N' Roll Party Tunes Of All Time*; *My Generation* on *Pebbles, Vol. 8* (LP); *Evil Hearted You* on *What A Way To Die* (LP), *Hang It Out To Dry* (CD) and *Highs In The Mid-Sixties, Vol. 9* (LP); *Evil Hearted You* and *Mr. Soul* (live) on *Filling The Gap* (4-LP). (GGI/MW/MMy/SR/NK/VJ)

The Human Equation featuring Jon Uzonyi

See **Peacepipe** entry.

The Humane Society

Personnel:	RICHARD MAJEWSKI	bs	A
	WOODY MINNICK	gtr	A
	JIM PETTIT	gtr	A
	BILL SCHNETZLER	drms	A
	DANNY WHEETMAN	gtr, vcls	A

45s:	Knock Knock (Who's There)/		
	Tiptoe Through The Tulips With Me	(Liberty 55968)	1967
	Lorna/Eternal Prison	(New World 2004)	1968

They hailed from Simi Valley in California and were originally called The Innocents. A demo of *Knock Knock*, recorded in 1966 at Golden State Recorders in San Francisco, led to a deal with Liberty where they re-recorded the song. A classic punker with a tight menacing feel, the 45 nevertheless failed to sell, and they were dropped leaving their proposed second 45 stranded at the acetate stage... They did later release another 45 on the New World label, the flip to which, *Eternal Prison*, is haunting soft garagey-psych.

The band have been well compiled: The demo version of *Knock Knock* can be found on the *Good Things Are Happening* CD, whilst the "Liberty" version is included on *Pebbles, Vol. 8* (CD), *Psychedelic Unknowns, Vol. 4* (LP & CD), *Son Of The Gathering Of The Tribe* (LP), *Mayhem & Psychosis, Vol. 3* (LP), *Mayhem & Psychosis, Vol. 2* (CD), *Nuggets Box* (4-CD), *Victims Of Circumstances, Vol. 1* (LP) and *Victims Of Circumstance, Vol. 2* (CD); *Eternal Prison* is also on *Acid Dreams, Vol. 2* (LP), *Prisoners Of The Beat* (LP) and *Fuzz Flaykes & Shakes, Vol. 1* (LP & CD). (MW)

The Human Expression

Personnel:	MARTIN ESHLEMAN	ld gtr	A
	JIM FOSTER	gtr	A
	TOM HAMILTON	bs	A
	ARMAND POULIN	drms	A
	JIM QUARLES	ld vcls	A

45s:	Readin' Your Will / Everynight	(Acetate Demo)	1966
	Love At Psychedelic Velocity/Everynight	(Accent 1214)	1966
	Optical Sound / Calm Me Down	(Acetate Demo)	1966
	Optical Sound/Calm Me Down	(Accent 1226)	1966
	Sweet Child Of Nothingness /		
	I Don't Need Nobody	(Accent 1252)	1967

Hailing from Westminster and Tustin, California, this psychedelic punk band were formed early in 1966 and played around the L.A. area, at clubs such as Gazzari's and USO clubs. An acetate *Readin' Your Will / Everynight* cut in the Summer of '66 got them a deal with Accent, who released two awesome acid-punk singles in the shape of *Love At Psychedelic Velocity* and *Optical Sound*. Both singles were mixed by Wally Heider who also worked for the **Grateful Dead**, and are now extremely sought-after and impossibly hard to find.

After *Optical Sound* proved too far-out for the Charts, the band's manager offered them the opportunity to record two tracks by what he described as "an up-and coming songwriter". The first demo *Sweet Child Of Nothingness* would become their third single, and the other track was turned down because Jim Quarles' didn't think lyrics like "Get your motor running / Head out on the highway" were any good. The song was of course Mars Bonfire's *Born To Be Wild* which **Steppenwolf** would later cover!!

By the time the *Sweet Child Of Nothingness / I Don't Need Nobody* single was recorded, both Jim Quarles and Martin Eshleman had left the band.

Both their first two singles *Love At Psychedelic Velocity* and *Optical Sound* are worthy of investigation and all their released material has now appeared on compilations. Even better, however, is the Collectables CD release *Love*

HUMAN BEINZ - Live In Japan 1968 CD.

At *Psychedelic Velocity*, which compiles all the band's singles, plus demos and four post-**Human Expression** solo tracks cut by Jim Quarles. The CD also includes excellent liner notes, from which this entry has largely been taken, and is recommended to fans of the band.

Jim Quarles is still active in the music business, working in a studio as a technical engineer, and writing and recording songs.

Compilation appearances have also included: *Optical Sound* on *Echoes In Time, Vol. 1* (LP), *Echoes In Time, Vol's 1 & 2* (CD), *Psychedelic Disaster Whirl* (LP) and *Nuggets Box* (4-CD); *Love At Psychedelic Velocity* on *Pebbles, Vol. 10* (LP), *Songs We Taught The Fuzztones* (Dble LP & Dble CD) and *Best of Pebbles, Vol. 3* (LP & CD); *Calm Me Down* and *Optical Sound* on *Green Crystal Ties, Vol. 6* (CD); *Everynight* and *Readin' Your Will* on *Green Crystal Ties, Vol. 9* (CD); *Who Is Burning?* (prev unreleased) on *Psychedelic Crown Jewels, Vol. 1* (Dble LP & CD); *Calm Me Down*, *Optical Sound* and *Your Mind Works In Reverse* (all previously unreleased demo versions) on *The Human Expression And Other Psychedelic Groups - Your Mind Works In Reverse* (CD); *Calm Me Down* and *Everynight* on *Highs In The Mid-Sixties, Vol. 3* (LP). (MW)

The Humans

Personnel incl: BILL KUHNS — ld gtr

45: Warning/Take A Taxi (Audition 6109) 1966

A typical garage-punk outfit with a real throaty vocalist. The cool looking six-piece formed whilst the members were in high school in Albion, New York in the Summer of 1964. They toured pretty extensively and got to open for the likes of The Animals, The Hollies, **The Standells** and The Stones and in the Summer of 1966, opened for **Mitch Ryder** at the Rheingold Festival in Central Park.

Compilation appearances include *Warning* on *Back From The Grave, Vol. 5* (LP) and *Back From The Grave, Vol. 2* (CD). (VJ)

The Human Situation

45: I Got Away/Mediocre Fred (Eclipse 4940) c1966

From Allentown, Pennsylvania. *I Got Away* is a fairly basic garage tune, but compelling nonetheless. You can also find it on *Sixties Rebellion, Vol's 1 & 2* (CD) and *Sixties Rebellion, Vol. 2* (LP). (VJ/MW)

The Human Zoo

Personnel:
JIM CUNNINGHAM — vcls — A
BOB DALRYMPLE — bs — A
LARRY HANSON — gtr, keyb'ds — A

THE HUMAN EXPRESSION & OTHER PSYCHEDELIC GROUPS CD.

THE HUMAN ZOO - The Human Zoo LP.

JOHN LUZADDER — gtr — A
KIM VYDAREMY — drms — A
ROY YOUNG — vcls — A

ALBUM: 1(A) THE HUMAN ZOO (Accent ACS 5055) 1969 R2

A California band whose album is extremely mediocre. The haunting finale, *The Time Was Over* is the best track. Despite my lack of enthusiasm, I must admit it's now a minor collectors' item.

The album fails because they're not sure what bag they're in. First there's some bits of good acid-guitar, some heavyish mainstream rock, but then some funk and the **Blood, Sweat and Tears**-like horns on top of some dirgeful material doesn't help. (VJ)

Ray Hummel III

45s: α Fine Day/Gentle Rain (Fenton 2188) 196?
Can't Keep A Good Memory Down/
Daily Grinds & Neon Signs (Renegade 5630) 196?
For Whatever It's Worth/
Don't Point Your Finger (Renegade 5651) 196?
From Adam's Rib To Woman's Lib/? (Renegade 5655) 196?

NB: α some copies of this 45 came with a picture sleeve, bumping up its asking price to $150+.

Originally from Grand Rapids, Michigan, this guy was vocalist with **The Ju Ju's**. His first 45, *Fine Day*, was his own composition and can be heard on both *Magic Carpet Ride* (LP) and *Project Blue, Vol. 1* (LP). Although not a particularly strong song it does give another airing to his vocal talents. The 45's flip, *Gentle Rain* has also been compiled on *Project Blue, Vol. 3* (LP), although reputedly after that 45 his material skips over the hills and far away into country / C&W territory. (VJ/MW)

Hung Jury

45: Buses/Let The Good Times In (Colgems 66-1010) 1967

Bouncy pop-psych with a warped guitar break and ending that saves it from anonymity, unlike the group, about whom we can reveal nothing. The flip is straight baroque-pop. (MW)

Hunger!

Personnel: BILL DAFFERN — vcls, drms — AB
STEVE HANSEN — gtr, vcls — ABC

MIKE LANE	vcls	ABC
JOHN MORTON	gtr, vcls	ABC
MIKE PARKISON	keyb'ds, vcls	ABC
TOM TANORY	bs, vcls	ABC
GENE GUNNELS	drms	C
(ED KING	gtr	B)

ALBUMS: 1(A) STRICTLY FROM HUNGER
(Public! Records P-1006) 1969 R4
2(B) HUNGER (No label) 1969 R6

NB: (1) reissued (Psycho 14) 1983 and counterfeited on CD (Afterglow 010) 1993. Reissued (Akarma AK 045) 1999 with one bonus track on vinyl and six bonus tracks on CD. (2) was only issued as a test pressing in a plain sleeve. Reissued on vinyl (Void 08) 1998. (1) and (2) reissued as *The Lost Album* a 2-LP package (Akarma 045/2) 1999.

45s: α She Let Him Continue/
     Mind Machine (Public! Records PR 101/2) 1968
     β No Shame/Not So Fine (Public! Records PR 103/4) 1968
     χ Colors/Mind Machine (Public! Records PR 1001) 1969

NB: α is non-LP versions. β as by **The Touch**. Both tracks figure on the *Strictly From* album, the 'B' side being re-titled, but the 45 versions are very different. χ same versions as on the *Strictly From* album.

Hunger! originated in Portland, Oregon but by 1968 they were based in Los Angeles, California and it was there that they issued their three singles and album on Public! Records, all of which are now rare collectors items.

Hunger! had a quintessentially sixties sound, and their recordings are recommended to readers of this book. Overall, their *Strictly From* album falls a bit short of its reputation, it being an early 'known' collectable from the West Coast rock scene fetching serous money even in the seventies. In retrospect, it's clear that the band wasn't quite ready to record. The album has an unfinished feel to it, punctuated by the inclusion of two versions of the same song, and several that, quite frankly, last longer than they should. One gets the impression that these shortcomings were necessary to flesh out the album's running time.

The reality of these observations come into focus upon hearing the re-recorded/alternate version of the album which turned up in 1995. According to members of the band, **Strawberry Alarm Clock** guitarist Ed King volunteered to re-arrange some of the material and contribute his lead guitar in the preparation of a new master. The results were truly stunning, and the remastered **Hunger!** album was immediately put into production and scheduled for release... but halted after only a handful of vinyl test pressings were made. This is the album reissued on the Void label, licensed from the band, that is highly recommended.

King's influence is most obvious on the opening track, *Colors* - transformed from a bouncy pop song (2'00") on the *Strictly From Hunger* album to a wicked hard-rocker similar to **Steppenwolf** with amazing dual lead guitar

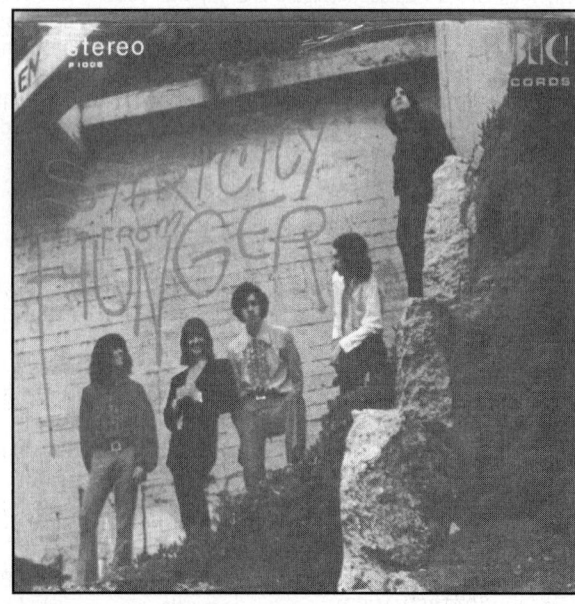

HUNGER - Strictly From CD.

HUNGER - Hunger (Void) LP.

parts (now stretching to 3'35"). *Portland '69* follows, this time radically remixed (i.e., it's the same recording, but hardly recognisable!) and what is a rather laboured instrumental on the *Strictly From Hunger* album is now a brutal tour-de-force that builds to an incredible intensity. The remaining tracks are remade and/or remodeled as well, rendering the released vesion obsolete. Really, this is the **Hunger!** album to have and had it been issued at the time, the band may well have survived into the seventies.

Bill Daffern left the band in 1969, which may be the reason the remastered album wasn't released - his distinctive lead vocals (heard on *She Let Him Continue* and *No Shame*) were part of the **Hunger!** sound from day one. He was replaced on drums by Gene Gunnels of the **Strawberry Alarm Clock**, and this final line-up played a few gigs before the band split for good.

Daffern pursued a career in rock for several years after leaving **Hunger!**. He was next heard playing drums in **Truk**, and was lead vocalist on the final Captain Beyond album (*Dawn Explosion* (Warner Bros.)) released in 1977.

Workshop was later covered by U.K. psych band Glass Keys (on *Rubble 9* (LP)).

Compilation appearances have included: *Colors* on *Love, Peace And Poetry, Vol. 1* (LP & CD) and *Highs In The Mid-Sixties, Vol. 3* (LP); *Workshop* on *Sixties Archive, Vol. 8* (CD), *Acid Trip From The Psychedelic Sixties* (LP), *Endless Journey - Phase Two* (LP), *Endless Journey - Phase I & II* (Dble CD) and *Glimpses, Vol. 3* (LP); and *Mind Machine* on *The Seventh Son* (LP). (VJ/MW/CF)

The Hungry I's

Personnel:	CHRIS DRAKE	gtr	AB
	NEIL HANEY	ld vcls, organ	AB
	ALLEN MARTIN	bs	A
	DANNY ROWDON	ld gtr	A
	LOU SHAWD	drms	AB
	RALPH CITRULLO	bs	B
	ALLEN DRESSER	ld gtr	B

45: Half Your Life / Comin' Round (Paris Tower PT-127) 1967

The Hungri I's were a garage band from Daytona Beach, Florida. Formed in the Spring of 1965, they named themselves after the famous San Francisco Folk nightclub. They performed mainly in Daytona Beach, as a house-band at the now defunct but world-famous Beachcomber Nightclub and at the equally renowned Surf Bar. Their only other Florida forays were to Titusville (The Vanguard Club) and Orlando, where they put down some demo songs at Eric Schabacker's Bee Jay Studio. These appeared on the Bee Jay Demo albums (one was a cover of *Hold On I'm Coming* on *Bee Jay Demo Vol. 2*); none made it onto 45.

During the Summer of 1967 they visited producer Robert Quimby in nearby Ormond Beach and cut a metal acetate of *Half Your Life*, written by Neil Haney, backed with the standard *How Come My Dog Don't Bark? (When You Come Around)*. In late 1967, Gil Cabot offered to make them famous if they paid to have *Half Your Life* released on his Tampa-based Paris Tower label. All that happened (as with all Paris Tower releases) was that 500 copies were shipped to them (to distribute themselves) ... and that was it!

So, off they went on a Winter tour of Wisconsin, Minnesota and Indiana to promote the single. They performed many **Hendrix** tunes which were unknown to many of the teens who came to see them but they were well received. Since they were from sunny Florida and the World's Most Famous Beach, the band thought it'd be cool to take a publicity photo in the snow whilst they were there - however it was the band that melted on their return home in the Spring of 1968. Haney joined **The 2/3rds**; Dresser and Citrullo were soon to follow; and they were reunited with Drake in 1969 when **The 2/3rds** became The Third Condition.

Half Your Life gets a new life on *Psychedelic States: Florida, Vol. 3* (CD). (MW/KCs)

Hungry Tiger

45: Fee-Fi-Fo-Fum/Tic Tac Toe   (White Whale WW-313) 1968

Another bubblegum psych pop single produced by **Kasenetz and Katz**, in the same "series" as **The Crazy Elephant** or **The Flying Giraffe**. This one was written by M. Moffit and arranged by "The Hawk and The Falcon"! (SR)

Tom Hunnicutt

ALBUM: 1 ESCAPING FROM TODAY
                                 (Hillside Country Records) c1969 ?

The liner notes of this scarce album indicates that "His songs embrace the folk style of the hill country music, but his lyrics are relevant to things that affect us all. He writes of love, war, pollution..." and adds "Regardless of where you might meet Tom, be it in a bar, church, in a concert hall or just sitting on a street corner playing his guitar, put out your hand and say Hi. He is your friend and brother". The songs include *The Environmentalist*, *To Fight A War*, *Brown Skin Girl*, *Potomac River Song* and the title track. A typical product from the late sixties. (SR)

The Huns

Personnel incl: ROBERT DEMPSEY   gtr   A
                DAVE GRUNDHOFFER vcls   A

45: Winning Ticket/Destination Lonely (Rock N Jazz 8668) 1966

Hailing from Arlington Heights, Illinois and often appearing in animal skins with bleached white hair this mob produced one of the best garage 45s to come from the Midwest. *Destination Lonely* is particularly notable for its powerful vocals and driving guitar.

Robert Dempsey took guitar lessons from Ted Nugent, who was also from Arlington Heights. He apparently helped his student by writing some of the guitar solos for the 45.

They later changed name to Greenwood County Farm and released a 45 for Ampex.

Compilation appearances have included: *Destination Lonely* on *The Midwest Vs. Canada* (LP) and *Garage Punk Unknowns, Vol. 5* (LP); and *Winning Ticket* on *Pebbles Vol. 6* (CD). (VJ/MW/BLg)

The Huns

45: Shakedown/You Know   (Pyramid 6646) 1966

There was a different **Huns**, from Concord, North Carolina, which was also home to **The Tamrons**, who issued just one 45.

Compilation appearances include: *Shakedown* on *Back From The Grave, Vol. 4* (LP) and *Back From The Grave, Vol. 2* (CD).

The Huns

EP: 1 THE HUNS - 1965   (Moxie M 1027) 198?

A New York outfit who don't appear to have released any 45s. The Moxie EP was put out in the mid-eighties and was taken from a dodgy tape (complete with skids and drop-outs). It comprises four tracks: the Kinks-like *I've Got You On My Mind*, a sneering *I Gotta Move*, jaunty thumper *Long Way Around*, and an untitled haunting garage-ballad - all cool stuff with neat farfisa vibes that deserves a proper reissue. (MW)

Huns Of Time

See **Attila and The Huns**.

Hunt and Dunk

ALBUM: 1 DID YOU EVER SING TO A MOUNTAIN?
                                 (Mountain LP-6110) 1974 -

From Arizona, a private pressing of ecological folk with delicate vocals. (SR)

The Hunted

An obscure band who's *Sinner* has resurfaced on *It's Finkin' Time!* (LP). (VJ)

The Huntsmen

45: So Long/Say What I Mean   (Sure-Shot SS 6704) 196?

This Massachusetts act was formed by a guy called Hunt. Their sole vinyl offering was this good double-sided punker - good beat, mouth harp, snarling vocals. Like their 'label-mates', **The Katz Kradle**, it's also rumoured that this is a bogus outfit put together by Erik Lindgren, the noted sixties enthusiast.

Compilation appearances have included: *Say What I Mean* on *Pebbles, Vol. 22* (LP); and *So Long* on *Follow That Munster, Vol. 2* (LP). (MW)

Michael Hurley

Personnel: MICHAEL HURLEY   vcls, gtr   ABCD
            ROBIN REMAILLY   fiddle, mandolin,
                                vcls   AB D
            EARTHQUAKE ANDERSON hrmnca   B
            JESSE COLIN YOUNG   bs, gtr   B
            MAGGIE HURLEY   harmony vcl   B
            MICHAEL KANE   bs, cornet   BC
            SCOTT LAWRENCE   piano   B
            JEFF MYER   drms   B
            BANANA   gtr, bs, piano, vcls,
                                claves   C
            JOE BAUER   drms   C
            PETER STAMPFEL   fiddle, vcls   D

ALBUMS: 1(A) FIRST SONGS   (Folkways FG 3581) 1964 -
        2(B) ARMCHAIR BOOGIE
                                (Raccoon 6 / Warner WS 1915) 1971 -
        3(C) HI FI SNOCK UPTOWN
                                (Raccoon 14 / Warner BS 2625) 1972 -
        4(D) HAVE MOICY   (Rounder 3010) 1975 -

NB: (4) With The Unholy Modal Rounders, Jeffrey Fredericks and the Clamtones. (4) reissued in 1987 by Rounder.

A strange folksinger closely associated with **The Holy Modal Rounders** and **The Youngbloods**. Born in 1941, he spent a part of his teenage years traveling in the South with Robin Remaillly. His first album was released in 1964 and contains his classic *Werewolf*.

The second and third albums were produced by **The Youngbloods'** **Jesse Colin Young** and **Banana** on their Raccoon label. Both albums are excellent, with very unusual lyrics but both are hard to find now. In 1975, he teamed up with Peter Stampfel and various other folk musicians to record *Have Moicy*. He kept on recording for Rounder and is still active on the music scene. **Hurley** is also a noted cartoonist, his main chracter being "Snocko", a strange "human dog". He drew most of his record sleeves, as well as the cover art for the **Holy Modal Rounders** album *Good Time Is Tasteless*. (SR)

The Hurricanes

See the **Johnny and The Hurricanes** entry.

Sandy Hurvitz

ALBUM: 1 SANDY'S ALBUM IS HERE AT LAST
(Verve/Bizarre V6-5064-X) 1968 SC

A good jazzy folk-rock singer and pianist, backed by Jeremy Steig, Donald McDonald and Eddie Gomez (all from **Jeremy and The Satyrs**) and **Jim Pepper**. **Sandy Hurvitz** was at the time the girlfriend of Cal Schenkel, the graphic designer for the **Mothers Of Invention** and her album was the first with the Bizarre logo on its cover, which also features **Zappa**'s head in a TV set. It was produced by Ian Underwood.

Sandy Hurvitz later changed her name to Essra Mohawk and record three albums on Reprise, Asylum and Private Stock between 1970 and 1977. (SR)

The Hush Puppies

45: Look For Another Love/Stop Messin' Around (Playboy 910) 196?

Back From The Grave, Vol. 7 (Dble LP) features both sides of this 45 by this unknown garage band. *Look..* is a wild rocker, with punchy organ and plenty of chops and changes in rhythm - it was probably more fun to record than listen to repeatedly. The flip has a driving beat and scorching guitar solo(s). California has been suggested as their home state but who were these guys? (MW)

The Hustlers

45: She Waits For Me/The Sky Is Black (Orlyn 1949) 196?

A Chicago garage band whose *The Sky Is Black* is on *The Essential Pebbles Collection, Vol. 1* (Dble CD). (VJ/MW)

The Hustlers

Personnel incl:	NICK FRESCA	drms
	BOB LEAVITT	gtr
	JOHNNY MCNICOL	gtr
	JOE ROMEO	bs

45s: α If You Try / My Mind's Made Up (Chelle 145) 1966
 β I Don't Know//Try To Forget Her/
  We Were In Love/Vivid In My Mind (Voice Inc. 8965) c1965

NB: α later appeared as a demo by 'Sweet Young Things'. β unreleased demo.

If You Try is a great punker with a powerful swagger that comes on initially like a fuzzed **Byrds** - crank this one up on *Psychedelic Crown Jewels Vol.2* (Dble LP & CD) - especially for the superb solo and Beatlesque harmonies. Jeff Lemlich, Mr. Florida, dug up their story and personnel for the liner notes.

My Mind's Made Up, composed by John McNicol, pops up again on *Psychedelic States - Florida Vol. 2* (CD) - it's a bouncey Beatlesque fuzz-popper. The accompanying booklet contains the story behind this track and the band as told by member Bob Leavitt.

Leavitt also co-wrote *You Can't Make Me* for the **Montells**. (MW/RM)

The Hustlers

Personnel:	TITUS FRENCHMAN	gtr	A
	TOMMY FRENCHMAN	bs	A
	TERRY HEWITT	drms	A
	SKIP MAGGIORA	gtr	A

45: Linda/Wipeout (Rich 113/4) 1965

From Sacramento, California. The rocking *Linda* can be found on *The Sound Of Young Sacramento* (CD). (VJ)

The Hustlers

Personnel:	JOHN BUSHONG	bs	A
	CRAIG FISCHER	ld vcls, gtr	A
	DAVE GRAFF	ld gtr, hrmnca	A
	STEVE WADE	drms	A

ALBUM: 1(A) THEIR FINEST ALBUM
(Caronet Recording Service 850C - 9455) 1965 R2

NB: (1) issued with a paste-on 'slick' cover.

A Columbus, Ohio, frat-rock/garage band. On offer are four clean-cut guys in suits playing straight forward R&B standards like *Carol*, *I Should Have Known Better*, *Tell Me Why*, *Tossin' And Turnin'*, *Searchin'*, *Route 66*, *You Can't Do That*, *Good, Good Lovin'*, and an instrumental version of *If I Fell* plus two neat ballads *I Can't Wait To Have You Meet My Baby* and the downer vibed *Tragedy*. No fuzz fest here, but there is some good guitar work and thumbs up for the fresh amateurish "were gonna make it" garage charm, which seems to keep these albums collectable. For fratheads and garage beat-completists, only. (CP)

Danny Hutton

45s: Roses And Rainbows / Monster Shindig (HBR 447) 1965 73
 Big Bright Eyes / Monster Shindig Part 2 (HBR 453) 1965 102
 Funny How Love Can Be/
 Dreamin' Isn't Good For You (MGM 13502) 1966 120

PSYCHEDELIC CROWN JEWELS Vol. 2 CD including The Hustlers.

The above were some of **Danny Hutton**'s early solo efforts. He may have also been involved with **The Bats**, before joining **Cory Wells and The Enemys**, and subsequently Three Dog Night with Cory Wells and Chuck Negron.

Compilation appearances include: *Roses and Rainbows* on *Even More Nuggets* (CD). (MW/TTi)

Laura Huxley

ALBUM: 1   RECIPES FOR LIVING AND LOVING
                                            (Columbia) c1969 ?

NB: (1) also issued in a plain white promo cover with name and title printed in blue.

From the wife of the famous and influential writer Aldous Huxley, comes this very meditative album of relaxation music, with two side-long tracks: *Your Favorite Flower* and *Rainbow Walk*. Prepare your incense vase! (SR)

Lee Hyatt

ALBUM: 1   WHAT IF WE GAVE A WAR   (Gigantic) 1969 SC

On the same label as **Hickory Wind**, a female folk-rock singer. Her album is rare. (SR)

Hydraulic Peach

45:        Reminiscence Of 'Lexa/
           Many, Many Possibilities   (Arpeggio A-1055) 1970

This band called Pennsylvania their home, and their 45 was produced by Dan Hartman of **Legends** fame. The 'A' side is a long, dark wailer, while the superior 'B' side brings Traffic to mind. (MMs)

The Hydraulic Raisins

Personnel:	RANDY BARNES	vcls, gtr	A
	DAN BRAYMER	drms	A
	JOHN GERODINI	bs	A
	LARRY OXENHAM	ld gtr	A

ALBUM: 1   WAILIN' IN WEST COVINA!!
                                       (Bacchus Archives BA 1128) 1998

NB: (1) CD retrospective which features **The Hydraulic Raisins**, The Rhythm Surfers and The Spectrums.

45:        Tragedy In Liverpool/The End   (Spectrum) 196?

Prior to joining **The Hydraulic Raisins**, Dan Braymer had drummed for the Ella Jones Varsity Show, the Teen Charmers (an all-girl accordion band!), and several incarnations of bands fronted by Del Pierce, including The Knockouts, The Masked Marvels, and The Squares. In 1963, he hooked up with the Rhythm Surfers, an instrumental surf band that released *502/Big City Surfer* on Daytona Records (D-6301).

Soon afterwards, Braymer formed the Spectrums, another instrumental band whose recordings have survived but were never officially released. Then, after the breakup of the Spectrums, Dan answered an ad for a local group based in Baldwin Park, California. After rejecting the name Hydraulic Kumquats(!), Braymer, Barnes Oxenham and Gerodoni decided on **The Hydraulic Raisins**.

The 'Raisins released one single on Spectrum Records (a label financed by Braymer's mother): *Tragedy In Liverpool / The End*. *Tragedy...* was yet another instrumental, whilst *The End* was folk-rock.

Since **The 'Raisins** always taped their rehearsals, several recordings remained in the can. Now all but one of these, *First Encounter*, have been included on the Bacchus Archives CD. Two of the tracks, *Travel The World*

HYDRO PYRO - Psychedelic Moods Part 4 CD.

and *Mountain Dew* were both used by the band as demos. In addition there's two group originals:- *Smog Song* (a clone of **Barry McGuire**'s *Eve Of Destruction* delivered in a similar manner to the original) and *Baby Boy*, plus a version of **The Rumblers**' *I Don't Need You No More*, which was recorded with some serious attitude.

The complete **Hydraulic Raisins** / Rhythm Surfers / Spectrums story, of which the above is a summary, can be found in the liner notes to the Bacchus Archives CD. (MDo)

Hydro Pyro

CD: 1   PSYCHEDELIC MOODS, PART 4: THE FINAL ACT
                                       (Collectables COL-CD-0653) 1995

NB: (1) is a retrospective, which also includes material by **The Deep**.

From upstate New York, they resided in Greenwich Village for part of 1967. On 24th April 1967, they entered the Mercury Sound Studios to cut six mind-expanding psychedelic numbers written by **Deep** members Mark Barkin and D. Blackhurst. None of the band were more than nineteen and they were heavily into acid. The six tracks:- *The House of Yesterday, Id, Hydro-Pyro, Purple Floating, Snow Petals* and *Little Tin Soldier* - sound like the **Deep** album and you'll find them all on *Psychedelic Moods - Part Two* (LP & CD).

Other compilation appearances include: *Hydro Pyro* and *Id* on *Green Crystal Ties Vol. 4* (CD). (MW/VJ)

H.Y. Sledge

Personnel:	MICHAEL EWBANK	organ, piano, vcls	A
	BILLY JONES	keyb'ds	A
	RICHARD PORTER	gtr, piano, harp, vcls	A
	JAN PULVER	bs, cowbell, vcls	A
	MONTE YOHO	drms	A

ALBUM: 1(A) BOOTLEG MUSIC   (SSS International SSS-22) 1971 -

Despite the colourful cover, this album has predominantly an early seventies rock sound. Its finest cuts include *Canadian Exodus* which starts abrasively but slows down and features some nice, mellow guitar playing and *Cellophane Lady*, which has some sixties style fuzz guitar. It was produced by Ewbank and Poner.

H.Y. Sledge came from Tampa, Florida. Jan Pulver had previously played in **Those Five**, and Monte Yoho and Billy Jones were also members of **The Outlaws**. (VJ/MW/SMR)

Hysterical Society

45s:	Come With Me/I Know	(United Artists 50147) 1967
	I Put A Spell On You/ Summertime (Variations)	(Tipton 100) 1968

A little behind the times down in Amarillo, Texas - their first 45 contains two fine chunky beat-punkers that have 1965 written across 'em. *I Put A Spell...* takes on a Doug Ingle and **Iron Butterfly** sound, with shades of light and heavy, doomy cathedral organ sounds and deep booming vocal. *Summertime* has a lighter jazzy feel (imagine Zombies meeting **Vanilla Fudge**). The band may have evolved out of The Hysterical Society Boys who issued another 45:- *Funny Face/I Got Shot* (EBR 620001) 1962?.

Compilation appearances have included: *I Know* on *Psychedelic Unknowns, Vol. 9* (CD), *Basementsville! U.S.A.* (LP) and *Incredible Sound Show Stories, Vol. 8* (LP). (MW)

Hysterics

Personnel incl: D. DISMUKES?   A

EP: 1 Won't Get Far/Everything's There/That's All She Wrote/ Why Should You Treat Me This Way   (Bing B-303) 1986

NB: (1) is a reissue. Its four tracks contain the band's two original 45s for Bing and Tottenham records.

45s:	That's All She Wrote/Won't Get Far	(Tottenham 500) 1965
	Why Should You Treat Me This Way/ Everything's There	(Bing B-303) 1965

A typical period punk band from the San Bernardino/Riverside area of California. Their finest moment was *Everything's There*. The lyrics were typical of the period - about the vocalist's infatuation with his girlfriend who's left him for another man.

The band also issued at least one 45 as **The Love Ins**, which coupled two of the above tracks: *Everything's There* and *That's All She Wrote*. The latter track has also been covered by Italy's **Others** on their 1995 EP *Going Around With...* .

Compilation appearances have included: *Everything's There* on *Mayhem & Psychosis, Vol. 1* (LP), *Mayhem & Psychosis, Vol. 1* (CD), *Pebbles, Vol. 8* (CD), *The Essential Pebbles Collection, Vol. 1* (Dble CD), *Pebbles, Vol. 7* (LP), and *Pebbles, Vol. 1* (ESD) (CD); *Won't Get Far* on *Pebbles, Vol. 9* (CD) and *I Was A Teenage Caveman* (LP); *Everything's There* and *Won't Get Far* on *Boulders, Vol. 1* (LP); *That's All She Wrote* on *Turds On A Bum Ride, Vol. 5* (CD), *60s Choice, Vol. 2* (LP) and *60s Choice, Vol's 1 & 2* (CD); and *Why Should You Treat Me This Way* on *Turds On A Bum Ride, Vol. 6* (CD). (VJ/MW)

HOLY MODAL ROUNDERS - 1 & 2 CD.

HP Lovecraft - 1 & 2 CD.

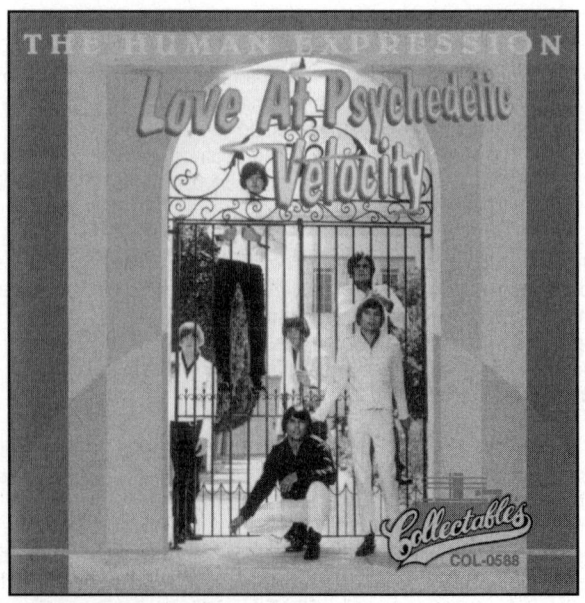

HOLY GHOST RECEPTION COMMITTEE No. 9 - Collected Works CD.

HUMAN EXPRESSION - Love At Psychedelic Velocity CD.

ICE - Melting Your Mind LP.

Ice

Personnel:	WAYNE BAKALAR	gtr, vcls	AB
	TIM KERESTES	drms, perc	AB
	BOB McKEE	bs	AB
	DAN NEFF	keyb'ds, flute, vcls	AB
	ALAN SHUPP	gtr, vcls	AB
	ROBIN YOUNG	vcls	A

ALBUM: 1(A) MELTING YOUR MIND (Bonny Records 1211L) 1972 R2

An Illinois band. Most of the members had been playing together in bands for several years; Bakalar and Kerestes since March 1965.

Ice began in October 1971. The band played local clubs and dances and was a popular live attraction for about a year. In March 1972, they recorded the tracks for their album at a local studio.

The *Melting Your Mind* album is a patchy affair, suffering mainly from poor material that does not serve to highlight the band's ability. The opening track, *Daughter Of Venus* is probably the record's most impressive piece, being the closest approximation of a vehicle for Young's female vocals. Most readers of this book will likely prefer *Five Card Draw* however, a loud bluesy jam that sounds like **Farm**. A couple of cuts are downright poor, with *In My Oldsmobile* leading the way. Sadly, no minds were melted by this album. (CF)

The Id

Personnel:	PAUL ARNOLD		A
	JERRY COLE	gtr	A
	ELIJAH		A
	?? ??		A
	?? ??		A

ALBUM: 1(A) THE INNER SOUNDS OF THE ID
(RCA Victor LSP 3805) 1967 SC

NB: (1) reissued on vinyl 199?

45s:	Short Circuit/Boil The Kettle, Mother	(RCA 47-9136) 1967
	Wild Times/The Rake	(RCA 47-9195) 1967

NB: Both 45s are taken from the album.

Paul Arnold was clearly the brainchild behind this San Diego band and produced their Beatles - influenced album. The title track is a strange voyage into the mysticism of Eastern-influenced music, which is not wholly successful. It does contain one outstanding cut, though, *Boil The Kettle, Mother*, which features some fine fuzztone guitar work and demented vocal style and lyrics, making it one of the classic psychedelic punk recordings.

Strangely, three versions of tracks from the *Inner Sounds* album: *Wild Times*, *Don't Think Twice* and *Boil The Kettle* turn up on the exploito-psych album *Give Me Some Lovin'* by **The Projection Company** (Custom CS 1113) 1967. The **Id**-entical (sic) first two also reappear as by **The Associated Soul Group** on the *Top Hits Of Today* album from 1968. They sound close enough to the originals at times, especially *Don't Think Twice*, to make one wonder whether **The Id** were behind these and perhaps other exploito tracks/albums credited to faceless (**Id**-less?) or fictitious groups.

Guitarist Jerry Cole had been in the Champs for a couple of years (he joined them in 1961) and also had several solo releases as well as session work.

Compilation appearances have included: *Boil The Kettle Mother* on *Mayhem & Psychosis, Vol. 1* (LP), *Mayhem & Psychosis, Vol. 1* (CD), *Mind Blowers* (LP), *Pebbles, Vol. 2 (ESD)* (CD), *Turds On A Bum Ride, Vol. 1 & 2* (Dble CD) and *Turds On A Bum Ride, Vol. 1* (Dble LP); (MW/VJ/GM)

Id

Personnel:	JAMES ALBERT	steel gtr	A
	RALPH JENKINS	drms	A
	KEVIN ORSON	bs	A
	DAVID OICKLE	gtr, keyb'ds	A
	GARY OICKLE	ld gtr	A

ALBUM: 1(A) WHERE ARE WE GOING (Aura AR 1000) 1976 R1

NB: (1) has had a limited repressing and has also been issued on CD (Flash 53) 199?.

This Glen Burnie, Minnesota, outfit is completely unconnected to the other Id(s). The album is spacey-sounding, largely instrumental and may be of interest to readers. It's full of feedback and sound effects. Most of both sides are taken up with the 30-minute long title track and the album was recorded in New York City in 1975.

Gary Oickle sadly died of ALS (Lou Gehrig's disease) in April 2000. (VJ/DCn/BK)

Id

45: Rotten Apple / Listen To Me (Jolly Roger 101/2) 1966

NB: first pressing, on a blue label, came with a pic sleeve.

Also from San Diego, California, but not the RCA bunch. This pre-pubescent quartet are pictured, in mournful contemplation around a headstone, on the rare 45 picture sleeve reproduced on the cover of *Diggin' For Gold, Vol. 7* (LP), which features their decent teen-punker *Rotten Apple*. (MM/MW)

THE ID - The Inner Sounds Of The Id CD.

THE IDES OF MARCH - Ideology LP.

The Id

The *Girls In The Garage, Vol. 1* (LP) compilation includes a previously unreleased track *Those Ever-Lovin' Baby Blues*, a raw bluesy sound from an all girl band.

The track has also made it onto CD on *Girls In The Garage, Vol. 1* (CD). (VJ)

The Ides

45: Psychedelic Ride/Only Your Love   (Ken-Del 5309) 196?

The Ides are thought to have came from Delaware. *Psychedelic Ride* is one of the classics of the psychedelic punk genre with discordant guitar and tormented vocals.

Compilation appearances include: *Psychedelic Ride* on *Psychedelic Unknowns, Vol's 1 & 2* (LP), *Psychedelic Unknowns, Vol. 1* (Dble 7") and *Teenage Shutdown, Vol. 13* (LP & CD). (VJ)

The Ides of March

Personnel:	BOB BERGLAND	bs	A
	MIKE BORCH	drms	A
	LARRY MILLAS	gtr	A
	JIM PETERIK	ld vcls, gtr	A

ALBUM: 1(A) IDEOLOGY   (Sundazed LP 5032) 2000

NB: (1) also issued on CD with the addition of the two unreleased tracks featured on the earlier Sundazed 45 and stereo versions of *Hole In My Soul* and *Girls Don't Grow On Trees* (Sundazed SC11067) 2000.

HCP

45s:	α	Like It Or Lump It /		
(up to		No Two Ways About It	(Epitome 7195)	1965 -
1969)	β	You Wouldn't Listen / I'll Take You Back	(Acetate)	1965 -
		You Wouldn't Listen /		
		I'll Keep Searchin'	(Harlequin 660412)	1966 -
	χ	You Wouldn't Listen/I'll Keep Searching	(Parrot 304)	1966 42
		Roller Coaster /		
		Things Aren't Always What They Seem	(Parrot 310)	1966 92
		Sha-La-La-La-Lee / You Need Love	(Parrot 312)	1966 -
		My Foolish Pride / Give Your Mind Wings	(Parrot 321)	1967 -
		Hole In My Soul /		
		Girls Don't Grow On Trees	(Parrot 326)	1968 -
		Nobody Loves Me / Strawberry Sunday	(Kapp 992)	1969 -

NB: α as Shon Dels Unlimited, just 200 pressed on their own label. β as The Shondels. χ as I'des of March. There's also a reisue 45: *I'm Gonna Say My Prayers / The Sun Ain't Gonna Shine Anymore* (PS) (Sundazed S 142) 1999.

The great commercial success as a top notch horn-rock outfit and Peterik's subsequent career as soloist and front-man of Survivor, have meant that the early period of this Chicago outfit has been overlooked, so here's a brief rundown on the pre-Warner Bros releases.

Originally known as Shon Dels Unlimited, and briefly The Shondels, they quickly became one of Chicago's top teen bands. Nearly all their material was group originals written by Peterik. Their style for this period was a vibrant blend of Invasion-influenced beat and mod sounds, brimming with melodic hooks, ringing guitars and commercial appeal but with strong vocals and harmonies and a tough edge - the result is some classic mid-sixties garagey pop.

The pre-Parrot releases are extremely hard to find these days but you can't go far wrong with the first three Parrot 45s. *I'll Keep Searching*, is great moody teenbeat not unlike **The Knaves**' *The Girl I Threw Away*. The classic *Rollercoaster* is a stunning Who-style mod-pop-punker and the mod theme continues with an excellent cover of the Small Faces' hit *Sha La La La Lee*. All the flips on these are decent beat-garage-pop too.

The next 45 brings early signs of change - *Give Your Mind Wings* is a smooth beat-ballad and *My Foolish Pride* has the first influx of brass (though it's still good pop). *Hole In My Soul* is upbeat brassy pop but *Girls Don't Grow On Trees* returns to form - a fine '**Raiders**-cum-**Monkees** style pop-punker. The transitional Kapp 45 features the soft ballad *Nobody Loves Me*, that would not be outta place on an **Association** album, even with the brass. The flipside *Strawberry Sunday* is more interesting - their sole attempt at a heavy psych-pop sound with distorted guitar, which comes off okay.

After that, well ... to each his own and it's well documented elsewhere ... check out "An American Rock History Vol. 3: Chicago and Illinois" for starters.

The Sundazed picture sleeve 45 dusts off an unreleased track from 1967 and an "Ides one-take wonder" from 1968 with notes and memories from Jim Peterik.

The fourteen-track *Ideology* album gathers the Parrot 45s tracks with the '65 Shon Dels Unlimited debut and The Shondels' acetate. The CD version adds the two unreleased tracks featured on the Sundazed 45 and stereo versions of *Hole In My Soul* and *Girls Don't Grow On Trees*.

Compilation appearances have included: *I'll Keep Searching* on *Pebbles, Vol. 7* (CD); and *Roller Coaster* on *Pebbles, Vol. 10* (LP). (MW/TTi)

The Ides of March

Personnel incl:	BOB WARD	vcls	A
	TIM WARD	gtr, vcls	A

45: Life Has Been So Good/
    Playthings - 5 x 5   (No label #1460) 1966

A different outfit from Bay City, Michigan who issued this privately pressed 45 before changing their name to **Blues Company**. (VJ)

Idle Few

Personnel:	RON BENNETH	A
	RON KNOOP	A
	DAN McLEAN	A
	PAUL ROMINE	A
	RICK WEBSTER	A

45s:	α	Farmer John/Another World	(Soma 1457) 1966
	β	Farmer John/?	(Dunwich 127) 1966
		Letter To Santa/Splishin' And Splashin'	(Not Known) 1967

NB: β is reissue of α. Although unconfirmed, the flip for Dunwich version is presumably *Another World*.

This was one of Indianapolis' top mid-sixties bands, although they'd originally formed back in 1958 as The Kingsmen but changed their name after the similarly-named Portland, Oregon, outfit had their *Louie, Louie* hit. They had a fine live reputation and fronted many big name acts like **The Byrds**, Beach Boys and **McCoys** on live bills. Their cover of *Farmer John* (made famous by **The Premiers**) can also be heard on *Hoosier Hotshots* (LP). (VJ/MW)

Idols

45:	True Luv Gone Astray / Haunted House	(Luv 201,306/7) 1967

NB: 'B' side as Ken Kerr (with The Idols).

An unknown New England outfit. Aram Heller describes *True Luv...* as "an excellent moody garage ballad" in his New England discography 'Till The Stroke Of Dawn'. The flip, *Haunted House*, with howls and manic vocals throughout, is simply demented.

Aram notes that this is not the Idols from Rhode Island who issued two 45s (on Dot and EZ) in the early sixties.

Compilation appearances have included: *True Love Gone Astray* on *New England Teen Scene* (CD) and *New England Teen Scene, Vol. 3* (LP); and *Haunted House* on *Sick And Tired* (LP). (MW/AH)

Iguana

Personnel:	ARTHUR BOD	gtr, oud, dumbeg, vcls	A
	KENNY BUTTREY	drms	A
	DON FALK	gtr, bs, pedal steel, vcls	A
	LIBERTY OVERMAN	drms	A
	JUDGE RUFFIN	keyb'ds	A
	DOLPHUS SHAW	gtr	A
	MORDECAI SILBER	violin	A
	BUDGE WITHERSPOON	gtr, vcls	A

ALBUM:	1(A)	THE WINDS OF ALAMAR	(Quadratrak A 101) 1975 R1

NB: (1) issued with insert. Later issued (United Artists 683) 1977 in the US, and in Europe (United Artists UAS 30130) 1977.

45:	Dream Song/ Happy One, Sad One	(United Artists XW 982) 1977

Ambitious and professional private pressing by this local Maryland group who recorded the album in genuine Quadrophonic sound at a studio in Nashville. The band play a highly competent FM-rock style, it reminds me of the **Big Lost Rainbow** album from the same area, only considerably more dynamic. The album was picked up by United Artists and saw an "official" release in 1977, along with a 45. (CF)

The Iguanas

Personnel incl:	A. MELINGER	A

45s:	Black Suit/Leaving You Baby	(Valerie 107) 1966
	I Can Only Give You Everything/ Leaving You Baby	(Iguana 101) 1967

An **Elevators** - inspired outfit from Baytown Texas, whose stage act often featured a live Iguana! Their most well-known song *I Can Only Give You Everything* was one of the best psychedelic tracks to come out of the State and has subsequently been well covered on compilations.

Melinger later played with **Endle St. Cloud**.

Compilation appearances have included: *Black Suit* on *Open Up Yer Door, Vol. 2* (LP); *Black Suit*, *I Can Only Give You Everything* and *Leaving You Baby* on *Texas Psychedelia From The Sixties* (LP) and *Sixties Archive, Vol. 6* (CD); *I Can Only Give You Everything* and *Leaving You Baby* on *Acid Visions - The Complete Collection, Vol. 1* (3-CD); *I Can Only Give You Everything* on *Texas Flashbacks, Vol. 2* (LP & CD), *Flashback, Vol. 2* (LP) and *Gone, Vol. 1 - Colour Dreams* (LP); *Leaving You Baby* on *Highs In The Mid-Sixties, Vol. 17* (LP); and *I Can Only Give You Everything* (alt. version) on *Houston Hallucinations* (LP). (VJ)

The Iguanas

Personnel incl:	JIM McLAUGHLIN	gtr, vcl	AB
	JIM OSTERBERG (aka IGGY POP)	drms	AB
	SAM SWISHER	sax, perc	AB
	NICK KOLOKITHAS	gtr, vcls	B
	DON SWICKERATH	bs	B

ALBUMS:	1(A/B)	JUMPIN' WITH THE IGUANAS (CD)	
			(Fuller Bosom 36024036) 1995
	2(A/B)	THE IGUANAS (LP)	(Norton ED-251) 1996

45:	Mona/I Don't Know Why	(Forte/Cosa Grande 201) 1965

Formative Michigan garage outfit whence Iggy got his moniker before going on to cult status with **The Stooges**. Formed by Iggy and Jim McLaughlin whilst in the 9th grade at school in Ann Arbor, Michigan, they played their first gig in '63 at a school dance. Within a few months Don Swickerath and Nick Kolokithas were recruited, and **The Iguanas** began building up a local following, playing at frat parties, high school dances and teen clubs.

In the Summer of '65 they became house band at the Club Ponytail in Harbor Springs, playing their own sets and also backing other acts - sharing the stage with the likes of **The Kingsmen**, The Guess Who, The Shangri-Las, Bobby Goldsboro, The Four Tops, The Reflections and others. The same year, they also went into United Sound Recording Studio and put three tracks down onto tape: *Mona* - their trademark and signature of live gigs, plus two band compositions, *I Don't Know Why* and *Again And Again*. The band released two of these on their own Forte label, and *Mona* received airplay in the Detroit/Ann Arbor region.

The following year Iggy left to join the Prime Movers and **The Iguanas** continued with a new drummer, playing clubs around Boston and New York. Columbia expressed an interest in the band, but when that failed to come to fruition they went their separate ways in 1967.

The *Jumpin With The Iguanas* CD retrospective, contains the three cuts recorded at the Winter '64/Spring '65 session at United Sound, plus material from a 1963 acetate (recorded by line-up 'A'), and 1964 rehearsals. Complete with photos, memorabilia, and sleeve-notes by Jim McLaughlin. For vinyl fans, there's also a similar collection on Norton.

Compilation appearances have included: *Mona* and *I Don't Know Why* on *A Journey To Tyme, Vol. 3* (LP); *Mona* on *Echoes In Time, Vol's 1 & 2* (CD) and *Echoes In Time, Vol. 2* (LP); and *Again And Again* (prev. unreleased) on *Highs In The Mid-Sixties, Vol. 19* (LP). (MW)

THE IGUANAS - Jumpin With... CD.

The Iguanas

Personnel:	VIC DIAZ?	A
	TONY MINICHIELLO?	A
	MANUEL SANCHEZ?	A

45s:	This Is What I Was Made For/?	(Dunhill 4004) 1965
	Meet Me Tonight Little Girl/?	(Dunhill ?) 1965

Another Sloan/Barry creation, who released two folk-pop singles. **The Iguanas** were probably the Matadors, a group who was previously working with Jan Berry at Colpix and on Jan and Dean records.

This Is What I Was Made For has been compiled on *Penny Arcade, Dunhill Folk Rock, Vol. 2* (LP). (SR)

Illinois Speed Press

Personnel:	MIKE ANTHONY	organ, piano	A
	PAUL COTTON	gtr, vcls	ABC
	KAL DAVID	gtr, vcls	AB
	ROB LEWINE	bs	A
	FRED PAGE	drms	A
	JOHN URIBE	gtr, vcls	C
	FRANK BARTOLI	bs	
	FRED PAPPALARDO	drms	

			HCP
ALBUMS:	1(A)	ILLINOIS SPEED PRESS (Columbia CS 9792) 1969	144 -
	2(B)	DUET (Columbia CS 9976) 1970	- -

NB: (1) has been reissued.

45s:	Right On Time/Night People	(Roulette 4687) 1969
	Get In The Wind/	
	Get In The Wind, Pt. II (PS)	(Columbia 4-44564) 1969
	Sadly Out Of Place/Country Dumplin'	(Columbia 4-45756) 1970

This Chicago-based quintet was formed in February 1968 by Paul Cotton and featured colleague Mike Anthony, whom Cotton had played with in another significant Chicago outfit, **The Rovin' Kind**, and Kal David, another important Chicago musician, after his spell in **H.P. Lovecraft**. The songs on their albums ranged from hard-rock to more mainstream rock with country influences and from blues towards folk-rock, very often with psychedelic references and some fine fuzz guitars.

The first album met with some commercial success, peaking at No 144 in the Album Charts during 1969. *Duet* failed to consolidate on this and the band, by now based in California, went their separate ways in late 1971.

David went on to play for **Fabulous Rhinestones** and Cotton to Poco, who were to become flagbearers for the country-rock movement. Earlier Fred Page had left for California where he played for various L.A.-based bands. (GG/VJ)

Illusion

Personnel:	CHUCK ADLER	bs	A
	RICHIE CERNIGLIA	gtr	A
	MIKE MANISCALCO	gtr, keyb'ds	A
	MICHAEL RICCIARDELLA	drms	A
	JOHN VINCI	vcls	A

				HCP
ALBUMS:	1	ILLUSION	(Steed 37003) 1969	69 -
	2(A)	TOGETHER	(Steed 37005) 1969	- -
	3(A)	IF IT'S SO	(Steed 37006) 1970	- -

NB: (1) to (3) also released in France by Dot. All of their albums have been reissued on CD on TRC, together with an album called *Madonna Blue*.

			HCP
45s:	Did You See Her Eyes?/Falling In Love	(Steed 712) 1969	-
	Run, Run, Run/I Love You, Yes I Do	(Steed 717) 1969	-
	Did You See Her Eyes?/Falling In Love	(Steed 718) 1969	32
	How Does It Feel?/Once In A Lifetime	(Steed 721) 1969	110

ILLUSION - Illusion LP.

α	Together/Don't Push It	(Steed 722) 1969 80
	Let's Make Each Other Happy/Beside You	(Steed 726) 1970 98
	Collection/Wait A Minute	(Steed 732) 1971 -

NB: α also released in France with a picture sleeve (Dot 2C00 690963) 1969.

An Italian - U.S. band, based in Long Island, New York. who played heavy-rock with some psychedelic influence. The band were formed by Bruce Brandt, who had also worked with **Faine Jade**. They enjoyed some minor chart success and their albums were produced by the famous Jeff Barry.

Michael Ricciardella went on to play in Barnaby Bye (1973) and in 1977 Cerniglia and Vinci formed Network.

You can also find *I Love You, Yes I Do* on *Psychedelic Crown Jewels, Vol. 1* (Dble LP & CD). (VJ)

Illusion

Personnel:	WENDELL ING	keyb'ds	A
	HANK LEANDRO	gtr	A
	DENNY MAEDA	gtr	A
	GREGG NUTT	drms	A
	BUTCH O'SULLIVAN	bs	A

ALBUM:	1(A)	ILLUSION	(Sinergia SR 7654) 1974 R1

A local Hawaii folk/rural album. It's sought - after mostly for its stunning sleeve design, as it's a bit too lightweight to have generated interest among collectors. (CF)

The Illusions

45:	City Of People/Wait Till The Summer	(Michelle 001-XX) 1966

A four piece from Detroit, Michigan. They started out as a frat band in 1964, but the following year got into the garage sound influenced by the likes of The Stones, The Pretty Things etc. They also got to appear on 'Milky's Party Time'- a TV show for kids. *City Of People* is a fine example of the garage genre - with great lyrics, good vocals and some catchy tinny guitar.

Compilation appearances have included: *Wait Till The Summer* on *Love Is A Sad Song, Vol. 1* (LP) and *Teenage Shutdown, Vol. 5* (LP & CD); *City Of People* on *Michigan Mayhem, Vol. 1* (CD), *Back From The Grave, Vol. 5* (LP), *Back From The Grave, Vol. 2* (CD), *Glimpses, Vol's 1 & 2* (CD) and *Glimpses, Vol. 1* (LP). (VJ)

The Illusions

45s:	I Know/Take My Heart	(ACP 375) 1966
	I Know/Take My Heart	(Columbia 43700) 1966

A different outfit from Palatka, Florida whose disc got picked up for nationwide release by Columbia. *I Know*, a folky pop-punk affair, can be heard on *The Midwest Vs. The Rest* (LP), *Pebbles, Vol. 11* (LP) and *Psychedelic States: Florida Vol. 1* (CD).

The only clue to the identities of band members might be the composer credit of Gardner, Touchman, Hewett, Williams. (VJ/MW)

The Illusions

Personnel?:	J. DOUGHERTY		A
	D. GILLON		A

45:	Rain, Shine, Or Snow/	
	Shadows Of You	(Chantain L-193-1/2) 1968

Yet another **Illusions**, who produced an above-average garage-beat ballad and an excellent garage folk-rocker. The above personnel, from the song credits, is listed in the hope of confirmation of their locality - believed to be Birmingham, Alabama.

Compilation appearances have included: *Shadows Of You* on *Psychedelic Crown Jewels, Vol. 2* (Dble LP & CD) and *Psychedelic States: Alabama, Vol. 1* (CD). (MW)

The Illusions

45s:	Impossibility/Her Own Way	(Cha Cha 744) 1966
	I've Had Enough/Boy-Girl	(Cha Cha 752) 1966

Another Chicago area group this time with two average beat-popsters on the second 45. (MW)

The Illusions

Personnel incl:	MARK SPENCER	gtr	A

45:	Tell Me No / Burning Embers	(Bar-Mar) c1967

Recorded at AAA studios in Dorchester, Massachusetts, *Burning Embers* is a wimpy ballad and *Tell Me No* is a typical New England moody song. The label name 'Bar-Mar' was derived from the surnames of two of the band members. (MKh)

The Ill Wind

Personnel:	KEN FRANKEL	ld gtr, banjo	A
	RICHARD GRIGGS		A
	(RICHARD ZVONAR)	gtr, vcls	A
	DAVID KINSMAN	drms	A
	CAREY MANN	bs, vcls	A
	CONNY DEVANNEY	vcls	A

ALBUM:	1(A)	FLASHES	(ABC S 641) 1968 R2

NB: (1) has been counterfeited at least twice on vinyl and on CD with six bonus tracks (Afterglow AFT 012) 1995. Reissued on vinyl and CD (Akarma AK 162) 2001, with three bonus tracks.

45s:	In My Dark World/Walkin' And Singin'	(ABC 11107) 1968
	In My Dark World/High Flying Bird	(ABC 11107) 1968

Originally known as The Prophets, with a singer called Judy Bradbury, this band were originally from Wellsley, Massachusetts but based themselves in Boston. Clearly, a hippie as opposed to a punk band, their album is a fine one, with their sound moulded by Conny Devanney's crystal clear vocals. On tracks like *Dark World* her voice is beautiful, while on others, notably the widely recorded *High Flying Bird*, *Hung Up Chick* and *Walkin' And Singin'*, it blends in beautifully with that of her male counterpart, Richard Griggs. Also of note is the unusual *People Of The Night* and the sleepy *Full Cycle*. This album is strongly recommended if you ever come across it. The band split up in December 1968, and Carey Mann went on to play with **Dirty John's Hot Dog Stand**.

The original album had an incorrect song order listed on the back cover. The second song on Side One was wrongly listed as *Sleep* rather than *People Of The Night*. Similary *Sleep* was wrongly listed as *People Of The Night*. The bonus tracks on the Afterglow and Akarma reissues are from demos for the album and these too miscredit the demo version of *People Of The Night* as *Sleep*. The majority of original copies of the album were also subject to a mastering fault on *High Flying Bird*, which also appears on both the 'counterfeit' and the 'legit' reissues.

Compilation coverage has included: *Full Cycle* on *Baubles* (LP); *In My Dark World* and *High Flyin' Bird* on *The Best Of Bosstown Sound* (Dble CD). (VJ/SR/RZ)

The Ill Winds

45s:	So Be On Your Way (I Won't Cry)/	
	Fear Of The Rain	(Reprise 0423) 1965
	I Idolize You/A Letter	(Reprise 0492) 1966

Fear Of The Rain can be heard on *Psychedelic Unknowns, Vol. 8* (LP & CD). Far from being a psychedelic outfit this was actually the Chantays under a pseudonym, a long way from *Pipeline*!

Ilmo Smokehouse

Personnel:	GERRY GABEL	keyb'ds	A
	CRAIG MOORE	bs	A
	SLINK RAND	gtr	A
	DENNIS TIEKEN	drms	A
	FRED TIEKEN	vcls	A

ALBUMS:	1(A)	ILMO SMOKEHOUSE (w/poster)	
			(Beautiful Sounds BS-3002) 1970 SC?
	2(A)	ILMO SMOKEHOUSE (remix of above)	
			(Roulette SR-3002) 1971 -

NB: (2) is a remixed issue of (1).

Formed in 1969 by the Tieken brothers from Quincy, Illinois. They'd previously been in the long-lived Freddy Tieken and The Rockers who'd been going at it since the late fifties. As **The Gonn** disintegrated in 1968, first Slink Rand and then Craig Moore joined 'The Rockers. Craig:- "Fred changed the name to The American Music Band, stealing it sort of from **The Electric Flag**. We played EVERYWHERE... Then when the horn guys all quit, we became **Ilmo Smokehouse**, heavy as hell, anti-war, pro-drug hippie all the way. When that eventually ended Slink, Dennis and I became

THE ILL WIND - Flashes LP.

'Smokehouse' as a really heavy progressive trio. Later on we had Micki Free on guitar (later with L.A. soul group Shalamar). We wore glitter and make-up *before* Kiss, but they made it we didn't. It's all nuts, convoluted, insane, I can't believe I did all of this crap!"

Their album was recorded in Memphis at 'Beautiful Sound' Studio, owned by Dan Penn of **Box Tops** fame (as a songwriter producer). He engineered part of the session, with his partner Jim Johnson. (MW/CMe)

Image

Personnel:	BARRY BRYAN	ld gtr	A
	JAMES DAWSON	vcls	A
	JERRY DYER	bs, vcls	A
	TIM JACOBSMEYER	keyb'ds	A
	ROGER PARKHAM	drms	A

The compilation *Dallas 1971 Part 1: A New Hi* (Tempo 2) 1971 features two songs, *The Out Station* and *Everybody's Laughin'*, by this Dallas band. Both are laid-back with nice guitar and keyboards. (VJ)

The Immigrants

Personnel:	RAY LEAVITT	ld gtr	A
	DAVE McKAY	bs	A
	NICK PERRON	drms	A
	DICK REILLY	vcls, gtr	A
	ED REILLY	keyb'ds	A

ALBUM: 1(A) IMMIGRANTS (Starburst SRA 9837) 1966 R3

NB: (1) reissued in 1994 as *The Immigrants '66*.

45: Time To Say Goodbye / ?? (Starburst 3121) 1966

A quintet of students based at Wesleyan University in Salina, Kansas though they hailed from New Jersey, Brooklyn and Staten Island, New York. More in the prep-rock than garage-rock genre they turn in some competent if uninspiring covers of *House Of The Rising Sun*, *Run For Your Life*, *She's Not There*, *Keep A Knockin'* and a *Kansas City/Route 66* medley. Influenced by U.S. rock 'n' roll and instrumental groups plus the U.K. beat invasion sounds, they could be mistaken for a U.K. outfit. No sign of a fuzzbox and their most garagey offering *2.25 Blues* has been compiled on *Oil Stains* (LP). (MW)

Impact

45: My World Fell Down/Could You Love Me (MGM K13726) 1967

An orchestrated pop version of the pop-psych classic immortalised by **Sagittarius**. If this outfit had made more of an impact, we'd probably know something about them. (MW)

Impact 5 (aka Impact IV)

45: Island Of Love/Riptide (Agar 7171) 1965

Riptide can also be heard on *Garage Punk Unknowns, Vol. 6* (LP). The band came out of Minneapolis, Minnesota and the 45 is now quite sought-after. The band were also known as **Impact IV**. (VJ)

Impacts/Impact Express

Personnel:	RON BALDWIN	vcls	AB
	HENRY BRUSCO	drms	A
	BRUCE FAROUHAR	ld gtr	AB
	BILL UHLIG	bs	AB
	DAN 'SPYDER' WHITE	keyb'ds	AB
	STEVE GREEN	drms	B

45s:	A Little More/Leavin' Here	(NWI 2660) 1965
	Don't You Dare/Green Green Field	(Lavender 2005) 1966
	I'm Gonna Change The World/	
	You Get Your Kicks	(Lavender 2006) 1967
	Sunshine Day/Don't You Dare	(Lavender 2007) 1967
	A Little Love/Fly With Me	(Lavender 2008) 1968

A Rainier, Oregon band who produced some enjoyable tunes - more pop than punk but with that solid Pacific Northwest beat. Baldwin and White had previously been with The Chessmen and this outfit would change its name to **Impact Express** after the second 45.

Compilation appearances have included: *Green Green Field* on *Sixties Rebellion Vol. 16* (LP & CD); *Don't You Dare* on *Tymes Gone By* (LP) and *Class Of '66!* (LP); *Green Green Field* and *Don't You Dare* on *Bad Vibrations, Vol. 2* (LP). (MW)

(Fabulous) Impacts

45s:	Get Out Of My Life Woman/Tell Me (PS)	(Dads 7-8001) 1967
	A Thousand Years/Cry Cry (PS)	(Dads 7-8002) 1967

Came out of Omaha, Nebraska. Both 45s were pressed in Minneapolis. (VJ)

The Impalas

Personnel:	RON MOEN	gtr	A
	JEFF MORETTI	vcls	A
	JERRY NORCIA	ld gtr	A
	MIKE PRICE	drms	A
	GENE SCHILLER	bs	
	JACK GEBHARDT	bs	
	STEVE KEPPEN	drms	
	JERRY KUEPER	vcls	
	CHUCK LOTH	gtr	
	DONNIE ROBERTS	drms	
	PHIL SHIELDS	keyb'ds	
	EMMITT SMITH	bs	

45s:	Spoonful/Talkin' About You	(Feature 817R-107) 1966
	The Great Pretender / Mary Lou	(Elaart 3001) 1975
	Teenager In Love /	
	I'm Gonna Love You Too	(Page 8083-26) 1977

A Milwaukee, Wisconsin act who formed in 1962. They took their name from Schiller's '58 Impala, unaware of other Impalas that were around. Their debut 45 was produced by Sam McClure of **The Legends**. *Spoonful* - a raw bluesy workout with a good snotty vocal has resurfaced on *Highs In The Mid-Sixties, Vol. 15* (LP).

Moretti had left by the time this was recorded but would reform **The Impalas** in the seventies and release two 45s. He moved to Florida in the eighties but was still returning for band reunions years later.

Phil Shields was also in **The Picture**. (MW/GM)

THE IMMIGRANTS - The Immigrants '66 CD.

Thee Impalas

45s:	Band Of Gold / ?	(Whittier 502) 1966
	Come On Up / Oh Yeah	(Whittier 506) 1967

From L.A.'s vibrant East Side scene, **Thee Impalas** released two 45s including a stomping cover of **The Young Rascals**' *Come On Up*. *Band Of Gold* was also compiled back in 1969 on the double-LP set *East Side Revue* (Rampart 3303).

Retrospective compilation appearances have included: *Oh Yeah!* on *Let's Dig 'Em Up, Vol. 1* (CD) and *Let's Dig 'Em Up, Vol. 2* (LP); *Come On Up* on *Basementsville! U.S.A.* (LP); and both *Oh Yeah!* and *Come On Up* on *The East Side Sound Vol. 2* (LP & CD). (MW)

Impala Syndrome

Personnel:	BERNARDO BALL	AB
	FRANCISCO BELISARIO	ABX
	RODOLFO MARQUEZ	ABX
	EDGARDO QUINTERO	ABX
	NERIO QUINERO	AB
	HENRY STEPHEN	A
	G. BUSNER	X
	F. CHANDRA	X

ALBUM: 1(X) IMPALA SYNDROME (Parallax P-4002) 1969 R2

NB: (1) also issued Venezuela (Palacio/Parallax LP - 7565), also later issued in Spain (Diresa/Parallax DLP 1053) 1973 and again on vinyl as a Spanish import (Wah Wah LPS 003) 2000. (1) has been reissued on CD. As Los Impala, they also had a Spanish only release: *Estos Son* (Marter M 30-056) 1968 R1 and an Argentinian LP *The Impala And Their Music* (Quinto Q 10.005) 1966

EP: 1 CADA VEZ + 3 (Sono Play SBP 10004) 1966

NB: (1) Spanish only release as **Los Impalas**.

Originally from Venezuela, where they were known as Los Impala, this group relocated to Madrid, Spain in 1965. After a few months, their singer Henry Stephens left to pursue a solo career, recording an EP as Lord Henry Con Los Impala.

After a few years the band moved to Chicago, releasing their *Impala Syndrome* album which is well worth checking out. An effective blend of melodic, laid-back songs (*Love Grows A Flower*, *Land Of No Time* and the superb Eastern-influenced finale, *Run (Don't Look Behind)*) combined with fuzz guitar numbers like *Too Much Time* and *Let Them Try*. *New Love Time* is also rather catchy but *Leave, Eve* sounds unashamedly like The Rascals' *Its Wonderful*.

The band recorded other EPs and 45s as Los Impala, not shown in the above discography. (VJ/CF/ML/MGi)

The Implicits

45:	Give Me Justice/She's Alright	(Atoll 100) 1965

This California outfit's eminently forgettable punk screamer *Give Me Justice* can also be heard on *Riot City!* (LP). (MW)

Improper Bostonians

Personnel incl:	DICK JEFFREY	ld gtr	A
	PAT O'CONNOR	drms	A
	PETER O'CONNOR	gtr	A
	DAVID PETERSON	bs	A

45s:	How Many Tears/I Still Love You	(Minuteman 207) 1966
	Set You Free This Time/ Come To Me Baby	(Minuteman 208) 1967
	Out Of My Mind/You Made Me A Giant	(Minuteman 209) 1967
	Gee I'm Gonna Miss You/ Victim Of Environment	(Minuteman 211) 1967

IMPALA SYNDROME - Impala Syndrome LP.

	Gee I'm Gonna Miss You/ Victim Of Environment	(Coral 62453) 1967

This outfit were the houseband at the Ebb-Tide, Revere Beach, Revere, Massachusetts, when Minuteman signed them up and paid for them to do a ten hour recording session in New York. Musically they played a hard **Byrds** sound. Indeed *Set You Free This Time* was actually a **Byrds** song.

Compilation appearances have included: *Victim Of Environment* on *Leaving It All Behind* (LP); and *How Many Tears*, *I Still Love You* and *Set You Free This Time* on *Bay State Rock* (LP). (VJ)

The In

45s:	In The Midnight Hour / You're So Fine	(Sonny 1002) c1966
	Just Give Me Time / You're So Fine	(Sonny 1004) c1966
	In The Midnight Hour/Just Give Me Time	(Hickory 1413) 1966

An obscure (probably from Tennessee) combo whose live frat-party rendition of the perennial *Midnight Hour* graces *Follow That Munster, Vol. 1* (LP). However it's *Just Give Me Time* that's the winner here - an outstanding fuzz-punker. (MW)

Inca

See **Maitreya Kali**.

The Incident

Personnel:	ALAN DAVID		A
	JOEL DAVIS	ld vcls	A
	CHARLIE FRASER	keyb'ds	A
	JIM FRASER		A
	STEVE LYONS		A

A quintet from Long Island, NY who evolved out of two earlier groups, the Changing Tyme and the King James Version. They played in the "Long Island" style and were regulars at Ondines in NYC, but do not appear to have released any 45s. (MW)

Incredible Broadside Brass Bed Band

Personnel:	VICTOR BERNADONI	drms	A
	MARK BIEBER	washboard, blues harp, water	A
	BILL COMEAU	vcls, gtr, blues harp	A
	JERRY DEVOKATIS	ld gtr	A
	PETE LEVIN	banjo, piano, kazoo	A
	THELONIUS LIPSCHITZ	bass skunk	A

	CRAZY MAX	bs, bass frogaphone	A
	PAUL OSSALA	bs	A
	VINCENT dePAUL		A
	LINUS PASTERNAK	ld gtr, noises	A

ALBUM: 1(A) THE GREAT GRIZZLY BEAR HUNT
(Poison Ring PRR 2240) 1971 -

45: Little Dead Surfer Girl/
Bullfrog Blues (Poison Ring PR-717) 1971

An album of good-timey folk-blues-hippie-rock and plain wackiness by a bunch of guys from Connecticut. For those who got lost on their way to Woodstock but still had a great trip.

The band was led by **Bill Comeau**, who wrote most of their songs and also had a solo career.

Three members later went on to **Fancy**. (MW/SR)

The In Crowd

Personnel incl:	JIM GLAVES		A
	BOBBY RAMBO	gtr	A

45: Big Cities/Inside Out (Abnak 121) 1967

NB: promo copies also exist on yellow vinyl.

Another Texas group from the Dallas/Fort Worth area, **The In Crowd** were produced by Dale Hawkins. The group reputedly sounds like another Abnak group, the **Five Americans**, and several members of these two groups played with **Jon and Robin**.

In 1968, Bobby Rambo would join the **Five Americans** and later became the guitarist of Jerry Jeff Walker. (SR)

Indelible Inc.

ALBUM: 1 FOR NOW (Concordia) 1972 ?

A Christian group playing a mix of folk-rock and heavy-rock with interestingly loud guitars. (SR)

Indescribably Delicious

Personnel:	MARK COHEN	drums, vcls	A
	JIM CONROY	vcls	A
	ART JOHNSON	gtr, vcls	A
	STEVEN SENCHIA	bs, vcls	A
	BRUCE TURNER	ld gtr, vcls	A
	(JACK BIELAN	keyb'ds	A)
	(GREG MUNFORD	ld gtr, keyb'ds, vcls	A)
	(GARY SOLOMON	sax, trumpet, vcls	A)

NB: Personnel shown in parenthesis weren't members of **Indescribably Delicious**. See main text for explanation.

ALBUM: 1 (A) INDESCRIBABLY DELICIOUS
(No Label AA-5743) 1969 R4

NB:(1) Test pressing only with blank labels, containing three tracks by **Indescribably Delicious**, with the remainder consisting of a later session including their vocalist Jim Conroy. (1) pirated as *Indescribably Delicious* (Fanny 20.08.92) 1994 and reissued "officially" on vinyl and CD (Akarma AK 046) 1999 as *Good Enough To Eat.*

45: Big Cities/
Inside Out Baby I Love You/ Brother, Where Are You 1969

Although **Indescribably Delicious** were a real band, their history and 'album' has been the subject of much speculation, with claims to be either a **Strawberry Alarm Clock** offshoot and/or to feature members of All-American label-mates **Big Brother (w/Ernie Joseph)**. The truth, however, is even stranger than fiction.

INDEX - INDEX (1967) LP.

The band formed in 1965 in Torrance, California, when Jim Conroy and Bruce Turner of garage band The Bountymen got invited to jam with another local band called Darkwaters. At some point in the jam, Jim and Bruce played with Darkwaters bassist and drummer, Mark Cohen and Steve Senchia. Jim:- "For the first time we all felt something magic and the next day quit our bands to form a new one. For a few weeks we didn't have a name, and then a friend suggested **Indescribably Delicious** and we went for it. Everyone ended up calling us the I.D. but **Indescribably Delicious** it was."

"From the start the band had an impact, our first gig was a battle of the bands which we won and our reputation grew quickly, to the point where we were soon the most popular band in our area. If there was a dance and the I.D. played it was packed. We then started to travel outside our area and usually got the same reaction. There was just something about the chemistry of the five of us together that created excitement. We couldn't even go to the local shopping malls because the girls would scream and chase us. It was our own mini-mania scene. Our manager, Ray Torrence, was just a kid down the block but one day we were approached by a guy named Gary Solomon (aka Gary Solo) who had Hollywood connections and we decided to go with him."

"He was kind of a shyster but he got us good gigs all over and made us polish up the act. We ended up being a well-oiled machine sometimes playing three different places in one night with our roadcrew going ahead of us to set up the next gig. The band performed with a light show with strobes and we put on a real show that most bands didn't have. Imagine a cross between James Brown and the Who. We played the Casey Kasem dances, traveled to Las Vegas and San Diego, opening for: **The Seeds**, **Music Machine**, **Thee Midniters**, Jimmy Reed, **Steppenwolf**, **Buffalo Springfield**, **The Turtles** and The Yardbirds. When we played in our hometown there were riots and we had to have police escorts a couple of times. At the time Bruce and I were 18, Art was 17 and Steve and Marc were 16."

"Then Gary told us we were going to record for Bill Holmes' All-American Records, the **Strawberry Alarm Clock** label. We went to Hollywood and recorded *Brother Where Are You*, *Baby I Love You*, and *The Kids Are Allright*. We were so green and naive and they didn't even let us in the mixdown session."

"Then came the 45 of *Brother, Where Are You* and *Baby I Love You*. We never even met Bill Holmes or had a contract when they started playing *Brother* on KRLA a bit. By the way, that silly noise at the end of *Brother* was not our idea. Anyway it didn't become a hit but I got to hear myself on L.A.'s biggest radio station. We continued playing and our musicianship got better, but times were a-changin quickly."

"Sometime afterwards I was asked to come up to Hollywood and sing on a demo that the lead singer of the **Strawberry Alarm Clock** and Gary Solo were making. I agreed to do it even though I didn't think the songs were very good, as I saw it as a chance to get some more recording experience. Bill Holmes had nothing to do with writing those songs, although he's credited as such on the Akarma release. Afterwards they made a small test pressing of the tunes and also put the three **I.D.** tunes on it. They gave me two of the test pressings, which I played for the guys and we all thought it was pretty funny. The tunes were bad, the playing was bad, and my singing was done in one pass, take it or leave it. I didn't really know the songs very well at all. The test pressing was jokingly called 'the Conroy' and we never listened to it again."

"About a year after we had done our recording Bruce Turner got the call to be the lead guitar player for the **Strawberry Alarm Clock** and decided to take it. At the time **The Strawberry Alarm Clock** had split in two and Bill Holmes had the lead singer with one band and the other members had another. Bruce joined the one with Bill Holmes and the lead singer which lasted about 6 months when the two factions sued each other and ended up in the courts for the next 15 years. So, that's what happened to the **Strawberry Alarm Clock** and I'm sure Bill Holmes had a lot to do with that. As for the **I.D.**, after Bruce left we broke up and that was that. It was the Fall of 1968."

So, the **Indescribably Delicious** 'album', isn't quite what quite what it's been rumoured to be over the last few years.

The two reissues feature the same tracks, although *Work Song* and *No Time To Answer* on the 'Fanny' release are titled *It's Been A Hard Hard Day* and *The World Is Ended Right Now* on the Akarma version. The music is a mixed bag, from melodic psych-pop (*Big Ben*, *Is It Love*, *The World Is Ended Right Now*) which will certainly appeal to fans of **Strawberry Alarm Clock**, through to heavy fuzz, psychy pop-rock with occasionally soulful vocals (*It's Been A Hard Hard Day*, *Take Me For One Last Ride*) and onto full-blown brassy soul-pop (Jerry Ragavoy's *Baby I Love You*).

Incidentally, Greg Munford, who was also on the "Conroy" session does get a backing vocals credit on **Big Brother Ernie Joseph**'s solo album *An All American Emperor*, and also gets writer credits on a couple of tracks. The mystery is not quite complete however, as *Brother, Where Are You* (which we now know as being by the real **Indescribably Delicious**) also crops up as the **Big Brother** 45 (All-American 5718-AA), and is the EXACT same track right down to the spacey outro...

Today, Jim Conroy is still a musician and has two recent CD releases of his own:- "I mostly play Jazz now and am still passionate about making music and hope to be for the rest of my life. Bruce and Mark are also still both musicians and we talk frequently."

As for the reissues, the band are still waiting for any kind or royalty or contract from Bill Holmes... (MW/VJ/JCy)

Index

Personnel:	JOHN FORD IV	ld gtr, ld vcls	AB
	GARY FRANCIS	bs (gtr)	AB
	JIM VALICE	drms	AB
	TOM BALLEW	bs	B

ALBUMS:	1(A)	INDEX	(DC Records) 1967	R5
	2(B)	INDEX	(DC Records) 1968	R6

NB: (1) black label. (2) red label. (1) reissued in a new sleeve (Voxx 200.023) 1984. (2) reissued on Sears (GRF 71413). (1) and (2) reissued on CD as *Anthology*, (Top Jimmy Productions 1995) 1995 together with nine previously unreleased tracks recorded in 1969.

From Grosse Pointe, Michigan, originals of their albums are extremely rare. Their first discordant acid-soaked folk album is well worth a listen. It opens with the band's own version of the **Byrds**', *Eight Miles High*, includes some interesting echo fuzztone guitar work on *Turquoise Feline*, their own arrangements of the traditional song John Riley and *You Keep Me Hanging On*, and three fuzztone instrumentals, *Shock Wave*, *Feedback* and *Israeli Blues*.

Their second album on the DC label, is musically very different to their first. They were obviously quite into the early (pre-disco) Bee Gees because it included covers of *I Can't See Nobody* and *New York Mining Disaster 1941*, as well as a rehash of **The Byrds**' classic *Eight Miles High* and Cream's *Spoonful*. This version of *Eight Miles High* and *Turquoise Feline* were also on the album issued by Voxx.

When Tom Ballew joined the band, Gary Francis switched from bass to guitar - this expanded line-up also recorded the bonus material included on the *Anthology* retrospective CD, which dates from 1969. The CD was produced and compiled by Jim Valice. (VJ/MW)

Indian Puddin' and Pipe

Personnel:	DAVE BURKE	bs	A
	PAT CRAIG	keyb'ds	A
	JEFF LABRACHE	drms	A
	KRIS LARSON	gtr, vcls	A
	STEVE MACK	ld gtr	A
	LYDIA MARENO	vcls	A

Originally from Seattle and known as **West Coast Natural Gas**, they relocated to San Francisco in 1968. It's a great pity that they did not release an album since their four tracks, *Hashish*, *Water Or Wine*, *Beyond This Place* and *Two's A Pair*, on *The 5th Annual Pipedream* album are arguably the best in that collection. They are well worth investigating and if you can't obtain a copy of that album, there are plenty of compilations featuring one or more of the tracks. They do not appear to have released any 45s, although they did make other recordings, including a 45 as **West Coast Natural Gas**.

Indian Puddin' and Pipe were one of several bands managed by Matthew Katz, along with **Moby Grape**, **It's A Beautiful Day**, **Tripsichord (Music Box)** and others. Due to the nature of his contracts with these bands, he was able to operate different versions of each, and it was therefore possible for three different audiences to watch "Moby Grape" playing live in Los Angeles, San Francisco and Seattle on the same night if he so wished!

The band that recorded the tracks on the *Fifth Pipedream - San Francisco Sound Vol. 1* various artists compilation, weren't in fact the "original" **Indian Puddin' and Pipe**, but today they are thought of as the definitive band due to the above album. In fact, whilst they were still known as **West Coast Natural Gas**, they played a gig in Seattle with the "original" **Indian Puddin' and Pipe** before the original band split-up with Katz and became **Easy Chair**. Reputedly, there was a third L.A. version of the band, put together by Katz to play gigs down South.

After their demise, Lydia Mareno went on to play with **Stoneground** and Craig and Mack later played with Pipe. Jeff LaBrache had earlier played with **The City Limits** and **Rocky and His Friends**.

Compilation appearances have included: *Two's A Pair*, *Beyond This Place*, *Hashish* and *Water Or Wine* on *Fifth Pipedream* (LP & CD); *Hashish* on *The Magic Cube* (Flexi & CD), *Acid Dreams - The Complete 3 LP Set* (3-LP), *Acid Dreams Testament* (CD); and *Water Or Wine* on *Gathering Of The Tribe* (LP). Recently Matthew Katz's *Then And Now, Vol. 1* (CD) has compiled *Planetary Road* and *Vol. 2* includes *Shadowlarks*. (VJ/CF/JLb)

INDIAN PUDDIN' & PIPE gig poster.

The Individuals

45:	I Really Do/I Want Love	(Raven 2018)	196?

This is the only known 45 by this Danville, Virginia band.

Compilation appearances have included: *I Want Love* on *Teenage Shutdown, Vol. 11* (LP & CD); and *I Really Do* on *Garage Punk Unknowns, Vol. 5* (LP). (VJ)

The Individuals

Personnel:	ANDY CAHN	organ	A
	RENO FRANZE	vcls	A
	LARRY KRAMER	gtr	A
	SANDY REINER	drums	A

EP: 1	Sky Is Falling/Satisfaction/She's Gone Away/ Monkey On My Back	(Moxie M-1028)	198?

The Moxie EP, subtitled *Johnny Farfisa's Greatest Hits*, comprises four tracks from 1965 by this NY combo. Some or all of these were apparently recorded in New Rochelle for an unreleased album. Musically we're talking frat-garage with a solid sound and reedy keyboards. Highlights are the moody and introverted *Monkey...* with its wailing harmonica and *She's Gone Away*, a dynamic fuzzy punk instrumental.

The band later evolved into The Euphorian River, who are reported to have had a very heavy organ and guitar-laden sound.

Compilation appearances include: *She's Gone Away* (previously unreleased 1966 version) on *Psychedelic Crown Jewels Vol. 2 - '60s Garage Unknowns* (Dble LP & CD); and *Monkey On My Back* on *Ya Gotta Have Moxie, Vol. 2* (Dble CD). (MW/RM)

Industrial Image

45:	Living In The Middle Ages/ Put My Mind At Ease	(Epic 5-10096)	1966

Folk-rockers from Texas with a lone stab at stardom. (MW)

The Inexpensive Handmade Look

45:	Ice Cream Man/What Good Is Up	(Brunswick 55334)	1967

This seems to have been a one-off venture on Brunswick. You'll also find the flip, a decent psych/garage number built around a repetitive riff, on the *Psychedelic Disaster Whirl* (LP), *30 Seconds Before The Calico Wall* (CD), *The Psychedelic Experience, Vol. 1* (LP) and *Psychedelic Experience* (CD) compilations. (VJ)

Infinite Companions

See **Glenn Saiger** entry.

The Infinite Pyramid

From the vaults of Rembrandt Records, *On A Windowsill*, taken from an 1968 unreleased acetate, has been included on the *Chicago Garage Band Greats* (LP), *The Cicadelic 60's, Vol. 3* (CD) and *Green Crystal Ties Vol. 3* (CD) compilations.

Infinite Staircase

Personnel incl:	BOBBY FLORES	bs	A

45:	Margaret/Long Hair	(Black Sheep BS-1337)	1967

A flower-power outfit from San Antonio in Texas, The 'A' side of their sole vinyl offering can also be heard on *Flashback, Vol. 4* (LP), *Texas Flashbacks, Vol. 4* (LP & CD) and *Texas Flashback (The Best Of)* (CD).

The line-up included Bobby Flores, who was formerly in **The Five Canadians**. (VJ/MW)

Influence

Personnel:	JACK GEISINGER	bs, gtr	AB
	ANDREW KEILER	vcls	AB
	LOUIS MCKELVEY	gtr	AB
	DAVE WYNNE	drms	AB
	BOB O ISLAND (BOB PARKIN)	keyb'ds	B
	WALTER ROSSI	gtr	B

ALBUM:	1(B)	INFLUENCE	(ABC ABCS 630)	1968 SC

Formed as a quartet in late 1966, this act have an interesting and almost global pedigree. English-born singer Andrew Keiler moved firstly to South Africa in 1964 and together with Irish-born guitarist Louis Campbell McKelvey played in the Johannesburg R&B outfit The Upsetters. McKelvey left this act in late '65, to join The A-Cads, although he was too late to appear on their album, despite being pictured on the sleeve. Andrew Keiler too left The Upsetters, recording a solo album in late 1965 before moving to Montreal in late 1966, along with McKelvey and fellow A-cad, Hank Squires.

In Canada, Squires moved into production working with The Haunted, amongst others, and McKelvey briefly played with Les Sinners and Our Generation before reuniting with Keiler in **Influence**. Czech-born bass player Geisinger came in from the Soul Mates and English-born drummer Dave Wynne was recruited from The Haunted.

To complete the line-up, two other former Soul Mates, Rossi and Island joined after playing on a Wilson Pickett tour in June 1967. The band then relocated to the US...

David Wynne recalls:- "We played Montreal in the Spring of '67, then went to Toronto Village and played one of the clubs there until September when we went to New York and cut the album with ABC. McKelvey was involved in production. Afterwards we were offered another deal by Columbia which was turned down by the band, and at that point I left and went back to Canada and school. You were right about the album, but it may have had a little impact. Our publicist at ABC was dating Peter Townshend and reportedly he liked the opera idea. As musicians and artists the **Influence** really outclassed anything else around - Walter Rossi as I said was a superb guitarist. You should have heard us live..."

"The entire band except me had done hard time with mature audiences. Not many Canadian musicians had had the experience of recording in or touring the U.S. as Wally, Jack and Bobo had with Wilson Pickett. They were also all seasoned musicians. (I heard, from Buddy Miles I think, that **Steve Cropper** had said he thought Wally the better guitarist). It was also innovative and had confidence that it was cutting edge and could compete on any stage. Toronto Village in Summer 1967 was great - lots of talent and a real buzz. The imbalance in the band was that we had two front men, Bobo and Andy, and while it was never pushed I think after I left that it became an issue - I bridged both sides and may have helped keep some of it together. At the time there seemed enough room for everyone, but it was really an amalgam of two bands in one - the Wally, Jack, Bobo and Louis and Andy. Yum Yum who replaced me was definitely associated with the former group. I had started the band with Louis, but felt much more at home musically with Wally, Jack and Bobo. I was not a fan of British drummers (Baker, Moon) but American black funk and jazz drummers. I think I mentioned the time at the Barrel, where watching and talking to Rashid Ali (Coltrane's second drummer with Elvin Jones) and hearing new wave drumming was a priceless clinic..."

Their album makes it easy to understand why they chose their name, as it is more or less a hodgepodge of styles without much consistency. Many satirical elements betray the strong influence of **Zappa**, on whom they clearly lean too heavily. Nevertheless their love of discordant riffs and 'wrong' modulations works brilliantly on at least two tracks: *We Are Here*, a sour masterpiece on lost love and *Natural Impulse*. Lyrically **Zappa** is omnipresent as becomes hearable in the choice of admittedly transitional subject-matter such as sodomy (on *County Fair*) and the longing of the gentry to mingle with the peasants (on *Sir Archibald*). Parodies on The Marcels, Little Richard and the hippie-movement in general sound dated, although they probably were modern in 1968. Worth trying, but don't pay too much.

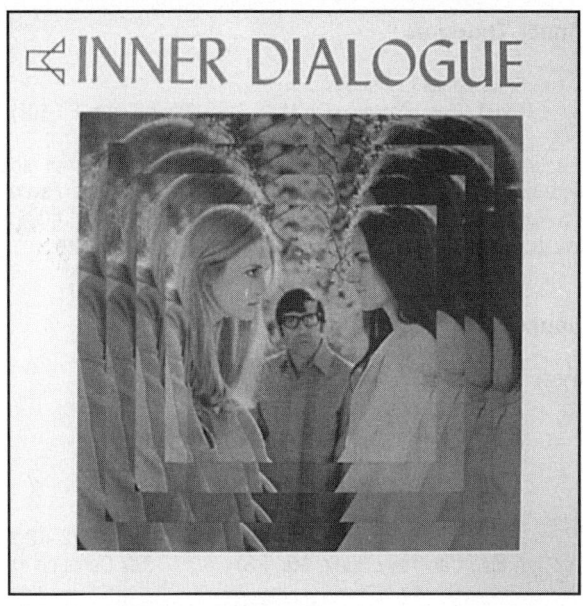

INNER DIALOGUE - Inner Dialogue LP.

After **Influence** broke up, McKelvey and Geisinger played in the Canadian band Milkwood. Geisinger later left Milkwood for Luke and The Apostles. Rossi meanwhile, played with **The Buddy Miles Express** briefly before joining Geisinger in Luke and The Apostles.

Walter Rossi later played with Charlee, Moonquake and Bombers. Jack Geisinger also later played with Moonquake, Rockers and Crescent Street Singers. Bob Parkin committed suicide in 1970.

Walter Rossi is also rumoured to have played on an album by **Thee Muffins** in 1966. (NW/MK/VJ/TLw)

The Ingredients

45:	Hey Who/Please Don't Leave Me	(Toddlin Town 3238) 1966

The work of a late sixties Chicago act. You'll also find the flip on *Psychedelic Unknowns, Vol. 6* (LP & CD), *Victims Of Circumstances, Vol. 1* (LP) and *Victims Of Circumstance, Vol. 2* (CD). (VJ)

The Initial Shock

Personnel incl:	MOJO COLLINS	organ	A
	GEORGE CROWE		A
	GEORGE WALLACE	ld gtr	A

45s:	You Been A Long Time Comin'/I Once Asked	(BFD 2022) 1967
	Mind Disaster/It's Not Easy	(BFD 0036) 1966

This five-piece formed out of the remnants of two earlier Missoula, Montana bands The Chosen Few and Mojo's Mark IV. They cut their debut 45 in Butte, Montana in 1966 and then relocated to San Francisco in 1967, where they played at the legendary Avalon Ballroom among other places. *Mind Disaster*, was quite an appealing psychedelic pop single and can now be heard on *Nuggets, Vol. 8* (LP). It also got a further airing, along with a post **Initial Shock** recording featuring Wallace and Crowe, *You Been A Long Time Comin'*, on the *California Halloween* album.

Wallace and Crowe later played together in Yellowstone, and also The Invaders, who issued one 45 *Long Time Comin'/Could You Would You* on an indie label in 1977. Another Invaders track was featured on the Bomp compilation *Waves*, and the pair also backed Gerrie Roslie on the *Sinderella* project for Bomp under **The Sonics** moniker. They also later did demo an album for Randy Bachman that went unissued. (VJ)

The In-Keepers

45s:	Daily News / Everytime	(RCA Victor 47-9713) 1968
	That Was Just His Thing/ The Cobweb Threads Of Autumn	(RCA 74-0229) 1969

Thought to be from New England, their first coupling (written by S. Burnett and produced by Pierre G. Maheu) is good rousing acoustic-harmony-folk-pop backed by hush-voiced vaudeville-style pap, sadly a-la-mode at that time. The second 45 fatures a doomy, quasi-religious 'A' side with whipping fuzztone and a sombre multi - voiced chorus. The 'B' side is totally different: strong melodic baroque pop with harpsichord, a middle eight with string quartet and elaborate and tricky contrapuntal harmonies. Excellent.

Compilation appearances include *That Was Just His Thing* on *A Fistful Of Fuzz* (CD). (MK/MW)

The Inmates

Personnel:	AL ASHETTINO	bs	A
	RON FLANNERY	gtr	A
	BOBBY NOLAN	ld vcls	A
	GORDON RHOADES	vcls	A
	SAMMY SALVO	drms	A

45:	Local Town Drunk/You Tell Lies	(Columbia 44032) 1967

From Long Branch in New Jersey, this outfit gained a contract with Columbia by virtue of winning a *Battle Of The Bands* competition in 1966. Sadly, when *Local Town Drunk*, (a novelty song) flopped, they were dropped from the label.

In addition to the 45, the band also recorded some other tracks that were unreleased at the time. Of these *More Than I Have*, is the highlight featuring some good guitar work and drumming.

Compilation appearances have included: *More Than I Have* and *Fakirs And Thieves* on *Pebbles Box* (5-LP) and *Trash Box*; *More Than I Have* on *Pebbles, Vol. 22* (LP) and *The Essential Pebbles Collection, Vol. 2* (Dble CD); and *You Tell Lies* on *Garage Punk Unknowns, Vol. 7* (LP). (VJ/MW)

Inn Crowd

Personnel incl:	HAL ELLIS	gtr	A

45s:	You Must Believe Me / Sun Arise	(Montel-Michelle MX-971) 1966
	Run Clarence Run / Baby You're So Fine	(Montel-Michelle 982) 1966
α	Go Away / Keep Your Hands Off My Baby	(Montel-Michelle MX 986) 1967

NB: α as Ye Olde Inn Crowd.

This particular **Inn Crowd** from Baton Rouge, Louisiana and latterly known as Ye Olde Inn Crowd, had a penchant for Invasion flavoured folk-rockers with cool harmonies. Their debut couples a lightweight cover of Curtis Mayfield's *You Must Believe Me* with a yearning Searchers-inspired ballad. The catchy uptempo folk-punker *Go Away* is probably their finest moment. (MW/AB)

Inner Dialogue

Personnel:	GENE DINOVI	dulcitron, piano	A
	LYNN DOLIN	vcls	A
	JIM GORDON	drms	A
	ROBERT LANNING	drms	A
	JERRY SCHEFF	bs	A
	B.J.WARD	vcls	A
	BARRY ZWEIG	gtr	A

ALBUM:	1	INNER DIALOGUE	(Ranwood R-8050) 1969 SC

NB: (1) reissued on CD and LP.

45s:	Little Children/Yesterday, The Dog	(Ranwood 851) 1968
	Friend/Loving	(Ranwood 878) 1969
	Too Much For Me/Cry, Baby, Cry	(Ranwood 883) 1969

Recorded in Hollywood, a pop-psych trio (two girls, one man) with songs like *Get Aboard A Dream*, *In Sequence*, *I Go To Life*, *The Touch*, *Within You* and *Inner Dialogue*. Some dealers describe it as mellow dreamy psych, but it's mainly pop with female vocals in the **Free Design** style, with lots of string arrangements as well.

Ranwood also released 45s by **Sounds of Sunshine**. (SR)

Inner Light

Personnel incl:	LARRY JOHNSON	vcls	A
	DICK STEFFES	vcls	A

45:	This Girl / Temptation	(Century 33685) 1969

Harvested in Page, North Dakota, *Temptation* is late'n'great sixties fuzz-psych and is featured on *A Lethal Dose Of Hard Psych*. The liners note that the 'A' side is "a slow insipid ballad with whiney sax". (ELn/MW)

Inner Lite

45s:	Hold On To Him/Tabula Rasa	(ssExx 666) c1970
	All The Way In/If I Only Know	(ssExx 667) 1970

A Marshalltown, Iowa, five-piece who released two 45s on ssExx and featured on the *Crown Production Sampler* - a booking agency record from 1967. They should **not** be confused with the **Innerlite** featured on the *Strangers From A Strange Land* (LP) compilation, who were in fact from Bombay, India... The Indian act were in fact featured on *Simla Beat '70*, the first of two rare compilations funded by the Simla Tobacco Company in '70 and '71. Subsequently the better tracks were combined onto *Strangers From A Strange Land* (LP) and mistakenly sold by dealers as being of U.S. origin.

Tabula Rasa and *All The Way In*, composed by Dave Robinette and Don Sullivan, are heavy freaky guitar instrumentals - check 'em out on *Buzz Buzz Buzzzzzz Vol. 2* (CD) and *Buzz Buzz Buzzzzzz Vol. 1* (CD) respectively. *Hold On To Him* is a cover of a Ritchie Cordell/ Sal Trimachi pop song and is dispensable. (MW)

Inner Scene

This Texas outfit have a previously unreleased cut *Communication Breakdown*, a clumsy version of The Led Zeppelin classic, included on *Epitaph For A Legend* (Dble LP). (VJ)

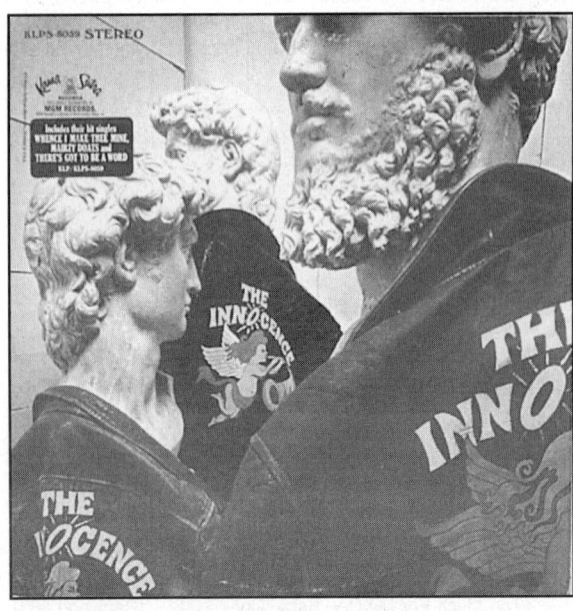

THE INNOCENCE - The Innocence LP.

The Inner Thoughts

45:	Smokestack Lightning /	
	1,000 Miles (Cheating On Me)	(Paris Tower PT-105) 1967

An obscure quintet from Clearwater, Florida. Promos of their sole 45 included inserts, declaring they'd be around for a long time. *Psychedelic States: Florida, Vol. 3* (CD) features their original composition *1,000 Miles*, a heavy punker with a great riff and some glorious fuzz. (MW/MM)

The Innkeepers

Personnel:	JIM ASPAAS	ld gtr	A
	RICH BALOGH	bs	A
	ERNIE CANTIBEROS	keyb'ds	A
	DON ROUSSIN	ld vcls	A
	RON ROUSSIN	gtr, backing vcls	A

45s:	?/?	(2 + 2) 196?
	A Man Can Tell / Hurtin' Me (PS)	(Six Cents no #) 1968

A quintet from Gardena, California who put out a brace of rarely seen 45s - details of the first remain shrouded in mist. Locomotive keyboard-led pop with keen harmonies and a pealing guitar solo, *A Man Can Tell* reappears on *Fuzz, Flaykes And Shakes, Vol. 3* (LP & CD) which reveals the personnel and instrumentation above... except for the drummer. (MW/TSz/LJ)

Innocence

Personnel:	PETER ANDERS	vcls, gtr	A
	VINNIE PONCIA	vcls, gtr	A

ALBUM:	1(A)	THE INNOCENCE	(Kama Sutra KLP-8059) 1968 -

EP:	1	Mairzy Doats/Lifetime Lovin You/There's Got To Be A Word/	
		I Don't Wanna Be Around You	(Kama Sutra 617 107) 1968

NB: (1) French release with picture sleeve.

This is in fact a new name for **The Tradewinds**, Peter Anders (Andreoli) and Vinnie Poncia. Another attempt by Kama Sutra to develop their "good time music" image together with **Sopwith Camel** and **The Lovin Spoonful**. (Indeed, **The Innocence** covers their *Do You Believe In Magic?*).

Several of the songs on the album were written by Don Ciccone of **The Critters**. (SR)

Innovation

45s:	α	This Ain't Real/Things Ain't The Same	(Ascot 2219) 1966
		Heartaches And Headaches/	
		I Can Make It Without You	(RCA Victor 47-9318) 1967
		Your Time's Gonna Come/	
		Things Ain't The Same	(Amy A-11, 032) 1968

NB: α released as In-Ovations.

Heartaches And Headaches can also be heard on *Victims Of Circumstances, Vol. 1* (LP). Brash pop-beat with a cheesed-off attitude towards the fairer sex, as you might guess from the title. *I Can Make It Without You*, a powerful DC5-type stomper with similar sentiments, can also be heard on *Lost Generation, Vol. 1* (LP). *Your Time's...* is fratty upbeat fuzz-pop but lacking the bite of its predecessors and *Things Ain't The Same* certainly ain't, being a comparatively toothless pedestrian effort.

Their stomping ground was the Elizabeth/Irvington area of New Jersey. (MW/MM)

The Innsmen

45:	Things Are Different Now/I Don't Know	(Wheel's 4 3611) 1966

From Michigan.

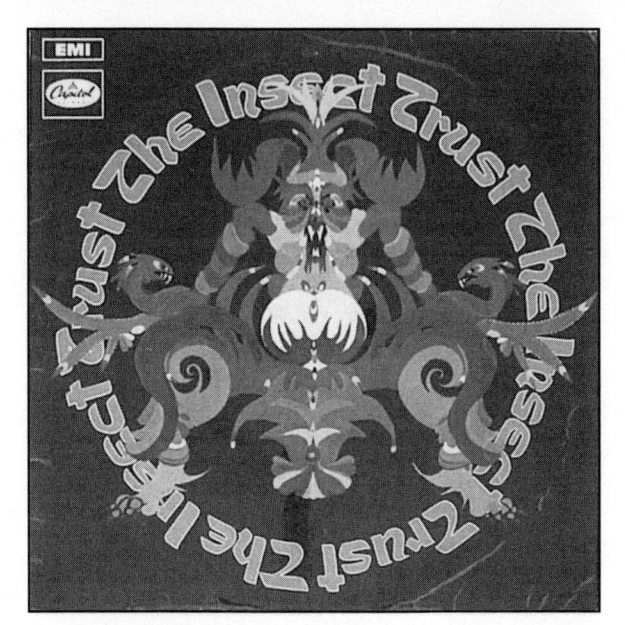

THE INSECT TRUST - The Insect Trust LP.

Compilation appearances have included: *I Don't Know* on *The Night Is So Dark* (LP); *Things Are Different Now* on *The Cicadelic 60's, Vol. 2* (LP) and *I Was A Teenage Caveman* (LP); and both *I Don't Know* and *Things Are Different Now* on *The Cicadelic 60's, Vol. 3* (LP), *The Cicadelic 60's, Vol. 1* (CD), *Green Crystal Ties, Vol. 8* (CD) and *The History Of Michigan Garage Bands In The 60's* (3-CD). (VJ/MW)

The Insane

45:	I Can't Prove It/	
	Someone Like You	(Allen Association 201,347/8) 1967

The band hailed from Plymouth, Connecticut. *I Can't Prove It* is an undistinguished garage punker.

Compilation appearances have included: *Someone Like You* on *New England Teen Scene* (CD) and *New England Teen Scene, Vol. 2* (LP); and *I Can't Prove It* on *New England Teen Scene, Vol. 3* (LP). (VJ/MW)

The In-Sect

ALBUM:	1 INTRODUCING THE IN-SECT DIRECT FROM ENGLAND	
		(RCA Camden 909) 1965 SC

A British Invasion album by a fake "English group" in denim shirts, with covers of the Beatles (*Ticket To Ride*, *Yes It Is*) and rock pop songs (*Can't You Hear My Heartbeat*, *Do The Freddie*, *You Were Made For Me*). (SR)

The Insects

45s:	She's A Pest / Girl That Sits There	(Earthy 101) 1966
	The L&H Song / Then You Came My Way	(Earthy) 1966/7
	Then You Came My Way /	
	Girl That Sits There	(Highland 1185) 1967

An obscure L.A. outfit who emerged from the Fontana and Pomona districts. Their debut featured the punker *She's A Pest*, compiled on *Teenage Shutdown, Vol. 15* (LP & CD). For their final 45 they repolished the 'B' sides from the earlier releases; it's the later version of *Girl That Sits There* that was chosen for *Fuzz, Flaykes And Shakes, Vol. 5* (LP & CD). (MW)

The Insect Trust

Personnel:	BILL BARTH	elec/acoustic gtrs, perc	A
	LUKE FAUST	banjo, perc, vcls	A
	NANCY JEFFRIES	vcls, perc	A
	TREVOR KOEHLER	bar sax, bs, thumb piano	A
	BOB PALMER	altosax, clarinet, perc, recorders	A

ALBUMS:	1(A)	THE INSECT TRUST	(Capitol SKA 01 09) 1968 R1
	2(A)	HOBOKEN SATURDAY NIGHT	(Atco SD 33-313) 1970 SC

NB: (1) has been reissued on vinyl. (1) also reissued on CD (Ascension ANCD 031) 2001.

45s:	Miss Fun City /	
	Special Rider Blues (Short Version)	(Capitol P-2386) 196?
	Been Here And Gone So Soon /	
	World War 1 Song	(Capitol P-2496) 1968
	Reciprocity/Reincarnations	(Atco 6764) 1969

The Insect Trust were an interesting group whose sound was based around the vocals of Nancy Jeffries. Jeffries and Barth had earlier played with Peter Stampfel (see **Holy Modal Rounders**) in an outfit called The Swamp Lillies.

The Insect Trust took their name from a newspaper called The Insect Trust Times, founded by Bill Levy, the original editor of International Times in England.

Their debut album was an amalgam of various strands of country music and most of the material was written by the band. They utilised a wide range of woodwind and stringed instruments. Their style was varied, ranging from the bluesy *Special Rider Blues* through the string instrumental *Foggy Bridge Riverfly*, to the harmonious *Been Here And Gone So Soon* and *Going Home*. Also of interest is the unusual instrumentation of another track *Mountain Song*.

In 1970, the band emerged on a different label, with their follow-up *Hoboken Saturday Night*. This continued their experimentation and included the unusual, brassy *Somedays*, successful ballads like *Our Sister The Sun* and *The Eyes Of A New York Woman*, the big band sound of *Reciprocity*, strange woodwind accompaniment of *Now Then Sweet Man*, strange attempts to merge stringed and woodwind backing in *Glade Song* and ends with a brassy instrumental jam, *Ducks*. Guests on the album include the well-known jazz musicians Elvin Jones, Bernard Purdie and Hugh McCracken.

The previous year, Trevor Koehler had also played on a couple of tracks on **Octopus**' sole album.

After the demise of **The Insect Trust**, Bob Palmer became a journalist. Sadly, Trevor Koehler later committed suicide.

Compilation appearances include *Miss Fun City* on *Rock A Delics* (LP). (VJ/CW/NK)

THE INSECT TRUST - Hoboken Saturday Night LP.

The In-Sex

45s: Space Man/Penitentiary Planet Blues (Hammer 3001) c1969
Alligator Wine/Action in The Streets (Hammer 3002) c1969

Late sixties psychy rock-soul from Philadelphia by an outfit made up of ex-**Down Children** members. *Alligator Wine*, the Leiber/Stoller track, which was originally recorded by Screaming Jay Hawkins, is done in a **Steppenwolf** style.

Compilation appearances include *Alligator Wine* on *Sixties Rebellion, Vol. 15* (LP & CD). (MW)

Inside Experience

45: Tales Of Brave Ulysses / Be On My Way (CEI no #) 1969

A Lakeside, Ohio, outfit covering Cream. Highly-rated by those lucky enough to have heard it.

The Inside Out

ALBUM: 1 BRINGING IT ALL BACK (Fredlo 6834) 1968 R2

A rare garage-punk album from Iowa. (VJ)

The Instincts

ALBUM: 1 THE LOVING SANDWICH (Private Pressing) c1967 R2
NB: (1) split album with one side by The Instincts, the other by Maiyeros.

A rare Connecticut prep school project housed in a purple and green psychedelic cover. On their side, **The Instincts** played some good garage tracks, notably *No No No*, while The Maiyeros recorded some strange songs on their side. (SR)

The Insurgents

Personnel:
RICH DYMALSKY — bs — A
BOB MELLICH — drms — A
JOE ORLANDO — gtr — A
RON ROBINSON — vcls — A
PAUL TIFT — ld gtr — A

45: Peppermint Man/Summertime (Zar 117/8) 1965

From Sacramento, California. Their spooky version of *Summertime* can be found on *The Sound Of Young Sacramento* (CD), Big Beat's collection of local bands from California's capital city.

Internal Canitery Sin

This Circleville, Ohio band didn't release any 45s in their own right but their cover of Hendrix' *Purple Haze* made it onto the *Hillside '67* (7" EP). The other bands featured were **The Gears**, Emeralds and Dedicated Followers.

Retrospective compilation appearances have included *Purple Haze* on *Relics, Vol's 1 & 2* (CD) and *Relics, Vol. 2* (LP). (MW/GGI)

International Bell

45: As Much As I Love You/
Lo Mucho Que Te Quiero (Mala 12030) 1968

Produced by Dale Hawkins (**Mouse and The Traps, Five Americans**), a chicano beat-pop 45 with organ. The flip is probably the same song with Spanish lyrics. (SR)

THE INSTINCTS - The Loving Sandwich (Split) LP.

International Brick

Personnel:
RANDY BENNETT — bs — A
DICK GERBER — gtr — A
CARL PETERS — drms — A
ANTHONY "TINY TONY" SMITH — vcls — A

45: You Should Be So High/Flower Children (Camelot 137) 196?

Formally members of **Tiny Tony and The Statics**, they formed **International Brick** when **Merrilee** and Neil Rush departed. They were also called The Bricks for a short time and operated out of Seattle in Washington State, opening for the likes of **The Doors** and **The Byrds**. Their nice, mellow slice of flower-power pop can be heard on *Highs In The Mid-Sixties, Vol. 16* (LP). (VJ)

The International Submarine Band

Personnel incl:
IAN DUNLOP — bs — A
MICKEY GAUVIN — drms — A
GRAHAM "GRAM" PARSONS — vcls — AB
JOHN NUESE — ld gtr — AB
BOB BUCHANAN — gtr — B
JON CORNEAL — drms — B
CHRIS ETHRIDGE — bs — B
(EARL "LES" BALL — piano — B)
(J.D.MANESS aka
GOOD OLE JAY DEE — steel gtr — B

ALBUM: 1(B) SAFE AT HOME (LHI 12001) 1968 R1
NB: (1) several counterfeit editions exist. Also reissued on vinyl by Shiloh with a new cover art, on CD (Magnum CDSD 071) 1991 and vinyl (Sundazed LP 5112) 2002.

45s: The Russians are Coming/
Truck Driving Man (PS) (Ascot 2218) 1966
One Day Week/Sum Up Broke (Columbia 43935) 1966
Blue Eyes/Luxury Liner (LHI 1205) 1968
I Must Be Somebody Else/Miller's Cave (LHI 1217) 1968

One of the very first groups to try to combine rock with country music, the **International Submarine Band** is now mostly remembered for being Gram Parsons' first significant group. He, of course, would later join **The Byrds** and form the Flying Burritos Brothers.

Formed in 1967, after two flop singles, the group (Parsons, Dunlop, Gauvin and Nuese) moved from New York to California responding to an offer of the actor Brandon deWilde to get them some film work. The **ISB** did appear in the film "The Trip" with Peter Fonda but their music was erased and replaced by the **Electric Flag**. The group also recorded an entire album of Beatlesque material at Los Angeles Gold Star Studios but the tapes, given to deWilde for safekeeping, disappeared in the "rock's black hole"!

In late Spring 1967, after a discussion over the direction the band was taking, Dunlop and Gauvin left the group and moved to Boston. Ian Dunlop would later record some solo records for small labels. Having decided to play with a country music sound, Parsons recruited a new drummer, Jon Corneal and, together with Nuese and a temporary bassist, auditioned successfully for Lee Hazelwood's label, LHI. Produced by **Suzi Jane Hokum**, the sessions began with the help of a new bassist, Chris Ethridge and a new singer/guitarist, Bob Buchanan. Two well-known country musicians, Maness and Ball, also helped the group. The album was finished in Christmas 1967 but in February 1968, Parsons joined **The Byrds**. The album, *Safe At Home*, was only released in late Spring 1968.

Without a real group to promote it (the remaining members tried to find a suitable substitute to Parsons, but were unable to!) and country-rock not being the hottest thing in 1968, the album logically flopped. It's however an interesting album if you are a fan of early country-rock, with good vocals and a fresh sound displayed on several Parsons compositions and covers of songs by Merle Haggard, Johnny Cash and Big Boy Crudup.

After the **Byrds**, the Flying Burritos Brothers and two solo albums, Gram Parsons died in 1973. His body was stolen by his manager Philip Kaufman and burned in the desert near the Joshua Tree... He is now revered as a kind of "country-rock icon" by many rock and country musicians. Among the other **ISB** members, John Corneal would also play for a short period with **The Byrds** and not surprisingly would team up again with Parsons and Ethridge in the Flying Burritos Brothers. He also drummed with Dillard and Clark and on the first album by **Warren Zevon**. Chris Ethridge went on to form **L.A. Getaway** and became a successful studio musician. Bob Buchanan and John Nuese apparently stopped recording.

The Magnum CD features a good history of the group written by Sid Griffin, that we've used for this entry. (SR)

Interns

45: I've Got Something To Say/The Trip (PS) (Eastwood 1213) 1967

This garage quintet formed in July 1965 in Akron, Ohio. The 'A' side is a typical girl put-down song with some effective farfisa organ, whilst the flip is a fuzzy instrumental. The 45 came with a picture sleeve and had two pressings - the first being mismastered with the effect that the drums and backing vocals are outta sync!

I've Got Something To Say has also resurfaced on *Back From The Grave, Vol. 3* (LP). (VJ/GGl/MW)

The Interns

| 45s: | Sally Met Molly/Have Mercy | (Paradise 1019) 1966 |
| | Don't Make Me No Mind/Life With You | (Paradise 1023) 1966 |

From Houston, Texas. According to Roy Ames, this lot were a bunch of medical students who used to like to play R&B covers and other favourites at clubs and frat parties.

Sally Met Molly can also be found on *Acid Visions - The Complete Collection Vol. 1* (3-CD).

The Interpreters

45: I Get The Message/Stop That Man (Gemini 100) 1965

A New England all-girl band. The vocals are very upfront on *I Get The Message* and there's some nice surfish guitar. You'll find it on *Girls In The Garage, Vol. 1* (LP). (VJ)

The Intruders

Personnel:	SHEP COOKE	bs	A
	LARRY COX	vcls	A
	TERRY LEE	gtr	A
	PETE SCHUYLER	drms	A
	TOM WALKER	gtr, vcls	A

45s:	Every Time It's You/Let Me Stay	(Gallant No) 1963
	Then I'd Know/My Name	(Moxie MRC 101) 196?
	Now She's Gone/Why Me?	(Moxie MRC 104) 1964

Started out playing surf instruments around Tucson, Arizona in 1963 but when The Beatles became popular they added Larry Cox on vocals. In 1964 they won a recording session having won a local Battle of the Bands competition. What they expected to be a real studio turned out to be the guy's living room! The Gallant 45 was the result and their manager Dan Peters issued two others on his Moxie label. In late 1964/early 1965, the success of a black Detroit outfit called The Intruders led them to change their name to **Quinstrells**. Later still they became The Beloved Ones and **The Dearly Beloved**. *The Dearly Beloved* (Voxx 200.018) 1984 compilation includes *Every Time It's You* and *Why Me?* which featured some ripping fuzz guitar.

Compilation appearances have included *Every Time It's You* and *Why Me?* on *Let's Talk About Girls!* (CD). (VJ)

The Intruders

Personnel:	ROD CROSBY	gtr, vcls	A
	PAUL DILLON	ld gtr, vcls	A
	LEFTY EISCH	drms	A
	PAUL WEST	bs, vcls, trumpet	A

This band from El Paso, Texas had four cuts:- *Our Love So Warm*, *Put Yourself In My Place*, *Coming On Home* and *Patrician Melody*, all from around 1969, on the compilation *I Love You Gorgo*. The compilation had a limited vinyl repress of 300 in 1997. (VJ)

The Intruders

45: I'll Go On/That's The Way (Marlo 1545) 196?

The band were a six-piece from the St. Louis area of Missouri and the Marlo label was a subsidiary of Cinema. *I'll Go On* featured some effective echoed guitar work and has resurfaced on *Monsters Of The Midwest, Vol. 4* (LP), which informs us of a second 45 with a picture sleeve on the Cinema label but gives no details of it.

Other compilation appearances include: *I'll Go On* on *Teenage Shutdown, Vol. 6* (LP & CD). (VJ)

The Intruders

Personnel:	BOB 'BUB' EVANS	gtr	A
	JEFF HALLOWS	drms	A
	LARRY LEMONS	bs	A

I LOVE YOU GORGO (Comp LP) including The Intruders.

| BILL MOBUS | ld gtr | A |
| DOUG OAKLEY | vcls | A |

| 45: | Now That You Know Me/She's Mine (PS) | (It 2312) 1966 |

From Pittsfield, Illinois, this 45 has been reissued on yellow/gold wax with a picture sleeve and detailed insert by Doug Oakley on Craig Moore's MCCM label (MCCM 9101). The 'A' side is a folk-punk ballad. The flip has some catchy fuzz guitar.

Compilation appearances have included: *She's Mine* on *Monsters Of The Midwest, Vol. 3* (LP); and *Now That You Know* on *Turds On A Bum Ride, Vol. 5* (CD) and *Teenage Shutdown, Vol. 5* (LP & CD). (VJ)

Intruders 5

| Personnel incl: | CHRIS WILLIAMS | vcls | A |

| 45: | Ain't Coming Back/I Don't Know You | (Grog 2201) 1966 |

Hailed from Greeneville, Tennessee and judging from *Ain't Coming Back*, which was originally put out on their own label, they were a typical snarling punk band - snotty vocals, organ backing and girl put-down lyrics. As a bonus, there's a bit of tasty guitar work too.

Ain't Coming Back can also be heard on *Back From The Grave, Vol. 3* (LP). (VJ)

The Invaders

Personnel:	STEVE DRUMHELLER	vcls, drms	A
	AIVARS OSVALDS	organ	A
	BOBBY POLLOCK	sax, vcls	A
	STEVE POLLOCK	gtr, vcls	A
	HAROLD ROBERTS	trumpets, drms, hrmnca	A

| ALBUM: | 1(A) | ON THE RIGHT TRACK | (Justice 157) 1967 R3 |

NB: (1) reissued on CD (Collectables COL-CD-0608) 1995.

A welcome reissue of this mythical album that most of us could never possibly afford on the rare occasion that an original copy might surface - a total eclipse is a more frequent event. Inevitably therefore, there is bound to be some disappointment, confirmed by the original liner notes describing their style accurately as 'rock and soul'. Hailing from Charlottesville, to the Northwest of Richmond, Virginia, this outfit presents ten competent covers plus two originals that encompass frat-rock, brassy soul sounds, soppy ballads and some decent garage nuggets. One of those originals, *Have You Ever*, can also be sampled on *Project Blue, Vol. 3* (LP). (MW)

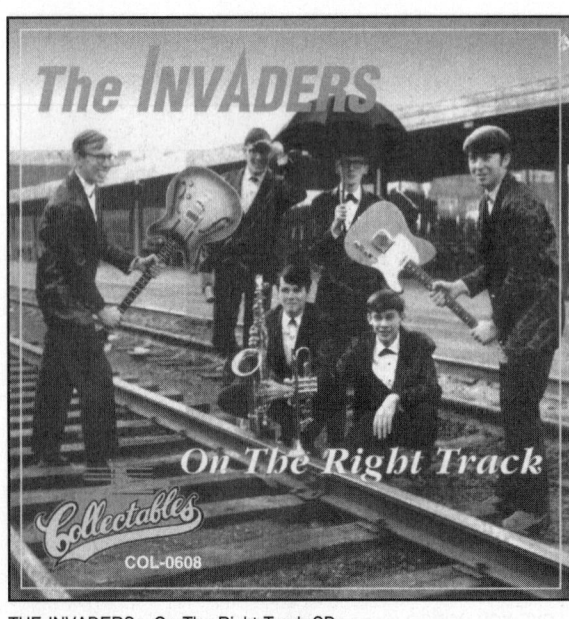

THE INVADERS - On The Right Track CD.

The Invaders

Personnel:	DAVE DAVIS	ld gtr	A
	JEFF GLASS	sax, horn	A
	DONNIE GOODSON	drms	A
	BOB HAAS	keyb'ds	A
	STEVE SEITZ	bs	A

| 45: | She's A Tiger / Honda Come Back | (Suncrest 3344) 1965 |

NB: the band is credited on the 45 label as **The Invaders of Burdine's Combo Castle**.

Miami's **Invaders** had already written and recorded two originals at Criteria studios when they entered, and won, the Burdine's Combo Castle Battle Of The Bands in 1965. However the prize of a 45 release came with a catch - the songs would have to be changed to suit the sponsors, Honda. And so it was that *She'll Come Back* became *Honda Come Back* and *Never Said Goodbye* became *She's A Tiger* (rewritten to appeal to WQAM "Tiger radio"). The original versions were never released, nor were two other songs that made it onto acetate, *Little Things You Do* (an original) and a cover of of *Keep A Knockin'*.

She's A Tiger rocks and roars on *Psychedelic States: Florida Vol. 3* (CD).

Goodson would join **The Echoes Of Carnaby Street** where he was reunited with an original member of **The Invaders**, Kenny Ahern. Haas joined **Sounds Unlimited** and went on to become a respected nutrition doctor and author, with the best-seller "Eat To Win" ... and of a biography of Cher (?!). (JLh/MW)

Invasion

Personnel:	DON GRUENDER	gtr	A
	MIKE JABLONSKI	drms	A
	MARK MILLER	bs	A
	GENE PERANICH	keyb'ds	A
	RICK CIER	keyb'ds	
	BRUCE COLE	drms	
	GARY FREY	bs	
	BOB McKENNA	gtr	
	TONY MENOTTI	gtr	
	P.T.PEDERSEN	bs	

| 45s: | The Invasion Is Coming/ I Want To Thank You | (Dynamic Sound 2004) 1967 |
| | Do You Like What You See?/ Do You Like What You See? | (Dynamic Sound 2009) 1967 |

A trendy-looking quintet from Milwaukee, Wisconsin who were previously known as **The Ethics**. They release two highly-rated 45s featuring meaty punkers like *The Invasion Is Coming* and *Do You Like What You See?*.

The original line-up ('A') lasted about a year; thereafter it was very fluid. Peranich, Gruender and Jablonski would form Raw Meat and recorded a 45 in the early seventies - *Standby Girl / Out In The Country* (Blue Hour 12661). Pedersen would later work with **Charlie Musselwhite**. Drummer Bruce Cole played in several Milwaukee acts in the sixties starting with the Grand Prix's in 1963, then The Triumphs (1963), Van-Tels (1964), Savoys (1965), Ricochettes (c1966), and **The Invasion** (c1967-8).

Compilation appearances have included: *Do You Like What You See* on *Psychotic Moose And The Soul Searchers* (LP) and *Back From The Grave, Vol. 7* (Dble LP); *The Invasion Is Coming* on *Vile Vinyl, Vol. 2* (LP), *Vile Vinyl* (CD) and *The Madness Invasion* (LP). (VJ/GM/MW)

The Invictas

Personnel:	MARK "MAX" BLUMENFELD	gtr	A
	HERB GROSS	vcls, ld gtr	AB
	DAVE HICKEY	drms	AB
	JIM KOHLER	bs	AB
	DAVE PROFETA	gtr	B

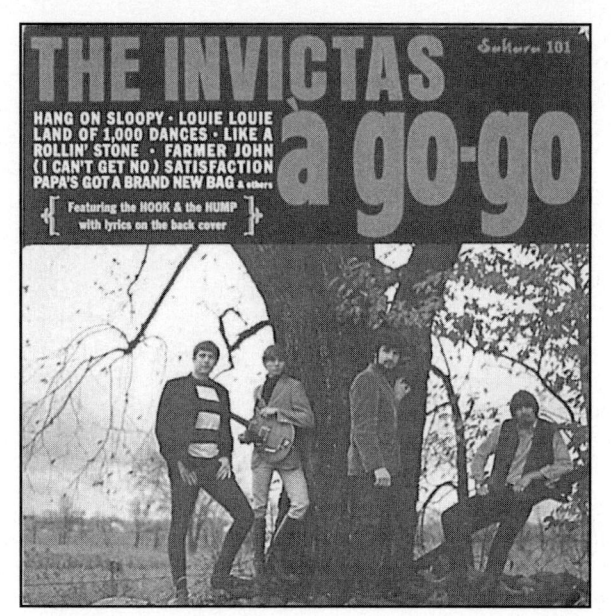

THE INVICTAS - A Go-Go LP.

ALBUM: 1(A)　A-GO-GO　(Sahara 101) 1965 R2

NB: (1) counterfeited on Eva (12016) 1983. Also of interest is the CD (A/B) *The Best Of Herb Gross And The Invictas* (Forevermore 5007) 1996.

45s:		
	I'm Alright / Stuff	(Bengel DIS-113) 1964
	The Hump/Long Tall Shortie	(Sahara 107) 1965
	Do It/The Hump	(Sahara 110) 1965
	Shake A Tail Feather/The Detroit Move	(Sahara 117) 1968

Based in Rochester, New York State, this band all attended Rochester Institute Of 1964 Technology and Syracuse University. They were 'discovered' while playing at Bengel's Inn hence the debut 45 label name. Their collectable album is choc full of garage-frat-dance classics - *Land Of 1,000 Dances*, *Farmer John*, *Louie Louie*, *Hang On Sloopy* - plus all the 45s listed. The twenty-track retrospective CD incorporates most of their released material, an interview, live and unreleased material, plus later eighties and nineties recordings featuring guitarist Dave Profeta (including *The Hump '95*).

There was also an EP released in 1980, title unknown, on Bengel DIS-1980.

Compilation appearances have included: *Do It* on *Oil Stains* (LP); and *The Hump* on *Garage Monsters* (LP). (VJ/MW)

Iota

45s:		
	Within These Precincts/Love Come Wicked	(Hi 2200) 1971
	Sing For You/R.I.P.	(MOC 678) 1972

From El Paso, Texas. Their second 45, *Sing For You*, features decent heavy sounds with some great guitar flourishes. The first, *Within These Precincts* consists of heavy and doomy psych-rock.

Compilation appearances have included: *Within These Precincts* on *Psychedelic Unknowns, Vol. 11* (LP) and *Slowly Growing Insane* (CD). (MW)

I.R.A.

45:　Dooley Vs. The Ferris Wheel/I'm A Woman　(Dot 45-17087) 1968

Compiled on *An Overdose Of Heavy Psych* (CD), the 'A' side appears to have also been released as *A Matter Of Fact* by **The Dominoes**. Basically it's a *Purple Haze* ripoff, with gutsy female(?) vocals. Recommended. (MW)

The Iris Bell Adventure

Personnel:	IRIS BELL	A
	BUTCH MILES	A
	DEREK PIERSON	A

ALBUM:　1(A)　THE IRIS BELL ADVENTURE　(Rubaiyat) 1969 SC

A live 'folkish' performance which was recorded at The Rubaiyat in Ann Arbor, Michigan. (VJ)

Iron Butterfly

Personnel:	DARRYL DeLOACH	vcls	ABCD
	DOUG INGLE	keyb'ds, vcls	ABCDE
	JACK PINNEY	drms	A
	DANNY WEIS	gtr	ABC
	GREG WILLIS	bs	A
	RON BUSHY	drms	BCDEF
	BRUCE MORSE	drms	B
	JERRY 'THE BEAR' PENROD	bs	BCD
	ERIK BRANN	gtr	DE
	LEE DORMAN	bs	EF
	MIKE PINERA	gtr	F
	LARRY REINHARDT	gtr	F

HCP

ALBUMS:	1(C)	HEAVY	(Atco 33227) 1967 78 -
(up to	2(E)	IN-A-GADDA-DA-VIDA	(Atco 33250) 1968 4 -
1972)	3(E)	BALL	(Atlantic 33280) 1969 3 -
	4(F)	IRON BUTTERFLY LIVE	(Atlantic 33318) 1970 20 -
	5(F)	METAMORPHOSIS	(Atlantic 33339) 1971 16 -
	6(-)	THE BEST OF IRON BUTTERFLY/EVOLUTION	(Atco 369) 1971 137 -

NB: (2) to (5) also released in France (Atco). (1) reissued in France by Midi (MID 20050). (1) and (5) reissued on CD by Repertoire. (1) reissued on CD by Rhino (8122-71521-2) 1993. (2) reissued on CD by Rhino with additional versions of the title track. (3), (4) and (5) reissued on CD by Rhino. (3) reissued on CD by Line (LECD 9.00950) 1990. (5) has also been repressed. There's also a 21-track CD compilation, *Light And Heavy - The Best Of Iron Butterfly* (Rhino RZ 71166) 1993, which is a pretty good introduction to the band featuring a selection of their 'A' and 'B' sides and cuts from their first three albums.

HCP

45s:		
	Unconscious Power/Possession	(Atco 6573) 1967 -
	In-A-Gadda-Da-Vida/Iron Butterfly Theme	(Atco 6606) 1968 30
	Soul Experience/In The Crowds	(Atco 6647) 1969 75
	In The Time Of Our Lives/It Must Be Love	(Atco 6676) 1969 96
	I Can't Help But To Deceive You Little Girl/	

IRON BUTTERFLY - Heavy CD.

To Be Alone	(Atco 6712) 1969	118
Easy Rider (Let The Wind Pay The Way)/ Soilder In Town	(Acto 6782) 1970	66
Silly Sally/Stone Believer	(Atco 6818) 1971	-

This band originated in San Diego and evolved out of Gerry and The Gerritones and The Palace Pages in mid-1966. Their line-up went through a number of changes with Pinney and Willis leaving in the Summer 1966, being replaced briefly by Penrod and Morse. After their first album Danny Weis left in August 1967, to form Nirvana, which never got off the ground. He then auditioned for Elektra's Project Supergroup. Penrod and DeLoach left the following month, with Penrod re-joining Weis in Project Supergroup and DeLoach recording a solo 45. Pinney, Willis, Morse and DeLoach all later played in various line-ups of **Glory**; whilst 'Project Supergroup' became **Rhinoceros** in February 1968.

Iron Butterfly's second and most successful album, *In-A-Gadda-Da-Vida*, was recorded by Brann, Dorman, Bushy (ex-Voxmen) and Ingle. This remained near the top of the U.S. album charts for over two years and is generally thought to be the first album to go platinum. The title track, a seventeen-minute composition of Doug Ingle's, comprised the whole of one side. Although the lyrics of the remaining tracks like *Flowers and Beads* and *Termination* sound dated today, they also accounted for the album's enormous popularity in the flower-power era. Ingle's organ work (his father had been a church organist which accounted for the classical influence in his writing), is always to the fore. This gave the group a similar sound to **The Doors** and his classical influence is particularly evident in *My Mirage*.

The album's phenomenal success proved too much for the group to live up to. In late 1969 Brann was replaced by twin guitarists Mike Pinera (ex-**Blues Image**) and Larry Reinhardt (a former associate of Duane Allman). This new line-up recorded the live album and *Metamorphosis* but was unable to arrest the group's decline. They eventually dissolved on a farewell tour in 1971. Like so many other West Coast groups, they were to reform to cut two unsuccessful albums in 1975.

Possession was included on *The Age Of Atlantic* compilation and both sides of their first 45 appeared on the *Savage Seven* soundtrack album.

As part of the promotion for *Metamorphosis*, a rarely-seen radio interview album was issued in a plain cover with title stamp - *Iron Butterfly Interview with Mitch Reed* (Atco PR-A-161)1970.

Mike Pinera went on to **Ramatam**, New Cactus Band and Thee Image.

Compilation appearances have included: *In-A-Gadda-Da-Vida* on *Nuggets, Vol. 9* (LP) and *Psychedelic Visions* (CD); and *Evil Temptation* on *Garagelands, Vol. 2* (CD). (VJ/NW/MW/RMe/CF)

The Iron Gate

Personnel:	MIKE CAMPBELL	A
	TOM CULLEN	A
	SAL GAMBINO	A
	BILL MOSER	A
	LOU WOLFENSON	A

45s:	Feelin' Bad/My Generation	(Marbell 1001) 1966
	Hold On I'm Coming	(one sided acetate) 1967

This Philadelphia-based outfit was formed in late 1965 by Tom Cullen and Mike Campbell, who were classmates at the Father Judge High School in the Mayfair area of town. They were originally known as the 5 Shades but soon changed name to **The Iron Gate**. They set out playing hard-edged blues-based music very much in the mould of British invasion bands like The Yardbirds, The Rolling Stones and The Animals. In November 1966 they were runners up to **The Scholars** in the P.A.L. Battle Of The Bands. In December 1966 they recorded their 45 and two unreleased tracks:- *Spoonful* and *Hit The Road Jack*. Only 500 copies of the 45 were pressed for sale at their gigs. *Feelin' Bad*, essentially consisted of a 'I Want My Baby Back' groan. The acetate is reputed to be of poor sound quality. When they graduated from High School in 1968 the band fell apart, although Tom Cullen and Mike Campbell performed together in several blues bands up to 1971. More recently Tom Cullen has become co-founder and director of The Bucks County Blues Society and a radio show presenter in Warminster, Pennsylvania.

IRON BUTTERFLY - In-A-Gadda-Da-Vida LP.

Compilation appearances include: *Feelin' Bad* on *Psychedelic Unknowns, Vol's 1 & 2* (LP), *Psychedelic Unknowns, Vol. 1* (7"), *Teenage Shutdown, Vol. 6* (LP & CD) and *Crude PA, Vol. 1* (LP). (VJ)

The Iron Gate

Personnel:	FRANK BENNETT	ld gtr, bkg vcls	A
	BARRY BETTS	drms, bkg vcls	A
	WADE HILMAN	bs, bkg vcls	A
	LARRY JANZACK	gtr, bkg vcls	A
	KARL KENNINGTON	ld vcls	A
	STEVE THULANDER	keyb'ds, bkg vcls	A

45:	Get Ready / You Must Believe In Me	(Mobie 3429) 1968

A Rockford, Illinois, group who evolved out of **The Cavemen**. The titles indicate a strong soul influence and the band utilised strong harmony vocals. Their rendition of *Get Ready* became a big seller in the Midwest, outselling another version by local rivals the **Missing Links**. It got played on all the top Chicago Radio Stations and garnered acclaim in Billboard.

After touring nationally, Mercury Records began to show interest as Karl Kennington explains:- "Mercury set a meeting with us and our Record Manager to buy our contract from Mobie and sign us up. But, when they found out that two of us were at draft age the deal was put on hold. I was drafted six months later and our lead guitarist, Frank Bennett, only four months later. We were set to release our first original single *Love Has Gone* backed with a live version of *Fever*, but Uncle Sam stepped in and that was the end of the first Rockford group that could have made it." (MW/GM/KH)

Iron Horse

EP:	1	THE IRON HORSE "6 UNRELEASED CUTS 1967-1968" (PS)	(Moxie M-1038) 1982

The EP comprises just five tracks - *Light My Fire, In My Own Time, 96 Tears, Time (Has Come Today)* and *Back In The U.S.S.R.*. From the San Gabriel Valley, California, and featuring future Surf Raider Bob Dalley, they are competent cover versions. (MW)

Iron Lung

Personnel:	ROD ANDERSON	drms	A
	BILL BOLTZ	ld gtr, vcls	A
	WAYNE PETERSON	bs	A
	ROGER REPP	gtr, vcls	A

ALBUM:	1(A)	HIGH BAIL	(K.D.R. BB 1063) 1975 R3

NB: (1) reissued on Casket in the U.K. in 1994.

A very rare and sought-after local Illinois blues - rock privately pressed album. It commands a high value despite being rather unexceptional in the style. The reissue, which had a pressing of 400, should enable those of you curious to hear it to do so. (CF/VJ/NK)

It's A Beautiful Day

Personnel:
DAVID LaFLAMME	flute, violin	ABCD
LINDA LaFLAMME	keyb'ds	A
VAL FUENTES	drms	ABCDE
PATTIE SANTOS	vcls	ABCDE
HAL WAGENET	gtr, vcls	ABC
MICHAEL HOLMAN	hrmnca, vcls, bs	ABC
FRED WEBB	vcls, horns, keyb'ds	BCDE
TOM FOWLER	bs	CD
BILL GREGORY	gtr	CDE
GREG BLOCK	violin	E
BUD COCKRELL	bs, vcls	E
DAVID JENKINS	ld gtr	
JOHN NICHOLAS	bs	

HCP
ALBUMS:	1(A)	IT'S A BEAUTIFUL DAY	(Columbia 9768) 1969	47 -
	2(B)	MARRYING MAIDEN	(Columbia 1058) 1970	28 -
	3(C)	CHOICE QUALITY STUFF	(CBS 30734) 1971	130 -
	4(D)	LIVE AT CARNEGIE HALL	(Columbia 31338) 1972	144 -
	5(E)	TODAY	(Columbia 32181) 1973	114 -
	6(A)	1001 NIGHTS	(Columbia 32660) 1974	- -
	7(-)	IT'S A BEAUTIFUL DAY	(San Francisco Sound SFS 11790) 1985	- -

NB: (1)-(6) were issued on CBS in the UK. (1) to (3) also issued in France by CBS. (6) is a reissue of (1). (1) has been reissued on vinyl and CD. (2) has been reissued on vinyl (San Francisco Sound) 197? and CD (San Francisco Sound SFS 04800). TRC have released (3) and (4) on CD, together with a *Greatest Hits* disc.

HCP
45s:	Bulgaria/Aquarian Dream	(San Francisco Sound 7) 1968	-
	White Bird/Girl With No Eyes	(San Francisco Sound) 1969	-
	White Bird/Wasted Union Blues	(Columbia 44928) 1969	118
	Soapstone Mountain/Good Lovin'	(Columbia 45152) 1970	-
	Anytime/Apples And Oranges	(Columbia 45536) 1972	-

One of the leading second-generation San Francisco bands, this group's music was dominated by the excellent violin playing of classically-tutored La Flamme, who also produced their records. Their debut album made an enormous impact and contained the stand out song *White Bird*. This was one of the classic albums of the era and the twin vocals of La Flamme and Pattie Santos blended together beautifully on tracks like *White Bird*, *Hot Summer Day* and *Girl With No Eyes*. Side Two is dominated by the sleepy, drug-influenced *Bulgaria* and the Eastern-influenced *Bombay Calling*, it is slightly marred, however, by a rather tedious drum solo on the final track *Time Is*.

IRON LUNG - High Bail LP.

IT'S A BEAUTIFUL DAY - It's A Beautiful Day LP.

Linda La Flamme then left the band and Fred Webb was also introduced on keyboards for follow-up *Marrying Maiden*. **Jerry Garcia** guested on this record, too, playing banjo and pedal steel guitar. Although inferior to their debut effort, this album contained some fine tracks too, *Don And Dewey* and *Hoedown* were effective instrumentals, whilst the laid-back harmonies of the first album were in evidence on *The Dolphins*, *Essence of Now*, *Let A Woman Flow* and *Do You Remember The Sun?*. However, the follow-up *Choice Quality Stuff* marked a clear downward turn. The laid-back mysticism of their earlier songs had been replaced by a rather unimaginative 'good time' sound. The album had its moments, however - *The Grand Camel Suite* was a competent instrumental - but it was enormously disappointing. The follow-up live album was unable to reverse this trend and further personnel changes reduced the band to a mere shadow of its former self, as did subsequent albums.

It's A Beautiful Day reformed for a performance at the Fillmore Auditorium in San Francisco on November 29th 1997. The line-up consisted of original members David LaFlamme, Mitch Holman, Val Fuentes and Hal Wagenet, plus long-time vocalist Linda Baker LaFlamme and new keyboardist Larry Blachshere.

Two tracks, *Bulgaria* and *Aquarian Dream* appeared on the *Fifth Annual Pipe Dream*, which was very rare prior to its reissue a few years back. More recently, Matthew Katz's *Then And Now, Vol. 1* includes *Girl With No Eyes*, *The Dolphins* and a 1980 tribute to John Lennon entitled *John*. *Then And Now, Vol. 2* also contains *Aquarian Dream* and *Wasted Union Blues*; and *Turds On A Bum Ride, Vol. 5* (CD) includes *Aquarian Dream*.

Bill Gregory had earlier played in New Orleans band Nectar. (VJ/PB)

It's Them

45s:	α	Don't Look Now / A Girl Like You	(King 5967) 1964
	β	Baby (I Still Want Your Lovin') / You Give Your Love To Me	(Toy Tiger 1001) 196?
	χ	Baby (I Still Need Your Lovin') / You Give Your Love To Me	(Toy Tiger 1001) 196?

NB: α issued as by **Them**. β issued as **It's Them**. χ second issue of β as **Tthheemm**. χ flip may be *What's A Girl Like You Doing In A Place Like This*.

This Cincinnati, Ohio group was actually called **Them** and continued to perform as such, but they chose to issue their second 45 under different names to prevent confusion or legal hassles when the Belfast U.K. bunch appeared on the scene. It was issued first as by **It's Them** and then as by **Tthheemm**.

Baby I Still Want Your Lovin' is British invasion styled, gritty, bluesy R&B, very much in the mould of The Animals.

Compilation appearances have included: *Baby I Still Want Your Lovin'* on *Highs In The Mid-Sixties, Vol. 21* (LP); and *Don't Look Now* on *Ho-Dad Hootenanny* (LP). (GGI/MW/VJ)

It's Us

45:	Don't Want Your Lovin'/?	(Arab) 1966

Came out of Kenellon, New Jersey, where they formed in 1965. This was their sole platter and they put it out on their own label. They recorded it at Roulette Studios in New York City. *Don't Want Your Lovin'*, is a rather appealing folk-punkish number.

Compilation appearances include: *Don't Want Your Lovin'* on *Punk Classics, Vol. 1* (7") and *Back From The Grave, Vol. 7* (Dble LP). (VJ)

Ivan and The Sabers

Personnel:
BILL ALBAUGH	drms	A
BILL BARTLETT	ld gtr	A
IVAN BROWNE	vcls	A
REG NAVE	bs	A
STEVE WALMESLEY	keyb'ds	A

45s:
Just Let Her Go / It's Not Like You	(Prism 1893)	1964
Listen To Me / I Want To Know	(Prism 1916)	1964
My Mind Cries Out /What's Rushing Through Your Mind Dear	(Counterpart C-2615/6)	1967
Think Of Me / Great Potato Famine Of '71	(Counterpart C-2623/4)	1968
Stereo / Cozy	(Counterpart C-2645/6)	1969

Originally from Centerville, Ohio this pop band relocated to Cincinnati and were given a second identity, **The Lemon Pipers**, by bubblegum impressarios Jerry Kasenetz and Jeffrey Katz. (GGI/MW/MB)

Peter Ivers

Personnel:
TONY ACKERMAN	gtr	A
PAUL BALMUTH	sax	A
YOLANDE BAVAN	vcls	A
PETER IVERS	vcls, hrmnca	ABCD
STEVE KOWARSKY	bassoon	A
R.FRANK POZAR	perc	A
JOE SEALE	intermodulator	A
HENRY SCHUMAN	oboe	A
RICHARD YOUNGSTEIN	contrabass	A
KATHY APPLEBY	violin	B
BEN BENAY	gtr	B
DAVID COHEN	gtr	B
ALICE DeBUHR	drms	B
ELLIOT INGBER	gtr	B
MARTY KRYSTALL	sax	B
PAUL LENART	gtr	B
BUELL NEIDLINGER	bs	BC

ALBUMS:
1(A)	KNIGHT OF THE BLUE COMMUNION	(Epic BN 26500)	1969 -
2(B)	TERMINAL LOVE	(Warner Bros. BS 2804)	1974 -
3(C)	PETER IVERS	(Warner Bros. BS 2930)	1976 -
4(-)	NIRVANA PETER	(Warner Bros. 25213-1)	1985 -

NB: (4) is a compilation of the Warner Bros. LPs with unreleased tracks.

45s:
α	Ain't That Peculiar/Clarence O'Day	(Epic 5-10681)	1971
	Eighteen And Dreaming/ Eighteen And Dreaming (mono)	(Warner Bros. WBS 8287)	1976
	Love Theme from Filmex/ Love Theme From Filmex (instr.)	(Filmex)	1980

NB: α as **Peter Ivers Group**.

Born in Boston in September 1946, **Peter Ivers** was a multi-talented artist: singer/songwriter, yoga master, actor, theater writer, experimental video director... A Harvard graduate, he began playing in the late sixties with the Street Choir which was part of "Boston's new sound". His first album *Knight Of The Blue Communion* is one of the strangest records of this period and can only be compared to the **United States of America** for mixing classical and rock instruments with electronic sounds (provided by an "intermodulator"), free jazz and classical singing (Yolande Bavan was a opera singer). The lyrics written by Timothy Mayer (future Associate Director of the American National Theater) have a strong religious content (*Gentle Jesus, Confession, Lord God Love, Dark Illumination...*) and the result is really "something else". The album was produced by Sandy Linzer.

Still with the same producer, his next project, *Take it Out On Me*, was recorded in 1971 although Epic shelved it and only a 45 was released. In the mid-'90s, One Way tried to license all the Epic recordings for a CD but this was rejected by Sony.

The second album from 1974, *Terminal Love* was totally different but is equally as interesting: high pitched voices, unusual songs structures and lyrics (*Holding The Cobra, Alpha Centauri, Felladaddio...*). The album was co-produced by **Ivers** and the free jazz bass player Buell Neidlinger. Elliot Ingber (ex-**Fraternity of Man**, **Zappa**, **Beefheart**) plays on some tracks.

The 1976 album was produced by Gary Wright (ex-Spooky Tooth) and is not as interesting.

Later **Ivers** wrote *In Heaven*, the theme of David Lynch's "Eraserhead". A final single was released in 1980, with Richard Greene (ex-**Seatrain**) and Falconer (Rod Taylor). He also performed with John Cale and created the New Wave Theater. He was murdered in 1983. (SR)

Ivory

Personnel:
CHRISTINE CHRISTMAN	vcls	A
MIKE McCAULEY	keyb'ds, vcls	A
KENNY THOMURE	gtr, vcls	A

ALBUM:
1(A)	IVORY	(Tetragrammaton T-104)	1968 SC

NB: (1) reissued on CD (Gear Fab GF-182) 2002.

This California trio had a sound similar to **Jefferson Airplane** (not surprising considering their producer was Al Schmitt, the **Airplane** producer) with powerful female vocals by Chris Christman. An excellent example of the American tough psychedelic sound with some great fuzz guitar / organ interplay on the best track *Silver Rains*. All their material was written by Chris Christman and Kenny Thomure, Mike McAuley being also credited for *Silver Rains* and Wark on *Last Laugh*. None of the group members appear to have played in any documented group before or after **Ivory**. Recommended.

Ken Thomure and Mike McCauley grew up together and played together in Boron, California. After high school the duo decided to go to Hollywood and form a band there. They bumped into Christman, who lived in Westchester, on Sunset Strip. They started out by playing small clubs then graduated to out-of-town gigs and set up a production company. Next they acquired manager Tony Christian, who got them auditions and a recording contract. After the album was recorded they got bigger gigs, a TV appearance on the Tonight and went on their first tour in Colorado. On their return to L.A., McCauley was drafted and sent to Vietnam where he was wounded and the band never recovered.

Silver Rains can also be found on *Journey To The East* (LP).

There was also another act by the same name who had a self-titled album on Playboy (115) in 1973. We had this listed as a reissue of the above album, but this is incorrect, the music is by a completely different group. (TA/EM/MW/SR/VJ)

The Ivymen

45:	La Do Da Da/Bo Diddley	(Twin Town 720) 1966

This very rare and sought-after 45 was the work of a Minnesota band from Coon Rapids, just North of the Twin Cities. They changed their name to The Buttons in 1968 but did not record under that name. (VJ)

The Jackals

Personnel:	PHIL CAMPBELL	drms	AB
	BILL LAWSON	vcls, harp	AB
	MIKE NEAL	gtr, vcls	A
	RON STERLING	bs	AB
	JOHN TALLEY	keyb'ds, vcls	AB
	WILLIAM WILLIAMS	gtr, vcls	B

45s: Love Times Eight/
A.F. Lament (Instr)   (Boyd Recording demo acetate) 196?
Love Times Eight/Taxman (PS)   (Caped Crusader CC-72) 1989

A Dallas guitar garage outfit whose unreleased gem *Love Times Eight* has finally seen the light of day on the Caped Crusader release which contains a full biography of the band. (MW)

Jack and The Beanstalks

Personnel:	JOHN CONRATH	ld gtr	A
	ROBERT KENNEDY	bs	A
	JOHN LYONS	drms	A
	JACK TATE (TADYCH)	gtr	A
	JIM DIETRICH	drms	
	PAT GLASS	piano	
	DOUG WERGINZ	drms	

45s: Don't Bug Me/So Many Times   (Le Ron 822L-3601) 1966
A Long Time Comin', A Long Time Gone/
Mood For Hurt   (Revolution 2914) 1968

This beat outfit came from Milwaukee, Wisconsin. There's a strong Yardbirds/Stones influence on their first 45, although the second is reputedly a more psychedelic affair.

Compilation appearances have included: *So Many Times* on *Teenage Shutdown, Vol. 9* (LP & CD); and both *Don't Bug Me* and *So Many Times* on *Highs In The Mid Sixties, Vol. 10* (LP). (VJ/MW/GM)

Jack and The Rippers

Personnel:	LARRY BERRY		A
	JOHNNY BROOKS		A
	JACK HAMMOND	ld gtr	A
	JIMMY STEPHENS		A

An obscure act with one 4-track EP on Jades Promotional Records. From Fort Worth, Texas, they used to rehearse at Jack's father's Texaco garage station (Hammond Garage!). (VJ/MPo)

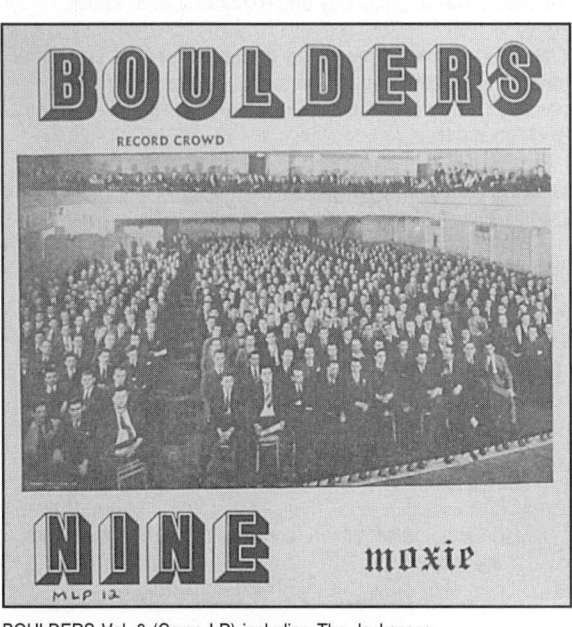

BOULDERS Vol. 9 (Comp LP) including The Jackasses.

The Jackasses

Personnel:	TERRY ANDERSON	gtr, vcls	AB
	LEE DITMER	drms, vcls	AB
	CHUCK EFFINGER	bs, vcls	A
	BUB FOLLEY	organ	AB
	MARK GENSMEN	sax	AB
	DAN LOWTHER	bs	B

45: Sugaree/Shake It Up   (Bray 2626) 1964

Formed in Vancouver, Washington in 1963 by former members of an outfit called The Gay Blades. They played as one of three paid acts at the first Portland Teen Fair along with **Paul Revere and The Raiders** and **Don and The Goodtimes**. Their sole 45 was popular in the Northwest. In 1965 they changed their name to The Mid-Night Sons.

Compilation appearances have included: *Sugaree* on *Ya Gotta Have Moxie, Vol. 2* (Dble CD), *Boulders, Vol. 9* (LP) and *Boulders, Vol. 7* (LP). (VJ)

John Roman Jackson

ALBUM: 1 JOHN ROMAN JACKSON
(Oak Records ORS-2001) c1971 -

A Californian folk-rock singer/songwriter with some country influences and an electric backing (drums, bass, guitar, occasional organ and harmonica) and, on two tracks, female background vocals. Some tracks are quite good, notably *Rosemary*, *Mary's Garden* and *Sometimes*, but the record suffers from the muddy production of Ernie Freeman and poor drumming. The album was recorded at the Goldstar Studios.

Oak Records was a short-lived label based on Sunset Bld, Hollywood. (SR)

The Jackson Investment Co.

Personnel:	TRACY ANDERSON	ld gtr	A
	GARY COOKE	ld vcls	A
	DANNY PROVINCE	keyb'ds	A
	MIKE ROLLER	bs	A
	GEORGE STEWART	gtr	A
	JIM STEWART	drms	A
	MIKE TRABUSLY	gtr	A

45: What Can I Do?/Not This Time   (Paris Tower PT-125) 1967

Lakeland, Florida, was home to this septet, who laid down two highly-rated folk-punkers from the pen of George Stewart. They are highly-rated by compilers: both sides adorn *Teenage Shutdown, Vol. 9* (LP & CD); *What Can I Do?* is on *Pebbles, Vol. 21* (LP); the pumping *Not This Time* is on *Sixties Rebellion, Vol. 6* (LP & CD) and *Psychedelic States - Florida Vol. 1* (CD). (VJ/MW/JLh)

Robert Jacobs

45: Blackbird/Time Of A Man   (Capitol P-2621) 1969

A cover of the Beatles done in the style of Joe Cocker, with Hammond organ and full orchestra. (SR)

Jacobs Creek

Personnel:	STEVE BURGH	vcls, gtr, organ	A
	TIM CASE	drms	A
	BRUCE FOSTER	vcls, gtr, piano, banjo	A
	DERREK VAN EATON	vcls, bs, gtr	A
	LON VAN EATON	vcls, gtr, sitar, harpsichord, sax	A
	(STEVE MOSLEY	drms	A)
	(DENNY STORLEY	perc	A)

ALBUM: 1(A) JACOBS CREEK   (Columbia CS 9829) 1969 SC

NB: (1) issued with lyric sheet.

Patient listeners will be rewarded with three quite stunning tracks closing Side One of the album. Sadly, the remainder is merely well-played country-ish rock with some religious lyrics and horns.

The Van Eaton brothers made solo albums and guested on many other artists records, including solo Beatles projects. Steve Burgh worked prolifically as a studio musician through the seventies and can be found on albums by Billy Joel, **Richie Havens**, David Bromberg, Judy Collins and many others. (CF/SR)

Jacob's Ladder

ALBUM: 1 IF I HAD A WISH   (Lovejoy) c1976 -

From San Francisco, a private pressing issued on a black and white cover. It has been described as "sleepy hippie music". (SR)

Jacob's Reunion

ALBUM: 1 JACOB'S REUNION   (Private Pressing) 1975 ?

From New Hampshire, a folk rock group with feminine vocals, mixing traditional and original material. Only 500 copies were pressed. (SR)

Jade

Personnel: JIM AUMANN   keyb'ds   A
             RANDY MORSE   gtr   A
             TIM NIXON   drms   A
             NICK ROOT   bs   A

ALBUM: 1(A) FACES OF JADE
              (General American Records GAR 11311) 1970/71 R1/R2

45:   My Honey/?   ( ) 1970/71
      Flying Away/
      Sunshine   (General American Records GAR 311) 1971

The album sports a sticker 'contains the hit single *My Honey*' - such a big hit that no trace of it can be found! From Cincinnati, **Jade** gave us a pleasant potpourri of late sixties Beatlesque pop - unfortunately dealers tout this as 'Rare Garage/Psych' to bump up the price. Rare it may be, garage or psych it certainly is not, You've been warned!

Compilation appearances include *Rest Of My Life* on *Pepperisms Around The Globe* (LP& CD). (MW/UB)

Jade

45:   I'm Leaving You/?   (Jade SS-769) 196?

This group came from Pueblo, Colorado and is thought to feature ex-members of **The Trolls**.

Compilation appearances include *I'm Leaving You* on *The Garage Zone, Vol. 1* (LP) and *The Garage Zone Box Set* (4-LP). (MW)

Jade

45:   They Call The Wind Mariah/
      Your Cheatin' Heart   (Master 1006) 19??

Released on a Houston, Texas label, this 45 has a good production. The 'B' side has an excellent quite chunky arrangement. The singer is a dead ringer for **Beacon St. Union**'s John Lincoln Wright. (SBn)

Jades

Personnel: ALEXANDER?   A
             C. CLARKE?   A
             D. SIEGEL?   A

JADE - Faces Of Jade LP.

45s: Confined Congregation/Please Come Back   (Fenton 2134) 1966
      Surface World / We Got Something Going   (Fenton 2208) 1967

A Sparta, Michigan, outfit whose 45s are keenly sought and command suitably steep prices. Swingin' folk-punk is their forte with just the occasional use of fuzz. No surprise that they've been well compiled:- *Confined Congregation* on the cassette-only *Best Of Michigan Rock Groups, Vol. 2* and *Destination Frantic!* (LP & CD); *Please Come Back* is on *Midnight To Sixty-Six* (LP); and *Surface World* on *Teenage Shutdown, Vol. 5* (LP & CD). (MW/MM)

Jades

Personnel: RAY DEMENT   drms   A
             TERRY HAILEY   keyb'ds   A
             JIM HUTCHCRAFT   gtr   A
             SHERRILL PARKS, Jr. vcls, harp A
             HORACE PHOEBUS   bs   A

45s: I A'int Got You / Rough House   (Renay 403) 1966
      When Shadows Fall / Blue Nocturne   (Renay 404) 1967

This Union City, Tennessee group were formerly known as **The Viscounts**, who had included all the personnel above except Phoebus. Both their 45s on Renay, recorded in Memphis, are well worth seeking out.

Parks moved onto several other groups including Kangaroo and Cymarron. Hailey is now Mayor of Union City and owner of a radio station.

I A'int Got You (the label misplaced the apostrophe) is on *Garage Punk Unknowns, Vol. 7* (LP) and *A History Of Garage And Frat Bands In Memphis* (CD). *When Shadows Fall* appears on *Mindblowing Encounters Of The Purple Kind* (LP).

Thanks to Jacqueline Sabri-Tabrizi for reminding us about this band. Read more about them in the Ron Hall's companion book to the Memphis CD mentioned above, 'Playing For A Piece Of The Door', published by Shangri-La Projects in 2001, ISBN 0-9668575-1-8. (MW)

The Jades

ALBUM: 1 LIVE AT THE DISC A GOGO   (Jarrett 21517) 1965 R2

45:   So Tough! / ?   (Ching no #) 196?

From Dallas, Texas, their album consists of early sixties rock meets mid-sixties punk. (VJ)

The Jades

45s:	Blue Black Hair/Surfin' Crow	(Gaity GA 2-23-64) 1964
	Blue Black Hair/Surfin' Crow	(Oxboro 2002) 1964
	Little Marlene / Shake Baby Shake	(Oxboro 2005) 1964

From Bloomington, Minnesota. *Blue Black Hair* a fifties-inspired rocker was issued on Gaity in very limited quantities. It was almost immediately picked up by Oxboro and became something of a local hit. Their second 45 is another great rocker.

The instrumental *Surfin' Crow* can be found on *Strummin Mental, Vol. 5*. (BM/MW)

The Jades

45:	I Cried/Once Upon A Time	(Holiday 101) c1966

This low key, defiant garage 45 was released on a Union, Kentucky label. (MW)

The Jades of Fort Worth

Personnel:	RONNIE BROWN		A
	GARY CARPENTER		A
	LARRY EARP		A
	JACK HENRY		A
	ALVIN McCOOL		A

ALBUM:	1(A)	INTRODUCING THE JADES	(Cicadelic 1000) 1982

45s:	α	I'm Alright/'Till I Die	(Ector 101) 1965
		Sha-La-La-La-Lee/I'm Coming Home	(Strawberry 10) 1966
	β	Little Girl/Mercy, Mercy	(Emcee 012/3) 1966

NB: α as **The Jades**. β originally released as by **Jade Of Stone** with a later pressing as **The Jades Of Fort Worth**.

A raw punk outfit from Fort Worth who were a popular local attraction in their day. Sometimes known as **The Jades Of Fort Worth**, their second 45 and later pressings of the third one were released under that name. Their third 45 was originally credited to Jades Of Stone. They specialised in cover versions, which they delivered in their own fiery style. On *I'm Alright* Gary Carpenter set a Rolling Stones song to new lyrics and the formula worked - they enjoyed a local hit. Next up was a Small Faces song and for their third and final effort they chose a Van Morrison composition. They finally called it a day in 1969, by which time only Carpenter and McCool remained from their original line-up. For the first half of the seventies Carpenter played in a showband called Colossus, and later he recorded an album which he decided not to release. After a spell as a DJ in Fort Worth he was last heard of managing the Sound Idea stereo store in Camp Bowie.

The most comprehensive guide to their material can be found on their retrospective album.

Compilation appearances have included: *I'm All Right* on *Flashback, Vol. 2* (LP) and *Texas Flashbacks, Vol. 2* (LP); *Sha La La La Lee*, *Don't Bring Me Down* and *Little Girl* on *20 Great Hits Of The 60's* (LP); *I'm Alright*, *Little Girl*, *Don't Bring Me Down* and *Mercy Mercy* on *The Fort Worth Teen Scene - The Major Bill Tapes Vol. 2* (LP); and *Little Girl* on *We Have Come For Your Children*. (VJ/MW)

Jagged Edge

Personnel:	DREW GEORGOPOLOUS	gtr, vcls	AB
	ELLIOT INGBER	ld vcls	AB
	RONNIE SHERMAN	drms	A
	ART STEINMAN	ld gtr, vcls	AB
	HARLEY WISHNER	bs	AB
	KENNY BENNETT	drms	B

45s:		You Can't Keep A Good Man Down/ How She's Hurtin' Me	(Gallant 3017) 1965
	α	A Change Is Gonna Come/Xanthia (Lisa)	(Jubilee 5542) 1966
	α	Reflections/Lies I Spoke	(acetate only) 1966
	α	Stop Feeling Sorry For Yourself/ Look in Her Eyes	(acetate only) 196?

NB: α as by **The Off-Set**.

From Brooklyn, New York, this band evolved out of The Jaguars who formed in 1963 and included Art Steinman and Harley Wishner. Probably the first band to use the **Jagged Edge** moniker, their first 45 was promoted heavily at DJ hops in the tri-state area, resulting in a hit in Buffalo and a piece in the June 1966 edition of "16" magazine.

By the time their second 45 was released, another Jagged Edge had appeared on the scene with a 45. A threatened law suit resulted in the Brooklyn act changing their name to **The Off-set**, but their second 45 wasn't as well promoted and subseqently didn't sell as well. They broke-up soon after.

Art Steinman continued to play music professionally and was signed to Atlantic after Ahmet Ertegun saw him and Wilbert Harrison perform at The Filmore East on Feb 9th 1970. No releases were forthcoming, although tapes are known to exist - indeed as are rehearsal tapes of **Jagged Edge** and the pre-**Jagged Edge**, Jaguars.

Of the unreleased demos: *Lies I Spoke* is the most promising - dramatic but fragmented pop-punk with psychy effects and raga-esque break; *Look In Her Eyes* is a strong and moody folk-rocker; *Reflection* and *Stop Feeling Sorry For Yourself* present the band's poppy side with the former winning out for the sweet harmonies which bring to mind **Curt Boettcher** confectionery.

Art Steinman: "One of the two managers of our group was Eric Van Lustbader (aka Eric Lustbader), who is the successful author of Ninja books and other thrillers. We played some WMCA Good Guy shows at tri-state high schools to promote our 45s and appeared with and backed up some of the leading bands of the mid-sixties - **Question Mark and the Mysterians**, **Music Machine**, **Critters**, Percy Sledge, Brian Hyland, **The Association** and **The Left Banke** to name a few."

Currently Art works for Lucent Technologies; Drew is a consultant for a software company in New Jersey and continues to write music; Elliot has his own high-end audio/video installation company in Manhattan; Harley is a urologist living in Van Nuys, California and Kenny Bennett works for the US post office in Brooklyn, New York.

As to one obvious factoid question - was Elliot Ingber the same guy who was with **Frank Zappa and the Mothers Of Invention**, then **Fraternity Of Man**, before becoming Winged Eel Fingerling in **Captain Beefheart**'s band? Art replies - "It is an amazing coincidence in names, but I am quite

TEXAS FLASHBACKS Vol. 2 (Comp CD) including The Jades Of Fort Worth.

certain that he was not the famous musician who performed with Beefheart and Zappa. I don't think our Elliot Ingber had a musical career beyond the Jagged Edge."

Art also played in another Brooklyn act 'Southern Socket' with **The Keepers**' member Barry Drimmer.

Compilation appearances include: *You Can't Keep A Good Man Down* on *Vile Vinyl, Vol. 2* (LP), *Vile Vinyl* (CD) and *Gone, Vol. 2* (LP); *How She's Hurtin' Me* on *From The New World* (LP); and *Xanthia (Lisa)* on *Brainshadows, Vol. 1* (LP & CD). (MW/ASn)

Jagged Edge

45:    Midnight To Six Man/How Many Times?   (Twirl 2024) 1967

This 45 was recorded in California although I can't confirm that the band originated from there... Michigan and Ohio have also been claimed as their stompin' ground.

Compilation appearances have include: *How Many Times* on *Open Up Yer Door! Vol. 1* (LP), *Sixties Choice, Vol. 1* (LP), *60's Choice Collection Vol's 1 And 2* (CD), *Teenage Shutdown, Vol. 6* (LP & CD); and *Midnight To Six* on *The Cicadelic 60's, Vol. 4* (CD) and *The Cicadelic 60's, Vol. 2* (LP). (MW)

Jagged Edge

45:    Madelynn Murphy / The Big Black Bird   (WGW 329) 196?
NB: split 45, with flip by The Time Masheen.

A split 45, *Madelynn Murphy* is thought to be by a New Jersey based **Jagged Edge**.

Jagged Edge

HCP
45:    Deep Inside/
       Baby You Don't Know   (RCA Victor 47-8880) 1966 129

Another **Jagged Edge** - anyone able to elaborate the details?

The Jaggers / Jaggerz

Personnel:	THOM DAVIS	keyb'ds, trumpet	A
	BENNY FAIELLA	gtr, bs, vcls	A
	DOMINIC IERACE	gtr, bs, trumpet, vcls	A
	BILLY MAYBRAY	bs, vcls, drms	A
	JIM PUGLIANO	drms, vcls	A
	JIMMY ROSS	bs, vcls, tuba, trombone	A

ALBUMS: 1( ) INTRODUCING THE JAGGERZ   (Gamble) 196? -
        2(A) WE WENT TO DIFFERENT SCHOOLS TOGETHER
                                   (Kama Sutra KSBS 2017) 1970 -
        3( ) COME AGAIN   (Wooden Nickel (S)1-0772) 1975 -
NB: (3) is a reunion album.

45s: α Feel So Good / Cry   (Executive no #) 1966
         Baby, I Love You (That's Why)/
         Bring It Back   (Gamble 218) 1968
         Gotta Find My Way Back Home/
         Forever Together, Together Forever   (Gamble 226) 1968
         Let Me Be Your Man/Together   (Gamble 238) 1969
         Higher And Higher/Ain't No Sun   (Gamble 4008) 1970
         Here's A Heart/Need Your Love   (Gamble 4012) 1970
         The Rapper/Born Poor   (Kama Sutra 502) 1970
         I Call My Baby Candy/
         Will She Believe In Me   (Kama Sutra 509) 1970
         Memories Of A Traveller/
         What A Bummer   (Kama Sutra 513) 1970
         I'll Never Forget You/
         Let's Talk About Love   (Kama Sutra 517) 1971
         Let's Talk About Love/Ain't That Sad   (Kama Sutra 583) 1973
         Two Plus Two/
         Don't It Make You Want To Dance (Wooden Nickel 10194) 1975

NB: α as **The Jaggers**.

From the Pittsburgh area, this band lasted into the seventies. Following a respelling to **Jaggerz**, they achieved a top-5 U.S. hit with *The Rapper* in 1970 and released several 45s for Kama Sutra.

According to two band members the first 45 listed above, *Feel So Good*, is by a different band. This features a Kinks-esque riff with great harmony vocals and a super-cool guitar break. It has also resurfaced on *Psychotic Reactions* (LP).

In 1970 Dominic Ierace, started a solo career as 'Donnie Iris'. He later joined Wild Cherry, who had a platinum single in '76 with *Play That Funky Music*. In the eighties, Iris still continued to tour and often performed *The Rapper* in his shows. (GGI/MW/SR/VZ/WM)

The Jaguars

45s: Dead Sea/Supersonic   (Dot 16723) 1965
      The Gorilla/You'll Turn Away   (Dot 16931) 1966
      You'll Turn Away/The Gorilla   (Jaguar 101) 1966
      Another Lonely Night/Night People Make It   (Jaguar 102) 1966
      St James Infirmary/Good Time   (Jaguar 103) 1967

This outfit operated in San Jose, California circa 1965-68. Another California Jaguars, assumed to be a different outfit, put out two 45s on Faro in 1964. (VJ)

The Jaguars

45:    It's Gonna Be Alright/I Never Dream Of You (Skoop 1067) 1967

A Kinks-influenced rock outfit from Michigan, although their sole vinyl offering was recorded in Santa Claus, Indiana.

Compilation appearances include: *It's Gonna Be Alright* on *Back From The Grave, Vol. 5* (LP) and *Back From The Grave, Vol. 2* (CD). (VJ)

The Jaguars

45s: Fine, Fine, Fine / It Finally Happened   (Rendezvous 216) 1963
        Where Lovers Go / Discover A Lover   (Faro 618) 1964
    α   The Return Of Farmer John / Love Is Strange   (Faro 619) 1964
NB: α flip by The Salas Brothers.

BRAIN SHADOWS Vol. 1 (Comp CD) including Jagged Edge.

An East Side Los Angeles outfit, whose *Where Lovers Go* was featured on the 1966 *East Side Revue, Vol. 1* (LP) and 1969 double-LP compilation *East Side Revue*.

Retrospective compilation appearances have included: *One Like Mine* and *The Return Of Farmer John* on *The West Coast East Side Sound, Vol. 2* (CD); *Love Is Strange* and *Where Lovers Go* on *The West Coast East Side Sound, Vol. 3* (CD); and *Where Lovers Go* on *The East Side Sound, Vol. 1* (CD). (MW)

The Jaguars

Personnel:	SANDY EDELSTEIN		A
	JIM KELLY	keyb'ds	A
	DAN MASYS	ld vcls, ld gtr	A
	JON RICKLEY	drms	A
	DAVE SAMPSON	bs	A

45s:	Two Can Play /		
	The Day You're Mine	(unreleased acetate)	1964/5
α	I'll Be Lonely /		
	You Are Your Only Mystery	(Ironbeat HR 1167)	1968

NB: α as **Baroque Monthly**.

Formed circa 1964 in Columbus, Ohio, whilst students at Bexley and Eastmoor high schools. From their 1964/5 acetate *Two Can Play*, a coy garage-beat charmer, can be heard on *Psychedelic Crown Jewels, Vol. 2* which also features their 1968 effort *You Are Your Only Mystery*, released under a one-off name - **The Baroque Monthly**.

Watch out for a two volume Get Hip retrospective collection of the Mus-I-Col label, of which Ironbeat was a subsidiary).

Today Dan Masys is Associate Clinical Professor of Medicine in California, Sampson is an engineer for Lockheed Martin, Kelly a gymnastics teacher in New Jersey, Rickley lives in Indiana, and Edelstein's whereabouts are unknown.

Compilation appearances include: *Two Can Play* on *Psychedelic Crown Jewels Vol. 2* (Dble LP & CD). (MW/GGI/RM)

Jaim

Personnel:	PAUL BISHOP	piano, organ, harpsichord	A
	JERRY CRONIN	vcls, 12 str gtr	A
	MARTIN HALL	gtr, vcls	A
	FAL OLIVER	drms	A
	GARY WOODS	bs	A

ALBUM:	1(A)	PROPHECY FULFILLED	(Ethereal Sunset 1001) 1969 R2

45s:	Ship Of Time / Running Behind	(Ethereal Sunset 101) 1969
	Pretty Woman /	
	Sparkle In Her Eyes Again	(Ethereal Sunset 107) 1969

Thought to be California (Los Angeles?) but not confirmed. The prevalent style here is gentle orchestrated non-electric folk-pop, often with piano. It should appeal to those who like **Gentle Soul**, **Bob Lind** and **The Love Generation**... music for beautiful people, definitely NOT 'psych' as has been touted before. (SR/MW)

Jake Jones

ALBUM:	1	JAKE JONES	(Kapp) c1971 -
	2	DIFFERENT ROADS	(Kapp) c1972 -

From Missouri, a forgotten band, between psychedelic and rural-rock, with good floating guitar work. Their second album contains several good tracks, notably *Tripping Down A Country Road* and *Lost In My Own Back Yard*. (SR)

PEBBLES Vol. 12 (Comp LP) including The Jam.

The Jam

45:	Loving Kind Of Way/Something's Gone	(Sire 5001) 1972

This seems to have been a one-off venture produced by Seymour Stein, who later discovered The Ramones. The flip, a fine example of baroque-pop with strong vocals, harmonies and some good upfront Hammond organ, has resurfaced on *Pebbles, Vol. 12* (LP). (VJ)

Steve Jam

ALBUM:	1	SONGS OF A SONGWRITER	(Private Pressing) 1975 ?

The title says everything! A folk singer with some psychedelic influences. (SR)

The Jam Band

Personnel:	TOM HAMILTON	bs, vcls	A
	JOE PERRY	gtr, vcls	A
	DAVID 'PUDGE' SCOTT	drms	A
	JOHN McGUIRE	hrmnca, vcls	

ALBUM:	1(A)	THE JAM BAND	(private pressing) 1969 ?

NB: (1) Just four copies are thought to exist.

Joe Perry a native of Hopedale, Massachusetts, was the fiery guitarist of this group and had played in local groups The Chimes Of Freedom (1964-65), Just Us (1965-66), The Flash (1967) and Pipe Dream in 1967 with Tom Hamilton (bass), David 'Pudge' Scott (drums), Kathy Lowe (vocals) and Perry on lead guitar. They worked the Boston and New Hampshire band circuit, but didn't gain any decent support gigs, which was considered the 'making' of a local act. Hamilton, Scott and particularly Perry were heavily influenced by British act The Yardbirds and the new spin-off of that group, The Jeff Beck Group. They split Pipe Dream to form Plastic Glass in mid-1967 with John McGuire (harmonica, vocals) which followed the heavy psych blues style laid out by the Jeff Beck Group and the **Jimi Hendrix Experience**, before splitting in late 1968.

In early 1969 Hamilton, McGuire and Scott formed a power outfit with Guy Williams on lead guitar, but before long Joe Perry worked his way into the group and they became known as **The Jam Band** and worked the New Hampshire scene in a heavy blues vein. Their further influences included the **MC5** and another British act, Fleetwood Mac; the latter group's *Rattlesnake Shake* was the **Jam Band**'s showstopper. John McGuire couldn't committ to the group full-time and eventually left. The remaining trio of Hamilton, Perry and Scott recorded one of their rehearsals via two microphones into a two track reel to reel recorder on August 30th, 1969.

The resulting tape was privately pressed as four albums in individual sleeve designs, apparently the three members got a copy, while the fourth was supposedly given to Elyssa Jerrett who recorded the set for the band. The resulting album featured the group's version of Jeff Beck's *Shapes Of Things*, *Let Me Love You Baby*, *Blues Deluxe* and *Rice Pudding*, as well as takes on *Red House*, *Ramblin' Rose*, *Milk Cow Blues* and *Gimme Some Lovin'* in a heavy psych-blues style.

In 1970, the group was in the position to back a Boston based singer Steve Tallarcio on a demo as an audition for the Jeff Beck Group. Tallarcio like the members of the **Jam Band** was a veteran of the Boston band scene, but with far greater credentials as he had played drums and sung with a variety of groups starting with The Mancis in 1963 and alternating between The Strangers and The Dantes in 1964.

The Rolling Stones influenced Strangers became a professional group in late 1964 and changed their name to The Stranguers, signing with CBS in 1966 and recording as the **Chain Reaction** for CBS subsidiary Date Records with little success, although they became regulars on the New York circuit and opened for the Yardbirds. **The Chain Reaction** folded in June 1967, Tallarcio then worked in the studio with the last version of **The Left Banke** before working the New York club scene with Chain in 1967-1968, then back to Boston where that group split in 1969. He then worked with Fox Chase (1969) and William Proud (1970) before trying out for the reforming Jeff Beck Group.

Tallarcio was teamed with **The Jam Band** by Henry Smith, a roadie and gofer not only for The Stranguers, but also the Yardbirds, The Jeff Beck Group and even Led Zeppelin. The resulting recordings did nothing towards the Beck venture, although Tallarcio was convinced that he should continue to work with the group which was on the verge of splitting with 'Pudge' Scott leaving. In September 1970, Joe Perry and Tom Hamilton joined Tallarcio in Boston and they rounded out the group with rhythm guitarist Ray Tabano, a childhood friend of Tallarcio's who had been in William Proud and had jammed with **The Jam Band** in 1969. In October 1970, the group was complete with drummer Joey Kramer and they named themselves **Aerosmith**.

In 1971, Tabano was replaced by Brad Whitford, and in 1972 this version of **Aerosmith** signed to Columbia Records; at this point Steve Tallarcio changed his last name to Tyler. They recorded their debut album in Boston in October 1972 and it was issued in 1973. Despite various line-ups through the years and the subsequent reformation of the 1971-79 version, **Aerosmith** are still active today and remain a chart band. (JO)

Michael J. James

45s:	She Needs The Same Things I Need / Thinking To Myself	(UNI 55096) 1968
	Get The Message / Love's Funny	(UNI 55140) 1969

Possibly from California, a flower-pop singer. *She Needs...* was penned by T. Powers and C. D'Errico. It was produced and arranged by John D'Andrea and Bob Marcucci, who later worked with **Griffin**. (SR)

Tommy James and The Shondells

Personnel:	EDDIE GRAY	gtr	A
	TOMMY JAMES	vcls	A
	MICK JONES	gtr	A
	PETER LUCIA	drms	A
	PAUL REANEY	vcls	A
	RONNIE ROSMAN	piano	A
	MIKE VALE	bs	A

ALBUMS:				HCP
1( )	HANKY PANKY	(Roulette 25336)	1966	46 -
2( )	IT'S ONLY LOVE	(Roulette 25344)	1967	- -
3( )	I THINK WE'RE ALONE NOW	(Roulette 25353)	1967	74 -
4( )	SOMETHING SPECIAL!	(Roulette 25355)	1968	174 -
5( )	GETTIN' TOGETHER	(Roulette 25357)	1968	- -
6( )	MONY MONY	(Roulette 42012)	1968	193 -
7( )	CRIMSON AND CLOVER	(Roulette 42023)	1968	8 -
8( )	CELLOPHANE SYMPHONY	(Roulette 42030)	1969	141 -
9( )	BEST OF...	(Roulette 42040)	1970	21 -
10( )	TRAVELIN'	(Roulette 42044)	1970	91 -
11( )	TOMMY JAMES	(Roulette 42051)	1971	- -
12( )	CHRISTIAN OF THE WORLD	(Roulette 42062)	1972	- -

TOMMY JAMES and THE SHONDELLS - 1+2 CD.

NB: (1),(3) and (5) to (10) were released in France on Vogue/Roulette. (4) is a 'best of'. There's also a French *Greatest Hits* (Roulette CLVLXR 362) 1969. (1) and (2) reissued on one CD (Repertoire REP 4425-WY). Rhino have also released a double LP 'Best Of' collection entitled *Anthology* which may interest collectors.

			HCP
45s:	Hanky Panky/Thunderbolt	(Red Fox 110)	1965 -
	Hanky Panky/Thunderbolt	(Roulette 4686)	1966 1
	Say I Am (What I Am)/ Lots Of Pretty Girls	(Roulette 4695)	1966 21
	It's Only Love/ Don't Let My Love Pass You By	(Roulette 4710)	1966 -
	It's Only Love/Yah Yah	(Roulette 4710)	1966 31
	I Think We're Alone Now/ Gone, Gone, Gone	(Roulette 4720)	1967 4
	Mirage/Run Run Baby Run	(Roulette 4736)	1967 10
	I Like The Way/ Baby I Can't Take It No More	(Roulette 4756)	1967 25
	Gettin' Together/Real Girl	(Roulette 4762)	1967 18
	Out Of The Blue/ Love's Closing In On Me	(Roulette 4775)	1967 43
	Get Out Now/Wish It Were True	(Roulette 7000)	1968 48
	Mony Mony/One Two Three And I Fell	(Roulette 7008)	1968 3
	Somebody Cares/Do Unto Me	(Roulette 7016)	1968 53
	Do Something To Me/Gingerbread Man	(Roulette 7024)	1968 38
	Crimson And Clover/(I'm) Taken	(Roulette 7028)	1968 -
	Crimson And Clover/Some Kind Of Love	(Roulette 7028)	1968 1
	Sweet Cherry Wine/Breakaway	(Roulette 7039)	1969 7
	Crystal Blue Persuasion/I'm Alive	(Roulette 7050)	1969 2
	Ball Of Fire/Makin' Good Time	(Roulette 7060)	1969 19
	She/Loved One	(Roulette 7066)	1969 23
	Gotta Get Back To You/Red Rover	(Roulette 7071)	1970 45
	Come To Me/Talkin' And Signifying	(Roulette 7076)	1970 47
α	Ball And Chain/Candy Maker	(Roulette 7084)	1970 57
α	Church Street Soul Revival/ Draggin' The Line	(Roulette 7093)	1970 62
α	Adrienne/Light Of Day	(Roulette 7100)	1971 93
α	Draggin' The Line/Bits And Pieces	(Roulette 7103)	1971 4
α	I'm Coming Home/Sing Sing Sing	(Roulette 7110)	1971 40
α	Nothing To Hide/Walk A Country Mile	(Roulette 7114)	1971 41
α	Tell' Em Willie Boy's A Comin'/ 40 Days And 40 Nights	(Roulette 7119)	1972 89
	Cat's Eye In The Window/ Dark Is The Night	(Roulette 7126)	1972 90
α	Love Song/Kingston Highway	(Roulette 7130)	1972 67
α	Celebration/The Last One To Know	(Roulette 7135)	1972 95
α	Boo, Boo Don'tcha Be Blue/ Rings And Things	(Roulette 7140)	1973 70
α	Calico/Hey, My Lady	(Roulette 7147)	1973

NB: α Released by **Tommy James**. There are also five French EPs with picture sleeves on Roulette (VREX 65044, 65045, 65048, 65049 and 65051).

Tommy James (real name Thomas Jackson) was born on 29 April 1947 in Dayton, Ohio. He formed his first group in Niles, Michigan when he was just nine and they cut a 45, *Long Pony Tail*, for a local label. Later in 1963, after hearing *Hanky Panky* performed in a night club in South Bend, Indiana, he recorded the song for DJ Jack Douglas' Snap label with an outfit called The Shondells. It sold quite well around Illinois, Michigan and Indiana - and you can now hear it on *Born Bad, Vol. 2*. Two years later when he'd just left college and was out of work Tommy received a call from a DJ in Pittsburgh, Pennsylvania, who had popularised the record. Tommy relocated there and, when the original Shondells refused to leave Indiana, he hired a local band, The Raconteurs, to become the new Shondells. The New York-based Roulette label picked up the disc from Red Fox for national release. It became a million-selling No 1 in the U.S. and also made No 38 in the UK. The debut album made No 46 in the U.S. Album Charts. The Roulette label arranged for songwriter/producers Bo Gentry and Richie Cordell to team up with the band in a partnership which produced a string of melodic and exhilarating hits. Their third LP *I Think We're Alone Now* reached No 74 in the U.S. Charts and their fourth - a compilation *Something Special! The Best of Tommy James And The Shondells* peaked at No 174. *Get Out Now*, their 10th single for Roulette, which made No 48, marked the end of their lightweight pop period.

Mony, Mony, still written by Gentry and Cordell, but with assistance from Bobby Bloom and **James** himself, heralded a new hardened dance beat sound. Not only did it make No 3 in the U.S. but more surprisingly, in view of their lack of previous success there, it was an U.K. No 1 for four weeks and the most popular dance record of the Summer of 1968. The album of the same name reached No 153 in the US. However, after their two *Mony, Mony* - style follow-ups, *Somebody Cares* and *Do Something To Me* were relatively unsuccessful, the group persuaded Roulette to let them produce their next album themselves.

This marked another change of direction and paid off in the short-term. Their next album *Crimson And Clover* made No 8 in the U.S. and an abridged version of the title track topped the U.S. Charts, becoming their biggest selling record and winning a gold disc. With its hints of psychedelia and complete web of instrumental and vocal sounds, *Crimson And Clover* and their next two 45s:- *Sweet Cherry Wine* and *Crystal Blue Persuasion* are their most relevant recordings to this book, but the album *Cellophane Symphony*, which made No 141, and the compilation *The Best Of Tommy James And The Shondells*, which peaked at No 21, are also worth a listen. Their later recordings reverted back to a R&B style and are less relevant. The act ended when **James** collapsed on stage in Alabama and The Shondells quit to become **Hog Heaven** while James recuperated on his farm in upstate New York. When he recovered he embarked on a reasonably successful solo career in the early seventies, producing **Neon**'s sole album with Bob King. He also had a minor resurgence when he signed to Millenium Records in the early eighties.

Crimson And Clover was covered by Joan Jett in 1982 and her version climbed to No 7 in the U.S. Charts prompting other acts to cover some of the band's old hits. Later in 1987 Billy Idol topped the U.S. Charts with a cover of *Mony, Mony* which also made No 7 in the UK. (VJ)

Bobby Jameson

Personnel: ROBERT PARKER JAMES (aka CHRIS LUCEY/ BOBBY JAMESON) hrmnca, vcls A

ALBUMS:
1. JAMESON, COLOR HIM IN (Verve 5015) 1967 SC
2. WORKING! (GRT 10004) 1969 -

NB: There was also a UK album *Too Many Mornings* on the President subsidiary (Joy JOYS 193) 1965. This was released in the US under the pseudonym **Chris Lucey**.

45s:
α I'm So Lonely / I Wanna Love You (Talamo 1934) 1964
Okey Fanokey Baby / Meadow Green (Talamo 1938) 1964
All Alone / Your Sweet Lovin' (Current 103) 1964
β All I Want Is My Baby / Each And Every Day (London 9730) 1965
χ I Wanna Know / Rum Pum (Brit 7001) 1965
Reconsider Baby / Lowdown Funky Blues (Penthouse 501) 1966
Gotta Find My Roogalator / Lowdown Funky Blues (Penthouse 503) 1966
δ New Age / Places, Times And The People (Verve 10509) 1967
Right By My Side / Jamie (Verve 10542) 1967
Palo Alto / Singing The Blues (GRT Records GRT 11) 1969

NB: α issued in the U.K. on London (HL 9921). β recorded with the Rolling Stones and issued in the U.K. on Decca (F 12032). χ issued in the U.K. on Brit (WI 1001). δ as by **Robert Parker Jameson**.

Little is known about this artist, but hopefully more will be revealed. Here's what's turned up so far... Born, Robert Parker James in Tucson, Arizona, he certainly spent some time in (or relocated to) L.A., where his first album was produced by the creative studio whizz **Curt Boettcher** (**Ballroom**, **Sagittarius**, **Millennium**...). Indeed, *Color Him In* is a must for **Boettcher** acolytes. **Jameson**'s strong, sometimes raw'n'bluesy, vocals are to the fore on his self-penned selection of folk-beat-hippie pop. On several cuts Curt B. wraps it in his trademark dreamy neo-psych aura with multi-layered sounds and effects. The angelic (verging on twee) backing vocals are there too. Both Verve 45s are taken from the album.

At least two of his 45s were regional hits, garnering airplay on Cleveland, Ohio and Detroit, Michigan stations. The biggest, *All I Want Is My Baby* was backed by The Rolling Stones. Andrew Loog Oldham recalls:- "**Bobby Jameson** figures reasonably in '2Stoned' - my book with **Kim Fowley**. As I recall **Jameson** turned up in England on the tails of P.J and Mr. Fowley. Keith (Richard) and I recorded him once. He wore one black glove... that and the fact he was game to record some ditty Keith and I had written as a cross between Crewe-Gaudio and **Shadow Morton** got him recorded."

Jameson also recorded an excellent album, *Songs Of Protest And Anti-Protest* under the alternative pseudonym **Chris Lucey**. This was also released in the U.K. as *Too Many Mornings*, but as by **Bobby Jameson**. To confuse matters further, the US labels show his name as "Chris Ducey" and under that moniker he was involved with **Maitreya Kali**'s *Inca* album. Some of the material on *Inca* appears to come from mid-sixties Capitol recordings, when "Chris Ducey" was working with Craig Smith as **Chris and Craig**.

Jameson's records were promoted by Tony Alamo, who also worked with many other artists and John and Bobby Kennedy. L.A. musician Denny Bruce recalls: "To introduce **Bobby Jameson** to the 'industry' Tony Alamo took out a 7-page fold out ad (four color in Billboard) that showed Bobby standing on top of a limo somewhere on the Pacific Coast Highway. With the ocean in the background, so he was not lit, you just saw this guy with a cowboy hat, with his staff next to the limo: very much like the Village People- wearing the very obvious uniforms of their jobs: chef, nurse, barber, bodyguard, driver, etc. There were at least 10 of them. Tony arranged for Bobby to be the opening act for another new act that had signed to Atlantic and were getting a buzz. The showcase was to be at lunch time, so with food being served, everyone came. The act was Caesar and Cleo, wearing togas with olive wreaths in their hair. They of course, became Sonny and Cher. They went on first. Needless to say, when Tony took the mike and had Bobby backlit, behind some see-through screen and was saying "Ladies and gentlemen, here's an act that can act as well as James Dean, sell as many records as the Beatles, on and on, everybody got up and started walking out while a four-track demo was playing, with Bobby is lip-synching to an almost empty house."

Okey Fanokey Baby has also been aired on *Scum Of The Earth, Vol. 1* (LP) and *Scum Of The Earth* (Dble CD) whilst *Vietnam*, a Bo-Diddley rave-up, with snarling vocal, can be heard on *Turds On A Bum Ride, Vol. 2* (Dble LP) or *Turds On A Bum Ride Vol. 1 & 2* (Dble CD). This track first appeared on the soundtrack album *Mondo Hollywood* (Tower T 5083). (MW/RK/JJs/MJ/CP/SBn/JFr/CF)

Jamison

45: We Got Love / Changes (Bell 45-103) c1970

Produced by the obscure "American Varied, Inc", a decent single of flower-psych sung and written by the equally obscure **Jamison**. (SR)

JAMME - Jamme LP.

Jamme

Personnel:	DON ADEY		A
	PAUL DOWNEY		A
	TERRY RAE		A
	TIM SMISER		A
	(JIM GORDON	drms	A)
	(LARRY KNECHTEL	bs, keyb'ds	A)

ALBUM: 1(A) JAMME (ABC Dunhill DS 50072) 1970 -

NB: (1) also released in Australia (Stateside SOSL-10082).

45: Poor Widow/She Sits There (ABC Dunhill 4231) 1970

A pleasant effort which spans Californian folk-rock and light psych. **John Phillips** (of **Mamas and Papas**) handled production duties and Terry Rae had previously played in **The Palace Guard**.

All their material was penned by the Adey brothers, with the help of P. Downey on two tracks.

Terry Rae: "Originally known as Strawberry Jam, the band started to fall apart after John found Michelle, Mia Farrow and myself under a table (high as kites.) Don Adey was the sole survivor bringing in his brother Keith to finish up the album. It was later released on John's own label "Warlock Records" a subsidiary of Dunhill records as **Jamme**. (VJ/SR)

The Jammers

45: You're Gonna Love Me Too/
     I Didn't Mean To Make You (Dearborn 519) 1965

This was this Michigan group's sole vinyl excursion. The 'A' side can be heard on *Michigan Mayhem Vol. 1* (CD) and *Highs In The Mid-Sixties, Vol. 5* (LP). It's a competent, fast-moving beat song. (VJ)

Jamul

Personnel:	RON ARMSTRONG	drms, vcls	A
	BOB DESNOYERS	gtr, vcls	AB
	JOHN FERGUS	bs, vcls	AB
	STEVE WILLIAMS	hrmnca, vcls	AB
	JEFF HOFFMOCKEL	gtr	B
	RICH ROBINSON	drms	B

ALBUM: 1(A) JAMUL (Lizard A-20101) 1970 SC

NB: (1) also released in France in 1971. (1) has been counterfeited on vinyl and on CD in 1996.

45s: Sunrise Over Jamul/ Tobacco Road (Lizard X-21001) 1970
      Movin' To The Country/Ramblin' Man (Lizard X-21004) 1970

NB: Both 45s contain mono, edited versions of LP tracks.

A San Diego group formerly known as The Jamul City Funk Band. **Jamul** (pronounced 'Ha-Mool') is a city in Eastern San Diego county. Armstrong was formerly with **The Misfits**, Desnoyers with **Joel Scott Hill** in The Friendly Grin, and Williams with Puzzle and The Voxmen. The Jamul City Funk Band was a trio until just a few months before recording, when Williams came aboard. This gave the band the distinct advantage of four lead singers trading off on individual tracks.

The band was signed by **Steppenwolf** producer Gabriel Mekler to his new Lizard Records label and it was at Mekler's insistence that they shortened their name to **Jamul**. For those interested in true minutae, "Lizard" was the name of Mekler's pet cat!

The **Jamul** album has much to recommend it, particularly to fans of loud hard-rock (**Euclid**, labelmates **Frantic**, **Yesterday's Children** bear some resemblance). Of the eleven tracks that make up the album, eight are original. There's also a brutal cover of *Tobacco Road*, a dirge-like *Jumpin' Jack Flash* and a bluesy *Long Tall Sally* with Williams wailing away on harmonica. If this album had not sold in excess of 75,000 copies in 1970, it would be fetching serious money today.

Jamul fell out with their management in 1971, and a split followed. Some months later, a reformed line-up ('B') recorded a second album, *Jamul II* which remains unreleased.

Since leaving **Jamul**, Ron Armstrong has made a number of recordings featuring other San Diego musicians like Jerry McCann (**Orfuns**, **Framework**, **Formerly Anthrax**), Jerry Raney (**Roosters**, **Glory**, The Beat Farmers), **Joel Scott Hill** (**Canned Heat**), **Bob Mosley** (**Misfits**, **Moby Grape**). These recordings (which extend from the seventies to the present) constitute an album-in-progress, a pet project of Armstrong's that he has steadily continued to work on when time and capital is available. (CF/VJ/SR)

Jan and Lorraine

Personnel:	JAN HENDIN	gtr, vcls, keyb'ds	A
	LORRAINE LEFEVRE	vcls, gtr	A

ALBUM: 1(A) GYPSY PEOPLE (ABC ABCS 691) 1969 SC

On their album, which is folky with a psychedelic taint rather similar to Trees who came a year later, the duo are backed by half a dozen session musicians. The better tracks include *The Assignment Song Sequence* and *Life's Parade*.

Their album was recorded in London, although it doesn't seem to have secured a U.K. release. The session musicians were Keshav Sathe (Cosmic Eye, Magic Carpet, John Martyn, etc.), Terry Cox (Pentangle,

JAMUL.

JAMUL - Jamul CD.

Humblebums, Sallyangie, Tudor Lodge, etc.), Clem Cattini (Brian Auger, Joe Cocker, P. J. Proby, etc.) and Brian Odgers (Sweet Tuesday, John McLaughlin, Al Stewart, etc.). Given the extensive U.K. connections it's doubtful they were American. (VJ)

Janey and Dennis

Personnel:	GREG ADAMS	trumpet	A
	GITRY BOYD	ld gtr	A
	PETER CHILDS	bs, banjo, dobro, gtr	A
	JERRY CORBITT	hrmnca	A
	GREG DEWEY	drms	A
	LAWRENCE HAMMOND	bs	A
	JOHN MCFEE	pedal steel	A
	JEFF MEYER	drms	A
	DENNIS PERECA	vcl, piano, gtr	A
	JANEY SCHRAMM	vcl, gtr	A
	VIC SMITH	bs	A

ALBUM: 1(A) JANEY AND DENNIS (Reprise RS 6414) 1970 -

Produced by **Jerry Corbitt** (ex-**Youngbloods**), this is a Californian folk-rock duo mainly interesting because of the presence of members of **Mad River** (Hammond and Dewey), **Grootna**/**Bodacious D.F.** (Smith) and Clover (McFee). It's unfortunately overproduced with strings and horns and therefore really disappointing. (SR)

January Tyme

Personnel:	WILLIAM BRANCACCIO	gtr, keyb'ds vcls	A
	STEVE CIANTRO	bs	A
	ALAN COOLEY	drms, vcls	A
	ANTHONY (MONY) IZZO	ld gtr, vcls	A
	JANUARY TYME	vcls, keyb'ds, perc	A

ALBUM: 1(A) FIRST TIME FROM MEMPHIS
(Enterprise ENS-1004) 1970 SC

NB: (1) reissued on vinyl and CD (Akarma AK 030) 1998.

Dominated by the strident, in-yer-face vocals of January Tyme this is late sixties bluesy-folk-rock in the **Jefferson Airplane**/**Big Brother** format and somewhere between those two reference points in musical style. Like so many others who chose to emulate this particular sound, they fail to establish their own identity despite their obvious competence and vitality, making them one of the "also-rans" in this category. (MW)

Cook E. Jarr

ALBUM:	1 PLEDGING MY LOVE	(RCA LSP-4159) 1969 -
45s:	Reason To Believe/	
	Do You Believe In Magic	(RCA 74-0182) 1969
	If I Were A Carpenter/Pleding My Love	(RCA 74-0119) 1969
	Red Balloon/Darling, Be Home Soon	(RCA 47-9708) 1969
	Cookie's Bag/Who Wears Hot Pants	(Epic 10735) 1971
α	Ain't No Use, Pt. 1/Pt. 2	(Roulette) 1975

NB: α by Cook E. Jarr and His Krums.

A bubblegum soul-pop singer that you'll find either awful or amusing (or both!). Produced by John Woram, this album contain no less than four compositions by **Tim Hardin** plus covers of Otis Redding, Eddie Floyd and the **Lovin' Spoonful**'s *Do You Believe In Magic?*. (SR)

Rick Jarrard

45s:	Constantly/Why	(Chattahoocie 657) 1964
	I Put A Spell On You/?	(Chattahoochie) c1965
	Traffic Jam/Time's Tomorrow	(Chattahoochie 700) 1966

Released on **Kim Fowley**'s label, **Rick Jarrard** would later become better known for his production work with **Loading Zone**, **Jefferson Airplane**, Harry Nilsson and **Stone Country**. (SR)

Jarvo Runga

ALBUM: 1 DEMO-DISC (No label) 1972 R3

A local New Jersey duo, whose privately - pressed album comprised primitive rockers. (CF/NK)

Jasper Wrath

Personnel:	ROBERT GENNETTE	A
	CHRISTOPHER HAWKE	A
	MICHAEL SOLDAN	A
	PHILIP STOLTIE	A

ALBUM: 1(A) JASPER WRATH (Sunflower SNF 5003) 1971 R1

NB: Also of interest is *Anthology 1969 - 1976* (Oxford Circus OXF 001) 1996, a double CD retrospective, including the best tracks from (1), unreleased material, live tracks and three new recordings.

JANUARY TYME - First Time From Memphis LP.

45s:	Did You Know That?/It's Up To You	(Sunflower 107) 1971
	Did You Know That (Mono/	
	Stereo) DJ promo	(Sunflower 107) 1971
	You / General Gunther	(Future Music FMI 101) 1976

This was a short-lived hippie-rock outfit whose album was produced with assistance from Joey Levine and Jim Carroll. The most upbeat number, *Did You Know That?* also appeared on a 45; the flip side of which was not from the album. For the most part the album comprises soft-rock with lots of electric and acoustic six and twelve string guitars, organ, harpsichord, celeste, percussion, theremin and variable frequency oscillators. It mostly works quite well with *Odyssey and Portrait: My Lady Angelina* probably the finest moments. The closing track, *Roland Of Montevere*, veers far more towards progressivism.

Their 1976 45, *You / General Gunther* is a comparatively disappointing typical mid-seventies prog effort. It was produced by Jeff Cannata.

The band were formerly known as Christopher Hawke, and before that Tri-Power, who'd included Joe Mendyk (later of The Better Days and **Nova Local**). They were based in Hamden, Connecticut. (VJ/MW/SR)

Robby Jay

| Personnel: | BOB EVESLAGE | A |

| 45: | The Days When I Knew Judy/ | |
| | Portrait Of My Dream | (Panorama 47) 1966 |

A one-off 45 by **Unbelievable Uglies** member Bob Eveslage, which was recorded at Audio Recording studios, Seattle: "I played all the instruments myself and multi-tracked it. Both sides took about three hours, 'cause it was my "nickel" and times were lean for me in those early Seattle years. Man, those are good memories, though!"

For more information on Bob Eveslage's career - see the **Unbelievable Uglies** entry.

The Jaybees

| 45s: | I'm A Loner/Do You Think I'm In Love | (RCA 47-8904) 1966 |
| | Think Of Her/Unbelievable | (RCA 47-9001) 1966 |

An obscure garage-rock group with frantic guitar parts. Produced by Joe Rene, the songs on their first single were written by A. Nicholls, F. Hill and A. Kaye.

Compilation appearances have included: *I'm A Loner* on *Pebbles, Vol. 22* (LP) and *The Essential Pebbles Collection, Vol. 2* (2-CD). (SR)

Jay Hawkers

45s:	Dawn Of Instruction/Searchin'	(Deltron 1227) c1965
	To Have A Love (As Sweet As You)/	
	Send Her Back	(Deltron 1228) c1965
	Love Have Mercy/Baby Blue	(Lyke Til 4147) 196?
	Come On/A Certain Girl	(Lucky Eleven 232) 1966

From the Detroit area, a band best known for *Dawn Of Instruction*, a riposte to Barry McGuire's *Eve Of Destruction*. Their other outings remain uncompiled but the Deltron 1228 45 is cool 'n' catchy Invasion-garage-beat backed by a sultry beat-ballad that has echoes of the Kinks' *Tired Of Waiting*. The band also made one 45 as **Dwight Douglas and The Jayhawkers**.

Compilation appearances include: *Dawn Of Instruction* on *Sixties Rebellion, Vol. 12* (LP & CD) and *Sixties Archive Vol. 7* (CD). (MW)

Jeanie, Jim, Tom And Bill

| 45: | Silly Whim/Devotion | (No label 5-5998) 1965 |

Mid-sixties punkers from Minnesota. The 'A' side has resurfaced on *Hipsville, Vol. 3*. (VJ)

JASPER WRATH - Anthology 1969-1976 CD.

The Jeans

| 45: | In My Own Time/To Love Somebody | (Zefco 4127) 1968 |

Hailing from Stanley, Kansas, this mob started life as Beatles imitators but later switched allegiance to the Bee Gees. Their Gibb brothers cover, *In My Own Time*, which featured some snarling fuzz guitar, can now be heard on *Monsters Of The Midwest, Vol. 3* (LP). (VJ)

Jefferson Airplane

Personnel:	SIGNE ANDERSON	vcls	AB
	MARTY BALIN	gtr, vcls	ABCDE
	BOB HARVEY	bs	A
	PAUL KANTNER	gtr, vcls	ABCDEFG H
	JORMA KAUKONEN	gtr, vcls	ABCDEFG H
	SKIP SPENCE	drms	AB
	JACK CASADY	bs	BCDEFG H
	SPENCER DRYDEN	drms	C
	GRACE SLICK	vcls	CDEFG H
	JOEY COVINGTON	drms	DEF
	PAPA JOHN CREACH	violin, vcls	EFG H
	JOHN BARBATA	drms	G
	DAVID FRIEBERG	vcls	H

HCP

ALBUMS:	1(B)	JEFFERSON AIRPLANE TAKES OFF		
(up to			(RCA LSP 3584) 1966	128 -
1975)	2(C)	SURREALISTIC PILLOW	(RCA LSP 3766) 1967	3 -
	3(C)	AFTER BATHING AT BAXTER'S		
			(RCA LSP 1511) 1967	17 -
	4(C)	CROWN OF CREATION	(RCA LSP 4058) 1969	6 -
	5(C)	BLESS ITS POINTED LITTLE HEAD		
			(RCA LSP 4133) 1969	17 -
	6(C)	VOLUNTEERS	(RCA LSP 4238) 1970	13 -
	7(-)	THE WORST OF JEFFERSON AIRPLANE		
			(RCA LSP 4459) 1970	12 -
	8(F)	BARK	(Grunt FTR 1001) 1971	11 -
	9(H)	LONG JOHN SILVER	(Grunt FTR 1007) 1972	20 -
	10(-)	THIRTY SECONDS OVER WINTERLAND		
			(Grunt FTR 0147) 1973	52 -
	11(-)	EARLY FLIGHT	(Grunt FTR 0437) 1974	110 -

NB: All titles have been reissued on CD. (2) reissued on vinyl (Sundazed LP 5135) 2002. (7) is a 'best of'. (10) is a live album containing a balance between old and new material. (11) includes previously unreleased material from the 1965-70 era. Recent releases which may interest collectors include *2400 Fulton Street* (a 'Best Of' collection also available on CD); *Great Society*, *Live Monterey*, *Collection* and *Crown Of Creation* (all CDs) and *Volunteers*, *Take Off On A Surrealistic Pillow* a bootleg of live material recorded in 1969. *Through The Looking Glass* (Almafame EFA 88905-2) 1998 is a messy CD compilation, which is not recommended, whereas *Jefferson Airplane* (Camden 74321 841022) 2001 is a good introductory CD to their music.

Ignition (RCA 07863 68032 2) 2001 is a 4-CD box set focusing on their first four albums and featuring both mono and stereo mixes of the first two. Other releases are detailed at the end of this article.

Paul Kantner Solo: HCP
ALBUM: 1   BLOWS AGAINST THE EMPIRE
                                          (RCA LSP 4448) 1970 20 -

Paul Kantner with Grace Slick: HCP
ALBUM: 1   SUNFIGHTER   (Grunt FTR 1002) 1971 89 -

EPs: 1   Bless It's Pointed Head - Open End Interview
                                                 (F.A.S. 369) 1969
        2   Stereo Review Sampler (4 Cuts)   (RCA 564) 1969

                                                                 HCP
45s: It's No Secret/Runnin' Round This World   (RCA 8679) 1966 -
         Come Up The Years/
         Blues From An Airplane   (RCA 8848) 1966 -
         Bringing Me Down/Let Me In   (RCA 8967) 1966 -
         My Best Friend/How Do You Feel   (RCA 9063) 1967 103
         Somebody To Love/She Has Funny Cars   (RCA 9140) 1967 5
         White Rabbit/Plastic Fantastic Lover   (RCA 9248) 1967 8
   χ   The Ballad Of You, Me And Pooneil/
         Two Heads   (RCA 9297) 1968 42/124
   χ   Watch Her Ride/Martha   (RCA 9389) 1968 61
         Greasy Heart/
         Share A Little Joke With The World   (RCA 9496) 1968 98
         Lather/Crown Of Creation (PS)   (RCA 9644) 1968 64
   χ   Plastic Fantastic Lover/
         Other Side Of This Life (PS)   (RCA 01 50) 1969 133
         Volunteers/We Can Be Together   (RCA 0245) 1969 65
         Mexico/
         Have You Seen The Saucers? (PS)   (RCA 0343) 1969 102
   α   Let's Go Together/A Child Is Coming (PS)   (RCA 0426) 1971 -
         Pretty As You Feel/Wild Turkey (PS)   (Grunt 0500) 1971 60
   β   Sunfighter/China (PS)   (Grunt 0503) 1972 -
         Long John Silver/Milk Train (PS)   (Grunt 0506) 1972 104
         Trial By Fire/Twilight Double Leader   (Grunt 0511) 1972 -

NB: α Paul Kantner. β Paul Kantner and Grace Slick. χ were also released in France with picture sleeves. There's also a rare French EP with picture sleeve: *Somebody To Love/My Best Friend/White Rabbit/How Do You Feel* (RCA 86560) 1967.

Jefferson Airplane had the advantage of a compulsive name. Previously groups had tended to name themselves after animals or insects but this name, which actually evolved from blues singer 'Blind Lemon Jefferson' really made you sit up and take note. The same was true of their music, you may love or hate it but you could not ignore it. They had so much to say and their music generated such urgency - a sort of direct channel of communication between the group and your brain.

JEFFERSON AIRPLANE - Takes Off CD.

JEFFERSON AIRPLANE - Surrealistic Pillow CD.

Jefferson Airplane was the foremost of the new San Francisco underground bands and also one of the earliest. Apparently only **The Charlatans** and **The Mystery Trend** predated them. More significantly they were the first of the new San Francisco bands to win a recording contract - a $20,000 advance from RCA to produce their first album *Takes Off*.

Marty Balin was the group's founder member. Although born in Milwaukee, his family moved to San Francisco because of Marty's childhood asthma. He became a lithographer and painter, with a penchant to sing, cutting two solo 45s for Challenge Records in 1962: *I Specialize* and *Nobody But You* and singing in a Los Angeles folk group, The Town Criers in 1964. After seeing The Beatles on the Ed Sullivan show earlier that year, he decided to start a rock and roll band and, when he met Paul Kantner at a local folk club in San Francisco, invited him to join his group (which had not been formed yet). Jorma Kaukonen, a friend of Kantner's, joined as a favour to him. Kaukonen had worked with Janis Joplin around the Bay Area, the strength of her vocals motivating him to buy his first electric guitar. Kaukonen recommended his old friend Jack Casady to come across from Washington DC and replace original bassist, Bob Harvey, in the group. With the addition of Signe Anderson, a girl singer, also originally from Washington DC, and **Skip Spence**, on drums, the show was on the road. **Spence** was not the band's original drummer, but he soon replaced Jerry Peloquin, who only lasted a few weeks. Balin had apparently recruited **Spence** while he was on his way to audition as guitarist for another important San Francisco band, **Quicksilver Messenger Service**.

In 1965 Marty Balin took over a folk and jazz club called 'The Honeybucket', which he rechristened as 'The Matrix Club' and **Airplane** became semi-resident there. They played at almost all the important early San Francisco music events, including the very first dance organised by the Family Dog (a group of hippie concert promoters who originated from Mexico) at the Longshoreman's Hall near the Fisherman's Wharf on October 16th, 1965.

Marty Balin designed three screenprint posters to publicise the event and **The Airplane** topped the bill, which included **The Charlatans**, **The Great Society** and **The Marbles** (one of the lost bands of San Francisco rock history, who were there at the beginning but then simply vanished). They played again at the first event held at the Fillmore by its new owner, Bill Graham, as a benefit for the Mime Troupe, a radical theatre group which also organised dances (they were rival promoters to the Family Dog). This time **The Airplane** played alongside **The Great Society**, **The Mystery Trend**, The Gentlemen's Band, The VIP'S, The Warlocks, (later to become **The Grateful Dead**) and many others.

In November 1965 **The Airplane** signed to RCA and four months later their debut single was issued, *It's No Secret/Runnin' Round This World*. The 'B' side contained the word 'trips' and RCA insisted that the track be omitted from their debut album, *Jefferson Airplane Takes Off*, which was issued a month later in the US, but a handful of copies did escape the factory with the song intact, and are now the rarest item in the **Jefferson Airplane** canon, fetching in excess of $8000. This incident marked the first souring of relationships between RCA and the band which would become a feature of

JEFFERSON AIRPLANE - After Bathing At Baxter's CD.

the following year. A second single *Blues From An Airplane/Come Up The Years*, was issued.

The album, although instrumentally shaky, went gold. It included the hippie anthem *Let's Get Together*, later a hit for **The Youngbloods**, which epitomised the peace and love message of the Summers of 1966 and 1967. It also created enough interest to attract a host of record company executives to San Francisco to sign up the new 'acid rock' bands. However, for the present, **Airplane**'s format was very much folk-rock, with Marty Balin's love songs to the fore. Shortly after the release of the first album, Signe Anderson left the group, having had a baby, and **Skip Spence**, who was never at ease playing the drums, left to set up another important San Francisco group, **Moby Grape**.

Spence was replaced by Spencer Dryden, an experienced jazz drummer, who was then playing with a Los Angeles based group, **The Ashes** (later to become **The Peanut Butter Conspiracy**). **The Airplane** had often gigged with **The Great Society**, another 'Frisco band, and Grace Slick who'd sometimes hung-out at **Airplane** rehearsals was recruited to replace Signe Anderson.

Grace brought with her a unique voice. It was rougher and more raucous than Signe Anderson's and complimented Marty Balin's smooth, sweeter tones. She combined with Kantner and Balin to produce strange harmonies which were superimposed on Casady's and Kaukonen's unpredictable and disturbing guitar rhythms. She also brought two songs from **The Great Society**, *Somebody To Love* and *White Rabbit* which **The Airplane** were to transform into their only big U.S. hits, reaching No's 5 and 8 respectively in the Billboard charts. Both songs were contained on the group's second album *Surrealistic Pillow*, although the British version of the album inexplicably omitted *White Rabbit* and *Plastic Fantastic Lover* in favour of three songs from the *Takes Off* album.

White Rabbit demonstrated Slick's meandering, weaving vocals and her use of unpredictable musical intervals admirably, a style which was to become a poignant feature of many of her songs. A drug song, and, therefore, banned by onshore radio in the U.K. at the time, *White Rabbit* appears to be based on the concept of Alice tripping in Wonderland.

"One pill makes you larger
One pill makes you small
And the ones that mother gives you
Don't do anything at all
Go ask Alice
When she's ten feet tall
And it you go chasing rabbits
And you know you're going to fall
Tell 'em a hookah-smoking caterpillar
Has given you the call"
(from *White Rabbit*)

From a gentle beginning the song builds into an impressive crescendo.

Like **The Byrds**, **Airplane** progressed through various musical phases and their change from Marty Balin's electrified folk rock songs like *Today* (apparently two songs merged into one), *My Best Friend* and *Comin' Back To Me* towards the 'acid rock' of subsequent albums is evident on *Surrealistic Pillow* in songs such as *White Rabbit* and *3/5ths Of A Mile in 10 Seconds*, representing the more electrified 'acid' rock.

The Airplane's next single *The Ballad Of You, Me and Pooneil/Two Heads* was superb. Both tracks were from their forthcoming album. Unfortunately, they were too complex for the singles market and it only reached No 42 in the States. Commercially, it was such a flop in the U.K. that their follow-up single *Watch Her Ride/Martha* was not released here.

Their next two studio albums *After Bathing At Baxter's* and *The Crown Of Creation* mark the pinnacle of their achievement and the consolidation of their 'acid' phase. Some of the songs on these albums are very weird indeed, and in their live appearances the band strived hard to superficially recreate the drug experience, using imaginative light shows and often drifting into lengthy, improvised meandering jams which lifted the psychedelic mood of the times. The *Baxter's* album contained one such nine minute long jam *Spare Chaynge*, while *Saturday Afternoon* was written in memory of the 'Be-In', a spontaneous gathering held in the Polo grounds of Golden Gate Park on 14th January 1967 which included the **Airplane**. This event attracted an estimated crowd of 20,000 and the concept of free music in parks had become part and parcel of the San Francisco rock scene. The 'Be-In' also inspired the 1967 Monterey Rock Festival, featuring the **Airplane** and many other leading San Francisco rock groups.

Airplane were playing in an era of considerable social change and this was often reflected in their lyrics, for instance in *Wild Thyme*, also on their third album, they sing:.

"It's a wild time
I see people all around with changing faces
It's a wild time
I'm doing things that haven't got a name yet......"

One of the most interesting songs of this album is *Rejoyce*. A particularly complex piece, this again highlights the effectiveness of Grace's meandering vocals and unpredictable musical intervals. Like many of **Airplane**'s songs, it echoes their anti-establishment, anti-Vietnam sentiments:-

"War's their business
So give your son
But I'd rather have my country die for me......"
(from *Rejoice*)

JEFFERSON AIRPLANE - Crown Of Creation CD.

The *Crown Of Creation* album features what is, arguably, their finest song *The House At Pooneil Corner*. The song has an impressive, spacey and very compulsive beginning and works towards a compelling climax. The title

JEFFERSON AIRPLANE - Bless Its Pointed Little Head CD.

song itself uses the lyrics from John Wyndham's The Chrysalids to re-emphasise **Airplane**'s interpretation of the conflict between the hippie movement and the American establishment:

"The old people are determined still that there is a final form to defend,
Soon they will attain the stability they strive for,
In the only form it is granted - a place among the fossils......"

and again

"In loyalty to their kind they cannot
tolerate our minds
In loyalty to our kind we cannot tolerate
their obstruction......"
(from *Crown Of Creation*)

The album contained many other impressive numbers such as *Greasy Heart* and *Ice Cream Phoenix* as well as *Chushingura*, a piece of Pink Floyd style psychedelia. It reached No 6 in the U.S. charts.

Their next album was a live one featuring reworked versions of their early songs and some new material, including Donovan's song *Fat Angel* (which made the phrase 'Fly Jefferson Airplane, getcha there on time' world famous) and *Bear Melt*, another trippy, drug influenced song.

But 1969 saw also the end of the hippie dream at Altamont, where **The Airplane** had played with The Rolling Stones, and also the demise of the Haight Ashbury peace-love scene. So **The Airplane** deserted 'acid rock' and the result was *Volunteers*, a strongly political album which developed the theme of conflict between the revolutionaries, **The Airplane** and the establishment, which had been introduced in the title track of *Crown Of Creation*. The title track *Volunteers*, and *We Can Be Together* contained the rallying cries: 'Got to Revolution, Got To Revolution' and 'Tear down the wall, motherfuckers'. Beyond this, lyrics were vague on how the revolution was to come about and it all sounds rather dated today. It does, however, contain a gorgeous version of *Wooden Ships* written by Kantner, **Crosby** and Steve Stills, which marks Kantner's first excursion into the realms of science fiction. The song assumes a post-nuclear age, permitting **The Airplane** to say 'We are leaving, you don't need us'- without having to confront the problems raised by their twin espousal of love and revolution. However, the theme of leaving Earth in a giant starship would return later.

A single, *Volunteers/We Can Be Together* was taken from the album and issued both in the US, where it was a minor hit, and in UK.

After *Volunteers* the group began to fragment. Marty Balin left and with Slick expecting Kantner's child ,further gigging was impossible. Kaukonen and Casady, therefore, began to spend more time with their own 'spin-off' group **Hot Tuna**, which had first taken shape in December '68 as an outlet for **Airplane** members to gig more frequently, whereas Kantner in particular disliked touring, other members were keen to play in front of a live audience. Marty Balin, too sang at early **Hot Tuna** gigs, and future **Airplane** drummer, **Joey Covington** was also involved with the outfit from

the beginning. There was also a need within the band to stretch themselves artistically and Slick and Kantner began work on solo albums.

Blows Against The Empire marked the development of Kantner's interest in science ficton. The plot suggested hijacking an interplanetary starship built on the earth and to make it suitable for practical travel to other solar systems. *Hijack* deals with this, *Have You Seen the Stars Tonite?* with an evening stroll on board the deck and *Starship* rejoices about the whole scheme. Interspersed between the tracks are space-like sounds creditably produced given the minimal instrumentation available at the time. Some U.S. promo copies of this album were pressed on clear vinyl and have become some of the most collectable **Airplane** - related items. Kantner's science fiction fantasies would emerge again on later Jefferson Starship albums.

In comparison with *Blows Against The Empire*, remaining **Airplane** studio albums were uninteresting. *Bark* was disappointing and *Long John Silver* not much better, although *Pretty As You Feel* from *Bark* was a minor hit. **Airplane**'s lyrics had always made them interesting - while most other groups and artistes sang the typical 'boy meets girl' love songs, **Airplane** always had a message to put across. But now with Kantner, the group's most prolific songwriter keeping the best material for his solo albums and the hippie dream discredited, **The Airplane** seemed to be running out of things to say. Nevertheless, *Long John Silver* has its moments, particularly with *Easter?* featuring Grace singing about its futility as a religious festival. Two 45s were issued from the album, *Long John Silver/Milk Train* and *Trial By Fire/Twilight Double Leader*. Neither met with chart success.

JEFFERSON AIRPLANE - Volunteers CD.

A number of compilations of **The Airplane**'s material exist. *The Worst Of Jefferson Airplane* issued in 1970 contained a fair cross-section of their material. *Early Flight* (Grunt APL1 0437), issued in 1974, contains unissued songs from the band, including *High Flying Bird*, which they performed in the 'Monterey Pop' movie. *Thirty Seconds Over Winterland* (Grunt APL1 0147), issued in 1973, was recorded 'live' and contained a balance between their old and new material. It also featured ex-**Turtle** John Barbata for the first time on drums (**Joey Covington** having departed to form his own outfit, Fat Fandango); and David Freiberg, who had joined from **Quicksilver Messenger Service**. Later compilations included *Flight Log* (Grunt 1255/RCA LSP 3766), and *Best Of* (RCA 42727). *Crown Of Creation* and *Volunteers* were reissued in a budget series in 1985 and *The Worst Of* followed in 1986.

1973 saw **The Airplane** finally disband, but they had indeed been a remarkable outfit. The most interesting and successful of the San Francisco bands. Just a year would elapse before they returned to the limelight as the enormously successful (in commercial terms) Jefferson Starship. 1987 saw the issue of *2400 Fulton Street* (RCA NL90036(2)) - an important double album compilation of their material. It featured 25 tracks put together by Bill Thompson, with an extra 10 tracks on the CD, which included a couple of previously unreleased Levi's tracks. The four sides were subtitled:- Beginnings, Psychedelia, Revolution and Airplane Parts and featured material from 1965 to 1971. *White Rabbit* and *Somebody To Love* were also reissued on a 45 and the 12 inch version featured *She Has Funny Cars* and *Third Week In Chelsea* as extra tracks.

1988 saw the release of *The Jefferson Airplane Collection* on Castle Records (CCSLP 200), licensed from BMG/RCA. Also available on CD, it contained no previously unreleased material but included some of their less well known recordings like *Meadowlands, Alexander The Medium* and a live version of *Have You Seen The Saucers*.

1989 saw a CD release of *Live At The Monterey Pop Festival* (Document Records (DR 023 CD)) and featured their full 39-minute set.

In August 1989, *Jefferson Airplane* got it all together again for an American tour and a new album (also available on CD). The line-up was the seminal quintet of Marty Balin, Grace Slick, Jack Casady, Jorma Kaukonen and Paul Kantner, which had recorded all their best albums with the help of the then sixth (line-up C) member, drummer Spencer Dryden. The album *Jefferson Airplane* (Epic OE 45271) had some fine moments. Four new Grace Slick contributions of which *Freedom* is the best but *Common Market Madrigal, Now Is The Time* and *Panda* all found her in fine voice. Other tracks like *The Wheel* confirmed that Kantner, Slick and Balin could still produce those superb three-part harmonies. Although the instrumentation suffered at times from the involvement of far too many "guest" musicians which undermined the traditional instrumental incisiveness of Casady, Kantner and Kaukonen, overall the album was a welcome testament for the short-lived relaunch.

The band's set at the Monterey Pop Festival which had previously only been available on the quasi-legal CD on Document finally got an official release, *Live At The Monterey Pop Festival* on Thunderbolt (THBL 074) in 1990. The same year saw a vinyl-only release of *Avalon Ballroom, 1969* (Kornyfone 006), which is actually a reissue of the *Up Against The Wall* bootleg from 1970. Also released in 1990 was the very misleadingly titled CD *The Woodstock Revival* (Pulsar PULS 002) in Holland. It actually features material which entirely predated Woodstock - a mixture of material from the Monterey Pop Festival, their *High Flyin' Bird* bootleg, *Takes Off, Surrealistic Pillow* and the four non-Airplane cuts which made up Side Two of the *High Flyin' Bird* bootleg.

Camden's 2001 repackaged CD compilation *Jefferson Airplane* is a good introduction to the band, featuring all their early singles, including their hits *White Rabbit* and *Somebody To Love*. Also of note are a version of *Wooden Ships*, Jorma Kaukonen's *Embryonic Journey* and two live 'B' sides.

Fans of **Jefferson Airplane** are strongly recommended to subscribe to the 'fanzine' **Holding Together** published by Bill Parry, 89 Glengariff Street, Clubmoor, Liverpool L13 8DW.

In 1999, original bass player Bob Harvey released a new CD with songs made from 1965 to 1999 with his current band San Francisco Blue.

Compilation appearances have included: *White Rabbit* on *Psychedelic Frequencies* (CD); *Somebody To Love* on *First Vibration* (LP); *The California Christmas Album* (LP) features live versions of *Kansas City* and *Fat Angel* from 1966 and three of the four Levi's Jeans commercials they did in 1967. *California New Year* includes versions of *White Rabbit, Please Come Back, She Has Funny Cars* and *Ride Jefferson Airplane*. Matthew Katz's *Then And Now, Vol. 2* (CD) compilation also includes a version of *Other Side Of This Life* recorded live at The Matrix in 1965, together with *It's No Secret* (from *Takes Off*) and Marty Balin's live *Summer Of Love*. *Then And Now, Vol. 2* (CD) also includes *Runnin' Round This World* and *Embryonic Journey* recorded live at the Matrix in 1965, and Marty Balin's *Always Tomorrow*. (VJ/BP/SR)

Jefferson Hankerchief

| 45: | I'm Allergic To Flowers/ | |
| | The Little Matador | (Challenge 59371) 1967 |

Recorded in California, this was a one-off venture by a group of Los Angeles session musicians. The 'A' side, *I'm Allergic To Flowers*, is laden with references to flower-power mythology, relating how the narrator would love to be a hippie but can't because of his allergy to pollen (dig?). The song was written by Dave Burgess, who'd previously played with The Champs, who'd enjoyed instrumental hits in the late fifties and early sixties and Keith Colley, who wrote for **The Knickerbockers** and The Magic Lanterns among others.

The song travelled well - it was picked up down-under in 1968 by Aussie duo Vicky & Dicky - sniffle along with their version on *No.8 Wire*.

Compilation appearances have included: *I'm Allergic To Flowers* on *Pebbles, Vol. 3* (CD), *Pebbles, Vol. 3* (LP), *Garagelands, Vol. 2* (CD) and *Mindrocker, Vol. 1* (LP); and *The Little Matador* on *Sixties Rebellion, Vol. 12* (LP & CD). (VJ/MW)

Jefferson Lee

Personnel incl: JEFF LEE

| 45s: | Book Of Love/Sorcerella | (Original Sound OS-88) 1969 |
| | Bubblegum Music/Pancake Trees | (Original Sound OS-93) 1970 |

A Californian act which may have just been a solo artist. *Sorcerella* is heavy melodramatic pop with fuzz and psychy guitar-work, whilst *Book Of Love* is a heavy 'psychedelic-soul' take on a Monotones song. The second 45 features catchy pop backed by an airy pop-psych ditty with flute and various effects that doesn't quite come off.

Compilation appearances have included: *Sorcerella* on *Son Of The Gathering Of The Tribe* (LP) and *Turds On A Bum Ride Vol. 3* (CD); and *Pancake Eyes* on *U-Spaces: Psychedelic Archaeology Vol. 1* (CDR). (VJ/MW)

Jekyl and The Hydes

| 45: | To Forgive Is Divine / | |
| | High Heeled Sneakers | (General American GAR 107) 1967 |

The label for this garage 45 was based in Columbia, MO. but it featured bands from Ohio, Arkansas, even the UK, as well as local Missouri acts.

There are at least two 45s by near-same-name outfits, that we presume are different bands:- Jekyll and Hyde (possibly from New England): *My Baby Loves Monster Movies / Theme From Whodunit* (Dcp 1111) 1964; and Jekyll's and The Hydes (from Dorchester, Massachusetts): *Diddley Daddy / You Can't Judge A Book* (Boss 200,899/900) May 1966. (BM/MW)

The Jelly Bean Bandits

Personnel:	JOHN (JACK) DOUGHERTY	ld gtr	A
	FRED (FABLES) BUCK	bs	A
	JOE (LAREDO LONDON) SCALFARI	drms	A
	BILLY (BREWSTER) DONALD	ld vcls	A
	MICHAEL (MR ADDAMS) RAAB	keyb'ds	A

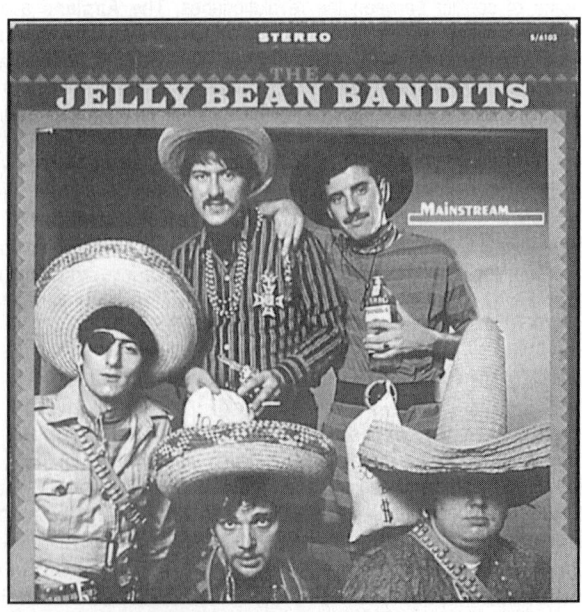

THE JELLY BEAN BANDITS - The Jelly Bean Bandits LP.

ALBUM: 1(A) THE JELLY BEAN BANDITS
(Mainstream S/6103) 1967 R2

NB: (1) also released in France (Vogue CLVLXMA 224) 1968. (1) has been pirated on CD.

45: Country Woman/Generation (Mainstream 674) 1967

Hailing from Newburgh in New York State with one of Mainstream's better albums came the **Jelly Bean Bandits**. More punk than psychedelic it includes some searing guitar and good effects. The album contains the classic *Generation*, which was arguably their finest moment with a bizarre intro about flying saucers giving way to a driving assault on the senses with searing guitar, powerful vocals and sound effects.

Originaly known as The Mirror, they managed to score a three-album deal with Mainstream on the basis of three demo tracks. Unbeknown to label boss Bob Shad, these were the only songs the band had written and a week-long marathon song-writing session ensued, before they were whisked into the cavernous Columbia Studio "A" to record the album in a generous twelve hours stretch.

Mainstream pulled the plug before the band could start on their second album, although a demo for one track, *Salesman* was recorded, and the other material written back in '68 may yet see the light... the band are still in touch and have released a second album in the same style & manner as they had intended to do thirty years ago... "look to the skies... the flying saucers will always be there!"

Mike Raab reports: "Initial recording sessions this past February went quite well. Billy Dee, is still lead singer in his band, Big Edsel, and so declined participation in the project. We went with the material we could do justice to. First cut is a power riff-rocker *Lover Wrapped In Leather*, which was written back in 1968 about the woman we all lusted for, Diana Rigg (Mrs. Peel of The Avengers). Also a bouncy pop number, *Happiness Is You*. The next leg of the sessions is coming up in October. Scheduled tunes: *Superhog* (about a daytime computer programmer / nightime biker - from 1968), *Salesman* (a 1998 re-make of the 1968 original) and a few others, such as a tongue-in-cheek lookback entitled *Back in '68*."

The new CD, which came out in Spring 2001 has been doing well, prompting the band to do their first gig in 33 years. **The Jelly Bean Bandits** are doing another reunion gig in 2002 to promote this year's release, *Mirror Music*, a CD of live music from 1967 featuring the original band doing a few originals but mainly covers.

The 1968 version of *Salesman* has recently arrived on *Psychedelic Crown Jewels, Vol.2* (Dble LP & CD) - a mighty slab of ravin' freakbeat. Other compilation coverage has also included: *Generation* on *Mayhem & Psychosis, Vol. 1* (LP), *Mayhem & Psychosis, Vol. 1* (CD), *The Essential Pebbles Collection, Vol. 2* (Dble CD) and *Pebbles, Vol. 2 (ESD)* (CD); *Superhog* on *Psychedelic States: New York Vol. 1* (CD); and *Poor Precious Dreams* on *Turds On A Bum Ride, Vol. 1 & 2* (Dble CD) and *Turds On A Bum Ride, Vol. 1* (Dble LP). (VJ/MW/MRb/BDe)

Jeremiah

45: Goin' Lovin' With You/No Sense Nonsense (Philips 40321) 1965

The flip, a Dylanesque obscurity, can be heard on the *Psychotic Moose And The Soul Searchers* (LP) compilation. The record was probably recorded in New York and sounds like a cross between **Mouse and The Traps** and **Godfrey**. (VJ)

Jeremiah

Personnel incl:	DAVID BROWN		A
	JOHN JEREMIAH	keyb'ds, vcls	A
	DENNY SEIWELL	drms	A

ALBUMS: 1(A) JEREMIAH (UNI 73098) 1971 -
2( ) I WANT TO BE WITH YOU (UNI 73128) 1972 -

These two albums consist of soft-flowing pop-rock. John Jeremiah went on to form **Aliotta Haynes Jeremiah** and **Acme Thunder** whilst Denny Seiwell later joined Paul McCartney's Wings.

JEREMY and THE SATYRS - Jeremy and The Satyrs LP.

Speculatively, David Brown may have also been in **The New Mix**, as both bands are in a similar musical style and share the same music publishing credits. (SR/RBn)

Jeremy and The Satyrs

Personnel:	WARREN BERNHARDT	keyb'ds	A
	EDDIE GOMEZ	bs	A
	ADRIAN GUILLERY	gtr	A
	DONALD McDONALD	drms	A
	JEREMY STEIG	flute	A

ALBUM: 1(A) JEREMY AND THE SATYRS (Reprise RS 6282) 1968 -

45: Let's Go To The Movie Show/
Lonely Child Of Tears (Reprise 0664) 1968

Fronted by Jeremy Steig, who'd earlier played with **Peter Walker**, this band's psychedelic rock album has now become a very minor collectors' item. It was produced by John Court who also worked with **Electric Flag** and the **Butterfield Blues Band**.

Jeremy was a cartoon artist like his father William Steig (New Yorker Magazine etc.), whilst Adrian Guillery was studying art in New Paltz / Manhattan.

The band backed **Tim Hardin** live, and some members did some recording sessions with him.

Donald McDonald later played with **Joe Beck** and is now dead. Jeremy Steig became a reknowned jazz musician, whilst Warren Bernhardt moved to Woodstock, NY and has continued recording. (VJ/SD)

The Jerks

45: Don't Make Me Sorry /
I'm Leaving You (Vaughn--Ltd VA-726) 1966

NB: label name is not a typo, it has two '-'s.

Gear Fab's *Psychedelic States: Alabama Vol. 1* (CD) revisits *I'm Leaving You*. Composed by M. Ellis, it's jaunty pop-beat with a **'Raiders'** flavour that's notable for the lengthy denouement where first the guitars then the drummer hit the accelerator pedal(s). Hopefully more details will come to light about this Alabama group. (MW)

The Jerms

| Personnel: | LARRY BURTON | | A |
| | MIKE DOYLE | | A |

	TOM JACOBY		A
	GALEN SENOGLES		A
			HCP

45s:	Love Light/That Word	(Casino 1322)	196? -
	Good Feelin' Yea/ Bald Headed Woman (PS)	(Jerms Inc. 2079)	1966 -
	Since You Went Away/ That's All She Wrote (PS)	(Del Mar 4)	196? -
	Not At All/Who's Green Door/I'm A Teardrop	(Shana 7195)	1968 -
		(Hon. Brigade 1) 1969	129
	Nobody/Baby, Baby, Love	(Hon. Brigade 4)	1969 -
α	Nobody/Baby, Baby, Love (PS)	(Exit 2541)	1969 -

NB: α was a Spanish Release.

From Topeka in Eastern Kansas, this outfit had a prolific output of variable releases. Among the quartet's best was *Since You Went Away*. It's rumoured that their manager, who owned the name, had two or three groups playing as 'The Jerms' in different parts of the State. In their later days they included a female singer known as Angel. The Shana 45 was produced by the **West Coast Pop Art Experimental Band**'s Shaun Harris, but the garage had been left far behind by then.

Compilation coverage has included: *Since You Went Away* on *Monsters Of The Midwest, Vol. 3* (LP); *Bald Headed Woman* on *Magic Carpet Ride* (LP) and *Gamma Knee Kappa* (LP); and *Love Light* on *Monsters Of The Midwest, Vol. 4* (LP) and *Midwest Garage Band Series - Kansas* (CD). (VJ/MW)

Bill Jerpe

ALBUM:	1	BILL JERPE	(Shortwheel SW-100)	1970 SC

A psych-folk singer, his album came with an insert. (SR)

Jerry and The Gems

Personnel incl?: JEFF BROWN   A

45:	Last Stop / Summertime	(Heigh-Ho 630)	1966

A Queens, New York, outfit whose *Last Stop* (written by Jeff Brown) uses lyrics about a ride on the New York Subway as a metaphor for the end of a relationship. Catch it on *Psychedelic States: New York Vol. 1* (CD). (MW)

Jerry and The Others

Personnel:	JERRY BEHRING	bs	AB
	ROBERT BUDELINEY	gtr	AB
	PAT SMITH	keyb'ds	AB
	BILL		A
	DANNY		A
	RON SKINNER	drums	B

A Dayton, Ohio, combo better known as The Others. Their sole gift to posterity under either moniker was the drum-bashin' tambourine-shakin' Diddleyesque pounder *Don't Cry To Me*, peformed by line-up 'A' and composed by guitarist Robert Budeliney. It's one of the best cuts on the album *WONE, The Dayton Scene* (Prism PR-1966), which showcased the top twelve groups from the WONE-sponsored three-day Daytonian battle of the bands in 1966.

Ron Skinner of **The Pictorian Skiffuls** joined later. The final Others line-up (B above) changed their name to the **Elders** in 1970, releasing the *Looking For The Answer* LP and 45 in 1971 on Audio Fidelity.

Retrospective compilation appearances include: *Don't Cry To Me* on *Back From The Grave, Vol. 3* (LP), *Back From The Grave, Vol. 2* (CD), *Echoes In Time, Vol's 1 & 2* (CD) and *Echoes In Time, Vol. 1* (LP). (GGI/MW)

ECHOES IN TIME Vol's 1 & 2 (Comp CD) including Jerry and The Others.

Jerry and The Playmates

Personnel incl:	BOWLING
	OLIVER
	SMITH

45:	She's The Kind/Want-A-Love You	(Alvera M-68)	1966

On a Tulsa, Oklahoma- based label. The flip, a pretty routine garage punker, has resurfaced on *Monsters Of The Midwest, Vol. 2* (LP). (MW/VJ)

Jesse J. and The Bandits

ALBUM:	1	TOP TEEN HITS '65	(Re-Car 2001)	1965
45:		Stomp Your Feet/Honey Love	(Re-Car 9003)	1964

Now hard to find, *Stomp Your Feet* is a punker, which is rated highly by some. The work of a Minneapolis- based studio group, the same bunch also put out a 45 as **King Krusher and The Turkeynecks**, the A-side of which (*King Krusher*) was also featured on the **Jesse J. and The Bandits** album.

They also recorded as **The Bandits**. (VJ/MW)

Jesse, Wolf and Whings

Personnel:	JESSE NEAL BARISH	ld vcls, gtr, flute, piano	A
	KENNY KAUFMAN	bs, vcls	A
	KEVIN KELLEY	drms, vcls	A
	BILL WOLFF	ld gtrs, vcls	A
	(GRANT JOHNSON	organ	A)
	(LARRY KNECHTEL	piano	A)

ALBUM:	1(A)	JESSE, WOLFF AND WHINGS	(Shelter SW 8907)	1972 -

NB: (1) also released in Holland (Philips 6369 109) 1972.

Jesse, Wolff and Whings was formed by Jesse Barish, a San Francisco singer/songwriter and Bill Wolff, the former **Peanut Butter Conspiracy**, **Sound Machine** and **Fusion** guitarist. Housed in a superb black and white sleeve with a mystic symbol on its front, their only album offered a very consistent choice of songs mixing West Coast guitars with good vocals and occasional flute playing from Barish. Their drummer, Kevin Kelley, had previously been with the **Rising Sons** and the **Byrds** and had already teamed up with Kenny Kaufman on a Phil Ochs album, *Gunfight At Carnegie Hall*. The album was recorded in Hollywood and produced by Denny Cordell.

Jesse Barish would later work with Jefferson Starship and also issued two bland solo albums which were produced by Marty Balin. (SR)

Glen Jester and The Mersey Men

45:   Hey What You Gonna Do / If I Were King   (Maarc 1506) 196?

A joint venture by solo artist **Glen Jester** from Canton, Ohio on the local Maarc (Mills Audio And Recording Company) label. On this 45 he's backed by Salem's **Mersey Men**, who had two 45s of their own.   (GGI/MW)

The Jesters

ALBUM: 1   THE JESTERS   (Audio House AH 466) 1966 R3

This garage outfit came from Kansas City in Eastern Kansas. Their album is full of covers of classics like *Gloria*, *We've Gotta Get Out Of This Place* and *She's Not There*.

Presumably the 1966 cover of *Gloria*, taken from a test pressing and credited to the **Jesters From Kansas** on the *Midwest Garage Band Series - Kansas* (CD), is by the same band.   (VJ)

The Jesters

Personnel:	JAMES DICKINSON	bs	A
	TEDDY PAIGE	hrmnca	A
	JERRY PHILLIPS	vcls, gtr	A
	EDDIE ROBERTSON	drms	A
	BILLY WULFERS	gtr	A

45:   Cadillac Man/My Babe   (Sun 400) 1966

This Memphis band was an early outing for **James Dickinson**. The 45 was recorded at Sun Studios in January 1966. The 'A' side has resurfaced on *The Best Of Sun Rockabilly, Vol. 2*, but it's certainly not rockabilly!   (VJ)

The Jesters

45s:	I'll Laugh At You/You Can Have Her	('no label') 1965
	I'll Laugh At You/Just Let Me Love You	(Jesters no #) 1965
	Leave Me Alone/Don't Try To Crawl Back	(Sidewalk 910) 1966
	Hands Of Time/	
	If You Love Her, Tell Her So	(Sidewalk 916) 1967
	Unchain My Heart/Blue Feeling	(Qualicon 5003) 1967

From Naples, Florida. This band were picked up by Mike Curb's Sidewalk label, home of all those exploitation movie soundtracks. One of these, the *Freakout U.S.A.!* soundtrack album, features one track by **The Jesters**, *Don't Try To Crawl Back*. Otherwise they remain uncompiled. *Hands Of Time* is an above average organ-punker worth picking up. The non-Sidewalk 45s are very elusive.   (MW)

The Jesters IV

Personnel:	LINDA CARTER	gtr	A
	LOU FACENDA	drms	A
	TONY FACENDA	bs	A
	ROBIN SIBUCAO	vcls, gtr	A

45:   (Bye Bye Bye Bye) So Long / She Lied (I Know Why)   (Fuller CFP-2684) 1966

From Tampa Florida, this band played the Maderia Beach Surfers Club, Big Mooses' saturday night St. Pete dances and also the Spot Night Club in Tampa...

Robin Sibucao recalls: "Three of the four members were under fifteen. Instrumentation was bass, drums, two guitars and one singer. Radio station WALT used to have a vote by postcard for your favorite tune.... both tracks were selected at the time **The Tropics** and **Roving Flames** had records out."

"Bye Bye So Long was an uptempo tune, two verses and chorus with a guitar solo (clean - no fuzz tone) verse and out".

"She Lied was a medium tempo tune with a power chord time guitar line that had no distortion or overload sound".

The band carried on until 1968 and spawned two local outfits, Southern Comfort and Toy Shoppe. In 1970, Robin Sibucao moved to L.A. and formed Shuffle, which included singer Rick Fitts, bassist Terry Cashburn, and former-**Nazz** drummer Thom Mooney.

Compilation appearances include *She Lied* on *Teenage Shutdown, Vol. 12* (LP & CD) and *Psychedelic States: Florida Vol. 3* (CD).   (MW/RSo)

Jesters of Newport

45:   Stormy/Where Have You Been?   (Solo 700) 1964

A four-piece from Santa Clara in California. They recorded their 45 in a back room studio of a record store there. The disc is an interesting crossover from surf to garage. Indeed the organist had earlier played in a surf group called The Crygons. *Stormy*, starting out with a crazy organ intro straight out of Grieg's "In the Hall of the Mountain King", is a fine garage cruncher with powerful vocals, interesting surf-influenced guitar, catchy organ and a very distinctive ending.

Compilation appearances include: *Stormy* on *Back From The Grave, Vol. 5* (LP).   (VJ)

Jesus Generation

ALBUM: 1   INSIDE-OUT   (J.G 10685) c1972 SC

From Houston, Texas, a Christian rock group singing their own material (*These Days*, *Peace*, *Trust*, *Satisfied*, *Rocks Will Cry*) in a mellow psych/pop/rock style. Only 500 copies were pressed.   (SR)

The Jet Stream

HCP
45:   All's Quiet on West 23rd/Crazy Me   (Smash 2095) 1967 101

An obscure rock group. Their 45 was a minor hit in 1967.   (SR/VJ)

Tommy Jett

45:   Groovy Little Trip/Send Me Some Lovin'   (Jox 060) 1967

This guy who worked out of San Antonio, accidentally ingested too much nutmeg one day and wrote the lyrics to *Groovy Little Trip* as an ode to the 'Psychedelic Sensation' that he experienced. Musically the result starts off

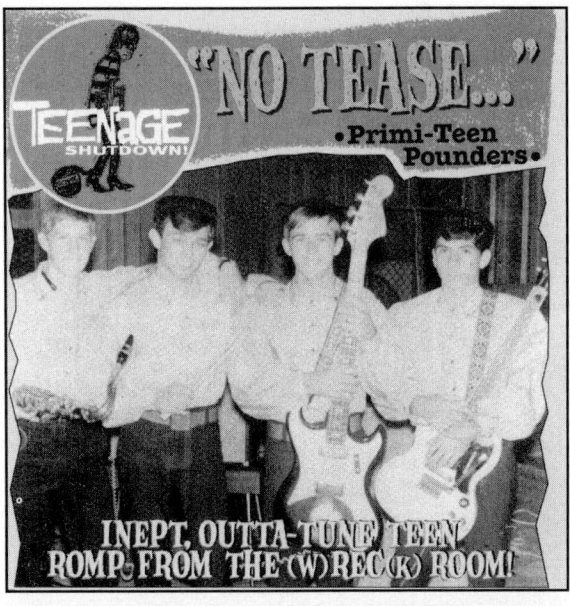

TEENAGE SHUTDOWN Vol. 12 (Comp CD) including The Jesters IV.

sounding like any other garage punk moan but towards the end is engulfed in a haze of fuzz guitar.

Compilation appearances include: *Groovy Little Trip* on *Psychedelic Experience* (CD), *The Psychedelic Experience, Vol. 2* (LP), *Texas Flashbacks, Vol. 5* (LP), *Flashback, Vol. 5* (LP) and *Highs In The Mid-Sixties, Vol. 12* (LP). (VJ)

J.H. and The Esquires

45:	Comin' On Strong / Stay By Me	(Mus-I-Col HR 1149)	1967

From Columbus, Ohio and more commonly known as the Esquires. More soul than garage. (GGI/MW)

The Jiants

45:	Tornado/She's My Woman	(Claudra CL-1 12)	196?

Hailed from Marion, Indiana. *Tornado* has since resurfaced on *The Madness Invasion, Vol. 3*, and both sides feature on a cassette-only compilation *Indiana Rocks!* (Roundtuit, 1991).

Jim and Dale

Personnel:	JIM CARTER		A
	DALE JARRED		A

ALBUM:	1(A)	86% OF US	(United Artists UAS 6706) 1968 -

45s:	Livin' On Love/Sounds Of The City	(Roulette 4755) 1967
	Richard Cory/Once Again	(United Artists 50527) 1969
	Past The State Of Mind/Serena	(United Artists 50569) 1969

An album with lots of orchestrated, at times almost baroque, arrangements. Almost all the tracks are of a good standard with *Past The State Of Mind* and a cover of Paul Simon's *Richard Cory* among the highlights. The duo hailed from Philadelphia, Pennsylvania. Their first 45 was a reasonable folk-pop effort.

Jim and Jean

Personnel:	STEVE BOOKER	drms	A
	HARVEY BROOKS	bs	A
	BOBBY GREGG	drms	A
	JIM GLOVER	vcls, gtr	AB
	JEAN GLOVER	vcls	AB
	PAUL HARRIS	keyb'ds, vibes	A
	AL KOOPER	gtr, harpsichord	A
	JOE MICHAELS	drms	A
	BOB ROSE	gtr	A
	TED SOMMERS	perc	A
	BOB SYLVESTER	cello	A
	LANCE WAKELY	gtr	A

ALBUMS:	1(A)	CHANGES	(Verve Folkways FTS-3001) 1966 -
	2(B)	PEOPLE WORLD	(Verve Forecast FTS-3015) 1967 -
	3( )	JIM AND JEAN	(Philips 600-182) 196? -

EP:	1	Changes/About My Love/Loneliness/ Strangers In A Strange Land	(Verve 519 901) 1967

NB: (1) French release with picture sleeve.

45s:	Stalemate / What's That Got to Do With Me	(Verve Forecast KF-5035) 1966
	People World / Time Goes Backward	(Verve Forecast KF-5073) 1967

Friends of **Phil Ochs**, who wrote the funny and clever liner notes and offered them four songs, **Jim and Jean** recorded their fine debut folk-rock album in 1966. They were helped by several of the musicians who played with Bob Dylan on *Highway 61 Revisited*: **Al Kooper**, Harvey Brooks and Bobby Gregg. The influence of Dylan can also be heard on their cover of his *Lay Down Your Weary Tune* and the album also contains three covers of **David Blue**: *Grand Hotel*, *About My Love* and *Strangers In A Strange Land*. Nothing exceptional but a pleasant album nonetheless.

Lance Wakely would later move to California and play with **Brewer and Shipley** before forming **Joyous Noise**.

The second album contains a few highlights, including the jerky *Success* with its strong psychedelic leanings, the vaguely Eastern *Time Goes Backwards* and the extremely eerie *Playground*. The acapella singing on *Sweet Water* is also quite convincing, as is the singing in general. Unfortunately there is also much discardable and inconsequential material in between, although the album never falls into the trap of getting too sweet for comfort. (SR/MK/NK)

Jimmy and The Offbeats

Personnel:	JIMMY BANKHEAD	vcls, gtr	A
	BILL POWELL	keyb'ds	A
	DONNY SHORT	gtr	A

45:	Stronger Than Dirt/ I Ain't No Miracle Worker	(Bofuz BF 1113) 1966

This Baton Rouge, Louisiana band took a commercial for Ajax Laundry Detergent and turned it into a punk single, with a cool cover of **The Brogues**' *Miracle Worker* on the flip. When John Haas was recruited from **The Barracudas** they renamed themselves **John Eric & The Isosceles Popsicles** and recorded *I'm Not Nice* on the USA label.

Compilation appearances include: *Miracle Worker* on *Louisiana Punk From The Sixties* (LP), *Sixties Archive Vol. 3* (CD) and *Best of Pebbles, Vol. 1* (LP & CD); *Stronger Than Dirt* and *I Ain't No Miracle Worker* on *Highs In The Mid-Sixties, Vol. 22* (LP). (VJ/MW)

J.K. & Co.

Personnel:	JAY KAYE	gtr, keyb'ds, vcls	AB
	RICK DEAN	drms	B
	JOHN KAYE	bs	B

ALBUM:	1(A)	SUDDENLY ONE SUMMER	(White Whale WWS-7117) 1968 R1

NB: (1) counterfeited on CD (Afterglow AFT 18) 1998 and as a 10" (Akarma AK 2015). Reissued officially in 2001 on 180gm vinyl (Beat Rocket BR 126) and CD (BRCD 126) 2001.

J.K. & Co. - Suddenly One Summer LP.

JK & Co. - French *Fly* 45 PS.

45:    Break Of Dawn / Little Children   (White Whale # Unkn) 1968
NB: There's also an extremely rare French 45 with PS: *Fly/Christine* (London) 1968.

The above album of dreamy soft psychedelia is something of an undiscovered gem for pop-psych enthusiasts. Recorded in Vancouver, Canada, until recently, nothing was known about the identity or true location of the band.

Housed in a delightful pop-art cover, this concept album was meant to "depict musically a man's life from birth to death" - it was written by Jay Kaye who was just 15 years old at the time. Heavily orchestrated with lush arrangements, silky vocals and backward effects, it is dreamy soft-rock that caresses psychedelia and flirts with the 'baroque'. It occupies a hazy territory somewhere between *Sgt. Pepper* and *The Magical Mystery Tour*, the **Left Banke**'s second album and The Zombies' *Odessey And Oracle*. Highlights include the delightful Eastern-influenced *Magical Fingers Of Minerva*, some superb, melodic slices of pop-psych like *Fly* and *Little Children*, the guitar-driven instrumental *Speed* and the prog-psych finale *Dead* which gives way to the opening bars of the album at the end. The yearning vocal style is appealing and evident throughout but particularly evident on *Crystal Ball* and *Nobody*.

Until recently nothing was known to collectors about the history behind the record or the artist - now thanks to Sundazed, Efram Turchick and the parties involved it can be told: - Las Vegan Jay Kaye was born into a musical family. His mother was pioneering guitarist Mary Kaye, of the Mary Kaye Trio and who had a Fender Stratocaster named after her. His uncle was famed ukelele player Johnny Ukelele.

Both Jay and his cousin John Kaye were bitten by the Beatle bug. Jay led a band called the Loved Ones and started to write his own material. In 1968, he accompanied his mother to Vancouver where she was making some appearances. On a visit to a studio, who wanted to record some tracks with his mother (she turned them down), a 15-year-old Jay proffered his material and played a couple of his songs to producer Robin Spurgin.

Spurgin had a great track record, from our retrospective perspective(?!) anyway, having produced the likes of the Collectors, Painted Ship, United Empire Loyalists and One Way Streets. He was impressed enough with Jay to start work on an album and agreed also to look after him (his mother was returning to Vegas). First off he brought in Robert Buckley from local band Spring, whom he'd also produced. Buckley was another prodigiously talented teenager who played numerous instruments; he took on the role of arranger. With the help of various session musicians, including members of Mother Tucker's Yellow Duck, the project was realized over the next few months.

The completed tape was touted around L.A. labels in the Summer of '68. It was jumped on by White Whale, whose president Ted Feigin christened it *Suddenly One Summer*. With the release imminent, Jay quickly assembled a trio to play live and promote it - his cousin John and drummmer Rick Dean (son of jazz drummer Jack Dean).

A period of heavy local promotion followed and it started to gather playtime on underground radio stations. At this point White Whale decided to release a 45. Strangely they didn't choose the stand-out *Fly*; instead they opted for the album's opener *Break Of Dawn*, a sound collage of barely half a minute. The 45 may only have made it to the promo stage... at that point the momentum sank without a trace, as did the 45 and the label's interest. The band carried on performing on the local teen circuit but were too young to go on tour or do nightclubs. Their brief moment in the limelight was gone.

Some tracks from the album were creatively recycled by White Whale, appearing on an album credited to Zager and Evans - *The Early Writings Of Zager & Evans & Others* (White Whale WWS-7123) - in 1969.

The young trio went on to various other bands. Latterly Jay Kaye moved to Majorca, Spain in 1987 where he plays blues guitar, sings and writes. John Kaye is back in Las Vegas with a band called The Overlords.

Two of the album's many highlights have turned up elsewhere - the superb dream-like *Fly* is on *A Heavy Dose Of Lyte Psych* (CD) and *Magical Fingers Of Minerva* graces *Electric Psychedelic Sitar Headswirlers, Vol. 1* (CD). (MW/VJ/ETk)

J. Michael and The Bushmen

45s: I Need Love / Little John's Revenge   (Corby CR 207) 196?
        I Need Love / Wine Wine Wine   (Corby CR 210) 1966

From Corvallis, Oregon - home to Oregon State University. The opening scream on *I Need Love* sets the tone for this punk song, which can also be heard on *Highs In The Mid-Sixties, Vol. 14* (LP), *Boulders, Vol. 11* (LP), *Ya Gotta Have Moxie, Vol. 2* (Dble CD) and *Riot City!* (LP). (MW)

The Jodarettes

45:    What's In De Box/?   (Jodica 302) c1966

An obscure garage 45 written by N. Nathan and B. Williams, it was a Rose Production. (SR)

Joey and The Continentals

45s: Lynda/Will Love Ever Come My Way?   (Komet 1001) 196?
        Sad Girl/Baby   (Laurie 3294) 1965
        She Rides With Me/Rudy Vadoo   (Claridge 304) 1965

You'll also find *Baby* on the *Pride Of Cleveland Past* (LP) compilation which places them as a Cleveland, Ohio band. The third 45 was later reissued on Claridge 312 but shown as by "The GTO's". (VJ)

Joey and Time Machine

Personnel incl: JOEY WELZ   A

45:    Caught By Love/Big City   (Rabbit RR 1001) 1991

A 1991 limited-edition of 300 consisting of two unreleased 1967 tracks by a Baltimore outfit led by Joey Welz.

Caught By Love has also reappeared on *Fuzz, Flaykes And Shakes, Vol. 4* (LP & CD). It reveals that Welz had played in the fifties with Bill Haley's Comets; in the sixties, he recorded and produced other Maryland teen bands. (MW/TSz/LJ)

John and Gunther

45:    Hey, Hey, Babe /
       That Was Yesterday   (Counterpart C-2585/6) 1967

A Peter and Gordon-style folk-beat duo from Cincinnati who also released an unaccompanied folk 45 as The Minutemen. (GGl/MW)

John Bunyan's Progressive Pilgrims

ALBUM: 1 APRICOT BRANDY AND ALBATROSS
(Alshire S-5154) 1969 SC

Subtitled "The Sound That Sent The Pilgrims On A Trip", this exploito album contains the following tracks: *Albatross, Apricot Brandy, Sabre Dance, Mozart's Dilemma, Spaced Out, Hot Shot, Summertime Blues, Winter Draws On, Song Without Words* and *Pecadillo*. (SR)

Johnny and The Hurricanes

Personnel incl:
LIONEL 'BUTCH' MATTICE	bs		AB
JOHNNY PARIS	vcls, sax		AB
PAUL TESLUK	keyb'ds		AB
DON STACZEK	drms		A
DAVE YOURKO	gtr		AB
BILL 'LITTLE BO' STAVICH	drms		B

ALBUM: 1 LIVE AT THE STAR CLUB (Atila 1030) 1965 R1?

45s: Saga Of The Beatles / Rene (Jeff 211) 1964
(selective) Saga Of The Beatles / Rene (Atila 211) 1964
I Love You / Judy's Moody (Atila 214) c1965
Wisdom's 5th Take /
Because I Love Her (Atila 215) 1966
The Psychedelic Worm / Red River Rock (Atila 216) 1967
What You Know About Love / Yes It's You (Atila 221) 196?

A surprising entry perhaps. This well-known Toledo, Ohio, group were a classy instrumental-rock'n'roll-dance band that hit big in the early sixties on both sides of the Atlantic with *Crossfire, Red River Rock, Reveille Rock* and *Rocking Goose* (a No.1 in the UK). Constantly touring and with only Johnny Paris surviving line-up changes into the Beatles era (the early personnel is shown above) their recorded music was pumped out even whilst they were on the road by session musicians - a fairly common practice of the times.

They released a total of five albums and over thirty 45s and EPs but the selective discography should be of interest here, with some of the later 45s being released as by **The Hurricanes**. George Gell has drawn attention to this period where "they did make the stylistic transition to a garage-pop sound and all their mid-sixties records are worth having". He points out that the 'Live' album isn't live but "features a solid garage sound of mostly hits of the day".

Wisdom's 5th Take (as by **The Hurricanes**) can be heard on *Garage Punk Unknowns, Vol. 6* (LP) to confirm this. 1959's *Reveille Rock* was included on the K-Tels *Juke Box Jive*, a seventies double album collection of fifties-sixties party/pop classics. (MW/GGI)

Johnny and The Nite Ryders

45: I Had A Girl/She's Gone (Perfection 558) 1966

From Smyrna, Georgia. You'll also find *I Had A Girl* on *Hipsville 29 B.C.* (LP) and *She's Gone* on the excellent 'desperate garage punker' comp *I Can Hear Raindrops* (LP). (VJ/MW)

Johnny Gee Men

10" Acetate: At The Party/She's True (Audiodisc) 1965

From Oklahoma, an obscure frat-rock/garage group, who possibly only recorded this acetate. (SR)

Johnnys Uncalled Four

45s: Shortnin' Bread / Day Dream (Wam 4001) 1964
Please Say / Every Time I Close My Eyes (Magic 1000) 1966

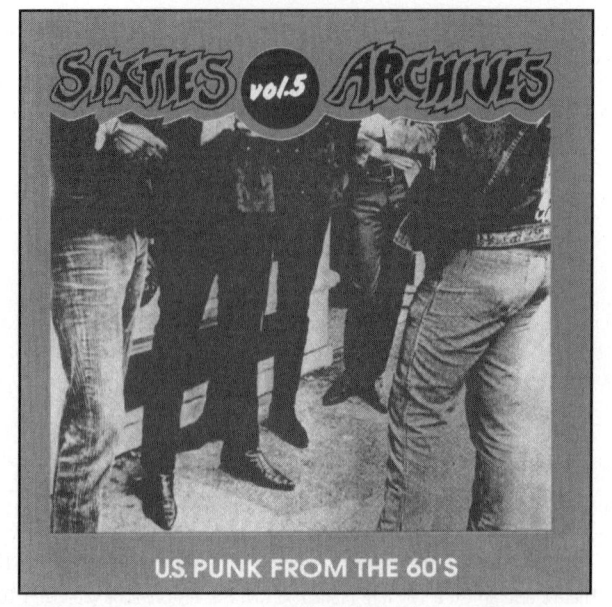

SIXTIES ARCHIVES Vol. 5 (Comp CD) including The Joint Effort.

From Columbiana, Ohio and sometimes known as **Johnny and The Uncalled Four**. Their version of *Shortnin' Bread* is to be found on the frat-garage comp *Ho-Dad Hootenanny* (LP), whilst *Please Say*, a decent garage effort, is on *Sixties Rebellion Vol. 14* (LP & CD). (GGI/MW)

Mike Johnson

ALBUM: 1 LORD DOCTOR (Freedom Light) 1970/1 R1

You may recognize this guy as an ex-Exkursion member - he played (and plays) lead guitar. The above album continues in that vein - nice countryish at times, guitar-based psych. Highlights include *Cause And Effect* and *Pride*. The cover is a simple picture of Mike appearing very introspective.

Johnson and Drake

Personnel:
GUY DRAKE		A
TOM JOHNSON		A

ALBUM: 1(A) CARRY IT ON (Ovation OVQD 1434) 1972 -

Produced by Herb Pilhofer, an album of rather mellow folk-rock. It isn't as good as their label-mates **Hollins and Star**, but came with a large insert. (SR)

Joint Effort

45: Theme From An Imaginary Western/Country (Deck 1004) 1968

Hailed from McAllen, Texas in the late sixties. The flip to their 45 is a really nice laid back song with strong vocals - you can also find it on *Punk Ballads Sampler* (LP) and *Sixties Archive, Vol. 5* (CD). (VJ)

Joint Effort

Personnel:
DAVE CALLENS	gtr, vcls	ABC
JEFF SALISBURY	drms	AB
ED VILLAREAL	gtr, vcls	ABC
TOMMY JACOBSON	drms	C
CLYDE KAYE	bs	BC
WANDA WATKINS	vcls	BC

45s: The Children/The Third Eye (JE-1) 1967
The Square/Mary On A Go Round/ (SpinIt 127) 1967
Loving You Could Be Magic/
Coming Home To You Baby (Ruby-Doo 10) 1968

Dave Callens, Edmund Villareal and Jeff Salisbury were originally from San Antonio, Texas, but relocated to Hollywood in February 1967. They were picked up by former boxer, apartment manager Bud "Babyface" Mathis and former bus driver Barry Cantor (Cantor-Mathis Management). More members were auditioned and added to the original trio, including vocalist/dancer Wanda Watkins from Garnerfield Saniatium (who became **The Brain Train** and finally **Clear Light**) and Clyde Kay on bass.

The Joint Effort became the house band at Gazzarri's on The Strip in the Summer of '67 and Cantor-Mathis released their debut to promote this. It hit the top ten in the Santa Barbara area.

I wish I'd been there - *The Children* is breezy California psych-pop whilst *Third Eye* is glorious folk-raga-psych with an unusual solo of one long feedback sustain. A rare and highly recommended 45, it was recorded at Original Sound Studios in Hollywood and engineered by the legendary Paul Buff. *The Children* was rated on American Bandstand and got a 75...

In the Spring of 1968 **The Joint Effort** became the touring version of **The Box Tops**. Bud Mathis booked them as impersonators and they toured with Del Shannon as opening act in Hawaii. The band broke up in late 1968 in Santa Barbara, California, days before they were to record their first album.

The band got to support **The Doors** in Santa Barbara, **The Strawberry Alarm Clock**, **Sweetwater**, **Peanut Butter Conspiracy** and also appeared as extras in the "hippie-burial scene" of the cult classic 'Psych-Out' movie with Jack Nicholson. Follow-up 45s moved into **Association** harmony-pop and flower-pop territory, with occasional use of brass, with producer John Marascalco who wrote *Good Golly Miss Molly* and others for Little Richard.

Check out *The Third Eye* on *Psychedelic Crown Jewels Vol. 2* (Dble LP & CD).

In 2000, a retrospective of Bud Mathis acts appeared. *Take The Brain Train To The Third Eye* (LP & CD) re-airs *The Third Eye*, *The Children* and *Mary On A Go Round*. It also features two unreleased tracks - *Broken Glass* and *Tomorrow's Yesterdays* - where **The Joint Effort** provide backing for Wolfgang (Dios). He was a songwriter signed by Mathis and is best remembered for writing *Black Roses*, recorded by **The Brain Train / Clear Light**. (MW/DCs/EDV/JSy)

The Jokers Wild

Personnel incl: PETE HUBER   A
                 DENNY JOHNSON   bs   A
                 LONNIE KNIGHT   A

45s: All I See Is You/
      I Just Can't Explain It   (Metrobeat 4451) 1968
      Sunshine/Because I'm Free   (Peak 4456) 1968
      Tomorrow/Peace Man   (Peak 4459) 1968

One of the better late sixties Minneapolis bands whose 45s are worth seeking. They split in 1970 and Johnson went on to record a solo pop 45 and Knight two solo LPs *Family In The Wind* (Flashlight/Symposium) 1974 and *Song For A City Mouse* (Flashlight/Symposium) 1975. They started out as a six-piece but ended up as a trio for their final recordings. They were clearly an experimental outfit.

The best source for their music is *The Best Of Metrobeat! Vol. 1* (LP) compilation which includes the psychedelic *All I See Is You*, *I Just Can't Explain It*, *Because I'm Free*, *Sunshine* and, perhaps best of all, a previously unreleased cut, *All The World's A Copper Penny*.

Lonnie Knight went on to play with various groups including the Hoopsnakes, and is currently performing with Lonnie Knight and Big Shoes.

Other compilation appearances have included: *All I See Is You* on *Psychedelic Experience, Vol. 2* (CD), *Garagelands, Vol. 1* (LP) and *Garagelands, Vol. 1 & 2* (CD). (VJ)

Pete Jolly

45: Little Bird/Sweet September   (Mainstream 699) 1969

Unexpectedly enough this Mainstream 45 contains an 'A' side with inspired but unkempt piano-jazz, very similar to the Ramsey Lewis Trio! The 'B' side features prominent orchestrion which utterly destroys the impression created by the 'A' side. Sadly, the Oscar Peterson-like solo comes too late to rescue. (MK)

The Jolly Beggars

45: The Last Step of Doom/
     Don't Walk On Me   (Pamela Rose PR-1) 196?

A mystery disc which appeared on a Florida label but is also reputed to have got an airing on the Roxbury, Massachusetts-based Step label with the artistes credited as The Rogues Of Roxbury. Either way *Last Step Of Doom* is a superb driving punker, well worth checking out on *Pebbles, Vol. 21* (LP). (VJ/LBp)

The Jolly Green Giants

45: Caught You Red Handed/Busy Body   (Redcoat 101) 1966

A Northwest band and clearly one influenced by **The Kingsmen** taking their name from their classic Top Ten hit. Both sides of the 45 were in a raucous dance style.

Compilation appearances have included: *Caught You Red Handed* on *Teenage Shutdown, Vol. 4* (LP & CD), *Vile Vinyl, Vol. 1* (LP) and *Boulders, Vol. 1* (LP); and *Busy Body* on *Teenage Shutdown, Vol. 1* (LP & CD) and *Highs In The Mid-Sixties, Vol. 7* (LP). (VJ/MW)

Jon and Robin

Personnel incl: JOHN "JON" ABDNOR   vcls, gtr   AB
                 JAVONNE "ROBIN" BRAGA vcls   AB
                 JOHN DURRILL   B
                 JIM GLAVES   B
                 JIM GRANT   B
                 MICHAEL RABON   B
                 BOBBY RAMBO   gtr   B
                 JIMMY WRIGHT   B

ALBUMS: 1(A) THE SOUL OF A BOY AND A GIRL
                                        (Abnak ABST-2068) 1967 -
         2(B) ELASTIC EVENT   (Abnak ABST-2070) 1967 -

45: Love Me Baby/I Want Some More   (Abnak AB-124) 1967

This Dallas pop-rock male-female duo was formed by **John Abdnor Junior** and Javonne Braga. As John Abdnor Senior was the owner of the record label Abnak, their records were naturally released on this small label.

VILE VINYL Vol. 1 (Comp LP) including The Jolly Green Giants.

Their first album contains many pop and soul hits cover versions (like *In The Midnight Hour* and *Hold On, I'm Coming*) but includes one good garagey track, *Love Me Baby*, with a *Gloria*-like guitar chord sequence and swirling organ.

Housed in a colorful cover with **Jon and Robin** wearing psychy clothes (now looking very kitsch!), *Elastic Event* was directed by **Michael Rabon**, the leader of the **Five Americans** who formed the backing group along with Bobby Rambo and Jim Glaves (from **The In Crowd**). The album contains cover versions of **Mouse and The Traps**' *Like I Know You Do*, and **The Youngbloods**' *Grizzly Bear*. Two other interesting tracks are *Doctor Jon* and *You Got Style*.

All in all, their two albums are rather patchy and probably too pop-oriented for most rock fans, but contain however some surprisingly good tracks.

Javonne Braga went on to marry Jimmy Wright, the **Five Americans** drummer in the seventies, while Jon went solo in 1969 as **John Howard Abdnor** for one album. (VJ/MW/TTi/SR)

Jonathan and Charles

Personnel incl: JOHN GUEST   A

ALBUM: 1(A)   ANOTHER WEEK TO GO   (IVR - Inner Varsity) 1967 SC

One of the first Catholic folk and folk-rock groups, with an organ, vocal harmonies similar to Simon and Garfunkel and the track *Why?*. Their record is beginning to attract attention amongst some collectors. (SR)

Jonathan and Leigh

Personnel incl:			
JONATHAN ALDEN	vcls, gtr	A
LEIGH	vcls, electric dulcimer	A
JAY BERLINER	electric gtr	A
RICHARD DAVIS	bs	A
VINNIE BELL	gtr	A
WILLIAM SALTER	bs	A
RUSS SAVAKUS	bs	A
WARREN SMITH	drms, perc	A

ALBUM: 1(A)   THIRD AND MAIN   (Vanguard VSD-79257) 1967 -
NB: (1) also exists in mono (VRS-9257). (1) reissued on CD and LP 2001.

Produced by Elmer Jared Gordon, an interesting folk, folk-rock and folk-blues male/female duo with good vocals plus electric and acoustic backing by famous session men from the New York scene: **Vinnie Bell**, Jay Berliner and Richard Davis (later with Van Morrison). Their rhythm section, Salter and Smith, also played on several albums of **Pearls Before Swine**. They were heavily influenced by Dylan and **Phil Ochs** (they cover his *Changes*) and they combine good self-penned material with *Cocaine Blues*, *Someday Baby* (by Muddy Waters) and *Going To Brownsville*. (SR)

JONATHAN and LEIGH - Third And Main LP.

DEL JONES' POSITIVE VIBES - Court Is Closed LP (1st Reissue).

Jerry Jones

ALBUM: 1   TELL IT NOW   (Crescendo Custom CCR 7002) c1971 ?

A weird album, between gospel music, garage and folk, with some psychy touches and Christian lyrics. It came with a booklet with the lyrics and music. *Tell It Now*, *We Have Something To Say*, *Status Quo* and *Man, My God Is Real* were recorded with electric guitars, organ, drums and choir. For fans of "incredibly strange" sounds. (SR)

E. Rodney Jones and The Prairie Dogs

See **King Harvest** entry.

Del Jones' Postive Vibes

ALBUM: 1   COURT IS CLOSED   (Hikeka HR 3331) 1973 R4
NB: (1) reissued twice on vinyl with different mixes, in different sleeve designs.

A Philadelphia black psych-rock group with flute and acid guitar. (SR)

Marc Jonson

ALBUM: 1   YEARS   (Vanguard VSD-6577) c1970 -

45:   I'm Coming Up To Boston/?   (Vanguard 35141) 1970

A forgotten psychedelic folk singer songwriter. His album was recorded with guitar, organ, harpsichord, autoharp, piano and cello. The lyrics are rather dark, with songs like *Autopsy* (about his own autopsy!). (SR)

Joplin Forte

Personnel:			
PAT BALL	gtr	A
GARY CARLSON	ld gtr	A
DENNIS COATS	banjo	A
MONTE PAPKE	bs	A

ALBUM: 1(A)   AIN'T MISBEHAVIN'   (Shamley SS 702) 1969 -

45s: Ain't Misbehavin'/You Might Be The One To
       Change My Mind   (Shamley 44010) 1969
       This Time/Changing Woman   (Shamley 44014) 1969

Ballad Of Butch Cassidy And The Sundance
Kid/? (Dunhill 4426) 1970

One of the four albums released on the short-lived Shamley label (along with **HMS Bounty**, **Moonrakers** and **Future**). The Original Joplin Forte's music was a kind of old-timey folk, like the **Cleanliness and Goodliness Skiffle Band** and certains cuts of Dan Hicks and the Hot Licks. The liner notes of their album, produced by George Fernandez, explain that "much of today's music is concerned with complex electronic loudness and computerized loudness. Our effort is toward an understandable clean sound". Dennis Coats wrote eight of the twelve tracks, the other being covers of Fats Waller (the title track), the often covered John Hartford's *Gentle On My Mind* and B. Russell's *Little Green Apples* plus the traditional *Sally Ann*. The group would disappear after two non-album singles.

Dennis Coats resurfaced in 1977 with the group Driver (one album for A&M), while Gary Carlson would play with the country singer Mason Williams during the early seventies. (SR)

Mark Jorg

ALBUM: 1 COME HOME MY SON
(Mt Abbey Angel Records NWI-2791) c1972 ?

Possibly from Oregon, a private pressing of folk and folk-rock songs. (SR)

Josefus

Personnel:	PETE BAILEY	vcls, harp	A
	DAVE MITCHELL	gtr	A
	DOUG TULL	drms	A
	RAY TURNER	bs	A

ALBUMS:	1(A)	DEAD MAN	(Hookah 330) 1970 R3
	2(A)	JOSEFUS	(Mainstream 6127) 1970 R2
	3(A)	GET OFF MY CASE	(Epilogue EPI 1002) 199? -

NB: (1) reissued by Eva (12010) 1983. (1) also reissued on vinyl (Texman Tex 1001) and on CD (Sundazed SC 11066) 1999 with bonus tracks from (3). (2) had a pirate repress circa 1986/87. (1) and (2) have been reissued on CD by TRC. (3) contains pre-*Dead Man* recordings including a lengthier *Dead Man*, *Crazy Man* and *Situation*. Further albums were *Son Of Dead Man* (Paradise Lost) 1990 and *Get Off My Case* (Epilogue) 1992. There's also a reunion LP *Son Of Dead Man* (Paradise Lost Records) 2000.

45s:	Crazy Man/Country Boy	(Dandelion) 1970
	Jimmy, Jimmy/Sefus Blues	(Mainstream 725) 1970

NB: There are also two later 45s: *Hard Luck/On Account Of You* (Hookah 78009) 1979 and *Let Me Move You/Big Time Loser* (Hookah 78010) 1979.

JOSEFUS - Josefus LP.

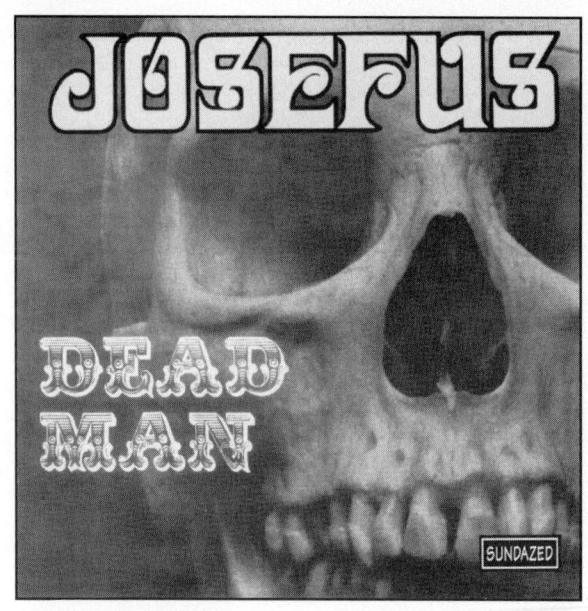

JOSEFUS - Dead Man CD.

From Houston, **Josefus** formed in September 1969, by Doug Tull after he'd been fired from United Gas (see **Christopher** entry). A couple of months later they attracted the attention of record producer Jim Musil, who invited them to Phoenix in Arizona to record under the name Come. However, the deal he was negotiating with Straight Records did not materialise and the sessions remained unreleased until the *Get Off My Case* retrospective.

The band reverted back to the name **Josefus** and returned to Houston. They went back to Phoenix, however, to record their 'first' album, *Dead Man*, which was recorded in just eight hours and mixed the next day. Comprised largely of originals it was probably their best work. It sold well in Texas and the highlight was the 17'5" minute title track. Two tracks from the album *Crazy Man/Country Boy* were also issued as a single.

Indeed the *Dead Man* release attracted the attention of Mainstream who signed them on a one album contract. The result was recorded at the Criteria Studios in Miami and produced by Bob Shad. This was in the same hard-rock vein as their first effort, but less imaginative and when neither the album or the 45 taken from it made any impression, they split in December 1970.

Pete Bailey and Ray Turner went on to play in a 1971 combo Stone Axe, together with guitarist Mike 'Wolf' Long and drummer Jerry Ontiverez. They had one 45, *Snakebite* on Rampart in the same year. Doug Tull later played for an outfit called **Christopher** and may also have backed power popper Tommy Keene in the mid to late eighties. Pete and Dave Mitchell were involved in an EP by Guitar Orchestra issued on Home Cooking Records in 1976.

In July 1978, Pete Bailey and Dave Mitchell reformed the band with a new line-up. This was short-lived but they did make the two 1979 45s listed.

In the nineties, *Get Off My Case* appeared, which contains their first efforts recorded in December 1969 prior to *Dead Man*. It's largely made up of different versions of songs that appeared on their first official album, including a lengthier version of *Dead Man, Crazy Man* and *Situation*. The release was accompanied by a booklet of the band's story.

Compilation appearances include *Dead Man* on *Gathering Of The Tribe* (LP). (VJ/SW/MW/RM)

Joseph

Personnel incl: JOSEPH LONGERIA gtr, vcls A

ALBUM: 1(A) STONED AGE MAN (Scepter SPS 574) 1970 R1/R2

NB: (1) also released on Scepter in France. The U.S. release also lists a mono version on the cover (SRM 574), but this is unlikely to exist. Also counterfeited on CD.

JOSEPH - Stoned Aged Man CD.

A wild album of heavy guitar blues - rock by this Tennessee guitarist. *Cold Biscuits And Fish Heads, I Ain't Fattenin' No More Frogs For Snakes*, etc.; crazy stuff! No other musicians are credited on the album.

Joseph Longeria also contributed the song *I'm Gonna Build A Mountain* to **Great Bear**'s eponymous album. (CF/RBn)

Ernie Joseph

Personnel:	CORY COLT	vcls, gtr, keyb'ds	A
	BRIAN FAITH	vcls, bs, drums	A
	ERNIE JOSEPH	vcl, ld gtr	A
	GREG MUNFORD	vcls	A

ALBUM: 1 (A)   AN ALL AMERICAN EMPEROR   197?

NB: (1) this may never have been released at the time, but has been 'reissued' on vinyl and CD (Akarma AK 042) 1999.

Ernie Joseph was a local hero on the Santa Barbara scene - as Ernie Orosco he fronted several outfits in the sixties including **Ernie and The Emperors**, **Ernie's Funnys**, **Giant Crab** and **Big Brother**. The content of this solo venture by the **Big Brother** mainman is not what one might expect from his group's style and indeed the axeman poses on the cover. Perhaps in an attempt to appeal to a more mainstream audience it is big production pop-rock of mainly Scott English (co-)compositions, often with beefy orchestration. **Ernie** was nothing if not adaptable and possesses a fine voice but don't be suckered by any garage or psych tags attached to this. It's more likely to appeal to fans of the **Association** - Cleo being one track that immediately brings that comparison to mind. In fact, as with some of the other Akarma 'reissues' of All American material, it may not have been released at the time.

Cory Colt was also a member of **Big Brother** whilst Greg Munford was with label-mates **Indescribably Delicious**. (MW/AP)

Joshua

Personnel:	QUINCY ROGERS	A
	SHELBY ROGERS	A
	TONY SENA	A

ALBUM: 1(A)   GOD SPOKE... AND SAID, "LEAD MY PEOPLE"
                                                     (Impact R 3228) 1973 R2/R3

NB: Also released in the U.K. (Key KL 014) 1973 R4.

From the Southwestern U.S., this religious hard-rock band's rare album also got a release in the U.K. on Key. For no particular reason, this is valued at R4. There are two U.S. pressings in existence; the original is black, the second has a red label. Tony Sena penned almost all of the material on their album, although three cuts: *New Life*, *Caterpillar* and *Free Me* were co-written with other band members. We're talking melodic rock with crisp guitar work and quite poignant lyrics here, but the stand-out track is the only non-original, *I Wish We'd All Been Ready*, a pleasant vocal harmony number. (CF/VJ)

Joshua Dyke

Personnel:	RON CLARK	ld vcls	A
	BUDDY DEHART	bs	A
	JOHN MARRIOTT	gtr, hrmnca	A
	GERALD PATTON	drms	A
	JOHN TSOTSOS	ld gtr	A

45:   Cheating / Confessin' The Blues   (Paris Tower PT-101) 1967

Formed by students at St.Petersburg Jr. College in Florida in 1966. Initially covering their favourite bands like the Rolling Stones, their immediate popularity led to a 45 on Paris Tower in 1967.

A menacing fuzzed-up cover of the Animals' *Cheating*, re-aired on *Psychedelic States: Florida Vol. 1* (CD), is backed by a blues standard also covered by the Stones.

Military call-ups and career choices splintered the group but they reunited 30 years later in Clearwater to record a CD. (MW/JLh/RM)

Joshua Fox

Personnel:	MIKE BOTTS	drms	A
	LARRY HANSEN	gtr	A
	JOE LA MANNO	bs	A
	TOM MENEFEE	gtr	A

ALBUM: 1(A)   JOSHUA FOX   (Tetragrammaton 125) 1968 SC

45s: Moontime Bore/
       Goin' Down For Big Numbers   (Tetragrammaton 1527) 1968
       It's Just Meant To Be You/
       Don't Tell Me A Story   (Tetragrammaton 1532) 1968

A hippie outfit from Los Angeles whose late sixties psychedelic folk album is now a very minor collectors item. Botts and La Manno were both top L.A. session men and Botts was later in Bread and Linda Ronstadt's roadband.

The Journey Back

Personnel:	BILL BROWN	gtr, organ	A
	LARRY BURNELL	bs	A
	STANLEY BURNELL	drms	A
	MICHAEL GENTILLINI	ld gtr	A
	BOBBY SUTTON	vcls	A

45:   Synthetic People /
      Run Away Baby   (Nottingham Disc Co. 849) 1968

Before the advent of the Beatles, the Burnell brothers were playing instrumentals with The Live Wires in their hometown of Plymouth, Virginia. Nothing was released but they also kept recordings on reel-to-reel, travelling widely to tape other local acts. One such trip into North Carolina was to capture the Creations just as that band was ending.

In 1967, they formed **The Journey Back** with Bill Brown and Bobby Sutton from the Creations. The following year they released their sole 45 (500 copies). The 'B' side, *Run Away Baby*, is a slow-burner with fiendish fuzz and powerful vocals like Eric Burdon. The flip, *Synthetic People*, is mighty fuzz-rock with a Cream-y riff and a nod in the direction of **Blue Cheer**.

Come the new millennium and the Burnell brothers are still playing together in a band called... **The Journey Back**.

Compilation appearances have included: *Run Away Baby* on *Sixties Rebellion, Vol. 3* (LP & CD); *Synthetic People* on *A Fistful Of Fuzz* (CD); and both *Run Away Baby* and *Synthetic People* on *Aliens, Psychos And Wild Things* (CD). (BHr/ST/MW)

The Journey Men

45:	She's Sorry/Short And Sweet	(Boss 008)	196?

From Tampa, Florida.

Compilation appearances include: *She's Sorry* on *Pebbles Box* (5-LP), *Acid Dreams - The Complete 3 LP Set* (3-LP), *Acid Dreams Epitaph* (CD) and *Trash Box* (5-CD). (VJ)

Joy

Personnel:	RALPH DESIMONE	drms	A
	BOB DI PIERO	gtr	A
	DON DI PIERO	bs	A
	BILLY JOE SHIVA	vcls	A
	RALPH VITELLO	organ, piano, acoustic gtr	A

ALBUM:	1(A)	THUNDERFOOT	(Paula LPS 2217) c1969 SC

45s:	Get Outta My Mind/Your Mama	(Paula 341) 1971
	Ride the World/For What It's Worth	(Paula 348) 1971
	Things Are Gonna Be Alright/Yes My Friend	(Paula 359) 1971

Recorded in Shreveport, Louisiana, by George W.Clinton (maybe the co-leader of **Timber**), this obscure album veers between hard prog and heavy rock, with decent vocals, lots of "churchy" organ and loud guitars. All their material was written by the group members but, despite sophisticated and often interesting introductions, the tracks are generally not strong enough to really retain attention. The best cuts are maybe *Cross Country Woman*, *Mother Nature* and *Ride The World*. (SR/MMs)

Joyfull Noise

Personnel:	DAVID W. HANNI	gtr	A
	WOLCOTT E. PUGH	piano	A
	DAVID M.ROWE	bs	A
	JOHN C.ROWE	gtr	A
	ERIC C. VON AMMON	drms	A

ALBUM:	1(A)	JOYFULL NOISE	(RCA VICTOR LSP-3963) 1968 -

45:	Animals, Flowers And Children / What, Me Worry	(RCA Victor 47-9516) 1968

ERNIE JOSEPH - An All American Emperor LP.

Orchestrated, sometimes brassy, pop-cum-soft-rock from a Northeastern quintet which strays occasionally into novelty territory. A charming but patchy collection for fans of pop, rather than garage or psych (despite sometimes being labelled 'psych' by dealers). (MW)

Joyful Noise

Personnel:	JOE GRIER	vcls, gtr, flute	A
	MARK GUNGON	vcls, keyb'd's, bs	A
	DEBBIE GUNGOR	vcls	A
	GAYLE HENSLEY	vcls	A
	LYNN ANN KIMBERLEY	drms	A
	BUBBA POLYTHRESS	gtr, bs	A
	PAUL SPENCER	vcls	A

ALBUM:	1(A)	NATIVITY	(Private S 200-38) 1970 ?

The band that created this Christian album has nothing to do with **Joyfull Noise**. It's so goddamn (sic) serious that it's easy to overlook its musical value. Titles such as *Love Is God's Command*, give the game away even before the listener has the chance to decide for themselves. So, every track drips of 'Jesus', but is otherwise a partly fine and mild progressive rock album with a sound at times close to **Kristyl** or **Titus Oates**. A respectably driving cut is *Make A Choice* by Grier with a pretty tempo change included and some fine guitar work. The intended main piece *Nativity*, which concludes the album, lasts over 10 minutes and tells the story of Christ being born. It includes flashes of greatly inspired playing alternating with rather stale and rigid music. Still worth hearing, I guess. (MK)

The Joyful Noise

Personnel:	NATHAN BOWMAN	A
	JOHN BURCH	A
	MARNEE HOLLIS	A
	NAOMI LYSO	A
	PAULA PUDWILL	A

ALBUM:	1(A)	THE DESIGNER	(Sound Preservers 74013) c1970 -

From Olympia, Washington, a Christian folk-rock group with male/female vocals and tambourine. Their album was produced by John Burch, who also wrote three songs. Several other Christian groups with the same name released albums of Jesus rock, folk-rock, psychedelic gospel... between 1968 and 1975. (SR)

Joyride

See **Friendsound**.

The Joyride

45s:	The Crystal Ship/Coming Soon	(World Pacific 77877) 1966
	Big Bright Green Pleasure Machine/ Coming Soon	(World Pacific 77883) 1967
	Land Of Rypap Papyr/His Blues	(World Pacific 77888) 1967

Probably from California and on the same label as **The Hardtimes**, an obscure psych-rock group. (SR)

The Joys of Life

Personnel incl:	JIM ALBRECHT	A

45:	Good Times Are Over/Descent	(Columbia 44188) 1967

Originally from Indianapolis, Indiana, this outfit moved to Chicago and played a paisley-styled garage rock with lots of fuzz guitar. The above 45 is thought to be their sole stab for stardom and on the flip, *Descent*, their psychedelic backing features a raving vocal and catchy organ.

Jim Albrecht was at Pike High School at the time their 45 became a big hit in the Midwest, and the band got to perform the song on a local TV show. Whilst Jim's single was playing all over the local airwaves and around the country, the principal at Pike High was at the time cracking down on long hairdos, even offering free haircuts in the schools front office for those students with 'Beatle'-like mops. Jim, however, was granted an exception and allowed to retain his long-hair!

A possible second 45 by this group, or another outfit with the same-name outfit is: - Everybody Wants To Fall In Love / Yesterday..(part-title) (Tomorrow 241) 196? Can anyone confirm details?

Compilation appearances include: *Descent* on *Sixties Archive, Vol. 8* (CD), *Acid Trip From The Psychedelic Sixties* (LP), *Chosen Few, Vol's 1 & 2* (CD) and *The Chosen Few, Vol. 2* (LP). (VJ/MW/TL)

Juarez

Personnel incl:	HAL BLAINE	drms	A
	JAMES BURTON	gtr	A
	LARRY KNECHTEL	keyb'ds	A

ALBUM: 1(A) JUAREZ (Decca DL 75189) 1970 -

A sophisticated male/female folk-rock trio backed by the usual L.A. session men. Their songs include such titles as *Acalpulco, Starfisher, Kyrie, St. Mary's Railroad, Langdon Street* and *Lauderdale Rain*. (SR)

Judge 'N' Jury

45: Roaches/Try Me (Verve 10486) 1967

This seems to have been a one off on Verve. You can check out the'A" side on *Garage Punk Unknowns, Vol. 6* (LP). (VJ)

The Judges

45: The Judge And Jury / Come On - Come On (Shurfine 018) 1966

Despite releasing their sole 45 on an Atlanta, Georgia label in the Summer of 1966, this band were from Birmingham, Alabama. *Judge And Jury*, penned by Walt Stewart, is a solid slab of dynamic sixties pop with pealing guitars and dramatic chords; judge for yourself on *Psychedelic States: Alabama Vol. 1* (CD). (MW)

The Ju-Ju's

Personnel:	MAX COLLEY		A
	BILL GORSKY		A
	RAY HUMMELL III	vcls	A
	ROD SHEPPARD		A
	RICK STEVENS	gtr	A

45s: You Treat Me Bad/Hey Little Girl (Fenton 1004) 1966
Do You Understand Me?/
I'm Really Sorry (PS) (United 121570) 1966

From Grand Rapids, Michigan, this band's vocalist sounded very much like David Surkamp (of Pavlov's Dog) although it was one **Ray Hummell III**, on the Fenton 45. **Ray Hummel III** also issued a solo 45 *Fine Day/Gentle Rain* on Fenton. Hummell left the group after the first 45 to form The Traffic Jams. They started out as a five-piece, though, and the second 45 suffered rather for Hummell's departure. Whilst with Fenton they recorded material for an album which remained unreleased, although a limited edition cassette was in circulation a few years back.

Rick Stevens had earlier played with The Paeans, who apparently recorded an unreleased 45 for Fenton.

Compilation appearances have included: *I'm Really Sorry* on *Let 'Em Have It! Vol. 1* (CD), *Psychedelic Unknowns, Vol. 8* (LP & CD), *Teenage Shutdown, Vol. 9* (LP & CD) and *Highs In The Mid Sixties, Vol. 19* (LP);

TEENAGE SHUTDOWN Vol. 9 (Comp CD) including The Ju-Ju's.

You Treat Me Bad on *Pebbles Vol. 1* (CD), *The Essential Pebbles Collection, Vol. 1* (Dble CD), *Pebbles, Vol. 1* (LP), *Teenage Shutdown, Vol. 2* (LP & CD), *Best of Pebbles, Vol. 3* (LP & CD), *Best Of Michigan Rock Groups Vol. 1* (Cass) and *Great Pebbles* (CD); *Hey Little Girl* on *Pebbles, Vol. 8* (LP); and *Do You Understand Me* on *Back From The Grave, Vol. 1* (LP) and *Garage Kings* (Dble LP). (VJ)

Jimmy Jukebox

45: Motor Boat/25 Hours A Day (Chattahoochee CH8) 196?

Another production of **Kim Fowley** (who also sings) and Michael Lloyd : classic and efficient "Fowley pop". According to the labels, the 'A' side was recorded in American Colony, Venus and the flip in Denny's Parking Lot!

Both sides can also be found on the **Fowley** retrospective *Living In The Streets*. (SR/WHn)

Jukin' Bone

Personnel:	DANNY COWARD	drms, perc	A
	JOHN DEMASO	bs, perc	A
	MARK DOYLE	gtr	A
	GEORGE EGOSARIAN	gtr	A
	KEVIN SHWARYK	drms	A
	JOE WHITTING	vcls	A

ALBUM:	1(A)	WHISKEY WOMEN	(RCA LSP 4261) 1972 SC
	2(A)	WAY DOWN EAST	(RCA LSP 4768) 1973 SC

This Upstate New York band was originally called Free Will. They were signed by RCA while some of the members were still in their teens, and renamed **Jukin' Bone**. Both records are very good hard, loud, bluesy rock, described in Creem magazine as "seminal classics of early '70s hard rock".

After the commercial failure of these releases the band members went their separate ways. Mark Doyle went on to play for Meatloaf, Andy Pratt, Cindy Bullens, Hall and Oates and many others. One reviewer said that Doyle's guitar "sounded like dinosaurs eating cars". Joe Whiting joined Bobby Comstock's band as saxophone player and would tour and perform with the likes of Little Richard, Chuck Berry and Jerry Lee Lewis. In the late seventies he replaced Ronnie James Dio in Elf (those recordings were eventually released in Europe on the Nibelung label), and in 1982 "Joe Whiting and The Bandit Band" toured as the opening act for Van Halen.

Doyle and Whiting would reunite and record together in the eighties as The Doyle-Whiting Band, in the nineties as Backbone Slip and finally in 2001 **Jukin' Bone** would reform and record under the original moniker Free Will. (HS)

Juletta's Valiants

Personnel:
DANNY		A
JOE		A
JULETTA		A
STEVE		A

A Dayton, Ohio, band whose only recorded legacy appears to be an earnest folk-rock rendition of John Stewart's *Love Me Not Tomorrow*. This appears on *WONE, The Dayton Scene* (Prism PR-1966), a souvenir album of the 1966 WONE-sponsored three-day battle of the bands which features one cut each from the top twelve Daytonian acts. (MW/GGl)

Julius Victor

Personnel:
LAWRENCE "ZEA" ENGSTROM	drms	A
JIM CUTSINGER	bs	A
KIMBALL LEE	organ, piano, vcls	A
MARK SCHNEIDER	gtr	A

ALBUM: 1(A) FROM THE NEST (AJP LPS-5160) 1970 R1

NB: (1) reissued on CD (Dodo DDR 517) 2001.

Probably from New York, this short-lived outfit was obviously influenced by **Iron Butterfly**. Their album features prominent organ and all their material was original and penned by Lawrence Engstrom (sometimes with the help of Kimball Lee). It was produced by the famous jazz musician Ahmad Jamal.

From The Nest is now rare and sought-after by some collectors. (SR/NK)

Jungle

ALBUM: 1 JUNGLE (No label CD 3027) 1969 R6

NB: (1) demo album issued in plain black sleeve. Reissued initially in a blue velveteen cover with all artwork and text embossed in silver foil (Little Indians #8) 1997. This limited repressing (450 numbered copies) sold out quickly and the record was re-released in a smaller edition (250 copies) on multi-coloured vinyl. These copies were issued in the same velveteen cover design, but in three different covers: the blue was augmented by black and red. All four versions of the Little Indians reissue are currently in the R1 category. The same label also produced a CD edition in 1999. The label on the original demo album is yellow with red print; the reissues have a yellow label with black print.

Nothing is currently known about the fine band responsible for this rare demo album. Both of the two known copies were found in plain black sleeves with no personnel or recording information.

Early Morning Rising, *Slave Ship*, *House Of Rooms* and *Gray Picnic* are all loaded with nice guitar and organ work, and could be positively labeled "hard-rock" were it not for the drummer's apparent jazz aspirations. The album as a whole has a relaxed, almost loose quality that somehow seems to underscore its "demo" classification but very little of the music seems unpolished... and the vocals are exemplary across both sides. It's not hard to imagine that these musicians pursued careers well into the seventies.

As originals are rather elusive, grab the reissue and check this one out.

An edited version of *Slave Ship* has also resurfaced on *Love, Peace And Poetry, Vol. 1* (LP & CD). (CF)

Roy Junior

45: Victim Of Circumstances/
Looks Like The Sun Ain't Gonna Shine (Hickory 1425) 1966

Junior is actually Roy Acuff Jr. from Nashville, Tennessee, and the son of the Grand Ole Opry legend. He had a few pretty decent folk-rock 45s on Hickory using his real name. Roy's producer was singer Don Gant, later of the **Neon Philharmonic**.

JULIUS VICTOR - From The Nest LP.

Compilation appearances have included: *Victim Of Circumstances* on *Back From The Grave, Vol. 2* (LP) and *Garage Kings* (Dble LP); and *Looks Like The Sun Ain't Gonna Shine* on *Every Groovy Day* (LP). (MW/JLh)

Just Luv

45: Valley Of Hate/Good Good Lovin' (M-S 216) 1966

A Detroit, Michigan, high school band, they combine folk and punk influences quite successfully on *Valley Of Hate*.

It has also been suggested they may have been from New England, but this is now known to be incorrect.

Compilation appearances include: *Valley Of Hate* on *Pebbles, Vol. 16* (LP), *Punk Ballads Sampler* (LP) and *Sixties Archive, Vol. 5* (CD). (VJ/MW/GGl)

Just Too Much

45: She Gives Me Time/
I Can Only Give You Everything (M-Gee) 1966

This band hailed from Los Angeles.

Compilation appearances include: *She Gives Me Time* on *Back From The Grave, Vol. 8* (CD) and *Back From The Grave, Vol. 8* (Dble LP). (VJ)

Just Us

ALBUM: 1 JUST A THOUGHT (Private Pressing) 1973? R1

A "real people" acid folk group, sometimes compared to **Bobby Brown**, with male and female vocals. The album came housed in a colour hand-drawn cover with an insert. (SR)

The Juveniles

ALBUM: 1 BO DIDDLY (Piccadilly PIC-3371) 1980 SC

45s:
α	Bo Diddley/Yes, I Believe	(Jerden 770)	1965
α	Baby, Baby/I've Searched	(Jerden 795)	1966
β	You Gotta Understand/Long Green	(Panorama 50)	196?

NB: α 'B' sides non-LP. β both sides non-LP.

JUNGLE - Jungle LP.

JEFFERSON AIRPLANE - Early Flight LP.

Originally from Norman in Oklahoma, they recorded some tracks there at the Shore Bird recording studios, before relocating to the Northwest.

The retrospective album is a collection of 'live' and unreleased recordings in a frantic frat-garage vein with some slower bluesy ballads, together with their superb fuzz-rockin' version of *Bo Diddly*. Raw and vibrant - if this was an original sixties local label or private press it would be in the mega-buck category.

They later became The Express.

Compilation appearances have included: *Bo Diddley* on *Northwest Battle Of The Bands, Vol. 1 - Flash And Crash* (LP & CD), *Dementation Of Sound* (LP) and *Wavy Gravy Vol. 1* (LP & CD); and *I've Searched* on *Northwest Battle Of The Bands, Vol. 2 - Knock You Flat!* (LP & CD) and *Northwest Battle Of The Bands, Vol. 1* (CD). (MW)

Jynx

Personnel:	CHRIS BELL	ld gtr	A
	BILL CUNNINGHAM	bs	A
	MIKE HARRIS	vcls	A
	DAVID HOBACK	gtr	A
	DEWITT SHY	drms	A

10" ALBUM: 1   GREATEST HITS!   (Norton TED-1003) 2000

The Norton 10" 45 presents the complete legacy of a forgotten Memphis garage quintet - four demos recorded at Sonic Studios in December 1965 in an attempt to get them onto 'Talent Party', the local TV talent show hosted by George Klein. The band chose covers - *Little Girl* (Them), *Just Like Me* (**Paul Revere and The Raiders**), *And My Baby's Gone* (Moody Blues) and *I'll Go Crazy* (James Brown, via the Moody Blues).

The Jynx splintered soon after and would have remained forgotten but for some members' further ventures. Bill Cunningham joined The Jokers and later toured with **The Box Tops**. Norton's scoop here is that these recordings capture the first forays of his friend and fellow Jynxer, the late Chris Bell, who would team up with ex-**Box Top** Alex Chilton to form Big Star. (MW)

PAUL KANTNAR - Blows Against The Empire CD.

JEFFERSON AIRPLANE - Long John Silver CD.

Kack Klick

45: One More Day And One More Night/
Lord My Cell Is Cold　　　　(House of Guitars H 1001) 1963

Both sides of this obscure 45 figured on *Glimpses, Vol. 4* (LP). This was later the **Church Mice**, see details under that entry. (VJ)

Kai-Ray and Crew

Personnel incl:　KAI-RAY

45s:			
	Jungle Talk/Trashman's Blues	(Lodestar 27-61)	1961
α	Living On Borrowed Time/Limbo Limbo	(Lodestar 39-61)	1961
	Limbo Limbo/Sugar Daddy	(Lodestar 74-62)	1962
	I Want Some Of That/		
β	Trashman's Blues	(Shooting Star 2267)	196?
	I Want Some Of That/		
	Trashman's Blues	(Brite Star KB 2267)	c1962

NB: α released as **Shane Kai-Ray**. β shown as by **Kai-Ray**.

This Minneapolis, Minnesota act's main significance may be that **The Trashmen** took their name from the *Trashman's Blues* song.

Compilation appearances include *I Want Some Of That* on *Scum Of The Earth* (Dble CD) and *Scum Of The Earth, Vol. 2* (LP). (VJ)

Kak

Personnel:	JOSEPH D DAMRELL	bs, gtr, sitar, tambourine	A
	CHRISTOPHER A LOCKHEED	drms, tabla, harp, vcls, maracas	A
	DEHNER C PATTEN	ld gtr, vcls	A
	GARY LEE YODER	ld vcls, rhythm gtr, acoustic gtr	A

ALBUM:　1(A)　KAK　　　　(Epic 26429) 1969 R2

NB: (1) counterfeited on vinyl in the UK circa 1982 and in Italy (Dino) 1998. Reissued officially on vinyl by Epic in 1998. Also issued on CD (Epic EK 48534) 199? counterfeited on Israphon (ISR 008). Better still, *Kak-Ola* (Big Beat CDWIKD 187) 1999, is a twenty-track compilation comprising: the original LP, 45 version of Rain, several demos plus five Gary Lee Yoder solo tracks including the *Flight From The East / Good Time Music* 45.

45s:	α	Everything's Changing/Rain	(Epic 10383) 1968
	β	Everything's Changing (mono)/(stereo)	(Epic 10383) 1968
		I've Got Time/Disbelievin'	(Epic 10446) 1969

NB: α 'B' side is no-album version. β promo only.

KAK - Kak LP.

This highly talented, underrated band from Davis in California produced what is now one of the most sought-after psychedelic albums. Mellow laid-back tracks like *I've Got Time* and *Flowing By* are merged with up-tempo numbers like *Disbelievin'* and *Electric Sailor*. The excellent guitar playing of Patten and Yoder is evident throughout the album. Most tracks, particularly the final one *Lemonaide Kid* had considerable commercial potential and the band was clearly a victim of under-exposure. They disbanded in 1970.

Yoder had earlier led **The Oxford Circle**, issued a solo 45 *Good Time Music/Flight From The East* (Epic 10560) in 1970 and then played for a while in **Blue Cheer**. Patten was also in **The Oxford Circle**, and Damrell in **Group "B"**. Lockheed joined forces with **Randy Holden** for his *Population II* album. Several years later, Chris Lockheed along John Cipollina played on the rare Stu Blank's *Under The Big Top* album from 1988.

The Big Beat reissue of the album, with a healthy dollop of bonus tracks, *Kak-Ola* is recommended.

Compilation coverage has so far included: *Trieulogy* on *Endless Journey - Phase Two* (LP) and *Endless Journey - Phase I & II* (Dble CD); *Lemonade Kid* and *Electric Sailor* on *Psychedelic Dream* (Dble LP); *Disbelievin'* on *Reverberation IV* (CD) and *Rockbusters* (LP); *Rain* on *California Halloween*; and *Flight From The East*, a Gary Yoder solo effort, on *Filling The Gap* (4-LP). (VJ/SR)

Kalapana

ALBUM:　1　KALAPANA　　　　(Private Pressing) c1974 -

A local prog-rock quartet from Hawaii. (SR)

Kaleidoscope

Personnel:	MARK FEEDMAN	hrmnca	A
	SOLOMON FELDTHOUSE	gtr, caz	ABCD
	DAVID LINDLEY	gtr, fiddle, harp, banjo	ABCD
	JOHN WELSH	gtr	A
	CHESTER CRILL (alias FENRUS EPP)	keyb'ds, violin, vcls	BCD
	CHRIS DARROW	bs, mandn	B
	JOHN VIDICAN	drms	B
	STUART BROTMAN	bs, vcls	C
	PAUL LAGOS	drms, vcls	C
	RON JOHNSON	bs	D
	JEFF KAPLAN	gtr, vcls	D

　　　　　　　　　　　　　　　　　　　　　　　　HCP
ALBUMS:	1(B)	SIDE TRIPS	(Epic 26304) 1967 - R1
	2(B)	A BEACON FROM MARS	(Epic 26333) 1968 - R1

KALEIDOSCOPE - Side Trips LP.

KALEIDOSCOPE - A Beacon From Mars LP.

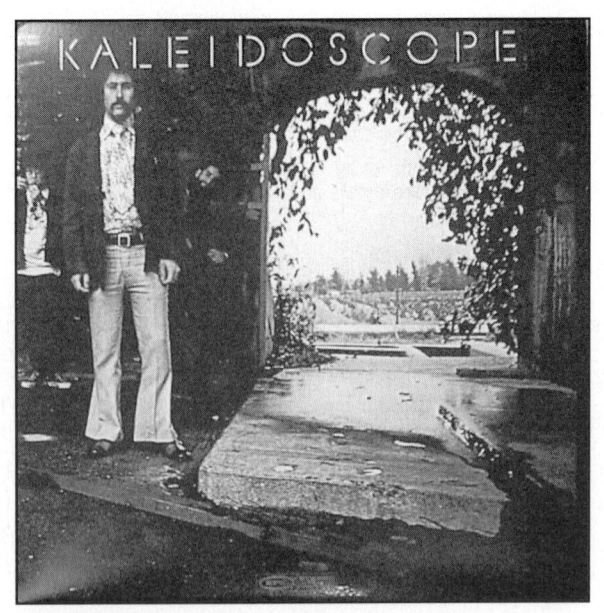

KALEIDOSCOPE - Incredible Kaleidoscope LP.

3(C)	INCREDIBLE KALEIDOSCOPE	(Epic 26467) 1968	139 SC
4(D)	BERNICE	(Epic 26508) 1970	- -

NB: (1) reissued on CD (Edsel EDCD 531) and (Epic EK 48513). (1) also reissued on vinyl by Epic 1998. (2)-(4) also now available on CD. (3) and (4) are also available on one CD (Head 3697). It should perhaps be noted that (1) was counterfeited early on, perhaps even in the late 1970s. This fake is easy to identify - the back cover on the original pressing is printed in blue, the fake in black. The discs, however, are very convincing. (1) and (2) were both issued in mono as white label promo issues (R1 and R2 respectively). (1) also reissued on vinyl by Edsel in 1988. Also of interest is the bootleg *Live At The Shrine* (Boot) 198?. Edsel have also issued a *Best Of Kaleidoscope*.

45s:
Please/Elevator Man	(Epic 10117)	1967
Why Try?/Little Orphan Nannie	(Epic 10219)	1967
I Found Out/Rampe Rampe	(Epic 10239)	1967
Nobody (with Johnny'Guitar'Watson & Larry Williams)/ Find Yourself Someone To Love	(Okeh 730)	1967
Hello Trouble/Just A Taste	(Epic 10332)	1968
Let The Good Love Flow/Lie To Me	(Epic 10481)	1969
Tempe Arizona/Lie To Me	(Epic 10500)	1969
Killing Floor/Lie To Me	(Epic 10500)	1969

Kaleidoscope's music was so wide-ranging that it is difficult to categorise. Not surprisingly therefore, all of their albums have become obscure collectors items. However, compilations of material from their first three albums are now available and all the original albums have been reissued on CD.

An explanation for the range of this group's music can be found in the backgrounds of its personnel. Lindley, born in L.A., had previously played with a number of bands, including The New Christy Minstrels and The Greenwood Singers and had also played banjo for several labels. He formed the group in September 1966. They initially called themselves The Baghdad Blues Band. Feldthouse originated from Ismit in Turkey and played a wide range of exotic instruments which included the saz, bouzouki, dobro, vina, doumbeg and dulcimer as well as the more mundane 12-string guitar and fiddle. He was responsible for the Eastern influence on tracks like *Egyptian Gardens*, *Why Try* and *Keep Your Mind Open* on their first album. Darrow was born in South Dakota, but raised in Claremont, California. His musical taste encompassed bluegrass, country, blues, jug band, R&B and old-time jazz. Percussionist Vidican grew up in Hollywood, and Epp was from Oklahoma City. Apart from the Eastern-influenced songs, other tracks on their first album included the traditional *Come On In*, *Oh Death* and the offbeat *Minnie The Moocher*. Another cut *Please* was chosen as the 'A' side for their first single with a non-album track, *Elevator Man*, a more straight-ahead rock track with some superb guitar playing from Lindley, on the flip. The single went nowhere. Next off they tried a remixed version of *Why Try* and a version of *Little Orphan Annie*, written by Darrow and Epp, which later turned up on the *Bernice* album in a very different form. However, this 45 made no commercial impression either.

A Beacon From Mars contained an incredible 12-minute 'live' version of the psychedelic title track and an 11-minute 'live' version of their Eastern-jam *Taxim*. Indeed, their 'live' performances were quite a show with a belly dancer performing to the latter track and flamenco dancers accompanying their Spanish guitar work. The remainder of the album comprised more traditional country-influenced songs like *Greenwood Sidee*, *Life Will Pass You By*, *Louisiana Man* and the goodtime rag *Baldheaded End Of A Broom*.

By the time of *Incredible Kaleidoscope*, Darrow and Vidican had left. Side One of *Incredible...* opens with the Eastern-influenced *Lie To Me* and the goodtime rag *Let The Good Times Flow*. The bluesy *Tempe Arizona* is followed by the country-influenced *Petite Fleur* and *Banjo*. Side Two contained the group's arrangement of the traditional ballad *Cuckoo* and the 11.30 minute *Seven-Ate Sweet*.

However, *Bernice* was comparatively weak and the group disbanded in 1970. The album was to have included many tracks which were censored by Epic, including three that were removed for taking stands on major political issues of the day, including the Chicago riots.

The group reformed in 1975 for a rather disappointing album *When Scopes Collide*, (Pacific Arts 102) and again in 1995 for the *Greetings From Kartoonistan* album.

Kaleidoscope also recorded some pre-Epic demos, which were produced by **Curt Boettcher** and Victoria Winston. Tantalisingly, these have recently resurfaced and the tape log indicates that the sessions included *Down The Line*, an early version of *Egyptian Gardens*, plus a reel apparently containing a number of songs labelled *Irish With Sitars*.

The first three albums are recommended, but the originals may be difficult to obtain at reasonable prices. More accessible are the CD reissues, and four compilations of their material, including: Sony's *Egyptian Candy* (CD), *Bacon From Mars* (Edsel XED 11 5), which features some of their best short compositions, *Rampe Rampe* (Edsel ED 138), which contains most of their longer cuts and 1993's *Blues From Baghdad* CD (Edsel EDCD 375), which basically comprised the earlier vinyl compilation *Bacon From Mars* with four additional tracks:- *Beacon From Mars*, *Seven Ate Sweet*, *Greenwood Sidee* and *Rampe Rampe*.

Darrow also played fiddle on **Morning**'s second album and went on to record a number of solo albums. He has also had a number of recent releases on the German Taxim label, played for a very short time with The Nitty Gritty Dirt Band and also backed Linda Ronstadt.

Kaleidoscope's other compilation appearances include:- *Keep Your Mind Open* on *Psychedelic Dream* (Dble LP) and *Psychedelic Frequencies* (CD); *Brother Mary* and *Mickey's Tune* on the *Zabriskie Point* soundtrack; *Nobody* (with Johnny Guitar Watson and Larry Williams) on *Mindrocker, Vol. 7* (LP); and *You Don't Love Me* on *Rockbusters* (LP). They also have three live tracks, *Oh Death*, *Taxim* and *Egyptian Gardens* on *California Acid Folk* (LP). Fans of the band will also want to seek of a free EP which came with

KALEIDOSCOPE - Bernice CD.

'Ptolemaic Terrascope Magazine No. 12', containing two 1965 acetate tracks by this band - *I'm A Hog For You* and *Little Orphan Annie*. (VJ/JFr)

Maitreya Kali

ALBUMS: 1 APACHE - SOUND TRACK FROM YOSEMITE, DEDICATED TO JIMI HENDRIX
(Akashic CF 2777) 1972 R5
2 INCA (United Kingdom Of America) 1972 R6
3 APACHE/INCA ( ) 197? R6

NB: (1) was issued with a booklet. (2) was issued with an insert and poster. (3) was a limited edition package comprising both records (original pressings) in a gatefold cover with the *Apache* front cover on the front of the gatefold, the *Inca* front cover on the rear of the gatefold and the two original back covers on the inner gatefold. The booklet from the *Apache* album and the insert and poster from *Inca* were included in the package. (1), (2) and (3) are credited to Satya Sai Maitreya Kali. (1) reissued as a single album circa 1989 in a limited edition of 300. (2) reissued as a limited edition circa 1991. (3) reissued as a double album with all three inserts, beautifully reproduced in limited edition, 180gm vinyl (Little Indian No. 2) 2000, later issued as a double CD (Normal Records) 2001.

Maitreya Kali (real name believed to be Craig Smith) left behind two of the rarest and most unusual private pressings from the California rock scene.

Apparently a young man of considerable wealth with more than a passing interest in rock music, these two albums are collections of recordings he financed from the mid-sixties to approximately 1971. Being without much in the way of liner notes or recording dates, much of what is known about the artist and the music on offer has been deduced from the arcane cryptology on the records (which must be seen to be believed). One collector actually managed to get close to finding the mysterious Mr. Smith in the late 1980s being connected by phone to a gentleman claiming to be the executor of his trust, who advised him in no uncertain terms that further pursuit of Mr. Smith would be inadvisable and unproductive.

All that aside, these are amazing records that should not be missed by anyone interested in sixties music. Not all of the material is of the same quality, but the earlier-sounding tracks on each album are mindblowing. These were made with a small, well-rehearsed rock band, and some of them (the ones on the *Inca* album) were written by Chris Ducey (aka **Chris Lucey**, aka **Bobby Jameson**), another Los Angeles-based artist about whom little is known. *Knot The Freize* is one such track, covering most of Side One of *Inca* as an intricate, engaging rock-folk suite. It is implied on the cover that this "Rock Opera" was written in 1965 and recorded by Capitol records with the involvement of Nick Venet! *Color Fantasy* and *Voodoo Spell* from *Apache* are obviously vintage sixties recordings and are the high point of the first release, the former having top-notch production values and being a swirling mass of treated guitars and trippy vocals. Smith apparently decided to switch gears and embrace folk music circa '69 (probably a necessity; the photos on the albums suggest that he travelled the world extensively around the turn of the decade) and roughly half the music on each album is acoustic guitar and vocal. Obviously, this material will be of less interest to readers of this book but these records are highly recommended nevertheless.

Apache was reissued as a single album circa 1989, and *Inca* followed in the early nineties. The double album version (with all three inserts!) was beautifully reproduced in limited edition by the Little Indians label (No. 2) in 1999. A double CD release was also made in 2001.

It seems likely that Craig Smith and **Chris Lucey** were responsible for the **Chris and Craig** indian-influenced 45: *Isha/I Need You* (Capitol 5694) 1966. (CF/VJ)

Mickey Kalis and The Bakersfields Blues Band

45: 2:10 to Yuma / Got No Time (United Audio 6003) 1969

A late sixties outfit from Youngstown, Ohio. *Got No Time*, a lengthy slab of blues-infused locomotion with a hint of **CCR**, is also featured on *Sick And Tired* (LP). (MW/GGI)

Kallabash Corp

Personnel:	ISH BRADY	ld vcls, bs	A
	TOM COLEMAN	drms, congas	A
	TED KEATON	ld vcls, organ	A
	RICK OATES	gtr	A
	MARK 'BIRD' WRENN	flute, alto flute, tenor sax	A

ALBUM: 1(A) KALLABASH CORP (Uncle Bill 311) 1970 R1/R2

NB: (1) reissued on CD (Free Records FR 2011) 2001.

Greenboro in North Carolina seems to have been home for this band. The album's not essential to fans of garage, psychedelia or hippie rock, but they do sound competent musicians. It's really a progressive with quite a lot of brass and woodwind and the occasional mellow instrumental like *Jimmy's Song* and *Rainbows*. (VJ)

Kama Del Sutra

45: She Taught Me Love/Come On Up (Zig Zag 273) 1967

Originally known as We The People, this outfit came from Duluth, on the Western bank of Lake Superior up in Minnesota. Needless to say their highly-touted punk 45 is now rare and sought-after.

MAITREYA KALI - Apache LP.

Compilation appearances have included: *She Taught Me Love* on *The Essential Pebbles Collection, Vol. 2* (Dble CD), *Pebbles, Vol. 1 (ESD)* (CD), *Root '66* (LP) and *Teenage Shutdown, Vol. 3* (LP & CD). (VJ)

The Kan Dells

Personnel:	GENE BEST	ld gtr, vcls	A
	JAY BEST	drms	A
	SAM BURCH	keyb'ds, vcls	A
	PETE VAN DER SCHAEGEN	bs, vcls	A
	BOB VAN DER SCHAEGEN	gtr	A

45s:	Cry Girl/Cloudburst	(Boss 6501) 1964
	I Want You To Know/Do You Know?	(Bear 1971) 196?
	I Want You To Know/ Shake It Baby (PS)	(Magnitude MA-1001) 1994
α	Lucky Day / I've Met Death (PS)	(Magnitude MA-1002) 1996

NB: α contains two unreleased tracks from 1966.

From Sandstone, Minnesota. The Bear 45 is particularly hard to find, having only been released as a promo 45. Fortunately, the 'A' side has recently been reissued, with a different flip. *Cry Girl* was originally compiled on *Top Teen Bands Vol. 1* (LP).

Retrospective compilation appearances include *Cry Girl* on *Root '66* (LP) and *Everywhere Chainsaw Sound* (LP).

Pete Van Der Schaegen later became an electrician but continued to play in bands. (VJ/MW/PVS)

Kane's Cousins

ALBUM:	1	UNDERGUM BUBBLEGROUND	(Shove Love ST-9827) 1968/9 - HCP

45s:	Take Your Love And Shove It/ Support Your Local Bands	(Shove Love 500) 1968/9 116
	Take Your Love And Shove It/ National Anthem (Red/Yellow Vinyl)	(Shove Love 0069) 1968/9 -

This mob came out of Fort Lauderdale, Florida. The music is mainly buried beneath the party going on in the studio, a veritable confusion of 'intermissions', noises, quips and general hilarity. They certainly had a lot of recording freedom. One track where they finally come together as an integrated unit is the tough rockin' ode to Jim Morrison suitably titled *Morrison*. This is followed by the long instrumental freak-out jam *Rushes*, which builds up to an impressive climax to close the album. Oh yes - the labels on the record are reversed too - so funny! Best avoided. (MW/VJ)

Kangaroo

Personnel:	JOHN HALL	gtr, bs, steel gtr, keyb'ds, vcls	A
	BARBARA KEITH	vcls	A
	N.D. SMART	drms, vcls	A
	TED SPELIES (TED SPELEOS)	ld gtr, vcls	A

ALBUM:	1(A)	KANGAROO	(MGM SE 4586) 1968 SC

45s:	I Never Tell Me Twice/ Such Long Long Time	(MGM 13960) 1968
α	Frog Giggin'/Maybe Tommorow	(MGM 13962) 1968

NB: α released as by N.D. Smart II and Kangaroo.

When **Barbara Keith** and N.D.Smart relocated from Boston to Washington DC, they teamed up with local heroes John Hall and Ted Speleos (ex-**British Walkers**), who were based in the downtown area. **Kangaroo** played at the Peppermint Lounge during their short lifespan.

MAITREYA KALI - Inca LP.

Basically their album's a country-rock influenced collection with some rather over-enthusiastic lead guitar. It does have two outstanding tracks which feature the beautiful vocals of **Barbara Keith** (the only two that do). Certainly an album that's worth a listen. John Hall was later with Orleans whilst, prior to **Kangaroo** N.D. Smart II had played with several bands including The Mark V, The Knights, Thee Rubber Band, **The Remains** {1966}, The Bait Shop and **Bo Grumpus** before joining **Kangaroo** in 1968. Whilst with **Kangaroo** he met the performance troupe **The Hello People** at the Cafe Wha? and worked with both groups for a while. In 1969 he left to work with **Leslie West** and was in the initial **Mountain** line-up, before joining Great Speckled Bird {1969-72}, and its Woodstock based spin-off Hungry Chuck {1971-72}. In 1972, he worked with **The Hello People** once again.

Barbara Keith wrote *Free The People*, the **Delaney and Bonnie** hit and also released two solo albums in 1969 (Verve Forecast) and 1972 (Reprise, with one of the best versions of *All Along The Watchtower*) and the participation of Lowell George and N.D. Smart II. Ted Speleos later played with **Holy Moses**. (MWh/VJ/CF/MW/SR/JO)

Kantones

45:	Lovn'g And Roses / In The Mood	(Maarc MA 1544) 1968

From Canton, Ohio and on the same local label as **Glen Jester and The Merseymen**, this 45 was described as "garage" but is actually the work of a harmony-pop lounge band. The flip is a cover of Judy Garland's *In The Mood*. Steer clear. (MW/GGI)

Kaper

45:	In Her Eyes/Daisy	(Le Bru) c1973

A mix of prog and psych from an obscure group from Lincolnwood, Illinois. They are also said to have released an album. (SR/KKz)

The Kaplan Brothers

ALBUMS:	1	THE KAPLAN BROTHERS	(Kap) c1972 SC
	2	NIGHTBIRD	(Quinton Record) c1973 R1

Probably from Illinois, this group played an unusual mix of symphonic prog rock and lounge music, with various covers and some original tracks. Their first album included a reworking of *Eleanor Rigby* and the second a cover of King Crimson's *Epitaph*. Their albums are held in high esteem by some collectors searching for unusual sounds and "sincere" projects. (SR)

The Kards

Personnel incl:
CLAYTON	vcls	A
J.W. HUGHES	vcls	A
D.P. WALLACE		A

ALBUM: 1(A) THE KARDS (12" metal acetate)
(Jaggar's Recording Studio) 196? R3

A Little Rock, Arkansas garage band performs covers of Yardbirds, Kinks and Animals songs with guitar/bass/drums line-up plus a few instrumentals where saxophone substitutes for lead guitar. Inept, but charming. Probably only a handful of these were made, as they have typed labels which are glued to the acetate. They were issued in a plain cover with a business card glued to the front. (CF)

Kartune Kapers

45: On The Plane/Knock On Wood (Space SR 00011/12) 1966

Hailing from the Albuquerque area of New Mexico both sides of this group's 45 were produced by **Lindy Blaskey**. *On The Plane*, is a particularly good fuzz-punk cover of the **Leaves** song.

Compilation appearances include: *Knock On Wood* and *On The Plane* on *Chicago 60's Punk Vs. New Mexico 60's Pop* (LP). (VJ)

The Kasenetz Katz Singing Orchestral Circus

Personnel incl: JOEY LEVINE ld vcls

ALBUMS:
1. THE KASENETZ KATZ SINGING ORCHESTRAL CIRCUS (Buddah BDS-2020) 1968 -
2. THE KASENETZ KATZ SUPER CIRCUS (Buddah BDS-5028) 1968 -
3. CLASSICAL SMOKE (THE KASENETZ-KATZ ORCHESTRAL CIRKUS) (Super K SKS 6001) 1968 -

NB: (3) also issued in Germany (Hansa 80389) 1968.

EP: 1 HOLIDAY SPECTACULAR (Buddah SP-1) 1968

45s:
			HCP
	Down In Tennessee/Mrs Green	(Buddah 52) 1968	124
	Quick Joey Small (Run Joey Run)/ Mr Jensen	(Buddah 64) 1968	25
α	I'm In Love With You/To You With Love	(Buddah 82) 1969	105
	Mrs Green/Embrassez Moi	(Buddah 90) 1969	-

NB: α credited to the Kasanetz Katz Supercircus.

This 'Bubblegum' rock group was assembled by producers Jerry Kasenetz and Jeff Katz and comprised members from **The Ohio Express**, **Music Explosion** and **1910 Fruitgum Company**. 'Bubblegum' was a short-lived, but extremely commercially successful fad in America between 1968-69. At its most basic it was characterised by a heavy, repetitive bass beat; simple lyrics and affected nasal vocals. It was particularly successful with teen audiences. Jerry Kasenetz and Jeff Katz are generally credited for inventing the phenomenon and *Quick Joey Small* with its heavy, repetitive bass beat was one of the better examples of the genre. Like so many other recordings of this ilk it was commercially successful reaching No 25 in the U.S. and No 19 in the UK.

The first album was a fake live album, though oddly the concert was actually recorded and is itself pretty good. The second album also features the **Shadows Of Knight**. Another album by **K-K Orchestral Circus**, called *Classical Smoke* reputedly sounds uncannily like a Joe Meek record.

Compilation apearances have included: *Quick Joey Small* on *Born Bad (Songs The Cramps Taught Us)* and *Pop Explosion* (1968, LP); *Quick Joey Small*, *We Can Work It Out* and *I'm In Love With You* all as **Kasenetz Katz Super Circus** on *Bubble Gum Music Is... The Naked Truth* (LP). (VJ/JFr/SR/VZ)

The Kasuals

45: Just Call My Name / Listen To The Rain (GMA 4) 1964

This unknown outfit's sole release on a Chicago label. *Just Call My Name*, a solid merseybeat stomper with piercing leads, is featured on *Sick And Tired* (LP). (MW)

Katmandu

Personnel:
BOB CALDWELL	bs	A
NORMAN HARRIS	organ, ld vcls	A
BOB JABO	gtr, vcls	A
KENNY ZALE	drms	A

ALBUM: 1(A) KATMANDU (Mainstream S/6131) 1971 R1

NB: (1) reissued on Merlin in 1979.

A keyboard dominated heavy album with the occasional good guitar piece but generally unimaginative and a marginal case for inclusion in this book. Not recommended.

Bob Jabo had earlier played in Miami based **Shaggs**, and **Kollektion**. (VJ)

Katz Kradle

45: Bad Case Of You/Bring It On Home (Sure-Shot 6609) 196?

Like the **Huntsmen** 45 this is rumoured to be garage collector, compiler and enthusiast Erik Lindgren in a bogus sixties garage project. They're the only known 45s on the label and were totally unknown until they started to suddenly appear on the specialist market. Great stuff though, and the flip is a good slow-burning Animals' punker.

Compilation appearances include *Bad Case Of You On My Mind* on *Gone, Vol. 2* (LP). (MW)

Peter Kaukonen

Personnel:
TERRY ADAMS	cello	A
NICK BUCK	organ, piano	A
JOE COVINGTON	drms	A
DIANE EARL	backing vcl	A
PETER KAUKONEN	vcls, gtr	A
PETER MARSHALL	bowed bs	A
MARK RYAN	bs	A

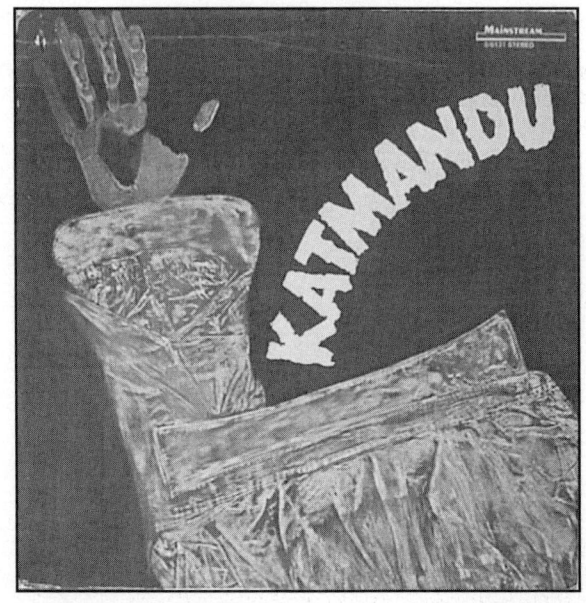

KATMANDU - Katmandu LP.

| | SHELLEY SILVERMAN | drms | A |
| | LARRY WEISBERG | bs | A |

ALBUM: 1(A) BLACK KANGAROO (Grunt FRT-1006) 1972 -

45: Prisoner/Dynamo Stranger (Grunt 65 0507) 1972

Brother of Jorma, **Peter Kaukonen** released his first solo album in 1972 on **Jefferson Airplane**'s label, Grunt. *Black Kangaroo* is a very convincing attempt at producing a **Hendrix** style album, a bit like **Randy California**'s *Kaptain Kopter* or **Velvert Turner**'s output. *Up Or Down*, *Prisoner* and *Dynamo Snackbar* are filled with electric guitar solos while *Barking Dog Blues* is a country blues track with funny lyrics. **Peter Kaukonen** wrote all the songs and produced the album. Definitely worth a spin.

Joe Covington had previously played and recorded with The Vibratones, the 'Airplane and the original Hot Tuna line-up. Mark Ryan played with **Quicksilver** and **Bodacious D.F.**. Larry Weisberg would later join **Spirit**. Nick Buck had previously played with Peter Green and would later play in Hot Tuna and SVT. Peter had previously been in the band Petrus who recorded an unreleased single for A&M. Peter had also been called upon to replace Bob Harvey in the **Jefferson Airplane**, but his parents wouldn't let him drop out of school! (Jack Casady was the second choice). Peter then played short stints with **Johnny Winter** as "Albino Kangaroo" (bootleg CDs of that band exist), Hot Tuna, and was the first Jefferson Starship bass player, being asked to leave the band before the first album was recorded. He then released two cassettes in the eighties.

Peter Kaukonen's career was not as prolific as his brother's. He later played with Grace Slick (*Manhole*) and Terry Allen (1975, *Juarez*) and did some session work too. (SR/HS)

Thee Kavaliers

45s:	α	Sea Weed/Pride	(Pharaoh 137) 1965
		That Hurts/Symbol Of Sin	(Pharaoh 146) 1966
		The Last Four Words/	
		Ballad Of Thee Kavaliers	(Pharaoh 150) 1966
		Congregation For Anti-Flirts Inc./	
		Back To You	(Pharaoh 154) 1967

NB: α as The Cavaliers.

From McAllen deep in the Texas Valley, they were originally known as The Cavaliers and *Texas Punk, Vol. 5* includes their first 45 and an earlier recording of *Congregation For Anti-Flirts, Inc.* under this name. Some band members later played with two other Texas outfits:- The Playthings and Transluscent Umbrella. (VJ)

Jimmy Kaye and The Coachmen

Personnel incl: JIMMY KAYE

45: Gloria/Debbie (Soma 1441) 1965

A band from Des Moines, Iowa who did a good cover of Them/**The Shadows Of Knight**'s hit *Gloria*.

THE KEEPERS.

Compilation appearances include *Gloria* on *Soma Records Story, Vol. 2* (LP) and *The Big Hits Of Mid-America - The Soma Records Story* (Dble CD). (VJ)

The Kee-Notes

Personnel:	MIKE BRANDT	gtr	A
	BREA BERRY	drms	A
	DANNY CURLER	bs	A
	DICK INSTNESS	organ	A
	CLIFF MAURER	ld gtr	A

45: Please Don't Tell Me No/
Quit Changing Your Mind (Esar 115/6) 1965

Vejtables-like folk-rock from Sacramento, California. Berry was later in the all-female seventies rock group **Fanny**. *Quit Changing Your Mind* can be found on *The Sound Of Young Sacramento* (CD).

Keepers

Personnel:	FRED ADINOLFI	bs	A
	BARRY DRIMMER	ld vcls	A
	RITCHIE MARCIANTI	gtr	A
	BILLY MARTIN	ld gtr	A
	JOE RUCHIO	drms	A

45: She Understands / Lost Love (Bravura 5003) 1965

A Canarsies, Brooklyn-based band whose sole 45 has come to the attention of compilers. *She Understands*, a frantic beat number, has appeared on *Brain Shadows, Vol. 1* (LP & CD) and *Psychedelic States: New York Vol. 1* (CD).. The forlorn *Lost Love* has also resurfaced on *Leaving It All Behind* (LP).

Barry Drimmer: "I joined in 1964 at the age of fourteen, and the band were together from 1963 to 1966. We were quite well known in Brooklyn through out these years, playing all over the borough, at the Flatbush Terrace (a great concert hall run by Mike Gaynor), and at the Midwood Friendship Club where we opened for a young **Mitch Ryder and The Detroit Wheels**. The band also got to perform at the Canarsie movie theater opening up for the 'A Hard Days Night' film. In 1965 we cut an acetate as Five Against The World (a brief alter ego suggested by a hot shot management team in Manhattan)."

Barry Drimmer also played in a Brooklyn band called Southern Socket with **Jagged Edge** member Art Steinman. (MW/BD)

The Keggs

45: To Find Out/Girl (Orbit 20959/60) 1967

A Detroit high school quartet who were strongly influenced by The Kinks. We're talking crude but powerful garage punk here. They recorded the 45 in a seedy part of Detroit in July 1967, only to discover the studio burnt to the ground in the Detroit race riots a couple of weeks later. Fortunately a tape was salvaged and the band pressed up a few copies for their friends.

Compilation appearances include: *To Find Out* on *Acid Dreams - The Complete 3 LP Set* (3-LP), *Acid Dreams Epitaph* (CD), *Back From The Grave, Vol. 5* (LP) and *Back From The Grave, Vol. 2* (CD); and *Girl* on *Back From The Grave, Vol. 6* (LP). (VJ)

Barbara Keith

Personnel:	JIM COLEGROVE	bs	A
	RICHARD CURTIS	gtr	A
	JEFFREY GUTCHEON	keyb'ds	A
	BARBARA KEITH	vcls, gtr, piano	AB
	BILL KEITH	pedal steel, banjo	A
	N.D. SMART II	drms	A

ALBUMS:	1(A)	BARBARA KEITH	(Verve Forecast FTS-3084) 1969 -
	2(B)	BARBARA KEITH	(Reprise MS 2087) 1972 -

NB: (2) also released in France (Reprise 44 232).

45s:	α	Only Thing I Had/Daydream Stallion	(MGM 13961) 1968
	β	Fisherman King/Good Lovin Man	(Verve Forecast 5108) 1969
	β	Rainmaker/Free The People	(A&M 1191) 1970
		All Along The Watchtower/ The Bramble and The Rose	(Reprise 1191) 1972

NB: α by **Barbara Keith** and **Kangaroo**. β are non album tracks. There's also a French 45 with PS, *All Along The Watchtower / Free The People* (Reprise 14240, 1973).

The brilliant vocalist of **Kangaroo**, Barbara Keith, went solo in 1969 and her first album was produced in New York by Peter Asher (ex-Peter and Gordon). Still working with N.D Smart from her previous group, she was also backed by Jim Colegrove (**Bo Grumpus**), Jeff Gutcheon (**Great Jones**), Bill Keith (**Jim Kweskin Jug Band**) and Richard Curtis. All her material was original, in a folk-rock vein with country-rock influences, nice vocals and strong instrumental parts, the highlights being *My Easy Days* and *The Big Black Deep*, with some additional vocals by the mysterious "Little Sabre". The album unfortunately suffers a bit from the similiarity of several slow tracks.

Her song *Free The People* became a hit for **Delaney and Bonnie** but she had to wait nearly three years to see the release of her second album. Produced by Larry Marks (**Phil Ochs**, **Thirty Days Out**), her vocals were still beautiful and her backing group included Lowell George, **Spooner Oldham**, Danny Kootch and Lee Sklar. The material, penned by **Barbara Keith** and D. Dibbles, is mainly in the country-rock style but this album is worth hearing for the exceptional electric version of Dylan's *All Along The Watchtower*, with Tony Peluso (**Abstracts**) and David Cohen (**Country Joe and The Fish**) on guitars.

Barbara Keith then apparently stopped her career, but re-surfaced a few years ago fronting a rock-n-roll outfit: The Stone Coyotes. Based out of Greenfield, Massachussetts they comprise of **Keith** (gtr, vcls), her husband Doug Tibbles (drums) and and step-son John Tibbles (bs). They describe their music as "Patsy Cline meets AC/DC" and that's not too far off the mark. So far they've released three CDs. (SR/JN)

Peter Kelley

Personnel incl:	DANNY FEDERICI	keyb'ds	A
	PETER KELLEY	vcls, gtr	AB

ALBUMS:	1(A)	PATH OF THE WAVE	(Sire SES-97009) 1969 -
	2(B)	DEALER'S BLUES	(Sire SI 4903) 1971 -

NB: (1) also released in the U.K. (London HAK 8402) 1969.

This East Coast singer songwriter went largely unnoticed at the time but his two albums are worth a spin. The first one is folk-psych with almost whispered vocals. Songs range from Dylanesque ballads to the monster cut *The Man Is Dead* (6'56") with fuzz guitar. Other cuts include *High Flyin' Mama*, *Childhood's Hour*, and a cover of **Rhinoceros**' *Apricot Brandy*.

Danny Federici went on to play with Bruce Springsteen and The E Street Band.

Housed in a nice textured cover, *Dealer's Blues* is, as its title indicates, more blues-orientated and is a superb album combining white blues, folk and rock. It was produced by Richard Gottehrer (ex-**Strangeloves**). (SR)

Dick "Wilde Childe" Kemp

45:	Get It On / Wilde Childe Freakout	(Cle-O 1000) 196?

A Cleveland area DJ with a solo mid-sixties release. *Get It On* is a strong rock novelty backed by an instrumental. (GGI/MW)

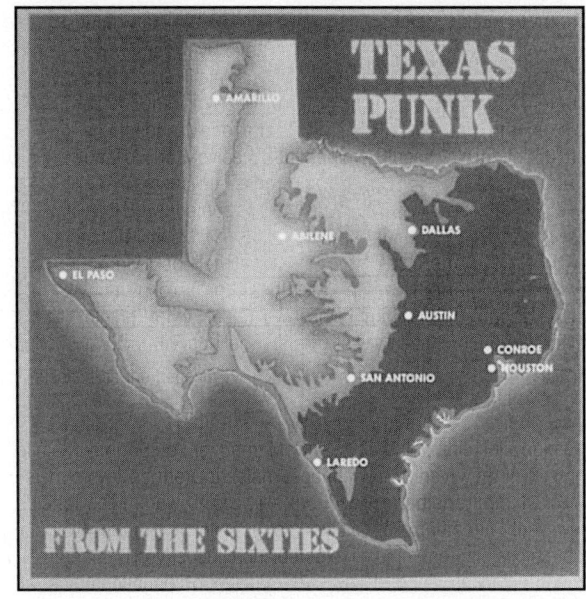

TEXAS PUNK FROM THE SIXTIES (Comp LP) including Kempy and The Guardians.

Kempy and The Guardians

Personnel:	DEAN BROWN	ld gtr	A
	GARY KEMP RAWLINGS	ld vcls	A
	ALAN ROTH	drms	A
	LARRY SAMFORD	bs, vcls	A
	GARY SEALS	gtr, vcls	A
	DAVID SMITH	organ	A
	E. PAT DAVIDSON		

45s:	Love For A Price/Never	(Lucky Sounds 1006) 1966
	Love For A Price/Never	(Romunda P-1) 1966

This Dallas outfit's finest moment was *Love For A Price*, which they got to record after winning first place in a Gibsons' Discount Center's "battle of the bands" contest. Shortly after, they also got to perform it on Ron Chapmen's "Sumpin' Else" TV show. The two versions of the 45 feature different versions of *Love For A Price*, with the Romunda recording including an additional blistering guitar break, with lead guitar on both being provided by Dean Brown.

Line-up 'A' features the band's main personnel circa 1966/67, although during their four year lifetime, some members did change. One such member, E. Pat Davidson, went on to record a solo 45, *Fools Pride/Stay With Me* (Sevens Internatios 11005).

The band originated in Oak Cliff, Texas, when Gary Seals and Dean Brown got together with their guitars in junior high school. Dean:- "I was 13 and he was 15. We found a drummer and entered a battle of the bands at our local Montgomery Wards store, but lost to Jimmy Vaughn's band, The Pendulums. They were good and deserved to win. After that we played school parties and dances as The Guardians for about a year. Gary Kemp (Kempy) Rawlings was at one of our parties and sang a song with us. He sang so well we asked him to join and we became **Kempy and The Guardians**. We eventually graduated from school parties and roller rinks to playing several local teenage clubs in the North Dallas area".

Kempy left the band sometime around 1968, but the band continued as The Guardians with Larry Samford switching from bass and vocals to lead vocals and David Johnson coming in on bass. This form of the Guardians lasted about a year or so, but by the time they had graduated from high school it was all but over.

Dean Brown still performs to this day, whilst Alan Roth became a local police officer.

Compilation coverage has included:- *Love For A Price* (Romunda version) on *Flashback, Vol. 6* (LP), *Sixties Archive Vol. 2* (CD) and *Garage Punk Unknowns, Vol. 2* (LP); *Love For A Price* (Lucky Sounds version) on *Highs In The Mid Sixties, Vol. 17* (LP); and both versions appear on *Texas Punk From The Sixties* (LP). (VJ/TDs/DBn)

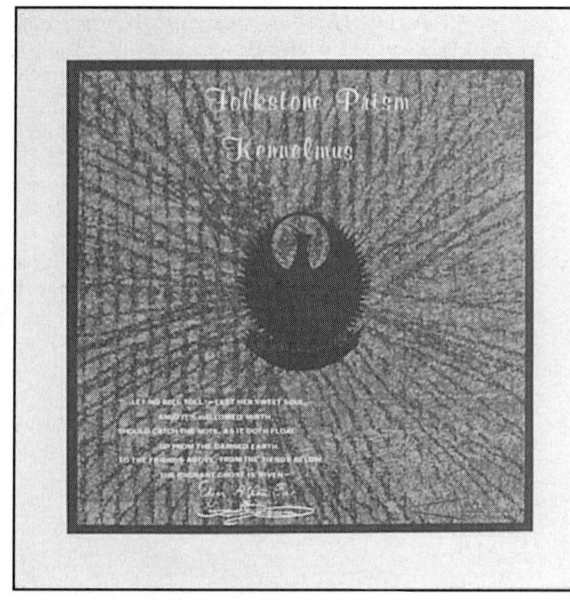

KENNELMUS - Folkstone Prism LP.

Ken and The 4th Dimension

Personnel incl: KENNETH JOHNSON   A

45:	See If I Care/Rovin' Heart	(Starburst 128)	1966

This was a raucous L.A.-based punk band. Ken (alias Kenneth Johnson) was a Los Angeles producer and writer for many obscure bands, including **Limey and the Yanks** and **The Avengers** who recorded on the Starburst label owned by his father. Like some other punk bands they set out as a surf band The Rockets and then changed names to Ken and The Ho-Dads issuing a surf instrumental 45 *Surf Dance*, before getting into punk.

Compilation appearances include: *See If I Care* on *Back From The Grave, Vol. 3* (LP) and *Everywhere Chainsaw Sound* (LP); and *Rovin' Heart* on *Highs In The Mid-Sixties Vol. 2* (LP). (VJ)

Rich Kendall

ALBUM:	1	FOOD FOR THOUGHT	(Unknown Records)	c1974 R1

A private pressing of folk-rock with some psychy touches. (SR)

Kennélmus

Personnel:	KEN E. WALKER	vcls, gtr, effects	ABCD
	TOM GILMORE	bs	C
	BOB NARLOCH	vcls, gtr, hrmnca, tamb	C
	MIKE SHIPP	drms	C
	KAREN GARDNER		D
	PHIL QUIROZ		D
	ROB ZELMER		D

ALBUM:	1(C)	FOLKSTONE PRISM	(Phoenix Int'l PIR 41271)	1971 R5

NB: (1) reissued on Rockadelic (RRLP 16) 1994 (R1) in a limited edition pressing of 300. It's an exact copy except for the label design. (1) reissued on CD (Sundazed SC 6129) 1999. Also of interest is (C) *Beyond Folkstone Prism* (OR RD 1) 1995, which is comprised of material recorded during 1971-72 but remained unreleased until 1995 in a limited edition of 400.

45s:	α	Alligator/A Song For Her	(Pirate 9-29-70)	1970
	β	Plastic Shadow/Black Sunshine	(Pirate 01-05-71)	1971
		No Way To Treat Your Man/ No Reply	(Phoenix Int'l PIR 10-8-71)	1971
		The Fool/Bumble Bee	(Phoenix Int'l ?)	1972

NB: α shown as by Rande Bell Soup. β shown as by Gray Ghost.

From Phoenix, Arizona, Ken Walker and Bob Narloch played as a duo originally in the sixties. **Kennélmus** was formed in 1970 and their two albums were recorded between 1970-72 in recording engineers' Chuck Hauke's studio using two Ampex 351-2 two track recorders. Even the Rockadelic reissue of the first album is becoming hard to find. This is the better of the two. Side one of the album is instrumental and while some of the tracks are in a primitive hard-rock style not unlike **Hootch**, others are very dense and beautiful. The vocal tracks are very quirky and strangely recorded - it's clear that **Kennélmus** spent a great deal of time knob-twiddling in the studio! While the results are obviously mixed, the album is recommended.

A number of additional musicians assist on the second album, which includes a couple of adequate Dylan covers, *I'll Be Your Baby Tonight* and *On The Road Again*, four Bob Narloch originals and three penned by Chuck Hauke among others. Of these, *Pickers On A Guitar* has a strong country feel. The most psychedelic is Chuck Hauke's *Black Sunshine* with some groovy guitar work and for me this is the stand-out track. Rather disappointing overall. The six 45 tracks are non-album cuts or different versions. (CF/VJ)

Kenny and The Friends

45s:	The House On Haunted Hill Pads 1&2	(Princess 51)	1963
	Last Night Was The Night/ She Kept Doing Him Wrong	(Princess 54)	1963
	The House On Haunted Hill/ The Green Door	(Princess 871)	1964
	The House On Haunted Hill Pads 1 & 2	(Dot 16568)	1964
	Moon Shot/One-Two-Three-Four	(Dot 16596)	1964
	The Raven (Part 1/The Raven (Part 2)	(Posea 80)	1965

A mid-sixties Los Angeles act whose loony freak-out *The Raven, Part 1* can also be heard on the *The Magic Cube* (Flexi & CD) compilation. (VJ)

Kenny and The Kasuals

Personnel:	DAVID BLACKLEY	drms	ABC
	KENNY DANIEL	vcls, gtr	ABCD
	LEE LIGHTFOOT	bs	ABC
	TOMMY NICHOLS	hrmnca	A
	PAUL ROACH	keyb'ds	AB
	JERRY SMITH	ld gtr	ABCD
	RICHARD BORGENS	ld gtr	C
	GREG DANIELS	bs	D
	DAN GREEN	gtr	D
	RON MASON	drms	D
	KARL TOMORROW	keyb'ds	D

ALBUMS:	1(A)	LIVE AT THE STUDIO CLUB	(Mark 500) 1966 R5
	2(D)	TEEN DREAMS	(Mark 6000) 1978 R3
	3(D)	GARAGE KINGS	(Mark 7000) 1979 -
	4(-)	4	(Mark) 1981 -
	5(A/B)	(A/B) NOTHING BETTER TO DO	(Eva 12011) 1982 -
	6(B)	THINGS GET BETTER	(Eva 12031) 1983 -

NB: (1) as by **Kenney and The Kasuals**, also reissued in 1977 (Mark LP 5000). (3) was also reissued in Germany by Line (LLP 5020 AS) 1982. (5) and (6) were recently issued on one CD.

EPs:	1(D)	THE KASUALS ARE BACK	(Mark 400) 1978
	2( )	THE BEST THING AROUND + 3	(EVA 2005) 1980s

NB: (2) ltd edition of 2000.

45s:		Nothin' Better To Do/Floatin'	(Mark 911) 1965
		Don't Let Your Baby Go/ The Best Thing Around	(Mark 1002) 1965
		It's All Right/You Make Me Feel So Good	(Mark 1003) 1966
		Raindrop To Teardrops/Strings Of Time	(Mark Ltd 1004) 1966
	α	Journey To Tyme/I'm Gonna Make It	(Mark Ltd 1006) 1967
		See Saw Ride/As I Knew	(Mark Ltd 1008) 1967
	β	Chimes On 42nd Street/ When Was Then	(Mark Ltd 1009) 1968

NB: α Leased to United Artists (UA 50085) for nationwide release. β as The Truth.

One of Texas' finest sixties bands, they were reputedly playing at the La Fontaine Club in Dallas one night as The Illusion Combo (another of their early names was The Ken Daniel Combo) when Mark Lee walked in and told them that they were now called **Kenny And The Kasuals** and he was their manager. Their first three 45s on Lee's label attracted little attention but during 1966 they started playing at the Studio Club in Dallas and the same year they recorded their first album just to be sold there as a promotion gimmick. It begins with a guy answering the telephone with music in the background telling a caller that **Kenny And The Kasuals** are playing the Studio Club that evening. In fact it was not a live album at all - it was the result of one afternoon's work in a recording studio, but it captured the band playing cover versions of some of the popular songs of the time like *Gloria, Baby Please Don't Go, You Better Move On, Money,* and *All Day And All The Night*. Just 500 copies were pressed in mono and around 400 sold, but it gradually acquired a legendary reputation among record collectors and by the mid-seventies copies were changing hands for megabucks hence its eventual reissue in 1977.

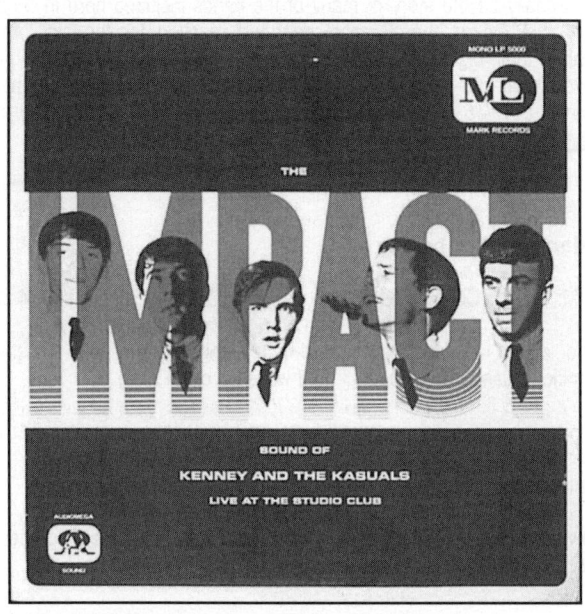

KENNY AND THE KASUALS - Live At The Studio Club LP.

After its release Jerry Smith replaced Tommy Nichols on lead guitar and started writing songs with Kenny. Their next 45, *Raindrop To Teardrop* was a local hit as was the follow-up *Journey To Tyme*, which marked their progression from punk to psychedelia and told the story of an acid trip. This was leased to United Artists for nationwide distribution. After a further, equally good 45, *See Saw Ride* they headed to New York with a new line-up. Jerry Smith, realising his limitations on lead guitar had switched to rhythm and Richard Bergens (previously with **The Briks**) filled the resulting vacancy. The organist, Paul Roach, also left because he didn't want to leave Dallas that Summer. They failed to make the break in New York, where Kenny and Richard Bergens were constantly arguing. Soon after their return from New York in September 1967 their fate was arguably sealed when Kenny got drafted, although they renamed themselves The Truth and soldiered on for a while releasing one further 45. Unfortunately their name was confused with the title of Jeff Beck's album and the 45 flopped. Kenny did return to make a farewell appearance with the band at the 'Flower Fair', a big show in Dallas in April 1968.

In 1977 their first album was reissued and the following year Kenny and Jerry Smith reformed the band with a new line-up (D). They recorded a new album, *Garage Kings*, and *The Kasuals Are Back* (EP). A year earlier a compilation of their 45s and some unreleased cuts were issued, *Teen Dreams*. In Europe this was circulated as the 'lost **Electric Prunes** LP'!

Both of the Eva releases are worth checking out. *Nothing Better To Do* contains their six singles and the Truth 45. *Things Get Better* included The Gator Shades Blues Band's *Down In Mexico* and previously unissued material and outtakes. (The Gator Shades Blues Band were a short-lived venture which consisted of The Kasuals minus Kenny. Their *Down In Mexico* 45 had a limited pressing of 100).

Compilation coverage has so far included: *Journey To Tyme* on *Nuggets, Vol. 12* (LP), *Mayhem & Psychosis, Vol. 3* (LP), *Nuggets Box* (4-CD), *Texas Music, Vol. 3* (CD) and *Songs We Taught The Fuzztones* (Dble LP & Dble CD); and *Everybody's Making It* on *Acid Visions - The Complete Collection Vol. 1* (3-CD). (VJ/MW)

Kensington Forest

45: Bells/Movin' On (Baysound 6901) 1967

The 'A' side is a lovely, ethereal electric folk composition with male and female tandem vocals that wouldn't sound out of place on the debut **It's A Beautiful Day** album, except for the constant Plastic Cloud - style fuzz guitar laid on top of it! The 'B' side is more standard sixties garage rock. The group are believed to have been based in Millbrae, California.

Bells can also be heard chiming on *Psychedelic Experience, Vol. 3* (CD). (CF/MW)

Keith Kessler

45: Don't Crowd Me/Sunshine Morning (MTW 102) 196?

A mid-sixties garage-sounding 45 from an outfit based in Seattle's University District. The 'A' side is superb. You'll find it on *The Essential Pebbles Collection, Vol. 1* (Dble CD), *Pebbles, Vol. 3 (ESD)* (CD), *Teenage Shutdown, Vol. 14* (LP & CD), *Best of Pebbles, Vol. 2* (LP & CD) and *Ear-Piercing Punk* (LP & CD). (MW)

Ken Kesey

ALBUM: 1 THE ACID TEST (Sound City 27690) 1967 R2

NB: (1) reissued on Psycho (4) 1983 in the UK.

This guy was one of the gurus of the psychedelic culture. His album was an extract of the original Acid Test and seeks to probe the psychedelic experience with help from **The Grateful Dead**, whose entry includes much more information about his relationship with them. The original album is now a rare and expensive item. The reissue on Psycho was a limited pressing of just 300 and is also likely to become rare in time. (VJ)

The Keymen

ALBUM: 1 KEYMEN LIVE (Goldust LPS 153) 1968 SC

NB: There's also a retrospective CD *The Keymen-Surf Party A Go-Go!* (Collectables Col-0685) 1996.

45: Walkin' Talkin'/What Am I To Do (PS) (Goldust 5019) 1967

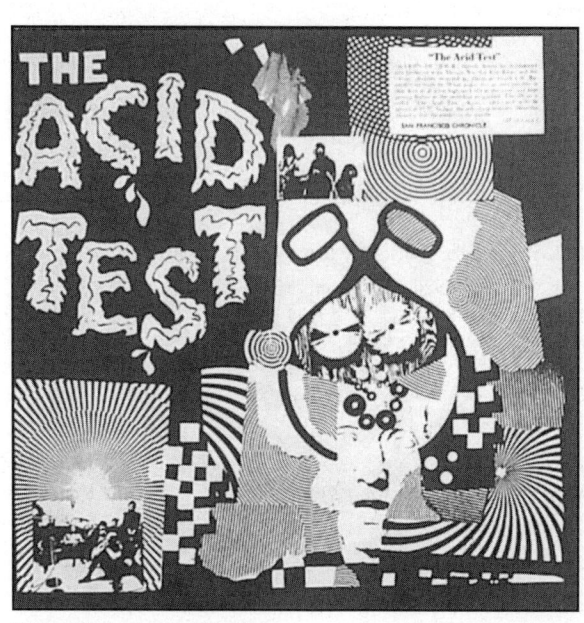

KEN KESEY - The Acid Test LP.

The Keymen were generally recognized as the premiere band in Las Cruces, New Mexico throughout the sixties. The Collectables CD serves as overview of the band's total output, and includes some early surf instrumentals, such as *A Yank In London* and *Thunder Bay*; some standard cover versions of popular tunes, such as *Little Latin Lupe Lu* and the Miracle's *Shop Around*; the band's only single, released in 1967; a couple of unreleased recordings; and four songs from **The Keymen**'s live album, recorded in 1968. Not garage or psych, and probably best avoided.

The Keymen also backed Pat and Dodie on their Goldust 45 - *The Doubles Of Our Hearts / He's Gone From Me*.

Compilation appearances have included: *What Am I To Do* on *Basementsville! U.S.A.* (LP); *Walkin' - Talkin'* and *What Am I To Do* on *The Goldust Records Story* (CD); *Little Latin Lupe Lu* and *Shop Around* on *Green Crystal Ties, Vol. 3* (CD). (MDo/MW)

Khazad Doom

Personnel:			
	JACK EADON	ld gtr, vcls, perc	A
	STEVE 'CROW' HILKIN	perc, vcls	A
	TOM SIEVERS	bs, vcls	A
	STEVE 'AL' YATES	vcls, keyb'ds	A

ALBUM: 1(A) LEVEL 6 1/2   (LPL 892) 1970 R4

NB: (1) originally limited to 180 copies. The album was later pirated in the late eighties and issued on CD in the nineties by the band as *Encore!* with eight bonus tracks.

From Morton Grove, Illinois, this band took its name from the mountain, "Khazad Dûm" in J.R.R. Tolkien's 'Lord Of The Rings' trilogy. A progressive rather than psychedelic or garage album, it's quite an interesting listen if you can get the reissue CD but don't fork out megabucks for an original. The finer moments include *Nothing To Fear*, quite a commercial song with appealing vocals and lots of atmosphere; *In This World*, a melodic harmony soft-rock song and *Excerpt From The Hunters, The Prelude*, a long progressive piece with lots of keyboards.

The group had their roots in an act called **The Laymen**, who formed back in 1964 and graduated from surf through soul to mild psychedelia. In late '69 they changed name to **Khazad Doom**, which with its Tolkien reference, reflected their penchant for concept-laden song-writing. Their *Level 6 1/2* album, which was recorded in Chicago and Gary, Indiana, was named after the seven internal levels of Tolkien's "Khazad Dûm" mountain, but modified slightly, to show that "there was still room for them to grow...".

Gigging at local teen clubs around Illinois, they also were featured in the Chicago "Walk For Hunger", where 15,000 people gathered in a parking lot in Skokie, Illinois one Saturday morning to walk 20 miles on behalf of the hungry.

KHAZAD DOOM - Level 6 1/2 LP.

The *Encore* CD retrospective includes two tracks by **The Laymen** recorded in '68, their *Level 6 ½* album, and five tracks recorded in 1971, shortly before a band disagreement caused them to split. One of these 1971 cuts, *Stanley's Visit To Kerkle Morff*, is a twelve-minute epic telling in three acts how Stanley invents and builds a flying machine, flys to Kerkle Morff, and eventually becomes King. With a catchy beat and original narrative, the track is reminiscent of Caravan's *In The Land Of Grey And Pink*. In fact the band used to help audiences understand the intricacies of the piece by handing out pamphlets explaining the storyline! The *Encore* CD also features a track by Jack Eadon from 1978, and all the bonus material is in a similar vein to the original release.

In 2001, Jack Eadon's autobiographical "Got To Make It" was published by Vantage Press. A kind of "That Thing You Do" but without the Hollywood glitz, the book is an eloquent account of how the band evolved throughout the sixties, from their earliest instrumental days as The Vibratos through to the early seventies. It is as much a study of the times and the changing relationships between family and friends, as it is about **Khazad Doom** and it could easily be the story of many of the bands included here in "Fuzz"... Groups that caught the 'Beatles' bug and reached for the sky. Almost inevitably, their big break was always just out of their grasp, but Jack's discovery some 25 years later of the collectors circuit and amazement that copies of *Level 6 1/2* were circulating in Europe is quite heartwarming. Overall a worthwhile read! (VJ/IT)

Kickland and Johnson

ALBUM: 1   CLAY COUNTY   (Effenar) 1974 SC ?

A rare album of Nebraska hippie-rock, ranging from folk to electric rural-rock, housed in a nice black and white art cover. (SR)

Kicks Inc.

A Cleveland sixties outfit who are thought to have recorded but had no releases. (GGI/MW)

The Kidds

Personnel incl:	LOUIE BENEVIDES	A
	STEVIE BENEVIDES	A

45:    Nature's Children/This Girl She's Mine   (Laurel 1096) 1968

Came out of Fall River, Mass. with a typical garage-punker soaked in plenty of fuzz, snotty vocals and anti-social lyrics, called *Nature's Children*. If it sounds a little familiar then it's because the track was later recorded by **Tangerine Zoo**.

Though not an earlier incarnation of the **Tangerine Zoo**, as was previously thought, **The Kidds** did indeed have a connection to the better known Mainstream recording artists. In addition to recording *Nature's Child*, a tune written by the **Zoo**'s Ron Medeiros and Don Smith, **The Kidds** line-up included Louie and Stevie Benevides, cousins to Bob Benevides, guitarist for **Tangerine Zoo**. **The Kidds** were a seven-man band, and included three horn players, guitar, bass, drums, and an organ.

Compilation appearances include: *Nature's Children* on *Pebbles Vol. 10* (CD) and *Pebbles, Vol. 21* (LP). (MW/MM/MDo/BBs)

The Kidds

45:    Straighten Up And Fly Right/
       See What My Love Means   (Big Beat BB 1017) 196?

A different outfit from Mississippi. Their 45 was produced by Tommy Bee. *Straighten Up...* is a decent garage-punker, now compiled on *Bad Vibrations, Vol. 2* (LP). The flip's a wimpy ballad. (MW)

KHAZAD DOOM - Encore! CD.

The Kidds

Personnel:	ANTOINE LEBLANC	keyb'ds	AB
	GERALD PATRIZI	drms	AB
	JOEY PATRIZI	gtr	A?
	JIMMY PHELEAN	gtr	A?
	JOHN SCHMIDT	bs	A
	JAKE TORTORICE	vcls	AB
	GLEN MOYER	bs	B
	JOHNNY SERIO	gtr	B

The Kidds out of Beaumont, Texas played extensively in Texas and Louisiana in the mid to late sixties. They were a good show / cover band popular with the high school and college crowds, primarialy booked and promoted by Al Caldwell of KAYC radio. They were due to record a 45, *Down To Middle Earth*, but the line-up 'A' dissolved before they reached the studio.

After another Beaumont act, **SJ and The Crossroads** split, two members, Johnny Serio and Glen Moyer joined **The Kidds**. This incarnation was short-lived, however, as Johnny soon joined the coast guard to avoid going to Vietnam. (IT/JSt/GMr)

Kids

Personnel:	PATRIC AMARANDO	ld gtr	A
	LOUIS MARULLO	gtr	A
	PAUL COLELLA	bs	A
	JOHN BERTONICA	drms	A

45:	Flipped Hair And Lace / Lovin' Everyday (PS)	(Chroma 45-1004) 1965

An almost pre-teen quartet from Auburn, NY. *Lovin' Everyday*, a slice of Beatlesque pop, appears on *Class Of '66!* (LP) with a picture which gives their ages, which ranged from 10 to 13. (MW)

Pat Kilroy

Personnel:	BOB AMACKER	tabla	A
	SUSAN GRAUBARD	flute, glockenspiel	A
	STEFAN GROSSMAN	gtr	A
	ERIC KAZ	hrmnca	A
	PAT KILROY	vcls, gtr, jews harp, glockenspiel, bs, finger cymbals	A
	MARC SILBER	gtr, bs	A
	JIM WELCH	conga drum	A

ALBUM:	1(A)	LIGHT OF DAY	(Elektra EKS-7311) 1966 -

According to **Pat Kilroy**'s liner notes he was influenced by writers like Herman Hesse, Aldous Huxley, and George Gurdjieff, making it literally interesting to this book. All compositions were by **Pat Kilroy** and the album was produced by Peter K. Siegel and supervised by Jac Holzman. Several of the musicians came from New York City so perhaps **Pat Kilroy** did too. Best known amongst the supporting cast is Stefan Grossman (earlier in **Even Dozen Jug Band**) and Eric Kaz (**Bear**, **Blues Magoos** and Happy & Artie Traum).

The album contains a mix of folk, strumming blues and some Eastern moves with lots of tabla. **Kilroy** had a very improvised, unusual vocal style that pre-dated **Tim Buckley**'s similarly avant-garde approach by two years. The final track, *Star Dance*, would have been at home on an Incredible String Band album. The best tracks are probably the dreamy/trippy folk songs, but the album is a highly original work and adventurous listeners will appreciate much of its content. (CP)

Kim and Grim

45:	You Don't Love Me/Lonely Weekend	(Flamingo 501) 1965

The band - an all girl one - were from Los Angeles. *You Don't Love Me* was a popular song with underground bands in the 1966-67 era and this is a pretty good cover

Compilation appearances include *You Don't Love Me* on *Pebbles, Vol. 1* (ESD) (CD) and *Girls In The Garage, Vol. 1* (LP & CD). (VJ)

Kim and The Characters

45:	Sinbad Stomp/Jawbone	(Kimley) 196?

This 45 lists **Fowley**-Zentmeyer and Characters with writing credits and Kim Fowley Music BMI as the publishers. The songs are short with a very early sixties sound.

Kindred

Personnel:	DAVID BLUEFIELD	keyb'ds	AB
	BOBBY COCHRAN	gtr	AB
	GLORIA GAIONE (GRINEL)	vcls	AB
	RON GRINEL	drms	A
	BERNIE MYSIOR	bs	AB
	MARTY RODGERS	keyb'ds, vcls	AB
	JIMMY ERICKSON	drms	B

ALBUMS:	1(A)	KINDRED	(Warner Bros. WS 1931) 1971 -
	2(B)	NEXT OF KIN	(Warner BS 2640) 1972 -

45s:	Get Small/Get It Together	(Warner 7407) 1970
	Rhoda/Rhoda (mono)	(Warner 7430) 1970

NB: Both 45s non LP tracks.

From Los Angeles, **Kindred** practiced an early seventies Californian sound with strong female/male vocals and good keyboards and guitar parts. Their main attractions were their blonde singer, Gloria Grinel-Gaione, their guitarist Bobby Cochran (ex-**Don Preston and The South**) and David Bluefield on keyboards.

Their discography began with a good single penned by Sandi Szigeti, who co-produced it with Steve Braverman. After another non-album single produced by Mike Melvoin and Braverman, their first album was released in 1971. Produced by Chuck Negron of Three Dog Night; it offered eight original tracks penned by Bluefield or Cochran, with the help of Mark Elder (for *Great Day*), Brent and Bobby Seawell (*Movin' On* and *Everything Is For Now*) and two covers: *Too Many People* written by Lydia Pence of **Cold Blood** and the funny *Captain Bobby Stout* (I came down to Wichita town, a pocket full of Mexican smoke, I sold it to a man I did not know, Captain Stout done found me, now I stay here in jail) composed by Lane Tietgen of **The Serfs**. The result is pleasant but not really distinctive.

Their drummer, Ron Grinel then left the group and became a session man (he would work with Joe Walsh and the Souther Hillman Furay Band). Jimmy Erickson replaced him and Gloria Grinel became Gloria Gaione. Produced by James Dennis Bruton, *Next Of Kin* was much better, being more rock-oriented. Three tracks were penned by Bluefield, two penned by Cochran with Casey Van Beek (another ex-member of **The South**) and several covers: *One More River To Cross* composed by **Daniel Moore**, two L. Goldsmith songs and another song titled *Movin' On*, this time written by Michael Smotherman of **Buckwheat**.

Overall recommended for fans of **Smith** or **Stoneground**.

Lisa Kindred

ALBUM: 1 I LIKE IT THAT WAY! (Vanguard) c1965 -

From Boston, a folk-blues singer who would later be part of the Mel Lyman Family, a local community which also included **Jim Kweskin**. (SR)

Kindred Spirit

45s:	Under My Thumb/Blue Avenue	(Intrepid 75016) 1969
	Clown/Peaceful Man	(Intrepid 75028) 1969
	Under My Thumb/Blue Avenue	(Moxie 201) 1969

An obscure Johnstown, Pennsylvania, sextet. Their finest moment *Blue Avenue* is notable for a memorable guitar riff and is a good example of the typical garage-punk farfisa organ sound.

Compilation appearances include: *Blue Avenue* on *Return Of The Young Pennsylvanians* (LP), *Acid Dreams - The Complete 3 LP Set* (3-LP), *Acid Dreams Epitaph* (CD), *An Overdose Of Heavy Psych* (CD) and *Gathering Of The Tribe* (CD).

Kinetics

45: I'm Blue/Feeling From My Heat (Studio City 1033) 1965

This outfit was from Michigan, although the 45 was recorded on the Minneapolis-based Studio City label. It's a rare and highly-touted punk disc. They are rumoured to have later been known as Kinetic Energy, though unconfirmed, who issued one decent hard-rocking 45.

Compilation appearances have included: *I'm Blue* on *Off The Wall, Vol. 2* (LP); and both *I'm Blue* and *Feeling From My Heart* on *When The Time Run Out* (LP & CD). (VJ)

Charlie King

ALBUM: 1 OLD DREAMS (Private Pressing) 1975 ?

A "real people" folk singer with songs such as *The Rats Are Winning* or *The Good Ole CIA*. Only 300 copies were pressed. (SR)

Denny King

Personnel:	JESSE BRIONES	bs	A
	AL CARR	congas	A
	ALEX St. CLAIRE	gtr, slide gtr, trumpet	A
	PETER DOLAN	flute	A
	GREG HAMPTON	drms	A
	DENNY KING	vcls, gtr, bs	A
	DOUGLAS MOON	hrmnca	A

ALBUM: 1(A) EVIL WIND IS BLOWING (Specialty SPS 5003) 1972 R1

| 45s: | α | She's My Girlfriend/Long Lonely Night | (Tide 1091) c1967 |
| | | Bessie Mae/Go Down Moses | (Specialty) 1972 |

NB: α is non-LP.

This rare and excellent psych/heavy blues album was produced by **Denny King**, Dillard Crume and Alex St.Clair. Recorded at White Tree Studios,

GATHERING OF THE TRIBE (Comp CD) including Kindred Spirit.

Palmdale, California, the liner notes written by Dr. Demento (Barry Hansen) are explicit about its content: "From the California high desert to your own sweet magic mind - may we present the blues band that makes you smile, **Denny King** and his B.O.Boogie Band. Yes sir, it's the true blues this **King** sings, while the B.O. blows a blue norther of sneaky slide guitar and howling harp. But there ain't no bringdowns in this here blues. May the truth be told - Denny has the greatest laugh on records! The High Desert is where the real funky sounds of Southern California come from. It's the primeval home of **Beefheart** and **Zappa**. Right now **Denny King** is the magic man, and he's called out the meanest cats between Lancaster and Mojave and recorded them right there on the desert, just to bring some sunshine soul into your heavy head. Touch your strongest stylus to these growling grooves and you'll soon know why they call that place the High Desert!"

The songs are really nice and often funny: *Evil Wind Is Blowing*, *Sunday Driver*, *Boogie Man*, *Bessie Mae*... All the tracks were composed by *Dennis King* except *Lucille* (Penniman/Collins) and *Desert Sand* (King / A St. Claire). Alex St Claire and Doug Moon were previously were in **Captain Beefheart's Magic Band** and Greg Hampton was in **Merrell and The Exiles** circa 1964/65.

Denny King was a native of Milwaukee, Wisconsin. and his real name was Ottenbacher. His first group was The Darnells, aka Denny and The Darnells, who lasted from 1959 until the end of 1963. The final line-up included a young drummer called Gary Myers. **King** settled in Los Angeles in the mid-sixties. He did session work for **The Monkees** and joined the Marketts for their final 1966 album. He then moved into business; first he started a booking agency, then he built a considerably successful business importing medical supplies. Sadly **Denny King** died of a massive heart attack in April 2000. (SR/GM)

King Arthur's Quart

Personnel incl: RUDI PROTRUDI A

EP: 1 LIVE AT ALLEN JR. HIGH SCHOOL
(Misty Lane 047) 1999

NB: (1) numbered ltd.edition of 700.

'Twas 1966 in Camp Hill, Pennsylvania and **King Arthur's Quart**, a young "buncha outcasts" including one Master Rudi Protrudi, played a local school dance which was captured on tape. Preserved in their lo-fi garage-grunge glory are two covers - *Hey Joe* and **Count Five**'s *Psychotic Reaction* - plus two Protrudi originals, *She's Got A Brand New* and *They're Gonna Take You Away*.

A decade or so later, having relocated to NYC and played in numerous bands, Rudi returned to these musical roots and "Class Of '66" sounds with the almighty Fuzztones, where those same originals were reborn as *Brand New Man* and *It Came In The Mail* respectively. (MW)

The King Bees

Personnel:	DICKIE FRANK	bs	A
	DANNY KORTCHMAR	gtr	A
	JOHN McDUFFY	organ, vcls	A
	JOEL 'BISHOP' O'BRIEN	drms	A

45s:	What She Does To Me/		
	That Ain't Love	(RCA Victor 47-8688)	1965
	On Your Way Down The Drain/		
	Rhythm And Blues	(RCA 47-8787)	1966
	Lost In The Shuffle/Hardly (Part 3)	(RCA 47-8979)	1966

The King Bees were a little ahead of their time, playing the blues in New York City before it became popular there. They recorded three singles for RCA between Autumn 1965 and late 1966, which consequently were not successful. Perhaps their best effort was *Lost In The Shuffle*, a cool blues number structured around the organ and deliberate vocals.

Frustrated by their lack of success, The King Bees split in the Autumn of 1966. Kortchmar and O'Brien joined James Taylor and The Flying Machine and in 1970 formed Jo Mama, whilst John McDuffy replaced Al Kooper in The Blues Project. Kortchmar also played with The Fugs and with City and later became a renowned session man.

Compilation appearances have included: *Lost In The Shuffle* on *Mindrocker, Vol. 9* (LP); *On Your Way Down The Drain* on *Hide & Seek Again* (LP); and *What She Does To Me* on *The Lost Generation, Vol. 3* (LP). (VJ/SR/MW)

The King Bees

45:	Keep Lovin'/I Want My Baby	(Pyramid 6217) 1966

From North Carolina, *Keep Lovin'* is a decent fast-paced punker, whilst the flip has a catchy chorus and Beatles inspired screams. Both sides were written by Larry Chapman.

Compilation appearances include: *Keep Lovin'* and *I Want My Baby* on *Sixties Rebellion, Vol. 5* (LP & CD); and *I Want My Baby* on *Teenage Shutdown, Vol. 8* (LP & CD). (MW)

The King Biscuit Entertainers

Personnel:	SCOTT ASHLEY	bs	ABC
	ROGER HUYCHE	drms	ABC
	RAY KENNEDY	gtr, vcls	ABC
	RON OVERMAN	ld gtr	A
	MARK WHITMAN	gtr	AB
	NEIL ANDERSON	gtr	C

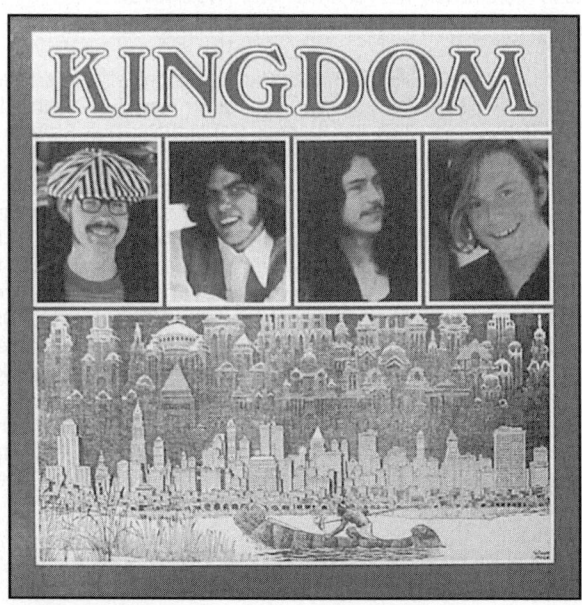

KINGDOM - Kingdom LP.

45s:	Stormy/Pride	(Burdette 7) 1968
	Ride My Soul Away/Take My Thoughts Away	(Burdette 9) 1968
	Courtship Of Priscilla Brown/	
	Now Baby I Love You	(KBE 45-KBE-1) 1968
	Rollin' Free Man/Sunset Blues	(Revue 11 066) 1968

A popular late sixties Portland, Oregon band which evolved out of an outfit called Genesis. Kennedy, Ashley and Huyche had also all previously played in The Wilde Knights and Ron Overman had once been in Don and The Goodtimes. The name change from Genesis to The King Biscuit Entertainers came about when Mark Whitman, a flashy guitarist, was added to the initial quartet. After they had recorded the two 45s for Burdette, Ron Overman was drafted. The KBE release was on their own label and Revue was a R&B subsidiary of Uni Records whose Russ Regan had heard a demo tape of the band and signed them up as a token white act. The record stiffed and shortly after Mark Whitman left. His replacement Neil Anderson had previously been in The Bootmen and The Wailers. With a slightly modified line-up they went on to record as American Cheese. *Now, Baby I Love You* can be heard on *Rough Diamonds: The History of Garage Band Muslc, Vol. 7* which includes detailed sleevenotes by Greg Shaw about The King Biscuit Entertainers and the bands that preceded them. According to these Kennedy now works in a record pressing plant in L.A., Scott Ashley now lives in South Carolina where he's active in the music scene and Roger Huyche drives a bus in Seattle. Mark Whitman now plays in The Mark Whitman Band.

Compilation appearances include: *Take My Thoughts Away* on *Acid Dreams, Vol. 3* (LP). (VJ)

King David and The Slaves

Personnel incl:	RANDALL BRAMBLETT	A
	J. BRINKLEY	A

45:	All I Can See Is Your Love /	
	I've Been Told	(Slave #442) 1967

A little known outfit from Athens, Georgia, featuring Randall Bramblett, who would go on to play sax with Steve Winwood. *Psychedelic States: Georgia Vol. 1* (CD) features *I've Been Told*, an exuberant swinging pop-punker with a superb rhythm section and cool leads. (MW/RM)

Kingdom

Personnel:	ED NELSON	vcls, bs	A
	JIM POTKEY	ld vcls, organ, gtr	A
	JOHN TOYNE	vcls, gtr	A
	GARY VARGA	drms	A

ALBUM:	1(A)	KINGDOM	(Specialty SPS 2135) 1970 R2

NB: (1) reissued on vinyl and CD by Akarma (AK 031) 1999.

45:	If I Never Was To See Her Again/	
	Seven Fathoms Deep	(Specialty 722) 1970

From Southern California, near Los Angeles. A West Coast heavy psychedelic rock outfit with two lead guitars and pretty incisive they are too at times. All bar one song (*Seasons*) were written by Jim Potkey. If you're into lots of heavy guitar work Side One's for you, but aside from the two 45 cuts the material's rather samey. *Seven Fathoms Deep* has a melodramatic intro and if *I Was Never To See Her Again* was altogether more commercial. Side two is more interesting and includes the magnum opus *Prelude* with some interesting percussion and the extended finale *Morning Swallow*. Worth investigation.

The 45 features abridged versions of the LP tracks. (CF/VJ/MW)

King Harvest

Personnel incl:	RONNIE ALTBACH	keyb'ds
	TONY CAHILL	bs
	LANCE HOPPEN	bs, vcls
	SHERMAN KELLY	vcls, keyb'ds
	WELLS KELLY	drms

DAVID ROBINSON	vcls, bs	
EDDIE TULEJA	gtr	

ALBUMS:
1. CONTRACTUAL BLUES (Concert Hall SPS1319) 1970 -
2. DANCING IN THE MOONLIGHT (Perception 36) 1972 -
3. LE FEU SACRE (soundtrack) ( ) 1972 -
4. KING HARVEST (A&M SP 4540) 1975 -

NB: (1) by E. Rodney Jones and The Prairie Dogs (2) also released in the UK by Pye and in France by Calumet.

45s: (partial list)
- α The Smile On Her Face/ Bookstore Blues (America AM 17017) 1970
- β Roosevelt And Ira Lee/ Marty And The Captain (Calumet 1675) 1971
- β A Train/Slide (Chuckanut 4700) 1971
- χ Dancing In The Moonlight/ Lady, Come On Home (America AM 17029) 1972
- β Give Me A Sign/Jesse's Going Away (Cart 75003) 1973
- Celestial Navigator/Angels Of Mercy (Perception PS-556) 1973

NB: α as Chin. α β χ French releases with PS. χ also released on Perception in the USA.

After **Boffalongo**'s second album, David Robinson, Lance Hoppen and Wells Kelly teamed up with some other New York musicians and moved to Europe. They spent nearly two years in England and France where they recorded some 45s on French labels. Originally known as Chin, they finally became **King Harvest**.

They also recorded an album as E. Rodney Jones and The Prairie Dogs for Concert Hall, a small French budget label. It includes a new version of *Dancing In The Moonlight* (a song also on **Boffalongo**'s second album), covers of Tony Joe White's *Roosevelt And Ira Lee*, **Creedence**'s *Lodi* and the Beatles' *Get Back* plus several originals. Their good guitarist, Eddie Tuleja, also played with US bluesmen like Willie Mabon for their recordings on French labels.

Partly recorded in France, their first album was released in the USA by **Jimmy Curtiss**' Perception label. It's a decent rock effort, with a third version of *Dancing In The Moonlight*, some prog rock and hard blues songs (*She Keeps Me High*, *I Can Tell*), an adaptation of Ennio Morricone but also some lame fillers. After more singles, a soundtrack and a second album, the group disbanded and the musicians returned to the USA.

Ronnie Altbach and Eddie Tuleja would later work with Mike Love and Dennis Wilson (Beach Boys). In 1975 the Hoppen Brothers would form Orleans with John Hall (ex-**Kangaroo**). (SR)

King Krusher and The Turkeynecks

45: King Krusher/Fuzzy (Hassler 9008) 1965

This was a Minneapolis-based studio group who also recorded a good stomping punker on the Re Car label as **Jessie J. And The Bandits** and were also known as **Wolfman Jack and The Wolfpack**. They produced quite a highly-rated garage 45.

Compilation appearances include: *King Krusher* on *Hipsville, Vol. 3* (LP). (VJ)

King Lizard

45: Big Bad Cadillac/ Man Without A Country (Original Sound Records OS-99) 1969

Another nom-de-plume for **Kim Fowley** who wrote and produced this rare single of garage rock. Both sides can also be found on the **Fowley** retrospective *Living In The Streets*. (SR/WHn)

King Richard and The Knights

Personnel:
BILL "CORKY" ANDERSON	drums		A
GARY BUTLER	bs		A
LARRY LONGMIRE	lead/rhythm gtr		AB
DICK "KING RICHARD" STEWART	ld gtr, vcls		AB
JACK PADEN	drums		B
LARRY REID	sax, vcls		
GARY SNOW	bs		

ALBUMS:
1. PRECISION! (CD) (Collectables COL-0684) 1996
2. I DON'T NEED YOU (Lance L-2000) 2000

45s:
- Precision / Cut Out (instrs) (Red Feather 18401) 1963
- Moonbeam / Lonely By The Sea (instrs) (Red Feather 20327) 1963
- Those Things You Do / I Want To Love You (Delta 2048) 1964
- Why / That's The Way It Goes (Delta 2115) 1965
- I Don't Need You / How About Now (Delta 2143) 1966
- Moonbeam (vocal version) / ?? (Jyck 102) 1990s

Starting as an instrumental outfit in Albuquerque, New Mexico, they hit big locally with *Precision*, a catchy Ventures-style instrumental with piano, which the majors failed to pick up. Led by Dick 'King Richard' Stewart, who wrote their material, they graduated to a vocal rockin'-fratrock-garage style in 1964 and so it's the three Delta 45s that are of the most interest to us. Their new style was an updated U.S. sound rather than British-Invasion influenced. A crisp clean sound and the odd use of sax points to their rock and instrumental roots. The vocals too are clean sounding and more like the Everlys than the Beatles. No dirty 'longhair' sounds in Stones or Animals vein, though *Why* treads close in its mean'n'moodiness. Other highlights are *I Want To Love You* with its *Louie Louie* beat, and a catchy *That's The Way It Goes* which a country-pickin' air.

KING RICHARD and THE KNIGHTS - I Don't Need You LP.

Drummer Corky would join local rivals **The Plague** and still plays today in Dark Horse. Replacement drummer Jack Paden moved to another local band the Sidewinders when the **Knights** split in 1966. Dick Stewart also produced the **Kreeg**'s now legendary *Impressin'*.

The *King Richard And The Knights - Precision!* CD is really an Albuquerque retrospective, starring **King Richard and The Knights**. It features all their sixties 45s above plus a nineties rerecording of *Moonbeam*. The CD then adds Delta/Look label 45s by **The Plague**, **Era Of Sound**, **Kreeg**, Sidewinders, Saliens and a new recording by Jason Stewart, one of Dick's two musician sons. With its wide range of sounds running from instrumental through beat, frat-rock, garage, folk-rock and psychedelia this package neatly encapsulates the musical evolution of a local scene in the early-to-mid-sixties. Liner notes and reminiscences are by Dick Stewart himself - which have helped to flesh out this entry and do it justice. I hope he doesn't mind because this package is to be commended, and heartily recommended.

Other compilation appearances have included: *I Don't Need You* and *How About Now* on *Green Crystal Ties Vol. 2* (CD). (MW)

THE KINGSMEN - In Person LP.

The Kings

45s:	It's The LCB/IF I Could Believe You	(Jox 045) 1965
	Baby, You're The One/Got Temptation	(Jox 049) 1965
	I've Got A License/Just A Little Bit Of You	(Jox 052) 1966

Came out of Kingsville, which is just Southwest of Corpus Christi in Texas. They had a liking for coloured promotional copies - their second 45 was promoted on green wax and the third on red.

Compilation appearances include *It's The LCB* on *Scum Of The Earth* (Dble CD) and *Scum Of The Earth, Vol. 2* (LP). (VJ)

The Kings Court

45:	Don't Put Me On/Midnight Hour	(Wheel's 4 WH 3613) 1966

From the Detroit suburbs, the 45 is from 1966 and fetches up to $400 these days.

Compilation appearances include: *Don't Put Me On* on *Let 'Em Have It! Vol. 1* (CD); *Don't Put Me On* and *In The Midnight Hour* on *The Cicadelic 60's, Vol. 1* (CD), *The Cicadelic 60's, Vol. 3* (LP), *Green Crystal Ties Vol. 7* (CD) and *The History Of Michigan Garage Bands In The 60's* (3-CD). (MW/VJ)

King's English

Acetate:	Doctor Hunger/She Lied To Me	(Mid Western no #) 1968

Monsters Of The Midwest, Vol. 4 (LP) features a previously unreleased recording called *Doctor Hunger* by these rasping garage punkers from Shawnee Mission, Kansas. Its best feature is some frantic guitar work which is marred by poor production. (MW)

King's English

From Worthington, Ohio. Their competent cover of The Yardbirds' classic, *Mister You're A Better Man Than I* appeared on the 1966 sampler of Columbus, Ohio bands *Hillside '66*. It has subsequently resurfaced on *Relics, Vol. 2* (LP). (GGI/MW)

King's English

45:	It Could Be Bad / Toys In Her Attic	(Prism 1950) 1966

From Ohio, maybe the Dayton area, but not the same outfit as either the Worthington, Ohio bunch who featured on the *Hillside '66* album, or the Bucyrus, Ohio bunch of the same name who also put out a 45.

It Could Be Bad, a vengeful folk-punker aimed at ex-girlfriends, is on *Psychedelic Crown Jewels, Vol. 3* (CD). (GGI/MW)

The Kingsmen

Personnel:	LYNN EASTON	drms, sax, vcls	ABC
	JACK ELY	gtr, vcls	A
	DON GALLUCCI	keyb'ds	AB
	MIKE MITCHELL	gtr	ABCDE
	BOB NORBY	bs	A
	GARY ABBOT	drms	B
	NORM SUNHOLM	bs	BC
	BARRY CURTIS	organ	CDE
	DICK PETERSON	drms	CDE
	FREDDIE DENNIS	bs	DE
	STEVE FRIEDSON	keyb'ds	D

NB: Line-up 'A' early 1963; 'B' mid-1963-1964; 'C' 1964-1967; 'D' 1972; 'E' 1982.

				HCP
ALBUMS:	1(C)	IN PERSON	(Wand WDS-657) 1964	20 -
	2(C)	THE KINGSMEN (MORE GREAT SOUNDS)	(Wand WDS-659) 1964	15 -
	3(C)	THE KINGSMEN, VOL 3	(Wand WDS-662) 1965	22 -
	4(C)	THE KINGSMEN ON CAMPUS	(Wand WDS-670) 1965	68 -
	-5(C)	15 GREATEST HITS	(Wand WDS-674) 1966	87 -
	6(C)	UP AND AWAY	(Wand WDS-675) 1966	- -
	7(C)	THE KINGSMEN'S GREATEST HITS	(Wand WDS-681) 1967	- -
	8(C)	A QUARTER TO THREE	(Piccadilly 3329) 19?	- -
	9(C)	YA YA	(Piccadilly 3330) 19?	- -
	9(C)	HOUSE PARTY	(Piccadilly 3346) 19?	- -
	10(C)	GREAT HITS	(Piccadilly 3348) 19?	- -
	11(C)	MAY DAY	(Heavy Weight?) 1967	- -
	12(C)	THE BEST OF THE KINGSMEN	(Scepter-Citation CTN.L 8002) 19?	- -
	13(C)	THE VERY BEST OF THE KINGSMEN	(Varese Vintage VSD 5905) 1998	- -

NB: (1), (2), (3), (4) and (6) reissued on CD by Sundazed with bonus tracks (SC 6004, SC 6005, SC 6006, SC 6014 and SC 6015 respectively) the fist three in 1993 and the other two in 1994. Sundazed have also released *Since We've Been Gone* (SC 6027) 1994, a previously unreleased album, recorded for Wand in 1967. There's also *A Best Of* CD with 18 tracks (included four previously unreleased ones and a *Best Of* LP on Rhino and a CD compilation on Jerden (JRCD 7004), *Live And Unreleased*. (9) was also reissued on Piccadilly (PIC 3371) in 1980. (1) was also released in France with a different sleeve as *Dansez Le Surf* (Vogue LD 655 30) 1964.

			HCP
45s:	Dig This/Lady's Choice	(Jalynne 108) 1961	-
	Louie, Louie/Haunted Castle	(Jerden 712) 1963	-
	Louie, Louie/Haunted Castle	(Wand 143) 1963	2
	Money/Bent Scepter	(Wand 150) 1964	16
	Little Latin Lupe Lu/David's Mood	(Wand 159) 1964	46
	Death Of An Angel/Searching For Love	(Wand 164) 1964	42
	The Jolly Green Giant/Long Green	(Wand 172) 1964	4
	The Climb/The Waiting	(Wand 183) 1965	65
	Annie Fanny/Give Her Lovin'	(Wand 189) 1965	47
	(You Got) The Gamma Goochee/ It's Only The Dog	(Wand 1107) 1965	122
	Little Green Thing/Killer Joe	(Wand 1115) 1966	77
	My Wife Can't Cook/Little Sally Tease	(Wand 1127) 1966	-
	If I Needed Someone/Grass Is Green	(Wand 11 37) 1966	-
	Trouble/Daytime Shadows	(Wand 1147) 1967	-
	Children's Caretaker/ The Wolf Of Manhattan	(Wand 1154) 1967	-
	Don't Say No/Another Girl	(Wand 1157) 1967	-
	Bo Diddley Bach/ Just Before The Break Of Day	(Wand 1164) 1968	128
	Get Out Of My Life/Since You Been Gone	(Wand 1174) 1968	-
	You Better Do Right/Today	(Capitol 3576) 1972	-

NB: There are also six French EPs with picture sleeves on Vogue.

The origins of this Portland, Oregon band go back to 1957 when Lynn Easton and some of his pals from David Douglas High School formed a band which played at local dances and fairs and was a little unusual for featuring a small church type organ in its act. This phase in their career lasted until about 1962 when they got one of their early breaks. Ken Chase, Musical Director for KISN spotted them playing at a Portland teen club called The Headless Horseman and offered them a residency at his own bigger club, The Chase. They remained the house band there for a whole year. Then in 1963 Ken Chase helped them cut some audition tapes at the Old Northwest Recording Studio. Among the cuts recorded was *Louie, Louie*. Recorded under extremely primitive conditions it gave them a No 2 in the U.S. and reached No 26 in the UK, although **Paul Revere And The Raiders'** version (recorded the same week in the same studio) actually fared better in the Northwest. Chase had originally persuaded Jerry Dennon to release the song on his own Jerden label but later the group were signed by Wand becoming the first white act on what had been an all black label.

Louie, Louie sold over seven million copies legally and a few more were pirated. **The Kingsmen** were extremely successful enjoying eight singles in the Top 100 and five Top 100 albums in the Billboard charts, selling over 20 million records in all. Of their albums (1), (2), (3), (4) and (5) peaked at Nos 20,15, 22, 68 and 87 respectively. All five are now becoming mini-collectables.

Lynn Easton left the group in July 1967, and the remaining members soldiered on until September 1968. There was a reformation in 1972 (line-up D) - Freddie Dennis had previously played with **The Liverpool Five** - and later in 1982 (line-up E), although they played mostly for fun. Norm Sunholm set up the Sunn Amplifier Company with his brother using **The Kingsmen** as a testing ground for their products. Jack Ely is still in the music business in Portland and, since leaving the band, Lynn Easton has hosted a teen dance show, worked in advertising and most recently as a printing salesman. The band's stature as America's premiere garage band shows no sign of diminishing. Don Gallucci went on to fame by forming **Don & The Goodtimes** and later **Touch**.

Compilation appearances have included:- *Louie Louie* on *Frat Rock! The Greatest Rock 'N' Roll Party Tunes Of All Time, Tough Rock, Highs Of The Sixties, History Of Norttthwest Rock, Vol. 1, We Have Come For Your Children, Wild Thing, Nuggets Box* (4-CD), *Nuggets From Nuggets* (CD), *Sundazed Sampler, Vol. 1* (CD) and *History Of Northwest Rock, Vol. 2* (CD); *Louie Louie* and *I Guess I Was Dreaming* on *Nuggets, Vol. 8* (LP); *C.C. Rider* on *Battle Of The Bands, Vol. 2* (LP) and *The History Of Northwest Rock, Vol. 3* (LP); *Twist And Shout* and *All The Little Animals* on *The Hitmakers* (LP); *Louie Louie* and *Jolly Green Giant* on *The History Of Northwest Rock, Vol. 1* (LP); and *J.A.J.* on *The History Of Northwest Rock, Vol. 2* (LP). (VJ)

Kings Ransom

Personnel incl:	BOB DOUGHERTY	vcls	A
	JIMMY SASSMAN	gtr	A
	BOB WERLEY	ld gtr	A
	?? HOMICK		A
	?? ZOSKI		A

45s:	Shame/Here Today Gone Tomorrow	(Integra 101) 1966/67
	Shadows Of Dawn/Street Car	(Integra 102) 1966/67

Their throne was Allentown in Pennsylvania. *Shadows Of Dawn* is a fairly routine punk single apart from some competent ringing guitar work.

Martin Torbert, formerly of Scranton's **Druids**, composed *Shadows Of Dawn* (though it is not known if he was a band member) prior to releasing his solo 45 on the same label in 1967 - *Magic Girl / All Of Tomorrow* (Integra 106). Anyone involved or interested in the Pennsylvania sixties scene should seek out the soft-back publication "Sounds From The Woods", a discographical odyssey by Mike Kuzmin, Jr.

Compilation appearances include: *Shame* on *Psychedelic Unknowns, Vol's 1 & 2* (LP), *Psychedelic Unknowns, Vol. 2* (Dble 7"), *Pebbles, Vol. 1* (ESD) (CD), *Sixties Choice, Vol. 1* (LP), *60's Choice Collection, Vol's 1 And 2* (CD) and *Teenage Shutdown, Vol. 9* (LP & CD); and *Shadows Of Dawn* on *Pennsylvania Unknowns* (LP). (VJ/MW)

HISTORY OF NORTHWEST ROCK Vol. 1 (Comp CD) including The Kingsmen.

King's Road

ALBUM:	1	WATKINS GLEN	(Pickwick LP SPC-3355) 1971 -

A exploito album with an unknown band trying to recreate "the heavy sounds of the Watkins Glen concert" - songs of the **Grateful Dead** (*Truckin'*, *Uncle John's Band*, *Casey Jones*), The Band (*Up On Cripple Creek*, *Stage Fright*, *The Weight*) and the **Allman Brothers Band** (*Statesboro Blues*, *You Don't Love Me* and *Whipping Post*). Largely dispensable as the original tracks are easy to find and much better. (SR)

Kings Verses

Personnel:	JIM BAKER	gtr, ld vcls	AB
	LLOYD BELL	gtr, keyb'ds	A
	BILL KUFIS	bs	AB
	BOB MELCHOR	drms	AB
	JOHN HOLLINGSWORTH	bs	B
	PHILIP HOLLINGSWORTH	keyb'ds	B

ALBUM:	1(A)	KINGS VERSES	(Beatrocket BR 105) 1998

Formed in 1966 in Fresno, California, this band soon peaked locally, winning the 1966 KYNO Battle Of The Bands, where the guest band was the **13th Floor Elevators**. Despite Bob Melchor's previous outfit being a local covers-band, the Trandells, this confident quartet performed originals only. It was inevitable therefore that after graduation they were drawn to the music mecca Los Angeles. Line-up B made the trip to the Strip in the Summer Of Love, playing openers and rubbing shoulders with established acts and gaining the interest of some labels. Before any contract had been signed however, the band was finished after they were blacklisted by L.A. clubs for daring to speak out against illegal club practices.

Luckily ten demos from 1966 and two live performances from the KYNO 1966 band battle both survive and are at last aired on Sundazed's subsidiary Beatrocket. The demos show that their repertoire ranged from upfront and uptempo garage-rockers (*Lights*), fuzz-rockers (*Ballad Of Lad Polo*, *A Million Faces*), and groovy keyboard-led instrumental workouts (*Mind Rewind*), to sultry folk-punkers and beat ballads from the **Beau Brummels-Byrds** canon (*It's Not Right*, *She Belonged To Me*, *It's Love*). *She Belonged To Me* and *Light* comprise the live couplet.

With pictures and memories from Bob Melchor and sleeve notes from Jud Cost, from which the above is extracted, this is a worthwhile and recommended release. (MW/Sundazed)

Kingtones (Dave Roberts and)

Personnel incl:	DAVE ROBERTS	A

45s:	Wish For An Angel/Don't Come Around	(Musitone 102/3) 1961

	Twins/Have Faith	(Derry 101) 1964
	Twins/Have Faith	(Kitoco 335) 1964
	A Love I Had/To Have A Little Girl	(Kitoco 104) c1964
	A Love I Had/Girl I Love You	(Drummond 105) 1965
α	Spicks And Specks/You...	(Eucalyptus 5928) 196?
	It Doesn't Matter Anymore/ How Can A Man	(Eucalyptus 002) 196?
	It Doesn't Matter Anymore/ How Can A Man	(Cotillion 44069) 1969/70

NB: α as **Dave Roberts and Kingtones**.

From Grand Rapids in Michigan, they were also known as **Dave Roberts and The Kingtones**. You'll find *Wish For An Angel* on *Best Of Michigan Rock Groups, Vol. 1* and *Twins* has resurfaced on *Vol. 2* of the same series. (MW)

Russ Kirkpatrick

ALBUM: 1 RUSS KIRKPATRICK (Altogether) 1971 ?

From Denver, Colorado, a folk/folk-rock obscurity housed in a nice psychedelic sleeve. (SR)

Kit and The Outlaws

Personnel incl: KIT MASSENGILL A

HCP

45s:	Worlds Apart/Fun, Fame And Fortune	(In 102) 196? -
α	Midnight Hour/Don't Tread On Me	(Blacknight BK-902) 1966 -
	Midnight Hour/Don't Tread On Me	(Philips 40428) 1966 131
	No Doubt About It/Mama's Gone	(Empire 1) 196? -

NB: α original pressing credited to **The Outlaws**.

This punk outfit hailed from the Dallas/Fort Worth area of Texas and were originally known as **The Outlaws** with their debut 45 and early copies of the second issued under this name. The second 45 attracted quite a lot of attention and got national distribution but did not make the national charts. Their version of *Midnight Hour* was ok, but the flip, *Don't Tread On Me* was their finest moment, and in the eighties the track was covered by numerous bands including Gravedigger V and The Nomads.

Compilation appearances have included: *Don't Tread On Me* on *Pebbles, Vol. 3 (ESD)* (CD), *All Cops In Delerium - Good Roots* (LP), *Texas Flashbacks, Vol. 5* (LP), *Trash Box* (5-CD), *Best of Pebbles, Vol. 2* (LP & CD), *Flashback, Vol. 5* (LP), *Highs In The Mid-Sixties, Vol. 11* (LP); and *Midnight Hour* on *Sixties Rebellion, Vol's 1 & 2* (CD) and *Sixties Rebellion, Vol. 1* (LP). (MW/DSt)

Kitchen Cinq

Personnel:	MARK CREAMER	A
	DALE GARDNER	A
	JIM PARKER	A
	DALLAS SMITH	A
	JOHNNY STARK	A

ALBUM: 1 EVERYTHING BUT (LHI 1200) 1967 R1

45s:	Determination/You'll Be Sorry Someday	(LHI 17000) 1967
	If You Think/ (Ellen's Fancies) Ride The Wind	(LHI 17005) 1967
α	Still In Love With You Baby/same	(LHI 17010) 1967
	Still In Love With You Baby/ (Ellen's Fancies) Ride The Wind	(LHI 17010) 1967
	The Street Song/ When The Rainbow Disappears	(LHI 17015) 1967
	Good Lovin'(So Hard To Find)/ For Never We Meet	(Decca 32262) 1968
	The Minstrel/She's So Fine	(Decca 32374) 1968

NB: α Promo only.

An Amarillo, Texas outfit despite the fact their album, which is pleasant pop and features some nice fuzz guitar, was produced by Lee Hazlewood and issued on his Hollywood-based label. They were earlier known as **Y'alls** and issued a 45 for Ruff under this name.

John Stark, Jim Parker and Mark Creamer were all later members of **Armaggedon** and Stark played on Them's U.S.-only album *In Reality*. (VJ/SR)

Kit Kats

ALBUMS:	1	DO THEIR THING LIVE	(Jamie) 1968 -
	2	IT'S JUST A MATTER OF TIME	(Jamie 3029) 1967 -
	3	THE VERY BEST OF	(Virtue LP-V-102067) 1968 -

45s:	Aba Daba Honeymoon/Good Luck Charlie	(Laurie 3186) 1964
	Cold Walls/You're No Angel	(Lawn 249) 1964
	That's The Way/Won't Find Better Than Me	(Jamie 1321) 1965
	Let's Get Lost On A Country Road/ Find Someone (Who'll Make You Happy)	(Jamie 1326) 1966
	You've Got To Know/Cold Walls	(Jamie 1331) 1966
	Won't Find Better Than Me/Breezy	(Jamie 1337) 1967
	Sea Of Love/Cold Walls	(Jamie 1343) 1967
	Distance/Find Someone	(Jamie 1345) 1967
	I Got The Feeling/That's The Way	(Jamie 1346) 1967
	I Want To Be//Need You	(Jamie 1353) 1968
	You're So Good To Me/Need You	(Jamie 1354) 1968
	Hey, Saturday Noon/That's The Way	(Jamie 1362) 1968

From Philadelphia, a garage group with fuzz guitars, interpreting the usual covers of the era: *Money, Sweet Little Rock'n'Roller, Good Lovin'* etc.

On *It's Just A Matter Of Time*, six of the twelve songs, are credited to Hausman and Stewart, and seem to be originals. These are quite good, sometimes reminiscent of **The Critters**. Most of the remainder, however, are disposable covers, including *Sea Of Love, Cotton Fields* and *Nut Rocker*. (SR/MMs)

Klansmann

ALBUM: 1 THE KLANSMANN (Audio House AHP 269) 196? R4

NB: (1) seen as both acetate and vinyl album.

A rare garage album from the Kansas label, so presumably the band was local to the state. Consisting mostly of covers (*My Back Pages, Hey Joe, Monkey Time, Don't Let The Sun Catch You Crying* etc.), the band sounds very young and amateurish. Justice label collectors will adore it, but it's best avoided unless you're a fan of that genre.

TEXAS FLASHBACKS Vol. 5 (Comp LP) including Kit and The Outlaws.

A counterfeit acetate was made by an enterprising thief in the late nineties but this is easily identified by the misspelled band name (The Clansmen). Beware! (CF)

Marc Klingman

ALBUM: 1 MARK MOOGY KLINGMAN (Capitol ST 11072) 1972 -

45: Making The Rounds At Midnight/
Liz, When You Waltz (Capitol) 1972

A musician and songwriter active on the New York scene between 1967 and 1973, **"Moogy" Klingman** recorded this solo album in 1972, produced by Todd Rundgren and featuring several guests: ND Smart (**Remains**), Rick Derringer (**McCoys**), Amos Garrett, Ben Keith, Joel Bishop O'Brien (**King Bees**)...

His songs has been covered by **Brethren** (*The Sun And The Moon*), **Buzzy Linhart** (*Friends*) and he played keyboards on albums by Rundgren, **Music** and **Al Kooper**. (SR)

The Klowns

ALBUM: 1 THE KLOWNS (RCA LSP-4438) 1970 -

45s: If You Can't Be A Clown/Lady Love (RCA 74-0395) 1970
Flower In My Garden/
I Don't Believe In Magic (RCA 74-0485) 1971

Produced by Jeff Barry, **The Klowns** were a pop sextet with male and female vocals, probably a product from the New York studios. The group wore white suits and painted faces, like **Hello People** but their record is rather lame and best avoided. All their material was penned by Barry, Slavin, Bobby Bloom, Renzetti, Goldberg and Soles. The Ringling Brothers & Barnum & Bailey Circus was associated with this short-lived venture. (SR)

The Knaves

Personnel:	HOWARD BERKMAN	ld gtr	ABC
	MARK FELDMAN	gtr	ABC
	GENE LUBIN	drms	ABC
	NEAL POLLACK	bs	AB
	JOHN HULBERT	ld gtr	BC
	STU EINSTEIN	bs	C

EP: 1(B) LEAVE ME ALONE (Sundazed SEP 10-166) 2001

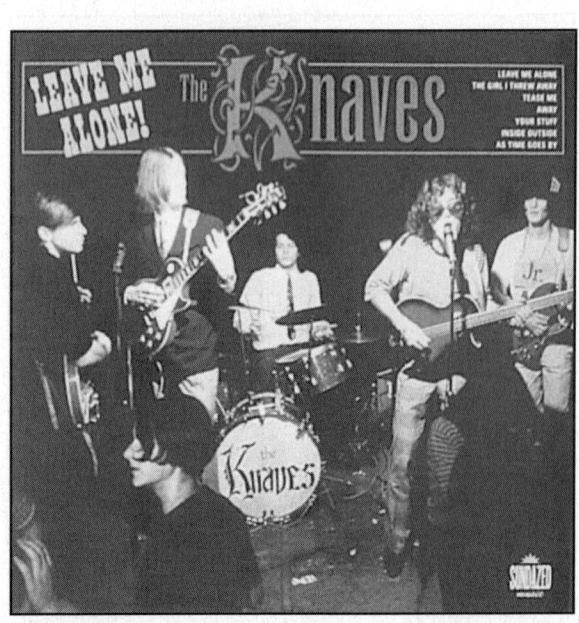

THE KNAVES - Leave Me Alone! 10" EP.

45s: Leave Me Alone/The Girl I Threw Away (Glen 8303) 1967
Leave Me Alone/The Girl I Threw Away (Dunwich 147) 1967
α Inside Outside/Your Stuff (Dunwich 164) 1967

NB: α unreleased.

This mid-sixties Chicago outfit attracted the interest of a major label but failed to break through commercially. Their first 45, *Leave Me Alone* is an uptempo rocker with lots of mouth organ and great lyrics - now regarded as among the finest U.S. sixties garage singles. The flip, *The Girl I Threw Away*, is a brooding pop-punk ballad.

The band evolved out of The Jesters in the Fall of 1964 and lasted through to 1967. Based in the Northern suburbs of Chicago, they were neighbours (and friendly competitors) with **The Flock**, although rumours that they escaped a freezing Northern Winter by touring California with them are false.

Gene Lubin:- "Both groups played the teen clubs around the suburbs and the so-called 'Old Town' district, a regentrified sort of Soho area near downtown Chicago... teen clubs, head shops, etc. Except **The Knaves** had started out in '64-65 playing go-go places on Rush Street and other tough joints on the city's mean streets, i.e. neighborhood bars. Clientel at the time were mostly still into Beach Boys and we were doing British Invasion stuff. In '64-65 there were not too many groups playing in an early punk style as we were... They were mostly Beach Boy clones like **The Flock** or Holiday Inn types, pseudo-Beatles, and maybe some Troggs like stuff. We emulated a Pretty Things demeanor and got our pictures in the newspapares a lot for looking outrageous. We wore undertaker frock coats and bell bottoms we bought at the army navy store before the love-ins began."

They also recorded a second 45 for Dunwich, which apparently owed more to the sexual suggestiveness of The Troggs than any other influences. Perhaps this is why Dunwich never released it.

In 1966, Neal Pollack was drafted and the band called it quits the following year.

Howard Berkman and Neal Pollack were later in Euphoria Blimp Works, an early seventies Chicago act which did not record, as well as in a related project **Yama And The Karma Dusters**, who cut an album in 1970. Gene Lubin has also released a CD *End Of The Spectrum* ( ) 2001, of vintage post-**Knaves** stuff recorded in 1974. He is now a personnel manager for local government in Chicago, and is still writing songs. Howard Berkman is still a full time musician.

Gene:- "This past year with the release of *Leave Me Alone* (35 years late) we've gotten a nice bit of coverage on the Web and some radio. Most of our studio/original stuff is now being labeled as vintage "folk-punk" by some, however, *Leave Me Alone* has already won us some "early punk-rock" acclaim from other quarters. So go figure."

Compilation appearances include: *The Girl I Threw Away* on *Mindrocker, Vol. 2* (LP), *Pebbles, Vol. 9* (LP) and *Pebbles, Vol. 1 (ESD)* (CD); *The Girl I Threw Away*, *Tease Me*, *Leave Me Alone*, *Inside Outside* and *Your Stuff* on *Oh Yeah! The Best Of Dunwich Records* (CD); *Leave Me Alone* on *Pebbles, Vol. 3 (ESD)* (CD) and *What A Way To Die* (LP); *Tease Me, Away, Leave Me Alone* on *The Dunwich Records Story* (LP); and *Away* on *If You're Ready - The Best Of Dunwich... Vol. 2* (CD). (VJ/MW/GLn)

The Knickerbockers

Personnel:	BEAU CHARLES	gtr	A
	JOHN CHARLES	bs	A
	BUDDY RANDELL	sax	A
	JIMMY WALKER	drms	A

HCP

ALBUMS: 1(A) LLOYD THAXTON PRESENTS.... (Challenge 1264) 1965 - SC
2(A) JERK & TWINE (Challenge 621) 1966 - SC
3(A) LIES (Challenge 622) 1966 134 SC

NB: (3) issued as London 8924 in the UK. (2) and (3) have been issued on CD by Sundazed with many bonus tracks (SC 6010) 1993 and (SC 6011) 1993 respectively. (2) has been reissued in Germany. *The Fabulous Knickerbockers* (See For Miles SEE 208) 1987 is a compilation comprised of the best of (3) and some

THE KNICKERBOCKERS - Knickerbockerism! CD.

non - LP gems. In addition, Sundazed also issued *20 Classic Tracks!* (SC 11002) 1992 and *Great Lost Album* (SC 11012) 1992 on CD. The latter was also issued on coloured vinyl in 1989 (5,000) and contains 14 rare and unreleased tracks, 'B' sides and demos. 1997 saw the release of *Knickerbockerism!*, a double CD (SC 11040) 1997 containing 36 tracks including many previously unissued versions. Collectables has issued *Golden Classics* (COL-CD-0531). More recently *A Rave-Up With The Knickerbockers* (Big Beat CDWIKD 122) combines the best of the band's original releases with the better cuts from Sundazed's recent rarities set, *The Great Lost Knickerbockers Album*. There's also a 20 track CD with rare and unreleased recordings and a book, *Presents The Fabulous Knickerbockers*. Finally, check out *Rockin' With The Knickerbockers* (Sundazed LP 5154) 2002.

HCP

45s:		
All I Need Is You/ Bite Bite Barracuda	(Challenge 59268)	1965 -
Jerktown/Room For One More	(Challenge 59293)	1965 -
Lies/The Coming Generation	(Challenge 59321)	1965 20
One Track Mind/ I Must Be Doing Something Right	(Challenge 59326)	1966 46
High On Love/Stick With Me	(Challenge 59332)	1966 94
Chapel In The Fields/ Just One Girl	(Challenge 59335)	1966 106
Love Is A Bird/ Rumors, Gossip, Words Untrue	(Challenge 59341)	1966 133
Please Don't Love Him/ Can You Help Me	(Challenge 59348)	1966 -
What Does That Make You/ Sweet Green Fields	(Challenge 59359)	1967 -
Come And Get It/Wishful Thinking	(Challenge 59366)	1967 -
I Can Do It Better/ You'll Never Walk Alone	(Challenge 59380)	1967 -
A Matter Of Fact/ They Ran For Their Lives	(Challenge 59384)	1968 -

NB: In 1992 Sundazed reissued the first two Challenge 'A' sides on one 7" *All I Need Is You/Jerktown* (Sundazed S 101). There's also a rare French EP with picture sleeves: *Lies/The Coming Generation/One Track Mind/I Must Be Doing Something Right* (London 10178) 1966.

The Knickerbockers took their name from Knickerbocker Avenue in Bergenfield, New Jersey, where they came from, but they moved to Los Angeles in 1965, where they recorded for Challenge Records. They followed the initial success of their Beatlesque rock number *Lies* with a succession of excellent pop-rock singles. *One Track Mind*, which was also covered by **The Gants** was a bit more punkish... whilst another of their finer moments, *High On Love*, was an energetic pop-rock 45.

Jimmy Walker later joined The Righteous Brothers.

Compilation coverage has so far included: *One Track Mind* on *Mindrocker, Vol. 1* (LP), *Nuggets, Vol. 4* (LP) and *Sundazed Sampler, Vol. 1* (CD); *Lies* and *One Track Mind* on *Nuggets Box* (4-CD); *High On Love* on *Nuggets, Vol. 5* (LP); *Lies* on *Highs Of The Sixties, Tough Rock, Wild Thing, We Have Come For Your Children, Nuggets* (CD), *Nuggets From Nuggets* (CD), *Nuggets - Original Artyfacts From The First Psychedelic Era 1965-1968* (Dble LP), *Nuggets, Vol. 3* (LP), *Battle Of The Bands* (CD) and *Excerpts From Nuggets* (CD); *It's Not Unusual* on *Out Of Sight* (LP); *Lies* (Demo) and *My Feet Are Off The Ground* (Demo) on *I Turned Into A Helium Balloon* (CD). (VJ/SR)

Terry Knight and The Pack

Personnel incl:			
	DON BREWER	drms	AB
	BOB CALDWELL	keyb'ds	A
	MARK FARNER	bs	AB
	CURT JOHNSON	gtr	A
	RICHARD TERRANCE KNAPP (TERRY)	vcls, keyb'ds	AB

HCP

ALBUMS:			
1(A)	TERRY KNIGHT AND THE PACK	(Lucky Eleven LE(S)-8000)	1966 127 -
2(A)	REFLECTIONS	(Lucky Eleven LE(S)-8001)	1966 - -
3( )	TRACK ON! THE BEST OF MARK FARNER, TERRY KNIGHT AND DONNIE BREWER	(Lucky Eleven LE 8001)	c1969/70 - -
4( )	MARK, DON AND TERRY 1966-67	(Abkco AB 4217)	1972 192 -

NB: (2) also issued as Cameo C(S)-2007 in 1967. (3) was released after the formation of Grand Funk Railroad and contains some of their 45 cuts plus some previously unreleased material. It appears to have the same catalogue number as (2), but only one title is duplicated. (4) is a compilation, also seen as *Funk-Off 1966-1967*.

HCP

45s:			
α	You Lie / Kids Will Be The Same	(A&M 769)	1965 -
	I've Been Told/How Much More?	(Lucky Eleven 225)	1966 -
	Better Man Than I/I Got Love	(Lucky Eleven 226)	1966 125
	Lady Jane/Lovin' Kind	(Lucky Eleven 228)	1966 -
	A Change On The Way/ What's On Your Mind?	(Lucky Eleven 229)	1966 111
	I (Who Have Nothing)/Numbers	(Lucky Eleven 230)	1966 46
	This Precious Time/ Love Love Love Love Love	(Lucky Eleven 235)	1967 120/117
	One Monkey Don't Stop No Show/ The Train	(Lucky Eleven 236)	1967 -
β	Harlem Shuffle/ I've Got News For You	(Lucky Eleven 003)	1967 -
χ	Wide Trackin'/ Does It Matter To You Girl	(Lucky Eleven 007)	1968 -
χ	Let Me Stand Next To Your Fire/ Without A Woman	(Capitol 2174)	1968 -
β	Tears Come Rollin'/The Color Of Our Love	(Wingate 007)	1968 -
δ	I (Who Have Nothing) / Lizbeth Peach	(Abkco 4005)	1975 -

NB: α is shown in Ken Clee's "Stak O'Wax" but existence is dubious/unconfirmed. β by The Pack without Terry. χ as The Fabulous Pack. δ reissue. There's also a rare French EP with picture sleeve *I (Who Have Nothing)/Numbers/This Precious Time/Love Love Love Love Love* (Stateside FSE 1002) 1967.

HCP

45s:		
Lizbeth Peach / Forever And A Day	(Cameo 482)	1967 -
Come Home Baby / Dirty Lady	(Cameo 495)	1967 -
Lullaby / Such A Lonely Life	(Capitol 2409)	1969 -
Saint Paul / William And Mary	(Capitol 2506)	1969 114
Lullaby / I'll Keep Waiting Patiently	(Capitol 2737)	1970 -

This garage-rock quintet from Flint, Michigan is probably most significant for containing DJ **Terry Knapp**, who formed, managed and produced Grand Funk Railroad, which also included Pack members, Don Brewer and Mark Farner. In the early sixties, Terry was a DJ in Detroit who played Pretty Things, Them, Zombies, Kinks etc long before any other radio station in the area had picked up on the U.K. bands, introducing The Rolling Stones on stage at their first New York gig and interviewing them during their first U.S. tour.

With the Pack, Terry had a few minor hits and their first two albums are now minor collectables. Prior to becoming Grand Funk Railroad and without

Terry, the group also recorded two 45s as The Pack and The Fabulous Pack. There is a picture sleeve one of these 45s, *Wide Trackin'*, that clearly shows a five-piece with him on keyboards. Whether it was a contemporary photo is another matter, of course. Another of their tracks (*I Got News For You*) was penned by Dick Wagner (of **Frost**), whilst *Love, Love, Love, Love, Love* was covered by **The Music Explosion** and later in 1973 by Brownsville Station.

In 1975, Terry left the music business.

Compilation appearances have included: *How Much More?* on *Michigan Mayhem, Vol. 1* (CD), *Pebbles, Vol. 3 (ESD)* (CD), *Chosen Few, Vol's 1 & 2* (CD) and *The Chosen Few, Vol. 2* (LP); *What's On Your Mind?* on *Michigan Nuggets* (CD) and *Michigan Brand Nuggets* (LP); *Harlem Shuffle* and *Wide Trackin'* on *Mindrocker, Vol. 11* (LP); *Numbers* on *Turds On A Bum Ride, Vol. 1 & 2* (Dble CD) and *Turds On A Bum Ride, Vol. 1* (Dble LP); and *The Color Of Love* on *Relics Vol. 1* (LP), *Relics, Vol's 1 & 2* and *Sixties Archive, Vol. 7*. (VJ/MW/OR/SR/EW)

Knight Riders

Personnel:	RYAN CLARK	ld gtr	A
	VIRGIL "BUTCH" DANIELS	gtr	A
	MIKE "MAD DOG" LENTOS	drms	A
	JAY MIERLY	vcls	A
	RODNEY PEARCE	bs	A

From Belmont, California, this band became better known due to the issue of their one unreleased June 1965 track *I* on *San Francisco Roots* (LP) in 1968 (the compilation was also reissued in 1975 on JAS). Clearly a popular number - it's appeared more recently on *The Autumn Records Story* (LP), *Pebbles, Vol. 13* (LP), *We Have Come For Your Children* and *Mindrocker, Vol. 10* (Dble LP). Basically, it's a infectiously catchy punker with a bit of extended guitar work in the middle.

More recently, *I* and the previously unreleased *I Don't Know* have also resurfaced on *Psychedelic Microdots Of The Sixties, Vol. 3* (CD), whilst Big Beats' *Dance With Me* (CD) (part of the *Nuggets From The Golden State* series) features *I* plus three unreleased tracks from 1965 - *Where Did I Fail*, *Torture And Pain* and *Won't You Be My Baby*. (MW/VJ)

The Knights (aka The Hermon Knights)

Personnel:	GRADY BENN	vcls, piano	X
	VARNEY HINTLIAN	bs	X
	DOUG HOUSTON	vcls	X
	CRAIG ROCHE	gtr	X
	MARC SOLOMON	drms	X
	BRAD WATERMAN	keyb'ds	X

ALBUMS:	1( )	1958 HERMON KNIGHTS	(Trans Radio TR 855)	1958	SC
	2( )	KNIGHTS ON THE ROAD, VOL. 2	(HK 1)	1962	R1/R2
	3( )	COLD DAYS - HOT KNIGHTS	(Ace 4763)	1963	R1/R2
	4( )	EXPRESSIONS	(Ace MG 79867/8)	1964	R1/R2
	5( )	OFF CAMPUS	(Co 1269)	1965	R1/R2
	6( )	ACROSS THE BOARD	(Ace MG 200854)	1966	R1/R2
	7(X)	THE KNIGHTS 1967	(Ace MG 201302/3)	1967	R1/R2
	8( )	HERMON KNIGHTS	(Ace 2323)	1968	R1/R2

NB: (7) counterfeited on CD (Flash 66) 1998.

This was a prep-rock outfit from Mount Hermon School, a boarding school in Northfield, Massachusetts. Because the band was made up of students, each "annual" album has a different personnel line-up. The earliest known album to emerge from the school is from 1958, and there may be even earlier issues.

Musically these range from early instrumental sounds to big-band jazz and by the mid-sixties, garage band covers. *The Knights 1967*, for example, reveals a collection of soul, R&B, beat and ballad covers ranging from sappy (*Unchained Melody*, *Under The Boardwalk*) to rockin' (*Bring It On Home*, *I'm Crying*), all done competently but rather uninspired.

Two of the members, Dan and John Cole of the 1964-5 line-up, later turned up in **Quill** (thereby applying what they learned in college on a professional level! No doubt their parents were thrilled.)

Brad Waterman recalls: "Students at the school were known as 'Hermonites' and the name **Hermon Knights** was a play on this. We dropped 'Hermon' in the 1966-1967 school year, and thus were known as **The Knights**. The first version of **The Knights** played long before 1961, I recall that the group started in the 1930s. The group was similar to other student groups like sports teams, yearbook, etc. in that new kids were added each Fall to replace seniors who graduated the previous Spring. The personnel listed above were the 1966 - 1967 members of the group."

"Mount Hermon had a sister school, the Northfield School, in Northfield, Massachusetts. (Both were combined into a single school, Northfield Mount Hermon, in the early seventies.) There were social events on the two campuses on most Saturday nights. **The Knights** were the school's dance band and we played dances, mixers, etc. On off weekends, we sometimes played at other schools. We always had a great time playing, boarding school was more than a little weird in those days and through our music, we were a link to the 'real' world."

"During my four years, and for at least a couple prior and subsequent years, the group made an album each Spring at Ace Recording Studios, Boston. We sold subscriptions during the Winter, used the subscription proceeds to make a downpayment to Ace, practiced at a band member's home for the first several days of Spring vacation, cut the album in a day (that's one day), distributed the records when they arrived in May, and paid off Ace with the balance of the sales proceeds...."

"The group underwent a significant transition during my four year tenure. That transition mirrored the development of rock in those years. In my freshman year, we had only one electric instrument (a guitar) and we played a mix of rock, jazz, big band, etc. By my senior year, we were fully electric, and we were a pure garage band. The jazz sound is in evidence on the 1964, 1965, and 1966 albums."

"Mount Hermon and Northfield produced some well-known musicians, including Will Ackerman (founder of Windham Hill) and Natalie Cole. As I recall, Ackerman was into folk, not rock. Natalie sang with us once or twice - if only I knew then what I know now! I do not believe that any of the Knights with whom I played became professional musicians."

"Marc Solomon, the drummer, and I played together in college, where we were into the Memphis/Stax - Volt sound of Booker T. and MGs, Otis Redding, Sam and Dave, etc."

Brad Waterman later became a tax lawyer working with Don Arden, Black Sabbath, Wayne Newton and briefly Jim Stewart (the co-founder of Stax/Volt!).

Compilation appearances have included their cover of Goffin/King's *Don't Bring Me Down* on *Oil Stains* (LP) and *You're Not Mine* from the *Off Campus* album can be heard on *Hipsville, Vol. 2* (LP). (VJ/MW/CF/BWn)

OLI STAINS (Comp LP) including The Knights.

Knight's Bridge

45:	C.J. Smith/Make Me Some Love	(Sea Ell 105) 196?

This band came from Odessa in West Texas, although their 45 was recorded at Robin Hoods Brians Studio in Tyler, Texas. *C.J. Smith* is pretty psychedelic, as is the flip which is much more keyboard orientated.

Compilation appearances have included: *C.J. Smith* and *Make Me Some Love* on *Texas Flashback (The Best Of)* (CD), *Texas Flashbacks, Vol. 2* (LP), *Flashback, Vol. 2* (LP) and *Green Crystal Ties, Vol. 4* (CD); *Make Me Some Love*, *C.J. Smith*, *C.J. Smith* (demo) and *I Need Your Love* (prev unreleased) on *The History Of Texas Garage Bands, Vol. 1* (Dble CD); (VJ/MW)

Knights Bridge Quintet

Personnel incl:	HAROLD HUTCHINSON		A

45s:	Sorrow In C Minor/Hits Don't Come Easy	(K 101) 1967
	Sorrow In C Minor/Hits Don't Come Easy	(TRC 2072) 1967
	Sorrow In C Minor/ Love Of A Different Flavor	(Mark VII 101 9) 1967

This psychedelic outfit hailed from Waco, Texas. Hutchinson was later involved in the classic sixties musical Hair.

Compilation appearances have included: *Sorrow In C Major* on *Psychedelic Experience, Vol. 2* (CD), *The Psychedelic Sixties, Vol. 1* (LP) and *The Cicadelic 60's, Vol. 4* (CD); *Sorrow In C Major* and *Love Of A Different Flavor* on *Texas Punk, Vol. 10* (LP). (VJ)

The Knights 5 + 1

ALBUM:	1 ON THE MOVE	(Justice 156) c1967 R2

NB: (1) reissued on CD (Collectables COL-0604) 1995.

Another unknown album on the rare Justice label, with covers of *Knock On Wood*, *West Sun*, *Mustang Sally*, *Tomatoes*, *In The Midnight Hour*, *Barefootin'*, *When A Man Loves A Woman*, *Land Of A 1,000 Dances*, *On The Move*, *Try Me*, *Don't Lose Your Cool* and *Ninety Nine And A Half (Won't Do)*. (SR)

The Knightsmen

Personnel:	DARRELL BALL	vcls	A
	KARL HINKLE	vcls	A
	GARY IRWIN	drms	A
	DAVID LEE	keyb'ds	A
	DON LEE	gtr	A
	ROB McCOY	vcls	A
	TOM REA	bs	A
	MARK TRIBBY	ld gtr	A

45:	Let Love Come Between Us/ Gimme A Little Sign	(Irwin Productions) 1966

Originally known as The Demensions, this Indiana band released only one 45 comprising two cover versions: James and Bobby Purify's *Let Love Come Between Us* and Brenton Wood's *Gimme A Little Sign*. Winners of the Pendleton Pike Drive-In Battle of the Bands, **The Knightsmen** became very popular locally, and appeared on 'Bandstand 13', a local television program. Their popularity led to their opening for Kenny Rogers and the **First Edition** and Tommy Roe, among others.

The band has since reformed, and has released a reunion CD. (MDo/KH)

The Knights of Darkness

Personnel:	MAC GREGORY	vcls	A
	KEITH HANSON	organ	A
	GRIFFIN LOVETT	drms	A
	TOM SIMMONS	bs	A
	JOEY WILLIAMS	ld gtr	A

45:	I Can't Look Down / Andromeda	(Key Recordings no #) 1968

Members of this Dublin, Georgia band had come via numerous other high school bands, including The Beachcombers, Confederates, Four Digits, Mineral Spirits and Sultans. Drummer Griffin Lovett's brother Billy ran the Lovett label with several artists on his books, including **The Solid Soul**. Although arrangements were made for the recordings via the label, it ended up being issued on a private imprint in 1968.

I Can't Look Down is one of those 'serious' and soulful '68 pop extravaganzas with big beefy arrangements, brass and piano passages... a sound that would come to be personified by **Blood, Sweat and Tears** - not what most would ever call garage or psych, you will find it on *Psychedelic States: Georgia Vol. 1* (CD). (MW/RM)

Knights of Day

45:	Then There's You/Mr. Pitiful	(Tee Pee 55/6) 1968

These **Knights Of Day** were not from Wisconsin despite their 45 appearing on the Tee Pee label. They were popular around Lincoln, Nebraska in the mid-sixties but are not believed to be from Nebraska either. (GM/MW)

Knights of Day

45s:	Hey Gyp/Distinguished Metal Salesman	(CMC 1,000,000) 196?
	Everybody Needs Somebody To Love/ Why Did You Treat Me So Bad?	(Tower 245) 1966

This band was from Orange County, California and one member went on to Adrian and The Sunsets. *Hey Gyp* was produced by Mike Curb.

Compilation appearances include: *Everybody Needs Somebody To Love* on *Of Hopes And Dreams & Tombstones* (LP) and *Psychedelic Unknowns, Vol. 7* (LP & CD); and *Hey Gyp* on *Follow That Munster, Vol. 2* (LP) (MW/GM)

The Knowbody Else

Personnel:	JIM "DANDY" MANGRUM	vcls	A

ALBUM:	1 THE KNOWBODY ELSE	(Hip Records HIS 7003) 1969 SC

A mix of heavy psych and hippie-rock, with fluid guitar and some good tracks: *After I Smoke I Like To Go To Sleep*, *Flying Horse Of Louisiana* and *No One And The Sun*.

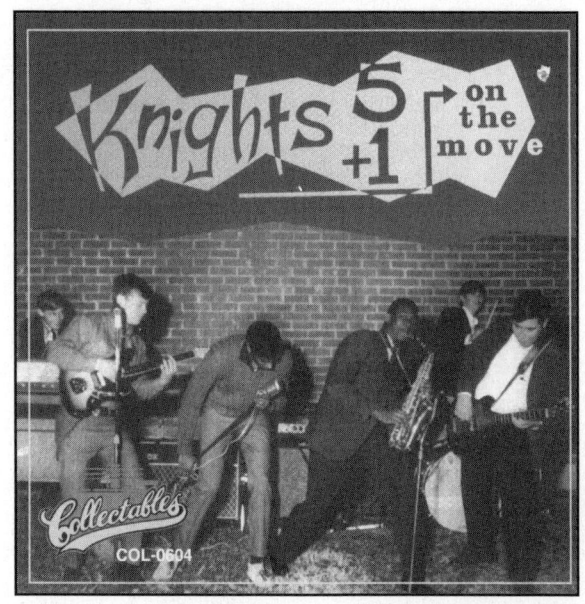

KNIGHTS 5 + 1 - On The Move CD.

Hip Records was a short-lived subsidiary label of Stax (two of their few other releases were **Southwest FOB** and **Paris Pilot**). In 1971, **Knowbody Else** became **Black Oak Arkansas**. (SR)

Koala

Personnel:	JOE ALEXANDER		A
	LOUIS CAINE	gtr	A
	JOEY GUIDO		A
	JOSE MALA		A
	ANTHONY WESLEY		A

ALBUM: 1(A) KOALA (Capitol SKAO 176) 1968 R2

NB: (1) also issued in Canada on Capitol with the same catalogue number

45:	Don't You Know What I Mean?/ Scattered Children's Toys	(Capitol 2365) 1968

The liner notes to this album suggest that this band were from Australia, a curious marketing ploy by Capitol that neither helped sell the record or impress the band (they didn't know a thing about being from 'Downunder' until they saw the record in the stores!). Actually, they were a New York garage punk band, and sound like one.

Not all the tracks are great, but more than half of the album will appeal to sixties enthusiasts. The band has a sound similar to **Druids Of Stonehenge** and **Autosalvage**. The record was produced by Bob Wyld and Art Polliemus (better known for discovering **The Blues Magoos**). Both sides of the 45 are taken from the album, which is made up of thirteen raw, punky cuts.

Louis Caine (aka Louis Dambra) later contributed his furious guitar to **Sir Lord Baltimore**.

A track from the album, *Poor Discarded Baby*, has resurfaced on *Turds On A Bum Ride, Vol. 1 & 2* (Dble CD) and *Turds On A Bum Ride, Vol. 2* (Dble LP). (CF/MW/VJ)

Dean Kohler

Personnel:	ROBERT CRAIG	organ	A
	JOHNNY JOHNSTON	drms	A
	DEAN KOHLER	vcls, gtr	A
	GEORGE NEWSOME	bs	A

45:	Gooseberry Pie / The Next Boy	(Elko 3001) 1968

Dean Kohler started out playing instrumentals in his hometown of Portsmouth, Virginia, with **The Satellites**. The group's orbit was halted by his call-up from Uncle Sam in 1966. Undeterred, Dean formed **The Electrical Banana** whilst on tour in Vietnam to entertain his comrades. In 1967 they recorded two folk-rockers live in an army tent and pressed up ten custom acetates.

Shortly after his safe return to Portsmouth, in time for Christmas 1967, he was back in the studio recording *Gooseberry Pie* - a catchy slice of fuzz-pop about "a trip to the drive-in with a girl". Success was elusive despite a lip-synched appearance on local TV show Disco Ten although it gave him the opportunity to form the show's house band (Soft Light) for the following season.

Gooseberry Pie has been served up again on *The Essential Pebbles Collection, Vol. 2* (Dble CD) and on the excellent Virginia compilation *Aliens, Psychos And Wild Things* (CD). The latter includes his earlier waxings with **The Satellites** and **Electrical Banana**. (BHr/ST/MW)

Kollektion

Personnel incl:	RICHARD 'RICHIE' BORKAN	organ	A
	BOB JABO	gtr	A
	ANGELA RISOFF	vcls	A
	GREGG SHAW	drms	A

45:	Savage Lost/ My World Is Empty Without You	(Heads-Up W 101) 1967

This classic slice of early 'heavy psych' can also now be heard by a wider audience via the excellent compilation *An Overdose Of Heavy Psych* (CD) and *Psychedelic Experience* (CD). *Savage Lost* is a great title too and Jeff Lemlich used it for his fascinating and worthy Florida Discography. The flip is not up to the same standard but a **Vanilla Fudge** type rework.

From Miami, Gregg Shaw had previously played with **The Shaggs** and when he joined **Kollektion** the prior drummer swapped drum roles (sic) and took his place in **The Shaggs**. Bob Jabo too had been with **Dr. T and The Undertakers**. He would later play in **Katmandu**, whilst vocalist Angela Risoff split in '68 to tour with **Blues Image**. Richard Borkan also played with **Sounds Unlimited**. (MW/JBn/MA)

The Kommotions

45:	She Won't See Me/It's Over	(Sams 101) 196?

This outfit came from Garland in Texas. There's a version of *Little Black Egg* on the *Ear-Piercing Punk* (LP & CD) compilation credited to **The Kommotions**, but this may be a mix up between **Kenny Wayne and The Kamotions**, who did not record this track, and **Wayne Lacadisi** who did. (VJ)

The Koo Krew

45:	Wet And Wild/Down To Earth	(Ascot 2225) 1967

A rare garage-rock group, *Wet And Wild* was written by M. Rubenstein. They were possibly from the Nashville area, as their producer was Wayne Moss, a local musician. (SR)

Al Kooper

HCP

ALBUMS: (selective)	1	SUPER SESSION	(Columbia CS 9701) 1968	12 -
	2	THE LIVE ADVENTURES OF MIKE BLOOMFIELD AND AL KOOPER	(Columbia KGP-6) 1969	18 -

NB: (1) by Bloomfield/Kooper/Stills.

Singer, guitarist, organist, arranger, producer, **Al Kooper** was an essential figure of the rock scene between 1965 and 1970. He formed the **Blues Project** in 1965 and **Blood, Sweat and Tears** in 1968. As an organist, he played on Bob Dylan's *Highway 61 Revisited* and *Blonde On Blonde*, helping to create a sound which was influential on groups like The Band or Procol Harum.

THE KNOWBODY ELSE - Knowbody Else LP.

Kooper was also an active session man playing with **Tom Rush, Jim and Jean, Jimi Hendrix**, the Paupers and **Moby Grape**. He was also one of the first musicians to record a session of rock jams with the commercially successful *Super Session* with **Mike Bloomfield** and Steve Stills in 1968. Although this was common with jazz or blues, the 'jam' album hadn't yet set root in the rock genre. This was followed in 1969 by *The Live Adventures* with **Bloomfield**, John Kahn, Skip Prokop, Carlos Santana and Elvin Bishop. In 1972, he formed his own label, Sounds Of The South, and produced the first three Lynyrd Skynyrd albums, one of the best Southern rock acts. He also produced several other rock and soul groups.

Between 1968 and 1978, **Al Kooper** recorded several solo albums which are mainly pop-oriented, generally weak and beyond the scope of this book. After a long legal procedure with Columbia, he came back in 1995 with a new album which failed to chart.

Compilation appearances include *I Stand Alone* on *Pop Revolution From The Underground* (LP). (SR)

Kopperfield

Personnel:			
	TOM CURTIS	drms, perc	A
	PAUL DECKER	vcls, perc	A
	CHUCK EAGAN	gtr, vcls, ld vcls	A
	JERRY OPDYCKE	bs, vcls	A
	JIMMEY ROBINSON	ld vcls	A
	KEITH ROBINSON	keyb'ds, vcls	A

ALBUM: 1(A) TALES UNTOLD (Kopperdisc 5014 N5) 1974 R3

NB: (1) reissued on CD with nine unreleased cuts, recorded between 1972 and 1975 (Gear Fab GF-164) 2001. Also reissued as a double-LP including the same bonus cuts (Gear Fab Comet GFC 412/2) 2001.

From Edwardsberg and Ann Arbor, Michigan. **Kopperfield** formed in 1971 from the ashes of Touch Of Blue, a local trio that released two singles in 1969/70. The line-up above that recorded the album was established by 1972, and they were a popular live attraction for several years before recording, opening for **The James Gang**, Foghat and Kansas, among others. By 1974 they had become a full-blown progressive rock band.

Most of the tracks are fronted by Robinson's distorted organ, which calls to mind early seventies European progressive rock bands like Brainticket or Virus. Typical of the progressive keyboard/guitar driven genre, it is held in high regard by some collectors, but unless skilled musicianship is your bag, it is best avoided. (VJ/SR/MW/CF)

The Kords

45: Boris The Spider/It's All In My Mind (Laurie 3403) 1967

A one-off venture on Laurie who came up with an interesting cover of *Boris The Spider*, which can also be heard on *Mindrocker, Vol. 3* (LP). (VJ)

The Artie Kornfeld Tree

Personnel incl:			
	FRANK HARRIS	keyb'ds	A
	ARTIE KORNFELD		A
	TONY LEVIN	bs	A
	HUGH McCRACKEN	gtr	A
	DONALD McDONALD	drms	A

ALBUM: 1(A) A TIME TO REMEMBER (Dunhill DS 50092) 1970 -

NB: (1) also released in the U.K. (Probe SPB 1022) 1970.

From the New York scene, this was a short-lived project lead by Artie Kornfeld, also a member of the **Changin' Times** and a renowned songwriter and producer. The album is mainly composed of original material penned by Kornfeld and played by a group of outstanding musicians: McDonald was in **Jeremy and The Satyrs** and played with both **Joe Beck** and **Tim Hardin**. **Hugh McCracken** (who was an in-demand session man on the New York scene then) filled the guitar parts with ease and bassist Tony Levin went on to King Crimson in the early eighties.

KOPPERFIELD - Tales Untold LP.

Artie Kornfeld production credits include 45s by the **Bassetts**, Carnival Connection, Guild Light Gauge, Tuneful Trolley and the Unclaimed (with Milan), **Bert Sommer**'s eponymous album on Kama Sutra in 1971, the **Wind In The Willows** and **Swampgas**. He also went on to be one of the quartet that created and organised Woodstock - with Joel Rosenman, John Roberts and Michael Lang. (SR)

K-otics

Personnel:			
	MIKE JOHNSON	ld gtr, ld vcls	A
	TOMMY MANN	ld vcls	AB
	WARREN MUNDY	drms	A
	BARNEY PARKER	bs gtr	A
	JOE TORRILLO	gtr, backing vcls	A
	RAY GOSS	bs, bcking vcls	B
	KIM VENABLE	drms	B
	MARK TRIBBY	ld gtr	A

45s:		
Charlena/They Don't Know	(Sea Cap 1000)	1966
Charlena/Ooh-Wee	(Rick 10276)	1966
I'm Leaving Here/ Double Shot (Of My Baby's Love)	(Fortune 1000)	1966
I'm Leaving Here/ Double Shot (Of My Baby's Love)	(Bang 521)	1966

From Alabama, **The K-Otics** were formed at Troy State University in Troy, Alabama U.S.A. in 1962. After all but one of the original members left college, the remaining member recruited players from around his hometown. Tommy Mann, Ray Goss and Marvin Taylor were from around Tallassee, Alabama and Tuskegee, Alabama.

I'm Leaving Here is a cool punker that wears its influences on its sleeve. Built around the Kinks' *All Day And All Of The Night* riff, the break also features the *Louie Louie* signature prominently on keyboards.

Kim Venable went on to play with Dennis Yost and the Classics Four.

Compilation appearances include *I'm Leaving Here* on *Everywhere Chainsaw Sound* (LP) and *Psychedelic States: Alabama Vol. 1* (CD). (MW)

The K-pers

Personnel incl?:		
	RICHARD CALHOUN	A
	MITCH GOODSON	A

45: The Red Invasion / Sweet Girl (Tiki 101) 1968

NB: There was also a second 45 from 1968 - details unknown.

The K-pers were from Dothan, Alabama and released two 45s. Their anthemic fuzz-punker *The Red Invasion*, written by (group members?) Goodson and Calhoun, can be heard on *Yeah Yeah Yeah* (CD) and *Psychedelic States: Alabama Vol. 1* (CD). (MW)

Kracker-Barrel Komplex

Personnel:			
	DENNIS CIESIELSKI	ld gtr	A
	TERRY GHIGHI	vcls	A
	MICHAEL MENTE	keyb'ds	A
	JACK SCMITZ	gtr	A
	DAVID URBANOWSKI	drms	A
	MARK URBANOWSKI	bs	A

45: The Red Invasion / Sweet Girl   My World / Different Than Me 1968

A short-lived sextet from Peru and Oglesby, Illinois - they just had time to put out one 45 on a Wisconsin label before the draft claimed both the drummer and their manager. *Different Than Me*, notable for its **Cryan' Shames**-like harmonies, is on *Psychedelic Crown Jewels, Vol. 2* (Dble LP & CD). (MW/RM)

Kreed

Personnel:			
	REED BOYD	ld gtr	A
	DAVID CANNON	vcls	A
	NIGEL COFF	gtr	A
	JOHN DIDIER	organ	A
	DOUG PARENT	bs	A
	DEAN SACK	drms	A

ALBUM: 1(A) KREED!   (Vision Of Sound 71-56) 1971 R4

This album was recorded by six 12-14 year olds whilst they were at St. James School, a military training school in Fairbault, 50 miles South of Minneapolis in Minnesota. Although it was recorded in the early seventies with the band being so young it sounds more like a mid-sixties effort. They chose the name because they were all going to an Episcopalian School - they took the word creed and replaced the 'C' with a 'K'. David Cannon wrote all the songs on the album (except for a cover of *In-A-Gadda-Da-Vida*) and he was clearly a talent. Between 1976-1982 he fronted No Cheese Please, Balderdash and The Fabulous Toasters. **Kreed** were together for just eight months from September 1970 until the Summer of 1971. Not many bands have produced an album of songs from such a brief association! (VJ)

The Kreeg

Personnel:			
	HAP BLACKSTOCK	bs, vcls	A
	LARRY INKS	ld gtr	A
	ROBERT STURTCMAN	gtr, vcls	A
	RUSS STURTCMAN	drms	A
	RAY TRUJILLO	bs	A

CD: 1(A) IMPRESSIN' (1966-1973)   (Collectables COL-CD-0689) 1995

45: How Can I/Impressin'   (Lance 2229/7094) 1966

The flip to their sole 45 has some good guitar leads. Both sides were written by Bob Sturtcman and produced by Dick Stewart of **King Richard and The Knights**.

The retrospective CD is most impressive. With an informative CD booklet with pictures, notes by Bob Sturtcman, a full track listing and personnel details, this is essential for anyone enchanted by this Albuquerque outfit's previously compiled 45. Superb folk-rock, garage and psychedelic sounds are to be enjoyed herein - fifteen quality tracks in all with just four covers (*Soul Kitchen, For Your Love, Better Man Than I, Hey Joe*). They went through several identities - Goldenaires, **Kreeg**, Mother Sturtcman's Jam And Jellies, and finally Albatross. To find out more, get this CD - you will not be disappointed.

I WANNA COME BACK FROM THE WORLD OF LSD (Comp CD) including The Kreeg.

Other compilation appearances have included: *Impressin'* on *King Richard And The Knights - Precision!* (CD) and *I Wanna Come Back From The World Of LSD* (CD); *How Can I* and *Impressin'* on *New Mexico Punk From The Sixties* (LP) and *Sixties Archive, Vol. 4* (CD); *How Can I, Impressin'* and *Jams And Jellies* on *Bands On Lance* (LP); *For Your Love* and *I'm Over You* on *Green Crystal Ties, Vol. 9* (CD). (MW)

Kristyl

Personnel:			
	DAVID ATHERTON	bs	A
	SONNY DEVORE	ld gtr	A
	BOB TERRELL	gtr	A
	BRUCE WHITESIDE	drms	A

ALBUM: 1(A) KRISTYL   (Private Pressing) 1975 R3

NB: (1) reissued in 1986 (Hype 01) and has also been issued on CD (Titanic 001).

This album is homemade guitar psychedelia from Kentucky. A nice mixture of gentle dreamy passages, heavier acid guitar and wah-wah fuzz along with charmingly teenage vocals. It had a limited repress in 1986 and if you can buy a copy cheaply do so. (VJ)

The Krums

Personnel incl: BRUCE BERNSTEIN   ld gtr   A

45: LSD/?   (Airplay 102) 196?

A late sixties Chicago outfit I'd like to know more about. Their lead guitarist also played in **The Underprivileged**. (VJ)

The Krystal Tones

45: Carol/Don't Cry   (Han-di) 1966

From Schiller Park, Illinois, a rare garage single. *Carol* is not the Chuck Berry song. (SR)

The Bob Kuban Explosion

HCP

ALBUMS: 1 THE BOB KUBAN EXPLOSION
       (Musicland 501) c1966 - -
2 LOOK OUT FOR THE CHEATER!
       (Musicland) c1967 129 -

NB: (1) by the Bob Kuban Explosion. (2) by Bob Kuban and His In-Men.

				HCP
45s:	α	The Cheater/Try Me Baby	(Musicland 20001)	1966 12
	α	Pretzel Baby/?	(Musicland 20003)	1966 -
	α	The Teaser/All I Want	(Musicland 20006)	1967 70
	α	Drive My Car/The Pretzel	(Musicland 20007)	1967 93
	α	Harlem Shuffle/ Theme From Virginia Woolf	(Musicland 20013)	1967 -
	α	Batman Theme/ You Better Run, You Better Hide	(Musicland 20017)	1967 -
		Soul Man/Hard To Handle	(Reprise)	1969 -

NB: α by Bob Kuban and his In-Men.

From St. Louis, Missouri, this singer recorded several 45s and at least two albums containing mostly covers of garage, pop and white soul covers, like *You Better Run*, *Little Girl*, *Drive My Car*, *Turn On Your Lovelight*, *Batman Theme*, *In The Midnight Hour*, *These Boots Are Made For Walking*... Quite rare but nothing essential. The second sold quite well, climbing to No. 129 during a five week chart stint. They also enjoyed three hit singles. The biggest *The Cheater* spent eleven weeks in the charts. Their third and final hit single was a cover of Lennon-McCartney's *Drive My Car*. (SR/VJ)

Kubla Khan

Personnel:	JEFF BURKE	ld gtr	A
	TOM ENGLE	bs	A
	CHRIS GERNIOTTIS	vcls, gtr	A
	MIKE GERSMANN	drms	A
	MIKE GREGORY	organ	A

CD:	1(A)	MYSTICAL CRYSTAL REVOLUTION	(Collectables COL-CD-0654) 1996

45:	Bad Side Of The Moon/Out In The Country	(Spearway 2) 1970

A short-lived, Corpus Christi rock and roll outfit included here because it was a late outing for Gerniottis who had earlier led **The Liberty Bell** and prior to that **Zakary Thaks**. You can hear their 45 on *The J-Beck Story, Vol. 3: The Liberty Bell* (Eva 12036) 1984, or check out the Collectables retrospective CD, which includes previously unreleased material.

Formed in February 1970 the band only lasted until September that year. They hardly played live at all but mainly spent their time rehearsing and recording at Studio B in Corpus Christi. Their 45, *Bad Side Of The Moon* was an early Elton John number while the other tracks on the retrospective CD range in style from the latin-rock of *Bossa Nova* through the broodingly atmospheric instrumental *Help Yourself* to gruff-voiced hard-rock and gospel. Unfortunately, it's a bit lacklustre compared to Gerniottis's earlier outings with **Zakary Thaks** and **The Liberty Bell**.

Compilation appearances have included: *Revolution II* and *Help Yourself* on *Green Crystal Ties, Vol. 1* (CD). (VJ/LP)

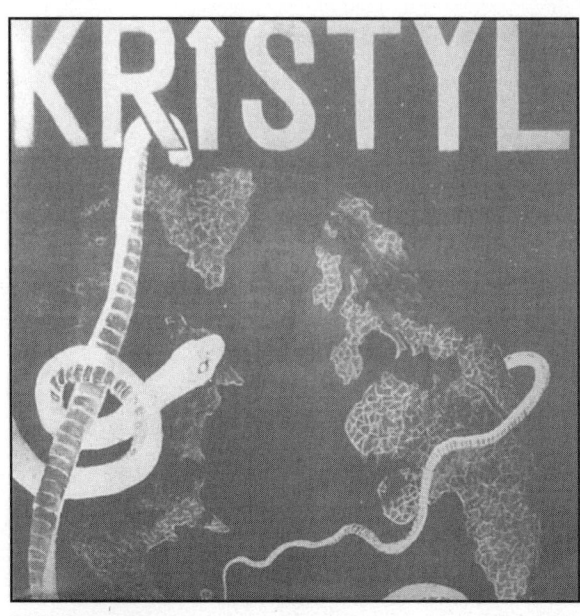

KRISTYL - Kristyl LP.

Tuli Kupferberg

ALBUM:	1	NO DEPOSIT NO RETURN	(ESP 1035) 1967 SC

A rare solo album by the co-leader of **The Fugs**. It came with an insert and some copies were pressed on gold wax. (SR)

Jim Kweskin Jug Band

Personnel incl:	JIM KWESKIN	vcls, gtr, comb	AB
	GEOFF MULDAUR	gtr, vcls, washboard, kazoo	AB
	FRITZ RICHMOND	jug, washtub bs	AB
	BOB SIGGINS	banjo, mandolin, steel gtr	A
	BRUNO WOLF	kazoo, hrmnca, vcls	A
	RICHARD GREENE	fiddle	B
	BILL KEITH	banjo, pedal steel, gtr	B
	MEL LYMAN	hrmnca	B
	MARIA D'AMATO (MULDAUR)	vcls, violin	B

ALBUMS:	1(A)	JIM KWESKIN AND THE JUG BAND	(Vanguard VSD-2158) 1963 -
	2	JUG BAND MUSIC	(Vanguard VSD 79163) 1965 -
	3	RELAX YOUR MIND	(Vanguard VSD 79188) 1966 -
	4	SEE OTHER SIDE FOR TITLE	(Vanguard VSD 79234) 1966 -
	5	JUMP FOR JOY	(Vanguard VSD 79243) 1967 -
	6	GARDEN OF JOY	(Reprise RS-6266) 1967 -
	7	WHAT EVER HAPPENED TO THOSE GOOD OLD DAYS	(Vanguard VSD 79278) 1967 -

45s:	Minglewood/Sheik Of Araby	(Reprise 0624) 1967
	I'll Be Your Baby Tonight/Circus Song	(Reprise 0675) 1968

A seminal group from the Boston scene, **Jim Kweskin and his Jug Band** appeared in 1963 and played a happy mix of folk, blues, jug band music, rock and old-timey songs. The personnel was quite unstable, having between four and eleven members, but they had a very good live reputation. Muldaur and Richmond also played with **Eric Von Schmidt** and are both present on the Elektra *Blues Project* album from 1964. Their records may interest fans of the early **Nitty Gritty Dirt Band**, **Dr. West's Medicine Show and Junk Band** or the **Lovin' Spoonful**.

When the group finally broke up in 1967, its various members kept on playing: Geoff and Maria Muldaur recorded, first as a duo, then with Paul Butterfield's Better Days and finally had solo careers. Fritz Richmond moved to California and become a renowned studio engineer. He also played with Norman Greenbaum, Ry Cooder and is still touring with **John Sebastian**. Jim Kweskin for many years became a devotee of "guru" Mel Lyman, although recently he has pursued a low-key career in the folk clubs and is now recording once again.

In 1969, Bill Keith and Richard Greene founded the Blue Velvet Band who released a good country-folk album produced by Erik Jacobsen, the producer of **Lovin' Spoonful** and Norman Greenbaum. Greene also joined **Seatrain** and took part in several groups and sessions (**Brewer and Shipley**, **William Truckaway**, **Pearls Before Swine**). Prior to joining the 'Jug Band' Bill Keith had played with Bill Monroe and The Bluegrass Boys. In the early sixties he revolutionised bluegrass banjo with his melodic style, adapted from arranging fiddle tunes for the banjo.

Compilation appearances include *Memphis* on *Pop Music Super Hebdo* (LP). (SR/JNa/CMn)

Kyks

Personnel:	MARK GIBSON	vcls	AB
	DAVE MOORE	drms	AB
	DAVE RIMMER	bs	AB
	STEVE RIMMER	ld gtr	AB
	MIKE WILLIAMS	keyb'ds	A
	BOB WILLIAMS	keyb'ds	B

45: Where Are You?/When Love Comes Searching
For Me (PS)   (RAF Productions 1001) 1966

From Marshall, Missouri and pronouncing their name 'Kicks' this quintet recorded an album in 1967 in Memphis. Titled *Bittersweet*, it was scrapped before release, although Collectables are promising a "reissue" in the near future. Their sole 45, which was recorded at Columbia studios in Nashville, came in a picture sleeve which featured a photo of the band in a field surrounded by their Vox Super Beatles, with their name superimposed in blue psychedelic lettering. The contents of the sleeve, a routine garage dirge, did not live up to sleeve's promise.

The group changed its name to Bittersweet some time around '68 or '69 and recorded the unreleased album at a recording studio outside Columbia, Missouri. The group remained the same with the exception of Bob Williams who replaced Mike Williams (no relation).

Compilation appearances have included: *Where Are You?* on *Monsters Of The Midwest, Vol. 2* (LP); *Where Are You?* and *When Love Comes Searching For Me* on *The Human Expression And Other Psychedelic Groups - Your Mind Works In Reverse* (CD). (VJ/MW/MGn)

The Kynd

45: Mr. America/Clouds   (Kynd Company 103169) 1969

Late sixties heavy-rock from New Jersey, though the 'B' side demonstrates a lighter more melodic touch. (MW)

KALEIDOSCOPE - Best Of CD.

KENNELMUS - Featuring Bob Narloch LP.

KALLABASH CORP - Kallabash Corp CD.

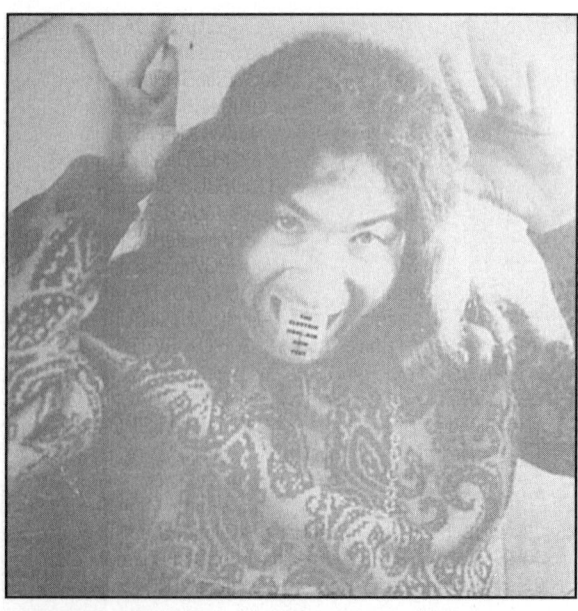

KEN KESEY - Acid Tests Vol. 1 CD.

KEN KESEY - Electric Kool Aid Acid Test (bootleg) LP.

Ken LaBrie

ALBUM: 1 LOST AND FOUND (American Artists AAS-1171) c1972 ?

An obscure album, in the Christian folk-psych style. (SR)

Wayne Lacadisi

45: Little Black Egg/Broken Hearts (Bell 630) 1965

Previously thought to have been the work of **Kenny Wayne**, this is now know to be incorrect. So, who was this guy?

Lacewing

Personnel:	DAVE ANDRESS	keyb'ds	A
	JEFF CURREY	bs	A
	MARK FRAZIER	drms	A
	MARY STEPKA	vcls	A
	BOB WEBB	gtr	A

ALBUM: 1(A) LACEWING (Mainstream S/6132) 1970 R1

45: Paradox/Paradox (Mainstream 731) 1970

NB: promo only release, with same cut on both sides.

From Kent, Ohio, this outfit formed out of the ashes of The Measles, who had once included Joe Walsh before his **James Gang** days and Joe Vitale, who was also in **Chylds** and Joe Walsh's Barnstorm. They reverted their name to The Measles after the Mainstream album in 1970.

Their album is a West Coast-influenced affair which ranges from folk tracks like *Time To Go* to more atmospheric numbers such as *Rebirth* and on to heavier rock cuts like *Epicycle* and *Play For You*. The 45 is from the album and is by far the best track. (VJ)

Gaylan Ladd

Personnel:	GAYLON LADD (GAYLAN LATIMER)		A

45s: α Don't Go In My Room Girl/
   It Belongs To You (Ventural 722) 1965
   Think About Me/Her Loving Way (MGM 13435) 1965
   Smokey Places/Think About Me (Ventural 723) 1965
   I Better Go Now/Painted Lady (Ventural 731) 1966
   β My Life, My Love/Repulsive Situation (Pacemaker PM-257) 1966

NB: α recorded with Bob Sharp as Bob and Gaylan. β released as **Gaylan Ladd & The East Side Transfer**.

This guy came from Waco in Texas and his real name was Gaylan Latimer. He was also based in Houston for a time and had earlier played in other Texas sixties punk outfits like **The Dawgs** (with Bob Sharp) and **The Silvertones**. He recorded the first of these 45s with Bob Sharp.

His producer, the infamous, Huey P. Meaux used a fake Gaylan Ladd for extra touring cash.

He later formed **Eastside Transfer** and then went on to **Heather Black**, a hippie-art folk band. His finest moment to readers of this tome will be *Repulsive Situation*, a brooding dynamic punker - his other material tended to be melodramatic ballads and moody folk-rock-cum-beat music.

Today Gaylan works in Austin selling audio and video gear and still plays music. Curiously he doesn't remember *Replusive Situation* but has said it was probably done when he was in high school.

Heather Black later became Christopher Cross.

Compilation appearances have included *Her Loving Way* and *Don't Go In My Room Girl* on *Austin Landing, Vol. 2* (LP); *Her Lovin' Way* on *Garage Punk Unknowns, Vol. 5* (LP); *Her Loving Way* and *Repulsive Situation* on *Highs In The Mid Sixties, Vol. 23* (LP). (VJ/MW/AB/NL)

AUSTIN LANDING Vol. 2 (Comp LP) including Gaylan Ladd.

The Ladds

Personnel:	ALEX CAMPBELL	keyb'ds	A
	CHUCK HOLZER	vcls	A
	ERIC MELBY	bs	A
	MARK MELBY	drms	A
	RALPH RUSSELL	gtr	A
	RANDY TAYLOR	bs	
	CLARE TROYANEK	bs	

45s: Keep On Running/
   Wild Angels Theme (PS) (Transaction 703) 1967
   Survival/I Found A Girl (Universal Audio 706) 1968
   Bring Back The Days/
   Goodness Gracious Baby (Teen Town no#) 1969
   α The Lone Ranger / No Name Boogie (Teen Town 115) 1970
   β Witchi Tai To / Bring Back The Days (Bang 577) 1970
   β Wanton Forest / You've Gone Away (Teen Town 118) 1971
   β Lifeless / Smile Away (Teen Town 125) 1972

NB: α as The Silver Bullets, β as Today's Tomorrow.

Led by the talented Campbell, who had earlier recorded with **The Fax**, **The Ladds** came from La Crosse and were considered to be one of Southwest Wisconsin's best sixties groups.

Bring Back The Days did well in their hometown so when they recorded a cover of **Everything Is Everything**'s *Witchi Tai Toi*, it was decided to push it out to a bigger label. It was released as by Today's Tomorrow and topped the WOKY charts in Milwaukee for four weeks. When it failed to pick up airplay outside of the region, the momentum was lost. Meantime they released an instrumental 45 as The Silver Bullets. They would stick with Today's Tomorrow for two further 45s before breaking up.

Campbell went to college, returning to music in the seventies with the Changing Times, before moving into the TV industry. Eric Melby was later with Ice and Flying Free. Later member Clare Troyanek had previously been in **The Unchained Mynds**.

Compilation appearances include *Survival* on *Psychedelic Unknowns, Vol. 8* (LP & CD). (GM/MW/VJ)

Lady and The Tramps

45: House Of The Rising Sun/Wearin' That
   Loved On Look (Universal Audio 547-49580) c1970

Recorded at Universal Audio, Winona, Minnesota. This excellent version of *Rising Sun* is a heavy bluesy blast with some burnin' leads but also notable for the forceful female lead vocals. The flip isn't half as good - piano boogie pop.

Compilation appearances include *House Of The Rising Sun* on *Girls In The Garage, Vol. 5* (LP). (MW)

The Ladybugs

| 45: | How Do You Do It?/Liverpool | (Chattahoochie 637) 1964 |

A Mersey influenced all girl band. A track called *Fraternity, U.S.A.* has resurfaced on *Girls In The Garage, Vol. 4* (LP). This astonishing slice of wax was conceived and produced in Norfolk, Virginia, by none other than Frank Guida, the mastermind who created Gary "U.S." Bonds in 1960. It was recorded in 1964. *Liverpool* was written by **Kim Fowley**.

Their version of Gerry and The Pacemaker's *How Do You Do It?* can also be heard on *Girls In The Garage, Vol. 1* (CD) and *Girls In The Garage, Vol. 2* (LP). (VJ/SR)

Ned Lagin and Phil Lesh

| ALBUM: | 1 | SEASTONES | (Round RX 106) 1975 SC |

Ned Lagin was a friend of Phil Lesh, the bassist of the **Grateful Dead**, and they were both into electronic music (they even played some during the '**Dead** shows and, to their amazement, the Dead Heads liked it!). This album is mainly an experimental effort and was recorded with the support of **Jerry Garcia**, David Freiberg, Glace Slick, David Crosby and **Mickey Hart**. (SR)

Lamb

Personnel:	BARBARA MAURITZ	vcls	ABC
	BOB SWANSON	gtr	ABC
	DAVID HAYES	bs	BC
	TOM SALISBURY	keyb'ds	C
	RICK SCHLOSSER	drms	C
	(ED BOGAS	violin	ABC)
	(BILL DOUGLAS	bs	AB)
	(JOHN McFEE	steel gtr	C)

ALBUMS:	1(A)	A SIGN OF CHANGE	(Fillmore 30003) 1970 -
	2(B)	CROSS BETWEEN	(Warner Bros. WS 1920) 1971 -
	3(C)	BRING OUT THE SUN	(Warner 1952) 1971 -

NB: (1) was also released by CBS (S 63954) in Holland. (2) with lyric insert. (3) as **Barbara Mauritz Lamb**. **Barbara Mauritz** had a later solo album *Music Box* (Columbia KC 31749) 1973, also issued in Holland (CBS S 65632).

| 45: | Isn't It Just A Beautiful Day/ | |
| | Winter In The Valley | (Warner WB 7562) 1973 |

NB: Promo copies with a mono verion of *Isn't It...* on the flip also exist.

From San Francisco, **Lamb** was primarily a hippie duo formed by Barbara Mauritz and Bob Swanson. Appearing at several concerts in the Bay Area, by the time of their third album, they were a quintet with a strong rhythm section, backing Barbara Mauritz' powerful voice. Their music is a mix of West Coast and soul with some oriental and jazzy influences.

From Beaumont, Texas originally, Barbara Mauritz was born into a very musical family that claims Gypsy blood. At the age of four she began playing piano and at fifteen started playing in the local clubs. There she met artists like Edgar and **Johnny Winter** and **Janis Joplin**, the latter being a close friend of Barbara's sister.

A year later, Barbara moved first to Houston, where she opened for Lightning Hopkins and **The American Blues**, and then New Orleans. Around this time she started playing guitar and composing songs, but it wasn't long before the attractive "new sounds" coming out from California led her to settle in San Francisco.

There she formed **Lamb** with Bob Swanson and after being spotted by producer David Rubinson, got to open for CSN & Y at the Winterland for four nights. Suitably impressed, Bill Graham took **Lamb** under his wing. In 1969 their first album for the Fillmore label, *A Sign Of Change* was released. Still today it has a unique and very distinctive sound, enhanced by the unusual instrumentation: classical guitars, upright bass, cello, flute, oboe and Barbara's beautiful voice. *Traveler's Observation*, *In My Dreams* and *The Odyssey of Ehram Spickor* are real gems of acoustic psych-rock.

After recording *Hello Friends* for the famous *Last Days Of The Fillmore* set, **Lamb** switched to Warner Bros., and produced two further albums. Both *A Cross Between* and *Bring Out The Sun* offered more haunting songs composed by both Barbara and Swanson, but with a fuller and sometimes elaborated sound due to the participation of many more talented musicians. These included **Jerry Garcia**, Ed Bogas, Bill Attwood, Mark Springer, John McFee and Tom Salisbury, to name a few. The best tracks probably remain the more acoustic numbers like *Sleepwalkers*, *While Waiting*, *The Vine*; or the lively *Ku*, *Milo And The Travelers* and *Live To Your Heart*.

In 1973, Barbara Mauritz became a solo artist and completed *Music Box*, a good - even if a little more mainstream - offering. Particularly noteworthy are two beautiful ballads, *Winter In The Valley* and the title track. The same year The Pointer Sisters went platinum with a cover of Barbara's *River Boulevard* (originally on *Bring Out The Sun*). In 1974 she wrote a music score for the movie "Where The Lilies Bloom", sharing the musical space with Earl Scruggs. The soundtrack was issued by Columbia (KC 32806).

In 1976, a bad road accident interrupted her live performances, major label recording deals and an eight year management contract with Bill Graham's Fillmore Management. Still in 1977 and 1978 Barbara collaborated with artists like Tom Salisbury and Chris Michie, but only in 1983 resumed writing again. More recently she has composed more than 150 commercials, including a Levi-Strauss one and you can hear her sing on albums by **Link Wray** (1973), Steve Douglas (1983) and Vince Wellnick (1998). Today she has plenty of new songs, runs an independent label called Citylife Records and a publishing company.

A new CD *Give Me Half A Chance* and a compilation of **Lamb** material are expected to be out soon.

David Hayes went on to work with **Jesse Colin Young** and Terry and The Pirates. (SR/GBi)

Lamb

| Personnel: | JOEL CHERNOFF | A |
| | RICK "LEVI" COGHILL | A |

ALBUMS:	1	LAMB	(Messianic LBA 1001) 1973 -
	2	LAMB II	(Messianic LBA 1002) 1974 -
	3	LAMB III	(Messianic LBA 1003) 1976 -
	4	SONGS FOR THE FLOCK	(Messianic LBA 1500) 1978 -

A Christian duo, unrelated to the other **Lamb** with Barbara Mauritz. They integrated rock with folk-rock, Jewish folk, pop, lamentations and even occasional hard-rock to produce a rather unique sound, with vocals in English and sometimes in Hebrew! (SR/KSt)

Lamp Of Childhood

Personnel:	JAMES HENDRICKS	gtr, vcls	AB
	BILLY MUNDI	drms	A
	FRED OLSEN	gtr	AB
	MIKE TANI	bs	AB
	GABRIEL MEKLER	perc, vcls	B

45s:	Season of The Witch/You Can't Blame Me	(Dunhill ?) 1967
	First Time, Last Time/	
	Two O'Clock In The Morning	(Dunhill ?) 1967
	Two O'Clock In The Morning /	
	No More Running Around	(Dunhill 4089) 1967

From L.A., this folk-rock group formed in the Autumn of 1966 and lasted through to June 1967. Their first single was a cover of the famous Donovan song. James Hendricks was married to Mama Cass from the **Mamas and Papas** and had been with her in the **Big Three** and the **Mugwumps**. Billy Mundi (ex-**Mastin and Brewer**) helped record the singles, but left in

October 1966 to join the **Mothers Of Invention**. He later played with **Rhinoceros** and on numerous sessions (**Stone Poneys**, **Fred Neil** etc.). A good guitarist, Fred Olsen would later play with **Mike Bloomfield** and **Brewer and Shipley**.

No More Running Around (co-written by Hendricks and Gabriel Mekler, the future **Steppenwolf** producer) has been compiled on *Penny Arcade, Dunhill Folk Rock, Vol. 2*. It's not certain if Gabriel Mekler was actually a band member, but he certainly helped out with the recordings and used the group's equipment to help start up **Steppenwolf**.

An unreleased **Lamp Of Childhood** track, *You're Gonna Get It In The End* was later covered by **The Nitty Gritty Dirt Band**. (SR/NW)

J.J. Lancaster

45:	Parade Has Passed Me By/So Unkind	(Date 1564)	1967

From Tulsa, Oklahoma, his *So Unkind* can also be heard on *Open Up Yer Door!, Vol. 1* (LP), whilst *Parade* is on the double cassette *Psychedelic Archives, Vol. 7: USA Garage*. (VJ)

Lance Romance

45:	California Summertime/Hollywood Nights	(Now)	1974

This 45 was one of **Kim Fowley**'s alter ego's - both sides can also be found on his *Living In The Streets* retrospective album. (WHn)

Lancers

45s:	The Witch/?	(Take 3 101)	196?
	See You In Seattle/?	(Lancelot)	196?
	Can't Help Falling In Love With You/ Head Of A Clown	(Lancelot 122)	196?
	True Blue/Your Summer Dream	(Lancelot)	196?

The Witch can also be heard on *Garage Punk Unknowns, Vol. 2* (LP). A Pacific Northwest outfit, possibly from Seattle, covering **The Sonics**' classic. (VJ)

The Lancers

Personnel incl:	IDOL	A
	TAYLOR	A

ALBUM:	1(A)	THE LANCERS	(Earsa 1003) c1965 ?

All the members of this band were Americans living in the Panama Canal Zone. Their rare album consists of instrumental tracks: *Hypo, Little Rockin' Greenie, Torture, Jack Rabbit, Ghost Freight*, combining covers and original material. (SR)

The Landlords

45:	I'll Return/I'm Through With You	(Reed 1069) 1967

From Boston. You'll find *I'll Return* on *New England Teen Scene, Vol. 2* (LP) and *New England Teen Scene* (CD). The flip, a diffident (despite the title) but affecting teen ballad, can be found on Arf! Arf!'s *No No No* (CD) compilation. (MW/LP)

Landslide

Personnel:	TOMMY CAGLIOTTI	drms	A
	ED CASS	vcls, perc	A
	BOBBY SALLUSTIO	bs	A
	BILLY SAVOCA	ld gtr	A

ALBUM:	1(A)	TWO SIDED FANTASY	(Capitol ST 11006) 1972 R2

LANDSLIDE - Two Sided Fantasy LP.

A New York band, they don't appear to have released any 45s for Capitol, but their album is an undiscovered gem. Kicking off with *Doin' What I Want* which featured slick rhythms and fine guitar, a high standard is set and equalled by *Creepy Feelin'* and the Johnny Winter-influenced *Everybody Knowns (Slippin')*, with its gruff vocals and fine guitar interplay. *Dream Traveler* rounds off Side One with some simply exquisite guitar work. Perhaps the album's finest moment is *Happy*, the closing track, which builds into an amazing climax. Recommended. (VJ)

Tony Lane and The Fabulous Spades

ALBUM:	1	TONY LANE AND THE FABULOUS SPADES	(Justice 133) c1967

Another Justice album. It probably contains beat/pop/frat rock or soul/lounge/club, or both.

Compilation appearances have included *Baby Please Don't Go* and *Baby, What You Want Me To Do* on *Green Crystal Ties, Vol. 7* (CD). (SR)

David Lannan

ALBUM:	1	STREETSINGER	(San Francisco SD 202) 1970 -

A hippie folksinger recorded in the streets, with cuts like *Hare Khrisna*. A kind of David Peel clone, but much weaker and best avoided.

Wait For The Light/Hare Khrisna and *Patterson's Song* also appear on a San Francisco sampler album, *San Francisco Sampler - Fall 1970*. (SR)

Laramie

ALBUM:	1	LARAMIE	(Mercury SR-61292) 1970 -

An obscure rural-rock group using banjo and fiddle. They covered *Ruby Tuesday* and **Tommy James**' *Crimson And Clover*. (SR)

Larry and The Blue Notes

Personnel:	BUDDY BATES	gtr	A
	DAN FLETCHER	bs	A
	MIKE GRIFFIN	drms	AB
	LARRY ROQUEMORE	vcls	AB
	LARRY SLATER	gtr	AB
	RANDY CATES	bs	B
	JACK HAMMONDS	keyb'ds	B

ALBUM: 1(A/B) THE MAJOR BILL TAPES, VOL 1 - LARRY
              AND THE BLUE NOTES   (Big Beat WIKM 33) 1985 UK

45s: All My Own/Night Of The Phantom   (Tiris 101) 1965
      All My Own/
      Night Of The Phantom   (20th Century Fox 573) 1965
   α The Phantom/She'll Love Me   (Charay 20) 1965
      Everybody Needs Somebody/She'll Love Me (Charay 20) 1966
   β Everybody Needs Somebody To Love/
      She'll Love Me   (Epic 9871) 1966
      Love Is A Beautiful Thing/In And Out   (Charay 44) 1966
      I'll Be True To You/In And Out   (Charay 44) 1966

NB: α issued as by The Mark Five. β Issued as by The Bad.

The first and one of the best garage bands to come out of Fort Worth in the sixties. Slater and Roquemore put the band together to play at a Halloween gig. Line-up 'A' dates from 1963, but line-up 'B' was the one that played on their 45s. Hammond had earlier played for Jack And The Rippers, a sixties Texan outfit that did not make it onto vinyl. Their first song was *Night Of The Sadist*, a spine-chilling recital of an attack by the Lake Worth Goat Monster whose legend the band fuelled. They took it to local entrepreneur Major Bill Smith, who feeling he had a hit on his hands, removed the word 'sadist' from the title and renamed the record *Night Of The Phantom*. It was soon leased to 20th Century Fox and gave the band a local hit. The group developed a penchant for recording under pseudonyms and later that year cut an inferior rehash of the song for a 45 released as by The Mark Five. For a latter 45 they used the pseudonym The Bad, and also toured as a bogus **Sir Douglas Quintet**.

In 1968 the band split when Slater and Roquemore went on to form a new outfit, Soul Purpose and Randy Cates joined Gypsy. Roquemore also had a solo 45, *Mrs Brown You've Got A Lovely Daughter/Just Stay* (Guyden 2124). The 'A' side was a U.S. No. 1 back in 1965 for Herman's Hermits.

Understandably, the band have been heavily compiled including: *Night Of The Sadist* on *Acid Dreams - The Complete 3 LP Set* (3-LP), *Acid Dreams Epitaph* (CD), *Back From The Grave, Vol. 4* (LP); *In And Out* on *Texas Flashbacks, Vol. 5* (LP), *Teenage Shutdown, Vol. 10* (LP & CD), *Flashback, Vol. 5* (LP), *Gathering Of The Tribe* (LP) and *Highs In The Mid-Sixties, Vol. 11* (LP); and *Night Of The Phantom* on *Back From The Grave, Vol. 1* (LP), *The Fort Worth Teen Scene - The Major Bill Tapes Vol. 2* (LP) and *Garage Kings* (Dble LP). (VJ)

Larry and The Loafers

45s: Panama City Blues / Til The End   (Reed 1061) 1961
(Partial   Panama City Blues / ??   (Heart # unkn) 196?
List)   Let's Go To The Beach / Who   (Shurfine 017) 1966
       α   Panama City Blues / ??   (Rock'n'roll Reunion 31041) 1980s

NB: α reissue 45.

HIGHS IN THE MID-SIXTIES Vol. 11 (Comp LP) including Larry and The Blue Notes.

From either Atlanta, Georgia or Pensacola, Florida. *Let's Go To The Beach* is a punk/surf number. Larry, their leader, was later involved in **The Thingies**.

Compilation appearances have included *Let's Go To The Beach* on *Victims Of Circumstance, Vol. 2* (LP), *Victims Of Circumstance, Vol. 2* (CD), *What A Way To Die* (LP) and *Hang It Out To Dry* (CD); *Panama City Blues '61* on *The Big Itch*; and the retake *Panama City Blues '62* on *The Big Itch, Vol. 2*. (VJ)

Larry and The Paper Prophets

45:   Can't Sit Around/Only One Thing   (Epic 10186) 1967

This was a one-off venture on Epic. The 'A' side, *Can't Sit Around*, has resurfaced on *Glimpses, Vol. 3* (LP). (VJ)

Lyn La Salle

45:   Randee Ram Jet / Takin' Life Easy   (A&M 889) 1967

A male singer, despite the name. *Randee Ram Jet* is a decent garage-punker with pounding drums and an interesting acid guitar, the flip is in **The Turtles** vein. Interesting but the 45 suffers from overproduction. (SR/HMa)

Laser Pace

Personnel: GEORGE BELL   perc   A
            W. G. CHRISTENSEN   drms, perc, vcls   A
            JIMBO DEE   synth   A
            D. DISTORTO   bs, mellotron   A
            MAUREEN O'CONNOR   gtr, vcls, mellotron   A
            LARRY PARSONS   keyb'ds   A
            CARL VANYOUNG   clarinet   A
            LARRY WOLF   soprano sax   A

ALBUM: 1(A) GRANFALLOON   (Takoma R 9021) 1973 SC

An experimental, avant-garde, progressive album also characterized by Maureen O'Connor's distinctive vocal style. Some of you could find this album 'psychedelic', but it's certainly not for garage fans. If progressive rock is your niche you could find this interesting and it's becoming rare. Lots of complex keys, mellotron and guitar and Maureen O'Connor's vocals are haunting.

The album cover is somewhat misleading, listing the band name and the album title in such a way that it's impossible to tell which is which. Consequently many dealers list the band as Granfalloon and title as *Laser Pace*. Chris Christensen (who is listed as W. G. Christensen on the cover), has however confirmed that **Laser Pace** was the bands name.

Christensen, who was married to Maureen O'Connor, had earlier played in **Opus 1** with Doug Decker (who may also be "D. Distorto" in the line-up above). (VJ/AMi)

Last Call Of Shiloh

Personnel incl: DIANNE MURRAY   A
                 JOHN MURRAY   A
                 JOHN ROSENBERRY   A

ALBUM: 1(A) LAST CALL OF SHILOH
                       (Last Call Records SRC 5136) c1970 R2

A super rare local Idaho religious guitar-rock album with male and female vocals and several long tracks (*Marriage Supper Of The Lamb*, *Great Day Of The Lord*). A number of copies turned up with no covers, the few others being housed in a b&w jacket featuring a pencil drawing of the face of Jesus.

The record was made circa 1969/70. The Murrays and Rosenberry went on to form **Living Sacrifice**, another Christian rock group. (CF/SR)

The Last Days

ALBUM: 1 THE LAST DAYS (LP 487) 1972 ?

A Christian folk-rock group from Texas, with guitars, flute, piano and ultra-frail vocals. Mostly acoustic tracks, but also some hard rock moments. (SR/KSt)

The Last Draft

45: It's Been A Long, Long Time/
Lovely To See You (PS) (Trans-Action 711) 1969

Late sixties 'soft-rock' from LaCrosse, Wisconsin, with a faithful cover of the Moody Blues on the 'B' side that could do with just a bit more oomph. (MW)

The Last Five

45: Kicking You/Weatherman (Wand WND 1122) 1966

Cool garage-beat from a Pacific Northwest outfit with a snappy and swingin' rhythm section. (MW)

Last Friday's Fire

See **Lynn Castle with Last Friday's Fire**.

Last Knight

45: Shadow Of Fear/? (Orlyn no #) 1968

A Chicago garage band. *Shadow Of Fear* features a fine fuzztone break and great drumming. Although the 45 had no Orlyn cat number, its RCA matrix dates it as 1968.

Compilation appearances include: *Shadow Of Fear* on *Pebbles Vol. 6* (CD) and *Psychedelic Disaster Whirl* (LP). (VJ/MW)

Last Nikle

Personnel:	ROGER BERTRAND	gtr	A
	LENNY McDANIEL	bs, vcls	A
	WALLY McDANIEL	keyb'ds	A
	CLAY MUSACCHIA	trombone	A
	JERRY ROUSELLE	drms	A
	GORDON SCHUMERT	trumpet	A
	MIKE SCORSONE	sax	A

ALBUM: 1(A) THE LAST NIKLE (Mainstream S/6122) 1969 -

45s: She's The One/? (Mainstream 706) 1969
Save Your Love For Me/? (Mainstream 708) 1969
Got To Be Somebody/
α I've Been Trying To Love You (Mainstream 712) 1969
α Confusion Road/
Groove On What You're Doin' (Mainstream 715) 1969

NB: α credited To Lenny McDaniel And The Last Nikle.

Beware! **The Nikle** were responsible for this horrid brass-rock album, which is just about the worst album on this interesting label. Collectors of psych and garage music steer clear. You have been warned! (VJ)

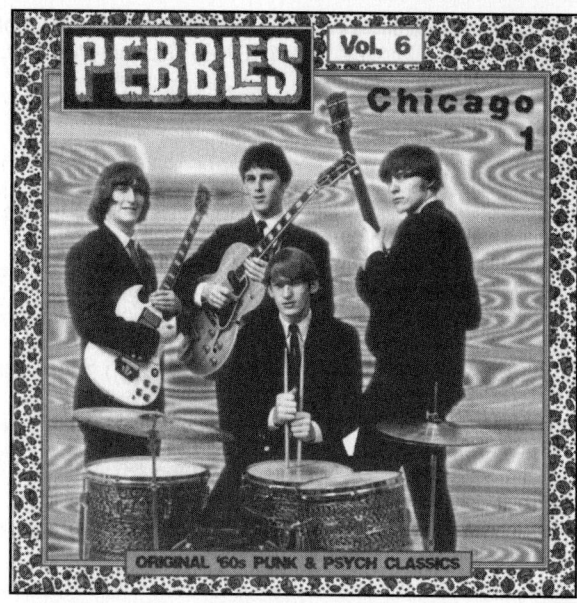

PEBBLES Vol. 6 (Comp CD) including Last Knight.

The Last Ritual

Personnel:	MICKEY DAVIS	piano, organ, harpsichord	A
	CHRIS EFTHIMIAN	drms	A
	GABRIEL	gtr	A
	KENNETH LEHMAN	alto sax, clarinet	A
	ROBERT LIGHTIG	bs	A
	SHARON MOE	french horn	A
	TONY SALVATORE	trombone	A
	JOHN SCARZELLO	trumpet, fluegel horn	A
	ALLAN SPRINGFIELD	vcls	A

ALBUM: 1(A) THE LAST RITUAL (Capitol SKAO 206) 1969 -

45s: Delighted, Strung Out And 25/
Talk About Time We're Wasting (Capitol 2495) 1969

NB: Both 45 cuts also appear on the album.

I've seen this minor collectable described as 'psychedelic' but it's really an experimental horn-rock album, with psychedelic influenced lyrics from Alan Springfield. It has a rather messy production, by **Tom Wilson** and unless you're a jazz or horn-rock connoisseur steer clear.

Springfield, Efthimian, Lehman and Scarzello ended up in a group called **Chelsea Beige**, who recorded a remake of **Last Ritual**'s *Heritage*. (VJ/LL/SR)

Last Times

45: Don't Tell Me / I Need Your Love (Togy 52866) 1966

From Marion, Ohio. Their garage ballad *Don't Tell Me* is on *Love Is A Sad Song, Vol. 1* (LP). (MW/GGI)

The Last Word

Personnel:	BERRY ABERNATHY	bs, vcls	A
	LEE HUGHES	gtr	A
	JERRY RUE	drms	A
	JOHNNY VASQUEZ	organ	A

45: Sleepy Hollow/Jump, Point, Shout (Downey 137) 1966

This classic record has now been revealed as the work of a studio group, comprising of players from Las Vegas. Abernathy and Rue had previously recorded for Downey as Sir Frog and The Toads. *Sleepy Hollow* is a spine-chilling punker, with snarling vocals telling of the singer's encounter with the headless horseman and a slow pulverising organ riff. You can find it, along with a great unissued punker, *Don't Call Me I'll Call You* on Big Beat's *Scarey Business* (CD).

Other compilation appearances have included: *Sleepy Hollow* on *Pebbles Vol. 8* (CD), *Best of Pebbles, Vol. 2* (LP & CD) and *Highs In The Mid-Sixties, Vol. 20* (LP). (VJ/RSe)

Last Words

Personnel:	MIKE BYRNES	ld gtr	A
	RICKY COOK	drms	A
	JOHNNY LOMBARDO	ld vcls, tambourine	A
	STEVE (SHROEDER) SECHAK	organ	A

ALBUM:	1(A)	LAST WORDS	(Atco SD 33-235) 1968 - HCP
45s:		Hot Summer Days/Bidin' My Time	(Boom BM 60014) 1966 -
		Can't Stop Loving You/Don't Fight It	(Atco 6498) 1967 78
		I Wish I Had Time/One More Time	(Atco 6542) 1967 105
		Mo'reen/Runnin' And Hidin'	(Atco 6579) 1968 -

A frustrating band that embraced many styles. Their debut 45 is moody beat-punk. Subsequently they'd vary from strident garage beat with some wicked guitar outbursts, to straight pop and brassy soul-tinged bombast. Their slightly fuzzy cover of **Paul Revere and The Raiders'** *Mo'reen* is O.K. but lacks conviction, whereas the flip is a much livelier affair with some excellent scorching guitar runs - the pick of the crop. Produced by Brad Shapiro and Steve Alaimo, the album is similarly patchy despite occasional fuzz outbursts. It features four originals and six covers: - Phil Spectors' *Be My Baby* (Ronettes) and *You've Lost That Lovin' Feelin'* (Righteous Bros) - the latter in overblown **Vanilla Fudge** style; the Beatles' *No Reply* is also ala **Fudge**; *The Kids Are Alright* (The Who); *Mo'reen* (**Raiders**); and an awkwardly beefed-up version of *A Basket Of Flowers* (by Florida folk-rockers **The Nightcrawlers**). They come across as a club/cabaret covers-band with an interesting choice of material but some clumsy re-arrangements. Two members were from Jersey City and other two from New York, where the band was based before relocating to Florida.

Compilation appearances include *Bidin' My Time* on *Acid and Flowers* (CD). (MW/SR)

James Late

Personnel:	JAMES LATE	vcls, acoustic gtr, hmca	A
	WOODY LEWIS	bs	A
	ALLAN NICHOLS	acoustic gtr	A
	BILLY SCHWARTZ	gtr	A
	JOHN SIOMOS	drms	A
	(EDDIE WILLIAMS	mellophonium	A)

| ALBUM: | 1(A) | FULTON FISH MARKET | (Metromedia) 1971 - |

Produced by Allan Nichols (who also worked with **Morganmasondowns**), this album is housed in a gimmick gatefold cover with a fish hook (!), as its songs are mainly centred around the New York Fulton Fish Market. **James Late** (real name Lategano) introduces his songs with some talking before every track and, if that was probably an original idea then, it makes the album quite difficult to listen to now. It's unfortunate as it contains some good folk-rock songs with acoustic guitars and harmonica plus some brilliant electric guitar parts played by Bill Schwartz (**Chelsea Beige**, Tom Fogerty). John Siomos was previously with **Chicago Loop** and **Buzzy Linhart**. (SR)

L.A. Teens

45s:	I'm Gonna Get You/	
	You'll Come Running Back	(Decca 31763) 1965
	All I Really Want To Do/Saturday's Child	(Decca 31813) 1965

Produced by Gary Usher, an L.A. outfit with a mixture of pop, beat and jangley folk-rock sounds hot on the trail of **The Byrds'** success.

Compilation appearances have included *All I Really Want To Do* on *Leaving It All Behind* (LP); *I'm Gonna Get You* and *You'll Come Running Back* on *Bad Vibrations, Vol. 2* (LP). (MW)

ACID AND FLOWERS (Comp CD) including Last Words.

Latter Rain

| ALBUM: | 1 | LATTER RAIN | (New Life Music 6102Q3) 1976 ? |

From Northern Kentucky, a rural progressive hard-rock group with wah-wah guitar and organ. Their album is comprised of eight original compositions with long guitar solos. Another rare private pressing, only 500 copies were pressed and it came housed in a nice sleeve. (SR/KSt)

The Laughing Kind

Personnel:	SOL CASSEB	drms	A
	BOB GEISSLER	bs, vcls	A
	KENT LIMING	gtr, vcls	A
	ABEL ORNELAS	keyb'ds, vcls	A
	JOHNNY SCHWERTNER	keyb'ds, vcls	A
	TOMMY SMITH	drms	A

45s:	Empty Heart/	
	I Could Have Showed You The Way	(Heat Wave 102) 1967
α	Empty Heart/	
	I Could Have Showed You The Way	(Orbit 1128) 1967
	I Who Have Nothing/Show Me	(Jox 066) 1967
	Shotgun/Sad Memories	(Jox 072) 1968

NB: α issued as by Tommy Smith.

This Texas outfit is most significant for including Tommy Smith later of **Red Crayola** and Johnny Schwertner of **Lavender Hill Express**. **The Laughing Kind** also made a 45 with Al Davis *Jeannie/Edge Of Love* (Dynamic 117).

Schwertner also played with **The Reasons Why** whilst both Bob Geissler and Kent Liming played with The Speidels and **The Swiss Movement**.

Compilation appearances include: *Empty Heart* on *The Cicadelic 60's, Vol. 4* (CD), *The Cicadelic 60's, Vol. 2* (LP) and *I Wanna Come Back From The World Of LSD* (CD). (VJ)

Andy Lauren

45:	I'm Too Big To Cry /	
	I Never Knew Such Happiness	(Kasper 105) 196?

A loungey singer from Cleveland, Ohio, who released several 45s. The above 45 recorded with the Persuaders has been described by dealers as 'garage' but is included here more as a warning - musically it's very borderline to our territory, being MOR-pop with a combo backing. (GGl/MW)

TEXAS FLASHBACK -THE BEST OF (Comp CD) including The Lavender Hour.

Lavender Country

ALBUM: 1 LAVENDER COUNTRY (Private Pressing) c1971 -

Released by a gay community center in Seattle, this album contains mostly country and country-rock sung by a guy with a really nasal voice, with very radical and militant lyrics. The exception is a folk-psych lesbian love song. Musically quite good and it's fairly easy to find. For curious collectors! (SR/JPn)

The Lavender Hill Express

Personnel:	LEONARD ARNOLD	gtr	A
	LAYTON DE PENNING	gtr	A
	JOHN SCHWERTNER	keyb'ds	A
	RUSTY WIER	drms	A
	JESS YARYAN	bs	A

45s:	Visions/Trying To Live A Life	(Sonobeat 102) 1967
	Watch Out/Country Music's Here To Stay	(Sonobeat 105) 1968
	Outside My Window/Silly Rhymes	(Sonobeat 110) 1968
	Mr. Peabody/Goin Back To Mexico	(MVL 101) 196?

One of Austin's most durable sixties outfits, they were formed in 1966 by Leonard Arnold and Layton DePenning from Baby Cakes, who had approached Rusty Weir and Jess Yaryan of **The Wig** and Johnny Schwertner from **The Reasons Why** to form a new band. Baby Cakes manager, booking agent and local D.J. Mike Lucas was chosen to be their manager.

The Sonobeat 45s, which were issued in picture sleeves, were actually recorded in a 'studio' set up at the famous Vulcan Gas Company club. Musically after an initial pop 45, they experimented in a country direction. Indeed when they split, Rusty Wier became an important figure in the local C & W scene and enjoyed a solo career. Schwertner was involved with **Plymouth Rock** who issued a 45 on Sonobeat and with the **Laughing Kind**. The remaining members went on to play in Genesee, a later Austin band. Most of them later achieved commercial success in other bands.

John Schwertner also played in **The Laughing Kind**. (VJ/MLs/JYn)

The Lavender Hour

Personnel:	JERRY COPE	drms	AB
	STEVE HEADLEY	ld gtr	A
	TOM PENA	bs	AB
	MIKE TEAQUE	vcls	AB
	SID TEMPLETON	gtr, keyb'ds	AB
	RONNIE SWONKE	ld gtr	B

45s:	I'm Sorry/Hang Loose	(Steffek 619) 1967
	I'm Sorry/Hang Loose	(Tribe 8323) 1967
	So Sophisticated/ I've Gotta Way With Girls	(Steffek 1929) 1967
	Ain't Too Proud To Beg/ Harry's Drive-In Church	(Steffek 1969) 1969

This outfit, which dates from December 1966, features among Houston's finest punk bands. Their first 45 was picked up by Huey P. Meaux's Tribe label and made No 65 on Billboard, but their finest moment was *So Sophisticated*. The flip to this 45 was later covered by The Chesterfield Kings. Their third and final effort was the work of line-up B. Swonke had previously played with Pena in The Coachmen, an earlier Houston act that did not record.

They disintegrated in 1969 and all except Swonke were invited to join **The Clique** although Teaque and Headley remained with them only briefly. They went on to record material for International Artists which remains unreleased and Teaque also played with an outfit called Just Us who made a 45 on Mod International. In 1982 Tom, Mike and Steve built their own recording stuido. They record progressive rock under the name Tiger's Claws and run Adonis Records.

Compilation appearances have included: *I've Gotta Way With Girls* on *Sixties Rebellion, Vol. 6* (LP & CD) and *Teenage Shutdown, Vol. 15* (LP & CD); and *So Sophisticated* on *Acid Visions - The Complete Collection Vol. 1* (3-CD), *Texas Flashback (The Best Of)* (CD), *Texas Flashbacks, Vol. 5* (LP) and *Flashback, Vol. 5* (LP). (VJ)

Arnie Lawrence and The Children of All Ages

ALBUM: 1 INSIDE AN HOUR GLASS (Embryo SD ???) 1970 -

An extremely strange album by a four-piece group plus a couple of small children, improvising on two side-long tracks for a mix of rock, jazz and pure weirdness. **Arnie Lawrence** would later become a session man, playing with Ian Hunter and **Blood, Sweat and Tears**.

Lawrence also played with Larry Coryell in the late sixties and has recorded some other albums, between jazz and rock. (SR)

Lawson and Four More

Personnel:	BILL DONATI	drms	A
	JOE GASTON	bs	A
	BOB LAWSON	gtr, vcls	A
	JOE LEE	ld gtr	A
	TERRY MANNING	keyb'ds	A

45s:	If You Want Me You Can Find Me / Back For More (PS)	(Ardent 105) 1966
	Half Way Down The Stairs / Relax Your Mind	(Ardent 107) 1967

A cool quintet from Memphis, Tennessee. Their first 45, *If You Want Me...*, is a fine Stones - cum - Pretty Things style shuffle-punker, whilst their second, *Half Way Down The Stairs* is a superb droning pop-punker.

After their first 45 they recorded a Batman cash-in 45 with Jim Dickinson as **The Avengers**.

Terry Manning had previously been briefly in the **Bobby Fuller Four** and stayed in Memphis where he became a respected sound engineer and producer for the Staples Singers, **Cargoe**, Isaac Hayes and ZZ Top. He also released a solo album.

Both tracks of the first single were written and produced by Jim Dickinson (it's the first record he ever produced), who was then working with several Memphis groups including: **The Jesters, Flash and The Memphis Casuals**.

After Lawson left the group the others carried on as the Goat Dancers and were involved in studio/session work (Lee, Gaston and Donati with **Honey Jug**) and several other groups.

Ardent was a short-lived local label managed by John Fry, the owner of the Ardent Studios, one of the more active Memphis studios. Fry later relaunched the label in the early seventies and signed a distribution deal with Stax. The best group of this second Ardent would be Big Star.

Compilation appearances have included: *If You Want Me You Can Find Me* on *Lost Generation, Vol. 1* (LP) and *The Essential Pebbles Collection, Vol. 2* (Dble CD); *Halfway Down The Stairs* (only partly featured - track cuts abruptly) on *Punk Classics, Vol. 3* (7" EP) and *Punk Classics* (CD); *Halfway Down The Stairs* (in it's full glory) on *Psychedelic Experience, Vol. 3* (CD) and *Electric Psychedelic Sitar Headswirlers, Vol. 7* (CD). (MW/SR/RHI)

The Laymen

45:   Practice What You Preach/Hey Joe   (Rise 101) 196?

An obscure band. The 'A' side, *Practice What You Preach*, has resurfaced on *60's Punk E.P., Vol. 4* (7" EP), *Moxie Punk EP Box Set*, and *Ya Gotta Have Moxie, Vol. 2* (Dble CD). (VJ)

Lazarus

Personnel:	GARY DYE	vcls, piano, organ	AB
	BILL HUGHES	vcls, gtr, piano	AB
	CARL KEESEE	vcls, bs	AB
	(NICK JAMESON	drms, perc	B)

ALBUMS: 1(A) LAZARUS   (Bearsville BR 2004) c1972 -
        2(B) A FOOL'S PARADISE (Bearsville BR 2135) 1973 -

This trio played soft-rock with vocal harmonies and some prog influences. After a first album, they recorded a final effort produced by Phil Ramone and Peter Yarrow (of Peter, Paul and Mary) recorded in New York and Minneapolis. For this, they were backed up by Nick Jameson (**American Eagle**), with orchestrations courtesy of Chris Dedrick (**Free Design**). It has not aged very well, to say the least.

Hughes, Keesee and Dedrick worked together again in 1977/78 for two obscure albums recorded by David Bradstreet. (SR)

The Lazy Eggs

Personnel:	TOM CARSON	ld gtr	AB
	BOB KRAUSE	drms	AB
	SAM MOCERI	(drms) keyb'ds	AB
	TOM POINT	ld gtr	A
	CLEM RICCOBONO	bs	AB
	GARY PRAUGE		B

45s: I'm Gonna Love You/
       As Long As I Have You   (Enterprise 5060) 1965
       I'm A Clown/Poor Boys Always Weep (Enterprise 5085) 1965

This Detroit area act started life as **TC and The Good Guys** in 1960 and were managed by Bob Swartz, who also managed **Bob Seger's Last Heard**. Indeed both bands knew each other well, although they never actually gigged together and Swartz failed to break either act... Still, **The Lazy Eggs**' superb blend of Beatlesque garage-beat helped them pack clubs in the Detroit / Michigan area and both 45s were local Top 10 hits. In particular *I'm A Clown* is an instantly likeable affair that bounces effortlessly along and oozes pure class - by rights it should have been a massive hit. The flip, *Poor Boys...* is more of a ballad with some simple effective guitar-work.

Sadly, their 45s were given little promotional support and in 1968, although still popular on the University circuit **The Lazy Eggs** split. A contributory reason, no doubt, was the unusual job Sam Moceri held, being a Police Officer by day and rock & roll musician by night could not have been an easy task - given the political turmoil of the time. Moceri and Carson later started a music business in 1970, the "Fiddlers Music Company" that lasted until 1980 and was well known in the Detroit area. (MW/BMi)

LAZY SMOKE - Corridor Of Faces CD.

Lazy Nickels

45:   35 Design / Struggle For Freedom   (Slug WR-5016) 1970

35 Design, which Erik Lindgren describes as a "hard psych thumper with thick flanging and tape regeneration effects", can be heard on his *A Lethal Dose Of Hard Psych* (CD) and *Seeds Turn To Flowers Turn To Dust* (LP & CD).

The flip is also described - "a lame swing ditty with blaring trumpet lines". The band is thought to have been based in Michigan. (MW/ELn)

Lazy Smoke

Personnel:	RAY CHARRON	drms	A
	BOB DOOR	bs	A
	RALPH MAZZOTTA	ld gtr, vcls	A
	JOHN POLLANO	ld vcls, gtr	A

ALBUM: 1(A) CORRIDOR OF FACES   (Onyx ES 6903) 1969 R5

NB: (1) counterfeited on vinyl (Heyoka HEY 206) 1986 and on CD (Afterglow 003) 1993. Reissued from the master tapes by the band on vinyl (Onyx 6803) 1993 (with booklet and bonus 45 in PS), and on CD (Arf! Arf! AA-065) 1997 with twelve bonus tracks.

This outfit came out of Northern Massachusetts with what some would argue is the ultimate psychedelic album, full of superb Beatles - like vocals and songs with great guitar work.

All the band's members had previously been in an outfit called The Road Runners, who released an acetate single, *You Don't Understand/One Light* and Charron, Mazzotta, Door and Pollano were helped out on the album by Joe Villanucci, who played electric piano on *Sarah Saturday*. Original copies of *Corridor Of Faces* now change hands for hundreds of dollars and are virtually impossible to find in the U.S. let alone elsewhere.

The album was recorded between 22nd June and 13th July 1968 on a budget of $1000 and emphasised the softer, more reflective side of the band, which was apparently a lot heavier live. Although lacking the range of the Beatles, the album perfectly establishes a mood - musing and introspective but not melancholy - with guileless vocals expressing a rapt, unhurried contentment. While not overtly psychedelic, the atmosphere strongly suggests the drug experience in its basking-in-the moment serenity. At times the band sound almost dead-ringers for Kaleidoscope (UK version) on tracks like *Salty People*, *How Was Your Day Last Night* and *Come With The Day*. *Under Skies* has all the evanescence and permanence of a hazy Summer's day, while *Sarah Saturday* and *How Did You Die* sound like parodies of Paul McCartney and John Lennon respectively. A beautiful album that keeps on improving with further acquaintance.

The Aggregation
MIND ODYSSEY
THE ELECTRONIC HOLE
THE AMERICAN DREAM
I Ain't Searchin'
Good News
THE BYRDS
EIGHT MILES HIGH
THE BUCKINGHAMS
BACK IN LOVE AGAIN
BLISS
OUT OF THE BACHS
The BACHS
Kind of a Drag
Lawdy Miss Clawdy
THE BUCKINGHAMS
The Dance At St. Francis
the BARRACUDA
"IT COULDN'T HAPPEN HERE"
STEREO
ASYLUM
"FIRST AND LAST"
THE BAROQUES
INCLUDES TWO EXTRA TRACKS
THE BLUE BEATS
EXTRA GIRL
She's the One
MONO

THE CYRKLE
ONE STEP BEYOND
THE CHOCOLATE WATCHBAND
STEREO
COUNTRY JOE & THE FISH
VANGUARD
Electric Music for the Mind
CIRCUS MAXIMUS
NEVERLAND REVISITED
STEREO
VAULT LP 117
TANYET
TRIBUTE TO
JIMI HENDR
JEFF COOPER AND THE STONED WINGS
Fire
Hey Joe
Git Some
Crossword
Blues For Jimi
Requiem For Jimi
& others
"Who Am I"
Country Joe and The Fish
THE CRITTERS
MR. DIEINGLY SAD
I KNOW
YOU CAN HAVE HIM
Chocolate Watch Band
Stereo
No Way Out
CHOCOLATE
WATCH BAND
THE CYRKLE
THE CYRKLE
"CAMARO"
PAUL REVERE & THE RAIDERS
"SS 396"
STEREO
The Inner Mystique Chocolate Watch Band

STEREO SP-7051
PSYCHEDELIC MOODS
A MIND EXPANDING PHENOMENA
SHADOWS ON THE WALL
YOUR CHOICE TO CHOOSE
WHEN RAIN IS BLACK
TRIP NO. 76
TURNED ON
IT'S ALL A PART OF ME
COLOR DREAMS
ON-OFF
PINK ETHER
PSYCHEDELIC MOON
CRYSTAL NIGHT
WAKE UP AND FIND ME
I'M A FOOL • SO MANY WAYS
DINO, DESI & BILLY
DINO, DESI & BILLY
The Rebel Kind
Don't Fight It
Straight Or Lame
UNITED INTERNATIONAL
THE DAISY CHAIN
LPM-13001 MONO
BREAK ON THROUGH
B/W END OF THE NIGHT
the doors
the doors
LIGHT MY FIRE
BREAK ON THROUGH
The Doors
PEOPLE ARE STRANGE
B/W UNHAPPY GIRL
the doors
ROCK 'N' ROLL MASS
THE EXCEPTIONS
THE FOREST OF BLACK
Worex Records
HARD ROCK
EARTHEN VESSEL
everlasting life
THE DAVID
ANOTHER DAY, ANOTHER LIFETIME
I Call My Baby STP
The Del-Vetts
A LITTLE RAIN MUST FALL
DON ... THE GOODTIMES
"I Could Be So Good To You"
A Gift From Euphoria
MIDNIGHT CONFESSIONS
THE EVER-GREEN BLUES
ELECTRIC
HAIR
DIRTY JOHN'S HOT DOG STAND
WITH KENNY PAULSON
RETURN FROM THE DEAD

HAiR
THE 31 FLAVORS
REAL FAR OUT • DISTORTIONS OF DARKNESS • FREE FUZZ • FREE DRUM
AQUARIUS/LET THE SUNSHINE IN • ONE-TWO-THREE-FOUR • PROTEST • HAIR

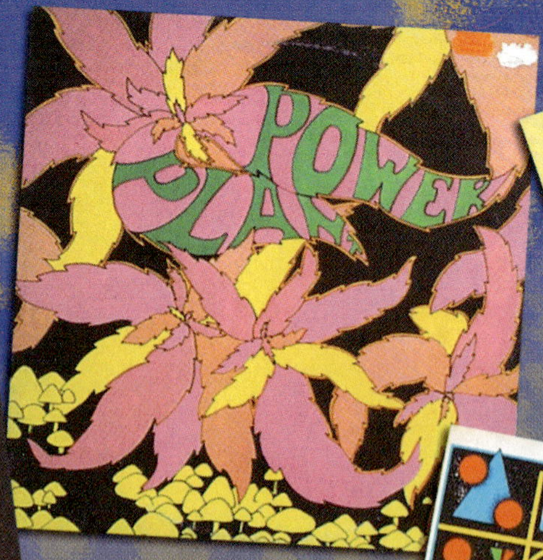
POWER PLANT

FRUMIOUS BANDERSNATCH

FIFTY FOOT HOSE
Cauldron

THE FREDRIC
PHASES AND FACES

STEREO
INTROSPECTION:
A FAINE JADE RECITAL

GANDALF

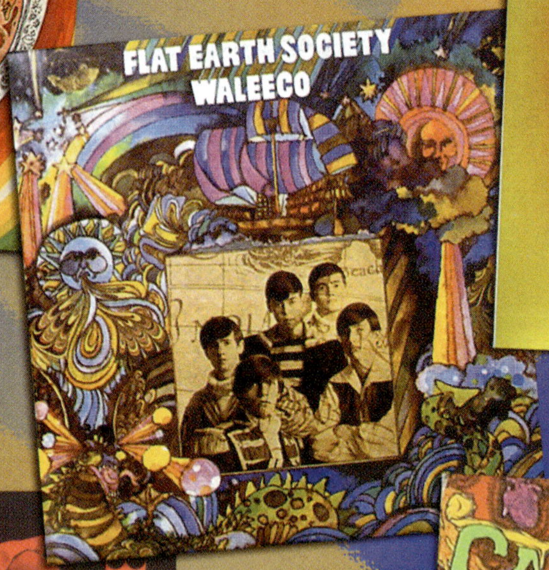
FLAT EARTH SOCIETY
WALEECO

LIGHT MY FIRE
THE FIREBIRDS

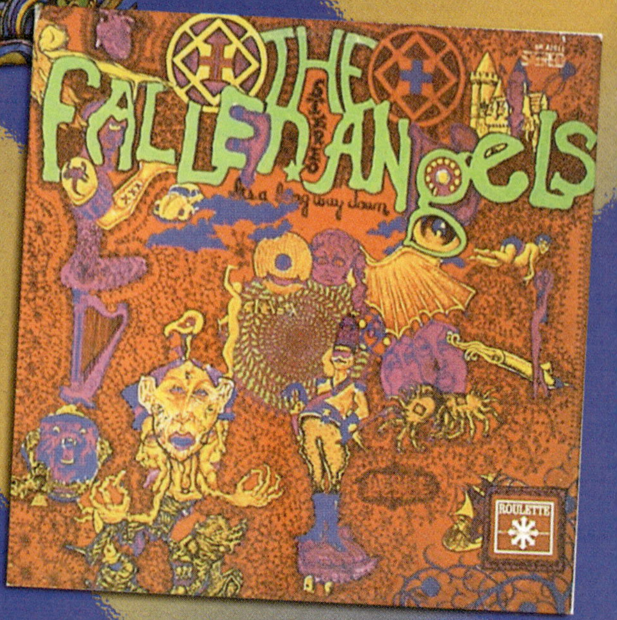
THE
FALLEN ANGELS
ROULETTE

stereo
PUBLIC RECORDS
STRICTLY FROM HUNGER
Accent
The Human Zoo
EMI
Capitol
The Insect Trust The Insect Trust The Insect Trust
FLASHES
ILL WIND
IMPALA SYNDROME
STEREO
THE JELLY BEAN BANDITS
MAINSTREAM
SPIRIT RECORDS STEREO
DANNY HERNANDEZ
& The ONES
BACK HOME
at
THE BREWERY
ICE
melting your mind

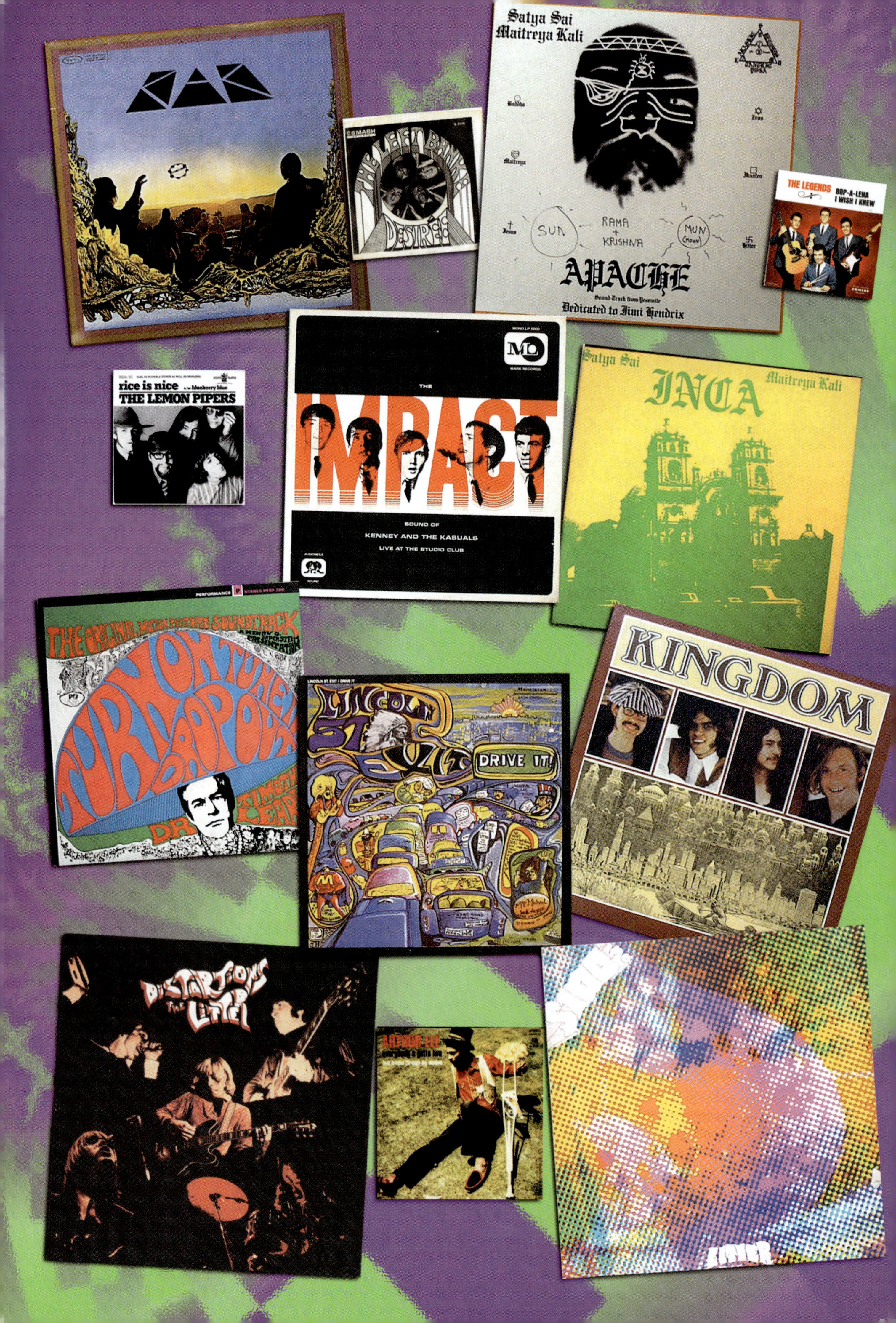

SITTING BY THE WINDOW
INDIFFERENCE
Mystic Siva
RFR-002
MAGIC
enclosed
MAXIMILLIAN
Neighb'rhood Childr'n
Love Special Delivery
Don't Go Away
"Sometimes You Just Can't Win"
"Mouse and the Traps"
BARRY McGUIRE
THIS PRECIOUS TIME
BARRY McGUIRE
DUNHILL
THE NEW COLONY SIX
CAN'T YOU SEE ME CRY
B/W SUMMERTIME'S ANOTHER NAME FOR LOVE
Flash
The Moving Sidewalks
MAGIC FERN
Something In The Air
Mandrake Memorial

Merryjuana
Pit Factor
THE ORIENT EXPRESS
The Other Half
STEREO
THE PEANUT BUTTER CONSPIRACY
IT'S A HAPPENING THING
PAPER GARDEN
Happy Trails
Quicksilver
Messenger Service
Capitol
THE OUTSIDERS
GIRL IN LOVE
WHAT MAKES YOU SO BAD, YOU WEREN'T BROUGHT UP THAT WAY
QUICKSILVER
Messenger Service
STAND BY ME
BEARS
EMI
QUICKSILVER
QUICKSILVER
Comin' Thru

THAT ACAPULCO GOLD
THE RAINY DAZE

THE ELECTRIC PRUNES

Relatively Clean Rivers
"RELATIVELY CLEAN RIVERS"

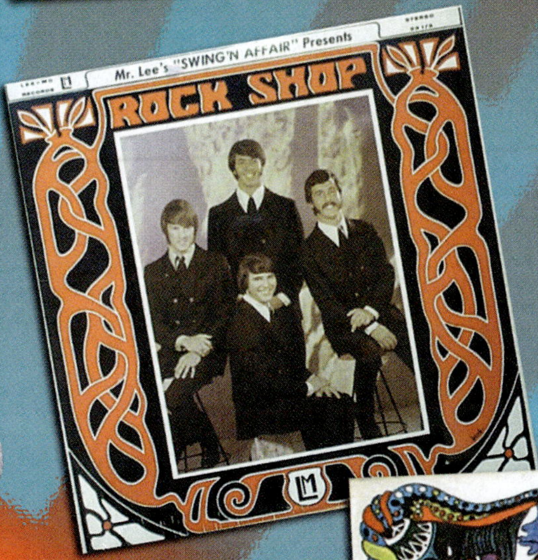
Mr. Lee's "SWING'N AFFAIR" Presents
ROCK SHOP

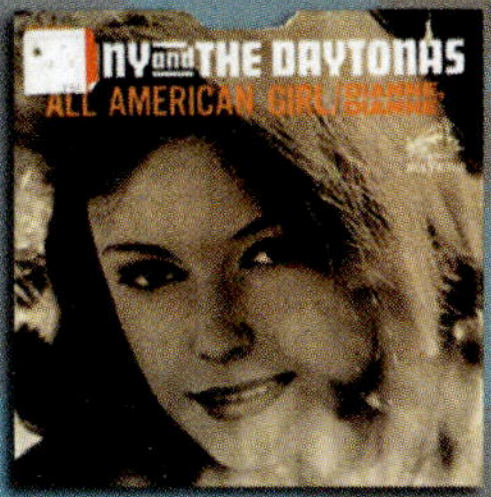
NY and THE DAYTONAS

THE RATIONALS

OPEN UP YOUR DOOR
RICHARD AND THE YOUNG LIONS

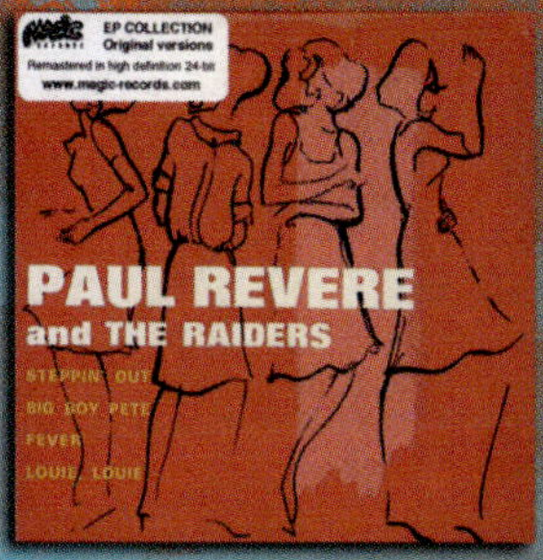
PAUL REVERE
and THE RAIDERS

the rising storm
calm before ...

Who is MRS. GRIFFITH
Ask THE RUBBER MAZE

THE RACKET SQUAD
TNT

THE STANDELLS
'LIVE' AND OUT OF SIGHT
SUNSET
POSTCARD FROM JAMAICA
B/W LITTLE ORPHAN ANNIE
THE SOPWITH "CAMEL"
THE SOPWITH CAMEL
SAGA OF THE LOW DOWN LET DOWN
THE SMOKE
The Smoke
STEREO
Pushin' Too Hard
Can't Seem To Make You Mine
THE SEEDS
HIP-POCKET
SEEDS
BORN TO LOVE/SRC
Big Casino Records
SPINDRIFT
LIBERATE
The Pirates of Penzance
IN THE NEW POP-ROCK SOUND
OF AN OPERETTA BY
GILBERT AND SULLIVAN
THE SONS OF CHAMPLIN LOOSEN UP NATURALLY
THE SAVAGE
RESURRECTION
THE SEEDS
A THOUSAND SHADOWS
the soothsayers
The Sneekers
Soul Sneaker
Sneaker Talk
THE STANDELLS
Can't Help But Love You
Ninety Nine And A Half
THE SACRED MUSHROOM

the time the album was released, the band had split up (Door had left
 oon after the album's recording that he wasn't included on the album
 , but Pollano cut one post-album 45 in a trio called **The Owl**, which is
  ilar style to the album. The twelve bonus tracks on the excellent Arf!
  CD, (which contains a full history of the band including many photos)
  mainly acoustic demos recorded in the Autumn of 1967, seven of which
  early versions of songs from the album.

 ano also recorded twelve further songs in Boston in the Winter of 1969
 n intended second album, but only two of them surfaced on a single,
 Always Seem To Know/It Happened Again that was included with the
 reissue on the Onyx label. Mazzotta later played with **Euclid** and was
  g in a country band in Massachusetts in the early-90s.

 recently a reunion album was recorded, *Pictures In The Smoke*.

 ilation appearances include: *There Was A Time* on *Love, Peace And
 , Vol. 1* (LP & CD); and *All These Years* on *The Arf! Arf! Blitzkrieg
 rack Sampler* (Dble CD). (VJ/LP)

and The Bishops Four

 nnel incl: R. ENGLAND   A
               L. STRIPLING   A

       I'm Gonna Show You Mary /
       It Doesn't Seem Fair   (Sevens International SI-1006) c1966

 om New Boston in the Northeastern corner of Texas, near Texarkana. *It
 Doesn't Seem Fair* is a cool minor-mood Searchers-style folk-rocker. The
  roup won through to the nationwide finals of the 1967 Battle Of The Bands
  mpetition held in Braintree, Massachusetts. They didn't make the Top 3
   their rendition of *Midnight Hour* was captured for posterity on
 N mandy's double (or 3-LP) compilation *Battle Of The Bands - Ridge
   ena*. (MW/AB)

Timothy Leary

ALBUMS: 1   THE PSYCHEDELIC EXPERIENCE
                                        (Broadside BRX 601) 1966 R1
          2   L.S.D.   (Pixie CA-1069)   1966 R1
          3   TURN ON, TUNE IN, DROP OUT (ESP 1027)   1966 SC
          4   TURN ON,TUNE IN, DROP OUT(soundtrack)
                                        (Mercury SR-61131)   1967 SC
          5   YOU CAN BE ANYONE THIS TIME AROUND
                                        (Douglas #1)   196? SC
          6   BEYOND LIFE WITH...   ( )   1998 -

NB: (2) counterfeited on CD. (3) has been reissued both on vinyl and CD, (4)
reissued on CD and vinyl (Performance PERF 389). (5) has also been reissued on
CD and vinyl by UFO in the U.K., and on CD by Rykodisc in the U.S.A.

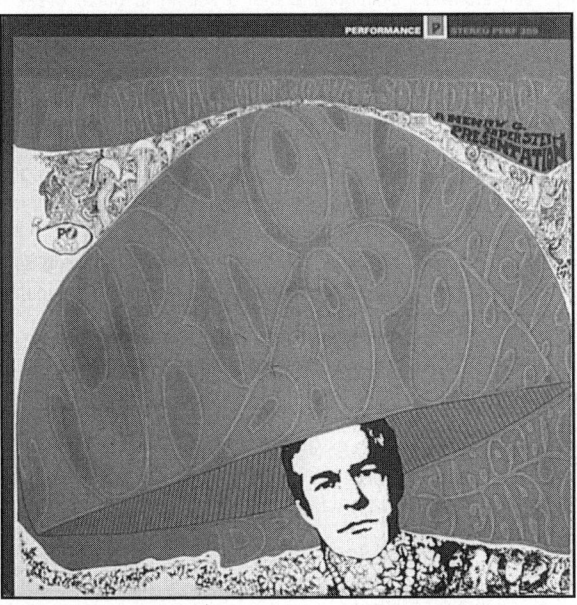

TIMOTHY LEARY - You Can Be Anyone This Time Around CD.

Leary was the 'high priest' of the psychedelic cult. Whilst Professor of Psychology at the University of Havard he had promoted the potential of psychedelic drugs as a vehicle for expanding the individual consciousness and for favourably modifying social attitudes. He was an extremely energetic writer and in his book, 'The Politics Of Ecstacy' as well as through a series of articles, reported speeches and interviews, he explained why he believed people should turn to psychedelic drugs to achieve a more humane and satisfying relationship with the universe and everyone and everything in it. Leary used every channel of communication open to him to expound the aims of the psychedelic movement and like his many other books, the above four albums, which are all now minor collectables, did just that. Needless to say that all this not only cost him his job but he was also imprisoned for ten years on the charge of possessing a very small quantity of 'pot'. The uncredited line-up on *You Can Be Anyone This Time Around* comprised **Hendrix** (bs), Stills, Sebastian and Miles.

Leary appeared on other acts albums, including Ash Ra Tempel and Dial-A-Poem Poets. He later escaped from prison, fled to North Africa and then to Switzerland, where his later publications continued to give him considerable influence as a 'high priest' of the psychedelic culture. He was a very important cult figure, indeed martyr, for very many young people.

Timothy Leary died on 31st May, 1996 at the age of 75. (VJ/BK)

The Leather Boy (aka Milan)

See **Milan** entry.

Leather-Coated Minds

Personnel: J.J. CALE   A
               ROGER TILLISON   A
               TERRYE TILLISON   A

ALBUM: 1(A)   A TRIP DOWN THE SUNSET STRIP
                                        (Viva V-36003)   1967 R2

NB: (1) issued on Fontana (5412) in the UK. Reissued on CD (Acid Symposium AS 001) 2001.

TIMOTHY LEARY - Turn On Tune In Drop Out (Soundtrack) LP.

This was a Los Angeles-based studio project involving J.J. Cale and the Tillisons, a folky couple who had migrated to L.A. and released one 45 as **Gypsy Trips** in 1965 which was subsequently covered by **The Electric Prunes** on their debut 45. The album, which was released on Amos "Snuf" Garrett's Viva label is notable for being Cale's first album appearance. He wrote the bands' original material and co-produced the album. It consists mainly of covers of the 'in' sounds of the time including *Eight Miles High*, *Psychotic Reaction*, *Over Under Sideways Down*, *Sunshine Superman*, *Kicks* (by **Paul Revere And The Raiders**), *Mr. Tambourine Man* and *Along Comes Mary*.

We previously had the Viva label down as being owned by **Leon Russell**, however this is incorrect as all the Viva 45s we've checked bear a logo and 'Snuff Garrett Productions'. **Leon Russell** did produce at least one 45 on the label - **The Shindogs** 45 on Viva 601- so perhaps he was an inhouse-producer for the label?

Roger Tillison later released a good solo album in 1970 *Roger Tillison's Album* with Jesse Ed Davis. (VJ/RAd/MW/SR)

The Leaves

Personnel:	JIMMY KERN	drms	A
	JIM PONS	bs	ABCD
	ROBERT LEE REINER	gtr	ABC
	BILL RHINEHART	gtr	AB
	JOHN BECK	sax, hrmnca, vcls	BCD
	TOM RAY	drms	BCD
	BOBBY ARLIN	gtr	CD

ALBUMS:
1(A) HEY JOE (Surrey) 1966 127 R1 HCP
2(C) ALL THE GOOD THAT'S HAPPENING (Capitol ST2638) 1967 - SC

NB: (1) also issued on Mira (3005) (SC), also issued in France (Festival FLOX 525) 1966. (1) and (2) reissued on CD by One Way, with the reissue of (1) including five extra bonus tracks. (2) was counterfeited during the eighties. There's also a French CD release *Leaves-1966* which includes some of their best known songs as well as previously unreleased and live material and a retrospective *The Leaves Are Happening* (Sundazed SC 11058) 2000.

45s: HCP
Too Many People/Love Minus Zero (Mira 202) 1965 -
Hey Joe/Be With You (Mira 207) 1965 -
You'd Better Move On/A Different Story (Mira 213) 1966 -
Be With You/Funny Little World (Mira 220) 1966 -
Hey Joe/Girl From The East (Mira 222) 1966 -
Hey Joe/Funny Little World (Mira 222) 1966 31
Too Many People/Love Minus Zero (Mira 227) 1966 -
Get Out Of My Life Girl/Girl From The East (Mira 231) 1966 -
Lemon Princess/Twilight Sanctuary (Capitol 5799) 1967 -

NB: There's also a reissue 45 *Hey Joe / Girl From The East* (Lost Nite LN 314) 197? and a French single with a group picture sleeve: *Too Many People/Girl From The East* (Festival SPX 143) 1966.

Beatlemania influenced Jim Pons to put together a band called The Rockwells, in 1964, whilst at San Fernando State College (California), using the $1,000 he was awarded following an automobile lawsuit. The original line-up soon set about performing classics like *Louie, Louie* and *Twist And Shout* at frat parties. The band's quest for self-improvement soon led them to add John Beck and replace Jimmy Kern with Tom Ray.

The band's break came when they got a residency at Ciro's in L.A. They then chose a new name **The Leaves** and had posters designed with pictures of themselves and a marijuana leaf saying 'The Leaves Are Happening'. **Pat Boone** heard them playing at the club one night and signed them for his Penthouse Production Company. Through this **The Leaves** were first signed to Mira and released their debut single *Too Many People/Love Minus Zero*. The 'A' side was a hit in Los Angeles.

The Leaves were the first band to release *Hey Joe* as a single. They made two previous recordings of *Hey Joe* before the third fuzztone version, which reached No. 31 in the U.S. charts. By now, Bobby Arlin had replaced Bill Rhinehart on guitar. **The Leaves** had now won a residency at the Whisky A Go Go in L.A., where they topped the bill, which on occasions included **The Grateful Dead**, **Big Brother and the Holding Company** and **Quicksilver Messenger Service**. In 1965 when they appeared at the Golden Bear in Huntington Beach, The Rolling Stones opened for them!

However, their follow-up single *Get Out Of My Life Woman* was less successful. 1966 saw Robert Lee Reiner become an acid casualty and he left the band. They continued as a quartet, but they lacked the fullness of sound necessary to make them click.

Then they signed for Capitol to produce a second album, augmented by studio musicians and strings. It contained some of their best material including *Lemon Princess* and *Twilight Sanctuary*, (issued on their last single), but it did not sell and Pons left during its recording to join **The Turtles**. Pons later did work with **Frank Zappa**. Beck and Arlin went on to produce a song called *Dead Time Bummer Blues* which was never released. Arlin later formed the power-trio, **The Hook**.

THE LEAVES - All The Good That's Happening LP.

Compilation appearances have included: *Hey Joe* on *Mayhem & Psychosis, Vol. 2* (LP), *Nuggets From Nuggets* (CD), *Nuggets - Original Artyfacts From The First Psychedelic Era 1965-1968* (Dble LP), *Nuggets, Vol. 1* (LP), *Excerpts From Nuggets* (CD), *Garage Monsters* (LP), *Tough Rock* and *Wild Thing*; *Love Minus Zero* on *Mindrocker, Vol. 5* (LP); *Hey Joe* and *Too Many People* on *Nuggets Box* (4-CD); *Too Many People* on *Nuggets, Vol. 2* (LP); and *Lemon Princess* on *Psychedelic Perceptions* (CD). (VJ/SR)

Leaves of Grass

Personnel:	DAVE EDEL	keyb'ds	AB
	BRADY FLOWERS	bs	ABC
	DON FREID	drms	A
	JERRY KOTEK	ld gtr	AB
	PAUL DURENBERGER	gtr	BC
	SHAG SMITH	drms	BC

45: Summertime/Crabs (MAAD 2668) 1968

The origins of this band lie in the Montgomery, Minnesota-based Uni-Qs who'd formed back in September 1965. The name change to **Leaves Of Grass** came in late 1966 and, given its association with marijuana, was well suited to the times. Their sole vinyl offering consisted of a very fast rendition of Gershwin's *Summertime* with a scorching guitar break in the middle backed by *Crabs*, which was penned by the band.

Don Freid got drafted in May 1968 with Jerry Kotek and Dave Edel departing soon after. Shag Smith and Paul Durenberger were recruited from Cambridge Heresy but by then the band was inescapably in the twilight of its career.

Compilation appearances include *Crabs* on *Hipsville, Vol. 3* (LP).

There was also another **Leaves Of Grass** based in L.A. and featuring Dennis Wilson's friend and collaborator Stephen Kalinich. Their name was a reference to Walt Whitman. (VJ/JFr)

Leaves of Grass

Personnel incl:	RONNIE CHASSNER	vcls	A
	JERRY COHN	gtr	A
	ALBERTO DeALMAR	ld gtr	AB
	BILL SABELLA	keyb'ds	AB
	DOUG DAMICO	ld vcls	B
	KENNY THOMAS	bs	B
	RICK THOMAS	drms	A? B

45:	All This Is Right /	
	City In The Rain	(Platinum PLP 2001) 1968

A Miami band formed by Sabella (ex-**Burgundy Blues**), DeAlmar (ex-**Pods**) plus ex-**Gents Five** members including Cohn and Chassner. Their sole 45 is bright harmony flower-pop. Sabella and DeAlmar later relocated to Gainseville and formed Celebration. (MW/JLh)

Barry Lee and The Actions

Personnel incl: BARRY LEE   A

45s:	Things Gotta Change / Make It	(Redda 13143/4) 1964
	Things Gotta Change / Make It	(Veep 1201) 1964
	Try Me / For Such A Little Wrong	(Wine And Roses 2002) 1966
	Try Me / For Such A Little Wrong	(Ascot 2226) 1966

From Cleveland, Ohio. Their catchy Invasion-pop effort *Try Me* features on *Let's Dig 'Em Up!!! Vol. 1* (LP). (MW)

Billy Lee and The Rivieras

Personnel:	JOHNNY "BEE" BADANJEK	drms	A
	EARL ELLIOTT	bs	A
	JOE KUBERT	gtr	A
	JIM McCARTY	ld gtr	A
	MITCH RYDER (BILLY La VERE)	vcls	A

45:	You Know / Won't You Dance With Me	(Hyland) 1964

NB: (1) reissued by Sundazed (S 117) in 1996 on blue wax with a PS.

The first and very rare 45 by a quintet from the Detroit suburbs who'd hit bigtime as **Mitch Ryder and The Detroit Wheels**. Available again thanks to Sundazed, *You Know* is a hand-clappin' frat raver whilst the flip's a mid-pace Merseybeat-flavoured mover. (MW)

Frankie Lee

45:	Another Love/	
	I Love The Go Go Girls	(International Artists IA-104) 1966

As there's a band Judas Priest, Bob Dylan will be glad to learn there's a singer **Frankie Lee** too! On the 'A' side there's a fairly succesful pop effort with a slight folk touch. The 'B' side is stolen from *Watermelon Man*, though not as overtly as **Future Shock**. (MK)

Terry Lee

ALBUM:	1	MAGIC MUSIC	(Stone) 1971 R1

From Pittsburgh, an acid garage psych singer with demented vocals. **Terry Lee** was previously the producer of the **Fantastic Dee-Jays**. (SR)

The Left Banke

Personnel:	MICHAEL BROWN (LOOKOFSKY)	piano	A CDE
	GEORGE CAMERON	drms, (vcls)	ABC EFG
	WARREN DAVID	drms	A
	TOM FINN	bs	ABC EFG
	STEVE MARTIN	vcls, drms	ABC EFG
	JEFF WINFIELD	gtr	B
	RICK BRAND	gtr	C E
	BERT SOMMER	gtr	D
	TOM FEHER	vcls, gtr	G

HCP

ALBUMS:	1(A/B/C)	WALK AWAY RENEE/PRETTY BALLERINA	
			(Smash SRS 67088) 1967 67 -
	2(E)	THE LEFT BANKE TOO	(Smash SRS 67113) 1968 - SC
	3(-)	AND SUDDENLY IT'S ... THE LEFT BANKE (UK)	
			(Bam-Caruso KIRI 021) 1984 - -
	4(-)	THE HISTORY OF THE LEFT BANKE	
			(Rhino RNLP 123) 1985 - -
	5(-)	VOICES CALLING (UK)	(Bam-Caruso KIRI 045) 1986 - -
	6(-)	WALK AWAY RENEE (mini-LP) (UK)	
			(Bam-Caruso PABL 036) 1986 - -
	7(-)	STRANGERS ON A TRAIN	( ) 1986 - -
	8(-)	THERE'S GONNA BE A STORM - THE COMPLETE RECORDINGS 1966 - 69	
			(Mercury 848 095-2) 1992 - -

NB: (3) reissued in 1988 with new cover and two additional tracks. (8) issued on CD.

EP:	1	Adverts: Coca Cola/Hertz/Toni Hair Spray	(Winfield Boot) 1990

HCP

45s:	Walk Away Renee/	
	I Haven't Got The Nerve	(Smash 2041) 1966 5
	Pretty Ballerina/Lazy Day	(Smash 2074) 1966 15
	Ivy Ivy/And Suddenly	(Smash 2089) 1967 119
	She May Call You Up Tonight/	
	Barterers And Their Wives	(Smash 2097) 1967 120
	Desiree/	
	I've Got Something On My Mind (PS)	(Smash 2119) 1967 98
	Dark Is The Bark/My Friend Today	(Smash 2165) 1968 -
	Goodbye Holly/Sing Little Bird Song	(Smash 2198) 1968 -
	Bryant Hotel/Give The Man A Hand	(Smash 2209) 1969 -
	Nice To See You/	
	There's Gonna Be A Storm	(Smash 2226) 1969 -
	Myrah/Pedestal (PS)	(Smash 2243) 1969 -
	Walk Away Renee/Pretty Ballerina	(Smash 1416) 1970 -
	Queen Of Paradise/And One Day	(Camerica CS 0005) 1978 -

The brainchild behind this band was Michael Brown, who'd been born in New York as Michael Lookofsky. He'd undergone a classical musical training and his father, Harry, was a respected musician who owned a recording studio and gave his son much encouragement in his career as a producer and pianist. Brown's first disc was a 45 in 1965, *It's Alright Ma (I'm Only Bleeding)/They Just Don't Care*, which was credited to an outfit called **Christopher and The Chaps**. The 'A' side was a Bob Dylan cover, the flip was written by M. Lookofsky and B. Jerome (whoever he was) and produced by Harry Lookofsky's World United Productions. However, it soon vanished without trace.

Brown resurfaced soon after with line-up 'A' of **The Left Banke**, although on their debut 45 *Walk Away Renee*, which appeared on Smash in July 1966 and eventually made it into the Top Ten in November that year, Harry Lookofsky made use of session musicians. It seems that the musical abilities of some group members were rather dubious. The song was later covered by The Four Tops giving them a massive U.K. hit. After the follow-up, *Pretty Ballerina*, had also made the Top 20, the band began work on their debut album. Around this time Jeff Winfield was replaced by Rick

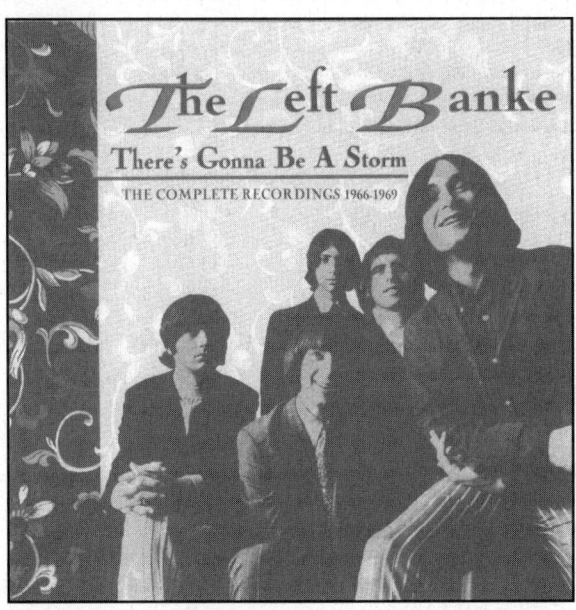

THE LEFT BANKE - There's Gonna Be A Storm CD.

Brand, a talented guitarist and songwriter. The album was a successful vehicle for Michael Brown's songwriting talents, his father's production skills (making use as it did of studio techniques and session musicians) and Steve Martin's haunting vocals. It's a very consistent album and, aside from the first two singles, it featured several other gems notably *Shadows Breaking Over My Head*, *She May Call You Up Tonight* and *I've Got Something On My Mind*, it's rather sad, therefore that the group subsequently collapsed when Michael Brown announced he wanted to experiment and compose in the studio and wouldn't tour with the band anymore. Hereafter, the band's history becomes rather complex with both the remaining four members and Brown (who'd put together a new line-up (D)) claiming the name. Brown and Tom Feher (from (C)) penned another lovely song, *Ivy Ivy*, which was released as a follow-up 45 and later withdrawn when the other four band members demanded that radio stations boycott the disc. *She May Call You Up Tonight* was released instead, but neither 45 made any commercial impression. An attempted reconciliation took place in September 1967 and another Brown/Feher composition *Desiree* was issued in the hope of relaunching the group. However, radio stations tended to steer clear of it and the anticipated commerical comeback just did not happen. At this point Brown quit the group but the remaining members soldiered on producing a brace of good 45s:- *Dark Is The Bark*, *Goodbye Holly* and *Bryant Hotel* - which came nearer to the 'group' sound as opposed to orchestrated backing that Brand and the other remaining members wanted. They also released a further album, *Too*, which suffered overall from Brown's absence but matched their earlier effort in its finest moments (particularly with *There's A Storm Coming*). It was generally ignored and after just one further 45, *Myrah* (which has become the band's rarest 45), the band (by now a trio (line-up E)) gave up the ghost, shelving plans for a projected third album with just one cut left in the can.

Brown went on to form **Montage** in 1969, which was really another vehicle for his songwriting and production skills and later he formed **Stories** (in 1972) and The Beckies (in 1976). More recently, circa 1998, he was responsible for producing / engineering / songwriting and providing keyboards on Yvonne Vitale's *On This Moment* CD. Sadly, the album, on the aptly named "Endangered" record label, was quickly withdrawn and less than 200 copies are thought to have survived. **Bert Sommer** became an actor in the Broadway production of "Hair", had a minor hit single with *We're All Playing In The Same Band* in 1970, and died of liver failure on July 23 1990.

The Bam-Caruso compilation, issued in 1982, rekindled some interest in the band. It was reissued in 1988 with two additional cuts, *Walk Away Renee* and a mono version of *Foggy Waterfall* (the one track in the can for the third and never completed album). *Voices Calling* was taken from the master tapes of a 1978 reunion of line-up E. This and all the other retrospective compilations except for *There's Gonna Be A Storm - The Complete Recordings 1966 - 69* (which contains both their original albums, as well as several rare bonus tracks) are now deleted. With their lavish orchestration and complex arrangements, this baroque-rock outfit is still lovingly remembered by many psychedelic rock fans.

Compilation appearances have included: *Walk Away Renee* on *Highs Of The Sixties*; *Desiree* on *More Nuggets* (CD); and *Pretty Ballerina* on *Nuggets, Vol. 11* (LP); The band's Coca Cola ad from 1967 can also be heard on *From The New World, Vol. 1* - one of three adverts they which has also featured on a recent bootleg EP. *From The New World Vol.1* also includes Christopher and The Chaps' *They Don't Care*.

Tom Finn had earlier been in **The Magic Plants**. (VJ/MW/LP)

Lefty and Leadsmen

45:	Wildwood Fun/Changing	(Go And Ce 103) 196?

An obscure Pittsburgh punk era band. You can check out *Wildwood Fun* on *Scum Of The Earth* (Dble CD) and *Scum Of The Earth, Vol. 2* (LP). (VJ)

Legend

Personnel:	E. BROOKS		A
	B. CORSO		A
	S. ROMANS		A

THE LEGENDS - High Towers CD.

ALBUM:	1(A)	LEGEND	(Megaphone M/S 101) 1968 R1/R2
45s:		The Kids Are Alright/Baby Blue	(Megaphone 701) 1968
		Portrait Of Youth/Enjoy Yourself	(Megaphone 703) 1968
	α	I Love The Little Girls/I Know	(Megaphone 705) 1968
	α	Shirley Temple Curls/ Shirley Temple Curls (instr)	(Megaphone 705) 1968

NB: α issued as by **Mike Kelly & Legend**, the *Shirley Temple* variation of the 45 may only have been issued as a promo.

Originally from Colorado, this five-piece band relocated to Los Angeles and later became **Dragonfly**, who also recorded for the same label.

The material on this album largely predates the psychedelic era and is full of cover versions (eg. Reg Presley's *With A Girl Like You*, Dylan's *Baby Blue* and Pete Townsend's *The Kids Are Alright*). A few cuts, like *Where Oh Where Is Mother* contain some good guitar playing with psychedelic undertones and the album ends with a little sitar solo.

All but the first 45 feature non-album tracks. *Enjoy Yourself* is on *A Lethal Dose Of Hard Psych* (CD), whilst *Portrait Of Youth* is also on *Boulders, Vol. 11* (LP) and *Ya Gotta Have Moxie, Vol. 2* (Dble CD). It was later re-recorded for their album as **Dragonfly**. (VJ/MW)

The Legends

Personnel:	DAN HARTMAN	electric piano, organ, gtr	ABCD
	DAVE HARTMAN	gtr	AB
	RALPH SWARTZ	drms	A
	DENNY WOOLRIDGE	bs	AB
	LARRY SADLER	drms	BCDE
	JOE CALEOIERO	bs	CDE
	LARRY SWARTZWELDER	gtr	C E
	DEAN LESCALETTE	gtr	E

ALBUM:	1	HIGH TOWERS (Dble CD)	(Arf! Arf! AA-086/7) 2001
45s:		Why/Baby Get Your Head Screwed On	(Bridge Society Up 2202-7-13) 1968
		Keep On Running/Cheating	(Bridge Society Up 2204) 1968
		High Towers/Fever Games	(Railroad House 12003) 1969
		Sometimes I Just Can't Help It/ Jefferson Strongbox	(Legends no #) 1969
		Rock And Roll Woman/Problems	(Heart CS 7672) 1973
		Rock And Roll Woman/Problems	(Epic 5-10937) 1973
	α	If I Had A Nickel / Remember What I Told You	(Frog FR-01) 1992

NB: α is a limited edition 45 of two Hartman-penned tracks from 1969.

Hailing from Harrisburg, Pennsylvania, **The Legends** set out as a soul band but soon got into rock. However, this soon led to the departure of their original drummer, Ralph Swartz, who hated rock, and his replacement by Sadler.

Soon after their debut single was released in early 1968 with the above-mentioned line-up. The 'A' side, *Why*, was a mellow, bluesy ballad - an attempt at commercialism and it was a local hit. The flip, *Baby Get Your Head Screwed On*, was an early Cat Stevens' composition, which the band rearranged into a driving rock song.

Their follow-up 45, did not stray much from the original versions. It featured Larry Swartzwelder on guitar as Dave Hartman was drafted for the Vietnam war. This also was a local hit.

Their third single, *High Towers*, was cut in 1969. Dan Hartman played guitar on this as Swartzwelder had gone into service. Joe Caleoiero had joined the band on bass. This was the band's most stable line-up and they sounded much like **The Jimi Hendrix Experience**, performing many of his songs in their live shows. *High Towers* included wah wah effects, electric piano, double tracked vocals and dreamy **Nazz**-like harmonies and was the band's most popular single. The 'B' side, is equally inspired by **Hendrix** / Cream.

The band was arguably on the verge of a breakthrough when its leader, Dan Hartman, departed to join The Edgar Winter Group and later embarked on a solo career. However, they soldiered on and were rejoined by Swartzwelder upon his return from service and added Dean Lescalette (rhthm gtr). The 'A' side of their final single, *Rock And Roll Woman* was nonetheless produced and written by Hartman. Initially issued on Heart Records (CS 7672), it was at Hartman's instigation later issued by Epic (5-10937). The band planned a single for Epic, but this did not materialise, although they carried on playing until 1975 before calling it quits: Caleoiero went on to play in a pop R&B band, The Class Act. Sadler became a session musician for Olivia Newton-John and John Miles among others and managed funk band, Positive Force, and co-managed Skyline Records.

The High Towers double-CD retrospective comes with a lavish 24-page booklet. The first CD includes nine tracks (seven previously unissued) cut in 1969 and two early 1968 singles (including a freakbeat cover of Double Feature's *Baby Get Your Head Screwed On*), a rare promo flexi, a 1972 radio spot and a CD-Rom bonus of a 1973 film short. The second CD mostly comprises 1965-66 demos of British invasion covers.

Compilation appearances have included: *High Towers* on *Psychedelic Patchwork* (LP) and *30 Seconds Before The Calico Wall* (CD); *Cheating* on *Sixties Rebellion, Vol. 15* (LP & CD); and *Fever Games* on *Brain Shadows, Vol. 2* (LP & CD). (VJ)

The Legends

45:	I'm Just A Guy/I'll Come Again	(Fenton 2512) 1967

A different band from Holland, Michigan, who formed in 1964 and won the Holland Battle Of The Bands in 1965. Two members later joined The Traffic Jams who used to back **Ray Hummel III** when he couldn't get **The Ju Ju's**.

Compilation appearances include: *I'll Come Again* on *Let 'Em Have It!, Vol. 1* (CD), *Back From The Grave, Vol. 1* (LP), *Chosen Few, Vol's 1 & 2* (CD), *The Chosen Few, Vol. 2* (LP), *Garage Kings* (Dble LP) and *Highs In The Mid-Sixties, Vol. 5* (LP). (VJ)

The Legends

Personnel incl:	BILLY JOE BURNETTE	vcls
	LARRY FOSTER	rhythm gtr
	SAM McCUE	vcls, ld gtr
	JOHN RONDEL	ld gtr
	JERRY SCHILS	bs
	JIM SESSODY	drms

ALBUMS:	1	LET LOOSE	(Ermine 101) 1962
	2	LET LOOSE	(Capitol 1925) 1962
	3	RUN TO THE MOVIES	(Capitol Custom No #) 1963

45s:	Lariat / Gail (PS)	(Key 1002) 1961
	Say Mama / My Love For You	(Ermine 39) 1962
	Lariat / Late Train	(Ermine 41) 1962
	Bop-A-Lena / I Wish I Knew (PS)	(Ermine 43) 1962
	Temptation / Marionette (PS)	(Ermine 45) 1962
	Run To The Movies / Summertime Blues	(Capitol 5014) 1963
	Here Comes The Pain / Don't Be Ashamed	(Warner Bros. 5457) 1964
	Just In Case / If I Only Had Her Back	(Parrot PAR 45010) 1965
	Alright / How Can I Find Her	(Parrot PAR 45011) 1965
	Raining In My Heart/How Can I Find Her	(Thames T-104) 1966
α	How Can I Find Her / Raining In My Heart	(Date 2-1521) 1966

NB: α released as the Legend.

Sometimes referred to as Sam McCue's Legends, this Milwaukee group were also known as the Canadian Legends whilst they were in Miami - why 'Canadian' I don't know unless, like the **Five Canadians** from Texas, it was a trick to get more interest as exotic foreigners in the wake of Invasion-mania. They spent considerable time in the mid-sixties down in Florida and continued to release 45s whilst there, causing them to be regarded as a Florida band too.

I've yet to hear any of their pre-64 material, but all their 45s from 1964 onwards are recommended to fans of pure sixties Invasion-flavoured beat-pop. Their use of melody, three-part harmonies and clear ringing guitars is more reminiscent of the Searchers than the Beatles - particularly *How Can I Find Her*, *If I Only Had Her Back*, *Here Comes The Pain* and their rendition of Buddy's *Raining In My Heart*. Yeah, for the most part they're sultry beat ballads but they can belt it out too - especially on their version of Ross-Vanadore's *Alright*, featured on *Off The Wall, Vol. 1* (LP). This song was previously done by Houston's **Coastliners** and later by Palmyra Wisconsin's **Madadors**. Sam McCue would later feature in **Crowfoot** in the early seventies.

Jerry Schills also played with Florida's **Birdwatchers**.

For fuller (and doubtless more accurate) details on this band seek out a book on Wisconsin bands 'Do You Hear That Beat' by Gary Myers. (MW)

J. Leland Braddock

ALBUMS:	1	EVIL IS ON MY MIND	(Private Pressing) 1975 SC
	2	THAT SECOND MILE	(Private Pressing) 1976 SC

A bluesy folk singer/songwriter, his privately pressed albums are beginning to be sought-after by some collectors. (SR)

LET EM HAVE IT! (Comp CD) including The Legends.

THE LEMON DROPS - Crystal Pure LP.

Lemon Drops

Personnel:			
	JEFF BRAND	bs	ABCD
	BOBBY LUNAIK	gtr	ABCD
	DANNY SMOLA	vcls	ABCD
	GEORGE SORENSON	ld gtr	A
	EDDIE WEISS	ld gtr	ABCD
	GARY WEISS	drms	ABCD
	RICKY ERICKSON	ld gtr	BC
	DICK SIDMAN	vcls	CD

ALBUMS:	1(-)	CRYSTAL PURE	(Cicadelic CIC 984) 1985
	2(-)	SECOND ALBUM	(Cicadelic CIC 982) 1987
	3(-)	CRYSTAL PURE	(Collectables COL-CD-0517) 199?

NB: (3) is a 24 track CD compilation.

45:	I Live In The Springtime/Listen Girl	(Rembrandt 5009) 1967

NB: *I Live In The Springtime* was issued on Rembrandt 5009 in two different ways: The more common issue (if a rare single like this could be considered common) is missing the drums and bass. The lesser seen pressing has the exact same label, but it has the drums and bass and the guitar is further down in the mix. We can only summise that they took the stereo mix and issued the left channel (in mono) on one pressing and the right channel (in mono) on the other pressing. It's not known if the two variations share the same dead wax markings.

This band formed in the Chicago, Illinois, suburb of McHenry in 1966. Despite its repetitive lyrics the band's only 45 *I Live In The Springtime*, has a strong enough melody to suggest that better things could have laid ahead.... but as it turned out, none of their other 1967-68 recording sessions were released on record until the mid-eighties.

Ricky Erickson (ex-**The Nuchez**) was brought in to do guitar on the 45 after the band's original guitarist (George Sorenson) had quit prior to the recording and *I Live In The Springtime* did get some airplay in New York. Consequently the **Lemon Drops** recorded a second 45, the hard-rockin' *It Happens Everyday* backed by a Ricky Erickson composition *Alone*, at the RCA Studios in Chicago, but it was never released. They then recruited a new 17-year-old singer Dick Sidman and began working on an ambitious new project with tablas, flowery harmonies and numerous special effects and ran up a studio bill of $1,200 that Reggie Weiss, the owner of Rembrandt Records couldn't pay. Only in 1985 were the master tapes from this session released as *Crystal Pure*.

In their quest for major label interest the band proceeded to record a live album over two evenings at Weiss' home. They took the tapes to several Hollywood labels but none were interested and losing heart the band actually split in 1968. However, the following month the Weiss family moved to Phoenix, Arizona, and by chance played their tape for Buena Vista Productions who offered to put up $250,000 to promote the group. Obviously they were thrilled and the **Lemon Drops** reformed with just Ricky Erickson missing from the new line-up. They recorded lots of new songs in Chicago's Sound Studios during November and December 1968, but ironically these efforts too proved to be in vain, for the owner of Buena Vista died in his sleep and the deal was cancelled! Devastated the band split up for good.

Gary and Eddie Weiss later formed **Watermelon** and then **Buzzsaw**. In 1972 Reggie Weiss, frustrated by their lack of success issued a stereo mix of *I Live In The Springtime* as **Buzzsaw**.

Compilation appearances include: *I Live In The Springtime* on *Nuggets Box* (4-CD), *Psychedelic Patchwork* (LP), *Pebbles, Vol. 8* (LP) and *I Wanna Come Back From The World Of LSD* (CD); *Talk To The Animals*, an unreleased cut with loads of fuzz guitar, on *Psychedelic Crown Jewels, Vol. 1* (Dble LP & CD); *Listen Girl* on *Time Won't Change My Mind* (LP); *Flowers On The Hillside, I Live In The Springtime, Listen Girl, Nobody For Me* on *Chicago Garage Band Greats* (CD); *Sometime Ago, My Friend (Theatre Of Your Eyes), Jennifer Ann, Crystal Pure, Maria* and *(Flower) Dream* (demos) on *The Cicadelic 60's, Vol. 5* (CD); *I Live In The Springtime* (unreleased version culminating in a guitar solo), *Alone* and *Jennifer Ann* on *Chicago Garage Band Greats* (LP); *It Happens Everyday* and *I Live In The Springtime* on *Green Crystal Ties, Vol. 9* (CD). **Buzzsaw**'s version of *I Live In The Springtime* can also be found on *Highs In The Mid-Sixties, Vol. 4* and *Pebbles, Vol. 6* (CD). (VJ/MW/BM)

Lemon Fog

Personnel:			
	TED EUBANKS	keyb'ds	A
	TERRY HORDE	ld gtr	A
	CHRIS LYONS	drms	A
	DANNY OGG	bs	A
	BILL SIMMONS	vcls	A

45s:	Lemon Fog/Echoes In Time	(Orbit 1117) 1967
	Summer/Girl From The Wrong Side-Of Town	(Orbit 1123) 1968
	Day By Day/The Prisoner	(Orbit 1127) 1968

In the Spring of 1963, The Bar Eights were formed, with Fillmore High School classmates Danny Ogg and Terry Horde on lead guitar and drums, respectively, Timmy Thorpe on bass, and Dale VanDeloo on saxophone and vocals. Essentially, The Bar Eights were a Rip Chords cover band, with a few Lou Christie covers mixed in for variety. Aside from a few coffee bar gigs and a sock hop, The Bar Eights failed to establish themselves even semi-professionally over the next two years. When VanDeloo reportedly attacked Ogg with a mic stand during an argument over who would get the taller riser, The Bar Eights were no more.

Then, one sweltering afternoon in the Summer of 1965 at Clem's Music in downtown Houston, it happened. Chris Lyons was hanging around the store recruiting talent for a new band he was forming. He had already earmarked drummer Eddie Sura and keyboardist Jimmy Spicher and was looking for a guitarist and bassist. Danny Ogg entered the store with hopes of trying out the new Danelectro that Clem had in. When Chris asked him to join, he

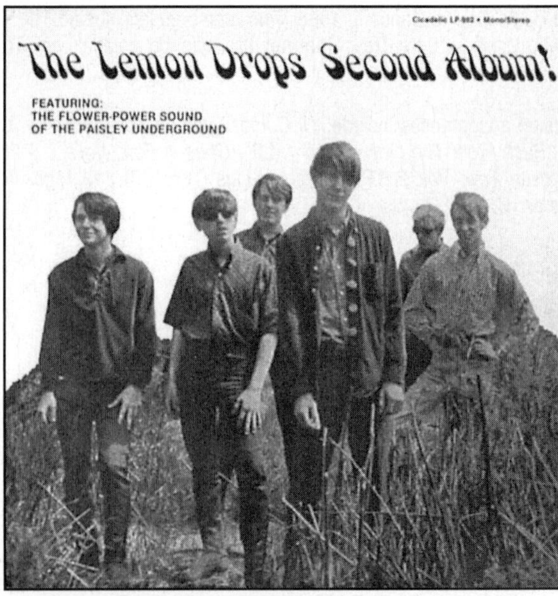

THE LEMON DROPS - Second Album! LP.

LEMON FOG/NOMADS - Three O'Clock Merrian Webster Time LP.

agreed, but only under the condition that his friend Timmy Thorpe, who had just gotten laid off from his job at the glass factory and was bored out of his mind, play bass for them. Lyons agreed, taking on Thorpe sight-unseen. After a few rehearsals, it became painfully obvious that Sura was not working out. According to Ogg, "Eddie kept yelling at everybody, particularly Timmy, 'cause he couldn't keep good time." When Ogg ran into former Bar Eight bandmate Terry Horde at Clem's the following week, Ogg offered him the drummer spot in the band. Horde agreed. By that weekend, The Pla-Boys were playing their first gig, at St. Regis College for the Arts. In the audience that night was a man who would change their lives...

Ted Eubanks, an avant-garde composer and fixture of Houston's mod scene, caught The Pla-Boys' act. Their set consisted mostly of covers of such garage greats as **Sam the Sham and the Pharaohs** and **? and the Mysterians**. As Eubanks puts it, "They were playing this garage crap! It was horrible. But something about them struck me... I think it was their chemistry". Eubanks immediately approached the band after the show and offered to take them over. They agreed. But Eubanks decided that before anything was to become of them, a few changes would need to be made. First, the music. Eubanks immediately began injecting original numbers into the group's repertoire and dissuaded them from the typical garage fare they had been playing. Second, the image. The Pla-Boys basically looked like something right out of a Frankie and Annette movie, with matching grey sport suits. But Eubanks got them good and "psychedelicised", dressing them in beads, mod suits, and the like. Finally, the name. From this moment forth,The Pla-Boys would be known as **The Lemon Fog**.

In short order, **The Lemon Fog** established themselves as one of the area's two premier bands, along with the well-established **Nomads**. The "all thumbs" Jimmy Spicher was substituted for fellow Fillmore High classmate Bill Simmons. At this point, Eubanks decided to also drop Timmy Thorpe, whom Ted felt was "an incompetent", and switch Danny Ogg to bass, while Chris Lyons assumed guitar duties. This line-up gained local celebrity status, and soon, **The Lemon Fog** were invited into the studio to cut a single.

Under Eubanks' guidance, **The Lemon Fog** entered the studio to create some of the most experimental recordings of the 1960's. Eubanks' ongoing experimentation with new electronic sounds became a hallmark of **The Lemon Fog** recorded legacy. From July of 1966 to February 1968, they recorded several albums worth of material. Little of this material was ever released, however, most of it having been stolen when Liquid Stereo Studios' vaults were raided in 1968. But two singles were released, *Echoes Of Time/The Prisoner*, and the compelling *Living Eye Theme/Summer*, and a self-titled EP containing these and three other songs, *Girl From The Wrong Side Of Town*, *Day By Day* and *So Sophisticated*, was released. *The Living Eye Theme*, also known as *The Lemon Fog*, was their biggest success, reaching the Top 8 regionally. The song's composer, Ted Eubanks explains, "The Living Eye was a huge club in Houston where we were the house band. I vaguely remember one night staring at the huge pulsating eye which sits in front of the door. As I sat there, suddenly the words and images of the song just started dancing around in my head. It's not the kind of thing one forgets". Aside from their studio work, **The Lemon Fog** enjoyed being one of the top club draws in the area. Besides the music, the Fog benefited from a spectacular stage presence. This was attributed largely to Chris Lyons' charisma and good looks. Also adding to the spectacle was Ted Eubanks, dancing on stage wearing a long, flowing, sequined cape, and occasionally chiming in a harmony or two, described by Ogg as "Chinese sounding." Off-kilter harmonies aside, Ted assumed the role of group leader, despite the fact that he himself played no instruments. Ted felt his presence was enough. In addition to live performances, **The Lemon Fog** also made television appearances on Sump 'n' Else and The Larry Kane Show, where they performed *Echoes Of Time* and *The Living Eye Theme*.

At the height of the Fog's heyday, problems began to arise. Eubanks was becoming increasingly demanding of the others, insisting that they practice every day they are not performing. In particular, the slothful Horde took exception to this. Furthermore, Eubanks' compositions began to become more and more self-indulgent and less accessible. The others tried to turn down his latest inclusions and attempted to inject some covers back into their repertoire to give their show more appeal. But Ted would have none of it. He insisted that his new material be considered. A power clash began to develop. At one point, Eubanks threatened to walk out on the group and leave them holding the bag for four gigs they had lined up that month. When the group proceeded with those engagements without him, Eubanks reluctantly grovelled back. Adding to this, acid casualty Bill Simmons began making himself scarce, sometimes for as long as a month, causing further tension in the group. Eubanks refused to substitute for Simmons, insisting that his on-stage role was too important to compromise. As a result, Chris Lyons was left to take up a "lyon's" share (pun intended) of the keyboard duties, in addition to guitar and vocals.

By 1970, the group was in disarray. A break-up seemed inevitable at this point. When Eubanks met with the others for rehearsal, planning to propose his latest composition, *Internal Combustion* (later titled *Bedroom War* and released by Eubanks as a solo single), he found the equipment packed away, and grim faces on his bandmates. They told him it was over. The four left the practice space that day, and each went their separate ways.

Cicadelic's first collectors' album in 1982 *Three O'Clock Merrian Webster Time* has one side devoted to them, which compiles all seven of their surviving tracks (*Summer, Echoes Of Time, Day By Day, The Prisoner, Yes I Cry, Girl From The Wrong Side Of Town* and *Lemon Fog*) - the same material has also been reissued on CD by Collectables as *Acid Visions - Complete Collection, Vol. 3* (3-CD), and *The History Of Texas Garage Bands, Vol. 2* (CD)- the latter featuring two additional takes of *Summer*.

Other compilation coverage has included: *Lemon Fog* and *Summer* on *The Cicadelic 60's, Vol. 2* (CD) and *Green Crystal Ties, Vol. 9* (CD), *Summer* and *Yes I Cry* on *Gathering Of The Tribe* (CD); *Summer* on *Acid Dreams Epitaph* (CD) and *Acid Dreams - The Complete Collection* (3-LP); *The Living Eye Theme* and *The Prisoner* on *Acid Visions - The Complete Collection Vol. 1* (CD). (VJ/??)

The Lemon Pipers

Personnel:	BILL ALBAUGH	drms	A
	IVAN BROWNE	vcls, gtr	A
	BILL BARTLETT	gtr	A
	REG NAVE	keyb'ds	A
	STEVE WALMSLEY	bs	A

HCP

ALBUMS:	1(A)	GREEN TAMBOURINE	(Buddah 2349 006) 1968 90 -
	2(A)	JUNGLE MARMALADE	(Buddah BDS 5016) 1969 - -
	3(A)	CHECKMATE	(Buddah BDS-5015) 1968 - -

NB: (3) is a split album with **1910 Fruitgum Co.**. Four CDs which may interest collectors are *Lemon Pipers*, a 20-track 'Best Of' CD (Sequel NEX CD 131) 1990, Collectables *Golden Classics* (COL-CD-0533), *Green Tambourine*, an 11-cut European release and *Green Tambourine: The Best Of The Lemon Pipers* (Buddah) 2001.

HCP

45s:	Quiet Please / Monaural 78	(Dana Lynn # Unkn) 1967 -
α	Turn Around And Take A Look/Danger	(Buddah 11) 1967 132
	Green Tambourine/No Help From Me	(Buddah 23) 1967 1
	Quiet Please / Monaural 78	(Carol 107) 1968 -
	Rice Is Nice/Blueberry Blue	(Buddah 31) 1968 46

Jelly Jungle (Of Orange Marmalade)/ Shoe Shine Boy	(Buddah 41)	1968 51
Lovely Atmosphere/Wine And Violet	(Buddah 63)	1968 -
I Was Not Born To Follow/Rainbow Tree	(Buddah 136)	1969 -

NB: α also released in France as by the *Citron Pressés* with a PS.

Ivan and The Sabers, from Centerville, Ohio, were a pop band who had been releasing 45s since 1964. In 1967, they were picked up by bubblegum maestros **Kasenetz-Katz**, relocated to Cincinnatti, and transformed into psychedelic bubblegem act **The Lemon Pipers**. They are best remembered for their single *Green Tambourine*, which topped the U.S. charts and reached No. 7 in the U.K. in early 1968. Ironically, this was one of the earliest drug songs to achieve chart success. Although the follow-up *Rice Is Nice* also made the U.S. Top 50 and No. 41 in the UK, like most other bubblegum bands they were not equipped to live up to their original promise and split after further single failures. Their singles were released by Pye Int. in the UK.

Thru' With You on their first album contrasts starkly with their bubblegum repertoire - being an awesome psychedelic guitar, extended freak-out. This album was later reissued by Buddah. It made No. 90 in the charts.

They appear to have led a double life, with 45s by **Ivan and The Sabers** continuing to appear during and after their time as **The Lemon Pipers**. Bill Bartlett went on to form Ram Jam, whose 1977 smash hit *Black Betty* was produced by **Kasenetz-Katz**.

Compilation appearances have included: *We Can Be Together* on *Pop Explosion* (Buddah 643 312) 1968; *Green Tambourine* on *Psychedelic Visions* (CD) and *Best Of '60s Psychedelic Rock* (CD); *Quiet Please* on *Echoes In Time, Vol. 1* (LP) and *Echoes In Time, Vol's 1 & 2* (CD); *Green Tamourine*, *Jelly Jungle* and *Rice Is Nice* on *Bubble Gum Music Is... The Naked Truth* (LP); and *The Shoemaker Of Leatherwear Square* on *Electric Psychedelic Sitar Headswirlers, Vol. 4* (CD). (VJ/MW)

Lemon Sandwich

45:	I Must Be Dreaming/Give Me Love	(La Salle L-371)	1967

A Long Island, New York, group who were spotted by local talent scout and producer Carl Edelson (also responsible for releases by **The Shandels** and **The Taboos**). Their sole release appeared on his La Salle label in late 1967.

The poppy *I Must Be Dreaming* was picked as the top side. Thirty-five years later it's the resoundingly moody flip *Give Me Love* that's the chosen cut for *Psychedelic States: New York Vol. 1* (CD). (MW)

Leo and The Prophets

45:	Tilt-A-Whirl/The Parking Meter	(Totem 105)	196?

A great Ronnie Weiss-inspired punk outfit from Austin, Texas. Their 45 is well covered on compilations. Check out the 'A' side, *Tilt-A-Whirl*, whose wacky lyrics deal with banana peelings and living in technicolour cinematic style, and the flip, which is equally bizarre and nonsensical.

Compilation appearances include: *Tilt-A-Whirl* on *Pebbles, Vol. 10* (LP), *Pebbles, Vol. 3 (ESD)* (CD), *Texas Flashbacks, Vol. 4* (LP & CD) and *Flashback, Vol. 4* (LP); and *Parking Meter* on *Highs In The Mid-Sixties, Vol. 12* (LP). (VJ)

Leon and Malia

ALBUM:	1	LEON AND MALIA	(Quadrum QS-2004)	c1970 SC

NB: Other albums exist by this duo.

A mellow male/female duo with mainly acoustic guitars plus some hand drums, electric guitar, bass and drums. Songs include *Funny Ways*, *Looking At The Sky*, *Sea Splashing Sadly*, *Stone Shepherds* and a cover of Donovan's *Hurdy Gurdy Man*. (SR)

GEORGIE LEONARD - One Man Band LP.

Georgie Leonard

ALBUM:	1	ONE MAN BAND	( )	197?

NB: (1) reissued on vinyl (American Sound AS-1006) with a bonus 7".

A strange hippie singer. His album has been reissued with two different covers. (SR)

Leonda

ALBUM:	1	WOMAN IN THE SUN	(Epic BN 26383)	1968 SC

A totally forgotten album of bluesy-rock, with some acid-folk tracks. *Blue Diamond To A Platinum Setting* was compiled on the Epic catalogue sampler *Rockbusters* (LP). (SR)

Perry Leopold

ALBUM:	1	EXPERIMENT IN METAPHYSICS	(No label)	1970 R5

NB: (1) issued in plain gold textured sleeve with small sticker on front. Counterfeited in the U.K. on vinyl (Psychedelic Archives AR 305) 1996 (R1), and reissued officially on CD (Gear Fab GF-122) 1998 with three bonus tracks, *Jets They Roar*, *The Prophesy* and *The Dawning Of Creation* recorded in the same era. A second (unreleased) album, *Christian Lucifer* (recorded in 1973) has also been released on CD (Gear Fab GF-141) 1999 and vinyl (Gear Fab/Comet GFC 401) 2001 with poster insert.

From Philadelphia, *Experiment In Metaphysics* is probably the most sought-after solo acoustic folk record in the world, with only 300 copies pressed in the Summer of 1970. **Leopold** handles the vocals and guitar and a dark atmosphere is obtained by this mysterious troubadour. The album sides are labelled 'Smoke' and 'Drop' with Side Two being bannered "ACID FOLK". This one delivers!

Perry Leopold later recorded material for two further albums. The Gear Fab CD reissue of *Experiment In Metaphysics* contains three tracks from one of these unreleased LPs included as bonus material (fantastic stuff - especially *The Dawning Of Creation*), and have already issued another in its entirety: *Christian Lucifer*, recorded in 1973.

An eponymous 7" EP was from 1978 also exists (No label), but isn't of the same standard and won't be of interest to readers of this book.

Anyone interested in checking out **Leopold**'s work (without obtaining a second mortgage first) should check out the Gear Fab CD's, which are made from **Leopold**'s tape archives.

Compilation appearances include *The Prophesy* on Gear Fab's *Psychedelic Sampler* (CD). (CF/MW)

Leviathan

Personnel:	SHOF BEAVERS	A
	WAIN BRADLEY	A
	PETER RICHARDSON	A
	JOHN SADLER	A
	DON SWEARINGEN	A
	GRADY TRIMBLE	A

ALBUM: 1(A) LEVIATHAN (Mach AMA 12501) c1974 SC

NB: (1) reissued on vinyl and CD (Akarma AK 110).

From Memphis, this group played a mixture of progressive and hard-rock. Their first album includes tracks like *Seagull*, *Angel Of Death*, *Quicksilver Clay* and *Endless Dream* and was released on a local label. A second album is known to exist but so far we've been unable to find any information about it. (SR)

Drake Levin

45: On the Road to Mexico/ ? (Parrot) 1966

A rare single by the guitarist of **Paul Revere and The Raiders**, who also played with **Lee Michaels** and formed **Friendsound** and **Brotherhood**. (SR)

Mark LeVine

Personnel:	BEN BENAY	gtr	A
	RY COODER	mandolin	A
	MIKE DEASY	gtr	A
	TOXEY FRENCH	drms	A
	PAUL HUMPHREY	drms	A
	LARRY KNECHTEL	piano	A
	MARK LeVINE	gtr, vcls	A
	JOE OSBORN	bs	A
	JERRY SCHEFF	bs	A

ALBUM: 1(A) PILGRIM'S PROGRESS (HogFat HLP-1) 1968 SC

This album is an an interesting example of West Coast rock with nice guitars, although the vocals could have been better. It is also a pretty rare private pressing, with Hogfat being "a Division of the Society for the Naturalization of Animals". Scheff, French and Benay were previously in **Goldenrod**, Cooder in the **Rising Sons** and **Captain Beefheart's Magic Band**.

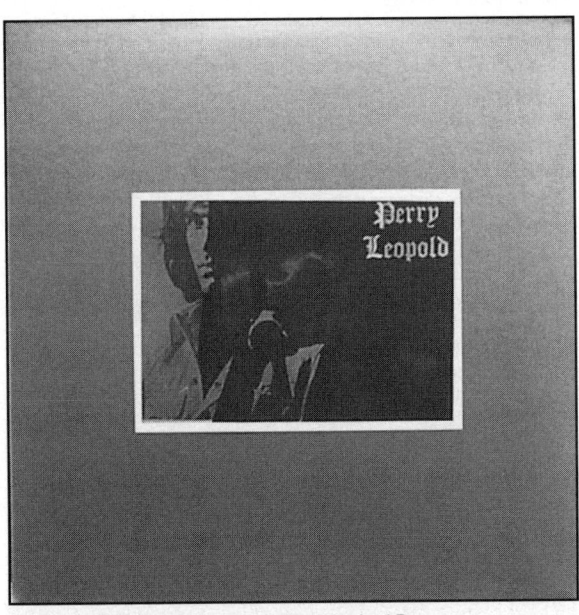

PERRY LEOPOLD - Experiment In Metaphysics LP.

PAUL LEVINSON - Twice Upon A Rhyme LP.

One of the first examples of artists "going (back) to the country". The liner notes are explicit: "So I'm off to the mountains, the sea, the earth of nature. I leave you my songs and my wealth of insights of THE SCENE. They are of some use to the narrow minded youth of tomorrow and some use to the narrow minded aged of yesterday. To me they are of no use any longer... The meaning to my life is to be found other than drugs/words/sex/money. Where? the glimpse I've had tells me to move: physically. So my move: where words are few, where money is not important, where drugs are surpassed by environment, where sex is children and love".

LeVine would inspire the lyrics of the **Floating House Band**'s *Shep's Goin To The Country*. (SR)

Paul Levinson

Personnel:	ED FOX	keyb'ds, vcls	A
	PAUL LEVINSON	keyb'ds, perc, vcls	A
	PETER ROSENTHAL	gtr	A

NB: Plus at least nineteen guests!

ALBUM: 1(A) TWICE UPON A RHYME (Happysad Records HS M 3000) 1972 R2

NB: (1) in mono!

A local New York private pressing recorded between July 1969 and October 1971. At their best, Levinson and his crew produce dark, druggy pop music remindful of neighbours **The Patron Saints** or bayou obscuros **Feather Da Gamba**. *Forever Friday*, *Looking For Sunsets* and *You Are Everywhere* fit this profile. *The Lama Will Be Late This Year* is probably the most intriguing cut on the album, having as it does an oddly Syd Barrett-like delivery of the lyrics and some pretty unorthodox music with fuzz guitar leads. If the other two-thirds of the album was on par with the aforementioned tracks, several labels would be arm wrestling for reissue rights.

The album contains over fifty minutes of music, so beware of high prices on less-than mint copies, these will likely be noisy! (CF)

The Levis

45: Hear What I Say/That's Not The Way (Fleetwood 4563) 1966

From Lynn, Massachussetts. **The Levis**' 45 is on the sought-after Fleetwood label, although it is a pretty average effort.

Compilation appearances have included: *That's Not The Way* on *New England Teen Scene, Vol. 3* (LP), *Teenage Shutdown, Vol. 8* (LP & CD); and *Hear What You Say* on *Garage Punk Unknowns, Vol. 5* (LP). (VJ/MW/GGI)

Levitt and McClure

Personnel:	DAN LEVITT	gtr, banjo	A
	MARC McCLURE	gtr	A

ALBUM: 1(A) LIVING IN THE COUNTRY (Warner Bros. WS 1807) 1969 -

Definitely not for garage fans, but it should interest **Beau Brummels** fans due to the involvement of **Ron Elliott**, who produced the album and provided three songs:- *Empty Boxes*, *Farewell To Sally Brown* and *Paradise* (co-written by Butch Engle, from **Butch Engle and the Styx**). Recorded at Sunwest Studios in Hollywood in August 1969, the album is a good mix of folk, country and West Coast sound with duet vocals, the liner notes indicating Flatts and Scruggs and **Buffalo Springfield** as their main influences.

Marc McClure (ex-**Wildflower**) co-wrote *Mercedes Blues* with **Janis Joplin** and went on to form **Joyous Noise**. Both worked again with **Ron Elliott** for his *Candlestickmaker* solo album, Levitt also working on the **Beau Brummels** 1975 album. (SR)

The Lewallen Brothers

Personnel:	DENNIS GAMBLE	drms	A
	BOBBY LEWALLEN	organ, vcls	A
	CARL LEWALLEN	bs, vcls	A
	KEITH LEWALLEN	ld gtr, vcls	A
	TIM LEWALLEN	gtr	A

CD: 1(A) HITCH-HIKE! (1964-1968) (Collectables COL-CD-0661) 1995

45s:	Tough He Was/That's All	(Mustang 3009) 1965
α	It Must Be Love/I Think I'm Glad	(Split Sound 1) 1967
β	Only A Dream/Somethin' On My Mind	(??) 1968
	It Must Be Love/I Think I'm Glad	(RPR R-109) 1969

NB: α recorded Dec. '66. β most probably released on Split Sound.

Originally called the Cokats, from Mt. Lemon, Arizona, their story is told on *Hitch-Hike!* a fourteen-track CD retrospective. Comfortable and competent in adopting the Invasion sounds, with some fine Beatlesque poppy numbers and Zombie-inspired minor-moodies, the CD features generally cool pop-beat fodder with excellent harmonies. The stand-out track is *It Must Be Love*, a reedy upbeat number with an unexpected edge due to an outburst of mean 'n' moody guitar. This is used similarly on an alternate version of *If I Was You* to end the collection with a buzz.

The band toured incessantly in the Southwest, opening shows for **The Beau Brummels**, **Paul Revere and the Raiders**, **The Turtles**, and backing performers such as the Rip Chords, Donna Lauren, Bobby Sherman, and Chris Montez. Their biggest commercial triumph came with their final 45 of the sixties, *Only A Dream / Something On My Mind*, which they mimed on the Dick Clark showcase, Happening '68. They continued to perform well into the nineties, despite the death of Bobby Lewallen in 1981, and retain a strong following in the Southwest with their brand of late-fifties and mid-sixties style rock & roll.

Other compilation coverage has included: *It Must Be Love* on *The Tucson Sound 1960-68*. *Cause You Want Me To*, *Don't Say Why*, *Dream*, *I'm Normal*, *Wine, Wine, Wine* and *You're Gonna Leave Me* (four unreleased and two live tracks) on *The Cicadelic '60s - Vol. 7* (CD); *Only A Dream* and *Tough He Was* on *Green Crystal Ties, Vol. 3* CD; and *Wine, Wine, Wine* on *Green Crystal Ties, Vol. 7*. (MW/BTs)

Lewis and Clarke Expedition

Personnel:	KEN BLOOM	ld gtr, autoharp, clarinet, sax, flute, organ	A
	BOOMER CLARKE (OWEN CASTLEMAN)	gtr, perc	A
	TRAVIS LEWIS (MICHAEL MARTIN MURPHY)	gtr, hrmnca	A
	JOHN LONDON	gtr, bs, perc	A
	JOHNNY RAINES	drums, perc	A

NB: Line-up 'A' 1966 - 1968.

ALBUM: 1(A) EARTH, AIR, FIRE AND WATER (Colgems COM 105) 1967 -

NB: (1) issued in mono and stereo.

45s:	Daddy's Plastic Child/Gypsy Song Man	HCP (Colgems) 1967 -
	Blue Revelations/I Feel Good (I Feel Bad) (PS)	(Colgems 1006) 1967 64
	Destination Unknown /? (PS)	(Colgems 1011) 1967 -
	Chain Around The Flowers/?	(Colgems 1022) 1968 131

Having enjoyed mammoth profits with their pre-packaged Beatles-clones **The Monkees**, it only made sense that Colgems (co-owned by RCA and Columbia) would attempt to manufacture a second corporate super group. That said, how many of you remember **The Lewis and Clarke Expedition**? Probably few of you. That's unfortunate since the band's sole album, 1967's *Earth, Air, Fire And Water* is nothing short of wonderful.

1966 found Travis Lewis (aka Michael Martin Murphey) and Boomer Clarke (aka Owen Castleman) paying their bills as songwriters for Screen Gems. Originally from Dallas, Texas, Lewis/Murphey was a passing acquaintance of Mike Nesmith. The connection helped the pair place one of their compositions *Hangin' Round* with **The Monkees**, in the process bringing them to the attention of Colgems which quickly recognized their potential and signed them to a recording contract. Produced by Jack Keller and built around the talent of Lewis and Clarke (the line-up rounded out by multi-instrumentalist Ken Bloom, guitarist John London and drummer Johnny Raines) actually debuted with an instantly obscure 1966 single for the small Chartmaster label. While parallels to **The Monkees** were apparent, there were also some major difference; notably the fact the band were all capable musicians and namesakes Lewis and Clarke were responsible for the majority of material. That said, their debut was easily as good as anything in **The Monkees** catalogue. Musically varied, the set included stabs at shimmering Top 40 pop (*I Feel Good (I Feel Bad)*), folk-rock (*This Town Ain't The Same Anymore*), vaudeville (*Everybody Loves a Fire*), psych (*House Of My Sorrow*), an ecological message (*Chain Of Flowers*) and **Byrds**-styled jangle-rock (*Blue Revelation*). Rounded out by strong melodies and tight harmonies, mid-sixties pop simply didn't get much better. Highlights included the goofy *Spirit Of Argyle High* and the extended suite *Memorial To The American Indian* which included one of the first covers of **J.D. Loudermilk**'s *(The Lament Of) The Cherokee Reservation Indian* we've ever heard (coming a full three years before **Paul Revere and The Raiders**' hit). Unfortunately, with Colgems devoting most of it's energy to marketing **The Monkees**, neither the band nor the album or much in the way of promotional support. Needless to say, it failed to chart.

Compilation appearances include: *I Feel Good (I Feel Bad)* on *Nuggets, Vol. 3* (LP). (SB/SR/MMs/VJ)

LEWIS and CLARK EXPEDITION - Earth, Air, Fire And Water LP.

Roger Lewis and The Moondawgs

45s:	Don't Let Him/Harriet	(Karate 517) 1966
	Wild About You/Pretty Little Ramblin' Rose	(PAL 889-W) c1967

A New York group with female background vocals. (SR)

Jeff Liberman

Personnel:	JEFFERY LIBERMAN	vcls, gtr, keyb'ds	ABCD
	TOM RADLOCK	drms	ABC
	PHIL UPTEMPLE	bs	ABC
	DAN LOMAS	moog, bs, gtr	BC
	BYRON K BOWIE	horns, flute	D
	BYRON GREGORY	rhythm gtr	D
	MORRIS JENNINGS	perc	D
	SOLOMON (KING) JOHNSON	vcl	D
	KOCO	keyb'ds	D
	PAUL RICHMOND	bs	D

NB: Line-up 'C' also includes Uncle Tom Cobbly 'n' all!

ALBUMS:	1(A)	JEFF LIBERMAN	(Librah No 1545) 1975 R2
	2(B)	SOLITUDE WITHIN	(Librah JL 6969) 1975 R2
	3(C)	SYNERGY	(Librah 12157) 1978 R1
	4(D)	INTO THE COMFORT ZONE	(Tasty Music?) 1989 -

NB: (1), (2) and (3) have had limited reissues. All four albums have also been released as a double CD *Then And Now* (Second Battle SB 034) 1996.

Liberman is Flossmoor, Illinois' favourite son. All four albums are brimmed full of guitar-based heavy psychedelia. All of his albums are now important minor collectors' items and all have seen limited reissues.

Compilation coverage has included: *Woman* on *Valley Of The Son Of The Gathering Of The Tribe* (LP); *I Can't Change, Rock Or Roll Me, Life Is Just A Show, Woman's Need* and *Boogie Blues* on *Gathering Of The Tribe, Vol. 4* (LP); and *Woman's Needs* on *Reverberation IV* (CD). (VJ)

Liberty Bell

Personnel:	CARL AEBY	drms	AB
	WAYNE HARRISON	bs	AB
	AL HUNT	ld gtr	AB
	RICHARD PAINTER	gtr	AB
	RONNIE TANNER	vcls	A
	CHRIS GERNIOTTIS	vcls	B

ALBUMS:	1(A/B)	THE J-BECK STORY, VOL 3 - THE LIBERTY BELL (LP) (Eva 12036) 1984
	2(A/B)	REALITY IS THE ONLY ANSWER (CD) (Collectables COL-CD-0651) 1995

45s:	The Nazz Are Blue/Big Boss Man	(Cee-Bee 1001) 1967
	For What You Lack/That's How It Will Be	(Cee-Bee 1002) 1967
	Al's Blues/Something For Me	(Cee-Bee 1003) 1967
	Thoughts And Visions/ Look For Tommorow	(Back Beat 595) 1969
	Naw, Naw, Naw/Recognition	(Back Beat 600) 1969

This Corpus Christi outfit was originally called The Zulus but when Carl Becker, who ran the J-Beck/Cee-Bee record labels, became their manager circa 1966/67 he persuaded vocalist Ronnie Tanner to join the band and changed their name to **Liberty Bell**. They quickly recorded a Yardbirds cover as their first 45 and with this line-up released two other 45s. They also recorded two versions of an Al Hunt composition entitled *I Can See* which was never released but was to have been Cee-Bee 1004. Chris Gerniottis came in from **Zakary Thaks** to replace Ronnie Tanner on vocals on their last two 45s. The band disintegrated whilst recording these, but the owner of the Back Beat label which concentrated on black artistes considered Chris one of the best vocalists he'd heard. Eva's retrospective album and the equivalent Collectables CD includes all the band's 45s (including the unissued one), *Eveline Kaye* an Al Hunt number and *Reality*

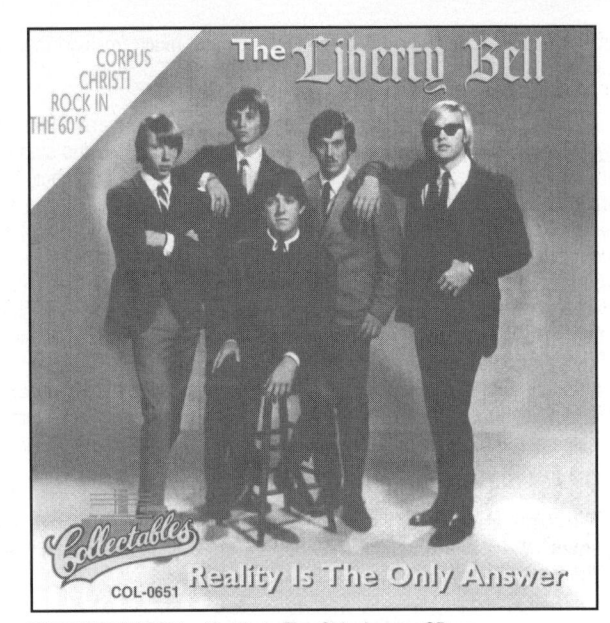

THE LIBERTY BELL - Reality Is The Only Answer CD.

Is The Only Answer, a superb psychedelic-punk song written by Chris. It also includes both sides of Gerniottis' next band's 45. They were called **Kubla Khan**.

The Lime Spiders later covered *That's How It Will Be* on *Slave Girl*.

Compilation appearances have included: *That's How It Will Be* on *Psychedelic Crown Jewels, Vol. 1* (Dble LP & CD); *For What You Lack, I Can See, Reality Is The Only Answer* and *Eveline Kaye* on *Texas Reverberations* (LP); *Something For Me* and *Reality Is The Only Answer* on *Green Crystal Ties, Vol. 1* (CD); *I Can See* and *Reality Is The Only Answer* on *The History Of Texas Garage Bands, Vol. 5* (CD). (VJ)

Liberty Lads

Personnel:	ANDY ARGUELLO		A
	JOHN LUJAN	drms	A
	MIKE MENDOZA		A
	GEORGE TOMELLOSO	vcls, gtr	A
	EDDIE WILLIAMS	bs	A

45:	Too Much Lovin'/I Need Believin'	(Dixon 111/112) 1965

A late sixties band from Liberty Island, California. Dixon was an Esar subsidiary. Williams was later in The Tears.

Compilation appearances include *Too Much Lovin'* on *The Sound Of Young Sacramento* (CD) and *Hipsville, Vol. 2* (LP). (MW/AP)

The Liberty Party

Personnel incl:	JERRY HAWKES	gtr, vcls	A
	GORDY "FLASH" KJELLBERG	gtr, vcls	A
	AL MALOSKY	drms	A
	BILL RIEBEN	bs	A
	MIKE ROBBINS	keyb'ds, vcls	A

45s:	Weep On/Get Yourself Home	(Jerden 787) 1966
	Send For Me/?	(Jerden 787) 1966

A Seattle five-piece, **The Liberty Party** were originally known as The Enchanters, with Vern Kjellberg (aka Joey Newman), Gordon Kjellberg, Ed Leckenby, Mike Robbins, Jerry Hawkes, Bill Rieben, and Al Malosky all playing in the final version of The Enchanters. When Ed Leckenby left to play drums for **Merrilee Rush** and the Turnabouts, and Vern Kjellberg left to play with **The Kingsmen**, the remaining members became **The Liberty Party**.

Their two 45s were recorded at Audio Recording studio in Seattle and Mike Robbins recalls that the band recorded *Get Yourself Home* and *Send For Me* under pressure from the label owner Jerry Dennon, as he liked those particular tunes although the band felt that they had much "rockier" material available...

Gordon was drafted to the National Guard and when he returned from the Army, although the group were sounding great with Mike Robbins standing in on vocals in his absence, something had been lost and the magic was never quite there again. Mike left to attend college, as did Bill Rieben and Jerry Hawkes whilst Al Malosky moved to L.A. and was in and out of the music scene for awhile. Gordon Kjellberg later played with **The Feelies** and Vern Kjellberg went on to **Don & The Goodtimes** and **Touch**. Sadly Jerry Hawkes had a very serious car accident many years ago and has never been able to play the guitar or sing again. Bill Rieben meanwhile has had a very successful career in finance and accounting, Al Malosky played with several successful bands after the **Liberty Party** including the **Emergency Exit** and **Easy Chair**, and today spends his time working in construction and helping troubled kids. Mike Robbins went on to become a Dr. of Clinical Psychology and a B&B owner in the Kitsap/Hood Canal area.

Mike Robbins also played in Jimmy Hanna and the Dynamics, **The Kingsmen**, **Merrilee Rush** and the Turnabouts and had one brief West Coast tour with Sonny and Cher.

Compilation appearances include: *Get Yourself Home* on *Northwest Battle Of The Bands, Vol. 2 - Knock You Flat!* (LP & CD); *Goodbye* (prev unreleased) on *Northwest Battle Of The Bands, Vol. 1* (CD); *Send For Me* on *Battle Of The Bands, Vol. 1* (LP) and *The History Of Northwest Rock, Vol. 4* (LP); *Weep On* on *The History of Northwest Rock, Vol. 6*; *Please Help The Man* (prev unreleased) on *Northwest Battle Of The Bands, Vol. 2* (CD). (VJ/DR/MW/MR)

The Liberty Street Ferry

Personnel incl:	KEN FREY	vcls	A

45:	Gloria/Baris Blues	(IGL Records 184)	1967

A good garage cover of the all-time classic, complete with gritty vocals and grungy guitar. The "B" side is a cool, bluesy vocal tune also with good guitar. (SR)

Licorice Schtik

45:	Flowers, Flowers/Kissin Game	(Dot)	c1967

A trippy pop single. (SR)

The Lidos

45:	Since I Last Saw You/Trudi	(Bandbox 359)	1964?

This Colorado band's *Since I Last Saw You* really pre-dates this book. It's a primitive dance hall thrash that even predated the British Invasion sound. It's eminently forgettable, but should you want to hear it, you'll find it on *Highs In The Mid-Sixties, Vol. 18* (LP) and on *Open Up Yer Door, Vol. 2* (LP) and *Mondo Frat Dance Bash A Go Go* (CD). (VJ/MW)

Lt. Garcia's Magic Music Box

Personnel:	HARRY J. BOYLE	ld vcls, ld gtr, keyb'ds	A
	RALPH DePALMA	vcls, drms	A
	TOM MORRISSEY	ld vcls, gtr, keyb'ds	A
	JAMES TRAGAS	ld vcls, bs	A

ALBUM:	1(A)	CROSS THE BORDER	(Kama Sutra klps-8071)	1968 -
45:		Latin Shake/Me Amor Es Verdadero	(Kama Sutra 246)	1968

Another **Kasenetz-Katz** production, for fans of bubblegum pop-psych in the mould of **Ohio Express** and **Crazy Elephant**. (SR/ET/HB)

ENOCH LIGHT - Spaced Out LP.

Light

Personnel incl:	GREG ECKLER	drms	A

45:	Back Up/Music Box	(A&M 873)	1967

From the San Bernardino/Riverside area of California. *Back Up* is a hard uptempo pop-rocker with occasional outbreaks of screeching guitar - planets away from the usual fare associated with A&M. The fact that the single was produced and arranged by Brian Ross, the man behind many Original Sound productions (**Mad Andy's Twist Combo**, **Music Machine**) has probably a lot to do with its unusual sound. *Music Box* is so different you wonder if it's the same outfit - an awful Seekers-type folk-ballad with female vocals, flute and soppy aura.

Greg Eckler had earlier played in **The Bush**, and later was found keeping the beat for eighties surf-instrumental outfit Jon & The Nightriders.

Back Up can also be found on *A Lethal Dose Of Hard Psych* (CD). (MW/SR)

Enoch Light

ALBUM:	1	ENOCH LIGHT PRESENTS SPACED OUT EXPLORATORY TRIPS THROUGH THE MUSIC OF BACH, BACHARACH AND THE BEATLES (Project 3 PR 5042SD) 1969 -

NB: (1) counterfeited on vinyl 2001.

Though largely forgotten today, **Enoch Light** was quite a talented guy. He started out in the mid-thirties as a band leader, recording and touring the States and Europe as Enoch Light and the Light Brigade. By the mid-fifties **Light**'s interests had migrated to the production and business sides of the house. He formed Command Records and leaping at the opportunities provided by the advent of stereo technology, recorded a string of big selling instrumental 'cash-in' albums. He also formed the Project Three label, using it as a base for less commercial experiments such as **The Free Design**.

Obviously most of his material isn't going to appeal to psych fans, but there's at least one exception. Released by **Light**'s Project 3 label, the cover notes were pretty accurate. "Enoch Light Presents Spaced Out Innovations in Stereo Sound" offered up a fascinating set of Bacharach and David, Beatles and Bach covers. Largely instrumental, the twelve selections were accompanied by occasional snippets of Up with People-styled smiley face vocals (check out *A Little Fugue For You And Me*). For his part, producer **Light** didn't really tamper with the original melodies. What actually makes this such a timepiece classic are the bizarre arrangements. Almost impossible to accurately describe, material such as *Norwegian Wood*, *Ob-La-Di, Ob-La-Da* and *What The World Needs Now Is Love* found **Light** mixing in equal parts of MOR/muzak moves and cutting edge (remember this was 1969), sounds (moogs, heavy fuzz guitar and some weird channel hopping effects - great headphone album). Anyone into **The Free Design** (one of **Light**'s side projects), or the recent Lounge revival is bound to find this a blast !!! (SB)

J.J. Light

ALBUM: 1 J.J. LIGHT (Liberty C062-91008) 1969 SC

NB: (1) German only release.

45s: α Heya/On The Road Now (Liberty 56111) 1969
      Na-Ru-Ka/Follow Me Girl (Liberty 2C00690888M) 1969
      Baby Let's Go To Mexico / It's A Sunshine Day (PBR 502) 1976

NB: α also issued in Italy, Germany, and the U.K. (Liberty LBF 15228) 1969, and in France with an art sleeve showing a drawing of the statue of liberty (Liberty 2C00690272M) 1969. (2) French release.

While in Los Angeles, he met **Bob Markley** of the **West Coast Pop Art Experimental Band**, who produced his album, recorded with other **WCPAEB** members. It's a superb record of tribal rock, mixing psych, rock and Navajo roots, with splendid guitar parts on several tracks.

The *Heya* 45 sold well in Europe, especially in France, Germany and Italy, precipitating a further 45 there, *Na-Ru-Ka*. *Heya* was covered in 1970 by the German group Jeronimo and in New Zealand by Zonk (this version was also released in the US by UA). In the eighties, Marc Tobaly (ex-Variations) released another version in France.

Circa 1970, Stallings and **Markley** recorded another album but it was shelved when Liberty went bankrupt and only some tapes are known to exist.

Their third 45, produced by Jim Stallings and P. Boyde is weak pop and best avoided. (MW/SR)

Lightmyth

45: Across The Universe/
     Quest Of The Golden Hord (RCA 74-0361) 1970

A cover of the Beatles song by an obscure group. (SR)

Lightning

Personnel: TOM 'ZIP' CAPLAN gtr A
            BERNIE PERSHEY perc A
            RONN ROBERTS gtr, vcls A
            MICK STANHOPE vcls, perc A
            WOODY WOODRICH bs A

ALBUM: 1(A) LIGHTNING (P.I.P. PP 6807) 1970 SC

NB: (1) reissued on CD (Anthology ANT 38.11) 1996. There's also *The Lost Studio Album* (American Sound Records AS-1003) 1996, an album of previously unreleased recordings.

45: Freedom/Hideaway (P. I. P. 8923) 1970

NB: contains edited versions of tracks taken from the P.I.P album.

Originally known as **White Lightning** the group was formed by Tom Caplan in Minneapolis, Minnesota, upon leaving **The Litter**. Musically their recorded output was decent hard-rock, not dissimilar from the Caplan-less **Litter**'s third album.

The *Lost Studio Album* contains two tracks by **White Lightning**, *Only Love* and *William Tell*, taken from an acetate and digitally cleaned, along with recordings made by **Lightning** in 1969, prior to the release of the P.I.P. album. Three of the songs featured are also on the P.I.P. album, but they are in a very different form on this limited edition release, which features some good guitar work and is well worth investigation.

Bernie Pershey had previously played in **Trilogy**.

In 2001, Zip Caplan released a new CD *Monsters And Heroes* as **Zip Caplan and Cast of Thousands**. Mostly instrumental it comprises 21 tracks of classic Horror movie, old Serials and fifties T.V. Series Soundtracks but recorded with 'rock' instruments. 48 different musicians are featured, with a different set of players backing Zip on each track. Some of the guests include Jim McCarty (The Yardbirds), Joey Molland (Badfinger), Nokie Edwards (The Ventures), Bobby Torres (Joe Cocker and Tom Jones), Doug Nelson (Jonny Lang Band), Bruce "Creeper" Kurnow **Mason Proffitt**), Denny Libby (**The Castaways**) plus guys from Edgar Winter, **Gypsy**, **The Litter**, **Stillroven**, **Underbeats**, **White Lightning** and **Crow**. (VJ/ZC)

The Light Nites

Personnel: AL CINER ld gtr A
            CHUCK COLBERT bs A
            LEE GRAZIANO drms, trumpet A
            GARY LOIZZO vcls A

45: One, Two Boogaloo/Same Old Thing (Dunwich 149) 1967

This outfit formed in 1965 and were originally known as **Gary And The Night Lights**, and also worked as **The Knight Lites**. Like **The Del-Vetts**, they had previously worked with Bill Traut cutting two low-budget jukebox singles for Seeburg. After a brief move to U.S.A. where they released an underrated soulful ballad, *I Don't Need Your Help* in late 1965, they appeared under dubious arrangement on Dunwich. After recording one single as **The Light Nites** they signed to Acta and changed their name to **The American Breed**.

All of the band came from Chicago except Al Ciner who was from Brookfield, Illinois.

Compilation appearances have included: *Take Me Back* (originally released as **Gary & The Knight Lites** on Kedlen (2002) 1965) on *Pebbles, Vol. 7* (CD); and *Same Old Thing* on *The Dunwich Records Story* (LP) and *If You're Ready - The Best Of Dunwich... Vol. 2* (CD). (VJ)

Lil' Boys Blue (aka Little Boys Blue)

Personnel incl: LARRY DIEHL A
                 DAVE WESTBERRY gtr A

45: Take You Away/I'm Not There (Batwing 2003) 1966

This outfit operated out of Sunnyvale, California in the mid-sixties. The pounding flip appears on *Back From The Grave, Vol. 3* (LP) and *Boulders, Vol. 11* (LP). The song was a hit in Monterey and was also very popular in San Jose. Dave and Larry had originally come together in the early sixties as The Ritones, an instrumental and hits covers band. They changed name to The Conquests in 1964 and became **Lil' Boys Blue** in 1965. (VJ)

LIGHTNING - Lightning CD.

LINCOLN ST. EXIT - Drive It! LP.

Lily and Maria

ALBUM: 1 LILY AND MARIA (Columbia CS 9707) 1968 SC

An acid-folk duo, like **Wendy and Bonnie**, that went totally unnoticed at the time and has yet to attract collectors' attention. The album includes several long cuts like *There'll Be No Clowns Tonight*, *Subway Thoughts* or *Melt Me*, all done in a very spooky and mellow way. (SR)

Lime

Personnel incl:	LARRY SANDERS	ld vcls	A
	RUSSELL SANDERS		A
	STEVEN SANDERS		A

45s:	Soul Kitchen / Love A Go-Go	(Westwood 12367) 1967
	Hey Girl / Love A Go-Go	(Chess 2045) 1967
	Beautiful Day / Satisfied	(Interpolation RPL 6569) 1969
	Satisfied / Beautiful Day	(Dot 17298) 1969

This outfit included three brothers from Akron, Ohio. Their 45s are upbeat pop, some of which border on garage. Both *Hey Girl* and *Beautiful Day* were written by local teen idol and lead singer Larry Sanders (not to be confused with the spoof TV talkshow host). He had a charismatic stage presence and was just 15-years-old when they recorded the first 45.

Soul Kitchen was a fabulous cool dark, garagey version of **The Doors** classic with some great organ and guitar work. On it, they changed the lyrics, saying "Let me sleep all night in your soul kitchen, we can work on GETTING STONED!"

Love A Go-Go turns up on *Every Groovy Day* (LP). (MW/RL/KSl/JKy)

Limey and The Yanks

45s:	Guaranteed Love/	
	Love Can't Be A One Way Deal	(Starburst 127) 1965
	Out Of Sight, Out Of Mind/	
	Gather My Things And Go	(Loma 2059) 1966
	Out Of Sight, Out Of Mind/	
	Gather My Things And Go	(Laurie 3356) 1966

From Los Angeles. The 'A' side of their first 45, *Guaranteed Love*, is a Stones/Bo Diddley styled rocker, with some fine lead guitar. *Out Of Sight, Out Of Mind* was a softer cover version of **The Marauders**' obscurity, complete with harpsichord.

Compilation coverage has included: *Guaranteed Love* and *Out Of Sight, Out Of Mind* on *Pebbles, Vol. 8* (CD); *Guaranteed Love* on *Highs In The Mid-Sixties, Vol. 1*(LP) and *Teenage Shutdown, Vol. 14* (LP & CD); *Out Of Sight, Out Of Mind* on *Highs In The Mid-Sixties, Vol. 3* (LP) and *Gather My Things And Go* on *Psychedelic Unknowns, Vol. 8* (LP & CD), *Ya Gotta Have Moxie, Vol. 2* (Dble CD) and *Boulders, Vol. 11* (LP). (VJ)

Lincoln Park Zoo

Personnel incl: TOM MURRAY A

ALBUM: 1 THE COWSILLS PLUS THE LINCOLN PARK ZOO
(Mercury-Wing 16354) 1968 -

45s:	Zoo's Blues/Woman Don't Let Me Down	(Fona 317) 1966 177
	If You Gotta Go, Go Now/	
	Love Theme Haight Street	(Mercury 72708) 1967
	Greatest Moments/Symphony Of My Soul	(USSA 912) 1968
	Kissy Face / My Baby ... (part-title)	(Twinight 127) 1969/70

This Chicago late sixties band is most notable for the inclusion of Murray, who was later in **Litter** and Straight Up. They also provided one side (four tracks) to the above album, a budget production, which is quite pleasant. (VJ/MW/JV)

The Lincolns

Personnel:	LONNIE ANDERSON	A
	ROBERT "BOBBY" BAXTER	A
	MICHAEL BRUMMEL	A
	BERNIE GRIFFITHS	A
	RICHARD S. KNIGHT	A
	DEAN NYGAARD	A

45s:	I Don't Understand/In The Back Of My Mind	(Topaz 1303) 196?
	We Got Some/Pop Kat	(Dot 16958) 1966
α	Girl/Listen	(Ripchord 45-0001) 1967
	Humpty Dumpty/Painted Picture	(Ripchord 0003) 196?
	Smile Baby Smile/Come Along And Dream	(Tripp 1000) 1969
	Summer Winds/In The Back Of My Mind	(Tripp 1002) 1970

NB: α as The Lincoln's.

This quintet hailed from Bonniville, Washington. *Come Along And Dream* which is very punkish with lots of fuzz, sounds straight out of 1966 but was actually one of their last recordings released in early 1969. *Girl* is a strong fuzz-popper with a screeching solo. *Listen* is dreamy **Association**-style harmony-pop with cooing female backing.

Compilation appearances have included: *Pop Kat* on *Riot City!* (LP); *We Got Some* and *Pop Kat* on *Vile Vinyl, Vol. 1* (LP) and *Vile Vinyl* (CD); *We Got Some* on *Garage Punk Unknowns, Vol. 1* (LP); *Come Along And Dream* on *Highs In The Mid Sixties, Vol. 7* (LP). (VJ/MW/DR)

Lincoln St. Exit

Personnel:	LEE HERRERA	drms	A
	R.C. GARISS	ld gtr	A
	MICHAEL MARTIN	ld gtr, vcls	A
	MAC SUAZO	bs	A

ALBUM: 1(A) DRIVE IT! (Mainstream S/6126) 1970 R2/R3

NB: (1) has been counterfeited on vinyl and also issued on CD (TRC 044), with both sides of the Ecco 45 as bonus tracks.

EPs:	1	Half A Dream/Sunny Sunday/Whatever Happened To	
		Baby Jesus	(Psych-Out 101) 1983
	2	I Wanna Come Back (From The World Of LSD)/	
		Double Crossin' Girl/Who's Been Driving My Little	
		Yellow Taxi Cab/Paper Place	(Lance/Bacchus) 2000

NB: (2) first two songs by **Fe Fi Four Plus 2**.

45s:	Who's Been Driving My Little Yellow Taxi Cab/	
	Paper Lace	(Lance 109/110) 1966
	The Bummer/Sunny Sunday Dream	(Ecco ER 1001) 1967

	Whatever Happened To Baby Jesus part 1 /part 2	(N/K) 196?
	Mississippi Riverboat Gamblin' Man/	
	St. Louis Mama	(Souled Out 104) 196?
	Soulful Drifter/	
	Time Has Come, Gonna Die	(Mainstream 722) 1969
Acetate:	Open Doorway/Orange Benevolent	(Audio Recording) 196?

A Sioux Indian band based in Albuquerque, New Mexico. *The Bummer* is a fine upbeat rocker, whilst *Sunny Sunday Dream* is much more trippy with lots of keyboards. Changing their name to **Xit** the band made several albums in support of the cause of the American Indian during the 1970's. The **Lincoln St. Exit** album is essentially blues-based and does not include their non-Mainstream 45s. It is now a very sought-after collectors' item and has been counterfeited. Much of their earlier material was officially reissued on the **Xit** LP *Entrance* (Canyon 7114) 1974, which has also become rare.

Compilation coverage has so far included: *The Bummer* and *Sunny Sunday Dream* on *New Mexico Punk From The Sixties* (LP) and *Sixties Archive, Vol. 4* (CD); *The Bummer*, *Sunny Sunday Dream* and *Whatever Happened To Baby Jesus, Part 1 & 2* on *Filling The Gap*; *Sunny Sunday Dream* and *Whatever Happened To Baby Jesus* on *Gathering Of The Tribe* (CD); *Sunny Sunday Dream* on *Garage Zone, Vol. 1* (LP) and *Garage Zone Box Set* (4-LP); *The Bummer* on *Everywhere Chainsaw Sound* (LP), *The Midwest Vs. The Rest* (LP); *Who's Been Driving...* on *Diana's Rootin' Tootin' Party*; *Paper Place* and *Who's Been Driving My Little Yellow Taxi Cab* on *Bands On Lance* (LP) and *I Wanna Come Back From The World Of LSD* (CD); and *Who's Been Driving My Little Yellow Taxi Cab* on *Diana's Rootin' Tootin' Wild Teenage Rock 'N' Roll Party!* (LP). (VJ/MW)

Bob Lind

ALBUMS:	1	DON'T BE CONCERNED		
		(World Pacific WPS 21841) 1966	148	-
	2	THE ELUSIVE BOB LIND		
		(Verve Forecast FTS-3005) 1966		-
	3	PHOTOGRAPHS OF FEELING		
		(World Pacific WPS 21851) 1966		-
	4	SINCE THERE WERE CIRCLES (Capitol ST-780) 1971		-
				HCP

45s:	Roads of Anger/To My Elders With Respect (Aura 88123) 1965	-
	Elusive Butterfly/	
	Cheryl's Going Home (World Pacific 77808) 1965	5
	Remember The Rain/Truly Julie's	
	Blues (I'll Be There) (World Pacific 77822) 1966	64/65
	Wandering/Hey Nellie, Nellie (Verve Folkways 5018) 1966	-
	I Just Let It Take Me/	
	We've Never Spoken (World Pacific 77830) 1966	123
	San Francisco Woman/	
	Oh Babe Take Me Home (World Pacific 77839) 1966	135
	White Snow/Black Night (Verve Folkways KF 5029) 1966	-
	It's Just My Love/	
	Goodtime Special (World Pacific 77865) 1967	-
	Goodbye Neon Lies/	
	We May Have Touched (World Pacific 77879) 1968	-
	She Can Get Along/	
	Theme From The Music Box (Capitol 3169) 1971	-
	Elusive Butterfly/	
	Truly Julie's Blues (United Artist XW032) 1972	-

An introspective folk-singer/songwriter, born in Baltimore on Nov. 25, 1942. The success of his song *Elusive Butterfly* in March 1966 opened up a space in the charts for a new kind of song, breathy and wispy, previously thought to be too slow to be commercial. Other folk singers, like **Tim Buckley** or **Tim Hardin**, benefited from this breakthrough, but **Lind** only charted again with his follow-up 45 *Remember The Rain*.

After two albums for World Pacific (both produced by Jack Nitzsche and the second engineered by Dave Hassinger), he retired temporarily from the music business, suffering from alcohol and drug abuse and moved to Santa Fe, New Mexico.

The Verve Forecast album was released to cash-in on **Lind**'s success. They bought an acoustic tape of Lind from his Denver days, overdubbed instruments and released it as an authentic album.

When **Lind** returned to L.A. in early 1971, Capitol Records signed him and he recorded a sombre, warts-and-all album, *Since There Were Circles*, backed by Doug Dillard, Gene Clark, Bernie Leadon and David Jackson plus **John Buck Wilkin**, Michael Lang, Ralph Grierson, Carol Kaye and Paul Humphrey. After that, he soon retired permanently, giving up music for a literary career.

Lind was managed by Charles Green and Brian Stone, who later worked with **Buffalo Springfield**, **Iron Butterfly** and **Dr. John**.

His song *Cheryl's Going Home* was covered by the **Blues Project** on their *Projections* album and by Switzerland's Les Sauterelles on their debut album. **The Turtles** also recorded his *Down In Suburbia* on their *You Baby* album, whilst The Yardbirds' Keith Relf recorded *Mr Zero*. (SR/LP)

Dennis Linde

ALBUM:	1	LINDE MANOR	(Intrepid IT-74004) 1969 SC

Released on the same short-lived label as **Underground Sunshine**, this album combines tracks with fuzz guitar (*The Fat Of The Land*) and psychedelic folk tunes (*Stormy Weather*) and may interest some readers.

In 1972, **Dennis Linde** would form Jubal, a boring country-rock group and later released several solo albums, out of scope and time-frame for this book. He is mostly remembered for having penned *Burning Love*, the last rock hit for Elvis Presley. (SR)

Mark Lindsay

45s:	First Hymn From Grand Terrace /	
(up to	Old Man At The Fair	(Columbia 4-44875) 1969
1969)	Arizona / Man From Houston	(Columbia 4-45037) 1969

The lead singer and co-leader of **Paul Revere and The Raiders** went solo in 1969 and met with some success, releasing 15 singles in seven years, mostly aimed at the pop and teen market. The first 45, however, contains two Jim Webb songs.

Lindsay also recorded with **The Unknowns**. (SR)

Lines End

45:	Hey Little Girl/Miss-Illusion	(Lompri 90599) 1969

Recorded at Natural Sound, Racine, Wisconsin. *Hey Little Girl* is a bouncy but wimpy garage-beat effort that sounds more like 1965 or 1966. *Misillusion* also sounds a little out of its time but is a haunting garage-folk ballad - with tearful guitars and subdued keyboards. (MW)

Buzzy Linhart

Personnel:	EYES OF BLUE		A
	BUZZY LINHART	vcls, gtr, vibes	ABCD
	KESHAV SATHE	tabla	A
	BIG JIM SULLIVAN	sitar	A
	LUTHER RIX	drms, vcls	BC
	BILL TAKAS	bs, vcls	B
	MARK KLINGMAN	keyb'ds	C
	PETER PLANSKY		C
	PETER PONZOL		C

ALBUMS:	1(A)	BUZZY	(Philips PHS600 291) 1968 -
(selective)	2(B)	THE TIME TO LIVE IS NOW	
			(Kama Sutra KBS 2037) 1971 -
	3(C)	BUZZY	(Kama Sutra KBS 2053) 1972 -
	4(D)	PUSSYCATS CAN GO FAR	(Atlantic) 1974 -
	(-)	THE BEST OF (dbl)	(Kama Sutra KSBS 2615-2) 1976 -

NB: (1) (2) (3) and (4) were also issued in England. There's also a later compilation *Tornado* (Accord SN 7130) 1981.

45s:	End Song/Yellow Cab	(Philips 40599) 1969
	Friends/?	(Kama Sutra 538) 1970
	You Got What It Takes/?	(Kama Sutra 548) 1971
	If You Gotta Break Another Heart/?	(Kama Sutra 561) 1972
	You Don't Have to Tell Me Goodbye/ A Tear Outweighs A Smile	(Atco 45-6959) 1974

From Cleveland, the singer and songwriter **Buzzy Linhart** was a veteran of the East Coast coffee house scene and formed the **Seventh Sons** in 1967. Between 1968 and 1974, he also released several interesting solo albums as well as forming **Music**.

His first album *Buzzy* was recorded in England in October 1968. On the first side he is backed by the Welsh group Eyes of Blue and performs his own songs (*Willie Jean*, *Step Into My Wildest Dreams*) and a fast cover of **Tim Hardin**'s *Yellow Cab*. The second side features *Sing Joy*, a long (18'45") raga with only Big Jim Sullivan on sitar and Keshav Sathe on tabla. A really interesting album, it deserves to be heard.

In 1971, after Music, *The Time To Live Is Now* was recorded in New York. Reduced to a trio, the group provide a solid album with a cover of *Get Together* plus several original songs. Rix was previously in **Group Image** and briefly with **Ten Wheel Drive** with Bill Takas.

The later albums are unfortunately not as interesting.

In addition to his solo career, **Linhart** was very active in the late sixties / early seventies, playing guitar or vibes with **Jimi Hendrix** (*Cry Of Love*), **Cat Mother**, **Jake and The Family Jewels**, Montreal and **Zephyr**. (SR)

Bob Linkletter

45:	The Out Crowd/ The Final Season	(Chattahoochee 702) 1965

On the Los Angeles label managed by **Kim Fowley**, an "answer" to the success of "The In Crowd" song. (SR)

Linn County

Personnel:	LARRY EASTER	wind	ABC
	DINO LONG	bs	ABC
	RAY 'SNAKE' MCANDREW	drms	A
	STEPHEN MILLER	vcls, keyb'ds	ABC
	FRED WALK	sitar, gtr	ABC
	CLARK PIERSON	drms	BC

ALBUMS:	1(A)	PROUD FLESH SOOTHSEER	(Mercury 61181) 1968 -
	2(A)	FEVER SHOT	(Mercury 61218) 1969 -
	3(B)	TILL BREAK OF DAWN	(Philips 600326) 1970 -

LISTENING - Listening LP.

45s:	Cave Songr/Think	(Mercury 72852) 1969
	Lower Lemons/Fast Days	(Mercury 72882) 1969
α	Girl Can't Help It/Fever Shot	(Mercury 72907) 1969
	Let The Music Begin/Wine Take Me Away	(Philips 40644) 1970
β	Sea Cruise/It's A Fact Of Life	(Philips 40669) 1970

NB: α Credited to Linn County Blues Band. β as by Stephen Miller.

Originally from Cedar Rapids, Iowa they moved to Chicago and then, like many others they migrated to San Francisco during the flower-power era. Musically they played a mixture of blues, rock and jazz, a bit like **A.B. Skhy** or **The Serfs** with psych influences. All three albums are now very minor collectables. The most interesting is maybe the first, which is housed in a very strange gatefold cover showing the group on the moon (!) with a Rick Griffin lettering.

They disbanded when **Stephen Miller** left to do a solo album, although most of them backed him on it. He later joined Elvin Bishop's band and from there went on to Grinderswitch. Clark Pierson joined Janis Joplin's Full Tilt Boogie Band and Ray McAndrew was involved with Gainsborough Gallery. (VJ/GH/SR)

Lion and The Leprechauns

45:	MouseTrap/ 2 Miles Over And 2 Miles Back	(Little Fort 8846) 196?

The Madness Invasion, Vol. 3 features *Mouse Trap*. The band spent time in Wisconsin and Illinois. (VJ)

Liquid Blue

45:	Henry Can't Drive/ A Pretty Good Day	(Texas Revolution 3) 1969

A rare 45 by an obscure Texas group. It was released on the same label as **Glory** and it's rumoured that both groups shared some members. (SR)

Liquid Smoke

Personnel incl:	MIKE ARCHELETA	bs	A
	VINCE FERSAK	gtr	A
	CHAS KIMBRELL	drms	A
	BENNY NINMANN	keyb'ds	A
	SANDY PANTALEO	ld vcls	A

ALBUM:	1(A)	LIQUID SMOKE	(Avco Embassy 33005) 1970 SC HCP

45s:	I Who Have Nothing/ Warm Touch	(Avco Embassy 4522) 1970 82
	Shelter Of Your Arms/ Let Me Down Easy	(Avco Embassy 4532) 1970
	Hard To Handle/?	(Avco Embassy 4546) 1970 -

The New York band's album of doom-laden heavy guitar/organ underground psychedelic rock is now a minor collectable. Consisting of original material written by Vince Fersak and some covers (*Hard To Handle*, *It's A Man's Man's World*), the album was produced by Vinnie Testa, who was then also working with **Frijid Pink**, to whom they can be compared.

The quintet also made No. 82 in the U.S. with *I Who Have Nothing*. Their *Lookin' For Tomorrow* was also covered by Peruvian band Gerardo Manuel and Humo on their debut 1970 album, *Apocallypsis*. (VJ/SR/CF)

Listening

Personnel:	ERNIE KAMANIS	drms, vcls	A
	PETER MALICK	gtr	A
	WALTER POWERS	bs	A
	MICHAEL TSCHUDIN	organ, keyb'ds, vcls	A

THE LITTER - Distortions LP.

ALBUM: 1(A) LISTENING   (Vanguard 6504) 1968 R1
NB: (1) reissued on CD and LP (Akarma AK 050) 1999.

45s: I Can Teach You/Cuando   (Vanguard 35077) 1968
      α Life Stories/Hello You   (Vanguard 35094) 1968
NB: α both sides non-LP.

From Boston and rated highly by some, this album includes some fine guitar and organ work on cuts like *Baby: Where Are You?*. Still an undiscovered gem this is worth searching out.

Most of the vocals were performed by drummer Ernie Kamanis, and Peter Malick who was 16 at the time the album was recorded. Walter Powers had previously been in the famed punk band **The Lost**.

A reworked version of the album's opener, Michael Tschudin's *You're Not There*, appears on the highly-touted album *...Setting Forth... Improvising Against The Future* by **Odyssey**.

Michael Tschudin later played with **Cynara** and produced the **Fort Mudge Memorial Dump** album. He became a session man and producer during the seventies, notably working with Tim Curry. Peter Malick played with the James Montgomery Band and is is still active, fronting his own Peter Malick Band playing blues / R&B influenced music in/around Boston. Walter Powers teamed up with his old **Lost** companion Willie "Loco" Alexander in the final incarnation of **The Velvet Underground**.

The uplifting baroque-pop of *Hello You* can be found on *Bring Flowers To U.S.* (LP), whilst one track from the album, *Stoned Is* has also resurfaced on *Marijuana Unknowns* (LP & CD). (VJ/MW/SR/PMk)

Lite Storm

Personnel incl: JOHNIMA P. BAHLU   A

ALBUMS: 1 WARNING   (Beverly Hills BHS-1 135) 1973 SC
         2 GOD IS LOVE   (Beverly Hills BHS-1136) 197? -

The label suggests that this was possibly a Los Angeles band. The five piece (three lads and two lasses) was led by Johnima, who takes all the credits on the first album - the others don't get a jot. An early seventies 'beautiful people' act, *Warning* is soft hippie-rock. *Hanana*, is probably the only 'psychedelic' track on the album. The unheard second album sounds even less encouraging.

One of the girls is possibly **Kali Bahlu** (Johnima's Wife? Sister?) who, in her persona of 'Gypsy Star Child', released an album entitled *Kali Bahlu Takes The Forest Children On A Journey Of Cosmic Rememberance* (World Pacific WPS- 21875) which says it all!

Compilation appearances include: *Hanana* on *Lycergic Soap* (LP), *Turds On A Bum Ride, Vol. 1 & 2* (Dble CD) and *Turds On A Bum Ride, Vol. 1* (Dble LP). (MW)

The Litter

Personnel: JIM KANE   bs, moog   ABCDE   H
            TOM MURRAY   drms   ABCDEFG H I
            DAN RINALDI   gtr, vcls   ABCDEFG H I
            BILL STRANDLOF   ld gtr   A
            DENNY WAITE   vcls, organ AB   H I
            TOM 'ZIPPY' CAPLAN ld gtr   B   H I
            LONNIE KNIGHT   ld gtr, vcls C
            MARK GALLAGHER   vcls   DEF   I
            RAY MELINA   ld gtr   D
            SEAN JONES   ld gtr   EF
            JOHN SUTFON   bs   F
            CASEY McPHEARSON   vcls   G
            JOHN KING   ld gtr   G
            ?? ??   G
            WOODY WOODRICH   bs   H
            MICK STANHOPE   vcls   I
            BOB HOOD   I
            RICK OTTUM   I

NB: Line-up (A) 1966-67, (B) 1967-68, (C) 1968, (D) 1968-70, (E) 1970, (F) late-1970, (G) 1971-72,(H) 1990, (I) 1992.

                                                           HCP
ALBUMS: 1(A/B) DISTORTIONS   (Warick WM-671-A) 1967 - R3
         2(B) $100 FINE   (Hexagon 681(S)) 1968 - R3
         3(D)   EMERGE THE LITTER (Probe 4504 S) 1969 175 SC
         4(H)   LIVE AT MIRAGE 1990 (Arf! Arf! AA-079) 1998 - -
         5(I)   RE-EMERGE   (Arf!Arf! AA-080) 1998 - -

NB: (1) and (2) counterfeited in the early eighties as limited editions and reissued officially on K-Tel. The K-Tel issues have not only been remastered but previously unavailable tracks have been added. *Distortions* (K-Tel 835-1) contains *The Egyptian* and *Blues One*, whilst *$100 Fine* also includes *Confessions (Of A Traveler Through Time)*. (2) was also reissued on Hick-cup in 1976. (1) and (2) reissued in 1999 by Arf! Arf! (AA-077) and (AA-078) respectively with even more bonus tracks. The Arf! Arf! *Distortions* CD adds the previously reissued *Confessions* and *Blues One*; two unreleased cuts - *Hey Joe* and *Harpsichord Sonata #1*; plus five cuts recorded live at the Electric Theatre on 18th June 1968. The bonus cuts on the Arf!Arf! *$100 Fine* CD comprise nineteen unreleased tracks - *Angelica* (with J.Frank Wilson) plus eighteen Zippy Caplan / Larry Loofbourrow demos from 1965 through 1968). (3) also issued as an 8-track cartridge (Columbia House 4504) and on cassette (Probe X-54504). (3) reissued on Big Beat (WIK 68) and One Way (CD).

45s: Action Woman/Legal Matter   (Scotty 803G-6710) 1967
      Somebody Help Me/I'm A Man   (Warick 9445-6711) 1967
      Action Woman/
      Whatcha Gonna Do About It?   (Warwick 6712) 1968

THE LITTER - $100 Fine LP.

Feeling/Silly People	(Probe 461) 1969
On Our Minds/Blue Ice	(Probe 467) 1970

The Litter came from Minneapolis, Minnesota and recorded two of America's finest psychedelic punk albums. *Distortions* and *$100 Fine* are both strongly recommended. *Distortions* contained high energy psychedelic rock versions of many classic songs, including *Action Woman* and their amazing (if over the top) psychedelic rework of *I'm A Man*. Play it Loud! Feedback appears to have been one of the main weapons in their repertoire and it is seldom used more effectively than on the aforementioned track. Also on the album are fine versions of Cream's *I'm So Glad*, The Small Faces' classic *Whatcha Gonna Do 'Bout It*, The Who's *Substitute* and *A Legal Matter*, Spencer Davis' *Somebody Help Me*, The Yardbirds' *Wrack My Mind*, Warren Kendrick's *Soul Searchin'* and **Buffy St. Marie**'s much recorded *Codine*. Strandlof played lead on *Action Woman*, *A Legal Matter*, and *Soul Searchin'* but his attempts to steer the band in a folk-rock direction caused friction with Kane who wanted the band to become heavier. In the Spring of 1967, he was replaced by Zippy Caplan, freshly back from a sojourn in California.

By their next effort *$100 Fine* the group were writing much of their own material. For this reason *$100 Fine* is probably the better album. Opening track *Mindbreaker* features fine fuzztone guitar work and culminates in a psychedelic haze. Their driving electric guitar work is well represented in tracks like *Tallyman* and *Here I Go Again* which has a catchy guitar riff intro. More vintage psychedelic guitar work is evident on *Morning Sun* and *(Under The Screaming Double) Eagle*. The side culminates with a piece of psychedelic nonsense *Apologies To 2069*, which ends with the intro to *Action Woman* - a track on their first album. However, the stand-out track is their cover of Procol Harum's *Kaleidoscope* on Side Two, featuring an early use of 'phasing'. The remainder of this side is comprised of an impressive extended version of The Zombies' *She's Not There* and the self-explanatory *Blues One*. If you ever get the chance to hear either of these two albums, take it!

Bad management decisions hampered the band's progress during 1968. Both Elektra and Columbia made offers to the band but were knocked back because of heavy touring commitments. In August 1968 they recorded numbers for the film 'Medium Cool' but only made about 20 seconds of the final cut with the **Mothers Of Invention** dubbed over them. Soon after, Waite (who was burnt-out) and Caplan (who formed **White Lightning** and then **Lightning**) dropped out of the band.

1969 saw the group sign to a major record company (ABC) for a third album - a good hard-rock effort that suffers only by comparison to the first two. Denny Waite had also departed and his place was taken by Mark Gallagher who'd previously been with **The Troys**.

Despite the band's legendary status there has often been confusion and misspeculation surrounding them and the other artistes under Warren Kendrick's guidance. **The Electras/Twas Brillig** outfit must be fed up by the constant claims that they were a **Litter** offshoot since they'd been around for some years beforehand - see their entry for details. This

THE LITTER - Emerge LP.

GATHERING AT THE DEPOT (Comp LP) including The Litter.

confusion was due to them also being under Warren Kendrick's wing apart from the fact they also recorded Kendrick's *Action Woman* and *Soul Searchin'*. No wonder the two outfits sounded similar. The confusion was aggravated by Eva's compilation, *Litter - Rare Tracks* (LP), which would have better been entitled 'The Best Of The Rest Of Warren Kendrick'. It features **Litter**'s *She's Not There* (short version), *On Our Minds*, *Little Red Book*, *Ungrateful Pig* and *Substitute*; **Electras/Twas Brillig**'s *Dirty Old Man*, *You Love*, *This Week's Children* and *Soul Searchin'*; **White Lightning**'s *William* and *Of Paupers And Poets*; **Zoser**'s *Together* and *Dark Of The Morning* and **Second Edition**'s *To Keep You*.

Denny Waite and Jim Kane had been in another Kendrick-produced group, **The Victors**, prior to **The Litter**. Five unreleased **The Victors** tracks have been aired on the Get Hip album *Electras vs. Scotsmen/Victors*, which was released in 1993, and repeated on *The Scotty Story* CD.

Before they called it a day **Litter** came together with other Minneapolis acts on the *Gathering At The Depot* (LP) compilation (Beta 580 47-14145) 1970, which features a live *Ungrateful Pig* (misspelled *Ungrateful Peg* on the LP!). After that Tom Murray went on to Straight Up who issued one 45 *Fire/So Blind* (Straight Up 1001).

Fans of the band should look out for no less than four new CD's on Arf! Arf! - the definitive versions of *Distortions* and *$100 Fine*, plus the storming *The Litter - Live At The Mirage 1990*, which captures the band on top form and a previously unreleased studio album from 1992, entitled, *Re-Emerge*. The Arf!Arf! *Distortions* CD adds much to the original album cuts: the previously reissued *Confessions* and *Blues One*; two unreleased cuts - *Hey Joe* and *Harpsichord Sonata #1*; and five cuts recorded live at the Electric Theatre on 18th June 1968. The bonus cuts on the Arf!Arf! *$100 Fine* CD comprise nineteen unreleased tracks - *Angelica* (with J.Frank Wilson) plus eighteen Larry Loofbourrow demos from 1965 through 1968.

The *Live At The Mirage* CD is highly recommended to all **Litter** fans. From a 20-year reunion concert in Minneapolis on September 19th 1990, it features the classic 'B' line-up, though Kane guests on just three tracks, plus bassist Woody Woodrich. They run through much of the material from the first two albums plus an excellent cover of the **Music Machine**'s *Talk Talk*. The years just roll back - if it weren't for the modern sound quality this could've been circa 1970.

Zippy Caplan's lost none of his dexterous zip; Denny Waite's vocals may have lost their adolescent timbre but are still in fine form, and Tom Murray's drumming is just awesome. Sounding like a classic car that's been lovingly preserved in a garage just waiting for the right time to be taken out again for a drive - all parts are still tight but well-oiled and as they warm up the throttle pedal goes down... and so the concert builds to a glorious climax - a stunningly powerful *Train Kept A-Rollin'* that can only be topped by the frenzied finale of *I'm A Man*.

The *Re-Emerge* CD is all new recordings including a reworking of *Action Woman* plus sixteen new numbers by the latest line-up and features guest appearances by Joey Molland (gtr, b.vcls, ex-Badfinger), James "Owl"

Walsh (keyb'ds, ex-**Gypsy**), Larry Wiegand (bass gtr, ex-**Crow**) and Andy Bailey (keyb'ds).

Bill Strandlof who played the electrifying solo on *Action Woman* died of leukaemia on March 4th, 1995.

In 2001, Zip Caplan released a new CD *Monsters And Heroes* as **Zip Caplan and Cast of Thousands**. Mostly instrumental it comprises 21 tracks of classic Horror movie, old Serials and fifties T.V. Series Soundtracks but recorded with 'rock' instruments. 48 different musicians are featured, with a different set of players backing Zip on each track. Some of the guests include Jim McCarty (The Yardbirds), Joey Molland (Badfinger), Nokie Edwards (The Ventures), Bobby Torres (Joe Cocker and Tom Jones), Doug Nelson (Jonny Lang Band), Bruce "Creeper" Kurnow (**Mason Proffitt**), Denny Libby (**The Castaways**) plus guys from Edgar Winter, **Gypsy**, **The Litter**, **Stillroven**, **Underbeats**, **White Lightning** and **Crow**.

Retrospective compilation appearances have included: *Action Woman* on *Nuggets Box* (4-CD), *Pebbles, Vol. 1* (CD), *Pebbles Box* (5-LP), *Pebbles, Vol. 1* (LP), *Songs We Taught The Fuzztones* (Dble LP & Dble CD), *Trash Box* (5-CD), *Excerpts From Nuggets* (CD) and *Great Pebbles* (CD); *I'm A Man* on *Pebbles, Vol. 2* (LP) and *Pebbles, Vol. 3 (ESD)* (CD); *Hey Joe* and *7 UP Commercial* on *The Scotty Story* (CD). (VJ/MW/LP/ZC)

Ken Little

Personnel:	JOHN CAMELOT	keyb'ds	A
	SUGARCANE HARRIS	violin, backing vcls	A
	KEN LITTLE	vcls	A
	RICK MACOWSKI	drms	A
	FRANK MUSTARI	gtr	A
	NORMA WAGNER	gtr	A

ALBUMS:	1(A)	SOLO	(Dharma D-801) 1972 -
	2(-)	LEANIN' ON THE BAR	(Dharma D-805) 1976 -

NB: (1) reissued on Breeder (RPR 006-2C-566) 1986.

Ken Little was a Chicago singer and a friend of **Harvey Mandel**. In 1972, he appeared on **Mandel**'s bluesy project *Get Off In Chicago* with two songs co-written with Norm Wagner, *High Test Fish Line* and *Springfield Station Theme*. The same year, **Mandel** co-produced **Little**'s *Solo* album. This is basically mainstream heavyish progressive rock with strong blues influences (Hubert Sumlin of Howlin' Wolf's band plays on one track and Sugarcane Harris on five). If that's your bag, it's not bad but don't be misled by dealers with limited descriptive abilities who describe it as 'psychedelic'.

Ken Little returned in 1976 with *Leanin' On The Bar*. In a totally different style, the music is a consistent mix of country and bar rock. (VJ/SR)

(A) Little Bit of Sound

45:	α	Incense and Peppermints/	
		I Want You To Know	(Carole 1002) 1967

NB: α also released on Vogue in France.

A cover of the **Strawberry Alarm Clock**'s classic by an unknown Los Angeles area act on GNP Crescendo's sister label.

Compilation appearances include: *Incense And Peppermints* on *Psychedelic Unknowns, Vol. 5* (LP & CD) and *Incense And Peppermints* on *Acid Dreams, Vol. 3* (LP). (VJ/MW/GT)

The Little Bits

45:	Girl Give Me Love/Spoofin'	(Tiger-Eye TE-101) 196?

This record was made by 8 or 9 year old kids from Jennings, Louisiana. The lyrics mostly consist of them screaming or singing *Girl Give Me Love*. This makes it an unique novelty.

LITTLE BOY BLUES - In The Woodland Of Weir CD.

Compilation appearances have included: *Girl Give Me Love* on *Louisiana Punk From The Sixties* (LP), *Sixties Archive, Vol. 3* (CD) and *Yeah Yeah Yeah* (CD); and *Spoofin* on *Acid Dreams, Vol. 2* (LP). (VJ)

Little Bits of Sound

Personnel:	JEFF EVANS	drms	A
	BOB GREENSTONE	ld gtr, vcls	A
	LARRY JACK	bs	A
	JEFF MORRIS	keyb'ds	A
	JERRY PRIESER	gtr	A

45:	What's Life About/	
	Girls Who Paint Designs	(Roulette 4744) 1967

Often confused with **(A) Little Bit Of Sound**, the 'B' side of this group's 45 is on *Of Hopes And Dreams & Tombstones* (LP) and *Psychedelic Unknowns, Vol. 7* (LP & CD).

Interestingly, *Girls Who Paint Designs* was mastered to the 45 faster than the original recording and can be heard changing keys after the first four bars.

The band came from Franklin Square, Long Island NY. Their 45 came about via Koppelman & Rubin Associates Chardon Music, Inc. where their manager (Stu Antzis)'s wife worked. The 45 was never promoted though and the band played only small local venues and school functions.

Larry Jack left the band after James Foley, from Koppelman & Rubin approached him with a song by Richard Fishbaugh called *A Little Rain Must Fall* asking him if he could get a band together to record it. Jack joined forces with a local group The Entire Thing, who in turn were renamed by the record company as **Epic Splendor** and *A Little Rain Must Fall* became a Top 30 hit in the region. (MW/MM/RJ)

Little Boy Blues

Personnel:	JAMES BOYCE	drms, vcls	ABC
	RAY LEVIN	bs, piano, organ, flute	ABCD
	PAUL OSTROFF	ld gtr	ABC
	LOWELL SHYETTE	gtr, hrmnca, vcls	AB
	BILLY McCOLL	vcls	B
	FRANK BINER	vcls, gtr	C
	MARK COPLON	vcls	D
	BILL MOONEY	drms	D
	PETER POLLACK	gtr	D

ALBUM:	1(D)	IN THE WOODLAND OF WEIR	
			(Fontana MGF-27578/SRF-67578) 1968 -

NB: (1) reissued on CD (Acid Symposium AS 002) 2001.

45s:	Look At The Sun/Love For A Day	(IRC 6929) 1965
	I'm Ready/Little Boy Blues Blues	(IRC 6936) 1966
α	I Can Only Give You Everything/ You Don't Love Me (PS)	(IRC 6939) 1966
	Great Train Robbery/Season Of The Witch	(Ronko 6996) 1967
	It's Only You/Is Love	(Fontana 1623) 1968

NB: α Issued in a limited edition (approx. 500 copies) with picture sleeve.

The 45s this Chicago punk outfit produced will be of more interest than their album. Of particular note were their interpretation of Donovan's *Season Of The Witch* and two fine fuzz punkers *Great Train Robbery* and *I Can Only Give You Everything*, which was recorded by several other bands in this era. The best source of these 45s is the compilation *Chicago 60's Punk Vs. New Mexico 60's Pop* (LP), which contains both sides of their first four 45s.

The album is a real hodgepodge of styles that doesn't hang together well. Most cuts feature orchestration and range from light *Sgt Pepper* chamber-pop through brassy R&B workouts to heavier fuzzed moments and pedestrian Fudge-like pomp... seriously arty and very '68. Two of the stronger album cuts were put out on the Fontana 45, which states that they are "from Fontana's album Can You Dig It (SRF-67578)" - presumably the original title for *Woodland Of Weir*. *Is Love?* is a punchy **Left Banke**-ish ditty except for a mid-point crescendo of noise, with gut-wrenching guitar. *It's Only You* is fuzzy acid-rock.

Original guitarist Lowell Shyette was drafted in September '66 shortly after the band appeared on Dick Clark's 'Where The Action Is'. He later worked as a sales rep for Fender and is still active musically. Frank Biner later played for a California outfit called Kingsnake.

Line-up 'C' also have a rock/soul effort *Ain't Too Proud To Beg*, from April 1967, on which they are assisted by a horn section of studio musicians, on the compilation *Early Chicago* (Happy Tiger HT-10107) in 1972.

The Greek CD reissue of the album collects their entire recorded output by adding the three IRC 45s, the Ronko 45, and *Ain't Too Proud To Beg* (from the *Early Chicago* compilation).

Retrospective compilation appearances have included: *Great Train Robbery* on *Mayhem & Psychosis, Vol. 2* (LP), *Mayhem & Psychosis, Vol. 1* (CD) and *Highs In The Mid-Sixties, Vol. 4* (LP); *The Great Train Robbery* and *I'm Ready* on *Off The Wall, Vol. 2* (LP); *It's Only You* on *Boulders, Vol. 11* (LP) and *Ya Gotta Have Moxie, Vol. 2* (Dble CD); *You Don't Love Me* on *Pebbles, Vol. 6* (CD), *Garage Punk Unknowns, Vol. 5* (LP); *Cathedral* on *Songs Of Faith And Inspiration* (CDR & CD); *I Can Only Give You Everything* on *Pebbles, Vol. 2* (CD), *Pebbles Box* (5-LP), *Pebbles, Vol. 2* (LP), *Trash Box* (5-CD) and *Great Pebbles* (CD); *The Great Train Robbery* and *You Dove Deep In My Soul*, a previously unreleased track on *Oh Yeah! The Best Of Dunwich Records* (CD); *Love For A Day, Look At The Sun, I'm Ready, Little Boy Blue's Blues, I Can Only Give You Everything, You Don't Love Me, The Great Train Robbery* and *The Season Of The Witch* on *Chicago 60's Punk Vs. New Mexico 60's Pop* (LP). (VJ/MW)

Little Caesar and The Conspirators

Personnel:	JIM 'LITTLE CAESAR' BARNHOLDT	drms	AB
	MARV HUNTINGTON	bs	AB
	BILL KLINKHAMMER	gtr	A
	GARY SORENSON	ld gtr	AB
	JOHN PUTNAM	gtr	B

45:	New Orleans/It Must Be Love	(Studio City 1023) 1965

This Owatonna, Minnesota-based group formed out of the ashes of another Owatonna band The Henchmen, who included Marv Huntington and Gary Sorenson and the Fairmont-based Reconstituted Lemons, whose leader had been Jim Barnholdt. Local dee-jay Bill Diehl took them under his wing and got them appearing on stage in Roman Style dress for what was reputed to have been a wild act. They financed a 45 on the Minneapolis-based Studio City label and their finest moment, *It Must Be Love*, got lots of airplay around Southern Minnesota at the time. In May 1965, a rift developed between Barnholdt and the rest of the band, so he left to join a Minneapolis-based folk-rock group called Id. The three remaining members went on to play for the Rochester-based Furys.

HIGHS IN THE MID-SIXTIES Vol. 4 (Comp LP) including Little Boy Blues.

Compilation appearances have included: *New Orleans* on *Grab This And Dance!!!* (LP) and *It Must Be Love* on *Hipsville, Vol. 3* (LP). (VJ)

Little John and The Monks

45:	Needles And Pins/Black Winds	(Jerden 775) 1965

This Blue River, Oregon group were originally known as The Nomads. Their cover of The Searchers' classic *Needles And Pins* can be found on *The History Of Northwest Rock, Vol. 5*. More recently *Black Winds*, a gentle folk-rock ballad has resurfaced on *Relics, Vol. 2* (LP), *Relics, Vol's 1 & 2* (CD), *Northwest Battle Of The Bands, Vol. 1* (CD) and *Tymes Gone By* (LP). (VJ/MW)

Little John and Tony

45:	The Beginning Of The End / All I Ask	(Volkano V-5001) 1965

A Detroit-area duo produced by **Dennis Coffey**. *The Beginning Of The End* is a fine tribute to **Barry McGuire**'s *Eve Of Destruction* - apocalyptic theme, even the gravelly vocals, over the classic Dunhill folk-rock sound (dramatic Spectoresque production wrapped around **Beau Brummels**' jangle).

It's been revitalised on the Misty Lane folk-flower-pop compilation *Every Groovy Day*. (MD)

Little Phil and The Night Shadows

See **The Nightshadow(s)** entry.

Little Willie and The Adolescents

Personnel:	TOM McLAUGHLIN	keyb'ds, vcls	A
	ERIC SCHABACKER	gtr, vcls	A
	BERRY VAUGHT	drms, vcls	A

45s:	α	Get Out Of My Life/Stop It	(Tener 1009) 1966
		Looking For Love/Push Song	(Tener 1013) 1967

NB: α 'B' side credited to The Starfires.

Starting out in a basement in Buffalo, New York in 1963 as **The Starfires**, the following year they put out an album *Play* on the O.R.S. (Ohio Recording Service) label, whose cover features several photos of the band, including one with the Isley Brothers.

The band relocated to Orlando and changed their name to **Little Willie and The Adolescents** with the above line-up. None of them was called Willie but they used to set up a small fluorescent-green metal man in front of the drums that they told people was Little Willie when they asked. Berry Vaught is remembered as a stand-up drummer and a renowned part of the band's repertoire was to stand on their heads whilst playing the instrumental *David's Mood* - don't ask why.

Get Out Of My Life, a really nasty punky song with snotty vocals and catchy keyboards, was good enough to make it onto *Back From The Grave, Vol. 3* (LP). *Looking For Love*, a frantic keyboard-led romp, first reappeared on the hellishly rare 1967 *Bee Jay Demo, Vol. 2* compilation. Thankfully it is available again on *Psychedelic States - Florida Vol. 2* (CD).

It was the enterprising Eric Schabacker himself who founded the Bee Jay booking agency and recording studios, and the associated record labels - Tener, Hype and Immunity. (MW/JLh/MM/RM)

The Live Five

Personnel:	CRAIG MARTELL	drms	A
	JERRY MEIER	ld gtr	A
	BILL O'BRIEN	vcls	A
	JOE SMITH	bs	A
	STAN STEINER	keyb'ds	A

45s:	Shake A Tail Feather/Yes You're Mine	(Panorama 31) 1966
	Shake A Tail Feather/Yes You're Mine	(Jerden 797) 1966
	Hunose/Let's Go, Let's Go, Let's Go	(Panorama 46) 1966
	Move Over And Let Me Fly/ Been Nice Knowin' You Baby	(Piccadilly 233) 1967
	I Must Move/I Must Move	(Piccadilly 236) 1967
	Take The Good And The Bad/Who Knows	(Piccadilly 248) 1967

Came out of Salem, Oregon, forming in 1965. Steiner, O'Brien and Smith had all previously played in an outfit called The Che-vels. Managed by dance promoter and radio station operator Ed Dougherty they got plenty of good live bookings appearing on bills with all the top acts that came to Salem. They also appeared with **The Knickerbockers** at the Seattle Teen Fair and with The Rolling Stones in Portland, Oregon in July 1966. They appeared in candy-striped trousers and played a blend of Northwest rock and Merseybeat. *Yes You're Mine* and *Hunose* were both big regional hits. *Move Over And Let Me Fly* is an irresistable jerker with 'call and response' style vocals which ought to have been a big hit.

They broke up in late 1967, although Joe Smith carried on with four new members for a further six months.

Compilation appearances have included: *Let's Go, Let's Go, Let's Go* on *Battle Of The Bands, Vol. 1* (LP), *Northwest Battle Of The Bands, Vol. 1 - Flash And Crash* (CD) *The History Of Northwest Rock, Vol. 4* (LP); *Move Over And Let Me Fly* on *Battle Of The Bands, Vol. 2* (LP), *Northwest Battle Of The Bands, Vol. 2 - Knock You Flat!* (LP & CD), *The History Of Northwest Rock, Vol. 3* (CD) *Highs In The Mid Sixties, Vol. 16* (LP), *The History Of Northwest Rock, Vol. 3* (LP) and *Northwest Battle Of The Bands, Vol. 2* (CD); *Yes You're Mine* and *Let's Go, Let's Go, Let's Go* on *Northwest Battle Of The Bands, Vol. 1* (CD); *Hunose* on *Sixties Rebellion Vol. 16* (LP & CD) and *History Of Northwest Rock, Vol. 2* (CD). (VJ/MW)

Liverpool Five

Personnel:	DAVE BURGESS	bs	A
	KEN COX	gtr	ABCD
	RON HENLEY	keyb'ds	AB
	STEVE LAINE	vcls	ABCD
	JIMMY MAY	drms, vcls	ABCD
	FREDDIE DENNIS	bs, vcls	BCD
	MARK GAGE	keyb'ds	C
	GARY MILKIE	keyb'ds	D

ALBUMS:	1(A)	TOKYO INTERNATIONAL	(CBS) 1965 ?
	2(A)	THE LIVERPOOL FIVE ARRIVE	(RCA Victor LSP- 3583) 1966 -
	3(A)	OUT OF SIGHT	(RCA Victor LSP-3682) 1967 -
	4(A)	EXCITEMENT IN STEREO SOUND	(RCA PRS 250) 1967 -
	5(A)	STEREO FESTIVAL (also featuring The Astronauts)	(RCA PRS 251) 1967 -

NB: (1) German only release as by The 5 Liverpools, reissued on CD (Ultravybe UVB 10042) 2001. (4) and (5) were promotional only releases.

EP:	1	OUT OF SIGHT	(TK 151) 1967

NB: There's also a French EP with picture sleeve: *If You Gotta Go, Go Now/Too Far Out/Heart/I Just Can't Believe It* (RCA 86493) 1967.

HCP

45s:	α	L'um D'Lum D'Lum High/ Good Golly Miss Molly	(Picadilly 1255 (UK)) 1964? -
		That's What I Want/ Everything's Al' Right	(RCA Victor 47-3578) 1965 -
		If You Gotta Go, Go Now/ Too Far Out	(RCA Victor 47-8660) 1965 -
		Heart/I Just Can't Belive It	(RCA Victor 47-8725) 1966 -
		Sister Love/She's Mine	(RCA Victor 47-8816) 1966 -
		New Directions/What A Crazy World (We're Living In)	(RCA Victor 47-8906) 1966 -
		Anyway That You Want Me/ The Snake	(RCA Victor 47-8968) 1966 98
	β	Cloudy/She's Got Plenty Of Love	(RCA Victor 47-9158) 1967 -

NB: α was a U.K. only 45 as by Liverpool 5. β some promo copies with 'A' side on both sides of disc, and same catalogue no.

Originally from the U.K. their German manager arranged for them to tour Europe and Asia, including a gig at the 1964 Olympic Games in Tokyo. On their return to Germany they recorded a 45 and rare German album as the 5 Liverpools then relocated to the States (Spokane, Washington) where they signed with RCA in 1965. Paul Handler became their new manager. When Dave Burgess left to get married in 1967 he was replaced by Freddie Dennis who had played in several Spokane groups. They played a mixture of folk-rock, beat, R'n'B and ballads as well as punk. They could imitate the best U.S. bands (**Remains, Standells**) but also retained their Englishness. *Broken Dreams, Vol. 4* (Line OLLP 5395 AS) 198? includes *She's Mine* and *Piccadilly Line*. *New Directions*, which contains some infectious guitar work, is included on *Mindrocker, Vol. 9* (LP). *Everything's Allright*, meanwhile, has resurfaced on *Hide & Seek, Vol. 1*. They even had a very minor hit with *Any Way That You Want Me*.

Later in 1969 they changed keyboard players twice before finally quitting in 1970. Freddie Dennis later joined the reformed Kingsmen. Only Jim May returned to the UK, all the other four original members remained in Northern California.

One track from their privately pressed *Out Of Sight* EP entitled *Gotta Get A Move On* has also resurfaced on *The Technicolour Milkshake* compilation. (VJ/HI/MW)

SIXTIES REBELLION Vol. 16 (Comp CD) including The Live Five.

The Liverpools

Probably from Dallas, Texas. *Soho* a Radio Spot ad originally aired on KLIF-AM, can be found on *Acid Visions - Complete Collection, Vol. 3* (3-CD) and on *Texas Punk, Vol. 9* (LP).

The Liverpools

Personnel incl:	BADERAK?	A
	MANN?	A
	RICHARDS?	A
	ROY STRAIGIS	A

ALBUMS:	1	BEATLE MANIA! IN THE U.S.A. (Wyncote W 9001) 1964 -
	2	THE HIT SOUNDS FROM ENGLAND (Wyncote W 9061) 1964 -

A Philadelphia studio-only outfit, according to Mike Kuzmin in his Pennsylvania book 'Sounds From The Woods', they also recorded as **The Emblems** and **The Haircuts**. No guesses as to influences and style - both albums unashamedly cashed in on the first wave of Beatlemania. The first includes four Beatles covers - *She Loves You*, *I Want To Hold Your Hand*, *I Saw Her Standing There* and *Please, Please Me*. The remaining tracks are good beat fodder mainly composed or co-composed by Straigis, including *Whenever I'm Feeling Low* previously aired on the **Emblems**' 1963 45. (MW)

The Livers

45:	Beatle Time/This Is The Night	(Constellation 118) 1964

Another attempt at cashing in on the Beatles' success, this 45 is instrumental. (SR)

Live Wires

45:	Keep It To Yourself/The Mask	(Boom 60,015) 1966

The above recording was produced by Richard Gottehrer of **Strangeloves** fame possibly placing this as a New York outfit. (VJ)

The Live Wires

45s:	Bona Vista Twist / Kickoff	(R.E.F. 110) 196?
	One Cycle Venture / A Rovin'	(R.E.F. 300) 196?
	Love / Being Alone	(R.E.F. 301) 1966

The first two 45s contain instrumentals and may predate the third by some time. A different outfit to that on Boom and thought to be from Pennsylvania - this has been confirmed by Mike Kuzmin's Pennslyvania sixties book 'Sounds From The Woods' which places them in Dubois.

Love, which illustrates the Anglophile influence on American garage bands, can be found on *The Essential Pebbles Collection, Vol. 2* (Dble CD) and *Pebbles, Vol. 7* (LP). (MW/VJ)

The Livin' End

45s:	Society / The World's Goin' Round	(Soft 1012) 1968
	Society / I Got To Have It Girl	(Soft 1012) 1968
	Gotta Get Back To My Baby / I Got To Have It Girl	(Soft 1012) 1968
	Your Kind Of Love / You Make Me Feel	(Soft 1031) 1968
	Today / You Don't Want Me	(Soft 1033) 1968
	Foolish People / Life Is A Search	(Shalimar 303) 1969

Although they formed in Wichita Falls this band moved to Burkburnett, Texas and recorded in Dallas. *Society*, which features some catchy organ and drumming and good fuzz guitar, probably captures them at their best. Compilation appearances have included: *Society* on *Punk Classics* (CD) and *Flashback, Vol. 6* (LP); and *Your Kind Of Love* on *The Fort Worth Teen Scene - The Major Bill Tapes Vol. 2* (LP). (VJ/MM/MW)

The Livin' End

Personnel:	WAYLAND HUEY	gtr	AB
	BILL LEITER	ld vcls	A
	ROBERT OLIVERA	gtr	AB
	BARRY ROBERTSON	bs	AB
	CAL STANTON	drums	A
	JOE MARTIN	drums	B
	LEE PENCE	keyb'ds, vcls	B
	TOMMY MARLIN	ld vcls	C

CD:	1	UNRELEASED TEXAS GARAGE SOUNDS (Collectables COL 0715) 1998

Previously assumed to be the other Texas **Livin' End**, thanks and kudos goes to Collectables for straightening out the facts and history behind this particular bunch. They were formed by Wayland Huey in Abilene, Texas after his previous outfit **The Coachmen** split in 1964 after issuing just one 45, also included on the CD. Though **Livin' End** never got to release a 45 during their lifespan, they would last until 1968 and recorded many unreleased nuggets between 1965 (*Get Off Of My Cloud*, *Friends*, *All Alone*) and 1967 (covers of *Baby Please Don't Go* and **The Doors**' *Love Me Two Times*).

The CD contains a further twelve **Livin' End** tracks including some live performances from a seventies reunion and the full lowdown on this band's story. Kicking off with an original garage-fuzz-punker *Pine Street Boys*, one of the highlights of this collection, there's a smattering of the usual covers (*Roadrunner*, *Talkin' About You*, *Empty Heart*, *Makin' Time* - this last probably their best cover) - all are competent if uninspiring. It's the originals that are more interesting even though very derivative - *All Alone* borrows the *I'm A Man* riff; *Friends* is Dylan via **The Byrds** ala *Chimes Of Freedom*; *My Destination* borrows a Beatles riff but transforms it into a tough garage-punker with a *Psychotic Reaction*-style rave-up break - most excellent indeed.

The band have also appeared on a number of other compilations, including: *Makin' Time*, *Captain Soul*, *Talkin' About You*, *Empty Heart* and *Unknown Destination* on *Texas Flashbacks Vol.1: Dallas* (LP); *All Alone*, and *Get Off Of My Cloud* on *Texas Punk: 1966, Vol. 1* (LP); *Roadrunner* and *Your Enemies* on *Texas Punk, Vol. 3* (LP); *All Alone*, *Get Off Of My Cloud*, *Roadrunner* and *Your Enemies* on *Acid Visions - The Complete Collection Vol. 2* (3-CD); and *Makin' Time*, *Empty Heart* and *Captain Soul* on *Psychedelic Microdots Vol. 2* (CD).

Barry Robertson is still active in the music business, playing with Slim Chance and The Survivors. (MW)

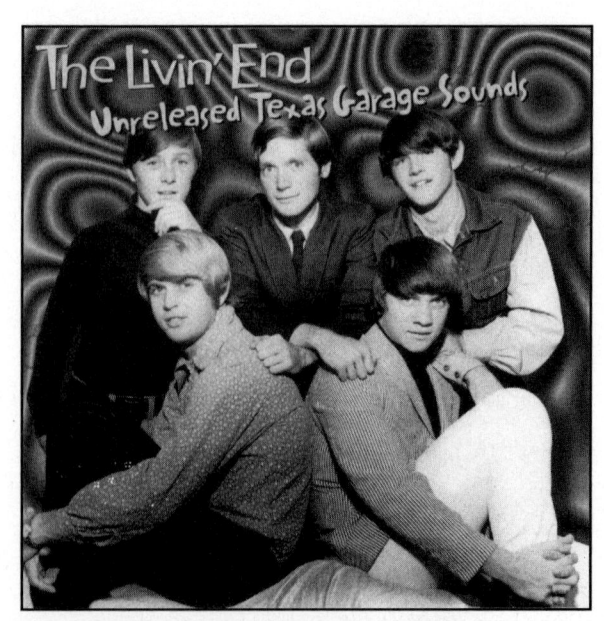

THE LIVIN' END - Unreleased Texas Garage Sounds CD.

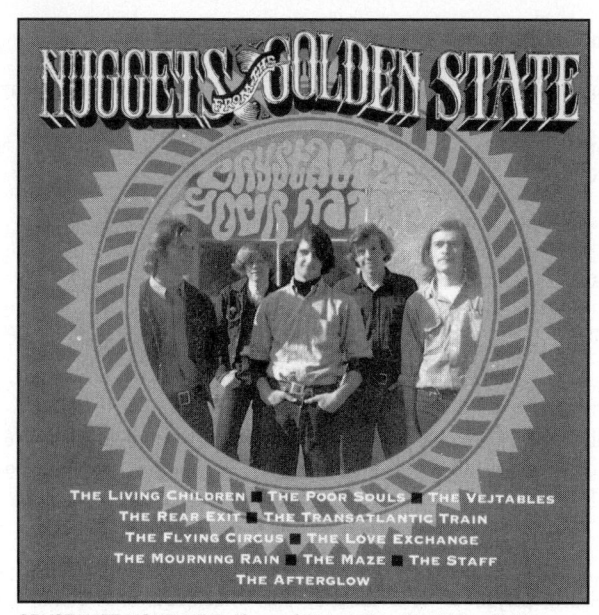

CRYSTALIZE YOUR MIND (Comp CD) including The Living Children.

The Livin' End

45: But I'll Live/
Don't Let Me Be Misunderstood (PS)   (KB 3008) 1968

From Centralia, Illinois. The 'A' side of their sole slightly psychedelic guitar driven disc is to be found on *Monsters Of The Midwest, Vol. 3* (LP). (VJ/MW/MM)

The Livin' End

45: You're My Woman /
Our Love Was Strong   (No label 1190, Rite #20211/2) 1967

A Dayton, Ohio band whose raw punker *You're My Woman* has reappeared on *Boulders, Vol. 11* (LP), *Ya Gotta Have Moxie, Vol. 2* (Dble CD) and *Sick And Tired* (LP). (MW/GGI/MM)

Liv'in End

45: She's A Teaser/
The Orange Rooftop Of My Baby's Mind   (Rickin 007) 196?

A West Coast outfit who have two cuts:- *Orange Rooftop Of My Baby's Mind* and *She's A Teaser* on *Boulders, Vol. 11* (LP) and *Ya Gotta Have Moxie, Vol. 2* (Dble CD). (MW/MM)

Livin End

45: Move Me/Time To Leave   (Murco No. 1054) 1969

The above 45 - on a Shreveport, Louisiana label - is a stately rock-ballad with vibrant bluesy vocals ala John Fogerty (**Creedence Clearwater Revival**) and some fluid fuzzwork, that sounds circa '67 or '68. The flip is okay pop-rock. (MW)

Livin' End

45: The Right Girl/You Cheatin' Heart   (Spontaneous 1001) 1967

From Camden, New Jersey, the band responsible for this soul-garage 45 achieved fame when they changed their name to **Crazy Elephant**. They may have also be responsible for the following 45:

45: Sheep / You Ain't No Friend Of Mine   (Di Venus 104) 196?

Sheep has been compiled on *World Of Acid* (LP). (MW/MM)

Livin' End

45: Round, Round / La-La   (Eceip 1005/6) c1966

An unheard Rochester, New York outfit on **Ron Wray**'s Eceip label. (MW)

Livin' End

45: What Now My Love / Hey, Come Here   (Domino D-101) 196?

MOR harmony-pop ballads from Columbus, Ohio. (MW)

Livin' Ends

45: I Love You More Than You'll Ever Know /
Jolyn   (Atlantic 2622) 1969

Rumoured to be from Texas, with this sole soul 45. (MW)

Livin' Ends

45: Hey Everybody /
Please Don't Hurt Me (Anymore)   (Patty 1347) 196?

Recorded on a susidiary label of New York's Holton Records, *Please Don't Hurt Me* was written by Vincent Sanpierto and Benjamin Galiani. (DJe/MW)

Livin' Ennd

45: Come To Me / Stop And Go   (M-6 69-1) 1969

A Michigan obscurity. Another 45 *White Horses / Remember When* (Sunday 1005) was released in the early seventies by an identically spelt **Livin' Ennd**. (MW/SR)

The Living Children

45: Crystalize Your Mind/Now It's Over   (MTA 140) 196?

An overlooked band from Fort Bragg, California. *Crystalize Your Mind* is good garage with psychy lyrics, a menacing riff and relentless beat. The flip is a superb slice of mellow **Love**-influenced psychedelia.

Compilation appearances have included: *Crystalize Your Mind* on *Sixties Rebellion, Vol. 3* (LP & CD); *Crystalize Your Mind* and *Now It's Over* on *Crystalize Your Mind* (CD). (VJ)

The Living End

45: I Need A Lot Of Lovin'/Turkey Stomp   (Mira 215) 1965

A Journey To Tyme, Vol. 5 (LP) includes both sides of this frat-beat stomper... From Brooklyn, New York. (MiW/MM)

Living End

Personnel: SCOTT LYMAN — bs — A
JOE MEYER — vcls, drms — A
JEFF RUNYON — organ — A
RAY WILKINS — gtr — A

45: A Night Like This / Brigitta   (Court ES 127/8) 1966

From Courtland, California. 'Court' was a personalised label on the Esar imprint.

Both sides of the 45 also appear on *The Sound Of Young Sacramento* (CD). (MW/MM/AP)

Living End

45:	Skyride / Jumpin' At The Lion's Gate	(Bolo 757) 1965

This **Living End** came from the Pacific Northwest. (MW)

Living End

Personnel:	JOHN	A
	LES	A
	MIKE	A
	MIKE	A
	STEVE	A

ALBUM:	1 (A)	POW	(GGM 001) 1999

This album contains fourteen demos recorded in L.A. in November 1966. It opens with a fine raw garage instrumental *The Street*, and a further highlight is the promising folk-punker *Baby I Love You*. However, only a handful of tracks feature the rhythm section. The majority are intimate folk ballads - just vocal(s) and acoustic guitar(s), more likely to appeal to followers of Bryan MacLean or **Bob Lind**. These are originals bar *Hey Joe* and *Wild Mountain Thyme*.

Whether this group is the same **Living End** who released the 45 on Mira is not known. (MW)

The Living Ends

45:	I Don't Mind / Self Centered Girl	(Hudson 707) 1966

A Patterson, New Jersey, group who were known as The Flames until late 1965. One of them later formed the Looking Glass who had success on Epic in the early seventies.

Compilation appearances have included: *Self Centered Girl* on *Teenage Shutdown, Vol. 15* (LP & CD); and *I Don't Mind* on *The Cicadelic 60's, Vol. 4* (CD), *The Cicadelic 60's, Vol. 5* (LP) and *Hang It Out To Dry* (LP & CD). (MM/MW)

The Living Example

45:	Jet Plane/Outside Window	(Atlantic 2541) 1968

A long forgotten mellow pop group. (SR)

The Living Legends

45:	Monkey Don't Care / Soul Supper	(RCA 8782) 1966

A flower-pop single with a lethargic instrumental on flip. (SR)

Living Sacrifice

Personnel incl:	DIANNE MURRAY	A
	JOHN MURRAY	A
	JOHN ROSENBERRY	A

ALBUM:	1	LIVING SACRIFICE	(LS 770816) c1973 R2

Formed by at least three members of **Last Call Of Shiloh**, the Idaho-based **Living Sacrifice** released only 200 copies of their debut album. Comprised of gentle acoustic ballads alongside some fine samplings of West Coast guitar psych in the style of **Azitis** or **Wilson McKinley**, with male/female harmonies. The lyrics are mainly about religious themes, notably the apocalypse and the prophecies.

In 1979/80, a renewed line-up, the Living Sacrifice Band, now established in New Jersey, released two other albums, *Beauty For Ashes* (Praise Jesus EARS-36) and *A Call To Brokeness* (Shekinah SHM-3019). (SR/KSt)

Toby Ray Lloyd

ALBUM:	1	TOBY RAY LLOYD	(0 and 9 Records) c1971 ?

A private pressing recorded in Village Sound Studios in Sommerville, New Jersey, it's supposedly interesting. (SR)

Load

Personnel:	DAVE HESSLER	gtr, bs (doubleneck gtr)	A
	STERLING SMITH	keyb'ds, moog bs	A
	TOM SMITH	drms, perc	A

ALBUM:	1(A)	PRAISE THE LOAD	(Owl Intermedia) 1976 R2

NB: (1) reissued together with an unreleased album *Load Have Mercy* from 1976/7 on CD (Lasers Edge) 1996.

The Load started in March 1973 in Columbus, Ohio. Sterling had previously played in **The Grayps**, **J.D. Blackfoot**, and **Osiris**; Dave Hessler in The Esquires and **Osiris**; and Tom Smith had been playing with The Bob Paas Blues Band who were schoolmates of **Raven**. Originally a trio with keyboards as the lead instruments, Dave built a double neck guitar in 1974 and Sterling added a minimoog synthesizer, enabling the band to play with different combinations of sound, switching at will between synthesized bass and bass guitar.

The Load played concerts around Ohio, and opened for **Bob Seger**, Brian Auger, The Michael Stanley Band, and Rick Derringer. **The Load** also shared a bill with Strongbow and Joy Token at the Ohio Theater in 1976. They moved to Los Angeles in 1977 and worked briefly with singer Meatloaf that Summer.

Returning to Los Angeles, the **Load** played gigs at The Troubador and the Fox Venice Theater and recorded with Dennis Wilson, The Beach Boys and Terry Reid. They also backed singer Baron Keith Stewart on an MCA album.

Unable to find a market for their "progressive rock," the band eventually split up, though they continue to collaborate and are planning a new CD sometime in the 21st century. Sterling is still a musician in Los Angeles, and Tom and Dave have a very successful band in Columbus, Ohio called, The Danger Brothers.

As part of the partnership that built and ran Owl Recording Studios, **The Load** recorded two albums. Only one was released on vinyl, but both are now out on CD. Other Owl releases included albums by **Raven** and **Tom Wachunas**. (SR/SGgS)

Loading Zone

Personnel:	PAUL FAUERSO	vcls, keyb'ds	ABCD
	BOB KRIDLE	bs	ABC
	GEORGE NEWCOM	drms	ABC
	PETER SHAPIRO	gtr	ABC
	STEVE DOWLER	gtr	BC
	LINDA TILLERY	vcls	CD
	STEVE BUSFIELD	ld gtr	D
	MIKE EGGLESTON	bs	D
	GEORGE MARSH	drms	D
	(TODD ANDERSON	woodwind, keyb'ds	C)
	(PATRICK O'HARA	trombone	CD)
	(PAUL TAORMINA	hrns	D)
	(STEVE KUPKA	hrns	)

ALBUMS:	1(C)	LOADING ZONE	(RCA 3959) 1968 -
	2(D)	ONE FOR ALL	(Umbrella 101) 1970 R1

NB: (1) reissued on CD (Acadia ACA 8012) 2001.

45s:		Don't Lose Control/Danger Heartbreak Ahead	(RCA 9538) 1968
	α	No More Tears/Can I Dedicate	(RCA 9620) 1968
		One For All/Time Stops	(Umbrella 1001) 1970

NB: α as Linda Tillery and The Loading Zone.

THE LOADING ZONE - The Loading Zone CD.

Really an R&B outfit, based in Oakland, California, their two mediocre jazz-blues albums are now of minor interest to 'psych' collectors. The band were formed by Paul Fauerso, after his jazz group The Tom Paul Trio had broken up and he soon recruited Pete Shapiro and Steve Dowler from **The Marbles**. Line-up 'B' remained stable for a long time, with the band playing around the Bay Area and as far away as Vancouver but gigging mostly in gyms and clubs in Berkeley, Oakland and San Francisco. They also played the Fillmore a number of times, thanks to their manager Ron Barnett's good connections with Bill Graham.

Gigs in San Francisco were slim except for the Fillmore because the other halls such as the Avalon and the California Ballroom were under control of the Family Dog and others that were more interested in the psychedelic sound than R&B stuff. Still, they did get to share the bill with Cream and **Big Brother** amongst others.

Linda Tillery joined after they ran an ad in the Chronicle looking for a lead singer. Steve Dowler:- "Bob and I drove to San Francisco one day to meet her and bring her back to our practice room which was the living room of the house we rented in Oakland on 14th street. After the first album came out we toured back East on Columbia's ticket, starting in Cleveland, going to Chicago and ending in NYC at the Fillmore East with **Vanilla Fudge**".

After the band went their different ways in late 1968, Paul Fauerso and Linda Tillery put together a new line-up ('D'). They had a much more 'hip' tighter and sometimes more jazzy sound than the original '**Zone** but they kept the R&B roots solidly in place too.

Steve:- "Pat O'Hara played with the '**Zone** for a number of gigs along with the rest of the horns, Todd Anderson and Steve Kupka when we could get them to join us and when there was room on the stage. Steve was in the band at Berkeley High playing baritone. The sound guy, Mike Ritter's sister Nancy and her friend Mary Hawkes knew him from Berkeley High and we eventually asked him to sit in on some gigs."

"Kup later played with the Motowns which evolved into the Tower of Power as you probably know. He was really good with tight horn section charts and along with Todd and Paul put together many of the fine horn sounds. We didn't use Steve as much as Todd and Pat, if I remember correctly but the combination of them with Paul on the B3 was dynamite."

Linda Tillery later played for Cesar 830 (a short-lived San Francisco-based jazz fusion outfit from 1975) and had a solo career, whilst Patrick O'Hara later played with Boz Scaggs.

Although musically a marginal case for inclusion in this book, **The Loading Zone** are still remembered fondly by fans of soulful R&B. (VJ/SDr)

Loading Zone

45:	Times Are Gonna Be Different/ I Couldn't Care Less	(Columbia 43938)	1967

A different band from Youngstown, Ohio. This **Loading Zone** only used the name for this particular record - they were in fact a popular local band called The Hi-Guys. Both songs, which contain good organ driven pop psych, were written by P. Pylypiw and arranged/produced by Charlie Calello. (GGl/SR)

Loadstone

Personnel:
BARRY ABERNATHY	bs	A
SAM CERNUTO	trombone	A
LARRY DEVERS	drms	A
STEVE DOUGLAS (aka HUSCZKA)	trumpet, fluegel horn	A
JOHN PHILLIPS	tenor sax, flutes, oboe, bassoon	A
TERRY RYAN	keyb'ds	A
JOHN STERLING	gtr	A

ALBUM: 1(A) LOADSTONE (Barnaby Records 21235004) 1969 SC

This album is of interest for *Flower Pot*, a long fifteen minute psychedelic suite which takes up the whole of Side Two. Complete with sound effects, phasing, screams, echo loops and bird noises, the track was recorded in one take, with the voices overdubbed later.

The group formed in Las Vegas, Nevada. Devers, Abernathy and Phillips were backing Bobby Darin at the time when he went on his hiatus to find himself, leaving them looking for a gig. Ryan, Douglas, Sterling and Cernuto were freelance musicians in Vegas looking for work. Thanks to a guitar player by the name of Mike Richards, who originally was in the group, they got together and formed a cover band to make some cash. The band worked a club in Vegas called 'The Pussycat A Go Go' where Andy Williams used to hang out. He signed the band to his label, Barnaby Records, because of the big following the band attracted to its live performances. Andy also got Dave Grusin to produce the album as well as play piano on one track, *Dayshine*. The album was recorded in a two week period in the Summer of 1969 and other than record promotion concerts and a few club gigs in L.A., the band never toured.

The album's lack of sales caused the group to slowly dissolve to working lounge gigs in Vegas. When that was over the band members went on to other groups. Today, all the members are still working as musicians in one capacity or another except for Douglas, who passed on in 1991.

The group's energy in live performance could never really be captured on record. The horn sound created by the trumpet, trombone and sax with the funky rhythm section was truly incredible.

Barnaby Records still owns the masters, with a few tracks never released. Dave Grusin is mostly known as a jazzman and soundtrack composer. (VJ/SR/SCo)

LOADSTONE - Loadstone LP.

LOCKSLEY HALL - Locksley Hall LP.

Locksley Hall

ALBUM:	1	LOCKSLEY HALL	(Or 013) 1996

NB: (1) Limited edition of 500 copies.

Locksley Hall was one of the better known psychedelic bands in the Pacific Northwest during their existence from 1967 until 1970. The album was recorded in 1969 at the legendary Audio Recorders in Seattle with long-time Northwest guitarist Ned Neltner (**Mark Five**, **Gas Company**, Junior Cadillac) producing and **Sonics** engineer Kearny Barton at the console. It remained unreleased until the limited edition came out in 1996. The album reminds us of every band who ever played the Fillmore West in the late sixties and blends together elements of **It's A Beautiful Day**, **Jefferson Airplane** and **Big Brother and The Holding Co**. Recommended. (VJ)

Locomotive

Personnel:	RUSS KAMMERER	drms	A
	SKIP MOREHOUSE	keyb'ds	A
	BILL STROUM	bs	A
	JOHN USSERY	ld vcl, ld gtr	A

ALBUM: 1(A) LOCOMOTIVE (MGM SE-4653) 1969/70 -

45s: Roberta/Big City Car (MGM 14102) 1969

Locomotive came from Seattle/Mercer Island, and recorded an album for MGM in late 1968, but because of management reshuffles at MGM, the release of the album was considerably delayed. **John Ussery** later made at least one solo album. (CBn/DR/MW)

Lode Star

Personnel:	MIKE BALLARD	bs	A
	PAT BLANKS	ld gtr, vcls	A
	ANDRE BONAGUIDI	drms, vcls	A
	FRANK SOTELO	ld gtr, vcls	A

Hailed from El Paso, Texas. They had four tracks: *Glympses*, *Raga*, *Bottom Of The Hill* and *It's Gonna Be There* on the *I Love You Gorgo* (Suemi 1090) 1969 compilation, which had a limited vinyl counterfeit reissue of 300 in 1997.

Frank Sotelo also contributed a solo, acoustic snippet to the closing moments of the album.

The band are of course, totally unrelated to Lodestar, a heavy psych hard-rock group from Ohio whose privately pressed album was released in 1979. (VJ/SR)

Logos

Personnel incl:	STEVE EPLEY	vcls, gtr	A
	CINDY WILLIAMS	vcls, piano	A

ALBUM: 1(A) FIRESIDES AND GUITARS (Audio House AHSPL 113L74) 197? R3

An early seventies folk album from the Kansas studio/label. Several of these cuts have an engaging pop feel, perhaps like acoustic demos of unreleased Badfinger songs. Two tracks are written and sung by Williams, the other ten by Epley. Very simple silkscreened cover. (CF)

The Lollipop Fantasy

45: Waiting For A Dream/ It's A Groovy World (ERA 3193) 1968

An obscure "groovy" pop-rock group. (SR)

The Lollipop Shoppe

Personnel:	BOB ATKINS	bs	A
	ED BOWEN	gtr	A
	RON BUZZELL	gtr	A
	FRED COLE	vcls	A
	CARL FORTINA	accordian	A
	JOHN THE GREEK	keyb'ds	A
	TIM ROCKSON	drms	A

ALBUM: 1(A) JUST COLOUR (Uni 73019) 1968 R2

NB: (1) was reissued legitmately in 1985 and has also been counterfeited on CD (Flash) 199?.

45s: You Must Be A Witch/
Don't Close The Door On Me (PS) (UNI 55050) 1967
Someone I Know/Through My Window (Shamley 44005) 1969

Orginally from Las Vegas, where they were known as **The Weeds** they migrated to Portland, Oregon and changed their name when **The Seeds**' manager Lord Tim took them on. Cole's vocals are very distinctive and your reaction to the album will largely be determined by how you respond to them. The opening cut *You Must Be A Witch* is reminiscent of **Love** at their most frantic. Other strong tracks on the album are the slower sensitive punk ballad *Underground Railroad*, *Don't Close The Door On Me* and the more commercial *Its Only A Reflection*. The album has been repressed, and pirated on CD.

They also had two tracks featured on the *Angels From Hell* soundtrack album (Tower 5128) - *Mr. Madison Avenue* and *Who's It Gonna Be*. The non-album Shamley 45 is a disappointing 'downer'.

LOGOS - Firesides And Guitars LP.

Band leader Fred Cole later formed seventies band **Zipper**. He remains active on the music scene with the highly regarded cult act Dead Moon.

Compilation appearances have included: *You Must Be A Witch* on *Nuggets Box* (4-CD), *Nuggets, Vol. 12* (LP), *Psychedelic Visions* (CD), *Pebbles, Vol. 8* (LP), *Baubles - Down To Middle Earth* (LP), *Excerpts From Nuggets* (CD), *Garage Monsters* (LP) and *We Have Come For Your Children*; *Mr. Madison Avenue* on *Turds On A Bum Ride Vol. 1 & 2* (Dble CD) and *Turds On A Bum Ride, Vol. 2* (Dble LP); *Who's It Gonna Be* on *Turds On A Bum Ride Vol. 4* (CD); and both *Mr. Maison Avenue* and *Who's It Gonna Be* on *Filling The Gap* (4-LP). (VJ)

The Lollipop Tree

| 45: | Hey Jude/ Peace | (B.T. Puppy 546) 1968 |

On the label managed by The Tokens, a forgotten pop-rock group probably from the New York area. (SR)

Robb London (and The Rogues)

45s:	α	Bitter Tears/Standing Under Big Ben	(Beckingham 1083) 1965
	α	Who'll Be The One/ It Should've Been Me	(Beckingham 1085) 1965
		Crazy Baby/Mary Jane	(Beckingham 1086) 196?
		Funny Situation/Gloria	(Suzuki 1000) 1967
	β	Good Natured Emma/The Children	(AV International 1065) 1971

NB: α backed by The Rogues. β Credited to The Robb London Company.

London recorded for quite a few San Antonio labels from 1965 onwards, with and without The Rogues, so the above discography is not complete. His best effort is usually considered to be his cover of Van Morrison's *Gloria* which can be heard on *Highs In The Mid-Sixties, Vol. 13* (LP). In fact his moody, bluesy voice sounds out of place on this punk 45 which is unrecognisable from the original. **London** also wrote and produced records for other Texas bands in this era. (VJ)

London and The Bridges

Personnel:	MARC FREEMAN	organ	AB
	MIKE LEVY	bs	A
	JON SHOLLE	ld gtr	AB
	JOHN WAXMAN	drms	AB
	RICHARD WEINTRAUB	gtr, vcls	AB
	JOHNNY MILLER	bs	B

45s:	α	It Just Ain't Right/Leave Her Alone	(Date 1502) 1966
		City I Was Born In/Tell It To The Preachers	(Date 1517) 1966
		I'll Probably Understand It When I'm Older/ Keep Him	(Date 1535) 1966

NB: α also issued in the UK (CBS 202056) 1966.

From Great Neck, New York, which is on the Northern end of Long Island. All of the guys went to school together and subsequently formed a group. Noted NYC producer Al Harvey got them a deal with Columbia records in early 1966, which resulted in the three 45s on the subsidiary Date label. Many of their gigs were teen parties, and several were performances for rich and famous folks, taking the group from Boston to Washington D.C.

All three 45s were produced by Al Harvey and Steven Scott. Five of the six sides were written by Richard Weintraub and Jon Scholle. The overriding style is slick accomplished upbeat or frantic pop-punk with an attitude and edge that retains some garage cred but is also very commercial - similar to **Paul Revere & The Raiders** perhaps. The one slower effort is a midtempo baroque-popper with shades of Dylanesque folk-rock. All good stuff!

When Richard Weintraub got married the group split, with Jon Sholle and Johnny Miller merging with **The Savages** to form **Today's Special**. They then cut a few songs written by Johnny Miller and Richard Weintraub (who also sang background on some of the recordings but never really joined the band).

THE LOLLIPOP SHOPPE - Just Colour LP.

Jon Sholle went on to become a bluegrass performer of some note with records such as *Catfish For Supper* and *Out Of The Frying Pan*. He later played with acts like Melissa Manchester and Meatloaf, performed with Bette Midler in the movie "The Rose" and is still doing his own thing, a combo of bluegrass and jazz, regularly in NYC.

Richard Weintraub moved to Hong Kong where he played with a band called AWOL that did lots of acid rock and hard rock (Hendrix, Cream, The Who, Deep Purple, etc).

Compilation appearances have included: *It Just Ain't Right* on *Sixties Choice, Vol. 1* (LP) and *60's Choice Collection Vol's 1 & 2* (CD); *City I Was Born In* and *Tell It To The Preachers* on *Psychedelic Archives Vol. 7* (cass); *Tell It To The Preacher* on *Sixties Rebellion Vol. 16* (LP & CD) and *Tell It To The Preacher* on *Victims Of Circumstances, Vol. 1* (LP); (MW/MM/RW)

London Fog

| 45: | Mr Baldi/Maudie | (Coulee 118) 1966 |

From Audubon, Iowa. This fine piece of keyboard-led psychedelia builds into a frantic climax. Check it out on *The Midwest Vs. The Rest* (LP) or *Son Of The Gathering Of The Tribe* (LP). (VJ)

The London Knights

| 45: | Go To Him/Dum Diddlee Dee | (Mike MK 4200) 1966 |

Go To Him is a dramatic and melodic beat ballad reminiscent of The Cascades. This was the only 45 by this Los Angeles outfit. *Go To Him* was also covered by Oregon's **Tymes Children** and earlier, in July 1965, by Aussie beatsters Ray Brown and The Whispers.

Compilation appearances include *Go To Him* on *The Cicadelic 60's, Vol. 3* (CD) and *The Cicadelic 60's, Vol. 5* (LP). (MW)

London Phogg

| 45: | The Times To Come / Takin' It Easy | (A&M 1010) 1968 |

Los Angeles is the likely locale for this group. Their sole California-pressed 45 was produced by artist-turned-writer-producer Keith Colley (who came from the Pacific Northwest but who also operated in L.A.) and arranged by Al Capps.

Takin' It Easy, possibly a group original (composed by J.Spitale, J.Painter, N.Corro and B.Luther), is laid-back sunshine harmony-pop. Described by Ben Chaput as "the Mamas And Papas on acid", the Keith Colley-Knox

Henderson-composed flip is a paean to world peace - galloping harmony folk-pop with sustained fuzz guitar and female vocals.

Compilation appearances include *Takin' It Easy* on *Bring Flowers To U.S.* (LP). (MW)

Londons

45:	Old Man-A Thing Of Age/?	(Pyramid 7211) 196?

A Greensboro, North Carolina band. You'll also find this song on *Garage Punk Unknowns, Vol. 7* (LP) and *Tobacco A-Go-Go, Vol. 2* (LP). (VJ)

TOBACCO A GO-GO Vol. 2 (Comp LP) including The Londons.

London Taxi

Personnel incl: RICHARD CORRIN — clarinet, sax
GARY McLAUGHLIN — gtr
JOEL NYE — bs

45:	Feelin' Down/Last Step	(Piccadilly 239) 1966

From Spokane, Washington, they were earlier known as The Runabouts. You'll also find *Feelin' Down*, their finest moment on *Battle Of The Bands, Vol. 2* (LP), *The History Of Northwest Rock, Vol. 3* (LP) and *Northwest Battle Of The Bands, Vol. 2* (CD). (VJ/MW/DR)

Long Island Sound

Personnel incl: ANGELO FRISKETTI — ld gtr
TOM HANION — gtr
FRED O'BRIEN — bs
BOB PASTERNACK — organ
TONY PRAGANO — vcls
JACK RUSSELL — bs

45:	One, Two, Three and I Feel/Skid Row	(Dyno Voice 903) 1968

The name is misleading because New Haven, Connecticut, was actually home to this band. They started life as a surf harmony group and had some 45s for Wonder Records, which aren't relevant to this book. After going through a folk-rock phase they wound up on the Dyno Voice label and recorded this 'bubblegum' style 45, which was produced by top bubblegum producers Bo Gentry and Richie Cordell. You'll find the 'A' side on *Nuggets, Vol. 4* (LP) and it's fairly typical of that genre, although it met with no commercial success. The 'B' side is a sort of blues jam with an incoherent vocal track. (VJ)

Long John and The Silvermen

Personnel incl: RANDY ECKART

45s:	Remember / I'll Come Back	(Wanted S-4581) 1965
	Heart Filled With Love / Wind In The Sky	(Wanted 001) 1966
	Cathy's Clown / One Time Loser	(MBS Recording Studios Acetate) 1966
α	Somebody / Remember	(MBS Recording Studios Acetate) 1965

NB: α as **Randy Eckart**.

A trio from Chicago. *Heart Filled With Love* is a highly-rated garage 45 about searching for love. It was recorded at M.B.S. studios and released on the bands own label.

Compilation appearances include *Heart Filled With Love* on *Back From The Grave, Vol. 6* (LP). (VJ/MW)

Lonnie and The Legends

Personnel incl: G. GRAH — A
LONNIE GRAH — A

45:	I Cried/Baby Without You	(Impression 109) 1966

From Sylmar, California. Snappy garage-beat British invasion sounds, from the label also graced by the **Grodes**, **Dirty Shames**, **Tangents** and **Mark Five** (pre-**Peppermint Trolley Co.**).

Both sides have been compiled - *I Cried* is on *Fuzz, Flaykes and Shakes, Vol. 3* and *Baby, Without You* is on *Basementsville! U.S.A.*. According to the latter their lead guitarist (Steve Rabe perhaps?) went on to form **Thee Sixpence**. (MW)

The Looking Glasses

Personnel incl: JERRY BERKE — A
L. NAKTIN — A

45s:	α	Kathy's Dream / ?Migada Bus? (promo only)	(Media 414) 1967
		Visions / Migada Bus	(Media 414) 1967
	β	Visions / Migada Bus	(Independence 82) 1967

NB: α promo-only release, 'B' side unconfirmed. β as by The Clouds.

From the environs of Los Angeles. This band's superb spacey acid punker *Visions* comes in three forms; the original version was entitled *Kathy's Dream*, before *Visions* appeared on the same label, then was picked up by Independence whereupon the band was rebilled as **The Clouds**. *Fuzz, Flaykes And Shakes, Vol. 1* revealed that members from this band and the **Just Too Much** teamed up to become the **Odyssey** who put out the excellent *Little Girl, Little Boy* 45 on White Whale in December 1967.

Bliss out to *Visions* on *Psychedelic Unknowns, Vol. 6* (as by **The Clouds**), *Pebbles, Vol. 11* (LP) and *30 Seconds Before The Calico Wall* (CD). *Migada Bus*, a swingin' baroque-flavoured instrumental (with an occasional fuzzy flourish) can be sampled on *Buzz Buzz Buzzzzzz, Vol. 2* (CD). (VJ/MW/MM/TSz)

The Loose Ends

Personnel incl: T-BONE BURNETT — A

45s:	He's A Nobody/A Free Soul	(Mala 538) 1966
	Dead End Kid/Verses	(Bell 671) 1967

This Fort Worth-based band was most significant for including T-Bone Burnett who wrote both of these Kinks imitation songs on their first 45. The second 45 is mellow Beatlesque pop with *Verses* being the better side.

Compilation appearances have included: *He's A Nobody* and *A Free Soul* on *Texas Punk, Vol. 9* (LP) and *Acid Visions - Complete Collection, Vol. 3* (3-CD); and *He's A Nobody* on *Texas Music, Vol. 3* (CD). (VJ)

ALAN LORBER ORCHESTRA - The Lotus Palace CD.

The Loose Ends

| 45: | Hey Sweet Baby/I Love You, Baby | (Meadowbrook 25069) 1969 |

From Nichols, Connecticut, *Hey Sweet Baby* is a frantic rocker with plenty of fuzz. The 'A' side has also resurfaced on *Sixties Rebellion, Vol. 3* (LP & CD). (VJ)

Loose Enz

45s:	A World Outside/	
	Mister You're A Better Man Than I	(DB 47667) 1967/8
	The Black Door/Easy Rider	(Virtue 2502) 1968

Hailing from York in Pennsylvania this punk quartet recorded during the mid-sixties. Some of their songs were obviously influenced by British bands like the Yardbirds and the Pretty Things. *You're A Better Man Than I* is a decent cover version with a pretty good guitar solo.

Compilation appearances have included: *The Black Door* on *The Psychedelic Experience, Vol. 1* (LP) and *30 Seconds Before The Calico Wall* (CD); *A World Outside*, *The Black Door* and *Easy Rider* on *Pennsylvania Unknowns* (LP); *Mister You're A Better Man Than I* on *Return Of The Young Pennsylvanians* (LP); *Mister You're A Better Man Than I* and *A World Outside* on *Stompin' Time Again!* (CD); *Easy Rider* on *An Overdose Of Heavy Psych* (CD); and *A World Outside* on *Crude PA Vol. 2* (LP). (VJ)

The Alan Lorber Orchestra

Personnel:
SEYMOUR BARAB	cello	A
VINCENT BELL	gtr, sitar	A
HOWARD HIRSCH	eastern & western perc	A
HUGH McCRACKEN	gtr	A
JEROME RICHARDSON	flute, bass clarinet, tenor sax	A
DONALD ROBERTSON	tambura	A
COLIN WALCOTT	sitar, tabla	A
Plus viola and violins		A

ALBUM: 1(A) THE LOTUS PALACE (Verve V6-8711) 1969 -

NB: (1) reissued on CD (Big Beat CDWIKD 172).

During the late sixties on the East Coast, **Alan Lorber** was a very active producer and the man behind the "Boss-Town Sound" hype (**Ultimate Spinach**, **Puff**, **Orpheus**, **Chamaleon Church**) as well as records by **Bobby Callender** and **The Groupies**. He also released this instrumental album to "play a subtle fusion of raga and pop". For it he recruited some excellent musicians (**Hugh McCracken**, Colin Walcott (later with **Oregon**), **Vincent "Vinnie" Bell**) and asked them to play two Beatles songs *Within You Without You* and *Lucy In The Sky*, the **Blues Project**'s *Flute Thing*, **Tim Hardin**'s *Hang On To A Dream* and various other "groovy" tunes with lots of sitar, tamboura and percussion. The only original track, *Roopaka Da Teri Dhin Dhin* was written was Colin Walcott.

The album's best feature is probably the liner notes, which warn you that "what you are going to hear on this record, the sounds that will be produced, are akin only to the sounds you may have heard inside the expanded consciousness of your own mind". (SR)

Lord and The Flies

| 45s: | You Made A Fool Of Me/Come What May | (USA 828) 1966 |
| | Echoes/Come What May | (USA 857) 1966 |

This outfit spent time in both Chicago and Indiana. Their finest moment, *Echoes* is also captured on *Pebbles Vol. 7* (CD) and *Mindrocker, Vol. 5* (LP). (VJ)

Lord August and The Visions of Life

Personnel incl: AUGIE MEYER — vcls, keyb'ds

45s:	Found Me A New Love/Gigolo	(Visions Of Life 132) 1967
	Mod Fashions/	
	Everybody's Always Putting Me Down	(AOK 1013/14) 196?
	Let Me Be Me/Get On Home	(SSS International 739) 196?
α	Let Me Be Me	(SSS International 739) 196?

NB: α promo only.

This was Texan Augie Meyer's outfit after Rocky and The Border Lords and prior to the **Sir Douglas Quintet**. *Let Me Be Me* is a fair psychedelic punker. (VJ)

Lord Beverley Moss and The Mossmen

Personnel incl:
LORD BEVERLEY MOSS	vcls	A
TOM GEBHEIM	gtr	A
BOB TIMMERS	ld gtr, bs	A
VIC WENDT	keyb'ds, bs	A

| 45: | The Kids Are Alright/ | |
| | Please Please What's The Matter | (Target 107/8) 1967 |

Whilst the band hailed from Appleton, Wisconsin, **Lord Beverley** was British-born and apparently recruited by placing ads in the U.K. music press - such was the power of Limey connections in that era! Their cover of *The Kids Are Alright* is disappointing, but the flip is a good blues-punker and culminates in quite a memorable solo guitar freak-out. You can hear it on *Highs In The Mid-Sixties, Vol. 10* (LP).

Moss departed soon after but the remaining members continued to play in local outfits. Tom Gebheim sat in on Target/Tee Pee and would also find employment there as an engineer and producer. (VJ/MW/RNo/GM)

Lord Led

ALBUM: 1 LORD LED (Dean Brown Productions) c1971 ?

From Artesia, California, a Christian trio with 12-string acoustic guitar, electric bass and drums, and occasional piano. They played a mix of folk-rock and lounge music. (SR)

Lords

Personnel incl: DAVE JOHNSON
WARREN MILLER

| 45: | Light Rain/Death Bells At Dawn | (Aldrich ALD 1001) 1966 |

A fabulous 45 from New Jersey. *Light Rain* is a sublime garage ballad with reedy keyboards and clean guitar - sorta slow folk-rock-beat. The flip, *Death Bells At Dawn*, is a doomy lament with atmospheric Eastern-influenced keyboard doodlings. No frantic fuzz thrash this - one to float away on.

Compilation appearances include: *Death Bells At Dawn* on *Sixties Rebellion, Vol. 11* (LP & CD), *Acid and Flowers* (CD), *30 Seconds Before The Calico Wall* (CD) and *Brain Shadows, Vol. 1* (LP & CD). (MW)

Lords

45:	She Belongs To Me/On The Road Again	(Valiant V-725) 1965

Decent Los Angeles area beat with harmonica. Both Dylan covers - presumably in an attempt to emulate **The Byrds**' success. (MW)

Lords

Personnel:	JOHN BLUE	bs	AB
	DANNY BORZELLINO	vcls	AB
	DENNIS MESSNER	drums	A
	TERRY PETERS	gtr	AB
	DEWEY WAHL	gtr	AB
	JIM PATTI	drums	B

45:	Young Sweetheart / Sweet Words	(Barclay 19679/10) 1967

Aristocracy from the Shillington area of Reading, Pennslyvania from 1966 until 1968. Their legacy has been preserved on Arf! Arf!'s *Eastern Pa Rock Part Two* (CD), which contains their story plus their 45 and two unreleased 1967 tracks *What Went Wrong* and *Tell Me*. An unreleased instrumental version of *Young Sweetheart* can also be heard on *30 Seconds Before The Calico Wall* (CD). (MW/ELn)

The Lorey's

45:	Goin' Downtown / Ready To Go	(Cathay 1202) 196?

From Sparta, Ohio, thirty miles Northeast of Columbus. They took part in the Third Annual Battle of the Bands at the Northland Shopping Center in Columbus in 1967, which was won by the **Four O'Clock Balloon**. **The Lorey's** didn't come in the Top 5 but their own contribution *Don't You Care* was captured on the resultant album (see the **Four O'Clock Balloon** entry for more details). (GGI/MW)

The Lost

Personnel:	WILLIE 'LOCO' ALEXANDER	electric piano, perc, vcls	A
	KYLE GARRAHAN	ld gtr, vcls	A
	LEE MASON	drms	A
	TED MYERS	gtr, vcls	A
	WALTER POWERS	bs, organ, vcls	A

CDs:	1	EARLY RECORDINGS	(Arf! Arf! AA-059) 1996
	2	THE LOST LOST TAPES	(Arf! Arf! AA-081) 1999

NB: Other relevant CDs include: *Flat Earth Society 'Waleeco'/ The Lost 'Space Kids'* (Arf! Arf! AA-063) 1993; and *Family Circle - Family Tree* (Big Beat CDWIKD 146)1996, which contains Lost and offshoot bands.

45s:		Maybe More Than You/Back Door Blues	(Capitol 5519) 1965
	α	Violet Gown/Mean Motorcycle	(Capitol 5708) 1966
	α	Violet Gown/No Reason Why	(Capitol 5725) 1966
	β	Who Do You Love/It Is I (PS)	(Stanton Park SRE 004) 1996

NB: α contain different versions of *Violet Gown*. β comprises 2 unreleased tracks circa 1966.

Related:
45s:	α	I Shall Be Released/Shame	(Janus 109) 1970
	β	Kerouac/Mass. Ave	(Garage 505) 1975/6

NB: α Kyle Garrahan solo 45 (as 'Kyle'), β Willie Alexander first solo 45.

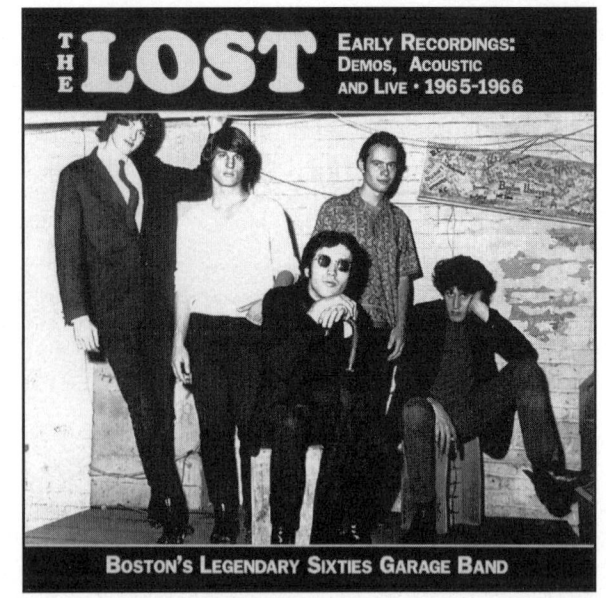

THE LOST - Early Recordings CD.

Formed in 1964 at Goddard College in Vermont, this band became part of a burgeoning Boston scene (well before the "Bosstown sound" hype). Contemporaries of, and often compared to, **The Remains** who were said to be Boston's answer to the Beatles, the **Lost** assumed the Stones' mantle. Musically however they were much more diverse. Whilst embracing the new Invasion sounds they did not discard their own heritage and influences - elements of rock & roll, folk and jazz were mixed into a dynamic stew by songwriters Ted Myers and Willie Alexander. Their unique strength however was having four vocalists in the band, each capable of taking the lead part. This added a new dimension to set them apart from others with an infusion of **Byrds** or Beach Boys influences into the melodies and finely structured vocal arrangements (coincidentally they supported the Beach Boys 1966 tour of the region).

The resultant Capitol 45s are great examples of New England's response to Olde England's "Invasion" - classy and timeless sixties beat-pop-rock nuggets. *Maybe More Than You* with Alexander's cutting put-down vocals to the fore, backed by the *Back Door Blues*' snappy rockin' beat. *Mean Motorcycle* continues in uptempo rockin' vein and backs the track that signposted Myers' future direction - the sublime *Violet Gown* with a haunting melody, ringing guitars and romantic lyrical imagery. This 45 was quickly followed by an alternate version of *Violet Gown* backed by the frenetic raver *No Reason Why* with screamin' guitars and screechin' harmonica.

No Reason Why was covered by California outfit Mondo Crescendo on the flip of their 1998 45 *A Boy And His Itch* 45 (Train Bridge Records).

The Lost CDs are highly recommended to those who want to investigate this band's legacy. *The Early Recordings* CD contains twenty-six previously unreleased recordings from 1965-6, and fans should also check out the Stanton Park 45. **The Lost** *Lost Tapes* CD unearths seventeen gems from the original Capitol tapes, remixed by Ted Myers and Erik Lindgren. *Family Circle - Family Tree* (CD) is a fascinating collection of **The Lost** and their offshoots:- nine tracks by **The Lost** - *Violet Gown, Maybe More Than You*, and seven unreleased/alternate tracks including *Mystic, Kaleidoscope* and *Everybody Knows*; eleven cuts by **Chamaeleon Church** (most of their 1968 MGM LP plus some alternate and unreleased tracks); *Back Door Blues* and *Happiness Child* by the Myers/Scheuren **Ultimate Spinach**; two more versions of *Everybody Knows* by the post-Lost Alexander/Mason outfit the **Bagatelle** and a further 1978 version by Willie Alexander & The Boom-Boom Band. A follow-up *The Best Of Bosstown Sound* (Dble CD), includes four **Lost** tracks: *Maybe More Than You, Everybody Knows, Mystic (Seven Starry Skies)* and *Violet Gown*, duplicating two from the earlier *Family Circle - Family Tree* (CD).

In 1967, **The Lost** were commissioned to provide the soundtrack to a children's sci-fi opera. The resultant albums worth of material can be heard on the Arf! Arf! CD coupled with the **Flat Earth Society** album reissue - three lengthy tracks *Space Kids Part 1, Space Kids Part 2* and *Incidental Music To Space Kids*.

By 1967, the band were being pulled in different musical directions - with

Alexanders, Powers and Mason pushing a move to jammin' jazz/funk climes. The split saw Alexander and Powers initially in the unrecorded Grass Menagerie, before Alexander joined Mason in the nine-piece funk-fusion **Bagatelle**. Powers joined prog-psychers **Listening**. Myers continued to write prodigiously and became a staff songwriter for **Alan "Mr.Bosstown" Lorber**. He formed the psychy soft-rock **Chamaeleon Church** with Garrahan plus Tony Scheuren and drummer Chevy Chase - the latter of course has achieved fame as a comedian and film star personality.

After one under-rated album and the haunting *Camillia Is Changing* 45, Myers and Scheuren were drafted into the post-Bruce-Douglas **Ultimate Spinach** for the third album, which also featured pre-Steely Dan and Doobie Brothers Jeff "Skunk" Baxter.

Kyle Garrahan went solo and released one 45 on Janus (note that he is not the **Kyle** who had releases on Paramount and Family around the same time) and moved to Europe where he spent much of the seventies living in France.

After **Listening**, Powers teamed up again with Alexander in Doug Yules' post-Lou Reed **Velvet Underground** from 1970-1971. This line-up toured and appeared in the U.K. but did not release any new studio recordings. Willie Alexander commented that they've never been forgiven for nor allowed to forget this episode in certain cliques.

Alexander continues to record to this day and is regarded as a living legend in New England. After **VU** he went solo with the Kerouac 45 in the mid-seventies - an updated version of this by his next outfit Willie and The Boom Boom Band is featured on the 1979 *Who Put The Bomp?* compilation. The Boom Boom Band issued two albums on MCA 1978-'79. In the early eighties Willie Loco Alexander And The Confessions saw him reunited again with bassist Walter Powers. His band in 1999 is Willie Loco Alexander And The Persistence Of Memory Orchestra.

Ted Myers was A&R Manager for Rhino Records in L.A. until 2000 when he left to "pursue my true passions: record production and artist development. I am currently working with three bands, all based here in the L.A. area, producing one and representing the other two."; Kyle Garrahan is a jazz guitarist living in Astoria, NY ; Walter Powers a librarian at M.I.T. and resides in Wellsley, Ma.; Lee Mason runs an airline business in Florida and was involved in mercy flights to hurricane-torn Central America in early 1999.

For a few days in March 1999, **The Lost** reunited for the ultimate Boston Tea-Party at the Paradise Club, to complete a dream line-up with **The Rising Storm** and Barry Tashian's **Remains**. Original drummer Lee Mason was unable to attend due to ill health but his stool was superbly filled by Alexander's current POMO drummer Jim Doherty. Convening at Erik Lindgren's new Sounds Interesting studios in Middleborough, it was soon obvious to privileged observers that the chemistry still worked and something special was brewing. After their final run-through all were treated to a preview of the *The Lost Lost Tapes*, which Ted Myers and Erik

LOST AND FOUND - Everybody's Here... LP.

THE LOST - The Lost Lost Tapes CD.

Lindgren had just remixed. Erik's reward would be to augment them on keyboards at the upcoming gig.

On Saturday March 20th, **The Lost** hit the stage after **The Rising Storm** had set the scene and spirit of the occasion, and MC Peter Wolf (J. Geils Band) had paid eloquent homage to **The Lost**'s influence on him. Their stage presence and rapport with the audience was immediate and generated much warmth and humorous repartee.

Kicking off their eleven-song set with *When I Call*, they strode through their repertoire with a vitality, tightness and confidence which belied the 30+ year gap since they'd played together and the mere day-and-a-half they'd had to rebuild their act. All the Capitol 45 tracks bar *Mean Motorcycle* were revisited with Myers' beautiful *Violet Gown* saved for last, earning them a rapturous response and an encore of *Who Do You Love* featuring stunning vocals from a vibrant Willie Alexander. The only other cover was *A Certain Chick* (aka *A Certain Girl*), featuring "younger than springtime" Kyle Garrahan on lead vocals. A beaming Walter Powers took his turn on lead vocals for the catchy swingin' *(You Send Me Through) Changes*. Original agent "Uncle Fred" Taylor, called onto the stage after **The Lost**'s tribute to him - *(No) Money In My Pocket* - to accept the band's and fans' plaudits, described it as "a great trip".

Other compilation appearances have included: *Back Door Blues* on *Sixties Choice, Vol. 2* (LP) and *60s Choice Collection Vol's 1 & 2* (CD); and *Changes* on *The Arf! Arf! Blitzkrieg 32 Track Sampler* (Dble CD). (MW/ELn/JFr/GBs/TMs)

The Lost Agency

45:   One Girl Man/Time To Dream   (USA 881) 1967

A Chicago band whose sole stab for stardom was *One Girl Man*, a pounding garage rocker with abrasive vocals and some fine guitar. *Time To Dream*, on the flip, has a raga-esque feel, pulsing bass and relentless drums,

Compilation appearances have included: *One Girl Man* on *Mindrocker, Vol. 2* (LP) and *Essential Pebbles Collection, Vol. 1* (Dble CD); *One Girl Man* and *Time To Dream* on *Pebbles Vol. 7* (CD). (VJ)

Lost and Found

Personnel:	PETER BLACK	gtr, vcls	A
	JIMMY FROST	ld gtr	A
	JAMES HARRELL	bs	A
	STEVE WEBB	drms	A

ALBUMS: 1(A) EVERYBODY'S HERE - FOREVER LASTING
        PLASTIC WORDS   (International Artists 3) 1967 SC

	2( ) NUMBER 2	(Tempo 7064) 1973 -

NB: (1) reissued on vinyl (Decal LIK 21) 1988, and on CD (Collectables COL-CD-0552). Eva too have counterfeited (1) on CD with an acoustic demo of *25 M.P.H.*. (2) remains unreleased.

45s:	Forever Lasting Plastic Words/	
	Everybody's Here	(International Artists 120) 1967
	When Will You Come Through/	
	Professor Black	(International Artists 125) 1968

Originally known as The Misfits, this band came together in Houston in 1965. They changed their name to **Lost And Found** just prior to commencing a six-month residency at Houston's Living Eye club. They became friendly with Roky Erickson, who introduced them to Lelan Rogers of International Artists, who signed them for an album. The result was further evidence of Roky's influence. They covered *Don't Fall Down* from **The Elevators**' first album and imitated their jug sound on *Let Me Be*. The album also included a couple of instrumentals of note; *Zig Zag Blues* dedicated to the founder of Zig Zag Magazine and *Living Eye* dedicated to Houston's Living Eye Teen Club. Their first 45 was taken from the album but the second, a non-album release, was much better. Both sides featured good fuzz guitar and the flip was very strange. This second 45 was intended to form part of a second album which never emerged because the band disintegrated after a 30-day Texas tour with **The Music Machine**. Two tracks also cut for the intended album: *Girl With A One Track Mind* and *25 M. P. H.* were subsequently included on a *Texas Archive Flashback* compilation. The latter, a bedroom demo, was also included on *Epitaph For A Legend* (Dble LP), along with count-ins where the solo was supposed to go. You'll find both sides of their second 45 on *International Artists Singles Collection* (LP) and the *Austin Landing* (LP) compilation. Their album, which was also available in 1979 as part of a boxed set of the first 12 International Artists LPs, is worth getting now that it's been reissued. *There Would Be No Doubt*, one of its best tracks, also appeared on Radarscope's 1978 promotional EP. (VJ)

Lost Chords

45:	I Won't Have To Worry/	
	I Want To Be Her Man	(Vaughn-Ltd. VA-725) 1966

Sultry garage from the South - Birmingham, Alabama to be precise. The 'A' side is a clumsy steal of **The Byrds**' *You Won't Have To Cry*, recredited to a J. Whitworth. The 'B' side sounds more like a J.W. original and is a fine, yearning garage-ballad.

Compilation appearances include: *I Want To Be Her Man* on *Leaving It All Behind* (LP) and *Class Of '66!* (LP); and *I Won't Have To Worry* on *Psychedelic States: Alabama Vol. 1* (CD). (MW/MM)

The Lost Generation

45:	Night Time (Makes You Lonely)/Baby!	(Tear Drop 3195) 1968

An obscure outfit with an unheard 45 from Freeport, Texas.

The Lost Generation

Personnel incl:	BRUCE BETTS	A

45:	I'd Gladly Pay/Milk Cow Blues	(Paris Tower PT-109) 1967

Just one cool 45 was put out by this Clearwater, Florida combo. *I'd Gladly Pay* is a lightweight Stones-like affair until an attack of schizophrenia in the middle-eight - an outburst of fuzz followed by feedback and a frenzied solo in *Psychotic Reaction* tradition - only to return to the original theme as if nothing had happened.

Compilation appearances have included: *I'd Gladly Pay* on *Garage Punk Unknowns, Vol. 1* (LP) and *Psychedelic States - Florida Vol. 2* (CD). (VJ/MW)

The Lost Generation

45:	Let Me Out / They Tell Me	(Bofuz BF-1114) 1966

A different outfit from Baton Rouge, Louisiana. This 45 features two excellent punk ballads.

Compilation appearances include: *They Tell Me* on *Highs In The Mid-Sixties, Vol. 17* (LP); and *Let Me Out* on *Highs In The Mid-Sixties, Vol. 23* (LP). (MW)

The Lost Legend

45:	Love Flight/Yes I'm Ready	(Onyx ES 6901) 1969

An obscure New England band, from Lowell, Massachusetts. Their *Love Flight*, which got further exposure on *New England Teen Scene, Vol. 3* (LP), is a little gem. Check out the fine upfront drumming and discordant guitar work. Unfortunately the flip is a dire horn-ballad. (VJ)

Lost Nation

Personnel incl:	RON STULTS	A
	CRAIG WEBB	A
	L. ZELANKA	A

ALBUM:	1(A) PARADISE LOST	(Rare Earth RS 518) 1970 -

Don't let the cover of this obscure Detroit album put you off - it depicts the band behind a balustrade on whose lower wall is graffiti on a predominantly ecological theme, but this is no hippie-rock, or back-to-nature concept album. This is serious progressive rock, soundwise somewhere between Uriah Heep and Rare Bird - busy keyboards, strong vocals, neo-classical movements and some excellent heavy guitar. Not strictly within the main thrust of this book, this quintet merit an entry for including Ron Stults, formerly of revered heavy garage kings **The Unrelated Segments**. Craig Webb also had a spell in **Frijid Pink**. (MW)

Lost Ones

45:	I Don't Believe You/I Wanna Know	(Mersey 002) 196?

An awful effort from a Pennsylvania band who were previously known as The Kruisers and would later be known as Lite Rain. If you want to hear how bad *I Don't Believe You* actually is, listen for yourself on *Garage Punk Unknowns, Vol. 3* (LP). (VJ)

LOTHAR and THE HAND PEOPLE - Presenting... CD.

LOTHAR and THE HAND PEOPLE - This Is It... LP.

Lost Souls

| 45: | My Girl/Lost Love | (Lepoard 100) 196? |

This outfit may have come from Florida.

Compilation appearances include: *Lost Love* on *No No No* (CD); and *My Girl* on *Garage Punk Unknowns, Vol. 3* (LP). (VJ)

Lost Souls

Personnel:	DENNY CARLETON	gtr	AB
	ED GAZOSKI	ld gtr	A
	CHUCK McKINLEY	bs	AB
	RICH SCHOENAUR	sax, flute	AB
	LARRY TOMCZACK	drms	AB
	DENNY MAREK	ld gtr	B

Another **Lost Souls** were active in Euclid, Ohio in the sixties. Although no 45s were released at the time, Denny Carleton had enough acetates to compile a retrospective on cassette in the mid-eighties. If his name sounds familiar it's because Denny also served time with sixties mod-supremos **The Choir**. (GGI/MW/MDo)

The Lost Souls

| 45: | Simple To Say/The Girl I Love | (Bang 509) 1965 |

This was a different outfit from New York City or New Jersey who had one 45 in 1965. They may be the group who marked the start of Billy Joel's career.

Compilation appearances include *Simple to Say* on *The Lost Generation, Vol. 2* (LP) and *Mindrocker, Vol. 6* (LP). (MW)

The Lost Souls

45s:	It's Not Fair/Enchanted Sea	(Gloria 778) 1966
	Artificial Rose/Sad Little Girl	(Dawn 808) 1968
	Artificial Rose/Sad Little Girl	(Liberty 56024) 1968

Yet another **Lost Souls** this time from Dickenson, North Dakota. The Liberty 45 was recorded at Kay Bank Studios in Minneapolis and produced by Dave Hoffman and Bob Eveslage (of **The Unbelievable Uglies**). *Artificial Rose* has a moody intro with a throbbing bass line that brings to mind the **Electric Prunes**' *Too Much To Dream*... but soon veers off into harmony-pop territory. *Sad Little Girl*, was originally recorded by **Beau Brummels** and *Artificial Rose* was written by Ernie Marcesca of *Shout Shout (Knock Yourself Out)* fame.

Compilation appearances have included:- *It's Not Fair* on *The Essential Pebbles Collection, Vol. 2* (Dble CD); and *Artificial Rose* on *Every Groovy Day* (LP). (MW)

The Lost Souls

Personnel:	FRANK DILORENZO	ld gtr, ld vcls	A
	JOE GAMBA	drms	A
	MIKE MacTAVISH	keyb'ds	A
	DENNIS PTAK	gtr	A
	RANDY ROY	bs	A

| 45: | Step Inside/Leaving | (Musicor 1436) 1967 |

Another bunch of **Lost Souls**, this time from the village of Darlington in the city of Pawtucket, Rhode Island. They were one of the best and most popular local bands of the era and their garage 45 is quite highly-rated and commands a price of $100+.

Randy Roy later entered the Navy, being replaced by Gary Graveline. Dennis Ptak and Mike MacTavish also left and Mike was replaced by Steve Lemos.

Frank Dilorenzo and Joe Gamba, who were the driving force behind the band, still live in the same area. Frank is now a CPA, still playing occasionally for his own enjoyment. Joe runs a moving company and was playing in Ladies Choice. Mike died of a drug overdose in '75 in Indiana and Randy was last reported living in New Hampshire. (MW/AMk)

The Lost Souls

From Dearborn, Michigan, with no known 45s, this **Lost Souls** have four unreleased efforts - *Diamond Head*, *On Broadway*, *Come Home* and *Don't Let The Sun Catch You Crying* on *History Of Michigan Garage Bands In The '60s* (3-CD). (MW)

Lost Tribe

| 45: | Walk One Way/Fools Live Alone | (United Artists UA 50465) 1969 |

This seems to have been a one-off venture on United Artists. The flip can be found on *Garage Music For Psych Heads, Vol. 1*. (VJ)

Lothar and The Hand People

Personnel:	PAUL CONLY	keyb'ds, moog	A
	JOHN EMELIN	vcls	A
	TOM FLYE	perc	A
	RUSTY FORD	bs	A
	KIM KING	moog, synth, gtr	A

| ALBUMS: | 1(A) | PRESENTING LOTHAR AND THE HAND PEOPLE | (Capitol 2997) 1968 R1 |
| | 2(A) | SPACE HYMN | (Capitol 247) 1969 R1 |

NB: Both albums have been reissued. (1) was counterfeited in the USA in the late seventies, and was subsequently reissued by Capitol circa 1980, on the yellow Capitol label. The first pressing has the black/rainbow Capitol label. (1) has been reissued on CD (One Way 17960) with six bonus tracks. There is also a 15-track U.K. vinyl and CD release *This Is It, Machines* (See For Miles SEECD 75).

45s:	L-O-V-E/Rose Colored Glasses	(Capitol 5874) 1967
	Every Single Word/Comic Strip	(Capitol 5945) 1967
	Have Mercy/Let The Boy Pretend	(Capitol 2008) 1967
	Machines/Milkweed Love	(Capitol 2376) 1968
	Midnight Ranger/Yes, I Love You	(Capitol 2556) 1969

This was one of the most interesting groups to emerge from America in this era. Originally from Denver, Colorado, they moved to New York to record their two albums. **Lothar** was actually the name they gave to the theremin, which, together with two moog synthesisers, Ampex tape decks, keyboards and a linear controller characterised the group's sound.

Their debut album was reissued in the U.K. a few years ago and is consequently not difficult to obtain. On most tracks like *This May Be Goodbye* and *That's Another Story*, the theremin's influence is confined to short intros to fairly conventional two or three-minute compositions. However, three exceptions to this are the weird *Machines*, the unusual *Sex And Violence* and final track *It Comes On Anyhow* - which is a foretaste of some of the psychedelic craziness which appeared on their follow-up album.

On *Space Hymn*, the theremin and other electronic gadgetry is generally used to better effect. The album is composed of a mixture of weird material and more commercial numbers, such as *Yes, I Love You*, *Heatwave*, and *Say I Do*. The lyrics are often full of the usual hippie cliches. For example, *What Grows On Your Head?* is, as one might expect, romanticising about the freedom and virtues of long hair, while *Midnight Ranger* sounds like the story of a ranger who has had one trip too many! Some of the other material is particularly weird, notably the keyboard instrumental *Wedding Night For Those Who Love*, *Sdrawkcab* and *Today Is Only Yesterday's Tomorrow*. The title track, however, reaches new heights of craziness when the vocalist sets about hypnotising his audience! Certainly an interesting album, this is recommended. Apart from *Heatwave*, all the material was written by the band and you won't hear anything more unusual from this era than that title track.

Kim King went on to become a producer and sound engineer, notably working with **Steeplechase**, **Holy Moses** and Colin Winski. He also toured with **Zephyr**, being the first replacement for Tommy Bolin, but did not record with the band. It's not clear if Tom Flye is the same Tommy Flye who was recording engineer for, among others, **Zappa**'s *Shut Up And Play Yer Guitar* albums.

Compilation appearances include *Standing On The Moon (Space Hymn)* on *Psychedelic Frequencies* (CD). (VJ/SR/RDk)

Louie and The Leprechauns

45:	Let's Move/Your Foolin' Babe	(Music 102) 1965

A highly-regarded garage 45 from Central Kansas. *Let's Move* has also resurfaced on the *Midwest Garage Band Series - Kansas* (CD). (VJ/MW)

Louie and The Lovers

Personnel:	LOUIE ORTEGA	vcls, gtr	A
	FRANK PARADES		A
	ALBERT PARRA		A
	STEVE VARGAS		A

ALBUM:	1(A)	RISE	(Epic E 30026) 1970 -

45:	I Know You Know/Driver Go Slow	(Epic ?) 1970

LOVE - Love LP.

Produced by Doug Sahm (**Sir Douglas Quintet**), Louie Ortega and his group came from the Mexican-American community of Salinas, California. With a good singer and brilliant guitar parts, the best tracks are probably *Sittin By Your River*, *Royal Oakie*, *Driver Go Slow*, *Rock Me Baby* and the only cover, **Kaleidoscope**'s *If The Night* (Ortega wrote the ten other tracks). The rock critic Greil Marcus described them as "clear and sharp, relaxed without being fashionably lethargic, the vocals have feeling without pain".

Ortega would keep on working with Doug Sahm and Merrell Fankhauser.

Love

Personnel:	ARTHUR LEE	vcls, gtr	ABCDEFG
	JOHN ECHOLS	gtr	ABCD
	KEN FORSSI	bs	ABCD
	BRYAN MACLEAN	gtr, vcls	ABCD
	ALBAN 'SNOOPY' PFISTERER	keyb'ds, drms	BC
	DON CONKA	drms	A
	MICHAEL STUART	drms	CD
	TJAY CANTRELLI	horns	C
	JAY DONNELLAN	ld gtr	EF
	FRANK FAYAD	bs	EFG
	GEORGE SURANOVICH	drms	EFG
	DRACHEN THEAKER	drms	E
	GARY ROWLES		FG
	NOONEY RICKET	vcls, gtr	G

HCP

ALBUMS:	1(B)	LOVE	(Elektra EKS 74001) 1966	57	-
	2(C)	DA CAPO	(Elektra EKS 74005) 1967	80	-
	3(D)	FOREVER CHANGES	(Elektra EKS 74013) 1967	154	-
	4(E)	FOUR SAIL	(Elektra EKS 74049) 1969	102	-
	5(F)	OUT HERE (dbl)	(Blue Thumb BTS 9000) 1969	176	-
	6(-)	REVISITED	(Elektra 74058) 1970	142	-
	7(G)	FALSE START	(Blue Thumb BTS 8822) 1970	184	-
	8(-)	REEL TO REEL	(RSO SO 4804) 1975	-	-
	9(-)	BEST OF ...	(Rhino RNLP 800) 1980	-	-
	10(-)	LOVE LIVE (pic disc)	(Rhino RNDF 251) 1981	-	-
	11(-)	STUDIO/LIVE	(MCA 27025) 1982	-	-
	12(-)	GOLDEN ARCHIVE (BEST OF)	(Rhino RNLP 70175) 1986	-	-

NB: (2) and (3) issued in France in 1968 (Vogue/Elektra CLVLXEK 249 and CLVLXEK 218 respectively). (3) reissued on CD (Elektra/Rhino 8122-73537-2) 2001. The Blue Thumb recordings were released on Harvest in the UK. (10) was also released on Line (625047/5153) in Germany. Two UK-only releases were *Love Masters* (Elektra K 32002) 1973 and *Out There* (Chiswick WIKA 69) 1988. Most of their albums are now available on CD. (1) was reissued on Edsel (ED 218) and later on CD (Rhino/Warners 8122 735 672) 2001, with the mono and stereo mixes side by side. (1), (2) and (3) reissued on vinyl (Sundazed/Elektra/Rhino LP 5100-5102) 2001. (2) reissued on CD (Rhino/Elektra 8122 73604 2) 2002, featuring both mono and stereo versions. (4) reissued on CD (Warner/Rhino R 4049) 2002 with three remixed bonus cuts. (6) reissued on vinyl (Sundazed LP 5104) 2001. Arthur Lee also had a couple of solo LP's:- *Vindicator* (A & M SP 4356) 1972 and *Arthur Lee* (Rhino RNLP 020) 1981 released on (Beggars Banquet BEGA 26) in the UK, which aren't particularly relevant to this book. Recent CD issues are: *Love Comes In Colours* (Raven) 1993, a 24-track CD compilation with three non-LP tracks and *Love Story: 1966-1972* (Rhino R2 73500) 1995, a 2-CD set with 44 tracks and many non-album sides. It includes most of their early work, all of *Forever Changes*, a selection of their 'A' and 'B' sides and some of their best post-1967 material. Also of interest is *Oncemoreagain* a live CD recorded in London in 1992 and 1994 and Eva's *Black Beauty & Rarities* CD, which compiles Arthur's pre-**Love** recordings, together with the "Black Beauty" LP and a couple of more recent unreleased cuts.

EPs:	1	My Little Red Book/Message To Pretty/Hey Joe/ Emotions	(Vogue INT 18072) 1967
	2	7 And 7 Is/No. Fourteen/And More/ You'll Be Following	(Vogue INT 18095) 1967
	3	Feathered Fish/Gethsemene/ It's The Marlin, Baby (PS)	(LSD 1) 1995

NB: (1) and (2) French releases with picture sleeves. There's also a 3 x 10" EP tribute, *We're All Normal And We Want Our Freedom* (Alias A-50) 1994, also on CD by Modern Underground and indie outfits.

HCP

45s:	My Little Red Book/

LOVE - Da Capo LP.

Born in Memphis, Arthur Lee later moved to Los Angeles where he first saw **The Byrds**. The folk-rock act represented a break with the usual rhythm and blues format previously played at the clubs and had an enormous influence upon him. Lee had formed and disbanded a number of groups since moving to L.A., including The VIP's and Arthur Lee and the Lags. After hearing **The Byrds** he formed The Grassroots which included former **Byrds** roadie, Maclean; Forssi (earlier with The Sufaris) and Memphis-born Echols. They began to play around the L.A. clubs, but Lee discovered that another band had got first rights to their name and it was changed to **Love**.

Love made their debut at the Brave New World in Spring 1965 and by the early Summer of that year, Jac Holzman (head of Elektra records) discovered them playing at the Hollywood club, Bido Lito's. Elektra were looking for one of the new folk-rock acts, and eventually signed them up. They quickly became a cult attraction and by 1966 had a residency at Bido Lito's.

Their debut album **Love** was impressive, containing the drug-orientated *Signed D.C.*, *Hey Joe* and *My Little Red Book*. *Signed D.C.* was dedicated to Don Conka, who would have been in the band but for his drug problem (ironically with most people presuming him dead he did turn up in a late eighties reformation line-up). The list of bands who subsequently recorded *Signed D.C.* included **December's Children**, **Rising Storm**, **Axis Brotherhood**, Jeff Dahl Group, **Fallen Angels**, Sidewinders and Dead Moon. Another of its finer moments was *Softly To Me*, a fine track with haunting vocals and clashing guitars, released briefly as a single.

Before the release of their follow-up album *Da Capo*, Lee bought in Michael Stuart (formally with L.A. band **The Sons Of Adam**) on drums and Tjay Cantrelli on horns. 'Snoopy' Pfisterer was transferred from drums to keyboards. This album contained their second hit single *7and 7 Is*, *The Castle* and *Stephanie Knows Who*. Whilst *Orange Skies* would set the style for their following album, the whole of Side Two was taken up by the highly ambitious but only partially successful twenty-minutes long *Revelation*. *7 and 7 Is* was perhaps their most influential track. It was later covered by Alice Cooper, Billy Bragg, Marshmallow Overcoat, Sidewinders, Fuzztones, Spiral Jetty, Barracudas and The Blues Inc. among others.

Pfisterer and Cantrelli had both departed before the band released the masterful *Forever Changes* as a five-piece. Both Bob Harris and Penny Valentine chose this as their favourite album of all time in Paul Gambaccini's book "Critics Choice: Top 200 Albums". Almost every track was a classic and *Alone Again Or* and *Andmoreagain* were further U.S. hit singles. *Alone Again Or* was later covered by The Damned and UFO. Many of the other songs flowed gently with muted guitar leads, soothing brass, sweeping strings and often nihilistic lyrics. Lee chose haunting surrealistic lyrics, often making play on words. The drug influence which helped inspire this album was also to be the group's undoing. They scarcely left their former horror movie set/house near Hollywood and when they did record another album it was too awful to release.

Lee broke the band up and formed a new one comprising Frank Fayad (bs), George Suranovitch (drms), and Jay Donnellan (gtr) (all from **Nooney**

Message To Pretty	(Elektra EK 45603)	1966 52
7 And 7 Is/No. Fourteen	(Elektra EK 45605)	1967 33
Stephanie Knows Who/Orange Skies	(Elektra EK 45608)	1967 -
She Comes In Colours/Orange Skies	(Elektra EK 45608)	1967 -
Que Vida!/Hey Joe	(Elektra EK 45613)	1967 -
Alone Again Or/ A House Is Not A Motel	(Elektra EK 45629)	1968 99
Your Mind And We Belong Together/ Laughing Stock	(Elektra EK 45633)	1968 -
Alone Again Or/Good Times	(Elektra EK 45700)	1970 -
Alone Again Or/My Little Red Book (Spun Gold Series)	(Elektra EK 45056)	197? --
I'll Pray For You/Stand Out	(Blue Thumb 106)	1970 -
Keep On Shining/ The Everlasting First	(Blue Thumb 7116)	1970 -
Time Is Like A River/ Time Is Like A River (promo only)	(RSO SO 502)	1974 -
Time Is Like A River/ With A Little Energy	(RSO SO 502)	1974 -
You Said You Would/ You Said You Would (promo only)	(RSO SO 506)	1975 -
You Said You Would/ Good Old Fashioned Dream	(RSO SO 506)	1975 -
α Girl On Fire/Midnight Sun (PS)	(Distortions DR-1017)	1994 -

NB: α The 'A' side is a newly recorded track, the flip is from the much talked about Arthur Lee and **Jimi Hendrix** sessions from 1970. There's also a French picture sleeve 45: *Stand Out / Listen To My Song* (Blue Thumb 2C006-91524) 1970.

Related:

45s:	α	The Ninth Wave/Rumble-Still-Skins	(Capitol 4980) 1963
	β	Luci Baines/Soul Food	(Selma 2001) 1964
		House Of The Rising Sun/ House Of The Rising Sun (instr)	(Blue Star 1000) 196?
	χ	It's The Marlin, Baby/ House Of The Rising Sun	(LSD 1001) 1964
		Everybody's Gotta Live/ Love Jumped Through My Window	(A & M 1361) 1972
	δ	Sad Song/You Want Change For Your Re-run (promo only)	(A & M 1381) 1972

NB: α An instrumental 45 by Arthur Lee and The Lags. Both were Arthur Lee compositions. β by **American Four**. χ This is the interesting one. The 'A' side credits the vocals to Arthur Lee and John Echols and this acid folk adventure extols the virtues of 'The Marlin', an obscure sixties dance. This seems to have been a very early **American Four** release or possibly even earlier, released on a Texas label, sometime later when **Love** were famous. It can also be heard on *Texas Psychedelia From The Sixties*. The flip side was credited to an outfit called The Hurricanes who also released it on another label. There is some speculation that they may also have been **Love** incognito. δ Arthur Lee solo releases.

Arthur Lee solo:

EP:	1	I Do Wonder/Just Us/Do You Want To Know A Secret?/ Happy You (PS)	(Da Capo CAP 1001) 1977 UK

LOVE - Forever Changes CD.

Rickett), although additional musicians were used on recordings. *Four Sail* was their last album for Elektra and subsequent albums were comparatively disappointing. They managed a tour of England in 1970, but after the failure of *False Start*, Lee split the group again and worked on his solo album. Later, he would try unsuccessfully to form another version of **Love**. Somehow Arthur Lee got mixed up with Robert Stigwood and the result was *Reel To Reel*, a disco-influenced album with a female backing group, The Blackberries and a horn section on many tracks. Best avoided!

It is unlikely, however, that the mellow blend of their first three albums will ever be repeated and **Love** are best left alone to be remembered as one of the very best of the L.A. rock bands. Material from their early years is thoughtfully compiled on Rhino's *Best of Love* (RNLP 800), which was repackaged in 1987. *Love Live* (Rhino RNDF 251) (1982) and (Line LLP 5152 AP) 1983 is a recording of a reunion concert at the Whisky A Go Go in 1978. It includes gorgeous versions of *Orange Skies* and *Old Man* but the rest is pretty inept.

Several former **Love** members went on to play with other groups: Tjay Cantrelli joined **Geronimo Black**, Jay Donnellan (aka Jay Lewis) formed **Morning** with Jim Hobson, Gary Rowles formed **Cottonwood** and joined Richard Torrance's Eureka.

Live/Studio (MCA 27025) 1982 consisted of previously unreleased material live from the Fillmore East in 1970 and eight remastered tracks from the *Out Here* album. The live side is an energetic performance by line-up G and notable for its inclusion of the otherwise unavailable *Product Of The Times*. *Out There* (Big Beat WIKA 69) 1988 includes the best of **Love**'s *Out Here* and *False Start* albums.

In 1987 Lee reformed the band as a four piece, backed by Berton Averre (ex-The Knack) (ld gtr), Sherwood Akuna (bs) and Joe Blocker (drms), as part of the 'Psychedelic Summer of Love' package. Their short half-hour sets featured mostly material from their Elektra period:- *7 And 7 Is*, *My Little Red Book* and *Andmoreagain*.

In 1992 and 1994 Lee again played to packed audiences, in one-off London gigs, which were captured for posterity on the *Oncemoreagain* CD. In particular the 1992 set is memorable for the admirable backing by **The High Llamas**, who provided lush orchestral backing on tracks taken from the first three **Love** albums. Arthur Lee subsequently stole the show at Creation records 10th anniversary bash at the Royal Albert Hall.

George Suranovich died of a heart attack in 1990.

Bryan MacLean's profile has been revived of late with Sundazed's 1997 album and CD collection *Ifyoubelievein*. This is highly recommended to those captivated by the wistful romantic side of **Love** - e.g. *Orange Skies*, *Old Man* and *Alone Again Or*. The follow-up collection *Candy's Waltz* (Sundazed SC 10076) 2000 is also of interest. Sadly, Bryan MacLean passed away on Christmas Day 1998 at the age of 52.

In 1992, New Rose issued a CD of new material *Arthur Lee And Love*, which is not listed in the discography at the start of this entry.

1994 saw the release of a tribute CD to Arthur Lee and Love *We're All Normal And We Want Our Freedom* (Alias A-058) from modern alternative, underground and indie outfits including Hypnolovewheel, H.P.Zinker, Teenage Fanclub and TV Personalities. One interesting **Love** cover of recent years is a dynamic nineties guitar-thrash version of *Alone Again Or* by the Boo Radleys, from a Peel session and featured on their *Learning To Walk* retrospective.

In 2001, Rhino co-ordinated the remastered reissue of *Forever Changes* which boasts seven bonus cuts: the unreleased *Hummingbird* and *Wonder People*, the *Your Mind.../Laughing Stock* 45, alternate versions of *Alone Again Or* and *You Set The Scene*, and a series of *Your Mind...* studio takes. There is absolutely no excuse for not having this classic album now.

Also in 2001, drummer Michael Stuart published a book about his time in the band.

And finally, TV and Love trivia buffs: the instrumental section of *The Castle* was the theme tune of the BBC TV 'Holiday' programme in the early seventies, when it was presented by Cliff Michelmore.

As one would expect **Love** have also featured on several compilations including:- *Alone Again Or*, *Andmoreagain*, *Hey Joe*, *My Little Red Book*, *7 And 7 Is*, *She Comes In Colors*, *Signed D.C.* and *Singing Cowboy* on *Elektrock The Sixties* (4-LP); *My Little Red Book* and *7 And 7 Is* on *The Golden Archive Series Sampler*; *My Little Red Book* on *Wild Thing* and *Nuggets, Vol. 2 - Punk* (LP); *7 And 7 Is* on *Highs Of The Sixties*, *Nuggets Box* (4-CD), *Nuggets From Nuggets* (CD), *Nuggets, Vol. 9* (LP), *Psychedelic Perceptions* (CD) and *Kings Of Pop Music Vol. 1* (LP); *It's The Marlin Baby* on *Sixties Archive, Vol. 6* (CD) and *Texas Psychedelia From The 60s* (LP); *Bummer In The Summer* and *Hey Joe* on *Kings Of Pop Music Vol. 2* (LP); *The Daily Planet* on *Hallucinations, Psychedelic Underground* (LP); *And Somebody* on *California New Years*; *If You Wanna Be Free*, *Stand Out*, *Andmoreagain* and *Singing Cowboy* from a Fillmore West concert 23/11/70 on *California Easter*; a 1974 version of *Singing Cowboy* is on the RSO 10" sampler *Prime Cuts*; and a pre-**Love** *Lucy Baines* by **The American Four** on *California Acid Folk*.

Also of interest is the recent compilation, *Sixties Rebellion, Vol. 8*, which collects together various sixties garage covers of **Love** classics including the likes of **Soul Benders**, **Flower Power**, **Five By Five**, **Noblemen** and Haunted. (VJ/MW/JFr/SR)

Lovechain

45: Step Out Of Your Window You Can Fly /
     Sadness In My Mind   (Westwood A-1008) 1969

A rarely-seen 45 on a Canton, Ohio label. The trippily titled and sounding *Step Out...* features on *A Lethal Dose Of Hard Psych* (CD) which informs us that the band was from Dover and New Philadelphia, Ohio. (ELn/MW)

Love Corporation

45: Love Corporation/Should I   (Pride 673) 1967

An Oklahoma band, who recorded an excellent beat-punk 45. *Love Corporation* can be heard on *Monsters Of The Midwest, Vol. 4* (LP). (VJ)

The Loved Ones

45: Surprise, Surprise (For You)/
     Another Time Or Place   (Ambassador TIF 212) 196?

Newark, New Jersey was home to this particular set of **Loved Ones**. The 'A' side is a typical punk put down song conducted at breakneck speed and featuring some snotty vocals and good guitar. Interested? Well, it has resurfaced on *Pebbles Vol. 10* (CD), *Attack Of The Jersey Teens* (LP), *Sixties Choice, Vol. 1* (LP) and *60's Choice Collection Vol's 1 & 2* (CD). (VJ)

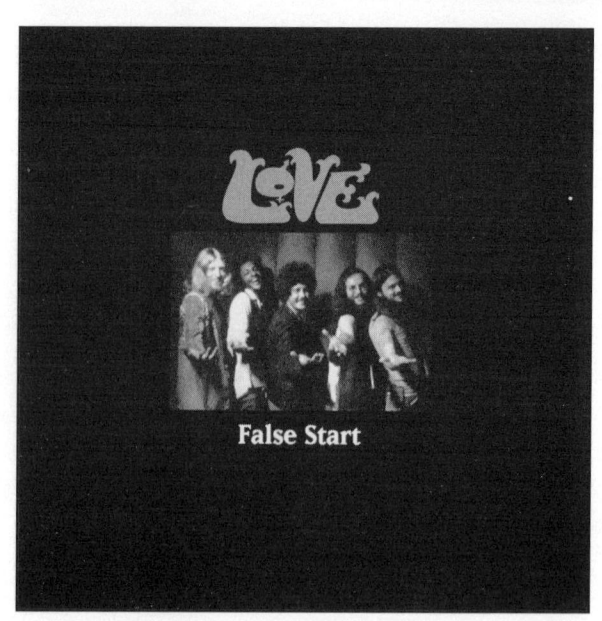

LOVE - False Start CD.

The Loved Ones

45:　　　Country Club Life/Together Together　　　(Brookmont 556) 196?

From New York. This excellent 45 lashes out at "rich swingers" on *Country Club Life* in a slowish but powerful number with effective Eric Burdon style rasping vocals and a twee baroquish chorus - neat. The flip is a psych-rocker reminiscent of the lighter side of **Iron Butterfly**.

Compilation appearances include *Together, Together* on *Sixties Choice, Vol. 2* (LP) and *60's Choice Collection Vol's 1 & 2* (CD). (MW)

Love Exchange

Personnel:　DAN ALTCHULER　　12 string gtr　　A
　　　　　　FRED BARNETT　　　gtr　　　　　　A
　　　　　　JEFF BARNETT　　　 drms　　　　　 A
　　　　　　RONNIE BLUNT　　　 vcls　　　　　　A
　　　　　　WALTER FLANNERY　organ　　　　　A
　　　　　　MIKE JOYCE　　　　bs　　　　　　　A

ALBUM:　1　LOVE EXCHANGE　　　(Tower ST-5115) 1968 -

NB: (1) reissued on CD with six bonus tracks (Sundazed SC 6113) 2001.

45:　　　Mellow Memory/Swallow The Sun　　　(Uptown 755) 1967

A flower-power group from Los Angeles who were produced by Larry Goldberg (who'd also worked with **Fire Escape**, **Mesmerizing Eye**, **Neighb'rhood Childr'n**, **Maze** and **The Other Half**). *Swallow The Sun* is actually a cover version of **The Peanut Butter Conspiracy**'s *Dark On You Now* with slightly modified lyrics. Typifying the freshness of L.A. rock in this period it's very listenable. Their album is a very minor collectable.

Most of the band had earlier played in **The Crusaders**. Walter Flannery was later in **Charity**.

Swallow The Sun is also on on *Highs In The Mid-Sixties, Vol. 3*, *Nuggets, Vol. 10* (LP) and *Crystalize Your Mind* (CD). (VJ/MW)

Love Flowers

Probably from Texas hence the inclusion of *Peace And Love*, *Near Vanna* and *Who Are You* on *Acid Visions - Complete Collection, Vol. 2* (3-CD). *Peace...* is a slow organ, Procol Harum-influenced melodic tune with flower-power lyrics and some fiery guitar towards the end; *Near Vanna* ('nirvana' geddit?) is similarly a slow-paced ballad, whilst *Who Are You* is a heavier early-Led Zepplin style rocker...

Other compilation appearances include *Peace And Love* and *Nirvana* (sic) on *Green Crystal Ties Vol. 6* (CD).

THE LOVE EXCHANGE - Love Exchange CD.

THE LOVE GENERATION - Love Generation LP.

The Love Generation

Personnel:　JOHN BAHLER　　　　　　　　　　　A
　　　　　　TOM BAHLER　　　　　　　　　　　 A
　　　　　　MITCH 'THE COUNT' GORDON　　　　A
　　　　　　MARILYN MILLER　　　　　　　　　 A
　　　　　　JIM 'LITTLE FLOWER' WASSON　woodwind　A
　　　　　　ANNIE WHITE　　　　　　　　keyb'ds　A

ALBUMS:　1(A)　LOVE GENERATION　　　(Imperial LP-12351) 196? -
　　　　　2(A)　A GENERATION OF LOVE　(Imperial LP-12364) 1968 -
　　　　　3(A)　MONTAGE　　　　　　　 (Imperial LP-12408) 1968 -

NB: There's also a compilation *Love And Sunshine: The Best Of The Love Generation* (Sundazed SC 11120) 2002.

HCP

45s:　Groovy Summertime/
　　　Playin' On The Strings Of The Wind　(Imperial 66243) 1967 74
　　　Meet Me At The Love In/
　　　She Touched Me　　　　　　　　　　 (Imperial 66254) 1967 -
　　　Mamam/WC Fields　　　　　　　　　　(Imperial 66275) 1968 -
　　　Love And Sunshine/Magic Land　　　 (Imperial 66289) 1968 -
　　　Consciousness Expansion/
　　　Montage From How Sweet It Is　　　 (Imperial 66310) 1968 86
　　　Catching Up On Fun/
　　　Let The Good Times In　　　　　　　(Imperial 66336) 1968 -

NB: There was also a UK 45: *She Touched Me/The Love In Me* (Liberty LBF 15018) 1967.

A harmony rich pop act from California who will appeal to lovers of The **Association**, **Mamas and Papas** or **Orange Colored Skies**. Prior to their collaboration all six members had kicked around the music scene, working as back-up singers and touring with various acts (White had actually been a member of The New Christie Minstrels).

1969's Tommy Oliver-produced *Montage* saw the crew expanded their heart warming (or mind-numbing) hip platitudes beyond Top 40 pop. Apparently intended to give the group a slightly more controversial edge, tracks such as *The Pill*, *Consciousness Expansion* and *A Touch Of Love* (complete with excerpts from John F. Kennedy speeches) saw them wrapping their ever cheerful tight knit harmonies around socially and politically-relevant themes. Not only that, but the Bahlers and company brought with them a certain cloying enthusiasm; almost evangelical fervour, in the knowledge that their insights could change the world. Highlights include the lead-off song *Montage from How Sweet It Is (I Knew That You Knew)* and they should've-been-a-hit slice of Top 40 pop *Candy*.

Not to be confused with **Montage**.

The Sundazed compilation is a fine 25-track collection, which comes with excellent sleevenotes. Highlights include *The Love In Me*, the original version of Jimmy Webb's *Montage* and two quasi-psychedelic offerings; *Meet Me At The Love-In* and *Consciousness Expansion*.

Brothers, John and Tom Bahler later wrote and arranged material for The Partridge Family, for whom they also acted as background vocalists. Tom Bahler also penned *She's Out Of My Life* for Michael Jackson. He and his brother also sang back-up for Elvis Presley and Frank Sinatra! (SR/MMs/SB/VJ)

The Love Ins

45:	Everything's There/ That's All She Wrote	(Curtis Bros 101)	196?

There had to be a band which took its name from this late sixties institution. *That's All She Wrote* is a pretty good pop-punk effort. If the titles sound familiar it's because this is **The Hysterics** from San Bernardino under a pseudonym; the same coupling was issued on Tottenham (500) as by **The Hysterics**.

Compilation appearances include: *That's All She Wrote* on *Sixties Choice, Vol. 2* (LP) and *60's Choice Collection Vol's 1 & 2* (CD). (VJ)

The Love Ins

45s:	It Was Yesterday/ You're Supposed To Be Mine	(Laurie 3415)	1968
	Grove Me/Red Light, Green Light	(Laurie 3456)	1968
	Love / ?	(NML 20)	196?

Another **Love-Ins**, this bunch specialised in harmony flower-pop. (VJ)

Love Is A Heart-On

ALBUM:	1	LOVE IS A HEART-ON	(Heavy)	c1972 -

NB: (1) reissued on CD (Cosmic Daze 102) 1998.

Rumored to be the same musicians who recorded the **Heavy Balloon** album, **Love Is A Heart-On** was sold only by mail-order with ads placed in the classified pages of men's magazines, as it's an X-rated album with pornographic lyrics (quite dated now). Although some tracks are decent hard-rock slammers, the album is rather boring and best avoided. (SR)

Love Machine

ALBUM:	1	ELECTRONIC MUSIC TO BLOW YOUR MIND BY!!!	(Design SDLP-282)	1968 SC

NB: (1) counterfeited on vinyl 2001.

LOVE IS A HEART-ON - Love Is A Heart-On CD.

LOVE MACHINE - Electronic Music To Blow Your Mind By!!! LP.

A budget label's attempt to cash in on psychedelia. Almost certainly this was just a bunch of studio musicans assembled to recycle some instrumentals. The cover is colourful and so are the titles - *Inner Ear Freakout*, *Asbury Tripper*, *Zenquake*, *Bells For Eternal Zoom*, *The Shadows Of Vibrate*, *Mindblower* and so on.

The trouble is... this is tacky intermission muzak with cheesy cinema keyboards, topped off with chimes, oscillators, 'way out' electronic effects, even Klanger-like noises (?!). An artifact of its time, this is more likely to split your sides than blow your mind; whoever thought this was psychedelic had clearly lost theirs. (MW)

Love, Serve, Remember

ALBUM:	1	LOVE, SERVE, REMEMBER	(ZBS)	1973 SC

A box set of mystic and religious folk music (one album contains only spoken word), issued in a black and white cover with a booklet. (SR)

Love Sitars

45:	Paint It Black/Paint It Black	(Soul Galore SG-2603)	1968?

Like Lord Sitar this act takes someone else's hit, removes the vocals and heads East. *Paint It Black* lends itself very well to this treatment - if you didn't already know the song you might think it was a rare example of Calcutta garage-psych!! (MW)

The Love Society

Personnel:	KEITH ABLER	ld vcls, gtr	A C
	MIKE DELLGER	drms, vcls	ABC
	STEVE GILLES	bs	ABC
	MIKE HOLDRIDGE	keyb'ds	ABC
	DAVE STEFFEN	ld gtr, vcls	ABC
	DUANE ABLER	gtr	BC

				HCP
45s:	Do You Wanna Dance?/Without You	(Tee Pee 3878)	1968	-
	Do You Wanna Dance?/Without You	(Scepter 12223)	1968	108
	Tobacco Road/Drops Of Rain	(Scepter 12236)	1968	-
	Let's Pretend (We're Making Love)/ You Know How I Feel (And Why)	(Target T 1006)	1969	-
	Don't Worry Baby/ You Know How I Feel (And Why)	(RCA Victor 0257)	1969	-
	Bang On Your Own Drum/ Candle Waxing	(RCA Victor 9821)	1969	-
	America/Wanda	(Mercury 73130)	1970	-

For the most part this Plymouth, Wisconsin, band played cover versions in competent harmony pop style. Two exceptions to this were *You Know How I Feel (And Why)*, a Dylan imitation, which got a further airing on *Highs In The Mid-Sixties, Vol. 10* (LP) and their cover of *Tobacco Road*, which was a heavier fuzzy effort most likely to be of interest to readers.

Keith Abler left for a while to join **Phase III**, returning in time for their final 45 on Mercury. He later issued a solo album, *Pilgrim* (Homegrown Records) 1975.

Members from both **Love Society** and **Phase III** would go on to form Sunblind Lion, who released three fine albums of melodic progressive rock in the seventies. (VJ/MW/GM)

Love Song

ALBUM: 1 LOVE SONG (Good News) 1972 ?

A Christian rock outfit. (SR)

The Lovin' Spoonful

Personnel:	STEVE BOONE	bs	AB
	JOE BUTLER	drms	AB
	JOHN SEBASTIAN	gtr, vcls	AB
	ZAL YANOVSKY	gtr, vcls	A
	JERRY YESTER	gtr, vcls	B

HCP

ALBUMS:
1(A) DO YOU BELIEVE IN MAGIC? (Kama Sutra 8050) 1965 32 -
2(A) DAYDREAM (Kama Sutra 8051) 1966 10 -
3(A) WHAT'S UP TIGER LILY? (Kama Sutra 8053) 1966 126 -
4(A) HUMS OF THE LOVIN' SPOONFUL (Kama Sutra 8054) 1966 14 -
5(A) THE BEST OF THE LOVIN' SPOONFUL (Kama Sutra 8056) 1967 3 -
6(A) YOU'RE A BIG BOY NOW (Kama Sutra 8058) 1967 160 -
7(B) EVERYTHING PLAYING (Kama Sutra 8061) 1968 118 -
8(A) THE BEST OF THE LOVIN' SPOONFUL, VOL 2 (Kama Sutra 8064) 1968 156 -
9(A) 24 KARAT HITS (Kama Sutra 750-2) 1968 - -
10(B) REVELATION: REVOLUTION' 69 (Kama Sutra 8073) 1969 - -
11(A) THE VERY BEST OF ... (Kama Sutra 2013) 19? - -
12(B) ONCE UPON A TIME (Kama Sutra 2029) 19? - -
13(B) THE BEST ... LOVIN' SPOONFUL (Kama Sutra 2608(2)) 1976 183 -

NB: Most of their albums have been reissued and many of them are now available in CD format. (1) and (2) (Sundazed LP 5159-51560) 2002 and (4) (Sundazed LP 5166) 2003. In addition, readers may be interested in a 26-track Euro CD, *Collection* and a 26-track U.S. CD, *Anthology*. See For Miles have also compiled EP tracks on their CD *The EP Collection* (See For Miles SEECD 229). Recent vinyl releases have included, *Jug Band Music: Great Years* (a French release) and *Good Time Music*, a 24-track compilation including some very rare tracks. A recent 'hits' collection is *Greatest Hits* (Buddha 74465 997 162) 2000.

EPs:
1(A) DID YOU EVER? (Kama Sutra KEP 300) 1966
2(A) JUG BAND MUSIC (Kama Sutra KEP 301) 1966
3(A) DAY BLUES (Kama Sutra KEP 303) 1967
4(A) NASHVILLE CATS (Kama Sutra KEP 304) 1967
5(A) LOVING YOU (Kama Sutra KEP 305) 1967
6(A) SOMETHING IN THE NIGHT (Kama Sutra KEP 306) 1967

NB: Eight EPs with picture sleeves were also released in France on Kama Sutra.

HCP

45s:
Do You Believe In Magic?/On The Road Again (Kama Sutra 201) 1965 9
You Didn't Have To Be So Nice/My Gal (Kama Sutra 205) 1965 10
Daydream/Night Owl Blues (Kama Sutra 208) 1966 2
Did You Ever Have To Make Up Your Mind?/Didn't Want To Have To Do It (Kama Sutra 209) 1966 2
Summer In The City/Butchie' Tune/Fishing Blues (Kama Sutra 211) 1966 1
Rain On The Roof/Pow! (Kama Sutra 216) 1966 10
Nashville Cats/Full Measure (Kama Sutra 219) 1966 8/87
Darlin' Be Home Soon/Darlin' Companion (Kama Sutra 220) 1967 15
Six O'Clock/The Finale (Kama Sutra 225) 1967 18
Lonely (Amy's Theme)/You're A Big Boy Now (Kama Sutra 231) 1967 -
α She Is Still A Mystery/Only Pretty, What A Pity (Kama Sutra 239) 1967 27
Money/Close Your Eyes (Kama Sutra 241) 1967 48
Never Goin' Back/Forever (Kama Sutra 250) 1968 73
(Til I) Run With You/Revelation Revolution '69 (Kama Sutra 251) 1968 128
Me About You/Amazing Air (Kama Sutra 255) 1968 91
Summer In The City/You And Me And Rain On The Roof (Kama Sutra 551) 1972
Daydream/Do You Believe In Magic? (Kama Sutra 608) 1976 -

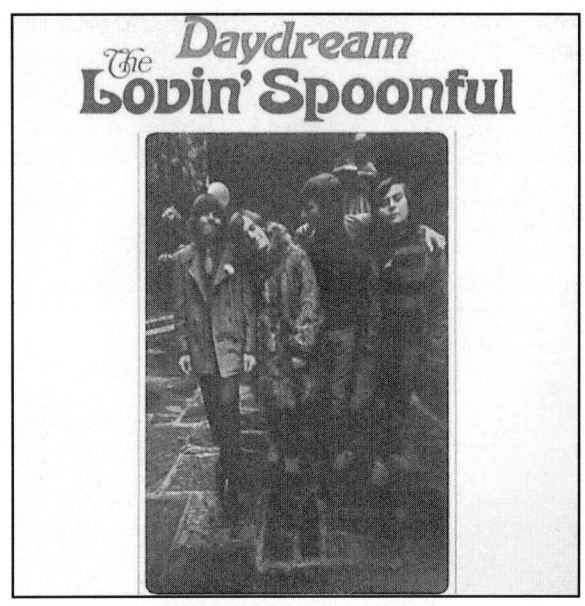

NB: α also released in France with a picture sleeve (Kama Sutra 718 110) 1968.

The core of this band were **John Sebastian**, who was born on 17th March 1944 in New York, and Zalman Yanovsky, who was born on 19th December 1944 in Toronto, Ontario, Canada. They'd first met as a number of guests invited to Cass Elliot's house to watch the Beatles' U.S. TV debut on the Ed Sullivan Show in February 1964. They played guitar together through the night and discussed the possibility of forming a rock group. At the time **Sebastian** was a Greenwich Village folkie and sometime member of the **Even Dozen Jug Band** and Yanovsky was guitarist with the Nova Scotia folk group, The Halifax Three. When this disbanded in June 1964 Yanovsky was briefly involved in the **Mugwumps** (with **Denny Doherty**, Cass Elliot and James Hendricks). This was a short-lived and unsuccessful venture, which soon disbanded, and, of course **Doherty** and Elliot went on to form one half of **The Mamas and The Papas**. With Yanovsky at a loose end again the seeds for a rock group with **John Sebastian** (along the lines they'd discussed earlier) were sewn in January 1965. The name **Lovin' Spoonful** was taken from a phrase in Mississippi John Hurt's *Coffee Blues* and Joe Butler (from Glen Cove, Long Island) and Steve Boone, who was born on 23rd September 1943 in North Carolina, were drafted in to be the other members.

They won a residency at the Night Owl in Greenwich Village and their producer Erik Jacobsen got them a deal with the newly formed Kama Sutra label. Playing their own brand of folk-rock/good-time music they enjoyed immediate commercial success. Their first 45 made No. 9 in the U.S. and their debut album of the same name peaked at No. 32. Follow-up *You Didn't Have To Be So Nice* peaked at No. 10 and *Daydream*, their lazy, laid back celebration of love on a Summer's day, was even bigger, reaching No. 2 in the U.S. and UK, becoming a million seller. Their second album of the same name made No. 10 in the U.S. and No. 8 in the UK. They also had four cuts included on the Elektra compilation *What's Shakin*, including one called *Good Time Music*, for them this is what music was all about.

THE LOVIN' SPOONFUL - Hums Of... LP.

Their next 45, *Did You Ever Have To Make Up Your Mind?* peaked at No. 2, but this was soon surpassed by what was arguably their finest moment, *Summer In The City*. Notable for its atmospheric streetnoise sound effects this topped the U.S. charts for three weeks and made No. 8 in the UK. It became their second and biggest million seller.

They went on to appear on the soundtrack of the cult movie *What's Up Tiger Lily?* (No. 126 in the US) and their third album of the year *Hums Of The Lovin' Spoonful* peaked at No. 14. *Nashville Cats* would be their last U.S. Top Ten hit (peaking at No. 8) - the flip side also made it to No. 87. In the U.K., it climbed to No. 26. They followed this with the heavily orchestrated *Darlin' Be Home Soon*, which peaked at No. 15 in the U.S. and No. 44 in the UK. (It would be their last U.K. Hit.) In March 1967, *The Best Of The Lovin' Spoonful* climbed to No. 3 in the U.S. Album Charts in which it spent a year in all. Their follow-up, *You're A Big Boy Now*, their second soundtrack album, was a minor U.S. Album hit peaking at No. 160.

After just one further U.S. hit, *Six O'Clock*, Zal Yanovsky left the band, following media coverage of a marijuana bust in San Francisco when he was accused of incriminating others to avoid prosecution under threat of deportation (as he was still technically a Canadian citizen) and the group were ostracised by their rock peers. He was replaced by **Jerry Yester**, who'd played in the **Modern Folk Quartet**. Although they enjoyed further minor 45 hits in the States with *She's Still A Mystery*, *Money* and *Never Going Back*, they rather lost their way and their next two albums *Everything Playing* and *The Best Of The Lovin' Spoonful, Vol. 2* could only manage No. 118 and 156 respectively. When **John Sebastian** left the group in October 1968 it soon crumbled. He went on to enjoy a reasonably successful solo career and made a memorable appearance at The Woodstock Festival the following year, performing *Younger Generation*, which became a highlight of the movie, and *I Had A Dream*, which opened the *Woodstock* album. The following year he appeared with Zal Yanovsky at the Isle of Wight Rock Festival in the U.K. (Yanovsky was there as part of Kris Kristofferson's band).

Yester too, made solo albums but none rose above cult success. In the 1980s he reformed the **Modern Folk Quartet** but became best known as a producer and string arranger. **The Lovin' Spoonful**'s original line-up did reform in October 1980 to appear in Paul Simon's movie *One Trick Pony*.

The band had two good years and are lovingly remembered by many for their zany image, wild sense of humour and their unique brand of good-time music, which combined traditional folk and blues influences with the rock and roll of their era.

Zal Yanovsky's solo album, *Alive And Well In Argentina* (Buddah BDS-5019) 1968 and (Kama Sutra KSBS-2030) 1971 is worth checking out as a good example of weird, deranged and wonderful sixties extravaganza. Nowadays, **Zal Yanovsky** operates a successful restaurant in Kingston, Ontario, called 'Chez Piggy'.

Compilation appearances include *She Is Still A Mystery* on *Nuggets Vol. 5* (LP). (VJ/SR/MJs)

Rob Lowrey and The Rock Collection

45:   Organized Confusion/
      Get Out Of My Life Woman   (Creative Family Records 25) c1969

A rare single. *Organized Confusion* was written by **Kim Fowley**. (SR)

Ted Lucas

ALBUM: 1   TED LUCAS   (Om 5374) 1975 R2

45:   Head In California / My Dog   (Zonk 1) 197?

Ted Lucas handles the vocals and guitar on this solo album. A local Michigan artist he was previously in the **Spike Drivers** and **The Misty Wizards**. Musically, we're talking underground folk. The album, which came with an insert, sported some stunning cover art by Stanley Mouse. **Lucas** also contributed two tracks to a local sampler, *Detroit Folk*, which pre-dates his album.

Lucas was killed in the late nineties. (CF/MW)

Tom Lucas

ALBUM: 1   RED LETTER DAY   (New Fate 500) 1976 R2

A New York artist whose album, which consists of strong, well-played, electric folk and rock, was issued with an insert. (CF)

Chris Lucey

Personnel: ROBERT PARKER JAMES
             aka CHRIS LUCEY/
             BOBBY JAMESON   hrmnca, vcls   A

ALBUM: 1(A)   SONGS OF PROTEST AND ANTI-PROTEST
                           (Surrey SS 1027) c1965/6 R2

NB: Mono and stereo versions exist. There were also two different label colors: red and purple, red being the somewhat rarer one and the purple label crediting "Chris Ducey". Mint copies can fetch upwards to $150-300. (1) also issued in the UK as by **Bobby Jameson**, but entitled *Too Many Mornings*. Also issued in Canada, some copies say "Chris Lucey" on cover and labels, some say "Chris Ducey" on cover and labels!

Robert Parker James was born in Tucson, Arizona, but took the pseudonym **Bob Jameson** and was most likely based in California. In the US, this album was released under the alternative pseudonym **Chris**

TED LUCAS - Ted Lucas LP.

TOM LUCAS - Red Letter Day LP.

Lucey, but in the U.K. it was released as *Too Many Mornings* as by **Bob Jameson**. Produced by ex-surfer Marshall Lieb and issued in the U.S. on the same budget label as **The Leaves** debut, no info is given on the cover other than the picture of a **Byrd** look-alike with his mouthharp(*). The album also includes an excellent version of *Girl From The East* similarly featured on the **Leaves** album.

The music is laid-back folk-rock with echoes of **Byrds**, **Tim Buckley**, **Steve Noonan** and **Lovin' Spoonful**. Many of the songs feature charming guitar parts, dreamy arrangements, jazzy even Lee Underwood-ish backing. Some of the highlights are *I'll Remember Them* and *Girl From Vernon Mountain*, both of which are excellent introspective pieces. Most of the album is filled with a haunting atmosphere and all the tracks are originals.

Collectors may wish to note that the Mono copies differ considerably to the Stereo ones.

Surrey was a sort-of subsidiary label of VeeJay operated by their West Coast promo team, led by Randy Wood and Steve Clark (the link between BJ and **Boettcher**). They cut **Hoyt Axton** and various others on the budding folk-rock club scene in L.A. According to **Axton**, he went over to the office one day, and everything was gone, even the desks and chairs!

Jameson's records were promoted by Tony Alamo, who also worked with many other artists and John and Bobby Kennedy. L.A. musician Denny Bruce recalls: "To introduce **Bobby Jameson** to the 'industry' Tony Alamo took out a 7-page fold out ad (four color in Billboard) that showed Bobby standing on top of a limo somewhere on the Pacific Coast Highway. With the ocean in the background, so he was not lit, you just saw this guy with a cowboy hat, with his staff next to the limo: very much like the Village People- wearing the very obvious uniforms of their jobs: chef, nurse, barber, bodyguard, driver, etc. There were at least 10 of them. Tony arranged for Bobby to be the opening act for another new act that had signed to Atlantic and were getting a buzz. The showcase was to be at lunch time, so with food being served, everyone came. The act was Caesar and Cleo, wearing togas with olive wreaths in their hair. They of course, became Sonny and Cher. They went on first. Needless to say, when Tony took the mike and had Bobby backlit, behind some see-through screen and was saying "Ladies and gentlemen, here's an act that can act as well as James Dean, sell as many records as the Beatles, on and on, everybody got up and started walking out while a four-track demo was playing, with Bobby lip-synching to an almost empty house."

NB: (*) This picture, according to Denny Bruce, was actually a photograph of Brian Jones, pictured at a Hollywood club called 'The Action'. (CP/JJs/MJ/JFr)

Lucifer

Personnel:	JOE BERTOLA	drms	A
	VINCENT "BUTCH" BIOCCA	bs	A
	JOE GALLO	piano	A
	JOE MATTIOLI	ld vcls	A
	PETE SKELTON	ld gtr	A

ALBUM: 1 LUCIFER (Gallo Records) 1970 R3/R4

NB: (1) reissued on LP (Void VOID 25) 2001. (1) reissued on LP and CD (Akarma AK 044) 2001.

This very rare album was the work of a Rochester, New York band. The album sleeve notes declare that their music is "hard rock in the style of Grand Funk Railroad and Uriah Heep". Overall, the album is nowhere near that heaviness - there's a notable lack of thunderous riffing or screaming solos. Uriah Heep influences are more obvious in the soaring Byron-esque vocals on the dramatic ballads but an underlying soulful vibe and keyboard dominance puts them in the class of those NYC and Long Island Italian-American bands influenced by **Vanilla Fudge** or the **Young Rascals**, rather than the proto heavy-metal set. On their lighter side, they deliver a fine flowing rendition of the **Youngbloods**' version of **Dino Valente**'s hippie anthem *(Let's) Get Together*.

The original is supposedly very rare and has been hyped by specialist dealers with asking prices reaching a dizzyingly silly level - one copy seen going for $900 in 2001 - surely guaranteed to disappoint. So, if this sounds like your bag and you're not stupidly rich, pick up the reissue.

Mattioli, Skelton and Gallo had previously played together in a band called Infirmary and Biocca joined them from Poor Heart. Lou Gramm, later with Foreigner, may have been in the band for a while. (VJ/SR/MW/CF)

Lucifer

ALBUM: 1 BLACK MASS (UNI 731 1 1) 1971 -

Mort Garson, the mind behind the unusual **Cosmic Sounds** *Zodiac* album, was also responsible for this rather good atmospheric electronic album.

Another **Lucifer** self-titled album (Invictus 7309) is by a different act. (VJ)

Jack Lucking

ALBUM: 1 LIFE (Artronics 7293) 1972 ?

A local Minnesota folk singer with psychedelic touches, his album is a concept album about the life cycle. (SR)

Lumbee

Personnel incl:	CAROL FITZGERALD	vcls	AB
	WILLIE FRENCH LOWERY	ld gtr, vcls	AB
	FORRIS FULFORD	drms, vcls	AB
	RONALD SEIGER	bs	A
	BOBBY PAUL	bs	B
	RICKEY VANNOY	gtr, vcls	B

LUCIFER - Lucifer LP.

LUMBEE - Overdose CD.

ALBUM: 1(B) OVERDOSE (Radnor R2003) 1970 R1

NB: (1) reissued on CD (Gear Fab GF-166) 2001.

45: Streets Of Gold / Get Ready (Radnor 104) 1970

Originally known as **Plant and See** (line-up 'A'), a four-piece from Fayetteville, North Carolina. They were enjoying some success with a 45 and album under their belt when their label White Whale went under and they were marooned. Determined to continue they got another contract which meant a change of name - so they chose to adopt the name of Lowery's native American tribe.

A strange album which came with a big cardboard insert for the 'Overdose' game, a kind of 'Monopoly' for stoned people! The lyrics are obviously drug-related (*You Gotta Be Stoned*, *Veronica High*) and the music is rather bluesy with some sound effects. Now rare and sought-after but probably more for the game than for the music itself, which is of minor interest. (SR/MW)

Lunar Madness

45s: The Exorcism/Msicroxe Eht (Pot Records) c1974

Probably from Texas hence the inclusion of *The Exorcism* on *Acid Visions - The Complete Collection Vol. 1*. (3-CD). According to the sleeve notes, "**Lunar Madness** consisted of **Johnny Winter**'s long-time bass player I.P. Sweat and songwriter Tom Lunar. After the movie 'The Exorcist' came out, they teamed up with guitarist David Kealy and made one record, *The Exorcism*, which was heavily influenced by psychedelic sounds and effects. They released the record on their own Pot label, and the flip side, *Msicroxe Eht*, was merely *The Exorcism* played backwards. Eventually Sweat turned to the Texas brand of country music known as 'honky tonk' and scored several big hits, while Lunar still writes songs today." (CV)

Garrett Lund

Personnel:			
	GLEN CAMPBELL	steel gtr	A
	DONNIE FERRO	bs	A
	ANGIE GUDINO	keyb'ds	A
	JIMMY JERVISS	gtr	A
	PHIL KELLY	bs	A
	DAVID LAUSER	drms	A
	GARRETT LUND	vcls	A
	MARION McCRARY	trumpet	A
	JEFF NICHOLSON	bs	A
	BILL OVERTURF	gtr	A
	HANK QUINN	perc	A
	PETE THOMPSON	sax	A

ALBUMS: 1(A) ALMOST GROWN (No label) 1975 R4
2(A) ALMOST GROWN (Terra Fertilis TFS 72549) 1976 R4

NB: (1) issued with lyric insert and "planet" label design. (2) issued with lyric insert, different label design shows black script titles on white background - this edition also has a large metallic gold title sticker on the front cover giving release date as 1976 and label name "Terra Fertilis". The album has also been reissued (World In Sound RFR-006) 2001 on heavy duty vinyl - It comes in a cloth-effect laminated gatefold and with a lyric sheet. A CD edition (World In Sound WIS 1006) has five bonus tracks.

45: Country Livin' (stereo)/(mono) (Tralfamadore T-1005) 1973

NB: LP track, but a very different mix.

A local California guitar-rock album, extremely well-played and produced. Only a handful of each of theses two versions have ever surfaced and it's considered one of the lost masterworks of the seventies West Coast scene. The single track also appears on the album with many added overdubs, suggesting that the album sessions took place over several years. Much mystery surrounds this private pressing... it's an unusually extravagant artifact, with a full colour gatefold jacket and labels, top-quality recording, mastering and pressing. Why is this record so hard to find? It seems unlikely that less than a thousand copies were pressed; what happened to them?

If in fact the mysterious Mr. Lund decided not to market the finished album and the entire pressing languishes in the cellar of some Hollywood mansion, that would be the only mistake he made... and a tragic one! This is a pretty cool album; despite being somewhat "too polished" to appeal to most readers of this book, it has much to recommend it. Most of Side One is powerful, ethereal guitar-based rock with **Lund**'s satisfying vocal soaring over the original songs. The album closes with the most resplendent version of Dylan's classic *(It's All Over Now) Baby Blue* ever heard - delicately orchestrated; if it was any prettier it couldn't be classified as rock.

The painting gracing the outside of the gatefold sleeve must be seen to be believed.

The most intriguing aspect of this mystery album is the phenomenal amount of money it must have taken to produce it. It's clear that **Garrett Lund** was somebody (talent notwithstanding) of considerable means who had an interest in music, but didn't necessarily want (or need) to make a career of it, which in turn suggests that he may have recorded this album for his own amusement and never intended to market it. Fueled (undoubtedly) by their quest to learn the answer to these burning questions, a number of collectors have hunted down the album's producer over the last fourteen years to be slipped the top-secret information that **Garrett Lund** is actually one Bruce Robertson and that a few well-placed phone-calls would result in just the vinyl bonanza they seek... a few treasure hunters have actually taken this as gospel and burned up the phone lines trying to connect with each of the six hundred "Bruce Robertsons" in the USA! Despite much sleuthing and speculation (I admit to being guilty of the latter myself!), the very mysterious Mr. Lund is still as anonymous as he intended to be from the start. (CF)

GARRETT LUND - Almost Grown LP.

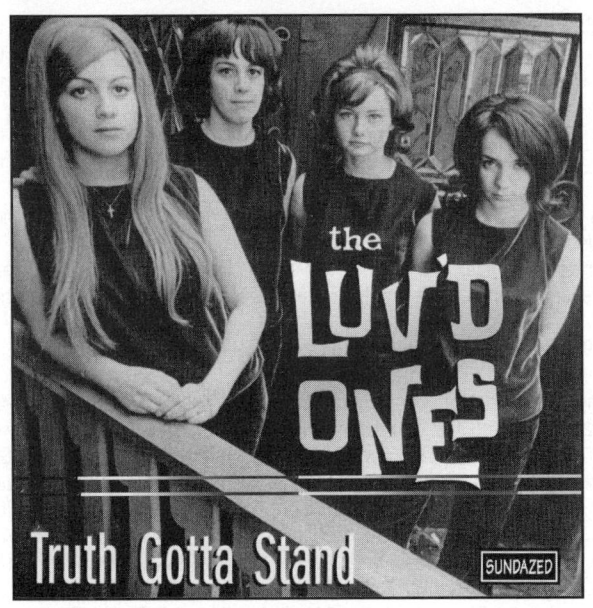

THE LUV'D ONES - Truth Gotta Stand CD.

Mary Catherine Lunsford

ALBUM: 1   MARY CATHERINE LUNSFORD   (Polydor) 1969 ?

A rare and good album in the Joni Mitchell school of folk. (SR)

The Luv Bandits

45:   Mizzer-Bahd/Blues No. 2   (Parrot 316) 1967

This is generally considered to have been a studio group (possibly from New York). *Mizzer-Bahd* is a superb amalgam of Middle Eastern sounds, raga rock, psychedelia and garage-pop.

Compilation appearances include *Mizzer-Bahd* on *Psychedelic Unknowns, Vol. 3* (LP & CD) and *Pebbles, Vol. 14* (LP). (VJ)

Luv'd Ones

CD: 1   TRUTH GOTTA STAND   (Sundazed SC 11050) 1999

NB: (1) also on vinyl (Sundazed LP 5033) 1999.

45s:	Walkin' The Dog/I'm Leaving You	(Dunwich 121) 1966
	Stand Tall/Come Back	(Dunwich 130) 1966
	Dance, Kid Dance/I'm Leaving You	(Dunwich 136) 1966
	Up Down Sue/Yeah I'm Feeling Fine	(White Oak 759101) 196?

An all-girl band from Chicago, previously known as **The Tremolons** who recorded two singles for a tiny local label. The White Oak 45 (*Up Down Sue*) was recorded while they were down in Dania, Florida for the holiday season. The 'A' side has good vocals and great fuzzy guitar and is worth a listen. The flip is average girlie-garage with more neat licks. Both sides of this 45 were composed by Charlotte Vinnedge.

Compilation appearances have included: *Up Down Sue* on *Girls In The Garage, Vol. 1* (LP & CD); *I'm Leaving You* and *Yeah, I'm Feelin' Fine* on *Girls In The Garage, Vol. 3* (LP); *I'm Leaving You, Walkin' The Dog, Dance Kid Dance* and *Stand Tall* on *If You're Ready - The Best Of Dunwich... Vol. 2* (CD). (VJ/MW)

Lyd

ACETATE: 1   LYD   (Metal Acetate) 1970 R5

NB: (1) reissued (Fanny 1 00592) 1992, on CD (Thorns S 532) 1997, and on CD (Akarma AK 913) and 10" (Akarma AK 2013).

Just three or four copies of this Hollywood band's acetate were cut originally, but it has been "reissued" several times since. The album, whilst short, is well worth seeking out for lots of superb psychedelic guitar work. (VJ)

The Lykes of Us

45:   7.30 Said/Tell My Why Your Light Shines   (Molt 6802) 1968

This band hailed from Dearborn Heights, Michigan.

Compilation appearances have included: *7:30 Said* and *Tell Me Why Your Light Shines* on *The Cicadelic 60's, Vol. 1* (CD), *The Cicadelic 60's, Vol. 3* (LP) and *History Of Michigan Garage Bands In The 60's* (3-CD). (VJ/MW)

Lyme and Cybelle

Personnel:	TULE LIVINGSTON	vcls	A
	WARREN ZEVON	gtr, vcls	A
			HCP

45s:	Follow Me/Like The Seasons	(White Whale 228) 1966 65
	If You Gotta Go, Go Now/I'll Go On	(White Whale 232) 1966 -
	Song No. Seven/	
	Write If You Get Work	(White Whale 245) 1967 -

Formed by a young **Warren Zevon** and his then girlfriend Tule Livingston (also credited as Violet Santangelo), this short-lived California male-female duo got a contract with White Whale after the **Turtles** took notice of their songwriting skills (they would later use their own version of *Like The Seasons* on the 'B' side of *Happy Together*). They are best remembered for *Follow Me*, a nice harmony folk-pop song which was a minor hit. Their second single was produced by Bones Howe (*If You Gotta Go* is a Dylan cover). The third, produced by **Curt Boettcher**, featured two **Zevon** originals, credited to "J. Glenn" for contractual reasons.

Zevon was later in **The Brothers** (a 1967 San Francisco-based act), played with **Smokestack Lightnin** and went on to achieve some success as an L.A.-based singer/songwriter, often working with Jackson Browne.

Follow Me was later covered by U.K. outfit The Californians (!) and their version can be heard on *Rubble, 11.* You can also find the original on *Nuggets, Vol. 4* (LP), *Nuggets Box* (4-CD) and *Mindrocker, Vol. 6* (LP). The White Whale retrospective, *Happy Together - The Very Best Of White Whale Records* (CD) also includes *Follow Me* and *If You Gotta Go, Go Now.* (VJ/SR)

Mike Lymon and The Little People

45:   A Message To Pretty/I Need You   (Emanon 101) c1967

An obscure group of teenagers who played in a garage rock style.

LYD - Lyd CD.

Compilation appearances include *Message To Pretty* on *Sixties Rebellion, Vol. 8* (LP & CD). (SR)

Lynn and The Invaders

| 45: | Boy Is Gone/Secretly | (Fenton 2040) 196? |

This all girl band came out of Michigan. *Boy Is Gone* can also be heard on *Best Of Michigan Rock Groups, Vol. 1*, *Girls In The Garage, Vol. 1* (CD) and *Girls In The Garage, Vol. 2* (LP). (VJ)

Kathy Lynn and The Playboys

| Personnel incl: | KATHY LYNN | | A |

45s:	Rock City/Rockin' Red River	(Swan 4175) 1964
α	My Special Boy/I Got A Guy	(Swan 4193) 1964
	Little Baby/He's Gonna Be My Guy	(Swan 4209) 1965

NB: α credited to Kathy Lynn.

An all-girl band whose *Rock City* has resurfaced on *Girls In The Garage, Vol. 2* (LP). (VJ)

The Lynx

| 45s: | You Lie/She's My Woman | (Thunderball 135) 1966 |
| | Something For You/Show Me | (Thunderball 137) 196? |

Hailing from Tyler in Texas, this band's vinyl zenith was *You Lie*, a catchy punk number.

Something For You composed by probable group members Bob Kindel and David Wade is a lighter pop effort backed by a good cover of Joe Tex's classic *Show Me*.

Compilation appearances include: *You Lie* on *Texas Flashbacks, Vol. 1* (CD), *The Cicadelic 60's, Vol. 2* (CD), *The Cicadelic 60's, Vol. 4* (LP) and *Flashback, Vol. 1* (LP). (VJ)

Jamie Lyons

45s:	Little Black Egg/Stand By My Side	(Laurie 3409) 1968
	Soul Struttin'/Flowers To Sunshine	(Laurie 3422) 1968
α	Gonna Have A Good Time/ Heart Full O'Soul II	(Laurie 3427) 1968
	Stoney/Rhapsody In F Minor	(Laurie 3465) 1969

NB: α credited to the Jamie Lyons Group.

This was the solo output by the former leader of Ohio's **Music Explosion**.

Compilation appearances include: *Stay By My Side* on *Mindrocker, Vol. 6* (LP). (VJ)

The Lyrics

Personnel:	BILLY GARCIA	ld gtr	ABCDE
	STEVE KHAILER	vcls	ABC
	MICHEAL ALLEN	gtr	BC
	CRAIG CARLL	vcls	BCDE
	DANNY GARCIA	bs	BCDE
	GREG LEINHART	keyb'ds	B
	GARY NEVES	drms	BC
	CHRIS GAYLORD	vcls, harp, keyb'ds	C
	CLAUDE MATHIS	drms	D
	DAVE COMPTON	keyb'ds	E
	JACK FLANARY	drms	E

NB: Line-ups: 'A' orig group 1959-64 pre-punk; 'B' 1964-65; 'C' 1965-66; 'D' 1966-67; and 'E' 1967-68.

45s:	So What!!/They Can't Hurt Me	(Era 3153) 1965
	My Son/So Glad	(GNP Crescendo 381) 1966
	Mr. Man/Wait	(GNP Crescendo 393) 1967
	Wake Up To My Voice/ Can't See You Anymore	(Feather 1968) 1967
	So What / Why'd He Go	(Feather 101) 196?

This California garage punk band originated from just North of San Diego, around Oceanside/Encinitas. *So What!!* is an excellent punker with prominent harmonica and raw vocals. By the time of their final release, however, they had discarded their rawness for a more harmonious sound.

In 1966 Allen and Gaylord left the band to join **Magic Mushroom**.

Compilation appearances have included: *So What!* on *Nuggets Box* (4-CD), *Pebbles, Vol. 2* (CD), *The Essential Pebbles Collection, Vol. 1* (Dble CD) and *Pebbles, Vol. 2* (LP), *Son Of The Gathering Of The Tribe* (LP), *Great Pebbles* (CD); *Wait* on *Mindrocker, Vol. 1* (LP), *Fuzz, Flaykes, And Shakes, Vol. 5* (LP & CD); *Wait* and *Mr. Man* on *Psychotic Reaction Plus Ten* (CD); *Mr. Man* on *Sixties Rebellion, Vol's 1 & 2* (CD), *Sixties Rebellion, Vol. 1* (LP), *Victims Of Circumstances, Vol. 1* (LP), *Brain Shadows, Vol. 2* (LP & CD), *Destination Frantic!* (LP); *They Can't Hurt Me* on *Back From The Grave, Vol. 2* (LP), *Highs In The Mid-Sixties, Vol. 1* (LP) and *Garage Kings* (Dble LP); and *Wake Up To My Voice* on *Highs In The Mid-Sixties, Vol. 3* (LP). (VJ/MW/PD)

Lyte

Personnel incl:	LEE DARK	ld vcls	A
	CLINT DeLONG	gtr	A
	BILL HOAK	bs	A
	CAROL SUFFRON	vcls	A
	?? ??	drms	A

NB: The drummer's name has been suggested as Chris Raffle, but this is probably incorrect.

| 45: | It's Gonna Work Out Fine/I Don't Believe You | (Bolo 761) 1968 |

A five-piece folk-rock outfit from Everett, Washington, who evolved out of **The Dimensions (Five)**. Their sole 45 is topped by a heavy version of a tune covered earlier by **The Starfires**. The flip by comparison is kind of **Monkees**-pop-punk (?!) punctuated by some fine Eastern fuzzy guitar warbles that are slightly at odds - somehow it works.

In 1968, Lee Dark had been in a bad auto accident and was flat on his back during this time (68/69). He later became a hairdresser.

The band also recorded a demo in Bill Hoak's basement. Their 45 was recorded in Vancouver, WA at Ripcord Studios. (MW/DR/RCn)

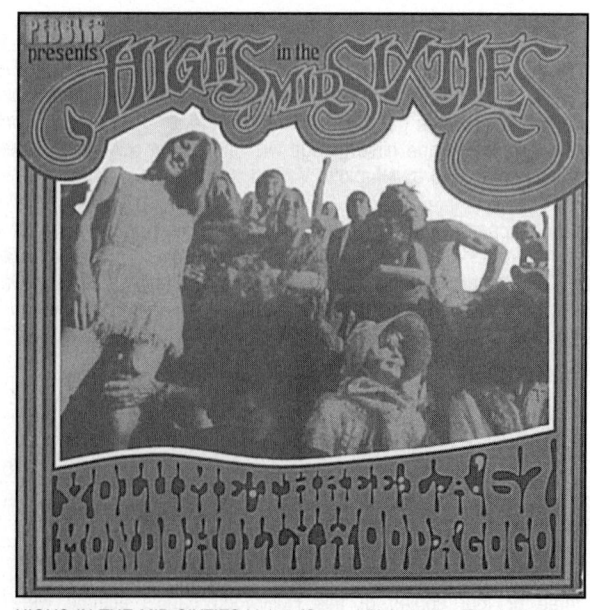

HIGHS IN THE MID-SIXTIES Vol. 3 (Comp LP) including The Lyrics.

Bobby Mabe and The Outcast

45s:	Tender Lovin'/How Many Times?	(Tab 102) 196?
	Tender Lovin'/How Many Times	(Audition Master 109) 196?
	Take A Step/I'm Lonely	(RoTab 101 3) 196?

This outfit came out of Galveston, Texas. *I'm Lonely*, a powerful punk cut can also be found on *Texas Flashback (The Best Of)* (CD), *Texas Flashbacks, Vol. 5* (LP) and *Flashback, Vol. 5* (LP). (VJ)

Macabre

45:	Be Forewarned/Lazy Lady	(Intermedia 003) 1974

From Arlington, Virginia, this outfit would later become **Pentagram**. This sole 45 under this incarnation has received good compilation coverage. *Be Forewarned* can also be heard on *Pebbles Box* (5-LP), *Acid Dreams - The Complete 3 LP Set* (3-LP), *Acid Dreams Testament* (CD), *Trash Box* (5-CD) and *Gathering Of The Tribe* (LP). The flip, *Lazy Lady*, has also resurfaced on *Turds On A Bum Ride, Vol. 1 & 2* (Dble CD) and *Turds On A Bum Ride, Vol. 1* (Dble LP). (VJ/MW)

The Mach V

Personnel incl:	ROBBIE ANDERSON	gtr, organ, ld vcls	A
	JIM BROOK	drms	A
	MITCH FREEMAN	bs, ld vcls	A
	JOHN TIEDEMANN	ld gtr, bckg vcls	A

45:	If I Could / I Want To Stay	(Associated Artists 102) 1967

This Savannah, Georgia, group started circa 1963 as The Fugitives. By 1967 they'd evolved into **The Mach V** with their most stable line-up (above) who recorded their sole 45 at Decca in Nashville late that year. *If I Could* is a straight-ahead fuzz-punker with pumping bass and keyboards; it would be classic Class Of '66 fare but for the occasional use of wah-wah.

Compilation appearances include: *If I Could* on *Pebbles, Vol. 10* (CD), *Scum Of The Earth* (Dble CD), *Scum Of The Earth, Vol. 1* (LP) and *Psychedelic States: Georgia Vol. 1* (CD). (MW/RM)

Larry Mack

45:	Last Day Of The Dragon/	
	Can't You See Me Crying	(Ty Tex 126) 1966

This artist came from Tyler, Texas. The 'A' side of his sole 45, a folk-punk number, can be heard on *Highs In The Mid Sixties, Vol. 23* (LP). (VJ)

Bruce MacKay

ALBUM:	1	BRUCE MACKAY	(ORO 1) 1967 SC

NB: (1) reissued on CD as *Midnight Minstrel* (ESP 1069-2).

45:	Feet Of Clay /	
	This Song About A Railroad Shack	(Oro 45-69) 196?

A self-penned singer/songwriter album. **MacKay** is assisted by his wife Tanya and various ESP label artists, Cyril Castor (ld gtr, piano), Lee Crabtree (organ, piano) (of **Pearls Before Swine**), Chuck Raney (bs), Bob Sanderson (flute, bs, clarinet), Peter Schubert (bs), Warren Smith (drms), and Richard Tyler (electric harpsichord, organ). Tracks like *In The Misty-Eyed Shores Of Morning* and *Geneva Brown* are a bit **Tom Rapp**-ish, but the strongest composition is *Feet Of Clay*. Pleasant but unexceptional (like most of these types of albums usually are). (VJ/MW)

Rabbit Mackay and The Somis Rhythm Band

Personnel:	MIKE FLEMING	gtr, vcls	A
	HARRY HELLINGS	tmpt	A
	WALK KUNNECKE	flute	A
	RABBIT MACKAY	gtr, hmnca, keyb'ds, vcls	A
	REJI PEKAR	gtr	A
	JOHN PILLA	gtr	A
	JOHN RAINES	drms	A
	BILL ST PIERRE	flute	A
	DAVID SUEYEREES	keyb'ds, vcls	A
	BOB THOMPSON	drms	A

ALBUMS:	1(A)	BUGCLOTH	(UNI 73026) 1968 -
	2(-)	PASSING THROUGH	(UNI 73064) 1969 -

NB: (1) also issued on MCA.

45s incl:	Candy/Big Sur Country	(UNI 55074) 1968
	Tendency To Be Free/Somebody Beat Me	(UNI 55112) 1969

NB: There was also a UK 45: *Candy/Hard Time Woman* (MCA MU 1041) 1968.

Issued two albums of soft breathy folk with a psychedelic tinge. They achieve rather a primitive amateurish sound very much in the spirit of dope smoking and the glorification of the Southern Californian hippie lifestyle. The end result is a blend of quite effective laid-back tunes alternating with light-hearted acoustic sing-along type celebrations. The best of the former style are reminiscent of the second **West** album.

Compilation appearances include: *West Grogan Dormitory Blues* on *Turds On A Bum Ride, Vol. 6* (CD) and *Turds On A Bum Ride, Vol. 2* (Dble LP); *Tendency To Be Free* on *Baubles - Down To Middle Earth* (LP), *Turds On A Bum Ride, Vol. 1 & 2* (Dble CD) and *Turds On A Bum Ride, Vol. 1* (Dble LP). (VJ)

Raun MacKinnon

ALBUM:	1	RAUN IS HER NAME	(Kapp KS-3556) c1967 -

A mellow female pop singer with some psychedelic influences and songs like *Color Wheel*, *Sugar In Your Soul*, *Sacrifice Of The Goat* and *Nickel And Dime World*. (SR)

The Madadors

Personnel:	JERRY ADAMS	bs	A
	GENE BELL	drms	A
	LARRY BLACK	keyb'ds	AB
	PHIL HOLZBAUER	gtr	AB
	RON BUCHEK	drms	B
	JERRY STEFANI	bs	B

45:	Girl Don't Leave Me / Allright	(Feature RPS-105) 1966

A quartet from East Troy and Palmyra, Wisconsin, who started in the early sixties as The Mad Madadors. *Girl Don't Leave Me* is a melodic garagey ballad, that sounds uncannily like the Everly Brothers' *When Will I Be Loved* on occasions. The flip is a brisk version of the Ross-Vanadore song, also covered by **The Coastliners** and **The Legends**.

In 1967, they changed their name to **Easy Street**.

Confusingly there was another 45 on Feature by **Matadors**, a totally different group from Sheboygan Falls. (MW/MM/GM)

Mad Andy's Twist Combo

Personnel incl: JOHN BRANCA — A
JEFF PASTERNAK — A
BRIAN ROSS — A
NEIL SINCLAIR — drms — A

45: X-Tra, X-Tra, Read All About It/
Painted Smile   (Original Sound OS-85) 1968/9

A rather strange, some might say psychedelic, 45 by a Los Angeles studio group that previously replied to the name of **Pasternak Progress** with the venerable Brian Ross (of **Music Machine** and **Friendly Torpedos** fame) at the controls. Plenty of sound effects and an odd feedback intrusion but leaning more towards **Zappa**/Bonzos. (MW)

The Mad Hatters

Personnel incl: TOM CURLEY — vcls — A
ALAN FOWLER — bs — A
BILLY HANCOCK — bs — A
RICHARD 'SPIDER' KUMER — drms — A
DAVE VITTEK — gtr — A

45s: I Need Love/Blowin' In The Wind   (Ascot 2917) 1965
I'll Come Running/Hello Girl   (Fontana 1582) 1966

Hailing from Annapolis, Maryland, this quartet played their own brand of Bob Dylan - **P.F. Sloan**-influenced folk-rock. They benefited from a strong management-production team of Tom Traynor and Barry Seidel. Their first 45 is very much in that mould. By 1966 and their second 45 they'd developed a fuller, more mature sound.

Drummer Richard 'Spider' Kumer later teamed up with Jack Bryant (who wrote *Hello Girl* for **The Mad Hatters**) in **The Fallen Angels**.

One side of *Washington D.C. Garage Band Greats!* is given over to the band. It includes their two 45s (a previously unreleased alternate take of *Hello Girl* and three previously unreleased tracks:- *Go Fight Alone*, *A Pebble In My Sand* and *Goodbye Babe*). Their finest moment? I guess that was *I'll Come Running*, a fine up-tempo folk-punk number, full of energy, enthusiasm and pulsating organ.

MADRIGAL - Madrigal LP.

MAD RIVER - Mad River CD.

There Goes The Neighborhood, Vol. 3 (CD) also contains four live tracks from 1965 - *Time Is On My Side*, *Satisfaction*, *Mickey's Monkey* and *What's Your Hurry* - plus two radio spots.

Other compilation appearances have included: *I'll Come Running* on *Pebbles, Vol. 12* (LP); *I Need Love* on *Signed, D.C.* (LP); *Go Fight Alone* and *A Pebble In My Sand* on *Green Crystal Ties, Vol. 10* (CD). (MW/BE)

The Madhatters

Personnel incl: DALE MENTON — A

45s: The Game Is Done/
You're Not A Big Man Any More   (Cardinal 0072) 1967
You May See Me Cry/Chicks Are For Kids (Cardinal 0077) 1967

Another band from Mankato in Minnesota which involved Dale Menton. He formed them after the break-up of **The Gestures** and they were also known as The Best Thing.

The first 45 is credited to Tommy Mason and The Madhatters. Mason, an all-American halfback with the Minnesota Vikings, had sung lead vocals on both sides of the disc.

The second 45 was picked up and released on United Artists 500027 as by The Best Things. The 'A' side, *You May See Me Cry* is a slow melancholy ballad with subdued organ.

Compilation appearances have included: *You May See Me Cry* on *No No No* (CD) and *Sixties Rebellion, Vol. 9* (LP & CD); and *Chicks Are For Kids* on *Root '66* (LP). (VJ)

The Madison Revue

Personnel incl: D. FISHER
R. ROUNTREE

45: Sad And Blue/Another Man   (Madison 4130) 1967

This band was based in San Antonio, Texas. The flip to their sole vinyl output, *Another Man*, is a pleasant garage number.

Compilation appearances include: *Another Man* on *Texas Flashbacks, Vol. 4* (LP & CD), *Flashback, Vol. 4* (LP) and *Highs In The Mid-Sixties, Vol. 13* (LP). (VJ)

The Mad Lads

Personnel incl?: BUTCH ROMANO — A
LARRY ROSSER — A

45:	Come Back To Me / Tossin' And Turnin'	(Prestige Productions PP66-152) 1966

This 45 was released on a collectible Birmingham, Alabama, label but the band's hometown remains unconfirmed. The imploring *Come Back To Me* has come back, on *Psychedelic States: Alabama Vol. 1* (CD). (MW)

Mad Mike and The Maniacs

45:	The Hunch/Quarter To Four	(Hunch 345) 1961

The 'A' side of this obscure New York 45 can also be heard on *Scum Of The Earth, Vol. 1* (LP) and *Scum Of The Earth* (Dble CD). The flip is also on *The Big Itch, Vol. 3*. (VJ)

Madrigal

Personnel:	WILLIAM BONKOSKI	bs	A
	WILLIAM HORN	gtr, theremin, oscillator	A
	(JOHN ACKERMAN		A)

ALBUM:	1(A)	MADRIGAL	(No label ARA/B 136) c1971 R4

An early seventies private press from New Jersey. Experimental rock music with electronic drums (an early drum machine - the Maestro). A very primitive affair; sounds like it was recorded live in a basement. The record is dominated by an "anything goes" attitude, epitomised by the 14'00" *Stoned Freakout* featuring druggy chatter and distorted screams. An acquired taste, this one. Fans of the long tracks on the first two **Velvet Underground** albums, should investigate further.

I'm told that Bill Horn released several later albums of either electronic music or keyboard-based rock, but I don't have details. (CF)

Mad River

Personnel:	RICK BOCHNER	gtr	AB
	GREG DEWEY	hrmnca, drms	AB
	LAWRENCE HAMMOND	keyb'ds, bs, vcls	AB
	TOM MANNING	vcls	A
	DAVID ROBINSON	ld gtr	AB
	(BANANA	steel gtr	B)
	(JERRY CORBITT	steel gtr	B)
	(RON WILSON	perc	B)

			HCP
ALBUMS:	1(A)	MAD RIVER	(Capitol ST 2985) 1968 - SC
	2(B)	PARADISE BAR AND GRILL	(Capitol ST 185) 1969 192 SC

NB: (1) reissued as Edsel ED 140 (1985) and (2) as Edsel ED 188 (1986). (1) and (2) also available now on CD (Edsel EDCD 651) 2000.

EP:	1(A)	MAD RIVER	(Wee 10021) 1967

NB: (1) - which is commonly referred to as 'The Wind Chimes' EP, was counterfeited in the late seventies/early eighties. It has since been included on *The Berkeley EPs* CD, (Big Beat CDWIKD 153) 1995, along with the EPs by **Country Joe and The Fish** (June 1966), **Frumious Bandersnatch** and **Notes From The Underground**. It features different recordings of two cuts which appear on their album, plus a third track unavailable elsewhere.

45s:	Amphetamine Gazelle/High All The Time	(Capitol 2310) 1968
	Copper Plates/Harfy Magnum	(Capitol 2559) 1969

This unique band were fronted by Lawrence Hammond, who was born in Berkeley, but spent much of his childhood in Nebraska. Bluegrass music was his main musical influence. The band was formed by Hammond (harp, vcls) and a series of fellow medical students (Robinson (gtr), Manning (bs), and Dewey (drms)), who all attended Antioch College in Yellow Springs, Ohio. They were originally known as **The Mad River Blues Band** - Mad River being a small tributary of the Ohio. The band, minus Manning, then moved to Washington D.C. for a while. In this period they began to write their own material and secured gigs at very disreputable dives. They then returned to Yellow Springs where Manning rejoined the band and Rick Bochner was added on guitars. In the Spring of 1967 the band quit college, headed for San Francisco, and soon became based in Berkeley. Soon afterwards Sam Silver, a friend of Ed Denson, manager of **Country Joe and the Fish**, became their manager. Consequently, they secured a number of gigs with **The Fish**. The band were befriended by Lonnie Hewitt and in 1967 recorded their legendary EP on his Wee label (10021). It's an interesting record, not easy to obtain, which contains an early version of *Amphetamine Gazelle* (simply called *Gazelle* on the EP), *Wind Chimes* and *Orange Fire*. The first two were re-recorded for their album. *Orange Fire* is a non-album track.

By the end of 1967 they had played a number of Fillmore and Avalon gigs and were signed to Capitol along with **The Quicksilver Messenger Service** and **The Steve Miller Band**. Their debut album was issued in 1968. Extremely uncommercial it was particularly noteworthy for Lawrence Hammond's distinctive quavering vocals and some superb interweaving acid guitar work (particularly on *The War Goes On* and *Eastern Light*. It has later transpired that during its making the recording and playback speeds were not the same - so everything came out higher and faster than they had played it!

Prior to the recording of their second album, Manning left the band and they got a new manager, Harry Sobol. They also asked Jerry Corbitt (of **The Youngbloods**), an acquaintance from their Yellow Springs days, to produce it. The album was an amalgam of different styles - short country rock tracks like *Paradise Bar and Grill*, *Love's Not The Way To Treat A Friend* and *Cherokee Queen* appear alongside a couple of long acid-influenced tracks, *Leave Me Stay* and *Academy Cemetery*. This album was greeted with more enthusiasm than their debut by the critics, but Capitol did nothing to promote it and did not release it in Britain.

Inevitably, then, **Mad River** split up in 1969. Bochner went to run a homestead in Canada. Dewey worked on Jerry Corbitt's first album and later had a spell with **Country Joe and the Fish**, **Grootna**, Eggs Over Easy and **Bodacious D.F.**. Robinson became a building contractor and Manning did occasional work for him and some session work.

Lawrence Hammond later formed The Whiplash Band, a bluegrass/country music group. Supported by this outfit (Alan Lane (bs), Janet Bryson (vcls), Al McShane (drms), and James Louis Parber (ld gtr)), Hammond recorded a country-rock album *Coyote's Dream* (Takoma C 1047) in 1976. Fellow **Mad River** members Dewey and Robinson also made guest appearances on the album.

As for **Mad River** - their output is essential for any collector of psychedelia.

Compilation appearances have included: *High All The Time* on *Rock A Delics* (LP); *A Gazelle*, *Orange Fire*, and *Windchimes* on *The Berkeley EPs* (CD); and *Orange Fire* on *Glimpses, Vol. 3* (LP). *California Easter* contains a live recording of *Wind Chimes* and *War Goes On* from Dr.Sunday's Medicine Show at Fairground Family Park, San Jose on 10th August 1967. (VJ/MW/SR)

MAD RIVER - Paradise Bar And Grill LP.

MAGI - Win Or Lose LP.

MAGIC - Enclosed LP.

Madson

The compiler of the *Gone, Vol. 1* (LP) included *I Saw What You Did* by a band of this name. Max Waller writing in 'Freakbeat' was first to discover that this was actually **The Olivers** track of the same name. See **The Olivers**' entry for details of this superb farfisa'n'fuzz punker which has resurfaced on a number of compilations. So what of **Madson**? Either **The Olivers**' also released the 45 under this name or, more likely, as Max suggests, the compiler of *Gone, Vol. 1* really was totally gone. (VJ)

Maelstrom

45: Organ Player/We Can't Go   (Counterpart C-2635/6) 1968

From Fairfield, Ohio, **Maelstrom** were actually **Us Too** under a pseudonym and this particular 45 was released without the bands knowledge!! *Organ Player* is nice slow pop-psych with a somewhat murky production. *We Can't Go* is more up-tempo, a pretty good sound - not punk, more pop-rock.

For more information see the **Us Too** entry. (GGI/MW)

Maffit and Davis

Personnel incl:	DAVIS	vcls, gtr	A
	MAFFIT	vcls, gtr	A

ALBUM: 1(A) THE RISE AND FALL OF HONESTY   (Capitol) 1967 -

A little-known folk-rock duo, their album contains a mix of originals and covers of Dylan and **Hoyt Axton**, some with only acoustic guitars, others with tablas, bass and piano.

Magi

Personnel:	JOHN GAUT	vcls	A
	TOM STEVENS	bs, vcls	A
	LARRY STUTZMAN	gtr, vcls	A
	STEVE VAN LANINGHAM	gtr	A
	JERRY WIGGINS	drms	A

ALBUM: 1(A) WIN OR LOSE   (Uncle Dirty's 6102 N13) 1976 R2
NB: (1) reissued on Breeder (RPR 001-IC-560) 1986.

45: Mama/Win Or Lose   (Magi) 1976

Drug-orientated high energy rock, featuring some excellent guitar work but lacking variety of material. The band recorded at Uncle Dirty's Sound Machine in Kalamazoo, Michigan, but the label was based in Milford, Indiana, which may well have been their home. (VJ)

The Magi

45: You Don't Know Me/Rock And Roll Lady   (Farr 71271) 1971

This is a great progressive 45 by an outfit from Daytona Beach, Florida. They sound like good musicians and you'll also find *You Don't Know Me* on *Pebbles Vol. 5* (CD) and *Pebbles, Vol. 5* (LP). (VJ)

Magic

Personnel:	CLYDE HAMILTON	organ	A
	GARY HARGER	drms	AB
	DUANE KING	ld vcls, gtr	AB
	NICK KING	bs	AB
	MIKE MOTZ	gtr	A
	JOEY MURCIA	gtr	B

ALBUMS:	1(B)	ENCLOSED	(Armadillo 8031) 1969 R4
	2(B)	MAGIC	(Rare Earth 527) 1971 -

NB: (1) reissued on vinyl (Hyp HYP 02) 1986, and counterfeited on CD (Flash 44) 1997. Better still is the legitimate reissue on Gear Fab - On CD (GF-116) 1998 with additional bonus material, and LP (GF-204) 1998.

45s:	I Think I Love You/		
	That's How Strong My Love Is	(Monster 0001) 196?
	Keep On Movin' On/One Minus Two	(Armadillo 0022) 1969
	Sound Of Tears Is Silent/California	(Armadillo 0023) 1970

This band spent time in both Michigan and Florida. Their first album, which was recorded in Florida, has become a collectors' item and is full of excellent dual guitar work with the extended track *Play* the stand-out song. The album is worth acquiring. They relocated to East Lansing, Michigan and Detroit to record their second album and whilst in Michigan they gigged with several local bands like **The Rationals**, **The Woolies** and **Ormandy**. Unfortunately, their second album is not as good as their first.

Joey Murcia was also connected with Florida bands. Ex-**Birdwatchers** and went on to play in Life. He later became a renowned studio musician, working with Jay Ferguson, Joe Cocker, the Bee Gees and Joe Walsh. Duane King moved to L.A. in 1972 and is still singing and writing songs. His brother Nick sadly died in a automobile accident in 1998.

Compilation appearances include *Keep On Movin'* on Gear Fab's *Psychedelic Sampler* (CD). (VJ/SR)

The Magic Circle

Personnel:	STEVE BARLEY	gtr	A
	STEVE CARTER	drms	A
	JIM RAST	gtr, vcls	A
	JIM ROOP	bs	A

| WINTON NEIL TAYLOR | keyb'ds | A |

45: I Put A Spell On You /
     She Means All The World To Me   (Paris Tower PT-119) 1967

A Florida quartet from the Wildwood/Leesburg area. Their sole 45 features a cover of Screamin' Jay Hawkins, backed by a Jim Roop original. The latter is of more interest - a moody Byrdsy folk-punker with *Bells Of Rhymney* chiming, compiled on *Psychedelic States: Florida Vol. 1* (CD). (MW/RM)

Magic Fern

Personnel:	BRIAN CONRAD	drms	AB
	TIM COOLEY	bs	A
	TOM SPARKS	ld gtr, vcls	AB
	MIKE WATERS	gtr, vcls	AB
	MIKE ALLAN	bs	B

ALBUM: 1( ) MAGIC FERN   (Piccadilly PIC 3386) 1980 R2

45s: Maggie/I Wonder Why   (Jerden 813) 1966
      Maggie/I Wonder Why   (Piccadilly 235) 1967
      Nellie/Cloudy Day   (Piccadilly 240) 1967

From Seattle, Washington, this mob were a bunch of students at the University of Washington and were very popular on campus. Their best known number, which displays some trappings of the psychedelic era, was *Beneath A Tree*. Their album contains all their 45 sides, plus unreleased sixties material, the best of which is the 11'00" *Solar Plexis* on which they sound like **Quicksilver** circa '68!

Mike Allan, who replaced Tim Cooley when Tim had an accident and broke his leg, had earlier been in **The Time Machine**.

Compilation appearances have included: *Beneath A Tree* on *Battle Of The Bands, Vol. 2* (LP) and *The History Of Northwest Rock, Vol. 3* (LP); *Maggie*, *I Wonder Why* and *Beneath A Tree* on *The History Of Northwest Rock, Vol. 3* (CD); *High Flyer*, a rare early track, appears on *Northwest Battle Of The Bands, Vol. 2* (CD). (MW/DR/TWg)

The Magicians

Personnel:	GARY BONNER	bs	A
	ALAN GORDON	drms	A
	ALLAN JACOBS	gtr	A
	JOHN TOWNLEY	gtr	A

CD: 1 AN INVITATION TO CRY : THE BEST OF THE
        MAGICIANS   (Sundazed SC 6133) 1999

MAGIC FERN - Magic Fern LP.

THE MAGICIANS - An Invitation To Cry CD.

45s: An Invitation To Cry/
      Rain Don't Fall On Me No More   (Columbia 4-43435) 1965
      Angel On The Corner/About My Love (Columbia 4-43608) 1966
      And I'll Tell The World (About You)/
      I'd Like To Know   (Columbia 4-43725) 1966
      Double Good Feeling/Lady Fingers (Columbia 4-44061) 1967

An East Coast band who are best known for their pop-rock rendition *Invitation To Cry* on Lenny Kaye's *Nuggets* compilation. They made three other reasonably good singles and an unreleased album, but although they seemed on the verge of success they never actually achieved much. Upon their demise, Allan "Jake" Jacobs went solo then joined someone called Bunky and became... **Bunky and Jake**, who released two albums and some 45s. Townley founded the Apostolic Studios in New York and was behind projects such as **Family of Apostolic** and **Gospel**. Bonner and Gordon were the force behind the group **Barracuda**, penning most of that group's output and later became a successful songwriting team, penning **The Turtles'** *She's My Girl*, *Me About You*, *You Know What I Mean*, *She'd Rather Be With Me* and *Happy Together*, among others. They also wrote *Celebrate* for 3 Dog Night, *Fancy Dancin' Man* for The Righteous Bros. and *Cat In The Window* for Petula Clark! One of their **Magicians** compositions, *And I'll Tell The World About You* was also covered by Joe Walsh on his *Barnstorm* album, whilst *Me About You* was covered by **The Mojo Men**, **Gandalf** and **Orpheus** amongst others. They also composed a classic pop-punker *Put The Clock Back On The Wall* which was done by the **E-Types** and later the **Parrots**.

Obviously a talented band who deserved bigger success (there was even a TV documentary on the band entitled *Four To Go*), they were also a good live act and are remembered as one of the best bands to play at the Night Owl Cafe in Greenwich Village.

More recently *Invitation* has been re-aired on *Nuggets, Vol. 11* (LP) and *Nuggets Box* (4-CD), whilst *Lady Fingers* is on *Psychotic Reactions* (LP). *Lady Fingers*, one of their best psychedelic folk-rock songs, was originally intended for an album of their material which was sadly never released. More recently a CD retrospective *An Invitation To Cry : The Best Of The Magicians* contains their four 45s plus five unreleased offerings and comes with a detailed history.

Gary Bonner is currently working with The Plantones, a traditional doo wop group with Kenny Vance. (VJ/MW)

The Magnificent Men

ALBUMS:	1	MAGNIFICENT MEN	(Capitol ST 2678) 1967 -
	2	THE MAGNIFICENT MEN LIVE!	(Capitol ST 2775) 1967 -
	3	WORLD OF SOUL	(Capitol ST 2486) 1968 -
	4	BETTER THEN A TEN CENT MOVIE	
			(Mercury SR 61252) 1970 -

45s:	Peace Of Mind/		
	All Your Lovin's Gone To My Head	(Capitol 5608)	1966
	I've Got News/Maybe, Maybe, Baby	(Capitol 5732)	1966
	Stormy Weather/		
	Much, Much More Of Your Love	(Capitol 5812)	1967
	You Changed My Life/I Could Be So Happy	(Capitol 5905)	1967
	Sweet Soul Music Pt. 1/Pt 2	(Capitol 5976)	1967
	Babe, I'm Crazy About You/		
	Forever Together	(Capitol 2062)	1967
	By The Time I Get To Phoenix/		
	Tired Of Pushing	(Capitol 2134)	1968
	Almost Persuaded/		
	I Found What I Wanted In You	(Capitol 2202)	1968
	Save The Country/So Much Move Waiting	(Capitol 2319)	1968
	Lay, Lady, Lay/		
	Holly, Go Softly-Open Up And Get Richer	(Mercury 72988)	1969

A white septet with a horn section, they played a mix of rock, pop and soul with occasional psychedelic influences. Their last album features covers of the Temptations' *Cloud Nine* and Dylan's *Lay Lady Lay*. (SR)

Magic Mushroom

Personnel incl:	MICHAEL ALLEN	A
	JOHN BUELL	A
	CHRIS GAYLORD	A
	GARY WILLIAMS	A

45:	Cry Baby/I'm Gone	(Warner Bros. 5846) 1966

From the 'North County' area near San Diego this band were joined by Allen and Gaylord from **The Lyrics**. Just one 45 was released before they moved to New York in late 1967 where they became known as Love Special Delivery.

I'm Gone, is a fine example of garage punk with snotty vocals and lots of mouth harp.

Compilation appearances have included: *I'm Gone* on *Mayhem & Psychosis, Vol. 1* (LP), *Mayhem & Psychosis, Vol. 1* (CD), *Pebbles Vol. 9* (CD) and *What A Way To Die* (LP); and *Cry Baby* on *Psychedelic Unknowns, Vol. 6* (LP & CD). (VJ/MW)

The Magic Mushrooms

Personnel incl:	SONNY CASSELLA (or CASELLA)	gtr, vcls	A
	STU FREEMAN		A
	DAVID RICE	gtr	A
	J. RICE		A

			HCP
45s:	It's A Happening/Never More	(A&M 815)	1966 93
	Look In My Face/Never Let Go	(Philips 40483)	1967 -
	Municipal Water Maintenance Man/		
	Let The Rain Be Me	(East Coast 1001)	1968 -

A Philadelphia outfit who have been much confused over the years with California's **Magic Mushroom**. Sonny Cassella was not only their producer and manager but played and sang on some of their tracks. Sonny "Casella" also co-produced the debut 45 by **The Snaps**. In view of previous errors, the long-running rumour that they have an unreleased album in some dusty vault should be regarded as pure speculation, until someone can prove otherwise.

Stu Freeman later appeared in the short lived Broadway show 'Hard Job Being God'. Later still he resurfaced, singing with 'Stars on 45'.

They've been well-compiled: the trippy-hippie-pop of *It's A Happening* is a fitting finale on Lenny Kaye's classic *Nuggets - Original Artyfacts From The First Psychedelic Era 1965-1968* (Dble LP) set, later on Rhino's *Nuggets Box* (4-CD); *Never More* on *Psychedelic Unknowns, Vol. 7* (LP & CD) and *Of Hopes And Dreams & Tombstones* (LP); *Never Let Go* on *Boulders, Vol. 2* (LP) and *Ya Gotta Have Moxie, Vol. 2* (Dble CD); *Let The Rain Be Me*, an enchanting folk-rocker, is on *Filling The Gap* (4-LP) and *Fuzz Flaykes & Shakes Vol. 1* (LP & CD). (VJ/MW/MMs)

The Magic Plants

Personnel incl:	TOM FINN	A

45s:	I Know She's Waiting There/		
	I'm A Nothing	(World United 104)	1966
	I Know She's Waiting There/I'm A Nothing	(Verve 10377)	1966

An obscure outfit whose 45 got a major label outing. The flip, *I'm A Nothing*, is a rather stark folk-punk offering.

The World United label was run by Harry Lookofsky, and his son Michael Brown also worked as engineer's assistant for the WU studio. Tom Finn met Michael Brown whilst recording the 45, and both would of course later play together in **The Left Banke**.

Compilation appearances include: *I'm A Nothing* on *Mayhem & Psychosis, Vol. 1* (LP), *Mayhem & Psychosis, Vol. 1* (CD), *Off The Wall, Vol. 1* (LP), *Pebbles, Vol. 3 (ESD)* (CD), *The Essential Pebbles Collection, Vol. 2* (Dble CD), and *Teenage Shutdown, Vol. 4* (LP & CD). (VJ/MW/LP)

Magic Reign

Personnel:	DUKE AIRES	gtr	AB
	MIKE BURKER	bs, vcls	ABC
	MIKE VOLK	vcls	ABC
	BOBBY WINKLER	drms, keyb'ds	ABC
	PICK KELLY	bs	B
	JOHNNY PETERSON	drms	BC
	STEVE SUMMERS	ld gtr	BC
	STEVE CROSSAN	gtr	C

45s:	Pop Goes The Weasel / Mirrors	(Jamie 1364)	1968
	Jefferson Street / Charcoal Sketch	(Jamie 1374)	1969

Winkler and Volk had been in The Chocolate Snowflake, based in Manassas, Va., and which had included at various times Charlie Johnson (**Fallen Angels**) and drummer Rocky Isaac (also from the **Fallen Angels**, later **Cherry People** and Joe Walsh's Barnstormer).

In 1968 Winkler and Volk left to form their own band, **Magic Reign**, relocating to Arlington, Va. Their bubblegum debut was followed by a strong late-sixties fuzz-popper *Jefferson Street* (their location in Arlington) which can also be heard on the bonus EP in Moxie's *The Garage Zone Box Set* (4-LP) and on *The Magic Cube* (CD). (BE/MW)

The Magic Ring

45s:	Like Me Like A Lover/Jane	(Tantara 3102)	1967
	Do I Love You?/Little Mary Sunshine	(Tantara 3105)	1967
	Do I Love You?/Little Mary Sunshine	(Music Factory 4O4)	1967

A Houston-based pop outfit. Written by Phil Spector with **Anders and Poncia**, *Do I Love You?* was included on a radio station sampler album issued in 1967/8 - *21 KILT Goldens Vol. 2* (Take 6 2027). *Little Mary Sunshine* has risen again on Misty Lane's flower-folk-pop compilation *Every Groovy Day*. (VJ/MW)

Magic Sand

Personnel incl:	V. GABRIELE	A
	A. KLEIN	A

ALBUM:	1(A)	MAGIC SAND	(UNI 73094) 1970 -

This is quite a varied album which hasn't as yet attracted much interest from collectors. The stand-out track is the psychedelic *Get Ready To Fly*. The title cut is a country-influenced instrumental jig and there's quite a lot of country banjo on *Down On My Knees* and *The Good Lord Willing*. The blues is an evident influence on *Thinking Out Loud* and *You'd Better Be Ready*. Worth a spin. You may be interested to know that *Get Ready To Fly* is the same song that was released by **The Hooterville Trolley** as *No Silver Bird*.

The **Hooterville Trolley** 45 lists an address in Mississippi on the label, which may be the home state of 'both' groups - especially as a another 45 produced by Tom Bee was by the Mississippi **The Trademarks**. Tom Bee could also be the same guy that led / produced **Xit** and **Lincoln St. Exit** and had earlier played in **Fe Fi Four Plus 2**, but that would imply that they were from Arizona or New Mexico.

As a further twist in this band's convoluted history, the same A. Klein and V. Gabrielle listed as **Magic Sand** personnel are also the main songwriters (along with a "Tom G") for Mud on Mudd on their self-titled album. Mud on Mudd were a septet (no personnel listed explicitly) and although the music isn't really psychedelic, it is very good rock-soul. The album is split between Traffic, Sam and Dave, and Beatles covers; and a handful of well-written originals. They also completely transform Porter Waggoner's country classic *Satisfied Mind* into a funky rocker (!).

The most interesting thing is that both albums came out on UNI, and the catalogue numbers indicate that they were released very close to each other. Was this in fact the same band? A UNI-manufactured studio group? Perhaps A.Klein and V.Gabrielle were staff writers? (VJ/CF/RBn)

Magic Sounds

Personnel:
- DUANE CLANTON — A
- LYNN REYNOLDS — A
- TOM STRINGFELLOW — A
- STEVE WELLS — A

45: Love Can Be So Fine/ In Love With You (The Magic Sounds 60801) 1966

From Hampton, Arkansas, a great minor-mood 45. Fine mid-tempo beat-garage backed by a slow and haunting Beatles/Zombies style ballad. A QCA pressing, for you dead-waxers.

Compilation appearances include *Love Can Be So Fine* on *Love Is A Sad Song, Vol. 1* (LP). (MW)

Magic Swirling Ship

45: Love In Your Eyes/He's Comin' Part II (Cadet 5642) 1969

An obscure Illinois outfit whose 45 was produced and written by the Kasenatz-Katz team.

Compilation appearances have included: *He's Coming Pt. 2* on *Lycergic Soap* (LP), *30 Seconds Before The Calico Wall* (CD), *Turds On A Bum Ride Vol. 6* (CD), *Turds On A Bum Ride, Vol. 1* (Dble LP) and *Glimpses, Vol. 4* (LP); and *Love In Your Eyes* on *Psychedelic Patchwork* (LP). (VJ)

The Main Attraction

Personnel incl:
- GENE SALO — vcls — A
- JEANNE SALO — vcls — A

ALBUM: 1(A) AND NOW (Tower ST 5117) 1968 -

45s:
- If I'm Wrong / I Remember Yesterday (Tower 420) 1968
- Every Day / One Must Cry (Tower 435) 1968
- Friends / Jonathan (Tower 464) 1969

A pop-rock quartet with a female singer, they had a contract to promote Wurlitzer instruments. Their album was produced by Lewis Merenstein and arranged by Jimmy Wisner and Herb Bernstein. Two of their tracks, *Everyday* and *If I'm Wrong* can be found on a rare promo 7" (Tower SPRO 4557) along with **Eternity's Children**, the Sunrays and **Davie Allan and The Arrows**. (SR)

Maitreya Kali

See under K (**Kali**).

MAJIC SHIP - Majic Ship CD.

The Maiyeros

See **The Instincts** entry.

Majestics

45: Smile Through My Tears/ Love Has Forgotten Me (MGM K13488) 1966

Fine dramatic Searchers-style folk-beat ballad with ringing guitars that would appeal to fans of early **Beau Brummels**. The flip is more pedestrian and far less impressive. (MW)

Majic Ship

Personnel:
- JEFF BILOTTA — keyb'ds — A
- ROB BUCKMAN — drms — AB
- MIKE GARRIGAN — vcls — AB
- TOMMY NIKOSEY — gtr, vcls — AB
- PHIL POLIMENI — ld gtr — AB
- COSMO (GUS) RIOZZI — bs, organ, vcls — AB

ALBUM: 1(B) MAJIC SHIP (Bel-Ami BA-711) 1970 R4

NB: (1) reissued on vinyl (Heyoka Hey 203) 1985 and counterfeited on CD (Afterglow 009) 1993. More recently the album has been reissued on CD officially by Gear Fab, as *The Complete Authorized Recordings* together with many bonus tracks (Gear Fab GF 107) 1997, and on double vinyl (Akarma AK 084/2) 2000.

45s:
- Night Time Music/To Love Somebody (Crazy Horse 1322) 1968
- Hummin'/It's Over (Majic L 519) 1969
- Hummin'/It's Over (Crazy Horse 1311) 1969
- And When It's Over/On The Edge (Crazy Horse 1317) 1969
- Green Plant/Nite Time Music (B.T. Puppy 548) 1969
- Wednesday Morning Dew/We Gotta Live On (PIP 8936) 1970

From Long Island, New York. The above album is rare and contains a stunning version of Neil Young's *Down By The River*, which merges into *For What It's Worth*. Many other tracks, such as *Free* contain some pulsating guitar work, but there are some mellow ones too. A highly recommended album, now available officially on CD by Gear Fab, together with many bonus tracks.

Majic Ship evolved out of The Primitives, an outfit formed by Ray Rifice and Tommy Nikosey whilst at Saint Anselm's school in New York at the tender age of thirteen! By June 1965, they had learned to play their instruments somewhat, recruiting Mike Garrigan on vocals and the following year recording an acetate of *On The Edge / Mustang Sally* at a local studio. When original bass-player John Kharouf quit, Gus Riozzi was introduced, and they became The New Primitives, performing locally and adding keyboardist Jeff Bilotta in the process.

As the Summer of '68 approached, the band's high school years were coming to an end, and Ray Rifice moved to Florida. Days before he moved, ex-fifties singer turned manager, Johnny Mann saw the band perform at a local gig and offered them a deal. Fortuitously, the day after the gig Philip Polimeni was found as a replacement for the departing Ray and with a new name given to them by their management company, **Majic Ship**, they recorded the *Night Time Music* 45.

Shortly after its release, *Night Time Music* was selected as WMCA's "Pick Of The Week" in Dec '68 and the soulful *Hummin'* was picked as its follow-up, charting regionally, and allowing the band to tour around the East Coast. After a further two singles, including the excellent *Green Plant*, Jeff Bilotta quit... and the band, wishing to return to their rock roots, went back into the studio to record their debut album.

Like many bands of the era, their album was largely overlooked at the time, although it is in retrospect a definite 'classic', with the years spent gigging and recording 45s resulting in a well-produced and 'rounded' album that flows with a graceful beauty absent in many chart acts. However also like many of their counterparts, their progress was brought to an untimely end when in 1971 their rented apartment in Staten Island burned down together with all their equipment. With no insurance, the band called it quits.

The Gear Fab retrospective includes The Primitives acetate, all of **Majic Ship**'s 45 cuts, the entire album and one new cut *Blow Me Away*, recorded by the band in 1997. It also comes with detailed liner notes, from which this article has been compiled, and many rare photos of the band. The package can only really be faulted in that the running order is a little dis-jointed, with the bonus tracks coming before the album cuts, and the band interview sections being too quiet. Still an essential reissue though!

Compilation appearances have included *Sioux City Blues* and *Life's Lonely Road* on *Psychedelic Crown Jewels, Vol. 1* (Dble LP & CD). (VJ/IT)

Major Arcana

Personnel incl: SIGMUND SNOPEK   A
JIM SPENCER   A

ALBUM: 1 MAJOR ARCANA   (A Major Label) 1976 R2
NB: (1) issued with poster.

On the same label as **Anonymous**, an album of West Coast psych-folk, with **Sigmund Snopek** of the **Bloomsbury People** and **Jim Spencer**.

Additional participants are thought to have included Jay Borkenhagen (ex-**Baroques**), Tom Ruppenthal and Rob Fixmer. **Jim Spencer**, now sadly deceased, had other Milwaukee releases. (SR/GM)

Majority of Six

45: I See The Light / Tears Like Rain   (CEI 134) 196?

From Bowling Green, Ohio - some or all of this band attended Bowling Green State University. (GGI/MW)

The Makers

45: Everlasting Love/?   (Kee Wee Records MS 3171) c1968

An obscure pop-rock group. (SR)

Malachi

Personnel: STEVE CUNNINGHAM   jew's harp   A
MALACHI   A

ALBUM: 1(A) HOLY MUSIC   (Verve Trident V6/5024) 1966 -

Subtitled "Evening Vibrations", this album was recorded Wednesday, August 17th, 1966 in San Francisco and its five tracks are named *Wednesday* (*Second*, *Sixth*, *Fourth*, *Fifth* and *Eighth*). Long meditative and instrumental ragas, with minimal instrumentation. The liner notes were written by **Allen Ginsberg** ("Malachi approach music in spirit of consciousness-meditation: altar, flowers, herb, incense, silence, communion with selves, hush and darkness and improvisation. Poe would have enjoyed his presence") and Michael Harner ("Malachi's music transcends the traditions of East and West and represents the new synthesis which is still being worked out by those participating in the psychedelic revolution").

Steve Cunningham later joined **Red Crayola**. (SR)

The Male

45: Over My Head/You're Playing With Fire   (Quinvy Q-7006) c1966

Released on a label better known for its Southern Soul productions, the flip of this an extremely rare 45 features highly energetic drumming, lots of fuzz guitar and good vocals. *Over My Head* is comparatively less interesting as it's a soul-rock song.

The Male was a local singer from Raleigh, North Carolina. (SR)

Malibus

45s: I'm Crying/Runaway   (Quill 104) 1965
Baby, Let Me Take You Home/La Da Da   (Orlyn 66312) 1966

Named after a California beach the band actually came from Chicago. *I'm Crying* is a short but sweet R&B raver with harmony vocals, and can also be found on *Pebbles Vol. 7 - Chicago 2* (CD). Another track, *La Da Da*, is a rather weak rocker and has also been compiled on *Highs In The Mid-Sixties, Vol. 4*. According to the *Pebbles* CD liner notes, the band also recorded a number of acetates. (VJ)

The Malibus

45s: Cry/I Miss You   (Malibu 1) 1966
Leave Me Alone/Cry   (Planet 58) 1966

This was a different outfit from Litchfield, Connecticut. The 'A' side of their second 45, *Leave Me Alone*, was based around the Zombies' *Leave Me Be* and had a muffled, surfy feel. The flip, *Cry* is a grinding punker, although there is also a later more psychedelic version.

Compilation appearances include: *Leave Me Alone* on *New England Teen Scene* (CD) and *New England Teen Scene, Vol. 1* (LP); *Cry* (later version) on *Son Of The Gathering Of The Tribe* (LP); *Cry* (earlier version) on *Back From The Grave, Vol. 1* (LP) and *Garage Kings* (Dble LP). (VJ/MW)

The Malibus

Personnel incl: DAVID LUCKIE   ld gtr   A

45: I've Gotta Go / I Want You To Know   (PJ 1004) 1966

Formed in Macon, Georgia, in 1964 by guitarist/writer David Luckie, this band released their sole 45 in the Spring of 1966. The **Byrdsy** *I Want You To Know* graces *Psychedelic States: Georgia Vol. 1* (CD) and both sides are included on *The Essential Pebbles Collection Vol. 1* (2-CD). (MW)

Lee Mallory

45s: That's The Way It's Gonna Be/
Many Are The Times   (Valiant V-751) 1966
Take My Hand/The Love Song   (Valiant V-761) 1967

Lee Mallory was a member of the **Millennium** and this rare single was produced by **Curt Boettcher**. *Take My Hand* was written by the Addrisi Brothers, the flip by **Mallory** and Randy Naylor, of **The Poor**. (SR)

The Maltees Four

45: All Of The Time/You   (Pacific Challenger 112) 1966

This outfit, who were probably from the Los Angeles area, have a cut called *You* on the *The Cicadelic 60's, Vol. 5* (LP) and *The Cicadelic 60's, Vol. 3* (CD) and the flip appears on *Tymes Gone By* (LP). (VJ/MW)

Malt Shoppe Gang

ALBUM: 1 MALT SHOPPE GANG   (Fleetwood BMC-5100) 1968 SC

From Massachusetts, a rather primitive garage band doing covers of fifties rock and doo-wop songs. (SR)

The Mama Cats

45: Miss You/My Boy   (Hideout 1225) 196?

An all-girl band from the Detroit area. *Miss You* has resurfaced on *Girls In The Garage, Vol. 2* (LP). (VJ)

Mama Lion

Personnel incl:
LYNN CAREY	vcls		AB
COFFI HALL	drms		AB
JIM HOWARD	keyb'ds		AB
NEIL MERRYWEATHER	gtr, bs, vcls		AB
ALAN HURTZ			B
ED MIKENAS			B
BOB ROSE			B

ALBUMS:
1(A) MAMA LION (PRESERVE WILDLIFE) (Family Productions FPS 27??) 1972 -
2(B) GIVE IT EVERYTHING YOU GOT (Family Productions FPS 2713) 1973 -

NB: (1) released in the U.K. by Philips.

45s: Ain't Too Proud To Beg/Cry (Family Productions 0903) 1973
α Give It Everything I've Got/Sister, Sister (Family Productions 0921) 1973

NB: α also released in France with PS (Philips 6078 015) 1973. There's also a UK 45 *Ain't Too Proud To Beg/Mr. Invitation* (Philips 6078 002) 1972.

The daughter of the actor and poet McDonald Carey, Lynn Carey grew up in Beverly Hills. A sculptural blonde beauty, in 1966 she played in the George Axelrod's comedy 'Lord Love A Duck' with Roddy McDowell and Tuesday Weld, and in 1969 formed her first rock group, **C.K. Strong**. After working on the soundtracks of two Russ Meyer's movies, as part of **Carrie Nations** in 'Beyond The Valley Of The Dolls' and performing with a group the song *Midnight Tricks* in the film 'The Seven Minutes', she met **Neil Merryweather** and began recording with him, first as **Vacuum Cleaner** and **Ivar Avenue Reunion**, and in 1972 as **Mama Lion**.

This group was clearly destined to show off the Joplinesque voice and the very impressive figure of Lynn Carey, and is maybe better remembered for the front cover of their first album, with Lynn Carey breastfeeding a lion cub. As often with **Merryweather**, the music was a rather loose mix of blues, pop, soul and rock. However it contains some decent tracks like *Be Bad With Me*, *Wildcat*, *Mr. Invitation* and a cover of Bill Withers *Ain't No Sunshine*.

The second album is in the same style, with *Crazy Place*, *Love Is Just A Four Letter Word* and a more 'classic' cover art. The group also recorded as **Heavy Cruiser**. It's basically a **Mama Lion** album sans Lynn Carey, even if she co-wrote some songs and sang background vocals. Circa 1973, Lynn Carey also appeared in Penthouse! She also appeared on some albums of **Charlie Musselwhite** and sang on an album by Eric Burdon.

For various reasons, after this busy period, her career went downhill. She disappeared from the scene for several years and got married. She came back in the eighties as a member of the L.A. Jazz Choir and did a lot of session work in the Californian and French studios, generally recording with mainstream pop artists. As part of the Flat Foot Floozies (!), Lynn Carey also spent three years on the Queen Mary, doing Andrew Sisters' style songs. In the nineties, she moved for a while to Russia where she recorded and wrote songs with several local groups. A video 'Lynn Carey In Moscow' was released and circa 1995 a CD titled *Good Times* offered a choice of jazzy pop, miles away from the **Mama Lion** days.

However in 2001 Lynn Carey was preparing a new CD *Mama Lion Roars Back*. (SR)

The Mamas and Papas

Personnel:
DENNY DOHERTY	vcls	ABC
CASS ELLIOT	vcls	ABC
JOHN PHILLIPS	vcls	ABC
MICHELLE GILLIAM PHILLIPS	vcls	A C
GILLIAN GIBSON	vcls	B

HCP

ALBUMS:
1(A) IF YOU CAN BELIEVE YOUR EYES AND EARS (Dunhill DS-50001) 1966 1 -
2(C) CASS JOHN MICHELLE DENNY (Dunhill DS-50010) 1966 4 -
3(C) DELIVER (Dunhill DS-50014) 1967 2 -
4(C) FAREWELL TO THE FIRST GOLDEN ERA (Dunhill DS-50025) 1967 5 -
5(C) THE PAPAS AND THE MAMAS (Dunhill DS-50031) 1968 15 -
6(C) GOLDEN ERA, VOL 2 (Dunhill DS-50038) 1968 53 -
7(C) 16 OF THEIR GREATEST HITS (Dunhill DS-50064) 1969 61 -
8(C) A GATHERING OF FLOWERS (dbl) (Dunhill DS-50073) 1971 - -
9(C) MONTEREY INTERNATIONAL POP FESTIVAL (Dunhill DS-50100) 1971 - -
10(-) PEOPLE LIKE US (Dunhill DS-50106) 1971 84 -
11(-) 20 GOLDEN HITS (dbl) (Dunhill DS-50145) 1973 186 -
12(-) THE ABC COLLECTION: GREATEST HITS (ABC 30005) 1976 - -

NB: In the UK, (1)-(3) and (5) released on RCA. (1) reissued on CD by MCA). (3) and (4) reissued on one CD (BGO BGOCD 462) 1999. *All The Leaves Are Brown: The Golden Era Collection* (MCA 088 112 653 2) 2001 is a 2-CD set, which features their original sixties albums in full plus their one non-album sixties 'B' side (*Glad To Be Unhappy*) and mono single mixes of *I Saw Her Again*, *Words Of Love* and *Creeque Alley*. (6) was released on Stateside. (8), (10) and (11) were issued on Probe and (10) and (11) were also released on ABC and Music For Pleasure. There's also a 2-CD compilation *Creeque Alley: The History Of The Mamas And Papas* (MCA MCADZ-10195) 1991. UK-only compilation releases include:- *Hits Of Gold* (Stateside SL 5007) 1969; *Monday Monday* (Music For Pleasure SPR 90025) 1974; *California Dreamin'* (Music For Pleasure SPR 90050) 1974; *The Best Of The Mamas And Papas* (Arcade ADEP 30) 1977; *Golden Greats* (MCA MCM 5001) 1985

THE MAMAS & THE PAPAS - 20 Greatest Hits LP.

(also issued on CD); *The Collection* (dbl) (Castle CCSLP 173) 1987; *The Very Best Of The Mamas And Papas* (Platinum PLAT 302) 1988; and *Elliot, Phillips, Gilliam, Doherty* (dbl) (Connoisseur Collection VSOPLP 119) 1988, which concentrates on **John Phillips**' original songs (also issued on CD). Also relevant is the 2-CD set *The Singles +* (BR Music BS 8125-2) 2000.

EPs:		
1	IF YOU CAN BELIEVE YOUR EYES AND EARS	(Dunhill 50006) 1966
2	PEOPLE LIKE US	(ABC 50106) 1972

NB: There's also *Four Tracks From The Mamas And Papas* (12") (ABC ABE 12006) 1977, which features *Monday Monday*, *Dedicated To The One I Love*, *California Dreamin'* and *Creeque Alley*. There are also five French EPs with picture sleeves on RCA

			HCP
45s:	Go Where You Wanna Go (promo only)	(Dunhill 4018) 1965	-
	California Dreamin'/Somebody Groovy	(Dunhill 4020) 1965	4
	Monday Monday/Got A Feelin'	(Dunhill 4026) 1966	1
	I Saw Her Again/Even If I Could	(Dunhill 4031) 1966	5
	Look Thru My Window/ Once There Was A Time I Thought	(Dunhill 4050) 1966	24
	Words Of Love/Dancing In The Street	(Dunhill 4057) 1966	5/73
	Dedicated To The One I Love/ Free Advice	(Dunhill 4077) 1967	2
	Creeque Alley/ Did You Ever Want To Cry?	(Dunhill 4083) 1967	5
α	Twelve-Thirty (Young Girls Are Coming To The Canyon)/ Straight Shooter	(Dunhill 4099) 1967	20/130
	Glad To Be Unhappy/Hey Girl	(Dunhill 4107) 1967	26/134
	Dancing Bear/John's Music Box (PS)	(Dunhill 4113) 1967	51
	Safe In My Garden/Too Late	(Dunhill 4125) 1968	53
	For The Love Of Ivy/ Strange Young Girls	(Dunhill 4150) 1968	81
	Do You Wanna Dance?/My Girl	(Dunhill 4171) 1968	76
	Step Out/Shooting Star	(Dunhill 4301) 1972	81

NB: α was released in France with a picture sleeve (RCA 49902). Another French single with picture sleeve is: *Creeque Alley/String Man* (RCA 49900).

The Mamas and Papas have been described as America's first hippies, which is primarily why they're included here. The quartet had originally formed in New York City back in 1963. **John Phillips**, who was to become their main songwriter was born in Parris Island, South Carolina on 30 August 1935. By the age of 15 he was playing in jazz outfits and he was later a member of the folk outfit, The Journeymen. Holly Michelle Gillian Phillips, born in Long Beach, California on 4th June 1945, had abandoned a promising modelling career to sing alongside him in The Journeymen and married him back in 1962. The Journeymen, incidentally, had also included **Scott McKenzie**, who would later join the reformed **Mamas and Papas** in 1985. Cass Elliot, born on 19 September 1943 in Alexandria, Virginia, had earlier been in **The Mugwumps** with the fourth member of the quartet, **Dennis Doherty**, (who'd been born on 29 November 1941 in Halifax, Nova Scotia, Canada), and future **Lovin' Spoonful** member Zal Yanovsky. After perfecting their vocal style in the Virgin Isles they settled in Los Angeles in 1964 and signed to Lou Adler's Dunhill label. They preferred the name **The Mamas and The Papas** to The Magic Circle (the other possibility they were considering at the time), 'Mamas' being what Hell's Angels called their girls.

They soon developed a very distinctive vocal style which was well suited to their hippie image - their songs tended to be about peace, love and doing one's own thing.

Their first 45, *Go Where You Wanna Go* only appeared as a promotional release and was quickly replaced by *California Dreamin'* which had been written by **John Phillips** back in 1963. Capturing the warmth and security of life on the U.S. West Coast with the lyrics, they achieved exquisite vocal harmonies with Michelle's soft, sweet voice contrasting with Cass's harsher, high-pitched voice. Meanwhile the two males provided the background harmonies. The result was a Top Ten hit in the U.S. and a No. 23 in the UK. The song was also recorded by **Barry McGuire** on his first album. The follow-up *Monday Monday* did even better earning them a Grammy. The single went to No. 1 in the USA and reached No. 3 in the UK. When they made a short tour in June 1966 to promote the single Gillian Gibson filled in for Michelle Phillips who had temporarily broken up with her husband John. The split did not last for long and once the couple were reconciled Gibson was ousted. Meanwhile *I Saw Her Again* maintained their chart success with another Top Ten hit in the US. It also reached No. 11 in Britain.

THE MAMAS & THE PAPAS - Best Of LP.

1966 ended with the release of their second album, which is generally considered to have been a marked improvement on their first. It provided them with another Top Ten U.S. hit, *Words Of Love*, which was also a minor No. 47 hit in the UK. 1967 was another good year for the band. They were undoubtedly one of the best acts at the Monterey Pop Festival, which **John Phillips** had actually organised. Their vocal harmonies reached near perfection at times. *Dedicated To The One I Love*, an old Shirelles song had given them a No. 2 hit on both sides of the Atlantic. Again it was characterised by simply delightful vocal harmonies. It was included on their third album, *Deliver*, which was by far their best to date, despite the fact that its recording was disrupted by Mama Cass's pregnancy. *Deliver* also included their autobiographical 45 *Creeque Alley* another Top Ten U.S. hit, it also achieved No. 9 in the UK, where it was their last hit. *Creeque Alley* was a real place, in St. Thomas in the Virgin Islands. The song was their first single in a more rock'n'roll format. It succinctly tells their story, of how from varied folk backgrounds these four unique talents gravitated to sunny California. The second half of the year was less successful for them commercially. Their next 45, *Twelve-Thirty (Young Girls Are Coming To The Canyon)*, could only manage No. 20 in the U.S. and missed out completely in the UK. What was interesting about it was that it was really two songs in one. **John Phillips** had written the first part whilst the band were living in the East Village in New York, which was grim and dirty, and there was a clock across the road from his apartment with its hands stuck on 12.30. He wrote the first part of the song then and abandoned it. He completed it six months later when they were in California, which was so idyllic, springlike, fresh and free in comparison. So he contrasted the two songs by putting them together. For their next 45, they used *Glad To Be Unhappy* from the 1936 Rodgers and Hart musical 'On Your Toes', but both this and follow-up, *Dancing Bear*, marked a downwards trend commercially.

During the Summer of 1967 **John Phillips** wrote *If You're Going To San Francisco* for **Scott McKenzie**. In the October they visited Britain to play at the Royal Albert Hall on 30 October and 1 November, although they pulled out of the concerts after Cass Elliot was arrested for stealing two blankets and keys from a Kensington hotel. The charges were later dismissed.

By now the band were past their prime and they actually split up during the recording of *The Papas and The Mamas* album but came back together to complete it. Overall it wasn't a bad effort but by 1968 their simple vocal harmonies were sounding rather dated - the rate of musical progression in the mid-sixties was very rapid indeed - with arrangements and instrumentation becoming even more elaborate, **The Mamas and Papas** found themselves one of countless bands whom progress had left behind. The album spawned three further minor U.S. hits of which *Safe In My Garden* was perhaps the best. This was really **John Phillips**' anti-Vietnam song. A song about marijuana being safe in your garden and doing the normal things you would do rather than going to far off foreign countries to kill complete strangers. This was one of their more under-rated songs.

When they split in 1968 Michelle Phillips embarked on quite a successful acting career. Her film credits included 'Dillinger' and 'Valentine' and she was part of the TV cast of 'Knots Landing'. She was also married to actor Dennis Hopper for eight days in 1970. Mama Cass Elliot went on to launch a pretty successful solo career. She put out seven albums and several singles, of which *Dream A Little Dream Of Me* was the best known and most successful, until her death in London from heart failure in July 1974. She even teamed up with Dave Mason from Traffic for one album in 1971. **John Phillips** and **Denny Doherty** also embarked on solo careers but with less success. **John Phillips**' *Wolfking of L.A* (Dunhill DX 50077) is extremely mellow and better avoided.

The Mamas and Papas reformed briefly in the early 1970s to fulfil their contract with Dunhill making one final album, *People Like Us*. *Step Out* gave them another minor hit off the album but the inter-group dynamics weren't at all good and it wasn't a terribly successful reunion. All the other albums listed in the discography are compilations or repackages.

There was another (permanent) reunion in 1981. The initial line-up was **John Phillips**, **Denny Doherty**, McKenzie Phillips (John's daughter) and Spanky McFarlane (formally lead singer with the successful sixties group Spanky and Our Gang). **Scott McKenzie** was added to the line-up in 1985 and **Denny Doherty** left in 1987. They toured and recorded an album in 1988, but it wasn't released for legal reasons.

John Phillips died of heart failure in Los Angeles on 18th March 2001.

If you're into vocal harmonies **The Mamas and Papas** are a must for you. All their original albums are now available on CD and perhaps the best of the compilations is Connoisseur Collection's double album, *Elliot, Phillips, Gilliam and Doherty*, which concentrates on **John Phillips**' songs rather than the many cover versions they also recorded.

Compilation appearances include: *California Dreamin'*, *Monday Monday*, *Look Through My Window* and *Creeque Alley* on *Dunhill Folk Rock Vol. 1*; *Strange Young Girls* and *No Salt On Her Tail* on *Penny Arcade - Dunhill Folk Rock Vol. 2*; and *Dedicated To The One I Love* on *Undersound Uppersoul* (LP). (VJ/MW/SR)

Mammoth

45:	The Mammoth/ Sensations Head To Toe	(United World 01970-001) 1970

The 'A' side is excellent garage guitar psych similar to **Morgen** with echoes of *Mr. Soul*. The label had a California distribution deal, but the group is believed to be from San Antonio, Texas.

Compilation appearances include *Mammoth* on *The Psychedelic Experience, Vol. 1* (LP), *A Lethal Dose Of Hard Psych* (CD) and *High All The Time, Vol. 1* (LP). (MW)

Man

Personnel:	DENNIS BELLINE	gtr, keyb'ds, vcls	A
	RICHIE CARDENAS	bs, vcls	A
	ANTONY KRASINSKI	drms, perc	A
	GILBERT SLAVIN	keyb'ds	A
	RICHARD SUPA	gtr	A

ALBUM:	1(A)	MAN	(Columbia CS 9803) 1969 -

45s:	Sister Salvation/ Sleepy Eyes And Butterflies (PS)	(Columbia 44806) 1969
	Girl From The North Country/ Riverhead Jail	(Columbia 44953) 1969

This outfit developed from the Long Island, New York outfit **Denny Belline and The Rich Kids**. When Denny went solo, the Rich Kids named themselves **Man**. Their album is one of varied styles ranging from melodic soft rock to more throwaway mainstream rock like *Sister Salvation*, which has a gospel-influenced introduction. It's worth a spin.

The band got to appear on the Ed Sullivan show with Peter Max - Max painted a picture while **Man** played a cut from their album.

Richard Supa later became a session man and recorded a solo album *Supa's Jamboree* (Paramount PAS 6009) 197?. (VJ/SR)

The Manchesters

ALBUMS:	1	BEATLERAMA	(Diplomat) 1964 -
	2	BEATLERAMA, VOL. 2	(Diplomat) 1964 -
	3	A HARD DAY'S NIGHT	(Diplomat DS-2335) 1964 -

45s:	I Don't Come From England/Dragonfly	(VeeJay 700) 1965

A fake English Invasion group, their albums were subtitled "The New Sound Of England" and included covers of the Fab Four (*I Want To Hold Your Hand*, *She Loves You*) plus other songs in the same style.

It's not confirmed that the 45 is by the same act. (SR)

Harvey Mandel

Personnel incl:	HARVEY MANDEL	gtr, vcls	A

				HCP
ALBUMS:	1	CRISTO REDENTOR	(Philips PHS 600281) 1968	169
(up to	2	RIGHTEOUS	(Philips PHS 600306) 1969	187
1974)	3	GAMES GUITARS PLAY	(Philips PHS 600325) 1970	- -
	4	BABY BATTER	(Janus 3017) 1971	- -
	5	GET OFF IN CHICAGO	(Ovation 14/15) 1972	- -
	6	THE SNAKE	(Janus 3037) 1972	198
	7	SHANGRENADE	(Janus 3047) 1973	- -
	8	FEEL THE SOUND OF	(Janus 3067) 1974	- -
	9	BEST OF	(Janus 7014) 1975	- -

NB: (1) to (7) were also released in the U.K.: (1) to (3) by Philips, (4) by Dawn. (5) by London, (6) and (7) by Janus. (4) was released as *Electronic Progress* in Holland by Janus and in Germany by Bellaphon. (4) reissued on CD (BGO BGOCD 252). (4) and (6) reissued on vinyl (Akarma) and on one CD (Akarma AK 075/6). (6) reissued on CD (BGO BGOCD 398). (7) reissued on CD (BGO BGOCD 410). (7) and (8) reissued on one CD (Akarma AK 166)

45s:	Wade In The Water, Pt 1/ Wade In The Water, Pt 2	(Philips 40579) 1970
	Moontang/Summer Sequence	(Philips 40627) 1970
	Midnight Sun/Baby Batter	(Janus J-144) 1972
	Pegasus/Uno Ino	(Janus J-198) 1973

Born in Detroit in 1945, **Harvey "The Snake" Mandel** is an excellent guitar player who began his career in 1964 on the Chicago Blues scene, playing on records and performing with **Charlie Musselwhite**, **Barry Goldberg** (he played on his first five albums) and **Neil Merryweather**. Playing in a very recognizable fluid style and specialized in sustain and controlled feedback, **Mandel** began his solo career in 1968 with *Cristo Redentor*. Housed in a stunning sleeve signed by Alton Kelley (of Mouse & Kelley), this largely instrumental album was produced by Abe "Voco" Kesh and contains a good cover of *Wade In The Water* (also recorded by **Clover**).

HARVEY MANDEL - The Snake LP.

Having relocated in Los Angeles, **Mandel** began to do some session work, notably with Graham Bond on his Pulsar albums produced by **Wayne Talbert** and with Jimmy Witherspoon.

After *Righteous*, **Mandel** teamed up with Russell DaShiell (**Crowfoot**) to release *Games Guitars Play*, which is probably his best album with strong guitars on *Dry Your Eyes* or *Leavin Trunk*. **Mandel** then replaced Henry Vestine in **Canned Heat** and played on *Future Blues* and *Historical Figures And Ancient Heads*. He also performed with them at Woodstock. **Mandel** then joined John Mayall for three albums (from *Back To The Roots* to *The Turning Point*).

He moved to Janus for whom he recorded four further albums, which are not as good as his Philips period but which still contain some interesting guitar parts (notably on *Shangrenade*). In 1972, he also produced and organized the bluesy project *Get Off In Chicago* with **Ken Little** and Freddy Fox. He then formed **Pure Food and Drug Act** with Sugarcane Harris, Paul Lagos and Larry Taylor. They released *Choice Cuts* in 1972 on Epic but the same line-up also worked on two Sugarcane Harris albums. **Mandel** was also briefly part of The Ventures and even recorded an album with them!

In 1973, **Harvey Mandel** produced both **Ken Little**'s *Solo* album and a Freddy Roulette album. He played on the *Music From Free Creek* project and on Dewey Terry's Big Chief. 1974 saw him playing with the Rolling Stones on *Black And Blue* (he was one of the possible substitutes for Mick Taylor). In the mid-seventies, he vanished from the music scene, but returned in the nineties and is still recording with Howard Wales (ex-**A.B. Skhy**, **Barry Goldberg** and Gary Sloan (**Proof**)). (SR)

The Man-Dells

Personnel:	KIT CRAWLEY	drms	A
	LARRY GRANT (aka LARRY McSEATON)	gtr	A
	NORMAN LOMBARDO	vcls, bs	A
	RICK RANDLE	vcls, keyb'ds	A

45:	Bonnie/Oh No	(Dandy 5308) 1964

A pop-rock British invasion influenced quartet from San Diego, California. They were a precursor to **The Other Four** and **Brain Police**.

Compilation appearances include *Bonnie* on *The Garage Zone, Vol. 4* (LP), *Ya Gotta Have Moxie, Vol. 2* (Dble CD) and *The Garage Zone Box Set* (LP). (CF/MW)

The Mandrake Memorial

Personnel:	CRAIG ANDERTON	gtr, sitar	AB
	MICHAEL KAC	keyb'ds, vcls	A
	J KEVIN LALLY	drms	AB
	RANDY MONACO	vcls, bs	AB

ALBUMS:	1(A)	THE MANDRAKE MEMORIAL	(Poppy 40002) 1968 -
	2(A/B)	MEDIUM	(Poppy 40003) 1969 SC
	3(B)	PUZZLE	(Poppy 40006) 1970 SC

NB: (1) has been counterfeited on vinyl, and all three albums have also been released on CD (1) (Collectables COL-0691) 1996, (2) (Collectables COL-0692) 1996, and (3) (Collectables COL-????) 1996. (3) has also been counterfeited in Europe on CD (MM 02371). (3) originally issued with a round insert sheet.

45:	Something In The Air/Musical Man (PS)	(Poppy 90103) 1968

The Mandrake Memorial began life with an unknown New York City band called The Novae Police, featuring Kevin Lally and Randy Monaco. They played in the Village for a while, opening for bands like **The Flying Machine** (featuring James Taylor), whilst Randy was also doing a lot of demo work, singing on the first demo of "Happy Together" which **The Turtles** later recorded.

Meanwhile, guitarist Craig Anderton was playing in a college band from the University of Pennsylvania called The Flowers of Evil, who played shows with **Woody's Truck Stop** (Todd Rundgren's first band). Keyboardist Michael Kac was also in Philadelphia's Cat's Cradle.

The Mandrake's came together through promoter Larry Schriver, who was working in conjunction with club owner Manny Rubin. Manny was looking for a house band for his club, The Trauma in Philadelphia. The band started playing the Philadelphia, New York, Boston and college circuits, even appearing with Pink Floyd on TV and through Manny obtained a deal with MGM subsidiary Poppy (their first two albums were issued by RCA in the UK).

Their debut album which was released in the Fall of '68 sold over 100,000 copies and is made up of short commercial rock compositions like *Bird Journey*, *Rainy May* and *Dark Lady* with Randy Monaco's pleasing, laid-back vocals and Michael Kac's keyboards usually to the fore. The strongest track on the album is possibly the haunting *Strange*, but a consistent standard is maintained throughout.

The simple pop format is dropped on the *Medium* album which is the group's first real excursion into the world of psychedelia. By the time of its release Michael Kac had left the band due to musical differences. Overall, it is less consistent but possibly more interesting than their earlier effort. Of particular interest is the opening track on Side Two, the haunting *After Pascal*, which has an unusual psychedelic intro, and the fuzztone guitar work on *Smokescreen*. Another track *Barnaby Plum* also has an unusual psychedelic intro and a pleasant autoharp piece in the middle. However, some of the other music on the album is frankly tedious.

As a three piece, the band came to England to record an album with Shel Talmy producing. However the resultant "intimate acoustic guitar" album was deemed too uncommercial and shelved. An acetate of the album still exists and many of the songs were later re-recorded for *Puzzle*.

Their third and final album, *Puzzle*, was their most ambitious. It had a most interesting cover. The mysterious opening track *Earthfriend Prelude* sets the tenor for the remainder of the album, which is their rarest and something of a collectors' item. But other tracks like *Just A Blur* were more in the style of their first album, while *Kyrie* finds the group playing quasi-religious material, as does *A Children's Prayer* on Side Two. *Volcano Prelude*, the opening track on Side Two commences with a slow orchestrated drum crescendo, while *Whisper Play* is possibly the strangest track on the album, based around the idea of quasi-religious music, superimposed with whispers. Overall, this amounted to an early concept album and, with a total playing time of almost 49 minutes, was excellent value when first released.

After *Puzzle* the group recorded a cover of Thunderclap Newman's *Something In The Air*, which was released as a 45 with picture sleeve, but this didn't "happen" and Kevin Lally left afterwards.

Randy Monaco later played with **The 1910 Fruitgum Co.** but sadly died in the late seventies from cirrhosis.

Craig Anderton went on to form Anomaly with musicians Charles Cohen and Jeff Kane. They backed Linda Cohen on her Poppy label albums in the early seventies. Anderton became well-known beginning in the seventies as

THE MANDRAKE MEMORIAL - Mandrake Memorial LP.

MANDRAKE MEMORIAL - Medium CD.

an author, writing the do-it-yourself books "Electronic Projects For Musicians" and "Home Recording For Musicians", as well as contributing a regular column to 'Guitar Player' magazine called "Electronic Guitar". He also participated in a newsletter available to musicians by mail-order called "Device" that provided tips on modifying guitars, amps and special effects boxes. In retrospect, while he might be a footnote in rock history for his musical talents, his contribution to rock music in general through his writing is phenomenal, certainly without measure.

Thanks to David L. Brown - whose sleeve notes from the Collectables reissues have been used for part of this entry. (VJ/LRd/CF)

Mankind

An obscure Texas band who performed *Little Girl* on the 'Sump 'n' Else' TV show in 1966. This track has been included on *Texas Flashbacks Vol. 1: Dallas*. A Rhodes Recording acetate of a track *Never* by **Mankind** may be this same outfit. (VJ)

Herbie Mann

| ALBUMS: | 1 | IMPRESSIONS OF THE MIDDLE EAST | (Atlantic) c1967 - |
| (very selective) | 2 | THE WAILING DERVISHES | (Atlantic) c1968 - |

Based on the East Coast and born in 1930, the jazz flutist **Herbie Mann** deserves a mention here for his late sixties material, as he worked with several rock musicians and some of his albums are inspired by the Middle East sounds.

Mann also produced the **Floating Opera** album. His later releases are in a soul/jazz/pop vein and consequently outside the scope of this book. (SR)

Terry Manning

ALBUM: 1   HOME SWEET HOME   (Enterprise) 1969 SC

A multi-talented man in the Memphis scene, **Terry Manning** was equally at ease with guitars and keyboards and had previously briefly been in the **Bobby Fuller Four**, **Lawson and Four More** and **The Avengers**. His only solo album contains lots of heavy guitar with various effects and a crazed version of *Savoy Truffle* with psyched vocals. **Manning** later became an engineer and producer for soul and rock acts (notably Isaac Hayes, ZZ Top, George Thorogood and Jason & The Scorchers). (SR)

Charles Manson

ALBUM: 1   LIE-THE LOVE AND TERROR CULT
                                                        (Awareness 22145) 1970 R2

NB: (1) also released on ESP (Disk 2003). Reissued on Awareness (AWARE 1) 1987. Reissued on CD (Grey Matter GM 05CD), with 14 demo tracks recorded in Van Nuys on the 9th of August, 1968, and 12 tracks of "The Manson Family Sings The Songs Of Charles Manson" recorded in 1970.

Yes, this is the notorious **Charles Manson**. The recordings on this album were made prior to the Tate-Labianca murders. It contains 14 original songs in an acid hippie-folk vein. The music mainly consists of **Manson** singing and playing guitar. On some tracks he's accompanied by sitar, tamboura, violin, strange percussion, electric guitar and voices. The sleevenotes to this now rare album give no indication of who the other musicians were. (VJ/SR)

The Marauders

Personnel:	BRIAN BARMBY	bs	A
	JACK GIERE	vcls, keyb'ds	A
	RICK JAGLA	drms	A
	GLENN STRAWN	ld gtr	A
	MIKE LILLMAN	gtr	
	ED SCHEID	gtr, vcls	

| 45s: | Something In The Air/ Musical Man (PS) | Since I Met You/I Don't Know How 1966 |
| α | Something In The Air/ Musical Man (PS) | Goin' Down / I Want You 1967 |

NB: α as **Waphphle**.

From Sacramento, California. An acetate of a fabulous psycho fuzz-punker with virtuoso vocals has been unearthed by Alec Palao and Joey D. *Our Big Chance* is a sparkling rough diamond set in *Psychedelic Crown Jewels, Vol. 2* (Dble LP & CD). The band were to rework and retitle this track - it appeared as *Goin' Down* in 1967 on their next 45 under the name **Waphphle**.

Brian Barmby won an audition to play with the Beach Boys, but his parents wouldn't let him join because he was only fifteen. Glenn Strawn's girlfriend, Nancy Ross was in a band called She and Glenn Strawn plays guitar on two home demos that appear on the *She* CD (Big Beat) 1999.

Watch out for a **Marauders** retrospective collection on Ace/Big Beat in 1999.

Brian Barmby died recently.

Other compilation appearances have included: *Since I Met You* on *Pebbles, Vol. 10* (LP); and *Our Big Chance* on Gear Fab's *Psychedelic Sampler* (CD). (MW/RM/JD)

THE MANDRAKE MEMORIAL - Puzzle CD.

MARBLE PHROGG - Marble Phrogg CD.

The Marauders

| 45: | Lovin'/Nightmare | (Lee 9449) 1965 |

From Saginaw, Michigan.

Compilation appearances have included: *Lovin'* on *Scum Of The Earth* (Dble CD) and *Scum Of The Earth, Vol. 2* (LP); and *Nightmare* on *Teenage Shutdown, Vol. 8* (LP & CD), *Glimpses, Vol's 1 & 2* (CD) and *Glimpses, Vol. 2* (LP). (VJ)

The Marauders

Personnel:	TERRY GARDNER	drms	A
	RICK MILLER	ld gtr	A
	RICK PERVISKY (PRZYWOJSKI)	gtr	A
	JIM YOUNG	bs	A

| 45s: | α | I Can Tell/Hi-Di Hi-Di | (Coulee 110) 1964 |
| | β | Bad Times / Girl Don't Tell Me | (Twin Town 714) 1965 |

NB: α issued on blue vinyl. β as by **The Satisfactions**.

Formed in 1963 in La Crosse, Wisconsin, this quartet marauded all over the Midwest. For their second 45 a name change was imposed by producer Dave Garrett, against the band's will. The reasoning behind it was that the Stones' *I Can't Get No Satisfaction* was riding high in the charts at the time. Both sides reappeared soon after on the Bud-Jet series of compilations released in 1965/6 - *Girl Don't Tell Me* on *Top Teen Bands, Vol. 2* and *Bad Times* on *Top Teen Bands, Vol. 3*.

The band split around the end of 1966. Rick Miller went on to achieve success and kudos as the owner of Harley Davidson Apparel.

Retrospective compilation appearances have included: *I Can Tell* on *Hipsville, Vol. 3* (LP); and *Bad Times* on *Everywhere Interferences* (LP). (MW/GM)

The Marauders

Another Marauders, this time from Iowa, whose *Warning* was originally released on the rare 'Heads' label, and has since resurfaced on *Garage Punk Unknowns, Vol. 8* (LP). (VJ)

The Marauders

| 45: | Bad Girl/She's So Fine | (Rockland 2) 1966 |

Again, another Marauders, this time from Maine.

Compilation appearances include: *Bad Girl* on *Teenage Shutdown, Vol. 12* (LP & CD). (VJ)

The Marauders

| 45: | Bad Girl/ | |
| | She's So Fine   Jugband Music/Out Of Sight, Out Of Mind | 1967 |

Probably from Chicopee, Massachusetts, *Out Of Sight, Out Of Mind* is an excellent pop-punker written by Dave Morris and Steve Duboff (the latter was one half of the **Changin' Times** of *How Is The Air Up There* fame). It was also covered by **Limey And The Yanks**, **Bit' A Sweet** and in the eighties by The Outta Place.

Compilation appearances include: *Out Of Sight, Out Of Mind* on *Mindrocker, Vol. 3* (LP), *Glimpses, Vol's 1 & 2* (CD) and *Glimpses, Vol. 1* (LP). (MW)

Marble Cake

An early seventies Kent, Ohio outfit who didn't release any vinyl. They included Joe Vitale after he left **The Chylds** and before he teamed up with Joe Walsh. (GG/MW)

Marble Collection

45s:	(What's So Good About) Love In Spring/	
	Glad You're Mine	(Cotique C-143) 1969
	A Friend Like You/Big Girl	(Marble Disc 2995) 1969

Late sixties ballads on the Cotique 45; the top-side in a **Young Rascals** style, the flip in a cool sultry mood with some atmospheric reeds and restrained lead. Not for the garage clan unless you like a touch of soul. From Ansonia, Connecticut. (MW)

Marble Phrogg

| ALBUM: | 1(-)   THE MARBLE PHROGG | (Derrick 8868) 1968 R4 |

NB: (1) counterfeited on vinyl and CD in the early nineties.

| 45s: | Love Me Again/? | (Derrick # unknown) 1968 |
| | Fire/There's A Girl | (Derrick 8568) 1968 |

This now rare and sought-after album was the work of a band from Tulsa in North-eastern Oklahoma. Although entirely embellished with cover versions collectors will pay hundreds of bucks for an original copy, the attraction being that many of the covers are as good, maybe even better than the originals. First off is *I'm So Glad* with some tasty fuzz guitar; next up is *Love Me Again* with more superb guitar work; this is evident too on Mars Bonfire's *Born To Be Wild* - every bit as good as **The Steppenwolf** version. There's a fine rendition of **The Byrds**' *I Feel A Whole Lot Better*, a very psychedelic treatment of Ingle-De Loach's *Fields Of Sun* with some excellent guitarwork and drumming and a fine **Hendrix** impersonation on *Fire*. Side Two isn't quite as good but it includes a rehash of Mick Jagger's *Connection*, a very fuzzy cover of *Strange Brew* and impressive reworks of Donovan's *Season Of The Witch* and Eric Burdon's *Sky Pilot*. Certainly any collector of psychedelia should snap up the recent repress. It has an interesting back cover too!

Compilation appearances have included *Love Me Again* and *Born To Be Wild* on *Kicks & Chicks* (LP). (VJ)

The Marbles

Personnel:	DAVID DOUGDALE	bs	A
	RAY GREENLEAF	drms	A
	STEVE DOWLER	gtr	A
	PETE SHAPIRO	gtr	A

This mid-sixties Berkeley, California, outfit played at the first gig at San Francisco's Longshoreman's Hall on 16th October 1965 along with

Jefferson Airplane, The Charlatans and The Great Society, but then apparently vanished from the scene.

In fact, The Marbles broke up when David Dougdale was deported to England. Pete Shapiro and Steve Dowler went on to Loading Zone, whilst Ray Greenleaf went to work for a politician running for the California Senate. (VJ/SDr)

Lydia Marcelle

45s:	Everybody Dance/		
	I've Never Been Hurt Like This	(Atco 6366)	1965
	The Girl He Needs/Come On And Get It	(Manhattan 805)	1967
	It's Not Like You/Imitation Love	(Manhattan 809)	1967

An obscure solo artist. Her aggressive garage-pop song *The Girl He Needs*, originally released on Mike Curb's Manhattan label, can also be heard on *Girls In The Garage, Vol. 1* (LP & CD). (VJ)

Marcia and The Lynchmen

45:	Won't Turn Back/		
	Ain't Gonna Eat My Heart Out	(Scotty 94456740)	1967

This rare 45, which was the work of a Minneapolis-based band, was written and produced by Warren Kendrick who worked with The Litter, too. They later became The Plastic Ice Cube.

An unreleased cover of *Very Last Day* from 1966 is also on the double album collection of Dove studio recordings *Free Flight* (Dble LP). (VJ/MW)

Marcus

Personnel incl: MARCUS UZILEVSKY (aka RUSTY EVANS) A

ALBUM: 1(A) MARCUS (Kinetic Z-30207) 1970 R2
NB: (1) reissued on CD (Collectables COL-CD-0571) 1994.

This was a later project in the expanding consciousness of Rusty Evans, the guru behind The Deep, Freak Scene and others. Musically, it's like psychedelic period Donovan.

The Collectables CD includes two demo tracks *Time Of Our Time* and *Children Of Aquarius*. You can also find more Marcus demos on the *Psychedelic Moods Part 5* CD (COL-CD-0690) 1996.

MARCUS - Marcus CD.

Marcus Uzilevsky later released a folk album, *Life's Railway To Heaven* (Folkways FTS 32440) 1979.

Compilation coverage has included:- *A Million Grains Of Sand*, from the Marcus album, but miscredited as Rusty Evans on *Filling The Gap*; 1983 and *The Life Game* on *Green Crystal Ties, Vol. 5* (CD). (VJ/MW)

Marcus

ALBUM: 1 FROM THE HOUSE OF TRAX (No label) 1979 R3
NB: (1) reissued on CD.

A different Marcus, who dealt in heavily phased, cosmic psych along the lines of Terry Brooks and Strange. The band was based in Indiana.

One track from their album, *A Trip In Time*, which includes lots of fuzz and swirling sound effects, later resurfaced on *Relics, Vol. 2* (LP) and *Relics Vol's 1 & 2* (CD). (VJ)

Mardi Gras

45:	Everyday I Have To Cry Some/The Days	(Map City)	1970

NB: also released in France with a PS (AZ SG 330).

Produced by Vinnie Poncia (Tradewinds) on his label, Mardi Gras came from the East Coast and are another example of white soul rock similar to Rascals (but not as interesting). They spent some time in France, where they recorded some singles circa 1972.

An album may have been released too. (SR)

Mariani

Personnel:	VINCE MARIANI	drms	ABC
	ERIC JOHNSON	gtr	BC
	?? NELSON		B
	JAY PODOLNICK	bs, vcls	BC
	DARRELL PEAL	vcls	C
	BILL WILSON	vcls	C

ALBUM: 1(C) PERPETUUM MOBILE (Sonobeat HEC 411/2) 197? R6
NB: (1) all known copies are in a sleeve labeled 'advance copy' and are numbered on the front by hand. It is believed that only 100 copies were made, and known copies are numbered in the double-digits, supporting this theory. (1) counterfeited (Hablabel HBL 11004) 1988, (Fanny 300894) 1997 and also on a CD with additional

MARIANI - Perpetuum Mobile LP.

material. More recently reissued as 10" (Akarma AK 140LP) and CD with both sides of the second 45 as bonus tracks.

45s:	α	Pulsar/Boots	(Sonobeat R-S 116) 1969
		Re-Birth Day/	
		Memories Lost And Found	(Sonobeat R-S 118) 1970

NB: α issued as Vince Mariani.

From Austin, Texas. They are now known more as a springboard for guitarist Eric Johnson, than for their collective efforts as a band. *Perpetuum Mobile* was pressed for demo purposes in 1970 or 1971 and shopped to major labels. Sonobeat had used this rather innovative means (presenting a finished album master to an established label for release) to place Johnny Winter with Imperial Records.

Musically they were very heavy with plenty of good guitar work but perhaps too much instrumentation. They won a good 'live' reputation, but sadly broke up before Sonobeat concluded their negotiations with United Artists. Eric Johnson was a brilliant 16-year-old guitarist who still has a considerable reputation as a guitarist in the 1980s with jazz/fusion instrumental band Electromagnetics. His guitar work was also much in evidence on their second 45. The first was a pair of drum solos backed by studio electronics. The reissue of their album is obviously welcome because copies of the promotional-only release were very rare indeed.

Memories and *Re-Birth Day* have also been compiled on *Filling The Gap* (4-LP). (VJ/RB/CF)

Mariano and The Unbelievables

ALBUM:	1	MARIANO AND THE UNBELIEVABLES	
			(Capitol ST-2831) 1968 -

In the same style as the **18th Century Concept**, a studio group with white wigs playing hits of the day (*Sunshine Superman*, *As Tears Go By*, *Wack Wack*, *There's A Kind Of Hush*, *Somethin' Stupid*...) in a baroque pop style. Better avoided! (SR)

Marjorine

45:	I Live/Loving Shrine	(Look 45.5025) c1967

A Tennessee group. As often, the 'A' side is a rather commercial pop-rock song with horns, while the flip, written by Grissin and Rison, is a good garage track.

Look was a small label distributed by Starday-King Records from Nashville and also released 45s by the **Berwick Players**. (SR)

Mark and The Escorts

45s:	Tuff Stuff/Get Your Baby	(GNP Crescendo 350) 1965
	Dance With Me/Silly Putty	(GNP Crescendo 358) 1965

Formed in 1963 in East Los Angeles and originally as The Escorts, **Mark and The Escorts** released two 45s on GNP Crescendo in 1965.

They remained active into the mid-seventies under a succession of identities:- in 1966 they became The Men From S.O.U.N.D.; around '68/69 they became **Nineteen Eighty-Four** and released one 45 on Kapp; by the seventies they were The Mudd Brothers; their final incarnation was Tango, with an album on A&M.

In the sixties they had one track, *Get Your Baby* on the *East Side Revue, Vol. 1* (LP) compilation in 1966 and the double-album set *East Side Revue*.

Retrospective compilation appearances have included: *Get Your Baby* on *Mindrocker, Vol. 1* (LP) and *The Magic Cube* (CD); *Get Your Baby* and *Dance With Me* on *Psychotic Reaction Plus Ten* (CD); *Get Your Baby* on *The West Coast East Side Sound, Vol. 2* (CD); *Tuff Stuff*, *Get Your Baby*, *Dance With Me*, *Silly Putty* and *Get Your Baby* on *The East Side Sound Vol. 2 Featuring Mark And The Escorts* (LP & CD). (MW/LJ/MGo)

Marke V

Personnel:	STEVE KELBURG	bs	A
	BILL MUFFET	ld gtr	A
	PETE SANCHEZ	gtr	A
	EDDY TRUMAN	drms	A
	DONNIE WOFFORD	vcls	A

45:	Pay/The Leader	(JCP 102) 196?

From Raleigh, N.Carolina, this 45 was recorded by a bunch of 9th, 10th and 11th graders. Both sides can be heard on *Tobacco A-Go-Go, Vol. 2* (LP).

Steve Kelburg later went into the military, retired and became a policeman, Bill Muffet works at a music store and Donnie Wofford has been involved in radio business. Ed Truman now owns a garage and has recently got back into playing music again.

Ed Truman (drums) and Lee Caplin (keyb'ds) later played as **The Castaways**, with original **Castaways** member Bob Folschow, who been drafted into service. At the time, Bob was using the surname Bob Leroy and was stationed in Fayetteville, North Carolina. This outfit played for two years, in and around Durham, Chapel Hill and points North and South, including schools, bars, public venues and a gig at Duke University. (MW/EDT)

The Marketts

ALBUM:	1	SUNPOWER	(World Pacific WPS 21870) 1967 -

From California, **The Marketts** were an instrumental group formed in the early sixties, playing a mix of surf music, rock and covers of current hits, in the same style as The Ventures or **The Challengers**. Like the other two groups, they kept on recording during the mid-sixties and tried to adapt their style to the flower-power era. Their line-up often changed and included some ace session musicians like Ben Benay (**Goldenrod**). (SR)

Mark Five (Mark V)

Personnel:	LES CLINKING BEARD	sax	AB
	MIKE CLOTHER	keyb'ds	AB
	WAYNE FREEMAN	drms	A
	HAL LOTZENHISER	bs	AB
	NED NELTNER	gtr	AB
	ED THOMAS		AB
	MIKE BUONO	drms	B

NB: Line-up 'A' 1961-63, 'B' 1963-65.

45s:	Ooh Poo Pah Doo/Get On Back	(Bolo 746) 1964
	It's Your Heart/48 LBs of Bad Luck	(Jani 1258) 1964/5
	Maggie's Farm/Who Made Lonely	(Jani 1265) 1965

A Spokane, Washington act. When original drummer Wayne Freeman was killed in an auto accident in 1963, he was replaced by Mike Buono. Ned Neltner later played in **Gas Company** and produced **Locksley Hall**'s album. Both he and Les Clinking Beard later played in the long-lasting outfit Junior Cadillac. (DR/MW/GGI)

Mark V

A raw tape demo of a heartfelt garage-ballad *Over You* by this unknown garage combo has been rescued for posterity on *Psychedelic Crown Jewels, Vol. 2* (Dble LP & CD). (MW/RM)

The Mark Five

Personnel incl:	DANNY FARAGHER	keyb'ds	A
	JIMMIE FARAGHER	bs, gtr, sax	A

45:	I'm Through With You/	
	I'll Keep On Trying	(Impression 102) 1965

Jangley beat-Invasion sounds backed by mid-tempo beat with the odd horn intrusion. From San Bernardino, California, and featuring the Faragher brothers, who went on to form **The Peppermint Trolley Co**. (MW)

The Mark Five

45:	Search Your Mind/Determination	(N.W.I. 2700) 1966

From Albany, Oregon. *Determination* can also be heard on *Garage Music For Psych Heads, Vol. 1*. (GGI/MW)

The Mark Four

45s:	Swingin' Hangout /	
	Just My Dream	(Pacific Challenger 102) c1965
	Forget It Baby/Go Away Now	(Pacific Challenger 1004/5) 1965

Forget It Baby later resurfaced on *A Journey To Tyme, Vol. 4* (LP). (VJ/MW)

Mark IV

Personnel incl: MIKE REILLY

| 45: | Better Than That/Hollow Woman | (Columbia 43911) 1966 |

From Connecticut, the Mike Reilly in this band was a different guy to he of Pure Prairie League fame. *Hollow Woman* on *Mindrocker, Vol. 7* (LP), which was recorded in late '66, contains some tasty fuzztone guitar. This, together with the lead vocalist's intriguing voice, are the main points of interest on the record. (MW/GGI)

Mark IV

Personnel?:	?? ACKERT	A
	?? GILROY	A
	?? LORETA	A
	?? RUGER	A

45s:	Hey Girl (Won't You Listen)/?	(Giant Star) 1966
	Would You Believe Me/	
	Don't Want Your Lovin'	(Giant Star GS-405) 1966
	Churches And Houses/?	(Giant Star) 1967

A quartet from Poughkeepsie, New York. The debut was a folk-pop outing. Their second came with a photo insert autographed by band members and is highly prized amongst collectors; even more so because *Don't Want Your Lovin'* is a primitive *I'm A Man*-style garage rave-up.

Compilation appearances include: *Don't Want Your Lovin'* on *Pebbles, Vol. 2* (CD), *Psychotic Reactions* (LP), *Best of Pebbles, Vol. 3* (LP & CD) and *Psychedelic States: New York Vol. 1* (CD). (VJ/MW/MM)

Mark Markham and The Jesters

Personnel incl: MARK MARKHAM

45s:	Goin' Back To Marlboro Country/	
	I Don't Need You	(Power 4225) 1966
	Goin' Back To Marlboro Country/	
	I Don't Need You	(RCA 8992) 1966

This Florida outfit's 45 got picked up by a major label despite its off key piano and guitars. Both sides are country-influenced punkers, the flip has lots of mouth harp and organ. Not bad.

Mark Markham is still a local legend around the Fort Lauderdale area, getting a namecheck on Charlie Pickett and The Eggs first two albums and providing them with a track *If This Is Love, Can I Have My Money Back?!*

Compilation appearances have included: *Goin' Back To Marlboro Country* and *I Don't Need You* on *Sixties Archive, Vol. 4* (CD) and *Florida Punk Groups From The Sixties* (LP). (VJ/MW)

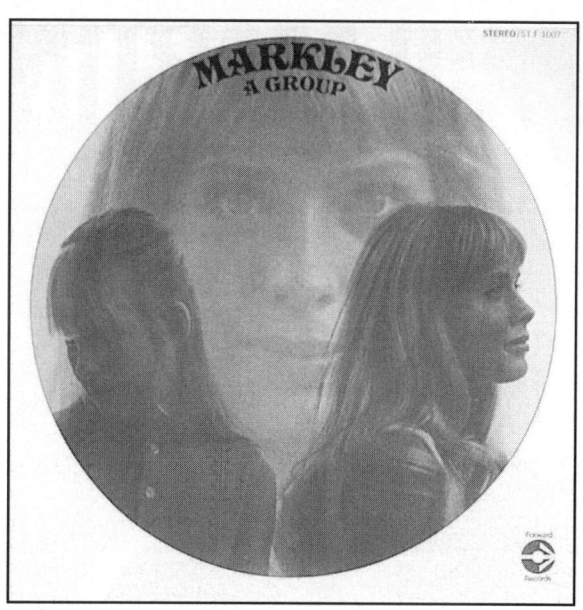

BOB MARKLEY - A Group LP.

Bob Markley

Personnel:	DAN HARRIS	A
	SHAUN HARRIS	A
	MICHAEL LLOYD	A
	BOB MARKLEY	A

| ALBUM: | 1(A) | A GROUP | (Forward ST-F-1007) 19?? SC |

NB: (1) shown as by **Markley**. (1) has been counterfeited on LP.

This is in fact the last **WCPAEB** album, produced by **Bob Markley** and Michael Lloyd. All the tracks are composed by the above personnel. Musically, it's not as good as the **WCPAEB** but contains some good tracks: *Next Plane To the Sun*, *Sweet Lady Eleven* and *Magic Cat*. Quite surprisingly, there are also several bubblegum-influenced tracks (*Zoom, Zoom, Zoom* being the worst). (SR)

Marlboros and The Jokers Six

| ALBUM: | 1 | REAL LIVE GIRL | (Justice 126) 196? R2 |

NB: (1) reissued on CD by Collectables (COL-CD-0610), 1995.

Very rare garage soul-rock - not a compilation of two bands, but two bands that play with each other (i.e. **Marlboros** is a black vocal group and **Jokers Six** a white teen garage combo behind them). (CF)

The Marquis

Personnel:	CHUCK BALBONI	ld gtr, vcls	A
	JOHN "MARVIN" COOK	bs	A
	BOB "STICK" DICKIE	drms	A
	PAT WEST	gtr, vcls	A
	MARK WHITWORTH	keyb'ds	A

| 45: | In This State Of Mind/ | |
| | Broken Mirror | (Teen Grove 201,159/60) 1967 |

NB: Vocal on *In This State...* by Pat West, vocal on *Broken Mirror* by Chuck Balboni.

A garage band from Boston. The 'A' side is a garage-style ballad, whilst the flip is a is a cool teenbeat garage shuffler with a guitar and organ riff. Mark Whitworth recalls:- "We were high school students in Canton, Massachusetts when we recorded our 45 at Ace Recording Studios ('Ace is the place ... to make recordings') in Boston. The 45 became a staple at the soda shop, The Family Treat (aka 'The Beat')." (AH/MM/MWt)

PAUL MARTIN - Paul Martin LP.

The Marsadees

Personnel:	BOBBY AREHART	gtr	A
	LARKIN CORLEY	gtr	A
	STACK HARMON	bs	A
	LARRY INGRAM	drms	A
	DENNIS STEELE	ld gtr	A

ALBUM: 1(A) THE MARSADEES (Justice 150) 1967

NB: (1) reissued by CD (Collectables Col-0619) 1997.

The members of **The Marsadees** all attended Lexington High School in Lexington, South Carolina. Aside from the group's original instrumental *Palisade*, their lone album contains the band's interpretations of songs that were staples of many of the bands on the Justice Records roster, including *Louie Louie*, *Walk, Don't Run*, *Little Latin Lupe Lu*, *Pipeline* and *Wipe Out*.

Compilation appearances include *Wipe Out* and *Lonely Sea* on *Green Crystal Ties, Vol. 10* (CD). (MDo)

Marshmallow Way

Personnel incl:	BILLY CARL	A
	REID WHITELAW	A

ALBUM: 1(A) MARSHMALLOW WAY (United Artists UAS 6708) 1969

45s: C'mon Kitty Kitty Let's Go To The City /
Michigan Mints (United Artists 50545) 1969
Good Day / Music, Music (United Artists 50611) 1969

Billy Carl had been around a while and putting out 45s since 1962, fronting Billy and The Essentials and The Heatwaves. This was a short-lived late sixties venture, trying to catch another wave, somewhere between rock and bubblegum pop. (MW/SR)

The Marshmellow Highway

45: I Don't Wanna Live This Way /
Loving You Makes Everything Alright (Kapp K-904) 1968

Produced by Claus Ogerman and Scott English. The flip was co-written by English and Kenny Young, the man behind the **San Francisco Earthquakes**. (SR)

The Marshmellow Steamshovel

45: Mr. Mold/Steamshovel (Head 1908) 1968

From Pittsburgh, Pennsylvania. The 'A' side, *Mr. Mold* is rather an appealing garage pop song and the heavy instrumental flip, comes complete with squeaky noises.

Compilation appearances have included: *Steamshovel* on *30 Seconds Before The Calico Wall* (CD); *Mr. Mould* on *Gone, Vol. 1* (LP); *Mr. Mold* and *Steamshovel* on *Burghers, Vol. 1* (LP & CD). (VJ)

Tom Martel

Personnel:	JIM BIEKER	organ, piano, vcls	A
	JACK COYNE	perc, vcls	A
	DOROTHY LERNER	vcls	A
	TOM MARTEL	gtr, vcls	A
	JOHN O'REILLY	acoustic gtr, vcls	A
	TOM TROXELL	bs, vcls	A
	JOE VALENTINE	ld gtr, vcls	A
	SUSIE WALCHER	vcls	A
	BOBBY WINGO	drms, vcls	A

ALBUM: 1(A) HARD JOB BEING GOD
(GWP Records GWP ST 2036) 1971 -

Slightly more than your run of the mill God rock, **Tom Martel**'s *Hard Job Being God* does indeed borrow heavily from "Jesus Christ Superstar" but has its moments. **Martel**'s songwriting takes less from Broadway and adds a bit more genuine rock, with at least one stunning fuzz guitar solo. Housed in a beautiful purple and pink gatefold sleeve, the album is well worth acquiring if cheap. The play apparently had a Broadway run that closed after only six performances. The stage presentation featured a slightly revised cast, including Stu Freeman who had previously played in the **Magic Mushrooms** and toured with Jesus Christ Superstar. (MMs)

Martians

This North Carolina band have a version of *Lawdy Miss Clawdy* on *Tobacco A-Go-Go, Vol. 2* (LP). (VJ)

Bill Martin

ALBUM: 1 CONCERTO FOR HEADPHONES AND
(selective) CONTRA-BUFFOON IN ASIA MINOR (Warner) 1970 -

Based in California, **Bill Martin** was a composer and arranger who worked with the **Modern Folk Quartet** and **Fred Neil**. His solo album is an extremely weird release (and one of the rarest Warner albums), mixing spoken word and strange sound effects. (SR)

Bob Martin

ALBUM: 1 MIDWEST FARM DISASTER (RCA) 1972 -

A rural counterculture folk-rock singer with songs like *Captain Jesus* and *Third War Rag*. (SR)

Paul Martin

ALBUM: 1 PAUL MARTIN (1966-1967) (Distortions DR 1028) 1996

45s: It Happened / Last Remnants Of Our Love (Impex 7-66) 1966
The Last Remains Of Our Love /
The Fairy Princess (PS) (Rodin RO 1303) 1967

Paul Martin (real name Myerberg) started off in New York influenced by the vibrant folk scene happening during the early sixties. By the mid-sixties he had diverted his attention to the British groups and emerging folk-rock scene in the U.S. It was around this time that he started to record some demos, some of which were released as 45s in 1966/1967. They are included on this album along with some material recorded later after he

MARY BUTTERWORTH - Mary Butterworth LP.

became a recording engineer at Bell Sound from 1968 to 1970. Some the of the recordings are heavily influenced by **The Left Banke**, and have an overall different flavour than the 45 tracks.

Dewey Martin and Medicine Ball

Personnel:	PETE BRADSTREET	piano, organ, gtr, vcls	ABC
	BILL DARNELL	gtr	AB
	BUDDY EMMONS	steel gtr	AB
	HARVEY KAGEN	bs	A
	DEWEY MARTIN	drms, vcls	ABC
	STEVE LEFEVER	bs	B
	RANDY FULLER	gtr, vcls	C
	TERRY GREGG	bs, vcls	C

ALBUMS:	1(-)	DEWEY MARTIN AND MEDICINE BALL		
			(Uni 73088)	1970 -
	2(-)	ONE BUFFALO HEARD	(Piccadilly)	198? SC

NB: (2) is a retrospective compilation of pre-**Buffalo Springfield** material featuring **Dewey Martin**.

45s:	α	Jambalaya (On The Bayou)/Ala-Bam	(Uni 55178)	1970
		Indian Child/I Do Believe	(Uni 55245)	1970
		Caress Me Pretty Music/		
		There Must Be A Reason	(RCA Victor 0489)	1971

NB: α promo-only credited to **Dewey Martin**.

The Canadian born **Dewey Martin** (ex-**Buffalo Springfield**) formed Medicine Ball in November 1969 upon leaving **New Buffalo**. Basically a country-soul aggregation, Kagen was ex-**Sir Douglas Quintet**; Darnell ex-Albert King's backing band and Bradstreet ex-Rock City Band (a Dayton, Ohio group). Line-up 'A' was probably responsible for their debut single, although it was credited just to **Dewey Martin**. Issued as a promo only, it comprised the country favourite *Jambalaya (On The Bayou)* and **Martin**'s *Ala-Bam*.

As sessions for the album commenced during April-May 1970, ex-Danny Cox bass player Stephen Lefever helped out until Terry Gregg joined full-time. Darnell left towards the end of the sessions and ex-**Blue Mountain Eagle** member Randy Fuller helped finish it, as did **Bruce Palmer**, who appeared uncredited on his own compostion *Recital Palmer*.

Their album which was produced by **Dewey Martin** with the help of Dave Hassinger, was released in a superb gatefold sleeve of native American sandpaints. It offered an energetic mix of psych, rock (an unusual version of *Yesterday*), country and raga. There's even a pedal steel fuzz solo on one track, *Race Me On Down*. The album also featured some excellent covers, particularly two Ron Davies' songs *Change* and *Silent Song Through The Land*. One track, *It Ain't Easy*, was also recorded by David Bowie.

The A-side to their second 45, *Indian Child* was used in the film "Angels Die Hard".

Steel guitarist Jay Dee Maness has also been reported at various times as a member of **Medicine Ball**, but he only rehearsed with them on a couple of occasions and never played a gig with them. After Buddy Emmons left for session work, another steel player helped fulfil their live dates.

In early '71, Bradstreet rejoined Darnell (who had played with Doug Kershaw in the interim) and his songwriting partner John Alden (co-author of *I Do Believe*) in Starbuck. Martin produced Truk and later became a mechanic. In the late seventies he also played sessions on a Hoyt Axton album. Buddy Emmons kept on recording hundreds of country sessions, Harvey Kegen rejoined Doug Sahm and Augie Meyer and Steve Lefever became a session man, notably with Alexander Harvey. Darnell, Bradstreet and Alden are currently playing in country-rock outfit The Electric Range. (VJ/JO/SR/NW)

The Mar-Vels

45:	Someone Else/When You're Gone	(Melbourne 1538) 1966

A New Hampshire band recording on a Manchester-based label. *Someone Else* is a good garage number and is featured on Aram Heller's *Relative Distance* (LP). (VJ)

Mary Butterworth

Personnel:	MICHAEL AYLING	bs, vcls, flte	A
	MICHAEL EACHUS	organ	A
	JIM GIORDANO	gtr	A
	MICHAEL HUNT	drms, vcls	A

ALBUM:	1(A)	MARY BUTTERWORTH		
			(Custom Fidelity CFS 2092)	1969 R3

NB: (1) bootlegged by Breeder in the early 1980s, also reissued officially on CD by the band themselves, 1998.

45:	Phase II/Week In 8 Days	(Custom Fidelity) 1969

From South Gate, California (a suburb of Los Angeles), **Mary Butterworth**'s album contains some fine progressive rock which maintains a good standard throughout. Featuring lashings of good keyboards and drums, *Phase II* and *It's A Hard Road* are perhaps the pick of the bunch, but really every track's a winner and the album is recommended. Originals are very rare but the official CD reissue will be easier to track down. Two of its finer moments, *Phase II* and *Week In 8 Days* (a bluesy number), can also be heard on *Valley Of The Son Of The Gathering Of The Tribe* (LP). (VJ)

Masalla

45:	Burning Feeling/?	(Private pressing) 1970

A Florida group, between heavy psychedelia and hard-rock. Their single was released in very limited quantities. (SR)

The Masked Marauders

ALBUM:	1	THE MASKED MARAUDERS	(Deity/Reprise 6378) 1968 -

NB: (1) also released in France, U.K. and Greece.

HCP
45:	Cow Pie/I Can't Get No Nookie	(Deity 0870) 1969 123

NB: also released in France with a picture sleeve.

After the appearance of the first rock bootleg, Dylan's *Great White Wonder* rock critic Greil Marcus wrote a tongue-in-cheek review in 'Rolling Stone Magazine' of a non-existant bootleg album featuring a band comprised of Lennon, Jagger and Dylan. The review actually fooled some readers into believing that this mythical album actually existed and record stores across the U.S. were flooded with requests. On reaction, Reprise quickly had the

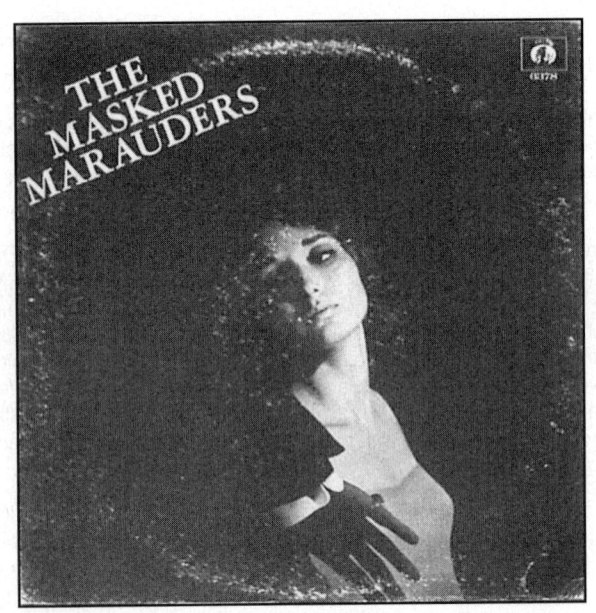

THE MASKED MARAUDERS - The Masked Maraauders LP.

Masked Marauders album recorded and it soon appeared on the "Deity" label (as the review had described).

Musically, it mixes some rock numbers with vocals similar to Jagger or Dylan, another cover of Donovan's *Season Of The Witch* and doo-wop classics (*Duke Of Earl*, *The Book Of Love*) and it cannot be recommended. The musicians were probably members of **The Cleanliness and Godliness Skiffle Band**. (SR)

Mason

Personnel:	STEVE ARCESE	organ, bs, ld vcls	A
	JIM GALYON	gtr, bs, sax, vcls	A
	MORGAN HAMPTON	drms, perc, vcls	A

ALBUM: 1(A) HARBOUR (Eleventh Hour 1001) 1971 R2

NB: (1) original pressing came with a paste-on cover. There is also a slightly later remixed pressing which came in a black and white printed cover with large booklet (R1). This version also has a different track running order. The re-mixed version of the album was also isued in New Zealand (Columbia SCX-5047) 1971, although no booklet is known to be included with this pressing. (1) reissued officially on CD (Gear Fab GF-137) 1999 and vinyl (Akarma AK 105) 2000.

Formed in Virginia in 1969, this power-trio shared the same stomping grounds as **Short Cross** in the Richmond-Norfolk-Virginia Beach area. This heavy rock album has now become a minor collectable. With strong vocals and lots of excellent instrumentation it's easy to see why. One track, *Golden Sails*, sounds uncannily like Jethro Tull, but all eight cuts are originals, six of them Jim Galyon compositions, the other two co-written with Steve Arcese. A must for heavy rock fans but worth a twirl for most collectors. They lasted until the mid-seventies and their legacy has been secured with the CD on Gear Fab.

Jim Galyon later released a disappointing privately pressed solo album in the late seventies. (CF/VJ/MW/RM)

Bonnie Jo Mason

Girls In The Garage, Vol. 4 (LP) includes a song called *Ringo, I Love You*, which was written by Phil Spector, Anders and Poncia and released on Spector's Annette subsidiary circa '64. According to the compilers, Sonny Bono worked for Phil Spector in the early sixties and had Cher sing back-up on records whenever they needed an extra voice. Sonny really wanted to record Cher as a solo, but either Spector didn't like Cher or didn't think she was talented enough for a solo disc. As a joke, Spector gave this song to Sonny for Cher to record, the joke being that Cher's voice was so low, people would think it was a guy singing about being in love with Ringo. So Sonny recorded Cher singing *I Love You Ringo* under the name **Bonnie Jo Mason**. It wasn't a hit, but it was the beginning of Cher's singing career. (ME)

Mason Proffit

Personnel:	TIM AYERS	bs	ABC
	RICK DURETT	piano	A
	ART NASH	drms	ABC
	RON SCHUETTER	gtr, vcls	AB
	JOHN TALBOT	gtr, vcls, banjo	ABC
	TERRY TALBOT	gtr, vcls	ABC
	(JOHN FRIGO	fiddle	A)

ALBUMS: (up to 1971)
1(A) MASON PROFFIT WANTED (Happy Tiger HT-1009) 1969 -
2(B) MOVIN' TOWARD HAPPINESS (Happy Tiger HT-1019) 1970 -
3(C) LAST NIGHT I HAD THE STRANGEST DREAM (Ampex A-10138) 1971 -

NB: (1) and (2) reissued as a double LP *Come And Gone* (Warner) 1974 and again (Line) 1984.

HCP
45s:
Voice Of Change / Rectangle Picture (Happy Tiger 545) 1970 -
Two Hangmen / Sweet Lady Love (Happy Tiger 552) 1970 -
Hard Luck Woman / Good Friend Of Mary's (Happy Tiger 570) 1970 -
α Hope/Jewel (Ampex 11048) 1971 108
β Lilly / I Saw The Light (Warner Bros. 7709) 1973 -
χ Easy To Slip / Trail Of Tears (Warner Bros. 7794) 1974 -

NB: α also issued as a double-sided promo. β and χ as The Talbot Brothers.

Recording in Chicago, **Mason Proffit** was formed out of **Sounds Unlimited** which included at various times Tim Ayres, Art Nash and the Talbot brothers. Their first three albums were produced by Bill Traut, the manager of the Dunwich label/production company. With their long-haired outlaw look and clothes, **Mason Proffit** was essentially a folk and country-rock group with vocal harmonies but some of their songs may interest readers, especially on the first album (also known as "Two Hangmen" because of its stunning cover) with *Voice Of Change* and *A Rectangle Picture* about a soldier sent to Vietnam:

"Janie is my lady, she walks my mind at night
I'm lying in this rice field, I know that it ain't right
Everything has turned around, I think I'll close my eyes
To shut out those machine gun sounds that muffle all the cries
Ever since they called me, my life ain't been the same
An old rectangle picture in an oval picture frame."

Led by John and Terry Talbot, **Mason Proffit** toured intensively and sometimes shared the bill with the **Grateful Dead**. After two more country rock albums for Warner in 1972 and 1973, **Mason Proffit** disbanded and The Talbot Brothers turned to Christian music, recording several albums for Myrrh and Sparrow.

MASON - Harbour LP.

In 1999, Swedish acid rock band Spacious Mind covered *Walk On Down The Road* on their *The Mind Of A Brother* CD. (SR/MW)

Mass

45:	Raining Sorrow/Without You	(Roulette R-7040) 1969

Late sixties downer rock-pop with liberal doses of fuzz and wah-wah - the flip is brighter with some solid solos. Whether this is the same outfit as the Chicago group who put out one 45, also in 1969, *I'll Meet You In My Dreams/Hear Me Out* (Neil 001), is unconfirmed.

Compilation appearances include *Raining Sorrow* on *U-Spaces: Psychedelic Archaeology Vol. 1* (CDR). (MW)

Paul Masse

ALBUM:	1	BUTTERFLY LAKE	(Liberty LST-7600) 1968 -
45:		Motels And Stations/High On A Hill	( ) 196?

Nifty singer-songwriter with pop leanings and heavy orchestration. Recorded in L.A., at times the album's sound compares favorably with the cotton candy folk-pop of **Timothy Clover** album, if that's the kind of thing you're into. (MMs)

Masters of Deceit

Personnel:	STEVE BLUM	gtr, bs	A
	GARY CAMPBELL	bs, tenor sax, vcls	A
	STAN GAGE	drms	A
	TOM HENSLEY	keyb'ds, vcls	A

ALBUM:	1(A)	HENSLEY'S ELECTRIC JAZZ BAND AND SYNTHETIC SYMPHONETTE	(Vanguard 6522) 1969 -

NB: (1) reissued on vinyl (Vanguard/Comet).

The album may interest fans of acid psychedelia with a strong jazzy haze. The group originated from Indianapolis and was fronted by Tom Hensley, an excellent keyboard player who would become a sought-after studio musician during the seventies, working with Leonard Cohen, Hall & Oates and **David Blue** to name but a few.

Their sole record features some fine guitar work, particularly on *Boxes* and *Long Hard Journey* but suffers somewhat from rather weak vocals. Hensley was aware of this problem, as he mentioned in the long, rather intellectual and often funny liner notes that "I was never able to work out the trick of singing as if I were black. So I compromised. I try to sound like a Jewish singer. I haven't done too well on that one either. So we like to think of ourselves as primarily a playing group."

An acetate recorded at Ultra Sound Studios in NY with some non-album tracks has recently resurfaced. (VJ/SR)

The Masters of Stonehouse

45:	If You Treat Me Bad Again/Please	(Discotheque 002) 1966

A completely unknown Michigan band. The 'A' side is a good folk-protest song, quite Dylanesque.

Compilation appearances have included: *Please* on *No No No* (CD) and *If You Treat Me Bad Again* on *Highs In The Mid-Sixties, Vol. 6* (LP). (VJ/MW)

Mastin and Brewer

Personnel:	MIKE BREWER	gtr, vcls	A
	JIM FIELDER	bs	A
	TOM MASTIN	gtr, vcls	A
	BILLY MUNDI	drms	A

45:	Need You/Rainbow	(Columbia 4-43977) 1966

In December 1965, after a few years playing together on the folk-circuit, **Mastin and Brewer** arrived in L.A.. Here they stayed with producer Barry Friedman and New Christy Minstrel, Randy Sparks, recording a three-song demo, comprising originals *Need You*, *Sideswiped* and *Bound To Fall*. The latter track was later covered by Stephen Stills's Manassas.

In early 1966, they formed a group with ex-**Skip Battin Group** drummer Billy Mundi and **Tim Buckley** sideman Jim Fielder. Rehearsing in the same house as **Buffalo Springfield**, they joined **The Byrds** and **Buffalo Springfield** on a tour of Southern California and also played at L.A.'s Whisky A Go Go and Ash Grove clubs.

In mid-1966 they changed name to the Elesian Senate and began work on an album. Mastin however, left during the sessions and the band subsequently fragmented. Mundi joined **The Lamp of Childhood** for a few months and then **The Mothers of Invention**, Fielder too joined **The Mothers** at the suggestion of Mundi, whilst Mastin moved to San Francisco to work in bars and later committed suicide.

Left without a band, Mike Brewer brought in his brother Keith to overdub his voice over Mastin's on the duo's lone single. The two brothers then began work on new material; Mike's *Truly Right*, written about Mastin was covered by **The Nitty Gritty Dirt Band** and the brothers' collaboration, *Love, Love* and Mike's *Truly Right* were later rerecorded by **Brewer and Shipley** on their debut album.

In the Summer, Mike took up a songwriting post at Good Sam Music, which ultimately led to the formation of **Brewer and Shipley**. (NW)

The Matadors

Personnel:	ROMAN "ROMY" BRUTZ	ld gtr	A
	GREG BUSCH	gtr	A
	LEE McGLADE	bs	A
	TOMMY RAML	drms	A
	RONNIE THONE	vcls	A

45:	You're A Better Man Than I / Bright Lights Big City	(Feature 109) 1966

Not to be confused with Palmyra, Wisconsin's **MADadors**, who had a 45 on the same label, this quintet had formed in 1962 in Sheboygan Falls, Wisconsin and were together for about five years.

Thone turned up in a band called Yazz, who were featured on a 1982 WAPL Battle Of The Bands album, *Apple Cellar Tapes*.

Drummer Tommy Raml was later in **Blue Feeling**. (MM/MW/GM)

MASTERS OF DECEIT - Hensley's Electric Jazz Band... LP.

Donnie Matchett

45:	Come On Baby/Runaway	(Scotty GQP 945) 1966

From Butler, Pennslyvania. You'll also find *Come On Baby* on *Glimpses, Vol. 3* (LP). (VJ/MW)

Matrix

Personnel: TOM BAIRD A
DINO FEKARIS A
NICK ZESSES A

ALBUM: 1(A) MATRIX (Rare Earth RS 542 L) 1972 -

A rock trio on the same label as **Xit**, **Magic** and **Sunday Funnies**. (SR)

Matrix

ALBUM: 1 MATRIX (Pro-Gress PGLP-5001) 1975 SC

This **Matrix** (probably unrelated to the other act) released an album comprised of jazz-rock, with tracks like *Jungle Rot*, *Barebottom* and the nine-minute *Count To Seven And Boogie*. The few known copies are in plain white "Advance Reviewer Copy" jacket. (SR)

The Mauds

Personnel: TIM CONIGLIO gtr, trumpet A
ROBERT (FUZZY) FUSCALDO gtr A
DENNY HORAN drms A
JIMMY RODGERS vcls A
BILL SUNTER bs A

ALBUM: 1(A) THE MAUDS - HOLD ON (Mercury SR 61135) 1967 - HCP

45s:
Hold On/C'mon And Move (Dunwich 160) 1967 -
Hold On/C'mon And Move (Mercury 72694) 1967 114
When Something Is Wrong/
You Make Me Feel So Bad (Mercury 72720) 1967 -
He Will Break Your Heart/
You Must Believe Me (Mercury 72760) 1967 -
Soul Drippin'/Forever Gone (Mercury 72832) 1968 95
Only Love Can Save You Now/
Sgt. Sunshine (Mercury 72877) 1968 -
Satisfy My Hunger/Brother Chickee (Mercury 72919) 1969 -
Man Without A Dream/
Forget It, I've Got It (RCA 47-0377) 1970 -

Quite a prolific Chicago-based rock quintet who did achieve minor commercial success with *Hold On* and *Soul Drippin'*. They have a recording of Dick Monda's *Drown In My Broken Dreams* from a session on 24th April 1968, on which they are assisted by the horns of Chicago (then known as The Chicago Transit Authority) included on Happy Tigers' *Early Chicago* (LP) compilation. More recently two previously unreleased cuts - *Searchin'* and *You Don't Know Like I Know* have appeared on Sundazed's CD compilation *Oh Yeah! The Best Of Dunwich Records*. (VJ)

The Maundy Quintet

Personnel incl: DON FELDER A
BERNIE LEADON A

45: 2's Better Than 3 / I'm Not Alone (Paris Tower PT-103) 1967

Trivia time of the rich and famous - this quintet were based in Gainesville, Florida and included two gents who'd both go onto global success in the seventies.

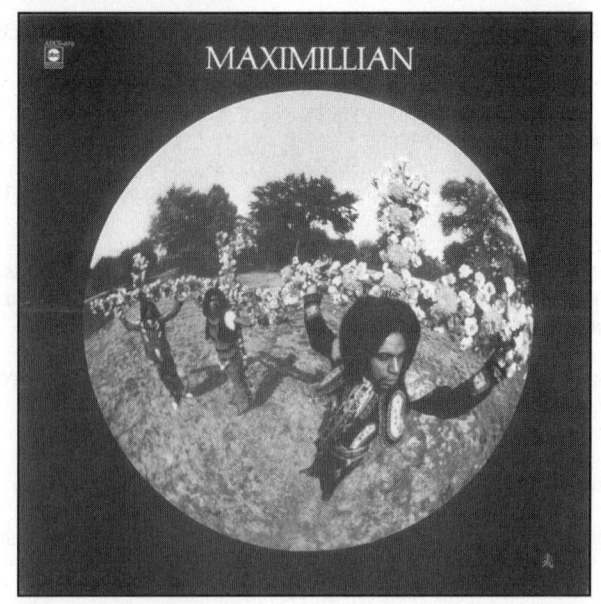

MAXIMILLIAN - Maximillian LP.

Don Henley moved on to a band called Flow (who put out a jazz-rock album on the CTI label) before goin' to Califonia and joining Linda Ronstadt's band, where he was reunited with Leadon and encountered other members of her band with whom he'd form The Eagles. Bernie Leadon had already been around in various outfits like the Scotsville Squirrel Barkers before his tenure in **The Maundy Quintet**. Leadon's route to the Eagles was less direct - via **Hearts and Flowers**, Dillard and Clark, **The Corvettes**, Linda Ronstadt's band and The Flying Burrito Brothers.

The Byrds-inspired *2's Better Than 3* can be heard on *Psychedelic States: Florida Vol. 1* (CD) and the breezy harmony-beat flip, *I'm Not Alone* is on *Psychedelic States: Florida Vol. 3* (CD). (MW/JLh)

The Mauve

45: You've Got Me Cryin/In The Revelation (Cori 31006) 196?

From the Framingham area of Massachusetts, this outfit was previously known as The Boss-Todes, whose *Sally The Pollywog* is featured on *The Cicadelic Sixties, Vol. 2* (LP).

Compilation appearances as **The Mauve** include *You've Got Me Cryin'* on *New England Teen Scene* (CD) and *New England Teen Scene, Vol. 1* (LP). (VJ)

The Mavericks

45: Life Ain't No Bucket Of Roses /
When I'm Gone (20th Century 595) c1967

An interesting 45 written by Steve and Eric Nathanson, who also worked with **Omnibus**, **Boffalongo** and **Music Asylum**. It was produced by Feldman and Gottehrer of **The Strangeloves** and arranged by Bassett Hand. (SR)

Maximillian

Personnel: MAXIMILLIAN (BUDDY BOWZER) ld vcls A
MOJACK MAXIMILLIAN gtr A
MOBY MAXIMILLIAN bs A

ALBUM: 1(A) MAXIMILLIAN (ABC ABCS 696) 1969 R1

From New York, produced and arranged by Teddy Vann, this is an album which gets a mixed response from collectors. Some like it, claiming that it's **Hendrix** inspired psych-soul-rock here, on tracks like *Rat Race* or *Kickin' 9 to 5*, and deserves to be heard. Others hate it, citing awful vocals and weak material.

Featuring a trio plus anonymous drums and occasional organ and violin, the album came housed in a gatefold sleeve with pictures of the trio being crucified on flower crosses and various religious symbols. The liner notes explained that "Golgotha music was one of the few surviving vestiges of truth. Its prophets of love and truth such as BB King, Bob Dylan, Donovan, Aretha Franklin, Arlo Guthrie and Joan Baez sang the psalms of time. The crucifixion of the social heroes of the day, Martin Luther King, John and Robert Kennedy, has made even bigger demands on the importance and value of music, thus creating new prophets of love and truth".

It is rare and therefore sought-after by some collectors, though others advise to avoid it at all costs. (CF/SR)

Maxx

45s:	200 Years/Castles	(Signal 1043) 1969
	200 Years/Castles	(Mainstream 714) 1969

More obscurities from Michigan who recorded a superb slice of psychedelia with lots of fuzz guitar and sound effects entitled *200 Years*.

Compilation appearances include: *200 Years* on *Lycergic Soap* (LP), *Relics Vol's 1 & 2* (CD) and *Relics, Vol. 2* (LP). (VJ/MW)

Judy Mayhan

ALBUM: 1 MOMENTS (Atco SD33-319) 1970 -

Judy Mayhan began her career in the early sixties as a traditional folk singer playing dulcimer. After several albums which are out of the scope of this book, she signed to Atco and turned electric. Her *Moments* album is mainly notable for *Walk Right In* with Mike Pinera (**Iron Butterfly**, **Ramatam**) on guitar, and three former members of **The Factory**: Lowell George on guitar and flute, Ritchie Hayward on drums and Warren Klein on sitar, plus Williama Charlton on bass and Aumashananda on aum drum. All the other tracks were recorded in Muscle Shoals with Duane Allman and Eddie Hinton, but are not as interesting. (SR)

Maypole

Personnel incl:	STEVE MACE	gtr	A
	JOHN NICKELS	bs	A
	DENNIS TOBELL	ld gtr, backing vcls	A
	KENNY ROSS	ld vcls	A
	PAUL WELSH	drms	A
	DENNY ROMANS	gtr	
	JEFF LUTZY	bs	

ALBUM:	1(A)	MAYPOLE	(Colossus CS-1007) 1970 R1
45:		Show Me The Way/Johnny	(Colossus CS 131) 1970

This anonymous outfit's album, which has been likened to outfits like **The Ill Wind** and **Neighborhood Childr'n**, is now a minor collectable. In fact it's far heavier than either of these two and doesn't feature female lead vocals either. It does however merge psychedelia and heavy rock, with some excellent **Hendrix**-inspired lead guitar work on *Johnny* and *Glance At The Past*. All their material was original and it was produced by Pat Perticone at New York's A&R studios.

The long liner notes, written by Paul Welsh, state that their name came from the Maypole erected by the people of Merrymount in New England in the 17th Century to break most of the Puritan laws, stating that "Maypole intends to combine the techniques of literature in lyrics and structure with the feeling generated by our music to communicate the "real" to an unlimited audience".

The band came from Baltimore and were founded by Paul Welsh and Dennis Tobell. Dennis was the mainstay of the band, writing or co-writing the bulk of their material. He is still playing professionally as Demian Bell and has played in Los Bravos amongst others. Prior to **Maypole** he was also a member of **The Barbarians**.

The band came from Baltimore. Lutzy was previously with **The Progressions** (on Scepter) and would be involved again with later incarnations of that band. Another member was in a group called A Taste (on Gazette). (VJ/SR/JV)

May Street Tops

ALBUM: 1 SOLD OUT (Private Pressing) 1974 R1?

From North Carolina, a hard-rock quintet with two guitars, two drummers and a bass. Only 300 copies were pressed. (SR)

The Maze

Personnel:	C. BOYD	A
	R. EITTREIM	A
	W. GARDNER	A
	J. JENSEN	A

ALBUM: 1(A) ARMAGEDDON (MTA MTS 5012) 1969 R2

NB: (1) counterfeited on vinyl in 1989 and reissued legitimately on CD (Sundazed SC 6060) 1995 with six previously unreleased tracks - a combination of outtakes from the album and earlier folk-rock offerings from 1967.

From Fairfield, California, this band were previously known as **Stone Henge**, who in turn had evolved out of **The Donnybrookes**. Their album was produced by Larry Goldberg and Leo (De Gar) Kulka who operated out of Golden State Recorders in San Francisco. The album starts out with the melodramatic *Armageddon* which comprises most of Side One, the rest is taken up with the more melodic and laid back *I'm So Sad*. The second side begins with the rather lightweight good-time *Happiness*, but *Whispering Shadows* opens with some great discordant guitar work which gives away to some good group harmonies and *Kissy Face* also features some great vocals, *Dejected Soul*, with its sleepy vocals and fine fuzz guitar work, is among the album's finer moments. The final track, *As For Now*, seems to return to the more melodic, laid-back style of *I'm So Sad*. An album well worth tracking down. The Sundazed CD bonus cuts include two unreleased efforts from 1967 as by **Stone Henge**.

Compilation appearances have included: *Whispering Shadows* on *Psychedelic Crown Jewels, Vol. 1* (CD); *As For Now* on *Sundazed Sampler, Vol. 2* (CD); and *Kissy Face* and *Dejected Soul* on *Crystalize Your Mind* (CD). (VJ/MW)

Cash McCall

Personnel incl:	CASH McCALL	A

ALBUM: 1(A) OMEGA MAN (Paula LPS-2220) 1970 -

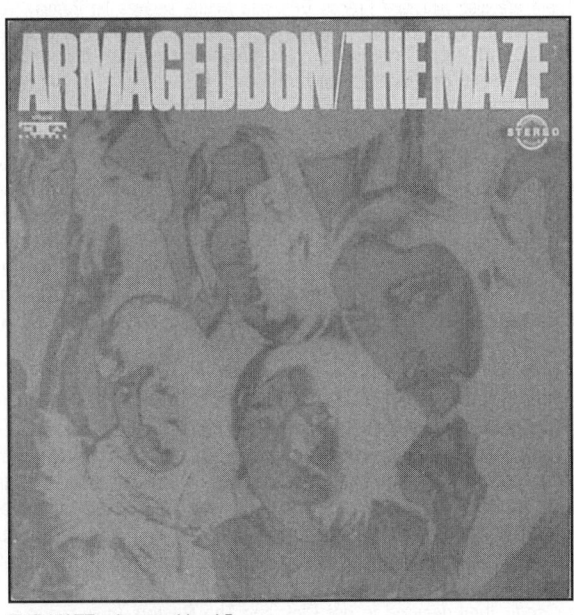

THE MAZE - Armageddon LP.

45: I Need Your Love/Junkie For Your Love (Paula 404) 1974

An interesting, but overlooked, album of psych-blues with fuzz guitar on tracks like *Blues 99*, *Junkie For Your Love*, *Hard Attack*, *Mojo Woman* and the title track. The album also contains a couple of lighter soul-funk tunes, notably a cover of Timmy Thomas' *Why Can't We Live Together*.

Cash McCall also had many other releases. He also did a lot of session work at Chess in the late sixties / early seventies. (SR/GM)

David McCallum

ALBUM: 1 MCCALLUM (Capitol ST-2748) c1969 -

Produced by **David Axelrod**, an album of psych-pop verging toward mainstream pop, with *White Daisies*, *Strawberry Fields Forever*, *98.6*, *Mellow Yellow*, *B.B.* and *Penny Lane*. **David McCallum** is better known for his actor's career in the TV series "Man From Uncle"! (SR)

The McCoys

Personnel:
DENNIS KELLY	bs	AB	
RANDY ZEHRINGER	drms	ABCD	
RICK ZEHRINGER (DERRINGER)	gtr, vcls	ABCD	
RONNIE BRANDON	keyb'ds	BC	
RANDY HOBBS	bs	CD	
BOBBY PETERSON	keyb'ds	D	

ALBUMS: (selective)
			HCP
1(C) HANG ON SLOOPY	(Bang 212)	1965	44 -
2(D) YOU MAKE ME FEEL SO GOOD	(Bang 213)	1966	- -
3(D) INFINITE MCCOYS	(Mercury SR-61163)	1968	- -
4(D) HUMAN BALL	(Mercury SR-61207)	1969	- -

45s:
			HCP
Hang On Sloopy/I Can't Explain It	(Bang 506)	1965	1
Fever/Sorrow	(Bang 511)	1965	7
Up And Down/If You Tell A Lie	(Bang 516)	1966	46
Come On Let's Go/Little People	(Bang 522)	1966	22
(You Make Me Feel) So Good/Runaway	(Bang 527)	1966	53
Don't Worry Mother-Your Son's Heart Is Pure/Ko-Ko	(Bang 532)	1966	67
I Got To Go Back (And Watch That Little Girl Dance)/Dynamite	(Bang 538)	1966	69
Beat The Clock/Just Like You Do To Me	(Bang 543)	1967	92
I Wonder If She Remembers Me/Say Those Magic Words	(Bang 549)	1967	-
Jesse Brady/Resurrection	(Mercury 72843)	1968	98
Daybreak/Epilogue	(Mercury 72897)	1968	-
Only Human/Love Don't Stop	(Mercury 72917)	1969	-
Don't Fight It/Rosa Rodriguez	(Mercury 72967)	1969	-

NB: There are also four rare French EPs with picture sleeves on Barclay, Atlantic and Bang, including *Dansez Le Monkiss with The McCoys and The Strangeloves* (Atlantic 850 010) 1966. Their French label tried to promote their records to dance "Le Monkiss", one of the forgotten sixties dances!

The McCoys formed as a trio in 1962 while the Zehringer brothers and Dennis Kelly were at high school in Fort Recovery, Indiana. They took their name from the Ventures 1960 rock instrumental 'B' side, *The McCoy*. However, in those early days they were also known as Rick and The Raiders and The Rick Z Combo. One 45, *You Know That I Love You/What Can I Do* (Sonic 76234) was released under the Rick and The Raiders name. Soon after keyboardist Ronnie Brandon was added to the original trio while Kelly left to go to college and was replaced by 17-year-old Randy Hobbs.

In July 1965, they signed to New York's Bang Records after opening for **The Strangeloves** at a gig in Dayton, Ohio. **The Strangeloves** (aka NYC record producers Feldman, Gottehrer, and Goldstein) had just cut a version of a little-known Bert Berns song *My Girl Sloopy*, which had been originally recorded by The Vibrations and were performing it on tour to extremely positive audience response. Concerned however that former tour-mates, The Dave Clark Five, were planning to record their own version of the song, and hesitant to release an immediate followup to their present hit, *I Want Candy*, they decided to get Rick and The Raiders (now renamed The Real McCoys and then **The McCoys**) to record the number. Using the original **Strangelove** tracks, they overdubbed vocals from the **McCoys** and a guitar solo by Rick and rush-released the single to immediate success and the No. 1 spot on the U.S. charts.

In September, they recorded their first album and their second single, a revival of Peggy Lee's 1958 hit *Fever*, made No. 7 in the U.S. and No. 44 in the U.K. Their debut album *Hang On Sloopy* also made No. 44 in the U.S. Album Charts. Meanwhile Bobby Petersen took over keyboard duties from Ronnie Brandon. Further minor hit singles followed in the US, although they enjoyed no further chart success in the UK. Initially they were still at school in Indiana because their parents forbade them to tour despite numerous offers. Finally they were persuaded by the **Strangeloves** to go on tour in the late spring of 1966 with ex-Token (of *Lion Sleeps Tonight* fame) Eddie Rabkin (who was a teacher) hired as their tutor. A few months later they toured with The Rolling Stones and began to jettison their image of youthful naivete with the psychedelic single *Don't Worry Mother (Your Son's Heart Is Pure)* in which they gave a tongue in cheek reassurance to their parents. However it fared disappointingly in terms of sales and the band returned briefly to their previous R&B style with their follow-up *I Got To Go Back*. A further psychedelic single *Beat The Clock* was issued to only minor success and the **McCoys** ended their association with Feldman, Gottehrer, and Goldstein and the ailing Bang records.

In 1968, in search of more recording freedom they signed to Mercury Records and produced *Infinite McCoys* which was really their psychedelic album and the prime reason for their inclusion in this book. Their 45 *Jesse Brady* briefly entered the U.S. Charts at No. 98 but their next album, *Human Ball* failed to chart. Both albums contain an eclectic (and beautifully played) mix of rock, jazz, blues, and psychedelia and are a far cry from the pure pop of their early releases.

In 1969, they became the house-band at Steve Paul's Scene Club in New York. Steve Paul became their manager and linked them with albino guitarist **Johnny Winter** who he also managed. By now Bobby Peterson had left the group, Rick Zehringer had changed his surname to Derringer and produced the album *Johnny Winter And...* on which the remaining **McCoys** were the backing group. It made No. 154 in the U.S. and No. 29 in the U.K.. This was effectively **The McCoys**' last venture. Rick then joined Edgar Winter's White Trash and went on to record eight solo albums. He was also an in-demand session guitarist.

Anyone interested in investigating their work might like to check out some of the compilations of their work: One Way have issued a CD titled *The Psychedelic Years* (30642). *Hang On Sloopy* is a 22-track CD (with rarities) on Rock Artifacts in 1995. There's also a 'Best Of' CD compilation of their material, *Hang On Sloopy: The Best Of The McCoys* (Columbia Legacy CK 480951 2) 1995.

Their compilation appearances to date have been:- *Don't Worry Mother* on *Mindrocker, Vol. 3* (LP), *Fever* and *Sorrow* on *Roots Of S. O. B., Vol. 2* and *Hang On Sloopy* on the *Battle Of The Bands* (CD) and *Frat Rock! The Greatest Rock N Roll Party Tunes Of All Time*. (VJ/SR/LP)

MC5 - Kick Out The Jams CD.

MC5 - '66 Breakout CD.

McDonald and Sherby

Personnel:	DAN DROPICK		A
	MONTY EDWARDS		A
	GUY McDONALD	gtr, keyb'ds, vcls	A
	DAN OLSON		A
	STAN SHERBY	gtr, vcls	A
	SLY WILLIAMS		A

ALBUM: 1(A) CATHARSIS (Omniscient Records S 80-1426S) c1976/7 -

NB: (1) reissued on vinyl (Rockadelic RRLP 7.5) 1992 with insert in different sleeve design.

A guitar-based progressive album recorded at Sound 80 in Minneapolis. Though undated, the record sounds of a mid-seventies vintage, not dissimilar to fellow Great Lakes prog-rockers **Kopperfield**. (CF/SR)

McDonald's Farm

45: Tis But I / Between The Lines   (Pulsar 2422) 1969

A California group, their single was arranged by Joe Leahy, produced by Mel Gordon and Bob Hamilton. Written by Larry Hosford (of **The E-Types**), *Tis But* is naff but the flip is a good heavy psych song, which you can also find on *U-Spaces Psychedelic Archeology, Vol. 6* (CDR). (SR/RD)

MC5

Personnel:	MICHAEL DAVIS	bs	AB
	WAYNE KRAMER	gtr	AB
	FRED 'SONIC' SMITH	gtr	AB
	DENNIS THOMPSON	drms	AB
	ROB TYNER	vcls, hrmnca	AB
	(PETE KELLY	keyb'ds	B)

HCP

ALBUMS:	1(A)	KICK OUT THE JAMS	(Elektra 74042) 1969	30 -
	2(B)	BACK IN THE USA	(Atlantic 8247) 1970	137 -
	3(A)	HIGH TIME	(Atlantic 8285) 1971	- -

NB: (1-3) have been reissued on vinyl (Sundazed LP 5092) 2001, (Sundazed LP 5093-5094) 2002 and on CD. There have also been numerous retrospectives including:- *Babes In Arms* (ROIR 122) 198?, first released on tape only and now available on CD, it contains alternate versions, their earliest 45s and an uncensored version of *Kick Out The Jams*; *Power Trip* (Alive 005) 1995 is a 10" (also on CD) with unreleased live and studio recordings. The 10" version has 3 bonus tracks; *Ice Pick Slim/Mad Like Eldridge Cleaver* (Alive 008) 19?? consists of a 10" (also on CD) with more than 30 minutes of unreleased material; *The American Ruse* (Total Energy NER 3001) 1995 10" (also on CD) with pre-production rehearsals for *Back In The U.S.A.*; *Looking At You* (Total Energy NER 3005) 19?? 10" (also on CD) mini album with six tracks; *Teenage Lust* (Total Energy NER 3008) 19?? recorded live New Years Day 1970, it contains the complete show and is available on vinyl and CD; *Live 1969/70* (Fan Club NRCD 4001) 19??; *Phun City* (1996) consists of eight previously unreleased live tracks, recorded in the U.K. in 1970; *Vintage Years* ( ) 199??, a collection of singles tracks available on CD and vinyl; *Live '69 and '70* on CD and vinyl; *Kick Copenhagen*, on vinyl only, a live 1972 limited edition European release; and *'66 Break-Out!* (Total Energy NER 3023) 1999. *Human Being Lawnmower/The Baddest And Maddest Of The MC5* (Total Energy NER 3032 2) 2002, also issued on a purple vinyl album, collects the besst of their semi-legitimate output over the years.

HCP

45s:	I Can Only Give You Everything/	
	One Of The Guys	(AMG AMG 1001) 1966 -
	Looking At You/Borderline	(A2 333) 1968 -
	Kick Out The Jams/	
	Motor City Is Burning	(Elektra 45648) 1969 82
	I Can Only Give You Everything/	
	I Just Don't Know	(AMG AMG 1001) 1969 -
	Tonight/Looking At You	(Atlantic 2678) 1969 -
	Shakin' Street/The American Ruse	(Atlantic 2724) 1970 -

The **MC5** met in school, forming back in 1964 in Detroit and by 1966 they were local favourites. Just 500 copies were pressed for their first 45, a driving version of Them's *I Can Only Give You Everything* which was backed by a group original, *I Just Don't Know*. The following year they formed an association with John Sinclair, a Detroit dee-jay, who soon became their manager and agent and was very influential indeed in setting the agenda for the rest of their career. A second 45 was recorded in January 1968 and came out on A2 Records in a picture-collage sleeve. Like their first effort this is now extremely rare, although it was bootlegged by Skydog in 1977 with the 'A' side misspelt *Bordeline* and catalogue numbers on the sleeve and cover which didn't correspond. The original sold out quickly and they were signed by Elektra in mid-1968. The resultant album *Kick Out The Jams* was probably one of the most significant high energy rock albums of all time and was also notable for the band's revolutionary political stance, which had been tailored under Sinclair's influence. Tracks like *Ramblin' Rose*, *Come Together*, *I Want You* and *Borderline* represented the loudest, most powerful music of their day. Original U.S. pressings contained an uncensored version of *Kick Out The Jams* containing the line *Kick Out The Jams, motherfuckers!*, which was later amended to *Kick Out The Jams, brothers and sisters!*, as well as a political manifesto from Sinclair printed on the inside gatefold which was removed from subsequent pressings (R1). The title track was issued as a 45 in the U.S. and the U.K. and a follow-up *Ramblin' Rose/Borderline* was only released in the UK, where their album was better received. Outside Michigan much reaction in America was unfavourable. The situation worsened when Hudson's, an Ann Arbor store refused to stock the album on the grounds it was obscene. In response the band took out an advert in the 'Ann Arbor Argus' which ran.. 'kick in the door if the store won't sell you the (MC5) album ... fuck Hudsons!' and included the Elektra logo on the bottom right hand corner. This resulted in the store withdrawing all the label's product and the band finding themselves without a contract with immediate effect. However, they were quickly snapped up by Atlantic. Meanwhile AMG had repackaged the group's first single but replaced *One Of The Guys* with *I Just Don't Know*.

Their first effort for Atlantic, *Back In The USA* was another classic, but its sound was cleaner, less frantic and more controlled than their work hitherto. With their manager jailed on a cannabis charge the group were now coaxed away from their left wing political stance with *The Human Being Lawnmower* being the only acknowledgement of this on the new release. The album was well-received by the critics and contained a number of fine hard-rock tracks like *Tutti-Frutti*, *Looking At You*, *Call Me Animal*, *The American Ruse* and *Shakin' Street*. Its sales, though, were relatively disappointing. Collectors might be interested to know that a withdrawn version of this album also exists: near the end of *Teenage Lust*, Rob Tyner can be heard to say "C'mon bitch - You got to get down" on the rare uncensored pressing (R1). Apparently, this version of the song also appears on the pre-recorded tape releases as well.

The follow-up *High Time* was an attempted compromise between the wild, arrogant style of *Kick Out The Jams* and the more controlled sound of *Back In The USA*. As such it failed, although some individual songs like *Poison* and *Over and Over* stood out. It did not sell well and the band planned to move to Europe. They embarked on a European tour and played some successful dates. They recorded a couple more tracks which appeared on a Soundtrack album called *Gold*, only released on Mother Records in the U.K. in 1972 (Mother MO 4001). The album is now very rare but mostly comprised of naff material. During and after the European tour the band disintegrated marking the end of an all-too-short career.

Wayne Kramer later formed a group with **Mitch Ryder** (of Detroit Wheels fame) called Kramer's Kreemers, which also used the **MC5** name. This ended when the band's guitarist was busted and imprisoned for five years. Later Kramer projects included Wayne Kramer's Gang War (1980) and Air Raid (1982). He also played on The Deviants live album *Human Garbage* recorded at a one-off reunion gig in 1984. The album included some songs, including *Rambin' Rose*, that Kramer had written in his days with the **MC5**. Since then he has played with U.S. bands Das Damen and G.G. Allin.

After the **MC5** split, Thompson, Smith and Davis formed Ascension, which didn't make it onto vinyl. Later Thompson worked for New Order, Motor City Bad Boys and, in 1981, he was involved with Ron Asheton (once guitarist with **The Stooges**) and three members of Radio Birdman in an outfit called New Race.

Fred Smith and Michael Davis were both involved in the Scott Morgan Group, which later became Sonic's Rendezvous Band, although by then Davis had left to join Destroy All Monsters. Fred 'Sonic' Smith sadly died of a heart attack on November 4th 1994, although Sonic's Rendezvous have subsequently had a posthumous CD entitled *Sweet Nothing* (Mack Aborn Rhythmic Arts) 199?.

Rob Tyner spent some time in the UK in the late seventies, writing and recording. He released one 45: *Till The Night Is Gone (Let's Rock)/Flip-Side Rock* (Island) 1977, shown as by Robin Tyner and The Hot Rods. He also issued a CD in 1990, *Bloodbrothers* (this time backed by Cub Koda's band). Tyner died in September 1991.

MC5 material continues to appear on the market. 1983 saw the release of a ROIR cassette *Babes In Arms* which includes the five pre-Elektra tracks, the uncensored version of *Kick Out The Jams*, four tracks from *Back In The USA*, five from *High Time* and a previously unreleased cut, *Gold*, from the film soundtrack. This cassette was reissued on album and CD in 1990 in France by Danceteria Records.

The Wayne Kramer compiled and annotated *'66 Breakout* is guaranteed to appeal to garage-niks, even those not into their later stuff. This collects their earliest live, studio and demo sounds, 1965-1966. Eleven tracks including *Looking At You, Black To Comm, Baby Please Don't Go, I'm A Man* and *I Can Only Give You Everything*.

Human Being Lawnmower/The Baddest And Maddest Of The MC5 collects the best of their semi-legitimate releases, which are a mixture of lo-fi live recordings and studio out-takes. The live material stems mostly from a dry-run for the recording of *Kick Out The Jams*. More interesting is the studio material, including the unedited take of *Skunk (Sonically Speaking)* (from *High Time*), the January '68 session for the *Looking At You/Borderline* single and Fred Smith's sparse acoustic demo of *Over And Over* (from *High Time*).

MC5 - Babes In Arms CD.

Compilation appearances have so far included: *Motor City Is Burning* and *Kick Out The Jams* on *Kings Of Pop Music, Vol. 1* (LP); *Looking At You, Borderline, I Can Only Give You Everything, One Of The Guys* and *I Just Don't Know* on *Michigan Nuggets* (CD) and *Michigan Brand Nuggets* (LP); *Kick Out The Jams* (uncensored version) on *Michigan Rocks* (LP); *Come Together, Starship* and *Ramblin' Rose* (all from their first LP), the 45 version of *Kick Out The Jams*, and *Motor City Is Burning* on *Elektrock The Sixties* (4-LP); *I Just Don't Know* and *Looking At You* on *Turds On A Bum Ride, Vol. 1 & 2* (Dble CD) and *Turds On A Bum Ride, Vol. 1* (Dble LP); *Kick Out The Jams* and *I Want You Right Now* on *Hallucinations, Psychedelic Underground* (LP).

MC5 have certainly never been identified with psychedelia. Their relevance here is as part of the garage band phenomena in their early days and, of course, their recordings, especially the first album, were enormously influential on the punk rock revival which started in Britain in the late seventies. (VJ/CRn/MW)

Bat McGrath and Don Potter

| Personnel: | BAT McGRATH | vcls, gtr | A |
| | DON POTTER | vcls, gtr | A |

ALBUM:	1(A)	INTRODUCING BAT McGRATH AND DON POTTER	(Epic BN-26499) 1969 -

45s:	Mister Cadillac/Walking Bird	(Epic 10562) 1969
	Me And Bobby McGee/	
	Get Yourself On A Farm	(Epic 10582) 1969
	Dear Christine/Song Of Long Ago	(Epic 10824) 1971

A forgotten folk-rock duo with a full backing band. Their album includes titles like *Jefferson Green, Someone Take Me Home, Lullaby To An Unborn Child, I Chose To Lose, Mr. Cadillac* and *The Parade*. Bat McGrath also recorded a single with D. Harvey in 1968 for RCA and later went solo and recorded several albums and singles, notably for Amherst between 1975 and 1978. (SR)

Suni McGrath

| Personnel: | RAYMOND BIASE | bass drm | A |
| | SUNI McGRATH | gtr | A |

ALBUMS:	1( )	CORNFLOWER SUITE	(Adelphi AD 1002) 1969 SC
	2(A)	THE CALL OF THE MORNING DOVE	(Adelphi AD 1014) 1971 -
	3( )	CHILDGROVE	(Adelphi AD 1022) 1973 -

All three albums are acoustic 6 and 12 string guitar efforts, very much influenced by other American guitarists of the time (**John Fahey**, Fred Gerlach, John Rosmini, Mark Spoelstra). But **Suni** differed from the guitarists that influenced him in that he managed to incoporate into his music other influences (English and Celtic folk, Bartok, and Bulgarian rhythms) with occasional percussion, electric guitar, vocals, or a second guitarist, creating music with a wider appeal. These records were quite popular with the college and hippie crowd of the time. He was also a big influence on other younger guitarists of the "pre-Leo Kottke" era. (HS/SR)

McGraw Bros

| ALBUM: | 1 | SCOTCH ON THE ROCKS A GO GO | (Tore) 196? R2 |

A New Jersey garage/frat-rock band with a mix of covers (*Twist And Shout, She's About A Mover, I'm Telling You Now* etc.) and original songs. The band was pictured in kilts (!) on the front cover of their extremely rare album. (SR)

Barry McGuire

HCP

ALBUMS:	1	EVE OF DESTRUCTION	(Dunhill 50003) 1966 37 -
(up to	2	THIS PRECIOUS TIME	(Dunhill 50005) 1966 - -
1971)	3	WORLD'S LAST PRIVATE CITIZEN	(Dunhill 50033) 1968 - -

| | 4 | BARRY McGUIRE AND THE DOCTOR | (Ode 77004) 1971 - - |

NB: There's also an 18-track CD compilation on One Way, *Anthology* (22094).

| EP: | 1 | THIS PRECIOUS TIME (PS) | (Dunhill DS 50005) 1966 |

NB: (1) came with juke strips and mini-covers. Tracks included: *Hang On Sloopy, Let Me Be, Yesterday, Hide Your Love Away, Just Like Tom Thumb's Blues, Do You Believe In Magic?* and *This Precious Time*.

HCP

45s:		Eve Of Destruction/			
		What Exactly's The Matter With You	(Dunhill 4009) 1955	1
	α	Upon A Painted Ocean/			
		Child Of Our Times	(Dunhill 4014) 1965	72/117
		Don't You Wonder Where It's At/			
		This Precious Time	(Dunhill 4019) 1965	-
		Cloudy Summer Afternoon (Raindrops)/			
		I'd Have To Be Outta My Mind	(Dunhill 4028) 1966	62
		There's Nothing Else On My Mind/			
		Why Not Stop And Dig It	(Dunhill 4048) 1966	-
		Masters Of War/			
		Stop And Dig It Now While You Can	(Dunhill 4098) 1967	-
		Inner Manipulations/Lollipop Train	(Dunhill 4116) 1968	-
		Grasshopper Song/Top O'The Hill	(Dunhill 4124) 1968	-
		Old Farm/ South Of The Border	(Ode 66010) 1970	-

NB: α some copies in PS. There's also two French EPs with picture sleeves: *Eve Of Destruction / Try To Remember Sloop John B. / Why Not Stop And Dig It While You Can* (RCA 86900M) 1966 and *Don't You Wonder Where It's At/This Precious Time/Child Of Our Time/Won A Painted Ocean* (RCA 86904M) 1966.

Barry McGuire was born on 15th October 1937 in Oklahoma and first came to attention as the gruff lead vocalist with the New Christy Minstrels, who enjoyed some success in the early 1960s. Before going solo he released an album with another ex-new Christy Minstrels member, Barry Kane, *Here And Now* (Horizon 1608) circa 1964/65 as Barry and Barry. The bassist on this is Jimmy Bond who played on **Tim Buckley**'s *Goodbye And Hello* album.

He met Lou Adler and **P.F. Sloan** at the **Byrds**' opening gig at Ciro's in L.A. and in Autumn 1965 he recorded **P.F. Sloan**'s *Eve Of Destruction*, which is rightly remembered as one of the protest songs of all time, rising to No. 1 in the U.S. and No. 3 in the UK. Its lyrics were chillingly pertinent in the days of the Vietnam War. This arguably was his finest moment, although his albums are worth investigation, especially *Barry McGuire And The Doctor*. Thereafter he discovered Christianity and proceeded to record several religious albums mostly on the Myrrh label. **McGuire** also appeared in the seventies film 'The President's Analyst', which included him singing lead vocals on **Clear Light**'s *She's Ready To Be Free*, which was originally the flip to *Black Roses*.

Compilation coverage has included: *Eve Of Destruction* on *Nuggets, Vol. 10* (LP); *Eve Of Destruction, Child Of Our Times* and *Let Me Be* on *Dunhill Folk Rock, Vol. 1*; and *This Precious Time* and a version of *California Dreamin'* with **McGuire** on lead vocals on *Penny Arcade: Dunhill Folk Rock, Vol. 2*. (VJ/MW/SR/EW)

Scotty McKay

45s incl:		Batman/All Around The World	(Claridge 309) 1966
		Waikiki Beach/I'm Gonna Love You	(HBR 495) 1967
		Truely True/Salty Waterman	(Atco Pompeii 66692) 196?
	α	The Train Kept A Rollin'/	
		The Theme From The Black Dog	(Falcon 101) 1968
		High On Life/	
		If You Really Want Me To I'll Go	(Charay 1001) 1970
		High On Life/	
		If You Really Want Me To I'll Go	(UNI 55205) 1970

NB: α 'A' side credited to The Scotty McKay Quintet, 'B' side credited to Scotty McKay's Bolero Band.

This Dallas-based artist's real name was Max Lipscomb and back in 1958 he had briefly been a member of Gene Vincent's Blue Caps. He released numerous 45s throughout the 1960s and also sang vocals on The Gator Shades Blues Band 45, a **Kenny And The Kasuals**-related venture.

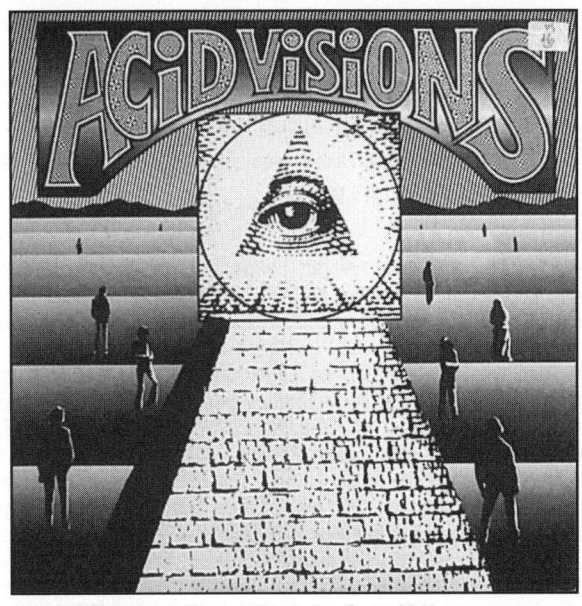

ACID VISIONS Vol. 1 (Comp LP) including Scotty McKay.

His most relevant release to this book was his storming rendition of *The Train Kept A Rollin'*. This was strongly rumoured to have featured Jimmy Page on lead guitar, although it was actually **Exotics** guitarist Blair Smith who was responsible for the blistering fretwork. Nevertheless, the track has subsequently been heavily compiled including: *Mindrocker, Vol. 4* (LP), *Acid Visions* (LP), *Acid Visions - The Complete Collection Vol. 1* (3-CD), *Texas Music, Vol. 3* (CD) and *James Patrick Page: Session Man Vol. 2*.

The compilers of *Acid Visions* also suggest that **Scotty McKay** came from Fort Worth rather than from Dallas. (MW/VJ)

McKendree Spring

HCP

ALBUMS:	1	McKENDREE SPRING	(Decca DL 7-5104) 1969 - -
(up to	2	SECOND THOUGHTS	(Decca DL 7-5230) 1970 192 -
1973)	3	THREE	(Decca DL 7-5332) 1972 163 -
	4	TRACKS	(Decca DL 7-5385) 1972 - -
	5	SPRING SUITE	(MCA 370) 1973 - -

One of the first American examples of progressive rock with the prominent electric violin of Michael Dreyfuss, plus moog and guitars. Led by Fran McKendree, the group also had some country influences. As with many other prog groups, you'll either like or hate their records. The second and third spent two and seven weeks respectively in the charts. (SR/VJ)

Scott McKenzie

Personnel incl:	MAX BENNETT	bs	B
	COLIN CAMERON	bs	B
	RY COODER	slide gtr	B
	CRAIG DOERGE	harpsichord, piano, organ	B
	CHUCK DOMANICO	bs	B
	MAC ELSENSOHN	drms	B
	WALTER FOUTZ	organ	B
	BUNK GARDNER	horns	B
	BARRY McGUIRE	vcl harmonies	B
	SCOTT McKENZIE	vcls	AB
	RUSTY YOUNG	pedal steel	B

HCP

| ALBUMS: | 1(A) | VOICE OF SCOTT MCKENZIE | (Ode 44002) 1967 127 - |
| | 2(B) | STAINED GLASS MORNING | (Ode 77007) 1970 - - |

HCP

45s:	α	No, No, No, No, No/I Want To Be Alone	(Epic 101 24) 1967 -
		San Francisco (Be Sure To Wear Some Flowers In Your Hair)/	
		What's The Difference	(Ode 103) 1967 4

Look In Your Eyes/All I Want Is You	(Capitol 5961)	1967 111
Like An Old Time Movie/ What's The Difference, Chapter II	(Ode 105)	1967 24
Holy Man/ What's The Difference, Chapter III	(Ode 107)	1967 126
Going Home Again/Take A Moment	(Ode 66012)	1970 -

NB: α credited to Scoff McKenzie's Musicians.

Born on 1st October 1944 in Arlington, Virginia, **Scott McKenzie** first came to public attention as a member of The Journeymen, which also included **John Phillips**. When **Phillips** relocated to California to start **The Mamas and Papas**, **McKenzie** remained in New York where he recorded a few ballads for Capitol. Later in 1967 he did relocate to L.A. to join the booming folk-rock movement. Indeed **John Phillips** produced his first 45 for Epic. However, it is for the next 45, *San Francisco (Be Sure To Wear Some Flowers In Your Hair)*, which **John Phillips** wrote, that **McKenzie** is best remembered. Arguably the hippie anthem, it became an international hit in 1967 when it appeared on Lou Adler's new Ode Records and inspired thousands of youngsters to head for San Francisco.

McKenzie was very closely associated with the flower-power philosophy and, save for one disappointing country-rock album in 1970 which also spawned a 45, did not record when the Summer Of Love ended. *San Francisco (Be Sure To Wear Some Flowers In Your Hair)* can also be heard on *Nuggets, Vol. 10* (LP) and many other sixties collections.

In the late sixties he worked hard to make young people aware of the dangers of drug taking and he is also a member of the reformed **Mamas and Papas**. (VJ)

Billy Wade McKnight

45:	I Need Your Lovin'/ Trouble's Commin' On	(International Artists 116) 1967

Given the Texas connection, this could be the same **Billy Knight** as in the following entry, but stylistically it is very different from their Custom 45. This release is like an inferior Righteous Brothers without the power of the singers and without Phil Spector's production. (MK)

Billy McKnight and The Plus 4

45:	You're Doin' Me Wrong/Time Wasted	(Custom 127) 1966

A punk outfit from Tyler, Texas. The 'A' side of their sole stab for stardom was a sneering punker, the flip was much slower.

Compilation appearances include *You're Doin' Me Wrong* on *Trash Box* (5-CD). (VJ)

McLuhan

ALBUM:	1	ANOMALY	(Brunswick SBL-754177) c1972 -

Housed in a strange gatefold cover, an album of psych-prog with two long cuts on each side: *The Monster Bride*, *Spiders (In Neals Basement)*, *Witches Theme And Dance*, and *A Brief Message From Your Local Media*. (SR)

Meadow

Personnel incl:	LAURA BRANIGAN	vcls	A

ALBUM:	1	THE FRIEND SHIP	(Paramount) 1972 -

45s:	Here I Am/ Something Borrowed, Something Blue		(Paramount 0187) 1972
	Cane And Able/ Something Borrowed, Something Blue		(Paramount 0208) 1972

A Christian progressive folk-rock group. Their singer, Laura Branigan, had a short pop star career in the eighties. (SR)

BACK FROM THE GRAVE Vol. 3 (Comp LP) including Me and Them Guys.

Me and Dem Guys

45:	Gone, Gone, Gone / She Cried	(Pyrenees Records MDG-5) c1968

An obscure garage group from Grand Rapids, Michigan. (SR)

Me and Them Guys

Personnel:	MARTY BAKER	organ	A
	ROD KERSEY	drms	A
	STEVE MICHAEL	gtr	A
	STEVE PRITCHARD	gtr	A
	CRAIG TERRY	bs	A

45:	I Loved Her So/Somethin' Else	(Gre-Tle 101) 1966

This mid-sixties high school outfit formed in Greencastle, Indiana and soon became a live attraction at nearby Purdue and De Pauw universities. They travelled to Indianapolis to record their 45. The 'A' side, which has a nice organ backing with spoken vocals, has resurfaced on *Back From The Grave, Vol. 3* (LP). The flip was a Kinks-influenced instrumental. (VJ)

Me and The Other Guys

Personnel:	BILL AERTS		A
	CHUCK DOUGHERTY		A
	KENT LAVOIE		A
	LEON MASSEY	drms	A
	DUTCH WALTON	vcls	A

ALBUM:	1 ( )	BE YOUNG, BE FOOLISH, BE HAPPY	(Copahog 00069/70) 1974 ?

45s:	Skinny Minnie / Crazy	(Hit Cat 102) 1966
	Runaround Girl / Everybody Knew But Me	(Boss 009) 1967

Jim Krist and The Delrays from central Florida (maybe Madeira Beach) evolved into **Me And The Other Guys**, joined by Bill Aerts from The Mark V along the way. Vocalist Dutch Walton (confusingly not from Holland, but Germany) kept the band going well into the seventies and recorded an album in Largo, Florida in 1974.

The others had moved on - notably Kent Lavoie. He was in The Sugar Beats and U.S. Male before finding major solo success in the seventies as 'Lobo', still accompanied by Aerts.

Everybody Knew But Me sounds somewhat dated for 1967. A fine tribute to the Searchers' school of sultry jingle-jangle, it can be heard anew on *Psychedelic States - Florida Vol. 2* (CD). (MW/JLh/MM/RM)

Me and The Rest

45: Mark Time/Dark Clouds (Brass City 2027) 196?

The band came from Waterbury, Connecticut.

Compilation appearances include *Mark Time* on *Vile Vinyl, Vol. 2* (LP) and *Vile Vinyl* (CD). (VJ)

The Measles

Personnel:	BUDDY BENNETT	drms	ABCDEFG H
	LARRY LEWIS	gtr	A
	BOBBY SEPULVEDA	ld vcls, bs	AB EFG H
	JOE WALSH	ld gtr, vcls	AB
	BILL LOHR	gtr	B
	TOM CLAPSADDLE	gtr	CDEF
	RICK LYTLE	bs	C
	DENNY SCOTT	organ	CDE
	CASS ??	vcls	CD
	BOB BAIRD	bs	DEFG
	RIK WILLIGER	keyb'ds, gtr, sax	FG H
	MIKE DELANEY	ld gtr	G H
	MARY STIRPKA	vcls	H

This seminal Ohio outfit was formed by Kent State University students. The original line-up 'A' above recorded several songs, but only three have subsequently been released: One unfinished track was issued under the title of *Maybe* as the flip to the **Ohio Express**' hit 45 *Beg Borrow Or Steal* and the remaining two (*And It's True* and *I Think Of You*) were released on the **Ohio Express** album on Cameo! When Larry and Bobby were drafted, the band broke up circa mid-67 so Bobby Sepulveda first learned about their release when he heard the **Ohio Express** album playing in his army barracks!

Joe Walsh briefly played in a couple other local bands. Amazingly, **The Measles** were not the most popular band in Kent, with The Counterpoints and the Turnkeys getting bigger followings. Joe was a very short-lived member of the Turnkeys, before hitting the road to success with the **James Gang**. After many personnel changes **The Measles** became **Lacewing** but later reverted to **The Measles** again. Buddy Bennett is the only member who stayed with the band.

Bobby Sepulveda did, in fact, rejoin **The Measles** after his stint in the military, and the band went on successfully for many years thereafter. They finally called it quits in 1978. He and Rik Williger later played with Magna and Badge. Today Rik is playing in Jonah Koslen and The Gentlemen Rockers. (GGl/MW/RWr)

Mechanical Switch

Personnel:	BART BACA	vcls, tamb	A
	BEN DUSEK	drms	A
	ALAN MEEK	ld gtr, vcls	A
	LEROY SHELTON	bs, gtr	A
	MARK WENGLAR	gtr, keyb'ds	A

45: Everything Is Red/Spongeman (PS) (Bag One Way 906) 1968

Thought to have originated from St. Louis, Missouri, they were later based in Houston, Texas. Their sole vinyl output was an excellent psychedelic punk 45. Both sides can be heard on *Texas Psychedelia From The Sixties* (LP), *Sixties Archive, Vol. 6* (CD) and *Human Expression And Other Psychedelic Groups: Your Mind Works In Reverse* (CD). *Spongeman*, in particular, is very catchy with immediate appeal.

For the full band low-down check the Collectables' *Human Expression And Other Psychedelic Groups: Your Mind Works In Reverse* sleeve-notes.

Spongeman was covered in the eighties by U.S. psych power trio **Wig Tortüre** on their *Just Say Flow* album. (VJ/MW)

Mecki Mark Men

Personnel:	MECKI BODEMARK	keyb'ds, vcls	AB
	BJORN FREDHOLM	drms	A
	THOMAS GARTZ	sitar, drms	A
	HANS NORDSTROM	flute, sax	A
	CLASS VANBERG	gtr	A
	PELLE EKMAN		B
	BELLA FEHRLIN		B
	KENNY HAKANSSON		B

ALBUMS:
1(A) MECKI MARK MEN (Limelight 86054) 1968 -
2(B) RUNNING IN THE SUMMER NIGHT (Limelight 86068) 1969 -

45: Love Feeling/Sweet Movin' (Limelight 3083) 1968

Originally from Sweden, these guys relocated to the USA and were pretty high on psychedelics when they recorded these two albums. Leader Mecki Bodemark was a former art student, who had also worked with several pop groups and as a studio musician. The other musicians on the first album had their musical roots in jazz and this was reflected in the music which was mostly rather avant-garde, jazzy and with lots of experimental keyboards. The vocals are ineffective and much of the material on their first album is rather disjointed.

Their second effort was a slight improvement with the title cut undoubtedly its finest moment. Other tracks of some note were *The Life Cycle* and *Help Me Somebody*, but I can't recommend either of these albums with much enthusiasm. (VJ)

The Medallions

Personnel incl:	BILL BISHOP	A
	RALPH MULLINS	A

45: Leave Me Alone/She'll Break Your Heart (Warped 1001) 1967

From Oak Park, Illinois, but also associated with Wisconsin, you'll find their version of **The Knaves**' *Leave Me Alone* on *Highs In The Mid-Sixties, Vol. 15* (LP). (VJ/MW/GM)

The Meditations

45: Transcendental Meditation / Beautiful Experience (World Pacific 77876) 1967

A rare West Coast psychedelic 45, both songs were written by Al Boniface. (SR)

TEXAS PSYCHEDELIA FROM THE 60's (Comp LP) includes Mechanical Switch.

MELANIE - Melanie (German) LP.

Medius

| 45: | Let Me Show You / Your Love | (Odessa 807C-4658) c1969 |

From Wisconsin, a S.E. Griffin production written by Gary Tanin. One garage side and a ballad on the flip. (SR)

Melanie

ALBUMS:	1	BORN TO BE	(Buddah BDS 5024) 1969 -
(up to	2	MELANIE	(Buddah BDS 5041) 1969 -
1970)	3	LAY DOWN	(Buddah BDS 5060) 1970 -
	4	LEFTOVER WINE	(Buddah BDS 5066) 1970 -

NB: There's also a German double LP compilation *Melanie* (Buddah DALP 2/3701) 1971.

Melanie Safka was the perfect symbol of the flower-child folksinger of the Woodstock period, with her firm faith in good vibes and her long hair/long dress/bright smile look. *Candles In The Rain* can be found on the Woodstock movie and records and she was also at the Isle Of Wight festival in 1970. Typical of the hippie values, her records sound terribly naive now. (SR)

Barry Melton

Personnel incl:	JOHN CIPOLLINA	gtr	X
	MICKEY HART	drms	X
	BARRY MELTON	vcls	X

ALBUMS:	1	BRIGHT SUN IS SHINING	(Vanguard VSD-6551) 1970 -
(up to	2	GAS-S-S-S	(AIR A-1038) 1970 SC
1975)	3	THE FISH	(United Artists UAS 29908) 1975 -

NB: (3) is a U.K. release.

| 45: | Teacher/Teacher | (Nasty Records X-1) 1973 R3 |

When **Country Joe and The Fish** disintegrated, their guitarist, **Barry Melton**, went solo. His first album *Bright Sun Is Shining* is not recommended, the songs being poor. **Melton** then signed with CBS and formed **Melton, Levy and The Dey Brothers**, which again is best avoided.

In 1970, he also recorded the soundtrack to an obscure Roger Corman movie 'GAS-S-S-S', with the help of **Country Joe** and Robert Corff (ex-**Purple Gang**); the album is extremely rare. In 1971/72 **Melton** played on **Mickey Hart**'s *Rolling Thunder* and also did some sessions with Otis Spann, the blues pianist.

His 1973 45 is very rare. As the lyrics are X-rated and an identical version of the song appears on both sides, it's a total mystery just who this record was made for, or even why it was pressed at all! If it only existed on tape, it could be surmised that *Teacher* (like The Rolling Stones' *Cocksucker Blues*) was recorded to fulfil a contractual obligation; but the fact that it exists on vinyl suggests a plan to market it somehow. The music is a 12-bar blues-rock improvisation of no particular distinction. No sleeve is known to exist for this item, and although no artist is listed on the label, the personnel is known to Bay Area collectors as line-up 'X' above. **Hart**'s wife is said to have provided the female "vocals" on the track.

His first really interesting album is *The Fish*, recorded in Wales with members of Help Yourself and Man. After that, **Melton** kept on recording on various labels and in the eighties formed the Dinosaurs with other Bay Veterans:- Spencer Dryden (**Jefferson Airplane**), John Cipollina (**Quicksilver**), Merl Saunders (**Jerry Garcia**'s jamming friend) and Peter Albin (**Big Brother**).

Barry Melton still lives and perform in San Francisco. A recent CD *The Saloon Years* illustrates his work in the local clubs. Quite surprisingly, he is also known as a lawyer. (SR/CF)

Melton, Levy and The Dey Brothers

Personnel:	RICK DEY	vcls, bs	A
	TONY DEY	vcls, drms	A
	JOEY LEVY	vcls, keyb'ds	A
	BARRY MELTON	vcls, gtr, trombone	A
	(MIKE BLOOMFIELD	gtr, slide gtr	A)
	(BRUCE BRYMER	drms	A)

| ALBUM: | 1(A) | MELTON, LEVY AND THE DEY BROTHERS |
| | | (CBS KC 31279) 1972 - |

This is **Barry Melton**'s second effort outside of **Country Joe and The Fish**. This is a good album with a loose West Coast feel, and will appeal to anyone who has an appreciation for **Melton**'s later solo efforts. Many of the songs were written or co-written by Rick Dey who had penned *Just Like Me* for **Paul Revere and The Raiders**. Rick, who later died of a laughing gas overdose at a party, previously played with **The Vejtables**, **The Wilde Knights** and **The Giant Sunflower**. Brother John Dey drummed with late versions of **The Daily Flash** and **The Stone Poneys** and would eventually join Van Morrison's band. (HS/SR)

David and Tina Meltzer

Personnel:	ED BOGAS	violin, viola, gtr, bs	A
	IVAN CUNNINGHMA	flute	A
	TOM HEIMBERG	viola	A
	DON IRVING	gtr	A
	SALLY KELL	cello	A
	DAVID MELTZER	gtr, mandolin	AB

DAVID and TINA MELTZER - Poet Song LP.

TINA MELTZER	vcls	AB
JIM MEYERS	snare drm	A
DON O'BRIEN	clarinet, sax	A
KREHE RITTER	french horns	A
NATHAN RUBIN	violin	A
EARL SAXATON	french horns	A
JOHN GUERIN	drms	B
SCOTT HAMBLY	mandolin	B
DAVID LINDLEY	violin	B
LYLE RITZ	bs	B
MICHAEL RUBINI	piano	B

ALBUMS: 1(A) POET SONG (Vanguard VSD 6519) 1968 R1
2(B) GREEN MORNING (RD Records RD5) 199? -

NB: (1) reissued on vinyl (Akarma AK 054). (1) reissued on CD with **Serpent Power**'s debut (Akarma AK 053/54). (2) later issued on CD (RD Records).

Produced by Sam Charters, the first album features six poems by **David Meltzer** plus nine melancholic songs sung by Tina or David. Like its predecesor, **Serpent Power**, it is worth investigating. The second album was recorded for Capitol Records circa 1970 with session musicians and remained unreleased until the RD Records release. It too is an interesting album with a distinctly period feel. It was produced by Vic Briggs in Hollywood and San Francisco.

Another album, *Faces*, was released in 1984 on Folkways. (VJ/SR/CF)

Mike Melvoin

ALBUMS: 1 KEYS TO YOUR MIND (Liberty LST-7485) 1968 -
2 THE PLASTIC COW GOES MOOOOG (Dot DLP 25961) 1969 -

45s: On Broadway/Promise Her Anything (Colpix 800) 1966
Lady Jane/One Man One Volt (Dot 17300) 1968

Based in Los Angeles, keyboard maestro and arranger **Mike Melvoin** was a busy session man who can be found on many albums relevant to this book (**Hourglass**, **Brewer and Shipley**, **Gabor Szabo**, **Tongue and Groove**, **Michele**). Not limiting his activities to rock, he also played on hundreds of albums of pop, jazz, soundtracks and easy listening records. His solo albums contain only covers of hits, notably from Dylan and the Beatles. The second one was recorded with **Beaver and Krause** and is one of the first moog exploito albums. (SR)

Members

Personnel incl: JAY LEE ANGELO A
JEFF NEIMAN A

45s: Wish I'd Never Met You / Jenny Jenny (Label LR-45-101) 1965
Come On Everybody /
I'll Get By Without You (Label LR-45-102) 1966

A St.Petersburg, Florida, band which included Jay Lee Angelo. Angelo was a co-founder of The Impacs who'd been on the Tampa scene since the start of the sixties and released at least two albums and ten 45s between 1961 and 1968. Their second 45 features a tame but faithful cover of the Eddie Cochran classic. The flip is an enchanting Neiman original, with an honours degree from the Searchers/**Beau Brummels**/**Byrds** academy of yearning jangle; check it out on *Psychedelic States: Florida Vol. 1* (CD). (MW/JLh)

The Menaces

Personnel:	DENNIS ALEXANDER	ld vcls, ld gtr	A
	BRIAN CASE	bs	A
	ROBERT PETLEY	drms	A
	JIM SCROEDER	gtr	A

45: 'Til I Met You / If You Want Me (Dramel ARA-22767) 1967

TINA & DAVID MELTZER - Green Morning LP.

Fuzz, Flaykes And Shakes, Vol. 4 (LP & CD) features the pleading *If You Want Me* and reports that this Phoenix, Arizona quartet were originally known as Dennis and The Menaces. (MW/TSz/LJ)

The Menagerie

A completely obscure Northwest outfit who have one unissued folk-rocker, *About Him*, on Big Beat's *Northwest Battle Of The Bands, Vol. 2* (CD). (VJ)

Mendelbaum (Blue Band)

Personnel:	GEORGE CASH	sax, perc, vcls	ABC
	KEITH KNUDSEN	drms, perc, vcls	ABC
	TOM LaVARDA	bs, piano, vcls	ABC
	RONNIE PAGE	organ	AB
	BOB SCHMIDKE	gtr	A
	STEVE SCHULTZ	hrmnca, vcls	A
	CHRIS MICHIE	gtr, vcls	BC
	J.D. SHARP	organ	C

ALBUM: 1(B/C) MENDELBAUM (dbl) (Shadoks Music 034) 2002

NB: (1) Germany-only limited edition containing live and studio tracks recorded 1969-1970. Also available on CD (Shadoks Music 034) 2003.

45: Try So Hard/
Can't Be So Bad (Smack Records, Ltd. J-6963) 1969

Originally from the Madison area of Wisconsin where their 45 was released, the band moved to the Bay Area in 1969 and gigged regularly at the San Francisco ballrooms and concert halls. Archive tapes included on the recent Shadoks release reveal that live, **Mendelbaum** was a high-energy blues band with Chris Michie's stunning lead playing to the fore. However, the first disc of the double album is all unreleased studio recordings from 1970, and this paints quite a different picture of the band as careful craftsmen with melodic sensibilities. This is the high point of the record for me, with tracks like the uptempo *All My Life*, the soaring vocal harmonies of *Walk With Me*, and the ethereal waltz-like *Blood Of The Nation* (all on Side Two) warranting repeat plays.

Keith Knudsen's name will be familiar to most readers as the longtime drummer of The Doobie Brothers. Both Chris Michie and Tom LaVarda went on to play with **Lamb**, and Michie continued with The Pointer Sisters, Boz Scaggs, **Link Wray**, Jerry Garcia, Van Morrison and others. He penned a book about his musical exploits, 'Name Droppings', which is a fun read. There are also currently four CDs of his work available, *Guitars And Oranges* (1993); *Tough Love* (1998); *Seven Rivers* (2000); and *The Goyer Golf Suite* (2001). Sadly, Michie passed away on 27th March 2003 after battling melanoma. (CF)

Menerals

Based in Denton, Texas, they recorded a demo at the WFAA-TV studio in 1966 of the **Love** song *My Flash On You*. It's subsequently been included on *Sixties Rebellion, Vol. 8* (LP & CD), *Psychedelic Microdots Of The Sixties, Vol. 2* (CD) and *Texas Flashbacks Vol. 1: Dallas* (LP) and is a *Hey Joe* styled guitar thrash. They were rumoured to have recorded for the Bismarck label but no vinyl has been discovered as yet. (VJ)

Menn

Personnel:
- DON BAGBY — A
- JOHN BARNETT — A
- MARVIN HALE — A
- DON GRAY — A
- FRED VANDERHEIDE — A

45s:		
A One Way Deal / Ian Fleming Theme	(Two & Two 1)	1966
Things To Come/What Ever Happened To	(Mod 1013)	c1967

An obscure combo, probably from California, whose 45 on Mod is worthy of note. *Things To Come* kicks off with a chiming fuzz intro then goes into a jangley '64/'65 **Beau Brummels** mode. Just when expectations are starting to shrink, comes a shout of 'hey' and glorious raving fuzz break. Then back to the beat-pop again and a short snarling fuzz coda to end. Strange, a split personality - check it out on *Psychedelic Crown Jewels, Vol. 2* (Dble LP & CD).

What Ever is a sultry beat ballad and both are published by Wickwire, whose label issued 45s by San Bernardino's **Emperors** and **Dave Myers and The Disciples**. One further 45 featuring one side by the **Menn** and one by Sunday, may or may not be connected - *Happy Happy Birthday / You Cheated* (Sidewalk 922) 1967. (MW/RM)

Mephistopheles

Personnel:
- DARYL BURCH — drms — A
- GORDON GRANT — piano, organ — A
- SKIP MOSHER — bs, flte — A
- BOB SILLER — gtr, vcls — A
- STEVEN SIMONE — gtr, vcls — A
- FRED TACKETT — gtr, piano, tpt, vcls — A

ALBUM: 1(A) IN FRUSTRATION I HEAR SINGING (Reprise 6355) 1969 -

45s: Cricket Song/Take A Jet (Reprise 832) 1969

This melodic soft-rock album is good background listening but lacks anything to differentiate it from the 'also rans'. Many of the tracks, including the two which were selected for the 45, have quite an immediate appeal. Recorded at The Sound Factory, Hollywood and produced by Dave Hassinger it is pleasant but not essential.

Fred Tackett later became a renowned session musician and played with the second formation of Little Feat. (VJ/SR)

The Merced Blue Notes

Personnel incl: GARY GRUBB (DUNCAN) — A

45s:			
(from 1962)	Rufus/Your Tender Lips	(Accent 1069)	1962
	Midnight Sessions(Part 1)/(Part 2)	(Tri-Phi 1011)	1962
	Whole Lotta Nothin'/Fragile	(Tri-Phi 1023)	1963
	Notes Thompin'/Rufus, Jnr.	(Galaxy 738)	1965
	Mama Rufus/Bad Bad Whisky	(Galaxy 744)	1965

From the East Bay of San Francisco, this band made other 45s for Frantic. This early to mid 1960s R&B outfit is of interest to fans of psychedelia only because Gary Grubb (nee Duncan) was a short time band member prior to his tenure in **The Brogues**. He does not appear on any **Merced Blue Notes** recordings and they were never known as The Merced Blues Band.

MERKIN - Music From Merkin Manor LP.

In the eighties, a private label anthology of the bands' recordings was issued with extensive liner notes and old photos; there is no mention of Gary Grubb or Gary Duncan anywhere on that album.

You'll also find *Rufus Jnr.* on *Sounds Of The Sixties San Francisco, Vol. 1* (LP). (VJ/HS)

Mercy

Personnel incl: JACK SIGLER Jr — vcls — A

45s:			
	Love (Can Make You Happy)/Fire Ball	(Sundi 6811)	1968
α	Love Can Make You Happy/ Happy As Can Be (La La La)	(Warner Bros. 7291)	1968
α	Forever/The Morning Comes	(Warner Bros. 7297)	1968
	Heard You Went Away/Hello Baby	(Warner Bros. 7331)	1969

NB: α also released in France with PS by Vogue.

This Florida pop-rock act with male/female vocals was fronted by a young student, Jack Sigler Jr. The group got noticed by a local producer and made a cameo in the movie 'Fireball Jungle', singing *Love Can Make You Happy*. That lead them to be signed to Warner Bros., who reissued the song. Their third single is rather poppish and was produced by Brad Shapiro and Steve Alaimo, two local businessmen and producers who also worked with the **31st of February** and several other local groups. (SR)

The Mercy Boys (aka The Mersey Boys)

Personnel:
- STEPHEN ALCOMBROCK — ld gtr — A
- JIM BRADY — ld vcls — AB
- FRED COOK — keyb'ds — AB
- STEVE GEDDIS — drms — A
- GARY PETERSON — drms — AB
- GARY SNYDER — bs — A
- TERRY CRAIG — gtr — B
- LARRY GADLER — bs — B

45s:		
Mercy, Mercy/Lost And Found	(Panorama 24)	1965
Long, Tall Shorty/This Girl	(Panorama 45)	1966
Spoonful/Gimmie Gimmie	(Merrilin 5300)	1967

From Everett, Washington, this band is notable for having two drummers. Prior to their formation, Gary Snyder had played with The Dynamics and Stephen Alcombrock had been in Tom Thumb & The Casuals. They split in November '67, when Jim Brady joined **The Sonics**.

Their finest moment *Long, Tall Shorty* is captured on *Battle Of The Bands, Vol. 1* (LP), *Northwest Battle Of The Bands, Vol. 1* (CD), *Northwest Battle*

Of The Bands, Vol. 1 - Flash And Crash* (CD) and *The History Of Northwest Rock, Vol. 4* (LP). Other compilation appearances include: *Mercy Mercy* on *Northwest Battle Of The Bands, Vol. 2* (CD); *Spoonful* on *The Garage Zone, Vol. 1* (LP) and *The Garage Zone Box Set* (4-LP); and an alternate version of *Lost And Found* on *Northwest Battle Of The Bands, Vol. 2* (CD). (DR/MW)

Merda

See the **Black Merda** entry.

The Merging Traffic

See **The Romans** entry for details.

Merkin

Personnel:	KENT BALOG	bs	AB
	ROCKY BAUM	gtr, vcls	AB
	RALPH HEMINGWAY	ld vcls	AB
	DOUG HINKINS	ld gtr	A
	ALAN NEWALL	drms	A
	GARY BALOG	drms	B
	ROBERT BARNEY	ld gtr	B
	RICHARD LEAVITT	keyb'ds	B

ALBUM: 1(B) MUSIC FROM MERKIN MANOR
(Windi WLP 1005 AB) 1973 R3

NB: (1) counterfeited on vinyl (Merkin MERK 1001) 1994 in the UK and 1999 in Italy, and reissued officially (Akarma AK 049) 1998 and on CD (Gear Fab GF-109) 1997, with three bonus tracks.

Only 200 copies of this album were pressed so it's now a rare collectable. There's some good guitar work on a few of the tracks, most notably *Walkin, Todaze, Watching Man* and *The Right One*, but much of material is light-weight. Worth a listen if you ever get the opportunity but don't fork out megabucks for a copy.

The band were formed in 1967 in the small town of Orem, Utah by Rocky Baum and Ralph Hemingway. By 1969, they'd recruited a full line-up and began playing local gigs. In 1970, with new guitar, drums and the addition of keyboardist Richard Leavitt, they cut two demos, *Maybe Someday* and *Cry On My Shoulder* at a Brigham Young University. Both of these have now resurfaced on the Gear Fab CD and are arguably better than the later album cuts.

The following year the band sent out a number of live tapes, in the hope of getting a deal, and sure-enough found themselves recording the album at an L.A. studio, although they were only given four days to complete the task! After a short tour of Colorado, the album was finally released in February 1973, but a dispute over the song-writing credits caused Rocky Baum to be ousted, and by 1974 the band had gone their separate ways.

Today Al & Ralph are now steelworkers, Robert plays in a band called Head First, Rocky is a chief organic chemist and Rod a business development manager.

Compilation appearances include *Maybe Someday* on Gear Fab's *Psychedelic Sampler* (CD). (VJ/SR)

The Merlynn Tree

Personnel:	ANDY BROWN	gtr	A
	BILL JOSEPH	ld gtr, vcls	A
	WAYNE McMANNERS	drms	A

45: Look In Your Mirror/How To Win Friends   (Dixietone 6794) 1967

Formed in Austin, Texas, in 1966. In the Summer of 1967 they went to Austin Studios and recorded two songs which were released on the local polka/C&W Dixietone label. They changed their name to **Troy** in 1969 and released a single before calling it quits after graduating in 1971.

Compilation appearances include *Look In Your Mirror* and *How To Win Friends* on *Back From The Grave, Vol. 8* (CD) and *Back From The Grave, Vol. 8* (Dble LP). (VJ)

Merrell and The Exiles

Personnel:	JEFF COTTON	gtr, vcls	A
	JOHN DAY	organ, vcls	A
	BILL DODD	gtr, vcls	A
	MERRELL FANKHAUSER	vcls, gtr	A
	JOHN FRENCH	drms	A
	JIM FURGUSON	bs	A
	GREG HAMPTON	drms	A
	DICK LEE	drms	A
	DAN MARTIN	drms	A
	JOHN OLIVER	bs	A
	MARK THOMPSON	gtr, keyb'ds	A
	LARRY WILLEY	bs, vcls	A

ALBUMS: 1(A) THE EARLY YEARS 1964-1967
(American Sound AS-1000) 1995
2( ) WILD IN THE DESERT   (Lance L-4001) 2000

NB: (1) also issued as (Legend LM9006) 1995. (1) and (2) may contain the same material.

45s: Sorry For Yourself/I Saw Suzie Crying   (Glenn 313) 196?
Please Be Mine / Too Many Heartbreaks (Glenn Records) 1964
Don't Call On Me / Send Me Your Love (Glenn Records) 1964
α Can't We Get Along /
That's All I Want From You   (Golden Crown) 1965

NB: α could be by another group.

Created by Merrell Fankhauser in 1964 after he arrived in Lancaster and the Antelope Valley area, **Merrell and The Exiles** are probably more interesting historically than for purely musical reasons. Born in Louisville, Kentucky on the 23rd of December, 1943, Fankhauser had previously lived on the California Coast, in Pismo Beach. There he began playing surf music, even winning the Arroyo Grande Battle of the Bands in March 1962 and being part of the Sentinals and the Impacts (one instrumental album *Wipe Out!* (Del-Fi 1234) 1963).

In Lancaster, Fankauser met Jeff Cotton, John French and Larry Willey and they became **Merrell and The Exiles**. Their first recordings took place in a small studio in Palmdale, California, Glenn Recording Studios, which were owned and directed by Glenn MacArthur. All the songs were recorded live on two track tape. In April 1964, *Please Be Mine* was No. 9 in the local Palmdale station KUTY charts! In all, three singles were recorded for Glenn Records and pressed in very limited quantities.

MERRELL and THE EXILES - The Early Years LP.

More **Merrell and The Exiles** sessions took place in Hollywood in 1966 at the Gary Paxton Studio and in 1967 at the Gold Star Studio with a changing line-up. Some of their songs (*Too Many Heartbreaks*, *Suzy Cryin*) were in fact released on the **Fapardokly** album, another Fankhauser creation. The other songs however, had to wait until the eighties before they were released in various forms.

Bill Dodd also played with Fankhauser in **Fapardokly** and **H.M.S. Bounty**. John French and Jeff Cotton left to join **Captain Beefheart's Magic Band**, another group from the High Desert area, but in 1970 Cotton rejoined with Merrell to form **MU** (also with Larry Willey). Greg Hampton also later played with Denny King.

The retrospective *Early Years* album consists largely of surf and garage rock tracks. Aside from the few 45 tracks, the majority were previously unreleased. *Don't Call On Me* is notable for featuring the first guitar solo ever recorded by then fledgling guitarist Jeff Cotton. *Yes I Love You*, another cut on this album was originally intended for inclusion on the **Fapardokly** album but wasn't used in the end. This album is primarily of archival interest, however. (SR/VJ)

Jerry Merrick

Personnel:
CHET AMSTERDAM	bs	A
HUGH McCRACKEN	gtr	A
JERRY MERRICK	vcls, gtr	A
ARTIE SCHROECK	drms	A

ALBUM: 1(A) FOLLOW   (Mercury SR 61208) 1969 -

Although Jerry looks quite rural on the front cover, his record is hitherto unnoticed downer folk (including some efficient rock implants) with a few rather moving melodies to the front. Tasteful orchestrations and a fairly subdued atmosphere make for unobtrusive, but agreeable listening. A track like *The Pond* crosses **Tim Buckley** with Donovan, but without the compelling force of the first or the fairy mood of the latter. Uneven, but worth a spin. (MK)

Merrie Motor Company

Personnel incl:
CINDY FITRO	A
PETE FULLENWIDER	A

45s:
Walkin' Down This Road To My Town/Dream Of You	(Scott 3050)	196?
Walkin' Down This Road To My Town/Dream Of You	(Decca 32320)	1967

A Michigan (Lansing) pop-psych group, with male/female vocals and a kind of "Wall Of Sound" production on the 'A' side, which was written by Al Shackman. (Al played guitar on some **Pearls Before Swine** albums). The flip, a Pete Fullenwider song, is slower, with nice guitar. The 45 was a Scott Production, picked up by Decca. (SR/DRt)

Bobby Merritt

ALBUM: 1 OUT OF THE CROWD   (Musicor MS 31??) 1969 ?

A strange mix of drug folk (*I'm So High*, *Poppin' Pills*) and arranged pop, with some fuzz guitars and flute. (SR)

Merry Airbrakes

Personnel:
BERT CAREY	bs	A
RAY ESSLER	drms	A
BILL HOMANS	vcls, gtr, hrmnca	A
PETER HOMANS	gtr	A
BOB O'CONNELL	gtr	A
(LINDLEY GOOLRICH	vcls	A)
(BILL HEILINGMANN	perc	A)
(TED LA BOMBARD	gtr, organ	A)
(KEN WARNER	piano	A)

ALBUM: 1(A) MERRY AIRBRAKES
                    (St. George International ST 06) 1973 R4

NB: (1) first pressing issued in plain white cover. Second pressing from 1979 including insert (R4). The covers on the second issue were decorated with a simple woodblock-print design, in various colours. Some of these were printed on both sides, some only on the front. The vinyl pressings are indistinguishable; the value therefore must be considered equal! (1) reissued on vinyl (Shadoks Music 002) 1999 and CD in 2000.

Merry Airbrakes is a collection of works by Bill Homans, with some assistance from his brother Peter. Homans recorded this album after his tour of duty in Vietnam, and subsequently joined up with an organisation called 'Vietnam Veterans Against The War' that travelled across the USA during the seventies. Most of the copies of this album were distributed by hand during his travels. Musically, the album is steeped in traditional American folk and blues that feature Homan's gritty vocals, harmonica and slide guitar prominently. The record is decidedly uncommercial lyrically, revealing its underground intent through the course of its ten tracks which read like snapshots of an unusual life.

St. George International was an East Coast label and the *Merry Airbrakes* album is a local Massachusetts release. (CF)

Merry Dragons

45: Let's Sail Away/Smokey/Universal Vagrant   (ABC 10838) 1966

A Los Angeles-based studio project assembled by producer Denny Lambert. You'll also find *Universal Vagrant* on *Pebbles Vol. 5* (CD) and *Pebbles, Vol. 5* (LP). (VJ)

Merry-Go-Round

Personnel:
GARY KATO	ld gtr	A
JOEL LARSON	drms	A
EMITT RHODES	keyb'ds, bs	A
BILL RINEHART	bs, gtr	A

                                                                        HCP
ALBUMS: 1(A) YOU'RE A VERY LOVELY WOMAN-LIVE
                                        (A&M 4132) 1967 190 -
        2(A) BEST OF MERRY-GO-ROUND
                                        (Rhino RNLP 125) 1985 - -
                                                                        HCP
45s:
Live/Time Will Show The Wiser	(A&M 834)	1966 63
We're In Love/Gonna Fight The War	(A&M 857)	1967 -
You're A Very Lovely Woman/Where Have You Been All My Life?	(A&M 863)	1967 94
She Laughed Loud/Had To Run Around	(A&M 886)	1967 -
She Laughed Loud/Come Ride, Come Ride	(A&M 889)	1967 -
Gonna Leave You Alone/Listen, Listen	(A&M 920)	1968 -

MERRY AIRBRAKES - Merry Airbrakes LP.

THE MESMERIZING EYE - Psychedelia... LP.

Listen, Listen/Missing You	(A&M 920)	1968 -
Highway/'Till The Day After	(A&M 957)	1968 -
You're A Very Lovely Woman/ 'Till The Day After	(A&M 1254)	1971 -

This Los Angeles soft-rock outfit contained some very talented musicians. **Rhodes** had played drums for **The Palace Guard**, an early to mid-sixties L.A. outfit, when he was just fifteen. Larson joined from **The Turtles** and Rinehart from the Gene Clark Group. All three went on to either solo careers or, in Larson's case, session work.

Their style was clearly influenced by British beat outfits like The Beatles and The Zombies but it did not suffer from this. *Time Will Show The Wiser*, in particular, was one of the lost pop masterpieces of the sixties with its backwards guitar intro, brilliant harmonies and catchy melody. Most of the later 45s weren't on the album but many are included on the Rhino compilation which is the most accessible source to their music.

Emitt Rhodes continued into the seventies as a solo artist issuing four albums and several 45s. If your bag is finely crafted pop then look no further.

Time Will Show The Wiser was also a keystone of Fairport Convention's early repertoire and you'll find a great version of the track on their eponymous debut album.

Compilation appearances include: *Live* and *You're A Very Lovely Woman* on *More Nuggets* (CD), *Nuggets Box* (4-CD), *Nuggets, Vol. 4* (LP) and *Excerpts From Nuggets* (CD); and *You're A Very Lovely Woman* on *Nuggets, Vol. 3 - Pop* (LP). (VJ/JFr)

The Mersey Beats U.S.A.

Personnel incl:			
STEVE FERGUSON	ld gtr		AB
CHAUCEY HOBBS	keyb'ds		A
DON SZYMANSKY	drms		ABC
BOB WEBB	bs		ABC
BOB YATES	vcls		ABCX
TERRY ADAMS	keyb'ds		B
GARY FUST	keyb'ds		C
RICK MICKA	ld gtr		C
RUDY HELMS	ld gtr		X
DUTCH KIRCHNER	drms		X
RON REED	keyb'ds		X
JOHN WILSON	bs		X

45s:			
You'll Come Back / Nobody Loves Me That Way		(Top Dog 2313)	1966
Does She Or Doesn't She / Stop, Look And Listen		(Top Dog)	1966
30 Second Lover / Nobody Loves Me That Way		(Top Dog 2322)	1967

Formed in Shively, Kentucky, circa 1963 as The Squires, the group Anglicized their name in 1965 to the **Mersey-Beats U.S.A.** and adopted the English Invasion sounds. *You'll Come Back* and *30 Second Lover* did well on the local charts.

In late 1966, Ferguson and Adams left and joined **The Seven Of Us**, a group of New Yorkers who'd relocated to Miami; a couple of years later they'd evolved into **NRBQ**. The **Merseybeats USA** continued until the end of the decade, going through a long succession of line-ups with Bob Yates the constant factor.

Compilation appearances include *Nobody Loves Me That Way* on *Bad Vibrations, Vol. 1* (LP & CD) and *Fuzz, Flaykes And Shakes, Vol. 3* (LP & CD). (MW/JLh)

The Merseylads

45:	What'cha Gonna Do/Jonny No Love	(MGM K 13481) 1965

A great garage-pop 45, produced by **Tom Wilson** and written by Kooper/Levine. The band featured Dave Heenan, a U.K. ex-pat from Newcastle, who'd later form **The Dave Heenan Set**.

Compilation appearances include: *What'cha Gonna Do Baby* on *The Lost Generation, Vol. 2* (LP). (VJ)

The Mersey Men

Personnel incl:	AL CATLOS	ld gtr	A
	RON FLORY	ld gtr, drms	A

45s:		
I Can Tell/Miss Ann	(Wildwoods 2001)	1965
Take A Heart/Hey Little One	(Wildwoods 2002)	1965

This group was from Salem, Ohio. Their manager moved from Salem to Lawton, Oklahoma and got the group on an extended tour through Oklahoma and Texas. The two records, which are fine 45s in garage-beat style, were recorded in Robin Hood Brians' studio in Tyler, Texas.

In addition to the two records, lead guitarist Al Catlos played in an earlier band called The Renegades who recorded a good instrumental 45. The group also backed a Canton, Ohio singer named Glen Jester on a record (credited as **Glen Jester and The Mersey Men**).

Probably their best effort *I Can Tell* has also resurfaced on *Boulders, Vol. 11* (LP) and *Ya Gotta Have Moxie, Vol. 2* (Dble CD). (VJ/GGl/MW)

Mersey Sounds

45s:		
Get On Your Honda And Ride / Honda Holiday	(Montel-Michelle 966)	1966
More Wrong Than Right / Two Lips	(Montel-Michelle 981)	1966
The Train / Young Lovers	(Mon-Art MM-992)	1967

A Baton Rouge, Louisiana, combo whose debut was in surf/hot-rod mode. Their cover of **The Five Americans**' *The Train* is in dramatic 'big ballad' style but retains a garagey aura with cheesy keyboards and a neat fuzz solo - you can also find it on *Basementsville! U.S.A.* (LP). (MW)

The Mesmerizing Eye

ALBUM:	1	PSYCHEDELIA - A MUSICAL LIGHT SHOW
		(Smash MGS 27090) 1967 R1

Another, obscure studio band whose only recording known to the author was the above mentioned album. A low budget cash-in on 'psychedelia', more wacky than weird sometimes, with effects like bagpipes (!?) cropping up. Some tracks stand out, notably *Requiem For Suzy Creamcheese* (a popular subject then), *Rain Of Terror* and *Dear Mom, Send Money*, which predates Pink Floyd's *Money* with the same cash register sounds. It makes **The Unfolding**'s album sound brilliant!

All the tracks on the album were written and produced by Hank Levine and Larry Goldberg, making it almost certainly some relation to the other phantom group **Fire Escape**. The remaining members are unknown, but the band were from Hollywood. Levine and Goldberg also produced **The Other Half** and **Neighb'rood Childr'n**. (VJ/SR)

The Messengers

Personnel incl:	PETER BARANS	gtr, bs	A
	GREG JENNINGS (JERESEK)	bs	A
	AUGIE JURISHICA	drms	A
	JESSE ROE	organ	A
	JEFF TAYLOR	vcls	A
	MIKE DEMLING	drms	
	ROB LESLIE	organ	
	MICHAEL MORGAN	organ	

NB: Above line-up as "Milwaukee Messengers".

ALBUM:	1( )	THE MESSENGERS	(Rare Earth 509) 1970 -

HCP

45s:	α	Midnight Hour/Hard Hard Year	(U.S.A. 866) 1967 -
	β	In The Midnight Hour/Up Til News	(U.S.A. 866) 1967 116
		Romeo And Juliet/?	(U.S.A. 874) 1967 129
		Window Shopping/California Soul	(Soul 35037) 1967 132
		I Gotta Dance / Right On	(Home Made 01) 1969 -
		That's The Way A Woman Is/	
		In The Jungle	(Rare Earth 5032) 1971 62

NB: β was a second pressing of α shown as by **Michael and The Messengers**.

Originally from Milwaukee, they cut *Midnight Hour/Hard Hard Year* (U.S.A. 866) at Chicago's U.S.A. Studios in 1967. Almost immediately afterwards they signed to Motown records, becoming the first white group to do so. However, with the U.S.A. 866 release doing pretty well, the record company needed someone to promote it, so they signed **Michael and The Messengers** from Boston and re-recorded *Midnight Hour* with a different flip side. The **Messengers** had a lean spell at Motown, but eventually re-emerged with further recordings on its Rare Earth label.

The personnnel listed comprise the "Milwaukee Messengers" who were responsible for the recordings above but who are also inextricably tangled up with the other Messengers/Michael and The Messengers groups, originating from Minnesota and Massachusetts. Gary Myers had made a comprehensive attempt to unravel this Gordian knot in his excellent book on Wisconsin fifties and sixties bands 'Do You Hear That Beat' (Hummingbird Pub. 1994, ISBN 0-9643073-9-1) and with whose permission the personnel and discography above has been clarified.

Both sides of their privately-pressed 45 on Home Made can be heard on *A Journey To Tyme, Vol. 5*. (VJ/MW/GM)

The Messengers

Personnel:	CHIP ANDREWS	keyb'ds	AB
	GREG BAMBENEK	ld gtr	A
	ROY BERGER	gtr	AB
	GREG JERESEK	bs	AB
	JIM MURRAY	drms	AB
	JOHN CARTER	ld gtr	B

45:	My Baby/I've Seen You Around	(Soma 1427) 1965

This crew formed in Winona, in South-Eastern Minnesota near the Wisconsin border in 1963. They took their name from a C.B. radio called the Viking Messenger. Predating **The Ferraris** by a few months they were actually Winona's first rock'n'roll band and were quite a spectacle at the time as they wore olive green woollen blazers on stage.

Early in 1965 they signed to the Minneapolis-based Soma Records. Just 1,000 copies of their 45 were pressed so it's now quite hard to find.

Greg Bambenek left the band in June 1965 to attend college to train to become a shrink and John Cader replaced him on guitar for the twilight days of the band.

Greg Jeresek started another band called The Messengers in Milwaukee, Wisconsin. They released an upbeat cover version of Wilson Pickett's *In The Midnight Hour* on 45 and an album on Motown (becoming the first white act to record on the label). Roy Berger later played in **New World Congregation** and went on to manage another Winona band, **The Ferraris**.

Compilation appearances have included: *I've Seen You Around* on *Root '66* (LP), *Soma Records Story, Vol. 2* (LP) and *Teenage Shutdown, Vol. 2* (LP & CD); and *My Baby* on *Soma Records Story, Vol. 3* (LP); *I've Seen You Around* and *My Baby* on *The Big Hits Of Mid-America - The Soma Records Story* (Dble CD). (VJ)

Metamorphosis

ALBUM:	1	DYNAMIC ARENA	(London) c1973 -

Previously known as **Symphonic Metamorphosis**, this obscure group played a mix of heavy prog with jazz influences.

Taro Meyer

ALBUM:	1	TARO MEYER	(RCA) 1973 -

Housed in a nice cover, a weird hippie-chick with songs like *The Penetration Limited*, *When The Lotus Was In Flower* and *Stripped Down To My Senses*. (SR)

M.H. Royals

Personnel incl:	B. FREIMUTH
	ERNIE LeBEAU
	TERRY LeBEAU

45s:	Tomorrow's Dead/She's Gone Forever	(ABC 10907) 1967
	Old Town/Now She's Crying	(ABC 10957) 1967

This bunch hailed from around Chicago and shared the same publishers (Pamco Music) and producer (Johnny Pate) as that of **The Trolls** (aka **Troll**). These are two fine 45s - the first is pleasant garage-beat but both sides of the second are excellent mid-tempo punkers with a ferocious fuzz solo in *Old Town*, a song about the city's club district.

Ernie LeBeau himself writes: "Thanks for listing my band from the sixties. I am quite busy performing and recording with my current band **Ernie LeBeau & The Beach Blasters**, and have a few records out including one called *Everybody's Shaggin'* which is sort of instrumental in bringing back a R&B style of music called Beach Music which was popular in the East from the forties - seventies. I'm also in the process of releasing a remake of

TEENAGE SHUTDOWN Vol. 2 (Comp LP) including The Messengers.

Sinatra's *It Had To Be You*. Producer Johnny Pate was also producer for The Impressions during their heyday with B.B. King on guitar, and was last heard of living in the U.K. working with old R&B acts." (MW/EB)

Micah

ALBUM:	1	I'M ONLY ONE MAN	(Sterling Award) 1970 R2/3

45:	I'm Only One Man/		
	So You Can See	(Sterling Award ST-103) c1969

The album features bluesy psychedelic guitar with organ jams. The 45 is interesting keyboard-dominated prog-rock 'psych' with many shifts and the occasional good solo. From New York City. (VJ/MW)

Michael

45s:	Will You Ever Change?/	
	Love Is Just Around The Corner	(Cinema 007) 1966
	Will You Ever Change?/	
	Love Is Just Around The Corner	(Cinema 11) 1967
	Arkansas/Checkerboard	(Cinema 23) 1967

This Houston-based quartet were originally known as The Glass Kans. Early copies of their first 45 came in a picture sleeve. The *Arkansa* 45 was a rock'n'roller. (VJ)

Michael

45s:	My Last Day/I'm Nobody's Man	(J-Beck 1007) 1966
	Gotta Make My Heart Turn Away/	
	People See It	(J-Beck 1008) 1967
	Gotta Make My Heart Turn Away/	
	I'd Only Laugh	(Roulette 4735) 1967

This was actually Mike Taylor who played in Corpus Christi in the mid-sixties with **The Bad Seeds** and later went on to **The Zakary Thaks** and **Bubble Puppy**. *The History Of Texas Garage Bands, Vol. 5 - Corpus Christi Rarities* (CD) (phew!) includes his 45 tracks - two in unreleased version form - plus an unreleased *If I Were A Man*.

Other compilation appearances include: *People See It* and *My Last Day* on *Green Crystal Ties, Vol. 1* (CD). (VJ/MW)

Al Michael and The Medallions

Personnel incl:	AL MICHAEL	vcls	ABC
	JERRY HENDERSON	vcls	C
	TOM LAICHE	vcls	C

45s:	α	I Wanna Talk To You / Better Forget Her	(Bragg B-222) 1965
	β	I Wanna Talk To You/	
		If I Had A Record Machine	(Apollo no #) 1965
	χ	Something You Said To Me /	
		Waiting For You	(Apollo AM-007/8) 1966

NB: α as **Michael and The Medallions**. β as **Al Michael and The Medallions** and features a different version of *I Want To Talk To You*. χ as **Swinging Medallions featuring Al Michael**.

I Wanna Talk To You is cool jangley beat - the Bragg 45 version is on *Leaving It All Behind*, the Apollo take is on Eva's *Louisiana Punk Groups From The Sixties, Vol. 2* (LP). Their compilers still disagree as to which is the better version.

Confusion reigns as to their origins too: - Eva's placement in Louisiana is probably due to this Apollo label being distributed by Dover Records out of New Orleans; some have connected them to (or confused them with) frat-kings **The Swingin' Medallions**, of *Double Shot* fame, who were from Greenwood (some say Greenville) South Carolina; another says they're a different outfit from Birmingham, Alabama.

Can anyone resolve this? (MW)

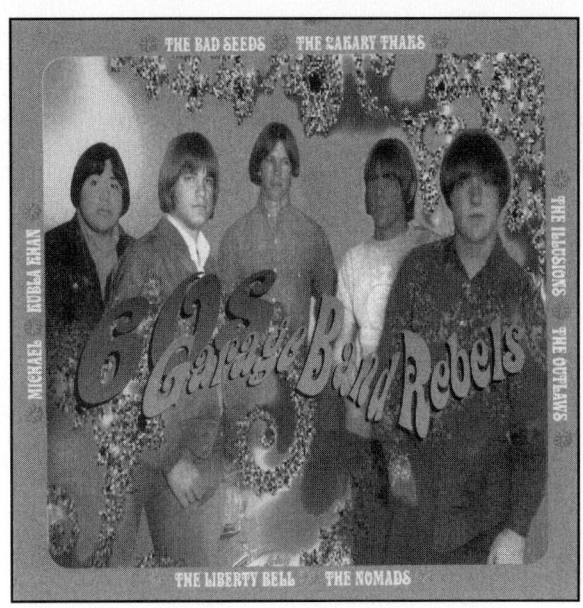

GREEN CRYSTAL TIES Vol. 1 (Comp CD) including Michael.

Michael and The Messengers

Personnel:	WAYNE BECKNER	vcls	A
	JACK DeCAROLIS	organ	A
	PAUL "MICHAEL" CORENZA	drms	A
	TOMO FINI	gtr	A
	RON GAGNON	bs	A
	JERRY GOODMAN	gtr	
	KEN MENEHAN	gtr	

				HCP
45s:	α	Midnight Hour/Hard Hard Year	(USA 866) 1967	-
		Midnight Hour/Up Till News	(USA 866) 1967	116
	β	(Just Like)Romeo And Juliet/		
		Lifs (Don't Mean Nothing)	(USA 874) 1967	129
		Run And Hide/She Was The Girl	(USA 889) 1967	-
		Gotta Take It Easy/I Need Her Here	(USA 897) 1968	-

NB: α recorded by the Milwaukee **The Messengers**, the other 45s recorded by group personnel above. The label for β misspells the 'B' side as 'Lifs' - presumably intended to be 'Lies'!

Originally from Milwaukee, and known simply as **The Messengers**, they cut *Midnight Hour/Hard Hard Year* at Chicago's U.S.A. Studios in 1967. Almost immediately afterwards they signed to Motown records, becoming the first white group to do so. However, with the U.S.A. 866 45 doing pretty well, the record company needed someone to promote it, so they signed so they signed another group. Gary Myers' book 'Do You Hear That Beat' reveals that this was the Del Mars (line-up 'A' above), who were originally from Leominster, Massachusetts. They were a club band on the New England/New York circuit who were heavily influenced by **The Rascals** and **The Vagrants**. Signed up by Premier Talent they re-recorded *Midnight Hour* with a different flip side and were responsible for the later singles on USA listed above. To get an idea of the tangled web surrounding the various **(Michael and The) Messengers** groups, look no further than the aforementioned 'Do You Hear That Beat'.

Their final 45, featured *Gotta Take It Easy* which was written by Bob Stanley of **The Bryds**.

Compilation appearances have included: *Romeo And Juliet* on *Nuggets Box* (4-CD), *Nuggets - Original Artyfacts From The First Psychedelic Era 1965-1968* (Dble LP); and *Life (Don't Mean Nothin')* on *Vile Vinyl, Vol. 2* (LP) and *Vile Vinyl* (CD). (MW/JSa/GM)

Michaelangelo

Personnel:	ANGEL	autoharp, vcls	A
	STEVE BOHN	gtr, vcls	A
	ROBERT GORMAN	bs, vcls	A
	MICHAEL JOHN HACKETT	drms	A

ALBUM:	1(A)	ONE VOICE MANY	(Columbia C 30686) 1971 -

45s:	300 Watt Music Box/Half A Tap	(Columbia 4-45328) 1971
	West/It's Crying Outside	(Columbia 4-45459) 1971

Delicate and melodic baroque soft-rock with a mellow hippie aura. Vocally not unlike the softer moments of the **Peanut Butter Conspiracy** or **Comfortable Chair**. Where they came from is unknown, though some of the credits hint at it being recorded in New York City. To be taken in the drawing-room with perfumed tea. (MW)

Lee Michaels

Personnel:	GARY DAVIS	organ	A
	EDDIE HOH	drms	A
	JOHN KESKI	bs	A
	LEE MICHAELS	piano, organ, harpsichord, bs, vcls	AB
	HAMILTON WESLEY WATT	gtr	A
	JOHN BARBATA	drms	B
	FRANK DAVIS	drms	B
	LARRY KNECHTEL	bs	B
	DRAKE LEVIN	gtr	B

HCP

ALBUMS:	1(A)	CARNIVAL OF LIFE	(A&M SP 4140) 1968 - SC
	2(B)	RECITAL	(A&M SP 4162) 1968 - -
	3( )	LEE MICHAELS	(A&M SP 4199) 1969 53 -
	4( )	BARREL	(A&M SP 4249) 19?? 51 -
	5( )	5th	(A&M SP 4302) 1971 16 -

NB: (2) also issued in Germany (A&M 212054) 1968.

45s:	Hello/Love	(A&M) 1968
(up to	Sounding The Sleepin/Tomorrow	(A&M) 1968
1969)	If I Lose You/My Friends	(A&M) 1968
	Goodbye/The War	(A&M) 1969

Born on the 24th of November, 1945 in Los Angeles, **Lee Michaels** began in the early sixties with The Sentinals, a surf group from San Luis Obispo. In 1966, he joined the **Joel Scott Hill Trio** and then **Family Tree**.

His first album is an excellent example of California psych-pop with inventive keyboards parts. One track, *Love* was also covered by **The Novells**, whilst the guitar player is Hamilton Wesley Watt of **Euphoria**.

Lee Michaels' later albums were commercially successful and more pop-oriented. On his second, he was assisted by **Drake Levin** (ex-**Paul Revere and The Raiders**), John Barbata (ex-**Joel Scott Hill and The Strangers**). Frank Davis also played drums with **Cold Blood** and **Loading Zone** but is not the same guy as the **Travel Agency** leader.

Compilation appearances include *Hello* on *Nuggets, Vol. 11* (LP). (SR)

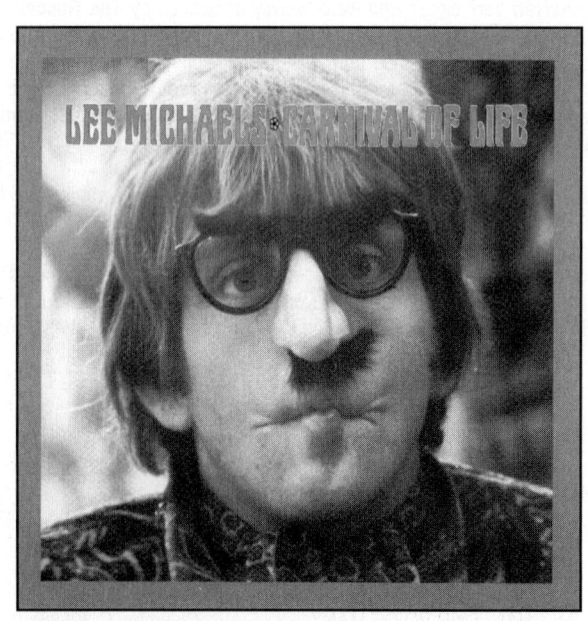

LEE MICHAELS - Carnival Of Life CD.

Nancy Michaels

ALBUM:	1 FIRST IMPRESSIONS	(Reprise RS 6380) 1969 -

A soft psych-folk singer with songs like *White Devil*, *It Slips Away*, *Tired Of Waiting* and *Fantasy*. Sometimes compared to **Linda Perhacs**, although it's not as interesting. (SR)

Michael's Mystics

45:	Pain/But It's All Right	(Charlie no #) c1969

An obscure Minnesota garage band, their single was reissued by Metromedia in 1970. (SR)

Michele

Personnel:	LOWELL GEORGE	flute, hrmnca	A
	ELLIOT INGBER	gtr	A
	MICHELE O'MALLEY	vcls	A
	MIKE MELVOIN	arrangements	A
	BOBBY NARCOFF (NOTKOFF)	elec. violin	A

ALBUM:	1(A) SATURN RINGS	(ABC ABCS-684) 1969 SC

Michele had previous been in **Ballroom** along with **Curt Boettcher**. Produced by **Mike Deasy**, the album also benefited from heavy **Curt Boettcher** involvement, as he wrote or co-wrote nine of the eleven songs (*Lament Of The Astro Cowboy*, *Musty Dusty*, *Misty Mirage*). Musically it's in a West-Coast psych-folk style with dreamy vocals, strange lyrics (*Song To Magic Frog*) and interesting instrumental parts. In particular, there are some Eastern trappings with tabla and electric violin on *Fallen Angel* and the 8'05" *Lament Of The Astro Cowboy*.

Three of the songs *Would You Like To Go* (B. Jameson), *Song To A Magic Frog* (M. O'Malley) and *Musty Dusty* (C. Boettcher and T. Almer) were also included on the Usher and **Boettcher** produced **Sagittarius** *Present Tense* album. Strangely enough *Would You Like To Go* was here credited to **Boettcher** and Gordon Alexander (of **Association** fame). Another track *Spin, Spin, Spin* was resurrected from their earlier **Ballroom** 45 and *Believe You* (**Boettcher**) also deserves a listen for its dreamy psych-vibed melody.

The album comes housed in a nice "astral" picture sleeve designed by Dean Torrence (ex Jan and Dean) of Kittyhawk Graphics.

Reputedly **Michelle** was also a witch of sorts, said by some witnesses to have flown over L.A. in company with **Boettcher** on one occasion. This story apparently scared the shit out of **Sandy Salisbury** at the time. Despite the writing credits, **Bobby Jameson** didn't compose *Would You Like To Go* but was involved with this album somehow, probably along with the **Millennium** crew, with uncredited vocal backings.

Lowell George was previously in the **Factory** and the **Mothers Of Invention**, Elliot Ingber in the **Mothers Of Invention**, **Captain Beefheart** and **Fraternity Of Man**, and Bobby Notkoff was in the **Rockets**. Mike Melvoin, apart from being a busy and talented session keyboardist, was also the man behind the exotica classic *The Plastic Cow Goes Moog*!

Michele who now teaches singing among other things in L.A. (SR/CP/JFr)

Mick and The Shambles

Personnel incl:	MICHAEL JOYCE	A

45:	Lonely Nights Again/ Girls Girls Girls	(Verve Folkways 5010) 1966

From Philadelphia, an obscure one-off venture on this label. Mike was Michael Joyce, who produced and co-wrote the 45 with Robert Youngs.

You can also find *Lonely Nights Again* on *Psychedelic Unknowns, Vol. 5* (LP & CD) and *Lost Generation, Vol. 1* (LP). (VJ/MW/SR)

MICHELE - Saturn Rings LP.

Middle Earth

45:	Bitter Sweet/About You	(Mutual 110) c1966

From Philadelphia, produced by Sam Hodge Jr at Virtue Studios, this obscure group covered a **P.F. Sloan**/Steve Barri song that was also recorded by **The Robbs**. (SR)

The Mid-Knighters

Personnel:	KEITH DREHER	gtr	A
	BILL HAKOW	bs	A
	CHARLIE LEWONDOWSKI	keyb'ds	A
	MEL LUNDIE (LEWONDOWSKI)	drms	A
	JIMMY ROSSETTI	vcls	A
	JOHNNY VEER (VERBRAKEN)	electric piano	A

45s:	Baby My Heart/More Than I Can Say	(Key 1003) 1961
	Charlena/Flower Of Love	(Paragon 814) 1962

Hailing from Milwaukee in Northern Wisconsin, this outfit was one of several to cover *Charlena*, an early sixties greasy R&B tune originally recorded by The Sevilles from the San Francisco area. The song was a minor hit in Canada for Richie Knight and The Mid-Knights and this crew probably thought they'd profit by putting out their own version and using a slightly modified version of the Canadian outfit's name.

Verbraken was later in (Ray Allen and) The Trendells who were based in the Racine/Kenosha area. Dreher moved on to (Big Louie and) The Renegades and then The Walking Sticks.

You'll also find their version of *Charlena* on *Highs In The Mid-Sixties, Vol. 15* (LP). (VJ/MW/GM)

The Mid-Night Sons

Personnel:	TERRY ANDERSON	ld gtr	A
	CHUCK EFFINGER	keyb'ds	A
	LEE DITMER	drms	A
	MARK GENSMEN	sax	A
	DAN LOWTHER	bs	A

45s:	Draft Time Blues/I'm Telling You	(KG 100) 1966
	Draft Time Blues/??same as above??	(Jerden ?) 1966

Evolved out of **The Jackasses** in Vancouver, Washington. They opened concerts for many top sixties acts and did a three month tour with Gary Lewis and The Playboys. The 45 was a rework of Eddie Cochran's *Summertime Blues* and got quite liberal airplay in the Northwest. The group ended when three of its members were drafted. Chuck Effinger was last reported playing for Vancouver band 10K Gold. (VJ)

Midknights

45s:	Mamie Lou / ?	( ) 1965
	Pain/Why	(Style 2001) 1966

A high school band who won their way into a regional tour and got themselves signed by Style Records of Chattanooga, Tennessee, although they were originally from Broken Pump, Iowa. This explains why their teen-rocker *Pain* has resurfaced on *Highs In The Mid-Sixties, Vol. 8 - The South* (LP) and *Teenage Shutdown, Vol. 2* (LP & CD). (VJ/MW/MM)

Midnight Sam

Personnel incl: MIKE CUSSACK

EP:	1	Heartbreak Survivor/Moonglow/My Imagination/ You Ain't Leaving Me	(Green Mountain 12165) 197?

A hippie foursome from Laurens, Iowa, whose EP released in the early seventies was notable for good guitar work. (VJ)

Midnight Snack

45:	Mister Time / Jenny Adaire	(Corby Cr-220) 1967

According to *Fuzz Flaykes & Shakes, Vol. 1* (LP & CD), this band hailed from Hawthorne, California (Beach Boys-ville). It compiles *Mister Time*, a decent pop-punker with **Doors**' keyboard vibes. The flip is a disjointed pop novelty with Vaudeville moves. Both sides were composed by Tom Sack. (MW)

Thee Midniters

Personnel incl:	GEORGE DOMINGUEZ	ld gtr	A
	JIMMY ESPINOZA	bs	A
	RONNIE FIGUEROA	organ	A
	WILLIE GARCIA	vcls	A
	ROY MARQUEZ	gtr	A
	ROMEO PRADO	trombone	A
	LARRY RENDON	sax	A
	GEORGE SALAZAR	drms	A

ALBUMS:	1(A?)	THEE MIDNITERS	(Chattahoochee CS-1001) 1965 SC/R1
	2( )	BRING YOUR LOVE SPECIAL DELIVERY	(Whittier W-5000) 1966 -
	3( )	UNLIMITED	(Whittier W-5001) 1966 -
	4( )	THE GIANTS	(Whittier W-5002) 1967 -
	5( )	BEST OF	(Rhino RNLP 063) 1983 -

HCP

45s:	Land Of A Thousand Dances (Parts 1 and 2)/ Ball Of Twine	(Chattahoochee 666) 1965 67
	Heat Wave/Sad Girl	(Chattahoochee 674) 1965 -
	Heat Wave/Sad Girl	(Chattahoochee 675) 1965 -
	Whittier Boulevard/Evil Love	(Chattahoochee 684) 1965 127
	I Need Someone/Empty Heart	(Chattahoochee 693) 1965 -
	It's Not Unusual/That's All Brother, Where Are You?/ Heat Wave	(Chattahoochee 694) 1965 - (Chattahoochee 695) 1965 -
	Are You Angry?/I Found A Peanut	(Chattahoochee 706) 1966 -
	Love Special Delivery/Don't Go Away (PS)	(Whittier 500) 1966 -
	It'll Never Be Over For Me/ The Midnite Feeling	(Whittier 501) 1966 -
	Dragon-Fly/The Big Ranch	(Whittier 503) 1966 -
	Never Knew I Had It So Bad/ The Walking Song	(Whittier 504) 1967 -
	Jump Five And Harmonise/ Looking Out A Window	(Whittier 507) 1967 -
	Chile Con Soul/Tu Despedida	(Whittier 508) 1967 -
	Breakfast On The Grass/ Dreaming Casually	(Whittier 509) 1967 -
	Make Ends Meet/	

	You're Gonna Make Me Cry	(Whittier 511) 1967 -
	The Ballad of Cesar Chavez (Part 1)/	
	(Part 2)	(Whittier 512) 1967 -
	Chicano Power/	
	Never Goin' To Give You Up	(Whittier 513) 1967 -
α	She Only Wants What She Can Get/	
	I've Come Alive	(UNI 55170) 1969 -

NB: α released as **Midnighters**

This Mexican-American band operated out of Los Angeles. They enjoyed some minor chart success early on with *Land Of A Thousand Dances (Part 1)* and *Whittier Boulevard*, before switching to their own Whittier label. All four albums are now minor collectors' items with *Bring Your Love Special Delivery* the most likely to interest readers of this book.

Both sides of their final 45 were penned by K. Morill, who is believed to have been a member of the Cascades.

Compilation coverage has so far included: *Dragon-Fly* on *Diana's Rootin' Tootin' Wild Teenage Rock 'N' Roll Party!* (LP); *Never Knew I Had It So Bad* on *A Journey To Tyme, Vol. 2* (LP); *House Of Wax* on *East Side Revue*; *I Found A Peanut* on *Teenage Shutdown, Vol. 3* (LP & CD); and *Jump, Jive, And Harmonize* on *Teenage Shutdown, Vol. 1* (CD). (VJ/JO/EW)

Midwest

Personnel incl:	DANNY HOLIEN		A
45:	Heaviness/Alibis	(Metrobeat 4460) 1970	

A Minneapolis-based project essentially for **Holien**'s benefit. They were essentially a power rock trio and *Heaviness*, which you'll find on the *The Best Of Metrobeat! Vol. 1* (LP), is a fine sample of the genre.

Holien had previously fronted another Minneapolis outfit, **The Shades**, in the mid-sixties. In 1971, he also recorded a solo album for Tumbleweed. (VJ/SR)

Jack Miffleton

Personnel incl:	JACK MIFFLETON	gtr, vcls	A
	SKIPP SANDERS		A
ALBUM:	1(A) SOME YOUNG CARPENTER		
		(WLSMFR-2242 SM) 1970 ?	

From Cincinnati, Ohio, a religious psychedelic folk album recorded with male/female vocals, acoustic and electric guitars, bass, drums and occasional organ. The album contains several protest songs, like the antiwar *Revolutionary Peace* with machine gun shots and ambulance sounds. (SR)

Mighty Manfred and The Wonderdogs

45:	Bo Diddley/		
	By The Time I Get To Phoenix	(Paris Tower 140) c1969	

An obscure garage group. The 'A' side is a good cover of this classic song, but the flip is rather lame. (SR)

Mij

Personnel:	JIM HOLBERG	vcls, gtr	A
ALBUM:	1(A) COLOR BY THE NUMBER	(ESP-Disk 1098) 1969 R1	

NB: (1) has been reissued on CD

Well, it's E.S.P. time and again strange doesn't begin to describe this. Basically a record of a man and his guitar, this album manages with the simple means of vocals, guitar playing, whistling and some studio effects (loads of echo everywhere) to create a compelling listening experience. Unlike on any other release by this label that I know of, the music is quite straightforward in itself. The opening *Two Stars* sounds common enough, but the seven-minutes plus *Grok* (martian love call), evidently partly sung in Martian too, sees the singer diving through inner space with dexterity and courage. At times vaguely reminiscent of the British songwriter Simon Finn, Jim journeys along through a set of disconcerting songs that all sound like far-out space-rock played on acoustic guitar only. Extremely soft passages turn up unexpectedly and odd dissonances occur. *Little Boy* has a slightly untuned guitar and jarring stops. *Never Be Free* has disquieting repetitive phrases and the long *Look Into The (K)Night* has a spectral and disjointed way of playing. Balancing precariously between terror and bliss, this is one of the still undiscovered psychedelic records that must be pigeon-holed like that on the strength of the uncompromisingly psychedelic inner attitude of the player. Practically incomparable to anything else, this comes recommended for adventurous listeners. (MK/SR)

Mijal and White

45:	I've In You/Reflections	(Zatop 2208) 196?	

A character called Mike Mijal later produced some 45s for **Salem Witchcraft**, but it's unknown if the two **Mijal**'s are in any way connected.

Compilation appearances include: *I've In You* on *Lycergic Soap* (LP), *Turds On A Bum Ride Vol. 1 & 2* (Dble CD), *Turds On A Bum Ride, Vol. 2* (Dble LP), *Echoes In Time, Vol. 2* (LP), *Echoes In Time Vol's 1 & 2* (CD). (MW)

Mike's Messengers

45:	Gone And Left Me/		
	Cause Of All Mankind	(EL-EZ-DE 122579) 196?	

The 'A' side of this obscure 45 deals with the singer's indifference to his woman's departure. You can also hear it on *Back From The Grave, Vol. 7* (LP). The flip is a more sensitive folk-punk exploration of society's troubles. (VJ)

Milan (The Leather Boy)

as 'Milan':

45s:	I Am What I Am/		
	Over And Over Again	(20th Century Fox 487) 1964	
	Angel's Lullabye/		
	Runnin' Wild	(20th Century Fox 552) 1965	
	Cry, Lonely Boy/Luva-Luva	(ABC Paramount 10718) 1965	

as 'World Of Milan':

45s:	Follow The Sun/I'm Cryin' In The Rain	(Brunswick 55292) 1966	
	One Track Mind/Shades Of Blue	(Brunswick 55298) 1966	

as 'Milan (The Leather Boy)':
45:     My Prayer/You Gotta Have Soul   (Flower FLO 100) 1966

as 'Leather Boy':
45s: Jersey Thursday/Black Friday   (Parkway 125) 1966
        I'm A Leather Boy/Shadows   (MGM 13724) 1967
        On The Go/Soulin'   (MGM 13790) 1967

Real name reportedly Rick Rondell, an interesting late-fifties/early-sixties style greaserocker whose 45s are sought-after. The later biker-rock 45s adopted some appealing garage sounds but purists should note that the earlier **Milan** and **World of Milan** 45s (prior to the Flower label 45s) are best avoided, though the *One Track Mind* 45 has its moments.

Based in New York City he also produced many other acts, e.g. **Downtown Collection** and **Head Shop**.

Compilation appearances have included: *I'm A Leather Boy* on *Mayhem & Psychosis, Vol. 1* (LP) and *Mayhem And Psychosis, Vol. 1* (CD), *Pebbles, Vol. 3 (ESD)* (CD); *I'm A Leather Boy* and *On The Go* on *Pebbles, Vol. 10* (CD); *Shadows, You Gotta Have Soul* and *I'm A Leather Boy* on *Pebbles, Vol. 11* (LP); *On The Go* on *Wavy Gravy, Vol. 1* (CD) and *Wavy Gravy, Vol. 2* (LP & CD); *On The Go* and *Soulin'* on *A Journey To Tyme, Vol. 5* (LP), *Garagelands, Vol. 1* (LP) and *Garagelands, Vol. 1* (CD); and *Shadows* on *Pebbles Box* (5-LP) and *Trash Box* (5-CD). (VJ/MW)

The Mile Ends

Personnel:
MIKE McFADDEN	vcls, gtr, hrmnca	ABC
GEORGE ALEXANDER	gtr	ABC
RICHARD MICKEL	gtr	ABC
STEVE "WALLY" FRESENER	bs	AB
?? ??	drms	A
DANNY PACHECO	drms	BC
ED BLACK	bs	C

EP: 1 THE MILE ENDS   (Sundazed SEP 151) 2000

45s: Candy Man / Bottle Up And Go   (Fifth Estate 8447) 1966
     Ferris Wheel (one-sided demo)   (no label) 1967

From Phoenix, Arizona, this band landed regular gigs in '66 at The Fifth Estate (in Tempe, near Arizona State University), run by Jim Musil Jr. who became their manager. They also got a slot at nearby JD's, run by Jim Musil Sr.. Primarily a Stones cover band they opened for many national acts who played The Fifth Estate including the **Doors, Leaves, Association, Music Machine, Count Five, Them,** and **(Young) Rascals**. In the Summer they released their own 45 and got to play The Hullabaloo in L.A. after manager Jim arranged a weekend band swap (they played with the **Yellow Payges**, whilst **The Palace Guard** played at the Fifth Estate).

MIJ - Color By The Number LP.

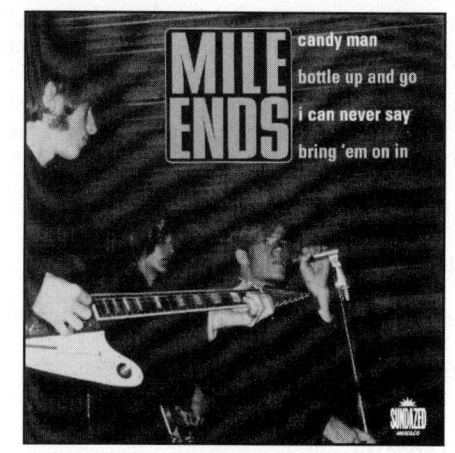

THE MILE ENDS - The Mile Ends 45 EP.

Late in '66 Fresener was replaced by Ed Black and the band's impetus was flagging. In December they started work on their first psychedelic effort, *Ferris Wheel*. Flute and strings were added in early '67 and **Mike Condello** was brought in by McFadden to help out on piano and vocals, but the rest of the band had faded away by then. 100 copies of a one-sided blank demo were pressed by Jim Musil.

It was the end of the **Mile Ends** but the beginning of **Superfine Dandelion**.

The R&B infused *Candy Man* has resurfaced on *Sixties Rebellion, Vol. 14* (LP & CD). The Stones-like and immensely catchy *Bottle Up And Go* is on *Ear-Piercing Punk* (LP & CD), *Best of Pebbles, Vol. 2* (LP & CD), *Trash Box* (5-CD) and *The Essential Pebbles Collection, Vol. 1* (Dble CD).

Both sides of the debut 45 plus the unreleased *I Can Never Say* (a Pretty Things cover) and *Bring 'Em On In* (a Them cover) are gathered together on the Sundazed EP. These also appear on Sundazed's **Superfine Dandelion** CD (Sundazed SC 11057, 2000) with two versions of *Ferris Wheel*. (MW)

Buddy Miles Express

Personnel incl:
BUDDY MILES	vcls, drms, gtr	ABC-
TERRY CLEMENTS	sax	A
MARCUS DOUBLEDAY	trumpet	A
VIRGIL GONSALVES	sax	A
JIM McCARTY	gtr	ABC
BOB McPHERSON	sax	A
BILLY RICH	bs	A
HERBIE RICH	organ	A
RON WOODS	drms	A
DUANE HITCHINGS	organ	BC
CHARLIE KARP	gtr	C
(BOB PARKINS		
(BOB ISLAND)	keyb'ds	C)
(WALTER ROSSI	gtr	C)

HCP
ALBUMS:
1(A) EXPRESSWAY TO YOUR SKULL
                              (Mercury SR 61196) 1968 - -
2(B) ELECTRIC CHURCH   (Mercury SR 61222) 1969 145 -
3(C) THEM CHANGES   (Mercury SR 61280) 1970 35 -
4(-) WE GOT TO LIVE TOGETHER
                              (Mercury SR 61313) 1970 53 -
5(-) MESSAGE TO THE PEOPLE
                              (Mercury SRM 1608) 1970 60 -
6(-) LIVE   (Mercury SRM 7500) 1971 50 -

NB: (1) to (6) also released in the U.K..

Born in August 1968 out of the **Electric Flag**, the **Buddy Miles Express** tried to pursue the direction started by the '**Flag**, with a mix of rock, blues, soul and jazz, clearly built around **Buddy Miles**' personality. Their records were commercially successful and they managed to release six albums in four years, although the management of the group was quite erratic. *Them Changes* is reputedly their best effort. **Miles** often used talented musicians like Jim McCarty (ex-**Mitch Ryder**, pre-**Cactus**), Duane Hitchings (pre-**Cactus**) or Bob Parkins (Bob Island) and Walter Rossi (ex-**Influence**).

Buddy Miles also played with **Jimi Hendrix** on *Band Of Gypsies* and with Carlos Santana on a live album in 1972. He spent part of the late seventies in jail and subsequently tried to make a comeback several times. (SR/NW)

Milk and Honey

45:	Have A Nice Day/White Bird	(Magic 541-17) c1970

An obscure single seen described as electric psych-rock. (SR)

Milkwood Tapestry

Personnel:	ROLAND G. ANTONELLI	gtr, vcls	A
	JOSEPH LOUIS RANSOHOFF	ld vcls, tamb, maracas	A

ALBUM: 1(A) MILKWOOD TAPESTRY (Metromedia MD 1007) 1969

NB: (1) reissued on CD with 7 bonus tracks (Gear Fab GF-179) 2001.

An intriguing and above-par acid-folk-rock odyssey by this New York duo. They journey from the manic (*Beyond The Twelve Mile Zone*) etched by some excellent acid-guitar, to minstrel-like folk and baroque ballads, and back into heavy rock territory. An acquired taste for the adventurous palate, this certainly deserves wider appreciation.

And it came to pass that in 2001 that Roger Maglio at Gear Fab answered the call, tracked down Joe Ransohoff, and presented the duo's legacy on CD. The liner notes reveal that **Milkwood Tapestry** wove their idiosyncratic sounds from 1968 to 1972. Multi-instrumentalist Joe Ransohoff had studied music since the age of 14. He'd finished college, quit law school soon after and placed an ad in the Village Voice for a folk-rock songwriter. Roland Antonelli responded from Poughkeepsie and the two hit it off; Antonelli relocated to NYC the following year.

Starting on the NY club and coffee house circuit, they were spotted by Donovan's manager, who helped get them a contract with Metromedia. Tours on the college circuit across New York and New England followed, where they opened for the likes of **Country Joe McDonald**, Four Seasons, **Phil Ochs**, **Ten Wheel Drive**, NRBQ, **Tim Hardin**, Johnny Winter, **Rhinoceros** and **The Velvet Underground**. They also got to perform live on FM radio several times on the Alex Bennett Show.

Their material took on a more mediaeval vibe with the use of cello, tambourine and recorder, examples of which are to be found amongst the seven unreleased cuts dusted off by Joe Ransohoff for the CD reissue. (MW)

MILLENIUM - Begin LP.

Millard and Dyce

Personnel incl:	DYCE	vcls	A
	MILLARD	vcls	A

ALBUM: 1(A) MILLARD AND DYCE (Century - Kamar KS 7-265) 1973 R2

A privately - pressed local acoustic folk album from Baltimore, Maryland.

The Millennium

Personnel:	CURT BOETTCHER	vcls	A
	RON EDGAR	drms	A
	MIKE FENNELLY	gtr	A
	LEE MALLORY		A
	DOUG RHODES	organ	A
	SANDY SALISBURY	vcls	A
	JOEY STEC		A
	(KEITH OLSEN		A)
	(JERRY SCHEFF	bs	A)

ALBUM: 1(A) BEGIN (Columbia CS-9663) 1968 R1

NB: (1) reissued in Holland in 1976. (1) also reissued on CD (CBS Special Products WK 75030) 1990, with two unreleased tracks *Blight* and *Just About The Same* (covered by **The Association**). Also relevant are *Again* (Poptones MC5012CD) 2001 (CD) and *Again* (Dreamsville YDLP 0050) 2001 (LP); and *Magic Time: The Millenium/Ballroom Sessions* (3-CD) (Sundazed SC 11002) 2001.

45s:	I Just Want To Be Your Friend/ It's You (PS)	(Columbia 4-44546) 1968
	5.A.M./Prelude	(Columbia 4-44607) 1968
	There Is Nothing More To Say/ To Claudia On Thursday	(Columbia 4-44674) 1968

Curt Boettcher was a prodigious talent (sadly he died in 1987 at age 43) whose studio wizardry produced sounds and arrangements way ahead of any at the time and **The Millennium** album was the culmination of this period. He'd started out with the folk group **The Goldebriars** (two albums on Epic in 1964) then formed a vocal duo, Summer's Children, before getting into production which included **The Association**'s first album *And Then Along Comes* and their million-selling *Along Comes Mary* 45. From then until **Millennium** he was involved in a plethora of groups and studio projects:- **Ballroom** (with **Sandy Salisbury** and **Lee Mallory**), Your Gang and **Friar Tuck** (both with **Mike Deasy**), culminating in **Sagittarius** (with Gary Usher) which put out a lot of unreleased **Ballroom** material. In the seventies Curt would issue a solo album and form California but it's for his creative outburst in the mid-late sixties and those heavenly multi-layered vocal arrangements that he will be remembered.

Millennium then, were put together as a vehicle for **Boettcher**'s ideas with the intention to weld Fennelly and Stec's rock background with the avant-garde pop of **Mallory** and **Salisbury**. **Boettcher** was to 'Lead the way'... and there was a kind of evangelical fervour about it, best heard on their first single *It's You*. **Goldenrod** who are thought to have acted as a backing group to **Lee Mallory**, formed the basis of the remaining personnel, originally becoming involved as part of the "Our Productions" house band led by **Mike Deasy**.

Boettcher wrote almost half of the tracks on their pleasant pop-rock album, **Salisbury**, Fennelly, and **Mallory** providing most of the remainder, with Jerry Scheff from **Goldenrod** contributing *Dandelion* (not on the album) to their repertoire. The album took a year to record and was only the second album ever done on 16-track (Simon and Garfunkel's *Bookends* being the first). Columbia Engineer Roy Halee had pioneered the technique by jerryrigging two eight-track recorders with a third machine feeding the two.

Stylistically, the album is in the mould of **Sagittarius**, with the standout cut being the astonishing *Karmic Dream Sequence #1*. A true voyage into the infinite and six of the most magical minutes that sixties music has to offer. Group member **Sandy Salisbury** describes the song: "This piece still evokes everything I felt in those days, from ecstacy to amazement to downright fear. Though I never used drugs, I always felt somehow out of touch when I heard this song - still do. The only explanation for that feeling is that *Karmic Dream Sequence* somehow tells me that Life is far, far deeper and more fascinating than my limited human mind can comprehend

- it makes me want to explore, to experience, to feel, no matter how scary it gets".

When it looked like **Millennium** might become a full-time band, the **Goldenrod** members departed due to session commitments, and Edgar, Rhodes and Keith Olsen all previously with **The Music Machine** came into the frame.

The **Music Machine** personnel had early ties with **Curt Boettcher** as Edgar had been the **Goldebriars** drummer, Olsen an old friend of **Boettcher** had played with Gale Garnett and Jimmie Rodgers, and briefly with The Wayfarers, at whose club in Charleston the **Goldebriars** often played. Olsen also married **Goldebriar**' Sheri Holmberg, whilst Sean Bonniwell was the **Goldebriars** tour manager, and migrated to L.A. with them adopting their all-in-black, dyed black beatlecut look lock, stock, and barrel for **The Music Machine**.

Though **Millennium** never toured, 'The Lee Mallory Group', which consisted basically of **Goldenrod**, **Mallory**, **Salisbury**, Rhodes, Fennelly and Stec debuted much of the *Begin* material at the Pasadena Icehouse on a couple of occasions in late 1967, as a dry run for the projected live **Millennium** shows.

After being dropped by Columbia, **The Millennium** stayed together as a songwriting/production team, with **Boettcher**, Olsen, **Salisbury**, and **Mallory** joining the relaunched **Sagittarius**.

The protracted sessions for **Sagittarius**' *Blue Marble* in fact included sessions for a solo album by **Salisbury** and various other projects which were recorded back to back, including tracks for "Midnight Cowboy" written by **Millennium** members (primarily Stec and **Salisbury**) and Harry Nilsson, which were scrapped when their publisher fell out with the film producers (an album by 'The Groop' *Sing Songs From Midnight Cowboy* includes covers of the songs). Nilsson of course sang **Fred Neil**s *Everybody's Talking* as the theme, because Neil ironically refused to speed the song up.

Another project concurrent with **Sagittarius**' *Blue Marble* was an attempt to launch another offshoot named "Big Shot" fronted by Fennelly and including former **Goldebriar** guitarist Murray Planta. This petered out fairly quickly... Stec took up an offer from old friends **The Blues Magoos** to join full-time. He later worked as a writer with Steven Stills/CSNY, and made a solo album with Jimmy Miller. Fennelly started **Crabby Appleton**, signing to Elektra and enjoying some success. He also later made a solo album, *Lane Changer*, which was produced by Rod Argent and Chris White. **Salisbury** was a jobbing arranger before becoming a best selling childrens author.

As an aside readers might note that **Mike Deasy** of Your Gang recorded the creepy live tapes of Charles Manson at Spahn Ranch which did the rounds in Hollywood and cut a couple of studio sessions too. Oddly, the **Millennium** guys were part of **Frank Zappa**'s clique rather than the folk-rock crowd.

At long last **Curt Boettcher** and **The Millennium** have begun to garner long-overdue praise and attention. The *Begin* album has been reissued at least twice to astound and entrance new generations. In 1998, a retrospective of **Ballroom** appeared, aptly titled *Preparing For The Millennium* (Rev-ola CREV 058 CD). At the dawn of the new millennium Poptones put together the *Again* CD, a collection of unreleased demos and live performances, and three accompanying CDs of solo ventures: **Curt Boettcher** - *Misty Mirage* (MC5007CD), a collection of demos and outtakes; **Sandy Salisbury**'s unreleased solo album (MC5008CD); and a self-titled Joey Stec CD comprising 1976 recordings (MC5005CD).

Also in 2001 Sundazed put together the almost-complete 3-CD package *Magic Time: The Millennium/Ballroom Sessions*. This includes much of the **Ballroom**'s Rev-ola material plus unreleased **Ballroom** versions of **Millennium** tracks, the entire *Begin* album plus singles and outtakes, a couple of Summer's Children and **Sagittarius** tracks, and a handful of **Curt Boettcher** demos (avoiding overlaps with the Poptones CD). (VJ/MW/JFr/LP)

Patti Miller

ALBUM: 1 PATTI MILLER (Custom) c1970 ?

A folky soft rock female singer. (SR)

THE STEVE MILLER BAND - Children Of The Future LP.

Stephen Miller

ALBUM: 1 STEPHEN MILLER (Philips PHS 600-335) 1970 -

Stephen Miller was formerly the leader of **Linn County**. A gifted keyboard player, he is sometimes credited as Steve Miller but is totally unrelated to the "Gangster Of Love". He went on to play with the Southern rock group Grinderswitch (formed by the former roadies of the **Allman Brothers Band**) and is also featured on many Bay Area records.

His first solo album is reputedly a good blues-rock effort and is becoming sought-after. (SR)

The Steve Miller Band

Personnel:			
JAMES 'CURLEY' COOKE	gtr, vcls	AB	
TIM DAVIS	drms, vcls	ABCDEF	
STEVE MILLER	gtr, vcls	ABCDEFG H	
LONNIE TURNER	bs	ABCDE	
JIM PETERMAN	organ	BC	
BOZ SCAGGS	gtr, vcls	C	
GLYN JOHNS	gtr, perc, vcls	D	
BEN SIDRAN	keyb'ds	D	
BOBBY WINKELMAN	bs, vcls, gtr	F	
JACK KING	drms	G	
ROSS VALORY	bs	G	
ROGER ALLAN CLARK	drms	H	
GERALD JOHNSON	bs	H	
DICK THOMPSON	keyb'ds	H	

HCP

ALBUMS:				
(up to 1972)	1(C)	CHILDREN OF THE FUTURE	(Capitol SKAO-2920)	1968 134 -
	2(C)	SAILOR	(Capitol ST-2984)	1968 24 -
	3(D)	BRAVE NEW WORLD	(Capitol 184)	1969 22 -
	4(E)	YOUR SAVING GRACE	(Capitol 331)	1969 38 -
	5(F)	NUMBER FIVE	(Capitol 436)	1970 23 -
	6(G)	ROCK LOVE	(Capitol 748)	1970 82 -
	7(H)	RECALL THE BEGINNING A JOURNEY FROM EDEN	(Capitol 11022)	1972 109 -

NB: (1) reissued (Capitol SF-718) with different cover. (2) reissued as *Living In The USA* with a different cover (Capitol SF-719). There are numerous compilation LP's, of which *Anthology* (Capitol 11114) is probably the best. The band are also featured on *Revolution Soundtrack* (UA 5185) with: *Mercury Blues*, *Your Old Lady* and *Superbyrd*. More recently there has been a double live CD from their 'King Biscuit Flower Hour' radio broadcasts, *On Tour 1973-1976* (King Biscuit) 2002.

HCP

45s:			
(up to 1972)	Sittin' In Circles/Roll With It (PS)	(Capitol 2156)	1968 -
	Living In The USA/Quicksilver Girl	(Capitol 2287)	1968 94
	Dear Mary/Sittin' In Circles	(Capitol 2447)	1968 -

My Dark Hour/Song For Our Ancestors	(Capitol 2520) 1968	126
Don't Let Nobody Turn You Around/ Little Girl	(Capitol 2638) 1968	-
Going To The Country/ Never Kill Another Man	(Capitol 2878) 1969	69
Steve Miller's Midnight Tango/ Going To Mexico	(Capitol 2945) 1969	117
Rock Love/Let Me Serve You	(Capitol 3228) 1971	-
Fandango/Love's Riddle	(Capitol 3344) 1972	-

A child music prodigy, **Steve Miller** was born in Milwaukee, Wisconsin, but raised in Texas. Coming from a musical family - his mother was a singer and his father a country fiddler - **Miller** was learning to play guitar at the age of five. At twelve he played with Boz Scaggs in a local band The Marksmen. His music hero at this time was T-Bone Walker and **Miller** developed a strong interest in black music. Whilst Scaggs and he were both attending Wisconsin University, they formed a soul and Motown group - The Ardells. **Miller** then headed for Chicago where be became involved in the white blues scene. There he played in bands which featured Junior Wells, Muddy Waters and Buddy Guy. Eventually, he met up with **Barry Goldberg** (of **The Electric Flag**) and formed a group called World War Three which recorded a single, *The Mother Song*. They were beginning work on an album when **Miller** quit because of managerial troubles. He headed for Texas and also spent a while at Copenhagen University, but in 1966, like Joplin and so many others, he was attracted by the exciting music developments taking place in San Francisco. There with **Tim Davis** (drms), Lonnie Turner (bs) and **Curley Cooke** (rhythm gtr) he formed the first **Steve Miller Band**. This line-up contributed three tracks to the Soundtrack of *Revolution*, a cult film at that time. They developed the raw, driving sound which characterised the early 'acid' bands, yet the blues remained a strong influence in their music. This was particularly evident on one of the tracks, *Mercury Blues* (which reappears in more sophisticated form on the band's 1975 *Fly Like An Eagle* album), whilst the instrumental *Superbyrd* and *Your Old Lady* captured that driving guitar and organ sound.

The band made a successful appearance at the Monterey Pop Festival in June, 1967 and were soon offered a recording contract by Capitol. By now, old pal Boz Scaggs had replaced **Curly Cooke** in the band and organist Jim Peterman was included in the new fivesome. Surprisingly, **Miller** decided to go to London to record their excellent debut album *Children of the Future*. This was produced by Glyn Johns, who had helped engineer The Beatles' *Sergeant Pepper* album. His influence is evident throughout the album, which entirely lacked the 'live' atmosphere of so many of the early West Coast acid-rock albums, but attained an unequalled standard of production at that time among San Francisco bands. Of particular significance is the early use of psychedelic sound effects throughout Side One, with Peterman's fine organ work to the fore. The band had temporarily dropped its driving, bluesy rock in favour of a series of beautiful 'acid' ballad type numbers such as *In My First Mind* and *Children of the Future*. The use of sound effects are particularly prominent in the side's closing track *The Beauty of Time Is That It Is Showing*. The material on Side Two is similar to what they were playing before they left San Francisco, with each track merging into the following one. *Junior Saw It Happen* and two

THE STEVE MILLER BAND - Sailor LP.

THE STEVE MILLER BAND - Brave New World LP.

bluesy numbers - the fast *Fanny Mae* and the slow *Key To The Highway* - are the stronger tracks in this side. Over all, the album was extremely varied.

The group was busted while in London and returned to San Francisco to work on the follow-up, *Sailor*. This was more consistent than their earlier effort and, possibly, the group's finest album. The opening track *Song For Our Ancestors* was an instrumental which commenced with the sound of San Francisco bay's fog horns. *Dear Mary* featured **Miller**'s high-pitched vocals which came to characterise their more sensitive numbers. However, the album's most popular tracks proved to be dance number *Living in the USA*, a song, as its title suggests, about American life, and the self-descriptive *Gangster Of Love*. Its most melodic was the beautiful *Quicksilver Girl*, which opens Side two, while *Overdrive* was a Stones-like R&B number.

Boz Scaggs and Jim Peterman left the band in 1968 with Ben Sidran (keyb'ds) and Glyn Johns (gtr, perc, vcls) coming in for the third album, *Brave New World*. Johns also co-produced the album with **Steve Miller**. The title track featured the sound effects of both a rain and a sandstorm, but overall the album lacked the imagination and consistency of the band's two earlier efforts. Most of the songs were up-tempo boogies, but two notable exceptions were the beautifully laid-back number *Seasons* and *Space Cowboy*, later to become something of a classic.

The band's fourth album *Your Saving Grace* was also released in 1969. Ben Sidran and Nicky Hopkins assisted with its production. This was the last album the band recorded in San Francisco. *Just A Passing Fancy In A Midnite Dream* and *Don't Let Nobody Turn You Around* were up-tempo country-influenced numbers. Another track, *Feel So Glad*, featured Nicky Hopkins' dynamic keyboard-playing. But it is really the slower tracks that stand out on this album - the title song and two other sensitive numbers *Baby's House* and *Motherless Children*. Although more consistent than their previous effort, this album did not attain the heights of the first two albums and Lonnie Turner left the band, being replaced by Bobby Winkelman (ex-**Frumious Bandersnatch**). Ben Sidran also quit to go into producing and Nicky Hopkins joined The **Quicksilver Messenger Service**.

Miller left San Francisco with this new line-up and *Number Five* was recorded in Nashville, Tennessee and released in July 1970. Various Nashville sessionmen assisted on this album. However, at the turn of the sixties the music scene was beginning to change and this album shows the band struggling to keep apace with developments. The opening track *Good Morning* is noteworthy for its psychedelic intro and unusual ending - a variation on the *Christmas Carol God Rest You Merry Gentlemen*. Inevitably, others like *Going To The Country* and the excellent *Hot Chilli* echoed the influence of the Nashville music scene. The other stand-out number on the album was *Jackson-Kent Blues* featuring **Miller** on echoplex guitars and culminating in an interesting ending. Two other slower numbers are of note, *Steve Miller's Midnight Tango* and closing track *Never Kill Another Man*. The remaining material was dispensable, though, and overall this album was on a par with the previous two.

Further personnel changes took place, with Winkelman and Davis leaving, the latter to start a solo career. Their replacements Ross Valory (bs) and Jack King (drms), (both of whom had earlier been with **Frumious Bandersnatch**) recorded the disappointing *Rock Love*, but Valory then departed with Dick Thompson (keyb'ds), Roger Allen Clark (drms) and Gerald Johnson (bs), playing on their 1972 release *Recall The Beginning* and Ben Sidran returning to help in its production. By the end of the 1972 the band was at its lowest ebb, with possibly its best work to come.

The title track of their next album *The Joker* would become a U.S. No.1 elevating the band to new heights of popularity. After a three year recording lay off they returned with the excellent *Fly Like An Eagle* (Capitol 11497) and the similar but equally successful *Book Of Dreams* (Capitol 11630) (1977). Later the band acquired considerable popularity in the discos with the title track in their 1982 album *Abracadabra* (Capitol 12216).

Retrospective compilation appearances have included: *Dime-A-Change Romance* and *Living In The U.S.A.* on *Rock A Delics* (LP); *Mercury Blues* on *Texas Music, Vol. 3* (CD); and *Living In The U.S.A.* on *In The Beginning* (LP). (VJ/MW/FT/DQ)

Miller Bros.

45:	Jump Jack Jump/?	(Layne 203)	1961

A very obscure 45 from a Virginia band. You'll also find *Jump Jack Jump* on *Garage Punk Unknowns, Vol. 6* (LP). (VJ)

Mill Valley Bunch

Personnel:	MIKE BLOOMFIELD	gtr	A
	SPENCER DRYDEN	drms	A
	NICK GRAVENITES	vcls	A
	IRA KAMIN	bs	A
	KATHI McDONALD	vcls	A
	MARK NAFTALIN	keyb'ds	A
	MICHAEL SHRIEVE	drms	A

ALBUM:	1(A)	CASTING PEARLS	(Verve V 8825)	1973 SC

NB: (1) has been reissued on CD.

The result of massive bluesy jams between Bay Area musicians, this album was produced by **Nick Gravenites**, **Mike Bloomfield** and Leo De Gar Kulka. (SR)

Milwaukee Iron

Personnel incl:	ROGENE	vcls	A

ALBUM:	1(A)	MILWAUKEE IRON	(Milwaukee Iron KM-2137)	c1973 SC

MIND GARAGE - Again LP.

An album of "biker-rock" with female vocals on some tracks and songs like *Get Down Biker Music, Turn Me Over, Don't Turn Me Out, If I've Ever Seen A Biker He Is I, Cheezy Rider, Shovel Man, Get Down Fade Out* and *Jerk Me Off.* (SR)

Mind Distortions

A Chicago garage band who signed to Rembrandt Records but didn't make it onto vinyl at the time. However, *Chicago Garage Band Greats* (LP) includes their unreleased version of *Who Do You Love?* from 1968. (VJ)

The Mind-Expanders

ALBUM:	1	WHAT'S HAPPENING	(Dot 25773)	1967 SC

NB: (1) released in both mono (Dot 3773) and stereo. The mono versions are rarer.

A 'psychedelic' cash-in album recorded at Regent Sound Studios, New York City, by faceless musicians. Using such exotic instruments as "Panther Combo Organ, ondoline, chromatic tom-toms, Hohner melodica, Chinese bell tree, harpsichord, autoharp, kazoos, 'electric guitar with squawk box'... and two ashtrays". What they achieve is sometimes akin to cinema organ intermission muzak or laughably 'groovy' soundtrack sounds.

An O.K. version of *Pictures At An Exhibition* and *"Downtown" Trip* (a 'psych' version of Petula Clark's hit with fuzz guitar and traffic noises!) are amusing - titles like *Sensory Overload, Pulsation, Love Syndrome* and *Euphoria* add to the mirth. (MW)

Mind Garage

Personnel:	JACK BONASSO	keyb'ds	A
	NORRIS N LYTTON	bs, sax	A
	LARRY McCLURG	vcls	A
	TED SMITH	drms	A
	JOHN VAUGHAN	ld gtr	A

ALBUMS:	1(A)	MIND GARAGE-AN ELECTRONIC ROCK MASS	(RCA LSP-4218)	1969 -
	2(-)	AGAIN-ELECTRIC LITURGY	(RCA LSP-4319)	1970 -
45s:		Reach Out / Asphalt Mother	(Morning Glori 1000)	1968
		What's Behind Those Eyes/ There Was A Time	(RCA Victor 47-9755)	1969
		Jailhouse Rock/Tobacco Road	(RCA Victor 47-9812)	1969

From Morgantown, West Virginia. Although some of their material is psychedelic rock-pop, much is '69 class-of-brass too. The *Electric Liturgy* is reportedly along the same lines as the **Electric Prunes**' *Mass In F Minor* although **Mind Garage** were not aware of *Mass In F Minor* and had been performing their *Electric Liturgy* in churches for several years before they released the above album.

Larry McClurg: "My own contributions were original, and I assumed the others were also. **Mind Garage** collaborated on the *Electric Liturgy* at the suggestion of Reverend Michael Paine and his wife Tori. The idea was to bring the contemporary music into the church while attracting the young people who might not otherwise ever visit a church. We started as "garage" musicians and were not into ministry. In fact we were very much a part of the 'street'. As I remember, Reverend Paine explained the church seemed too far away from real life... "you shouldn't leave your humanity at the door" when you enter church."

"I believe we made a difference. At the time of our recording there was no Christian rock music industry. We played *Electric Liturgy* as a real Mass, live in churches in New York, D.C., even in the Princeton University Chapel, N.J., and in numerous other cities. Communion was given. Reverend Paine presided, and traveled with us, and convinced churches to allow us inside. There were also guest ministers.... As far as I know we were the only rock band doing that. It was unique. I have always felt we were the first. If there were any others we were not aware of them. If that is not true, we were certainly instrumental in the creation of Christian rock and roll, and hopefully examples to some of the Christian Rock musicians who followed. We were called Communists, devils, and many other names by our detractors, which included many people in the church, but we were also very much appreciated by a large following."

Their heaviest and finest moment, *Asphalt Mother*, has been re-aired on *A Lethal Dose Of Hard Psych* (CD) and *U-Spaces: Psychedelic Archaeology Vol. 1* (CDR).

Jack Bonasso continues his musical career and in recent years provides the entertainment on the Carribean cruise ships. Ted Smith spent years as tour drummer with The Spinners and still performs occasionally. John Vaughn finished college and still gigs. (MW/LM)

The Mind's Eye

Personnel:	BILL ASH	gtr	A
	LOUIS CABAZA	bs, keyb'ds	AB
	CHRIS HOLZHAUS	gtr	AB
	STEVE PERRON	vcls	AB
	ANDY SZUCH	drms	AB
	BENNY TRIEBER		AB
	(GAYLEN NILES	gtr	B)

45:   Help I'm Lost/Still In Love With You Baby   (Jox 058) 1967

An excellent, but sadly too short-lived psychedelic outfit from San Antonio, Texas. Perron, Cabaza and Holzhaus had all played with the band when they were earlier known as **The Argyles**. Bill Ash of **The Stoics** was also with the band for about eight months in 1967, although Chris Holzhaus played on their 45. The 'A' side was a psychedelic gem with swirling guitar/organ/violin crescendos and melodramatic vocals.

Gaylen Niles, who helped out on the 45, was a member of **The Outcasts**.

Towards the end of '67 the band became **The Children**.

Steve Perron co-wrote ZZ Top's hit *Francine* before his death in the early 1970s.

Compilation appearances include: *Help I'm Lost* on *Acid Dreams - The Complete 3 LP Set* (3-LP), *Acid Dreams Testament* (CD), *Acid Dreams, Vol. 1* (LP), *Texas Flashbacks, Vol. 3* (LP & CD)), *Flashback, Vol. 3* (LP) and *Highs In The Mid-Sixties, Vol. 12* (LP). (VJ)

The Mind's Eye

45:   Mind's Eye Theme /
          Donna, Where Can You Be   (Arlingwood 9567) 1967

All that has come to light so far is that this Jacksonville, Florida outfit released just one 45 produced by J. Atkins. The groovy fuzz-a-go-go *Mind's Eye Theme* with it's hip exhortations and hyena-like laughter can be heard on *Psychedelic States - Florida Vol. 2* (CD). It'd fit well on one of those Tower/Sidewalk exploito movie soundtrack albums. (MW/JLh/RM)

Mindy and The Complex

Personnel incl: MINDY DALTON   A

45:   Any Way That You Want Me / ?   (Athena 5011) 1969

This 45 featured Mindy Dalton from **The Feminine Complex**. (SR)

Minets (Of England)

45s: α   Secret Of Love/Together   (Rock It 200,054/5) 1964
          β   Wake Up/My Love Is Yours   (DCP Int'l DCP 1129) 1965

NB: α as Minets, β as Minets Of England.

British invasion garage-beat from the Boston area. The first 45 features a pair of tame ballads, but things pick up on the second 45 with the uptempo hand - clappin' *Wake Up*. They go back to sleep again with a sombre ballad on the flip. (MW)

The Minimum Daily Requirements

45:   I'm Grounded/
          If You Can Put That In A Bottle   (Tower 372) 1967

A one-off venture on Tower. You'll also find the 'A' side on *Psychedelic Unknowns, Vol. 6* (LP & CD). (VJ)

The Minitmen

45:   Smokin' In The Boys Room/Rollin' In Money   (Rust 5103) 1965

A short-lived New York outfit. The 'A' side is a little unusual with percussion work and humming guitar, indeed it features some quite elaborate solo trade-offs between the lead guitar and drummer, but it doesn't really come off overall. You'll also find it on *Mindrocker, Vol. 8* (LP). Rust was a subsidiary of Laurie Records. (MW)

Minnesoda

Personnel incl: DON LEHNHOFF   trombone   A

ALBUM: 1   MINNESODA   (Capitol ST-11102) 1972 -

This album was recorded by a Minnesota group called Copperhead, but before it's release, they learn't of the ex-**Quicksilver Messenger Service Copperhead** and changed names to **Minnesoda**.

Trombonist Don Lehnhoff had settled in Minnesota after being auditioned by **Mitch Ryder**. **Ryder** first came to Baltimore in 1966 to put together a replacement for **The Detroit Wheels**. He auditioned several well-known Towson (a North Baltimore suburb) blue-eyed soul bands to form a new group which he called the Mitch Ryder Show. Eventually they all disbanded, but the trombonist Don Lehnhoff made his home in Minnesota. (SR/JV)

Minnie and The Kneebones

Me and My Miniskirt, which has resurfaced on *Girls In The Garage, Vol. 4* (LP), was written by Bill Martin and Phil Coulter, who wrote hits for The Troggs and other English groups. It was released on a small L.A. label in July 1966. To further confuse matters, there's a French EP by Karen Young and the Kneecaps which includes the same two titles on the 45. A fairly well - known Karen Young was recording in England around this time, and although her other stuff sounds nothing like this, I suspect a connection.

MINT TATTOO - Mint Tattoo LP.

The Minority

| 45: | Where Was My Mind?/High Flyer | (Hyperbolic 105) 1969 |

Nothing has come to light so far about **The Minority**. The Hyperbolic ("presents Underground") label was run by Mike Archer, formerly of Fort Lauderdale's Busy Signals.

Where Was My Mind? is on *Psychedelic Unknowns, Vol. 5* (LP & CD). The chaotic fuzz freakout *High Flyer*, composed by Luther Robinson, is on *Psychedelic States: Florida Vol. 3* (CD). (VJ/MW)

The Mint

Personnel:	DANNY BAUCUM	bs	A
	CLAY CUNNINGHAM	drms	A
	RANDALL PHILLIPS	vcls	A
	STEVE SAINTON	keyb'ds	A
	JIMMY WALLACE	ld gtr	A

This teenage outfit came from Dallas. They recorded two tracks, *Can't Be Free* and *We're Friends*, which both feature sleepy vocals superimposed on an effective guitar and organ backing. They originally appeared on the rare *A New Hi - Dallas 1971 - Part 1* compilation.

Retrospective compilation appearances have included: *Can't Be Free* and *We're Friends* on *Endless Journey - Phase Two* (LP) and *Endless Journey - Phase I & II* (Dble CD). (VJ)

Mint Tattoo

Personnel:	RALPH BURNS KELLOGG	bs, keyb'ds, vcls, perc	A
	BRUCE STEPHENS	gtr, vcls, kazoo	A
	GREGG THOMAS	drms, perc	A

ALBUM: 1(A) MINT TATTOO (Dot DLP 25918) 1969 -
NB: (1) also issued on CD (Akarma AK 015).

| 45: | Talking About You/Mark Of The Beast | (Dot 17242) 1969 |

The album was produced by James William Guercio and recorded at A&R Studios, New York. The two 45 cuts are taken from the album, which I've never rated highly. It's a blues - influenced offering with occasionally good guitar work but it rarely ascends above mediocrity. During 1969 Kellogg and Stephens departed for **Blue Cheer** and Gregg Thomas later played with **The Fabulous Rhinestones**. (VJ)

The Minute Men

| 45: | Good Things Must End/Disillusion | (TMM no. #) 1968 |

A Houston outfit whose *Disillusion* doesn't quite gel and lives up to its name. Some great fuzz but after a great intro of crashin' chords that promises a ravin' fuzz-rocker it immediately drops down a coupla gears to a midtempo pace with tweeting *96 Tears* keyboards. Reprises of the intro break in again but the clumsy time changes can't recover the initial impetus. Good but it could have been great. The flip is a more accomplished minor-mood garage ballad. Both sides sound more they're from '66 rather than '68.

Compilation appearances have included *Disillusion* on *Punk Classics* (CD) and *Flashback, Vol. 6* (LP). (MW/AB)

The Minute Men

| 45: | Yes I Will/Lat-In-Da | (Minutemen Records) 1965 |

From the Boston suburbs, this 45 from 1965 has the moody organ complete with girl gone bad lyrics. (BB)

Mirthrandir

ALBUM: 1 FOR YOU THE OLD WOMEN (No label) 1976 R2

From New Jersey, an album of progressive rock with flute, keyboards, long tracks and lots of rhythm changes. (SR/CF)

The Misfits

| 45: | Mess Around/Bari Blues | (Agar 7130) 1964 |

From Minneapolis, this act were one of the more popular Minnesota live acts of 1964. *Mess Around* captures their lively enthusiasm for pre-invasion beat, with great driving power and a cool sax break. (BM)

The Misfits

Personnel:	RONNIE ARMSTRONG	drms, vcls	ABCDEF
	EDDIE DUNN	gtr, vcls	AB EF
	BOB MOSLEY	gtr, vcls	ABCD
	EARL STEELY	bs, vcls	A F
	CLIFF WHITT	bs, vcls	B E
	MIKE LAWSON	bs, vcls	CDEF
	"RANK FRANK" SMITH	keyb'ds	C

| 45s: | This Little Piggy/Lost Love | (Imperial 66054) 1964 |
| | α The Uncle Willie/Big Bad Wolf | (Troy 222-101) 1965 |

NB: α shown as by The San Diego Misfits.

This seminal San Diego, California band is best known for containing **Moby Grape** founding member **Bob Mosley**. Initially called The Hooters, the band changed their name when they secured a residency at the prestigious Red Coat Inn - significant in that they were the first rock group to break into San Diego's upscale nightclub scene, in the Summer of 1964.

Closely tied to local contemporaries **Joel Scott Hill** and The Invaders (their drummer Willie Kellogg was the inspiration for the second **Misfits** 45!), it was the inevitable merging of these two groups, along with **Hill**'s friend Peter Lewis, that created the first pre-**Moby Grape** line-up in Los Angeles and came to the attention of Matthew Katz. **The Misfits** and The Invaders played together often in the mid-sixties, including a riotous show with The Rolling Stones in 1964.

The Misfits are remembered more for their wild performances than their singles, which (while competent) are somewhat burderned with overdubbed applause and do little to support their reputation as rowdy punks. **The Misfits** was an apt name for these guys - Dunn and Steely were known to start fights with each other just for entertainment (the "sandwich incident" got particularly ugly) and **Mosley** once leapt into the audience and choked a guy that wasn't paying attention when he was rendering a ballad! Apparently this was one wild band.

THE MISFITS (San Diego).

THE MISFITS (San Diego) and THE ROLLING STONES.

The Misfits played live extensively up and down the West Coast into 1966 and have no shortage of funny stories to tell of their adventures. For example, after **Mosley** made Armstrong the object of ridicule on stage one night, Armstrong hid a tape recorder recorder under **Mosley**'s bed and captured his tryst with a groupie... which he later played at a party for everybody to hear!

Ron Armstrong (diminutive and ordinarily mild-mannered but nicknamed "Knuckles" by **Mosley** after landing a rare punch directly to the mouth of a heckler, knocking him out cold) went on to the Jamul City Funk Band, later known simply as **Jamul**.

Frank Smith was previously with **The Vejtables**. Mike Lawson joined "Uncle Willie" Kellogg in **The Five # Grin**, and later still was a member of The Docker Hill Boys (see **Joel Scott Hill** entry).

Compilation appearances have included *The Uncle Willie* on *California Acid Folk* (Dble LP). (CF)

Missing Links

45: Where Were You Last Night?/
Get Out Of My Life   (Paris-Tower 115) 1967

From Tampa, Florida. You'll also find *Where Were You Last Night?* on *Garage Punk Unknowns, Vol. 5* (LP). (VJ/MW)

Missing Links

Personnel incl: SAM DeSANTOS   keyb'ds, vcls   A

ALBUM: 1(A) AT THE 5 O'CLOCK LOUNGE (Fleetwood 3012) 1965 R2

A prep-rock style album of garage/soul covers including the obligatory *Louie, Louie* and *For Your Love*. The band were a five piece from Salisbury Beach, Massachusetts and the album, which was produced by Bobby Herne, is now extremely rare. It wasn't however recorded live as the title suggests.

After the album, DeSantos went on to **The Ones**. He and MacPherson (also from **The Ones**) later formed Atlantis in 1970 with Bobby Herne. (MW/AH/JC)

Missing Links

45: You Hypnotize Me /
Makin' Up And Breakin' Up   (Signett no #) 1966

Jim "Soul" Holvay, the main force behind **The Mob** and the composer of *Kind Of A Drag* for **The Buckinghams**, wrote and produced both sides of this 45 as a demo. Holvay has confirmed that this is not the Rockford, Illinois outfit (as reported in Tom Tourville's Chicago book) but were a local Chicago band and that at least three members went on to form **Chicago (Transit Authority)**. The 45 is very rare - to the extent that Holvay was not even aware that it had been released. Thankfully, You Hypnotize Me can be found on Arf! Arf!'s *No No No* (CD) compilation. (MW/GM)

Missing Links

45: Under My Thumb / Get Ready   (Marek 676) 1967

And another **Missing Links**, this time from Rockford, Illinois and not connected to the pre-Chicago group above. Tom Tourville reports that this was one of the best Rockford 45s of the period and is very hard to find - neither side has been compiled to-date. Another version of *Get Ready*, by Rockford rivals **Iron Gate**, was released almost simultaneously. (MW/GM)

The Missing Links

Personnel: GEORGE MESECKE   organ   A
            JOE PARISI   drms   A
            DENNIS RAFFELOCK bs   A
            LARRY RUBENSTEIN ld gtr   A
            AL VERTUCCI   gtr, ld vcls A

45s: I Told You I Loved You/When I See My Baby (Jowar 105) 1966
      I Told You I Loved You/When I See My Baby (Amy 960) 1966

These **Missing Links** came from Brooklyn and Long Island. Al Vertucci went on to join **The Naturals** original line-up, which soon became **Tea Company**. He recalls that the 12-string on the Jowar 45 was a Danelectro, a "baseball bat - very, very thick neck"!

"The Jowar (45) was recorded at Ultra-Sonic in Hempstead, Long Island. Four tracks and the owner/engineer was Bill Stahl who did all of the '**Fudge** and Shangri-Las stuff there. One of the great engineers ever!! He did with four tracks what people can't do today with 48. **Tea Company** and all **The Naturals** stuff (*Maiden In The East* was recorded on the first 8-track Scully SN 0001) was also done at Ultra-Sonic by Bill Stahl."

"On the Amy re-recorded version was a Rickenbacker 12, you could really hear the difference. It was recorded at Stea Phillips in NYC right after a **McCoys** and right before a 4 Seasons session. I guess they didn't rub off on us! "

He confirms that another Missing Links, reportedly from Brooklyn and who released a 45 in 1968 - *Don't Hang Me Up / Show Me The Way* (Sock-It 2003), were a different band. (MW/AV)

Missing Links

45: Run And Hide / I Really Ought To Go   (Bamboo No #) 1966

Yet another **Missing Links** who remain true to their name - all that is known is that they hailed from Quincy, Florida. Their 45 on Bob Carson's Bamboo label was engineered by Glen M. Wetherington. A growling Stones-like riff (echoes of *Last Time*) permeates their cantering pop-punker *Run And Hide*, which can be reappraised on *Psychedelic States - Florida Vol. 2* (CD). (MW/JLh/MM/RM)

Missing Lynx

45: Behind Locked Doors/Anymore   (Dynovoice 227) 1966

From Cleveland, Ohio, this was sadly their sole 45. *Behind Locked Doors* is a fabulous catchy punk-popper with powerful vocals, haunting keyboards and dynamic two-fisted drumming. The flip is solid but more poppy.

Compilation appearances include: *Behind Locked Doors* on *Psychedelic Experience, Vol. 3* (CD), *Sixties Rebellion Vol. 16* (LP & CD) and *Son Of The Gathering Of The Tribe* (LP). (VJ/GG/MW)

Missing Lynx

Personnel incl: CALDWELL DAVIS Jr   A

45:         Hang Around / Louie Go Home   (United Sound 100) 1967

Hang Around is well popular with compilers, having resurfaced on *The Essential Pebbles Collection, Vol. 1* (Dble CD), *Let's Dig 'Em Up* (LP), *No No No* (CD) and *Killer Cuts* (LP).

The flip is a swingin' cover of **Paul Revere and The Raiders** and has popped up on *Teenage Shutdown, Vol. 7* (LP & CD), which reveals that the band were from Lawrenceburg, Tennessee and that a coupla members graduated to **The Ravenz**. (MW/MM)

The Mission

ALBUM: 1   VIRGIN   (Paramount PAS-8000) 1972 -

A Christian rock group with songs like *No More Silence*, *Kyrie Eleison*, *Sign In The Darkness*, *Got To Know*, *No Choice* and *My Child*. Their album was a kind of conceptual rock opera and came in a box with a booklet. (SR)

The Mission Singers

ALBUM: 1   EVERYTHING'S JUST FINE OR IS IT ??
                                                (Catholic Relief Services) c1967 R1

This four piece folk/folk-rock group made an educational record designed to be used by Catholic Youth Groups. The record is quite good and is notable for ending with a fuzz garage track, *Reconciliation*. (SR)

Miss Nikki and The No Names

Personnel incl: NIKKI SULLIVAN   gtr, vcls   A

45:         Got A Message/Boni Maronie   (Infinity 1) 1961

Nikki and The No Names were formed in Roosevelt - Jefferson High School(s) in Cedar Rapids, Iowa. Their 45 was produced by Bobby Bare, with *Got A Message* being written by Nikki Sullivan (not The Crickets member). She eventually settled in California where she worked with Li'L Bit Country, Nite Life and the County Hoedowners. (MBp/EW/MW)

Missouri

ALBUM: 1   MISSOURI   (Panama) 1972 -

An undistinguished hard-rock outfit, presumately from Missouri! (SR)

Mr. Christian

45:         Conquistador/You're A Better Man Than I   (Tamm T-2019) 196?

Heavy vibes from Lafayette, Louisiana with two competent covers. Procol Harum's *Conquistador* is done faithfully but is less poppy and more moody than the original. Mike Hugg's *Mister...* is in a '67 or '68 heavy rock vein with some **Blue Cheer** style drumming, though the vocals and harmonies point towards **Vanilla Fudge**. Still pretty impressive all in all. (MW)

Mr. Flood's Party

Personnel: TOM CASTAHNARA   A
            MIKE CORBETT   A
            JAY HIRSCH   A
            RICK MIRAGE   A
            FRED TESCANO   A
            MARCEL THOMPSEN   A

ALBUM: 1(A) MR FLOOD'S PARTY   (Cotillion SD 9003) 1969 SC

45s: Deja Vu/Alice Was A Dream   (Cotillion 44017) 1969
            α   Compared To What/Unbreakable Toy (GM 714) 1969/7?

NB: α also released in Germany (Metronome M 25 374). All 45 cuts are non-LP, except *Deja Vu*.

An unheralded psychedelic rock album which is worth investigating. Its better tracks include: - *The Liquid Invasion*, *Garden Of The Queen* and *The Mind Circus*. Their second 45 was a Larry Douglas production, produced by Royce M. Hyatt, but is reputedly "soul".

It's suggested that the band were from Michigan but that may be a premise due to the label. Their album was produced by Hirsch, Corbett and Tescano and probably recorded in New York. In 1971, **Corbett and Hirsch** released another album in the same vein.

They may be the same outfit who had an earlier 45 on the same label as by Now:-

Now
45s: Deja Vu/Having A Hard Time   (Cotillion 44005) 1968
            I Want/Like A Flying Bird   (Embassy 1968) 1968
(VJ/SR)

Mr. Lucky and The Gamblers

Personnel: BUD GARRISON   bs   ABC
            MIKE PARKER   organ   AB
            DENNY RANDALL   sax   A
            WILLY REINER   gtr, vcls   A
            NORM SMITH   drms   A
            JIM GRAZIANO   drms   BC
            ALAN GUNTER   gtr, vcls   BC
            DAVE MAITLAND   gtr   BC
            JIM DUNLAP   vcls   C
            GREG PERRY   organ   C
            JEFF HAWKS   vcls
            CARL WILSON   gtr

45s: New Orleans/Searching   (United International 1001) 1965
            New Orleans/Searching   (Kasino 1001) 196?
            I Told You Once Before/
            Koko Joe   (United International 4404) 1966
            Take A Look At Me/I Told You Once Before   (Jerden 799) 1966
            Take A Look At Me/I Told You Once Before (Panorama 37) 1966
            Take A Look At Me/I Told You Once Before   (Dot 16930) 1966
            Alice Designs/You Don't Need Me   (Panorama 52) 1967

This band started out in Newport, Oregon and were originally known as The Blazers. Bud Garrison persuaded Mike Parker to consider the merits of the name change in 1964. They decided on **Mr. Lucky** (a popular TV character at the time) because Mike being tall with dark hair looked like

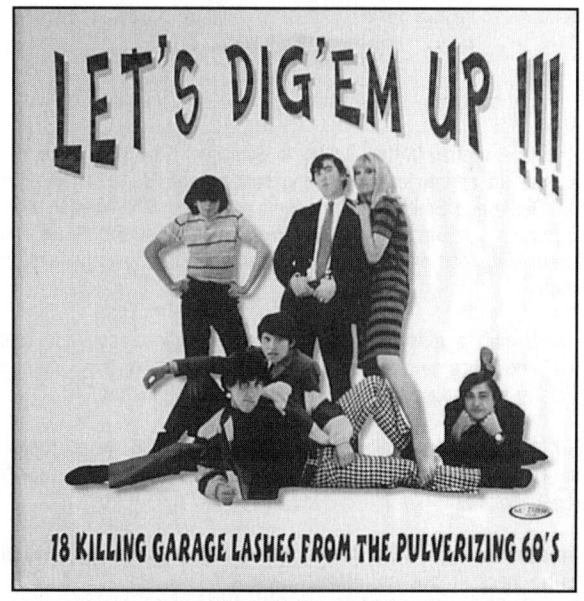

LET'S DIG 'EM UP!!! (Comp LP) including Missing Lynx.

him. They performed locally and attracted the attention of local dee-jay Tom Mix and Hal Branson (who managed a local club called The Chase at that time). Chase and Branson decided to form their own record company to promote the act and the result was *New Orleans*, which became a local hit in Portland. In late 1965, Garrison and Parker changed **The Gamblers** line-up merging with a Portland group The Rogues for whom Graziano, Gunter and Maitland had all previously played. By now the band had perfected a harsh garage-punk sound and were one of the major dance circuit attractions in the Northwest (having relocated to Portland, Oregon). On New Years Day, 1966, they shared the bill with **Don and The Goodtimes** at Portland's Oriental Theatre and Don and the lads were so impressed they helped get **Mr. Lucky and The Gamblers** a record deal with Jerry Dennon's Panorama label. Two regional hits resulted:- *Take A Look At Me* (a really catchy punker, written and produced by Bob Holden and Don Gallucci (of **Don and The Goodtimes**)) and *Alice Designs (LSD Signs)*, which was produced by Bob Holden and written by **Tandyn Almer** of *Along Comes Mary* fame. *Alice Designs* is **Union Gap** style commercial upbeat pop, whilst its brass-pop flip was also written by Bob Holden.

Early in 1967 Mike Parker left the band and Greg Perry joined on keyboards. Jim Dunlap (formerly of Gentleman Jim and The Horsemen) came in on vocals. However, in July 1967 the band split. Dunlap, Graziano, Maitland and Perry all went on to form a new band, **The Sound Vendor**. Mike Parker joined a local blues band, Carl Wilson joined **Merrilee Rush and the Turnabouts** and Jeff Hawks became a member of **Don and The Goodtimes**. In the late eighties, Norm Smith became the State Representative from Tigard, Oregon and Greg Perry later played for Johnny and The Distractions.

The superb *Take A Look At Me* has resurfaced on *Teenage Shutdown, Vol. 1* (LP & CD), *Boulders, Vol. 3* (LP), *History Of Northwest Rock, Vol. 2* (CD) and *Highs In The Mid-Sixties, Vol. 7* (LP); *I Told You Once Before* (written by group member Alan Gunter) can be found on *Northwest Battle Of The Bands, Vol. 1* (CD), *Battle Of The Bands, Vol. 1* (LP) and *The History Of Northwest Rock, Vol. 4* (LP); *Take A Look At Me* and *I Told You Once Before* on *Northwest Battle Of The Bands, Vol. 1 - Flash And Crash* (LP & CD); and *Alice Designs* on *Northwest Battle Of The Bands, Vol. 2 - Knock You Flat!* (LP & CD) and *Northwest Battle Of The Bands, Vol. 2* (CD). (VJ/MW)

Mister's Virtue

| 45: | Summernight/Captured | (Vector V 211) 196? |

A good garage psych 45, from Washington, D.C..

The Mistics

Personnel:	MIKE CREDNO	keyb'ds	ABC
	JOHN REALE	bs	ABC
	FRITZ SMITH	drms, ld vcls	ABC
	ED VANDERWATER	gtr	AB
	'JOSE' ??	ld gtr	A
	RICH CARRINO	ld gtr	BC

| 45: | About Love / Why Baby Why | (Wide Art 101) 1967 |

The Knights 5 formed in high school in Syracuse, New York State in 1964 and served an apprenticeship playing schools and Battle of The Bands. Credno, Reale and Smith had the opportunity to join **The Mistics** who had a club residency in Baldwinsville, New York State. They soon took over the band, replacing Jose with Carrino, who had been their lead guitarist in the Knights 5.

They performed a mixture of Top 40 covers, oldies, soul, and Motown classics and became very popular, especially when they were once mis-billed at a Syracuse University frat house as The Miracles.

In 1967, they recorded their sole 45. They split in 1968 when Smith was drafted. On his return Smith teamed up again with Carrino in a new band, called the Mystics.

The insistent refrain of *Why Baby Why* would have gone down well at frat parties - check it out on *Sixties Rebellion, Vol. 14* (LP & CD) and *Psychedelic States: New York Vol. 1* (CD). (MW)

The Misty Blues

| 45: | Still In Love With You Baby/ I Feel No Pain | (Stature 66-5-7) 1966 |

A Chicago punk band. *I Feel No Pain* can also be found on *Highs In The Mid-Sixties, Vol. 4*. It's a pretty lame garage pop effort. (VJ)

Misty Wizards

| Personnel incl: | RICHARD KEELAN | A |
| | TED LUCAS | A |

| 45: | It's Love/Blue Law Sunday | (Reprise 0616) 1967 |

It's Love is scintillating psychedelic pop - an ideal start to Erik Lindgren's top - drawer CD compilation *A Heavy Dose Of Lyte Psych* on Arf! Arf!, with its irresistible uptempo swingin' rhythm, cool male - female vocals, topped with maelstroms of dizzying effects. Garage purists will hate it - psych heads will levitate, but come back to earth on hearing the comparatively dull flip.

The band were based in Detroit and at least two members were also in the better known **Spike Drivers**.

Other compilation appearances include *It's Love* on *The Arf! Arf! Blitzkrieg 32 Track Sampler* (Dble CD). (MW/PMz)

Billy Mitchel

| ALBUM: | 1 | MIGHT BE HOPE | (Mercury SR-61335) 1970 - |

Housed in a nice cover, an obscure hippie singer combining folk-rock and jazzy tracks. (SR)

Chad Mitchell

| ALBUM: | 1 | CHAD | (Bell) 1969 SC |

Previously known as the leader of the Chad Mitchell Trio, a traditional folk group, **Mitchell** went solo in 1968 after his group had broke up. His only solo album contains a good selection of songs by **Jake Holmes**, **Tim Buckley**, **Dino Valente**, **H.P. Lovecraft** or Joni Mitchell, sung in a dark and melancholic voice, with a large studio backing. (SR)

MOBY GRAPE - Moby Grape (with DJ Strip) LP.

The Mixed Emotions

| Personnel incl?: | J. BOWERS | A |
| | J. SIMMONS | A |

| 45: | Can't You Stop It Now /
I'll Fade Away | (Kustum Kut 45-001) 1968 |

This 45 has enjoyed something of a revival in the last few years - never heard of until the mid-late nineties, it suddenly started appearing on several garage/psych specialists' lists. At around the same time their driving fuzz-rocker *Can't You Stop It Now* began to pop up on compilations - *The Essential Pebbles Collection, Vol. 1* (2-CD), *Bad Vibrations, Vol. 1* (LP), *Project Blue Vol. 5* (LP) and most recently *Psychedelic States: Alabama Vol. 1* (CD). Hmmm, was this another bogus sixties garage record like **The Huntsmen** or **Katz Kradle**?

Not according to the *Psychedelic States: Alabama Vol. 1* (CD) liners. The band had formed in 1965 in the small town of Coden, near Southern Mobile in Alabama, and operated under several names, eventually releasing their sole 45 in the Summer of 1968. They sold only a handful of copies at the time but one member had the foresight (and perhaps a nose for investment) to store the remaining copies safely... until he was tracked down by a collector. Members have reportedly been in contact again thanks to the regenerated interest, though they're too shy to reveal their identities. (MW/RM)

The Moanin' Glories

Personnel:	KARL BERKEBILE	keyb'ds	A
	ANDY GORE	bs	A
	RITCHIE KUNKLE	gtr	A
	MARC MOURNING	drms	A

| 45: | She Took The Rain Out Of My Mind/
You Better Watch Out For That Girl | (Yorkshire YR-1001) 1967 |

This garage rock quartet operated out of Wichita in Southern Kansas. Their sole vinyl offering is highly-rated and you can also find *She Took The Rain...* on *The Midwest Vs. Canada* (LP) and on Tom Tourville's *Midwest Garage Band Series - Kansas* (CD).

The Moanin' Glories formed out of another Wichita act, The Candelles. Formed in 1965 by Ritchie Kunkle and Andy Gore, The Candelles underwent several personnel changes and after Karl Berkebile and Marc Mourning joined in 1966, they changed names to **The Moanin' Glories**. Andy Gore:- "We actively toured throughout the Midwest U.S.A. and were later based in the Boston, Mass. area around 1970. We even toured Japan in late 1970 but then disbanded in early 1971".

After the group split, Kunkle and Mourning formed Crank and were active for several more years. Kunkle was on the verge of a career rebound in 1994 in Nashville when he sadly passed away. Mourning is active today in Christian Music, whilst Berkebile has a solo act in Dallas, Texas. Andy Gore is in business in Wichita and has written a book about his experiences with the band during those heady days. (VJ/MW/AGe)

Moby Grape

Personnel: (up to 1971)	PETER LEWIS	gtr, vcls	ABCD
	JERRY MILLER	gtr, vcls	ABCD
	BOB MOSLEY	bs, vcls	AB D
	SKIP SPENCE	gtr, vcls	A D
	DON STEVENSON	drms	ABCD
	BOB MOORE	bs	C
	GORDON STEVENS	mandolin, dobro, violin	D

HCP

ALBUMS: (up to 1972)	1(A)	MOBY GRAPE	(Columbia CS 9498) 1967	24 -
	2(A)	WOW	(Columbia CS 9613) 1968	20 -
	3(A)	GRAPE JAM	(Columbia CXS 3) 1968	- -
	4(E)	MOBY GRAPE '69	(Columbia CS 9696) 1969	113 -
	5(C)	TRULY FINE CITIZEN	(Columbia CS 9912) 1970	157 -
	6(G)	20 GRANITE CREEK	(Reprise 6460) 1971	177 -

MOBY GRAPE - Wow LP.

NB: (1) also issued in mono (Columbia CL 2698) SC. Original copies do not list song titles on front cover, and Don Stevenson's middle finger is visible on washboard. Poster included also shows the finger on the washboard. Second pressing also has no song titles listed on front cover, but the finger has been removed from the cover and poster. Subsequent issues list the song titles on the front cover alongside the censored band photo. Mono version reissued on vinyl (Edsel ED 137) 1984. (2) and (3) were issued concurrently and stock copies were initally sold shrinkwrapped together as a "double album" in two separate covers. (2) was later available as a separate album. (2) and (3) were coupled together with a paper band for promo distribution and a special white label mono edition exists of the promo set (CL 9613/MGS 1) (R2). Mono stock copies of (2), (4) and (5) do not exist in the USA, but all three were issued in mono in the UK on CBS. (6) reissued on vinyl (Edsel ED 176) 198?. (2) has also been reissued and all of the above albums have been reissued on CD. Also of interest are: *Live Grape* (Escape JAM 95018) 1978, issued on both purple and black vinyl; *Moby Grape* (San Francisco Sound SFS-04830) 1983; and *Vintage - The Very Best Of Moby Grape* (Columbia Legacy C2K 53041) 1993, a double-CD set including many rare and unreleased material.

HCP

| 45s: | α | Fall On You/Changes (PS) | (Columbia 44170) 1967 - |
| | α | Sitting By The Window/
Indifference (PS) | (Columbia 44171) 1967 - |
| | α | 8:05/Mister Blues (PS) | (Columbia 44172) 1967 - |
| | α | Omaha/Someday (PS) | (Columbia 44173) 1967 88 |
| | α | Hey Grandma/
Come In The Morning (PS) | (Columbia 44174) 1967 127 |
| | | Can't Be So Bad/Bitter Wind | (Columbia 44567) 1967 - |
| | | Trucking Man/
If You Can't Learn From My Mistakes | (Columbia 44789) 1968 - |
| | | Ooh Mama Ooh /
It's A Beautiful Day Today | (Columbia 44885) 1968 - |
| | β | Gypsy Wedding/Apocalypse | (Reprise 1040) 1971 - |
| | | Goin' Down To Texas/About Time | (Reprise 1055) 1971 - |

NB: α were all issued in the same picture sleeve with different titles. β also issued in Germany: *Gipsy Wedding/Apocalypse* (PS) (Reprise REP 14114) 1971.

One of San Francisco's best-loved bands, **Moby Grape** was formed in late 1966 by San Diego native **Bob Mosley** (ex-**The Misfits**) and Peter Lewis (ex-Peter and The Wolves, **The Cornells**) from Los Angeles. **Mosley** and Lewis had already made several trips to the Bay Area in hopes of putting a band together there, but it was not until **Skip Spence** (who had left **Jefferson Airplane** because he wanted to play guitar instead of the drums!) and the ex-**Frantics** Don Stevenson and Jerry Miller came aboard, that they relocated there permanently.

The pre-history of **Moby Grape** is very complex, involving a number of Southern California musicians (**Joel Scott Hill**, John Barbata of **The Leaves** and **The Turtles**, Kent Dunbar and Bob Newkirk) each of whom played temporarily in pre-album line-ups but were not actually members of the group. Stevenson and Miller had migrated to the Bay Area from Seattle and Miller had also spent time in Texas where he played on the first version of **The Bobby Fuller Four**'s *I Fought The Law*. **Spence** had moved to the East Bay with his family in 1959 but was born in Canada... so in actuality, none of the members of **Moby Grape** were originally from the Bay Area!

The band played its first concerts at the end of 1966 and soon attracted a large local following. Their all-original repertoire was made up of tightly-structured, short, high-energy songs - the very antithesis of the current trend in San Francisco. They were soon offered a record contract by Columbia and their debut album was issued in June 1967. To their credit, Columbia spared no expense in promoting **Moby Grape**, producing special press kits in fuzzy purple folders, issuing five singles in picture sleeves simultaneously, throwing elaborate press parties wherever the band played, and of course packaging the album in a full-colour sleeve with a huge poster. Despite their best intentions, all this shameless promotion served only to alienate the band from the hippie culture, who perceived it as arrogant commercialism. Columbia steadfastly continued to support the band, who were now trashing hotel rooms and conducting their affairs on the road in a very unprofessional manner. When several of the band members were busted partying late into the night with some teenage girls, the label finally took a big step back. The record did pretty well on its own, reaching the Top 30, but it surely deserved better. There are some great tracks on the album - hard-rockers like *Hey Grandma* and *Omaha* appear alongside laid-back tracks like *Someday*, *8:05* and *Sitting By The Window*. The group had three fabulous lead guitarists and all five members sang. The end result was a structured album with diverse vocal harmonies and some fine interweaving acid guitar work. It's as close to a masterpiece as any American band produced in the late sixties and its power and influence has not diminished over the years, unlike many records from the psychedelic era.

The next album *Wow* contained a number of short compositions with melodic guitar work, and the opening tracks on each side, *The Place and the Time* and *He*, both contained orchestral arrangements which was uncommon among San Francisco bands at that time (although in England groups like The Beatles and The Moody Blues were using them regularly). *Three-Four* was a sensitive, beautiful song:-

"Cause I love you all
Even though my heart is far away
It's here I'll stay
Until my life is through
When I'm dead and gone
And my life has passed beyond your view
There inside of you
My life goes on and on..."
(from *Three-Four*)

Rose Coloured Eyes and *Bitter Wind* are equally memorable, whilst *Can't Be So Bad*, a faster rockier number, demonstrated their musical diversity. One track, featuring Lou Waxman and his orchestra and starring Arthur Godfrey on banjo and ukelele has to be played at 78 rpm! A free bonus album *Grape Jam* was issued with *Wow* and this featured **Mike Bloomfield** and **Al Kooper** on keyboards. Commercially, *Wow* made little impact - the group could not recover from their earlier over-exposure. Towards the end of 1968 they split - but by 1969 they had reformed again as a foursome without **Skip Spence**. They released the competent *Moby Grape '69* and did a series of live gigs, but generated little interest outside of California. So 1970 saw them split for the second time and **Mosley** left to join the Marines. Later that year, the remaining three reformed, adding Bob Moore (bs) to produce *Truly Fine Citizen*. Inevitably they split again, later reforming as a five-piece band to produce an disappointing album *20 Granite Creek*.

Moby Grape's talented members spawned a number of solo projects. The first and rarest of these is **Skip Spence**'s *Oar* (Columbia CS 9831) 1969, which was also released in Holland (CBS S 63919). This is an expensive item nowadays but has been reissued on vinyl (Columbia LP 5030) and CD (Sundazed SC 11075) (with ten bonus tracks) and (Sony WK 75031) with five bonus tracks. There's also a 7" *All My Life/Land Of The Sun* (Sundazed S 153) recorded in 1966/1972. **Bob Mosley** had a solo album *Bob Mosley* (Reprise MS 2068) and a single, *Gypsy Wedding/Gone Fishin'* (Reprise 1096), both in 1972. There's also an acoustic mini-album, *Wine And Roses* (Nightshift) 1987 on which he is assisted by percussionist Willie Kellogg (**Joel Scott Hill**'s bands, **The Time Machine**, **The Five # Grin, Pale Fire**; Willie was also the drummer of **Moby Grape** in the late seventies), and Bob Mosley and Mosley Grape: *Live At Indigo Ranch* (San Francisco Sound SFS-04880) 1989. Peter Lewis also issued a good solo album in 1995 *Peter Lewis* (Taxim TX-2008-2), featuring Stu Cook (**Creedence**), John McFee (**Clover**, Doobie Brothers), Cornelius Bumpus (**Moby Grape**, Doobie Brothers) and Keith Knudsen (**Mendelbaum**, Doobie Brothers, **Lee Michaels**). Finally Jerry Miller has issued *Life Is Like That* (Messaround Records MRSCD004) 1995, a bluesy album with John Oxendine (**Moby Grape**, **Sir Douglas Quintet**) and Tiran Porter (Doobie Brothers), **Merl Saunders** and Michael Carabello (**Santana**, Elvin Bishop, Boz Scaggs).

Ultimately **Moby Grape** never attained their true potential on record, but their first two albums are recommended as offering a glimpse of their real ability. There are also a number of 'Best of' compilations, including the excellent *Vintage - The Very Best Of Moby Grape* (Sony 53041) 1993, a double CD compilation of album tracks, live recordings and alternate takes. There's also an interesting bootleg CD, *Dark Magic*, with live cuts, though the Peter and The Wolves tracks it contains are not by Peter Lewis' pre-**Moby Grape** outfit, but another band with the same name. Lewis had also been in The Cornells, a surf band that issued a hideously rare album in 1963 on the Garex label that was reissued by Sundazed with bonus tracks.

Moby Grape issued a cassette-only album in 1990 *The Legendary Moby Grape* (Herman Records), but this was quickly withdrawn when their former manager took legal action, and the tape was repackaged shown as by The Melvilles.

Skip Spence sadly passed away on April 16th 1999.

Compilation appearances have included: *Hoochie* on *Pop Revolution From The Underground* (LP); *War In Peace* and *Omaha* on *Psychedelic Frequencies* (CD); *Omaha* and *Hey Grandma* on *Sixties Years, Vol. 2 - French 60's EP Collection* (CD); *Om-Aha, Mr. Blues*, a 1983 recording *Hard Road To Follow* and *Say You Want To Leave Me* on *Then And Now, Vol. 1* (CD); and *Hey Grandma*, a 1983 recording *Silver Wheels* and a 1988 recording *Lonesome Highway* on *Then And Now, Vol. 2* (CD).
(VJ/CF/SR/CW)

MOBY GRAPE - Grape Jam LP.

Mod and The Rockers

Personnel:			
	STEVE DORMAN	organ	A
	GARY McINTYRE	drms	A
	RICKY OATES	ld gtr	A
	EDWIN (BOO) SNIDER	bs	A

ALBUM: 1(A) ...NOW (Justice 153) c1966 R3
NB: (1) reissued on CD (Collectables COL-CD-0618) 1996.

45: You Got Me Hummin'/
Always By My Side (Kay Mar # unknown) 196?
NB: as Joy.

MOBY GRAPE - Truly Fine Citizen LP.

One of the better albums on the Justice label. Although they stray into cabaret/lounge territory with their choice of material (*It's Not Unusual, Walk On By, Goin' Out Of My Head*) and the soulful (*Love Is A Beautiful Thing, Ninety-Nine And A Half*), strong raucous vocals and an aggressive vitality shine through.

Their glorious swingin' fuzz-punker *Gonna Love You Every Day*, a faithful version of *Gloria*, and savage assaults on *Come On Up* and the **Beau Brummels**' *Just A Little*, are worth the price of admission alone. Apparently members went on to become Joy, with the 45 listed above. (MW)

Modds

45: Leave My House/
All The Time In The World   (American National 3041) 1967

A true garage recording! *Leave My House* is a really crude recording. This guy is really struggling to play some simple guitar riffs overloading his amp whilst someone bangs idly on a tambourine in the background. Rumoured to have been based in Memphis, Tennessee though one suspects that they probably just recorded there.

Compilation appearances include: *Leave My House* on *Pebbles, Vol. 11* (LP) and *Teenage Shutdown, Vol. 13* (LP & CD). (VJ/MW)

The Modds

Personnel:	DEWEY BOND	drms	A
	DEAN LIAPIS	vcls	A
	JOHN MASCARO	gtr	A
	BOB NIMER	ld gtr	A
	DON RICKETTS	vcls, bs	A

45: Don't Be Late / So In Love   (Dukoff Studios Acetate) 1965

After Miami's Deltonas split at the end of 1964, John Mascaro and Don Ricketts formed **The Modds** with vocalist Dean Liapis, lead guitarist Bob Nimer and drummer Dewey Bond. They built a repertoire of thirty covers and two originals and honed their sound at teen hall dances and frat parties, before they entered Dukoff Studios and captured the originals on acetate. One was presented to WFUN radio where *Don't Be Late* was spun by Morton "Doc" Downey Jr. and received positive responses. The group's manager contacted Columbia, who were keen, but insisted that the tracks be rerecorded. In the interim they were impressed enough to ask **The Modds** to perform at their upcoming convention at the Americana Hotel in Miami Beach where attendees would include **The Byrds**, **Paul Revere and The Raiders** and other nationally known acts.

All seemed to be set for a promising future, then Uncle Sam delivered an untimely draft notice to John Mascaro ... and that was that.

Thankfully copies of the acetate survived. Their resounding beat-punker *Don't Be Late* can be enjoyed again, on *Project Blue Vol. 5* (LP) and *Psychedelic States: Florida Vol. 3* (CD), the latter providing the band's story which is summarised above.

One member is thought to have gone onto another outfit called Asbury Park. (MW/JLh)

The Models

45: Bend Me Shape Me/
In A World Of Pretty Faces   (MGM 13775) 1966

This all girl band seem to have recorded the original version of *Bend Me, Shape Me*, pre-dating The **American Breed** by about four months. It's notable also for some pretty psychedelic guitar effects.

The band comprised some leggy Vogue models (hence the name) and may have had some connection with The Vogues who recorded a 45 a little later on the same label:- *Brighter Days/Lovers Of The World Unite* (MGM 13813) or (MGM 13831).

Compilation appearances include *Bend Me, Shape Me* on *Open Lid* (7" EP) and *Girls In The Garage, Vol. 1* (LP & CD). (VJ/GG)

Modern Folk Quartet

Personnel:	HENRI "TAD" DILTZ		AB
	DOUGLAS FARTHING HATELID	bs	AB
	CYRUS FARYAR	vcls, gtr	AB
	JERRY YESTER	vcls, gtr	AB
	EDDIE HOH	drms	B

ALBUMS: 1( ) MODERN FOLK QUARTET
(up to   (Warner Bros. WS-1511) 1963 -
1976) 2( ) CHANGES   (Warner Bros. WS-1546) 1964 -

NB: (1) also released in Germany on Teldec. (1) reissued on CD in Japan (Warner Bros. WPCP-3423) 1990. (2) reissued on CD in Japan (Warner Bros. WPCP-3423) 1990. Later albums include: *Moonlight Serenade* (Homecoming Records HC-00400) 1985; *Live In Japan* (Pony Canyon, D25Y0318) 1989; *Bamboo Saloon* (Pony Canyon, PCCY-00061) 1990; *Christmas* (Pony Canyon, PCCY-00165) 1990; *Wolfgang* (Pony Canyon, PCCY-00284) 1991; and *Highway 70* (Polystar PSCW-5094) 1999.

HCP

45s: It Was A Very Good Year/
Road To Freedom   (Warner Bros. 5387) 1963 -
The Love Of A Clown/If All You Think   (Warner 5481) 1964 -
Every Minute Of The Day/
That's Alright With Me   (Warner Bros. 5623) 1965 -
Night Time Girl/Lifetime   (Dunhill 4025) 1966 122
Don't You Wonder/
I Had A Dream Last Night   (Dunhill 4137) 1968 -

A seminal folk-rock group from Los Angeles. **Faryar** had been in the Whiskeyhill Singers and **Yester** had been in the Inn Group. Both quit their respective bands and formed the **Modern Folk Quartet** with Hatelid and Diltz. *Night Time Girl* was produced by Jack Nitzsche and written by **Al Kooper** and Irwin Lewine. A pop raga with oriental instruments, it is quite interesting. Another 45, *Don't You Wonder* was composed by Hatelid and Bill Martin.

When the group broke up, Douglas Hatelid, who was then known as Chip Douglas, joined **The Turtles** and Gene Clark for a short spell, before becoming a producer (**Monkees**, **Turtles** etc.). He also played with **Fred Neil**. Henry Diltz became a photographer and Eddie Hoh a session drummer (**Barry Goldberg**, **Lee Michaels**, **Kim Fowley** etc.). **Jerry Yester** joined the **Lovin' Spoonful**, replacing Zal Yanovsky. He also cut two solo singles and two albums with his wife, Judy Henske, before becoming a renowned producer and engineer (notably for **Tim Buckley** and Tom Waits). **Cyrus Faryar** became a session musician, notably with **Fred Neil** and **Stone Poneys** and was also the voice of the **Cosmic Sounds**. In 1972 he cut a solo album on Elektra before moving to Hawaii where he produced local acts.

In the mid-eighties a reformed band had quite a successful run in Japan with several further albums.

Compilation appearances have included: *Night Time Girl* on *Nuggets, Vol. 10* (LP); and *Don't You Wonder* and *Night Time Girl* on *Penny Arcade, Dunhill Folk Rock, Vol. 2* (LP). (SR)

The Modern Sounds

ALBUM: 1 FAMOUS SONGS OF HANK WILLIAMS,
A RETURN TRIP (Alshire S-5136) 1969 SC

Another 'exploito' album from the budget label who were also responsible for **The Animated Egg** etc. This effort consists of cover versions of Hank Williams' classics (*Jambalaya, Kaw-Liga, Cold Cold Heart, Hey Good Lookin...*) with loads of fuzz guitar, and delivered 'in Modern Rock-Acid Sound and with exciting vocals'. For curious listeners! (SR)

The Mod 4

45s:	Midnight Hour/Funny...	(The Mod 4 6723) 1967
	Open Up Your Mind/?	(The Mod 4 6833) 1968

Unknown girl band from either Michigan or Iowa. *Open Up...*, a rough 'n' ready punker, has also resurfaced on *Sixties Rebellion, Vol. 4* (LP & CD). (VJ)

The Mods

Personnel:	SCOTT FRASER	drms	A
	CHRIS HAWKINS	gtr	A
	EDDIE LIVELY	vcls, gtr	A
	DON McGILVERY	bs	A

45: It's For You/Days Mind The Time (Cee Three 1000,01) 1966

This band hailed from Fort Worth. The 'A' side of their 45, a folk-rock ballad, was originally written by Lennon-McCartney for Cilla Black, whilst the flip had similarities to The Beatles' *If I Needed Someone*. Scott Fraser, incidentally, was a multi-instrumentalist who taught the rest of the band to play. In 1969, he would form **Whistler, Chaucer, Detroit and Greenhill** with Lively and in 1969 **Space Opera**.

Compilation appearances include: *It's For You* on *Acid Visions - Complete Collection, Vol. 3* (3-CD) and *Texas Punk, Vol. 9* (LP); *Days Mind The Time* on *The Cicadelic 60's, Vol. 3* (CD) and *The Cicadelic 60's, Vol. 5* (LP). (VJ/MW/SR)

The Mods

45s:	High School Days/The Broken Hip	(Kool 1024) 1964
	My Baby's Gone/Stone Henge	(Kool 1028) 1965
	Opp-Sy-Do/Stay With Me	(Kool 1029) 1965
	Only The Young/?	(Kool 1032) 1966

Routine garage fare from a different Houston band. *My Baby's Gone* can be heard on *Texas Flashback (The Best Of)* (CD), *Texas Flashbacks, Vol. 3* (LP & CD) and *Flashback, Vol. 3* (LP). The flip was an instrumental. (VJ)

The Mods

45: I Give You An Inch (And You Take A Mile)/
You've Got Another Thing Comin' (Peck 331) 1966

A raw garage band from Toledo, Ohio. The flip, the story of a guy warning his cheating girl, features some raunchy harp and powerful guitar.

Compilation appearances include: *I Give You An Inch (And You Take A Mile)* on *Teenage Shutdown, Vol. 10* (LP & CD), *Chosen Few Vol's 1 & 2* (CD) and *The Chosen Few, Vol. 1* (LP); *You Got Another Thing Comin'* on *Back From The Grave, Vol. 3* (LP) and *Back From The Grave, Vol. 2* (CD). (VJ/MW/GGI)

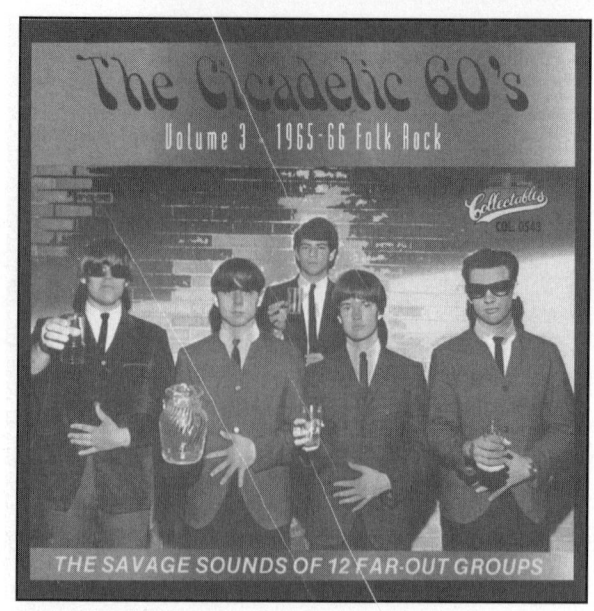

CICADELIC 60's Vol. 3 (Comp CD) including The Mods.

The Mods

Personnel:	STEVE KATH	drms	AB
	PAT PETIT	organ, gtr	AB
	SUE PETIT	gtr, organ, vcls	AB
	BILL WHITE	bs	A
	DAVE FRANZEN	ld gtr	B
	TOM McNEIL	bs	B

Acetate: Lost Again/
Till The End Of The Day (Welhaven Recording Co.) 1965

Formed in 1964 in the Plainview area of Minnesota. They were originally known as The Impalas and their musical repertoire initially consisted of Beatles, Rolling Stones and Kinks covers. They recorded a Sue Petit/Steve Kath composition, *Lost Again* along with a cover of The Kinks' *'Till The End Of The Day* to which they added a frantic garage style climax, in the Summer of 1965, but it didn't get beyond the acetate stage. In the Fall of 1965, Bill White left to go to Mankato State University and Tom McNeil came in as a replacement. Dave Franzen, a talented lead guitar player was drafted in too. The group finally fell apart when Sue Petit left to become female vocalist with a R&B group, The Happy Go Luckies. Later still she joined a Miami, Florida, band called The Faculty. (VJ)

The Mods

45s:	Ritual /Everybody Needs Somebody	
	To Love	(Revilation VII # Unkn) 1965
	Ritual / Candid Camera Theme (Instr)	(Mod 116) 1965
	Satisfaction / Ford Mustang	(Revilation VII R 104) 1966

This outfit from Allenhurst, New Jersey were a popular attraction on the teen-club circuit of Monmouth County, New Jersey. Their cover version of The Stones' *Satisfaction* has some surfish-styled guitar but the flip side is more in the Beach Boys genre. Their first 45, *Ritual* is more punkish.

Compilation appearances have included: *Satisfaction* on *Back From The Grave, Vol. 2* (LP) and *Garage Kings* (Dble LP); and *Ritual* on *Hang It Out To Dry* (LP & CD). (MW)

The Mods

Personnel:	BRUCE CAMERON	keyb'ds	A
	ROBBIE GONZALES	drms	A
	JERRY TILLMAN	ld gtr	A
	BILL WILKES	bs, ld vcls	A

45: Empty Heart/Sweets For My Sweet (Knight 105) 1966

A teen quartet from Tampa, Florida, whose exuberant cover of the Stones' *Empty Heart* takes pride of place on *Psychedelic States - Florida Vol. 2*

(CD). The liners reveal that they were billed as Tampa's youngest pro band - they were barely in their teens.

There's some fine ringing guitar in their cover of The Searchers' *Sweets For My Sweet*.

Other compilation appearances include *Empty Heart* and *Sweets For My Sweet* on *Sixties Archive, Vol. 4* (CD) and *Florida Punk Groups From The Sixties* (LP). (VJ/MW/JLh/RM)

The Mods

Personnel:	TOM BOLES	vcls	AB
	DAN HECKEL	gtr	A
	DANN KLAWON	drms, hrmnca, gtr, vcls	ABCDE
	DAVE SMALLEY	gtr, vcls	ABCDE
	WALLY BRYSON	gtr	BCDE
	DAVE BURKE	bs	DE
	JIM BONFANTI	drms	E

This outfit came from Mentor (near Cleveland), Ohio who and formed in the Fall of 1964. They recorded a demo in 1966. Two originals, *In Love's Shadow* and *I'm Slippin'*, turned up on the Sundazed album *Choir Practice*. When they signed with Cleveland label Claridge, in 1966, they changed their name to **The Choir**. (VJ/GG)

The Mod VI

45: What Can I Do/
Show Me How You're Lovin's Gonna Be   (Emerald 127) 196?

An obscure band from South Carolina. *What Can I Do* features some blistering fuzz guitar and an unusual 'circus' ending. On the flip, the fuzz is knocked down a notch, but there's a promising lead near the end.

Compilation appearances have included: *What Can I Do* and *Show Me How (Your Lovin's Gonna Be)* on *Sixties Rebellion, Vol. 4* (LP & CD); and *What Can I Do* on *Yeah Yeah Yeah* (CD). (MW)

The Modulation Corporation

45:    What To Do/Worms   (Atom 1001) 1967

Undistinguished garage punk, this time from San Marcos in Texas. The 'A' side later resurfaced on *Texas Flashback (The Best Of)* (CD) and *Texas Flashbacks, Vol. 4* (LP). (VJ)

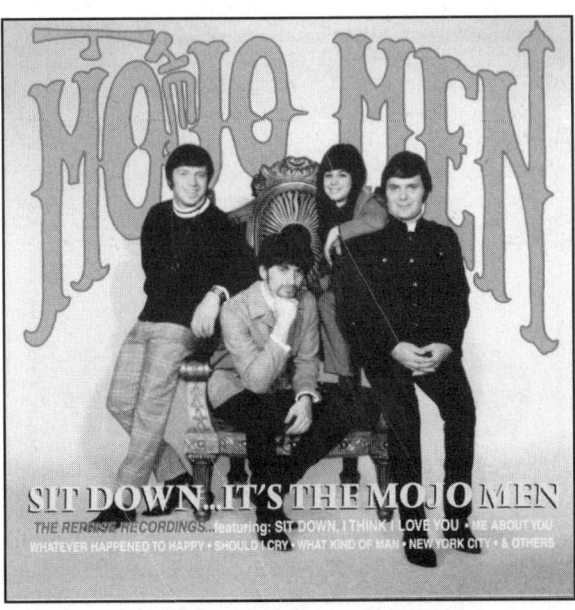

THE MOJO MEN - Sit Down... It's The Mojo Men CD.

Moguls

Personnel incl:	SKIP BIGGS	drms
	JEFF BLOOMQUIST	bs
	"ROUND RANDY" BRYSON	keyb'ds, vcls
	DENNY JOHNSON	drms
	JOHN MOORE	drms
	GREG NANCE	bs
	JOHN STARKEY	sax
	PAUL STARKEY	ld gtr

45s:	Ghost Slalom/Avalanche	(?) 1965
	Ski Bum/Try Me	(Panorama 27) 1966
	Another Day/Round Randy	(Tork 1095) 1966

Hailing from Eugene, Oregon, this outfit were originally known as The Centurians but they changed their name to The Moguls in December 1964. Their manager was convinced that after 'surf' music, 'ski' music would be the next big thing. So he hired two go-go dancers in ski-bunny outfits and clad the group in ski pants, turtlenecks and ski boots.

Their first 45 was a double-sided instrumental with snow sound effects. They performed it at a local Battle Of The Bands competition and won, getting to record their next 45 free!

Their second 45, *Ski Bum*, which was produced by a member of **Don and The Goodtimes** is quite a pounder. Their third, *Another Day*, came out on the Tork label named after the Tork Club where they were regulars. This was a faster number with lots of mouth harp - probably their finest moment. They later became known as Music Prism but only lasted for about a year under that moniker.

Compilation appearances include: *Ski Bum* on *Northwest Battle Of The Bands, Vol. 1 - Flash And Crash* (LP & CD); *Try Me* on *Northwest Battle Of The Bands, Vol. 2 - Knock You Flat!* (LP & CD) and *Northwest Battle Of The Bands, Vol. 2* (CD); *Another Day* and *Ski Bum* on *Back From The Grave, Vol. 7* (Dble LP); and *Round Randy* on *Ho-Dad Hootenanny* (LP). (VJ/MW/DR/SC)

The Mo Joes

45:    Night Train/
Is There Something On Your Mind   (Northeast 202) 196?

Hailed from Worcester, Massachusetts, with this sole frat/garage 45. (VJ)

The Mojo Men

Personnel:	JIMMY ALAIMO	vcls, bs	ABC
	PAUL CURICO	gtr	ABC
	JAN ERRICO	drms, vcls	ABC
	DON METCHIK	organ	AB
	SLY STONE	keyb'ds, gtr, vcls	A

ALBUM: 1 MOJO MAGIC   (GRT 10003) 1968 -

NB: There have also been three compilations:- *Dance With Me* (Eva 12049) 1984, is a 16 track compilation of their 1965-1966 material; *Why Ain't Supposed To Be* (Sundazed SC 11028) 1996, concentrates on their period at Autumn, 1965-6, including nine previously unreleased tracks; *Sit Down... It's The Mojo Men* (Sundazed SC 11032) 1996, similarly concentrates on their period at Reprise, 1966-8 including many previously unreleased tracks.

HCP

45s:	Off The Hook/Mama's Little Baby	(Autumn 11) 1965 -
	Dance With Me/Loneliest Boy In Town	(Autumn 19) 1965 61
	She's My Baby/Fire In My Hean	(Autumn 27) 1966 -
	She's My Baby/Do The Hanky Panky	(Reprise 0486) 1966 -
	Sit Down, I Think I Love You/ Don't Leave Me	(Reprise 0539) 1967 36
	Me About You/When You're In Love	(Reprise 0580) 1967 83
	What Ever Happened To Happy/ Make You At Home	(Reprise 0617) 1967 -
	New York City/ Not Too Old To Start Cryin'	(Reprise 0661) 1968 -
	Should I Cry/You To Me	(Reprise 0689) 1968 -

	Sit Down, I Think I Love You/		
	Me About You (reissue)	(Reprise 0707)	1968 -
α	Don't Be Cruel/Let It Be Him	(Reprise 0759)	1968 -
β	I Can't Let Go/Flower Of Love	(GRT 5)	1969 -
β	Candle To Burn/Make You At Home	(GRT 8)	1969 -
β	Everyday Love/There Goes My Mind	(GRT 10)	1969 -

NB: α as The Mojo. β as Mojo. There's also a rare French EP with picture sleeve: *Off The Hook/Mama's Little Baby/Dance With Me/Loneliest Boy In Town* (Vogue INT 18050) 1966.

Although this band was based in San Francisco some members originated from Florida. The original band formed in Coral Gables, Florida as The Valiants. Singer Jim Alaimo (cousin of singer Steve Alaimo) had early releases under the names Jimmy Sumers and The Slicks and Jimmy Paris. The Valiants also back Steve Alaimo on his 1961 album *Twist With Steve Alaimo*. It was pretty much the same line-up that moved to San Francisco in 1964 and became *The Mojo Men*. For much more info, see the liner notes of the Sundazed compilation *Why's Ain't Supposed To Be*.

Sly Stone had left the band (to form **Sly and The Family Stone**) by the time the band signed to Reprise and achieved some success with Steve Still's *Sit Down I Think I Love You*. Their diminiutive female vocalist Jan Errico had earlier achieved much popularity on the West Coast as drummer and lead vocalist for **The Vejtables**.

In late 1967 the band became known as **Mojo** because Jan Errico got tired of being known as a Mojo Man. They also changed labels to GRT so that they could record an album. Released in 1968 it was produced by Dave Hassinger. It contained their *New York City* 45, which suffered from sounding too much like **The Mamas and Papas** and overall contained a number of mildly psychedelic, post-*Sgt. Pepper* pop-rock songs. The band finally split in 1969 when they realised their era had ended.

There remains a lot of unissued material from both eras of **The Mojo Men**. From their time with Autumn fifteen tracks remained unissued although some of these later appeared on Eva's *Dance With Me* compilation and the superior Sundazed retrospective *Why Ain't Supposed To Be*. A further nineteen tracks were recorded but not released during their spell with Reprise. These include the long and experimental *What Kind Of Man*, which was reputed to be a latter-day venture into psychedelia by the band.

Jim Alaimo later resurfaced in a seventies funk band called Jammer that recorded for the Avco-distributed Honey label. He later died of heart failure.

Compilation coverage has so far included: *Sit Down, I Think I Love You* and *She's My Baby* on *Nuggets Box* (4-CD); *Sit Down I Think I Love You* on *Nuggets Vol. 5* (LP), *Nuggets - Original Artyfacts From The First Psychedelic Era 1965-1968* (Dble LP) and *Sundazed Sampler, Vol. 2* (CD); *Off The Hook* on *Sounds Of The Sixties San Francisco, Vol. 1* (LP); *Dance With Me* on *Sound Of The Sixties* (Dble LP), *Sixties Archive, Vol. 1* (CD) and *We Have Come For Your Children*; *Dance With Me* and *She's My Baby* on *San Francisco Roots* (LP), *The Autumn Records Story* (LP) and *Nuggets, Vol. 7* (LP). All three of their Autumn singles also figure on the *Autumn Single Box*. More recently much of their material has featured on Big Beat's *Nuggets From The Golden State* series:- the *Dance With Me* CD contains *Dance With Me* plus a demo and six unreleased cuts from 1965 (*She Goes With Me*, *Off The Hook*, *Something Bad*, *My Woman's Head*, *Can't You See That She's Mine*, *Why* and *As I Get Older*); *Someone To Love* features four 1966 cuts - *She's My Baby*, *Fire In My Heart* and the unreleased *Why Can't You Stay* and *Girl Won't You Go*. (VJ/MW/SR/JLh)

The Mojos

45:	Love Does Its Harm/I Like It	(Mojo 1) 1965

From Fairfield, Connecticut. You'll also find *Love Does Its Harm* on *New England Teen Scene, Vol. 1* (LP) and *New England Teen Scene* (CD). (MW/MM)

The Mojos

45:	What She's Done To Me/Go	(Mojo 88/124) 1966

From Hurricane, West Virginia, both sides of this **Mojos'** 45 are fine Brit-Invasion inspired originals written by Joe Clatworthy.

Compilation appearances have included: *What She's Done To Me* and *Go* on *Sixties Rebellion, Vol. 14* (LP & CD); and *What She's Done To Me* on *All Cops In Delerium - Good Roots* (LP).

They were later known as **The Muffetts**. (MW)

Moloch

Personnel:	LEE BAKER	ld gtr, vcls	AB
	PHILLIP DURHAM	drms, vcls	A
	FRED NICHOLSON	organ	A
	STEVE SPEAR	bs	A
	GENE WILKINS	ld vcls	A
	MICHAEL BUSTA JONES	bs	B
	BOBBY DODDS	drms	B
	JIMMY SEGERSON	gtr	B

ALBUM:	1(A)	MOLOCH	(Enterprise/Stax ENS 1002) 1970 SC

NB: (1) reissued on CD (Lizard Records LR 0712-2).

45:	Cocaine Katy/Terrorization Of Miss Nancy	(Booger 1001) 1972

Formed in Memphis in 1968 by Baker, who'd fronted local faves The Blazers, the initial line-up evolved to include drummer Durham, who'd been with The Group and The Rapscallions. Produced, written and arranged by **Don Nix** (ex-Mar-Keys and **Paris Pilot**) in Memphis, *Moloch* is an excellent blues-rock album with some sound effects, noises and superb acid guitar solos by Lee Baker. Their single was recorded after the album with a later line-up and is extremely rare.

Cocaine Katy has been compiled on *It Came From Memphis* (Upstart 022) 1995.

A close friend of **Jim Dickinson**, Lee Baker would later work with Big Star and Alex Chilton and various other Memphis acts before forming Mud Boy and The Neutrons. He was tragically murdered in the late nineties.

Their last bassist, Busta Jones, would later front **White Lightnin'**. (SR/MW/RHI)

Moms Boys

The totally demented 1967 fuzz punker *Up And Down* has resurfaced on *Turds On A Bum Ride, Vol. 2* (Dble LP), *Turds On A Bum Ride, Vol. 1 & 2* (Dble CD) and *Pebbles, Vol. 9* (CD). Thought to have been a California-based act, both this track and *Yellow Pill* were on the *Freakout U.S.A.!* (LP) Soundtrack album. Another track, *Children In The Night* is also featured on the *Riot On Sunset Strip* (LP) Soundtrack album. (VJ/MW)

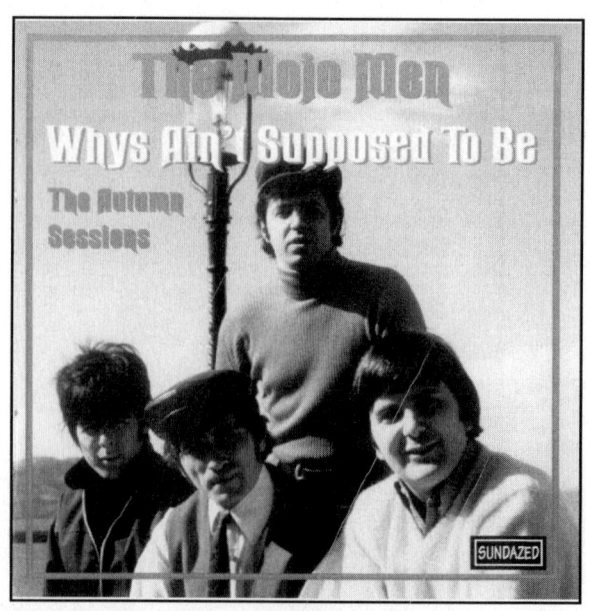

THE MOJO MEN - Whys Ain't Supposed To Be CD.

MOLOCH - Moloch CD.

Monacles

Personnel:	PHIL GRAY	drms	AB
	SKIP HAHN	gtr, organ	A
	JIM NEWBY	bs, vcls	AB
	MARLOW STEWART/HENDRIX	ld gtr	AB
	JOE CUNNINGHAM	organ	B

ALBUM: 1 THE MONACLES (Arcania International LP #1) ???? ?

45s: I Can't Win/Headaches For Me (PS) (Variety Films 301) 1965
You'll Do It Again/Debbie (PS) (Variety Films 401) 1966
I Found The Way/
The Way You Smile (PS) (Variety Films 501) 1967
Everybody Thinks I'm Lonely/
Now That I'm Here (Variety Films 601) 1967

NB: There's also a retrospective 45: (A) *I Can't Win / Heartaches For Me* (Norton 100) 2002, which reproduces the first 45, with art sleeve and pressed on golden-yellow wax, but presents two alternate takes.

Marlow Stewart and His 4 Guitars
45: Riptide / Sky Surf N (Variety Productions) 1963

Marlow Stewart and The (Frantic) Illusions
45: Earthquake /
Ooh Poo Pah Doo (PS) (Variety Prod. VP-201) 1964

Orange County in California was home to this teen-beat quartet whose ages ranged from 11 to 16. They started life as The Masters and were later known as The Laurels before they finally settled on **The Monacles** as their name. *I Can't Win*, is a typical teen punk number written by Jim Newby. Marlow Hendrix had previously fronted two surf instrumental 45s on the same label, under the name Marlow Stewart.

The Arcania Int'l album presents: three different takes of both sides of **The Monacles** debut, which are their strongest brat-pack punky-poppers; both sides of the follow-up; one cut each from the last two 45s; two unreleased 1966 cuts; and the top sides from the earlier 'Marlow Stewart' 45s.

Compilation appearances have included: *Heartaches* and *I Can't Win* on *Sixties Rebellion, Vol. 6* (LP & CD); *I Can't Win* on *Back From The Grave, Vol. 3* (LP) and *Everywhere Chainsaw Sound* (LP); and *Everybody Thinks I'm Lonely* on *Bad Vibrations, Vol. 1* (LP). (MW)

Stephen Monahan

ALBUM: 1 STEPHEN MONAHAN (Kapp KL-1528) 1968 -

45s: α City Of Windows/Lost People (Kapp 835) 1967
Play While She Dances/ The Iron Horse (Kapp 857) 1967
Long Live The King/Newberry Barn Dance (Kapp 872) 1967
The Flying Machine/A Little Bit (Jamie 1392) 1970
Gonna Build Me A World/
You Didn't Mean To Make It Rain (Jamie 1404) 1972

NB: α also issued in the UK (London HLR 10145) 1967.

Although sometimes described as a mix of Donovan and **Darius** by imaginative dealers, this album is in fact composed of universally weak orchestrated pop tunes, written by Monahan and T. Lazoros.

The album was recorded at the Gold Star Studios in Hollywood, arranged by Don Peake and produced for their York/Pala company by Charles Greene and Brian Stone, the managers of **Buffalo Springfield** and **Iron Butterfly**.

The first two (and maybe the third) Kapp singles are from the album.

The Flying Machine 45 was a "Trip Universal" production and might have appeared originally on that Miami label. Trip Universal had also placed the Heroes of Cranberry Farm and later co-owner Bill Stith with Jamie.

Monahan also recorded (in a Roy Orbison style) for Vee Jay in the early sixties. His whereabouts are unknown. (SR/JLh)

(Florian) Monday and His Mondos

45s: α Mondo / Mondo Moe (FM 1214) c1961
β Mondo / Mondo Moe (Realm 006) 1964
χ Rip It, Rip It Up / Lovin' (Realm 007) 1964
δ Minnie Ha Ha / (I'm) Crying (Columbus 1040/1) 1965

NB: α as **Junior and His Mondos**. β 'B' side also seen as **The Way Of The Mondo** - confirmation anyone, please. χ as **Florian Monday and His Mondos**. δ as **Monday's Mondos**.

This was an early sixties garage rock'n'roll outfit from Woonsockett, Rhode Island. They recorded under at least three different names. On the **Monday's Mondos** 45 they sounded very much like **The Kingsmen**.

I'm Crying was a cover of The Animals track.

Compilation appearances have included: *I'm Cryin'* on *New England Teen Scene, Vol. 2* (LP) and *Teenage Shutdown, Vol. 2* (LP & CD); *Mondo* on *Garage Punk Unknowns, Vol. 6* (LP); and *Rip It Up* on *Hipsville, Vol. 2* (LP). (VJ/MW)

Monday Rain

45: It's All Too Much/I Gotta Get Back To You (A&M 1107) 1969

Their cover of the Fab Four's *It's All Too Much* is heavy pop with a 'White Album' - period - Beatles feel, and a withering guitar break - unexpectedly good for this label. The flip reverts to laid - back folk - pop, more the A&M norm. (MW)

The Monkees

Personnel:	MICKEY DOLENZ	gtr, drms, vcls	ABC
	DAVY JONES	vcls	ABC
	MICHAEL NESMITH	gtr, vcls	AB
	PETER TORK	gtr, bs, vcls	A

ALBUMS:
1(A) THE MONKEES (Colgems 101) 1966 1 -
2(A) MORE OF THE MONKEES (Colgems 102) 1967 1 -
3(A) HEADQUARTERS (Colgems 103) 1967 1 -
4(A) PISCES, AQUARIUS, CAPRICORN AND JONES LTD
     (Colgems 104) 1967 1 -
5(A) THE BIRDS, THE BEES AND THE MONKEES
     (Colgems 109) 1968 3 -
6(A) HEAD (Colgems 5008) 1968 45 SC
7(A) INSTANT REPLAY (Colgems 113) 1969 32 SC
8(A) GREATEST HITS (Colgems 115) 1969 93 -
9(B) THE MONKEES PRESENT (Mickey, Davy, Michael)
     (Colgems 11 7) 1969 100 SC

10(C)	CHANGES	(Colgems 11 9) 1970 - SC
11(A)	GOLDEN HITS	(Colgems 329) 1970 - -
12(A)	BARREL FULL OF MONKEES	(Colgems 1001) 1970 - SC
13(-)	THE MONKEES (dbl)	(Laurie House 8009) 197? - -
14(-)	THE MONKEES GREATEST HITS	(Arista 4089) 1976 58 -

NB: All of **The Monkees** original albums have been repackaged on CD by Rhino, each with bonus tracks and copious liner notes. (1), (2), (3), (4) and (5) also reissued in 1996 by Sundazed on limited edition coloured vinyl (SC 5045/6/7/8 respectively). (14) is a reissue of (8) but with some different tracks. Several collectable items have also appeared on vinyl recently. These include *Monkeyshines* (an ultra rare "Fan Club" edition of previously unreleased material); 1986 *Philadelphia* (a limited edition interview picture disc); *Live L.A. '86* (their 20th Anniversary Tour); *Original Formula* (Live '89, a limited edition release with Mike Nesmith); *Revolutions* (featuring their previously unreleased TV soundtrack and live material) and *Talk Down Under* (an interview LP from Australia). Recent CD releases include:- *Listen To The Band* (a 4-CD set featuring 80 of their classic songs); *Live '67* (a 16-track CD on Rhino); *Pool It* (a reunion CD on Rhino) and a series called *Missing Links, Vol. 1, Vol. 2* and *Vol. 3* which contain previously unavailable tracks.

HCP

45s:	Last Train To Clarksville/		
	Take A Giant Step	(Colgems 1001) 1966 1
	I'm A Believer/		
	(I'm Not Your) Stepping Stone	(Colgems 1002) 1966 1/20
	Little Bit Me, Little Bit You/		
	Girl, I Knew Somewhere	(Colgems 1004) 1967 2/39
	Pleasant Valley Sunday/Words	(Colgems 1007) 1967 3/11
α	Daydream Believer/Goin' Down	(Colgems 1012) 1967 1/104
	Valleri/Tapioca Tundra	(Colgems 101 9) 1968 3/34
	D.W. Washburn/		
	It's Nice To Be With You	(Colgems 1023) 1968 19/51
	Porpoise Song/As We Go Along	(Colgems 1031) 1968 62/106
	Tear Drop City/A Man Without A Dream	(Colgems 5000) l969 56
	Listen To The Band/Someday Man	(Colgems 5004) 1969 63/81
	Good Clean Fun/		
	Mommy and Daddy	(Colgems 5005) 1969 82/109
	Oh My My/I Love You Better	(Colgems 5011) 1970 98

NB: α also released in France with a picture sleeve (RCA 49952). There are also four French EPs with picture sleeves on RCA.

In 1966, Bob Rafelson (writer, director and producer) teamed up with Bert Schneider to produce for Screen Gems a new TV comedy series about the life of a mythical pop group using the Beatles' film *A Hard Days Night* as its framework. An ad was placed in L.A.'s 'Daily Variety' for 'four insane boys' between the ages of 17-21 and 437 hopefuls were auditioned. The chosen four were Davy Jones, a British child TV star who'd been born in Manchester on 30 December 1945 and had released a solo album and 45 in the US; Michael Nesmith, who'd been born in Houston, Texas on 30 December 1942, he was a member of L.A.'s folk circuit and using the name **Michael Blessing** had released 45s on the Colpix label; Mickey Dolenz, who'd been born in L.A. on 8 March 1946 and was a child star of the American TV show 'Circus Boy' and Peter Tork, born in Washington, D.C. on 13 February 1945 and also involved in the L.A. folk circuit as a member of the Au Go Go Singers. Among those rejected were Stephen Stills (allegedly because of bad teeth) and future Three Dog Night leader, Danny Hutton. **Charles Manson** too is often said to have been rejected, but he is also said to have been in jail at the time.

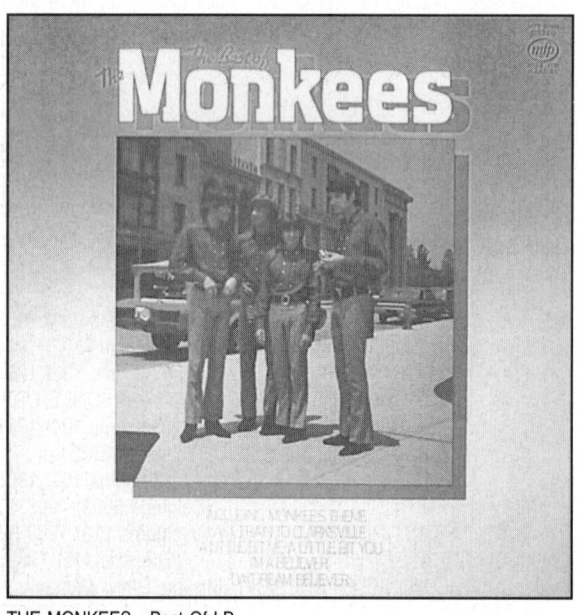

THE MONKEES - Best Of LP.

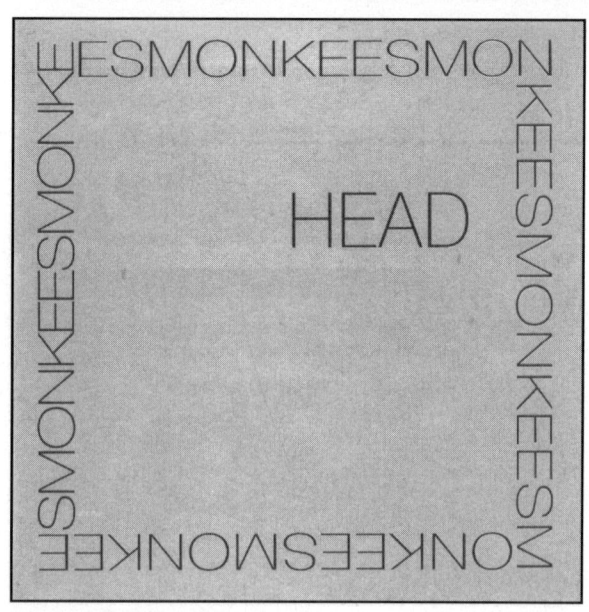

THE MONKEES - Head CD.

Once recruited the acting and grooming lessons began and the groups' development was very carefully managed. They were told what to sing, how to sing, weren't allowed to play their own instruments on recording sessions and the head of Screen-Gems Music, Don Kirshner, who was responsible for the musical supervision of the series, signed seasoned songwriters like Gerry Goffin, Carole King, Neil Diamond and Neil Sedaka to write their songs.

Over the next two to three years **The Monkees** were extremely successful in commercial terms - almost a match for The Beatles. Their debut 45 hit the No. 1 spot in the USA and later in 1967 made No. 23 in the UK. Their first album went gold in the USA where it topped the charts for 13 weeks. Their next 45 *I'm A Believer* also hit No. 1 in the USA and the U.K. and *Monkeemania* was now equalling Beatlemania. Their next album *More Of The Monkees* also topped the U.S. charts for 18 months and later reached the zenith of the U.K. Charts too. Strengthened by all this success and with the band gaining confidence as musicians following a successful U.S. tour, **The Monkees** insisted that they should be permitted to play on their own records and write more of their own songs and eventually they won the day on this with Don Kirshner resigning as Chief Executive of Screen Gems Music. He went on to manufacture another TV pop group, The Archies, who existed only in cartoon form. After **The Monkees**' next 45 *A Little Bit Me, A Little Bit You* had made No. 2 in the US, they themselves recorded their next LP *Headquarters* assisted by just three outsiders. It topped the U.S. Album Charts for just one week before being displaced by The Beatles' *Sgt. Pepper*. It reached No. 2 in the U.K. where it was kept from the top by *Sgt. Pepper*. They continued to enjoy further 45 chart success with *Alternate Title* (No. 2 in the UK - not issued in the USA), *Daydream Believer* (No. 3 in the U.S. and No. 1 1 in the UK), *Words* (the B side to *Daydream Believer* (No. 1 1 in the US) and *Valleri* (No. 3 in the U.S. and No. 12 in the UK).

The Monkees continued to press for more artistic freedom and on their next album *The Birds, The Bees and The Monkees* each group member contributed individual tracks. This didn't seem to undermine the project's commercial success because it still made No. 3 in the U.S. Album Charts and they were now enthusiastically working on a feature film *Head*. This was directed by Bob Rafelson assisted by Jack Nicholson for Columbia Pictures. Whilst all this was going on there were signs of a downturn in their popularity. In June 1968 their TV series, which had run successfully since its inception was scrapped, and the following month their revival of The Coasters' *D.W. Washburn* made only No. 19 in the U.S. Charts and No. 17 in the UK. The follow-up *Porpoise Song* peaked at just 62 in the U.S. and didn't chart in the U.K. at all. *Head* was the most relevant of their projects in terms of this book but in box office terms it was a disaster. Far from the standard teen film they had expected Columbia found themselves presented with an imaginative, bizarre and disjointed mixture including scenes of the band committing suicide by jumping from a bridge and a concert intercut with Vietnam war atrocities. The album only managed No. 45 in the album charts; despite its relatively disappointing commercial showing the album was by far the group's most creative and interesting venture. After this the band began to slowly disintegrate. Peter Tork bought out his contract at considerable cost ($160,000 to be precise) in December 1968 and later in March 1970 Mike Nesmith, having stayed on to fulfil his contractual obligations, left to start his own group, The First National Band. Whilst in 1969 the group had continued to enjoy some chart success as a trio, the Changes album recorded by Dolenz and Jones (after the departure of the other two) in 1970 chalked up very disappointing sales. By June that year Dolenz and Jones had also decided to call it a day.

There was a reformation in 1975 involving Jones and Dolenz (Tork and Nesmith weren't interested) who revived the band with Tommy Boyce and Bobby Hart, who'd written many of their early songs. They began a two year tour "The Golden Great Hits Of The Monkees Show - The Guys Who Wrote 'Em And The Guys Who Sang 'Em", signed a new deal with Capitol who issued an album *Dolenz, Jones, Boyce And Hart*, whilst the compilation *The Monkees Greatest Hits* made No. 58 in the U.S. Charts. Since then there have been various (often successful) attempts to revive the band, most notably in 1986 when to celebrate the group's 20th anniversary MTV in the U.S. showed a 22.5 hour 'Pleasant Valley Sunday' marathon of every **Monkees** TV programme. This prompted Dolenz, Jones and Tork to reform the group in February of that year for a Summer tour and during a **Monkees** convention in August that year in Philadelphia they enjoyed no fewer than seven albums in the U.S. Top 200 Album Charts.

The *Head* project did receive more acclaim in retrospect. In March 1977, in response to cult demand, the U.K. National Film Theatre imported a copy of the film and it ran for a season in London's Electric Cinema.

A further reunion of the four original Monkees occurred during 1996. An album was recorded and released, followed by a tour.

You'll also find *Porpoise Song* on *Nuggets, Vol. 9* (LP) and *Pleasant Valley Sunday* and *Valleri* both appear on the *Nuggets* (CD). (VJ/CB/SR)

The Monks

Personnel:	GARY BURGER	vcls, gtr	A
	LARRY CLARKE	organ	A
	DAVE DAY	banjo	A
	ROGER JOHNSTON	drms	A
	EDDIE SHAW	bs	A

ALBUM: 1(A) BLACK MONK TIME (Polydor 249900) 1966 R5

NB: (1) German only issue. (1) Reissued on CD by Israphon 199?, and later by Repertoire (REP 4438-WP) 1994 with their two non-LP 45s as bonus tracks. The definitive CD reissue however is 1998's Infinite Zero Archive release (9 43112-2), which also includes both non-LP 45s and demo versions of *I Hate You* and *Oh, How To Do Now*, plus a detailed band history / interview with the band. (1) has also been counterfeited on LP. There's also a CD of early demos *Five Upstart Americans* (Omplatten FJORD 005).

45s:	Complication/		
	Oh, How To Do Now	(Polydor International 52952)	1966
α	I Can't Get Over You/		
	Cuckoo (PS)	(Polydor International 52957)	1966
α	Love Can Tame The Wild/He Went Down		
	To The Sea (PS)	(Polydor International 52958)	1967

NB: α non LP cuts.

A U.S. band stationed in Europe. They consisted of five serving soldiers in the U.S. army in Frankfurt who formed a band and hit the German beer club halls. Far from singing twee songs about love and cars **The Monks** used a riffing style and lyrics concerned with war, death and hate. This highly unusual image got them lots of bookings, a tour with The Easybeats and, after they'd quit the army in early 1966, a record deal with Polydor. They got to appear on German pop TV shows like "Beat Club" to promote their records but they didn't sell, probably because the public didn't know how to react to a punkish band ahead of their time. Their album now commands a small fortune on the collectors' market but the various CD reissues are now a cheaper way to get to hear it.

Eddie Shaw has also published a book entitled 'Black Monk Time' about the band's exploits.

With continued interest in **The Monks**, the band reformed for a couple of appearances at the New York 'Cavestomp' festival (5-7th November 1999), performing alongside luminaries such as **The Chocolate Watchband** and **The Standells**.

Compilation appearances have included: *Cuckoo* on *Magic Carpet Ride* (LP); *Complication* on *Nuggets Box* (4-CD), *Turds On A Bum Ride, Vol. 1 & 2* (Dble CD) and *Turds On A Bum Ride, Vol. 1* (Dble LP). A live track *Monks Chant* has also subsequently resurfaced on *Hide & Seek Again* (LP). (VJ/MO)

The Monocles

Personnel:	ROBB CASSEDAY	AB
	JOE FLOTH	AB
	DON HIRSHFIELD	AB
	RICK HULL	AB
	KEVIN McILHENNY	A

45s:	Psychedelic (That's Where It's At)/		
	Boogie Man	(Denco 926)	1966
	The Spider And The Fly/		
	The Other Side of Happiness	(Chicory 407)	1966

This band operated out of Greeley, Colorado, whose Chicory label apparently issued a number of mutated psychedelic punk singles circa 1966-67. Their *Spider And The Fly*, is a re-creation of someone's nightmare. Falsetto shrieks of *Help Me, Help Me*, are superimposed upon a booming bass, mysterious organ and echo effects. The end result is a most unusual single. Prior to this they'd recorded an earlier 45. The 'A' side *Psychedelic (That's Where It's At)* has some effective percussion and guitar backing which gives way to an instrumental freak-out.

The band actually formed in 1964 and Kevin McIlhenny died in early 1966 before they started recording. Their repertoire consisted of the popular hits of the day as well as their own more demented originals and they used to drive around Boulder in a hearse!

In 1967, the band changed name to **The Higher Elevation**, backing **Dave Diamond** on his amazing "bubbly-fudge" *Diamond Mine* (a reworking of the instrumental track to their *Spider And The Fly*) before releasing three 45s on Liberty.

Compilation appearances have included: *The Spider And The Fly* on *Mayhem & Psychosis, Vol. 1* (LP), *Mayhem & Psychosis, Vol. 1* (CD), *Pebbles, Vol. 3* (CD), *Pebbles Box* (5-LP), *Pebbles, Vol. 3* (LP), *Pebbles, Vol. 2 (ESD)* (CD) and *Trash Box* (5-CD); *Psychedelic (That's Where It's At)* on *Highs In The Mid-Sixties, Vol. 18* (LP), *Psychedelic Experience, Vol. 2* (CD) and *The Psychedelic Experience, Vol. 2* (LP). (VJ/MW)

THE MONKS - Black Time LP.

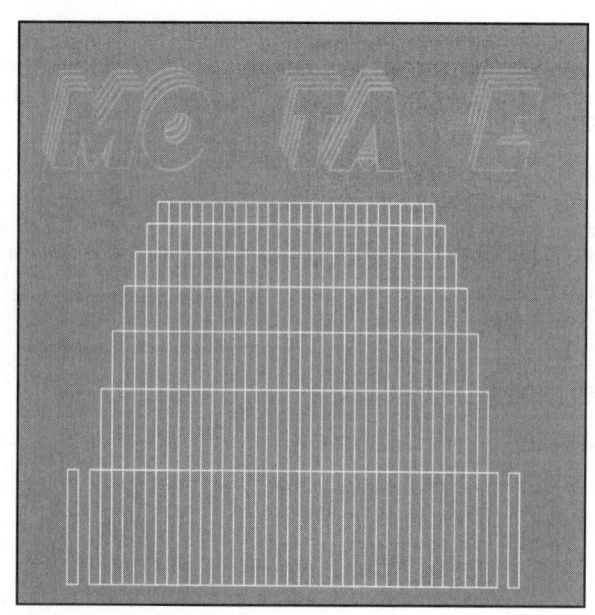

MONTAGE - Montage CD.

Jeff Monn

Personnel incl: JEFFREY MONN (JEFFREY NEUFELD) vcls, gtr   A

ALBUM: 1   REALITY   (Vanguard VSD 65??) 1968 -

Jeff Monn was in fact Jeffrey Neufeld, the former singer of the **Third Bardo**. He probably had some kind of identity problems, as he would also record as **Chris Moon**!

This album is rather disconcerting as Monn/Neufeld sang and played guitar in front of a classical orchestra conducted by Peter Shickele, of P.D.Q. Bach "fame". The concept would be used by several groups in the following decades, and you'll either be enthusiastic about it or hate it completely. The songs were written by Neufeld who also selected two Rolling Stones covers *I'm Free* and *Back Street Girl* plus *Think I Care*, written by Skip Prokop and Adam Mitchell of The Paupers and a Jimmy Reed song. (SR)

Montage

Personnel: MICHAEL BROWN   keyb'ds   A
             VANCE CHAPMAN   drms   A
             LANCE CORNELIUS   bs   A
             MIKE SMYTH   gtr   A
             BOB STEURER   vcls   A

ALBUMS: 1(A) MONTAGE   (Laurie SLP 2049) 1969 SC
         2(-) HOT PARTS   (Kama Sutra KSBS 2054) 1972 -

NB: (1) reissued in the U.K. on Bam-Caruso (KIRI 055) in 1987. (1) reissued on CD (Sundazed SC 6172) 2001.

45s: I Shall Call Her Mary/
       An Audience With Miss Priscilla Gray   (Laurie 3438) 1968
       Wake Up Jimmy/Tinsel and Ivy   (Laurie 3453) 1968

Michael Brown, who had previously played with New York-based **Left Banke**, wrote nine of the ten tracks on the above album by this New York band, arranged them and played all the keyboards. The album characterised by melodic vocal harmonies and either stringed or keyboard accompaniment had considerable commercial potential and it's surprising that **Montage** did not enjoy greater success. The album included a ghostly version of *Desiree*, which had earlier been an unsuccessful single for **The Left Banke**, and *I Shall Call Her Mary*, an absolute gem that was also released as a 45. A second, equally strong 45, *Wake Up Jimmy* was also released. Later, after Brown had signed for Kama Sutra, he played on and wrote both cuts on Steve Martin's only solo single (he'd played with Martin in **Left Banke**), *Two By Two/Love Songs In The Night*. This was released on Buddah (219) in 1971. The two tracks later reappeared, along with three cuts from the **Montage** album and a few other items on the Soundtrack to *Hot Parts*, which starred Ultra Violet, famed for her movie work with Andy Warhol. Brown later formed **Stories**, which he left after their second album.

I Shall Call Her Mary has resurfaced on *Nuggets, Vol. 11* (LP) and you'll also find *Tinsel and Ivy* on *Illusions From The Cracking Void*. (VJ)

Montells

Personnel: JEFF ALLEN   drms
             GEORGE HALL   bs
             DANNY MURPHY   vcls, bs, gtr, perc
             CARTER RAGSDALE   vcls
             GEORGE WALDEN   ld gtr
             JOHN WEATHERFORD   gtr

ALBUM: 1   THE MONTELLS / THE EVIL   (Corduroy CORD 027) 1997

45:          Daddy Rolling Stone/You Can't Make Me   (Thames 102) 1966

NB: There's also a split 45, *I'm Movin' On/You Can't Make Me* (Norton 826) 1999, with the 'A' side by **Evil**.

Hailing from Miami in Florida this youthful five piece began life as The Impalas before changing name to the **Montells**. Between 1965 and 1968 they were arguably the premier garage outfit to play in Florida and South Georgia, at venues like the Surf Club in Daytona Beach, headlining over acts like the pre-**Allman Brothers**, **Allman Joys**. Unashamedly influenced by The Pretty Things and The Kinks, their drummer Jeff Allen regularly travelled to London to see the Pretty Things play and hung out with Viv Prince. Changing name again to **H.M. Subjects** they went on to record a good cover of The Pretties' *Don't Bring Me Down* which was a local hit, although they reverted back to The **Montells** moniker again later.

You Can't Make Me, which is one of the finest primal R'n'B blasts you could ever wish for, has also appeared on *Back From The Grave, Vol. 3* (LP), *Back From The Grave, Vol. 2* (CD) and *Psychedelic States: Florida Vol. 3* (CD). The track was written by Danny Murphy and **The Hustlers'** Bob Leavitt. It was recorded at Criteria Studios with Bill Lachmiller guesting at the last minute on guitar (for an unavailable George Walden) and laying down that blistering solo.

Jeff Allen later went on to play with **Evil**, and a compilation featuring both bands has just been released on Corduroy. It features the 45 sides, both versions of *Don't Bring Me Down* (as by **H.M. Subjects**) plus two tracks from May 1965, *Can't Explain* and *Watch Out For That Guy*. (VJ/MW/JLh)

Monuments

Personnel incl: HOWARD COLLINGS   A

45:          I Need You/African Diamonds   (Alvera M-65) 1966

Tulsa in Oklahoma was home to this mob. The flip side, *African Diamonds*, can also be heard on *Monsters Of The Midwest, Vol. 3* (LP). It's innocuous enough with some effective upfront keyboards. (VJ)

The Mood

45:          In The Amber Fields/Erica   (B & G 101) 196?

An extremely obscure 45. You can also find *In The Amber Fields*, which is eminently forgettable on *Pebbles, Vol. 16* (LP). (VJ)

The Moods

ALBUM: 1   LIVE AT TURNER HALL   (ACR hrs-33-6933) c1968 R1

From Texas, a frat-rock/garage group, with the usual covers of *Hey Joe, Gloria, Suzy Q, What'd I Say, Wine Wine Wine*... Some fuzz breaks, but also some country ballads. (SR)

Ron Moody and The Centaurs

45:          If I Didn't Have A Dime/The New Breed   (Columbia 44908) 1969

An obscure rock group. The 45 was produced by Tom Maeder and Charlie Bradshaw. (SR)

Moogie Woogie

Personnel:	PAUL BEAVER	moog	A
	FAST FINGERS FINKELSTEIN		
	(MICHAEL BLOOMFIELD)	gtr	A
	NORMAN DAYRON		A
	ERWIN HELFER		A
	MARK NAFTALIN	keyb'ds	A

ALBUM: 1(A) MOOGIE WOOGIE (Chess 1545) 1969 SC

An attempt at using the moog to create some psychedelic blues and boogie with titles like *Angel Dust Boogie*, *Moogie Boogie* or *Boogie Loo*. Paul Beaver (from **Beaver and Krause**) was one of the first American specialists of the synthesizer. **Bloomfield** and Naftalin were previously in the **Paul Buttterfield Blues Band**.

The album is getting hard to find. Beaver and **Bloomfield** had previously worked together with the **Electric Flag** and would team up again on **Beaver and Krause**'s *Gandharva*. (SR)

Moolah

ALBUM: 1 WOE YE DEMONS POSSESSED (Private Pressing) 1974

A very strange album of spaced-out psychedelic electronics with trippy effects, which may interest fans of the German group Faust. (SR)

The Moon

Personnel incl:	LARRY BROWN	drums	A
	DAVID JACKSON	bs, vcls	A
	DAVID MARKS	gtr, vcls	A
	MATTHEW MOORE	keyb'ds, gtr, vcls	A

ALBUMS:	1	WITHOUT EARTH	(Imperial LP 12381) 1968 -
	2	THE MOON	(Imperial LP 12444) 1969 -

45s:	Mothers And Fathers / Someday Girl	(Imperial 66285) 1968
	John Automation / Faces	(Imperial 66330) 1968
	Pirate / Not To Know	(Imperial 66415) 1969

NB: There's also a French 45 with PS, *Pirate/The Good Side* (Liberty 2C00691346M) 1969.

A late sixties pop-rock supergroup from Los Angeles. David Marks had been with the Beach Boys and **The Band Without A Name**; Matthew Moore was with **Matthew Moore Plus Four** and did solo work before joining the Mad Dogs; David Jackson came from **Hearts and Flowers** and was later with Dillard and Clark; Larry Brown had drummed with **Davie Allan and The Arrows** (and no doubt on many other combos behind film soundtracks and those Sidewalk/Tower releases produced by Mike Curb) and would later turn up in **Gunhill Road**.

Their albums are rated highly by some - not really psychedelic but with psychy touches and imagery, and more pop than rock - their sound has been compared to the Beatles and the Bee Gees from that period. Certainly well-crafted, dare one say, progressive-pop. Almost all their material was written by the band (MW/VJ/HM/BCr/SR)

The Moon-Dawgs

Personnel:	RAY GENOVESE	vcls	A
	FRANK SPENCER		A
	JOHNNY SPENCER		A

45s:	Baby As Time Goes By / You're No Good	(Bofuz BF-1115) 1966
	Keep On Pushing / Devil's Season	(Round 69) 1968/9

Formed in Summer '65 in New Orleans after the arrival of the Spencer brothers from Key West, Florida. The first 45 is a moody mid-tempo punker with strong raw vocals and screams from Genovese but a rather wimpy guitar break, where some biting fuzz would have been more suitable. *You're No Good* is a great Kinks-inspired punker with strong drumming, good yearning vocal style and a short frantic break - ideal for one of those 'desperate garage punker' compilations.

The band split up in 1967 but a year or so later got together again to record the TOTALLY AWESOME *Keep On Pushing*. Kicking off with some evil distortion, Genovese's vocals are in superb form for this aggressive testosterone-fuelled punker with vicious outbursts of distorted fuzz, driving beat, a psychotic break, and the climax-of-rage that has Genovese shouting incoherently. In my 'umble opinion this is an all-time top acid-punk classic and certainly No.1 on the shivers-down-the-spine and hairs-standing-on-the-neck scale, even beating out the **Calico Wall**'s *Living Sickness* - yeah, it's THAT incredible!

Compilation appearances have included: *You're No Good* on *The Lost Generation, Vol. 2* (LP) and *Let's Dig 'Em Up, Vol. 2* (LP); *Keep On Pushing* on *Louisiana Punk Groups From The Sixties, Vol. 2* (LP), *Punk Classics, Vol. 3* (7" EP) and *Sixties Archive, Vol. 3* (CD); *Baby As Time Goes By* on *Highs In The Mid-Sixties, Vol. 13* (LP). (MW/AB-"Brown Paper Sack")

Glen Mooney and The Ferraris

45: The Big Surf / You Lied To Me (Cenna Tawni 101) 1964

Midwest surf-garage on a Marion, Ohio label whose name must have a great story behind it. About as far from the coasts as you could get, catch *The Big Surf* on *The Big Itch (Vol.1)*. (GGI/MW)

Chris Moon Group

Personnel incl:	CHRIS MOON (JEFFREY NEUFELD)	vcls, gtr	A

ALBUM: 1 THE CHRIS MOON GROUP (Kinetic) 197? -

45: Good/ Give It To Me (Kinetic 6000) 1970

NB: also released with a PS in Holland by CBS.

An early seventies release on the same label as **Marcus**, by the singer from **The Third Bardo**. (SR)

The Moon Men

45: Other Side Of The Moon/? (Southern Sound 114) 196?

From Washington D.C., this is actually the legendary **Link Wray and The Raymen** under one of the many pseudonyms they used during the

THE MONTELLS/EVIL - Split LP.

early-to-mid-60s. Their instrumental *Other Side Of The Moon* can also be heard on *Signed, D.C.* (LP). (VJ/MW)

The Moonrakers

Personnel:	JOEL BRANDES	bs	AB
	DENNIS FLANAGAN	keyb'ds	AB
	BOB MacVITTIE	drms	A
	VEEDER VAN DORN	vcls, rhythm gtr, elect. banjo, hmnca	A
	BOB WEBBER	gtr	A
	BOB SAUNER	drms	B
	RANDY WALRATH	gtr	B
	(JERRY CORBETTA	drms, keyb'ds	B)

ALBUM: 1(A/B) TOGETHER WITH HIM (Shamley SS 704) 1968 -

45s:
You'll Come Back/I Was Wrong (Tower 157) 1965
I'm Alright/Come On, Let's Move (Tower 180) 1966
Trip And Fall/Time And A Place (Tower 222) 1966
Baby, Please Don't Go/I Don't Believe (Tower 239) 1966
Love Train/
He's A Coming My Way Lord (Shamley 44012) 1967/8
No Number To Call/Together With Him (Shamley 44015) 1969
Not Hidin' Anymore/
Seventh Star (B Side non-LP) (Shamley 44021) 1969

From Denver, Colorado, this outfit started out as a fine punk band releasing four 45s for Tower. Amongst these are the frantic garage-punker *You'll Come Back*, plus excellent covers of *I'm All Right* and *Baby, Please Don't Go*. The flip to their fourth 45 was also a cover of The Guilloteens' folk-rocker.

The Moonrakers evolved out of surf act The Surfin' Classics, when vocalist/guitarist Doug Dolph was replaced by Denny Flannigan. As The Surfin' Classics, they'd performed a lot of Beach Boys/Ventures material, but their name change came about when they got matched in a Battle of The Bands with Colorado's **Astronauts** and needed a more 'with-it' name. Bob MacVittie thus renamed themselves after the book he was reading at the time, Ian Fleming's novel "Moonraker".

The band obtained their deal with Tower through their manager Roger Christian, a well-known L.A. disc jockey. Christian (who co-wrote *Little Deuce Coupe* and *Don't Worry Baby* with Brian Wilson), had 'connections'... **The Moonrakers** thus got to open for many major groups in Denver, including The Dave Clark Five, the Righteous Brothers and Sonny and Cher. They even got to meet The Beatles and Bill Haley and The Comets when they played for 50,000 screaming fans at Red Rocks Amphitheatre, in the Foothills of the Rocky Mountains.

The band also helped promote a Denver concert with **The Byrds** around the time of *Mr. Tambourine Man* in the Ballroom at Lakeside Gardens Amusement Park, home of one of the greatest old-time rollercoasters in the world. Veeder Van Dorn:- "The Byrds parked their tour bus at the Moonraker's bass player's parents house for a few hours while they prepared for the concert, but when they all arrived at the Amusement Park, Joel's hair was dyed orange and he was mumbling 'the colors are flowing.... can you see them... can you see them?' about all the rainbow colors flowing around the Concert Hall!"

With the onset of the psychedelic era came a dramatic charge of style in **The Moonrakers** music which is apparent on their album. Full of psychedelia with religious overtones, the cover shows the group below an altar and there is some good psychedelic guitar work plus great lyrics on *The Pot Starts To Boil*.

Veeder Van Dorn, also claims to be the first person to play an electric banjo in a rock band:- "I purchased a steel-rimmed Ode banjo at the Denver Folklore Center from the owner Harry Tufts and installed a simple magnetic pickup under the wooden bridge. It was used on the Moonrakers' Tower release *Time And A Place*, which was selected by the radio stations in Colorado Springs, sixty miles South of Denver, as the A side instead of *Trip And Fall* and went to No. 1 there".

During the recording of the album, Webber (ex-**The Soul Survivors**) and MacVittie left being replaced by Randy Walrath and Bob Sauner. Van Dorn also quit to join **The Poor**, where he got to know **Bruce Palmer** at a gig with **Buffalo Springfield** at Hollywood's 'Whisky A-Go-Go'. Shortly afterwards, Van Dorn, MacVittie, Corbetta and Webber formed **Sugarloaf**, although Van Dorn left after a few months (he wrote one song *Things Gonna Change Some* on their debut album *Spaceship Earth*). He then formed Mescalero Space Kit with Sam Fuller and Kip Gilbert (both ex-**Rainy Daze**), and Mark Kincaid (ex-**Electric Prunes**). Van Dorn:- "Kip Gilbert's brother Tim, who'd had a songwriting hit with *Incense And Peppermints*, arranged a demo session with Saul Zaentz at Fantasy Records in Berkeley. At the time Fantasy was having a huge success with **Creedence Clearwater Revival**. One of the original songs we recorded *Earth Ain't A Jail* was soon translated into *I'm Just A Singer In A Rock And Roll Band* by the Moody Blues...".

Joel Brandes later went on to manage Eric Burdon and War.

Compilation appearances have included: *Baby Please Don't Go* on *Mayhem & Psychosis, Vol. 3* (LP), *Mayhem & Psychosis, Vol. 2* (CD), *Psychotic Moose And The Soul Searchers* (LP), *Victims Of Circumstances, Vol. 1* (LP), *Victims Of Circumstance, Vol. 2* (CD); *You'll Come Back* on *Pebbles, Vol. 10* (LP); *I'm All Right* on *Everywhere Interferences* (LP); *I Don't Believe*, *Baby Please Don't Go* and *Highs In The Mid-Sixties, Vol. 18* (LP). (VJ/MW/VD)

Bill and Ron Moore

ALBUM: 1 LO AND BEHOLD (Private Pressing) 1969 ?

From Kentucky, a Christian folk duo with cuts like *Look To Your Soul* or *Buffalo*. (SR)

Bob Moore

ALBUM: 1 VIVA (Hickory) 1968 -

45s:
Only the Lonely/Skokian (Hickory 1357) 1965
Hell's Angels/I Can't Stop Loving You (Hickory 1372) 1966
Elephant Rock/Spanish Eyes (Hickory 1407) 1966
Acapulco/Parade Of The Matadors (Hickory 1426) 1966
Amigo No. 1 /White Sport Coat (Hickory 1437) 1967
River/Fastest Guitar Alive (Hickory 1480) 1967
Amigo No. 1 /You Sit Around All Day (Hickory 1521) 1968

The album is reputed to be psychedelic and is now a minor collectors' item. (VJ)

Jerry Moore

ALBUM: 1 LIFE IS A CONSTANT JOURNEY HOME (ESP) 1969 ?

45: Winds Of Change/? (ESP-Disk 4561) 1969

Another ESP oddity, this one combines folk psych and spacy jazz. (SR)

THE MOONRAKERS - Together With Him LP.

STEVE MORGEN - Morgen LP.

Matthew Moore (Plus Four)

45s:	α	I've Been Lonely Before/	
		I Know You Girl	(GNP Crescendo GNP 343) 1965
	α	Codyne (She's Real)/	
		You've Never Loved Before	(White Whale 223) 1965
	β	Face In The Crowd/St. James Infirmary	(Capitol 5668) 1966
	β	White Silk Glove/Come On	(Capital 5720) 1967

NB: α as **Matthew Moore Plus Four**. β Matthew Moore solo.

Excellent outfit featuring **Matthew Moore** prior to his formation of **Moon**. The GNP 45 kicks off with a vibrant beat - punker with strong vocals and wailing harp, whilst the flip is a brooding menacing affair. An accomplished first outing... and it gets better. Their version of *Codyne* is quite frankly, difficult to top, with forceful vocals and powerful backing in a beat - punk setting. The flip is back to cool folk - beat but the standard remains very high. If this outfit has more (unreleased) material, it certainly merits a retrospective collection!

Compilation appearances include: *Codine* on *Mindrocker, Vol. 5* (LP) and *Happy Together - The Very Best Of White Whale Records* (CD). (MW)

Moorpark Intersection

45: I Think I'll Just Go And Find Me A Flower/
Yesterday Holds On   (Capitol 2115) 1968

Infectious flower-pop produced by **David Axelrod** (**Electric Prunes** producer, **Pride**, solo concept albums). The flip is more in the **Axelrod - Prunes** 'Mass' mould - monastic chanting, muffled lines of twisting psychy guitar, oblique lyrics (albeit not in Latin) - unusual and strangely atmospheric. (MW)

More-Tishans

45: (I've Got) Nowhere To Run/
(I've Got) Nowhere To Run (instr.)   (Peak P-4453) 1967

This was a rock quintet from Stillwater in Minnesota. The 'A' side, is completely unconnected to the Martha and The Vandellas song. In fact it was the only song the band had ready to record, so the record company put an instrumental version of it on the flip side. It was the first release on the Peak label.

Compilation appearances include: *(I've Got) Nowhere To Run* (unreleased stereo version) on *Psychedelic Microdots Of The Sixties, Vol. 1* (CD); *(I've Got) Nowhere To Run* on *Root '66* (LP) and *The Best Of Metrobeat! Vol. 1* (LP). (VJ)

Chris Morgan and The Togas

Personnel incl:	CHRIS MORGAN	A
	N. RISI	A

45: There She Goes/
Would You Believe (Love Is Dead)   (Challenge 59330) 1966

From California and an excellent slice of 1966. The 'A' side is an excellent stomper with a little fuzzy guitar. The flip, a powerful folk-rock ballad. A previous 45 was released as by The Togas - *Hurry To Me/Baby, I'm In The Mood For You* (Challenge 59309) in August 1965, but is unfortunately inferior beat-folk-pop.

Compilation appearances have included:- *There She Goes* on *Mindrocker, Vol. 1* (LP); *Would You Believe (Love Is Dead)* on *Boulders, Vol. 11* (LP), *Ya Gotta Have Moxie, Vol. 1* (Dble CD) and *Psychedelic Archives, Vol. 7*; *Babe I'm In The Mood For You* on *Every Groovy Day* (LP). (VJ)

Morganmasondowns

Personnel incl:	DOWNS	A
	MASON	A
	MORGAN	A

ALBUM: 1(A) MORGANMASONDOWNS   (Roulette SR-42047) 1970 -

A folk-psych trio with a female singer produced by Allan Nicholls. (SR)

Steve Morgen

Personnel:	RENNIE GENOSSA	bs	A
	BOB MAIMAN	drms	A
	STEVE MORGEN	gtr, vcls	A
	BARRY STOCK	gtr	A

ALBUM: 1(A) MORGEN   (ABC Probe CPLP 4507S) 1969 R2

NB: (1) with poster insert. (1) reissued on vinyl (GMG) in the eighties and counterfeited on CD by Eva in the nineties.

45: Of Dreams/She's The Nitetime   (ABC Probe 474) 1969

NB: 'A' side is an edited version of an LP track.

This rare album from Long Island, New York, contains some superb psychedelic guitar work and powerful drumming on tracks like *Of Dreams, Purple* and *Love*. All the material was written by **Steve Morgen** and he also co-produced the album with Murray Shiffrin. It's not brilliant, but is worth obtaining and is now quite collectable.

The 45 version of *Of Dreams* has also resurfaced on *30 Seconds Before The Calico Wall* (CD). (VJ/MW)

Morgus and The Daringers

45: Werewolf/?   (Fulton 2458) 1964

Garage Punk Unknowns, Vol. 6 (LP) includes *Werewolf*, from this Michigan outfit. (VJ)

Mor-Loks

Personnel incl:	JOHNNY HARTIGAN	A
	SAMMY HALL	A

45s:	α	Elaine/There Goes Life	(Loks 1/2) 1965
		What My Baby Wants/	
		Lookin' For A New Day	(Decca 31950) 1966

NB: α later issued as (Living Legend 100) 1965.

From Fort Lauderdale, Florida and previously known as the Impressions (V). They followed their local debut with an excellent uptempo fuzz -

punker, backed by an impressive beat - punker. Johnny Hartigan would turn up in a seventies outfit called Truth.

Sammy Hall wrote a song called *A Little Bit of Lovin'* which was a candidate for the follow-up to *There Goes Life*, but he left and was with The Trolls briefly before joining **The Birdwatchers**; the latter got to record the song.

Compilation appearances have included: *There Goes Life* on *Love Is A Sad Song, Vol. 1* (LP); and *What My Baby Wants* on *Realities In Life* (LP). (MW/JLh)

Morly Grey

Personnel:	TIM ROLLER	gtr	AB
	MARK ROLLER	bs, vcls	AB
	PAUL CASSIDY	drms	A
	BOB LaNAVE	drms, perc, vcls	B

ALBUM: 1(A/B) THE ONLY TRUTH   (Starshine 6900) 1971 R3

NB: (1) counterfeited on vinyl in 1986. Reissued on CD and LP (Akarma AK 109) 2000, the LP version including a reprint of the original poster.

45s:	Who Can I Say You Are/ You Came To Me	(Starshine 7201) 197?
	After Me Again/A Feeling For You	(Starshine 7202) 1972

The highlight of this Youngstown, Ohio band's otherwise over-rated album is the seventeen-minute title track which is full of acid guitar work and incorporates the group's own arrangement of *When Johnny Comes Marching Home*. A free poster came with the album which was convincingly counterfeited in 1986.

Curiously, on the label of the first single it says both of these songs are "from the L.P. *The Last Supper*". This was the working title for the album during the recording sessions.

Original drummer Paul Cassidy was replaced by Bob LaNave, and a new side was recorded containing the 17-minute *The Only Truth*.

Compilation coverage appears to have been limited to *The Only Truth* on *Reverberation IV* (CD). (MMy/VJ/GGl/MRr)

Morning

Personnel:	BARRY BROWN	gtr, drms, vcls	AB
	JIM HOBSON	piano, organ, theremin, vcls	AB
	TERRY JOHNSON	gtr	AB
	JIM KEHN	drms, gtr, vcls	AB

MORNING - Morning LP.

MORLY GREY - The Only Truth LP.

	JAY LEWIS	gtr, banjo, vcls	AB
	BRUCE WALLACE	bs	A
	STUART BROTMAN	bs	B
	(AL PERKINS	steel gtr	A)
	(CHRIS DARROW	fiddle	B)

ALBUMS:	1(A)	MORNING	(Vault 138) 1970 -
	2(B)	STRUCK LIKE SILVER	(Fantasy 9402) 1972 -

45:	Tell Me A Story/Easy Keeper	(Vault 972) 1972

A fine Los Angeles-based group, originally known as The Morning and The Evening. The group was formed after Jay Lewis, also known as Jay Donnellan, had been fired from **Love** by Arthur Lee. Jim Hobson also appeared on **Love**'s *Out Here*. When the band signed a recording contract with Vault they retained complete control of the writing, engineering, arranging and producing of their first album, which is an underrated folk-influenced gem. It has a crisp, yet often sleepy sound, which is at its best on *And I'm Gone* and *Sleepy Eyes*. The album closes with a ninety second country gem *Dirt Roads* (the only track written by Jim Kehn) which is worthy of comparison with the title track of Quicksilver's *Happy Trails*.

The line-up then changed; Bruce Wallace being replaced by the former **Kaleidoscope** member Stuart Brotman and Terry Johnson only playing on one track. Vault was bought by Fantasy and the follow-up *Struck Like Silver* continues in similar vein, though the drug-influenced sleepiness has made way for a more acoustic sound epitomised by *Only To Say Goodnight* and *Now I Lay Me Down*. *Understand My Ways* on Side two particularly highlights Jay Lewis' harmonious vocals and Jim Hobson's melodic piano work, whilst *Comin' In Love* features Chris Darrow (another ex-**Kaleidoscope**) on fiddle. *Jay's Movie Song* is a beautiful instrumental while *Now I Lay Me Down* and **Hoyt Axton**'s *Never Been To Spain* merge more sensitive guitar work with artistic piano playing.

When the group broke up, Jim Hobson and Jay Lewis became session musicians and worked with Delaney Bramlett, **Country Joe**, Danny O'Keefe and Rabindra Danks. (VJ/SR)

Morning After

Personnel:	JAY ENOS	keyb'ds, gtr	A
	JIMMY GRANDMONT	drms	A
	CRAIG HERRICK	bs	A
	DON JOHNSON	ld gtr	A

45:	Things You Do / If You Love	(Tam 201,369/70) 1967

From Braintree, Massachusettes, Enos and Grandmont were originally with the Vandels who played the South Shore from 1963. After they split Grandmont formed **The Bourbons** with other Vandells but would team up with Enos again, when the latter formed **Morning After** whilst at Dean Junior College in Franklin. *Things You Do*, a punk-pop gem, can also be heard on *Psychotic Moose And The Soul Searchers* (LP) and *New England Teen Scene, Vol. 3* (LP). More recently, it has reappeared on the *New England Teen Scene* CD, whose detailed story of this band provided the member details above, alongside an unreleased version. The flip, by the way, is a ballad. (MW/ELn)

Morning Dew

Personnel:	DON ANDERSON		A
	BLAIR HONEYMAN		A
	MAL ROBINSON	ld gtr, vcls	A
	DON SLIGAR		A

ALBUMS:	1(A)	MORNING DEW	(Roulette 42049) 1970 R3
	2(-)	CUT THE CHATTER	(Caped Crusader 121) 1988 SC

NB: (1) has been counterfeited on vinyl. (2) issued on CD as *Second Album* by Collectables (COL-CD-0655), with four bonus tracks, which were left over from the first album. There is also a CD compilation of seventeen tracks by Collectables called *Definitive Collection* (COL-CD-0592).

45s:	Winter Dreams/	
	Touch Of Magic	(Audio House Acetate no #) 1966
	No More/Look At Me Now	(Fairyland 1001) 1967
	Go Away/Be A Friend	(Fairyland 1003) 1967

This outfit came from Topeka, Kansas. Their Roulette album is well worth obtaining particularly for the superb opening cut *Crusader's Smile* although many of the other cuts like *Cherry Street* feature good guitar work. Their 45s were made prior to the album and are much more punkish. *Go Away* has a good catchy guitar riff.

They had a good live reputation and performed great cover versions of many of the punk classics of the era, which were full of fuzz and feedback.

Compilation coverage has so far included: *Sing Out* on *Psychedelic Crown Jewels, Vol. 1* (Dble LP & CD); *No More* on *Monsters of The Midwest, Vol. 1* and *Pebbles, Vol. 14* (LP); and *Go Away* on *Monsters Of The Midwest, Vol. 2* (LP); An unreleased 1966 stereo demo of *Winter Dreams* is also on *The Cicadelic 60's, Vol. 5* (CD); *A Touch Of Magic* and *No More* on *Green Crystal Ties, Vol. 5* (CD); *Someday* and *Flying Above Myself* on *Green Crystal Ties, Vol. 6* (CD); *Sycamore Dreamer* and *Our Last Song* on *Green Crystal Ties, Vol. 9* (CD); Eight more tracks (*No More, Look At Me Now, Be A Friend, Go Away, Sycamore Dreamer, Then Came The Light, Sing Out* and *This Sportin' Life*) including some demos appear on *The Thingies Have Arrived!!* (CD), which also features **The Thingies** and The Exotics. (VJ/MW)

Morning Glory

Personnel:	BOB BOHANNA	bs, gtr, vcls	A
	LARRY GERUGHTY	organ, piano, harpsichord, vcls	A

MORNING DEW - Morning Dew LP.

MORNING GLORY - Two Suns Worth LP.

	GINI GRAYBEAL	ld vcls, cymbals, tamb	A
	ALLEN WEHR	drms	A

ALBUM:	1(A)	TWO SUNS WORTH	(Fontana SRF 67573) 1968 -

45:	Need Someone/I See The Light (PS)	(Fontana 1613) 1968

A hippie-rock outfit formed in San Francisco in 1967. Their album comprises ten originals, mostly penned by Bob Bohanna. The standard of the material is inconsistent to say the least making a positive recommendation difficult but one cut *Jelly Gas Flame* is a superb piece of acid rock with layered vocals, sound effects and catchy guitar - a pity it isn't all this good. *I See The Light* and *Hey Little Girl* also catch the ear. Side Two wins out over Side One which is more in a hard-rock vein. The album was produced by Abe "Voco" Kesh.

Bob Bohanna later played with **Pure Love and Pleasure**.

Need Someone and *So Glad Being Here* also featured on the 1968 compilation *Electric Food* (LP). (VJ/GG)

Morninglory

Personnel:	JIM DRAPER	gtr, keyb'ds	A
	JIM GRUDEN	bs, gtr	A
	PHIL MEDEIRA	drms	A
	CRAIG THOMAS	gtr, keyb'ds	A

ALBUM:	1(A)	GROWING	(Toya TSTLP 2001) 1972 SC

45:	Happiness To The Homeland/	
	Face To The West Wind	(Toya 100) 1972

Unconnected with **Morning Glory**. This is backwater rock with hippie undertones. In places it gets too close to the group America - acoustic guitars and close harmonies wrapped in smooth orchestral arrangements - at other times they kick out and rock in a countrified fashion. (MW)

Morning Song

ALBUM:	1	LISTEN TO A SUNRISE	(Private Pressing) c1974 ?

A Christian psychedelic group inspired by Pink Floyd. (SR)

Morningstar

45:	Virgin Lover/	
	If I Didn't Want to See You Anymore (PS)	(Lion 1003) 1969

Released on the same small label as **Chessman Square**, this 45 has been described as psychedelic rock on some lists. From Missouri, the group were composed of four men and one female singer. (SR)

Morning Sun

45:	Together/Little Girl You're A Woman	(VMC V1238)	1968

A obscure psychedelic rock band from California, whose album was produced and arranged by Tony Harris (from **Eastfield Meadows**). *Together* is a song written by Duke Baxter and Harry Nilsson. (SR)

The Morning Tymes

45:	Every Day/On Top	(MAAD 522768)	1968

A garage band from Osage, Iowa, who recorded a 45 for a Minnesota label. Reputedly great garage.

Compilation appearances include: *On Top* on *It's A Hard Life* (LP). (VJ)

Morocco

45:	Opa Kukla/Ela'Tho	(MGM Kl 3496)	1967

For those into the **Kaleidoscope**, **Orient Express**/**John Berberian**, Eastern trip, here's a 45 to watch out for. Full of (middle) Eastern promise, *Opa Kukla* gently sways in the desert breeze but turn over and we get serious gyrations complete with ululating females. A delight. (MW)

Kent Morrill

ALBUM:	1	THE DREAM MAKER	(Cream)	c1972 -

NB: (1) came with a big poster.

An overproduced album, by the former singer of **The Wailers**. (SR)

The Morrison

Personnel incl: C. MORRISON   A

45:	Every Part Of You/Gonna Have That Girl	(Viking 376)	c1965

From Jacksonville, Florida, a local group, between sixties rock and garage. (SR)

Bob Morrison

Personnel incl:	HAL BLAINE	drms	A
	BOB MORRISON	vcls	A
	JOE OSBORNE		A

ALBUM:	1(A)	FRIENDS OF MINE	(Capitol)	1969

Recorded in California, a decent album of folk-rock and rural rock songs with the backing of ace studio musicians.

Compilation appearances have included: *Hey Puppet Man* and *I Looked In The Mirror* on *Turds On A Bum Ride, Vol. 4* (CD). (SR)

The Morticians

45s:	Little Latin Lupe Lu/Baby Darlin'	(Mortician 101)	196?
	Louie Louie/Twist And Shout	(Mortician 102)	196?

You'll also find *Little Latin Lupe Lu* on the cassette compilation *Monsters Of The Mid-west, Vol. 1*, although they were from Waco, Texas. (VJ)

The Morticians

45:	Now That You've Left Me/Marie, Marie	(Roulette R 4702)	1966

Cool 'n' classy garage - folk - rock buried in Phillipsburg, New Jersey and worthy of exhumation. (MW)

Mortimer

Personnel incl:	GUY M. MASSON	gtr	A
	TOM SMITH	gtr	A
	TONY VAN BENSCHOTEN	gtr	A

ALBUM:	1(A)	MORTIMER	(Philips PHS 600-267)	1968 -

45s:	Dedicated Music Man/		
	To Understand Someone (PS)	(Philips 40524)	1968
	Slicker Beauty Hints/Ingenue's Theme	(Philips 40567)	1968

A trio from upstate New York. Their poppy-rock mix comes from a folk-rock direction, with some psychy moves reminiscent of the Beatles and the Hollies. Their album contains one good psychedelic track *Where Dragons Guard The Doors*, but the remainder (including tracks like *Singing To The Sunshine* and *Life's Sweet Magic*) is more in the soft-rock/Bee Gees vein.

All the songs written and arranged by Smith/Masson/Van Benschoten/Conga and their album was produced by Daniel Secunda for B.B.&D. Productions. (SR/VZ/MW)

Moses Lake

Personnel incl:	MIKE BALZOTTI	keyb'ds, vcls
	BOB GALLOWAY	drms, vcls
	MARDI SHERIDAN	ld gtr, vcls
	CHUCK WARREN	bs, vcls

CD:	1	THE BARDS RESURRECT "THE MOSES LAKE RECORDINGS"	(Gear Fab GF-183)	2002

45:	Oobleck/Moses	(Together T-113)	1969

From Moses Lake, Washington and originally known as **The Bards**, they moved to L.A. in 1969 and teamed up with **Curt Boettcher** and Keith Olsen. Under this auspicious production team they recorded an unreleased album and the above 45. After the album's completion however **Curt Boettcher** wanted to go back to the Northwest to sing with the band which delighted Mike and Mardi but not Bob and Chuck who wanted to get back on their old gig circuit and preserve their autonomy. They split and Mike and Mardi left, ultimately heading back to L.A. to pursue writing and recording careers.

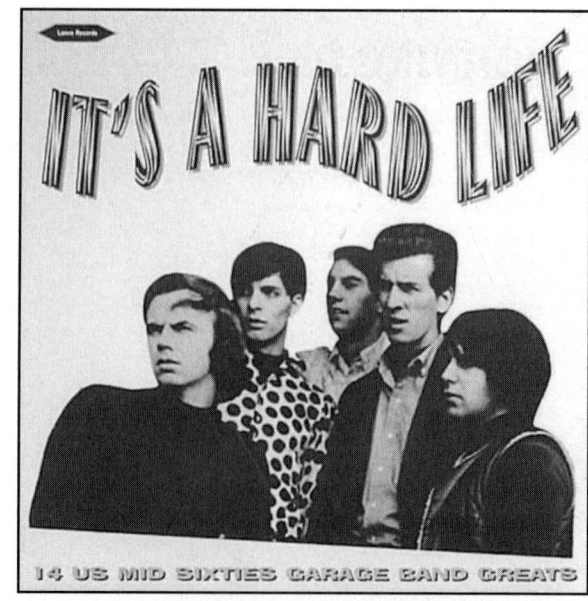

IT'S A HARD LIFE (Comp LP) including The Morning Tymes.

The **Boettcher**/Olsen produced material has finally been released on the Gear Fab CD above and includes both sides of the 45. For more information see **The Bards** entry. (MW)

Mo-Shuns

| 45: | Way She Walks/What Can I Say? | (20th Century 6645) 1966 |

Long Island was home to this mob. They put out just one teenbeat raver with the 'A' side having pounding drums, a neat guitar outburst, and a vocalist intent on telling us how he likes the way his girlfriends' hips swivel... The flip also features a good guitar break but is most notable for the gong that ends the song.

Compilation appearances include: *The Way She Walks* on *Destination Frantic!* (CD); and *What Can I Say* on *Garage Punk Unknowns, Vol. 4* (LP). (VJ/MW)

Bob Mosley

Personnel:	WOODIE BERRY		A
	BOB MOSLEY	bs, vcls	A
	FRANK SMITH		A
	ALLEN WEHR	drms	A
	(ED BLACK	pedal steel	A)
	(MEMPHIS HORNS	horns	A)

ALBUM:	1(A)	BOB MOSLEY	(Reprise MS 2068) 1972 -
45:	α	Gypsy Wedding/Gone Fishin'	(Reprise REP 1096) 1972

NB: α double headed promos also exist.

Born in December 1942 at Paradise Valley, California, James Robert "Bob" Mosley played bass with the **Misfits** and **The Strangers** before joining **Moby Grape** in 1966. In 1969, **Mosley** left the group to join the US Marines (one of the very few San Francisco musicians to do this!) but after nine months and a fight with an officer, he had to return to civil life. He rejoined **Moby Grape** in 1971 for their fifth album and, when the group disbanded again, he went solo and co-produced his first album with Michael O'Connor (a friend of Chris Darrow). The sessions were held in November 1971 in Hollywood with a backing group including Allen Wehr, the former drummer of **Morning Glory**, and Ed Black (ex-**Superfine Dandelion**). The Memphis Horns also played on three tracks. The album is interesting overall, with good vocals and strong instrumental parts displayed on various styles: rock, West Coast, country-rock and white soul. The best moments are probably *The Joker* and *Gone Fishin*. The album included a new version of *Gypsy Wedding* also recorded on **Moby Grape**'s *20 Granite Creek*.

After this, **Mosley** played for a while with Chris Darrow but nothing was released. In October 1973, he teamed again with the **Moby Grape** guitarist Jerry Miller to play the Californian bars and clubs circuit under various names (Maby Grope, Original Grape...). The group finally managed to get a contract with Polydor and released a decent album as **Fine Wine** in 1976. For obscure reasons, the album was only released in Germany. Miller then left **Mosley** to play with the other ex-**Grape** members Lewis and **Spence**.

In 1977/78, **Mosley** returned playing the clubs circuit with John Craviotto and Jeff Blackburn (ex-**Blackburn and Snow**) as The Ducks. During several weeks, they were joined by Neil Young (some tapes and bootlegs exist). Between various **Moby Grape** reformations, **Mosley** would later have severe personal problems (he spent several years homeless) and had to wait until the late eighties to release some other solo records: *Wine And Roses* (Niteshift) 1986, *Mosley Grape, Live at Indigo Ranch* (San Francisco Sounds) 1989 and *Never Dreamed* (Taxim) 1999. In recent years, he has played several live dates with **Moby Grape**. (SR)

Moss and The Rocks

Personnel:	DAVID HOUSTON	vcls, gtr, keyb'ds, hrmnca	A
	JIM MATHEWS	gtr	A
	RON McMASTER	drms, vcls	A
	PAT MINTER	bs, vcls	A

MOSS AND THE ROCKS.

45s:	There She Goes/Please Come Back	(Ikon 181-182) 1965
	There She Goes/Please Come Back	(Chattahoochee 703) 1966

Rare garage-pop sounds from this Sacramento, California outfit. Despite having identical titles, these two singles contain different recordings. The Ikon single (in-house label of Ikon Studios in Sacramento) is so rare that only one copy is currently known to exist. The Chattahoochee single was recorded at Gold Star in Hollywood.

The band was originally known as The Jaguars, changing their name to **Moss and The Rocks** in 1965. The same line-up became known as **Public Nuisance** in 1966, recording two albums in 1968-1969 that only recently have been made available (*Gotta Survive* LP/CD, see **Public Nuisance** entry for details). Both formats include the four **Moss and The Rocks** sides as bonus material. (CF/JD)

Mother Earth

Personnel:	JOHN 'TOAD' ANDREWS	ld gtr	ABCD
	BOB ARTHUR	bs	AB
	MARTIN FIERO	horns	A
	MARK NAFTALIN	keyb'ds	A
	TRACY NELSON	vcls, piano	ABCD
	GEORGE RAINS	keyb'ds	A
	R POWELL ST JOHN	vcls, harp	AB
	LONNIE CASTILLE	drms	B
	CLAYHORN BUTLER		
	COTTON	keyb'ds	B
	REV RONALD STALLINGS	horns	B
	BOB CARDWELL	ld gtr	CD
	KARL HIMMEL	drms	CD
	ANDY McMAHON	keyb'ds	CD
	DAVE ZETTNER	bs	C
	TIM DRUMMOND	bs	D
	JAMES DAY	slide gtr	

HCP

ALBUMS:	1(A)	LIVING WITH THE ANIMALS		
(up to			(Mercury SR 61194) 1969	144 -
1972)	2(B)	MAKE A JOYOUS NOISE	(Mercury SR 61226) 1969	95 -
	3(B)	PRESENTS TRACY NELSON COUNTRY		
			(Mercury SR 61230) 1969	- -
	4(C)	SATISFIED	(Mercury SR 61270) 1970	- -
	5(D)	BRING ME HOME	(Reprise 6431) 1971	199 -

45s:	Revolution/		
(up to	Stranger In My Own Home Town	(United Artists 50303)	1968
1972)	Wait, Wait, Wait/		
	I Wanna Be Your Mama Again	(Mercury 72943)	1969
	Good Night Nelda Grebe/Down So Low	(Mercury 72878)	1969
	Satisfied/Andy's Song	(Mercury 73116)	1970
	I'll Be Long Gone/Bring Me Home	(Reprise 1041)	1971

Mother Earth originated in Texas, (Andrews, Rains and Arthur had earlier played with Wigs), but were one of a number of bands who were attracted by the San Francisco music scene and it was there they made their home.

They first came to attention nationally in the film *Revolution*, which featured them singing three tracks *Without Love*, *Stranger In My Own Home Town*, and the title track.

With their roots in the blues, Tracy Nelson's harsh voice was **Mother Earth**'s prime strength. **Powell St. John** too was a talented songwriter and friend of Janis Joplin. He also wrote some songs for **The Thirteenth Floor Elevators** and both his *Monkey Island* and *Living With The Animals (Down In Jungle Land)* share common themes - the latter commenting on the thickheaded redneck Texans who would regularly chase the local artsy types and pound their heads for their drunken amusement.

The band ended their career in Nashville and their later albums were very much in a country vein.

Naftalin, who had joined from **The Butterfield Blues Band** went on to play with **Electric Flag** and **The Wizards From Kansas**. Fiero played with the **Sir Douglas Quintet**. McMahon later played for Commander Cody.

A track from their first album *Sorry Heidi Neldi, The Telephone Company's Cut Us Off* was also featured on the *Blues Package* compilation. (VJ)

The Mother Love

ALBUM: 1 CAROUSEL OF DAYDREAMS (Epic BN 26520) 1969 -

45s: Flim Flam Man/
Where Do We Go From Here (20th Century 6687) 1967
Goodbye Mary/Sidewalks Of My Mind (Epic 10379) 1968

A forgotten hippie group. (SR)

The Motifs

45: Molly/If I Gave You Love (PS) (Selsom 107) 1966

Open Up Yer Door, Vol. 2 (LP) features *If I Gave You Love* by this New Jersey band. Other Motifs also popped up in Minneapolis and the Pacific Northwest. (VJ)

The Motion

45: The Thief/Granny Goose (Dore 781) 1967

A little known band. The 'A' side has resurfaced on *Moxie Punk EP Box Set* and *60's Punk E.P., Vol. 4* (7" EP). (VJ)

The Motions

45s: Big Chief/Where Is Your Heart (ABC-Paramount 10529) 1964
Beatle Drums/Long Hair (Mercury 72297) 1964
I Can Dance/Land Beyond The Moon (Mercury 72368) 1964
Bumble Bee 65/Motions (Mercury 72413) 1965

In those crazed early days of Beatlemania when anything that wasn't English didn't seem to matter, **The Motions** still held sway as a top band in the Cleveland area. They had the local scene sewn up in '64, playing Beatles rallies to thousands of screaming teens, and going on to open for every top act of the day. *Land Beyond The Moon*, their third of four releases, was a torrid chunk of reverb insanity. Wilder still is the fact that the oldest guy in the band was fourteen!

Compilation appearances have included: *Bumble Bee '65* on *Wavy Gravy, Vol. 1* (CD); and *Land Beyond The Moon* on *Hipsville 29 B.C.* (LP). (VJ)

The Motivations

45: The Birds/Motivate (Pride 301) 1964?

You can also hear *The Birds* on *Garage Punk Unknowns, Vol. 6* (LP), *Scum Of The Earth, Vol. 1* (LP) and *Scum Of The Earth* (Dble CD). Glendale, California was their home turf. (VJ)

The Motleys

45s: I'll See Your Light / Louisiana (Valiant V-724) 1965
You/My Race Is Run (Valiant V 739) 1966

Their second 45 contains brisk L.A. folk - rock/beat sounds.

Compilation appearances include: *You* on *Turds On A Bum Ride, Vol. 5* (CD); and *My Race Is Run* on *Turds On A Bum Ride, Vol. 6* (CD). (MW)

Motor City Bonnevilles

45s: High School Sally/Wrong Side (Red Rooster 310) 196?
Make Up Your Mind/That Lonely Feeling (Patlow 7009) 196?

This outfit was from Detroit as the name suggests. *Make Up Your Mind*, a fairly typical garage-punker with a Kinks-influenced guitar riff, can also be heard on *Garage Punk Unknowns, Vol. 3* (LP). (VJ)

The Mott's Men

45: She Is So Mean/Comin' Or Goin' (Loren 105) 1966

An obscure band from St. Johnsbury, Vermont. The 'A' side, a primal rocker, has also resurfaced on *Sixties Rebellion, Vol. 3* (LP & CD) and *Teenage Shutdown, Vol. 15* (LP & CD). (IT)

Mountain

Personnel: STEVE KNIGHT keyb'ds A
CORKY LAING drms AB
FELIX PAPPALARDI bs, vcls ABC
LESLIE WEST gtr, vcls ABC
DAVID PERRY gtr B
BOB MANN gtr, keyb'ds C
ALAN SCHWARTZBERG drms C

HCP
ALBUMS: 1(-) MOUNTAIN (Windfall 4500) 1969 72 -
(up to 2(A) CLIMBING! (Windfall 4501) 1970 17 -
1974) 3(A) NANTUCKET SLEIGHRIDE (Windfall 5500) 1970 16 -
4(A) FLOWERS OF EVIL (Windfall 5501) 1971 35 -
5(A) LIVE (THE ROAD GOES EVER ON)
(Windfall 5502) 1972 63 -
6(A) THE BEST OF MOUNTAIN (comp)
(Columbia-Windfall PC 32079) 1973 72 -
7(B) AVALANCHE (Columbia-Windfall PC 33088) 1974 102 -
8(C) TWIN PEAKS (Columbia PG 32818) 1974 142 -

NB: (1) a **Leslie West** solo album. (2) also issued in the UK (Bell SBLL 133) 1970,

MOUNTAIN - Nantucket Sleighride CD.

MOUNTAIN - Twin Peaks LP.

and reissued on CD (CBS CK 47361) and (BGO BGO 112) 1997. (3) originally issued with a booklet and two B&W photos of the band. (3) also issued in the UK (Island ILPS 9148) 1971, and reissued on CD (BGO BGOCD 33) 1989 and 1997, and (CBS CK 47362). (4) also issued in the UK (Island ILPS 9179) 1971, and reissued on CD (BGO BGOCD 113) 1991. (5) reissued on CD (BGO BGOCD 111) 1997. (6) This compilation LP includes the studio version of *Roll Over Beethoven*, the only time this cut has appeared. (6) also issued in the UK (Island ILPS 9236) 1973, and reissued on CD (BGO BGOCD 32) 1989, (CBS CK 32079), and (CBS 4663352) 1992. (7) also issued in the UK (Epic EPC 80492) 1974, and reissued on CD (Castle CLACD 136X) 1987. (6) and (7) also issued in Quadrophonic. (8) also issued in the UK (CBS CBS 88095) 1974, and reissued on CD (CBS CGK 32818) 1986.

			HCP
45s:	Missisippi Queen/The Laird	(Windfall 532) 1970	21
	For Yasgur's Farm/To My Friend	(Windfall 533) 1970	107
	Animal Trainer And The Toad/ Tired Angels	(Windfall 534) 1971	76
	Silver Paper/Travelin' In The Dark	(Windfall 535) 1971	-
	Roll Over Beethoven/Crossroader	(Windfall 536) 1972	-
	Waiting To Take You Away/?	(Windfall 537) 1972	-

NB: They also had some early UK 45s:- *Dreams Of Milk And Honey/Wheels In Fire* (Bell BLL 1078) 1969; and *Sittin' On A Rainbow/My Friend* (Bell BLL 1125) 1970. (1) also issued in the UK (Bell BLL 1112). (5) also issued in the UK (Island WIP 6119) 1972. There were also two French 45s with picture sleeves:- *Roll Over Beethoven/Crossroader* (Island 6138009) 1972 and *The Animal Trainer And The Toad/Don't Look Around* (Island 6123002) 1972.

Formed in 1969 by Felix Pappalardi after the demise of Cream (he was their producer) and **Leslie West** (ex-**Vagrants**), **Mountain** was one of the first successful hard-rock acts, in the same style, not surprisingly, as Cream.

Although their apparent leader was the huge **Leslie West**, Pappalardi was in fact the bands musical director, producer and main songwriter. A respected musician, he began working in the mid-sixties on the New York folk scene and played with **Fred Neil**, **Tom Rush**, **Richard Farina** and **Richie Havens**. He was also a producer and worked with **The Youngbloods**, **Apple Pie Motherhood Band**, **Bo Grumpus**, **Hot Tuna**, **Devil's Anvil** and Canada's Kensington Market.

One of their first appearances was the Woodstock Festival and two songs: *Blood Of The Sun* and Jack Bruce/Pete Brown's *Theme For an Imaginary Western* appeared on the *Woodstock* compilations.

Their first album *Climbing* was "made to be played loud" and sold well, *Mississippi Queen* also being released as a 45. It's probably their most interesting effort, the songs being well-structured and penned by West, Laing, Pappalardi and his wife Gail Collins.

Mountain toured constantly and three more albums were released in two years, still in the same vein: loud guitar, bass in the style of Jack Bruce, plus heavy percussion and keyboards, with occasional "lighter" cuts. The vocals were shared between Pappalardi and **West**.

The group first broke up in 1972. **West** and Corky Laing attempted to revive Cream with Jack Bruce forming West, Bruce and Laing for three albums. In 1974, **Mountain** reformed without Steve Knight for two best avoided efforts. **Leslie West** then went solo and released two uninspired albums for Phantom in 1975: *Leslie West Band* and *The Great Fatsby*, the latter with Mick Jagger.

Corky Laing later released *Makin' It On The Streets* (Elektra 7E-1097) 1977 with Clapton and played with various Canadian hard-rock groups. Pappalardi recorded two solo records in 1976 (*Pappalardi And Creation*) and 1979 (*Don't Worry Mum*). He was shot to death in 1983 by his second wife (Gail Collins - designer of **Mountain**'s album covers).

From time to time, **Mountain** have reformed and issued new albums (the last one in 1998). (SR/SBi/VJ)

Mountain Bus

Personnel:	TOM JURKENS	vcls	A
	BILL KEES	electric, acoustic, 12-string, bottleneck gtr	A
	STEVE KRATER	drms, perc	A
	ED MOONEY	electric and acoustic gtr	A
	LEE SIMS	drms, perc	A
	CRAIG TAKEHARA	bs, banjo	A

ALBUM: 1(A) SUNDANCE (Good Records G 101) 1971 R2

NB: (1) has had a limited counterfeit repress and has also been counterfeited on CD by Eva. Reissued officially on CD with five bonus tracks (Gear Fab GF-115) 1998 and on double vinyl (Akarma AK 066/2) 1999.

This Chicago-based outfit were sued by **Mountain** for stealing the name. In actual fact they had the name first but never really recovered from the law suit which required them to state on their album cover that they were in no way connected with **Mountain**. If you like **The Grateful Dead** you should like this album because it's very similar in style. The title cut, in particular, includes some beautiful ringing guitar work but almost all the tracks are good and the album, which is now rare, is recommended listening.

Ed Mooney recalls that "Our plan, when we recorded, was to have a seamless transition between the last three songs - *I Know You Rider - Apache Canyon - Hexahedron*. That idea never made it onto the LP but we often did this for live shows, with the three songs often ending up being 45 minutes to an hour long, depending on the quality & quantity of substances we ingested!" Incidentally, the new Gear Fab CD features these final three tracks run together as originally intended.

Compilation appearances have included: *Sundance* on Gear Fab's *Psychedelic Sampler* (CD); and *I Know You Rider* on *Reverberation IV* (CD). (VJ/EM)

MOUNTAIN BUS - Mountain Bus LP.

Mount Rushmore

Personnel:	MIKE BOLAN	ld gtr	A
	TRAVIS FULLERTON	drms	A
	TERRY KIMBALL	bs	A
	GLEN SMITH	vcls	A

ALBUMS: 1(-) HIGH ON MOUNT RUSHMORE (Dot DLP 25898) 1968 -
         2(-) '69   (Dot DLP 25934) 1969 -

45: Stone Free/(Cause) She's So Good To Me   (Dot 17l58) 1968

A San Francisco band of no particular merit whose albums are not recommended. Fullerton later played with Sylvester and The Hot Band. (VJ)

The Mourning Reign

Personnel:	JOHNNY BELL	ld gtr	A
	STEVE CANALI	rhythm gtr	A
	CHARLIE GARDEN	bs	ABC
	BEAU (FRANK) MAGGI	vcls	ABC
	CRAIG MAGGI	drms	ABC
	JAY GARRETT	gtr	BC
	THOMAS O'BONSAWIN	ld gtr	BC

ALBUM: 1(-) THE MOURNING REIGN (Beat Rocket BR 102) 2001

EP: 1 Satisfaction Guaranteed/Our Fate/Light Switch/
        Cut Back   (Sundazed SEP 115) 1996

NB: (1) *Light Switch* and *Cut Back* are two previously unreleased tracks from 1967 recorded by line-up 'C'.

45s: Satisfaction Guaranteed/Our Fate (PS)   (Link-MR 1) 1966
      Evil Hearted You/Get Out Of My Life Woman (Link MR-2) 1966
      Evil Hearted You/Get Out Of My Life Woman (Contour 601) 1966

A mid to late sixties five-piece band from San Jose, California. Both of their 45s are sought-after, containing good pop efforts with great **Byrds**-style guitar work. More recently there's been a retrospective compilation, on Sundazed subsidiary Beat Rocket, which includes all of their 45 cuts, unreleased tracks and mono / stereo versions.

Steve Canelli left the group when it was still known as The English and later played with a house band call The Housepets.

Compilation coverage has included: *Satisfaction Guaranteed* and *Our Fate* on *Finest Hours Of U.S. Sixties Punk* (LP), *Sixties Archive, Vol. 5* (CD) and *Good Things Are Happening* (CD). The unreleased *Light Switch* and *Cut Back* also appear on *Crystalize Your Mind* (CD). (VJ/SG)

Mourning Son

45: Make My Day / Make My Day   (Arpeggio 1061) c1966

An obscure garage psych 45 written by Stan Blair and produced by Don Whitticar and B. Rohrbach. (SR)

Mouse and The Boys

Personnel:	LARRY DREGGORS	ld gtr	AB
	BILL HARDEN	bs	AB
	LESTER LANGDALE	keyb'ds	AB
	TED ROWLAND	drms	A
	MAURICE "MOUSE" SAMPLES	vcls	AB
	TED VAUGHN	drms	B
	(FRANK CRUMPLER	trumpet	?)
	(JIMMY MOORE	trumpet	?)

45s: α Dancing To The Beat /
         Tears In My Eyes   (Wild Moose # Unkn) 1967
      α Dancing To The Beat / Tears In My Eyes (SSS Int'l 716) 1967
      β Xcedrin Headache #69 / Love Is Free   (Rubiat 68-1043) 1968

NB: α as Mouse and The Boys and Brass. β as Mouse and The Boys.

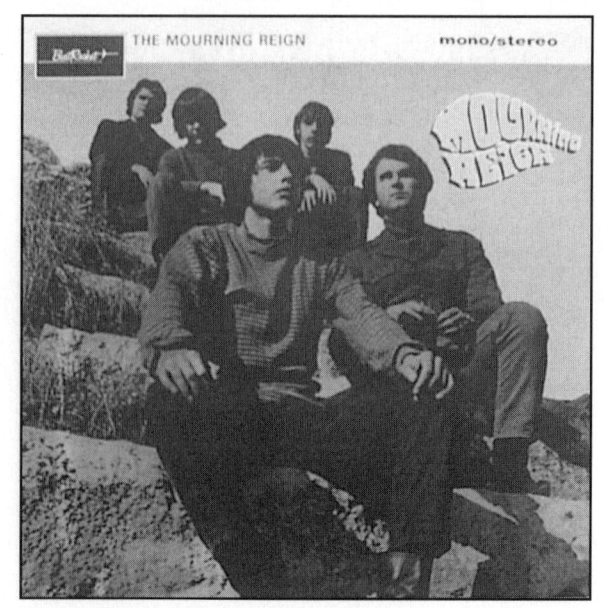

THE MOURNING REIGN - The Mourning Reign LP.

45s: Knock On My Door / Where's The Little Girl   (Bell 870) 1970
      Woman Or A Girl /
      I Can Only Touch You With My Eyes   (Bell 918) 1970

NB: as "M.O.U.S.E.".

A Jacksonville, Florida, group who rose from the ashes of The Deep Six (aka Florida Deep Six) and **The Boys**. Their first two 45s were issued as Mouse and The Boys and Brass, with the brass portion provided by Moore and Crumpler. Their finest moment is the acid-punker *Xcedrin Headache #69*, which can be enjoyed once more on *Psychedelic States: Florida Vol. 1* (CD). It's actually a rip-off of Ellie Greenwich's *I Want You To Be My Baby* but they add **Vanilla Fudge** harmonies, Creamy riffs, wah-wah and phasing. It works well - indeed it hit the #1 spot in Jacksonville in October 1968.

Maurice "Mouse" Samples later released two solo 45s as "M.O.U.S.E.". (JLh/MW)

Mouse and The Traps

Personnel:	BUDDY 'BUGS' HENDERSON	ld gtr	A
	JERRY HOWELL	keyb'ds	AB
	KEN MURRAY	drms	ABCD
	DAVE STANLEY	bs	ABCD
	RONNIE WEISS	gtr, vcls	ABCD
	DOUG RHONE	ld gtr	BC
	BOBBY DALE	keyb'ds	C
	BOBBY DELK		D

ALBUM: 1 THE FRATERNITY ALBUM   (Fraternity) 196? ?

NB: (1) not issued. There are also two retrospective compilations: *Public Execution* (LP) (Eva 12001) 1981, later issued on CD, and *Fraternity Years* (CD) (Big Beat CDWIKD 171) 1997.

HCP

45s: α A Public Execution/All For You   (Fraternity 956) 1966 121
         Maid Of Sugar, Maid Of Spice/
         I Am The One   (Fraternity 966) 1966 -
         Would You Believe?/Like I Know You Do (Fraternity 971) 1966 -
         Do The Best You Can/
         Promises Promises   (Fraternity 973) 1967 -
         Cryin' Inside/Na Ya   (Fraternity 989) 1967 -
      β L.O.V.E. Love/same   (Fraternity 1000) 1967 -
         L.O.V.E. Love/
         Lie, Beg, Borrow and Steal   (Fraternity 1000) 1967 -
         Sometimes You Just Can't Win/
         Cryin' Inside (some PS)   (Fraternity 1005) 1968 125
      β I Satisfy/
         I Satisfy (long and short versions) (Fraternity 1011) 1968 -
         I Satisfy/Good Times   (Fraternity 101 1) 1968 -

Requiem For Sarah/Look At The Sun	(Fraternity 101 5) 1968 -
Wicker Vine/And I Believe Her	(Bell 850) 1969 -
Knock On My Door/Where's The Litte Girl	(Bell 870) 1969 -

NB: α Flip as Mouse. β promo only.

This band played in Tyler, Texas between 1965-69. Their founders Ronnie Weiss and Dave Stanley and Jeff Howell had all previously played together in an outfit called Jerry Vee and The Catalinas. Weiss had also done studio work for Robin Hood Brians studio. Lead guitarist Bugs Henderson joined from an instrumental combo called The Sensors and played on some of **The Cast of Thousand's** 45s. Their first 45, a Dylan soundalike, actually made the Billboard charts climbing to No. 121. The follow-up was as good, if not better, but poorly marketed and failed to repeat their early chart success. A later 45 *Sometimes You Just Can't Win* (Fraternity 1005) did spend one week at No 125 and was also a regional hit in Tyler and Louisville, Kentucky.

The band also recorded a couple of 45s under pseudonyms:- *I've Got Her Love/As Far As The Sea* (Fraternity 983) 1967 was issued as Chris St. John and in the same year they issued *Psychotic Reaction/13 O'Clock Theme For Psychotics* (HBR 500) 1967 with the singer Jimmy Rabbit as **Positively Thirteen O'Clock**. Their two Bell 45s were produced by Dale Hawkins and the band were included on two of his 45s and his LP, *L.A., Memphis and Tyler, Texas* (Bell 6036).

The Eva compilation includes all of their 45s except *Satisfy/Good Times* and has also been issued on CD, but even better is the legitimate *Fraternity Years* CD (Big Beat CDWIKD 171) 1997, which includes 25 tracks, including seven unreleased cuts and detailed analysis from Alec Palao and Robin Hood Brians.

The band split late in 1969. There was a very brief reformation in 1972 (line-up 'D') and Weiss, Stanley and Murray then went on to play together in another Texas band, **Rio Grande**.

Buddy 'Bugs' Henderson now has a pretty fair reputation in Texas as a "legendary blues guitarist." He currently records for a Colorado indie named Flat Canyon Records, and has solo album releases that fall outside the scope of this book.

Compilation appearances have included: *A Public Execution* on *More Nuggets* (CD), *Nuggets - Original Artyfacts From The First Psychedelic Era 1965-1968* (Dble LP), *Nuggets, Vol. 6* (LP), *Texas Music, Vol. 3* (CD) and *Excerpts From Nuggets* (CD); *A Public Execution* and *Maid Of Sugar - Maid Of Spice* on *Nuggets Box* (4-CD); *Maid Of Sugar, Maid Of Spice* on *Nuggets, Vol. 12* (LP), *Acid Dreams - The Complete 3 LP Set* (3-LP), *Acid Dreams Testament* (CD), *Glimpses, Vol's 1 & 2* (CD) and *Glimpses, Vol. 1* (LP); *I Satisfy* on *Psychedelic Unknowns, Vol. 4* (LP & CD); *I Satisfy* and *Good Times* on *Sixties Archive, Vol. 2* (CD) and *Texas Punk Groups From The Sixties* (LP). (VJ/MW/PMt)

MOUSE AND THE TRAPS - Public Execution LP.

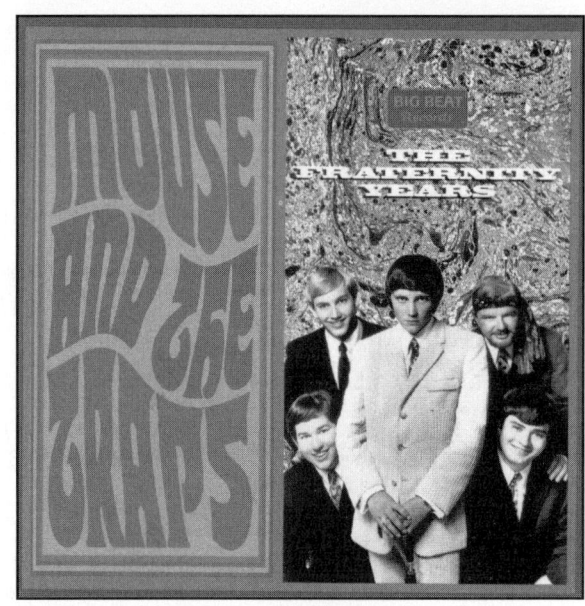

MOUSE AND THE TRAPS - The Fraternity Years CD.

Mouzakis

Personnel:	FRED DAWSON	sax, keyb'ds	A
	EDDIE STEVENSON	drms, vcls	A
	SAM STIPO	gtr	A

| ALBUM: | 1(A) | MAGIC TUBE | (British Main) 1971 R2 |

| 45: | Hey Hey Hey / Lady | (British Main 101472) c1972 |

From Delaware, this album is the work of a rare garage psych group. It was recorded and pressed on low-fi equipment.

The band, who stayed together under various names for thirteen years, were built around the nucleus of Eddie Stevenson and Fred Dawson. Twenty-three guitarists passed through their ranks, over the years and the group played support slots for **Poco**, **Seatrain**, **Redbone**, Dr. Hook, Chicago, Stylistics, Jo Jo Gunn and many others. They also got to appear on several TV shows including Kirby Scott in Baltimore, Jerry Blavatt in Philadelphia (the day after Martin Luther King was assassinated), and **Pat Boone** in Hollywood.

Prior to becoming **Mouzakis**, Eddie and Fred played as **The Fabulous Pharaohs**, and as such recorded many 45s. After **Mouzakis**, they ended up using the name Capone.

Of **Mouzakis**, Fred Dawson says:- "After trying to get 4 - 5 people to agree on 'stuff to play' we ended up as a three-piece band. What we lacked in personnel, we made up for in amplification! There are many fond memories and happenings. It was fun, but Peter Pan finally went away and I am now a successful financial Planner in Wilmington, Delaware. In the past few years I have performed with my sax hero "yakety sax-man" Boots Randolph, and play occasionally from time to time."

Today, Sam Stipo is now teaching guitar here in Wilmington, DE and not playing or performing with any band. Eddie Stevenson's whereabouts are unknown. (SR/MW/FD)

The Movement

45s:	Green Knight /	
	Stinking Peanut Butter Love	(Tinker No #) 1968
	Just-A-Driftin' / Dear Abby	(Hemphill No #) 1968

An unknown group from Midfield, Alabama. After a stop-start intro, *Green Knight* swings into a keyboard-led groove, with Jaggeresque vocals and a short harmonica break, culminating in a fuzz solo. *Just-A-Driftin'*, is a sultry ballad telling the tale of a vagrant, well-evoked by whiskey-roughened vocals and whistled break.

Compilation appearances have included: *Green Knight* on *Open Up Yer Door! Vol. 1* (LP) and *Psychedelic States: Alabama Vol. 1* (CD); *Stinking*

Peanut Butter on *Sixties Rebellion, Vol. 12* (LP & CD); and *Just A Driftin'* on *Psychedelic Crown Jewels Vol. 3* (CD). (MW/MM)

The Movement

| 45: | Combination Of The Two / | | |
| | Riding On A Sunday | (Century 34180) | 1969 |

Another **Movement** from Buffalo, New York State. Both sides of their 45 appear on *Seeds Turn To Flowers Turn To Dust* (LP & CD). (MW)

The Movers

			HCP
45s:	Birmingham/Leave Me Loose	(123 1700) 1968	116
	Hello L.A. (Bye Bye Birmingham)/		
	Hey You, Hey Me	(123 1705) 1968	-

A solid and bouncy version of *Birmingham* in a **Paul Revere** style (shame about the horns) with a meaner flip - raucous vocals, wicked guitar and NO horns - a definite improvement. *Hello L.A....* returns to bounce and brass but the rampant fuzz - rock flip rules again and is the pick of these tracks. It did get to No. 116 in the national charts. The band hailed from New Port Richey, Florida and were known previously as The Intruders.

Compilation appearances include *Leave Me Loose* on *Sixties Rebellion, Vol. 16* (LP & CD). (MW/VJ)

The Moving Sidewalks

Personnel:	BILLY GIBBONS	gtr, vcls	AB
	TOM MOORE	organ, piano	A
	DAN MITCHELL	drms	AB
	DON SUMMERS	bs	AB
	LANIER GREIG	keyb'ds	B

| ALBUM: | 1 | FLASH | (Tantara 6919) 1969 R4 |

NB: (1) was counterfeited on vinyl in the eighties and on CD (Afterglow 002) 1993 and (TRC Records 041) 1994. (1) reissued on double vinyl (Akarma AK 117/2) and CD (Akarma AK 117) 2000 in a lavish package containing the LP and all the non-LP 45 sides. (1) plus 45 tracks was earlier pirated on vinyl as *99th Floor* (Eva 12002) 1982.

| EP: | 1 | 99th Floor/What Are You Going To Do?/Need Me/ | |
| | | Every Night A New Surprise | (Moxie Mutt 1030) 1980 |

45s:	99th Floor/	
	What Are You Going To Do?	(Tantara 3101) 1967
	99th Floor/What Are You Going To Do?	(Wand 1156) 1967
	Need Me/Every Night A New Surprise	(Wand 1167) 1967
	I Want To Hold Your Hand/Joe Blues	(Tantara 3108) 1968
	Flashback/No Good To Cry	(Tantara 3113) 1968

Hailing from Houston this was one of Texas' premier psychedelic bands. Their first 45 topped the Texas chart for five weeks and was selected for national distribution by Wand. It was not a national hit and nor were any of their subsequent efforts, but all are now sought-after collectors' items. The album was also full of excellent psychedelic rock cuts like *Flashback*, *Scoun da Be*, *You Make Me Shake* and *Pluto-Sept 31st*. With Gibbons' **Hendrix**-like guitar work and freaky lyrics some of these are very trippy indeed. Others like *Eclipse* and *Reclipse* on the end of Side Two were very experimental. The album remains rare although there were pirate repressings a few years back. The Eva compilation included all the album, and non-LP 45 sides, but does have the disadvantage of poor sound quality. The Akarma edition is vastly more palatable.

The band lasted until 1970 when Moore and later Summers were drafted. Lanier Greig came in from **Neal Ford and The Fanatics** to fill the keyboard slot but by the end of 1970 the three remaining members had become the first ZZ Top line-up - Gibbons and Mitchell having enrolled at the University of Texas to avoid the draft. Gibbons' earlier bands had been Billy and The Ten Blue Flames, The Saints and The Coachmen.

Naturally the band has featured prominently on compilations, including:- *99th Floor*, *What Are You Going To Do?*, *Need Me* and *Every Night A New Surprise* on *Mindrocker, Vol. 4* (LP); *99th Floor* on *Pebbles, Vol. 2* (LP), *Pebbles, Vol. 2* (CD), *Songs We Taught The Fuzztones* (Dble LP & Dble CD), *Great Pebbles* (CD) and *21 KILT Goldens, Vol. 2*; *Need Me* and *Every Night A New Surprise* on *A Journey To Tyme, Vol. 1* (LP); *I Want To Hold Your Hand* on *Endless Journey - Phase One* (LP), *Endless Journey - Phase I & II* (Dble CD), *Texas Flashbacks, Vol. 5* (LP), *Flashback, Vol. 5* (LP) and *30 Seconds Before The Calico Wall* (CD); *Every Night A New Surprise* on *Houston Post - Nowsounds Groove-In* (LP) and *Mayhem & Psychosis, Vol. 3* (LP); *Need Me* on *We Have Come For Your Children* and *Crimson Witch* on *Reverberation IV* (CD). (VJ)

Moving Violations

45s:	This Time/Three For Love	(Gem 101) 196?
	You'd Better Move On/	
	In The Deep Blue Sea	(SSS International 733) 196?

A Chicago garage band. *Three For Love* was a cover of a **Shadows of Knight** 'B' side. I can't confirm for sure that the second 45 is by the same band, it was produced by Huey P. Meaux so Texas is a more likely location. (VJ)

Movin' Morfomen

Personnel:	DANNY GAVURNIK	trumpet, gtr, vcls	A
	RUDY MAESTAS	gtr, vcls	A
	ANTHONY MARTINEZ	bs	A
	DAVE RARICK	gtr, keyb'ds, vcls	A
	ED VALDEZ	drms	A

| CD: | 1 | FLASHBACKS! | (Collectables COL-0696) 1997 |

45s:	When You Were Mine/Run Girl Run	(Delta 2242) 1967
	Don't Go Baby / Only The Young	(Lance 2242) 1967
	Write Me A Letter / ?	(Tewa 1001) 1967
	We Tried, Try It / Distant Drums	(Nel-Ric 301) 1967
α	Thinking Of You /	
	What I'm Going Through	(Goldust GR-45-5306) 1969

NB: α released as by **The Morfomen**.

A five-piece pop outfit with a punky edge from Espanola, New Mexico. After the first two 45s the line-up underwent constant changes, apparently breaking up and reforming at frequent intervals - the end finally came officially in 1969 although Dave Rarick did record several songs in 1971 (featured on the Collectables CD) with a new band using the same name. Three original members - Rarick, Gavurnik and Valdez - are back together performing in the nineties as the Flashbacks and contribute the final five tracks, and the title, to the retrospectve CD.

THE MOVING SIDEWALKS - Flash CD.

TEENAGE SHUTDOWN Vol. 13 (Comp CD) including The Moxies.

Run Girl Run, written by Dave Rarick, is compiled on *Pebbles, Vol. 8* (LP), *New Mexico Punk From The Sixties* (LP) and *Sixties Archive, Vol. 4* (CD). *We Tried, Try It* - made famous by **The Standells** - can be found on *Diana's Rootin' Tootin' Wild Teenage Rock 'N' Roll Party!* (LP) and *Garage Music For Psych Heads, Vol. 1*. *What's Happened To Me?*, one of the unreleased 1971 tracks with backwards guitar effects and lyrics about a bad trip, has also resurfaced on the *Psychedelic Crown Jewels, Vol. 1* (Dble LP & CD); *Try It* and *What's Happened To Me* on *Green Crystal Ties, Vol. 5* (CD); *Don't Go Baby* on *I Wanna Come Back From The World Of LSD* (CD); and both sides of the Goldust 45 (*Thinking Of You* and *What I'm Going Through*) appear on Collectables' *The Goldust Records Story* (CD). (VJ/MW)

Mowoody

| Personnel: | GARY PAREDES | A |
| | ROYAL SCANLON | A |

ALBUM: 1(A) SIGNING OUR LIVES AWAY
(Missouri Woodlands 1553) c1972

A rare album of hippie-folk from Missouri, with a full band playing acoustic and electric instruments on a selection of original material. Only 500 copies were pressed. (SR)

The Moxies

Personnel incl: GEORGE CORYELL   A

EP: 1   FOUR BY THE MOXIES   (No label #20932) 1964
NB: (1) features *I Feel Happy, I Must Apologize, Passout, Jazzmine*.

45s:	α	I Feel Happy/I Must Apologize	(Monza C-1124) 1965
		Please Don't Go/Get A Move On	(Monza C-1126) 1965
		I'm Gonna Stay/Drinkin' Wine (PS)	(Century 26070) 1966

NB: α flip is an edited version of the EP track.

From Paducah, Kentucky. Their first 45, *I Feel Happy* is fine garage-beat backed by a charming but soppy garage-ballad. The 'A' side of the third, *I'm Gonna Stay*, is their fuzz garage peak.

Compilation appearances have included: *Get A Move On* on *Teenage Shutdown, Vol. 2* (LP & CD); *I'm Gonna Stay* on *Teenage Shutdown, Vol. 13* (LP & CD) and *Highs In The Mid-Sixties, Vol. 8* (LP); *Please Don't Go* on *Diggin' For Gold, Vol. 7* (LP). (MW)

Mu

Personnel:	JEFF COTTON	gtr, vcls, sax	ABCD
	MERRELL FANKHAUSER	gtr, vcls	ABCD
	LARRY WILLEY	bs	A
	RANDY WIMER	drms	ABCD
	JEFF PARKER	bs	CD
	MARY LEE	violin	D

ALBUM: 1(A/C) MU   (RTV 300) 1972 R2/R3

NB: (1) copies on RTV were issued with a lyric sheet. (1) also issued in the U.K. by United Artists as *Lemurian Music*. (1) reissued on CAS in 1974 (R1) and on Reckless (RECK 4) 1988 in the UK. Later retrospective releases include:- (D) *The Last Album* (Appaloosa AP 017) 1981, an Italian release; (D) *Children Of The Rainbow* (Blue Form BF1) 1985; (D) *End Of An Era* (Reckless RECK 7) 1988, which was recorded in Maui in 1974; and (-) *The Band From The Lost Continent* (Xotic Mind XMCD-1) 1995, a double CD which includes the first album, three singles tracks from 1971 and another 20 songs which were recorded in 1974. This was later issued on Sundazed (SC 11037) 1997 and there's also an 18-track U.S. CD, *Best Of*.

45s:	α	I'm Flying Home/Girl	(Shamley 44008) 1968
	α	Tampa Run/Everybody's Talking	(Shamley 44019) 1969
		Ballad of Brother Lew/ Nobody Wants To Shine	(Mantra 101) 1971
		One More Day/You've Been Here Before	(Mu 101/2) 1971/2
		Too Naked For Demetrius/ On Our Way To Hana	(Mu 103/4) 1973

NB: α were solo Fankhauser singles before **Mu**.

Fankhauser formed this band after the demise of **H.M.S. Bounty**. Cotton and Willey had earlier played with Fankhauser in **The Exiles**.

Mu initially lived on a half acre estate in Canoga Park, California and were heavily into meditation and vegetarianism. Their debut album, recorded on a small Beverly Hills label, was both inventive and imaginative. **Mu**'s sound was a departure from all of Fankhauser's earlier projects, being an earthy blues and folk group centred on Cotton's fabulous slide guitar work.

After Willey's departure the remaining trio moved to the island of Maui in Hawaii in 1974, where they recorded two singles for their own Mu label and, with the addition of Mary Lee and Jeff Parker, a second album, which was shelved when they split up. In 1981 Fankhauser remixed it, added two singles and it was released in Italy.

Many other tapes of **Mu** exist and *Children Of The Rainbow* is an excellent album of material recorded live on Maui in 1974. It's full of well-structured, often mystical songs and also includes some tasty laid-back guitar work from Fankhauser and Jeff Cotton (who had earlier played with **Captain Beefheart**). It also features a brief interview with the band by Lew Irwin.

MU - The Band From The Lost Continent CD.

Fankhauser, one of the West Coast's most interesting musicians, went on to make three solo albums, including one in 1976 (Maui M 101) and Mary Lee continued to play in his band. Parker remained in Hawaii, where he purchased an orchid plantation and Wimer became a youth counsellor in Los Angeles.

Like all of **Fankhauser**'s bands, **Mu** were interesting and worth investigation.

You can also find **Merrell Fankhauser**'s *Pot* on *Reverberation IV* (CD). (VJ/CF)

Maury Muehleisen

Personnel:	DAVID BROMBERG	gtr	A
	GARY CHESTER	drms	A
	SAL DETROIA	gtr	A
	JOE MACHO	bs	A
	MAURY MUEHLEISEN	vcls, gtr, keyb'ds	A
	AL RODGERS	drms	A
	JIM RYAN	gtr	A
	TOMMY WEST	keyb'ds, vcls	A

ALBUM: 1(A) GINGERBREAD (Capitol ST 644) 1970 -

A set of original songs, carried by the fine voice of **Maury** with elegant and sympathetic backing and above par lyrics. The pace is quiet and almost all the songs radiate serenity and calm. What's missing is any real highlights. Apart from *Winter Song*, with it's Left Banke echoes and parts of *That's What I Like*, which is tasteful folk-rock, the compositions are just a pinch too average to really excite. A nice late evening record, but no lost masterpiece.

Muelheisen would later join **Jim Croce**'s backing group. (MK/SR)

Muffets

45: Cold Winds / My Money (Counterpart C-2621/2) 1968

From Germantown, Ohio, they previously put out a 45 in 1965 as the **Muphets**. (GGI/MW)

Muffetts

45: Lost/Heather Girl (Counterpart C 2629/30) 1968

Late sixties garagey pop from Hurricane, West Virginia. Snaking leads and a simple fuzzy break bring an average number up a notch. The subdued flip is enhanced solely by a fluid wah-wah break - other than that it's pretty ordinary pop - rock.

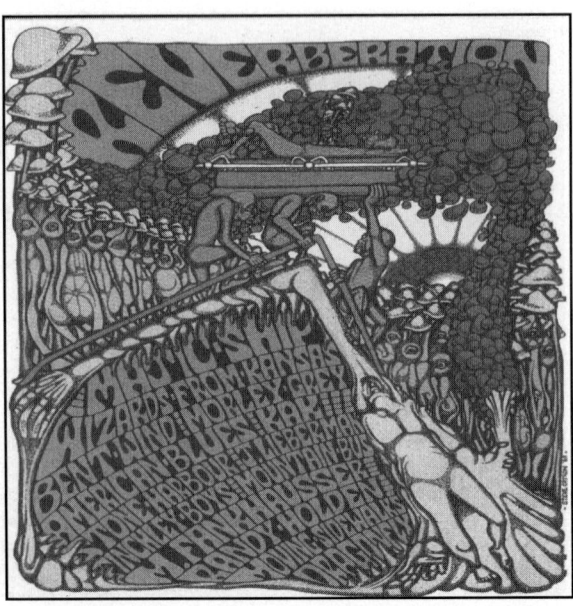

REVERBERATION IV (Comp CD) including Merrell Fankhauser.

The band had earlier recorded as **The Mojos**.

Lost can be found on *Lost Gems From The '60s, Vol. 1* (EP), *Acid Dreams, Vol. 2* (LP) and *Psychedelic Crown Jewels, Vol. 3* (CD). The latter reveals how **The Mojos** became **The Muffets**, ended up in Ohio, and released two further 45s (whose details remain elusive) - the final one on Rondo in 1970 as "A.G.Pygmie and The Muffet Company". (MW/GGI/MM)

Thee Muffins

ALBUM: 1 POP UP! (Fan Club # unknown) 1966 R2

A very obscure outfit probably from Lake George, New York (though Tennessee has also been cited). The album, though exceedingly rare, is disappointing soulful beat-ballad music in the same mould as **Skip and The Creations**. Predominantly covers including *Surprise Surprise, Don't Let The Sun Catch You Crying, Do You Love Me?, I Feel Good, Crying Over You, Oo Poo Pah Doo* and *Not Fade Away*. Only two tracks are notable, the Hank Williams cover *Caliga* and an instrumental version of Mel Torme's *I'm Comin' Home*. The album has not been reissued or pirated yet and given the prices it fetches, can't be recommended to garage fans.

Walter Rossi (of Charlee / **Influence**) is rumoured to have played on their album.

Compilation appearances include *Not Fade Away* on *Oil Stains* (LP). (VJ/CLy/TM)

Mugwumps

Personnel:	DENNY DOHERTY	vcls	A
	CASS ELLIOT	vcls	A
	JAMES HENDRICKS	vcls, gtr	A
	ZAL YANOVSKY	vcls, gtr	A
	(JOHN SEBASTIAN	hrmnca	A)

ALBUMS:	1	THE MUGWUMPS	(Warner 1697) 1967 -
	2	HISTORICAL RECORDINGS	(Valiant VS 134) 196? -

45s:	I'll Remember Tonight/I Don't Know	(Warner Bros. 5471) 196?
	Searchin'/Here It Is Another Day	(Warner Bros. 7018) 1967

Formed by the former **Big Three** members Cass Elliot and **Denny Doherty**, the **Mugwumps** were a folk-rock group who were completely unsuccessful during their time together, circa 1964/65. Most of the above records were released when their members later found fame. Mama Cass and **Denny Doherty** went on to form the **Mamas and The Papas**, James Hendricks (Cass' husband) the **Lamp Of Chilhood** and Zal Yanovsky the **Lovin' Spoonful** with **John Sebastian**.

For those wondering about their name, "Mugwump" is an Indian word meaning "a person who is neutral in a controversial issue"! (SR)

The Mugwumps

45s:	Bald Headed Woman/Jug Band Music	(Sidewalk 900) 1966
	My Gal/Season Of The Witch	(Sidewalk 909) 1967
α	Bo Weevil/I Can't Keep From Cryin'	(Sidewalk 931) 1967

NB: α released as by The Mugwump Establishment.

Unconnected to the earlier **Mugwumps**, this was almost certainly a L.A.-based studio group and they played a sort of jug-punk music. Mike Curb's Sidewalk label was most notably for producing Soundtracks for teen movies. They managed a pretty good cover of *Bald Headed Woman*, which can also be heard on *Highs In The Mid-Sixties, Vol. 20* (LP) and you can also find *Sunset Sally* on *Riot On Sunset Strip* (LP); *Season Of The Witch* on *Freakout U.S.A.!* (LP); *Mondo Hollywood (City Of Dreams)* and *Mondo Hollywood Freakout* on *Mondo Hollywood* (LP); and *Mondo Hollywood Freakout* on *Buzz Buzz Buzzzzzz, Vol. 1* (CD). (VJ/MW)

The Mulberry Fruit Band

Personnel:	PETER ANDERS		A

VINNIE PONCIA		A
45:	The Audition/Yes, We Have No Bananas	(Buddah 1) 1967

A pop single by **Anders** and Poncia, better known as **The Tradewinds**. (SR)

Barbara Muller

ALBUM:	1	DOUBLE PREMIERE	(Quote Records Q2) 1964 ?

A rare album of femme folk with dark overtones. (SR)

Munx

45s:	Sometimes I Dream /	
	It's Too Late For Love	(Clevetown CTXP-280) 1966
	Our Dream / Girls, Girls, Girls	(Clevetown CTXP-400) c1968
	Our Dream / Girls, Girls, Girls	(Jubilee 5612) 1968
	So Much In Love / Why Did You Run Away	(Jubilee 5634) 1968

This band were from Lorain, Ohio. They would later be known as Sheffield Rush. (MW/GGI)

Muphets

45:	Why Can't You Go / All I Want	(Sound Spectrum 36001) 1965

From Germantown, Ohio, they'd correct their spelling and release another 45 as the **Muffets** in 1968. (GGI/MW)

Murietta

ALBUM:	1	MURIETTA	(Cherry Red CR-5103) 1971 -

An obscure rock quintet with female vocals. (SR)

Murmaids

Personnel:	CAROL FISCHER	A
	TERRY FISCHER	A
	SALLY GORDON	A

45s:	α	Why Can't You Go / All I Want	(Chattahoochee CH 628) 1963
		Heartbreak Ahead/	
		He's Good To Me	(Chattahoochee CH 636) 1964
	β	Wild And Wonderful/Bull Talk	(Chattahoochee CH 641) 1964
		Stuffed Animals/	
		Little White Lies	(Chattahoochee CH 668) 1965
		Little Boys/Go Away	(Chattahoochee CH 711) 1966

NB: α also issued in the UK (Stateside SS 247) 1963. β also seen listed as (Chattahoochee CH 650).

Produced by **Kim Fowley**, the 'A' side to their first 45 was written by David Gates (pre-Bread) and is average female pop. The flip, credited to **The Murmaids Band**, was written by **Fowley** / Harris (possibly one of the **WCPAEB** brothers) and is an early sixties instrumental track.

Both sides of their second single were also produced by **Fowley**.

It's believed that members Carol and Terry Fischer were the daughters of pianist Carl Fischer, who worked with Frankie Laine and co-wrote a couple of hits. (SR/GM/JW)

J.F. Murphy and Free Flowing Salt

Personnel:	RON ALLARD	sax, bagpipes, flute	A
	GEORGE CHRIST	hrmnca, bs, perc	A
	BOBY KURTZ	drms	A
	J.F. MURPHY	ld vcls, piano, bs, gtr	A
	JOE PARRINO	ld gtr, bs, flute	A

ALBUMS:	1( )	J.F. MURPHY	(Verve Forecast FTS-3085) 1969 -
(selective)	2(A)	ALMOST HOME	(MGM SE-7408) 1970 -
	3( )	THE LAST ILLUSION	(Columbia 32539) 1973 -

After a rarely seen first album on Verve Forecast, this New York band signed with MGM and released an album produced by Vinny Testa (who also worked with **Group Image**). They had quite an unique sound, veering from hard-rock (on *Rock'n'Roll Band*) to almost avant-garde jazz with its use of saxophone, piano and flute (on *The First Born* and *Trilogy*). All their material was original, penned by Murphy and the album definitely has its moments. It may interest some curious collectors, but be aware that they also used bagpipes on some tracks (not all of them luckily!).

J.F. Murphy with Salt (a renewed line-up) also released one live album on Elektra in 1972; but the continuous use of bagpipes with sax and guitars is not an easy taste to acquire! (SR)

Murphy and The Mob

45:	Because You Love Me/Born Loser	(Talisman 1823) 196?

A garage-punk outfit from Tyler in Texas. The flip, *Born Loser*, included some catchy guitar work. It can also be found on *Acid Dreams - The Complete 3 LP Set* (3-LP), *Acid Dreams Testament* (CD), *Texas Flashbacks, Vol. 3* (LP & CD), *Back From The Grave, Vol. 3* (LP), *Best of Pebbles, Vol. 1* (LP & CD), *Back From The Grave, Vol. 2* (CD) and *Flashback, Vol. 3* (LP). (VJ)

The Mushrooms

Personnel incl:	GLENN FREY	gtr, vcls	A

45:	Burned/Such A Lovely Girl	(Hideout) c1967

An obscure Detroit garage band featuring Glenn Frey, who would later move to California to form Longbranch Pennywhistle in 1970 and later The Eagles. After leaving **The Mushrooms** he was in a band called the Heavy Metal Kids, who were managed by Ed "Punch" Andrews. Other members of the Heavy Metal Kids included Lance Dickerson (later of Commander Cody), Jeff Alborell (bs ex-**Four of Us**), Steve Burrows (keyb'ds) and Paul Kelcourse (ex-**Fugitives**, also guitarist with **Four of Us** and bass with Billy C. and the Sunshine).

Compilation appearances have included: *Burned* on *Realities In Life* (LP); *Such A Lovely Child* on *Sixties Archive, Vol. 7* (CD); and both *Burned* and *Such A Lovely Child* on *Best of Hideout Records* (CD). (SR/PK)

Music

Personnel:	(DAVID BROMBERG	dobro	A)
	(MARK KLINGMAN	keyb'ds	A)
	BUZZY LINHART	vcls, gtr, vibes	A
	DOUGLAS RAUCH	bs, gtr, perc	A
	DOUG RODRIGUEZ	ld gtr	A
	JON SIOMOS	drms	A

ALBUM:	1(A)	MUSIC	(Eleuthera Records ELS 3601) 1971 -

NB: (1) also released in England (Buddha 2318028) 1972.

45:	Talk About A Morning/	
	Kilpatrick's Defeat	(Kama Sutra 526) 1970

Produced by Eddie Kramer and recorded in New York, this is an interesting album with **Buzzy Linhart** (ex-**Seventh Sons**), Doug Rauch and Doug Rodriguez (**Santana**). Covers of **Fred Neil**, **Tim Hardin** and several **Linhart** songs with good vocals and guitars. (SR)

Music Asylum

Personnel:
	LOUIS ARGESE	keyb'd's, vcls, various horns	A
	LEONARD ARGESE	gtr, vcls	A
	LEONARD CONFORTI	drms, perc	A
	LUIS LUZZI	bs, vcls	A

ALBUM: 1(-) COMMIT THY SELF (United Artists UAS 6776) 1970 -

45s: I Need Someone (The Painter)/
Yesterday's Children (Ascot 2238) 1967
α I Need Someone (The Painter)/
Yesterday's Children (United Artists UA 50274) 1968

NB: α not released.

This album of U.S. psychedelia, which is a very minor collectable, was also issued in Germany. Produced by Steve and Eric Nathanson who also produced **Boffalongo** and **Omnibus**, all the tracks are written by the Argese brothers, except a strange cover of Dylan's *Million Dollar Bash*. An interesting album if you like melodic psychedelia influenced by jazz. Its best track is *In My World*. (SR/VJ)

The Music Combination

45s: Mechanical People/
Bambi (American Music Makers AMM-0012) c1966
Lonely Shore/The Story Of
My Life (American Music Makers AMM-0013) c1966
Crystal/Holding On For
Dear Love (American Music Makers AMM-0013) c1967

Produced by Lou Guarino, three singles of psych-pop. (SR)

The Music Emporium

Personnel:
	CASEY COSBY	organ, vcls	A
	CAROLYN LEE	bs gtr, piano, acoustic bs, organ, vcls	A
	DAVE PADWIN	ld gtr, vcls, acous bs gtr	A
	DORA WAHL	perc, drms	A

ALBUM: 1(A) MUSIC EMPORIUM (Sentinel 100) 1969 R4

NB: (1) counterfeited on vinyl (Psycho 11) (ltd to 700 copies in mono and with the inner gatefold used, rather than the proper cover) 1983, (Sentinel PC 69001-1) 1991, (No label) 1997, (Fantazia Music 4-501) 2000, (Action Records AR 304) (in die-cut sleeve) 2001 and on CD by (Afterglow 001) 1992 and (Flash) 1997. Reissued officially on vinyl (Sundazed LP 5078) 2001 and CD with bonus tracks (Sundazed SC 6166) 2001.

45: Nam Myo Renge Kyo/Times Like This (Sentinel 4-501) 1969

This group's leader, Casey Cosby, won the Frank Sinatra Award Competition at UCLA in 1967 and performed in both classical and jazz media prior to forming **The Music Emporium**. Padwin had previously played for several Midwest country-rock groups. In Dora Wahl the band had one of rock's few woman drummers at the time. All songs on their album were written by the band. The album is one of different moods, from the quasi-religious chants of *Nam Myo Renge Kyo* and *Day Of Wrath* to gentle ballads, such as *Velvet Sunsets* and *Gentle Thursday*, which are both noteworthy for Carolyn Lee's soft, smooth vocals, to the haunting introduction of *Catatonic Variations*. The album is a significant collectors' item and originals change hands for quite a considerable sum.

Of the various reissues, the Psycho version lost something in the process (like one channel!), but a recent reissue on 'Sentinel' has corrected that. Later 'reissues' include a vinyl version on Action Records, that reproduces the original die-cut sleeve and an official reissue on Sundazed - the CD version of which, includes bonus tracks.

Compilation appearances include: *Nam Myo Renge Kyo* on *Love, Peace And Poetry Vol. 1* (LP & CD), *Sixties Archive Vol. 8* (CD), *Acid Trip From The Psychedelic Sixties* (LP) and *Gathering Of The Tribe* (LP). (VJ/CF)

THE MUSIC EMPORIUM - Music Emporium LP.

Music Explosion

Personnel:
	DON ATKINS	ld gtr	A
	BOB AVERY	drms	A
	JAMIE LYONS	vcls, perc	A
	RICHARD NESTA	gtr	A
	BURTON SAHL	bs	A

HCP
ALBUM: 1(A) LITTLE BIT OF SOUL (Laurie SLLP 2040) 1967 178 -

NB: (1) reissued on CD. In addition, One Way has issued the CD *Anthology* (18260). There's also *Little Bit Of Soul: The Best Of* CD (Sundazed SC 11119) 2002.

HCP
45s: Stay By My Side/Little Black Egg (Attack A-1 404) 1967 -
Road Runner/Sunshine Games (Attack) 1967 -
α Little Bit O'Soul/I See The Light (Laurie 3380) 1967 2
Sunshine Games/Can't Stop Now (Laurie 3400) 1967 63
β We Gotta Go Home/Hearts And Flowers (Laurie 3414) 1967 103
What You Want/Road Runner (Laurie 3429) 1968 119
Where Are We Going?/Flash (Laurie 3440) 1968 -
Yes Sir/Dazzling (Laurie 3454) 1968 120
Jack In The Box/Rewind (Laurie 3466) 1968 -
χ What's Your Name/Call Me Anything (Laurie 3479) 1969 -
Stay By My Side/Little Black Egg (Laurie 3500) 1969 -

NB: α some early copies show *I See The Light* as the 'A' side and *Little Bit O'Soul* as the flip. β and χ were also released in France by Vogue with picture sleeves. There's also a French EP with picture sleeve: *Little Bit O'Soul/I See The Light/Let Yourslf Go/La La La* (Vogue INT 18140).

This pop-soul quintet hailed from Mansfield, Ohio. Their records were produced by Jerry Kasenetz and Jeff Katz, who founded the short-lived but commercially successful bubblegum movement. **Jamie Lyons** also enjoyed a brief solo career and played for Capital-City Rockets and Bob Avery later went on to **Crazy Elephant**, a top bubblegum group. They enjoyed commercial success with *Little Bit Of Soul* which can also be heard on the *Battle Of The Bands* (CD), *Nuggets Box* (4-CD) and *Wild Thing* compilations. Their cover of **Question Mark and The Mysterians'** *96 Tears*, which appeared on their album, has also resurfaced on Eva's *Sound Of The Sixties* (Dble LP) and *Sixties Archive, Vol. 1* (CD) compilations. Other compilation appearances include:- *Road Runner* and *Sunshine Games* on *Mindrocker, Vol. 5* (LP) and *Stay By My Side* on *Everywhere Chainsaw Sound* (LP).

They were previously known as the Chosen Few but with no release under that name - thank heavens, there are too many Chosen Few's as it is.

Their album sold quite well, spending two weeks in the charts and peaking at No. 178. (VJ/MW/SR/KSI/SBn)

Music Fair

45:	I'll Be Back Up On My Feet Again/		
	Councilman Jones	(Epic 5 10569)	1969

NB: a later pressing was credited to Jimmy Druiett and The Music Fair.

An awful bouncy pop version of the Linzer - Randell track covered by **The Monkees** on *The Birds, The Bees...* album. The flip is of greater interest here - late sixties pop-psych that can be heard on the *Slowly Growing Insane* (CD) and its vinyl counterpart *Psychedelic Unknowns, Vol. 11* (LP). (MW)

The Music Machine

Personnel:	SEAN BONNIWELL	rhythm gtr	AB
	RON EDGAR	drms	A
	MARK LANDON	ld gtr	A
	KEITH OLSEN	bs, vcls	A
	DOUG RHODES	organ, vcls	A

HCP

ALBUMS:	1(A)	TURN ON	(Original Sound 8875)	1966	76	SC
	2(B)	BONNIWELL MUSIC MACHINE	(Warner Bros. 1732)	1967	-	R1
	3(B)	CLOSE	(Capitol ST 277)	1969	-	-

NB: (1) reissued on vinyl (Big Beat WLK 17) in 1983 in the U.K. and later on CD and vinyl by (Performance PERF 0397). (2) also released in France (Warner CLPW 1545) 1968. (3) Sean Bonniwell Solo LP. There's also a number of retrospective releases:- *Best Of* (Rhino RNLP 11 9) 1984; *Turn On - The Very Best Of* (CD) (Collectables COL-CD-6044) 199?; *Beyond The Garage* (CD) (Sundazed SC 11030) 1996, a reissue of the second album from 1967 with two previously unreleased and bonus tracks; and *Ignition* (LP/CD) (Sundazed SC 11038 / LP 5038) 2000 a decent collection of rarities and unreleased material.

HCP

45s:	Talk, Talk/Come On In	(Original Sound 61)	1966	15
	The People In Me/			
	Masculine Intuition	(Original Sound 67)	1967	66
	Double Yellow Line/			
	Absolutely Positively	(Original Sound 71)	1967	111
	The Eagle Never Hunts The Fly/			
	I've Loved You	(Original Sound 75)	1967	-
	Hey Joe/Taxman	(Original Sound 82)	1968	-
	Hey Joe/Wrong	(Original Sound 82)	1968	-
	Bottom Of My Soul/			
	Astrologically Incompatible (PS)	(Warner Bros. 7093)	1967	-
	Me, Myself And I/Soul Love	(Warner Bros. 7162)	1968	-
	You'll Love Me Again/			
	In My Neighborhood	(Warner Bros. 7188)	1968	-
	You'll Love Me Again/To The Light	(Warner Bros. 7199)	1968	-
	Tin Can Beach/			
	Time Out For A Daydream	(Warner Bros. 7234)	1968	-
	Advice And Consent/			
	Mother Nature Father Earth	(Bell 764)	1969	-
	Where Am I To Go?/Sleep	(Capitol 2551)	1969	-

NB: The Warner Bros and Bell 45s are as the Bonniwell Music Machine. The Capitol 45 is taken from Sean's solo LP. (11) released in France with picture sleeve (Warner WV 5110). A rare French EP with picture sleeve also exists: *Talk, Talk/Come On In/The People In Me/Wrong* (Vogue INT 18121). There's also a reissue 45: *Point Of No Return / King Mixer* (PS) (Sundazed S 131) 1997.

Centred around Bonniwell, who had earlier sung with sixties folk group The Wayfarers, this Los Angeles band developed out of a trio called the Ragamuffins, which had featured Bonniwell, Edgar and Olsen. Edgar had earlier drummed for **The Goldebriars** with **Curt Boettcher**, whilst Olsen who was an old friend of **Boettcher**, had played with Gale Garnett and Jimmie Rodgers and also briefly with the Wayfarers, at whose club in Charleston the **Goldebriars** often played. He later married Goldbriar Sheri Holmberg.

Bonniwell disillusioned with straight folk, became the **Goldebriars** tour manager and migrated to L.A. with them. Olsen meanwhile had run into another old friend, Doug Rhodes and Bonniwell grabbed them for his new band, **The Music Machine**, adopting **The Goldebriars** all-in-black, dyed black Beatlecut look in the process, lock, stock, and barrel.

The Music Machine's debut album contained the U.S. hit *Talk Talk* and a number of other strong original compositions, notably *Masculine Intuition*, *Wrong* and *Trouble*. Bonniwell's harsh voice was ideal for much of this material and for a while the group achieved some success. Their debut album also featured competent versions of *Hey Joe*, **? and The Mysterians**' *96 Tears*, the Beatles' *Taxman* and Neil Diamond's *Cherry Cherry*.

The People In Me/Masculine Intuition 45 was also taken from their debut album and *Hey Joe* was subsequently issued as a 45. However, not everything was presumably going smoothly and the second album was issued after the band had split. Recorded in Muscle Shoals, Alabama and New Mexico it comprised three outtakes from the earlier album and some new material.

The band also made some other recordings, acetates of which have recently surfaced with the following tracks: Side One *Everything Is Everything/You'll Love Me Again/This Should Make You Happy/Black Snow/Mother Nature, Father Earth/Dark White*; Side Two *No Girl Gonna Cry/King Mixer/Advise And Consent/Tell Me What Ya Got/Citizen Fear/Point Of No Return*.

After the split Edgar, Rhodes and Olsen all reunited again with **Boettcher** in **Millennium** and appeared on the first **Sagittarius** album. Keith Olsen later became a studio engineer and producer.

Bonniwell went on to record a solo album *Close*, a moody, rather introverted effort. After that he dropped out and got religious, resurfacing in the 1980s fronting Heaven Sent, a Christian band. In 1982, he re-recorded *Talk Talk*.

In 1984, Rhino issued a *Best Of* compilation, which comprised many of their best known cuts and some unissued masters. One interesting and rare spin off from the band was *Nothin's Too Good For My Car/So Long Ago* (Original Sound 95) which Bonniwell recorded with Paul Buff and Brian Ross under the name **Friendly Torpedos** shortly before leaving Original Sound. It was released in 1970. Warner Bros 7188 also from 1968 was withdrawn soon after being issued and is now highly sought-after.

A 1997 picture sleeve 45 from those fine folks at Sundazed features two more unreleased tracks from 1966 - *Point Of No Return* and *King Mixer*. Hopefully many more corpses from the moody men in black are still to be exhumed.

In 1998, Sean Bonniwell joined the Fuzztones on 45 for an updated rendition of *The People In Me* (Misty Lane 046). More recently he has published an autobiography called *Beyond The Garage*.

Compilation appearances have included: *Talk Talk* on *Battle Of The Bands* (CD), *More Nuggets* (CD), *Nuggets From Nuggets* (CD), *Excerpts From Nuggets* (CD) and *Nuggets, Vol. 1* (LP); *Talk Talk* and *Double Yellow Line* on *Nuggets Box* (4-CD); *Talk Talk* and *96 Tears* on *20 Great Hits Of The 60s* (LP); *No Girl Gonna Cry* on *Turds On A Bum Ride, Vol. 1 & 2* (Dble

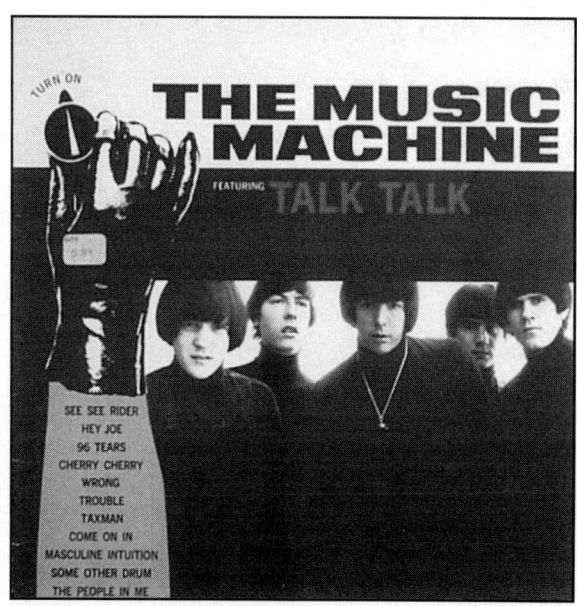

THE MUSIC MACHINE - Turn On LP.

CD) and *Turds On A Bum Ride, Vol. 1* (Dble LP); *You'll Love Me Again* on *Acid Dreams - The Complete 3 LP Set* (3-LP), *Acid Dreams Testament* (CD) and *Acid Dreams, Vol. 1* (LP); *Double Yellow Line* and *The Eagle Never Hunts The Fly* on *Nuggets, Vol. 2* (LP); *Double Yellow Line* on *Sundazed Sampler, Vol. 2* (CD) and *Garage Music For Psych Heads, Vol. 1*; *Double Yellow Line*, *Absolutely Positively*, *The Eagle Never Hunts The Fly* and *I've Loved You* on *Mindrocker, Vol. 10* (LP). (VJ/MW/JFr/SR)

The Musics

| 45: | It's The Little Things / | |
| | You Sure Fall Down A Lot | (Columbia 43634) c1966 |

A mixed vocal commercial folk-rock pop offering similar to **Mamas and The Papas**. (SR)

The Mussies

Personnel incl: MARK SHELDON   A

45: Louie Go Home/12 O'Clock July   (Fenton 2216) 1966

The above 45 was the sole vinyl offering from this obscure West Michigan group. The flip, *12 O'Clock, July*, is an over-the-top psych-punk instrumental with lots of fuzz and feedback.

Mark Sheldon later issued a 45 as **Smoke**.

Compilation appearances have included: *Louie Go Home* on *Let 'Em Have It! Vol. 1* (CD) and *Chosen Few, Vol's 1 & 2* (CD); *Louie Go Home* and *12 O'clock July* on *The Chosen Few, Vol. 2* (LP); *12 O'Clock, July* on *Everything You Always Wanted To Know...* (CD) and *Highs In The Mid-Sixties, Vol. 5* (LP). (VJ/MW)

Mustache Wax

45: I'm Gonna Get You/On My Mind   (Inner 501/2) 1965

Highs In The Mid-Sixties, Vol. 13 - Texas Part Three (LP) includes the rather uninspired effort, *I'm Gonna Get You*. Despite being on a 'Texas' compilation however, the band came from the Queens/Bronx in New York. You can also find the flip to their 45 on *Sixties Rebellion, Vol. 5* (LP & CD). (VJ/MM/MW)

Mustang

| ALBUM: | 1 ORGAN FREAKOUT | (Somerset) c1967 - |
| | 2 BEATLES SONGBOOK | (Somerset SF 23000) c1967 - |

An anonymous cheesy exploito group, they may have released other albums. (SR)

The Mustang

45: Why/Here There And Everywhere   (Ascot 2231) 1967

This seems to have been their sole vinyl offering. You'll also find the 'A' side on *Diana's Rootin' Tootin' Rock 'N' Roll Party*. The flip was a Beatles cover. (VJ)

The Mustangs

45: That's For Sure/Nova Blues   (Nero 1002) 1965

Hailed from Riverside, California. They were originally known as The Ressacs. The 'A' side to their sole 45, *That's For Sure* is a snarling fuzz-punk effort which made little impression at the time. By the end of 1966 they were no more.

Compilation appearances include *That's For Sure* on *Back From The Grave, Vol. 7* (Dble LP) and *Boulders, Vol. 3* (LP). (VJ)

The Mustangs

45: Baby Let Me Take You Home/
     Davie Was A Bad Boy   (Keetch 6002) c1965

Another group with this name, this one came from the New York area. Both songs were produced by Bert Berns and written by Wes Farrell and Russell.

The Keetch label was distributed by Atlantic. (SR)

The Mustard Family

Personnel:	BILL CARTIER	drms	A
	BOB DEPALMA	flute, sax	A
	DON DEPALMA	keyb'ds	A
	BILL DURSO	vcls, gtr	A
	GIL NELSON	bs	A

45: Yesterdays Folks/African Sunshine   (Buddah 101) 1969

This was the Connecticut outfit **U.S. 69** under a different name. Both cuts also figure on the **U.S. 69** album.

The Mustard Men

Personnel:	STAN KELLICUT	ld gtr	A
	KEITH PAPLHAM	gtr, ld vcls	A
	GEORGE WELIK	drms	A
	WARREN P. WIEGRATZ	sax, organ	A
	JERRY WIMMER	bs	A

45: Another Day/I Lost My Baby   (Raynard 10036) 1965

NB: 'A' side by Don Grady, backed by **The Mustard Men**, flip by **The Mustard Men**.

From the suburbs of Brookfield and New Berlin, Milwaukee, Wisconsin. **The Mustard Men** formed at Brookfield Central high school and judging by *I Lost My Baby* had a primitive punk sound.

Warren Wiegratz:- *"Another Day* written and sung by Don Grady with backing by **The Mustard Men**. The 'B' side, *I Lost My Baby* was a collaboration between all the members of the band. We were popular in the Southeastern part of Wisconsin from 1964 to 1967, and won the WRIT Radio 'Battle of the Bands' in 1965 and 1966."

Compilation appearances have included: *I Lost My Baby* on the *Mind Blowers* (LP), and *Highs In The Mid-Sixties, Vol. 15* (LP). (VJ/MW/WW)

THE MUSIC MACHINE - The Bonniwell Music Machine LP.

Mustardseed

ALBUM: 1 MUSTARDSEED (Spectrum) c1972 R1

From California, an interesting Christian psychedelic rock outfit with organ and fuzz guitar. Issued in a plain cover with dayglow yellow stickers, the few known copies were made in Canada but the label has a Californian address. (SR)

Mustard Seed Faith

Personnel:
PEDRO BUFORD	vcls, flute, piano	A
PRESTON "ODEN" FONG	ld vcls, gtrs	A
ALEX McDOUGALL	perc, drms	A
LEWIS McVAY	vcls, drms, acoustic gtr	A
BILL SOROUSE	electric piano, keyb'ds	A
JAY TRUAX	bs, vcls	A
(FRED FIELD	mandolin, violin	A)
(DARREL GARDNER	trumpet	A)
(ERICK NELSON	handclaps, inspiration	A)
(AL PERKINS	banjo	A)
(BRYAN SHAW	trumpet	A)

ALBUM: 1(A) SAIL ON SAILOR (Maranatha MM001 BA) 1975 -

Housed in a splendid Rick Griffin cover (it's in fact often sought-after for the cover alone!), this was a Californian Christian rock group produced by Tom Coomes, with some good guitars and harmony vocals. Lewis McVay later recorded a similar sounding album *Spirit of St Lewis*, also on this Christian label and Jay Truax worked with Richie Furay (from **Buffalo Springfield/Poco**) on his first solo album. (SR)

Mutha Goose

ALBUM: 1 MUTHA GOOSE 1 (Alpha Omega LP 264-01) 1975 R2/R3

A rare local Indiana privately pressed hard rock/guitar psych/progressive album. Similar in style to **Sweet Toothe**. (VJ)

Mutzie

Personnel:
ANDEE LAVENBURG	organ	A
BARRY LAVENBURG	bs	A
E. 'MUTZIE' LAVENBURG	gtr, vcls	A
NICK PALISE	sax, flte	A
MARC WHITE	drms	A

ALBUM: 1(A) LIGHT OF YOUR SHADOW (Sussex 7001) 1970 -

A Detroit outfit who span heavy rock, jazz, blues, soul and psychedelic influences on their album, which was produced by Theo-Coff. There's also a promo-only 33rpm 7" *LP Sampler* (Sussex SP 24) 1970 clocking in at about sixteen minutes. It features *Highway* (a blast of fuel-injected hard rock with fluid intertwining leads), *Because Of You* (a rock ballad that starts off rather leadenly before picking up in mood and tempo), *Cocaine Blues* (a series of diverse styles from funky to fuzzy, then a drum solo and toy effects - strange) and finally *Daily Cycles* (back to guitar squealin' hard rock). A good appetiser. (VJ/MW)

The Myddle Class

Personnel:
CHARLES LARKEY	bs	A
DANNY MANSOLINO	keyb'ds	A
DAVE PALMER	vcls	A
RICK PHILP	ld gtr	A
MYKE ROSA	drms	A

45s:
Gates Of Eden/Free As The Wind	(Tomorrow 7501)	1966
Don't Let Me Sleep Too Long/ I Happen To Love You	(Tomorrow 7503)	1966
Wind Chime Laughter/Don't Look Back	(Tomorrow T-912)	1967
Don't Let Me Sleep Too Long/ I Happen To Love You	(Buddah 150)	1969

Started out as a Summit, New Jersey prep-rock outfit, The Four Classics featuring Mansolino (vcls), Philp, Rosa and Kurt Gabrook (bs). By 1965 they'd become The King Bees, after adding Dave Palmer and Charlie Larkey, only to discover late that year than Danny Kortchmar's New York City group had already bagged that name. They adopted the moniker of **Myddle Class**. Already a popular draw around the Summit/New Providence/Berkeley Heights area they were put in touch with New Jerseyans Gerry Goffin and Carole King. This famous tin-pan alley team not only provided material and co-wrote (with Palmer/Philp) but also provided the means for the band to appear on vinyl via their Tomorrow label.

The results are three high quality releases of garagey folk-rock ballads that have stood the test of time remarkably well. Of these the second, *I Happen To Love You*, is regarded as their best. A superb punk ballad it was later recorded by **The Electric Prunes** and Them. *Don't Let Me Sleep Too Long* was also 'adapted' by the **Blues Project** as *Wake Me Shake Me* and covered by many others including Australia's Vacant Lot (*Ugly Things, Vol. 1*), Canada's Power of Beckett (*Nightmares From The Underworld, Vol. 2*) and the **Wrongh Black Bag**. The track also bears lyrical similarity to the Coasters *Wake Me, Shake Me*, but the roots of all these seem to be an old black church him *Heaven's Door's Gonna Be Closed*.

Still, success was elusive. A move to Buddah in 1969 resulted in a reissue of the second 45 and the recording of an album which sadly was never released, although *Lovin' Season* did make it onto the 1970 *Rock And Roll With Buddah* sampler. After this disappointment the band disintegrated. Fate dealt a further blow when Rick Philp was murdered by a college roommate. The rest regrouped as the **Quinaimes Band**. Charlie Larkey would team up with rival **King Bees**' Danny Kortchmar in **The City** and was married to Carole King for several years. He now lives in Austin, Texas and recorded with two songs with Carole King on her recent album.

A sad demise for a band of undoubted talented - perhaps some adventurous spirit may see fit one day to put out the unreleased album and 45s to redress the balance.

The band may also have helped Carole King record a 45 as **Bachs Lunch**, one side of which was written by Palmer/Philp.

Compilation appearances have included: *I Happen To Love You* on *Mindrocker, Vol. 3* (LP); *Lovin' Season* on *Psychotic Reactions* (LP); *I Happen To Love You* and *Don't Let Me Sleep Too Long* on *A Journey To Tyme, Vol. 3* (LP); and *Don't Let Me Sleep Too Long* on *Boulders, Vol. 3* (LP). (MW/BM/ReJ)

Dave Myers and The Disciples

ALBUMS:
1	HANGIN' TWENTY	(Del-Fi DFST 1239)	1963 SC
2	GREATEST RACING THEMES	(GNP Carole CARS 8002)	1967 SC

NB: (1) as Dave Myers and The Surftones. (1) reissued on CD.

DAVE MYERS and THE SURFTONES - Hangin' Twenty! CD.

45s:	Church Key/Passion	(Impact 27) 1962
α	Blue Soul/Exotic	(GNP Crescendo 196) 1963
	Let The Good Times Roll/Gear!	(Wickwire 13008) 1964
	C'mon Love/?	(Harmony Park?) 1965/6

NB: α as Dave Myers and The Rhythm Kings.

According to Tim Warren's *Back From The Grave Vol. 8* sleeve-notes, California guitarist **Dave Myers** first started making music at the age of 8, in 1951. He spent a few years playing the folkie circuit and one night during a show at a pad called Cafe Frankenstein, Dave strolled along and was exposed to the insane rattle emerging from the nearby Rendezvous Ballroom, where Dick Dale was cutting loose with his insane reverbed frenzy. He then formed the Surf-Tones in 1961. By Spring 1962, they issued their first single, *Church Key/Passion* on the Impact label and a bunch of cuts on various 'battle of the bands' albums. In early 1963 their first album, *Hangin' Twenty*, was released on Del-Fi. 1964 saw their sharp *Gear* 45 and in 1965 *C'Mon Love* (with vocals) and a second album on Carole (*Greatest Racing Themes*) was released. The band kept at it, up the end of the decade, before calling it quits.

Compilation appearances have included: *C'mon Love* on *Back From The Grave, Vol. 8* (CD), *Back From The Grave, Vol. 8* (Dble LP) and *Boulders, Vol. 3* (LP). (VJ/GG)

The Myrchents

45:	Indefinite Inhibition/All Around	(Mus-i-Col 1094) 196?

From Columbus, Ohio, you'll also find *Indefinite Inhibition* on *Scum Of The Earth* (Dble CD) and *Scum Of The Earth, Vol. 2* (LP). (MW)

Mysterians

45s:	Ram Charger/Loraine	(Sterian 691) 196?
	Wild Man/A-Bomb	(Zordan 801) 1965
	Theme From The Fuzzy Ones/Pure Distortion	(Jorel 101) 196?

Came out of Chicago in the late sixties. *Wild Man* can also be heard on *Ho-Dad Hootenanny* (LP) compilation, and *A-Bomb* on *Strummin' Mental, Vol. 5*. (VJ)

Mysteries

Personnel:	TOM BENNETT	drms	A
	HENRY SEYMOUR	bs	A
	TOM "KARL" ZACKTON	ld gtr	A

45s:	My True Love / Pink Panther	(JDL 3554) 1965
	Please Agree / I Find It's True Love	(Manhattan 815) 1967
	I Can't Wait For Love / Satisfaction Guaranteed	(Manhattan 817) 1968

These **Mysteries** aren't. They were an Orlando, Florida, trio who issued three interesting poppy 45s between 1965 and 1968.

Their debut is very rare. *My True Love* is bouncy pop-beat and was included on a rare 1966 sampler album - *12 Groovy Hits, 12 Florida Bands* (Tener 154). The second 45 is their best. *Please Agree* steams along at locomotive pace - catchy and well-produced pop with a unique sound and a few touches of fuzz. It ain't garage, but deserves its inclusion on *Psychedelic States: Florida Vol. 1* (CD). Its flip is slow harmonious pop.

I Can't Wait For Love kicks off their final 45 with some fine fuzzy guitar that promises so much but.... thereafter it's almost buried under a wash of sweet harmonies. The result is decent mid-tempo pop, but a big disappointment. Tom Bennett's *Satisfaction Guaranteed* is lightweight fluff with Everlys-style harmonies, sounding out-of-date for '68. (MW/JLh)

The Mystery Trend

Personnel:	LARRY BENNETT	bs	ABCD
	BOB CUFF	gtr	ABC
	JOHN LUBY	drms	ABCD
	RON NAGLE	vcls	ABCD
	LARRY WEST	ld gtr	B
	JOHN GREGORY	gtr		D

CD:	1	SO GLAD I FOUND YOU	(Big Beat CDWIKD 190) 1999

EP:	1	Mambo For Marion/Words/ Empty Shoes	(Sundazed SEP 118) 1996

NB: (1) contains previously unreleased tracks from 1966.

45:	Johnny Was A Good Boy/ House On The Hill	(Verve VK 10499) 1967

This band were one of the first generation San Francisco sound groups, with only **The Charlatans** pre-dating them. Formed in 1965, and originally known as The Terrazzo Brothers (minus West), they soon became known as **The Mystery Trend**. The name was apparently taken from the line in Dylan's *Like A Rolling Stone* where he sings 'the mystery tramp', although the band apparently thought his words were 'the mystery trend'. They played at the very first Bill Graham Benefit for The San Francisco Mime Troupe on November 6th, 1965. Later that month (27th Nov) they played a gig at Peter Voulkos' studio. Both were apparently very successful. They also played at some of the early Fillmore gigs. However, their music, which consisted of two - three minute tightly-structured songs, ran against the predominant tide of long, loose, free-flowing jams, which were so popular in the city in this era. They were managed by Mike Daly.

The band signed to Verve in mid-1966, which was around the time Larry West left. Originally an album was projected and seven tracks were recorded, (*There It Happened Again, Carl Street, Words You Whisper, One Day For Two, Johnny Was A Good Boy, A House On The Hill* and *Carrots On A String*). In the end only a 45 appeared. This came out in March 1967. The 'A' side is a fast, frantic number (which was originally mastered too fast) which included some vintage 'Frisco guitar work. The 'B' side is an interesting slower number written by Bob Cuff. Cuff left the band in June 1967, later joining **Serpent Power**. He was replaced by John Gregory, who later played with **Seatrain**.

The band struggled on to 1968, but then fizzled out largely because they could not secure enough live gigs to survive. **Nagle**, who later became one of the United States' top ceramicists, put together a band called Marlow, before forming Fast Bucks in 1969. He also produced a solo album *Bad Rice* in 1970.

In 1979, **Ron Nagle** formed the duo Durocs with Scott Matthews. They made one album, *Durocs* (Capitol ST 11981) 1979.

The Big Beat CD collects together twenty-one tracks - all their known studio recordings plus five home-taped efforts. It confirms the hearsay evidence over the years - that this band produced a varied selection of intelligent and artful pop.

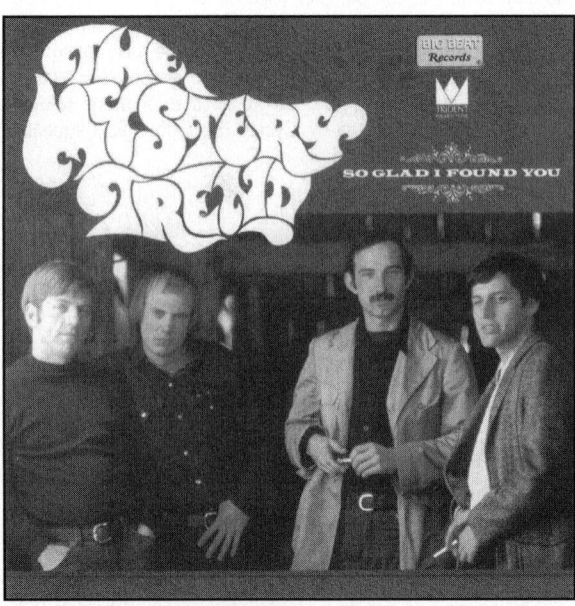

THE MYSTERY TREND - The Mystery Trend CD.

Johnny Was A Good Boy has also resurfaced on: *Nuggets Box* (4-CD), *Psychedelic Unknowns, Vol. 5* (LP & CD), *Sounds Of The Sixties San Francisco, Vol. 1* (LP), *Turds On A Bum Ride, Vol. 4* (CD) and *California Acid Folk* (Dble LP). (VJ/MW)

The Mystic Astrologic Crystal Band

Personnel:	STEVE HOFFMAN	keyb'ds, bs, gtr	A
	JOHN LEIGHTON	bs, gtr	A
	JOHN MORELAND	ld gtr	A
	BOB PHILLIPS	drms	A
	RON ROMAN	vcls, perc	A
	PHIL ALAGNA	bs	A
	GARY MYERS	drms	

ALBUMS:	1( )	MYSTIC ASTROLOGIC CRYSTAL BAND	(Carole 8001) 1967 SC
	2( )	CLIP OUT, PUT ON BOOK	(Carole 8003) 1968 SC

NB: (1) and (2) also issued in France by Vogue in 1969.

45:	Flower Never Cry/Early Dawn	(GNP Carole 1004) 1967

Musically their albums were Los Angeles psychedelic pop which has its moments. A 22 track CD compilation of their two albums (*Flowers Never Cry* on Dropout (DO 1993) released in 1992, is worth checking out.

It turns out that two members on the 45 line-up were from The Portraits. Gary Myers recalls:- "The MAC Band was being produced by Clancy B. Grass III, the same guy who was producing us (the Portraits) for Mike Curb's Sidewalk label. The Carole label was named after Curb's sister. "We had met Steve Hoffman a couple of times and, for whatever reason, two of his guys could not do this session. I think they might have been leaving the band, but I'm not sure. At any rate, Clancy had Phil Alagna (aka Phil Anthony) and me came in to do the session. The other musicians were Hoffman (guitar) and his organist (who coughed on the end of one take, requiring us to re-do it). The liner notes of the second album include The Portraits among those being thanked (although our help came before that LP)."

Steve Hoffman and Ron Roman later went on to **Proposition**. (VJ/MW/GM)

Mystic Blue

45:	Mr. McKenzie/Shelia	(Planet No 80) 1969

Simple garage - pop from Rhode Island, sounding like it was recorded in someone's living room circa 1965. For all that it has a certain charm. The flip is called *Sheila* but misprinted as 'Shelia' on the label. (MW)

The Mystic Five

45:	Are You For Real, Girl?/ I'm Gonna Love You Too	(Go-Go's 26,000) 1966

This crew formed in Venetia, Pennsylvania, in 1965 and put out the above 45 the following year. The 'A' side is a rather routine crunching garage-punker and the flip was a Buddy Holly cover. The Go-Go's label was based in Wintersville, Ohio.

Compilation appearances have included *Are You For Real, Girl?* on *Back From The Grave, Vol. 7* (Dble LP), *Chosen Few Vol's 1 & 2* (CD) and *The Chosen Few, Vol. 1* (LP). (VJ)

The Mystic Five

45:	It Doesn't Matter/Walking The Nose (?)	(Mystic 1) 1966

This was a different outfit from Hope, Rhode Island. *It Doesn't Matter* can also be heard on the *New England Teen Scene, Vol. 1* (LP), *New England Teen Scene* (CD) and *Garage Music For Psych Heads, Vol. 1*. (MW)

THE MYSTIC ASTROLOGIC CRYSTAL BAND - Flowers Never Cry CD.

The Mystic Number National Bank

Personnel:	RUSS BOOTH	bs	A
	DAVE LORENZ	gtr	A
	BOB SEBBO	gtr	A
	GLENN WALTERS	drms, vcls	A

ALBUM:	1(A)	MYSTIC NUMBER NATIONAL BANK	(Probe CPLPS 4501) 1969 -

45s:	Good Time Music/I Put A Spell On You	(Brass 421) 1968?
	Beautician Blues/St James Infirmary	(Probe 457) 1969

A late sixties Kansas City outfit, who'd originally intended to call themselves The After Life Carnival Singers. Walters went on to join Stoneface and **The Hoodoo Rhythm Devils**. The album is not recommended though their rendition of *I Put A Spell On You* is quite respectable and can also be found on the *The Garage Zone Box Set* (bonus EP) and *Ya Gotta Have Moxie, Vol. 2* (Dble CD). (VJ)

The Mystics

45s:	Snoopy/Ooh Poo Pah Doo	(Future Talent 13893/4) 1964
	Snoopy/Ooh Poo Pah Doo	(Black Cat 501) 1964

Snoopy, a punk-style reinterpretation of The Vibrations old R&B hit, was also a big hit for **The McCoys** in 1965. These 45s were the work of a Tallahassee, Florida, band and it's rumoured that their version, which is thought to have been recorded in September 1964, got played in Akron, Ohio, where **The McCoys** heard it and recorded the tune, turning it into a big commercial success.

This **Mystics** later changed name to The Many Others recording one 45, *(Tell Me Why) I'm Alone / Can I Get A Witness?* (Orchid 504) circa 1965, the 'A' side is reputedly a **Byrds**-influenced folk-rocker.

Compilation appearances include: *Snoopy* on *Back From The Grave, Vol. 2* (LP) and *Garage Kings* (Dble LP). (MW/GGI)

The Mystics

45s:	Didn't We Have A Good Time / Now And For Always	(Spectra S-707-1) 1965
	Didn't We Have A Good Time / Now And For Always	(Dot 16862) 1966

This 45, produced by Dale Hawkins, features a good uptempo rocker. This band, from Dallas, later became **The New Breed**.

Didn't We... can also be found on *The Lost Generation, Vol. 3* (LP). (BM/MW)

The Mystic Siva

Personnel:	MARK HECKERT	organ, vcls	A
	DAVE MASCARIN	drms, ld vcls	A
	AL TOZZI	gtr	A
	ART THIENEL	bs, vcls	A

ALBUM: 1(A)   THE MYSTIC SIVA   (V.O. 19713) 1972 R4/R5

NB: (1) counterfeited on vinyl in the eighties and on CD (Anthology Ant 16.11) 1994. Reissued officially on CD (World In Sound WIS-1002) 2001 and vinyl in a deluxe gatefold cover (World In Sound RFR 002).

This outfit from Michigan produced an excellent psych-rock album, which comes in an amazing sleeve and is as rare as hell. The *Gathering Of The Tribe, Vol. 4* (LP) compilation features three tracks, *Supernatural Mind*, *Keeper The Keys* and *Spinning A Spell*, which demonstrate the band's superb guitar work. (VJ)

The Mystic Tide

Personnel:	JOE DOCKO	gtr, ld vcls	AB
	PAUL PICELL	bs, vcls	AB
	JIM THOMAS	gtr, vcls	A
	JOHN WILLIAMS	drms	AB

ALBUMS: 1(A/B)   IT COMES NOW   (Distortions DB-1 006) 1991
         2(A/B)   SOLID SOUND/SOLID GROUND   (Distortions ?) 1994

NB: (2) is an eighteen-track CD compilation, including all single tracks and an unreleased acetate of their first song from 1965. Seven songs are not on (1) which is now out of print.

45s:	Stay Away/Why	(Esquire 4677) 1965
	Mystic Eyes/I Search For A New Love	(Esquire 719/720) 1966
	Frustration/Psychedelic Journey Pt 1	(Solid Sound 156/7) 1966
	Running Through The Night/Psychedelic Journey Pt 2	(Solid Sound 158/9) 1967
	Mystery Ship/You Won't Look Back	(Solid Sound 321/2) 1967

Out of the Woodbury suburb of New York City, this band made some outstanding recordings. They started life combining their own compositions with Them, Searchers and Zombies originals. They went very much against the tide of most Long Island bands, who were heavily into soul. By early 1966 they were becoming more adventurous. For their second 45, they covered a Them song, *Mystic Eyes*. Indeed, this slow punk ballad was party responsible for their name, as their leader Joe Docko liked it so much. Their third 45 was their magnum opus. *Frustration* was a haze of dementia with superb guitar leads from Docko. They played 10-minute versions of it live and each was different. The flip, *Psychedelic Journey Pt 1* was a stunning psychedelic instrumental which once again contained some superb guitar playing from Docko. The song continued on the flip to their fourth 45, which featured fine discordant clashing guitars and a striking ending. After this Jim Thomas left and they continued as a trio for one final effort:- *Mystery Ship*, another punk ballad - a tale of death and the futility of life, backed by the more optimistic, *You Won't Look Back*. This lacked the 'fullness' of sound of their previous two, now they were only a trio.

The band are well represented on compilations. You can find *Psychedelic Journey Pts 1 & 2* on *Endless Journey - Phase One* (LP) and *Endless Journey - Phase I & II* (Dble CD); *Frustration* on *Acid Dreams, Vol. 1* (LP); *Mystery Ship* and *Mystic Eyes* on *Sixties Archive, Vol. 5* (CD) and *The Finest Hours of U.S. '60s Punk* (LP); *Psychedelic Journey, Part 1* on *Son Of The Gathering Of The Tribe* (LP); *Mystery Ship* on *Glimpses, Vol's 1 & 2* (CD) and *Glimpses, Vol. 2* (LP); *Runnin' Through The Night* on *Ear-Piercing Punk* (LP) and *Pebbles, Vol. 2 (ESD)* (CD); *You Won't Look Back* on *Boulders, Vol. 11* (LP); *Stay Away* on *Psychedelic States: New York Vol. 1* (CD); and finally *You Know It's True* on *Psychedelic Crown Jewels, Vol. 1* (Dble LP & CD). The band also appear on Eva's *E-Types vs Mystic Tide* 1984 retrospective with the following tracks:- *Frustration*, *Psychedelic Journey (Pts 1 and 2)*, *Running Through The Night*, *Search For A New Love*, and *You Won't Look Back*. All tracks were written by Joe Docko.

The recent Distortions retrospectives include all their 45s plus an early effort, *I Wouldn't Care*, a gentle Merseybeat-influenced song. The later CD release includes seven extra tracks. Forget all the compilations and get this excellent legitimate collection of their 45s.

An absolute 'must' for connoisseurs of psychedelia, they were at the forefront of experimentation and ahead of their time. (VJ)

The Mystifying Monarchs

45:   Soldier Of Fortune/I'm In Misery   (Century 27913) 1967

This 45 had a nice garage style sixties sound with fuzz guitar and organ. The band came from Fargo in North Dakota.

Compilation appearances include: *I'm In Misery* and *Soldier Of Fortune* on *When The Time Run Out, Vol. 1* (LP & CD). (VJ)

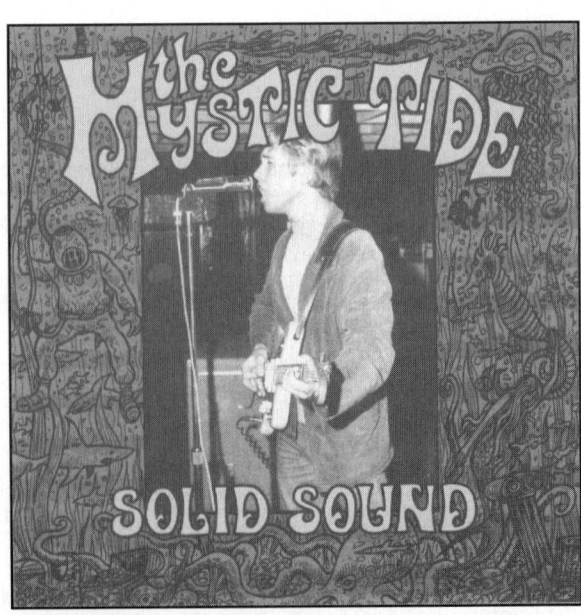

MYSTIC SIVA - Mystic Siva LP.

THE MYSTIC TIDE - Solid Ground CD.

Ron Nagle

Personnel:
	JIM BARNETT	bck vcl	A
	JOHN BLAKELEY	gtr, perc	A
	RY COODER	gtr	A
	JIMMY GETZOFF	strings	A
	RON NAGLE	keyb'ds, vcls	A
	JACK NITZSCHE	perc	A
	GEORGE RAINS	drms	A
	BRAD SEXTON	bs	A
	SAL VALENTINO	bck vcl	A
	MICKEY WALLER	drms	A

ALBUM: 1(A) BAD RICE (Warner Bros. WS 1902) 1970 -

NB: (1) reissued on vinyl (Edsel ED204) 1986.

Produced by Jack Nitzsche and Tom Donahue, this was the only solo album by the former **Mystery Trend** leader. Tracks like *Marijuana Hell* or *61 Clay* are full of excellent guitar solos and the backing group is outstanding: **Sal Valentino** (**Beau Brummels**, **Stoneground**), John Blakeley (**Stoneground**), George Rains (**Mother Earth**, **Sir Douglas Quintet**), Mickey Waller (**Pilot**, **Silver Metre**)...

In the liner notes to the Edsel reissue, **Nagle** explains that his memories of the 1969/70 period are mostly vague, due to experimenting with "the combo plate", a mixture of drugs and alcohol. The songs are about repressed teenagers killing their moms, gypsy faith healers, astrology...

Nagle later continued writing songs for Leo Kottke, The Tubes and **Stoneground**. Together with Scott Matthews he formed the Durocs who recorded one album for Capitol in 1979 and became a renowned producer (working with John Hiatt, Non Fiction). A multi-talented artist, **Nagle** is also known as one of the top American ceramicists and has also written the score for "The Exorcist", "The Sorcerer" and "Cat People". (SR)

Naked Truth

45s: Shing-A-Ling Thing/The Stripper (RCA Victor 47-9327) 1967
The Wall/If I Needed Someone (Jubilee 5642) 1968

The Wall is a cover of a Fruit Machine track and is slightly bent soft psych with suitably phased vocals. The band are thought to be a New York or Philadelphia outfit, but there was also a Rhode Island act by this name.

Compilation appearances include: *The Wall* on *Pebbles Box* (5-LP), *Pebbles, Vol. 2 (ESD)* (CD) and *Trash Box* (5-CD). (VJ/MW/EL)

Napoleon XIV

Personnel incl: JERRY SAMUELS A

ALBUM: 1 THEY'RE COMING TO TAKE ME AWAY
(Warner Bros. W 1661) 1966 R1

NB: (1) also issued in stereo (WS 1661). Reissued (Rhino RNLP 816) 19??.

EP: 1 They're Coming To Take Me Away/Aaahah, Yawa Em Ekat Ot Gnimoc Er'yeht/Doing The Napoleon/I'm In Love With My Little Red Tricycle (Warner 108) 1966

NB: (1) French release.

HCP

45s: They're Coming To Take Me Away/Aaahah, Yawa Em Ekat Ot Gnimoc Er'yeht (Warner Bros. 5831) 1966 3
I'm In Love With My Red Tricycle/
Doin' The Napoleon (Warner Bros. 5853) 1966 -
They're Coming To Take Me Away/Aaahah, Yawa Em Ekat Ot Gnimoc Er'yeht (Warner Bros. 7726) 1973 -

They're Coming To Take Me Away was a novelty song, later recorded by **Kim Fowley**. When released on 45 the flip side, *Aaahah, Yawa Em Ekat Ot Gnimoc Er'yeht* was the title track played backwards, an idea also used by the **Yellow Balloon** on their *Yellow Balloon* 45.

BEYOND THE CALICO WALL (Comp CD) including The National Gallery.

The album contains all of the single tracks and several more, including *I Live In A Split-Level Head* and one of several "replies" by "Josephine XV" (*I'm Happy They Took You Away, Ha Ha!*).

Samuels also wrote for other artists including Sammy Davis Jr's MOR hit *The Shelter of Your Arms*.

Compilation appearances have included *They're Coming To Take Me Away, Ha-Haaa!*, *The Place Where The Nuts Hunt The Squirrels* and *They're Coming To Get Me Again, Ha-Haaa!* on *Napoleon Complex* (CD). (SR/BR)

Napoleonic Wars

45s: Little Sally Tease /
Lonely Lonely Boy (Hunch 45-GQP-824) 1966
I Can't Explain It/
The Singer Not The Song (20th Century 6659) 1966

From Greensburg, just South East of Pittsburgh, they were earlier known as The Starfires. *The Singer Not The Song* has also resurfaced on *Burghers, Vol. 1* (LP & CD). (MW)

Nanette Natal

ALBUM: 1 THE BEGINNING (Evolution) 1971 -

An obscure hippie-folk singer with some freaky arrangements, a song titled *Iron Butterfly* and some psychedelic guitar leads on some tracks. (SR)

The National Gallery

ALBUM: 1 THE NATIONAL GALLERY (Philips PHS 600-266) 1968 -

Literally an 'art-rock' concept album from Cleveland, inspired by the works of artist Paul Klee (1879-1940) and complete with a glossy leaflet with lyrics and pictures of some of his paintings.

A fusion of harmonious folk, pop and avant-garde with some psychy touches, culminating in its most memorable track *Long Hair Soulful* with stoned vocals and acid-etched guitar. This had been released on 45 in 1967 in an abridged form and credited to **Bhagavad Gita**, backed by an instrumental version of the same (Philips 40485, with PS). The instrumental take can be heard on *Beyond The Calico Wall* CD (not on the album version).

The musicians themselves don't get a name-check, just a picture - three guys and a gal.

Composers Roger Karshner and Charles Mangione were involved with several other Cleveland area acts and Karshner was manager of one of the city's more successful sixties bands, **The Outsiders**.

It's worth noting that several tracks on this album were also recorded, in jazzier versions, by the Gap Mangione Trio on the album *Diana In The Autumn Wind* (GRC 9001) 1968, with Charles Mangione, Steve Gadd and Tony Levin. Mangione kept on recording throughout the seventies, with at least three albums on A&M between 1976 and 1979. (VJ/MW)

The Naturals

Personnel incl:	FRANKIE CARRETTA	vcls, gtr	AB
	JOE DeGREGORIO	drms	A
	AL FRAZIA	bs, vcls	A
	JOE SANTOS	ld vcls	A
	AL VERTUCCI	vcls, gtr	AB
	MIKE LASSANDRO	drms	B
	JOHN VANCHO	bs	B

45s:	Internationally Me/Say Hay-Ha-Ha	(Jowar 120) 1967
α	Maiden From The East/ Theme From A Natural	(Jowar 123) 1967

NB: α Lead vocal on *Maiden From The East* by Al Frazia.

A garage band from Queens, New York, whose 45s were tinged with psychedelia. Shortly after Mike Lassandro and John Vancho joined in 1967, they became the Lip-Tin Tea Company and then **Tea Company**.

John and Mike had previously played in The Summa-Sets, who formed in 1965, whilst Al Vertucci had previously been with **The Missing Links**.

Al Vertucci recalls that the **Missing Links**' debut "was recorded at Ultra-Sonic in Hempstead, L.I. Four tracks and the owner/engineer was Bill Stahl who did all of the **Fudge** and Shangri-Las stuff there. One of the great engineers ever!! He did with four tracks what people can't do today with 48. **The Tea Company** and all **The Naturals** stuff (*Maiden In The East* was recorded on the first 8-track Scully SN 0001) was also done at Ultra-Sonic by Bill Stahl". (MW/AV)

Natural Tendency

ALBUM:	1 SOMETHING GOOD IS HAPPENING	(No label) 1972 -

A melodic folk album with mystic content, it was recorded by supporters of the Maharishi Mahesh Yogi. (SR)

The Nautiloids

Personnel:	GREG 'MAC' BELL	drms	A
	RICK FULTON	ld gtr	A
	GLENN SHAEFFER	gtr	A

45:	α	Nautiloid Reef/ Nautiloid Surf	(Edgewood Studios acetate) 1965

NB: α may have also been released on (Octopus), although this now seems very doubtful.

From the Rockville/Montgomery County, Maryland area, the *Signed, D.C.* (LP) compilation includes their instrumental *Nautiloid Reef* and both sides can be found on the 1991 compilation *Concussion*. Their sole 45 was recorded at Edgewood Recording Studio on March 16th 1965.

Rick Fulton:- "I was the group's founder (1964), songwriter and lead guitarist. The group only recorded two songs (*Nautiloid Reef* and *Nautiloid Surf*) before it dissolved with the members going to other groups. The group only had three regular members; Greg "Mac" Bell (drummer), Glenn Shaeffer (rhythm guitar) and myself on lead guitar. There was no bass guitarist." (MW/RF)

NAZZ - Nazz LP.

The Navarros

Personnel:	RICK BOLZ	gtr, vcls	AB
	GARY CAMPBELL	ld gtr	AB
	DIANE (CARTER) HOFFMAN	keyb'ds, vcls	AB
	GEORGE GLEIM	bs	AB
	JOHN MORRISON	drms, vcls	A
	TOM RYAN	drms	B

45s:	Moses/Ikie	(Corby CR-204) 196?
α	I'll Be Back/Last Kiss Goodbye	(Acetate) 196?
	Tomorrow Is Another Day/ Too Many Times	(Golden State Recorders Acetate) 1966
	Please Leave Me Alone/ Sad Man	(Golden State Recorders metal acetate) 1966

NB: α only one metal acetate is known to exist.

From Phoenix, Arizona, and Talent, Oregon, **The Navarros** began in 1960 playing in a Pacific Northwest style. Carter, Bolz and Morrison shared lead vocals, backing the others in turn for three-part harmonies. On the group's best known recording, *Moses*, all three sing and it is Morrison's high pitched scream that is heard on the chorus echo. The two voices heard at the end of the record are Morrison and Carter. The flip side, *Ikie*, features Bolz on lead vocal with Carter and Morrison providing harmony back-up.

The group began its metamorphosis into the psychedelic-sounding **Neighb'rhood Childr'n** when Morrison was drafted and sent to Vietnam. His replacement, Tom Ryan influenced the group away from its original Pacific Northwest roots toward a mix of British Invasion/San Francisco sounds. It was at this time that the line up of Bolz, Campbell, Carter (now married and using the name Hoffman), Gleim and Ryan changed their name to the **Neighb'rhood Childr'n**. After about a year, this line-up broke up with the departure of Campbell, Gleim and Ryan. Bolz and Hoffman then were joined by central California musicians W.A. Farrens on drums and Ron Raschdorf on lead guitar to form the quartet that recorded most of the group's psychedelic album, although Campbell, Gleim and Ryan can be heard on some of the early work.

There is also one unreleased recording (two songs) recorded by the original band in Portland, Oregon shortly before Morrison's departure for the army. Both show the group beginning to move away from its earlier party-rock sound roots. *I'll Be Back*, a slow blues number with some distinctive rhythm twists, was written and sung by Morrison as his farewell. The flip, *Last Kiss Goodbye* is a medium tempo somewhat haunting three-part harmony with Bolz singing lead and Morrison and Carter in support.

The Corby label was based in Corvalis, Oregon.

Compilation appearances have included:- *Moses* on *Mondo Frat Dance Bash A Go Go* (CD); *Tomorrow Is Another Day* on *Highs In The Mid-Sixties, Vol. 16* (LP); and both *Tomorrow Is Another Day* and *Sad Man* on *Good Things Are Happening* (CD). (MW/DR)

NAZZ - Nazz Nazz LP.

Navasota

Personnel:	STEVE LONG	gtr	A
	LINDSEY MINTER	drms	A
	PAUL MINTER	bs	A
	RAY PAWLIK	gtr, vcls	A
	(JEFF BAXTER	gtr	A)
	(DONALD FAGEN	keyb'ds	A)
	(BYRON BERLINE	fiddle	A)
	(FLO & EDDIE	backing vcls	A)
	(CLYDIE KING	backing vcls	A)
	(SHIRLEY MATTHEWS	backing vcls	A)
	(JACKIE WARD	backing vcls	A)

ALBUM: 1(A) ROOTIN'   (ABC ABCX 757) 1972 -

Housed in a memorable sleeve with a warthog head, a decent album of bluesy hard-rock with rasping vocals and strong guitar parts. Some tracks have background vocals. It's now sought-after as it features two Steely Dan members, Don Fagen and Jeff Baxter. (SR)

The Nazz

Personnel:	ROBERT 'STEWKEY' ANTONI	piano, vcls	AB
	THOM MOONEY	drms	AB
	TODD RUNDGREN	ld gtr	A
	CARSON VAN OSTEN	bs	AB
	RICK NIELSON	gtr	B
	TOM PETERSSON	gtr	B

				HCP
ALBUMS:	1(A)	NAZZ	(SGC SD 5001) 1968	118 SC
	2(A)	NAZZ NAZZ	(SGC SD 5002) 1969	80 SC
	3(A)	NAZZ III	(SGC SD 5004) 1971	- -
	4( )	THE BEST OF NAZZ	(Rhino RNLP 119) 198?	-
	5( )	NAZZ FROM PHILADELPHIA	(Distortions DR-1037) 1997	-
	6( )	13th AND VINE	(Distortions DR-1044) 1998	-

NB: (1) - (3) reissued (Rhino RNLP 109 to 111) 1983, and reissued on CD (Rhino R2 70109 to 111). (5) & (6) are retrospective collections of outtakes, demos and alternate versions on vinyl and CD respectively. *Open Your Eyes: The Anthology* (Castle Music CMEDD 593) 2002 is a 2-CD set featuring the entire contents of their three albums, plus their cover of *Train Kept A-Rollin'*.

			HCP
45s:	Open My Eyes/Hello It's Me (PS)	(SGC 001) 1968	112
	Hello It's Me/Crowded	(SGC 002) 1969	66
	Not Wrong Long/Under The Ice	(SGC 006) 1969	-
	Magic Me/Some People	(SGC 009) 1969	-
	Sydney's Lunch Box/It Must Be Everywhere		
	Sydney's Lunch Box #2 (PS)	(Distortions DR-1035) 1997	

Nazz were not really Todd Rundgren's first band, both he and Van Osten had earlier played with **Woody's Truck Stop**, who were basically a white blues band and released their own album on Smash in early 1969.

Essentially a British-influenced mod band, the Philadelphia-based **Nazz** were quickly signed by Screen Gems Columbia who were looking for a replacement for **The Monkees**. 1968 saw the release of their debut album and a single *Open My Eyes*. Both were superb. The single was a high energy rocker with a compulsive beginning (which begged comparison to The Who's *I Can't Explain*), and beautifully blended harmonies. It received a lot of airplay in Britain, but inexplicably was not a hit. In the U.S. it was only a minor hit. It may well have been a much bigger hit, but many stations preferred to play its flip side *Hello It's Me*, which was also a minor hit when re-issued as the 'A' side to *Crowded* in 1969.

The album was full of variety - aside from the stunning *Open My Eyes*, it contained a number of fine rock ballads such as *See What You Can Be*, *Hello It's Me*, and *If That's The Way You Feel* and other dynamic hard-rock numbers such as *Back Of Your Mind*, *When I Get My Plane* and *She's Goin' Down* (the latter showing a distinct **Hendrix** influence). Despite its acclaim, in retrospect, as a superb album, *Nazz* did not sell, either in the U.S. or the UK. Released at the height of the American West Coast's heyday, perhaps it cut across the general musical tide that year. However, it became a sought-after collectors' item.

Nazz Nazz, recorded in Los Angeles, was a more consistent album and arguably the band's best. It was originally planned as a double album, but relationships within the group, particularly between Rundgren and Mooney were beginning to deteriorate to such an extent that only a single album was possible. (*Nazz III* was later released after the band split and made up of left-overs from the earlier recording sessions.) Opening track, *Forget All About It* was a cohesive, melodic number. *Not Wrong Long* was the band's third U.S. single - the final one to be released in the UK. *Under The Ice* and *Rain Rider* were further examples of their heavier brand of rock. *Gonna Cry Today* and *Letters Don't Count* were melodic ballads, whilst *Meridian Leeward* was a rather strange number about a piloting human-eating pig. The final track, an eleven-minute extravaganza entitled *A Beautiful Song*, married together all of **The Nazz**'s musical styles as well as many of the influences on them. The album was not released in the UK, although all three **Nazz** albums were reissued by Rhino in 1983, making original SGC copies of this and the third (US-only) album much sought-after by collectors.

Nazz III is not as good as the first two albums. It lacked the consistency of their second one, but had its moments. It contains quite a good version of Paul Revere's *Kicks* and a number of rock ballads, such as *Only One Winner*, *Resolution*, *It's Not That Easy* and *You Are My Window*, on which Todd sang lead vocals, but lacks any killer cuts. Indeed, the best of the harder-rock numbers *Christopher Columbus* was written by Van Osten rather than Rundgren.

When Todd Rundgren left in 1970 he was replaced by Rick Nielson and Tom Petersson, who were later both members of **Fuse** and Cheap Trick.

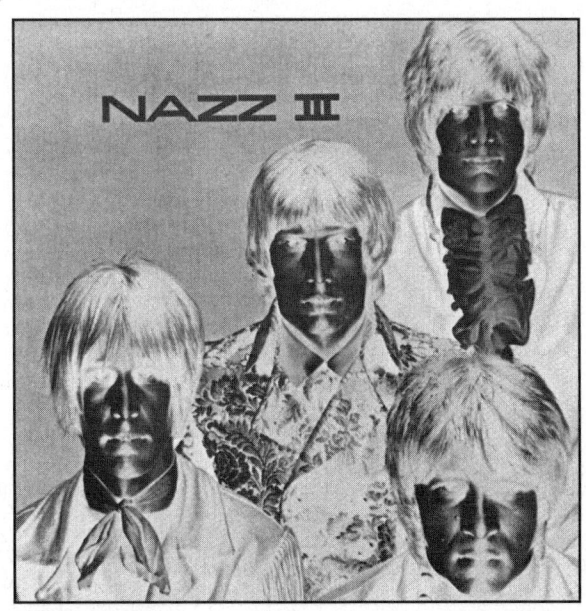

NAZZ - Nazz III CD.

The Nazz are certainly well worth listening to but their greatest significance is as an early musical songwriting venture for Todd Rundgren. Rhino have issued a *Best Of Nazz* compilation which is a good starting point for their material. Fans of the band will also be interested in the *Sydney's Lunch Box* 45, which contains two studio outtakes by the band, and the *Nazz From Philadelphia* retrospective, which compiles unreleased and alternate versions of **Nazz** classics.

Compilation appearances have included: *Open My Eyes* on *Nuggets Box* (4-CD), *Nuggets* (CD), *Nuggets - Original Artyfacts From The First Psychedelic Era 1965-1968* (Dble LP), *Nuggets, Vol. 1* (LP) and *The Seventh Son* (LP). (VJ/MW)

The Nazz

Personnel:	MIKE BRUCE	gtr, keyb'ds	A
	GLEN BUXTON	ld gtr	A
	DENNIS DUNAWAY	bs	A
	VINCENT FURNIER (ALICE COOPER)	vcls	A
	NEAL SMITH	drms	A

45:	Wonder Who's Loving Her Now/ Lay Down And Die Goodbye	(Very Record S-001) 1967

Formerly known as The Earwigs and then **The Spiders**, Neal Smith was added to the line-up for **The Nazz**, Cooper's third and final Arizona-based band before they relocated to L.A. and became known as Alice Cooper. The 45 resurfaced on an EP along with **The Spiders**' 45 made available by Blitz magazine in 1980 and a very different version of *Lay Down And Die Goodbye* appeared on Alice Cooper's *Easy Action* album.

Compilation appearances have included *Lay Down And Die, Goodbye* on *Garagelands, Vol. 1* (LP) and *Garagelands, Vol. 1* (CD). (VJ)

Ted Neeley

Personnel:	JERRY LE MIRE		A
	TED NEELEY	vcls	AB
	BILLY PATTON	ld gtr	A
	LYNN READY	gtr	A
	PAUL TABET	drms	A

ALBUMS:	1(A)	TEDDY NEELEY	(Capitol T-2774) 1968 -
	2(B)	1974 AD	(RCA APLJ 0317) 1974 -

45s: α (up to 1969)	You Must Believe Me/Love Her	(Capitol 5781) 1967
	Autumn Afternoon/ Always Something There To Remind Me	(Capitol 5781) 1967
	Contact/Where You Are	(Capitol 5967) 1968
	Bring The Whole Family/New In Town	(Capitol 2025) 1968
	Autumn Afternoon/One More Tear	(Capitol 2159) 1968

NB: α by the Teddie Neeley Five, non LP tracks.

Originally from Ranger, Texas, Teddy Neeley first sang in a local rock band before recording with **A 440**. Graced with a pleasant face and a good voice, he moved to Hollywood where he signed contracts with Capitol and Mosrite and assembled the Teddy Neeley Five for two pop singles produced by Nik Venet and Ernie Freeman.

Aged 22, he recorded his first album with his group. Produced by Trade Martin and Lee Holdridge for Koppelman-Rubin Associates, with liner notes by Bobby Darin, *Teddy Neeley* sounds now very pop-orientated and rather commercial. The material is, however, interesting with some good tracks: two songs by Bonner and Gordon (ex-**Magicians**), *Look Here Comes The Sun* and *Bring The Whole Family* written by John and Terence Boylan (of **Appletree Theatre**), two Dobyne/Jones compositions and a cover of David Blue's *Grand Hotel*. The drummer Paul Tabet would later play in **White Duck**.

Neeley then became an actor and specialised rock operas and musicals, playing in the stage versions of 'Hair', 'Tommy', 'Sgt. Pepper', 'Ulysses: The Greek Suite' and 'Jesus Christ Superstar' and in several movies, notably Robert Altman's 'A Romance' in which he was the leader of a rock band.

In 1973/75, he recorded another album and four singles for RCA and UA and later worked with Meat Loaf and Bo Diddley. (SR)

Negative Space

Personnel incl:	ROB RUSSEN	A

ALBUM:	1(A)	HARD, HEAVY, MEAN AND EVIL	(Castle NS1001) 1969 R5/R6

NB: (1) counterfeited on vinyl in 1995. Also counterfeited on CD and reissued officially as *The Living Dead Years* (Monster MCD009).

45:	The Long Hair/Light My Fire	(Castle 106) 1969

From either the Philadelphia, Pennsylvania or New Jersey area. Their album may not be considered psychedelic, but the music is plenty raw and not too polished, being in a heavy garage rock vein. It was apparently sent out to local venues around 1971 for booking purposes and was issued in both plain white jacket, and white jacket with group name and label/number stamped on it in blue ink. Some copies contained a biography and cover letter.

The 45 was non-album. It is also rumoured that they backed El John, an Elvis impersonator on his album *Caught In The Act* (private pressing, circa 1972).

All songs were written by their leader Rob Russen.

Compilation appearances include *Light My Fire* on *Filling The Gap* (4-LP). (AM/CF/MW/SR/NK)

NEGATIVE SPACE - Hard, Heavy, Mean & Evil CD.

Tommy Nehls

Personnel:	DICK BAILLARGEON	gtr, perc	A
	DOROTHY BENHAM	vcls	A
	BRETT FORBERG	drms	A
	JIM GREENBERG	sax	A
	CRAIG GUDMUNDSON	vcls, bs	A
	STEPHANIE MARLIN	flute	A
	TOM NEHLS	gtr, keyb'ds	A
	DAVE SLETTEN	keyb'ds	A

ALBUM:	1(A)	I ALWAYS CATCH THE THIRD SECOND OF A YELLOW LIGHT	(No label) 1973 R2

NB: (1) issued with lyric booklet.

Dedicated to all of the Beatles, **Frank Zappa**, J.R.R. Tolkien, M. Sandberg and D. Stoyke, this rare album comes in a handmade black and white cover with an insert, and includes cuts like: *The Under Water Symphony Dream*, *No People in The Forest*, *Your Death*, *Words Can't Explain*, *Clean Air*, *All I Need*, *Reminiscing*, *Hot Wind*, and *Dawn In The Park*.

Judging by this odd private press with occasionally jazzy experimentations, the Winters in Minnesota are very, very cold. (SR/CF)

The Neighborhood

ALBUM:	1 DEBUT	(Dot) 1969 -	HCP
45s:	Children On Our Way/Woman Think	(Dot 17238) 1969 -	
	Big Yellow Taxi/		
	You Could Be Born Again	(Big Tree BT 102) 1970	29
	Laugh/Now's The Time For Love	(Big Tree BT 106) 1971	104

A soft pop group with some light psychy touches. Produced by Jimmy Bryant, their second single included covers of songs written by Joni Mitchell and by Chris Dedrick of **Free Design**, a group exploring similar territory. (SR)

Neighborhood Of Love

45:	Count Yourself Out Of Bounds / Miss' Blue Three Quarter	(Trip 102) 1969

Nothing has been uncovered yet on this Southern Florida outfit. According to the liners for *Psychedelic States: Florida Vol. 1* (CD), which features *Miss' Blue Three Quarter*, a double-length version of this wild freak-out exists ... where the song is repeated twice. (MW/JLh/RM)

Neighb'rhood Childr'n

Personnel:	RICK BOLZ	12 string gtr, tamb, hrmnca, vcls	AB
	GARY CAMPBELL	ld gtr	A
	GEORGE GLEIM	bs	A
	DYAN HOFFMANN	vcls, organ, tamb	AB
	TOM RYAN	drms	A
	W. A. FARRENS	drms, hrmnca, tamb, vcls	B
	RON RASCHDORF	gtr, tamb, vcls, hrmnca	B

ALBUMS:	1( )	THE NEIGHB'RHOOD CHILDR'N		
		(Golden State Recorders acetate)	1967	R5
	2( )	THE BOOK OF CHANGES		
		(Golden State Recorders acetate)	1968	R4
	3(B)	NEIGHB'RHOOD CHILDR'N (Acta A-38005)	1968	R2
	4(-)	LONG YEARS IN SPACE (dbl)		
		(Sundazed LP 5023)	1997	-

NB: (1) is a 12" metal acetate album. Some tracks appear on the Acta album, most don't. (2) is a one-sided 12" metal album acetate of Acta album tracks with different mixes. *Chocolate Angel* has a longer intro. (3) pirated in 1989 and also on CD. (4) is an essential retrospective collection, also issued on CD (SC 11041) 1997.

EP:	1	THE NEIGHB'RHOOD CHILDR'N	
		(Vegas Productions 863)	1967

NB: (1) issued with press kit by the group's booking agency. This promo-only 7" EP was not issued in a sleeve. It contained non-album cuts/versions of *Up, Down, Turned Around World*, *Maggie's Farm*, *That's What's Happening* and *Please, Please Leave Me Alone*.

45s:	α	Little Black Egg/Louie Louie	(Golden State Recorders)	1967
		Maintain/Just No Way (as 'The Neighborhood')	(Acta 813)	1967
	β	Please Leave Me Alone/Happy Child	(Acta 823)	1968
		Behold The Lilies/I Want Action	(Acta 828)	1968
		Woman Think/On Our Way	(Dot 17238)	1969

NB: α is a One-sided 8" metal acetate. Only β is from the Acta album.

NEIGHB'RHOOD CHILDR'N - Neighb'rhood Childr'n LP.

One of the many forgotten bands gigging in the 'Frisco area, **Neighb'rhood Childr'n**'s sole album on Acta is a psychedelic 'gem'. But, alas, after its release they simply vanished from the scene. Back in '68 with comparatively crude instrumentation available they created some very spacey sounds on tracks like *Long Years In Space*, while *Chocolate Angel* is something of a psychedelic jam. *Feeling Zero* appears to have been specially written to bring you down after another trip, while tracks like *Happy Child* and *Patterns* feature Dyan Hoffmann's crystal clear vocals. Indeed on *Long Years In Space* she complements the other vocalists to give the band a **Jefferson Airplane**-type sound. They even perform a re-creation of *Over The Rainbow* from Wizard of Oz.

Neighb'rhood Childr'n also recorded a couple of acetate albums in addition to the album on Acta. Much of this material has been compiled on the excellent *Long Years In Space* retrospective on Sundazed and this together with the 'Acta' album is strongly recommended to connoisseurs of psychedelia.

The band evolved out of Oregon's **Navarros**, when their original drummer John Morrison was drafted. After about a year Campbell, Gleim and Ryan quit too and Bolz and Hoffman were then joined by central California musicians W.A. Farrens on drums and Ron Raschdorf on lead guitar.

Collectors should note that a DJ 45, with *Dancing In The Street* on both sides (N.A.M.I. 2014) 1974, is actually by a different Neighborhood Children, and sounds similar to early Jackson brothers.

Compilation appearances include *Changes Brought To Me* on *Turds On A Bum Ride, Vol. 1 & 2* (Dble CD) and *Turds On A Bum Ride, Vol. 2* (Dble LP). (VJ/CF/DR/SR)

Fred Neil

Personnel:	VINCE MARTIN	gtr, vcls	A E
	FRED NEIL	vcls, gtr	ABCDE
	PETE CHILDS	gtr, dobro	BCD
	FELIX PAPPALARDI	bs	B
	DOUGLAS HATELID	bs	B
	JOHN SEBASTIAN	mouth harp	B
	JAMES E. BOND	acoustic bs	CD
	CYRUS FARYAR	magic bouzouki, gtr	CD
	RUSTY FARYAR	finger cymbals	C
	JOHN T. FORSHA	gtr	C
	BILLY MUNDI	drms, perc	C
	NICK VENET	lightning, thunder	C
	AL WILSON	harp	C
	ERIC GLEN HORD	gtr	D
	BRUCE LANGHORN (aka LANGHORNE)	gtr	D
	MONTE DUNN	gtr	E
	LES McCANN	piano	E
	GRAM PARSONS	vcl, piano	E

ALBUMS:
- 1(A) TEAR DOWN THE WALLS (Elektra EKS-7248) 1964 R1
- 2(B) BLEECKER AND MACDOUGAL (Elektra EKS 7293) 1966 R1
- 3(C) FRED NEIL (Capitol ST 2665) 1967 SC
- 4(D) SESSIONS (Capitol ST 2862) 1968 SC
- 5(C) EVERYBODY'S TALKIN (Capitol SM 294) 1969 SC
- 6(B) LITTLE BIT OF RAIN (Elektra EKS 74073) 1970 -
- 7(E) OTHER SIDE OF THIS LIFE (Capitol ST 657) 1971 -

NB: (1) shown as by Martin and Neil. (6) is a retitled reissue of (2) with a new sleeve. (5) is a retitled reissue of (3) with a new sleeve. Some albums have been reissued on CD, including (2) on (Elektra AMCY-2693). (2) also reissued on vinyl (Sundazed LP 5107) 2002. There's also a double CD compilation *The Many Sides Of Fred Neil* (Collector's Choice CCM 070) 1999.

45s:
- Dolphins/Badi-da (Capitol 5786) 1966
- Dolphins/I've Got A Secret (Capitol 2047) 1967
- Felicity/Please Send Me Someone To Love (Capitol 2091) 1968
- Everybody's Talkin/That's The Bag I'm In (Capitol 2256) 1968
- Candy Man/The Water Is Wide (Elektra EKSN 45036) 1968
- α Everybody's Talking/Badi Da (Capitol 2604) 1969

NB: α also issued in various European countries including a French 45 with picture sleeve (Capitol 2C00680188) 1969.

A folk, folk-jazz and blues singer, guitar player and songwriter, **Fred Neil** was a very important figure in the sixties music scene, although he never reached a high level of public awareness.

Born in Florida in 1937, **Neil** came from the late fifties folk Village scene and began writing songs which have been popularized by many, many groups: *Other Side Of This Life* has been recorded by **Jefferson Airplane**, **Lovin' Spoonful**, Eric Burdon, the **Youngbloods** and several other acts, *Blues On The Ceiling* by **Tim Hardin**, *Everybody's Talkin* by Harry Nilsson, *Dolphins* by **Tim Buckley**...

Managed by Herb Cohen (**Frank Zappa** business associate), **Fred Neil** began recording in 1964 and his first songs can be found on live folk compilations (*Hootenanny Live At The Bitter End*, *World Of Folk Music*). After a rare first album (*Tear Down The Walls*) with Vince Martin, *Bleeker And MacDougal* was recorded with **John Sebastian**, Felix Pappalardi and Pete Childs and produced by Paul Rothchild (**Tim Buckley**, **Doors** etc.). It contains an excellent mix of folk and folk-blues and his classic songs *Blues On The Ceiling*, *Candy Man* and *Other Side Of This Life*. For an unknown reason, Elektra reissued this album in 1970 under the new title of *Little Bit Of Rain*.

In 1967, **Neil** left Elektra, signed a new contract with Capitol and released one of his best records, *Fred Neil* with *Sweet Cocaine*, *The Dolphins*, *I've Got A Secret* and the superb acid folk raga *Cynicrustpetefredjohn Raga*. Produced by Nick Venet, he is accompanied by Al Wilson (**Canned Heat**), Billy Mundi (**Mothers Of Invention**), Cyrus Faryar (**Modern Folk Quartet**, **Cosmic Sounds**) and Peter Childs. This album would be reissued under a new title after his song *Everybody's Talkin* was chosen for the theme of 'Midnight Cowboy' and became a huge hit sung by Nilsson.

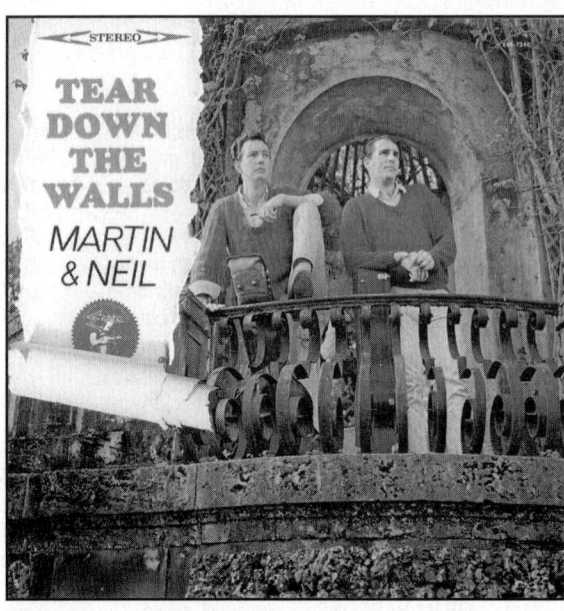

FRED NEIL - Tear Down The Walls CD.

The next album *Sessions* is once again excellent and was recorded in October 1967 live in the studio: four acoustic guitars, one bass and Nick Venet producing.

Finally released in 1971 but probably recorded before, *Other Side Of This Life* is composed of one live side of his classics recorded with **Monte Dunn** at the Elephant Club in Woodstock and one studio with Gram Parsons on one track (*You Don't Miss Your Water*).

Jefferson Airplane wrote two songs about **Neil**: *House At Pooneil Corners* and *Ballad Of You And Me And Pooneil*.

Refusing to play the game of promotion, interviews and tours, **Neil** never had much commercial success and retreated by the late sixties to Coconut Grove, Florida, where he engaged himself in dolphin research. The recent CD reissues have helped to relaunch the interest in his music.

Sadly, **Fred Neil** died of cancer in July 2001. (SR/GBi)

Neon

Personnel:
- PETER BRANNIGAN — gtr, vcls — A
- FRANCIS CRABTREE — keyb'ds, vcls — A
- RUSSELL LESLIE — vcls, perc — A
- FUNG PORTER — bs, vcls — A

ALBUM: 1(A) NEON (Paramount PAS 5024) 1971 -

45s:
- Dark Is The Night/Hold Back My Tears (Paramount 0061) 1970
- Movin'/Darling Before I Go (Paramount 0121) 1971

An obscure outfit whose output might interest readers. Their sole album was produced by Tommy James and Bob King of **Tommy James and The Shondells** fame. (VJ)

Neon Philharmonic

Personnel:
- DON GRANT — vcls — A
- TUPPER SAUSSY — keyb'ds — A

ALBUMS:
- 1(A) THE MOTH CONFESSES (Warner Bros. WS 1769) 1968 -
- 2(A) NEON PHILHARMONIC (Warner Bros. WS 1804) 1969 -

NB: (1) reissued on CD (Sundazed SC 6084) 1996. (2) reissued on CD.

HCP

45s:
- Morning Girl/Brilliant Colors (Warner Brothers 7261) 1969 17
- No One Is Going To Hurt You/You Lied (Warner Brothers 7311) 1969 120
- Clouds/Snow (Warner Brothers 7355) 1969 -
- Heighty - Ho Princess/Don't Know The Way Around Soul (Warner Brothers 7380) 1970 94
- Flowers For Your Pillow/To Be Continued (Warner Brothers 7419) 1970 -
- Something To Believe In/A Little Love (Warner Brothers 7457) 1971 -
- Gotta Feelin' In My Bones/Keep The Faith In Me (Warner Brothers 7497) 1971 -
- Making Out The Best You Can/So Glad You're A Woman (Trx 5039) 1972 -
- Annie Poor/Love Will Find A Better Way (MCA 40518) 1976 -

Beware of opportunistic dealers who describe this studio creation duo as psychedelic, they are more poppish really. The project consisted of Nashville Symphony Orchestra musicians and was headed by Grant and Saussy. They have their moments though, on tracks like *Are You Old Enough To Remember Dresden?* from their second album. Their debut 45 *Morning Girl* was a Top 20 hit and they enjoyed a couple more minor hits.

Grant later died on 6th March 1987, aged only 44. (VJ/GG)

Nepenthe

45: Good Morning Baby/Slow It Down (Direction 4003) 196?

A mid-sixties San Francisco-based outfit. (VJ)

NEON PHILHARMONIC - The Moth Confesses CD.

The Nervous Breakdown

45: I Dig Your Mind/Seeds Of Love   (Take 6 1001) 196?

This outfit is thought to have been Californian, based in L.A. The 'A' side of their 45, *I Dig Your Mind*, is quite a good effort where the vocals blend with the organ backing and moderate echoes are used to good effect. The flip is apparently nothing more than an instrumental version of the 'A' side.

Compilation appearances include: *I Dig Your Mind* on *Pebbles, Vol. 9* (CD), *Psychedelic Unknowns, Vol's 1 & 2* (LP), *Psychedelic Unknowns, Vol. 1* (Dble 7"), *Pebbles, Vol. 1 (ESD)* (CD), *Sixties Choice, Vol. 2* (LP) and *60's Choice Collection, Vol's 1 & 2* (CD). (VJ)

Nervous System

45s: Make Love, Not War / Bones   (Jambee 1001/2) 1967
     Make Love, Not War / Oh!   (Jambee 1001/4) c1967

Both California and Chicago have been suggested as this band's origins. *Make Love...* is waltzing harmony pop except for some acidic guitar in the last few bars. *Oh!* is brassy pop with keening guitar. (MW)

Neurotic Sheep

45s: Season Of The Witch/I'm Free   (Bofuz BF-1117) 1967
     Drive My Car/?   ( ) 1968

Originally from Houston, Texas they relocated to Baton Rouge, Louisiana and released the Bofuz 45 in 1967 during their stay. Returning to Houston they recorded *Drive My Car* around 1968, legend has it, for a 45 on Capitol which never appeared.

Drive My Car has subsequently resurfaced on *The Cicadelic 60's, Vol. 2* (CD) and *The Cicadelic 60's, Vol. 4* (LP). (VJ/MW/AB)

Never Mind

See **Damin Eih, A.L.K. and Brother Clark** entry.

The New Arrivals

45s: Take Me For What I Am /
     You Know You're Gonna Be Mine   (South Bay SBM 102) 1966
     Scratch Your Name /
     Just Outside My Window   (South Bay SBM 103) 1966
   α Just Outside My Window /
     Let's Get With It   (South Bay SBM 104) 1967

NB: α also issued on Macy's 7-UP (104) 1967.

The second 45 is a superb stompin' fuzz - punker in a folk - rock vein, from the San Jose area, complete with a great rave-up outro in the **Count Five** *Psychotic Reaction* style for good measure. The 'B' side is lighter pop, but is still good harmony 'n' jangle folk - rock full of California sunshine vibes. Recorded at the now - legendary Golden State Recorders, this is a nugget of some pedigree. *Scratch Your Name* was written by Tom Talton - yes, he of **We The People** fame, confirmed by Alec Palao: "the bands manager was a friend of **We The People**'s producer Tony Moon, hence their access to the song". Alec adds -"All their singles are worth getting, but tend to be mostly instrumentals".

Compilation appearances include: *Let's Get With It* on *Acid Dreams, Vol. 3* (LP). (MW/AP)

The New Breed

45s: Sunny/P.M. Or Later   (In Crowd 001) 1967
     Sunny/P.M. Or Later   (Jamie 1341) 1967
     Big Time/Summer's Comin'   (In Crowd 1234) c1967
     Little Bit Of Soul/Someone   (In Crowd 1235) c1967
     I'd Like To See Her Again/
     High Society Girl   (Fraternity 1003) 1968

This Dallas band were earlier called **The Mystics**. Their finest moment was *Big Time*, which had a catchy guitar riff. The 45 was also released on Cottonball (1 235) as by Tim and Bill.

Compilation appearances have included: *Big Time* on *Punk Classics* (CD) and *Flashback, Vol. 6* (LP); and *High Society Girl* on *A Journey To Tyme, Vol. 2* (LP). (VJ)

The New Breed

Personnel: RON FLOGEL   gtr, vcls   A
            GEORGE HULLIN   drms   A
            TOM PHILLIPS   gtr, keyb'ds, vcls   A
            TIM SCHMIDT   bs, vcls   A

ALBUM: 1(A) WANT AD READER   (Cicadelic CICLP 985) 1985

NB: (1) has been reissued on CD by Collectables (COL-CD-0524) together with **Basement Wall**'s *The Incredible Sound Of....*

45s: Green Eyed Woman/I'm In Love   (Diplomacy 22) 1965
     Leave Me Be/I've Been Wrong Before   (Mercury 72556) 1966
     Want Ad Reader/
     One More For The Good Guys   (World United 001) 1966
     Want Ad Reader/
     One More For The Good Guys   (HBR 508) 1966
     Fine With Me/The Sound Of The Music   (World United 003) 1967

Sacramento, the State Capital of California, was home to this band and their finest moment *Want Ad Reader* is recommended to garage fans. After a few 45s they changed name again beginning work on an album using the name Never Mind, although the album was later issued under the name **Glad**, who later evolved into Redwing. Tim Schmidt would go on to The Eagles and **Poco** amongst others.

The retrospective album on Cicadelic is worth checking out - it contains all 45 tracks bar *Fine With Me* plus nine unreleased gems.

Compilation appearances have included:- *Want Ad Reader* on *Psychedelic Unknowns, Vol. 7* (LP & CD), *Of Hopes And Dreams & Tombstones* (LP) and *Sounds Of The Sixties San Francisco, Vol. 1* (LP); *One More For The Good Guys* on *Buzz Buzz Buzzzzzz, Vol. 1* (CD); *Woman* and *I'll Come Running* on *Green Crystal Ties, Vol. 2* (CD); and *Green Eyed Woman* on *All Cops In Delerium - Good Roots* (LP). (VJ)

New Breed

45: Wasting My Time/It's Love (Polaris 711) 1966

From Worcester, Massachusetts.

Compilation appearances have included *Wasting My Time* on *New England Teen Scene, Vol. 1* (LP) and *Gone, Vol. 2* (LP); *Wasting My Time* and *It's Love* on *The Polaris Story* (CD). (VJ)

The New Brick Window

45: Little Girl / Baby, Come Running (Vendetta 126) 1968

A bunch of teens from Jamestown, New York, released their sole 45 in 1968. Bouncey pop with a fuzzy edge and a guitar-rave-up outro, *Little Girl* has been unearthed on *Psychedelic States: New York Vol. 1* (CD). (MW)

New Buffalo (Springfield)

Personnel:			
	BOB APPERSON	bs	A
	DEWEY MARTIN	vcls	ABC
	DON PONCHER	drms, vcls	ABC
	DAVE PRICE	gtr, vcls	ABC
	JIM PRICE	hrmnca	A
	GARY ROWLES	gtr	AB
	RANDY FULLER	bs	BC
	BOB JONES	gtr	C

After **Buffalo Springfield** disintegrated, **Dewey Martin** put together **New Buffalo Springfield**, with line-up 'A' including Gary Rowles (ex-**Nooney Ricket and The Pure**) in October 1968. The band made its debut in Hawaii in November 1968 and the following month played at San Francisco's Holiday Rock Festival alongside **Canned Heat** and **Steppenwolf**. Early in 1969 however, they were forced to shorten their name to **New Buffalo**, and shortly afterwards Apperson was replaced by ex-Randy Fuller Four leader Randy Fuller and Jim Price left to join **Delaney & Bonnie**.

Bob Jones then replaced Rowles, who later joined **Love** and a recording deal was obtained with Atco. Before they could fulfil this, however, **Martin** left for a solo deal with UNI in July and the group added Joey Newman (ex-**Don and The Goodtimes / Touch**) to become **Blue Mountain Eagle**.

Bob Apperson the bass player also worked with Jose Feliciano, the cuban jazz guitarist who covered *Light My Fire*. Apparently he played on a lot of his early work. Bob also played with Wilson Pickett, Glenn Campbell and The Lettermen. (NW)

Curt Newbury

Personnel:			
	RICHARD APLANALP	clarinet	A
	MIKE DEASY	gtr, dobro, mandolin	A
	COFFI HALL	perc	A
	HOWARD JOHNSON	tuba	A
	RON JOHNSON	bs	A
	JEFF KAPLAN	gtr, organ, bs, piano	A
	PAUL LAGOS	drms	A
	RICK MATTHEWS	perc	A
	CURT NEWBURY	vcls, gtr	A
	TEMPLETON PARSLEY (MAX BUDA)	electric violin, hrmnca	A
	PAT SMITH	bs fiddle	A

ALBUM: 1(A) HALF A MONTH OF MAY DAYS (Verve Forecast FTS-3087) 1969 -

Texan born, **Curt Newbury** began picking folk guitar in the coffee houses then became a flying instructor and a licensed hypnotist. He recorded his only solo album in 1970 at The Sound Factory in Hollywood, produced by Don Hall. Backed up by four members of **Kaleidoscope**:- Lagos, Kaplan, the enigmatic Parsley/Budha (aka Fenrus Epp or Chester Crill) and Ron Johnson, plus **Mike Deasy** and some other players, **Newbury** composed and sang all the tracks resulting in an interesting album of West Coast folk-rock with some brilliant guitar solos. (SR)

THE NEW COLONY SIX - Attacking A Straw Man LP.

Newbury Park

ALBUM: 1 NEWBURY PARK (Cream) c1972 -

A "groovy" soft-rock quartet with female vocals. (SR)

New Colony Six

Personnel:			
	RAY GRAFFIA	vcls, tamb	ABCD
	CHIC JAMES	drms	ABC
	CRAIG KEMP	organ	A
	WALLY KEMP	bs	AB
	JERRY VAN KOLLENBERG	gtr, vcls	ABCD
	PAT McBRIDE	hrmnca, vcls, perc	ABCD
	RONNIE RICE	vcls, gtr, keyb'ds	BCD
	CHUCK JOBES	keyb'ds	CD
	LES KUMMEL	bs	CD
	BILLY HERMAN	drms, vcls	D

HCP
ALBUMS: 1(A) BREAKTHROUGH (Sentar 101) 1966 - R3/R4
2(B) COLONIZATION (Sentar SST-3001) 1967 172 -
3(C) REVELATIONS (Mercury 61165) 1968 157 -
4(D) ATTACKING A STRAW MAN (Mercury 61228) 1969 179 -

NB: (1) reissued on Eva (12008) 198? and on Sundazed (LP 5106) 2002. (1) reissued by Sundazed as *At The River's Edge* on LP (LP 5007) and on CD (SC 11016), 1993, with eight additional tracks. (2) reissued by Sundazed on CD (SC 6026) 1994 with two additional tracks - alternate versions of *Accept My Ring* and *Rap-A-Tap* which earlier appeared on the Sundazed 7" EP below. (3) and (4) reissued on one CD as *The Best Of New Colony Six* in Japan (Mercury PHCR 1436) 1996. There's also a "greatest hits" CD entitled: *Colonized! Best Of The New Colony Six* (Rhino CD: R2 71188) 1993.

EP: 1 FOUR BY SIX (Sundazed SEP 107) 1993

NB: (1) contains *Last Nite*, *Accept My Ring*, *Cadillac* and *Rap-A-Tap*. *Accept My Ring* and *Rap-A-Tap* are previously unreleased alternate versions.

HCP
45s: I Confess/Dawn Is Breaking (Centaur 1201) 1965 80
(up to α I Lie Awake/
1974) At The River's Edge (Centaur/Sentaur 1202) 1966 111
Cadillac/Sunshine (Sentar 1203) 1966 -
β (The Ballad of the) Wingbat Marmaduke/
The Power Of Love (Sentar 1204) 1966 -
Love You So Much/Let Me Love You (Sentar 1205) 1966 61
You're Gonna Be Mine/Woman (Sentar 1206) 1967 108
I'm Just Waiting/Hello Lonely (Sentar 1207) 1967 128
Treat Her Groovy/Rap-A-Tap (PS) (Mercury 72737) 1967 -
I Will Always Think About You/
Hold Me With Your Eyes (Mercury 72775) 1968 22

Can't You See Me Cry/Summertime's Another Name For Love (PS)	(Mercury 72817)	1968 52
Things I'd Like To Say/ Come And Give Your Love To Me	(Mercury 72858)	1968 16
I Could Never Lie To You/ Just Feel Worse	(Mercury 72920)	1969 50
I Want You To Know/Free	(Mercury 72961)	1969 65
Barbara, I Love You/Prairie Grey	(Mercury 73004)	1969 78
People And Me/ Ride The Wicked Wind	(Mercury 73063)	1970 116
Close Your Eyes Little Girl/ Love, That's The Best I Can Do	(Mercury 73093)	1970 -
Roll On/If You Could See	(Sunlight 1001)	1971 56
Long Time To Be Alone/ Never Be Lonely	(Sunlight 1004)	1971 93
Someone, Sometime/Come On Down	(Sunlight 1005)	1972 109
Never Be Lonely/Long Time To Be Alone	(MCA 40215)	1974 -
I Don't Really Want To Go/Run	(MCA 40288)	1974 -

NB: α was originally released as (Centaur 1202) but after a threatened copyright lawsuit, it was reissued as (Sentaur 1202). This too resulted in a copyright problem and subsequent singles came out on "Sentar"! The 'A' side to β, *(The Ballad of the) Wingbat Marmaduke* is actually the same track as *Elf Song* from their *Colonization* album.

This Chicago band started out as The Patsmen in 1964 playing a British invasion sound. The travelled to California in 1965, but returned to Chicago forming their own Centaur (later Sentar) label. In 1966, they sounded very punkish with a strong Animals - Them influence. Their first album in particular is very much in this vein and originals are very rare and sought-after. Its reissue by Eva has made it more accessible. The second is more poppy, but contains a fine cover of The Yardbirds' classic *Mister You're A Better Man Than I*. Later they signed to Mercury and developed into a successful harmony ballad-soft rock act which continued recording well into the 1970s. Over the years they enjoyed much minor chart success and one Top Twenty hit, *Things I'd Like To Say*.

In 1967, Ray Graffia produced a single for **The Prophets**. In 1969, Graffia and Chic James left the **New Colony Six** and joined up with former member Craig Kemp to form the **Raymond John Michael Band**, which eventually released three singles. Patrick McBride later worked at Plynth Studios in the Chicago area. In 1975, the **New Colony Six** finally stopped rockin'.

Ray Graffia and **Ronnie Rice** re-formed **The New Colony Six** for a one-time reunion at Chicago's Park West in 1988. Subsequently Ray Graffia has also performed with a new line-up of the band, doing selected shows throughout the nineties. **Ronnie Rice** also now performs as a solo artist and still makes occasional appearances with **New Colony Six**. Anyone interested in **Ronnie**'s solo material should check out *Refried Rice ('61-'86)* on Sunlight Records (SU-5007) 1997.

Les Kummel and Chuck Jobes had earlier been in **The Revelles**, whilst Billy Herman had been in **Aorta**. Sadly Les Kummel died in an auto accident on 19th Dec, 1978.

In the eighties and nineties Ray Graffia has been busy running his company Arbortech, which deals with cleaning up environmental problems in industry, primarily focusing on wastewater.

Compilation appearances have so far included:- *At The River's Edge* on *Pebbles, Vol. 9* (LP); *At The River's Edge* on *Pebbles, Vol. 4 (ESD)* (CD); *At The River's Edge* on *Nuggets Box* (4-CD); *I Will Always Think About You* on *45s On CD, Vol. 3 ('66 - '69)*; *I Will Always Think About You* on the 8-track *Sound Singles Best of '68: Volume One*; *Things I'd Like To Say* on *Rock 'N' Roll Relix, 1968-1969* (CD) (reissued in 1998 as as *Whole Lotta...Rock, 1968-1969*); *Things I'd Like To Say* on *Sunshine Days: Pop Classics Of The Sixties, Vol. 5* (CD); *Cadillac* on *Mindrocker, Vol. 12* (LP) and *Sundazed Sampler, Vol. 1* (CD); and *Love You So Much* on *Sundazed Sampler, Vol. 2* (CD). (VJ/BSw/CM/MW)

The New Dawn

Personnel:	BILL	A
	BOBBY	A
	DAN	A
	JOE	A
	LARRY	A

ALBUM: 1(A) THERE'S A NEW DAWN
  (Hoot (Garland GR) 70-4569) 1970 R3

NB: (1) pressed in Canada. (1) has been counterfeited on vinyl and on CD (Synton 809972). (1) reissued officially on CD in mini card sleeve (Akarma AK 152) and LP (Akarma AK 152) 2001.

45: Tears/Why Did You Go? (Garland 2020) 1970

Salem, Oregon was home turf for this soft-rock quintet whose rare album has been reissued. The opening cut *New Dawn* begins with an unusual spoken intro, but is essentially a soft-rock ballad; *I See A Day* has some good fuzz guitar and *Its Rainin'* couples this with sound effects; there's some upfront organ on *Hear Me Cryin'* and Side One closes with *Dark Thoughts*, a more uptempo song with lots of fuzz guitar. Side two is disappointing by comparison and very samey with a country-style rhythm section that never excites.

Other 'New Dawn' acts abound, including one on Imperial.

You can also find *Dark Thoughts* on *Love, Peace And Poetry Vol. 1* (LP & CD). (VJ)

The New Dawn

45s:	If I Can't Have Your Love/Loser	(Mainstream 652) 1967
	Slave Of Desire/	(Mainstream 664) 196?

The first 45 is rather disappointing multi-voiced pop, a few intelligent harmonies notwithstanding. The second, *Slave of Desire* has been compiled on *Sixties Choice, Vol. 2* (LP) and *60's Choice Collection, Vol's 1 & 2* (CD). (MK/MW)

The New Dawn

45: Listen To The Music / Someday (RCA 47-9569) 1968

A garage-pop song with lots of fuzz and "mind-expanding" lyrics. The flip is a ballad. (SR)

New Directions

Personnel:	CHIP GOLDEN	drms	A
	BOB JONES	vcls	A
	LOUIS JONES	vcls	A
	STEVE KORMAN	bs	A
	STEVE PEPPOS	gtr	A
	JIMMY WHITE	gtr	A

THE NEW DAWN - There's A New Dawn LP.

45:   Springtime Lady / Swlabr   (Nottingham Disc Co. 850) 1969

Formed in Virginia Beach, Virginia, circa 1965 as the Directions. In early 1969 they recorded their sole 45 - a laid-back rock original backed by a Cream cover. An initial pressing of 500 copies was successful enough in the Petersburg charts to warrant a second helping.

Aliens, Psychos And Wild Things (CD) features two versions of *Springtime Lady* - the 45 version is above-par late sixties rock with a West Coast vibe in the vocal arrangements. The instrumental version is a different unreleased take, introduced as "Springtime Lady music track one", and highlights the soothing quality of the twin-guitar workout where wah-wah snakes in and out of fluid runs and sustains. It's the final "bonus track" on the CD and a great way to wind down. (BHr/ST/MW)

New Folk

ALBUM: 1   BORN YESTERDAY - I CONQUERED DEATH!
(Campus Crusade For Christ) 19?? -

An above-average Christian rock record, including the blistering psych cut *Love Comes Down*. Religious and secular. Also includes the fuzzed-out *Let's Get Together* plus the medley *Windy/Never My Love*.

The band came from Arrowhead Springs, Oklahoma. (MMs/SR)

The New Fugitives

45:   She's My Baby/That's Queer   (GLO 5241) 1966

The New Fugitives, from Meriden, Connecticut, were formed in early 1965 by two high-school pals. According to Tim Warren's *Back From The Grave* liner notes, at the suggestion of The Rogues' label boss they hit Soyka Studios in the late Summer of 1966 and cut four tunes. RCA then offered to sign them if they dropped their lead singer, but they declined. Their manager worked out a deal with the studio owner to press up 300 copies of the above 7" but they had to add New to their name because some New York City lawyers representing a group named The Fugitives threatened to sue if they used that name. The group split up in mid-1967 when the guitarist was drafted and the rest went off to college.

Compilation appearances have included *That's Queer* and *She's My Baby* on *Back From The Grave, Vol. 8* (CD) and *Back From The Grave, Vol. 8* (Dble LP). (VJ/GG)

The New Generation

Personnel incl: TOMMY CALDWELL   bs   A
                  DOUG GRAY   vcls A

45:   Because Of Love (It's All Over) /
      That's The Sun   (Sonic SR 1002) 1968

From Spartanburg, South Carolina, this band released two 45s before Gray and Caldwell found success with The Marshall Tucker Band. *That's The Sun*, a breezy garage-pop ditty, has re-emerged on *Basementsville! U.S.A.* (LP). (MM/MW)

The New Hope

45:   Won't Find Better (Than Me)/
      They Call It Love   (Jamie 1381) 1967

Probably from Philadelphia, an anglophile pop group with harmonies. Their single was produced by "Mike" and the songs respectively penned by Hausman/Stewart and Lamp/Apsey. The result is rather commercial. (SR)

New Hudson Exit

Personnel incl: PHIL KEAGGY   A

45s: Come With Me/Waiting For Her   (Date 1576) 1967
      Fantasy Day/Too Many People   (Peace 222) 196?

This band featured Phil Keaggy from Ohio, who was also in **The Squires** and, later, in **Glass Harp**. Previously known as Volume IV, the power-poppy *Come With Me* was also written by Phil and the band also made several acetates of original material.

Their second 45 was recorded after Phil Keaggy had left the band and suffers from poor production. (GGI/MW)

The New Life

ALBUM: 1   SIDEHACKERS (Original Soundtrack)
(Amaret ST 5004) 1968 -

45s: Ha Lese Cle Di Khana/Backwoods Annie   (Amaret 103) 1968
      Strollin' Sunday Mornin'/
      Only For Our Minds   (Amaret 107) 1968
      All Aboard/Sidehacker   (Amaret 115) 1969

This hippie quartet is thought to have originally been based in Minneapolis although they relocated to San Francisco, as did so many bands in the late sixties. They also had a cut, *Why Now Girl?* included on the rare *San Francisco International Pop Festival, Vol. 1* (Colstar 5001). Mike Curb discovered them in California and used them on the "Sidehackers" Soundtrack. Most of the album tracks are written by Curb collaborator Jerry Styner. Three tracks from the Amaret singles are included (*Ha Lese Cle Di Khana*, *Strollin' Sunday Mornin'* and *Sidehacker*). The best tracks are *Ha Lese...*, a killer garage-psych rocker written by C. Semenya, and *I Wanna Cry*, written by Fred Perry. Semenya and Perry were probably both members of the group. Larry Goldberg was also an associate producer on this album.

Compilation appearances have included: *Why Now Girl* on *Pebbles, Vol. 13* (LP); and *Ha Lese (Le Di Khanna)* on *Acid Dreams, Vol. 3* (LP) and *Garagelands Vol. 2* (CD). (VJ/GG)

The New Life

45:   Canterbury Road/Up Grade   (Epic 10538) 1969

Probably the work of a different **New Life** to **The New Life** on Amaret, this 45 was the brainchild of Bob Goldstein, a showbiz/Broadway type who was involved in the **Goldebriars** management and also with Lou Christie's management. *Canterbury Road* is a re-write of *There Is Nothing More To Say* from **The Millennium** *Begin* album with an additional songwriting credit for Lou Christie. The track was intended as part of a Broadway show / Rock opera based on Chaucer, but who is featured on the record is anyone's guess. It could be the Millennium and Lou Christie, a multi-tracked **Sandy Salisbury** (always a good sport with these things) or maybe the band on the Amaret records were involved after all. The 45 was produced by Sandy Linzer, who also worked with the Bostonian **Peter Ivers**.

ACID DREAMS Vol. 3 (Comp LP) including The New Life.

A solo version of *Canterbury Road* often shows up on Lou Christie compilations. (JFr)

The New Look

| 45: | East Of The Dawn / | |
| | What Did You Take Me For | (TRX 5011) c1968 |

An over-produced garage-pop single. (SR)

Newluvs

| 45: | It's All Over/Be My Girl | (Barclay N 196713/4) 1967 |

Invasion-influenced reedy garage-beat that may have sounded dated by 1967 in Reading, Pennsylvania. It still has a certain charm and Barclay releases are becoming much harder to find. Both sides of the 45 are also featured on Arf!Arf!'s 1998 Barclay compilation CD *Eastern Pa Rock Part Two (1966-'69)*. (MW)

The New Mix

| ALBUM: | 1 | THE NEW MIX | (United Artists UAS 6678) 1968 - |

NB: (1) reissued on 10" (Akarma AK 2016) 2001.

A fresh-sounding psychedelic rock-pop album. The opening cut, *While We Waited*, has a melodramatic intro and wailing guitar, but for the most part the album consists of pleasing vocal harmonies and nicely blended keyboards. The music is quite Beatle-ish at times, particularly on Side Two. Recommended.

All the material on this album was written by D. Brown and H. Steele, but the group still remain enigmatic. No 45s can be found by this band on United Artists or elsewhere. It may explain why their album seems to have made little impact and remains obscure and unappreciated.

Compilation appearances include *While We Waited* on *Songs Of Faith And Inspiration* (CDR & CD). (VJ/MW)

The New Order

Personnel incl:	B. BARBERIS		A
	ROGER JOYCE	vcls	A
	WEINSTEIN		A

45s:	You've Got Me High/Meet Your Match	(Warner Bros. 5816) 1966
	Why Can't I/Pucci Girl	(Warner Bros. 5836) 1966
α	Had I Loved Her Less/Sailing Ship	(Warner Bros. 5870) 1966

NB: α as **The New Order Featuring Roger Joyce**. There's also a French EP with picture sleeve: *You've Got Me High/Meet Your Match/Why Can't I/Pucci Girl* (Warner 113) 1966.

Combining U.S. and U.K. influences, New England's **New Order** belt out a healthy mix of raunchy Beatlesque beat with some Four Seasons-like harmonies on *You've Got Me High*, which can now be heard on *Psychotic Reactions* (LP). The flip is a slow moody ballad with a touch of Dylan about it but is more garage than folk-rock.

The second 45 is the killer, a glorious slice of moody garagey pop with ringing guitar chords and a neat solo - sorta like the early **Ides Of March** in style - great 'teenbeat'. *Pucci Girl* is a decent beat ballad.

Their third 45, however is very different from its predecessors, having crossed the tracks into big production pop ballad territory - blue-eyed soul with a nod to the Four Seasons.

Dum Dum, a Joyce/Barberis bubblegum song, was released by **Carrot Tree** in 1970 though it is unknown if the duo were group members. (MW/SR)

THE NEW MIX - The New Mix LP.

The New Phoenix

Personnel incl:	LARRY BYROM	A
	BILL RICHARDSON**	A
	RUDY ROMERO	A

NB: ** Not confirmed.

| 45: | Give To Me Your Love/Thanks | (World Pacific 77884) 1968 |

This would appear to be a one-off project between the demise of San Diego's **Hard Times** and the birth of **T.I.M.E.** A mellow workout with some laid-back guitar that presages the sounds that **T.I.M.E.** would treat us to. Bill Richardson and Larry Byrom would go on to form **T.I.M.E.** whilst Rudy split for a solo career. Thanks is purely an instrumental of the 'A' side. The 45 was produced by Mama Cass Elliot. (MW)

The Newports

| Personnel incl: | WILLETT | A |

| 45: | The Trouble Is You/I Want You | (Laurie 3327) 1966 |

Maryland was home to this band. The 'A' side is a decent garage band effort with good vocals, effective drumming and distinctive harpsichord playing. It can also be heard on *Mindrocker, Vol. 8*. (VJ)

The New Roadrunners

Personnel:	GARY PNUNN	A
	DON POWELL	A
	TOME RENDERS	A
	BOB SIMONETTI	A

| 45: | Tired Of Living/Love Is | (AOK 1036) 1967 |

This West Texas outfit was put together by Simonetti who'd earlier made a 45 with Bob and His Agents and one as The Venturas. This quartet included Gary P. Nunn who was in many sixties bands and emerged as a solo artist during the eighties. Their semi-psychedelic 45 can be heard on *Highs In The Mid-Sixties, Vol. 12* (LP) and both sides of the 45 are compiled on Collectables' *The History Of Texas Garage Bands, Vol. 3 - The AOK Records Story* (CD) (snappy title, eh?). (VJ/MW)

The New Rock Band

| 45: | Rock Steady/Little David | (Laurie LR 3480) 1968 |

Inoffensive and catchy pop-rock with some smooth guitar - the 'B' side is just an instrumental take of the 'A' side. Significant only in that it is Florida's **Birdwatchers** with Duane Allman. (MW)

The News

Personnel incl: DAYV BUTLER   A

45s:		
If I Had A Girl / Does Your New Boy Cry	(JCP 1032)	196?
She's A Baby / I'll Be Your Friend	(JCP 1044)	196?
Blue Shoes / Follow My Footsteps	(MU MUL-5578)	1968

NB: (1) & (2) as Dayv Butler and The Delmars. A third 45 under the same name may also exist on the Freak Out label.

Blue Shoes, by this obscure North Carolina band, has resurfaced on *30 Seconds Before The Calico Wall* (CD). It's got some great fuzz guitar. The flip is bouncey harmony-pop. Both sides of this 45 were written by Dayv (note the spelling!) Butler. (MW/ELn)

The News

ALBUM: 1 HOT OFF THE PRESS   (Private Pressing) 1974 SC

A New Haven, Connecticut, hippie group in a West Coast style. Their album was recorded between 1971 and 1974. (SR)

The New Society

Personnel incl:			
BILL CHADWICK	gtr, vcls		AB
MICHAEL MARTIN MURPHY			AB
MICHAEL NESMITH	gtr, vcls		A
TED ANDERSON	ld vcls, gtr		B
LARRY HICKMAN	harpsichord, gtr, banjo, vcls		B
CAROL KIMZEY	autoharp, clave, maracas, vcls		B
GARY MILLER	gtr, vcls		B
ALAN PARKER	gtr, banjo, vcls		B
DEL RAMOS	bs, gtr, vcls		B
CAROL STROMME	vcls, tambourine		B

ALBUM: 1(B) THE BAROCK SOUND OF   (RCA LPM-3676) 1966 -

NB: (1) also released in Canada.

45s:		
(I Prithee) Do Not Ask For Love/ Buttermilk	(RCA 47-8807)	1966
Dawn Of Sorrow/We Have So Little Time	(RCA 47-8958)	1966
Love Thee Till I Die/ I've Been Thinkin' About You, Baby	(RCA 47-9149)	1967

From Texas, this group included Michael Nesmith for a while before his incarnation as **Michael Blessing** and his fame with **The Monkees**. They played a mix of folk, folk-rock and novelty songs (like *Buttermilk*, recorded in 1964 and the only track with Nesmith).

The line-up changed in 1965 and the band relocated to California, where they recorded their album. They were managed and produced by Randy Sparks, the man behind the New Christy Minstrels and the Back Porch Majority, two "straight" folk-pop groups.

Arranged by Lincoln Mayorga, their second single starts with an Eastern vibe before finishing with orchestrated folk.

Carol Stromme would later have a solo career. (SR)

The New Survivors

Personnel incl: TONY TEEBO   A

THE NEW TWEEDY BROS! - The New Tweedy Bros! LP.

45s:		
The Pickle Protest/Little One	(Kanwic 147)	1968
The Pickle Protest/But I Know	(Scepter 12227)	1968

A Pittsburg/Fort Scott, Kansas combo put out the poppy *Pickle Protest* that still retains a garage feel with some reedy doodlings. Teebo would go on to a solo career in the seventies. (MW)

The New Troubadours

ALBUM: 1 WINDS OF BIRTH   (Lorian) 1974 SC

A rare folk album with male/female vocals and some psychedelic touches. The album was released in a white or a blue sleeve, both equally rare. (SR)

The New Tweedy Bros!

Personnel:			
STEVEN EKMAN	gtr, vcls		AB
DENNIS FAGALY	bs, vcls		A
DAN LACKAFF	drms, vcls		AB
FRED LACKAFF	gtr, vcls		AB
DAVE McCLURE	bs, vcls		B

ALBUM: 1(B) THE NEW TWEEDY BROS!   (Ridon SLP 234) 1968 R5

NB: (1) originally issued in oversized hexagonal silver foil-coated paper sleeve. Significantly fewer sleeves exist than original vinyl discs and therefore it should be noted that the disc alone is currently in the R3 category. (1) counterfeited on vinyl in the early nineties and on CD (Afterglow 004) 1993. More recently, it has been reissued legitimately (Shadoks Music 018) 2000, in an exact cover reproduction. This deluxe issue also included an insert of photographs and concert flyers. The band members supplied a master proof and original negatives to aid in the reproduction of this highly elaborate sleeve and the results were so impressive that additional covers were manufactured to house the bands' leftover vinyl discs from the original pressing. Shadoks Music have also issued the album on CD (Shadoks Music 018) 2001 from the recently discovered master tapes. This CD has a triple gatefold hexagonal sleeve and three bonus tracks.

45: Good Time Car/Terms Of, You Love Me   (Dot 16910 1966

Originally based in Oregon, this band began playing regularly in San Francisco by 1966. The 45 they recorded that year for Dot Records is a good-timey **Lovin' Spoonful** style, bearing little resemblance to most of the material on their 1968 album.

Produced by omnipresent Northwest figure Rick Keefer, the album has long captured the interest of collectors world-wide. It is perhaps most notorious for its highly unusual oversized cover - too large to fit into a standard bin in the shops; many were damaged straight away and finding one now in pristine condition is close to impossible! It was a fantastically expensive

THE NEW YORK ROCK & ROLL ENSEMBLE - Reflections CD.

item to produce, even back in the sixties. Although 1,000 covers were printed to match the 1,000 albums pressed, only 500 covers were picked up from the printer (these were delivered flat, incidentally - and the band members folded them and glued them up by hand), the plan being to distribute the initial batch and use the money to pay the printer for the balance of the order. Sadly, when they returned for the remainder of the jackets, the shop was out of business. The music, however, suffers from none of this trivia and is highly recommended, especially the recent legitimate CD on Shadoks which was made from the original master tapes! The album's highlights are many and include the opening track *Somebody's Peepin'*, with its nice vocal harmonies; *I Can See It*, a folk-rocker with unusual raga-like segments; *Wheels Of Fortune*, which has a catchy chorus and winds down with a psychedelic guitar jam; *I See You're Lookin' Fine*, another mildly psychedelic number with interesting echoed vocals and the amazing *Her Darkness In December (Drone Song)*, which is arguably the most psychedelic track on offer. The recent CD includes a slightly earlier but no less effective alternate take of this number that is not to be missed! Both sides of the Dot 45 are included as well. All connoisseurs of psychedelia should make it a point to hear this band's material now that it's readily available.

The New Tweedy Bros! left behind additional live and studio recordings and future releases are in the works.

Producer Rick Keefer was a very busy man during the sixties; his name can be found on records by **The Wallflowers**, **The Phantoms**, **Wheels Of Fortune**, **The Sound Vendor**, **United Travel Service**, **The Easy Chair** (their 45), The Bystanders, The Fire and many others.

Sadly, Steve Ekman lost his battle with cancer in May 2001.

Compilation coverage has been limited to: *Danny's Song* on *Love, Peace And Poetry, Vol. 1* (LP & CD) and three album cuts:- *What's Wrong With That*, *Someone Just Passed By* and *Darkness In December* on the bootleg compilation *California Halloween*. (CF/VJ)

The New Wave

Personnel incl:	TOMMY ANDRE		A
	REID KING	vcls, gtr	A

ALBUM:	1(A)	THE NEW WAVE	(Canterbury CLPM-1501) 1967 SC

45s:	Where Do We Go From Here/	
	Not From You	(Canterbury C503) 1967
	Little Dreams/Autre Fois	(Canterbury C512) 1967

On the same Californian label as **Yellow Balloon**, a rare album produced by Ken Handler. Reid King would later play with **Papa John Creach**. (SR)

New Wine

ALBUM:	1 NEW WINE	(Prestige) 1973 ?

An obscure Christian folk group. (SR)

The New Wing

45s:	The Thinking Animal/My Petite	(Pentacle 101) 1967
	Brown Eyed Woman/I Need Love	(Pentacle 104) 1968

A raw sounding L.A.-based punk band which evolved out of **The Sons of Adam** who provided the music, fronted by one Davy Peters on vocals.

It's rumoured that *I Need Love* was also put out on the Take 6 label but this remains unconfirmed. The first 45, at least, is for **Sons Of Adam** completists only - the material sounds like it's from some third-rate musical show or exploitation movie.

Compilation appearances include *I Need Love* on *Ya Gotta Have Moxie, Vol. 2* (Dble CD) and *Boulders, Vol. 1* (LP). (VJ)

New World Congregation

Personnel:	ROY BERGER	ld gtr	A
	BO BRIDEN	bs	A
	JAY EPSTEIN	drms	A
	DAVE HEYER	keyb'ds	A

45s:	Day Tripper/	
	My World Is Empty Without You (PS)	(Coulee 123) 1967
	Day Tripper/My World Is Empty Without You	(Atco 6667) 1967

From Winona, Minnesota - this lot blast through two covers in true '69 post-**Vanilla Fudge** bombastic style. Actually *Day Tripper* isn't all that bad but it's not one for garage purists so beware the garage or psych tags touted by none-too-discerning dealers. Roy Berger had earlier been with another Winona band **The Messengers** and he later managed **The Ferraris**. (VJ/MW)

The New York Rock (& Roll) Ensemble

Personnel:	BRIAN CORRIGAN	gtr	A
	MARTIN (MARTY) FULTERMAN	drums, oboe	ABC
	MICHAEL (MIKE) KAMEN	keyb'ds, oboe	ABC
	CLIFTON (CLIFF) NIVISON	lead guitar	ABC
	DORIAN RUDNYSTSKY	bs, cello	ABC
	(HANK DEVITO	oboe	B)

ALBUMS:	1(A)	THE NEW YORK ROCK AND ROLL ENSEMBLE	(Atco SD33-240) 1968 -
	2(A)	FAITHFUL FRIENDS...	(Atco SD 33-294) 1969 -
	3(A)	REFLECTIONS	(Atco SD 33-312) 1970 -
	4(B)	ROLL OVER	(Columbia C 30033) 1970 -
	5(C)	FREEDOMBURGER	(Columbia KC-31317) 1972 -

NB: (4) and (5) released as **The New York Rock Ensemble**. (3) reissued on CD (Atlantic 75678 06352). (4) and (5) issued on one CD.

			HCP
45s:	Biji/Biji Rock	(Atco 6467) 1967	
	Kiss Her Once/Suddenly	(Atco 6501) 1967	
	The Thing To Do/Pick Up In The Morning	(Atco 6584) 1968	-
	Wait Until Tomorrow/The Brandenburg	(Atco 6671) 1969	-
	Running Down The Highway/ Law And Order	(Columbia 45242) 1970	-
	Beside You/The King Is Dead	(Columbia 45288) 1970	123
	Fields Of Joy/Ride, Ride My Lady	(Columbia 45367) 1971	-
	Roll Over/A Whiter Shade Of Pale	(Columbia 45574) 1972	-

The story goes that three members of this act were classically trained at Juilliard Music Conservatory (arguably the most prestigious American music school) and that at some point they "realized" that they could make more money being rock stars than classical musicians. The music on their first two albums is distinctive in that they used classical instruments (usually oboes and string quartets) in their rock songs and then might play a classical Bach piece using modern rock instruments. Their third album was a unique collaboration with Manos Hadjidakis, who is best known for composing the music for the movie "Never On Sunday". This album has a distinctive Greek flavor and is quite unique - very beautiful, relaxing. After their third album, they shortened their name to become **The New York Rock Ensemble**, switched record companies (from Atco to Columbia), and Brian Corrigan left.

The fourth album was less original, but was ironically their best selling album. I have a personal theory that this was related to a free or inexpensive sampler album, called *Different Strokes*, that Columbia distributed and which featured a cut from this album. In my humble opinion, their fourth and fifth albums were much less interesting and qualify only as average rock music.

Michael Kamen went on to have a successful career producing film scores, working with artists such as Pink Floyd, Roger Waters etc. In 1991, he won two Grammy's: "Best Pop Instrumental Performance" for the *Robin Hood: Prince Of Thieves* album conducting the Greater Los Angeles Orchestra and "Best Song Written Specifically For A Motion Picture Or For Television" for *(Everything I Do) I Do It For You* from *Robin Hood: Prince Of Thieves*. (CO/LP)

The New Yorkers

Personnel:	KEN FILLMORE	drms	A
	WILLIAM HUDSON	gtr, vcls	AB
	BRETT HUDSON	bs, vcls	AB
	MARK HUDSON	gtr, vcls	AB
	BOB HAWORTH	drms	B

45s:	α	Things Are Changing/City Girl	(Santana 6602) 1966
		When I'm Gone/You're Not My Girl	(Scepter 12190) 1967
		Mr. Kirby/Seeds Of Spring	(Scepter 12199) 1967
		Show Me The Way To Love/Again	(Scepter 12207) 1967
		Ice Cream Wodd/Adrianne	(Jerden 906) 1968
		Michael Clover/Land Of Ur	(Jerden 908) 1969
		Lonely/There'll Come A Time	(Warner Bros. 7319) 1969
		I Guess The Lord Must Be In New York City/ Do Wah Diddy	(Decca 32569) 1969
	β	Love Is The World/Laugh, Funny Funny	(Decca 732634) 1970

NB: α *City Girl* was by The Fury Four. β Credited to Everyday Hudson, promo copies have *Laugh, Funny Funny* as the 'A' side.

Despite their name, this outfit came out of Portland, Oregon, where they won some local "Battle Of The Bands" contests early in 1967 when they were known as My Sirs. Based around the three Hudson brothers they changed name to **The New Yorkers** when asked to do a promotional tour by the Chrysler company, who required them to use the name of one of the company's cars. Musically they were very influenced by The Beatles and they did enjoy some regional success with their early recordings. Later 45s, especially those on Jerden, leaned towards an Anglophile pop-psych sound.

Mr. Kirby is a fine psychedelic raga style punker, with lots of fuzz.

Years later the three brothers signed to Elton John's Rocket label achieving some commercial success as The Hudson Brothers and even having their own TV show!

Compilation appearances have included: *Again* on *Mindrocker, Vol. 8* (LP), *History Of Northwest Rock, Vol. 5* and *Northwest Battle Of The Bands, Vol. 2 - Knock You Flat!* (CD); *Mr. Kirby* on *Northwest Battle Of The Bands, Vol. 1 - Flash And Crash* (LP), *Psychedelic Unknowns, Vol. 4* (LP & CD), *Garagelands, Vol. 1 & 2* (CD), *Garagelands, Vol. 2* (LP), *The History Of Northwest Rock, Vol. 3* (CD) and *The History Of Northwest Rock, Vol. 2* (LP); *Mr. Kirby* and *Seeds Of Spring* on *Northwest Battle Of The Bands, Vol. 1 - Flash And Crash* (CD); *You're Not My Girl* on *Northwest Battle Of The Bands, Vol. 1* (CD); *Lazy Meadow*, a previously unreleased psychedelic track, on *Northwest Battle Of The Bands, Vol. 2* (CD); and both *Adrianne* and *Ice Cream World* on *Bring Flowers To U.S.* (LP). (VJ/MW/DR/MAy)

New Zealand Trading Company

ALBUM: 1 NEW ZEALAND TRADING COMPANY (Memphis 1001) 1970 -

A quintet of uncertain origin. The music is group-penned (except for an inventive cover of *Hey Jude*) in a soft psych-jazz vein, reminiscent of the *Wake Up, It's Tomorrow* era **Strawberry Alarm Clock**. The song *Jam And Anti-freeze* is particularly fine. There are also very nice harmonies on several cuts, most notably *Winnifred Jellicoe*, and one cut (*Ruo Moko*) which seems to be sung (as near as I can tell) in Portugese. (RBn)

Next Five

Personnel:	MARK BUSCAGLIA	keyb'ds	A
	ERIC OLSON	gtr	A
	TOM "STEWIE" STEWART	drms	A
	STEVE THOMAS	ld gtr	A
	GORDON WAYNE (OLSKI)	bs	A
	GARY COOPER	drms	
	JOHN CROOK	drms	
	JOHN PETER	gtr	

45s:		He Stole My Love / Little Black Egg	(Destination 637) 1967
		Mama Said / Talk To Me Girl	(Wand 1170) 1967
	α	Sunny Sunny Feeling / What's The Melody	(Jubilee 5668) 1969

NB: α as Toy Factory.

From Brookfield, Wisconsin. Their version of **The Nightcrawlers**' *Little Black Egg* is noteworthy for harmonious vocals and tasty organ chord changes. Another of their tracks, *Talk To Me Girl*, is more commercial power-pop than garage. After another label change and some personnel shuffles they released a final 45 as by the **Toy Factory**.

Compilation appearances have included: *He Stole My Love* on *Mindrocker, Vol. 3* (LP); and *Talk To Me Girl* on *Pebbles, Vol. 10* (LP). (VJ/MW/GM)

Next Morning

Personnel:	EARL ARTHUR	keyb'ds	A
	BERT BAILEY	gtr	A
	HERBERT BAILEY	drms	A
	LOU PHILLIPS	vcls	A
	SCIPIO SARGEANT	bs	A

ALBUM: 1(A) THE NEXT MORNING (Calla SC 2002) 1971 R1/R2

NB: (1) also issued in France on Roulette (R1). Reissued on CD (Sundazed SC 6150) 1999.

THE NEXT MORNING - The Next Morning LP.

INCREDIBLE SOUND SHOW STORIES Vol. 8 (Comp LP) including NGC-4594.

A black group based in New York play **Hendrix** - style heavy rock with great acid fuzz organ jams and wild fuzz bass on this album.

The band members actually came from Trinidad in the Caribbean and St. Croix in the Virgin Islands, according to Jud Cost's liner notes to the Sundazed CD, which is recommended. (CF/MW)

NGC-4594

Personnel:	DAVID BLISS	piano	A
	MINTY COLLINS	electrified flute, hrmnca	A
	BOB DE VOS	drms	A
	CHAS MIRSKY	gtr	A
	DANNY SHANOK	bs	A
	STEVE STARGER	organ	A

45: Going Home/Skipping Through The Night (Smash S-2104) 1967

Formed in Storrs, Connecticut in 1967, they chose a truly astronomical moniker in their search for stardom (NGC-4594 being otherwise known as the 'Sombrero' galaxy). Their 45 features very pleasant psychy soft-rock with the odd jazzy feel. *Going Home* is the more commercial, slightly more upbeat. *Skipping* is the gem here with its mellowed-out aura and trilling flute - somewhere between Boston's **Freeborne** and UK's Caravan. Delightful.

Incredible Sound Show Stories, Vol. 8 (LP) and *Psychedelic Experience, Vol. 1* (CD) both include *Skipping*. (MW/CW/SS)

'N' Group

45: Keep On Runnin'/Words Of Love (Wes Mar 1021) 196?

The titles may sound familiar but these are not covers of the Spencer Davis Group and Buddy Holly. From Akron, Ohio, this bunch do two originals - one upbeat and one ballad - in a competently soulful **Young Rascals** style. Not likely to get aired on any 'garage comp' but not at all bad for the much maligned 'soul - garage' sub - genre.

This was their only 45 and they were previously known as The Ingroup. (MW/GGI)

Chet Nichols

Personnel:	LEO COLLIGNON	gtr	A
	DAVE GARIBALDI	drms	A
	NICKY HOPKINS	piano	A
	CHET NICHOLS	vcls, gtr	A
	PETE SEARS	bs	A

ALBUM: 1(A) TIME LOOP (Kama Sutra KSBS 2057) 1972 SC

A California folk singer/songwriter, whose album is beginning to interest collectors. Most tracks were written between 1967 and 1970 and were produced by Steve Barncard and **Nichols**. The title track was produced by **Nick Gravenites** and is the only one with an electric backing (Sears, Hopkins, etc.).

A good album but definitely more folk than psychedelic. Don't spend what some dealers ask for it! (SR)

Penny Nichols

ALBUM: 1 PENNY'S ARCADE (Buddah) 1968 -

45: Look Around Rock/Farina (Buddah BDA-28) 1968

An overlooked figure of the San Francisco sixties scene, **Penny Nichols** began on the folk circuit. In 1966, she was in a short-lived band with Spencer Perskin (later in **Shiva's Headband**) and eventually released a solo album in 1968, produced by Artie Ripp and Billy James. We haven't heard *Penny's Arcade* yet, but it may be an undiscovered gem if it contains more tracks like *Look Around Rock*, a superb song with a long instrumental intro like *Eight Miles High* and powerful echoed vocals, truly nice. *Farina* is more in a trad-folk vein, again with good vocals. In March 1968, she played the Fillmore with Traffic, **Blue Cheer** and **H. P. Lovecraft**.

During the seventies, she became a session singer in the Californian studios (**Arlo Guthrie**, Jackson Browne, **Nitty Gritty Dirt Band**, Linda Ronstadt) as well as a producer and educator specialized on pitch perception (she has a doctoral degree from Harvard's School of Education). She continued releasing records for children and educational videos. (SR)

Roger Nichols and The Small Circle of Friends

ALBUM: 1 AND THE SMALL CIRCLE OF FRIENDS (A&M) 1968 -

NB: (1) reissued in Japan (Lexington LEX9311) 1993.

45s:	α	Don't Go Breaking My Heart/ Our Day Will Come	(A&M 801) 1966
	α	Love Song, Love Song/Snow Queen	(A&M 830) 1967
	α	I'll Be Back/Just Beyond Your Smile	(A&M 849) 1968
		Let's Ride/Love So Fine	(A&M 946) 1968

NB: α by Roger Nichols Trio.

A California soft-rock group with some "groovy" moments, typical of the A&M sound. Roger Nichols was a friend of Paul Williams (**Holy Mackerel**) and together they wrote several songs recorded by other California pop and soft-psych acts. (SR)

Nickel

Personnel:	NAUMANN	A
	POOR	A
	RESNICK	A

ALBUM: 1(A) NICKEL (Musicor MS-3205) 1971 -

45: Saturday Night At The Movies / ? (Musicor 1430) 1971

Little is known about the band but the album ranges from reasonable psych pop to more guitar-orientated early seventies style rock. (VJ/GG)

The Nickel Bag

45: The Woods/Come On Back (Rembrandt 5004) 1966

A Chicago punk band previously known as The Nite Owls. *The Woods*, is a pounding rocker.

Compilation appearances have included: *Come On Back*, *The Woods* and *It's A Hassle* on *Chicago Garage Band Greats* (CD); and *Come On Back* and *The Woods* on *Chicago Garage Band Greats* (LP); *Come On Back* on *Garage Punk Unknowns, Vol. 7* (LP). (VJ)

The Nickel Bag

ALBUM: 1 DOING THEIR LOVE THING
(Kama Sutra KPLS-8066) 1968 -

Between pop-psych and bubblegum music. The front cover of their album shows them wearing oriental outfits, with a pretty girl waiting on a chair and a tree with human skulls on the branches in the background. Strange! (SR)

The Night

45: To Realize My Mind/Too Much Loneliness (Elite 163/4) 1967

A Sacramento area outfit with a cool minor key psych-pop release. Both sides are featured on *The Sound Of Young Sacramento* (CD). (MW)

The Nightcrawlers

Personnel:			
CHUCK CONLAN	bs, vcls		A
ROBBIE ROUSE	vcls, hrmnca, tamb		AB
TOMMY RUGER	drms		AB
PETE THOMASON	gtr, vcls		ABC
SYLVAN WELLS	ld gtr		ABC
BOB KELLER	bs		B
BOBBY GILL			C
VAN HARRISON			C
RICK HOLLINGER			C
MARSHALL LETTER			C

ALBUM: 1(A) THE LITTLE BLACK EGG (Kapp KS 350) 1967 R2

NB: (1) counterfeited (Eva 12042) in 1984/5, with several 45-only tracks added. Much better is the official 24-track *The Black Egg* CD (Big Beat CDWIKD 203) 2000.

HCP
45s: Cry / Marie (Lee 101) 1965 -
The Little Black Egg / If I Were You (Lee 1012) 1965 -
The Little Black Egg/
You're Running Wild (Kapp K-709) 1965 85
Washboard / A Basket Of Flowers (Marlin 1904) 1966 -
A Basket Of Flowers / Washboard (Kapp K-746) 1966 -
I Don't Remember / What Time Is It (Scott 28) 1966 -
The Little Black Egg /
You're Running Wild (Kapp KE-110) 1966 85 -
My Butterfly/Today I'm Happy (Kapp K-826) 1967 -

by Conlan and The Crawlers
45s: I Won't Tell / You're Comin' On (Marlin 16006) 1967 -
Won't You Say Yes To Me Girl /
Midnight Reader (Marlin 16007) 1967 -

Charles Conlan solo
45s: α When God Comes To Call /
He'll Understand (Tropical 112) 1965 -
Mighty Lighty Moon /
I Wish I Could Have Told You (Warner-Curb 8136) 1975 -
You Are A Woman / Keys To The City (Wheel 001) 1984 -

NB: α Flip is by Charles Vickers.

It's Daytona Beach, Florida in 1964. Wells, Thomason and Rouse were in band at school called The Group, whose guitarist George Brown had recently moved to the area from Louisville, Kentucky, where he'd been in a band called the NightCrawlers. When they graduated to college in the Fall, the trio decided to start another band and connected with Charles "Chuck" Conlan. Conlan had been playing folk in a group called The Craftsmen and was already writing and doing demos for Lee Hazen's National Songwriters Guild. He knew drummer Tommy Ruger and got him into the group.

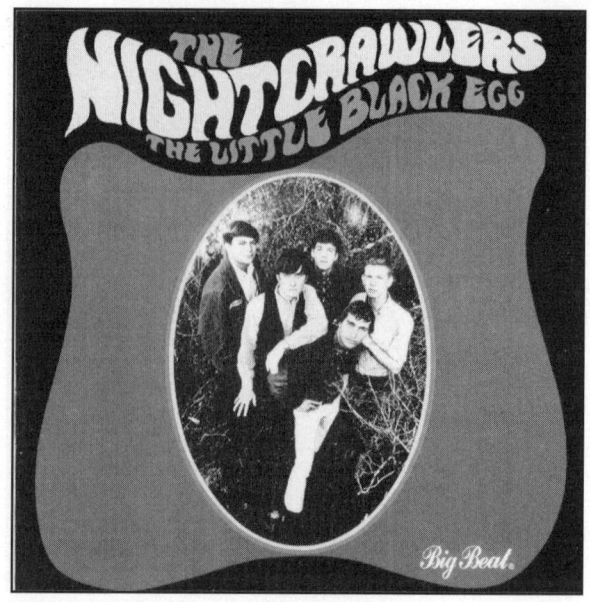

THE NIGHTCRAWLERS - The Little Black Egg CD.

So began **The Nightcrawlers**, who are best remembered for the haunting and cryptic folk-rocker *Little Black Egg* which personifies their sound - a sultry garage version of the **Beau Brummels**, with their plaintive Searchers-like melodies and a hint at the Stones' shake and rattle in the more upbeat material. *Little Black Egg* became a local hit and the band got plenty of gigs. Live most of the songs featured Rob Rouse on lead vocals and they performed more upbeat and soulful material, whereas Conlan sang lead on his compositions in the studio with Rouse or Thomason on harmonies. When Kapp picked up on the band they pushed to get more material out of a band that was raw but had obvious hit potential. *Little Black Egg* was re-released and started picking up in other regions; it would be pushed for a third time and eventually hit the Billboard charts in early 1967, long after the original band who recorded it had split.

In fact Conlan had been fired by the band in early 1966 - his heart was less with band rehearsals than with a young lady. He was replaced by Bob Keller from **The Allman Joys**. Kapp were still pushing for follow-ups but the band already knew that they'd be splitting for college in the Summer of 1966 and were not willing to be pushed around by producer Brad Shapiro. In the event, they split in June 1966.

Shortly after Wells and Thomason decided they wanted to get another band together but Kapp insisted on them forming a new **Nightcrawlers** if they wanted to record again. Eventually, they were persuaded by their friend and "6th member" Mike Stone to reform (line-up 'C' above). This band went on tour and the album was released, despite the fact that the band's sound had moved on considerably since the material it showcased. Mike Stone would keep the band going through numerous personnel changes until 1970, when it became Orion.

Meantime, Conlan had enrolled at the University of Miami. In 1967, he signed up with Henry Stone and released two 45s in 1967 as "Conlan and The Crawlers". He went on to work with **The Birdwatchers**, producing *Girl I Got News For You* and had songs covered by the **Proctor Amusement Co**.

This is just the bare bones of a fascinating history recounted in person by all the major players in the Big Beat CD liners. The CD contains 24 cuts: all the original band's 45 cuts except *Marie*, from their debut; alternate versions of *Washboard* and *If You Want My Love*; four unreleased originals; and seven unreleased covers which include some cool Stones and Kinks covers. A mighty fine package that is unreservedly recommended - there may be no fuzz guitars but for fans of evocative sixties Invasion-inspired beat/garage sounds this is hard to top.

The Little Black Egg has come to be regarded by many as a sixties classic and has been featured on *More Nuggets* (CD), *Nuggets Box* (4-CD), *Nuggets, Vol. 6* (LP) and *Excerpts From Nuggets* (CD). It remains popular to this day and has been frequently covered by a variety of bands including **Music Explosion**, Margins (on the 1966 Columbus, Ohio *Hillside Promotion* LP), **The Kommotions**, Tonebenders (*Northland Third Annual Battle Of The Bands*, 1967 2-LP), **Neighb'rhood Childr'n** (*Long Years In Space* retrospective), **Bourbons** (*House Party* CD which also features a cover of

A Basket Of Flowers), later still by The Cars and also nineties bands like The Others (from Italy) and Seattle's Minus 5 (with REM's Peter Buck). *A Basket Of Flowers* has also been covered by the **Last Words** (1968 s/t Atco LP), and by the Cynics (1988 LP, *Twelve Flights Up*). Finally, *If You Want My Love* was revived by The Lyres in 1986 on their *Lyres Lyres* LP.

Jimmy Pitman was also a briefly member at some point, prior to moving to L.A. and joining **The Strawberry Alarm Clock**. Drummer Tommy Ruger subsequently played with Duane and Gregg Allman. (VJ/MW/JZ/MMe/JLh/AP)

The Night Crawlers

| 45: | Let's Move/Hiding | (Shadow 101) 196? |

A garage band from Lubbock, Texas who may have included a young Marc Benno. T 'A' side of this raw, poorly recorded 45 can be heard on *Vile Vinyl, Vol. 1* (LP), *Vile Vinyl* (CD) and *Highs In The Mid-Sixties, Vol. 13* (LP). There was no connection with the Florida outfit of *Little Black Egg* fame. (VJ)

The Night Crawlers

Personnel:	BARRY GILLESPIE	vcls	A
	MARK HEADINGTON	bs	A
	MIKE JINES	ld gtr	A
	BILL REDEKER	drms	A
	MARC REIGEL	keyb'ds	A

45s:	You Say/Night Crawlin'	(MAAD 51166) 1966
	You Say/Night Crawlin'	(Joel 1566) 1966
	(I) Feel So Fine/Want Me	(Acetate) 1966

Yet another band of this name, this time they were students at Carlton College in Northfield, 30 miles South of Minneapolis in Minnesota. This highly-touted garage 45 came out on two different colour labels. Both pressings are hard to find, the one with the green label was the earlier of the two. The flip, *Night Crawlin'* is a raw Stones-style recording.

Later in 1966, they travelled to the CBS Studios in Chicago for another recording session. Six songs in all were recorded:- *Dandelions* (a Marc Reigel original); *(I) Feel So Fine* (a cover of Johnny Preston's classic); *Want Me* (a fuzz guitar original); *Chimes Of Freedom* (a **Byrds** cover); *Just Like Romeo and Juliet* (a Reflections song) and *Shoulder Of A Giant* (a **Prince and The Paupers** cover). Acetates of *(I) Feel So Fine/Want Me* were cut, but no actual records materialised from the session and the band disbanded in the Fall of 1967.

Their drummer Bill Redeker later became a TV journalist for ABC News and 20/20.

Compilation appearances have included: *Night Crawlin'* on *Pebbles, Vol. 17* (LP); *Want Me* on *Back From The Grave, Vol. 8* (CD) and *Back From The Grave, Vol. 8* (Dble LP); and *You Say* on *Hipsville, Vol. 3* (LP). (VJ)

The Night People

Personnel:	BOB HOLCEPL	vcls	A
	GREG PAUL	drms	A
	TERRY PAUL	gtr	A
	RON PEITLE	organ	A
	FRANK ROSE	theremin, recorder	A
	JOE ROSE	bs	A

| 45: | We Got It/Erebian Borealis | (Del-Nita 1002) 1967 |

This group were responsible for a superb two-sided garage-psych 45. The 'A' side features an early Theremin solo which is pretty unusual for a garage 45. The flip side is a psychy instrumental. All of the band came from the West side of Cleveland, except for Ron Peitle who came from Parma, Ohio.

Compilation appearances have included: *We Got It* and *Erebian-Borialis* on *Sixties Rebellion, Vol. 6* (LP & CD); and *We Got It* on *It's Finkin' Time!* (LP). (MW/GP)

Night Riders

| 45: | Don't Say/? | (Bublo 110) 1965 |

From Detroit, Michigan - *Don't Say* can also be heard on *Garage Punk Unknowns, Vol. 2* (LP). (VJ)

The Night Riders

Personnel:	MONTE ALLISON	keyb'ds, vcls	A
	RAY ATWATER	rhythm gtr, vcls	A
	JON (TWO GUN) JOHNSON	drms, vcls	A
	MAC LEWIS	rhythm gtr	A
	DAVID MARLETTE	ld gtr, vcls	A
	STEVE ROGERS	bs, drms	A

| ALBUM: | 1(A) | INTRODUCING THE NIGHT RIDERS | (Justice 157) 1967 |

NB: (1) reissued on CD (Collectables Col-0603) 1995.

After finishing as second runner-up in a local high school Battle of the Bands, **The Night Riders** were contacted by a correspondent for the Justice Records Company, whom they later recorded their sole album for in 1967. Typical Justice fare, the album includes cover versions of *Double Shot Of My Baby's Love*, *Twist & Shout*, *Night Train*, *Little Latin Lupe Lu* and *Louie Louie*, among others.

The band were from North Carolina and were all sixteen (except 15-year-old Mac Lewis) at the time of recording. The sole original on the album, a keyboard-led instrumental entitled *Journey To The Stars* has subsequently resurfaced on *Oil Stains, Vol. 2* (LP), *Relics, Vol. 2* (LP) and *Relics, Vol's 1 & 2* (LP). (MDo/MW)

The Nightriders

45s:	With Friends Like You, Who Needs Friends/?	(Star-Bright) 1965
α	With Friends Like You, Who Needs Friends/?	(Modern) 196?
β	Satisfaction Guaranteed/Whatever's Right	(Star-Bright 3054) 196?

NB: α as The Composers. β as Niteriders.

With Friends Like You... is a guitar/organ pounder which most likely came out of the Portland, Oregon area as it was issued on a local label there. The second issue was released on a Los Angeles R&B label and credited to **The Composers**.

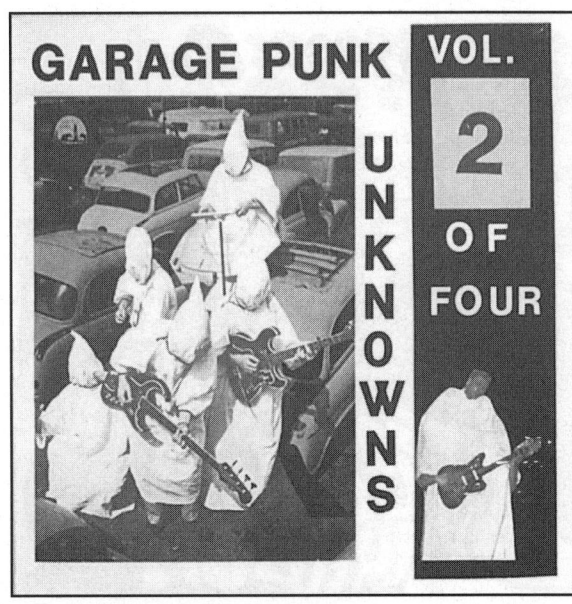

GARAGE PUNK UNKNOWNS Vol. 2 (Comp LP) including Night Riders.

Compilation appearances include *With Friends Like You, Who Needs Friends* on *Back From The Grave, Vol. 8* (CD) and *Back From The Grave, Vol. 8* (Dble LP). (VJ)

The Nightrockers

Personnel incl: RONNY KNIGHT   A

45:     Junction No.1 / Run Mary Run (PS)   (Arco SC-105) 1966

The Arco label from New Bedford, Massachusetts put out some notable 45s by the Bad Manners, Circle Of Friends, Dandelion Army, the pre-**Tangerine-Zoo Ebb Tides**, Northeast Expressway, Reign, Van Goghs, and Your Own Kind.

This **Nightrockers** 45 also came in a rare colour picture-sleeve, reproduced on the front of the *Yeah Yeah Yeah* (CD) booklet and in b&w on the front cover of *Midnight To Sixty-Six* (LP). Both these compilations feature *Junction No. 1*, a fab garage stomper. (MW)

The Nightshadow(s)

Personnel: RONNIE FARMER   gtr   A
            ALECK JANOULIS   bs   A
            BOBBIE NEWELL   keyb'ds   A
            LITTLE PHIL (ROSS) vcls   A
            CHARLIE SPINKS   drms   A

ALBUMS: 1(A) THE SQUARE ROOT OF TWO
                                     (Spectrum Stereo) 1968 R5
        2(A) THE SQUARE ROOT OF TWO
                                     (Hottrax ST 1414) 1978 R1
        3(-) LIVE AT THE SPOT   (Hottrax ST 1430) 1981 -
        4(-) INVASION OF THE ACID EATERS (Hottrax) 1982 -
        5(-) A ROCK ANOMALY   (Roft) 1988 -

NB: (2) was remixed in stereo and is much superior in sound to (1).

45s: α The Way It Used To Be/So Much   (Dot 16912) 1966
      α Hot Dog Man/Hot Rod Song (800 pressed) (Banned 6T9) 1966
      α 60 Second Swinger/
         In The Air (500 pressed, 250 with PS)   (Gaye 3031) 1966
      β Turned On/
         Don't Hold Your Breath (500 pressed)   (Baja 4504) 1967

NB: α as Little Phil & the Night Shadows. β as 'Square Root of 2'.

The **Nightshadows**, who were also known as **Little Phil And The Nightshadows**, were one of the Old South's few acid-punk bands and something of a rock anomaly. They started playing in the late fifties and their 27 or so members apparently included Barry Bailey (later of The Atlanta Rhythm Section). The artists listed above were those who recorded their 1968 album which was pieced together from an assortment of tapes recorded on portable cassette machines. The band, who came from Atlanta, Georgia, in the heart of Dixieland, never achieved the recognition they might have because of the Vietnam War, which prevented them touring for fear of losing their draft deferments.

Of particular note on their album is the psychedelic intro to *In The Air* and *The Hot Rod Song*. Another track *I Can't Believe* has a Spoonful-type beat and others like *Illusions* sounded rather a racket. Overall, the album is probably best forgotten. The most sought-after of their recordings is the original release of *The Square Root Of Two* on Spectrum Stereo. They recorded over a long period under various names and backed numerous other artists so the 45s shown are highly selective and only cover their garage-psych period.

Compilation appearances have included: *The Way It Used To Be* on *Pebbles Vol. 5* (CD) and *Pebbles, Vol. 5* (LP); and *So Much* on *Psychedelic States: Georgia Vol. 1* (CD). (VJ/MW)

The Night Walkers

Personnel: DICK CARASCO   drms   A
            DAVID HOOPER   ld gtr   A
            BOB KALAL   bs   A
            JERRY McCASLAND   ld vcls, gtr A
            JIM SPRINGER   sax   A
            DARRELL BOYLES   drms
            MANNY PALAZZO   drms
            BOB THURMAN   keyb'ds

45:     Sticks And Stones/Give Me Love   (Detroit 2648) 1965

This outfit formed in Longview, Washington, when a bunch of high school kids came together for fun on the crest of the wave of Beatlemania that swept across America in 1963/64. They recorded their sole 45, a garage-sounding recording, at Northwestern Studios in 1965. It was offered to major labels but rejected, so the group released it on their own label.

None of the band remained in the music business. Bob Kalal was last reported to be a pharmacist in Longview where Dave Hooper also works. Carasco works in construction and lives in Portland, Oregon and Springer owns a bowling alley in Kalama.

Compilation appearances include *Sticks and Stones* on *Highs In The Mid-Sixties, Vol. 7* (LP).

Nightwalkers

45:     It'll Only Hurt For A Little While/?   (JCP 1058) 196?

Came out of Raleigh in North Carolina with this Dave Clark Five cover, *It'll Only Hurt For A Little While*, which can also be heard on *Tobacco A-Go-Go, Vol. 1* (LP). It's nothing special. (VJ)

Nineteen Eighty-Four

45:     Three's A Crowd/Amber Waves   (Kapp 2003) 1969

Garage and psych collectors often discover that the 'B' side of a seemingly bland pop 45 can reveal a cool nugget that betrays a band's garage roots. This is more frequent on a national label where the producer's will and commercial considerations ruled on the plug side; in some cases the flip is where some bands were given leave to make their original statements. Here's another example - the top side is a typical '69 brassy belter; the flip is a harmonious folk-rock ballad punctuated by some heavy acidic fuzz.

Formed in 1963, this East Los Angeles combo was originally **Mark and The Escorts**, releasing two fine 45s on GNP Crescendo in 1965. They lasted until the mid-seventies via a succession of identities - The Men From S.O.U.N.D., **Nineteen Eighty-Four**, The Mudd Brothers, Tangos - the last of which released an album on A&M. (MW/LJ/MGo)

NIGHT SHADOW - The Square Root Of Two CD.

PSYCHEDELIC UNKNOWNS Vol. 7 (Comp LP) including 1910 Fruitgum Co.

1910 Fruitgum Co.

Personnel:
	MARK GUTKOWSKI	vcls, keyb'ds	A
	FRANK JECKELL		A
	PAT KARWAN		A
	FLOYD MARCUS		A
	STEVE MORTKOWITZ		A
	JIMMY CASAZZA	drms	B
	DON CHRISTOPHER	gtr, vcls	B
	RALPH COHEN	trumpet	B
	RICHIE GOMEZ	gtr, vcls	B
	JERRY ROTH	sax	B
	PAT SORIANO	gtr, vcls	B
	BRUCE SHAY	bs	
	CHUCK TROIS		

HCP
ALBUMS:					
1( )	SIMON SAYS	(Buddah BDS 5010)	1967	162	-
2( )	CHECKMATE	(Buddah BDS 5015)	1968	-	-
3( )	A RED LIGHT	(Buddah BDS 5022)	1968	163	-
4( )	GOODY GOODY GUM DROPS				
		(Buddah BDS 5027)	1968	-	-
5( )	INDIAN GIVER	(Buddah BDS 5036)	1969	147	-
6( )	HARD RIDE	(Buddah BDS 5043)	1969	-	-
7(-)	JUICIEST FRUITGUM	(Buddah BDS 5057)	1970	-	-

NB: (1) reissued on CD by Repertoire. (2) is a split album with **The Lemon Pipers**. There is also a *Golden Classics* CD compilation on Collectables.

HCP
45s:				
	Simon Says/			
	Reflections From The Looking Glass	(Buddah 24)	1967	4
	May I Take A Giant Step (Into Your Heart)/			
	(Poor Old) Mr Jensen	(Buddah 39)	1968	63
	1-2-3 Red Light/Sticky Sticky	(Buddah 54)	1968	5
	Goody Goody Gumdrops/Candy Kisses	(Buddah 71)	1968	37
	Indian Giver/Pow Wow	(Buddah 91)	1969	5
	Special Delivery/No Good Annie	(Buddah 114)	1969	38
	The Train/Eternal Light	(Buddah 130)	1969	57
	When We Get Married/Baby Sweet	(Buddah 146)	1969	118

This 'bubblegum' outfit came from Linden, New Jersey. Their records were produced by Jerry Kasenetz and Jeff Katz, who masterminded the 'bubblegum' movement and were behind other key acts like **The Music Explosion** and **Ohio Express**. Essentially a 'singles' band they made an immediate impact with *Simon Says*, which has become a classic party song and, in addition to being a Top Ten hit in America, it also made No. 2 in the U.K. (although it was their only major hit here). They enjoyed other success in the US, particularly with *1-2-3 Red Light* and *Indian Giver*. Their *Hard Ride* album was by an entirely different line-up. There may come a time when collectors take an interest in their first four albums.

Bruce Shay was their bass player on their second, third and fourth albums and **Chuck Trois** (ex-**Soul Survivors**) was also in the band at some point.

Mark Gutkowski sang the lead vocal on the first two 45s and plays organ, whilst his brother played rhythm guitar. One interesting thing about this group is that the following 45s, *Goody Goody Gumdrops* and *1-2-3 Red Light*, were entirely sung by members of the Philly-based doo-wop group Billy and The Essentials, who had a few 45s out in the early and mid-sixties.

Compilation appearances have included: *Reflections* on *Of Hopes And Dreams & Tombstones* (Dble LP) and *Psychedelic Unknowns, Vol. 7* (LP & CD); *Goody Goody Gumdrops* on *Pop Explosion* (Buddah 643312) 1968. *Simon Says*, *1, 2, 3, Red Light*, *May I Take A Giant Step* and *Goody Goody Gumdrops* on *Bubble Gum Music Is... The Naked Truth* (LP). (VJ/MM)

The '1900' Storm

45s:	A Beautiful Day/Lila	(Cinema 003,04) 196?
	Sympathy Stone/Lila	(Texas Revolution 2) 1969
α	Fireside Song/Slow Down	(American Worm 710) 196?

NB: α as Storm.

This Houston outfit recorded on collectable labels. Their final effort, a rock'n'roller, was issued as by simply Storm. (VJ)

90th Congress

Personnel incl:	DAVE HANSEN	ld vcls	A
	BOBBY HERNE	ld gtr	A

45s:	The Sun Also Rises /	
	Does It Make You Feel Better	(Right RRM-6613) 1967

From Manchester, New Hampshire and previously known as Skid Mark and The Victims, both sides of the sole 45 appear on Collectables' *You Ain't Gonna Bring Me Down To My Knees* (CD), with an unreleased *You Make Me Shake Off The Blues*.

Bobby Herne was previously with **The Outside In**. (MW)

The 98% American Mom and Apple Pie 1929 Crash Band

ALBUM:	1	THE 98% AMERICAN MOM AND APPLE PIE		
		1929 CRASH BAND	(LHI)	c1968 -

A weird Lee Hazlewood project released on his own label. (SR)

The Ninth Street Bridge

45:	Wild Illusions/Hey Baby	(Cecile 5-1968) 1968

The 'A' side, of this Houston band's 45 *Wild Illusions* is a catchy garage song with some good guitar work. It's been heavily compiled, making appearances on *Texas Flashbacks, Vol. 3* (LP & CD), *Flashback, Vol. 3* (LP), *Glimpses, Vol's 1 & 2* (CD) and *Glimpses, Vol. 1* (LP). The flip, has also resurfaced on *Relics Vol's 1 & 2* (CD) and *Relics, Vol. 1* (LP).

In addition, *Houston Hallucinations* (LP) includes two hitherto unreleased efforts of theirs:- an appalling bluesy version of *Heartbreak Hotel* and one of *2120 South Michigan* with lyrics added. (VJ)

9th Street Market

45:	I'm A Baby/You're Gone(?)	(Fenton 2136) c1967

From Michigan, the flip title of the above 45 is speculative. *I'm A Baby* is passable garage, whilst *You're Gone* is the better track, with a repetitive guitar refrain bubbling throughout the song.

Compilation appearances have included *I'm A Baby* and *You're Gone* on both *Michigan Mayhem Vol. 1* (CD) and *Michigan Mixture, Vol. 2* (LP). (MW)

Nirvana Banana

45:      Lovin' Man/Rainy Day Stagedoor Mama   (Atlantic 45-2422) 1967

Lovin' Man is thumpin' good raucous pop - beat with that infectious choppy rhythm from the Beatles' *She's A Woman* and updated to a **Monkees**-styled belter. The flip is solid pop with gravelly vocals. The 'A' side was penned by 'Matt Moore - Dan Moore' - whether Matt is our man from **Matthew Moore Plus Four** and **Moon** is not known. Produced by **Dan Moore** and Jeff Thomas. (MW)

The Nite Owls

Personnel incl: GARY MILLER   vcls

45:      Boots Are Made For Talking/It's A Hassle   (Rembrandt 1) 1966

Came out of South Illinois University, where they formed in 1965. Just 500 copies of the 45 were pressed making it the rarest Rembrandt 45. On the 'A' side, the band simply substituted 'Talking' for 'Walking' on the old Nancy Sinatra hit! However, its lack of originality did not prevent it getting some airplay. Rembrandt's owner, Ronnie Weiss, later changed their name to Nickel Bag - not the band who recorded on Kama Sutra - but they remained in oblivion.

Compilation appearances have included: *The Hassle* and *Boots Are Made For Talking* on *Chicago Garage Band Greats* (CD); *Boots Are Made For Talking* and *The Hassle* (two versions) on *Chicago Garage Band Greats* (LP); and four unreleased cuts from 1966 - *Something You Got*, *Ooh Poo Pa Doo*, *The Woods* and *The Hassle* on *The Cicadelic 60's Vol. 6* (CD). (VJ/MW)

The Nite Walkers

45:      High Class/You've Got Me   (Russell 43107) 1966

Another raw punk outfit judging by *High Class*. They came from Downey, California.

Compilation appearances include: *High Class* on *Teenage Shutdown, Vol. 6* (LP & CD) and *Highs In The Mid-Sixties Vol. 2* (LP). (VJ/MW)

NITZINGER - Nitzinger LP.

Nitzinger

Personnel incl:	CURLY BENTON	bs, vcls	AB
	JOHN NITZINGER	gtr, vcls	AB
	LINDA WARING	vcls, perc	AB
	BUGS HENDERSON	gtr	B

ALBUMS:	1	NITZINGER	(Capitol SMAS 11091) 1972 -
	2	ONE FOOT IN HISTORY	(Capitol SMAS 11122) 1973 -
	3	LIVE BETTER ELECTRICALLY	
			(20th Century 518) 1976

NB: (1) counterfeited on CD (Buy Or Die BOD 107) and reissued on vinyl (Akarma AK 163) 2001. (2) reissued on vinyl (Akarma AK 172). (3) also released in England. (1) - (3) reissued on CD as a Box set (Akarma AK 163/3) 2001.

45s:	Earth Eater/One Foot In History	(Capitol 3559) 1973
	Yellow Dog/Are You With Me	(20th Century 2311) 1976

This Texas guitarist began with **The Barons** and formed his group in the early seventies. Bugs Henderson (ex-**Mouse and The Traps**) plays on the second album.

Their three albums are mostly in a bluesy hard-rock style and are sought-after by some collectors.

John Nitzinger would later form PM, a short-lived group which released an album on Ariola in 1980, and also record with Alice Cooper in 1982. (SR)

Don Nix

ALBUMS:	1	IN GOD WE TRUST	(Shelter SHE 8902) 1971 -
(up to	2	LIVING BY THE DAYS	(Elektra EKS 74101) 1971 -
1976)	3	THE ALABAMA STATE TROUPERS ROAD SHOW	
			(Elektra EKS-75022) 1972 -
	4	HOBOS, HEROES AND STREET CORNER CLOWNS	
			(Enterprise ENS 1032) 1973 -
	5	GONE TOO LONG	(Cream 1001) 1976 -

NB: (2) also released in the UK (Elektra K42096).(3) also released in France (Elektra 62010).

45s:	α	I Saw Her Yesterday/	HCP
		Ain't About To Go Home	(Winrod 1001) c1964 -
	β	Olena/Going Back To Iuka	(Elektra 12026) 1971 94

NB: α as Donnie Nix.β is a French single with PS.

Originating from Memphis, **Don Nix** is an important figure of this local scene, comparable to two other Memphis musicians, **Steve Cropper** and **Jim Dickinson**, as the three men produced, arranged and played on hundreds of records.

His presence here is justified by his participation on several rock albums.

Nix began his career in the late fifties with **Cropper** in the Mar-Keys, responsible for the instrumental hit *Last Night*. Nix was originally a sax player with this group but he soon developed an interest in songwriting, arrangements and production, and that lead him to produce several groups and singers: **Paris Pilot**, **Delaney and Bonnie**, **Charlie Musselwhite**, as well as some blues artists (Albert King, Furry Lewis...). Most of these albums were co-written by **Nix**.

After some months spent in Tyler, Texas with Dale Hawkins and Robin Hood Brians (the producers of **Mouse and The Traps**) and several Texan groups), **Nix** moved to Los Angeles where he became friend with **Leon Russell** and the "Oklahoma Mafia" musicians. His first contract as a solo artist (he was also able to sing, with a good warm voice) was naturally with Shelter, the new label created by **Russell** but the sales of *In God We Trust* were extremely limited and the album is now hard to find.

Don Nix then moved to Elektra releasing three albums combining rock, country, blues and gospel influences, always with good musicians. After the success of **Leon Russell**'s "Mad Dogs And Englishmen" troup, he formed The Alabama State Troupers Road Show with Furry Lewis and **Brenda Patterson** and the resulting double live album has its moments.

In 1971, **Nix** was also the choir master for George Harrison's "Concert For Bangladesh".

In 1970/73, he kept on producing albums for Lonnie Mack (*Hills Of Indiana*), the French group the Variations, and Beck, Bogart and Appice, this trio also recording his song *Goin' Down* (also covered by Freddie King, Moloch, J.J. Cale...).

Don Nix was also by then one of the managers of Enterprise, the rock subsidiary label of Stax and his Memphis productions included **Sid Selvidge**, **Dallas County**, **Moloch**, Larry Raspberry and The Highsteppers (ex-**Gentrys**).

Nix also spent several months with John Mayall (the album *Ten Years Are Gone*) and in 1975, invited by Keef Hartley, he went to England to produce Michael Chapman's *Savage Amusement*.

Totally exhausted and suffering from serious drug problems, **Nix** then seriously reduced his activities, with only two albums in 1976 (*Gone Too Long*) and in 1979 (*Skyrider*).

In 1996, **Nix** released a new solo CD and published an interesting book "Road Stories And Recipes" with his adventures in the music business plus sixty pages of cooking recipes given by people like J.J. Cale, **Sam The Sham**, **Jim Dickinson**, Delbert McClinton and John Mayall! (SR)

Noah's Ark

Personnel:	BOBBY CALDWELL	drms	AB
	RONNY ELLIOTT	bs	AB
	BILL MANN	gtr	AB
	BUDDY RICHARDSON	ld gtr	AB
	RODNEY JUSTO	vcls	B

45s:	Love In/I Get All The Luck	(Decca 32153) 1967
	Paper Man/	
	Please Don't Talk About Yesterday	(Decca 32217) 1967
α	Purple Heart/Stormy	(Liberty 56157) 1970

NB: α as **Noah's Ark featuring Rodney Justo**.

Well, someone just had to make a record called *Love-In*. You'll find this likeable psychedelic ditty on *30 Seconds Before The Calico Wall* (CD) and *Boulders, Vol. 11* (LP). Strangely, *Paper Man* appears on *Rubble, Vol. 15* where it's somehow surmised that the band were from the U.K. despite the 45 getting no U.K. release (huh?!). *Paper Man* has since appeared on *Psychedelic States: Florida Vol. 3* (CD), which sets the record straight.

The band was from Tampa, Florida and Elliott and Richardson had previously been in other local groups including the Raveons, **Outsiders** and **Soul Trippers**. Their first two 45s are recommended. The Liberty 45 is totally different; augmented by ex-**Candymen** Rodney Justo and in a final attempt at commercial success they switched to the overblown soul'n'brass bombast of **Blood, Sweat and Tears** that was then in fashion. Both sides were written and produced by the Buie/Cobb team, who would work with Justo again when he formed The Atlanta Rhythm Section.

Bobby Caldwell had earlier drummed for The Go-Mads, prior to forming **Noah's Ark** with Buddy Richardson and Ronny Elliott. Both Elliott and Bill Mann also played in **The Outlaws**. Caldwell then was recruited by **Johnny Winter** and, later the UK/US outfit Captain Beyond. Caldwell also drummed on the New Englander's tracks found on the Tener Bee-Jay sampler albums. When Caldwell left The Go-Mads, the remaining members became, **Plant Life**.

Noah's Ark later re-grouped as Duckbutter and Buddy Richardson would later form **White Witch**.

Info on all the bands on the Florida sixties scene are covered in Jeff Lemlich's essential 1992 book 'Savage Lost' (Distinctive Publishing, ISBN 0-942963-12-1). (MW/RE/RT/SR/SMR)

Noah's Ark

45:	I Think I Wanna Love You Baby/	
	Hold Back The Sun	(Roulette 4703) 1966

Unconnected to the Tampa, Florida act, this 45 is OK harmony-pop produced by one Bob Feldman. This band could possibly then originate from New York. (MW)

The Noblemen

ACETATE:	1	THE NOBLEMEN	(Audiodisc) 196? R3

NB: (1) one-sided 12" metal acetate.

45s:	Stop Your Running Around/Bend It	(CJL 1001) 196?
	My Flash On You/	
	Here's Where You Belong	(Kaleidoscope 001) 196?

Came out of Dallas in the mid-sixties, although they also spent time in Oklahoma City. *Stop Your Running Around* is a fast dance number delivered in a typical garage punk style, whilst for their second 45 they opted for a reasonable cover of **Love**'s *My Flash On You*.

The 12" acetate, which sounds circa 1966, contains a cover of The Yardbirds' *You're A Better Man Than I* plus three untitled originals, all with thick fuzztone. It's not confirmed that this was recorded by the same **Noblemen**, but it was cut in Oklahoma.

Compilation appearances include: *My Flash On You* on *Sixties Rebellion, Vol. 8* (LP & CD); and *Stop Your Running Around* on *Texas Flashback (The Best Of)* (CD), *Texas Flashbacks, Vol. 4* (LP & CD) and *Flashback, Vol. 4* (LP). (VJ/MW)

The Noblemen

Personnel incl:	JIM PEARIE	gtr	A

45:	Short Time/?	(Orlyn ?) 1967

A quartet of freshmen from The University of Chicago they had all previously played with high school bands, in Pearie's case back home in Pennsylvania with The Marauders. They played during 1967 and 1968 and their screeching version of *Short Time* is worth investigating on *Back From The Grave, Vol. 7* (Dble LP). (VJ)

The Noblemen

45:	Things Aren't The Same/Night Rider	(IGL 130) 1967

A garage outfit from Albert City, Iowa. Their finest moment, *Things Aren't The Same*, is a raucous if melancholic song and comes with a surf-styled guitar break.

SIXTIES REBELLION Vol. 8 (Comp CD) including The Noblemen.

Compilation appearances have included *Things Aren't The Same* on *Monsters Of The Midwest, Vol. 2* (LP) and *The Arf! Arf! Blitzkrieg 32 Track Sampler* (Dble CD). (VJ/MW)

The Noblemen

Personnel incl:	JOE CALDWELL	gtr	A
	CHRIS CALVIN	bs	A
	DAVE CULP	vcls	A
	RANDY HUFF	drms	A
	FRANK MARSHALL	ld gtr	A
	JEFF WELLS	organ	A

From Grandview Heights, a village just Northwest of Columbus, Ohio, these **Noblemen** inspired by local heroes **The Dantes**, were active between 1966-68. Their main claim to fame was their inclusion on the rare *Hillside '66* (LP) compilation, with a cover of The Who's *Under My Thumb*. Chris Calvin recalls: "Hillside Records was run by a guy called Larry McKenzie, who we used to hire amplifiers from for our gigs. The track was recorded about a month after we formed in the Fall of '66 and we were all fifteen at the time. Larry had a good two-track Ampex or Scully machine and the track was recorded in Larry's house, with band members spread through his front room, dining room and kitchen. The *Hillside '66* record itself came with phone numbers under each band's name and was meant to be a demo for each band... it ended up being a snapshot of his customer base for 1966!"

Retrospective compilation appearances include *Under My Thumb* on *Oil Stains, Vol. 2* (LP). (IT/CC)

The Noblemen

Personnel:	LARRY BURCH	ld vcls, organ, gtr	AB
	JERRY COMPTON	bs	AB
	CHUCK LARUE	drms	AB
	RICK WILHELM	gtr	A
	MICKEY SMITH	gtr	B

45:	Satisfied/She Thinks I Still Love Her	(Prism 1930) 1965

Formed in 1965 these **Noblemen** came from Indianapolis, Indiana. Rick Wilhelm and Brian Crouch co-wrote the 'A' side of their record, *Satisfied*. Larry Burch recalls: "I was the oldest (20) and Chuck the youngest (17), was still a senior in high school. The band was managed by Chucks' Dad Ramon and his brother Gene. We worked all over Indy and most of the state.... playing at a lot of small town armorys and teen dances, etc. We sold our 45 and 8"x 10" glossys for a buck each and developed a pretty good local following. One gig that stands out was playing for a Summer stock cast party of which Edie Adams was the main star. It was our only association with a major star at that time and I can remember we thought it was a pretty deal at the time. After about a year or so we cooled off somewhat and Rick left the group first and was replaced by Mickey Smith."

"After a few more weeks Mickey and I moved on to play in house bands in nightclubs playing in a group called **Melting Pot**. I left that group and went to the West Coast and the **Melting Pot** gravitated toward Florida. They did one album, *Burn Fire, Cauldron Bubble* (Capricorn Records) before they disbanded. The drummer of that group (Jerry Thompson) went on to work some with Dickey Betts, but I don't know what they're doing now. After I discovered that **The Noblemen** were on a compilation record, I did locate Rick Wilhelm and he's still in the Indy area into real estate."

"As far as I know I'm the only one of the original group who has stayed in music all their life. I stayed in the San Francisco bay area for about five years working with a trio (The Company) and we worked from Portland, Ore. down past San Bernandino, Ca. and most points in between with a few trips to Reno and Tahoe. (Those gigs always payed well, and still do I guess) However this was the late sixties and in to the early seventies and I (plus the band and everyone else) were very much into "hippiedom" so a lot of the gigs remain kind of 'purple hazy' if you know what I mean. One thing that was constant until about 15 years ago was being on the road. I had met Woody Herman at a gig in Ohio and he was such a gentlemen and complimentary towards me that it gave me enough confidence to move to Nashville. It was there that I joined a R&B group called Pure Pleasure.

We were managed by Ed Leffler from L.A. who was also at the time managing Sammy Hagar and a couple of lesser known groups. He went on to manage Van Halen until he passed away in '93 I believe. But he got us a deal with A&M Records and we did shows mostly around the South with acts like Cameo and The Commodores. etc."

"I've been in the Columbus area since '88 and have found it to be a good home base for gigs. One days drive in any direction has hundreds of places for musicians to work. I've had a band called Larry B and The Real Deal for the last ten years. We're fairly well known in the area and have done shows with the likes of Tower Of Power, Clarence "Gatemouth" Brown and most every one in between in that musical genre."

Compilation appearances have included *She Still Thinks I Love Her* on *Fuzz, Flaykes, And Shakes, Vol. 5* (LP & CD). (GGI/MW/LB)

The Noblemen

45s:	Two Faced Woman /	
	You Didn't Have To Be So Nice	(Paris Tower PT-110) 1967

An obscure and uncompiled band from Clearwater, Florida. (MW)

The Noblemen

Personnel:	CHUCK LALICATA	gtr	A
	RAYMOND OJEDA	sax	A
	BRUCE "ACE" RUDAN	bs	A
	BRAND SHANK	ld gtr	A
	BOB STRANGE	sax, accordion	A
	JERRY SWORSKE	drms	A

45s:	Thunder Wagon / Dragon Walk	(USA EM-1213) 1959
	Dirty Robber / Forever Lonely	(USA 1222) 1960
	Dirty Robber / Forever Lonely	(Profile 4012) 1960

Seminal Milwaukee rock'n'rollers whose debut was a modest hit - popular enough to merit a U.K. release in both 45 and 78 format (Top Rank JAR 155). They backed other artists including Tony Majestro and Little Sir Ryland, the latter on his 1959 release *My Worried Lover* (USA 1214). You can hear their *Dirty Robber* on *Highs In The Mid Sixties, Vol. 10* (LP). (VJ/GM/MW)

The Noblemen

45:	Tiddle Winks / Vibratin'	(Bee 1826) 1963

From Reading, Pennsylvania. (MW)

The Noblemen

45:	Little Girl You Look So Fine / Together	(Epic 9723) 1964

Any of the above? Heaven knows. (MW)

Noblemen 4

45s:	Get Out Of My Life Woman /	
	What's Your Name	(Recap R.R. 291) 1967
	I Can Hear Raindrops /	
	Hang It In Your Ear	(Recap R.R. 292) 1967
	Beach Umbrella World / Lady Flora	(Mercury 72828) 1968

Mike Kuzmin's discography of Pennsylvania, 'Sounds From The Woods', reveals that this band hailed from Greensburg/Irwin. *I Can Hear Raindrops*, a superb garage ballad with great rainstorm effects and a salute to the Cascades, is to be found on *I Can Hear Raindrops* (LP). Confusingly it turns up again, with the last verse repeated, as *I Can Hear The Rain Drops*

GARAGE PUNK UNKNOWNS Vol. 5 LP including Nobody's Children.

by **The Aces** on *Thee Unheard Of*, supposedly a collection of Michigan acetates on the Punch label (a Hideout subsidiary). However, it turns out that the reason they were "unheard of" is that many of these acetates were modern forgeries, manufactured by a fraudster who duped the compiler.

Similarly, *Hang It In Your Ear* also appears on *Thee Unheard Of*, but credited to "The Underdogs"! (MW/MM)

The Nobles

45: Something Else/
I Hope I Don't Get Hurt Again (Marquis 4991) 1966

This quartet was out of Wilmington in Delaware and earlier known as The Sting Rays and The Cobras. *Something Else* was a pretty frantic garage punker with vibrant guitar and lots of organ. The local radio station banned it because they thought the song was about sex and it sank without trace. The group soldiered on until 1968, when the draft and college led to their demise.

Compilation appearances include: *Something Else* on *Psychedelic Unknowns, Vol's 1 & 2* (LP), *Psychedelic Unknowns, Vol. 2* (Dble 7") and *Back From The Grave, Vol. 5* (LP). (VJ)

Nobody's Children

45: Good Times/Somebody To Help Me (GPC 1944) 1968

From Dallas, this outfit's 45, with its monster guitar riff, psychedelic fuzz and rampaging punk vocals is rather special.

Compilation appearances have included: *Good Times* on *Psychedelic Microdots Of The Sixties, Vol. 1* (CD), *Pebbles, Vol. 3 (ESD)* (CD), *Trash Box* (5-CD), *Texas Music, Vol. 3* (CD), *Best of Pebbles, Vol. 1 - Get Primitive* (LP & CD), *Flashback, Vol. 6* (LP) and *Highs In The Mid-Sixties, Vol. 11* (LP); and *Good Times* and *Somebody To Help Me* on *Sixties Archive Vol. 8* (CD) and *Acid Trip From The Psychedelic Sixties* (LP). (VJ)

Nobody's Children

45: Girl I Need You/
Girl I Need You (instr) (Kiderian 45112) 1967

A mid-sixties garage band from Chicago. *Girl I Need You* is an uptempo blast, with plenty of fine fuzz guitar and harmony vocals. You can also find it on *Pebbles, Vol. 6* (CD) and *Let's Dig 'Em Up!!!* (LP), whilst the instrumental 'b' side version appears on *Buzz Buzz Buzzzzzz, Vol. 1* (CD). (MW)

Nobody's Children

45: Baby - I Tried/St. James Infirmary (Delta 2207) 1966

St. James Infirmary, a blues-influenced song written by G. Primrose, can also be heard on *New Mexico Punk From The Sixties* (LP) and *Sixties Archive, Vol. 4* (CD). (VJ)

Nobody's Children

Personnel:	DENNIS BOONE	ld vcls, rhythm gtr	A
	MARK MOUHTOURIS	drms	A
	LEE TRAVERS	ld gtr, vcls	A
	JAN ZUKOWSKI	bs, vcls	A

45s: Junco Partner (Worthless Cajun)/
Let Her Go (United Artists 50090) 1966
α I Told Santa Claus I Want You/
Stuck In The Chimney (Scepter 12180) 1966
I Can't Let Go/Don'tcha Feel Like Crying (Bullet 1000) 1967
I Can't Let Go/Don'tcha Feel Like Crying (Buddah 36) 1968

NB: α released under the moniker **The Surf Boys**.

Yet another outfit of this name, this time from Prince George's county Maryland. The band were managed by Washington Radio station WPGC DJ Harv Moore and the horns featured on *I Can't Let Go* were courtesy of another DC group called The Arabians. The flip, *Don'tcha Feel Like Crying* is perhaps more interesting, with some fuzz guitar.

Whilst under contract to United Artists they recorded a Christmas single under the moniker **The Surf Boys**. *Junco Partner (Worthless Cajun)* can be found on *Garage Punk Unknowns, Vol. 5* (LP).

Jan Zukowski who also played with **The Cherry People** in 1967, is currently playing with an outfit called The Nighthawks. (VJ/SR/MW)

Nobody's Children

45: Colours And Shapes / ? (Deek 1021) 196?

Colours And Shapes is an awesome 'bad trip' punker with screeching fuzzed guitar and snarling vocalist, comparable to the brooding magnificence of **The Unrelated Segments** or **The Chocolate Watchband**. The lyrics come in clotted couplets of syllabic triplets, as if being extracted by forceps -

"I see blue - you're all green.
It's all lonely - nothin' seen.
Outside world - too bad, square.
It's too bad - you're still there.
(chorus) I'm alive - I'm alive.
You're so cold - growing old.
There's no time - you're my mind"

Crank it up on *Open Lid EP* (7"), *Turds On A Bum Ride Vol. 5* (CD) or *Mayhem & Psychosis, Vol. 1* (CD). No idea yet whence they hailed - no one's lettin' on and the writer credits (Sterling, McKenzie, Spitale) is the only clue to hand. (MW)

Nobody's Children

Personnel:	JOHN HAAS	vcls	A
	TOMMY McNABB	bs	A

Formed in 1967 in Bunkie, Louisiana, by the above after the break-up of their previous group, **The Barracudas**. However, this was a short-lived outfit, who don't appear to have recorded. Instead John Haas was nabbed by **Jimmy and The Offbeats** and released a brace of 45s with them after a name change to John Eric and The Isosceles Popsicles. (AB/MW)

Noises N' Sounds

Personnel incl: TERRY DALE   vcl   A

45:     Yum Yum Eat 'Em Up/How Much Lovin'   (Piccadilly 222) 1966

Most likely a studio group, produced by Tex Hughes and featuring members of **The Page Boys**. The fuzz-filled *How Much Lovin'* can be found on Big Beat's *Northwest Battle Of The Bands, Vol. 2* (CD). (VJ)

The Nomadds

Personnel:
TONY CANNOVA	drms	A
LEE GARNER	gtr	A
GREG JOHNSON	vcls, gtr	A
DEAN KUEHL	vcls, hrmnca	A
DENNY KUHL	bs	A

ALBUM: 1(A)   THE NOMADDS   (Radex MLP 6521) 1965 R3

A rare pop-rock garage album from Freeport, Illinois. Rather inept like all records of the genre that are sought - after. (CF/MW)

The Nomads

Personnel:
JOHNNY COLEMAN	vcls	A
BILL HAM	gtr	A
WESLEY HARRIS	gtr, vcls	A
HARRY LARSON	drms	A

45s: I Saw You Go/I Really Do   (Soft 958) 1965
Be Nice/Empty Heart (PS)   (Spotlight 5019) 1966

This wild garage band was based in Fort Worth, Texas. After an initial ballad-punk 45, they issued the only garage 45 from Fort Worth to appear in a picture sleeve. Wesley Harris and Bill Ham left not long afterwards to form The Rocks and later Bill teamed up with Bob Barnes (from **Those Guys**) in **The Yellow Payges**.

Compilation appearances include *Be Nice* on *Back From The Grave, Vol. 4* (LP) and *Back From The Grave, Vol. 2* (CD). (VJ)

The Nomads

Personnel incl: BILL KIRBY
JAMES MANLOVE
JOHNNY ORVIS   vcls, gtr
FRANK ZIGEL

45s: I Walk Alone/I'll Be There   (Damon 101) 1967
Three O'Clock Merrian Webster/Situations   (Orbit 1121) 1968

A different Houston outfit who started out as a folk-rock band but progressed into a bizarre psychedelic outfit. Their development is well-documented on the compilation *Three O'Clock Merrian Webster Time* (LP) which includes the above 45s, two 1967 outtakes:- *My Little Red Book*, *New Generation* and a cut from a 1968 45 on Orbit (1126) called *Mainstream* by which time they had changed their name to **The Smoke**. In 1969 they relocated to California and recorded two albums for UNI.

Situations, quite an interesting garage punk number, can also be heard on *Acid Visions - The Complete Collection, Vol. 1* (CD), *Flashback, Vol. 6* (lp) *Gathering Of The Tribe* (CD); and *My Little Red Book* was included on *The Cicadelic Sixties, Vol. 2*. The six tracks featured on *Three O'Clock Merrian Webster Time* (LP) have also been recompiled on Collectables' 3-CD set - *Acid Visions - Complete Collection, Vol. 3* (CD), and five are repeated again on *The History Of Texas Garage Bands, Vol. 2 - The Orbit Records Story* (CD). *My Little Red Book* and *Situations* also appear on *Green Crystal Ties, Vol. 1* (CD). (VJ/MW)

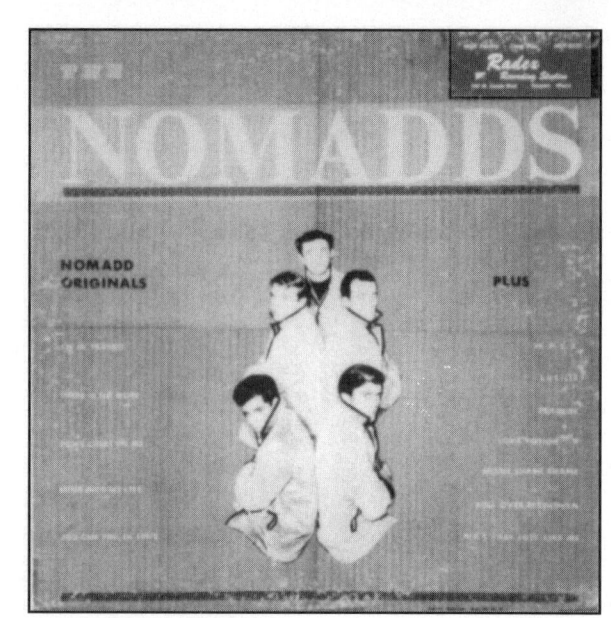

THE NOMADDS - The Nomadds LP.

The Nomads

Personnel:
MIKE BADGETT	drms	A
GARY BEESON	gtr, keyb'ds	A
BRUCE EVANS	ld gtr, vcls	A
LARRY DEATHERAGE	vcls	A
JERRY MARTIN	bs, vcls	A

ALBUM: 1(A)   THE NOMADS: FROM ZERO DOWN   (Crypt 006) 1985

45s: Not For Me/How Many Times   ( ) 1966
Thoughts Of A Madman/From Zero Down   (Tornado 159) 1966/7

A five-star garage combo from Mount Airy, North Carolina. *Thoughts...* is regarded by many as a classic and it's flip, is also a typical primal, grungy fuzztone scream about partying. The excellent and thoroughly worthwhile retrospective LP on Crypt is a must for garage-heads everywhere.

Some members went on to an outfit called **Blu-Erebus** who released one 45 in September 1968. *Plastic Year*, "a prime example of four-star late sixties psychedelia" (Erik Lindgren), can be heard on *An Overdose Of Heavy Psych*.

Also a mystery outfit, Willow Green, put out a 45 - *Fields Of Peppermint* (a Deatherage-Evans composition), backed by an instrumental version of the same, on Whiz #619 circa 1968. Another **Nomads** offshoot?

As **The Nomads** compilation appearances have included: *From Zero Down* on *Pebbles, Vol. 12* (LP) and *Teenage Shutdown, Vol. 10* (LP & CD); *Thoughts Of A Madman* on *Vile Vinyl, Vol. 1* (LP), *Vile Vinyl* (CD), *Chosen Few Vol's 1 & 2* (CD) and *The Chosen Few, Vol. 1* (LP). (VJ/MW/LP)

The Nomads

45:     I Need Your Love/Willow Wind   (Discotek 70646) 1967

From Sylvania, Ohio. *I Need Your Love* can also be heard on *Everywhere Interferences* (LP) and *Fuzz, Flaykes, And Shakes, Vol. 5* (LP & CD). (MW/GGI)

The Nomads

45:     Time Remains/?   (J&S 1002) c1967

Yet another different combo whose raw folk-rock rendition of *Time Remains* can be heard on *Highs In The Mid-Sixties, Vol. 22* (LP). The band may be from Louisiana, as the label is thought to have been based in Metarie, Louisiana. (VJ/AB/MW)

The Nomads

A Philadelphia band who recorded two songs as a demo at that city's Magna Sound studios. The songs - *Point Five* and *I Need Your Energy* - are both crudely recorded but have a certain charm about them, particularly their pounding drumming and you'll find them both on the *Crude PA, Vol. 1* (LP) compilation. A later version of *Energy* was released on Romain records under the name **One Way Street Band**. (VJ)

The Nomads

45:	I (Need Your Love)/Please Be True	(Samter 216)	1965

George Gell informs us that this **Nomads** were a different act to The Nomads from Sylvania, who had a similarly named 45. Anyone out there know details of this bunch? (MW)

Nomadz

Personnel:	JOHN MIKOVICH	A
	J. OBERMAN	A
	P. RUCHTIE	A
	D. TACSIK	A
	PAUL TACSIK	A

45:	She Ain't Lovin' You No More / Wait Till The Midnight Hour	(WAM 5980)	1967

An Ohio garage band who left behind two competent covers. The 'A' side being a **Distant Cousins** track and the flip, the often covered soul-garage-fave *In The Midnight Hour*. (MW)

No-Na-Mee's

45:	Gotta Hold On/Just Wanna Be Myself	(Era 3165)	1966

From the label that gave us **The Lyrics**' debut 45 came this terrific waxing from an unknown L.A. combo. The 'A' side can be found on *Highs In The Mid-Sixties, Vol. 2* (LP) and the flip on *Highs In The Mid-Sixties, Vol. 20* (LP). They had quite a wide musical range taking in flowery-pop, folk-rock and punk. (VJ)

The Non Conformists

45:	A Two Legged Big Eyed Yellow Haired Crying Canary/ Bird Walk	(Scepter 12184)	1967

A studio group from New York. Their single is mostly pop, written and arranged by Hutch Davie and Vance, both men being then active with the Bob Crewe productions. The flip is instrumental. (SR)

Steve Noonan

ALBUM:	1 STEVE NOONAN	(Elektra EKS-74017)	1968 -

A young Californian singer/songwriter who wrote *Buy For Me The Rain*, the first hit for **Nitty Gritty Dirt Band**. The material on his sole album was co-written with Jackson Browne and Greg Copeland and was described as "folk flavored art song" by Lillian Roxon in her 1969 Rock Encyclopedia.

The songs are generally good but **Noonan**'s voice has nothing to retain your attention. (SR)

Noonan Levi and Houshmand

Personnel:	HOUSHMAND	A
	LEVI	A
	NOONAN	A

ALBUM:	1 EAST RIVER	(Universal Dynamics Corporation)	197? SC

Hailing from Kansas City, this acoustic trio released a rare album of progressive folk with violin, acoustic guitars and good "drifting" vocals. (SR)

Dave Nordin

ALBUM:	1 IN MY MIND	(SPECifications Records)	1971 R2

From California, an introspective folk singer/songwriter, whose only album was released in very small quantities on SPECifications Records, a label from Kentfield, California. Tracks like *Voyage, Maryjane* (with obvious lyrics), *Rosemary* or *You Make Me Feel Like Someone* may interest some readers. (SR)

North Atlantic Invasion Force (N.A.I.F.)

Personnel incl:	P. BIRCH	A
	GEORGE MORGIO JR.	A

45s:	Sweet Bird Of Soul/ Elephant In My Tambourine	(Majestic 998)	1967
	Blue And Green Gown/ Fire, Wind And Rain	(Congressional 999)	1967
	Black On White/The Orange Patch	(Mr.G. 808)	1968
	Rainmaker/Elephant In My Tambourine	(Mr. G. 819)	1968
	Love's No Game/Elephant In My Tambourine	(Staff 1006)	1969

An obscure Connecticut combo, more frequently known as **N.A.I.F.**. The intriguingly titled *Elephant In My Tambourine* is unfortunately not off-the-wall psych but a catchy cornball novelty complete with jew's harp - you've been warned!

Their four singles plus six unreleased tracks form half of Collectables' 2CD set *The History Of Connecticut Garage Bands In The 60's*, which they share with **Yesterday's Children**.

Other compilation appearances include: *Blue And Green Gown* on *New England Teen Scene* (CD) and *New England Teen Scene, Vol. 2* (LP); *Elephant In My Tambourine* on *Sixties Rebellion, Vol. 12* (LP & CD); *Blue Light In The Window* and *I Won't Be Back* on *Green Crystal Ties, Vol. 5* (CD). (MW)

North Bridge Company

Personnel:	SCHULLER	A
	DENNIS STEWART	A

45:	Strange Land, Strange People/ Crying All Alone	(Sand "G" 840G-3111)	1968

NEW ENGLAND TEEN SCENE (Comp CD) including N.A.I.F.

Uptempo psychy soft folksy rock with echoey vocals and evocative reedy keyboards - the flip is also uptempo despite the title and features some winsome guitar. From Peoria, Illinois.

Compilation appearances have included:- *Strange Land, Strange People* on *Psychedelic Crown Jewels Vol. 2* (Dble LP & CD) and *Every Groovy Day* (LP); *Crying All Alone* on *Basementsville! U.S.A.* (LP). (MW)

The Northern Front

ALBUM: 1   THE FURNITURE STORE   (Kader K 4321) 1975 R1

Recorded in Maywood, Illinois, this obscure group recorded a very eclectic mix of psych, garage, avant-garde, folk-rock, satire and poetry. Their album came with handwritten-style inserts. (SR)

Nosy Parker

Personnel:			
	TONY ABBATE	bs, keyb'ds	A
	JOSEPH CELANO	vcls, gtr, clarinet	A
	THOMAS VIOLA	vcls, gtr	A
	WILLIAM VIOLA	drms, keyb'ds	A

ALBUM: 1(A)   NOSY PARKER   (No label) 1975 R2

NB: (1) reissued on CD (Gear Fab GF 189) 2002.

A local New York electric folk album. It was issued with a lyric sheet. (CF)

The Notations

45:   Everything's All Right/Miserlou   (Beverly 1555) 196?

Coming from Amarillo in Texas the 'A' side of this 45 sounds a crossover between rock'n'roll and mid-sixties garage punk. The flip was an instrumental.

Compilation appearances include *Everything's Allright* on *Texas Flashback (The Best Of)* (CD), *Texas Flashbacks, Vol. 4* (LP & CD) and *Flashback, Vol. 4* (LP). (VJ)

Notes From The Underground

Personnel:			
	JOE LUKE	drms	A
	MARK MANDELL	acoustic gtr, gtr, vcls	ABCD
	JOHN MILLER	keyb'ds	A D
	MIKE O'CONNOR	bs, vcls	ABC
	FRED SOKOLOW	gtr, banjo, mandn, tamb, vcls	ABCD
	PETER OSTWALD	drms	BC
	JIM WORK	piano	B
	SKIP ROSE	piano, harp, elec. piano, organ	C
	FURRY GRASSO	drms	D
	BING NATHAN	bs	D

ALBUM: 1(C)   NOTES FROM....   (Vanguard VSD 6502) 1968 SC

NB: (1) reissued on vinyl and CD (Akarma AK 032) 1999.

EP: 1(B)   NOTES FROM THE UNDERGROUND
                                              (Changes 601) 1966

NB: (1) is a four track EP which can now be heard on CD, along with three bluesier outtakes, on *The Berkeley EPs* (Big Beat CDWIKD 153) 1995, which also features the EPs by **Frumious Bandersnatch**, **Mad River** and the June 1966 effort from **Country Joe and The Fish**.

45:   Down In The Basement/
       I Wish I Was A Punk   (Vanguard 35073) 1968

This Berkeley-based band were one of the first wave of Bay Area rock bands. Sokolow came from a very musical family and owned a five string banjo by the time he'd reached High School. Mandell was an old High School friend of his, who earlier played with a band called The Dune Patrol in Santa Barbara. Joe Luke was the drummer in the original line-up, which played at the first Family Dog Longshoreman's Hall concert. With folk musician O'Connor on bass they started gigging at the Jabberwock where Berkeley's only other rock band at the time, **Country Joe and the Fish**, were the houseband. Through **The Fish** they met Chris Strachwitz who had earlier recorded their *Rag Baby EP*, and Chris subsequently recorded **The Notes** for their own EP, which was released in 1966. This is now rare. The tracks were *Where Does Love Go, Down In The Basement* (which was later re-recorded for the album), *What Am I Doing Here?* (also on the album), and *I Got To Get Out Of This Dream*. By this time Ostwald, who'd played with various blues and jazz outfits, had replaced Luke on drums.

The Notes later became the houseband at The New Orleans House (Berkeley), and built up a strong local following playing lots of benefits around The Bay Area. They got a manager, Dan Carey in 1967 (he'd earlier been a road manager for Junior Wells in Chicago) and then a contract with Vanguard for the above album. Ex-jazzman, Skip Rose came in to replace the original keyboard player, John Miller, who fell ill just before it was recorded. The album, which was cut in New York, reflects the diverse musical backgrounds of the band's members. Its most psychedelic cut was *Why Did You Put Me On?* which had a fine fuzztone solo and swirling organ. Their lightheartedness is best represented by *Follow Me Down (To The Underground)*, *I Wish I Was A Punk* and *Mainliner*. Other notable tracks were *Where I'm At, Cantaloupe Island* and *What Am I Doing Here?*

Sadly, after O'Connor and Ostwald left the band, Vanguard, fearing they would disintegrate, became unwilling to provide them with the necessary financial backing and eventually dropped them. Further personnel changes ensued before they left Berkeley for Taos in New Mexico and finally disintegrated. Fred Sokolow and Mark Mandell later formed Prince Bakaradi in Berkeley in 1970. In the late seventies, when Sokolow and Mandell were collaborating on a book about their sixties music experiences, they re-assembled the band with a new line-up recording one album, *Prince Bakaradi* (Appaloosa AP 006) 1980, using mostly material written back in 1970 and 1972. Prince Bakaradi was the villain of a fifties Sci-fi TV series.

Sokolow also recorded a bluegrass album, *Bluegrass Banjo Inventions* (Kicking Mule) 1977. Skip Rose went on to play on a number of **Charlie Musselwhite** albums. Mandell now writes fiction and non-fiction full-time. Sokolow still plays music and writes guitar instruction books for many publishers.

Compilation appearances include: *Follow Me Down (To The Underground)* on *The New Sound Of Underground* (LP); and *Where Does Love Go, Down In The Basement, What Am I Doing Here, Got To Get Out Of This Dream, You Don't Love Me, Let Yourself Fly* and *Where I'm At Today* on *The Berkeley EPs* (CD). (VJ)

NOTES FROM THE UNDERGROUND - Notes From The Underground EP.

NOTES FROM THE UNDERGROUND - Notes From The Underground LP.

The Notorious Noblemen

Personnel:	J.B. ANDERSON	gtr	A
	MIKE BUCHHOLZ	bs	ABC
	JONNIE JOHNSTON	gtr	A
	MIKE McCORMICK	keyb'ds	ABCD
	DOUG SMITH	drms, vcls	ABCD
	STEVE SMITH	sax	A
	JOE SCHMITT	gtr	BC
	KEITH BROWN	gtr	D
	DENNIS CARLBERG	drms	D
	SUE HENRY	vcls	D
	JOE KAISER	bs	D
	LARRY LIND	bs	D

45: Yellow Canary/If I Needed Someone (Bedell 80405) 1967

While based in Iowa (members hailed from Storm Lake, Albert City and Fort Dodge), **The Norious Noblemen**'s only 45 *Yellow Canary* (an original written by the entire band) b/w a cover of the Beatles' *If I Needed Someone* was recorded at the Lynn Recording Studio in Rochester, Minnesota in 1967. Only 500 copies were pressed and because a guy called Tom Bedell helped fund the 45 his name was put on as the record label name.

The band's live set list consisted of many of the "Top 40" songs of the era, ranging from the Rolling Stone's *Get Off Of My Cloud*, **Sam The Sham and The Pharaohs**' *Wooly Bully* and the Beatles' *Ticket To Ride*, to more latter day fare such as covers of songs by Crow, **Blood Sweat and Tears** and Jimi Hendrix. Keyboardist Mike McCormick has stated that the band's "legacy was doing tunes that were either too hard or too weird for other bands of (the) time to do. Yet we had to remain popular and danceable... earlier we were more mainstream, but later we evolved into a more eclectic band". The band was locally reknown for playing everything from *Harlem Shuffle* to the *Rocky And Bullwinkle* theme!

It should be noted that this is an entirely different to Iowa's other **Noblemen**. (MDo/MMc)

Novac

Personnel:	JOHN DZUBAK	drms	A
	BUZZY FEITEN	gtr	A
	ERIC GALE	gtr	A
	JERRY LEE NOVAC	vcls, keyb'ds	A

ALBUM: 1(A) THE FIFTH WORD (Embryo SD 527) 1970 -

Recorded in New York, *The Fifth Word* is a mix of jazz and psych with good keyboards and guitars and titles like *I Am/Classified Speed Freak/I Am/Saturday Night Approval*. Embryo was a subsidiary label of Cotillion/ Atlantic and mostly specialized in fusions of rock and jazz (**Jim Pepper**, **Herbie Mann**, **Floating Opera** etc.). (SR)

Nova Local

Personnel:	PHIL LAMBETH	gtr	A
	BILL LEVASSEUR	drms	A
	JOE MENDYK	ld gtr	A
	JIM OPTON	bs	A
	CAM SCHINHAN	organ	A
	RANDY WINBURN	gtr	A

ALBUM: 1(A) NOVA I (Decca DL 74977) 1967 R1

NB: (1) issued on MCA (MUPS 377) 1969 in the UK.

45s: Games/If You Only Had The Time (Decca 32138) 1967
Other Girls/
John Knight's Body (I Wanna Get Out) (Decca 32194) 1967

This band were students at University of North Carolina in Chapel Hill. Their album, which was recorded in New York in December 1966, is definitely worth investigating and is a minor collectable. Its very Anglophile sound garnered it a U.K. release, although the band had split by April 1967.

Bassist Jim Opton told U-Spaces:- "We were a band that was making a pretty good living playing fraternity parties around the campus, and a few cellar clubs in Chapel Hill. My fraternity, Phi Mu Alpha, was sponsoring a charity concert for our scholarship fund, and we decided to go for broke that year and book a big name. We contacted William Morris Agency in New York, and booked **Chad and Jeremy**. We needed an opening act, so I booked my own band... got us real cheap. The deal was that Rob Heller, who was with the Morris Agency would come and hear us play. He signed us immediately after the concert. A week later he hooked us up with Elliot Mazer, who became our producer. Elliot also worked as a song peddler for E.B. Marks Music, who published the music. We got a recording contract with Decca, I don't know how, but Rob put that deal together with Elliot, and the next thing I know, we are in the studio with all kinds of famous people that had us in awe for the first 35 seconds or so. I do know that somebody thought we were kind of special, because the studio was absolutely closed to visitors while we were there, and we were not allowed to take home raw tape to play for anyone. We did a lot of things that were pretty advanced for our time. Listen carefully to *Morning Dew* for example. The strange vocal effects were done by feeding the vocals through a Leslie Tone Cabinet from a Hammond B3. Also, the bass lead is the first bass feedback lead I think I can remember in a rock song. I blew up the amp doing it!! Cost me $750 (a LOT of money I didn't have in 1966)!! But, it was a hell of a lick. The album was essentially recorded by five of us: Randy, Bill, Joe, Cam and me. Phil had departed for law school. I believe he is alive and well, and practicing law in Charlotte, N.C."

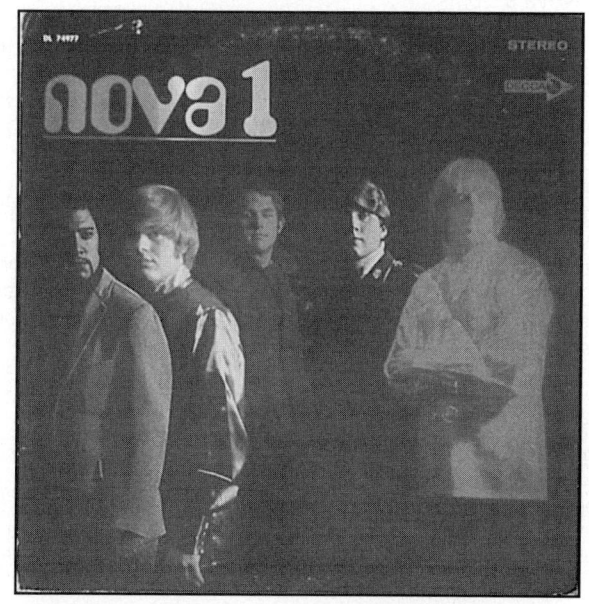

NOVA LOCAL - Nova 1 LP.

"Actually, there is one little piece or two of rock and roll history that goes with that album. It was the first ever recorded using the very new, and relatively unknown, Dolby NR System. It took up a good size room at the time. The engineer for the album, Fred Catero, was also the engineer for Simon and Garfunkel."

Joe Mendyk had earlier played in Tri-Power, The Better Days and The Warlocks (with an excellent 45 on Decca). The 'A' side of their first 45, excellent harmony pop-punk, can be heard on *Echoes In Time, Vol. 2* (LP) and *Echoes In Time, Vol's 1 & 2* (CD), the flip is on the album. *Forgotten Man*, also from the album, has resurfaced on *Baubles - Down To Middle Earth* (LP). (VJ/MW)

The Novas

Personnel:	DAVID BROWNE	vcls, gtr	A
	DAVID DENNARD	bs	A
	GARY MADRIGAL	drms, vcls	A
	JOHN SALIH	ld gtr, keyb'ds, vcls	A

ALBUM: 1( ) WILLIAM JUNIOR: THE SUMPIN' ELSE TAPES
(Distortions DR 1026) 1996

NB: There's also a CD on Collectables titled *Sump 'n' Else Tapes* which presumably covers the same material.

45s:	William Junior/And It's Time	(S.T.A.R. 001) 1966
	Coronado's Puzzle/Lakeside Lot	(GPC 1946) 1967

From Dallas in Texas they started out in 1964 covering Astronauts' songs but developed into a tightly knit pop band issuing a folk-rock 45 on S.T.A.R. Dennard later headed for L.A. joining The Ravers. Then, after a spell in The Low Numbers, he ended up in fellow Texan Gary Myrick's band.

The Distortions album is a compilation of the recorded output by this mid-to-late sixties Dallas band. The title track falls into the folk-rock vein which is also where some of their other material lands. It also contains some really cool tracks which were recorded specially for lip-syncing to on the 'Sumpin' Else' TV show. These include a fuzz-frat version of *Shake*, the Mersey sounding *Help*, a cool version of *Bus Stop* which quite possibly outdoes the original as well as the obligatory **Byrds** cover *Feel A Whole Lot Better*. There are a few other tracks from an unreleased 45 and some demos. But while they did some stellar versions of other bands' songs, in the end, it's their originals from their 45, *William Junior/And It's Time* that really shine.

Compilation appearances have included: *And It's Time* and *William Junior* on both *Acid Visions - Complete Collection, Vol. 3* (3-CD) and *Texas Punk, Vol. 6* (LP). (VJ/MW)

The Nova's

EP:	1 THE CRUSHER (PS)	(Norton 075) 1999

45s:	The Crusher/Take 7	(Parrot 45005) 1965
	Nova's Coaster/On The Road Again	(Twin Town 713) 1965

A punk band from Edina, Minnesota who are worth investigating. They were a high school four-piece. Their debut 45 consisted of a Trashmen-inspired novelty song *The Crusher*, backed by a primitive but worthwhile surf instrumental. Their second 45 included their grungy-style interpretation of Bob Dylan's *On The Road Again*. This was featured on the Bud-Jet mid-sixties Minneapolis compilation *Top Teen Bands, Vol. 2*, whilst *Nova's Coaster* appeared on *Top Teen Bands, Vol. 3*.

Billy Miller's welcome Norton reissue EP features the Parrot 45 plus 1965 Dove demos of Dylan's *On The Road Again* and a cover of the **Astronauts'** *My Sin Is My Pride*.

Compilation appearances have included:- *Take 7* on *Pebbles, Vol. 17* (LP) and *Strummin Mental, Vol. 2*; and *The Crusher* on *We Have Come For Your Children, Born Bad (The Songs The Cramps Taught Us), Back From The Grave, Vol. 2* (LP) and *Garage Kings* (Dble LP). (VJ/MW)

The Novas

Personnel:	JOHN BERNARD	drms	AB
	RICK CALABORO	gtr	AB
	BILL CAMPBELL	vcls	A
	JIM LeFEVRE	bs	AB
	KENNY WYNN	ld gtr	AB

45:	Whenever You're Ready / Please Ask Her	(Chelle PH 162) 1967

One of several local bands to come out of the Palmetto High School in Miami, Florida. Their adversaries included the Summits, Squires, Travellers, Collegians and Nightwalkers (w/Bobby Caldwell). They entered Criteria Studios in 1966 and under the controls of Steve Kimball (who also oversaw recordings by **The Hustlers** and **Cavemen**) they put down the overtly Merseybeat-styled *Please Ask Her*, notable for some fab harmonies. It was arranged by the **Hustlers'** Bob Leavitt and has been reaired on *Psychedelic States: Florida Vol. 3* (CD). They also recorded an unreleased track called *Frogs Eyeballs*!

Kenny Wynn was later in the New York Square Library. (MW/JLh)

The Novells

Personnel:	BOB ARCHER	ld gtr	A
	ED BENSON	bs	A
	CHIP MOORE	drms	A
	TERRY TIBBETS	keyb'ds	A

ALBUM: 1(A) THAT DID IT! A HAPPENING, INC.
(Mothers Records MRS-73) 1968/9 SC/R1

45:	Almost There/Sunshine Of Your Love	(Mothers 1312) 1968/9

A L.A.-based outfit whose album is at present only a very minor collectable. Seriously arty pop it mixes soft melodies with searing acidic guitar - tracks like *Love* (a **Lee Michaels** cover) owe a heavy debt to the **Vanilla Fudge** school. With covers of *Sitting On The Dock Of The Bay* and Cream's *Sunshine Of Your Love* amongst freshly-scrubbed harmony-pop, this group seemed to be in a quandary - "are we just another pop group or a serious rock band?" The resulting dichotomy won't convince fans of either genre, so the album is disappointing and best described as patchy.

Love has also resurfaced on *Sixties Archive Vol. 8* (CD), *Turds On A Bum Ride, Vol. 1 & 2* (Dble CD) and *Turds On A Bum Ride, Vol. 1* (Dble LP). (VJ/MW/SR)

Len Novy

Personnel:	SAM BROWN	gtr	A
	RALPH CASALE	gtr	A
	PAUL HARRIS	keyb'ds, arrangements	A
	HERB LOVELLE	drms	A
	LEN NOVY	vcls, gtr	A
	CHUCK RAINEY	bs	A
	BYARD RAY	fiddle	A

ALBUM: 1(A) NO EXPLANATIONS   (Atco SD 33-274) 1969

Produced by Arthur Gorson (**Phil Ochs**, **David Blue**) and Jerry Schoenbaum (**Blues Project**), *No Explanations* is the sole album by **Len Novy**. Recorded in New York with some renowned session men, the material comprises covers of **Ars Nova**'s *Round Once Again*, **Eric Andersen**'s *Think About It*, Stevie Wonder's *You're The One For Me* and several originals penned by **Novy** often helped by Bonnie McCullough or Michael Thomas. Although the album suffers from often insipid arrangements by Paul Harris, it does contains three good tracks: *Tucson* (with some tasteful guitar parts), *Shy Ann* and *Rain And Snow* (both with Byard Ray's fiddle). The music is a mix of electrified folk and rock, graced by **Novy**'s distinctive voice. (SR)

Now

Personnel:	RANDY GUZMAN		
	(aka RANDY GORDON)	drms	A

	OLIVER McKINNEY	keyb'ds	A
	FRANK STRAIGHT	ld gtr	A
	DAVID ZANDONATTI	bs, vcls	A

| 45: | I Want/Like A Flying Bird | (Embassy 1968) 1967 |

Previously known as **The Ban**, from Lompoc, California, they changed names when their lead guitarist Tony McGuire was drafted and David Zandonatti came aboard to play bass/vocals. Subsequently the group moved to Los Angeles, signed with Embassy (owned by comic Milton Berle) and changed their name to **The Now**.

Their 45 contains straight pop-rock on *I Want* backed by a pleasant harmony-pop number in a baroque vein that may appeal to fans of **The Left Banke**.

Managed by Randy Guzman's parents, (hence his stage name Gordon), the band were shopped around to all of the L.A. labels and promoters. They'd played great gigs at the Sea Witch and Pandora's Box on the Sunset Strip, building up a stong following and generally playing the same circuit as the **Seeds**, **Strawberry Alarm Clock**, **Yellow Payges** etc... They also moved to San Bernardino East of L.A..

Finally they caught the attention of Matthew Katz in San Francisco. Katz had just lost contractual control of **Jefferson Airplane** and was looking for new groups to bolster his roster. **The Now** moved to San Francisco and were 'given' the name **Tripsichord Music Box**.

Another unconnected group called **Now** put out one 45 - *Deja Vu/Having A Hard Time* (Cotillion 44005). Origins unknown. (MW/GMy)

Now

| Personnel incl?: | ?? RESICO | | A |
| | ?? SELPH | | A |

| 45: | Deja Vu/Having A Hard Time | (Cotillion 44005) 1970 |

An obscure psych-rock group, their single was arranged and produced by Charles Chalmers. Selph and Resico wrote *Deja Vu*. (SR)

Now Generation

| Personnel incl: | JIMMY BUFFETT | vcls | A |

ALBUMS:	1(A)	NOW GENERATION	(Spar Premiere 4803) 1968 -
	2(A)	COME TOGETHER	(Spar 4806) 1969 -
	3(A)	HITS ARE OUR BUSINESS	(Spar 4807) c1970 -

This 'exploito' pop group (five men, two gals) recorded several albums of covers of current hits, generally pop oriented, sometimes with instrumental tracks. Their line-up included a young Jimmy Buffett and, because of this, their albums are becoming sought-after by some collectors. (SR/MMs)

NRBQ

Personnel incl:	TERRY ADAMS	keyb'ds, vcls	A
	STEVE FERGUSON	ld gtr, vcls	A
	FRANKIE GADLER	vcls	A
	JODY ST NICHOLAS	bs, vcls	ALL
	TOM (GT) STANLEY	drms	A
	LEE TIGER	gtr	A
	DON ADAMS		
	AL ANDERSON	gtr, vcls	

ALBUMS:	1	NRBQ	(Columbia CS-9858) 1969 -
(up to	2	BOPPIN' THE BLUES	(Columbia CS-9981) 1970 -
1973)	3	SCRAPS	(Kama Sutra KSBS 2045) 1971 -
	4	ALL HOPPED UP	(Kama Sutra) 1972 -
	5	WORKSHOP	(Kama Sutra KSBS-2065) 1972 -

NB: (2) featuring Carl Perkins. (3) and (4) repackaged in 1976 as a 2-LP set (Annuit Coeptis 1001).

THE NOVELLS - That Did It! A Happening, Inc. LP.

HCP

45s:	Stomp / I Didn't Know Myself	(Columbia 4-44865) 1969 122
(up to	C'mon Everybody / Rocket No. 9	(Columbia 4-44937) 1969 -
1974)	Sure To Fall (In Love With You) / Down In My Heart	(Columbia 4-45019) 1969 -
	α All Mama's Children / Step Aside	(Columbia 4-45107) 1970 -
	α State Of Confusion / My Son, My Sun	(Columbia 4-45132) 1970 -
	α What Every Little Boy Ought To Know / Just As Long	(Columbia 4-45253) 1970 -
	α Me Without You / Red Headed Woman	(Columbia 4-45347) 1971 -
	α Cotton Top / About All I Can Give You Is My Love	(Columbia 4-45466) 1971 -
	Howard Johnson's Got His Mojo Workin' / ?	(Kama Sutra 544) 1971 -
	Magnet / Only You	(Kama Sutra 549) 1972 -
	C'mon If You're Comin' / ?	(Kama Sutra 575) 1973 -
	Get That Gasoline Blues / Mona	(Kama Sutra 586) 1974 70

NB: α Carl Perkins 45s - we're not sure which feature **NRBQ**.

The New Rhythm and Blues Quintet evolved from **The Seven Of Us**, originally a New York-based band who had relocated to Miami in 1966, where they were joined by Adams and Ferguson, from Kentucky outfit **Mersey Beats U.S.A.**. Shortly after adopting their new identity in 1968/9 they returned North to Passaic, New Jersey, finally ending up back in New York City and hitting the big time. **NRBQ** is an interesting good-time bluesy rock band with a quirky sense of humour. Its members were renowned for their musicianship and they had played on many studio sessions as well as short-lived groups before forming the group circa 1969. Their first single *Stomp* was a minor hit in 1969, but they had to wait five years to chart again, when *Get That Gasoline Blues* climbed to No. 70 and spent six weeks in the Top 200 in 1974.

Their second album was recorded with the rock pioneer Carl Perkins and is an interesting (and good humored) attempt at mixing "new" and "old" sounds.

In 1971, they were joined by Al Anderson from the **Wildweeds**.

A kind of cult group on the East Coast, **NRBQ** kept on recording and touring intensively, mainly on the New York area. In 2001, the group still exists, playing live and releasing albums. (SR/MW/JLh/VJ)

The Nuchez's

| Personnel incl: | RICKY ERICKSON | ld gtr | A |

| 45: | Open Up Your Mind/ B.G.'s One Eye | (Rembrandt 818R-5001) 1966 |

A psychedelic masterpiece from a Chicago-based band with a strong Anglophile influence which probably explains why both sides of the 45 were erroneously included on the U.K. compilation *Chocolate Soup For Diabetics*. The 'A' side has some fine organ and frantic guitar-work, the flip is an instrumental.

Ricky Erickson later joined **The Lemon Drops** who also recorded for Rembrandt Records.

Compilation appearances have included: *Open Up Your Mind* (alt version) on *Chicago Garage Band Greats* (CD) and *Chicago Garage Band Greats* (LP); *B.G.'s One Eye* and *Open Up Your Mind* on *The Cicadelic 60's, Vol. 5* (CD); and *Open Up Your Mind* on *Green Crystal Ties, Vol. 9* (CD). (MW)

Nu-Dimension

45:    Another Side/Look Thru Any Window   (Burdette 1) 1967

Often described as 'psych', the 'A' side is actually decent pop with some good keyboard moves, the odd baroque touch and weird effects - all said, an interesting effort by this Pacific Northwest outfit. It's backed by a slightly slowed down version of The Hollies' hit with lotsa echo.

Compilation appearances include *Another Side* on *Northwest Battle Of The Bands, Vol. 2 - Knock You Flat!* (LP & CD). (MW)

Stu Nunnery

ALBUM: 1   STU NUNNERY   (Evolution 3023) 1973 -
NB: (1) also issued in the UK (Crest CREST 6) 1973.

A New York soft-rock singer. His album was recorded with the best local studio musicians including: **Elliott Randall**, **Hugh McCracken**, John Tropea and Paul Griffin. It was also released in the UK, where a 45 was also issued (*Madelaine/Sally From Syracuse* (Mooncrest MOON 17) 1973. (SR)

NAZZ - From Philadelphia LP.

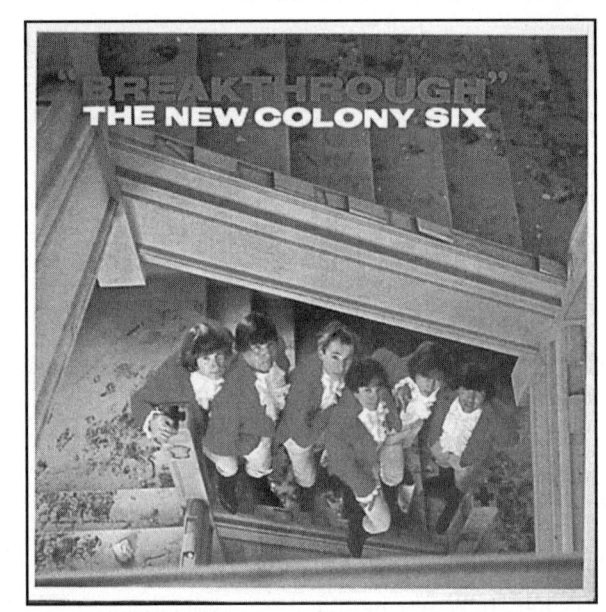

THE NEW COLONY SIX - Breakthrough LP.

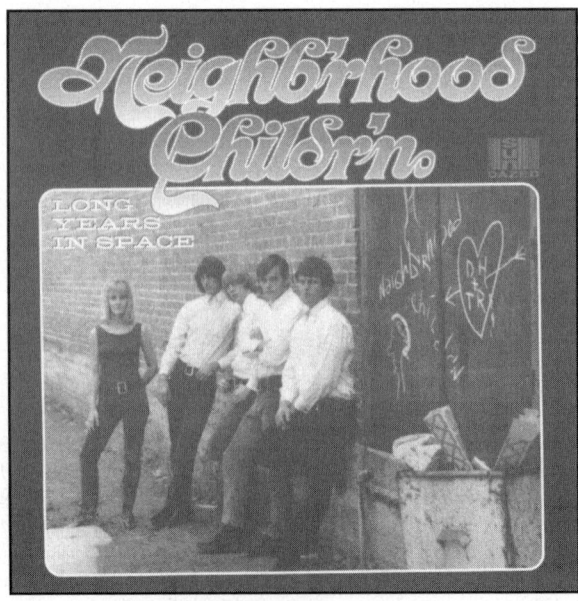

THE NEW COLONY SIX - Revelations LP.

NEIGHB'RHOOD CHILDR'N - Long Years In Space CD.

Oasis

Personnel:	STEPHEN BARNCARD	bs, producer	A
	KELLY BRYAN	bs	A
	SHERRY FOX	vcls	A
	JOEL SIEGEL	vcls, gtr	A
	CARL TASSI	drms	A
	TED TEIPEL	keyb'ds, flute	A
	JOHN YAGER	vcls, gtr	A

ALBUM: 1(A) OASIS (Canada/Cranbus No #) 1973 R3

Although this album was pressed in Canada and lists no home base for the group on the cover, it is known that they were based in Marin County, California. The album, which is pop-rock with male and female vocals, sounds like a cross between Pablo Cruise and later-day **It's A Beautiful Day** - which is defined as "psychedelic" by some record dealers in Europe. The group was previously known as RJ Fox, who saw a double CD issue of their early seventies material issued in Summer 1994: *RJ Fox: Retrospective Dreams* (Black Bamboo).

Sherry Fox was previously in **Cookin Mama** and Stephen Barncard also worked with **Chet Nichols** and **David Crosby**. Kelly Bryan had earlier been in the short-lived **Grootna** and later played on a couple of albums by **Jesse Colin Young**. (CF/SR)

Phil Ochs

HCP

ALBUMS:	1	ALL THE NEWS THAT'S FIT TO SING (Elektra EKS-7269) 1964 - -
	2	I AIN'T MARCHIN' ANYMORE (Elektra EKS-7287) 1965 - -
	3	IN CONCERT (Elektra EKS-7310) 1966 149 -
	4	PLEASURES OF THE HARBOR (A&M 133) 1967 168 -
	5	TAPE FROM CALIFORNIA (A&M SP4148) 1968 - -
	6	REHEARSALS FOR RETIREMENT (A&M 4181) 1969 167 -
	7	GREATEST HITS (A&M SP4253) 1970 194 -
	8	GUNFIGHT AT CARNEGIE HALL (A&M SP 9010) 1971 - SC
	9	CHORDS OF FAME (A&M SP 5611) 1976 - -
	10	A TOAST TO THOSE WHO ARE GONE (Rhino ?) 1986 - -

NB: (6) also released in the U.K. (AMLS 934). (8) only released in Canada and Japan. (9) is a compilation with rare tracks. (10) are early demos, also released in the U.K. (Edsel ED242) 1988

HCP

45s:	Cross My Heart/Flower Lady	(A&M 881) 1967 -
	Miranda/Outside A Small Circle Of Friends	(A&M 891) 1967 118
	Harder They Fall/War Is Over	(A&M 932) 1968 -
	My Life/?	(A&M 1070) 1969 -
	My Kingdom For A Car/ One Way Ticket Home	(A&M 1180) 1970 -
	Gas Station Woman/Kansas City Bomber	(A&M 1376) 1972 -
	Here's To The State Of Richard Nixon/ Power And Glory	(A&M 1509) 1974 -

Born in Texas in 1940, **Ochs** was a journalist student in Ohio before he started singing in the early sixties. He arrived in Greenwich Village in 1962, began writing political folk songs and soon got a contract with Elektra. His first album established him as the first of the singing journalists, with songs about the Bay Of Pigs, the escalation in Vietnam and also an inspired adaptation of Edgar Allan Poe's *The Bells*. **Danny Kalb** (pre-**Blues Project**) played guitar and Bob Gibson helped to write some tunes.

The second album, *I Ain't Marchin Anymore*, was even more political, with *That Was The President* being about the Kennedy Assassination and there are also two anti-war songs (the title track and *Draft Dodger Rag*). Both albums were produced by Paul Rothchild, the future **Doors/Love** producer. After a good live album, with *There But For Fortune* (a later hit for Joan Baez), **Ochs** moved to California and signed with A&M, Larry Marks producing his three next albums.

Pleasures Of The Harbor was his most ambitious project to date and marked an attempt to become a major songwriter/poet in the mould of Dylan. Two tracks are oustanding: the long *The Crucifixion* about Kennedy's Death, with an electronic score arranged by Joseph Byrd (two years before his **United States Of America** project) and *Outside Of A Small Circle Of Friends*, which could have been a hit if it wasn't for the censorship which chopped up the single.

Ochs then teamed up with **Van Dyke Parks** for *Tape From California*. His most successful album notable for the title track and the 13-minute *When In Rome*, a rewritten history of the USA. Ramblin Jack Elliott and Lincoln Mayorga backed him on some tracks.

Ochs then went to Chicago for the Democratic Convention in August 1968. He was involved in the violent riots, even spending a night in jail. He never recovered from this trauma and his next album *Rehearsals For Retirement* showed a gravestone with the inscription: "Phil Ochs (American). Born El Paso, Texas, 1940. Died Chicago, Illinois, 1968". Musically it was very sad and depressing, with songs like *The World Began In Eden But Ended In Los Angeles* and *I Kill Therefore I Am*. Bob Rafkin and Mayorga helped him on this project.

For his next album, **Ochs** bought a gold lamé suit, posed like Elvis Presley and titled the project *Greatest Hits*, with a subtitle: "50 Phil Ochs Fans Can't Be Wrong". Produced by **Van Dyke Parks** it featured a prestigious back-up group: two **Byrds** (Clarence White and Gene Parsons), Ry Cooder, James Burton, Tom Scott and Dick Rosmini. Unfortunately, the album is also one of his weakest, with the heavy arrangements being unsuitable.

The next album *Gunfight At Carnegie Hall* was released only in Canada and Japan and contains two rock medleys of Elvis Presley and Buddy Holly songs. **Phil Ochs** then began traveling to Chile, Australia (where he recorded a single) and Africa, notably Tanzania, Nigeria, South Africa and Kenya, where he recorded a single in Swahili.

Back in the U.S.A. and after a period of depression, he released a final single *Here's To The State Of Richard Nixon/Power And The Glory*. A tormented character, **Phil Ochs** killed himself in 1976.

Two albums with previously unreleased tracks have subsequently been released: the essential double album *Chords Of Fame* with an extensive biography by **Ed Sanders** (of **The Fugs**), and a collection of early demos, *A Toast To Those Who Are Gone*, in 1986.

His brother, Michael Ochs, has founded the 'Michael Ochs Archives', one of the biggest collections of music related items: records, sleeeves, posters etc., and published a marvelous book of photographs of musicians from the 1940s - 1960s called "Rock Archives" (Doubleday, 1984). (SR)

October Country

Personnel:	EDDIE BERAM	drms	A
	CARYLE DE FRANCA	vcls	A

OASIS - Oasis LP.

	JOE DE FRANCA	vcls	A
	MARTY EARLE	gtr	A
	BRUCE WAYNE	gtr	A
	BOB WIAN	keyb'ds	A

ALBUM: 1(A) OCTOBER COUNTRY (Epic BN 26381) 1968 R1

NB: (1) reissued by Quadrant.

45s: October Country/Baby What I Mean (Epic 10252) 1968
Just Don't Know/My Girlfriend Is A Witch (Epic 10320) 1968
Cowboys and Indians/I Wish I Was A Fire (Epic 10373) 1968

A Los Angeles-based six-piece harmony-pop group. *October Country* is a quite delightful piece of orchestrated harmony-pop and showcased Michael Lloyd's talents as a producer and composer. Check it out on *Nuggets, Vol. 3* (LP).

He also worked with the **West Coast Pop Art Experimental Band**, **Smoke**, and as an arranger or producer (or both, often with **Kim Fowley**) with **Fire Escape**, **St. John Green**, **American Revolution**, **A.B. Skhy** and **Grains Of Sand**. He was also a member of Laughing Wind, a band who recorded for Tower and masterminded an album called *Cream Songbook* (GTR 10000) 1969, which was credited to **The Rubber Band**, as well as Cotton, Lloyd and Christian, before becoming an even more successful producer and songwriter. (VJ)

Octopus

Personnel:	LANNY BROOKS	bs, vcls	A
	DION GRODY	keyb'ds, gtr, vcls	A
	CRAIG JUSTIN	drms	A
	TOM MILLER	sax, vcls	A
	(TREVOR KOEHLER	sax	A)

ALBUM: 1(A) OCTOPUS (ESP 2000) 1969 -

NB: (1) has been reissued on CD by ESP.

The New York band's album has blues and jazz leanings. The second side is the strongest containing two long tracks: the unbluesy *U.S. Blues*, an anti-war song with wild vocals and free-jazz sax and the jazzy-psych *Fruk Juice*.

Trevor Koehler was a member of **Insect Trust** and was just an assisting musician with this band playing on two of the album tracks. (VJ/GG)

Oda

Personnel:	KEVIN ODA	drms	A
	RANDY ODA	ld gtr, organ	A
	ART PANTOJA	ld vcls, gtr, congas	A
	KYLE SCHNEIDER	bs	A

ALBUM: 1(A) ODA (Loud LD 80011) 1973 R3

NB: (1) reissued on vinyl (Void 010) 1998 and CD (Hallucinations HCD 01) 2000.

This hard-rock album is now of minor interest to collectors. Randy Oda was later in a late seventies band, Ruby, with Tom Fogerty. This album probably won't be of any interest to fans of garage, psych or 'hippie-rock' but is a very competent hard rock album with some incisive lead guitar work from Randy Oda.

They were based in the San Francisco Bay Area. (VJ)

The Odds and Ends

45s: Be Happy Baby/Cauz, You Don't Love Me (SouthBay 102) 1966
Before You Go (Hey Little Girl) /
Never Learn (Red Bird 10-083) 1967

OCTOPUS - Octopus CD.

This California outfit started out as a Bay Area folk-rock band. *Cauz, You Don't Love Me* was also recorded by **The Tormentors** on their *Hanging 'Round* album, although it's not known who wrote the song. *Be Happy Baby* is a very Stones-influenced effort. *Cauz You Don't Love Me* is a more upbeat folk-punk effort.

Compilation appearances have included: *Cauz, You Don't Love Me* on *Boulders, Vol. 2* (LP) and *Garage Punk Unknowns, Vol. 4* (LP); and *Be Happy Baby* on *Garage Punk Unknowns, Vol. 3* (LP). (VJ/MW)

Kevin Odegard

ALBUM: 1 WOOF (Private Pressing) 1974

A folk-rock singer from Minneapolis. Nothing really interesting. (SR)

Noel Odom and The Group

45: I Can't See Nobody/
Pardon My Complete Objection (Uptown 763) 1969

The 'A' side is indeed a cover of the Bee Gees song, but much less sentimental and thus better to my ears. The 'B' side is really fine: an organ-guided gloomy observation on the dismal sides of life and the uselessness of striving anywhere. Stylish and worth while. (MK)

Odyssey

Personnel:	FRED CALLAN	gtr	A
	VINCENT E. KUSY	keyb'ds	A
	JAY SHARKEY	drms	A
	LOUIS YOVINO	ld vcls	A

ALBUM: 1(A) ...SETTING FORTH..... IMPROVISING AGAINST
THE FUTURE! (Organic) 1971 R4/R5

NB: (1) repressed in 1990 on (Trip T 1000) and on CD by Timothy's Brain (TB 103) 1995.

This is a very rare psychedelic/progressive collectors' item, from a Brentwood, Long Island, New York group and certainly the recent repressing/CD issue is well worth seeking out. The album is of a pretty consistently high standard. There's lots of heavy psychedelic guitar, upfront keyboards and very expressive vocals. The stand-out tracks include *Society's Child*, *Church Yard* and *Angel Dust* (although this last one is partly marred by a rather boring drum solo).

Michael Tschudin's composition *You're Not There*, was a reworked version of a track that appears on **Listening**'s album. Original copies were issued in a plain white cover, some of which were emblazoned with a title sticker reflecting the album title above. Most were in plain covers and this title does not appear on the record label.

Compilation coverage has been limited to: *Churchyard* on *Psychedelic Crown Jewels, Vol. 1* (Dble LP & CD). (VJ/CF/MW)

Odyssey

Personnel incl:	JERRY BERKE?		A
	SYDNEY QUEEQUE?		A

45:	Little Girl, Little Boy/		
	Little Orphan Annie	(White Whale WW-263)	1968

This 45 was reported as **The Turtles** using a pseudonym, however *Fuzz Flaykes & Shakes, Vol. 1* (LP & CD) reveals that the group was not **The Turtles** but comprised of ex-members of L.A. oufits **Just Too Much** and the **Looking Glasses**. The credits - a Media production and *Visions* composer J./Jerry Berke appear to bear this out. Well-spotted, but deduct two brownie points for billing it as *Little Boy, Little Girl.*.

As to the 45, *Little Girl...* is one great pop-punk belter. A driving punchy beat, some great girl put-down lyrics and delivered with a slight snarl and oozing testosterone. The flip is cute and uninspiring by comparison. (MW)

Odyssey

Personnel:	C. MALCOLM	A

45:	California / Jethro (promo only)	(ESP-ODY-1) 1968

Another **Odyssey** - this time a three piece, rumoured to be from California, with a promo-only release on the New York label, so no wonder they get confused with either of the previous oufits. *California* can also be found on *High All The Time, Vol. 2* (LP). (MW)

Oedipus and The Mothers

Personnel incl:	J. BLINDERMAN		A
	DON PASSMAN	ld gtr	A

45:	(I Remember) How It Used To Be/		
	Lonesome	(Beacon 1001)	1967

Came out of Austin, Texas, with this highly thought of 45. You'll find the 'A' side on *Texas Punk From The Sixties* (CD). An interesting psychedelic effort with some good guitar, though it does come across as a little disjointed.

Don Passman was studying law at the University of Texas. When he gave a demo of the band to legendary record producer (and family friend) Snuff Garrett, the producer smiled and said, "Don, go to law school," which is exactly what he did. In fact, he went to Harvard!

The band should not be confused with the **Oedipus and The Mothers** (1963-66), who performed at frat parties at RPI, Cornell, and Albany State, but did not record. (VJ/SR/MW/RMh)

Off-Beats

Personnel incl:	BILL HOPKINS		A
	RICKY SIMON	vcls	A

45:	Tired Of Crying/Tell Me Baby	(Rhythm 100) 1967

Probably unrelated to The Off-Beats on Guyden and Tower, this West Monroe, Louisiana release boasts a moody punker modelled loosely on *Harlem Shuffle*, backed by a bluesy garage ballad. *Tired Of Crying* has subsequently resurfaced on *Psychedelic Crown Jewels Vol. 2* (Dble LP & CD). (MW)

The Offbeats

45s:	I Feel Fine/Crying	(Fairday 1001) c1966
	I Feel Fine/Love...	(Crown Ltd. 106) 196?

Some good ole boys from Birmingham, Alabama run through one of the best swingin' versions of this Beatles song from the era - really classy, especially the nifty lead. Their cover of Roy Orbison's *Crying* is less successful but not bad. (MW)

The Offbeets

Personnel:	DAVID DUFF	gtr	AB
	DENNIS MESSIMER	gtr	A
	JIM ROBINSON	bs	AB
	TOM WYNN	drms	AB
	TOMMY TALTON	gtr	B

45:	α	Double Trouble / I Wanna Do It	( ) April 1964
		Double Trouble / She Lied	(Tropical 109) 1964

NB: α acetate only, as **The Nonchalants**.

From the Orlando / Winter Park area of Florida, **The Offbeets**' manager, Ron Dillman managed to score them their recording sessions, as well as getting them into a 'B' movie - "Daytona Beach Weekend". Their main claim to fame, however, is that they they would later evolve into the seminal **We The People**.

The acetate version of *Double Trouble* and *I Wanna Do It* have subsequently resurfaced on the great Sundazed **We The People** retrospective, *Mirror Of Our Minds*, together with a previously unreleased track, *Drivin' Me Out Of My Mind*.

Like many bands of the era, their destiny was shaped by the Vietnam War - when Dennis Messimer was drafted, Tommy Talton was recruited from The Chessmen. Soon afterwards Jim Robinson got called up and with their band evaporating fast, Ron Dillman organised a jam session with Wayne Proctor and Randy Boyte from **The Trademarks** - who he also managed. Within the week **We The People** had cut their first session and the rest, as they say, is history... (IT)

Off-Set

Personnel:	KENNY BENNETT	drms	A
	DREW GEORGOPOLOUS	gtr, vcls	A
	ELLIOT INGBER	ld vcls	A
	ART STEINMAN	ld gtr, vcls	A
	HARLEY WISHNER	bs	A

ODYSSEY - Setting Forth... CD.

45:	A Change Is Gonna Come/Xanthia (Lisa)	(Jubilee 5542) 1966
	Reflections/Lies I Spoke	(acetate only) 1966
	Stop Feeling Sorry For Yourself/	
	Look in Her Eyes	(acetate only) 196?

This is Brooklyn's **Jagged Edge** who were forced to change their name for this, their second 45. A double-sided gem, *A Change Is Gonna Come* is a chiming folk-rocker with subtle fuzz in the background and momentarily brings to mind **The Dovers**. *Xanthia*, meanwhile, is a glorious Eastern raga-type concoction with mewling guitars, 'sitars' and suitably cool vocals - one for the connoisseur.

Art Steinman recalls - "We were all set to go into the studio with our version of *It Ain't Me Babe* by Dylan, when **The Turtles** released their version. Ours was quite similar to theirs so we scuttled the plans when they beat us to the punch. *A Change Is Gonna Come* was recorded as a substitute. It was a big hit for and written by Sam Cooke, the famous R&B singer, who did such great singles as *Chain Gang*, *Another Saturday Night*, *Cupid* and many others. That's me playing surfer twelve string on the tune and singing harmony. The fuzz is Harley on bass through my Maestro fuzz box, one of the first ever made, I think".

"Drew Georgopolous, second guitar in Jagged Edge to my lead guitar, wrote *Xanthia*. I'm playing the psychedelic slide guitar on my Gretsch Tennessean with a Zippo lighter."

Compilation appearances include: *Xanthia (Lisa)* on *Brain Shadows, Vol. 1* (LP & CD); and an unreleased version of *A Change Is Gonna Come* on *Psychedelic States: New York Vol. 1* (CD). (MW/ASn)

Ofoedian Den

Personnel:	D. AFRICA	flute	A
	G. GAVIN	keyb'ds, vcls	A
	K. MAYER	gtr	A
	M. MENDELSON	bs	A
	P. MILLER	drms, vcls	A
	S. OPPENHEIM	vcls	A
	(Plus Chorus!		A)

ALBUM:	1(A)	THE BIRDS	(Rock Bottom CFS-2151) 1970 R1

A marginal case for inclusion here, as this album is the soundtrack to a college play and includes a large chorus that distracts mightily. Largely, the musical accompaniment is of a jazzy nature and only a couple of tracks tread in either rock or folk territory. This album is very rare, having only been sold at the performances which were staged at the College Of Marin in May 1970. (CF)

Oganookie

Personnel:	TIMMY ACKERMAN	drms	A
	JACK BOWERS	gtr	A
	BRUCE FRY		A
	GEORGE STAVIS	gtr, vcls	A
	BOB STERN	bs, vcls	A

ALBUM:	1(A)	OGANOOKIE	(Oganookie DSW-4154) 1973 SC

Stavis, Ackerman, Stern and Bowers were all previously in **Federal Duck**. A communal hippie-rock band, **Oganookie** was apparentky based in California, as their only album was released in Brookdale, California. It came with an insert and included songs recorded between 1970 and 1973, like *Oganookie Farm Song*, *Your Woman Is Ugly*, *Blues Ain't Nothin' But A Bad Dream* and *Play It Cool*. (SR)

Carl Oglesby

ALBUMS:	1	CARL OGLESBY	(Vanguard VSD-6527) 1969 -
	2	GOING TO DAMASCUS	(Vanguard VSD-6569) 1971 -

Carl Oglesby was initially known as an ex-Weavermen and Pete Seeger sideman. He went solo and released at least two albums. The first is a good psychy folk-rock effort, which is beginning to attract attention amongst collectors. Surprisingly, the lyrics are pseudo-Dylanesque rather than political with nice instrumentation, including guitars, woodwinds and cello. The second is probably in the same style and has a Dave Sheridan comics on its front sleeve plus an insert. (SR)

OFOEDIAN DEN - The Birds LP.

Ognir and The Night People

Personnel:	GINO ANDREUZZI		A
	THOMAS MARUSAK		A
	JOHN McMENAMIN		A
	RICHIE MOLONARO		A
	SKIP NEHRING	ld vcls	A

45s:	I Found A New Love/All My Heart	(Samron 102) 1965
	I Found A New Love/All My Heart	(Warner Bros. 5687) 1965

This 45 was good enough to get picked up by a major label and was a No. 1 hit in the Hazleton area. The band hailed from Hazleton, Pennsylvania and later recorded a further 45 as **The Cartunes**.

Lead singer Richie Molonaro is reputedly some sort of lounge singer now and occasionally still sings *I Found A New Love* live.

Compilation appearances include: *I Found A New Love* on *Open Up Yer Door! Vol. 1* (LP), *Psychedelic Unknowns, Vol. 3* (LP & CD) and *Teenage Shutdown, Vol. 3* (LP & CD). (MW/JWa/MM)

Ohio Express

Personnel:	DOUGAL ASGRASSEL	gtr	A
	TIM CORWIN	drms	A
	DEAN KASTRAN	bs	A
	JOEY LEVINE	vcls	A
	JIM PLAYLER	keyb'ds	A
	DALE POWERS	gtr	A

HCP

ALBUMS:	1(-)	BEG, BORROW AND STEAL	(Cameo 20000) 1968 -
	2(-)	OHIO EXPRESS	(Buddah BDS 5018) 126
	3(-)	SALT WATER TAFFY	(Buddah BDS 5021) 1968 -
	4(-)	CHEWY, CHEWY	(Buddah BDS 5026) 1968 191
	5(-)	MERCY	(Buddah BDS 5037) 1969 -
	6(-)	VERY BEST OF THE OHIO EXPRESS	
			(Buddah BDS 5058) 1969 - -

NB: There is also a Best Of CD available now and two compilations on Collectables: *Super K* Collection (COL-CD-0579) and *Golden Classics* (COL-CD-0535).

HCP

45s:	Beg Borrow And Steal/Maybe	(Cameo 483) 1967 29
	Try It/Soul Struttin'	(Cameo 2001) 1967 83

Yummy Yummy Yummy/Zig Zag	(Buddah 38) 1968	4
Down At Lulu's/She's Not Comin' Home	(Buddah 56) 1968	33
Chewy Chewy/Firebird	(Buddah 70) 1968	15
Sweeter Than Sugar/Bitter Lemon	(Buddah 92) 196?	96
Mercy/Roll It Up	(Buddah 102) 196?	30
Pinch Me (Baby Convince Me)/Peanuts	(Buddah 117) 196?	99
Sausalito (Is The Place To Go)/ Make Love Not War	(Buddah 129) 196?	86
Cowboy Convention/ The Race (That Took Place)	(Buddah 147) 1969	101
Peanuts/Love Equals Love	(Buddah 160) 1970	-

This was one of the number of bubblegum acts put together by producers Jerry Kasenetz and Jeff Katz. From the start this was more of a 'project' rather than a single band. *Beg, Borrow Or Steal* was recorded by **The Rare Breed**. The outfit that first went on the road as **Ohio Express** was another Mansfield, Ohio group Sir Timothy and The Royals, led by Tim Corwin. They were involved in many of the earlier studio recordings and Corwin stayed on through later personnel shifts. Other early tracks were recorded by the **Measles** (who included Joe Walsh and were later known as **Lacewing**), before Levine took control of the project.

They are best remembered for their hits *Yummy, Yummy, Yummy* and *Chewy, Chewy*, which were typical of the bubblegum genre (heavy repetitive bass beat, simple lyrics and nasal vocals), but they also enjoyed several other minor hits. Two of their albums made the Top 200:- *Ohio Express* (which included *Yummy, Yummy, Yummy* climbed to No. 126 and *Chewy, Chewy* peaked at No. 191, but bubblegum music was really aimed at the singles market. Their first seven 45s were sung and written by Joey Levine, who was on Buddah's staff, but Buddy Bengert was lead singer on *Pinch Me* and Graham Gouldman (later of 10cc fame) performed the vocal honours on *Sausalito (Is The Place To Go)*.

On their eponymous second album whilst the studio musicians performed songs like *Yummy Yummy Yummy* and *Down At Lulu's*, they left the rest of the material to the band pictured on the cover. Tucked away on this album are some very pleasant surprises. For fans of pop-psych with beautiful harmony vocals, *She's Not Coming Home* is simply exquisite and the breezy pop of *Winter Skies* may appeal too. *Into This Time* has a great psychedelic guitar ending, *First Grade Reader* showcases a harsher side to their music - it also features some fine guitar work. *Turn To Straw* is a superb slice of psychedelia and the jewel in the crown is garage-popster *The Time You Spent With Me*, which contains some great psychedelic guitar passages.

Compilation appearances have included:- *Chewy, Chewy* and *Firebird* on *Pop Explosion* (Buddah 643 312) 1968 (LP); *Yummy, Yummy, Yummy*, *Down At Lulu's*, and *Chewy, Chewy* on *Bubble Gum Music Is... The Naked Truth* (LP); and *First Grade Reader* on *Turds On A Bum Ride, Vol. 1 & 2* (Dble CD) and *Turds On A Bum Ride, Vol. 2* (Dble LP).

Do check out some of their albums - you'll be pleasantly surprised. (VJ/MW/MM)

Ohio Knox

Personnel:	PETER GALLWAY	vcls, gtr	A
	PAUL HARRIS	keyb'ds	A
	RAY NEOPOLITAN	bs	A
	DALLAS TAYLOR	drms	A
	(LYNN BLESSING	vibes	A)
	(RUSS KUNKEL	perc	A)
	(JOHN SEBASTIAN	gtr, hrmnca	A)
	(DANNY WEIS	gtr	A)

ALBUM: 1(A) OHIO KNOX (Reprise RS 6435) 1971 - -
NB: (1) also released in the U.K. (Reprise RSLP 6435).

Led by Peter Gallway, the former **Fifth Avenue Band** leader, **Ohio Knox** was a lightweight **Lovin' Spoonful**-like group. To reinforce this impression, **John Sebastian** played guitar and harmonica on several tracks.

Danny Weis (ex-**Iron Butterfly**) plays guitar on one of the best tracks, *Baby Sox Knox*.

PSYCHEDELIC UNKNOWNS Vol. 3 (Comp CD) including Ognir and The Night People.

Paul Harris was a very active session man, Ray Neopolitan played in studio with the **Doors** and Dallas Taylor was previously with **Clearlight** and Crosby, Stills and Nash. Pete Gallway has recently released a solo album, *Redemption* (Gadfly 255). (SR/FH)

Oho

Personnel:	STEVEN MICHAEL HECK	A
	MARK O'CONNOR	A
	JOSEPH O'SULLIVAN	A
	(JAY GRABOSKI	A)
	(RAYMOND INDIANA	A)

ALBUM: 1(A) OKINAWA (NR 4579) 1975 R1
NB: (1) reissued in Germany on Little Wing (LW 3044) in 1995.

A really weird psychotic local Baltimore, Maryland progressive band who released a truly demented album in 1974. There's some clear **Zappa** influence here and a very free-form approach. Certainly not for everyone, but if you like highly experimental music, this could be for you. The album's quite a collectors' item and Greg Shaw listed it in his Top 10 "Acid Punk" review in one of the Bomp issues of 1978 or 1979. The reissue contains all sixteen tracks from the original plus another fifteen the group had recorded in the same sessions. The reissue consisted of four 10" albums in a can (like the old metal boxes for films).

Later **Oho** became a more disciplined progressive band in 1975-76. Their never released *Vitamin Oho* album was finally put out in 1992 by Little Wing (LW 3023).

Most, or all, of the members of **Oho** later released at least one album as The Dark Side, *Rumours In Our Own Time, Legends In Our Own Room* (Gohog Records) 1980. It's quite a good album, much more in the "punk" or new wave style of the time, but still recognisably strange and weird enough to be quite interesting. The original band line-up has a non-album cut on *The Best Of Baltimore's Buried* compilation. (VJ/ESn/BK)

Okiextremist Moon Dog

ALBUM: 1 OKIEXTREMIST MOON DOG (Private Pressing) c1976 SC
NB: Other albums exist.

From Oklahoma, a group of "Okies" doing rural-rock influenced by the **Grateful Dead**. (SR)

Old Hickory and The Pirate

Personnel incl:	ASHISH KHAN	sitar	A
	MICHAEL MATHIS		A
	ED VILLAREAL		A

ALBUM:	1	FEATURING MICHAEL MATHIS AND WHITE LIGHTENING	(Hakim HR 1001) 1977 R1

From California, Michael Mathis (born 1948) was the son of Bud Mathis, a boxer-turned-music-entrepreneur based on the Sunset Strip in the sixties. Bud managed several groups including the **Brain Train**, the **Joint Effort** and the **Fairviews**. Michael started singing with his brother Mark and recorded a 45 on the Blue River label in 1962. A voice change ruined his hopes of teen career and he had to wait until 1977 to release an album. Produced by his Dad, *Old Hickory And The Pirate* is in fact a very patchy compilation of songs recorded over a twelve year period. It includes some sixties pop songs recorded by **Paul Buff** at Original Sound Studios and a version of *Discomboomber* also recorded by the **Fairviews**. The real highlights of the album are a superb track *The Third Eye*, which approaches Merrell Fankhauser's best moments, and two excellent sitar psych cuts with Ashish Khan (of **Shanti**). The overall result is extremely interesting, but the album is very hard to find. (SR)

Olivers

Personnel incl:	MIKE MANKEY	A

45s:	Beeker Street/I Saw What You Did	(Phalanx 1022) 1966
	Beeker Street/I Saw What You Did	(RCA-Victor 47-9113) 1967
α	I Saw What You Did/?	( ) 1967

NB: α as **Madson**.

This Indiana outfit has received much compilation coverage with *Beeker Street* included on *The Psychedelic Sixties, Vol. 1* (LP) and the flip side appearing on *Michigan Mayhem Vol. 1* (CD), *Garage Music For Psych Heads, Vol. 1*, *Mind Blowers* (LP), *Sixties Choice, Vol. 1* (LP) and *60's Choice Collection Vol's 1 & 2* (CD). The flip's a typical garage effort with some catchy organ and guitar work. A second recording, *I Saw What You Did*, under the name **Madson**, was also cut in Chicago and this can be heard on the *Gone, Vol. 1* compilation - ha, but wait. *I Saw What You Did*, also appears on *The Cicadelic 60's, Vol. 2* (LP) though erroneously credited (on the LP sleeve only) to The Nomads - a bit of a mix-up, i.e. if you mix-up the letters of **Madson** you get Nomads - is this a private joke by *Gone, Vol. 1* compiler? No one seems to have heard of a **Madson** 45. (VJ/MW)

Dennis Olivieri

Personnel:	RONNIE BROWN	bs	A
	JACK ELLIOTT	gtr	A
	EDDIE GREENE	drms, perc	A
	DENNIS OLIVIERI	piano, vcls	A
	TOMMY SCOTT	sax	A
	TANDYN ALMER	rocksichord, Thomas Celebrity Organ, autoharp	
	JACK MARGOLIS	vcls	

ALBUM:	1(A)	COME TO THE PARTY	(VMC VS 130) 1969 -
45:		Sad Song #1/Come To The Party	(VMC V 733) 1969

On the short-lived Californian label which also released **David** and **Pacific Ocean**, *Come To The Party* can only be described as "extremely strange". Housed in a weird collage cover showing **Olivieri** naked and showing the palms of his hand full of people, surrounded by strange colors, it's a kind of concept album with the sides titled "Before" and "After".

Produced by **Tandyn Almer** (the man also behind **Paper Fortress**), the music is extremely messy, with loads of keyboards, percussion and bass with almost no melody. It provides a rather appropriate background to the hallucinated lyrics and vocals of **Olivieri**, who sounds sincere in what he sings, even if it's completely absurd or banal. *Fuzzy Soft Thing*, *I Cry In The Morning*, *Yesterday Was Nuthin' Like Today* and *Lady Fair* are some examples of this weird production. (SR)

Ol' Paint

ALBUM:	1	OL' PAINT	(GWP) 1971 -
45:		I Am A Natural Man/?	(GWP 526) 1970

Possibly from California, an obscure melodic rock group on the same label as **Sarofeen and Smoke**. (SR)

Hans Olson

Personnel:	DICK FURLOW	bs	A
	JIM HAAPALA	drms, vcls	A
	PLATO JONES	perc, vcls	A
	BOB MEIGHAN	vcls	A
	HANS OLSON	vcls, gtr, hrmnca	A

ALBUM:	1(A)	WESTERN WINDS	(Joplin Records 3266) 1973 R1

NB: (1) reissued on vinyl (Marshall Records 10320) 1980.

Based in Tempe, Arizona, **Olson** released three fine albums in the seventies. The above is probably his finest work and it sold well enough locally to warrant a repressing in 1980. Other releases include *The Blonde Sun Album* (1976 live recordings, issued in 1977 in a stunning Rick Griffin-style cover), *Hans Olson Sings The Blues* (studio recordings, issued in 1980), and *The Aspen Tapes* (a 7" EP recorded in 1981 with such luminaries as Albert Lee, Mark Naftalin, **Al Kooper** and Linda Tillery). Each album contains a mixture of electric and acoustic blues-based material, comparable perhaps to Bill Homans' **Merry Airbrakes**, although **Olson**'s material is decidely more topical.

Olson continues to perform and release CD's in Arizona, and makes trips regularly to Europe where his uniquely American folk style has found favour. (CF)

Omegas

Personnel incl:	JOE TRIPLETT	vcls	A

45:	I Can't Believe / Mr. Yates	(United Artists 50247) 1968

Triplett was formerly vocalist for **The Reekers**, who became the **Hangmen** after his departure. On this 45, written and produced by **Reekers/Hangmen** founder Tom Guernsey, he's backed by female vocal group the Jewels.

HANS OLSON - Western Winds LP.

I'M TRIPPIN' ALONE (Comp LP) including Omegas.

I Can't Believe, a punchy fuzz-popper which hit the local top ten, can be heard on *I'm Trippin' Alone* (LP).

Guernsey also produced a 45 by **The Piece Kor** in 1968. He was back performing with his brother John in the early seventies in a band called Claude Jones. (MW/BE)

The Omen

45:	Once Upon A Taste/		
	Melancholy Moonlight Minded Dreamer	(Ascot 2227)	1967

From Lake Mahopac, New York. The 'A' side, which is a superb slice of psychedelia, has resurfaced on *30 Seconds Before The Calico Wall* (CD). (MM/MW)

The Omen and Their Luv

45:	Maybe Later / Need Some Sunshine	(Daisy no #)	1967

A Tuscaloosa, Alabama, group whose 45 is sought-after. Why? Well, check out *Maybe Later*, composed by Tommy Stewart, and give it a few spins. On the surface it's a cool, almost-catchy fuzzy pop-punker; what makes it stand out is an expressive and versatile vocalist plus some creative and seemingly off-the-cuff guitarwork. It is a fitting finale on *Psychedelic States: Alabama Vol. 1* (CD). (MW)

The Omens

Personnel:	GENE COOPER	ld gtr	AB
	TIM JONES	drms	AB
	DUANE O'DONNELL	organ	A
	DON REVERCOMB	vcls, gtr	AB
	BRAD RUSSEL	bs	AB
	AL PATKA	organ	B
	(CAROL BUEHLER	vcls	AB)

45s:	Searching/Girl Get Away	(Cody 007)	1965
α	Searching / As Tears Go By	(Cody # unkn)	1965

NB: α 'B' side by **Carol with The Omens**.

From Hammond, Indiana, a suburb of Chicago. This band anthemic garage 45 is well worth 'searching' out... Duane O'Donnell:- "The 45 was recorded in the Summer of 1965, I remember playing a lot of gigs, but can't remember making any money. In retrospect, however, it was tremendous fun."

Compilation appearances include: *Searching* on *Off The Wall, Vol. 2* (LP), *Pebbles Vol. 6* (CD), *The Essential Pebbles Collection, Vol. 1* (Dble CD), *Trash Box* (5-CD), *Best of Pebbles, Vol. 2* (LP & CD) and *Highs In The Mid-Sixties Vol. 4* (LP); and *Girl Get Away* on *Sixties Rebellion, Vol. 7* (LP & CD).

Duane:- "I was 15 years old when I joined **The Omens** in 1964. Carol Buehler was the girlfriend and later wife of Don Revercomb who wrote and sang *Searching*; they were married when Don was 16 and Carol had just turned 15. She sang only one song, *As Tears Go By*, at our gigs. We recorded the three songs one Saturday in East Chicago, Indiana in a tiny apartment onto an Ampex reel to reel. Two 45's were cut, with *Searching* being the 'A' side on both. My only copy of the 45 had *Tears* on the 'B' side. I gave the 45 as a birthday present to Al Patka, who played organ with **The Omens** after I had to quit in the Summer of 65."

"The sixties were a great time to be in a rock & roll band. I still gig occassionaly, and it's still just as much fun".

As to the other **Omen** members "I have no idea... I saw the drummer, Tim Jones, at a muffler shop in 1990, the day before leaving for the West Coast". Come 2002, Duane works for the Sacramento County Environmental Management Department regulating the operation of underground fuel storage tanks. His oldest son has got the rock & roll bug, playing bass with a group from Santa Cruz named A Burning Water, who are doing the California college circuit and about to release their first CD. (MW/DOI)

Omnibus

Personnel:	J. POLT	A
	A. RAIMONDI	A
	R. WEGRZYN	A

ALBUM:	1(A)	OMNIBUS	(United Artists UAS 6743)	1970 SC

NB: (1) was pirated in 1996.

45:	It's All In Your Heart /		
	Man Song	(United Artists 50631)	1970

This trio hailed from Boston. The album, which was recorded in New York and produced by Steve and Eric Nathanson (who were the producers of **Boffalongo**), has recently been pirated. All the songs on the album were written by R. Wegrzyn. It's really pretty mediocre, the most psychedelic thing about it being the cover. (VJ/MW)

Om Shanti

ALBUM:	1	WE ARE HOME	(Solace SSR-1001)	c1973 ?

A psychy hippie-folk male/female duo from Houston, their rare album includes tracks like *Namrie*, *Jellyfish*, *Om Mani Padme Hum*, *Another Step* and *Om Shanti Triad*. It was recorded with 6 and 12-string guitar, tablas, autoharp and mandolin. (SR)

Oncomers

Personnel:	BILLY CAPRANICA	bs	A
	JACK O'NEILL	drms	A
	WAYNE SCHILLINGER	gtr	A

45:	Every Day Now /		
	You Let Me Down	(Gateway Custom 45-G-103)	c1965

From McKeesport, Pennsylvania, this band formed around 1962 and lasted until early 1965 after which they became known as Grant Street Exit.

In 1968, O'Neill joined Soul Congress, who would relocate to Detroit. This band featured vocalist Billy Sha-Ray from Uniontown Pennsylvania., and two former **Arondies** - Jim Pavlack (guitar) and Gary Pittman (bass).

O'Neill revived **The Oncomers** circa 1997 as Splash and did a few local (McKeesport area) club shows.

Compilation appearances include: *You Let Me Down* on *Love Is A Sad Song, Vol. 1* (LP) and miscredited to **The Shieks** on *Thee Unheard Of* (LP). (BSj/MW)

One

Personnel:
MARK BAKER	drms	A
REALITY D. BLIPCROTCH	vcls, perc	A
ROGER CRISSINGER	keyb'ds	A
DONALD ENSSLIN	gtr, banjo	A
FRANK TREVOR FEE	bs	A
MARV GRANAT	gtr, sitar, dulcimer	A
SARAH OPPENHEIM	vcls, autoharp	A
LAURIE PAUL	vcls, tampura	A
THEODORE TEIPEL	flute, hrmnca, piano	A

ALBUM: 1(A) ONE (Grunt FTR 1008) 1972 -

45: Free Rain / One Of A Kind (PS) (Grunt 0509) 1972

This album is rather naive, but a precious document of the hippie community, mixing jazz with country and western, Eastern and renaissance sounds.

Roger Crissinger had earlier been in **Pearls Before Swine**; Sarah Oppenheim with **Ofoedian Den**. (VJ/SR/MW)

One Eyed Jacks

Personnel incl:
B. FASMAN		
G. HARVEY		
W. SCHNEIDER		
MICHAEL MURPHY		X

45s:
Die Today/ Somewhere They Can Find Me	(Lake Side 1981)	1967
Sun So High/Love	(White Cliffs 265)	1967
α Another Lonely Day / Get Yourself Ready	(Bang 548)	1967
California's Callin'/ Together We're In Love	(Roulette 7025)	1968
Sky Of My Mind/Gettin' In The Groove	(Roulette 7035)	1969

NB: α as **Dave Armstrong and One Eyed Jacks**.

They may have originated in Florida but became based in Champaign, Illinois and later evolved into **Fat Water**. *Love*, which was released on a Louisiana label, features some rather discordant psychedelic guitar work and good vocals (and a rarity - enhancing sax!).

GARAGE ZONE Vol. 2 (Comp LP) including One Eyed Jacks.

Michael Murphy, who played on the last Roulette release went on REO Speedwagon.

Compilation appearances include: *Love* on *Ya Gotta Have Moxie, Vol. 2* (Dble CD), *Garage Zone, Vol. 2* (LP) and *The Garage Zone Box Set* (4-LP). (MW/GM)

One Man's Family

Personnel:
JOHN BELAND	gtr, vcls	A
KENNY HODGES	bs, vcls	A
THAD MAXWELL	drms	A
NIGEL PICKERING	gtr, vcls	A
SUE RICHARDS	vcls	A

One Man's Family originated from guitarist Nigel Pickering and bassist Kenny Hodges, members of **Spanky and Our Gang** who were seeking to work together in a similar line-up after Spanky had left to go solo in 1969. John Beland (ex-Wheatstraw), auditioned and got the job as guitarist, vocalist. Also brought in was vocalist Sue Richards and Thad Maxwell as the band's drummer, fresh from a stint with the A&M band **Tarantula** with whom he had played guitar. Although no tapes of **One Man's Family** exist the group mixed five-part harmonies singing a blend of pop and country as an early country-rock outfit. Their arrangement of *When Will I Be Loved* inspired Linda Ronstadt's version.

One Man's Family toured with **The Byrds**, Hollies and **Steppenwolf** and had received rave reviews. While touring with the comedy troupe 2nd City and hanging out with John Prine and Steve Goodman they split mid-tour in Chicago. After the band split up, Thad Maxwell and John Beland returned to L.A, where in December 1969 Beland was hired by Linda Ronstadt to help replace her backing group The Corvettes. Beland merged forces with three quarters of The Reasons, Eric White on bass, Gib Guilbeau on fiddle, vocals and guitar, and Stan Pratt on drums. This outfit became Swampwater and in early 1970 Eric White became their road manager with Thad Maxwell joining to play bass. They recorded their debut album in 1970 and followed with a second in 1971. After backing Ronstadt for a year and a half they backed **Arlo Guthrie** before folding in 1972 while recording their third album.

Nigel Pickering reunited with Spanky McFarlane for a 1975 **Spanky And Our Gang** album. Eric White had worked with The Kentucky Colonels in the sixties with brothers Roland and Clarence White, including their 1973 European reunion tour. Gib Guilbeau and John Beland worked as backing musicians for a variety of pop and country artists, both recorded solo albums in the 1970's and teamed up in The Flying Burrito Brothers, Sierra and The Burrito Brothers. Beland currently leads the Flying Burrito Brothers. (JO/JBd)

One Mile Ahead

Personnel incl?: ALBERT A. SIMBALLA   A

45: There Ain't No Use In Crying / Contribution (Santiago 2633) c1968

Both sides of this Elkton, Virginia band's 45 were written by Albert A. Simballa and produced by Jim Gallegos. *There Ain't...* is a strong Cream-like rocker with generous doses of fuzz and flowing wah-wah passages. The flip is restrained pop-rock until the final minute or so when it disintegrates into a free-form guitar freakout. (MW)

The Oneness Space

Personnel incl: MARK ALLEN   A

ALBUM: 1 THE ONENESS SPACE (Living Love) 1975 -

The offering of a hippie community with Mark Allen. Housed in a stunning gatefold cover, it mainly contains psych-folk tracks. (SR)

ONE ST. STEPHEN - One St. Stephen CD.

One of Hours

Personnel incl:	BOGLIOLE
	FLYNN
	FOREMAN
	WILLCUTT

45s:	It's Best/Trifolia	(Chetwyd CW-45001) 1967
	Psychedelic Illusion/Feel The Pain	(Chetwyd CW-45005) 1967

This band came from the Lexington area of Kentucky. Their first 45 sounded very **Byrds**-influenced. The 'A' side to the second was excellent chiming soft psychedelia, whilst the flip was guitar-laden pop-punk.

Trifolia can be heard on *I Can Hear Raindrops* (LP), a compilation of vulnerable and frail 'loser' garage-ballads. *Psychedelic Illusion*, a coy garagey hippie-psych ditty that brings to mind the **Venus Flytraps**' *Have You Ever*, is on *Psychedelic Experience, Vol. 3* (CD). (MW)

The Ones

Personnel:	JEFF COSTELLO	gtr	AB
	RICK McPHERSON	vcls	AB
	MARIS NEIBURGERS	bs	AB
	BOB SHEARER	vcls	A
	DICKIE STAMM	drms	AB
	SAM DeSANTOS	vcls, keyb'ds	B

ALBUM:	1(A)	THE ONES	(Ashwood House AH-1105) 1966 R3

This group originated in Unionville, Connecticut, and worked extensively in the Lake George/Albany NY, region, before taking up residence in Boston. They became known as one of the hottest outfits to come out of the city in the era, but success eluded them probably because they concentrated on cover songs rather than originals. Their album, nonetheless, is now a significant collectors' item and hasn't yet been reissued. For a taster of how they sounded you can find *Didi-Wa-Didi* on *Pebbles, Vol. 13* (LP), *Mister You're A Better Man Than I* on *Oil Stains* (LP), and *I Can't Explain* on *Psychotic Reactions* (LP).

The album was recorded in NYC, and included one original, *Maybe It's Both Of Us*, written by the producer Clay Pitts. After its release, Sam DeSantos was recruited from **Missing Links**, who the band had met previously when working in Salisbury Beach, MA.

Jeff Costello:- "**The Ones** broke up in 1968. Jon Landau, who later became Bruce Springsteen's manager, reviewed our group in Crawdaddy, saying we were a "competent, soulful club band but not originaters." It was true."

Sam DeSantos and Rick McPherson later formed Atlantis in 1970 with legendary producer Bobby Herne. (MW/AH/JC)

One St. Stephen

Personnel:	BILL BLECHSCHMID	A
	TERRY FINNERAN	A
	DANNY LAWSON	A
	DAVID PIERCE	A
	FRANKLIN REYNOLDS	A
	BRUCE ROBERTS	A
	CHARLES SQUIRES	A

ALBUM:	1(A)	ONE ST. STEPHEN	(No label) 1975 R3/R4

NB: (1) counterfeited in 1988 also issued on CD (Mind's Eye Records MER 32-175) 199?.

A mellow rock album, with vocals reminiscent of **The Doors**' Jim Morrison. They came from Ohio. **One St. Stephen** have however sometimes been confused with **St. Steven**, mainly due to incorrect sleeve notes on the *Filling The Gap* compilation. In fact the two tracks featured on this compilation were recorded by **Front Page Review**, prior to Steve Cataldo having a short stint in **Ultimate Spinach**. Subsequently the **One St. Stephen** reissues have also included these bonus tracks due to an incorrect assumption that the two artists were the same.

One Way Street

Personnel incl:	DOUG FAIRBAIRN	gtr	A
	BOB HIRTLE	keyb'ds	A
	GREG JOHNSTONE	bs	A
	RICK WANZELL	vcls	A
	JIM WARREN	drms	A

45s:	α	Listen To Me/Tears	(VanTown VT 101) 1966
	β	I See The Light/Tears In My Eyes	(Paula 281) 1967

NB: β features the same recordings as α, but with the track titles renamed.

Although this band were from Vancouver, Canada, we're including them here to help avoid confusion with a different Louisiana act who issued a 45 on Apollo and two on Smash. This **One Way Street** only recorded one 45, which was originally issued on Tom Peacock's VanTown label and subsequently licensed to the U.S. Paula label, who reissued it with different track titles.

Presumably because of the Paula release, people have assumed that the band came from Louisiana and indeed you can find both tracks on Eva's *Louisiana Punk Groups From The Sixties, Vol. 2* (LP) and its CD equivalent *Sixties Archive Vol. 3*. In addition, *I See The Light* has resurfaced on *Psychedelic Unknowns, Vol. 7* (LP & CD) and *Of Hopes And Dreams & Tombstones* (LP); *Tears In My Eyes* on *Psychedelic Unknowns, Vol. 9* (CD), whilst *The History Of Vancouver Rock & Roll, Vol. 4* includes both tracks taken from the master tapes, with liner notes from band member Doug Fairbairn. (GGI/MW)

One Way Street

45s:	Yard Dog/Girls Girls	(Apollo) c1966
	Yard Dog/Girls Girls	(Smash 2155) 1967
	If You're Looking For A Fool/ What's Your Name	(Smash 2187) 1967

A Louisiana garage group. A local hit, *Yard Dog* was written by Miller Evan and was re-released by Smash. The group disappeared after his second 45. (SR)

The One-Way Street

Personnel incl:	J.E. CHEANEY	A
	D.L. GRAHAM	A

45s:	I Know, I Love/With Love Untrue	(Deeek DK-101) 1967
	Illusions/Never End	(Deeek DK-102) 1967
	Joy And Sorrow/Falsely Presented Society	(Deeek DK-103) 1968

From Pharr, near McAllen, Texas. *Joy And Sorrow* is catchy and notable for upfront drumming. The second 45 is also noteworthy - *Illusions* is an insistent fuzzy garage-popper and *Never End* is a silky garage-ballad with sweet harmonies.

Compilation appearances include: *Joe And Sorrow* on *Texas Flashbacks, Vol. 2* (LP & CD), *Texas Flashback (The Best Of)* (CD) and *Flashback, Vol. 2* (LP). (VJ/AB/MW)

One-Way Street Band

45: Energy / Time Of Temptation (Romain 1011) 1967

From Philadelphia, this band were previously known as **The Nomads**. (MW)

The One Way Streets

45: Jack The Ripper/We All Love Peanut Butter (Sunrise 103) 1966

This was recorded by an Ohio teen quartet at the Sunrise Studios in Hamilton in the Summer of 1966. Although they credited *Jack The Ripper* to themselves it was actually a Screaming Lord Sutch composition. Their version is a pretty demented teen thrash although the flip is eminently forgettable.

Compilation appearances have included: *We All Love Peanut Butter* and *Jack The Ripper* on *Back From The Grave, Vol. 1* (LP) and *Garage Kings* (Dble LP). (VJ)

Only Ones

Personnel incl: LARRY CALDER A

45: Find A Way/You're The Reason (Panik 5112) 1965/6

Both sides of this Detroit 45 are excellent examples of Merseybeat-styled garage. *You're The Reason* is to be found on the Eva *Sixties Archive, Vol. 7* (CD). (MW)

On The Seventh Day

ALBUM: 1 ON THE SEVENTH DAY (Mercury SR-61248) 1970 -

This was a concept album rather than a band. It was written and produced by Alan Bernstein and Victor Millrose in New York. Leroy Glover was the arranger and conductor. There's a note on the album sleeve which says:- "It took God six days to create a perfect world. On the seventh day he rested. That was a big mistake for on the seventh day we took over." The album begins with a narrator reading these sentences and then gives way to a collage of sounds/documents and musical "Hair" - like songs. The bombing of Hiroshima, political speeches, black activists, civil rights, the Vietnam War, Chicago and Paris 1968 riots - all are mixed.

The album was released in two different sleeves (like the **Asylum Choir** Mercury album). The first has two naked kids (a boy and a girl). This controversial cover was immediately withdrawn and replaced with a tree cover, which is much more common. (VJ/GG)

Onyx

ALBUM: 1 FEATURING WILDWOOD (Private Pressing) 1974 ?

Housed in a black and white charcoal sleeve, a private pressing with a cover of **The Doors'** *Roadhouse Blues* and good guitars, between psych and Southern rock. (SR)

MICHAEL OOSTEN - Michael Oosten LP.

Michael Oosten

Personnel:	ALGIS BYLA	bs	A
	TOM HENNICK	keyb'ds	A
	MICHAEL OOSTEN	gtr, vcls	A
	JAN REEK	vcls	A

ALBUM: 1(A) MICHAEL OOSTEN (Hub City Music KS 5191) 1974 R2

NB: (1) reissued officially on CD (Gear Fab GF-132) 1999 and on vinyl (Gear Fab Comet GFC 411) 2001.

An excellent local Wisconsin electric folk album in a stunning silk-screened cover. (CF)

Operations

45: Reincarnation/
The Ever Gentle Presence (Of Your Love) (Chance 1301) 1968

From Cincinnati, Ohio. You'll also find *Reincarnation* on *Punk Classics, Vol. 3* (7") and the equivalent *Punk Classics* (CD). (MW/GGl)

The Opposite Six

Personnel:	JACK ANDROVICH	drms	A
	ED DUNK	ld vcls	A
	HAL HANEFIELD	gtr	A
	BRENT MACINTOSH	bs	A
	LARRY McGLADE	ld gtr	A
	DON WRIGHT	gtr	A

45: I'll Be Gone/Why Did You Lie? (Spectra 119/120) 1966

Teen punk from Sacramento, recorded at Bill Rase's studio. Leader Wright later had a release as **Don Wright and The Head Set**.

Compilation appearances have included: *I'll Be Gone* on *Off The Wall, Vol. 1* (LP), *The Sound Of Young Sacramento* (CD) and *Teenage Shutdown, Vol. 4* (LP & CD). (MW)

The Opposite Six

45: Church Key(Part 68)/Continental Surf (South Shore 721) 1964

Thought to be a different **Opposite Six**, and sometimes put down as from San Luis Obispo, California. *Church Key (Part 68)* can also be found on *Scum Of The Earth* (Dble CD), *Scum Of The Earth, Vol. 1* (LP). (MW)

The Opposite Six

Personnel:	RON ARNSMEYER	sax	A
	TIM CAIN	sax	A
	BILL CHAMPLIN	organ	A
	DON IRVING	gtr	A
	ROB MOITOZA	bs	A
	DICK ROGERS	drms	A

45: All Night Long / Come Straight Home (Dot 16700) 1965

From Marin County, this R&B act regrouped as the **Sons Of Champlin** at the end of 1965. Irving later played in **The Beau Brummels**. (MW)

Opus IV

Personnel incl:	BILL GUNION	drms	A

45s: α Give Me A Chance/When We're Apart (Process 146) 1965
Mess Around/About Her (MGM K 13731) 1967

NB: α credited to Epiks.

From Steubenville, Ohio and previously known as the Epiks. *Mess Around*, featured on *Victims Of Circumstances, Vol. 1* (LP), is a party-dance popper, like a hybrid of *Shake* and *Land Of 1,000 Dances*. The vocalist has a strange drawl to his voice and on the slow ballad flip with Animals - style keyboards, he sounds strangely slurred in his attempts to do a Scott Walker deep 'n' moody style. (MW/DMr)

Opus 1

Personnel:	CHRIS CHRISTENSEN	drums, vcls	A
	BRIAN DECKER	ld gtr, vcls	A
	DOUG DECKER	bs, vcls	A
	PETE PARKER	organ, vcls	A

45: Back Seat '38 Dodge/In My Mind (Mustang 3017) 1966

A young quartet from Long Beach, California were playing teen clubs like The Cinnamon Cinder, city and radio-sponsored youth dances, and the occasional bar gig (even though they were all under age). At one such bar, The Brass Lantern, they were plied with drinks early in the evening... by the end of the night they'd all switched instruments!

In March 1966 they presented themselves at Del-Fi's Hollywood studios. They'd already recorded a session at Western Recorders with the famed producer/engineer Bones Howe (**Association**, **Turtles**, **Mamas and Papas**) which yielded two tracks - *In My Mind* and the never-to-be-released *Birds Of Passage*. Del-Fi liked what they heard and laid on a day's recording session.

During one of the breaks, discussions came around to the controversy surrounding a sculpture by L.A.-based avant-gardist Ed Kienholz which was being shown at the Los Angeles County Art Museum. Entitled "Back Seat '38 Dodge", this was a '38 Dodge car, cut in half, with beercans on the floor and two pairs of leg sticking out from the backseat - one pair of feet pointing up, the other down! Seems it was all too much for moralists, who thought it depicted what was wrong with teens at the time. Newspaper editorials abounded and it was declared obscene by the Museum board, but it remained on show ... with the car's doors closed!

With this in mind, they took one of the group's songs called *Why Did I Lie* (also known as *Song*), changed the lyrics ("what goes on in the back seat? I really wanna know"!) and tweaked the arrangement. Paired with the already-completed *In My Mind*, a dynamic upbeat pop-punker, *Back Seat 38 Dodge* was released on Mustang in April. It's a hyrid of throttling hot-rod and garage, a pulsating punker with crashing chords - check it out on *Highs In The Mid-Sixties Vol. 2* (LP) and crank up the volume.

This was to be their sole release. Del-Fi had just signed a deal with the Yardley Black Label company to provide the music for a TV commercial. They asked the group to record a song called *Some Guys Get It* as "Limey and the Yanks" but the producer wasn't happy with the vocals and the chorus lyrics ("It's bitchin'... It's bitchin' ... when you get it, you got to get it"). He over-dubbed the vocals replacing the offending "bitchin'" with "bewitchin'" (hence the full page ad in KRLA Beat which said that the *Back Seat '38 Dodge* single was 'Bewitchin'). When Doug Decker and Chris Christensen heard the new vocals, they were not happy and the band quit the label.

Opus 1 later made an appearance on The Perry Mason TV show, in one of the last black and white episodes ('The Case Of The Avenging Angel'). They were supposed to be playing themselves, but were called Gabe and His Angels and had to mime to some real fruity movie-rock-and-roll version of *The Jersey Bounce*. They also were supposed to appear in the Dean Martin movie 'Murderer's Row' but, typically Hollywood (where nepotism ruled), they were cut out and replaced by **Dino, Desi, and Billy**.

They broke up soon after. Christensen got his draft notice; he sold his car, cut his hair, put the drums in storage, and held a farewell party.... only to be turned down. He eventually went back to drumming, singing and playing guitar and bass and has done some film and video scoring. 35 years on, he teaches music and is the director of a youth band and choir for a Catholic church. Doug Decker became a successful recording engineer and worked with Johnny Cash, the Beach Boys, Band of Gypsies, Roger Miller, and John Fahey amongst others. Come the new millennium he was doing the sound for a cable TV show called 'Win Ben Stein's Money'.

The Back Seat '38 Dodge sculpture is still on show at the L.A. County Art Museum in their permanent collection and continues to cause a stir. (MW/BTs)

The Oracle

45: The Night We Fell In Love/
Don't Say No (Verve Forecast KF 5075) 1967

Dreamy harmony - pop confections from Los Angeles. Produced by the team of **Curt Boettcher** (here spelt Kurt) and Keith Olsen (of **Music Machine**, later **Millennium** and **Sagittarius** with Curt B.). For fans of these latter two groups, this is a must, especially *Don't Say No* with its sitar, tablas, vocal and wind effects and those unmistakable heavenly **Boettcher** harmonies. A little gem. (MW)

Orange Colored Sky

Personnel incl:	TONY BARRY	vcls	AB
	HAROLD LITTLE	drms	AB
	NEAL MYERS	gtr	AB
	JOEL CHRISTY	bs	A
	WALTER SLIVINSKI	organ	AB
	LARRY YOUNGER		
	(LOREN COPE)	vcls	AB
	JACK SKINNER	bs	B

VICTIMS OF CIRCUMSTANCES Vol. 1 (Comp LP) including Opus IV.

	ERNIE HERNANDEZ	gtr	
	BOB WILSON	bs	
	DAVE DICKEY	bs	
	LARRY PARKER	bs, vcls	

ALBUM: 1(B) ORANGE COLORED SKY (UNI 73031) 1968 -

45s:	Orange Colored Sky/		
	The Shadows Of Summer	(UNI 55088)	1968
	Another Sky/Happiness Is	(UNI 55115)	1969
	Mr. Peacock / Knowing How I Love You	(UNI 55140)	1969
	Sweet Potato/The Sun And I	(UNI 55156)	1969
α	Help/Press A Rose	(People)	19??
β	Morning Light / Who Are You Foolin'	(MGM K 14578)	1973

NB: α label listings seem to give this 45 as both People #1004 and #1007, with release date somewhere between '69 and '71. Ernie Hernandez, however tells us that the tracks were recorded at the same sessions as β.

Joel Christy (or 'Christie') solo
45s:	It's All Right Now / See That Girl	(Imperial 66128)	1965
	Angels In The Sky / Lead Me On	(Imperial 66142)	1965
	It's All Right Now / Since I Found You	(Imperial 66198)	1966

A bright 'n' breezy pop outfit from Los Angeles, Slivinski, the organist, also wrote and arranged all eleven songs on the album which was produced by Norman Ratner, although Larry Younger was the group's leader. The album, which is quite highly orchestrated, is a typically polished L.A. production with pleasing vocal harmonies, but it cannot be described as psychedelic. Their second 45 and *Sweet Potato* are not on the album.

Mr. Peacock the band's third 45 was also featured in the movie, "The Love God", starring Don Knotts.

In addition to the personnel listed above, Walter Slivinski's half-brother Ron Guzak was added at some point as second keyboardist. Ernie Hernandez (gtr) joined in 1970:- "MGM also released *Simon Zealots*, a cover of an album track from the rock musical "Jesus Christ Superstar". This received some great DJ reviews and airplay in Los Angeles. It also featured backing vocals by The Mike Curb Congregation, although politically, we made the mistake of not wishing to grant them co-credit on the record's label - an oversight that may have cost us substantial chart success, and lack of MGM promotional support".

"*Help/Press A Rose* was recorded during the same time, as *Morning Light*, which features myself (guitar), and also Bob Wilson (bassist from Cincinnati, OH). **Pat Boone** was also in the studio, as a guest of producer Don Costa. In those days, young MGM artists, like Marie and Donny Osmond, would also pop by our recording sessions, as they were in recording themselves, next door".

In 1974 Larry Parker (bs, vcls) joined, but **Orange Colored Sky** finally called it quits in the early eighties. They reformed in 1996 with Ernie Hernandez (gtr), Larry Younger (vcls), Larry Parker (bs, vcls), Ron Guzak (kyb'ds, vcls) and Andrea Carol-Libman (drms, vcls). Michael Chanslor replaced Ron Guzak in 1998 and Larry Younger left in December 1999. Michael Chanslor: "In April, 2000, we shot a scene in the movie "Ghost World" in which we performed two songs, *Mister Magic* and *Where Is The Love?*. "Ghost World" stars Thora Birch and Steve Buscemi and will be released in Spring, 2001, by... here's some irony...MGM!"

After leaving the band, Jack Skinner pursued a career in acting and commercials, becoming very successful locally, in Southern California; Joel Christy went on to play one of the lead roles in the first Hollywood production of "Hair"; and Dave Dickey (bassist from Oklahoma, from 1972-73) went on to be the bassist with America (of "A Horse With No Name" fame).

Joel Christy had a solo career prior to **OCS**, releasing at least three 45s on Imperial in 1965-6. (VJ/MW/SPr/GM)

ORANGE COLORED SKY - Orange Colored Sky LP.

The Orange Groove

ALBUM: 1 CRYSTAL BLUE PERSUASION AND OTHER SOUNDS OF RODAY (Somerset SF-34000) 1969 -

Subtitled "The Sounds Of The New Generation", a rare exploito album similar to **Firebirds** or **California Poppy Pickers**. Nine of the ten songs are original material, with cuts like *A Bad Trip Back To '69*, *Poppy's To Be Picked*, *Sockerina* and *Land Of Fusan*. (SR)

The Orange Wedge

Personnel:			
	DAVE BURGESS	keyb'ds	A
	GREG COULSON	vcls, perc	AB
	DON COWGER	bs	AB
	JOE FARACE	gtr	AB
	TOM RIZZO	drms	AB
	JAY GRABOSKI	gtr	B
	GENE INGHAM	bs	B
	GENE MEROS	flute	B
	MARK O'CONNOR	keyb'ds	B

ALBUMS:	1(A)	WEDGE	(Contraband)	1972 R3
	2(A)	NO ONE LEFT BUT ME	(No label)	1974 R3

NB: (1) also appears more commonly as a 'No label' pressing. Both albums have also been officially reissued as a double vinyl package (Little Wing LW 3051/2) 1997.

Hailed from Baltimore, Maryland, where they formed in 1968. Both albums are full of guitar-oriented heavy rock gems and are recommended. The first features songs like *Love Me*, *Death Comes Slowly* and *Keep On Livin*, full of driving guitar and strong vocals. *Comfort Of You* has some nice jazzy piano playing, but perhaps the finest track is the finale, *Revenge*, which features some superb Neil Young-influenced guitar playing.

The second album is more of the same but slightly more aggressive vocally, particularly on the title track, and with more guitar exhibitionism on *Hungary Man*. *Dream* is a pleasant instrumental and *Whisky And Gin* pays its dues to the blues. *The Gate* provides a stunning finale much in the style of John Cipollina's **Copperhead**, but the first album seems marginally the better of the two. (VJ/CF)

The Orange Wedge

45:	From The Tomb To The Womb/		
	Morning Dew	(Blue Flat Owsley Memorial 95097)	1968

A different outfit from Grand Rapids, Michigan. This 45 is now very rare and sought-after. *From The Tomb To The Womb* features some superb heavy guitar work. Check it out on *An Overdose Of Heavy Psych* (CD), *Highs In The Mid-Sixties, Vol. 19* (LP), *Best of Pebbles, Vol. 2* (LP & CD), *Trash Box* (5-CD), *Let 'Em Have It! Vol. 1* (CD) or *Michigan Mixture, Vol. 1* (LP). (MW)

THE ORANGE WEDGE - 1+2 LP reissue.

Oregon

Personnel:	PAUL MCCANDLESS	oboe, english horn	A
	GLEN MOORE	bs, flute	A
	RALPH TOWNER	gtr, piano	A
	COLIN WALCOTT	sitar, tamboura, tabla	A

ALBUMS:	1(A)	MUSIC OF ANOTHER PRESENT ERA		
(up to			(Vanguard VSD 79326)	1972 -
1974)	2(A)	DISTANT HILLS	(Vanguard VSD 79341)	1973 -
	3(A)	WINTER LIGHT	(Vanguard VSD 79350)	1974 -

Born in New York in 1945, Colin Walcott was a disciple and sitar student of Ravi Shankar and a tabla student of Ustad Alla Rakha. He worked with the Society Of Contemporary Music in New York and, being one of the few American players really able to understand indian music, began to be used as a session musician on many records from the late sixties, from **Bobby Callender** to **Elyse Weinberg**, from the soundtracks of **John Simon** to the **Alan Lorber Orchestra**.

In 1969, he started working with Ralph Towner (b.1940 in Chehalis, Washington) and Glen Moore, who both had played with **Tim Hardin** and were also interested by jazz and oriental music. Towner was originally a trumpet and piano player who discovered the guitar in 1962 and moved to New York in 1968, where he teamed up with Jeremy Steig (from **Jeremy and The Satyrs**). In 1970, Walcott, Moore and Towner joined the Winter Consort, one of the first groups combining jazz, rock and classical music and met Paul McCandless, an oboe major from the Manhattan School Of Music, who was already in the group. In 1972, they released their first album as **Oregon**. They also played **Cyrus Faryar**'s album.

The music of **Oregon** was largely based on the combination of indian ragas with jazz, rock and chamber music influences and was comprised of meditative tracks with mystic titles (*Baku The Dream Eater*, *The Silence Of A Candle*, *Ghost Beads*) with an unusual instrumentation: sitar, oboe, bass, guitar, piano and light percussions. Their material was mainly original, one of the very few covers being the classic "Witchi-Tai-To" by **Jim Pepper**.

This influential group was successful, both artistically and commercially and would later work with Elektra and ECM. Walcott died in a car accident in 1984.

Their early records should interest people who enjoy **Sandy Bull**, **Peter Walker** or **Paul Horn**. (SR)

Orfeus

ALBUM:	1	LYING TO THE WALL	(Lemco) 1972 R2

A local Kentucky group which specialized in hard-rocking numbers. (SR)

(Little Annie and) The Orfuns

Personnel:	KEITH BRANVILLE	bs	A
	RON CARLSON	sax	ABC
	JERRY McCANN	gtr, vcls	ABC
	SKIP RUDOLPH	gtr	ABC
	CARL SPIRON	drms	ABC
	PATRICIA SPIRON	vcls	A
	LEONARD EDINGTON	bs	B
	DON GARDNER	bs	C

DISCOGRAPHY:
- α Gettin' It On/Put You Down (Shore Bird 1004) 1966
- β Bobby, Don't Laugh At My Beatle Bangs/ Get Up And Go (Fairmount no #) 1964
- χ The Animal In Me/ I Can't Be Treated This Way (Audiodisc no #) 1965
- δ The Animal In Me/ I Can't Be Treated This Way (Harmony Recorders no #) 1965
  In The Back Of My Mind (Audiodisc no #) 1965

NB: α 10" one-sided metal acetate, shown as by Little Annie and The Orfuns. β 10" two-sided metal acetate, first version of unreleased 45. χ two-sided metal acetate, second version of unreleased 45. δ 10" one-sided metal acetate.

From San Diego, California, **The Orfuns** were a British Invasion/Surf-Hot Rod influenced garage band of high school students. Their first recording was made on a wire recorder (!) at a band member's house, where they backed drummer Carl Spiron's sister Pat on a Beatle novelty tune. They also recorded an instrumental and both cuts were transferred to acetate. Fans of **Randy Alvey**'s *Green Fuzz* will become incontinent upon hearing this! **The Orfuns** got serious about their music after this initial recording. The second acetate contains two stunning garage-punk numbers, again recorded by the band. A copy of the acetate was sent to White Whale records, who immediately invited the band to Los Angeles to record a few tracks. They laid down three McCann originals; the two on the second acetate were updated and *In The Back Of My Mind*, the third was a brooding Them/Rolling Stones - influenced number. White Whale didn't release the recordings but the acetates supplied to the band survive and will see release soon. **The Orfuns** continued to play live locally and recorded a rehearsal, but shortly after their last line-up change, McCann got into trouble with the law in San Diego and the band was forced to pack it in.

McCann and Spiron later dominated the two incarnations of **Framework** (1967-9), and then McCann was with **Formerly Anthrax** (1970-1). McCann continues to be active in the San Diego music scene. (CF)

The Organgrinders

Personnel:	FRANK EVENTOFF	woodwind, flute, sax, ld vcls	A
	NISAN EVENTOFF	piano, organ, accordion, synth, keyb'd-bs, ld vcls	A
	PAUL EVENTOFF	drms, vcls	A
	HENRY MELCHER	gtr, bs, vcls	A
	JAMES ROCK	bs, vcls	A

ALBUM:	1(A)	OUT OF THE EGG	(Mercury SR 61282) 1970 -

45s:	Daylight/Mirror Images	(Smash S-2227) 1969
	Babylon/Precious Time	(Smash S-2242) 1969

A flower-pop quintet from Baltimore. Their to date unheralded album is a fine example of this genre. There are very few weak cuts on it, but mostly bright and breezy pop with some delightful woodwind, like *Shady Tree*. Not garage or psychedelic music, but it's typical late sixties melodic flower-pop similar to albums like **Orange Colored Sky**. Most of the finer moments come on Side One on tracks like *Halls Of Hours*, *New Day Holiday*, *Reach For The Sky* and *8th Day In Heaven*, although *Smile For The Sun* on Side Two is also a gem. Side Two does included one throwaway cut, *And I Know What Love Is*, and ends with an experimental instrumental *Kama Kazie Woman*, which doesn't really come off.

Frank Eventoff had earlier been in **The Seventh Sons**. Nisan Eventoff:- "With my four brothers, Richard, Franklin, Paul, and Maury, and with my parents, Joseph and Ethel Eventoff, we had a music and magic show. We called ourselves The Seven Evens and our theme song was called *The Magic Genie*. We all studied at the Peabody Conservatory of Music and had scholarships".

"I am the youngest, then Richard (he played stand up bass), Frank (woodwinds), Paul (drums) and Maury (piano). Mom still plays piano at 93 years old. Dad played piano, violin, mandolin and danced. He passed away when I was 14."

On **The Organgrinders** Nisan tells us:- "Frank played woodwinds, flute, sax, and he also invented several instruments that were used. Frank and I did most of the lead vocals, however the whole band sang. Henry also sings *Honey Bee* on the album. After the **Organ Grinders** we formed a "gypsy rock" band called Romany. We sent demos out and Mercury was interested as were a few others including Decca. Maury, my oldest brother called Bob Reno who was head of A & R at Mercury and convinced him we were the next Beatles. They signed us and we ended up as opening act for many name groups. We played at colleges, clubs, arenas, Strawberry Fields Festival and did some T.V. and movie work. We stayed together for 15 years. At my moms 90th birthday, we all played together, it was great!"

Nowadays Nisan is a professional magician, balloon sculptor and musician. (VJ/NE)

Organised Confusion

45:	Makes Me Sad/Tell Me Why	(Golden-Records 104)	1968

Great garage-punk. Mike Markesich tracked this group down to a "small town South of Detroit, Michigan"; the record label was from a long way further South (Baton Rouge, Louisiana). *Makes Me Sad* kicks off in the vein of *I Who Have Nothing* and by the end you're convinced he hasn't even got that. *Tell Me Why* is a moody mid-tempo fuzz - punker about a guy being stood up. I hope they put out some more 45s yet to come to our attention. (MW)

Organized Confusion

Personnel:	JOE FRAILY	gtr	A
	RANDY RICHARDSON	ld gtr, vcls	A
	BILL TOLLAND	bs	A
	DAVE WILHITE	drms	A

45:	That I Love You/You Are My Sunshine	(Star Dust 161/2) 1967

Another act of the same name, this time from Citrus Heights, California, whose 45 was issued on this Esar subsidiary.

Compilation appearances include: *That I Love You* on *The Sound Of Young Sacramento* (CD). (MW)

Orient Express

Personnel:	GUY DURIS	sitar, electric oud, vcls	A
	BRUNO GIET	electric minitar, vcls	A
	FARSHID GOLESORKHI	electric melodica, dumbek, tympani, vcls	A

ALBUM:	1(A)	ORIENT EXPRESS	(Mainstream S/6117) 1969 R1

NB: (1) counterfeited on vinyl in the late eighties and on CD (Head 2796) 199?.

Originally from Europe this band moved to the States. Guy Duris was actually born on the Left Bank and later met Golesorkhi, who had been decorated by the Shah of Iran for his drumming and was interested in applying Eastern rhythms to Western music, in Iran. They met Bruno Giet, a Belgian pilot and guitarist, in Paris while travelling around Europe. Soon the three members headed for America and settled in New York's East Village initially but ended up in California where their album was recorded. It's powerful Eastern-influenced psychedelia similar to **Kaleidoscope**. Particularly fine examples of their marriage of Eastern and Western music are *Train To Bombay* and *For A Moment*. This album is highly recommended. They did not release any singles on Mainstream.

This act should not be confused with Liz Damon's Orient Express, who were from Hawaii and played cabaret music. They issued one album *Liz Damon And The Orient Express* (Anthem) 1970, and at least three singles: *Loneliness Remembers/Quiet Sound* (Anthem 51005) 1970, *All In All/Walking Backwards Down The Road* (Anthem 51006) 1970, and *1900 Yesterday/You're Falling In Love* (White Whale).

Compilation appearances have included: *For A Moment* and *Train To Bombay* on *Turds On A Bum Ride, Vol. 1 & 2* (Dble CD); *For A Moment* on *Turds On A Bum Ride, Vol. 1* (Dble LP); and *Train To Bombay* on *Turds On A Bum Ride, Vol. 2* (Dble LP). (VJ/MW)

The Original Dukes

Personnel incl:	CHARLES BEST
	JAMES HICKMAN
	JAMES SONODAY

45:	Ain't About To Lose My Cool/ It Looks Like	(Down Home 106) 1966

Recorded in Nashville by an obscure and raw-sounding Southern outfit *Ain't About To Lose My Cool* has some really aggressive vocals and upfront guitar.

Known as The Dukes since the early sixties, they changed their name to **The Original Dukes** when they heard about another set of **Dukes** around Indianapolis, Indiana.

Compilation appearances include: *Ain't About To Lose My Cool* on *Pebbles, Vol. 3 (ESD)* (CD), *Everywhere Chainsaw Sound* (LP) and *Highs In The Mid-Sixties, Vol. 8* (LP). (VJ/MW/MM)

The Original Joplin Forte

See **Joplin Forte**.

The Original Sinners

Personnel:	JACK FINNELL	drms, vcls	A
	STEWART METZ	ld gtr, vcls	AB
	RICHARD ROBINSON	bs	AB
	BRENT SMITH	gtr, vcls	AB
	ARTHUR KIDD	drms, vcls	B

45:	You'll Never Know/I'll Be Home	(Discotech 1001/2) 1966

THE ORIENT EXPRESS - The Orient Express LP.

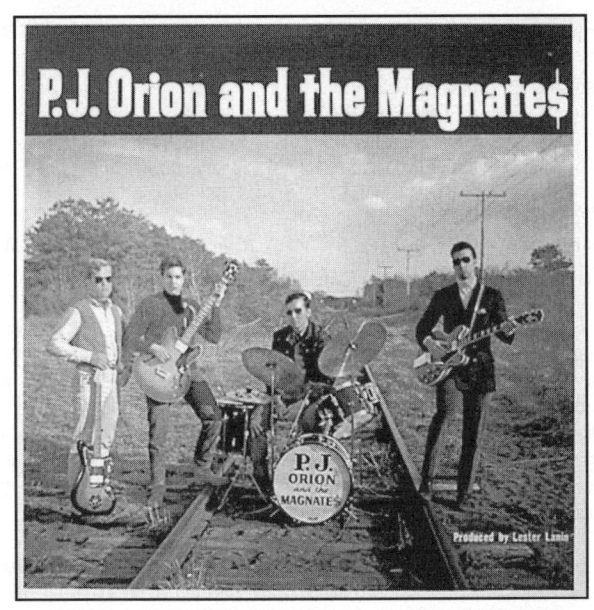

P.J. ORION and THE MAGNATES - P.J. Orion and The Magnates LP.

Formed by Yale University students in the Fall of 1964. The 'A' side to their sole 45, *You'll Never Know*, is a rip off of *Empty Heart*, one of the classics of the punk era. The flip is no slouch either.

The group played mostly college parties and private gigs, didn't play the local club scene. They did however travel up to the Boston area quite a bit, sharing some bills with **The Remains**, which led to some believing the group to be a Boston-based band.

Their 45 was recorded at the Music Box Record Shop in Hamden, Connecticut in early 1966, with funds provided by three Yale pals as an "investment" in the group's potential. The four guys recorded the song in the back room of the store. A local harmonica playing whiz kid named Mark McHugh, a 15-year-old, happened to be in the store and saw the guys setting up. He heard them play their originals and suggested adding some 'harp' to fill-out the sound. After running thru the songs a few times, Mark joined in for the session - but he was never a member of the group. He later joined **Bone**. Likewise, the guys had been trying to convince Steve Stack to join the group as their lead singer. He also was involved at the session, singing the lead vocal on both songs, but similarly was not a member of the group.

The 45 was issued in March, 1966 and received some local airplay, and notoriety in the Boston area. They were invited to play a high profile gig at the legendary Boston club the Rat, and won the crowd over with their set. They signed a management deal with Music Productions, and moved to Cambridge for the Summer of 1966 to gig. They returned to studies in the Fall back at Yale, then back to Cambridge in the Summer of 1967.

Two further songs exist as an unreleased acetate, although the titles are not yet confirmed. Richard Robinson would graduate from the group, move to New York City, where he became a scenester of importance and started his career in the Music business by founding the underground rock mag called Creem.

Compilation appearances have included: *You'll Never Know* on *The Essential Pebbles Collection, Vol. 2* (Dble CD) and *Pebbles, Vol. 13* (LP); and *I'll Be Home* on *Sixties Rebellion, Vol. 6* (LP & CD). (MW/AH/MM)

Original Wild Oats

| 45: | Comic Guy Heroes / | |
| | Comic Guy Heroes Part Two | (Link CGL 1) 1966 |

In late February 1966, this Nevada City, California group visited Golden State Recorders in San Francisco and laid down four tracks. The lilting jangley garage ballad *My Chance Will Come* has been unearthed on *Good Things Are Happening*, from the excellent 'Nuggets From The Golden State' series of CDs on Big Beat. Compiler Alec Palao reports that the other tracks were novelty numbers - the 45 tracks plus one possibly titled *World Of Darkness* (only the 'D' of the first word can be seen in the photo of the tape box). (MW)

P.J. Orion and The Magnates

Personnel:
ARISTEDES GEORGE EMBIRICOS	bs	A
PETER JOHN GOULANDRIS	gtr, ld vcls	A
PETER NICHOLAS GOULANDRIS	drms	A
JEREMIAH MILBANK III	ld gtr, vcls	A

ALBUM: 1(A)   P.J. ORION AND THE MAGNATES
(Magnate XTV 122459) 1967 R4

NB: (1) counterfeited on vinyl (Eva 12023) 198?.

One of those gloriously rare garage albums. It contains nine covers in a somewhat pedestrian folk-rock garage style with vocals that occasionally stray into unknown keys - the strained and wavering 'harmonies'at the end of *Bells Of Rhymney* are worth the price of the reissue alone! Good clean fun as witness the 'for best results, remove the needle and play at 78 r.p.m.' tag!

The Eva counterfeit, suggests that the band came from Ohio, but this is incorrect as the album was recorded by four students who were based at Groton boarding school in Massachusetts. The school was a very strict place - with no radios allowed, and so whenever the band played they had a captive audience. Three members of the band are all cousins (all except Jerry Milbank) and still play together occasionally. Their album was recorded at Columbia Studios in New York.

Compilation appearances include *We Gotta Get Out Of This Place* on *Oil Stains* (LP). (MW/AE)

The Orkustra

Personnel:
BOBBY BEAUSOLEIL	gtr, bouzouki	A
DAVID LA FLAMME	violin, vcls	A
JAIME LEOPOLD	bs	A
HENRY RASOF	oboe	A
TERRY WILSON	drms	A
JESSE BARISH	gtr, vcls, piano	
EMMET GROGAN	vcls	

NB: The above line-up is not exact.

Formed in 1965, this seminal San Francisco "avant-garde" band never released any records although all its members, went on to play with other groups or found fame for various reasons. When they disbanded in 1967, Terry Wilson joined **The Charlatans** and David LaFlamme founded **It's A Beautiful Day** (after a brief stint with the first line-up of Dan Hicks and The Hot Licks). Jaime Leopold too joined Dan Hicks and The Hot Licks in 1968, whilst Jesse Barish, who was friends with Marty Balin became a song writer and went on to form **Jesse, Wolff and Whings** in 1971. Bobby Beausoleil also joined several local groups (including The Powerhouse Of Oz who performed for film-maker Kenneth Anger) before teaming up with **Charles Manson** and being associated with his murders.

The leader of the San Francisco 'Diggers', a legendary activist organization, Emmet Grogan later wrote his semi-romanced memories, "Ringolevio", which is recommended reading about San Francisco life in the mid-sixties. He also worked with Rick Danko of The Band contributing lyrics for his *Rick Danko* album in 1976. Sadly Grogan died in the late seventies.

Henry Rasof recalls:- "I joined the group in the Summer of 1966 after seeing an ad in the Psychedelic Shop on Haight St. There were a lot of people in the band at that time. By Christmas, when we played our first gig at St John's the Evangelist Episcopal Church, there were, as I recall, six people and instruments:- guitar, drums, violin, acoustic bass, flute and oboe. I played the oboe, amplified with a harmonica pickup. I have a tape of that concert, which I got long ago from David LaFlamme. The flute player then dropped out, and there were five of us. The group disbanded the next year. The big gigs, at least for me, were playing at the Avalon on **Big Brother** and the **Sir Douglas Quintet** and at the Rock Garden club, near Ocean (on April 11th 1967) with the **Buffalo Springfield**."

"Emmet Grogan, founder of the Diggers, never played in the group whilst I was in it. Possibly there was a version of the **Orkustra** later on, or before I joined. I also don't know the Jesse mentioned in your article."

"CBS or NBC taped us for a new program, but I never saw it. Ahmet Ertegun heard us play but never recorded us for Atlantic. There were many fantasies and some possibilities."

Henry Rasof is now a publicity consultant in Louisville. (SR)

Ormandy

45s:	Good Day/Sparrow's Corner	(Kasaba 100) 1970
	Good Day/Sparrow's Corner	(Decca 32741) 1970

From Ann Arbor, Michigan. This outfit's 45 was picked up by Decca for national release. Despite the catchy hand-clapped chorus on *Good Day* it still sounds like a 'serious' rock outfit trying to go commercial - definitely not garage. For **Blood, Sweat and Tears** fans maybe.

Compilation appearances include *Good Day* on *Michigan Nuggets* (CD) and *Michigan Brand Nuggets* (LP). (VJ/MW)

Orphan

Personnel:	STEVE ABDU		A B
	DAN ADRIEN	gtr, vcls	A B C
	ERIC LILLJEQUIST	gtr, vcls	A B C
	STUART SCHULMAN	keyb'ds, bs	A B
	(JEFF LABES	keyb'ds	A B)
	(RICHARD ADELMAN		B)
	(BILL KEITH		B)

ALBUMS:	1(A)	EVERYONE LIVES TO SING	(London XPS-614) 1972 -
	2(B)	ROCK AND REFLECTION	(London XPS-630) 1973 -
	3(C)	MORE ORPHAN THAN NOT	(London XPS-645) 1974 -

NB: (1), (2) and (3) also released in the UK by London.

45s:	Easy Now / Lonely Day	(London 185) 1972
	Smilin' River / Sit Down Rock And Roll Man	(London 192) 1973
	It's A Good Day / Lovin' You	(London 195) 1973
	When All Helpers Fail /	(London 201) c1974
	I've Been Working /	(London 210) 1975

Formed as The Allurs in an Avon high school in the mid-sixties, this band relocated to Brockton, released two 45s on Epic in 1967 as **The Orphans**, then moved to Boston. Only Eric Lilljequist would still be around when they evolved into **Orphan** in the early seventies. Their albums were produced by Peter Casperson and they were backed up by session musicians like Bill Keith (**Jim Kweskin Band**) and Jeff Labes (**Applepie Motherhood Band**).

They often played with Jonathan Edwards, the former leader of **Sugar Creek**. (SR/MW/AH)

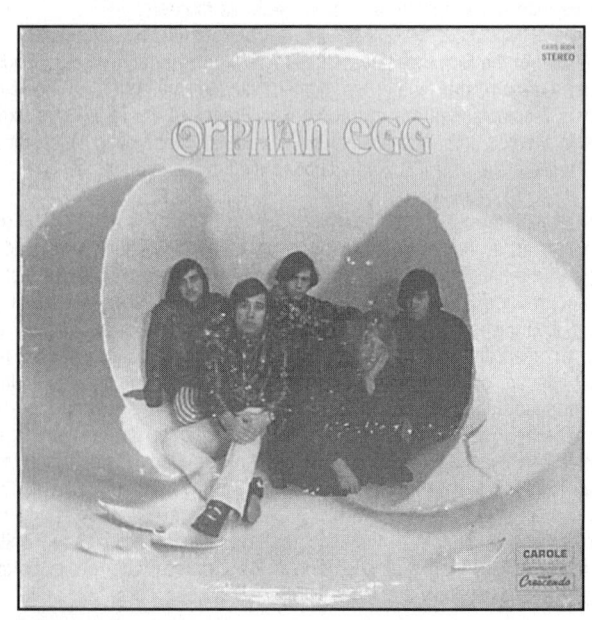

ORPHAN EGG - Orphan Egg LP.

Orphan Egg

Personnel:	JIM BATES	vcls	A
	GEORGE C. BRIX	drms	A
	PAT GALLAGHER	ld gtr, vcls	A
	DAVE MONLEY	keyb'ds, gtr	A
	BARRY SMITH	bs	A

ALBUM: 1(A) ORPHAN EGG (Carole CARS 8004) 1968 R1/R2

NB: (1) also released in Germany (Carole 9621).

A San Jose band who formed at Saratoga high school. They played at local dances and won a battle of the bands contest at their school, which led to the above album. Produced by Guy Hemric and Jerry Styner, it is quickly becoming a significant collectors' item. Probably the two most promising tracks on a rather disappointing album are *Falling* and *It's Wrong*. *Circumstance* is also notable for some wild, early **Blue Cheer**-style guitar pyrotechnics.

The band also had tracks on the Original Soundtrack of *Cycle Savages* and there's rumours of an album called *Don't Say No* (OMI M-7002) in 1980 (although this could easily be the work of a different band).

Compilation appearances include: *Falling* and *It's Wrong* on *Turds On A Bum Ride, Vol. 1 & 2* (Dble CD); *Falling* on *Turds On A Bum Ride, Vol. 1* (Dble LP); and *It's Wrong* on *Turds On A Bum Ride, Vol. 2* (Dble LP). (VJ/SR/DCr)

The Orphans

Personnel incl:	WALLY CRAWFORD		A
	ERIC LILLJEQUIST	gtr, vcls	A

45s:	There's No Flowers In My Garden /	
	One Spoken Word	(Epic 10288) 1967
	This Is The Time / Deserted	(Epic 10348) 1967

Formed in high school in Avon, Massachusetts, as The Allurs, this band relocated to Brockton and changed their name to **The Orphans**. Both 45s were produced by Denny Randell and Sandy Linzer (whose compositions include *I'll Be Back Up On My Feet Again*, covered by **The Monkees** and **Music Fair**). Their material is slick mainly-orchestrated sixties pop. *There's No Flowers...* is classic Summer-of '67 fare with floral tributes to San Francisco.

They eventually settled in Boston and would last into the mid-seventies, releasing several 45s and three albums on the London label, as **Orphan**. By that time Crawford had moved on to the Spectres and later **Sugar Creek**.

Eric Lilljequist wrote a bunch of songs on a 1970-ish Jonathan Edwards album and apparently played guitar on it. (MW/AH/JNa)

Orphans

45:	Bad Apple / Typical Flip Side	(Normandy 12267) 1967

A Newport, Rhode Island group who do a rousing version of Burton-Sawyer's *Bad Apple*, covered by **The Pilgrimage** just a few months previously. *Typical Flip Side* is yer groovy intermission instrumental led by cheesy keyboards, that brings to mind those go-go club scenes in hip sixties movies. (MW)

Orpheus

Personnel:	BRUCE ARNOLD	vcls, gtr	A B
	ERIC GULLIKSEN	vcls, bs	A
	JACK McKENES	vcls, gtr	A
	HARRY SANDLER	vcls, drms	A
	K.P. BURKE	hrmnca	B
	HOWARD HERSCH	bs	B
	STEVE MARTIN	vcls	B
	BERNARD PURDIE	drms	B
	ELLIOT SHERMAN	piano, clavinet	B

ALBUMS:
1(A)	ORPHEUS	(MGM (S)E-4524)	1968 -
2(A)	ASCENDING	(MGM SE-4569)	1968 -
3(A)	JOYFUL	(MGM SE-4599)	1969 -
4(B)	ORPHEUS	(Bell 6061)	1971 -

NB: There is also a double CD set *The Best Of Orpheus* (Big Beat CDWIK 2 143) 1996, which contains 34 tracks from all four albums and a pre-**Orpheus** cut by **The Villagers** circa 1966. All four albums have also been reissued as a double CD set (Akarma AK 155/2) 2001 and there's also a 'best of' *The Very Best Of Orpheus* (Varese Sarande 302 066 236 2) 2001.

45s:
		HCP
Can't Find The Time/Lesley's World	(MGM K 13882) 1968	80
I've Never Seen Love Like This/ Congress Alley	(MGM K 13947) 1968	-
Brown Arms In Houston/ I Can Make The Sun Rise	(MGM K 14022) 1969	91
By The Size Of My Shoes/Joyful	(MGM K 14139) 1970	-
Big Green Pearl/Sweet Life	(Bell 45 128) 1971	-

NB: There have also been some reissue 45s: *Can't Find The Time / Brown Arms In Houston* (MGM Golden Circle MVG 529) and (Polydor Band Of Gold MVG 529); and *Can't Find The Time* (Rock 'n Mania RMGD-2424A).

From Worcester, Massachusetts, **Orpheus** were formed by ex-**Villagers**, Arnold and McKenes, Gulliksen from **The Blue Echoes** and Harry Sandler from The Mods. McKenes and Gulliksen had earlier worked together in a few folk groups, including **The College Boys**, who had one 45 *The Man* (Swan S-4166) 1963. Gulliksen: "This was a Kennedy tribute record; the group name was selected by Swan to remove commerciality from the record!".

Under the guidance of **Alan Lorber**, who produced all their albums, **Orpheus** became part of the "Boss-town Sound" movement but cultivated an almost singer-songwriter styled soft-rock sound with folkie elements, at variance with the overtly psychedelic sounds and image of most of their stablemates. Possibly a marginal case for inclusion here therefore and not recommended to either garage or psych fans, although some of their material could be classified as 'hippie-rock' at a stretch.

Check out their contributions to the double CD set *The Best Of Bosstown Sound*: *Can't Find The Time To Tell You* (1967), *Walk Away Renee* (1968), *Brown Arms In Houston* (1969), *Tomorrow Man* (1971) - and decide for yourself.

They should be given credit for having a wider appeal and more output than most of their regional stablemates which saw them survive most of the hype and subsequent critical backlash. One of their songs, *Can't Find The Time*, was also covered by sixties instrumental band Groovin' Strings on their 1969 album *Groovin' Strings And Things*, and Rose Colored Glass, who had a Top 40 hit with the song. Other covers have included *Brown Arms In Houston* by the Plastic Cow on an album called *The Plastic Cow Goes Moog* (!?!?) and a very interesting cover of *Congress Alley* by a New York jazz funk group called "Congress Alley" on their album *Congress Alley*.

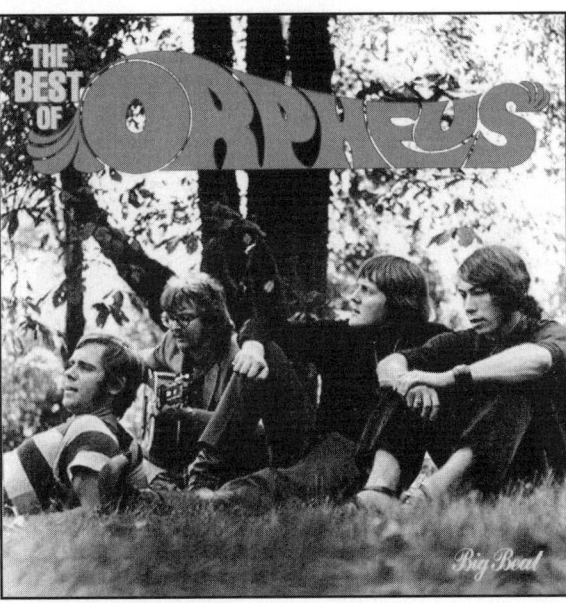

ORPHEUS - The Best Of CD.

Fans of the band might be interested to know that legendary studio drummer Bernard "Pretty" Purdie was used on some material on the early albums but as was the industry standard at the time, he did not receive credit for the work.

Orpheus also performed the theme song for the MGM movie "Marlowe", starring James Garner, called *Little Sister*. Jack McKenes and Bruce Arnold can also be heard on a 45 by **The Alan Lorber Orchestra**, *Massachusetts / Congress Alley* (MGM K-13926SS).

You can do a lot worse than invest in Akarma's excellent double CD set. Alternatively, for a general introduction to the band *The Very Best Of Orpheus* draws material from all four of their albums and showcases the talents of Bruce Arnold (their co-writer) and Jack McKenes.

Can't Find The Time was covered more recently by Hootie and The Blowfish and this version was included on the soundtrack for the 2000 Jim Carrey movie "Me, Myself and Irene". Eric G's verdict - "It's not bad at all, certainly better than the one by The Rose Colored Glass back in the seventies". (MW/GDh/EGn/BA/VJ)

The Orphuns

Personnel incl:	WAYNE PAV	vcls	A
	ROGER L. VAIL		A

45s:
	I.F.O.C./ This Stock, Merely Arranged	(No label SS-7867-01)	1966
α	Oh, Mona / Bring It On Home	(PAV 650)	1967

NB: α as **Wayne Pav and The Orphuns**.

I.F.O.C. - It's Four O'Clock - is a swaying hypnotic jangly folk-punker with a bathroom-echo sound. *This Stock...* is dreamy laid-back folk-punk, with a nod in **The Byrds** direction and quite compelling after a few plays. The Wayne Pav-led 45 covers Bo Diddley's *Mona* via the Stones' *Not Fade Away*, with raucous upfront vocals and a brief but brilliant guitar solo. The flip looks to the Animals for a rendition of Sam Cooke's *Bring It On Home To Me*. It's no wonder that both 45s are sought-after and amazing that they remain mostly uncompiled.

Other band members included Roger Vail from Macomb, Illinois, who had been in **The Vectors** (with a pre-**Shadows Of Knight** Joe Kelley) and went on to **Osgood**.

Compilation appearances include *Oh Mona* on *Bad Vibrations, Vol. 3* (LP). (MW)

Oscar and The Majestics

Personnel incl:	OSCAR HAMOD	ld gtr, vcls	A
	SAM HAMOD	bs	A
	AL PAGE	sax	A
	JOHNNY TODA	drms	A

45s:
α	Why-O/?	(Ark)	1963
	Come On Willie/Top Eliminator	(Score 1964)	196?
	I Can't Explain/My Girl Is Waiting	(USA 851)	1966
	Got To Have Your Lovin'/Soulfinger	(USA 878)	1967
	My Girl Is Waiting / Jungle Beat	(Ark 7638)	1967??
	House Of The Rising Sun 1969 Part I / Part II	(Soulful 200)	1969
	House Of The Rising Sun 1969 / Dawn	(Soulful 200)	1969
β	No Chance Baby /?	(unknown)	196?

NB: α as by Oscar Hamod and The Majestics, 'B' side might be *No Chance Baby*. β flip could possibly be *Jackie, Jackie*, which the band are known to have recorded.

From Gary, Indiana originally where they were the mainstay act in the locale, this band later operated out of Chicago and played with a strong Anglophile influence. Led by Oscar Hamod, his Gibson Firebird guitar was fitted with a flat piece of sheet metal over the neck of his guitar, so people couldn't see what chords he was playing!

Phil Swan recalls: "Everyone in the Gary area in the mid-sixties knew Oscar as the King of the Marquette Park Pavilion at Miller Beach. Oscar's drummer John Toda was sort of a pioneer in the drumming arena. He was very innovative, as well as talented. On *Why-O* John played mostly on his tom-toms... it was a haunting song with sort of a slow jungle beat, just right for seductive dancing. All of the "garage bands" in the area began playing it at parties. Then one day - lo and behold - I find the song on Natalie Cole's *Take A Look* album and the song is titled *Calypso Blues*. *Come On Willie* is a take-off of *Hang On Sloopy*. *Top Eliminator* was an instrumental that let Oscar show off his ability to double-pick on up-tempo songs. He wrote a song called *Jackie Jackie* that was a spin-off of *Louie Louie*."

Drummer Johnny Toda was also the band's comedian and when they would perform *Top Eliminator* live, he would do the revved-up engine sound by mouth. He also used to sing Ian Whitcomb's *You Really Turn Me On*, copying the falsetto voice.

Their garage-punk interpretation of *I Can't Explain*, with chopped rhythm and distorted guitar, can be heard on *Pebbles, Vol. 7* (CD) and *Mindrocker, Vol. 2* (LP). *No Chance Baby* is on *Tougher Than Stains* (LP), whose secretive compiler reveals only that it was issued on a 'semi-big label' (USA perhaps?); *House Of The Rising Sun '69* is on *Let's Dig 'Em Up, Vol. 2* (LP); *Come On Willie* on *Psychedelic Unknowns, Vol. 9* (CD); and *Got To Have Your Lovin'* on *Teenage Shutdown, Vol. 13* (LP & CD). (MW/PS)

The Oscar Five

45:   ? / I Won't Be Your Fool   (D&C DC 25) 1966

Upstate New York punkers on the Schenectady label that put out **The Chancellors** and **The Continentals**. *I Won't Be Your Fool*, penned by J.Massia and J.Ramsey, is a heartfelt garage-ballad with vocals full of pain and outrage, a mood amplified by some wicked fuzz.

Compilation coverage has included:- *I Won't Be Your Fool* on *Midnight To Sixty-Six* (LP) and *Ear-Piercing Punk* (CD) (albeit incorrectly titled as *No More*). (MW)

Osgood

Personnel incl: ROGER L. VAIL   A

45:   You'll Survive/Everybody Sing   (Golden Voice 834G-5434) 1968

Catchy and melodic, mid-fast folk-rock-pop backed by driving jangley pop, both sides of this 45 were written by Roger Vail, from Macomb, Illinois. He was previously in **The Vectors** (with a pre-**Shadows Of Knight** Joe Kelley) and **The Orphuns**. (MW)

Oshun

45:   Ridin' With The Milkman/Rattle Of Life   (Mercury 72687) 1967

An obscure combo whose *Ridin'* is pleasant pop fare backed by a wacky concoction of sound effects, street noises and sorta fairground hustler vocals instructing the listener to 'swim in your rainy mood, crystallizing your dehydrated food'. Tune into this dementia on *Pebbles Box* (5-LP), *Trash Box* (5-CD), *Pebbles, Vol. 3* (CD) or *Only In America* (CD). (MW)

Other Five

45:   Better Come Home/You Really Got Me   (BAUS 855B-5887) 1967

A garage combo from Indiana with two competent covers. *Better Come Home* suffers from a slight intrusion of brass whilst *You Really Got Me* is strangely restrained and not the wild rave-up with raucous screams one normally expects. (MW)

The Other Four

Personnel:			
	LARRY GRANT (aka LARRY McSEATON)	gtr	A
	NORMAN LOMBARDO	vcls, bs	ABC
	KENNY PERNICANO	drms, vcls	ABC
	RICK RANDLE	vcls, gtr, keyb'ds	A
	CRAIG PALMER	vcls, keyb'ds, bs	BC
	DON SPARKS	vcls, gtr	BC

45s: Why/Searching For My Love   (Musette 6517) 1965
These Are The Words/
Once And For All Girl   (P.L.A.Y. 711) 1966
How Do You Tell A Girl/
Your Ma Said You Cried   (Decca 32050) 1966

A local San Diego, California, teen combo formed out of **The Man-Dells**. Their first two singles attracted so much attention locally that Decca signed them and (unfortunately) rushed in a staff producer to supervise the third release, which fails to capture the exuberance of the first two pop - rock charmers. The group was featured in the March 1966 issue of 'Teen Screen' magazine, and in 1967 Rick and Norman reunited in **The Brain Police**. The singles were recorded at Western Sound Studios and Gold Star in Hollywood.

Your Ma Said You Cried was previously covered by Chicago's **Thunderbirds**.

Compilation appearances have included: *Once And For All Girl* on *Fuzz, Flaykes, And Shakes, Vol. 3* (LP & CD); *Searching For My Love* on *Fuzz, Flaykes, And Shakes, Vol. 2* (LP & CD); and *Why?* on *Fuzz, Flaykes, And Shakes, Vol. 5* (LP & CD). (CF/MW)

The Other Half

Personnel:			
	LARRY BROWN	bs	A
	RANDY HOLDEN	ld gtr	A
	JEFF KNOWLEN	vcls, hrmnca, gtr	A
	GEOFF WESTERN	rhythm gtr	A
	DANNY WOODS	drms	A
	RON SAURMAN	drms	B
	MIKE PONS	bs	
	CRAIG TARWATER	gtr	

ALBUM: 1(A)   THE OTHER HALF   (Acta 38004) 1968 R2

NB: (1) also released in Germany with a totally different sleeve (Die Volks Platte) 1968. (1) counterfeited on CD and on vinyl as *Mr. Pharmacist* (Eva 12003) 198?. Housed in a different sleeve, the Eva album contains additional 45 cuts.

45s: Wonderful Day/Flight Of The Dragon Lady   (Acta 801) 1967
No Doubt About It/I Need You   (Acta 806) 1967
Oz Lee Eaves Drops/Morning Fire   (Acta 825) 1968
Mr Pharmacist/I've Come So Far   (GNP Crescendo 378) 1968

THE OTHER HALF - The Other Half (Acta) LP.

NB: There's also a rare French EP with picture sleeve: *Mr Pharmacist/I've Come So Far/It's Too Hard/I Know* (Vogue INT 18112) 1968.

The above album was a competent effort, composed of original numbers aside from an interesting version of Arthur Lee's *Feathered Fish*. **Holden**'s fine psychedelic guitar work stands out throughout and is at its best on *Morning Fire* plus the finale *What Can I Do For You?*. Another number, *Oz Lee Eaves Drops* had an interesting beat, whilst the band's best known track, the non-album *Mr. Pharmacist*, is a classic psych-punker and well worth checking out.

This group contained **Randy Holden** who, on **The Other Half**'s demise, replaced **Leigh Stephens** in the better known **Blue Cheer**. Craig Tarwater (gtr) and Mike Pon (bs), both ex-**Sons Of Adam**, were also members of the band, but did not feature on the album.

Carolyn White, who used to live with the band in Mill Valley, California, recalls that they may have recorded a second album entitled *The Other Half And How To Get It* - Anyone have further info? Carolyn also tells us "Things came to an official end in L.A. when Jeff and Larry and Ron decided to move to Northern California, however I think Randy was the first to want to break up. It happened right after they recorded the theme to 'Mod Squad', a sixties cop show".

Compilation appearances include: *Mr. Pharmacist* on *Mayhem & Psychosis, Vol. 2* (LP), *Mindrocker, Vol. 1* (LP), *Nuggets Box* (4-CD), *Nuggets, Vol. 12* (LP), *Sound Of The Sixties* (Dble LP) and *Sixties Archive, Vol. 1* (CD); *Mr. Pharmacist* and *I've Come So Far* on *Psychotic Reaction Plus Ten* (CD); and *Feathered Fish* on *Sixties Rebellion, Vol. 8* (LP & CD). (VJ/SR)

The Other Half

Personnel:	BOB COLLETT	vcls	AB
	JOHN HAWKINS	bs	A
	ANDREA INGANNI	vcls	AB
	DON KARR	keyb'ds (bs)	AB
	REX LAMB	ld gtr	AB
	DOMINICK PUCCIO	gtr (bs)	AB
	CRANLEIGH SAMMIS	drms	A
	ROBERT POTTER	drms	B

ALBUM: 1(A) THE OTHER HALF (7/2 Records HS-1 /2) 1966 R4

NB: (1) reissued on (Resurrection CX 1266) 1984.

45: A Lot To Live For / Aspens Of The Night (7/2 P-1 1/2) 1966

An obscure garage combo who formed at The Hill School, a prep school in Pottstown, Pennsylvania, with members originating from all over the locale - Long Island, central Jersey, just outside Philly etc. Both Hawkins and Sammis were previously in **The Half Tribe** (of Mannasseh) whose equally rare private album was also reissued on Resurrection. Covers, including *Gloria*, *Satisfaction* and *Time Won't Let Me*, make up the bulk of the material with the odd 'original' done in a competent frat-cum-garage style. The original is beyond all but the fanatics' pocket so grab the reissue.

The Other Half lasted two years: the academic years of 1965-66 and 1966-7. Their album was made in the Spring of 1966, recorded on the top floor of the Oasis Hotel in Camden New Jersey (just across the river from Philadelphia) in a small for-hire recording studio.

Don Karr recalls:- "Two members, the bassist and drummer (Hawkins and Sammis), carried over from **The Half Tribe** to **The Other Half**. They both graduated in 1966. For **The Other Half** Mk.2, the following academic year, a new drummer was added, Robert Potter. Puccio and I took over the bass (Puccio played Fender Bass; I played either Fender Bass or bass keys on the Farfisa Combo Compact). Inganni, Lamb, Puccio, and Collett all graduated in 1967. Potter, who was class of '68, went on to graduate; I was class of '69 (indeed, a mere freshman when I joined) and left The Hill after the '66-'67 school year (my second year)."

"A second album was planned, to be recorded Spring of 1967, but one of the members was expelled from school just days before the recording was to take place."

Don Karr later played in The Trojans and **Sleepless Knights**. (MW/DKr)

PEBBLES Vol. 8 (Comp LP) including The Others.

The Others

Personnel incl:	MIKE BRAND		A
	JOHN COSTA		A
	PETE SHEPLEY		A

45s:	I Can't Stand This Love Goodbye/ Until I Heard It From You	(RCA 47-8669) 1965
	The First Time I Saw You/Lonely Street	(RCA 47-8776) 1965
	My Friend The Wizard/Morning	(Jubilee 4550) 1967

From Rhode Island. Their debut 45, *I Can't Stand This Love Goodbye*, couples smooth harmonies with upbeat dance rhythms, and is backed by a harmonious folk-rocker. Their second, *The First Time I Saw You* is a pleasant pop-rock song, coupled with a chiming pop-ballad. Their final effort, *My Friend The Wizard*, features a more psychedelic sound and the uncompiled *Morning* is a dreamy harmony ballad. The consistently high quality of their garage-pop output, blending Beatles and **Byrds** influences with mellow harmonies, surely indicates there's more to be heard. Ripe for a retrospective?

Compilation appearances have included: *Lonely Street* on *Leaving It All Behind* (LP); *My Friend The Wizard* on *Mindrocker, Vol. 12* (LP) and *New England Teen Scene, Vol. 2* (LP); *I Can't Stand This Love, Goodbye* on *Pebbles Vol. 10* (CD), *Pebbles, Vol. 8* (LP), *Pebbles, Vol. 1* (ESD) (CD) and *Garage Monsters* (LP); *I Can't Stand This Love, Goodbye, Until I Heard It From You* and *(I Remember) The First Time I Saw You* on *Mindrocker, Vol. 9* (LP). (MW)

The Others

Personnel:	JOHN DUNS	drms	A
	MIKE GOTCHER	vcls	A
	MONTY HARPER	keyb'ds	A
	TIM MYERS	bs	A
	JOHN POPA	gtr	A
	MARTY PRUE	ld gtr, vcls	A

45s: Revenge/I'm In Need (Mercury 72602) 1966

NB: reissued with PS (Sundazed S 137) 1998.

From the Lancaster-Palmdale area of California, they were a surf band until bitten by the Invasion bug and joined by Prue from the folkie Townsmen. Their story is revealed by Jud Cost on the very welcome Sundazed reissue. The 'A' side is pretty good fuzz-punk.

Compilation appearances include: *Revenge* and *I'm In Need* on *Pebbles, Vol. 17* (LP) and *Good Things Are Happening* (CD). (MW)

The Other Side

Personnel:
TOM ANTONE	bs, vcls		AB
KEN MATTHEWS	drms, vcls		AB
JIM SAWYERS	ld gtr, vcls		A
SKIP SPENCE	gtr		A
DAVE TOLBY	gtr, vcls		A
JO KEMLING	organ		B
DAN PHAY	gtr, vcls		B
NED TORNEY	ld gtr, vcls		B

45: Streetcar/Walking Down The Road (Brent 7061) 1966

Skip Spence, later of **Jefferson Airplane**, was a transitory member of this San Jose outfit, originally a surf act known as The Topsiders, who were close friends of **The Chocolate Watch Band**. Indeed, in 1965 both bands underwent a change around in personnel with Phay, Torney and Kemling all joining **The Other Side** from **The Watchband** and Dave Tolby moving across to join **The Watchband**. Mark Loomis also had a brief spell with **The Other Side** after Jim Sawyers had joined **The Vejtables**, and **Watchband** bassist Rich Young had been drafted.

Although **The Other Side** did not record an album, they drew thousands to local dances in the San Jose area... Their 45, which was included on the Mainstream *A Pot Of Flowers* (LP) compilation, is sadly their only vinyl epitaph.

Retrospective compilation appearances have included *Streetcar* and *Walking Down The Road* on *Mindrocker, Vol. 10* (Dble LP) and *Sound Of The Sixties: San Francisco Part 2* (LP). (VJ/CKg)

The Other Two

45s:
Look Around/Don't Lock Me In (Jerden 777) 1965
Don't Say No/When I Sleep (Panorama 40) 1966

This duo sound like the Pacific Northwest's answer to Peter and Gordon, especially on the mellow folk - rocker *Look Around*. The flip is solid punchy British invasion - styled beat with ringing guitars - a charming debut. *Don't Say No* features a catchy Latin shuffle, like a subdued Concrete and Clay, whilst *When I Sleep* is a soporific beat - ballad. Invasion and beat fans will cherish these. All four tracks were composed by Curt Bartholomew and Nicholas Richardson. (MW)

Otter Creek

ALBUM: 1 OTTER CREEK (Bolt B3234) c1972 ?

From the NorthEast area, a quintet of hippie country-rock in the tradition of the **Grateful Dead**/New Riders, with songs like *High Country*, *Baby Blues* and *Hangman's Day*. Only 500 copies were pressed. (SR)

Our Gang

45: Careless Love/Heartbeat (Warrior 166) 1966

Careless Love, which has resurfaced on *Highs In The Mid-Sixties, Vol. 18* (LP), is a raving punk effort with lots of mouth organ. This was confirmed by the Colorado Springs **Our Gang** as not being them and neither is it Norman Petty's Warrior label. Yet more same-name games.

Mike Markesich has since traced both to California - Warrior was owned by Tom Sawyer, who also operated the Trident label and was based in North Hollywood. The band were from Buena Park, a suburb of Los Angeles. (VJ/MSk/MW/MM)

Our Gang

45: Rapunzel /
Here Today Gone Tomorrow (Round & Round RR-4503) 1967

From Colorado Springs, this was the band's sole release. (MSk/MW)

MAYHEM & PSYCHOSIS Vol. 2 (Comp LP) including The Outcasts.

Our Patch of Blue

45: Zoom Zoom Zoom / Lily White (Warner Bros. 7257) 1969

Another Italian-American group from the East Coast. The first side was written by Zampe and de Caesar and is a decent psych-pop track. It sounds overall like several other Map City Productions of Vini Poncia (ex-**Tradewinds**), such as **The Blue Jays** or **Mardi Gras**. (SR)

Our Village Sound

ALBUM: 1 OUR VILLAGE SOUND (Private Pressing) c1970

From Queens Village in New York, a Christian folk group with a female singer. (SR)

The Outcasts

Personnel:
EUGENE 'BUDDY' CARSON	keyb'ds, hrmnca	ABC
DENNY TURNER	gtr	AB
RICKY WRIGHT	drms	ABC
JIM CARSTEN	gtr	BC
JIM RYAN	bs	BC
GALEN NILES	gtr	C

CD: 1 I'M IN PITTSBURGH AND IT'S RAINING
(Collectables COL-CD-0591) 1995

45s:
Nothing Ever Comes Easy/Oriental Express (Outcast 6865) 1965
I'm In Pittsburgh (And It's Raining)/
Price Of Victory (Askel 102) 1966
I'll Set You Free/Everyday (Askel 104) 1966
Route 66/Everyday (Askel 107) 1966
1523 Blair/Smokestack Lightning (Gallant 101) 1967

Based in San Antonio, this was one of the very best psychedelic/punk bands to come from Texas. Their two best known songs were *I'm In Pittsburgh (And Its Raining)*, a Jim Carsten composition with catchy drumming and some effective mouth organ, and *1523 Blair*, the zenith of their career. This has a superb psychedelic beginning which gives way to high speed guitar work culminating in a psychedelic haze.

For you curious completists, their first 45 comprises a rather lame beat ballad backed by a rockin' instrumental with no real hint as to what was to follow. It is however notable for being written and produced by Mike Post, who was in basic training at Lackland Air Force Base at the time. He went on to write music for many great TV series, including: "The Rockford Files" and "Hill Street Blues" etc. **The Outcasts'** manager at the time was Maj.

John Carson who arranged for Mike and Jimmy Hawkins (Donna Reed Show, Leave It To Beaver, Elvis movies actor also in training) to do a series of shows at local military bases with **The Outcasts** as a back-up unit. Mike had worked as an arranger / band coach for Gary Lewis and the Playboys before this and put the show together. Exposure to Mike's professional attitude and working with him in the studio was an important factor in tightening the group into a working unit that went on to bigger and better things.

Of their other recordings, the flip to their final 45, *Smokestack Lightning* features a stunning performance and the unreleased *What Price Victory*, is a protest song about the Vietnam War.

Over 10 years on the band turned up singing *I'm In Pittsburgh* on the 'A' side to a 45 *I Feel So Bad/Undecided* (Grease FUN 2) credited to The Kicks, which was supposed to be released as a new wave record in Europe! A few picture sleeve recordings did apparently get circulated.

The CD compilation *I'm In Pittsburgh And It's Raining* contains all of their 1966-7 singles, unreleased material and later recordings when they were in Houston.

Galen Niles, who played guitar on *1523 Blair* and was later a founding member of **Homer**, recalls:- "I also did two recordings with my friend Steve Perron - *Still In Love With You Baby* (**The Argyles**) and *Help I'm Lost* (**The Mind's Eye**). I was never a member of these groups, as I was involved with other bands at the time. Steve just asked me to play on these tracks, so I did. Both were recorded at Abe Epstien's Studio in San Antonio circa 1967."

Compilation appearances have included: *1523 Blair* on *Mayhem & Psychosis, Vol. 2* (LP), *Songs We Taught The Fuzztones* (Dble LP & Dble CD), *Acid Dreams - The Complete 3 LP Set* (3-LP), *Acid Dreams Testament* (CD), *Acid Dreams, Vol. 1* (LP) and *Teenage Shutdown, Vol. 4 - I'm A No-Count* (LP & CD); *I'm In Pittsburg (And It's Raining)* on *Pebbles, Vol. 1* (CD), *Pebbles, Vol. 1* (LP), *Texas Flashbacks, Vol. 2* (LP & CD), *Flashback, Vol. 2* (LP), and *Great Pebbles* (CD); *1523 Blair* and *Smokestack Lightning* on *Texas Punk Groups From The Sixties* (LP), *Sixties Archive, Vol. 2* (CD) and *Texas Psychedelic Punk, Vol. II* which wasn't released, but for which metal acetates exist; *I'm In Pittsburgh (And It's Raining)*, *Smokestack Lightning*, *Sweet Mary*, *I'll Set You Free*, *Route '66* and *The Birds* on *Texas Punk: 1966, Vol. 2* (LP); *Smokestack Lightning* on *Endless Journey - Phase One* (LP) and *Endless Journey - Phase I & II* (Dble CD); *I'm In Pittsburg And It's Raining*, *Smokestack Lightning*, *Sweet Mary*, *I'll Set You Free*, *The Birds*, *My Love*, *Every Day* (prev. unreleased mix), *Rout '66* and *What Price Victory* on *Acid Visions - Complete Collection, Vol. 2* (3-CD); *I'm In Pittsburg (And It's Raining)* and *Route '66* on *Green Crystal Ties, Vol. 8* (CD); and *My Love, Everyday* (prev. unreleased mix) and *What Price Victory* on *Texas Punk, Vol. 3* (LP) (Another track featured on the comp, *Hard Lovin' Babe* with Linda Pierre King on vocals, is by a different **Outcasts**...). (VJ/MW/JRy)

ACID DREAMS TESTAMENT (Comp CD) including The Outcasts.

The Outcasts

45: People/ You're Teaching Me (Sola 12) 1966

From Arizona, this **Outcasts** just managed one 45, *People*, which is a reasonable garage number.

Compilation appearances include: *People* on *Legend City, Vol. 1* (LP & CD) and *Sixties Rebellion, Vol. 14* (LP & CD). (VJ)

The Outcasts

Personnel incl: M. MCCARTY   A

45: I Wanted You/Little Bitty Man (Shore Bird 1005) 1966

A more rock-orientated 45 from Warren's Norman-based studios. An Oklahoma band, this time based in Norman, *I Wanted You* can also be found on *The Essential Pebbles Collection, Vol. 2* (Dble CD). (VJ/MW)

The Outcasts

45: You Do Me Wrong/Love Eternal (Studio City 1040) 1965/6

This particular band came from Grand Rapids in Northeast Minnesota in the mid-sixties, though I can't confirm that the 45 was in the garage genre. (VJ)

The Outcasts

Personnel:	MARK FOLEY	vcls, gtr	A
	BOB MARTIN	drms, vcls	A
	BRIAN WHELAN	bs, gtr	A
	BRUCE WILLIAMS	vcls, ld gtr	A

ALBUMS: 1(-) THE OUTCASTS LIVE! STANDING ROOM ONLY
                                                     (Cicadelic CICLP 988) 1985
              2(-) MEET THE OUTCASTS! (Cicadelic CICLP 987) 1985

NB: (1) available on CD (Collectables COL-CD-0545) with two previously unreleased singles from 1967. (2) issued on CD with the **Arkay IV**'s *The Mod Sound Of The Arkay IV 1966-1968* as *Battle Of The Bands* (COL-CD-0519). It contains 26 tracks including previously unreleased demos.

45s: You'd Be Surprised/Set Me Free (Decca 32036) 1966
      Today's The Day/
      I Didn't Have To Make Her Anymore (Cameo 477) 1967

An excellent Long Island, New York garage combo who started out as The Radiations in 1965. The same foursome became **The Outcasts** in 1966 and were expanded to a five piece with Chuck Thatcher on organ and vocals for their debut 45. Whilst the 'A' is pleasant beat-pop it's the plaintive tones, imaginative drumming and haunting keyboards that make the flip *Set Me Free* just a bit special.

Chuck Thatcher was replaced by Jimmy Williams and this line-up features on the *Standing Room Only* collection of live tracks from their '66-67 period and which recorded the second 45. *I Didn't Have To Love Her Anymore* is a catchy and commercial minor-key folk-rock-punker with an irresistible beat.

Paul Brokan was the next keyboardist brought in until the demise of the group in 1968. *The Meet The Outcasts!* album includes two Radiations tracks, the 45 tracks, a live *Today's The Day* and more excellent live material, plus several unreleased tracks. As with many of the bands of the era the live stuff is predominantly fave covers, though they also include rather good versions of *Walk On By* and the Good Rats' *Groovy* in their repertoire. Do yourself a favour and pick up the Cicadelic albums if you come across them.

Compilation appearances have included: *I Didn't Have To Love Her Anymore* on *Mindrocker, Vol. 11* (LP), *Pebbles, Vol. 12* (LP) and *A Journey To Tyme, Vol. 2* (LP); *Set Me Free* on *Acid Dreams - The Complete 3 LP Set* (3-LP), *Acid Dreams Testament* (CD), *Echoes In Time Vol's 1 & 2* (CD) and *Echoes In Time, Vol. 2* (LP); *Boom Boom Boom* and *Gloria* on *Green Crystal Ties, Vol. 7* (CD); *Walk On By* on *Green Crystal Ties, Vol. 9* (CD); *Nothing But Love* and *Something About You* on *Green Crystal Ties, Vol. 10* (CD). (MW)

The Outcasts

Personnel:	BOB BROWN	bs, vcls	ABC
	JIMMY MARINO	drms	A
	GARY PUCKETT	gtr, organ, vcls	ABC
	TOMMY KENDALL	drms	B
	DWIGHT BEMENT	keyb'ds, sax	C
	WILLIE KELLOGG	drms	C
	BOB SALISBURY	sax	C

45s:	Run Away/Would You Care	(Prince 1265) 1965
	I Can't Get Through To You/	
	I Found Out About You	(Karate 531) 1966

Formed in San Diego, California, line-up 'A' was known as The Ravens before changing their names to **The Outcasts** in early 1965. The band picked up speed when Kendall joined and the two singles this line-up recorded sold well locally and found their way onto San Diego radio. *Run Away* has a nasty fuzz riff coursing through it and is probably their finest moment. The Karate 45 is reasonable garage beat with strong vocals, but nothing to write home about.

Line-up 'C' was decidedly less garage and the demo they recorded in 1966 was all the proof Columbia needed to offer the group a contract, but several members of the band would have nothing to do with Puckett's personal manager and wouldn't sign on. A new group was quickly assembled and subsequently recorded for Columbia as **The Union Gap** (later '**Gary Puckett and The Union Gap**'), dressed in Civil War uniforms (no doubt inspired by **Paul Revere and The Raiders**).

Kellogg went on to **The Five # Grin**, **Pale Fire**, The Friendly Grin (see **Joel Scott Hill** entry), The Survivors, and **Moby Grape**. Dwight Bement (who went on to **The Union Gap**) is currently in Colorado with Flash Cadillac.

Compilation appearances include *I Can't Get Through To You* on *Let's Dig 'Em Up, Vol. 1* (CD); and *Run Away* on *Follow That Munster, Vol. 2* (LP). (MW/CF)

The Outcry

45:	Can't You Hear (My Heartbeat)/	
	Gravey Covered Fruitcake	(Rileys 8785) 196?

Can't You Hear (My Heartbeat) from this obscure Detroit combo, is a nicely understated garage piece featuring a neat guitar break and pounding beat.

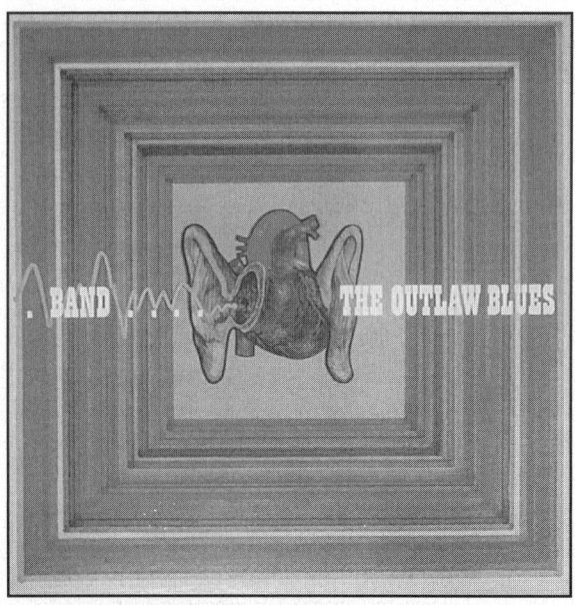

THE OUTLAW BLUES BAND - The Outlaw Blues Band LP.

Compilation appearances include: *Can't You Hear (My Heartbeat)* on *Michigan Mayhem Vol. 1* (CD), *Scum Of The Earth* (Dble CD) and *Scum Of The Earth, Vol. 2* (LP). (VJ)

Outer Edge

45:	Help Each Other / Pushin'	(Zazz #2781) 1970/1

An obscure group from the Pacific Northwest. The 'A' side is a weak ballad but the flip is a very heavy psych track. (SR/MW)

The Outer Limits

Personnel:	J. BACHMAN	A
	P. HERCKER	A
	JIM WESTBROOK	A

45:	Don't Need You No More/Walkin' Away	(Goldust 5014) 1966

A garage punk combo based in University Park, New Mexico. The 'A' side, *Don't Need You No More*, has got pretty vocals and several changes of pace.

Compilation appearances have included: *Don't Need You No More* on *New Mexico Punk From The Sixties* (LP) and *Sixties Archive, Vol. 4* (CD); *Walkin' Away*, *Don't Need You No More*, *The Waves*, *Don't Leave Me*, *Alone And Crying* and *Begin Your Crying* (i.e. both sides of the 45, plus four original unreleased cuts recorded in 1966) on *The Goldust Records Story* (CD); and *Walkin' Away* and *The Waves* on *Green Crystal Ties, Vol. 5* (CD). (VJ/MW)

Outlaw Blues

45:	Non-Stop Blues/Mustafa	(Era 3171) 1967

The 'A' side to this obscure single can also be heard on the *Ear-Piercing Punk* (LP & CD) compilation. (VJ)

The Outlaw Blues Band

Personnel:	VICTOR ALEMAN	drms, perc	AB
	JOE FRANCIS GONZALES	bs, vcls	A
	PHILLIP JOHN	ld gtr, ld vcls	AB
	LEON RUBENHOLD	hrmnca, vcls	AB
	JOE WHITEMAN	sax, flute, vibra harp	AB
	LAWRENCE DICKENS	bs	B

ALBUMS:	1(A)	OUTLAW BLUES BAND	(Bluesway BLS 6021) 1968 SC
	2(B)	BREAKING IN	(Bluesway BLS 6030) 1969 SC

NB: (1) reissued on CD and LP (Akarma 108 CD/LP). (2) reissued on CD and LP (Akarma 107 CD/LP).

As their name suggests, this was a blues-rock outfit but they were a pretty good one at that. From California, they were one of the several new acts signed by Bob Thiele, the producer of several interesting jazz artists (Coltrane, **Gabor Szabo**) and rock groups (**Eden's Children**, **Free Spirits** etc).

Their first album features lots of fluid guitar and you should enjoy this if blues-rock is your thing. Even if it isn't you might still like it. Certainly *I've Got To Have Peace On My Mind* is very imaginative with interesting sound effects and it extends far beyond the usual blues-rock format. The band also have strong jazz influences, particularly in the drumming and the sax (or flute) interludes. Other highlights include an interesting reinterpretation of **John D. Loudermilk**'s *Tobacco Road*, the instrumental *Death Dog Of Doom*, *Tried To Be A Good Boy (But I'm Worse Than A Nazi)*, *Two 'Tranes Running* (not a mispelling but an an homage to Coltrane!) and the catchy *Lost In The Blues*.

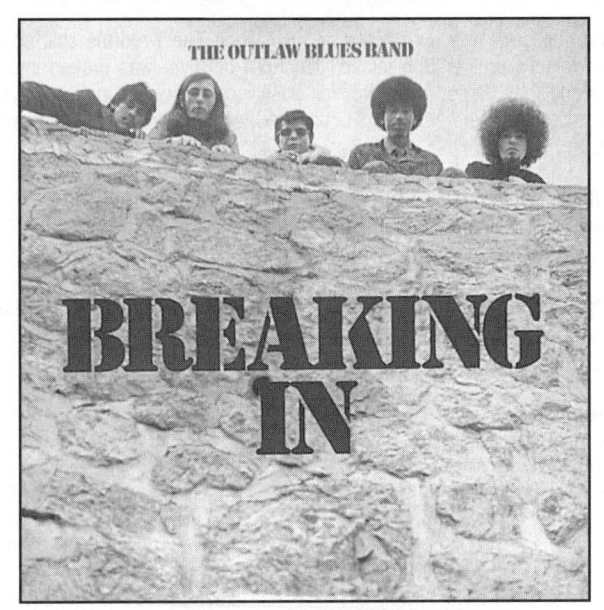

THE OUTLAW BLUES BAND - Breaking In LP.

After Gonzales, their bass player, was replaced by Dickens (who would later play with Willie Hutch, a soul/funk singer), they recorded a second album in the same style, still mixing blues covers (*Stormy Monday Blues*) with original material (*Mano Pano Shhhh*, *Plastic Man*, *Day Said...*).

They can easily be compared to the best moments of the **Paul Butterfield Blues Band** or **The Blues Project**, although their albums are only very minor collectables at present.

Leon Rubenhold had previously played in Rosie And The Originals, in the early sixties and later did a lot of uncredited session work in the Hollywood studios. Equally at ease with guitar and harmonica, he reappeared in 1980 with Rainbow Red Oxidiser, a short-lived L.A. group formed by Michael Neal (a friend of Sky Saxon) with Mars Bonfire, Ed Cassidy (**Spirit**) and Gary Marker (**Rising Sons**, **Fusion**).

Bass player, Joe Francis Gonzales died recently of liver cancer. (SR/VJ)

The Outlaws

45:	Worlds Apart/Fun, Fame, And Fortune	(In 102)	1966

A sixties Dallas, Texas band who are better known under their later moniker **Kit & The Outlaws**.

Compilation appearances have included: *Fun, Fame, And Fortune* on *Punk Classics, Vol. 4* (7"); *Fun, Fame And Fortune* and *Worlds Apart* on *Green Crystal Ties, Vol. 1* (CD) and *The History Of Texas Garage Bands, Vol. 4* (CD). (VJ/MW)

The Outrage

ALBUM:	1	OUTRAGE	(Kama Sutra KLPS-8074) 1969 ?

45s:	The City / Be My Baby	(Kama Sutra 252) 1968
	The Letter / The Letter (Edit)	(Kama Sutra 259) 1969
	The Letter / The Way I See It	(Kama Sutra 259) 1969

This outfit recorded a heavy psychedelic version of *The Letter* (slowed down in the style of **Vanilla Fudge**). Thought to have come from San Francisco, they were probably however from New York, where their producer, John Linde (Community Production) also worked with **Group Image**, **GNP** and the **New York R&R Ensemble**. (TA/MW/SR)

The Outside In

Personnel incl:	FRED DANE	vcls	A
	BOBBY HERNE	ld gtr	A
	ANDY MURTON	bs	A

45:	You Ain't Gonna Bring Me Down To My Knees/ Sometimes I Don't Like Myself	(Right RRM-6612) 1966

York in Maine was home to this crew. According to the accompanying notes to *You Ain't Gonna Bring Me Down To My Knees* (CD), Herne was the guitarist on the **90th Congress** 45. He also crops up on numerous Northeast recordings as producer/arranger (**Missing Links**, **Shaggs**, **Flat Earth Society**, **Lazy Smoke**, **Euclid**) and was in numerous bands from the late fifties.

In the sixties Herne's outfits include The Exotics (on Coral), OJ and The Soulbeats and **The Cobras**. In 1970 he formed Atlantis. He died suddenly in May 1998 and some of his legacy is revealed in Aram Heller's zine 'Banjo Room Revisited #2'.

Bassist Andy Murton went on to be Sunday editor for the Boston Globe.

Compilation appearances have includes: *You Ain't Gonna Bring Me Down To My Knees* and *Sometimes I Don't Like Myself* on *You Ain't Gonna Bring Me Down To My Knees* (CD); *You Ain't Gonna Bring Me Down To My Knees* on *The Cicadelic 60's, Vol. 4* (CD), *The Cicadelic 60's, Vol. 2* (LP) and *Green Crystal Ties Vol. 4* (CD). (MW/AH)

The Outsiders

Personnel:	BILL BRUNO	ld gtr	A B
	SONNY GERACI	vcls	A B
	TOM KING	gtr	A B
	MERDIN MADSEN	bs, hrmnca	A B
	RICKY BAKER	drms	B

				HCP
ALBUMS:	1(A)	TIME WON'T LET ME	(Capitol 2501) 1966	37 -
	2(B)	ALBUM 2	(Capitol 2568) 1966	90 -
	3(B)	IN	(Capitol 2636) 1967	- -
	4(B)	HAPPENING LIVE	(Capitol 2745) 1967	103 -

NB: There are also two retrospective compilations: *The Best Of The Outsiders* (Rhino) 198? and *The Outsiders* (CD) (Collectables COL-5686) 1996.

			HCP
45s:	Time Won't Let Me/Was It Really Real?	(Capitol 5573) 1966	5
	Girl In Love/		
	What Makes You So Bad? (PS)	(Capitol 5646) 1966	21
	Respectable/Lost In My World	(Capitol 5701) 1966	15
	Help Me Girl/You Gotta Look	(Capitol 5759) 1966	37
	I'll Give You Time/		
	I'm Not Trying To Hurt You	(Capitol 5843) 1967	118
	Gotta Leave Us Alone/		
	I Just Can't See You Anymore	(Capitol 5892) 1967	121
	I'll See You In Summertime/		
	And Now You Want My Sympathy	(Capitol 5955) 1967	-
	Little Bit Of Lovin'/I Will Love You	(Capitol 2055) 1967	117
	Oh How It Hurts/We Ain't Gonna Make It	(Capitol 2216) 1968	-
	Changes/Lost In My World	(Bell 904) 1970	107

NB: There are also three French EPs with picture sleeves: *Time Won't Let Me/Was It Really Real/Girl In Love/What Makes You So Bad?* (Capitol EAP 120804); *Respectable/Lost In My World/Help Me Girl/You Gotta Look* (Capitol 120879); *I'll Give You Time/I'm Not Trying To Hurt You/Oh How It Hurts/Since I Lost My Baby* (Capitol 120948).

A rather ordinary pop outfit from Cleveland, Ohio. They enjoyed short-term success, including a Top Ten hit with *Time Won't Let Me*. It was the zenith of their career, which then took a slow downward spiral.

Tom King initially formed the Starfires, a rock'n'roll/soul band, recording numerous records on his uncle's Pama label. Seeking greater success with a major label after acquiring Sonny Geraci as vocalist led to family friction resulting in (and reflected by) the band's new name, **The Outsiders**. *Time Won't Let Me* secured a deal with Capitol via Roger Karschner, whose name crops up on many other sixties Cleveland recordings. He became their manager too.

The flip to their cover of The Isley Brothers' *Respectable*, *Lost In My World*, was rerecorded in 1970 by singer Sonny Geraci's his new band Climax. Based in Los Angeles, they enjoyed a Top Ten hit with *Precious and Few*. Geraci went on to become a pretty atrocious ballad singer.

The Outsiders CD retrospective on Collectables is a 25-track odyssey of recordings spanning 1965 through 1968 and is accompanied by a well-researched and detailed booklet.

Compilation appearances have included: *Time Won't Let Me* on *Nuggets Box* (CD), *Nuggets From Nuggets* (CD), *Nuggets, Vol. 3* (LP) and *Pride Of Cleveland Past* (LP); *Lost In My World* on *Nuggets Vol. 4: Pop Part Two* (LP); and *I'm Not Trying To Hurt You* on *Pebbles, Vol. 9* (LP). (VJ/MW/SR)

The Outsiders

Personnel:	HARDY DIAL	vcls	A
	RONNIE ELLIOT	bs	AB
	SPENCER HINKLE	drms	AB
	BUDDY RICHARDSON	ld gtr	AB
	RONNIE VASKOVSKY	gtr	AB
	JOHN DELISE	vcls	B

45s:	She's Coming On Stronger/Just Let Me Be	(Knight 103) 1965
	Summertime Blues/Set You Free This Time	(Knight 104) 1966

A different five-piece from Tampa, Florida, which formed in 1964. Bassist Ronny Elliot joined in 1965 from another Tampa band The Raveons and Hinkle had played in early line-ups of Tampa's Tropics. They developed a lot of local support and cut their first 45 at Tampa's H & H Avenue. *She's Coming On Stronger* is a pretty good pop/punk piece with some upfront drumming and they followed it with a ripping cover of Eddie Cochran's *Summertime Blues*. By now John Delise had replaced Hardy Dial on vocals. In 1966, they were signed to the Laurie Records subsidiary label Providence who changed their name to **The Soul Trippers** because of the better-known Ohio Outsiders. Then, in 1967, they changed name again to **Noah's Ark** releasing two 45s for New York's Decca label.

Buddy Richardson went on to form White Witch who released two albums on Capricorn 1973-4. John DeLise also had spells in **The Rovin' Flames** and **Those Five**.

Compilation appearances include *She's Comin' On Stronger* on *Psychedelic States - Florida Vol. 1* (CD). (VJ/MW/JLh)

The Outsiders

45:	Go Go Ferrari/Big Boy Pete	(Cha Cha 724) 196?

From Michigan City, Indiana. You'll also find the 'A' side, *Go Go Ferrari* on *Hipsville, Vol. 2* (LP). (VJ/MM)

The Outspoken Blues

Personnel:	BILL KIRCHMEYER	ld gtr	A
	JIM KORN	bs, vcls	AB
	BILL LEVAK	drms	ABC
	TOM NELSON	gtr	ABC
	JOHN PENCAK	keyb'ds	ABC
	JAMES STANLEY	bs, vcls	ABC
	BOB STANLEY	ld gtr	BC

45:	Mister, You're A Better Man Than I/	
	Not Right Now	(Orlyn) 1966

From Chicago, the 'B' side to this bands 45 *Not Right Now* was recorded in June 1966 and is a moody rocker, with fiery lead guitar, a relentless throbbing beat and spine-chilling organ.

The band's roots lay in frat rock combo The Empires (Bill Levak - drms; Tom Nelson - gtr; 14-year old Bob Stanley - vcls, ld gtr; Jim Stanley - gtr, vcls; and Tim Wagner - bs). When Jim left the band for college, they continued for a while as a four-piece, but he soon returned after damaging his knee and then Tim Wagner was drafted. The Empires subsequently split in 1965, with Bob Stanley joining **The Bryds** and the remaining members joining forces with Jim Korn and Bill Kirchmeyer from Beat Incorporated.

The group grew to a six-piece in 1967 when **The Bryd(e)s** split up and Jim Stanley's brother Bob joined. Jim Korn however was drafted into the army and then James took over full bass/vocal duties. In their later years they adopted a more white-soul sound and recorded an unissued album for Mercury.

Bill Kirchmeyer and Jim Stanley later formed a group called The Prod with bassist Herb Eimerman. Bob Stanley also later formed Hot Mama Silver with Herb Eimerman.

Compilation appearances include *Not Right Now* on *Back From The Grave, Vol. 8* (CD) and *Back From The Grave, Vol. 8* (Dble LP). (VJ/JSa)

Owen-B

Personnel:	JIM KRAUSE	hrmnca, vcls, perc	A
	BOB TOUSIGNANT	drms, vcls, conga	AB
	TERRY VAN AUKER	gtr, vcls	AB
	TOM ZINSER	bs, vcls, piano, gtr	AB
	TONY MARTUCCI	bs	B
	STERLING SMITH	keyb'ds	B

ALBUM:	1(A)	OWEN-B	(Mus-I-Col 101 209/101210) 1970 R1

NB: (1) reissued in the late eighties. Line-up 'B' also recorded a further album outside of this books timeframe *Old Happy Places* (Owl 7093N6) 1978.

HCP

45s:	Mississippi Mama/Nowhere To Run	(Janus 107) 1970 97
	Never Goin' Home/Zig Zag Man	(Janus 123) 1970 -

Their debut is an early seventies privately-pressed rock album with some good guitar moments. It has become a significant collectors' item and was repressed in the late eighties. Recorded in Columbus, Ohio, it achieves a good standard throughout. The material was written, arranged and produced by the band themselves. There are some good rock numbers like *Daily News, Mellow Meadow, My Friends* and *Out On Our Own*, some nice vocal harmonies on *Share* and *All We Are Asking* is a more sensitive psychedelic folk number. Well worth a listen. Both 45s feature non-album tracks and they rock.

You can also find *Zig Zag Man* on *Marijuana Unknowns* (LP & CD) and *Mississippi Mama* on *Acid Dreams, Vol. 2* (LP). (VJ/MW/CW)

Owl

Personnel incl:	BRIAN CHASE	A
	JOHN LOWELL	A
	JOHN POLLANO	A

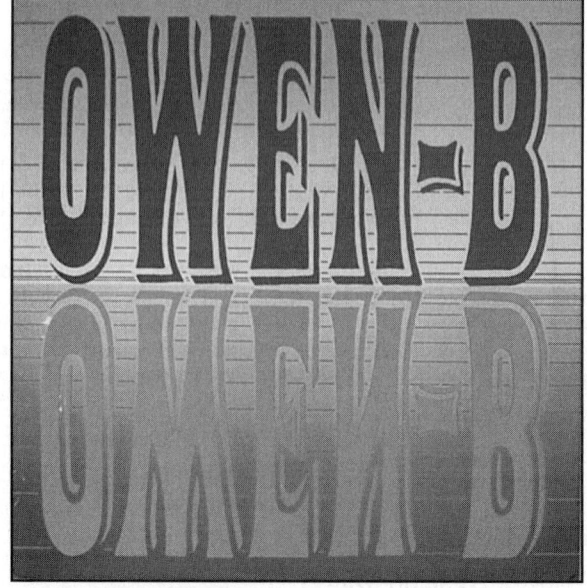

OWEN-B - Owen-B LP.

45:	Aunt Cate Is Dead/		
	As The World Keeps Turning		(Onyx No #) c1971

Early seventies light 'psych' - rock from Massachusetts by an outfit who had evolved out of **Lazy Smoke** and **The Shadows Of Time**. That fact alone makes this 45 quite collectable, though it's certainly not up to their earlier incarnation's standards. (MW)

The Oxford Circle

Personnel:	JIM KEYLOR	bs	A
	DEHNER PATTEN	gtr	A
	PAUL WHALEY	drms	A
	GARY YODER	rhythm gtr, vcls	A

CD:	1	LIVE AT THE AVALON '66	(Big Beat CDWIKD 178) 1998

45:	Foolish Woman/Mind Destruction	(World United 1002) 1966

An historically significant outfit from Sacramento, California. They included Gary Yoder (later of **Kak** and **Blue Cheer**) and gigged regularly as support to bands like **The Grateful Dead**. Jim Keylor was in some groups with Bob Segarini after **Family Tree** and in the embryonic **Roxy**. He was also involved in assembling **Blue Cheer** for their *Oh! Pleasant Hope* album and in 1978 started BSU studios whose products included Dead Kennedys, Suspects and True West. Patten also went on to play for **Kak**.

What of their music? The recent Big Beat retrospective shows a band that was pushing back the barriers of psychedelia in much the same way as The Yardbirds were. They should have gone on to better and bigger things in their own right. It includes fourteen live tracks, plus four studio cuts, including both sides of their exceptional 45. Also included are a detailed history of the band. Donnie Jupiter of the cult seventies psych/punk band **The Twinkeyz** recalls: "The first time I saw them I was blown away - they looked cooler than hell with their long hair, hippie beads and somewhat surly attitude. Their drummer, Paul Whaley, nailed his kit to the floor with screwdrivers and flailed away like a madman through the whole set. When they were finished playing his hands were bleeding." The Big Beat CD is probably the next best thing to having been there and comes highly recommended.

World United Records was owned by fellow Sacramento-based band **The New Breed** who had set up the label when they were dropped by Mercury.

Compilation appearances have included: *Foolish Woman* on *Pebbles Box* (5-LP) and *Trash Box* (5-CD); *Mind Destruction* on *Everything You Always Wanted To Know* (CD); and *Foolish Woman* and *Mind Destruction* on *Endless Journey - Phase One* (LP) and *Endless Journey - Phase I & II* (Dble CD). (BS/VJ/MW)

The Oxford Circus

45:	Tracy/4th Street Carnival	(Zig Zag 101) 1967

From Houston, Texas. The flip features some some fine up-front bass and can also be found on *Texas Flashback (The Best Of)* (CD), *Texas Flashbacks, Vol. 2* (LP) and *Flashback, Vol. 2* (LP). (VJ)

The Oxford Circus

Personnel:	DAVE BARFIELD	bs	A
	WINSTON LOGAN	drms	AB
	STEVE BRAUNSTEIN	gtr	B
	BRIAN CUMMINGS	bs	B
	GENE SMITH	gtr	B

Another, apparently different, Texas outfit from Waco, have six live tracks from 1968 featured on **The Headstones** *24 Hours (Everyday)* CD. Heavy acid-psych covers of *Splash 1* (**13th Floor Elevators**), *99th Floor* (**Moving Sidewalks**), *Time Has Come Today* (**Chambers Bros**), *59th Street Bridge Song* and *You Keep Me Hanging On*. According to the CD liners, they'd formed in 1966 after Logan had left McAllen's **Headstones** (hence their inclusion on the CD). In 1969, line-up 'B' decided to concentrate on original compositions only, acquired a young guitarist called Rene Best and changed their name to **Watermusic**, who also feature on the CD. (MW)

The Oxford 5

45:	The World I've Planned/	
	Out Of Love For You	(Sidra 9009) 1965/6

From around Birmingham, Michigan, this act's *The World I've Planned* is regarded as a classic. They band also contributed three tracks (*Gloria*, *The World I've Planned* and *All Really Want To Do*) to the mega-rare 1965 sampler *Friday At The Cage A Go Go*, later known as *Long Hot Summer* and reissued in 1989 (Hide The Sausage HTS-001).

Other compilation appearances include: *The World I've Planned* on *Oil Stains* (LP); and *Gloria* on *Highs In The Mid-Sixties, Vol. 19* (LP). (VJ)

The Oxfords

Personnel:	JIM GUEST	drms	ABCDE
	CHRIS HUBBS	gtr	A
	JIM McNICOL	bs	A
	STEVE McNICOL	ld gtr	A
	DANNY MARSHALL	gtr	B
	JAY PETACH	keyb'ds, ld gtr	BCDEFGHI
	BILL TULLIS	ld vcls, gtr	BCDE
	BILL TURNER	bs	B
	RAY BARRICKMAN	bs, vcls	C
	RONNIE BROOKS	gtr, bs	CD
	GARY JOHNSON	bs	E
	DILL ASHER	bs	F
	JILL DEMARCO	gtr, vcls	FGHI
	DONNIE HALE	drms	F
	LARRY HOLT	bs	GH
	PAUL HOERNI	drms	GH
	JERRY CANTER	gtr	H
	BOBBIE JONES	drms	I
	QUENTIN SHARPENSTEIN	bs	I
	TONY WILLIAMSON	ld gtr	I
	(KEITH SPRING		F)

NB: Line-ups:- 'A' - 1965, 'B' 1965-6, 'C' 1966, 'D' 1966-7, 'E' 1967-8, 'F' 1968-9, 'G' 1969-71, 'H' 1971-2, 'I' 1972.

ALBUM: 1(F/G) FLYING UP THROUGH THE SKY
(Union Jac LH 6497) 1970 R2

NB: (1) reissued on CD with additional tracks (Gear Fab GF-168) 2001.

THE OXFORD CIRCLE - Live At The Avalon '66 CD.

45s:	Time And Place/	
	Always Something There To Remind Me	(Our Bag 103) 1966
	Time And Place/	
	Always Something There To Remind Me	(Mala 550) 1967
	Sunflower Sun/Chicago Woman	(Mala 563) 1967
	My World/Sung At Harvest Time	(Union Jac 5632/3) 1969
	Come On Back To Beer / Your Own Way	(Paula 331) 1970

This Louisville, Kentucky band's album is now beginning to interest some collectors. Bright 'n' breezy pop very much in the same mould as **Orange Coloured Sky** is on the Side One menu. Side two isn't quite as good, but is more experimental. *Young Girl's Lament* is the stand-out cut on this side with powerful female vocals and fuzz guitar; *Come On 'Round* is marred by a tedious drum solo and *Good Night* sounds gospel-influenced. Worth a spin if you come across a copy.

Originally formed in 1964 by Jim Guest, the band became very popular and influential on the Louisville scene, where they were the first group to adopt the British sound and look. In 1965, a rift developed between Guest and the rest of the band. Being friends with another local band The Spectres (Jay Petach, Bill Tullis, Bill Turner, Danny Marshall and drummer Glenn Howerton) the problem was resolved by trading drummers. The Spectres joined Guest in **The Oxfords** whilst Howerton teamed up the ex-**Oxfords** to form **The Rugbys** (their preferred stage attire being rugby shirts). Over the next couple of years **The Oxfords** released a couple of 45s including the superb fuzz-punker *Time And Place*. In 1968, Guest left; Jay Petach took the reins and built a new group which included Jill DeMarco, lead singer from girl group The Hearby. This line-up set about recording an album though it wasn't released until 1970 when, despite label offers, the band chose to put it out with a showcase 45 on their own label. They also released a 45 on Paula featured the **Zappa**-inspired *Come On Back To Beer*, which hit the No. 1 spot in Louisville. In 1971, Petach composed a musical called 'Grease', which was performed by **The Oxfords** in Louisville, Atlanta and Kansas. The following year he got involved in studio engineering. **The Oxfords** appeared to be going nowhere fast so they finally called it a day in the Summer of 1972.

In 1997, **The Oxfords** had a "reunion" gig in Louisville for a charity function. Jill DeMarco:- "After 25 years of not playing together, we actually did pretty well! Everyone looked much the same as they did way back when, believe it or not - full sets of hair and no potbellies. Only the acne was gone!"

"Today, Jay Petach is still in the music business as a producer in a studio in Cincinnatti, Ohio. He has made numerous commercials over the years and has even released an all-instrumental CD of songs played on the ocarina! (He was the multi-talented member of the group). Larry Holt sadly suffered a severe back injury and was out of commission for a while, but he is back to playing bass around Louisville, Paul Hoerni continues to play drums around Louisville and works for UPS, whilst I'm the only one who hasn't stayed in music to any great degree. I moved to Chicago in 1973 and did some recording, music copyrighting, and jazz studies for six years. Then moved to Seattle in 1979 and played solo gigs up through the mid-eighties, but it was not lucrative enough to survive. So, I found full-time work as a Technical Writer for the U.S. government (Federal Aviation Administration), and have been working at it ever since. I'm still in Seattle and do sing in the shower!"

The Gear Fab retrospective CD gathers together the complete album and all 45 tracks with several unreleased cuts from 1969 to 1972.

Compilation appearances have included *Time And Place* on *Sixties Rebellion Vol. 16* (LP & CD), *Victims Of Circumstance, Vol. 2* (LP) and *Victims Of Circumstance, Vol. 2* (CD). (MW/LDwiththankstoJDo)

The Oxfords

45:	I Ain't Done Wrong/Cheatin' Little Girl	(Soul 001) 1966

From Tulsa, Oklahoma. The 'A' side is a Yardbirds song and **The Oxfords** version of this rave-up isn't bad. The flip is in a slower beat/ballad vein.

Compilation appearances have included: *I Ain't Done Wrong* and *Cheatin' Little Girl* on *Sixties Rebellion, Vol. 4* (LP & CD); and *I Ain't Done Wrong* on *Teenage Shutdown, Vol. 10* (LP & CD). (MW)

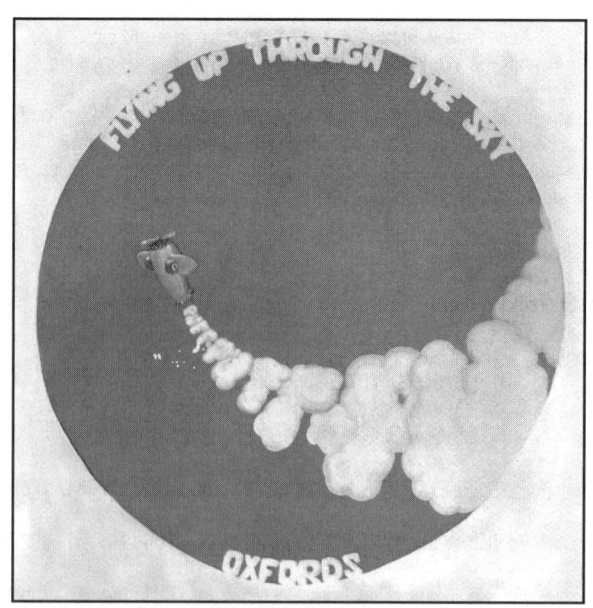

OXFORDS - Flying Up Through The Sky LP.

The Oxfords

45:	Don't Be A Dropout/Don't Play That Song	(Strand) c1967

Written by Stanley and Taub, a garage group with interesting guitar breaks, but for once the lyrics are anti "high school dropouts". They are unrelated to the two other bands of this name. (SR)

Oxford Watchband

45:	Diagnosis (One Way Empty And Down)/	
	Welcome To The World	(Hand 496) 1969

From Rochester, New York. A remarkable top side kicks off like it's going to be **Vanilla Fudge** before a heavy blast of fuzz and bombast. Midway a peal of thunder fades to return as a barrage of gun and fighting effects. A strange and disjointed trip, with some wicked guitar on the outro and vocals reminiscent of Don Gallucci's **Touch**. The '**Fudge** influence is more to the fore on the pedestrian flip, though it does feature some quiet flute passages between the ponderous keyboard vibes, soulful vocals and brassy outbursts. (MW)

The Oxpetals

Personnel incl:	DANIEL "ACE" ALLISON	drms	X
	BENJAMIN HERNDON	vcls, gtr	X
	STEVEN PAGUE		X
	GUY PHILLIPS		X
	ROBERT WEBBER	keyb'ds	X
	D. FLOWERS		

ALBUM:	1(X)	THE OXPETALS	(Mercury 61289) 1970 -

45s:	Prune Growing In June/	
	Walking Down The Sunny Side	(Musicor MU 1274) 1967
	Down From The Mountains /	
	What Can You Say	(Mercury 73143) 1970

From upstate New York. *Prune...* is psychedelic pop with a twist. Ignoring the awful square sounding male - female vocals and stupidly hip lyrics, there's some strangely warped pop with phasing, acidic guitar and chiming keyboards that'll please Rubble-ites, but not garage-psych fans. The flip is harmony - folk - pop.

By 1970 they had evolved into a five-piece, commune-based band. The album comes in a gatefold of pastoral serenity. Pasted-in leaves of photos and lyrics fail to give details of the band personnel and instrumentation, other than writer credits. Very laid-back and with pleasing harmonies, this is uplifting soft-rock that incorporates boogie, folk and country influences.

Likely to be labelled "hippie-rock" but that's not to denigrate it - it doesn't ramble and the varied selection shows that they can rock.

Daniel "Ace" Allison sadly died of cancer recently. (MW)

The Oz Band

45:   I Am Not The Same/Winter Rain   (Cub 9158 SS) 1968

An obscure outfit with a meritorious 45 in a restrained but haunting folk-psych style, like a softer **Jefferson Airplane** with cool male - female vocals that intertwine well. *Winter Rain* in particular has a persistent and hypnotic quality that demands repeated playing. Both sides are credited to Morris - Freeman and produced by Lamont Johnson for Downeast Productions. (MW)

Oz Knozz

Personnel: RICHARD HEATH   gtr, vcls   A
            BILL MASSEY
            (aka NEWT BILDO) bs   A
            DUANE MASSEY   keyb'ds, horns   A
            MONTY NAUL   drms   A

ALBUM: 1(A) RUFF MIX   (Ozone OZ-1 000) 1975 R2

NB: (1) has counterfeited on vinyl. Later reissued on CD (Black Rose BR 146) 2001.

A much-vaunted album, which has become a minor collectors' item. A private-press by a Bellaire, Texas band and recorded in Houston, this commands a high price tag (in Europe anyway). It's actually quite good, but not really psychedelic in the sixties sense. It certainly varies in style from heavy to soft, jazzy to funky and is of a high standard of musicianship but it has more in common with, say, Led Zeppelin (especially *Led Zepp III*). The stand-out track is the superb *Second Time Blues* - an anguished bluesy-rock ballad whose comparison to Led Zepp tour-de-force *Since I've Been Loving You* is, I'm afraid, unavoidable, The main problem with the album, though, is that the songwriting lacks any real flair.

Incredibly, the band is still active, and Duane Massey recalls: "Richard Heath left the band shortly after *Ruff Mix* was released, and was tragically killed in an auto accident several years later while playing with Vince Vance and The Valients. Although there have been several personnel changes and two "dormant" periods, we are back performing on a limited basis in regional halls. Marty, Bill and I still make up the nucleus of the band, with a guitarist, Bill Mojelsky, and a singer, Milton Coronado."

"I agree with your observation on the songwriting on *Ruff Mix*, as the material in that period of the band was restricted by my own vocal limitations. We added a vocalist in 1979 (the first of several) and my composing boundaries were greatly increased."

"The band also released a two-song EP with this line-up but never really marketed it and only pressed 500 copies. Incidentally, *Ruff Mix* was limited to two pressings of 1,000 copies each, but was bootlegged in Italy at some time in the eighties, I believe. The cover has "Made in Italy" printed on it. (CF/MW/VJ/DMa)

Ozone

45:   Ways Of Living/Tornado   (Wildflower 001) c1970

A totally obscure group, presumably in the garage style. (SR)

ODA - Oda CD.

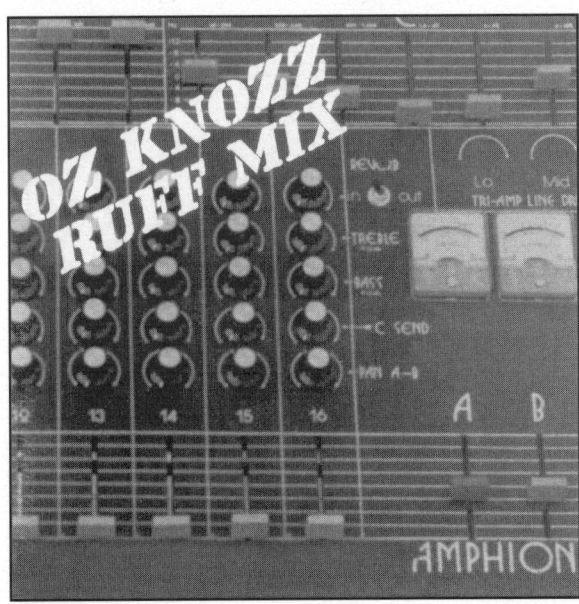

OZ KNOZZ - Ruff Mix CD.

OTHER HALF - Mr Pharmacist CD.

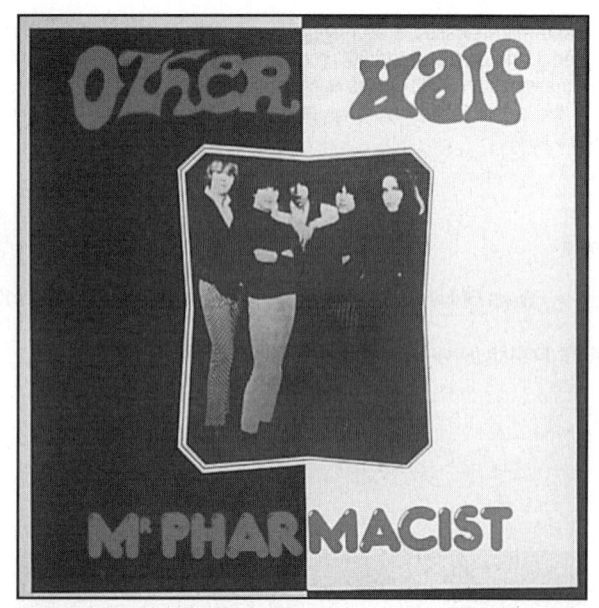

OTHER HALF - Mr Pharmacist LP.

ENDLESS JOURNEY PHASE 1 (Comp LP) including Oxford Circle.

ENDLESS JOURNEY PHASE 1 & II (Comp CD) including Oxford Circle.

EVERYTHING YOU ALWAYS WANTED... (Comp CD) including Oxford Circle.

TRASH BOX (Comp CD) including Oxford Circle.

SIXTIES REBELLION Vol. 4 (Comp CD) including The Oxfords.

The Pack

45: Time/Baby I Ask You Why   (Sound Tex 650529) 1965

Out of San Antonio, Texas in the mid-sixties. The flip can also be found on *Texas Punk From The Sixties* (LP), and *Sixties Archive, Vol. 2* (CD). (VJ)

The Pack

45: The Tears Come Rollin'/
The Colour Of Our Love   (Wingate 007) 1968

This 45 was the work of the Michigan outfit, previously **Terry Knight & The Pack**. When Terry decided to quit the limelight and manage the group they released this 45 and three more as **The Fabulous Pack** before being guided onto infamy and fortune as Grand Funk Railroad. The R&B styled flip, *The Colour Of Love*, can be heard on *Relics, Vol's 1 & 2* (CD), *Relics, Vol. 1* (LP) and *Sixties Archive, Vol. 7* (CD). (VJ)

The Pagans

Personnel:			
JEFF SULLIVAN	bs		ABCD
KIP SULLIVAN	ld gtr, ld vcls		ABCD
JAY THOMPSON	drms		ABC
JIM RUSHTON	gtr, vcls		BCD
JERRY HUITING	gtr		CD
STEVE ROSSI	drms		D
CHRIS HOLLENBECK	keyb'ds		

45: Ba Ba Yaga/Stop Shakin' Your Head   (Studio City 1034) 1965

Rochester in Southeast Minnesota was home turf to this outfit, which gradually came together during 1963-64. Steve Rossi took over on drums in August 1964 after Jay Thompson (who had once filled in for Gordy Scudamore on drums in **The Mustangs**) committed suicide. They travelled to Minneapolis during Easter 1965 to record the two original compositions which comprised their 45. The 'A' side veers towards folk-rock and 500 copies of the 45 were pressed.

Chris Hollenbeck was a member of the band only briefly - he was killed in a car crash sometime after leaving the band. His main claim to fame was that his father was a distinguished surgeon who had removed LBJ's gall bladder. The band disintegrated after Kip Sullivan left to go to Pomona College in California in the Fall of 1965. They later reformed into The Downchilds and then The Downchild's Blues Band but these later incarnations produced no vinyl. The Sullivan brothers and Steve Rossi were later involved in a late eighties reformation of the band.

Compilation coverage has so far included: *Ba Ba Yaga* on *The Midwest Vs. Canada* (LP) and *Teenage Shutdown, Vol. 3* (LP & CD). (VJ/MW)

Page Boys

45: All I Want/Sweet Love   (Rum 1020) 1967

From Amarillo, Texas. There's a laid-back vocal over a fuzz-punk backing on the 'A' side. (VJ)

The Page Boys

Personnel:			
SPENCER CLARK	bs		A
DAN DAZELL	drms		A
JACK WHITE	vcls, gtr		A
BOB WIKSTORM	organ		A

45: Our Love/Things Are Going To Break Up   (Camelot 114) 1965

Came out of Moses Lake, Washington, where they formed in 1963. Their single was a popular regional hit in 1965. They were short-lived at the time but re-united in 1985 and still perform around the Northwest periodically. (VJ)

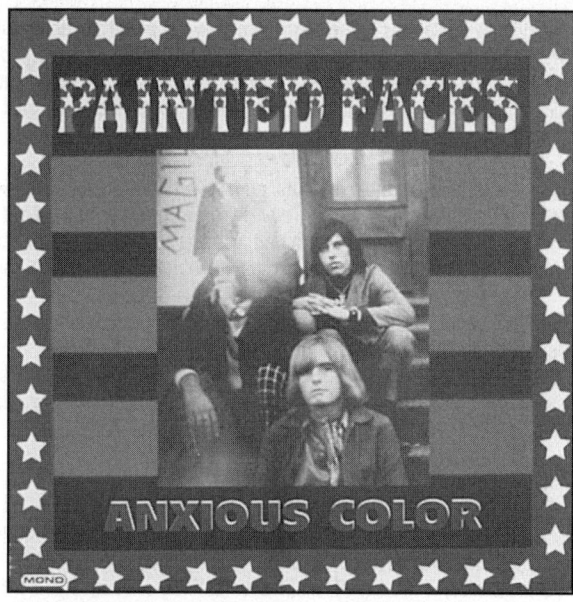

PAINTED FACES - Anxious Color LP.

The Page Boys

45: When I Meet A Girl Like You/
I Have Love   (Seville 45-135 V) 1965

A New York area outfit's sole stab at fame. Punchy British Invasion sounds with oh-too-short garagey guitar breaks on both sides. (MW)

The Pagens

45: Mystic Cloud/Someone Like You   (Ish-Koom 6901) 1966

This outfit came from Dearborn, Michigan. *Mystic Cloud* is a superb poppy slice of garage-psych.

Compilation appearances include: *Mystic Cloud* on *Michigan Mayhem, Vol. 1* (CD) and *Green Crystal Ties, Vol. 9* (CD); *Mystic Cloud* and *Someone Like You* on *The Cicadelic 60's, Vol. 1* (CD), *The Cicadelic 60's, Vol. 3* (LP) and *The History Of Michigan Garage Bands In The 60's* (3-CD). (MW)

Painted Faces

Personnel incl:			
HARRY BRAGG	drms		ABCD
CRAIG GUILD	bs		A
JOHN McKINNEY	gtr/bs		ABC
JACK O'NEIL	vcls		ABCD
JERRY TURANO	ld gtr		ABC
GEORGE SCHULE	bs		C
BRUCE MORFORD	bs		D

ALBUM: 1(-) ANXIOUS COLOR   (Distortions DR 1020) 1994

NB: (1) is a reissue of all the 45s plus a ton of unreleased material.

45s:		
Things We See/I Want You	(Qualicon 5002)	1967
Anxious Color/Things We See	(Manhatten 803)	1967
I Think I'm Going Mad/		
I Lost You In My Mind	(Manhatten 811)	1968
Don't Say She's Gone/		
In The Heat Of The Night	(Manhatten 818)	1968
The Letter//I Need You		
Shovel Song/Time Goes On (PS)	(Distortions DR 0031)	1997

This band came from Fort Myers in Florida and not Los Angeles as had previously been suggested. Turano and McKinney were eventually forced to quit the band as they travelled increasingly to play in New York City and they were replaced by various musicians, but the heart of the band remained Jack O'Neill, George Schule and Harry Bragg. It was during a spell at a bar called 'A Place In The Sun' on the Virgin Islands that they began painting their faces. In the same era they recorded an entire album of *Today's Hits*, featuring covers of songs like *The Letter*, *Brown Eyed Girl* and *Incense And Peppermints*, which was supposed to come out on Sidewalk or Tower as a budget album, but which never got past the acetate stage.

Thanks to Distortions all their 45 cuts and several previously unreleased cuts are now compiled on *Anxious Color*. In *Anxious Color* and *I Lost You In My Mind*, in particular, they recorded some stunning slices of sixties garage-psych, making this collection a 'must have' for all fans of the genre.

An influential band on the "next generation" of garage artists, cover versions have included: *Anxious Color* by The Birdmen Of Alkatraz on their *From The Cage* LP; *Anxious Color* by the Mutts in 1984 on the Voxx comp *Battle Of The Garage III*; and *Don't Say She's Gone* by Italian garage-folk-rockers the Others on their 1997 *So Far Out* 10".

Compilation appearances have included: *I Lost You In My Mind* on *The Magic Cube* (Flexi & CD), *Sixties Archive, Vol. 8* (CD), *Acid Trip From The Psychedelic Sixties* (LP) and *Psychedelic States: Florida Vol. 3* (CD); *Anxious Color* on *Pebbles, Vol. 3* (CD), *Pebbles, Vol. 4 (ESD)* (CD), *The Psychedelic Sixties, Vol. 1* (LP), *Acid Dreams - The Complete 3 LP Set* (3-LP), *Acid Dreams Testament* (CD), *Acid Dreams, Vol. 1* (LP) and *Garagelands Vol. 2* (CD); *Black Hearted Susan* on *Psychedelic Crown Jewels, Vol. 1* (Dble LP & CD); *Anxious Color* and *Things We See* on *A Journey To Tyme, Vol. 1* (LP); and *I Think I'm Going Mad* on *Highs In The Mid-Sixties Vol. 3* (LP). (VJ/MW)

The Paisleys

ALBUM: 1 COSMIC MIND AT PLAY
(Audio City/Peace 9445-2809) 1970 R2

NB: (1) counterfeited on vinyl (Psycho 7) 1983 and on CD (Afterglow 007) 1993. Also reissued on CD as *Cosmic Mind At Play Plus* with later bonus material.

From Minneapolis in Minnesota came **The Paisleys**. The most interesting tracks on their significant album are *Rockin*, notable for its use of echoes and sound effects, and the haunting *Wind*. Side two of the album consists entirely of the ambitious, though not entirely convincing *Musical Journey*.

There's also an Italian CD entitled *Beyond The Cosmic Mind* (Cosmic Mind Records 001) that is said to contain outtakes from the original album. However, the material is recorded some ten - twelve years later as is easily discovered when listening to the drumbeats (by a machine) and the track *Dear John*, about the murder of John Lennon. Still it's a pleasant collection of songs.

Compilation appearances have included: *Now!* on *Acid Trip From The Psychedelic Sixties* (LP) and *Sixties Archive, Vol. 8* (CD); *Something's Missing* on *The Scotty Story* (CD); *Wind* on *Endless Journey - Phase Two* (LP) and *Endless Journey - Phase I & II* (Dble CD). (VJ/CF)

THE PAISLEYS - Cosmic Mind At Play LP.

The Palace Guard

Personnel:
DAVE BEAUDINE	vcls	AB
DON BEAUDINE	vcls	AB
JOHN BEAUDINE	vcls	AB
TERRY RAE		AB
EMITT RHODES	drms	A
CHUCK McLUNG	ld gtr	B
RICK MOSER		B
MIKE CONLEY	vcls	
(DON GRADY	drms, keyb'ds, vcls	)

45s: α Summertime Game/
Little People (Orange Empire OE 91647/8) 1965
All Night Long/Playgirl (Orange Empire OE 331) 1965
A Girl You Can Depend On/
If You Need Me (Orange Empire OE 332) 1965
Falling Sugar/Oh Blue (Orange Empire OE 400) 1966
Falling Sugar/Oh Blue (Verve 10410) 1966
Saturday's Child/Party Lights (Parkway 111) 1966
Greed/Calliope (Parkway 124) 1966

NB: α as **Don Grady and The Palace Guard**.

This L.A.-based band is most significant for the inclusion of **Emitt Rhodes**. He joined the band when he was just fifteen, having already been in an outfit called The Emeralds. Musically they served up an amalgam of the British invasion sound and the burgeoning L.A. folk-rock style. After Emitt left the group they acquired considerable popularity as the houseband at Dave Hull's 'Hullaballoo Club', where they opened for touring bands who visited L.A. from The Yardbirds to Sonny and Cher. Their finest moments, *Falling Sugar* and *All Night Long* are both pleasant folk-pop renditions and it's surprising that they achieved no chart success and attracted little attention outside of Southern California. They certainly paid homage to the British invasion, often wearing uniforms and tall fur hats in an attempt to emulate the guards outside Buckingham Palace. Although their later material consisted of originals they also played some Beatles' covers, like *Norwegian Wood* and *Its Only Love* in their live act.

The Palace Guard also backed Don Grady (**Agrati**) before he joined **The Yellow Balloon**, recording a 45 for Orange Empire under this name. After leaving the band **Emitt Rhodes** went on to form **Merry-Go-Round**, whose sound was defined by the harmonious beat ballad *A Girl You Can Depend On*... Terry Rae also played in **Jamme**.

Party Lights was an excellent cover of the Claudine Clark hit with quite a novel arrangement.

Compilation appearances have included: *Falling Sugar* on *Nuggets Box* (4-CD), *Excerpts From Nuggets* (CD); *Falling Sugar* and *All Night Long* on *Nuggets, Vol. 4* (LP); *All Night Long* and *A Girl You Can Depend On* on *From The New World* (LP); *Greed* on *Fuzz Flaykes & Shakes, Vol. 1* (LP & CD). (VJ/MW/SBn/TR)

The Palace Guard(s)

Personnel incl:
R. FABER?	A
L. GRAY?	A
JEFF MILLER	A
ED VOLKER	A

45s: α Sorry / Better Things To Do (U-Doe 104) 1966
α No Comin' Back / Barbara (White Cliffs 269) 1967
α Never Be Lonely / ? (White Cliffs 278) c1967
α Christmas Would Be Nothing ?Flip To Above?/
Christmas Would Be Nothing
?Flip To Above? (White Cliffs #unkn) ??
Lookin' Everywhere /
β Gas Station Boogaloo Downtown (White Cliffs 286) 1968
Sideshow / Mr.Greene (rAe #1003) 1969

NB: α as by **The Palace Guards**, β as by **The Palace Guard**.

From Metarie, Louisiana, this bunch were active between '65 - '69. *No Comin' Back* is a screaming psychedelic-punker with a great guitar break and plenty of fuzz. *Gas Station Boogaloo Downtown*, is a poppier number with a psychedelic feel to it.

LUCIA PAMELA - Into Space With...

Sideshow, written by Ed Volker, is upbeat acid-rock-pop. The Jeff Miller composed flip is lighter, pop-psych. Both sides have an anglophile essence, especially lyric-wise and would not be out of place on a *Rubble* volume.

Compilation appearances have included: *No Comin' Back* and *Gas Station Boogaloo Downtown* on *Sixties Archive, Vol. 4* (CD) and *Florida Punk Groups From The Sixties* (LP); and *No Comin Back* on *Trash Box* (5-CD). (MW/JRe/MM)

Pale Fire

Personnel:	DAVID DORAN	vcls, gtr	A
	WILLIE KELLOGG	drms	A
	MIKE LAWSON	vcls, gtr	A
	MALCOLM McCASSY	vcls, bs	A

| 45s: | α | Never Hurt Again/Eye Girl | (Feather PF-4822) 1968 |
| | | Ups And Downs/Back Home | (Feather 72621 (PF-4826)) 1968 |

NB: α some copies have labels on wrong sides.

Late sixties orchestrated 'psych' obscurities, so dubbed mainly due to some outbursts of heavy searing guitar on the first 45. Unfortunately brassy sounds are in evidence along with soulful vocals especially on *Never Hurt Again*. *Eye Girl* has a dreamy vibe with baroque flashes until an explosive acid-drenched finale. Unlikely to appeal to either garage or psych purists initially, but after a few plays they do grow on you.

This San Diego, California, bunch were also known as **Five # Grin** and had a rawer version of *Never Hurt Again* which made it onto acetate - this can be heard on *Brain Shadows, Vol. 2* (LP & CD). (MW/CF)

Lucia Pamela

| ALBUM: | 1 | INTO OUTER SPACE | (No label) 1969 R3 |

NB: (1) reissued on vinyl (Gulfstream) 197? and on CD (Arf! Arf! AA 037).

Her truly eccentric album can be described as free-spirited bebop stuck in insterstellar overdrive. She came from Florida and sings about 'moon people' who abducted her Cadillac! The second pressing was on a different label and is the version the reissue was taken from. It originally appeared as a 'No label' issue.

Curiously, it turns out **Lucia Pamela** may also have been psychic! In the closing song on her album, the eccentric *In The Year 2000*, she proclaims "they will still be playing football in the year 2000". Not only are they still playing football, but Pamela's daughter, Georgia Frontiere, is at the top of the (U.S.) football world; the team she owns, the St. Louis Rams, won the Super Bowl in 2000!

Frontiere, also a show girl and psychic, apparently takes after her mother! It turns out **Lucia Pamela** was voted Miss St. Louis way back in 1926. She may have also recorded under the name Kathy Kent on both the Gulfstream and YG labels and there is a rumored duet between Pamela and Walter Scott (ex-Bob Kuban and The In-Men)... (JLh/MW)

Pan

Personnel:	KEITH BARBOUR	vcls	A
	RON ELLIOTT	gtr, vcls	A
	DON FRANCISCO	drms, vcls	A
	SHERMAN HAYES	bs, vcls	A
	ARTHUR RICHARDS	gtr, vcls	A

| ALBUM: | 1(A) | PAN | (CBS 32062) 1973 - |

Formed by Ron Elliott (ex-**Beau Brummels**) and Don Francisco (ex-**Highway Robbery**), **Pan** was a short-lived Californian group whose only album rarely turns up for sale. (SR)

The Pandas

| 45: | Walk/Girl From New York City | (Swingtime 1001) 196? |

Early copies of this 45 were released on red vinyl. The 'A' side, *Walk*, was a great dance number with fine fuzztone guitar and a great pulsating beat.

From Alamo City, Texas, they were originally known as **The Centurys** and later became Giant Smiling Dog, but did not record under that name.

Compilation appearances have included: *Walk* on *Mindrocker, Vol. 4* (LP) and *Acid Visions* (LP); and *Walk* and *Girl From New York City* on *Acid Visions - The Complete Collection Vol. 1* (3-CD). (VJ)

Pandemonium Shadow Show

Personnel:	KERRY NARF	gtr	A
	JANET WAGNER	vcls	A
	TIM ?	bs	A
	?? ??	ld gtr	A
	?? ??	keyb'ds	A
	?? ??	drms	A

| 45: | Sunshine Summer Day / Tender Is The Girl | (Teen Town 177) 1970 |

From Milwaukee, Wisconsin, this late sixties/early seventies band issued at least one single and opened for a bunch of big acts who played the Milwaukee Arena at that time including **The Association**. They had a very

PAN - Pan CD.

First Edition / Association / Left Banke sound. Fantastic breezy paisley pop band full of harmonies!

Kerry Narf recalls that he sang on some sessions with Tony's Tigers. (JKn/MW/GM)

Pandora and The Males

45:	Kiddie A-Go-Go / Kiddie A-Go-Go	(Fibra No #)	1965

Themes for a syndicated TV kiddie show. The flip is a different largely instrumental version credited to 'The Males'. With great vocals and cool organ, this good-timey kids 45 was recorded in Chicago, musicians included a young Ted Nugent! (BM/MW)

The Panicks

45s:	Work/Treat Me Right	(Dupree 102)	1965
	You're My Baby/Lots Of Pretty Girls	(Dupree 200)	1966

Obscure Stones-inspired teen-punk from Brecksville and Boston Heights, Ohio, two communities between Cleveland and Akron. Originally known as Panics, they had to change their name to **The Panicks** to avoid confusion with another act. Consequently their first 45 has a pasted on "Panicks" tag over their original moniker. They only cut the two 45s listed.

Compilation appearances include: *You're My Baby* on *Vile Vinyl, Vol. 1* (LP), *Vile Vinyl* (CD) and *It's A Hard Life* (LP); and *Treat Me Right* on *Highs In The Mid-Sixties, Vol. 21* (LP). (GGl/MMy/MW)

The Panics

45:	I Pretend/No More	(Shoestring SHO 107)	1965

Richmond, Virginia was home to this particular **Panics**. Both sides were penned by Bill Lyell and Bill Larue and performed in a lively and enthusiastic British Invasion - beat style with Beatlesque harmonies. (MW)

Papa Nebo

Personnel:	KEN ADAMS	drms	A
	SANDY ALLEN	vcls, bs	A
	SAL CONSTANZO	keyb'ds	A
	BRENDAN HARKIN	gtr, vcls	A
	AL LEATHERS	violin	A
	BOB MINTZER	horns	A
	MICHAEL PACKER	gtr, vcls	A

THE PAPER GARDEN - The Paper Garden LP.

ALBUM: 1(A) PAPA NEBO (Atlantic SD-8280) 1971 -

Produced by **Alan Lorber**, **Papa Nebo** was formed by Brendan Harkin, who had previously recorded with **Bamboo**. Their only album went totally unnoticed but the musicians kept working together and, in 1975, Packer, Allen, Harkin and Mintzer formed Free Beer for three albums of mainstream rock on Southwind and RCA. In 1976, Harkin left them to front Starz, an awful hard rock group a la Kiss (1976/79) and Mintzer became a session man. (SR)

Paper Fortress

45:	Butterfly High/Sleepy Hollow People	(VMC V 719)	1968

L.A. area harmony-pop with flower - power lyrics about caterpillars and butterflies, produced and arranged by **Tandyn Almer** and Eddie Hodges. Ultimately rather messy with constant interjections of various different instruments and the odd effect in an attempt to turn it into 'psych' - it doesn't really work. The flip, too, is more harmony-pop. (MW/SR)

The Paper Garden

Personnel:	JIMMY	perc	A
	JOE	bs	A
	JOHN	keyb'ds	A
	PAUL	ld gtr	A
	SANDY	gtr	A

ALBUM: 1(A) THE PAPER GARDEN PRESENTS... (Musicor MS 3175) 1969 R2

NB: (1) reissued (Antar 3) 1986 in new sleeve. Later reissued in original sleeve 2002.

A varied album of Eastern-style psychedelia but with some jazz influence too. It's become a minor collectors' item and the reissue in 1986 is worth a listen. The group were from the New York area.

Compilation appearances include: *I Hide* on *Pepperisms Around The Globe* (LP & CD); and *Man Do You* on *Electric Psychedelic Sitar Headswirlers Vol. 2* (CD). (VJ/MW)

Paper Mind

Personnel:	ALAN 'CUBBY' BAIR	ld vcls, ld gtr	A
	STAN KHANZADIAN	ld vcls, gtr	A
	BOB MORPHIS	drms	A
	MIKE TORRES	vcls, bs, recorder, clarinet, flute, gtr, perc	A

45:	Will She Ever/Far Away From Here	(Resound PRS 4101)	1966

A quartet from Hollywood perform two mid-sixties harmony teen-pop numbers. The 45 comes enveloped in an orange-brown open-out cover that contains a picture and info on the boys. "Nice" pop and definitely not garage, despite being touted as such. (MW)

Paper Train

45:	Brother/Time Waits For No One (Especially The Young)	(Capitol 2464)	1969

An intro and outro nicked off the **Cosmic Sounds** *Zodiac* sandwiches a heavy and fuzzy acid-rock belter by this obscure band. The flip is a tedious ballad about war, sacrifice and death. (MW)

The Parade

Personnel:	MURRAY MacLEOD		A
	JERRY RIOPELLE	keyb'ds, vcls	A
	SMOKEY ROBERDS		A

			HCP
45s:	Sunshine Girl/This Old Melody	(A&M 841) 1967	20
	She's Got The Magic/		
	Welcome, You're In Love	(A&M 867) 1967	-
	Frog Prince/Hallelujah Rocket	(A&M 887) 1967	-
	Radio Song/I Can See Love	(A&M 904) 1968	127
	She Sleeps Alone/ A.C./D.C.	(A&M 950) 1968	-
	Hallelujah Rocket/Laughing Lady	(A&M 970) 1968	-

This Los Angeles-based pop trio made the Top 20 with their debut recording *Sunshine Girl*, that had a light, summery feel which epitomised the Summer of peace and love. Comprised of aspiring actors for the most part rather than serious musicians, they never got beyond the studio and this meant they never built up much of a following. The band was master-minded by **Jerry Riopelle**, who wrote, arranged and produced their music and recorded solo albums in the seventies. The group recorded an album that was never released.

Jerry Riopelle also worked with **The Black Sheep**.

Actor Stuart Margolin (later "Angel" in the Rockford Files) was apparently also a member.

Compilation appearances have included: *Sunshine Girl* on *More Nuggets* (CD) and *Nuggets, Vol. 3* (LP); and *She Sleeps Alone* on *Nuggets, Vol. 4* (LP). (VJ)

Paragons

45s:	Abba/	
	(flip probably) Better Man Than I	(Paragons # unknown) 196?
	Abba/Better Man Than I	(Bobbi no #) 1967

From Charlotte, North Carolina, *Abba* later got a further airing on *Tobacco A-Go-Go, Vol. 2* (LP) and *Teenage Shutdown, Vol. 5* (LP & CD). The existence of the first 45 is unconfirmed. (VJ/MW)

Paraphernalia

45:	Never/Watch Out	(St. George I. 7-202, 440 /1) 1968

From Lowell, Massachusetts. *Never* is a late sixties rock - prog ballad that's melodic but doesn't quite gel. *Watch Out* is a heavyish rocker with some inventive and intense guitar effects that can be sampled on *An Overdose Of Heavy Psych* (CD). (MW)

Paraphernalia

45:	Sunny Days (And Good Living)/	
	Sea Of No Return	(Time 501) c1969

A different outfit, reported to be from Michigan. This is very good anthemic pop - rock with a U.K. Nirvana feel thanks to some melodic piano runs and slightly drippy but phased vocals. However, it's not all soft 'n' sweetness - a superb guitar break erupts mid-song which reappears on the outro. This should appeal to fans of Rubble-type psych. The flip remains unheard as I've only managed to obtain the double 'A' side promo version of this 45. (MW)

Parish Hall

Personnel:	STEVE ADAMS	drms	A
	JOHN HADEN	bs	A
	GARY WAGNER	vcls, gtr, piano	A

| ALBUM: | 1(A) | PARISH HALL | (Fantasy 8398) 1970 SC |

NB: (1) issued in the U.K. on Liberty (LBS 83374) 1970 and in France on America (30 AM 6041). Reissued on CD and LP by Akarma (AK 037) 1999.

PARISH HALL - Parish Hall LP.

This is an excellent, underrated local Bay Area hard-rock/blues-rock power trio. Their album is recently beginning to gain the recognition of some collectors in Europe. It's likely that Gary Wagner was connected to the **Chosen Few**, as he is credited as songwriter on their North Beach (1003) 45. (CF/MW)

Paris Pilot

Personnel:	DAVID MAYO	vcls	A
	JIMMY TARBUTTON	gtr	A
	KEN WOODLEY	keyb'ds	A
	RAY SANDERS	bs	A
	LARRY WALL	drms	A

| ALBUM: | 1(A) | PARIS PILOT | (HIP HIS 7004) 1969 - |

| 45: | Miss Rita Famous / Overton Park Flip | (Hip 8017) 1969 |

HIP Records were a division of Stax Records aimed at the white "pop" market. They also released the **Southwest F.O.B.** album. **Paris Pilot**'s sole album was produced, arranged and engineered in Memphis by **Don Nix** (ex-Mar-Kays), who also co-wrote most of the songs and took the photographs on the sleeve! The four other members are not credited.

Musically interesting, it's a kind of lightweight **Vanilla Fudge** with a cover of *The Beat Goes On*, lots of heavy organ, guitar and drums and good vocals. *Don't Let It* was co-written by Nix and Delaney Bramlett, and *Shades Of Doubt* by **Don Preston** and Joe Cooper, two members of **Leon Russell**'s "Oklahoma Mafia".

Don Nix would later become a solo artist, a friend of **Leon Russell** and George Harrison and a successful producer (Beck, Bogert & Appice, Lonnie Mack, Albert King, Variations...). (SR/MW/RHI)

Park Avenue Playground

Personnel:	BOB ANTON	bs	A
	GEORGE EDER	bs, gtr	ABC
	RON HOWARD	ld gtr	ABC
	MIKE JONES	organ	ABC
	PAUL KOVAK	drms	AB
	DOUG MAXEINER	drms	C

| 45: | I Know/The Trip | (USA 919) 1968/9 |

A late sixties Lansing, Illinois act. *The Trip*, a classic piece of punk dementia with driving organ, lots of fuzz, swirling sound effects and psychedelic lyrics like: 'You Say There's No Beginning/I Say You're Wrong/This Trip Is Never-Ending/It Won't Be Long', can now be heard on *Beyond The Calico Wall* (LP & CD).

George Eder recalls:- "The band arose from the ashes of my first band, The U.S. Males (Lansing, IL '65-'67). Because we had gone through some personnel changes, we needed a new name. I lived on Park Ave in Lansing IL. and one of the playgrounds of the local grade school was on my block. We'd always meet on the Park Ave. playground, so that's how I got the name."

"In the year and a half we were together ('67 - '69), we went through several bass players, but none stuck so I'd play bass live and in the studio as well a rhythm guitar the on recordings."

"We recorded *The Trip* in Lansing, MI in an old theatre that a lot of bands were using in those days. **The Rotary Connection** had just wrapped their recording so the vibe was in the room. There was a Hammond B3 for Mike so we put it on the record. The majority of the psychedelic sounds were added after the fact by our manager and the studio engineer."

Mike Jones wrote the 'A' side, *I Know* whilst I wrote *The Trip*. After the session, Paul Kovak had to leave the band due to parental pressure and another ex-U.S. Males member Doug Maxeiner was rehired. Most of the 45s were used by their manager, who took them to radio stations on the mid-west and East Coast, the remainder being distributed between the band members.

The U.S. Males also recorded an earlier 45, *She Cried* with to quote George: "a truly bad original on the B side, we had about 100 copies made and gave them to all our friends."

George:- "My name is now George Michael. I was born George Eder but changed my name legally in '79 for professional reasons. What a mistake that turned out to be... That kid from the UK has ruined my name (at least in CA)!" (VJ/GMI)

Parliament

Personnel incl:	GEORGE CLINTON	vcls	A
	BOOTSY COLLINS	bs, vcls	A
	TIKI FULWOOD	drms	A
	EDDIE HAZEL	gtr	A
	GARY SHIDER	vcls	A
	BERNIE WORRELL	keyb'ds	A

ALBUM: 1 OSMIUM (Invictus 7302) 1970 R2
(up to 1970)

Parliament was in fact another moniker for George Clinton and the musicians of **Funkadelic**. They played a powerful mix of psych and funk, maybe a bit more soulish than **Funkadelic**. After their first album, which is now rare and sought-after, Clinton reused this name after 1974 for a long series of funk albums on Casablanca. (SR)

Paul Parrish

ALBUM: 1 THE FOREST OF MY MIND (Music Factory MFS-12001) 1969 -

NB: (1) reissued on vinyl and CD (Akarma).

45s: Walking In The Forest Of My Mind/
White Birds Return To Warm Seas (Music Factory MU 407) 1968
Haynie / When They Return (Warner Bros. WB 7522) 1971
Numbers/Nathan (Warner Bros. WB 7556) 1971
Nathan/American (Warner Bros WB 7601) 1972

Paul Parrish's album was recorded at Tera Shirma Studios in Detroit and features slight 'loner' vibes. The very simple - but effective- drums and vocals are the most interesting aspects of the album, with *English Sparrows*, *Walking In The Forest (Of My Mind)*, *Dialogue Of Wind* and *Lover* being the most interesting tracks on Side One, which also concludes with a laid back, melodic cover version of the Beatles' *You've Got To Hide Your Love Away*. The other three songs are filled with fragile vocals and folky guitars backed with nice, psychedelic orchestrations. Most of Side Two is not of the same quality but on *Flowers In The Park* a sparkling magic atmosphere can be heard. Not bad!

The first 45, which is taken from the album features orchestrated folk-pop on the 'A' side, with lots of phasing and fuzzy effects, like a psychedelic pop version of **Bob Lind**. Pure confection but enjoyable. The flip is more melodic Lind-esque folk-pop with harpsichord. Arranged and conducted by Mike Theodore and **Dennis Coffey** (aka Theo-Coff Invasion).

Parrish would later release three 45s for Warner, the second being produced by Dan Dalton in an early Bee Gees vein. **Parrish** then became a session man. (JTk/MW/SR)

Parrish and Wilde

45: Don't Take This Love Away/Don't Fight It (Invader 407) 1965

They hailed from San Francisco. The flip can also be heard on *Mindrocker, Vol. 12* (LP). (VJ)

The Parrots

45: Put The Clock Back On The Wall/
Why All Got Carried Away Hey (Mala 558) 1967

The above 45 was the sole vinyl offering from this obscure outfit thought to have come from Florida. The 'A' side was a sort of psychedelic/garage grinder which can also be heard on *Psychedelic Unknowns, Vol. 4* (LP & CD). The same year it was redone with melodic harmonies by San Jose's **E-Types** who achieved a minor hit with the song in Northern California. (VJ)

Tom Parrott

ALBUM: 1 NEON PRINCESS (Folkways) 1968 ?

An interesting mix of acoustic folk and fuzz-guitar psych with tracks like *Groovy & Linda*. (SR)

Passing Clouds

Personnel:	JOE FINEMAN	vcls	A
	HERSCHEL FREEMAN	bs, vcls	A
	BOB KARAPETIAN	drms, vcls	A
	STEVE ROSS	keyb'ds, vcls, gtr	A
	KEITH STEIN	gtr, vcls	A

ALBUM: 1(A) HAWKS AND DOVES (Pete S1106) 1970 SC

Produced by Dick Glasser for a small Californian label, this rare and little known album contains eleven short cuts with keyboards-driven tracks like *Dr. Bernstein's Dream* and *Clock Upon The Sky*. Their material, rather jazzy in places, was inspired by the Chinese I Ching and written by Ross and Fineman. Competently arranged and with some thrilling time/measure changes plus great vocal parts, *Touch And Go* arguably dominates the record. The title track too, is in the same excellent vein and shows considerable musical wit and feeling. At times **The Association** come to mind, but unfortunately there's just a shade too much filler. Still there's room for another outstanding feature: the very cool atmosphere of *I'd Be Lying* and the heavy fuzz on *At The Head Of The List*. Uneven, but a nice listen nonetheless.

The front sleeve shows a picture of the group bare chested with a dove (it was probably to dangerous to picture an hawk too!).

Herschel Freeman also played with the **Sir Douglas Quintet** on their *1+1+1=4* album. (SR/MK)

The Passions

45: Lively One/You've Got Me Hurtin' (Pic 1117) 1965

From Sherman, Texas, this 45 was a Huey P. Meaux production. The 'A' side, *Lively One*, is a real stomper with sneering vocals and good harmonica.

Compilation appearances have included: *Lively One* on *Sixties Archive, Vol. 2* (CD), *Texas Punk From The '60s* (LP) and *Teenage Shutdown, Vol. 4* (LP & CD); and *You've Got Me Hurtin'* on *Ho-Dad Hootenanny* (LP). (VJ/MW)

The Pastels

Personnel incl: CHARLIE ROMANS   A

45s:	Weird Sounds/I Can Tell	(Push 110) 1967
α	Come Back Home/24 Hour Service	(Hickory 1438) 1967

NB: α as Charlie Romans.

Also known as Charlie Romans and The Pastels this band released two 45s on local Houston labels and recorded two tracks - *Yeah I Wanna Know* and *Weird Sounds* (their best effort), both of which have subsequently appeared on *Houston Hallucinations* (LP).

An outfit called Charlie Romans 7th Plane who released one 45, *There's A Place/?* on Spar (305) may have been related to this project. (VJ)

The Pastels

45s:	Why Don't You Love Me?/	
	What Can I Say?	(Century 22103) 1964
	Circuit Breaker/How Many Nights	(Century 22698) 1965
	Mirage/Where Is The Answer	(Century 23507) 196?

An Anglophile-influenced outfit from Pasco, Washington. Two members later went on to **The Rock-N-Souls**. *Why Don't You Love Me?* features a vocalist with a fake British accent, a practice which was not uncommon in the British invasion era. A pretty ordinary song, though.

Compilation appearances have included: *Where Is The Answer* on *Class Of '66!* (LP); and *Why Don't You Love Me* on *Highs In The Mid-Sixties, Vol. 7* (LP). (VJ/MW/GGI)

The Pastels

45:	'Cause I Love You/Don't Ya Know	(Phalanx 1006/7) 1966

This was the work of a different and unknown Michigan group, whose label was based in Portage Michigan.

Compilation appearances have included: *'Cause I Love You* on *Sixties Archive Vol. 7* (CD), *When The Time Run Out (Minnesota vs Michigan)* (LP & CD), *Glimpses, Vol's 1 & 2* (CD) and *Glimpses, Vol. 2* (LP). (VJ/MW)

Pasternak Progress

Personnel incl: JOHN BRANCA   A
                  JEFF PASTERNAK   A
                  NEIL SINCLAIR   drms   A

45:	Flower Eyes/Cotton Soul	(Original Sound 77) 1967

A Southern California outfit. Both sides of their 45 can also be heard on *Mindrocker, Vol. 13* (LP). This duo would team up with Original Sound's engineer and **Music Machine** technical whiz Brian Ross to produce a rather odd 45 under the name **Mad Andy's Twist Combo**. (VJ)

Patrick

45s:	Move/Five Different Girls	(RSVP 1117) 1966
	All Over Again/	
	Don't Let This Room Become Your World	(RSVP 1119) 1967
	Where You Gettin' Your Kicks Now?/	
	We Gotta Stick It Out (PS)	(RSVP 1122) 1967

A young black singer, who was featured on "Hullabaloo" for a while. Produced by Gilligan and Hutch Davie (who co-wrote both songs with R. Alfred), his first single is folk-rock with funny lyrics and a "wall of sound" production including harmonica, harpsichord, guitar, horns, male and female vocals. It's rather interesting.

RSVP was a small label from New York, which also released **Faine Jade**'s classic *Introspection* LP. (SR)

The Patriots

45:	What A Drag It Is/Blankets And Candles	(Murbo M-1025) 1968

A New York City outfit on the same label that brought us **The Household Sponge**. The 'A' side is a pleasant mid-tempo Beatlesque pop effort whilst the flip is an insistent minor-mood ballad. Not for yer fuzz'n'snarl brigade - this will appeal to those who dig Zombies, **Choir**, etc. (MW)

The Patriots

45:	I'll Be There/The Prophet	(Mainstream 631) 1966

This seems to have been a one-off venture on Mainstream. Thought to hail from the Louisville, Kentucky area and not connected with New York City's Patriots on Murbo or another Patriots on White Cliffs.

Compilation appearances include: *Last Time* on *The Louisville Scene* (LP); and *The Prophet* on *Mindrocker, Vol. 13* (LP). (VJ)

Patron Saints

Personnel:	ERIC BERGMAN	gtr, bs, perc, vcls	ABC
	PAUL D'ALTON	drms, perc	A
	JONATHAN TUTTLE	gtr, piano, bs, vcls	AB
	JOHN DOERSCHUK	gtr, vcls	BC
	KIRK FOSTER	bs, vcls	BC
	JOE IRVINS	drms, perc	BC

ALBUM: 1(A)   FOHHOH BOHOB   (No label PS-JT 1001) 1969 R4/R5

NB: (1) originally issued in thick white sleeve with front and rear paper 'slicks' glued on by hand. Some copies came with booklet (R5). Counterfeited in Austria in 1994 (300 copies with photocopied booklet), and in 1997 an official reissue was produced from the master tapes (American Sound 106202-3), 500 numbered copies with booklet and bonus 7" of unreleased material. In addition, (1) has been issued on CD with three bonus tracks (Patron Saint PSCD-101) 1997. More recently two compilations of unreleased recordings have appeared: *Proto Bohob* (Patron Saint PSCD-104) 1999, consisting of early demos from 1969, and *The Latimer Sessions* (Patron Saint PSCD-105/6) 2000, which is unreleased material from 1970-3 by line-ups 'B' and 'C'.

THE PATRON SAINTS - Fohhoh Bohob LP.

"Fohhoh Bohob" is slang for 'blow job' so now you know. *Fohhoh Bohob* was produced by the band over the course of a few weeks in the Summer of 1969 and it doesn't sound too much like anything else. There are moments where it could be **The Velvet Underground**, perhaps **Pearls Before Swine**, maybe Sidetrack or even **Faine Jade** influencing them, but one gets the impression that these guys made their own maps. There are a few places where the band seems to flounder, but other passages where their ability to impress is apparent. The album isn't a masterpiece, but it is a very unique and unusual record, and many collectors rate it very highly as a result - others think it is amateurish rubbish. Only 100 copies were pressed originally, but the reissues are quite easy to find.

Of their compilations of unreleased material, *The Latimer Sessions* (a double CD release) is the better of the two. **The Patron Saints** definitely improved over the years - the quirky, underground vision is still there, but their ability to render ideas as a band is markedly improved. With well over two hours of material on offer, this is remarkably consistent throughout. *Proto Bohob*, however, is similar to their original *Fohhoh Bohob* and consequently has less to recommend it.

Eric Bergman also issued two solo albums that fall outside the scope of this book: *Modern Phonography* (Patron Saint PS-1) 1978, and *Sending Out Signals* (Patron Saint PS-2) 1982. Both albums have been compiled on CD with bonus material (Patron Saint PS CD-102/3) 1998.

John Tuttle passed away in 1994.

Compilation appearances include *Reflections On A Warm Day* on *Love, Peace And Poetry, Vol. 1* (LP & CD). (CF/VJ)

The Pattens

| 45s: | Shame Shame Shame/Say Ma, Ma | (Pattens 1001) 196? |
| | You Should Know/Jump | (Stature 1102) 1966 |

This band operated out of Wheaton, Illinois, for the second half of the sixties. The flip to their first 45, *Say Ma, Ma*, was a Gene Vincent cover.

Compilation appearances include: *Say Ma, Ma* on *Pebbles Vol. 6* (CD) and *Highs In The Mid-Sixties Vol. 4* (LP); *You Should Know* and *Jump* on *A Journey To Tyme, Vol. 5* (LP); and *Jump* on *Glimpses, Vol. 3* (LP). (VJ)

The Patterns

A Texas outfit who were an early version of **Thursdays Children**. They have a pleasant cut *In My Own Time* on *Epitaph For A Legend* (Dble LP). (VJ)

Paulist Folk Singers

ALBUM: 1 PRAISE THE LORD IN MANY VOICES (Avant Garde) 196? ?

The **Paulist Folk Singers**' folk mass comprises one side of this album. The other features live material from John Ylvisaker. (GG)

The Pawnbrokers

45s:	Someday/This Fine Day	(IGL 143) 1967
	Realize/Smell Of Incense	(Big Sound 1003) 1968
	Dime-A-Dance Romance/	
	It's Been A Long, Long Time	(Big Sound 1004) 1969

Students at the University of Northern Iowa formed this outfit. Their second 45 couples the Cream-y riffer *Realize* with a slightly laboured acid-rock version of **West Coast Pop Art Experimental Band**'s *Smell Of Incense*. Their final release also looks to a heavy Cream / **Blue Cheer** sound, especially the excellent fuzz-crunchin' cover of the **Steve Miller Band**'s *Dime-A-Dance Romance*. The flip is in a blues-rock vein. To find out the full low-down, including personnel and minutiae, get yourself a copy of the excellent, but sometimes xenophobic, 'Lost And Found no. 4'.

Compilation appearances include: *Someday* on *The Best of IGL Folk Rock* (LP) and *The IGL Rock Story: Part Two (1967 - 68)* (CD). (MW)

Pawnee Drive

| 45s: | Break My Mind/Ride | (Forward F-103) 1969 |
| | Little Girl/Homeward Bound | (Forward 115) c1969 |

Their first 45 is very catchy bubblegum/punk and almost certainly the work of a studio group. *Ride* was also released as *Love Tunnel*, which is what the lyrics were all about and was apparently suppressed because someone considered it pornographic! The same song was also released as *Take A Ride* by an outfit called River Deep on Bell (791). *Break My Mind* was a pop cover of **John D. Loudermilk**. The 45 was produced by a George Tobin, who also produced the **Roads End** 45 on Brahma. Ohio has been suggested as the band's locale but hasn't been confirmed.

Pawnee Drive's *Ride* can also be heard on *Pebbles, Vol. 12* (LP). (MW)

P.B. and The Staunchmen

Personnel incl: PAUL BEECHER A

45: Mean Willie/Lost Generation (Lee 100) 196?

An obscure band from Hornell, New York, whose *Mean Willie* was included on *Garage Punk Unknowns, Vol. 8* (LP). (MW)

Peabody Co.

Acetates:
- α Tobacco Road (ODO) 196?
- β Sunny Daze/People Go (ODO) 196?
- β Love/Live For Today (ODO) 196?
- β This Better Life/Sleep (ODO) 196?
- β Can't Explain/A Hundred Percent Of Nothing (ODO) 196?
- β Mountain High/Effigy To A One Eyed Banana (ODO) 196?

NB: α one-sided 10" metal acetate, 33 1/3 rpm. β two-sided 10" metal acetate, 45 rpm.

A set of acetates comprising an unreleased album by a New York band. They play a typical late sixties garage style with the surprising addition of theremin on their extended version of *Tobacco Road*, which you can check out on *A Fistful Of Fuzz* (CD). (CF)

Joe Peace

Personnel:	MIKE HUFFMAN	bs, ld gtr	A
	TOM LANHAM	drms, perc	A
	JOE PEACE	vcls, ld gtr	A

ALBUM: 1 FINDING PEACE OF MIND (Rite 29917) 1972 R3

NB: (1) reissued on CD (World In Sound WIS 1005).

JOE PEACE - Finding Peace Of Mind CD.

Cincinnati, Ohio, was home to this singer-songwriter, who wrote, produced and arranged all ten tracks on the above album. Essentially of the folk-rock genre it's a pleasing collection of varied guitar styles from the fuzz guitar of Reflections *I See*; to the jangly guitar of *It's Been So Long* and *Goodbye*; the wailing guitar and catchy percussion of *Sad Surprise*, the melody of *High Time We Made Love* and *Love Me Like A Stranger* and the crisp guitar style of *Hello My Lady Friend*. Already a very rare album it is worth checking out if you find a copy. (VJ)

Peace and Quiet

Personnel:	ROGER PAVLICA	gtr	A
	RICK STEELE	vcls	A
	JIM TOLLIVER	bs	A
	GREG WILLIAMS	drms	A
	CHUCK WITHEROW	keyb'ds	A

ALBUM: 1(A) PEACE AND QUIET (Kinetic Z 30315) 197? -

From Miami, an overlooked act on the same label as **Marcus**. Their album sported a wonderful front cover and contained six self-penned compositions. On one, *Margo's Leaving Song*, **Flock**'s Jerry Goodman helped out on violin. The best track is the finale, the lengthy instrumental jam *Looney Tunes*. Not a psychedelic album but an interesting mainstream rock effort with lots of good organ and guitar work and a few country-rock and jazz rock passages.

Some members had early played with: **The Birdwatchers**, **Razor's Edge**, **The Villagers**, and The Convairs. (VJ/RBc/SR)

Peace Bread and Land Band

Personnel incl:	SID BROWN	gtr	A

ALBUM: 1(A) LIBERATION MUSIC (No label) 1969 R2

NB: (1) was a 10" album issued in a silk-screened paper envelope cover with an insert booklet. (1) due to be reissued on CD and vinyl, along with later material from 1973 and 1978, *Liberation Music 1969 - 1978* (Retroll Records) 2002.

A local Washington band who made albums into the seventies. This major collectable from the Northwest underground scene was distributed by the band. It consists of political electric folk-rock, with appealing female lead vocals and is highly-rated.

Sid Brown had earlier been in **The Spike Drivers**. He now directs and produces a cable TV show called "PrimeTimers" which gives voice and inspiration to older adults. (CF/SBn)

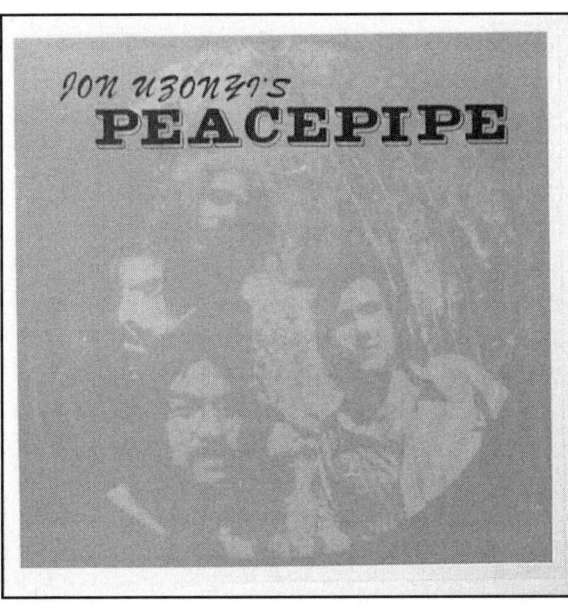

PEACEPIPE - Jon Uzonyi's Peacepipe LP.

Peacepipe

Personnel:	RICK ABTS	keyb'ds	A
	GARY TSURUDA	drms	A
	JON UZONYI	gtr	A

ALBUM: 1(A) THE HUMAN EQUATION FEATURING JON UZONYI
 (Rockadelic RRLP 18) 1995

NB: (1) with insert. (1) reissued on CD as *John Uzonyi's Peacepipe* (Normal/Shadocks Music NSM 029) 2002 with three bonus tracks.

45: The Sun Won't Shine Forever/
 Lazy River Blues (Accent ACS 1279) 1968

Uzonyi formed the band with Tsuruda in the mid-sixties whilst they were still at High School. In 1968, they headed for Hollywood and recorded two tracks; the absolutely stunning *The Sun Won't Shine Forever* and *Lazy River Blues*, which were released on a rare 45 by Accent. After school Uzonyi joined the U.S. Air Force and was based in Tucson, Arizona. There he met Rick Abts who joined Jon and Gary to form The Human Equation. They gigged around the U.S. West but disbanded in 1969 to pursue non-musical careers. Shortly after, though, they reformed to record the tunes, which 26 years later found their way onto Rockadelic's *Peacepipe* album. (Jon shelved the project at the time). The result is some stunning psychedelic rock with the opening track *Sea Of Nightmares* especially ear-catching. On Side Two, *A Biker's Tune* features some superb psychedelic guitar work and *Open Your Mind* culminates in more guitar histrionics. The final track *Love Shine* is much more mellow by contrast.

The CD reissue includes three bonus cuts; both sides of their rare late sixties single and a toe-tapping pop song called *Keep A-Smilin' Cari*.

Compilation appearances include *The Sun Won't Shine Forever* on *Incredible Sound Show Stories, Vol. 7* (LP) and *For A Few Fuzz Guitars More* (CD). (CF/VJ)

The Peanut Butter Conspiracy

Personnel:	AL BRACKETT	bs	ABCDEF
	LANCE FENT	hrmnca, gtr	A
	JOHN MERRILL	gtr	ABCD
	BARBARA "SANDI" ROBINSON	vcls	ABCDEF
	JIM VOIGT	drms	ABC
	MIKE KALLENDER	gtr	B
	BILL WOLFF	gtr	C
	MICHAEL NEY	drms	E
	RALPH SHUCKETT	keyb'ds	EF
	PETE MCQUEEN	drms	F
	MICHAEL STEVENS	drms	F

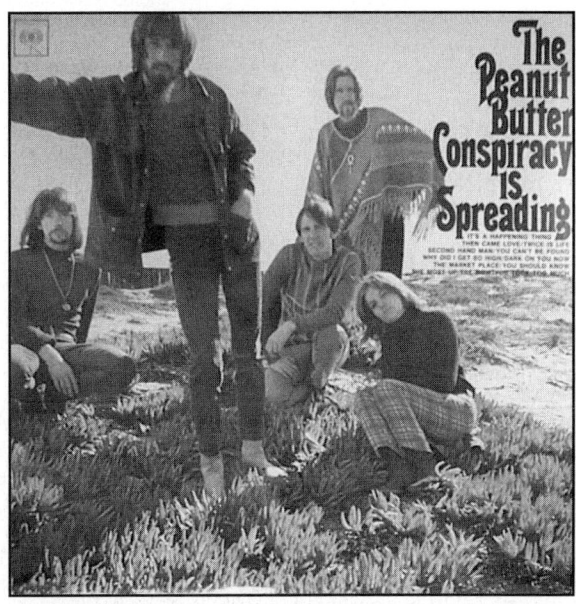

THE PEANUT BUTTER CONSPIRACY - Is Spreading LP.

PEANUT BUTTER CONSPIRACY - The Great Conspiracy LP.

				HCP
ALBUMS:	1(A)	THE PEANUT BUTTER CONSPIRACY IS SPREADING	(Columbia 9454) 1967	196 -
	2(B/C)	THE GREAT CONSPIRACY	(Columbia 9590) 1967	- -
	3(F)	FOR CHILDREN OF ALL AGES	(Challenge 2000) 1969	- SC

NB: (1) and (2) reissued on CD. (3) reissued by Line in 1981 and on CD by Collectables (COL-0529) with seven extra tracks. There is also a compilation of their first two LPs called *Turn On A Friend* (Drop Out) in 1988.

			HCP
45s:	Time Is After You/Floating Dream	(Vault 933) 1966	-
α	It's A Happening Thing/Twice Is Life	(Columbia 43985) 1967	93
	Dark On You Know/Then Came Love	(Columbia 44063) 1967	-
	Turn On A Friend/Captain Sandwich	(Columbia 44356) 1967	-
	I'm A Fool/It's So Hard	(Columbia 44667) 1968	125
β	Back In L.A./Have A Little Faith	(Challenge 500) 1969	-

NB: α some promo copies in PS. β also issued in Belgium in a picture sleeve (London 5 662) 1968. Both tracks were written/produced by Alan Brackett.

Evolving out of the remains of **The Ashes**, which had included Brackett, Merrill and Robinson, they recorded their first 45 for Vault before signing with the major-label Columbia in November 1966. Much of their material was written by Brackett and Merrill and produced by Gary Usher. It was well produced and often orchestrated. Their first album was a fine debut. The stand-out track was *Then Came Love*, a beautiful love song on which Sandy's gorgeous voice was supported by excellent orchestration. Also of note were the goodtime sounds of *You Took Too Much* and *Why Did I Get So High?* which sounds like an anti-drug song. The chorus lyrics to this one were:-

"Why did I get so high?
Just to fall from the sky
Why did I get so high?
Just to see our love die
Oh, why did I get so high?"
(from *Why Did I Get So High?*)

The second album was in similar vein, bursting with ravishing harmonies and psychedelic lyrics (e.g. "Everyone has a bomb / In their mind / And when it explodes / Blows your mind" from the transcendent *Living, Loving Life*). The single off the album, *Turn On A Friend* found its way on to the *Rock Machine Turns You On* compilation.

However, the end of the flower-power era sounded the death knell for the band. Their third album dispensed with the folk-rock and psychedelia in favour of gospel-rock and gruff male vocals fronting horns and girlie choruses (the CD bonus tracks, however, do include a couple of glorious Barbara Robinson vocal performances). After the album's failure, Al Brackett went into session and production work, Lance Fent played for Randy Meisner and Bill Wolff (who'd also played with **Sound Machine**) later joined **Fusion**. Sadly, Sandy Robinson died a few years back.

Compilation coverage has so far included: *It's A Happening Thing* on *Nuggets, Vol. 10* (LP) and *Psychedelic Visions* (CD); *Time Is After You* on *Mindrocker, Vol. 1* (LP); *Too Many Do*, from their second album, on *Psychedelic Dream: A Collection of '60s Euphoria* (LP); *Angels From Hell* on *Turds On A Bum Ride, Vol. 4* (CD); *Time Is After You*, *One-Nine-Six-Seven*, *Big Bummer* and *Floating Dream* on *West Coast Love-In* (CD); *Angels From Hell*, *Crystal Tear* and *No Communication* on *Filling The Gap* (4-LP); and *Roses Gone* on *First Vibration* (LP).

In addition, **Love Exchange**'s *Swallow The Sun*, featured on *Nuggets, Vol. 10* and *Highs In The Mid-Sixties, Vol. 3* is actually **Peanut Butter Conspiracy**'s *Dark On You Now* with slightly altered lyrics - **Peanut Butter Conspiracy** under a pseudonym or a faceless studio outfit? Drop me a line if you know. (VJ/LP/SR)

Pearl Divers

According to the liner notes to *Acid Visions - The Complete Collection Vol. 1* (3-CD), which includes *Terminal Loser*, *Riding On A Rainbow* and *She Was The Doctor*, this band came from Houston, Texas. The three tracks were recorded at ACA studios in 1968. (GG)

Pearls Before Swine

Personnel:	ROGER CRISSINGER	organ	A
	WAYNE HARLEY	autoharp, banjo, mandolin	ABC
	LANE LEDERER	bs, gtr, horns	AB
	TOM RAPP	gtr, vcls	ABCD
	WARREN SMITH	drms	AB
	JIM BOHANNON	keyb'ds, marimba	B
	ELIZABETH RAPP	vcls	CD
	(LEE CRABTREE	piano, organ, flute	B)
	(JOE FARRELL	flute, french horn	B)
	(BILL SALTER	bs	BC)
	(AL SHACKMAN	gtr	B)
	(JIM FAIRS	gtr	C)
	(RICHARD GREENE	violin	C)
	(GRADY TATE	drms	C)

				HCP
ALBUMS:	1(A)	ONE NATION UNDERGROUND	(ESP 1054) 1967	- SC
	2(B)	BALAKLAVA	(ESP 1075) 1968	- SC
	3(C)	THESE THINGS TOO	(Reprise RSLP 6364) 1969	200 -
	4(D)	THE USE OF ASHES	(Reprise RSLP 6405) 1970	- -
	5(D)	CITY OF GOLD	(Reprise RSLP 6442) 1971	- -
	6(D)	BEAUTIFUL LIES YOU COULD LIVE IN	(Reprise RSLP 6467) 1971	- -

NB: (1) and (2) have been reissued on CD by ESP (ESP 1075-1 and 1075-2 respectively). (2) reissued on vinyl by Base in Germany. There's also a good CD compilation, concentrating on the 1969-72 era *Constructive Melancholy* (Birdman BMR 021) 1998.

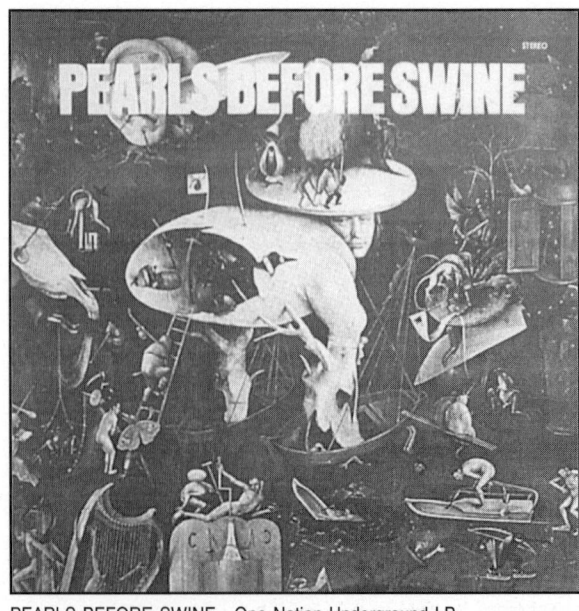

PEARLS BEFORE SWINE - One Nation Underground LP.

45s:	Drop Out!/Morning Sun	(ESP 4554) 196?
	These Things Too/If You Don't Want To	(Reprise 0873) 1969
	The Jeweller/Rocket Man	(Reprise 0949) 1970

This group focused on **Tom Rapp**, who had apparently once finished ahead of Bob Dylan in a local New York talent contest. Although the group's original line-up is listed above, after their first two albums it became much more flexible, consisting of whoever **Tom Rapp** could gather around him in the studio. The group's acid sound seems almost certain to have been drug-inspired and their music was always mystical, innovative and mysterious.

Their debut album was released on the avant-garde ESP label, and characterised by **Rapp**'s gentle vocals and a woodwind musical accompaniment. *Morning Song* and *The Surrealist Waltz* were two of the stronger tracks, although a consistently high standard was maintained throughout. The album's lyrics were often inquisitive and philosophical; for example:

"Where have you been to?
Where did you go?
Did you follow the Summer out
When the Winter pushed its face
In the snow?
Or have you come by again
To die again?
Try again another time."
(from *Another Time*)

Another track, *Shall Not Care* has a strange Eastern sound. The follow-up *Balaklava* was in similar vein, and based around the concept of the charge of the Life Brigade at Balaklava in 1852. It also includes a beautiful version of the Leonard Cohen song *Suzanne*. All the other compositions are **Rapp**'s, including the final track *Ring Thing*, which is possibly the strangest of all - taken as it is from the cornerstone verse of J.R.R. Tolkien's *Lord Of The Rings*.

Rapp abandoned his use of abstract themes for his remaining albums which were more conventional. He also signed for the better known Reprise label. Although possibly less interesting than those first two albums, the remaining four **Pearls Before Swine** LPs are still well worth hearing.

The *Use Of Ashes* album and part of the follow-up, *City Of Gold* were recorded in Nashville. The remainder and *Beautiful Lies You Could Live In* were made in New York. In 1972, **Tom Rapp** started recording under his own name, although his first solo album was largely comprised of re-recordings of songs from his earlier albums.

Fans of the band and **Tom Rapp** will also be interested in a tribute album *For The Dead In Space*, including Fit And Limo, Bevis Frond, Mourning Cloak and even an exclusive track by **Tom Rapp** himself. More recently **Tom Rapp** gave a mesmerising performance at Ptolemaic Terrascope's 'Terrastock III' and released a fine solo album, *A Journal Of The Plague Year*.

Roger Crissinger was later in **One**. (VJ/JOl)

Pearly Gate

| Personnel: | RON DANTE | A |

45s:	Free/Carole's Epic Song	(Decca) 1969
	Daisey/	
	What Do You Hear From Your Head	(Decca 32663) 19??

Whilst *Free* is standard pop rock tune, the flip is a cool trippy instrumental. *Free* charted in (at least) New York on WMCA at a high of #50 on Nov 5, 1969. (SR/MC)

The Pebble Episode

| 45: | Tripsy / The Plum Song | (J-2 1300) 1967 |

From Brooklyn, New York. Their haunting and rather trippy psychedelic instrumental called *Tripsy* can also be found on the *Beyond The Calico Wall* (LP & CD) compilation. Worth a spin.

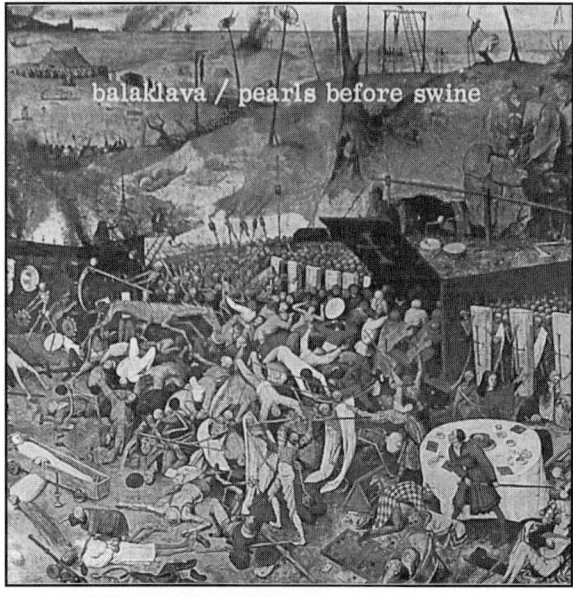

PEARLS BEFORE SWINE - Balaklava LP.

Some copies of the 45 were miscredited to Vincent Oddo, the owner of the recording studio where the 45 was cut. (VJ/MW/MM/RMh)

The Pebbles

| 45: | Love Me Again/It's Alright With Me Now | (Dot 16746) 1965 |

An anonymous Mersey-folk outfit who we thought were from the Texas/New Mexico border, but actually were from Belgium! You'll also find *Love Me Again* on *Pebbles, Vol. 13* (LP) but it's really very ordinary.

The Pebbles

| Personnel incl: | CHUCK BLACKWELL | drms | A |
| | JOEY COOPER | vcls, gtr | A |

| 45: | Don't Come Running To Me/ | |
| | Don't Hide It | (Prince P-6707-1/2) 1967 |

NB: some copies came with a PS.

Great fuzzy garage-pop, not rough enough presumably to make it onto compilations so far, but given the band name, a natural for that classic series. The flip is straight bouncy pop fodder with some brass. Produced by Brian Ross (of **Music Machine** fame), both sides are composed by Cooper / Blackwell who played with Leon Russell and Delaney Bramlett in **The Shindogs**. **The Pebbles** may well have been a pseudonym for that band. (MW/RAd)

The Pebbles

Personnel:	BILL BIRTHOLD	drms	A
	JOE CAMUCCIO	vcls, trumpet	A
	DENNY DOWNEY	gtr	A
	RALPH STRAIGHT	ld gtr	A
	RAY ??		A

| 45: | Endless Tears / Vicki (PS) | (RPH 2001) 1965 |

A quintet from St.Petersburg, Florida. Originally the Satins, they lost their original bassist to **Tommy Roe and The Roemans** and by 1965 were known as **The Pebbles**. Recorded in Tampa in early '65, their sole 45 was released on manager Ralph P. Hitchcock's vanity label. *Endless Tears*, a Merseybeat style ballad, is included on *Psychedelic Crown Jewels Vol. 3* (CD). (MW/JLh/RM)

DAVID PEEL & THE LOWER EAST SIDE - Have a Marijuana LP.

Pebbles

45s:	Forty Miles/Get Around	(Mainstream 695) 1969
	Mother Army/Some Days Are Gone	(United Artists 35 380) 1972

Yet another **Pebbles**? The first of these 45s is orchestrated pop on both sides, the 'B' side as usual much better, but still quite unexciting. Therefore it's a nice surprise that *Mother Army* is punchy pop-rock rock with a strangely bouncing backdrop and some good guitar work. Its flip again veers into melodic pop, too bloody relaxed to delight, unfortunately. A certain Mr. Bobbot co-wrote all four tracks here. (MK)

Peck's Bad Boys

45s:	Crazy World/Cloud Seventy-Six	(Scepter 12176) 1966
α	Girl In Chains/Silver Dawn	(Scepter 12182) 1967

NB: α as **Pex's Bad Boys**.

The first 45, released as by **Peck's Bad Boys**, is rare and sought-after for the frenzied *Crazy World*. Their second 45 however, as **Pex's Bad Boys** tends towards garagey pop with *Silver Dawn* winning out with its mesh of jangling guitars and waltzing rhythm.

Compilation appearances include *Crazy World* on *Tougher Than Stains* (LP) and *Teenage Shutdown, Vol. 11* (LP & CD). (MW)

The Pedestrians

Personnel incl: TONY COOPER A

45s:	It's Too Late/My Little Girl	(Fenton 2116) 1968
	Think Twice/Snyder's Swamp	(Fenton 2102) 196?
	The Unpredictable Miss Kinsey/ You Aren't Going To Say You Know	(Fenton 2226) 196?
	It's Too Late/Think Twice	(Buy-It 2556) 1966
	It's Too Late/Think Twice	(Atco 6567) 1968

From Michigan. *Think Twice* is a haunting garage ballad with an early sixties feel (Shadowy guitars chiming) with an intro whistled a-la spaghetti westerns! *It's Too Late* harks back to 1965 garage beat sounds - definitely 'out' in '68. It was featured on a 1968 radio sampler EP, *WLAV Memory Pack Vol. 1*.

Compilation coverage has so far included:- *Its Too Late* on *Psychedelic Patchwork* (LP), *Psychedelic Unknowns, Vol. 5* (LP & CD) and *Every Groovy Day* (LP); and *Think Twice* on *Best of Michigan Rock Groups, Vol. 1*. (MW)

David Peel and The Lower East Side

Personnel:	LARRY ADAM	gtr	A
	HAROLD C. BLACK	vcls, tamb	AB
	GEORGE CORI	bs	A
	DAVID PEEL	vcls, gtr	ABC
	BILLY JOE WHITE	gtr	AB
	TONY BARTOLI	drms	B
	HERB BUSHIER	bs	B
	DAVID HOROWITZ	organ	B
	HAROLD FISHER	drms	C
	EDDIE MOTRAU		C
	CHRIS OSBORNE		C
	EDDIE RYAN		C

HCP
ALBUMS:	1(A)	HAVE A MARIJUANA	(Elektra EKS-74032) 1968	186 SC
(up to 1972)	2(B)	THE AMERICAN REVOLUTION	(Elektra EKS-74069) 1970	- SC
	3(C)	THE POPE SMOKES DOPE	(Apple SW-3391) 1972	191 -

This New York-based 'hippie' rock group may interest readers. They developed quite a cult following and continued to record albums into the eighties. The above three have become collectable. *I Like Marijuana* from their first album can also be heard on *Elektrock The Sixties* (4-LP). It was the highlight of a musically poor album, which has not stood the test of time well, but the songs which mostly dealt with dope and getting 'stoned' were popular with hippie audiences at the time.

He was a friend of John Lennon and Yoko Ono and they sometimes performed together. He's celebrated on Lennon's song *New York City* on the *Sometimes In New York City* album and they also produced his final album.

David Peel still resides on the lower East side and is today involved with Cures Not Wars and the Marijuana legalisation movements. (VJ)

The Steve Peele Five

Personnel incl: STEVE PEELE vcls, gtr A

45:	Frankie's Got It! / Today She Didn't Want To	(FGI 1000) 1969

A one-off studio assemblage in Norfolk, Virginia, dashed off this 45 as a promo for the *Frankie's Got It* record store. It's quite memorable - a novelty of sorts, affected verging-on-manic lead vocals with background keening that gives it a ghoulish B-movie flavour. I guess it didn't make it onto the soundtrack for High Fidelity so you'll have to seek it out on *Pebbles, Vol. 16* (LP) or *Aliens, Psychos And Wild Things* (CD). (BHr/ST/MW)

The Peepl

Personnel?:	PETER ALONGI	A
	JOSEPH De JESUS	A
	ROBERT TURNER	A

45:	Freedom / Please Take My Life	(Roaring Records 801) 1968

Freedom is a sombre pleading folk-rocker ballad with keening falsetto harmonies. The flip, composed by Joseph De Jesus, is a laboured instrumental where the guitarist attempts some resounding John Cippolina chops, giving it a West Coast vibe. Maybe that's why it has been suggested that the band are from California. All we know for sure is that it was produced by Jim Kemper and Pete Glick, for Boy Wonder and Kama Sutra Productions. (MW)

Peers

45:	Once Upon A Time/Palasades Park	(Le Jac 3005) 1966

A Minneapolis, Minnesota combo. You'll also find *Once Upon A Time* on *Hipsville, Vol. 3* (LP). (VJ)

Pembrook Ltd

Personnel incl: J. BUCHANAN
L. LAYTON

45:	Love's So Easy/Sleepyjohn	(Debutone 779)	1967

This was actually a Canadian band although they seem to have gigged a lot in the Pacific Northwest hence their appearance on *Highs In The Mid-Sixties, Vol. 16 - The Northwest Part 3* (LP). *Sleepyjohn*, which figures on that album, was a frantic sort of effort. This 45 seems to have been their sole vinyl excursion. (MW/DR)

Pendulum

ALBUM:	1	PENDULUM	(Baldwin CS 7948)	c1973 ?

A local Pennsylvania band formed in 1961 by "Bob" which apparently didn't record until the early seventies. Their album contains covers of Uriah Heep's *Easy Livin* and Jethro Tull's *Locomotive Breath*, plus some original tracks like *Journey To Nowhere* and *Black Cloud*. (SR)

The Pendulum

45s:	Silly Sally Sunday / I Do You	(Kama Sutra KA-253)	1968
	Now I'll Cry / Dead Dog	(Kama Sutra KA-257)	1968
	She Can Blow Your Mind / High On A Hill	(Kama Sutra KA-257)	1968

An obscure rock group. Both songs on their second 45 were produced by David Lucas and George Grast, and penned by Billy Alessi, who would form the Alessi Brothers with his twin Bobby in 1976. (SR)

Pendulum & Co.

Personnel:	STAN BOOTHBY	bs, vcls	A
	STEVE HOWARD	gtr, vcls	A
	BRIAN IMHOFF	drms	A
	DON LEVESQUE	gtr, vcls	A
	TOM PERKINS	gtr, vcls	A

ALBUM:	1(A)	PENDULUM & CO.	(Perception PLP 23)	1971	SC

Late-sixties sounding pop/rock from this Massachusetts band. A rather mixed bag, actually. At their best, they are reminiscent of early **Buffalo Springfield**, with *Tell Me You're Free* being an uptempo rocker and *Loneliness* owing a great deal to both *For What It's Worth* and Neil Young's *Down By The River*. A number of tracks are orchestrated which will not endear most listeners perusing this book, but be advised that this album has its moments. Those interested in a more druggy, introspective rock sound will appreciate their approach.

PENDULUM & Co. - Pendulum & Co. LP.

Pendulum & Co., like everything else in the Perception/Dwarf catalogue, is rare on the West Coast and the only copies I have seen are designated promo. (CF)

William Penn and The Quakers

Personnel:	JEFF BLANSKMA	A
	JO ANN GUNTHER	A
	LONNY GUNTHER	A
	JIM SLADE	A
	DAN WHITE	A

45s:	Ghost Of The Monks/Goodbye My Love	(Twilight 410)	1966
α	Care Free/Coming Up My Way	(Duane 104)	1968
	Little Girl/Somebody's Dum Dum	(Hush 230)	1968

NB: α recorded Dec. 1967.

Thanks to Alec Palao's liner notes to *Hush Records Story* (CD), we now know that this act were led by Lonny Gunther and were from Boise, Idaho. They are therefore unconnected to the Californian **William Penn Fyve** and you can check out *Believe Me*, *Hey Hey Hey Hey*, *Ghost Of The Monks*, *Care Free* (demo), *Coming Up My Way* and their version of **Syndicate Of Sound**'s *Little Girl* on Big Beat's *Hush Records Story*.

The confusion doesn't end here however as we have record of one more 45 as **William Penn and The Quakers**: *Philly/Santa Needs Ear Muffs On His Nose* (Melron 5024), which was also issued with a different 'A' side, *Sweet Caroline*... There's also another **William Penn and The Quakers** track, *California Sun* on *Grab This And Dance* (LP)... answers on a $100 note please.... (LP/MW)

The William Penn Fyve / William Penn & His Pals

Personnel:	RON COX	drms	AB
	NEIL HOLTMANN	vcls	A
	STEVE LEIDENTHAL	bs	AB
	GREG ROLIE	organ	AB
	MIKE SHAPIRO	gtr	AB
	JACK SHELTON	gtr	AB

NB: Other early personnel include Dave Lovell (keyb'ds) who was replaced by Greg Rolie, Mike Dunn, and possibly Steve Sweet.

45:	Swamii/Blow My Mind	(Thunderbird 502)	1966

From San Mateo, California, they were originally known as **William Penn & His Pals**, and as such recorded demos for Fantasy Records including an early version of *Blow My Mind*. Following a name change, line-up 'B' recorded the single which was licences to a New York label for release.

Swamii has become an acid punk classic due to its inclusion on *Pebbles, Vol. 3* (LP).

Gregg Rolie later went on to play keyboards for **Santana** and Journey!

Compilation appearances have included: *Swami* on *Pebbles, Vol. 3* (LP), *Pebbles, Vol. 3* (CD), *The Essential Pebbles Collection, Vol. 1* (Dble CD), *Pebbles, Vol. 2* (ESD) (CD), *Punk Classics, Vol. 3* (7") and *Great Pebbles* (CD); *Blow My Mind* and *Swami* on *Pebbles Box* (5-LP), *Sound Of The Sixties: San Francisco Part 2* (LP) and *Trash Box* (5-CD). As **William Penn & His Pals** you can also find *Gotta Get Away*, *Blow My Mind* and *Far And Away* on *The Scorpio Records Story* (CD). (VJ/LP/SR/CF/DLI/BPn)

The Penny Arcade

Personnel:	PETER ANDERS	A
	VINNIE PONCIA	A

45s:	Francine/Me And My Piano	(UA 50221)	1967
	Bubble Gum Tree/Tears In My Heart	(Smash 2190)	1968

Two 45s of bubblegum pop by **The Tradewinds** in disguise. (SR)

Penny Candy Machine

45: Lollipop/Ode To Midnight (Strobe) c1967

A totally unknown group produced by **Milan**. The 'A' side is a horrid fifties cover, but the flip is great downer folk. (SR)

Pentagram

Personnel:
	BOBBY LIEBLING	vcls	A
	VINCENT McALLISTER	gtr	A
	GEOFF O'KEEFE	drms	A
	GREG WAYNE	bs	A

ALBUM: 1(A) 1972-1979 (Peace) 1992

45s:
Be Forewarned/Lazy Lady	(?)	1972
Hurricane/Earth Flight	(Boffo Socko 13859)	1973
Under My Thumb/When The Screams Come	(Gemini 002)	1974
Living In A Ram's Head/		
When The Screams Come	(High Voltage 666)	1979

This was a later version of **Macabre**, from Arlington, Virginia. The *1972-1979* album is best described as a psychedelic hard-rock album. It includes 1972 versions of *Be Forewarned* as well as covers of *Little Games* and *Under My Thumb*.

They went on to record two heavy metal albums in the eighties. *Pentagram* in 1985 was later re-mixed and reissued as *Relentless* on Peaceville and *Day Of Reckoning* (Napalm) in 1987 (also re-mixed on Peaceville).

In 2000, a further album of death metal appeared *Review Your Choices* (Black Widow BWR 031).

They still play live occasionally. (VJ/BK)

The Penthouse Five

Personnel:
	JUSTIN BROWN	gtr	A
	ROB GRAHAM	vcls	A
	RICHARD KEATHLEY	ld gtr, vcls	A
	BILL KOONEY	bs, vcls	A
	MARK PORTER	drms	A
	JON WILLIAMS	vcls	A
	STEVE WOOD	gtr	A

45s:
Bad Girl/In His Shadow	(Solar 7665-4211)	1966
You're Gonna Make Me/		
Don't Mess Around With My Dream	(Hawk H,2-67)	1967

A psychedelic band from Dallas whose second 45 was credited simply to Penthouse.

Compilation appearances have included: *Vertigo Blue Sometime*, *It's All My Own Bizarre Dream*, *You're Gonna Make Me*, *Bad Girl*, *In His Shadow* and *Don't Mess Around With My Dream* on *Texas Punk, Vol. 4* (LP) and *Acid Visions - Complete Collection, Vol. 2* (3-CD); *The Years Have Passed* (prev. unreleased) on *Texas Punk, Vol. 6* (LP) and *Acid Visions - Complete Collection, Vol. 3* (3-CD); *It's All My Own Bizarre Dream* on *The Cicadelic 60's, Vol. 2* (CD) and *Green Crystal Ties, Vol. 9* (CD); *In His Shadow* on *From The New World* (LP); and *You're Gonna Make Me* and *You're Always Around* on *Green Crystal Ties, Vol. 2* (CD). (VJ)

People

Personnel:
	DENNY FRIDKIN	drms	ABCD
	JEOFF LEVIN	gtr	ABC
	ROBB LEVIN	bs	ABCD
	GENE MASON	vcls	AB
	LARRY NORMAN	vcls	A
	SCOTT (BRUCE) EASON	vcls	C
	ALBERT RIBISI	organ	ABCD
	JOHN TRISTAO	vcls	D
	TOM TUCKER	gtr, vcls	D

ALBUMS:
1(A)	I LOVE YOU	(Capitol ST 2924)	1968	128 SC
2(B)	BOTH SIDES OF PEOPLE	(Capitol ST 151)	1969	- SC
3(D)	THERE ARE PEOPLE AND THERE ARE PEOPLE			
		(Paramount PAS 5013)	1970	- -

NB: (1) reissued on CD in Korea (Si Wan SRNC 6010).

HCP

45s:
Organ Grinder / Riding High	(Capitol 5920)	1967	-
I Love You /			
Somebody Tell Me My Name	(Capitol 2078)	1968	14
Apple Cider / Ashes Of Me	(Capitol 2251)	1968	111
Ulla / Turnin' Me In	(Capitol 2449)	1969	-
Turnin Me In' / Ulla	(Capitol 2499)	1969	-
Love Will Take Us Higher and Higher /			
Livin' It Up	(Paramount 0005)	1969	-
Sunshine Lady / Crosstown Bus	(Paramount 0011)	1969	-
For What It's Worth / Maple Street	(Paramount 0019)	1970	-
One Chain Dont Make No Prison /			
Keep It Alive	(Paramount 0028)	1970	-
Chant For Peace /			
I Don't Carry No Guns	(Polydor 14087)	1971	-

A San Diego, California band who made two slightly psychedelic albums. Larry Norman, later known for his Christian beliefs and records in that vein, was an early member and shares lead vocals on their first album. The group had a small hit with a cover of the Zombies *I Love You*. Besides that track, their first album contains some tracks with a slight psychedelic influence, notably *1000 Years B.C.*, *Nothing Can Stop The Elephants*, and *Ashes Of Me*. Side two of the album contains the sidelong *The Epic*, which changes shape several times and tells the tale of the maid Tori Kincaid. It also sold quite well, climbing to No. 128 and spending eight weeks in the charts.

By the second album Larry Norman had left the group, but it still contains several of his compositions. Like their first album, their sound is somewhat similar to **Iron Butterfly**, but quirkier, with lots of Hammond organ to the fore. Their vocal harmonies sometimes make you think of **Vanilla Fudge**, but the group make it all part of their own sound. *Both Sides Of People* covers many styles (there's even a country song!), and on this album there's more excellent guitar work than on their first. Side two is particularly excellent, with only three tracks, the first of which, *Lucky John*, contains some sitar, and some snakey fuzz. *She's A Dancer* contains great wah-wah and searing fuzz. Lastly *Pirate Bill* is another example of their humourous style and somewhat reminiscent of parts of *The Epic*. By the third album, the group had been revamped, and had lost their lead vocalist as well as their lead guitarist. There was also added brass, so consequently their sound had changed a lot and the reason for its inclusion here is minimal.

PEOPLE - I Love You LP.

In between the second and third albums, Bruce Eason sang for in the band for about three months:- "I appeared as lead singer for the band on American Bandstand and Sam Riddle's 9th Street West. I used the stage name Scott Eason on the shows because Geoff and Robby didn't like my real first name. I also participated in some unreleased studio recording which we did at Rainbow Studios in Hollywood as well as the arrangement of several songs for which I never received credit."

Compilation appearances include: *I Love You* on *Nuggets, Vol. 3* (LP). (CBe/VJ)

People of Sunset Strip

45:	Sunset Symphony/Trippin'	(Atco 6458)	1967

Following the riots, **Sonny Bono** (of Sonny and Cher) put together *Sunset Symphony*, a track of noises and comments of the strip transplanted onto a musical background. It can also be heard on *Highs In The Mid-Sixties, Vol. 2* (LP). (VJ)

People's Victory Orchestra and Chorus

ALBUMS:	1	THE SCHOOL	(People's Music Works)	c1971 R1
	2	WELTSCHMARZEN	(People's Music Works)	c1972 R2

From the New York area, and maybe the output of a community, this group issued two rare albums mixing rock in the mould of the Rolling Stones with psych and prog influences. (SR)

Jim Pepper

Personnel:	BILLY COBHAM	drms	A
	LARRY CORYELL	gtr	A
	TOM GRANT	piano	A
	JERRY JEMMOT	bs	A
	GILBERT PEPPER	vcls	A
	JIM PEPPER	sax, vcls	A
	RAVIE PEPPER	flute	A
	CHUCK RAINEY	bs	A
	SPIDER RICE	drms	A

ALBUM:	1(A)	PEPPER'S POW WOW	(Embryo SD 731)	1971 SC

Jim Pepper was a Kaw and Creek Indian as well as a jazz and rock musician. In 1967 he formed **Free Spirits** with Larry Coryell and Chris Hills and pursued a jazz career. He also wrote *Witchi Tai To* which was covered by Chris Hills and Danny Weiss's **Everything Is Everything**, **Harpers' Bizarre** and **Brewer and Shipley**. *Witchi Tai To* was inspired by a religious Peyote chant from the Kaw tribe.

Released in 1971 and recorded at Apostolic Studios in New York, *Pepper's Pow Wow* is a strange mix of Indian songs (*Witchi Tai To, Slow and Fast War Dance, Squaw Song, Newly-Weds Song* have Kaw origins, *Rock Stomp Indian Style* and *Nommie-Nommie* are Creek inspired), folk (two Peter LaFarge songs), jazz, country and rock, with some excellent guitar solos by Coryell. The album was produced by **Herbie Mann** and Danny Weiss.

After releasing some jazz albums, **Pepper** died in the nineties. (SR)

Pepper and The Shakers

45s:	Need Your Love/?	(Chetwyd CW-45002)	196?
	Semi-Psychedelic (It Is)/		
	I'll Always Love You	(Coral 62523)	1967

Semi-Psychedelic, by this unknown band, has resurfaced on *30 Seconds Before The Calico Wall* (CD) and *Sixties Rebellion, Vol. 11* (LP & CD). They are thought to have come from Michigan and / or Kentucky and / or New York and their first 45 is rare soul. (GG)

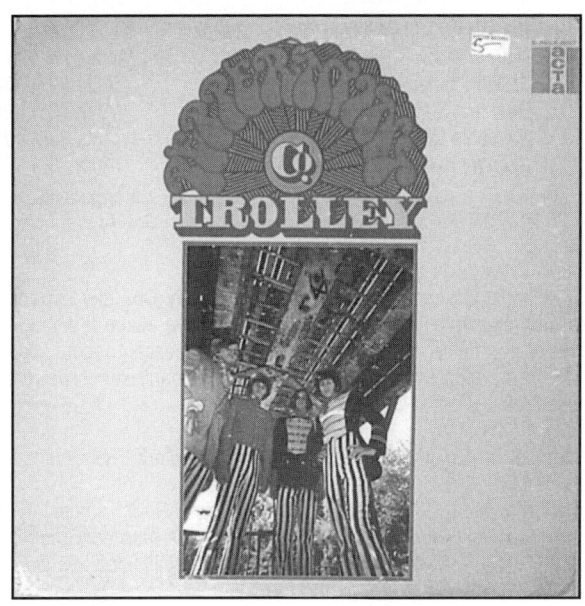

THE PEPPERMINT TROLLEY Co. - The Peppermint Trolley Co. LP.

Peppermint Rainbow

Personnel incl:	SKIP HARRIS		A
	PAT LAMDIN	vcls	A
	BONNIE LAMDIN	vcls	A
	DOUG LEWIS	gtr	A

					HCP
ALBUM:	1	WILL YOU BE STAYING AFTER SUNDAY?			
			(Decca DL-75129)	1969	106 -

NB: (1) also released in Canada.

				HCP
45s:	Pink Lemonade /			
	Walking In Different Circles	(Decca 32316)	1968	-
	Will You Be Staying After Sunday /			
	I'll Be There	(Decca 32410)	1968	32
	Don't Wake Me Up In The Morning Michael/			
	Rosemary	(Decca 32498)	1969	54
	You're The Sound Of Love / Jamais	(Decca 32562)	1969	-
	Good Morning Means Goodbye/			
	Don't Love Me Unless It's Forever	(Decca 32601)	1969	-

A quite successful late sixties pop band from Baltimore, Maryland. They were formed by Skip Harris, previously with **The Progressions**, and Doug Lewis. Both had played together in an earlier teen-pop outfit.

They were discovered and promoted by the producer/songwriter Paul Leka and *Will You Be Staying After Sunday* was a Top 35 hit in April 1969. The album also sold quite well, spending nine weeks in the charts and climbing to No. 106. Leka had previously worked with **The Lemon Pipers** and the album contains a reworked version of their *Green Tambourine*. Largely forgotten now, it may appeal to fans of the softer aspects of the **Mamas and Papas** or **Spanky and Our Gang**.

After they split in 1970, Doug Lewis joined **The Better Half**. (VJ/MW/JV/SR)

The Peppermint Trolley Co

Personnel:	CASEY CUNNINGHAM	gtr, flute	A
	DANNY FARAGHER	keyb'ds	A
	JIMMIE FARAGHER	bs, gtr, sax	A
	GREG TORNQUIST	drms	A

ALBUM:	1(A)	PEPPERMINT TROLLEY CO.	(Acta 38007)	1968 -

			HCP
45s:	Lollipop Train/Bored To Tears	(Variant 752)	1966 -
	She's The Kind Of Girl/Little Miss Sunshine	(Acta 807)	1967 -
	It's A Lazy Summer Day/Blue Eyes	(Acta 809)	1967 -

α	Baby You Come Rolling Across My Mind/ Nine O'Clock Business Man	(Acta 815)	1968 59
	Trust/I Remember Long Ago	(Acta 829)	1968 -
	Beautiful Sun/I've Got To Be Going	(Acta 831)	1968 -
	Memphis City Letter/Last Thing On My Mind	(Acta 834)	1969 -
	Spinnin' n Whirlin' Around/New York City	(Acta 835)	1969 -

NB: α also issued in U.K. on Dot 110. A Portuguese EP with picture sleeve also exists:- *Trust / Sunrise / I Remember Long Ago / I've Got To Be Going* (Dot EP-44-3) 1969

From Redlands, California, **The Peppermint Trolley Co.** later evolved into **Bones** and later The Faragher Brothers. The above album is full of bright and breezy pop tunes. It's nothing special, but a pleasant record. Some of their 45s are apparently far superior, and in particular *Nine O'Clock Business Man* is a great slice of psych-pop.

The Faragher brothers had previously been in **The Mark Five**.

Compilation appearances include: *Baby You Come Rollin' Across My Mind* on *From The New World* (LP); *9 O'Clock Business Man* on *Garagelands, Vol. 1* (LP), *Garagelands, Vol. 1 & 2* (CD) and *Incredible Sound Show Stories, Vol. 6* (LP). (VJ/MW/SR)

Pepper Swift

45: Pinto The Wonder Horse Is Dead (stereo)/
(mono) (Metromedia DJH0-007) 1972

Produced by Gary Paxton (**California Poppy Pickers**) and Danny Davis, this is a rare 45 of hippie-rock. (SR)

Linda Perhacs

Personnel: LINDA PERHACS — vcls, gtr, electronics — A
(STEVE COHN — gtr — A)
(MILT HOLLAND — perc — A)
(BRIAN INGOLDSBY — effects — A)
(SHELLY MANN — perc — A)
(JOHN NEUFELD — flute, sax — A)
(REINIE PRESS — bs, gtr — A)
(LEONARD ROSENMAN — electronics — A)

ALBUM: 1(A) PARALLELOGRAMS (Kapp KS 3636) 1970 R2

NB: (1) reissued on CD (Ace Of Discs WILD005).

A drifting femme fatale folk-psych album which is highly-rated by some. The best tracks are the few where **Perhacs** is augmented by the guest musicians, as on *Moons And Cattails* which has Eastern percussion and is rather psychedelic. **Perhacs'** voice is actually very reminiscent of Ann Wilson's (Heart)... very lovely. (CF/VJ)

The Perils

45: Hate/Baby, Do You Love Me (Velva 7484) 1966

Came out of Hart in Texas. The 'A' side of this 45, *Hate*, is a catchy garage moan.

Compilation appearances include: *Hate* on *60's Punk E.P., Vol. 3* (7"), *Texas Flashback, Vol. 4* (LP & CD), *Ya Gotta Have Moxie, Vol. 2* (Dble CD) and *Flashback, Vol. 4* (LP). (VJ)

Periscopes

Personnel: RICHARD GOLDEN — drms — A
JIM HUNGERFORD — bs — A
JIM KAPLAN — keyb'ds — A
TED KRUGER — sax — A
JOHN NICHOLSON — gtr — A

45: Beavershot / I'm Happy To Be (Desett Wells W.D.R.2274) 1965
NB: reissued in a limited (1000) pic sleeve edition (Bacchus Archives BA 1144) 2000.

LINDA PERHACS - Parallelograms CD.

A rare'n'raw frat-rock 45 whose reissue comes with a seal of approval from Crypt's Tim Warren and reveals their history... **The Periscopes** started playing at Van Nuys High School, California in 1964 and by 1965 the line-up had settled to the quintet above. Their biggest gig was at the L.A. Coliseum for the UCLA-SC football games, with an audience of over 80,000. In the Summer of '65 they recorded the raunchy *Beavershot* at RCA studios in Hollywood. It got some airplay and appeared briefly on the Sight & Sound charts before being banned by the FCC for being "overly suggestive". Producers Wells and DeSett not only ripped off *Louie Louie* for the flipside but did a runner, so the band never got paid either.

Only Kruger still plays professionally, Nicholson and Golden reside in the San Fernando Valley, Hungerford lives in Washington state and Kaplan passed away. (MW)

Perpetual Motion Workshop

Personnel incl: SIMON STOKES — A

45: Infiltrate Your Mind/Won't Come Down (Rally 66506/7) 1967

From the 1966/67 era and based in Los Angeles. The 'A' side, *Infiltrate Your Mind*, written by **Simon Stokes**, sounds similar to **The Music Machine**. The 'B' side has a kinda psychedelic turbulence and its Sky Saxon-style vocals beg the inevitable comparisons to those revered L.A. kings of the garage, **The Seeds**.

Compilation appearances have included: *Won't Come Down* on *Pebbles Vol. 9* (CD) and *Psychedelic Experience, Vol. 3* (CD); *Infiltrate Your Mind* on *Psychedelic Experience Vol. 4* (CD); *Won't Come Down* and *Infiltrate Your Mind* on *Psychedelic Disaster Whirl* (LP). (VJ/MW)

Pep Perrine

ALBUM: 1 1. LIVE AND IN PERSON - HUMORNUCLEOSIS
(Hideout HLP-1003) 1969 R2

Perrine was drummer for **Bob Seger's Last Heard**. This was reputedly a comic psych-rock album. (VJ/SR)

The Persian Market

Personnel incl: L. DEHART — A
T. RANSON — A

45: Flash In The Pan/Sometimes Good Guys
Don't Wear White (Lightning LR-103) 196?

A Louisiana combo. *Flash In The Pan*, is a rather good quasi-psychedelic pop song.

Compilation appearances have included: *Flash In The Pan* on *Louisiana Punk Groups From The Sixties, Vol. 2* (LP) and *Sixties Archive, Vol. 3* (CD); *Flash In The Pan, Sometimes Good Guys Don't Wear White, The Gamma Goochie* and *The Wind Calls Her Name* on *The Cicadelic 60's, Vol. 2* (CD) and *The Cicadelic 60's, Vol. 4* (LP). (VJ)

Perspective

ALBUM: 1   SYLLABUS   (No label) 1970 ?

A high school folk-psych effort. The album came with an insert. (GG)

The Persuaders

45:      (Tiny Little) Seeds/This Girl   (Achillean 501) 196?

An obscure 45, touted as 'garage', but in truth bright folk-pop and pop-beat with reedy keyboard solos. (MW)

Peter and The Prophets

Personnel incl: BOYLAN
                     SAMUELSON

45:      Don't Need Your Lovin'/Johnny Of Dreams   (Fenton 2050) 1966

This 45 was the sole platter by this Detroit, Michigan folk-rock outfit for whom **The Byrds** were a clear influence. You'll also find *Don't Need Your Lovin'* on *Highs In The Mid-Sixties, Vol. 5* (LP) and *Best Of Michigan Rock Groups, Vol. 2*. (VJ)

Peter and The Rabbits

45:      Bless You Little Girl/
        Someone I've Got My Eyes Upon   (Bell 670) 1967

Thought to have been a Tennessee band they seem to merge folk-rock, punk and bubblegum on *Someone I've Got My Eyes Upon*, a pretty commercial effort which can also be heard on *Pebbles, Vol. 12* (LP). (VJ)

Peter and The Wolves

45:      Hey Mama/Only Everything   (P.W. 500) 196?

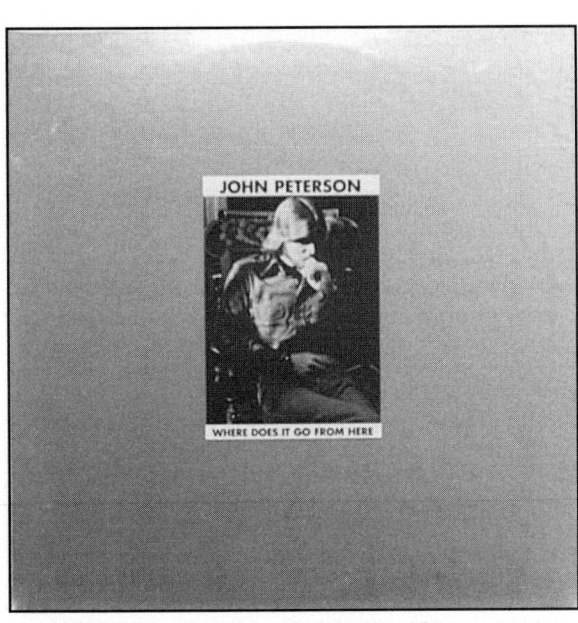

JOHN PETERSON - Where Does It Go From Here LP.

This Los Angeles-based outfit operated in 1965 and '66 and were thought to include future **Moby Grape** members Peter Lewis and Bob Newkirk, however Peter Lewis has confirmed that his **Peter & The Wolves** never recorded.

Compilation appearances have included: *Hey Mama* and *Only Everything* on *Off The Wall, Vol. 1* (LP) and *The Essential Pebbles Collection, Vol. 1* (Dble CD); and *Only Everything* on *Teenage Shutdown, Vol. 3* (LP & CD). (VJ/CMn)

Peter Pan and The Good Fairies

Personnel incl: JIMMY GORDON   A

45:      Balloons/Kaleidoscope   (Challenge 59373) 1967

Two glorious baroque-psych instrumentals from **Jim Gordon** that'd fit right onto the **Cosmic Sounds** *Zodiac* album or a hip sixties film soundtrack.

You can also find *Balloons* on *Buzz Buzz Buzzzzzz, Vol. 1* (CD) and *Kaleidoscope* on *Buzz Buzz Buzzzzzz, Vol. 2* (CD). (MW)

Peter Pipers

45s: Airplane/I Didn't Believe Her   (Philips 40518) 1968
       Groovy Weekend/Helping You Out   (Philips 40543) 1968
       The Magic Book/
       I Don't Know What You're Waiting For   (Philips 40568) 1969

Hailed from Pittsburgh, Pennsylvania. *I Don't Believe Her* and *Helping You Out* can both be heard on *Burghers, Vol. 1* (LP & CD). (VJ)

John Peterson

ALBUM: 1   WHERE DOES IT GO FROM HERE
                                         (Private Pressing) 1976 SC

NB: (1) has been counterfeited on LP.

A recently discovered "real people" folk singer/songwriter. (SR)

Kris Peterson

ALBUM: 1   A CHILD'S DREAM   (Stormy Forest SFS 60??) 1972 -

On **Richie Havens**' label, a female folk-pop singer. (SR)

Petra

ALBUM: 1   PETRA   (Myrrh MST-6527) 1974 -

A good Christian hard-rockin group, with *Walkin' In The Light, Wake Up, Lucas McGraw, Storm Comin* and *I'm Not Ashamed*. (SR)

Petrified Forest

Personnel incl: WARREN SCHATZ   vcls, gtr   A

45:      So Mystifying/She's The Only Thing
        That's Kept Me Going   (Fontana 1596) 1967

A New York group formed by **Warren Schatz**. *So Mystifying* was a cover of the Kinks' number (also recorded by **The Shapes Of Things**).

Compilation appearances include: *So Mystifying* on *60's Punk E.P., Vol. 3* (7") and *Ya Gotta Have Moxie, Vol. 2* (Dble CD). (VJ/MW/SR)

PHAFNER - Phafner LP.

Pex's Bad Boys

45s:	Crazy World/Cloud Seventy-Six	(Scepter 12176) 1966
α	Girl In Chains/Silver Dawn	(Scepter 12182) 1967

NB: α as **Peck's Bad Boys**.

The first 45, released as by **Peck's Bad Boys**, is rare and sought-after for the frenzied *Crazy World*, which can also be found on *Tougher Than Stains* (LP) and *Teenage Shutdown Vol. 11* (LP & CD). Their second 45 however, as **Pex's Bad Boys** tends towards garagey pop with *Silver Dawn* winning out with its mesh of jangling guitars and waltzing rhythm. (MW)

Caroline Peyton

Personnel:	BRUCE ANDERSON		A
	MARK GRAY		A
	MARK INGHAM		A
	BILL NOLL		A
	CAROLINE PEYTON	vcls	AB

ALBUMS:	1(A)	MOCK UP	(Bar-B-Que BRBQ-1) c1972 -
	2(B)	INTUITION	(Bar-B-Que BBRQ-8) c1974 -

Originating from Bloomington, Indiana, **Carolyn Peyton** was a member of the **Screaming Gypsy Bandits**. Her voice sounded like a cross between Joni Mitchell and Carole King and she released at least two solo albums (there may be more). The first was housed in a home-made yellow cover with graffiti and drawings and was recorded with the help of Anderson and Ingham, two members of the **'Bandits**. It includes songs like *The Sky In Japan Is Always Close To You, Hook, Sweet Misery, Pull, Come For A Day*, the strongest track being possibly *Lor el iii*. The next album, *Intuition*, included *Brister, Light-Years, All This Waiting, Donkey Blues, Together, Call Of The Wild* and *You Too* and can be described as hippie-folk rock.

Carolyn Peyton later relocated to the West Coast, where she has recorded Celtic music and done major-movie voice-overs for animated features. (SR)

The Phaetons

45s:	Dancing In The Street/Where Are You	(Warner Bros. 5892) 1967
	She Came Like The Rain/Three Weeks, Four Days And Fifteen Hours	(Warner Bros. 7082) 1967
	You'd Better Come Home/ Leave It To Me	(Warner Bros. 7205) 1968

An obscure outfit whose second 45 is good pop-psych. The third 45 harmony-pop 45, produced by Jerry Ragovoy, covers *You'd Better Come Home* by UK songsmith Tony Hatch (not the oft-covered Bert Russell song of the same name) and a Pomus-Schuman composition. (SR/BM/MW)

Phafner

Personnel:	STEVE 'GUS' GUSTAFSON	drms	A
	DALE SHULTZ	gtr, vcls	A
	TOMMY SHULTZ	bs	A
	GREG "SMITTY" SMITH	vcls, harp	A
	STEVE "SPIDER" SMITH	ld gtr	A

ALBUM:	1(A)	OVERDRIVE	(Dragon no #) 1971 R5

NB: The Rockadelic-related label Animus Ochlus LP titled *Phafner* (AOLP 101) 1990 collected six of the eight tracks on the *Overdrive* album plus two unreleased demos. More recently, Akarma have issued their own **Phafner** album (AK 009) 1998 on vinyl and CD but this version contains only the six tracks from *Overdrive* that were included on the Animus Ochlus collection and duplicates the sleeve created for the Animus Ochlus collection. To date, neither the original sleeve or the complete music of (1) have been reissued.

45:	Overdrive/Plea From The Soul	(Dragon 1001) 1971

This band formed in Marshalltown, Iowa, in 1969 playing a form of hard-edged, drug-induced rock'n'roll. Their album was recorded in a basement studio in 1971 and just 50 copies were pressed on the Dragon label. In 1972, they recorded some rough cuts for what was to be their second album, *Meathook*. Sadly the band fell apart before the album was completed but two of these previously unreleased tracks, *Breakdown* and *Cat Black Claw*, can now be heard on the Animus Ochlus retrospective album - which is not a straightforward reissue of *Overdrive*, as it omits some of the original material. *Overdrive* features some pretty fine and varied guitar work. The opening cut, *Plea From The Soul*, has lots of fuzz and mouth harp; *Uncle Jerry* and *Rock n Roll Man* feature breakneck guitar work, whilst by contrast *Whiskey Took My Woman* is slower and bluesy. Recommended. (VJ)

Phananganang

Personnel:	DALE DUCKETT	bs, vcls	A
	ERNIE ENOCHSON	drms	A
	LEIA KELLS	keyb'ds	A
	CARLOS NEWCOMB	bs	A
	MARK QUINN	vcls, gtr	A
	ROSS WINETSKY	vcls, gtr	A

45:	The Clowns Are Coming/ Two A Little One	(San Francisco Sound) 196?

A rare 45 of guitar-based pop-rock, which was recorded in Boston by Tom Foley. This act performed in the San Francisco area between 1969 and 1972 and were managed by Matthew Katz. In their time they got to open for the likes of **The Grateful Dead** and **Jefferson Airplane** and also performed on the same bill with **Clover**.

Both sides of the 45 can also be found on *California Halloween*. More recently Mark Quinn has recorded a solo CD. (VJ/JLi)

PHANTASIA - A Psychedelic By... LP.

Phantasia

Personnel incl: J. De PUGH A
D. JOHNSON A
R. WALKENHORST A

ALBUMS: 1(A) PHANTASIA (Damon D-12918) 19?? R5
2(A) WALKENHORST - DE PUGH (Damon D-12969) 19?? R5

NB: (1) and (2) are promo-only demo albums issued without covers. (2) is one-sided. Material from both albums, plus the equally rare **Trizo 50** demo album has been compiled as *A Psychedelic By Phantasia* (Ton Um Ton LP ST-641), 1994, *I Talk To The Moon* (Ton Um Ton 1096) 1996, and CD *A Psychedelic By* (Synton 1610974) 1997.

These two rare demo albums were recorded at Damon Recording Studios in Kansas City, Missouri, in approximately 1970. As they are virtually unobtainable, the Ton Um Ton/Synton collections are the only currently accessible source for the material.

The *A Psychedelic By* collection on vinyl and CD has the edge over the *I Talk To The Moon* release, with highlights including the siren effects on the rocky *Ride Me* and the phasing and bubbling sounds on *I'm Alive* (which have an almost **13th Floor Elevator** aura). The sound on these releases is predominantly gentle psychy hippie-rock but with the odd heavier moment like the excellent slow burnin' *A Stumbling Dragon*. This latter track also appears on the *I Talk To The Moon* collection as the second half of the wistful *Genena*. Another track, *Chasing Now The Flying Time*, also gets an airing on both vinyl releases.

The same band continued to record well into the seventies and another demo album appeared circa 1974 as by **Trizo 50**.

You can also find **Trizo 50**'s *Graveyard* on *Love, Peace And Poetry, Vol. 1* (LP & CD). (VJ/CF)

Phantom

Personnel: JOHN BDANJECK drms A
TOM CARSON vcls, gtr, piano A
DENNIS CRANER bs A
MIKE DeMARTINO key'ds A
GARY MEISNER gtr A

ALBUMS: 1( ) PHANTOM'S DIVINE COMEDY, PART ONE (Capitol 11313) 1974 R1
2(A) THE LOST ALBUM (Ghost) 1990 -

NB: (1) reissued in 1989, and also available on CD (One Way 56842). (2) is a bootleg, that has also recently appeared on CD (Flash 49).

45: Calm Before The Storm/
Black Magic, White Magic (Hideout 1080) 1973

NB: also exists as a doubled sided promo *Calm Before The Storm* (stereo) / *Calm Before The Storm* (mono) (Hideout 1080) 1973. Reissued on Capitol red label (3857) 1974.

Originally known as **Walpurgis**, *The Lost Album* is supposed to have been recorded by line-up 'A' in Los Angeles and predates the official *Divine Comedy* release. We have been told that the band were re-named by their manager as **Phantom** and we know that the line-up which recorded *Divine Comedy* definitely came from Rochester, a small town about 30 miles from Detroit.

On both albums the vocalist sounds like Jim Morrison and indeed Capitol Records issued a statement that it *was* leading to legal action by Elektra.

What of the music? *Divine Comedy* is highly-rated by many, it has a mystical sound and is recommended. *Tales From A Wizard* and *Welcome To Hell*, which are both rather melodramatic, are arguably the strongest tracks but a consistent standard is maintained throughout.

The *Divine Comedy* line-up made a second self-titled album in 1978 under the name **Happy Dragon Band** (Fiddlers 11 57) 1978, This is more electronic.

The *Lost Album* contains previously unreleased material. Musically it's similar to their first effort though not as good. (VJ/RMn/SR)

PHANTOM - Phantom's Divine Comedy, Part One LP.

The Phantom Raiders

Personnel: DOUG ALMOND bs A
RANDY LEE ld gtr A
RICKY LEE gtr A
MITCH MILLER drms A
EDDIE SMITH gtr A

ALBUM: 1 NEW SOUND '67 (Justice 146) 1967 R2

NB: (1) reissued on CD (Collectables COL-0612) 1995.

A true teen combo, with members all between the ages of eleven and fourteen, **The Phantom Raiders**' 1967 album was released on Calvin Newton's Justice Records label. As opposed to many of the label's other acts, who concentrated on mostly soul and R&B covers, the **Phantom Raiders**' leaned towards pop/Top 40 material. As such, their lone album includes the band's versions of **The Monkees**' *I'm Not Your Stepping Stone* and *I'm A Believer*, the Beatles' *Day Tripper*, J. Frank Wilson's *Last Kiss*, Mitch Ryder & The Detroit Wheels' *Devil With A Blue Dress On/Good Golly Miss Molly*, and Them's *Gloria*, which the band seemingly improvised lyrics on. The album is also heavy on instrumentals, and features versions of *Stick Shift*, *Pipeline*, *Wipeout*, *Walk, Don't Run*, and *New Sound '67*, a group original. (MDo)

The Phantoms

Personnel incl: BRYAN ASHBAUGH A
MULLER brothers A
GEOFF SOENTPIET A

45s: Hallucinogenic Odyssey /
Sixty Minutes To Nine (Graves 1104) 1967
Story Of A Rich Man / Our Great Society (Ridon 859) 1968

From Portland, Oregon and on the same label as the **United Travel Service**, *Story...* is excellent catchy UK/Beatles-infused psych-rock, produced by Rick Keefer, best known to readers of this book for his collaboration with **The New Tweedy Bros!**. Check it out on *Psychedelic Crown Jewels, Vol. 2* (Dble LP & CD) whose liners reveal (via Mike Markesich) that the band started as a three-piece with the Muller brothers in 1965. They were later known as Prime Mover having been augmented by Indonesian nationals, Soentpiet and Ashbaugh, who composed both sides of the Ridon 45.

Our Great Society is a moody off-the-wall psych gem that goes off on its own amazin' freak-out trip and doesn't come back! Well overdue for a compilation or reissue. The first 45 remains elusive, but is said to be good psych too. (MW/CF/GGl/MM)

Phase III

Personnel incl: KEITH ABLER   A

45: I'm Not A Fool Anymore/
     Back In The U.S.A.   (Target T 1007) 1969

This would be a below-par late sixties pop-rock 45 from Wisconsin but for some white-hot fuzz throughout the 'B' side.

Keith Abler also played with **The Love Society**, and both members of that group and **Phase III** went on to Sunblind Lion. (MW)

Phil and The Frantics

Personnel: STEVE FORMAN   ld gtr   A
            PHIL KELSEY   vcls, sax   ABC
            JOHN LAMBERT   bs, vcls   AB
            BILL POWELL   gtr, vcls   AB
            RICK ROSE   keyb'ds   AB
            JOE MARTINEZ   drms   BC
            STEVE DODGE   gtr   C
            TED HARCHEK   keyb'ds   C
            DON SNIDER   bs   C
            FRANK UVEDS

ALBUM: 1(A/B) ROUGH DIAMONDS: HISTORY OF GARAGE
               BAND MUSIC, VOL. 3: PHIL AND THE FRANTICS
                                (Voxx VXM 200.001) 1985

45s: She's My Gal/Ko-Ko Joe   (La Mar 100) 1964
      New Orleans/To Me   (Sounds Ltd 1216) 1965
      Say That You Will/
      Till You Get What You Want   (ARA 1968) 1965
      I Must Run/Pain   (Rabbit 1219) 1966
      I Must Run/What's Happening   (Ramco/ARA 1970) 1966

Phil Kelsey was born into a musical environment in Dallas, both his parents had jazz and gospel experience. His family later moved to Phoenix, Arizona, where in his last two years of school he fronted The Four Gants, a fifties rock combo. Kelsey put together line-up 'A' of **Phil And The Frantics** in 1963. Jim Musil discovered the band playing at their own Phoenix club, The Cave, and became their manager and producer. Phil renamed the club The Frantic Den and enlisted his mother's assistance to run it. Their early recordings were much influenced by the British invasion sound. The first 45 made no impact at all, the second was a local hit and the third a smash hit in Phoenix. Both sides, particularly the flip, featured haunting minor key melodies making this their best record so far. However, *I Must Run*, which was produced by Waylon Jennings and largely based on *I Must Move*, an early Zombies 'B' side, went one better charting in many parts of the country, although it was not a national hit. After its success they toured with Peter and Gordon and also played with other big name acts, but the band fell apart when Lambert and Powell left to join **Beethoven Soul**, a California band who had an album on Dot. Kelsey put together a new line-up (C), but their now dated British invasion sound could not survive the psychedelic era.

The Voxx compilation traces the band's musical development superbly and has excellent liner notes part of which have been summarised here. The first side concentrates largely on fast R&B rockers, the flip on their British invasion sound. All their 45s are included.

Upon the demise of **Phil And The Frantics** Phil Kelsey and Steve Dodge drifted between L.A., Las Vegas and Phoenix. They changed their name to Phil Mark Five and then with the addition of Bobby Blood on trumpet to The Babies. An album was recorded after a deal with ABC - Dunhill in 1969. They toured with Three Dog Night, **Blues Image** and other popular bands of the time but, increasingly beset by drug problems and after three 45s had flopped, they then learnt that their album was shelved. Shortly afterwards, when Phil broke his leg, the band sacked him!

Back in L.A. Phil became an active session musician and songwriter. He worked with Earth Wind and Fire, Billy Preston and Brenton Wood among others. In 1979, he changed his name to Devin Payne and recorded an album, *Excuse Me*, which was scheduled for release on Casablanca but shelved when the company went bust in 1980. Later he produced a record for Blow-Up, a sixties-inspired new wave band.

Compilation appearances include: *I Must Run* on *Pebbles Vol. 2* (CD) and *Pebbles, Vol. 2* (LP); *I Must Run* and *Til You Get What You Want* on *Pebbles Box* (4-LP), *Acid Dreams - The Complete 3 LP Set* (3-LP), *Acid Dreams Epitaph* (CD) and *Trash Box* (5-CD); and *Pain* on *Garage Music For Psych Heads, Vol. 1*. (VJ)

Samy Phillip

45s: When I Say I Love You I Mean It, And Don't Change
      My Mind/?   (Infinite 2001) 196?
      Magic Fly/I Wander Freely (PS)   (Infinite 2002) 196?

When I Say .... has resurfaced on *Boulders, Vol. 2* (LP), but nothing else is known about this artist. (VJ)

Glenn Phillips

Personnel: JERRY FIELDS   drms   A
            JOHN CARR HARRIMAN   cello   A
            MIKE HOLBROOK   bs   A
            GLENN PHILLIPS   gtr   A
            JIMMY PRESMANES   drms   A
            BILL REA   gtr   A
            SANT RAM SINGH   keyb'ds A

ALBUM: 1(A) LOST AT SEA   (Snow Star 1) 1975 SC

NB: (1) also issued in the U.K. on Caroline - Virgin (1519) 1975 SC.

The first solo album by the former lead guitarist of the Hampton Grease Band. This is his only album that fits within the time frame of the book. The Atlanta, Georgia artist is still making CDs and performing today. The album, which comprises instrumental progressive guitar rock, is often described as 'psychedelic' by record dealers. (CF)

John Phillips

                                                        HCP
ALBUM: 1 JOHN PHILLIPS, THE WOLF KING OF L.A.
                                (Dunhill DS 50077) 1970 181 -

45s: α Topanga Canyon/Holland Tunnel   (Stateside) 1970
         Mississippi/April Anne   (Dunhill 4236) 1970

NB: α Australian release.

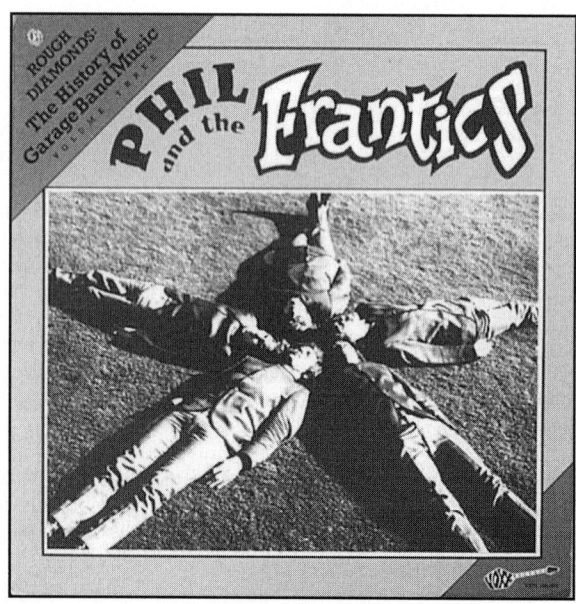

PHIL and THE FRANTICS - Rough Diamonds... LP.

THE PHILOSOPHERS - After Sundown LP.

This solo album by the former **Mamas and Papas** leader was recorded with **Hal Blaine**, Darlene Love and James Burton. Some rate it highly, but many find it rather boring. It sold reasonably well, reaching No. 181 during a nine week chart sojurn. After many problems with drugs, **Phillips** sadly died in 2001, two weeks before the release of his second solo album. This compiles recordings done over 25 years, including some with members of the Rolling Stones. (SR)

The Philosophers

Personnel incl: HAROLD P. JOHNSON

ALBUM: 1   AFTER SUNDOWN - GETTING DOWN
                          (Philo Spectrum PS 1001) 1970 R2

45:   The Law Of Love/Do Fuga   (Philo Spectrum PS 31180) c1969

An early seventies Los Angeles based group produced this blues-rock album with some biting leads. There's also lots of keyboard dominance, including some instrumentals, but musically it's not terribly memorable. The album's produced by J. Gibson and arranged by Harold P. Johnson (who also seems to have been part of the multi-racial quintet, which included two blacks). All bar one track (*Baby I Care* was credited to Harold Johnson) were co-written by J. Gibson and Harold Johnson.

The 45 is often described as 'psych', presumably due to *Do Fuga*, a piece of backwards mayhem that appears to be just the 'A' side in reverse, and probably more interesting for that.

The front cover of the album uses the same picture as **White Light**'s album. This was because both albums were pressed by Century records. If customers didn't have their own artwork, then the company had a selection of non-copyrighted cover art blanks from which they could choose. The odd art (resembling the contents of a fish aquarium under coloured lights) was picked up by both **White Light** and **Philosophers** coincidentally. Century also offered an outdoor scene showing an old mill wheel, which was used on many different records - the **Victims Of Chance**: *Goin' Home Blue* and **Fifth Flight**: *Into Smoke Tree Village*, to name two. Most of Century label's customers seem to have been schools / marching bands. (CF/VJ/MW)

Phineas and The Lemon Fogg

45:   Anything Can Happen (When You're Lonely)/
        Love Is A Groovy Feeling   (Scepter SCE 12225) 1968

Multi-gender harmony flower-pop for lovers of the **Association**, **Love Generation** or Fifth Dimension. (MW)

Phinx

ALBUM: 1   SOMETIMES   (Crazy Cajun CCLP-1059) 1978 SC

45s: My Baby Don't Care/Sometimes   (Pic 1 139) 1966
         Duke of Earl/House Of The Rising Sun   (Pic 1 144) 1967

Houston's answer to **The Gants**. A mystery outfit produced by Huey P. Meaux, who eventually released the 10-track compilation of their material, though omitting *House Of The Rising Sun*. Like **The Gants** their stuff is almost all covers, competent but lightweight garagey beat/folk-rock - good but not that good. They even cover **The Gants**' own *My Baby Don't Care* alongside regular faves like *Feel A Whole Lot Better*, *You Make Me Feel Good*, etc. (MW)

Phlegethon

Personnel: JEFF BOUGHNER   gtr   AB
                  TOM DAVIS   drms   A
                  ARIS HAMPERS   keyb'ds, tympani, vcls   AB
                  DAVE PRYCE   gtr   A
                  JOE SARNICOLA   bs   A
                  L.C. DAVIS   bs, flute   B
                  RANDY MARSH   drms   B

CDs: 1   THE SOULBENDERS/PHLEGETHON: THE
            MICHIGAN TAPES 1967-1971 (CD)   (Arisdisc no #) 2000
          2   THE SOULBENDERS/PHLEGETHON:
            BONUS DISC (CD)   (Arisdisc no #) 2000

45s: You're No Good / The Sun   (Pre-Heat 200) 1970
     α   Last Voyage Home /
          Prelude To An Odyssey   (Pre-Heat 202) 1971

NB: α was pressed on red vinyl and in stereo.

Phlegethon was the next musical venture for Hampers and Boughner after Grand Rapids, Michigan's mighty **Soulbenders**.

Aris: "Phlegethon was more of an "art-rock" band than garage, at least the last incarnation... it was the times. But some of the earlier stuff definitely borders on garage... particularly the organ and guitar sounds."

They disbanded a couple of months after the second release - "Actually the friction had begun before the recording session. I knew we were about to give it up... that's pretty much why I titled the tune *Last Voyage Home* even though the lyrics don't allude to that."

Aris Hampers released two CDs of material from both bands in 2000.

Compilation appearances include: *You're No Good* on *Sixties Archive, Vol. 6* (CD) and *Brain Shadows, Vol. 2* (LP & CD). (MW)

PHLUPH - Phluph LP.

Phluph

Personnel:	BENSON BLAKE IV	A
	LEE DUDLEY	A
	JOEL MAISANO	A
	JOHN PELL	A

ALBUM: 1(A) PHLUPH (Verve 5054) 1968 SC

NB:(1) reissued on LP and CD (Akarma AK 147) 2001.

45s:	Another Day/Doctor Mind	(Verve 10564) 1967
	Patterns/In Her Way	(Verve 10576) 1968

This Boston band made an excellent psychedelic album full of trippy lyrics, catchy organ work and, at times, fine guitar work. Almost all the tracks are interesting so it's difficult to single out individual ones. This is more commercial than most of the Bosstown Sound's offerings in 1968 and is now a very minor collectors' item. All the 45 cuts are taken from the album. (VJ)

Phoenix

Personnel:	CHUCK McCABE	gtr, vcls	A
	TIRAN PORTER	bs, vcls	A
	HOMER SWAIN	drms, vcls	A
	MIKE WALCH	perc, vcls, piano	A

ALBUM: 1(A) PHOENIX (ABC ABCS-703) 1969 -

45s:	Baby, I'm Sorry/Postmark : N.Y.C.	(ABC 11249) 1969
	Postmark : N.Y.C./Julia's Face	(ABC 11263) 1969

Produced by Bob Todd, **Phoenix** was a California rock quartet whose album is only of minor interest. The musicians are good, but the songs are weak and the production is direction-less, with ballads with strings, rock songs with horns. The best tracks are the ones used for the 45s, plus *I'm Leaving, You Arrived*.

Their young black bassist, Tiran Porter, would later join the Doobie Brothers. (SR)

Phoenix Bird

Personnel:	GEORGE GORDON	gtr, vcls	A
	KEITH HART	bs, vcls	A
	MIKE McINNIS	drms	A

45: F.T.C./Parchman Farm (PS) (American Sound AS 1001) 1996

A Lincoln, New Hampshire, band who recorded for the Onyx label (**Lazy Smoke**) but whose recordings were never released at the time. The tracks on the 7" above are from an acetate recorded in 1970 and remind a lot of **Blue Cheer**. It's been released in a picture sleeve of 500 copies only. (MW/VJ)

Phoenix Trolley

45: When Charlie's Doin' His Thing/
Three-Part Invention (Capitol 2227) 1968

An obscure harmony-pop 45 that reeks of L.A. and would have remained obscure but for Erik Lindgren featuring the flip on his weird 'n' wacky odyssey *Only In America*. The top-side is pretty ordinary pop but the 'B' side is a haunting dirge that combines a **Curt Boettcher** type vocal collage and adds a **David Axelrod** backing track. Not psych, just extra-ordinary.

Compilation appearances include *Three Part Investigation (Too Many Trees In The Forest)* on *Only In America* (CD). (MW)

PH PHACTOR - Merryjuana LP.

Phorenbach Delegation

45: Tall Grass/? (Fahrenheit FAH-100) 1968

Came out of Chicago. *Glimpses, Vol. 4* (LP) includes *Tall Grass*. (VJ)

PH Phactor (Jugband)

Personnel:	PAUL BASSETT	washboard, drms, kazoo, jug, jews harp	A
	JOHN BROWNE	gtr, hrmnca, vcls	A
	DAVY COFFIN	gtr, mandolin	A
	JOHN HENDRICKS	mandolin, kazoo, jug	A
	NICK OGILVIE	gtr, hrmnca	A
	STEVE MORK	bs, jug	A
	CHRIS ROBINSON	gtr, vcls	A
	MIKE RUSH	drms	A

ALBUM: 1 MERRYJUANA (Piccadilly PIC 3343) 1980 R2

45: Minglewood Blues/Barefoot John (Piccadilly 241) 1967

A five-piece from Portland, Oregon, they moved to San Francisco in the flower-power era to record the above 45. An album collecting their material, entitled *Merryjuana*, was put out in the early eighties but is extremely elusive and is similar to early **Charlatans**, **Kaleidoscope** and **Country Joe and The Fish**. Note that the group's name is spelled "Factor" on the cover, but "Phactor" on the label.

Paul Bassett became a poster artist and like Nick Ogilvie now lives in Portland. John Browne resides near Seattle and Steve Mork lives in Sacramento, California. A video *"The Life And Times Of The Red Dog Saloon"* which is due for release, includes extensive footage of a Red Dog reunion featuring the **P.H. Phactor Jugband**, **Charlatans** and others, as well as a soundtrack of period **P.H. Phactor Jugband** material and footage from the sixties.

You'll also find their version of *Minglewood Blues* on *Battle Of The Bands, Vol. 2* (LP) and *The History Of Northwest Rock, Vol. 3* (LP); *Minglewood Blues*, *Merryjuana* and *Barefoot John* on *The History Of Northwest Rock, Vol. 3* (CD); another cut, *Rain Island*, also features on the *California Halloween* compilation. (VJ/DR/MCn/NK)

The Pictorian Skiffuls

Personnel incl: RON SKINNER drms A

45: In A While/You've Done Me Wrong (Skifful 15587/8) 1965

Hailed from Dayton, Ohio. *In A While*, a folkish Merseybeat offering can also be heard on *Highs In The Mid-Sixties, Vol. 21* (LP). This 45 seems to have been their sole vinyl offering.

Ron Skinner went on to **Jerry and The Others**. (VJ/MW/DJe)

Picture

Personnel:	WAYNE BABICH	bs	A
	MIKE BEASTER	drms	A
	MIKE MILEWSKI	ld gtr	A
	JIM MILEWSKI	gtr/bs	A
	PHIL SHIELDS	keyb'ds, sax	A
	BILL AIKEN	gtr, keyb'ds	
	MIKE HOULIHAN	bs	
	WAYNE LaPENE	drms	
	BOB McKENNA	vcls	
	LON OMITT	drms	

45s:	Reach Out/Evolution	(Nasco 002) 1969
	Universal Soldier / Dance Of Love	(WRN WRN-45-101) 1970

Formed in Milwaukee in 1967 by the Milewski brothers after the break-up of the **Richochett(e)s**, their first 45 is well-regarded for the acid etched *Evolution*. Erik's Lindgren' description can't be topped - "Excessive flanging, searing guitar leads and heavily echoed drums add up to one far out enchanted musical journey". The 'A' side is a cover of the Four Tops' *Reach Out (I'll Be There)*.

The band was together for around five years although latterly the personnel was apparently very fluid.

Compilation appearances include *Evolution* on *A Heavy Dose Of Lyte Psych* (CD), *Psychedelic Experience* (CD), *The Psychedelic Experience, Vol. 2* (LP) and *Acid and Flowers* (CD). (MW/GM)

Pidgeon

Personnel:	CHERI GAGE	autoharp, ld vcls	A
	RICHARD T. MARSHALL	poetry	A
	JOBRAITH SALISBURY	keyb'ds, gtr, ld vcls	A
	BILL STRONG SMITH	drms, perc	A

ALBUM:	1(A)	PIDGEON	(Decca DL 75103) 1969 -

45:	Prison Walls/Rubber Necks	(Decca 32545) 1969

Thanks to Mike Warth of Leighton Buzzard for drawing this album, which has attracted little interest from collectors to date, to my attention. It's a typical West Coast-sounding album with some nice female vocals from Cheri Gage, although most of the tracks feature harmony vocals. Mostly soft-rock it includes one good rocker, *The Dancer*. The 45 was not on the album. (VJ)

The Piece Kor

Personnel:	MICKEY BALL	hrmnca, gtr, vcls	A
	JACK BANDONI	gtr	A
	CHARLEY CLARK	drms, vcls	A
	DANNY MOORE	ld gtr	A
	BARRY SCOTT	bs	A

45:	All I Want Is My Baby Back/ Words Of The Raven	(Laray 2556) 1968

A garage band from Bel-Air, Maryland. The 45 was produced by Tom Guernsey of **The Hangmen**. *All I Want Is My Baby Back* is a pretty late piece of teen honk, whilst the flip is quite a classy slab of garage-psych with a superb reverb style guitar break.

Compilation appearances have included: *Words Of The Raven* on *Sixties Rebellion, Vol. 14* (LP & CD); *All I Want Is My Baby Back* on *Back From The Grave, Vol. 8* (CD) and *Back From The Grave, Vol. 8* (Dble LP). (MW/MM)

Pied Pipers

Personnel incl:	DICK BELLEY	A
	DENNIS SESSONSKY	A

45s:	Hey Joe/Hold On I'm Coming	(Wam 5948) 1967?
	Stay In My Life/ You Don't Know Like I Know	(Hamlin 2510) 1967?

From the Youngstown, Ohio area. **The Pied Pipers** had quite a following on the local scene, and were second only in the pecking order to the **Human Beinz**. They played at teen dances locally and recorded at Wam studios in Youngstown (long shut-down) who cut many local bands.

Led by Dennis Sessonsky, who co-wrote *Stay In My Life*, the group lasted until 1970, and had many personnel changes. The last version, when they were known as The Pipers, also included Dick Belley, who had played with the **Human Beinz**.

Sessonsky was a bizarre character to be sure. He later metamorphised into Dennis T. Menass and fronted Left End, the top Youngstown band throughout the seventies and early eighties. Left End also cut a few local singles and one album on Polydor.

The flip to their second 45, *You Don't Know Like I Know*, was a Porter/Hayes Stax composition.

Compilation coverage to date has included: *Stay In My Life* and *You Don't Know Like I Know* on *Everywhere Interferences* (LP); *Hey Joe* on *Highs In The Mid-Sixties, Vol. 9* (LP); *Stay In My Life* on *Midnight To Sixty-Six* (LP) and *Victims Of Circumstance, Vol. 2* (CD). (GGl/MMy/MW/VJ)

Pierce Arreau

Personnel:	ROD RUSSELL	A

45:	Let Me Take A Ride/Chandelier Ball	(Mark Ltd 1010) 1967

Pierce Arreau was actually Rod Russell, an accomplished Dallas musician. This was officially the last release on Mark. (VJ)

(Mark Stein and) The Pigeons

Personnel incl:	TIM BOGERT	A
	VINCE MARTELL	A
	MARK STEIN	A

ALBUM:	1(A)	WHILE THE WORLD WAS EATING VANILLA FUDGE	(Wand 687) 1968/69 SC

NB: (1) also issued in Germany on the Metronome subsidiary 2001 (08) in 1970.

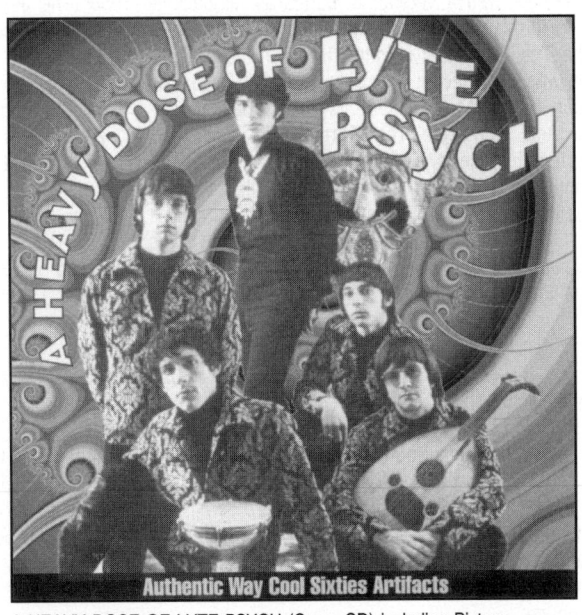

A HEAVY DOSE OF LYTE PSYCH (Comp CD) including Picture.

| 45: | (In The) Midnight Hour/ Stay In My Corner Baby | (Musicor MU-1199) 1966 |

An album of third rate **Rascals** imitations, which appeared on the back of Stein, Martell and Bogert's success as **Vanilla Fudge**. The album mostly comprised soul covers, but originals are *Upset The People* and *About Me*.

The band were discovered by former UK Undertakers, Chris Huston, who introduced the band to Atlantic... (VJ/MW/AHr)

Piggy Bank

Personnel:	VIC GABRIELE	vcls, bs	A
	DON GLEICHER	ld gtr	A
	BENJIE MARTINEZ	drms	A
	GEORGE ORANA	gtr	A
	WES SMYTHE	organ	A

| 45: | Thoughts Of You/Play With Fire | (Lavette LA 5017/18) 1966 |

This 45 was produced by Lindy Blaskey and recorded on his Albuquerque-based label. Also known as the Monkey Men this band had local hits on the Q-Q label. (VJ/MW/MDo)

Pig Iron

Personnel:	MARTY FOGEL	sax	A
	ADAM IPPOLITO	keyb'ds, vcls	A
	BILL PETERS	gtr, vcls	A
	PAUL SQUIRE	drms	A
	GARY VAN SCYOC	bs	A

| ALBUM: | 1(A) | PIG IRON | (CBS CS 1018) 1970 - |

NB: (1) also released in Holland (CBS 54044).

From New York, an urban blues-rock band using horns. The album has its moments. Van Scyoc and Ippolito would later join **Elephant's Memory** and Marty Fogel went on to play with Lou Reed. (SR)

Travis Pike's Tea Party

Personnel:	GEORGE BROX	gtr	A
	KARL GARRETT	ld gtr	AB
	TRAVIS PIKE	vcls	AB
	MIKEY HOE VALENTE	bs	AB
	PHIL VITALI	drms	AB
	LONNIE HILLARD		B

| 45: | If I Didn't Love You Girl/The Likes Of You | (Alma) 1967 |

Travis Pike was a veteran of bands as far back as 1959 (The Jesters) prior to forming the **Tea Party**. A prolific writer, he wrote numerous songs for the **Tea Party** that unfortunately were never released. The band's sole single was recorded at Joe Sawyer's AAA Recording Studio in Boston. In addition to composing music for and appearing on a local TV program, 'Here And Now', the **Tea Party** joined **The Rockin' Ramrods** on a promotional cruise for WRKO Radio. Despite a trip to California in 1968 to try and jump start the band's career, the **Tea Party** dissolved shortly thereafter.

Compilation appearances have included *If I Didn't Love You Girl* on *Sixties Rebellion, Vol. 7* (CD & LP) and *Tougher Than Stains* (LP). (MW)

Pilgrimage

| 45s: | Bad Apple/You Satisfy Me | (Mercury 72631) 1966 |
| | Do You Love Me?/Hey | (Mercury 72706) 1967 |

From Long Island, New York. The 'A' side to their first 45, *Bad Apple*, is the pick of the crop - a thumpin' singalong punker. The flip, *You Satisfy Me*, is an R'n'B-influenced pounder, graced with rippling keyboards and the odd lead phrase.

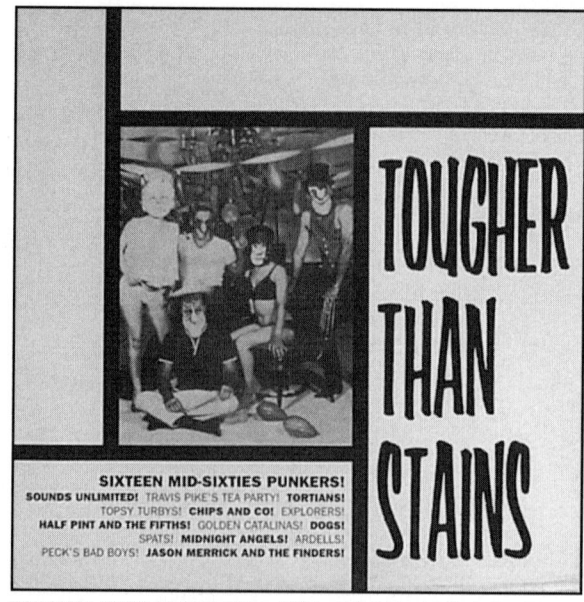

TOUGHER THAN STAINS (Comp LP) including Travis Pike's Tea Party.

The follow-up is not quite so impressive though their cover of Berry Gordy's *Do You Love Me?* is solid and probably inspired by the Dave Clark Five version.

Compilation appearances have included: *Bad Apple* on *60's Punk E.P., Vol. 3* (7"), *Teenage Shutdown, Vol. 3* (LP & CD) and *Victims Of Circumstance, Vol. 2* (CD); and *You Satisfy Me* and *Bad Apple* on *Victims Of Circumstances, Vol. 1* (LP). (VJ/MW/MM)

Pilot

Personnel incl:	MARTIN QUITTENTON	gtr	A
	BRUCE STEPHENS	gtr, keyb'ds, vcls	A
	LEIGH STEPHENS	gtr, vcls	A
	MICK WALLER	drms	A
	NEVILLE WHITEHEAD	bs	A

| ALBUMS: | 1(A) | PILOT | (RCA LSP-4730) 1972 - |
| | 2(A) | POINT OF VIEW | (RCA LSP-4825) 1973 - |

| 45: | Rider/Miss Sandy | (RCA 74-0770) 1972 |

Leigh Stephens and Mick Waller had already played together on **Stephens**' solo album and in **Silver Metre**. **Pilot** was an Anglo-American hard-rock "supergroup" as its line-up also included Bruce Stephens (ex-**Blue Cheer** and **Mint Tattoo**) plus Martin Quittenton from Steamhammer.

They were of course completely unconnected with the UK pop act of the same name. (SR)

Pinkiny Canandy

| Personnel incl: | MICHAEL CHAIN | vcls | A |

| ALBUM: | 1(A) | PINKINY CANANDY | (UNI 73049) 1969 - |

Produced by Mike Post, this is a strange concept album written and sung by Michael Chain which tells the adventures of **Pinkiny Canandy**, a super hero in pink clothes. Musically it's a mix of pop, pop-psych and rock with good guitars and unusual lyrics (*Christopher Centipede, Mutual Indemnity Insurance Company* etc.). One of the best tracks is *Hello Hello* (not the **Sopwith Camel** song).

The album came in a gatefold sleeve with two pages of Marvel-like cartoons. (SR)

Pinnochio and Puppets

45:	Fusion/Cowboys And Indians	(Mercury 72659)	1967

The absolutely ultimate awesome East-meets-West fusion instrumental that blows everything else away. Uncompiled until recently and now featured on the Erik Lindgren's instrumental mayhem compilation *Everything You Always Wanted To Know About '60s Mind Expanding Punkadelic Garage Rock Instrumentals But Were Afraid To Ask* (CD) (phew), *Slowly Growing Insane* (CD), *The Arf! Arf! Blitzkrieg 32 Track Sampler* (Dble CD) and *Psychedelic Unknowns, Vol. 11* (LP). It turns out that this is none other than New York City's **Teddy Boys**. The flip is another instrumental that's more rocky and in a slightly 'twangy' vein, but is pretty tasty too. (MW)

The Pirates

45s:	Big Boy Pete/Little Boy Sad	(Deaux DEA-1 150)	1965
	Naughty Girl/Cuttin' Out	(Back Stage 5001)	1965

An unexceptional garage punk outfit from Houston, Texas. They sound like a frat-party outfit on *Big Boy Pete* though *Little Boy Sad* is more garagey though nowhere near **The Gants**' version. They later became **Their Singing Bodies**.

Compilation appearances include *Cuttin Out* on *Sixties Archive, Vol. 2* (CD) and *Texas Punk From The Sixties* (LP). (VJ)

Pitche Blende

45:	My World Has Stopped/Stop	(Valley 1102)	196?

Michigan Mixture, Vol. 1 (LP) features both 45 cuts by this outfit. The first, *My World Has Stopped*, is a pleasant enough harmony-pop effort. The second, *Stop*, is much faster and punkier with some good guitar moments. (VJ)

The Plague

Personnel incl:	BILL "CORKY" ANDERSON drms	A

45:	Go Away/Money	(Epidemic 2164)	196?

This band came from Albuquerque in New Mexico and drummer "Corky" Anderson had previously been with **King Richard and The Knights**. Their punkish 45 was clearly influenced by The Kinks. The 'A' side, written by S. Erickson and Bill Anderson, can also be heard on *King Richard And The Knights - Precision!* (CD), *New Mexico Punk From The Sixties* (LP), *Pebbles Vol. 5* (CD), *The Essential Pebbles Collection, Vol. 1* (Dble CD), *Pebbles, Vol. 5* (LP), *Sixties Archive Vol. 4* (CD) and *Teenage Shutdown, Vol. 4* (LP & CD). (VJ/MW)

PEBBLES Vol. 5 (Comp LP) including The Plague.

The Plague

This Plague from Bismarck, New Delaware, has a previously unreleased version of *Money* on *Hipsville, Vol. 2* (LP). (VJ)

The Plague

45:	Mr. White Collar Man/		
	When I See That Girl Of Mine	(Wright W 6863)	1968

Poppy "garage" from Milwaukee, Wisconsin, that sounds more like '65 or '66 and has too many sha-la-la's - it's nearer to teeny-pop sounds despite the moody keyboards. The 'B' side, *When I See That Girl Of Mine*, is a cover of the Kinks and has popped up on *Leaving It All Behind* (LP). (MW)

The Plague

45:	Brighter Side/Cherry Road	(Nottingham Disc Co)	c1970

From Virginia, near Norfolk, this obscure group released a single with a good flip in the heavy garage style, with organ. (SR)

Plague

Personnel:	SCOTT DONALDSON	gtr	A
	ED MOSS		A
	JOHN PALMER	gtr	A
	PETE RAINE		A

A group of punky rebels on the Richmond, California, scene in 1966 who have come to be regarded as a local legend by virtue of their exploits and tough image. They released no records but two members would end up in bands whose legacy has been preserved. Scott Donaldson joined Berkeley's **Haymarket Riot** (formerly The Livin' End) in late 1966. John Palmer had previously been in The Boys (with Randy Hammon) and would be in **The Boys Blue** and Lincoln's Promise before teaming up with Hammon again in the highly-regarded **Savage Resurrection**. (MW)

Plague

ALBUM:	1	THE PLAGUE	(No label)	c1969	R1

45:	Somebody Help Me / Hard To Wait	(Smitty's 1293)	197?

From Michigan, a garage band with organ and guitar, recorded with primitive equipment judging by the result. All copies came in a plain white cover.

The band weren't connected to the earlier Michigan outfit **The Plagues**. (SR/MW)

The Plagues

EP:	1	THROUGH THIS WORLD (PS)	(Quarantined 41369)	1987

45s:	Why Can't You Be True/		
	Through This World	(Fenton) 2020)	1966
	I've Been Through It Before/		
	Tears From My Eyes	(Fenton 2070)	1966
	That'll Never Do/Badlands	(Quarantined ?)	1966

A Michigan outfit whose *I've Been Through It Before* is a good melodic beat ballad with fuzz and their only strong track if truth be told - the rest are lightweight but dirgeful ballads.

The EP collects all tracks from the three 45s except *Badlands*. It's hard to find nowadays - the original 45s are nigh on impossible to obtain. Isn't it time some enterprising soul put out a legal compilation of Fenton's finest moments?

Compilation appearances include: *I've Been Through It Before* on *Teenage Shutdown, Vol. 2* (LP & CD) and *The Chosen Few, Vol. 2* (LP); *(Clouds Send Down) Tears From My Eyes* on *Teenage Shutdown, Vol. 5* (LP & CD); *Why Can't You Be True* on *Destination Frantic!* (LP & CD). (MW)

The Plagues

45:	To Wander/Cherry Pie	(Ronn 1000) 1966

A Taunton, Massachusetts combo whose *To Wander* also appeared in a very rare picture sleeve - one copy fetched $500!!

Compilation appearances include *Cherrie Pie* on *Mondo Frat Dance Bash A Go Go* (CD); *To Wander* on *New England Teen Scene* (CD) and *New England Teen Scene, Vol. 2* (LP). (VJ/?)

Plain Jane

Personnel:	DON GLEICHER	gtr, vcls	A
	BARRY RAY	gtr, vcls	A
	DAVID SCHOENFELD	drms	A
	JERRY SCHOENFELD	keyb'ds, vcls, bs	A

ALBUM:	1(A)	PLAIN JANE	(Hobbit H.B. 5000) 1969 R1

A pleasant and largely undiscovered dreamy rural-rock album. Their dreamy organ sound, fragile harmonies and backwards fuzz guitar is best represented on tracks like *Who's Drivin' This Train*, *You Can't Make It Alone* and *Mrs. Que*. Others veer more towards pop, particularly the beautiful *Silence* and pleasant pop-rock of *Not The Same*. Certainly no lost gem, but its ten cuts all are originals and the album's worth checking out.

Their album was produced by Les Brown from **Rockin' Foo**. (MW/CF/SR)

Planet of The Apes

ALBUM:	1	A MUSICAL TRIP	(TPI) 1974 R1

A Connecticut group mixing psych, pop and rock with lots of wah-wah guitar and some decent tracks (*People Sure Do Make Funny Noises* and *Hey Pet*). Due to their primitive facilities, this private pressing is quite noisy. (SR)

Planned Obsolescence

Personnel:	GERALD IRVING	keyb'ds	A
	BILL LIPSCOMBE	ld gtr	A
	DOUG McGUINN	drms	A
	TOM McGUIRE	vcls	A
	JOE RODRIGUEZ	bs	A

45:	Still In Love With You Baby/ Exit Sticky Icky	(JetSet 4296) 1967

This band met while attending high school in Santa Barbara, California. They played local battle of the bands, dances and club dates, eventually attracting the attention of The Sufaris' management team.

Interestingly, the flip side to their sole 45, *Exit Sticky Icky* was originally written with the intention of using it as advertising for a soft rubber toy (the toy manufacturing company ultimately backed off the idea).

To capitalise on the 45, the band spent a couple of months touring Southern California. Their gimmick was playing with bags over their heads and in black capes. At the Univerity of California, Santa Barbara they played the world's longest song - literally hour after hour of *Exit Sticky Icky* (with members of Ernie and the Crabs aka **Giant Crab** and other friends helping out).

Compilation appearances include *Still In Love With You Baby* on *Vile Vinyl, Vol. 2* (LP) and *Vile Vinyl* (CD). (SB/VJ)

Plant and See

Personnel incl:	WILLIE LOWERY	gtr, vcls	A

ALBUM:	1(A)	PLANT AND SEE	(White Whale WW 7120) 1969 -

From Fayetteville, North Carolina, a mix of psych and folk-rock with some interesting guitar work. When White Whale disappeared, they became **Lumbee**. (SR)

Plant Life

Personnel:	GEORGE CLARK	A
	LOUIE GOLD	A
	TOM HARASZMIS	A
	MIKE PASTERNAK	A
	RANDY WILIFORD	A

45:	Flower Girl / Say It Over Again	(Date 2-1572) 1967

Originally known as the Go-Mads, some members of this Orlando, Florida quintet were later in Cowboy (which also included Tom Talton and Tom Wynn of **We The People**).

Flower Girl is excellent **Turtles**-like garage-pop and was a local hit - it should be hauntingly familiar since it borrows heavily from the Easybeats' *Friday On My Mind*. The flip is noisy pop with grating falsetto harmonies.

The band used to play regularly at Winter Park Youth Center in Orlando.

Flower Girl was compiled in 1968 on the rare sampler album *Bee Jay Video Soundtrack* (Tener 1014) but has blossomed again on *Psychedelic States - Florida Vol. 2* (CD). (MW/JLh/RM)

Plaster Casters Blues Band

ALBUM:	1	PLASTER CASTERS BLUES BAND	(Flying Dutchman) 1968 SC

On Bob Thiele's label, a rare exploito album. The **Plaster Casters** was the name of a few groupies who built a collection of plaster castings of famous rock stars penis' and this album was aimed to cash in on their name. (SR)

Plastic Ax

Personnel incl:	ERNESTO DA GAMA	A

45:	White Smoke - Part 1 / White Smoke - Part 2	(Custom Sound SC-155) c1969

PLAIN JANE - Plain Jane LP.

A lengthy fuzz-laden instrumental workout with busy percussion and latterly some brass - by a band reported to be from Dickens, Texas. (MW)

Plastic Blues Band

Personnel:
- JOHNNY BEAR — drms — A
- RALPH RICHOUX — bs, vcls — A
- JAY WOLFE — gtr — A

45s:
- Gone/Country Food (Busy-B ZAP 8) 196?
- You're Gonna Get Burned/Dead Seed (Busy-B ZAP 13) 196?
- A Thing You Gotta Face/One Week Ago Today (Busy-B) 196?

A New Orleans, Louisiana-based psychedelic rock outfit. Their 45s have lots of fuzz and wah-wah pedal. Both *Gone* and *Dead Seed* are pretty decent.

Jay and Johnny are thought to now live in Florida.

Compilation appearances include: *Gone* and *Dead Seed* on *Sixties Archive, Vol. 4* (CD) and *Florida Punk Groups From The Sixties* (LP); and *Gone* on *Trash Box* (5-CD), *Garagelands, Vol. 1* (LP) and *Garagelands, Vol. 1 & 2* (CD). (VJ/RC)

The Plastic Ice Cube

45: Won't Turn Back (Warick 6750) 1967

The Litter's producer Warren Kendrick produced this Minneapolis band's song which they had first recorded under an earlier name, **Marcia and The Lynchmen**. The flip was by a different artist, Andrea Forrest, so it isn't shown here. (VJ)

Plastic Mushroom

45: Baby I See/Whistle Stop Review (ssExx 668) 196?

The work of the late sixties outfit from Des Moines, Iowa, presumably later known as The Wild Cherries likewise from Des Moines, who also put out *Baby I See/You Know Whatcha Want* on Kapp (2113) in 1970, followed by *Wigwam/Whistle Stop Review* on Kapp (2137), sometime later. (VJ)

Plastik Peeple

45: Wait / Work (Sanfris SF-31) 1968

From the Bayside area of Queens, New York. Their sole release appeared on an obscure label owned by a Miss Santa Friscia, which also put out 45s by the **Tides In** and Upward Movement.

Psychedelic States: New York Vol. 1 (CD) features *Wait*, which sounds more like 1965-6 than 1968 with its jerky danceable rhythm, *Taxman*-like chops and hesitant keyboard solo. (MW)

Plato and The Philosophers

Personnel:
- MIKE IMBLER — ld gtr — ABC
- BARRY ORSCHELN — keyb'ds — ABCD
- KEN TEBOW — bs, vcls — ABCD
- MARK VALENTINE — drums — AB
- BEN WHITE — bs — BC
- STEVE VAN CLEVE — drms — CD
- KEN WOLVERTON — gtr — C
- BRUCE RENFRO — gtr — D

NB: Line-up 'C' 1967, Line-up 'D' 1999.

CD: 1(A/B/C) THIRTEEN O'CLOCK FLIGHT TO PSYCHEDELPHIA (Collectables COL 0714) 1998

45s:
- I Don't Mind/C. M. I Love You (It 2313) 1966
- I Don't Mind/
- C.M. I Love You (General American GAR 104) 1966

PLATO and THE PHILOSOPHERS - Thirteen O'Clock... CD.

- 13 O'Clock Flight To Psychedelphia/Wishes (Fairyland 1002) 1967

From Moberly, Missouri. This band formed in 1962 as the Checkmates but changed name to **Plato and The Philosophers** in 1965 and lasted until 1970. The *Thirteen O'Clock Flight To Psychedelphia* (CD) retrospective features the band's story, from which the personnel is confirmed, and features fourteen tracks: the It 45 and many unreleased goodies - two versions of *Thirteen O'Clock...*, *Wishes*, the proposed third 45 *Doomsday Nowhere City / I Knew*, and seven others from 1968 onwards, which include some excellent heavy acid-punkers. Other artists feature on the CD - **Something Wild**, **Smoke** (Houston's ex-**Nomads**) and the Fortunes.

Their first 45 was a routine garage effort. You'll also find the 'A' side, *I Don't Mind*, on *Monsters Of The Midwest, Vol. 3* (LP). *Monsters Of The Midwest, Vol. 2* (LP) includes the 'A' side of the Fairyland 45, *Thirteen O'Clock Flight To Psychedelphia*. It doesn't live up to its name but does feature some arresting double lead guitar breaks and rather haunting harmonies.

Tebow and half of the original line-up still gig occasionally! (VJ/MW/BSw)

The Playboys Of Edinburg (P.O.E.)

Personnel:
- VAL CURL — keyb'ds, bs, gtr — A
- DON FAIRES — drms — A
- JERRY McCORD — ld gtr, piano, bs — A
- MICHAEL WILLIAMS — perc, vcls — A
- JAMES WILLIAMS — gtr — A

ALBUM: 1(A) UP THROUGH THE SPIRAL (UNI 73099) 1971 -

NB: (1) as **P.O.E.**.

HCP

45s:
- Wish You Had A Heart/Understand Me (Pharaoh 141) 1965 -
- Look At Me, Girl/News Sure Travels Fast (Pharaoh 142) 1966 -
- Look At Me, Girl/
- News Sure Travels Fast (Columbia 43716) 1966 108
- Dream World/One-Way Ticket (Columbia 43933) 1966 -
- Sanford Ringleton V Of Abernathy/
- Mickey's Monkey (Columbia 44093) 1967 -
- Suzy Walker/Fair-Haired Lady (123 1715) 1968 -
- Let's Get Back To Rock And Roll/
- Homemade Cookin' (123 1722) 1969 -
- La Bamba/Happy Train (123 1729) 1970 -
- La Bamba/Happy Train (Capitol 2890) 1970 -
- α Up Through The Spiral/There Is A River (UNI 73099) 1971 -

NB: α as **P.O.E.**.

This Texas band originated from McAllen but were later based in Houston and played between 1965-70. Their music was a mixture of punk, folk-rock and rock'n'roll with their first two singles best described as garage-folk. By the time of their three 45s for "123" they had become more rock-orientated. In 1970, they changed their name to **P.O.E.** making an album and a 45 for UNI. A decent album in a heavy-psych vein, *Up Through The Spiral* is a concept album based on the life of Edgar Cayce.

All of **The Playboys Of Edinburg** 45s listed above are non-album.

The Williams brothers later recorded a 45, *When I Think Of You/Springtime* (JSM 101), as James and Michael which was also leased to London (257) for nationwide distribution.

Compilation coverage has so far included: *Wish You Had A Heart* on *Texas Flashbacks, Vol. 1* (LP & CD) and *Flashback, Vol. 1* (LP); *News Sure Travels Fast* on *Mindrocker, Vol. 7* (LP); *Look At Me, Girl*, *News Sure Travels Fast* and *Wish You Had A Heart* on *Texas Punk, Vol. 5* (LP) and *Acid Visions - Complete Collection, Vol. 2* (3-CD). (VJ/MW/JRe)

Playful Pups

45:	Palpatations/Dinosaur	(Intrepid 75008)	1969

Produced, like **Year 2000**, by a young Rupert Holmes, a bubblegum pop single on the same label as the **Leer Brothers**. (SR)

The Playgue

Personnel:	WAYNE CHAPMAN	gtr	A
	LEWIS MOYSE	bs, vcls	A
	DON MYRICK	drms	A
	CHARLES HENRY SHERBURNE	ld gtr	A
	DANNY TILLOTSON	organ	A

45:	Baby No More/I Gotta Be Goin'	(Rebic BNB-19653)	1965

Baton Rouge, Louisiana was home to this teen band who came up with the pretty frantic *I Gotta Be Goin'*, unfortunately the 'A' side is a rather lame garage ballad with two left feet!

The 45 was produced by Nick Benedetto with his brother and recorded at on 14th August 1965 at La Louisiane Studio in Lafayette, Louisiana. Rebic was their label and the brothers also handled bookings for the band, getting them gigs all over the South, including Texas, Louisiana, Mississippi, Alabama and elsewhere. Nick remembers:- "We sometimes travelled with them while holding down day jobs and raising families. It was quite a time. They opened for **Johnny Rivers**, and played on the stage between showings of the Beatles movie "Help". When Moyse left, Wayne Chapman took over the vocals and another musician was added".

For more information there is an excellent article about the band in 'Brown Paper Sack'. Write to Andrew Brown, Post Office Box 1622, Houston Texas 77251-1622.

Compilation appearances have included:- *I Gotta Be Goin'* on *Louisiana Punk Groups From The Sixties, Vol. 2* (LP), *Sixties Archive, Vol. 3* (CD) and *Teenage Shutdown, Vol. 15* (LP & CD); and *Baby No More* on *Shutdown '66* (LP). (VJ/MW)

Pleasure (featuring Billy Elder)

Personnel incl:	BILLY ELDER		A

45s:	Born A Girl / It Ain't Right	(Revue R 11057)	1969
α	Poor Old Organ Grinder/		
	Don't Take The Night Away	(Tower 506)	1969

NB: α also released as by Billy Elder (Pathway 101).

The first 45 is pleasant late sixties pop but it's the Tower 45 that's a real (ahem) pleasure - Sgt.Peppery pop backed by a haunting and heavily echoed 'baroque-psych' ballad. The latter can be heard by lucky owners of the *Slowly Growing Insane* compilation, which is a CD version of Billy Synth's *Psychedelic Unknowns, Vol. 11* (LP). (MW)

THE PLEASURE FAIR - Pleasure Fair LP.

Pleasure Fair

Personnel:	MICHAEL COCHRANE	vcls	A
	STEVE COHN		A
	TIM HALLINAN		A
	ROB ROYER	keyb'ds	A

ALBUM:	1(A)	PLEASURE FAIR	(UNI 73009) 1967 SC
			HCP

45s:	Morning Glory Days/Fade In, Fade Out	(UNI 55016) 1967 134
	(I'm Going To Have To) Let You Go/Today	(UNI 55078) 1968 -

A foursome from Los Angeles, The album, which is poppy with some psychedelic influence, was produced by David Gates shortly before he formed Bread, with Roger and James Griffin.

Compilation appearances include *Morning Glory Days* on *The Magic Cube* (CD). (VJ/MW/JLt/CF)

The Pleasure Seekers

Personnel:	DIANE BAKER	keyb'ds	A
	MARY-LOU BALL	gtr	ABCD
	NAN(CY) BALL	drms	AB
	PATTI QUATRO	ld gtr	ABCD
	SUZI QUATRO	bs	ABCD
	PRISILLA WENSER	keyb'ds	BCD
	?? ??	drms	C
	ARLENE QUATRO	keyb'ds	D

45s:	What A Way To Die/		
	Never Though You'd Leave Me	(Hideout 1006)	1965
	Light Of Love/Shame	(Mercury 72542)	1967
	Light Of Love/Good Kind Of Hurt	(Mercury 72800)	1968

Out of Detroit, Michigan, this was a rather special all girl band in that it figured on bass a teenage Suzi Quatro. Suzi along with her friends and sisters used to attend Harper Woods clubs to watch local bands such as **The Fugitives** and **Underdogs** and one evening a comment to the club's owner Dave Leone that the current band playing "were crap" led to an invitation to do better. So it was that, towards the end of '64 Suzi and her friends put together **The Pleasure Seekers** and trundled through versions of *Loopy Lou*, *Louie Louie* and *Twist And Shout* at the club. Leone subsequently offered them a one-off deal with his Hideout label, penning *What A Way To Die* - a crude homage to beer, whilst the band wrote the flip - an altogether more melodic folk-rocker.

The Pleasure Seekers soon found themselves playing gigs up and down the East Coast, from South Carolina to New York, playing everying from Teen Hops to Strip Clubs. In New York, future New York Doll Jerry Nolan even helped out on drums for a short while when Nancy Ball had to quit due to family pressure... In those days Rock'n'Roll was far from an acceptable 'career path'!

In 1967, the band signed to Mercury and released a more pop-soul orientated 45 - they also flew out to Vietnam to play for the troops there, but with the music scene rapidly changing and the emergence of the 'heavier' sound they decided to call it quits, with Suzi moving on to an outfit called Cradle.

The Pleasure Seekers 45s are rare and obviously sought-after.

Another **Pleasure Seekers**' 45, *If You Climb On The Tigers Back/(Theme from) Valley Of The Dolls* on Capitol (2050) from 1967 is almost definitely by a different outfit.

Thanks to Dave Tulloch/Faren Short and Jon 'Mojo' Mills from 'Shindig' mag for allowing us to plunder their info and help get the facts straight!

Compilation appearances include: *What A Way To Die* on *Michigan Mayhem, Vol. 1* (CD); *What A Way To Die* and *Never Thought You'd Leave Me* on *What A Way To Die* (LP) and *Hang It Out To Dry* (CD); and *Never Thought You'd Leave Me* on *Best Of The Hideouts* (LP), *Best of Hideout Records* (CD) and *Highs In The Mid-Sixties, Vol. 6* (LP). (VJ/MW)

Bill Plummer and The Cosmic Brotherhood

See **The Cosmic Brotherhood** entry for details.

Plum Nelly

Personnel:			
	PETER HARRIS	bs, vcls	A
	CHRISTOPHER LLOYD	drms, perc	ABC
	RIC PRINCE	keyb'ds, ld vcls	ABC
	STEVE RESS	gtr, vcls	ABC
	JOHN E. (EARL) WALKER	ld gtr	ABC
	BOB FEIT	bs	B
	JOHN MURPHY	bs, vcls	C

ALBUM: 1(A) DECEPTIVE LINES (Capitol ST 692) 1971 SC

For the most part this album's pretty typical early seventies progressive/hard-rock with strong vocals, good guitar and quite a lot of woodwind. It may interest fans of the progressive/hard-rock genre.

This five-man band began playing under the name "Creedmore State" until Nicky and Arnie Ungano of the famed defunct New York City rock club of the same name took them under their wings and signed the band to Capitol Records under the name **Plum Nelly**. They either played with or opened for many famous acts such Bo Diddley, B.B. King, Buddy Guy, **Jimi Hendrix**, The Kinks, Savoy Brown, John Mayall, Fleetwood Mac, Rod Stewart and The Faces, Joe Cocker, **Dr. John**, Muddy Waters, Terry Reid and notibly at Carnegie Hall with **The James Gang**.

The band recorded the album *Deceptive Lines* at Capitol East, November through December 1970 along with producer Kenneth Cooper. Guests on the album included Jeremy Steig (of **Jeremy and The Satyrs**) on flute and The Sweet Inspirations were featured on the background vocals of *Lonely Man's Cry*. The Sweet Inspirations were led by Cissy Houston who is Whitney Houston's mom. They also were Elvis Presley's and Aretha Franklin's back-up singers during this period. Dave Bash Johnson played conga's on the song *Carry On*.

The group toured the US during the early seventies and relocated in Los Angles in 1974. It was at this time that John Murphy replaced Bob Feit, who went on to become Tina Turner's bass player.

Plum Nelly disbanded in 1976. It was during this time that Walker formed the first incarnation of "The John Earl Walker Band," circa late seventies to early eighties.

In the late seventies, Walker and Murphy played clubs such as Gildersleeves and The Electric Circus and in the early eighties performed as The Rockers with more of a new wave sound.

At present John Murphy still plays with Walker in The John Earl Walker Band, a New York blues outfit. Coincidentally he replaced bass player Peter Harris in Walker's band yet again, in 2001.

This act should not be confused with the Texan-based outfit who later became known as Mother of Pearl. (VJ/EHs)

The Plunkers

45: Night Time Love/Hippy Lippy Goosey (HBR 479) 1966

NB: Also released in Australia (Astor AP 1287).

The 'B' side of this 45 is a fantastic grungy R&B number. It was also released in Australia but is thought to be the work of an L.A.-based act. The 45 was produced by the well-known John Marascalco, who was a musician in his own right and who also produced Harry Nilsson among others.

Both songs on the 45 were also recorded by **The Liverpool Five**. (CPe/MW)

Plymouth Rock

Personnel incl:			
	DONNIE DOLAN	drms	A
	JOHN INMAN	ld gtr	A
	JOHN SCHWERTNER	keyb'ds	A

45: Memorandum/Just A Start (Sonobeat 114) 1969

A quintet from Austin, Texas. Inman and Dolan were previously with South Canadian Overflow and later in Lost Gonzo Band. Schwenner was in **Lavender Hill Express**. Their hard-rock 45 was highly-touted and they were on the verge of signing to Epic before they split. (VJ)

The Plymouth Rockers

Personnel:			
	CHUCK DESILVA	drms	A
	LARRY HICKMAN	gtr	A
	AL PARKER	ld gtr	A
	GARY VALLETRE	bs	A

45s:	Around And Around/	
	Brown Eyed Handsome Man	(Warner Bros. 5475) 1964
	Roll Over Stephen Foster/	
	Girl From The North Country	(Valiant V-729) 1965
	Don't Say Why/Walk A Lonely Mile	(Valiant V-737) 1966

You can also check out *Don't Say Why* on *New England Teen Scene, Vol. 2* (LP). These may be two different outfits - normally one would associate Valiant with L.A. acts so why does, this crop up on a New England

HIGHS IN THE MID-SIXTIES Vol. 6 (Comp LP) including The Pleasure Seekers.

compilation? There was certainly a **Plymouth Rockers** in L.A. in 1966 playing the Whisky A Go-Go, comprising the personnel listed and the Warner Bros 45 was produced by David Gates indicating L.A. again. Who knows - an itinerary troupe or just another compilation cock-up?

Who cares anyway - decent garagey folk/rock'n'roll beatsters is where they were at. *Don't Say Why* (an Addrissi brothers composition) is a great fuzzy pop-punker, whilst the flip is excellent folky-beat-pop and sounds remarkably like the early **Association** stuff - (L.A. again!). This 45 was produced by Don Dalton and **D. Moore**. (MW/SR)

Plynth

45: Life Beyond The Clouds/Wondering (Castle 111) c1970

Turn-of-decade keyboard dominated rock from Camden, New Jersey that should appeal to prog-rock fans. *Wondering* is rather fragmented by the time and mood changes. *Life Beyond The Clouds* has some solid riffin' interrupted by lighter passages that may work for some listeners. The band sound like they want to let loose but never do, even on the solos.

The 45 was recorded at MSI studios in Camden, New Jersey and both tracks were written by Sanson / Siganuk. (MW/DJe)

P-nut Butter

45s:
Please Don't Ever Leave Me/? (P-Nut 101) 196?
On The Road Again/I'm Glad I Knew You (Mascot 113) 1966
Still In Love With You Baby/
What Am I Doin' Here With You (Mascot 114) 1966
Still In Love With You Baby/
What Am I Doin' Here With You (Tower 265) 1966
Look Out Girl/Yes Your Honor (Mascot 115) 1967
Golden One/The Girl From Chelsey (Mascot 117) 1967
Conquistador/One More Chance (Mascot 119) 1967

A pop-beat outfit from Phoenix, Arizona. Their cover of **John Sebastian**'s *On The Road Again* is snappy and competent whilst *I'm Glad I Knew You* is excellent Beatlesque beat. Their next 45, a folk-rock-pop Sloan-Barri cover backed by an uptempo version of the **Beau Brummels**' classic, proved popular enough to be picked up and released by Tower in November 1966. Not strictly garage, they remain uncompiled to date, but shouldn't be overlooked by those who enjoy good sixties beat and pop. (MW)

Polyphony

ALBUM: 1 WITHOUT INTRODUCTION
(Eleventh Hour 1003) c1971-3 R2

NB: (1) has been pirated on CD.

POLYPHONY - Without Introduction CD.

A hard-rock progressive outfit from Virginia whose album reputedly features psych / prog jams with guitar and keyboards interplay. It came in a stunning sleeve. The album is undated but believed to date from circa 1971 - 1973. The other known album on Eleventh Hour, **Mason**, was released in 1971. (CF/SR)

Erica Pomerance

Personnel:
ERICA POMERANCE vcls, gtr, hand drms A
(DION BRODY ld gtr A)
(LANNY BROOKS bs A)
(D. COOPER SMITH perc A)
(MICHAEL EPHRAIM piano A)
(RICHARD HEISLER gtr, chanting A)
(CRAIG JUSTIN perc A)
(BILL MITCHEL ld gtr A)
(TOM MOORE flute A)
(GAIL POLLARD sitar, chanting, flute A)
(RON PRICE ld gtr A)

ALBUM: 1(A) YOU USED TO THINK (ESP 1099) 1969 R2

NB: (1) has been reissued on CD (ESP ESP 1099-2)

From the New York scene, an acid-folk poetess with some jazz influences and feminist lyrics. It was allegedly recorded after dropping a tab and subsequently deteriorates the further you go into the record. It was recorded with local musicians like Trevor Koehler, then with the **Insect Trust**. (SR)

David Pomeranz

ALBUM: 1 NEW BLUES (Decca DL-75274) 1971 -

A forgotten blues-rock singer, his album was produced by Ray Ellis with the help of Sandy Nassan, Steve Mendel, Paul Simon, Donald MacDonald and Ronnie Zito. (SR)

Pony Express

45: What You Done Done/I Dream Of Pennies (Reprise 0650) 196?

The 'A' side, a strange combination of rough 'n' ready rock with **The Association**, leaves the impression that maybe they could have achieved more than they did on this cut. The 'B' side is just as intelligent, has nice vocal harmonies and a shrewd arrangement. Some unexpected discordant effects towards the end are very pleasing and lift the song into the category of interesting flip-sides. (MK)

Poobah

Personnel: JIM GUSTAFSON gtr, vcls, keyb'ds A
(up to PHIL JONES bs, vcls A
1976) GLENN WISEMAN drms, vcls A

ALBUM: 1(A) LET ME IN (Rite-Peppermint PP 1015) 1972 R3

NB: (1) has been counterfeited.

45: Rock City/Bowleen (Peppermint - Fireball) 1973

A brutal garagey hard-rock item from Youngstown, Ohio. Rock City does not figure on their album, which is a very important collectors' item for hard-rock fans. There's lots of driving, sometimes fuzzy guitar on tracks like *Mr. Destroyer, Live To Work* and the finale title track *Let Me In*, which also has the obligatory drum solo. *Bowleen* has some interesting guitar and percussion. Unlikely, though, to interest psych fans.

They recorded beyond the time span of this book. In addition to *U.S. Rock* (Anchor) 1976, which came with a poster insert and *Steamroller* (Peppermint) 1979, which had a lyric insert, there's also a late seventies test pressing *Live At Snug Harbor, Chittaqua, New York* (Cleveland Recording Company), which circulated without a cover and is rarely ever seen. (VJ/GG)

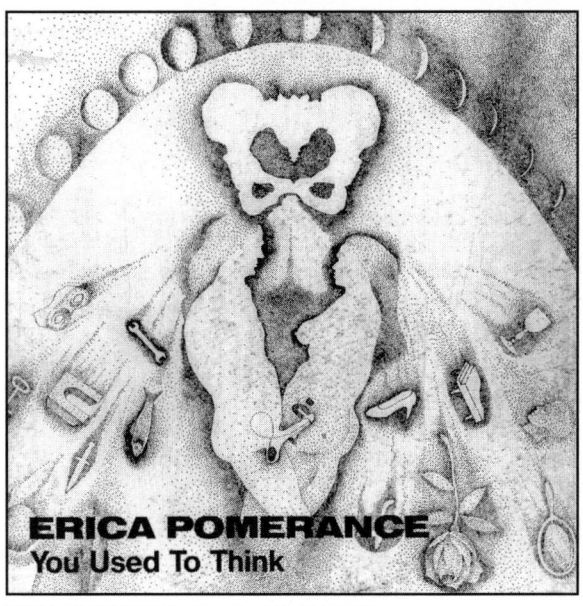

ERICA POMERANCE - You Used To Think CD.

Pookah

Personnel:
	PAT CUPO	keyb'ds	A
	JOHN IPPOLITO	bs, gtr	A
	DAVE RANALETTA	drms, perc	A

ALBUM: 1(A) POOKAH (United Artists 50604) 1969 -

45: Blue and Peaceful/Merein's Party (United Artists 50604) 1969

An album which brings to mind **Autosalvage**. Unfortunately the vocals often detract from what would otherwise be a good album. (VJ/GG)

The Poor

Personnel:
	JOHN DAY		A
	ALLEN KEMP	gtr	ABC
	RANDY MEISNER	bs	ABC
	PAT SHANAHAN	drms	ABC
	RANDY NAYLOR	gtr, keyb'ds	B
	VEDER VAN DOREN		C

HCP
45s: Once Again/How Many Tears (Loma 2062) 1966? -
She's Got The Time (She's Got The Changes)/
Love Is Real (York 402) 1967 133
My Mind Goes High/
Knowing You, Loving You (York 404) 1967 -
Come Back Baby/Feelin' Down (Decca 32318) 1968 -

Another interesting group, this time from Colorado. Not only did they include Nebraskan Randy Meisner, who as you probably all know was later in **Poco** and The Eagles, but Tom Shipley and Mike Brewer (of **Brewer and Shipley** fame) both wrote for the group.

Formed in late 1963 out of the ashes of **The Soul Survivors**, John Day left before the singles were recorded and returned to Denver. His replacement was Randy Naylor who was likewise replaced in late '67 by Veder Van Doren (ex-**Moonrakers**). The band also got to open for **Buffalo Springfield** in December 1966.

She's Got The Time (She's Got The Changes) is usually considered their best effort. Tom Shipley wrote it and evidenced by this they played a kinda folk-pop with lots of hooks and melodies, refined vocals and chiming guitars. *She's Got The Time* was also covered in the U.K. by a group called Afex. The song was popular around the Midwest and in search of fame and fortune the band relocated to Los Angeles, where they worked as The North Serrano Blues Band.

Of their other recordings, Mike Brewer wrote *Feelin' Down*, Allen Kemp wrote *How Many Tears*, Naylor composed *Love Is Real* and Meisner penned *Come Back Baby*.

Whilst in L.A., Jim Bell of the **Ballroom** was also involved with the band to the extent that **Curt Boettcher** produced some material for them and was introduced to future **Millennium** member Joey Stec through them... Randy Naylor also co-wrote some songs with **Boettcher** during the **Ballroom** period, whilst Meisner, Young and Shanahan were also employed by **Boettcher** for his **Millennium** projects.

The band split in 1968 when Kemp and Shanahan went on to join Rick Nelson's Stone Canyon Band.

Curiously many unusual guitar riffs used by various incarnations of all these guys up to and including The Eagles were apparently inspired by their drummer Pat Shanahan's attempts to play various cliche Rock'n'Roll riffs!!

Compilation appearances have included:- *She's Got The Time (She's Got The Changes)* on *Highs In The Mid Sixties, Vol. 18* (LP); and *Feelin' Down* on *Every Groovy Day* (LP). (VJ/MW/JFr/NW)

The Poor Boys

45: I Will Be Free/Over The Hill And Down
In The Valley (General American 005) 196?

Obscurities, purportedly Californian, whose *I Will Be Free* can also be heard on *Psychedelic Unknowns, Vol. 8* (LP & CD). Another Poor Boys from Chicago had a 45 on Flame. (VJ)

The Poor Boys

45: Still Love You/
Coco Loco (Coconut Tequila) (Sutter S 100) 196?

One of the few **Poor Boys** outfits around at the time, this bunch's brand of 'garage' is soulful and brassy with a thinly disguised remake of *Shake*, backed by another derivative brassy instrumental. Best avoided. (MW)

The Poor Boys

ALBUM: 1 AIN'T NOTHING IN (Rare Earth RS 5??) 1970 -

An obscure rock group. Rare Earth was the rock label of Tamla Motown and also issued **Xit** and **Power of Zeus**. (SR)

Poor Little Rich Kids

Personnel:
	MIKE BLEEKER	drms	A
	PHIL BLEEKER	vcls	A
	WAYNE CROOK	gtr, vcls	A
	BILL RENNIE	bs	A

POOBAH - Let Me In LP.

45s:	She's The Best Girl In Town/	
	Stop - Quit It	(Exodus 2007) 1966
	She's The Best Girl In Town/	
	Stop - Quit It	(H.I.P. H 102) 1966

Catchy Brit Invasion influenced beat-pop with the 'B' side winning out on attitude, as well as for the harmonica break. They were from Memphis and originally known as The Saints. (MW/RHI)

Poor Richard

ALBUM:	1	PLACE OF THE SUN	(Kazoo) 197? R1

A Michigan outfit whose relaxed folky/jamming album is hard to track down. The opening cut sounds like it belongs on the first Mighty Baby album. (CF)

Poor Richard's Almanac

45:	Baby Bring A Way / Never Again	(Jody A-9000) c1966

Thought to be from New York City, **Poor Richard's Almanac** released a seldom-seen 45 on the equally obscure Jody label. *Baby Bring A Way* is a forlorn garage ballad full of heartbreaking minor chord changes, soaring ooh's and grieving la-la-la's; it has turned up again on *Psychedelic States: New York Vol. 1* (CD). (MW)

The Poore Boys

45s:	Give/It's Love	(Summer 181) 1967
	Give/It's Love	(Uptown 739) 1967

Conflicting reports place this band in Arizona or Minneapolis. *Give* is a low key garage ballad that tells a tragic tale whilst the flip is a decent garagey folk-rocker with a harp solo. (MW)

Poother Unlimited

45:	Tastee Freeze (Not Going To Wait Any Longer)/	
	Maggie	(Cadet 5653) 1968

Fuzz-laden mayhem from the Midwest. Both sides of the 45 were written by Joel Schbofsky and produced by Bobby Whiteside, an important behind-the-scenes-figure in the Chicago rock scene at this time. The 'A' side, *Tastee Freeze*, is pretty good and you can also check it out on *Mindrocker, Vol. 8* (LP). (VJ)

Popcorn Blizzard

Personnel incl:	MARVIN LEE ADAY		
	PETER WOODMAN	drms	A
	SUSIE WOODMAN	keyb'ds, vcls	A

45:	Once Upon A Time/Hello	(Magenda 7411) c1967

Hailed from Michigan and *Michigan Mixture, Vol. 1* (LP) showcases their 45 cuts:- *Once Upon A Time*, which has some pleasant woodwind and *Hello*, a keyboard-driven song, which has its moments.

One historically significant fact that has come to light is that the Magenda 45 represents the first released waxing of Marvin Lee Aday, known to the world as Meat Loaf. 5,000 copies were pressed in all so its not very rare - but no doubt there'll be a stampede for any copy that appears and its price will soar.

After this group, Meatloaf played in **Stoney and Meatloaf**. (VJ/MW)

Popcorn Blizzard

ALBUM:	1	EXPLODE!	(De-Lite DE-2004) 1968 SC

45s:	Good Thing Going/My Suzanne	(De-Lite 516) 1968/9
	Good Good Day/I Just Saw A Face	(De-Lite 522) 1968/9

Unconnected to the Michigan **Popcorn Blizzard**, this album is reputedly dreamy melodic pop with pleasant harmonies. (SR)

The Popcorn Generation

45:	Kitchy Kitchy Koo/Shake It	(HIP 8004) 1968

Released on a Memphis label, another bubblegum pop single similar to **Ohio Express**. (SR)

Port Authority

Personnel:	JIM ALLEN	keyb'ds	A
	LEONARD CUDDY	drms	A
	SKIP HARDING	sax	A
	RON PORTEE	bs	A
	JOHN SHERIDAN	keyb'ds	A
	MIKE TAYLOR	vcls	A
	MIKE VACCARO	gtr	A
	plus a horn section		A

ALBUM:	1(A)	PORT AUTHORITY	(U.S. NAVY 71001) 1971 -

Created by the U.S. Navy, **Port Authority** played "a funky blend of hard-rock and brass rock that reflects the pace and excitement of today's Navy". Not for sale, their record was an aid to Navy recruiting. Strongly influenced by Chicago and **Blood, Sweat and Tears**, it offers cover versions of *We've Only Just Begun*, **The Box Tops'** *The Letter* and **Dino Valenti**'s classic *Get Together* (certainly not written for that purpose!), plus seven compositions by Skip Harding. (SR)

Jerry Porter

ALBUM:	1	DON'T BOTHER ME	
		(Mirror/Capitol Custom SWB 1220) c1966 ?	

Produced by Armand Schaubroek (**Church Mice**) on his label, *Don't Bother Me* is a twisted folk album with wailing harmonica and strummed guitar. It deserves an inclusion here for tracks like *LSD Fixation* and *Losin' My Traction*. (SR)

Positively Thirteen O'Clock

45:	Psychotic Reaction/13 O'Clock Theme	(HBR 500) 1967

This was actually the work of **Mouse and The Traps** recording under a pseudonym with the singer Jimmy Rabbit and without Bugs Henderson or Doug Rhone on lead guitar. The 45 also appeared on a French EP issued on Vogue (18099). The other two tracks were by an outfit called TV and The Tribe Men. Incidentally, Jimmy Rabbit was actually known as a big-time AM DJ in Dallas; singing was only a side project for him.

Compilation appearances include: *Psychotic Reaction* on *Pebbles, Vol. 1* (CD), *Pebbles Box* (5-LP), *Pebbles, Vol. 1* (LP), *Songs We Taught The Fuzztones* (Dble LP & Dble CD), *Trash Box* (5-CD) and *Great Pebbles* (CD. Both sides of the 45 also feature on Eva's **Mouse and The Traps** collection *A Public Execution* (Eva 12001) 1981. (VJ)

Possum River

Personnel incl:	LENNY KERLEY	bs, vcls	A

ALBUM:	1	POSSUM RIVER	(Ovation 14) 1969 -

45s:	Girl, You Make Me So Happy / Right Back	(Ovation 1007) 1969
	Let The Good Times Roll /?	(Ovation 1013) 1969

This forgotten group featured Lenny Kerley, formerly of **The Cryan' Shames**. (SR)

The Possums

From Columbus, Ohio. **The Possums** were featured on the highly valued and sought-after compilation *Hillside '66*, performing *She Don't Care About Time* and *Stepping Stone*. The latter, is quite an interesting echoey interpretation of the **Boyce and Hart** composition, made famous by **The Monkees**.

Other local bands featured on the comp. were the Grim Reapers, New Breeds, Penetrations, Terry Davidson and the Barracudas, Brick Walls, **Kings**, Geers, Eggs, **Noblemen**, Margins and **The Deadlys**. Nothing was spared technically - it sounds like they were playing in the bathroom - expect it to cost both arms and legs!

Compilation appearances include *Stepping Stone* on *Highs In The Mid-Sixties, Vol. 9* (LP).

The Possums

45: She's Loving Me/King In This World   (JM 3824) 1966

This unknown band came from Scottsdale, Arizona. Their bright 'n' breezy 'A' side, *She's Loving Me*, has neat staccato rhythm guitar/organ, a catchy chorus and fine fuzz lead.

Compilation appearances have included *She's Loving Me* on *Sixties Rebellion, Vol. 3* (LP & CD) and *Teenage Shutdown, Vol. 2* (LP & CD); and *King In His World* on *Shutdown '66* (LP). (VJ)

Pot Liquor

Personnel:
- JERRY AMOROSO — drms, vcls — A
- GEORGE RATZLAFF — keyb'ds, gtr, vcls — A
- GUT SCHAEFFER — bs, vcls — A
- LES WALLACE — gtr, vcls — A

ALBUMS:
1(A) FIRST TASTE (Janus) 1971 -
2(A) LEVEE BLUES (Janus 3033) 1972 -
3(A) LOUISIANA ROCK 'N' ROLL (Janus 3036) 1972 -

45s:
Down The River Boogie/Riverboat (Janus 139) 1970
Chattanooga/Cheer (Janus 179) 1971
Beyond The River Jordan/? (Janus 186) 1972
Waitin' For Me At The River/? (Janus 195) 1972

A Louisiana blues-rock and boogie group formed by George Ratzlaff after the demise of **The Basement Wall**. The group released further 45s on Capitol and Capricorn. (SR)

Potter St. Cloud

Personnel:
- DANNY BAKER — vcls, organ — A
- JAMES HARRELL — vcls, bs, gtr — A
- D.F. POTTER — vcls, drms — A
- ENDLE ST. CLOUD — vcls — A
- GENE TREEK — vcls, gtr — A

ALBUM: 1(A) POTTER ST. CLOUD (Mediarts 41-7) 1971 -

This project, formed by St. Cloud and Potter, was a continuation of **Endle St. Cloud**. Their only album was recorded in Los Angeles with the assistance of Sneaky Pete Kleinow, Eddie Fisher and Billy Caldwell. It contained ten original compositions which varied from psychedelia to country-folk and were essentially in the same mould as the earlier material recorded by **Endle St. Cloud**. (VJ/GG)

Potters Clay

ALBUM: 1 POTTERS CLAY (Audio Lab AP 2083) c1971 ?

A large group (six men and two girls), playing soft-rock with vocal harmonies and Christian lyrics. (SR)

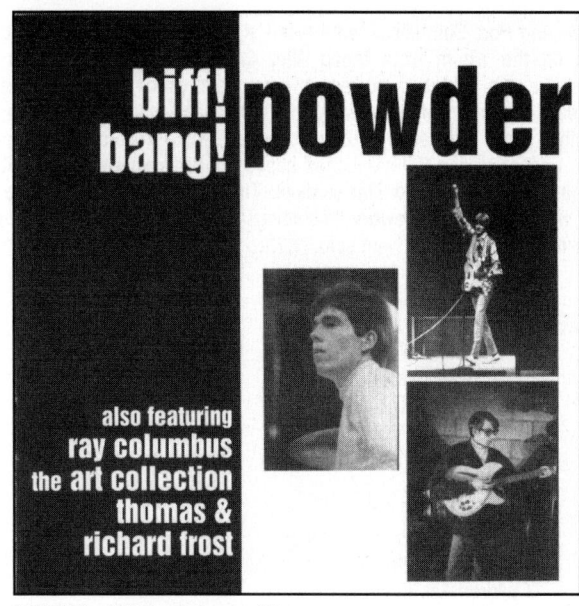

POWDER - Biff! Bang! Powder CD.

Pound

Personnel:
- CHUCK ARCHER — gtr — A
- DAVE BITHER — ld vcls — A
- DAVE FRANSON — vcls — A
- JACK GALLAGHER — gtr — A
- PAT GALLAGHER — slide gtr — A
- BERT GEISMAN — bs — A
- STEVE KORASIDAS — perc — A
- DAN O'CONNOR — synthesizer — A
- LARRY O'CONNOR — bs — A
- PAM PETROS — vcls — A
- GREG SHANNON — piano, vcls — A
- JEFF SHANNON — effects — A

ALBUM: 1(A) ODD MAN OUT (Audio Mixers AMS 74840) 1974 R2

This album, which was recorded at Audio Mixers Recording Company in Chicago, has its moments, most notably on the title cut, which starts with a sensitive instrumental introduction, leads into some great hard-rock midway and also features a memorable ending. The rest of the material ranges from country-rock to harder rock and rock'n'roll and is worth a spin.

They evolved out of a garage band called Down From Nothing. (VJ)

Poverty Five

45: Cry Cry Cry (Over You)/Sorrow (Thumbs Down 45 1002) 1966

From Centralia Washington. More Invasion sounds, with Searchers-style guitars. Uptempo beat backed by a cover of the Mersey's hit. Strangely negative label name! Overall, I'd give it the thumbs up. (MW/GGI)

Powder

Personnel incl:
- SCOTT ARBULICH — bs, vcls — A
- STEVE CHRIEST — drms — A
- RAY COLUMBUS — vcls — A
- RICHARD FROST — gtr — A
- THOMAS FROST — gtr — A

ALBUM: 1 BIFF! BANG! POWDER (Distortions DR 1015) 1996

NB: (1) also issued on CD with fifteen bonus tracks including side projects by Ray Columbus and **Art Collection**.

Hailing from San Mateo on the San Francisco peninsula, **Powder** evolved out of **The Art Collection**, who teamed up with visiting New Zealand singer Ray Columbus for the demonic garage fuzz thrash, *Kick Me* - which is joined on the album by the then unreleased and far more commercial *Snap*

Crackle And Pop. Both songs were taped at the start of 1967. The next five tracks on the album were taped after Columbus' departure, when the band's live set confused audiences who were used to the blossoming psychedelia of the time. By early 1968 the band had evolved into the altogether more satisfactory **Powder**, whose entire recorded legacy (16 tracks) appear on the CD mentioned above (mostly from an aborted album taped at Hollywood's Gold Star studios). The final four tracks wrap up the story with some post-**Powder** recordings from 1969 by **Thomas and Richard Frost**, who later went solo. (VJ/GG)

Power

Personnel:	ROBIN JOHNSTON	ld gtr, vcls	A
	JOE RODRIGUEZ	drms, vcls	A
	JOE ROMERO	bs, vcls	A
	JOHN ROMERO	ld vcls, gtr	A
	JIM SANCHEZ	keyb'ds, vcls	A

45s:	Children Ask (If He Is Dead)/ She Is The Color Of	(Showplace WS 218) 1967
	Children Ask (If He Is Dead)/ She Is The Color Of	(MGM K 13815) 1967

A strange one indeed. Whilst *She Is The Color Of* is a whimsical pop ballad, the topside is difficult to bag - it could be described as early MOR-ish **Iron Butterfly** with its quasi-religious keyboard doodlings similar to Doug Ingle. Add to that deep manly vocals like Ingle (again) or Sean Bonniwell, religious lyrics and occasional fuzzy guitar and... well, it's touted as 'psych' by specialist dealers - but make up your own mind!

Robin Johnston recalls:- "The band was originally called The Wild Ones, and we were from the South Bay, mainly Torrance and Hawthorne, having started out as a surf band in the very early sixties. We worked our way into being one of the house bands at the Hullabaloo in Hollywood, playing there with some of the biggest acts in the world. The other house bands were **The Palace Guard**, **The Yellow Payges** and **The East Side Kids**. The Hullabaloo was owned by Gary Bookasta, who was the manager of **The Palace Guard** and us, and I think **The Yellow Payges**. He worked very hard to mold all of us into hit bands and brought in professional songwriters to give us songs to record. Gary later bought KROQ radio station, but I don't know where he is now, maybe in Washington, D.C., as a lobbyist."

"*Children Ask* and *She Is The Color Of* were written by **Bernie Schwartz** who is given credit on the 45, but also by Morgan Cavett. We were presented the songs and rehearsed them at The Hullabaloo and recorded them at Paramount studios on Santa Monica Blvd., I think in the Spring or early Summer of 1967. The original title was *Children Ask If God Is Dead*, but we were told we couldn't use the name 'God' on the radio like that so we had to go back in and re-record the lyrics to say, *Children Ask If He Is Dead*. We then did a Summer tour from Southern to Northern California with **The Standells** and **The East Side Kids**. On the tour we passed through San Francisco and Haight-Ashbury, right in the middle of The Summer Of Love."

"Then, a small-time DJ from L.A. joined the Navy and became stationed at the Naval Base in Biloxi, Mississippi, and had taken our record with him where he started playing it on the air. It got some response so in November of '67 we went to Biloxi for four weeks and played there in clubs, also in New Orleans, including a couple of TV spots."

"Then we came back and played at the Hullabaloo for two more months and then broke up because of the draft, the bass player and I both going into the military."

"We had a good time back then, and as I look back now, we were only 16, 17, and 18 years old, so young and naive."

Compilation appearances include *Children Ask* on *Garagelands, Vol. 2* (CD). (MW/SR/RJn)

Power of Zeus

Personnel:	BILL JONES	bs	A
	BOB MICHALSKI	drms	A
	JOE PERIANO	gtr	A
	DENNIS WEBER	keyb'ds	A

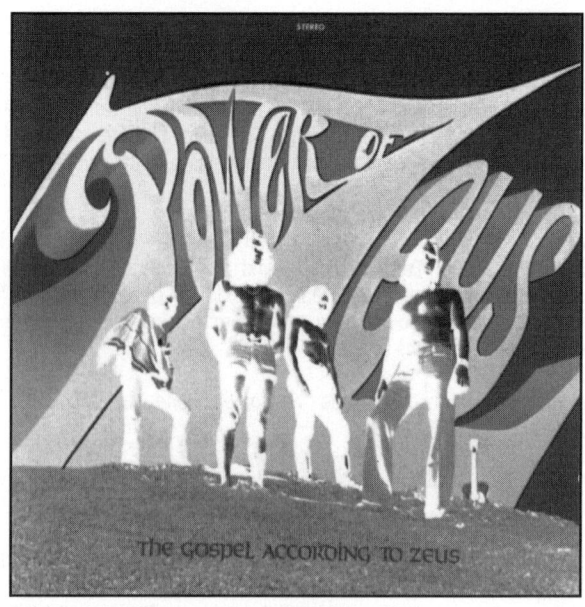

POWER OF ZEUS - Gospel According To Zeus CD.

ALBUM:	1	GOSPEL ACCORDING TO ZEUS	(Rare Earth 516) 1970 R1

NB: (1) reissued on CD by Buy Or Die.

This heavy keyboard and guitar-dominated album, which is becoming a minor collectable, may interest some readers, though I certainly wouldn't recommend it to garage or psych purists. They did not record any 45s for this label.

The band were from Detroit, Michigan. (VJ/NK)

Powers of Blue

ALBUM:	1	FLIP OUT	(MTA 5002) 1967 SC

45s:	Good Lovin'/(I Can't Get No) Satisfaction	(MTA 113) 1966
	Cool Jerk/You Blow My Mind	(MTA 118) 1967

This was a New York studio project featuring **Hugh McCracken**, a session guitarist, who later did work for Paul Simon (1975), Henry Gross (1976), Paul McCartney (1971) and Gary Wright (1970-71), to name but a few.

A regular on the New York sixties scene he was in several groups and released two 45s on Congress as **Hugh McCracken and The Funatics** in 1965 and 1966.

The album consists of instrumental covers of some of the 'hip' sounds of the times - *Paper Back Writer*, *The Midnight Hour*, *Cool Jerk*, *Bang Bang*, *Got My Mojo Working*, *The Tracks Of My Tears* and *Satisfaction* - almost entirely devoid of fuzz. A sorta Duane Eddy goes garage! Not recommended.

You Blow My Mind is a passable garage punk instrumental and has recently been compiled on the *Everything You Always Wanted To Know...* (CD). (MW)

The Powers Uv Purple

Personnel incl:	TIPPY SMITH	vcls	A

45:	Story Book Plays / Miss Dove	(Sandal Wood 0007) 1969

An obscure outfit from Jacksonville, Florida, whose *Miss Dove* has resurfaced on *Psychedelic States: Florida Vol. 3* (CD).

They are credited on the CD track listing and liners as **The Powers Uv Purple** despite the depicted 45 label showing that they were credited as The Blues Uv Purple (though this was a sticker over the original band name). Anyone know the story behind this? (MW/MM)

The Preachers

Personnel:
- JAMES 'ZEKE' CAMARILLO — bs — ABC
- RICHARD FORTUNATO — gtr, ld vcls — A
- RUDY GARZA — piano, hrmnca — ABC
- STEVE LAGANA — drms — ABC
- HAL TENNANT — ld gtr, hrmnca — ABC
- BURKE REYNOLDS — ld vcls — B
- JOHN ENGLISH — ld vcls — C

CD: 1( ) MOANIN' (Bacchus Archives CD BA 1181) (2-CD) 2001

NB: (1) also on vinyl.

45s:
- Who Do You Love?/Chicken Poppa (Moonglow 240) 1965
- The Zeke/Quit Talkin' 'Bout Him (Pep 102) 1965
- Stay Out Of My World/Pain And Sorrow (Moonglow 5006) 1965

NB: A French EP on Barclay (70890) features the four tracks from the first two 45s.

A raw L.A. punk band from the Hollywood area. They are best known for their version of Bo Diddley's *Who Do You Love?*. **The Preachers** gave it gritty treatment with snarling vocals and a wild chorus.

According to *Pebbles*, three of these guys went on to the final line-up of **The Vejtables** (after Jan Errico and Ned Hollis had left) to record the excellent *Shadows/Feel The Music* psypunk 45 and five other unreleased tracks. Richard Fortunato co-wrote both 45 tracks and was one of the three. He'd later turn up in the post-**Bees W.C. Fields Memorial Electric String Band**, **ESB** and **Fields** and may have been in **The Bees** too.

Rudy Garza recalls:- "Hal Tennant did all of the guitar leads on all the records and the inital line-up gave us our best sound. I always thought of the band as a hard-rock blues band. Punk hadn't been invented then. The band's line-up was pretty stable, except for vocalists. After Richard Fortunato we switched to a guy named Burke. He didn't last too long as his voice was too pure and we soon hired **John English**. This gave us our punkish sound and punkish lyrics. When we broke up Hal joined the **W.C. Fields Memorial Electric String Band** not Richard. I think Richard joined **The Vejtables**. Just before we broke up **The Preachers** recorded *Moanin'* (a jazz tune done in a rock style) and *Just Don't Complain* (another punk tune written by me and **John English**). The label, Moonglow then released this as **John English III**."

The *Moanin'* compilation compiles the three singles they recorded as **The Preachers** and one further one as **John English and The Lemondrops**.

Compilation appearances include: *Who Do You Love?* on *Pebbles, Vol. 1* (CD), *The Essential Pebbles Collection, Vol. 1* (Dble CD), *Pebbles Box* (5-LP), *Pebbles, Vol. 1* (LP), *Punk Classics, Vol. 5* (7"), *Acid Dreams - The Complete 3 LP Set* (3-LP), *Acid Dreams Epitaph* (CD), *Trash Box* (5-CD) and *Teenage Shutdown, Vol. 1* (LP & CD); *Stay Out Of My World* on *Project Blue, Vol. 3* (LP) and *Fuzz, Flaykes, And Shakes, Vol. 3* (LP & CD). (VJ/MW/MDo/RG)

The Preachers

45s:
- α Inspiration/Who's That Hiding In The Closet (Righteous Enterprises Re-1001) 1965
- Dedicated / Girls, Girls, Girls (Righteous Enterprises RE 491) 1966
- Hallowed Ground /What's Happ'nin Pussy Cat (Righteous Enterprises RE-1002) 1966
- α Inspiration / Hallowed Ground (Righteous Enterprises RE-1003) 1966

NB: α 'A' side is the same version.

A different outfit from Birmingham, Alabama, who released their 45s on a label run by the Righteous Brothers. Mike Markesich reports that their strongest track is *Inspiration*, a Dylan-inspired rant, and that *Hallowed Ground* is "a big production number, supposedly used in a movie soundtrack (but you can't believe everything you read on labels!)".

Dedicated is a slow soulful rendition of *Dedicated To The One I Love*, whilst the flip is upbeat sax-y pop. (MW/MM/PRd)

ACID DREAMS EPITAPH (Comp CD) including The Preachers.

The Premiers

Personnel:
- GEORGE DELGADD — gtr — A
- 'FARMER' JOHN PEREZ — drms — A
- LAWRENCE 'BOY' PEREZ — gtr — A
- PHILIP RUIZ — sax — A
- JOE URZUA — sax — A
- FRANK ZUNIGA — bs — A

ALBUM: 1(A) FARMER JOHN (Live) (Rampart) 1964

NB: (1) also issued on Warner Bros (WC 1565) 1964.

HCP

45s:
- Farmer John/Duffy's Blues (Faro 615) 1964 -
- Farmer John/Duffy's Blues (Warner 5443) 1964 19
- Annie Oakley/Blues For Arlene (Warner 5464) 1964 -
- So Fine/Little Irene (Warner 5488) 1964 -
- I'm In Love With Your Daughter Pt. 1 /Pt. 2 (Faro 620) 1965 -
- Get Your Baby/Little Ways (Faro 621) 1965 -
- Come On And Dance/Get On The Plane (Faro 624) 1966 -
- Ring Around My Rosie(Part 1)/(Part 2) (Faro 627) 1967 -

NB: There's also a French EP with picture sleeve: *Farmer John/Cross My Heart/Anymore/Feel Like Dancing* (Warner WP 1437) 1966.

This outfit from San Gabriel, California predate the psychedelic era, but may be of interest to readers in view of the inclusion of *Farmer John* - their most famous song - on several compilations.

Back in 1966, *Farmer John* appeared on the compilation *East Side Revue, Vol. 1*, and with *Get On This Plane* on the clear wax double compilation *East Side Revue* (Rampart 3303).

Dressed in matching suits they were atypical of their era.

Larry Tamblyn (of **The Standells**) produced at least the last two Faro 45s. John Perez later played for the **Sir Douglas Quintet**.

Retrosepctive compilation appearances have included: *Farmer John* on *Nuggets Box* (4-CD), *Nuggets - Original Artyfacts From The First Psychedelic Era 1965-1968* (Dble LP) and *The West Coast East Side Sound, Vol. 3* (CD); *Get On This Plane* on *Boulders, Vol. 2* (LP), *Psychedelic Experience* (CD), *The Psychedelic Experience, Vol. 1* (LP) and *The West Coast East Side Sound, Vol. 4* (CD); *Farmer John* and *Get On This Plane* on *The East Side Sound, Vol. 1* (LP); *Farmer John, Duffy's Blues, Get On This Plane*, and *Come On And Dream* on *The East Side Sound, Vol. 1* (CD); *Come On And Dream* on *The West Coast East Side Sound, Vol. 1* (CD); and *Little Ways* on *The East Side Sound Vol. 2 Featuring Mark And The Escorts* (LP & CD). (VJ/SR)

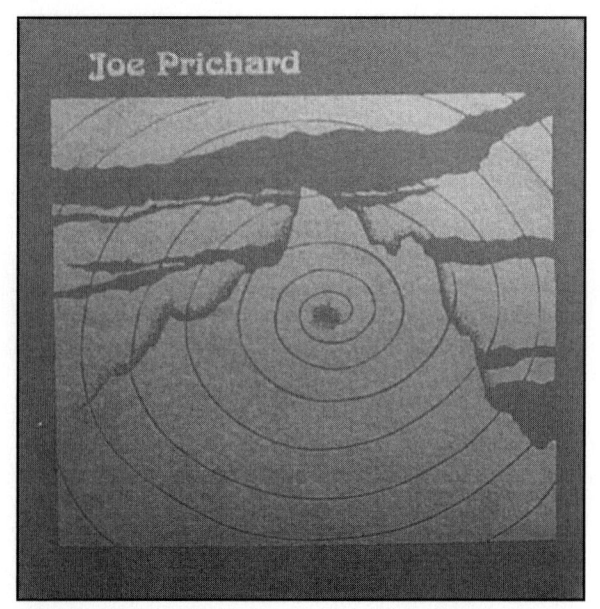

JOE PRICHARD and GIBRALTAR - Joe Prichard and Gibraltar LP.

Prentice and Tuttle

ALBUM: 1 EVERY LOVING DAY (R.P.C.) 1972 R1

From Massachusetts. A sort of druggy garage folk duo. (VJ/GG)

Preparations

45: Nobody But You Girl/
That's When He Remembers (Mainstream 720) 1970

Mainstream completists beware, as this is features devastatingly ill-advised calypso-meets-soul-trash on the 'A' side with some of the worst horns in history. The flip is just simply chaotic and banal, which in this case is a deliverance... (MK)

Pressed Down, Shaken Together and Running Over

ALBUM: 1 PRESSED DOWN, SHAKEN TOGETHER
AND RUNNING OVER (Almond Tree) 1972 SC

A good Christian psych group with a fine sleeve. Some cuts are featured on the *Holy Fuzz* compilation. Some group members went on to play with **Selah**. (SR)

Preston

45: This World Is Closing In On Me/
Waterfall (Orange vinyl) (Sound Patterns 110) 1967/8

The work of a Detroit, Michigan, group. The 'A' side, *This World Is Closing In On Me*, is rather interesting, a sort of haunting piece of psychedelia with some orchestration. This 'outfit' was persistent to say the least - the 45 was later released on three other labels, all as by **Chris Carpenter** (Oceanside, Sidra and United Artists). The **Preston** version is much hotter, with the fuzz guitar and mysterious organ higher in the mix.

Compilation appearances include *This World Is Closing In On Me* on *Magic Carpet Ride* (LP), *Psychedelic Unknowns, Vol. 11* (LP), *Slowly Growing Insane* (CD) and *Sixties Archive, Vol. 6* (CD). (VJ/MW/KBn)

Pretty People

Personnel:	MIKE ANTHONY	gtr	A
	PAT BRITT	flute/sax	A
	DENNY GORE	piano, vcls, arranger	A
	LYNSEED LAVENDER	vcls	A
	JUDY MOSS	vcls	A
	MILO PEERPOINT	ld vcls	A
	STEVE VENEM	vcls	A
	(DANNY BRYANT	hrmnca	A)
	(JAY DAVERSA	trumpet	A)
	(JIM GANNON	bs	A)
	(BOBBY MORIN	drms	A)

ALBUM: 1 THE PRETTY PEOPLE (Crestview CRS-3056) 1970 SC

Housed in a green and red "psychedelic" cover, a large group (two female singers and five men) singing light pop-psych in the style of **Free Design** or **The Association** with songs like *Song Rider*, *Hard Luck Stories*, *Just For Today* and *Lady Melinda*. Recorded at Sound Factory West, Hollywood, their album was produced by Randall Wood and all their material was original.

A short-lived label, Crestview also released the album by **Victims Of Chance**. (SR/VJ)

Joe Prichard and Gibraltar

Personnel incl: JOE PRICHARD vcls A

ALBUM: 1(A) JOE PRICHARD AND GIBRALTAR
(Kendall - Lee 74201) 1974 R3

NB: (1) has had a limited edition vinyl counterfeit of 300 in 1996.

A rare hard-rock/blues/progressive album from a Missouri outfit. The recent European counterfeit incorrectly dates the album to 1970! (CF)

Nancy Priddy

ALBUM: 1 YOU'VE COME THAT WAY BEFORE
(Dot DLP-25893) 1968 SC

45s: Ebony Glass/You've Come This Way Before (Dot 17164) 1968
Take Care Of My Brother/Feelings (Warner Bros. 7350) 1969

A beautiful blonde California singer in a folk-psych/soft-rock style, with tracks like *Epitaph*, *Ebony Glass* and *Mystic Lady*.

Her voice can also be heard on the series of **Mort Garson**'s "Signs Of The Zodiac". (SR)

Pride

Personnel:	DAVID A. AXELROD	A
	M.T. AXELROD	A

ALBUM: 1 PRIDE (Warner Bros. 1848) 1970
NB: (1) repressed 1998.

Primarily remembered (and cursed by many) for hijacking **The Electric Prunes** and turning them into a faceless concept band with *Mass In F Minor* and *Release of An Oath*, **David Axelrod** was to continue in this vein for a couple more years with a trilogy of albums before this release. An acoustic sound is to the fore and a decidedly Spanish feel, it's rather stretching the term psychedelic but for those who enjoyed the feel (and pretentiousness) of *Mass* it could be of interest. **David Axelrod** also produced a 45 for **Moorpark Intersection** and David McCallum albums for Capitol. (MW/JFr)

Adrian Pride

45: Her Name Is Melody/I Go To Sleep (Warner 5867) 1966

This 45 was in fact **Bernie Schwartz** with the Everly Brothers. *Melody* is an astounding hypnotic raga/sitar beauty, the flip is a Ray Davies song. (SR)

Pride and Joy

Personnel incl:
- JACK BURCHALL — bs
- ROGER DEATHERAGE — drms
- BOB GOOD — gtr, vcls
- JIM LAUER — gtr, vcls

45s:	Girl/If You're Ready	(Dunwich 152) 1967
	We Got A Long Way To Go/ That's The Way It is	(Acta 817) 1967

A Chicago punk band previously known as **The Del-vetts**. *If You're Ready* has an R&B style harp and some nice guitar.

Compilation appearances have included: *If You're Ready* on *Mindrocker, Vol. 2* (LP), *The Dunwich Records Story* (LP) and *If You're Ready - The Best Of Dunwich... Vol. 2* (CD); and *Girl* on *Oh Yeah! The Best Of Dunwich Records* (CD). (VJ)

The Primates

Personnel incl: JOHN DEMETRIOUS — A

45s:	Knock On My Door/She	(Marko M 923) 1965
	Don't Press Your Luck/Cathy	(Marko M 924) 1966

Schoolmates in Astoria, New York, formed this punk outfit in 1964. They combined Merseybeat with the more usual garage-punk sound and the results are quite accessible.

Compilation appearances have included: *Knock On My Door* on *Teenage Shutdown, Vol. 15* (LP & CD), *Chosen Few Vol's 1 & 2* (CD), *The Chosen Few, Vol. 2* (LP) and on *Psychedelic States: New York Vol. 1* (CD); *She* on *Glimpses, Vol. 3* (LP) and *Fuzz, Flaykes, And Shakes, Vol. 4* (LP & CD); and *Don't Press Your Luck* on *Garage Punk Unknowns, Vol. 1* (LP). (VJ/MW/MM)

Prime Mover

Personnel incl:
- JOHN PASTOR — A
- TONY PASTOR Jr. — A

45:	When You Made Love To Me / Shadows Of A Day Gone By	(Sock-O PRS-45-2002) 1967

An obscure NYC outfit's gift to posterity. *When You Made...* is a gloriously simple but effective garage ballad with tambourines, bells and chimes to the fore and a restrained guitar solo - check it out on *Psychedelic Crown Jewels, Vol. 2* (Dble LP & CD) where it's better described as "...great Eastern sound to the guitar, chimes blending well with a heavily staggered stepping crescendo chorus". Disappointingly the flip is a Coasters-style lounge-ballad. (MW/RM)

PRIDE - Pride LP.

PRIMEVIL - Smokin' Bats At Campton's LP.

Primevil

Personnel:	DAVE CAMPTON	vcls, hrmnca, perc	A
	MEL CUPP	drms	A
	LARRY LUCAS	ld gtr, vcls	A
	MARK SIPE	bs	A
	MO WHITTEMORE	keyb'ds	A
	JAY WILFONG	ld gtr	A

ALBUM: 1(A) SMOKIN' BATS AT CAMPTON'S
(700 West 740105) 1974 R2/R3

NB: (1) has been counterfeited in a reverse-image sleeve (the original has black art on a red background).

This is an example of seventies hard-rock at its best with some superb twin lead guitar work from Larry Lucas and Jay Wilfong. Some dealers describe this as psychedelic. The band came from Indiana and the album was issued privately and had a limited vinyl reissue.

The group were also responsible for the anonymous Buccaneer album and 45s released circa 1980. (VJ/CF)

Primrose Circus

45:	P.S. Call Me Lulu/In My Mind	(Mira 246) 1968

A hopelessly obscure but rather good L.A. pop group judging by this sole 45. Perhaps they were a studio group. *P.S Call Me Lulu*, is a decent enough harmony pop effort, whilst *In My Mind* really is a very good ballad.

Compilation appearances have included: *P.S. Call Me Lulu* on *Mindrocker, Vol. 10* (Dble LP) and *P.S. Call Me Lulu* on *Nuggets Vol. 5* (LP); and *In My Mind* on *Sixties Punk Ballads Sampler* (LP). (VJ)

Prince and The Paupers

Personnel:	STEVE CHRISTIANSEN	keyb'ds	AB
	EDDIE HELDER	vcls, gtr	AB
	BOB LEE	bs, gtr	AB
	RON LEE	drms	AB
	GARY SANDS	gtr	A
	DAN DUFFY	bs, gtr	B

45:	Shoulder Of A Giant/Exit	(JRJ 2115) 1965

This outfit came from Mankato in Southern Minnesota. Their 45 was recorded in an old schoolhouse in 1965. 1,000 copies were made originally, with a later repress of 5,000. It's the flip side, *Exit*, an energetic punk-style instrumental, which now attracts interest. The 'A' side was a bit of a bummer.

Eddie Helder went on to a solo career releasing two 45s in the early seventies. Bob Lee and Steve Christiansen both later moved to Las Vegas, whilst Bob's identical twin Ron still lives in Mankato.

Compilation appearances include: *Exit* on *Mondo Frat Dance Bash A Go Go* (CD), *The Midwest Vs. Canada* (LP) and *The Arf! Arf! Blitzkrieg 32 Track Sampler* (Dble CD). (VJ/MW/CT)

The Princemen

45:	Love Is A Beautiful Thing/ Don't You Even Care?	(IGL 137) 1967

The work of a garage band from Des Moines, Iowa.

Compilation appearances include *Love Is A Beautiful Thing* on *The IGL Rock Story: Part Two (1967 - 68)* (CD). (VJ)

The Princetons

45s:	Georgianna/Killer Joe	(Princeton 1465) 1965
	Georgianna/Killer Joe	(Colpix 793) 1965
	Little Miss Sad/Bony Moronie	(Wand 193) 1965
	Gone/You're My Love	(Philips 40379) 1966

Decent garagey frat-beat from a bunch of students at Iowa State University, Ames. *Georgianna* is an early **Critters**' track whilst *Killer Joe* is a lightweight *Louie, Louie*-style shuffler; the second 45 covers two popular party movers. The Wand 45 couples two garage-frat faves; both are performed with verve and rockin' competence.

You're My Love is catchy garage, full of throbbing organ.

Compilation appearances include *You're My Love* on *Sixties Rebellion, Vol. 5* (LP & CD). (MW)

Private Property Of Digil

Personnel:	STEVE GERTSCH	drms	AB
	DAN JACKLIN	gtr	AB
	CHUCK POSNIAK	organ, vcls	A
	DOUG YANKUS	gtr, keyb'ds	AB
	DAVE FAAS	bs	B
	GARY SCHIBILSKI	keyb'ds	B

ALBUM:	1	SOUP	(Gear Fab GF-144) 2000

NB: (1) by **Soup** but with all the **PPOD** 45s.

45s:	Look At Me (The Mantlepiece Martyr)/ To My Friends	(Target 109/10) 1967
	Destination Nowhere/The Patch Of Brick	(Tee Pee 115/6) 1967
	Sunshine Flames/Princess	(Tee Pee 23/4) 1967
	Jewelry Lady/I'm Looking At You	(Tee Pee 35/6) 1967

Led by the talented Doug Yankus, this Appleton, Wisconsin, outfit formed in 1966. Doug's previous groups included Ritchie Dino and The Dukes (Ritchie Dino was a stage-name Yankus adopted), The Versatones and The Strangers From Digil. 'Digil' was the name given to the basement room in the Yankus household that was used for music, parties and band practice.

Chuck Posniak was previously in The Memories. He left **PPOD** in mid-1967. His elder brother Al Posniak had started the Target and Tee Pee labels after leaving the **Golden Catalinas**.

Their 45s mix beat, folk-rock and multi-part harmonies with a quirky aura. On *Look At Me* the harmonies are unsettling and deliberately off-key. The melodic and jangley *Destination Nowhere* is a stand-out despite the Four Seasons-style falsettos. *Patch Of Brick* is a haunting and sombre ballad with interesting time changes, marred by an annoying glitch on the master tape, whose passage of hiss seems worse on the CD than on the original 45. The *Sunshine Flames* and *Jewelry Lady* 45s are probably their strongest, comprising upbeat Byrdsian folk-rock.

PPOD folded in 1968. Doug Yankus formed **Soup** with Dave Faas and Doug Griffith. They released one 45 and a sought-after album, that have been reissued on the above CD with the **Private Property Of Digil** 45s. They lasted until the mid-seventies.

Doug Yankus later formed Soft Touch and the Doug Yankus Band. He has appeared on recordings by John Hiatt, Ry Cooder, Roseanne Cash, Tracy Nelson, and **Mother Earth** amongst others. He passed away in 1982 due to complications arising from diabetes. The *Soup* CD is dedicated to his memory with proceeds going to the Diabetic Foundation.

Compilation coverage has included:- *Sunshine Flames* on *Every Groovy Day* (LP); and *Princess* on *Leaving It All Behind* (LP). (RM/SY/MW)

Privilege

Personnel:	TOMMY BRANNICK	drms	A
	JACK DOUGLAS	bs	A
	EDWARD LEONETTI	ld gtr, vcls	A
	PAUL VENTURINI	organ, vcls	A

ALBUM:	1(A)	PRIVILEGE	(T.-Neck TNS 3003) 1973 -

NB: (1) reissued on CD (Lizard LR 0711-2) 2001.

Venturini and Leonetti had previously been in the **Soul Survivors** and, according to the liner notes, **Privilege** was formed to mix the influence of **Hendrix** with the Isley Brothers and **The Soul Survivors**. The resulting album has its moments, especially because of its good guitar parts with loads of effects (fuzz, wah wah etc.). Tracks like *Purple Dog* and *Traitor* also have effective vocals with a good rhythm.

T. Neck was a subsidiary label of Buddah. (SR)

Probable Cause

45:	Tailspin / Chain Reaction	(GRT 17) 1969

From Philadelphia, this was one of a handful of Philly bands picked up on a scouting trip by the Los Angeles label. A great psych single with eerie organ and a swirly climax with sound effects. Both sides were composed by Gary Brauner and Steve Carpenter.

Mike Kuzmin suggests in his 'Sounds From The Woods' book that this could be the same Steve Carpenter who had put out two solo 45s: *You're Putting Me On / Something Good Is Happening To Me* (Brunswick 55322) 1967, and *Am I Lost / Sweet Talk* (Impex 368) 1968. (BM/MW)

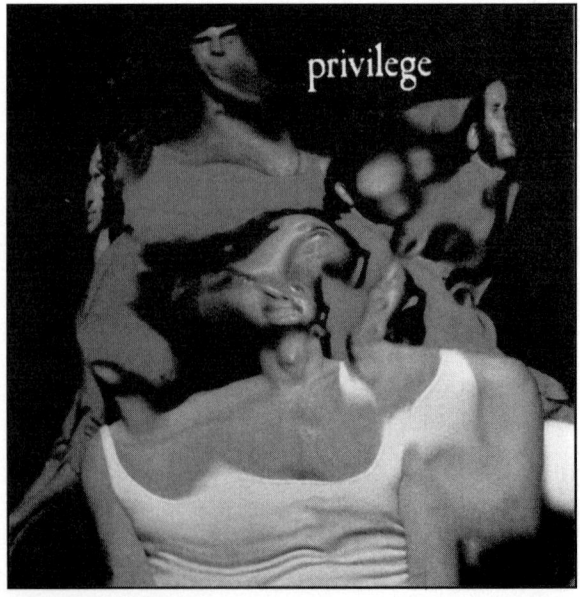

PRIVILEGE - Privilege CD.

PROBE - Direction CD.

Probe

Personnel:	JOHN FURLAND	bs, vcls	A
	HENRY LAMARCA	drms, vcls	A
	DAVE NELSON	gtr, vcls, hrmnca	A
	MIKE OLSON	gtr, organ, vcls	A

ALBUM: 1(A) DIRECTION (Eborp SS 21396) 1969 R4

NB: (1) has been counterfeited and reissued on CD.

From Rockford, Illinois, this band released an extremely rare album on their own label. It contains eight tracks. They are mostly hard-rock, although some of the songs are blues-tinged. Among them are a cover of **The Steve Miller Band**'s *Living In The U.S.A.* and the traditional *Rock Me*. The most psychedelic track is *Carol*. (VJ/GG)

Proctor Amusement Co.

Personnel:	KEN BYERS	keyb'ds	AB
	GARY CARTER	gtr	AB
	CHUCK KIRKPATRICK	gtr/ld gtr	ABC
	SANDY MEYER	drms	AB
	GEORGE TERRY	bs, vcls	ABC
	CLEVE JOHNS	vcls	B
	EDDIE KEATING	gtr, vcls	C
	SCOTT KIRKPATRICK	drms, vcls	C
	LES LUHRING	keyb'ds, vcls	C

NB: 'A' Gas Company. 'B' 1966-68. 'C' 1968-9.

45s:	Heard You Went Away/Call Out My Name	(Scott 168) 1967
	Heard You Went Away/Call Out My Name	(Laurie 3396) 1967
	You Don't Need A Reason / Two Wonderful Girls	(Scott 31) 1967

Formed around 1966 and originally known as The Gas Company (also line-up 'A'), this group were based in Fort Lauderdale, Florida. *Heard You Went Away*, composed by **The Birdwatchers**' Bobby Puccetti, is *Pet Sounds* cloned harmony-pop. The equally summery flip was penned by **The Nightcrawlers**' Chuck Conlan.

Kirkpatrick had earlier been in the Aerovons. Kirkpatrick and Terry's next outfit was The Game in 1970. Ex-members of **Proctor Amusement Co.** and The Game regrouped in the late seventies as The Crane.

Jeff Lemlich's sixties Florida book 'Savage Lost' (Distinctive Publishing, ISBN 0-942963-12-1) reveals the line-up details and that there may be an albums worth of unreleased '68 material on a Criteria Studios acetate.

Compilation apearances include: *Heard You Went Away* on *Bring Flowers To U.S.* (LP). (MW/JLh/CKp)

The Prodigal

45: Reality/You've Got Me (Mercury 72688) 1967

This seems to have been their sole platter. Los Angeles has been suggested as their stomping ground.

Compilation appearances include: *Reality* on *A Fistful Of Fuzz* (CD); and *You've Got Me* on *Boulders, Vol. 9* (LP), *Ya Gotta Have Moxie, Vol. 2* (Dble CD) and *Hipsville 29 B.C.* (LP). (VJ)

The Prodigies

Personnel incl:	ROGER FRANCISCO	vcls	A
	HOWIE SMITH	vcls	A

45: I Want To Do It/What'd I Say (Rofran ER 1013) 1966

No frills R&B tinged garage-beat from Urbana, Illinois, preluded by a seriously spoken intro about the "philosophy of life that has taken root in the very heart of America" and describing the **Strangeloves**-penned 'A' side as a "moving serenade".

Roger "RoFran" Francisco was later in experimental psychsters **Spoils Of War**. (MW)

Professor Morrison's Lollipop

HCP

45s:	You Got The Love/Lady	(White Whale 275) 1968 88
	Angela/Duba Duba Do	(White Whale 288) 1968 -
	Oo Poo Pah Susie/You Take It	(White Whale 293) 1969 -

This was in fact **The Coachmen** playing bubble gum music. Their first two singles were produced and written by Resnick, Levine, **Kasenetz and Katz**, the usual team responsible of the Super K productions: **Crazy Elephant**, **Lemon Pipers** and **1910 Fruitgum Co.**. The first *You Got Love* spent three weeks in the Top 100, peaking at No. 88. It's worth noting that *Duba Duba Do* is a totally unlistenable backwards track!

Before this incarnation, they also recorded one further 45 as **Alexander's Rock Time Band**.

Compilation appearances include *You Got The Love* on *Happy Together - The Very Best Of White Whale Records* (CD). (SR/VJ)

Progressions

Personnel incl:	SKIP HARRIS		A
	JEFF LUTZY	bs	A

45: The Love Train / What I Gotta Do To Satisfy You (Scepter 12146) 1966

This Baltimore, Maryland group may not have achieved commercial success but it proved to be a launching pad for several members.

Lutzy turned up in **Maypole** who put out a fine album and 45 on Colossus in 1970. He would return to later incarnations of **The Progressions**. Skip Harris had previously been in a teen band with Doug Lewis and would rejoin him to form **The Peppermint Rainbow**, who enjoyed success in 1968-9 with several 45s and an album on Decca. After **The Peppermint Rainbow** split in 1970, Lewis joined **The Better Half**. (JV/MW)

The Projection Company

ALBUM: 1 GIVE ME SOME LOVIN' (Custom) c1968 SC

In the same style as the **Firebirds**, another 'exploito' group recording for a budget label, with heavy fuzz and sitar. (SR)

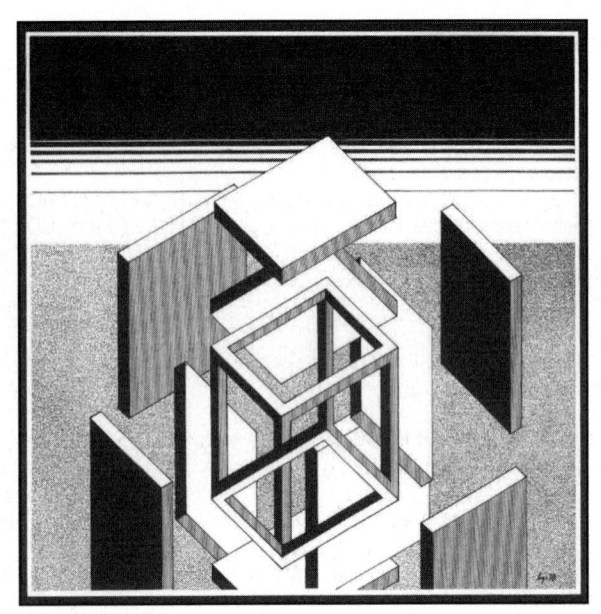

PROOF - Proof LP.

The Promissory Notes

45: Flowers / Purple Haze   Claw CR-1220/1 196?

Believed to be from Connecticut or Rhode Island, this outfit's 45 couples a heavy late sixties rocker with a competent version of the Hendrix classic. (MW)

Proof

Personnel:			
MIKE CAPORALE	drms	A B	
DEAN FORBES	gtr, vcls	A	
JOHN LEE	gtr, vcls	A C	
PETE NOLFI	bs	A	
GARY SLOAN	vcls, hrmnca	A B C D E F	
LINDY RAINES	gtr, vcls, bs	B F	
STEVE TYLER	bs, hrmnca, gtr	B	
RUFUS REID	gtr, vcls	C D	
ROGER	drms	C	
CURT CUNNINGHAM	gtr	D E	
TED LUTHER	drms, vcls	D E	
SPIKE	bs	D E	
MARK THOMPSON	vcls	E	
GORDIE CANYON	drms	F	
DON MACKEY	gtr	F	
LARRY RAINES	bs	F	

NB: Line-up 'A' May 1966 to January 1968. 'B' November 1968 to June 1969. 'C' June 1969 to February 1970. 'D' May to June 1970. 'E' August to November 1970. 'F' March to May 1971.

ALBUMS: 1(D/E) PROOF   (No label) 1971 R3
2(A-F) 5th ANNIVERSARY PHONOGRAPH RECORD
    (No label) 1972 R4

NB: (1) live recordings from two concerts in Anchorage, Alaska during the Summer of 1970. It was issued with an insert, and 300 copies were pressed. (2) is a collection of live and studio tracks recorded from 1966-71. 125 copies were pressed.

Proof's two albums are amongst the rarest blues rock records from the USA. Only a couple of copies of their second have ever surfaced.

5th Anniversary Phonograph Record is a sampler produced by Sloan for the band and the Proof family and it is extremely rare. Containing "snapshots" of the various line-ups of the band, it begins with a July 1966 live track and traces the evolution of the band to mid-1971. At each stop on the journey, Proof is revealed to be purveyors of gritty blues-based rock. It is the 1970-era material that will have the most appeal to readers of this book, with Leavin' Trunk and the lovely City Line being the pick of the offerings on this engaging album.

The first Proof album, recorded in concert during this same era, has great versions of Love's Made A Fool Of You, Highway 61 Revisited and Ridin' On The L + N. Much of Proof's early repertoire consisted of covers, a direct reflection of Gary Sloan's interest in record collecting. That Proof's two album have such a strong collector appeal is therefore appropriate; they were assembled by one!

Gary Sloan continues to record and has produced many albums which fall outside the scope of this book. Gary Sloan and Clone - Gary Sloan And Cloan (Proof Records No. 3) 1979 was cassette-only; Harmonitalk (Proof Records No. 4) 1980 contains a fantastic extended track called Together Again that features several former Proof members and may be their finest moment; South Side Blues (Proof Records No. 5) 1981; Nightraid (Proof Records No. 6) 1983 was issued on album and cassette; Harmonitalk/South Side Blues (Proof Records No. 7) 1985 was a cassette-only reissue of his 1980/1 albums; Techno-Blue (Proof Records No. 8) 1987 was cassette-only; This One's For Us (Proof Records No. 9) 1988 was cassette-only and shown as by Southside Blues; Iditarod Blues (7" single) (Proof Records 002) 1988; Blue Shoes (Proof Records No. 11) 1992 was made available on CD and cassette. It was reissued in 1996 with some tracks re-recorded, Skull (Live) (Proof Records No. 12) 1994 was CD and cassette; Polar Bear-Hug Blues (Proof Records No. 14) 1995 was CD and cassette, and Live Arkansas To Yugoslavia (Proof Records No. 15) 1997 was cassette only. Many Proof alumni appear on these later releases, and both Blue Shoes and Skull feature legendary axemen Freddy Robinson and Harvey Mandel on extended jams that will have you double-checking the recording dates! (CF)

Proof of The Puddin'

45: Color Wheel/Flying' High   (RCA Victor 47-9332) 1967

An intriguing name and titles to whet psychedelic collectors' appetites. However, Color Wheel is a rambling melodic pop ditty in the 'baroque' style. Flyin' High is a much better upbeat melodic power-popper - beware the 'psych' tag on collector lists! (MW)

Prophecy

45: Goddess Of Love/Take A Look At Mary   (Airborne AB 711) 1968

An obscure Long Island outfit, who unsurprisingly get their brand of melodramatic soulful pop-rock sounds from the local Vanilla Fudge and Young Rascals school. A decent 45 for all that might imply, you can check out Take A Look At Mary on Marijuana Unknowns (LP & CD). (MW)

The Prophets

Personnel incl: TOM KUBAZEK   A
RAY WATSON   A

45: Yes I Know/Sad On Me   (Twin-Spin 3000) 1967

Came out of Iowa with this haunting garage ballad, Yes I Know. Produced by Ray Graffia of New Colony Six fame, it didn't take off and they were never heard from again.

Compilation appearances have included: Yes I Know on Pebbles Vol. 10 (CD), Pebbles, Vol. 22 (LP); Yes I Know and Sad On Me on The Quill Records Story (CD). (MW/BSw)

The Prophets

Personnel incl: LEON FRAZIER   A

45: I Still Love You/Baby   (Shell 1005) 1965

Out of Fredericksburg, Virginia, where they were known to dress in togas and leather thongs which criss-crossed at the knees, these garage punkers were a popular local attraction and once one of three finalists at the Lambertsville, New Jersey Music Circus in 1965. I Still Love You is a typical garage-punk effort.

Compilation appearances include I Still Love You on Signed, D.C. (LP).

Thee Prophets

Personnel:
JIM ANDERSON	ld gtr		A B
BRIAN LAKE	keyb'ds		A B C
DAVE LESLIE (STIMAC)	bs		A B C
CHRIS MICHAELS (MICHAEL MASHOCK)	drms		A B C
TONY GAZZANA	vcls		B
JOE KOPECKY	sax		B
JERRY GEORGE	sax		B
JOSE SALAZAR	trumpet		B
MARK SANDUSKY	ld gtr		C
LEE JOHNSON	gtr		
DAVE MACIOLEK	bs		

ALBUM: 1 PLAYGIRL (Kapp KS-3596) 1969 163 -

45s:
To Be With You / If You Would Leave Me (Tee Pee 29/30) 1967
Playgirl / Patricia Ann (Kapp 962) 1968 49
Some Kind Of Wonderful /
They Call Her Sorrow (Kapp 997) 1969 111
Rag Doll Boy / It Isn't So Easy (Kapp 2038) 1969
A Little Bit Of Love / Come To Me Girl (Kapp 2087) 1970
Some Kind Of Wonderful /
They Call Her Sorrow (Kapp 2097) 1970

Four friends in West Allis, Wisconsin got together and formed a group in 1962. They played a brand of upbeat teen-pop which acquired an R&B flavour over the next few years. Around 1966 they expanded to an eight-piece with a vocalist and brass section, including Tony Gazzana and Jerry George from Milwaukee's Triumphs. By the time they came to record their debut 45 in 1967 however, they had reverted to a quartet.

The breezy teen-pop follow-up was their commercial peak, eventually climbing to No. 49 in Billboard after a few months of hitting hot spots in several regions. The rush to find a follow-up and cash in on the success with an album inevitably led to to the perennial pitfalls. The band were wanting to go in a heavier, rock direction (they'd moved onto playing Cream and **Hendrix** material in their live shows) yet the producers and label wanted more teen-pop and bubblegum chart fodder to cash in on their investment. Bearing this in in mind, it comes as no surprise that the album doesn't work.

This scenario and the band's full story is recounted by Brian Lake in Gary Myers' book 'Do You Hear That Beat'. Tied to a five year contract and having reached an impasse with both producer and label, the band chose to forego the pleasure of making further recordings in an incompatible style. They returned to the clubs and touring, finally splitting at the end of 1972.

Latter-day members included Dave Maciolek of Milwaukee's Dynastys. (MW/SR/GM)

PROOF - 5th Anniversary Phonograph Record LP.

Proposition (aka Ron Roman and...)

Personnel incl: STEVEN HOFFMAN A
RON ROMAN A

45s: Two Faced Madonna/
The Ways Of Love Are Strange (Dot 17186) 1968
I'll Be Your Baby Tonight/
Just Let Rosemary Know (Dot 17264) 1969

Featuring at least two ex-members of the **Mystic Astrological Crystal Band**. Inoffensive summery Los Angeles soft psychy-pop with some orchestration that should appeal to fans of the **M.A.C.B.**. (MW)

Prospectus

ALBUM: 1 PROSPECTUS WITH FRIENDS (dbl) (Bristol) 1971 R1

A double album of hippie-rock covers. (GG)

The Proverbial Knee Hi's

Personnel:
EDDIE HALL	drms		A B
DALE PATE	organ		A B
BUTCH POWELL	bs		A B
CHARLES SMITH	gtr		A B
WILLIE T.	vcls		A

45: Crying For Her / Watch Out (Beachcomber 11) 1967

Managed by Buddy Eisen, owner of the chain of Beachcomber clubs on the East Coast (hence the label name), this Virginia outfit formed in late 1966 and released their sole 45 a year later, after the departure of original fron-man Willie T.. *Crying For Her* is like a garage take on a big production ballad - impassioned vocals, dramatic swirling keyboards and just a hint of the Zombies. *Watch Out* is a beaty belter with a catchy refrain and defiant mood.

Compilation appearances include *Crying For Her* and *Watch Out* on *Aliens, Psychos And Wild Things* (CD). (BHr/ST/MW)

The Pseudos

45: A Long Way To Nowhere/
Back Door Man Bites The Dust (Fink 122) 1966

Garage quartet out of Utica, Michigan. The 'A' side, *A Long Way To Nowhere* has resurfaced on *Back From The Grave, Vol. 8* (CD) and *Back From The Grave, Vol. 8* (Dble LP). (VJ)

Psychedelic Sounds

45: Stars Seas To Shine/
Sorry Baby, Goodbye (Sunny-Side 0014) 1967

A very rare, psychedelic 45. Aram Heller's New England bible 'Till The Stroke Of Dawn' places them in Bridgeport, Connecticut but another source has placed them in Poughkeepise and Newburgh, New York. Could somebody settle this?

Compilation appearances include *Sorry Baby - Goodbye* on *Class Of '66!* (LP). (SR/MW)

Psychedellic Guitars

ALBUM: 1 PSYCHEDELLIC GUITARS (Custom CS-1078) c1968 SC

Another exploito album with tracks like *Psychedelic Ripple*, *Way Out*, *Love In*, *Flowers* and *Take A Trip*. Note the dubious spelling of PsychedeLLic! (SR)

Psychic Motion

Personnel:	RONNIE BAXLEY	gtr, vcls	A
	DICKIE BRITT	keyb'ds	A
	JOHNNY HAYES	bs, vcls	A
	JIMMY SOSSAMON	drms	A
	CARLTON WARWICK	vcls, gtr	A

45: Big Teaser/It's You (Mu Records ZTSB 125277) 1967

This was actually The Young Ones from North Carolina. The band released this, their second 45 as **Psychic Motion** when they heard that another band in the Northeast was using the "Young Ones" moniker.

Jimmy Sossamon was later the driving force behind The Cycle.

You can check out both sides of the **Psychic Motion**'s garage pop 45 on the Gear Fab CD reissue of *Cykle* (GF-106), where they are included as bonus tracks.

Compilation appearances have included *Big Teaser* on *Tobacco A-Go-Go, Vol. 2* (LP). (CF)

The Psychopaths

Personnel incl: DAVID ARVEDON   A

45s:	Till The Stroke Of Dawn/		
	See The Girl	(David Lloyd Co 201438/9)	1966
α	There Is No Woman (For This Broken Man) /		
	Fancy Woman	(WRECKED Record Co. W-1001/2)	c1970

NB: α released as High Voltage.

A Boston, Massachusetts, outfit. **David Arvedon** also made solo recordings with a double CD on Arf! Arf!, collecting together much of his later wanderings and solo psychopathic weirdness: *In Search Of The Most Unforgettable Tree We Ever Met (1969-1974)* (Arf! Arf! AA-053/4) 1995.

Only one copy of the second 45 has been found, which features different versions to the ones included on the retrospective Arf! Arf! release.

Compilation appearances have included: *See The Girl* on *No No No* (CD); *'Til The Stroke Of Dawn* on *New England Teen Scene* (CD) and *Gone, Vol. 1* (LP); *'Til The Stroke Of Dawn* and *See The Girl* on *New England Teen Scene, Vol. 1* (LP). (MW)

The Psychos

Personnel:	TERRY BACON	vcls, ld gtr, hrmnca	A
	BILL GREEN	organ, gtr, vcls	A
	JERRY JAMES	bs	A
	CLARKE THRASHER	drms	A

45: Black River #3 / Pebbles And Stones (Tiki 68-11/12) 1968

Formed in Norfolk, Virginia in 1964, the **Psychos**' debut 45 didn't appear until their final year. Bacon and James had appeared on other local acts recordings by then, notably on *Workin' For My Baby* - a local hit for **Lenis Guess** in the Summer of '66. *Black River #3* is a slow folk-rocker with wailin' harp, waltzing rhythm and pastoral vibe. It can be heard on *Aliens, Psychos And Wild Things* (CD) which documents the Tidewater sixties scene in Virginia and, in addition to all the info above, notes that this band mastered a somewhat unique skill - skateboarding whilst playing!

The flip is an upbeat organ-dominated number that sounds more like '65 than '68. (BHr/ST/MW)

The Psychotics

45:	I'm Determined/		
	Still, The Time Will Come	(Uptown 7-7666)	1967

NB: some copies appeaed in a picture sleeve.

A rather sought-after fuzz-punk 45 recorded in Minneapolis, Minnesota. A sextet, the band came from Charlotte, North Carolina. *(I'm) Determined* is accessible again via *When The Time Run Out Vol. 1* (LP & CD) and *Psychedelic Crown Jewels Vol. 3* (CD). (VJ/MW/MM)

The Psychotics

45:	If You Don't Believe Me, Don't/		
	School Boy Blues	(Acid 24975/6)	196?

This bunch of **Psychotics** came from Michigan and recorded an extremely rare and expensive bluesy psycher on the Acid label.

Compilation appearances include: *If You Don't Believe Me Don't* on *Michigan Mayhem, Vol. 1* (CD), *Sixties Rebellion, Vol. 15* (LP & CD) and *Sixties Archive, Vol. 7* (CD). (VJ/GG)

Public Nuisance

Personnel:	DAVID HOUSTON	vcls, gtr, keyb'ds,	
		hrmnca, theremin	A
	JIM MATHEWS	gtr	A
	RON McMASTER	drms, perc, vcls	A
	PAT MINTER	bs, vcls	A

ALBUM: 1(A) GOTTA SURVIVE (Shadoks Music 040) (dbl) 2002

NB: (1) also released on CD (Frantic Records 1313) 2002.

An amazing late sixties rock band from Sacramento, California. The core band originally formed in 1964 as The Jaguars and played concerts using this moniker but did not record. During 1965, the line-up shown above was fixed and they made their first recordings as **Moss and The Rocks**. One of the two 45s by this band was made at Ikon Studios in Sacramento, which at the time was home to engineer Eirik Wangberg. Readers of this book will recognise at least two of the projects that Wangberg handled at Ikon, the 45 by **The Oxford Circle** and the album by **Glad**. The relationship between **Moss and The Rocks** and Wangberg continued for over three years, during which time Wangberg relocated to Southern California and helped the group record two remarkable albums of British-influenced rock that have to be ranked amongst the finest ever produced in the State. Their release is the basis for the band's inclusion here.

During 1966, **Moss and The Rocks** adopted what are now considered quintessential "punk" pretensions; the more aggressive music and the unorthodox fashion sense. As they moved their local campaign into high gear, they changed name to the more appropriate **Public Nuisance**, which surely must have cost them some concert opportunities in the relatively staid community of Sacramento! The band spent a great deal of time and energy on visual propaganda during this period, staging photo sets and producing rather provocative handbills and holiday greeting cards for fans on their mailing list. In time, the band was invited to record a demo for Fantasy Records. Sessions took place at Fantasy's studios in San Francisco during 1967 that resulted in a finished master. Sadly, a recent search of the company's archives proved fruitless and the demo appears to

PUBLIC NUISANCE.

PUBLIC NUISANCE.

be lost. It was eventually apparent to the group that the label wasn't interested in pursuing a contractual agreement, however.

In 1968, **Public Nuisance** recorded a new demo on a four-track machine operated by Eirik Wangberg at his new center of operations, Sound Recorders in Hollywood. This is an album-length recording, produced by the band, that makes up disc-two of the *Gotta Survive* double set. In even a cursory review of this music, it is apparent that Fantasy made an enormous blunder in letting this band get away! Punishing fuzz guitars, pummeling drums - it's like someone commanded **The Savage Resurrection** to record a follow-up to *The Who Sell Out*! Aside from a cover of The Beatles' *I'm Only Sleeping*, the material is all original and is not to be missed by any and all fans of late-sixties rock. *Time Can't Wait* sounds like a '66 punk 45 side with better production; *Pencraft Transcender* has thick fuzz reminiscent of the Canadian Plastic Cloud album; *Darlin'* and *Katie Shiner* have a distinctly British underground feel that readers will associate with the *Chocolate Soup For Diabetics* UK compilation series. For a self-produced demo tape, it's a phenomenal achievement. Wangberg thought so, too - and in the course of playing it for visitors to the studio, brought it to the attention of producer Terry Melcher (**Paul Revere and The Raiders**, **The Byrds**) who envisioned **Public Nuisance** as (indeed) an American-made British rock band. He had the group back to Sound Recorders and under the watchful eye of Wangberg in 1969, with a simple prime directive: make a British rock album. This new recording (disc one of the double set) is every bit as powerful as the 1968 demo. *Love Is A Feeling* and *Small Faces* are violent freakbeat like Creation/Who/Pretty Things, while *Evolution Revolution* could fit on Tomorrow's album. *Strawberry Man* is pleasant power-pop until the last minute, when it explodes into a maelstrom of druggy pyrotechnics. The only noticeable difference between the two sessions is a hint of a British accent on the vocals on this later recording. None of the material from the 1968 demo repeats here - this is a completely original album-length master that, due to Melcher's self-imposed exile following the **Manson** incident in August, was shelved and forgotten. Not long after, the band split.

Dave Houston opened a recording studio in the seventies, producing a number of albums that fall outside the scope of this book. One band that readers may be familar with, The Twinkeyz, did all their records with Houston. Ron McMaster works for Capitol Records and is responsible for remastering albums by Badfinger, The Beach Boys and the Blue Note jazz catalogue amongst others. Eirik Wangberg turned knobs on a number of projects that readers will be familiar with (Paul McCartney's *Ram* album, John Mayall, **Peacepipe**, Joan Baez) before returning to his native Norway and (presumably) abandoning music-orientated pursuits. (CF/JD)

Gary Puckett and The Union Gap

See **The Union Gap** entry.

Puddin' Heads

45:	Now You Say We're Through/ You Don't Have To Be Lonely		(Catch 111) 1964

A Los Angeles outfit whose pounding punker *Now You Say We're Through* can be heard on *Back From The Grave, Vol. 7* (Dble LP). Strangely enough there was an early sixties outfit of the same name in San Antonio, Texas (four 45s on the Menard and Gallant labels). (VJ)

Puff

Personnel:	VIN CAMPISI	ld gtr	A
	ROBERT HENDERSON	drms, vcls	A
	JIM MANDELL	piano, organ, flute	A
	DAVID-ALLEN RYAN	bs, vcls	A

ALBUM:	1(A)	PUFF	(MGM SE-4622) 1968 -

45:	Looking In My Window/Rainy Day	(MGM 14040) 1968

NB: (1) 'A' side is a non LP track.

This band's album, which reflected the psychedelic era in some of its music, is beginning to interest some collectors. Another example of the 'Bosstown' sound produced by **Alan Lorber** (**Ultimate Spinach**, **Chamaeleon Church**) and recorded in New York on August 26/27th, 1968, this pleasant psych-prog album is of note since **Puff** were formed out of the ashes of **The Rockin' Ramrods**: Vin Campisi and Henderson, as well as Ronn Campisi (who wrote all the songs but doesn't play on the album), were all previously in this group.

Housed in an awful sleeve (photographed at Phil's Thrift Shop Fur Annex!), the album contains well-structured songs with good vocals and harmonies and occasional guitar leads (especially on *Dead Thoughts Of Alfred*). A light jazz influence is evident, with baroque-jazz pointillist piano lines on *Trees* and echoplexed flute textures on the trance-like *I Sure Need You*.

The Big Beat compilation *The Best Of The Rockin' Ramrods* includes the entire **Puff** album plus the non-album 45 - eleven tracks in all.

In 1982, Jim Mandell would release on Elektra a solo album in the mould of Billy Joel *No More Illusions*. Ronn Campisi is now a publications designer; Vin Campisi works in record distribution; Bob Henderson became a recording engineer; Jim Mandell a L.A. studio musician; and David Allen Ryan later played with Sha Na Na.

Compilation appearances include: *Vacuum, Go With You* and *Looking In My Window* on *The Best Of Bosstown Sound* (Dble CD). Their commercial harmony-pop effort (and non-album) *Looking In My Window* also reappears on *Bring Flowers To U.S.* (LP). (VJ/MW/SR/LP)

Pugsley Munion

Personnel:	THOMAS "DUCKY" BELLIVEAU	gtr, bs, vcls	A
	JOHN SCHULLER	keyb'ds, bs, gtr, vcls	A
	EDWARD KELLY	drms, vcls	A
	STAN HARRIS		
	GARY IANUZZI	bs	

ALBUM:	1(A)	JUST LIKE YOU	(J & S Records SLP 0001) 1970 -

NB: (1) reissued officially on CD (Gear Fab GF-143) 2000, with three bonus cuts - a 1971 live version of *What's Right For Me*, and two demos from 1970.

45:	Just Like You/Slumberland Blues	(J & S 00002) 1970

Schuller was clearly the creative force in this Fitchburg, Massachusetts, band. He either wrote or co-wrote with Belliveau every track on their album. This album contains some tasty guitar on *I Don't Know Who To Blame* and thundering organ on *What's Right For Me*.

They were not a garage or psych band as such but were influenced by Cream, Procol Harum and other late sixties bands. It's a unique record in that it is an unabashed portrait of the band's music.

The value of the record has dropped considerably due to a sizeable warehouse find some ten years ago. In the 'States this album is considered to be in the SC rather than R2 category.

Recently, Gear Fab reissued the album with notes from John Schuller, who reveals that the band was formed in 1969 as Mask until it was found that another band had registered the name. He points out that the initial album jackets came with "3 In 1 Records" printed on the spine. The title was to be *Three In One*, but the label lost the original artwork, dropped Kelly's last name and retitled the album after the single that had been released. Worst of all, the band learnt that the label was putting out the album using the rough session mixes (which they expected to mix and redo some bass and vocal parts) but were unable to stop its release. The Gear Fab CD adds three bonus cuts - two 1970 demos and a live *What's Right For Me* from February 1971 featuring bassist Gary Ianuzzi.

Schuller reports that all three original members remain active on the music scene: he has his own band, produces/engineers local Massachusetts acts and has worked with members of Boston and Heart; "Ducky" Belliveau is an in-demand pedal steel session player, working and touring with many well-known acts including Terence Trent D'Arby and J.Geils' Peter Wolf; Ed Kelly remains the choice drummer for area bands' projects and gigs. (VJ/MW)

The Pullice

Personnel incl:	DON BANDUCCI	drms	A
	BRUCE BRYMER	drms, vcls	A
	RICH HAINES	keyb'ds	A
	DAVE SCHALLOCK	bs, vcls	A
	BRUCE WALFORD		A

This mid-sixties group from Santa Rosa, California have two cuts on Big Beat's *Good Things Are Happening* (CD), culled from an audition tape made at Golden State Recorders in San Francisco. Both *Little Girl* and *I'm A Lover, Not A Fighter* have raw early garage appeal.

Schallock and Brymer later played in **Freedom Highway**. (CF)

The Pulsating Heartbeats

45s:	Talkin' About You/?	(Pace-Setter Internationale) 1966
	Wait 'Till Then/?	(?) 196?

Northwest flavoured R&B punk band from Anchorage, Alaska.

Compilation appearances include: *Talkin' About* on *Back From The Grave, Vol. 8* (CD) and *Back From The Grave, Vol. 8* (Dble LP). (VJ/GG)

The Pulse

Personnel incl:	CARL AUGUSTO		ABCD
	RICH BEDNARCZYK		ABCD
	LANCE GARDNER BIESELE		A
	PETER NERI		ABCD
	BENNET (BEAU) SEGAL		ABCD
	TOMMY VIOLANTE		ABC
	PAUL ROSANO		BCD
	JEFF FULLER	hrmnca	CD

ALBUM:	1	PULSE	(Poison Ring 2237) 1969 R1

NB: (1) reissued on CD (Black Rose BR 144).

45s:	Can Can Girl/Burritt Bradley	(Atco 6530) 1967
	Another Woman/My Old Boy	(Poison Ring 711) 1969

From New Haven, Connecticut, **The Pulse** evolved out of **The Bram Rigg Set** and **The Shags**, and were originally known as **The Pulse Of Burritt Bradley**. The track, *Burritt Bradley*, is a surreal slice of psychedelic madness, which can also be found on the *Beyond The Calico Wall* (LP & CD) compilation.

By contrast, their album is a furious heavy rock affair and rated highly by some collectors.

Tommy Violante left in 1969, although the band soldiered on until '72, playing mostly rehashed Cream-type stuff.

PUGSLEY MUNION - Just Like You CD.

The excellent Gear Fab label are currently researching a legit CD release of **The Shags** material. (VJ)

Pulse

Personnel:	RICHIE GOGGIN	gtr, vcls	A
	BILL GOLDEN	organ, piano	A
	CARLO MASTRANGELO	drms, kazoo, ld vcls	A
	KENNY SAMBOLIN	bs, vcls	A
	(CHRIS GENTILE	organ	A)

ALBUM:	1(A)	PULSE	(Thimble TLP-1) 1972 -

Another **Pulse**, this one from New York and produced by Herman Gimbel (**Sacred Mushroom**) and Orrin Keepnews, a respected jazz producer. Musically, it's a decent early seventies hard-rock group with driving organ and fuzz guitar. All their material was penned by their leader, Carlo Mastrangelo (who also played with Dion and The Belmonts!), sometimes helped by Kenny Sambolin or Jimmy Demitrack. It's probably one of the few hard-rock albums listed here which features a kazoo solo! (SR)

Punch

Personnel:	DEE	vcls	A
	KATHY	vcls	A
	STEVE	vcls	A
	CHARLES MERRIAM	vcls	A
	(ZAVIER	12-string gtr	A)
	(BOB ALCIVAR	piano	A)
	(MIKE ANTHONY	gtr	A)
	(HAL BLAINE	drms	A)
	(DENNIS BUDIMIR	gtr	A)
	(MIKE DEASY	gtr	A)
	(JIM HORN	flute	A)
	(BONES HOWE	tamb	A)
	(GARY ILLINGWORTH	piano, organ, harpsichord	A)
	(LARRY KNECHTEL	piano, organ	A)
	(JOE OSBORN	bs	A)
	(JIMMY ROWLES	organ	A)
	(FRED TACKETT	gtr	A)

ALBUM:	1(A)	PUNCH	(A&M SP4307) 1970 -

Produced by Bones Howe (**Smokestack Lightnin**, Tom Waits), this is a deceptive attempt at launching another **Mamas and The Papas**. Led by Charles Merriam who wrote five songs, the group also covers material by the Beatles, Dylan, Paul Simon and Paul Williams. Except for a decent cover of *While My Guitar Gently Weeps* and its fine guitar solo by **Mike Deasy**, the album is better avoided. (SR)

The Puppets

| 45: | Ain't Gonna Eat Out My Heart/ | |
| | Love Is A Beautiful Thing | (Red Rooster 311) 196? |

An all-girl group from Michigan who did two **Young Rascals**' covers on this their sole disc. Their version of *Ain't Gonna Eat Out My Heart* is excellent.

Compilation appearances include *Ain't Gonna Eat Out My Heart* on *Girls In The Garage, Vol. 1* (LP & CD). (VJ)

Pure Food and Drug Act

Personnel:	VICOR CONTE	bs	A
	SUGARCANE HARRIS	violin	A
	PAUL LAGOS	drms	A
	HARVEY MANDEL	gtr	A
	RANDY RESNICK	gtr	A

| ALBUM: | 1(A) | CHOICE CUTS | (Epic KE 31401) 1972 - |

| 45: | Eleanor Rigby/ My Soul's On Fire | (Epic 10907) 1972 |

A short-lived group formed by **Harvey Mandel**, Paul Lagos (ex-**Kaleidoscope**) and Sugarcane Harris (ex-Don and Dewey and **Frank Zappa** band) with Victor Conte and Randy Resnick. Their only album was recorded live at the Fresh Air Tavern in Seattle, with some studio overdubs. Produced by Skip Taylor (who also worked with **Canned Heat**), it includes a long version of *Eleanor Rigby* and several soul-rock tracks, largely instrumental. The album may interest those who like early seventies blues rock with a large dose of soul.

Mandel, Conte, Resnick and Lagos kept on working with Sugarcane Harris on several of his solo albums between 1972 and 1975. All these musicians, bar Conte, can also be found on several albums of John Mayall recorded between 1970 and 1975. (SR)

Pure Jade Green

According to the liner notes to *Acid Visions, The Complete Collection, Vol. 1* (3-CD): "**Pure Jade Green** was a reincarnation of the earlier Jades, from El Campo, Texas. The leader was the same Freddie Koenig as before, but accompanied by a different line-up of musicians. Like the Sonics from nearby Rosenburg, the Jades/Pure Jade Green drew enormous crowds to their live concerts and made a staggering number of records but never lucked out with a national hit."

One of the **Pure Jade Green** tracks on the CD is awesome. *Into The Sun* is a laid-back slice of psych with heavily flanged vocals, very trippy effects, and a wonderfully druggy feel throughout. (VJ/GG)

PULSE - Pulse LP.

Pure Love and Pleasure

Personnel:	JOHN ALLAIR	organ, piano, vcls	A
	BOB BOHANNA	gtr, bs, vcls	A
	PEGGE ANN MAY	vcls	A
	DAVID McANALLY	vcls	A
	DICK ROGERS	drms, perc, vcls	A

			HCP
ALBUM:	1(A)	A RECORD OF PURE LOVE AND PLEASURE	
		(Dunhill DS 50076) 1969 195 -
			HCP
45:	All In My Mind/?	(Dunhill 4232) 1970 104

A San Francisco outfit whose album ranged from hippie-rock to more lightweight flower-power. A kind of mixture of **Cold Blood** and **The Mamas and Papas**. The better tracks are *The Lord's Prayer, Too Scared To Go* and *Hard Times*. Bob Bohanna had earlier been with **Morning Glory**. It spent two weeks in the chart with a best position of No. 195.

Compilation appearances have included *All In My Mind* on *Undersound Uppersoul* (LP). (VJ)

Purple Avalanche

| 45: | Oh-Bah-Um-Dee-Dum/When I Saw Her | (Roulette R 7046) 1969 |

A decent fuzz bubble-gum topside, backed by a sober rock ballad, by an unknown bunch. (MW)

Purple Canteen

| 45: | Brains In My Feet/ | |
| | If You Like It That Way | (Alley AS 1049) 1967 |

An obscure combo, possibly from the Arkansas region. The flip is a good slow psychedelic folk number.

Compilation appearances include *Brains In My Feet* on *World Of Acid* (LP) and *Glimpses, Vol. 4* (LP). (VJ)

Purple Fox

Personnel:	ALEX "PURPLE FOX" BOGGS	gtr, vcls	A
	BOB GRAY	bs	A
	RAFF WITKIN	drms	A

| ALBUM: | 1(A) | TRIBUTE TO JIMI HENDRIX | |
| | | (Stereo Gold Award MER 340) 1971 |

NB: The above release is a U.K. one. The album was also issued in Germany (on Sonic) and in Canada (Summit). Another Canadian pressing (Stereo Gold Award GA-40), manufactured by Arc Sound Ltd., Toronto, exists, but this edition does not include the *Palamatoon* track.

A mysterious record not issued in America but possibly of American origin as Clark Faville feels the group sound remarkably similar to the Chicago-area band **The Exkursions**, which may or may not be a coincidence. The bulk of the tracks on this album were also issued on another German-only album **Jeff Cooper and The Stoned Wings**, so it's possible the personnel listings on both albums are ficticious. One track, *Palamatoon*, also appears on Funky Junction's album *Tribute To Deep Purple* (Stereo Gold Award MER 373) 1973, featuring UK band Thin Lizzy, Dave Lennox and Benny White. Can anybody confirm if the two versions are the same?? Curiously, *Palamatoon* is omitted from one of the Canadian pressings of the album...

According to the sleeve notes, to *Tribute To Jimi Hendrix*, leader and **Hendrix** acolyte Alex Boggs hailed from St. Louis, Missouri and is joined by two sidemen from New Orleans. Lashings of heavy guitar psych featuring decent, though sometimes leaden, covers of some **Jimi** classics. Whether this could "possibly fill the void left by Jimi" was optimistic beyond doubt - a worthy tribute but lacking something in the *Fire* department by trying to be too faithful and reverent, right down to the vocal mannerisms. It should still have appeal for staunch **Hendrix** fans, completists and air guitarists.

Compilation appearances have included: *Acid Test* on *Lycergic Soap* (LP), *Turds On A Bum Ride, Vol. 6* (CD) and *Turds On A Bum Ride, Vol. 1* (Dble LP); *Are You Experienced* on *The Stars That Play With Dead Jimi's Dice* (LP); and *Patch Of Grass* on *Turds On A Bum Ride, Vol. 3* (CD). (CF/VJ/MW/JP/AS)

Purple Gang

45s:	Answer The Phone/I Know What I Am	(Jerden 794) 1966
	Bring Your Own Self Down/ One Of The Bunch	(MGM KI 3607) 1966

A Southern California five-piece outfit who debuted at a gas station (and presumably coined the phrase 'what a gas'!) - a new breed of garage band perhaps. Both sides of the MGM 45 are upbeat bombastic pop with liberal doses of strident guitar and fuzz - infuriatingly infectious after a few spins. The topside is in reality rather good with an excellent 'off-beat' and a great pseudo-psychedelic break. Unfortunately the Jerden 45 doesn't live up to further expectations.

Compilation appearances have included: *One Of The Bunch* on *The Lost Generation Vol. 3* (LP); and *I Know What I Am* on *Northwest Battle Of The Bands, Vol. 2* (CD). (MW)

The Purple Haze

45:	It's Getting Harder All The Time/ Electrocution	(JMS 120867) 1967

A highly-touted 45 by a Corpus Christi (Texas) act. The flip was an instrumental and both sides have resurfaced on *Acid Visions - The Complete Collection Vol. 1* (3-CD). (VJ)

The Purple Haze

Personnel incl:	JERRY BEADLECOMB	vcls	A

45:	Shades of Blue/Someday Baby	(Plaza 1001) 1969

Both sides of this Montgomery, Alabama band's 45 were written and sung by Jerry Beadlecomb. *Shades Of Blue* is an excellent fuzz-rocker. The flip is a sappy ballad.

Compilation appearances have included *Shades Of Blue* on *The Essential Pebbles Collection, Vol. 2* (Dble CD), *Psychedelic Unknowns, Vol. 9* (CD) and *Acid Dreams, Vol. 3* (LP). (VJ/MW)

Purple Image

Personnel:	WARREN ADAMS	vcls, piano, organ	A
	WILLIAM ADAMS	vcls, perc	A
	DIANE DUNLAP	vcls	A
	DEL MORAN	bs	A
	RICHARD PAYNE	drms	A
	KENNETH ROBERTS	vcls, gtr	A
	FRANK SMITH	gtr	A
	(ED SNODGRASS	sax	A)

ALBUM:	1(A)	PURPLE IMAGE	(Map City) 1970 R1

45:	(Marching To A) Different Drummer/Why	(De-Lite 526) 1970

From Cleveland, Ohio, this black group played a mix of soul-funk and psych-rock with fuzz and wah-wah guitars, clearly influenced by **Hendrix**. After some tracks like *Living In The Ghetto*, *We Got To Pull Together* or *What You Do To Me*, the album ends with fifteen minutes of guitar jams. The album also has really nice cover art.

Map City was the New York label managed by the ex-**Tradewinds**, **Anders** and Poncia. (CF/SR)

TURDS ON A BUM RIDE Vol. 6 (Comp CD) including Purple Fox.

Purple Passage

45:	Lost Childhood / Beyond Reality	(Sound Associates 1001) 1970

A very obscure 45 on a one-off Grand Rapids, Michigan, label is the sole evidence of this mystery outfit. Writer credits of H. Martinez, P. Martinez and G. Clark are the only other clues. *Beyond Reality* is upbeat acid-rock with meandering guitar solos - compiled on *Psychedelic Crown Jewels, Vol. 3* (CD). (MW)

Purple Prism

45:	Hold On/Purple Jam	(Fulltone 1001) 196?

This group came from Estherville in Iowa, but their 45 was recorded at the United Artists Studios in Sioux Falls, South Dakota. (VJ)

Purple Rock

Personnel incl:	SID MYERS Jr		A

45:	News / Everything	(Crodon 101) 19??

Riff-heavy acid-rock recorded in Carthage, Texas circa 1969-1970. (AB/MW)

Purple Smoke

ALBUM:	1	PURPLE SMOKE, VOL. 1	(Mark) 196? SC

A garage pop band whose album is now very rare and had a hand painted paste-on cover. (GG)

The Purple Underground

Personnel:	JIM CARLTON	bs	A
	HALSEY LaFRANDRE	drms	ABC
	JON LaFRANDRE	keyb'ds	ABC
	TOM NAY	ld gtr	AB
	JOHN KERAMIDAS	gtr	C

45s:	On Broadway/Rain Come Down	(Boss 009) 1966/7
	Count Back/Soon	(Boss 010) 1967

Starting out as a sextet called The Spades, by 1967 this Winter Haven, Florida band had slimmed down to a quartet and adopted a more original moniker.

Their finest moment is *Count Back*, a unique and stunning example of garage-psych. Pulsing with spacey effects (including a short wave radio tuned to cosmic noise), rapid-fire drumbursts and distorted vocals, it culminates in a passage of nightmarish whispering that dissolves into an alien miasma.

One memorable highlight for the band was their appearance at the Palm Beach Pop Festival, where they did a turn immediately after **Spirit** on the main stage that would also accomodate the Stones later that evening.

Unfortunately nothing more made it onto vinyl, although the band lasted until 1971.

Tom Nay now lives in Sarasota Florida and is in realtor, Halsey Lafrandre lives in Auburndale, Florida and Jon Lafrandre still lives in Winter Haven. Thirty years on Jon and Halsey LaFrandre were still playing together in the local band Second Nature.

Compilation appearances include *Count Back* on *Mayhem & Psychosis, Vol. 2* (LP), *Mayhem & Psychosis, Vol. 2* (CD), *Off The Wall, Vol. 1* (LP), *Psychedelic Experience, Vol. 2* (CD) and *Psychedelic States: Florida Vol. 2* CD. (VJ/MW/RM)

Purpose

Personnel:	FLUFFER HIRSCH	gtr	A
	JOHN JOHN McDUFFY?	vcls, keyb'ds	A
	JOHNNY MITCHELL	sax, vcls	A
	CHOCOLATE WRIGHT	drms	A
	SAM WRIGHT	bs	A

ALBUM: 1(A) PURPOSE (ABC) 1969 -

Similar in style to **Group Therapy**, Puzzle and **Vanilla Fudge**, this was a psychedelic/bluesy-soul act from New York. An integrated quintet, with five black members. Two tracks, *Hippie Chick* and *Hog For You Baby*, were compiled on *Tom's Touch*, an album dedicated to **Tom Wilson** productions.

Both songs are good examples of psych-soul. (SR/NK)

Purpose

Personnel incl: J. PHILLIP LANDGRAVE A

ALBUM: 1 PURPOSE (Boardman Records 452-109) 1966 ?

A Christian rock musical written by J.Phillip Landgrave, who later became a music theory professor at the Southern Baptist Seminary!. Oddly enough, if the album offers some muzak tracks, it also contains some good garage and hip rock tracks. For curious collectors! (SR)

Joseph Pusey

ALBUM: 1 IN MY LADY'S CHAMBER (Private Pressing) c1976 R1

An introspective acid-folk singer. (SR)

Puzzle

Personnel:	CURT JONNIE	bs, vcls	A
	(EDDIE KRAMER	keyb'ds	A)
	TONY GRASSO	gtr, vcls	A
	MIKE ZACK	drms	A

ALBUM: 1(A) PUZZLE (ABC ABCS 671) 1969 -

45: Hey Medusa/Make The Children Happy (ABC 11181) 1969

A blues-influenced outfit from Washington D.C. who sometimes had a psychedelic taint to their music. Produced by Eddie Kramer, the album has its moments, on tracks like *Hey Medusa*, *I've My Head Right Yesterday* and *Working For The Rich Man*.

Zack and Johnnie had previously played together in Wild Honey and Zack was previously with Lawrence and The Arabians, **The British Walkers**, and the Reasons Why. In the seventies he moved onto the Cherry People and Nils Lofgren's band.

Not to be confused with another Puzzle led by John Livigni and Joseph Spinazola who issued two albums of white soul-rock with horns on Motown in 1973 and 1974 (*Puzzle* and *The Second Album*). (VJ/MW/SR)

Pynk Peach Mob

45: No Tears/
     Love Captured Me (Night Owl No # (Cuca # 1558)) 1969

An uninspiring pop pair, penned by a Rex Jackson, on a collectable Wisconsin label, though I'm told the band was from Michigan.

The 45 may be as late as 1971/2 (MW/GM)

The Pyramids

45: I Don't Wanna Cry/I'm - A Love Ya (Archer 102) 196?

An obscure band. The 'A' side, *I Don't Wanna Cry*, has a soul-ish beat and some fine vocals. Hear it on *Sixties Rebellion, Vol. 9* (LP & CD). (GG)

THE PSYCHEDELIC EXPERIENCE Vol. 2 (Comp CD) including The Purple Underground.

MAYHEM & PSYCHOSIS Vol. 2 (Comp CD) including The Purple Underground.

PATRON SAINTS - Proto Bohob CD.

PEANUT BUTTER CONSPIRACY - For Children Of All Ages CD.

PEANUT BUTTER CONSPIRACY - Turn On A Friend CD.

PEARLS BEFORE SWINE - The Use Of Ashes LP.

PHANTOM - Lost Album CD.

THE PHANTOM RAIDERS - New Sound '67 CD.

Quadrangle

Personnel incl:	JAY FISHMAN	A
	MICHAEL KONSTON	A

45:	She's Too Familiar Now/No More Time/	(Philips 40408) 1966

A studio-only outfit from New York. Produced by the ubiquitous **Artie Kornfeld**, **Quadrangle** included Jay Fishman and Michael Konston and released their sole 45 in the Fall of 1966.

She's Too Familiar Now is a wondrous slab of resounding Invasion-inspired teen-punk. Take some Alan Price keyboard moves and the bass-line from The Animals' *We Gotta Get Out Of This Place*, then add strong, bawling vocals and rampaging guitars... and you have a classic sixties nugget.

It's become more familiar now thanks to compilation appearances on *Chosen Few Vol's 1 & 2* (CD), *The Chosen Few, Vol. 2* (LP) and *Psychedelic States: New York Vol. 1* (CD). (VJ/MW)

The Quantrill Raiders

45:	I'm Going/Sad Eyed Lady	(Tema PTX-1 50) 196?

Ohio was this mob's stomping ground and you can also check out *I'm Going* on *Victims Of Circumstances, Vol. 1* (LP), *Follow That Munster, Vol. 1* (LP) and *Glimpses, Vol. 4* (LP). (VJ/MW)

Quatrain

Personnel:	JIM LEKAS	drms	A
	BUFF LINDSAY	bs	A
	ERIC PEASE	gtr	A
	DON SENNEVILLE	ld gtr	A

ALBUM:	1(A)	QUATRAIN	(Tetragrammaton T 5002) 1969 -

The band were from L.A. but their rather inconsistent album was not one of the best on the label.

Senneville went on to play for **Simon Stokes and The Nighthawks**.

Michael Quatro and The Jam Band

ALBUMS: (up to 1976)	1	PAINTINGS	(Evolution 3011) 1972 -
	2	LOOK DEEPLY INTO THE MIRROR	(Evolution 3021) 1973 -
	3	IN COLLABORATION WITH THE GODS	(UA LA 420) 1975 -
	4	DANCERS, ROMANCERS AND DREAMERS	(UA 587) 1976 -

NB: (3) and (4) also released in England by UA and Prodigal.

			HCP
45s: (up to 1976)	Circus/Time Spent In Dreams	(Evolution 1062) 1972	108
	Natural Way/Prelude In AB Crazy	(Evolution 1077) 1973 -	
	Tomorrows/?	(Evolution 1083) 1973 -	
	Neptune's Nicromea/ In Collaboration With The Gods	(UA XW-672) 1975 -	

A largely forgotten musician, whose albums range between ambitious prog-rock, heavy-psych and pop. His records feature several well-known musicians including: on the two Evolution albums, Ted Nugent (**Amboy Dukes**); on *In Collaboration* Rick Derringer (**McCoys**), Mark Volman and Howard Kaylan (**Turtles**). **Michael Quatro** kept on recording until the early eighties and released at least four other albums. (SR)

Queen Anne's Lace

Personnel incl:	ANNE PHILLIPS	vcls	A
	WILLIAM PHILLIPS		A

ALBUM:	1(A)	QUEEN ANNE'S LACE	(Coral CRL 757509) 1968 -

? and THE MYSTERIANS - Action LP.

45s:	You Have Turned Me Every Way But Loose / Windows And Doors	(Mona-Lee 218) 1968

Recorded at Bear Brook Sound Studio, a flower-pop album with original songs (*Power Of The Flower*, *The Happiest Day Of My Life*) and covers of the Beatles (*The Fool On The Hill*, *Ticket To Ride*), Paul Simon (*Dangling Conversation*) and **The Box Tops** (*Neon Rainbow*). Named after the flower **Queen Anne's Lace** the liner notes mention that you can "Weave It, Pluck It, Touch It, Smoke It". It's not psych at all, although it's often described as such by unscrupulous dealers. (SR/MW)

Queen's Nectarine Machine

Personnel:	JIMMIE JERSIE	vcls, perc	A
	JOE RIBAUDO	gtr	A
	GUY RIGANO	drms	A
	DREW TROEDER	bs, vcls	A

ALBUM:	1(A)	THE MYSTICAL POWERS OF ROVING TAROT GAMBLE	(ABC ABCS 666) 1969 SC

45:	I Got Trouble / Gypsy Lady	(ABC Paramount 11172) 1969

From New York, their album was a "Super K" production by Kasenetz-Katz, with a psychedelic side and a bubblegum side. Among its better tracks are *4th Dimension* and *Seance* and overall it's worth hearing.

One of the tracks, *The Seance* started when Jeff Katz came into the studio whilst the engineer was trying to get a volume and EQ level. As usual, the band were goofin-off - playing dissonant jibberish to irritate and annoy the engineer, but Jeff thought that THAT SOUND was just what he was looking for to finish the album...

One track from the album, *Mysterious Martha* has been compiled on *Psychosis From The 13th Dimension* (CDR & CD). (VJ/MW/DTr)

The Quest

45:	The Last Days/Love	(Gramaphone 1270) 1970

This later fuzz 45 is worth a spin. The band came from Winona in South-East Minnesota. (VJ)

? and The Mysterians

Personnel:	BOBBY BALDERAMMA	gtr	AB
	FRANK LUGO	bs	AB
	RUDY MARTINEZ	vcls	AB
	FRANK RODRIGUEZ	organ	AB
	EDDIE SERRATO	drms	A

	ROBERT MARTINEZ	drms	B
	LARRY BORJAS		
	MEL SCHAEFER	bs	

ALBUMS:
1. 96 TEARS (Cameo Parkway C 2004) 1966 66 R1 — HCP
2. ACTION (Cameo Parkway C 2006) 1967 - R1

NB: (1) and (2) have been released on CD, with (1) including four bonus tracks. There's also a CD compilation entitled *30 Original Recordings*, which includes both their original albums, plus extra material (Campark QMATM 01) 1995. Also of interest is (B) *Re-Union* (Roir A-1 37) 1984, a live cassette release, later issued as a double LP *96 Tears Forever* (Roir DANLP 032) 198?.

45s: HCP
- 96 Tears/Midnight Hour (Pa-Go-Go 102) 1965 -
- 96 Tears/Midnight Hour (Cameo Parkway 428) 1966 1
- I Need Somebody/"8" Teen (Cameo Parkway 441) 1966 22
- Can't Get Enough Of You, Baby/Smokes (Cameo Parkway 467) 1967 56
- Girl (You Captivate Me)/Got To (Cameo Parkway 479) 1967 98
- α Do Something To Me/Love Me Baby (Cameo Parkway 496) 1967 110
- α Make You Mine/I Love You Baby (Capitol 2162) 1968 -
- α Ain't It A Shame/Turn Around Baby (Tangerine Record Corp 989) 1969 -
- α Sha La La/Hang In (Super K 102) 1969 -
- α Talk Is Cheap/She Goes To Church On Sunday (Chicory 410) 1972 -
- β Hot' N Groovin'/Funky Lady (Luv 159) 1973 -
- 96 Tears/I Can't Get Enough Of You Baby (Abkco 4020) 19? -
- 96 Tears/Got To (Million Seller 800) 19? -

NB: α and β all non-LP. Only 100 copies of β were pressed. There are also three French EPs with picture sleeves: *96 Tears/Midnight Hour/I Need Somebody/"8" Teen* (Columbia ESRF 1825); *Can't Get Enough Of You, Baby/Smokes/Tellin Lies/Upside* (Stateside FSE 105); and *Girl (You Captivate Me)/Got To/Don't Tease Me/Why Me* (Stateside FSE 106).

Question Mark (Rudy Martinez) was born in 1945 and raised in Saginaw, Michigan. The band of Mexican/Americans were initially based in Corpus Christi, hence their inclusion here, although they were based for much of their career in Flint, Michigan, where they issued *96 Tears* on their own label before it was picked up by Neil Bogart for release on Cameo. A relentless 'punk' two note organ sound ran throughout the record which quickly became a classic of its genre making No. 1 in the U.S. and No. 37 in the UK. They enjoyed some subsequent chart success but were never quite able to recapture the magic of *96 Tears* or shake off the 'one hit wonder' tag, although it wasn't quite true. Robert Martinez and Larry Borjas were also original members of the band but they were in the U.S. Army when the first album was recorded.

Splitting in 1968, Martinez has made various attempted reformations. A 45 was issued in 1973 and new demos were recorded with **Kim Fowley** in 1978. They also played a reunion concert at the Dallas Arcadia in early 1985 and have continued to perform into the nineties. The Michigan band Inflight included ex-members of **The Mysterians**.

Mel Schaefer would later form Grand Funk Railroad.

Compilation appearances have included *Can't Get Enough Of You Baby* on *Michigan Nuggets* (CD) and *Michigan Brand Nuggets* (LP); (VJ/MW/MO/SR)

Questors

A very obscure outfit from Dearborn, Michigan. They appear not to have made it onto vinyl during their time but a septet of unreleased covers feature on *The History Of Michigan Garage Bands In The 60's - The Wheels Four Label Story* (3-CD) - *Are You A Boy Or Are You A Girl*, *Little Red Rooster*, *She Was Mine*, *The Last Time*, *Tarantula '65*, *We Gotta Get Outta This Place* and *You Can't Sit Down*. (MW)

The Quest's

45s:
- Scream Loud/Psychic (Fenton 2032) 1966
- Shadows In The Night/I'm Tempted (Fenton 2086) 1966
- α Shadows In The Night/What Can I Do (Fenton 2174) 1967

NB: α also seen listed with a 'B' side *Sometimes I'm Tempted*.

A West Michigan high school band, whose raw and savage garage ravers are highly-regarded. All their 45s are amongst the most keenly sought on the Fenton label and enjoy hefty 3-figure price tags.

Compilation appearances have included: *Shadows In The Night* on *Let 'Em Have It! Vol. 1* (CD), *Trash Box* (5-CD), *Best of Pebbles, Vol. 3* (LP & CD) and *Highs In The Mid-Sixties, Vol. 5* (LP); *Scream Loud* and *I'm Tempted* on *Michigan Mayhem, Vol. 1* (CD), *Chosen Few Vol's 1 & 2* (CD) and *The Chosen Few, Vol. 2* (LP); *Scream Loud* on *Teenage Shutdown, Vol. 2* (LP & CD); *I'm Tempted* on *Teenage Shutdown, Vol. 8* (LP & CD); and *Psychic* on *Strummin Mental, Vol. 2*. (VJ/MW)

The Quick

Personnel:
ERIC CARMEN	vcls, gtr	A
DANNY KLAWON	gtr	A
RANDY KLAWON	gtr	A
MICHAEL McBRIDE	drms, vcls	A

45: Ain't Nothing Gonna Stop Me/Southern Comfort (Epic 10516) 1969

Heavy passionate Cleveland pop-blast collectable mainly as this was one of Eric Carmen's pre-Raspberries ventures, following his stint with Cyrus Erie. The 'B' side in particular points towards the Stones-influenced stompers that would feature heavily in The Raspberries' repertoire.

Brothers Danny and Randy Klawon had previously been with **The Choir**. Michael McBride had been in Cyrus Erie with Eric Carmen and would be called on again for the Raspberries fourth and final album. Ken Sharp's book "Overnight Sensation: The Story Of The Raspberries" (Power Pop Press) gives further details of the numerous pre-Raspberries groups and their tangled personnel histories. (MW)

Al Quick and The Masochists

45: Theme From The Sadistic Hypnotist/? (Ciao 001) 196?

An obscure band most likely from Los Angeles because they recorded for a label which was housed on Sunset Boulevard.

Compilation appearances include *Theme From Sadistic Hypnotist* on *60's Punk E.P., Vol. 4* (7") and *Moxie Punk EP Box Set*. (VJ)

Quicksilver Messenger Service

Personnel:
JOHN CIPOLLINA	gtr	ABCDEF
DAVID FRIEBERG	bs, vcls	ABCDEFG
JIM MURRAY	hrmnca, vcls	AB
CASEY SONOBAN	drms	A

QUICKSILVER MESSENGER SERVICE - Quicksilver Messenger Service LP.

SKIP SPENCE	gtr	A
GARY DUNCAN	gtr, vcls	BC EFG H
GREG ELMORE	drms	BCDEFG H
NICKY HOPKINS	piano	DE
DINO VALENTI (aka VALENTE)	gtr, vcls	EFG H
MARK NAFTALIN	keyb'ds	FG
MARK RYAN	bs	H
CHUCK STEAKS	keyb'ds	H

ALBUMS: (up to 1975)

			HCP
1(C)	QUICKSILVER MESSENGER SERVICE	(Capitol 2904) 1968	63 -
2(C)	HAPPY TRAILS	(Capitol 120) 1969	27 -
3(D)	SHADY GROVE	(Capitol 391) 1969	25 -
4(E)	JUST FOR LOVE	(Capitol 498) 1970	27 -
5(F)	WHAT ABOUT ME?	(Capitol 630) 1971	26 -
6(H)	QUICKSILVER	(Capitol 819) 1971	114 -
7(H)	COMIN' THRU	(Capitol 1002) 1972	134 -
8(-)	SOLID SILVER	(Capitol 11 462) 1975	89 -

NB: (1) and (2) originally issued on the rainbow label, these are in the (SC) category. (1) reissued on Edsel ED 200 (1986) and on CD (EDCD 648) 2000 and (3) on Edsel XED 208 (1987). Most of these have been reissued now and are also available on CD. There's also a two CD set *Sons Of Mercury* of 31 tracks 1969-75. The band are also featured on the *Revolution Soundtrack* (UA 5185) with two tracks: *Babe I'm Gonna Leave You* and *Codine*. There have been a number of **Quicksilver** compilations including:- *Anthology* (dbl) (Capitol 11165) 1978; *Best Of..* (Capitol EURO 054 80691) 1976; *Hit Road* (EMI EURO 048 51874) 1976; *Ultimate Journey* (a U.K. compilation) (See For Miles SEECD 61) and *First Album Demos* (a bootleg which also includes live material from 1976). All of these contain a fair selection of their material. There is also an excellent 'live' album, *Maiden Of The Cancer Moon* (Psycho 10) 1983, which contains material from a 1968 concert at the Fillmore East in June 1968 and from a Pacific High recording studio broadcast also of 1968, which included a complete version of *Gold and Silver*. Unreleased, *Lost Gold And Silver* (Collectors Choice/EMI-Capitol Music CCM-109-2) is a 2-CD set, but note that the first duplicates the *Maiden Of The Cancer Moon* album.

45s:

		HCP
Pride Of Man/Dino's Song	(Capitol 2194) 1968	-
Stand By Me/Bears	(Capitol 2320) 1968	110
Who Do You Love?/ Which Do You Love?	(Capitol 2557) 1969	91
Holy Moly/Words Can't Say	(Capitol 2670) 1969	-
Shady Grove/ Three Or Four Feet From Home	(Capitol 2800) 1970	
Fresh Air/Freeway Flyer	(Capitol 2920) 1970	49
What About Me?/ Good Old Rock And Roll	(Capitol 3046) 1971	100
Hope/I Found Love	(Capitol 3233) 1971	-
Doin' Time In The USA/Changes	(Capitol 3349) 1972	-

Quicksilver were another of the finest San Francisco bands. Like **The Grateful Dead** their music was instrumentally orientated. It was led by the twin guitars of Gary Duncan and John Cipollina in true virtuoso style. Their main musical influence had been Bo Diddley. Prior to forming the band each of the members had played either independently as folk singers or as part of a band. They appeared on the Soundtrack to the film *Revolution*, although by the time the album was released Murray had left the band to go to Hawaii and study the sitar. **Dino Valenti** was also to have been included in the group but inconveniently he was busted and indisposed somewhere in a California jail. Incidentally, Elmore and Duncan had both earlier played together in an unsuccessful group - **The Brogues**.

Quicksilver contributed two tracks to *Revolution*. *Codine* was recorded by many other Bay Area groups, including **The Charlatans**. This was arguably the finest version of the song, with Duncan's vocals very much to the fore. Their second song, *Babe, I'm Gonna Leave You* provided a promising glimpse of the fine guitar work to come. The group soon developed a cult following in the Bay Area and were always in demand for 'live' gigs. Wary, perhaps, of the fate of some of their contemporaries, they seemed in no hurry to win a recording contract. Indeed, they were one of the last important San Francisco bands to sign up. Eventually Capitol made them the right offer and their two debut albums can be regarded as the purest examples of the San Francisco Sound in this era.

The first album contained some fine material. The outstanding track is probably the melodic Bo Diddley derivative *Gold And Silver*, one of the most melodic guitar suites ever, featuring some gorgeous ringing guitar work. Most of Side Two was taken up with the long, ambitious composition

QUICKSILVER MESSENGER SERVICE - What About Me LP.

The Fool which again featured adventurous guitar work from Duncan and Cipollina. Other tracks such as *Light Your Windows* and *Dino's Song* featured mellow vocal harmonies. The drug influence in their music was clear too.

Some of **Quicksilver**'s albums have astonishing covers. *Happy Trails* is possibly the best of all. Many critics also regarded the album as one of the best rock, let alone psychedelic rock, albums ever made. A 'live' recording Side One is composed entirely of the *Who Do You Love? Suite*, a guitar masterpiece. However, this is overshadowed by Cipollina's decisive, cutting work on some of the songs on Side Two, particularly *Mona*.

Meanwhile, **Dino Valenti**, who wrote the classic hippie anthem *Get Together*, had been released from jail and started gigging and writing songs, eventually recording a solo album for Epic in October 1968. In January 1969 **Valenti** persuaded Duncan to leave the group and accompany him to New York to form a band called The Outlaws. But they failed to find the personnel they wanted and returned to rejoin the band a year later.

With Duncan gone, Elmore, Frieberg and Cipollina were left in limbo for a while until pianist Nicky Hopkins, having left Jeff Beck, joined the band. As a foursome they recorded *Shady Grove*, but without Duncan their distinctive twin guitar sound had gone. The album was disappointing in comparison to their two earlier gems, although it still contained some fine songs. The virtuoso keyboard playing of Nicky Hopkins on tracks like *Joseph's Coat* and *Edward the Mad Shirt Grinder* was particularly noteworthy. Also of interest were the sleepy slow acid-influenced compositions like *Flute Song* and *Flashing Lonesome*. The sentiments of the title track - *Let's Quit The Pressures of City Living For Greener Pastures* - were an essential part of the hippie philosophy.

"I used to walk on the city streets
Now I wander far and wide
I never found my happiness
Till I moved to the countryside..."

and later in the same song:

"If you've been watching the city streets
They don't seem to get much greener
But I know where we're going to
Our heads will feel much cleaner..."
(from *Shady Grove*)

With both **Valenti** and Duncan in the band, they got back on the road as a sextet and started work on their fourth album *Just For Love*. However, Nicky Hopkins left the band in July 1970 before its release to join The Rolling Stones and do session work. This album, and part of the next, was recorded in Hawaii. The group was dominated more and more by **Valenti**'s laid-back vocals - you either love them or hate them. Unfortunately, the diminished influence of Duncan and Cipollina meant the demise of their celebrated acid-rock guitar sound. This cost **Quicksilver** many of their previously diehard fans. Nevertheless, in its own way *Just For Love* was a fine album. The opening and closing track *Wolf Run* was a successful attempt to re-create the sounds of the jungle, whilst *Just For Love* also in two parts, following and preceding *Wolf Run*, demonstrated **Valenti**'s vocal dexterity. Among the tracks sandwiched between these were two classics. The drug song *Fresh Air*:-

"Have another hit of California sunshine..."

was also performed by the band in the *Last Days Of The Fillmore* Soundtrack. But over-shadowing it was the mellow *Gone Again* (an early insight into the laid back West Coast music of the seventies?).

The follow-up album *What About Me?* marked the arrival of Jose Reyes (congas, vcls) and was also Cipollina's last with the band. The title track poses the question of how the U.S. Establishment could come to terms with the growing rebellion of American youth:

"I feel like a stranger
In the land where I was born
And I live just like an outlaw
I'm always on the run
And though you may be stronger now
My time will come along
You keep adding to my numbers
As you shoot my people down..."
(from *What About Me?*)

It also contained two beautiful love songs *Baby, Baby* and *Long Haired Lady* which, together with *All In My Mind*, captured **Valenti**'s vocals at their best. As **Valenti**'s influence increased, Cipollina's, unfortunately, diminished, with the rather lame instrumental *Local Colour* his only credit on this album. This probably influenced his departure in October 1970. In the Fall of 1971, however, he started a new group, **Copperhead**, which recalled the kind of sound associated with the early **Quicksilver** - rock and roll with intricate instrumentals and a trace of harshness. This included Jim Murray and Nicky Hopkins for a while. **Copperhead** successfully captured this sound on their 1973 Columbia album, particularly on tracks like *Roller Derby Star*, *Kibitzer*, *Spin Spin*, *Wang Dang Do* and the excellent *Making A Monster*.

September 1971 brought further disaster for **Quicksilver** when David Frieberg was convicted for marijuana possession for the third time, fined $200 and jailed for two months. He did not rejoin the band after his release, but did session work, playing on **Mickey Hart**'s solo album *Rolling Thunder* before ending up with **Jefferson Airplane**. When Frieberg became involuntarily indisposed the band was halfway through a new album. Mark Ryan, (ex-**Country Joe and the Fish**) was brought in to replace Frieberg on bass and Chuck Steaks was introduced on organ.

This line-up recorded the band's next two efforts, *Quicksilver* and *Comin' Thru*, which showed it to be a mere shadow of its former self. Three years later, in 1975, Duncan, Cipollina, Frieberg, Elmore and **Valenti** got together for an unsuccessful reunion album *Solid Silver*. Nonetheless, **Quicksilver**'s acid guitar sound on those first two albums was the finest to come out of San Francisco and their next three albums also contained some excellent material.

John Cipollina went on to play in numerous other Bay Area bands. Born a chronic asthmatic, he also suffered from emphysema in later life and tragically died after being admitted to hospital during 1989. David Frieberg went on to play for Jefferson Starship.

Compilation appearances have included:- *Got My Mojo Working* and *The Fool* on *The California Christmas Album* (LP) and *Smokestack Lightning*, *Pride Of Man* and *Gold and Silver* on *California New Years*; *Pride Of Man* on *Psychedelic Visions* (CD); and *Pride Of Man* and *Dino's Song* on *Rock A Delics* (LP). (VJ)

Quill

Personnel:	DAN COLE	A
	JOHN COLE	A
	ROGER NORTH	A
	BILL ROGERS	A
	PHIL THAYER	A

ALBUM: 1 THE QUILL (Cotillion SD 9017) 1970 -

At present this is very minor psychedelic/progressive item but it could grow in significance. The opening cut *Thumbnail Screwdriver* is a fine guitar progressive and *The Tube Exuding* captures the band at their most psychedelic. Compared to these the final track on Side One *They Live The Life* is very disappointing. On Side Two *Yellow Butterfly* is a slice of mellow psychedelia, but the remainder of the record is rather ordinary.

The band came from Massachusetts and the two Coles attended Mount Hermon Academy where they were in prep-rock outfit **The Knights** from 1964 to 1965, appearing on their *Off Campus* album. (VJ/MW/AH)

Paul Quinlan S.J.

Personnel:	PAUL QUINLAN	vcls, gtr	A
	RICH REGAN	gtr	A
	STEVE SEERY	perc	A

ALBUM: 1(A) RUN LIKE A DEER (F.E.L. Church 7101-M) 1967 ?

Subtitled "Folk-Rock Psalms", this album is one of the first attempts at creating Christian folk-rock, aimed at "the young Christians of the Sixties". The liner notes say that "the music roams from folk sound to lush, smooth Beatle-like harmonies, to hard-rock sound". Their definition of hard-rock was clearly not the same as Led Zeppelin's, but the album is interesting overall. (SR)

The Quinstrells

Personnel:	SHEP COOKE	bs	A
	LARRY COX	vcls	A
	TERRY LEE	gtr	A
	PETE SCHUYLER	drms	A
	TOM WALKER	gtr, vcls	A

45: I Got A Girl/Tell Her (Moxie MRC 105) 1965

This name was used briefly by **The Intruders** in 1965 to record the above 45. They did not gig under this name and by the end of the year had become **The Dearly Beloved**. The 'A' side of the 45, which was recorded at Audio Sound Recorders in Phoenix, Arizona, began with a fifties style intro leading into a sixties love song with wild leads and four part harmonies. An alternate take of the song from 1966 appears on the album *Rough Diamonds: History Of Garage Band Music, Vol. 6 - The Dearly Beloved* and *Think Of The Good Times* (LP). (VJ/MW)

Quintette Plus

| 45s: | Shop Around / Grits And Grease | (SVR 1003) 1965 |
| | Work Song / Summertime | (SVR 1004) 1965 |

An instrumental teen quintet from Detroit who recorded two workman-like 45s, bolstered by Motown staff musicians - according to *S.V.R. Rock Hits Of The Sixties* (LP & CD) which features *Work Song*. Other compilation coverage has included: *Shop Around*, an unreleased version of *Grits And Grease*, *Work Song* and *Summertime* on *The Cicadelic 60's, Vol. 8* (CD). (MW)

Jimmy Rabbit and The Karats

45s:	Pushover/Wait And See	(Knight 1049)	1965
	Pushover/Wait And See	(Southern Sound 200)	1965
α	Wishy Washy Woman/My Girl	(Knight 1052)	1965
α	Wishy Washy Woman/My Girl	(Josie 947)	1965

NB: α as by **Jimmy Rabbit**.

One of the Texan singer's sixties outfits. *Pushover* is a highly infectious punker.

Jimmy released a further 45 with members of **Mouse and The Traps**, covering **Count Five**'s *Psychotic Reaction*, under the name **Positively 13 O'clock**.

Compilation appearances have included: *Pushover* on *Texas Flashback (The Best Of)* (CD), *Texas Flashbacks, Vol. 2* (LP & CD) and *Flashback, Vol. 2* (LP); and *My Girl* on *Follow That Munster, Vol. 2* (LP). (VJ/MW)

Michael Rabon and Choctaw

Personnel:	RANDY FOUTS	keyb'ds	A
	JERRY McDONALD	bs	A
	MICHAEL RABON	ld vcls, gtr	A
	JIM WRIGHT	drms	A

ALBUM:	1(A)	MICHAEL RABON AND CHOCTAW	(Uni/Abnak 73102) 1971 -

Rabon and Wright were previously in **The Five Americans** and stayed together when their old group disbanded. Produced by **Rabon** and Robin Hood Brians, this album offers only original compositions, lying between early seventies rock-pop and country-rock. Not bad, but nothing really important.

One of the songs, *Texas Sparrow*, was re-recorded in 1973 by Gladstone, another Texan group featuring Randy Fouts.

Michael Rabon also produced the second album by **Jon and Robin**. (SR)

Racket Squad

Personnel:	SONNY DI NUNZIO	vcls, keyb'ds, gtr, tpt	A
	GENE	drms, perc	A
	HOP	ld gtr	A
	RONNIE	bs, tenorsax	A

ALBUMS:	1(A)	THE RACKET SQUAD	(Jubilee JGS 8015)	1968 -
	2(A)	CORNERS OF YOUR MIND	(Jubilee JGS 8026)	1969 -

NB: (1) and (2) reissued on one CD (Collectables COL-CD-6217).

45s:	Hung Up/Higher Than High	(Jubilee 5591)	1967
	Romeo And Juliet/Little Red Wagon	(Jubilee 5601)	1967
	The Loser/No Fair At All	(Jubilee 5613)	1968
	Let's Dance To The Beat Of My Heart/ Higher Than High	(Jubilee 5623)	1968
	That's How Much I Love My Baby/Movin' In	(Jubilee 5628)	1968
	Suburban Life/A Loser	(Jubilee 5638)	1968
	I'll Never Forget Your Love/ Maybe Tomorrow	(Jubilee 5657)	1969
	In Your Arms/Coal Town	(Jubilee 5682)	1969
	Roller Coaster Ride/Coal Town	(Jubilee 5694)	1970

NB: Most of the above released as double-A promos.

From Apollo, Pennsylvania, this band were previously known as **The Fenways** and released numerous 45s between 1964 and 1966 including some with other acts (Tawny Sims, the Vogues) and under assumed names (Townsmen, Four Chaps). Certainly no teenage garage combo, they look like a bunch of seasoned session men cobbled together and told to try and look and sound 'groovy'!

THE RACKET QUAD - The Racket Squad LP.

Technically competent, they at times lacked that certain passion. Covers include *(Just Like) Romeo And Juliet*, *No Fair At All* (**Association**) *Let It Out* (*Let It All Hang Out*)(**Hombres**), *Get Out Of My Life Woman* and *Little Wing* (**Hendrix**). The latter track is probably one of their best if you ignore the vocals - a mellow version with fine non-distorted guitar. Their second album is the stronger of the two. *The Minstrel* has good effects and a certain charm, *Sweet Little Smoke* is quite a successful sensitive ballad, the title track is a good slice of pop-psych and *You Turn Me On* is a reasonable attempt at the same. *Ain't Nobody Gonna Love You* and *Suburban Life* raise the tempo, but the reprise to *Get Out Of My Life Woman* is simply awful.

Sonny Di Nunzio went on to Sebastian.

For the full story check out Mike Kuzmin's well-researched book on sixties Pennsylvania, "Sounds From The Woods". (VJ/MW)

Mark Radice

ALBUM:	1	MARK RADICE	(Paramount) 1972 -

45s:	Save Your Money/Wooden Girl	(RCA 47-9420)	1972
	You Took The Words Right Out/ Natural Morning	(Decca 32349)	1968
	Ten Thousand Year Old Blues/ Three Cheers	(Decca 32411)	1968
	Richest Man In The World/ Girl By The Meter	(Decca 32525)	1969
	Your Love Is Like Fire/Hey My Love	(Paramount 0170)	1972

A forgotten folk-rock and pop singer with a significant output. (SR)

Raga and The Talas

Personnel incl:	RANDY MYERS	ld vcls	A

45:	My Group And Me/ For Old Times Sake	(World Pacific 77847)	1966

A Los Angeles-based mid-sixties studio project. Randy Myers was Jackie DeShannon's brother and she wrote and produced both tracks. It's an aggressive folk-rocker, which is rather discordant and suffers from slighty inadequate vocals.

My Group And Me has subsequently been compiled on *Pebbles, Vol. 10* (LP). (VJ/BG)

RAIN - Live, Christmas Night LP.

The Raggamuffins

45s:	Four Days Of Rain/	
	It Wasn't Happening At All	(Seville SEV 141) 1967
	Hate To See A Good Thing Have To Go/	
	Parade Of Uncertainty	(Seville SEV 143) 1967

Four Days... is a top-drawer folk-rocker with vibrant vocals and dramatic guitar chords - sounds more like San Francisco than New Bedford, Massachusetts. The flip's lighter airy folk-pop. *Hate...* continues in the lighter vein, but *Parade...* returns to form with **Airplane**-like vocals and more intense guitar. Immensely appealing. (MW)

Raging Winds

Personnel:	BILL	A
	BOB	A
	DAVE	A
	PATRICK HUTCHIN	A
	JOE	A

A quartet from Dayton, Ohio whose recorded legacy is only available on *WONE, The Dayton Scene* (Prism PR-1966), the souvenir album of the WONE-sponsored three-day Daytonian battle of the bands in 1966, where the top twelve bands get one cut apiece.

Tell Me Who is their selection. Ploughing the moody Merseybeat furrow of The Searchers, it sits well alongside the contributions of **The X-cellents**, **Warlocks** and **Dawks**. (MW)

Raik's Progress

Personnel incl:	TONIO KRIKORIAN	A

45:	Why Did You Rob Us, Tank?/	
	Sewer Rat Love Chant	(Liberty F-55930) 1966

Both sides of this Fresno band's 45 feature chiming psychedelic Eastern-influenced folk-rock at its best. The 'A' side, *Why Did You Rob Us Tank?*, was composed by Krikorian, Olson, Scott, Shapazian and Van Maaoh, and the flip by John Kates. It was produced by Dallas Smith.

Krikorian, of **Raik's Progress**, later become better known as Tonio K.

Compilation appearances include: *Why Did You Rob Us Tank?* on *U-Spaces: Psychedelic Archaeology Vol. 1* (CDR); and *Sewer Rat Love Chant* on *Beyond The Calico Wall* (CD). (MW/PS)

Rain

ALBUM:	1	LIVE, CHRISTMAS NIGHT	
			(Whazoo! USR 3046) 1971 R2

NB: (1) had a limited numbered reissue of 300 in 1991.

A local New York area band. Their album contained lots of heavy bar-band covers of Stones numbers and is worth checking out, if that's your bag. (VJ/CF)

Rain

Personnel poss. included:		LARRY SELF	

45s:	ESP/Outta My Life	(A.P.I. 336) 1966
	ESP/Outta My Life	(London 107) 1966
	Hear You Cry/Substitute	(A.P.I. 337) 1967
	Hear You Cry/Substitute	(London 111) 1967

A Hollywood, California-based outfit. *ESP* was a rework of The Pretty Things' *LSD*, whilst *Outta My Life* mimics *I Can Only Give You Everything*. The *ESP* 45 was produced by Brian Ross of Original Sound/**Music Machine/Friendly Torpedos** fame.

It's thought that this outfit may in fact be an embryonic **Big Brother Featuring Ernie Joseph**.

Compilation appearances have included: *Hear You Cry* on *Turds On A Bum Ride, Vol. 3* (CD); *Outta My Life* on *Ya Gotta Have Moxie, Vol. 2* (Dble CD); *Outta My Life* and *E.S.P.* on *Boulders, Vol. 2* (LP); and *E.S.P.* on *Highs In The Mid-Sixties, Vol. 20* (LP), *Mayhem And Psychosis, Vol. 2* (LP) and *Mayhem And Psychosis, Vol. 2* (CD). (VJ/MW/MM)

Rain

Personnel:	COBB BUSSINGER	vcls, organ, pianos, celeste, synth	A
	RIC CRINITI	bs, vcls	A
	MICHAEL KENNEDY	ld gtr, vcls	A
	FRANK SCHALLIS	drms, vcls, acoustic gtr	A

ALBUM:	1(A)	RAIN	(Project 3 PR 5072 SD) 1972

For those into early seventies U.K. progressive rock like Yes, Genesis etc., this may interest you. Shades of light and dark, jazzy signatures, oodles of keyboards, the odd guitar solo and harmony vocals. Not many American bands embraced the prog-rock genre - this outfit occasionally bask in it though they tend towards lighter moods rather than heavy pomposity. All four members were previously with Rock Island, suggesting they were a Chicago-area band. (MW/CF)

Rain

Personnel incl:	JAN EGELSON	A
	NORMAN	A
	SAGNER	A
	SCHUBERT	A

45:	Take It Away/City Lovin'	(MGM 13622) 1966

Apparently unconnected to the many other Rain's... any information on this act would be much appreciated - the personnel listed comes from the 45s song-writing credits, although Jan Egelson was definitely in the band and later became a film director in Cambridge, Massachusetts. (MW/DC)

Rain

45:	Show Me The Road Home/	

Funky Junky Blues   (Paramount 0087) 1970

Another unconnected and unknown Rain... email us if you can help fill in the gaps!

The Rain

45s: Love Me And Be Glad / Little Boy Blue   (Webb 5667) 1967
London / I'm Free   (Kanwic 151) 1967

Another **Rain** - from Osage City, Kansas. Their earthy punker *I'm Free* with its moody fuzz break and underpinned by some Kinks-like riffing can be heard on Tom Tourville's *Midwest Garage Band Series - Kansas* (CD) and *Basementsville! U.S.A.* (LP). *London* is revisited on *Leaving It All Behind* (LP). (MW)

Rainbow

Personnel:	DARRELL DEVLIN	drms	A
	BOB GAY	bs	A
	W DAVID MOHR	keyb'ds	A
	HARRY VAVELA	ld gtr	A

ALBUM: 1(A) AFTER THE STORM   (GNP Crescendo GNPS 2049) 1968 SC

NB: (1) has been reissued on CD (Lyrical Sound Device CW 5003).

A short-lived Los Angeles-based project. Their album has a great cover. The contents incorporate several different styles. All the music is written by W. David Mohr and much of it is heavy with lots of fuzz guitar reminiscent of **Iron Butterfly**. It ranges from heavy-soul (*I Just Want To Make Love To You*); hippie-pop (*Leaf Clover*); a West Coast sound which seems in places distinctly similar to **Fever Tree**'s *San Francisco Girls* (well-spotted, Max!); pretentious pop with lots of keyboards (*Midnight Candle*); gimmickry with lots of sound effects (*Does Your Head Need Straightening?*) to the very pleasant *After The Storm*, which has some delightful soothing piano. (VJ)

The Rainbow Band

ALBUM: 1 THE RAINBOW BAND   (Elektra EKS-74092) 1971 -

45: Simple Song/Midnight Sun   (Elektra 45730) 1971

An obscure hippie duo, the front cover shows them wearing oriental clothes, one of them meditating in lotus position! (SR)

RAINBOW - After The Storm CD.

Rainbow Press

Personnel:	MARC ELLIS	gtr	A
	JOE GROFF	vcls, perc	A
	LARRY MILTON	keyb'ds, gtr	A
	CHARLIE OSBORN	keyb'ds	A
	DAVE TROUP	bs, vcls	A
	BILLY VERGIN	drms	A

ALBUMS: 1(A) THERE'S A WAR ON   (Mr G 9003) 1968 R1
2(A) SUNDAY FUNNIES   (Mr G 9004) 1969 R1

NB: (1) and (2) have been reissued on one CD (Hipschaft no #) 199?

45s: There's A War On/Better Way   (Mr G 817) 1968
The Last Platoon/Great White Whale   (Mr G 821) 1969

Both albums are excellent soft rock with touches of psychedelia, particularly the first one, which is beginning to become a minor collectable. (VJ)

Rainbow Promise

Personnel:	RIC BOWERS	gtr	A
	LEONARD BRANNON	bs	A
	DENNIS JONES	drms	A
	STEVE POWELL	gtr	A
	RICHARD SLATON	gtr	A

ALBUM: 1(A) RAINBOW PROMISE   (New Wine - Wine Press LPS 259-01) 1972 R3

NB: (1) reissued as Steve Powell and Rainbow Promise (Wine Skin) 1975 R2.

This is religious rock very much in the same mould as **Agape**. The front cover quotes from the book of Revelations and depicts Christ surrounded by seven candlesticks. There are some naff country tracks on this extremely rare album which does have some good tracks. What might interest readers is the fuzzy guitar work on *Someone You Need* and the more melodic guitarwork on *Get Ready* and *I've Got The Rebirth*.

The band was based in Texas, their album was recorded in Illinois and released on a Missouri label. (VJ/CF)

Raindear Army

45: Subterranean Sunset/?   (Ledger 18811) 1968

From Peoria, Illinois. *Subterranean Sunset* is a strange and disjointed slab of psychedelic rock that kicks off with a bubbling cauldron of keyboards and fuzz, veers off into strident hard-rock territory before fragmenting with a trippy break and floating flute interludes. A joint is a pre-requisite here. (MW)

The Rainmakers

45s: Jeanie Green Bean/
My Home Town Girl   (Cross-Winds CW 101) 1965
Sinner Man/The Treasure Of Your Love   (Bonjo B 3152) c1966

The first 45 on a Lake Elsinore, California, label contains catchy garagey folk-beat, especially the moody flip with its finger ringing break, credited to Tim Elmer and Dale Harris. *Sinner Man* and Barry DeVorzon's *Treasure...* are covered in a tough folk-rock vein with almost raucous vocals. All in all, two worthy platters of the genre by an obscure New Jersey band (far from the label's locale) about whom we should know more. (MW)

The Rainmakers

Personnel?:	D. EICKENROTH		A
	?? RANEY		A

45s: Don't Be Afraid /
I Won't Turn Away Now   (Discotheque 875) 196?

House Of The Rising Sun /	
Do You Feel It	(Lee no # (matrix 867L-9178)) 196?
Tell Her No / You're Not The Only One	(Phalanx 1029) 1966

Lower-profile Michigan garage out of Traverse City. The Lee 45 features some decent fuzz guitar work, but the Phalanx 45 is their best. *Tell Her No* is not the Zombies classic but a bittersweet garage-ballad with sultry vocals punctuated by the odd blast of rasping fuzz. The flip is more overtly Searchers-influenced jangly garage-beat sounds with keening harmonies. A true nugget.

Compilation appearances include: *Tell Her No* and *You're The Only One* on *Time Won't Change My Mind* (LP). (MW/KBn)

Bob Rains

ALBUM: 1 LIGHTEN UP PEOPLE
(Joint Artists Records JA-331) 1975 ?

A scarce album of folk-rock with some psychedelic influences. Joint Artists also released the album of **Bill Clint**. (SR)

Rainy Days

Personnel incl: ALAN HAFELI   gtr   A

45s:	I Can Only Give You Everything /	
	Go On And Cry	(Panik 7566) 1966
	Turn On Your Lovelight / Go On And Cry	(Panik 7542) 1967

From the University of Detroit high school in Detroit, Michigan, this band rendered one of the better versions of *I Can Only Give You Everything*. Guitarist Alan Hafeli was 21 when this was recorded and the remaining of the band were still at high school, the youngest being their 16-year old singer.

A third single was recorded but never released.

I Can Only Give You Everything has also been compiled on *Mayhem & Psychosis, Vol. 3* (LP), *Mayhem & Psychosis, Vol. 2* (CD), *Michigan Mixture, Vol. 2* (LP), and *Sixties Archive, Vol. 7* (CD). (MW/JT/DGn)

Rainy Daze

Personnel:	MAC FERRIS	ld gtr	A
	SAM FULLER	bs	A
	KIP GILBERT	drms	A
	TIM GILBERT	vcls, gtr	A
	BOB HECKENDORF	keyb'ds	A

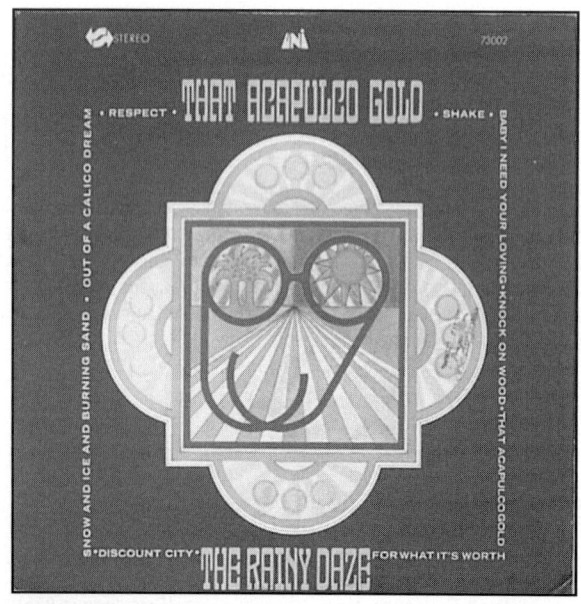

RAINY DAZE - That Acapulco Gold LP.

ALBUM:	1(A) THAT ACAPULCO GOLD	(UNI 73002) 1967	SC
			HCP
45s:	That Acapulco Gold/		
	In My Mind Lives A Forest	(Chicory 404) 1967	-
	That Acapulco Gold/		
	In My Mind Lives A Forest	(UNI 55002) 1967	70
	Discount City/Good Morning Mr. Smith	(UNI 55011) 1967	-
	Fe Fi Fo Fum/Stop Sign	(UNI 55026) 1967	-
	Blood Of Oblivion/Stop Sign	(UNI 55026) 1967	-
	Make Me Laugh/		
	My Door Is Always Open	(White Whale 279) 1968	-

A great pop-punk-psychedelic outfit from Denver, Colorado. Only the first 45 appears on their album, which is recommended. They first formed in 1965 when they specialised in playing beat and R&B and they were a regular attraction at local frat parties. Almost unbelievably they were unearthed by Phil Spector who signed them to a management contract and a giant publicity campaign was planned but never really materialised.

A year or so later *That Acapulco Gold* appeared on the local IP label and Frank Slay, a local producer, bought the rights and released it on his Chicory label. However, it was quickly leased to UNI and became the band's best known song making the No. 70 spot. Although they never again equalled this commercial success they continued to make some excellent 45s. One of the best, a beautifully crafted piece of pop-psych was originally released as *Fe Fi Fo Fum*, but was almost immediately withdrawn and reissued with a different title *Blood Of Oblivion*, even securing a U.K. release (Polydor 56737).

Tim Gilbert, the main songwriter, also released a solo 45 *Early October/If We Stick Together* (UNI 55045) 1967 - folkie fare which has been compared to **Tim Buckley**. He would go into songwriting and his compositions (with J. Carter) would appear on **Hardwater** (fellow Coloradans The Astronauts in disguise), **Yankee Dollar**, **Horses** and **Strawberry Alarm Clock** albums.

Their album includes the first 45 and *Discount City*, a kind of bluesy honky tonk, which was the 'A' side of their third 45. Aside from an almost four minute medley of *Shake, Knock On Wood* and *Respect*, other notable songs include a pretty good cover of Stephen Stills' *For What Its Worth*, a fuzzy *Taxman*-like song called *Weatherman* and an Eastern-style slice of psychedelia, *Snow And Ice And Burning Sand*. However, the album's finest moment was *In My Mind Lives A Forest* (the flip to their first 45) - an exquisite slice of pop-psychedelia. Recommended.

Compilation appearances have included: *Absurd Bird* on *Kicks & Chicks* (LP); *Make Me Laugh* on *Of Hopes And Dreams & Tombstones* (LP) and *Psychedelic Unknowns, Vol. 7* (LP & CD); *That Acapulco Gold* on *Psychedelic Visions* (CD); *In My Mind Lives A Forest* on *Psychedellc Archives, Vol. 6* and *Acid and Flowers* (CD); and *Fe Fi Fo Fum* on *Highs In The Mid Sixties, Vol. 18* (LP). (VJ/MW)

Ram

Personnel:	DENNIS CARBONE	piano, tamb, vcls	A
	JOHN DEMARTINO	sax, flute, clarinet	A
	RALPH DEMARTINO	gtr, vcls	A
	MICHAEL RODRIGUEZ	bs, vcls	A
	?? STEELER	drms	A

ALBUM: 1(A) WHERE? (IN CONCLUSION) (Polydor 24-5013) 1972 SC
NB: (1) reissued on CD (Lizard Records LR 0710-2).

This heavy progressive album by a New York progressive outfit is becoming rare and in demand. It consists of five long tracks (one occupies the whole of one side). The music's full of complex arrangements, with lots of mellotron and flute as well as some vicious guitar leads. (VJ/NK)

Ramadas

Personnel incl: NEAL FORD   A

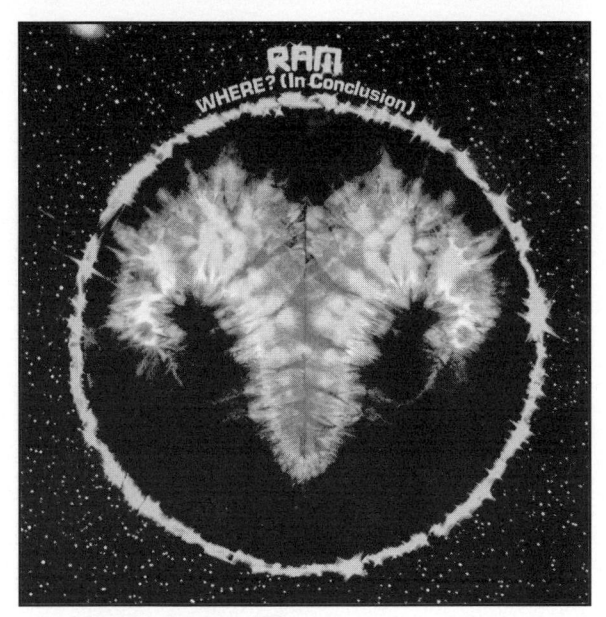

RAM - Where? (In Conclusion) CD.

45s:	Teenage Dream / My Angel Eyes	(Philips 40097) 1963
	Summer Steady / Lonely Tears	(Philips 40117) 1963
	Walking Down The Hall / I'm Gonna Be Blue	(New World 2000) 1964
	Cindy / Sweet Valentine	(New World 2007) 1964
	Life Is So Tough / The Very First Time	(New World 2008) 1965

Pre-Invasion style teen ballads, not garage, by a Houston outfit whose only relevance here is that **Neal Ford** would later team up with the Fanatics. (MW)

Ramatam

Personnel:	APRIL LAWTON	ld gtr	AB
	MITCH MITCHELL	drms	A
	MIKE PINERA	gtr	A
	RUSS SMITH	bs, vcls	A
	TOMMY SULLIVAN	keyb'ds, reeds, vcls	AB
	JIMMY WALKER	perc, vcls	B

ALBUMS:	1(A)	RAMATAM	(Atlantic SD 7236) 1972 -
	2(B)	IN APRIL CAME THE DAWNING OF THE RED SUNS	(Atlantic SD 7261) 1973 -

Mike Pinera was of **Blues Image** and **Iron Butterfly** fame and Mitch Mitchell was the ex-**Jimi Hendrix Experience** drummer.

Their first album, recorded in Florida, was mainstream rock which veered towards hard-rock and jazz-rock in places. There's a good guitar solo from April Lawton on *She's A Woman* and also a brass section.

After the first album Pinera departed for The New Cactus Band and later formed Thee Image. The second album, recorded by new line-up (B), is much better. It was recorded in New York. Highlights include *The Land/Rainy Sunday Evening*, an imaginative melancholic song in a progressive style with great string orchestration; *I Can Only Love You*, a fast tempo song with horns and a great guitar solo by Lawton and *Stars And Stripes Forever*, which has a carnival-like orchestration. There are also a couple of hard-rockers and some fine fifties style material like **Rhinoceros**. (VJ/GG)

The Ramrods

Personnel:	TOM CARTER	ld gtr	ABCD
	L. NOWICKI?		A
	R. SELBY?		A
	CATHY KAHLER	vcls	B
	PATSY STEVENS	vcls	C
	BOB HEY	bs	C
	JOHNNY BOGGS	keyb'ds, vcls	C
	DAVE CLELLAND	drms	C

CD:	1 SHOUT	(Gear Fab GF-170) 2001

NB: (1) by **The Soundsations**, but including 15 tracks by **The Ramrods**.

45s: (selective)	Flyin' Saucer Twist (instr) / Twistin' Boogie (instr)	(Northway Sound 1005) 1961
	Teen Love / Frankie And Johnny (instr)	(Carram JC 102) 1962
	Runaround Boy / Cotton Candy	(Carram JC 103/4) 1962
	Love's A Game / El Cumbanchero	(Carram JC 106) 1963
	I Remember / You Know I Love You	(Fenton 2014) 1965

Formed in 1961 by a 13-year old Tom Carter, this Kalamazoo, Michigan, band released several 45s on local labels and performed on the teen night club circuit. Carter composed/co-composed almost all their early output - initially instrumentals before they graduated to cute early-sixties teen-pop with the addition of a female vocalist.

By 1964, the personnel had stablilised with line-up 'C' above. The next year they released a 45 on the now-revered Fenton label - the top side features Sonny and Cher style vocals and background chimes. Both sides were composed by Boggs, who'd taken on the mantle of main songwriter as they embraced post-Invasion styles.

At the start of 1966 Stevens, Hey, Boggs and Clelland left en bloc to form **The Soundsations**. Tom Carter soldiered on but no further records appeared.

The reissue of the **Soundsations**' album *Shout* reunites them by adding the complete recorded legacy of **The Ramrods** (15 tracks). (MW/RM)

Elliott Randall

Personnel:	TERRY ADAMS	keyb'ds	A
	GEORGE ANDREWS	piano	A
	ALLEN HERMAN	drms	AB
	ANDY MUSON	bs	A
	BOB PIAZZA	bs	A
	POT	piano	A
	ELLIOTT RANDALL	gtr, vcls	AB
	GARY KING	bs	B

ALBUMS: (up to 1973)	1(A)	RANDALL'S ISLAND	(Polydor 24 4044) 1970 -
	2(B)	ROCK'N'ROLL CITY	(Polydor 5026) 1973 -

NB: (1) also released in the UK (Polydor 2489 004).

From New York, and originally in **Tingling Mother's Circus**, guitarist **Elliott Randall** is mostly known for his session work in the studios during the seventies. He also released some solo albums recorded with local musicians like Terry Adams (**NRBQ**), Bob Piazza (**Grinder's Switch**) and Pot (**Dave Van Ronk**). Any additional information welcomed! (SR)

Terry Randall

45:	S.O.S./Tell Her	(Valiant 756) 1966

This previously unknown artist wrote *S.O.S.*, a classic teen protest song, which was his musical comment on the series of Sunset Strip riots of November 1966, and then faded back into obscurity.

The 'A' side can also be found on *Pebbles Vol. 8* (CD) and *Highs In The Mid-Sixties, Vol. 2* (LP). (VJ)

Randy and The Holidays

Personnel incl:	?? ACREE	A
	RANDY LITTLE	A

45:	Paul Revere 250 / Living Doll	(Hickory 1465) 1967

A group from Alabama whose pounding, fuzzy popper *Paul Revere 250* can be heard on *Psychedelic States: Alabama Vol. 1* (CD). The uncompiled flip, composed by Randy Little, is bouncy pop-beat. (MW)

Randy and The Radiants

Personnel:	HOWARD CALHOUN	bs	AB
	MIKE GARDNER	drms	AB
	RANDY HASPEL	gtr, vcls	AB
	ED MARSHALL	ld gtr	AB
	BOB SIMON	vcls	AB
	BILL SLAIS	sax	AB
	TONY ROSSINI	vcls	B

45s:	Peek-A-Bo/Mountain's High	(Sun 395) 1965
	My Way Of Thinking/The Truth From My Eyes	(Sun 398) 1965
	Just Like You/I Need A Vacation	(ABC 12394) 1977

This Memphis group had started around 1962, but college split the band in 1966 soon after they'd released their 45s. They were part of the same scene as the Devilles (pre-**Box Tops**), the **Gentrys**, the **Scepters** and **Tommy Burk and The Counts**. With the **Jesters**, they were one of the few garage outfits on Sun (Rossini had recorded several solo 45s on Sun and as part of the duo **Toni and Terri**). Their first single was produced by Sam Philips. On the second, *My Way Of Thinking* is a rip-off of the Kinks *You Really Got Me* and was written by Donna Weiss (later co-writer of *Bette Davies Eyes*). The group was very popular locally and a tentative tour of the South was planned but finally collapsed.

Members got back together again in the late seventies and even got to release another 45. Randy Haspel went on to become a successful songwriter for Rufus Thomas, George Jones and Moe Bandy, while Bob Simon worked in the Memphis studios. In the nineties, the group was still playing occasionally in the local clubs.

Compilation appearances have included *My Way Of Thinking* on *Boulders, Vol. 9* (LP) and *Ya Gotta Have Moxie, Vol. 2* (Dble CD). (MW/RH/SR)

Randy and The Rest

45s:	Confusion/Dreaming	(Jade JA 767) 1967
	The Vacuum/Dreamin'	(SSS International 720) 196?
	The Vacuum (2:12)/	
	The Vacuum (2:48)	(SSS International 720 PROMO) 196?

These are the work of an Alabama outfit. *Confusion* is poppy psychedelia complete with sounds effects, the flip is straight pop. *The Vacuum* starts off as a reasonably normal 'pop' tune, before the vacuum cleaner 'solo' and war siren/bugle kicks in leading to a freak-out style ending. This track is also one of the more 'normal' entries on the hilarious *Only In America* (CD). (VJ/MW)

Randy and The Ring

Personnel incl:	NEIL SCHWARTZ	A
	RANDY SCHWARTZ	A

45:	Good Time Merry-Go-Round/	
	Caverns Of My Mind	(Tangy SS 101) 1967

Another obscure California outfit with a passable uptempo garage-pop ditty backed by a tougher outing that loosens up towards the end, but is not psychedelic despite its title. (MW)

Rapid Richard Group

Personnel incl:	RICHARD GREENBURG	gtr, bs	A
	MIKE JUNGKMAN	drms	A
	(FRED CABAN	keyb'ds	A)
	(JIM HESS	keyb'ds	A)

ALBUM:	1(A)	DID I SEE WHAT I THOUGHT I SAW?	
			(Home Spun RG 1000) 1977 ?

Rapid Richard was in fact Richard Greenburg and his backing musicians include three members of **Agape**, the Christian hard-psych group. This rare Christian hard-prog private pressing comprises several long tracks with lots of inventive guitars and keyboards. (SR/KSt)

TOM RAPP - Sunforest CD.

Tom Rapp

Personnel incl:	TOM RAPP	vcls, gtr	ABC

ALBUMS:	1(A)	FAMILIAR SONGS	(Reprise MS 2069) 1972 -
	2(B)	STARDANCER	(Blue Thumb BTS-44) 1972 -
	3(C)	SUNFOREST	(Blue Thumb BTS-56) 1973 -

NB: (3) reissued on CD (Edsel EDCD 548) 1998.

After **Pearls Before Swine**, **Tom Rapp** started recording under his own name, although his first solo album was largely comprised of re-recordings of songs from his earlier albums (hence its title). Produced by Peter Edminston, the second was recorded in Nashville with all the local musicians and is clearly disappointing, although it contains new songs and uses another Breughel The Elder painting on its sleeve.

His third solo album, *Sunforest* marked a return to form, containing some good tracks.

Fans of **Tom Rapp** will also be interested in a tribute album *For The Dead In Space*, including Fit And Limo, Bevis Frond, Mourning Cloak and even an exclusive track by **Tom Rapp** himself. More recently **Tom Rapp** has performed at Ptolemaic Terrascope's 'Terrastock III' and released a fine solo album, *A Journal Of The Plague Year* (Woronzow) 1999. (SR)

Rapunzel

Personnel incl:	RAPUNZEL (MICHAEL MILITECA)	ld vcls	A

45:	Mornin' Sunrise/The Riddler	(Corn) 1973

An unknown heavy organ/guitar group. The flip is instrumental with crazed laughter over it. (SR/TDk)

The Rare Breed

CD:	1	THE RARE BREED SUPER "K" COLLECTION	
			(Collectables Col-0580) 1994

45s:	Beg, Borrow And Steal/Jeri's Theme	(Attack AR-1401) 1966
	Come And Take A Ride In My Boat/	
	Take Me To This World Of Yours	(Attack AR-1403) 1966

Still somewhat of a mystery group, this New York or New Jersey band, discovered by producers **Jeffrey Katz and Jerry Kasenetz** - later to be acknowledged as two of the originators of "bubblegum" music - was presented as an Ohio group since it was believed at the time easier to break a record out of the Midwest. After recording the instantly likeable *Louie Louie* ripoff *Beg, Borrow and Steal*, the band supposedly grew reluctant in giving any more control to **Katz and Kasenetz**, and were shortly thereafter dismissed by the producers - but not before leaving behind at least nine additional songs, all included on the Collectables release.

The bands second 45, *Come And Take A Ride In My Boat* was re-titled and recorded by **Every Mothers' Son** as *Come On Down To My Boat* and became a huge hit for them. For the **Rare Breed** it seemed another case of almost, but not quite.

Aside from *Beg, Borrow and Steal* (reportedly, **Katz and Kasenetz** would later take a true Ohio group, Sir Timothy and the Royals, and re-release the exact same single under the band's new moniker, **The Ohio Express**), the CD includes a cover of **The Grodes'** *I Won't Be There*, the garagey *Where Are You Going To*, and two **Monkees**-ish songs: *Bad Girl* and *City Girl*.

Beg, Borrow and Steal has been comped on Rhino Record's 1998 *Nuggets Box* (4-CD). (MDo/SNs/DJ)

The Rare Breed

Personnel:	BILL CARTER	ld gtr	AB
	JIMMY GARCIA	gtr	AB
	RON GAUSE	organ	AB
	PAUL McARTHUR	drms	AB
	RANDY McDANIEL	bs	AB
	RANDY ?	vcls	A
	PUD	vcls	B

NB: Randy ? was just 16, he was replaced by a guy who went just by the name of Pud!

45s:	I Need You / In The Night	(Cool As A Moose 012) c1965
	I Talk To The Sun / Don't Blow Your Cool	(Cool As A Moose Fr-3250) 1965

From Gainesville, Florida - this outfit started out in 1962 as The Playboys, changing their name to **The Rare Breed** in 1965. *I Talk To The Sun*, is a melodic garage-power-popper with swirling keyboards and prominent bass. The band later signed with Mainstream Records, but nothing ever came of the deal.

Carter moved to West Palm Beach and joined The Eighth Day. Jimmy Garcia went on to become an attorney in Houston, while McDaniel became an occupational therapist at Auburn University.

The correct title of *I Talk To The Sun* is actually *I Talked To The Sun*, the title was messed up on the label! The band also backed soul singers Gene Middleton (on D&B) and Linda Lyndell (on Volt), who did the original version of *What A Man*, the song made famous three decades later by Salt 'N' Pepa/En Vogue.

Compilation appearances include: *I Talk To The Sun* on *Psychedelic States - Florida Vol. 1* (CD) and *Destination Frantic!* (LP & CD); and *In The Night* on *Psychedelic States: Florida Vol. 3* (CD). (MW/JLh)

Rare Earth

Personnel incl:	GIL BRIDGES	flute, vcls
	KENNY JAMES	keyb'ds
	RAY MONETTE	gtr
	ROD RICHARDS	gtr, vcls
	PETE RIVERA	drms, vcls

				HCP
ALBUMS:	1	DREAM ANSWERS	(Verve 5056) 1968	- SC
(up to	2	GET READY	(Rare Earth RS 507) 1970	12 -
1973)	3	ECOLOGY	(Rare Earth RS 514) 1971	15 -
	4	ONE WORLD	(Rare Earth RS 520) 1971	28 -
	5	IN CONCERT	(Rare Earth RS 534) 1972	29 -
	6	WILLIE REMEMBERS	(Rare Earth RS 543) 1973	90 -

			HCP
45s:	Get Ready/Magic Key	(Rare Earth 5012) 1970	4
(up to	(I Know) I'm Losing You/		
1971)	When Joanie Smiles	(Rare Earth 5017) 1970	7
	Born To Wander/ Here Comes The Night	(Rare Earth 5021) 1971	17
	I Just Want To Celebrate/The Seed	(Rare Earth 5031) 1971	7
	Hey Big Brother/?	(Rare Earth 5038) 1971	19

A mediocre white soul-rock band in the style of **Vanilla Fudge** with long versions of soul hits (e.g. twenty minutes of *Get Ready*). Their records are not recommended but were successful enough to allow Tamla Motown to launch a rock label imaginatively called Rare Earth for other white rock acts like **Power Of Zeus** or **Xit**. Rare Earth were, of course, based in Detroit, Michigan. Their records sold well commercially, resulting in several hit albums and singles.

Ray Monette had previously been with **Scorpion**.

Rod Richards left in 1971 to form Road with Noel Redding. The band kept on recording during the seventies.

Compilation appearances include *Hey Big Brother* on *Michigan Rocks, Vol. 2* (LP). (SR/VJ)

The Rascals

See **The Young Rascals** entry.

John Rasmussen

ALBUM:	1	RASMUSSEN	(Reprise 6440) 1971

45:	Love Song/Johnny Got His Gun	(Reprise 1037) 1971

An obscure bearded singer/songwriter. (SR)

Rajput and The Sepoy Mutiny

ALBUM:	1	FLOWER POWER SITAR	(Design SDLP 280) c1967 -

One of those gloriously stupid cash-in budget albums for 'turned-on' grannies - file under novelty' or 'comedy', sounds like a middle-aged session man on sitar backed by a local muzak outfit! Put it on when you want the party to end. (MW)

Rasputin and The Mad Monks

Personnel incl:	ROLAND BOISJOLY	bs	A
	BOB RAYMOND (RASPUTIN)	vcls	A
	BOB URZI	ld gtr	A

Operated out of Lawrence, Massachusetts. On 16th December 1967, they cut a four track demo. Three of the tracks:- *Don't Let The Sun Catch You Crying*, *The Rain, The Park and Other Things*, and *See You In September* were pretty sluggish and will be of little interest to readers. The fourth was a completely over the top version of **The Electric Prunes'** hit, *I Had Too Much To Dream Last Night*, full of tape manipulation and sound effects. It's really bizarre.

Compilation appearances include *I Had Too Much To Dream Last Night* on *Beyond The Calico Wall* (LP & CD). (VJ)

Rasputin and The Monks

Personnel:	BAKER	vcls	A
	FREEMAN	drms	A
	GARDNER	vcls	A
	HARRISON	gtr	A
	LUTKINS	bs	A
	TAYLOR	ld gtr	A

ALBUM:	1(A)	SUN OF MY SOUL (one side only)	(Trans Radio 200836) 1965/6 R3

NB: Other side featured The Octet. (1) reissued as *Rasputin And The Monks* (one-sided) on Resurrection (CX 1227 AO) in the mid-eighties.

On the above album a grungy New Hampshire garage combo ran through seven cover versions:- *I Want To Be Your Man*, *You'd Better Move On*, *Gotta Get Away*, *You Didn't Have To Be So Nice*, *19th Nervous Breakdown*, *As Tears Go By* and *Roadrunner*. In the 'prep-rock' genre along with all those Phillips Academy bands' albums and the Justice releases, this is for the hard-core collector and the original album is priced accordingly. (MW)

Billy Rat and The Finks

Personnel incl: WALLY 'THE ZOMBIE' SHOOP   gtr   A

45:    Little Queenie/All American Boy   (IGL 122) 1967

Came from Spirit Lake, Iowa. Shoop had an earlier 45 release for Soma as Wally Shoop and The Zombies, and later recorded as **Wally Shoop and Fubar**.

Compilation coverage has included *Little Queenie* on *The Midwest Vs. The Rest* (LP); and both *Little Queenie* and *All American Boy* on *The IGL Rock Story: Part One* (CD) and *The Best Of IGL Garage Rock* (LP). (VJ/MW)

Ratchell

Personnel:	LARRY BYROM	gtr	A
	CHRIS COUCHOIS	gtr	A
	PAT COUCHOIS	drms	A
	HOWARD MESSER	bs	A

ALBUMS: 1(A) RATCHELL   (Decca DL-75330) 1973 -
         2( ) RATCHELL II   (Decca 75365) 1973 -

45s: Lazy Lady/Problems   (Decca 32893) 1971
       Julie, My Woman/Out Of Hand   (Decca 32958) 1972
       My, My/Peace Of Mind   (Decca 32981) 1972

Pat Couchois and Larry Byrom were together in **T.I.M.E** before Byrom joined **Steppenwolf**. When Byrom left **Steppenwolf** in 1970, they teamed up again to form **Ratchell**, a short-lived hard-rock group.

Larry Byrom became a session man, while, in 1979, the Couchois brothers and Howard Messer formed Couchois, an insipid hard FM group (with two albums on Warner Bros.). (SR)

The Rationals

Personnel:	STEVE CORREL	ld gtr, vcls	A
	BILL FIGG	drms	A
	SCOTT MORGAN	vcls, gtr	A
	TERRY TRABANDT	bs, vcls	A

ALBUM: 1 THE RATIONALS   (Crewe 1334) 1969 -

NB: (1) reissued on CD with twelve bonus tracks (Flash 46). Also of interest is *Temptation 'Bout To Get Me* (Total Energy NER 3004) 1995, a 10" recorded live at the Grande Ballroom, November 1968. It has also been issued on CD.

                                                               HCP
45s: α Turn On/Irrational   (Danby's 125850/1) 196? -
         Look What You've Done/Gave My Love   (A² 101) 196? -
         Feelin' Lost/Little Girls Cry   (A² 103) 1966 -
         Respect/Leavin' Here   (A² 104) 1966 -
         Feelin' Lost/
         Leavin' Here (special double 'A' release) (A² 103/4) 1966 -
         Respect/Leavin' Here   (Cameo 437) 1966 92
         Hold On Baby/Sing   (A² 105) 1967 -
         Hold On Baby/Sing   (Cameo 455) 1967 -
      β I Need You/Get The Picture   (A² 402) 1967 -
         Leavin' Here/Not Like It Is   (A² 106) 1968 -
         Leavin' Here/Not Like It Is   (Cameo 481) 1968 -
         I Need You/Out In The Streets   (A² 107) 1968 -
         I Need You/Out In The Streets   (Cameo 2124) 1968 -
         Guitar Army/Sunset   (Genesis # 1) c1969 -
         Handbags And Gladrags/Guitar Army   (Crewe 340) 1969 -

NB: α was a Danby's Men's Shops promo-only release. β The flip side was by **SRC**.

RASPUTIN and THE MONKS - Sun Of My Soul LP.

Out of Ann Arbor, this was one of Michigan's top sixties bands. Essentially an R&B outfit, they often covered popular songs and *Respect* was actually a minor U.S. hit in late 1966, after it was leased to Cameo Parkway for nationwide distribution. They signed to the Crewe label for an album, which may become a minor collectors' item before long.

The flip *Out In The Streets* was the same song as *Sing* minus the vocal track.

Compilation coverage has so far included: *Feelin' Lost* on *The Cicadelic 60's, Vol. 2* (LP) and *A Journey To Tyme, Vol. 2* (LP); *Feelin' Lost*, *Sing* and *Leavin' Here* on *Mindrocker, Vol. 11* (LP); *Turn On* and *Little Girls Cry* on *Highs In The Mid-Sixties, Vol. 5* (LP); *Little Girls Cry* and *I Need You* (alternate take) on *Michigan Mayhem, Vol. 1* (CD); *Respect* on *Turds On A Bum Ride, Vol. 4* (CD) and *Michigan Rocks, Vol. 1* (LP); *I Need You* on *Boulders, Vol. 2* (LP); *Respect*, *Sing!*, *Leavin' Here* and *I Need You* on *Michigan Brand Nuggets* (LP) and *Michigan Nuggets* (CD); In addition *Highs In The Mid-Sixties, Vol. 5* includes their rarest recording, a promo 45 for Danby's Men's Shop. Their cover of the Kinks' *I Need You* (a different song to the previous one mentioned) is on *Nuggets Box* (4-CD). Finally *Let 'Em Have It! Vol. 1* (CD) features *Look What You're Doin' (To Me Baby)*, the unreleased track *Poor Dog* and *Gloria*, from a rare Fan Club LP. (VJ/MW)

The Rats

45:   Rats Revenge (Part One)/(Part Two)   (Black Cat 502) 1963

This was actually the work of an Akron, Ohio, group called **The Decades** who'd released a spacey instrumental 45 *Come On Pretty Baby/Strange Worlds* earlier in 1963. *Rats Revenge* is an awful, crudely recorded, garage punker, which you'll either love or loathe.

Compilation appearances include: *Rats Revenge* (both parts) on *Back From The Grave, Vol. 1* (LP) and *Garage Kings* (Dble LP). (VJ)

The Ravelles

45:   Psychedelic Movement/
      She's Forever On My Mind   (Mobie 3430) 1968

A good heavy acid-rocker from Rockford, Illinois, that's really messed up by some truly awful trilling female vocals. Otherwise this would be a classic. The flip too isn't bad but for the vocals again (male this time). Some MOR group going psychy? A shame.

Psychedelic Movement can also be heard on *Brain Shadows, Vol. 2* (CD). (MW)

The Raven(s)

Personnel:	BRIAN EGAN	bs	AB
	JOHN HOWENSTEIN	keyb'ds	A
	MARK MACONI	ld vcls	ABCDEF
	PAUL PURCELL	drms	ABCDEF
	AL SCHWEIKERT	ld gtr, vcls	ABCDE
	CHRIS KRAWCZYN	keyb'ds	BC
	BEAU FISHER	bs	C
	KEN SPIVEY	bs	D
	KENT PEARSON	bs	EF
	TOMMY ANGARANO	organ, vcls	F
	CHARLIE BAILEY	gtr	F

45s:	α	Reaching For The Sun/Things We Said Today	(Boss 003) 1966
	β	Calamity Jane/Now She's Gone	(Rust 5123) 1968

NB: α credited to The Ravens, β to The Raven.

The debut waxing by this Pinellas County, Florida, quintet hit the stores in the Summer of '66. *Reaching For The Sun* is moody jangley folk-punk with yearning harmonies - this has resurfaced on *Psychedelic States - Florida Vol. 2* (CD).

The second 45 features a couple more tunes from Al Schweikert. Bright 'n' breezy pop with an RKO-radio-blip intro and some fuzz is slightly marred by some brass. The flip is an introspective lovelorn ballad with keyboard doodlings. *Calamity Jane* was co-composed with Karl Lamp with whom Albert Schweikert also composed **The Tropics**' classic *As Times Gone?*

The Ravens were managed by A.J. Perry, who was 'the' regional concert promoter at the time. They opened for every major act that came to town during that time, including The Hollies, The Yardbirds, The Who, Hermans Hermits, **Blues Magoos** and Sonny and Cher.

Kent Pearson: "Albert Schweikert and I reformed the band after it had split up in 1968. Shortly before the band ended for good, Albert left and we brought on Charlie Bailey and Tommy Angarano, both from St. Petersburg bands The Tempests and Pink Anacin. At that point, we were doing lengthy and complex arrangement in the style of **Vanilla Fudge**, as well as copping the some of the styles of New York's The Child. The band broke up for good in late 1969. At that time, I relocated to Boston, put the bass behind me and began playing guitar with The Soul Blenders, Buck, and later, the band which was to become John Butcher Axis. I'm still performing with The Electric Blues Band, as vocalist-guitarist.

Some members went on to form Manitoba who released a couple of 45s on RCA in the early seventies. For more on the sixties Florida scene, pick up Jeff Lemlich's 1992 book 'Savage Lost' (Distinctive Publishing, ISBN 0-942963-12-1). (MW/KPn)

Raven

ALBUM:	1	BACK TO OHIO BLUES	(Owl) 197? R3/R4

NB: (1) reissued on Rockadelic (RRLP 15.5) 1994.

Another **Raven**, probably from Ohio, whose highly-rated and ultra-rare album had a reissue by Rockadelic in 1994. It consists of five hard-rock tracks with some blues leanings and slight psychedelic overtones. The title cut is a powerful blues-rock jam that took up most of Side Two. No personnel details unfortunately. (VJ/GG)

Raven

Personnel:	TOMMY CALANDRA	bs	A
	JAMES CALIRE	keyb'ds, vcls	A
	TONY GALLA	vcls, hrmnca	A
	GARY MALLABER	drms	A
	JOHN WEITZ	gtr	A

ALBUMS:	1	LIVE AT THE INFERNO	(Discovery 36133) 1967 R2
	2	RAVEN	(CBS CS 9903) 1969 -

45s:	Feelin' Good/Green Mountain Dream	(CBS 4-44988) 1969
	Children At Our Feet/Here Come A Truck	(CBS 4-45163) 1970

THE RATIONALS - The Rationals LP.

Originating from Buffalo, New York, **Raven** recorded a good and rare live blues-rock album in 1967. After an undistinct album and a brace of 45s on Columbia, which had moved into **Blood, Sweat and Tears** style, they broke up. Gary Mallaber (or Mallabar) would later join the **Steve Miller Band** and also have a successful career in the Californian studios, whilst James Calire would play with America.

Of the other members, Tommy Calandra passed away around five years ago, Jim Calire's son Mario plays (or played) with Jakob Dylan's band the Wallflowers, Gary Mallaber has been working with local musicians in Buffalo recently and Tony Galla now successfully performs old Italian love songs. (SR/PF/MW)

Ravenz

Personnel incl:	CALDWELL DAVIS Jr	A

45:	Just Like I Want Her/?	(Crockett 5030) 1968

The above killer organ/fuzz track was by a Waynesboro, Tennessee, band and recorded in June 1968 at the Kecoata Studio in Wayne County, Tennessee. The 'A' side has resurfaced on *Back From The Grave, Vol. 8* (Dble LP), where Tim Warren tells us that the band originally formed in 1965 and played around mid-Southern Tennessee and Northern Alabama for a few years, until their wild, fast-living lead singer was killed in an auto accident. They then reformed with three new members, including Caldwell Davis Jr. who had previously led **The Missing Lynx** who'd issued the killer two-sider *Hang Around/Louie, Go Home* in 1967. College and Vietnam signalled **The Ravenz** demise not too long after the release of the above single. (VJ/GG)

The Rave-Ons

Personnel:	LONNIE KNIGHT	gtr	A
	HARRY NEHLS	drms	A
	DICK WIEGAND	gtr	A
	LARRY WIEGAND	bs	A

ALBUM:	1(-)	THE RAVE-ONS	(Dove Acetate no #) 1965/66 ?

NB: (1) remains unreleased.

45s:	The Line/Baby Don't Love Me	(Re-Car 9016) 1965
	I Want You To Love Me/	
	Everybody Tells Me	(Twin Town 702) 1965
	Whenever/Love Pill	(Twin Town 710) 1965

A Richfield, Minnesota, group who formed in the early sixties as the Knights. Around 1964 they became **The Rave-Ons** and embraced the Invasion sounds. They released three quality 45s, mainly original compositions, before breaking up in 1967. Members went on to **Jokers**

Wild, **South 40** and **T.C. Atlantic**. Dick and Larry Wiegand would achieve success with **Crow**, releasing four albums and a pile of 45s. Larry remains an in-demand bassist - in 1996, he worked worked with the reformed **Canoise** on their *Plugged In* CD.

Whenever, *Love Pill* and *I Want You To Love Me* feature on the mid-sixties Bud-Jet label Minneapolis sampler albums *Top Teen Bands, Vol. 1* (LP, *Top Teen Bands, Vol. 2* (LP) and *Top Teen Bands, Vol. 3* (LP) respectively. *Baby Don't Love Me* is on *Root '66* (LP) and an unreleased 1965 Lonnie Knight composition *I'll Come Back To You* has resurfaced on *Project Blue, Vol. 5* (LP).

It has been confirmed by Lonnie Knight that they are NOT the Rave-Ons who feature on several Columbine label albums including *The Now Sounds Of Today* (CRH-14) 197?. This was a Hollywood label who specialized in song-poem music and employed the services of mainly local area acts. Any information about the Columbine Rave-Ons would be appreciated.

Lonnie Knight had earlier been a founder member of **The Castaways**. (VJ/MW/PMs)

The Raves

| Personnel incl: | D. JIMENEZ | A |
| | M. JIMENEZ | A |

45s:	Mister Man/Mother Nature	(Smash 2088) 1967
	Don't Chop Down My Tree/	
	Think Of Your Love	(Smash 2105) 1967
α	Everything's Fire/Sing Children Sing	(Smash 2162) 1968

NB: α also issued as DJ promo featuring mono and stereo versions of *Everything's Fire* (Smash DJS-15).

A Brooklyn, New York outfit, whose *Mother Nature* is a catchy and uplifting psych-pop tune with crisp production, cool fuzz, thrumming bass runs, great percussion and a swirling Middle Eastern influenced break.

All songs on the above 45s were composed by M. and D.Jimenez.

Compilation appearances include: *Don't Chop Down My Tree* on *Psychedelic Unknowns, Vol. 9* (CD); *Mother Nature* on *Beyond The Calico Wall* (CD), *Echoes In Time, Vol's 1 & 2* (CD) and *Echoes In Time, Vol. 1* (LP). (VJ/MW)

Ravin' Blue

Personnel incl:	R. BERNARD	A
	A. CHRISTOPHER Jnr.	A
	L. NIX	A

| 45s: | It's Not Real/Love | (Monument 968) 1966 |
| | Colors/In My Sorrow | (Monument 1034) 1967 |

This high school combo recorded these two 45s for a Nashville, Tennessee, label. They played folk-punk with a psychedelic tinge. The 'A' side to their first 45 has a Dylan-type blues harmonica, while the flip has a mod pop feel.

Compilation appearances include: *Love* on *Pebbles, Vol. 10* (CD), *Mayhem And Psychosis, Vol. 2* (LP) and *Mayhem And Psychosis, Vol. 1* (CD); *It's Not Real* on *The Essential Pebbles Collection, Vol. 2* (Dble CD); *Love* and *It's Not Real* on *Highs In The Mid Sixties, Vol. 8* (LP). (VJ/MW)

The Raving Madd

| 45: | I Said Oh No No (What's In It For Me)/ | |
| | Boundaries | (Goldstar 1) 196? |

From Florida.

Compilation appearances include: *Boundaries* on *Psychedelic Experience, Vol. 2* (CD); and *I Said Oh No No No (What's In It For Me)* on *Vile Vinyl, Vol. 2* (LP) and *Vile Vinyl* (CD). (VJ/MW)

The Ravons with Bobby Roberts

| Personnel incl: | BOBBY ROBERTS | A |

45s:	Little Flirt/I'll Never Leave You Alone	(GMA 3309) 196?
	How Can I Make Her Mine?/I'm In Love Again	(GMA 10) 1965
	How Can I Make Her Mine?/	
	I'm In Love Again	(Cameo 339) 1965
	I Want You To Be/Sweet Little Girl	(GMA 13) 196?
	Jenny Jenny/Red Hot	(GMA 15) 196?

A mid-sixties Chicago-based outfit.

Compilation appearances have included: *How Can I Make Her Mine* on *Vile Vinyl, Vol. 1* (LP), *Vile Vinyl* (CD) and *Garage Punk Unknowns, Vol. 1* (LP). (MW)

Raw Edge

| 45: | October Country/?? | (Sidewalk 936) 1968 |

A wonderful baroque pop song from the **Smoke** album, issued under a pseudonym. Sensitive strings and an arching melody make this obligatory for **Left Banke** aficionados. (MK)

Raw Honey

| ALBUM: | 1 | RAGWEED | (No label RH 1057) 1974 R1 |

An obscure hippie-folk offering with male and female vocals. The album came in a cool black and white cover. (CF)

Bob Ray

Personnel:	HAL BLAINE	drms	A
	JIM GORDON	drms	A
	JIM HORN	flute, sax	A
	LARRY KNECHTEL	bs, keyb'ds	A
	JOE OSBORNE	bs	A
	BOB RAY	vcls	A

| ALBUM: | 1(A) | INITIATION OF A MYSTIC | (Soul City SCS-92007) 1968 - |

A Californian singer/songwriter, influenced by Donovan and similar artists. Produced by **Johnny Rivers** during his psychy period, his album is rather mellow but nonetheless pleasant. Arranged with flute and strings, songs like *City Of Toys*, *Money Tree* and *Smog Song* will clearly be of interest to fans of melancholic singers. **Bob Ray** was backed by the usual group of L.A. session musicians: **Hal Blaine**, Larry Knechtel, Jim Horn...

RAW HONEY - Ragweed LP.

Soul City Records was a sub label of Liberty and also released the single of the **Fourth Way**. (SR)

Burch Ray (and The Walkers)

45s:	Well, All Right / Play Ground	(Lavender 2306)	195/6?
(select α	Waitin' Around / Time Trap	(Soma 1187)	1962
-ive)	Love Questions / Blues Stay Away From Me	(Sully 915)	1965
	Love Questions / Love Was Made For Two	(Ruff 45-1017)	1966

NB: α as **Burch Ray and The Walkers**.

Itinerant performer **Burch Ray** originated from Miles City in Montana. Although most of his material falls outside the remit of this book, one track has found favour with garage collectors. In the mid-sixties he was in Oklahoma City long enough to record *Love Questions*, a dramatic teen-beater with ringing guitar, released first on the Sully label and later on Ruff. It certainly merits a place on the excellent *Fuzz, Flaykes And Shakes, Vol. 5* (LP & CD) compilation.

Burch Ray released an album and several 45s on the Yellowstone label in the seventies. (MW)

Jerry Raye and Fenwyck

See **Fenwyck**.

The Raymarks

Personnel:	GAIL DAVIES	vcls	A
	KEN HUFF	gtr	A
	GREG PETTIT	sax	A
	MIKE SPOTTS	keyb'ds	A
	TERRY SELVIDGE	drms	A
	LARRY TRUDEAU	bs	A
	TERRY CARTER	sax	
	CHUCK SNYDER	gtr	

45s:	Work Song/Backfire	(Panorama 6)	1964
α	Dollar Bill/Louise	(Jerden 752)	1965
	I Believe/Dr. Feelgood	(Jerden 774)	1965

NB: α Misprinted as by Paymarks.

From Bremerton, Washington, they played a pretty standard sort of R&B with lots of raw guitar and organ. They were originally known as The Orbits and changed name to The Galaxies in 1962, but this had to be changed again in 1964 when they learnt of the better-known and similarly named Tacoma-based band. Their first record was a re-make of Cannonball Adderley's *Work Song*. Their finest moment, though, was probably *Louise*, a pretty standard R&B howl.

The band ended when Huff and Selvidge were drafted in 1966 but Spotts went on to form The Icemen and was later in **The Wailers** and **Crome Syrcus**. Greg Pettit also went on to play in Superband.

Gail Davies went on to have a country music career during the seventies and eighties and is still actively singing and recording albums. She was born in Oklahoma but raised in the Pt. Orchard - Bremerton, Washington. She also sang with The Coming Generation and a few other small time groups during her high school days at South Kitsap. She moved to Los Angeles in 1967 and eventually settled in Nashville in 1975.

Compilation appearances include: *Louise* on *Northwest Battle Of The Bands, Vol. 2 - Knock You Flat!* (LP & CD), *Northwest Battle Of The Bands, Vol. 1* (CD), *Highs In The Mid-Sixties, Vol. 14* (LP) and *The History of Northwest Rock, Vol. 5*; *Louise* and *I Believed* on *History Of Northwest Rock, Vol. 2* (CD); *Work Song* on *Highs In The Mid-Sixties, Vol. 16* (LP); and *Hard Times* (prev unreleased) on *Northwest Battle Of The Bands, Vol. 2* (CD). (VJ/MW/DR/RPe)

Raymond John Michael Band

Personnel:	RAY GRAFFIA	rhythm instruments, ld vcls	A
	CRAIG KEMP	organ	A
	CHIC JAMES	drms	A
	GREG NASHAN	ld gtr	A
	TERRY STONE	bs	A
	JEFF TUCKMAN	bs	A

45s:	Let There Be Love/Feel Free	(Ivanhoe 1-501)	1970?
	Let There Be Love/Feel Free	(London 136)	1970
	Rich Kid Blues/Hitch-Hiker	(London 145)	1971

The **Raymond John Michael Band** (RJM), named by its founder Ray Graffia, Jr. was formed in 1969 when Graffia left the **New Colony Six**. They recorded three singles (or more?) on the Ivanhoe and London labels and disbanded in 1971. In addition to Graffia, the band included two of further original **New Colony Six** members, Craig Kemp and Chic James. **RJM**'s sound was heavier than the **NC6**, yet retained the harmonious sound of the former group. *Let There Be Love* was written by the Bee Gees and *Rich Kid Blues* was penned by Terry Reid. Unreleased **RJM** tracks includes such songs as *Gwendolyn*, *Bobby And Georgia*, *I Confess* (a new version of the **NC6** classic!), *I Can't Believe That We're Alone*, *I Never Dreamed*, *People In Search Of* and *Splendid Friends/Dining In Film*. No albums were released and to my knowledge, none of these songs has been compiled. (BSw)

Rayne

Personnel:	FRANK SAUCIER	gtr, vcls	A
	GEORGE SAUCIER	bs	A
	JOHNNY SAUCIER	gtr	A
	MIKE SAUCIER	drms	A

ALBUM:	1(A) RAYNE	(No label)	1979 R4

NB: (1) Reissued on OR Records (OR 002) 1994.

This ultra-rarity is strictly speaking outside the time-span of this book but sounds like it's from the early seventies. The group came from New Orleans and the album was recorded in their living room, with nothing remixed or overdubbed. The high energy album with psychedelic tinges had a limited reissue (500 copies) in 1994. The reissue contains an insert with some information on the group. (CF)

Razor's Edge

Personnel:	BILL ANDE	ld gtr	A
	TOM CONDRA	gtr	A
	DAVE HIERONYMUS	drms	A
	JIM TOLLIVER	bs	A

			HCP
45s:	Let's Call It A Day Girl/Avril (April)	(Pow 101)	1966 77
	Don't Let Me Catch You In His Arms/ Night And Day	(Pow 103)	1966 -
	Night And Day/The Patron Of The Arts	(Pow 103)	1966 -
	Baby's On His Way/The Patron Of The Arts	(Pow 105)	1967 -
	Get Yourself Together/Cloudy Day	(Power 4932)	1967 -

A West Palm Beach, Florida outfit whose *Get Yourself Together* is full of lots of psychedelic sitar and fuzz. They were previously known as **The American Beetles** and may also have recorded as The Queen City Show Band. Their other 45s are pop/ballads of minor interest here, but *Let's Call It A Day Girl* was a minor hit.

Compilation appearances include *Get Yourself Together* on *Garage Zone, Vol. 2* (LP) and *The Garage Zone Box Set* (4-LP). (VJ/MW)

Razor's Edge

Personnel incl: PAT FARRELL (PATRICK HENRY SICKAFUS)   A

45:	Gotta Find Her/War Boy	(Kingston E-1 967)	1967

Previously known as **The Triumphs** (with a couple of 45s on Barclay), this Reading, Pennsylvania, outfit was forced to change their name to **Pat Farrell and The Believers** when it was discovered that this moniker was already in use. This 45 was duly reissued on Diamond D-236. *Gotta Find Her* can also be heard on *Psychedelic Unknowns, Vol. 3* and is a bouncy ditty but really not in the psych or garage genres. The flip is a slow crooner ballad!! (MW)

Reactions

45:	In My Grave/Love Is A Funny Thing	(Rock 5810) 1968

A campus band from the University of Missouri's Engineering School at Rolla. *In My Grave* can also be found on *Monsters Of The Midwest, Vol. 4* (LP). Its best point is some enthusiastic guitar work. (VJ)

Reactors

Personnel:
	DONNIE GUMS	bs	A
	STEVE HICKS	bs	A
	BUTCH HOLLAND	drms	A
	EDMUND MORRIS	vcls, gtr	A
	STEVE PRIVOTT	ld gtr	A
	GORDON TWINE	organ	A
	BILLY WALKER	sax	A

45s:	She's A Queen / Please Tell Me	(Ablaze 651) 1965
	1-A / Do That Thing	(Ablaze 662) 1966
	Do That Thing / 1-A	(Cameo C-446) 1966

From the Suffolk area of Virginia. Their debut has a pre-Invasion flavour, coupling a cool saxy frat-jerker with a slow last-dance ballad. They updated their sound considerably for the follow-up which was picked up by Cameo Parkway. *Do That Thing* is a natural progression from *She's A Queen*, still retaining a frat flavour but incorporating beat and dance elements and relegating the sax to a background role.

Of most appeal here is *1-A*, a moribund folk-rocker with swirling keyboards on the theme of the Vietnam war, destruction and death - reared on *Aliens, Psychos And Wild Things* (CD).

Latterly the band included bassist Steve Hicks who'd move on to the Hustlers, a Sandston, Virginia outfit who changed their name to **Short Cross** around the turn of the decade. (MW/BHr/ST)

The Readymen

EP:	1	THE READYMEN MEET THE YETTI-MEN
		(Norton 037) 19??

NB: (1) contains two tracks by **The Readymen**: *Shortnin' Bread* and *Disintegration*.

45:	Surfer's Blues/Shortnin' Bread	(Bangar 665) 1965

The Readymen, from Minneapolis, weren't the only rock 'n' rollers willing and able to slam into the old folk/children's song *Shortnin' Bread* but their version is the most gone. Perhaps it's got something to do with the air in Minneapolis that makes people sing with such a raw growl as can be heard in **The Trashmen**'s *Surfin' Bird* and **The Novas**' *The Crusher*.

Compilation appearances include *Shortnin' Bread* on *Pebbles Vol. 4 - Various Hodads* (CD) and *Born Bad, Vol. 5*. (VJ/GG)

Real People

Personnel incl:
	ALAN	A
	PARKS	A

45:	Sea of Reality/The Man	(Rev 119-68/120-68) 1968

An example of one of the numerous **Jefferson Airplane** clones that blossomed as part of the 'West Coast sound' replete with Grace Slickesque vocalist stridently belting it out, especially on the uptempo flip. *Sea Of Reality* is a very slow atmospheric dirge with suitably tiresome lyrics. (MW)

Rear Exit

45:	Excitation/Miles Beyond	(MTA 132) 1967

A sixties punk outfit from the San Francisco area. Basically we're talking an amalgam of psychedelia and punk, with *Excitation* similar in style to **The Music Machine** and *Miles Beyond* having some neat chops and changes. There were rumours of a retrospective album of their material but I can't confirm that it appeared.

Another Rear Exit, presumably from the Wisconsin area, had a 45 *Thinking Of You/Summertime* on Cuca (1527).

Compilation appearances have included *Excitation* and *Miles Beyond* on *Psychedelic Moods - Part Two* (LP & CD), *60's Punk E.P., Vol. 3* (7"), *Boulders Punk EP Box* and *Crystalize Your Mind* (CD). (VJ/MW)

Reason

Personnel:
	TOMMY DILDY	keyb'ds, vcls	A
	TERRY GORKA	bs	A
	J. JENSON	bs	A
	BILL MANNING	drms, vcls	A
	BILLY WINDSOR	gtr, vcls	A
	(DANNY GATTON	gtr	A)

ALBUM:	1(A)	THE AGE OF REASON	
			(Georgetowne TRS 1002) 19?? R2

NB: (1) labels show band name as 'Reason', whereas it often appears on dealer lists as Age Of Reason.

On a Washington D.C. label, this band is thought to have come from Virginia. The album is now rare and sought-after by collectors. It kicks off with the band's own individualistic cover version of Bob Dylan and Rick Danko's *This Wheel's On Fire*, which is probably their magnum opus. Like most of the album, the music is very keyboard driven - **Sony Bono**'s *Bang Bang* and Ike Turner's *I'm Blue* get similar treatment. It also contains a couple of originals with Bill Manning and Tommy Dildy's *Letter To Home* the pick. It starts with some cool bluesy piano but then becomes very country-influenced.

On the album, the late Danny Gatton is credited as playing on at least two cuts. Many years later Billy Windsor was the singer in Gatton's band that gigged around Washington in the late eighties / early nineties. Terry Gorka was also in **The Telstars**. (VJ/ED/MW/CF)

The Reasons Why

Personnel:
	DONNIE DOLAN	drms	ABC
	JOHN INMAN	ld gtr	ABC

ALIENS PSYCHOS & WILD THINGS Vol. 1 (Comp CD) including Reactors.

FRANK KALENDA	vcls		A
RONNIE MILLER	bs		AB
JOHN SCHWERTNER	keyb'ds		BC
TOMMY LANGFORD	bs		C

45: Melinda/Don't Be That Way (Sound Track 2000) 1966

Based in Temple North of Austin in Texas, this group was managed by a Waco businessman Carl Sachs who tried hard to promote their 45, but due to a small pressing and limited distribution it never took off. If the 'A' side was an unmemorable ballad, the flip was a **13th Floor Elevators**-influenced rocker. The band split in the Autumn of 1967 when Schwertner left to fill the vocal spot in the newly formed **Lavender Hill Express**. Later still, he was reunited with Dolan and Inman in **Plymouth Rock**. In the short-term Inman, Dolan and Miller played in a blues trio called Feast Of Stephen which later evolved into South Canadian Overflow.

Compilation appearances include: *Don't Be That Way* on *Acid Visions - The Complete Collection Vol. 1* (3-CD), *Austin Landing, Vol. 2* (LP), *Texas Flashbacks, Vol. 1* (LP & CD), *Flashback, Vol. 1* (LP) and *I Was A Teenage Caveman* (LP). (VJ/MW)

The Reasons Why

45s:	Johnny Come Home/The Game Of War	(Cha Cha 780)	1966
(selective)	All I Really Need Is Love/ Night Time-Daytime	(KM727-1/2)	1967

A Chicago-based outfit. *All I Really Need Is Love*, a lighthearted punk thrash, can also be heard on *Back From The Grave, Vol. 2* (LP), *Garage Kings* (Dble LP) and *Highs In The Mid-Sixties, Vol. 4* (LP). (VJ)

The Reasons Why

Personnel:	STEVE BECKMEYER	bs	A
	BUZZY FEITEN	gtr	A
	DANNY (FING) HORTON	gtr	A
	AL STEGMEYER	drms	A

45s:	Games/Why Pack Up	(Amy 962)	1966
	Tell Her One More Time/Try And See Me	(Amy 970)	1966
	Same Old Worries/ I Don't Care If You Don't Care	(Amy 980)	1967

This was a different outfit, from Syosset, Long Island who formed at Syosset High School. Their first two 45s were great dynamic pop-punk, kind of **Monkees**-style garagey-pop.

Al Stegmeyer's younger brother played bass in the Billy Joel Band between 1975-1990.

Compilation appearances have included *One More Time* on *Teenage Shutdown, Vol. 11 - Move It!* (LP & CD). (MW/SBr)

The Reasons Why

45: Dark Side / Today Is Here (acetate) c1966

A Tucson, Arizona, band later known as the Revelation. *Dark Side*, taken from an acetate (it's unknown whether a 45 was released) can be heard on *Think Of The Good Times*.

Another Reasons Why 45 (connections unknown)
45: That Girl/Stop, Think of Me (Happy 688H-7360) c1966 (MW)

Rebecca and The Sunnybrook Farmers

Personnel:	ERNIE EREMITA	bs, vcls	A
	MICKEY (MARK) KAPNER	keyb'ds, sitar	A
	KIKI	vcls	A
	CLIFFORD MANDELL	drms	A
	ILENE NOVOG	viola	A
	ILENE RAPAPORT	vcls, gtr, recorder	A

THINK OF THE GOOD TIMES (Comp LP) including The Reasons Why.

ALBUM: 1(A) BIRTH (Musicor MS-3176) 1969? SC
NB: (1) some copies with photo insert.

An interesting and rather imaginative Pittsburgh-based act judging from this album. There's lots of interesting string arrangements, Kiki's seductive vocals and for the most part strong material, although Side Two becomes more experimental. Obviously not for garage fans, but if experimental psychedelic/progressive rock is your niche this minor collectable may be of interest.

Kapner had previously played with **Group Image** and was later in **Country Joe and The Fish**. Ilene Rappaport, Ilene Novog and Ernie Eremita were later known as Chunky, Novi and Ernie, a late seventies Los Angeles-based band. This latter act released three albums on Warner Bros which are reputedly very eclectic and progressive in nature. Ilene Rappaport (aka Chunky), later became Lauren Wood who has had some top hits like *Fallen* on the 'Pretty Woman' soundtrack.

All the members of **Rebecca and The Sunny Brook Farmers** were old high school friends. (VJ/SBn/RB)

Rebirth

ALBUM: 1 REBIRTH (Lefevre Sound) 196? -
NB: (1) reissued in 1971 on Avantgarde Records (135).

An obscure and minor psychedelic collectable. The original Lefevre Sound and Avant Garde reissue, which appeared a few years apart include some different tracks. (VJ/AGI)

The Rebounds

45: Since I Feel For You/ I'm Not Your Stepping Stone (Tower 288) 1966

From Columbus, Ohio, this band also recorded a demo of **The Nightcrawlers**' *Little Black Egg*. Their cover of *I'm Not Your Stepping Stone* has also resurfaced on *Boulders, Vol. 2* (LP) and the *Boulders Box Set.* (MW/BKr/GGl)

The Rebs

Personnel:	CRAIG DeGEAR	drms	A
	JOHN HERRIG	vcls	A
	KEN KEIL	bs	A

	GLEN KILBURG	gtr	A
	STEVE NORPEL	organ, vcls	A
	JERRY TILL	gtr	A
	(GERALD HYLER	drms	A)

ALBUM: 1(A) 1968 A.D. BREAKTHROUGH (Fredlo 6830) 1968 R3

The Rebs were a high-school sextet from Bellevue, Iowa. They played local "sock hops" and teen dances, alongside acts such as **Grandma's Rockers**, without intending to turn "professional". Band member Ken Keil recalls: "We had fun. We weren't good, but we had guts. None of us went on to professional musicianship, but some of us, including myself, still play."

Just 200 copies of this album were pressed and it was impossible to locate until around 50 copies were found a few years back. Evidently songwriting wasn't one of the band's strengths, as their album consists of generally inferior cover versions of many of the popular songs of the era - sometimes little changed from the original, whilst some bear the band's own interpretation. The vocalist is powerful and particularly suited to ballads - so the magnum opus is arguably the cover of The Classics IV hit *Spooky*, but among the other songs to get **The Rebs** treatment were *My Back Pages*, *Lady Madonna*, *Mony Mony*, *Dream Dream*, *Sugar And Spice* and *Chains* and there's an almost laughable version of Eddie Cochran's *Summertime Blues*.

Although not an essential part of any garage or psychedelic collection, it is well worth a few spins and will shortly be reissued by the band on CD.

What became of the band? Well, Ken Keil is now a physician living in West Monroe, Louisiana; Glen Kilburg works as a building contractor and is based in Seattle, Washington; Craig DeGear lives in the Milwaukee area and is a school counsellor; Jerry Till is a business man in Dubuque, Iowa; John Herrig also lives in Dubuque, Iowa and is a real estate agent; Steve Norpel resides in Bellevue, Iowa and Gerald Hyler, who was an unoffical part-time member is a school teacher in Correctionville, Louisiana. (MW/KKI)

Red Beard and The Pirates

45:   Go On Leave/Don't Be A Loser   (Gaye 3043) 1966

An obscure garage punk outfit from Atlanta, Georgia. *Go On Leave* has just about all the classic garage-punk ingredients; frantic beat, pumping bass, fuzz outbursts, girl-put-down lyrics, and raw vocals. Rediscover that teen-angst on *Back From The Grave, Vol. 4* (LP), *Back From The Grave, Vol. 2* (CD) and *Psychedelic States: Georgia Vol. 1* (CD). (MW)

Red Bud Thunder

ALBUM: 1 AMERICAN ROCK AND ROLL (Private Pressing) 1977 SC

From Wisconsin, a decent hard-rock outfit, interesting for its acid guitar leads, although strictly outside the time frame of this book. (SR)

Red Cheek

Personnel:	RON BOGDON	bs	A
	GENE CORMAN	gtr, vcls	A
	BOBBY RADELOFF	drms, vcls, gtr	A
	(BOBBY PUCCETTI	keyb'ds	A)

ALBUM: 1(A) RED CHEEK   (Armadillo 8032) 197? R1

Acoustic/electric rural-rock and folk from a Florida-based band. This same label also issued the **Magic** *Enclosed* album circa 1969; this record sounds circa 1970-1. A rare item, to be sure... but it's appeal will be somewhat limited due to the lightweight material. Fans of **Big Lost Rainbow** or **Gabriel Gladstar** should investigate further.

The production was handled by Steve Alaimo. (CF)

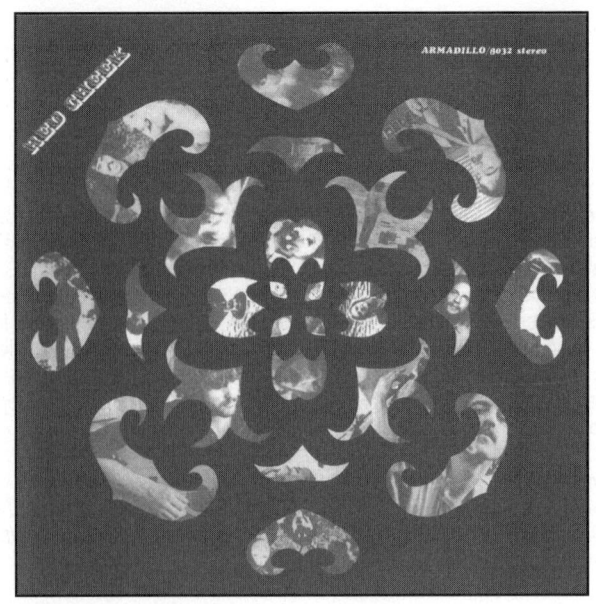

RED CHEEK - Red Cheek LP.

Redcoats

Personnel:	RANDY BOCELLE	bs, ld vcls	A
	ZACK BOCELLE	gtr, ld vcls	A
	MIKE BURKE	ld gtr	A
	JOHN SPIRIT	drms	A

ALBUM: 1(A) MEET THE REDCOATS - FINALLY!
               (Dionysus/Bacchus Archives BA 1157) 2001

45:   The Dum Dum Song / Love Unreturned   (Laurie 3319) 1965

This Beatlesque band's tragic story is finally told on the Dionysus album. Briefly...

Formed in 1964 in Wildwood, New Jersey by composer and drummer John Spirt and his school-friend Mike Burke, they were joined by the Bocelle brothers. In 1965, they released their debut 45; it went nowhere. They recorded several other tracks but their producer was unable to get the band a recording contract because they sound too much like the Beatles. Following his departure, the band were 'sponsored' to the tune of $10,000 by a society dame referred to (for legal reasons they say) as Madam X. The contract they signed gave her exclusive management over them for 10 years. They did get to release an album and several 45s, but under another name. They were not allowed to play on the studio recordings and the material was selected for them - just four of the twelve tracks on the album were Spirt-Burke originals. Apparently, even after it flopped and madam lost interest in the band, she refused to release them from the contract, effectively gagging them.

So, at long last, the real **Redcoats** emerge. Seven Rappaport-produced tracks (including both 45 sides) and five of the unreleased cuts that the band produced from their sponsorship.

Some scars and bad feelings are in evidence (or is someone still gagged?). The story is told by the band's first producer, Steven Rappaport. Still peeved at Laurie's lack of effort perhaps, he refers to them as "a small New York label". More glaringly, absolutely no mention is made of the new identity that the band donned for their 'major label' releases. Okay okay, for those who don't know, check out the **Sidekicks**. (AR)

Red Crayola

Personnel:	RICK BARTHELME	drms	AB
	STEVE CUNNINGHAM	bs	ABC
	BONNIEE MERSON	gtr	A
	DANNY SCHACT	hrmnca	A
	MAYO THOMPSON	gtr, vcls	ABC
	TOMMY SMITH		C
	JESSE CHAMBERLAIN		
	GUY CLARK		

ALBUMS:
1(B) THE PARABLE OF ARABLE LAND (International Artists 2) 1967 SC
2(C) GOD BLESS THE RED KRAYOLA AND ALL WHO SAIL WITH IT (International Artists 7) 1968 SC

NB: (1) reissued on Radar (RAD 12) 1978 and Decal (LIK 20) 1988. (2) reissued on Radar (RAD 16) 1979 and Decal (LIK 29) 1989. (1) and (2) have also been issued together on a European CD and in the U.S. by Collectables. Later releases include:- *Soldier Talk* (Radar RAD 18) 1978, *Black Snakes (with Art and Language)* (Recommended) 1983; *Three Songs On A Trip Across The U.S.* (mini) (Recommended) 1985; *The Male Factor Die* (Glass) 1989. There is also a very strange, live album recorded in 1967, (B) *Coconut Hotel* (DC 62) 1996.

Red Crayola were established in Houston in September 1966. line-up 'A' was very much embryonic. They began playing straight rock numbers like *Hey Joe* but by December 1966 they had developed the improvised music style - the Freeform Freak-out - that they are best remembered for. All interested parties were invited to perform in their shows and in effect a companion group (known as The Familiar Ugly) was established. When International Artists invited **Thompson**, Barthelme and Cunningham to record their debut album in March 1967 The Familiar Ugly were featured in the Freeform Freak-outs between each track. Quite aside from the Freak-outs the album included some very strange material - formless and improvised, the psychedelia of tracks like *Hurricane Fighter Plane* (which Roky Erickson played organ on), *Transparent Radiation* (which Roky played harmonica on) and *Pink Stainless Tail* was very different to that of other Texas bands of the era. On stage, too, the **Red Crayola** were very much an acquired taste. Lacking natural rhythms and structure their music was practically impossible to dance to. They were once paid ten dollars (to split three ways) and asked to leave a gig at the New Orleans House in Berkeley after 20 minutes! They were, however, invited to play at the Berkeley Folk Festival in the Summer of 1967. Once again their performance did not go down well and the band fell apart with **Thompson** spending time in New York and Los Angeles. One of their live performances was released in the nineties as *Coconut Hotel*, but it isn't recommended unless you're into avant garde/ambient noises.

In 1968, Thompson and Steve Cunningham returned to Texas and along with a new drummer Tommy Smith, who had briefly played with **Bubble Puppy**, began recording their second album, which consisted of numerous one and two minute tracks of simple but experimental acoustic weirdness. They were now spelling Krayola with a k. Surprisingly perhaps, this album was even less successful than their first and the band became dormant for many years. They did apparently record a double album with guitarist **John Fahey** but the tapes were lost.

Mayo Thompson has continued to enjoy an active solo career. He fronted a temporary group called **Saddlesore** and recorded a solo album. He met Jesse Chamberlain in New York in the Winter of 1974/75 and later reformed **Red Krayola** with Jesse as a two-piece. This line-up gigged in London in 1978. The band were signed by Radar who reissued (1) and (2) and put out (3), an album of new wave material. On (3) the two-piece was assisted by Lora Logic and Pere Ubu. Indeed **Thompson** went on to join Pere Ubu until they temporarily dissolved. **Thompson** has also worked as or with Art and Language who straddle his other projects, indeed Art and Language assisted on their fourth album Black Snakes which is full of **Thompson**'s dramatic vocals and included Allen Ravenstine (of Pere Ubu) on sax and synthesizer.

Compilation appearances have been confined to:- *Hurricane Fighter Plane* on *Austin Landing* (LP) and *Born Bad, Vol. 4*; *Hurricane Fighter Plane* (demo) on *Acid Dreams Vol. 2* (LP); plus five cuts on the *Epitaph For A Legend* (Dble LP) compilation. Two - *Nickle Niceness* and *Vile Vile Gross* - were previously unissued. The other three were different recordings of *Hurricane Fighter Plane*, *Pink Stainless Tail* and *Transparent Radiation*. They do also have *Hurricane Fighter Plane* on a 7" flexi-disc (Radar SFI.347) issued in 1978. The other three cuts are by the **13th Floor Elevators**. They also have one cut *Pink Stainless Tail* on a 7" promotional release (Radar SAM-88) that came out the same year. Copies were given away at a 1978 reunion concert along with the magazine 'Howdy From Texas The Lone Star State'.

Jesse Chamberlain is also a member of Necessaries and Steve Cunningham later played for Malachi. (VJ)

The Reddlemen

45: I Can't Go This Way/ I'm Gonna Get In That Girl's Mind (Custom 131) 1967

Came out of Tyler in Texas. The flip, *I'm Gonna Get In That Girls Mind*, has some typical screeched vocals with catchy guitar.

Compilation appearances include: *I'm Gonna Get In That Girls Mind* on *Sixties Archive, Vol. 2* (CD), *Texas Punk From The Sixties* (LP), *Teenage Shutdown, Vol. 4* (LP & CD) and *Flashback, Vol. 6* (LP). (VJ/MW)

The (Roaring) Red Dogs

Personnel incl: STEVE ELLIOT gtr
DAVE JEWELL
JERRY KNACK

45s: Open Up/We're Gonna Hate Ourselves In The Morning (Atco 6497) 1965/6
Tomorrow/Fix It (Veritas 71969) 1969
Tomorrow/Family Tree (by Macy & Co) (Kansas Bankers Weekly no #) 1969

This eight-piece outfit formed in Lawrence, Kansas, in the mid-sixties and continued giging into the 1970s. They were originally known as The Limits. Considered to have been one of the best acts to have graced the Midwest, their music ranged from fuzz-rock to horn-rock. A good example of the former was *Open Up*, which you'll also find on *Monsters Of The Midwest, Vol. 1* or *Boulders, Vol. 3* (LP). A recent compilation *Midwest Garage Band Series - Kansas* (3-CD) from 1993 also includes both sides of their Atco 45 plus a live *But It's Allright* from 1967.

Some band members later played for Smoke Rings, a Norfolk, Nebraska band. (VJ)

Redemption

Personnel incl: BEKAH CRABB vcls A
KEMPER CRABB A

ALBUM: 1(A) LOOK UP (Evan/Comm) 1975 SC

From San Antonio, Texas, a rare Christian folk-psych with twelve string guitar, bass, drums and male/female vocals and occasional organ and fuzz guitar.

Kemper and Bekah Crabb would later play in another Texan group, Arkangel. (SR)

RED CRAYOLA - The Parable Of Arable Land LP.

RED PONY - Red Pony LP.

Redeye

Personnel:	BOB BEREMIAN	drms	AB
	DAVE HODGKINS	gtr, vcls	AB
	BILL KIRKHAM	bs, vcls	AB
	DOUGLAS "RED" MARK	ld gtr, vcls	AB
	(JIM GORDON	drms	A)

HCP

ALBUMS:	1(A)	REDEYE	(Pentagram PE 10003) 1970 113 -
	2(B)	ONE MAN'S POISON	(Pentagram PE 10006) 1971 - -

NB: (1) also released in New Zealand (Festival SFL-93397).

HCP

45:	Games/	
	Collections Of Yesterday And Now	(Pentagram P204) 1970 27
	Red Eye Blues/?	(Pentagram P 206) 1971 78
	Just A Little More/Same (mono)	(Pentagram P20?) 1973 -

Produced by Al Schmitt, a California group mixing CSN&Y harmonies and excellent West Coast guitars, courtesy of Douglas Mark. Dave Hodgkins (ex-**Sunshine Company**) was their leader and wrote all their songs. The first album's best tracks are probably *Games*, *Dadaeleus' Unfinished Dream* and *Collections Of Yesterday And Now*. It spent twelve weeks in the Top 200, peaking at No. 113.

One Man's Poison is a bit bluesier and the guitars are more prominent. Cuts like *The Seeker* (not the Who song), *Cold In The Night* and *Walter Why Knott* are the best moments of a record which may interest some. (SR/GM/TJH/VJ)

The Red House

Personnel:	JAMES COCO	vcls	A
	JIM HOWARD	gtr, vcls	A
	JAMES NOE	bs, vcls	A
	STEVE SCHULTZ	drms	A

45:	Sunflower/Mary Jane	(Big 'K' 1004) 1969

A later version of **Stereo Shoestring** who were based in Corpus Christi in Texas from late 1968 until 1969. Their 45 was a rock'n'roller. (VJ)

The Red Lite District

Personnel incl?:	M. CHRISTIAN	A
	C. CLAYTON	A

45s:	Mr. Feelgood/I Gotta Know	(Mae # unknown) 196?
	Mr. Feelgood/I Gotta Know	(Scepter 12250) 1969

An obscure band whose upfront riffin' brassy pop-rocker *Mr.Feelgood* can be heard on *I'm Trippin' Alone* (LP). *I Gotta Know* is on *Psychedelic Unknowns, Vol. 5* (LP & CD). (VJ/MW)

Red Mountain

Personnel:	ROD MOXIE	bs	AB
	CHRIS OESCH	gtr	A
	LARRY OTIS	gtr	AB
	BRICE SULLIVAN	vcls, hrmnca	AB
	LLOYD WICK	drms	AB
	STEVE AVERY	gtr	B

ALBUM: 1(A/B) RED MOUNTAIN AND THE CHOSEN FAMILY
(Rockadelic RRLP 41) 2003

Red Mountain was the house band at The Chosen Family commune at Rancho Olompali in Novato, California, in 1968-69, after **The Grateful Dead** had moved out. The site is now a State Park, but from the mid-sixties to the early seventies it was (much to the chagrin of the residents of upscale Marin County) a notorious hippie haven and magnet for runaway teenage girls who managed to misplace their clothing shortly after arriving.

Red Mountain held daily rehearsals in the loft of a barn on the property, the hay loading doors flung wide open to the communal landscape. A few informally-recorded reel to reel tapes reveal the band as purveyors of a primitive, evil, distorted blues sound; tailor-made for the Rockadelic label. No awards will be given for high-fidelity here, but the San Francisco sound is so thick that it renders most professionally-recorded albums from the era impotent by comparison. The retrospective album has extensive liner notes documenting the communal debauchery and a lovely nude cover.

Red Mountain recorded a demo at Sierra Sound Labs in 1969 that got them an invitation to make an album in Los Angeles with the producer Roger Dollarhide (Randy Californias' *Kapt. Kopter And The Fabulous Twirly Birds*) and they left Rancho Olompali in the Fall of 1969 to pursue that opportunity. The next chapter in the band's history was also documented by Rockadelic (see **Born Again** entry). (CF)

Red Pony

Personnel:	CARL GAUGER	bs, vcls	A
	HANK LAAKE	drms, vcls	A
	BRIAN McVEY	gtr, vcls	A
	TIM MURRAY	keyb'ds, vcls	A
	KATHY TURNER	vcls	A

ALBUM:	1(A)	RED PONY	(Artco LPR 1123) 1975 R1

A local Oklahoma private press, featuring very aggressive hard-rock with Turner's gutsy lead vocals to the fore. All the material is original except for a cover of Janis Joplin's *Move Over*. (CF)

Red Roosters

Personnel:	MARK ANDES		A
	ED CASSIDY	drms	A
	JAY FERGUSON		A
	MIKE FOURNIER		A
	RANDY WOLFE	gtr	A

If the names seem familiar this L.A. band was a pre-**Spirit** line-up. No known releases. (MW)

Red Shadow

ALBUM:	1	THE ECONOMICS ROCK AND ROLL BAND
		(Physical 21-005) 1975 -

An unusual political rock album with tracks like *Stagflation*, *Movement Lovers*, *Understanding Marx* and *Ass With The Class*. (SR)

RED, WILDER, BLUE - Red, Wilder, Blue LP.

Red, Wilder, Blue

Personnel:	MIKE BALLEW	gtr, vcls	A
	LUCKY FLOYD	drms, vcls	A
	MACK TUBB	gtr, vcls	A
	DANNY WILDER	bs, piano, vcls	A

ALBUM: 1(A) RED, WILDER, BLUE (Pentagram PE 10007) 1971 -

A California group who mixed CSN&Y harmonies and West Coast guitars with good folk and country. The highlight of their album is an excellent and long cover of the **Youngbloods**' *Darkness, Darkness* beginning with Indian chants.

All their other songs were written by Danny Wilder and Mike Ballew (who later played with Rusty Wier). It was produced by Al Schmitt.

Originating from Texas, Lucky Floyd was previously in **The Sparkles**. (SR)

The Redwoods

45: Tell Me / Little Latin Lupe Lu (Phalanx 1030) 1966

Fuzz, Flaykes And Shakes, Vol. 3 (LP & CD) features *Tell Me*, not the Stones hit but a moody strummin' original. Nothing has been uncovered about this Michigan outfit whose sole 45 was the final release on the highly collectable Phalanx label out of Portage, Michigan. (MW/TSz)

The Reekers

Personnel incl:	JIM DANIELS	drms	A
	TOM GUERNSEY	gtr	AB
	JOE TRIPLETT	vcls	AB
	BOB BERBERICH	drms	B
	MIKE GRIFFIN	bs	B

45:	Don't Call Me Flyface / Grindin'	(Ru-Jac 13) 1965
	What A Girl Can't Do/	
	The Girl Who Faded Away	(Edgewood acetate) 1965

An aggressive surf-oriented instrumental combo from Montgomery County, Maryland. - check out *Don't Call Me Flyface* on the *Signed, D.C.* (LP) compilation. Led by Tom Guernsey, they evolved into **The Hangmen**, who also included Bob Berberich. **The Hangmen** quickly re-recorded two **Reekers** songs, *The Girl Who Faded Away* and *What A Girl Can't Do*, although you can still find the original acetate version of *The Girl Who Faded Away* on *Garage Dreams Revisited* (EP).

Tom Guernsey would turn up post-**Hangmen** as the writer and producer of the sole 45 by another Montgomery County band **The Omegas**, featuring fellow **Reeker** Joe Triplett. (VJ/MW/BE)

Reets

Personnel:	TEDDY BUCKLEY	bs, vcls	AB
	RICKY McWHORTER	gtr, vcls	AB
	ALSTON MEEKS	ld gtr, vcls	A
	JIMMY PAMBANCHI	ld vcls, hrmnca, tambourine	AB
	MIKE TURNIPSEED	drms	AB
	JOHN DANRUTHER	ld gtr	B
	RICHARD MUNS	bs, gtr	B

45:	When You Brought Me You /	
	Why Can't Time Stand Still	(Dimac 1001) 196?

Cool garagey sounds from the Mississippi Delta. *When You Brought Me You* is a catchy soulful pop number with raw heartfelt vocals and atmospheric keyboards. *Why Can't Time Stand Still* is a haunting beat ballad.

Sid Herring of **The Gants** occasionally deputised on vocals. The band lasted into the seventies and eighties and got together again in 1999 for a celebratory gig in Clarksdale, Missouri. with the Curb Service Band featuring ex-**Gants** Johnny Jennings and John Freeman. (MW/JK/JJeandRMs)

The Reflections

Personnel:	DAVID BELLAH	gtr	A
	ROBBIE HOLCOMB	drms	A
	ED CALDERONE	ld gtr	A
	STEVE LINDQUIST	bs	A

45: Let Me Go/A Little Bit More (Reflections 141/2) 1967

From Roseville, California. Both sides of their crude sounding 45 can be found on *The Sound Of Young Sacramento* (CD).

The Reflections

Personnel:	DAN BENNIE		A
	PHIL CASTRODALE		A
	JOHN DEAN		A
	TONY MICALE	ld vcls	A

		HCP
45s:	Just Like Romeo And Juliet/Can't You Tell	
	By The Look In My Eyes	(Golden World GW-8) 1964 6
	Like Columbus Did/?	(Golden World GW-12) 1964 96
	Oowee Now/?	(Golden World GW-15) 1964 -
	(I'm Just A) Hen Pecked Guy/	
	?	(Golden World GW-16) 1964 124
	Shabby Little Hut/	
	You're My Baby	(Golden World GW-19) 1964 121
	Poor Man's Son/Comin' At You	(Golden World GW-20) 1965 55
	Wheelin' And Dealin'	(Golden World Gw-22) 1965 -
	Out Of The Picture/?	(Golden World GW-24) 1965 -
	Girl In The Candy Store/?	(Golden World GW-29) 1965 -
	Like Adam And Eve/?	(ABC 10794) 1966 -
	Long Cigarette/?	(ABC 10822) 1966 -

A forgotten garage pop group, who enjoyed quite a lot of chart success. (SR/VJ)

The Regents

45s:	When I Die, Don't You Cry/	
	She's Got Her Own Way Of Lovin'	(Reprise 0430) 1965
	Summer Time Blues/You Don't Love Me	(Peoria 008) 1966
α	Words/Worryin' Kind	(Penthouse 502) 1966
	Russian Spy And I/Bald-Headed Woman	(Dot 16970) 1966

NB: α also released in the UK (CBS 202247) 1966.

One of a few **Regents** around at the time, this bunch were based in L.A. The Reprise 45 is ok, a folk-rock ditty backed by catchy beat-pop with harmonica. Their subsequent efforts are definitely meritorious - kickin' off with a swingin' version of Eddie Cochran's classic, backed by a handclappin' brassy version of a popular song covered by the likes of the **Sinners**, **Kim and Grim**, **Starlets**, and **Kaleidoscope**.

Next up, a great cover of *Words*, also recorded by **The Monkees** and the **Boston Tea Party**. This deep-throated version adds a quick burst of fuzz and a touch of Eastern promise, whilst the flip is good rockin' beat-pop. *Russian Spy...* is solid pop-beat with a touch of humour - also a hint of novelty in the Russian-dance-meets-Dick Dale guitar-break that sounds better than this lame description can convey. *Bald...* is a raucous party blast too.

Two more 45s - *Me And You/Playmates* (Blue Cat 110) 1965 and *That's What I Call A Good Time/??* (Kayo 101) 196? may or may not be connected to this group.

Compilation coverage has so far included: *Words* features on *Killer Cuts* (LP); *Worryin' Kind* on *Acid Dreams, Vol. 3* (LP); and *Russian Spy And I* is on *Psychedelic Unknowns, Vol. 9* (CD). (MW)

The Regents

Personnel: SAL CUOMO A
CHUCK FASSERT A
TONY GRAVAGNA A
DON JACOBUCCI A
GUY VILLARI A

ALBUM: 1(A) LIVE AT THE AM/PM DISCOTHEQUE
(Capitol KAO-2153) 1964 -

An early sixties rock quintet with sax, recorded live. They cover the classics *Mojo Workout*, *Blue Suede Shoes*, *Hully Gully* and *Linda Lu*.

The album was produced by **David Axelrod**. (SR)

The Regiment

Personnel incl: EVERETT R. AMUNDSON keyb'ds A
PETE MILIO drms A
WAYNE PURSELL bs A
JOE REAM A
RALPH vcls, gtr A
RICK vcls, gtr A

45: My Soap Won't Float/The Sinking Violet (G&G #305) 1967

Formed originally as "The". Wayne Pursell had been one of the founding members of **The Shadows Of Knight** and formed this act whilst at the University Of Illinois in Urbana. Wayne:- "Instead of just saying 'The' people would say 'the The' or they would spell the letters. This didn't have the right ring to it so I changed the name to something less clever and more commercial, **The Regiment**. The band wore old WWI army uniforms and easily became the most popular local band at the university inside two years. This became a problem, because I had quit the previous band to study at the Univ. and found that I was working every day with the band and had no time to study. So, I had to quit **The Regiment**, too".

All the band members originally came from Chicago, (with the exception of a lead guitar player from Falls Church, West Virginia) and Joe Ream had earlier played in **The Rip Tides**. Before Wayne quit in late 1966, he wrote *My Soap Won't Float*, which the band later recorded and released in the Summer of '67.

My Soap Won't Float is definitely worth checking out, with its way out lyrics:- (MW/MM/WP)

The Rehabilitation Cruise

Personnel incl: L. OWEN

45: Don't Care What They Say/Mini Skirts (Rondon 2119/20) 196?

A very obscure folk protest outfit from Wisconsin. Side 'A' is actually an anti-protest song exhorting the virtues of fighting for ones country in some faraway paddie field. It's pretty awful but you'll find it on *Highs In The Mid-Sixties, Vol. 10*. *Highs In The Mid Sixties, Vol. 15 - Wisconsin, Part 2* (LP) of the same series includes the flip - a put down of mini skirts! It's actually rather catchy, though. (VJ)

KILLER CUTS (Comp LP) including The Regents.

Rejects

Personnel incl: JERRY De MARCO Jnr.

45s: All Of My Life/Just A Little Bit Of You (Cabell 107) 196?
Black Is Black/Down This Street Before (Cabell 113) 196?

An obscure, possibly Virginian outfit.

Compilation appearances have included: *Down This Street Before* on *The Lost Generation, Vol. 2* (LP); *All Of My Life* on *Sixties Punk Ballads Sampler* (LP); and *Just A Little Bit Of You* on *It's A Hard Life* (LP). (VJ/MW)

Rejoice!

Personnel: NANCY BROWN A
TOM BROWN A

ALBUM: 1(A) REJOICE! (Dunhill DS 500??) c1970 -
HCP

45s: Sonora/Spring Flew In Today (Dunhill D-4152) 1968 -
Golden Gate Park/Sonora (Dunhill D-4158) 1968 96
α November Snow/Quick Draw Man (Dunhill D-4176) 1969 126
Sausalito Surprise/
Spring Flew In Today (Dunhill D-4189) 1969 -

NB: α also issued in the UK (Stateside SS 8010) 1969.

An obscure and forgotten husband and wife folk/rock duo. Their best known song *Golden Gate Park* spent one week in the Top 100 at No. 96. (SR/MMs/VJ)

Reknown

45s: It Ain't All Right With Me / Summertime (E&M 2904) 1966
You And Me / Leave (General American GAR 108) 1967
I Can't Go On/Can't Get Enough Of Your Love (My 2928) 1967

A Little Rock, Arkansas outfit whose second 45, recorded in Chicago, features a melodious yearning **Byrdsy** jangler backed by a catchy beat-punker with attitude. Composer credits are Delane Campbell and Campbell-Quattelbaum. The other 45s are unheard but the third 45 has been described as "horn pop". (MW/MM)

Relatively Clean Rivers

Personnel:
	KURT BAKER	vcls, gtr	A
	DWIGHT MOROUSE	drms	A
	PHIL PEARLMAN	vcls, gtr, bs, sahz, hrmnca, keyb'ds	A
	(JOHN ALABASTER	perc	A)
	(HANK QUINN	perc	A)

ALBUM: 1(A) RELATIVELY CLEAN RIVERS
(Pacific Is PC 17601) 1976 R3

NB: (1) issued in two different sleeve designs. One has lyrics printed on the inner gatefold, the other doesn't. Both pressings include a photo insert.

Former **Beat Of The Earth** leader Phil Pearlman assembled this band in the early seventies and eventually recorded this magnificent rural-rock album in 1975. The *Relatively Clean Rivers* album stands with the very best albums of the era, possessing a purely American sound and walking confidently past the shadow of its previous incarnation. Amazingly well produced for a private pressing, it is the very antithesis of his earlier releases that could be classified as garage (at a stretch, perhaps - they are not without a certain tangible sophistication). No measurable degree of time or expense was spared in the creation of the *Relatively Clean Rivers* album, which took over a year to assemble and is the most flawless snapshot of the California seventies underground scene you will ever hear.

While it should be easy to describe the sound the band produced, it most definitely is not. There are moments where they sound like **The Grateful Dead** at their most ethereal, for example like *Box Of Rain* from *American Beauty*; but other tracks on *'Rivers* are utterly psychedelic in the **Damin Eih** way (although this album smells more like thai stick than acid). *The Persian Caravan* is as Eastern as the title suggests; Pearlman's collection of ethnic instruments used by the band to good effect. The lyrics are both funny and thought-provoking, especially when addressing religion:

"Could I believe if I had nothing to gain?
Would I walk away to paradise,
Or keep on playin' the game?"

Famed poster artist Jim Evans was enlisted for the cover, which must be seen to be believed. Imagine a cross between **The Chocolate Watchband**'s *No Way Out* and one of those dayglo head shop posters and you'll have some idea. (Some of Evans' other rock-orientated commissions include **The Cosmic Travelers** album cover, the movie poster for *A Sea For Yourself*, and **The Allman Brothers**' *Wipe The Windows* album cover.)

There were two pressings of the album (500 each) and Pearlman hand-distributed them throughout California for a couple of years, even leaving copies on college campuses (under trees; on benches, etc!) and used a special technique that he referred to as "reverse shoplifting" to get them into record shops (use your imagination!).

RELATIVELY CLEAN RIVERS - Relatively Clean Rivers LP.

Of the (known) private pressings that Phil Pearlman was involved with, *Relatively Clean Rivers* is the easiest one to acquire and is recommended to anyone even remotely interested in seventies music. None of his albums have been reissued as of yet. (CF)

The Rel-Yea's

Personnel:
	JIMMY BISSET	bs	AB
	JIMMIE BOLADO	gtr/ld gtr	AB
	ZEKE GREEN	ld gtr	A
	?? ??	drms	A
	JIM FRIZZELL	gtr, keyb'ds	B
	EDDIE GUIERRO	drms	B

45s:
The Rugged Rock/ Good, Good Lovin'	(Kaye Records KY-101)	196?
You Know How/Julida Polka	(Kaye Records KY-102)	196?
The Crawl/Tu-Ber-Cu-Las (And The Sinus Blues)	(Kaye Records KY-103)	196?

From San Antonio, Texas, this band featured members from MacArthur, Highlands and Edison High schools. Despite being only aged 13-16 they played all over Texas and in and around San Antonio, opening for Roy Orbison in Corpus Christi, and at the premier of The Beatles 'Hard Day's Night' film at the Texas Theatre in downtown San Antonio. They also played at the Joe Freeman Collisium Rolling Stones concert, along with a few other 'unknown' British groups including Gerry and The Pacemakers, as Jim Frizzell recalls:- "That was before they had released any music in the U.S. so nobody had heard of them yet... We had a great time backstage talking to each other, they liked our Texas accents and we like their British accents... go figure".

Other gigs included performing at the Grand Ol' Opera in Nashville with Minnie Pearl, Little Jimmie Dickens, and a few others.

Jim:- "We also did lots of sock hops for Disc Jockey Rickey Ware and Bruce Hathaway (KTSA), Teen Canteen and Officer Clubs around S.A. We played lots of Proms and Senior dances in just about every small town within 300 miles of San Antonio."

Jim Frizzell later joined **The Chayns**. (IT/JF)

The Remaining Few

Personnel:
	ROBERT GLODT	drms	A
	MIKE JONES	gtr	ABC
	FROSTY McKEE	bs	ABC
	JOEL MULKEY	vcls	ABC
	ROBERT SPECHT	ld gtr	ABC
	CHARLES USERY	drms	BC
	LARRY LOGAN	keyb'ds	C

45: Painted Air/In The Morning (Askel 112) 1967

Formed in San Angelo, Texas, as a foursome of fourteen year olds in 1964 called The Boys, they had changed their name to **The Remaining Few** and stabilised into line-up 'A' by 1966, They were the house band at San Angelo's top 13th Hour club for two years. Their 45 was produced by Ron Newdoll and only 300 copies were pressed. The 'A' side was brilliant garage psychedelia, commencing with a screeching intro which gradually slows down in tempo. The lyrics are sung to minimum instrumentation with each verse sandwiched by further screeching guitar work.

The flip, *In The Morning*, turns out to be a moody garage ballad with a melody reminiscent of Gerry and The Pacemakers' *Ferry Cross The Mersey*.

They spent some time in San Francisco before disbanding in 1970.

Compilation appearances have included: *Painted Air* on *Acid Dreams - The Complete 3 LP Set* (3-LP), *Acid Dreams Testament* (CD), *Austin Landing, Vol. 2* (LP), *Acid Dreams, Vol. 1* (LP) and *Highs In The Mid-Sixties, Vol. 12* (LP); and *In The Morning* and *Painted Air* on *The Human Expression And Other Psychedelic Groups - Your Mind Works In Reverse* (CD). (VJ/MW)

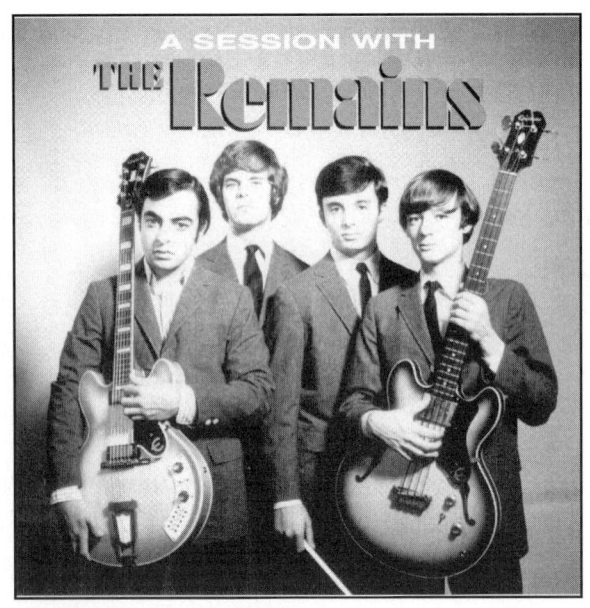

THE REMAINS - A Session With CD.

The Remains

Personnel: WILLIAM BRIGGS   keyb'ds   AB
            CHIP DAMIANI   drms   A
            VERN MILLER   bs, gtrs, horns AB
            BARRY TASHIAN   gtr, vcls   AB
            N.D. SMART II   drms   B

NB: There was also a fill-in bass player with **The Remains**, David Sherman (originally from Brookline, MA, and Boston University), who is in the photo on the cover of the Epic LP: second from the right.

ALBUMS: 1(A)   REMAINS   (Epic 24214) 1967 R2
        2(A)   REMAINS   (Spoonfed 3305) 1978 -
        3(A)   DIDDY WAH DIDDY   (Eva 12007) 1982 -
        4(A)   LIVE IN BOSTON   (Eva 12024) 1983 -
        5(A)   THE REMAINS (dbl.)   (New Rose ROSE FC 012) 1985 -
        6( )   A SESSION WITH THE REMAINS
                                         (Sundazed LP 5015) 1996 -

NB: (2) is a reissue of (1) with additional material. (2) reissued on vinyl (Sundazed LP 5055) 1998. (3)-(6) are all posthumous releases and their most accessibly recordings. (6) is an album of demos and features the same material as (4) but with the fake applause removed. It is also available on CD (SC 6069). For CD collectors, there's also a 26 cut 'Best Of' CD and a CD on Epic entitled *Barry And The Remains*.

10" EP: 1 THE REMAINS   (Sundazed SEP 10-162) 2000

NB: (1) is a six-pack of '65-'66 recordings making their vinyl debut, including a previously unheard alternate version of *All Good Things*.

                                                               HCP
45s: I'm Talking About You/
       You Say You're Sorry   (Epic 9777) 1965 -
       But I Ain't Got You/
       I Can't Get Away From You   (Epic 9872) 1965 -
       Diddy Wah Diddy/Once Before   (Epic 10001) 1966 129
   α   Diddy Wah Diddy / Diddy Wah Diddy (Epic) 1966 -
       Don't Look Back/Me Right Now   (Epic 10060) 1966 -
   β   Why Do I Cry/Mercy Mercy (PS)   (Spoonfed 4505) 1978 -

NB: α white label promo 45 on red wax. β 'A' side previously appeared on a promo-only release in 1965. They also recorded four unissued singles for Spoonfed.

A highly-regarded Massachusetts punk band, who were originally known as Barry and The Remains. They had quite a reputation in the Boston area in the late sixties and opened for The Beatles last tour in the Summer of 1966.

The Sundazed *A Session With* retrospective is an albums worth of demos they recorded for Capitol in May 1966. The demos had earlier been released by Eva as *Live In Boston* but the only thing 'live' about it is that the tracks were recorded live in the studio in one take. The Eva version included fake applause and isn't recommended - get the Sundazed issue instead... Strong covers and one stellar original, *Why Do I Cry*, prove once again that **The Remains** were one of the very best. It also contains a never-before-heard version of *Walkin' The Dog* plus five more alternate/rehearsal tracks.

Briggs and Tashian were later part of an embryonic Flying Burrito Brothers line-up and Barry was also connected with **Chirco** who released one rather rare album *The Visitation* on Crested Butte. He's still an active musician on the folk circuit and has published a book 'Ticket To Ride' - his diary of The Beatles last U.S. tour on which **The Remains** were a support act.

Although Billy Vera wrote *Don't Look Back* **The Remains** made it their own. The song was also recorded by The Instincts, (to be found on *New England Teen Scene Vol.III*) and by **The Rising Storm** on their *Calm Before* LP (also featured on *Endless journey - Phase 1*). A couple of **The Remains**' original tunes have also been covered, including *I Can't Get Away From You* - in 1967 by Don Craine's New Downliners Sect (hear it on *Voyage Through The Sugarcube*) and The Cynics on their 1986 LP *Blue Train Station*. *Why Do I Cry* was also covered by Australia's Vyt and The World (*Ugly Things Vol.2*).

In 1998 Barry, Billy, Vern and original pre-Beatles-Tour drummer Chip Damiani were invited to Spain, where they still enjoy a fanatical following, for a reunion event. This was followed by the Cavestomp '98 event nearer to home in NYC in November and turned out to be a warm-up for a historic homecoming at the Paradise Club in Boston on 20th March 1999. Headlining with a reformed **Lost** and **The Rising Storm**, this was the ultimate Boston tea-party.

The Remains were in smokin' form, tight and rockin', with Barry's vocals in fine fettle. The band seemed to get as much of a buzz as the 600+ sell-out crowd, whose age-range attested to their timeless appeal. They included several covers (*My Girl Sloopy*, *Lonely Weekend*, *Walkin' The Dog*, *My Babe* and for an encore *I'm A Man*) but most importantly many of their best originals (which Barry pointed out they'd not performed live very often) - *Why Do I Cry*, a wonderful *Thank You*, a stunning *Ain't That Her*, and *All Good Things*. Of course Billy Vera's *Don't Look Back* was reserved for the climax of a truly memorable gig for all concerned.

Compilation appearances have included: *I Can't Get Away From You* on *Mayhem & Psychosis, Vol. 3* (LP); *Don't Look Back* and *Why Do I Cry* on *Nuggets Box* (4-CD);   (VJ/AGI/MW/JNa)

The Renagades

Personnel incl: LORIN RUGGIERO   A

45:       Waiting For You/Tell Me What To Say   (Polaris 501) 1966

A New Hampshire outfit, they weren't connected to **Richie's Renegades** who also recorded for Polaris.

Compilation appearances include *Waiting For You* on *New England Teen Scene, Vol. 2* (LP); *Waiting For You* and *Tell Me What To Say* on *The Polaris Story* (CD). (VJ)

The Renegades (IV/V)

Personnel: ALLDAY
             DEBAUB
             HAUFLER
             SCHWARTZ
             SHINE

45s: α   Greensleeves/Autumn Night   (Fenton 945) c1964
      β   Wine, Wine, Wine/Love And Fury   (Duboney 982) c1965
          She's Your Find / Raving Blue   (Cambridge 121103/4) 1966

NB:b α as Renegades IV. β as Renegades V.

A Grand Rapids, Michigan, quartet who started out in 1963 as **The Renegades IV**. By the time of their second release they'd expanded to a quartet and were duly billed as **The Renegades V**; by the time of their final 45 in the Summer of 1966 they'd stopped counting.

The second 45 on the Fenton custom label 'Dubonay' uncorks the frantic rocker *Wine, Wine, Wine* featuring some wild surf guitar.

Compilation appearances include: *Autumn Night* on *Best Of Michigan Rock Groups, Vol. 2* (Cassette); *Wine Wine Wine* on *Wild! Wild!! Wild!!!* (LP) and *Highs In The Mid-Sixties, Vol. 6* (LP); and *She's Your Find* on *Let 'Em Have It! Vol. 1* (CD) and *Fuzz, Flaykes, And Shakes, Vol. 5* (LP & CD). (VJ/MW/TSz)

Rennaissance Fair

Personnel incl: WOODY LEFEEL   A

45s:	It's Still Her / ?	(Princeton 108) 196?
	In Wyrd/Simple Love	(Princeton 111) 196?

NB: A third 45 may be by the same band - *Always Love You / She's A Woman* (Astral Projection 170) 19??

A late sixties band from Michigan, possibly Jackson. Rumoured to include 2-ex Brambles. Woody Lefeel was apparently later in Black Rose, **Granicus** and Believe.

Their amazin' bad-trip garage-psych monster *In Wyrd* has been compiled on *Michigan Mixture, Vol. 1* (LP) and *Psychedelic Experience, Vol. 3* (CD). Their 45s are rarely seen and even less affordable. The patchy data is unconfirmed and presented in the hope that someone with better knowledge will come forth. (MW)

Mike Renolds and The 'Infants of Soul'

Personnel incl: MIKE RENOLDS   A

45s:	When Will I Find Her/It's Judy	(Frog Death 66-3) 1966
α	When Will I Find Her / Maybe I'll Be Seeing You Again	(Gum 1005) 1966

NB: α as **Mike Renolds and Bill Payne**.

A Texan garage band, possibly from El Paso. *When Will I Find Her* is quite catchy.

Compilation appearances include: *When Will I Find Her* on *Open Up Yer Door, Vol. 2* (LP), *Texas Flashbacks, Vol. 4* (LP & CD) and *Flashback, Vol. 4* (LP). (VJ/MW)

Research 1-6-12

Personnel:	DICK BOZZI		A
	DON BURNS		A
	MORRIE YESS	gtr	A

ALBUM:	1(A)	1-6-12 IN RESEARCH	(Flick City FC 5001) 1967 SC

45s incl:	I Don't Walk There No More/Juicy	(Flick City 3005) 1967
	Can You Baby/Lip Smackin' Good	(Flick City 3007) 1967

This folk-oriented band was based in Hollywood, Los Angeles. They recorded for Flick City Records who only issued three albums, were connected to cult figure **Kim Fowley** and whose records were distributed by MGM. The album is mediocre.

Aside from the above-mentioned album, they recorded three singles. One of these, *I Don't Walk There No More* is notable for some catchy guitar work and growling vocals.

Compilation appearances include *I Don't Walk There Anymore* on *Highs In The Mid-Sixties Vol. 3* (LP). (VJ)

The Restless Feelin's

45:	Hey, Mama, You've Been On My Mind/ A Million Things	(United Artists 50053) 1966

A sole major label outing for this obscure outfit. You could check out *A Million Things* on *Glimpses, Vol. 3* (LP). (VJ)

The Restless Knights

A Wichita, Kansas band who cut a Medley of songs which has resurfaced on *Hipsville, Vol. 2* (LP). It was previously unreleased. (VJ)

Retreds

45:	Black Mona Lisa/Johnny Be Good	(R&T RP 6601) 1966

A cool five piece from Acton, Massachusetts who were originally known as The Avanties. A very blues-influenced outfit they developed a strong local following in Eastern Massachusetts. Their parents loaned them the money to press and record the 45 in a small basement studio in Newton, Massachusetts. Their bluesy ode to a local femme fatale *Black Mona Lisa* can also be heard on *Back From The Grave, Vol. 7* (Dble LP), whilst the flip - a re-spelt cover of Chuck Berry's old nugget and can be found on *Teenage Shutdown, Vol. 11* (LP & CD). (MW)

Revelation

ALBUM:	1	REVELATION	(Mercury SR-61301) 1970 -

A mellow hippie sextet dressed in colorful tie-dye saris, with mixed male/female vocals and tracks like *Psalm 150*, *Beyond Myself*, *Someone Is Standing Outside* and *Pocketful Of Keys*. (SR)

The Revelation

45s:	Kiss Your Mind Goodbye / Dorplegank	(Combine 11/12) 196?
	Cotton Candy Weekend / Wait And See	(Music Factory MU 412) 1968

The first 45 listed above by this obscure California outfit is bouncy, almost 'toytown', Anglophile pop-psych - with both sides, written by Duke Baxter. More groovy but heavier pop-psych sounds abound on the Mike Post-produced Music Factory 45 where Baxter shares writer credits with arranger Kerry Hatch.

Compilation appearances include: *Kiss Your Mind Goodbye* and *Dorplegank* on *Sixties Rebellion, Vol. 11* (LP & CD). (MW)

RESEARCH 1-6-12 - 1-6-12 In Research LP.

Reveliers

Personnel incl: DON BECKWITH   ld gtr   A

45: Hangin' Five/Patch   (G-Clef 702) 1963

An obscure outfit, mainly from Newton, Massachusetts, who existed between 1960-64. Both sides of their hard rocking 45 can be found on the *Bay State Rock* (LP) compilation. (VJ)

The Revelles

Personnel incl: FREDDIE GLICKSTEIN
CHUCK JOBES
LES KUMMEL
B. MATTEY?

45s:
One More Day/I Know   (Freeport FR 1004) 1965
One More Day/
You Don't Love Me No More   (Freeport FR 1005) 1965
That's How Strong My Love Is/
Out Of Sight   (Jim Ko 41105) 1966
Something Good About Living/Little Girl   (Jim Ko 41106) 1966

This band was based in Chicago between 1965-67. Les Kummel and Chuck Jobes, both went on to **New Colony Six** and Freddie Glickstein also later played with **Flock**. The 'A' side of their third 45, was also coupled with the 'B' side of their 4th, and issued by L.A. label "RPR" as by **The Shady Days**.

Les Kummel sadly died in an auto accident on 19th Dec, 1978.

Compilation appearances include: *Little Girl* on *Pebbles Vol. 7* (CD); and *You Don't Love Me No More* on *Hipsville, Vol. 2* (LP). (VJ/MW/BSw)

Reverbs

45: Lie In The Shade Of The Sun/I Got The Need (Repro 425) 1968

From Georgia, this outfit didn't have any connection with the Connecticut act who put out an album entitled *Chalk-Up* in 1965.

Compilation appearances have included: *Lie In The Shade Of The Sun* on *Psychedelic Experience Vol. 4* (CD), *Victims Of Circumstance, Vol. 2* (LP & CD) and *Everywhere Chainsaw Sound* (LP). (VJ/MW)

Paul Revere and The Raiders

Personnel:
BILL HIBBERT	bs	A	
JERRY LABRUM	drms	A	
MARK LINDSAY	sax, vcls	ABCD	
PAUL REVERE	keyb'ds	ABCD	
RICHARD WHITE	gtr	A	
ROBERT WHITE	gtr	A	
ROSS ALAMANG	bs	B	
CHARLIE COE	gtr	B D	
MIKE HOLIDAY	bs	B	
PIERRE OULETTE	gtr	B	
MIKE SMITH	drms	BC	
STEVE WEST	gtr	B	
DRAKE LEVIN	gtr	C	
JIM VALLEY	gtr	C	
PHILIP VOLK	bs	C	
JOE CORRERRO	drms	D	
FREDDY WELLER	gtr	D	

NB: line-up 'A' 1961; B 1963-64; C 1964-67, D 1968.

ALBUMS: (up to 1972)
HCP
1(A) LIKE LONG HAIR   (Gardena LP-G 1000) 1961 - R2
2(B) PAUL REVERE AND THE RAIDERS
    (Sande S-1001) 1963 - R1/R2
3(B) HERE THEY COME   (Columbia CL-2307) 1964 71 -
4(C) JUST LIKE US   (Columbia CL-2451) 1965 5 -
5(C) MIDNIGHT RIDE   (Columbia CL-2508) 1966 9 -
6(-) IN THE BEGINNING   (Jerden JRL-7004) 1966 - -
7(C) THE SPIRIT OF '67   (Columbia CL-2595) 1967 9 -
8(-) PAUL REVERE AND THE RAIDERS GREATEST HITS
    (Columbia KCL-2662) 1967 15 -
9(C) REVOLUTION!   (Columbia CL-2721) 1967 25 -
10(C) A CHRISTMAS PRESENT ... AND PAST
    (Columbia CL-2755) 1967 - -
11(D) GOIN' TO MEMPHIS   (Columbia CL-2805) 1968 61 -
12(D) SOMETHING HAPPENING
    (Columbia CQ-1026) 1968 122 -
13(-) HARD'N HEAVY (with Marshmallow)
    (Columbia CO-1 074) 1969 51 -
14(-) PAUL REVERE AND THE RAIDERS
    (Columbia GP-1 2) 1969 166 -
15(-) ALIAS PINK PUZZ   (Columbia HC-1 214) 1969 48 -
16(-) PAUL REVERE AND THE RAIDERS FEATURING
    MARK LINDSAY   (Harmony KH-30089) 1970 - -
17(-) RAIDER'S COLLAGE   (Columbia KG-39964) 1970 154 -
18(-) GOOD THING   (Harmony KH-30975) 1971 - -
19(-) PAUL REVERE AND THE RAIDERS GREATEST
    HITS, VOL 2   (Columbia CS-30386) 1971 - -
20(-) INDIAN RESERVATION   (Columbia CS-30768) 1971 19 -
21(-) MOVIN' ON   (Harmony KH-31183) 1972 - -
22(-) COUNTRY WINE   (Columbia KC-31196) 1972 - -
23(-) ALL TIME GREATEST HITS
    (Columbia KG-31464) 1972 143 -

NB: (1) has been illegally reissued on white vinyl as *Rock 'n' Roll With Paul Revere And The Raiders*, with additional tracks. (4), (5), (7), (9), (11), (12), (13) and (15) reissued on CD by Sundazed (SC 6127, SC 6135, SC 6095, SC 6096, SC 6136, SC 6097, SC 6137 and SC 6138 respectively). All contain bonus tracks. The *Mojo Workout!* double-CD retrospective (Sundazed SC 11097) 2000, collects 44 tracks from their earliest years with Columbia, 1963 to 1965. It contains 15 unreleased cuts and rehearsals plus a couple of alternate versions served up with live studio takes, early 45 and LP cuts. There's also a 55-track double CD collection including ten previously unreleased cuts. *The Essential Ride '63-'67* was issued on the Rock Artifacts label in 1995 which contains twenty tracks, five of which are alternate previously unreleased versions. It has also appeared in the U.K. on Columbia (480954 2). Edsel have also issued a compilation in 1983 entitled *Kicks* and there is also a fine double LP bootleg called *Rarities* (Raring Records D-539).

HCP
45s:
Beatnik Sticks/Orbit (The Spy)   (Gardena 106) 1960 -
Paul Revere's Ride/Unfinished Fifth   (Gardena 115) 1961 -
Like Long Hair/Sharon   (Gardena 116) 1961 38
Like Charlestown/Midnight Ride   (Gardena 118) 1961 -
All Night Long/Groovy   (Gardena 124) 1961 -
Like Bluegrass/Leatherneck   (Gardena 127) 1962 -
Shake It Up(Pt 1)/Shake It Up (Pt 2)   (Gardena 131) 1962 -
Tall Cool One/Road Runner   (Gardena 137) 1962 -
So Fine/Blues Stay Away   (Jerden 807) 1963 -
Louie Louie/Night Train   (Sande 101) 1963 -
Louie Louie/Night Train   (Columbia 4-42814) 1963 103
Louie-Go Home/
Have Love Will Travel   (Columbia 4-43008) 1964 118
Over You/Swim   (Columbia 4-43114) 1964 133

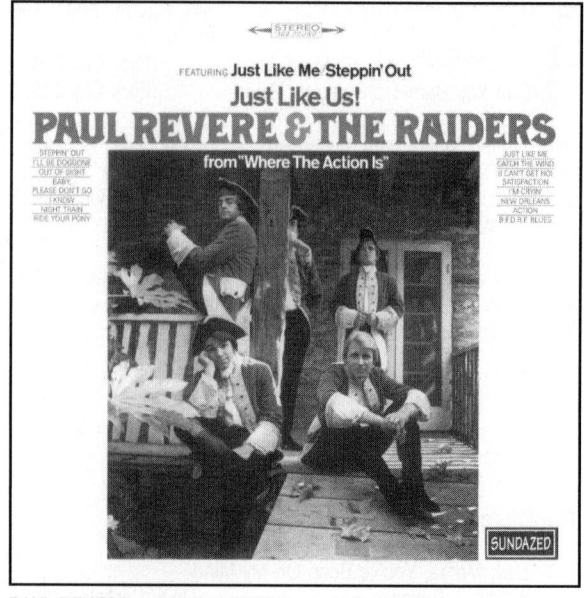

PAUL REVERE and THE RAIDERS - Just Like Us CD.

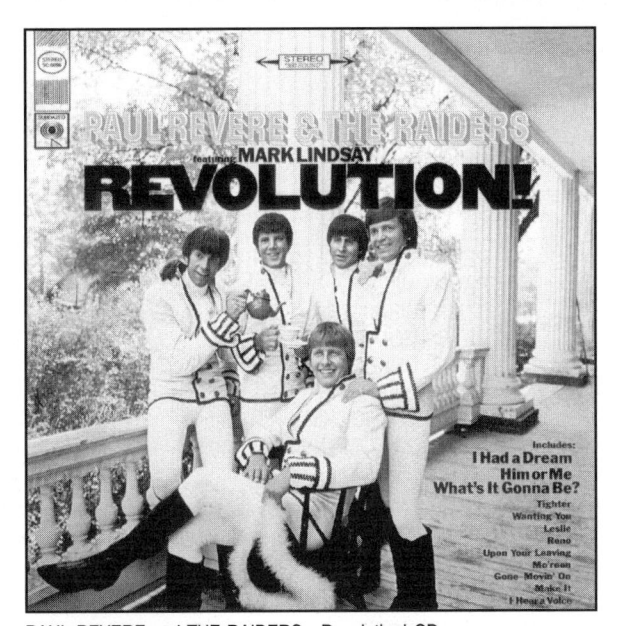

PAUL REVERE and THE RAIDERS - Revolution! CD.

	Oh Poo Pah Doo/Sometimes	(Columbia 4-43273) 1964	131
	Steppin' Out/Blue Fox	(Columbia 4-43375) 1965	46
	Just Like Me/B.F.D.R.F. Blues	(Columbia 4-43461) 1965	11
	Kicks/Shake It Up	(Columbia 4-43556) 1966	4
	Kicks/Kicks (promo only)	(Columbia 4-43556) 1966	-
	Hungry/There She Goes	(Columbia 4-43678) 1966	6
α	The Great Airplane Strike/ In My Community	(Columbia 4-43810) 1966	20
	Good Thing/Undecided Man	(Columbia 4-43907) 1966	4
	Ups And Down/Leslie	(Columbia 4-44018) 1967	22
α	Him Or Me, What's It Gonna Be/ Legend of Paul Revere	(Columbia 4-44094) 1967	5
	I Had A Dream/Upon You Leaving	(Columbia 4-44207) 1967	17
β	Io Sogno Te (aka I Had A Dream)/ Little Girl (aka Little Girl In The 4th Row)	(CBS) 1967	-
	Peace Of Mind/ Do Unto Others	(Columbia 4-44335) 1967	42/102
	Rain, Sleet, Snow/Brotherly Love	(Columbia 4-44376) 1967	-
	Too Much Talk/Happening	(Columbia 4-44444) 1968	19
	Don't Take It So Hard/ Observation From Flight 285	(Columbia 4-44553) 1968	27
	Cinderella Sunshine/ Theme From It's Happening	(Columbia 4-44655) 1968	58
	Mr Sun, Mr Moon/Without You	(Columbia 4-44744) 1969	18
	Let Me/I Don't Know	(Columbia 4-44854) 1969	20
	We Gotta All Get Together/ Frankfort Side Street	(Columbia 4-44970) 1969	50
	Just Seventeen/ Sorceress With Blue Eyes	(Columbia 4-45082) 1970	82
	Gone Movin' On/Interlude	(Columbia 4-45150) 1970	120
	Indian Reservation/Terry's Tune	(Columbia 4-45332) 1971	1
	Birds Of A Feather/The Turkey	(Columbia 4-45453) 1971	23
	Country Wine/ It's So Hard Gening Up Today	(Columbia 4-45535) 1972	51
	Powder Blue Mercedes Queen/ Golden Girls Sometimes	(Columbia 4- 45601) 1972	54
	Simple Song/Song Seller	(Columbia 4-45688) 1972	96
	Love Music/?	(Columbia 4-45759) 1973	97
	Gonna Have A Good Time/ Your Love	(Columbia 3-10126) 1975	-
	The British Are Coming/?	(20th Century 2281) 1976	-

(Columbia Hall Of Fame)
45s:

	Louie Louie/Louie Go Home	(Columbia 33082) 197?	-
	Kicks/Just Like Me	(Columbia 33098) 197?	-
	The Great Airplane Strike/Hungry	(Columbia 33106) 197?	-
	Ups And Downs/Goodthing	(Columbia 33111) 197?	-
	Steppin' Out/ Him Or Me, What's It Gonna Be	(Columbia 33126) 197?	-
	Don't Take It So Hard/ Cinderella Sunshine	(Columbia 33137) 197?	-
	Cinderella Sunshine/ Mr. Sun, Mr. Moon	(Columbia 33162) 197?	-

NB: α also released in France with picture sleeves (CBS 2411 and 2737). β Italian only 45, with both songs sung in Italian. There is also a rare French EP with picture sleeve: *Steppin Out/Big Boy Pete/Fever/Louie, Louie* (CBS 5930)

Paul Revere formed his first band in Boise, Idaho in 1958 soon after getting kicked out of school. He originally called them The Downbeats but later **Paul Revere and The Raiders**. Whilst he owned a drive-in restaurant he befriended an 18 year old bakery delivery man **Mark Lindsay** whom he eventually recruited to his band on vocals. In the Spring of 1959 Paul headed for L.A. with a taped arrangement of an instrumental called Beatnik Sticks by his band. He was turned down by several companies but eventually got a contract from a guy who owned a pressing plant and put out recordings he liked on his own Gardena label. Later in April 1961 Gardena released an instrumental that made it into the national charts. However, the following year Paul was drafted and the group fell apart.

When he returned from service Paul decided to change his base to Portland, Oregon. **Mark Lindsay** joined him there but the other band members couldn't so he set about forming a new line-up (B). Eventually they got a manager Roger Hart who eventually got them signed to Columbia as its first rock act. They soon moved to L.A. and became regulars on the show 'Where The Action Is', which put them in the public eye. Just prior to their move to California they had also begun wearing the uniforms they became famous for, for the first time. They also hired the services of former Beatles publicity agent Derek Taylor and their albums were benefiting from first class production by the likes of Terry Melcher (the **Byrds**' producer) and Bruce Johnson (of The Beach Boys). From 1966 when they burst into the national charts with *Just Like Me* and *Kicks* (one of the first anti-drug songs) until well into the seventies they enjoyed considerable chart success. In later years they underwent several personnel changes. Although they began in the garage tradition, their exposure following their signing to 'Where The Action Is' killed off their underground appeal pointing them in a pop direction.

Raiders' members **Drake Levin**, Mike Smith and Phil Volk all later played in **Brotherhood** and **Friendsound**. Pierre Ouelette went on to **Don & The Goodtimes** and **Aesop & The Fables**, whilst Charlie Coe had earlier played in **Jack Eely & The Courtmen**. **Lindsay** and Alliso also recorded two singles as **The Unknowns**.

In 2001, the **Raiders** released a new CD *Ride To The Wall 2001* with three new songs and nine re-recordings of classics - profits from the CD go to Vietnam Veterans 'Ride To The Wall' foundation.

Compilation appearances have included: *Steppin' Out* and *Just Like Me* on *Nuggets Box* (4-CD); *Steppin' Out* on *Nuggets, Vol. 12* (LP); *Over You* and *Just Like Me* on *Nuggets, Vol. 8* (LP); *Like Charleston* on *Out Of Sight!* (LP); *Kicks* and *Shake It Up* on *Sixties Years, Vol. 2 - French 60's EP Collection* (CD); *Kicks* and *There She Goes* on *The Best Of Beat, Vol. 3* (LP); *Kicks* on *Wild Thing*; *Mojo Workout*, *Shake Rattle And Roll* and *Linda Lu* on *The Hitmakers* (LP); *Kicks* and *Night Train* on *The History Of Northwest Rock, Vol. 2* (LP); *Hungry* on *Born Bad (Songs The Cramps Taught Us), Vol. 2*; *Hungry* and *Just Like Me* on *Frat Rock! The Greatest*

PAUL REVERE and THE RAIDERS - Hard 'N' Heavy (with Marshmallow) CD.

Rock'N'Roll Party Tunes Of All Times (CD); Beatnik Sticks (1960) on Welcome To The Beat Generation; Like Charleston (1961) on Out Of Sight! - a 1968 compilation on the budget Design label; Shake It Up Pt. 1 (1962) on History Of Northwest Rock 7 (Cass); Louie Louie (1963) on The Best Of Louie Louie Vol. 2; and SS 396 (1966) on Mexican Rock & Roll Rumble.

Paul Revere & The Raiders are still going strong today. (VJ/PV/MW/SR)

Revival

| ALBUM: | 1 | REVIVAL | (Kama Sutra KSBS-2047) 1972 - |

45s:	α	Let Him In/Take A Lesson From Jesus	(A&M 1293) 1971
		One Too Many Goodbyes/	
		To No One In Particular	(Kama Sutra 550) 1972

NB: α may be by a different group.

An early seventies rock group with psychy touches. Judging by the cover of their only album, it may have been a Native American group like Redbone or **Xit**. (SR)

The Revlons

| 45: | Sugaree/So In Love | (Shurfine 006) 196? |

An Atlanta, Georgia, band whose good cover of Marty Robbins' Sugaree can also be found on Garage Zone, Vol. 2 (LP) and The Garage Zone Box Set (LP). (VJ)

Revolution

| 45: | A Guide For Living/Revolt | (Revolution RRP 8112) 196? |

A good primitive garage 45. (GG)

The Revolvers

45s:	Like Me/When You Were Mine	(Ty Tex TT-127) 196?
	Good Lovin' Woman/	
	Land Of 1,000 Dances	(Ty Tex TT-128) 196?
	I Love Lovin' You/Green Unicycle	(Ty Tex TT-131) 196?

Like Me is pleasantly jangly folk-pop like **Beau Brummels** whilst the flip is a haunting moody folk-rock dirge with a melodic structure loosely modelled on House Of The Rising Sun. If the later 45s are up to this standard they are well worth acquiring. The third 45 was apparently released as by Stan Gorman and The Revolvers. They hailed from Tyler, Texas. (MW)

L. J. Reynolds

| 45s: | Call On Me/Intruder | (Mainstream 717) 1969 |
| | Please Don't Set Me Free/Down On Me | (Mainstream 718) 1969 |

Four heavy slices of a soul-blues amalgam that do not offer anything which has not been done better elsewhere. Only Call On Me, an atmospheric blues-ballad, cries for attention. Three of the four were written by members of **Big Brother and The Holding Company**. (MK)

RFD

Personnel incl:	DAN GERMAIN	gtr	A
	RUSS McILLWAIN	gtr, keyb'ds	A
	DEBBIE McKEE	vcls	A

| ALBUM: | 1(A) | LEAD ME HOME | (Private Pressing) 1971 R2/R3 |

A private pressing offering some soft hippie-folk with mixed male/female vocals and tracks like He Is Coming, Loner, Long Time In The Rain and the title track. Most songs have a Christian content. (SR)

Rhinoceros

Personnel:	JOHN FINLEY	vcls	ABCDEF G
	MICHAEL FONFARA	keyb'ds	ABCDEF G
	ALAN GERBER	perc, vcls	ABC
	DOUG HASTINGS	gtr	ABC
	BILLY MUNDI	drms	ABC
	JERRY 'THE BEAR' PENROD	bs	A
	DANNY WEIS	gtr, perc	ABCDE
	STEVE WEIS	bs	B
	PETER HODGSON	bs	CDEFG
	EDDIE 'DUKE' EDWARDS	drms, vcls	D
	LARRY LEISHMAN	gtr, vcls	DEFG
	RICHARD CROOKS	drms	E
	MALCOLM TOMLINSON	drms	F
	ERIC JOHNSON	drms	G

NB: Although Pete Hodgson is shown in line-up 'C' onwards, he was also briefly in the initial band, prior to line-up 'A'.

				HCP
ALBUMS:	1(A)	RHINOCEROS	(Elektra 74030) 1968	115 -
	2(C)	SATIN CHICKENS	(Elektra 74056) 1969	105 -
	3(D)	BETTER TIMES ARE COMING	(Elektra 74075) 1970	178 -

NB: (1) reissued on CD (Collectors Choice Music CCM 284 2) 2002.

			HCP
45s:	You're My Girl/I Will Serenade You	(Elektra 45640) 1968	-
	Apricot Brandy/		
	When You Say You're Sorry	(Elektra 45647) 1969	46
	I Need Love/Belbeukus	(Elektra 45659) 1969	-
	Back Door/In A Little Room	(Elektra 45677) 1969	-
	Let's Party/Old Age	(Elektra 45691) 1970	-
	Better Times/It's A Groovy World	(Elektra 45694) 1970	109

Assembled by **Doors/Love** producer Paul Rothchild, this Los Angeles outfit was largely composed of ex-members of well-known bands and is hence regarded as one of the first 'supergroups'. In fact they evolved out of Elektra Records Project Supergroup, formed between November '67 and February '68. Danny Weis and Jerry Penrod were from the **Iron Butterfly**, Michael Fonfara the **Electric Flag**, Billy Mundi the **Mothers Of Invention**, and Doug Hastings the **Daily Flash** and (briefly) the **Buffalo Springfield**.

As a result of this pedigree and some strong early live performances, expectations amongst the L.A. cognoscenti were high and Elektra quickly financed the band to the tune of $80,000 (big money in 1968). Recorded in live takes, their debut album garnered favourable reviews in the music press at the time, but tends to get slagged off today as a fairly nondescript blend of blues/jazz/funk/gospel-tinged late sixties rock. One short catchy instrumental Apricot Brandy was a minor hit single, later used by the BBC as a Radio One programme-link. After this debut however, things started to go downhill.

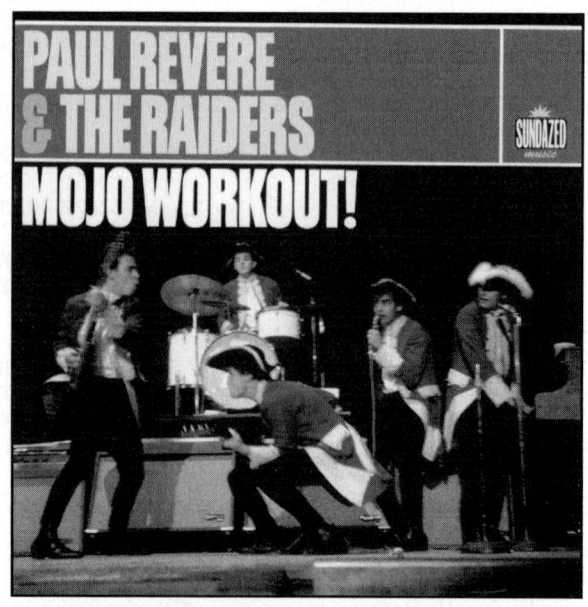

PAUL REVERE and THE RAIDERS - Mojo Workout! CD.

Jerry Penrod left soon after to be briefly replaced by Danny Weis's brother, Steve, and finally by Peter Hodgson. In fact Hodgson had been the original bass player, but was only with the initial line-up briefly.

Their second album met with a muted commercial and critical response and Mundi, Gerber, and Hastings soon quit (Gerber releasing a solo album in 1971 on Shelter records.)

The revised line-up released a follow-up album in a similar vein (and to similar indifference) and the band decided to leave Elektra (against Jac Holzman's wishes). The band split in October 1971, but reformed with slightly different personnel in July 1972 as Blackstone and moved to Canada. Fonfara, Finley, Hodgson, and Leishman were all Canadians and in the sixties had played together in a Toronto band, Jon and Lee and the Checkmates. In 1972, they released an album *On The Line* (produced by Paul Rothchild) on a Canadian label (GRT 92301025). Hodgson rejoined after having had spells with David Clayton-Thomas and Jackson Browne. Leishman and Edwards came in from The Duke Edwards Cycle, whilst Crooks had played on **Dr John**'s Autumn 1969 tour alongside ex-member Doug Hastings. He later played with White Cloud and Loudon Wainwright III.

After a number of personnel changes Blackstone became the Blackstone Rangers and ended up backing Lou Reed in the mid-70's, with Michael Fonfara becoming Reed's right-hand man for a number of years.

Weis left in late 1970 and replaced Buzzy Feiten in **The Rascals**. Hastings left in June 1969 and joined Pam Polland. He later did sessions with David Ackles, Danny O'Keefe and Bill Cowsill. Tomlinson came in from Montreal bands Milkwood and Damage. He later played with Bearfoot.

Weis and Tomlinson later played with Rick James before his Motown deal and Weis also led Bette Midler's 'Rose' band.

Compilation appearances have included: *Apricot Brandy* and *I Need Love* on both *Kings Of Pop Music Vol. 1* (LP) and *Elektrock The Sixties* (4-LP); and *Apricot Brandy* and *The Pledge* on *Hallucinations, Psychedelic Underground* (LP). (LP/NW)

Rhode Hog and The Nuisances

45:   The Pflashsong!/The Pflip Side of Pflash   (Fina 123705) 1967

Fina hired this Texas band to sing a petrol commercial in punk style! (VJ)

Emitt Rhodes

				HCP
ALBUMS:	1	AMERICAN DREAM	(A&M SP 4254) 1970	194 -
	2	EMMITT RHODES	(Dunhill DSX 50089) 1971	29 -
	3	MIRROR	(Dunhill DSX 50111) 1971	182 -
	4	FAREWELL TO PARADISE	(Dunhill DSX 50122) 1972	- -

NB: (1) also released in the UK (A&M AMLS64254), (2) on (Probe SPBA 6256), (3) on (Probe SPBA 6262) and (4) on (Probe SPBA 6266). (4) reissued (ABC ABCL 5041) 1974.

45s: You Take The Dark Out Of The Night/
      Fresh As A Daisy   (Dunhill 4267) 1971
      Live Till You Die/Promises I've Made   (Dunhill 4274) 1971
      With My Face On The Floor/A Lullaby   (Dunhill 4280) 1971
      Really Wanted You/Love Will Stone You   (Dunhill 4295) 1971
      Take You Far Away/Golden Child Of God   (Dunhill 4303) 1972
      Golden Child Of God/Tame The Lion   (Dunhill 4315) 1972

The Californian **Emitt Rhodes** began his recorded career with the **Palace Guard** in 1964 before forming the **Merry-Go-Round** in 1966. His four solo albums will interest readers who like well crafted pop-rock similar to early Paul McCartney. The first was recorded with the assistance of **Drake Levin**, **Hal Blaine**, Don Randi, **Emil Richards**, Lyle Ritz and the three other members of the **Merry-Go-Round**. It spent one week at No. 194.

The Dunhill albums were recorded by **Rhodes** alone, playing all the instruments on most of the tracks. Of these his eponymous album was the most successful commercially, spending twenty weeks in the Top 200 and peaking at No. 29. (SR)

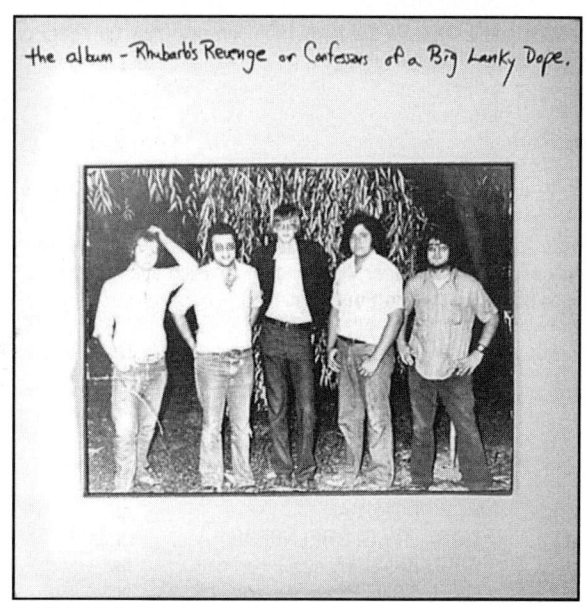

RHUBARD'S REVENGE - The Album... LP.

Rhubarb's Revenge

Personnel: CHRIS BREETVELD   vcls   A
             M. PARMENTER   A
             G. SHUSS   A

ALBUM: 1(A) THE ALBUM - RHUBARB'S REVENGE or
              CONFESSIONS OF A BIG LANKY DOPE
                                    (Pink Grass) 1972 R3

NB: (1) reissued on CD (Gear Fab GF-128) 1999 and LP (Gear Fab/Comet GFC 416 LP) 2001, with four bonus tracks.

This very home-made record, recorded 1970-71 is an acquired taste, to be sure. Side one is all covers, including *Mr. Spaceman*, *Victoria*, *Time Of The Season* and others, all very strangely interpreted. Side two is all originals where the band's true dementia is revealed on tracks like *When I Feed My Prize Hog*, *Nice Spot In The Dark* and *Avon Girl*. Not for all, but definitely all for some of you weirdos. File next to Underground Failure, **Hot Poop** or Crazy People as a point of reference. They hailed from Kendall Park, New Jersey and the album wasn't issued with a cover.

Compilation appearances include *Time Of The Season* on Gear Fab's *Psychedelic Sampler* (CD). (CF/MW)

Rhythm Rockers

45:   Three Strikes/Surf Around   (Fenton 944) c1964

A Michigan band. *Three Strikes* has since resurfaced on *Best Of Michigan Rock Groups, Vol. 1.* (VJ)

Randy Rice

ALBUM: 1   TO ANYONE WHO'S EVER LAUGHED AT
             SOMEONE ELSE (dbl)   (Private Pressing) 1974 R3

A folk-psych album which is extremely rare and seldom seen. (GG)

Ronnie Rice (and The Gents/Silvertones)

This Chicago-based artist released several 45s during a career which spanned at least from 1962-78. They were mostly pop or country singles but *Pebbles, Vol. 22* (LP) includes one of his recordings, *I Want You To Be My Girl*, which may interest readers being a cover of the Frankie Lymon and The Teenagers' hit done garage style. Our friends in Chicago will also no doubt remember him primarily in his other role as a member of the excellent **New Colony Six**.

Warm Baby and *La Do Da Da* from 1966 can also now be heard on *The Quill Records Story* (CD). (VJ/MW)

Cathy Rich

45:	Wild Thing/Paper Tiger	(World Pacific 77913)	1969

This was Buddy Rich's teenage daughter who recorded two songs:- a reputedly poor cover of *Paper Tiger* and an amusing attempt at *Wild Thing*, both were produced by **Kim Fowley** in 1969.

Compilation appearances include *Wild Thing* on *Girls In The Garage, Vol. 1* (LP). (VJ)

Richard and The Young Lions

Personnel:	BOB FREEDMAN	gtr	AB
	MARK 'TWIG' GREENBERG	drms	AB
	FRED RANDALL	bs	A
	RICHARD TEPP	vcls	AB
	LOUIE VLAHAKES	ld gtr	AB
	LARRY SMITH	bs	B

HCP

45s:	Open Up Your Door/		
	Once Upon Your Smile (PS)	(Philips 40381)	1966 99
	Nasty/Lost And Found	(Philips 40414)	1966 -
	You Can Make It/To Have And To Hold	(Philips 40438)	1967 -

This five-piece hailed from Newark, New Jersey. They actually enjoyed minor chart success with *Open Up Your Door*. The follow-up *Nasty* flopped but *You Can Make It* was a rather appealing high energy garage-punker, which is usually considered their best effort and also the hardest of their 45s to find.

Compilation appearances have included: *Open Up Your Door* on *Nuggets Box* (4-CD), *Open Up Yer Door! Vol. 1* (LP) and *Boulders, Vol. 9* (LP); *You Can Make It* on *Pebbles, Vol. 12* (LP), *What A Way To Die* (LP) and *Hang It Out To Dry* (CD). (VJ/MW/MDo)

Emil Richards and The Microtonal Blues Band

Personnel:	DENIS BUDIMIR	gtr	A
	DAVE MACKAY	piano	A
	RAY NEAPOLITAN	bs	A
	JOE PORCARO	drms	A
	EMIL RICHARDS		A
	MARK STEVENS	perc	A
	TOMMY TEDESCO	gtr	A

ALBUMS:	1	JOURNEY TO BLISS	(Impulse A-9166)	1968 SC
(selective)	2	SPIRIT OF 1976	(Impulse A-9182)	1969 -
	3	STONES	(Uni 3008)	1969 SC

45:	No Place I'd Rather Be/Bo Diddley	(UNI 55027)	1967

NB: as Emil Richards and The Factory.

Born in Connecticut in 1932 as Emilio Joseph Raddochia, **Emil Richards** was one of the best vibes and percussion players operating in the Hollywood studios. Apart from his countless rock and pop sessions (notably with **The Factory**, **Russ Giguere** and Ry Cooder), he also recorded some albums with his group, the Microtonal Blues Band. A disciple of the Maharishi Yogi and a master of weird and exotic instruments, **Emil Richards** was primarily a jazz player fascinated by Indian music and odd rhythms.

His late sixties albums may interest some curious readers, especially *Journey To Bliss*, subtitled a "Meditation Suite in Six Movements" with cuts like *Mantra*, *Bliss*, *Maharimba* and the eighteen-minute title track. Really innovative and faithful to its title, this album was produced by Bob Thiele, who also worked with **Salvation**, **Eden's Children** and John Coltrane.

The UNI album was recorded with **Bill Plummer** and Dave McKay and also combines psych, jazz and experimentation.

Richards is one of these jazz players who were interested by Indian music and crossed over to the rock scene. He can be compared to **Bill Plummer**, **Charles Lloyd** or **Gabor Szabo** (they all played together on some albums). (SR)

Warren S. Richardson

Personnel:	DAVID BIRKETT	bs	A
	OTIS EUGENE HALE	sax	A
	RICHARD LEWIS	keyb'ds, trumpet	A
	MICKEY McGEE	drms	A
	WARREN S. RICHARDSON Jr	vcls, gtr	A
	JOSEPH RAY TRAINER	sax	A

ALBUM:	1(A)	WARREN S. RICHARDSON	(Cotillion SD 9013)	1969 SC

There is some mystery surrounding this album, which is a hard-rocker with a couple of excellent tracks... the band is from Arizona, it was produced by **Mike Condello** and the cover features four photographs of **Condello** guitarist (and future Tubes guitarist) Bill Spooner! Spooner's name does not appear anywhere on the record which begs the question - is **Warren S. Richardson** his twin brother, or is it "Bill Spooner"'s real name? (CF)

Karl Richey

Personnel:	KARL RICHEY	vcls, gtr, hrmnca	A

ALBUM:	1(A)	KARL RICHEY	(Studio 10 DBX 102)	1969 -

45:	Black Fleeced Lamb/People's Park	(Studio 10 R2502)	1969

Born in Seattle in 1950, **Karl Richey** moved to San Francisco in 1963 and began playing folk and blues in the coffee houses. His only album was issued on the small Studio 10 label (which also released **Day Blindness**) and is a pleasant bluesy folk album graced by his warm voice and good harmonica. Except for a cover of Nat Adderley's *Work*, he penned all the tracks: *Stoned Livin'* ("all the food in the house has been seasoned with pot"), *Mary Jane*, *Fast Last Night*, *Pussy Cat* etc. Pleasant, but getting hard to find.

His album was produced by Tom Preuss. (SR)

Richie's Renegades

Personnel:	BILLY DUNN		A
	BOBBY LEDGER	gtr	A
	BRIAN MICHAELS	bs	A
	BOBBY PECK	drms	A

PSYCHOTIC MOOSE... (Comp LP) including Richie's Renegades.

	RICHIE REYNOLDS	vcls	A
	KEVIN R. (ROBICHAUD?)		A

NB: Kevin R. / Kevin Robichaud not confirmed.

45:	Don't Cry / Baby It's Me	(Polaris 002)	1966

From Lynn, Massachusetts. Winning a 1966 Battle Of The Bands won them a contract to release their sole 45 on Polaris. *Don't Cry*, a mid-tempo punk ballad with some nice backing harmonies, has since been compiled on *Psychotic Moose And The Soul Searchers* (LP) and *Tymes Gone By* (LP). Their complete recorded output - two versions of both 45 tracks and a 'Pepsi' commercial - have also been collected together on *The Polaris Story* (CD). (MW)

Rich Mountain Tower

ALBUM:	1	RICH MOUNTAIN TOWER	(Ovation)	1971 -

45:	Thank You, Maggie/Uncle Bobwhite	(Ovation 1014)	1971

A local Illinois group, with acoustic, electric and steel guitars, moog, keyboards, drums and harmonica. They sounded a bit like the **Grateful Dead** circa *American Beauty*, with tracks like *Song Of The Sea*, *Circle Sky*, *Moon Mix* and *Our Passage Home*. (SR)

Rick and Ronnie

Personnel:	RONNIE SCAIFE	bs, gtr, vcls	A
	RICK YANCEY	gtr, vcls	A
	PERRY YORK	drms	A

45:	Don't Do Me This Way/Misty Eyes	(Sprite 5001)	1966

A Memphis group whose *Don't Do Me This Way*, sounds strongly influenced by The Kinks and Zombies. Ronnie Scaife had been in the Travis Wamack Band and the Us Group; he and York would form Shylo. Rick Yancey went on to form Cymarron.

Compilation appearances include: *Don't Do Me This Way* on *The Lost Generation, Vol. 2* (LP) and *Highs In The Mid-Sixties, Vol. 22* (LP). (VJ/MW/RHI)

Rick and The Ravens

Personnel:	ROLAND BISCALUZ	bs	A
	JIM MANZAREK	organ, hrmnca	A
	RAY MANZAREK	vcls, piano	A
	RICK MANZAREK	gtr	A
	PAT STONNER	sax	A
	VINCE THOMAS	drms	A

45s:	Soul Train/Geraldine	(Aura 4511)	1965
	Henrietta/Just For You	(Aura)	1965
	Big Bucket "T"/Rampage	(Posae)	1965

From Los Angeles, this act is best remembered as featuring a pre-**Doors** Ray Manzarek. They played at the Turkey Joint in Santa Monica and at the Port O Call in San Pedro, where they once supported Sonny and Cher. Four of the six songs were original compositions, written and sung by Ray Manzarek.

The Aura label was a subsidiary of World Pacific.

In September 1965 they returned to the studio, with Jim Morrison and John Densmore in tow and recorded a 6-song demo acetate. Shortly after, Ray Manzarek's brothers left the band and **The Doors** were born. (RFn)

Rick and The Riots

45:	Big Murph/?	(Shazzamm 111)	1961

You can hear *Big Murph* on *Garage Punk Unknowns, Vol. 6* (LP). Rick and his riotous friends were based in Indianapolis, Indiana. (VJ)

THE LOST GENERATION Vol. 2 (Comp LP) including Rick and Ronnie.

Nooney Rickett

Personnel:	KENTON DUNBAR	drms, vcls	A
	TOM FUNK	sax, vcls	AB
	JONI LYMAN	vcls	AB
	NOONEY RICKETT	gtr, vcls	AB
	?? RUCKER	bs	A
	TOM POOLE	bs, trumpet, vcls	B

45:	Bye Bye Baby / Maybe The Last Time	(Dimension 1051)	1966

NB: credited to **Nooney Rickett and The Nooney Rickett Four**. Both tracks also released on a French EP with a picture sleeve (Colpix 8007 M) 1966. The other side of the EP was by **Gamma Goochee**.

From Los Angeles and previously known as the V.I.P's (with Arthur Lee), **Nooney Rickett** (the name of the band and their leader) recorded two tracks which appeared on a domestic 45 and a rare French EP in 1966. Penned by Rickett and Poole, *Bye Bye Baby* is strongly reminiscent of the Beatles and Wayne Fontana, while *Maybe The Last Time* is a cover of James Brown.

The band existed between 1964-7 and also appeared in two movies, 'Pajama Party' and 'Winter A Go Go'.

Their occasional singer, Joni Lyman, also sang with **The Strangers** led by **Joel Scott-Hill**.

Compilation appearances have included: *Bye Bye Baby* on *Mindrocker Vol. 12* (LP); *She's Not There* on *12 Groovy Hits, 12 Florida Bands* (LP); and *This Is The Time* on *Garagelands Vol. 2* (CD). (SR/SBn/TomFunk)

The Ricochettes (Ricochetts)

Personnel incl:	JOHN JOHN GALOBICH	drms	A
	HERB HOHNKE	bs, keyb'ds	A
	A.R. STEVENS (KRIEGEL)	ld gtr	AB
	JERRY WOLLENZIEN	gtr	A
	JIM MILEWSKI	bs, tamb	B
	MICK MILEWSKI	gtr	B
	BOB "HUMPTY" NEUHOFER	drms	B
	BRUCE COLE	drms	

45s:	I'll Be Back/Can I Be Sure	(Raynard RS 10030)	1964/65
	Come In My Love (Out Of The Rain)/ Losing You	(Quill 102)	1966
	Find Another Boy/ Don't Waste Your Time	(Continental 500)	c1966
	Find Another Boy/I Don't Want You	(Destination 629)	1966

NB: There's also a much later 45 on a reissue label credited to AR and The Rockin' Ricochettes: *Rock On/Carl's Rockabilly Roll* (PS) (Mean Mountain 1424) 1982.

A Milwaukee-based outfit who put out some decent pop-beat. The Destination 45 is good mid-sixties teen-beat with a nod towards other area artists like **The Robbs** and Chicago harmony popsters like the **Cryan' Shames** and **Saturday's Children**. Credit to Tom Tourville's Wisconsin book for pointing out that they became the **Picture**, with one great psychedelic 45 on Nasco.

The Continental 45 was a different version of *Find Another Boy*, recorded by a group called 'Mickey, They and Them', which included the Milewski brothers and Neuhofer. They were by then in the **Ricochettes** so someone decided to credit it to the better-known group.

When several members were called up, the Milewski brothers and Stevens formed The Picture. Stevens was drafted in the Summer of 1968 before that group recorded. In the eighties he formed a new Ricochettes, releasing one 45 in 1982 and an album as Ar Stevens and The Rockin' Ricochettes - *Ain't Rock And Roll Pretty* (Ottertail 1235) 1985.

Further details can be found in 'Do You Hear That Beat', the definitive book on Wisconsin fifties and sixties rock by Gary Myers (Hummingbird, 1994, ISBN 0-9643073-9-1), who kindly permitted us to use it.

You can also find *Losing You* on *The Quill Records Story* (CD). (MW)

LET'S DIG 'EM UP Vol. 1 (Comp CD) including Riders Of The Mark.

The Riddles

Personnel:	LEE ADAMS	bs, vcls	A
	WESTON DOBSON	gtr	A
	RONALD FRICANO	drms	A
	PATRICK HARPER	ld gtr, vcls	A

45s:	Sweets For My Sweet/It's One Thing To Say	(Quill 116) 1967
	Sweets For My Sweet/ It's One Thing To Say	(Mercury 72669) 1967

From Crystal Lake, Illinois, comes this very poppy cover of The Searchers' hit. Turn it over however and there's a rather good moody punk-popper with some tasteful if understated licks... check it out on *The Quill Records Story* (CD). Nice. (MW)

Riders of The Mark

45:	The Electronic Insides And Metal Complexion That Make Up Herr Doktor Krieg/ Gotta Find Somebody	(20th Century Fox 6694) 1967

The work of an obscure band the record was composed by John Hill and Don Cochrane. They're thought to have emanated from Arizona with this maelstrom of pumping electronic psych. The flip is pop with a hard edge.

Compilation appearances have included: *Gotta Find Somebody* on *Let's Dig 'Em Up, Vol. 3* (LP) and *Let's Dig 'Em Up, Vol. 1* (CD); *The Electronic Insides And Metal Complexion That Make Up Herr Doktor Krieg* on *Mayhem & Psychosis, Vol. 1* (CD), *Open Lid EP* (7") and *Beyond The Calico Wall* (CD). (VJ/MW)

The Riffs

45s:	Tell Her / I Been Thinkin'	(Lubee 304) 1965
	Tell Her / I Been Thinkin'	(Jamie 1296) 1965

Bright and instantly likeable Invasion-beat from a Phoenix, Arizona band. (MW/MM)

The Riffs

45:	Outside That Door/Holy Ravioli	(Cori 31005) 1965

Another **Riffs**, this time from Newton, Massachusetts. (MW/MM)

Rig

Personnel:	BUFFALO BUTTREY	A
	TOM CERONE	A
	KENDELL KARDT	A
	DON KERR	A
	WELDON MYRICK	A
	ARTIE RICHARDS	A

ALBUM:	1(A)	RIG	(Capitol ST-473) 1969

45:	Quiet Lady/Sister Liza Bookman	(Capitol) 1970

A rare and obscure album, combining bluegrass, melodic rock, pop and hippie country-rock. Some dealers describe it as psychedelic, but that is way off mark. Still a decent album though! (SR/ScottYoung)

Rigor Mortis

Personnel:	BRUCE MEGLIO	drms	A
	RUDI PROTRUDI	ld gtr	A
	CRAIG STOUFFER	vcls, gtr	A
	BIGLER	vcls	A
	BEN ?	bs	A

Originally known as **King Arthur's Quart** and based in Harrisburg, Pennsylvania, **Rigor Mortis** came to life in 1966 and was one of the earliest oufits in the long history of Rudi Protrudi, who'd return to his garage roots a decade or so later with the mighty Fuzztones. Read Rudi's reminiscences in 'Misty Lane #17', then slap *Basementsville! U.S.A.* (LP) on your turntable and crank up the volume for a stormin' **Blue Cheer**-infused blast called *Bandit*, taped live in the late sixties but never before on vinyl. (MW)

The Ringers

Personnel:	STANLEY BONACCORSO ('REX PARIS')	ld vcls, bs	ABCD
	KEITH JOHNSON	gtr, vcls	ABCDEF
	BILL LYNN	drms, vcls	ABCDEF
	TOM CROCKETT	ld gtr	B
	PAUL INDELICATO	ld gtr, vcls	C
	DAVID TURNER	ld gtr, vcls	E

ALBUMS:	1(D/E)	BEFORE AND AFTER	(Virrey DVS 708) 1970 R1
	2	LET THEM BE KNOWN (LP)	(Break-A-Way 001) 2001
	3	LET THEM BE KNOWN (CD)	(Break-A-Way 002) 2001

NB: (1) released in Peru. (2) 10-track retrospective with insert. (3) 22 track retrospective with 10 page booklet.

45s:	Mersey Bounce / Graduation Doll	(Bil-Lou 1001) 1965
	α Let It Be Known /	
	Never Too Young	(Velvet Tone VTR-105) 1966
	Daydream / Not The Marrying Kind	(Amp ANX-119/120) 1966

NB: α by as by "The TR-4" (Tommy Rettig 4).

Stan Bonaccorso was from San Jose, California and started playing folk and rock'n'roll in the mid-fifties, when he graduated from guitar to electric bass. He was in several outfits (Original Galaxies, Ernie and The Fanatics, Royals) before relocating to Hollywood in 1963. Soon after his arrival an agent pointed him to an audition. Dick Gabriel (sax/keyb'ds), Bill Lynn (drums) and Keith Johnson (gtr) were looking for a bassist; Bonaccorso got the nod but they quickly discovered that he was in a different musician's union to the rest of the band; adopting a stage name of Rex Paris got around that potential pitfall. The group became Richard and The Bowmen and decked themselves out in Robin Hood attire.

Drummer Bill Lynn had also been playing since the mid-fifties. In 1960, he become the session drummer for Paramount in Nashville, where he met and played with Elvis Presley. He would continue to play for him occasionally throughout the sixties.

Richard and The Bowmen started playing at clubs on Sunset Strip. Here they encountered the nascent Sonny and Cher, who asked Dick Gabriel if he and his band would like to be their road band. Without consulting the others, Gabriel turned them down; unimpressed, the other three took their leave.

In 1964, with Beatlemania in full swing, the trio had the mop-tops and could also sound like the Fab Four - so they adopted the name Dead Ringers. In the late Summer they found guitarist Tom Crockett to complete the format and drop the "Dead" from their name. Their first 45 in 1965 did little and they brought in Tommy Rettig (an actor who played Jeff in the Lassie TV series) as co-manager. Several tracks were laid down but none were released until the brief chance to record a theme for a new soap opera resulted in the rush-recording of *Never Too Young*, with Larry Bropsky filling in for an out-of-town Bill Lynn. This would be their second release in 1966 and was credited to the TR-4 (Tom Rettig 4). Though a cool pop tune, **The Ringers**' version was ultimately rejected by the TV company in favour of a song composed by the show's producer's nephew!

Crockett was replaced by Indelicato in 1966 and their third 45 appeared soon after. *Daydream* is an excellent swingin' garage rocker with mean licks; the flip is a soppy last-dance ballad. Indelicato left in 1967 and **The Ringers** were back to the original trio. Four more tracks were recorded before Rex decided to leave in 1968 and was replaced by David Turner. Two more cuts were laid down - *Bandsong* and *Another Day* - then they departed for a tour of Central and South America.

They eventually wound up in Peru, where they became a regular attraction at clubs and on TV. Signed by the Virrey label to produce an album, they used the two 1968 cuts and added some reworkings of earlier recordings; it was released in 1970.

Soon after they returned to the US. David Turner joined Poco; Johnson and Lynn carried on until 1972, occasionally rejoined by Paris. Bill Lynn who'd earlier played with The Champs, was a highly successful staff drummer for ABC Paramount Records in Nashville. In 1964, he began working often with Elvis Presley, and appeared in a handful of the King's films. In the seventies, he did studio work with Dallas Smith of Liberty Records.

As to the music: they may have played covers live but their recordings appear to be all originals. Mersybeat is to the fore on their earlier mop-top shakers (*Mersey Bounce*) and beat ballads; they also took on pre-beat teen-pop (*Graduation Doll*), a brief hi-five to the surf scene (*Never Too Young*) then moved on to Stones-like raunch (*Let It Be Known*), fuzz-garage (*Ask Me No Questions*) and pop... like a documentary of the pre-psychedelic sixties.

The CD retrospective contains 22 tracks, just about all their recorded output; the album version features their ten best 1965-1967 garage/beat recordings for garage purists. Both contains the band's full history from which this entry has been composed.

As **Tr-4**, *Let It Be Known* has also resurfaced on *The Night Is So Dark* (LP). (MW/MDo/WV/BLn)

The Ringers

| ALBUM: | 1 PLAY FOR TODAY'S DANCE-IN | |
| | | (Unart M-20013) 1967 SC |

Housed in a psychedelic sleeve, an instrumental 'exploito' band with organ and guitar. Covers include *Let's Spend The Night Together* and *Friday On My Mind*. (SR)

Jerry Riopelle

ALBUMS:	1 JERRY RIOPELLE	(Capitol) 1971 -
	2 SECOND ALBUM	(Capitol) 1972 -
	3 TAKE A CHANCE	(ABC) c1973 -
45s:	Darlin' Daughter/?	(Capitol 3125) 1971
	Livin' The Life/?	(ABC 12025) 1974
	You And I/?	(ABC 12042) 1974
	Walkin' On Water/?	(ABC 12129) 1975

California based, **Jerry Riopelle** began his career circa 1966 with the **Black Sheep** and the **Parade**. He also produced the first album by **Brewer and Shipley** and worked with **Leon Russell** in **Asylum Choir**. His solo albums are reputedly pleasant, in a singer/songwriter vein. (SR)

The Riots

| 45: | You're My Baby/I Can Go On | (X Records 661389) 1966 |

I Can Go On, a booming garage-ballad by this West Tennessee band, is on *Garage Punk Unknowns, Vol. 8* (LP). The 'A' side, *You're My Baby*, is also on *Diggin' For Gold, Vol. 7, In The USA* (LP). (MW/MM)

The Rip Tides

| Personnel incl: | JOE REAM | A |
| 45: | She Set Me Free / Stay With Me | (Spin-A #101) 1966 |

From Chicago, Joe Ream later went to the University Of Illinois in Urbana, where he played in **The Regiment** (of *My Soap Won't Float* fame). (MM)

Rising Hope

ALBUMS:	1 FAREWELL TO THE SHADOWLANDS	
		(Private Pressing) 1975 ?
	2 WHERE THE SONG CAME FROM	
		(Private Pressing) 1978 ?

THE RISING SONS - The Rising Sons (Israphon) CD.

A rare Christian folk-psych trio (two women, one man) sometimes compared to **All Saved Freak Band** or **Spiritwood**, with tracks like *Secret Of The Stars* and *Lead Me On* on the first album and a West Coast vibe on the second. (SR)

The Rising Sons

Personnel:	ED CASSIDY	drms	A
	RY COODER	ld gtr	AB
	JESSE LEE KINCADE	gtr, vcls	AB
	TAJ MAHAL	vcls	AB
	GARY MARKER	bs	AB
	KEVIN KELLY	drms	B

ALBUMS:	1	THE RISING SONS	(Groucho) 19?? SC
	2	THE RISING SONS	(Israphon ISR 009 CD) 199? -
	3	THE RISING SONS FEATURING TAJ MAHAL AND RY COODER	(Sony) 199? -
	4	THE RISING SONS	(Sundazed LP 5054) 2001 -

NB: (1) Italian LP. (2) is an eighteen-track pirate CD release, but (3) is an official release with twenty-two tracks.

45:	Candy Man/ The Devil's Got My Woman	(Columbia 4-43534) 1966

This California band, which formed in L.A. in April 1965, has assumed legendary status because many of its personnel went on to far greater things. For example, Gary Marker recorded a 45 with **Sound Machine** and an album with **Fusion**; Ed Cassidy was a founder member of **Spirit**; Kevin Kelly later joined **The Byrds** for a while and Cooder and Taj Mahal both had very successful solo careers.

Although their version of *Candy Man* on the 'A' side of their 45 is good, it's the flip which is the killer cut, featuring the now familiar slide guitar of Cooder and Taj Mahal on lead.

The band also recorded an album for Columbia, which was not released at the time, although it has subsequently been pirated twice, and posthumously released by Sony on CD. Produced by Terry Melcher, who was also responsible for one Columbia's hottest acts, **The Byrds**, their recordings are a melting pot of rock / folk / electric blues and old-style country blue-grass.

Presumably, when Columbia pulled the plugs, the band split up.

Compilation coverage has also included *Candy Man* and *The Devil's Got My Woman* on *Mindrocker, Vol. 7* (LP).

Another **Rising Sons**, from Macomb, Illinois issued at least one 45 - *Have Some Patience Girl / Hold On I'm Coming* (Max 6719), circa 1967. (VJ/SR/MW)

THE RISING SONS - The Risng Sons (Sundazed) LP.

The Rising Sons

45:	(So) In Love (With You)/?	(Swan) 1964

A forgotten group from Buffalo, New York State. (SR)

The Rising Sons

45:	Talk To Me, Baby/Try To Be A Man	(Amy 931) 1965

Another **Rising Sons**, this one was possibly from the South. (SR)

The Rising Storm

Personnel:	BOB COHEN	ld gtr	A
	TODD COHEN	bs	A
	CHARLIE ROCKWELL	organ	A
	TOM SCHEFT	drms, bongos, tamb	A
	TONY THOMPSON	rhythm gtr, vcls	A
	RICH WEINBERG	vcls, hrmnca, tamb, cowbell	A

ALBUM:	1(A)	CALM BEFORE...	(Remnant BBA-3571) 1966 R5/R6

NB: (1) reissued as Eva 12012 (1984). Now available again as an exact legal reissue on Stanton Park (SRE-001) 1992 and on CD with their 1983 re-union (Arf! Arf! AA-034). Also relevant are:- *Alive Again At Andover* (Arf! Arf! 007) 1983, a limited edition of 1000, capturing their 1983 reunion; and *Second Wind* (Arf! Arf! AA-083) 2000, which gathers together new studio and live material.

45:	FROZEN LAUGHTER	(Stanton Park STP-021) 1993

NB: a double single set featuring two new songs, the Arthur Lee tune *Signed D.C.* and *Trying To Fool*, plus two bands doing covers of previous **Rising Storm** tracks.

Recorded whilst the aforementioned were attending Phillips Academy, Andover, Massachusetts, the *Calm Before...* album was an ultra-rare collectors' item prior to its reissue. It's easy to see why. The album contains fine versions of hard-rockers *Don't Look Back*, *In The Midnight Hour* and *Baby Please Don't Go*, alongside Arthur Lee's *A Message To Pretty* and a number of self-penned compositions, such as the driving *I'm Comin Home* and slow, sensitive numbers like *Frozen Laughter* and *The Rain Falls Down*. This is an album of variation and contrast and the recent Stanton Park/Arf! Arf! reissues are recommended.

Alive Again At Andover was a reunion concert recording and is surprisingly good. Brought back together for the 15th Reunion of Andovers' Class of '67 ten of their gymnasium gig numbers are captured plus a version of *Baby Please Don't Go* from their first reunion stint at the Flowermarket Cafe, Boston in October '81. The original line-up is intact bar Todd Cohen whose place is filled by the ubiquitous Andy Paley. Unlike other reunion albums which cash in on past glories this one stands up well on its own and, although these guys had done nothing in the music sphere since graduation, the spirit and fun of those heady days is reincarnated.

In 1999, the original sextet again minus Todd Cohen, but with Aram Heller (Mr. Stanton Park) bounding into the bassist role, had the chance to appear on the same bill as Boston legends **The Lost** and **The Remains**. The latter were one of the **'Storm**'s inspirations of course, as their cover of *Don't Look Back* testifies. Naturally they grabbed the opportunity with aplomb, indeed they played for free.

Despite some pre-gig nerves they proved to be the perfect openers of this historic event on Saturday 20th March 1999 at the Paradise Club in Beantown and they set the tone for what turned out to be a magical and memorable evening. Opening with their own *I'm Coming Home*, the half-hour set comprised many of the upbeat numbers from their album. **The Rockin' Ramrods**' *Bright Lit Blue Skies*, *Signed T.T.* and *Baby Please Don't Go* went down very well - another original *She Loved Me* with its Charlie Rockwell Hammond organ solo and great vocal arrangements was outstanding. It was a performance full of fun, vibrance and enthusiasm which quickly infected and was appreciated by the audience. Having played their part, the buoyant members joined the 600+ throng with as much eagerness to await the appearances of **The Lost** and **The Remains**.

THE RISING STORM - Calm Before... CD.

The *Second Wind* CD gathers together new studio material (primarily from 1992 and 1998 sessions) with live renditions of *Midnight Hour* and *Baby Please Don't Go*. Other covers are *Signed D.C.* and John Lee Hooker's *Don't Look Back*. The remainder are originals, split between strong rockers and the **Storm**'s trademark haunting, melancholy folk-rockers.

Compilation appearances have included: *Frozen Laughter* on *The Magic Cube* (Flexi); *To R.S. - Who Won't Know* on *New England Teen Scene, Vol. 3* (LP); *A Message To Pretty* on *Sixties Rebellion, Vol. 8* (LP & CD); *She Loved Me* on *The Arf! Arf! Blitzkrieg 32 Track Sampler* (Dble CD); *Baby Please Don't Go*, *Message To Pretty* and *Don't Look Back* on *Endless Journey - Phase One* (LP); and *Message To Pretty* on *Endless Journey - Phase I & II* (Dble CD). (MW/VJ)

Rising Tides

Personnel incl:	PEARSON		A
	SABINE		A

Came out of Morristown, New Jersey. They were heavily into the British R&B scene and their live act included lots of Stones' covers, Pretty Things and Kinks. They went up to New York to record an acetate containing *Take The World As It Comes* and a cover of The Animals' *I'm Crying*. It remained unreleased at the time but their competent original *Take The World As It Comes* can now be found on *Back From The Grave, Vol. 5* (LP). (VJ)

The Rising Tides

Personnel:	DAN CARLISLE	ld gtr	A
	PHIL CLARK	gtr	A
	JOHNNY JOHNSON	drms	A
	PAUL KINSELLA	ld vcls	A
	JOHN PREY	bs	A

A quintet whose members hailed from LaSalle, Peru, Oglesby and Tonica, Illinois. In 1968, they contributed two tracks, along with five other local acts, to the sampler LP *A Psychedelic Six-Pack Of Sound* (LP).

The liners note that the band formed in 1965 and appeared at the Illinois State Fair in 1967, placing 9th out of 90. Certainly they provide some of the best moments on this album, thanks to the songwriting skills of Phil Clark, although psychedelic they are not.

Little Girls is a fine '66-sounding pop-punker with a short fuzzy solo and a solid swingin' beat that brings to mind early **Creedence**. *The Girl Made Good* is a classy minor-mooder reminiscent of **The Cyrkle** or **The Critters**.

Phil Clark remembers: "It was a stark recording setting. On a cold Winter evening we set up in a 'storage room studio' located in the back of a meager storefront musical instrument shop in the town of Streator, IL. Our two songs were recorded in single takes after a ten minute warm-up using three microphones and a single track. We were in and out in less than an hour, as was the other band that was leaving as we came in. John Prey had electronics training and built what was at the time a very advanced flourescent strobe light system for our performances. We wore flourescent capes and did covers of popular psychedelic songs, Kinks and Yardbirds etc. After taking a few decades off to raise a family and teach in the public schools, I'm now writing songs again." (MW)

Peter Ritchie

ALBUM:	1	ALICE'S RESTAURANT MASSACREE - COMPLETE
		(Design) 1968 -

As you can guess, Side one is a side-long note for note cover of **Arlo Guthrie**'s song. Why somebody would buy such a record is questionable. Side two contains some decent folk-rock tracks. Design was an exploito label, also responsible of the awful **Rasput and The Sepoy Mutiny**. (SR)

Ritchie's Renegades

See **Richie's Renegades**.

The Rites

Personnel:	ROBERT AZZARELLO	drms	A
	JAMES CAHN	organ	A
	PETER FELLER	gtr	A
	THOMAS B. FITZPATRICK	bs	A
	PETER KEREZMAN	gtr	A

45:	Things/Hour Girl	(Decca 32218) 1967

A pop-psych 45 worthy of your attention. *Things* is an uptempo outing with some neat backwards guitar whilst *Hour Girl* is a mellow folk-psych ballad. Both sides were written by Peter Kerezman and *Things* can also be heard on *Fuzz Flaykes & Shakes, Vol. 1* (LP & CD). The band had come together in NYC. Pete Feller lived in Rockland County, a Northern suburb; Tom Fitzpatrick was from the Boston area, attending Columbia University; Jimmy Cahn was in New Rochelle NY in Westchester County, another Northern suburb; Bob Azzarello was from Northport, Long Island, suburb East of NYC, attending New York University; Peter Kerezman grew up on 161 St. and Broadway in Upper Manhattan, a few blocks from the George Washington bridge.

Peter Kerezman recalls:- "We played a lotta frat parties and some dances around Columbia University, some bars and clubs in the suburbs, and rich kid private parties. Our biggest gig was the Clairol Caravan, Summer of 1967. A total of thirty-three, I think it was, free concerts w/fashion show in various parks of the five boroughs, sponsored by Clairol, Inc. If you look at a fiche (or a copy if you got one) of Time magazine for June 30, 1967, you can see a Clairol Caravan photo on page 21. Jimmy Cahn's on the right, dancing with amateur fashion model Patsy Sabline. I'm the guy with the eyepatch (car wreck) all the way on the left, bangin' on a D-21. Still got that guitar but I lost the eyepatch."

"The Decca-supplied producer was Milt Gabler, and our former manager Bob Prescott brought in his own guy, Steve Hammer to 'help out'. The record did not do very well for us, to put it mildly (less than 1,000 copies sold). I did quite a few demo sessions on bass for other folks, but nothing else was released. Me, Jimmy and Bob stuck together for quite a while but didn't achieve much due to lack of focus. I'm now the owner of a small bicycle shop in a rural community deep in Southernmost Texas, still playing bass and guitar in the clubs occasionally". (MW/PKm)

Rites of Spring

Personnel:	MICHAEL GUNNELS		A
	RONALD PARR		A

45:	Why/Comin' On Back To Me	(Cameo Parkway 109) 1966

This Birmingham, Alabama, group were originally known as **The Hard Times**. A change of name was precipitated, due to the national exposure of the San Diego **Hard Times** on ABC-TV'S 'Where The Action Is', when they were recording their second 45 (with **Terry Knight** producing) at Frankford Wayne Recording Labs in Philadelphia. An acetate exists of two tracks, *Why* and *No Name*, credited to the **Hard Times**; both would appear on the eventual Cameo Parkway 45, as by the **Rites Of Spring** - *No Name* having become *Comin' On Back To Me* with the addition of vocals.

Why is a melodic folk ditty with music-box chimes; *Comin' On Back To Me* is a stompin', hand-clappin', hook-laden fuzz-popper and the stronger cut from our viewpoint. Compilers agree; it's on *Turds On A Bum Ride, Vol. 5* (CD) and *Psychedelic States: Alabama Vol. 1* (CD).

Confusingly there were other, unconnected **Rites Of Spring** around in the sixties who released 45s: *The King In Your City/Happy Feet* (La Fra # unknown) by a group thought to be from Massachusetts; and an MOR harmony-pop outfit of unknown locale - *If You Let Me Make Love To You Then Why Can't I Touch You / Gettin' Into A Good Thing* (Generation 113) 1969. (MW/JLh)

Rittenhouse Square

Personnel:	MITCH EASTER	vcls	A
	PETER HOLSAPPLE	vcls	A
	BOBBY LOCKE	drms	A
	CHRIS STAMEY	vcls, gtr	A

ALBUM: 1(A) RITTENHOUSE SQUARE
            (R² Records CCSS-1214) 1972 R4

NB: (1) 12" mini-album issued in paper sleeve printed on one side, with a hole in the center through which the label can be viewed.

A very rare North Carolina release. Easter, Holsapple and Stamey all followed this short-lived venture with prolific careers in power pop as performers and producers - and each of them are now quick to dismiss their **Rittenhouse Square** record as garbage. Truth be told, this is an interesting guitar/progressive effort that will be universally favoured over their later work by readers of this book.

Rittenhouse Square play an infectious hard-rock, comparable perhaps to Big Star at their heaviest, or to the loud uptempo material that SVT produced at the end of the decade. This is unpolished, though - and it is probably the raw character of the record that has led the band to dismiss it in recent years. Ignore the warnings and check it out, if you get the chance... but don't hold your breath waiting for the band members to reissue it! (CF)

Rituals

45: Surfers Rule/She's Gone   (Arwin) c1963

A rare Californian surf single, deserving an inclusion here as *Surfers Rule* was written by **Kim Fowley**, while *She's Gone* is a Bruce Johnston and Terry Melcher song. Coincidentally, **Fowley** and Johnston/Melcher would later record as the Rogues in two different groups! (SR)

River City Street Band

Personnel:	TOMMY BYRD	ld vcls, gtr	A
	FUZZ FOSTER	ld gtr, vcls	A
	RANDY GARDNER	drms, perc	A
	BLAN HEATH	organ, piano	A
	ETHRIDGE HILL	trumpet	A
	DICK JOHNSON	bs, vcls	A
	TOM JONES	trombone	A
	DALE MARLOW	trumpet	A

ALBUMS: 1(A) RIVER CITY STREET BAND
              (Enterprise ENS-1024) 1970 -
        2(A) ANNA DIVINA
              (Enterprise ENS-10??) c1971 -
NB: (2) as River City.

This obscure Memphis group released two albums on Enterprise, the subsidiary rock label of Stax. Their sound was rather specific, with the nice guitar solos of Fuzz Foster, a gritty lead singer, a dynamic rhythm section and a prominent horn section (very irritating on some tracks). The result is a mixture of good rock, R&B, hard-rock and big band sounds (!), somewhere between **The Rugbys** and the Memphis sound and may interest some readers.

Produced by Tim Riley and recorded at the famous Ardent Recording Studios, their first album contains some good tracks, notably *Some Other Man*, *So Many Things*, *If You Can* and the nine minutes of *Lamp Of Love*.

The engineers were all active members of the Memphis scene: John Fry (the Ardent Studios owner), Richard Rosebrough (later in Alamon and Big Star) and **Terry Manning** (also playing moog, ex-**Avengers** and **Lawson and Four More**).

Their second album, released under a shortened moniker, contains *The Pimp Song* and *Roll Another Joint-Fuzz*. (SR)

Johnny Rivers

ALBUM: 1 REALIZATION   (Liberty LP-12372) 1968 -
NB: (1) reissued on CD along with his 1967 *Rewind* album (BGO BGOCD 401).

This singer/guitarist found fame and fortune during the early sixties after intensively playing in the California clubs where he developed a specific "sing along" style. As several other older Californian musicians (**Sonny Bono**), Ventures, **Pat Boone**...), he also recorded his psychy album, with covers of Dylan, **Scott McKenzie**, James Hendricks (**Lamp Of Childhood**)) and a fair and surprising version of *Hey Joe*.

Rivers kept on recording but all his other albums are clearly outside the acope of this book. He also produced the sole album by **Bob Ray**. (SR)

River Styx

Personnel:	PRESTON HARRISON	bs, vcls	ABCDE
	JIM HORNER	drms	ABCD
	CHARLIE MILLER	gtr	AB D
	TOM MILLER	ld gtr	AB
	TOM CHAPMAN	bs	B
	P. THOMAS	piano	C E
	TED ROMEJITO	ld gtr	D
	KERRY RAIVEL	sax	E
	MIKE ZARRILLI	drms	E

ALBUM: 1(A/B) RIVER STYX   (Distortions DR 1027) 1996

45s: Holding For Me / Now   (Capitol Acetate) 1967
      Dolly Nighttime / Lo   (Fete Greats Of 1967 No #) 1968
      Bike Writer / Holding For Me (Joey Lu # Unkn) 1971

RITTENHOUSE SQUARE - Rittenhouse Square LP.

THE RIVER STYX - River Styx LP.

This one spans quite a bit of territory, musically speaking. It starts off in the garage zone with some of their tracks from 1967, but most will be standing in line for the long psych freak-out of *Let Them All Excite You*, that's easily on par with any of those West Coast jam bands of the time. The album features tracks (most of them previously unreleased) from 1967-1971 by this Trenton, New Jersey band. Overall, this record leans more to the later sixties stylings, some of the material like *Understanding Is Hard To Come By* is quite bluesy.

Four of the cuts on this album - *Let Them All Excite You, Understanding Is Hard To Come By*, *Dolly Nighttime* and *Lo* - were previously recorded on a Hagens studio one-sided acetate album. Two others - *Holding For Me* and *Now* were from a 1967 Capitol New York City Studios acetate.

They also went under the name of **River Styx Blues Emporium**. (VJ/MW)

Road

Personnel incl:	NICK DISTEFANO	drms	B
	JIM HESSE	organ	B
	JOSEPH HESSE	bs	B
	JERRY HUDSON	ld vcls	B
	PHIL HUDSON	ld vcls	B
	RALPH PARKER	ld gtr	B

HCP
ALBUMS:	1	THE ROAD	(Kama Sutra KSBS 8075) 1969 - -
	2(B)	THE ROAD	(Kama Sutra KSBS 2012) 1970 199 -
	3	COGNITION	(Kama Sutra KSBS 2032) 1971 - -

HCP
45s:	She's Not There / A Bummer	(Kama Sutra KA 256) 1969 114
	The Grass Looks Greener On The Other Side / In Love	(Kama Sutra KA 266) 1969 -
	Mr.Soul / I Can Only Give You Everything	(Kama Sutra KA 267) 1969 -
	Mr.Soul /The Grass Looks Greener On The Other Side	(Kama Sutra 504) 1970 -
	If I Ever Needed A Woman / Alone	(Kama Sutra 531/2) 1971 -
	Night In The City /	(Goodtime 4504) 197? -
α	She's Not There / A Bummer	(Radio Active Gold 67) 197? -

NB: α reissue.

From Buffalo, New York, they were previously known as The Mellow Brick Rode, who released one 45 in 1968 - *Don't Put All Your Eggs In One Basket / Other Side Of This Life* (United Artists UA 50333).

On their 1970 album they come across as a club/covers band with occasional **Vanilla Fudge** mannerisms in their heavyish treatments. They tackle the Zombies' *She's Not There* (one of their better offerings and a minor hit), **Buffalo Springfield**'s *Mr.Soul* and *Rock'n'Roll Woman* (credit points for good taste if not the results) and **Sly Stone**'s *Dance To The Music*, *Love-itis* (tough R&B pop also done by **The Sonics**). Despite occasional heavy or fuzz guitar noises it's a patchy album - on the down side, they deliver a funky brassed-up version of garageband fave *I Can Only Give You Everything* and an uptempo lounge-style *Taste Of Honey*. The album spent two weeks in the chart, peaking at No. 199. (VJ/MW/CI)

Road

Personnel incl:	NOEL REDDING	bs, vcls	A
	ROD RICHARDS	gtr, vcls	A

ALBUM:	1(A)	ROAD	(Natural Resources 105) 1972 -

NB: (1) reissued on CD.

After Fat Mattress, Noel Redding returned to the power trio scheme he had practiced with **Jimi Hendrix**. This time the guitarist was Rod Richards from **Rare Earth** and the result is obviously not as inventive as the Experience.

Natural Resources was a subsidiary label of Tamla Motown. (SR)

The Road

45s:	You Rub Me The Wrong Way/ It's So Hard To Find	(Lemon-Lime 101) 1969
	You Rub Me The Wrong Way/ It's So Hard To Find	(Blue Onion 106) 1969

Recorded by a group of students from Akron, Ohio, *You Rub Me The Wrong Way* is a good example of the influence of the British beat movement on mid-sixties American bands. They were previously known as the Hard Road and the Lemon-Line 45 may have been released under that name.

No relation to the **Road** on Kama Sutra or the UK/US **Road** featuring a certain Noel Redding.

Compilation appearances include *You Rub Me The Wrong Way* on *Pebbles Vol. 2* (CD), *Pebbles Box* (5-LP), *Pebbles, Vol. 2* (LP) and *Trash Box* (5-CD). (VJ/MW)

The Road Home

Personnel:	DEE ARCHER	vcls	A
	GREG SHANNON	gtr	A
	JIMMY SIMS	drms	A
	WILLY SPROUSE	keyb'ds, vcls	A
	PETER WICKERSHAM	vcls	A

ROAD - Road (Natural Resources) CD.

ALBUM: 1(A) PEACEFUL CHILDREN (Dunhill DS 50104) 1971 -

Produced by Dennis Lambert and arranged by Jimmy Haskell, an obscure Californian album with male/female vocals. (SR)

The Road Runners

Personnel:
DENVER CROSS	gtr, vcls	AB
OZZIE GEORGENER		A
LARRY KARAGOZIAN		A
DAVE MENDOZA	gtr	A
DALE SAMUELIAN	keyb'ds, vcls	ABC
KELLY ?	drms	A
RANDY HALL	ld vcls, bs	BC
STEVE HEITKOTTER	drms	BC
BOB TRIPPELL	sax	BC
BRUCE CONTE	gtr	C

ALBUM: 1(B) THE ROAD RUNNERS (Beat Rocket BR 104) 1998

45s:
I'll Make It Up To You / Take Me	(Miramar 116) 1965
I'll Make It Up To You / Take Me	(Reprise 0418) 1965
Tell Her You Love Her / Goodbye (Yellow Wax)	(Morocco 001/2) 1966
Pretty Me / Baby Please Don't Go	(Morocco 121) 1966
Pretty Me / Sleepy Friend	(Morocco 122) 1966

This band hailed from Fresno, California. Their debut 45 is a catchy beat-folk-rocker notable for crisp upfront percussion, backed with a melodic beat ballad with some barely audible fuzz.

Beat Rocket's retrospective album contains one side of (7) studio tracks (3 unreleased) plus 7 live tracks preserved by the band's #1 fan Neil Hopper. The studio material is predominantly Invasion-inspired folk-rock, with a strong Searchers/**Beau Brummels** influence, occasionally topped off with fuzz. The live material includes their own *Goodbye* and *I'll Make It Up To You*, and shows off the band in meaner and rockier mood - especially on a great version of the Animals' *Don't Bring Me Down*, a rockin' *Train Kept A Rollin'*, and a bluesy take of *Baby Please Don't Go*.

Samuelian's story and Hoppers' photos, tied up neatly by Jud Cost's notes, round off a fine package.

Compilation appearances have included: *I'll Make It Up To You* on *Prisoners Of The Beat* (LP); *Goodbye*, an average folk-punk effort, on *60's Punk E.P., Vol. 3* (7") and *Highs In The Mid-Sixties, Vol. 1* (LP). (VJ/MW/AP)

The Road Runners

45: Do The Temptation/So Hard (Champ) 1966

A Wisconsin group, between rock, soul and pop. (SR)

The Roadrunners

45s:
Tell Her You Love Her / Roadrunner Walk	(Michigan Nickel MNC 003) c1968
Roadrunner Baby / Beautiful	(Michigan Nickel MNC 007) 1970

A Jackson, Michigan band whose raw version of *Roadrunner Baby* can also be heard on *Highs In The Mid-Sixties, Vol. 5* (LP). The song was made famous by Bo Diddley and also recorded by The Pretty Things. This is a very basic and raw cover version. (VJ/MW)

The Roadrunners

45: Woman Woman/? (Colossus C106) 1969

Produced by Art Wayne, a cover of the **Gary Puckett and The Union Gap** hit done in a white soul rock style, with horns and Hammond organ. (SR)

Road's End

Personnel:
TONY LANZA	drms	A
RICK SEPULVEDA	ld vcls, tamb	A
GLENN SWIADON		A
PETER SWIADON		A
BRUCE TEOLIS		A

45: When I Look At You / Why (Brahma 621661/2) 1966

From New York, this band described their music as a cross between "the Rascals, Vagrants, and Animals... a real bluesy sound". Strangely the 'A' side to their 45 is a slow smoochy affair, whilst the flip contains harmonious garage pop with guitars buried in the mix. The Brahma label was owned by George Tobin, the bands manager.

Compilation appearances include: *Why* on *Of Hopes And Dreams & Tombstones* (LP), *Psychedelic Unknowns, Vol. 7* (LP & CD) and *A Journey To Tyme, Vol. 4* (LP). (MW/MDo)

The Roamin' Brothers

ALBUM: 1 LISTEN TO THE SILENCE (FEL) c1970 ?

A decent Christian garage-folk album, housed in a "flames" cover. (SR)

Roamin' Togas

Personnel:
PETE ADAMS	vcls	A
RAYMOND DECOUX	gtr	A
DAVID JACKSON	drms	A
STEVE PEARSON	keyb'ds	A
DARYEL PRUST	gtr	A
RONNIE RAUBER	bs	A

45s:
	Bar The Door / You Must Believe Me	(Lightning LR-101) 1967
α	I Can't Find Love / Happy Lovin' Time	(Robe # Unkn) 1968

NB: α as Black Box.

Formed by Adams and Prust in 1966 at the University of Southwestern Louisiana in Lafayette, they were initially known as the Pete and The Playmates, later the Batmen, before settling on the **Roamin' Togas** and a stable line-up in 1967.

In 1968 the band were whisked off to Bakersfield, California to record an album. Just one 45 resulted and that wasn't even released under the band's name, but as by the Black Box. The band folded in 1969 after most of their equipment was wrecked in a road accident.

HIGHS IN THE MID-SIXTIES Vol. 5 (Comp LP) including The Road Runners.

Compilation appearances have included: *Bar The Door* on *Louisiana Punk From The Sixties* (LP), *Sixties Archive, Vol. 3* (CD) and *Teenage Shutdown, Vol. 3* (LP & CD).

Check out their eventful story in issue #1 of "Brown Paper Sack". (VJ/MW/AB)

Robbie The Werewolf

| ALBUM: | 1 | LIVE - AT THE WALEBACK | (No label) 1964 | R3 |

Pretty much unsurpassed in its level of incredible strangeness, this ultra rare album from the early sixties California coffee-house circuit is like no other. **Robbie** is a folksinger of the frantic variety with a fetish for monsters. This inspires some of the most bizarre original songs ever committed to vinyl!

Robison later turned up in **The Brain Train**. (CF)

ROBBIE THE WEREWOLF - At The Waleback LP.

The Robbs

Personnel:	DICK GONIA	ld gtr	ABC
	BRUCE ROBB		
	(ROBERT DONALDSON)	keyb'ds, vcls	ABCD
	DEE ROBB		
	(DAVID DONALDSON)	gtr, vcls	ABCD
	JOE ROBB		
	(GEROGE DONALDSON)	sax, vcls	ABCD
	DENNIS SACHSE	drms	A
	TEDDY (SALVATORE)		
	PEPLINSKI	drms	B
	CRAIG ROBB	drms, vcls	CD

					HCP
ALBUM:	1(D)	THE ROBBS	(Mercury SR 61130)	1967	200 -

					HCP
45s:	α	The Prom / Bye Bye Baby	(Argo 5349)	1963	-
	β	Surfer's Life / She Cried	(Todd 1089)	1963	-
	χ	Say That Thing / He's Got The Whole World In His Hands	(Score 1006)	1964	-
		Race With The Wind/ In A Funny Sort Of Way	(Mercury 72579)	1966	103
		Next Time You See Me/ I Don't Feel Alone	(Mercury 72616)	1966	-
		Bittersweet/End Of The Week (PS)	(Mercury 72641)	1966	-
		Rapid Transit/Cynthia Loves	(Mercury 72678)	1967	123
		Girls, Girls/Violets Of Dawn	(Mercury 72730)	1967	-
		Jolly Miller/?	(Mercury)	1967	-
		Castles In The Air/ I Don't Want to Discuss It	(Atlantic 2511)	1968	-
		Changin' Winds/A Good Time Song	(Atlantic 2578)	1968	-
		Movin'/Write To You	(Dunhill 4208)	1969	131
		Last Of The Wine/Written In The Dust	(Dunhill 4233)	1970	114
		I'll Never Get Enough/ It All Comes Back	(ABC Paramount 11 270)	1970	106

NB: α as Dee Robb, β as Robby and The Robins, χ as Dee Robb and The Robins.

The three Donaldson brothers began performing as a group at the start of the sixties. After three 45s under a variety of names, several drummers and the loss of guitarist Gonia to the draft, the line-up settled on the quartet (the brothers and Craig Kampf) that would produce some very enjoyable music over the next several years. A dynamic amalgam of harmony-pop and folk-rock with garagey pretensions, they were Milwaukee's answer to **The Monkees** or **Paul Revere and The Raiders** and, like the aforementioned points of reference, a borderline inclusion here. Purists may look down at these mid-sixties 'pop' outfits but don't forget that the golden age of garage and psychedelia was a memorable epoch for pop too (so there!) - just tune into any 'golden oldies' station. The Robbs would become Cherokee in the early seventies.

A detailed history of the band is in the book 'Do You Hear That Beat' book by Gary Myers (Hummingbird, 1994, ISBN 0-9643073-9-1), which graciously provided the early 45 and personnel details. (MW)

Derek "Derrik" Roberts

| 45: | World Without Sun/ There Won't Be Any Snow | (Roulette 4656) 1966 |

A weird pop singer with fuzz guitar, possibly from the New York area. Both sides were written and produced by P.J. Vance and Lee Pockriss, who were also responsible for the **Two Dollar Question** 45. (SR)

Howard Roberts

Personnel:	MAX BENNETT	bs	A
	BOBBY BRUCE	violin	A
	MIKE DEASY	gtr	A
	BRIAN GAROFALO	bs	A
	JOHN GUERIN	drms	A
	LARRY KNECHTEL	keyb'ds	A
	BOB MORIN	drms	A
	HOWARD ROBERTS	gtr	A
	PETE ROBINSON	keyb'ds	A
	MIKE WOFFORD	keyb'ds	A
	JOE WALSH	optimization of time-space energy transformation	A

| ALBUM: | 1 | ANTELOPE FREEWAY | (Impulse AS-9207) 1970 - |

Howard Roberts was an established jazz guitarist who released this interesting album in 1970. Produced by Bill Szymczyk and Ed Michel, it is a good example of "psychedelic instrumental jazz". Mostly instrumental and "Made Loud to be played Loud", it contains lots of excellent guitar parts using different effects (Energy Bow, Ring Modulator...) mixed with various instruments. The result is interesting, mixing jazz, psychedelic and free form music. Best tracks: *Five Gallons Of Astral Flash Could Keep You Up For Thirteen Weeks*, *Dark Ominous Clouds*, *That's America Fer Ya* and *De Blooz*.

The sleeve mentions special thanks to the **Firesign Theater**, John and Terence Boylan (from **Appletree Theater**), BB King, **Jimmy Haskell**, **Leon Russell** and the **James Gang**. (SR)

Billy Roberts and Grits

Personnel:	HAROLD ACEVES	drms	A
	PETER ALBIN	bs	A
	JOHN BESHARIAN	gtr	A
	STEVEN GURR	gtr, bs	A
	BILLY PHILADELPHIA	keyb'ds	A
	BILLY ROBERTS	vcls, hrmnca, gtr	A

ALBUM: 1(A)   THOUGHTS OF CALIFORNIA   (Tulip TLPS-2001) 1975 -

Billy Roberts is the folk-singer who wrote *Hey Joe*, one of the most covered songs of the sixties (**Leaves**, **Hendrix**, **Ant Trip Ceremony** to name but a few). He seems to have recorded very few albums. Produced by Allan Pierce and recorded in San Francisco, this album from 1975 is rather disappointing, with a first side clearly country-oriented and a second side quite patchy, with some good guitar on the title track. His main interest relies in the musicians involved: his backing group, Grits, featured Peter Albin from **Big Brother and The Holding Company** and the guests included John McFee from **Clover** (on "peddle steel guitar"!), Leo Collignon and Bobby Flurie.

Aceves and Flurie would later work with **Barry Melton**. (SR)

Don Robertson

Personnel incl:	MICHAEL DAHLGREN	drms, gong	A
	RAND ELIAS	bs	A
	DON ROBERTSON	gtr, keyb'ds, tablas, bells	A
	MARCIA	flute, vcls	A
	SUZIE	hand drum, vcls	A

ALBUM: 1(A)   DAWN   (Limelight LS 86067) 1969 SC

From San Francisco, this was a typical hippie outfit. **Don Robertson** wrote all their highly meditative and mystic tracks: *Dawn*, *Where*, *Why*, *Gateless Gate*, *When*, *Belief*, with strong oriental and religious influences and use of various noises (birds, bells etc.). Their album was released on Limelight, a subsidiary of Mercury which specialized in experimental albums: **Beaver and Krause**, **Fifty Foot Hose**, **Mecki Mark Men**. **Don Robertson** kept on recording meditatition records and logically became a pioneer of the "New Age" movement in the eighties. (SR)

Robin and The Three Hoods

45s:	α I Wanna Do It/The Marauder	(Fan Jr FJ-1003) 196?
	We The Living /	
	A Day You'll Never Forget	(Fan Jr. 5678) 196?
	I Wanna Do It/That's Tuff	(Fan Jr 5680/1) 196?
	I Wanna Do It/That's Tuff	(Hollywood 1110) 196?

NB: α also issued on Fan Jr.1003 as by Marrell's Marauders.

Reportedly from Madison, Wisconsin. *I Wanna Do It* is a bouncy effervescent cover of a Feldman, Goldstein, Gottehrer (**Strangeloves**) track. *That's Tuff* is an echoey uptempo beat ballad with hints of *Land Of 1,000 Dances*.

Compilation appearances have included: *I Wanna Do It* on *Pebbles, Vol. 1 (ESD)* (CD); *I Wanna Do It* and *That's Tuff* on *Garage Zone, Vol. 2* (LP) and *The Garage Zone Box Set* (4-LP). (VJ/MW)

The Robin Hoods

45s:	Wait For The Dawn/Love You So (PS)	(Mercury 72445) 1966
	Everything Is Alright/	
	Baby Let Down Your Hair	(Mercury 72526) 1966

A Chicago garage band whose first 45 came in a picture sleeve. (VJ)

Andy Robinson

ALBUM: 1   PATTERNS OF REALITY   (Philips PHS 600289) 1968 SC

Acoustic folk with a downer psych vibe, backed by the cream of the Los Angeles studios (Carol Kaye, Jim Gordon, Al Casey, Licoln Mayorga and Earl Palmer).

Now a rare album. (SR)

Chris Robison

ALBUM: 1   MANCHILD   (Gypsy Frog) 1974 ?

A rare private pressing from New York mixing melodic rock, folk and hard rock. **Chris Robison** was also in the last line-up of **Elephant's Memory**. (SR)

The Rob Roys

45s:	Judge Me Not/?	(Accent 1198) 1966
	Do You Girl?/Yes I Do	(Accent 1213) 1966
	Roses Are Red/Do You Girl	(Accent) 1966
	Goodbye To You/It's Wrong	(Accent 1216) 1967

Originally from Santa Rosa in Northern California, they were formerly known as the Malibus, but did not record under that moniker. *Pebbles, Vol. 22* (LP) includes their *Do You Girl?*, a reasonable effort with some snarling fuzz guitar. From the same label that brought forth the **Human Expression** and **Silk Winged Alliance**. (VJ/MW/CF)

The Rock & Roll Revival

ALBUM: 1   THE GREAT OLDIES DONE HEAR AND NOW
                                                                   (Dunhill) c1968 -

An 'exploito' style album, with doo wop hits done in an acid-rock style. A strange idea, but the result is quite decent. (SR)

Rock Candy

ALBUM: 1   ROCK CANDY   (MGM SE-4703) c1970 -

A hard-rock group with organ and wha-wha and fuzz guitars. The slow tracks are rather lame. (SR)

Rock Collection

Personnel:	CHUCK DOTON	drms	AB
	MARK EUBANKS	gtr, sax, keyb'ds, bassoon	AB
	BOB KOCH	ld gtr	AB
	BOB LOWERY	ld vcls	AB
	RON RUSARD	sax	AB
	JIM SANSTEAD	bs	A
	RANDY SCHEPPER	gtr	AB
	KEN HAKANSON	bs	B

NB: Line-up 'A' 1966-67, 'B' 1967-68.

45:   A Sunny Day/Get Ready   (Piccadilly 243) 1967

From Tacoma, Washington, they were originally known as **The Galaxies** but changed their name to **Rock Collection** in 1967 in a quest for a hipper image. Lowery departed to **The Surprise Package** in 1967 but the band lasted until 1968. Chuck Doton also played with Tacoma's Regents between 1965-67.

Compilation appearances include *A Sunny Day* on *Battle Of The Bands, Vol. 2* (LP). (VJ/MW/DR)

The Rockets

Personnel:	RALPH MOLINA	drms	A
	BOBBY NOTKOFF	electric violin	A
	BILLY TALBOT	bs	A
	LEON WHITSELL	vcls, gtr	A
	GEORGE WHITSELL	vcls, gtr	A
	DANNY WHITTEN	vcls, gtr	A

ALBUM: 1(A)   THE ROCKETS   (White Whale WWS 7116) 1968

NB: (1) has been reissued on CD (Varese Sarabande 302 066 269 2) 2001.

| 45: | Hole In My Pocket/Rockets | (White Whale WW 270) 1968 |

NB: double sided promo copies of *Hole In My Pocket* exist, with deep red colour label.

The Rockets are in fact the first version of Crazy Horse, the "classic" backing-group of Neil Young. From California, they managed to get a record deal in 1968 with White Whale, the **Turtles** label. Produced by **Barry Goldberg** (who knew Notkoff from the recording of the **Electric Flag**'s *The Trip*), their only album is a now minor collectable. All the tracks on the first side were composed by Danny Whitten (except a Talbot /Molina song) and the second side was written entirely by the Whitsell brothers.

A mix of rock and West Coast vibes, the best tracks are probably *Hole In My Pocket* (later used by **Goldberg** for one of his solo albums), *Pills Blues* and *Let Me Go*. The vocals are not always outstanding but the guitar and electric violin parts are good. The lyrics of *Pills Blues* are quite explicit about their habits...

In 1969, Whitten, Talbot and Molina met Neil Young, began playing with him and became Crazy Horse. *Everybody Know This Is Nowhere*, the first album they recorded with Young contains the superb *Running Dry (Requiem for the Rockets)* with Notkoff's haunting violin. *Crazy Horse*, their first "solo"album, with Cooder, Lofgren and Nitzsche, is excellent too. Whitten died of an heroin overdose in 1972 and the following Crazy Horse albums are best avoided.

Compilation appearances include *Hole In My Pocket* on *Happy Together - The Very Best Of White Whale Records* (CD).

Not to be confused with the other Rockets! (SR/EW)

Rock Garden

Personnel:	BRIAN BRIAN	bs, vcls	A
	STEVE CLAUNCH	drms	A
	ROBERT GARNER	vcls, gtr	A
	JIM JOHNSON	ld gtr	A
	SUSAN JOHNSON GARNER	organ	A
	CHARLES TUBERVILLE	gtr, vcls	A

EP:	1	ROCK GARDEN (PS)	
		(Dionysus/Bacchus Archives BA 1160) 2001
45:	Super Stuff/The Wind Is My Keeper	(Revise 300) 1967

Originally called The Ravin' Blues, all the band came from Camden, Arkansas, except for drummer Steve Claunch (from Memphis, Tennessee). Their rare and sought-after 45 features the immediately appealing *Super Stuff*, recorded at Sam Phillips Studios in 1967.

In total the band recorded four tracks in Memphis between 1966-67, with one session in Sonic Studios (1966) and the other at Sam Phillips'. The two unreleased tracks *Rainy Daze* and *You Got Me Signed* have finally resurfaced along with the 45 tracks on the Bacchus Archives EP. All have been lovingly restored and presented with a full history of the band.

Other **Rock Gardens** include the post-**Fredric** outfit also known as Garden with two 45s on Capitol, and an unknown bunch with one 45 - *Sweet Pajamas / Perhaps The Word Of Giving* (B.T. Puppy 536) 1967.

Compilation appearances include: *Super Stuff* on *Pebbles, Vol. 13* (LP) and *Teenage Shutdown, Vol. 13* (LP & CD). (VJ/MW)

The Rock Garden

Personnel:	LARRY BOWIE	vcls, keyb'ds	A
	BILL BRINKLEY	vcls, ld gtr	A
	JOE BURTON	vcls, drms	A
	DOUG GILL	vcls, bs	A

| 45: | Starry Eyed Woman / New Hope | (Prophet 6977) 1968 |

From Pine Mountain and West Point in Georgia, **The Rock Garden** formed in 1965. Their sole 45 appeared shortly before their dissolution in 1968, by which time their line-up included Larry Bowie from **The Continentals**.

Starry Eyed Woman appears on *Psychedelic States: Georgia Vol. 1* (CD). (MW/RM)

Rockin Foo

Personnel:	LESTER BROWN Jr	drms	A
	WAYNE ERWIN	gtr	A
	MICHAEL RACOON	piano, organ	A

| ALBUM: | 1(A) | ROCKIN FOO | (Hobbit HB 5001) 1969 - |
| 45: | Rochester River/Stanger In The Attic | (Hobbit 42001) 1969 |

A Californian hippie-rock trio, **Rockin Foo** released their album on the same label as **Sapphire Thinkers**. Housed in a rather intriguing sleeve with a black and white front cover with the ying/yang symbol and a seagull and a back cover with a Chinese ideogram, the album was produced by Les Brown, their drummer.

Clearly a minor group, their songs combined pseudo poetic lyrics with second rate melodies. Only some instrumental parts (organ and guitar) are of interest. All the songs were written by Wayne Erwin, save *Old Friends* co-written by Erwin and M.Clark.

The overall result sounds a bit like a lightweight version of **Morning**.

Les Brown also produced **Plain Jane** on the same label.

It's not clear whether a further album, *Rockin Foo* (Uni Records 73115) 1971, is by the same act. (SR)

The Rockin' Ramrods

Personnel:	RONN CAMPISI	bs	AB
	VIN CAMPISI	gtr	AB
	JESSE HENDERSON	drms	AB
	BILL LINANE	ld gtr	A
	LENNY CARELLI	ld gtr	B

ALBUMS:	1(A/B)	THE ROCKIN' RAMRODS	(Eva 12015) 198?
	2(A/B)	THE BEST OF THE ROCKIN' RAMRODS
			(Big Beat CDWIKD 151) 1995

NB: (2) is a 25 track CD which traces their career from 1963 onwards and includes tracks from their incarnation as **Puff**.

45s:	Jungle Call/Indian Giver	(Explosive F 101/2) 1963
	She Lied/Girl Can't Help It	(Bon-Bon 1315) 1964
	I Wanna Be Your Man/	
	I'll Be On My Way	(Plymouth 2961/2) 1964
	Wild About You/Cry In My Room	(Southern Sound 205) 1965

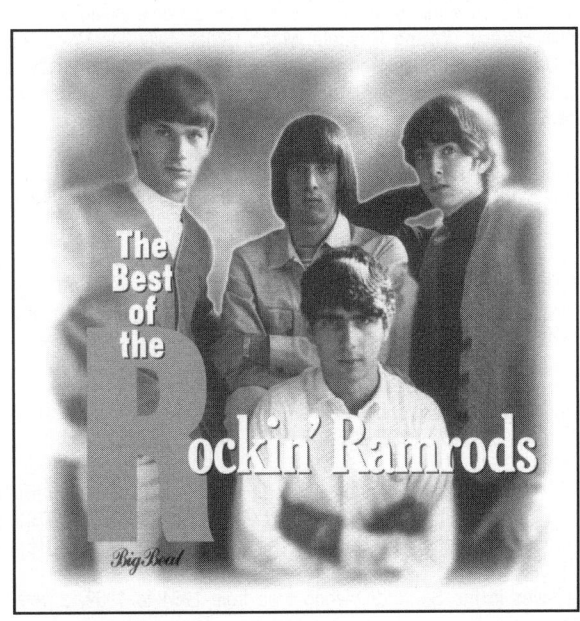

THE ROCKIN' RAMRODS - Best Of CD.

	α	Don't Fool With Fu Manchu/ Tears Melt The Stones	(Claridge 301) 1965
	α	She Rides With Me/Rudy Vadoo	(Claridge 312) 1966
		Play It/Got My Mojo Working	(Claridge 317) 1966
		Bright Lit Blue Skies/Mr. Wind	(Plymouth 2963/4) 1966
		Flowers In My Mind/Mary, Mary	(Plymouth 2965/6) 1966

NB: α as The GTO'S.

This Boston band started out playing instrumentals, backing Freddie Cannon early in their careers. Indeed, he went on to produce their first 45, an instrumental *Jungle Call*. They became the house band at the Surf Ballroom on Nantasket Beach on Boston's South Shore for a while. Later they progressed through influences ranging from The Beatles, punk, folk-rock, psychedelia and soft-rock. One of their cuts *She Lied* pursued a popular theme of American garage bands in this era - the lying and cheating of their girlfriends.

Bright Lit Blue Skies and *Mr. Wind* were written by Ron Campisi and covered by **The Rising Storm** on their album.

The group figured on early tours with The Stones and **The Kingsmen** and made an appearance in a rock'n'roll exploitation movie, *East Is East*. They also appeared on another 45: *Baby, Baby, Go Go/East Is East* (Claridge 308) 1966 backing Casey Paxton.

They later became **Puff** and released an eponymous soft psychedelic album on MGM (SE-4622) in 1969.

Compilation coverage has so far included *She Lied* on *Pebbles, Vol. 8* (LP); *I Wanna Be Your Man*, *Bright Lit Blue Skies* and *Mr. Wind* on *Bay State Rock* (LP); *Bright Lit Blue Skies* and *Can't You See*, misleadingly on the *The Best Of Bosstown Sound* (Dble CD) - both tracks are from 1966 and **The Rockin' Ramrods** predated the Bosstown hype. An unreleased track, *Merry Go Round* can also be found on *New England Teen Scene, Vol. 3* (LP). (VJ/MW)

The Rockin Rebellions

Personnel:	DONALD BARBEE	keyb'ds, gtr	A
	RONALD BARBEE	bs	A
	RICK FORTENBERRY	ld gtr	A
	ROSS GAGLIANO	drms	A
	HENRY LOVOY	ld vcls	A

45s:	By My Side / Run For Your Life	(Vaughn-Ltd VA-751) 1966
	Don't Let Go / Anyway The Wind Blows	(Gold Groove 111) c1967
	Drums And Other Things (Instr) / Would You Like To Go	(Gold Dust 300) 1967
	I Said No More / Oh What A Change	(Gold Dust 302) c1967

A quintet from Birmingham, Alabama, who released a total of four 45s. They played across the Southeast, opening for big acts including the Who, Herman's Hermits, **Young Rascals**, **Mitch Ryder**, Billy Joe Royal and the **Union Gap**. In 1967 they won the coveted Southeast Region Title at the Atlanta Battle Of The Bands, beating off competition from Georgia, Florida and the Carolinas.

By My Side is on *Psychedelic States: Alabama Vol. 1* (CD). It's a jerky upbeat number with pumping cheesy keys and nimble pickin'. (MW/RM)

Rockin' Roadrunners

Personnel:	STEVE GRIER	drms	A
	RUSS HAMILTON	ld gtr	A
	JACK LANDER	keyb'ds	A
	CHARLIE LYTLE	gtr	A
	DAVE MORRIS	bs	A

45s:	Go Away / My Window	(Lee C. 696) 1966
	King Of The Jungle / You Ain't Gonna Cry	(Lee C. 970) 1966
	Urban Meadows / Down	(Tener T1015) 1967

Florida faves in the Sanford/Orlando area from 1964 to 1969, a couple of members were later in an outfit called Yak. Their debut *Go Away* is a chiming and charming folk-rocker, perhaps influenced by the **Byrds**' debut album and especially *Here Without You*.

Their second 45, *King Of The Jungle*, was a novelty song that actually charted very high in Florida... it was a takeoff on a character that was a cross between George of the Jungle and Tarzan.

With street and storm effects, stately head-swirling organ, evocative lyrics and haunted vocals, their third effort, *Urban Meadows*, is both impressive and intensely addictive. Comparisons to Procol Harum's *Whiter Shade Of Pale* are inevitable but, given a vote, this'd get mine every time. *Down*, a cantering power-poppin' punker has a U.K. mod/freakbeat flavour. It's no wonder that the Tener 45 is much sought-after.

The Yak was Charlie Lytle's band after the **Rockin' Roadrunners**. They were a very popular band because they were one of the first bands in Orlando with a drummer with a double bass kit.

Compilation appearances include:- *Go Away* and *Urban Meadows* on *Psychedelic Crown Jewels Vol. 2* (Dble LP & CD); and *Down* on *Yeah Yeah Yeah* (CD) and *Psychedelic States - Florida Vol. 2* (CD). (MW/RM/SMR)

Rock Island

Personnel:	BOB 'COBB' BUSSINGER	keyb'ds, vcls	A
	TONY CURCIO	bs	A
	MIKE KENNEDY	gtr, vcls	A
	FRANK SCHALLIS	drms, perc	A
	B.J. TAYLOR	ld vcls	A

ALBUM:	1(A)	ROCK ISLAND	(Project 3 PR 4005 SD) 1970 R1

45:	Babe I'm Gonna Leave You / Hard And Never Easy	(Project 3 1382) 1970

A great band from Chicago whose album combined psychedelia, acid, rock and R&B. The best tracks are *Running Through My Mind* and *When I Was A Boy*. They released a second album on Project 3 as **Rain**. (VJ/MW)

The Rock-N-Souls

Personnel incl:	JIM KENFIELD	bs	A
	STEVE ROGERS	gtr	A

45:	Not Like You/Got No Love	(Rich Tone 2369/70) 196?

From Pasco, Washington. *Not Like You*, is a rather unusual recording.

Jim Kenfield later played in **Gas Co.**. Two members were previously in **The Pastels**.

HIGHS IN THE MID-SIXTIES Vol. 7 (Comp LP) including The Rock-N-Souls.

Compilation appearances include: *Turn And Run* (a previously unreleased cover of **The Wailers** track) on *Northwest Battle Of The Bands, Vol. 1* (CD); and *Not Like You* on *Highs In The Mid Sixties, Vol. 7* (LP). (VJ/MW/GGI)

Rocks

45:	Because We're Young / My Only Love	(Woodrich WR-1249) 1965

Because We're Young, a superb brooding R&B punker based around a solid *I'm A Man* riff, features moody sax interwoven with some cool but raw guitarwork and builds slowly in intensity without crossing into rave-up territory. *My Only Love is* one of those reverb'n'jangle lovelorn garage ballads that have started to find favour on compilations. **The Rocks** are thought to have come from Alabama but this is unconfirmed. Songwriter credits of Walter Sims (*Because...*) and Randy Duck/Johnny Harbin may help establish this, if they were band members.

Woody Richardson's predominantly gospel and country label recorded in Nashville and featured some other garage bands, also showcased on the *The Cicadelic '60s - Vol. 7*, the Shadows and the Shandells Inc.. According to the liner notes these 45s were pressed in limited quantities (about 500) and were not distributed or sold by the label but by the bands themselves at gigs.

There's another 45 by **The Rocks** on White Cliffs 239 circa 1966 featuring *Who Do You Love*, flip title unknown. The same band?

Compilation appearances include *Because We're Young* on *Yeah Yeah Yeah* (CD), *Bad Vibrations, Vol. 1* (LP) and *The Cicadelic '60s - Vol. 7* (CD). (MW)

Rock Shop

Personnel:	ALAN CLARK	vcls, ld gtr, bs, organ	A
	JOHN DALBECK	gtr	A
	PAT EDWARDS	bs	A
	PETE STEVENS	drms	A

ALBUM:	1(A)	MR. LEE'S "SWING 'N AFFAIR" PRESENTS THE ROCK SHOP	(Lee-Mo) 1968 R3

NB: (1) pirated on vinyl and CD. Reissued legitimately on vinyl and CD (Bacchus Archives BA 1115) 1997.

45:	Is That Your Halo?/State Of Your Mind	(Rowena 853) 1967

From Monterey, California. A very rare album of fuzz guitar-led blues and pop-rock. It has a very funny cover depicting the group as the next Beatles and hairdresser-cum-rock promoter "Mr. Lee" as God!

According to Tony Sanchez in the liner notes to *Fuzz, Flaykes, And Shakes, Vol. 4* (LP & CD), the above 45, both sides of which appear on the comp, is by a different band to the one who recorded the album - can anyone confirm this? *Is That Your Halo* is an intensely menacing punker that rumbles into Yardbirds' rave-up territory at the bridge where incendiary leads battle with rasping harmonica; *State Of Your Mind* is an almost equally powerful acid-punker - truly a double-whammy of a 45. (VJ/CF/MW/AP/MMs/NK)

Rocky and His Friends/and The Riddlers

Personnel:	JEFF BEALS	bs	A
	DAN DENTON	sax, vcls	A
	DAVE FAST	tpt	A
	CHRIS GASPARD	keyb'ds	A
	JEFF LABRACHE	drms	A
	ROCKY RHOADES	vcls, perc	A
	RIC ULSKY	keyb'ds	A

45s:	α	Surfer Plus/You're Not Wrong (unissued)	(Jerden 761) 1965
	β	Flash And Crash/Batman	(Panorama 28) 1966
	α	Riot City/You're Not Wrong	(Tower 178) 1966

NB: α as Rocky and His Friends. β as Rocky and The Riddlers.

ROCK SHOP - Mr. Lee's "Swing 'N Affair" Presents... LP.

From Seattle, Washington, they started out as The Imperials. Jeff LaBrache:- "The Imperials had much the same cast - Alan Parks, Dan Denton, Jeff Beals, Jim Wolf and myself. We did one record through Jerry Dennin (Jerden Records), but we were in our early teens, and it's not very good."

Their second 45, as **Rocky and The Riddlers**, *Flash And Crash* is a real bone-crunchin' punker and for fans of the very rawest, aggressive punk only. The follow-up, *Riot City*, is a frantic guitar-organ instrumental.

After recording these three mid-sixties 45s they changed names again to **The City Limits**.

Jeff Beals also played with **The Kingsmen** and Ric Ulsky later joined **The Association** in 1974. Jeff LaBrache later played with **West Coast Natural Gas** and **Indian Puddin' and Pipe**.

Compilation appearances have included: *Flash And Crash* on *Magic Carpet Ride* (LP), *Northwest Battle Of The Bands, Vol. 1 - Flash And Crash* (LP & CD), *Back From The Grave, Vol. 4* (LP) and *Back From The Grave, Vol. 2* (CD); *Riot City* on *Riot City!* (LP) and *Highs In The Mid-Sixties, Vol. 16* (LP); and *You Weren't Using Your Head* (a previously unreleased cover of **The Wailers** track) on *Northwest Battle Of The Bands, Vol. 2* (CD). (VJ/MW/JLb)

Rocky and The Border Kings

45:	Gulf Of Mexico / Michoacan	(Epic 10901) c1970

An obscure group lead by **Kim Fowley**, who wrote both songs. The flip, originally written for the 'Cisco Pike' movie, was also recorded by Doug Sahm and by **Atwood Electric Iceman**. (SR)

Rod and The Satalites

45:	She Cares/I'm Telling You Right Now	(Irish 4336/7) 1964

NB: 100 copies were issued with a rare picture sleeve.

A primitive punk outfit from Quincy, Illinois. The closing chord of *She Cares* sounds like the start of *A Hard Days Night*.

Compilation appearances include: *She Cares* on *Monsters Of The Midwest, Vol. 4* (LP); *She Cares* and *I'm Telling You Right Now* on *Drink Beer! Yell! Dance!* (LP). (VJ/MW)

Sixto Rodriguez

Personnel:	BOB BABBITT	bs	A
	DENNIS COFFEY	gtr	A

	SIXTO RODRIGUEZ	acc. gtr	ABC
	ANDREW SMITH	drms	A
	MIKE THEODORE	keyb'ds	A
	TONY CARR	perc	B
	PHIL DENNYS	keyb'ds	B
	CHRIS SPEDDING	ld gtr	B

ALBUMS:	1(A)	COLD FACT	(Sussex SXBS 7000) 1970 SC
	2(B)	COMING FROM REALITY	(Sussex SXBS7012) 1971 R1

45s:	α	I'll Slip Away/You'd Like To Admit It	(Impact 1031) 1967
		Forget It/Inner City Blues	(Sussex 204) 1970
		To Whom It May Concern/ I Think Of You	(Sussex 234) 1970

NB: α released as Rod Riguez. Possibly Promo only.

Until recently a mysterious figure, **Sixto Rodriguez** was born in Detroit, Michigan, in 1942 to Mexican immigrant parents - his first name chosen because he was their sixth child. Possessed of an distinctive voice, **Rodriguez** was a singer / songwriter steeped in the folk and blues traditions of his times and comparisons with Dylan and Donovan are inevitable and not undeserved. However, a profoundly working class upbringing in this industrial - and musical - heartland helped to make his work quite unique.

In April 1967, he recorded five original songs for the local Impact label. The 'A' side of the resulting single, *I'll Slip Away* (later re-cut in the mid-seventies), was an atmospheric number with considerable commercial potential, the 'B' side, *You'd Like To Admit It*, a contrasting folk-rocker in which the singer berated an ex-girlfriend for going off with a 'hick'. Unfortunately it became Impact's penultimate release before the label went under. Of the remaining tracks *Forget It* would later be re-recorded for his first album and *To Whom It May Concern* for the second, but the intriguingly titled *That Discoteque* remains unreleased in any form.

Undaunted, two years later **Rodriguez** found himself signed to the newly founded Hollywood label, Sussex (Bill Withers' first label), and the classic *Cold Fact* album emerged as their first release. Recorded in 1969 and skilfully produced by two other Impact refugees, Mike Theodore and Dennis Coffey, it opened with the trippy but dark *Sugar Man*. Over a subtle backing of acoustic guitar and electronic effects **Rodriguez**'s lyrics were starkly honest:

"Sugar man, met a false friend
On a lonely dusty road
lost my heart when I found it
it had turned to dead black coal.
Silver magic ships you carry
Jumpers, coke, sweet Mary Jane
Sugarman, you're the answer
That makes my question disappear
Sugarman, 'cos I'm weary
Of those double games I hear."

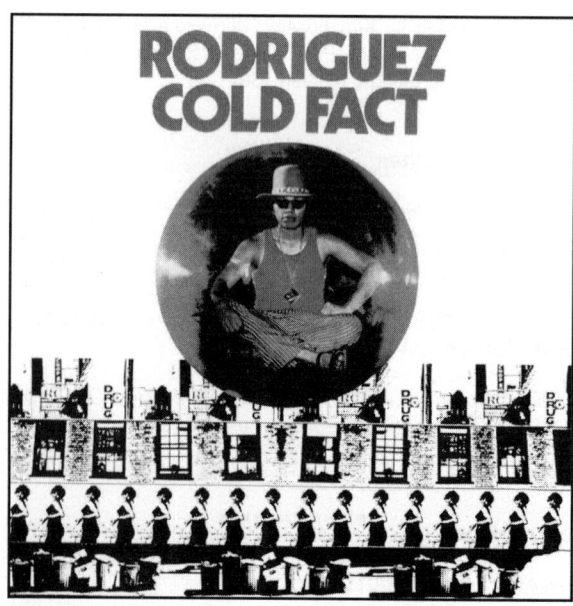

RODRIGUEZ - Cold Fact CD.

The themes of many other songs on the album can be gleaned from the titles alone: *Crucify Your Mind* (drugs), *This Is Not A Song, It's An Outburst: Or, The Establishment Blues*, *Inner City Blues* and *Rich Folks Hoax* (social unrest and political apathy), but there were also beautiful, bittersweet love songs in *Forget It* and *Jane S. Piddy*. Rumour has it (although **Rodriguez** has denied the connection) that *Like Janis* was inspired by **Janis Joplin**. The brutally direct *Only Good For Conversation* stands out as a great fuzz rocker, but for the most part the album gives prominence to **Rodriguez**'s acoustic guitar and powerful lyrics.

Coming From Reality, which was recorded at London's Lansdowne Studios, came in a striking die-cut gatefold sleeve. However, despite featuring some excellent musicianship - especially the lead guitar work courtesy of ace session man Chris Spedding - it somehow contrived to be less interesting than its predecessor. The most immediately striking tracks are undoubtedly those where the band is in full flight - *Climb Up On My Music* and *Heikki's Suburban Bus Tour* for instance - but the more restrained acoustic numbers repay repeated listening. *Sandrevan Lullaby - Lifestyles* (the title is a conflation of the names of **Rodriguez**'s two daughters) and *Cause* were both subtly orchestrated and their lyrics echoed the dark emotional themes of the debut album.

Three further tracks recorded in the mid-seventies - a new version of the Impact single *I'll Slip Away*, *Can't Get Away* and *Street Boy* - were each the equal of any of his previous works, but none were released at the time. After neither album made any impact in the States, **Rodriguez** seemed to simply disappear. That, however, was really only the beginning of the most extraordinary phase of his career. When, in 1970, some enterprising folk at Festival Records imported 400 copies of *Cold Fact* to Australia they rapidly sold out. The album was subsequently issued by A&M in 1971 and, as its fame spread, it gradually acquired a cult following amongst the disaffected youth both there and in countries like New Zealand and South Africa. When it was finally issued on CD in those markets it went platinum and **Rodriguez** was so well known by the beginning of the eighties that he even toured Australia with Midnight Oil. After disappearing into temporary obscurity once more - during which increasingly bizarre rumours circulated about his demise - he recently travelled to South Africa for a sell-out stadium tour. Both albums have subsequently been reissued in all formats in those countries, while a CD *Rodriguez: At His Best* (Blue Goose VPCD 6748) collects together highlights from both albums and adds the three unreleased mid-seventies tracks for good measure.

Compilation appearaces include *I'll Slip Away* on *The Best Of Impact Records* (CD). (TF)

The Roemans

Personnel:	BO GLOVER	ld gtr	AB
	BERTIE HIGGINS	drms	AB
	LANNY LANGFORD	ld vcls	AB
	JOE PAPPALARDO	bs	A
	RONNIE SWARTZKOPF	gtr	AB
	BARRY OAKLEY	bs	B

45s:	Your Friend/Give Me A Chance	(ABC Paramount 10583) 1964
	Miserlou/Don't	(ABC Paramount 10671) 1965
	Universal Soldier/ Lost Little Girl	(ABC Paramount 10723) 1965
	Listen To Me/ You Make Me Feel Good	(ABC Paramount 10757) 1965
	When The Sun Shines In The Mornin'/ Love (That's All I Want)	(ABC Paramount 10814) 1966
	All The Good Things/ Pleasing You Pleases Me	(ABC Paramount 10871) 1966

Tommy Roe's backing band put out the above 45s and were not reticent about their British Invasion-style 'folk-rock' influences to the extent that you'd swear they were The Searchers!

The Roemans formed in November 1963 with the original name Lanny and The Impressions. In early '64 an A&R man from ABC Paramount heard the group playing at a "Clearwater Star-Spectacular" concert and signed them to the label. Since Paramount already had a group named 'The Impressions' they changed their name to The Romans. A few weeks later ABC hooked them up to Tommy Roe... and so naturally they changed the spelling of their name to **The Roemans**.

THE ESSENTIAL PEBBLE COLLECTION Vol. 1 (Comp CD) including The Rogues.

The group toured the globe but eventually suffered the same demise as many groups of the era, with members having to be replaced due to the draft. By 1970, only Bertie Higgins (drums) and Bob (Bo) Glover (guitar) from the original line-up were left and the group dissolved totally that year.

Bertie went on to a solo career and later achieved fame in 1982 with a huge hit, *Key Largo*. Bob (Bo) bounced around the country leading different groups, one of the most intriguing names being 'Bojicada', a latin flavor band in the vein of **Santana** and a Southern rock group named 'Bo and Arrow' in the late seventies. Bo went on to a solo career and recorded albums titled *After The Lovin'* and a Gospel album *Amazing Grace*. Both Bertie and Bo are still performing and writing.

Barry Oakley, who replaced Joe Pappalardo after he was drafted in '66 was later in **The Second Coming** and **The Allman Brothers Band**. (MW/BGr)

Rog and The Escorts

| Personnel: | ROG BOOTH | drms, vcls | A |
| | ZELDA | keyb'ds | A |

45s:	Main Drag / Judy Or Joann	(Soma 1144) 1960
	I Found A Love / I Wanna Do It	(Fredlo 6311) 1963
	The Wobble Drum / On Top Of Old Smokey	(Fredlo 6403) 1964
	Heart Of Mine / Twelfth Of Never	(Fredlo 6416) 1964
	Space Walk / You're The One	(Zorch 101) 196?
α	I Wonder / Our Love May Not Live Again	(Zorch 102) 1966

NB: most of the early 45s probably as by 'The Escorts'. α as **Rog & The Escorts**.

From Ely, just South of Cedar Rapids in Eastern Iowa, this outfit was originally known as **The Do's and Don'ts**. A very clean cut band they recorded a number of records including *I Wonder* on Zorch Records circa 1966. This commercial pop song, which with better promotion may have charted, can also be heard on the *Dirty Water* (LP) compilation. (VJ)

The Rogues

Personnel incl:	KIM FOWLEY		A
	SHAUN HARRIS		A
	MICHAEL LLOYD		A

| 45: | Wanted: Dead Or Alive/One Day | (Living Legend 723) c1966 |

This was a L.A.-based studio-only project. Shaun Harris was later a member of the **West Coast Pop Art Experimental Band**. They recorded *Wanted: Dead Or Alive* in 1966, which is actually a slow re-write of *Hey Joe*.

Compilation appearances include *Wanted Dead Or Alive* on *Kim Fowley - Underground Animal* (LP & CD), *Pebbles Vol. 8* (CD), *Pebbles, Vol. 17* (LP), *Trash Box* (5-CD) and *Best of Pebbles, Vol. 2* (LP & CD). (VJ)

The Rogues

Personnel:	JOHN BONAR	bs	AB
	GLEN HEBERT	drms	AB
	MARK MacDIARMID	vcls, ld gtr	AB
	MIKE SCHWARTZ	gtr	AB
	FRED BECHTEL	vcls	B
	TOMMY WITHROW	keyb'ds	B

45s:	Put You Down / Stormy Monday Blues	(MBM 2002) 1966
α	You're Through / She's A Drag	(Montel-Michelle 959) 1966
	I Don't Need You / Tonight	(La Louisianne 8094) 1967

NB: α as by **The Dry Grins**.

A classy punk band from Lafayette, Louisiana. Their debut, *Put You Down*, is revisited on *Teenage Shutdown, Vol. 7* (LP & CD). *I Don't Need You*, a typical punk screamer, is on *Highs In The Mid-Sixties, Vol. 8* (LP).

They changed their name to **The Dry Gins** for one 45, produced by the **Greek Fountains**' Cyril Vetter. *You're Through* is re-aired on *The Essential Pebbles Collection, Vol. 1* (Dble CD), *She's A Drag* was dug up for *Back From The Grave, Vol. 8* (CD) and *Back From The Grave, Vol. 8* (Dble LP). (MW/AB)

The Rogues

| 45: | Love Is A Beautiful Thing/The Sound | (Wasp 102) 196? |

NB: released as The R./Rogues.

From Tacoma, Washington, this band were actually called **The Royal Rogues**, but their 45 is credited to the R./Rogues - so I guess they ran out of letters at the label paste-up (that's an attempted joke, not history!). You'll also find *The Sound* on *Boulders, Vol. 9*. (GGl)

The Rogues

| 45: | Summertime/Anything You Say | (Action 6.6400) 1966 |

Omaha in Eastern Nebraska was home to this band. The 'A' side was a much recorded ballad, but it's the flip, *Anything You Say*, which may interest readers. A typical post British invasion, pre-punk recording, pressed in Minneapolis, you could check it out on *Monsters Of The Midwest, Vol. 2* (LP). (VJ)

The Rogues

| Personnel incl: | DENNY FRY | vcls, bs | A |
| | NICK RADCLIFFE | drms | A |

This garage band operated out of Muscatine, Iowa, but did not record. Both the members listed were later in **Depot Rains**. (VJ)

The Rogues

| 45s: | Night Time/No Lies | (Boss City 160) 1969 |
| | Tobacco Road/Heavy | (Boss City 166) 1970 |

This New London, Connecticut, band produce a late-but-great screeching uptempo blast of *Tobacco Road* with some wicked guitar throughout. It's almost on a par with the **Blues Magoos** rendition. The flip is a brief up-tempo workout. (MW/MM)

The Rogues

45:	Good Lovin'/Set Me Free	(Talent Associates No #)	197?

This time from Brookfield, Wisconsin. The two covers on this 45 are competently executed in a straight garage-beat vein. Apparently the 45 dates from the seventies but has a very sixties sound and feel. (MW)

The Rogues

45s:	α You Better Look Now / Train Kept A Rollin'	(Audition 6110)	1966
	Say You Love Me / Secondary Man	(Thunderbird 507)	196?
	Should You Care / The Rest Of The Way	(Thunderbird 511)	196?

NB: α was reissued in the early eighties on Moxie (M 104).

From Buffalo, New York, this act were previously known as The London Fogs. Their *You Better Look Now*, a haunting folk-rock garage ballad, was covered in 1982 by Rochester NY's Chesterfield Kings on their debut *Here Are* album. The flip, a cover of *Train Kept A Rollin* is also excellent.

Compilation appearances have included: *The Train Kept A Rollin* on *Pebbles Box* (5-LP), *Pebbles, Vol. 4 (ESD)* (CD), *Acid Dreams - The Complete 3 LP Set* (3-LP), *Acid Dreams Epitaph* (CD), *Trash Box* (5-CD) and *Train Kept A Rollin'* on *Teenage Shutdown, Vol. 14* (LP & CD); and *You Better Look Now* on *Teenage Shutdown, Vol. 5* (LP & CD) and *The Cicadelic 60's, Vol. 5* (LP). (MW/MM)

The Rogues

45:	It's The Same All Over The World / Oh No	(Peyton P-1001)	1966

Produced by **The Blue Echoes**' Tom Zagryn this was **The Squires**' first vinyl outing... Tom later produced their classic *Going All The Way*, before selling the rights to Atco.

The Rogues

45:	How Many Times / Shout	(Lyn Lou 1126)	196?

Another **Rogues**, possibly from Memphis. Their *How Many Times* is on *The Essential Pebbles Collection, Vol. 2* (Dble CD). (MW/AB)

The Rogues

45:	Don't Follow Me / Mr. Sandman	(Compass 1857)	c1966

From Mercersberg, Pennsylvania, *Don't Follow Me* is on *Sixties Rebellion, Vol. 7 - The Backyard Patio* (LP & CD). (MW)

The Rogues

Personnel incl:	BRUCE JOHNSTON	A
	TERRY MELCHER	A

HCP

45s:	Every Day / Roger's Reef	(Columbia 4-43190) 1964	101
	Come On, Let's Go / Roger's Reef	(Columbia 4-43253) 1965	-

From L.A., Bruce Johnston and Terry Melcher also recorded some surf-pop singles as "Bruce and Terry" and produced several surf groups. Their studio group **The Rogues** deserves a mention here. *Everyday* is a catchy and uptempo adaptation of the Norman Petty/Hardin song, with a trace of the *Louie Louie* riff, which missed the Top 100 by just one place. *Roger's Reef* is an instrumental with wild B3 organ a lá Dave "Baby" Cortez. The son of Doris Day, Melcher is mostly known for his production work with **The Byrds**, **Paul Revere**, **The Rising Sons**, **Gentle Soul**... He also released two West Coast/Country-rock albums in 1974 and 1976. Johnston joined the Beach Boys and also had a solo career. (SR/MW/VJ)

The Rogues

Personnel:	JOHN CASETELLANO	vcls	A
	CASEY DUTCAVICH	bs	A
	LARRY KRZEMINSKI	ld gtr	A
	RON OLENIK	drms	A
	RICK REBSTOCK	keyb'ds	A

45:	Pearl Girl / The Secret	(Night Owl 67102)	1967

These **Rogues** hailed from Milwaukee. They lasted about five years, playing teen gigs and CYO dances and released just one 45. (MW/GM)

Rogues, Inc.

Personnel:	JODY DAWSON	drms	A
	GARY PEARSON	ld gtr	A
	GEORGE RODY	keyb'ds	A
	JIM RODY	bs	A
	CHARLIE STAFFORD	vcls	A

45:	People Say / Your Kind Of Man	(Associated Artists 101)	1967

People Say is an enchanting folk-punker with vibratin', not fuzzed, guitar from a Savannah, Georgia quintet. Clearly enounced vocals add an Anglophile air. Featured on *Psychedelic Crown Jewels Vol. 2 - '60s Garage Unknowns* (Dble LP & CD) and *Psychedelic States: Georgia Vol. 1* (CD) whose liners reveal that George Rody resides there still and owns a record store.

A **Rogues Inc** also had a track, *Dixie* on the Braintree National *Battle Of The Bands* double/triple album set - see the **Gents** entry for further details. (MW/RM)

Rohrbacker, Hendren and Kingen

ALBUM:	1 ROHRBACKER, HENDREN AND KINGEN	
	(Private Pressing)	c1975 ?

NB: (1) according to Ken Scott's "Vintage Vinyl Jesus Music" guide, only 500 copies were pressed.

A Christian rock trio, ranging from hard to melodic rural-rock, mostly notable for its good lead guitar work. (SR/MKy)

The Roks

Personnel incl:	MILTON KIRKPATRICK	A

45:	Transparent Day/Hey Joe	(Mark VII 1012)	1967

NB: labels credit band as **The Rox**.

A Texas band whose cover version of *Hey Joe* was delivered at breakneck speed. Presumably the 'A' side is a cover of the **West Coast Pop Art Experimental Band**'s ditty.

We're not sure whether the band name was **The Roks** or **The Rox** - can anyone confirm?

Compilation appearances include: *Hey Joe* on *Pebbles, Vol. 4 (ESD)* (CD), *Texas Flashbacks, Vol. 4* (LP & CD), *Flashback, Vol. 4* (LP) and *Highs In The Mid Sixties, Vol. 17* (LP). (VJ/MW)

PSYCHEDELIC CROWN JEWELS Vol. 2 (Comp CD) including Rogues Inc.

Rolling Ramsax(s)

45: You've Hurt Me So/Many Nights Go By   (Boot 330-3ja) 196?

From London Ohio, this band were actually known as **Rolling Ramsax**, but their 45 was miscredited as the **Rolling Ramsaxs** and *Garage Punk Unknowns, Vol. 3* (LP) (which includes *You've Hurt Me So*) credits them as **Rollin' Ramsaxes**. The 45 was recorded at Magnetic Studios in Columbus, Ohio and *You've Hurt Me So* is an unexceptional folk-punker. (VJ/GGI/MW)

The Romancers

Personnel incl: MAX UBALLEZ   A
                ROBERT UBALLEZ   A

45s: Don't Let Her Go/I Did The Wrong Thing   (Linda 117) 1964
     My Heart Cries/Tell Her I Love Her   (Linda 119) 1965
     Do You Cry / Love's The Thing   (Linda 120) 1965
     Took My Heart/She Gives Me Love   (Linda 123) 1966
     She Took My Oldsmobile/
     That's Why I Love You   (Linda 124) 1966
   α Love's The Thing / She Gives Me Love   (Prospect 101) 1966
   α Love's The Thing / She Gives Me Love   (Dot 16975) 1966

NB: α as by **The Smoke Rings**.

This outfit ranks amongst the best on the sixties Mexican-American scene in East Los Angeles, frequently referred to as the East Side Sound (other top dogs being **Cannibal and The Headhunters**, **Thee Midnighters** and **The Premiers**). **The Romancers** were led by prolific songwriter Max Uballez who composed nearly all of their material and plenty for other East Side bands - including *Get On This Plane* (**Premiers**), *Nau Ninny Nau* (**Cannibal and The Headhunters**) and *Beaver Shot* (**Atlantics**).

Their finest moment is *Love's The Thing*, a tremendous pumped-up punker with strong raw vocals and raging guitars that races to a breath-taking halt. **Count Five**'s producer Irwin Zucker liked it so much that he struck a deal with **Romancers** producer Eddie Davis, resulting in the 45 being put out again as by the **Smoke Rings**, first on Prospect and then on Dot. Pump up the volume on this one.

She Took My Oldsmobile is another fine punker.

Ballads were also part of their repertoire - *My Heart Cries* appears on the 1966 comp *East Side Revue, Vol. 1*; and both *My Heart Cries* and *That's Why I Love You* feature on the 1970 double album retrospective *East Side Revue* (Rampart).

Retrospective compilation appearances include: *Love's The Thing* on *Sixties Choice, Vol. 1* (LP), *60's Choice Collection, Vol's 1 & 2* (CD) and as **Smoke Rings** on *Boulders, Vol. 1* (LP); *She Took My Oldsmobile* on *Victims Of Circumstance, Vol. 2* (LP & CD), *The East Side Sound, Vol. 1* (LP), *It's Finkin' Time!* (LP), *Chosen Few, Vol's 1 & 2* (CD) and *The Chosen Few, Vol. 2* (LP); *Don't Let Her Go* and *Tell Her I Love Her (No Other Love)* on *The West Coast East Side Sound, Vol. 1* (CD); *Took My Heart* and *My Heart Cries* on *The West Coast East Side Sound, Vol. 2* (CD); *That's Why I Love You* and *She Took My Oldsmobile* on *The West Coast East Side Sound, Vol. 3* (CD); *She Gives Me Love* and *Love's The Thing* on *The West Coast East Side Sound, Vol. 4* (CD); *She Took My Oldsmobile* and *Love's The Thing* on *The East Side Sound, Vol. 1 - 1959-1968* (CD). (MW)

Murray Roman

ALBUMS: 1 YOU CAN'T BEAT PEOPLE UP AND HAVE
(very   THEM SAY I LOVE YOU   (Tetragrammaton T-101) 1968 -
selective) 2 A BLIND MAN'S MOVIE   (Tetragrammaton T-120) 1969 -

A California comedian, whose inclusion here is deserved partly because of the subjects of his sketches:- drug busts, banana smoking (!), the Vietnam war, religion, riots and all the other counterculture subjects. He also deserves an entry because his albums use a lot of music between or during his talks.

Produced by David Briggs (then the in-house producer of Tetragrammaton and in charge of **Summerhill**, **Quatrain** etc.), the two albums mentioned above reveal some surprisingly good versions of *Shake*, *Mojo Workout* and *Land Of 1000 Dances* treated in a very energetic way.

Murray Roman can also be heard on **Geronimo Black**'s debut album. (SR)

Roman Rebellion

45s: What Summer Brings / Now I'm Missing You   (Mr.G. 818) 1968
     The Weather's Getting Bold /
     Every Groovy Day   (RCA Victor 47-9443) 1968

A sunshine-pop outfit possibly from New York. All their material was co-written by Thomas Alessandro - *Now I'm Missing You* with Salvatore Pate and the rest with Rosario Rizzo. *Every Groovy Day* is featured on, and provides the title for, Misty Lane's flowery folk-pop compilation *Every Groovy Day* (LP). (MW)

The Romans

Personnel incl: JERRY BLACKLAW   A
                RICHARD E. SHOOK   A

45s: I'll Find A Way/You Do Something To Me (PS)   (My 2905) 1966
     I Just Had To Fall (In Love)/
     He Don't Love You   (My 2908) 1966
     Think It Over/You Won Your Victory   (My 2913) 1967
     Something Special /
     Ain't No Need (In Me Fooling Myself)   (My 2930) 1967

NB: (4) released as by Merging Traffic.

All togged up in their togas this Little Rock, Arkansas five-piece certainly cut a dashing figure - the drummer must've had lots of female admirers or a large bass drum! *I'll Find A Way* is a decent Searchers/**Byrds** inspired garage ballad but the flip is the showpiece here - a bouncy mid-tempo piece with evocative keyboard and a very short neat guitar solo but all underpinned by the earliest example of 'phasing' discovered to date, and it all comes off superbly - hats off to Little Rock.

Their remaining 45s are relatively disappointing after this: The second is a pleasant Zombies-inspired minor-mooder backed by a party mover with funky strutting. The third is a crooning lounge ballad and the flip is a brassy James Brown style number a-la *Ninety Nine And A Half*. The band evolved into The Merging Traffic and released one final soul-infused 45.

Other My label releases that are now attracting collectors' interest include those by the Egyptians, Culls, Spires Of Oxford and Dutch Masters. Pick'em up while you can.

Compilation appearances include *You Do Something To Me* on *Fuzz, Flaykes, And Shakes, Vol. 3* (LP & CD). (MW)

Jonny Rome and The Second Thought

See **Second Thought**.

Ron and Shirley

ALBUM: 1   ROCK AND SCROLL   (Private Pressing) c1976 SC

A New Jersey folk-psych duo with male/female vocals, fuzz guitar and keyboards. Their album came housed in a nice homemade cover with an insert. (SR)

Ron and The Starfires

Personnel:	CHARLIE BROWN	gtr	A
	CARL CHAMBERS	gtr	A
	GERALD (JESSE) CHAMBERS	bs	A
	ALLEN KEEFER	drms	A
	RON WHITNEY	ld vcls	A

45s:	Why Did You Cry / The Grass Is Greener	(Lee C. 1014) 1965
	Midnight Reader /	
	Be Sincere / The Grass Is Greener	(Tener 1024) 1966

Originally formed in 1959, the first **Starfires** broke up in 1963 but Whitney and Brown formed another group and retained the name. Shortly after, this Tampa/Auburndale, Florida band became **Ron and The Starfires** to prevent confusion with the numerous other Starfires, including one in North Florida.

Their 1965 debut *Why Did You Cry*, reaired on *Psychedelic States - Florida Vol. 2* (CD), is a tender beat ballad. They'd release another 45 on Eric Schabacker's Tener label the following year. An otherwise unavailable cover of Neil Diamond's *Solitary Man* turned up on the rare 1968 label sampler album, *Bee Jay Video Soundtrack* (Tener 1014).

Carl Chambers would join **We The People** in the late sixties. The band lasted until around 1970; some members were later in Cinnamon. (MW/JLh/RM)

The Rondells

From Louisville, Kentucky, this band had one track on the rare *The Louisville Scene* compilation, circa 1966 (Rod 'n' Custom 3001). The song in question, *One More Chance* takes the riff from *Just Like Me* and adds a Zombies flavour. A rather raw haunting punker, you can also find it on *Highs In The Mid Sixties, Vol. 22* (LP). (VJ)

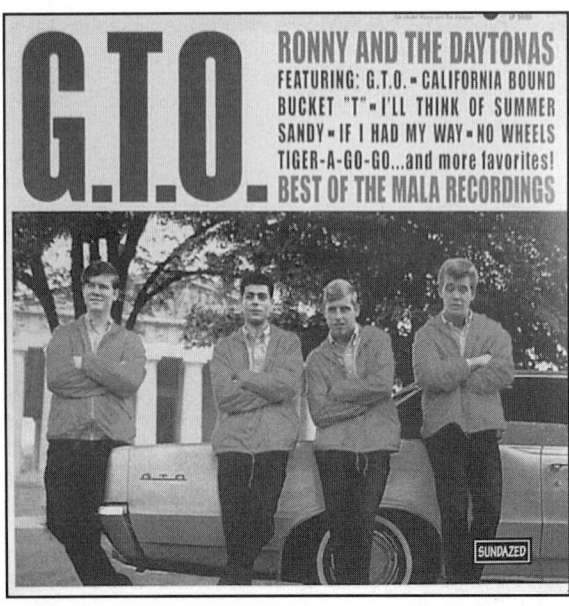

RONNY and THE DAYTONAS - G.T.O. LP.

THE ROOKS (Northwest).

The Ron-dels

Personnel incl:	RONNIE KELLY	A
	DELBERT McLINTON	A

ALBUMS:	1(A)	DELBERT McLINTON AND THE RON-DELS, VOL 1
		(Le Cam) 196?
	2(-)	DELBERT McLINTON AND THE RON-DELS, VOL 2
		(Le Cam) 196?
		HCP

45s:	Diddley Daddy/?	(Brownfield 13) 196? -
	Just When You Think You're Somebody/	
	Lover In Demand	(Brownfield 16) 1965 -
	If You Really Want Me To, I'll Go/	
	Walk About	(Brownfield 18) 1965 -
	If You Really Want Me To, I'll Go/	
	Walk About	(Smash 1986) 1965 97
	She's My Girl/It's Over	(Smash 2002) 1965 -
	Lose Your Money/Picture Of Me	(Smash 2014) 1965 -
	I Lost My Love/Crying Over You	(Brownfield 33) 196? -
	Matilda/Tina	(Le Cam 306) 1969 -
	Matilda/Tina	(Dot 17323) 1969 -

A Fort Worth-based combo fronted by McLinton (previously with Straightjackets and later Bright Side) who later became a country star. They were never able to capitalise on the success of their first 45 which was a semi-hit, locally and disintegrated at the end of the sixties.

Lose Your Money, is a Moody Blues cover with some Texan grit added, and *Lost My Love Today*, a folk-country pop number.

Compilation appearances have included: *If You Really Want Me To, I'll Go* on *Texas Music, Vol. 3* (CD); *Lost My Love Today* and *Lose Your Money* on *The Fort Worth Teen Scene - The Major Bill Tapes Vol. 2* (LP). (VJ)

Ron-De-Voos

45:	The Maid/Pipeline'66	(Cycle no #) 1966

This outfit from Indiana were known in earlier garage incarnations as The Blue Flames and The Rendezvous. *The Maid* can also be heard on *Back From The Grave, Vol. 7* (Dble LP) but it's a pretty routine rock'n'roller. The flip has also resurfaced on *Strummin' Mental, Vol. 5*.

The band finally folded in 1968. (VJ)

Ron-De-Vous

45:	Trip So Wild/Run Run Run	(Mastertone 4023) 196?

Trip So Wild is a breezy folk-rocker with fragile lyrics inspired by a psychedelic experience.

Compilation appearances include *A Trip So Wild* on *Psychedelic Unknowns, Vol. 5* (LP & CD), *Turds On A Bum Ride Vol. 1 & 2* (Dble CD) and *Turds On A Bum Ride, Vol. 1* (Dble LP). (VJ)

Ronny and The Daytonas

Personnel incl:	BUZZ CASON	gtr, vcls	A
	JOHN "BUCKY" WILKIN	gtr, vcls	A

ALBUMS:	1(A)	G.T.O.	(Mala) 1964 -
	2(A)	SANDY	(Mala) 1965 -

NB: (1) reissued on 12" vinyl (Beat Rocket BR 119) 2000 and CD. (2) reissued on 12" vinyl and CD (Beat Rocket BR 120) 2000. Also relevant is *G.T.O. The Best Of* (Sundazed SC 11046/LP 5051) 1997.

			HCP
45s:	G.T.O/Hot Rod Baby	(Mala 481) 1964	4
	California Bound./Hey Little Girl	(Mala 490) 1964	72
	Bucket "T"/Little Rail Job	(Mala 492) 1964	54
	Little Scrambler/Teenage Years	(Mala 497) 1965	-
	No Wheels/Bach Boy	(Mala 503) 1965	-
	Sandy/Sandy (instr)	(Mala 513) 1965	27
α	Tiger A Go-Go /Bay City	(Mala) 1965	-
	Somebody To Love Me/Good Bye Baby	(Mala 525) 1966	115
	Then The Rains Came/ Antique '32 Studebaker Dictator Coupe	(Mala 531) 1966	-
	I'll Think Of Summer/Little Scrambler	(Mala 542) 1966	133
β	Hey Little Girl/Please Go Away	(Amy 961) 1966	-
	Dianne, Dianne/All American Girl	(RCA 47-8896) (PS) 1966	69
	Winter Weather/Young	(RCA 47-9022) 1966	-
	Walk With The Sun/The Last Letter	(RCA 47-9107) 1966	-
	Hold Onto Your Heart/ Brave New World	(RCA 47-9253) 1967	-
	The Girls And The Boys/Alfie	(RCA 47-9435) 1968	-

NB: α by Buzz and Bucky, also released in the UK (Stateside SS428). β by The Daytonas.

Produced by Bill Justis and based in Nashville, **Ronny and The Daytonas** were fronted by **John "Buck" Wilkin** (aka Ronnie) and Buzz Cason. Although based very far from California, the group released several songs which can be compared to the best sides of the Beach Boys or Jan and Dean. Benefiting from the excellent songriting skills of Wilkin, they got a national hit in 1964 with *G.T.O.*, still a hot rod classic. Their subsequent singles sold quite well too and they became so popular that several fake "Ronny and the Daytonas" were touring in the Southwest.

Although their most successful period was 1964/65, when they were signed to the local Mala/Amy label (also in charge of **The Box Tops**), they kept on recording for RCA until 1968. Their line-up was not very stable and, in 1967, some of The Daytonas became **The Hombres**.

In 1969, when the group finally broke up, **John Buck Wilkin** formed the short-lived **American Eagles**. He would also release two interesting solo albums and do a lot of session work with rock and country acts. Buzz Cason became a well-known producer and worked with **The Hangmen, Us Four, White Duck** and **Jay Bentley**. (SR/EW)

THE ROOKS (Northwest).

The Rooks

Personnel:	RICHIE DANGEL	ld gtr	A
	JOEY JOHNSON	bs	A
	JOE RICHIE	gtr	A
	LARRY THOMPSON	drms	A
	BILLY WEBB	gtr	A

45s:	I'll Be The One/Believe In You	(Etiquette 14) 1965
	Bound To Lose/Gimme A Break	(Mustang 3008) 1965

This band is probably most notable for the involvement of **Wailers**' axeman Rich Dangel, although despite their Northwest connections, they were in fact based in L.A.. Their first 45 was weakish British Invasion-inspired beat but both sides of the second are worth a listen and you'll find them on *Highs In The Mid-Sixties, Vol. 14* (LP). We're talking Mersey-influenced rock here.

Billy Webb and Larry Thompson had both earlier played with the **Bobby Fuller Fanatics**, whilst that group was still back in El Paso in the early sixties. They later moved to Los Angeles, as did Richie Dangel (from Tacoma) circa mid-1964. When they met up they formed **The Rooks** in Los Angeles, whilst Dangel's ties with the Tacoma, Washington scene got the group their first release on Etiquette.

A second 45 followed on the same label as the **Bobby Fuller Four**. Just after its release Dangel quit, due to an argument with Richie. Dangel and Johnson then played in **The Time Machine**, and Dangel later re-emerged in 1969 with **The Floating Bridge**. **The Rooks** carried on, were joined for a period by a lead vocalist Brady Sneed (a dancer on Shindig!) and latterly appeared on **Paul Revere and the Raiders**' "Happening '68" TV show. After they split, they followed Dangel back to the Seattle area. Webb and Randy Fuller joined **Dewey Martin** and "Sarge" West in the **New Buffalo Springfield**.

30-odd years on ... Billy Webb resides across the street from Randy Fuller in the Eastern Los Angeles County area. They still play together, most recently in The Bobby Fuller Drive. Plans are afoot to team up again with drummer Larry Thompson, now based in Tacoma and tour under this name as a Bobby Fuller Four tribute band of sorts. (MW/DR/MM/BTs/LTn)

The Rooks

Personnel incl?:	THOMAS A. ENGEL	A
	JOHN B. SZMAGALSKI	A

45s:	A Girl Like You / Empty Heart	(Mercury 72644) 1966
	Ice And Fire / Turquoise	(Jo-Way 5000) 1968
	Free Sunday Paper / ?	(Twinight 115) 1969

A Chicago area band.

Compilation appearances have included: *A Girl Like You* on *Pebbles Vol. 10* (CD); *Empty Heart* and *A Girl Like You* on *Pebbles, Vol. 17* (LP); *Ice And Fire, Turquoise* and *Free Sunday Paper* on *The Quill Records Story* (CD). (VJ/MW)

THE ROOKS (Northwest).

The Roosters

45s: α   One Of These Days/
       You Gotta Gun   (Progressive Sounds Of America 1151) 1966
       Ain't Gonna Cry Anymore/Rosebush   (Enith 125) 196?

NB: α some copies of this 45 came in green vinyl.

A mid-sixties Los Angeles-based combo. Their vinyl zenith *One Of These Days* consists of glorious jingle-jangle garage folk-rock which spirals up and down your vertebrae. The overlooked flip is a melodic folk-rock ballad with harmonica and rather reminiscent of **Fenwyck** - a great 45.

Compilation appearances include: *One Of These Days* on *Highs In The Mid-Sixties, Vol. 2* (LP), *Pebbles, Vol. 8* (CD) and *A Journey To Tyme, Vol. 2* (LP); and *You Gotta Run* on *The Essential Pebbles Collection, Vol. 1* (Dble CD) and *Destination Frantic!* (CD). (VJ/MW)

The Roosters

Personnel incl:			
JOE GONZALES	gtr		A
BOBBY HIJER	gtr		A
RICHARD PURCHASE	organ, trumpet, gtr, bs		AB
SID SMITH	drms, vcls		A
JACK PINNEY	drms		B
JERRY RANEY	gtr, vcls		B

45:   Shake A Tail Feather/Rooster Walk   (A&M 746) 1964

'The Roosters' was the name given to the various line-ups of the house band at San Diego's Cinnamon Cinder club beginning in the late fifties. The two versions listed above are significant to this book as they spawned important local bands: Sid Smith was with **The Brain Police**, and then joined **Roy Head**'s band. Jack Pinney and Jerry Raney were the most steadfast members of **Glory**, thought to be San Diego's longest-lived underground band, lasting from 1967 until Raney formed The Beat Farmers in the eighties. Pinney was also the original drummer with **Iron Butterfly**. (CF/MW)

The Roosters

Personnel incl:		
MIKE GORDON		A
JAMES GRIFFIN		A

                                                HCP
45:   Love Machine / I'm Suspectin'   (Philips 40504) 1968 106

A Los Angeles psych-pop 45 with distinctive guitar work. James Griffin also worked with the Travel Agency and with Mike Gordon and David Gates would later form Bread. (SR)

Rooter

ALBUM: 1   ROOTER   (Founders Annex) 1970 ?

An album recorded by students of the Harveford College, in the same vein as the **Firesign Theater**. (SR)

The Roots

45:   It's Been A Long Journey/Lost One   (Brownfield 22) 1966

From Dallas, Texas, came this blues-punk 45 written by Rudy Wyatt, who may have been a band member. Later in 1966 the band returned as **The Wyld** with a new recording of *Lost One*. The band originally hailed from Greenville, South Carolina, but recorded the 45 in Texas under the guidance of Major Bill Smith, a colourful character behind many fine Texas outfits (**Jades**, **Larry and The Blue Notes**, **Elite**, **Electric Love**, **Livin' End**, **Ron-Dels**).

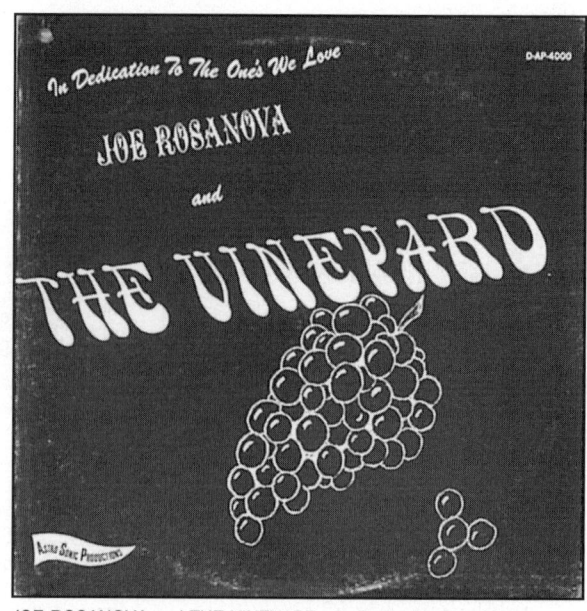

JOE ROSANOVA and THE VINEYARD - In Dedication To... LP.

Compilation appearances have included: *Lost One* on *Teenage Shutdown, Vol. 3* (LP & CD) and *Highs In The Mid-Sixties, Vol. 13* (LP); and *It's Been A Long Journey* on *Teenage Shutdown, Vol. 7* (LP & CD). (VJ)

Joe Rosanova and The Vineyard

Personnel:			
JOE ROSANOVA	drms		A
BART FIORI	vcls, gtr		A
MARK TORPEY	bs		A
DON VITALLE	keyb'ds		A

ALBUM: 1(A)   IN DEDICATION TO THE ONES WE LOVE
                                   (Astro Sonic D-AP-4000) 1968 SC

This outfit operated from the Nashville area. Their album, late sixties rock with a psychedelic feel, is disappointing overall. The stand-out track *Dreams Of You* has haunting vocals and a good backing.

Compilation appearances include *Dreams Of You* on *Lycergic Soap* (LP) and *Magic Carpet Ride* (LP). (VJ/MW)

Biff Rose

ALBUMS:	1	THE THORN IN MRS ROSE'S SIDE	
(partial			(Tetragrammaton T-103) 1968 -
list)	2	CHILDREN OF LIGHT	(Tetragrammaton T-116) 1969 -
	3	BIFF ROSE	(Buddah BDS 5069) 1971 -
	4	UNCLE JESUS AND AUNTY CHRIST	
			(UA I A 009 F) 1972 -

NB: (2) reissued (Buddah BD 5076).

A witty and oddball Californian singer, pianist and songwriter, typical of the counterculture values. His first two albums were produced by Art Podell and Nick Woods and benefited from the participation of **Van Dyke Parks** and **Beaver and Krause** on Moog synthesizer. **Biff Rose**'s songs, like *Communist Sympathizer*, *Spaced Out*, *Buzz The Fuzz* and *Who's Gnawing At Me* (covered by **Pat Boone**!), were mainly popular in the Californian clubs.

After a long break, only interrupted by a private pressing in 1978, *Roast Beef* (Down Pat), **Biff Rose** released a come-back album, *Bone Again* (Fast Eddie Records), in 1997. (SR)

Tim Rose

Personnel incl: TIM ROSE

ALBUMS:	1	TIM ROSE	(Columbia 9577) 1967	-
	2	THROUGH ROSE COLOURED SPECS		
			(Columbia 9772) 1969	-
	3	LOVE A KIND OF HATE STORY	(Capitol 673) 1970	-
	4	TIM ROSE	(Playboy PB 101) 1972	-

NB: (1) also issued in the UK (CBS CBS 63168) 1967. (1) reissued (Edsel ED 267) 1988 and on CD. (2) also issued in the UK (CBS CBS 63636) 1969. (4) also issued in the UK (Dawn DNLS 3062) 1974. He later had a U.K. only release *The Musician* (Atlantic K 50183) 1975.

45s:		I'm Bringing It Home/		
		Mother, Father, Where Are You	(Columbia 43563) 1966	
	α	Hey Joe/The Lonely Blue King	(Columbia 43648) 1966	
		I Gotta Do Things My Way/Where Was I	(Columbia 43722) 1966	
		I'm Gonna Be Strong/		
		I Got A Loneliness	(Columbia 4-43958) 1966	
	β	Morning Dew/		
		You're Slipping Away From Me	(Columbia 4-44031) 1967	
		Come Away Melinda/Long Time Man	(Columbia 4-44387) 1967	
		Long Haired Boy/Looking At A Baby	(Columbia 44603) 1968	
		Angela/Whatcha Gonna Do	(Columbia 4-44792) 1969	
	χ	Roanoke/Babe Do You Turn Me On	(Columbia 4-44849) 1969	
		I've Gotta Get A Message To You/		
		Jamie Sue	(Capitol 3001) 1970	
		It Takes A Little Longer/		
		Hide Your Love Away	(Playboy 50005) 1972	
		Goin' Down In Hollywood/?	(Playboy 50012) 1972	

NB: α some promo copies in red wax. β also issued in the UK (CBS 202631) 1967. χ also issued in the UK (CBS 4209) 1969. There were also UK 45s: *I Guess It's Over/Hello Sunshine* (CBS 3478) 1966; *I've Gotta Get A Message To You/Ode To An Old Ball* (Capitol CL 15664) 1970; *Hide Your Love Away/If I Were A Carpenter* (Dawn DNS 1085) 1974; and *Musician/7.30 Song* (Atlantic K 10667) 1975.

Born in September 1940, **Rose** grew up in Washington D.C. and was part of the quasi-folk singing movement of the late sixties, which was heavily influenced by Bob Dylan. Prior to launching his solo career on Columbia **Rose** was a member of **The Big Three** along with Mama Cass Elliot.

His debut album made quite an impression, being a powerful singer his gritty voice was well suited to his bluesy themes. His songs too were full of drama and contrast and his best known song *Morning Dew* was covered by several other artists in the era. The album also contained an arrangement of a traditional song called *Hey Joe*, which was subsequently covered and made internationally famous by **Jimi Hendrix**. Typical of his style too was *Come Away Melinda*, also on his debut album, which was taken to a wider audience by its inclusion on the compilation, *The Rock Machine Turns You On*.

He later moved to Britain and teamed up briefly in an unsuccessful duo with **Tim Hardin**. A marginal case for inclusion here but that first album is well worth a listen.

Some relevant covers of *Morning Dew* include: Id (Pre-**Euphoria's Id**) - 1965, on *New England Teen Scene* CD; **The Grateful Dead** - 1967, *Grateful Dead* LP; **Frantic** - 1968, *Frantic* LP; **Group Therapy** - 1968, *People Get Ready For* LP; **Nova Local** - 1968, *Nova 1* LP; **Sons Of May** - 1968 45; **Sweet Smoke** - 1968 45, *Texas Flashbacks 3* and *Highs In The Midsixties Vol. 23*; Tongue - 1969 *Keep On Truckin'* LP; **Damnation Of Adam Blessing** - 1969 45 and *The Damnation Of Adam Blessing* LP; Sound Foundation - 1969 45; Spectrums - 1960s, *Wailin' In West Covina* 1998 retrospective album; also covered by U.K. outfits Episode Six, The End and Jeff Beck. (VJ/MW/EW)

Rose Garden

Personnel:	BRUCE BOWDIN	drms	A
	BILL FLEMING	bs, vcls	A
	JAMES GROSHONG	gtr, vcls	A
	JOHN NOREEN	ld gtr, vcls	A
	DIANA DE ROSE	gtr, vcls	A

| | | | | HCP |
| ALBUM: | 1(A) | ROSE GARDEN | (Atco SD33-255) 1968 | 176 - |

				HCP
45s:	Next Plane To London/Flower Town	(Atco 6510) 1967	17
	Here's Today/If My World Falls Through	(Atco 6564) 1968	-

A lightweight pop outfit. Four members came from California, one West Virginia and the band were based in the Los Angeles area. Their best known song *Next Plane To London*, with Diana De Rose on lead vocal made No. 17 in the U.S. charts. It was written by Kenny Gist Jnr. (aka Kenny O'Dell).

The album, which is certainly not psychedelic although I've seen it described as such, contains a cover of Bob Dylan's *She Belongs To Me* and two nice Gene Clark compositions *Till Today* and *Long Time*. One of its better cuts is *February Sunshine*, a bright'n'breezy piece of flower-pop, which had been a minor hit for **The Giant Sunflower**. Their second 45 was non-album.

The Rose Garden's roots were in a teen act formed by Bruce Bowdin, John Noreen and Jim Groshong in around '64. They chose an "anglophile" name, The Blokes, to reflect their repertoire of Beatles covers and, by 1965, had recruited 15-year-old Bill Fleming on bass. Bill remembers: "The guys had been heavily influenced by the **Byrds** about this time. We literally had every **Byrds** tune from their first three albums in our repertoire. John was an accomplished 12-string guitar player."

Sometime in late '66 or early '67 Jim Groshong met Diana De Rose, in Hollywood and she asked him to join the band that she was in at the time. Instead, Diana ended up joining **The Blokes**. Bill: "With her came a fellow named David Hanson who fancied himself as a manager. He got us a lot of non-paying gigs in Hollywood and eventually through him we met **Kim Fowley**. We hung out at his place, but none of us ever lived there that I was aware of. The guys still lived at home with their parents. It is possible that Diana may have stayed there for brief periods of time."

"Dunhill Records, who I think was run by Lou Adler at the time, had recorded *February Sunshine* with a band called **Giant Sunflower** - Everything was flower-power at that time - but the band was not under contract. When the song started to climb they need a band to go with it, so we became **Giant Sunflower**, but that only lasted for about a month. We felt that we would probably get sued and really preferred to make it on our own, so we left that arrangement."

"Through David the manager we then met Charles Greene and Brian Stone. They had "discovered" Sonny & Cher and had produced some early songs for **Buffalo Springfield**. Their promotional man was Pat Pipolo, and Kenny Gist, Jr. (Kenny O'Dell) was a relative of his - that's how we got to record *Next Plane To London*."

With *Next Plane To London* riding high in the charts, **Rose Garden** began the promotional circuit... They had aleady played many of the local clubs such as Gazzarri's on the Strip (with **The First Edition** that later sent Kenny Rogers on his way to fame), Bito Lito's, The Cheetah (with Eric Burdon) - described by Bill as "a weird truly psychedelic place that was on a pier on Santa Monica Beach".

"We did most of the teen TV shows: American Bandstand was the only national show, but there were many local and syndicated shows: 9th Street

ROSE GARDEN - Rose Garden LP.

West (with **Canned Heat**), Groovy, and The Woody Woodbury Show (with Bobby Vee). These were all Los Angeles shows, and usually local shows in many of the towns where we toured."

"We were booked on many package tours and played several dates with **Tommy James and The Shondells**, Neil Diamond, **The Box Tops**, **The Association**, Chuck Berry, Little Richard, Glen Campbell, **Ohio Express**, Billy Joe Royal, Jay and The Techniques, **Canned Heat**, and **Stone Poneys** at various times. New Year's Eve 1967 in Fort Worth was particularly memorable with both Chuck Berry and Little Richard being on the same bill. Most of these tours went through the South, Southeast and Midwest states, probably because our agent was based in Texas..."

When the second single didn't make it and with friction between Diana and the other band members reaching critical mass, the band broke up in late '68. They later reformed in 1969 without Diana and Bruce (he had married and moved to Texas), with Bill Fleming's brother Ed joining as drummer. But after a few local gigs they split for good.

John Noreen went on to be a respected studio musician in Nashville, playing steel guitar for virtually everybody there. He also toured with Highway 101 (a country act) in the eighties, was a member of John Davidson's nightclub band in the seventies, and was in a band called Rotondi. Bruce Bowdin settled in Texas. Jim Groshong played solo in small clubs in Southern California and Bill Fleming has been a Police Officer in the Los Angeles area (NOT LAPD!) since 1973.

Bill: "We were approached about a big sixties revival three day festival to be held in Southern California about ten years ago. Bruce was in Texas, but agreed to participate; Jim, John and I got together, but then John had a commitment to finish a tour with Highway 101. Jim and I thought that John's 12-string was too important to our sound, so that ended that." (VJ/BF)

Charles Ross III

45s:			
α	Sidewalks Of The Ghetto/Look Away	(Tower 476)	1969
β	A Railroad Trestle In California/		
	My Happiness Day (some PS)	(Tower 477)	1969
	Laughing Girl/Little Boy	(Tower 499)	1969

NB: α 'A' side credited to **Eternity's Children**. β as by Charles E. Ross III

The work of former **Eternity's Children** member, the 'A' side, to the second 45, *A Railroad Trestle...* is a Chips Moman-produced track presumably cut in Memphis. It's flip-side is a mono mix of the track from the **Eternity's Children** debut, but released here as by **Charles E. Ross III**.

The 'split' debut single, the immediate solo follow-up and the parallel release of *Laughing Girl* with **Eternity's Children**'s *Blue Horizon* 45 (Tower 498), all point to a marketing campaign, which probably aimed at launching a solo career for **Charles Ross III** on the back of the more familiar **Eternity's Children** moniker. (JG)

The Rouges

45:	Next Guy/Faces On The Wall	(Waverly 109-03/4) 1966

From Watertown, Massachusetts, *Faces On The Wall* has some pleasing mouth harp, relaxed guitar chimes and lots of tempo changes. Worth a listen.

Compilation appearances include: *Next Guy* and *Faces On The Wall* on *New England Teen Scene* (CD); *Next Guy* on *New England Teen Scene, Vol. 1* (LP); and *Faces On The Wall* on *New England Teen Scene, Vol. 3* (LP). (VJ)

The Rousers

ALBUM:	1	IN CONCERT	(Fredlo 6520) 1965 R2

An extremely rare garage album thought to have come from a Cedar Rapids, Iowa, band. (VJ)

The Rovin' Flames

Personnel:	HARDY DIAL	vcls	A
	JERRY GOFF	drms	A
	J.R. MIETTA	bs	AB
	JIMMY "MOUSE" MORRISON	ld gtr	AB
	JOHNNY ROGERS	organ	AB
	JOHN DELISE	vcls	B
	DAVE TABAK	drms	B
	PAUL BATTLE	gtr, vcls	

45s:	Gloria/J.J.J.P.	(Fuller 2627) 1965
	I Can't/I'm Afraid To Go Home	(Boss 002) 1966
α	Now That Summer Is Here /	
	It's Nothing New	(Tampa Bay BC-1110) 1966
	Bo Diddley/Seven Million People	(Tampa Bay BC-1111) 1966
	How Many Times/Love Song No. 6	(Decca 32191) 1967

NB: α is a connected 45 - the 'A' side is by "The Forvus featuring Brooke Chamberlain with the Rovin' Flames", whilst the flip is "Brooke Chamberlain with the Forvus and the Rovin' Flames and Harvey Swadnungle"!!

A Tampa, Florida, band whose best known song *How Many Times*, is a typical punk protest song bemoaning girlfriends and society. Composed by Uncapher and Delise it would later be covered by the new psychedelic outfit Plan 9 on their *Frustration* album.

The Rovin' Flames 45s are uncommonly elusive. *Love Song No.6* also appeared on the very rare *Bee Jay Video Soundtrack* sampler album (Tener 1014) in 1968.

They also backed **The Forvus, featuring Brooke Chamberlain**, on their sole 45.

Hardy Dial was also in **The Outsiders/The Soul Trippers** as had his replacement, John DeLise, who would go on to **Those Five**.

Retrospective compilation appearances have included: *How Many Times* on *Pebbles, Vol. 3 (ESD)* (CD), *Pebbles, Vol. 8* (LP), *Best of Pebbles, Vol. 3* (LP & CD) and *Psychedelic States: Florida Vol. 3* (CD); *Bo Diddley* on *Teenage Shutdown, Vol. 15* (LP & CD); and *I Can't* on *Hang It Out To Dry* (LP & CD). (VJ/MW/JLh/HT)

The Rovin' Kind

Personnel:	MIKE ANTHONY	keyb'ds	A
	PAUL COTTON	gtr, vcls	A
	FRANK BARTOLI	bs	A
	KAL DAVID	gtr, vcls	A
	FRED PAPPALARDO	drms	A

45s:	Everybody/Bound To Roam	(Contrapoint 9006) 1965
	Night People/Right On Time	(Roulette 4687) 1966
	My Generation/Girl	(Dunwich 146) 1966
	She/I Didn't Want To Have To Do It	(Dunwich 154) 1967
α	You Can't Sit Down/	
	You Really Turn Me On	(Smash S-2102) 1967

NB: α flip with Barney Pip.

Came out of Chicago - the compilation *Early Chicago* contains their recording from February 1967 of a nice laid-back **John Sebastian** song, *I Didn't Want To Have To Do It*. All five members were later in **Illinois Speed Press** (which was really the same band) and David, Bartoli and Pappalardo all had brief spells as back-up musicians for **H.P. Lovecraft**. Kal David had earlier fronted **The Exceptions**. Avoid the first 45 - it's insipid soul - Four Seasons inspired stuff. Their subsequent covers are competent but not that inspiring, sad to say.

The band were briefly known as the Gentrys. In 1965 with the assistance of Billy the Kid Emerson they cut an acetate 45 at MBS studios: *Doo Doo Pah/Everybody*. *Everybody* was later recorded as the 'A' side for the first **Rovin' Kind** 45. The band also cut two versions of a radio jingle for Wrigleys chewing gum, which exists on acetate.

Compilation appearances have included: *My Generation* and *She* on *Oh Yeah! The Best Of Dunwich Records* (CD); *My Generation* on *The Dunwich*

Records Story (LP); and *Girl* and *Didn't Want To Have To Do It* on *If You're Ready - The Best Of Dunwich... Vol. 2* (CD). (MW/RMh)

Roxy

Personnel:	RANDY BISHOP	vcls, bs, gtr, keyb'ds	A
	JIM DE COCQ	ld gtr, keyb'ds	A
	JOHN McDONALD	drms	A
	JAMES MORRIS	keyb'ds	A
	BOB SEGARINI	ld vcls, gtr, bs, perc	A

ALBUM: 1(A) ROXY (Elektra EKS 74063) 1969

Formed when Segarini and De Cocq left **Family Tree**, **Roxy**'s album is very disappointing. Although the musicianship is competent, the songs are not inspired, the lyrics quite dumb and Segarini vocals not really good.

All the songs were written by Segarini except "I Got My Friends" by Randy Bishop and the album was produced by John Haeny.

After this failure, Bishop and Segarini formed **The Wackers**.

Compilation appearances include *Rock And Roll Circus* on *Elektrock The Sixties* (4-LP). (SR)

Royal Aircoach

45: Wondering Why/Web Of Love (Flying Machine 8868) 1968

From Boston, Massachusetts, this outfit only appears to have recorded this one, now sought-after 45. *Wondering Why* is notable for its ending admidst a barrage of sound effects.

Compilation appearances include: *Wondering Why* on *Psychotic Moose And The Soul Searchers* (LP) and *Relative Distance* (LP). (VJ/MW)

The Royal Caste

45: Blues Lovin' Woman/
Can't You See I'm Crying (Living Sound Custom LSM 6) 196?

Two superb low-down bluesy garage ballads with a sixties grunge sound, penned by a Gary Caldwell. No other info to hand yet. (MW)

The Royal Flairs

Personnel incl:	RICK BROWN	drms	AB
	DAVE BRUBECK	bs	ABC
	BOB EVERHART	sax, vcls, hrmnca	ABC
	JERRY FLEETWOOD	trumpet	A
	DARYL HILL	accordian, organ	AB
	DICK HODGES	vcls	A
	DAVE KRIVOLAVEK	gtr	ABC
	BRIAN SALLOZO	sax	A
	BRAD STARR	ld gtr	A
	MIKE NELSON	ld gtr	B
	MIKE DONION	drms	C
	MEL MATTHEWS	ld gtr, organ	C

ALBUM: 1(-) RARE RECORDINGS (Unlimited Productions UPLP 1007) 1988

EP: 1(A) SURFIN WITH THE ROYAL FLAIRS (PS) (Unlimited Productions UPEP 1) 1984

45s: α Dream Angel / Let's Go (instr) (Sam 119) 1962
Suicide/One Pink Box (Marina 503) 1966
β Feelings/Gone Away (Marina 506) 1966
χ Hat On Tie/My Baby Cries (Tonorous 018) 1966

NB:. α as Nelson Royal, Bobby Williams and The Royal Flairs' β as **The Unlimited**. χ 'A' side as Bobby and Dave, 'B' side as Bobby Williams.

This act started life as support band for vocalist Dick Hodge in the Omaha-Council Bluffs area of Iowa in 1961. The following year they progressed to becoming the housebard at the Milrose Ballroom, just outside of Omaha. At this time they were a surfing band. Over the next few years their music and line-up underwent considerable changes. Brad Star left the group to go to college and was sadly later killed in a water skiing accident. In early 1965, they headed for Chicago and recorded *Suicide*, which had a frantic guitar break and some atypical harmonica playing and is now a garage classic. The flip was a tasteless number complete with sound effects of nails being driven in and dirt thrown out on the grave. Originally titled *One Pine Box* a printing error at the pressing plant titled it *One Pink Box*!

They changed name to **The Unlimited** for a second 45. The 'A' side, *Feelings*, has a thundering beat backed up by slashing guitar, screaming vocals and pounding organ - it's worth hearing. When this failed to make any impact they changed name again to Bobby and Dave for a folk-rock number with a funky soul routine on the flip.

Their retrospective album contains their three 45s, eight reasonable cover versions and an interview with band leader Bob Everhart.

Compilation appearances have included: *Suicide* on *The Midwest Vs. Canada* (LP), *Back From The Grave, Vol. 3* (LP), *Back From The Grave, Vol. 2* (CD) and *Gathering Of The Tribe* (CD); and *Feelings* as **The Unlimited** on *The Midwest Vs. The Rest* (LP). (VJ)

The Royal Guardsmen

Personnel:	BILL BALOUGH	bs	A
	CHRIS NUNLEY	vcls	A
	TOM RICHARDS	ld gtr	A
	BILLY TAYLOR	organ	A
	BARRY WINSLOW	vcls, gtr	A

ALBUMS:
1(A) SNOOPY vs THE RED BARON (Laurie 2038) 1967 44 -
2(A) THE RETURN OF THE RED BARON (Laurie 2039) 1967 - -
3(A) SNOOPY AND HIS FRIENDS (Laurie 2042) 1967 46 -
4(A) SNOOPY FOR PRESIDENT (Laurie 2046) 1968 189 -

HCP

45s: Baby Let's Wait/Leaving Me (Laurie 3359) 1966 -
Snoopy vs The Red Baron/I Needed You (Laurie 3366) 1966 2
Snoopy vs The Black Knight/I Needed You (Laurie 3374) 1967 -
Return Of The Red Baron/
Sweetmeats Slide (Laurie 3379) 1967 15
Airplane Song (My Airplane)/Om (Laurie 3391) 1967 46
Wednesday/So Right (To Be In Love) (Laurie 3397) 1967 97
Snoopy's Xmas/it Kinda Looks Like Xmas (Laurie 3416) 1968 -
I Say Love/I'm Not Gonna Stay (Laurie 3428) 1968 72

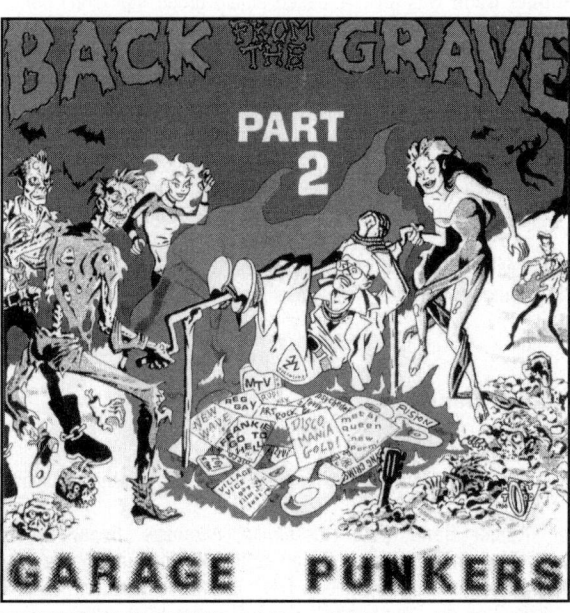

BACK FROM THE GRAVE Part 2 (Comp CD) including The Royal Flairs.

Snoopy For President/		
Down Behind The Lines	(Laurie 3459)	1968 85
Baby Let's Wait/Biplane Ever More	(Laurie 3461)	1968 -
Baby Let's Wait/		
So Right (To Be In Love)	(Laurie 3461)	1968 35
Mother Where's Your Daughter/		
Magic Window	(Laurie 3494)	1969 112
Snoopy For President/Sweetmeats Slide	(Laurie 3646)	1976 -

NB: There's also a French EP with picture sleeve: *Snoopy vs The Red Baron/Bears/Alley Oop/Roadrunner* (Vogue INT 11818) 1967.

This novelty-pop sextet came from Ocala, Florida. Classic 'one-hit wonders' their gimmicky tribute to Charles Schulz's famous cartoon character sold over three million copies worldwide. It made No. 2 in the U.S. and No. 8 in the UK, where it was released on Stateside. What followed was largely predictable and relatively unsuccessful although *Return Of The Red Baron* made No. 15 in the U.S. and No. 37 in the UK. Their debut album made No. 44 in the U.S. Album charts and their third effort made no. 46. As their popularity declined their final effort could only managed the 189 spot. The R&B tinged pop songs from their first 45 were perhaps their best efforts before they were labelled with the corny Snoopy tag. *Baby Let's Wait* was reissued in 1968 and made No. 35 in the U.S. charts.

Compilation appearances include: *Leaving Me* on *Mindrocker, Vol. 10* (Dble LP); *Baby Let's Wait* on *Nuggets, Vol. 4* (LP); and *Om* on *Buzz Buzz Buzzzzzz, Vol. 1* (CD). (VJ/SR)

The Royal Knights

45: I Wanna Know/Matilda (PS) (Nite 1005) 1965

From Arlington, Texas.

Compilation appearances have included: *I Wanna Know* on *Acid Visions - Complete Collection, Vol. 2* (3-CD), *Texas Punk: 1966, Vol. 1* (LP) and *Teenage Shutdown, Vol. 15* (LP & CD). (VJ)

The Royal Rogues

45: Love Is A Beautiful Thing/The Sound (Wasp 102) 196?

NB: released as The R./Rogues,

From Tacoma, Washington. Although this band were called **The Royal Rogues**, their 45 was credited to the R./Rogues - so I guess they ran out of letters at the label paste-up (that's an attempted joke, not history!). You'll also find *The Sound* on *Boulders, Vol. 9* (LP) and *Ya Gotta Have Moxie, Vol. 2* (Dble CD). (GGI)

The Royal Shandels

Personnel incl: DON GLADDEN keyb'ds A

45: Be Careful With Your Carful /
Be Careful With Your Carful (MDI 1000-28B) 1966

NB: 'A' side is by Merle Alvey's Dixieland Band.

Hidden away on the 'B' side of this Michigan Auto Safety Council sponsored 45, **The Royal Shandels** do a frat-punk rendition of *Be Careful With Your Carful*. Check it out, cautiously, on *Highs In The Mid-Sixties, Vol. 19* (LP). (VJ/MW)

The RPM's

45s:	White Lightnin' (It's Frightnin')/Down	(P. B. D. 102) c1965
	White Lightnin' (It's Frightnin')/	
	Down	(Ambassador 214) c1965

This snarlin' punk outfit came out of Newark, New Jersey. Their classy *White Lightnin'* features thumpin' drums, powerful guitars and typically snotty punk vocals.

Compilation appearances include: *White Lightnin (It's Frightnin')* on *Pebbles, Vol. 10* (CD) and *Pebbles, Vol. 17* (LP). (VJ)

RPS

ALBUM: 1 RPS (Mars) 1976 -

A hard-rock trio in the **James Gang** mould. (SR)

Rubayyat

Personnel incl:	DANNY GALINDO	bs	A
	BILL HALLMARK	gtr, vcls	A

45: If I Were A Carpenter/
Ever, Ever Land (International Artists 124) 1967

Based in Houston during 1967-68 this band, which was later known as Electric Rubayyat, included Galindo who had briefly been bassist with the **13th Floor Elevators** and Bill Hallmark who'd played with **Golden Dawn**. A later recording of the 'A' side of their 45, which was produced by Fred Carroll, can be heard on *Endless Journey - Phase Three* (LP) and *Epitaph For A Legend* (Dble LP). *Ever, Ever Land* a folk-rocker can also be heard on *International Artists Singles Collection* (LP).

Craig Malek writes: A friend played *If I Were A Carpenter* on KTRU in Houston around 1992, Bill Hallmark called in and said that he had never heard it before, 'though he remembered recording it at Gold Star in Houston. The band only lasted a few months, and were Houston/San Antonio based. Bill recently moved back to Austin from Kemah and was at least until recently, active in the music business. (VJ/CM)

Rubber Band

Personnel:	STAN AYEROFF	gtr	A
	STEVE BAIM	drms	A
	MICHAEL LLOYD	keyb'ds, bs, vcls	A

ALBUMS:	1(A) CREAM SONGBOOK	(GRT 10000)	1968 -
	2(A) HENDRIX SONGBOOK	(GRT 10007)	1969 -
	3(A) BEATLES SONGBOOK	(GRT 10015)	1969 -
	4( ) DOORS SONGBOOK	( )	19?? ?
	5( ) CREEDENCE SONGBOOK	( )	19?? ?

NB: (4) and (5) credited to The Waterfall but it really was **The Rubber Band**. It was just a different label. (1) and (2) were issued in the U.K. on Major Minor.

45: Deserted Cities Of The Heart/
Sunshine Of Your Love (GRT 1) 1968

The Rubber Band was an L.A.-based studio group that didn't perform or travel. A Michael Lloyd creation it actually consisted of the same personnel as **The Smoke**. All four of their albums comprised cover versions of some of the original artists' best known songs, though tucked away on the *Hendrix Songbook* is a Michael Lloyd composition *Rubber Jam*.

Their third album, *Beatles Songbook*, was produced by Stan Farber who later worked with **Frantic**. Entirely instrumental, some consider it a total waste of vinyl, with the use of neo classical orchestrations and clarinet.

Manic Depression from the *Hendrix Songbook* has also been aired on the **Hendrix** tribute compilation *The Stars That Play With Dead Jimi's Dice* (LP). (SR)

The Rubber Band

45: Below Up, Above Down /
?Forever Friday? (Richlin # unkn) 1968

Another **Rubber Band**, from Russellville, Arkansas. *Below Up, Above Down* and *Forever Friday*, unconfirmed as the 45 flip, can both be heard on the Collectables CD compilation *The Human Expression And Other Psychedelic Groups - Your Mind Works In Reverse* (CD). (MW)

THE RUBBER MEMORY - Welcome LP.

The Rubber Band

Personnel:
TIPPY ARMSTRONG	vcls, gtr		A
DENNY GREEN	vcls, sax		A
JACKIE SIMS	drms		A
JOE SOBOTKA	keyb'ds		A
TOMMY STUART	sax		A
JOHNNY TOWNSEND	vocals, sax		A
JOHN D. WYKER	vcls, trumpet, bs		A

45s: Charlena/Let Love Come Between Us (Columbia 4-43796) 1966
In And Out Of My Life /
Bring Your Love (Columbia 4-44013) 1967
Messin' Up The Mind Of A Young Girl /
I'm Gonna Make It (Reprise 0637) 1967
Laude Maude/I Know You (Gram-O-Phone 45725) 1975

This soulful-pop band came from Alabama, probably Tuscaloosa. Led by Tippy Armstrong the band lasted well into the seventies and Armstrong went on to play on many sessions in Muscle Shoals, Alabama, backing artists ranging from Wilson Pickett to Roy Orbison. Sadly he died at the age of 32.

John Wyker later played in the seventies Elektra band Sailcat who had a hit with *Motorcycle Mama*. A **The Rubber Band** song *Let Love Come Between Us* was also a big hit for James and Bobby Purify, the soul duo from Pensacola, Florida.

Bill Connel, drummer of the **Allman Joys**, played on the later **Rubber Band** recordings.

They may also be responsible for another 45 - *Plastic Soul / Let's Sail Away* (ABC Paramount 10849) 1966. (MW/JLh)

The Rubber Maze

45s: Mrs. Griffith/Won't See Me Down (Ruff 1098,99) 1968
Mrs. Griffith/Won't See Me Down (PS) (Tower 351) 1968

A West Texas quartet whose Tower release came in a picture sleeve.

Compilation appearances have included: *Mrs. Griffith* on *Mindblowing Encounters Of The Purple Kind* (LP) and *Psychedelic Unknowns Vol. 8* (LP & CD); and *Won't See Me Down* on *Let's Dig 'Em Up, Vol. 2* (LP). (VJ/MW)

Rubber Memory

Personnel:
BILL BABBIN	drms		AB
DAVID GREENE	ld gtr, vcls		A
TED HAAS	gtr, vcls		AB
DAVID PARKER	bs, vcls		AB
PARK SEWARD	keyb'ds, perc, vcls		A
JOE MONTELEPRE	keyb'ds, vcls		B

NB: Line-up 'A' 1967 - 70. 'B' known as **Rubber Memory 2**, Sept. 1970 - 71.

ALBUM: 1(A) WELCOME (RPC AZ 69402) 1970 R5
NB: (1) reissued in 2000 on vinyl (Loopden #2P-002) with three inserts.

A super-rare album by a New Orleans garage band. Although it contains several great cuts, more than half of the album comprises uninspired filler where primitive heavy rock (with the obligatory post-*In-A-Gadda-Da-Vida* drum solo) alternates with lounge sounds. (CF/SR/MW/MDo/TH)

Roger Rubin and Rotfree Anderson

ALBUM: 1 ATLANTA UNDERGROUND - FREEK MUSIC
(Purple Haze) 1971 R3/R4

A privately-pressed album by an Atlanta, Georgia band, which is full of rather twisted, weird folk music. (CF)

Ruby

45: Confusion/The Painter (Mid-Town 273) 196?

Psychedelic punkers from Michigan. The above 45 is speculative, as both cuts:- *Confusion* and *The Painter* appear on *Michigan Mixture, Vol. 2* (LP) and *Confusion* was released on a 45 by Mid-Town, and has also resurfaced on *Michigan Mayhem Vol. 1* (CD) and *Let 'Em Have It! Vol. 1* (CD). The track is also by far the best of the two. It comes with a rather catchy intro, a good beat and lots of fuzz. (VJ/MW)

Rude Awakening

45: A Certain Girl / Fortune Teller (Sounds Int'l 634) c1967

Thought to have been based in the Tidewater, Virginia area - hence the inclusion of their excellent fuzzed version of *A Certain Girl* on *Aliens, Psychos And Wild Things* (CD). (BHr/ST/MW)

The Rugbys

Personnel:
DOUG BLACK	sax		A
GLEN HOWERTON	drms		AB
CHRIS HUBBS	gtr		A
STEVE MCNICOL	ld gtr		AB

ROGER RUBIN and ROTFREE ANDERSON - Atlanta Underground... LP.

	JIM McNICOL	bs	A
	MIKE HORNEI	bs	B
	ED VERNON	keyb'ds	B

ALBUM:	1(B) HOT CARGO	(Amazon 1000) 1969 -

NB: (1) has been reissued.

45s:	Walking The Streets Tonight/Endlessly	(Top Dog 2315) 1966
	You, I/Stay With Me	(Tara # unknown) 1969
	You, I/Stay With Me	(Amazon 1) 1969 24
α	Wendegahl The Warlock/The Light	(Amazon 4) 1969 -
	Rockin' All Over/Juditha Gina	(Amazon 6) 1970

NB: α also issued in Spain with a picture sleeve (Exit 2-555-B) 1969.

A Louisville, Kentucky, band whose early blues rocker *Walking The Streets Tonight* was penned by Doug Sahm. The group formed in 1965 when Steve and Jim McNicol and Chris Hubbs left **The Oxfords** and continued until 1970.

In 1969, they signed to Amazon and recorded an album in Nashville, which is quite good. The best tracks, *King and Queen Of The World* and *Wendegahl The Warlock* are dominated by heavy organ work and veer towards the progressive genre. Three 45s were also released on the same label, although they were all taken from the album. (Although curiously *Stay With Me* isn't listed on the sleeve). One of their 45s *You, I* is a frantic and catchy 'heavy' rock number with some raucous distorted guitar - a sorta uptempo poppy **Blue Cheer** (?!). It even climbed to No 24 in the Billboard charts.

After they split in 1970, Jim McNicol formed **Lazarus** who recorded an album (Amazon 1001) in Nashville the same year. Steve and Jim later teamed up with their younger two brothers to form, you'll never guess, the McNicol Brothers. The younger McNicol then formed a band with a younger Hubbs, called The Weads, no doubt to compete with their elders. They had one 45 on the Trump label.

Steve McNichol reformed **The Rugbys** around 1988 with three original members, and garnered a good reputation for performing carbon copy covers in the Louisville area.

Compilation appearances have included: *You, I* on *The Seventh Son* (LP); and *Walking The Streets Tonight* on *Highs In The Mid Sixties, Vol. 8* (LP). (VJ/MW/LD/SR)

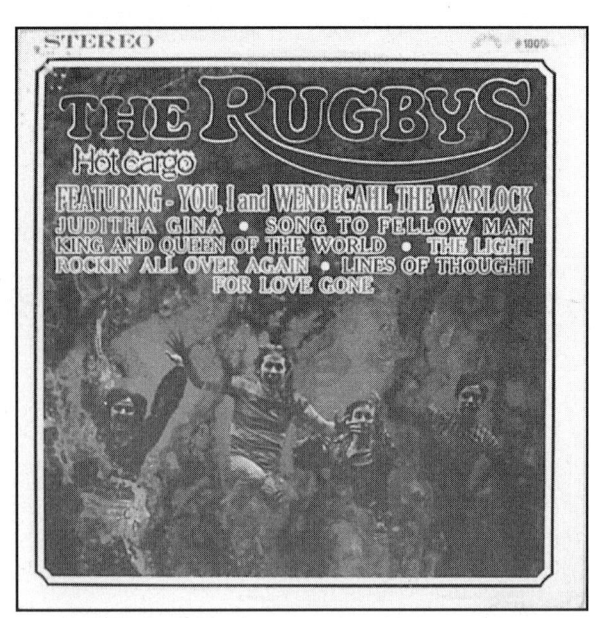

THE RUGBYS - Hot Cargo LP.

The Ruins

45:	The End /Take My Love (And Shove It Up Your Heart)	(Mutt M 27319) 1967

A surprisingly obscure Michigan band considering that *The End* is a really superb organ/guitar-led psychedelic punker with great vocals. The flip, *Take My Love...* was a cover of the **Blues Magoos**' song.

Compilation appearances include: *The End* on *Mayhem & Psychosis, Vol. 2* (LP), *Mayhem & Psychosis, Vol. 1* (CD), *Glimpses, Vol's 1 & 2* (CD), *Glimpses, Vol. 1* (LP) and *Garage Monsters* (LP); and *Take My Love* on *Follow That Munster, Vol. 2* (LP). (VJ/MW)

The Rumblers

Personnel:	BOB JONES	sax	A
	MIKE KELISHES	gtr	A
	JOHNNY KIRKLAND	gtr	A
	ADRIAN LLOYD	drms	A
	WAYNE MATTESON	bs	A

ALBUM:	1(A) BOSS	(Downey 1001) 1963 R1

NB: (1) reissued (Dot 25509) 196?.

			HCP
45s:	a Stomping Time/Intersection	(Highland 1026) 1962 -
	Boss/Don't Need You No More	(Downey 103) 1962 -
	Boss/Don't Need You No More	(Dot 16421) 1963 87
	Boss Strikes Back/Sorry	(Downey 106) 1963 -
	Boss Strikes Back/Sorry	(Dot 16455) 1963 -
	Angry Sea/Bugged	(Downey 107) 1963 -
	Bugged/Angie	(Dot 16480) 1963 -
	It's A Gas/Tootenanny	(Downey 111) 1963 -
	It's A Gas/Tootenanny	(Dot 16521) 1963 -
	The Hustler/Riot In Cell Block #9	(Downey 119) 1964 -
	Soulful Jerk/Hey-Did-A-Da-Do	(Downey 127) 1964 -
	Feel All Right Pt. 1/ Pt. 2 (as 'Bel-Cantos')	(Downey 128) 1965 -
	Boss Soul/Till Always	(Downey 133) 1966 -

This was essentially an instrumental rock group from Norwalk, California, whose album is now a minor collectors' item and who charted with *Boss*, a surf instrumental. However the flip of this, *Don't Need You No More*, is a putdown song with vocals and musically and lyrically a precursor of the garage punk sound of the mid-sixties which is why I've included the band here. Check it out on *Highs In The Mid Sixties, Vol. 20* (LP).

Boss has also resurfaced on *Born Bad, Vol. 4*. It provided the riff for The Cramps' *Garbageman*. (VJ)

The Rumbles

Personnel:	JOE BRUNNWORTH	gtr	A
	RICH CLAYTON	gtr	A
	STEVE HOUGH	drms	AB
	BUD PHILLIPS	bs	AB
	BOB FORD	keyb'ds	B
	LANCE HANCOCK	gtr	B

ALBUMS:	1(B) HOW CAN THIS BE	(Magic 28124) 1980 -
	2(B) RUMBLES LIVE	(Rumbles Records 30765) 1983 -
	3(A) THE RUMBLES 1964-70	(Rumbles Records 304009) 1983 -

45s:	α Wail It/Flip Side	(Dawn Cory 1003) 1964
	Everybody's Talkin'/The Truth Hurts (PS)	(Dads 101) 1965
β	The Echoing Past/I'll Be Gone	(Soma 1448) 1966
	14 Years/It's My Turn To Cry	(Mercury 72600) 1966
	Out Of Harmony/It'll Be Alright	(Mercury 72690) 1967
	Jezebel/The Music In Me	(Mercury 72723) 1967
	99% Sure/Everyday Kind Of Love	(Mercury 72815) 1968
	The Wildest Xmas/	
χ	Santa Claus Is Coming To Town (PS)	(Dads 103) 1968
χ	Push Push/First To Know	(Sire 4110) 1969
χ	Try A Little Harder/California My Way	(Lemon 101) 1969
χ	Try A Little Harder/ California My Way	(GNP Crescendo 430) 1969
χ	Hey Lenora/I Really Need You	(Capitol 2903) 1970
χ	Don't Let The Sun/Wipe Out	(Magic MXS 105,10034) 1980

χ	The Wildest Xmas/		
	Santa Claus Is Coming To Town (PS)	(Rumbles 210032)	1982

NB: α Shown as by Rich Clayton and The Rumbles. β As by The Fabulous Rumbles. χ As by Rumbles Ltd.

From Omaha, **The Rumbles** were undoubtedly Nebraska's top sixties band. They started out as Rich Clayton and The Rumbles, a surfing band. Their debut release was actually a double-sided surf instrumental. By the time of their third 45 they were calling themselves The Fabulous Rumbles. *Echoing Past* was another instrumental. From 1969 onwards they operated under the name Rumbles Ltd. LP (3) collects all their 45s from 1964-70.

Three of their cuts:- *Fourteen Years*, *Hey Lenora* and *Push Push* can now be heard on the cassette compilation *Monsters Of The Midwest, Vol. 1*. Other compiled cuts include *I'll Be Gone* on *Soma Records Story, Vol. 3* (LP), *The Echoing Past* on *Soma Records Story, Vol. 2* (LP), *Fourteen Years* on *Tymes Gone By* (LP) and *It's My Turn To Cry* on *Psychedelic Unknowns, Vol. 9* (CD).

They reformed in 1980 (line-up B) releasing a 45 and two albums. (MW)

Rumor(s)

45:	Hold Me Now/Without Her	(Gemcor 5002) 1965

A Los Angeles-based mid-sixties punk band. The 'A' side is very punkish, the flip more flower-folkish and very L.A.-sounding.

Compilation appearances include: *Hold Me Now* on *Nuggets Box* (4-CD), *Pebbles, Vol. 8* (CD), *Boulders, Vol. 1* (LP) and *Highs In The Mid-Sixties Vol. 1* (LP); *Without Her* on *Nuggets, Vol. 4* (LP) and *The Cicadelic 60's, Vol. 2* (LP); and *Hold Me Now* and *Without Her* on *The Cicadelic 60's, Vol. 8* (CD). (VJ/MW)

Rums and Coke

The Dave Clark Five's *Glad All Over*, by this girl-group, has resurfaced on *Girls In The Garage, Vol. 4* (LP). (GG)

The Run-a-Rounds

45s:	Oh Why/Such A Night	(Hyland 3018) 196?
	I Couldn't Care Less/I Can't Take You Back	(Manel 100) 196?

An obscure Owosso, Michigan, group who had two 45s including *I Couldn't Care Less*, which is a little monotonous but has a catchy guitar riff.

Compilation appearances include: *I Can't Take You Back* on *No No No* (CD) and *The Night Is So Dark* (LP); and *I Couldn't Care Less* on *Highs In The Mid-Sixties, Vol. 5* (LP). (VJ/MW)

The Runarounds

45:	You Lied/My Little Girl	(MGM K 13763) 1967

Frantic pop-beat thrash backed by a superb Diddleyesque shuffled rework of *Bony Maronie* with some mean guitar. (MW)

The Runaways

45:	18th Floor Girl/	
	Your Foolish Ways	(Alamo Audio 105) 1966

The intro to this San Antonio outfit's garage-inspired 45 is rather unusual, with pounding drums, booming bass and slide guitar building to a crescendo - before switching to a typical 'girl-put-down' type punker, with some rock 'n' roll guitar.

Compilation appearances include: *18th Floor Girl* on *Texas Flashback (The Best Of)* (CD), *Texas Flashbacks, Vol. 2* (LP & CD) and *Flashback, Vol. 2* (LP). (VJ)

The Runaways

45:	I'm A Runaway/It Can't Be Long	(Cle Town C 101) 1965

Catchy mod garage-beat from Cleveland with some real cool moody guitar. Both sides written by Howard Chizek. (MW)

Rural

ALBUM:	1	ONE BY ONE	(Mole MR-1) 1974 SC

As their name says, a rural-rock outfit influenced by the **Grateful Dead** and The Band. They were from Iowa. (SR)

Merrilee Rush

Personnel incl:	TERRY GREGG	bs
	VERN KJELLBERG	gtr
	CARL PETERS	drms
	MIKE ROBBINS	
	MERRILEE RUSH	
	NEIL RUSH	
	PETE SACK	drms

			HCP
45 incl:	Reach Out / Love Street	(AGP 107)	1968 79

NB: Several other singles and one LP released, but not relevent here.

Merrilee Rush from Seattle, Washington, is best known for the top 10 U.S. hit *Angel Of The Morning*. She was also responsible for creating an underground classic, *Reach Out*.

An intense gothic re-working of the Holland-Dozier-Holland song made famous by the Four Tops, it's slow, tense and has a pervading atmosphere of fear and evil. The sound is not unlike early Procol Harum and culminates in an amazing guitar solo in the style of Robin Trower. The arrangement is even more astounding when you consider how out of character it is compared with the country flavoured material she recorded before and after this record. The song reached No. 79 in the U.S. Charts and stayed just outside the top 40 in Australia.

Merrilee Rush and Neil Rush had earlier been in **The Statics** and Pete Sack hit the skins in **The Trolley**. Mike Robbins and Vern Kjellberg also played in **The Liberty Party**.

PEBBLES Vol. 8 (Comp CD) including Rumors.

Compilation appearances include *It's Alright* and *Party Song* on *Girls In The Garage, Vol. 8* (LP). (TA/DR/BSe)

Tom Rush

Personnel:	TOM RUSH	vcls, gtr	ABCDEF
	FRITZ RICHMOND	bs	B
	DADDY BONES	gtr	C
	JACK ELLIOTT	gtr	C
	BILL LEE	bs	CD
	FELIX PAPPALARDI	gtr	C
	JOHN SEBASTIAN	hrmnca	C
	HARVEY BROOKS	bs	D
	BOBBY GREGG	drms	D
	AL KOOPER	gtr, keyb'ds	D
	BRUCE LANGHORNE	gtr	DE
	HUGH MCCRACKEN	gtr	E
	ERIC GALE	gtr	E
	PAUL HARRIS	keyb'ds	E
	HERBERT LOVELLE	drms	E
	BERNARD PURDIE	drms	E
	JONATHAN RASKIN	gtr, bs	E
	RITCHIE RITZ	drms	E
	DON THOMAS	gtr	E

ALBUMS: (up to 1969)
1(A) AT THE UNICORN (Ly Cornu SA-70) 1962 R1
2(B) MIND RAMBLIN (Prestige 7536) 1963 SC
3(B) BLUES, SONGS AND BALLADS (Prestige 7374) 1963 SC
4(C) TOM RUSH (Elektra EKS-7288) 1965 -
5(D) TAKE A LITTLE WALK WITH ME (Elektra EKS-7308) 1966 -
6(E) THE CIRCLE GAME (Elektra EKS-74018) 1968 -
7(F) TOM RUSH (CBS CS9972) 1969 -
8(C/D/E) CLASSIC RUSH (Elektra EKS-74062) 1969 -

NB: There's also a French EP with picture sleeve: *Long John/Poor Man/Solid Gone/I'd Like To Know* (Vogue INT 118040) 1966.

Originating from Merrimack County (Portsmouth), **Tom Rush** came out of the flourishing Boston and Cambridge folk scene. Influenced by **Eric Von Schmidt**, his first three albums are excellent examples of blues-folk, **Rush**'s rich and clear voice being backed up only by Fritz Richmond from the **Jim Kweskin Jug Band**. **Rush** then got signed to Elektra and his first album for his new label was more of the same, but with a stronger backing, notably **John Sebastian** and Felix Pappalardi.

The big breakthrough occurred with his next album *Take A Little Walk With Me*, produced by Mark Abramson, with a side of rock and blues songs with **Al Kooper** (also credited as Roosevelt Gook on piano), Harvey Brooks, Langhorne and Gregg, basically the same group used on Dylan's *Highway 61 Revisited*. The versions of *Who Do You Love* or *Love's Made A Fool Of You* are excellent and **Tom Rush** was also present on the album *What's Shaking* with **Paul Butterfield Blues Band**, **Al Kooper**, **Lovin' Spoonful** and Eric Clapton.

Produced by Arthur Gorson, 1968's *The Circle Game* was his first fully arranged album but some of Paul Harris' orchestrations now sound a bit dated. The best moments were his long version of *Urge For Going* plus two songs by the then unknown Joni Mitchell. **Rush** also helped the career of James Taylor and Jackson Browne by singing their *Something In The Way She Moves* and *Shadow Dream Song*. Interested readers should try to get the *Classic Rush* album which compiles the three Elektra albums. **Tom Rush** then moved to CBS and started working with Trevor Veitch, the gifted Canadian guitarist of Three's A Crowd and Warren Bernhardt (ex-**Jeremy and The Satyrs/Tim Hardin**). *Tom Rush* contains several good songs with fine electric guitars, notably *Drop Down Mama* and **Fred Neil**'s *Wild Child*, but also some slow country-rock numbers.

The three subsequent CBS albums were increasingly mellow and **Rush**'s contract wasn't renewed and his career halted. He returned in 1982/1984 with two albums on a small label and apparently disappeared again, to return again only recently. Since 1998, **Tom Rush** has been on tour and CBS/Legacy have just released a double CD anthology, *No Regrets*.

Compilation appearances include: *Who Do You Love* on *Kings Of Pop Music Vol. 2* (LP). (SR)

Rush Hour

45: Set Me Free/Before I Die (Philips 40592) 1969

A dreamy and somewhat doomy re-work of the Kinks via **Vanilla Fudge**, with some heavy guitar. The flip adds some phased drums to a keyboard dominated sound but retains a dreamy feel. Overall above-average late sixties pop-rock from Chicago. (MW)

The Rustics

Personnel:	SCOTT DAVISON	bs	A
	FAINE JADE	gtr	A
	JEFF JADE	drms	A
	NICK MANZI	ld gtr	A

45: Can't Get You Out Of My Heart / Look At Me (Ye Old King 1000) 1966

Lynbrook High schoolmates **Faine Jade** and Nick Manzi had been writing and playing together around Long Island, New York, since 1959. They had been involved in various groups including The Cavaliers in 1962 and were playing as a duo in local pubs and clubs when they were signed to Laurie Records as writers and occasional studio musicans in 1965.

In 1966, they formed **The Rustics** with Faine's brother Jeff on drums and bassist Davison from East Rockaway. Manzi would form **Bohemian Vendetta** the following year and still be on hand to provide a backing band for **Faine Jade** on his subsequent solo recordings.

The upbeat garage-beat *Can't Get You Out Of My Heart* is featured on *Psychedelic States: New York Vol. 1* (CD). (MW)

Rustix

ALBUMS:
1 BEDLAM (Rare Earth RS-508) 1970 -
2 COME ON PEOPLE (Rare Earth) 1971 -

45s:
Leaving Here / When I Get Home (Cadet 5628) 1969
Can't You Hear The Music Play / I Guess This Is Goodbye (Rare Earth 5011) 1970
Come On, People / Free Again (Rare Earth 5014) 1970
My Peace Of Heaven/? (Rare Earth 5034) 1971
We All End Up In Boxes/ Down, Down (Rare Earth 5037) 1971

An undistinct hard-rock group, on the same label as **Power Of Zeus** and **Rare Earth**. (SR)

Ruthanne and The Invictas

A Michigan outfit who have *Little Angel* (originally issued on Mavis (220) and Fenton) on *Best Of Michigan Rock Groups, Vol. 1* and a previously unreleased cut (or possibly the flip), *I Met Him At The Dance* on *Vol. 2* of the same series. (VJ)

Mitch Ryder and The Detroit Wheels

HCP

ALBUMS: (up to 1969)
1 TAKE A RIDE (New Voice (S) 2000) 1966 78 -
2 BREAKOUT!!! (New Voice (S) 2002) 1966 23 -
3 SOCK IT TO ME (New Voice (S) 2003) 1967 34 -
4 WHAT NOW MY LOVE (Dynovoice (3)1901) 1967 - -
5 ALL MITCH RYDER HITS! (New Voice (S) 2004) 1968 37 -
6 MITCH RYDER SINGS THE HITS (New Voice S 2005) 1968 - -
7 THE DETROIT MEMPHIS EXPERIMENT (Dot DLP 25963) 1969 - -

NB: (5) reissued in 1968 on Crewe (CR 1335). The following albums were reissued on CD by Sundazed: (1) as (SC 6007), (2) as (SC 6008) (also on vinyl Sundazed

LP (5083), 2002), (3) as (SC 6009) (also on vinyl Sundazed LP 5084) 2003) all in 1993 and (5) as (SC 6033) 1996. There were other albums as well: *Greatest Hits* (Bellaphon) 1972, *How I Spent My Vacation* (Seeds & Stems 7801) 1978, *Rock 'n' Roll Live* (Line) 1979, *Naked But Not Dead* (Seeds & Stems 7804) 1980, *We're Gonna Win* (Line) 1980, *Look Ma No Wheels* (Quality) 1981, *Greatest Hits* (Roulette) 1981, *Live Talkies* (Line) 1982, *Never Kick A Sleeping Dog* (Riva 7503) 1983 (No. 120), *Wheels Of Steel* (PRT) 1983, *Rev-Up: The Best Of Mitch Ryder And The Detroit Wheels* (Rhino) 1990 and *Devil With The Blue Dress On* (Rhino) 1995. (1)-(5) were also released in the U.K. There's also a 50-track double CD, *Detroit Breakout! - The Ultimate Anthology* (West Side WESD 202) 1997.

			HCP
45s:	I Need Help/I Hope	(New Voice 801) 1965	-
	Jenny Take A Ride/Baby Jane	(New Voice 806) 1966	10
	Little Lapin Lupe Lu/I Hope	(New Voice 808) 1966	17
	Break Out/I Need Help	(New Voice 811) 1966	62
	Takin' All I Can Get/ You Get Your Kicks	(New Voice 814) 1966	100
β	Devil With The Blue Dress On - Good Golly Miss Molly/ I Had It Made	(New Voice 817) 1966	4
	Sock It To Me Baby/ I Never Had It Better	(New Voice 820) 1967	6
	Too Many Fish In The Sea - Three Little Fishes/ One Grain Of Sand	(New Voice 822) 1967	24
	Joy/I'd Rather Go To Jail	(New Voice 824) 1967	-
	You Are My Sunshine/Wild Child	(New Voice 826) 1967	-
	Come See About Me/ Face In The Crowd	(New Voice 828) 1968	113
	Ruby Baby/You Can Get Your Kicks	(New Voice 830) 1968	106
α	What Now My Love/ Blessing In Disguise (PS)	(Dynovoice DY 901) 1967	-

NB: α 'B' side non-LP, also issued in Denmark (Stateside KSS 4) 1967. β also released in France with a picture sleeve (Columbia CF 105). There are also four French EPs with picture sleeves (Columbia ESRF 1745, ESRF 1804, ESRF 1849 and Stateside FSE 1005).

Mitch Ryder and The Detroit Wheels blended the motown-soul sound with over-revved Midwestern rock & roll. **Mitch Ryder**'s (born William Levise) gutsy soul shouting and superhuman screams were some of the most electrifying sounds to charge AM radio in the mid-sixties, landing somewhere between **The Rascals**' Felix Cavaliere and Wilson Pickett. **The Wheels** sported two strong lead guitarists in Joe Cubert and Jim McCarty (later in **Cactus** and **Detroit**), and they were pushed along by one of the great unsung rock drummers of all time, John ("Johnny Bee") Badanjek.

It was producer Bob Crewe who signed the band to his New Voice label, releasing a string of high-octane rave-ups in *Jenny Take A Ride* (#10), *Little Latin Lupe Lu* (#17), *Devil With A Blue Dress On - Good Golly Miss Molly* (#4), *Sock It To Me Baby!* (#6), and *Too Many Fish In The Sea* (#24). In spite of all the hits and visibility, **Mitch Ryder and The Detroit Wheels** were victims of the era, making loads of money for Crewe and New Voice, but ending up broke. Around 1969 **Ryder** retreated to Detroit, where he formed the band Detroit: recording one fine album *Detroit*, (Paramount PAS-6010) 1971) before fading out of the public's gaze. The echoes of **Ryder**'s music lingered on in the Motor City madness of the **MC5** and the guitar sound of Alice Cooper, whilst **Ryder** himself has become an influential cult figure for a generation or two or rock bands and fans alike.

More recently **Ryder** has hit fine form with some outstanding tunes on his Mellencamp produced album in '83 called *Never Kick A Sleeping Dog*. Of these, Prince's *When You Were Mine* is noteworthy, as is a classic duet with Marianne Faithfull, *Thrill's A Thrill* plus a tremendous cover of Solomon Burke's *Cry To Me*... **Mitch Ryder** has also had a number of releases on the German Line record label since '79 and is still touring to this day.

Compilation appearances have included:- *Long Hard Road* on *Michigan Rocks, Vol. 1* (LP); *Turn On Your Lovelight* on *Sound Of The Sixties* (Dble LP) and *Sixties Archive, Vol. 1* (CD); and *Little Latin Lupe Lu* on *Sundazed Sampler, Vol. 1* (CD). (VJ/GMh/RAd/SR)

John Rydgren

ALBUM:	1	SILHOUETTE SEGMENTS (dbl)	
		(American Lutheran Church 8-8531)	c1968 R1

Housed in a colourful psychedelic gatefold cover, a strange double album, with tracks like *Hippie Version Of Creation*, *Plea Of A Lonely Girl*, *Music To Watch Girls By*, *Hippie Version Of The 23rd Psalm*, *Groovin' On A Saturday Night* and *Dark Side Of The Flower* (with sitar). It sounds a bit like the "word-jazz" spoken word records of Ken Nordine, but with psychedelic and pop music instead of a jazz background.

Rydgren was the director of media of the American Lutheran Church and he recorded this album to turn the hippies onto his religion. (SR)

Rye

ALBUM:	1	THE BEGINNING	(Beverly Hills) 1969 -

A pop-psych group with guitar and organ, comparable to the **New Mix**. Beverly Hills was a small label from Los Angeles which also released albums by **Lite Storm**. (SR)

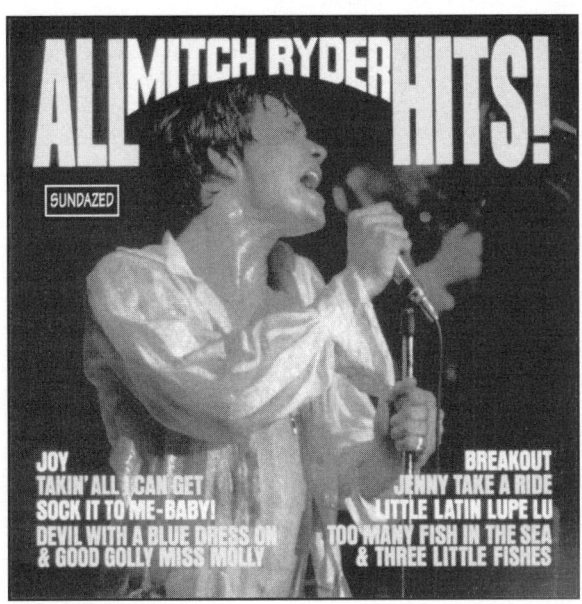

MITCH RYDER - All Hits CD.

THE RACKET SQUAD - Corners Of Your Mind LP.

THE RED CRAYOLA - God Bless... LP.

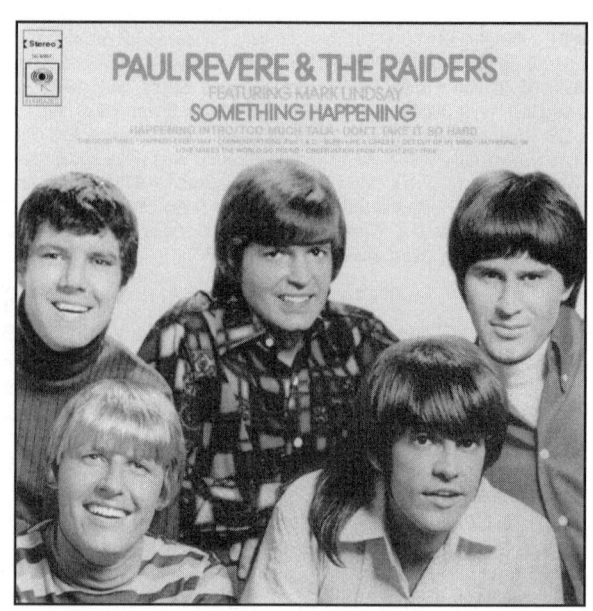

PAUL REVERE & THE RAIDERS - Something Happening CD.

PAUL REVERE & THE RAIDERS - Alias Pink Puzz CD.

PAUL REVERE & THE RAIDERS - Goin' To Memphis CD.

THE REMAINS - Barry and The Remains CD.

THE REMAINS - 10" EP.

Sabana Breeze

From Houston, Texas, with the unreleased track *Slave* on *Acid Visions - The Complete Collection Vol. 1* (3-CD). Any additional info anyone can give on this act would be much appreciated!

Sacred Irony

An early Mitch Easter band from Winston-Salem, North Carolina. Their *I See Love* can be heard on *Tobacco A-Go-Go, Vol. 2* (LP). (VJ)

The Sacred Mushroom

Personnel:	LARRY GOSHORN	ld gtr, vcls	AB
	FRED FOGWELL	gtr	B
	DANNY GOSHORN	vcls	B
	DOUG HAMILTON	drms	B
	JOE STEWART	bs	B
	(RUSTY YORK	hrmnca	B)

ALBUM: 1(B) THE SACRED MUSHROOM (Parallax P-4001) 1969 R2

NB: (1) counterfeited on vinyl in 1984 and on CD (Eva 852125) 1993.

45: Break Away Girl/Yellow Fellow (Minaret MIN-131) 196?

This band operated for several years in the Cincinnati, Ohio area. Their 45, which sounds circa 1967, is melodic pop-rock. Both sides were composed by group leader Larry Goshorn. Their album, which comes housed in a stunning "mushroom" art cover, finds the band playing a heavy blues style which proves an efficient vehicle for Goshorn's distorted guitar leads. The music is all original except for a cover of Ray Davies' *I'm Not Like Everybody Else*. Often advertised as psychedelic rock, which it simply isn't.

Larry Goshorn later played with The Pure Prairie League, and briefly with Kingfish. (VJ/CF)

Saddhu Brand

Personnel:	MICHAEL BELL	gtr, sarod	A
	HEIDI BOERGER	vcls	A
	MARYBETH BOERGER	vcls	A
	JOSH COLLINS	tabla, perc	A
	PAM CRANE	vcls	A
	JEANNE EHRHART	vcls	A
	DIANA EVANS	vcls	A
	ANN HARRISON	vcls	A

THE SACRED MUSHROOM - The Sacred Mushroom CD.

	CAROL NEWTON	vcls	A
	SIDNEY PAINTER	vcls	A
	LAUREL STEIN	vcls	A
	PETER VAN GELDER	sitar, guruji	A
	PAM WEST	vcls	A
	KENNY WILSON	esraj, flute	A

ALBUM: 1(A) WHOLE EARTH RHYTHM (Anna Chakraborty's Musical Sewing Machine Record Co. MSM 101) 1970 R2

NB: (1) Reissued on Uni (73116) 1971. (R1)

This band came from Fairfax, California. Their privately-pressed album was released originally in a primitive black and white cover design. The cover was re-designed for the later Uni reissue, which came in a colour sleeve. The album of Eastern music sung in English and Hindi is one of the hardest to find on the label. Peter Van Gelder had earlier been a member of **The Great Society** who had journeyed to India "to soak up the 'dreamy and vaporous atmosphere'" and, apparently, learn to play the sitar properly. The private press is a significant collectable from the Bay Area scene and is recommended to anyone appreciating Eastern sounds of a traditional nature. (CF)

Saddlesore

Personnel:	RICK BARTHELME	drms	A
	FRANK DAVIS	ld gtr	A
	MAYO THOMPSON	vcls, gtr	A
	CASSELL WEBB	vcls, bs	A

45: Old Tom Clark/Pig Ankie Strut (Texas Revolution 9) 197?

A short-lived and rather odd Texas outfit from the early seventies featuring former **Red Krayola** men **Mayo Thompson** and Rick Barthelme. Cassell Webb had been with **The Children** and Frank Davis with The Frank Davis Foundation. All four members went solo when they split up shortly after the 45. Cassell Webb headed for Britain.

Compilation appearances include: *Pig Ankle Strut* on *'69 Love-In* (CD) and *Acid Visions - The Complete Collection Vol. 1* (3-CD); and *Old Tom Clark* on *Filling The Gap* (4-LP). (VJ/GG)

Sage and Seer

Personnel:	DON BECKMANN	ld gtr, vcls	A
	DAVID REA	ld vcls, gtr	A

ALBUM: 1 SAGE AND SEER (Stylist SA-600) 1969 R1

THE SACRED MUSHROOM - Business Card (both sides).

45s:	Pictures Through A Sunday Afternoon /		
	Clarissa	(Stylist 45-601)	c1968
	She Died Again / Candle	(Stylist 45-602)	c1968
α	Calling/I Can't Take You Home	( )	1968

NB: α featured in Billboard magazine, but did not chart. Both sides of this 45 were non-LP.

Folk-pop-psych is one label that's applied by dealers and collectors to this duo on the few occasions that their releases have surfaced. Recorded in Denver, Colorado, their medium-rare album is appealing folkish pop with orchestration and a few tape effects. The front cover is more psychedelic than the music and it was issued with a poster insert. The first two 45s feature tracks taken from the album, but the third listed is probably chronologically earlier and both sides are non-album.

David Rea:- "**Sage and Seer** started in 1966. Don was 16 and I was 15. We played only original material our entire four-year career (except in rehearsal, where we warmed up with The Beatles' *When I Get Home*.) I sang lead on most of the songs and Don played lead guitar and sang harmony. Don's lead vocal on the album was *I've Cried*, a song he pretty much wrote alone. Songs I wrote alone included *Candle* and *She Died Again*. The two songs I remember us really writing together were *Be Still When You Cry* and *Pictures On A Sunday Afternoon*."

"We were supposed to record our album in L.A. six months before we finally did. When we got to L.A. with the rep from our label, we motored off to an appointment at Warner Bros. only to discover our chosen producer had just suffered a nervous breakdown. We had to go home, dejected and embarrassed, not knowing what our next step would be. I decided to take matters into hand, so I went off to find an arranger who could help us with the instrumentation. His name was Dan Goodman. (I recently saw his Web site. He's recording a jazz guitar CD of his own.) Then we pretty much made the decision to produce the thing ourselves, with Al Davis as the named producer. Al worked for our label and was a classically trained trumpeter. He always helped us notate our songs. When the album came out, the label went bankrupt and the inventory found its way to a creditor, who distributed it as a budget cut-out, I guess."

"When **Sage and Seer** broke up in 1970, Don and I went our separate ways. I moved to Mexico and performed with a Mexican rock band in the town of San Miguel de Allende, then returned to the States as a solo artist. I recently began recording on my own again in Los Angeles, produced by Mark Governor. I've also written music for television commercials and make my living as a creative director."

"Over the years the album, which we always thought could have been a lot better, found a small following from adventurous people who took a chance on buying an unknown entity. I've received calls over the years from people who've tracked me down. People in Texas and Seattle and New York. One caller owned a record label in Seattle and wanted to buy the master of the LP. Unfortunately, that disappeared when the company went bankrupt. She then said should I ever start recording again, she'd like me to consider her label. At the time I wasn't contemplating recording again. I lost her number. Now I'm recording again (slowly, it's expensive the way I do it) and I don't know who she was. Isn't life strange?"

The David Rea in this band is not the same guy who became a backing musician for Gordon Lightfoot. (MSk/CF/MW/DRa)

The Sages

Personnel incl:	JOHNNY KEITH	A
	DEREK WEBB	A

45:	In The Beginning/		
	I'm Not Going To Cry	(RCA Victor 47-8760)	1965

A mystery outfit with a strangely compelling 45 - the 'A' side is a quasi-religious but haunting folk-rock pop ballad that belongs more to the flower-power genre. The flip is a decent folk-beat ballad that has now reappeared on *Leaving It All Behind* (LP). (MW)

Sagittarius

Personnel:	CURT BOETTCHER	keyb'ds, vcls, gtr	A
	RON EDGAR	drms	A
	MIKE FENNELLY	gtr	A
	LEE MALLORY	gtr, vcls	AB
	DOUG RHODES	keyb'ds, gtr	A
	JOEY STEC	vcls	A
	SANDY SALISBURY	vcls	AB
	CHUCK GIRARD		B
	GARY USHER	keyb'ds	B

ALBUMS:	1(A)	THE PRESENT TENSE	(Columbia/CBS 9644)	1968 R1
	2(B)	THE BLUE MARBLE	(Together 1002)	1969 R1

NB: (1) reissued on CD with many bonus tracks (Sundazed SC 11053) 1997. (2) reissued on CD (Poptones MC 5036 CD) with five bonus tracks.

HCP

45s:	My World Fell Down/Libra	(Columbia 44163)	1967 70
	Hotel Indiscreet/Virgo	(Columbia 44289)	1967 -
	Another Time/Pisces	(Columbia 44398)	1967 -
	Truth Is Not Real/		
	You Know I've Found A Way	(Columbia 44503)	1968 -
	Keeper Of The Games/		
	I'm Not Living Here	(Columbia 44613)	1968 -
	In My Room/Navajo Girl	(Together 105)	1968 86
	I Guess The Lord Must Be In New York City/		
	I Can Still See Your Face	(Together 122)	1969 135

SAGE and SEER - Sage And Seer LP.

SAGITTARIUS - Present Tense LP.

Sagittarius were a studio group created by producer Gary Usher (who had earlier produced albums by **The Byrds**, Gene Clark, **Chad & Jeremy**, **The Millennium** and **The Peanut Butter Conspiracy**). **Curt Boettcher** helped with the arrangements and Terry Melcher was also involved in the projects. Both albums were of particular interest for their high degree of orchestration and polish. In this respect, they were ahead of their times.

Glen Campbell and Bruce Johnston (later of The Beach Boys) were involved in the first single, *My World Fell Down*, which came from a bunch of John Carter demos intended for **Chad & Jeremy**, who refused to cut the vocal... Usher made the backing track a bit freakier (i.e. adding more stops and starts, using **The Firesign Theatre**) and recorded it himself. Glen Campbell sings lead on the recording with Bruce Johnston and Terry Melcher providing backing. It's possible that Chuck Girard and some other Beach Boys etc. are in there too, although only Bruce and Glen are on the contract card for the session. *My World Fell Down* received considerable airplay in New York, although it failed to make the Top 40.

Their second 45 *Hotel Indiscreet* was arranged by **Boettcher** for outrageous multipart vocals and also features the writers Jim Griffin, (later in Bread), Michael Z. Gordon and **The Firesign Theatre**... Another couple of tracks on the first album were created by similarly unique associations, featuring the nascent **Millennium** and such unlikely figures as Angelo Badalamente (of "Twin Peaks" fame) as players and writers... the remainder being basically a combination of unused **Ballroom** tracks, and new songs which were worked up for the **Millennium** and consequently bumped up to "Grandiose Stereo" mixes. The singles are entirely and radically different versions to the album ones... with the first two minus the 'sound collages' in their album form.

The second album was recorded on Usher's own Together label and contained some beautiful love songs such as *Will You Ever See Me*, *I Still Can See Your Face* and *I See In You*. More coherent in theme though not as immediate as the first, ecology and religion/philosopphy are to the fore, as they were in Usher's next project, Celestium, which carried the sound and themes of *Blue Marble* into a more somber, almost Krautrock vein.. kind of like Gary Usher meets Bowie's *Low*!

The non-album 'star' tracks *Virgo*, *Libra* and *Pisces* are weird 'n' wonderful instrumental freakouts full of Eastern promise. *Pisces* can be heard on the *Everything You Always Wanted To Know...* (CD). You can also hear *My World Fell Down* on *Nuggets Box* (4-CD), *Nuggets - Original Artyfacts From The First Psychedelic Era 1965-1968* (Dble LP) and *Excerpts From Nuggets* (CD). (VJ/MW/DM/JFr)

The Saharas

45s:	This Mornin'/I'm Free	(Fenton 2016) 1966
	Debbie / They Play It Wild	(United 1033) 196?
	Here Comes Jody / ?	(United 3704) 196?

SAGITTARIUS - The Blue Marble CD.

This Michigan outfit got to record the Fenton 45 by virtue of coming second in a 1966 'Battle Of The Bands' competition. They also got a free set of instruments. *This Mornin'*, a half decent rocking reinterpretation of a **P.F. Sloan** composition which could have benefited from better vocals, can be heard on *Highs In The Mid Sixties, Vol. 19* (LP). A previously unreleased recording by the band, *Send Her To Me*, has also resurfaced on *Thee Unheard Of* (LP) compilation, although it's poorly recorded and of little merit.

They were also known as Ron Shannon and The Saharas. (VJ/MW)

Glenn Saiger/Infinite Companions

Personnel:	MIKE BEAVERS	flute, sax	A
	EMIL GEORGE	bs	A
	PAUL GIACALONE	keyb'ds	A
	T.J. ROLLER	perc	A
	GLENN SAIGER	gtr, vcls	A

ALBUM: 1(A) SANITY RESTS IN THE ABILITY TO FLY
(No label 30101-2) 1972 R2

NB: (1) issued with lyric sheet.

This local Ohio studio project was coordinated by **Saiger**. Most of the tracks fall into a progressive folk category, sometimes sounding like mid-seventies Pink Floyd. The closing track on the album, *Epic (Aren't We All)* sounds like a druggy Americanised version of *Fat Old Sun*; the lyrical phrasing being particularly similar to Roger Waters' performance. Overall, a very interesting album 'though probably too eclectic for wide acclaim. (CF/SR)

Endle St. Cloud

Personnel:	PETE BLACK	gtr	A
	A. MELINGER		A
	D.F. POTTER		A
	ENDLE ST. CLOUD		A

ALBUM: 1(A) THANK YOU ALL VERY MUCH
(International Artists 12) 1968 SC

NB: (1) Reissued by Decal (LIK) 1988.

45s:	Tell Me One More Time/	
	Quest For Beauty	(International Artists 129) 1968
	She Wears It Like A Badge/	
	Laughter	(International Artists 139) 1970

GLENN SAIGEN/INFINITE COMPANIONS - Sanity Rests In... LP.

Came together in 1968 in Texas. Their 45 that year was released under the name Endle St. Cloud In The Rain. Black joined from **The Lost And Found**, D.F. Potter had been with **East Side Kids** and Melinger with **The Iguanas**. Their album's two strongest tracks:- *Come Through* and *Professor Black* had first appeared on a **Lost And Found** 45 which Black presumably persuaded them to re-record. Ranging from acid-rock to country with each track linked by piano pieces the album is worth checking out. The second 45 credited simply to Endle was taken from it. Their first 45, a non-LP release, is one of the more sought-after International Artists singles. After this project **Endle St. Cloud** teamed up with D.F. Potter, James Harrell and others to form **Potter St. Cloud** who issued an album on Mediarts in 1971.

Compilation appearances include: *Tell Me One More Time (What's Happening To Our World)* on *Austin Landing* (LP); *Tell Me One More Time (What's Happening To Our World)* and *Quest For Beauty* on *International Artists Singles Collection* (LP). (VJ/MW)

ENDLE ST. CLOUD - Thank You Very Much LP.

Sainte Anthony's Fyre

Personnel:
TOMM NARDI — bs, vcls — A
GREG OHM — gtr, vcls — A
BOB SHARPLES — drms, perc — A

ALBUM: 1(A) SAINTE ANTHONY'S FYRE (Zonk ZP 001) 1971 R4

NB: (1) has been counterfeited on vinyl (Breeder RPR 004-IC-563) and reissued on CD. Reissued officially on vinyl (Void) 2001.

An unexceptional hard-rock guitar driven album. The guitar's OK but the material is very unimaginative with *Lone Soul Road* probably the pick of a poor bunch. More an album for hard-rock fans than garage or psychedelic enthusiasts. Sounds like the fire's gone out!

The band were from New Jersey. (VJ)

Buffy Sainte-Marie

ALBUMS: (up to 1971)
1 IT'S MY WAY (Vanguard VSD-79142) 1964 -
2 MANY A MILE (Vanguard VSD-79171) 1965 -
3 LITTLE WHEEL SPIN AND SPIN (Vanguard VSD-79211) 1966 -
4 FIRE, FLEET AND CANDLE LIGHT (Vanguard VSD-79250) 1967 -
5 I'M GONNA BE A COUNTRY GIRL AGAIN (Vanguard VSD-79280) 1968 -
6 ILLUMINATIONS (Vanguard VSD-79300) 1970 SC
7 SHE USED TO WANNA BE A BALLERINA (Vanguard VSD-79311) 1971 -

Born in Maine in 1941, **Buffy Sainte-Marie** is a Cree Indian folksinger/songwriter who was involved in the folk revival of the early sixties and the various movements for the rights of the Native Americans. An excellent writer, her songs have been covered by several groups, especially *Codine* (**Charlatans**, **Quicksilver Messenger Service**, **Wizards Of Kansas**), *Until It's Time For You To Go*, *Now That The Buffalo's Gone* or the anti-war *Universal Soldier* (Donovan).

Her first few albums may interest some readers, as she played guitar, piano and mouth bow, was backed by good musicians (Bruce Langhorne, Eric Weissberg, **Monte Dunn**) and even experimented with electronic scores (on *Illuminations*). Her voice, a powerful soprano with a heavy vibrato, is however quite disconcerting.

She also played on the soundtrack of Nicholas Roeg's *Performance* with Mick Jagger, Randy Newman, Jack Nitzsche and Ry Cooder (Warner BS 2654) 1970.

After 1972, **Buffy Saint-Marie** turned country, trying to change her image and subsequently her records are out of the scope of this book.

Compilation appearances include *Until It's Time For Me To Go* on *Pop Music Super Hebdo* (LP). (SR)

St. George and The Dragons

Personnel:
KURT BISCHOFF — drms — A
GEORGE CASTILLO — gtr — A
SID CUNNINGHAM — bs — A
JOHN SHARP — vcls, gtr — A

45: Trust Me/Donna Alone (Dragon 131/2) 1966

A popular mid-sixties outfit in Sacramento California, where they recorded this single after winning a local Battle Of The Bands. *Trust Me* is featured on *The Sound Of Young Sacramento* (CD).

St. George and Tana

ALBUM: 1 IS NOW (Kapp) 1967 -

A folk rock-pop duet, with a decent version of *High Flying Bird*. (SR)

Saint Jacques

ALBUM: 1 SAINT JACQUES (GRT 30005) 1970 -

On the same label as the Mojo, a soft-rock hippie trio with some trippy moments. (SR)

Rod St. James

ALBUM: 1 HAS ANYBODY SEEN THE SUPERSTAR (Paula/Jewel) 1972 -

A hippie singer with organ and fuzz guitar. (SR)

St. John Green

Personnel:
MIKE BAXTER — keyb'ds, vcls — A
ED BISSOT — bs, vcls — A
BILL KIRKLAND — A
VIC SABINO — hrmnca, vcls — A
SHEL SCOTT — drms — A

ALBUM: 1(A) ST. JOHN GREEN (Flick Disc FLS 45,001) 1967 SC

This Hollywood-based quintet were a popular attraction around L.A.'s bars and clubs for some years. Their album attracts some interest among collectors of psychedelia. Offbeat hippie-psych - 'canyon music' might be an apt description recalling the post 'flower power' scene exhorted by **Kim Fowley** as the next 'in-thing'. Indeed **Kim Fowley** produced the album. Unfortunately it didn't catch on. The album came in a wonderfully colourful cover. (VJ)

Alan St.Pierre

45:	Footsteps / Golden Bands	(DMO 2001)	1967

A one-off solo 45 by **The Unbelievable Uglies'** vocalist. (VJ)

The Saints

45:	Don't Make Me Wait Around/ Girl Forgive Me	(Raydin R 101)	1967

Moody keyboard dominated garage-pop but rather wimpy in the vocals department. From The Bronx, NYC.

Compilation appearances include: *Girl Forgive Me* on *Project Blue, Vol. 5* (LP) and *Class Of '66!* (LP). (MW)

Thee Saints and The Prince of Darkness

45:	Hey Girl/Running Away From You (PS)	(Champ 2006)	1967

Another Tennessee obscurity. *Hey Girl* has resurfaced on *Garage Punk Unknowns, Vol. 7* (LP). (VJ)

Mike St. Shaw and The Prophets

Personnel:	RAY GARCIA	bs, vcls	A
	CHUCK HATFIELD	gtr, vcls	A
	HAROLD LOGAN	sax, vcls	A
	MIKE ST. SHAW	vcls	A
	DANNY TAYLOR	drms, vcls	A

This combo were based in Tuscon in the mid-sixties. They had two cuts:- *Good Lovin'* and *Papa's Got A Brand New Bag* on the 1966 compilation *Where It's At: 'Live' At The Cheetah* (Audio Fidelity) and according to its liner notes were working on a film 'Step Out Of Your Mind'. I'm unable to confirm whether this was ever completed. They were a big-beat club band with soulful intentions and of no interest to garage purists. Mike St. Shaw would go solo and had at least one vinyl outing *Feel It/Hurry Sundown* on Capitol (2033) in 1967. (VJ)

Saint Steven

Personnel incl:	STEVE CATALDO		A
ALBUM: 1(A)	SAINT STEVEN	(Command-Probe-ABC CPLP 4506S)	1969 R1

NB: (1) also released in Peru (ABC Probe). (1) counterfeited on CD (Buy Or Die BOD 102).

45:	Ay-Aye-Poe-Day/Louisiana Home	(Probe 463)	1969

These recordings are the work of a Steve Cataldo (ex-**Front Page Review**) and the album certainly is rather interesting and highly-rated by many. The band seem to have been based in the New York/Massachusetts area.

The two sides of the album are titled "The Bastich" and "Over The Hills", which is why the latter is often referred to as the title in dealers' lists. The bonus cuts erroneously added to the reissue of the **One St. Stephen** album are actually by Steve Cataldo's previous outfit **Front Page Review**.

The U.K. See For Miles reissue label tried to buy the rights to this album but MCA deny all knowledge of the tapes!

Oddly, **Whalefeather** cover *The Bastich* on their second album!

Aye-Aye-Poe-Day has also been compiled on *Sixties Archive, Vol. 8* (CD). (VJ/CF/MW)

The Salados

45:	Got No Love/Spider Walk	(T.S.M. 9623)	1966

Taking their name from their home town of Salado in Texas and fronted by **Dick Treadway**, this 45 was their sole bid for stardom. They also have a track *1 To 10* on *Garage Punk Unknowns, Vol. 7*. (VJ)

Salem Mass

Personnel:	JIM KLAHR	keyb'ds	A
	MIKE SNEAD	ld gtr, vcls	A
	STEVE TOWERY	drms, vcls	A
	MATT WILSON	bs, vcls	A

ALBUM: 1(A)	WITCH BURNING	(No label SLP 101)	1971 R3

NB: (1) initially counterfeited on vinyl and later reissued officially on CD by Gear Fab (GF-117) 1998.

This group seems to have originated from Caldwell, Idaho. The title cut is certainly the highlight with lots of extended guitar and keyboard (organ and synthesizer) instrumentation. If you like early moog work done with enthusiasm this is a bit of a corker. More for fans of progressive rock, though.

The album was recorded on 2-Track, in a bar called "Red Barn" in 1971, which was temporarily turned into a studio. The mini moog used was serial no. 1023, (according to A.R. Moog, this was the 23rd Moog to be manufactured)... The album had a limited edition 'pirate' reissue a while back, but it has also been reissued officially on CD by the excellent Gear Fab label.

Compilation appearances include *Bare Tree* on Gear Fab's *Psychedelic Sampler* (CD). (VJ)

Salem Witchcraft

45s:	Just Looking/ Prostyle 3 (w/bumper sticker)	(Chaos 0715/6)	196/7?
	Onward/Rock 'n' Roll Lover	(Chaos 7629/30)	196/7?
	Keep On Rollin'/Sandman	(Chaos 543/44)	196/7?

Early seventies sounding Michigan "garage" rock that's in reality straight melodic rock with some tasty guitar breaks or keyboard workouts. Nothing exceptional though. Produced by Mike Mijal (of **Mijal and White**), writer credits to Arlen Viecelli, Ken Foster and Mark Johnston. (MW)

SAINT STEVEN - Saint Steven LP.

Sandy Salisbury

ALBUM: 1 SANDY (Poptones MC5008CD) 2000

NB: (1) CD release of an album recorded in 1968/9. Also relevant is *Falling To Pieces* (Rev-Ola CR REV 5) 2002.

45: Come Softly To Me/
     Once I Knew A Little Dog (Together 125) 1969

A 'solo' effort by **Sandy Salisbury** who is better known as a member of **Sagittarius**, **Millenium** and **Ballroom**. This rare 45 probably includes other musicians from the talented **Curt Boettcher** clique.

Salisbury also recorded a 1968/9 unreleased album, which finally saw light of day as *Sandy* (Poptones MC5008CD) CD 2000. (SR)

Salloom, Sinclair and The Mother Bear

Personnel:
JOHN BOLLING	bs		A
TOM DAVIS	ld gtr		A
PHIL MONTGOMERY	drms		A
DICK ORVIS	piano		A
ROGER SALLOOM	vcls, gtr		AB
ROBIN SINCLAIR	vcls		AB

ALBUMS: 1(A) SALLOOM, SINCLAIR AND THE MOTHER BEAR
                                (Cadet Concept 316) 1968 -
        2(B) SALLOOM-SINCLAIR (Cadet Concept 327) 1969 -

45: Sleep/Animal (Cadet Concept 7024) 1968

Originally from Texas, Roger Salloom and Robin Sinclair moved to Chicago to take a part on the local Blues scene. The first album, which is a very minor collectors' item, was recorded there in 1968 for the Chess subsidiary Cadet Concept. The killer cut is a drug song called *She Kicked Me Out Of The House Last Night (After This One)*. It features freaked-out vocals, a full organ sound and some good psychedelic guitar work. Salloom wrote seven of the eight tracks, the last one *Griffin* being authored by Robin Sinclair, a powerful female singer.

Recorded in Nashville and produced by Charlie McCoy, Wayne Moss and Norman Dayron (Michael Bloomfield manager), their second album, *Salloom-Sinclair* is more country-rock than psychedelic and includes both sides of the 45 listed.

When the group disbanded, Roger Salloom went back to Texas where he formed Roger Salloom and the Vest Pocket Players, releasing an album on a local label. In 1983, he recorded *Would You Like To Meet Someone* on Yellow Plum Records. Robin Sinclair went on to become the lead vocalist of **Gold** from 1971 to 1973, appearing with them at Winterland and Fillmore. (AT/VJ/SR/RCI)

Sonny Salsbury

ALBUM: 1 REFLECTION (Word WST68534) c1969 ?

A Christian rock singer with mixed harmonies, organ and some interesting guitar licks. (SR)

Salt

45: Long Way To Go/Old Comedy (Sandwich 0596) 1970

From Youngstown, Ohio with a lush-vocalled light-rock reading of the Mann-Weil number covered by, amongst others, **Pride and Joy** and the **Stained Glass**. This version comes alive with a killer guitar break. The flip, an anti-war song is harder rock with more mean guitar.

Two band of the band were brothers (surname Carver), who are thought to have gone on to play for a lounge act in Colorado. (MW/MMy)

SALEM MASS - Witch Burning LP.

Salt Water Taffy

ALBUM: 1 FINDERS KEEPERS (Buddah) 1968 -

45: Finders Keepers/He'll Pay (Buddah) 1968

NB: also released in France with a PS (Buddah 610010).

Another bubblegum pop group on the Buddah catalogue. (SR)

Salvation

Personnel:
AL LINDE	vcls		ABC
TEDDY STEWART	drms		AB
JOE TATE	gtr		ABC
ARTIE McLEAN	bs		BC
ART RESNICK (US of ARTHUR)	organ, harp		BC
RICK LEVIN	drms		C

ALBUMS: 1(B) SALVATION (ABC S623) 1968 SC
        2(C) GYPSY CARNIVAL CARAVAN (ABC S653) 1968 SC

NB: (1) issued in mono in non-gatefold sleeve, this may be promo-only. (2) was also released in Holland with a different sleeve as *Under Ground Music*, (ABCS 19502) 1969.

45: Think Twice/Love Comes In Funny Packages (ABC-1 1025) 1968

This San Francisco band was formed when former harpoon sharpener and garbage collector at the University of Washington Seattle, Al Linde, met Joe Tate, a cesspool driver and former student at the School of Mining and Minerology. Joe later met the group's drummer, Teddy Stewart, outside a bar in Sausalito. The other two members joined later. The band were featured in a series of three concerts in Golden Gate Park and eventually ABC offered them a recording contract.

The first album, released by United Artists in the UK, reflects the spontaneity of their music. Its front cover shows the converted bus they moved around in! The songs on the album are all originals ranging from hard rock songs like *She Said Yeah* and *Cinderellato* to good time songs like *The Village Shuck*, *What Does An Indian Look Like?* and the psychedelic *Think Twice*. Their second LP was more experimental. There's some keyboard wizardry from Art Resnick on *Handles Of Care* and *What'll I Do*, the latter was the album's most psychedelic track; *Salvation Jam* was an experimental instrumental, whilst *Come On Over Here* veered towards country music.

Art Resnick recalls:- "I was the last to join the band in the Spring of '68. That Summer in San Francisco was, as you know, the apex of the times and everything that the hippie generation represented (and more) was happening in the streets of Haight Ashbury. I had hitched a ride from

Minnesota to SF and got dropped off on some corner near H.A. where I stepped into a phone booth to call the one phone number I had on a piece of paper. This had been given to me by my ex-University of Iowa buddy, David Sanborn. He was supposed to be hanging out there and maybe playing around town. It was the number of Teddy, the drummer of the New Salvation Army Banned. When I called, this guy (turned out to be Al the lead singer) picked up the phone and I asked for David. In the background there was a very loud rock band playing so after shouting the name David Sanborn a few times he finally said David had been there but was out of town with **Paul Butterfield** and who was I?"

"I told him I was a keyboardist from Minneapolis who had just arrived and David was the only person I knew. He said that they were a band on the scene and their keyboard player had, 'that morning', packed up his gear and moved back to Minnesota where he came from! Weird. Anyway, he invited me over and it turns out they occupied a house right on Fredrick & Haight, within walking distance. When I arrived I was escorted in through a hallway into a room that was filled with posters and blacklight with two guys, each talking in one of my ears at the same time. Thus began my sojourn with the band. The rest is a somewhat risque history of Sex, Drugs, and Rock and Roll, and, oh yeah, ripoffs in New York's Filmore East... There's some really funny stories about that, like getting busted by the NYC police right on stage in the middle of a set, for non-payment of the hotel room (which is when our management team decided to take off with our advance from ABC Impulse). Anyway that's another story."

"The band started out as The New Salvation Army Banned and the name change was made because the record company was afraid of being sued by Colonel Hartog of the Salvation Army, SF chapter. It was changed when we signed our contract (which ABC later broke, although they did have good reason)."

"All of our gigs that Summer in San Francisco were notable since we were on the second echelon right beneath **Big Brother and The Holding Co.**, **Jefferson Airplane**, **The Doors**, etc. We played gigs being the warmup act (or following) all of the great bands. One time when we played for **The Doors** at the Winterland Arena when they came out and sat down on the stage in front of a TV and watched themselves on the 'Tonight' Show with Johnny Carson (I think, could be wrong about that - but it was some major network show) before a fully packed house of thousands. We also played the Avalon Ballroom with Chuck Berry, Janis Joplin, **The Doors**, and hosts of others."

"We also played, as part of a promo tour for our first album (which was incidentally produced by the way by Bob Theile - the producer of John Coltrane on all his ABC Impulse recordings) the Fillmore East and the Village Gate which was billed as from the Golden Gate to the Village Gate...."

"What destroyed the band was the fact that our managers left us high and dry in NYC, without a penny, absconding with our advance money (I think it was $10,000 if I'm not mistaken). Also, and probably the biggest reason for our gradual demise, is that members of the band acted so incredibly wild at the main offices of ABC In in NYC when going there to meet all the top execs. It was totally insane! Wilder than any rock movie I've ever seen."

"The most exciting gig I can remember was the gig we played in front of over 10,000 fans at the Malibu Rock Festival. They were mostly high on acid and other psychedelic mixures, and there we were on stage, outside in the sunny California afternoon, just following **Canned Heat**.... Seems like a dream now, but the feelings never die."

Teddy Stewart is thought to have become a postman in San Francisco. Art Resnick went on to record 12 albums, some solo, and some with rather well known jazz artists such as Benny Golson, Nat Adderly, Freddy Hubbard, Bobby Shew, etc. He was not the same guy as in **Third Rail**.

More Than It Seems also from their first album resurfaced on *Baubles - Down To Middle Earth* (LP). Another track, *I Don't Live Today* is on *The Stars That Play With Dead Jimi's Dice* (LP). (VJ/ARk)

Sam Samudio

Personnel:	SAMMY CREASON	drms	A
	JIM DICKINSON	piano, gtr	A
	CHARLIE FREEMAN	gtr	A
	FREDDY HESTER	bs	A
	MEMPHIS HORNS	horns	A
	TOMMY McCLURE	bs	A
	SAM SAMUDIO	gtr, mouth harp	A
	MIKE UTLEY	organ	A
	(DUANE ALLMAN	dobro, gtr	A)

ALBUM: 1(A) SAM, HARD AND HEAVY (Atlantic SD 8271) 1971 -

Sam Samudio had previously been the leader of **Sam The Sham and The Pharaohs**. His only solo album is an excellent mix of blues, rock and soul, with an exceptional backing group: **Jim Dickinson**, Duane Allman, Charlie Freeman etc. Recorded in Miami and produced by Tom Dowd, the songs are five originals plus five covers (Boz Scaggs, John Lee Hooker, Doc Pomus, Randy Newman and Otis Rush).

The album is particularly noteworthy for the really long thanks section, totally different from the usual "Thanks to my dear producer": he thanks the people who rejected him because of the color of his skin and texture of his hair, the people who broke his nose, the ones who mistreated him as a child, his friends the prostitutes...

Sam Samudio then apparently disappeared from the music scene, only to come back in 1982 on the soundtrack of *The Border* with Ry Cooder. He married the Memphis singer Brenda Patterson. (SR)

SALVATION - Salvation LP.

SALVATION - Gypsy Carnival Caravan LP.

TOBACCO A GO GO Vol. 1 (Comp LP) including The Sands.

Sam The Sham and The Pharaohs

Personnel: BUTCH GIBSON   strings   A
             DAVID MARTIN   bs   A
             JERRY PATTERSON   drms   A
             SAM SAMUDIO   keyb'ds, vcls A
             RAY STINNET   gtr   A

				HCP
ALBUMS:	1(A)	SAM THE SHAM - WOOLY BULLY		
			(MGM SE 4297) 1965	26 -
	2(A)	THEIR 2ND ALBUM	(MGM SE 4314) 1965	- -
	3(A)	ON TOUR	(MGM SE 4347) 1966	- -
	4(A)	LIL' RED RIDING HOOD	(MGM SE 4407) 1966	82 -
	5(A)	THE BEST OF SAM THE SHAM AND THE PHAROAHS		
			(MGM SE 4422) 1967	98 -
	6(-)	TEN OF PENTACLES	(MGM SE 4526) 1968	- -
	7(A)	REVUE/NEFERTITI	(MGM SE 4479) 1967	- -

NB: (6) Sam Samudio mostly. Readers may also be interested in a hits compilation *Pharaohization* that has appeared on Rhino.

			HCP
45s:	Betty and Dupree/Man Child	(Tupelo 2982) 1963	-
	Haunted House/		
	How Does A Cheating Woman Feel?	(Dinyo 001) 1964	-
	The Signifyin' Monkey/Juimonos	(XL 905) 1964	-
	Wooly Bully/Ain't Gonna Move	(XL 906) 1965	-
	Wooly Bully/Ain't Gonna Move	(MGM 13322) 1965	1
	Ju Ju Hand/Big City Lights	(MGM 13364) 1965	26
	Ring Dang Doo/Don't Try It	(MGM 13397) 1965	33
	Red Hot/Long Long Way	(MGM 13452) 1966	82
	Lil' Red Riding Hood/Love Me Like Before	(MGM 13506) 1966	2
	The Hair On My Chinny Chin Chin/		
	(I'm In With The) Out Crowd	(MGM 13581) 1966	22
	How Do You Catch A Girl?/		
	Love You Left Behind	(MGM 13649) 1966	27
	Oh That's Good, No That's Bad/		
	Take What You Can Get	(MGM 13713) 1967	54
	Black Sheep/My Day's Gonna Come	(MGM 13747) 1967	68
α	Banned in Boston/Money's My Problem	(MGM 13803) 1967	117
α	Yakety Yak/Let Our Love Light Shine	(MGM 13863) 1967	110
	Old MacDonald Had A Boogaloo Farm/		
	I Never Had No One	(MGM 13920) 1968	-
	I Couldn't Spell !!*/		
	The Down Home Strut	(MGM 13972) 1968	120

NB: α as by The Sam The Sham Revue. An EP, *Red Hot* (MGM EP794) 1966, was also issued in the UK through EMI containing *Wooly Bully, Ring Dang Doo, Red Hot* and *Lil' Red Riding Hood*. There are also six French EPs with picture sleeves.

Sam The Sham, christened Samudio Domingo, was a Mexican-American who was born in Dallas, Texas. He formed this outfit with the Pharaohs, (who were also of Tex-Mex origin and musical inspiration), in Memphis, Tennessee in the early sixties. Their early recordings included *Haunted House*, a cover version of Gene Simmons' novelty rock hit. *Wooly Bully*, a real sixties rocker was then leased to MGM in 1965 by Stan Kesler's Pen Records in Memphis. It gave the band a U.S. No. 1 and also reached No. 11 in the UK. The band relocated to Dallas and for a time were very successful indeed.

Eventually the hits dried up and they disbanded in 1970. *Ten Of Pentacles* had essentially been a solo effort from **Samudio** and in the seventies he embarked on a solo career.

Wooly Bully is one of the Soundtrack songs to the 1979 MCA film 'More American Graffiti'. Earlier in 1965 the band had performed *Monkey See Monkey Do* in the Soundtrack to the 1965 MGM production 'When The Boys Meet The Girls', which was a weird re-make of the Gershwin brothers' musical 'Girl Crazy'.

Readers may also be interested in a hits compilation *Pharaohization* that has appeared on Rhino.

Sam The Sham's backing singers **The Shamettes** also made some recordings in their own right.

Compilation appearances include: *Wooly Bully* on *Nuggets Box* (4-CD), *Nuggets From Nuggets* (CD) and *Frat Rock! The Greatest Rock'n'Roll Party Tunes Of All Time* (LP & CD); *A Long Long Way* on *Turds On A Bum Ride, Vol. 6* (CD); *Ju Ju Hand* on *Texas Music, Vol. 3* (CD). (VJ/SR/JRi)

Sanctuary

ALBUM: 1   SANCTUARY   (Veritas) 1971 R1 ?

An early progressive outfit with a strong Yes influence, melodic parts and soaring organ. Housed in a nice silver cover. (SR)

Sand

Personnel: RICK GOOCH   bs, vcls   A
             JACK MEUSSDORFFER ld vcls, ld gtr   A
             DAN ROSS   steel gtr, ld gtr   A
             STEVE WILLIAMS   drms   A
             DAN WILSON   vcls   A

ALBUM: 1(A)   SAND   (Barnaby BR 15006) 1973

Produced by Ken Mansfield, this Oregon group mixed two fluid electric guitars with vocal harmonies like CSN&Y. The musicianship is competent and all their material was original but is not strong enough to retain attention. The album was pressed on two one-sided discs to allow continuous play on an automatic record changer! The band had another album, a private pressing from about the same time.

In the eighties, a couple of the members were in FM-rockers Quarterflash. (SR/CF)

The Sandals / Sandells

ALBUMS:	1	SCRAMBLER	(World Pacific WP 1818) 1964 SC
	2	THE LAST OF THE SKI BUMS	
			(World Pacific WPS 21884) 1969 SC

NB: (1) was also released in stereo on red vinyl (ST 1818) and was credited to The Sandells. It was reissued in 1966 as *The Endless Summer* (World Pacific (WP)(ST) 1832).

45s:	α	Scrambler / Out Front	(World Pacific 405) 1964
	α	6-Pak / Endless Summer	(World Pacific 415) 1964
	α	Always (I Will Remember) /	
		All Over Again	(World Pacific 421) 1964
	α	School's Out / Wild As The Sea	(Aura 4501) 1965
	α	School's Out / Wild As The Sea	(World Pacific 4501) 1965
		Six Pak /	
		Theme From Endless Summer	(World Pacific 77840) 1966
		Tell Us Dylan / Why Should I Cry	(World Pacific 77852) 1966

| Cloudy / House Of Painted Glass | (World Pacific 77867) 1967 |
| Ski Bum / Winter Spell | (World Pacific 77907) 1969 |

NB: α as The Sandells.

Greg Shaw informs us that they were originally from Belgium and migrated to L.A. This might explain how they picked up on *Dis-Nous Dylan* by Marseilles outfit 5 Gentlemen (compiled on *Pebbles, Vol. 12* (CD)) and translated it into the cheeky folk-rocker *Tell Us Dylan*. The same track was reworked by U.K. outfit Darwin's Theory as *Daytime* (*English Freakbeat Vol. 5*).

Probably their most appealing 45 couples *House Of Painted Glass*, a novelty psych-pop number, with a cover of Paul Simon's *Cloudy*.

The group also had some of their songs featured on a soundtrack *The Endless Summer* (World Pacific).

Compilation appearances include: *All Over Again* and *Always (I Will Remember)* on *Realities In Life* (LP); *House Of Painted Glass* on *U-Spaces: Psychedelic Archaeology Vol. 1* (CDR); and *Tell Us Dylan* on *Highs In The Mid-Sixties Vol. 2* (LP). (VJ/MW/SR)

Don Sanders

Personnel:	DON JACKSON	A
	KIRK RAY	A
	DON SANDERS	A
	JOHN SAYLES	A
	JIM UNERLED	A

| EP: | 1 LIMITED EDITION (PS) | |
| | | (Private Pressing, 77002) 1974 - |

From Houston, Texas, a rare EP with Picture Sleeve with four original tracks: *Cruiser*, *Head Full Of Reds*, *Cocaine Ragin'* and *You And Me*, recorded live at Anderson's Fair Retail Restaurant, with slide guitar, juice harp (sic!), xylophone, slinky (?) and mandolin. The music is a mix of folk, folk-rock and blues. 1,000 copies were pressed, so it's not very hard to find. (SR)

Ed Sanders

| ALBUM: | 1 SANDERS' TRUCKSTOP | (Reprise 6374) 1970 SC |
| | 2 BEER CANS ON THE MOON | (Reprise 2105) 1972 - |

Two solo albums by the co-leader of **The Fugs**. Don't expect too much musically, as they mostly content country-rock and folk-rock with sarcastic lyrics. (SR)

The Sandmen

| 45: | I Can Tell/You Can't Judge A Book By Looking At The Cover | (Studio City 1025) 1965 |

From Minneapolis, Minnesota, this 45 contains a powerful, mid-tempo pair of covers. (BM/MW)

Sands

| Personnel incl: | EDDIE EVERETT |
| | TOM SMITH |

| 45: | Open Your Eyes/Can't Find A Way | (Capri 522) 1967 |

From Texas. *Open Your Eyes*, was strongly influenced by **The Seeds'** *Pushin' Too Hard* containing similar fuzztone guitar and the same vocal style. The flip was a garage-style teen ballad, rather appealing with quietly piercing keyboards.

Compilation appearances include: *Open Your Eyes* and *Can't Find A Way* on *Sixties Archive, Vol. 5* (CD) and *The Finest Hours of U.S. '60s Punk* (LP). (VJ)

The Sands

| 45: | Mister You're A Better Man Than I/? | (JCP 1042) 1967 |

Out of Raleigh, North Carolina and heavily influenced by the British invasion sound. You'll find their good cover of The Yardbirds' classic *Mister You're A Better Man Than I* which has a fine guitar solo in the middle, on the *Tobacco A-Go-Go, Vol. 1* (LP) compilation. (VJ)

The Sands of Time

| 45s: | Red Light/I Want To Thank You Girl | (Sterling 109) 196? |
| | Come Back Little Girl/ When She Crys For Me | (Stearly 8167) 1967 |

From Philadelphia. *Red Light*, a garage pop song with a decent guitar break, has been compiled on *Pebbles, Vol. 16* (LP), *Vile Vinyl, Vol. 2* (LP) and *Vile Vinyl* (CD); *Come Back Little Girl* on *Crude PA, Vol. 1* (LP) and *When She Crys For Me* on *Sixties Rebellion, Vol. 4 - The Go-Go* (LP & CD). (VJ/MW)

The San Francisco Earthquakes

| Personnel incl: | KENNY YOUNG | A |

45s:	I Feel Loved/That Same Old Fat Man	(Smash S-2117) 1967
α	Fairy Tales Can Come True/Su Su	(Smash S-2157) 1968
	Bring Me Back A Little Water/ March Of The Jingle Jangle People	(Smash S-2179) 1968
	Hold The Night/Sophia	(Smash S-2203) 1969
	Everybody Laughed/ The Day Lorraine Came Down	(Smash S-2218) 1969

NB: α also issued in UK (Mercury MF 1036) 1968.

An obscure group led by Kenny Young, who wrote and arranged both songs on their first 45, which are strongly influenced by the Beatles. *That Same Old Fat Man* is quite interesting, with cello, bells and harpsichord and "Lennonesque" vocals, while the flip features an awful whistling part. This single was produced by Steve and Bill Jerome for Real Good Productions. (SR/BR)

Tom Sankey

| ALBUM: | 1 SINGS THE SONGS THE GOLDEN SCREW | |
| | | (Atco SD 33-208) 1967 - |

Mostly topical folk, but some tracks feature backing group 'Inner Sanctum' and are in the folk-rock vein with weird lyrics (*Trip Tick Talking Blues*, *That's Your Thing Baby*, *Flippin' Out - Little White Dog*). (SR)

The Sanshers

| 45: | Gonna Git That Man / Kansas City | (Kweek No #) 196? |

An all-girl band.

Compilation appearances include: *Kansas City* on *The Garage Zone Box Set* (bonus 7"); *Gonna Git That Man* on *Girls In The Garage, Vol. 1* (CD) and *Girls In The Garage, Vol. 2* (LP). (VJ/MW)

Santa Fe

| ALBUMS: | 1 SANTA FE | (Ampex A-10135) 1970 - |
| | 2 THE GOOD EARTH | (RTV 301) 1971 - |

| 45: | Blue Bus/? | (Ampex 11035) 1970 |

A rural hippie outfit with good guitars and vocal harmonies. Their second album is rarer and was released on the same label as **Mu**. (SR)

Santana

Personnel:	DAVID BROWN	bs	ABCD
	TOM FRAZER	gtr	A
	ROD HARPER	drms	A
	GREG ROLIE	organ, vcls	ABCD
	CARLOS SANTANA	gtr	ABCD
	CHEPITO ARIAS	perc, trumpet	BCD
	MIKE CARABELLO	perc	BCD
	MARCUS MALONE	perc	B
	MIKE SHRIEVE	drms	BCD
	NEIL SCHON	gtr	D

				HCP
ALBUMS:	1(C)	SANTANA	(Columbia 9781) 1969	4 -
(up to	2(C)	ABRAXAS	(Columbia 30130) 1970	1 -
1971)	3(D)	SANTANA III	(Columbia 340595) 1971	1 -

NB: Also from this era is *The San Mateo Sessions* (Purple Pyramid LLP 12102) 2002, a 2-CD set and *Soul Sacrifice* (Abraxas GET 618) 2002 is a 3-LP set.

			HCP
45s:	Jin-Go-La-Ba/Persuasion	(Columbia 45010) 1969	56
(up to	Evil Ways/Waiting	(Columbia 45069) 1970	9
1970)	Black Magic Woman/		
	Hope You're Feeling Better	(Columbia 45270) 1970	4
	Oye Como Va/Samba Pa Ti	(Columbia 45330) 1970	13

Born in Mexico in 1947, Carlos Santana came to San Francisco in the sixties and formed the Santana Blues Band, soon known as **Santana**. Greg Rolie, ex-**William Penn Fyve**, was their organist and the group began playing their mix of blues, funk and latin rock at the Fillmore West in 1968.

In the beginning of 1969, their personnel changed. The young Mike Shrieve, ex-**Glass Menagerie** became their drummer and three afro-cuban percussion players reinforced the group. One of them, Marcus Malone, was soon sent to jail and wouldn't return until 1973.

A popular act, led by Carlos' characteristic guitar sound, **Santana** played Woodstock in August 1969 and soon after, their first album *Santana* was released and sold very well. The band also played at Altamont.

Many of the tracks on the 2-CD set *The San Mateo Sessions, 1969* were instrumental in landing them their deal with Columbia. The opener *Soul Sacrifice* was recorded at the 'Woodstock' festival and has been released on various collections and bootlegs. The triple album set *Soul Sacrifice* includes many pre-Columbia demos mostly recorded live in their studios. Included are long work-outs of the title track and other subsequent classics like *Coconut Grove* as well as a version of *With A Little Help From My Friends*.

In October 1970, *Abraxas* was published and soon reached No. 1 in the charts. Containing *Oye Como Va*, *Samba Pa Ti* and their cover of Peter Green's *Black Magic Woman*. The Marti Klarwein sleeve obviously helped the success of this album.

For the third album, a new guitarist, Neil Schon, was added. Soon after that David Brown was arrested in a drug bust and Chepito Arias sent to hospital with serious health problems. Carlos Santana later turned mystic and became "Devadip", a disciple of the guru Sri Chinmoy. His next albums fall out of the scope of this book.

Neil Schon and Greg Rolie would soon leave to form Journey with Ross Valory and George Tickner, both ex-**Faun**. Carlos' brother, Jorge, also had his own latin rock group, Malo, and later went solo. (SR/VJ)

SANTANA - Abraxas LP.

David Santo

ALBUM:	1	SILVER CURRENTS	(Phoenix 001) 1967 -
45:		Rising Of Scorpio/Jingle Down A Hill	(Phoenix PH1) 1967

This folkie from New York City cut an outstanding psychedelic folk track in *Rising Of Scorpio*. The album is nowhere near as good but has its moments. It was produced by **The Strangeloves**' Richard Gottehrer. Phoenix was a subsidiary of Sire.

Compilation appearances include *Rising Of Scorpio* on *Psychedelic Experience, Vol. 3* (CD) and *All Cops In Delerium - Good Roots* (LP). (GG/MW)

The Sants

Personnel incl:	CIRRINCIONE
	WIMBERLEY

45:	Leaving You Baby (On The Midnight Train)/	
	High Tide	(Format 118) 1966

From Paris, Tennessee, their snotty punk grunge was released on a Nashville label.

Compilation appearances include *Leaving You Baby* on *Teenage Shutdown, Vol. 2* (LP & CD) and *Highs In The Mid-Sixties, Vol. 8* (LP). (MW/MM)

The Sapiens

Personnel:	RONNIE BLACK	bs, vcls	A
	PATRICK HEARNS	ld gtr, vcls	A
	STEVE PETERS	drms, vcls	A
	GUY WHITE	gtr, vcls	A

45:	Love Ain't Makin' It No More/	
	Ask Yourself Why Babe	(Mercury 72502) 1965

An obscure 45, from a Newburgh, New York act that couples a waltzing folk-rocker with what sounds like The Stones doing a Dylan number. Interesting folk-punk.

Patrick Hearns later relocated to Florida and recorded as **Hopney**. Sadly, Ronnie Black the original bass player and vocalist for **The Sapiens**, died on 21st December 2000, in Vancouver, Canada. He was only 52 years old. (MW/KMn)

Sapphire Thinkers

Personnel:	TIM LEE	bs, vcls	A
	BILL RICHMOND	vcls, keyb'ds, gtr	A
	PEGGY RICHMOND	vcls, flte	A
	STEPHEN RICHMOND	vcls, drms, perc	A
	CHUCK SPEHEK	ld gtr	A

ALBUM:	1(A)	FROM WITHIN	(Hobbit 5003) 1969 R1

NB: (1) reissued on CD (Summer Of Love SOL 2000-2).

SAPPHIRE THINKERS - From Within CD.

45: Melancholy Baby / Blues On You (Hobbit HB 42002) 1969

A very U.S. West Coast sounding group who seemed similar to **Jefferson Airplane**, **Peanut Butter Conspiracy** etc. on their album. Since Hobbit Records were a subsidiary of GRT Records they were probably Californian. The album contains some pleasant vocal arrangements/harmonies and nice touches of acid and fuzz guitar and is recommended. It is becoming a minor collectable. (VJ/MW)

Sarofeen and Smoke

Personnel incl:	ANNE SAROFEEN	ld vcls	AB
	BILL PEVEAR		B
	LARRY SLACK		B

| ALBUMS: | 1(A) | SAROFEEN AND SMOKE | (GWP 2029) 1970 - |
| | 2(B) | LOVE IN A WOMAN'S HEART | (GWP 2039) 1971 - |

NB: (2) by Sarofeen.

45: Susan Jane/Tomorrow (GWP 523) 1970
NB: also released in Japan with a PS (GWP 274).

Anne Sarofeen, from the central New York town of Auburn, was a powerful bluesy rock singer, somewhere between **Joplin** and Ellen McIllwaine of **Fear Itself**. Her first album, co-signed with her backing group Smoke, reputedly contains several good bluesy psychedelic tracks.

Released in 1971, *Love In A Woman's Heart* should interest fans of West Coast bluesy rock, with some interesting guitar parts and impressive vocals, especially on *Fire In Me*, *Confrontation* and the cover of Jackie Lomax's hit *Sour Milk Sea* penned by George Harrison. This album was produced by Andy Wiswell and, except for the cover version, all the songs were written by Anne Sarofeen, Larry Slack or Bill Pevear. (SR/PMn)

Satan and The Deciples

| Personnel incl: | R. O. BATES | A |
| | D. DENSON | A |

| ALBUM: | 1 | UNDERGROUND | (Goldband GRLP 7750) 1969 SC |

45: Mummies Curse/Cats Meow (Goldband 1188) 1969

The sleevenotes to this album state that the band, who came from the South, have one of the greatest original interpretations of the new dimension of psychedelic sound! In fact, they were from Louisiana and this album surely deserves a place in any chamber of the worst records ever made. The opening cut, *Satan's First Theme*, is so bad it's laughable. The vocals are practically spoken, 'Satan' punctuates these with a laugh that is so unconvincing it's pitiful and in response to the vocalist's assertion 'I'm The Devil', there's a chorus retorting 'he's the booger-man'. Not psychedelic, not garage, simply garbage and the subsequent tracks are only marginally better.

Freddy Fender may have had some involvement with this album, but it's best avoided, unless you have a perverse curiosity to hear how bad that opening cut is. *Mummies Curse* is not on the album. (VJ/MW)

The Satans

45: Makin' Deals/Lines And Squares (Manhattan 801) 1965

From Fullerton, California, this was a raw sounding garage band whose 45 is regarded as a punk classic.

Compilation appearances have included: *Makin' Deals* and *Lines And Squares* on *Louisiana Punk Groups From The Sixties, Vol. 2* (LP) and *Sixties Archive Vol. 3* (CD); *Makin Deals* on *Pebbles Vol. 2* (CD), *Pebbles, Vol. 2* (LP), *Great Pebbles* (CD); *Lines And Squares* on *Highs In The Mid-Sixties Vol. 2* (LP). (MW/AB)

Satan's Breed

Personnel incl:	A. AUBIN	
	R. LEMME	
	D. MORETTI	A

| 45: | Little Girl/ | |
| | Laugh Myself To The Grave | (A.L.M. 201,129/130) 1966 |

A Rhode Island band. The 'B' side, *Laugh Myself To The Grave*, is pretty mediocre.

Compilation appearances include *Laugh Myself To The Grave* on *Magic Carpet Ride* (LP) and *Relative Distance* (LP). (VJ/MW)

Satan's Chyldren

According to Tim Warren, this mysterious mob roamed around Houston's South side for a while in 1966/7, yet the only source of info is from local promoter/coolster C.L. Milburn who recorded some demos of the band in late 1966. One of those tracks, *Don't Go*, has recently resurfaced on *Back From The Grave, Vol. 8* (CD) and *Back From The Grave, Vol. 8* (Dble LP). (GG/VJ)

The Satellites

Personnel:	CECIL BAINES	bs	A
	CLIFF EATON	organ, vcls	A
	LYNNE GILLIAM	drms	A
	DEAN KOHLER	gtr, ld vcls	A

| 45: | When Will You Stay / | |
| | The Next Boy | (unreleased acetate) 1964/5 |

A Portsmouth, Virginia, quartet called Dean and The Mustangs started out in 1962/3 performing instrumentals. With the British Invasion in full swing in 1964 they drafted in Eaton to replace a guitarist and became **The Satellites**. Shortly after, they cut two tracks at a local studio and this pairing kicks off the Tidewater sixties scene compilation *Aliens, Psychos And Wild Things* (CD). *When Will You Stay* is a robust punker based on the Kinks' *I Need You* riff. *The Next Boy* is a midtempo garagey ballad that infuses a Zombies mood with Searchers chordings and a hint of the emerging Dylan-derived folk-rock sounds in the chorus.

The Satellites time was up in 1966 when **Dean Kohler** was drafted but he'd be back again with two further 45s, one solo and the other as **The Electrical Banana** - also featured on the *Aliens, Psychos And Wild Things* (CD) compilation. (BHr/ST/DSU/MW)

OH YEAH! The Best Of Dunwich Records (Comp CD) including Saturday's Children.

The Satisfactions

Personnel:	TERRY GARDNER	drms	A
	RICK MILLER	ld gtr	A
	RICK PERVISKY (PRZYWOJSKI)	gtr	A
	JIM YOUNG	bs	A

45:	Bad Times/Girl Don't Tell Me	(Twin Town 714) 1965

This was **The Marauders** from La Crosse, Wisconsin, recording under another name. *Girl Don't Tell Me* was also featured on *Top Teen Bands Vol. 2* and *Bad Times* on *Top Teen Bands Vol. 3*, put out on the Bud-Jet label in 1965/6.

The name change was forced on the band by producer Dave Garrett because the Stones' *I Can't Get No Satisfaction* was riding high in the charts at the time.

The band split around the end of 1966. Rock Miller went on to achieve success as the owner of Harley Davidson Apparel.

Retrospective compilation appearances include *Bad Times* on *Everywhere Interferences* (LP). (VJ/MW/GM)

The Satisfied Minds

45:	I Can't Take It / Think About Me	(Plato PL-9001-45) 1968

From St. Albans near Charleston in West Virginia, this band issued just one 45 on the short-lived Plato label out of Milton, West Virginia, whose roster included the Outcasts, Kickin' Mustangs and King James and The Royal Jesters. *Fuzz, Flaykes And Shakes, Vol. 3* (LP & CD) features *I Can't Take It*, a jerky mover punctuated by several fuzz attacks. (MW)

Satori

45:	1,000 Micrograms Of Love/Time Machine	(Steffek 621) 196?

This guy's real name was Dennis Warkentin and he was a multi-instrumentalist from Houston, Texas. He was a virtuoso guitarist and the 'A' side of this acid rock 45 has some fine guitar leads. The flip is an **Elevators**-like psychedelic haze.

Compilation appearances include: *Time Machine* on *Mindrocker, Vol. 4* (LP), *Pebbles Box* (5-LP), *Acid Visions - The Complete Collection Vol. 1* (3-CD), *Acid Visions* (LP) and *Trash Box* (5-CD); *1,000 Micrograms Of Love* on *Sixties Archive, Vol. 6* (CD) and *Texas Psychedelia From The Sixties* (LP). (VJ)

Saturday's Children

Personnel:	JEFF BOYAN	bs, vcls	A
	DAVE CARTER	gtr	A
	RON HOLDER	gtr, vcls	A
	RICK GOETTLER	organ	A
	GEORGE PALUCH	drms	A

EP:	1	SATURDAY'S CHILDREN	(Sundazed SEP 2 126) 1997

NB: (1) is a double 7", which contains their three Dunwich 45s plus *A Man With Money* and *Tomorrow Is Her Name*.

45s:	You Don't Know Better/Born On Saturday	(Dunwich 139) 1966
	Deck Five/Christmas Sounds	(Dunwich 144) 1966
	Leave That Baby Alone/I Hardly Know Her	(Dunwich 156) 1967

Popular in their hometown of Chicago and almost unknown elsewhere, the band were previously known as **Dalek/Engam: The Blackstones**, and as such, also recorded a version of *You Don't Know Better*.

Deck Five, is a rip-off of Dave Brubeck's 1961 hit *Take Five* and even includes a melody line from *We Three Kings Of Orient Are*. Nonetheless, it contains some nice three part harmonies and some pleasing organ. You'll also find their otherwise unreleased recording of The Everly Brothers' song *Man With Money* on the *Early Chicago* compilation. This recording dates from an August 1966 session, which also produced their first 45.

The 'A' side of their last single, *Leave That Baby Alone*, was written by Randy Newman.

Jeff Boyan went on to join **H.P. Lovecraft** and relocated with them to California. He later played for Hezikah. Dave Carter also later played with **The Cryan' Shames**.

Retrospecive compilation appearances have included: *Deck Five* on *Mindrocker, Vol. 2* (LP); *Wisconsin Electric Co. Radio Spot*, *Man With Money* and *Leave That Baby Alone* on *Oh Yeah! The Best Of Dunwich Records* (CD); *Tomorrow Is Her Name* and *Man With Money* on *The Dunwich Records Story* (LP); and *Born On Saturday*, *You Don't Know Better*, *Tomorrow Is Her Name* and *Deck Five* on *If You're Ready - The Best Of Dunwich... Vol. 2* (CD). (VJ/KBn/MW)

Saturday's Garbage

Personnel:	ROBERT CIANCI	drms	A
	JIM DENNISON	bs, vcls	A
	GERRY KARR	keyb'ds, vcls	A
	ALLAN PARILLO	vcls	A
	MIKE NOWICKI	gtr, vcls	A

45:	The River Of Styx / In The Midnight Hour	(Creative Productions acetate) 1967

Forming out of a band called The Vandals which included Allan Parillo, Mike Nowicki, and Bob Cianci, **Saturday's Garbage** were formed at Bloomfield High School, Bloomfield, New Jersey in September 1967. They took their name from their favourite post-**Vandal** rehearsal activity - kicking over people's garbage cans, and played the usual round of church dances, school dances, a few private parties, swim club parties, and the occasional teen dance club (e.g. Clay Cole's Disk-O-Teen and the Monkey Club).

Bob Cianci: "Our best gig was the end of season teen dance at Green Pond, N.J. Community Center, in August 1968. We had just experienced a couple of bad gigs, and the kids there loved us. Girls screamed, and the guys dug the Cream and Hendrix stuff. Bloomfield, New Jersey was and probably still is a real greaser town; lots of blue-collar types, and they never liked us at all. We had the longest hair, wore Mod clothes, and played hard rock. We got hassled all the time for our appearance."

"We were never the most happening band around, because we played very little commercial material. We were true punks in that we did what we wanted: Rolling Stones, Yardbirds, Them, Animals, and later, **Steppenwolf**, Cream, Hendrix, **Doors**, **Rascals**, **Vanilla Fudge**, and toward the end, we began experimenting with jazzy stuff like **Spirit**."

In November 1967, the band recorded two tracks; *River Of Styx* - a strange number with Farfisa organ, a heavy drum beat and tortuous vocals; and a version of *In The Midnight Hour*. Bob: "The lyrics to *River Of Styx* were supplied by a guy named Ted Dunn who wanted to manage us. We wrote the two-chord riff, went into a studio and cut it, with *In The Midnight Hour* on the B-side. We only had one hour of studio time booked, but we did it. Ted had these big plans to pull us out of school and send us on tour but our parents said "no way!" and after our record was turned down by a few major labels, we never saw him again."

The band broke up in January 1969 after two members were busted for bringing marijuana to school. Bob: "Our parents called it quits for us. I had tried grass at a couple of gigs, and when my father found out, he dragged me to the barber for a very short haircut, one of the most humiliating experiences of my life. I still have never forgiven him for it."

"It's too bad it ended so suddenly. We were always good, but we were getting very good by the end. We copped the song *Gramophone Man* by **Spirit** note for note, and that's not an easy tune, with its extended jazzy thing in the middle. Gerry was a very accomplished keyboard player, and we had no trouble with it. I had been into jazz for years by then."

"Today, I'm still a working drummer and am proud to say, playing better than ever. I used to smash my drums up like Keith Moon, but have curtailed that activity. Mike played in band called Black Rose that had a single out on RCA records around 1974-75. He used a Gibson Melody Maker and used to throw it around a lot onstage-just short of smashing it. Gerry moved to California and may still be playing. He later switched to guitar, and became a very fine guitarist also. Just a natural talent for music. Jim gave up the bass and Allan hasn't been heard from in years."

"Mike, Allan, and I put together a new band in the Summer of 1971 while I was in college, called Suicide. We played some old Elvis, Jeff Beck/Rod Stewart, and some other cover stuff, but it went no farther than the garage and I went back to college in September. I'd love to play with those guys again for fun someday."

Compilation coverage has so far included *River Of Styx* on *Mindrocker, Vol. 8* (LP) and *Attack Of The Jersey Teens* (LP). (VJ/BCi)

The Satyrs

45:	Yesterday's Hero/Marie	(Spectrum 2668) 1968

From the Philadelphia area, **The Satyrs**' *Yesterday's Hero* is notable for its prominent organ work.

Compilation appearances include: *Yesterday's Hero* on *Pebbles Vol. 5* (CD), *Pebbles Box* (5-LP), *Trash Box* (5-CD), *Pebbles, Vol. 5* (LP), *Acid Dreams - The Complete 3 LP Set* (3-LP) and *Acid Dreams Epitaph* (CD). (VJ)

Rick Saucedo

ALBUM:	1	HEAVEN WAS BLUE	(Reality) 1976 R3

An album of psych-folk with long tracks, acid guitars and odd vocals, highly regarded by some. **Saucedo** became a well-known Elvis imperonator. (SR)

Merle Saunders

ALBUMS:	1	HEAVY TURBULENCE	(Fantasy) 1971 -
(up to	2	FIRE UP	(Fantasy) 1972 -
1973)	3	LIVE AT THE KEYSTONE	(Fantasy 79002) 1973 -

NB: (1) and most of (2) reissued on CD as *Fire Plus* (Fantasy FCD 7711). (3) reissued on CD.

45s:	Five More/How's That	(Fantasy 588) 1965
	High Heel Sneakers/?	(Fantasy 600) 1966
	Julia/Five More	(Fantasy 620) 1968
	Save Mother Earth, Pt. 1/Pt 2	(Fantasy 668) 1972
	My Problems Got Problems/	
	Welcome To The Basement	(Fantasy 678) 1972

SAVAGE GRACE - Savage Grace LP.

A figure of the San Francisco scene, **Merle Saunders** is a black keyboard player and singer who can be found on the albums by **Nick Gravenites**, Bonnie Raitt, **Danny Cox** and dozens of other rock, jazz and soul groups. His solo albums are a rather loose mix of rock, blues and jazz and were recorded with **Jerry Garcia**, **Tom Fogerty**, John Kahn and Bill Vitt, David Grisman (**Earth Opera**) and Martin Fierro (**Sir Douglas Quintet**).

A close friend of **Jerry Garcia** and **Tom Fogerty**, he also played on their solo albums and with the **Grateful Dead**. In 1988, he formed the Dinosaurs with four other Bay Area veterans, John Cipollina, **Barry Melton**, Spencer Dryden and Peter Albin. (SR)

Robert Savage

Personnel:	DON PARISH	bs, vcls	A
	TOMMY RICHARDS	drms	A
	ROBERT SAVAGE	gtr, vcls	A

ALBUM:	1(A)	THE ADVENTURES OF ROBERT SAVAGE, VOLUME 1	
			(Paramount PAS 6016) 1971 -

From California, **Robert Savage** was obviously influenced by **Hendrix** and his album is recommended to fans of hard-rock trios with inventive guitar parts. It comes in an unusual mediaeval style cover featuring a dragon. We are still, however, waiting for the volume 2... (SR)

The Savage Generation

Personnel incl:	RAY DEANGELIS
	R. FRUSCIANTE

45:	You're Not Going To Change My World/	
	Mr. Sun	(Senate S-2113) 1968

A Wes Farrell produced sole effort. The 'A' side, *You're Not Going To Change My World*, is notable for its heavy doses of phasing that lift it from being an ordinary latter-day punker. The flip is an awful lounge ballad!

Compilation appearances include: *You're Not Going To Change My World* on *Acid and Flowers* (CD) and *Turds On A Bum Ride, Vol. 3* (CD). (MW)

Savage Grace

Personnel:	AL JACQUEZ	vcls, bs	A
	RON KOSS	vcls, ld gtr	A
	JOHN SEANOR	piano, keyb'ds	A
	LARRY ZACK	drms, perc	A
	(BERNIE KRAUSE	moog	A)

ALBUMS: 1(A) SAVAGE GRACE (Reprise RS 6399) 1970 182 -
        2(A) SAVAGE GRACE 2 (Reprise RS 6434) 1971 - -

NB: (1) and (2) reissued on one CD, *The Complete Savage Grace* (33 & 1/3 Records TT 9801) 1998.

HCP

45s: Come On Down / Hymn To Freedom (Reprise 0924) 1970 104
      Come On Down/
      All Along The Watchtower (Reprise 0952) 1970 -
      Ivy/Save It For Me (Reprise 0988) 1971 -
      Yonder/Friends (Reprise 1022) 1971 -

From Ann Arbor, Michigan, this band evolved out of **Scarlet Letter**. Produced by Joe Wissert (**Lovin' Spoonful**, Flo & Eddie), the first album contains an excellent version of *All Along The Watchtower* and an interesting cover of *Hymn To Freedom* (an Oscar Peterson theme). The remaining songs were written by Ron Koss and *Dear Lenore, Night Of The Hunter* and *Turn Your Head* in particular, feature oriental percussion and interesting rhythms. Bernie Krause from **Beaver and Krause** also assisted on moog. The album climbed to No. 182, spending eight weeks in the Top 200.

Savage Grace 2 opens with *Mother's Son*, a **Hendrix**-inspired song and is more hard-rock than psychedelic. Both albums contain fine musicianship from **John Seanor and Ron Koss**, who later combined their talents on the album *Seanor And Koss* (Reprise 2091) 1972, in particular.

Both albums have been reissued on one CD from the master tapes as *The Complete Savage Grace*. The CD also includes the non-album *Ivy* as a bonus cut.

Larry Zack later became a session drummer and played with **Warren Zevon** and Jackson Browne.

Compilation appearances include *All Along The Watchtower* on *Psychosis From The 13th Dimension* (CDR & CD). (VJ/MW/SR)

Savage Resurrection

Personnel: RANDY HAMMON A
          BILL HARPER A
          STEVE LAGE A
          JEFF MYER drms A
          JOHN PALMER gtr A

ALBUM: 1(A) SAVAGE RESURRECTION (Mercury SR 61156) 1968 R1
NB: (1) has been bootlegged. Also reissued officially on CD (Mod Lang ML-007) 1998, with extra material.

45: Thing In 'E'/Fox Is Sick (Mercury 72778) 1968

One of the West Coasts 'forgotten' bands. Their album was a competent effort with tracks like *Every Little Song* and *Talking To You* containing some promising early psychedelic guitar work. John Palmer wrote (or co-wrote) all but one of the tracks on the album. Its closing cut *Expectations* features some fine Eastern-influenced electric guitar jamming. The 45 was taken from the album. Recommended by none other than Bevis Frond!

From Richmond, California the band was formed from members of two local outfits Button Willow (Hammon, Lage) and Whatever's Right (Myer, Harper) plus John Palmer. Randy Hammon, cousin of **Oxford Circle/Blue Cheer** drummer Paul Whaley, had been in the Boys with John Palmer, who'd then moved on to the **Plague**, Chico punk-legends **The Boy Blues** (of *Coming Down To You* fame) and Lincoln's Promise.

The Randy Hammon/Alec Palao produced CD reissue contains the entire album plus three rehearsals:- *Thing In E, Tahitian Melody* and *River Deep, Mountain High* - and a comprehensive history of the band.

Compilation appearances include *Fox Is Sick* and *Thing In 'E'* on *Electric Food* (LP). (VJ/MW)

THE SAVAGE RESURRECTION - Savage Resurrection LP.

The Savages

Personnel: DON HOOPER gtr, vcls A
          RICKY LAZUS drms A
          NEIL PORTNOW bs A
          LOUIS SEIGAL organ A

45: Cheating On Me/Best Thing You Ever Had (Red Fox 111) 1966

From Great Neck, Long Island. This act were friends with **London and The Bridges** and after that band had split, Neil Portnow and Louis Seigal, together with '**Bridges** members Jon Sholle and Johnny Miller formed **Today's Special**.

Compilation appearances include *Cheating On Me* on *The Cicadelic 60's, Vol. 4* (CD) and *The Cicadelic 60's, Vol. 5* (LP). (VJ/MW)

Savages

Personnel incl?: BARRINGTON A

45s: Everynight/So Much In Love (National NTL-2001) 1965
      Little Miss Sad/If You Left Me (National NTL-2002) 1965
      Little Miss Sad/If You Left Me (National NTL-2002) 1966

From Tampa, Florida, an anglophile rock group. Although the first single could have been sung by Cliff Richard, the second is truly nice, with big drums, ringing guitars and good vocals. *Everynight* was penned by Ware and Young, *Little Miss Sad* by the Addrisi brothers and the two flips by Barrington, who may have been a member of this little known group. (SR/MW)

The Savages

Personnel: PAUL MUGGLETON gtr A
          JIMMY O'CONNER gtr A
          HOWIE REGO drms A
          BOBBY ZUILL gtr A

ALBUM: 1(A) LIVE 'N WILD (Duane 1047) 1966 R2
NB: (1) reissued (Resurrection CX 1330) 1984.

45s: No No No/She's Gone (Duane 1043) 1965
      Roses Are Red My Love/Quiet Town (Duane 1049) 1966
      The World Ain't Round It's Square / ? (Duane 1054) 1966

Operating out of Bermuda their album is a mixture of cover versions and impressive originals. Most of their 45 cuts have been featured on compilations including: *No No No* on *No No No* (CD) and *Valley Of The Son Of The Gathering Of The Tribe* (LP); *Quiet Town* on *Oil Stains* (LP); *The World Ain't Round, It's Square* on *Open Up Yer Door! Vol. 1* (LP) and *Teenage Shutdown, Vol. 10* (LP & CD); and *Roses Are Red My Love* on *Garage Punk Unknowns, Vol. 2* (LP). (MW)

The Savoys

| 45: | Can it Be/? | (Summit 403) 1965 |

Named after the Plymouth Savoy they drove to gigs in, this Chicago band's fuzzy, distorted song with its rock'n'roll style vocals can also be found on *Back From The Grave, Vol. 6* (LP). (VJ)

Sawbuck

Personnel:
STARR DONALDSON	gtr, vcls	A
STEPHAN HATLEY	keyb'ds, gtr, vcls	A
MOJO	gtr, vcls	A
CHUCK RUFF	drms, vcls	A
NINE YEAR	bs	A

ALBUM: 1(A) SAWBUCK (Fillmore 31248) 1972 -

From California, a little known group between prog and early seventies rock, featuring Ronnie Montrose on guitar on two tracks. In 1973, Chuck Ruff became the drummer for the Edgar Winter Band. (SR)

Sawdust

| 45: | I Shall Try/Sunbeam | (EAB 1110) 1969 |

Hailed from Lewiston, Maine. The 'A' side is a soft psychedelic number. (GG)

The Saxons

Personnel incl: ART GROOM vcls A

| 45s: | Everybody Puts Her Down / Carol Ann | (Yorkshire YO-102) 1964 |
| | Things Have Been Bad / The Way Of The Down | (Yorkshire YO-127) 1966 |

From West Palm Beach, Florida. Art Groom later played in an outfit called Monopoly, who recorded for Power. *Things Have Been Bad* is by far the better of the two songs on the second 45 with some good fuzz guitar work. *The Way Of The Down* seems to have been a fake live recording.

Compilation appearances have included: *The Way Of The Down* and *Things Have Been Bad* on *Relics Vol's 1 & 2* (CD), *Relics, Vol. 2* (LP) and *Sixties Rebellion, Vol. 3* (LP & CD); *Things Have Been Bad* on *Teenage Shutdown, Vol. 3* (LP & CD). (VJ/MW/JLh)

The Scandal

Personnel:
CAROL FERRANTE	vcls	A
LEN "CROW" RENFRO	gtr, vcls	A
BRUCE SMITH	gtr, vcls	A
KATHY THORNTON	vcls	A

| 45: | There's Reasons Why/ Girl, You're Goin' Out'a My Mind | (Pepper 432) 1967 |

Len Renfro and Bruce Smith liked to sing with their girlfriends when they weren't playing with their Memphis, Tennessee, group The Sands. As their vocal arrangements became more accomplished they started performing around town and were heard by **The Gentrys'** Larry Raspberry, who thought they should put out a 45.

The Raspberry-produced 45 appeared at the end of 1967. It was well received - echoey harmonies over organ and tambourine. Both songs were written by Renfro and Smith. They split soon after when Renfro joined the Navy in the Spring of 1968.

Renfro later married Kathy Thornton. Carol Ferrante would become Mrs. Larry Raspberry. The full story is in Ron Hall's book 'Playing For A Piece Of The Door: A History Of Garage & Frat Bands In Memphis 1960-1975' (SR/MW)

Jim Scannell and The Believers

ALBUM: 1 SONGS FOR THE BEAUTIFUL PEOPLE TO GET READY BY (People's Music Works) c1970 ?

A very crude Christian folk group with flute, produced by no other than Jesus Christ (at least that's what the cover says!). (SR)

Scarlet Letter

Personnel incl:
| RON KOSS (KOSSADJA) | vcls, gtr | A |
| JOHN SEANOR | keyb'ds | A |

| 45s: | Macaroni Mountain / Outside Woman | (Mainstream 691) c1968 |
| | Mary Maiden / Timekeeper | (Mainstream 696) c1968 |

From Ann Arbor, Michigan, this outfit would become **Savage Grace**. Like many Mainstream 45s, stock copies are harder to find than white label double-A promos. Both *Macaroni Mountain* and *Mary Maiden* are pop-rock, not garage or psych. The former is lightweight, the latter piano-driven rockin' pop with keen guitar passages and use of wah-wah. (MW)

The Scavengers

Personnel incl:
| GRANT GILMORE | bs | A |
| JIM JOHANN | gtr | A |

| 45: | It's Over/But If You're Happy | (IGL 106) 1965 |

Byrds imitators from Sutherland, Iowa, whose one single was penned by the group's resident Jim McGuinn, Jim Johann and is included along with their previously unreleased version of **The Byrds'** *She Don't Care About Time* on *The IGL Rock Story, Part One* (CD) and *The Best of IGL Folk Rock* (LP).

They also have two more folk-rock numbers, *Always Traveling Around* and *Wandering Kind* included on the *IGL Dance Jamboree '66* (Dble CD).

Johann and Gilmore went on to join **Dee Jay and the Runaways**. (LP/VJ/MW)

TEENAGE SHUTDOWN Vol. 3 (Comp CD) including The Saxons.

Scepters

45:	Little Girls Were Made To Love/	
	Love You Baby All The Time	(MOC 661) 1965

Both sides of this Memphis outfit's sole 45 resurfaced on the rare 1982 French compilation *Everywhere Chainsaw Sound* (LP). *Little Girls...* reappeared in 2000 on *Leaving It All Behind* (LP). (VJ/MW/MM)

The Sceptres

45:	But I Can Dream / The Last Time	(Orlyn No #) 1966

From Chicago, the flip was a cover of the Rolling Stones' classic.

Compilation appearances have included: *But I Can Dream* on *Mindblowing Encounters Of The Purple Kind* (LP) and *Teenage Shutdown, Vol. 13* (LP & CD); *The Last Time* on *Teenage Shutdown, Vol. 15* (LP & CD). (MW)

Leonard Schaeffer

Personnel incl:	LEONARD SCHAEFFER	vcls, gtr	A
	(MARTIN BEARD	bs	A)
	(RICHARD GREENE	violin	A)
	(DAN HICKS	hrmnca	A)
	(NORMAN MAYELL	drms	A)
	(TERRY McNEIL	piano	A)
	(MARK NAFTALIN	keyb'ds	A)
	(RICHARD OLSEN	flute	A)
	(ROBERT "BOB" RAFKIN	banjo, organ, gtr, bs	A)
	(WILLIAM TRUCKAWAY	brass, recorders	A)
	(and several others		A)

ALBUM:	1(A)	A BOY AND HIS DOG	(Warner Bros. WS 1756) 1968 -

Produced in San Francisco by Erik Jacobsen and Bob Rafkin (a folk guitarist who also worked with **Tim Buckley**, **David Blue** and **Phil Ochs**), the only album by **Leonard Schaeffer** should interest fans of Californian good-time music. The songs, all self-penned, are not outstanding but the arrangements and the backing group make them pleasant (especially *The Artist* and *Smile On The Outside*). More than for **Schaeffer**'s voice (very similar to **Norman Greenbaum**'s, another Jacobsen's protegé), the record is in fact interesting for the musicians involved: two **Charlatans** (Hicks and Olsen), Richard Greene (**Jim Kweskin Jug Band**, **Seatrain**), Bill Douglas, Dan Patiris, Mark Naftalin (**Butterfield Blues Band**) and no less than four members of **Sopwith Camel**. (SR)

Warren Schatz

ALBUMS:	1	WARREN SCHATZ	(CBS S 64681) 1971 -
	2	WARREN SCHATZ	(Love Records ?) 1973? -

NB: (1) Dutch pressing, (2) also issued in Poland by Muza (XL 0937).

45:	Pattern People / Before He Took You	(Warner Bros. 7167) 1968

A little known but significant singer/songwriter/producer/engineer on the New York '66-'71 scene. Born in Brooklyn on November 3rd, 1945, **Schatz** originally performed as **Ritchie Dean** and had a hit with *Goodbye Girl*. He then organized a succession of groups for live dates and recordings and formed The Pendants, **The Petrified Forest**, **The Warmest Spring**, **The Shapes Of Things** and The Whispers. At the same time he was beginning to handle recording sessions as an engineer (**Unspoken Word**) and producer (**Yesterday's Children** and **Banchee**). In the early '70's he began singing under his own name and toured in Japan.

His CBS album was recorded in New York, Los Angeles and San Francisco. **Schatz** wrote all the material and produced it with sessionmen (Jerry Cole, Hugh McCracken, Al Gorgoni, Pretty Purdie). Marred by too many female background vocals, it's better avoided. **Schatz** then went to Finland to record his second album, which is much better, particularly the fantastic version of **David Crosby**'s *Long Time Gone* with lots of electric guitars. Strangely, this record was also pressed in Poland! (SR/MW)

Schield Sisters

ALBUM:	1	FRIENDS	(Schield 10860) 1969 ?

A hippie Christian folk group: three Schield sisters plus additional musicians. (SR)

The Scholars

45:	I Need Your Lovin'/Please Please	(Ruby Ray A-OK-1) 1967

I Need Your Lovin' has resurfaced on the *Pennsylvania Unknowns* (LP) and *Sick And Tired* (LP) compilations. What we do know is that they hailed from the Port Richmond area of Philadelphia and that they were a quintet attending Drexel and Temple Universities when their 45 came out in February 1967. Another cut left over from this session that never got beyond the acetate stage was *I'm Gonna Make It*, which can now be heard on the *Crude PA, Vol. 1* (LP) compilation. It combines the garage sound with group harmonies and has consequently been referred to as 'garage doo-wop'! (VJ/MW)

The Schoolboys

ALBUM:	1	BEATLE MANIA	(Palace 778) 1964 SC

As the title shows, this was another attempt to cash-in on the Beatles success in America. The album was issued with two different covers: a rare pink one and a more common white one. (SR)

Cherrie and Jim Schwall

Personnel:	CHERRIE SCHWALL	vcls	A
	JIM SCHWALL	vcls, gtr	A

ALBUM:	1(A)	A WEDDING PRESENT FROM	
			(Private Pressing) 1970 R1

A folk and folk-blues album recorded at home with a tape recorder by the co-leader of the **Siegel-Schwall Band** and his wife. It's quite interesting but copies rarely turn up. (SR)

Bernie Schwartz

Personnel:	KENNY EDWARDS	A
	GENE GARFIN	A
	GRANT JOHNSON	A
	KEVIN KELLY	A
	BILL LINCOLN	A
	BERNIE SCHWARTZ	A
	WESLEY WATT	A

ALBUM:	1(A)	THE WHEEL	(CoBurt CO-1001) c1969/70 -

45s:	α	She'll Break Your Heart/	
		Forever Please Be Mine	(Tide 1099) 1963
		Questions I Can't Answer/It Isn't Right	(Tide 2002) 1964
		Baby Bye Bye-Oh/Something's Wrong	(Warner Bros. 5651) 1965
	β	Her Name Is Melody/I Go To Sleep	(Warner Bros. 5867) 1966

NB: α as Don Atello, β as **Adrian Pride**.

Born in October 1945 in Hollywood, **Bernard Schwartz** took guitar lessons from the session musician Ray Pohlman in 1962 and through him met Sharon Sheeley, writer of hits for Ricky Nelson and other singers. He started writing with her and with Dale Bobbitt for various labels. In 1963, as Don Atello, he released his first single on Tide Records and a second one in 1964, this time as **Bernie Schwartz**.

Through Sharon Sheeley, he met Phil Everly and did a single for Warner Bros. on which Everly sang harmony and wrote the 'B' side, Sheeley co-writing the 'A' side with Jackie DeShannon. A second single was released using the same session musicians (Billy Preston, Jim Gordon, James Burton and the Everly Brothers) but this time under the name **Adrian Pride**. The 'B' side was a Ray Davies (Kinks) song.

Pursuing his songwriter career, **Bernie Schwartz** had his songs recorded by the **Yellow Payges**, **Power** and **The East Side Kids** in 1967.

In 1968, he formed **Comfortable Chair** but the group broke up after some concerts and one album produced by Krieger and Densmore from the **Doors**.

When **Schwartz** got his draft notice, he filed as a conscientious objector and was required to work at Goodwill. Sharon Sheeley called him up to tell him she had a new writing deal with CoBurt (Pierre Cosette and Burt Sugarman). **Schwartz** did three demos for them which ended up on his only album, *The Wheel*, which featured **Euphoria**'s Wesley Watt and Bill Lincoln, in addition to **Comfortable Chair** member Gene Garfin. Produced by **Schwartz** and Euphoric Productions, the album contains ten tracks, including a cover of **Euphoria**'s *Sunshine Woman* which ends with one minute of fuzz and feedback guitars! The album also features good covers of Neil Young's *Round And Round*, Randy Newman's *Think It's Gonna Rain Today*, **Fred Neil**'s *Candy Man* (with "frantic" guitar parts), former **Stone Poneys**' Kenny Edwards *Follow Me* and Gene Garfin's *Lost My Wings*. A really interesting album, especially if you like **Euphoria**.

Another **Schwartz** song was chosen for the soundtrack of "The Magic Garden Of Stanley Sweetheart" (MGM 1ST-20ST, 1970) which starred a young and unknown Don Johnson.

Schwartz later graduated from UCLA and went on to finish a masters degree program. He now teaches psychology, does seminars and writes books (the most recent is "Are You A New-Rotic?") (SR/GM)

John Scoggins

ALBUM: 1 PRESSED FOR TIME (Tiger Lily 14???) 1976 R2

45: Growing Pains/? (New World 80006) c1973

A melodic rock singer with good guitar playing similar to George Harrison. Tiger Lily was managed by Morris Levy, the New York producer more famous for his business abilities than for the music he produced. (SR)

Scorpio Ascendants

45: Billy B. Moanin (stereo)/(mono) (Gamble 227) 1969

A strange single produced by Bob Crewe on his label. (SR)

SCORPION - Scorpion LP.

Scorpion

Personnel:	BOB BABITT	bs	A
	MIKE CAMPBELL	vcls	A
	RAY MONETTE	gtr	A
	ANDREW SMITH	drms	A

ALBUM: 1(A) SCORPION (Tower S 171) 1969 R1

A strong local Detroit, Michigan, band's only album, containing hard-rock with a funky edge. Bob Babitt and Andrew Smith became well-known session musicians in the seventies, playing on albums by Alice Cooper, **Jimi Hendrix**, Yoko Ono, Alexis Korner, Four Tops, Temptations and many others. Ray Monette joined **Rare Earth** for several albums. (CF)

Scorpion

Personnel ?:	KENNY JEREMIAH	perc, theremin	A
	RICK KISSINGER	gtr	A
	BOBBY MARTORELLA	drms	A
	BILL NOCELLA	keyb'ds, vcls	A
	JOE YOUNG	bs, vcls	A

45: Can't Get Blood From A Stone/ I'm Only Human (American AR 701) 1969

Tough rockin' topside with vibrant guitar and 'proggy' keyboards. What makes this 45 noteworthy is *I'm Only Human* - an incredibly atmospheric piece of almost funky psych-prog with ethereal vocals. Whilst not to everyone's taste perhaps, it's quite unique.

The leader of this band, Kenny Jeremiah, had earlier achieved success with **The Soul Survivors**. After **Scorpion** broke up, he played in a Disco group called Shirley And Company (Shirley being Shirley Goodman of Shirley and Lee fame!) and then a Top 40 band called Full House. Kenny was last heard of playing the Casino circuit with a band called Jeremiah Hunter. Bobby Martorella went on to play drums for several soul recording artists, and Bill Nocella became a studio musician and worked in his fathers music shop in the Philadelphia area. Rick Kissinger went into business for himself, and Joe Young later played in a Top 40 band on the Holiday Inn circuit.

Compilation appearances include: *I'm Only Human* on *Psychedelic Experience* (CD) and *All Cops In Delerium - Good Roots* (LP). (MW/PC)

Scorpio Tube

45: Yellow Listen/White Birches (Vita V-001) 1967

This 45 was issued on a small Hollywood label so I assume the band to have been Californian. Produced, co-written and published by H. Eugene MacDonald, *Yellow Listen* utilises echoed guitar to good effect.

Compilation appearances include: *Yellow Listen* on *Psychedelic Disaster Whirl* (LP) and *Psychedelic Experience, Vol. 3* (CD). (MW)

The Scotsmen

Personnel:	RICHARD LAWSON	drms	A
	DAVID LUCAS	bs	A
	GARY REYNOLDS	vcls	A
	ROBERT SHOMER	gtr	A
	TOM YOOK	keyb'ds	A

45: Sorry, Charlie/Tuff Enough (Panorama 22) 1965

This band formed at college in Ellensburg, Washington, though their members were all originally from Seattle. They are famously remembered for wearing kilts on stage. *Sorry, Charlie* spoofed **The Kingsmen**'s *Jolly Green Giant* and was the band's sole recording.

Organist Yook later went on to **The Statics**, **International Brick** and The Joint Assembly.

Compilation appearances include: *Sorry, Charlie* on *Northwest Battle Of The Bands, Vol. 2 - Knock You Flat!* (LP) and *Northwest Battle Of The Bands, Vol. 1* (CD); and *Sorry, Charlie* and *Tuff Enough* on *Northwest Battle Of The Bands, Vol. 2 - Knock You Flat!* (CD) and *Highs In The Mid-Sixties, Vol. 14* (LP). (VJ/MW/DR)

The Scotsmen

Personnel:	DAN DAILEY	gtr	A
	JIM KANE	bs	A
	WARREN KENDRICK	gtr	A
	TERRY KNUDSEN	keyb'ds	A
	GARY LEACH	drms	A
	PETE LOKKEN	vcls	A

45:	Beer Bust Blues/Scotchmist	(Scotty 1803) 1965

Warren Kendrick's first project for Scotty. Minus Lokken and Kendrick they recorded several more unreleased tracks as **The Victors** before Warren got hot with **The Electras** and **The Litter**, the latter of whom of course included Jim Kane. For vinyl buffs both **Scotsmen** and five **Victors** tracks are included on Get Hip's recent *Electras Vs. Scotsmen / Victors* (1993) album and the same tracks also form part of Erik Lindgren's *The Scotty Story* (CD). Both are naturally highly recommended. You can also check out *Beer Bust Blues* on *Garage Punk Unknowns, Vol. 6* (LP). (MW)

Scott Bedford Four

Personnel incl:	JOHN DIPROPERZIO	drms	A

45s:	Manhattan Angel/	
	You Turned Your Back On Me	(Congress 247) 1965
	Sweets For My Sweet/How Does It Feel	(Congress 250) 1965
	Last Exit To Brooklyn/	
	Now I'm At The Top (How Do I Stay Here)	(Joy 296) 1965

From Northampton, Pennsylvania. The flip to the first 45, *You Turned Your Back On Me*, is a memorable pop-punker. According to Mike Kuzmin's 'Sounds From The Woods' Pennsylvania book they were originally known as the Corvairs and also released a 45 as **The Elusives**.

Their final 45, *Last Exit To Brooklyn*, with its 'Gene Pitney'-like vocals, was a Top 40 hit in Chicago and possibly several other Midwestern cities.

Compilation appearances include *You Turned Your Back On Me* on *Kicks & Chicks* (LP), *Punk Classics* (CD) and *Punk Classics, Vol. 2* (7"). (VJ/MW/BR)

Scoundrels

Personnel incl:	JIMMY ??		A
	HARRY J. BOYLE?		A
	T. MORRISSEY?		A

45s:	La Bola/Come Home With Me	(Verve 10389) 1966
	Devil's Daughter/Up There	(ABC Paramount 10834) 1966
	Easy/The Scoundrel	(ABC Paramount 10892) 1966

Rumoured to be a New York-based outfit, they were originaly called The Echoes. *Up There* is a great dance number with plenty of reverb-injected fuzz that even got airplay and a brief interview on the US Army radio service program "In Sound", compered by Harry Harrison.

Come Home With Me is a psychedelic harmony affair.

Compilation appearances have included: *Up There* on *Punk Classics* (CD) and *Punk Classics, Vol. 2* (7"); and *Come Home With Me* on *Psychedelic Unknowns, Vol. 11* (LP) and *Slowly Growing Insane* (CD). (VJ/MW)

Screaming Gypsy Bandits

Personnel incl:	BRUCE ANDERSON	gtr	
	MARK BINGHAM	gtr	
	TINA LANE	vcls	
	BOB LUCAS		
	CAROLINE PEYTON	vcls	A
	DALE SOPHIEA	bs	

ALBUMS:	1(A)	IN THE EYE	(BRBQ 22185) 1973 R1/R2
	2( )	THE DANCER INSIDE YOU	(BRBQ 04) 1974 SC

NB: (1) reissued (375 copies only) on OR (014) in 1996. (2) was a Bob Lucas solo album.

More progressive than psychedelic, the first album is worth seeking out but the best tracks are the folky ones with soft female vocals like *Junior*, *All This Waiting*, *Path Of Light* and *White Teeth*. When the violin's in evidence they sound a little like the U.K. band Curved Air. The more upbeat cuts, like the title track and *Prematurely (Fly Me Away)*, just don't come off so well. The album was recorded at Jack Gilfoy Studios in Bloomington, Indiana, which is where the band were from. At the time, columnist and Bloomington resident Michael Bourne gave them a very favorable review in Downbeat Magazine, which was their only brush with national exposure.

The bands personnel fluctuated wildly over the years and some members also backed Tina Lane on a couple of 45s. Sophiea and Anderson later played in MX-80 who recorded a local EP *Big Hits* which resulted in larger label releases *Hard Attack* and *Crowd Control*. They eventually moved to San Francisco. **Caroline Peyton** went solo, releasing at least two albums (*Caroline Peyton* and *Intuition*). She later relocated to the West Coast, where she has recorded Celtic music and done major-movie voice-overs for animated features. Mark Bingham went on to form the Brain Sisters (in Bloomington) and played with New York art-punk band the Social Climbers. While in Athens, Georgia he contributed strings to an REM album (*Automatic For The People?*). He eventually landed in New Orleans as engineer of Boiler Room Studios.

The Dancer Inside You was a Bob Lucas solo album, although Bingham produced and engineered (with Mark Hood).

Other Barbeque Records issues included *Mock-Up* and the eponymous *Intuition* by Caroline Peyton. The 1975/6 *Bloomington 1* compilation, included both a **Bandits** track and a Caroline Peyton track. The **Bandits** cut on this was taken from a legendary, never-released album called *Kryptonite*. A few acetates of this are also known to exist. (VJ/SR/CLn/EDn)

The Screaming Wildmen

45:	Good Old Days/St. Louis Here I Come	(USA 868) 1967

Chicago punkers. Sadly I've not heard the 45. (VJ)

The Sea Dogs

45s:	Blow My Mind / I'll Be There	(Tapestry T-1001) c1968

From Michigan, a rare psychedelic rock single. (SR)

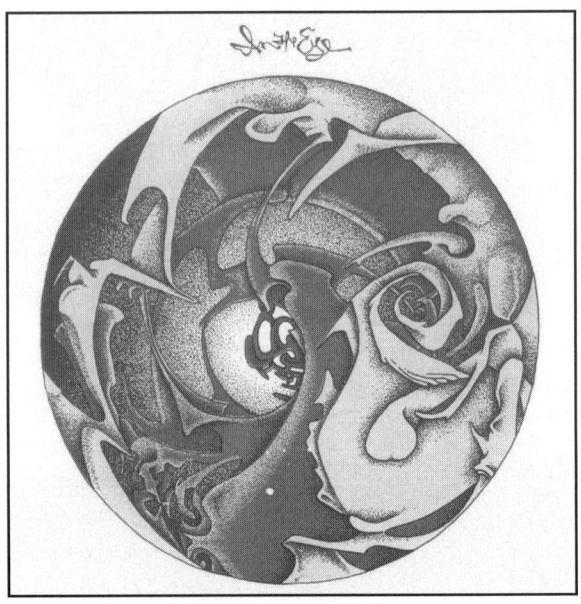

SCREAMING GYPSY BANDITS - In The Eye LP.

Sean and The Brandywines

45:	She Ain't No Good/Codine	(Decca 31910)	1966

A Los Angeles-based combo, whose 45 was produced by Gary Usher. The 'A' side, *She Ain't No Good*, is a cover of the U.K. Clique's song although it's a pretty lame effort. The flip is one of the weaker covers of *Codine* I've heard.

Compilation appearances have included: *She Ain't No Good* on *Pebbles Vol. 8* (CD), *Pebbles, Vol. 4 (ESD)* (CD) and *Highs In The Mid-Sixties, Vol. 1* (LP); *Codine* on *Sixties Punk Ballads Sampler* (LP) and *Sixties Archive, Vol. 5* (CD). (VJ/RR/MW)

Seanor and Koss

Personnel:	KENNY ALTMAN	bs	A
	KING ERRISON	congas	A
	RON KOSS	ld vcls, gtr	A
	JOHN SEANOR	keyb'ds	A
	JOHN SEBASTIAN	hrmnca	A
	JOH SEITER	drms	A

ALBUM:	1(A)	SEANOR AND KOSS	(Reprise MS 2091)	1972 -
45:		Babylon/Mystery Train	(Reprise 1114)	1972

Seanor and Koss were previously in **Savage Grace** and kept on working together when their group disbanded. Their only album was produced by Shel Talmy and was recorded in Hollywood with **John Sebastian** and Kenny Altman (**Fifth Avenue Band**). It's quite a good rock album with decent vocals, guitar and keyboard parts, all the songs being penned by Koss or Seanor. (SR)

The Search

Personnel incl:	JIM MANNINO	A
	PAUL MANNINO	A

45s:	Everybody's Searching/Too Young	(Era 3181)	1967
	Mr Custer/Climate	(In-Sound 404)	1967

An obscure San Diego, California, band led by the two Mannino brothers. The flip to their second 45, *Climate*, is notable for its change of tempo. The 'A' side was a punk-style cover of *Mr. Custer*.

Compilation appearances include: *Climate* on *Fuzz Flaykes & Shakes Vol. 1* (LP & CD) and *Highs In The Mid-Sixties, Vol. 3* (LP); *Mr. Custer* on *Fuzz, Flaykes, And Shakes, Vol. 2* (LP & CD). (VJ)

Search Party

Personnel:	PETE APPS	gtr, vcls	A
	JIM CARVALHO	bs, gtr, vcls	A
	NICHOLAS FREUND	keyb'ds	A
	JOANIE GOFF	vcls, gtr	A
	TIM KING	drms	A

ALBUM:	1(A)	MONTGOMERY CHAPEL	(Century)	1969 R4/R5

NB: (1) reissued on vinyl (Rapture(delic) RR 6.8) 1994 and counterfeited on CD (Flash) 1998 and again on vinyl.

A rare religious rock album by a from Wisconsin band who relocated to Sacramento, California. Many of the tracks feature lovely female vocals, although part of Side Two is more acoustic and folky with male vocals. Unless you're into singer/songwriting acoustic folk these are not as good. At its best the album is superb. A mystical atmosphere is created by the floating, melodic psychedelia of songs like *When He Calls*, *So Many Things Have Got Me Down* and *The News Is You*. Just listen and drift away. (VJ/CF)

THE SEARCH PARTY - Montgomery Chapel LP.

Seatrain

Personnel:	ROY BLUMENFELD	drms	A
	RICHARD GREENE	violin	ABC
	JOHN GREGORY	gtr, vcls	A
	ANDY KULBERG	bs, flte	ABCD
	DON KRETMAR	sax, bs	AB
	JIM ROBERTS	vcls	AB
	TEDDY IRWIN	gtr	B
	EOBBY MOSES	drms	B
	RED SHEPHERD	vcls	B
	LARRY ATAMANUIK	drms	C
	LLOYD BASKIN	keyb'ds, vcls	CD
	PETER ROWAN	vcls, gtr	CD
	JULIO CORONADO	drms	D
	BILL ELLIOT	keyb'ds	D
	PETER WALSH	ld gtr	D

HCP

ALBUMS:	1(A)	SEA TRAIN	(A&M 4171)	1969 168 -
	2(C)	SEA TRAIN	(Capitol SMAS 659)	1970 48 -
	3(C)	MARBLEHEAD MESSENGER	(Capitol SMAS 829)	1971 91 -
	4(D)	WATCH	(Warner Bros. BS 2692)	1973 - -

NB: (1) reissued on Edsel (ED 196) 1987 and on CD (Edsel EDCD 676) 2000. (2) and (3) were reissued in 1980 as SN-16102 and SN-16103. One Way have also reissued (2) and (3) on CD (57341 and 57661) and they've been reissued on a 2-CD set (Beat Goes On BGOCD 465) 2000. (2) and (3) have also been compressed into one album *The Best Of Seatrain and Marblehead Messenger* (See For Miles SEE 96) 1987. (1) and (4) have also been issued on CD.

HCP

45s:	Let The Dutchess Know/As I Lay Losing (PS)	(A&M 994)	1969 -
	Caroline, Caroline/Suite For Almond	(A&M 1106)	1969 -
	13 Questions/		
	Oh My Love - Sally Goodin'!	(Capitol 3067)	1971 49
	Song Of Job/Waiting For Elijah	(Capitol 3140)	1971 -
	Marblehead Messenger/Despair Tire	(Capitol 3201)	1971 108
	How Sweet Thy Song/Gramercy	(Capitol 3275)	1972 -
	I'm Willin'/Broken Morning	(Capitol 3421)	1972 -
α	Pack Of Fools/Abbeville Fair	(Warner Bros. PRO-562)	1973 -
	Flute Thing /		
	Freedom Is The Reason	(Warner Bros. 7696)	1973 -

NB: α promo only.

The band were formed by Kulberg and Blumenfeld in Marin County, California, after they quit New York's much loved **Blues Project**. John Gregory had previously played with **Mystery Trend**. However, it was Greene's virtuoso violin playing (he'd earlier been with **Jim Kweskin's Jug Band**) which dominated their debut album. Their next two efforts were recorded in London with ex-Beatle producer George Martin. By now, however, only Greene, Kulberg and writer Roberts survived from the original line-up. For *Marblehead Messenger* the remaining line-up was Larry Atamanuik (drms), Lloyd Baskin (keyb'ds,vcls) and Peter Rowan (vcls,gtr). This album was again dominated by Greene's excellent violin playing, particularly on the closing track *Despair Tire* and on the title track - a plea for pacifism:

"Take a message to the island
Take a message to the shores
Take a message cross the nation -
Put an end to war......"
(from *Marblehead Messenger*)

It also contained a number of other fine rock ballads, notably *The State Of Georgia's Mind*, *Protestant Preacher*, *London Song* and *Mississippi Moon*.

Perhaps it was its lack of stability which prevented the group from attaining the success one might have expected from the quality of its line-up. At any rate after one further album for Warner Brothers, which included many session musicians, they passed on without much publicity or acclaim.

Red Shepard also recorded as **Red Shepard and The Flock**.

Andy Kulberg passed away in January 2002. (VJ)

John B. Sebastian

ALBUMS:	1	JOHN B. SEBASTIAN	(Reprise RS 6379)	1969 -
	2	JOHN B. SEBASTIAN	(MGM SE-4654)	1970 -
	3	CHEAPO CHEAPO PRODUCTION PRESENTS	(Reprise MS 2036)	1971 -
	4	CHEAPO CHEAPO PRODUCTION PRESENTS	(MGM SE-4720)	1971 -
	5	THE FOUR OF US	(Reprise MS 2041)	1971 -

NB: (2) and (4) were withdrawn.

45s: (up to 1970)	She's A Lady/The Room Nobody Lives In	(MGM 14122)	1968
	She's A Lady/ The Room Nobody Lives In/	(Kama Sutra 254)	1968
	Magical Connection/Fa-Fana-Fa	(Reprise 0902)	1970
	What She Thinks About/Red-Eye Express	(Reprise 0918)	1970
	Welcome Back/?	(Reprise 1349)	1970

A gifted songwriter, singer, harmonica and guitar player, **John B.Sebastian** began his career in the early sixties recording with **Fred Neil**, **Tom Rush**, the **Mugwumps**, **Jesse Colin Young**, Judy Collins and **Eric Andersen**. In 1965 he formed the **Lovin' Spoonful** and, when the group disbanded in 1968, he started a solo career and signed with two record labels, MGM and Reprise. The following legal battle didn't help to promote his records. He also worked with Mama Cass and wrote Broadway musicals.

In 1969, **Sebastian** was invited to the Woodstock festival and his song *I Had A Dream* is featured in the movie and on the record. Produced by Paul Rothchild, his first album was recorded with the help of Crosby, Stills and Nash, **Buzzy Linhart**, Harvey Brooks, Danny Weiss, Bruce Langhorne and Paul Harris but is very deceptive. The sleeve shows several pictures taken at Woodstock. **Sebastian** was obviously having a good time but the material is weak and the playing uninspired. The following album was live and also issued by MGM, which finally had to withdraw its records. Recorded with Mac Rebennack (**Dr. John**), *The Four Of Us* contains two good bluesy tracks but is very self-indulgent and better avoided.

Very active in the studios, **Sebastian** can also be found on records by **Ohio Knox**, **The Doors** (he plays the stunning harmonica on *Roadhouse Blues* but was credited as Gary Pugliese), Rita Coolidge and Aztec Two Step. **John Sebastian** recorded two other albums in 1974 and 1975 and after that kept a low profile, as his solo career never obtained the success he had with the **Lovin' Spoonful**. He came back in the nineties to play jug band music with Fritz Richmond, the former **Jim Kweskin Jug Band** member. He is still touring today. (SR)

Don Sebesky

Personnel incl:	JOE BECK	gtr	A
	LARRY CORYELL	gtr	AB
	CHUCK RAINEY	bs	AB
	DON SEBESKY	keyb'ds, moog	AB

ALBUMS:	1(A)	DON SEBESKY AND THE JAZZ-ROCK SYNDROME	(Verve V6-8756)	1968 -
	2(B)	THE DISTANT GALAXY	(Verve V6-5063)	1969 -

NB:(2) as the The Distant Galaxy

Don Sebesky was primarily a jazz musician and arranger who released these two albums with musicians equally at ease with jazz, rock or pop, like **Joe Beck** and Larry Coryell.

Released in 1968, the first album contains tracks like *Somebody Groovy*, *Banana Flower*, *The Word*, *Meet A Cheetah*, *Big Mama Cass* (about the **Mamas and Papas**' singer) and is housed in a gatefold sleeve with psych cover art.

The following year the same musicians released a second album of mellow psychedelia under the name of "The Distant Galaxy" with covers of *Lady Madonna* and *The Sounds Of Silence* plus original material with "groovy" titles: *Guru-Vin*, *Cosmic Force* and *The Distant Galaxy*. (SR)

Second Chapter of Acts

ALBUMS:	1	WITH FOOTPRINTS	(Myrrh)	1974
	2	VOLUME OF THE BOOK	(Myrrh)	1975

SEATRAIN - Seatrain CD.

SEATRAIN - Marblehead Messenger LP.

A Christian folk trio with psychedelic edges on songs like *Which Way The Wind Blows, Goin' Home, With Jesus, The Devil's Lost Again, Love, Peace, Joy, Easter Song* or *He Loves Me*. (SR)

The Second Collection

ALBUM: 1 LOOK BEYOND ...THE SECOND COLLECTION
(Master Track MT-1003) c1973 ?

A California hippie pop-rock group with male/female vocals. Their material included *The Circle, Pass It On, Tell All The Earth* and *For Baby* plus covers of *Oh Happy Day, Put Your Hand In The Hand* and *Day By Day*. Some songs have a Christian content. One for fans of the **Free Design** and their ilk. (SR)

Second Coming

Personnel:
	BILL DINWIDDIE	trombone, perc	A
	LES KING	drms	A
	JACK KRAMER	trumpet, flugelhorn, valve trombone	A
	DAVE MILLER	keyb'ds	A
	TOM PALMER	bs, gtr, vcls	A
	BOB PENNY	gtr, vcls	A
	RICK RUDOLPH	sax, flute, trombone	A
	BUDDY STEPHENS	trumpet, vcls	A

ALBUM: 1 SECOND COMING (Mercury SR-61299) 1970 -

45s: Requiem For A Rainy Day/? (Mercury 73147) 1970
747/Take Me Home (Mercury 73184) 1970
Anthem/Palmyra (Mercury 73263) 1971

This band were part of San Francisco's 'second generation' movement along with **It's A Beautiful Day**, **Indian Puddin' and Pipe** and **Black Swan**. However, they were very much 'also rans'. Previously known as Buddy and The Citations, they actually originated from Chicago but had followed the group-goldrush to where it was happening.

Their album should be avoided by garage and psych fans, it's below-par horn-rock. (VJ/MW)

Second Coming

Personnel:
	DICKEY BETTS	gtr, ld vcls	A
	DALE BETTS	keyb'ds, vcls	A
	JOHN MEEKS	drms	A
	BERRY OAKLEY	bs	A
	REESE WYNANS	organ	A
	LARRY 'RHYNO' RHEINART	gtr	

45: I Feel Free/She Has Funny Cars (Steady HG 001) 1969

NB: Pressings on the Hourglass label, with the same HG 001 number, also exist.

Originally named The Blues Messengers and formed in the late-sixties in Sarasota, Florida, the band relocated to Jacksonville in 1968 and changed their name to **The Second Coming**.

Dickey Betts had previously been a member of The Jokers (immortalised by Rick Derringer in his song *Rock And Roll Hoochie Coo*) with Dan Joe Petty (later in Grinderswitch). Berry Oakely had been a member of Tommy Roe's road band (ex-**Roemans**).

The 45 was financed by the band's manager to be used as a marketing tool. It was originally intended only to be mailed to clubs in an attempt to generate gigs, but was later pressed in fairly large quantities. The 45 is a good example of material they played live, covers of songs by Cream and **Jefferson Airplane**.

Larry Rheinhart left **The Second Coming**, before the 45 was recorded, to form his own band The Load. When **The Second Coming** broke up due to Oakely and Betts joining the **Allman Brothers Band**, John Meeks would join The Load, Reese Wynans would join Ugly Jellyroll and then reunite with both Rheinhart and Meeks in The Load. Later Rheinhardt would briefly be a member of **Iron Butterfly**, then he and Reese Wynans would play together once again in **Captain Beyond**. Reese Wynans would eventually play with Delbert McClinton, Stevie Ray Vaughn and many others.

Faine Jade also had some involvement with this band, when following his Introspection album, he moved to Florida. (HS/MW)

The Second Edition

Personnel incl: B. WINTHER A
D. WINTHER A

45: To Keep You/Life... (Scotty 6730) 1967

Winsome melodic folk-pop from Minneapolis. Because of the involvement of Warren Kendrick, in producing the 45 and composing *To Keep You*, someone assumed that there was a connection to **The Litter** and the track was duly featured on Eva's *Litter - Rare Tracks* album. Hmmphh! The flip *Life..* is more akin to Peter, Paul and Mary than **The Litter**!

You can also find *To Keep You* on *The Scotty Story* (CD). (MW)

The Second Helping

Personnel incl: KENNY LOGGINS gtr, vcls A

45s: Hard Times/Let Me In (Viva 603) 1968
Floating Downstream In An Inflatable Rubber Raft/
On Friday (Viva 605) 1968
Children Of The Night/
Don't You Remember The Good Times (Viva 613) 1969

This Los Angeles band issued three excellent punky singles all written by Kenny Loggins, who it is thought was their leader. One of them, *Let Me In*, is on both *Pebbles, Vol. 9* (CD) and *Highs In The Mid-Sixties, Vol. 2* (LP) and is recommended listening. Loggins went on to play in **Gator Creek** and later in the mid-seventies embarked on a successful solo career. (VJ)

The Second Summers

45: Sad Vibrations/Remember The Days (Conn 777/8) c1966

An evocative garage ballad in Zombiesque mould from the New York area. Unfortunately backed by one of those silly UK-style 'music-hall' type pastiche songs, complete with kazoo and mock applause at the end. (barf). (MW)

Second Thought

45s: α The Museum/Sad Little Eyes (Brite Leaf 1801) 1968
Get Ready/Slingshot (Brite Leaf 1803) 1968

NB: α as Jonny Rome and The Second Thought.

A Minnesota band. *The Museum* was later included on the *Changes* (LP) compilation, a rare 1980 French compilation of sixties psychedelia from Minnesota. This is jaunty keyboard-dominated pop with the merest hint of music-hall, echoey vocals and ghostly outro, about uncovering old junk and heirlooms in the basement - "come on down and see 'em, it's a museum"! The flip is a slow, last-dance ballad with Fours Season styled backing vocals.

This outfit, also known as 'Jonny Rome and Second Thought', may have been a later incarnation of Duluth's Second Thought, who were formed out of The Devilles. The Duluth outfit's 45s are listed below:-

45s: When I'm In Love/If Only You Loved Me (Gloria 777) 1966

	Santa's Yellow Ski Doo/Ski Doo	(Gloria 779) 1966
	It's You I Love/Three Days Of Travellin'	(Gloria 780) 1966/7

(VJ/MW)

Second Time

ALBUM:	1	LISTEN TO THE MUSIC	(Tower 5146) 1968 ?
45:		Listen To The Music/Psychedelic Senate	(Tower 432) 1968

NB: flip side by The Senators.

A psychedelic pop outfit. Both sides of the 45 featured in the film 'Wild In The Streets' and on the resultant soundtrack album (Tower ST-5099/Capitol SKAO 5099), which includes another offering by the **Second Time**, *Sally Le Roy*. (VJ/MW)

Secrets

45:	I Know It's You/I Don't Know	(Raynard RS 10047) 1966

Charming but low-key garage-beat ballads from Green Bay, Wisconsin. (MW)

Section Five

Personnel:	MIKE GOFF	gtr	A
	CHUCK KALINOWSKI	drms	A
	DONNY THAYER	bs, vcls	A
	PAUL TRINGUK Jr	ld gtr, piano, vcls	A

45:	Pusher's Route/Please Don't Go (Audio Dynamics AD 105) 196?

NB: Initial pressing of the 45 labels show *Pusher's Route* as the 'A' side. This was an error and at the time *Please Don't Go* was 'pushed' as the main track.

From Massachusetts, circa 1967. *Pusher's Route*, composed and sang by Donald B. Thayer, is outstanding lo-fi garage-folk-psych with one larynx-wrenching scream and occasional fuzz and reverb effects. Paul Tringuk Jr's similarly composed/sung *Please...* is by contrast a sad garage ballad.

Paul and Donny later worked together in another Massachusetts band, Pretty Poison with Louis Santoro, and Jimmy D'Angelo. They had some local success for a few years before breaking up. Paul Tringuk also helped back his cousin, Kevan Michaels on two albums *Transatlantic Connection* and *How Long Can You Rock*, before retiring from the music biz. Donny Thayer moved to L.A. and went into acting.

THE SEEDS - The Seeds LP.

Pusher's Route can also be followed on *Psychedelic Experience, Vol. 3* (CD). (MW/KMs)

The Seeds

Personnel:	RICK ANDRIDGE	drms	A
	DARYL HOOPER	keyb'ds, vcls	A
	JAN SAVAGE	gtr, vcls	A
	SKY SAXON	vcls, piano, organ, sitar	A

HCP

ALBUMS:	1(A)	THE SEEDS	(GNP 2023) 1966	132	-
	2(A)	WEB OF SOUND	(GNP 2033) 1966	-	-
	3(A)	FUTURE	(GNP 2038) 1967	87	-
	4(A)	A FULL SPOON OF SEEDY BLUES	(GNP 2040) 1967	-	-
	5(A)	RAW AND ALIVE IN CONCERT	(GNP 2043) 1967	-	-

NB: (2) & (3) also on Vocalion (8062) and (8070) respectively. (1) issued in U.K. by Sonet in 1977. (1) and (2) are reissued on one CD (Edsel DIAB 8039) 2001 and (3) and (4) reissued on one CD (Edsel DIAB 8040) 2001. (1) - (5) reissued on vinyl by GNP Crescendo, together with *Fallin' Off The Edge* compilation. (3) also issued in Brazil (Som Maior SM -1550). CD. Compilations include *New Fruit From Old Seeds / Bad Part Of Town* (LP) (Eva) 1983 and *Evil Hoodoo* (Bam-Caruso KIRI 082) 1988. *Travel With Your Mind* (GNPD 2218-2) is a CD compilation only. 1996 also saw the release of *Flower Punk*, a 3-CD compilation on Demon (FBOOK 16) with 62 tracks, including rare and live material. Also relevant is Sky Saxon's *Lover's Cosmic Voyage* (private press) 1977.

HCP

45s:	Can't Seem To Make You Mine/ Daisy Mae	(GNP Crescendo 354) 1966	-
	Can't Seem To Make You Mine/ I'll Tell Myself	(GNP Crescendo 354) 1966	41
	(You're) Pushin' Too Hard/ Out Of The Question	(GNP Crescendo 364) 1966	-
	The Other Place/ Try To Understand	(GNP Crescendo 370) 1966	-
	(You're) Pushin' Too Hard/ Try To Understand	(GNP Crescendo 372) 1966	36
	Mr. Farmer/Up In Her Room	(GNP Crescendo 383) 1967	-
	Mr. Farmer/No Escape	(GNP Crescendo 383) 1967	86
	A Thousand Shadows/March Of The Flower Children (PS)	(GNP Crescendo 394) 1967	72
	Six Dreams/ The Wind Blows Your Hair	(GNP Crescendo 398) 1967	-
	Satisfy You/900 Million People Daily Making Love	(GNP Crescendo 408) 1967	-
α	Pushin Too Hard/ Can't Seem To Make You Mine	(Philco HP-26) 1968	-
	Wild Blood/Fallin' Off The Edge Of My Mind (PS)	(GNP Crescendo 422) 1969	-
	Bad Part Of Town/Wish Me Up	(MGM 14163) 1971	-
	Love In A Summer Basket/Did He Die?	(MGM 14190) 1971	-

THE SEEDS - Web Of Sound LP.

THE SEEDS - Future LP.

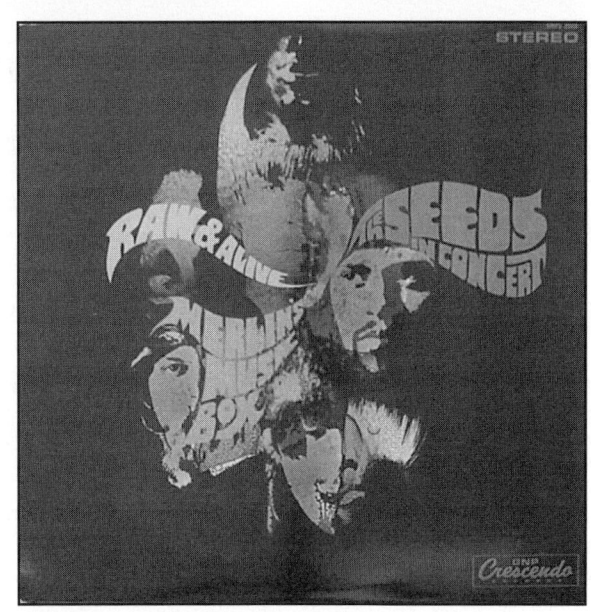

THE SEEDS - Raw And Alive In Concert LP.

Shuckin' And Jivin'/
You Took Me   (Surprise Productions Unlimited AJ-22) 1974 -

NB: α Hip-Pocket 4" (10cm) release in picture envelope. There are also three rare French EPs with picture sleeves on Vogue (INT 18022, 18077 and 18125).

This Los Angeles-based group was the inspiration of Sky Saxon (real name Richard Marsh) who formed them in 1965. Earlier outfits included Sky Saxon and the Soul Rockers and the Amoeba. They were extremely popular locally and their records sold quite well. Their debut single *Can't Seem To Make You Mine* made little impression as did *(You're) Pushin' Too Hard* when it was first issued. Their music was raw and often simple, but Saxon's growling vocals and their pummeling repetitive rhythms gave them a unique sound. When the debut album was issued a local DJ gave *Pushin' Too Hard* extended airplay and it was reissued climbing to No. 36 in the Billboard Hot 100. Their second album was also issued in the U.K. by Vocalion. It opened with the vibrant *Mr. Farmer* which became their next single and featured rampant rockers like *Rollin' Machine* and *Tripmaker* and a few gentler numbers. **The Seeds** were now hugely popular in L.A. and appointed a new manager, Tim Hudson who was apparently largely responsible for their nationwide success by pushing their flower-power aspect at the right time. In fact, much of their music was punky and only the *Future* album can really be called 'psychedelic'. This was an 'over the top' production and included a sheet of flowers to be cut out and pasted to the cover!

Rick Andridge recalls that their next album, *A Full Spoon Of Seedy Blues* was never meant to be a **Seeds** album which is why they went by **The Sky Saxon Blues Band** moniker. They never played any of those blues songs at any concert and Sky has said he recorded it to try and break their contract with GNP. Rick: "I did it because I learned to love the blues. I still believe to this day that it is one of the best albums we ever did. Really great for a group of white guys."

The Seeds name returned for the *Raw and Alive* album and two of the new tracks, on this credible blend of old and new - *Satisfy You/900 Million People Daily Making Love*, were issued as a 45 in a full colour art sleeve. It flopped but has now become the band's most collectable item. Sadly after one further 45, written by **Kim Fowley**, the band fell apart.

The band's demise came with the collapse of the flower-power culture in 1969, although Sky Saxon has continued to record spasmodically since. He re-appeared for two disappointing singles using the name 'The Seeds' in 1971 - *Bad Part Of Town* and *Love In A Summer Basket*. Slightly later a privately pressed heavy rock single, *Shuckin' and Jivin'* (Productions Unlimited 22) surfaced. He has also been connected with **Ya Ho Wa 13** and recorded an album with them for Psycho Records in 1982. This was previously issued on an eight-track tape. Only 300 copies of the Psycho issue were pressed and it is now deleted.

All of **The Seeds**' albums have subsequently been issued in Germany, by Line Records, including their 1977 compilation *Fallin' Off The Edge* (GNP 2107), which featured rare and previously unissued material.

Other items of interest to **Seeds** collectors will be Eva's 1983 compilation *New Fruit From Old Seeds/Bad Part Of Town* and *Starry Ride* Sky Saxon (Psycho 29) 1984, a mini LP. There's also a 1981 release *Purple Electricity* recorded live at the Cavern Club. The backing band includes members of Red Kross and The Primates.

Evil Hoodoo 1988 is another compilation. It contains all their best known tracks, but also includes the rare *Chocolate River*, previously only on a posthumous compilation and the Country and Western epic *Fallin' Off The Edge Of My Mind*. *Travel With Your Mind* is a CD compilation with many rare cuts/mixes and 1996 also saw the release of *Flower Punk* a 3-CD set.

Compilation appearances have included: *A Thousand Shadows* on *Mindrocker, Vol. 1* (LP); *Mr. Farmer* on *More Nuggets* (CD); *Pushin' Too Hard* and *Can't Seem To Make You Mine* on *Nuggets Box* (4-CD) and *Nuggets* (CD); *Pushin' Too Hard* on *Highs Of The Sixties*, *Tough Rock*, *Wild Thing*, *Best Of '60s Psychedelic Rock* (CD), *Battle Of The Bands* (CD), *Excerpts From Nuggets* (CD), *Nuggets From Nuggets* (CD), *Nuggets - Original Artyfacts From The First Psychedelic Era 1965-1968* (Dble LP) and *Nuggets, Vol. 1* (LP); *Can't Seem To Make You Mine* on *Nuggets, Vol. 2* (LP); *Try To Understand* on *Nuggets, Vol. 6* (LP); *The Wind Blows Her Hair* on *Nuggets, Vol. 9* (LP) and *Its Only A Passing Phase*; *Bad Part Of Town* on *Psychedelic Unknowns, Vol. 5* (LP & CD), *Pebbles, Vol. 3* (ESD) (CD) and *Psychedelic Patchwork* (LP); *Two Fingers Pointing On You* on *Psych-Out* (LP); *A Faded Picture* on *Microdelia*; and *Wild Blood* on *Filling The Gap* (4-LP). (VJ/EW/RAe)

The Seeds Of Time

45:    She's Been Travelin' 'Round The World /
       Gina   (Morgan 9060) 1966

NB: They also released a further 45 in 1967.

She's Been Travelin' is a glorious crudely-recorded thrash that would have elicited a more colourful and descriptive outpouring from Tim Warren, had it graced one of his *Back From The Grave* volumes. It didn't, but it has been unearthed on *Psychedelic States: Alabama Vol. 1* (CD).

The band were from Monroeville, Alabama and released another 45 in 1967 (reportedly soul with horns) whose details continue to elude. (MW/RM)

Bob Seger

ALBUMS: 1   BRAND NEW MORNING   (Capitol ST 731) 1971 -
(up to   2   SMOKIN O.P.'S   (Palladium MS 2109) 1972 -
1972)

NB: (2) reissued (Capitol) 1978.

| 45s: (up to 1972) | Who Do You Love?/ Turn On Your Love Light | (Reprise 1117) 1972 |

Brand New Morning is an excellent solo album in which **Seger** plays all the instrumental parts (piano and acoustic guitars). A very intimate atmosphere and an interesting production, totally different from his previous or subsequent work, it hasn't been reissued.

After *Brand New Morning* **Seger** joined **Teegarden and Van Winkle** and recorded *Smokin O.P.'s* with them and Mike Bruce on the new Palladium label managed by Punch Andrews.

Smokin O.P.'s (for "Smoking Other Person's Cigarettes", the cover art representing a cigarette pack) is a really good blues and rock album, with covers of **Tim Hardin**, Bo Diddley and Steve Stills. There's also a new recording of *Heavy Music*, the **Bob Seger and The Last Heard** song.

In 1974, **Seger** formed the Silver Bullet Band with Drew Abbott (ex-**Third Power**), and went on to sell millions of singles and albums of classic and well structured U.S. rock. These are, however, totally outside the scope of this book. (SR/EW)

Bob Seger and The Last Heard

Personnel:	DOUG BROWN	organ, gtr	A
	BOB EVANS	drms	A
	DAN HONAKER	bs	A
	PEP PERRINE	bongos	A
	BOB SEGER	vcls	A

| ALBUM: | 1 | BOB SEGER 66-67 | (KWR 7033) 197? ? |

NB: (1) an unauthorised retrospective compiling all the 45s. The same tracks have also been released on CDs of dubious origin and on *The Best Of Hide Out* compilation..

			HCP
45s:	East Side Story/East Side Sound	(HideOut 1013) 1966	-
	Persecution Smith/Chain Smokin'	(HideOut 1014) 1966	-
	East Side Story/East Side Sound	(Cameo 438) 1966	-
	Sock It To Me, Santa/Florida Time	(Cameo 444) 1966	-
	Persecution Smith/Chain Smokin'	(Cameo 465) 1966	-
	Vagrant Winter/Very Few	(Cameo 743) 1967	-
α	Heavy Music/Heavy Music, pt 2	(Cameo 494) 1967	103

NB: α also released in France with a picture sleeve (Stateside).

Born in Dearborn, near Ann Arbor, Michigan on May 6th, 1945, **Bob Seger** began his career with a school band, the Decibels in 1961. In 1963, he joined the Town Criers and later the Omens led by **Doug Brown**, the most popular Ann Arbor group. Backed by the Omens, he released a 45 as **The Beach Bums** and finally formed **Bob Seger and The Last Heard**.

Their debut 45 was released in May 1966 on the local Hide Out label (owned by Punch Andrews) and sold locally more than 50,000 copies. With fuzz, acid organ and heavy percussions, *East Side Story* and *Persecution Smith* are excellent and soon Cameo decided to distribute the first two singles nationally.

Sock It To Me, Santa was a James Brown inspired Xmas song and the 'B' side of the **Beach Bums** single was reused for the flip. The fifth 45, *Heavy Music*, began to sell really well and was even pressed in France.

Cameo however suddenly went bankrupt, provoking the end of the Last Heard, one of the first and best Detroit rock groups, with **Seger**'s powerful vocals, good songwriting and excellent guitars and rhythm section. **Bob Seger** then signed with Capitol and formed the **Bob Seger System** with Honaker and **Perrine**, who also issued a solo album for Hide Out.

Compilation appearances have included: *East Side Story, Persecution Smith, Chain Smokin', Heavy Music, Part 2* and *Sock It To Me Santa* on *Michigan Nuggets* (CD) and *Michigan Brand Nuggets*; *East Side Sound* on *Buzz Buzz Buzzzzzz, Vol. 1* (CD); *East Side Story, Heavy Music, Persecution Smith, Chain Smokin', Vagrant Winter, Florida Time, East Side Sound, Heavy Music, Part 2* and *Sock It To Me, Santa* on *Best of Hideout Records* (CD). (SR)

MICHIGAN BRAND NUGGETS (Comp CD) including Bob Seger System.

Bob Seger System

Personnel:	DAN HONAKER	bs	ABC
	PEP PERRINE	drms	ABC
	BOB SEGER	gtr, keyb'ds, vcls	ABC
	DAN WATSON	keyb'ds	C
	(MIKE ERELWINE	hrmnca	A)
	(BOB SCHULTZ	keyb'ds	AB)
	(TOM NEME	vcls, gtr	B)

ALBUMS:	1(A)	RAMBLIN' GAMBLIN' MAN	(Capitol ST-172) 1969	62 SC
	2(B)	NOAH	(Capitol ST-236) 1969	R1
	3(C)	MONGREL	(Capitol ST-499) 1970	171 SC

NB: (1) and (3) have been reissued several times. (2) was also released in France.

			HCP
45s:	2+2=?/Death Row	(Capitol 2143) 1968	-
	Ramblin' Gamblin' Man/ Tales Of Lucy Blue	(Capitol 2297) 1968	17
	Ivory/Love Needs To Be Loved	(Capitol 2480) 1969	97
	Noah/Lennie Johnson	(Capitol 2576) 1969	103
	Lonely Man/Innervenus Eyes	(Capitol 2640) 1969	-
	Lucifer/Big River	(Capitol 2748) 1970	84

NB: all 45s are album cuts.

After the demise of **Bob Seger and The Last Heard**, **Seger**, Honaker and **Perrine** formed the **Bob Seger System**. Their first 45 was released in January 1968 and was an excellent anti-war song backed with a fantastic tune about the prisons' death rows, with a memorable riff. It was a local success in Michigan but their second single sold nationally and reached No. 17 in the national charts.

Their debut album *Ramblin' Gamblin' Man* is a good example of Detroit Sound psychedelia and is highly recommended. Its follow-up, *Noah* saw the permanent inclusion of Bob Schultz on keyboards (he had already guested on the first album) and the influential arrival of a singer/songwriter, Tom Neme. More psychedelic (the long *Cats*) and less structured, the album is somewhat disappointing and its sales were poor, prompting Neme and Schultz to leave the group. Tom Neme would come back in 1979 with the Barooga Bandits. Even today **Bob Seger** still refuses to reissue *Noah*.

Dave Watson then joined the group and the last **Bob Seger System** album marked a return to a powerful rock with excellent guitars and great vocal parts on *Lucifer, Teachin' Blues* and *River Deep, Mountain High*. All three albums were produced by **Seger** and Punch Andrews, the former Hide Out label owner, who went on to work with **Seger** on all the subsequent output.

Bob Seger then disbanded his group and went to spend a year at Michigan University. He would return to the music scene at the end of 1971.

In 1970 British pop singer James Royal covered *Noah*. In the nineties *Lucifer* was covered by Jeff Tarlton on his *Sinner* EP.

Compilation appearances include: *Lookin' Back* on *Best of Hideout Records* (CD), *Michigan Nuggets* (CD) and *Michigan Brand Nuggets* (Dble LP); *Heavy Music* on *Michigan Rocks* (LP); *2+2* on *The Seventh Son* (LP). (SR)

Selah

Personnel:	ED FISHER	vcls, gourds	A
	MIKE LEB	bs, vcls	A
	KRISTINA LINDER	vcls, hrmnca	A
	JOE MAESTRI	drms, tamb, vcls	A
	PAUL VERGILIO	piano, organ, bells, vcls, gtr	A

ALBUM: 1(A) CONSIDER THESE WORDS (Almond Tree) c1972 SC

From Ohio, a Christian rock group, who shared the label and some members with **Pressed Down, Shaken Together and Running Over**. (SR/MMs)

The Semi-Colons?

45: Beachcomber/Set Aside (Cameo 468) 1967

An instrumental 45 recorded by **? And The Mysterians** under a pseudonym. (VJ)

The Senders

45: Sometimes Good Guys Don't Wear White/She Told Me (IGL 149) 196?

This Pocahontas, Iowa, band's cover of **The Standells**' hit is pretty decent. They reformed during the eighties to play sixties hits on the dance circuit.

Compilation appearances include: *Sometimes Good Guys Don't Wear White* on *Monsters Of The Midwest, Vol. 3* (LP); and *She Told Me* and *Sometimes Good Guys Don't Wear White* on *The Best Of IGL Garage Rock* (LP) and *The IGL Rock Story: Part Two (1967 - 68)* (CD). (VJ)

The Senders

45s:	Party Line/Love Me Too	(Leopard 201) 1966
	Chintz And Rubies/What's Your Sisters Name?	(Marlin 1910) 196?

Another **Senders**, this time from Tampa, Florida, whose *Party Line* was included on *Garage Punk Unknowns, Vol. 8* (LP). (GG)

Seompi

Personnel:	BILL REID	drms	ABC
	PAT ROCKHILL	bs	ABC
	DAVE WILLIAMS	bs	ABC
	MITCH WATKINS	gtr	B
	'SKID' ROWE	gtr	C

ALBUMS:	1(B)	SUMMER'S COMIN' ON HEAVY	(Rockadelic RRLP 33) 1998
	2(B)	SEOMPI (dbl)	(Akarma AK-089/2) 2000

NB: (1) issued in standard printed jacket with insert which was encased in a printed soft vinyl outer cover. (2) is a reissue and repackage of (1) also on CD as *AWOL* (Gear Fab GF-136) 1999.

45s:	α	Summer's Coming On Heavy/Lay On The Floor	(Blackstar S-101) 1970
	α	Summer's Coming On Heavy/Lay On The Floor	(Yin Yang S-101) 197?
		Almost In The Whole/Slide Slide	(Blackstar S-102) 197?

NB: α contain different versions of the same songs.

Seompi are on a very short list of Texas bands that successfully embraced the emerging heavy rock sound at the turn of the decade, using it (as did **Mariani** and, to a lesser degree, **Josefus**) to create provocative original music.

Created by Williams in 1969 as a power trio with no guitarist, it was this unusual line-up that recorded the first single on Blackstar. When both the 45 and the dual-bass guitar line-up were met with public indifference, Williams wisely ended the experiment and brought in Watkins on guitar. It was this more traditional quartet line-up that recorded all the music heard on the two full-length collections listed above, which are recommended. Both contain the band's second and third single releases, and are fleshed out with period rehearsal tapes of varying quality.

Fans of dark hard-rock should investigate this band's music.

Williams had earlier been with **The Headstones** and their retrospective CD *24 Hours (Everyday)* also includes **Seompi**'s second and third 45s.

Compilation appearances have included:- *Slide Slide* and *Summer's Coming On Heavy* on *Green Crystal Ties, Vol. 6* (CD); and *Almost In The Whole* on *Brainshadows, Vol. 1* (LP & CD). (CF)

Sequoiah

Personnel:	BILL JOHNSON	A
	BOB JOHNSON	A
	TOM MOBLEY	A

ALBUM: 1(A) SEQUOIAH (700 West 760605) c1973 SC

Released on the same label as **Zerfas**, Modlin and Scott and **Primevil**, **Sequoiah** was a trio playing 6 and 12-string acoustic and electric guitars, bass and percussion. Their music is mainly rural folk-rock and their material include *Trail Of Tears*, *Now She's Gone*, *I Can't Make It Any Better* and *The Sun Shines For You*. Their album was housed in a cover depicting the head of an Indian chief covered with eagles feathers. (SR)

The Serfmen

45s:	Chills And Fever/(I Want You) Back Again	(Nemfres 101) 1964
	A Man Can't Live Without Love/Cry	(Nemfres 101) 1964

An obscure band from Rhode Island. Both 45s had the same catalogue number.

SEOMPI - Seompi LP.

Compilation appearances include: *Cry* on *Time Won't Change My Mind* (LP); *Chills and Fever* on *Garage Punk Unknowns, Vol. 8* (LP). (GG/VJ)

The Serfs

Personnel:
- KENNY BLOOMQUIST — drms — A
- LARRY FAUCETTE — conga — A
- MIKE FINNEGAN — keyb'ds, vcls — A
- FREDDY SMITH — sax, vcls — A
- LANE TIETGEN — gtr, bs, vcls — A
- MARK UNDERWOOD — trumpet, french horn — A

ALBUM: 1(A) THE EARLY BIRD CAFE (Capitol SKAO 207) 1969 -

45: Early Bird Cafe/I'm A Man (Capitol P-2493) 1970

From San Francisco, **The Serfs** were a quite popular live act on the Bay Area scene between 1968 and 1969. Produced by **Tom Wilson**, their album is an interesting blend of psych-blues with some jazz influences. The best moments are the covers (Miles Davis' *All Blue*, Spencer Davis Group's *I'm A Man* and Dylan's *Like A Rolling Stone*), as their original compositions tend to use too much brass.

Their leader, **Mike Finnegan**, had previously released a single on Parkway. He would later work with Dave Mason, became a session man and also released several albums, alone, with Dudek and Kruger or with Jerry Wood.

Larry Faucette played conga on **Hendrix**'s *Electric Ladyland*, while Lane Tietgen would become a songwriter, notably for **Kindred**. (SR)

Serpent Power

Personnel:
- CLARK COOLIDGE — drms — AB
- DENNY ELLIS — ld gtr — A
- DAVID MELTZER — hrmnca, gtr, vcls — AB
- TINA MELTZER — vcls — A
- JOHN PAYNE — organ — A
- JEAN-PAUL PICKENS — banjo — AB
- DAVID STENSON — bs — A
- BOB CUFF — gtr — B
- DAVID MOORE — zhenei — B
- JIM MOSCOSO — bs — B

ALBUM: 1(A) SERPENT POWER (Vanguard VSD 79252) 1967 R1

NB: (1) has had a limited repressing in the eighties and again (Akarma AK 053) 2000. (1) reissued on CD by (Vanguard VMD 79252) 198?. (1) also issued on CD together with **David and Tina Meltzer**'s *Poet Song* (Akarma AK 053/054). A second album was also recorded but not released until 1998 *Green Morning* ( ).

A San Francisco band led by poet **David Meltzer**. He formed the band with his wife Tina in 1966. Ed Denton (then manager of **Country Joe And The Fish**) recommended them to Vanguard after hearing their first gig, a benefit for the Telegraph Group Neighborhood Centre on 27th November 1966. Stenson and Ellis had earlier played with The Grass Roots. The album is notable for some tasty mellow guitar work on tracks such as *Gently Gently* and *Open House*, whilst Tina's beautiful vocals are to the fore on *Flying Away*, a beautiful mellow song. However, the group are probably best remembered for the album's closing track *Endless Tunnel*, an ambitious amalgam of Western and Eastern musical styles. Now a mini collectors' item this album is recommended.

A second album, *Green Morning*, was recorded for Capitol but shelved until its release in 1998.

After the demise of **Serpent Power**, the **Meltzer**'s made a further album, *Poet Song*, which is also worth obtaining.

Bob Cuff later joined the band from **Mystery Trend**. Moscoso later played for The Cleveland Wrecking Co. and eventually became a carpenter in Marin County.

Jean-Paul Pickens, who was one of San Francisco's legendary 'Diggers', and his friend Gene Estribou released an unusual and rare folk album, *Intensifications* (MEA Records) circa 1967. (Pickens plays banjo solos on Side Two!) (VJ/SR/CF)

Sertified Sounds

45: Everyday/Love Is Strange (Tee Pee 25/6) 1967

Strange garage-pop cover of Buddy Holly, from Wisconsin. Produced by Alan Posniak, formerly with the Phaetons and **Golden Catalinas** and the driving force behind Target and Tee Pee records. (MW)

7 Dwarfs

45: Stop Girl/One By One (Ideal 1168) 1967

A fabulous 45 from a Norvelt, Pennsylvania. band who really dug the **Blues Magoos**' style. The 'B' side is a great cover of one of the **Magoos**' better-known ditties but it's *Stop Girl* that's the winner being an astounding pounding poppy fuzzer.

Compilation appearances include: *Stop Girl* on *Sixties Rebellion, Vol. 6* (LP & CD) and *Fuzz, Flaykes, And Shakes, Vol. 5* (LP & CD). (MW)

The Seven of Us

Personnel incl:
- J. (JOHNNY?) DeROBERTIS — — AB
- FRANKIE GADLER — vcls — ABC
- JODY SPAMPANATO — bs — ABC
- TERRY ADAMS — keyb'ds — BC
- STEVE FERGUSON — ld gtr — BC
- TOM (G.T.) STALEY — drms — C
- LEE TIGER — gtr — C

45s: How Could You /
The Way To Your Heart (Red Bird 10-069) 1966
Jamboree / It's Not Easy To Forget (Red Bird 10-080) 1966

A bunch of New Yorkers who put out two very collectible 45s that command high asking prices. Why? Well, these are garagey R&B/soul belters in the style so beloved by "Northern Soul" collectors. *Jamboree* in particular is an incredible stomper that it's absolutely impossible to sit still to.

Another reason for their desirability is that around the end of 1966 the band relocated to Miami, where they were joined by Adams and Ferguson (formerly of Kentucky outfit **Mersey Beats U.S.A.**). In 1968-9 they returned North after changing their name to The New Rhythm and Blues Quintet (**NRBQ**). (MW/JLh)

17th Avenue Exits

45: A Man Can Cry/
Ain't Gonna Eat Out My Heart Anymore (Modern 1035) 1967

THE SERPENT POWER - Serpent Power LP.

A mid-sixties punk band from Mobile, Alabama, managed to get their sole fuzzed-out 45 released by an independent Los Angeles label better known for blues and R&B. Both sides have reappeared on *Sixties Rebellion, Vol. 9 - The Nightclub* (LP & CD) and the *Scarey Business* (CD); the latter Big Beat compilation unearths garage-punk nuggets on the Modern, Titan and Downey labels. (VJ/MW/AP)

7th Cinders

45: You Take Me For Rides/One Day (Greezie 502) 1966

Came out of Newark, New Jersey in the mid-sixties with this pretty good folk-punk 45. *You Take Me For Rides* can also be heard on *Garage Punk Unknowns, Vol. 3* (LP). (VJ)

Seventh Dawn

Personnel:
ANN MUNSON	vcls, acoustic gtr, synth	A
BIL MUNSON	vcls, gtr	A
ERIC MUNSON	vcls, bs	A
HEFF MUNSON	vcls, keyb'ds, synth, drms	A

ALBUM: 1(A) SUNRISE (Fantasy Worlds Unlimited) 1976 R3

NB: (1) Just 200 copies were pressed originally, but it has been reissued (Project Aquarius PA 001) in 1995 as a limited numbered edition of 275.

The tracks comprising this Virginia album date from 1970 thru' 1976. It varies from very soft female-vocal 'folk-psych' to melodic keyboard dominated proggy-rock with flowing guitar. Nothing heavy at all about this quartet. File in the 'hippie-rock' genre because of its gently drifting feel and odes to nature (*The Snail and Robin*), not necessarily as a put-down.

Their album was recorded as a project for an electronic music course at Virginia Commonwealth College. A second album called *Dreams* was recorded but not released. This was a more progressive effort.

The band soldiered on until the early eighties, playing their farewell gig at a college for the deaf! (MW/VJ/JSo)

Seventh Seal

Personnel:
WILLIAM CRAUN	drms	A
MARC FARLEY	bs, vcls	A
DANNY LEGGE	gtr	A
ED "SHRED" SCHROEDER	ld gtr, vcls	ABC
LARRY TRAITOR	vcls	A
BOB ALTIC	organ	B
STEVE HALE	vcls	BC
BRUCE PETERSON	drms	BC
STEVE UPDIKE	bs	BC
RICHARD PRICE	organ	C

ALBUM: 1(A) REFLECTIONS (Justice JLP - 0) 1999

45: People Grow On You/
The Day Before Love (Gama 45-676) 1968

NB: credited to "The 7th Seal".

The quintet, attending college in Bridgewater, Virginia, were previously known as **The English Muffins**. Their album, a limited edition of 400, is taken from tapes for an unreleased Justice album recorded in Winston-Salem, NC in 1967. Whilst many on the Justice label suffer from a dearth of originals and a similar selection of cover material, several originals are included here, which occupy minor-mood introspective garage-ballad territory. *Well I Know* is a fine example and their reworking of *It's My Pride*, from their **English Muffins** repertoire, is very Zombiesque in the vocal arrangements. *Proud Reflections* is a moody jangler. The dark horse and arguably the best track is *Make Your Bed*, a low-key folk-punker that ends surprisingly in a crescendo of drums and feedback.

SEVENTH SEAL - Reflections LP.

Of the covers, *Till The End Of The Day* and *Mister You're A Better Man Than I* are above-par with searing lead guitar. Soulful aspirations are aired in *Midnight Hour* and the **Rascals**' *Come On Up*, whereas blues reign in the near five-minute finale *I've Got A Mind To Give Up Livin'*.

Numerous photos and an insert with the band's history complete a welcome release, certainly one of the most interesting and rewarding from the Justice stable.

By April 1968 and the Gama 45, Schroeder was the sole survivor of the album line-up. Organist Bob Altic had been an early member of the **English Muffins**; he was replaced soon after the 45 by Richard Price. *People Grow On You* is great psych with whispering vox at the beginning and end (sans music) and nice guitar work. The flip, composed by Steve Hale, is a ballad - adequate but nothing exceptional. (MW/FU/BHr)

Seventh Sons

Personnel:
FRANK EVENTOFF	flute	AB
SERGE KATZEN	drms	AB
BUZZY LINHART	vcls, gtr	AB
STEVE DE NAUT	bs	A
JACK ROCK	bs, vcls	B

ALBUM: 1(B) 4.00 AM AT FRANK'S (ESP 1078) 1967 -

NB: (1) sometimes listed as *The Seventh Sons*. Later reissued on CD as *Raga* (ESP 1078) 199? and on 180 gram vinyl (Get Back GET 1038) 1999.

The music on this album is a long raga with voices, flute, guitar and percussions. You either like it or you hate it! The "Frank's" referred to in the album title was not a club but Eventoff's house in Baltimore. **Linhart** later recorded another raga *Sing Joy* on his first solo album. Frank Eventoff was later involved with **The Organgrinders**. (SR/VJ/MW)

Shadden and The King Lears

Personnel:
NORMAN BROWN	ld gtr	ABCD
LARRY COOPER	bs	ABCDE
TERRY HOLDER	keyb'ds	ABCD
PRESTON WILLIAMS	drms	ABCDE
SHADDEN WILLIAMS	vcls	AB
RICHARD BRYANT	keyb'ds	BC
DON SINGLETON	gtr	BCDE
JACK HOLDER	gtr, keyb'ds	DE
JIM BRASHER	trumpet	E
MIKE CREPER	sax	E
DARRELL VENABLE	trumpet	E

45s:	Come Back When You Grow Up Girl /		
	All I Want Is You	(Arbet 1016)	1967
	Knock On Wood / Baby It's Too Late	(Arbet 1017)	1967
	Goodtime Mary-Go-Round / Goodbye Little Girl	(Bell 717)	1968
α	These Changing Times /		
	There Will Be No Tomorrow	(Trump 2829)	1970
α	Come On Down To Earth /		
	New Orleans Ruth	(Trump 2966)	1970

NB: α as Piccadilly Circus

A popular Memphis, Tennessee, pop group who were formed in 1966 by brothers Shadden and Preston Williams. Their debut featured a cover of a Marsha Sharp song and it started to do well in The South. Then teen-crooner Bobby Vee did a near carbon-copy of their version and ended up with a million-seller hit. Ain't life unfair. Two more 45s were released but didn't do so well. After the third, the band expanded with the arrival of Bryant and Singleton from The Funny Company. Then Shadden suddenly quit the band one night at a show following a religious experience and the band were forced to soldier on without him. Some months later they added a horn section, changed their name to Piccadilly Circus and issued two brassy pop 45s on Trump. For much much more on this band and the Memphis sixties scene, pick up Ron Hall's book 'Playing For A Piece Of The Door' (Shangri-La Projects, 2001, ISBN 0-9668575-1-8).

The band's best moment from our viewpoint is *All I Want Is You*. It can be found on the book's companion compilation *A History Of Garage And Frat Bands In Memphis* (CD) and had previously appeared on *The Garage Zone Vol. 3* (LP) and *The Garage Zone Box Set* (4LP + 7"). (MW/RHI)

The Shades (and variations of)

45s:	α	Lookie-Lookie-Lookie/		
		That's The Way The Cards Fall	(Mat 0003)	196?
	β	Tenderly I'll Love You/You Keep Me Coming	(Hub 0001)	196?
		Ginger Bread Man/The Hip	(AOK 1028)	1967
	χ	Search The Sun/		
		Bring Your Love	(International Artists 132)	1969
	χ	Third Number/		
		Profitable Dream	(International Artists 137)	1969

NB: α as KC Grand and The Shades. β as Mack Tubb and The Shades. χ as The Shayds.

This West Texas group changed their name five times in the course of as many records. They started out on their first 45 as K.C. Grand And The Shades. By the time of the follow-up - the 'A' side was a punky ballad, the flip an instrumental - they'd become Mack Tubb And The Shades. Their next incarnation as **The Shades** produced a credible punk-soul song *Ginger Bread Man*. This attracted the attention of International Artists who released their next two efforts under slightly different names. The first of these - a psych/pop 45 - is usually considered their finest moment. The band then underwent a more drastic name change to **Sweet Briar**.

Compilation appearances include: *Ginger Bread Man* on *Punk Classics* (CD), *Flashback, Vol. 6* (LP) and *Green Crystal Ties, Vol. 10* (CD); *Search The Sun* on *Highs In The Mid-Sixties, Vol. 23* (LP); *Ginger Bread Man* (alt. mix), *You Can't Do That* (previously unreleased) and *You Keep Me Going* on *The History Of Texas Garage Bands, Vol. 3 - The AOK Records Story* (CD). (VJ/MW)

The Shades

Personnel incl: D. MEYER
B. SEABOCH
T. WHITING

45s:	When You Said Goodbye/		
	Ballot Bachs	(Princeton PD 7012)	1968
	When You Said Goodbye/Ballot Bachs	(Cadet 5608)	1968

The work of a Chicago-recorded outfit, from Webster City, Iowa. *Ballot Bachs* is an instrumental notable for its mesmerising over-fuzz feed-back guitar and stop-start changes. The uncompiled top-side is an uptempo harmony-pop ditty without a trace of menace - a real Jekyll and Hyde 45.

SEVENTH SONS - 4 A.M. At Franks LP.

Compilation appearances include: *Ballot Bachs* on *Mindrocker, Vol. 3* (LP), *Everything You Always Wanted To Know...* (CD), *Garagelands, Vol. 1 & 2* (CD) and *Garagelands, Vol. 2* (LP). (VJ/MW)

The Shades

Personnel:	DAVID KOCHIE	ld gtr	AB
	TIM OLSON	drms	ABC
	BRYAN SKILLESTAD	gtr	A CD
	DANNY HOLIEN	gtr, vcls	BCD
	DARRELL WIDHOLM	bs	B
	DOVE DOFFING	bs	C
	MIKE LALLY	drms	D

45s:	Please, Please, Please/Summer's Here	(Soma 1437)	1965
	I Feel So Fine/Down The Road Apiece	(Welhaven 4957)	1965

From Cannon Falls in South-East Minnesota, this was the first of two bands fronted by **Holien**. The second being **Midwest**. They later became known as Clover in 1969 and evolved into a power trio.

Compilation appearances include: *Down The Road Apiece* on *The Essential Pebbles Collection, Vol. 1* (Dble CD); *Please, Please, Please* on *Soma Records Story, Vol. 3* (LP); *Summer's Here* on *The Big Hits Of Mid-America* (Dble CD). (VJ/MW)

The Shades

Personnel:	FRANCE ??	A
	NULL ??	A
	SWIDER ??	A

45s:	α	Cry Over You /		
		5th Of September	(RKO Sound Studio)	1964
	α	I Need You / Are You A Boy	(RKO Sound Studio)	196?
		Cry Over You / The 5th Of September	(Rapa 2010)	1964
		I Need You / With My Love	(Encore 1002-ARC)	1966
		Everybody Needs Somebody / Walk On By	(France 45-39)	1967

NB: α acetate only.

The 45s above may be by two different bands but the acetates listed had appeared to tie them together. The following is still to be untangled: Previously this was thought to be one band from Corona, NY who released another unconfirmed 45 (*Nowhere Man* / *Malaguena*) and whose members were in the **Go-Betweens**. More recently, however, Mike Markesich traced the band to Akron, Ohio, but this **Shades** apparently released only the 45s on Encore and Frances.

Until this conflicting info is finally resolved, enjoy *I Need You* (moody fuzz'n'farfisa with jangley shades of the **Leaves**' *Hey Joe*) and *With My*

Love (a mean stompin' punker with echoes of Them's *Gloria*) - both are on *Psychedelic Crown Jewels, Vol. 3* (CD); *I Need You* on *The Night Is So Dark* (LP); and *With My Love* on *Yeah Yeah Yeah* (CD) and *It's A Hard Life* (LP). (MW/MM)

The Shades

45:	Fire / Come On Up (+ 1)	(Joslin 1) 196?

Another **Shades** from Michigan this time with a rare three-track 45 that fetches big bucks and reportedly features a pre-pubescent vocalist. They may also be responsible for another 45 - *Sower And His Seeds / ?* (Out-Of-Site 2454). (MW)

Shades, Inc.

Personnel:	MARIO COMBO	drms	A
	TOM MURASSO		A
	PAT SMITH	bs	A
	JIM STATES	gtr	A
	SPIKE WARNER	ld gtr	A
	RANDY WOOLEY	ld vcls	A

45s:	Who Loved Her/Sights	(Abstract 4604) 1966
	Don't Run My Life /	
α	There Goes My Life	(Criteria Studios) c1966
α	Just Walk Away	(Criteria Studios) c1966

NB: α acetate only.

From Miami, Florida. *Who Loved Her*, a cool slab of minor-mood jangle-beat from the Searchers school, is featured on *Psychedelic States: Florida, Vol. 1* (CD). *Sights* is a psychy pop-punker with a mandolin solo, and is on *Psychedelic States: Florida Vol. 3* (CD). A subsequent line-up included Tom Murasso, who went on to The Heat Machine and The Sault Shaquer.

Spike Warner later played in **Southern Steel**. (MW/JLh)

Shades of Black Lightning Soul

Personnel incl:	BILLY FORD	vcls	A

ALBUM:	1	SHADES OF BLACK LIGHTNING SOUL
		(Tower ST 5129) 1968 SC

45:	Love In/Got Myself Together	(Tower 450) 1968

A Californian short-lived combo who is sometimes described as psychedelic. Produced by Freddie Piro and Billy Ford (their leader and songwriter), it's in fact a R&B quintet heavily influenced by Sam and Dave, the early **Chambers Brothers** and other similar groups. The cover depicts their black silhouettes on a green background and two of them are holding trombones! (VJ/SR)

The Shades of Blue

ALBUM:	1	HAPPINESS IS THE SHADES OF BLUE
		(Impact 1001) 1966 -

NB: There's also a compilation *Golden Classics* (Collectables) 199?.

			HCP
45s:	Oh, How Happy/Little Orphan Boy	(Impact 1007) 1966	12
	Lonely Summer/With This Ring	(Impact 101 4) 1966	72
	Happiness/The Night	(Impact 1015) 1966	78
	How Do You Say A Dying Love?/		
	All I Want Is Love	(Impact 1026) 1967	-
	Penny Arcade/Funny Kind Of Love	(Impact 1028) 1967	-

Edwin Starr discovered this Detroit-based quartet (three men, one woman) who enjoyed some minor chart success. Their album, which was of the psychedelic pop genre, is now a minor collectors' item but the recent Collectables retrospective is probably easier to obtain.

Oh How Happy, *Lonely Summer*, *How Do You Save A Dying Love* and *Penny Arcade* can be heard on another Collectables CD, *The Best Of Impact Records*. (VJ/MW)

The Shades of Blue

Personnel:	TIM FRAZIER	ld vcls, bs	A
	RICK MILLER	drms	A
	CHUCK OLMSTED	ld gtr, brass, vcls	A
	CLOYD SHANK	gtr, vcls	A
	MICHAEL SUPP	ld vcls, keyb'ds	A

45s:	You Must Believe Me/That's Not The Way	
	That Love Should Be	(Shades 836R-1030) 1967
	The Time Of My Life / Turn Turn Turn	(Shades 600) 1969

A different **Shades Of Blue** from Danville, Illinois, with a frantic garage cover of Curtis Mayfield's *You Must Believe Me*. They were together between 1965-69 and were known mostly for and prided themselves in their multiple-part harmonies. Their original manager and high school friend, Irving Azoff later went on to manage amongst others REO Speedwagon and The Eagles. (MW/MSp)

Shades of Darkness

Personnel:	NICK BATTAGLIA	drms	A
	PETER CHIMENTO	ld vcls, gtr	A
	TOM CONTI	bs	A
	JIM GLOFF	ld gtr	A

45:	She Ain't Worth All That /	
	Someone Better	(Shades 71031) 1967

Members of this previously unheralded quartet came from the communities of Fredonia and Dunkirk, New York. *She Ain't...* is an excellent garage-pop swinger with plaintive vocals and a dexterous workout on keening guitar. It is featured on *Psychedelic States: New York Vol. 1* (CD) whose liners reveal that the band used to make regular trips across the border to Toronto to check out the likes of The Ugly Ducklings. (MW)

The Shades of Night

45:	Such A Long Time/Fluctuation	(Alamo Audio 111) 1966

A Dallas garage band.

Compilation appearances include: *Fluctuation* on *Open Up Yer Door, Vol. 2* (LP), *Pebbles, Vol. 3 (ESD)* (CD), *Texas Flashbacks, Vol. 3* (CD) and *Flashback, Vol. 3* (LP). (VJ)

The Shadow Casters

45s:	It'll Be Too Late/Goin' To The Moon	(JRP 002) 1966
	Cinnamon Snowflake/But Not Today	(JRP 003) 1966

Hailed from Aurora, Illinois. *Cinnamon Snowflake* is a laid back folk-rocker, whilst both *It'll Be Too Late* and *Goin' To The Moon* are rather primitive and lightweight affairs.

Compilation appearances include: *Cinnamon Snowflake* on *Psychotic Moose And The Soul Searchers* (LP); *It'll Be Too Late* on *Garage Zone, Vol. 2* (LP) and *The Garage Zone Box Set* (4-LP). (VJ/MW)

Shadow Mann

ALBUM:	1	COME LIVE WITH ME
		(Tomorrow's Productions TPS 60001) 1968 SC

45s:	Come Live With Me/	
	One By One	(Tomorrow's Productions TP 0001) 1968

NB: released in the U.K. on Roulette (RO 504) 1969.

Late sixties New York freak-attack one might think from the tracks featured on *Turds On A Bum Ride, Vol. 3* (CD) (*Shadow Mann* and *You Gotta Be Me*). However, the 45 shows the other side - insipid orchestrated studio cash-in pop. Both sides were written by Art Wayne and arranged by Paul Harris.

Shadow Mann is actually Shadow Morton, Phil Spector's only real rival, who produced The Shangri-Las amongst others. The album is a more than uneven affair but I'm told it has its moments. (VJ/MW/SR)

The Shadows Four

Personnel incl:
RON BORELLI	ld gtr, bs, vcls	A
DONNIE GELAIDES	bs, gtr, vcls	A
JOEY SALEMI	drms, vcls	A
BILL TRAINOR	ld gtr, vcls	A

45s:		
Follow Me/Heart Of Wood	(Fleetwood 4553)	1966
I'm Beggin' You/Summertime	(DME 200,964/5)	1966

From Woburn and Revere, Massachusetts, they took their name from the U.K. Shadows, of whom lead guitarist Bill Trainor was (and still is) a big fan. The first 45 was never actually issued and the band did not get copies, even though they ended up suing Fleetwood Recording. Some copies were pressed, however and a few are in the hands of collectors.

The band were also sponsored by Vox instruments and toured with the movie 'How To Stuff A Wild Bikini' in the Summer of 1965. The following October, they became the first instrumental group to perform at 'The Boston Music Hall'

Bill Trainor had to join the service before the second record was recorded, which accounts for the lightweight sound. After he returned from service the band lasted for a few more years, recording several demos of cool late sixties pop-rock. The early line-up also made many unreleased recordings of rock instrumental standards.

Compilation appearances have included: *Heart Of Wood* and *I'm Beggin' You* on *New England Teen Scene* (CD); *Heart Of Wood* and *Follow Me* on *New England Teen Scene, Vol. 1* (LP); *I'm Beggin' You* on *New England Teen Scene, Vol. 2* (LP). (GGI/MW/BT)

The Shadows of Knight

Personnel:
NORM GOTSCH	gtr	AB
WAYNE PURSELL	bs	A
WARREN RODGERS	gtr, bs	AB
TOM SCHIFFOUR	drms	ABC
JIM SOHNS	vcls	ABCD
JOE KELLEY	bs, ld gtr	BC
JERRY McGEORGE	gtr	C
DAVE WOLINSKI	bs, keyb'ds	C
DAN BAUGHMAN	gtr	D
JOHN FISHER	bs	D
KENNY TURKIN	drms	D
WOODY WOODROFF	ld gtr	D
ERIC BLOMQUIST		E
JACK DANIELS	ld gtr	E
BOB HARPER		E
CHARLIE HESS		E
GARY LEVIN		E

HCP
ALBUMS:				
1(C)	GLORIA	(Dunwich SD 666)	1966	46 SC
2(C)	BACK DOOR MEN	(Dunwich SD 667)	1966	- SC/R1
3(D)	SHADOWS OF KNIGHT	(Super K SKS 6002)	1969	- -
4(-)	GEE-EL-O-AIRE-I-AY	(Edsel ED157)	1985	- -
5( )	LIVE	(DONE 5CD)	199?	- -
6( )	RAW 'N' ALIVE AT THE CELLAR CLUB 1966	(Sundazed 5006)	1992	- -
7( )	SUPER K COLLECTION	(COL-CD-0581)	199?	- -
8( )	ONE WAY, SHAKE	(COL-CD-30331)	199?	- -
9( )	DARK SIDES - THE BEST OF...	(Rhino R2 71723)	1994	- -

THE SHADOWS FOUR.

NB: (1) reissued on Radar (RAD 11) 1979 in the UK. (1) reissued (Sundazed LP 5034) 1998, also on CD (Sundazed SC 6155) 1998. (2) reissued (Sundazed LP 5035) 1998, also on CD (Sundazed SC 6156) 1998. (5) is a 7-track mini CD. (6) is a previously unreleased live album. Also on CD (SC 11013).

HCP
45s:				
	Gloria/Dark Side	(Dunwich 45-116)	1966	10
	Oh Yeah/Light Bulb Blues (PS)	(Dunwich 45-122)	1966	39
	Bad Little Women/Gospel Zone (PS)	(Dunwich 45-128)	1966	91
	I'm Gonna Make You Mine/ I'll Make You Sorry	(Dunwich 45-141)	1966	90
	Willie Jean/The Behemoth	(Dunwich 45-151)	1967	-
	Someone Like Me/Three For Love	(Dunwich 45-167)	1967	-
	The Potato Chip Record(5" Columbia S.P. Cardboard Disc)/ The Potato Chip Record(5" Columbia S.P. Cardboard Disc)	(Auravision)	1967	-
α	Shake/From Way Out To Way Under	(Team 520)	1968	46
	My Fire Dept. Needs A Fireman/Taurus	(Super K SK-8)	1969	-
	My Fire Dept. Needs A Fireman/ Run Run Billy Porter	(Super K SK-1 0)	1969	-
β	Gloria '69/Spaniard At My Door	(Atco 6634)	1969	-
	I Am The Hunter/Warwick Court Affair	(Atco 6776)	1970	-
	Gloria/Dark Side (reissue)	(Atlantic 13138)	1971	-
χ	I Got My Mojo Working/ Potato Chip + Interview	(Sundazed S 123)	1996	-

NB: *Gospel Zone* was also released as a one-sided promo in 1966. χ contains two previously unreleased tracks. The 'A' side is a rare alternate version while the 'B' side is a radio ad with interview. α and β also released in France (Buddah 610 020 and Atco 81). There's also a French EP *Oh Yea* (with the typo!) /*It Always Happens That Way*/*Gloria*/*Dark Side* (Atco 113) and a French single, *Gospel Zone*/*Bad Little Woman* (Atco 28). These four French releases have picture sleeves with photographs of the group.

A garage band from Chicago, formed in 1964 by Warren Rodgers, Norm Gotsch and Wayne Pursell, who went to Prospect High School in Mt. Prospect, Illinois. They took their name after the UK act The Shadows, adding the "Knight" reference from their high school mascot and recruited Jim Sohns. Strongly influenced by the Brit-Invasion sounds, they even started a teen-club The Cellar, named in honour of The Cavern Club.

The original line-up was discovered playing a showcase concert at the Cellar Club in Chicago's Arlington Heights which was being staged to attract talent spotters from record companies. Bill Traut and George Badonsky of Dunwich Records bit the bait and the band was signed up and went on to give this hitherto obscure label its major national success.

Before the release of their debut 45, however, Wayne Pursell was replaced by Joe Kelley (ex-**The Vectors**) in September 1965, and in December, Norm Gotsch was also replaced by Jerry McGeorge.

Their restrained version of Van Morrison's classic song with Them, *Gloria*, was chosen for their debut 45 because it was the band's showstopper. It made No. 10 in the charts, giving them their only Top 20 hit. Tom

THE SHADOWS OF KNIGHT - Gloria LP.

Schiffour's machine-gun drumming over the final choruses perhaps gave it a distinctive edge. By contrast the flip, *Dark Side* was a haunting melodic piece, in contrast to the bands other material... it turns out that this track was written by Wayne Pursell, but copyrighted in Warren Roger and Jim Sohns names, after Wayne had left the band. Shortly after the 45s release, Warren Rogers and Jerry McGeorge swapped bass/lead guitar roles.

The Shadows Of Knight's debut album, recorded during March/April 1966, was flush with cover versions of classics like *I Got My Mojo Working*, *Hoochie Coochie Man* and *Oh Yeah*. The album climbed to No. 46 in the U.S. Album Charts and provided their second single, *Oh Yeah*, a Bo Diddley cover. **The Shadows Of Knight**'s version climbed to a tremendous climax of blasting fuzz guitars and just made it to the lower reaches of the U.S. Top 40. Their third 45, *Bad Little Woman*, a reinterpretation of a very obscure British R&B single by The Wheels was another guitar extravaganza and coupled with its rather weird-sounding 'B' side *Gospel Zone*, which was dominated by wildly overechoed percussion, some regard this as their finest hour. In commercial terms, however, it was less successful peaking at No. 91.

The band's second album, *Back Door Men* was a mixture of cover versions and originals. It provided more examples of their Bo Diddley-inspired sound and of Joe Kelley's superb guitar work. However, the band were now beset again by personnel problems with Dave Wolinski, (of The Males), who'd played keyboards on some tracks on the second album joining to replace Warren Rogers, who was kicked out of the band after a gig and subsequently drafted into the U.S. Army. This line-up cut a raw version of *I Got My Mojo Working* in December 1966, which was later included on the 1972 compilation *Early Chicago* (Happy Tiger (HT 101 7). Two more 45s were recorded, *Willie Jean* and *Someone Like Me*, but neither enjoyed any commercial success. Indeed the last one didn't feature the group at all, as the band had disbanded in July 1967, but was the work of Jim Sohns and a group of session musicians. Of the departing members, Wolinski and Schiffour formed **Bangor Flying Circus** and Jerry McGeorge joined **H.P. Lovecraft**. This concluded their first musical phase during which they played punkish and R&B numbers.

Next, Jim Sohns (who'd had the band's name copyrighted in his name) put together an entirely new line-up (D) which recorded the album for Super K and lasted through until mid-1970. During this 'bubblegum' phase they enjoyed another minor hit with the Kasenetz-Katz produced *Shake*, which was also very big regionally. When they fell apart Sohns got together line-up (E) which played heavy metal music. Indeed Sohns kept the band together gigging on the local circuit with various personnel for most of the seventies. With the dawning of the 'punk' era of the late seventies came a new interest in mid-sixties garage bands of the first 'punk' era. Passport were keen to sign them in 1977, but only if they reverted back to their sixties image and style, which they refused to do.

Compilation appearances have included: *Someone Like Me* on *Mindrocker, Vol. 2* (LP), *The Seventh Son* (LP); *Oh Yeah*, *I'm Gonna Make You Mine* and *Bad Little Woman* on *Nuggets Box* (4-CD); *Oh Yeah* on *Nuggets - Original Artyfacts From The First Psychedelic Era 1965-1968* (Dble LP) and *Nuggets, Vol. 6* (LP); *Gloria* and *I'm Gonna Make You Mine* on *Nuggets, Vol. 2* (LP); *Oh Yeah* (LP version), *Light Bulb Blues*, *Uncle Wiggly's Airship* (unreleased) and *Interview/Potato Chip* on *Oh Yeah! The Best Of Dunwich Records* (CD); *Potato Chip* (which was originally issued on a 5" cardboard record and given away with Fairmont Potato Chips in 1967 as part of a potato chip promotion campaign) on *Pebbles, Vol. 1* (CD), *Pebbles Box* (5-LP), *Pebbles, Vol. 1* (LP), *Great Pebbles* (CD) and *Trash Box* (5-CD); *Bad Little Woman* on *Songs We Taught The Fuzztones* (Dble LP & Dble CD); *I Got My Mojo Working* on *The Dunwich Records Story* (LP), *Sundazed Sampler, Vol. 1* (CD); *I'm Gonna Make You Mine* on *Turds On A Bum Ride, Vol. 1* (Dble LP) and *Turds On A Bum Ride, Vol. 1 & 2* (Dble CD); *Taurus* on *Turds On A Bum Ride, Vol. 4* (CD) and *Filling The Gap* (4-LP); *Shake* on *Battle Of The Bands* (CD), *Bubble Gum Music Is... The Naked Truth* (LP) and *Pop Explosion*; *Gloria* on *Even More Nuggets* (CD) and *Highs Of The Sixties*; *I'm Gonna Make You Mine*, *Bad Little Woman* and *I Got My Mojo Working* on *If You're Ready - The Best Of Dunwich... Vol. 2* (CD).

The Sundazed *Raw 'N' Alive At The Cellar Club 1966* is an amazing slab of raw R&B and shows why this band are so revered, but there are several other retrospectives and their material is well worth investigating.

Of the best known line-up, Joe Kelley departed to form his own blues band, which also included Tom Schiffour; Jerry McGeorge joined **H.P. Lovecraft** and Dave Wolinski firstly went on to the **Bangor Flying Circus** and later Rufus. He has also worked with Quincy Jones and Michael Jackson. Wayne Pursell started a band called "The" which later became **The Regiment**. (VJ/LP/SR)

The Shadows of Time

Personnel:	BRIAN CHASE	keyb'ds, vcls	A
	RICK ECK	bs, vcls	A
	JOHN "SHORTY" HILL	ld gtr, vcls	A
	JOHN LOWELL	rhythm gtr, vcls	A
	BILL ROBERTS	drms	A
	OODY SMITH	vcls	A

45:	Search Your Soul/My Girl	(Sol 201) 1969

A Boston-based band whose superb *Search Your Soul*, originally released on the Sol label in the Fall of '69, was written and sung by Brian Chase. It's a superb garage disc with lots of fine guitar, fuzz and echo. The 45 was produced by Ray Fournier, who was also responsible for engineering much of the music for the Cambridge-based Polaris label.

The original name of the band was "The Shadows" - but fearing a lawsuit from the better known British act, was soon changed. John "Shorty" Hill:- "The band had been together for about five years when *Search Your Soul* was recorded (we stayed together through high school, and then a bit beyond). We broke up shortly after that. Brian, John Lowell and I then

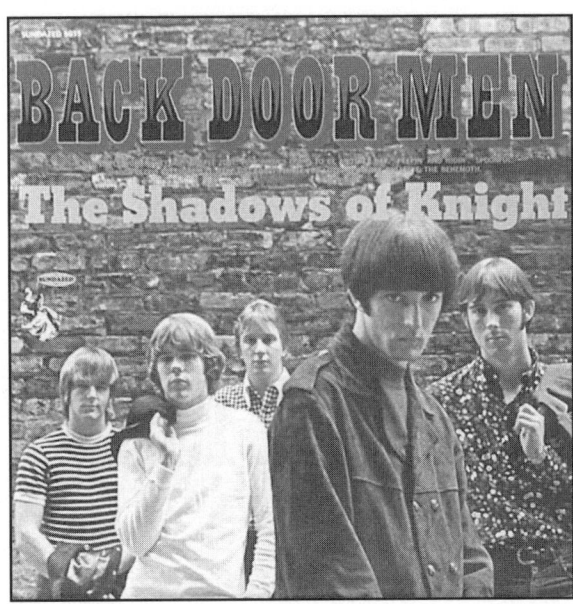

THE SHADOWS OF KNIGHT - Back Door Men LP.

formed Lord Timothy, and as such we played together throughout Northern New England for several more years. Brian and John also later played together in **Owl**".

"After Lord Timothy I played the New England club scene with various rock bands - American Stone, Sugarbear and The Full Moon Travelling Band. In 1976 I formed Shorty Hill and The Longhaulers, which built quite a following playing small combo swing music. I'm still actively playing guitar - now with A Little On The Side."

Search Your Soul can also now be heard on *An Overdose Of Heavy Psych* (CD) and *New England Teen Scene, Vol. 3* (LP). (MW/VJ//BE/JH)

Shadrack

Personnel:	DAN DODGER	drms	A
	STEVE FOX	gtr, bs, vcls	A
	(RANDY BERKA	gtr, vcls	A)
	(JOHN BRANSGARD	gtr	A)
	(JON PORTER	organ	A)
	(ARTIE STRUTZENBERG	drms	A)

ALBUM: 1(A) CHAMELEON (IGL 4051-5) 1971 R2/R3

NB: (1) had a limited vinyl repress in 1987 (STLP 132). Later reissued officially on CD with bonus tracks by Gear Fab (GF-110) 1997 and on vinyl in replica sleeve by Gear Fab (GF-202) 1997.

45: It Was Me/I Wonder Why (Sonic 202) 1971

This outfit came from Humboldt, Iowa and this album is one of only three rock albums issued on the IGL/Sonic labels, which were based in Milford, Iowa. Musically, it has that early seventies progressive feel (although some collectors describe it as a Neil Young type rural rock-folk). Pleasant guitar folk with some psychedelic influences. Earlier Steve Fox and Randy Berka issued a 45 on Sonic.

The prolific reissue label, Gear Fab have recently reissued the album on CD with bonus tracks, as well as a vinyl version.

This group has no relation to another "Shadrack" who recorded an eponymous LP (GRT 8024) 1977, a country/folk trio with female vocals.

Compilation appearances include *Granite Feast* on Gear Fab's *Psychedelic Sampler* (CD). (VJ/SR)

Shady Days

Personnel incl:	FREDDIE GLICKSTEIN	A
	LES KUMMEL	A

45: That's How Strong My Love Is/Little Girl (RPR 104) 1967

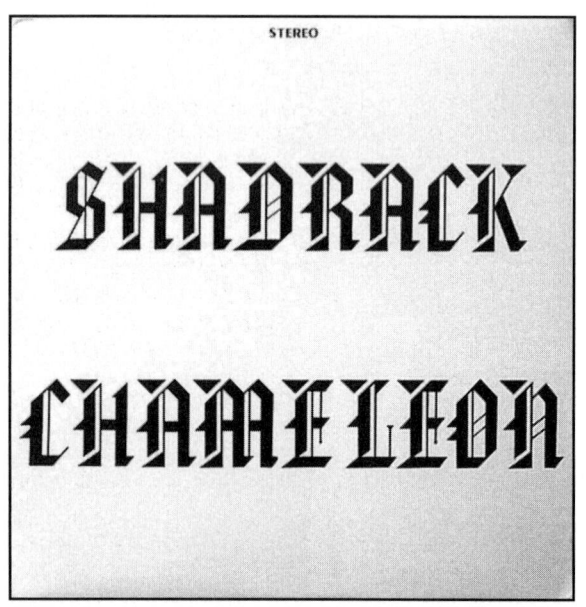

SHADRACK - Chameleon LP.

A soulful garage 45 backed by a light folk-rocker on the same label as **The Beautiful Daze**. This was in fact the work of **The Revelles**, from Chicago, and was a reissue of two early 45 cuts originally released on the "Jim-Ko" label. (VJ/MW)

Shady Daze

Personnel:	MARK DRZIEWICKI	drms	AB
	KURT GORE	bs	A
	BILL JORDAN	vcls	AB
	GREGG OWEN	keyb'ds	AB
	GLENN RUPP	gtr	AB
	GREG BIELA	bs	B

EP: 1 I'll Make You Pay/Love Is A Beautiful Thing/
Dennis Dupree From Danville/
You Don't Know Like I Know (Sundazed SEP 110) 1996

45s: Love Is A Beautiful Thing/I'll Make You Pay (USA 883) 1967
Dennis Dupree From Danville/
You Don't Know Like I Know (It's A Gass 6831) 1968

The **Shady Daze** were formed in the Summer of 1966, out of the remnants of the Travel-Aires (Gore and Owen) and the Silhouettes (Drziewicki, Jordan and Rupp). Kurt Gore had earlier played in the Roustabouts in 1965, prior to joining the Travel-Aires with Gregg Owen in 1965-66.

Best known for their original fuzz punker *I'll Make You Pay* (co-written by Drziewicki, Jordan and Rupp), the '**Daze** were more adept at playing the top 40 fare of the day, citing the **Young Rascals** as particular favorites. In fact, it was a '**Rascals** cover that comprised the 'A' side of the band's first single, *Love Is A Beautiful Thing* b/w the aforementioned *I'll Make You Pay*. Though the 'B' side is now rightly considered a classic of the garage punk era, the 'A' side did manage to chart in '67 in such locales as Green Bay, Wisconsin and St. Joseph, Michigan. During this time, the **Shady Daze** were regularly booked at the Blue Village in Westmont, Illinois, a club (owned by the band's manager, Robert Chappelow) that advertised itself as "The Home Of The Shady Daze".

Kurt Gore:- "We (The Shady Daze) were friends with other contemporary Chicago groups including **Saturdays Children**, **The Cryan' Shames**, **The Mauds** and **The Shadows of Knight**. In fact, for a while **The Cryan' Shames** also rehearsed at The Blue Village and taught us how to play their hit *It Could Be We're In Love*."

During its three year existence, the **Shady Daze** played alongside the **Music Explosion**, **Buffalo Springfield** and **The Doors**, among others. They also appeared on the Chicago TV programs "Kiddie A-Go-Go" and "Swinging Majority", where the band lip-synching *I'll Make You Pay* live on-air. Before disbanding in 1969, the group released their second and final single on the It's A Gass label (also owned by Chappelow), *Dennis Dupree From Danville* b/w *You Don't Know Like I Know*.

Kurt Gore, Bill Jordan, Gregg Owen, Glen Rupp and Greg Biela all went on to play in later line-ups of **The American Breed**. Kurt Gore also played with Bonnie Kolac in 1970.

Sundazed has released an EP containing both of the band's singles and *I'll Make You Pay* has been compiled on the *Mindrocker, Vol. 2* (LP) and *Pebbles, Vol. 6* (CD). *Dennis Dupree* is a cover of a **Cryan' Shames** ditty. (MDo/MW/KGe)

The Shag(s)

Personnel:	PAUL "GREEN" GREENWALD	drms	A
	MIKE LAMERS	gtr	A
	DON LUTHER		A
	JOHN SAHLI	gtr	A
	GORDY ELLIOT	ld gtr	
	RAY McCALL	gtr	

45s: α Cause I Love You/Dance Woman (Raynard 10034) 1965
Stop And Listen/Melissa (Capitol 5995) 1967

NB: α as by **The Shags**.

From Milwaukee, Wisconsin, this band were originally known as The Shags. On December 30th 1965, they appeared at the Milwaukee Auditorium amongst a dozen local outfits for the Milwaukee Sentinel Rock'n'Roll Revue. Captured on the lo-fi compilation album of that name (Century 23214, 1966) is their version of the Stones' *Get Off Of My Cloud*. Their *Stop And Listen* was an above average punk song with a catchy guitar riff and lyrics that were indicative of the times:-

"Everybody's goin'
Everybody's tripping,
Everybody tells you what you've been missing."
(From *Stop And Listen*)

Compilation appearances have included: *Stop & Listen* on *Pebbles, Vol. 5* (CD), *Pebbles Box* (5-LP), *Acid Dreams - The Complete 3 LP Set* (3-LP), *Acid Dreams Epitaph* (CD), *Trash Box* (5-CD), *Boulders, Vol. 1* (LP), *Great Pebbles* (CD) and *Highs In The Mid-Sixties, Vol. 10* (LP). (VJ/MW/AB/GM)

The Shaggs

Personnel:	BETTY WIGGIN	drms	A
	DOROTHY WIGGIN	gtr	A
	HELEN WIGGIN	gtr	A

ALBUMS:	1(A)	PHILOSOPHY OF THE WORLD	(Third World 3001) 1972 R4
	2(A)	SHAGGS OWN THING	(Rounder/Red Rooster) 1982 -

NB: (1) later reissued on Rounder (3032) and Red Rooster (103) in 1980. (1) and (2) have also been reissued on one CD by Rounder.

From Fremont, New Hampshire and completely uncommercial, **The Shaggs** are quite unlike any other group. Their father, Austin Wiggin, rented time in a recording studio so the girls could sing their songs and paid for the pressing of 2,000 copies of their debut album.

The instrumental backing on their album is fractured, the guitars sound out of tune, the harmonies warped and the lyrics innocent and childlike. However, it's precisely the amateurishness of their records that give them their curiosity value. Musically, they are so bad as to be a novelty item, which is probably why it was so sought-after by collectors prior to its reissue in 1982.

A live version of *My Pal Foot Foot* has subsequently resurfaced on *Only In America* (CD). (VJ)

The Shaggs

Personnel incl:	CRAIG CARAGLIOR	gtr, ld gtr, vcls	ABCD
	RICHIE CHIMELIS	vcls	AB
	CLEVE JOHNS	gtr, vcls	ABCD
	MIKE LATONA	bs	A
	DENNIS O'BARRY	ld gtr	A
	GREGG SHAW	drms	AB
	DON RICKETTS	bs	BC
	JACQUES HEIDEIER	vcls, perc	CDE
	DOUG ROMANELLA	drms	CDE
	MARK WATSON	keyb'ds	CDE
	CHRIS DIEGUEZ	bs	D
	TERRY McCAREY	ld gtr	E
	LARRY O'CONNELL	bs	E

45s:	It's Too Late/Anytime	(Abco 1002) 1965
	The Way I Care/Ring Around The Rosie	(Palmer 5010) 1966
	Hummin'/I Who Have Nothing	(Power P-103) 1967
	Mean Woman Blues/She Makes Me Happy	(Capitol 2511) 1969

From Miami, Florida, they apparently spelt **Shaggs** with two "g's" after drummer Gregg Shaw's last name. In 1967, they had a personnel swaparound with **Kollektion** and, by 1968, no original members were left.

Their third 45 on Power adopted the sound favoured by those infamous Long Island-sound outfits. *Hummin'* bridges the gap twixt the strident tones and electricity of **The Blues Magoos** and the blue-eyed soul of **The Young Rascals** - and comes off well. The flip is a 'power ballad' in **Vanilla Fudge** style.

HIGHS IN THE MID-SIXTIES Vol. 10 (Comp LP) including The Shag.

There's an interesting story behind the Capitol 45.... The Miami **Shaggs** spent much of 1966 touring Michigan and became very popular in Detroit, where they played alongside many of the Hideout-type bands. This explains why their second 45 came out on the Palmer label. They returned to Florida where they would cut their final 45 on Power in late 1967. Meanwhile their manager Ray Skop had elected to stay in Detroit. He assembled a completely new **Shaggs** from local musicians and would eventually secure a deal with Capitol.

Mean Woman Blues has been described as Roy Orbison fronting a garage band. The flip is highly-rated, described by Mike Markesich as "killer power pop/garage".

Skop was a former teacher at Southwest Miami Senior High School and also the manager of **The Modds**.

Ring Around The Rosie can also be found on *From The New World* (LP). (JLh/MW/JBn)

Shaggs

Personnel:	GEOFF GILLETTE	keyb'ds, gtr, vcls	A
	FRANKLIN KRAKOWSKI	drms	A
	RICK MEDICH	vcls	A
	TED POULOS	gtr, vcls	A
	RAY WHEATLEY	bs, vcls	A

ALBUM:	1(A)	WINK	(MCM 6311) 1967 R3

NB: (1) reissued on Resurrection (CX 1295) in the mid-eighties.

Despite the year this album could have come from '65-'66. One of those mega-rare releases that serious collectors will kill for, it fits into the 'prep-rock' niche, though this is not yet another Phillips Academy outfit but a five-piece from the campus of Notre Dame University, South Bend, Indiana. The liner notes tell us that it was recorded on March 14th, 1967 at the International Recording Studio in one 20-hour session. "Engineers Perry Johnson and Verner Ruualds amazed. Probably recording history". 'Fraid not chaps but a nice try!! 10 predictable covers and two originals in a soft melodic folk-rock style - no fuzz 'n' farfisa ravers here - though they do get more frantic on *My Generation* and *Let's Spend The Night Together*.

Probably successful businessmen, professionals or brain surgeons now(*), the quintet may curl up with embarrassment when reminded of this platter but they'll surely scour the attic for lost copies when they hear what collectors will pay for an original! And, with this entry, they've a place in history too.

NB: (*) Geoff Gillette is thought to subsequently have a had a career as a producer/recording engineer. (MW/JSs)

The Shags

Personnel:
- CARL AUGUSTO — ld gtr — A
- BILL HALL — bs — A
- FRANK PERKINS — ld vcls — A
- JOHNNY TANDREDI — drms — A
- TOMMY VIOLANTE — gtr — A

45s:
- It Hurts Me Bad/Wait And See (Nutta 101) 1965
- By My Side/'Cause Of You (Sammy SA-1 01 /2) 1965
- Don't Press Your Luck/Hey Little Girl (Taurus 1881) 1966
- I Call Your Name/Hideaway (Laurie 3353) 1966
- As Long As I Have You/Tell Me (Kayden 407) 1967
- Breathe In My Ear/Easy Street (Kayden 408) 1967
- As Long As I Have You/Tell Me (Cameo 470) 1967

Formed in late 1963 by Tommy Violante with a few high school friends: Carl Augusto, Rich Ventura, and Jeff Cannata. This initial line-up never played professionally, although the **Shags** quickly began to gig including an appearance at Frankie's Restaurant in Orange at a wedding, with Tommy, Carl, Jeff, and Mike Goodwin on bass.

In '64 they were known as The Deltons and absorbed Beatles influences. By '65 they had reverted to **The Shags** moniker and over the next couple of years had a number of hits locally in New Haven, Connecticut. These included *Wait And See* (1965), *By My Side*, (1966) and *I Call Your Name* (1966). Though most of their material is pop-beat, but *Breathe In My Ear* is a tougher punker with some ear-splitting guitar and pounding keyboards.

In 1967, Tommy Violante and Carl Augusto formed **The Pulse**, along with members of **The Bram Rigg Set**.

Today Violante still performs with the "Key West Trio", a Jimmy Buffett cover band that also does Beach Boys and a few fifties and sixties covers, doing gigs mainly in the Northeast area. The excellent Gear Fab label may be compiling a retrospective of **The Shags** material in the not too distant future... watch this space!!

Compilation coverage to date has included: *Hide Away* on *Mindrocker, Vol. 3* (LP); *Don't Press Your Luck* on *New England Teen Scene* (CD) and *New England Teen Scene, Vol. 1* (LP); *Hey Little Girl* on *Sixties Rebellion, Vol. 6* (LP & CD); *Tell Me* on *Realities In Life* (LP); *Wait And See* on *Bad Vibrations, Vol. 3* (LP); and *Breathe In My Ear* on *Fuzz Flaykes & Shakes, Vol. 1* (LP & CD). (VJ/MW)

The Shags

Personnel:
- JOHN GINKEL — drms — AB
- TOM GINKEL — ld gtr — AB
- BRUCE MELZER — bs — AB
- JOHN VOLINKATY — gtr — A
- JIM HUGHES — bs — B

45: Louis Louis/Summertime News (Concert 1-78-65) 1965

New Ulm in Southern Minnesota was home to the makers of this raw garage 45, the 'A' side being one of several covers of **The Kingsmens**' legendary song. The flip side was actually a cover of Eddie Cochran's *Summertime Blues* but the Concert label, which was one guy working out of a basement, managed to misspell it as *Summertime News*. **The Kingsmen**'s song was misspelt too! Eventually Bruce Melzer left to join the Navy and was replaced by Jim Hughes. They soldiered on for about a year until John Volinkaty moved up to Minneapolis at which point John Ginkel became drummer in another New Ulm band, **The Depressions**. Tom Ginkel became a school teacher in 1970 and formed a weekend band called Clover, who went on to record a 45 and an album.

Compilation appearances include *Louis Louis* on *Mondo Frat Dance Bash A Go Go* (CD) and *When The Time Run Out* (LP & CD). (VJ)

The Shags

Personnel incl:
- PAUL BOOE — AB
- BILL MELTON — AB
- CARL MEURN — AB
- TOM MORGAN — AB
- SCOTT SOMERVILLE — A
- DICK WESSELS — AB

45s:
- α It Ain't Easy / What Am I To Do (PS) (Golden Voice no #/3112) 1967
- β Did I Say (That I Love You) / Talk To A Sidewalk (PS) (Golden Voice 3114) 1967

NB: α has no # on the record label other than the matrix - '3112' appears only on the pic sleeve if you're lucky enough to have one. α and β reissued in 1999 as a pic-sleeve EP on clear wax and with a factoid-friendly insert (CMP records CMEP 9901).

A sextet from Peoria, Illinois. Both 45s came with picture sleeves which are very pricey in good condition 30+ years on. The band's music was in tune with their image - clean-cut harmony beat ballads with a romantic air .... no rebellious stances here.

Talk To A Sidewalk is on *Every Groovy Day* (LP), incorrectly billed as *Talk To A Stranger*. (MW)

Shakey Legs

Personnel:
- JACK BRUNO — drms — A
- TED DEMOS — gtr — A
- TOM ENRIGHT — bs — A
- NICK LAURITZEN — keyb'ds, vcls — A
- JOHN MASTORY — gtr — A

ALBUM: 1(A) SHAKEY LEGS (Paramount PAS 6022) 1971 -

Ted Demos and Jack Bruno were previously in the **Apple Pie Motherhood Band**. **Shakey Legs**, also known as **Shakey Legs Blues Band**, was essentially a bluesy bar-rock band, their best moment being a version of *Say You Love Me*. (SR)

The Shames

45: The World Is Upside Down/The Special Ones (RFT 310) 1966

From Northeastern Massachusetts, this outfit originally formed as The Dimensions in 1964 later changing name to The Cryin' Shames, but when the similarly-named Chicago band got big they dropped the Cryin' from their name becoming simply **The Shames**. Their 45 was a pretty standard garage grunge.

Compilation appearances include: *My World Is Upside Down* and *Special Ones* on *Back From The Grave, Vol. 6* (LP); *The World Is Upside Down* on *Chosen Few, Vol's 1 & 2* (CD); and *Special Ones* on *The Chosen Few, Vol. 1* (LP). (VJ)

The Shamettes

Known as **Sam the Shams**' back-up singers, these girls also made at least three records on their own in 1966 and 1967. One of them, *Big Bad Wolf* has resurfaced on *Girls In The Garage, Vol. 4* (LP). (GG)

The Shandells

Personnel:
- JIM CROGGINS — drms — A
- (CHARLES) GRANT GILBERTSON — gtr — A
- JEFF GOTTHEARDT — ld gtr — A
- MICK ZIRNGIBLE — bs — A

45s:
- Here Comes The Pain/ Summertime Blues (Studio City 1037) 1965
- α Gorilla/Hey Little One (Bangar 0659) 1965

NB: α only 100 copies pressed.

Eau Claire in Northwest Wisconsin was home to these punkers. *Gorilla*, their finest moment, can also be found on *Pebbles, Vol. 4 (ESD)* (CD), *Root '66* (LP), *Teenage Shutdown, Vol. 1* (LP & CD) and *Wavy Gravy, Vol. 1* (CD). (VJ/MW/GM)

ANANDA SHANKAR - Ananda Shankar LP.

The Shandells

| 45: | Chimes/Little Girl | (Bridge Society 112) c1966 |

A different outfit from Middletown, Pennsylvania, whose *Chimes* later resurfaced on *Pennsylvania Unknowns* (LP). (VJ)

Shandells, Inc.

| 45: | Say What I Mean / Just Cry | (Woodrich WR-1265) 1967 |

This Huntington, Alabama band's rare 45 came out on Woody Richardson's gospel/country label and was probably recorded in Nashville. *Just Cry*, with squeaky-thin fuzz sound and *Psychotic Reaction* style break, can be heard on *Basementsville! U.S.A.* (LP). Both sides are aired on *The Cicadelic '60s - Vol. 7* (CD), which notes that the label left the distribution to the artists and only pressed up small quantities (about 500). The CD features two other garage bands that cropped up on this label - **The Rocks** and the Shadows.

Other compilation appearances include *Say What I Mean* and *Just Cry* on *Green Crystal Ties, Vol. 8* (CD). (MW/MM)

The Shandels

| 45: | Mary, Mary/Caroline | (Sizzle 5130) 196? |

A teen combo from Chicago. *Caroline*'s a teen pounder, but the 'A' side has a little more to it.

Compilation appearances include: *Caroline* and *Mary Mary* on *Back From The Grave, Vol. 6* (LP). (VJ)

Shandels / Shan Dels

Personnel incl: JOHNNY MELNICK — A
ERIC STERN — A

45s:	No Way Out / Treat Me Like A Man	(Carldell C-510) 1965
	α Please Stay / Treat Me Like A Man	(Showcase S-404) 1965
	Fifteen Children / Shades Of Blue	(La Salle L-381) 1967
	Barnyard Blues / ?	(La Salle) 1967
	β Gypsy / Try A Little Tenderness	(La Salle 25) 1968

NB: α as by **Shan Dels**. β by **Ellen and The Shandels**.

A band from the Long Island, New York, communities of Levittown and Wantaugh. They specialized in subdued beat-pop and garagey ballads with a unique twist. Instead of a lead guitar they employed a Cordovox, a small keyboard-like organ, whose accordion-like strains enhances the moodiness and infuses a Gallic flavour.

Produced by NYC impressario Carl Edelson (also responsible for release by **The Lemon Sandwich** and **The Taboos**), they would release several interesting 45s over a three year period, culminating in a 1968 recording where they backed a female singer called Ellen on a torrid psychedelic soul rendition of the Moody Blues' *Gypsy*.

No Way Out is a harmonious midtempo charmer; *Treat Me...* is coy bouncy pop; *Please Stay* is a minor-mood garage ballad with a nod to the Zombies' school of wistfulness.

Compilation appearances include: *Shades Of Blue* on *Teenage Shutdown, Vol. 5* (LP & CD); and *Please Stay* on *Shutdown '66* (LP) and *Psychedelic States: New York Vol. 1* (CD). (MW/MM)

The Shane

| 45: | Don't Turn Me Off/That Girl Of Mine | (Brent 7047) 1965 |

This 45 seems to have been their sole venture for the label. Both sides can now be heard on *Mindrocker, Vol. 13* (LP). (VJ)

Shango

Personnel:
JOE BARILE	drms	A
MALCOLM EVAN	bs	A
RICHIE HERNANDEZ	gtr	A
TOMMY REYNOLDS	keyd's, perc	A

| ALBUM: | 1(A) | TRAMPIN' | (Dunhill DS 50082) 1970 - |

| 45: | Some Things A Man's Gotta Do / Walking In The Sunshine | (ABC Dunhill D-4242) 1970 |

A Californian psychedelic soul group similar to early **Santana**. Their song *The Time Has Come* can be found on the Dunhill 1970 catalogue sampler *Undersound Uppersoul*.

Barile would later play with the Ventures.

This outfit is apparently not connected to the Shango on A&M (*Mama Lion*/? (A&M 1060) c1970). (SR/MW)

Anandar Shankar

Personnel:
MICHAEL BOTTS	drms	A
PRANISH KHAN	tabla	A
DRAKE LEVIN	gtr	A
PAUL LEWINSON	keyb'ds, moog, arranger	A
JOE POLLARD	drms	A
DICK ROSMINI	gtr	A
JERRY SCHEFF	bs	A
ANANDA SHANKAR	sitar	A
MARK TULIN	bs	A

| ALBUM: | 1(A) | ANANDA SHANKAR | (Reprise RS 6398) 1970 - |

NB: (1) reissued on vinyl and CD (WEA/Reprise 936247 2631 / 2632) 1998.

Although Ananda Shankar came from India, this album was recorded in L.A. and the involvement of several respected L.A. rock/session musicians justifies its inclusion here - apart from the musical content, which should appeal to sitar-lovers and fans of East-West fusions. Notable cohorts include: **Drake Levin** formerly of **Paul Revere and The Raiders**, **Brotherhood** and **Friendsound**; Mark Tulin of **The Electric Prunes**; seasoned sessioneers Mike Botts (later in Bread) and Jerry Scheff (numerous **Curt Boettcher**-related groups including **Ballroom**, **Millennium** and **Goldenrod**). The Associate Producer is James Lowe - possibly THE James (Jim) Lowe who went into studio engineering and production work after leaving the **Electric Prunes**.

As to the music - all are instrumentals apart from *Raghupati* and the Stones' *Jumpin' Jack Flash*. The only other rock cover is the **Doors'** *Light My Fire* and these are the most Western and least interesting - the sitar merely meanders along the vocal melody line. **Shankar** states on the album notes that only *Sagar* (the Ocean), a beautiful soothing piece, is played in classical style - the sitar is otherwise used as "a medium of expression". The tracks composed with Lewinson are the strongest. Oriental curlicues over a subtle Western backing (Latin American in the case of *Mamata*) that flow easily, coming across as neither tacky nor exploitative - a bridge between the classical sitar music of Ravi Shankar and Western 'rock with sitar' albums, e.g. the **Folkswingers** and Lord Sitar. Levinson's occasional keyboard and electronic effects create a unique blend which works surprisingly well. Highlights are: the delicate melancholy of *Snow Flower*, which can be tasted on *Journey To A Higher Key: The Best Of Sitar Psychedelia, Vol. 1* (LP); the aforementioned *Sagar*; and *Metamorphosis*, where a **Zodiac Cosmic Sounds** style evolves into a swirling raga freakout.

Two other tracks have been compiled. *Renunciation* and *Cyrus* are on *Electric Psychedelic Sitar Headswirlers Vol. 4* and *Vol. 5* respectively. Both add flute to the mix and the latter a cooing female vocal with the melody and feel of a French sixties film soundtrack. Neither are on this album, despite what the comp liner notes state, so where are they from? (MW)

Shanti

Personnel:	STEVE HAEHL	vcls, gtr	A
	ZAKIR HUSSAIN	tabla, sholak	A
	ASHISH KHAN	sarod	A
	PRANESH KHAN	tabla, naal	A
	STEVE LEACH	vcls, gtr	A
	FRANK LUPICA	drms	A
	NEIL SEIDEL	ld gtr	A

ALBUM: 1(A) SHANTI (Atlantic SD 8302) 1971 -

From San Francisco, this Californian-meets-India group played a very relaxed mystic blend of music, alternating instrumental cuts with vocal songs. Titles like *We Want To Be Free*, *I Do Believe* and *Innocence* illustrate their work. Zakir Hussain also played with **Mickey Hart** of the **Grateful Dead** on his *Rolling Thunder* album. (SR)

The Shapes of Things

45: So Mystifying/Last Night Wasn't There (Laurie 3351) 1967

This band was assembled in New York for their sole recording, a rework of Ray Davies' *So Mystifying*, by singer/producer **Warren Schatz**. It can also be heard on *Mindrocker, Vol. 3* (LP) and *We Have Come For Your Children*. It features typical snotty-nosed vocals, punk-style guitar and jangling tambourines. **Schatz** named his studio group after The Yardbirds' psychedelic hit single.

So Mystifying was also recorded by **The Petrified Forest**. (VJ/SR)

The Shaprels

Personnel:	DON HRNJAK	drms	A
	BOB MEHRING	bs, organ	A
	JIMMY MEIER	vcls	A
	TOM RICHARDS	gtr	A
	BOB SCZWEDA	ld gtr	A

45s:		A Fool For Your Lies / You're Cheating On Me	(Feature 817R 103) 1966
	α	Dare I Weep, Dare I Mourn / Rock-A-Boo	(Chess 1993) 1967
		Clara Broomtree / Desert Maiden	(Tee Pee 39/40) 1967
		A Fool For Your Lies / You're Cheating On Me	(P.K.C. 846P-1017) 1968

NB: α Both sides also appeared on one-sided promos - it may also have been released on the Feature label.

Milwaukee, Wisconsin was home to this band. They released several high quality 45s with excellent vocals and resounding, often fuzz, guitarwork. *A*

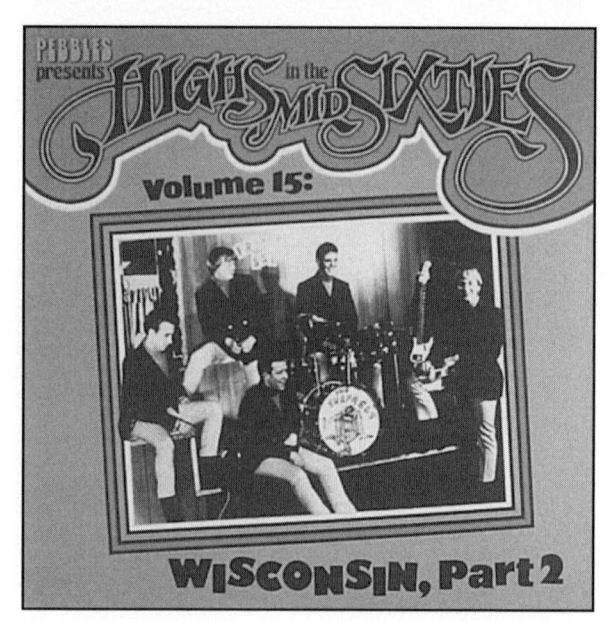

HIGHS IN THE MID-SIXTIES Vol. 15 (Comp LP) including The Shaprels.

Fool For Your Lies, a Mersey-influenced folk-rocker, can also be heard on *Highs In The Mid Sixties, Vol. 15* (LP). *Dare I Weep, Dare I Mourn*, later resurfaced on *Highs In The Mid-Sixties, Vol. 4* (LP), and also *Desert Maiden* appears on the *30 Seconds Before The Calico Wall* (CD). By now the influence of the psychedelic era was evident in their music and this was probably their finest moment. Well worth a listen. (VJ/MW/GM)

The Shatters

ALBUM: 1 THE SHATTERS (Welhaven Acetate no #) 1966 ?

This album by a raw garage band from Austin, in South-East Minnesota, remains unreleased. It contains covers of classic songs like *Gloria*, *Midnight Hour*, *Latin Lupe Lu*, *So Fine*, *Bo Diddley* and *I'm Free*. (VJ)

The Shattoes

Personnel:	BOB ALLISON	bs	A
	HOWARD ERNST	ld gtr	A
	WILLARD ERNST	gtr	A
	TERRY RAMEY	gtr	A
	ROGER PURSELL	drms	A

45: Surf Fever / Do You Love Me (Studio City SC 1010) 1965

In 1963 the Galaxies came together in Vermillion, South Dakota. When Howard Ernst joined from The Vibratos, they became **The Shattoes**. Just one 500-press 45 was released under this name.

In 1967 they amended the spelling to **Chateaux** (the near-phonetic French equivalent, meaning 'castles'). (MW)

Shawkey Seau and The Muffins

Personnel incl: SHAWKEY SEAU A

45: Just One More Time/Walk Alone (Planet 59) 1966

A crudely-recorded effort from a Rhode Island combo. *Garage Punk Unknowns, Vol. 3* (LP) and *Mondo Frat Dance Bash A Go Go* (CD) both include *Just One More Time*. (VJ)

The Shaynes

45s:	You Tell Me Girl/Motown Workout	(Pee Vee 140) 1966
	I'll Always Be/From My Window	(Pee Vee 142) 196?
	Valleri / Let's Hold Steady	(Pee Vee 5000) 196?

A Lancaster, Pennsylvania combo.

Compilation appearances have included: *From My Window* on *Psychedelic Unknowns, Vol. 4* (LP & CD), *Teenage Shutdown, Vol. 6* (LP & CD) and *Gathering Of The Tribe* (CD); *You Tell Me Girl* and *From My Window* on *Return Of The Young Pennsylvanians* (LP); *From My Window, You Tell Me Girl* and *Valarie* on *Stompin' Time Again!* (CD). (VJ/MW/MM)

She Devils

A Michigan band who sound very influenced by early Pink Floyd on *Red The Signpost*, which can be found on *Michigan Mixture, Vol. 1* (LP). Their song, which is a cover of the **Fifty Foot Hose** classic, is full of fuzz and distortion and well worth a listen. (VJ)

The Sheep

45s:	Hide And Seek/Twelve Months Later	(Boom 60,000) 1966	HCP 58
	I Feel Good/Dynamite	(Boom 60,007) 1966	130

The *Gone, Vol. 2* (LP) and *Boulders, Vol. 3* (LP) compilations both include a previously unreleased cut, *Thinkin' About It*, by this band, whilst *Hide And Seek* is on *Garage Monsters* (LP). This first 45 is pretty decent, with the 'A' side being a Bunker Hill song, whilst the flip is written by Felman / Goldstein / Gottehrer.

Strong rumours claim that this is none other than New York City's **Strangeloves**. (VJ/SR)

Sheffields

45s:	My Only Wish/Nothing I Can Do	(Fenton 980) 1965
	Fool Minus A Heart/Blowin' In The Wind	(Fenton 2118) 196?
	Please Come Back To Me/	
	My Lovin' Days Are Through	(Destination 613) 1966
	Do You Still Love Me/Nothing I Can Do	(Destination 621) 1966

Fool Minus A Heart is rather lightweight British Invasion - beat sounds. From Grand Rapids, Michigan, they had no connection to the Sheffields on Ssexx who hailed from Des Moines, Iowa and were rather soulful.

Compilation appearances include: *Do You Still Love Me* on *Realities In Life* (LP); *Fool Minus A Heart* on on *Best Of Michigan Rock Groups, Vol. 1*. (VJ/MW)

Sheffield's Gate

45:	Tell Her No / No Reply	(Prestige Productions PP67-235) 1967

Despite their name, Sheffield has not been confirmed as the home of this Alabama band whose 45 appeared on a Birmingham label. Their winsome rendition of the Zombies' *Tell Her No* is featured on *Psychedelic States: Alabama Vol. 1* (CD). The flip is a Beatles cover. (MW)

Gilbert Shelton Ensemble

Personnel incl:	TOM BRIGHT	drms	A
	BOB BROWN	gtr	A
	ED GUINN	bs	A
	GILBERT SHELTON		A

45:	If I Was A Hell's Angel/	
	Southern Stock Car Man (PS)	(ESP 4501) 196?

From Austin Texas, **Gilbert Shelton** was of course the reknowned Wonder Wart-Hog comics artist, later responsible for the ubiquitous *Furry Freak Brothers* empire. This appears to be his sole recording, on which he was backed by members of **The Conqueroo** and Tom Bright, who later played with **Black Swan**.

You can also find *Hell's Angel* on Collectables' *'69 Love-In* (CD). (IT/MW)

Shep

See **Shep Cooke** entry.

Red Shepard and The Flock

Personnel incl:	RED SHEPARD	vcls	A

45:	She's A Grabber/I Can't Hold On (PS)	(Philips 40398) 1966

A five-piece (the 45 came in a picture sleeve). *She's A Grabber* is very punkish grunge.

Red Sheppard also had a spell in **Seatrain** and performed in the Hollywood version of the musical 'Hair'. He was quoted in "Easyrider" magazine circa 1970 as also being a sometime member of **Salvation**.

Compilation appearances include: *She's A Grabber* on *Victims Of Circumstances, Vol. 1* (LP), *Garage Zone, Vol. 2* (LP) and *The Garage Zone Box Set* (LP). (VJ/RMh)

The Sheppards (aka Rickford Ziockowsky and The Sheppards)

Personnel incl:	RICKFORD ZIOCKOWSKY		A

45:	Poor Man's Thing/	
	When Johnny Comes Marching Home	(Help) 196?

NB: reissued (Impact 1018) 1967.

This 45 was first issued on the Detroit-based Help label and later leased to Impact. The 'A' side is a protest folk-rocker with throaty vocals.

Compilation appearances have included: *Poor Man's Thing* on *Pebbles, Vol. 21* (LP), *The Best Of Impact Records* (CD) and *Follow That Munster, Vol. 2* (LP); *When Johnny Comes Marching Home* on *From The New World* (LP) and *Garage Punk Unknowns, Vol. 5* (LP). (VJ)

The Sherwoods

Personnel:	JOHNNY CLARRY	drms	ABC
	MIKE CLAXTON	vcls	ABC
	JIM FRYE	gtr	ABC
	RANDY WEBER	bs	AB
	DAVE FRANKLIN	ld gtr	BC
	KENNY BLANCHETTE	bs	C

CD:	1	LIVE 1968 - 1969	(Collectables COL-CD-0589) 1994

45s:	If I Could See/I Know You Cried	(Nowsound 1001) 1968
	No Deposit No Return/Ride Baby Ride	(Smash 2252) 1969

Formed in 1965 by a bunch of high school pals playing for fun. They played a lot in the Houston area and by 1966 their line-up had stabilised to 'A' above, but a little later Dave Franklin joined from local group, The Upper Level. On a gig at the Safari-A-Go-Go in Baytown they met The Runaways' manager Jack Sims, who became their manager too. Early in 1968 they cut their first 45 at the ACA studios in Houston. 500 copies were pressed. Both songs were written by Mike Claxton and, after he'd finished recording them, he and Sims added the explosion at the end of the flip side from a sound effects album they found in the studio. In particular *I Know You Cried* was a rip roaring psychedelic number.

Like many of their compatriots they had a number of run-ins with Southern rednecks. For a while they rented a house in Houston, inherited from **Fever Tree**, and once played an all night jam with **The Doors** when they were in Houston for a show. While they were playing a show in early '69 a talent scout for Mercury spotted them and they went to Los Angeles in May that year to record a second 45. It didn't make much impression and it may have been a tax write-off for Smash. When two of the band joined the revived **Fever Tree** early in 1970, the rest called it a day.

They also recorded a couple of other cuts which have resurfaced on compilations, including *Bless Me Woman*, a slow number with haunting vocals, and a different version of *Ride Baby Ride*.

Three of the band's original members apparently still play together and Voxx did have plans to release an album of their material.

Compilation appearances include: *Ganada* on *'69 Love-In* (CD); *Bless Me Woman*, *I Know You Cried*, *I'll Be Gone* and *Ride Baby Ride* (unissued version) on *Acid Visions - The Complete Collection Vol. 1* (3-CD); *Bless Me Woman* and *I Know You Cried* on *Acid Visions, Vol. 2* (LP); *I Know You Cried* on *Texas Flashbacks, Vol. 1* (LP & CD) and *Flashback, Vol. 1* (LP); and *I'll Be Gone* (live) and *Ride Baby Ride* (live) on *There Goes The Neighborhood, Vol. 1* (CD). (VJ)

She's

45:	Ah Gee!! Maurie/The Fool	(International Artists 104) 1966

The sorry inane pop of the 'A' side constrasts starkly with the garagey flip where teeny feelings are expressed in a convincingly innocent manner. This track maybe super lightweight, but is gratifying anyway.

You can also find *The Fool* on *Girls In The Garage, Vol. 2* (CD) and *Girls In The Garage, Vol. 7* (LP). (MK)

The Shieks

The punk ballad, *You Let Me Down*, on 1989's 'unreleased Michigan' compilation *Thee Unheard Of* (LP), is not what it appears to be. It turns out that a gullible compiler was duped by some fraud who manufactured false acetate discs which were actually recordings copied from real 45s by obscure bands; this track is actually by the **Oncomers**, whilst another example is *I Can Hear The Raindrops* by "The Aces" - actually *I Can Hear Raindrops* by **The Noblemen 4**. (MW)

The Shillings

45s:	Just For You Baby/Laugh	(Fontana 1543) 1966
	Children And Flowers/	
	Lying And Trying	(Three Rivers 701) 1966
	Goodbye My Lady/	
	The World Could Stop	(Three Rivers 6778/9) 1967
	Strawberry Jam/Wild Cherry Lane	(Virtue 2504) 1968

Hailing from Allentown, Pennsylvania, their *Laugh* is a melodic and plaintive punk ballad with ringing guitars.

A cover of the Beach Boys *Barbara Ann* also made it onto a Fontana acetate. *Children & Flowers* was a cover of **The Critters** track.

Compilation appearances include: *Laugh* on *The Psychedelic Sixties, Vol. 1* (LP) and *The Cicadelic 60's, Vol. 3* (CD). (MW/GGI)

The Shillings

45s:	Yesterday's Dawn/	
	Just-Like-A-Girl	(Dayton Band Co. EU-946470/948496) 1967
	I Call For Her /	
	Forgive Me My Love	(Dayton Band Company EU-980808) 1967

This Dayton, Ohio bunch released two 45s which'll appeal to lovers of primitive garage-invasion beat ballads.

Compilation appearances include: *Forgive Me My Love* on *The Night Is So Dark* (LP). (MW)

The Shillings

Personnel:	PEPPER ARADA	bs	A
	GREG CAHILL	ld gtr	A
	PHIL CANTOR	vcls	A
	DAVID GUIDER	gtr	A
	RICH McDONALD	drms	A

45:	Not The Least Bit True /	
	It Was My Mistake	(Fantasy 594) 1965

Also known as the English Shillings, this band were from Oakland, California. After the Fantasy 45 they made several unreleased recordings that have been unearthed by Alec Palao, along with the band's personnel details, on Big Beat's essential *Nuggets From The Golden State* CD series. *It's Up To You* and *Made You Cry* from June 1965 are on *The Scorpio Records Story*, *I'm Over You* and *Part Time Man* from April 1966 are on *Good Things Are Happening*. (MW)

Shiloh

Personnel:	MIKE BOWDEN	bs	A
	RICHARD BOWDEN	gtr	A
	DON HENLEY	drms	A
	JIM ED NORMAN	keyb'ds	A
	AL PERKINS	pedal steel gtr, gtr, vcls	A

ALBUM:	1(A)	SHILOH	(Amos 7015) 1970 SC

45s:	Jennifer/Tell Me To Get Out Of Your Life	(Amos 140) 1970
	Simple Little Down Home Rock And Roll Love Song For Rosie/	
	Down On The Farm	(Amos 162) 1970

Apart from Al Perkins, the other four had all played with **The Felicity** which operated in Texas between 1964-68. They played as **Shiloh** from 1969-71. They relocated to L.A. where the album was recorded and became very influential on the early country rock movement there. Perkins later played with The Flying Burrito Brothers. Jim Ed Norman became string arranger for The Eagles and the other three all played for Linda Ronstadt. Henley was also in The Eagles and the Bowden brothers were in Cold Steel. (VJ)

Shiloh Morning

ALBUM:	1	SHILOH MORNING	(TRC TRCS-51053) 1974 -

A mix of rural and soft-rock with male/female vocals, their album contains mostly covers (**It's A Beautiful Day**'s *White Bird*, Moody Blues' *Nights In White Satin*) plus some original tracks (*Too Far Behind*). Not psychedelic, as some dealers tend to describe it. (SR)

The Shilos

45:	Lonely Town/Cause I Love You	(Norfolk 201268/9) 1967

Hailed from Stoughton, Massachusetts. The flip side is a strong garage number which can also be found on *New England Teen Scene, Vol. 3* (LP). (GG)

Shindogs

Personnel incl:	CHUCK BLACKWELL	drms	
	DELANEY BRAMLETT	gtr, vcls	
	JAMES BURTON	gtr	
	JOEY COOPER	gtr, vcls	
	DON PRESTON	gtr	
	LEON RUSSELL	piano	

45s:	Someday Someday / Why	(Warner Bros. 5665) 1965
	Who Do You Think You Are /	
	Yes I'm Going Home	(Viva 601) 1966
α	Don't Come Running To Me /	
	Don't Hide It (PS)	(Prince P-6707-1/2) 1967

NB: α as **The Pebbles**. Some copies came in a special PS.

A Los Angeles studio group and the house-band for TV's 'Shindig' show, with an interesting repertoire of mixing rock 'n' roll with country music. The roots of the group go back to the Palomino Club, a country music hotspot in North Hollywood that had first opened in 1949, and by 1960 featured Gene Davis, a country and rockabilly performer heading the

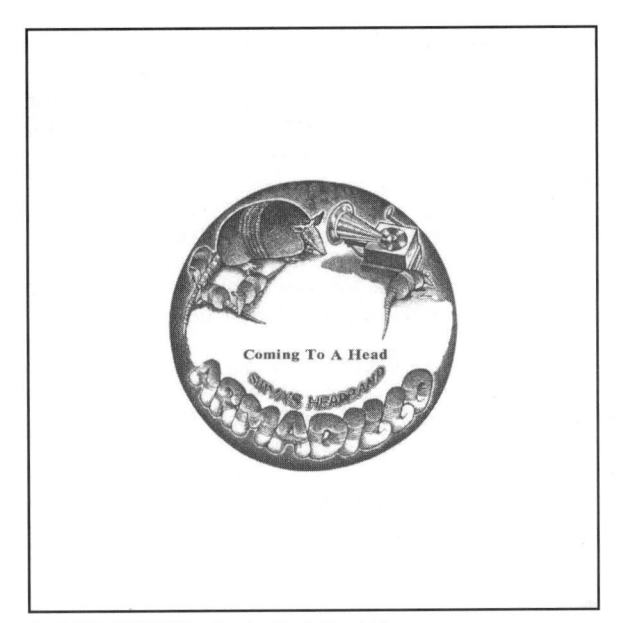

SHIVA'S HEADBAND - Coming To A Head LP.

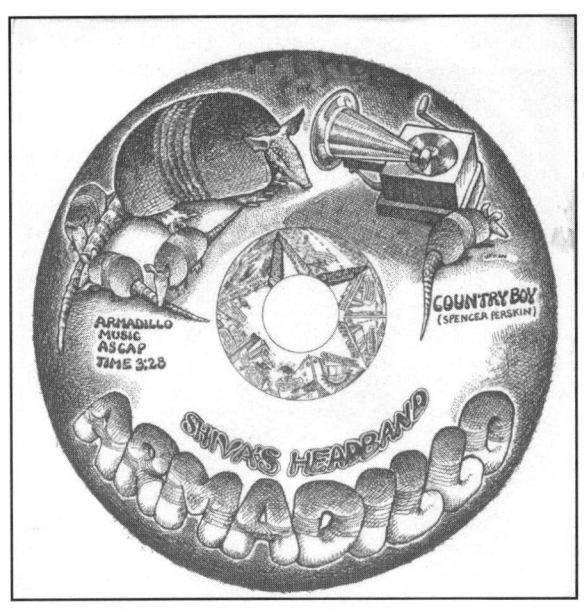

SHIVA'S HEADBAND - Country Boy 45 PS.

houseband. Throughout the early sixties the Gene Davis band had a steady flow of members including drummers Mel Taylor (later with The Ventures), Jan Curtis Skugstadt, Archie Francis, guitarists Jimmy Snyder, Jerry Inman, Bobby Durham, Glen Campbell and even James Burton who although not a member used to sit in informally when not touring with Rick Nelson. Other members included piano players Clyde Griffin, **Leon Russell** and Glen D. Hardin (ex-Crickets), bassists Norm Raleigh, Delaney Bramlett and the mainstay from 1960 to 1969, pedal steel guitarist and later bandleader Red Rhodes.

By late 1964 Jack Good had organised his new show 'Shindig' and **Leon Russell** was chosen to lead the group for the show which included James Burton, drummer Jim Gordon and Delaney Bramlett on bass.

Originally known as The Shindiggers, by 1965 **The Shindogs** had quickly evolved into the main line-up of Glen D. Hardin (piano), Delaney Bramlett (guitar, vocals, bass), James Burton (lead guitar), Joey Cooper (guitar, vocals) and Chuck Blackwell, an old Oklahoma bandmate of **Leon Russell**'s on drums. **Leon Russell** led the show's orchestra and would sometimes take a spot with **The Shindogs** to sing and play piano. **The Shindogs** line-up was also augmented by members of the other Shindig band, the Ray Pohlman Band which included guitarist Jerry Cole (ex-Champs) and Larry Knechtel on bass. While horn players like Jim Horn were called into the studio group when the need arose, others like Glen Campbell and Billy Preston became semi-regulars on the show. Both Bramlett and **Russell** had solo singles issued in 1965.

When 'Shindig' was cancelled in late 1965, the last show was aired in January 1966 and the group subsequently split. Most members went on to greater things - **Leon Russell** to **Asylum Choir** and a solo career; Cooper and Preston to Mad Dogs, both had solo releases; Delaney Bramlett briefly returned to the Palomino Club with Red Rhodes Detours in 1966 into 1967, married Bonnie, and is best remembered as half of **Delaney & Bonnie**. The original version of their group, Friends, included J.J. Cale on lead guitar in 1967.

While Chuck Blackwell joined the Taj Mahal Band (1966-1970), both Cooper and Blackwell played with **Russell**'s tour band in the seventies. The highly-regarded guitarist James Burton who'd recorded with Dale Hawkins in the fifties, and throughout the sixties and seventies backed Ricky Nelson, now backed Gram Parsons and **Delaney & Bonnie** before a long stint in Elvis Presley's show band.

Whether all the famed **Shindogs** played on the sessions is debatable; indeed the final 45 may well have been a studio group attempt to cash in on the group's fading fame.

The first 45 comprises bright'n' breezy Invasion pop, where the Beatles meet the Searchers. The second **Russell**-produced 45 is also good harmony-beat. The final 45 as **The Pebbles** was produced by Brian Ross (of **Music Machine**, **Friendly Torpedoes** etc.) drops the Invasion influences and turns to US garage sounds for *Don't Come Running To Me*, a slick fuzz-popper. (MW/RAd/JO)

The Ship

Personnel:
TODD BRADSHAW	bs		A
STEVE COWAN	gtr, vcls		A
MARC HAMBY	keyb'ds, vcls		A
STEVE MELSHENKER	gtr		A
STEVE REINWAND	gtr, vcls		A
TIM SCOTT	cello		A

ALBUM: 1(A) A FOLK MUSIC JOURNEY (Elektra EKS 75036) 1972 -
NB: (1) also released in the U.K. (Elektra K 42122) 1972.

Produced by Gary Usher (**Sagittarius**, **Byrds**), an ambitious folk-rock concept album housed in a gatefold sleeve. Dreamy and melodic.

The band were largely a regional act with a following at the Univeristy of Illinois. (SR/SCu)

Shira

45:   Shira/Frank's Ant Farm   (Jamie 1413) c1972

A psychedelic rock single with good guitar and an instrumental flip. (SR)

Shiva's Headband

Personnel:
JERRY BARNETT	drms	A D
KENNY PARKER	bs, gtr, vcls	ABC
SPENCER PERSKIN	violin, gtr, hrmnca, recorder, vcls	ABCDEF
SUSAN PERSKIN	perc, keyb'ds, vcls	ABCDEF
BOB TONREID	gtr	AB
SHAWN SIEGEL	keyb'ds, vcls	BCDE
JERRY STORM	drms	B
RICHARD FINNEL	drms	C
ROBERT GLADWIN	gtr, bs	C
MIKE COOPER	bs	D
ISIAH "IKE" RITTER	gtr, vcls	D
STEVE NAVARRO	bs	E
STEVE ROBB	drms	E
MAUREEN SIEGEL	vcls	E
SKIP SORELLE	gtr	E
JERRY BAZIL	drms	F
ROBERT FLYNN Jr.	gtr	F
BRIAN "RED" MOORE	bs	F
(ED VIZARD	sax	D)
(ALLEN McADAMS		F)
(DENNIE TARNER		F)

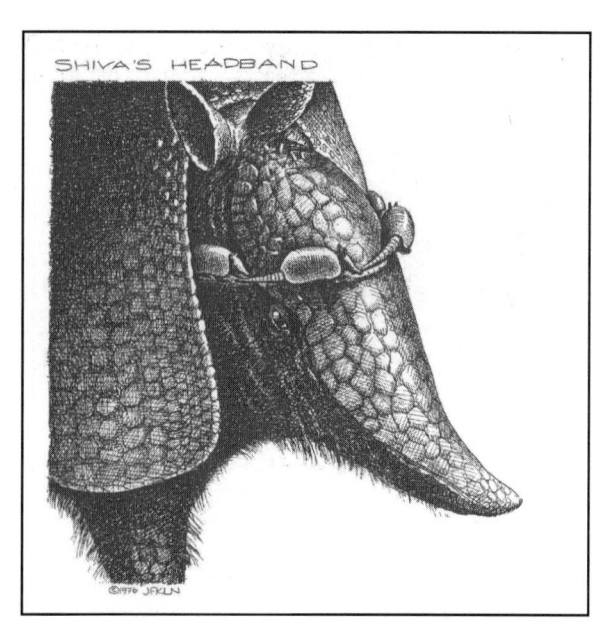

SHIVA'S HEADBAND - Extension 45 PS.

ALBUMS:
1(C)	TAKE ME TO THE MOUNTAINS	(Capitol ST 538) 1970	R1
2(D)	COMIN' TO A HEAD	(Armadillo 3301) 197?	R2
3(E)	PSYCHEDELIC YESTERDAY	(Ape 1001) 1978	SC
4(-)	IN THE PRIMO OF LIFE	(Moontower ?) 1984	-

NB: (1) like the original issue of **The Sons Of Champlin** debut, *Take Me To The Mountains* had to be "mechanically censored" when a Capitol staff member noticed that in the second panel of the cartoon back cover, artist Jim Franklin had surreptitiously used the word "cunt" on a storefront sign! Most copies known have this word scratched out of the sleeve, but some uncensored copies exist. (1) reissued on CD. (2) original copies have plain black labels on disc and were issued in a thick white jacket with front and rear 'slicks' pasted on by hand. It was reissued in 1980 in a standard printed cover. There's also a limited edition cassette-only release, *Now And Then* (Moontower 1002) that was made available by mail-order in 1988. The "Now" side was recorded live at the Austin Opera House in 1986, and "Then" was a live recording from Jubilee Hall in Houston in 1969.

45s:
α	Kaleidescoptic/Song For Peace	(Ignite 681)	1968
β	Take Me To The Mountains/ Lose The Blues	(Armadillo 811)	1968
χ	Country Boy/Such A Joy (PS)	(Armadillo 3-71426)	1972
δ	Don't Blame Me/Extension (PS)	(Armadillo AR6-HS 155)	1976

NB: α shown as by **Shiva's Head Band**. Both sides feature different versions than those appearing on the Capitol album. β first pressing has standard label, second pressing from 1969 has Jim Franklin artwork on labels. Both pressings were made from the same stamper, and consequently contain the same versions. The 'A' side is non-LP and the 'B' side is a different version to that appearing on the Capitol album. χ both sides feature different versions than those appearing on the Armadillo album. δ both sides non-LP tracks.

Founded in July 1967 by classically-trained violinist Spencer Perskin, **Shiva's Headband** have proved to be one of Texas' most durable outfits. Earlier, in 1966, Perskin had spent some time in San Francisco where he had briefly played in a band which included folkie **Penny Nichols**. He returned to Austin to form **Shiva's Headband** much influenced by his experiences in San Francisco. Their debut 45 sold well locally and is now a collectors' item. Their follow-up attracted wider attention and that year they relocated to San Francisco and signed for Capitol. They hated San Francisco but remained there to record *Take Me To The Mountains*, a fine album which included new versions of their first two 45s. Perskin's violin is prominent throughout the first album, particularly on the beautiful *Song For Peace* and standout track *Kaleidoscoptic*. During their spell in California they played a few gigs at the Avalon. They were also the resident band at the New Orleans House in Berkeley for a while. It was during this time that Spencer Perskin played on **Mother Earth**'s debut album *Living With The Animals* and also turned down the opportunity of joining the band. Shawn Siegel had similarly refused a spot in **The Thingies** prior to joining *Shiva's Headband* in 1968.

Having made little money from their Capitol deal, the band returned to Texas. As only 1,000 copies of their second album *Coming To A Head* were pressed on the small Armadillo label, it has become a rare collectors' item. Different versions of two of the album's tracks, *Country Boy/Such A Joy* were issued as a 45 in a picture sleeve. They spent a while in Las Vegas in a vain attempt to set up a string of music clubs before returning to Texas to issue a 45 *Don't Blame Me/Extension*, which appeared in another Jim Franklin picture sleeve. Sadly, this appears to have concluded their long relationship with Franklin, who provided the band with their distinctive armadillo imagery.

In 1978, the band issued *Psychedelic Yesterday*, by far their hardest-rocking album. This is the only **Shiva's Headband** album with up-front electric guitar and it also finds the band in rare form vocally. This album has also become very difficult to locate in recent years.

Their 1984 album *In The Primo Of Life* saw the band moving into jazzy and even reggae territory. This album garnered them considerable local accolades and in 1986 they were choses "Band Of The Year" in a local magazine poll. The band continue to perform to this day.

Compilation appearances include: the excellent *Song For Peace* on *The Psychedelic Experience, Vol. 1* (LP); and *Kaleidescoptic* (45 version) on *Texas Flashback (The Best Of)* (CD), *Texas Flashback, Vol. 3* (LP & CD) and *Flashback, Vol. 3* (LP). (VJ/CF)

Shiver

Personnel:
DON PECK	drms	AB
NEIL PERON	bs	AB
TERRY "HOOK" SALUGA	vcls	A
FRANK TWIST	ld gtr, vcls	AB

ALBUM: 1(B) SHIVER (Rockadelic) 2000

NB: (1) reissued on CD (Shadoks Music 023) 2001.

Based in San Francisco, this group recorded some tapes in 1972, which were finally released by Rockadelic in 2000. Five long jamming guitar cuts with screaming vocals on *Fixer* and *Bone Shaker* and an amazing track called *Alpha Man*, fifteen minutes of flowing West Coast guitar leads combined with heavy rock riffs.

The CD reissue contains four bonus cuts and a liner where Don Peck recounts the band's history.... His first real band was in Dallas in 1967 - The Hungry Freaks who adopted a heavy "badass" image and covered the likes of The Animals, Them, Stones and **13th Floor Elevators**. When they split, he joined the black R&B combo Les Watson and The Panthers who recorded on Ike Turner's Vesuvius label.

He'd been flitting back and forth between Dallas and San Francisco, where his sister lived and, in 1969, he decided to settle there. At the end of the year **Shiver** came together and over the next three or so years became a popular attraction, particularly with the biker fraternities.

Vocalist Saluga was known for his short fuse and wasn't averse to using the metal arm appendage that gave him his nickname. As a result he was fired numerous times, whereupon Frank Twist would take up vocal duties. During their lifespan they also went under the names Pacific Thrust, Kid Courage and Terry Saluga's Riff Raff. (SR/MW)

Wally Shoop and Fubar

Personnel incl: WALLY SHOOP gtr A

45: Evening In The City/ Words In My Head (AJS New Horizon International 1001) 1971

A little known band from Spirit Lake, Iowa, who recorded the above screaming psycher. They were previously known as **Billy Rat and The Finks** and Wally Shoop and The Zombies.

Compilation appearances include: *Words In My Head* on *Psychedelic Experience, Vol. 4* (CD); *Evening In The City* on *Sixties Rebellion, Vol. 15* (LP & CD); and as Wally Shoop and The Zombies: *Summertime, Memphis* and *Okoboji* on *The IGL Rock Story: Part One (1965 - 67)* (CD). (VJ/GG)

The Shoremen

Personnel:
- BRIAN ALLAN (DAVE KALMAN) — ld gtr, vcls — A
- KIP KURZMAN — bs — A
- DAVE MARK (DAVE BUCKMAN) — gtr, ld vcls — A
- BOB REINCKE — drms — A

45s:
- Look Into Her Eyes/She's Bad (Wynwood WR 1956) 1965
- The Wonder Of Christmas/ Day All My Dreams Come True (Wynwood WR 2062) 1965
- Dance U.S.A.! / I Expect Too Much (Wynwood WR 2088) 1966
- α The Time Of The Year/Cumberland Railroad (Bomar 401) 1967

NB: α by Brian & Dave "Tomorrow People.

In 1963, Dave Kalman from Rockdale, Maryland, was heavily into the Beach Boys, Jan & Dean, etc. The following year he met Dave Buckman, a displaced Baltimorean who'd just returned from California. The two immediately hit it off and began to create a sound that would develop into both **The Shoremen** and **Brian & Dave "Tomorrow People"**. Buckman's smooth voice and gift for harmony provided a unique styling and a competitive sound and amazingly the duo cut nearly 100 songs over a five-year period at David C. Smith's Marmon Avenue garage studio.

Prior to the first release Dave Kalman began using the pen name of Brian Allan as an artist, writer and arranger. All of his label credits through that period carried the Brian Allan moniker. Dave Buckman too shortened his name by using his middle name for his surname. He became David Mark. They began calling themselves **The Shoremen**, a name suggested by WCAO disc jockey, Les Alexander.

Their first release, *Look Into Her Eyes*, met with modest success in the Baltimore/Washington area and was selected as a "Hometown Sound" on WCAO. The group followed this with a seasonal song *The Wonder Of Christmas*, which unfortunately was released too late into the holiday season to have any impact. Their final **Shoremen** release *Dance, USA!* again had modest local airplay, but was highly-regarded by the group's growing fan base. *Dance USA!* was an interesting combination of the Liverpool sound and surf music.

Around early 1967, Brian and Dave started creating more philosophic and folk-rock oriented material and changed their name to **Brian & Dave "Tomorrow's People"**. They played many coffee houses in town, including the Peabody Beer and Book Stube, UMBC's "Collage," as well as numerous local TV appearances on Johnny Dark's TV Show, a regular spot on New Wind Blowin' and the Kerby Scott Show. They also auditioned for the Mike Douglas Show in Philadelphia. The only recording released under this name was *Time Of The Year* on the Bomar label, which got considerable airplay in the Baltimore area, but was only a modest success.

As a band, **The Shoremen** included line-up 'A' for the vast majority of Brian and Dave's music, except for the recording of *Dance, USA!* where Chris West played drums and Neil Ulman played bass.

A little known accomplishment of Brian and Dave was their writing of Catonsville Community College's Alma Mater by Dave Kalman and the demo production of the song sung by Dave Buckman.

Today, Dave Buckman is a psychologist in Tallahassee, Florida, where he still enjoys playing guitar. Dave Kalman is a consultant, photographer and continues as a very active songwriter with much material in Nashville and associated publishing houses. Dave's song *Can't We Start Over Again* by the O'Roark Brothers was a pick hit in Billboard, Cashbox and Record World magazines in 1983 and has earned national and international radio play.

Compilation appearances have included: *She's Bad* on *Teenage Shutdown, Vol. 2* (LP & CD) and *Yeah Yeah Yeah* (CD). (MW/MM/JV/DK)

Short Cross

Personnel:
- GRAY McCALLEY — drms, ld vcls — A
- BUTCH OWENS — organ, piano, moog — A
- VELPO ROBERTSON — gtrs, vcls — A
- BIRD SHARP — bs, vcls — A

ALBUM: 1(A) ARISING (Grizly S-160-13) 1972 R2

NB: (1) reissued on CD (Gear Fab GF-119) 1998 and on double vinyl (Akarma AK 079/2) 2000.

45: On My Own / Marching Off To War (Colpar 54-1005) 1970

From Sandston, Virginia, this band evolved out of the Hustlers, whose members included, at various stages, ex-Reactors(*) Steve Hicks and ex-Outlaws Butch Owens alongside core members Velpo Robertson, Gray McCalley and Ben Luck. The latter left to join the **Barracudas**, of *A Plane View* album fame.

Their rare album can best be described as heavy psychedelic blues, at its purest on *Suicide Blues*. There's plenty of good guitar work throughout, *Wastin' Time*, *Just Don't Care*, *Till We Reach The Sun* and *Hobo Love Song* all have their share, whilst *Ellen* is a slow bluesy ballad. The album lacks sufficient originality to make it special but if this musical genre is where you're at you shouldn't be disappointed.

For the band's detailed history, check out the reissues.

Compilation appearances include: *Bomb* on Gear Fab's *Psychedelic Sampler* (CD).

NB: (*) Steve Hicks, played with The Reactors from Sandston, Virginia who are unrelated to the **Reactors** from Suffolk, Virginia. (VJ/MW/RM)

SHIVER - Shiver LP.

SHORT CROSS - Arising LP.

The Short Cuts

| 45: | Hold It Baby/Broke Down | (Pepper) c1968 |

A pop garage outfit. (SR)

Shotgun Ltd

Personnel:
BUZZIE BUCHANAN	drms, perc	A
RUBEN DOMINGUEZ	bs, congas, backing vcls	A
JOE GUTIERREZ	ld vcls	A
DAVE NORUP	organ	A
JACK SCHOOLAR	ld gtr, dobro, backing vcls	A

ALBUM: 1(A) SHOTGUN LTD (Prophesy SD 6050) 1971 -

This group of young Californian musicians were all aged between 17 and 21 at the time of their album. They were discovered by Delaney Bramlett (from **Delaney and Bonnie**) who arranged for a recording deal with Prophesy and for his DelBon company to produce the album. With Jim Gordon (the keyboard/sax player, not the drummer of Derek and The Dominos) at the controls, the result was a powerful mix of heavy/prog-rock with lots of guitar/organ interplay and good vocals. Jim Gordon, Ben Benay (ex-**Goldenrod**) and the sax-player Jerry Jumonville provided some support. All their material was penned by the group members, with the help of J. Loppnow on two tracks and R. Lawson on one. Three cuts (*Number Two*, *Against The Wall* and *Feelin' Bad*) are over five minutes long and, with the opening *Bad Road*, are among the better moments.

The album appears to have sank without a trace, but in hindsight deserves to be rediscovered.

Buzzie Buchanan later reappeared in the late seventies as a studio musician, working with Commander Cody and Juice Newton. (SR)

The Showmen

| 45: | Make Up Your Mind/ Almost There | (Texas Record Co. 2068) 1966 |

This outfit came from Waco in Texas. A 45 called *Tubby Tina* on Campo Records may also have been by the band. Other Showmen turned up in Chicago, Boston, Minneapolis and Pennsylvania.

Compilation appearances include *Almost There* on *The Cicadelic 60's, Vol. 4* (CD) and *The Cicadelic 60's, Vol. 5* (LP). (VJ)

The Showmen

| 45: | Big Daddy Don/Judy | (Soul Kitchen SK 0014) 196? |

'68 sounding, garagey-rock about a dragster, with lots of great drag racin' FX, wah-wah guitar and brass. A soppy clubby ballad is on the flip of this obscure Cleveland label 45. (MW)

Show of Hands

See the **Formerly Anthrax** entry.

The Shy Guys

Personnel:
RANDY BOWLING	bs, vcls	A
WAYNE CEYNOWA	ld gtr, ld vcls	A
TIM DONAHOE	drms, vcls	A
BENNY FUTRELL	gtr, vcls	A
LARRY STEAD	keyb'ds, vcls	A

| 45s: | Black Lightening Light/Goodbye To You | (M-U 5941/42) 1968 |
| | α Just Can't Quit / She Don't Need No Other | (King 6331) 1970 |

NB: α as Miami.

From Sanford, Florida, *Black Lightening Light* is a pretty devastating piece of mindblowin' psychedelia. The flip is a haunting laid-back ballad. Both sides are recommended listening.

Wayne Ceynowa recalls: "*Black Lightening Light*, was for the most part, a group collaboration. It came together one stormy Florida evening while the band was rehearsing in the back of a Sanford music store, Music Unlimited (MU). The song was actually titled *Black Lightning Light*, but those in charge of the MU label design changed the song title's spelling. This was not discovered until after the pressing. The "B" side, *Goodbye To You*, was written by me. Unfortunately, I didn't get credit due to another similar label layout error".

"Both songs were recorded along with two further tracks in Nashville, Tennessee in one evening during the Summer of 1968. They were used as demos to present to record labels in hope of securing a contract and the band members were between the ages of 15-17 at the time. The MU label was our own and the 45 was the label's one and only release. The record number being made up."

"The band members did continue through our remaining high school years. We changed keyboardist a couple of times, finally settling on Teofilo Bautista."

"In late July, or early August 1970, we landed a contract with King Records (James Brown's label) and recorded thirteen songs for an album. The company insisted on changing our name to Miami (because we were from Florida) and a single was released (*Just Can't Quit/She Don't Need No Other*). The 45 was mentioned in Billboard magazine. I was even told we charted the top 100. Unfortunately, the album was never released and the band eventually disbanded in early 1971."

"In late 1971, myself, together with our drummer and bass player, reformed and have continued playing music (clubs, parties, etc.) to this day. We just can't seem to get it out of our systems!"

Compilation appearances include: *Black Lightening Light* on *Sixties Archive, Vol. 4* (CD), *Acid Dreams - The Complete 3 LP Set* (3-LP), *Acid Dreams Testament* (CD), *World Of Acid* (LP) and *Psychedelic States - Florida Vol. 2* (CD); and *Black Lightening Light* and *Goodbye To You* on *Florida Punk Groups From The Sixties* (LP). (VJ/MW/WC)

The Shy Guys

Personnel:
MARK FINN	drms, vcls	A
STU HOWARD (HIRSHFIELD)	gtr, vcls	A
RON NELSON (LEFKO)	ld gtr, vcls	A
MARTY LEWIS	bs, vcls	A

45s:	The Burger Song/?	(Burger 5004) 196?
	Lay It On The Line/We Gotta Go	(Palmer 5005) 1966
	Lay It On The Line/We Gotta Go	(Panik 5111) 1966
	A Love So True/Where You Belong	(Palmer 5008) 1966
	Without You/Feel A Whole Lot Better	(Canusa 503) 1967

This was an entirely different outfit who came from the Detroit suburb of Oak Park, Michigan. They played together for about three years, between '65 to '67, and opened for The Dave Clark Five and **Sam The Sham & The Pharaohs** in Detroit in 1966. *We Gotta Go* was a enough of a local hit to encourage DJ Scott Regan to get them to re-record the track with different lyrics as *Burger Song*, as a kind of promotion for his show.

Without You is a strong competent garage-style offering, the flip is a **Byrds**' song.

Compilation appearances include: *We Gotta Go* on *Michigan Nuggets* (CD), *Michigan Brand Nuggets* (Dble LP), *Garagelands, Vol. 1 & 2* (CD) and *Garagelands, Vol. 2* (LP); *We Gotta Go* and *Lay It On The Line* on *Sixties Archive Vol. 7 - Michigan Punk* (CD); and *Lay It On The Line* on *Vile Vinyl, Vol. 1* (LP) and *Vile Vinyl* (CD). (VJ/SG/MW/RNe)

The Shy Guys

| 45: | No Flowers On My Mind/Payin' My Dues | (Dunhill D-4167) 1968 |

A garage-rock 45 with farfisa organ, produced by Al Schultz and written by L. King. (SR)

The Shy Ones

| 45: | How Strong My Love Is / Twelve Months Later | (Disca/Tech 804 D-6137) 1967 |

From Ashland, Ohio. The flip to their sole 45, *Twelve Months Later* can also be heard on *Hipsville, Vol. 2* (LP). (GGl/MW)

The Shyres

Personnel:	KENNY BAXTER	drms	A
	BILLIE COX	bs	A
	JOSEPH HEALY	gtr	A
	BOBBY ?	keybds	A
	STEVE?	ld gtr	A

| 45: | Where Is Love?/My Girl | (Cori 31011) 1967 |

Originally known as The Bostonians (or possibly New Bostonians), the band changed names to **The Shyres** because of the local, but more famous **Improper Bostonians**. Billie Cox remembers: "Joseph Healy started the band with his cousin Bobby. I joined the band as a bassist and songwriter/arranger and wrote *Where Is Love*. The flip side, *My Girl* was an original by Joe Healy. The band didn't last too long after this, we did some Catholic Youth Organisation gigs and then went our separate ways. I haven't seen these folks since then but I think only I stayed in the biz, mostly doing theater work as a composer, sound designer and director".

The band was mostly located in a suburb of Boston, Massachusetts called Allston (a small area; it's sometimes thought of as a part of Brighton). The recording was made in Framingham, another town near Boston, where the Cori label was based. Incidentally, Cori also issued some collectable 45s by the likes of The Balladeers, Royals, Mauve, Sole Survivors and C.C. and The Chasers.

Where Is Love was later covered by Rhode Island eighties psychedelic band Plan Nine.

Compilation coverage has included *Where Is Love?* on *New England Teen Scene* (CD) and *New England Teen Scene, Vol. 2* (LP). (MW/BCx)

Siddha

| Personnel incl: | IAN UNDERWOOD | | A |

| ALBUM: | 1(A) | A VERY GENTLE FORCE | (Private Pressing) 1975 - |

Led by Ian Underwood (ex-**Mothers Of Invention**), an album mixing breezy West Coast sounds and light psychedelia with a combination of guitars, keyboards and percussions. (SR)

The Sidekicks

Personnel:	RANDY BOCELLE	bs	A
	ZACK BOCELLE	vcls	A
	MIKE BURKE	gtr	A
	JON SPIRIT	drms	A

| ALBUM: | 1(A) | FIFI THE FLEA | (RCA Victor 3712) 1966 SC HCP |

45s:	α	Suspicions/Up On The Roof	(RCA Victor 47-8864) 1966	55
		Fifi The Flea/Not Now	(RCA Victor 47-8969) 1966	115
		He's My Friend/Miss Charlotte	(RCA Victor 47-9079) 1967 -
		Sight And Sound/ You Gave Me Somebody To Love	(RCA Victor 47-9174) 1967 -

NB: α also released in the UK (RCA RCA 1538) 1966.

A LETHAL DOSE OF HARD PSYCH (Comp CD) including Si-dells.

Monkee-esque teen pop from Wildwood, New Jersey, they achieved some commercial success with their 45s. *Not Now* has also been compiled on the EP, *Garage Dreams Revisited* (7").

And now, turn to the **Redcoats** entry for the real story. (VJ/MW)

Si-dells

| 45: | She's The Only Girl For Me / Watch Out Mother | (East Coast Sound CO-101) 1968 |

This psychedelic outfit came out of Durham in North Carolina. *Watch Out Mother*, is a superb slice of psychedelia with lots of tempo changes, Eastern guitar riffs and surreal vocals. Recommended.

Compilation appearances include: *Watch Out Mother* on *A Lethal Dose Of Hard Psych* (CD) and *Tobacco A-Go-Go, Vol. 1* (LP). (VJ/MW)

The Side Show

| ALBUM: | 1 | THE SIDE SHOW | (Atlantic SD 82??) 1970 - |

Produced by Arif Mardin, a strange soft-rock/psych studio effort, with moog, lysergic vocals and very trippy effects. (SR)

The Sidewalk Skipper Band

Personnel incl:	JOE BALESTRIERI	A
	DAVE McDOWELL	A
	RICK NOVAC	A
	TOM YOAKUM	A

45s:	Strawberry Tuesday / Cynthia At The Garden	(Capitol 2127) 1968
	It's Raining Flowers In My House/ Seventeenth Summer	(Capitol 2205) 1968
	Jeanne At The Circus/Sidewalk Skipper	(TeenTown 113) 1969

Apparently from the Milwaukee area though they recorded in Chicago. Their material is mainly flowery harmony-pop with forays into psychedelia. Their debut and most memorable 45, *Strawberry Tuesday* kicks off with strong fuzz'n'effects then saunters towards dreamy **Association** territory; the baroque flavoured flip should appeal to fans of Anglophile toytown pop-psych.

Brian Balestrieri would still be around as a solo artist in the late seventies.

Compilation appearances include: *Strawberry Tuesday* on *Brain Shadows, Vol. 1* (LP & CD); and *Strawberry Tuesday* and *Cynthia At Her Garden* on *Bring Flowers To U.S.* (LP). (MW)

The Sidewinders

Personnel:	LEIGH LISOWSKI	bs, vcls	A
	ANDY PALEY	vcls, hmca	A
	MIKE READ	gtr	A
	ERIC ROSENFELD	gtr, vcls	A
	HENRY STERN	drms, vcls	A

ALBUM: 1(A) THE SIDEWINDERS (RCA LSP- 4696) 1972 -

Produced by Lenny Kaye in New York City, this was one of the first groups featuring Andy Paley. Still teaming up with Rosenfeld, he would also record with his brother Jonathan as "The Paley Brothers" in 1978 and later work with the Ramones. (SR)

Siegel Schwall Band

Personnel:	RUSS CHADWICK	drms	AB
	JACK DAWSON	bs	A
	JIM SCHWALL	gtr, mandolin, vcls	AB
	CORKY SIEGEL	hrmnca, piano, vcls	AB
	ROLLOW RADFORD	bs	B

ALBUMS: 1(A) SIEGEL SCHWALL BAND (Vanguard VSD-79235) 1966 -
(up to 2(A) SAY SIEGEL SCHWALL (Vanguard VSD-79249) 1967 -
1972) 3(A) SHAKE (Vanguard VSD-79289) 1968 -
4(A) SIEGEL SCHWALL 70 (Vanguard VSD-6562) 1970 -
5(B) THE SIEGEL SCHWALL BAND
 (Wooden Nickel WNS 1002) 1971 -
6(B) SLEEPY HOLLOW (Wooden Nickel WNS 1010) 1972 -

NB: (1) and (3) reissued on one CD (Vanguard VCD 79235/89).

This was Chicago's "other" white blues group of the sixties. **Siegel-Schwall** emphasized a kind of neo-psychedelic improvisation on blues themes that has not aged as well as the **Butterfield Blues Band**. Samuel Charters produced most of their Vanguard albums which are considered to be their best output. Recorded in New York, their second album, *Say Siegel Schwall* is quite consistent, with its long *I.S.P.I. Blues (Illinois State Psychiatric Institution)*. **Siegel Schwall** kept on recording during the seventies and Corky Siegel and his harmonica also guested on many blues albums. (SR)

The Sights and Sounds

Previously known as **Carroll's Mood** with one 45, this late sixties psychedelic outfit came from Texas and released a 45 which I don't have details of. However *Texas Punk, Vol. 3* (LP) and *Acid Visions - Complete Collection, Vol. 2* (3-CD) include four previously unreleased cuts by the band:- *Mystical Bells*, *Plastic People*, a cover of **The Buckingham's** hit, *Kind Of A Drag* and of The Supremes' classic *You Keep Me Hangin' On*. Their four unreleased tracks are also featured on Collectables' *History Of Texas, Vol. 3* and *4* CDs. (VJ/MW)

Silent Partner

ALBUM: 1 HUNG BY A THREAD (Lucky Boy LB-SP-32779) 1975 R1

From Georgia, and issued on a local label, an album of long melodic songs with electric and acoustic guitars on tracks like *The Better Half*, *Reunion*, *From The Diary Of H.R.H. 1975* and *Just Sail Around*. (SR)

The Silhouettes

ALBUM: 1 THE SILHOUETTES (Segue SEG-1001) c1970 ?

From Pittsburgh, an album mixing pop with female vocals (a cover of *Norwegian Wood*, *Conversations*, *Hashi Baba*, *Sesame*) with two wild psychedelic cuts with mega-fuzz guitar *Fonky First* and *Lunar Invasion*. (SR)

SILVER APPLES - Contact CD.

Silk

Personnel:	MICHAEL GEE (MICHAEL STANLEY)	bs	A
	CHRIS JOHNS	gtr, vcls	A
	COURTNEY JOHNS	drms	A
	(HARRY PALMER	gtr	A)
	RANDY SABO	keyb'ds	A
	(BILL SZYMCZYK	perc	A)

ALBUM: 1(A) SMOOTH AS RAW SILK (ABC ABCS 694) 1969 -

A hard organ/guitar quartet produced and arranged by Bill Szymczyk. The album has become a very minor collectable and contains several good tracks: *Foreign Thing*, *Skitzo Blues*, *Walk In My Mind* and *Scottish Thing* which is one of the few psychedelic tracks to end with bagpipes!

The songs were written by the group members and Bill Szymczyk, except a cover of Tim Rose's *Long Haired Boy* which was "dedicated to groupies everywhere" and *Custody* written by Steve Karliski and Larry Kolber. Harry Palmer of **Ford Theater** played guitar and percussion on some tracks and is also credited for production work.

Michael Gee later changed his name to Michael Stanley. He then formed the Michael Stanley Band, who were was popular, especially in the Ohio/Pennsylvania area, during the seventies and eighties. (SR/VJ/RP/EJ)

Silk Winged Alliance

45: Flashback/Hometown (Accent ACS 1277) 1968

A fine double-sided psychedelic offering by a sadly unknown band. Check it out! Great fuzz guitar on *Flashback*, but the flip may be the stronger song. (Someone else has recorded *Hometown* under another name). Does anyone know their hometown? The Accent label points to Los Angeles.

Compilation appearances have included: *Hometown* on *Turds On A Bum Ride Vol. 1 & 2* (Dble CD), *Turds On A Bum Ride, Vol. 1* (Dble LP); *Hometown* and *Flashback* on *The Garage Zone, Vol. 1* (LP), *The Garage Zone Box Set* (4-LP) and *The Human Expression And Other Psychedelic Groups - Your Mind Works In Reverse* (CD). (VJ/MW)

Silver

Personnel: anonymous A

ALBUM: 1(A) CHILDREN OF THE LORD
 (Grammi Fonics GPS 8322) 1975 R2

A local Wisconsin group. This is the best album in the series of obscure items issued in the plain (generic) covers emblazoned with "Advance Reviewer Copy - Confidential" during the early - mid seventies. A strong local effort with heavy guitar on about half of the cuts, garagey edge and strange mastering (a tape splice on the title track was done so badly, it sounds like a skip!). *Tail Dragger* is a loud, bluesy riffer that has universal appeal. (CF)

Silver Apples

Personnel:	SIMEON	electronics, vcls	A
	DAN TAYLOR	vcls, perc	A

			HCP
ALBUMS:	1(A) SILVER APPLES	(Kapp 3562) 1968	193 SC
	2(A) CONTACT	(Kapp 3584) 1969	- SC

NB: (1) and (2) have been reissued on one CD by TRC and officially on one CD by MCA (MCD-11680) 2002.

45s:	Oscillations/Whirly Bird	(Kapp 923) 1968
	Confusion/You And I	(Kapp 956) 1968

This New York duo began as a 5-piece band called The Overland Stage Electric Band, which gradually dwindled to two as a result of the other members' dislike of Simeon's increasing preoccupation with electronic sounds. The pair immediately changed their name to **Silver Apples** after a W.B.Yeats poem they liked. Simeon kept adding to his collection of electronic paraphernalia - dubbed the "simeon" - until it included over a dozen oscillators, six of them being tuned to bass-notes, which were played by his feet (as only six notes were available, this accounts for the monotony of the basslines).

Their first gig was in front of 30,000 people at an all-day concert in Central Park along with the **Mothers of Invention**, **The Fugs**, **Steve Miller Band** and others. The resultant glowing press-notices ("...absolutely mind shattering music...") helped land them a recording contract with Kapp Records.

They were one of the very first groups along with **The United States Of America** and **Fifty Foot Hose** to experiment with electronic music. The result was two interesting, but totally uncommercial albums. The music sounds partly drug-induced and is often discordant. In many ways it is possibly more acceptable now, in the wake of artists like Ultravox and Orchestral Manoeuvres In The Dark, than it was in 1968. Whilst their music was undoubtedly innovative, their lyrics were sometimes irritatingly repetitive. Both albums are worth hearing, however, with the second probably the stronger of the two. The intro to the second's opening track *You And I* successfully recreates the sound of an airplane taking off.

An obviously influential band, they were the subject of a tribute album by contemporary experimental psychedelic acts, *A Tribute To* in 1997. Simeon has also "reformed" the band, recording a 45, two albums, *Beacon* (1997) and *Decatur* (1998), as well as performing a few gigs. At one gig on Sept 14th 1997 in London, a various artists CD sampler was given away to the audience, which includes a **Silver Apples** track.

More recently *The Garden* - a CD of sessions dating from 1968/69 has surfaced. (VJ/LP)

Silver Bullets

See **The Ladds** entry.

Silver Fleet

45:	Come On Plane/Look Out World	(UNI 55271) 1971

This band's *Look Out World* typified the wave of protest sounds in 1965-66 in America. The vocalist growls about the threats to his freedom - his girl that's left him and an unsympathetic world. Musically, the recording predates the influence of psychedelics, comprising raucous vocals superimposed upon a 'my baby left me' guitar moan. It was much later covered by The Margin Of Insanity on their EP.

What's so strange about this 45 however is that it was issued in 1971 and this outfit has somehow been linked to 10cc (?!!).

Compilation appearances include *Look Out World* on *Pebbles, Vol. 10* (CD), *Pebbles, Vol. 3 (ESD)* (CD) and *Pebbles, Vol. 7* (LP). (VJ/MW)

Silver Metre

Personnel:	JACK REYNOLDS	vcls	A
	PETE SEARS	bs, keyb'ds	A
	LEIGH STEPHENS	gtr	A
	MICK WALLER	drms	A

ALBUM:	1(A) SILVER METRE	(National General NG-2000) 1970 -

NB: (1) counterfeited on CD and reissued legitimately on vinyl and CD (Akarma AK 072) 1999.

45s:	α Superstar/Now They've Found Me	(National General 001) 1970
	Now They've Found Me/ Compromising Situation	(National General 010) 1970

NB: α On first pressing *They've Found Me* is misspelt *Theyze*....

A short-lived San Francisco-based outfit whose album was partly recorded in London. **Stephens** had previously been with **Blue Cheer** and two musicians were British: Pete Sears was a session musician and Waller had come from The Jeff Beck Group. The album is basically heavy rock with splatterings of psychedelia. It included three Elton John/Bernie Taupin compositions: *Country Comfort*, *Now They've Found Me* and *Sixty Years On*.

Leigh Stephens also had a solo career and in 1972 would form **Pilot** with Waller. Pete Sears would later play with Rod Stewart but also with **Stoneground** and Jefferson Starship. He also played with John Cipollina and **Hot Tuna**.

National General was one of the many Buddah group subsidiary-labels. (VJ/SR)

Silver, Platinum and Gold

45:	La La Love Chains/ Yes, You Are	(Warner Bros. 8057) 1974

A rare California pop 45, of interest here as it was written and produced by Gary Zekley of **Yellow Balloon** fame and Mitch Bottler. (SR)

SILVER METRE - Silver Metre LP.

The Silvertones

Personnel incl: GAYLON LATIMORE (GAYLAN LATIMER)   A

45:	Something Is Strange/		
	Get Out Of Town	(Texas Record Co 2099)	1965

One of Latimore's sixties Texan bands, just prior to his solo career as **Gaylon Ladd**. Don't expect an early *Repulsive Situation* sound, the 'A' side here is pre-beat style crooning and the flip is more uptempo but still nightclub rather than garage fayre. (VJ)

Jeff Simmons

Personnel:	JEFF SIMMONS	gtr	AB
	RANDY STEIRLING		A
	JOHN KEHLIOR	drms	B
	CRAIG TARWATER	gtr	B
	IAN UNDERWOOD	gtr	B
	RON WOODS	drms	B
	FRANK ZAPPA	gtr	B

ALBUMS:	1(A)	NAKED ANGELS (Original Movie Soundtrack)		
			(Straight 1056)	1969 R1
	2(A)	LUCILLE HAS MESSED UP MY MIND		
			(Straight 1057)	1969 R1

NB: (2) also issued in the UK on Straight with the same catalogue number.

Simmons relocated to Los Angeles after splitting **The Easy Chair** and **Zappa** put him to work. Two albums were issued together with sequenced catalogue numbers in 1969, both are rather unstructured guitar-led inventions of a self-indulgent nature. While **Simmons** was obviously a very talented player, his ability to assemble his music into coherent structures was undeveloped. These are among the rarest records on the Straight label and yet are still only in the R1 category. (CF)

Simpson

ALBUM:	1	SIMPSON	(Columbia)	1971 -

A forgotten hippie country-rock group. (SR)

John Simson

ALBUM:	1	WE CAN BE EVERYTHING	(Perception)	1971 ?

From New York, a good folk-rock singer. Perception was the label founded by **Jimmy Curtiss** and this album was recorded in London with members of Spooky Tooth, Juicy Lucy, Adrian and Paul Gurvitz.

John later went to law school, but stayed in the music industry as an attorney and manager. He is currently the Executive Director of SoundExchange, the U.S. equivalent of PPL (in the U.K.). (SR/JSn)

The Sinners

Personnel:	EMANUEL ??	A
	TONY ??	A
	VIC ??	A

ALBUM:	1(A)	Unreleased acetate title unknown on Gold Star.	
			196?

NB: (1) cuts consist of:- *Mystic Woman, I've Had It, I'm A Man, You're The One, It's Not Unusual, Ya Done Me Wrong, I Go Crazy, That's My Little Suzy, Here Comes The Night, Suzie Q, Don't Let Me Be Misunderstood, Concrete And Clay*.

45s:	You Don't Love Me/		
	I Like The Look Of You	(Mercury 72388)	1965
	A Change/Goin' Out Of My Mind	(Mercury 72453)	1965

A California beat-pop outfit who produced a couple of decent punkers in *You Don't Love Me* and *Goin' Out Of My Mind*. The latter is notable for catchy riffs and a guitar sounding like a dying seagull(?!), whilst the former is a DC5-type stomper with fuzz. Both Nick Venet and Mike Curb had a hand in the two 45s - it's a shame the album, which consists of covers done in a beat style, never got past the acetate stage.

They were the house band on Hollywood A-Go-Go and performed mainly cover tunes. The show ran from December 1964 until mid-65; it was broadcast on KHJ TV Channel 9 in Los Angeles, but was syndicated nationally to a bunch of cities. (MW/JRe/BC)

Sin Say Shuns

Personnel:	BOBBY COTTLE	drms	A
	BILL EIDSON	gtr	A
	PAUL INDELICATO	bs	A
	TONY VISCO	keyb'ds	A

ALBUM:	1(A)	I'LL BE THERE	(Venett VS 940)	1966 ?

45s:	I'll Be There/You Said To Me	(Venett 106)	1966
	All My Lonely Waiting/?	(Venett 108)	1966
	You Said To Me/		
	Bring Back My Good Times	(American 3367)	Jun. 196?

Formed in 1965 in Southern California around Pasadena, they gigged around L.A. and Las Vegas. The LP was recorded live at P.J.'s in Hollywood, famous as the venue for the **Standells**' debut album. Unsurprisingly there are further comparisons - this is definitely not psych but 'big-beat' club sounds. With covers of *Midnight Hour*, *Big Boss Man*, *Good Loving* and *Stand By Me*, you get the gist? The originals, penned by Bill Eidson, fall mainly into the beat-ballad category with the notable exception of *You Said To Me* - a catchy uptempo beat - folk-rocker. Dealers who describe this as garage or psych should be fed into the nearest CD player!

The band were still going a decade or more later. Their cover of the Stones' *Jumpin' Jack Flash*, featured on *Kicks & Chicks* (LP), is from their 1978 album *Live At P.J.'s Vol. 3* (West One 028). (MW)

Sir Douglas Quintet

Personnel:	JACK BARBER	bs	A
	LEON BEATTY	vcls, perc	A
	AUGIE MEYER	keyb'ds	ABCDE
	JOHN PEREZ	drms	A CDE
	DOUG SAHM	gtr, flte, vcls	ABCDE
	WHITNEY FREEMAN	bs	B
	FRANK MORIN	sax	BC
	GEORGE RAINS	drms	B
	WAYNE TALBERT	keyb'ds	B
	HARVEY KAGAN	bs	C
	JIM STALLINGS	bs	C
	ALVIN CROW	gtr	D
	SPEEDY SPARKS	bs	DE
	LONIE ORTEGA	gtr	E

NB: Line-up 'A' late 1964-1967; 'B' 1967-late 1968; 'C' late 1968-December 1970.

HCP

ALBUMS:	1(A)	THE BEST OF THE SIR DOUGLAS QUINTET		
(up to			(Tribe 37001)	1966 - R1
1972)	2(B)	HONKY BLUES	(Smash SRS 67108)	1968 - -
	3(C)	MENDOCINO	(Smash SRS 67115)	1969 81
	4(C)	TOGETHER AFTER FIVE	(Smash SRS 67130)	1970 - -
	5(C)	1+ 1 + 1 = 4	(Philips 600.344)	1970 - -
	6(C)	ROUGH EDGES	(Mercury SRM 1-655)	1973 - -

NB: (1) is not a 'best of' album. There is a U.K. CD Collection which compiles 17 tracks. It's also available on vinyl as a double album. Also of interest to collectors will be the 2-LP set *Recording Trip*, which compiles some of their best and rare material from 1968-70. (6) is a collection of previously unreleased tapes from 1968/69 plus a non-album single. Also of interest are *Best Of* (LP/CD) (Beat Rocket BRCD 123) 2000, a reissue of (1) but with 2 bonus cuts; and *Is Back* (LP/CD) (Beat Rocket BRCD 124). *She's About A Mover: The Best Of Doug Sahm & The Sir Douglas Quintet* (Edsel NESTCD 918) 1999 is disappointing and repeats material previously issued on Edsel's 1999 *The Crazy Cajun Recordings*. *The Best Of The Sir Douglas Quintet.... Plus!* (Westside WESA 862) 2000 comprises the groups first album plus all the group's singles from that period.

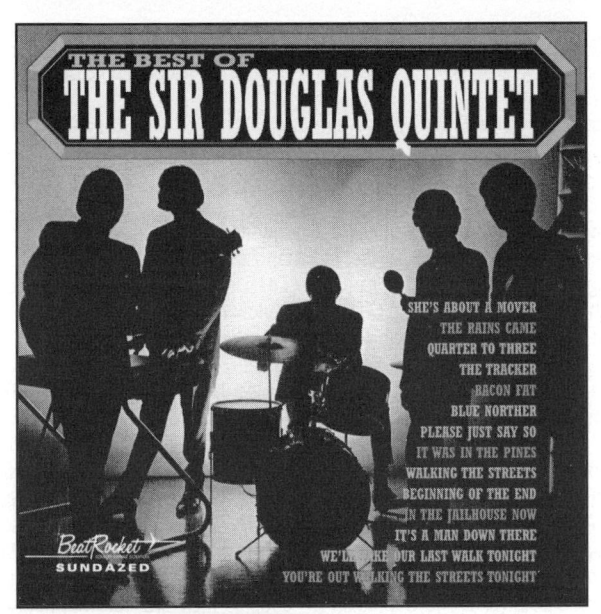

SIR DOUGLAS QUINTET - Best Of CD.

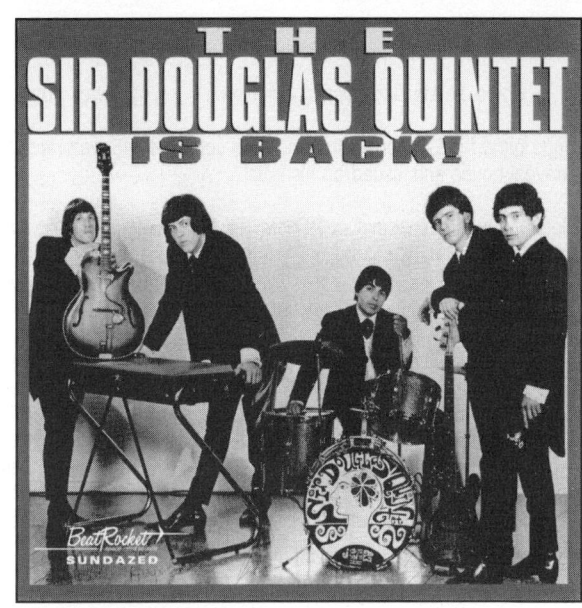

SIR DOUGLAS QUINTET - Is Back CD.

			HCP
45s: (up to 1972)	Sugar Bee/Blue Norther	(Pacemaker 260)	1964 -
	She's About A Mover/ We'll Take Our Last Walk Tonight	(Tribe 8308)	1964 13
	The Tracker/Blue Norther	(Tribe 8310)	1964 105
	The Story Of John Hardy/In Time	(Tribe 8312)	1965 -
	The Rains Came/Bacon Fat	(Tribe 8314)	1965 31
α	Quarter To Three/She's Gotta Be Boss	(Tribe 8317)	1965 129
	Beginning Of The End/ Love Don't Treat Me Fair	(Tribe 8318)	1966 -
α	She Digs My Love/ When I Sing The Blues	(Tribe 8321)	1966 132
	We'll Take Our Last Walk Tonight/ (b) Walking the Streets	(Teardrop 3070)	1966 -
β	It's A Man Down There/4 A.M.	(Teardrop 3074)	1966 -
χ	Wine, Wine, Wine/Joey's Guitar	(Pic One 11 1)	1966 -
	Are Inlaws Really Inlaws?/Sell A Song	(Smash 2169)	1968 -
φ	Mendocino/ I Wanna Be Your Mama Again	(Smash 2191)	1968 27
	It Didn't Even Bring Me Down/ Lawd I'm Just A Country Boy	(Smash 2222)	1969 108
γ	Dynamite Woman/ Too Many Docile Minds	(Smash 2233)	1969 83
	At The Crossroads/Texas Me	(Smash 2253)	1969 104
	Nuevo Laredo/I Don't Wanna Go Home	(Smash 2259)	1970 -
δ	Be Real/I Don't Wanna Go Home	(Mercury 73098)	1970 -
	What About Tomorrow?/A Nice Song	(Philips 40676)	1971 -
	Catch The Man On The Rise/ Pretty Flowers	(Philips 40687)	1971 -
ε	Michoagan/West Side Blues	(Mercury 73257)	1972 -
	Me And My Destiny/ Wasted Days, Wasted Nights	(Philips 40708)	1972 -

NB: α by Sir Douglas; (b) instrumental recorded by Don Goldie with Sir Douglas Quintet; β credited to Him. Recorded by Sahm with members of the Quintet and Houston guitarist Joey Long; χ credited to The Devons. The 'B' side is an instrumental featuring Joey Long again; δ a Doug Sahm solo effort credited to Wayne Douglas; ε the 'A' side was from the Movie 'Cisco Pike'. φ also released in France with a picture sleeve. γ also released with picture sleeve in Germany and Belgium. Non Lp until its inclusion in *Rough Edges*. There's also a rare French EP: *She's About A Mover/We'll Take Our Last Walk Tonight/The Tracker/Blue Norther* with a picture sleeve (London REU 10171).

Doug Sahm was born on 6th November 1941 in San Antonio, Texas. After some solo recordings in his youth, he formed The Sir Douglas Quintet in 1964 when he met producer Huey P. Meaux. Their first 45, *Sugar Bee*, flopped but the follow-up, *She's About A Mover*, which was an attempt to imitate the British beat groups of the era and featured an insistent organ riff from Augie Meyer, reached No. 13 in the U.S. Charts in the Summer of 1965. It later peaked at No. 15 in the UK. It remained their most successful song and had a raw harshness that was typically Texan.

The Rains Came gave the band a minor U.S. hit in the Spring of 1966 but the novelty of the band soon wore off and their debut album, *The Best Of The Sir Douglas Quintet* (which was not in fact a 'best of') attracted little interest when it was released. By 1966 Sahm had gotten into the drug scene and after getting busted in Texas he broke up the band (line-up 'A') and moved to San Francisco. The *Honky Blues* album was recorded by line-up B with the help of session musicians as *The Sir Douglas Quintet + 2*, although the following year he reformed the original Quintet with a modified line-up (C) and got the band a new recording deal with Mercury's Smash label. In the Spring of 1969 they enjoyed a Top 30 hit with *Mendocino* and an album of the same name was issued too. (Mendocino is a picturesque Northern California coastal town). Raw and unsophisticated it included some strong songs in addition to the title track, most notably *At The Crossroads*, which was later covered by Mott The Hoople. The album helped establish the band as an important part of the San Francisco Sound and they also had a good reputation as a 'live' band. *Dynamite Woman*, which peaked at No. 82 in the Autumn of 1969, was their final U.S. hit and with their fourth and fifth albums largely unnoticed, Sahm broke up the band in late 1972. By then he'd formed his own band which included several **Sir Douglas Quintet** personnel. **The Sir Douglas Quintet** also played and recorded without Sahm using the name El Quintet between January 1971 and August 1972. They recorded two albums for United Artists (*Future Tense* and *El Quintet 2*), although the second was never formally released.

Among the members of the **Quintet**, Augie Meyers created the Texas Re-cord label for his own solo records during the seventies, Jim Stallings was also known as **J.J. Light** and **Wayne Talbert** was also recording under his name. Harvey Kagan joined **Dewey Martin's Medicine Ball**.

In 1970, Doug Sahm produced the album of **Louie and The Lovers**. It's also worth mentioning that, during the seventies, Doug Sahm tried constantly to help Roky Erickson, by producing his demos, recording his songs (*You're Gonna Miss Me* is on *Border Wave*) and playing live with him (some taped surfaced on *The Reunion Of The Cosmic Brothers* with Freddie Fender (Crazy Cajun, CC-LP-1013) 1980.

At the start of the 1980s Sahm reformed the **Sir Douglas Quintet** with John Perez and Augie Meyer from the original line-up and two newcomers Alvin Crow and Speedy Sparks (line-up D). They released an album called *Border Wave* on Takoma in 1981 and at least five other albums of **Sir Douglas Quintet** material were released on Takoma during the 1980s.

Compilation appearances include *She's A Mover* on *Nuggets Box* (4-CD), *Texas Music, Vol. 3* (CD), *Wild Thing* and *21 KILT Goldens, Vol. 2*.

Doug Sahm died of a heart attack in Taos, New Mexico, in November 1999.

In 2000 Sundazed trawled **SDQ**'s Crazy Cajun/Tribe period, 1964-1966. First off is a reissue of *The Best Of The Sir Douglas Quintet* LP with two bonus tracks (*Bacon Fat* and *Blue Norther*). Its companion is *The Sir Douglas Quintet Is Back!* which gathers together various 45 sides (on Pacemaker and Tribe plus their cover of *Wine, Wine, Wine* as "The Devons") with outtakes from the 1965-6 Pasadena Sounds sessions. (VJ/SR/NL)

The Sires

| 45: | Come To Me Baby/Don't Look Now | (Graves 1094) 1966 |

A teenage band from Eugene, Oregon. Their sole "lo-fi" 45 was recorded at Alan Graves' house and issued on his label.

Compilation appearances include *Come To Me Baby* on *Highs In The Mid-Sixties, Vol. 7* (LP). (GGI/MW)

Sir Michael and The Sounds

| 45: | Can You/Love Your Fellow Man | (Dig 333) 1967 |

An obscure Clearwater, Florida outfit whose *Can You* can also be heard on *Teenage Shutdown, Vol. 9* (LP & CD), *The Chosen Few, Vol. 2* (LP) and *Chosen Few Vol's 1 & 2* (CD). According to the CD's liner notes, Dig records was run by Allen Diggs. (MW/MM)

Sir Raleigh and The Coupons

Personnel:
?? HARRIS		A
"SNEAKY" PETE KLEINOW	gtr	A
JOHNNY MEEKS	bs, gtr	A
WALTER DWAYNE MIDKIFF (aka SIR WALTER RALEIGH & DEWEY MARTIN)	ld vcls	AB
NORMAN RALEIGH	(?)	A
STEVE GREEN	ld gtr	B
J.C. RIECK	keyb'ds	B
LYALL SMITH	drms	B
?? ??	bs	B

NB: Line-up 'A' 1964-65, Line-up 'B' 1966.

45s:	White Cliffs Of Dover/Somethin' Or Other	(A&M 757) 1965
	Tomorrow's Gonna Be Another Day/Whitcomb Street	(Jerden 760) 1965
	While I Wait/Somethin' Or Other	(A&M 764) 1965
	Tell Her Tonight/If You Need Me	(Tower 156) 1965
	I Don't Want Her To Cry/Always	(Tower 220) 1966

From Seattle, Washington, **Sir Raleigh** was also known as Sir Walter Raleigh and **Dewey Martin**, but his real name was Walter Dwayne Midkiff, and he later became the drummer for **Buffalo Springfield**. Together with line-up 'A' of the Coupons he recorded a string of singles and his finest moment is usually considered to be his version of the Steve Venet/Tommy Boyce composition *Tomorrow's Gonna Be Another Day*. This sort of grungy pre-punk typified the Northwest in this era and this particular recording predated **The Monkees**' version by over a year. The flip *Whitcomb Street* was an instrumental - perhaps it was a tribute to influential Northwest pop/rock figure Ian Whitcomb.

Sir Raleigh sacked his original backing band after the recording of their final 45, but prior to its release. "Sneaky" Pete Kleinow went on to the Flying Burrito Bros. and Lyall Smith had previous been in The Stingrays (from Olympia, Washington).

Compilation appearances include: *Tomorrow's Gonna Be Another Day* on *Northwest Battle Of The Bands, Vol. 1 - Flash And Crash* (LP & CD), *Northwest Battle Of The Bands, Vol. 1* (CD), *The Hitmakers* (LP) and *Highs In The Mid-Sixties, Vol. 14* (LP); *Things We Said Today* and *Tomorrow's Gonna Be Another Day* on *The Hitmakers* (LP); and *White Cliffs Of Dover* on *The History Of Northwest Rock, Vol. 1* (LP). (DR/MW/VJ)

Sir Winston and The Commons

Personnel:
DON BASORE		A
HERBIE CRAWFORD		A
RONNIE MATELIC		A
JOHNNY MEDVESCEK		A
JOE STOUT		A

EP:	1(A) SIR WINSTON AND THE COMMONS (PS)	(Sundazed SEP 144) 1999
45s:	Come Back Again/We're Gonna Love	(Soma 1454) 1965
	Not The Spirit Of India/One Last Chance	(Nauseating Butterfly 2207) 1966

This Indianapolis band developed a large local following - indeed they once opened for **The Byrds** at the Indianapolis Coliseum in July 1966. Their stage shows were wild! *We're Gonna Love* is a real grungy garage number with lots of fuzz. *One Last Chance* is a slow melodic folk-rock ballad, whilst *Not The Spirit Of India* is an Eastern-style piece of psychedelia.

The band had evolved out of an outfit called The Pickups back in 1963 and Ron Matelic and John Medvescek later went on to **Anonymous**.

Compilation coverage has included: *We're Gonna Love* on *Back From The Grave, Vol. 3* (LP), *Back From The Grave, Vol. 2* (CD), *The Big Hits Of Mid-America* (Dble CD) and *Soma Records Story, Vol. 1* (LP); *One Last Chance* on *Hoosier Hotshots* (LP); *Not The Spirit Of India* on *Sixties Rebellion, Vol. 15* (LP & CD); and *Come Back Again* on *Soma Records Story, Vol. 2* (LP). The Sundazed EP couples their two 45s with notes from Jud Cost and quotes from Ron Matelic. (MW/VJ)

The Sirs

Personnel:
MIKE MEYERS	bs	A
ARTHUR SALAZAR	gtr	ABC
EVERETT SIMILA	gtr	ABC
DICK YANDELL	drms	ABC
RANDY CULCANGO	vcls	BC
ROY IHADA	keyb'ds	BC
ROGER STUART	bs	BC
PEGGY ADAMS	keyb'ds	C

| 45s: | Off In A Daydream/Help Me | (Amreco M 103) 1965 |
| | I'm In Love/Drop Me A Line | (Amreco M 106) 1966 |

Formed in 1965 at Roosevelt High School, Portland, Oregon. They got a contract with Amreco Records as a prize for coming second in a Portland teenfair band battle. Dan Gordon, who owned the label became their manager. *Off In A Daydream* got a lot of local airplay in Portland but the follow-up was less successful. Then, at the suggestion of Bobby Holden (**Don and The Goodtimes**), they changed their name to Atlantis, recording one 45 under this name before they dissolved in 1970/71. Most members still live in the Portland area.

Compilation appearances include *Help Me* on *Let's Dig 'Em Up, Vol. 3* (LP) and *Bad Vibrations, Vol. 3* (LP). (VJ)

SIX FEET UNDER - In Retrospect CD.

Six Feet Under

Personnel:
JERRY DOBB	keyb'ds, vcls	ABC
SCOTT JULIAN	gtr	ABC
DUANE ULGERAIT	bs	ABC
RICHIE	drms	A
HECTOR "TICO" TORRES	drms	B
JAY CRYSTAL	drms	C
NANETTE DeLAUNE	vcls	C

CD: 1 IN RETROSPECT 1969-70 (Arf! Arf! AA-074) 1998

45s: Inspiration In My Head/In Retrospect (Scepter 12289) 1970
  Fields/Freedom (Scepter 12324) 1971

Jerry Dobb and Scott Julian formed the Marc 5 in 1966 in Colonia, New Jersey. Later known as the Sonix, they decided to change musical direction in 1968 and new personnel were secured to form **Six Feet Under**. The first drummer didn't last long, his seat being taken by Hector Torres. By 1970, seeking a recording contract, another shake-up resulted in the exit of Torres and the acquisition of a young female vocalist to strengthen that department.

The CD retrospective comprises nineteen tracks - eight studio, five home recordings plus live and radio spots. It showcases the width of the bands hippie-acid-psych repertoire, sounding like **Ill Wind** one minute and **Iron Butterfly** the next. An excellent and welcome release with a fascinating history and track-by-track breakdown from Jerry Dobbs. And as Jerry points out, ironically it was only ousted drummer Torres who found real success and fame. After returning home to Sayerville, he'd bounce back after teaming up with a promising youngster called Jon Bon Jovi...

Six Feet Under Theme, an unreleased '68 effort, resurfaced on *30 Seconds Before The Calico Wall* (CD) and their unreleased cover of **Iron Butterfly**'s *In-A-Gadda-Da-Vida* on *Beyond The Calico Wall* (CD). Their first 45 occupies similar territory - heavy acid-rock with hippie undertones. (MW)

The Six Pack

45s: Tombstone Shadow/Vuela (Gordo) c1968
  Bring 'Em On Home/Weep No More (Gordo 704) c1968

A forgotten group, possibly from the Los Angeles chicano scene. Gordo also released some singles by El Chicano. (SR)

Six Pence

Based in Louisville, Kentucky this band's *Got A Girl* has resurfaced on *Oil Stains, Vol. 2* (LP). The track had originally appeared on a rare 1965 various artist album *The Louisville Scene* (Rod'N Custom LLP 3001). (MW)

Thee Sixpence

Personnel:
LEE FREEMAN	vcls, hrmnca, gtr	ABCD
GENE GUNNELS	drms	AB D
ED KING	gtr	ABCD
GARY LOVETRO	bs	ABCD
MIKE LUCIANO	tamb, vcls	AB
STEVE RABE	ld gtr	A
MARK WEITZ	vcls, keyb'ds	BCD
RANDY SEOL	drms	CD
GREG MUNFORD	vcls	D

ALBUM: 1(-) STEP BY STEP (Akarma AK 034) 1998

45s:
α	In The Building/Hay Joe	(All-American 333) 1966
	Long Days Care/Can't Explain	(All-American 303) 1966
	Fortune Teller / My Flash On You	(All-American 313) 1966
	Fortune Teller / My Flash On You	(Dot 16959) 1966
	Heart Full Of Rain/	
χ	(Gotta Get The) First Plane Home	(All-American 353) 1967
β	Heart Full Of Rain/Fortune Teller	(All-American 353) 1967
δ	Incense And Pepermints/ The Birdman Of Alkatrash	(All-American 373) 1967

THEE SIXPENCE - Step By Step LP.

NB: α as by The Sixpence, 'B' side title is a mis-spelling of HEY Joe. β is a second press of χ with *Fortune Teller* replacing *(Gotta Get The) First Plane Home*. δ 'A' side also has a 'p' missing from 'Peppermints'.

From Glendale, California, this band is best known for being the early incarnation of the **Strawberry Alarm Clock**, arguably one of the most famous, colourful, and doubtless the most commercially successful U.S. flower-power psychedelic-pop band.

Some band members were earlier in a sixties surf outfit called the Irridescents who released a 45 back in 1963. The adaptable and durable Ed King would find success again in the seventies with Lynyrd Skynyrd. *Incense...* vocalist Gregg Munford was a member of label-mates **Indescribably Delicious**, leading to speculations ever since as to their identity, which have finally been clarified with another Akarma reissue - see the **Indescribably Delicious** entry.

Thee Sixpence's line-up was pretty fluid - Ed King joined after the first 45. Following *Heart Full Of Rain* the group recorded *Incense And Peppermints*, but before it was released, their name was changed by management to the **Strawberry Alarm Clock**. The group played Santa Barbara quite a bit, leading to speculation that they were based there, but all but Lee Freeman came from Glendale.

Step By Step gathers together all their All-American 45s above and adds one bonus track, *The World's On Fire*, an awesome rambling garage-psych workout from **Strawberry Alarm Clock**'s debut album. Indeed this album is essential listening for garage, psych and **Strawberry Alarm Clock** fans and is unreservedly recommended. It bristles with raw fuzzy garage and psych gems which, with the obvious exception of *Incense And Peppermints*, barely hint at the subsequent transformation into **Strawberry Alarm Clock** and their wider-appealing kaftan-and-beads psychedelic pop. Covers include faithfully raucous versions of **Love**'s *Can't Explain* and *My Flash On You* and the oft-visited *Hey Joe* and *Fortune Teller*. *Heart Full Of Rain* was later covered by label-mates **Big Brother**.

Many of their tracks had previously been compiled *In The Building*, with its hypnotic drum fill, on *Psychedelic Disaster Whirl* (LP); (MW/VJ/MM)

The Sixpence

45: You're The Love/What To Do (Impact 1025) 1967

An obscure Detroit combo whose *You're The Love* is a frantic hand-clappin' frat-party-style rocker, backed by a harmonious mellow popper.

Compilation appearances include: *You're The Love* and *What To Do* on *The Best Of Impact Records* (CD). (MW)

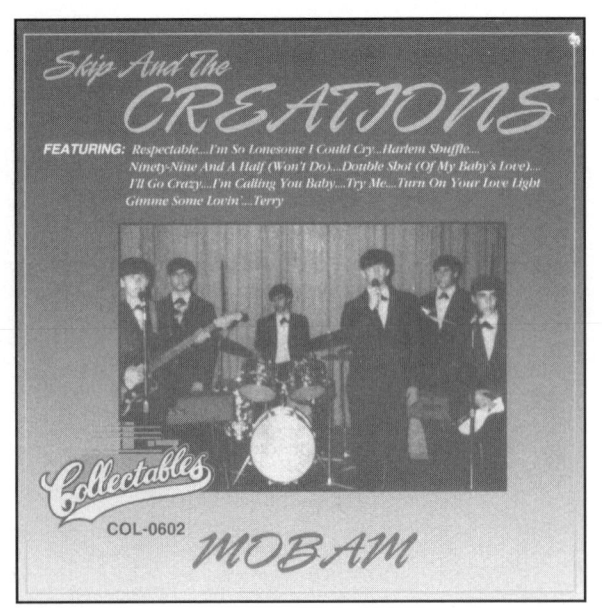

SKIP and THE CREATIONS - Mobam CD.

The Six Pents

Personnel:	RICHARD BAIN	vcls	A
	JOHN T. BONNO	bs	ABC
	MIKE CEMO	drms	AB
	D.J. GREER	piano, gtr, vcls	ABC
	PAUL GUILLET	ld gtr	ABC
	ROCK ROMANO	gtr, vcls	ABC
	SAM IRWIN	vcls, tamb	BC
	CARSON GRAHAM	drms	C

45s:	α	I'll Be Good/I Didn't Start Living	(Geer 5267) 1965
	β	Good To You/Your Girl Too	(Matrix 9 5268) 1965
		Summer Girl/She Lied	(Kidd 1335) 1966

NB: α some copies came with *I'll Be Good* crossed out and replaced with *Good To You* - the same track as on β.

Also known as the Six Pents, the nucleus of this Texas group: Rock Romano, Mike Cemo, Paul Guillet and John Bonno had previously played together in a high school R'n'R band. Most of their 45s were recorded at Andrus studios in Houston and in particular, *She Lied*, has some fine vocals, and a Beatles/Invasion influence.

The band later signed a contract with Bobby Shad of Mainstream Records, and became **The Sixpentz**. When they then discovered the similarly named **Sixpence** they opted for the more distinctive **The Fun And Games Commission**.

Sam Irwin later formed Phoenix and now plays in Duck Soup out of Austin Texas. Rock Romano went on to form Doctor Rockit and the Sisters of Mercy. He and the Sisters split and he continued to front Doctor Rockit. He also played guitar and bass with The Sheetrockers and even played bass with Duck Soup for a while. He now has a recording studio in Houston. Carson Graham played drums for several other groups and Paul Guillet retired from the professional music scene.

Compilation appearances have included: *She Lied* on *Acid Visions - The Complete Collection Vol. 1* (3-CD), *Texas Flashback (The Best Of)* (CD), *Texas Flashbacks, Vol. 2* (LP & CD), *Flashback, Vol. 2* (LP) and *Houston Post - Nowsounds Groove-In* (LP). (VJ/MW)

The Sixpentz

Personnel:	JOHN T. BONNO	bs	A
	CARSON GRAHAM	drms	A
	D.J. GREER	piano, gtr, vcls	A
	PAUL GUILLET	ld gtr	A
	SAM IRWIN	vcls, tamb	A
	ROCK ROMANO	gtr, vcls	A

45s:	Please Come Home/Imitation Situation	(Brent 7062) 1967
	Twinkle Talk/Don't Say You're Sorry	(Brent 7064) 1967

A later version of Houston outfit **The Six Pents**, renamed after they they signed a deal with Bobby Shad of Mainstream. When they discovered the similarly named **Sixpence** they opted for the more distinctive moniker **The Fun And Games Comission**.

Imitation Situation was written by local scenemakers Scott and Vivian Holtzmann with Rob Landes of **Fever Tree**. **Fever Tree** put out their own version on their 1968 debut album. The second 45 is pretty sugary pop.

Compilation appearances include: *Imitation Situation* on *Mindrocker, Vol. 13* (LP). (VJ/MW)

60,000,000 Buffalo

ALBUM:	1	NEVADA JUKEBOX	(Atco SD33-384) 1972 -

An obscure rural-rock group. (SR)

S.J. and The Crossroads

Personnel:	PHILIP BATTAGLIA	bs	ABC
	MIKE DALEO	gtr	ABCD
	SAM MESSINA	vcls	AB
	JOHN SERIO	ld gtr	ABCDE
	S.J. SERIO	drms	ABCDE
	SAM GIGLIO	organ, piano	BCDE
	GARY MOUTON	vcls	CDE
	GLENN MOYER	bs	DE
	W.C. LANGTON	drms	E

45s:	Breakdown/The Darkest Hour(Pt. 2)	(Deuce 101/2) 1966
	The Darkest Hour(Part 1)/(Part 2)	(Salmar 100) 1966
	Ooh-Poo-Pah-Doo/This Love Of Mine	(Salmar 101) 1966
	Breakdown/The Cryin' Man	(Salmar 102) 1966
	Night Time/The Darkest Hour(Part 2)	(Salmar 103) 1967
	Get Out Of My Life Woman/Play Your Game	(Salmar 105) 1968

Led by S.J. Serio, who had earlier recorded two songs *Funny Woman/London Girl* which remained unreleased until their inclusion on *Texas Punk, 1966: Vol. 10*, they formed in early 1966 in Beaumont. All of the original band were students at Kelley High School and only Sam Giglio, who joined a little later in June 1966, had any musical training.

Late in the Summer of 1966 the band entered the studio to record *The Darkest Hour-Part 1* and *Night Time* (later to be released as the group's fifth single). *The Darkest Hour-Part 2* was an instrumental version recorded at the same time to fill up some remaining tape and studio time. *The Darkest Hour (Part 1)/(Part 2)* was released and made the local Beaumont charts in September 1966.

The band also played live at many school and civic dances. Their material was largely British. Most of their gigs were confined to Southeast Texas and centred on Port Arthur and Orange as well as Beaumont. An influential DJ, Al Caldwell, who worked for KAYC, a local top 40 radio station in Beaumont, helped arrange their second 45. It climbed to No. 4 in the local charts.

Their third effort, a frantic raver, *Breakdown/The Cryin' Man* did not meet with the same success and a little later their competent version of *Night Time*, recorded in their first studio session, was issued backed by *The Darkest Hour (Part 2)*.

In late 1967, Messina left the band to be replaced by Gary Mouton. Philip Battaglia was drafted and similarly replaced by Glen Moyer. Then, early in 1968 when Mike Daleo quit W.C. Langton, a second drummer, joined. They disintegrated after one final competent upbeat 45.

Glen Moyer:- "By that time our repertoire had turned more to blue-eyed soul - lots of Sam and Dave and my favorite, Archie Bell and The Drells' *Tighten Up*. (I remember the first song I learned with the guys - while practicing in the Serio's garage on Major Drive in Beaumont - was **BS&T**'s *You've Made Me So Very Happy*.) With the advent of two drummers, SJ sometimes moved down front to share lead vocals with Gary Mouton."

"Prior to joining the Crossroads I was playing with another Beaumont garage band called The Past Tymes(*). As school chums since elementary school, Gary was familiar with me and the band and thus approached me about replacing Battaglia. I had grown up as a kid in the neighborhood where SJ & Johnny's Dad, Sal, operated his grocery store and trailer park, and where he opened the original SalMar record store, so I had hung around the band almost from the beginning."

"In fact, the band only broke up when SJ left, also facing service with the armed forces. At that point, his little brother Johnny Serio and I joined another band with its roots in Kelly High School called **The Kidds**. That incarnation of the **Kidds** didn't last long as Johnny soon joined the coast guard to avoid going to Vietnam and that group split."

Compilation appearances have included: *Ooh Poo Pah Doo* and *The Darkest Hour* on *Acid Visions - The Complete Collection Vol. 1* (3-CD); *Funny Woman* and *London Girl* on *Acid Visions - Complete Collection, Vol. 3* (3-CD) and *Green Crystal Ties, Vol. 5* (CD); *Get Out Off My Life Woman* on *Texas Flashbacks, Vol. 2* (LP & CD) and *Flashback, Vol. 2* (LP); *The Darkest Hour, Night Time, Ooh Poo Pah Doo, The Darkest Hour - Part 2, Breakdown, Get Out Of My Life Woman, Play Your Game, Funny Woman* and *London Girl* on *Texas Punk, Vol. 10 - With S.J. And The Crossroads!* (LP); *Ooh Poo Pah Doo* on *Flashback, Vol. 6* (LP); *The Darkest Hour* on *Garage Punk Unknowns, Vol. 5* (LP); *Ooh Poo Pah Doo* and *Darkest Hour* on *Highs In The Mid-Sixties, Vol. 17* (LP).

NB: (*) The Past Tymes did not record, however their single claim to fame was that lead vocalist, Bubba Busceme, had won four consecutive National Golden Gloves boxing titles and went on to box for the US at the '72 Olympics. (VJ/GMr)

The Skeptics

Personnel incl: JERRY WAUGH   vcls

45s:	α	For My Own/I Told Her Goodbye	(Thrush 1002) 1965
		Apple Candy/Ride Child (PS)	(Kampus 814) 1966
		Stripes/Certain Kind Of Love (PS)	(Kampus 815) 196?
		She's A Gas/Turn It On	(Sho-Boat 106) 196?
		Bit O'Honey/ East Side Tenement House (PS)	(Scratch 7823) 1967

NB: α as by Jerry Waugh and The Skeptics.

Bartlesville, in Northeast Oklahoma, was home to this band who played a raw guitar-driven pop/punk hybrid with considerable commercial potential. Primarily based around a group of brothers named Shevill (?) they were signed to Kampus by Rodney Lay, the leader and founder of Rodney and The Blazers.

Fortunately some of their finer moments have been captured on posthumous compilations:- *Certain Kind Of Girl* on *Let's Dig 'Em Up, Vol. 3* (LP) and *Let's Dig 'Em Up, Vol. 1* (CD); *Apple Candy* on *Monsters Of The Midwest, Vol. 2* (LP); *Bit O' Honey* on *Monsters Of The Midwest, Vol. 4* (LP); *Ride Child* on *Psychedelic Unknowns, Vol. 4* (LP & CD); *For My Own* on *Shutdown '66* (LP); *I Told Her Goodbye* on *Tymes Gone By* (LP); and *Turn It On* on *Highs In The Mid-Sixties, Vol. 8* (LP).

Another, presumably different, **Skeptics** have a track called *Wondering* on *Yeah Yeah Yeah* (CD). (VJ/MW/RL,Jr.)

Skip and The Creations

ALBUM: 1   MOBAM   (Justice 152) 1966 R2/R3

NB: (1) reissued on CD by Collectables (COL-CD-0602) 1995.

From Colonial Heights, just outside of Richmond, Virginia. This band's album is a rare and sought-after collectable. The album is garagey frat-rock of the soulful sort - covers include *Harlem Shuffle, 99.5, Double Shot, Turn On Your Lovelight, Respectable, Gimme Some Lovin'* and *I'm So Lonesome I Could Cry* - you get the picture? *I'm Calling You Baby* is the most uptempo offering here - a jerky and infectious ditty, but overall not recommended for garage fans.

Compilation appearances included *I'm Calling You Baby* on *All Cops In Delerium - Good Roots* (LP). (VJ/MW)

Skip Juried

ALBUM: 1   THE COMING OF THE DANCER
                                    (Blue Book LP-4000) 1968 -

A strange orchestrated folk-pop album from the New York area, its rather elaborated (but amateurish) production is an acquired taste. (SR)

Skunks

Personnel:	RICK ALLEN (SUTHERLAND)	keyb'ds	A
	TONY KOLP	sax, organ	AB
	DUANE LUNDY	drms	A
	LARRY LYNNE (real name OSTRICKI)	gtr	ABCD
	TEDDY PEPLINSKI	drms	BC
	JACK TAPPY	bs	BCDE
	RANDY KLEIN	gtr	CDE
	PAUL EDWARDS (FREDERICKS)	drms	DE

ALBUM: 1(E)   GETTIN' STARTED   (Teen Town TTLP 101) 1968 -

45s:	α	Ring Rang Roo/There's A Little Bit Of Heaven	(Era 3155) 1965
		Elvira / The Journey	(USA 865) 1966
		Don't Ask Why / Do The Duck	(Quill 120) 1967
		It's Only Love / Little Angel	(Quill 121) 1967
		I Recommend Her / I Need No One	(Teen Town 103) 1968
		I Recommend Her / I Need No One	(World Pacific 77889) 1968
		Small Town Girl / You Better Hold On To Me	(Teen Town 106) 1968
		Listen To The News Today / Doing Nothing	(Teen Town 110) 1969
		Doing Nothing / Listen To The News	(White Whale 322 and 325) 1969
		Heart Teaser / You, Me And Happiness	(Sheri 100) 1970

NB: α as by the Unbelievables.

Originally a Milwaukee rock'n'roll combo called The Bonnevilles, they got the British Invasion bug and adopted the name and hairstyle of, **Skunks**. Their debut 45 was recorded during a brief period in California but was released as by the Unbelievables, possibly because they caught the whiff of other Skunks around at the same time (one such had a 45 in 1965 - *Youthquake / A Girl Like You*, on Mercury).

The album is a patchwork of disparate styles - from pop covers and crooners to folk-rockers (the **Byrds**-like I Need No One). They do venture into garage and psych territory so the highlights, from our viewpoint, are a cover of **Jefferson Airplane**'s *Somebody To Love* (with psychedelic guitar

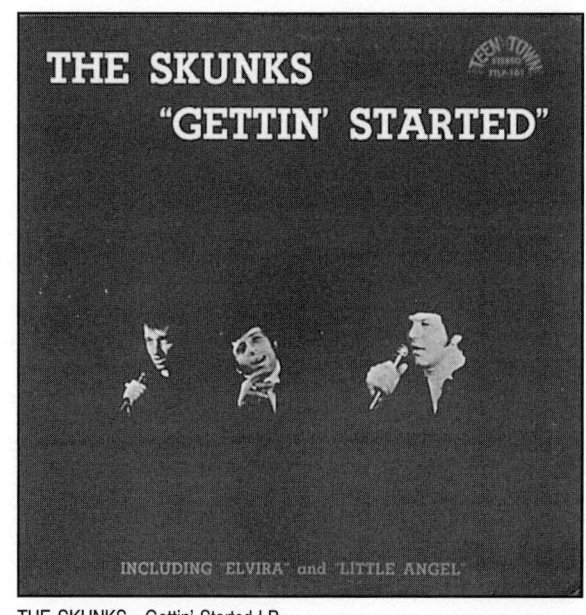

THE SKUNKS - Gettin' Started LP.

work), *When I Need Her* (good punk-psych) and *The Journey* (chiming folk-rock tinged with psychedelia).

Small Town Girl also appeared on a 1968 compilation EP *W-RIT* (W-Rit Radio 1340) alongside fellow Wisconsin acts Tony's Tygers and **The Robbs**.

Larry Ostricki went on to form the Larry Lynne Band.

A detailed history of the band can be found in the book 'Do You Hear That Beat' by Gary Myers (Hummingbird, 1994, ISBN 0-9643073-9-1).

Retrospective compilation appearances include: *Don't Ask Why* on *The Quill Records Story* (CD) and *Acid Dreams, Vol. 3* (LP); *Listen To The News Today* on *Boulders, Vol. 9* (LP); and *The Journey* on *Echoes In Time Vol's 1 & 2* (CD) and *Echoes In Time, Vol. 1* (LP).

The **Skunks** on Mercury also have their: *A Girl Like You* featured on *Searching For Love* (LP). (MW/VJ/GM)

Sky

Personnel:	DOUG FIEGER	bs, gtr, vcls	AB
	BOB GREENFIELD		A
	ROB STAWINSKI	drms	AB
	JOHN COURY	gtr, keyb'ds, flute, vcls	B
	(BOBBY KEYS	horns	AB)
	(JIM PRICE	horns	AB
	(IAN STEWART	piano	B)
	(JOHN URIBE	gtr	B)

ALBUMS: 1(A) SKY (RCA) 1971 -
2(B) SAILOR'S DELIGHT (RCA LSP-4514) 1971 -

NB: (1) also released in the UK (RCA SF 8168) 1972.

Formed by Douglas Fieger, **Sky** was one of many groups deeply influenced by the Rolling Stones. They managed to work with Jimmy Miller, the Stones producer, who got them the support of several Stones stalwarts: Jim Price and Bobby Keys on horns, Ian Stewart on piano, PP Arnold and Doris Troy on background vocals. The second album was even recorded in London. Lacking strong material (they wrote all their songs), the group disbanded when their second album flopped.

Several years later, Fieger would form The Knack, of *My Sharona* fame. (SR)

The Sky

45: I'm Not A Fool/I Know What's Up (Dynovoice 224) 1966

A pop-rock group, this single was arranged and produced by Peter Antell. (SR)

Patrick Sky

ALBUMS: 1 PATRICK SKY (Vanguard VSD-79179) 1965 -
2 A HARVEST OF GENTLE CLANG (Vanguard VRS-9207) 1966 -
3 REALITY IS BAD ENOUGH (Verve Forecast FRS-3052) 1968 -
4 PHOTOGRAPHS (Verve Forecast FTS-3079) 1969 -
5 SONGS THAT MADE AMERICA FAMOUS (Adelphi AR 4101) 1973 -
6 TWO STEPS FORWARD ONE STEP BACK (Leviathan 2006) 1975 -

45s: Love Will Endure/Keep on Walking (Vanguard 35045) 1966
Reason To Believe/Guabi, Guabi (Vanguard 35048) 1966
She/Pinball Machine (Verve Forecast 5111) 1967
Lucky Me/One Too Many Mornings (Capitol 2797) 1970

SLEEPY HOLLOW - Sleepy Hollow LP.

Patrick Sky is a folk singer, songwriter and guitarist. His albums of interest here are the ones released in the sixties. His later albums are outside the scope of this book, as the Adelphi album is a failed attempt at recording "funny" offensive songs and the Leviathan album is a traditional folk effort.

His most famous song, *Many A Mile*, was notably covered by John Kay (**Steppenwolf**) and by **Buffy Sainte-Marie,** who invited him to play on several of her albums. (SR)

Skyeros

ALBUM: 1 SKYEROS (No label) 1975

From Missouri, an unknown quintet combining prog-rock, psych and Southern boogie on tracks like *Daily Dreams* and *Don't Give Me No Alibis*. (SR)

The Skymonters

ALBUM: 1 WITH HAMID HAMILTON CAMP (Elektra EKS 75073) 1973 ?

A forgotten folk-rock group, their album was recorded with **Hamilton Camp** and copies very rarely turn up for sale. (SR)

Sleepless Knights

Personnel incl:	BOB HANNA		A
	DON KARR	keyb'ds	A

45: You're Driving Me Crazy/
Don't Hide Your Love From Me (Jerroc JR 1000) c1967

A sadly obscure 45 from a Philadelphia, Pennsylvania band. *You're Driving Me Crazy* has strong vocals and a really commercial backing. It could easily have been a pop-punk hit instead it sank without trace

Don Karr has previously been in **The Other Half** and The Trojans.

They opened for **Lothar and The Hand People** at The Trauma (in Philly) and for **Mandrake Memorial** at The Spot After (in the Philly suburb of Lower Moreland).

Compilation appearances include *You're Driving Me Crazy* on *Garage Zone, Vol. 2* (LP) and *The Garage Zone Box Set* (LP). (VJ/MW/DKr)

Sleepy Hollow

Personnel:	RICHARD BILLAY	vcls, gtr, piano	A
	RICHIE BREMEN	bs	A
	ESSRA MOHAWK	vcls	A
	JOE ZUCCA	drms	A

ALBUM: 1(A) SLEEPY HOLLOW (Family Productions FPS 2708) 1972 -

45: Hades/Sincerely Yours (Family Productions 0916) 1972

This outfit sound uncannily like The Beatles. The album must be one of the most blatant (and best) Beatle imitations around from the *Let It Be* period. It's full of variety and every track's a fine example of their versatility. It was recorded at Sigma Sound Studios in Philadelphia, Pennsylvania, although the label was based in Los Angeles. Richard Billay wrote all the songs and they are well worth hearing. The 45 tracks are from the album.

The album was produced by John Madara and Tom Sellers. (VJ/SR)

The Slightest Idea

ALBUM: 1 BRING YOUR OWN (Pit SI 1019) c1974 R1

An amateur band from Iowa, their album was recorded at the Cherrywood Studios and contains covers of hits like *Born To Be Wild*, *We're An American Band*, *Brown Sugar*, *Smoke On The Water*, and some original songs, most of them with fuzz guitar. (SR)

P.F. Sloan

ALBUMS:	1	SONGS OF OUR TIME	(Dunhill 50004) 1965 -
	2	12 MORE TIMES	(Dunhill 50007) 1966 -
	3	MEASURE OF PLEASURE	(Atco 33268) 1968 -
	4	RAISED ON RECORDS	(Epic 3120) 1972 -

NB: There's also a couple of compilations: *Precious Time*, a collection of his best and some previously unreleased material on Rhino and an 18 track CD compilation on One Way, entitled *Anthology* (22097).

HCP

45s:	α	All I Want Is Loving/	
		Little Girl In The Cabin	(Aladdin 3461) 1959 -
	β	If You Believe In Me/She's My Girl	(Mart 802) 1960 -
		The Sins Of A Family/This Mornin'	(Dunhill 4007) 1966 87
		Halloween Mary/	
		I'd Have To Be Out Of My Mind	(Dunhill 4016) 1966 -
		From A Distance/Patterns	(Dunhill 4024) 1966 109
		City Women/Top Of A Fence	(Dunhill 4037) 1966 -
		A Melody For You/I Found A Girl	(Dunhill 4054) 1966 -
		Sunflower Sunflower/	
		The Man Behind The Red Balloon	(Dunhill 4064) 1967 -
	χ	Karma (A Study Of Divinations)/	
		I Can't Help But Wonder, Elizabeth	(Dunhill 4106) 1968 -

NB: α as Flip Sloan. β as Phil Sloan. χ as Philip Sloan. There are also three French EPs with PS: *Sins Of A Family/This Mornin'/I Get Out Of Breath/Take Me For What I'm Worth* (RCA 86901); *The Man Behind The Red Balloon/From A Distance/Halloween Mary/Let Me Be* (RCA 86903); and *City Women/Here's Where You Belong/Patterns seg 4/This Precious Time* (RCA 86908).

Originally from Los Angeles but based in New York initially, **Sloan** was undoubtedly a talented songwriter. He was just 15 when he recorded his first 45 as Flip Sloan. The following year he issued another as Phil Sloan and he also belonged to an outfit called The Storytellers whose 45 *When Two People* for Ramark was later picked up by Dimension.

In 1963, he moved to L.A., teamed up with Steve Barri (real name Steve Lipkin) and began a successful songwriting partnership. The first group they wrote for was Round Robin and their second effort *Kick That Little Foot Sally Ann* made No. 61 in the U.S. Charts. Among the better known people they wrote for were Jan and Dean, Bruce (Johnston) and Terry (Melcher) and **Sloan** later wrote the classic protest song *Eve Of Destruction* for **Barry McGuire**. They also released their own recordings under pseudonyms like Philip and Steven, The Trash Cleaners, Willie and The Wheels and The Imaginations. Then, when Lou Adler formed Dunhill Records in 1965, they wrote much of the early folk rock material for the label. Sloan also embarked on a solo career which was less successful in commercial terms than one might have expected. Only *Sins Of A Family* sold well climbing to No. 87 in the U.S. and No. 37 in UK, but his first two solo albums, which were full of protest songs with commercial hook lines and simple acoustic backing, were well received. He also sang lead vocals on the first three Grassroots' singles which he wrote with Steve Barri. His final 45 in 1968 was full of echoes and sitars - rather interesting but after this he returned to New York. He was never as influential thereafter and his later albums were disappointing but he was a very significant member of the sixties folk-rock boom both as a performer and songwriter. His finest moment commercially *Sins Of A Family* is captured on *Nuggets, Vol. 10* (LP). (VJ/SR)

Sloths

45: Makin' Love/? (Impression 004) 196?

A mid-sixties punk combo from Los Angeles. *Makin' Love* is a really raunchy and primitive recording which sounds rather similar to *I Want Candy*.

Compilation appearances include *Makin' Love* on *Back From The Grave, Vol. 4* (LP) and *Back From The Grave, Vol. 2* (CD). (VJ)

Sly and The Family Stone

Personnel:	GREG ERRICO	drms	A
	LARRY GRAHAM	bs	A
	JERRY MARTINI	sax	AB
	CYNTHIA ROBINSON	trumpet	AB
	FREDDIE STONE	gtr, vcls	AB
	ROSIE STONE	keyb'ds	AB
	SLY STONE	vcls, keyb'ds, gtr	AB
	RUSTY ALLEN	bs	B
	ANDY NEWMARK	drms	B

HCP

ALBUMS:	1(A)	WHOLE NEW THING	(Epic BN 26324) 1967 - -
	2(A)	DANCE TO THE MUSIC	(Epic BN 26371) 1968 142 -
	3(A)	LIFE	(Epic BN 26397) 1968 195 -
	4(A)	STAND!	(Epic BN 26456) 1969 13 -
	5(A)	GREATEST HITS	(Epic KE 30325) 1970 2 -
	6(A)	THERE'S A RIOT GOING ON	(Epic KE 30986) 1971 1 -
	7(B)	FRESH	(Epic KE 32134) 1973 7 -
	8(B)	SMALL TALK	(Epic KE 32930) 1974 15 -

NB: (5) also issued in quadrophonic (Epic EQ 30325) 1973. (8) also issued in quadrophonic (Epic PEQ 32930) 1974.

HCP

45s:	α	Buttermilk/Buttermilk, pt 2	(Autumn 14) 1964 -
(up to		I Ain't Got Nobody/	
1973)		I Can't Turn You Loose	(Loadstone 3951) 1967 -
		Dance To The Music/	
		Let Me Hear It From You	(Epic 5-10256) 1967 8
		Life/ M'Lady	(Epic 5-10353) 1968 93
		Everyday People/Sing A Simple Song	(Epic 5-10407) 1969 1
		Stand/I Want To Take You Higher	(Epic 5-10450) 1969 22 & 60
		Hot Fun In The Summertime/Fun	(Epic 5-10497) 1969 2
		Thank You/Everybody Is A Star	(Epic 5-10555) 1970 1
		Family Affair/Luv n'haight	(Epic 5-10805) 1971 1
		Runnin' Away/?	(Epic 5-10829) 1972 23
		Smilin'/?	(Epic 5-10850) 1972 42
		If You Want Me To Stay/	
		Thankful 'n' Thoughtful	(Epic 5-11017) 1973 12
		Frisky/?	(Epic 5-11060) 1973 79

NB: α as Sly.

Born in Dallas in 1944, Sylvester "Sly" Stewart began singing gospel in his local church. In the fifties, the Stewart family moved to San Francisco and Sylvester and his younger brother Fred learned solfeggio and trumpet in a local college. They formed their first groups and Sly was also a DJ. Another DJ, Tom Donahue recruited him to work for his new label and he soon became an engineer and producer for Autumn, working with the **Mojo Men**, Bobby Freeman, the **Beau Brummels** and the **Great Society**.

In 1966, Stewart changed his name to Sly Stone and formed the Stoners with his brother and a trumpetist, Cynthia Robinson. The Stoners soon became **Sly And The Family Stone**, with the adjunction of Greg Errico on drums, Jerry Martini on sax, Larry Graham (another expatriate Texan) on bass, and finally Rosemary "Rosie" Stewart, his younger sister on keyboards.

Sly and The Family Stone started gigging around San Francisco and their mix of soul and psychedelic rock immediately won them a local following. After a debut 45 for a local label, they signed to Epic and their first album was released in October 1967. Its sales were not very high but *Dance To The Music* was issued as a single and soon charted. After this first commercial success, the Family Stone kept on recording well-received albums, still mixing dancing rock and soul tracks with psychedelic sounds (especially on the guitars and distorted keyboards) and intelligent lyrics. Sly wrote about civil rights, groupies, counter-culture movements and the riots, always with punch and good humor. His unusual band (a sexually and racially integrated group of multi-instrumentalists) provided perfect backing with inventive rhythms.

Sly And The Family Stone appeared at Woodstock (*Dance To The Music* and *I Want To Take You Higher* were included on the records and movie) and were an important part of the San Francisco sound, often playing live and one of the very few groups to attract both white and black fans. Most of the other record labels tried to launch their own psychedelic soul groups (ABC had **Bagatelle**, United Artists - War and Kent - **Pacific Gas and Electric** for instance) but few were able to reach the commercial and artistic success of the Family Stone.

In 1970, Rose Stone recorded a good 45 on Atlantic as Little Sister, *You're the One, pt 1/2* 1971, which was produced by Sly Stone. Unfortunately, drug problems hit the group in 1971 and Sly began cancelling shows, sometimes at the very last minute, or even forgetting to be on stage. Greg Errico and Larry Graham left in 1972, to be replaced by Andy Newmark and Rusty Allen and their subsequent records are not as good.

In 1974, Sly Stone went bankrupt and began doing sessions to get some money (he can be found on records by Elvin Bishop, New Riders Of The Purple Sage and even REO Speedwagon). He also tried unsuccessfully to get rid of his drug addiction. He tried to make a comeback in 1979 with *Back On The Right Track* (Warner) and in 1984 finally managed to get on top of his drug problem. After the Family Stone, Larry Graham went solo and formed Graham Central Station with Freddie Stone. He tried to carry on in the same direction but his records are not as inventive and dropped most of the psychedelic aspects.

Greg Errico joined **Santana** in 1971, did sessions and worked with Bill Kreutzmann and **Mickey Hart** from the **Grateful Dead** on several of their drum recordings. Jerry Martini and Andy Newmark both became session men.

Compilation appearances have included: *Love City* on *Rockbusters* (LP); *Buttermilk - Part 1* on *Sounds Of The Sixties San Francisco, Vol. 1* (LP); and *Scat Swim* and *Buttermilk* on *The Autumn Records Story* (LP). (SR)

THE SMACK (outside recording studio).

THE SMACK - The Smack LP.

Sly Boots

| Personnel incl: | DAVID GREENBERG | A |
| | MICHAEL WENDROFF | A |

ALBUM: 1(A)   NOTES ON A JOURNEY
                    (Faithful Virtue FVS-2002) c1971 SC

A decent folk-rock album. Wendroff would later have a solo career with two albums on Buddah (1974 and 1977) and also worked with Lou Reed. (SR)

The Smack

Personnel:	PHIL BROWN	gtr, vcls	A
	ALVIN HAYWOOD	bs, vcls	A
	LEE OVERSTREET	drms	A
	JIM UHL	gtr, vcls	A

ALBUM: 1(A)   THE SMACK   (Audio House no #) 1968 R4

NB: (1) had a limited reissue of 300 (TE 91004) in 1994. Also reissued on CD.

This short-lived four-piece was born at the yearly six-week "Midwestern Band and Art" camp in Lawrence, Kansas. In July 1967, hundreds of teenagers attended this event. Many of them were into folk-rock as well as classical music. In July 1968, many of the same teenagers who'd attended the 1967 camp attended the 1968 camp too. **Smack** was formed at the 1968 camp and since there were less than five of the six weeks to go after their formation they practised cover versions, mostly of Cream and **Jimi Hendrix** songs. They played dances and gigs at the camp and their fellow students got together a sign-up list for those who wanted a **Smack** album for posterity. So, a few days after the camp they went into a local studio and recorded nine cuts - four **Hendrix** covers: *Purple Haze*, *Fire*, *Manic Depression* and *Foxey Lady* (their spelling!); three Cream covers: *Sunshine Of Your Love*, *I'm So Glad* and *Swlabr*; a re-hash of The Kinks' *Set Me Free* and **Buffalo Springfield**'s *For What It's Worth*. The vocals were then dubbed over the music. The studio struck a deal with RCA to have 100-150 albums pressed. They were sent to the students who signed the purchase sheet - hence the rarity.. Worth a spin? Definitely, a few wrong notes were hit, the vocals are flat in places and some of the songs a bit slow, but some of the **Hendrix** covers, particularly the finale (and their tour de force) *Foxey Lady*, are great. Given the rarity of the original release, the limited reissues are particularly welcome and will have taken copies into a few more homes.

As to what became of the band, Jim Uhl lives on Long Island (NY) and has continued to play with other obscure acts (Little Wilson Band and Willie Steele's Terraplane). Alvin Haywood is thought to have become a minister in Philadelphia and Phil Brown lives in Roswell New Mexico and Lee Overstreet in Iowa.

We presume that a cover of *Suzie Q* on *Brain Shadows, Vol. 1* (LP & CD) is by a different **Smack**. (CF/JU)

Small Society

45:	Live For A Real Good Sound/ Somebody Help Me	(Westchester 277) 1968

Real good late sixties garage from Virginia, Minnesota, especially the fuzzy throbbing cover of the Spencer Davis Group classic *Somebody Help Me*. As yet uncompiled since many compilers deliberately steer clear of cover versions - this is a case for an exception. (MW)

Smith

Personnel:
JERRY CARTER	bs	A
JAMES RICHARD CLIBURN	gtr	A
BOB EVANS	drms, perc	AB
GAYLE McCORMICK	vcls	AB
LARRY MOSS	keyb'ds	AB
JUDD HUSS	bs	B
ALAN PARKER	gtr, vcls	B

ALBUMS:
				HCP
1(A)	A GROUP CALLED SMITH	(Dunhill DS 50056)	1969	17 -
2(B)	MINUS - PLUS	(Dunhill DS 50081)	1970	74 -

45s:
		HCP
Baby It's You/I Don't Believe It	(Dunhill 4206) 1969	5
Take A Look Around/Majalesky Ridge	(Dunhill 4228) 1969	43
What Am I Gonna Do/Born In Boston	(Dunhill 4238) 1970	73
Coming Back To Me/Minus-Plus	(Dunhill 4246) 1970	101

A West Coast band from Los Angeles whose sound was characterised by Gayle McCormick's great voice. She was from St. Louis originally. Both their albums were produced by Steve Barri. Most of the songs on their first album were cover versions and they are also well remembered for their version of *The Weight* in the Soundtrack to *Easy Rider*. Almost all of the material on *Minus - Plus* was written by well known sessionman Alan Parker and their keyboardist Larry Moss. *Baby It's You* got to No 5 in the U.S. Charts and *Take A Look Around* and *What Am I Gonna Do* were both minor hits peaking at No's 43 and 73 respectively. Gayle McCormick later went solo. Alan Parker, who'd previously been in **Summerhill**, later fronted his own band.

Compilation appearances include *The Last Time* and *Comin' Back To Me* on *Undersound Uppersoul* (LP). (VJ/GG)

Bob Smith

Personnel:
LARRY CHAPMAN	violin	A
JAMES CURTIS	hand drm	A
MIKE DEGREVE	rhythm gtr	A
STAN KEISER	flute	A
CAPTAIN KEYBOARD (DARYL DRAGON)	keyb'ds, vibes	A
JOHN LATINI	bs	A
DON PRESTON	moog, mellotron	A
SKIP SCHNEIDER	drms	A
BOB SMITH	gtr, vcls	A

ALBUM:	1	THE VISIT (dbl)	(Kent KST-551)	1970 R2

NB: (1) some copies issued with colour poster, which significantly increases the value of the LP (R2/R3). (1) counterfeited on CD (Virgo CD1518) 1996. Also legitimately reissued (RD Records RD 6) 2000, digitially remastered from the original 1/2" tapes, as a triple vinyl LP set *Stop For A Visit Down Electric Avenue*. The box set also contains selections from his *Stop* (1971) and *Electric Avenue* (1972) albums. Along with the three LP's, the box set includes a re-issue of "The Visit" poster, and a band history along with several photos.

Another significant collectable from the California rock scene that will interest readers. Not really a solo album at all, as **Smith** is backed by eight very capable musicians. Much of the music is instrumental, achieving a mystical and 'psychedelic' atmosphere, although there are a few more mainstream tracks and some nice bluesy guitar work in places. Interesting and a must for fans of psychedelia. The original pressing (especially with the amazing psychedelic poster) has skyrocketed in value in recent years; as such, the recent reissue is most welcome. It includes a bonus disc of material recorded by Stop, Bob's later band from the early seventies.

Prior to the Kent album, Bob was with Silverskin, and before that, Lid (not to be confused with **The Lyd**), who recorded an album in 1968 which remains unissued.

Don Preston was a member of Frank Zappa's **Mothers Of Invention** and Daryl Dragon was with **The Dragons**. Daryl worked on various projects with his brothers Doug and Dennis (**Farm**, *A Sea For Yourself*, et. al.) before finding fame and fortune as the 'Captain' in Captain and Tenille. **Bob Smith** continues performing locally in Florida and has finished a new recording, *The Visit - Destiny 2000 From Bob Smith* which he will make available on his own Southern Rose label.

Bob would also appreciate it if the Virgo chaps could contact him about royalties.... (VJ/CF/BSh)

Jojo Smith

45:	Find This Woman/Make Mine Coffee	(Stature 1103) c1966

Produced by Pete Stienberg, a rare garage 45 with a strange "druggy" flip. (SR)

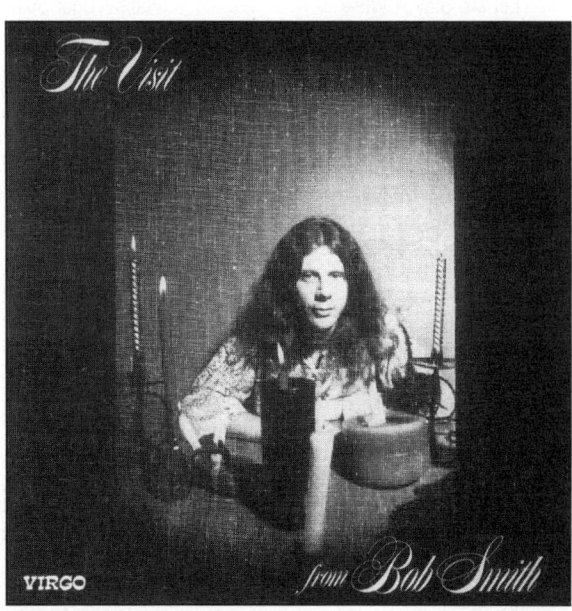

SMITH - A Group Called Smith LP.

BOB SMITH - The Visit CD.

Kathy Smith

ALBUM:	1	KATHY SMITH	(Stormy Forest) 1972 -
	2	SOME SONGS I'VE SAVED	(Stormy Forest 6003) 1973 -

45s:	Circles Of Love/?	(Stormy Forest 654) 1970
	Seven Virgins/?	(Stormy Forest 662) 197?
	For Emile/?	(Stormy Forest 665) 197?

On **Richie Havens**' label, a good female psychedelic-influenced folk-rock singer with a very rich and varied backing, including guitar, violin, flute, sitar and tabla. Her albums were recorded with excellent musicians, notably Colin Walcott (**Oregon**), Jeremy Steig and Warren Bernhardt (both ex-**Jeremy and The Satyrs**), Artie Traum, **Monte Dunn**, Jim Fielder (**Blood, Sweat and Tears**) and Bill LaVorgna.

In the eighties, **Kathy Smith** became friends with John Belushi and is rumoured to be the last person to have seen him alive. (SR)

Tedd Smith

Personnel incl:	JOAN HETTENHOUSER	vcls	A
	TEDD SMITH	keyb'ds, vcls	AB
	JOHN BAHLER	vcls	B
	KIM CARMICHAEL	vcls	B

ALBUMS:	1(A)	SMASH AND GRAB WORLD	
			(Word WST-8479-LP) c1969 ?
	2(B)	NEW VIBRATIONS: A QUEST IN FOLK ROCK	
			(Light LS-5561) 1971 ?

A conceptual folk-rock singer and pianist with Christian overtones. His first album is extremely rare and contains flower pop (*Circles*), powerful psychedelic tracks (*Smash And Grab World*), rock (*Jump For Joy*), classical-tinged tracks with woodwinds and strings (*Games, A Little Understanding*), the long *Running Man* with piano jamming and even some poetry readings. Except for the female singer, the group backing Tedd Smith is not credited.

The second album was recorded with The Young People and is more pop-oriented, even if its contains some good rock tracks, like *Life Is Why*, *Love And Understanding* and *Searching*. Tedd Smith may have later been the pianist of the televangelist Billy Graham! (SR/KSt)

Smithsonian Institute

45s:	Lively Played The Combo /	
	Oh, It's Gonna Rain	(Tamborine 45-4) 1968
	Dream For Tomorrow / Boston Bay	(Tamborine 45-5) c1968
	Where Will You Be When The World Changes /	
	Sunshine, Mustard Seed & Rainbows	(Happy Tiger 533) 1970
	Why Have You Been Gone So Long /	
	Let Me Stay A While	(Happy Tiger 554) 1970

Shiny happy folkie-pop people from Hendersonville, Tennessee. *Lively Played The Combo* is funny (ha ha) upbeat pop with smatterings of sitar-like effects but in no way psych. *Boston Bay* is a pleasantly hippie-ditty and can be found on the aptly titled *Every Groovy Day* (LP). *Dream For Tomorrow* is quite **Association**-like and *Sunshine, Mustard Seed And Rainbows* (written by Wayne Proctor of **We The People**) is overtly so - think *Birthday*-album period flower-pop. (MW/MM)

The Smoke

Personnel:	EDDIE BEYER	keyb'ds	A
	RICHARD FLOYD	bs, gtr, vcls	A
	EARL FINN	bs, keyb'ds, gtr	A
	JOHNNY ORVIS	vcls, gtr, banjo	A
	PHIL PARKER	drms	A

ALBUMS:	1(A)	CARRY ON YOUR IDEA	(UNI 73052) 1969 -
	2(A)	AT GEORGE'S COFFEE SHOP	(UNI 73065) 1969 -

45s:	Mainstream/Church House Blues	(Orbit 1126) 1968
	Choose It (Part 1)/Choose It (Part 2)	(UNI 55154) 1969

Originally known as **The Nomads** and based in Houston, Texas, this band issued two 45s under that name. They became known as **Smoke** in mid-1968. They later moved on to San Francisco where they gigged mainly at biker venues.

Led by John Orvis, who composed all their material, their music can best be described as "psychedelic boogie", epitomised by the nineteen-minute *M.C. Boogie* on the first album and nine-minute *Greased Lightnin* on the second. Loads of energy, jiving vocals, good guitar solos and powerful organ parts. The second album was produced by Jimmie Haskell, one of the best producers/arrangers operating in the California studios in the sixties. Beyer remained in California to play for Smith and **Canned Heat** and then in fellow Texan Gary Myrick's band. Phil Parker went on to play with the bluesman Shakey Jake Harris.

Compilation coverage has so far included: *Choose It (Part 1)* on *Sounds Of The Sixties San Francisco, Vol. 1* (LP); *Church House Blues* on *Thirteen O'Clock Flight To Psychedelphia* (CD); *Mainstream* on *Three O'Clock Merrian Webster Time* (LP), which also contains their recordings as **The Nomads**; and *Mainstream* on *Acid Visions - The Complete Collection, Vol. 3* (3-CD), *Gathering Of The Tribe* (CD) and *The History Of Texas Garage Bands, Vol. 2* (CD). (MW/SR)

The Smoke

Personnel:	STAN AYEROFF	gtr	A
	STEVE BAIM	drms, perc	A
	MICHAEL LLOYD	bs, keyb'ds	A

ALBUM:	1(A)	THE SMOKE	(Sidewalk 5912) 1968 SC

NB: (1) also released as Tower ST-5912.

This West Coast band's excellent album was co-produced by Michael Lloyd, who wrote most of the songs, and **Kim Fowley**. An album of mild psychedelia it contains a fair degree of orchestration and was probably influenced by The Beatles' *Sergeant Pepper* LP, released the previous Summer. Some tracks, like *Fogbound* and *Umbrella*, had considerable commercial potential. Others, like *Song Thru' Perception* are notable for their crispy, clear vocals and *October Country* for some beautiful string arrangements.

The Smoke formed when Michael Lloyd met Steve and Stan through some mutual friends. They played with a few other guys as The Laughing Wind, **Max Frost and The Troopers**, and worked together on Michael's project as **Rubber Band**. Michael Lloyd had previously been working - scoring some motion pictures and producing records - with a young business executive named Mike Curb. They had met four years previously when Michael was looking for some songs for a group he was recording. Michael started to work for Mike's company (Sidewalk Productions) about 1967. Mike liked the concept and songs for **The Smoke** album and agreed to sign the group and release the album on his Sidewalk label.

Towards the end of the project, Michael Lloyd's old friend Jimmy Greenspoon became interested in joining the band. They had been playing together for many years in outfits such as The New Dimensions. Jimmy didn't participate in the recording, but he did appear in the pictures and album cover art! While waiting for **The Smoke** to be released, Jimmy was offered the opportunity to become a founding member of Three Dog Night, which he wisely seized.

After recording **The Smoke** album (and briefly travelling on the road with **The West Coast Pop Art Experimental Band**), Stan Ayeroff studied composition at the California Institute of the Arts and classical guitar at California State University Northridge. He played with Delbert and Glen (legendary R&B pioneer Delbert McClinton, who taught John Lennon how to play harmonica). In 1971, he was a founding member of Oingo Boingo, at the time, a surrealistic musical theatre group. He's gone on to write books on pioneer guitarists Django Reinhardt and Charlie Christian as well as clarinetist Benny Goodman for the *Jazz Master* series. He's also written six solo guitar books for Warner Brothers Publications. In the late seventies he toured with Vicki Carr and Dory Previn as guitarist and arranger. Recently, he was orchestral supervisor for Rod Stewart's 1993-94 World Tour and the Page/Plant 1994-95 World Tour. In 1966 he was musical supervisor and conductor for Heart's concert video "The Road Home".

THE SMOKE - The Smoke (Sidewalk) LP.

Drummer Steve Baim (aka Braim) continued to write music and poetry, and was a performance artist in 1970-71 at Fresno State College. He's currently an upscale architect and builder in Los Angeles and plays accordion and writes poetry.

In the Fall of 1969 Mike Curb became President of MGM Records and Michael Lloyd (then 20 years old) Vice-President of A&R. Over the years he produced records and wrote for many television shows and motion pictures. His credits include Lou Rawls, The Osmonds, The Burrito Brothers, Shaun Cassidy, Belinda Carlisle, The New Seekers, Eric Carmen, Stryper, kids songs on TV and video, the music from "Dirty Dancing", The Bellamy Brothers, Debby Boone, the late George Burns, Barry Manilow etc. and he became one of the most successful American record producers. His recordings have earned over 100 gold and platinum awards, several Grammys, Academy Awards, Dove Awards, Golden Globes and American Music Awards. (VJ/JM)

Smoke

Personnel incl: MARK SHELDON   A

45:   Half Past The End / My Mama   (Smoke 1316) 1968

Mark Sheldon of Michigan's **The Mussies** recorded this 45 as by **Smoke**. You can also find *Half Past The End* on *Sixties Archive Vol. 6* (CD). (MW)

The Smoke Ring

Personnel:			
JERRY BENJAMIN	drms, gtr	A
TOM BENJAMIN	drms	A
JIM CASEY	sax, gtr	ABC
DAVE DOHREN	Trumpet	ABC
BOB HUPP	ld gtr	ABC
LITTLE JOE HUPP	organ	AB
NICK HUPP	bs	ABC
JOHN SCHRAD	tenor sax	AB
CHUCK ASMUS	drms	B
ROGER VOLK	drms	BC
GREG GOODMAN		C
RON McCLURE	trumpet	C
MIKE SEMRAD	trumpet, gtr	C

HCP
45s:
α Yogi Twist/B.B. Limbo   (Soma 1403) 1962 -
α Hurtin' Inside/Somebody Touched Me   (Studio City 1014) 1963 -
α Ooh Poo Pah Doo/
     We Belong Together   (Studio City 1019) 1964 -
     That Girl Was My Girl One Time/
     Her Love's A Lie   (Mala 568) 1967 -
     No Not Much/
     When Marty Throws A Party   (Gold Dust 317) 1968 -
     No Not Much/
     How'd You Get To Be So Wonderful?   (Buddah 77) 1969 85
     Portrait Of My Love/
     Waiting For Love To Come My Way   (Buddah 112) 1969 -
     High On A Rainbow/First Reaction   (Certron 10008) 1969 -
     Heavy Metal Whale/Triangle   (Shue 1988) 1972 -

NB: α as **Little Joe and The Ramrods**.

Two Norfolk, Nebraska bands, **Little Joe and The Ramrods** and **The Strollers** (no recordings), combined forces in 1965 to form the group that would eventually become known as **The Smoke Ring**. Originally retaining the **Little Joe and The Ramrods** moniker, line-up 'A' would move from the traditional "guitar-organ-bass-drum" garage band format to a larger horn-oriented band in 1967, then adopted the **Smoke Ring** name in 1968. It was also in 1968 that McClure and Semrad - formerly of the University Of Nebraska band J. Harrison and The Bumbles (Fremont, Nebraska's first rock band) - replaced Asmus and Schrad. Though not part of the line-up ('B') that recorded the first Buddah single, McClure and Semrad joined in time for the band to release the second Buddah single and make an appearance on "American Bandstand". Besides "Bandstand", where the group performed *No Not Much*, a cover of a Four Lad's tune that sold over 800,000 records for **The Smoke Ring**, the band also made television appearances on George Klein's local Memphis WHBQ-TV show, as well as appearances on regional rock shows in Cleveland, Boston and Los Angeles. In 1969, the band trekked to Sam Phillips' Sun Recording Studio in Memphis to record an album whose masters, according to Mike Semrad, "have never been found" (third generation copies, however, are still in the band's possession).

Appearing Tonite! - The Smoke Ring is a cassette-only release featuring both issued and otherwise unreleased material. It was released in 1995 by Ace Brothers Records and limited to 1,000 copies.

No Not Much was also released as part of Buddah's *Dial-A-Hit* compilation (Buddah 5039) 1969. More recently, the track has also appeared on the *Complete Buddah Chart Singles, Volume II* CD (Buddah 75517-49517-2, 1996). (MDo/MSd)

Smoke Rings

Personnel:	MAX UBALLEZ	A
	ROBERT UBALLEZ	A

45s: Love's The Thing/She Gives Me Love   (Prospect 101) 1966
         Love's The Thing/She Gives Me Love   (Dot 16975) 1966

Love's The Thing, is a superb rockin' punker with strong raucous vocals and clangorous guitars, that builds to a rave-up climax and a final breath-taking vocal 'whoop'. A true classic - play at full volume - it's guaranteed to cure head colds! The flip is a melodic pop ballad.

The band is actually East L.A.'s **Romancers** and these re-release 45s, under a new name, resulted from a deal between the band's producer Eddie Davis and **Count Five**'s Irwin Zucker, who thought *Love's The Thing* ought to be a hit. And so it shoulda been.

Compilation appearances include *Love's The Thing* on *Boulders, Vol. 1* (LP). (VJ/MW)

Smoke Rise

Personnel:	RANDY BUGG	bs	A
	GARY RUFFIN	gtr	A
	HANK RUFFIN	keyb'ds	A
	STAN RUFFIN	drms	A

ALBUM: 1   THE SURVIVAL OF ST. JOAN - A ROCK OPERA (dbl)
                                                            (Paramount PAS 9000) 1971 -

NB: There was a also a promotional box set of four 45s (Paramount DJ 5/6/7/8), with material from (1).

45s:	I Need A Woman/Late Last Friday Night	(Atco 6851) 1972
	I Need A Woman (Mono/Stereo) (Promo)	(Atco 6851) 1972

This is a double concept album which is musically in a progressive rock style. All the lyrics are written by James Lineberger. "Despite the well documented story of Joan of Arc, legends persist that the Bishop of Beauvais offered Joan the opportunity to be spared her life by the simple method of substituting another girl, similar in size and appearance to her". For the whole story you must read the booklet that follows the record. (VJ/GG)

Smokestack Banana

45:	F. Me//Get Out Of My Life Woman	
	The Pusher (PS)	(Sizzletone ENP 082) 1993

Sizzling heavy garage-psych recorded live at the Silverbell Club, Pontiac, Minnesota in January 1968. Their rework of *Fever* entitled *F. Me*, kicks off in expletive mood and is followed by savage workouts of two evergreens. A numbered limited edition of 500. If you see one, grab it. (MW)

Smokestack Lightning

Personnel:	RONNIE DARLING	vcls, perc	A
	RIC EISERLING	ld gtr	A
	KELLY GREEN	bs	A
	ART GUY	drms	A
	(WARREN "SANDY" ZEVON	piano, gtr	A)
	(MIKE DEASY	gtr, fine wines	A)
	(LARRY KNECHTEL	organ, piano	A)
	(HAL BLAINE	perc	A)
	(THE BLOSSOMS	backing vcls	A)
	(WILD BILL HOLMAN	horns	A)

HCP

ALBUM:	1(A)	OFF THE WALL	(Bell 6026) 1969 200 -

NB: (1) also released in England (Bell SBLL 116) and in France (with a totally different sleeve).

45s:	α	Nadine/Crossroads Blues	(White Whale 243) 1967
	α	Look What You've Done/	
		Got A Good Love	(White Whale 256) 1967
		Light In My Window/Long Stemmed Eyes	(Bell 755) 1968
		Something's Got A Hold On Me/I Idolize You	(Bell 777) 1969
	β	Baby Don't Get Crazy/The Blue Albino Shuffle	(Bell 836) 1969
	α	Hello L.A., Bye Bye Birmingham/Well Tuesday	(Bell 861) 1970

NB: α and β are non LP tracks. β was also released in France with a picture sleeve (Bell 2C 00690797).

A minor Los Angeles outfit whose bluesy-rock may be of interest here but who don't really fall into the psychedelic or garage genres despite *Look What You've Done*, which is a powerful garagey ballad with a short but searing guitar solo.

All their records were produced by Bones Howe and four of their six singles are not on their only album, which was recorded with the help of other California musicians, including **Warren Zevon** and **Mike Deasy**. Their song *Well Tuesday* was used in the motion picture 'Dreams Of Glass'.

Compilation appearances have included: *Look What You've Done* on *Of Hopes And Dreams & Tombstones* (LP), *Psychedelic Unknowns, Vol. 7* (LP & CD); *Light In My Window* on *Songs Of Faith And Inspiration* (CDR & CD); and *Nadine* on *Happy Together - The Very Best Of White Whale Records* (CD). (MW/SR)

Smokey and His Sister

ALBUM:	1	SMOKEY AND HIS SISTER	(Warner WB 1763) 1967 -

HCP

45:	Creators Of Rain/?	(Columbia 43995) 1967 121

Born in 1948 in Cincinnati, **Smokey** (real name unknown) met Dylan after a local concert in 1965 and "it just opened up his brain" according to the long liner notes to his only album. Shortly after, as with millions of other US teenagers, he began writing songs and playing guitar. In 1966, he moved to Greenwich Village with his sister Viki and their songs and harmonies scored them a contract with Columbia. Their single got a good review in 'Crawdaddy' and made a brief chart appearance at No. 121. They moved to Warner for an album which was produced, arranged (and ruined!) by Paul Harris, a busy session man (**Tom Rush**, **Jim and Jean**). If the songs are average folk-rock with male and female vocals, they were all recorded with rich strings arrangements and the album, which is now rare, is far from being collectable. (SR/VJ)

Smokey John Bull

ALBUM:	1	SMOKEY JOHN BULL	(Avco Embassy AVE 33020) 1971 -

45:	Do Me Like Like You Did Before/	
	Gotta Get Away	(Avco 4561) 1971

A large inter-racial group with nine members, who recorded this album combining horn-rock, soul, blues and gospel rock with some psychedelic touches. Their material included covers like Dylan's *The Mighty Quinn* and **The Byrds**' *He Was A Friend Of Mine* plus original material. (SR)

Smokin' Willie

ALBUM:	1	SMOKIN' WILLIE	(Ulrich) 1970 R3

NB: (1) Limited reissue of 375 on OR (006) 1994.

Smokin' Willie provided the tuneage for many Southern Indiana high school sock hops and biker gatherings in the late 1960s. Their only album was privately pressed and sank without a trace. 1,000 copies were pressed. Their fiery basement-thud approach to the hits of the day is well documented on the record, which features versions of *Get Ready*, *A White Shade Of Pale*, *House Of The Rising Sun* and others like you've never heard them before, plus a sizzling original *Hot Blooded Mama*. (GG/VJ)

Smubbs

Personnel incl:	J. BRAUNREUTHER	A
	JERRY DAVIS	A
	RICHARD SEGALL	A
	GEORGE UTTER	A
	?? ??	A

ALBUM:	1(A)	THIS IS THE END OF THE NIGHT	
			(Monument SLP 18112) 1969 -

45s:	Down On The Corner /	
	Don't Come Close	(ABC Paramount 10797) 1966
	It Can't Be Too Late / Her Love	(Spring SK 703 SS) 1968
	Rosary Anne / Mr. Open Minded	(Monument MN 45-1110) 1968
	Wait Another Heartache /	
	White Paper Sail	(Monument MN 45-1141) 1969
	Un-Pollution (Complete) /	
	Un-Pollution (Short)	(Monument MN 45-1191) 1970

A quintet from Lake Ronkonkoma, Long Island, NY. Their album, recorded at Syncron Sound Studios in Wollingford, Connecticut, is mainly in a poppy soft-rock vein, although they delve into R&B on *Momma's Blues*. The highlight is undoubtedly the haunting *White Paper Sail*, but it's a patchy and disappointing album overall. (VJ/MW)

Snails

45s:	Snail's Love Theme / When I Met You	(Perfection #360) 1966

From Smyrna/Marietta in Georgia this mob were just 11 -13 year olds when they started playing in 1964. They recorded their sole vinyl offering in 1966, inviting some of the neighbourhood teens into the studios by tempting them with free food. The result was far from a love theme; more a horrible noise - one of the worst records I've ever heard.

Compilation appearances include: *Snails' Love Theme* on *Back From The Grave, Vol. 7* (Dble LP); and *When I Met You* on *It's A Hard Life* (LP). (VJ)

Snakegrinder

ALBUM: 1 ... AND THE SHREDDED FIELDMICE
(Alligator Shoes) 1977 R1

From Delaware, a rural-rock outfit mixing acoustic, electric and pedal steel guitars with keyboards. Their album offers seven original songs with long fluid guitar jams a lá **Allman Brothers** or the **Grateful Dead** and some prog and jazz fusion influences. Their songs include *Jesus Was A Plumber*, *Better Late Than Frozen* and *Nothing's Very Easy When Your Baby's In The Lake*. (SR)

The Snaps

45s: You Don't Want Me/You're All Mine (Cuppy C 103) 196?
      Polka Dotted Eyes/The Voice (East Coast C- 1022/3) 196?

From the Folcroft/Collingdale area of Pennsylvania, their first 45 features a superb slice of Bo-Diddley via the Rolling Stones fuzz-garage ala *Not Fade Away*. The flip is also catchy garage-beat with a cool break. Even cooler, the 45 was co-produced by **The Magic Mushrooms**' Sonny Casella, with John Grande. The 'A' side of their second 45, *Polka Dotted Eyes*, is a mid-slow punker with Animals/Them influences and can also be found on *Psychedelic Unknowns, Vol. 6* (LP & CD) and *Crude PA, Vol. 1* (LP).

The band were later known as **Underground Balloon Corps** and then **The Balloon Corps**. (MW)

Sneakers

45s: Mary Lou/You Belong To Me (Delta 1868) 1966
      It's Just Not Funny Anymore/
      I'm Nothing As Of This (Delta 2141) 1966

The label suggests this was a New Mexican outfit - anyone out there able to supply more info?

The Sneakers

45: Whatcha Gonna Do/I'm Goin' Back (Hot Line 119) 1964/5

This band hailed from New Orleans. Both tracks on their sole 45 are heavily influenced by early Merseybeat sounds and, with a wonderfully sparse production, ooze with period charm. Not strictly garage but a good example of the U.S. response to 'the invasion' before the advent of the fuzz-pedal. (MW)

The Sneekers

45: Soul Sneeker/Sneeker Talk (Columbia 4 43438) 1965
NB: some copies in PS.

Lively rockin' frat-dance beat 45. Both sides written by J. Savage and T. Heck. No idea as to their origins, though Mike Kuzmin's excellent Pennsylvania discography 'Sounds From The Woods' wonders whether they might be a Philadelphia outfit. (MW)

Tony Snell

ALBUM: 1 MEDIEVAL AND LATTER DAY DAYS (ESP) 1973 -

Another weird folk singer from the ESP catalogue. (SR)

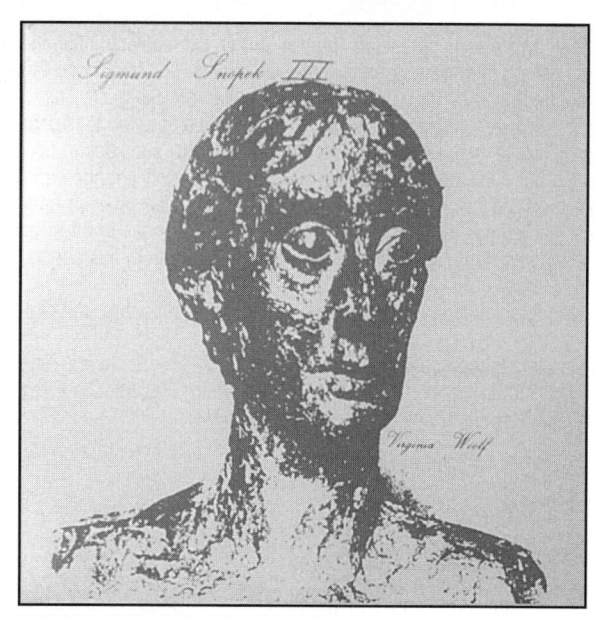

SIGMUND SNOPEK III - Virginia Woolf LP.

Alva Snelling

45: Clock On The Wall/? (Golden-Records 102) 1967

From Baton Rouge, Louisiana, this artist's *Clock On The Wall* shouldn't be confused with the **E-Types** or **Sounds Like Us** songs.

The lyrics to *Clock On The Wall* foretell the threat of a nuclear holocaust. A metronomic garage-punker, it's an interesting song which can now be heard on *Beyond The Calico Wall* (LP & CD). According to the compilation's sleevenotes **Snelling**, who works as a clinical social worker, is still active in the Louisiana music scene as a member of The Frenge. His previous combo (The Luv - Rackers) recorded a new version of *Clock On The Wall* on a 1986 45 and in 1967 he had another 45, a cover of Arthur Alexander's *Anna* under the **Alva Starr** moniker. (VJ/MW)

Sigmund Snopek III

ALBUM: 1 VIRGINIA WOOLF
(Water Street Records WST-1001) 1972 SC
NB: (1) reissued on CD (Gear Fab GF-160) 2000 and vinyl as a double LP (Gear Fab/Comet GFC 421 DLP) with two extra tracks.

Previously in **The Bloomsbury People**, his first solo album offers a mix of prog and psych. Based in Wisconsin, **Snopek** kept on recording during the seventies and eighties, with Major Arcana and solo. (SR)

Snow

Personnel incl: WILL RYAN   A

ALBUM: 1(A) SNOW (Epic BN 26435) 1968 R1

45: Where Has My Old Friend Billy Jones Gone/
     Caterpillar (Epic 5 10425) 1968

From Cleveland, Ohio, this band were originally known as the Muther's Oats. The awful folk-ballad 'A' side can be ignored here. The flip however is an incredibly strange slab of psych-pop which is somewhere between The Beatles' *I Am The Walrus* and **Sweetwater**'s *My Crystal Spider*. Truly a relic of the era. Both 45 cuts also appear on their eponymous album, of which *Catapillar* and *Song Of The Sirens* are the standout tracks. The band's female singer was recruited by the record producers to change their sound.

On the album, the first three tracks are pretty bland multi-voiced folk-rock, although the short guitar incisions are promising. What follows on Side One is strangely melodic acid-rock with oblique harmonies on the brilliant

Engelbert and a kind of twisted **Peanut Butter Conspiracy** influence, with a sharp tempo change and toytown psych on *You Let Me Know*. Side two is even better, starting with the piercing guitar on *Song Of The Sirens*, another track reminiscent of **PBC**. A coiled waltz similar to **Aorta**, *The Flying Miraldos* follows suit, whilst *Sweet Dreams* and *Bab's Song* are pompous but cultivated baroque harmony pop with lush arrangements. The venom is in the tail where the tour de force *Caterpillar* pulls all stops and ushers the listener through more effects and key changes in three minutes and sounds as boldly experimental today as anything from this period.

Will Ryan later recorded as Willio And Phillio in the seventies and eighties.

Compilation appearances have included: *Song Of The Sirens* on *Psychosis From The 13th Dimension* (CDR & CD); and *Where Has My Old Friend Billy Jones Gone* on *Rockbusters* (LP). (MW/JRe/GGl/MK)

The Society

Personnel incl:	SAMMY PIAZZA		A
45s:	High And Mighty/Summer Sunset	(Mark VII D-1 005)	1966
	Together/Love And Laughter DEMO	(Signet no #)	1971

A Texas group from Waco who produced one acid-inspired 45, the second being a demo by a much later incarnation. The 'A' side of the first sounds like a cross between **The 13th Floor Elevators** and **The Seeds**. The flip is a weird instrumental. Sammy Piazza also played with **The Chessmen** and was later with **Hot Tuna**.

Compilation appearances include: *High And Mighty* and *Summer Sunset* on *Sixties Archive, Vol. 2* (CD) and *Texas Punk Groups From The Sixties* (CD); *High And Mighty* on *Fuzz Flaykes & Shakes, Vol. 1* (LP & CD), *The Garage Zone, Vol. 1* (LP) and *The Garage Zone Box Set* (4-LP). (VJ)

Society's Children

45s:	Mr. Genie Man/Slippin' Away	(Cha Cha 775)	1968
	White Christmas / I'll Let You Know	(Atco 6538)	1967
	Count The Ways/Golden Child	(Atco 6553)	1968

An all-girl garage band from Chicago.

Compilation appearances include: *Mr. Genie Man* on *Off The Wall, Vol. 1* (LP) and *Girls In The Garage, Vol. 4* (LP). (VJ)

Society's Children

45:	I'll Find A Way / You Baby	(Empire No #)	1968

Reported as hailing from either NY or Cresson, Pennsylvania. *I'll Find A Way* found its way onto *Oil Stains, Vol. 2* (LP). (VJ)

Bill Soden

45s:	Echo In Your Mind/Rainy Day	(Compass CO-7004)	1967
	My Mermaid And Me/ Stop In The Name Of Love	(Compass CO-7012)	1967
	Old Time Movies/Soakin' Up Sunshine	(Epic 10363)	1968
	Monday Morning Rose/ Urge For Going	(Cotillion 44019)	1969

A little known but interesting singer songwriter, his first 45 was produced by John Hill. *My Mermaid And Me* is a superb flower-pop number, with sitar and strings and can be found on *U-Spaces: Psychedelic Archeology, Vol 5* (CDR).

Solenoid

Personnel:	JEFF BRODNICK	sax, flute	A
	CHAS CARLSON	synth	A
	ROGER DUMAS	synth	A
	ALAN DWORSKY	organ, clarinet	A
	DOUG EBERT	electric gtr	A
	WEST FOSTER	bs, gtr	A

PSYCHOSIS FROM THE 13th DIMENSION (Comp CD) including Snow.

TOM GARVIN	vcls	A
STEVE HILT	drms	A
LONNIE KNIGHT	gtr	A
BRUCE MORGAN	gtr	A
BOB RIVKIN	perc	A
MICHAEL MIDDLEMARK	dulcimer	A
BRUCE McCABE	piano	A
DICK ROBY	bs, vcls	A
SCOTT SANSBY	drms	A

ALBUM: 1(A) ALMOST TENDER (Rufert Records RR 1016) 1977 SC

A loose-knit group from St. Paul, Minnesota whose personnel included former members of **The Castaways** and Cain. The album was produced by Jeff Roberts and is strictly speaking outside the timespan of this book. Some collectors rate this highly - it didn't do a lot for me! (GG)

The Sole Survivors

Personnel:	DENNIS CORMIER	ld vcls, gtr	A
	RICHARD CORMIER	bs	A
	BRUCE McDONALD	ld gtr	A
	RALPH PIERONI	elec. piano, organ	A
	ROCKY STONE	drms	A
45:	Love Her So/There Were Times	(Cori CR 31008)	1966

Formed in high school in 1965 this Massachusetts band, from Fitchburg and Leominster, released just one 45 in 1966. They survived into the mid-eighties, performing in the central New England area. Reunited for the Dance Under The Stars benefit for the American Cancer Society in 1996, they continue to gather for an annual bash.

Love Her So is a moody garage-ballad that reaches a dramatic conclusion punctuated by some growling guitar chords. The vocals are too 'clean' and somewhat at odds with the music - they sound more like an accomplished vocal group. Still this is a 45 whose particular charm grows after several spins.

Love Her So can also be found on *Psychedelic Crown Jewels, Vol. 3* (CD). (MW)

Solid Ground

Personnel:	ROSS HERRICK	A
	DAVID REEDY	A
	RANDY WELLS	A
45:	Sad Now/She Played With Love	(Apro 1) 1966

From Arizona, a superb folk-rock garage-psych outing by an outfit from Mesa, Arizona who were also known as Sounds, Inc. *Sad Now* is a melodic garage folk-rock ballad with yearning vocals that suddenly erupts with a wonderful burst of warped off-the-wall guitar that returns to leave one stunned at the end. *She Played With Love* is cool **Byrds** garage jangle.

Compilation appearances have included: *Sad Now* and *She Played With Love* on *Legend City, Vol. 1* (LP & CD); and *Sad Now* on *High All The Time, Vol. 2* (LP).

Randy Wells was later in **Twentieth Century Zoo**; Ross Herrick would be in the folk-comedy act The Galahads; David Reedy moved onto Floyd and Jerry (& The Counterpoints). (MW/DN)

The Solid Soul

Personnel:	TOMMY DEANE	bs	A
	DOUG FREEDMAN	drms	A
	BOBBY LEVINSON	gtr	A
	STEVE SHERWOOD	keyb'ds	A
	BOB WADE	ld gtr	A

45s:	I've Been Hurt / The Price Of Loving You	(Lovett 69712) 1969
	I've Been Hurt / The Price Of Loving You	(123 1709) 1969

When Greg Presmanes left Atlanta's **Fly-Bi-Nites** in the Spring of 1969, it precipitated some major changes. Freedman took over as leader and they became **The Solid Soul**, reflecting their switch to a funkier R&B sound. Just one 45 was released in the Summer on the local Lovett label; it garnered enough interest to be picked up for national exposure by the Capitol subsidiary 123. (MW/RM)

Solid State

Personnel incl:	J. WALKER?	A

45:	The Lynching / Wait And See	(Elpa 101) 1968

Both sides of this excellent psychedelic 45 on an El Paso, Texas, label were composed by J. Walker. The band came from Bandera, Texas.

Compilation apearances have included: *The Lynching* and *Wait And See* on *Brainshadows, Vol. 1* (LP & CD); and *Wait And See* on *Fuzz, Flaykes & Shakes Vol. 5* (LP & CD). (MW/JI/TSz/LJ)

The Solitary Confinement

45:	A Winner Never Quits / You Send Me	(Sound Impression 6803/4) 1968

From the Detroit suburbs, their sole and rare 45 appeared on a subsidiary of the Wheel's 4 label. *A Winner Never Quits* has appeared subsequently on *The Cicadelic 60's, Vol. 3* (LP) and *The Cicadelic 60's, Vol. 1* (CD), itself repackaged and expanded to the 3-CD *The History Of Michigan Garage Bands In The 60's - The Wheels Four Label Story*. (VJ/MW)

Somebody's Chyldren

45:	Shadows/I'm Going Back To New York City	(Uptown 727) 1966

This was probably a Mike Curb studio group, although it might have been a backing band because both Ian Whitcomb and Mae West used them in this capacity in 1966. A little later that year they put out their sole platter - a powerful and rather folk-flavoured punk disc which had quite a lot of commercial potential.

Compilation appearances include *I'm Going Back To New York City* on *Highs In The Mid-Sixties Vol. 3* (LP). (VJ)

Some Other Animal

45:	Alone On the Highway / I Don't Need Anybody	(Cypher 103) 196?

Although the location of this band is unknown, they are thought to have come from New York or Massachusetts. The 45 was produced by Don Oriolo, and both sides were written by M. Papa (with D. Mullins for the 'A' side). The flip is a bluesy ballad, whilst the 'A' side is similar to **Steppenwolf** with a heavy sound and good vocals. (SR/MW)

Something Else

45:	Let Me Say Now Love / I Can't Believe	(Gama 45-707) c1967

An obscure band from the Washington, DC area. *I Can't Believe* is a punchy pop-punker.

Compilation appearances include: *Let Me Say Now Love* on *No No No* (CD); and *I Can't Believe* on *Garage Punk Unknowns, Vol. 8* (LP). (MW)

Something Wild

Personnel:	KAL BLUE	vcls	A
	BILL EVANS	ld gtr	A
	JOE GEPPI	bs	A
	BILL PAYNE	keyb'ds	A
	RED LIBBEN	drms	A

45:	Trippin' Out/She's Kinda Weird	(Psychedelic 1691) 1967

NB: reisued in green wax / PS by Sundazed (S 136) 1998.

The 'A' side of this outfit's 45, which relates to the influx of hallucinogenics onto the high school campuses of America and some of their virtues and perils, is quite a compulsive number with an effective harmonica intro and good fuzz guitar which culminates into a psychedelic haze.

Originally known as The Hustlers, **Something Wild** came from Santa Maria, California and played between 1965 and early 1967. They also recorded an earlier acetate *Hole In My Soul/The Blues*, which was recorded at Stars International Studios in Hollywood early in 1966.

Bill Evans is still active on the local music scene, penning Rickenbacker 12-string electric material with **Byrds**y licks and simple arrangements with local musicians.

Karl Gebhardt (Kal-X-Blue) had previously been in **The Gremlins**. Billy Payne went on to play with Little Feat.

NO NO NO (Comp CD) including Something Else.

Compilation appearances have included: *Trippin' Out* on *Pebbles, Vol. 7* (LP); *She's Kinda Weird* on *Boulders, Vol. 2* (LP); and *Trippin' Out*, *She's Kinda Weird* and *Hole In Her Soul* on *Thirteen O'Clock Flight To Psychedelphia* (CD). (VJ/MW/BEs)

Bert Sommer

ALBUMS:	1	INSIDE BERT SOMMER	(Eleuthera ELS 3600) 1968/9 -
	2	BERT SOMMER	(Buddah BDS 5082) 1971 -
	3	ROAD TO TRAVEL	(Capitol) c1971 -
	4	BERT SOMMER	(Capitol ST-11684) 1977 -

NB: (1) also released in France (Sava SV 45551) 1969. (2) also released in the UK (Polydor 2318 031) 1971.

ALBUM:	1	LP SAMPLER	(Eleuthera SP-16) 1968/9 -

45s:	α	We're All Playing In The Same Band / It's A Beautiful Day	(Eleuthera 470) c1969
		The Battle Of New Orleans/ On The Other Side	(Eleuthera 472) c1969
		Hold The Light / She's Gone	(Capitol 2434) 1969
		She Knows Me Better / The People Come Together	(Buddah 243) 1971
		Dance The Night Away / When You Feel It	(Capitol 4480) 1977
		The Song's In Me / I Got A Woman	(Capitol 4602) 1978

NB: α also released in France (Sava SV 45551) 1969.

Based in New York, **Sommer** was a folk-rock singer and songwriter who was the **Left Banke**'s vocalist on the February 1967 recording of the *Ivy Ivy/And Suddenly* 45 (Smash S-2089). *And Suddenly*, covered by **The Cherry People** on their debut 45 and album the following year, was composed with Michael Brown - their paths would cross again during his solo career over the next decade.

The 33rpm promo-only EP features four cuts from the *Inside Bert Sommer* album; a cover of Paul Simon's *America*, *Friends*, *Smile*, and *The Grand Pianist*. The latter could be from the **Left Banke**'s second album were it not for **Sommer**'s slightly quavering vocals, as opposed to the smooth and assured tones of Steve Martin.

The Buddah album was produced by **Artie Kornfeld**, of **Changin' Times** and Woodstock fame. Michael Brown shares credits and performs on one track, *Magic Elixir*. Other musicians on the album include Ron Frangipane (k'bds), David Spinozza (gtr), Tony Levin (bass), Donald McDonald (drms), Mike Miniere (perc) and former Funatic and renowned sessioneer **Hugh McCracken** (gtr).

Two of his songs can also be found on the soundtrack of *UltraViolet*, an album also featuring some tracks by **Montage** with Michael Brown.

THE SONICS - Here Are The Sonics!!! CD.

One of his best-known compositions is *And When It's Over*, covered by **Majic Ship**, **Aesop's Fables** and a stunning version by **The Vagrants**. (SR/MW)

Song

Personnel:	CLARK GARMAN	ld gtr	A
	ROB LEWINE	bs	A
	MICKEY ROONEY Jr	gtr	A
	TEDDY ROONEY	gtr, vcls	A
	SHELLY SILVERMAN	drms	A

ALBUM:	1(A)	THE SONG ALBUM	(MGM SE 4714) 1971 -

This Los Angeles band evolved out of a San Francisco group called Tsong. Rob Lewine had previously been with **Illinois Speed Press**. Their album was produced by **Curt Boettcher**. It's a simple rock offering with some pop influences, vocal harmonies and lots of guitar passages, though not outstanding ones. The better tracks include *Medicine Man*, a jazz-inspired song marred by a long drum solo, the psychedelically - tinged *I'm Not Home* and *Banana High Neon*. Mickey Rooney Jr. later went solo and Shelly Silverman went on to session work. (GG)

Songs For The Masses

ALBUM:	1	SONGS FOR THE MASSES	(Private pressing) 1971 ?

A Christian six-piece group, which may please readers who're interested by **The Holy Ghost Reception Committee** . (SR)

The Sonics

Personnel:	BOB BENNETT	drms	A
	ROB LIND	sax, vcls, hrmnca	A
	ANDY PARYPA	bs, gtr	A
	LARRY PARYPA	ld gtr, vcls	A
	GERRY ROSLIE	organ, piano, ld vcls	A
	JIM BRADY	ld vcls	
	RON FOOS	bs	
	RANDY HAITT	keyb'ds, vcls	
	DOUG HEATH	gtr	
	DANNY HOEFFER	ld gtr	
	STEVE MOSIER	drms	

NB: line-up 'A', 1964-67.

ALBUMS:	1(A)	HERE ARE THE SONICS!!!	(Etiquette 024) 1964 R2
	2(A)	THE SONICS BOOM	(Etiquette 027) 1965 R2
	3(A)	INTRODUCING THE SONICS	(Jerden 7007) 1966 R2
	4(-)	EXPLOSIVES	(Buckshot 001) 1973 SC

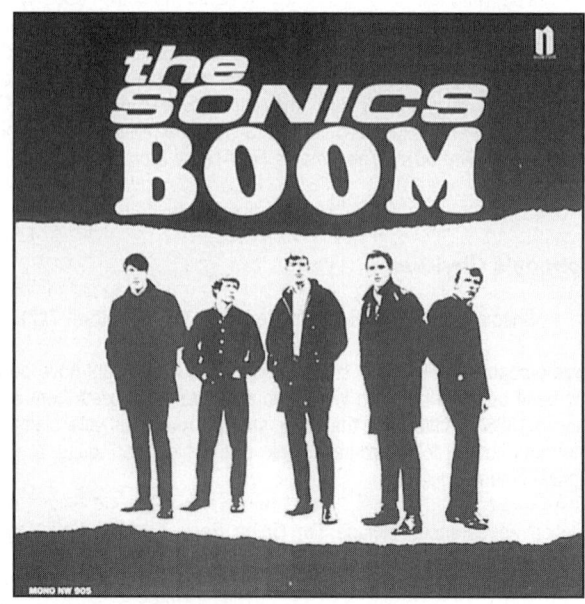

THE SONICS - Boom LP.

5(-)	THE SONICS	(First American 7719)	1978 -
6(-)	SINDERELLA	(Bomp 4011)	1979 -
7(-)	UNRELEASED	(First American FA-7719)	198? -
8(-)	FIRE AND ICE	(First American 7779)	1983 -
9(-)	FULL FORCE	(Etiquette 11 84)	1985 -
10(-)	LIVE FANZ ONLY	(Etiquette)	198? -
11(-)	MAINTAINING MY COOL	(Jerden JRCD 7001)	199? -
12(-)	FIRE AND ICE: THE LOST TAPES, VOL. 1	(Jerden JRCD ????)	1996 -
13(-)	FIRE AND ICE: THE LOST TAPES, VOL. 2	(Jerden JRCD ????)	1996 -

NB: (1) reissued (Norton CD CNW 904) 1999, also on vinyl. (3) reissued on First American Records (First 7715) in 1977 and again on vinyl (BeatRocket BR 114) 1999. (2) reissued on Fan Club (FC 020) 1987. (6) issued in Europe on Line (LILP 4.00249) in 1980 on white vinyl. (1) and (2) are now available on one CD, as well as being issued on CD as *Psycho Sonics*, together with some rarities. (9) is also now available on CD. (12) is a CD compilation. (13) and (14) contain their final recordings from 1966-1968. Also of interest to readers may be a tribute album, *Here Ain't The Sonics*, featuring cuts by Nomads, Cynics, Marshmallow Overcoat and Mojo Nixon among others. This is also available in CD format. *The Young Savage Sonics* (Norton NW 909) 2001 compiles extremely primitive recordings of the band found in an attic! *The Jerden Years 1966-69* (Munster MR CD 204) 2002 (also on vinyl double-album) includes the whole of their 1966 album and much more.

45s:	Keep A Knockin'/The Witch	(Etiquette 11)	1964
	Boss Hoss/The Hustler	(Etiquette 16)	1965
	Shot Down/Don't Be Afraid Of The Dark	(Etiquette 18)	1965
α	Love Lights/Like No Other Man	(Jerden 809)	1966
	Love Lights/ You Got Your Head On Backwards	(Jerden 809)	1966
	The Witch/Like No Other Man	(Jerden 810)	1966
	Don't Believe In Christmas/ (B side by The Wailers)	(Etiquette 22)	1966
	Psycho/Maintaining My Cool	(Jerden 811)	1966
	Louie Louie/Cinderella	(Etiquette 23)	1966
α	Love-itis/You're In Love	(Jerden 909)	1967
	Lost Love/Any Way The Wind Blows	(Piccadilly 244)	1967
	Love-Itis/You're In Love	(Piccadilly 255)	1967
	Any Way The Wind Blows/Lost Love	(UNI 55039)	1967
	Dirty Old Man/Bama Lama Bama Loo	(Burdette 106)	1975
	The Witch/Bama Lama Bama Loo	(Great Northwest 702)	1979

NB: α unreleased.

Tacoma, Washington was their home town and they were one of the finest punk bands to come from the Northwest in this era. *The Witch* was an enormous hit in the Pacific Northwest, indeed **The Sonics** were immensely popular there. Their follow-up *Psycho* was also a local hit. Most of their material was original and written by Gerry Roslie, although they also did cover versions of tracks like *I'm A Man*. Arguably they were left behind in the San Francisco-based rock renaissance of 1967.

Their debut album was full of power and energy. Roslie's screamed vocals and the thundering drumming of Rob Lind characterised a punk venom rarely matched in the sixties and this album included classic numbers such as *The Witch*, *Psycho*, *Boss Hoss* and *Strychnine*.

Their second album *Boom* sounded even tougher with highlights like *Cinderella*, *He's Waitin'*, *Shot Down* and a frenetic version of **The Kingsmen**'s *Louie Louie*.

Their third album, which was produced by Jerry Dennon, was called *Introducing* because it was their first on a major label. This album was later re-released in the late seventies under the title *The Sonics' Original Northwest Punk*. The last 45 recorded by the original line-up was *Any Way The Wind Blows*. After this members departed to go to college or join other bands - with Rob Lind being the last original to leave in 1968.

Jim Brady came in on lead vocals in 1967, from **The Mercy Boys**, and by 1968 was leading the band. From *Love-itis* onwards they perfected a new sound adding strings and horns but it didn't go down with their fans and they slowly faded out of the limelight.

Jerry Roslie reformed the band in 1979 with a new line-up to record (6) for Bomp.

Doug Heath and Ron Foos formed **The City Zu** and Danny Hoeffer went on to play for Tower Of Power. Rob Lind now lives in L.A. where he is involved in the film industry. Gerry Roslie still records and writes songs today.

As one would expect the band are featured on a number of compilations, including:- *The Witch* and *Psycho* on *The History Of Northwest Rock, Vol. 1* (LP); *Any Way The Wind Blows* and *You've Got Your Head On Backwards* on *The History Of Northwest Rock, Vol. 2* (LP); *High Time* on *The History Of Northwest Rock, Vol. 3* (LP), *Battle Of The Bands, Vol. 2* (LP) and *History Of Northwest Rock, Vol. 2* (CD); *Like No Other Man* on *The History Of Northwest Rock, Vol. 4* (LP); *Santa Claus* on *Back From The Grave, Vol. 4* (LP); *Any Way The Wind Blows* on *Baubles - Down To Middle Earth* (LP); *Cinderella* and *Louie Louie* on *A Journey To Tyme, Vol. 3* (LP); *Boss Hoss* and *He's Waitin'* on *Nuggets, Vol. 8* (LP); *Like No Other Man* on *Battle Of The Bands, Vol. 1* (LP); *The Witch*, *Shot Down* and *The Hustler* on *The Northwest Rock Collection, Vol. 1* (LP); *Strychnine* on *Born Bad (Songs The Cramps Taught Us), Nuggets, Vol. 2* (LP) and *Songs We Taught The Cramps*; *The Witch* on *Excerpts From Nuggets* (CD); *Louie Louie* on *The Best Of Louie Louie*; *Strychnine*, *Psycho* and *The Witch* on *Nuggets Box* (4-CD); *Like No Other Man* and *Maintaining My Cool* on *Northwest Battle Of The Bands, Vol. 1 - Flash And Crash* (LP & CD); *High Time* on *Northwest Battle Of The Bands, Vol. 2 - Knock You Flat!* (LP) and *Northwest Battle Of The Bands, Vol. 2* (CD); *High Time* and *You've Got Your Head On Backwards* on *Northwest Battle Of The Bands, Vol. 2 - Knock You Flat!* (CD); *You've Got Your Head On Backwards* and *Like No Other Man* on *Northwest Battle Of The Bands, Vol. 1* (CD); *Cinderella*, *Strychnine* and *The Witch* on *Songs We Taught The Fuzztones* (Dble LP & Dble CD); and finally the instrumental rarity *Goodhard Rock* appears on *Turds On A Bum Ride Vol. 6* (CD). The compilers of the last compilation sumise that this track is "probably" an outtake from material recorded for their third album.

They also contributed three tracks alongside **The Wailers** and The Galaxies to an early compilation *Merry Christmas* (Etiquette ETALB 025) 1965. The tracks were:- *Santa Claus*, *The Village Idiot* and *Don't Believe In Christmas*. (VJ/MW/KSI)

THE SONICS - Introducing The Sonics LP.

The Sonics

45s:	You Make Me Feel So Good/ Introduction To The Sonics	(Cha Cha ?)	1965
	Sherry/She Can't See Me	(Courtin' 5013)	196?

This mob issued the first 45 for members of their fan club and the flip recently re-emerged on the *Ho-Dad Hootenanny* (LP) compilation. They were unconnected to the Pacific Northwest combo. (VJ)

Sonics Inc.

45:	Diddy Wah Diddy/Nobody To Love	(no label SP 0003)	1966

This band might have come from Ohio 'cause the label design strongly resembles the Ironbeat label out of that state. The 'A' side is not the Bo Diddley tune.

Compilation appearances include *Nobody To Love* on *Teenage Shutdown, Vol. 5* (LP & CD); *Diddy Wah Diddy* on *Back From The Grave, Vol. 8* (Dble LP). (VJ/GG)

The Sons of Adam

Personnel:			
MARCUS DAVID			
RANDY HOLDEN	gtr		A
JOE KOOKEN			AB
MIKE PORT	bs		A
MICHAEL STUART	drms		AB
CRAIG TARWATER	gtr		B

CD: 1 RANDY HOLDEN - EARLY WORKS '64-'66
(Captain Trip CTCD-056) 1997

NB: (1) features Holden's period with The Fender IV and **Sons Of Adam**.

EP: 1 SONS OF ADAM (Moxie 1032) 1980

NB: (1) contains all three of their 45s.

45s: Take My Hand/
Tomorrow's Gonna Be Another Day (Decca 31887) 1966
You're A Better Man Than I/Saturday's Son (Decca 31995) 1966
Feathered Fish/Baby Show The World (Alamo 5473) 1966

One of the best of the L.A. garage bands. All three of their 45s can be heard on the Moxie *Sons Of Adam* retrospective, whilst Captain Trip's *Early Works '64 - '66* CD includes both Decca 45s and three previously unreleased cuts, *Without Love, I Told You Once Before* and a cover of the Zombies' *You Make Me Feel Good*. Their 45s were produced by Gary Usher.

Sometime in 1966, Randy Holden quit and was replaced by Craig Tarwater, who Joe Kooken and Michael Stuart spotted backing Jackie DeShannon at a club in San Jose, California.

Towards the end of 1967 they evolved into **New Wing** releasing two 45s for Pentacle. Stuart and Holden later played for **The Other Half**, Michael Stuart was in **Love** and Tarwater later played with the **The Other Half**, **Daily Flash**, **Frank Zappa**, **Buddy Miles** and **Love**'s Arthur Lee.

Joe Kooken later changed his name to Jack Ttanna and it was by this name that he led L.A.-based **Genesis** in the late sixties. He later went into a restaurant venture with **Lee Michaels** in Marina Del Ray, California. Craig Tarwater now lives in Walla Walla, Washington and operates a mail order business called Video School of Guitar as well as his local music store, Blue Mt. Music Inc.

Sons of Adam also played a song in the Sidney Poitier/ Anne Bancroft movie 'The Slender Thread' in the scene where Anne Bancroft goes to a go-go club with her husband. **The Sons of Adam** are identified in the film credits, but the name of the track is not known.

Compilation appearances have included: *Feathered Fish* on *Pebbles, Vol. 2* (CD), *Pebbles Box* (5-LP), *Trash Box* (5-CD), *Pebbles, Vol. 2* (LP), *Great Pebbles* (CD) and *Sixties Rebellion, Vol. 8* (LP & CD); *Baby Show The World* on *Turds On A Bum Ride, Vol. 1 & 2* (Dble CD) and *Fuzz, Flaykes, And Shakes, Vol. 5* (LP & CD); *Mr. You're A Better Man Than I* on *Turds On A Bum Ride, Vol. 4* (CD); *Tomorrow's Gonna Be Another Day* and *Take My Hand* on *Turds On A Bum Ride, Vol. 5* (CD); and *Mr. You're A Better Man Than I* and *Baby Show The World* on *Turds On A Bum Ride, Vol. 1* (Dble LP). (VJ/CTr/RR/JRo/MW)

The Sons of Barbee Doll

45: Psychedelic Seat/Lie To Them (Code 1) 1967

Wacky psychedelia from Port Arthur in Texas. It certainly sounds like it's recorded in someone's garage. Worth checking out if you're into light-hearted psychedelia.

Compilation appearances include *Psychedelic Seat* on *Sixties Archive Vol. 6* (CD), *Texas Psychedelia From The Sixties* (LP) and *Flashback, Vol. 6* (LP). (VJ)

The Sons of Champlin

Personnel:	JIM BEEM	trumpet	A C
(up to	TIM CAINE	sax	ABC
1973)	BILL CHAMPLIN	vcls	ABCDE
	TERRY HAGGERTY	gtr	ABCDE
	JIM MYERS	drms	A
	GEOFF PALMER	keyb'ds, horns, vcls	ABCDE
	AL STRONG	bs	ABCD
	BILL BOWEN	drms	BCD
	DAVE SCHALLOCK	bs	DE
	BILL VITT	drms	D
	MIKE ANDREAS	hrns	E
	MARK ISHAM	hrns	E
	JIM PRESTON	drms	E
	PHIL WOODS	hrns	E

HCP

ALBUMS: 1(B) LOOSEN UP - NATURALLY (dbl)
(up to (Capitol SWBB 200) 1969 137 -
1975) 2(C) THE SONS (Capitol SKAO 322) 1969 171 -
3(D) FOLLOW YOUR HEART (Capitol 675) 1971 - -
4(-) MINUS SEEDS AND STEMS
(No label CFS-2126) 197? - -
5(E) WELCOME TO THE DANCE
(Columbia/CBS 32341) 1973 186 -
6( ) THE SONS OF CHAMPLIN
(Goldmine Ariola America ST-50002) 1975 - -

NB: (1) first pressings contained the phrase "Big Fuckin' Deal" in the artwork on both sides of the cover, most of which were censored by scratching the offending word off! A handful of uncensored copies have turned up. (1) has been reissued on CD (See For Miles SEECD 441) in the U.K. and (One Way 18463) in the USA. (4) was a private pressing produced by the band themselves, made up of live tapes from the era. This album was issued with no song titles on the cover or labels, leading to speculation that an insert must exist, but none has materialised. (4) reissued on CD (Acadia ACA 8007) 2001. This album was reissued in the early nineties. There are also a couple of recommended compilations. *Marin County Sunshine* (Decal LIK 21) 1988, contains material from their first three albums, whilst *Fat City* is a good CD collection of the band's pre-Capitol recordings (Big Beat CDWIKD 188) 1999. The band recorded three further albums: *Circle Filled With Love* (Ariola) 1976; *Loving Is Why* (Ariola) 1977 and *Sons Of Champlin Live* (Grateful Dead Records) 1998.

EP: 1(B) JESUS IS COMING, PART I/PART II (PS)
(Capitol 4667/8) 1969

NB: (1) promotional issue only.

THE SONS OF CHAMPLIN - Fat City CD.

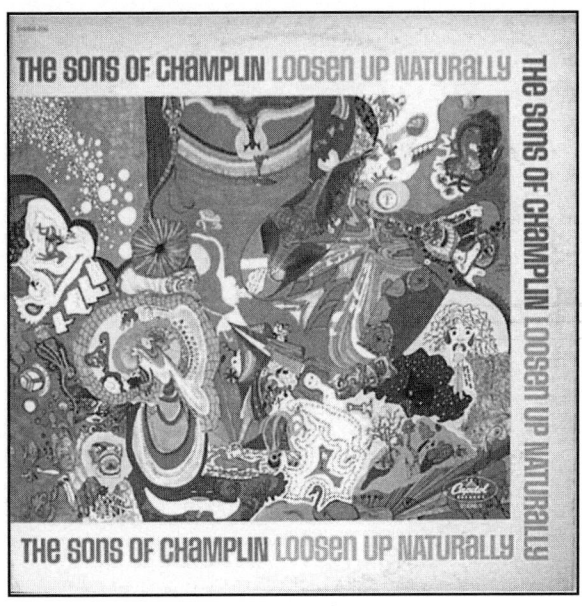

THE SONS OF CHAMPLIN - Loosen Up Naturally LP.

			HCP
45s:	Sing Me A Rainbow/Fat City	(Verve 10500) 1967	124
(up to	1982-A/Black And Blue Rainbow	(Capitol 2437) 1969	-
1973)	Freedom/Hello Sunlight	(Capitol 2534) 1969	-
	It's Time/		
	Why Do People Run From The Rain	(Capitol 2663) 1969	-
α	Terry's Tune/You Can Fly	(Capitol 2786) 1970	-
	Welcome To The Dance/Swim	(Columbia 45872) 1973	-

NB: α as by The Sons.

One of San Francisco's most durable 'second division' bands **The Sons Of Champlin** were clearly a product of the city's drug culture. They formed in the Autumn of 1965 out of the ashes of The Masterbeats (who had included Champlin, Haggerty and Caine) and the **Opposite Six**. After a debut gig at The College Of Marin they soon built up a strong 'live' reputation. They recorded a number of tracks during 1966-7, but only one 45 was ever released on Verve. In 1967, Myers left and was replaced by Bill Bowen from **Electric Train**. They signed to Capitol in 1969.

Their debut double album *Loosen Up - Naturally* successfully captures their live sound. By this time Myers had left the band to join the army and Jim Beem had also left. Essentially a loose jazz and drug influenced band, commercial success eluded them. Later in '69 they changed their name to The Sons and their second album saw a return of Jim Beem on trumpet.

Like so many Bay Area bands they split up in 1970, only to reform before the year was through, minus Caine. This format issued their third album which is worth a listen. However, further splits began to emerge and since their album sold badly Capitol dropped the band. After issuing *Minus Seeds And Stems* themselves they changed name to Yogi Phlegm for a while but entered a dormant spell on the recording front. They did, however, appear on the penultimate night of the closure of The Fillmore West on 3rd July 1971. They re-emerged with an album on Columbia in 1973 and thereafter playing a sort of funky style soul, recorded an album on their own Goldmine label. This was reissued by Ariola and several more albums followed for that label.

Bill Champlin went on to record solo albums in 1978 and 1982, before joining Chicago later that year. In 2000, he sang on *Who Said* a track on Los Angeles based guitarist Marino's album. Tim Caine played with **Good Dog Banned** after he left **The Sons Of Champlin**. Mark Isham is now a music arranger for the film industry and has scored music a number of movies.

The Big Beat CD, part of Alec Palao's 'Nuggets From The Golden State' series, collects twenty tracks from their 1966 Trident recordings - only the debut 45 was released at the time. This pre-Capitol period displays their initial pop influences - smooth harmony-pop, folk-rock, R&B and soul are prevalent but there's some good punky fuzz-pop too. The collection highlights their attention to, and competence in, harmonies and background vocal arrangements. The songs are nearly all originals. Just three covers appear apart from *Sing Me A Rainbow* - **The Beau Brummels'** *Don't Talk To Strangers*, Mann/Weils' *Shades Of Grey* and Paul Simon's *I Wish You Could Be Here*, later covered by the **Cyrkle**. (VJ/MW/CF/AP/CK/BHe)

Sons of Joseph

Personnel incl: RITCHARD POTOCZEK   A

45: It Won't Rain On Me / ? (Richard Joseph) 1968

A crudely recorded and insistent keyboard-dominated ditty. It makes up for its lack of polish with a naive charm that belies its release date. Featured on *Psychedelic Crown Jewels Vol. 2* (Dble LP & CD) who've tracked the band down to Wyandotte, Michigan. (MW/RM)

Sons Of Keystone Cops

45: Chain Gang Man/I Laughed You Cried (Public! 1003) 1969

From the Los Angeles label that also features **Hunger!**, a fuzzy blues-rock number backed by catchy late sixties pop-rock. (MW)

Sons Of May

Personnel incl: RICH SMITH   A

45: Morning Dew (And The Light Turned Red)/
Tossin' And Turnin' (Sonic 826A 2746) 1968

A fragmented fuzz-psych rework of **Tim Rose**'s *Morning Dew* from this Rhinelander, Wisconsin outfit. The flip sounds like a much earlier effort - an almost frat-style *Tossin' And Turnin'*.

Rich Smith also played in a band called Screamin Bob. (MW/JSh)

Sons of Thunder

ALBUMS:	1 TILL THE WHOLE WORLD KNOWS	(Zondervan) 1968 ?
	2 LIVE AT VIRGINIA BEACH	(Private Pressing) 1973 ?

The first album is housed in a nice sleeve and is by an obscure Christian folk-rock group comprising three girls and two men, with guitar and organ. Presumably the second is by the same Christian bunch. (SR)

The Soothsayers

45s:	I Don't Know/Please, Don't Be Mad (PS)	(Acropolis 6601) 1966
	Black Nor Blue/Do You Need Me? (PS)	(Acropolis 6612) 1966

Previously known as The Statesmen, this five piece hailed from Greeley near Denver in Colorado. They recorded for the obscure Acropolis label, which only had three releases and was owned by a Kansas University student who it was later discovered was an older brother of one of the band. Both their 45s came in picture sleeves. The first one *I Don't Know*, released in early 1966, made quite an impression locally and resulted in them getting quite a lot of touring engagements around the Midwest. Essentially it was in the folk-rock mould, whilst the second has a more 'garage' edge.

One of the former members is now dead and another became a jazz musician.

Compilation coverage has so far included: *I Don't Know* on *Highs In The Mid-Sixties, Vol. 18* (LP); *Please, Don't Be Mad* on *Monsters Of The Midwest, Vol. 2* (LP) and *Tymes Gone By* (LP); *Do You Need Me?* on *Monsters Of The Midwest, Vol. 3* (LP); and *Black Nor Blue* on both *Teenage Shutdown, Vol. 8* (LP & CD) and *Psychedelic Unknowns, Vol. 9* (CD). (VJ)

The Sopwith Camel

Personnel:	ROD ALBIN	bs	A
	FRITZ KASTEN	drms	A
	PETER KRAEMER	vcls, sax, synthophone, flute	ABCD
	TERRY MacNEIL	piano, gtr	ABCD
	MARTIN BEARD	bs	BCD
	NORMAN MAYELL	hrmnca, drms, perc, sitar	BCD
	WILLIAM SIEVERS	gtr	B
	JIMMY STRINGFELLOW	gtr, vcls	(C)D

				HCP
ALBUMS:	1(B)	SOPWITH CAMEL	(Kama Sutra KLPS 8060) 1967	191 -
	2(B)	HELLO HELLO	(Kama Sutra KSBS 2063) 1973	- -
	3(C)	THE MIRACULOUS HUMP RETURNS FROM THE MOON	(Reprise MS 2108) 1973	- -

NB: (2) is a reissue of (1). (1) has been reissued on CD by One Way (29311). (3) reissued on vinyl (Edsel XED 205) 1986 and on CD (Generic Type Records) April 2001. There's also a compilation *Frantic Desolation* released on vinyl (Edsel ED 185) 1986.

			HCP
45s:	Hello Hello/Treadin'	(Kama Sutra 217) 1966	26
	Postcard From Jamaica/ Little Orphan Annie (PS)	(Kama Sutra 224) 1967	88
	Saga Of The Low Down Let Down/ Great Morpheum (PS)	(Kama Sutra 236) 1967	-

NB: There's one rare French EP with PS: *Hello Hello/Treadin'/Postcard From Jamaica/Little Orphan Annie* (Kama Sutra 617 109).

Formed in San Francisco in 1965. Although Kama Sutra tried to portray them as a 'good time' band, they also gained the reputation as a good live act which placed emphasis on guitar work. This dual-identity is also in evidence on their 1967 album; although the bulk of the material follows Kama Sutra's obvious intention to turn the **Sopwith Camel** into a West Coast **Lovin' Spoonful**, tracks like the ethereal, classically-influenced *Maybe In A Dream* and the raucous *Cellophane Woman* are quintessentially San Francisco underground. This album was later reissued in 1973 as *Hello Hello*.

Their second and final album was a vast improvement on their earlier work. Many of the tracks, notably *Sleazy Street* and *Coke, Suede and Waterbeds* had a distinctly jazzy influence, whilst *Orange Peel* had some stand-out flute playing and *Dancin' Wizard* was a slower, Eastern-influenced number. The strongest track, however, was probably *Fazon* - the opening cut - which typified the soothing, laid back sound for which **The Sopwith Camel** had become known by the early seventies.

Rod Albin, who had been in their pre-album line-up had earlier played for Liberty Hill Aristocrats. He left before the album to join Roadhog, and Kasten also departed to Joy Of Cooking. Norman Mayell went on to play for Norman Greenbaum and **Blue Cheer**. William Sievers later recorded as **William Truckaway**.

In 2001, the bands drummer Norm Mayell reissued *Miraculous Hump* on CD.

Hello Hello is included on *Incense And Oldies* a budget sixties pop compilation which is nowhere near as good as the title suggests. You can also find *Frantic Desolation* on *Psychedelic Frequencies* (CD). (VJ/SR)

The Roy Sorensen Group

Personnel:	DAVE BOLSON	bs, vcls	A
	TERRY HOFFMEYER	gtr, vcls	A
	MICHAEL MANION	drms, perc	A
	ROY SORENSEN	electric piano, vcls	A

45s:	My Conscience Is Dead/Mack's Jazz	( ) c1969/70
	If You Could Read Me/ Life's Short Span (Part II)	(Cold Wart 78) c1970/71

From Grand Rapids, Michigan, this band formed in 1969. Michael Manion recalls:- "We formed just after I had returned from a concert tour of Europe with the American Youth Symphony. I had been in a couple of other bands with Hoffmeyer before. He knew Sorensen and Bolson, and that's how we got together. It was a somewhat unusual band for that area, in that we did almost exclusively original material, written by Sorensen. Since we didn't do covers, or not many, we were not a bar band, and so had trouble getting gigs. But there were some locals DJs, such as Johnny Mack (*Macks' Jazz*) and Jay Walker who were supportive. Also studio owner and producer Phil Roberts, who was in a well known group in that area called **The Kingtones**. We were pretty loud for the time, having large "Custom" amplifiers - the ones covered in padded naugahide, and I played a large, double bass drum set, a la Ginger Baker."

"We never really broke up, but sort of fizzled. I think that Hoffmeyer and Sorensen are still in the Grand Rapids area. I've heard that Hoffmeyer is in the health care field, and Sorensen is directing a chorus. I think Bolson was studying to be a lawyer. I was, even then, getting into 'New Music'; Feldman, Stockhausen, Cage, etc.. and 'am a composer. I moved to Cologne after grad school and lived there for most of the eighties, worked for Stockhuasen for a while. I lived in London for a few months, on Highbury Hill, just down the road from the Arsenal. Now I'm dividing my time between Southern California and Europe, I also continue to perform, now New Music on electronic percussion. But I just bought a really cool set of vintage Slingerlands..."

In addition to the two 45s, the band also recorded an album, the master tapes for which were lost by Roy Sorensen on a trip to LA.

Compilation coverage has so far included *If You Could Read Me* on *Glimpses, Vol's 1 & 2* (CD) and *Glimpses, Vol. 1* (LP). (VJ/MW/MMa)

S.O.S.

Personnel incl?:	M. EULBERG	A

45:	Hey Jim / To The Woods	(Cinema 6913) c1971

Hey Jim is a tribute to **Hendrix** following his death and is actually a medley of *Hey Joe* and *Purple Haze* with amended lyrics. *To The Woods* is also a hefty fuzz-rocker. Both sides are credited to M.Eulberg and were recorded in St.Louis, Missouri. It's not known whence this band hailed - another address of Belleville, Illinois on the label may offer a clue. (MW)

Sot Weed Factor

Personnel incl:	JEFF ADDISON	ld gtr	A
	GEORGE ARNTZ	gtr	A
	MIKE MONTEIL	drms	A
	CURL SLARSON	hrmnca	A
	JIM WALTERS	vcls	A
	BILL WHEATON	bs	A
	FITO DE LA PARRA	drms	

45: Bald Headed Woman/Say It Isn't So   (Original Sound 76) 1967

After forming in Tuscon in 1966 they moved to L.A. to record the above 45, before returning to Tuscon in 1968, where they disintegrated.

In the eighties the Marshmallow Overcoat payed homage to the band with a cover of *Say It Isn't So* on their *Try On* album.

Mexican drummer, Fito De La Parra went on to play with Bluesberry Jam (pre-**Pacific Gas and Electric**) before joining **Canned Heat** in 1967.

Compilation appearances have included: *Say It Is Not So* on *Psychedelic Unknowns, Vol. 4* (LP & CD); and *Bald Headed Woman* and *Say It Is Not So* on *The Tucson Sound 1960-68* (LP). (VJ/SR)

The Soul

Out of Colorado Springs in Colorado, this outfit had a good local live reputation but never made it onto vinyl at the time. *Highs In The Mid-Sixties, Vol. 18* (LP) includes a previously unreleased acetate by the band *Have It All Your Way*, which is competent but nothing special. (VJ)

Soulbenders

Personnel:	JEFF BOUGHNER	gtr		AB
	ARIS HAMPERS	ld vcls, keyb'ds, bs		AB
	STEVE JOHNSON	drms		AB
	DEL MAYER	gtr		A
	PETE SMITH	bs		B
	DICK STEIMLE	gtr		B

CDs:	1	THE SOULBENDERS/PHLEGETHON: THE MICHIGAN TAPES 1967-1971		
		(Arisdisc no #, private CD) 2000
	2	THE SOULBENDERS/PHLEGETHON: BONUS DISC		
		(Arisdisc no #, private CD) 2000

45s:	Hey Joe/I Can't Believe In Love (PS)	(Phantasm 2530) 1967
	Seven And Seven Is/Petals (PS)	(Phantasm 2568) 1968
	Seven And Seven Is/Petals	(Mala 596) 1968

Formed in 1966 in Grand Rapids, Michigan, by best friends Aris Hampers and Jeff Boughner, their first gig the line-up included classmate Del Mayer and a friend from Ottawa on drums, Steve Johnson. By 1967 Del Mayer had been replaced by Dick Steimle, a talented guitarist from another local band whom Hampers had approached after seeing him play.

They were just starting to get popular locally when they spotted an ad for a Battle Of The Bands that would culminate in a National finals. They entered and also won the State finals held on their home-turf in Grand Rapids.

So, in 1967, **The Soulbenders** made it to the grand final of a nationwide battle of the bands competition held in Braintree, Massachusetts which was recorded for posterity on *Battle Of The Bands - Ridge Arena*, issued as both a double album and triple album set on the Normandy label. Bands who placed outside the top three only got one track apiece preserved on vinyl but **The Soulbenders**' rendition of *House Of The Rising Sun* is one of the highlights, from our biased viewpoint. **The Gents** from Provo, Utah won top honours and have six tracks preserved, second and third (Action Brass and Tony's Tygers) have two tracks apiece.

Aris Hampers recalls that they shared a table with **The Gents**, who lived up to their name and got on really well with them. He was knocked out by their switch to classical sounds (*Moonlight Sonata*) which obviously impressed the judges. He found out afterwards that **The Soulbenders** had placed fifth - quite an achievement.

Encouraged, the band returned to Grand Rapids and recorded their first 45. *Hey Joe* went to the top of the local charts, staying at No. 1 on WLAV for six weeks before being toppled by the Beatles. Three months later they put out their follow-up, a cover of **Love**'s *Seven And Seven Is*. It was doing well locally when Bell Records' president happened to be in town, heard it, and signed the band up for the 45 with an option of more if it sold well. It did do well in several places but not enough to dent the national charts, so the option was dropped.

As the band prepared for the next 45, members started to leave. In the end it was back to the duo of Hampers and Boughner. Time for a change - they recruited new members and became **Phlegethon**, who released two 45s on the Pre-Heat label. A third world loan is required to obtain any of their original vinyl! Luckily Aris has combed the archives of both bands and released the CDs listed above, accompanied by a hefty booklet detailing the bands' histories and material.

Compilation coverage has so far included: *Hey Joe* on *Echoes In Time, Vol. 2* (LP) and *Echoes In Time, Vol's 1 & 2* (CD); *Seven And Seven Is* on *Sixties Rebellion, Vol. 8* (LP & CD), *Relics, Vol. 1* (LP), *Relics, Vol's 1 & 2* (CD), *Sixties Archive, Vol. 7* (CD) and *Songs We Taught The Fuzztones* (Dble LP & CD); and *House Of The Rising Sun* on *Michigan Mixture, Vol. 2* (LP) and *Battle Of The Bands* (LP). *Hey Joe* also turned up on a sixties radio station EP, *WLAV Memory Pack Vol. 1*. (VJ/MW/AHs)

The Souldiers

45: Lemon Sun / Would You Kiss Me   (Boss 007) 1967

Thought to be from the Tampa/St.Petersburg area of Florida. Jeff Lemlich, author of the indispensible Florida tome 'Savage Lost', has a possible clue in the form of a band business card where the name "The Blues Syndicate" has been amended to "The Soul Jers". The contact name is Bob Conn; can anyone shed any light on this?

Would You Kiss Me, a Lewis/Swilley composition with lilting lead guitar and Four Season harmonies, can be found on *Psychedelic States - Florida Vol. 2* (CD).

For more on the sixties Florida scene, pick up Jeff Lemlich's 1992 book 'Savage Lost' (Distinctive Publishing, ISBN 0-942963-12-1). (MW)

Soules of The Slain

Personnel:	DANIELSON	A
	HUTCHINSON	A
	KLAUSE	A

45: Seven And Seven Is/Can't Go On   (Rickshaw 101) 196?

Thought to be from New Orleans, this Louisiana outfit were clearly fans of Arthur Lee's **Love**. Their version of *Seven And Seven Is* is certainly different from **Love**'s, much more aggressive and punkish. The flip side is Lee's *Signed D.C.*, which the band have put to different lyrics and claimed the credit for. Actually it's pretty stunning stuff, very laid-back and trippy with some lovely flute.

Compilation appearances have included: *Can't Go On* and *7 And 7 Is* on *Sixties Rebellion, Vol. 8* (LP & CD), *Louisiana Punk From The Sixties* (LP) and *Sixties Archive Vol. 3* (CD).

SOPWITH CAMEL - Miraculous Hump Returns LP.

The Soul Generation

45: I Can't See You/Big Boss Man (Dater DT-1301) 1966

From Reading, Pennsylvania, this band were originally known as **The Starlites** with two 45s on Barclay. At the suggestion of their producer they changed name to **The Soul Generation** for their third 45 and recorded a different version of *I Can't See You* (which has been **The Starlites**' second 45 and a local hit). This later version, notable for its piercing organ 'wall of sound', can also be heard on the *Crude PA, Vol. 1* (LP) compilation. After this they changed name again to **Beatin' Path** recording the classic *Original Nothing People* 45. (VJ)

Soul Inc.

Personnel:			
	EDDY HUMPHRIES	sax	A
	TOM JOLLY	trumpet	A
	MARVIN MAXWELL	drms	AB
	JIMMY ORTON	bs, vcls	A
	WAYNE YOUNG	gtr	AB
	FRANK BUGBEE	gtr	B
	WAYNE McDONALD	vcls	B
	JIM SETTLE	bs	B

CDs:
1(A/B) SOUL, INC. VOL. 1 (Gear Fab GF-134) 1999
2( )   SOUL, INC. VOL. 2 (Gear Fab GF-138) 1999

NB: (1) and (2) also issued as a double vinyl set (Akarma AKLP 096) 2000.

45s:
Don't You Go/The Alligator (Fraternity 962) 1966
Who Do You Love/727 (Boss 9917) 1966
Midnight Hour/The Leaves Of Grass (Boss 9918) 1966
α Poppin Good Part 1 / Poppin Good Part 2 (Star #981) 1967
Stronger Than Dirt/60 Miles High (Boss 9920) 1967
I Belong To Nobody/
Love Me When I'm Down (Counterpart) 1968
I Belong To Nobody/
Love Me When I'm Down (Laurie 3430) 1968
Been Down So Long/
Get Right With Your Man (Rondo no #) 1969
Satisfied/Ready, Willing And Able (Rondo 106) 1969

NB: α was put out by the Southern Star Meat Co. and the 45 was redeemable via coupons in packets of their Southern Star Weiners.

Probably because of their moniker, this excellent Louisville, Kentucky outfit has been criminally overlooked - we'll try to set the record straight. Although the first 45 features the depressing brassy ballad *Don't You Go*, flip it over for a wild'n'raucous frat dance number with strangely distorted vocals, scorching guitar and a drum solo, later covered by **Us Four** and **The Dawnbreakers**. Changes were in the wind and the second line-up came to force in 1966. Despite the tendency for vocals with a soulful tinge they would produce some sounds worthy of your attention. *Stronger Than Dirt* is a moody punk version with fuzz and backward guitar effects, whilst the flip *60 Miles High* is a midtempo folk-punker with a laid-back but rough-edged feel. *Love Me When I'm Down* is a tough belter with commercial potential but still it retains garagey sensibilities with raw guitar interludes. Frank Bugbee's *I Belong To Nobody* is a softer melodic pop ballad which signalled the end of their peak (so far as this book is concerned), although it was a regional hit that year, and led to them touring with the "Dick Clark Caravan of Stars". Bugbee would later depart with Maxwell and Settle to form the **Elysian Field** and he was subsequently in a studio outfit Friendly Room.

Although **Soul Inc.** had temporarily petered out by the end of the decade, some members are still going strong performing and recording to this day as the **Shufflin' Grandads** including a CD *Southern Fried* CD.

Compilation appearances have so far included: *The Leaves Of Grass* on *Destination Frantic!* (CD); *60 Miles High* on *Mindblowing Encounters Of The Purple Kind* (LP) and *Fuzz Flaykes & Shakes, Vol. 1* (LP & CD); *Stronger Than Dirt* on *Fuzz, Flaykes, And Shakes, Vol. 2* (LP & CD); *Love Me When I'm Down* on *Bad Vibrations, Vol. 1* (LP); and *I Belong To Nobody* on *Acid Dreams - The Complete 3 LP Set* (3-LP) and *Acid Dreams Epitaph* (CD).

Another track, *You Better Get A Move On* by a different **Soul Inc.** can be found on *Teenage Shutdown, Vol. 7* (LP & CD). (MW)

SOUL INC. - Volumes 1 & 2 LP.

Soul, Inc.

Personnel:			
	LARRY BOWIE	vcls, organ, gtr	A
	LAVONNE MOON	vcls, drms	A
	JOHN WHITLEY	vcls, bs, gtr	A
	PAUL WHITLEY	vcls, ld gtr	A

45: Ode To A Girl / Work It On Out (Trepur 1019) 1966

A quartet From Pine Mountain and West Point, Georgia, who had formed in 1962 as **The Continentals**. They switched name circa 1965 to reflect their predilection for soul and R&B sounds. Recorded at Lefevre Studios in Atlanta, *Ode To A Girl* is a reedy garage ballad with sultry harmonies and appears on the compilation *Psychedelic States: Georgia Vol. 1* (CD).

Prior to their dissolution in the Summer of 1966 they were known briefly as **The Buckinghams**, before the Chicago act came to prominence. Larry Bowie was later in **The Rock Garden** and would eventually become a producer, songwriter and publisher in Atlanta. (MW/RM)

Soul Patrol

ALBUM: 1 SOUL PATROL
(White Horse Records WRRNP-SP-256) c1973 -

Another private pressing, this one was recorded by a group of ten musicians, between rock and blues-rock, with a cover of John Lee Hooker's *Use The Rod*. (SR)

The Soul Seekers

45: Good Revelations/Tears (Revelation 1001) 1966

Hailing from Corpus Christi in Texas. *Good Revelations* mixes snotty punk with harmony-pop. You can find it on *Highs In The Mid Sixties, Vol. 12* (LP). (VJ)

Soul Society

45s: What Cha Gonna Do/I've Been Dreaming (Showco no #) 1967
Get Out Of My Life Woman/Knock On Wood (Showco 001) 1967

These two 45s are the work of a Dallas garage band. *Sixties Rebellion, Vol. 11* (LP & CD) and *Brain Shadows, Vol. 2* (LP & CD) both include *Psychedelic Cycle* by a band of the same name, which was originally released as *Psychedelic Cycle / Leave Them Alone* Universal (2019/20) - does anyone know if they are the same mob? (VJ/MW)

The Souls Of Britton

45s:	I'll Be On My Way/Make A New Light	(CEI 129) 196?
	J.J. Come Back To Me/?	(Ken-Del) 196?

A little known band from Delaware whose *J.J. (Come Back To Me)* was included on *Garage Punk Unknowns, Vol. 8* (LP). The first-listed 45 above is by the same act, and was issued on an Ohio label. (MW/GGI)

Souls Of The Slain

Personnel:	DANIELSON	A
	HUTCHISON	A
	KLAUSE	A

45:	7 And 7 Is / Can't Go On	(Rickshaw 101) 1967

Thought to be from New Orleans, this Louisiana outfit were clearly fans of Arthur Lee's **Love**. Their version of *Seven And Seven Is* is certainly different from **Love**'s, much more aggressive and punkish. The flip side is Lee's *Signed D.C.*, which the band have put to different lyrics and claimed the credit for. Actually it's pretty stunning stuff, very laid-back and trippy with some lovely flute.

Compilation appearances have included: *Can't Go On* and *7 And 7 Is* on *Sixties Rebellion, Vol. 8* (LP & CD), *Louisiana Punk From The Sixties* (LP) and *Sixties Archive, Vol. 3* (CD). (MW/AB)

The Soul Survivors

Personnel:	JOEY FORGIONE	drms	AB
	RICHARD INGUI	vcls	AB
	CHARLES INGUI	vcls	AB
	KENNY JEREMIAH	vcls	AB
	CHUCK TROIS	gtr	A
	PAUL VENTURINI	keyb'ds	AB
	EDDIE LEONETTI	gtr	B

HCP

ALBUMS:	1(A)	WHEN THE WHISTLE BLOWS ANYTHING GOES WITH THE SOUL SURVIVORS	(Crimson LP-502) 1967	123	-
	2(A)	TAKE ANOTHER LOOK	(Atco SD 33-277) 1969	-	-
	3(B)	THE SOUL SURVIVORS	(T.S.O.P. K2 33186) 1974	-	-

NB: (1) reissued on CD by Collectables (COL-CD-0502).

HCP

45s:	Expressway To Your Heart/Hey Gyp	(Crimson 1010) 1967	4
	Explosion (In My Soul)/ Dathon's Theme	(Crimson 101 2) 1968	33
	Impossible Mission/Poor Man's Dream	(Crimson 101 6) 1968	68
	Turn Out The Fire/Go Out Walking	(Atco 45-6627) 1968	-
	Mama Soul/Tell Daddy	(Atco 45-6650) 1969	115
	Still Got My Head / Temptation's About To Get Me	(Atco 45-6735) 1970	-
	The Best Time Was The Last Time / City Of Brotherly Love	(TSOP ZS8-4756) 1974	-
	What It Takes / Virgin Girl	(TSOP ZS8-4760) 1975	-
	Lover To Me / Your Love	(TSOP ZS8-4768) 1975	-

From Philadelphia, this outfit took its inspiration from white soul. Their second album was recorded partly in Alabama in the Fame Studios and co-produced by Rick Hall. There have been rumours that Duane Allman played on it but Rick Hall denied them. The other tracks were produced by the Philly Soul specialists Gamble and Huff. Housed in a nice cover, it's quite patchy and the horn arrangements defintely belong to soul music. Their third album was totally soul-oriented.

Chuck Trois formed his own group and went on to play for Amazing Maze, Great Train Robbery and **1910 Fruitgum Co**. Kenny Jeremiah later played with **Scorpion**, and both Venturini and Leonetti went on to form **Privilege** in 1973. Charles Ingui is still touring and recording. (VJ/SB/SR/BR/PC/MW)

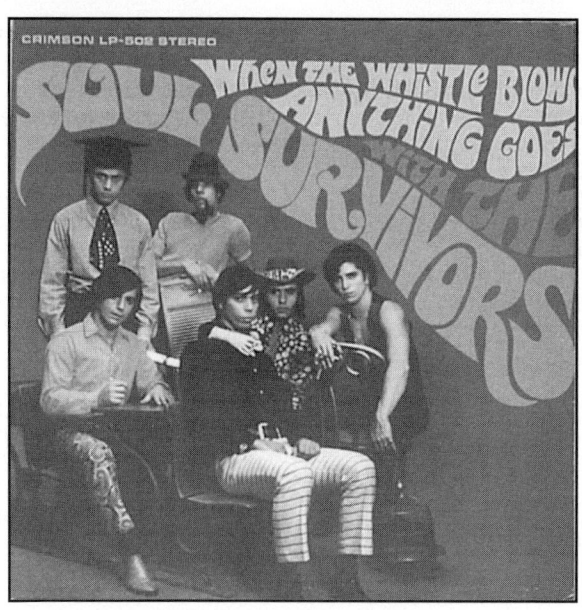

THE SOUL SURVIVORS - When The Whistle Blows... LP.

The Soul Survivors

45:	Devil With A Blue Dress On/ Shakin' With Linda	(Decca 32080) 1966

From Pittsburgh, Pennsylvania, their *Shakin' With Linda* was a fine dance number and was also reputedly a 'cold turkey' report.

Compilation appearances include *Shakin' With Linda* on *The Essential Pebbles Collection, Vol. 2* (Dble CD) and *Pebbles, Vol. 7* (LP). (VJ/MM)

The Soul Survivors

Personnel:	GENE CHALK	A
	ALLEN KEMP	A
	PAT SHANAHAN	A
	BOB WEBBER	A

45s:	Look At Me/ Can't Stand To Be In Love With You	(Dot 16793) 1965
	Hung Up On Losing/Snow Man	(Dot 16830) 1966

These 45s were the work of a different outfit from Denver. Bob Webber went on to join **The Moonrakers**, Kemp and Shanahan headed for L.A. in 1966 where together with Randy Meisner and Randy Naylor they formed **The Poor** and produced four fine 45s between 1966 and 1968. Naylor later got into country and western and Meisner joined The Eagles. Kemp and Shanahan went on to become part of Rick Nelson's Stone Canyon Band.

Compilation appearances include *Can't Stand To Be In Love With You* on *Fuzz, Flaykes, And Shakes, Vol. 3* (LP & CD). (VJ/MW)

The Soultons

45s:	Baby I Don't Know / Rain Down Soul	(Bay Town BT005/6) 1968
	Proud Mary / Cloud Nine	(Jaguar J-105) 1970

For some reason this Hayward, California band are billed as **The SoultAns** on *Fuzz, Flaykes And Shakes, Vol. 4* (LP & CD), which features their funereal punk ballad *Rain Down Soul*. The compilers make amends by nailing the perfect description to it - the Animals' *House Of The Rising Sun* meets **Love**'s *Signed D.C.*. (MW)

The Soul Trippers

Personnel:	JOHN DeLISE	ld vcls	A
	RONNIE ELLIOT	bs	A
	SPENCER HINKLE	drms	A
	BUDDY RICHARDSON	ld gtr	A
	RONNIE VASKOVSKY	gtr	A

45:	King Bee/Girl Of Mine	(Providence 415)	1966

From Tampa, Florida, **The Soul Trippers** were previously known as **The Outsiders**, but when they changed labels to Laurie subsidiary Providence, they were persuaded to change their name in order to avoid confusion with the **Outsiders** from Ohio.

Their rootsy blues-punk take of James Moore's *(I'm A) King Bee* is so cool and convincing that it shifted 20,000 copies before it was discovered they were a white band, which resulted in it getting pulled from local radio station playlists (so how good was it?). Judge for yourself - it has reappeared on *Mindrocker, Vol. 5* (LP) and *Psychedelic States - Florida Vol. 2* (CD).

The band would evolve into **Noah's Ark**. Buddy Richardson would form **White Witch** who released several 45s and two albums on Capricorn in the early seventies.

John DeLise also played in **Those Five** and **The Rovin' Flames**. (GGI/MW/SR/JLh/RM)

The Soul Twisters

45:	Swinging On A Grapevine/?	(Romat 1002)	1967

A black act from Greenville in North Carolina whose sole vinyl adventure seems to have been this 45. You can also hear *Swinging On A Grapevine* on the *Tobacco A-Go-Go, Vol. 1* (LP) compilation. (VJ)

The Souncations

45:	Respect/Exit	(Head 1001)	196?

The flip to this, *Exit*, is a pretty impressive punk ballad and can also be found on *Highs In The Mid-Sixties, Vol. 17* (LP). The band came from Dallas in Texas. (VJ)

The Sound Barrier

Personnel incl:	PAUL HESS	ld gtr, vcls	A

45s:	(My) Baby's Gone/Hey Hey	(Zounds 1004)	1967
	I Can't Explain/Greasy Heart (PS)	(United Audio 904111)	1969

From Salem, Ohio. *(My) Baby's Gone* has an unusual fuzztone intro but then degenerates into a routine, if rather meaty, punker. The flip is a pounding frat rocker with a continuous **Strangeloves**' style beat throughout. The best thing about this quintet's second effort was the picture sleeve it came in picturing the band in paisley-style mod outfits. The vinyl consisted of disappointing covers of The Who's *I Can't Explain* and **Jefferson Airplane**'s *Greasy Heart*.

Compilation appearances include *Hey Hey* on *Off The Wall, Vol. 2* (LP), *Teenage Shutdown, Vol. 10* (LP & CD) and *Highs In The Mid Sixties, Vol. 9* (LP). (VJ/MW/GGI)

Sound Extraction

Ear-Piercing Punk (LP & CD) and *Teenage Shutdown, Vol. 2* (LP & CD) all include *I Feel Like Crying* by this band about which nothing is known, except that the 45 was issued on J-Three (509). (GG)

The Sound Foundation

ALBUM:	1	SOUND FOUNDATION	(Smobro Records)	c1969 -

45:	Magic Carpet Ride/Morning Dew	(Smobro 401)	c1968

A multi-racial pop-rock sextet with a horn section, notable for the long instrumental *Soul Foundation* but also for bubblegum covers of **Steppenwolf** and Bonnie Dobson's songs.

Smobro was a short-lived label distributed by Buddah, their only other release seem to have been the **Two Brothers**' 45. (SR)

The Sound Investment

Personnel incl:	NEAL FORD	vcls	A

45s:	Don't Stop The Carnival/Like My Girl	(Laurie 3398)	1967
	Come Back Baby/The Beat	(Laurie 3442)	1968

One of **Ford**'s many Houston-based sixties bands which succeeded the Neal Ford Factory. After these two 45s **Neal Ford** teamed up with Rick Mensik. (VJ)

Sound Machine

Personnel incl:	ED CASSIDY	drms	A
	CLEM FLOYD		A
	GRANT JOHNSON	piano	A
	JACK LAKE	drms	A
	GARY MARKER	bs	A
	BILL WOLFF	gtr	A

45:	Gotta Ease My Mind/Spanish Flash	(Canterbury C 511)	1967

A Los Angeles combo who included ex-**Rising Sons** member Gary Marker. Their sole 45 has a cool jazzy vibe that permeates throughout, making them sound not too dissimilar to Ed Cassidy's **Spirit** in their more laid-back jazzy moments. Neither garage nor psych, just a cool West Coast breeze.

Gary Marker recalls working with **Sound Machine** on and off for about a year, but was surprised to learn that anything had been released... Gary Marker has also confirmed that Ed Cassidy (also with the **Rising Sons**) was a member of this band at one point. Bill Wolff later joined the **Peanut Butter Conspiracy** for their second album, *The Great Conspiracy*.

Both Bill Wolff and Gary Marker also played in **Fusion**. (MW/SR)

Sound of Feeling

Personnel:	PAUL BEAVER	moog	A

ALBUM:	1(A)	SPLEEN	(Limelight LS 86063)	c1969 -

45:	Hurdy Gurdy Man/Along Came Sam	(Limelight L-3088)	c1969

NB: both sides taken from the album.

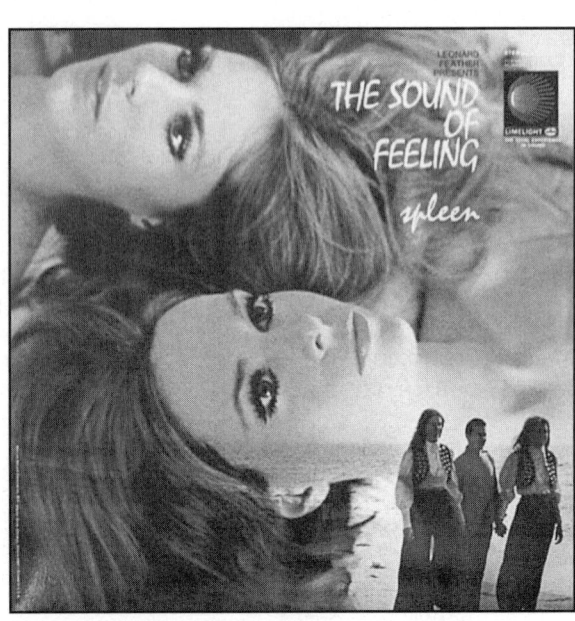

THE SOUND OF FEELING - Spleen LP.

Another project of Paul Beaver (from **Beaver and Krause**), with electronic sounds, moog and harmonious female/male vocals. (SR/SBn)

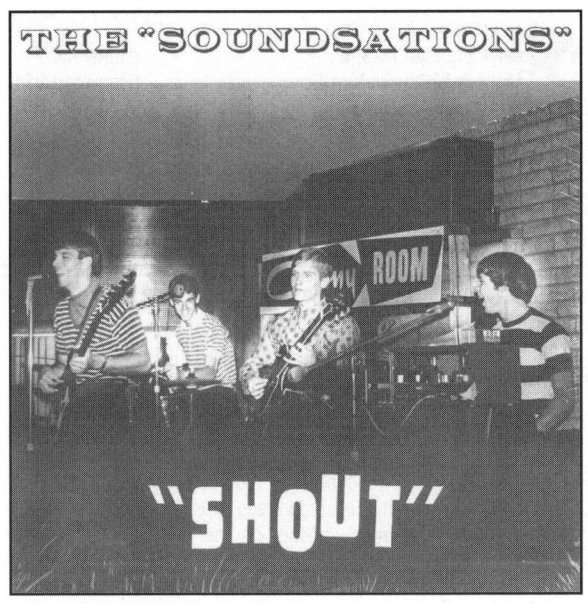

THE SOUNDSATIONS - Shout LP.

The Sound Offs

| 45: | The Angry Desert/Working Up A Steam | (Era 3100) 1963 |

This seems to have been their sole vinyl adventure and it certainly predated the psychedelic era although *The Angry Desert* can be heard on *Psychedelic Unknowns Vol. 8* (LP & CD). (VJ)

Sound Of Fury

Personnel:	JERRY KASZYNSKI	gtr	A
	JACK SADOWSKI	organ	A
	BILL WANGLER	bs	A
	MARK WANGLER	ld vcls	A
	JOE ZEMAN	ld gtr	A
	JOHN ZODKAL	drms	A

From the LaSalle/Peru area of Illinois, a band whose sound doesn't live up to their name. They don't appear to have released any 45s but contributed two cuts to the 1968 Illinois sampler *A Psychedelic Six-Pack Of Sound*. *I Don't Need You* and *I Can't See You* are fragile folk-rockers which look back to the 1965 sound of the Searchers and **Beau Brummels**.

I Don't Need You has also since appeared on *Project Blue, Vol. 3* (LP). (MW)

Sound Of The Seventh Son

| Personnel incl: | JIMMY GREENSPOON | | A |

| 45: | I Told A Lie / I'll Be On My Way | (Tower 169) 1965 |

A house band at the Stratford club on Sunset Strip in L.A., they included Jimmy Greenspoon, formerly of the surf band the New Dimensions. He's better known, here at least, for his later work with the **West Coast Pop Art Experimental Band** and **The East Side Kids**.

Compilation appearances include *I Told You A Lie* on *Love Is A Sad Song, Vol. 1* (LP). (DPe/MW)

Soundpeace

| 45: | Strawberry Pie Lounge/ Leaves Of Nellen Niaviv | (Taurus T-381) c1968 |

A faceless New York outfit who produced a nifty bit of pop-psych punctuated by warped fuzz-guitar on *Strawberry Pie Lounge*. (MW)

The Sound Sandwich

| 45s: | Apothecary Dream/Zig Zag News | (Viva 615) 1967 |
| | Tow Away/Mister Sunshine Man | (Viva 625) 1968 |

A psychedelic outfit out of Los Angeles. The 'A' side to their first 45, *Apothecary Dream*, is a well-produced slice of psychedelia with some fine fuzztone guitar, a hypnotic two note organ sound and crystal clear vocals which implore the audience to 'escape into a dream...'. *Zig Zag News* is a punky popper that starts slowly, accelerates to double-quick time for a rousing chorus with a crescendo of pizzicato guitar, then repeats the formula once more. *Tow Away* is rather messy pop with too many time changes but has a good chaotic guitar break; *Mister Sunshine Man* is a sentimental harmony-pop ballad. All four cuts were written by Johnny Cole and produced by Cole and Gil Garfield for Snuff Garrett Productions.

Compilation appearances include: *Apothecary Dream* on *Psychedelic Unknowns, Vol's 1 & 2* (LP), *Psychedelic Unknowns, Vol. 1* (Dble 7") and *30 Seconds Before The Calico Wall* (CD); and *Zig Zag News* on *U-Spaces: Psychedelic Archaeology Vol. 1* (CDR). (VJ/MW)

Soundsations

Personnel:	JOHNNY BOGGS	keyb'ds	AB
	DAVE CLELLAND	drms	AB
	TOM CORDLE	bs	AB
	BOB HEY	ld gtr	A
	PATSY STEVENS	vcls	AB
	DEXTER BELL	ld gtr	B

| ALBUM: | 1(B) | SHOUT | (Phalanx PH-001) 1966 R3 |

NB: (1) limited to 1000 copies. (1) reissued on CD (Gear Fab GF-170) 2001, with 15 bonus tracks by **The Ramrods**.

Kalamazoo, Michigan's, **Soundsations** were formed at the start of 1966 by the mass exodus of Stevens, Hey, Boggs and Clelland from **The Ramrods**. They'd just started a long-term residency at the Colony Room when Bob Hey got his draft notice - his replacement was Dexter Bell. The local Phalanx label approached the band to do a live party album featuring favourite covers (*Unchained Melody*, *Johnny B.Goode*, *Shout*, *Midnight Hour*...) and a Boggs original *Moody Love*. The final cut is a 5-minute handclappin' rave-up version of *Shout* which soon breaks into a rampaging drum solo/party accompanied by screams and squeals. 1,000 copies were pressed up and sold by the band at gigs who continued on the club circuit, with no further releases, until it all ended in a bust-up between Boggs and Cordle in Green Bay, Wisconsin.

Boggs recorded several country CDs and is occasionally joined in performances by Patsy Stevens. Clelland played drums full-time until the mid-nineties. Bob Hey returned from Vietnam and moved to Goshen, Indiana. Dexter Bell also got the call but did not make it back; the CD is dedicated to his memory. (MW/RM/CF)

Sounds Like Us

| Personnel incl: | JIM PATRICK | ld vcls | A |

45s:	Clock On The Wall/Outside Chance	(Jill-Ann 101) 1966
	Clock On The Wall/Outside Chance	(Fontana 1570) 1967
	It Was A Very Good Year/ The Other Side Of The Record	(Soma 8108) 1967

This outfit from Duluth, on the banks of Lake Superior in Minnesota, is best known for *Clock On The Wall* which was picked up by Fontana for nationwide release.

Compilation appearances have included: *Clock On The Wall* and *Outside Chance* on *Boulders, Vol. 3* (LP); *Outside Chance* on *Teenage Shutdown, Vol. 5* (LP & CD); *The Other Side Of A Record* on *Soma Records Story, Vol. 3* (LP) and *Everything You Always Wanted To Know...* (CD); and *It Was A Very Good Year* on *The Big Hits Of Mid-America - The Soma Records Story* (Dble CD). (VJ/MW/RPk)

Sounds Ltd.

Personnel incl: PHILIP JACKSON   A

45:    Slimy Sue/?   (Peak 108) 196?

Fronted by Philip Jackson this teen band were based in St. Joseph, Missouri. Jackson wrote *Slimy Sue*, a crudely recorded teen ditty, which can be heard on *Monsters Of The Midwest, Vol. 4* (LP). However, arguably he went on to better things as a member of the **Jefferson Airplane**-influenced White Eyes and the country-rockers White Rock Prairie Band. He also performed a duo with his wife and as a solo folky. (VJ)

The Sounds Of Dawn

45s: Walkin' Out On You/Stephanie Says   (Dot 17025) 1967
      How Many Times/If I Had My Way   (Twin Stacks 125) 1967
      She Said You Said/It Takes...   (Twin Stacks 128) 1968

The first 45 is pleasant L.A. harmony pop - the later ones go into a soulful ballad direction. *Walkin' Out On You* was written by Joey Stec, who'd team up with **Curt Boettcher** and ex-**Music Machine** members in super harmony pop-psych outfit **Millennium**. (MW)

Sounds Of Modification

Personnel: JOE CAVALEA   vcls, trombone, trumpet   A
           MIKE CAVOUTO   drms   A
           BOB DORSA   bs, vcls   A
           PETE MALETTA   keyb'ds   A
           FRANK PORCELLI   ld gtr, vcls   A

ALBUM: 1(A)   SOUNDS OF MODIFICATION   (Jubilee JGS 8013) 1967 -

From New York, an Italian-American pop-rock album produced and arranged by Bob Gallo, who previously created **The "You-Know-Who" Group**. The album is overproduced, uniformly weak and best avoided! Gallo would later produce **Aesop's Fable** and **Sum Pear**. (SR)

Sounds Of Our Times

ALBUM: 1   HEY JUDE   (Capitol ST-117) 1968 -

45s: Look Of Love/A Whiter Shade Of Pale   (Capitol 2109) 1968
      Hey Jude/Harper Valley PTA   (Capitol 2291) 1968

Housed in a nice psychedelic cover, an album of orchestral covers of songs by the Beatles, The Doors and Simon & Garfunkel (*Hey Jude, Light My Fire, The Fool On The Hill, The Sounds Of Silence*). (SR)

Sounds Of Randall

Personnel incl: JAY RANDALL   A

45:    Wasting My Time / Wasting My Time   (Carl C-101) 1966

Jay Randall was big in Church Point, Louisiana. He released several 45s under his own name and with the bands he fronted - Jay and The Driving Wheels, The Jay Randall Group and Jay Randall and The Epics. Mainly soulful beat or ballads, some described as "Gulf sound", he occasionally he poked his head into garage territory....

Wasting My Time is sultry beat with strong impassioned vocals and can be heard on *Leaving It All Behind* (LP) and *The Lost Generation, Vol. 2* (LP). (MW)

Sounds Of Sunshine

Personnel incl: WARNER WILDER   vcls   A

45s: Linda The Untouchable/ Love Means   (Ranwood 896) 1968
      I Do All My Crying In The Rain/
      It's Hard To Say Goodbye Forever   (Ranwood 912) 1968
      Yesterday Keeps Getting In The Way/
      Anything Can Happen   (Ranwood 913) 1969
      Make It Happy/Nature Boy   (Ranwood 921) 1969
      Make Believe Saturday Night/
      Today Is The First Day   (Ranwood 925) 1969
      End Of The World/Over And Over   (Ranwood 932) 1970
      Sea Gull/She Takes Care Of Me   (Ranwood 940) 1970

A soft pop group with elaborate harmony vocals. Most of their 45s were produced by Randy Wood and written by Warner Wilder. Ranwood also released records by **Inner Dialogue** and Turn Of The Century. (SR)

The Sounds of Tyme

45:    To Understand Mankind/Sold-Out Show   (Bow Mar 1001) 1967

From North Carolina, this obscure band recorded a great single. Written by V. Collins and M. Bowden, *To Understand Mankind* is an anti-war protest song with **Byrds**-like harmony vocals on the chorus, phased acid lead guitar and wild rolling drumming. The flip is mid-tempo, mostly notable for the active drumming. It was produced by M. Collins and Bowie Martin, the owner of this small label based in Wilson, North Carolina.

Compilation appearances include *To Understand Mankind* on *Of Hopes And Dreams & Tombstones* (LP) and *Psychedelic Unknowns, Vol. 7* (LP & CD). (VJ/SR/RD)

Sounds Of Us

Personnel: BRIAN GUNDERSON   gtr, vcls   A
           JOE HALTERMAN   drms, vcls   A
           GREG LOWERY   bs, trumpet, sax, vcls   A
           JIM TRAVIS   bs, vcls   A

A clubby band from the Ottawa/Marseilles area of Illinois. All they left behind are two cuts on the 1968 Illinois sampler *A Psychedelic Six-Pack of Sound*, which features five other local outfits doing two tracks each - **Coming Generation**, Eighth Day, Mavricks, **Rising Tides** and **Sound Of Fury**.

Despite the title, most of the material featured is in no way psychedelic or even garagey - this bunch's *True* is a very pedestrian sax-led lounge instrumental, whilst *What Would You Say* is tame beat-pop. (MW)

Sounds Unlimited

45:    Keep Your Hands Off Of It/About You   (Solar 101) 196?

A Dallas punk outfit.

Compilation appearances have included: *Keep Your Hands Off It* and *About You* on *Acid Visions - Complete Collection, Vol. 2* (3-CD), *Texas Punk: 1966, Vol. 1* (LP) and *Green Crystal Ties, Vol. 2* (CD). (VJ)

Sounds Unlimited

Personnel: PHIL BRANDT   ld gtr   A
           STEVE FOSTER   gtr   AB
           KEN MAHLKE   bs   A
           WAYNE WILSON   drms   AB
           JOHN TALBOT   gtr, vcls   B
           TERRY TALBOT   ld gtr, vcls   B

EP: 1   SOUNDS '66   (Sundazed SEP 104) 1992

NB: (1) contains *She, You Did It Before, Gotta Get Away* and *Our Love Is Gone*, which were recorded in 1966 before they signed with Dunwich.

45:    Little Brother/A Girl As Sweet As You   (Dunwich 157) 1967

A different outfit which formed in Indiana in 1966 but relocated up to Chicago the same year. Their music and stage act were strongly Anglophile - they regularly smashed their instruments! However, the flip to their Dunwich 45 was in the **Harpers Bizarre** style, and this can be heard on

Mindrocker, Vol. 2 (LP). An excellent unreleased version of **Blues Magoos'** *Gotta Get Away* has lately appeared on the CD compilation *Oh Yeah! The Best Of Dunwich Records*, as well as *A Girl As Sweet As You*. *Gotta Get Away* was part of a session arranged at Philadelphia's Cameo-Parkway Studios by Columbia-Screen Gems intended as an audition for 'The Monkees' by line-up 'A'. Several months later Terry Talbot replaced Brandt when he was injured in a motorcycle accident and John Talbot came in for Mahlke who quit for college. Steve Foster switched to bass in this line-up (B), which recorded the Dunwich 45. They evolved into **Mason Proffit** in 1969 and proceeded to release half a dozen albums and a similar number of 45s in the 1970s.

The Sundazed retrospective EP contains material they recorded prior to signing to Dunwich, of which only *She* was previously released. Another unreleased cut *You're Gonna Lose That Girl* has also resurfaced on *If You're Ready - The Best Of Dunwich... Vol. 2* (CD). (VJ)

Sounds Unlimited

Personnel:	GEORGE BENNETT	bs	A
	RICHARD BORKAN	keyb'ds	A
	RICHARD DOW	gtr	A
	RANDY RHODES	drms	A
	PAUL ROSE	ld gtr	A
	LARRY HINES	bs	

45s:	Nobody But You /		
	Why Doesn't She Believe Me	(ABC Paramount 10803)	1966
α	A Love That's Real / Take A Bus	(Columbia 4-45029)	1969

NB: α as **Stix & Stonz**.

Members of this Florida band hailed from Miami and Hialeah. Rose and Rhodes would adopt the moniker of the **Stix & Stonz** after the original Miami group of that name had disbanded.

The catchy Borkan-composed pop-punker *Nobody But You* is to be found on *Psychedelic States - Florida Vol. 2* (CD). *Why Doesn't She Believe Me* has also turned up on *The Lost Generation, Vol. 2* (LP).

Richard Borkan also played in **Kollektion**.

Another **Sounds Unlimited**, reportedly from the "South East", put out a 45 on the SWAL label, featuring *Cool One*, compiled on *Tougher Than Stains* (LP). (MW/RM/JLh)

The Sound Symposium

ALBUM:	1 PAUL SIMON INTERPRETED	(Dot DLP-25871) 1968 -

45s:	Mrs. Robinson/Bookends	(Dot 17115) 1968
	The Mighty Quinn/I'll Be Your Baby Tonight	(Dot 17296) 1969

In the same style as the **Rubber Band**, an 'exploito' group who specialised in instrumental covers of songs by Paul Simon and Bob Dylan. (SR)

Sound System

Personnel incl:	RAY BARNS	bs	A
	ROGER HAYES	drms	A
	LYNN JENKINS	vcls	A

45:	Take A Look At Yourself/Serenade	(Romat 1001) 1967

An obscure combo recorded this 45 in Greenville, North Carolina. *Take A Look At Yourself* is typical garage psychedelia with lots of fuzz and organ.

Some members went to school with Ed Truman (from Raleigh's **Marke V**), and later played in a group with Lynn Jenkins.

Compilation appearances include *Take A Look At Yourself* on *A Lethal Dose Of Hard Psych* (CD) and *Tobacco A-Go-Go, Vol. 1* (LP). (MW/ET)

The Sound Track

45:	I See The Light / ?	(Trail TSRC-1706) 1967

NB: There may be another 45: *Face The New Day / People Say* (Action 101) 196?

An unknown Tennessee outfit. Their cover of *I See The Light* can be heard again on *Sick And Tired* (LP). This isn't the **Five Americans**' hit but a slick punky popper written by E. Chiprut, who wrote the bubblegum smash *Simon Says*. (MW)

The Sound Vendor

Personnel:	JIM DUNLAP	vcls	A
	JIM GRAZIANO	drms	A
	ALLEN GUNTER	gtr	A
	DAVE MAITLAND	gtr	A
	GREG PERRY	keyb'ds	A

45s:	Mister Sun/In Paradise	(Liquid Stereo LS-25) c1967
	It's Snowing / She Knows	(Ridon 857) 1968

Portland, Oregon's **Sound Vendor** was formed in 1967 when **Mr.Lucky and The Gamblers** fragmented - all five had been in that outfit. Maitland and Gunter had originally been in the Stingrays, and with Graziano in the Rogues, before merging with the **Gamblers**. Jim Dunlap was previously with Gentleman Jim and The Horsemen.

Mister Sun is a wonderfully weird and brash anglophile psychedelic ditty. Imagine a cross between psych-era Who and The Move and stick a minute of glorious effects on the end - modern psych-popsters Kula Shaker ought to have had a crack at this.

The flip is laid-back and a square affair by comparison. (MW)

Soundz

45:	Freak Out Part 1/	
	Freak Out Part 2	(Crown Psychedel*Lite No #) 1967

Sounding more like The Ventures' *Super Psychedelics*, this exploito-psych 45 is pleasantly trippy with lots of echo, reverb and effects to tickle one's grey matter. Sponsored and released by the Crown Lamp Co. out of Greensburg, Pennsylvania, I guess this was one mind excursion that they recommended you experience with all the lights ON!

You can also find *Freak Out Part 2* on *Buzz Buzz Buzzzzzz, Vol. 1* (CD). (MW)

SOUP - Soup LP.

Soup

Personnel:	DAVE FAAS	vcls, bs	AB
	ROB GRIFFITH	vcls, drms, hrmnca	AB
	DOUG YANKUS	vcls, gtr	AB
	JIM PETERMAN	piano	B

ALBUMS: 1(A) SOUP (Arf Arm Artists 1) 1970 R2
2(B) THE SOUP ALBUM (Big Tree 2007) 1971 -

NB: (1) reissued officially on CD, together with bonus tracks (the 45, plus all the previous 45s as **Private Property Of Digil**, (Gear Fab GF-144) 2000. Also counterfeited on vinyl and reissued offically as a Double LP (Gear Fab/Comet GFC 403) 2001.

45: Big Boss Man/Veronica (Target T 1005) 1969

A local Appleton, Wisconsin band, formed after the demise of the **Private Property Of Digil** in 1968. Their first album was a privately pressed affair issued in a plain cover with a yellow insert sheet, which was, in some cases, glued to the front cover. One side has five studio tracks, the other a long live jam.

Their later album, which included Jim Peterman (from the **Steve Miller Band**) was Recorded at Brunswick Recording Studio and engineered by Bruce Swedien. All the tracks were composed by Doug Yankus and the album is an excellent mix of psychedelia, blues and hard-rock, with some jazz and country-rock influences. The best tracks are *Dance Magic Woman*, *Black Cadillac* and *Many Dancers Dance Inside Your Head*. Three of the ten tracks are over six minutes, leaving plenty of time for Doug Yankus to show off his guitar skills.

The 45 includes a rockin' late sixties version of *Big Boss Man* with some nimble guitar licks, while the flip is a yearning romantic paean.

Doug Yankus also guested on the Nashville-based band **White Duck** second album, whose line-up included songwriter John Hiatt. He also played on Hiatt's first solo album, *Hangin' Around The Observatory* (1974), and later on *Slug Line* (1979). After **Soup** split, Doug went on to form Soft Touch and the Doug Yankus Band. He passed away in 1982 due to complications arising from diabetes. The Gear Fab CD is dedicated to his memory with proceeds going to the Diabetic Foundation.

Beware of a recent counterfeit version of their first album and go for the legitimate Gear Fab CD version instead, which includes a number of pre-**Soup** tracks by **Private Property Of Digil** and comes with detailed liner notes. (CF/MW/SR/CD/RM/SY)

The Soup Greens

45: Like A Rolling Stone/That's Too Bad (Golden Rule 5000) 1965

An obscure sixties punk band from Rochester, New York. Their cover of Dylan's classic number *Like A Rolling Stone* attracted some attention when it was included on *Pebbles, Vol. 1* (LP) and it resurfaced again later on the *Pebbles Vol. 1* (CD), *Pebbles Box* (5-LP), *Pebbles, Vol. 4 (ESD)* (CD) and *Trash Box* (5-CD). The flip is also on *Psychotic Reactions* (LP), but is nothing special. (VJ)

The Source

45s: Phantom In The Air /
Yesterday Is Gone (American International A-141) c1969
It's Me I'm Running From /
Gone Tomorrow (American International A-156) c1970

Written and produced by Robert Gilly, Richard Bowen and Harold Finch, a dark orchestrated psychedelic single with harpsichord, organ, violin, marracas... (SR)

Joe South

ALBUM: 1 INTROSPECTIVE (Capitol ST 108) 1968 -

This Southern singer, songwriter, guitarist and producer deserves to be mentioned here for his *Introspective* album (whose cover could have been used for a WCPAEB album !). It offers a very decent mix of mainstream pop, rock and folk with some psychy touches. Several of his songs were recorded by other groups including: *Hush* (Deep Purple, **Five By Five**), *Down In The Boondocks*, *Games People Play*, *I Never Promised You A Rose Garden*, *Walk A Mile In My Shoes*... Working in Atlanta and Nashville, **Joe South** also co-produced **Friend and Lover**'s album and later became a successful country-pop singer. (SR)

Southbound Freeway

Personnel incl:	MARC CHOVER	ld gtr, vcls	ABC
	JIM MOHLER	drms	A
	JOHN MORIER		A
	LENNY SOMBERG	bs, vcls	ABC
	LARRY MILLER		B
	JIM WIEJECHA	drms	BC
	MARTY SOMBERG	ld vcls, gtr	C

NB: Pete Woodman also played drums for the band, after Jim Mohler had been drafted, and when they relocated to L.A. in early 1968.

45s: α Crazy Shadows/Revelations (Swan 4272) 1967
Psychedelic Used Car Lot Blues/
Southbound Freeway (Terashirma 67001) 1967
Psychedelic Used Car Lot Blues/
Southbound Freeway (Roulette 4739) 1967

NB: α also released in Canada (Quality 1852) in 1966.

A Detroit, Michigan act. Marc Chover recalls: "We were one of the earliest psychedelic bands. However, our producer (Fred "Saxon") wouldn't record our psychedelia because he thought it was on the way out. This was around the time of **Jimi Hendrix**' *Are You Experienced* release in the U.S...".

"For the record we may have appeared on the same bill with **The Spike Drivers** a couple of times, however, we were all close friends and played many of the same venues. Ted, Sid Brown, and I all taught music at Fava studios. The band also got to open for **Bob Seger** at the Roseville Theater."

Psychedelic Used Car Lot Blues has since resurfaced on *Michigan Brand Nuggets* (Dble LP) and *Michigan Nuggets* (CD), but it's more novelty than psychedelic! The band later moved to California where they split. Today, Marc Chover is still writing / playing and is an independent manufacturer's sales rep in the Pro Audio business. Lenny Somberg, who formed the band with Marc sadly died in the early seventies, whilst Marty Somberg has a graphics firm in Ann Arbor, Michigan. Jim Wiejecha later changed his surname to Surell and was Paul Anka's staff music copyist for many years - he currently works at Warner Bros. as a copyist.

SOUTHERN COMFORT - Southern Comfort LP.

Marc Chover has just released his first solo CD entitled *Geezerphoelia* by his virtual band Sleazy Geezer:- "It includes one tune I wrote with Ted when we were partners in The Horny Toads (never recorded) from 1969 to 1971. Marty Somberg did the graphic design and Jim Surell wrote the horn arrangements." The Horny Toads where regulars at the Unitarian Church and got to open for Crosby and Nash at a 'Winter Soldier Investigation' benefit concert held at University of Detroit stadium. It was their only 'major' gig.

It's worth noting that Larry Miller, who was an early member of **Southbound Freeway** was primarily a DJ in Detroit, with WDTM, a Fine Arts/Classical station. His "Promenade" show based on thematic programming of folk, cabaret, spoken word and miscellaneous stuff, is regarded as a precursor of sixties FM format. Miller later created the all night show on KMPX in San Francisco in February of 67, as an electrified extension of Promenade.

There was a later and unconnected Canadian act of this name whose sole 45 was also released in the US: *Roll With It/Don't Go Cryin'* (Atco 6690) in 1969. (MW/RR/MC)

John Southern

ALBUM:	1 EQUINOX		(Boyd) 1975 ?

A folk-rock singer with psychedelic influences, playing various instruments, including one he himself invented. (SR)

Southern Comfort

Personnel:	JEROME ARNOLD	bs, vcls	A
	"BIG" WALTER "SHAKEY" HORTON	vcls, hrmnca	A
	JESSIE C. LEWIS	drms, vcls	A
	MARTIN STONE	gtr	A

ALBUM:	1(A) SOUTHERN COMFORT	
		(Sire-London SES 97011) 1969 R1

NB: (1) also issued in the U.K. (London SHK 8405) 1969 (R2).

A U.K.-produced one-off album by three well-known black blues musicians from the U.S.A., plus ex-Savoy Brown Blues Band / pre-Mighty Baby guitarist Martin Stone. While the album is mostly short, unrehearsed blues songs, it closes with an amazing twelve-minute Eastern-fuzz-raga track that will appeal to browsers of this book. (CF)

Southern Comfort

Personnel:	STEVE FUNK	organ, piano	A
	(BOB HUBERMAN	bs	A)
	BON JONES	drms	A
	(JOHN KAHN	piano	A)
	FRED OLSON	gtr	A
	(GERALD OSHITA	flute, sax	A)
	(CHARLEY SCHONING)	piano	A)
	RON STALLINGS	sax, vcls	A
	ART STAVRO	bs	A
	JOHN WILMETH	trumpet	A

ALBUM:	1(A) SOUTHERN COMFORT	(CBS CS1011) 1970 -

NB: (1) also released in Holland (CBS S64125) 1970.

Not to be confused with the British Ian Matthews' **Southern Comfort**, nor Martin Stone's **Southern Comfort**, this group was created by San Francisco musicians working with **Mike Bloomfield** and **Nick Gravenites** (who produced their only album). Musically, it tries to explore the same territory as **The Electric Flag**: a combination of soul, blues and Bay Area sound, with a brass section and some good guitar parts. All the songs are original except for a cover of the Beatles' *Get Back* and Arthur Conley's *Love Got Me*.

Bob Jones was previously in **We Five**, John Wilmeth played bass with **The Fourth Way**, Steve Funk was in Wayne Nitro and the Whispering Shadows and also with the Debonairs. Ron Stallings was in **Mother Earth** and with The Mystic Knights Of The Sea. In 1972, Bob Jones and Steve Funk were in Snake, the backing group of **Alice Stuart**. Most of these musicians kept on working with **Nick Gravenites** and can be found on many of his solo records and productions (Otis Rush, **Brewer and Shipley**). (SR)

Southern Steel

Personnel:	JIM GOODMAN		A
	ED OLSZEWSKI		A
	GREG ORSINI	drms	A
	SPIKE WARNER		A

ALBUM:	1(A) GET ON THROUGH	(Earth E-00003/4) c1968/69
45:	San Francisco Man/24 Hours A Day	(Earth 4444) c1968/9

Although little is known about this group, it is similar in style to **The Byrds** circa *Notorious Byrd Brothers* / *Dr. Byrds And Mr. Hyde*. Issued on a North Miami, Florida label, both the cover and label are printed in black and white and have a very "home-made" feel.

Spike warner had earlier played in **Shades, Inc.** (DSv/JBn/JLh)

South 40

Personnel:	HARRY NEHLS	drms	A
	DAVE "KINK" MIDDLEMIST	keyb'ds	A
	DAVE WAGGNER	vcls	A
	DICK WIEGAND	ld gtr	A
	LARRY WIEGAND	bs	A

ALBUM:	1 LIVE AT SOMEPLACE ELSE!	
		(Metrobeat MBS 1000) 1968 SC

Recorded live at the Someplace Else Club in Minneapolis, this competent psych garage group played cover versions of **Hendrix** (*Fire*) plus various R&B numbers (*Ride Your Pony*, *Show Me*, *99 And 1/2* etc.) and their own compositions (*I Want Sunshine*, *What's Happening*). Pleasant, but nothing essential.

Harry Nehls was later replaced by Denny Casswell and **South 40** became **Crow**. Dave Waggoner had earlier been in **The Aardvarks** and Larry Wiegand **The Rave-Ons**.

Compilation appearances include: *I Want You To Love Me* on *Roof Garden Jamboree* (LP); and *Penny Song* on *The Best Of Metrobeat! Vol. 1* (LP). (SR)

Southwest F.O.B.

Personnel incl:	JOHN "LASSIE" COLEY	keyb'ds, vcls	ABC
	TONY "ZEKE" DURRELL	drms	ABCD
	(ENGLAND) DAN SEALS	ld vcls, sax	ABC
	LARRY "OVID" STEVENS	gtr, vcls	ABCD
	MIKE "DOC" WOOLBRIGHT	bs, vcls	AB
	RANDY BATES	trumpet	B
	SHANE KEISTER	keyb'ds	CD
	BOYD WILLIAMS	bs, vcls	CD

ALBUM:	1(A) THE SMELL OF INCENSE	(Hip HIS 7001) 1968 SC

NB: (1) has been "reissued" on vinyl (Big Beat WIK 81) and CD (Sundazed SC 11060) 1998. The original Hip LP contains just eight tracks, the Big Beat version thirteen (including a medley of two from the Hip LP *Baytown* / *And Another Thing*), and Sundazed twenty, including two versions of *And Another Thing*.

HCP

45s:	The Smell Of Incense/Green Skies	(GPC 1945) 1968 -
	The Smell Of Incense/Green Skies	(Hip 8002) 1968 56
	Nadine/All One Big Game	(Hip 8009) 1968/9 -

α	As I Look At You/Independent Me	(Hip 8015) 1969 -
α	Feelin' Groovy/Beggar Man	(Hip 8022) 1969 115

NB: α are non-LP.

This Dallas outfit was originally called **Theze Few** and included England Dan and John Ford Coley, who went on to achieve considerable success as a duo. In 1967, they played a gig in Dallas with visiting L.A. outfit, the **West Coast Pop Art Experimental Band**. Impressed by the latter's tune, *Smell Of Incense*, they decided to record it, shortening it for AM radio consumption and adding superbly-executed five-part harmonies. The result was a hit single which reached No. 56 in the Billboard chart.

Their pleasant soft-rock album was recorded at Robin Hood Brians studios in Tyler, Texas on October 25/27th, 1968, and has some psychedelic influences as well as a risque (for 1968) cover shot of four naked women enclosed in a plexiglass box (calling Dr. Freud!). *And Another Thing* is an interesting extended track, much in the *In-A-Gadda-Da-Vida* mould, with echoing drums rolling back and forth across the stereo mix over a bass ostinato. There are also good versions of **Buffalo Springfield**'s *Rock 'N' Roll Woman* and Chuck Berry's *Nadine* as well as a few harbingers of England Dan and John Ford Coley's somewhat bland future sound.

Southwest F.O.B were apparently a killer live act to the extent that they reportedly blew Led Zeppelin off stage in August 1969 (a gig which culminated in Zeke setting his cymbals on fire and throwing his drumkit all over the stage). They generally opened with a set of soul covers then, after a costume change, did a set of Cream-like hard-rock and finished with a set of original material. They were also known for their attire (powder blue double-breasted suits with high collars) which were designed by their guitarist, Ovid.

After Woolbridge and Bates left the band, ennui set in and sessions for a proposed second album were aborted (in Coley's words, "Everyone was pretty disorganized; people were drunk and passed out.") Soon after, Seals and Coley left and the remaining quartet settled into playing a Southern blues-styled music but the group fell apart a year later when Zeke got married and pulled out of a tour.

On the Big Beat release *And Another Thing* was edited down to just over two minutes. This release also substitutes the weaker album cuts with the singles and three otherwise unreleased tracks *You're Looking So Fine*, *Monday's World*, and *I'm Coming*. These seem to date from late in the group's career. Curiously the Sundazed CD omits these three tracks but includes all the rest of their output including *Mercy, Mercy, Mercy* from the Soul Explosion album and both sides of the **Theze Few** single.

The Smell Of Incense has also resurfaced on *Psychedelic Microdots Of The Sixties, Vol. 1* (CD). The non-album flip, *Green Skies*, has resurfaced on, *Psychedelic Microdots Of The Sixties, Vol. 2* (CD).

The "F.O.B." apparently stood for "Freight On Board". (VJ/JMe/LP)

Space Cadets

Personnel:	BUD BUDDARD	A
	RUDY HERNANDEZ	A
	GARRET HILLIARD	A

This group came from San Antonio, Texas, but recorded in Houston in the late sixties. Two previously unissued tracks:- *Nothing'll Stand In My Way* complete with the false start and finished take of the same song and *Love-itis* have both resurfaced on *Acid Visions Vol. 2* (LP) and *Acid Visions - The Complete Collection Vol. 1* (3-CD). (VJ)

Space Opera

Personnel:	DAVID BULLOCK	ld gtr, vcls	A
	SCOTT FRAZER	ld gtr, keyb'ds	A
	PHILIP WHITE	keyb'ds, bs	A
	BRETT WILSON	drms	A

ALBUM:	1(A)	SPACE OPERA	(Epic 32117) 1973 -

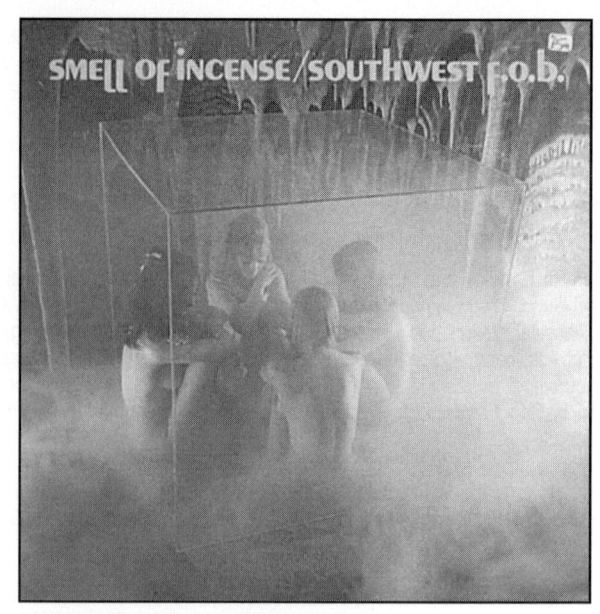

SOUTHWEST F.O.B. - Smell Of Incense LP.

45:	Country Max/Prelude No. 4	(Epic 10971) 1973

Although they recorded their album in Toronto, Canada and Hollywood and are frequently quoted as Canadians, **Space Opera** originated from Texas, and relocated in 1971 to Williamsville, New York, which remained their home-base. Bullock and Fraser had earlier played with **Whistler, Chaucer, Detroit and Greenhill**, a well-known sixties Texas outfit. The Country Max 45 is a great drug-influenced song and at its best their album featured some superb twin guitar work, but sadly it wasn't all of a high standard. All the 45 cuts were from the album. (VJ)

The Spacemen

Personnel:	GENE FONDLOW	ld gtr	A
	BOB JILEK	keyb'ds	A
	TOM McMAHON	gtr	A
	JOHN SCHUSTER	bs	A
	LOREN SKAARE	drms	A

45s:	The Spacewalk/Please Please Me	(Gemini 5-5566) 1965
	Modman/Retro	(Big Sound 303) 1966
	Run For Your Life/Same Old Grind	(Big Sound 309) 1966

This Antigo, Wisconsin band was in orbit from 1965 until 1967 and released three eagerly-sought 45s.

Compilation appearances include: *Same Old Grind* on *Highs In The Mid-Sixties, Vol. 15* (LP); and *Modman* on *Badger Beat Chronicles* (LP). (VJ/GM/MW)

The Space Walrus

45:	Searchin'/ Grazin' In The Grass	(Athena 5019) 1969

On the same label as the **Feminine Complex**, a rare 45 by an obscure group probably from the Nashville area. (SR)

The Spades

Personnel incl:	ROKY ERICKSON	gtr, vcls
	JOHN VERNEY	

45s:	I Need A Girl/Do You Want To Dance	(Zero 10001) 1965
α	You're Gonna Miss Me/We Sell Soul	(Zero 10002) 1965

NB: α reissued in 1975, later pirated in the 1980s.

Formed in Austin, Texas in 1965. Roky Erickson joined after the first 45 from The Fugitives, a garage band which he played in with George Kinney later of **Golden Dawn**. He wrote and sang vocals on *You're Gonna Miss Me* and when he went on to the **13th Floor Elevators** they re-recorded it and enjoyed a minor U.S. hit.

Both sides of the second 45 have resurfaced on *Epitaph For A Legend* (Dble LP), *Austin Landing* (LP), *Trash Box* (5-CD). *You're Gonna Miss Me* on *Mayhem & Psychosis, Vol. 2* (LP), *Mayhem & Psychosis, Vol. 1* (CD) and *Best of Pebbles, Vol. 1* (LP & CD);

The 45 itself was earlier reissued in 1975, and again in 1986. (VJ)

The Sparkles

Personnel:			
	GUY BALEW	sax	A
	JESSE BALEW	sax	A
	GARY BLAKEY	drms	AB
	BOB DONNELL	bs	A
	CARL HUCKABY	gtr	A
	STANLEY SMITH	gtr	ABC
	JOHNNY WALLER	piano	A
	CHARLIE HATCHETT	gtr	B
	LUCKY FLOYD	drms	CDE
	DONNIE ROBERTS	gtr	C
	BOBBY SMITH	bs	CDE
	LOUIE HOLT	gtr	D
	JIMMY MARRIOT	drms	DE
	GARY P. NUNN	gtr	D
	STEVE WEISSBERG	ld gtr	E

45s:		
The U.T./He Can't Love You	(Caron 94)	1962
The Hip/Oh Girls, Girls	(Hickory 1364)	1966
Something That You Said/ Daddy Gonna Put The Hun On You	(Hickory 1390)	1966
Jack And The Beanstalk/Oh Girls, Girls	(Hickory 1406)	1966
No Friend Of Mine/ First Forget (What Has Made You Blue)	(Hickory 1443)	1967
Hipsville 29 B.C./I Want To Be Free	(Hickory 1474)	1967

This was a very popular combo in West Texas between 1957 and 1972. Forming in Levelland in 1957, line-up 'A' did some recording at Norman Petty's studios in 1958 but nothing made it onto vinyl. They broke up for a while but later reformed with line-up 'B' and an unknown bassist. They underwent several further personnel changes. When Charlie Hatchet relocated to Lubbock to start a new outfit The Raiders he took Gary Blakey with him and a new line-up (C) resulted. For a while in 1965 (line-up D) they used two drummers, although Lucky Floyd was also used as a vocalist too.

Their first 45 really predates this book. *U.T.* stood for 'untitled' and was recorded in a garage in Clovis, New Mexico. Later in 1962 they signed for Hickory and Larry Parks, a drummer for Roy Orbison became their producer. They enjoyed some success with the resulting singles, particularly *The Hip*.

When Louie Holt and Gary P. Nunn left the band, Bobby Smith and Lucky Floyd headed to California changing the band's name to The Pearly Gate. This was around 1968. In fact they were scheduled to play a benefit for Robert F. Kennedy at the Americana Hotel the night he was shot. The band were involved with Al Perkins at this time and did a TV show called 'Judge For The Defense'. They later returned to Austin reverting back to **The Sparkles** and around 1970/71 Steve Weissberg, who had played lead guitar for John Denver, was in the band.

In 1972, Lucky Floyd was invited back to California to join **Red Wilder Blue**. **The Sparkles** disintegrated soon afterwards. An early sixties line-up played some reunion gigs in West Texas early in 1985.

The band frequently crop up on compilations. Check out any of these below:- *The U.T.* on *Highs In The Mid-Sixties, Vol. 17* (LP); *Hipsville 29 B.C. (I Need Help)* on *Mayhem & Psychosis, Vol. 2* (LP), *Mayhem & Psychosis, Vol. 2* (CD) and *Hipsville 29 B.C.* (LP); *No Friend Of Mine* on *Nuggets Box* (4-CD), *Pebbles, Vol. 1* (CD), *Pebbles, Vol. 1* (ESD) (CD), *Songs We Taught The Fuzztones* (Dble LP and CD), *60's Punk E.P., Vol. 1* (7"), *Acid Dreams - The Complete 3 LP Set* (3-LP), *Acid Dreams Testament* (CD), *Trash Box* (5-CD), *Best of Pebbles, Vol. 1* (LP & CD) and *Ear-Piercing Punk* (LP); and *I Want To Be Free* on *Turds On A Bum Ride, Vol. 1 & 2* (Dble CD) and *Turds On A Bum Ride, Vol. 1* (Dble LP).

Their excellent *No Friend Of Mine* (credited to 'Roy Junior') was covered in 1967 in Pittsburgh's legendary **Swamp Rats** and has been revitalised by The Fuzztones (*Leave Your Mind At Home* LP 1984) and The Cynics (*Blue Train Station* LP, 1988). (VJ)

Sparks of Life

45:		
La Bomba/Stay With Me	(Marek 681)	1968

The work of a garage band from Rockford, Illinois, this 45 was on the same local label as the **Missing Links**. (VJ)

The Sparrows

| ALBUM: | 1 | THAT MERSEY SOUND | (Elkay) 1964 ? |

These **Sparrows** were presented as being part of the English Invasion but were in fact a Californian studio group. Contrary to many similar records presented with a dubious claim to be 'recorded in England', this is quite good. Instead of poor "English harmonies with beat" it includes some good guitar and lots of dynamic vocals.

Rick Griffin did the cover art. (SR)

The Spartans

Personnel incl:	GARY CRAIG		A

| 45: | I Won't Be Taken/Who Told The Lie | (Keltone Int'l 1002) 1964 |

Produced by Fred Bonamici, a good Brit-Invasion beat sounds effort on a Van Nuys, California label from January 1964. Whether this is the same outfit who put out a 45 on Audio Int'l and another featured on *Bug Out, Vol. 1 - Can You Waddle Pt. 1/2* (Web 1) 1962 - is unconfirmed. (MW)

The Spats

Personnel:			
	MYRON CAPRINO	ld gtr	A
	BOB DENNIS	sax	A
	BUD JOHNSON	gtr	A
	DICK JOHNSON	vcls	A
	RONNIE JOHNSON	bs	A
	CHUCK SCOTT	piano	A
	MIKE SULSONA	drms	A

EPITAPH FOR A LEGEND (Comp LP) including The Spades.

ALBUM: 1(A) COOKING WITH THE SPATS
                              (ABC Paramount ABCS 502) 1965 -
                                                            HCP

45s: Gator Tails And Monkey Ribs/The Roach   (Enith 1268) 1964 -
        Gator Tails And Monkey Ribs/The Roach   (ABC 10585) 1964 96
        There's A Party In The Pad Down Below/
        She Kissed Me Last Night   (ABC 10600) 1964 -
        Tell Ya All About It Baby/
        Billy The Blue Grasshopper   (ABC 10640) 1965 -
        Scoobee Doo/She Done Moved   (ABC 10790) 1966 -
      α Have You Ever Seen Me Crying? /
        Go Go Yamaha   (ABC-Paramount 10711) 196? -

NB: α credited to **The Spats featuring Dick Johnson**. It may not have been issued although white label promos exist.

Hailing from Garden Grove, California, this band set out playing R&B in the early sixties but became more punkish with time. Ronnie Johnson was not the same guy as the Ron Johnson from **Kaleidoscope**. Their most successful song commercially was *Gator Tails And Monkey Ribs*, which spent a week at No. 96.

Compilation appearances have included: *She Done Moved* on *Nuggets, Vol. 12* (LP), *Sixties Choice, Vol. 2* (LP), *60's Choice Collection, Vol's 1 & 2* (CD) and *Boulders, Vol. 3* (LP). (MW/DDn/SR/VJ)

Special Delivery

45:     Hello Love/Love Is Contagious   (Verve 10606) 1967

A good flower-pop single. (SR)

Specktrum

Personnel incl: K. JEREMIAH   A
                 R. MOORE   A
                 R. SCHMEISSER   A

45:     Confetti/I Was A Fool   (Somethin' Groovy SG-500) 1967

The sole 45 from this Abington, Massachusetts band. *Confetti* is a wistful jangly folk-rocker whilst the flip is a subdued Zombies-style ballad. If you were lucky enough to subscribe to Dave Bass' "King's Ransom" 'zine, he uncovered a box of them and they were on offer in issue #1 at $3 a throw. That was in '81 and the 45 is just a shade more expensive now (add a zero!).

Recently *I Was A Fool* has appeared on *Tymes Gone By* (LP), and *Confetti* was thrown onto *Mayhem & Psychosis, Vol. 2* (CD). In 2000 the compilation *Leaving It All Behind* (LP) featured *Confetti* and reported that the band were really from Cranston, Rhode Island. (MW/MM)

The Speckulations

Personnel: FLOYD GREEN   gtr, vcls   A
             ROBERT HUBBS   bs, vcls   A
             DAVID HUMB   vcls, tamb   A
             HAROLD JOHNSON   drms, vcls   A
             TONY MEYERS   keyb'ds   A

ALBUM: 1(A) WALKING THE DOG IN THE MIDNIGHT HOUR
                                         (Justice 132) 1967 R2

NB: (1) reissued on CD (Collectables Col-0621) 1997.

45:     Hulu Hoop / ?   (Speck no #) 1966

Another Justice label rarity exhumed for collectors to pick over the bones. You'll either love it or cringe to it. The usual bag of soul, R&B and ballads also covered by several of the other local acts on this North Carolina label, they range from quite good (*House of The Rising Sun*) to downright sloppy and embarrassing (*Try Me*, *Midnight Hour*). The empty gym sound of the recording doesn't help nor do some very weak vocals - the band deciding to give everyone bar Tony Myers the chance to perform lead - their inadequacies are evident on the soul numbers and ballads. *Wipe-Out* comes as a welcome relief for that reason and is a most spirited rendition with clean ringing guitar.

The non-album *Hulu Hoop*, featured on *The Big Itch, Vol. 6*, was recorded at Arthur Smith Studios in Charlotte, North Carolina - the same venue used by the Voxmen. (MW/MDo)

The Specters

45:     Depression / 8 2/3   (Melbourne 3230) 1966

Doom'n'gloom garage sounds from Worcester, Massachusetts. *Depression* can be experienced on *Teenage Shutdown, Vol. 6* (LP & CD) and the *No No No* (CD) compilation. According to the *Teenage Shutdown Vol. 6* liners, it was done tongue-in-cheek as a replacement for a song about the local whorehouse, which had suffered a parental ban. (MW/MM)

The Spectrum

45:     Baby Let Me Take You Home/
        Bald Headed Woman   (Udell 61219) 196?

This Houston-based covers band had a good live reputation. The 'A' side was originally by The Animals, the flip by The Who.

Compilation appearances include *Bald Headed Woman* on *Highs In The Mid-Sixties, Vol. 17* (LP). (VJ)

Jimmie Spheeris

ALBUM: 1   ISLE OF VIEW   (CBS KC30988) 1972 -
(up to   2   JIMMIE SPHEERIS   (CBS KC32157) 1973 -
1973)   3   THE ORIGINAL TAP DANCING KID
                                         (CBS KC32157) 1973 -

A long-haired singer with hippie values. His records, which sold quite well, are mainly of interest for the interventions of Geoff Levin, the guitarist of **People** and **Elephant**. The third album was produced by Felix Cavaliere, the former leader of **The Rascals** and is rather mellow.

Spheeris kept on recording during the seventies. (SR)

Alexander "Skip" Spence

ALBUM: 1   OAR   (Columbia CS 9831) 1969 R2

NB: (1) also released in Holland (CBS S 63919). Reissued on vinyl (Columbia LP 5030) and CD (Sundazed SC 11075) 1999 (with ten bonus tracks) and (Sony Legacy WK 75031) with five bonus tracks.

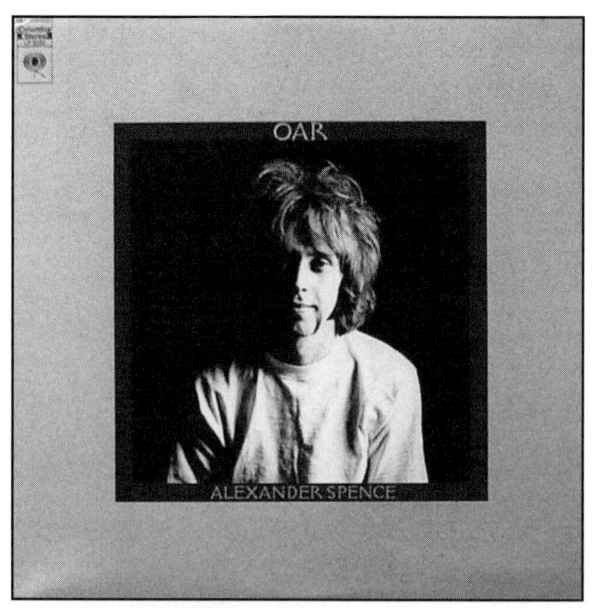

ALEXANDER "SKIP" SPENCE - Oar LP.

45:	All My Life/Land Of The Sun	(Sundazed S 153) 2000

NB: recorded in 1966/1972.

Born on the 18th April 1946 in Windsor, Ontario, **Alexander "Skip" Spence** moved to the Bay Area with his parents in 1959. The story goes that he was on his way to an audition for the band that became **Quicksilver Messenger Service** when he was spotted by Marty Balin of the nascent **Jefferson Airplane**. Balin decided just from his appearance that **Spence** was the drummer he wanted and although he had never played the drums before, **Spence** joined the 'Airplane in 1966 and wrote some of their early songs.

Some months later as a singer/guitarist he joined the fledgling **Moby Grape**, who released their debut album in June 1967. During recording sessions in July 1968, suffering from various personal problems, **Spence** tried to attack other members of the band with a fire axe. He was jailed at the Tombs and then committed to Bellevue Hospital. At the end of 1968, he was discharged and went to Nashville on a motorbike. There, in December 1968, he recorded *Oar*, on which he played all the instruments.

The result is extremely strange and very raw album. Tracks like *Grey/Afro*, *War In Peace* and *Lawrence Of Euphoria* are among the more interesting moments. Ignored at the time (and one of CBS' worst sellers), *Oar* has since gained a cult following and is now recognised as a kind of masterpiece, in the same special category as Syd Barrett's albums.

After this solo album, **Spence** rejoined **Moby Grape** on various occasions, as well as helping the Doobie Brothers (he got a special thanks on their first album). Unfortunately, due to persistant personal problems, he also spent long periods of time in various California social institutions.

Spence died in April 1999 of advanced lung cancer. Quite ironically, at the same time, a tribute album *More Oar* was released with cover songs from *Oar* by Robert Plant, Beck, Tom Waits, Mudhoney and others.

Compilation appearances have included *War In Peace* on *Psychedelic Frequencies* (CD). (SR)

Jim Spencer

Personnel:	JIM SPENCER	ld vcls, acoustic gtr	AB
	JAY BERKENHAGEN	gtr, sax, flute	B
	KENT CARPENTER	gtr	B
	ALAN EK	hrmnca	B
	ROB FIXMER	drms	B
	GARY KEMP	gtr	B
	JOHN NEBI	gtr	B
	MIKE PAGEANT	gtr	B
	TOM RUPPENTHAL	bs	B
	SIGMUND SNOPEK	keyb'ds, flute, strings, vcls	B
	RICHARD THOMAS	gtr, vcls	B

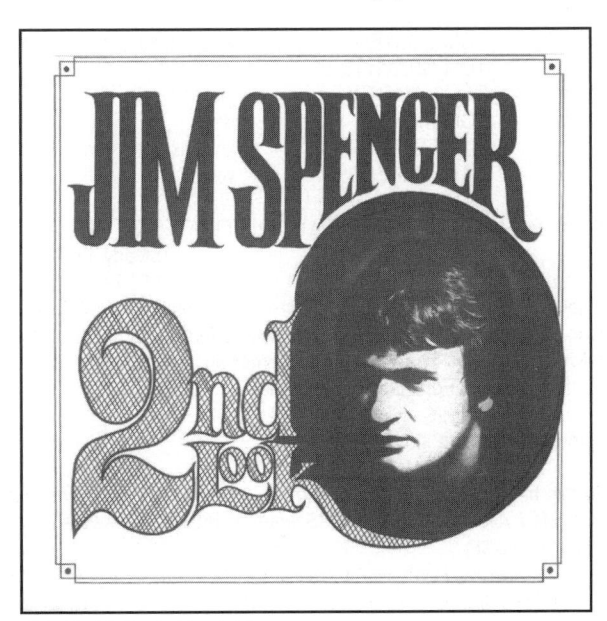

JIM SPENCER - 2nd Look LP.

ALBUMS:	1(A)	LANDSCAPES	(Thoth) 1973 R2
	2(B)	2nd LOOK	(Akashic AST 1001) 1974 R1

Well respected songwriter / musician / producer / studio owner best known as the man who recorded the Indiana group **Anonymous** in his Milwaukee, Wisconsin studio in 1976. His own records are also rare, and good in a straight electric / acoustic folk direction. He recorded a third album in 1976 as **Major Arcana**. Sadly, **Spencer** died in the eighties which was a great loss to the local scene. It's obvious by the large number of musicians on his records that he was a magnet for Milwaukee talent. (CF)

The Spi-Dells

ALBUM:	1	I'M COMING HOME	(Demco DRS-1003) c1967 ?

From New England, an obscure garage band with harmonies covering *Beggin'*, *Hully Gully*, *Gee But I Wish*, *I'm Comin' Home* and *You Make Me Feel So Good*. (SR)

Spider

Personnel:	MIKE DEASY	gtr	A
	(CARL RADLE	bs	A)
	(LEE SKLAR	bs	A)

ALBUM:	1(A)	LABYRINTHS	(Capitol ST-11046) 1972 -

45s:	Little Love Song / May Sixteenth	(Capitol 3325) 1972
	Burnin'/ May Sixteenth	(Capitol 3393) 1972

An interesting West Coast folk-rock album formed by two ex-New Christy Minstrels musicians. Their female singer is quite good and the song selection includes material written by **Dan Moore** and **Hoyt Axton**.

Mike Deasy played guitar and wrote several songs on the album. (SR)

Spider and The Mustangs

45:	So Long Child / You Ask Me Why	(Sands 10662) 1966

A punk outfit from Hemet in California. *So Long Child* resurfaced on *Garage Punk Unknowns, Vol. 7* (LP). (VJ)

The Spiders

Personnel:	GLEN BUXTON	ld gtr	AB
	DENNIS DUNAWAY	bs	AB
	VINCENT FURNIER	vcls, hrmnca	AB
	JOHN SUPER	drms	AB
	JOHN TATUM	gtr	A
	MICHAEL BRUCE	gtr	B

EP:	1	SPIDERS (PS)	(Sundazed SEP 141) 1998

45s:	Why Don't You Love Me / Hitch Hike	(Mascot 112) 1965
	Don't Blow Your Mind / No Price Tag	(Santa Cruz SCR 003) 1966

From Phoenix, Arizona and originally known as the Earwigs, this band would later become the **Nazz** before a final name-change and global success as Alice Cooper. Consequently these pre-stardom 45s have become extremely sought-after, and not just by rabid fans of Alice - they're darnn good too.

Compilation coverage has included: *Don't Blow Your Mind* on *Garagelands, Vol. 1* (LP) and *Garagelands, Vol. 1 & 2* (CD); Both *Don't Blow Your Mind* and *No Price Tag* also appear on *Back From The Grave, Vol. 7* (Dble LP) and *Back From The Grave, Vol. 4* (CD). Both sides of the Santa Cruz 45 are also compiled with the **Nazz** 45 tracks, on an EP put out by Blitz magazine in 1980.

The Sundazed retrospective EP features both sides of the Mascot 45, an unreleased instrumental take of *Why Don't You Love Me* and an unreleased version of *Don't Blow Your Mind*, featuring Michael Bruce previously of the **Wildflowers**.

Glen Buxton sadly passed away in October 1997. (VJ/MW/JB/DCa)

The Spiders

Personnel:	CHUCK BENNETT?	vcls	A
	SHORTY HORTON	bs	A
	JOHNNY SNEED	gtr	A
	DOUG WRAY	drms	A
	LINK WRAY	gtr	A

45:	Baby Doll / Run Boy Run	(Lawn 234) 1964

Yes, this **Spiders** was actually Washington DC's legends **Link Wray** and The Wraymen putting out a Beatles-influenced 45 under a suitable pseudonym. Issue 3 of Bob Embrey's fanzine "D.C. Monuments" is devoted to **Link Wray**, the man who made the world 'Rumble'.

Compilation appearances include *Baby Doll* on *Everywhere Chainsaw Sound* (LP). (MW/BE)

Spiffys

Personnel:	STEVE FAGAN	vcls, trumpet	A
	LARRY O'CONNELL	bs	A
	TOM O'CONNER	vcls	A
	DICK OTTO	drms	A
	MIKE IMESON	bs	AB
	MIKE MAY	vcls, organ	AB
	JOHN MILNER	vcls, drms	AB
	RICH PETRINO	vcls, sax, perc	AB
	LARRY PURDY	vcls, gtr	AB

ALBUMS:	1(A)	THE SPIFFYS	(No label # WB 242) 1967 R2
	2(B)	68 - THE U.S. NAVAL ACADEMY	(No label # R 12597) 1968 R2

Two rare garage pop-rock albums made by midshipmen at the U.S. Naval Academy at Annapolis, Maryland. Their first album mostly contains covers (*Gloria*, *Knock on Wood*, *Satisfaction*, *Along Comes Mary*) plus *No Pain*, a good original. One of their tracks *Dreams*, from the second album, also appears on *Oil Stains, Vol. 2* (LP). (CF/MW/SR)

The Spike Drivers

Personnel:	STEVE BOOKER	drms	A
	MARY CAROL BROWN	vcls	ABC
	SID BROWN	ld gtr, banjo	ABC
	RICHARD KEELAN	ld vcls, 12-string, bs	AB
	TED LUCAS	vcls, gtr	AB
	LARRY CRUSE	drms	BC
	RON COBB	bs, keyb'ds	C
	MARSHALL RUBINOFF	ld vcls, gtr	C

NB: Joel Myerson was the band's lyric writer and friend, but didn't perform with the band.

45s:	High Time/Often I Wonder	(Om 1000 (1 676)) 1966
	High Time/Baby Won't You Let Me Tell You How I Lost My Mind	(Reprise 0535) 1966
	Strange Mysterious Sounds/ Break Out The Wine	(Reprise 0558) 1967

Four groovy guys and a gal made up this outfit who hailed from Detroit, Michigan. Their material is in the soft psychedelic folk-rock mould - very hip, very San Francisco and they were produced by the Koppelman-Rubin team on *Break Out The Wine* and Jerry Ragovoy on the other Reprise tracks.

The band were also featured prominently on WDTM-FM's folk/eclectic show, "Promenade", hosted by Larry Miller, who is to be given some credence as one of the founders of sixties FM format (Miller created the San Francisco KMPX all night show in February '67, as an "electrified extension" of thematic "Promenade").

The Spike Drivers were semi-regulars at the Chessmate Coffee House in Detroit, a mostly folk venue that also hosted bands like **Southbound Freeway**, **Siegel-Schwall Blues Band** and **Blues Magoos**. They also got to open for The Animals in New York's Central Park in 1966.

After they signed with New York Manager Leonard Stogel, he decided that the two songwriters, Keelan and **Lucas** were where the money lay, so they split from the rest of the group and released a 45 as **Misty Wizards**.

Keelan then split for Canada (draft troubles) and formed Perth County Conspiracy. **Lucas** formed a band called the Horny Toads with Marc Chover (ex-**Southbound Freeway**), and later released a solo album back in Michigan in 1975. Sid Brown, departed for Berkeley California, before settling in Vancouver, Washington. He later led **Peace, Love and Land Band** and **Modality Stew** and nowadays directs and produces a cable TV show called "PrimeTimers" which gives voice and inspiration to older adults.

A retrospective album/CD is due to be released by World In Sound/RD Records, with great sleevenotes by Sid Brown.

Compilation appearances have included: *Baby Won't You Let Me Tell You How I Lost My Mind* on *Mind Blowers* (LP); and *High Time* on *Sixties Archive, Vol. 7* (CD). (VJ/PMz/SR/SCh/SBn)

The Spindle

45s:	α	Little Lies/Til The End Of Time	(Burdette 4) 1968
		Little Lies/Til The End Of Time	(Piccadilly 252) 1968
		Because I Love You/That's The Time	(Jerden 911) 1969

NB: α was not released.

From Bremerton, Washington, this band were basically folk-rockers with some psychedelic pretensions. Their finest moment however, was probably *Little Lies*, an uplifting slice of folky-harmony-pop with a San Francisco hippie vibe. The flip, *Til The End Of Time*, is a chiming melodious ballad with ringing Spanish guitar runs. This 45 was produced by **Gil Bateman**.

Compilation appearances have included: *Little Lies* on *The History Of Northwest Rock, Vol. 3* (CD) and *Northwest Battle Of The Bands, Vol. 2* (CD); and *That's The Time* on *The History Of Northwest Rock Vol. 6*, a 1984 cassette-only release. (VJ/MW)

Spindrift

Personnel:	TOM COSTELLO	vcls, bs, keyb'ds	A
	TOM GRAVITTE	vcls	A
	DOUG MARTIN	gtr, trumpet, vcls	A
	TOM PRINCE	drms	A
	JOHN SAPUTO	keyb'ds, sax, vcls	A
	DAVE ZAREFOSS	vcls	A

ALBUM:	1(A)	SPINDRIFT LIBERATE THE PIRATES OF PENZANCE	(Steady 111) 19?? SC

The album is a take-off on the operetta of the same name by Gilbert and Sullivan. This has everything - psychedelic effects, fuzz bass and even harpsichord (hints of **The Mandrake Memorial**). The cover is a painting using the 'Pirates of Penzance' as a theme.

The group were based in New York.

Could this be the same **Spindrift** who put out a 45 in 1966:- *Time Stands Still For Me / Alice In Wonderland* (Scepter 12168) ??? Answers on a £50 note please! (VJ/CF)

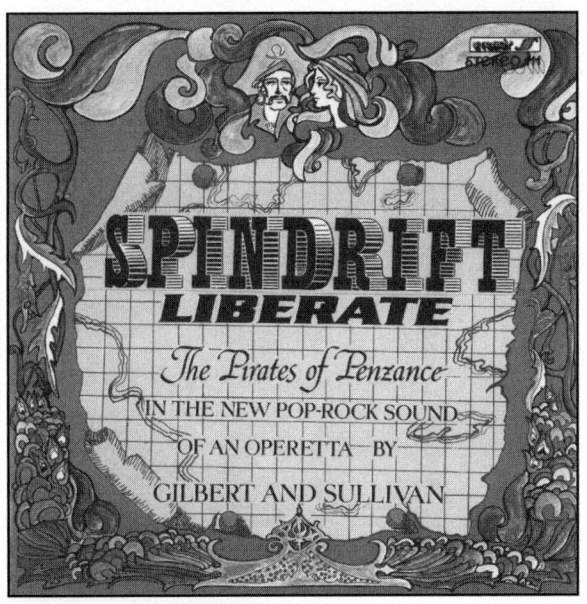

SPINDRIFT - Liberate The Pirates Of Penzance LP.

The Spiral Starecase

Personnel:	BO BRAYMOND	bs	A
	HARVEY KAYE	organ	A
	DICK LOPES	sax	A
	VINNY PARELLO	drms	A
	PAT UPTON	vcls, ld gtr	A

HCP

ALBUM: 1(A) MORE TODAY THAN YESTERDAY
(Columbia CS 9852) 1969 79 -

HCP

45s:
Baby What I Mean/
Makin' My Mind Up (Columbia 44442) 1968 111
I'll Run/
Inside, Outside, Upside Down (Columbia 44566) 1968 -
More Today Than Yesterday/
Broken Hearted Man (Columbia 44741) 1969 12
No One For Me To Turn To/
Sweet Little Thing (Columbia 44924) 1969 52
She's Ready/
Judas To The Love We Know (Columbia 45048) 1970 72

This outfit originally came together in Sacramento, California, in 1964 but later moved to Las Vegas. Their most successful record was clearly *More Today Than Yesterday* but one of their best was *Baby What I Mean*, which you can check out on *Nuggets, Vol. 3* (LP). It's a kind of **Rascals**-influenced soul-pop rendition. (VJ/MW)

Spireno

Personnel:	BILL LANDERS	gtr, vcls	A
	DAVE SMITH	gtr, vcls	A

45: I Have Often Wandered/Come And See For
Yourself If It's Real (PS) (Private Pressing) c1968

Spireno (for "Spiritual Revolution Now"!) was a Christian folk duo with "a fresh new sound that communicates the gospel of Jesus to this 'Now' Generation" if we must believe the liner notes of their rare single issued in a stunning red and yellow picture sleeve. (SR)

Spires Of Oxford

45: But You're Gone / I Really Do (MY 2923) 1967

One of the more sought-after 45s on this Little Rock, Arkansas, label. The band is thought to have come from Concord, Arizona, but this is unconfirmed. *But You're Gone* is featured on *The Essential Pebbles Collection, Vol. 2* (Dble CD). (MW/MM)

Spirit

Personnel:	MARK ANDES	bs, vcls	A
	ED CASSIDY	drms, perc	AB
	RANDY CALIFORNIA	gtr, vcls	AB
	JAY FERGUSON	keyb'ds, vcls	A
	JOHN LOCKE	keyb'ds	AB
	AL STAEHELY	bs, vcls	B
	CHRISTIAN STAEHELY	bs, vcls	B

HCP

ALBUMS: (up to 1973)
1(A) SPIRIT (Ode ZI 2 44003/Mono 44004/Stereo) 1968 31 -
2(A) THE FAMILY THAT PLAYS TOGETHER
(Ode ZI 2 44014) 1968 22 -
3(A) CLEAR SPIRIT (Ode ZI 2 44016) 1969 55 -
4(A) TWELVE DREAMS OF DR SARDONICUS
(Epic 30267) 1970 63 -
5(B) FEEDBACK (Epic KE 31175) 1972 63 -
6(-) KAPT. KOPTER AND THE (FABULOUS)
TWIRLY BIRDS (Epic KE 31755) 1972 - -
7(A/B) THE BEST OF SPIRIT (Epic KE 32271) 1973 120 -
8(A) SPIRIT (dbl) (Epic KEG 31457) 1973 191 -

NB: (1)-(3) reissued circa 1970 on Epic. (2) reissued 1972 (Epic KE 31461). (8) is a reissue of (1) and (3). In the U.K. Nos (1)-(3) were issued by CBS. (1) - (4) reissued on CD by Sony in 1996 with bonus tracks. (2) reissued on Edsel (XED 162) and on vinyl (Sundazed LP 5085) 2002. (3) also reissued on Edsel (ED 268) 1988 and on vinyl (Sundazed LP 5082) 2003. Most of the remaining albums are also now available on CD. (6) solo album by Randy California. Also of interest are two vinyl compilations of outtakes:- *Now Or Anywhere* (Sundazed LP 5067) 2001 and *Eventide* (Sundazed LP 5068) 2001.

HCP

45s:
But You're Gone / I Really Do (MY 2923) 1967 -
Mechanical World/Uncle Jack (Ode 257-108) 1968 123
I Got A Line On You/She Smiled (Ode 257-115) 1968 25
Dark Eyed Woman/New Dope In Town (Ode 257-122) 1969 118
1984/Sweet Stella Baby (Ode 257-128) 1970 69
Animal Zoo/Red Light Roll On (Epic 5-10648) 1970 97
Nature's Way/Mr. Skin (Epic 5-10701) 1970 111
Mr. Skin/Soldier (Epic 5-10701) 1970 92

Hearing **Spirit**'s records now, it seems surprising that they did not achieve greater success back in the late sixties. Certainly they have stood the test of time well.

Evolving out of an earlier Los Angeles band, **The Red Roosters**, **Spirit** were formed in 1967. They were one of the first bands to successfully combine rock and jazz, undoubtedly due to the jazz roots of their personnel. Drummer Ed Cassidy had been a modern jazz player in the fifties with the likes of Gerry Mulligan, Cannonball Adderley and Thelonious Monk. He married in the late sixties a lady whose son was **Randy California**. Randy was playing in a high school band, **The Red Roosters**. Jay Ferguson and Mark Andes also played in this band, Eventually Ed Cassidy joined his stepson and the other ex-**Red Roosters**, with the

SPIRIT - Spirit CD.

addition of jazz-influenced keyboard player, John Locke, to form Spirits Rebellious in early 1967, the name taken from the book of the same name by Kahlil Gibran.

Between the time of **The Red Roosters** and the formation of **Spirit**, **Randy California** spent some time in New York as part of a band called The Blue Flames, whose leader was **Jimi Hendrix**. **Hendrix** of course, was to be spotted by ex-Animal Chas Chandler, who bought him to Britain and, as his manager, produced a string of hits. Meanwhile, Mark Andes had been playing in an earlier version of what would later become another fairly successful L.A. rock-blues group, **Canned Heat**.

Spirit got a residency at The Ash Grove Club in Los Angeles, during 1967, where Cassidy had earlier played with **The Rising Sons**. The same year they recorded a demo tape comprised of such tunes as *Elijah*, *Hey Joe*, *Darlin'* and others which they sent, without much success, to several record companies.

They were on the point of folding when Lou Adler signed them to his Ode Records label, which had a distribution deal with CBS. Their debut album contained a number of fine tracks which displayed their flair for combining jazz and rock. *Fresh Garbage*, *Elijah* and *Gramophone Man* consisted of vocal numbers sandwiching piano pieces, while their first single, *Mechanical World* issued in 1968, was particularly interesting, but too uncommercial to become a hit.

Their second album *The Family That Plays Together* was released in December 1968 and did even better than their debut. One track, the more commercial rock number *I Got A Line On You* was issued as a single with *She Smiled* on the flip, and became a smash hit in the States. This marked a surge in their popularity, which progressed with each album they made. The album was also notable for three particularly melodic Jay Ferguson compositions, *Silky Sam*, *The Drunkard* and *Dream Within A Dream*.

Prior to the issue of their third album *Clear*, they had worked on an abortive movie project "The Model Shoppe" with French film producer, Jacques Demy. Although the soundtrack album never materialised two tracks from the film, *Ice* and *Clear* were released on their third album. A single *Dark Eyed Woman* was released from this album, but did not chart.

A further single *1984* was issued prior to their next album. This initially attracted considerable airplay but, shortly after its release, radio stations were urged not to play it as it was 'too politically orientated'. Consequently, it did not chart and has become one of their most collectable items, although the 'A' side is also featured on their *Greatest Hits* album.

Also around this time there was considerable friction between **California** and Ferguson about the direction of the band. The former favoured a loose improvisational format; the latter, a more commercial rock approach. Lou Adler also switched the Ode label from Columbia to A&M and, as part of the deal, gave **Spirit** to Epic. Despite all this, their fourth album, *The Twelve Dreams Of Dr. Sardonicus*, is generally considered their finest work. Far more commercial than their earlier albums, it contains a number of

SPIRIT - The Family That Plays Together... CD.

SPIRIT - 12 Dreams Of Dr. Sardonicus CD.

finely-structured rock songs like *Nature's Way*, *Animal Zoo*, *Mr. Skin* and *Morning Will Come*. Side two also contained some less structured but more ambitious numbers, such as *When I Touch You* and *Life Has Just Begun*, together with a jazzy instrumental, *Space Child*. However, the band split after the recording of this album, which was subsequently pieced together by producer David Briggs. The album did not sell at all at first, but gradually became more successful and went gold four years after the band had split. Ironically, had it sold better, the band might have stayed together longer.

A series of singles issued from the album - *Animal Zoo*, *Nature's Way* and *Mr. Skin* - all flopped. The first of these singles has become extremely collectable, as few were pressed and the flip has never appeared on any of their albums.

Andes and Ferguson went on to form Jo Jo Gunne, while **California** convalesced after a riding accident. The remaining members, Locke and Cassidy, continued, adding twins Al and Christian Staehely (**The Staehely Brothers**). The line-up produced the disappointing *Feedback* after which the two original members left. The band was later revived more successfully by Cassidy and **California** in 1974, and has subsequently produced a string of successful albums, which are less relevant to this book.

Returning to 1972, for a while though - **California** back in L.A., having recovered from his riding accident, formed a new band and released a **Hendrix** style album called *Kapt. Kopter and The (Fabulous) Twirlybirds*. This group included Larry Knight (bs) and Tim McGovern (drms) when they played live. However, Noel Redding played on the album under the pseudonym Clit McTorius and Ed Cassidy also played on a couple of cuts. This outfit also recorded an extremely rare non-album 45, *Walkin' The Dog/Live For The Day* (Epic 5-10927), which was only issued as a promo for radio stations. They also recorded the *Potatoland* album, which was not released until 1981 by Rhino (RNSP 303). Epic refused to release it at the time.

Tragically **Randy California** drowned on January 2nd 1997 after he and his son were hit by a freak wave in Hawaii.

The band's music has aged well and is well worth listening to. Ed Cassidy who is now in his mid-seventies still plays with Merrell Fankhauser in the Fankhauser-Cassidy band. They have a new album *Further On Up the Road* (Akarma AK 099/2) (Dble LP & Dble CD) 2001.

In 2001, Sundazed released two compilations of outtakes on vinyl, *Now Or Anywhere* comprises cuts from the 1967 album *Spirit* and the 1969 album *The Family That Plays Together*, but it does contain some lengthy instrumental tracks. *Eventide* comprises outtakes from *Clear* and *The Twelve Dreams Of Dr. Sardonicus*, three cuts from the 1968 soundtrack 'The Model Shop' (which are all mellow jazzy instrumentals) and two singles.

Compilation appearances have included: *Dream Within A Dream* and *Topanga Windows* on *Psychedelic Dream: A Collection of '60s Euphoria*

(CD); *I Got A Line On You* on *Pop Revolution From The Underground* (LP); and *Dream Within A Dream* on *Psychedelic Visions* (CD). (VJ/RS)

Spirit

45: Man Enough For You/No Time To Rhyme (Roulette 4757) 1967

A lesser known **Spirit** from Flushing in Queens, New York, who recorded this fabulous 45. Legend has it that they gave up their name to the L.A. band in true sixties spirit!

Compilation appearances include: *No Time To Rhyme* on *Pebbles, Vol. 10* (CD) and *Psychedelic Unknowns, Vol. 8* (LP & CD); *Man Enough For You* on *The Essential Pebbles Collection, Vol. 2* (Dble CD); and *Man Enough For You* and *No Time To Rhyme* on *Pebbles, Vol. 13* (LP). (MW)

Spirit In Flesh

Personnel:	JOHNNY AMERICA	drms	A
	NANCY COLE	vcls	A
	KAREN GRANTHAM	vcls	A
	MARK HOLLAND	piano	A
	TATER HOWES	gtr	A
	GLENN HUTCHINSON	organ	A
	POD LESLIE	ld gtr	A
	MICHAEL METELICA	ld vcls	A
	KATHY MURPHY	vcls	A
	TOM SNYDER	vibes	A
	DANE	vcls	A

ALBUM: 1(A) SPIRIT IN FLESH (Metromedia MD 1041) 1971 -

Very much a hippie outfit, their album was produced by Peter K.Siegel and Susan Leonard and all the selections were written by M. Metelica, T. Howes and A. Hinx.

Their rarely seen album contains some good guitar, organ and bass parts, but the vocals (especially the female vocalists) are the weakest aspect. Lyrically there's a christian influence on some tracks: *Blind Leading The Blind* and *The Meek Shall Inherit The Earth*, whilst the sleeve shows what looks like a rural community, all posing in front of a building covered with snow. (SR)

The Spirits

45: Double Shot/Rosalyn (Scene no #) 196?
NB: Flip side by **The Undertakers**.

A little known band from Hawaii who had three tracks on the 1966 *Live At The Funnyfarm* compilation, *Double Shot*, *Dancing In The Street* and *Almost There*.

Retrospective compilation appearances have included: *Almost There* on *Teenage Shutdown, Vol. 14* (CD) and *Garage Punk Unknowns, Vol. 8* (LP); and *Double Shot* on *Diana's Rootin' Tootin' Wild Teenage Rock 'N' Roll Party!* (LP). (VJ)

Spirits and Worm

Personnel:	CARLOS HERNANDEZ	ld gtr	A
	ARTIE HICK	jnr. drms	A
	ADRIANNE MAURICI	vcls	A
	TOMMY PARRIS	bs, gtr, vcls	A
	ALFRED SCOTTI	gtr, vcls	A

ALBUM: 1(A) SPIRITS AND WORM (A&M SP 4229) 1969 R4
NB: (1) was also released in the U.K. on Decca, which is now very rare. (1) counterfeited on vinyl (Water Serpent LIH 3388/9) 1995 in a limited edition of 375. (1) reissued on LP and CD (Akarma AK 141).

45: Fanny Firecracker/You And I Together (A&M 1104) 1969

This album is well worth searching out. Adrianne's powerful vocals are certainly an asset and although brass makes an occasional and unwelcome intrusion on the album it contains some fine guitar work, which on the title cut and *Sunny Please Hold Me* becomes quite psychedelic. Other highs include *You And I Together* and the final cut, *She's So Good*. Recommended. Both 45 tracks feature on the album, which was recorded at Ultra-Sonic Studios in Long Island, New York. (VJ/CF)

Spirits of Blue Lightning

45: Love Muscle/Well Baby (Lavendar 2009) c1968

A five-piece from the Pacific Northwest, probably Oregon.

Compilation appearances include: *Love Muscle* on *Victims Of Circumstance, Vol. 2* (LP) and *Victims Of Circumstance, Vol. 2* (CD). (VJ/MW)

Spiritwood

ALBUM: 1 SPIRITWOOD (Private Pressing) c1974 ?

A rare Christian folk album, sought-after now. (SR)

Split Ends

Personnel:	DAN ELIASSEN	vcls, bs	A
	BRUCE KNOX	gtr, vcls	A
	MIKE MYCZ	gtr, vcls	A
	JIM O'BROCK	drms, vcls	A

45: Rich With Nothin'/Endless Sea (CFP 4) 1966
NB: (1) reissued in 1995 by Spindle with picture sleeves on both black (101-7) and coloured (102-7) vinyl.

This band were from Tampa, Florida and their *Rich With Nothin'* is catchy garage punk at its best.

Formed by Dan Eliassen and Jim O'Brock in 1962, they were initially known as The Kingsmen. When *Louie Louie* became a hit for the more well known **Kingsmen**, they changed names to The Allusions, playing high school dances and teen centres. However, they did not record.

In 1966, they changed name again to **The Split Ends** to reflect the changing times. Jim: "We started writing more and recorded *Rich With Nothin'* and *Endless Sea*. The 45 was a moderate local (Tampa Bay area) success and we began playing larger venues and traveling across Florida. In 1967, we opened for a Dick Clark tour and were picked up to finish the tour: 'Happening '67'. The next year we were invited to Los Angeles to play on Dick Clark's nationwide band contest T.V. show: 'Happening '68'. We

SPIRITS AND WORM - Spirits And Worm LP.

lost, but while in L.A. we played a couple of local gigs with **Steppenwolf** and **Iron Butterfly**".

"In 1969 we changed name again to **B.O.O.T.**, an acronym for 'Blues Of Our Time', and released two albums in the early seventies".

Compilation appearances include: *Rich With Nothin'* on *Pebbles, Vol. 1* (CD), *Pebbles Box* (5-LP), *Pebbles, Vol. 1* (LP), *Psychedelic Unknowns, Vol's 1 & 2* (LP), *Pebbles, Vol. 3 (ESD)* (CD), *Psychedelic Unknowns, Vol. 1* (Dble 7"), *Acid Dreams - The Complete 3 LP Set* (3-LP), *Acid Dreams Epitaph* (CD), *Trash Box* (5-CD) and *I Was A Teenage Caveman* (LP). (MW/JOk)

Split Level

Personnel:	AL DANA	vcls, bs, sitar	A
	MICHAEL LOBEL	gtr, recorder	A
	HERBERT LOVELLE	drms	A
	LENNY ROBERTS	vcls, gtr	A
	LIZ SENEFF	vcls	A

ALBUM: 1(A) DIVIDED WE STAND (Dot DLP-25836) 1968

NB: (1) also seen listed as *Split Level* with same catalogue number.

45s:	I Don't Know Where You Are/Looking At The Rose Through World Colored Glasses	(Dot 17036) 1967
	Hangin' Out / Right Track	(Dot 17085) 1968
	Can't Complain / Love To Love You	(Dot 17142) 1968

A very lightweight 'pop-psych' group from NYC, actually more folk-pop than psych, with male/female vocals and occasional use of electric sitar and flute. The title of the record is apt: sweet sunny rock with strings and smoothness alternate with far more adventurous tracks. Clearly there are interests in classical music, which make themselves evident in the application of advanced choral composition techniques. Tracks like *You Can't Go* and *Equipment* (with sitar) sound strongly like **Peanut Butter Conspiracy**, though, and include fine flutes and strong harmonies. These are evidently the highlights of this album. An odd Japanese flavour is added to *Looking At The Rose Through World Colored Glasses*. The rest is enjoyable enough, but a bit bland too. A strange and schizophrenic record. (MK/SR/MW)

Mark Spoelstra

Personnel incl:	MARK SPOELSTRA	vcls, gtr	ABCDE
	ROY BLUMENFELD	drms	D
	HARVEY BROOKS	bs	D
	MIKE DEASY	gtr	D
	MITCH GREENHILL	organ, gtr	D
	DOUG CLIFFORD	drms	E
	STU COOK	gtr, bs	E
	DUCK DUNN	bs	E
	STEVE MILLER	piano, organ	E
	STOVALL SISTERS	vcls	E

ALBUMS:	1(A)	SONGS	(Folkways 2449) 1964 -
	2(A)	THE TIMES I'VE HAD	(Verve Folkways FVS-9018) 196? -
	3(B)	5 AND 20 QUESTIONS	(Elektra EKS-7283) 1965 -
	4(C)	STATE OF MIND	(Elektra EKS-7307) 1966 -
	5(D)	MARK SPOELSTRA	(CBS 9793) 1969 -
	6(E)	THIS HOUSE	(Fantasy 8412) 1971 -

NB: There are also two tracks, *France Blues* and *She's Gone* on *The Blues Project* (Elektra) 1964 and some on the soundtrack of *Electra Glide In Blue* (CBS) 1970.

45: Walking Around Town/Corinna (Folkways F45001) 1964

NB: as Two Time Mark.

In the sixties blues-folk movement, **Mark Spoelstra** was known was having done alternative service time as a conscientious objector long before the Vietnam war. A talented white blues-folk singer and 12-string guitar player, he is typical of these folkies who had many skills but somehow failed when folk became electrified under Dylan's influence. **Spoelstra** moved to New York in the early sixties and began singing in the Greenwich folk scene with Bob Dylan and was finally booked by Gerde's Folk House. He took an active part in the burgeoning Urban Blues Scene and recorded two tracks on the seminal *Blues Project* album, an Elektra project aiming at presenting these new musicians (others were Geoff Muldaur, **Eric Von Schmidt**, **Danny Kalb**, **John B.Sebastian** and Bob Landy (better known as Dylan!).

Spoelstra then secured a recording deal with Folkways and released two albums of folk-blues, which are too traditional to retain attention. After that, he got signed to Elektra for two records which are supposedly his best work but we have been unable to hear them. **Spoelstra** then moved to California and signed a management contract with Jim Guercio (**Buckinghams**, Chicago). Produced by Guercio, the 1969 CBS album benefited from the help of Roy Blumenfeld (**Blues Project/Seatrain**), Harvey Brooks (**Electric Flag**) and various L.A. sessionmen (Knechtel, Jim Gordon, **Mike Deasy**, James Burton), but the result is not really convincing. **Spoelstra** also appeared on the soundtrack of another Guercio project, *Electra Glide In Blue*.

In 1971, he signed to Fantasy and *This House* was produced by Doug Clifford of **Creedence**, with the help of Steve Miller (Lynn County), Stu Cook and Duck Dunn (Booker T and The MGs). The album offers a pleasant but lightweight choice of original electrified bluesy folk numbers, the best one being *Dirty Movie Show*.

Spoelstra then apparently vanished from the music scene. (SR)

Spoils Of War

Personnel:	JAMES CUOMO	keyb'ds, sax, recorder, clarinet, dobro	ABCD
	ROGER "RoFran" FRANCISCO	bs, vcls	AB
	FRANK "Big City Frank" GARVEY	perc	AB
	AL "Ral-Eardi" IERARDI	gtr, vcls	AB D
	JAMES STROUD	lights, trombone, FX	AB
	ANNE WHITEFISH/ WILLIAMS	vcls, gtr, organ	BC
	CHARLIE BRAUGHAM	drms	CD
	PAUL CHOUINARD	viola	C
	BOB WITMER	bs	CD
	CAL DRAKE	bs	D
	LARRY DWYER	trombone	D
	STEVE LARNER	vcls	D

DISCOG:	1(A)	THE SPOILS OF WAR	(RoFran Enterprises) 1968
	2(B)	YOU'RE INVITED TO HEAR SPOILS OF WAR	(Rofran XALS-2605) 1969

THE SPOILS OF WAR - The Spoils Of War LP.

	3(C)	JAMES CUOMO	(No label)	1970
	4(D)	CUOMO'S RECORD	(Depot Records RoFran 0608)	1970

NB: (1) 7" reel tape in box with sticker. (2) 7" EP with sleeve. (3) 5" reel tape in box with sticker. (4) 7" EP with sleeve. (1) and (3) reissued on LP as *The Spoils Of War* (Shadoks Music 001) 1999 which included a reissue of (2) as a bonus 7". A very small number of these vinyl albums were issued in an embossed red velvet sleeve. The regular printed cover edition was limited to 450 copies. (1) - (4) reissued on CD as *The Spoils Of War* (Shadoks Music 001) 1999.

Weird'n'wonderful sounds emanated from Urbana, Illinois in 1968 and 1969 thanks to this previously unheralded assemblage. The reissue contains a mixed bag of cerebral sounds - electronic collages interspersed or combined with jazzy vibes, acid-rock, and dreamy folk-rock. Some highlights:- *Walk In, Walk Out* opens with an electronic barrage before turning to more standard fuzz-psych with (for a change) good use of brass; the astounding *E-Thing* could be a soundtrack to 'Apocalypse Now' - a backdrop of whining, pulsing helicopter-like effects onto which is etched a heavy acid jam; *Rit Yellow Of The Sun* builds to a delicious Spanish-flavoured guitar freakout then degenerates into fuzz and electronic mayhem.

This should appeal especially to fans of experimental or elecronic psychedelia by the likes of **Fifty Foot Hose** and the **United States Of America**.

Roger Francisco was previously with **The Prodigies**. (MW/CF)

The Spokesmen

Personnel incl:	VINNIE BELL	gtr	A
	RAY GILMORE		A
	JOHN MADARA		A
	DAVID WHITE		A

ALBUM:	1	THE DAWN OF CORRECTION	(Decca DL-74712) 1965 - HCP
45s:		The Dawn Of Correction/For You Babe	(Decca 31844) 1965 36
		Have Courage, Be Careful/It Ain't Fair	(Decca 31874) 1965 -
		Michelle/Better Days Are Yet To Come	(Decca 31895) 1966 106
		Today's The Day/Enchante	(Decca 31949) 1966 -
		I Love How You Love Me/Beautiful Girl	(Decca 32049) 1966 -
		Flashback/Mary Jane	(Winchester 1001) 1967 -

In 1965 people were into happiness and hair, so when **Barry McGuire**'s *Eve Of Destruction* came out, it was regarded as something of a party-pooper and generated a lot of debate over its 'message' and mood. Apart from ensuring that this backlash against the protest folk-rock (sic) scene improved its sales somewhat, other groups responded with reply-songs, piss-takes, etc. The Jayhawkers' *Dawn Of Instruction* could be put into the latter category whilst this outfit's debut *The Dawn Of Correction* is in the former. *Better Days Are Yet To Come* continues this optimistic viewpoint whilst *Have Courage, Be Careful* touches on fighting abroad without either condoning or condemning it. All done in a tame folk-rock-pop mode including the chunky uptempo *Mary Jane* featured on *Everywhere Chainsaw Sound* (LP) which, despite the title, has no druggie connotations.

Session guitarist **Vinnie Bell** was responsible for inventing the electric sitar, on the back of which he released an album. The band were possibly Philadelphia-based. (MW/ET)

Spontaneous Generation

Personnel:	LARRY COLE	bs	A
	BILLY HOUSE	drms	A
	TERRY KINDALL	gtr, organ	A
	TERRY LAWSON	ld vcls	A
	JAN WHITTEN	ld gtr	A

45:	Up In My Mind / Pictures Of Lily	(Fevre 8680) 1968

Formed in 1966, this high school quintet from Atlanta played the local clubs frequently, opening for the likes of **Paul Revere and The Raiders** and **The Electric Prunes**, and included the latter's *I Had Too Much To Dream Last Night* in their repertoire. Indeed, it was one of the **'Prunes** who encouraged Kindall's father to get them into one of the area's better studios, LeFevre, hence the labelname of their sole 45 that was recorded there in late 1968.

Up In My Mind is an excellent opener on *Psychedelic States: Georgia Vol. 1* (CD) - heavy garage-psych with pulsing washes of fuzz and some wah-wah. You can also find it on *Pebbles, Vol. 2 (ESD)* (CD, *Beyond The Calico Wall* (LP & CD). The flip is a cover of The Who's hit given a **Litter**-esque treatment.

The 45 mades waves locally but the end of their tenure at high school sent them off in separate directions. Kindall remained in the music biz and was still playing professionally in 2002. (VJ/CW/MW)

Spooner and The Spoons

45:	Wish You Didn't Have To Go/ Hey, Do You Wanna Marry?	(Fame 6405) 1964

From Alabama. A very early attempt as a blue-eyed soul group, influenced by the British Invasion, but still basically a white soul record. Features legendary **Spooner Oldham**, with Dan Penn, one of the primary writing teams of some of the best soul compositions to come out of the South. (BM)

Sportin Life

Personnel:	RICHARD BABEUF	A
	JOHN HOMENICK	A
	MICHAEL SWERDLOW	A
	RONALD WEISSMAN	A

45:	I Can't Wait Till Tomorrow / I Can Feel It (Servant To The Sky)	(Riba R-1004) 1968

Produced by Richard Babeuf on his own RIBA label, this is the legacy of a group from Jericho in Long Island, New York. *I Can Feel It*, a cantering rock-popper with fleeting echoes of **Love**, can be heard on *Psychedelic States: New York Vol. 1* (CD). (MW)

Spring Fever

45:	Stop!/You Made My Life	(Capitol 2337) 1968

A late sixties San Francisco-based outfit. A moniker also used by Tuscon's **Grodes**. (VJ)

The Springfield Rifle

Personnel:	JEFF AFDEM	sax	A
	TERRY AFDEM	keyb'ds	A
	JOE CAVENDER	drms	A
	BOB PERRY	bs	A
	HARRY WILSON	gtr	A

ALBUM:	1(A)	THE SPRINGFIELD RIFLE	(Burdette 5159) 1968 SC
45s:		Stop And Take A Look Around/100 Or Two	(Jerden 812) 1966
		All She Said/It Ain't Happening	(Jerden 815) 1966
		The Bears/There Is Life On Mars	(ABC 10878) 1966
		I Love Her/That's All I Really Need	(Tower 455) 1968
		What Kind Of Day/Big Fat Mama	(Jerden 900) 1968
		I'll Be Standing There/ Will You Love Me Tomorrow	(Jerden 901) 1968
		Left Of Nowhere/I Must Go For A Walk	(Jerden 902) 1968
		That's All I Really Need/I Love Her	(Jerden 905) 1968
		That's All I Really Need/I Love Her	(Burdette 455) 1968
		He Will Break Your Heart/My Girl	(Burdette 475) 1968
		Angelene/Start At The Bottom	(Burdette 577) 1969
		That's The Way It Is/What We Will Be	(Jerden 925) 1971
		Keep On Loading/If You Live	(Jerden 926) 1971

Seattle, Washington was their home and they evolved out of The Dynamics (the Afdem brothers and Harry Wilson had all been members). Their most successful 45 was *That's All I Really Need*, a soft-rocker. Upon their demise Jeff Afdem formed a jazz group called The Springfield Flute, who recorded an album for Seattle's First American Records, but it flopped.

Will You Love Me Tomorrow was a cover of the old Shirelles' hit.

Compilation appearances include: *100 Or Two* on *The History Of Northwest Rock, Vol. 3* (LP) and *Battle Of The Bands, Vol. 2* (LP); *I Love Her* and *Start At The Bottom* on *The History Of Northwest Rock, Vol. 3* (CD); *That's All I Really Need* on *The History Of Northwest Rock, Vol. 1* (LP); *Will You Love Me Tomorrow* on *The History Of Northwest Rock, Vol. 2* (LP); and *100 Or Two* and *Nordstrom* on *Northwest Battle Of The Bands, Vol. 2* (CD). (VJ)

Sproton Layer

Personnel:	HAROLD KIRCHEN	trumpet	A
	BEN MILLER	ld gtr, vcls	A
	LARRY MILLER	drms	A
	ROGER MILLER	bs, ld vcls	A

ALBUM: 1(A) WITH MAGNETIC FIELDS DISRUPTED
(New Alliance NAR 055) 1991

45: Lost Behind Words//Space Red
Jam From Outer Space (PS) (New Alliance NAR 802) 1991

The above album and clear wax 45 comprise the recordings of an Ann Arbor, Michigan, outfit who lasted from 1969 through 1970. There's no mention of any original vinyl released at the time. Musically a mix of free-form, heavy acid-rock and cosmic noise - disturbing but often enthralling, cerebral rather than psychedelic and a treat for the musically adventurous. (MW)

Spruce

ALBUM: 1 SPRUCE
(Out to Lunch Productions OLP 1001) c1973 SC/R1

From Maryland, an obscure rock group in the mould of early **Allman Brothers Band**. (SR)

The Sprytes

45: Please Don't Stop It/
Land Of 1,000 Dances (Mortician 104) 196?

A New Mexico garage band.

Compilation appearances include: *Land Of 1,000 Dances* on *Punk Classics* (CD) and *Punk Classics, Vol. 5 - Six Wild Covers!* (7" EP). (VJ)

Spur

Personnel:	STAN BRATZKE	vcls, gtr	A
	JIMMY FEY	vcls, ld gtr	A
	EDD KALOTEK	vcls, keyb'ds	A
	STIX MAXWELL	drms, perc	A
	RICK WILLARD	vcls, bs	A

ALBUM: 1(A) SPUR OF THE MOMENT (Cinema CSLP 1500) 1969 R1
NB: (1) There was a limited repressing in the mid-eighties.

A quite appalling album which some books and dealers erroneously describe as 'psychedelic'. Beware, it's crap, full of badly done thirty second rehashes of rock'n'roll classics and country music. Apparently originals change hands for quite a lot of money. God help the people buying them. Things do improve a little on Side Two which includes three tracks which are half decent:- *Why Girl No 2*, *Mind Odyssey*, and *Modern Error*, but then concludes with a pitiful cover version of *River Deep Mountain High*.

The band came from St Claire county, Illinois and also provided the musical backdrop to a spoken word religious album by **Father Pat Berkery**.

Compilation appearances include *Don't Ever Trust A Woman* on *Yee-Haw! The Other Side Of Country* (CD). (VJ)

Square Root of Nine

ALBUM: 1 SQUARE ROOT OF NINE (Private Pressing) 1967?

A folk trio (two men, one woman) from Michigan. Their album contains covers of *Early Morning Rain* and *House Of The Rising Sun* and was pressed in very small quantities (maybe 500 copies). (SR)

Squiremen Four

Personnel:	BENNIE BUCHACHER	drms	ABC
	JERRY MOLINA	gtr	ABC
	JIM OLIVER	keyb'ds	ABC
	DON O'CONNELL	bs	ABC
	SANDY TORANO	ld gtr	A
	JACK VINO	gtr	C

45s: What's On Your Mind / Bitter End (Squire 14-15) 1967
α Who In The World / Secrets (Trip 110) 1969
NB: α as by The Squiremen.

A Miami quintet who had some local success with their self-released debut. *Bitter End*, a bouncy garage-pop ditty penned by Jim Oliver, can be heard on *Every Groovy Day* (LP). They continued as a foursome after Torano left. In 1969, after releasing a second 45 as **The Squiremen** and restored to five with guitarist Jack Vino, they became The Heroes Of Cranberry Farm and released at least seven 45s over the next two years.

Who In The World is a wonderful piece of piano-led melodrama where soft harmonious verses alternate with hard fuzz work-outs. Be sure to check this out on *Psychedelic States: Florida Vol. 1* (CD). (MW/JLh)

The Squires

Personnel:	MIKE BOUYEA	drms, violin, vcls	A
	TOM FLANIGAN	ld gtr	A
	JOHN FOLCIK	bs	A
	JIM LYNCH	gtr	A
	KURT ROBINSON	keyb'ds	A

ALBUM: 1(A) THE SQUIRES (Crypt 008) 1986

45: Going All The Way/Go Ahead (Atco 6442) 1966

SPUR - Spur Of The Moment LP.

SRC - SRC LP.

This outfit came from Bristol, Connecticut, and were earlier known as **The Rogues**. Their 45 has become something of a punk classic by virtue of the 'A' side's inclusion on *Pebbles, Vol. 1* and it has subsequently been heavily compiled. The Crypt album is a retrospective collection of their material. Both sides of the 45 were recently covered on the Remayns EP (Bam-Caruso 029).

Compilation appearances include: *Going All The Way* on *Nuggets Box* (4-CD), *Pebbles, Vol. 1* (LP), *Psychedelic Unknowns, Vol's 1 & 2* (LP), *Psychedelic Unknowns, Vol. 2* (Dble 7"), *Best of Pebbles, Vol. 1* (LP & CD) and *Excerpts From Nuggets* (CD); and *Go Ahead* on *Pebbles, Vol. 2* (LP). (VJ)

The Squires

Personnel incl: JACK EELY — gtr, vcls — A

45: Don't You Just Know It/Big Boy Pete (Northwestern 2506) 196?

From the Pacific Northwest, they were also known as **Jack E. Lee and The Squires** and included Jack Eely who'd earlier led **The Courtmen**. You can check out the 'A' side, which is a raw early rock version of Huey 'Piano' Smith's song on *Highs In The Mid-Sixties, Vol. 7* (LP). (MW/DR)

The Squires

Personnel incl: PHIL KEAGGY — ld gtr — A

45: Batmobile/I Don't Care (Penguin IG 1612) c1966

A different outfit from Youngstown, Ohio, who were influenced by The Beatles. *Batmobile* is an uncharacteristic spacey instrumental which later resurfaced on *Highs In The Mid Sixties, Vol. 9 - Ohio* (LP). Phil Keaggy later played in Volume IV, who later became **New Hudson Exit** and went on to front **Glass Harp** before becoming a Christian music star.

The Squires also recorded several acetate recordings that feature Phil Keaggy's early attempts to write Beatles-style garage-pop. (VJ/GGI/MW)

The Squires

An unknown outfit, possibly from the San Francisco Bay Area, whose only legacy is two unreleased tracks recorded in November 1966 - *Anyhow Anwhere* and *It Must Be Love*. They're described as "killer punk" and 'jangly folk-pop" respectively by Alec Palao, who unearthed them on Big Beat's CD compilation *The Scorpio Records Story* (CD). (MW)

SRC

Personnel:			
ROBIN DALE	bs, vcls		A
STEVE LYMAN	gtr, vcls		AB
SCOTT RICHARDSON	vcls		ABC
GARY QUACKENBUSH	ld gtr		AB
GLEN QUACKENBUSH	organ		ABC
E G CLAWSON	drms, vcls		BC
AL WILMOT	bs, vcls		BC
RAY GOODMAN	gtr		C

ALBUMS:
1(A) SRC (Capitol 2991) 1968 147 R1
2(B) MILESTONES (Capitol 134) 1969 134 SC
3(C) TRAVELER'S TALE (Capitol 273) 1970 - SC

NB: (1) - (3) have all been reissued on CD by One Way with bonus tracks. (1) & (2) have also been reissued on one CD. Also of interest are *Revenge Of The Quackenbush Brothers* (Bam-Caruso KIRI 054) 1987, which compiles material from their three Capitol albums including the classic *Black Sheep*; *Black Sheep* (RPM RPMBC 201) 2000; and *Lost Masters* (One Way 29219) 199?, a CD compilation which includes 21 tracks from singles and otherwise unreleased stuff.

45s:
I'm So Glad/Who Is That Girl (A2 301) 1967
α Get The Picture/I Need You (A2 402) 1967
Black Sheep/Morning Mood (Capitol 2327) 1968
Turn Into Love/Up All Night (Capitol 2457) 1969
My Fortune's Coming True/
Never Before Now (Capitol 2726) 1970
Born To Love/Badazz Shuffle (PS) (Big Casino 1001) 1971
β Out In The Night/Gypsy Eyes (Rare Earth 5040) 1972

NB: α as Scot Richard Case. The 'B' side is by **The Rationals**. β as **Blue Scepter**.

SRC were part of the wave of Detroit-based heavy rock groups which emerged in the late sixties and included bands like **The Amboy Dukes** and **The MC5**.

Originally from Birmingham, they started out as the Tremelos and later **The Fugitives** and issued four 45s (two on D-Town and two on Westchester) and an album, *The Fugitives At Dave's Hideout* (Hideout HLP-1001) 1965. Three of their tracks are on the sixties compilation, *Friday At The Cage A Go Go* (Westchester 1005) 1965. *Friday At The Cage A Go Go* has recently been reissued under its alternate title *Long Hot Summer* on Hide The Sausage (HTS-001) 1989. As **The Fugitives** they have cuts on *Oil Stains* (*Said Goodbye*) and *Glimpses 3* (*On Trial*). **The Fugitives** tracks on *Mindrocker, Vol. 7* and *Back From The Grave, 3* are by a different band.

SRC's debut album contained one stand-out track, *Black Sheep*, on which Glen Quackenbush's organ playing gave the band a similar sound to **The Doors**' *Light My Fire*. The track received considerable airplay from John Peel in England. However, the band failed to capture the interest of the American public at large and disbanded after two further good albums.

SRC - Traveler's Tale CD.

Compilation appearances have included: *Black Sheep* on *Rock A Delics* (LP); *Badazz Shuffle* on *Echoes In Time, Vol. 2* (LP), *Echoes In Time, Vol's 1 & 2* (CD) and *Gathering Of The Tribe* (CD); *I'm So Glad* on *Turds On A Bum Ride, Vol. 4* (CD) and *Michigan Rocks, Vol. 1* (LP); *Marionette* from their first album can also be heard on *Illusions From The Crackling Void*. As **Scot Richard Case** you can find their competent, snarly version of *Get The Picture* on *Michigan Mayhem, Vol. 1* (CD), *Sixties Archive, Vol. 7* (CD) and *Boulders, Vol. 2* (LP).

They also recorded a 45 in 1972 as **Blue Scepter** (*Out In The Night/Gypsy Eyes*) (Rare Earth 5040) - the 'B' side is on *Echoes In Time, Vol. 1* (LP) and *Echoes In Time Vol's 1 & 2* (CD). (VJ)

Stack

Personnel:	CHUCK BERRY		A
	JIM DOLE	gtr, vcls	A
	KURT FEIERABEND	gtr, vcls	ABC
	RICK GOULD	ld gtr, vcls	ABC
	KIRK HENRY		A
	RON THOMASON		A
	BUDDY CLARK	bs	BC
	BILL SHEPPARD	vcls	BC
	ROBIN WILLIAMS	drms	B
	BOB ELLIS	drms	C

NB: Line-up 'A' 1967.

ALBUM: 1(C) ABOVE ALL (Charisma CRS-303) 1969 R6

NB: (1) was counterfeited in Europe circa 1988. Reissued legitimately on vinyl (Void 06) 1998, and CD (Gear Fab GF-111) 1997. More recently reissued on vinyl (Akarma AK 057) 1999, with markedly superior sound to all previous reissues.

A local Californian release and one of the rarest and probably the most significant American private press hard-rock album of the era. *Above All* was 'discovered' by collectors in the mid-eighties and since then only a half-dozen original copies have turned up.

Stack were a figurehead group in a busy hard-rock scene exploding out of the Los Angeles area in the late sixties. Formed out of a surf band called The Vandells (which included Gould) and Wabash Spencer (with Ellis and Sheppard) in 1967, **Stack** enjoyed a prolific concert itinerary for over two years, playing with such notables as **Buffalo Springfield**, **Fields**, **Hook**, **Things To Come**, Rockin' Foo, **Iron Butterfly**, **Illinois Speed Press**, Three Dog Night, **Frank Zappa** and Alice Cooper. During 1968, they signed a long-term contract with Mike Curb's Sidewalk Productions and recorded an album in off-hours at local studios.

Above All is a brutal hard-rock album with a distinct British influence in several of the better tracks. *Cars* and *Only Forever* are remarkably effective showcases for Ellis' propulsive drumming style, which sounds like a cross between Paul Whaley (of **Blue Cheer**) and Keith Moon. There are a couple of tracks on the album that sound merely typical by comparison; a lengthy blues, and a cover of *Poison Ivy* that was rather unfortunately chosen as the opening cut on Side One, but overall it's a killer and highly recommended to hard-rock fans.

For reasons unknown to the band, *Above All* was never marketed and very few copies of the finished album escaped from Sidewalk. Producer Clancy Grass abandoned musical pursuits proper for film work over the next couple of years, beginning with "The Velvet Vampire" (see **Born Again** entry). **Stack** was mystified as to their stalled momentum, but lacked the financial wherewithall to escape their eight year exclusive contract, eventually breaking up and pursuing non-musical careers.

Drummer Bob Ellis was previously with Wabash Spencer, who issued a 45 and recorded an unreleased demo in 1967. He was also with **The Fabs** and plays on their rare Cotton Ball 45 from 1966. Bob passed away in January 1999.

Compilation appearances include *Only Forever* on Gear Fab's *Psychedelic Sampler* (CD). (CF)

STACK - Above All LP.

The Staehely Brothers

Personnel:	KING ERRISON	perc	A
	STOOP HAIRY	drms	A
	JOHN LOCKE	keyb'ds	A
	AL STAEHELY	ld vcls, gtr, bs	A
	JOHN CHRISTIAN STAEHELY	gtr, keyb'ds, bs	A

ALBUM: 1(A) STA-HAY-LEE (Epic KE 32385) 1973 -

The **Staehely Brothers** were in **Spirit** for the *Feedback* album. Afterwards they went solo and recorded this decent hard-rock album. John Locke from **Spirit** also played on it and wrote some songs and Ed Cassidy also plays, but uncredited (he may be "Stoop Hairy"). An underrated album, several tracks deserve to be heard: *Captain Zombie Meet Unfellini*, *Rockin In The Bush*, *Future Shock*... The album was produced by Alex Kazanegras and came housed in a superb sleeve with drawings of skeletons.

In 1982, Al Staehely released a solo album *Stahaley's Comet* (Ranger Records). He also went on to play with John Cipollina and **Nick Gravenites** in the early eighties under the names Thunder & Lightning and the Gravenites-Cipollina Band. He is now an attorney in Houston, Texas. (SR)

The Staffs

45: I Just Can't Go To Sleep/Another Love (Pa-Go-Go 118) 1966

A punk outfit from San Antonio in Texas. The flip, a rather off beat punk number can also be heard on *Highs In The Mid-Sixties, Vol. 11* (LP). The 'A' side was a Kinks cover version. (VJ)

Stained Glass

Personnel:	DENNIS CARRASCO(*)	drms	AB
	JIM McPHERSON	bs, vcls	AB
	BOB ROMINGER	gtr	A
	TOM BRYANT	gtr	B

NB: (*) shown as 'Carriasco' on second album.

ALBUMS:	1(B)	CRAZY HORSE ROADS	(Capitol ST 154) 1969 R1
	2(B)	AURORA	(Capitol ST 242) 1969 R1/R2

NB: (1) reissued by Capitol in Greece (1987).

45s:	If I Needed Someone/		
	How Do You Expect Me To Trust You	(RCA 47-8889) 1966
	My Buddy Sin/Vanity Fair	(RCA 47-8952) 1966

We Got A Long Way To Go/Corduroy Joy	(RCA 47-9166)	1967
A Scene In Between/Mediocre Me	(RCA 47-9354)	1967
Lady In Lace/Soap And Turkey	(Capitol 2178)	1968
Fahrenheit/Twiddle My Thumbs	(Capitol 2372)	1969
Gettin' On's Gettin' Rough/ The Necromancer	(Capitol 2521)	1969

More of a folk-rock band than a psychedelic band **Stained Glass** started out in 1966 playing Beatles cover versions in San Jose. Originally recording for RCA they issued a series of singles. The first two, which were a mixture of folk and Merseybeat, met with some local success. The best was *We Got A Long Way To Go*, a driving rock song with immediate appeal, which was a big hit in San Jose during April 1967.

They moved to Capitol in the Spring of 1968, issuing three singles and two albums. Of the six 45 sides on Capitol only *Lady In Lace* is non-LP. Both albums were quite highly-rated, but failed to make much impact and the band disbanded in November 1969, although McPherson went on the play with **Copperhead**.

Either of their albums are worth a listen if you can acquire them cheaply. The first was reissued by Capitol in Greece.

Compilation appearances include: *My Buddy Sin* and *We Got A Long Way To Go* on *Mindrocker, Vol. 9* (LP); *A Scene In Between* on *Of Hopes And Dreams & Tombstones* (LP), *Psychedelic Unknowns, Vol. 7* (LP & CD), *Acid Dreams, Vol. 3* (LP) and *Fuzz Flaykes & Shakes, Vol. 1* (LP & CD). (VJ)

Stained Glass Window

ALBUM: 1 STAINED GLASS WINDOW (Sycamore) 1975 SC

On a small Chicago private label, an acoustic loner/downer folk singer with unusual pessimistic lyrics. (SR)

The Stains

45: Now And Then/
Did You Ever Have To Make Up Your Mind (Lotus 1000) 1967

These **Stains** were Yale University students. You can also find their *Now And Then* on *Open Up Yer Door! Vol. 1* (LP) and *Teenage Shutdown, Vol. 3* (LP & CD). (MW/MM)

The Stairsteps

ALBUM: 1 THE STAIRSTEPS (Buddah BDS 5061) c1969 -

An obscure group mixing Beatles-influenced songs and soul. Their album contains covers of *Dear Prudence* and *Getting Better*. (SR)

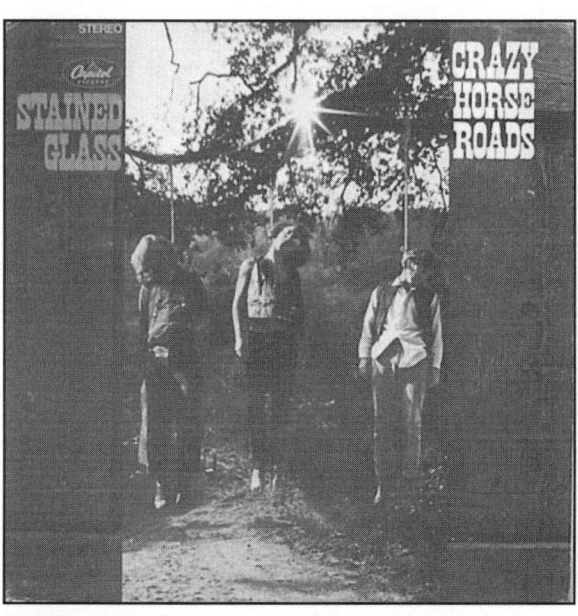

STAINED GLASS - Crazy Horse Roads LP.

Stalk - Forrest Group

Personnel:			
	ERIC BLOOM	gtr, vcls	A
	ALBERT BOUCHARD	drms	A
	ALLEN LANIER	keyb'ds, gtr	A
	DONALD ROESER	gtr, vcls	A
	ANDY WINTERS	bs	A

ALBUMS: 1(A) ST. CECILIA - THE CALIFORNIA ALBUM
(No label no #) 1998 R1
2(A) ST. CECILIA - THE ELEKTRA RECORDINGS
(Rhino Handmade RHM2 7716) 2001

NB: (1) is a deluxe vinyl-only release, containing material recorded for Elektra Records in New York in 1969 and in Los Angeles in 1970. (2) is a numbered limited edition (of 5000) CD-only release of the same material, from the master tapes.

45: What Is Quicksand?/Arthur Comics (Elektra 45693) 1970

NB: promo-only. At least two counterfeit editions exist - the original has a shiny black and white label and all printing is clear. One counterfeit has matte labels, the other looks more convincing but has a bit of "invisible" surface noise.

Stalk-Forrest Group (aka Oaxaxa; previously known as The Soft White Underbelly) recorded material in 1969 and again in 1970 for Elektra Records. An album was assembled by the label from these sessions, but never commercially released. However, it has long been rumoured, and is still possible, that acetates of the album exist. At this point, only the 45 listed above is confirmed to have been issued at the time.

Most of the music recorded by the band has been circulating on cassette for twenty years or more - in varying degrees of fidelity. In 1998, a vinyl album appeared that collected all the material in the hands of the band's admirers and ostensibly brought it to the attention of a much wider audience. This likely inspired Rhino to assemble their recent CD-only collection, which includes every known recording by the band over the course of two incarnations: as **The Stalk-Forrest Group** (Los Angeles recordings, early 1970) and as Oaxaca (New York recordings, 1969), all of which were languishing in Elektra's vaults.

The material possesses both the sophistication of their highly-regarded seventies work as The Blue Oyster Cult and the ethereal, druggy late sixties sound associated with West Coast bands like **Tripsichord Music Box** and **Quicksilver Messenger Service**, it's no stretch to say that **The Stalk-Forrest Group** will find wide acceptance with readers of this book. Don't miss this!

Compilation appearance have included *Arthur Comics* on *Elektrock The Sixties* (4-LP). (CF)

The Standells

Personnel:			
	DAVE BURKE	gtr, bs	ABC
	GARY LANE	bs	AB
	GARY LEEDS	drms	A
	LARRY TAMBLYN	keyb'ds, vcls	ABCD
	TONY VALENTINO	ld gtr	ABCD
	DICK DODD	bs, drms	BCD
	JOHN FLECK	bs	D

HCP

ALBUMS:			
1(B)	THE STANDELLS IN PERSON AT PJ'S	(Liberty LST 7384)	1964 - R1
2(B)	LIVE AND OUT OF SIGHT	(Sunset 5136)	1964 - SC
3(C)	DIRTY WATER	(Tower ST 5027)	1966 52 -
4(C)	WHY PICK ON ME-SOMETIMES GOOD GUYS DON'T WEAR WHITE	(Tower ST 5044)	1966 - SC
5(C)	THE HOT ONES!	(Tower ST 5049)	1966 - SC
6(D)	TRY IT	(Tower ST 5098)	1967 - SC

NB: (1) was also released as (2) in abridged form. (3), (4) (5) and (6) reissued on CD with previously unreleased and bonus tracks (Sundazed SC 6019/20/21/22 respectively). (3) and (5) reissued on one CD (Eva B5) 1990. (4) and (6) reissued on one CD (Eva EV 300) 1990. (5) and (6) reissued on one CD (Big Beat CDWIKD 112) 1993. Big Beat have also released the *Riot On Sunset Strip* soundtrack together with a *Rarities* album on one CD (Big Beat CDWIKD 113) 1993. There also a 19 track CD *Best Of* (Rhino), and three vinyl compilations, *Rarities* (Rhino RNLP 115) 1984, *The Standells* (Avi) 1982, and *The Best Of The Standells* (Rhino RNLP 107) 1983 (later repackaged in 1987). Also relevant is Eva's reissue of *Riot On Sunset Strip* (Eva 12043) 1984. There's also a 10" *The Live Ones* (Sundazed SEP 10-165) 2001, with live tracks from 1966.

EP: 1 POOR BOYS BORN IN A RUBBLE
(Sundazed SEP 108) 1995

NB: (1) Contains *Sometimes Good Guys Don't Wear White* (long version), *Riot On Sunset Strip* (Soundtrack version), *I Hate To Leave You* (previously unreleased) and *Why Pick On Me* (instrumental backing track). All tracks are in mono and the EP was issued on dark red vinyl.

			HCP
45s:	α	You'll Be Mine Someday/Girl In My Head	(Linda 112) 1964 -
		Peppermint Beatles/The Shake	(Liberty 55680) 1964 -
		I'll Go Crazy/Help Yourself	(Liberty 55722) 1964 -
		So Fine/Linda Lou	(Liberty 55743) 1964 -
		Zebra In The Kitchen/Someday You'll Cry	(MGM 13350) 1965 -
		The Boy Next Door/B.J. Quetzal	(Vee Jay 643) 1965 102
		Don't Say Goodbye/Big Boss Man	(Vee Jay 679) 1965 -
		Dirty Water/Rari	(Tower 185) 1965 11
		Sometimes Good Guys Don't Wear White/Why Don't You Hurt Me?	(Tower 257) 1966 43
	β	Help Yourself/Ooh Poo Pah Doo	(Sunset 61000) 1966 -
		Why Pick On Me?/Mr. Nobody	(Tower 282) 1966 54
		Try It!/Poor Shell Of A Man (PS)	(Tower 310) 1967 -
	χ	Don't Tell Me What To Do/When I Was A Cowboy	(Tower 312) 1967 -
		Riot On Sunset Strip/Black Hearted Woman	(Tower 314) 1967 133
		Can't Help But Love You/Ninety-Nine And A Half	(Tower 348) 1967 78
		Animal Girl/Soul Drippin'	(Tower 398) 1968 -

NB: α as by Larry Tamblyn and The Standells. β issued to 'cash-in' on their chart success, both tracks are taken from their earlier *Live At PJ's* album. χ as by Sllednats (Standells spelt backwards). There are two French EPs with picture sleeves: *The Shake/I'll Go Crazy/Help Yourself/Bony Moronie* (Liberty LEP 2211); and *Dirty Water/Rari/Why Don't You Hurt Me?/Little Sally Tease* (Capitol EAP 122009).

Formed in Los Angeles in 1962, by Larry Tamblyn and Tony Valentino, they started life as a twist type discotheque group as **Larry Tamblyn and The Standells**, but soon became an archetypal punk band. Ed Cobb wrote much of their classic material and ensured that their lyrics articulated the resentments of America's youth against their parents and society. They are perhaps best known for the classic punk-rock single *Dirty Water*, their first single for Tower, which Cobb had written about the Charles river in Boston.

Larry Tamblyn recalls:- "Although Ed Cobb did write much of the material, a few of the more memorable songs were written by members of the band such as *Mr. Nobody* (Larry Tamblyn), *Riot On Sunset Strip* (Tony Valentino / John Fleck) and *Why Did You Hurt Me* (Tony Valentino). **The Standells** had written and recorded material similar to *Dirty Water* before Ed Cobb (eg *Help Yourself* from the *Live At PJ's* album and *Big Boss Man* from the VJ recording). When Ed Cobb presented *Dirty Water* to us, it was not much more than an R&B song. He asked us to record it with the agreement we could arrange it. Tony V. came up with the famous guitar riff. Dick D. created the chant in the beginning "I'm going to tell you a story..." so it was more like a combined effort. Later, Mr. Cobb took over more and more control, until we no longer sounded like **The Standells**. Eventually, we were not even allowed to play on our own songs. He was trying to take us in a direction of a White Soul sound (evident in the departure of our sound on *Can't Help But Love You*). It was for this reason, we decided to part company with Cobb."

Prior to their association with Cobb, the band had recorded a 45 on Linda in 1964 as Larry Tamblyn and The Standells, three singles and an album for Liberty and a 45 for MGM who also included two tracks from their first album on the Soundtrack to *Get Yourself A College Girl* (MGM SE 4273) in 1965.

After two 45s for Vee Jay, produced by Sonny Bono (*The Boy Next Door* and *Don't Say Goodbye*) the band met Cobb. He was sufficiently impressed with them to have them signed to Tower and *Dirty Water*, released in November 1965, became a smash hit. Curiously, Dewey Martin substituted for **Dick Dodd** at this time, for four months after *Dirty Water* was recorded, but before it became a hit.

The *Dirty Water* album was also strong, providing another hit single, *Sometimes Good Guys Don't Wear White*, which was issued in June 1966. It was full of strong tracks like *Medication*, *There Is A Storm Comin'* and some good covers such as *Hey Joe* and *19th Nervous Breakdown*.

The Standells never equalled this commercial success again. The *Why Pick On Me* album sold quite well and included a track *Have You Ever Spent The Night In Jail?* which was apparently written from Cobb's experience whilst in Texas.

The Hot Ones! is best avoided, consisting as it does of cover versions of other artists' classic hits like *Sunny Afternoon*, *Wild Thing* and *Eleanor Rigby*. It flopped badly when it was released in November 1966, and according to the band was recorded only because of Cobb's and Greengrass Production's insistence that they do so.

Later, in 1967, they attracted more attention when *Try It* was banned because it was alleged to have disgusting lyrics. This was a real injustice because a cover version of the song by **Ohio Express** in 1968 wasn't. Yet, despite this, the release of their next single *Don't Tell Me What To Do* with their name spelt backwards as a publicity-seeking gimmick and the inclusion of two tracks, *Riot On Sunset Strip* and *Get Away From Her*, on the soundtrack to *Riot On Sunset Strip*, they never quite achieved their early promise.

Larry:- *"Try It* we loved and considered closer to the true **Standells** sound. *Can't Help Love You* was our next release, which saw Cobb trying to move the sound more towards white soul. *Don't Tell Me What To Do*, *Riot On Sunset Strip* and *Get Away From Here* (from the movie *Riot On Sunset Strip*) were all recorded and released earlier."

Keen to write and perform their own material, but frustrated by Cobb's increasing manipulation of the band, their association with him ended in

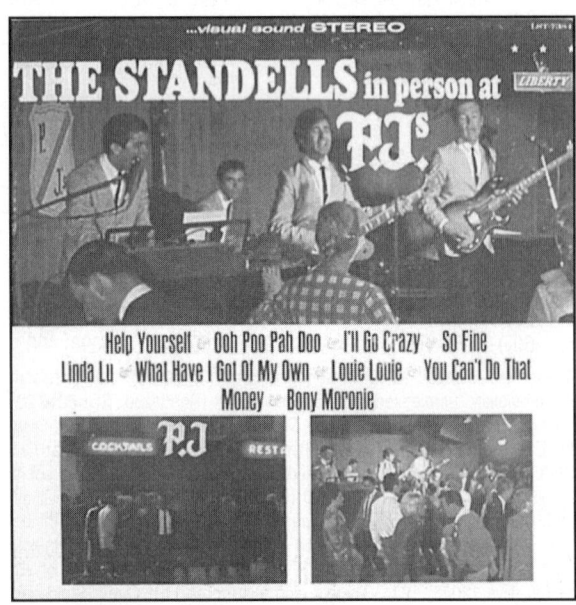

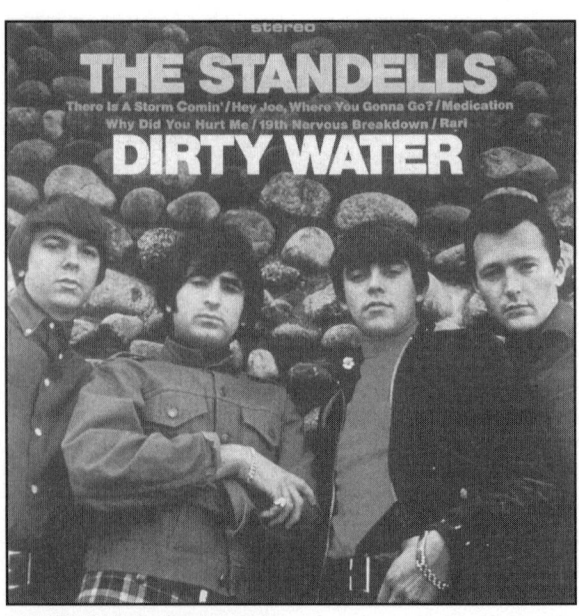

THE STANDELLS - In Person At PJ's LP.

THE STANDELLS - Dirty Water CD.

1968 and they split up later that year.

In their latter days it's been reported that they co-opted old friend Joey Stec of **Millennium**, first as a co-writer, later as a full member, but Larry disagrees:- "I don't recall Joey Stec. As far as I know, he was not a member of **The Standells**."

Prior to replacing Gary 'Walker' Leeds in **The Standells**, **Dodd** was "resting" from being an original Mouseketeer/**Blues Magoo**. He later recorded an unsuccessful solo album, *The First Evolution Of Dick Dodd* (Tower ST 5142) in April 1968 and later played for Joshua.

After Dick Dodd's departure, Lowell George (from **The Factory**) was recruited, but the band split soon afterwards, reforming again later without Lowell.

Larry Tamblyn, who was the brother of Russ Tamblyn, also made three singles for Faro prior to forming **The Standells**. Larry: "In the late fifties and early sixties, I was signed to Faro and Linda Records, owned by Eddie Davis, who later spearheaded the Chicano music movement with groups like El Chicano, Los Lobos, Cannon Ball and The Headhunters, etc. I had several singles out, including *Dearest* and *This Is The Night*. I am told the Salez Brothers sang backup on the latter." He also produced the third 45 by the **East Side Kids**.

A further Larry Tamblyn 45 followed in 1968 - *Summer Clothes Pts 1 & 2* (Sunburst) 1968. Larry:- "*Summer Clothes* (Side One, vocal by Larry Tamblyn; Side Two Instumental) was actually performed by **The Standells** and produced by Ed Cobb. But like *Don't Tell Me What To Do*, it was so different from the group's sound, that it was credited as 'Larry'."

Of the other members, Gary Leeds left the band prior to the recording of the *Live At PJ's* album and had a brief spell with The Walker Brothers before forming Gary Walker and The Rain. Dave Burke was previously bassist with **The Tropics**, from Tampa and went on to join **Indian Puddin' and Pipe**.

The Standells understandably have figured on several compilations, including:- *Someday You'll Cry* on *Pebbles, Vol. 9* (CD) and *Highs In The Mid-Sixties, Vol. 1* (LP); *Big Boss Man* on *Mindrocker, Vol. 5* (LP); *Dirty Water* on *Battle Of The Bands* (CD), *Nuggets From Nuggets* (CD), *Nuggets - Original Artyfacts From The First Psychedelic Era 1965-1968* (Dble LP), *Nuggets, Vol. 1* (LP), *Sundazed Sampler, Vol. 1* (CD), *Tough Rock* and *Wild Thing*; *Sometimes Good Guys Don't Wear Whlte* on *Highs Of The Sixties*; *Try It* and *Sometimes Good Guys Don't Wear White* on *Nuggets, Vol. 2* (LP); *Try It!* on *Born Bad, Vol. 4*; *Dirty Water* and *Why Pick On Me* on *Nuggets* (CD) and *Golden Archive Series Sampler*; *Sometimes Good Guys Don't Wear White* and *Try It* on *More Nuggets* (CD); *You'll Be Mine Some Day* on *The East Side Sound, Vol. 1 - 1959-1968* (CD); *Girl In My Heart* on *The West Coast East Side Sound, Vol. 3* (CD); *Dirty Water*, *Sometimes Good Guys Don't Wear White* and *Why Pick On Me* on *Nuggets Box* (4-CD); and there's an unnamed bonus track on *What A Way To Die* which sounds like it dates from very early in their career.

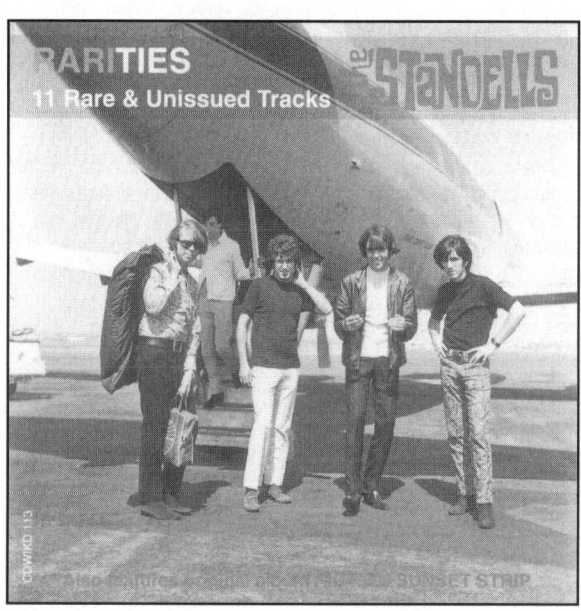

THE STANDELLS - Rarities CD.

In November 1999, **The Standells** reformed for a live gig at the 'Cavestomp '99!' festival in New York. Other bands which appeared included **The Chocolate Watchband** and **The Monks**!! Their set, which drew acclaim from gig-goers was later issued on CD *Ban This!* ( ) 200?. (VJ/MW/JFr/GSw/SR/GGc/LT)

Stanley Steamer

| Personnel incl: | HOLLY VAUGHN | ld vcls | A |

ALBUM: 1(A) STANLEY STEAMER (Jolly Rogers JR 5002) 1972 -

A California group in the style of **Ten Wheel Drive**, with a horn section. Holly Vaughn had earlier sang in the **First Edition** with Kenny Rogers who produced this album on his label. It tries to combine prog rock and soul with powerful female vocals, notably on the side long *Three Humours Of Man*. (SR)

Stapleton-Morley Expression

Personnel incl:	HAL BLAINE	drms	A
	MIKE DEASY	gtr, sitar	A
	LARRY KNECHTEL	bs	A

ALBUM: 1(A) THE MAMAS AND THE PAPAS BOOK OF SONGS (Dunhill) c1966 -

45: Dedicated To The One I Love/ Straight Shooter (Dunhill 4111) 1967

An album of instrumental covers of **The Mamas and Papas** recorded by a group of ace session musicians including **Hal Blaine**, Larry Knechtel, **Mike Deasy** etc. (SR)

Starbuck and The Rainmakers

45: I Who Have Nothing/ Let Your Hair Hang Long (Valiant V 744) 1966

An anthemic pop melodrama with powerful vocals backed by crashin' fuzz guitar - a strange but appealing hybrid. (MW)

The Starchiefs

Personnel:	STEVE (SKELTON) KELLY	drms	A
	WILLIAM "SONNY" LYLE	bs	A
	HUEY P. MEADOWS	gtr	A
	KENNY WAYNE	ld vcl, gtr	A

45: Blast-Off/ Your Love's So Hard To Understand (Orbit 2040) 1964

NB: 'B' side as by **Kenneth Hagler and The Starchiefs**.

This was **Kenny Wayne**'s first outing on vinyl. *Blast Off* was an instrumental and the band recorded a further 45, which was eventually released as by **The Grapes Of Wrath**, following a change of drummer.

Kenny Wayne came from Redwater, Texas and they were based in the Texarkana area. The Orbit label was based in Dekalb, Texas.

Starfire

ALBUM: 1 STARFIRE (Crimson 4476) 1974 R3

A furious hard-rock/progressive offering by a Californian quintet. Not very good, but very sought-after by collectors of this style. (CF/SR)

The Starfires

Personnel:	DAVE ANDERSON	ld gtr	A
	CHUCK BUTLER	ld vcls, tamb, claves	A
	JACK EMERICK	drms	A
	FREDDY FIELDS	bs	A
	SONNY LATHROP	gtr	A

ALBUM: 1(A) TEENBEAT A GO GO (La Brea LS 8018) 1965 SC

45s:	Fink/Work Out Fine	(Triumph 61) 1965
α	I Never Loved Her/Linda	(G.I. 4001) 1965
	No More/Rockin' Dixie (Goin' Down)	(G.I. 4002) 1965/6
	Cry For Freedom/Won't Die Away	(G.I. 4004) 1966
	There's Still Time/Unchain My Heart	(Yardbird 4005) 1966
	Something You've Got/The Hardest Way	(Yardbird 4006) 1966

NB: α reissued in 1997.

Hailing from the Los Angeles area, they started off as an early sixties beat band doing cover versions and their album, a live album of cover versions (*Around And Around, Walkin' The Dog, Farmer John, Peter Gunn, Hold Me, Justin, Money, No Reply, Great Balls Of Fire, Apache* and *Stand By Me*) was in this mode. Thereafter they became very punkish, performing mainly original compositions written by their bassist Freddy Fields. *I Never Loved Her* in particular stands out as a classic garage number, with a twist in the tail to its lyrics and one of the all-time great riffs. Other tracks also have merit too, with *Cry For Freedom* being notable as an early Vietnam protest.

Their final 45 features a reasonable version of the Chris Kenner song but tucked away on the flip is *The Hardest Way*, a stunning low-key moody droning pop-punker from Freddy Fields with dynamic drumming, lashings of choppy guitars and mean fuzz.

Sonny Lathrop, was later rhythm guitarist in a slick club band called Mickey And The Invaders in 1967 and later went on to form **Sweet Marie**.

G.I. 4003 is known to exist, but does not contain material by **The Starfires**.

Compilation coverage has included: *I Never Loved Her* on *Pebbles, Vol. 8* (LP), *Pebbles, Vol. 8* (CD), *The Essential Pebbles Collection, Vol. 1* (Dble CD), *Best of Pebbles, Vol. 3* (LP & CD), *Psychedelic Unknowns, Vol. 2* (Dble 7") and *Psychedelic Unknowns, Vol's 1 & 2* (LP); *Linda* on *Highs In The Mid-Sixties Vol. 1* (LP), *Psychedelic Unknowns, Vol. 3* and *Mondo Frat Dance Bash A Go Go* (CD); *There's Still Time* on *Acid and Flowers* (CD) and *Basementsville! U.S.A.* (LP); and *Cry For Freedom* on *Pebbles, Vol. 9* (CD).

In the 1980s *I Never Loved Her* was covered by Austria's Vogues on *A Doll Spits Cubes* and The Cynics on *Twelve Flights Up*. (VJ/MW/GGI)

The Starfires

Personnel incl:	TOM McLAUGHLIN	keyb'ds, vcls	A
	ERIC SCHABACKER	gtr, vcls	A
	BERRY VAUGHT	drms, vcls	A

ALBUM: 1(A) THE STARFIRES PLAY (Ohio Recording Service ORS-34) 1964 ?

Formed in 1963 by students from Rollins College who started out playing in a basement in Buffalo, New York. The following year they put out an album. One of the photos on the cover shows them with the Isley Brothers.

They relocated to Orlando, Florida and in late 1966 changed their name to **Little Willie and The Adolescents**. (MW)

The Starfires (Steve Ellis and)

Personnel:	JIM BRANDENBURG	gtr	AB
	RON BUTLER	bs, organ	ABC
	STEVE ELLIS	gtr, vcls	ABCDE
	CLEM 'BUTCH' HATTING	drms	ABCD
	BUTCH JERGINS	bs	B
	BARRY HANSON	gtr	CDEF
	BILL STORIE	bs	CD
	MIKE MULLIGAN	bs	EF
	DEAN "ZEKE" SENFNER	drms	EF
	JIMMY GROTH	ld gtr	F

STEVE ELLIS and THE STARFIRES - Steve Ellis Songbook LP.

ALBUM: 1(E) STEVE ELLIS SONGBOOK (IGL 105) 1967 R3

NB: (1) reissued on vinyl as *Songbook* (Get Hip GHAS 5003) 1994.

45s:	Walking Around/That's How It Feels	(Century Records Test Pressing 22355) 1965
	Walking Around/That's How It Feels	(Decima 2001) 1965

Steve Ellis was born in Pipestone, Minnesota on 23rd December 1944. He was a great lover of music, cars and motorbikes. By the age of 12 he'd learnt to play guitar, at 14 he'd joined his first local band The Squires. Later, he briefly played with another local band, The Sabres, before forming **The Starfires** in 1963. They were named after a car and Steve was in every respect the leader of the band, he even did all their bookings. They soon established themselves as a very popular live act in the Midwest. In 1964 Ron Butler switched to organ and Butch Jergins came in on bass. Later Barry Hanson replaced Jim Brandenburg on rhythm guitar and Bill Storie replaced Butch Jergins on bass. By mid-1965 Ron Butler had left the group and the remaining four players went to Sears Recording Studio in Omaha, Nebraska to cut a demo disc using two Steve Ellis original compositions *Walk Around/That's How It Feels*. The pressing is now rare. The songs weren't punk, but veered towards folk rock. Ellis headed out to California with the demo and tried to attract the attention of a major label, but he returned empty-handed. Despite this setback the band never gave up, they re-recorded the 45 in Dodge City, Kansas and it was issued on the Decima label. This was a far superior version. Butch Hatting left the band soon after the 45 was released and a new line-up (E) was put together. In the Summer of 1967 this line-up travelled to the IGL Recording Studio in Milford, Iowa to begin recording several new Steve Ellis compositions. Five were recorded - *On My Mind, Her Face, Looking Thru Me, Pride Of A Man* and *Baby's Gone* - plus *Since I Fell For You*, a cover of a Skyliners' song released in 1963. Then tragedy struck, before the other five songs could be completed, Steve was killed in a freak motorcycle accident on 31st August 1967, when his rear tyre blew, He was just 22. The *Songbook* album was pieced together after his death. It consisted of the six finished songs cut at IGL Studios, the two songs from the previous 45 and narration from a friend of his, Tom Rambler and is now very rare. **The Starfires** soldiered on for a while without Steve before calling it a day.

Pride Of A Man was also included on the rare *Roof Garden Jamboree* compilation released in 1967 and more recently seven tracks from the IGL sessions have been compiled on *The IGL Rock Story: Part Two (1967 - 68)* (CD). (VJ)

The Starfyres

Personnel:	ANDY ??		A
	FLAKE ??		A

	PADDY ??		A
	SEP ??		A

45:	Captain Dueseldorph /		
	No Room For Your Love	(Burr BU 45-1001)	196?

Just 500 copies of this 45 were pressed up by this Lansford, Pennsylvania quartet. They're even harder to acquire (and afford) since *Captain Dueseldorph*, a submarine sludge-fest modelled loosely on Gloria, appeared on Distortion's 1990 compilation *Crude Pa., Vol. 1* (LP). (MW)

Peter Stark

Personnel:	WENDALL BIGELOW	drms	A
	HAL DAVIS	gtr	A
	DAVE MASON	gtr	A
	RICK ED ROB	perc	A
	PETER RUTH	hrmnca	A
	WILLARD SPENCR	banjo	A
	BEN STARK	gtr, vcls	A
	PETER STARK	gtr, vcls	A

ALBUM:	1(A)	MUSHROOM COUNTRY	(Montage) 1976 SC

From Ann Arbor, Michigan, this album contains acid-folk music, with a cover of Donovan's *Hey Gyp*, some ragas (*Ragas For Bayleaf*) and fluid guitars. It's also housed in a nice sleeve. (SR/CF)

Stark Naked

Personnel:	RICHARD BELSKY	ld gtr	A
	LYNE BUNN	vcls, perc	A
	JOHN FRAGOS	drms, perc, gong	A
	JIM MONAHAN	vcls, gtr	A
	TOM RUBINO	bs	A
	PAUL VENIER	vcls, keyb'ds, perc	A

ALBUM:	1(A)	STARK NAKED	(RCA Victor LSP 4592) 1971 -

45:	Done/Sins	(RCA Victor 0588) 1971

From Levittown, Long Island, New York. This outfit's album is a superb and very under-rated progressive album with long organ tracks, fuzz, pleasant piano interludes and some effective female vocals in places. The opening cut, *All Of Them Witches*, is one of those long extended, elaborate tracks that characterised the progressive era, but the whole of Side One in particular is excellent. (VJ)

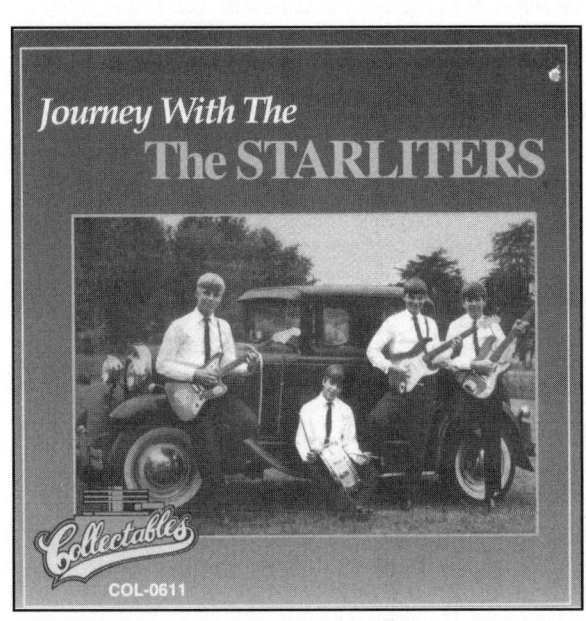

THE STARLITERS - Journey With The Starliters CD.

Stark Naked and The Car Thieves

ALBUM:	1 STARK NAKED & THE CAR THIEVES (AVI 8021) 196? -

45s:	Mixed Emotions/?	(Attarack 101) 196?
	Maria/The Pleasure Of Your Company	(Sunburst 771) 1968?
	Look Back In Love/Contact	(Sunburst 774) 196?
	Can't Stop Thinkin' About The Good Times/	
	Now A Taste...	(Sunburst 776) 196?

From the Los Angeles area **Stark Naked And The Car Thieves** have been variously described as 'garage' or 'soul tinged rock'.

Gary Myers (Mojo Men/Portraits) remembers this band:- "Stark Naked and the Car Thieves came from S.F. to L.A. in late '65 and they were doing a lot of the same material as our band (the Mojo Men, as we hadn't yet changed our name to the Portraits) - 4 Seasons and other pop harmony things, along with soul/dance stuff like *Knock On Wood*, etc. They had three lead singers. They also did the Flamingo in L.V. (dance room, not the lounge or the show room), and they either preceded or followed us at a club in San Jose in '67." (VJ/GM)

The Dave Starky Five

45s:	α	Hey Everybody/Stand There	(Shazam 112) 1966
		Used To Be/Brass Jam	(Mod International 456) 1971
		Used To Be/	
		Oh Woman (I Really Know The Blues)	(Atlantic 2831) 1971

NB: α released as Just Us.

British guitarist/R&B fanatic Dave Starky moved to Houston in late 1964 and with the help of some local boys soon started up **The Dave Starky Five**. In 1965, they caught the eye of a shady local record guy called Ray Rush, who took them into the ACA-Goldstar Studios to record the above two originals, both excellent garage pounders. Before the record could be released, however, Starky flew the coop and returned to England. The band more or less broke up at this point, but Rush wanted to release the record, cooking up a crazy promo scheme with a local radio station in a "rename the recording group" contest. The winner was chosen to be Just Us and that's how the record was released in January 1966. The original singer and bass player got some other guys and got back together at this point, but they hated the new name, so they went back to calling themselves **The Dave Starky Five**. Unfortunately, they never regained their momentum.

Compilation appearances include: *Stand There* on *Teenage Shutdown, Vol. 7* (LP & CD); *Hey Everybody* on *Back From The Grave, Vol. 8* (CD) and *Back From The Grave, Vol. 8* (Dble LP) (the sleeve-notes to which have provided the information for this entry). (VJ/GG)

The Starlets

45:	You Don't Love Me/I've Had It	(Tower 144) 1965

Davie Allan played guitar on this 45 which featured female vocals.

Compilation appearances include *You Don't Love Me* on *Girls In The Garage, Vol. 1* (CD) and *Girls In The Garage, Vol. 2* (LP). (VJ/AMn)

The Starliters

Personnel:	LARRY JONES	bs	A
	GARY ROGERS	drms, vcls	A
	MIKE ROGERS	ld vcls, ld gtr	A
	KEN WILKINS	gtr	A

ALBUM:	1(A)	JOURNEY WITH THE STARLITERS	
		(Justice JLP 124) c1967 R2/R3	

NB: (1) reissued on CD (Collectables COL-CD-0611) 1995.

A quartet of students from South Stokes High School, North Carolina, who have a great deal of talent to offer - so said Calvin Newton on the original liner notes to this rare album. A smattering of Invasion covers (Beatles, Animals) plus some clubby ballads and instrumentals (the obligatory *Wipe*

Out). Undoubtedly competent, but the band doesn't really swing, snap or bite and the vocals tend to be flat (in sound rather than key). Perhaps just doing covers meant they weren't able or willing to assert their own identity, creativity or let loose. Like some others on this Justice series, they sound stuck somewhere around 1964 to 1965 too - no sign of a fuzztone. The reissue satisfies curiosity but not the palate. (MW)

The Starlites

Personnel incl: MALINOWSKI
MUSSER

45s:	Stagger Lee/Everybody Needs Somebody	(Barclay 15016) 1965
	I Can't See You/Baby Set Me Free	(Barclay 17134) 1965
α	I Can't See You (diff. vers)/ Big Boss Man	(Dater DT- 1301) 1966
β	The Original Nothing People/ I Waited So Long	(Fontana 1583) 1967

NB: α as by **The Soul Generation**. β as by **The Beatin' Path**.

A five piece from Reading, Pennsylvania. Their first waxing of *I Can't See You* features on *Pennsylvania Unknowns* (LP) and *Psychedelic Disaster Whirl* (LP) and the second version as by the **Soul Generation** is on *Crude Pa. Vol. 1*. Both sides of their first 45 are also featured on Arf! Arf!'s *Eastern Pa Rock Part One (1961-'66)* (CD) whilst their second 45 is on *Eastern Pa Rock Part Two (1966-'69)* (CD).

Their best known incarnation is as **The Beatin' Path** whose *Original Nothing People* has been captured on *Boulders, Vol. 1* (LP), *Mayhem & Psychosis, Vol. 1* (LP), *Mayhem & Psychosis, Vol. 1* (CD) and *Ya Gotta Have... Moxie, Vol. 1* (Dble CD). (VJ/MW)

The Starlites

45: Wait For Me / ? (Zap 8015) 1965

A different and unknown **Starlites**, whose guitar and sax riffer *Wait For Me* is on *Teenage Shutdown, Vol. 7* (LP & CD). (MM)

Alva Starr

45: Anna/Light Of A 1,000 Years (Golden-Records 103) 1967

From Baton Rouge, Louisiana, **Alva Starr** also recorded as **Alva Snelling**. *Anna* is a keening ballad backed by a moody folk-punker. (MW)

Starvation Army Band

Personnel incl: DUKE DAVIS   bs   A

This band are thought to have recorded 45s on London in the 1960s. Duke Davis played bass for the **13th Floor Elevators** for a short while in early 1968. They also recorded material for International Artists but had nothing released. (VJ)

The State of Mind

Personnel incl: JAMES BOOTH   A

45s:	Move/If He Comes Back	(Chavis 1038) 196?
	Goin' Away/Make You Cry	(Chavis 1041) 196?

A punk outfit from Wilmington, Delaware. *Move* is usually considered their finest moment and features a wonderful 'shuffle' rhythm and superb guitar break.

Compilation appearances include: *Move* on *Pebbles, Vol. 5* (CD), *Psychedelic Unknowns, Vol. 3* (LP & CD), *Pebbles Box* (5-LP), *Pebbles, Vol. 5* (LP), *Trash Box* (5-CD) and *Great Pebbles* (CD); and *Make You Cry* and *Goin' Away* on *A Journey To Tyme, Vol. 5* (LP).

The State of Mind

45: Time Will Tell / City Life (Tener 1017) 1967

A different **State Of Mind** from the Orlando area of Florida. In addition to the 45 they have one track, a cover of **The Byrds**' *My Back Pages*, on the 1967 sampler album *Bee Jay Demo, Vol. 2* (Tener 1014). (MW)

Statesiders

45: Patterned The Sand/ She Belonged To Another (Providence 410) 1965

Thought to be an East Coast band, their origins remain a mystery. Both sides are composed by Carnaby and Shakepeare and have resurfaced on *Mindrocker, Vol. 12* (LP). The single was produced by Steve Rappaport. (VJ)

The Statesmen

45: Stop And Get A Ticket/Stick With Me Baby (Tema 137) 1967

This is thought to have been **The Baskerville Hounds**, a Cleveland, Ohio, band operating under a different name. This version of *Stop And Get A Ticket*, which was actually a hit for the **Clefs Of Lavender Hill**, can be heard on *Highs In The Mid-Sixties, Vol. 9* (LP). (VJ)

The Statics (with Tiny Tony)

Personnel:	RANDY BENNETT	bs	AB
	DAVE ERICKSON	drms	A
	RICHARD GERBER	gtr	AB
	MERRILEE RUSH	keyb'ds, vcls	AB
	NEIL RUSH	sax	AB
	ANTHONY "TINY TONY" SMITH	ld vcls	AB
	CARL PETERS	drms	B

45s:	Buster Brown Part 1 /Part 2	(Bregg 1000) 196?
	The Girl Can't Help It/Harlem Shuffle	(Camelot 110) 196?
	Tell Me The Truth/Rinky Dink	(Camelot 115) 196?

This act from Seattle had backed Tiny Tony on his 1962 regional hit *Hey Mrs. Jones*. Their three 45s are said to have been fine examples of the raw Northwest sound in this era and the act is notable for including **Merrilee Rush**, who later had a successful solo career. Neil Rush later played with **Merrilee Rush** and The Turnabouts, and the remaining members were later in **International Brick**.

Compilation appearances include: *Hey Mrs. Jones* on *Bolo Bash* (LP); and *Tell Me The Truth* on *Highs In The Mid-Sixties, Vol. 14* (LP). (DR/MW)

Status Cymbal

45s:	Blang-Dang (Yesterday And Tomorrow)/ Taking My Time	(RCA 47-9344) 1967
	Having Fun Again/In The Morning	(RCA 47-9419) 1967
	With A Little Love/From My Swing	(RCA 47-9598) 1968

A breezy flower-pop group with male and female vocals and electric sitar. (SR)

Status Quo

45: They All Want Her Love/All My Trials (Grant 45-690) 1966

Unrelated to the world famous U.K. band, this act came from Phoenix, Arizona. The 'A' side to their 45, *They All Want Her Love*, with its slightly discordant guitar, can also be found on *Sixties Archive, Vol. 2* (CD) and *Texas Punk From The Sixties* (LP). (VJ)

George Stavis

Personnel:	TIM ACKERMAN	perc	A
	GEORGE STAVIS	5 string banjo	A

ALBUM: 1(A) LABYRINTHS (Vanguard VSD-6524) 1969 -

Stavis released this acoustic psychedelic album in 1969 with the support of the drummer from his previous group, **Federal Duck**. Subtitled "Occult Improvisational compositions for 5-string banjo and percussion", it offers five long tracks, *Winter Doldrums*, *Finland Station*, *Firelight*, *Cold Spring* plus a cover of *My Favorite Things*. (Coltrane is cited as a strong influence in the liner notes, along with Earl Scruggs and Ravi Shankar.)

Like the **Peter Walker** albums, where Vanguard was obviously tryig to find another **Sandy Bull**, this album does not always hit the mark. But other than the **Serpent Power** album, I don't know where else one can find psychedelic banjo excursions. For fans of **Sandy Bull**, **John Fahey**, **Peter Walker**, J.P. Pickens, etc. it is well worth the effort in tracking down a copy.

Stavis was later with a Santa Cruz, California band called Oganookie that released a live album in 1973. (SR/DMo)

Steel

Personnel incl: DUANE HITCHINGS keyb'ds, vcls A

ALBUM: 1 STEEL (Epic) 1971 SC

45: Never On A Monday/Rosie Lee (Epic 10753) 1971

A hard-rock quintet, with three black and two white musicians, they went totally unnoticed. Duane Hitchings went on to play with Cactus. (SR)

Steeplechase

Personnel:	DEAN	ld vcls, backing vcls, gtr	A
	JOEY	drms, perc, backing vcls	A
	BOBBY SPINELLA	keyb'ds, backing vcls	A
	TONY	12 string gtr, ld vcls, backing vcls, organ	A
	(PAUL FLEISCHER	horns	A)
	(KIM KING	gtr	A)
	(EDDIE KRAMER	piano, backing vcls	A)

ALBUM: 1(A) LADY BRIGHT (Polydor 24-4027) 1971 -

Produced by Eddie Kramer, a hard-edged rock outfit from New York, strongly influenced by Uriah Heep, with lots of guitar/keyboards interplay and good vocals. All their material was penned by the group members (Radicello, Spinella and Parrish) and some tracks are quite good, notably *Wrought Iron Man* and *Lady Bright*, this one with the guitar of Kim King (from **Lothar and The Hand People**) who also engineered the album.

Bob Spinella was previously in **The Critters**. (SR)

Steeple Peeple

45: Ol' Man River/Green Plant (B.T. Puppy BTP 534) 1967

Unfortunately the 'A' side is a dire pop version of that *Ol' Man River*. So stick to the 'B' side - *Green Plant* - yes, the same track later covered by the **Majic Ship**, as featured on *Psychedelic Unknowns, Vol. 5*, and coincidentally released on the same label (B.T. Puppy 548) in 1968. The version here is lighter but excellent cool fuzzed-pop. And there's more...

The identical fuzz-pop track turns up again behind soulful songstress Amanda Ambrose on B.T. Puppy 539. And there's an earlier version of it - a cool jazzy instrumental with melodious sax by Shenny "Goofy" Brown on B.T. Puppy 531. Four different and all pretty good versions. (MW)

THE STENCH BAND - Pray For The Fred LP.

Gene Steiker and Larry Chenges

ALBUM: 1 STRAYWINDS (Shayn-Alexus EU-413504) 1973 SC

Vocal recitations with fragile instrumentation (piano, violin, acoustic guitar and light percussion). For late night listening! (SR)

David Steinberg

ALBUM: 1 THE INCREDIBLE SHRINKING GOD (Uni 73013) 1971 SC

Housed in a colorful cover, a counterculture comedian "inspired" by the Bible, with tracks like *Onan And Jonah*, *Cain And Abel* and *Moses*. (SR)

The Stench Band

Personnel incl: CHUCK St. LUCAS A

ALBUM: 1(A) PRAY FOR THE FRED (1971-73) (Zero Street Records STENCH 002) 2000

NB: (1) limited to 300 signed and numbered copies.

EP: 1(A) PRAY FOR THE DEAD ( ) 1972

NB: (1) 7" EP limited to 300 copies, 200 in oversized PS and some with inserts.

The Stench Band played and recorded in Lincoln, Nebraska from 1971-1973 and released one 7" EP (*Pray For The Dead*) in 1972.

The retrospective album shows the band to have been heavily influenced by **Captain Beefheart** and **Zappa**, with several strange and experimental cuts augmenting the original EP tracks.

Stephen and The Farm Band

See: **The Farm Band**.

Leigh Stephens

Personnel:	ERIC ALBRONDA		A
	NICKY HOPKINS	keyb'ds	AB
	LEIGH STEPHENS	gtr, vcls	AB
	IAN STUART		A

LEIGH STEPHENS - Red Weather LP.

MICKY WALLER	drms		A B
KEVIN WESTLAKE	drms		A
BOB ANDREWS			B
TONY ASHTON	keyb'ds		B
GLEN CORNICK	bs		B
KIM GARDNER			B
DICK MORRISSEY	sax		B
PETE SEARS			B

ALBUMS: 1(A) RED WEATHER (Philips PHS 600-294) 1969 R1
2(B) AND A CAST OF THOUSANDS (Philips/Charisma CAS 1040) 1971 ?

NB: (1) also issued in the UK (Philips SBL 7897) R1. (1) has been counterfeited on vinyl and CD, later reissued in both formats (Akarma AK 059) 2000. (2) UK only issue. (2) reissued on vinyl and CD (Akarma AK 094) 2001.

Originally from San Francisco, **Leigh Stephens** had previously been in **Blue Cheer** and **Silver Metre**. He moved to England in 1969 and recorded two interesting albums, the first being the better of the two. *Red Weather* is a good mix of psychedelia and progressive rock with effects on the guitars and voices. The second is more traditional, with a cover of *Jumpin' Jack Flash* and too many female background vocals.

Stephens went on form **Pilot** with Waller and Bruce Stephens (ex-**Blue Cheer**), releasing two albums in 1972 and 1973. (SR)

Steppenwolf

Personnel:
(up to 1976)

MARS BONFIRE (DENNIS EDMONTON)	gtr, vcls		X
JERRY EDMONTON	drms, vcls		XABCDEFGH
JOHN KAY (JOACHIM KRAULEDAT)	vcls, gtr, hrmnca		XABCDEFGH
GOLDY McJOHN	keyb'ds, vcls		XABCDEF
NICK ST NICHOLAS	bs		X BC
MICHAEL MONARCH	gtr		AB
RUSHTON MOREVE (aka JOHN RUSSELL MORGAN)	bs		A
LARRY BYROM	gtr		CD
GEORGE BIONDO	bs, vcls		DEFGH
KENT HENRY	ld gtr		E
BOBBY COCHRAN	gtr, vcls		FGH
ANDY CHAPIN	keyb'ds, vcls		G
WAYNE COOK	keyb'ds		H

NB: Line-up 'X' is actually Sparrow, listed here as they were responsible for the *Early Steppenwolf* album. Line-up 'A' is the first **Steppenwolf** personnel formed July 1967.

STEPPENWOLF - Line-up 'A'.

HCP
ALBUMS: 1(A) STEPPENWOLF (ABC-Dunhill DS-50029) 1968 6 -
(up to 2(A) STEPPENWOLF THE SECOND
1976) (ABC-Dunhill DS-50037) 1968 3 -
3(B) AT YOUR BIRTHDAY PARTY (ABC-Dunhill DSX-50053) 1969 7 -
4(X) EARLY STEPPENWOLF (ABC-Dunhill DS-50060) 1969 29 -
5(C) MONSTER (ABC-Dunhill DS-50066) 1970 17 -
6(C) STEPPENWOLF LIVE (dbl) (ABC-Dunhill DSD-50075) 1970 7 -
7(D) STEPPENWOLF 7 (ABC-Dunhill DSX-50090) 1970 19 -
8(-) STEPPENWOLF GOLD (comp) (ABC-Dunhill DSX-50099) 1971 24 -
9(E) FOR LADIES ONLY (ABC-Dunhill DSX-50110) 1971 54 -
10(-) REST IN PEACE (comp) (ABC-Dunhill DSX-50124) 1972 62 -
11(F) SLOW FLUX (CBS-Mums PZ-33093) 1974 47 -
12(G) HOUR OF THE WOLF (CBS-Epic PE-33583) 1975 155 -
13(H) SKULLDUGGERY (CBS-Epic PE-34120) 1976 - -

NB: (1) first pressing does not mention "Born To Be Wild" on front cover. Also issued in mono (R1). Reissued circa 1970 in non-metallic sleeve. (2) stock mono edition thought to exist, but all known mono copies are promo (R2). (3) was issued in Southern California in a non-diecut gatefold sleeve at the request of the Walt Disney Corp. who didn't like the idea of Mickey Mouse figures surrounding a photo of **Steppenwolf** through the diecut hole! (R1). (4) was not **Steppenwolf**, but a May 1967 live concert by Sparrow. (6) original issues in gatefold sleeve have only the words "Steppenwolf Live" on front cover. (8) original pressing has poster attached to cover by perforation, designed to be torn off. Later marketed in standard gatefold sleeve. (9) was originally issued with an amazing photo insert. White label promo editions exist of all the ABC-Dunhill albums, the first two in both mono and stereo. In the UK and most of Europe, albums (1)-(5) were issued on Stateside and (6)-(10) on Probe. Many compilations of **Steppenwolf** material exist from all over the world. Probably the rarest and earliest is the Japanese *All About Steppenwolf* (Stateside HP-8565) 1968, containing only tracks from the first two albums and pressed on red vinyl. Three US compilations fit within the time-frame of this book: *16 Greatest Hits* (ABC-Dunhill DSX-50135) 1973 (No. 152), *Steppenwolf - The ABC Collection* (ABC AC-30008) 1976 (these both cover the 1968-71 period with rather sloppy liner notes) and *Reborn To Be Wild* (CBS-Epic PE-3482) 1976 which collects material from their CBS albums in an inexcusably bad sleeve; thankfully this is rare. All of the ABC-Dunhill albums have been issued on CD.

EP: 1(A) STEPPENWOLF THE SECOND (PS) (ABC-Dunhill DS-50037) 1968

NB: (1) mini-album with six tracks from the second album; also described as a "jukebox EP".

HCP
45s: α A Girl I Knew/The Ostrich (ABC-Dunhill D-4109) 1967 -
(up to Sookie, Sookie
1976) Take What You Need (ABC-Dunhill D-4123) 1968 -
Born To Be Wild/
Everybody's Next One (ABC-Dunhill D-4138) 1968 2
Magic Carpet Ride/Sookie, Sookie (ABC-Dunhill D-4160) 1968 3
Rock Me/Jupiter Child (ABC-Dunhill D-4182) 1969 10
Jupiter Child/She'll Be Better (ABC-Dunhill D-4182) 1969
It's Never Too Late/
Happy Birthday (ABC-Dunhill D-4192) 1969 51
Born To Be Wild/

	Magic Carpet Ride	(ABC-Dunhill D-1433)	1969	-
β	Born To Be Wild/The Pusher (PS)	(ABC-Dunhill D-1436)	1969	-
	Move Over/Power Play	(ABC-Dunhill D-4205)	1969	31
	Monster/Berry Rides Again	(ABC-Dunhill D-4221)	1969	39
χ	Hey, Lawdy Mama/Twisted	(ABC-Dunhill D-4234)	1970	35
	Screaming Night Hog/Spiritual Fantasy	(ABC-Dunhill D-4248)	1970	62
	Screaming Night Hog/Corina	(ABC-Dunhill D-4248)	1970	-
	Who Needs Ya/Earschplittenloudenboomer	(ABC-Dunhill D-4261)	1970	54
	Snowblind Friend/Hippo Stomp	(ABC-Dunhill D-4269)	1971	60
η	Ride With Me (mono)/(stereo)	(ABC-Dunhill D-4283)	1971	-
δ	Ride With Me/For Madmen Only	(ABC-Dunhill D-4283)	1971	-
ε	Ride With Me/Black Pit	(ABC-Dunhill D-4283)	1971	52
η	For Ladies Only (mono)/(stereo)	(ABC-Dunhill D-4292)	1971	-
	For Ladies Only/Sparkle Eyes	(ABC-Dunhill D-4292)	1971	64
η	Straight Shootin' Woman (mono)/(stereo)	(CBS-Mums ZS8-6031)	1974	-
φ	Straight Shootin' Woman/Justice Don't Be Slow (PS)	(CBS-Mums ZS8-6031)	1974	29
η	Get Into The Wind (mono)/(stereo)	(CBS-Mums ZS8-6034)	1974	-
	Get Into The Wind/Morning Blue	(CBS-Mums ZS8-6034)	1974	-
η	Smokey Factory Blues (mono)/(stereo)	(CBS-Mums ZS8-6036)	1974	-
	Smokey Factory Blues/A Fool's Fantasy	(CBS-Mums ZS8-6036)	1974	108
η	Caroline (Are You Ready For The Outlaw World) (mono)/(stereo)	(CBS-Mums ZS8-6040)	1975	-
	Caroline (Are You Ready For The Outlaw World)/Angeldrawers	(CBS-Mums ZS8-6040)	1975	-

NB: α was almost certainly promo-only and contains embryonic versions of two tracks re-recorded for the first album. These early versions are very different and quite psychedelic (with backwards guitar solo!). β issued in picture sleeve with amazing band photo (line-up 'B' - oops!) and banner: "As Featured In The Sound Track Of The Motion Picture Easy Rider". χ both sides are the versions appearing on the *Steppenwolf Live* double album but without the audience noise overdubbed, proving rather conclusively that the album was (at least partially) assembled from studio recordings, like most "live" albums from the era. ε was probably a replacement for δ, the 'A' side is an album track from *For Ladies Only*, but the 'B' side of δ is a studio freakout! Clocking in at 8'46" it's also one of the longest 45 sides extant. Obviously not intended for the album, the track is instrumental, composed mostly of feedback from the bass guitar and creepy organ sounds. Edmonton/Biondo/McJohn are credited as writers on the label and they must have been buzzed to come up with this! φ 'B' side is non-LP. Many of **Steppenwolf**'s US singles were issued in Europe and Japan with picture sleeves. η promo only.

Steppenwolf evolved out of the Canadian group Jack London and The Sparrows, who made an album in 1965 for Canadian Capitol. Jerry Edmonton, Dennis (Mars Bonfire) Edmonton, Nick St. Nicholas and Goldy McJohn all came from this band, which was a very hot property in Toronto in the mid-sixties. It was a mutual interest in blues music that led these four to join forces with the German-born John Kay, who was playing clubs as an acoustic solo act in Canada and the USA. Now known simply as The Sparrow, the Kay-led band recorded singles for Columbia which were later compiled on an album *John Kay and The Sparrow* (Columbia CS 9758) 1969 and more recently on CD *The Best Of John Kay And Sparrow: Tighten Up Your Wig* (Columbia Legacy CK 53044) 1993. The Sparrow spent most of their time in the 'States by 1966 - first in New York, and then California. They settled in Mill Valley, and played all the ballrooms in nearby San Francisco in May-June 1967. When money got tight, Dennis Edmonton and Nick St. Nicholas left the band and moved to Los Angeles, where St. Nicholas set up a new group, **T.I.M.E.** and Edmonton pursued a solo career as Mars Bonfire. John Kay, Jerry Edmonton and Goldy McJohn also made the move South, but set up their own new band, **Steppenwolf** (after the Herman Hesse novel) with local musicians Rushton Moreve and Michael Monarch (who was just seventeen!). They spent the next six months rehearsing material for their album, which was recorded in little more than one day in January 1968. (Their first Dunhill 45 certainly pre-dates the album sessions, but exactly when these rather psychedelic early tracks were recorded is unknown.)

The initial 45 release from the album, *Sookie, Sookie* didn't make much impression, but radio stations started playing *Born To Be Wild* from the album and when Dunhill issued it as a single, it spent the Summer of 1968 at the top of the charts.

Steppenwolf is an astoundingly good debut album. It will probably always be remembered for containing *Born To Be Wild*, but it was John Kay's original compositions that gave the record real depth and colour. *Desperation* (covered by Humble Pie on their debut album), reprised largely from *Chasin' Shadows* by The Sparrow but given new life by Kay's re-arrangement and new lyrics, *Take What You Need*, *Your Wall's Too High*, *Everybody's Next One* (a song about groupies, covered by Ambrose Slade), *A Girl I Knew* and *The Ostrich* are all quite amazing and make up the real meat of the album.

The Ostrich featured provocative lyrics concerning ecological and (especially) political matters, a subject Kay would focus much of his imagination on throughout his career.

"You're free to speak your mind, my friend
As long as you agree with me
Don't criticise the fatherland
Or those who shape your destiny
'Cause if you do
You'll lose your job, your mind,
And all the friends you knew
We'll send out all our boys in blue
They'll find a way to silence you."

The album shot up the charts (deservedly so), and **Steppenwolf** threw themselves into a frantic touring and recording itineray. While this may well have contributed to their considerable commercial success over the next few years, in retrospect it wasn't particularly healthy for the creative process. While *Steppenwolf The Second* had some fine tracks like *None Of*

STEPPENWOLF - Steppenwolf LP.

STEPPENWOLF - At Your Birthday Party LP.

STEPPENWOLF - Monster LP.

Your Doing and *Don't Step On The Grass, Sam* alongside the smash hit single *Magic Carpet Ride*, it also reflected a marked downturn in creative dynamics. *At Your Birthday Party* was even less focused, and hindsight being 20/20... it appears that the band was subsituting quantity for quality, which, to be fair, may have been necessary vis-a-vis the terms of their contract with ABC-Dunhill. All these records sold very well, however and their producer Gabriel Mekler did well enough on his own royalties to start his own label, Lizard Records (**Jamul**, **Frantic**).

The second half of 1969 saw the theatrical release of two youth-orientated motion pictures featuring the music of **Steppenwolf**; "Candy" (with *Rock Me*) and the mega-hit "Easy Rider" which prominently featured both *Born To Be Wild* and *The Pusher*. The original soundtrack album of "Easy Rider" reached Gold status, further solidifying **Steppenwolf**'s own stature as a commercial entity, and the band toured as headliners thereafter.

Monster represented a dramatic return to focus, and the new line-up with Larry Byrom (from **T.I.M.E.** and **The Hardtimes**) was the most efficient and poweful version of the band yet. The title track, which clocked in at over nine minutes on the album, traced America's evolution from colonisation through to the current conflict in Vietnam with the controversial view that the nation's political fabric had become corrupt and the public at large was helpless to bring about change. This being a more acute problem for the youth of the nation who were being indiscriminately sent to Asia to fight, the song's chorus was a plea to their elders for help:

"America, where are you now?
Don't you care about your sons and daughters?
Don't you know we need you now
We can't fight alone against the monster".
(From *Monster*)

The anti-war/anti-establishment theme courses through the album. *Draft Resister* is a real gem, probably the strongest track on the record. Quite amazing from both an instrumental and engineering perspective, it has an edgy energy carried largely by Jerry Edmonton's various brilliant percussion overdubs and evocative, sympathetic lyrics from Kay:

"Shame, disgrace and all dishonour
Wrongly placed upon their heads
Will not rob them of the courage
That betrays the innocent."

Byrom's guitar work is dark and searing throughout the album, particularly on *Power Play*, the intense *Move Over*, and the aforementioned *Draft Resister*. The cover art is pretty mindblowing; said to be the work of famed poster artist Rick Griffin but it is uncredited.

The band toured extensively to promote *Monster* and in mid-1970 Dunhill issued a hastily-assembled "Live" album that went top ten. This allowed the band more time to fine-tune material for their next album, perhaps the first time since their debut that they had been afforded that luxury. Correspondingly, *Steppenwolf 7* represented their creative zenith, and it

remains one of American music's most majestic landmarks. Here **Steppenwolf** revealed that they had developed an unparallelled command of the language of rock. Jerry Edmonton's drumming, in particular is spectacularly inventive and dynamic, and John Kay's voice never sounded more confident. Tracks like *Renegade* (Kay's autobiography of his escape from East Germany as a child, chillingly told with a stunning instrumental section in the middle) and *Foggy Mental Breakdown* (so influential in composition that scores of Italian progressive bands used it as a blueprint for years) made it clear that **Steppenwolf** was one of America's best.

Following a Summer tour to promote *7*, work was begun back in Los Angeles on both *For Ladies Only* and John Kay's first solo album. *For Ladies Only* was finished first, and although a bit less consistent than *7*, not surprisingly it contains some fine music. Goldy McJohn, whose keyboards were consistently mixed under the guitars on all the group's albums really takes a front seat here, especially on the title track where he plays a remarkable classically-influenced spotlight piece. The album really shines on Side Two, though - *The Night Time's For You*, *Sparkle Eyes*, *Ride With Me* and the creepy instrumental *Black Pit* are all on par with the best material the band produced. New guitarist Kent Henry (previously with L.A. bands **Genesis** and **Charity**; he also did session work with **Blues Image** and Screaming Lord Sutch, appearing on the *Heavy Friends* album) adds some fine lead fills although he lacks the amazing fluidity of Larry Byrom, who was now with a band called **Ratchell**.

Steppenwolf did not launch a tour to promote the new album, as Kay was still working on his solo project. Kay told the band that he had decided to pursue a solo career when his album was released in the Summer and in February 1972 they announced that their upcoming tour would be their last. Kay continued work on his album with Henry and George Biondo, while Jerry Edmonton and Goldy McJohn formed a band with Rod Prince and Roy Cox of **Demian** called Manbeast that was short-lived and apparently did not record.

Kay's first solo album, *Forgotten Songs And Unsung Heroes* (ABC-Dunhill 50120) was released in June and Kay toured to promote it as the opening act for **Steppenwolf** on their farewell tour. His album did reasonably well, based mostly on the appeal of a nearly **Steppenwolf**-sounding cover of Hank Snow's *I'm Movin' On*, but Dunhill also released a compilation of some of **Steppenwolf**'s best album tracks that eclipsed it. *Rest In Peace* is a dynamic collection, proving conclusively that the best material in the band's canon were *not* the hits! Kay followed this with *My Sportin' Life* (ABC-Dunhill 50147) in 1973 and even before it was released, a **Steppenwolf** reunion was in the works. (John Kay's solo records are very listenable, but it was to the confusion of the public at large that they came to exist. It seemed quite unthinkable then, as it does now, that a band as magnificent and successful as **Steppenwolf** would be sacrificed for Kay's pursuit of any other style of music, simply because his dark, gritty voice was so perfectly suited to the hard-rock medium.)

Free of their contract with ABC, the band was now recording on their own schedule at John Kay's studio (a commercial enterprise owned and operated by Kay for many years!) and their ninth album appeared in 1974.

STEPPENWOLF - 7 LP.

Slow Flux held the promise of an inexorable return to public consciousness; long-time fans of the band were drunk with joy at hearing Kay's trademark growl on *Gang War Blues* and the blistering lead guitar of new member Bobby Cochran (L.A. session veteran; he later worked with The Flying Burrito Brothers). *Slow Flux* also has a wonderful underlying humour, best evidenced in the politically-orientated material ("Sure must be fun to watch a President run - just ask the man who owns one!"). **Steppenwolf** toured and played live on television in support of *Slow Flux*, which sold well initially but didn't have much staying power. Their new label didn't throw much support behind the follow-ups *Hour Of The Wolf* or *Skullduggery*, but admittedly these final two albums by the band are less interesting by comparison. Not coincidentally, these albums from their CBS period are the hardest to locate now.

Kay released another solo album, *All In Good Time* (Mercury SRM-1-3715) 1978, before forming a new L.A.-based "Steppenwolf" to tour and record with in the eighties. This band has produced at least five albums, the first issued in the USA only as a promotional radio show called *Retro Rock* (Show RR-82-44) 1982. This was issued commercially in Australia under the title *Live In London*. Other albums include *Wolftracks* (1982), *Paradox* (1984), *Rock & Roll Rebels* (1987) and *Rise & Shine* (1990). The albums produced by this band were shown as by John Kay and Steppenwolf, a name change that, while subtle, was likely adopted in respect to the conspicuously absent Jerry Edmonton. Edmonton's drumming and Kay's vocals are the only consistents through the course of **Steppenwolf**'s eleven albums and clearly they share responsibility for much of the magic the band produced. Edmonton's incredibly musical and intuitive ensemble playing is without parallel in hard-rock; his ability to create and build tension using restraint and flawless technique gave the band's best music a mature and sinister feel which has not diminished with time. It's hard to imagine a band called **Steppenwolf** without him, as much as John Kay. Jerry Edmonton was killed in an automobile accident in November, 1993. He was preceded in death by original bassist Rushton Moreve (also a car accident) in July, 1981 and by keyboardist Andy Chapin, who died alongside singer Rick Nelson in a plane crash on the last day of 1985.

John Kay moved his center of operations to an estate in Tennessee in 1989. He hosts an annual "Wolf-fest" there where band alumni meet with fans and perform live.

Steppenwolf's original albums (1968-71) remain essential to collections of rock music from the era outlined in this book, and are not difficult to acquire. As stated earlier, exploring the original releases as opposed to the many 'hits' compilations available will reveal much of their most ambitious music. Many of these are housed in wonderful sleeves as well, often with elements of wry humour that permeated their music. **Steppenwolf** will be remembered as one of America's pre-eminent rock bands, and in particular, one that helped bring respectability to rock by making it a vehicle for intelligent thought and communication.

Compilation appearances have included: *Sookie, Sookie* on *Nuggets, Vol. 6* (LP); *Magic Carpet Ride* on *Nuggets, Vol. 9* (LP), *Psychedelic Perceptions* (CD), *Best Of '60s Psychedelic Rock* (CD) and *Wild Thing*, and *Screaming Night Hog* and *Hey Lawdy Mama* on *Undersound Uppersoul* (LP). (CF/VJ)

The Stepping Stones

Personnel incl:	JOHN DELMATIER	sax		A

45s:	Little Girl Of Mine/		
	I Only Want To Dance With You	(Diplomacy 15)	1964
	So Tough/Pills	(Diplomacy 21)	1965
	Walk On By /		
	My World Is Empty (Without You)	(Flair 200)	1968

These 45s were the work of a mid-sixties California outfit, thought to have come from Sacramento or San Jose. *I Only Want To Dance With You* can also be heard on *Sounds Of The Sixties San Francisco, Vol. 1* (LP). This was an enthusiastic popish garage effort with powerful drumming. The follow-up *So Tough* was an adequate cover of a Casuals' song. (MW)

Stepson

Personnel:	LEN FAGAN	drms	A
	(DON GALLUCCI	piano	A)
	(JIMMY GREENSPOON	organ	A)
	BRUCE HAUSER	bs, vcls	A
	JEFF HAWKS	ld vcls	A
	JOEY NEWMAN	gtr, vcls	A
	(JEFF SIMMONS	harp	A)

ALBUM:	1(A)	STEPSON	(ABC ABCX-826) 1974 SC

An excellent hard-blues album, with Jeff Simmons on one track. Most of the songs were written by the group and the vocals and guitar parts are especially interesting (*Rude Attitude, I Apologize, Burnin' Hurt*). Arthur Lee of **Love** and Chris Hillman of **The Byrds** get "special thanks" on the cover.

Hawks, Newman and Gallucci had all previously been in **Don and the Goodtimes** and later with Hauser in **Touch**.

Compilation appearances include *It's My Life* on *Songs Of Faith And Inspiration* (CDR & CD). (SR)

Stereo Shoestring

Personnel:	JAMES COCO	vcls	A
	JIM HOWARD	ld gtr	A
	RICHARD LALOR	gtr	A
	JAMES NOE	bs	A
	STEVE SCHULTZ	drms	A

45:	Tell Her No/On The Road South	(English 1302) 1968

A superb psychedelic outfit from Corpus Christi, Texas who were sadly only together from early to late 1968. The 'A' side of their sole 45 is a Zombies cover, whilst the flip is a superb psychedelic punker, being an adaptation of The Pretty Thing's *Defecting Grey*.

The band were introduced to the Pretties' track by Ashley Johnson, who had earlier played with Lalor in **Clockwork Orange**. In late '68, minus Lalor, the band became **The Red House**.

Compilation appearances have included: *On The Road South* on *We Have Come For Your Children*, *Acid Dreams - The Complete 3 LP Set* (3-LP), *Acid Dreams Testament* (LP), *Austin Landing, Vol. 2* (LP), *Acid Dreams, Vol. 1* (LP), *Texas Flashbacks, Vol. 3* (LP & CD), *Best of Pebbles, Vol. 2* (LP & CD), *Flashback, Vol. 3* (LP), *Garagelands Vol. 2* (CD) and *Highs In The Mid Sixties, Vol. 12* (LP). (VJ)

ST4

45:	Trouble / Do It	(Perception) 1969

On **Jimmy Curtiss**' label, an early hard-rock single. (SR)

The Sticks and Stones

45:	Try/Live To Be Free	(Coral 62524) 1967

Produced by James Crane and Paul Leka, this 45 is good, fairly powerful pop with good guitar and a driving beat. The band locale is unknown, but Paul Leka was later involved in the Bubble-Gum movement. (BM/MW)

The Stillroven

Personnel:	PHIL BERDAHL	drms	ABCDE
	DAVE DEAN	keyb'ds	ABCDE
	JOHN HOWARTH	ld gtr	ABCD
	DAN KANE	gtr	A
	ROCK PETERSON	bs	A
	DAVE BERGET	bs	B DE
	JIM LARKIN	gtr	B
	MIKE FLAHERTY	bs	C
	MIKE O'GARA	gtr	CDE
	DAVE RIVKIN	ld gtr	E

ALBUM:	1(-)	CAST THY BURDEN UPON...	(Sundazed 5020) 1996

NB: (1) colour vinyl retrospective which contains all of their singles plus many previously unreleased tracks. Also released on CD (SC 11029) 1996 with extra tracks.

45s:	She's My Woman/		
	(I'm Not Your) Steppin' Stone (promo)	(Falcon 6-7296)	1966
	Hey Joe/Sunny Day	(Falcon 69)	1967
	Hey Joe/Sunny Day	(Roulette 4748)	1967
	Little Picture Playhouse/		
	Cast Thy Burden Upon The Stone	(August 101)	1968
α	Come In The Morning/Necessary Person	(August 102)	1968
	Have You Ever Seen Me?/Necessary Person	(August 102)	1968

NB: α withdrawn.

Formed in 1965 as The Syndicate in the Minneapolis suburb of Robbinsdale, Minnesota, they changed their name to **The Stillroven** in early 1966 when rhythm guitarist Dan Kane replaced Mark Moorhead from The Syndicate's earlier line-up.

The Falcon promo, *She's My Woman/(I'm Not Your) Steppin' Stone*, only had a limited pressing of 50 copies and like many of their singles is very sought-after. The superb *Little Picture Playhouse/Cast Thy Burden Upon The Stone* 45 features pure Anglophile pop on the 'A' side with its quaint theatrical metaphors and piano-based arrangement. The track was originally recorded by U.K. outfit Simon Dupree and The Big Sound and together with the flip, where John Howarth's electric sitar playing adds that hallucinogenic flavour, is arguably their creative zenith.

Following this 45, their manager Peter May moved to Tucson, Arizona, although he still continued his manager / producer role from a distance. More damaging was the departure of talented vocalist Phil Larkin and Dave Berget (although he later rejoined the band). In June 1968, they cut a fourth single, *Come In The Morning/Necessary Person*. The 'A' side was a **Moby Grape** cover, but May decided shortly after its release to pull the 'A' side and replace it with a more convincing rendition of The Small Faces' *Tell Me Have You Ever Seen Me*. By now Dave Berget had rejoined to provide the lead vocal on the song. Only 100 copies of *Come In The Morning* are thought to have left the factory, making it another highly collectable 45. The flip of both versions of this 45 was a pleasant Mike O'Gara original.

The *Cast Thy Burden Upon The Stillroven* retrospective features:- *And My Baby's Gone*, an obscure early Moody Blues track; *Have You Got A Penny*, a nice pop number; *Cheating*, a raw Animals' cover; *Little Games*, a failed 1967 Yardbirds' single and concludes with a slice of improvised psychedelia aptly named *Freakout*.

They also provided a track (*Hey Joe*) on *Money Music*Money Music (August 100), a rare 1967 compilation which itself had a limited pressing. In late 1968, they recorded an entire album for A&M Records which was never released... Sundazed have also promised to unearth that too!

The Stillroven have also been readily compiled. Their version of *Hey Joe*, which features superb guitar work by John Howarth and is reckoned to be one of the best, has resurfaced along with *Cast Thy Burden Upon The Stone* on *Garage Music For Psych Heads, Vol. 1*; their excellent cover of the Small Faces' *Have You Ever Seen Me?* can be heard on *Changes* (LP), and *(I'm Not Your) Steppin' Stone* re-emerged on *Root '66* (LP). Two of their finest moments, *Hey Joe* and *Sunny Day* are also compiled on *Psychedelic Microdots Of The Sixties, Vol. 3* (CD). (VJ/MW)

The Stingrays

Personnel:	JOHN PAULSON	sax	A
	DAVE SPITTELL	gtr	AB
	JOHN SPITTELL	bs, vcls	AB
	BOB THOMPSON	drms	A
	JIM McBEAN	bs, vcls	B
	TOM PAULSON	gtr	B
	BRIAN PETERS	gtr, bs	B
	GENE PETERS	gtr, vcls	B

45:	The Cat Came Back/Shaggy Dog	(Welhaven 8852) 1967

This 45 was the work of a band from Rochester in South-East Minnesota. They underwent further line-up changes in their final months but fell apart

THE STILLROVEN - Cast Thy Burden Upon LP.

in 1968. Gene Peters went on to play in several bands including Therica (1969-71), Willow Lane (1975-79), Fools Gold (1982-84), and DC5 (1987 onwards).

Compilation appearances include: *Shaggy Dog* and *The Cat Came Back* on *Root '66* (LP); and *Shaggy Dog* on *Teenage Shutdown, Vol. 8* (LP & CD). (VJ)

Sting-Rays of Newburgh

Personnel:	TONY DeVILLEO	ld gtr	A
	OCTAVOUS GRAHAM	vcls	A
	STEVE KINSLER	gtr	A
	RONNIE MOSKAWITZ	drms	A
	BRUCE SHAPIRO	bs	A

45s:	If I Needed Someone/Fool	(Columbia 4-44085) 1967
	(What Did I Do To Be So) Black And Blue/	
	Friday's Gone	(Columbia 4-44235) 1967

From Newburgh, New York. *If I Needed Someone* is a good Searchers-style Beatles cover but rather out-of-time by '67. The flip likewise, but it's a good garage popper with ringing guitar and a tough edge. The second 45 is very disappointing and mellower pop fodder and with brassy intrusions.

The Sting-Rays of Newburgh also did the music for a "Lifesavers Sours" commercial and Bruce Shapiro's mother would later become Mayor of the City of Newburgh!

Compilation appearances include *Fool* on *Fuzz, Flaykes, And Shakes, Vol. 3* (LP & CD). (MW/KMn)

Stix and Stones

45s:	Rouge Plant Blues/	
	Rouge Plant Instrumental (PS)	(Bump Shop 131) 1970
	Rouge Plant Blues/	
	Rouge Plant Instrumental	(Capitol 3865) 1974

A Detroit, Michigan band whose 45 was picked up Capitol for nationwide release. You'll also find *Rouge Plant Blues* on *Michigan Rocks, Vol. 2*. (MW)

Stix and Stones

45:	Sometimes Good Guys Don't Wear White / ?	(Impex 1225) 196?

A rare 45 from the Philadelphia area, covering **The Standells**' classic. (MW)

Stix & Stonz

Personnel incl: L.SHARP   A

45s:	Bad News / Gator Tails And Monkey Ribs	(Pat 100/1) 196?
	The World / I Can't Quit	(Pat 101/2) 196?

According to *Psychedelic Crown Jewels, Vol. 2* (Dble LP & CD), which highlights their classy put-down punker *Bad News*, this obscure Miami-area outfit recorded the first two 45s above before disbanding. It's uncertain that the latter was actually released.

Their name was subsequently adopted up by Rose and Rhodes, of Miami's **Sounds Unlimited**, who recorded a further (unconnected) 45 as **Stix and Stonz**. (MW/RM/JLh)

Stix & Stonz

Personnel incl: RANDY RHODES
PAUL ROSE

45:	A Love That's Real / Take A Bus	(Columbia 4-45029) 1969

Previously known as **Sounds Unlimited**, they nicked the **Stix and Stonz** moniker following the breakup of the otherwise unconnected **Stix and Stonz**. (JLh/MW)

Val Stoecklein

ALBUM:	1	GREY LIFE	(Dot DLP 25904) 1968

45s:	Sounds Of Yesterday/Say It's Not Over	(Dot 17200) 1968
	All The Way Home/	
	I Wonder Who I'll Be Tomorrow	(Dot 17234) 1969

Originating from Kansas, **Val Stoecklein** (or Stecklein) began with **The Bluethings** and, after that group disbanded, suffered from depression after the end of a love affair. He worked the Oklahoma oil fields, became a cowboy in Wyoming and finally recontacted Ray Ruff, a Texas producer who was now working in Los Angeles. **Stoecklein** moved to California and recorded his solo album. *Grey Life*, is a very sad folk album with self-penned songs about his lost love. Still working with Ray Ruff, **Stoecklein** would later form **Ecology** and record with **Truth Of Truths**.

Sadly, **Val Stoecklein** died in May 1993. (MW/SR)

The Stoics

Personnel:	AL ACOSTA	vcls	A
	SAM ALLEN	drms	A
	BILL ASH	ld gtr	A
	MIKE MARECHAL	bs	A
	ROY QUILLIAN	gtr	A

45:	Enough Of What I Need/Hate	(Brams 101) 1967

This band came out of San Antonio, Texas and just 150 copies of this garage gem were pressed on their own label. A popular local live attraction, they formed in the Spring of 1965 but split by February 1967. Quillian and Ash had wanted to play Kinks songs but the rest wanted instead to reproduce a Rolling Stones sound. Bill Ash went on to play briefly with **The Mind's Eye** although he didn't play on their 45. Curiously, **The Mind's Eye** became **The Children**, who also recorded a version of **The Stoics** *Enough Of What I Need*.

Compilation appearances include: *Enough Of What I Need* and *Hate* on *Mindrocker, Vol. 4* (LP), *Acid Visions - The Complete Collection Vol. 1* (3-CD) and *Acid Visions* (LP); *Enough Of What I Need* on *Pebbles, Vol. 1 (ESD)* (CD); and *Hate* on *Trash Box* (5-CD), *Teenage Shutdown, Vol. 10* (LP & CD) and *Best of Pebbles, Vol. 2* (LP & CD). (VJ)

Simon Stokes and The Nighthawks

Personnel:	RANDALL KEITH	gtr	AB
	ROBERT LEDGER	bs	AB
	DON "BUTCH" SENNEVILLE	gtr	ABC
	SIMON STOKES	vcls	ABCD
	JOE YULE Jr	drms	AB
	HARRY GARFIELD	keyb'ds	C
	BILLY GOODNICK	drms	C
	JOHN LOCKE	keyb'ds	C
	KATHI MCDONALD	vcls	C
	CHRISTIAN PENNICK	gtr	C
	NATHAN PINO	keyb'ds	C
	MARTY TRYON	bs	C

ALBUMS:	1(A)	SIMON STOKES AND THE NIGHTHAWKS	(MGM SE-4677) 1970 SC
	2(A)	OUTLAW RIDERS (soundtrack)	(MGM I SE-26 ST) 1971 SC
	3(B)	THE INCREDIBLE SIMON STOKES AND THE BLACKWHIP THRILL BAND	(Spindizzy KZ32075) 1973 -
	4(D)	THE BUZZARD OF LOVE	(UA UA-LA769-G) 1977 -

45s:	α	Truth Is Stronger Than Fiction / Big City Blues	(HBR 487) 1966
	β	Infiltrate Your Mind / Won't Come Down	(Rally 66506/7) 1967
		Cobwebs / ?	(In-Sound 406) c1968
		Voodoo Woman pt. 1/ Voodoo Woman pt. 2	(Elektra 45670) 1969
	χ	Southern Girl/Rhode Island Red	(MGM 14115) 1970
		Big City Blues / Jambalaya	(MGM 14135) 1970
		Ballad Of Little Fauss And Big Halsy / Where Are You Going	(MGM 14189) 1970

NB: α as by Simon T.Stokes, β by **Perpetual Motion Workshop**. There was also a French 45 with picture sleeve *Voodoo Woman/Can't Stop Now* (Elektra INT 80218) 1970, also released in Holland (Elektra EKS 45670). χ was from the first album.

Produced by Michael Lloyd (**WCPAEB**, **Smoke**...), designed by Cal Schenkel (**Zappa**) and dedicated to Jack Kerouac, **Simon Stokes**' first album is an excellent psychedelic blues album similar to **Captain Beefheart**. *Big City Blues*, *Voodoo Woman*, *Ride On Angel* and *Which Way* are fast blues-rock numbers with the growling voice of **Stokes** and the inventive guitar of Butch Senneville (ex-**Quatrain**). Almost all of the songs were composed by **Stokes** and Randall Keith and five tracks also appeared on the soundtrack of "Outlaw Riders", a bikers movie.

In 1973, **Stokes** was back with Senneville for a new album *The Incredible Simon Stokes And The Blackwhip Thrill Band* produced by David Briggs. Its sleeve designed by Pacific Eye and Ear shows mad monks whipping girls and S&M scenes. Weird! The songs have strange lyrics too (*The Boa Constrictor Ate My Wife Last Night*, *The Wolf Pack Rides The Night*, *The Devil Just Called My Name* and *She's Got The Voodoo*) and there's a new version of *Ride On Angel*. John Locke of **Spirit** plays keyboards on this album.

The fourth album contains a new version of *Big City Blues* but is not as interesting, being orientated more toward mainstream rock. This album is generally thought to be his last one, but, in 1996, Simon Stokes came back with no other than **Timothy Leary** to release as Leary and Stokes, *Right To Fly* (Psychorelic Records), a CD with twelve new songs co-written with Randall Keith. This year saw also the release on Baloney Shrapnel Records of *Ride On* by Conqueror Worm, a group formed by members of various US alternative groups (Rancid Vat, Poison Idea, Alcoholics Unanimous). They covered twelve of **Stokes**' songs, including *Big City Blues*, *Hot Summer Nights*, *Wolfpack Rides The Night* and *Voodoo Woman*.

Prior to forming the Nighthawks, **Stokes** released some solo 45s and was in **Perpetual Motion Workshop**, who released one sought-after 45. Robert Ledger was previously in **Armageddon** and Harry Garfield had been in Gary Lewis and The Playboys. (SR/MW/VJ/HM)

The Stolen Children

Personnel:	LARRY ANDREWS	gtr	AB
	DARRIS KNOWLES	ld gtr	AB
	TOM LEDFORD	keyb'ds	AB

	RONNIE YARBOROUGH	drms	AB
	?? ??	bs	A
	RANDY WIGGINS	bs	B

| 45s: | Set Me Free / I'm Alive | (Tomahawk 1002) 1967 |
| | I Need You / Never Be Right | (Tomahawk 113) 1967 |

From the town of Valley, Alabama, on the border with Georgia, this quintet released two 45s in 1967 on the Tomahawk label based in Columbus, Georgia. Managers Shawn Murphy and Bruce Andrews thought up the band's name and secured gigs for them in the area. They opened for the likes of **The Box Tops**, **Tommy James and The Shondels** and Billy Joe Royal.

I Need You is bright-eyed Beatlesque pop, 1964-5 vintage. It was written by replacement bassist Wiggins (who was several years younger than the other members) and can be found on *Psychedelic States: Alabama Vol. 1* (CD). (MW/RM)

The Stompers

| 45s: | I Know/Hey Baby | (Studio City SC 1028) 1965 |
| | I Still Love You/You're Gone | (Stomp 5477) 1965 |

A garage rock quintet from Mount Vernon, Iowa. You'll also find *Know* on the *Root '66* (LP) and *Teenage Shutdown, Vol. 11* (LP & CD). (VJ)

Sly Stone and The Family Stone

See **Sly and The Family Stone**

Stone Canyon Rock Group

| ALBUM: | 1 | MacARTHUR PARK | (Custom ?) 1970 - |

Another example of these exploito albums. No credits but some good guitars. (SR)

Stone Circus

Personnel:	MIKE BURUS	drms	A
	JONATHAN CAINE	keyb'ds	A
	SONNY HAINES	ld gtr	A
	DAVID KEELER	bs	A
	RONNIE PAGE	vcls	A

| ALBUM: | 1(A) | THE STONE CIRCUS | (Mainstream S/6119) 1969 R1 |

NB: (1) pirated on CD 1998.

STONE CIRCUS - Stone Circus LP.

| 45: | Mister Grey/? | (Mainstream 694) 1969 |

Thought to have been Californian, this band was responsible for one of the rarer and stranger Mainstream releases, which incorporates many diverse influences. Sometimes it doesn't always gel but it certainly makes interesting listening. All the cuts are originals, written either by Jonathan Caine or a guy called Murphy, who presumably had some connection with the band, since some tracks are co-written by Caine and Murphy. The material is wide-ranging from the accessible psych-pop of *Sara Wells*, laid-back, melodic opening cut *What Went Wrong* and uptempo *Inside-Out Man* to the highly experimental *People I Once Knew*, which starts with spoken lyrics over melodic piano and later descends into lots of fuzz and organ work. The *Mister Grey* 45, which is also on the album, is interesting too. Recommended for fans of psychedelia and/or progressive rock but not for garage purists.

Jonathan Cain was later a member of Journey. (VJ)

Stone Country

Personnel:	DANN BARRY	bs, vcls	A
	DON BECK	12 string gtr, banjo	A
	DOUG BROOKS	gtr	A
	DENNIS CONWAY	perc	A
	RICHARD LOCKMILLER	gtr	A
	STEVE YOUNG	ld gtr	A

| ALBUM: | 1(A) | STONE COUNTRY | (RCA LSP-3958) 1968 SC |

NB: (1) also issued in mono (LPM 3958).

45s:	Life Stands Daring Me/	
	Time Isn't There (Anymore)	(RCA 47 9301) 1967
	Ballad Of Bonnie & Clyde (Pt. 1)/(Pt. 2)	(RCA 47 9397) 1967
	Love Psalm/Magnolias	(RCA 47 9472) 1968
	Wheels On Fire/Million Dollar Bash	(RCA 47 9534) 1968

A truly excellent, but difficult to categorise, psychedelic album, at times country-oriented with strong lead vocal and beautiful harmonies and at times similar to some tracks by **Ars Nova** or **Kaleidoscope**. Produced by Rick Jarrard (**Loading Zone**, **Jefferson Airplane**, Harry Nilsson), it was recorded in Hollywood and is worth searching for.

In her 1969 rock encyclopedia, Lilian Roxon mentioned that "they played a combination of rock, folk, country-rock, pop, country that just covers everything and even has its own name: mod country". A gifted singer and songwriter, Steve Young shortly afterwards went solo and recorded a long series of critically acclaimed albums in the country-rock style, his most well known song being *Seven Bridges Road*. Don Beck went on to join Dillard and Clark, whilst Denny Conway became a session man.

The 'B' side to their first 45, and both sides of their last 45 were non-album cuts.

Compilation appearances include *Wheels On Fire* on *Mindrocker, Vol. 9* (LP). (SR/LG)

Stoned Circus

| ALBUM: | 1 | STONED CIRCUS | (Rockadelic RRLP 12.5) 1994 |

A fine hippie quintet with male-female vocals in the **Jefferson Airplane** mould. They recorded their only album, on 4th September 1970 at Cavern Sound Studios, Missouri and were originally from Independence (Harry Truman's birthplace). This is the same studio where **The Wizards From Kansas** and **Burlington Express** laid down their first tracks. The album, which remained unissued until 1994, contains an excellent cover version of the traditional *Babe I'm Gonna Leave You*. (VJ/GG)

Stone Garden

Personnel:	DAN MERRELL	bs, vcls	ABC
	GARY SPEER	gtr, ld vcls	AB D
	NEAL SPEER	drms	ABCD
	PAUL SPEER	ld gtr	ABCD

	JOHN PURVIANCE	sax, hrmnca	B
	RUSS PRATT	organ, ld vcls	C
	JOHN HELTON	bs	D
	DAVID LEE	elec. piano	D

ALBUM: 1(A-D) STONE GARDEN (Rockadelic RRLP 29) 1998

NB: (1) reissued on CD (Gear Fab GF 188) 2002.

45: Oceans Inside Me / Stop My Thinking (Angelus WR 4819) 1969

NB: just 300 copies were pressed.

The Rockadelic album comprises studio and live recordings by this Idaho band from 1969 through 1971 and comes in a gatefold sleeve with numerous photos plus an insert where Paul Speer tells their story ....

Lewiston, Idaho, was home to the Speer brothers and they started pre-teen groups in the early sixties, first as the Three Dimensions and later the Knights Of Sound. Renamed **Stone Garden** in 1967, they were influenced by the Doors, **Hendrix**, Cream, Beatles and Creedence Clearwater Revival.

In 1969, local support led to their first recording forays resulting in their now-rare 45 and several unreleased tracks recorded by Rick Keefer at Ripcord Studios in Vancouver, Washington. All are aired on the album, which consists predominantly of heavy acid-rock with Cream influences to the fore.

Graduations would force line-up changes and the band relocated to Seattle in 1971, only to break up a year later.

Oceans Inside Me was earlier compiled on *Filling The Gap* (4-LP). (MW)

Stoneground

Personnel:	TIM BARNES	gtr, vcls	ABC
(up to	LUTHER BILDT	vcls, gtr	A
1972)	JOHN BLAKELY	gtr, bs	ABC
	MICHAEL MAU	drms	AB
	MARIO CIPOLLINA	keyb'ds, bs	B
	ALAN FITZGERALD	bs	B
	LYNNE HUGHES	vcls	BC
	DIEDRE LAPORTE	vcls	BC
	LYDIA PHILLIPS	vcls	BC
	ANNIE SAMPSON	vcls	BC
	PETE SEARS	keyb'ds, bs	B
	SAL VALENTINO	perc, gtr, vcls	BC
	BRIAN GODULA	bs	C
	CORY LEROIS	keyb'ds	C
	STEVE PRICE	drms	C

ALBUMS:	1(A)	STONEGROUND	(Warner Bros. WS 1895) 1971 -
(up to	2(B)	FAMILY ALBUM (dbl)	(Warner Bros. WS 1956) 1971 -
1972)	3(C)	STONEGROUND THREE	(Warner Bros. BS 2645) 1972 -

45s:	Queen Sweet Dreams /	
(up to	Total Destruction	(Warner Bros. 7452) 1971
1972)	Looking For You /	
	Added Attraction (Come And See Me)	(Warner Bros. 7496) 1971
	You Must Be One Of Us /	
	Corrina, Corrina	(Warner Bros. 7535) 1972
	Passion Flower / Super Clown	(Warner Bros. 7546) 1972

Prior to their first album this band recorded an album that was never issued. Warner Bros reputedly have the tapes. They became the touring band for Warner Bros. Medicine Ball Caravan, a multi-circus group which toured Canada and the USA and journeyed to London between the Summer of 1970 and February 1971. During this time they produced demos for Columbia, which later emerged in Italy on Blue Velvet records. Reputedly pretty good despite their marginal sound quality, they include several tracks not included on later albums. For reasons better known to them the label called the album *Stoneground-On Stage* (Blue Velvet FCP 001), although none of the tracks are live.

After their tour they settled in their native San Francisco, where they rapidly established a reputation as a fine live band. Their debut album was notable for fine guitar work by Barnes and used several vocalists to good effect. The follow-up was a double album consisting of one studio side and three live sides from a San Francisco radio FM broadcast. After one further album with the full size band internal friction led to the departure of all of the original members except Barnes and Sampson. They too, split for a while, but Barnes returned in 1973 with a new line-up.

The band were also featured in the soundtrack to the Peter Cushing film 'Dracula A.D. 1972'. They can be seen performing *Alligator Man* in a party-scene at the beginning of the movie.

An historically important band in the tapestry of West Coast rock (for example, **Sal Valentino** had earlier been with **Beau Brummels** and later formed Valentino which included Blakely and Phillips; Lydia Phillips had earlier played with **Indian Puddin' And Pipe**; Pete Sears joined from **Silver Metre** and later played with **Copperhead** and Jefferson Starship, and Price, Godula and Lerois were all previously in Together). The band were also featured on the closing days of the Fillmore album. They were still recording albums, too, in the early eighties.

Very much a hippie outfit, they may be of interest to readers. (VJ/MW/CGo)

Stone Harbour

| Personnel: | RIC BALLAS | gtr, keyb'ds, perc, vcls | A |
| | DAVE McCARTY | vcls, drms, perc | A |

ALBUM: 1(A) EMERGES (No label) 1974

NB: (1) counterfeited on vinyl in 1991 and later on CD. Also of interest is *Re-Emerges* (Void 20) 2001, an album containing re-recorded and new material.

A mysterious duo from Youngstown, Ohio produced this sole album. Despite the ridiculous prices that the original fetches along with a plethora of superlatives from dealers eager for "mega-bucks", this is one album that justifies the hype. A mixed-bag of seventies "psych" to be sure, but it's a wonderfully atmospheric album that veers from folk-acoustics through acid and heavy rock and everywhere in between with fluid acidic and often over-the-top manic guitar.

Compilation coverage has so far included: *Rock & Roll Puzzle* and *Thanitos* on *Kicks & Chicks - Original 1960s Acid Punk* (LP) and *R & R Puzzle* on *Reverberation IV* (CD). (MW)

Stone Henge

A group from Fairfield, California, who evolved out of the **Donnybrookes** and later changed their name to the **Maze**, releasing the heavy-psych album *Armageddon*. Sundazed's CD reissue of the album (Sundazed SC 6060) 1995 includes two previously unreleased **Stone Henge** tracks - *Right Time* and *Rumors*. (MW/AP)

STONE GARDEN - Stone Garden LP.

Stonehenge

45:	(For The Love Of A) Sweet Woman Like You/		
	Big Wheel	(Renegade R-1204)	c1970

An unknown heavy rock group with fuzz guitar, bluesy organ and grumbling vocals on the 'A' side. The flip is comparativly disappointing. (SR)

The Stonemen

45:	No More/Where Did Our Love Go	(Big Topper 107)	196?

A significant 45 by a Fall River, Massachusetts band. The 'A' side, a moody garage ballad, has resurfaced on *New England Teen Scene, Vol. 3* (LP) and the *No No No* compilation CD. (MW/ELn)

Stonepillow

ALBUM:	1	ELEAZAR'S CIRCUS	
		(London Phase4 #SP-44123)	1969 -

NB: (1) also released in England (Phase 4 Stereo PFS 4163) 1969 SC.

An obscure album, which was the work of Lor Crane and Jay Zimmet. The lyrics occasionally suggest psychedelic undertones but the music is very poppy and the album is not recommended although it is pleasant enough on the ear. It has a sort of poor man's **Mamas and The Papas / Association** pop feel about it. Their album was also released in the U.K. on the Decca subsidiary, Phase 4, and the band are thought to have been based in the U.K..

Stone Poneys

Personnel:	KEN EDWARDS	gtr, vcls	A
	BOB KIMMEL	gtr, vcls	A
	LINDA RONSTADT	vcls, finger cymbals	A
	(JAMES E. BOND	bs	A)
	(PETE CHILD	gtr	A)
	(CYRUS FARYAR	bouzouki, gtr	A)
	(JOHN T.FORSHA	gtr	A)
	(BILLY MUNDI	drms	A)

					HCP
ALBUMS:	1(A)	THE STONE PONEYS	(Capitol ST-2666)	1967	- -
	2(A)	EVERGREEN Vol 2	(Capitol ST-2763)	1968	100 -
	3(-)	STONE PONEYS AND FRIENDS			
			(Capitol ST-2863)	1968	- SC
	4(A)	THE STONE PONEYS FTG RONSTADT			
			(Capitol ST-11383)	1974	172 -

NB: (4) is a reissue of (1) with a new sleeve. There's also a compilation *Stoney End* (Pickwick SPC 3298) 1972.

				HCP
45s:	So Fine /			
	Everybody Has Their Own Ideas	(Sidewalk 937)	1966	-
	Sweet Summer Blue And Gold/			
	All The Beautiful Things	(Capitol 5838)	1967	-
	Evergreen/One For All	(Capitol 5910)	1967	-
	Different Drum/I've Got To Know	(Capitol 2004)	1967	13
	Up To My Neck In High Muddy/			
	Carnival Bear	(Capitol 2110)	1968	93
	Some Of Shelley's Blues/			
	Hobo (Morning Glory)	(Capitol 2195)	1968	-

An interesting California folk-rock outfit. Originally a duo of Linda Rondstadt and Bob Kimmel known as The Kimmel Brothers, they soon adopted the **Stone Poneys** moniker and recruited Ken Edwards. Both Ken and Bob were already respected songwriters and studio musicians.

Their first album was produced by Nick Venet (**Mad River**, **Leaves**, **Euphoria**) and is really good. The material is strong (*Wild About My Lovin'*, *Train And The River*, *Sweet Summer Blue And Gold*) and the music and vocals extremely consistent. All the songs were written by Edwards and Kimmel, except for Tom Campbell's *2.10 Train* and *Orion*, and *Little Bit Of Rain* by **Fred Neil**. It is worth noting that all the backing musicians and Venet also worked with **Fred Neil** on his two albums recorded in 1967.

After two other albums, the trio disbanded although *Stone Poneys And Friends* was basically the original group in the studio with session players. When *Different Drum* became a hit, Linda went on the road with Bobby Kimmel (gtr), **Shep Cooke** (bs) and other sidemen. By that time, the group was defunct but Ronstadt needed the money and to support the single, they played a four-month tour as 'Linda Ronstadt and the Stone Poneys'.

This group was dropped as soon as the tour finished and by November 1968 the **Stone Poneys**, were John Forsha (gtr), John Ware (drms), John Keski (bs), Herb Steiner (steel gtr) and Bill Martin (piano). Herb Steiner recalls: "In 1968, Linda Ronstadt hired me for the **Stone Poneys** band as a dobroist/mandolinist. When she found out I could play a little steel guitar (mostly non-pedal), she encouraged me. Michael Nesmith was a friendly acquaintance of mine, and graciously loaned me a steel guitar until I could purchase one of my own. In the year I played with her we had several band incarnations, but the one that toured most was myself on steel, John Forsha on guitar, John London on bass, Johnny Ware on drums and Bill Martin on piano. My first gig after the **Stone Poneys**' was to move to Connecticut and join the **Wildweeds**, whose band leader, Al Anderson, went on to the **NRBQ**."

Kenny Edwards went on to the Los Angeles band Bryndle alongside Peter Bernstein, Wendy Waldman, Andrew Gold and Karla Bonoff. They played their first show at McCabe's in Santa Monica in 1969 and in 1970 recorded what should have been their debut album for A&M Records with newcomer producer Chuck Plotkin. Only a single, *Woke Up This Morning*, was ever released and was a regional hit in Northern California before disappearing. Bryndle soon disbanded with Andrew Gold and Kenny Edwards then forming the Rangers with Peter Bernstein (bassist of Bryndle and son of composer Elmer Bernstein) and Gene Garfin on drums (ex-**Comfortable Chair**). They made demo after demo, but never got a deal. In 1973, Andrew Gold joined Linda Ronstadt's band, then Kenny followed suit in time for her *Heart Like A Wheel* album. Kenny Edwards also kept on working in the California studios, notably with **Bernie Schwartz** and **Warren Zevon**.

John London (real name John Kuehne) and John Ware went on to join the **Corvettes**, who also featured Bernie Leadon and Chris Darrow and cut two 1969 singles for the Dot label. **The Corvettes** became Linda's backing band in 1969 but folded in December '69 when Leadon joined the Flying Burrito Brothers. London and Ware both joined Michael Nesmith's First National Band in late 1969, London had previously played with Nesmith in 1966, before relocating to L.A. in 1966. Sadly, he passed away in 2000. Ex-**Stone Poneys**' Shep Cooke and Bob Kimmel later formed the **Floating House Band**, a studio project for their 1972 album, although the duo did play at McCabe's alongside Bryndle. Andrew Gold also assisted on the album.

Cyrus Faryar was also in **Modern Folk Quartet** and Billy Mundi in **Lamp Of Childhood**.

STONEWALL - Stoner LP.

Compilation appearances have included: *Evergreen Parts's 1 & 2* on *Journey To A Higher Key, Vol. 1* (LP); *Some Of Shelly's Blues* and *Different Drum* on *In The Beginning* (LP). (SR/JO/CAn)

Stone Sypher

Personnel:
CHRIS LAWRENCE	drms		A
RANDY KOUNAS	ld gtr		A
A.D. RAY	vcls		A
ROBERT WARE	bs		A

A Dallas-based hard rock band responsible for two tracks:- *Who Do You Love?* and *You've Changed* on the compilation *A New Hi - Dallas 1971 - Part 1* (Tempo 2) 1971. Lawrence later joined Effect, another Texas band in 1983. (VJ)

Stonewall

ALBUM: 1(-) STONEWALL (Tiger Lily) 1974 R6

NB: (1) reissued in 1992 as a limited press of 300 copies. Later reissued and retitled as *Stoner* on vinyl and CD (Akarma AK 116) 2000.

An extremely rare, hard-rock album with some psychedelic trappings. This type of album is far more likely to interest hard rock enthusiasts than connoisseurs of psychedelia. *Solitude* and *Atlantis* are probably the most relevant tracks to this book.

The band are thought to have been based in New York, although the personnel listed on the Akarma reissue are ficticious. (VJ/NK)

Stoney and Meatloaf

Personnel:
MARVIN LEE ADAY "MEATLOAF"	vcls	A
STONEY	vcls	A

ALBUM: 1(A) STONEY AND MEATLOAF (Rare Earth R-528) 1971 -

45s: What You See Is What You Get/
Lady Be Mine (Rare Earth 5027) 1971
It Takes All Kinds Of People/
The Way You Do The Things You Do (Rare Earth 5033) 1971

A pop-rock male/female duo, with songs like *Lady Be Mine*, *Jessica White*, *Game Of Love*, *As Heavy As Jesus* and *What You See Is What You Get*. Marvin Lee Aday had previously recorded with **Popcorn Blizzard** and, after starring in the 'Rocky Horror Picture Show' movie, would launch a successful solo career in the late seventies. (SR)

The Stony Brook People

45: Easy To Be Hard/There's Tomorrow (Columbia 44866) c1968

A hippie-pop group. There's some acid guitar on the flip of their only single. (SR)

The Stooges

Personnel:
RON ASHETON	gtr	ABCDEFG
SCOTT ASHETON	drms	ABCDEFG
IGGY POP	vcls	ABCDEFG
DAVE ALEXANDER	bs	BCD
BILL CHEATHAM	gtr	CDE
STEVE MacKAY	sax	CDE
JAMES WILLIAMSON	gtr	DEF
ZEKE ZETTNER	gtr	E
SCOTT THURSTON	keyb'ds	G

HCP
ALBUMS: 1(C) THE STOOGES (Elektra EKS-74051) 1969 106 -
2(D) FUN HOUSE (Elektra EKS-74701) 1970 - SC
3(F) RAW POWER (Columbia KC-32111) 1973 182 -

NB: All of their material, including later albums, have been issued on CD. (1) reissued on vinyl (Sundazed LP 5149) 2002. (2) reissued on vinyl (Sundazed LP 5150) 2002.

45s: I Wanna Be Your Dog/1969 (Elektra EK 45664) 1969
Down On The Street/I Feel Alright (Elektra EKM 459695) 1970
Search And Destroy/Shake Appeal (Columbia 45877) 1973

The central figure in this band was Iggy Pop whose real name was James Jewel Osterburg. He was born on 21 April 1947 at Muskegan, Ann Arbor in Michigan. His first band was The Iguanas whom he drummed and sang for. They released a cover of Bo Diddley's *Mona*. He met Ron Asheton and James Williamson whilst he was with **The Iguanas**, whom he soon left to join the Prime Movers, who for a very short while also featured Ron Asheton on bass. It was around this time that he adopted the name Iggy Pop (Iggy after **The Iguanas** and Pop after Jim Popp, a local junkie). His stay with The Prime Movers was a brief one and he spent most of 1966 in Chicago before returning to Michigan to form The Psychedelic Stooges (line-up (A)) in 1967. At the end of the year bassist Dave Alexander joined the band. They gigged regularly around the Michigan area and having shortened their name to simply **The Stooges** caught the eye of an Elektra employee who was in Detroit to sign **The MC5**. **The Stooges** were snapped up too and advanced $25,000 to record their debut album which made No. 106 in the U.S. Album Charts. Produced by John Cale, it was recorded over four days and issued in a sleeve reminiscent of **The Doors** first album. The red labelled original Elektra releases are the most sought-after. Full of banal, three chord rock'n'roll the album was classic punk-rock and in retrospect years ahead of its time. Their debut 45, taken from the album, is extremely rare. Rarer still is an Italian issue which coupled *I Wanna Be Your Dog* with another cut from the album *Ann* which appeared on Vedette (VRN 34101) in a full colour picture sleeve. Equally rare is a French picture sleeve release which coupled *1969* with *Real Cool Time*.

Early in 1970 Steve Mackay and Bill Cheatham joined the band and they set about recording *Fun House*, which was produced by Don Gallucci (ex-**Don and The Goodtimes**) whose production credits had included **The Kingsmen**'s *Louie, Louie*. Many regarded the album as superb but the month it was released Dave Alexander went missing and later the band quit in August 1971 after a freeway accident. They had been disintegrating anyway amid drug-related problems that plagued many bands in this era. Their second 45 is also extremely rare, consisting of two cuts from *Fun House*. Rarer still is a French release with a stage shot of Iggy but there was also a mega-rare Japanese picture sleeve issue of their 45. *Down On The Street* can also be found on an Elektra various artists sampler, *Garden Of Delights*, which came out in 1971. After the split Iggy moved down to Florida where he improved his golf and took a job cutting lawns and it was a chance meeting with David Bowie in a New York bar which led to the band's reformation, at Bowie's instigation, for a final fling. Line-up F was

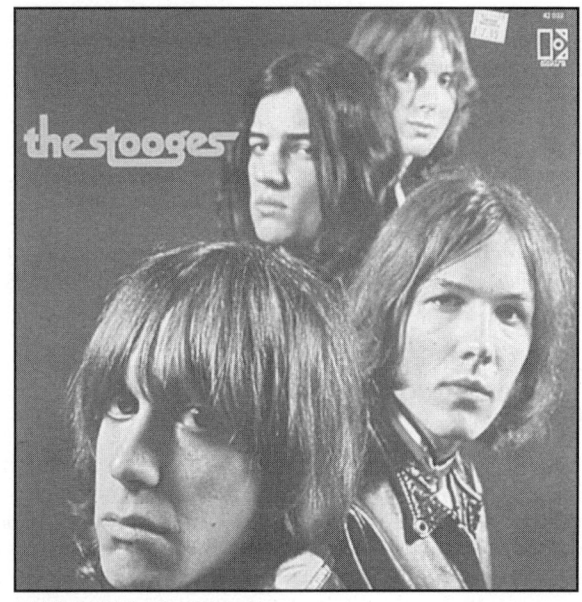

THE STOOGES - The Stooges LP.

THE STOOGES - Funhouse LP.

signed to his management company Mainman and flown over to England to record a two album deal with CBS. However, Tony De Fries (Bowie's manager) considered most of their initial output too violent to be associated with Bowie and most of it was scrapped at his insistence. Eventually the album was released, but it was disappointing overall. It did however, make No. 182 in the Album Charts. *Search And Destroy*, one of the few surviving tracks from their first session, also found its way onto a very rare 45 with *Shake Appeal* (which was a modified version of *Tight Pants* also from the first session). The second projected album never materialised because of differences of opinion between management and the band. De Fries then proceeded to sack Williamson because of the latter's drug problem and after a U.S. tour which ended in violence at two gigs in Detroit **The Stooges** split from Mainman and later disbanded. One of the shows, recorded on cassette, was later issued as *Metallic K 0.* (Skydog SGI 5 008) in France in 1976. A live version of *1969* (a song from their first album), recorded at the 1970 Cincinnati Pop Festival, later appeared on the 1977 *Michigan Rocks* compilation and two further tracks from this performance appeared on a bootleg single, *TV Eye/I Feel Alright*.

The Stooges were an important influence on the 'punk-rock' phenomena of the late seventies and in 1977 their first three albums were reissued in the U.K. and *Metallic KO.* got a U.S. release. The French label New Rose's Fan Club subsidiary released six tracks that Iggy and The Stooges had recorded as studio demos after the failure of *Raw Power*. 1977 also saw the release on Bomp (BLP 4001) in the U.S. and Radar (RAD 2) in the U.K. of the *Kill City* album, which had actually been recorded back in 1975 when journalist Bob Edwards and songwriter Jimmy Webb pooled their resources to bring Iggy Pop, James Williamson and Scott Thurston together to record it. Also of note is *Rubber Legs* (Fan Club FC 037) issued in France in 1987 along with a free 45. The album was a collection of previously unreleased studio material. More recently, Rhino have issued a limited edition eight CD set of all known recordings made during the *Fun House* sessions at Elektra in 1970.

Since their split back in 1973 Iggy Pop has enjoyed a reasonably successful solo career, Williamson became a recording engineer in L.A. and Ron Asheton formed a short-lived U.S. band called The New Order before joining Destroy All Monsters with various **MC5** members.

Compilation appearances have included: *I Wanna Be Your Dog*, *1969*, *1970*, *No Fun* and *T V. Eye* on *Elektrock The Sixties* (4-LP); and *1969* on *Michigan Rocks Vol. 1* (LP). (VJ)

Stop

45:	Cathy's Clown/Hip Girl	(Garland 2010)	1969

From Oregon, a group mainly of interest for 'B' side to their 45, an organ driven pop-garage song with a psychedelic guitar break. The 'A' side is a slow pop version of the Everly Brothers track. (SR)

Jeremy Storch

ALBUM:	1	FROM A NAKED WINDOW	(RCA)	c1970 -

A rarely seen album by the former organist of **The Vagrants**. (SR)

Stories

Personnel incl:	MICHAEL BROWN	keyb'ds	A
	IAN LLOYD	bs, vcls	A
	STEPHEN LOVE	gtr, vcls, bs	A
	BRYAN MADEY	drms	A

ALBUMS:	1	STORIES	(Kama-Sutra KSBS 2051)	1972 -
	2	ABOUT US	(Kama-Sutra KSBS 2068)	1973 -
	3	TRAVELLING UNDERGROUND		
			(Kama-Sutra KSBS 2078)	1973 -

			HCP
45s:	I'm Coming Home/?	(Kama Sutra 545)	1972 42
	Darling/?	(Kama Sutra 566)	1973 111
	Brother Louie/What Comes After	(Kama Sutra KA 577)	1973 1
	Mammy Blue/?	(Kama Sutra 584)	1973 50
	If It Feels Good, Do It/?	(Kama Sutra 588)	1974 88

Stories were formed after Michael Brown had left the **Left Banke** and **Montage**. After two album, he left **Stories**, who disbanded after one further album. Ian Lloyd then went solo, Bryan Madey would play with the Earl Slick Band and Stephen Love went on to join Rick Nelson and later the New Riders Of The Purple Sage.

At least one of their 45s charted with *Brother Louie* reaching No. 1 in the Billboard charts in September 1973. (SR/TC)

The Storybook

45:	Beads Of Innocence/Psych-Out	(Sidewalk 940)	1968

Two songs from the soundtrack to the cult 'Psych-Out' movie. The soundtrack *Psych-Out* album includes both cuts along with a further three tunes by the band. (SR)

The Story Tellers

Personnel:	BILL CHINNOCK	A
	BILLY	A
	JIM	A
	LARRY	A
	DANNY FEDERICI	A

45:	Cry With Me/Little Boy Sad	(Trystero 101)	1967

An obscure New Jersey outfit. *Cry With Me* is notable for its soulful vocals, and 'flea-farting' fuzz guitar.

Chinnock got quite ill at age 19 and after being away from the band for nearly six months the band decided they needed a new guitar player. Chinnock's replacement was a guy named Bruce Springsteen.... the band became the "E Street Band".

Bill Chinnock later had a country solo career in the seventies. He now lives in Maine, producing films and still performs once or twice a year to sellout crowds at small (600 or so) venues.

Compilation appearances include *Cry With Me* on *Psychedelic Disaster Whirl* (LP) and *The Cicadelic 60's, Vol. 5* (LP). (MW/SR/TCe)

David Stoughton

ALBUM:	1	TRANSFORMER	(Elektra EKS-74034)	1968 -

A weird album mixing baroque psychedelic and avant-garde styles. Still to attract the attention of collectors. (SR)

The Stowaways

Personnel:	KEN KNIGHT	bs	A
	TOMMY O'NEAL	ld gtr	A
	PAUL QUICK	rhythm gtr	A
	KEN TANNER	drms	A
	TIM TATUM	vcls	A

ALBUM: 1(A) IN OUR TIME (Justice 148) c1967 R2

NB: (1) Reissued on CD (Collectables COL-CD-0607) 1995.

From Charlotte in North Carolina. Apart from their original *Just A Toy* we have competent beat and Brit Invasion covers that don't quite take off. Slightly more inspiring than label-mates **The Starliters**, this outfit do engage in some charming garagey folk-rock with a decent version of **The Byrds**' *It Won't Be Long*. They tackle *C.C. Rider* with verve but they also dabble in soul and ballads where their vocal shortcomings are revealed. This is still one of the better Justice offerings - just don't expect a goldpan of nuggets.

Compilation appearances have included: *Just A Toy* on *Oil Stains, Vol. 2* (LP); and *What A Shame*, *It Won't Be Wrong* and *It's Only Love* on *Green Crystal Ties, Vol. 4* (CD). (MW)

The Strange Fate

45: Hold Me Baby/Love Is Like (Car CAR-S-2002) 1967

A Detroit, Michigan outfit.

Compilation appearances include *Hold Me Baby* on *Psychedelic Disaster Whirl* (LP) and *Sixties Archive, Vol. 6* (CD). (VJ)

The Strangeloves

Personnel:	BOB FELDMAN	vcls	A
	JERRY GOLDSTEIN	vcls	A
	RICHARD GOTTEHRER	vcls	A

HCP
ALBUM: 1(A) I WANT CANDY (Bang 211) 1965 149 -

NB: (1) reissued on Line (1966). There's also a CD *I Want Candy: The Best Of The Strangeloves* 1995.

HCP
45s: Love, Love (That's All I Want From You)/
I'm On Fire (Swan 4192) 1964 122
I Want Candy/It's About My Baby (Bang 501) 1965 11
Cara-Lin/(Roll On) Mississippi (Bang 508) 1965 39
Night Time/Rhythm Of Love (Bang 514) 1965 30
Hand Jive/I Gotta Dance (Bang 524) 1966 100
Just The Way You Are/Quarter To Three (Bang 544) 1967 -
Honey Do/I Wanna Do It (Sire 4102) 1968 120

NB: There are also for French EPs with PS on Barclay and Atlantic. With **The McCoys**, their records were used to dance "le monkiss", a short-lived craze.

From Brooklyn, New York. As recording artists they are best known for their pulsating versions of *I Want Candy* (which had been a hit for Brian Poole and The Tremeloes in the UK) and *Night Time*. Both are fine rockers.

The Strangeloves also recorded under the name **The Merry Dragons** and **Sheep**. Under the latter moniker they also enjoyed a No. 58 U.S. hit with *Hide And Seek* in 1966, whilst a later effort *I Feel Good* made No. 130. They're also rumoured to have recorded a 45 as **The Beach-Nuts**.

The band also recorded a version of *Hang On Sloopy* which they produced for one of their big discoveries - **The McCoys**. Other production credits by the trio included The Angels' *My Boyfriend's Back* (which had been a No. 1 for this New Jersey-based female pop trio) back in 1963.

Richard Gottehrer later became a partner in Sire Records, which the band helped to form, producing The Go-Go's first two albums and Blondie's debut. Jerry Goldstein's production credits included **The Druids Of Stonehenge**, Eric Burdon and War and **Tim Buckley**'s *Greetings From L.A.*. His Far Out Productions company were based in L.A. from 1969.

Later in 1974, basing themselves in New York, they issued an album as The Strange Brothers.

Compilation appearances have included: *Night Time* and *I Want Candy* on *Nuggets Box* (4-CD); *I Want Candy* on *Nuggets From Nuggets* (CD), *Frat Rock! The Greatest Rock N Roll Party Tunes Of All Time* and *Wild Thing*; *Night Time* on *Nuggets - Original Artyfacts From The First Psychedelic Era 1965-1968* (Dble LP); and *I Want Candy* and *Hang On Sloopy* (previously unreleased) on *Roots Of S.O.B. Vol. 2*. (VJ/SR)

The Strangers

Personnel:	HILARY BLOCKSOM	bs	A
	SUZY DAVID	gtr	A
	RUBY HOWARD	drms	A
	BARBARA McLORNDA	gtr, keyb'ds	A
	JEANETTE WOOD	tamb	A

45: Summertime/Restless Ribbon (Mistake 0001) 196?

Out of Tulsa, in Oklahoma, they were the State's only all-girl band to record a disc in the 1960s. The disc, a raw garage recording, actually details their full line-up. (VJ)

The Strangers

45: Easy Livin'/Tell Me (Linda 118) 1964

Probably from the Los Angeles area, this 45 seems to have been their sole vinyl venture. *Tell Me* has resurfaced on the *Everywhere Chainsaw Sound* (LP) compilation, a decent cover of a Stones' ditty. The flip is eminently forgettable! (VJ)

The Strangers

45: Lonely Star / What A Life (Oriel No #) 1965

From Newton, Massachusetts. The B side, described as 'basic garage' in Aram Heller's 'Till The Stroke Of Dawn', appears on the *The Essential Pebbles Collection, Vol. 1* (Dble CD) and *Teenage Shutdown, Vol. 12* (LP & CD). (MW)

Marcia Strassman

45: The Flower Children/Out Of The Picture (Uni 55006) 1967

A female hippie singer, her single was co-written and produced by Jerry Goldstein. *The Flower Children* has been compiled on the *Hippie Goddesses* CD.

Marcia Strassman later pursued a career as a TV actress. (SR)

The Strawberry Alarm Clock

Personnel:	GEORGE BUNNELL	bs	AB
	LEE FREEMAN	hrmnca, vcls, gtr	ABCDE
	ED KING	ld gtr, (bs), vcls	ABCDE
	GARY LOVETRO	bs	A
	RANDY SOEL	drms, vibes, bongos, vcls	AB
	MARK WEITZ	organ, vcls, piano	ABCD
	MARTY KATIN	drms	C

JIMMY PITMAN	gtr, vcls		CD
GENE GUNNELS	drms		DE
PAUL MARSHALL	gtr, vcls		E

ALBUMS:
					HCP
1(A)	INCENSE AND PEPPERMINTS	(Uni 73014)	1967	11	
2(B)	WAKE UP IT'S TOMORROW	(Uni 73025)	1968	-	-
3(B)	WORLD IN A SEASHELL	(Uni 73035)	1968	-	-
4(D)	GOOD MORNING STARSHINE	(Uni 73054)	1969	-	-
5(-)	BEST OF	(Uni 73074)	1969	-	-
6(-)	CHANGES	(Vocalion 73915)	1971	-	-

NB: (1) reissued on CD in Japan (Universal MVCE 22007). (2) reissued on CD in Japan (Universal MVCE 22008). (3) reissued on CD in Japan (Universal MVCE 22009). (4) reissued on CD in Japan (Universal MVCE 22010). There's also a CD compilation on One Way, *Anthology* (22083) and another: *Strawberries Mean Love* (Big Beat WIK 56) 1987. The later CD version featuring eight additional tracks.

45s:
			HCP
	Incense And Peppermints/		
	The Birdman Of Alcatraz	(All American 373) 1967	-
	Incense And Peppermints/		
	The Birdman Of Alcatraz	(Uni 55018) 1967	1
	Tomorrow/Birds In My Tree	(Uni 55046) 1967	23
	Sit With The Guru/		
	Pretty Song From Psych-Out	(Uni 55055) 1968	65
	Barefoot In Baltimore/Angry Young Man	(Uni 55076) 1968	67
	Sea Shell/Paxton's Back Street Carnival	(Uni 55093) 1968	-
	Stand By/Miss Attraction	(Uni 55113) 1969	-
α	Good Morning Starshine/		
	Me And The Township	(Uni 55125) 1969	87
	Desires/Changes	(Uni 55158) 1969	-
	Starting Out The Day/Small Package	(Uni 55185) 1969	-
	I Climbed The Mountain/Three	(Uni 55190) 1970	-
	California Day/Three	(Uni 55218) 1970	-
	Girl From The City/Three	(Uni 55241) 1970	-

NB: α 'A' side from the musical 'Hair'.

This Glendale, California-based band was originally known as the Irridescents, a surf combo with one 45 in 1963 and later as **Thee Sixpence**, who issued several 45s under this name. The name change came with the release of the 45 *Incense And Peppermints* because of other similarly-named groups. This was picked up by UNI and the rest is history as they say. **Strawberry Alarm Clock** were very much a product of their era and their commercial brand of psychedelia was more acceptable to the general public than that of the more interesting underground bands. Like **The Seeds** they were very much geared to the flower-power scene, and both bands were featured in a cult movie of that era, *Psych-Out*. One advantage they possessed over **The Seeds** was their catchy name, although later with the demise of flower-power, this would prove to be more of a disadvantage. Efforts the band made to tailor themselves a 'psychedelic' image are evident from the apparel they wore on the front cover of their best album *Incense and Peppermints*, which was released on

THE STRAWBERRY ALARMCLOCK - Incense And Peppermints LP.

STRAWBERRY ALARMCLOCK - Wake Up It's Tomorrow LP.

Pye (28106) in the UK. Aside from the ultra-commercial title track, this contained a number of prominently instrumental quasi-psychedelic jams, with Mark Weitz's organ usually to the fore.

Line-up 'A' above includes two bass players, of which Gary Lovetro was the original, being in both **Thee Sixpence** and **Strawberry Alarm Clock**. In mid-1967 after *Incense* had started to climb, their manager Bill Holmes and UNI decided to make an album. George Bunnell was drafted in to the sessions because of his song writing abilities, along with his best friend Steve Bartek (later in Oingo Boingo). George was friends with Randy Seol and that is how he was introduced into the band (they were both in Waterfyrd Traene prior to the **Strawberry Alarm Clock**). George joined the group and more than half of the first album's songs were Bunnell/Bartek compositions. Steve couldn't however join the band as he was still in high school and his parents wouldn't let him travel. Because George was a great song writer and a great bass player, by the end of 1967 Gary Lovetro was fired.

Further albums and more hits followed before **The Strawberry Alarm Clock** became a victim of the changing times. Ed King and Gene Gunnels both later played with **Hunger!**. King recorded with them and played live dates; Gunnels played live with the band when their original drummer Bill Daffern left to join **Truk**. Ed King went on to Lynyrd Skynyrd. A 1981 line-up was reportedly gigging around California. A good introduction to the band is the 1987 compilation *Strawberries Mean Love*.

After the *World In A Sea Shell* album was released a fellow by the name of Marty Katin came aboard on drums for about four months. He was never on any recordings but was an "official" member of the band and toured nationally with them. At the same time as Marty joined, Jimmy Pitman (ex-**The Nightcrawlers**) was recruited on guitar with Ed King movin temporarily onto bass. Marty was replaced shortly before recording commenced on the *Good Morning Starshine* album by former **Sixpence**/**Strawberry Alarm Clock** member, Gene Gunnels (who had previously drummed on the *Incense And Peppermints* 45 A-Side only!).

Original **Beauchemins** songwriter/lead vocalist Paul Marshall later joined **The Strawberry Alarm Clock**, circa '69, around the time of their final UNI album, *Good Morning Starshine*. He also appeared during a party scene in Russ Meyers' 'Beyond The Valley Of The Dolls' singing his self-penned *Girl From The City*, later issued on the *Beyond The Valley Of The Dolls* soundtrack album.

We asked Paul what working on this cult film was like:- "It was a lot like working on any movie set as an actor or sideline musician. We had ridiculously early call times. I seem to remember having to be on the Fox lot at 6:00 A.M. We had our own trailer into which we'd pile our belongings and head for the breakfast buffet or the makeup trailer or the wardrobe department. That whole process took several hours. After we were ready for our big scene, we'd wait around in the trailer or on the set. If we were in the trailer, at least two of us were getting semi-obliterated on one of a number of popular mind-altering substances. It's amazing I don't look more wiped out in my close-up. If we were on the set, we were often standing on the stage for hours while they'd do lights and blocking and then shoot our main scenes and our background scenes."

"The set was the party at the mansion, so all the actors and extras that were in that scene were around all the time. It was a pretty nutty collection of characters, so much so that the party in the movie is not an inaccurate portrayal of the assemblage. The stars were pretty nice to us too, as was Russ Meyer. The sweetest of all was Dolly Read, who I'd love to see again sometime. Lee had better social skills than I did and he shmoozed up Dolly and everybody else. I tried to do a good job, whatever that meant, and just focused on being where I was supposed to be. I probably gained 5 lbs that week just from the food. On movie shoots, there is always food. And then you go to lunch in the commissary. I remember seeing Charles Nelson Reilly in the commissary every day. So basically it was: eat, get high and wait around. Not very thrilling. I guess it was different from most movies at that time in that there were more scantily clad, large busted starlets than usual, but except for the extra who dances through the party in a flesh colored body suit, I was not presented with any truly X-rated sights."

"Around 6:00 p.m. they'd call it a wrap and we'd make our way back home and try to get our lives in order and get some sleep and do it again the next day. We got an invitation to Russ Meyer's wedding after the movie was over. We attended and were seated at a table with Hugh Hefner and Barbi Benton. That was fun."

Compilaton coverage has so far included: *Incense And Peppermints* on *Best Of '60s Psychedelic Rock* (CD), *Nuggets, Vol. 9* (LP), *Nuggets Box* (4-CD), *Nuggets From Nuggets* (CD), *Psychedelic Visions* (CD), *Even More Nuggets* (CD) and *Excerpts From Nuggets* (CD; *Tomorrow* on *Nuggets Vol. 5* (LP); *Nightmare Of Percussion* on *Baubles - Down To Middle Earth*; *Girl From The City* and *I'm Comin' Home* on *Beyond The Valley Of The Dolls* (LP); *In Relation* (as by 'Strawberry Sac') on *Mindblowing Encounters Of The Purple Kind* (LP); a seventies re-recording of *Incense..* appears on *Psychotic Reactions* (a compilation LP on U.K. budget label Topline, not the Planet X comp); and *Black Butter* on *Electric Psychedelic Sitar Headshrinkers, Vol. 3* CD. (VJ/MW/JZ/PMI)

Strawberry Tuesday

A Reading, Pennsylvania band who don't appear to have released any 45s but had one crude garage punker, *Return Of The Walrus*, featured on the local sampler LP *Reading '68* (Empire WWR 868-585). This has subsequently reappeared on *Crude PA Vol. 2* (LP). (MW)

Strawberry Window

Personnel incl:	JACK ESKRICH	gtr	A
	STEVE WILSON	gtr	A

STRAWBERRY ALARM CLOCK - The World In A Sea Shell CD.

An Oakland, California group who never got to release a 45 but did lay down some tracks at Leo De Gar Kulka's Golden State Recorders circa 1967. Two of the best cuts from their session tapes, *Purple Orange* and *Eyes*, have been resurrected by Alec Palao on *What A Way To Come Down* (CD). (MW)

The Straywinds

Personnel:	LARRY S. CHENGGES	A
	GENE F. STEIKER	A

ALBUM: 1(A) THE STRAYWINDS (Shanyn Alexus EU-413504) 1973 SC

A local Michigan duo released this rare album of spooky songs, with spoken word passages backed by spacey acoustic jamming on guitar, violin and percussion, and titles like *In Green Pastures*, *Some Old Town* and *Love Out Of The Crumbling Forge*. (SR)

The Street

Personnel:	WILL BETZ	gtr	A
	AL CAMARDO	perc	A
	TOM CHAPSON	drms	A
	ANYA COHEN	vcls, perc	A
	MICHAEL LYNNE	gtr, bs, vcls	A
	JOHN WILLIAMSON	gtr, bs, vcls	A

ALBUM: 1(A) STREET (Verve Forecast FTS 3057) 1969 -

45s: α There's One Kind Favor /
  Boeing 707 (PS) (Verve Forecast 5084) 1968
  β Apollo... Amen /
  It's Hard To Live On Promises (Verve Forecast KF 5103) 1969
  Apollo... Amen/
  Why Concern Yourself (PS) (Traffic Records TR 1001) 1969

NB: α French 45 issued as **Anya's Street**. α - β also issued in France (Verve Forecast 518907) 1968.

This New York group fronted by Anya Cohen, a fairly raunchy vocalist, was first known as Anya's Street. Produced and managed by Rick Shorter, who wrote or co-wrote six of the tracks, their album is an interesting combination of R&B with psychedelia. *There's One Kind Favor* is lively and *What A Strange Town* is unusual incorporating sound effects like buses, trains, footsteps and snoring in a folky format.

Apollo... Amen is a decent song marred only by "the actual voices of the Astronauts," as boasted by the back of the picture sleeve and a brief foray into *He's Got The Whole World In His Hands*. The 'B' side is quite nice folk-rock, reminiscent of the better moments of the **Rose Garden** album.

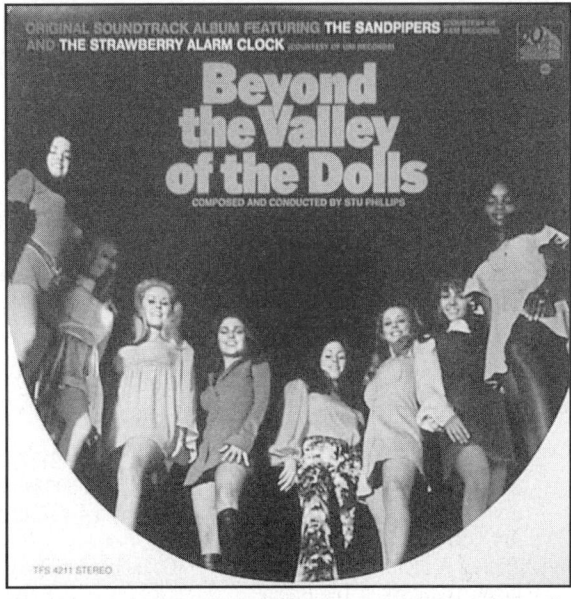

BEYOND THE VALLEY OF THE DOLLS (Soundtrack) LP including The Strawberry Alarm Clock.

Why Concern Yourself was also recorded by **Seth Connors**. (VJ/SR/MMs)

The Street Boys

| Personnel incl: | MICHAEL BISHOP | A |
| | RAYMOND BISHOP | A |

| 45: | Rusty Nail/Out of the Running (PS) | (AZ SG 453) 1973 |

NB: French pressing.

A decent rock single written by the Bishop brothers and produced by **Pat and Lolly Vegas** from **Redbone**. (SR)

Street Christians

| ALBUM: | 1 | IT'S BEEN A LONG TIME COMIN' | (PIP) c1970 - |

An obscure Christian rock group, their album came with a songbook. (SR)

The Street Cleaners

| Personnel: | STEVE BARRI | A |
| | P.F. SLOAN | A |

| 45: | That's Cool, That's Trash/Garbage City | (Amy 916) 1964 |

A one-off mess around venture for **P.F. Sloan** and Steve Barri. You'll also find the 'A' side, *That's Cool, That's Trash*, on the *Riot City!* (LP) and *Garbage City* on *Wail On The Beach*. (VJ)

Street People

| ALBUMS: | 1 | JENNIFER TOMKINS | (Musicor MS-3189) 1969 - |
| | 2 | THE STREET PEOPLE | (Pickwick) c1972 - |

				HCP
45s:	Jennifer Tomkins/All Night Long	(Musicor 1365) 1968	36
	Thank You Girl/		
	The World Doesn't Matter Anymore	(Musicor 1401) 1968	96
	I Remember/		
	I Wonder What Happened To Sally	(Musicor 1412) 1969	-

An obscure pop and bubblegum studio outfit with songs like *Ginsgersnap, She Lets Her Hair Down* and another cover of Tony Joe White's *Rainy Night In Georgia*. The Pickwick album contains mostly covers of rock and pop songs (Lennon's *Power To The People*, Ocean's *Put Your Hand In The Hand* and *Booty Butt*) but may be by a different group. It has an unusual cover, with three hands pictured doing the peace sign, the "black power" fist and "showing the finger".

They enjoyed some commercial success with *Jennifer Tomkins* and *Thank You Girl*. (SR/VJ)

Streys

| 45: | She Cools My Mind/I'm Feeling Lovey | (B-W 635) 1968 |

A garage band from Wooster, Ohio. *She Cools My Mind* has a certain amount of urgency about it and a couple of effective touches. It's since resurfaced on *Pebbles, Vol. 16* (LP). (GGI/VJ)

The Striders

45s:	Give Me A Break/Say You Love Me	(Delta 2137) 1966
	Sorrow/When You Walk In The Room	(Lavette LA 5007/8) 1966
	Sorrow/Say You Love Me	(Columbia 4-43738) 1966
	Am I On Your Mind?/	
	There's A Storm Comin'	(Columbia 4-43948) 1966
	When You Walk In The Room/	
	Do It Now	(Columbia 4-44143) 1967

The first two 45s by this pop outfit were on Albuquerque-based labels. From their covers they were fans of Invasion beat in the style of the Searchers - both *Sorrow* and *Say You Love Me* are done competently in this style. Their chunky version of **The Standells**' *There's A Storm Comin'* is more pop than garage, whilst the **Lindy Blaskey** composed flip is reminiscent of early Yardbirds/Animals. Probably of more interest to beat rather than garage enthusiasts but none the less enjoyable. (VJ/MW)

String and The Beans

| Personnel incl: | CRAIG FULFORD | gtr | A |
| | R. ROBINSON | | A |

| 45: | Come Back To Me/ | |
| | When I Get That Feeling | (Fat City 6 6130) 1966 |

A wonderful example of the garage-ballad genre, *Come Back To Me* is choc full of heartbreak but manages to include some glorious tortured guitar. The flip is much more upbeat and the fuzzed-guitar much more to the fore. Although the 45 is a Kaybank pressing outta Minneapolis, the band were local heroes in Birmingham, Alabama and struck out Northeast into Georgia and the Carolinas.

At long last *Come Back To Me* can be more widely appreciated via *Psychedelic Crown Jewels, Vol. 3* (CD). (MW/MM)

String Cheese

Personnel:	GREG BLOCK	violin	A
	LOUIS CONSTANTINO	bs	A
	WILLIAM DALTON	ld gtr, keyb'ds	A
	JOHN MAGGI	drms	A
	SALLY SMALLER	vcls	A
	LAWRENCE W. WENDELKEN	gtr, vcls	A

| ALBUM: | 1(A) | STRING CHEESE | (Wooden Nickel WNS 1001) 1971 - |

NB: (1) also released in France by RCA with a different sleeve.

A sort of poor man's **It's A Beautiful Day** from Chicago. Indeed electric violinist Greg Block, who contributed much to their album was later in **It's A Beautiful Day** and drummer John Maggi was earlier with **Turnquist Remedy**. This album features some nice lead guitar work and is definitely worth a spin. It was produced by James Golden.

Greg Block would later play with Mark-Almond and the Italian prog-rock group P.F.M. (VJ/SR)

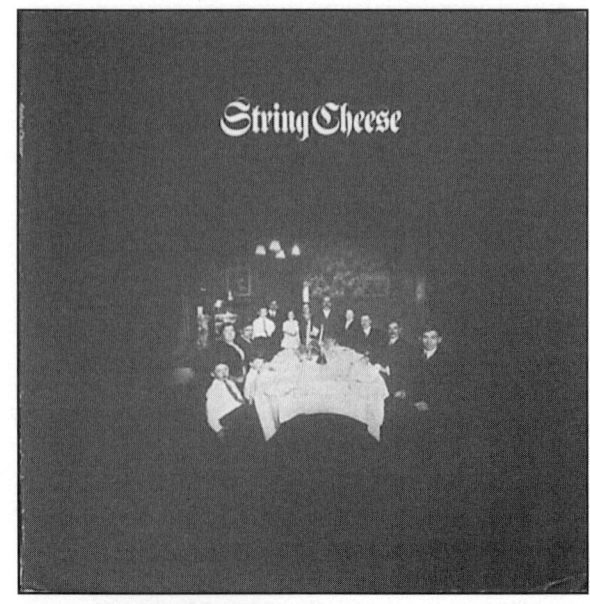

STRING CHEESE - String Cheese LP.

Carol Stromme

ALBUM: 1 THE SOFT SOUND OF (Pete Records S110?) 1970 -

A totally obscure soft-rock singer, whose album came in a nice psychedelic cover. Pete Records was a short-lived Los Angeles label. (SR)

Alice Stuart and Snake

Personnel:
ALICE STUART	vcls, gtrs, keyb'ds	AB
STEVE FUNK	keyb'ds	B
BOB JONES	drms, marimbas, vcls	B
KARL SEVARIED	bs, vcls	B
(BOBBY BLACK	steel gtr	B)
(FRED BURTON	gtr	B)

ALBUMS:
1( ) ALL THE GOOD TIMES (Arhoolie) 1964 -
2(A) FULL TIME WOMAN (Fantasy) 1970 -
3(B) BELIEVING (Fantasy 9142) 1972 -

45: Freedom's the Sound/
Full Time Woman (PS) (America/Fantasy AM 17024) 1970

NB: French release.

Based in California but originally from Chelan, Washington, **Alice Stuart** was one of the very few white female blues-rock guitarists and singers of the late sixties/early seventies. She began recording in Seattle with the **Upper U District Singers** and began her solo career in 1964 with a rare album. She had a very brief stint with the **Mothers Of Invention** circa 1966 and then began touring the bikers circuit, where she built up a strong following. That helped her to get signed to Fantasy for two albums.

After an elusive second effort, her third album was produced by Russ Gary, the house producer of Fantasy (**Redwing**, **Tom Fogerty**...). Notable for its good guitar parts and vocals, it features eight of her original compositions, plus two covers: the classic Blind Willie McTell's *Statesboro Blues* and Hank Snow's *Golden Rocket*. Her backing group, Snake, included the active drummer Bob Jones (from **We Five**, **Nick Gravenites**, **Southern Comfort**), plus a horn section. Andy Stein from Commander Cody guested on one track.

Both albums flopped and are hard to find now. Some years later, **Alice Stuart** made a come back attempt with a "rock queen" image but was unable to get a new recording contract.

She still performs and records locally blues in the Seattle area. (SR)

The Stuarts

45: Just A Little Bit More/Bringing It Home (Ascot 2209) 1966

Just A Little Bit More, is a ravin' piece of garage-pop and the rockin' garagey flip is good too. Both sides are produced and written or co-written by the Feldman, Goldstein, Gottehrer trio better known as **The Strangeloves**.

Compilation appearances include: *Just A Little Bit More* on *Vile Vinyl, Vol. 2* (LP) and *Vile Vinyl* (CD). (VJ/MW)

Stud

Personnel:
PAUL DAVID	vcls, gtr, keyb'ds, bs	A
GEORGE RUNDEL	vcls, drms	A
TIM WILLIAMS	vcls, bs, gtr	A

ALBUM: 1(A) STUD (Baron LP 002) 1975 R4

Only 300 copies of this local Texas album were pressed, and aside from a half-dozen copies discovered with the label owner in 1998, it's never turned up or been offered for sale. This is a big one for hard-rock fans; it's a dark, heavy blues-based guitar extravaganza. The 14'00" *War Song* goes *out there*! (CF)

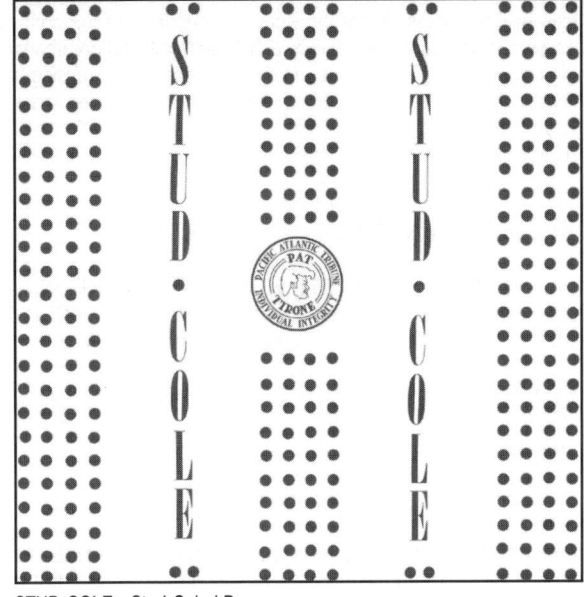

STUD COLE - Stud Cole LP.

Stud Cole

Personnel incl: PATRICK TIRONE vcls A

ALBUM: 1(A) STUD COLE (Pacific Atlantic Tribune PAT 1123) 196? R6

45: Burn Baby Burn/
Always And Always (Pacific Atlantic Tribune PAT 1123) 196?

Yet another amazing California discovery; certainly one of the most exciting and unique artifacts to be uncovered in recent years. Both records are undated and sound too arcane to fix a year on.

Tirone, who was originally from New York, moved to Los Angeles in the very early sixties. While admittedly obsessed with early rock 'n' roll heroes, particularly Elvis Presley, what makes this record so far outside the scope of the pomp and pompadour scene is that his band sounds like The Yardbirds circa *Roger The Engineer*! The resulting music sounds like an experiment gone horribly awry and will make readers of this book incontinent.

The album peaks on *The Devil's Comin'*, an insistent, up-tempo twelve bar blues wherein "Stud" urgently whispers creepy warnings in a brutally out-of-sync call and response style:

"The Devil's comin' to put his hands on you
He'll be walkin' in your step
He'll be watchin' every rule you break
The Devil's comin' to put his rope on you"

Much of the album (which includes both sides of the single release) has the same possessed, creepy feel. It's so dark that it's scary. Highly recommended!

A reissue is in the works by Loopden Records on vinyl and by Norton Records on CD. (CF)

Stuffin'

ALBUM: 1 STUFFIN (A&M SP41??) 1969 -

This obscure bluesy psych group with good guitars sound like they could have come from California. (SR)

Stuffy and His Frozen Parachute Band

ALBUM: 1 STUFFY AND HIS FROZEN PARACHUTE BAND
(Water Street WST 100) 1973 -

NB: (1) reissued (Paramount PAS-6070) 1973.

Produced by Tom Gress, this is the work of a rather weird folk-rock singer and songwriter. The first side sounds a bit like **Norman Greenbaum**, the second is more varied. The Paramount reissue came in an amusing "frozen food" cover and the slogan "Tired of canned music? Frozen music can change your life!!". (SR)

The Stumbling Blox

From Abilene in Texas. You'll find *Its Alright*, a previously unreleased recording, on *Acid Visions - Complete Collection, Vol. 2* (3-CD), *Texas Punk: 1966, Vol. 1* (LP) and *Green Crystal Ties, Vol. 3* (CD). (VJ)

The Stumps

45:	Think Of The Good Times/My Generation	(Boyd 159)	c1966

A garage band from New Mexico who recorded this 45 in Phoenix, Arizona. The 'A' side has some pretty effective guitar and organ work but suffers from poor vocals. The flip was a cover of The Who's classic sixties anthem.

Compilation appearances include *Think Of The Good Times* on *Let's Talk About Girls!* (CD), *The Midwest Vs. The Rest* (LP) and *The Tucson Sound 1960-1968* (LP). (VJ)

Dane Sturgeon

Personnel:	DAVID COSBY	vcls	A
	DON RALKE		A
	DANE STURGEON	vcls	A
	FREDDIE THOMAS	gtr	A

ALBUM:	1(A)	WILD'N TENDER	(Stur-geon TS-100) c1968 SC

From California, this album was produced with the help of Don Ralke. **Sturgeon** sings on the "Wild Side" while David Cosby sings lead on the "Tender Side". Although the liner notes of this rare album describe it as "Folk Rock in a Stone Groove", it is in fact mainly composed of anecdotal ballads and country-folk songs with occasional use of a fuzz guitar. Not recommended. (SR)

Styx

Personnel:	JOHN CURULEWSKI	gtr	A
(up to	DENNIS DE YOUNG	keyb'ds	A
1974)	CHUCK PANOZZO	bs	A
	JOHN PANOZZO	drms	A
	JAMES YOUNG	gtr	A

ALBUMS:	1(A)	STYX	(Wooden Nickel BXL1 1006) 1972 -
(up to	2(A)	STYX II	(Wooden Nickel BXL1 1012) 1973 -
1974)	3(A)	SERPENT IS RISING	(Wooden Nickel BXL1 0287) 1973 -
	4(A)	MAN OF MIRACLES	(Wooden Nickel BWL1 0638) 1974 -

NB: (1) - (4) reissued in the U.K. by RCA in 1980.

45s:	Winner Take All/?	(Wooden Nickel 0065) 1973
(up to	Best Thing/?	(Wooden Nickel 73 0106) 1975
1975)	I'm Gonna Make You Feel It/?	(Wooden Nickel 73 0111) 1973
	Lady/?	(Wooden Nickel 73 0116) 1973
	Unfinished Song/?	(Wooden Nickel 0252) 1974
	You Better Ask/?	(Wooden Nickel 10272) 1975

Originally known as TW4, the nucleus of this group was formed in 1964. They became **Styx** in 1971 and the front cover of first album shows them naked, surrounded by red smoke and fire. It's a decent art-rock effort, strongly influenced by British groups like Yes. They would keep on recording and touring and, after 1974 and their contract with A&M, they finally became very popular, as a "stadium rock act", especially with the American teenagers. This latter-day career is of course outside the scope of this book! (SR)

SUB ZERO BAND - Sub Zero Band LP.

The Styx

Personnel:	BUTCH ENGLE	vcls	A
	LARRY GERUGHTY	keyb'ds	A
	RICK MORRISON	drms	A
	HAPPINESS SMITH	bs	A
	BOB ZAMORA	gtr	A

45s:	My Girl / Stay Away	(Frantic CR-2125/6) 1967
	Hey I'm Lost/Puppetmaster	(Onyx 2200) 1967

From Mill Valley, California, just North of San Francisco - they were previously known as **Butch Engle and The Styx**. Both sides of the Onyx 45 feature on *Sound Of The Sixties: San Francisco Part 2* (LP); *Hey I'm Lost* is also on *Pebbles, Vol. 17* (LP) and an unreleased 1966 version is on the *Good Things Are Happening* CD. (MW/AP)

Substantial Evidence

Personnel:	ARTIE DESPORTE	gtr	A
	PAT GILL	bs	A
	MARK SIMON	keyb'ds, vcls	A
	TED TIERCE	ld gtr, vcls	A
	RAY ZOLLER	drms, vcls	A

45:	Death Angel // Please Walk On By	
	Hang Loose Mother Goose	(Groovy Grape GL102) 1968

Death Angel, written by Ray Zoller's brother Rusty, is one gem amongst a cluster on *Psychedelic Crown Jewels, Vol. 2* (Dble LP & CD), whose liners reveal the band's details. Their other recordings were originals despite them being primarily known for doing covers of the current popular dance tunes in the late 60s, especially along the Gulf Coast.

The group was based in Biloxi, Mississippi. (MW/RM/CF)

Subterranean Monastery

45:	Curiosity / Realistic Patterns	(RCA Victor 47-9512) 1968

A mystery one-off guaranteed to catch the eye of psych collectors scanning lists of obscurities in the hope of digging up an 'undiscovered' nugget. The trouble is that, too often, the wackier the group name or titles the more likely it is to be banal exploitation studio-pop from the mind of the trendy 'hip' producer. This sounds like a group but it's melodic pop, though *Realistic Patterns* is pleasantly laid-back with some psychedelic touches - judge for yourself on the *Justafixation* compilation. (MW)

SUDDEN DEATH - Suddenly LP.

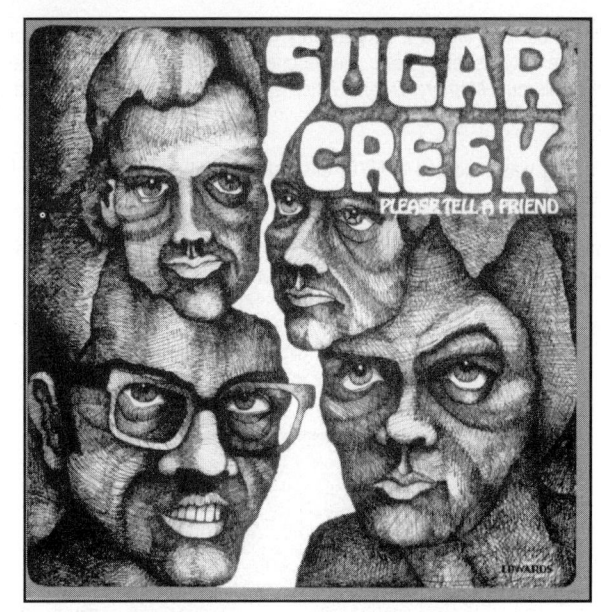

SUGAR CREEK - Please Tell A Friend LP.

Suburban 9-5

Personnel incl: GARY RICHRATH   A

45s:	Walk Away/Elevator Operator	(Ledger 18810) 1968
	I Wanna Be There/	
	Flying On The Ground Is Wrong	(Golden Voice 5778) 1968
	Sunshine Becomes You/	
	Capt. Kangaroo	(Golden Voice 2630) c1968

This garage band from Peoria, Illinois, was most notable for including Richrath, who later played with REO Speedwagon. Their debut couples an uptempo garagey popper with a fine rockin' version of former-**Byrd** Gene Clark's *Elevator Operator*. (MW)

Sub Zero Band

Personnel:	LARRY CAFFO	gtr, bs	A
	JOHN CORDES	fiddle, violin, mandolin	A
	JOHN GLICK	gtr, bs, banjo, steel gtr	A
	ANN HUDSON	vcls, keyb'ds	A
	GERRY McDONALD	drms, vcls	A
	CHRISTY SEALS	vcls	A
	ROBERT "GREEN BEAN" SEALS	vcls, gtr	A

ALBUM: 1(A) SUB ZERO BAND   (No label) 1972 R3

NB: (1) issued in a plain sleeve with a 'slick' on the front cover. Reissued on Void (Void 18) 1999, as a limited edition of 600 copies.

45: Flapjacks/Angel Lady   (Lavender 2017) 1972

NB: shown as by **Sub-Zero Band**.

This Chico, California, band spent much of their time playing in Oregon, where both of their records were recorded. Robert Seals recalls that 1,000 copies of the album were pressed, but the 45 is so rare that he's never owned one. The group play a rootsy, West Coast style country-rock similar to **Shiva's Headband** on tracks like *Home Is Where Your Head Is*, *Too Many Religions* and *Forty Shades Of Blue*. It was produced by Jay Webster. Robert recently reformed the band and they are recording and touring under the new moniker Bob Seals and The Wayhigh Patrol and have finished a new demo tape. The 45 contains two non-album cuts. (CF/SR)

Sudden Death

ALBUM: 1   SUDDENLY SUDDEN DEATH
                                             (Rockadelic RRLP 19) 1995

A Led Zeppelin - inspired early hard-rock, which was issued by Rockadelic in 1995 from previously unissued tapes from circa 1971. The two exceptions are the opening track, *My Time Is Over* and *Fugit Orchard*, which are much mellower with some good laid-back guitar moments. (GG)

The Suedes

45:     13 Stories High/My Girl   (Psychadelic 113) 1966

This outfit came from San Antonio in Texas and their 45 was also released as **The Botumles Pit**, with stickers over "The Suedes" band name.

Compilation appearances include *13 Stories High* on *Back From The Grave, Vol. 4* (LP); *Back From The Grave, Vol. 2* (CD); *Scum Of The Earth* (Dble CD) and *Scum Of The Earth, Vol. 2* (LP). (VJ/MT)

Sufi Choir

ALBUMS:	1	SUFI CHOIR	(Private Pressing) c1974 -
	2	STONE IN THE SKY	(Private Pressing) c1976 -

A San Francisco outfit, mixing folk and Eastern music, with flute, piano, tabla, bass with male/female choral sound. The first album came in a mandala cover with a poster. (SR)

Sugar Bear

Personnel:	IVAN BAILEY	bs, hrmnca, vcls	A
	JOHN McLAUGHLIN	gtr, hrmnca, vcls	A
	H.C. PERRYMAN	gtr, hrmnca, vcls	A
	TRENT SLEMMER	drms	A

ALBUM: 1(A) SUGAR BEAR   (No label NR 5392) 197? R3

Local Florida rural-rock private press from the early-mid seventies. Peaks on the long *Seasons For Love* and the ethereal *The Garden*. Recommended, but not easy to find! (CF)

Sugar Creek

Personnel:	JOHN EDWARDS	A
	GARY GANS	A
	MALCOLM McKINNEY	A
	TOD McKINNEY	A

ALBUM: 1(A) PLEASE TELL A FRIEND
                                             (Metromedia MD 1020) 1969 R2

NB: (1) counterfeited on CD (Lyrical Sound Device DU-5004) 1999. Reissued on vinyl and CD (Akarma AK 151) 2001.

For the most part this is a very average blues-rock album, but there are a few more psychedelic cuts:- the opener, *A Million Years* is a heavy psychedelic cut; *Memory Tree*, a much softer slice of psychedelia and the finale, *Night Flash*.

The album was recorded in NYC, although the band is thought to be from Massachusetts.

Jonathan Edwards later a long solo career of singer/songwriter in the mould of James Taylor, recording more than fifteen albums.

Compilation appearances include *A Million Years* on *Psychosis From The 13th Dimension* (CDR & CD). (VJ/MW/SR)

SUGAR CUBE BLUES BAND - Sugar Cube Blues Band LP.

Sugar Cube Blues Band

Personnel:
- BUDLEY BAYS — acoustic and electric gtrs — A
- BILL CROWDER — vcls, hrmnca — A
- DANNY LANCASTER — bs — A
- DEVO LANCASTER — drms — A
- TONY PORTERA — organ — A

ALBUM: 1(A) SUGAR CUBE BLUES BAND (Rockadelic RRLP 21) 1995

45: My Last Impression // Corinna Corinna
A Hard Rain's Gonna Fall (Black Crow 100) 1967

From Grenada, Mississippi, this act recorded an album in 1967 which finally saw the light of day in 1995. There are some good songs included, especially *My Last Impression*, which is very much in the garage-psych vein. Indeed the band's title is misleading as the songs aren't really bluesy at all. The material, which was all written by Bill Crowder, spans garage, psychedelia and more melodic rock and is well worth seeking out.

My Last Impression can also be heard on the vinyl version of *The Psychedelic Experience, Vol. 1*, whose liner notes state that some of the band members had recorded a 45 way back in 1959 as the Sundowners. (VJ)

Sugarloaf

Personnel:
- JERRY CORBETTA — piano, organ, vcls — ABC
- BOB MacVITTIE — drms — ABC
- BOB RAYMOND — bs, vcls — AB
- VEEDER VAN DORN — gtr, vcls — A
- BOB WEBBER — ld gtr, vcls — ABC
- ROBERT YEAZEL — gtr, vcls — C

HCP

ALBUMS: 1(B) SUGARLOAF (Liberty LST-7640) 1970 24 -
2(C) SPACESHIP EARTH (Liberty LST-11010) 1971 - -
3(D) I GOT A SONG (Brut-Buddah 6006) 1973 - -
4(E) DON'T CALL US, WE'LL CALL YOU
(Claridge 1000) 1975 - -

NB: (1) also issued in the U.K. (Liberty LBS 83415). (2) also issued in the U.K. (United Artists UAS 29165). (4) also issued in the U.K. (Polydor 2310 394).

HCP

45s: α Green-Eyed Lady/West Of Tomorrow (Liberty 56183) 1970 3
Tongue In Cheek/Woman (Liberty 56281) 1971 55
Mother Nature's Wine/Medley: Bach Doors
Man - Chest Fever (United Artists 50784) 1971 88
Round And Round/Colorado Jones (Brut 805) 1973 -
Don't Call Us, We'll Call You/
Texas Two-Lane (Claridge 402) 1974 -
Stars In My Eyes/? (Claridge 405) 1974 -

NB: α also issued in the U.K. (Liberty LBF 15401).

After they left **The Moonrakers**, Jerry Corbetta and Bob Webber formed Chocolate Hair with two original **Moonrakers** Bob MacVittie and Veeder Van Dorn plus Denver musician Bob Raymond. The band signed with Liberty Records and were coerced into changing their name, as Liberty insisted that Chocolate Hair would be interpreted as racist. They renamed themselves **Sugarloaf** after the Sugarloaf Mountain area North of Boulder where some of the members lived. After a few months, Veeder Van Dorn left, for Mescalero Space Kit, although his song *Things Gonna Change Some* was recorded for **Sugarloaf**'s debut album.

Their first album sold very well, reaching No. 24 in the national charts and their single, *Green-Eyed Lady* written by Jerry Corbetta, reached No. 3. Produced by Frank Slay (**Strawberry Alarm Clock**) and J.C. Phillips and engineered by Paul Buff (**Buff Organization**), their debut album contains five interesting long tracks full of organ and guitars and a good cover of the Johnny Burnette's *Train Kept A Rollin*. Van Dorn from **The Moonrakers** co-wrote *Things Gonna Change Some*, the other cuts being penned by Corbetta, Webber and Raymond, sometimes helped by Myron Pollock and J.C. Phillips.

The second album was inspired by and named after the Buckminster Fuller novel "Spaceship Earth". By this time the band had been bolstered by another guitarist Robert Yeazel (ex-**Beast**). This second effort was solid but did not repeat the success of their debut.

A third album, *I Got A Song*, credited to **Sugarloaf**/Jerry Corbetta was released in 1973. By this time both Yeazel and MacVittie had left and Larry Ferris (ex-**Beast**) had joined on drums. This was much more commercial than their earlier efforts but failed to make an impact.

In 1974, without a label, and frustrated with the record companies, Corbetta wrote the song *Don't Call Us, We'll Call You*. The band recorded it and with a few other new songs they re-released the *I Got A Song* album in 1975 as *Don't Call Us, We'll Call You*. The title track became their last Top 10 hit, and the band broke up in 1978. Corbetta pursued a solo career and eventually joined The Four Seasons. Webber and Yeazel continued to play guitar together in the Denver R&B outfit The Freddi-Henchi Band. (HS/CF/SR)

Sultans Five

Personnel:
- TIM MICHNA — A
- RAY PLAUSKE — A
- VIC WEINFURTER Jr. — A
- KEN — A
- LEN — A

45s: Tonight Is The Night/Hey Little Girl (Ral 1754-03) 1965
Tonight Is The Night/With You (Raynard RS 10052) 1966
Daisy/Life Is Like A River (Raynard RS 10053) 1966
α You Know, You Know/Calico (Enterprise 812E-1 066) 1966

NB: α came with a special "Enterprise Thirteen presents The Sultans Five" company sleeve.

An undistinguished Wisconsin outfit who released four 45s the best of which *You Know, You Know* can also be found on *Garage Punk*

Unknowns, Vol. 4 (LP). Whilst lyrically repetitive, it's worth checking out for interesting guitar work.

The band came from Racine, Wisconsin and were previously known as the Sultans IV they issued one 45 on the RAL label in 1964 - *Walk With Me / Who's At Fault*. (VJ/MW)

Summer Sounds

Personnel:	DAVE	gtr	A
	JOE	organ	A
	PAUL	bs	A
	RALPH	sax	A
	ROY	drms	A

ALBUM: 1(A) UP-DOWN (Laurel 331098) 1969 R4

NB: (1) reissued in 1996 with red paste-on sleeve. 100 copies with splash vinyl, 300 without.

This five-piece originally came from Dartmouth, Massachusetts. The album is worth around $650 and had a limited vinyl reissue during the nineties. It has been compared to **All Of Thus**.

Certainly their speciality is pleasant garage ballads. There's a cover of The Spencer Davis Group's hit *Gimme Some Lovin'*, but the remaining material is self-penned. The stand-out cut is *The Leaves Are Turning Brown* with some really cheesy organ and an earnest vocal performance. Also a little different from the rest is the catchy guitar and drum work on *I Love You*.

Oil Stains, Vol. 2 includes their version of *Oil Stains, Vol. 2* (LP). Another track *First Date* has appeared on *New England Teen Scene, Vol. 3* (LP). (VJ/GG)

Summerhill

Personnel:	DOUG BURGER	keyb'ds	A
	LARRY HICKMAN	bs	A
	ALAN PARKER	ld gtr	A
	DEL RAMOS	drms	A

ALBUM: 1(A) SUMMERHILL (Tetragrammaton T-114) 1968 -

NB: (1) also issued in the U.K. on Polydor (583 746).

45: Last Day/Soft Voice (Tetragrammaton 1528) 1969

This inconsistent album was recorded in Hollywood. It's difficult to categorise ranging from good psychedelia (*Friday Morning's Paper*) to heavier rock (*Bring Me Around*) and country (*The Last Day*). Not really recommended.

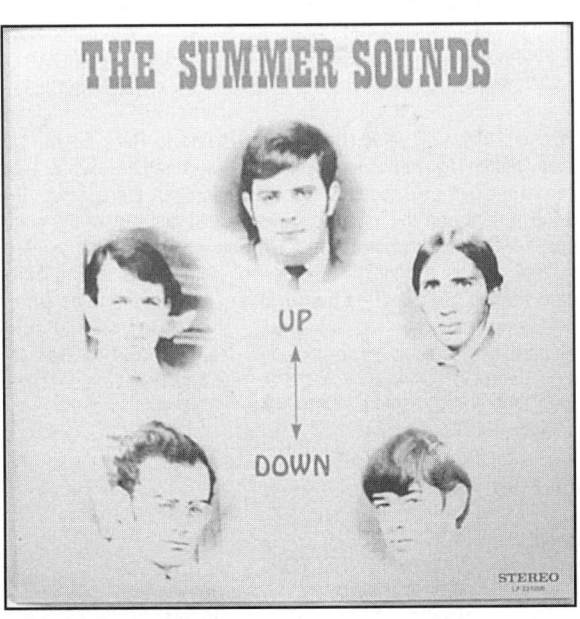

THE SUMMER SOUNDS - Up-Down LP.

Both 45 cuts are featured on the album and Alan Parker had earlier played in **Smith**. (VJ)

Sum Pear

Personnel:	SONNY HAHN	gtr, harpsichord, organ, piano	A
	DOUG MILLER	piano, organ, ld vcls	A
	(KATHY ALSON	bcgd vcls	A)
	(TOMMY CASTAGNARO	drms	A)
	(JOHN CAVALEA	trombone	A)
	(RICHIE CRUZ	trumpet	A)
	(BOB DORSA	bs	A)
	(STEVE HABER	sax	A)
	(ANDY RAGANO	wah wah pedal	A)
	(BILLY RASVANIS	drms	A)
	(JOHN SCADUTO	drms	A)
	(MIKE SEGALL	bcgd vcls	A)
	(BARRY TAYLOR	piano	A)

ALBUM: 1(A) SUM PEAR (Euphoria EST 1) 1971 SC

NB: (1) came with lyric sheet.

45: Better Get Down / Got Me Tragedy (Euphoria 202) c1971

A largely unknown album which has its moments in terms of heavy fuzz psychedelic guitar work, particularly on Side One, where *Hey Sun* is one of the stand-out tracks. Side two is relatively disappointing in comparison, but overall an album worth investigation. All the songs (except for Micky Newbury's *Down On Saturday*) were written by Sonny Hahn and Doug Miller, who performed them with the help of several session men. The album was recorded at Soundview Environmental Studios.

Bob Gallo and Louis Cofredo, who produced the album, had earlier worked with **Aesop's Fables**. Euphoria was a New York based subsidiary of the Jubilee Group. (VJ/MW/SR)

Sumpin' Else

45s:	Baby You're Wrong/ I Can't Get Through To You	(Liberty 55873) 1966
	Here Comes The Hurt/You're Bad	(Liberty 55900) 1966

Los Angeles punky pop featuring John Merrill-composed titles on the first 45 - presumably the same chap later in **The Peanut Butter Conspiracy**. *Baby You're Wrong* is a worthy inclusion on *Vile Vinyl, Vol. 2* (LP) and *Vile Vinyl* (CD), whilst both sides of the second 45 feature tough fuzzy pop. There may be another 45 since a French EP (Liberty LEP 2268) features the first 45 above plus *Toy Boy Girl* and *Danger*. (MW)

Sunday Funnies

Personnel:	RONALD AITKEN	gtr, vcls	A
	RICHARD FIDGE	vcls	A
	RICHARD KOSINSKI	keyb'ds, vcls	A
	RICHARD MITCHELL	drms, perc	A

ALBUMS:	1(A)	SUNDAY FUNNIES	(Rare Earth RS 526) 1971
	2(A)	BENEDICTION	(Rare Earth R 538L) 1972 -

45s:	Heavy Music/Path Of Freedom	(Hideout 1070) 1970
	Walk Down The Path Of Freedom/ It's Just A Dream	(Rare Earth 5035) 1971

From Detroit and unrelated to the L.A. outfit of *A Pindaric Ode* fame. Their two albums were produced by Andrew Oldham and are more progressive and gospel rock than psychedelic. The first features organ dominated rock with softer numbers like *It's Just A Dream* and *You And I* amongst its better offerings. The *Benediction* album is an improvement, with a strong religious content and a fine sleeve by Matti Klarwein (Abraxas, Miles Davis etc.).

Get Funkey, from their second album, can be heard on *Michigan Rocks, Vol. 2* (LP).

Richard Kosinski would later form the Big Wha Koo with Danny Douma from the Hello People. (VJ/SR)

The Sunday Funnies

45:	Headlines/Another Time, Another Place	(Capitol 5614) 1966

An unknown folk-rock Californian group, whose songs were written and produced by Perry Botkin and Garfield, with Johnny Cole and Nilsson. The 'A' side sounds a bit like *Eve Of Destruction* with a singer doing a Dylan imitation, complete with harmonica. The flip is also folk-rock, but with some fuzz guitar and even mariachi brass at the end!

Perry Botkin later worked with **Thorinshield**. (SR)

Sunday Funnies

45:	A Pindaric Ode/Whatcha Gonna Do (When The Dance Is Over)	(Valhalla 671) 1967

This group of Mexican-Americans came from Los Angeles. Their *A Pindaric Ode* is one of numerous examples of the influence of acid on garage bands. The almost-spoken lyrics relate their disorientation and disinterest for coming to terms with the real world and the song's got a pretty unusual ending too. They are unconnected to the Detroit outfit. Nebraska's Dynamic Impacts also used the name Sundae Funnies for a 45, *Get Out Of My Life Woman/Tell Me* (Dads 603) in 1968. There's yet another unknown Sunday Funnies on Mercury and a Tennessee mob covering *Poison Ivy* on the Orchid of Memphis label. For non-US readers, 'Sunday Funnies' are comic strip magazines included as supplements in some Stateside Sunday papers, hence the popular moniker.

Compilation coverage has so far included: *A Pindaric Ode* on *Pebbles, Vol. 7* (LP) and *The East Side Sound, Vol. 1 - 1959-1968* (CD); and *Whatcha Gonna Do...* on *East Side Revue, The West Coast East Side Sound, Vol. 1* (CD) and *The East Side Sound, Vol. 1* (LP). (VJ/MW)

Sunday Group

45:	Edge Of Nowhere/Pink Drapes	(Downey 129) 1965

Angst-ridden garage from this famous Los Angeles label. *Edge Of Nowhere* is featured on the *Scarey Business* (CD) compilation.

Sunday Servants

Personnel:	SKIP KNAPE	vcls, keyb'ds, bs	AB
	DAVE TEEGARDEN	drms, vcls	AB
	CARL DAY	vcls	B
	TOMMY TRIPPLEHORN	gtr	B

45:	Who Do You Love/ I'm Puttin' You On	(World Pacific 77825) 1966

This is the first record by **Teegarden and "Van Winkle" Knape**, produced in **Leon Russell**'s L.A. studio by J.J. Cale who also composed the flip. **Leon Russell** got them signed to World Pacific.

Who Do You Love is a cool 'live' version. The flip is great laid-back garage that takes a few plays to appreciate - understated fuzz and simple *96 Tears*-style keyboards underpinned by a cantering beat that's different-'n'classy.

After their single, Teegarden and Knape (whose idol was Garth Hudson from the Hawks, pre-Band) landed a job playing behind a singer guitarist named Denny White in Nevada and at the charmingly named Pussycat-A-Go-Go in Lake Tahoe. Once White left, they were sometimes reinforced by a black singer called Tommy Tex.

They finally returned to Tulsa, were spotted by a Detroit talent scout and became **Teegarden and Van Winkle**. (MW/SR)

Sundog Summit

ALBUM:	1	PRESENTING SUNDOG SUMMIT ON SUNDOG HILL	(Audio Mixers) 1976 R1

From the Chicago area, a freak-rock outfit. Their only album contains covers of *White Light, White Heat, Reefer Madness*, and *Jackson*, plus some twisted originals. (SR)

Sundowners

Personnel:	GEORGE BIANCHI	vcls, perc	A
	EDDIE BRICK	vcls, perc	A
	DOMINICK DE MIERI	bs, keyb'ds, vcls	A
	BOOBY DICK	bs, vcls	A
	BENNY GRAMMATICO	drms, vcls	A
	EDDIE PLACIDI	organ, ld gtr, vcls	A

ALBUM:	1(A)	CAPTAIN NEMO	(Decca DL 75036) 1968 -

45s:	Always You / Dear Undecided	(Decca 32171) 1967
	Sunny Day People / Easy Does It Baby	(Decca 32296) 1968
	Let It Be Me/Blue-Green Eyes	(Decca 32497) 1968

Probably from the New York area, this interesting album mixes Beatles inspired vocals with distorted guitars on tracks like *Plaster Casters* or *Sunny Day People*. The sleeve is unusual, with a strange drawing. (SR/MW)

Sun Lightning Incorporated

Personnel incl:	PHILLIP R. ARMSTRONG		A

45:	Quasar 45/There Must Be Light (PS)	(Whap WH-319) 1969

From the Sangralea Valley area of Indiana on the label that also put out a 45 by The Sangralads, *Quasar 45* is a post-Hendrix *Telstar* and, according to the sleevenotes, was inspired by (21-year-old) Phillips namesake, Neil, stepping out on the moon. "Listen carefully and you will hear the roar of a rocket launched, the monotonous din of radio signals from afar, the haunting and beautiful bass runs signifying the endless eternity of space itself". Yes well, it's good but won't put anyone into orbit. The flip is end-of-decade pop-rock and drags on like the sleeve-notes!

Quasar 45 is also on the freaky fuzzy instrumental compilation *Buzz Buzz Buzzzzzz, Vol. 1* (CD) and *High All The Time, Vol. 1* (LP). (MW)

Sunliners

Personnel incl:	PETE HOOTELBEKE	drms, ld vcls	A

45s:	Hully Gully Twist/Sweet Little Girl	(Hercules 182) 196?
	Hit It/The Islander	(Hercules 183) 196?
	So In Love/Little Girl Charm	(Hercules 184) 196?
	Swingin' Kind/All Alone	(Golden World GW31) 1965
	Land Of Nod/Well One	(MGM K13809) 1967

From Detroit, this outfit later changed their name to **Rare Earth**. *Land Of Nod* was written by Pete Hootelbeke and is a rather excellent slab of commercial cash-in psychedelia, full of fuzz and 'out there' lyrics. It would easily find a home on the *Rubbles* series. A different mix of the song later appeared on Rare Earth's first album *Dreams/Answers*, which came out on Verve. *Well One* is a chunky 'intermission' instrumental with a funky feel but some searing guitar and backward vocals. An odd one to be sure.

Compilation coverage has so far included:- *Land Of Nod* on *Garagelands, Vol. 2* (LP) and *Garagelands, Vol. 1 & 2* (CD); and *Well One* on *Buzz Buzz Buzzzzzz, Vol. 1* (CD). (MW)

Sunny Funny Co.

Personnel:	DICK ALBRECHT	drms	A
	WALLACE R. HELTON	keyb'ds, vcls	A
	RICK HOUCHIN	bs, vcls	A
	MIKE LOVELESS	gtr, vcls	A

45:	Alone/Move On	(Stanal 712-5661)	1969

This obscure late sixties garage 45 is reputedly good. From Kearney, Nebraska, this group were active in the Midwest between 1967-1972. Touring mainly around Denver, Colorado and Kearney, Nebraska, they played a mixture of psychedelic soul and original prog-blues music.

Rick Houchin: "The band toured with **Steppenwolf**, **Frijid Pink**, **The Lemon Pipers**, **The Royal Guardsmen**, and Seventh House (who included **Zephyr**/Firefall members). The pictures include a fifth member, Al Paez, who was only with the band very briefly. He played guitar and did some vocals. The main foursome was together for about five years and travelled all over the Midwestern U.S. We were one of those bands that went everywhere in a big school bus converted to be a travelling motel. It was a party on wheels - What a riot! The biggest gig we did was with Seventh House and **Steppenwolf** and we opened in our hometown of Kearney, Nebraska with about 4,500 in attendance. It was kind of a homecoming for the band, which had been on the road all Summer in 1969."

The only member to still play actively is Mike Loveless, who is in a horn/retro band called Blackberry Winter. (VJ/RH)

The Sunrays

Personnel:	BYRON CASE	gtrs, drms, vcls	A
	MARTY DIGIOVANNI	electric piano	A
	RICK HENN	drms, vcls	A
	VINCE HOZIER	bs, vcls	A
	EDDIE MEDORA	ld gtrs	A

ALBUM:	1(A)	ANDREA	(Tower ST 5017) 1966 -

NB: (1) reissued on CD by Collectables (COL-CD-0598). The same label have also put together a 58 track, 3 CD retrospective called *Vintage Rays*.

HCP

45s:	Outta Gas/Car Party	(Tower 101) 1964 -
	I Live For The Sun/Bye Baby Bye	(Tower 148) 1965 51
	Andrea/You Don't Phase Me	(Tower 191) 1965 41
	Still/When You're Not There	(Tower 224) 1966 93
	I Look Baby I Can't See/	
	Don't Take Yourself Too Seriously	(Tower 256) 1966 -
	Hi How Are You?/	
	Just 'Round The River Bend	(Tower 290) 1966 -
	Loaded With Love/Time (A Special Thing)	(Tower 340) 1967 -

A Californian post-surf band, two of whom had earlier issued 45s as The Snowmen. The above album was produced by Murry Wilson. (VJ)

Sunrisers

45:	I Saw Her Yesterday / No One	(Patty 101) 1966

A Little Neck/Whitestone, NY band who recorded one further 45 as the **What Four**. *I Saw Her Yesterday*, a yearning garage-ballad, is on *Fuzz, Flaykes, And Shakes, Vol. 2* (LP & CD). (MW/MM)

SUNNY FUNNY Co.

Sunset Love

CD:	1	THE HISTORY OF TEXAS GARAGE BANDS VOL. 6: PSYCHEDELIC FLOWER POWER WITH SUNSET LOVE
		(Collectables COL-CD-0665) 1995

Fourteen unreleased tracks recorded in Odessa, Texas in 1968 for a proposed album on the AOK label that never materialised. Quaint folky-flower-pop with male-female harmonising influenced by the likes of **Mamas and Papas** and soft West Coast sounds similar to **Ashes** / **Peanut Butter Conspiracy**... there is a very occasional psychy touch but nothing to get too heady about. No details of the group are given, just a track-by-track synopsis. The liner notes comparing this to The Zombies' *Odessey And Oracle* is pushing it way too far, especially since they misspelt it as "Oddysey...".

Compilation appearances include *Run To The Sun* and *Reach Out* on *Green Crystal Ties, Vol. 6* (CD). (MW)

Sunshine

45:	Niki Hoeky/Dreams Selection	(Bumpshop 1102) 1970

A Detroit area 45. *Niki Hoeky* features lashings of waspish fuzz and wah-wah against a catchy boogie-rock backdrop. Even the brass in the backing doesn't spoil it all. *Dreams Selection* is in mellow prog-psych mode, like a soft Uriah Heep, with trilling keyboards and more waspish fuzz. A shame this appears to be their sole 45. (MW)

Sunshine Buggs

ALBUM:	1	SUNSHINE BUGGS	(Astro 4104) c1966 -

Released on the small Astro label, this album contains mostly original material in the white boy garage/soul/frat "Justice" style. Songs include *I'm Chasing A Dream*, *Bourbon Street*, *Soul Minuet*, *She Said Yeah* and Chuck Berry's *Sweet Sixteen*.

It's not known if this is the same 'Astro' label as that responsible for Texas' **Blackwell** 1969 release. (SR)

The Sunshine Company

Personnel:	MERLE BREGANTE	drms, vcls	AB
	MAURICE MANSEAU	vcls, keyb'ds, gtr	AB
	DOUGLAS MARK	gtr, violin, vcls	AB
	MARY NANCE	vcls, perc	AB
	LARRY SIMS	gtr, vcls	AB
	DAVE HODGKINS	gtr	

HCP

ALBUMS:	1(A)	HAPPY IS THE SUNSHINE COMPANY	
			(Imperial 12359) 1967 126 -
	2(A)	SUNSHINE COMPANY	(Imperial 12368) 1968 - -
	3(B)	SUNSHINE AND SHADOWS	(Imperial 12399) 1968 - -

NB: There's also a compilation *The Sunshine Company* (Rev-Ola CREV 061CD), reissued again (Rev-Ola CR REV 13) 2002 with additional sleevenotes.

HCP

45s:	Up Up And Away/Blue May (unreleased)	(Imperial 66241) 1967 -
	Happy/Blue May	(Imperial 66247) 1967 50
	Back On The Street Again/	
	I Just Want To Be Your Friend	(Imperial 66260) 1967 36
	It's Sunday/	
	Reflections On An Angel (unreleased)	(Imperial 66278) 1968 -
	Look Here Comes The Sun/	
	It's Sunday	(Imperial 66280) 1968 56
	Let's Get Together/	
	Sunday Brought The Rain	(Imperial 66298) 1968 112
	On A Beautiful Day/Darcy Farrow	(Imperial 66308) 1968 106
	Willie Jean/Love Poem	(Imperial 66324) 1968 111
	Only Thing That Matters/Bolero	(Imperial 66399) 1969 -

THE SUNSHINE COMPANY - Sunshine Company LP.

This Los Angeles-based harmony pop group's music was characterised by happy harmonies. They enjoyed some minor chart successes including *Back On The Streets Again* and *Happy*.

Produced by Joe Saraceno and arranged by George Tipton, their third album offered 14 tracks including covers of Chet Powers's *Let's Get Together* and **Hoyt Axton**'s *Willie Jean* and *On A Beautiful Day*, a song penned by Gene Stashuk before he formed **The Unspoken Word**. Larry Sims and Maury Manseau wrote most of their original material.

They won't be of interest to garage and psych fans though.

Doug Mark had earlier recorded one 45 with **The Grains Of Sand**, whilst Merle Brigante and Larry Sims went on to form Loggins and Messina's rhythm section. Dave Hodgkins' next venture was **Red Eye**.

Compilation appearances include: *Back On The Street Again* on *Nuggets, Vol. 10* (LP) and *Even More Nuggets* (CD); and *Happy* on *Nuggets, Vol. 11* (LP). (VJ/SR/GM)

The Sunshine Trolley

45:	Cover Me Babe / It's Gotta Be Real	(Trump 2890)	1970

Possibly a Los Angeles studio aggregation, *Cover Me Babe* is silky smooth **Mamas and Papas**-style harmony-pop and a film theme song, co-written by Randy Newman.

Trump was a Capitol subsidiary label.

Compilation appearances include: *Cover Me Babe* on *Bring Flowers To U.S.* (LP). (MW)

Sunshine Ward

Personnel:	MARK BRETZ	gtr	A
	RICHARD OTIS FIFIELD	vcls, gtr	A
	ROBERT CARL MCLERIAN	bs	A
	TONY MURILLO		A
	PETER M. WYANT		A

45:	Sally Go 'Round The Roses / Pay The Price	(RCA Victor 47-9227)	1967

A late incarnation of **The Astronauts**. When Bretz left, they became **Hardwater**. (SR)

Super Band

Personnel:	ROGER BRYANT	bs	A
	JIMMY GREENSPOON	keyb'ds	A
	RON MORGAN	gtr	A
	MYRON POLLOCK	drums	A
	BOB YEAZEL	gtr	A

45:	I Ain't Got Nobody / Acid Indigestion	(Capricorn CA-100)	1967

A fascinating and previously unheralded Denver group whose history has been unravelled by Michael Stelk.

Super Band, who issued one very rare single around September 1967, were a spin-off from the **West Coast Pop Art Experimental Band**. It seems that when Denver-ite and guitarist Ron Morgan was a member of the group (for the three Reprise albums, most notable is the song *Smell of Incense* which he co-wrote with **Bob Markley**) he put the call up to Denver for musicans to help the **WCPAEB** perform, in the Winter of 1966. After several months the nucleus of Morgan, Yeazel, Greenspoon and Bryant (the latter pair from Southern California) returned to Denver as **Super Band** and acquired local drummer Myron Pollock.

After a successful run at the hot rock club in town, The Exodus, the owner arranged for the recording session for the single. It seems that Morgan didn't make the session and that Yeazel played the guitar on it. Late in the Fall of 1967, Jimmy Greenspoon was called back to California when the foundation of Three Dog Night was jelling. He pulled Morgan with him and into the early version of the group, leaving Yeazel and Bryant behind to form **The Beast**.

The Beast issued two albums in 1969/70 and on the second they play a track that they wrote and performed with the **WCPAEB** called *Communication*, a "long jam" that was edited down for the final release; it may still exist in the Norman Petty archives in Clovis, New Mexico, where both albums were recorded.

Ron Morgan withdrew from Three Dog Night as they were getting ready to record and he is not on the first album, although it's said that the guitar work is based on his arrangements. He'd turn up next in the **Electric Prunes**. Originally he'd been a member of a Denver group called The Wild Ones (1965-6). Although they did not release any 45s, there are some recordings that exist. They must have been a fine group - they opened for the **Mothers of Invention** at the Whisky in late 1965, played in Hawaii and opened for several big shows in Denver. Sadly Ron Morgan passed away circa 1980.

Both Yeazel and Pollock later played in **Sugarloaf**. (MSk/MW/HS)

SUNSHINE COMPANY - Sunshine & Shadows LP.

THE SUPERFINE DANDELION - The Superfine Dandelion LP.

SURPRISE PACKAGE - Free Up LP.

Superfine Dandelion

Personnel:	RICK ANDERSON	bs, gtr	A
	ED BLACK	gtr, keyb'ds	A
	MIKE COLLINS	drms	A
	MIKE McFADDEN	gtr, vcls	A

ALBUM: 1(A) SUPERFINE DANDELION (Mainstream S/6102) 1967 R1

NB: (1) pirated on CD (no label), later reissued officially (Sundazed SC 11057) 2000. The Sundazed version comprises the original album, plus 45s, unreleased track/alternate takes and four cuts by the **Mile Ends**.

45s:	The Other Sidewalk/Ferris Wheel	(Rook no #) 1967
	The Other Sidewalk/Don't Try To Call Me	(Rook no #) 1967
	People In The Street/ ?	(Mainstream 672) 1967
	CrazyTown (Move On Little Children)/ Janie's Tomb	(Mainstream 673) 1967

This outfit was based in Phoenix, Arizona between 1966-68 and were earlier known as **The Mile Ends**. Their first 45 contains the fine psychedelic punk of *The Other Sidewalk*, and the flip features sitars and has a mellow trippy feel, with the vocalist wishing that he'd never come down...

After such an interesting start, they went on to chart regionally with their *People In The Street* 45, but their album had a strong country influence and is largely dispensable.

Most of the band later went on to greater things - Ed 'The Creeper' Black went on to play with the **Goose Creek Symphony**, Commander Cody, Linda Ronstadt, Chris Darrow and later became a Nashville session musician. Mike McFadden also briefly played with the **Goose Creek Symphony**. Anderson later joined Beans who evolved into The Tubes.

Compilation appearances include: *The Other Sidewalk* on *The Lost Generation, Vol. 2* (LP); *The Other Sidewalk* and *Ferris Wheel* on *Psychedelic Moods - Part Two* (CD); and *Janie's Tomb* on *Songs Of Faith And Inspiration* (CDR & CD). (VJ/HS)

The Surf Boys

Personnel:	DENNIS BOONE	ld vcls, gtr	A
	MARK MOUHTOURIS	drms	A
	LEE TRAVERS	ld gtr, vcls	A
	JAN ZUKOWSKI	bs, vcls	A

45:	I Told Santa Claus I Want You/ Stuck In The Chimney	(Scepter 12180) 1966

This Christmas single was by Washington DC's **Nobody's Children**, using a pseudonym to avoid contractual wrangles with United Artists.

The Surf Knights

45s:	Broken Hearts/You Lied	(Surf 100) 1966
α	Anyway/The Way It Is	(Surf 101) c1966
	In The Summer/Midnight Surf	(Tiki 1001) 1967
β	Broken Hearts/Houdini	(Decca 32205) 1967

NB: α As The Shandels. β As Dream Machine.

A Houston, Texas, outfit who went under different names. Two unreleased offerings have been compiled: There's *No Girl Like My Girl* on *Acid Visions - The Complete Collection Vol. 1* (3-CD) and *Stains Of Love* on *Houston Post - Nowsounds Groove-In* (LP). The latter album also gives *In The Summer* a welcome airing. (MW)

Surprise Package

Personnel:	GREG BECK	gtr, vcls	AB
	KIM EGGERS	sax, vcls	A
	MICHAEL ROGERS	keyb'ds, bs, vcls	AB
	FRED ZEUFELDT	drms, vcls	AB
	ROB LOWERY	ld vcls	B

ALBUM: 1(B) FREE UP (LHI S-12005) 1968 -

NB: (1) reissued on CD (Flash 57) 199?.

45s:	Out Of My Mind/Everything Fine	(Columbia 43922) 1966
	The Other Me/The Merry-Go Round Is Slowing You Down	(Columbia 44292) 1967
	I'll Run/East Side West Side	(Columbia 44460) 1968
	Free Up Pt. 1/2	(LHI 10) 1969
	New Way Home/MacArthur Park	(LHI 15) 1969

From the Pacific Northwest the origins of this band lie in **The Viceroys** (who also included Jim Valley before he joined **Paul Revere and The Raiders**). They operated mainly around the Seattle-Tacoma area of Washington state and were later known as **The American Eagle**. However, with the onset of the psychedelic era Columbia decided to market them as **The Surprise Package** and as their management were based in San Diego, they often played in California.

The album is rarely seen and worthwhile only for the extended freaky title track which is not unlike *In-A-Gadda-Da-Vida* in structure. *Out Of My Mind*, a nice slice of psychedelia produced by Terry Melcher, can also be heard on *Mindrocker, Vol. 7* (LP) or *Nuggets, Vol. 8* (LP) - Its flip is a tough Pacific Northwest guitar instrumental, but the other Columbia 45s are rather bland pop fayre.

Rob Lowery had previously been in **The Rock Collection** and that bands' earlier incarnation, **The Galaxies**. Mike Rogers also produced a 45 for **The Bumps**. (VJ/MW/DR/JA)

Surprize

Personnel:	PETE ACCARDI	vcls, hrmnca	A
	FRANK BISSEL	keyb'ds, vcls	A
	FRED KIEFFER	drms, perc	A
	RICK MARTIN	bs, vcls	A
	MARK SHAPIRO	ld gtr, vcls	A

ALBUM: 1(A) KEEP ON TRUCKIN'
(East Coast Records EC 1049) 197? R2

NB: (1) some copies with a plain white sleeve. Later reissued on vinyl.

Like **Mountain Bus**, this was a **Grateful Dead** influenced group from Pennsylvania, whose album is now sought-after. It was produced by Tony Riccia and H. Stein, who also both wrote the six cuts.

Compilation appearances include: *Earth Odissey* on *Journey To The East* (LP) and *Psychosis From The 13th Dimension* (CDR & CD). The track reappeared originally on the *Changes* (LP) compilation as the final unlisted track. (SR/MW)

The Surprize

Personnel:	ROGER FUENTES	drms	A
	BUDDY GOOD	bs, vcls	A
	JAMES MARVELL	ld vcls	A
	PAUL PARIS	ld gtr	A

45: Too Bad / I Will Make History (Cent no #) 1967

A Tampa band managed by John Centinaro, who booked bands in the Tampa area and managed some notable acts including **The Robbs**, **The Mysterians** and Neil Diamond. Released on Centinaro's own label in the Summer of '67, *I Will Make History* has done so... by appearing on *Psychedelic States: Florida Vol. 1* (CD). It's an imperious pop-punker with a hypnotic fuzz refrain.

Drummer Roger Fuentes was previously with The Early Americans. (MW/JLh/RM)

The Surrealistic Pillar

Personnel incl:	ED FUTCH	gtr, vcls	A
	EDDIE SMITH		A

45: I Like Girls/Mexican Calliope (Tamm T 2027) 1967

From Lafayette, Louisiana, this act presumably took its name from **The Jefferson Airplane**'s second album. *I Like Cars* is actually pretty good, with appealing lyrics and an effective backing.

Ed Futch is better known as Eddy Raven.

Compilation appearances include: *I Like Girls* on *Louisiana Punk Groups From The Sixties, Vol. 2* (LP), *Sixties Archive, Vol. 3* (CD) and *Highs In The Mid-Sixties, Vol. 8* (LP). (VJ/MW/AB)

Sur Royal Da Count & The Parliaments

45: Scream Mother Scream/
Sgt. Ralf Yore U.S.M.C. (Villa Yore 60617) 196?

This is a guy called Joe Yore, probably from Colorado, recording a ridiculously crude, oddball anti-parent protest. A possible candidate for the worst record ever made?

Compilation appearances include: *Scream Mother Scream* on *Highs In The Mid-Sixties, Vol. 18* (LP) and *Boulders, Vol. 1* (LP); *Sgt. Ralf Yore U.S.M.C.* on *Turds On A Bum Ride, Vol. 2* (Dble LP) and *Turds On A Bum Ride, Vol's 1 & 2* (Dble CD).

SURPRIZE - Keep On Truckin' LP.

Sutters Mill

45: I Live Today/? (Superstar 472) c1970

A hippie country-rock group with male and female vocals and harmonies, influenced by CSN&Y. (SR)

The Swagmen

45: Mendocino/So Long Baby (Americana 1205) 1969

A label out of Mishawaka, Indiana, provide us with a reedy rendition of the **Sir Douglas Quintet** classic, backed by a tame garagey rocker that sounds more like the mid-sixties. (MW)

Swallow

Personnel:	MICK ARANDA	drms	A
	BOB CAMACHO	keyb'ds	A
	PHIL GREEN	gtr	A
	GEORGE LEH	vcls	A
	VERN MILLER	gtr, vcls	A
	(JEFF BAXTER	gtr	A)

ALBUM: 1(A) OUT OF THE NEST (Warner Bros. WS 2606) 1972 -
NB: (1) also released in the U.K., (Warner K56174).

Possibly from Vermont, a powerful rock group with a gutsy singer and a horn section. Jeff "Skunk" Baxter, of **Ultimate Spinach**/Steely Dan fame, guested on some tracks. (SR)

Swampgas

Personnel:	JOCK DAVIS	bs	A
	BAIRD HERSEY	gtr	A
	KIM ORNITZ	vcls	A
	RICKY SALTER	drms	A

ALBUM: 1(A) SWAMPGAS (Buddah BDS 5102) 1971 R1

A superb and little-known album, produced by the group members and Artie Kornfeld (**Wind In The Willows**, Artie Kornfeld Tree...) and engineered by Shelly Yakus at A&R Studios, NYC. A psychic chiropractor, Charlie Tuna, is also credited on the album!

Consisting of eight long tracks, all but one are composed by Baird Hersey. A mixture of some fast numbers (*Patato Strut*, *Don't*), some melancholic ballads, two complex tracks (*Eulogy, Trapped In The City*) and a raga with sitar (*Egg Shell*). Baird Hersey was obviously influenced by **Hendrix**, but goes further than his influences and the guitars (electric and acoustic) are especially interesting. Kim Ornitz's voice sounds a bit like **Henry Tree**'s vocalist.

Baird Hersey released at least two solo albums: *Lookin' For That Groove* in 1978, consisting of jazz rock (Novus/Arista) and *ODO OP8 FX* in 1980 (Bent), which was very experimental, with tape loops.

Artie Kornfeld had previously played with **The Changin' Times**. (SR)

The Swamp Rats

Personnel incl:	BOB HOCKO	vcls	AB
	DICK NEWTON	gtr	AB
	DENNY NICHOLSON	bs	A
	DAVE GANNON	drms	B
	PAUL SHALAKO	bs	B
	DON SHRINER	gtr	B
	GREG DETTORE	drms	

ALBUM:	1	DISCO SUCKS	(Keystone K111541-3A) 1979 -

45s:	Louie Louie/Hey Joe	(St Clair MF 69) 1966
	Psycho/Here There And Everywhere	(St Clair 2222) 1966
	Two Tymes Two/Mr. Sad	(St Claire 3333) 1966
	No Friend Of Mine/It's Not Easy	(St Clair 711-711) 1966
	In The Midnight Hour/It's Not Easy	(Co and Ce 245) 1967
	Brown Sugar/Brown Sugar	(Segue 107) 1972

Originally known as **The Fantastic Dee Jays**, (line-up 'A'), this was Pittsburgh's top punk band. They specialised in doing really wild covers of some of the classic songs of the era. Most of their finest moments can be heard on Eva's *Swamp Rats vs. Unrelated Segments* (LP) album which includes their covers of *Louie Louie, Hey Joe, Psycho, No Friend Of Mine, It's Not Easy, In The Midnight Hour, Here There And Everywhere* and a previously unreleased version of *Til The End Of The Day*.

A picture of the classic line-up 'B' circa 1966 can be seen in Crypt's *Back From The Grave Vol. 1* - the on-stage shot was taken at manager Terry Lee's "Night Train" club in Elizabeth, P.A.

By the early seventies only Bob Hocko would be left and they became **Galactus**, whose album was a lacklustre trudge through Stones' covers and beer-hall rock fayre.

In 1979, Bob Hocko put out the *Disco Sucks* album which has one side of 1966-7 tracks (six of 'em) and one side of five 1970s tracks (three 'Stones covers, one Kinks and one original).

SWAMPGAS - Swampgas LP.

Compilation appearances have included: *Louie Louie* on *Acid Dreams - The Complete 3 LP Set* (3-LP) and *Acid Dreams Testament* (CD); *It's Not Easy* on *Terry Lee Show WMCK* (LP); *No Friend Of Mine* and *It's Not Easy* on *Burghers, Vol. 1* (LP & CD); *Psycho* on *Back From The Grave, Vol. 1* (LP) and *Garage Kings* (Dble LP); *Hey Joe* on *The Cicadelic 60's, Vol. 2* (LP); and *Ain't No Friend Of Mine* on *Gone, Vol. 2* (LP). (MW/VJ/DMr/BSy)

Swaydes

45:	Anymore/Why	(Paris Tower 108) 1967

From Tampa, Florida, this act had just one single. A mere 500 copies were pressed and most were destroyed eventually by the band when sales proved disappointing. Luckily, *Anymore* has since been preserved on *Sixties Rebellion, Vol. 7* (LP & CD). (TJH/MW)

Sweathog

Personnel:	BOB JONES	gtr, vcls	A
	LENNY LEE GOLDSMITH	keyb'ds, vcls	AB
	BARTHOLOMEW SMITH		
	FROST "FROST"	drms	AB
	DAVID LEONARD		
	JOHNSON	bs, vcls	A

ALBUMS:	1(A)	SWEATHOG	(CBS 30601) 1971 -
	2(B)	HALLELUJAH	(CBS 31144) 1972 -

NB: (2) also released in the UK (CBS 64784).

45:	Hallelujah/Still On The Road	(CBS) 1972

From California, a rock-pop outfit with organ/guitar/drums interplay formed by experienced musicians, as "Frosty" was previously the drummer for **Lee Michaels**, Goldsmith was in Wolfgang and Jones and Johnston had played in **Blue Mountain Eagle**. Their second album came with a giant poster and both are best avoided. When the group broke up, Goldsmith became a studio musician and later played with the last line-up of **Stoneground**. (SR)

The Sweetarts

Personnel:	DWIGHT DOW	drms, vcls	A
	MIKE GALBRAITH	vcls, perc	A
	ERNIE GAMMAGE	gtr, ld vcls	A
	TOM VAN ZANDT	keyb'ds, vcls	A
	PAT WHITEFIELD	bs	A
	ERBIE BOWSER	organ	

45s:	So Many Times/ You Don't Have To Hurt Me	(Vandan 609 V-8195) 1966
	A Picture Of Me/Without You (PS)	(Sonobeat 101) 1967

This Austin five-piece became the first band to sign to the Sonobeat label run by Bill Josey and his son late in 1966. The resulting 45, written by Gammage was an excellent pop single and sold quite well.

Gammage and Dow were originally members of the Fabulous Chevelles prior to their stint in **The Sweetarts**. The majority of the **Sweetarts** would later morph into Fast Cotton. According to Ernie Gammage, later members did NOT evolve into the **Lavender Hill Express** or **Plymouth Rock**, as we previously had thought. Gammage did however go on to play for another Texas band, **Plum Nelly**.

Compilation coverage has so far included: *A Picture Of Me* on *All Cops In Delerium - Good Roots* (LP) and *I'm Trippin' Alone* (LP); and *So Many Times* on *Texas Flashback (The Best Of)* (CD), *Texas Flashbacks, Vol. 1* (CD) and *Flashback, Vol. 1* (LP). (VJ/MW/MDo)

The Sweet Acids

45:	That Creature/ Gonna Live Another Day Or Two	(Unique. A-14-1940-10) 1969

Released on a Carrollton, Georgia, label which may indicate their homebase, their 45 includes a rather commercial pop song. It features moog-like noises and pleasant harmonies that are at odds with vitriolic female-put-down lyrics probably considered un-PC these days, e.g. "Leave that ugly creature from another planet" and "a creature from the local zoo".

Compilation appearances include: *That Creature* on *Pebbles Box* (5-LP), *Pebbles, Vol. 22* (LP), *The Essential Pebbles Collection, Vol. 2* (Dble CD), *Acid Dreams - The Complete 3 LP Set* (3-LP), *Acid Dreams Epitaph* (CD), *Trash Box* (5-CD) and *Psychedelic States: Georgia Vol. 1* (CD). (VJ/MW)

Sweet Briar

45s:	We Can Work It Out/Slow Down	(Butter Sound 42076)	196?
	We Can Work It Out/Slow Down	(Heaven 72x7O)	196?

A West Texas outfit who had formed in the early sixties, issuing several 45s under different spellings of the name The Shayds. As **Sweet Briar** they put out two different versions of this rock'n'roll boogie 45. (VJ)

Sweet Cherry

Personnel:	MARK CARLI	ld vcls, sax	A
	GREG CHAIVRE	bs, bcking vcls	A
	RAY SOUCIE	ld gtr, bcking vcls	A
	PAUL ???	drms	A

45:	Eight Day Blues / Funny Things Floating	(Stop S-101-A/B) 1967

Sweet Cherry hailed from Trenton, Michigan, one of the 'down-river' suburbs a few miles from Detroit. Their sole single was recorded in a local 2-track studio as a demo disc, while they were still in high school. It was cut 'live' with no overdubs or studio sweetening, other than a bit of reverb on the vocals. The recording was self financed and 500 copies were pressed up by the band - many were given away at their live shows at local schools and dance clubs, although a large number were destroyed by 'sailing' them frisbee style off a mountain in Kentucky following a road trip... Surviving copies are consequently rare!

The story goes that the band used such a primitive PA system that they were never able to hear the vocalist, Carli, (whose girlfriend incidentally was a dancing regular on a Windsor, Canada teen show called "Swingin' Time") until they heard the playback of the 7". Subsequently they decided to become a strictly instrumental band, playing all original compositions and extended jams, with Carli on sax instead of vocals.

Without the constraints of the pop-song format, they became well respected as musicians and praised for their originality, but opportunities to play live dwindled and following school graduation (1968/69) the group quietly disintegrated.

Their two cuts:- *Eight Day Blues* and *Funny Things Floating* can be found on *Michigan Mayhem Vol. 1* (CD) and *Michigan Mixture, Vol. 1* (LP). The second of these is very garagey with some good guitar work in places. (SG/VJ)

Sweet Magnolia Band

Personnel:	JOHN GOOD	fiddle, banjo, gtr, sax, mandolin, drms, vcls	A
	WAYNE PIMBERTON	keyb'ds, vcls	A
	DAVID RADDLE	bs, gtr, vcls	A
	GARY RAY	perc, gtr, mandolin, keyb'ds	A
	PHIL SCHLENKER	steel gtr, gtr, keyb'ds, trumpet	A
	MIKE SCOGGINS	ld vcls, gtr, hrmnca	A

ALBUM:	1(A)	SWEET MAGNOLIA BAND (Lardbucket Records 0001LP) 197? R2

From Little Rock, Arkansas. There's no date on the album, but it looks/sounds 1974 or so. Less hillbilly than one might expect by the label name, this is very competent rural-rock with some fine lead guitar and all but a couple of tracks have a distinctly weedburning feel. The band looks particularly wasted on the cover picture - and the back cover sports some of the strangest typographical errors ever seen! (CF)

Sweet Marie

Personnel:	WILLY BIMS	drms	A
	SONNY LATHROP	gtr, vcls	A
	PRINCE TEDDY	bs, vcls	A

ALBUMS:	1(A)	SWEET MARIE # 1 (Yardbird Records YDBS 770) 1970 SC
	2(A)	STUCK IN PARADISE (Yardbird Records YDBS 771) 1971 SC

NB: (2) reissued on CD (Gear Fab GF-172) 2001.

HCP

45s:	Remember Mary/Don't You Understand	(Yard Bird 8009) 1970 -
	Remember Mary/Don't You Understand	(Liberty 56215) 1970 -
	Do You (Find Me A Way)/ I Got That Feelin'	(Yard Bird 8011) 1970 -
	My Little Angel/Stuck In Paradise	(Yard Bird 8012) 1971 -
	Stella's Candy Store/Another Feelin'	(Yard Bird 8013) 1971 123

This band resided in Honolulu, Hawaii, although Sonny Lathrop had previously been in California bands Mickey and The Invaders and **The Starfires**. Their albums contained acid-rock, exotic rhythms and hard-rock and both have been reissued. (VJ/MW)

SWEET MAGNOLIA BAND - Swet Magnolia Band LP.

SWEET MARIE - Sweet Marie #1 LP.

SWEET MARIE - Stuck In Paradise LP.

SWEET PANTS - Fat Peter Presents LP.

Sweet Nothings

45s:	Baby Please/Cry Baby Cry	(Marina 501) 1965
	Baby Please/Cry Baby Cry	(Destination 611) 1965
	A Girl In Love Forgives/ Wish He'd Let Me Be	(Marina 505) 1966

A short-lived all girl trio from Chicago. They were literally 'picked up' by Marina, which was **The Royal Flairs**' own label, since a couple of the lads got romantically involved with these sweet young thangs! The suitors' wish to impress resulted in the girls' first release and the label's first too. Whether romance continued to blossom after their third and final release we may never know. (VJ)

Sweet Pain

Personnel:	FRANK DEMME	vcls, bs	A
	MARTY FOLTZ	drms, perc	A
	CARL JOHNSON	ld gtr	A
	J.C. PHILLIPS	vcls, perc	A
	DAVID RIORDAN	vcls, gtr	A
	BOB SPALDING	ld gtr, special effects	A
	(JOE JULIAN	double bs, organ	A)
	(MEL TAX	flute	A)

ALBUM: 1(A) SWEET PAIN (UA UAS-6793) 1970 -

45s:	Berkeley Lady/ Upside Down, Inside Out Woman	(UA 50761) 1970
α	Chain Up The Devil/ Timber Gibbs	(UA 50808) 1971

NB: α has a non LP flip.

Produced by Frank Slay (**Strawberry Alarm Clock**, **Boenzee Cryque**...), this group should interest fans of Californian sounds with good guitars, like **Redwing** or **Redeye**.

Sweet Pain was fronted by Riordan and Phillips and the highlights of their very consistent album include the long *Joy* with its twin guitars, *Richard And Me* (the only cover, a Pistilli and West song from 1967) and *The Lover*. Their music was mainly comprised of free flowing West Coast rock with shared vocals and interesting guitar solos but also included a melancholic instrumental track with 12-string guitar.

The same year, Phillips and Slay produced the first album by **Sugarloaf**. In 1974, Marty Foltz drummed behind Tim Weisberg and, in 1979, Demme and Johnson formed the obscure Rock Rose who recorded one album on CBS. (SR)

Sweet Pants

Personnel:	MICHAEL CARR	drms	A
	TONY MOLLA	gtr	A
	MERK MOZZONE	bs	A
	MIKE MULLONEY	keyb'ds, vcls	A

ALBUM: 1(A) FAT PETER PRESENTS (Barclay LP 1141) 1971 R2

An interesting album from this outfit from Penna, although the vocals do sound rather flat in places. It was obviously recorded with rather primitive equipment. (VJ)

Sweet Pie

ALBUM: 1 PLEASURE PUDDING (ESP) c1969 -

Another obscure hippie-folk act on this eclectic New York label. (SR)

Sweet Revival

Personnel incl: DON HILL gtr, vcls A

ALBUM: 1 SWEET REVIVAL
(SSS International Records SSS-16) 1970 -

From the South (Tennessee, Alabama ?) and produced by Fred Burch, a Christian rock trio with some good guitar and organ parts, but the overall result is best avoided, the songs being inconsistent, with the exception of *Mr. Soul Saving Man*.

Other SSS albums include U.S. Apple Corps, H.Y. Sledge and **Arnold Bean**.

Sweet Smoke

Personnel:	RAY BOE		A
	SAMMY BOE		A
	GARY MILLER		A
	RON THIBERT		A

45s:	Morning Dew/Mary Jane Is To Love	(Jan-Gi 101) 1968
	Morning Dew/Mary Jane Is To Love	(Amy 1 1,042) 1968
	You've Got To Hide Your Love Away/ You Don't Know Like I Know	(Amy 11,0053) 1969
	Baby Sweet Baby (What You Doing To Me)/ I Want You	(Jan-Gi 102) 1969

Originally from Minot in North Dakota this band then known as **The Tracers** relocated to Amarillo in Texas and issued a 45 for Sully. Moving on to Fort Worth and calling themselves the Try-Cerz they then issued a 45 for Jan-Gi before a further change of name to **Sweet Smoke**. *Morning Dew* was a fine garage version of a classic folk-rocker and also had a fine dope inspired flip, with a superb hammond break. The 45 was leased to Amy for wider distribution and in an attempt to break through the group recorded a Beatles cover for the next 45. However, it was not to be and they disbanded late in 1969. The quartet still reside in Fort Worth.

Check out *Mary Jane Is To Love* on *Marijuana Unknowns* (LP & CD) and *Morning Dew* on *Texas Flashbacks, Vol. 3* (LP & CD), *Flashback, Vol. 3* (LP) and *Highs In The Mid Sixties, Vol. 23* (LP). (VJ)

Sweet Toothe

Personnel:	P.D. BRATTON	bs	A
	MICHAEL CHILCO	drms	A
	EMERSON R. CONLEY	ld gtr	A
	MICHAEL HOPKINS	vcls	A
	DAVID M. LEEDY	gtr	A

ALBUM: 1(A) TESTING (Dominion N R 7360) 1975 R3

NB: (1) reissued on vinyl by Void in a limited edition of 400.

This album by a local band from Bluefield, West Virginia, is well worth investigation. Consistently good throughout it oozes with superb heavy progressive guitar work. *All The Way Home* is one of the most 'psychedelic' tracks and the opening cut, *Karen*, is a melodic pop-rock number. An under-rated, largely unknown album which may get greater recognition in time. (VJ)

Sweet Vengeance

45: Tomorrow/She Said (MGM 14177) c1969

An obscure heavy psych group. (SR)

Sweetwater

Personnel:	AUGUST BURNS	cello	AB
	R.G. CARLYLE	gtr, bongos, vcls	A
	ELPIDIO PETE COBIAN	perc	AB
	ALEX DEL ZOPPO	keyb'ds	AB
	FRED HERRERA	bs, vcls	AB
	ALAN MALAROWITZ	drms	AB
	ALBERT MOORE	flute, vcls	AB
	NANSI NEVINS	ld vcls, acc. gtr	AB

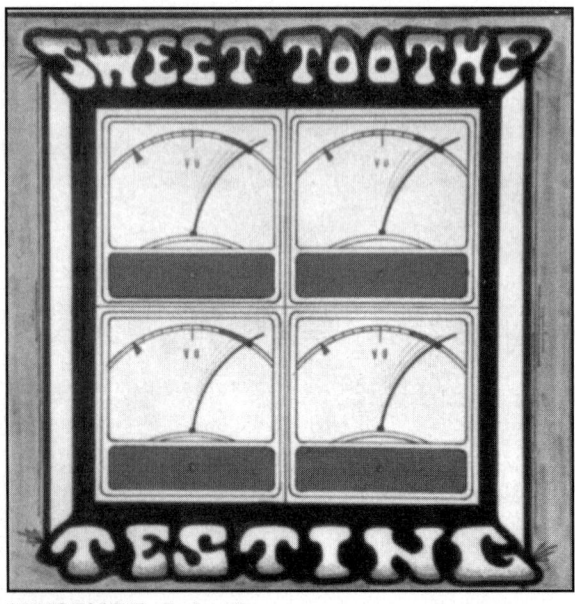

SWEET TOOTHE - Testing LP.

ALBUMS:	1(A)	SWEETWATER	(Reprise RS 6313) 1969	200 - HCP
	2(B)	JUST FOR YOU	(Reprise RS 6417) 1970	- -
	3(B)	MELON	(Reprise RS 6473) 1971	- -

45s:	What's Wrong/My Crystal Spider	(Reprise 0787) 1968
	Motherless Child/Why Oh Why	(Reprise 0816) 1969
	For Pete's Sake/Rondeau	(Reprise 0835) 1969
	Just For You/Look Out	(Reprise 0987) 1970
	Day Song / Without Me	(Reprise 1002) 1971
	Join The Band Part 1 / Join The Band Part 2	(Reprise 1076) 1972

A communal hippie band the San Fernando Valley area of Los Angeles who played an amalgam of psychedelia, classical, folk, jazz and latin styles. Their first album (produced by Dave Hassinger) is the best. The band's original drummer Alan Malarowitz appears only on two tracks of *Melon*, their third album:- *I'm Happy Today* and *Join The Band*. The rest of the album was recorded with session drummer Ricky Fataar, most famous for his appearance in the "rockumentary" *The Rutles: All You Need Is Cash* (he's The Rutles' drummer Stig O'Hara), and touring with The Beach Boys in the early seventies. It spent two weeks at No. 200 in the charts.

Before the first album, Nancy (not yet Nansi) Nevins also recorded one 45, *Don't Hold Back* (Tom Cat Records 10291), produced by Tom Catalano.

They were the first group on stage on the opening day of Woodstock, following **Richie Havens**, but nothing from their set made it onto the movie or soundtrack.

Following the band's split, Nansi (now Nancy) Nevins issued a self-titled solo album (Tom Cat Records BYL-1-1063) 1975. (VJ/RKt/NR/MW/SR/EG)

T. Swift and The Electric Bag

ALBUM: 1 ARE YOU EXPERIENCED? (Custom 1115) 1967 SC

NB: (1) reissued on CD (Gear Fab GF-173) 2001.

Nothing is known about this band, although the album sounds similar to **Animated Egg** or **Underground** but better. The title track is an interesting and different interpretation of the **Hendrix** classic. The last track on Side Two, *Expo In Sound*, also has some inspired jamming. The album had a vocal and an instrumental side.

A San Antonio outfit, Tom Swift and The Electric Grandmothers, who had a 45 on Sound Tex in 1964, could well be the forebears of this bunch.

Compilation appearances include *Are You Experienced?* on *Endless Journey - Phase Three* (LP). (VJ/MK/MW)

Swift Rain

Personnel:	ANDRE "SEAWEED" BONAGUIDI	drms, perc, vcls	A
	MIKE "CHICK" CICCARELLI	gtr, vcls	A
	FRANKIE "THE DUCK" SOTELO	gtr, keyb'ds, perc, vcls	A
	PAUL "WRANGLER" WEST	bs, perc, vcls	A

ALBUM: 1(A) COMING DOWN (HI SHL-32064) 1969 25 - HCP

Recorded in Memphis, Tennessee this album has been described as 'psych' in some quarters but turns out to be engaging late-sixties guitar-dominated power-rock, with light'n'heavy moods and some ripping solos. Certainly not for garage or psych fans, but recommended to admirers of early Joe-Walsh-period James Gang. (MW)

The Swingin' Apolloes

See **The Apolloes**.

T.SWIFT and THE ELECTRIC BAG - Are You Experienced? LP.

Swinging Machine

Personnel:	DICK BOCOCK	drms	A
	LEE CARAWAY	gtr	A
	BOB FISHER	sax	A
	EVAN PIERCE	bs	A
	GARY RICHARDSON	vcls	A
	BILL STALLINGS	organ	A

45:	Do You Have To Ask?/		
	Comin' On Back Home	(SPQR 1101)	1966

Formed in 1964 in the Churchland area of Portsmouth, Virginia. this versatile band were well-respected amongst their rivals on the Tidewater scene. Richardson had a wide range of styles. His soulful quality, sounding like a cross between Eric Burdon and Mick Jagger, can be heard on the so-cool punker *Do You Have To Ask?*. Underpinned by a tight but swingin' rhythm section and a simple but effective piercing guitar refrain and pizzicato solo, it's both unique and unforgettable. Two versions are featured on *Aliens, Psychos And Wild Things* (CD) where it is accompanied the flip, a reedy pop-punker.

The band came to an unfortunate end with the death of Gary Richardson in July 1968.

Compilation appearances have included: *Do You Have To Ask?* (two versions) and *Comin' On Back Home* on *Aliens, Psychos And Wild Things* (CD); and *Do You Have To Ask?* on *What A Way To Die* (LP) and *Hang It Out To Dry* (CD). (BHr/ST/MW/VJ)

Swingin' Medallions

Personnel:	CARROLL BLEDSOE	trumpet	A
	STEVE CALDWELL	sax, drms, keyb'ds	A
	JIM DOARES	gtr	A
	BRENT FORTSON	keyb'ds, woodwind	A
	JOHN McELRATH	keyb'ds, vcls	A
	JOE MORRIS	drms	A
	JIM PERKINS	sax, bs	A
	CHARLIE WEBBER	trumpet	A

HCP

ALBUM:	1(A)	DOUBLE SHOT (OF MY BABY'S LOVE)			
			(Smash SRS 67083)	1966	88 -

NB: (1) also issued in mono (MGS 27083). There's also a CD retrospective entitled *Anthology*.

HCP

45s:	Bye Bye Silly Girl / I Want To Be Your Guy	(Dot 16721)	1965 -
	Double Shot (Of My Baby's Love)/		
	Here It Comes Again	(4 Sale 002)	1965 -
	Double Shot (Of My Baby's Love)/		
	Here It Comes Again	(Smash 2033)	1966 17
	She Drives Me Out Of My Mind/		
	You Gotta Have Faith	(Smash 2050)	1966 71
	I Don't Want To Lose It For You Baby/		
	Night Owl	(Smash 2075)	1966 -
	I Found A Rainbow/Don't Cry No More	(Smash 2084)	1967 107
	Summer's Not The Same This Year/		
	Turn On The Music	(Smash 2107)	1967 -
	Where Can I Go To Get Soul/		
	Bow And Arrow	(Smash 2129)	1967 -
	We're Gonna Hate Ourselves In The Morning /		
	It's Alright	(1-2-3 1723)	1969 -
	Rollin' Rovin' River /		
	Don't Let Your Feet Touch The Ground	(1-2-3 1732)	1970 -

(Michael and The Medallions)
45:	I Wanna Talk To You / Better Forget Her	(Bragg B-222)	1965

(Swinging Medallions Featuring Al Michael)
45:	Something You Said To Me /		
	Waiting For You	(Apollo AM-007/8)	1966

NB: It has not been confirmed that the Bragg and Apollo 45s were by this group.

An eight man frat-rock outfit from Greenwood, South Carolina, who enjoyed some limited chart success and whose album has become a minor collectable and made No. 88 in the U.S. Album Charts back in 1966. They released numerous 45s, in addition to those listed, on 1-2-3 and Capitol and would still be wowing punters in The South in the new millennnium.

In 1967, Caldwell and Forston broke away to form The Pieces of Eight and released 45s on Action, A&M and Mala, including a new version of *Double Shot* in 1969.

Steve Caldwell died of pancreatic cancer on January 28th 2002 at the age of 55. He'd left the band in 1969, got a master's degree in chemistry at the University of South Carolina before returning to his native Atlanta, where he ran the Norell temporary staffing agency until starting his own company in 1976.

Compilation coverage has so far included: *Double Shot (Of My Baby's Love)* on *Frat Rock! The Greatest Rock N Roll Party Tunes Of All Time*, *Highs Of The Sixties*, *Wild Thing We Have Come For Your Children*, *Nuggets Box* (4-CD), *Nuggets From Nuggets* (CD) and *Excerpts From Nuggets* (CD). (VJ/MW/LS/SM)

(Swingin') Yo Yo's

Personnel:	RICK ALLEN	organ	A
	RAY DOTY	drms	A
	TED MARSHALL	ld gtr	A
	DENNY MORGAN	vcls	A
	RUSTY TAYLOR	vcls	A
	BILL VANCE	bs	A

45s:	α	Leaning On You/I Can't Forget You	(Goldwax 303)	1966
	α	Gotta Find A New Love/		
		I've Got Something In My Eye	(Goldwax 310)	1966
		Have You Ever / Do Something	(Jubilee 5569)	1967

NB: α as The Yo Yo's.

From Memphis, Tennessee and originally known as The Yo Yo's, they added the "Swingin'" prefix for the final 45 to avoid clashing with the NYC **Yo-Yo's**, since that bunch's hyphen was not a notable difference. They also shared management with **Sam The Sham**. *Leaning On You* was written by **Joe South**, recorded at Muscle Shoals in Alabama and engineered by Rick Hall who also worked with Otis Redding.

The band also played in New York and Atlanta.

Their full story is told in Ron Hall's book on the Memphis scene (1960-1975) - 'Playing For A Piece Of The Door', published in 2001 by Shangri-La Projects, ISBN 0-9668575-1-8.

Compilation coverage has included: *Gotta Find A New Love* on *Project Blue, Vol. 1* (LP) and *Teenage Shutdown, Vol. 3* (LP); and *Leaning On You* on *A History Of Garage And Frat Bands In Memphis* (CD).

A similarly named Yo Yoz from California recorded on Sacramento's Ikon label. (MW/MM)

The Swiss Movement

Personnel:	GREG CHESSE	ld vcls	A
	GENE COLEMAN	drms	A
	BOB GEISSLER	bs, vcls	A
	KENT LIMING	gtr	A

45:	Spoonful/Inside Of Me	(Perky 101) 1968

Originally known as The Speidels this outfit came from San Antonio in Texas and won the 1968 battle of the bands in Austin. Their 45 was a **Hendrix**-styled heavy fuzz effort and they were connected to another Texas outfit called The Runaways.

Bob Geissler and Kent Liming had earlier played with **The Laughing Kind**.

An act of this name had at least three 45s on RCA in the seventies, but Bob Geissler informs us that they were the work of a different band. The Speidels also had a couple of 45s under their own name. (VJ)

Symphonic Metamorphosis

ALBUM:	1 SYMPHONIC METAMORPHOSIS	(London) c1971 -

45:	Creation/Reach Out	(London 45-133) c1971

An obscure early heavy progressive outfit with acid guitar, keyboards and some horns. They later shortened their name to **Metamorphosis**. (SR/EW)

Syndicate

45s:	My Baby's Barefoot/Love Will Take Away	(Dore 743) 1965
	Egyptian Thing/She Haunts You	(Dot 16807) 1965

A really raw and frantic punk band from the Los Angeles County suburbs of Whittier and Long Beach. They formed in 1964 and had consolidated into a five piece by January 1965. Their first 45, *My Baby's Barefoot*, is characterised by slashing guitar and the vocalist's ravings about a mean woman. Their second, *Egyptian Thing*, is another frantic punk assault on the senses.

Not surprisingly, they were a popular live attraction and, aside from the usual high school and college dances in the area, appeared at Ciro's LeDisc (*) and the Sea Witch in Hollywood, the Marina Palace in Seal Beach and The Cinnamon Cinder in Long Beach. After signing to Dot Records they were to have recorded an album of originals *Five The Hard Way*, but the project ran into problems and they split in mid-1966.

Compilation appearances have included: *She Haunts You* on *No No No* (CD); *The Egyptian Thing* and *My Baby's Barefoot* on *Back From The Grave, Vol. 7* (Dble LP); and *The Egyptian Thing* on *Chosen Few, Vol's 1 & 2* (CD) and *The Chosen Few, Vol. 2* (LP).

NB: (*) probably after the club changed names to "It's Boss". (VJ/DPe)

The Syndicate of Sound

Personnel:	DON BASKIN	sax, flute	A
	JOHN DUCKWORTH	drms	A
	BOB GONZALEZ	bs	A
	JIM SAWYERS	ld gtr	A
	JOHN SHARKEY	keyb'ds, gtr, vcls	A

HCP

ALBUM:	1(A) LITTLE GIRL	(Bell 6001) 1966 148 SC

NB: (1) released on Stateside (SSL 101 85) in the U.K. Reissued in the late eighties and later on vinyl (Sundazed LP 5051) 1997 and CD (Sundazed SC 6120) 1997. Also of interest is *Syndicate Of Sound* (Performance PERF 388) 1988, also released on CD; *Little Girl - The History Of* (Performance) 1995, a CD release which contains 22 tracks; and *Collection Of Rare Tracks* (Performance) 199?, a compilation which comprises mostly single tracks that were released after the band's initial success but never quite caught on. The styles vary from cut to cut. Liner notes outline their story which spanned from 1964 all the way to 1970s.

HCP

45s:	Prepare For Love/Tell The World	(Scarlet 503) 1965 -
	Prepare For Love/Tell The World	(Del-Fi 4304) 1965 -
	Little Girl/You	(Hush 228) 1966 -
	Little Girl/You	(Bell 640) 1966 8
	Rumours/The Upper Hand	(Bell 646) 1966 55
	Good Time Music/Keep It Up	(Bell 655) 1966 -
	That Kind Of Mari/Mary	(Bell 666) 1967 -
	Brown Paper Bag/Reverb Beat	(Buddah 156) 1967 73
	Mexico/First To Love You	(Buddah 183) 1967 -
α	Little Girl/Rumors (PS)	(Hip Pocket HP-29) 1967 -
	You're Looking Fine/Change The World	(Capitol 2426) 1968 -

NB: α 4" flexi. There's also a retrospective 45: *Who'll Be The Next In Line/The Spider And The Fly* (PS) (Sundazed S 116) 1996, which contains two previously unreleased live tracks from 1965 at the Silver Dollar Saloon, San Jose.

This garage-rock quintet formed in San Jose in 1965 and are best known for their Top Ten hit *Little Girl*. By 1968 they were aiming at underground audiences and, although they achieved no further commercial success, they remained a popular live attraction. Their album (*Little Girl*) made No. 148 in the U.S. Album Charts and has become quite collectable.

In April 1965, just off a short tour headlining the Pacific Northwest with **Paul Revere and The Raiders**, they descended upon the San Mateo County Fairgrounds for The Teenage Fair (in April of 1965) and won the top prize at the Battle of the Bands competition - studio time at Del-Fi studios and a contract to release one Del-Fi single. The label passed on the option to release the single; instead they pressed up fifteen hundred promo copies of the single and gave them to the band, who took them back home to San Jose to sell at their shows. The 'A' side is an Animals copy, while the 'B' side is a lightweight, almost Beach Boys-like pop tune written by Sharkey. After the band had a minor hit on the Billboard charts with *Little Girl* Del-Fi reconsidered and decided to officially issue the earlier single, this time on the Scarlet label. However this was pulled quickly after objections from the band's recording manager (and Hush label-owner) Garrie Thompson.

The Syndicate of Sound toured constantly for the latter half of 1966, taking time off to tape TV shows like American Bandstand and Where the Action Is. Soul singer James Brown, who appeared with them on one of the TV shows, was so impressed that he invited them to open his theatre show in San Francisco. Success was short for the band; a year or so later drummer Duckworth was drafted at the height of the Vietnam conflict, the band went through several other changes from its original line-up and recorded three singles at the end of 1969. Baskin then moved to Los Angeles in 1970, where he and Gonzalez (the only other remaining original member of the band) mounted an unsuccessful attempt at recording another album for Capitol Records. It didn't do much, so they disbanded.

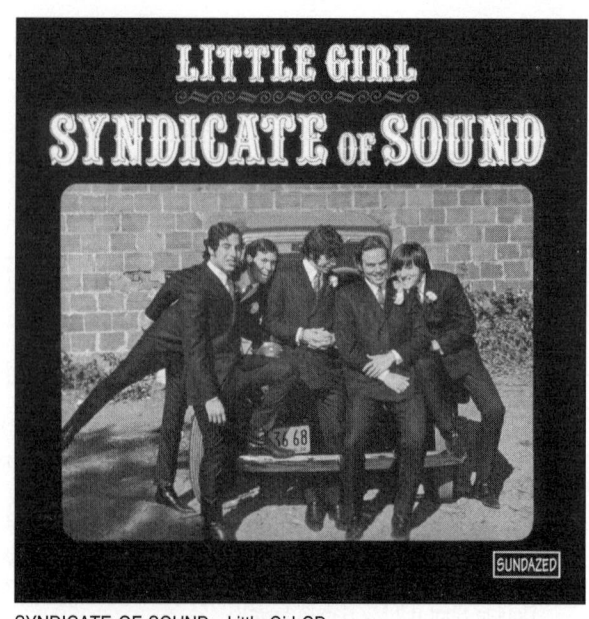

SYNDICATE OF SOUND - Little Girl CD.

The *Syndicate Of Sound* retrospective album features two unreleased cuts, the last three 45s and other selected 45 and album cuts.

Compilation coverage has so far included: *(We Ain't Got) Nothin' Yet* on *Nuggets Box* (CD); *Little Girl* on *Wild Thing*, *Nuggets* (CD), *Nuggets From Nuggets* (CD), *Nuggets, Vol. 12* (LP), *Sound Of The Sixties* (Dble LP), *Sixties Archive, Vol. 1* (CD), *Excerpts From Nuggets* (CD). Big Beat's *Hush Records Story* (CD) includes nine tracks by the band (*Little Girl*, *Get Outta My Life*, *Looking For The Good Times (The Robot)*, *That Kind Of Man*, *Rumors*, *Say I Love You*, *Mary (alternate version) (Marrie)*, *Games* and *Saturday Night*), many unreleased. A live rendition of *Louie Louie* from 1966 appears on the flexi 45 that came with 'Cream Puff War #2'. The San Jose *Todaze Yesterday* CD includes three tracks by the 1996 line-up - *Shakin' All Over*, *My Lonely Sad Eyes* and *Off The Hook*. (VJ/MW/BTs/EDW)

Synod

ALBUM: 1 NOBODY'S JUKEBOX (Private Pressing RS-21375) c1972 -

A local Illinois quintet whose album is in a pop-psych mould with some fuzz guitar and original and rather mellow material. *To A Californian*, *Future Shock*, *Touch A Clown* are some of the best tracks of this album, which came housed in a gatefold sleeve. (SR)

The System

45: Katheraynne/One In A Million (Vineyard 444) 196?

This rock quintet worked out of Minneapolis, Minnesota, in the mid and late sixties. They also have a cut, *Smiling Eyes*, on *Gathering At The Depot* (LP). (VJ)

Gabor Szabo

ALBUMS:			
1	GYPSY '66	(ABC Impulse! AS-9105)	1965 -
2	SIMPATICO	(ABC Impulse! AS-9122)	1965/6 -
3	SPELLBINDER	(ABC Impulse! AS-9123)	1966 -
4	JAZZ RAGA	(ABC Impulse! AS-9128)	1966 SC
5	THE SORCERER	(ABC Impulse! AS-9146)	1966 -
6	WIND SKY AND DIAMONDS	(ABC Impulse! AS-9151)	1967 -
7	LIGHT MY FIRE	(ABC Impulse! AS-9159)	1967 -
8	MORE SORCERY	(ABC Impulse! AS-9167)	1967 -
9	BACCHANAL	(Skye SK-3)	1968 -
10	DREAMS	(Skye SK-7)	1968 -
11	1969 (comp)	(Skye SK-9)	1969 -
12	BLOWIN' SOME OLD SMOKE	(Buddah BDS-20-SK)	1970 -
13	MIZRAB	(CTI 6026)	c1973 -
14	RAMBLER	(CTI 6035)	1974 -
15	NIGHTFLIGHT	(Mercury 1091)	1976 -
16	FACES	(Mercury 1141)	1977 -

NB: (1) with Gary McFarland and Co. (6) with The California Dreamers.

45s:		
	Walk On By / Yesterday	(ABC Impulse 45-244) 1965
	Gypsy Queen / Bang Bang	(ABC Impulse 45-248) 1966
	Witchcraft / Spellbinder	(ABC Impulse 45-254) 1966
	Paint It Black / Sophisticated Wheels	(ABC Impulse 45-257) 1966
	The Beat Goes On / Space	(ABC Impulse 45-263) 1967
	Saigon Bride /12:30 (Young Girls Are Coming To The Canton)	(ABC Impulse 45-268) 1967
	Sunshine Superman / (Theme From) Valley Of The Dolls	(Skye 451) 1968
	Bacchanal / Book Of Love	(Skye 454) 1968
	Fire Dance / Ferris Wheel	(Skye 459) 1968
	Dear Prudence / Stormy	(Skye 4515) 1968/9
	Sealed With A Kiss / Both Sides Now	(Skye 4517) 1969
α	Rocky Raccoon / That's What Happens	(Buddah 215) 1971
	Close To You / Love Theme From Spartacus	(Blue Thumb 7118) 197?
β	Breezin' / Azure Blue	(Blue Thumb 200) 197?
	It's Going To Take Some Time / ?	(CTI OJ-14) 1973
	Baby Rattle Snake / Keep Smiling	(Mercury 73840) 1976

NB: α with Lena Horne, β with Bobby Womack.

Born in Hungary in 1936, jazz guitarist **Gabor Szabo** arrived in the U.S.A. in 1956 with Louis Kabok (**The Advancement**) and began playing on records by Chico Hamilton. A very gifted guitarist with a specific touch and sound, he became influenced by Indian mysticism and began a solo career in 1965. Recording albums on ABC mixing jazz, rock, Indian music (with sitar) and pop, his records sold well and he was one of the few jazz musicians to influence the rock and psych market. **Insect Trust** recorded his *Walkin On Nails*, **A.B. Skhy** wrote the track *Gazebo* about him, **Dr. John** cited him on *The Lonesome Guitar Strangler* and **The Eden's Children** quoted him on their liner notes. He also played San Francisco's Fillmore on the same bill as **Hendrix**.

Gabor Szabo recorded intensively, notably on ABC with the famous producer Bob Thiele (John Coltrane, **Free Spirits**, **Salvation**) and on Skye with Gary McFarland. The musicians who usually played with him included Louis Kabok, Jim Keltner, Bill Plummer (of **Cosmic Brotherhood**), Hal Gordon and Jim Stewart. Their material was mostly instrumental and ranged from versions of Beatles, Stones, Sonny & Cher and Donovan to Manuel de Falla's *Fire Dance*, plus originals penned by **Szabo**. Live recordings from the period are also extremely interesting.

Readers should however avoid the two ABC records with the California Dreamers, these are an awful experience aimed at the adult market and are completely marred by insipid choir vocals. The California Dreamers were a vocal 9-piece who included John and Tom Bahler, better known as **The Love Generation**.

Szabo returned to the jazz style after 1970. He died in 1982.

Compilation appearances include *Walking On Nails* on *Journey To A Higher Key: The Best Of Sitar Psychedelia, Vol. 1* (LP). (SR/MW)

JOURNEY TO A HIGHER KEY (Comp LP) including Gabor Szabo.

SADDHU BRAND - Whole Earth Rhythm LP.

SAINTE ANTHONY's FYRE - Sainte Anthony's Fyre LP.

LEIGH STEPHENS - And A Cast Of Thousands LP.

STEPPENWOLF - Live LP.

STEPPENWOLF - The Second LP.

STRAWBERRY ALARM CLOCK - Good Morning Starshine LP.

The Taboos

| 45: | All My Life / So Sad | (La Salle L-382) 1967 |

A bunch of Long Island teens discovered by local talent spotter Carl Edelson, whose sole 45 appeared in 1967 on his La Salle label. Edelson was also responsible for releases by the **Shandels** and **Lemon Sandwich**. *All My Life* reappears on *Psychedelic States: New York Vol. 1* (CD) - it would be an average garage ballad but for a discordant outburst of acidic guitar. (MW)

The Talismen

Personnel:
	JOE BRITT		A
	JACK COOPER		A
	LEON JEFFREY		A
	JOHN WOOD		A

| 45s: | She Was Good/ Lonely (by Deviie and Gayliss) | (Julian 105) 1966 |
| | I Know A Girl/I'll Take A Walk | (Julian 109) 196? |

Hailed from Wenatchee, Washington, *She Was Good*, a superb punker, can also be found on *Highs In The Mid-Sixties, Vol. 14* (LP) and *Teenage Shutdown, Vol. 3* (LP & CD). (VJ/MW/DR)

The Talismen

Personnel:
	PAUL "RABBIT" BENEKE	gtr	A
	JOHN JAVORSKY	bs	A
	RUSS LONIELLO	drms	A
	BILL SHEREK	bs, gtr	A

| 45: | Glitter And Gold / She Belongs To Me | (Rampro R-115) 1966 |

Bill Sherek formed **The Talismen** in Wisconsin in 1966, after the breakup of his previous band **The Tikis**. In late 1966, this Madison/Janesville group recorded their sole 45, augmented on guitar by producer/artist **Dick Campbell**.

Glitter And Gold finally appeared on the 2001 compilation *Badger Beat Chronicles* (LP). (MW/GM)

The Tallysmen

| 45: | Little By Little/You Don't Care | (Tally 200,688) 1965 |

From Dorchester, Massachusetts. They also recorded an alternative version of *You Don't Care About Me* and another song, *Only Girl In The World*, which still exist as acetates.

One member was later in the Tweeds.

Compilation appearances include: *Little By Little* on *New England Teen Scene* (CD) and *New England Teen Scene, Vol. 1* (LP); and *You Don't Care* on *New England Teen Scene, Vol. 2* (LP). (VJ/MW)

The Talula Babies

| 45: | Hurtin' Kind/Mine Forever | (Mar no #) 196? |

This 45 was a bootleg of **The Tulu Babies** first 45 on Tema. For more information see the **Tulu Babies** and **Baskerville Hounds** entries. (GGl/MW)

Tamalpais Exchange

Personnel:
	RONNIE BEDFORD	drms	A
	PENELOPE ANNE BODRY	vcls	A
	MIKE BRANDT	gtr, vcls	A
	SUSAN KAY	gtr, vcls	A
	MICHAEL KNIGHT	gtr, vcls	A
	BUCKETS LOWERY	vcls	A
	RALPH ROST	bs	A
	PAMELA TALUS	keyb'ds, vcls	A
	(DON PAYNE	bs	A)

| ALBUM: | 1 TAMALPAIS EXCHANGE | (Atlantic SD 8263) 1970 - |
| 45: | Flying Somehow/Wish | (Atlantic 2747) 1970 |

Produced by Adrian Barber and recorded in New York, this mix of hippie folk, rock and pop with vocal harmonies has lyrics with religious or quasi-philosophical content. Overall weak and better avoided. (SR)

Tamrons

Personnel incl:
| | PETTUS |
| | WALTERS |

| 45s: | Wild-Man/Stop, Look, Listen | (Clay # unknown) 1966 |
| | Wild-Man/Stop, Look, Listen | (Pyramid 7-7381) 1967 |

These teen-punkers hailed from Concord in North Carolina and evolved out of the remains of two junior-high bands The Kings and The Night Raiders. *Wild-Man* is a fine example of the teen-punk genre and well worth a listen.

Compilation appearances include: *Wild-Man* on *Back From The Grave, Vol. 4* (LP) and *Back From The Grave, Vol. 2* (CD). (VJ)

James T and The Workers

| 45s: | Who Can I Turn To?/That's All | (SS 6368-01) 1966 |
| | I Can't Stop/ Let... (title incomplete) | (Prophonics 2026) 196? |

This band hailed from the wilds of the Northern Michigan peninsula near Bay City. *That Is All*, in *Louie Louie* style, has recently resurfaced on *Sixties Archive, Vol. 7* (CD), *Back From The Grave, Vol. 8* (Dble LP) and *Back From The Grave, Vol. 8* (CD). *I Can't Stop* can be heard on the *Michigan Mayhem, Vol. 1* (CD). Both 45s are incredibly rare - incredibly expensive anyway, as are many Michigan "nuggets". (VJ/GG)

The Tangents

| 45s: | Good Times/Till I Came Along | (Impression 105) 1965 |
| | Hey Joe (Where You Gonna Go?)/ Stand By Me | (Impression 111) 1966 |

Los Angeles was home turf for this mid-sixties outfit. Their first 45 was lightweight orchestrated pop-beat and is best avoided. Their finest moment, *Hey Joe (Where You Gonna Go ?)*, is captured for posterity on *Highs In The Mid-Sixties, Vol. 2* and *Boulders, Vol. 8* (LP). (VJ)

TANGERINE - The Peeling Of... LP.

Tangerine

Personnel:	DENNIS DEFELICE	bs	A
	AL FERRARO	ld gtr, vcls	A
	LYNN (CRASH) FERRARO	congas, gtr, vcls	A
	DENNIS KOSTLEY	drms	A

ALBUM: 1(A) THE PEELING OF TANGERINE (Stephen Productions SPST 001) 1971 R2

NB: (1) was pirated in 1991 and has been reissued officially on CD (Gear Fab GF-131) 1999 and vinyl (Akarma AK 137) 2001.

A rare album recorded in Pittsburgh, Pennsylvania. It contains five original songs. All of Side Two is taken up with *My Main Woman*, a thirteen minute jam on which each band member shows his playing skills. Overall an interesting album which ranges from hard-rock, guitar-orientated jazz-rock, tinges of psychedelia and lots of drums. The sleeve notes mention that one track *The Hutch* was written during a live performance of the group at The Hutch in Vienna, West Virginia on 28th February 1971.

Compilation appearances include *A.J.F.* on Gear Fab's *Psychedelic Sampler* (CD).

The band came from Latrobe, Pennsylvania. (MW)

Tangerine Roof

45: Back In My Arms/All We Need Is Love (Roof 1) 196?

A little known band from California. *Back In My Arms* has quite a poppy feel and can also be found on *Sixties Rebellion, Vol. 4* (LP & CD). (VJ)

Tangerine Zoo

Personnel:	ROBERT BENEVIDES (*)	ld gtr, bs, vcls	AB
	WAYNE GAGNON	gtr, vcls	AB
	RONALD MEDEIROS	hrmnca, organ, vcls	AB
	DONALD SMITH	drms, vcls	AB
	TONY TAVARES	bs, gtr	A

NB: (*) shown as Benevedes on the second album.

ALBUMS: 1(A) THE TANGERINE ZOO (Mainstream S6107) 1968 R1
2(B) OUTSIDE LOOKING IN (Mainstream S6116) 1968 R2

NB: (2) has been counterfeited on vinyl. (1) and (2) have also been counterfeited on one CD (Fingerprint CDTZ 2173).

45s: α One More Heartache/A Trip To The Zoo (Mainstream 682) 1968
β Like People/? (Mainstream 690) 1968

NB: α both sides taken from their debut album. β both sides taken from their second album.

From Newport, Rhode Island. Although their first album contains some impressive swirling organ work and occasional fuzztone guitar, its material, which is largely written by the band, lacks originality. Their second effort, *Outside Looking In* is the better of the two. Tavares departed prior to its recording and the remaining quartet produced wilder and more imaginative music which translated to vinyl quite effectively. On this, *Wake Up Sun*, *Can't You See*, *Confusion* and a cover of The Moody Blues' *Another Morning* are all excellent. It's a pity that the group didn't recruit a new lead vocalist, however, as shortcomings in this department are occasionally obvious.

Tangerine Zoo evolved out of **The Ebb Tides**, and Wayne Gagnon later played in an outfit called **Wadsworth Mansion**. Tavares was later in the seventies disco act of the same name.

Pebbles, Vol. 21 includes a version of one of their better tracks *Nature's Children* as by **The Kidds**, a previous incarnation of this outfit. (VJ/CF)

Gary Tanin

ALBUM: 1 LOVE CHANGES ALL (Private Pressing) 1972

A singer and multi-instrumentist (mostly playing piano), with songs about life and love. Housed in a black and white cover, it's not a particularly good album, but it may however interest people searching for "real people" sounds. (SR)

Taos

Personnel:	JEFF BAKER	gtr, vcls, keyb'ds	A
	KIT BEDFORD	keyb'ds, vcls, bs	A
	ALBIE CIAPPA	drms, vcls	A
	BURT LEVINE	gtr, bs	A
	STEVE OPPENHEIM	gtr, keyb'ds, vcls	A

ALBUM: 1(A) TAOS (Mercury 61257) 1970 -

45: Everybody's Movin'/? (Mercury 73032) 1970

Based in Taos, an Arizona town famous for the several hippie communities which settled there in the late sixties, this quintet played a melodic mix of folk, country and blues with vocal harmonies and some decent guitars. Nothing essential. (SR)

Tarantula

Personnel:	OZ BACH	bs, vcls	A
	MIKE EDELMAN	electric flute, sax, vcls	A
	TOM GRASSO	piano, prgan, vcls	A
	THAD MAXWELL	ld gtr, vcls	A
	STEVE SWIRN	drms	A

ALBUM: 1(A) TARANTULA (A&M SP-4202) 1968 -

45: Love Is For Peace/Billy The Birdman (A&M 1158) 1969

Produced by Chad Stuart (of **Chad & Jeremy**), **Tarantua** were a California group strongly influenced by **Zappa** and jazz. Tracks like *Electric Guru*, *Red Herring*, *Love Is For Peace*, *Peach*, *Fuzz And Peppermints* have lots of acid organ, fuzz guitar and strange vocals and lyrics, plus various noises and onomatopeas. The single tracks are from the album.

Oz Bach had previously been in **Spanky and Our Gang** and then in Wings, another California group similar to **Mama and The Papas** who released an album for Dunhill. Thad Maxwell went on to play with country-rock bands (Swampwater, Sierra) and **Arlo Guthrie**. (SR)

TANGERINE ZOO - Tangerine Zoo LP.

TANGERINE ZOO - Outside Looking In LP.

Tartaglia

ALBUM: 1 TARTAGLIAN THEOREM (Capitol ST 166) c1968 -

45s: Abraham, Martin And John/Poto Flavos (Capitol 2528) 1969
Classical Gas/Good Morning Starshine (Capitol 2577) 1969

A rare album mixing early electronic music with psychedelic sounds, it contains a cover of the Beatles' *I Am The Walrus*. **Tartaglia** also worked with **Richard Christensen**. (SR)

Tasmanians

Personnel incl: MIKE CARNES
ROBIN THOMPSON

45s: Love, Love, Love/Baby (Conda 101) 1967
I Can't Explain This Feeling/If I Don't (Power 4933) 1967

From West Palm Beach, Florida and another good double-sided debut 45. The 'A' side is a pleasant pop love song and the flip's a much wilder punker with some fine harmonica and guitar riffs.

Robin Thompson played with Bruce Springsteen's E Street Band in the seventies and now runs his own recording studio in Virginia.

Compilation appearances have included: *I Can't Explain This Feeling* on *Lost Generation, Vol. 1* (LP); *Baby* and *Love Love Love* on *Florida Punk Groups From The Sixties* (LP) and *Sixties Archive, Vol. 4* (CD); and *Baby* on *Teenage Shutdown, Vol. 14 - Howlin' For My Darlin'* (LP & CD) and *Psychedelic States: Florida Vol. 3* (CD). (VJ/MW/JLh)

Tayles

Personnel:			
	SCOTT EAKIN	flute, vcls	A
	RICK MARKSTROM	drms, vcls	A
	PAUL PETZOLD	organ	A
	BOB SCHMIDTKE	gtr, vcls	A
	JEREMY WILSON	bs, vcls	A

ALBUM: 1(A) WHO ARE THESE GUYS (Cinevista CU 1001) 1972 SC
NB: (1) reissued officially on CD by Gear Fab (GF-121) 1998 and on vinyl (Akarma AK 122/2) as a double LP with four extra tracks.

45s: α She Made Me That Way/
Bizzaro Man (Age Of Aquarius 1548) 1971
α Funny Paper Sun/It's High Time (Age Of Aquarius 1548) 1971
NB: α released early 1971 as a double gatefold.

The album was recorded live at the Nitty Gritty, Madison, Wisconsin on 18 March 1972. It's becoming sought-after by collectors. The songs are all originals and the band competent musicians. The music on Side One for the most part is R&B/bar blues, certainly not for garage or psychedelic purists. Side two is more interesting - *Angry With My Friend* has some experimental guitarwork, *Master Of The Arts* is a good track and *Guitar*, as its title suggests, features some pretty frantic and melodramatic guitarwork. Certainly Side Two has its moments.

The CD reissue comprises the 45 tracks and the live album and provides a detailed history of the band. **The Tayles** were formed in 1966 after two members of Jeremy Wilson's previous outfit (the Canterbury's) were killed in a car crash. This determined the name of the successor band.

The Tayles split in 1972 with members going onto the Shakers or the Beans, but they reunited as **The Tayles** in 1976. The name was finally retired in the late seventies and, as the Shakers again, they continued power-poppin' into the nineties.

Bob Schmidtke passed away in 1984 and the band have dedicated the reissues to his memory.

Compilation appearances include *She Made Me That Way* on Gear Fab's *Psychedelic Sampler* (CD). (VJ/MW)

James Taylor and The Original Flying Machine

Personnel:			
	AL GORGONI	harpsichord	A
	DANNY "KOOTCH" KORTCHMAR	vcls, gtr	A
	JOEL O'BRIEN	drms	A
	JAMES TAYLOR	vcls, gtr	A
	ZACHARY WIESNER	bs	A
	JERRY	bs	A

ALBUM: 1(A) JAMES TAYLOR AND THE ORIGINAL
FLYING MACHINE (Euphoria EST-2) 1971 -

45: Night Owl/Rainy Day Man (Euphoria) 1971
NB: reissued in France in 1972 with a PS (Jubilee 2C006-93296).

Produced by Al Gorgoni and Chip Taylor and designed to look like a bootleg, this album comprises the first recordings by **James Taylor** in 1967 whilst he was working the folk-rock circuit with Kortchmar and O'Brien from the **King Bees**. Only seven tracks are included with *Night Owl, Rainy Day Man* (covered by **Tom Rush** on his *Circle Game* album) and two takes of the catchy *Knocking Round The Zoo*, complete with false starts and studio dialogue. Musically it can be compared to the **Lovin' Spoonful** or early **Youngbloods**. Kortchmar went on to form **City** and with O'Brien **Jo Mama**, before becoming a session man. **Taylor** signed a contract with Apple enjoying a successful singer/songwriter career in the seventies.

TAOS - Taos LP.

Euphoria was a short-lived subsidiary of Jubilee and also released the album by **Sum Pear**. (SR)

T.C. Atlantic

Personnel:	ROD EATON	drms	A
	FREDDIE FREEMAN		A
	JOE KANAN		A
	BOB WELLS		A

ALBUM: 1(A)   LIVE AT THE BEL RAE BALLROOM
(Dove M 4459) 1967 R1

NB: (1) pirated on Eva (12014) in 1983. Also relevant is *The Best Of T.C. Atlantic* (Dionysus BA 1169) 2002.

45s:
Once Upon A Melody/
I Love You So Little Girl   (Aesops 5-6044) 1965
Mona/My Babe   (B-Sharp 272) 1966
Faces/Baby Please Don't Go   (Turtle 1 1 03) 1966
Shake/Spanish Harlem   (Turtle 11 05) 1966
20 Years Ago (In Speedy's Kitchen)/
I'm So Glad   (Candy Floss 101) 1968
Twenty Years Ago (In Speedy's Kitchen)/
I'm So Glad   (Parrot 330) 1968
Love Is Just/Faces   (Parrot 338) 1969
Judgement Train/Shine The Light   (Paramount 0098) 1971
α   The Countess/I Can't Love You Anymore   (Sire 4101) 1969

NB: α Recorded as Eric Marshall and The Chimes.

This band recorded in Minneapolis, Minnesota between the mid-sixties and early seventies and, aside from the above-mentioned album, issued several 45s including the one for Sire as Eric Marshall and The Chimes. They also had a cut on the *Money Music* compilation (*Faces*). Drummer, Rod Eaton, later played with The Underbeats, an early version of *Gypsy*.

The live album, which was reissued on the French Eva label in 1983, contains some fine drivin' renderings of such sixties classics as *Lovelight, Mona, Baby Please Don't Go, Shake, I'm So Glad* and *Smokestack Lightning*, as well as fine covers of more sensitive numbers like *Spanish Harlem* and *I Love You So, Little Girl*.

With the possible exception of *Love Is Just*, their post-'66 output is disappointing given that *Faces* is rightly regarded as one of THE best examples of psychedelic punk. Be warned that the version of *Faces* on the Parrot 45 is an orchestrated mellow version and, sad to say, sucks!

Some of this band's material was produced and written by Harley Toberman, who also recorded with **Blue Sandelwood Soap**.

T.C. ATLANTIC - Live At The Bel Rae Ballroom LP.

Compilation appearances have included: *Faces* on *Pebbles, Vol. 3* (CD), *The Essential Pebbles Collection, Vol. 1* (Dble CD), *Pebbles Box* (5-LP), *Pebbles, Vol. 3* (LP), *Pebbles, Vol. 2 (ESD)* (CD), *Faces* on *Trash Box* (5-CD) and *Great Pebbles* (CD); *Faces* and *Mona* on *Sixties Archive, Vol. 5* (CD) and *The Finest Hours of U.S. '60s Punk* (LP); and *Love Is Just* on *Changes* (LP). (VJ/JSz)

TCB

ALBUM: 1   OPEN FOR BUSINESS   (Traffic) c1970 -

From New York, an album with organ and female vocals, lying somewhere between psychedelia and horn-rock. (SR)

The Tea Company

Personnel:	FRANKIE CARRETTA	gtr, ld vcls	A
	MIKE LASSANDO	drms, backing vcls	A
	JOHN VANCHO	bs, backing vcls	A
	AL VERTUCCI	gtr, ld/backing vcls	A

ALBUM: 1(A)   COME AND HAVE SOME TEA WITH THE TEA
COMPANY   (Smash 67105) 1968 SC

NB: (1) has been counterfeited on LP and CD. There is also a superior CD edition, released by band member Mike Lassandro - see main text for details.

45:   Come And Have Some Tea With Me/
Flowers   (Smash 2176) 1968

Tea was another word for marijuana, so with a name like **The Tea Company**, it is clear what to expect from their sole album. It is an interesting effort, with the title track and ten-minute cut, *Flowers* outstanding. The latter sounds Beatles-influenced psychedelia, with high-pitched guitar notes superimposed upon a typical psychedelic backing. It sounds rather like an extended version of the ending to *Strawberry Fields Forever*. Aside from a slowed-down version of The Supremes' hit *You Keep Me Hanging On*, all the compositions are originals and some are full of the usual hippie cliches and social commentary, for example, *Love Could Make The World Go Round* and *Make Love Not War*. Their sole 45 contained shorter versions of two cuts from their album, with *Flowers* being a drastically edited and remixed version.

The group, who were originally called The Lip-Tin Tea Company, came from Queens, N.Y. and evolved out of **The Naturals**. They played mostly in New York City, Long Island, New Jersey and Connecticut.

Al Vertucci recalls:- "**The Tea Company** and all **The Naturals** stuff was done at Ultra-Sonic by Bill Stahl". Ultra-Sonic was "in Hempstead, Long Island, and the owner/engineer was Bill Stahl who did all of the '**Fudge** and Shangri-Las stuff there. One of the great engineers ever!! He did with four tracks what people can't do today with 48. **The Tea Company** album (which was recorded on 8 tracks) was then re-mixed and ruined at A&R Recording, 7th Avenue in NYC by Mercury's Dick Corby."

Frankie Carr's All Natural Band later turned up in 1977 with a same-titled album on the Tribute label.

The **Tea Company** album has also been reissued on CD by band member Mike Lassandro and is superior to the counterfeit "no label" CD which is also in circulation.

The freaky hubbly-bubbly instrumental *Don't Make Waves* has also turned up on *Buzz Buzz Buzzzzzz, Vol. 1* (CD). You can also find *Flowers* (45 version) on *A Heavy Dose Of Lyte Psych* (CD). (VJ/MW/AV/MLo)

Teardrops

Personnel incl:	RON MYERS	A
	ERNIE WATTA	A

45s: Sweet, Sweet Sadie /
You Go Your Way (PS)   (004 45-004.1/2) 1966
Armful Of Teddy Bear / Who Are You (PS)   (004 NPS-101) 1966

A quartet from Pueblo, Colorado - home of **The Trolls**. Their best effort is considered to be *Sweet, Sweet Sadie* - a catchy pop-punker produced by Norman Petty. Somewhere between **Paul Revere and Raiders** and **Sir Doug's** *She's About A Mover*. The flip is a lame pre-beat teen ballad.

Their second 45, *Armful...*, is a tame pop ballad distinguished only by its carnival theme and evocative merry-go-round keyboard sounds, but the flip is a surprisingly tight'n'bouncy novelty-cum-punker.

Compilation appearances include: *Sweet, Sweet Sadie* on *Monsters Of The Midwest, Vol. 3* (LP), *Victims Of Circumstance, Vol. 2* (LP) and *Victims Of Circumstance, Vol. 2* (CD). (VJ/MW)

The Tears

Personnel:	JIM BRACKETT	drums	A
	EDDIE GILHERME	bs	A
	BOB SALAZAR	organ, gtr, vcls	A
	RICK SALAZAR	gtr, vcls	A

45s:	Weatherman/Read All About It	(Scorpio 409) 1966
	Rat Race/People Through My Glasses	(Onyx 2201) 1968

Originally thought to be from Sacramento, California, the band were actually headquartered in the Bay Area town of Alameda. They won the State Fair Battle of the Bands in 1966, thereby getting the opportunity to cut *Weatherman*. The 45, which is most notable for some fuzzy instrumental and a good vocal, got a lot of airplay in Northern California in late 1966 and the band consequently toured heavily in that area, with gigs with **Grateful Dead**, **Music Machine**, **Mojo Men**, **The Seeds** etc.

The second 45 didn't come out until early '68, by which time the group had split - only the Salazar brothers feature on the flip *People Through My Glasses*. Two unissued killers, *Taxi Driver* and *No Time For Tears* are also to be featured on an upcoming *Nugget from The Golden State* volume, however and today Rick Salazar's son Arion is the bass player in Third Eye Blind.

Compilation coverage has so far included: all four sides on *The Scorpio Records Story* (CD) although the version of *People Thru My Glasses* appears here in remixed form, whilst the 45 version graces *Psychedelic Experience, Vol. 3* (CD); *Weatherman* and *Read All About It* on *Sound Of The Sixties: San Francisco Part 2* (LP); and *Weatherman* on *The Psychedelic Sixties, Vol. 1* (LP), *Sixties Choice, Vol. 2* (LP), *60's Choice Collection Vol's 1 & 2* (CD) and *The Cicadelic 60's, Vol. 4* (CD). Scorpio was a subsidiary label of Fantasy records. (VJ/MW/AP)

Teddy and His Patches

45s:	Suzy Creamcheese/From Day To Day	(Chance 668) 1967
	Haight And Ashbury/I Ain't Nothin'	(Chance 669) 1967

An interesting San Jose-based group which existed for too short a time. *Suzy Creamcheese* is a superb slice of mayhem and dementia and has rightly become an acid-punk classic on account of its inclusion on several compilations. All their material is essential stuff in any garage-psych collection.

Compilation appearances have included: *Suzy Creamcheese* on *Mayhem & Psychosis, Vol. 2* (LP), *Pebbles Vol. 3 - The Acid Gallery* (CD), *The Essential Pebbles Collection, Vol. 1* (Dble CD), *Pebbles Box* (5-LP), *Pebbles, Vol. 3* (LP), *Pebbles, Vol. 2 (ESD)* (CD), *Acid Dreams - The Complete 3 LP Set* (3-LP), *Acid Dreams Testament* (CD), *Acid Dreams, Vol. 1* (LP), *Trash Box* (5-CD) and *Great Pebbles* (CD); *From Day To Day* on *Sixties Rebellion, Vol. 6* (LP & CD), *Filling The Gap* (4-LP), *Victims Of Circumstances, Vol. 1* (LP) and *Victims Of Circumstance, Vol. 2* (CD); and *Haight Ashbury* on *60's Punk E.P., Vol. 2* (7"), *A Heavy Dose Of Lyte Psych* (CD) and *Boulders, Vol. 2* (LP). (VJ)

Teddy and The Pandas

Personnel:	JOE DALY	gtr	A
	AL LAWRENCE	perc, vcls	ABC
	DICK GUERRETTE	keyb'ds	ABC
	TEDDY DEWART	gtr	AB
	BILLY "SONNY" CORELLE	bs	ABC
	JERRY LABRECQUE	drms	ABC
	PAUL RIVERS	gtr, vcls	C

ALBUM: 1(C) BASIC MAGNETISM (Tower ST 5125) 1968 -

NB: (1) Teddy Dewart had left the band by the time of recording this album, but appears on it as special guest. The band have also released two CD retrospectives.

HCP
45s:	Once Upon A Time/Out The Window	(Coristine 574) 1966 -
	Once Upon A Time/Out The Window	(Musicor 11 76) 1966 134
	We Can't Go On This Way/Smokey Fire	(Musicor 1190) 1966 103
	Searchin' For The Good Times/Sunnyside Up	(Musicor 1212) 1966 -
	Lovelight/Day In The City	(Timbri 101) 1967 -
	Childhood Friends/68 Days Till September	(Tower 433) 1968 -

NB: There are also two Musicor acetates in existence *We Can't Go On This Way/Games* and *Sunnyside Up/Willie Dum Dum*. Both *Games* and *Willie Dum Dum* appear to be unissued songs. Acetates of unissued *Spring Came Early This Year* and *City Woman* also exist.

Originally from Beverly, Massachusetts, they were later based in nearby Boston. They first attracted attention when *Once Upon A Time* was transferred from Coristine to the Musicor label. It gave them their second local Top Ten hit, but national success always eluded them. Their leader Teddy Dewart had left the band by the time of their album and their earlier garage sound was surrendered for a bubblegum style. Their album is not recommended, but many of their 45s have resurfaced on compilations:- The *Lovelight* and *Once Upon A Time* are also on *Bay State Rock* (LP) and they have four tracks:- *Once Upon A Time*; *(Bye Bye) Out The Window*, *Smokey Fire* and *We Can't Go On This Way* on *Mindrocker, Vol. 10* (Dble LP). *We Can't Go On This Way* can also be heard on *Nuggets, Vol. 4* (LP) and is a rather pretty pop song. They also contributed two song on a Various Artists collection, *The Gene Pitney Show* (Musicor 2101).

Their producer Bruce Patch was also responsible for the **Timothy Clover** album and went on to establish Spoonfed Records who reissued some of Boston's classic albums like **The Remains**' Epic album.

In March 2002, the band released a CD EP *Rarities And Forgotten Gems* which contains seven unreleased and rare Pandas songs - tracks which were all recently discovered from long lost and forgotten demo acetates, audition pressings and rare singles. (VJ/HI/BW)

Teddy Boys

45s:	Jezebel/It's You	(MGM 13515) 1966
	Where Have All The Good Times Gone/La La	(Cameo 433) 1966

Mona/Good Morning Blues	(Cameo 448)	1967
Don't Mess With Me/?	(No label #1 616)	1967

From Hyde Park, New York, their finest moment was arguably their pretty offbeat version of Bo Diddley's *Mona*. *Jezebel* was a raw, vitriolic cover, and *Don't Mess With Me* a rock'n'roller which they put out themselves. *Where Have All The Good Times Gone* is pretty fine too, a solid Kinks-like swinger; the flip is a tad ponderous but has some raunchy guitar in the break and finale. All their 45s are worth picking up should you come across them.

They also had a 45 as **Pinnochio and Puppets**.

Compilation appearances include: *Mona* on *Pebbles Vol. 10* (CD), *Pebbles, Vol. 12* (LP), *Pebbles, Vol. 4 (ESD)* (CD) and *Trash Box* (5-CD); *Don't Mess With Me* on *What A Way To Die* (LP) and *Hang It Out To Dry* (CD); *Jezebel* on *Garage Punk Unknowns, Vol. 1* (LP). (MW/MM/VJ)

Teegarden and Van Winkle

Personnel:

SKIP "VAN WINKLE" KNAPE	vcls, keyb'ds, bs	ABCD
DAVE TEEGARDEN	drms, vcls	ABCD
MIKE "MONK" BRUCE	ld gtr, slide gtr, vcls	CD
BOB SEGER	vcls, perc	C
JACK ASHFORD	tambourine	D
DAMON REINHOLD	hypnotist	D
PAT "TACO" RYAN	sax, flute	D
(MERLENE DRISKELL	vcls	BC)
(BUDDY EMMONS	pedal steel	B)
(JO ANN HILL	vcls	BC)
(BRENDA KNIGHT	vcls	BC)
(JERRY PAUL	conga	B)
(JAY PENI	horns	B)
(STEVE BASSETT	vcls	C)
(ERNIE FIELDS	sax, bagpipes	C)
(TRACY NELSON	backing vcl	C)
(JERRY SMITH	piano	C)
(BOB GOODSITE		D)
(LAFAYETTE LEAKE	keyb'ds	D)
(DENNIS THOMPSON		D)

ALBUMS:
1(A)	AN EVENING AT HOME WITH...	(Plum ?)	1968 -
2(A)	AN EVENING AT HOME WITH...	(Atco SD33-272)	1968 -
3(A)	BUT, ANYHOW	(Atco SD33-290)	1969 -
4(B)	TEEGARDEN AND VAN WINKLE	(Westbound WB 2003)	1970 -
5(C)	ON OUR WAY	(Westbound WB 2010)	1972 -
6(D)	EXPERIMENTAL GROUNDWORK	(Westbound WB 2019)	1973 -

NB: (2) is a reissue of (1) with a simple sleeve instead of the original gatefold.

HCP

45s:
God, Love And Rock And Roll/Work Me Tomorrow	(Plum 68102)	1970 -
God, Love And Rock And Roll/Work Me Tomorrow	(Westbound 170)	1970 22
Everything Is Going Be Alright/You Do	(Westbound 171)	1970 84
Passing Gas/Ride Away With Me	(Westbound 200)	1971 -
Carry On/Ride Away With Me	(Westbound 210)	1971 -

From Tulsa, Oklahoma, this duo of drummer/organist began playing in the mid-sixties with a locally famous Elvis manque named Gene Crose, who figures in the career of practically all the members of the Oklahoma Mafia, including Leon Russell and J.J. Cale. When they quit Crose after Teegarden was fired, they formed a band called Skip and The Blue Tones. After a while, Knape hooked up with a regional outfit called Rodney and The Blazers led by Rodney Lay (later with Roy Clark). Eventually, Knape and Teegarden ended up in the L.A. home of Leon Russell and released a single as the **Sunday Servants**, produced by J.J. Cale.

The pair finally returned to Tulsa, complemented by local musicians including Tommy Tripplehorn (who would later join the Leon Russell influenced Gary Lewis and The Playboys) and Carl Day. They began playing around town as LSD and C (for Love, Skip, Dave and Carl!) when they were spotted by a Detroit college student and Robert Kennedy campaign worker named Jim Cassily, who was on his way to California. After the Kennedy assassination, Cassily moved back to Detroit and persuaded Teegarden and Knape to take up residence with him. Cassily, who was to produce all their albums, had a lot of enthusiasm and devised a plan for the two to record their debut album live at a local Detroit club. He also renamed Knape "Van Winkle". Released on the independent Plum Records label, the disc quickly attracted the attention of Atlantic Records executive Jerry Schoenbaum, who offered them a contract. They sold about 10,000 copies of *An Evening At Home* and Atco gave them the green light for a second album, *But Anyhow*, recorded in March 1969 in GM Studios in Detroit. This features some original cuts, Donovan's *Season Of The Witch* plus R&B covers of *Bright Lights, Big City*, *She Caught The Katie*, *Annie Had A Baby*, before ending with *All About My Ole Bitch*.

They sold about 20,000 copies but their Atco contact wasn't renewed. Teegarden and Knape failed to get a contract with another label and their career was on the downhill slide. Then came along Leon Russell who had put together the Mad Dogs And Englishmen with all the Tulsa Mafia. He called them and they ended up on stage, but they refused to go on the tour and appear in the Mad Dogs movie.

The pair stayed in Detroit instead and recorded the initial version of *God, Love And Rock 'n' Roll* on a Revox. With their own money, they pressed 500 45s and finally got a contract with a local label, Westbound, who had just signed a distribution deal with Janus Records. Westbound did a lot of promotion with this single and *God, Love And Rock 'n' Roll* became a national hit. Unfortunately, the album *Teegarden And Van Winkle* wasn't ready and arrived too late to cash on the 45s success. It's a good album, however, with creative arrangements of *Eleanor Rigby* and Merle Haggard's *Okie From Muskogee*.

Among the people who became interested in the duo was fellow Detroiter **Bob Seger**. They formed a trio and finally took on Mike "Monk" Bruce, a killer guitarist (also from Tulsa). The four men cut an album that was finally released as **Bob Seger**'s *Smokin O.P's*, released on Punch Andrews' label Palladium.

At the same time *On Our Way* was released and is arguably their best record, probably because of Bruce's guitar parts. Tracy Nelson of **Mother Earth** guests on some tracks recorded in Nashville, the others being recorded in Toronto and Detroit. It contains good covers of Gregg Allman's *Midnight Rider*, Mose Allison's *If You Live* and **Don Nix**'s *Going Down* plus eight original songs.

Experimental Groundwork, their final record, is supposed to have been recorded under hypnosis! Cassily found an hypnotist, Damon Reinhold, and came up with the idea of using him to hypnotize the band in the studio, inviting the press to watch. That allowed the group to get a lot of national promotion in Newsweek, Time etc.. but when the story came out, once again, the record wasn't done. When it was finally released, no one cared anymore and the duo had broken up. *Experimental Groundwork* is in fact an excellent rock 'n' roll album with various covers and originals. Both sides

HOOSIER HOTSHOTS (Comp LP) including Teen Tones.

begin with an induction and end with a band dehypnotization and the sleeve mentions that "You are advised to read the booklet included before playing the record". The said booklet is a must read, the writer (Gemini III !) explaining that hypnosis is a little like smoking grass and that, in case the record player malfunctions, you will merely fall asleep and wake up soon...

After 1973, Knape put together a big band with horns and female backing vocals and stayed around Detroit before moving to California in the late seventies to work with Eric Burdon and Doug Kershaw. Teegarden headed back to Tulsa and finally joined **Bob Seger**'s Silver Bullet Band at the height of his visibility.

Teegarden and Van Winkle reunited in 1997, did some concerts in Tulsa and recorded a new album, *Radioactive*.

God, Love And Rock And Roll was later included on *Michigan Rocks, Vol. 2* (LP). (SR/VJ/MW)

The Teemates

Personnel:	BOBBY LUNDUN	ld gtr	A
	BOB POLHEMUS	gtr	A
	BRYAN POST	drms	A
	RICHARD STAFF	bs, ld vcls	A

ALBUM: 1(A) JETSET DANCE DISCOTHEQUE
(Audio Fidelity DFS-7042) 1964 SC

45s:	Dream On Little Girl/Movin' Out	(Audio Fidelity 104) 1964
	Night Fall/No More Tomorrows (PS)	(Audio Fidelity 105) 1964

Another obscure New York/New Jersey outfit. Produced by Sidney Frey, the album is extremely hard to find and is not really for garage purists - it's competent frat-dance-beat featuring several beat covers *A Hard Day's Night*, *And I Love Her*, *Do Wah Diddy Diddy*, *Walk Don't Run* and dance numbers like *Cmon And Swim* and *Mashed Potatoes Yeah*. There are also four original songs written by their manager Josef Shefski. The liner notes mention "For the best possible reaction, this record can and should be played at maximum level".

Movin' Out can also be found on *Hipsville, Vol. 2* (LP). (VJ/SR)

Teenbeets

45:	I Should Wait / Oh Baby	(unknown) 1965

From Winston-Salem, North Carolina. *Tobacco A-Go-Go, Vol. 2* (LP) includes the previously unreleased *I Guess That's Why You're Mine* and a 45 cut *I Should Wait* from this North Carolina combo. (MW/VJ)

Teen Tones

45s:	Fortune Teller/Poison Ivy	(Don & Mira 6269) 196?
	Do You Wanna Dance/	
	Long Cold Winter Ahead	(T&T 2487/8) 1965

From South Bend, Indiana. *Punk Classics, Vol. 5* (7") includes *Fortune Teller*, whilst *Long Cold Winter Ahead* has resurfaced on *Hoosier Hotshots* (LP). (VJ)

The Telstars

Personnel:	JIMMY CARTER	gtr	A
	TERRY GORKA	bs	A
	GARY JOHNSON	gtr	A
	RONNIE WILSON	drms	A

45:	Keep On Running/Hold Tight	(Columbia 4-44141) 1967

Longhair Productions, who brought us **The Blues Magoos**, were behind this Washington D.C. band's sole 45. A pair of good fuzz-popsters with a competent version of the Spencer Davis Group classic though lacking the vibrant punch of the original. *Hold Tight* is not the Dave Dee, Dozy, Beaky, Mick and Tich hit.

Jimmy Carter and Steve Lacey had previously been with **The British Walkers**, whilst Terry Gorka was also in the **Reason**. (MW/BE/VJ)

The Tempests

45s:	Prancer / Rockin' Xmas Goose	(Fujimo 4630) 196?
	Look Away / Carousel Blues	(Fujimo 6946) 1963
	The Love I'm In / Pink Elephants	(Fujimo 7701) 196?
	Boppin' The Blues /	
	Whole Lotta Shakin'	(Fujimo # Unkn) 196?
	Searchin' / Come On Everybody	(Fujimo # Unkn) 196?
	Brainstorm / The Love I'm In	(Fujimo # Unkn) 196?
	Zip A Dee Do Dah /	
	Lookin' Out The Window	(Fujimo # Unkn) 196?

NB: 45s not listed in order of release.

From Elkhart, Indiana. *Look Away*, a good early sixties rocker also appears on *Highs In The Mid-Sixties, Vol. 19 - Michigan Part 3* (LP) but Fujimo was a North Indiana label. The song later got a further airing on the *Riot City!* (LP) compilation. (VJ/MW)

The Tempos

Personnel:	TERRY BARNETT	gtr	A
	LARRY COOK	gtr	A
	BILL MOORE	drms	A
	MIKE SHELL	gtr	A

ALBUMS:	1(A)	SPEAKING OF THE TEMPOS	(Justice 104) 1966 R3
	2(A)	THE TEMPOS	(Crypt 010) 1987 -

NB: (1) reissued on CD by Collectables (COL-CD-0601).

The Justice album changes hands for lots of bucks. A Sylacauga, Alabama, garage band whose *You're Gonna Miss Me* (not the **13th Floor Elevators** song), one of the tracks from the album, can also be heard on *Oil Stains* (LP), whilst the instrumental *Heart Beat* graces *Strummin' Mental, Vol. 2*.

Tim Warren's excellent compilation not only brings the album back from the grave (Cryptic pun intended!) but adds four live tracks - *Hey Joe*, *I'm Cryin*, *Good Lovin'* and *Twist And Shout* - and also two 'practice session' tracks *Scratchy* and *Louie Louie*. (VJ/MW)

Tennessee Farm Band

See: **The Farm Band**.

Tension

45s:	It's A Fact/Does Anybody Really Know	
	What Time It Is?	(Poison Ring PR-713) 1971
	Life Is A Beautiful Thing/	
	Run To Nowhere	(Poison Ring PR-715) 1971

From Connecticut, an obscure hard-rock group, on the same label as **Fancy**. They may have also released an album. (SR)

Terminal Barbershop

Personnel:	WYATT DAY	gtr, keyb'ds, vcls	A
	JOE FARRELL		A
	JOE HUNT	drms	A
	DICK HURWIT		A
	JIMMY OWENS	trumpet	A
	JON PIERSON	trombone, vcls	A
	JONATHAN RASKIN	bs, gtr, vcls	A
	ERIC WEISBERG		A

ALBUM:	1(A)	HAIR STYLES	(Atco) 1969 -

From New York, this short-lived studio group was put together after **Ars Nova** had split. The album, which is mediocre, consists of cover versions from the musical 'Hair' performed in the same style as **Ars Nova**. (VJ/NK)

The Termites

45: Carrie Lou/Give Me Your Heart (Bee 1825) 196?

An all-girl combo who have a cut called *Tell Me* on *Girls In The Garage, Vol. 1* (CD) and *Girls In The Garage, Vol. 2* (LP). (VJ)

Terra Nauticals

45: Black Friday/Hangin' On Me (Viber-Sound 105) 1967

An obscure Texas band. The 'A' side opens with some promising organ and soon develops into a bouncy punker. It has also resurfaced on *Sixties Rebellion, Vol. 9* (LP & CD). (GG)

The Terrifics

45: Lovers Plea/On The Sea Shore (Fig 301) 196?

A little known band from Kentucky. The 'A' side, a rocker with wild vocals, has also resurfaced on *Sixties Rebellion, Vol. 3* (LP & CD). (GG)

Terry and Tommy

45: It Ain't No Good To Love Anybody/
I'm No Fool (AOK 1030) 1967

A folk-rock duo based around West Texas.

Compilation appearances include: *It Ain't No Good To Love Anybody* on *The History Of Texas Garage Bands, Vol. 3* (CD) and *Highs In The Mid-Sixties, Vol. 11* (LP). (VJ)

Terry and The Chain Reaction

Personnel incl: TERRY WOODFORD   ld vcls   A

45s: Keep Your Cool/Stop Stopping Me (United Artists 50199) 1967
Take Me To Your Heart/
You Made Me (United Artists 50271) 1968

More a pop than garage combo, nevertheless *Keep Your Cool* may appeal to some. It's a catchy laid back strutter with 'cool' spoken vocals, *Green Onions* keyboard moves and an arrogance reminiscent of **006**'s *Like What, Me Worry*. From Alabama, they featured lead singer **Terry Woodford** who'd previously cut several solo releases. In high school Terry played in the Mystics, who included legendary Muscle Shoals player David Hood on bass. Supposedly they also recorded. Terry hooked up with **The Chain Reaction** right out of high school, and recorded at Fame Studios with producer Rick Hall. The follow-up *Take Me To Your Heart* is a powerful beat-stomper, sounding like something **Paul Revere and The Raiders** would have done a couple of years earlier. The flip is rather more typical of Fame sounds - soulful, strutting pop with brass.

Keep Your Cool was covered in 1985 by Plan 9 on their *Keep Your Cool And Read The Rules* album. (JLh/MW)

Joel Tessler

45: Why (Criteria acetate) c1966

Recorded at Criteria Studios in Miami, Florida. *Why*, a sombre jangley garage-ballad with a nod to **The Byrds** and a wink at Dylan, is featured on *Psychedelic Crown Jewels, Vol. 2* (LP & CD). (MW/RM)

Thackeray Rocke

Personnel: PAUL BUYS   drms, vcls   A
MIKE KESSLER   ld gtr   A
FRANK LACEY   vcls   A
AL QUINLAN   bs, vcls   A
SHELDON SKINKLE
(aka BUNKER HUDDLE/
Jr. ELLIS)   gtr, vcls   A

45s: Bawling/Season Of The Witch (Castalia 10671) 1967
Tobacco Road/Can't You See (Castalia 268) 1968

A mid-sixties outfit from Phoenix, Arizona. Featured on *A Fistful Of Fuzz* (CD), *Bawling* is notable for some frantic buzzin' fuzz though the track leans more towards 'heavier' rock than garage punk. Their version of *Tobacco Road* is also in a heavy acid-rock vein, this time coupled with a gentler rock ballad.

Jr. Ellis also played on some unreleased tracks by another Phoenix outfit **The Grapes Of Wrath**, which can be heard on the latter's retrospective CD on Gear Fab. (MW/JH/VJ)

Their Eminence

45: Mary Had A Little Lamb /
Go Ahead And Hurt Me (Limited Editions 001) 196?

From Southern California, a very rare 45 which may only exist in acetate form. *Mary...* is a new take on the nursery rhyme - a fuzz garage version to the tune of *House Of The Rising Sun*. Hear it on *Seeds Turn To Flowers Turn To Dust* (LP & CD). (MW)

Their Singing Bodies

Personnel incl: C.C. COURTNEY   A
LEW "KING" KIRBY   A

45s: Diagnosis-Neurosis/
You're Gotta Feel It (Back Stage 5002) 1965
α What Am I Gonna Do With You?/
Maybe Baby (Chase 4000) 196?

NB: α as by The Singing Bodies.

The band was a result of two New Orleans DJs teaming up with **The Pirates** to disrupt a Herman's Hermits concert in the Municipal Auditorium. Courtney and Kirby had their bodies painted gold and were dressed in baggies!

THESE TRAILS - These Trails LP.

Diagnosis-Neurosis is an amalgam of comedy, punk and Vietnam protest about the onset of paranoid schizophrenia. By the second 45 they were cured and delivered a faithful version of Buddy Holly's *Maybe Baby*. (VJ/MW/AB)

These Prosperous Times

Personnel incl: THOMAS BARTELLO   drms   A

45:   Baby's Comin' Back/
       The Time Has Come To Cry   (20th Century Fox 45-6660) 1966

Baby's Comin' Back can also be heard on *A Journey To Tyme, Vol. 4* (LP). (VJ)

These Trails

Personnel:	DAVE CHOY	recorder	A
	PATRICK COCKETT	gtr, tabla, vcls	A
	MARGARET MORGAN	gtr, dulcimer, vcls	A

ALBUM: 1(A)   THESE TRAILS   (Sinergia 4059) 1973 R2

NB: (1) has been reissued on CD by Gates Of Dawn.

This is an excellent album of folk-psychedelia with male/female vocals from Hawaii (musically it is reminiscent of The Incredible String Band and C.O.B. with dulcimer, tablas, slide guitar and sitar). The creative force behind the album was Margaret Morgan who composed most of the tracks. (VJ/GG)

These Vizitors

Personnel:	MICHAEL CURTIS	vcls, bs	A
	PATTI CURTIS	vcls, tamb	A
	RICK CURTIS	vcls, gtr	A
	TOM CURTIS	vcls, gtr	A
	TRAVIS ROSE	drms	A

45:   For Mary's Sake/Happy Man   (Capitol 2163) 1968

Originally from Indiana, **These Vizitors** lived up to their name, travelling widely, eventually settling in the sunny climes of West Palm Beach, Florida. Centred around the Curtis Family (Rick, Micheal, Patti, and Tom), their sole 45 is as rare as any garage 45. They were a great psychedelic folk band and played opening gigs with **Hendrix**, **Canned Heat**, etc.. They went on to be vocalists on the Crazy Horse album *At Crooked Lake* in 1972, their song *Blue Letter*, was covered on 1975 eponymous *Fleetwood Mac* album (their first with Buckingham/Nicks) and their largest grossing song *Southern Cross* was recorded by Crosby, Stills and Nash on their 1982 release *Daylight Again*.

The band actually recorded five songs in the '68 New York City session that produced the 45: *Happy Man*, *For Mary's Sake*, *Rippling Road*, *Duetime*, and *Reacher Teacher*. The first two were chosen for the 45 because they were more commercial - both are upbeat Monkee-esque garage-pop written by brothers Richard and Michael Curtis. The others had a slightly harder edge and were never released. *Reacher Teacher* is reportedly the best of the bunch and is slated for release on the forthcoming *Hoosier Hotshots, Vol. 2*.

The band subsequently appeared on a local Chicago version of the "Bozo" show, lip-syncing both sides of the 45, standing on the top of their road van. Amazingly, this footage has survived!

Micheal Curtis has also played and sang with **Hoyt Axton**, Gene Clark's (Byrds), **Dewey Martin**'s (Buffalo Springfield) etc... (PY/BC/JLh/MW)

Theze Few

Personnel:	JOHN "LASSIE" COLLEY	keyb'ds, vcls	A
	BUDDY LAY	drms, vcls	A
	DAN SEALS	vcls, sax	A
	LARRY "OVID" STEVENS	gtr, vcls	A
	MIKE "DOC" WOOLBRIGHT	bs, vcls	A

45:   I Want Your Love/Dynamite   (Blacknight 901) 1966

This Dallas outfit had been known as the Playboys 5 until 1966. An enforced name change in 1967 and they were **Southwest F.O.B.** whose retrospective CD 'Smell Of Incense' includes both sides of the **Theze Few** 45 and a full history of this band.

Dynamite can also be found on *Highs In The Mid-Sixties, Vol. 13 - Texas Part Three* (LP). It's an unexceptional **Kenny and The Kasuals** type effort. (VJ/MW)

The Thingies

Personnel:	BOB COLE	gtr, vcls	AB
	JOHN DALTON	gtr, vcls	AB
	GORDON MARCELLUS	drms	AB
	LARRY MILLER	bs, vcls	AB
	ERNIE SWISHER	organ	A
	PHIL WEAVER	ld vcls	AB

CD: 1(-)   THE THINGIES HAVE ARRIVED   (Collectables COL 0716) 1998

45s: It's A Long Way Down/
         Merry-Go-Round Of Life   (Casino 2305) 1966
         Mass Confusion/Rainy Sunday Morning   (Sonobeat 104) 1968

Passing through Austin, Texas en route from Topeka, Kansas to California this band were offered a one-off recording deal by Sonobeat. The result was an English-influenced hard-rocker, *Mass Confusion*.

Bob Cole tells us that Ernie Swisher played on the earlier 45, but quit before the band left Topeka. He later became a successful corporate lawyer. Cole also confirms that **The Things** did not contain two former members of **The Thingies**. John Dalton and Bob Cole were the only two **Thingies** to return to Topeka, but neither of them played professionally again. John still lives in Topeka. The other four are scattered from Florida to Texas (two), to Nevada, and they still keep in touch.

The Thingies Have Arrived!! CD gathers both 45s plus four unreleased cuts - *English Eyes* and three versions of *I'm Going Ahead*. Larry Miller had previously been in the TR4 and their 45:- *Peter Rabbit / Surfin' TR* (Exclusive 1007) 1963, is also included on the CD. The remainder of the album features fellow Topekans the **Morning Dew** and **The Exotics**, from Dallas.

Other compilation coverage has so far included: *It's A Long Way Down* and *Merry-Go-Round Of Life* on *The Monsters Of The Midwest, Vol. 1* (cassette); *It's A Long Way Down* on *Sixties Rebellion, Vol. 7* (LP & CD), *Midwest Garage Band Series - Kansas* (CD); *Mass Confusion* on *Monsters Of The Midwest, Vol. 2* (LP), *Vile Vinyl, Vol. 2* (LP) and *Vile Vinyl* (CD); and *Mass Confusion* and *Rainy Sunday Morning* on *High All The Time, Vol. 1* (LP). (MW/HI/BCe/VJ)

THE THINGIES - The Thingies Have Arrived CD.

THINGS TO COME - I Want Out LP.

The Things

| 45: | Jazz Rock With Soul/Believe | (Ray Pro 267) 1967 |

There have been rumours that this band contained two former members of **The Thingies**, but this is incorrect. The 45 is said to consist of wild rock. (VJ)

The Things

Personnel:
- FLOYD 'CHILLI' CHILDERS — A
- DAVID HOFFMAN — A
- GREG JONES — A
- DAVE TURNER — A

A Houston-based sixties outfit who didn't make it onto vinyl at the time. They originally called themselves String 'N Things and although the "strings" referred to their guitars, people imagined the name referred to a pop group with violins, so they shortened their name to **The Things**. Two of their recordings:- *I Don't Believe It* and *In Your Soul*, both contained fine fuzztone guitar and Farfisa organ work which characterized many late sixties Texas punk bands. Two further unissued cuts:- *Loveless Lover* and *Another Girl Like You* were cut at Andrus Studios on 12th July 1967.

Compilation appearances have included: *I Don't Believe It* on *Mindrocker, Vol. 4* (LP); *I Don't Believe It* and *In Your Soul* on *Acid Visions* (LP); *Loveless Lover* and *Another Girl Like You* on *Acid Visions, Vol. 2* (LP); *I Don't Believe It, In Your Soul, Loveless Lover* and *Another Girl Like You* on *Acid Visions - The Complete Collection Vol. 1* (3-CD). (VJ)

The Things

| 45: | Take It From Me / My Love | (DJ 102) c1966 |

Another, apparently different, **Things** from El Paso, Texas. *My Love* is also included on *The Garage Zone Vol. 3* and *Garage Zone Box Set* (4-LP). (MW)

Things To Come

Personnel:
BRYAN GAROFALO	bs		ABC
RUSS KUNKEL (aka RUSS WARD)	drms		ABC
LARRY ROBINSON	gtr		ABC
LYNN ROMINGER	gtr		A
STEVE RUNOLFSSON			ABC
MICHAEL MIGLIARO	gtr		BC

| ALBUM: | 1 | THINGS TO COME | (Century) 1978 R5 |

NB: (1) Contains previously unreleased recordings from 1966/7 plus their first 45. *I Want Out* (Sundazed 5008) 1993, is a coloured vinyl release which contains the first single and many previously unreleased tracks, recorded between 1965 and 1967. It has also been released on CD (SC 11017) with extra tracks.

45s:	Sweetgina/Speak Of The Devil	(Starfire 103) 1966
	Come Alive/Dancer	(Warner Bros. 7164) 1968
	Hello/Good Day	(Warner Bros. 7228) 1968

A Los Angeles outfit who had some fine moments. The group recorded a wealth of material in 1966/7, mostly in the typical L.A. acid-punk vein and of a really outstanding quality. Some of these recordings were released on the *Things To Come* album, issued apparently as a tax loss scam, as only 50 copies were pressed. Originals currently sell for $1500+, but thankfully the recent Sundazed retrospective means this excellent L.A. group's work is now accessible by all.

Their first 45 *Sweetgina* is a quite excellent bouncy organ/fuzz rework of *Gloria*. Specialists should note that the version of *Speak Of The Devil* included on the album is longer than on the 45 release. *Speak Of The Devil* is a superb slice of brooding menacing punk with ranting growling vocals, atmospheric vibes and feedback.

The chief songwriter behind the group was Steve Runolfsson, who the other members unwisely booted out in mid-1967. *Come Alive*, their second 45, is notable for excellent percussion and Eastern psychedelic guitar moves whilst the flip *Dancer* is a heavy cruncher straight out of The **Blue Cheer**/Cream school. Slightly mellower but passable heavy sounds feature on the **David Crosby**-produced *Hello* 45.

Garofalo later played for Californian solo artist John Stewart and Kunkel went on to do session work and played for Crosby, Stills, Nash and Young.

Compilation coverage so far includes: *Sweetgina* and *Speak Of The Devil* on *The Chosen Few, Vol. 1* (LP) and *Chosen Few, Vol's 1 & 2* (CD); *Sweetgina* on *Boulders, Vol. 9* (LP), *I Was A Teenage Caveman* (LP), *Sundazed Sampler, Vol. 1* (CD); *Come Alive* on *Slowly Growing Insane* (CD) and *Psychedelic Unknowns, Vol. 11* (LP); and *Dancer* a track which was first compiled on the 1969 LP *First Vibration* has more recently resurfaced on *Garage Zone, Vol. 3* (LP), *The Garage Zone Box Set* (4-LP) and *Lycergic Soap* (LP). (VJ/MW)

Things To Come

Personnel:
KEN ASHLEY	vcls		A
CLIFF HARRISON	drms		A
GEORGE HEATHERTON	bs		A
KEITH ST. MICHAELS	gtr		A

| 45: | I'm Not Talkin'/Til'The End Of Time | (Dunwich 124) 1966 |

A Chicago combo. The 'A' side, *I'm Not Talkin'*, is a fast and furious Yardbirds' cover, the flip, a folk-punk song with some appealing guitar work.

It's rumoured they recorded an album's worth of material for Dunwich which remains in the can.

Compilation appearances have included: *I'm Not Talkin'* on *Pebbles, Vol. 10* (LP), *Pebbles, Vol. 4 (ESD)* (CD) and *The Dunwich Records Story* (LP); *'Til The End* on *Pebbles, Vol. 21* (LP); and *I'm Not Talkin'* and *'Til The End* on *If You're Ready - The Best Of Dunwich... Vol. 2* (CD). (VJ)

The Third Bardo

Personnel:
BRUCE GINSBERG	drms		A
RICKY GOLDCLANG	ld gtr		A
DAMIAN KELLY	bs		A
JEFFREY MOON (real name: NEUFELD)	vcls, gtr		A
RICHY SESLOWE	gtr		A

| EPs: | 1(A) | LOSE YOUR MIND (7") | (Sundazed SEP 106) 1993 |
| | 2(A) | THE THIRD BARDO (10") | (Sundazed SEP 10-160) 2000 |

NB: (1) contains *Five Years Ahead Of My Time, Lose Your Mind, I Can't Understand Your Problem* and *Dawn Of Tomorrow*. The latter three are previously unreleased. The EP was released on yellow vinyl. (2) gathers all their 1967 recordings - essentially adding two versions of *My Rainbow Life* (one previously unheard) to the 7" EP tracks.

45:	I'm Five Years Ahead Of My Time/	
	My Rainbow Life	(Roulette 4742) 1967

A New York outfit. Their name, chosen by lead singer **Jeffrey Monn** and extracted from the 'The Tibetan Book of the Dead', refers to a "return to reality". The inclusion of *I'm Five Years Ahead Of My Time* on *Pebbles, Vol. 3* (LP) has made it something of a classic among collectors of psychedelic punk. Deservedly so in view of its haunting intro and fine fuzztone guitar work. Subsequently it has resurfaced on other compilations:- *Born Bad (The Songs The Cramps Taught Us)*, *Songs We Taught The Cramps*, *Nuggets Box* (4-CD), *Pebbles Vol. 3* (CD), *Trash Box* (5-CD) and *Best of Pebbles, Vol. 1* (LP & CD). **Rusty Evans** of **The Deep/Freak Scene** wrote the 45 for **The Third Bardo** along with songwriter Victoria Pike, who was married to **The Third Bardo**'s producer Teddy Randazzo (of Roulette Records) at the time. The excellent flip side of the 45 can also be heard on *Vile Vinyl, Vol. 2* (LP) and *Magic Carpet Ride* (LP) whilst another version of it appears on **Freak Scene**'s *Psychedelic Psoul* LP. If that wasn't enough, David Walters (author of the excellent "Children of Nuggets" book) has pointed out that the version of *My Rainbow Life* on *Glimpses, Vol. 4* (LP) is an acetate version, 20 seconds shorter than the final single and with a different mix! Both sides of the 45 can also be now heard on *Psychedelic Microdots Of The Sixties, Vol. 3* (CD).

In the early seventies, their lead singer Neufeld released an album under another pseudonym, **Chris Moon**. In the 1980s The Nomads did a fine cover version of *I'm Five Years Ahead Of My Time* and Kenne Highland's Majestic Gizmos reworked it into *He's Five Beers Ahead Of Your Time* (!) on the album of that name.

In 1999, **Rusty Evans** has helped re-record *I'm Five Years Ahead Of My Time*, *My Rainbow Life* and a number of other tracks with his son's band **Kaos**. Although currently unreleased, the new recordings are great, capturing the spirit of the originals. Rusty may also be writing some new material for **The Third Bardo** themselves, who played live again on May 16th 1999 with a line-up of Jeff Moon aka Neufeld, Damian Kelly and Ricky GoldClang from the original band. As for former drummer Bruce Ginsburg, his whereabouts are unknown - somewhere in California, whilst Richie Seslowe sadly died of a drug overdose in the eighties. (VJ/MW/JMz)

Third Booth

Personnel incl:	J.C. CLORE		A

45s:	Mysteries/Sound Incorporated	(Thunder 8346) 1967
	I Need Love/Mysteries	(Independence 86) 1968

Came out of Peoria, Illinois. Both *I Need Love* and *Mysteries* contain good vocals and guitar parts, were written by J.C.Close and produced by Jerry Milam.

Compilation appearances include: *I Need Love* on *Best of Pebbles, Vol. 3* (LP & CD), *Ear-Piercing Punk* (LP), *Garagelands, Vol. 1* (LP) and *Garagelands, Vol. 1 & 2* (CD); *Mysteries* on *Diana's Rootin' Tootin' Wild Teenage Rock 'N' Roll Party!* (LP). (VJ/MW/SR/PY)

The Third Condition

See **The 2/3rds** entry.

Third Degree

45s:	When Does Happiness Begin/	
	Someday We'll Walk In The Sunshine	(Music Factory 401) 1967
	Your World's Gonna Be My World/	
	My Guy	(Music Factory 413) 1968

An orchestrated flower-pop group with female vocals. They obviously liked long song titles! (SR)

The Third Edition

ALBUM:	1	TAKE ONE	(Rapture) 1973 ?

A late period garage-punk combo with organ and fuzz guitar. (SR)

Third Estate

ALBUM:	1	YEARS BEFORE THE WINE	
			(Private Pressing TTE 1000) 1976 R2/R3

NB: (1) reissued in 1991 and also on CD. Later reissued on CD (Mellow Records MMP 309).

A delightful and extremely rare item prior to its very limited reissue a few years back. The album is full of melodic guitar and some exquisite, often haunting female vocals on the title track. The group were from Louisiana. Recommended. (VJ/MW)

The 3rd Evolution

Personnel:	LOUIS BONILLA	bs, gtr	A
	MANNY COLON	drms	A
	RON LUPI	ld gtr	A
	ARGOT MEYER	vcls	A
	MIKE "HENDERSON" SAGLIMBERI	gtr, vcls	A

45s:	Gone, Gone, Gone/Don't Play With Me	(Dawn 306) 1966
	Everybody Needs Somebody (To Love)/You're Gonna	
	Lose The Only Love You Ever Had	(Dawn 312) 1966

In 1963 singer Argot Meyer formed a doo-wop style band, drawing members from the local community in The Bronx, New York. He christened them the Hi-Dells and doubled up as manager as well as providing his basement for band rehearsals. The neighborhood record stores, Cousins Music and Music Makers, were known then for supporting local bands and it was the latter whose Dawn label would provide the outlet for two 45s, released in 1966 after the band had updated their style and changed their name to **The 3rd Evolution**.

Gone, Gone, Gone is a rather routine 'my baby left me' number. *Don't Play With Me* is noteworthy despite the poor production - starting off slow and moody with sneering punk vocals, it features some deceptive changes of pace. *Everybody Needs...* is cool solid beat with a resounding *Day Tripper*-like riff and some Jaggeresque tambourine bashing.

The band's material was written by Henderson and multi-instrumentalist Lupi; they would write and record over 100 songs for the band over the next two decades. They band continued to evolve and become known as The Trolley, who released some 45s in the mid-to-late seventies on the Laurie label.

Nearly 40 years on, the band still get together every 4th of July.

Compilation appearances have included: *Gone, Gone, Gone* and *Don't Play With Me* on *Pebbles, Vol. 11* (LP); *Don't Play With Me* on *Off The Wall*,

THE THIRD BARDO - The Third Bardo 10" EP.

Vol. 2 (LP), *The Cicadelic 60's, Vol. 4* (LP) and *Teenage Shutdown, Vol. 7* (LP & CD); *Gone Gone Gone* on *Teenage Shutdown, Vol. 15* (LP & CD); and *Everybody Needs Somebody (To Love)* on *Psychedelic States: New York Vol. 1* (CD). (MW/MM)

Third Power

Personnel: DREW ABBOTT   gtr, vcls   A
            JIM CRAIG   drms, vcls   A
            JEM TARGAL   bs, vcls   A

ALBUM: 1(A) BELIEVE   (Vanguard VSD 6554) 1970 HCP 194 R1

NB: (1) has been counterfeited on vinyl and CD (Lizard Records LR 0701-2) 1998. Reissued officially on vinyl and CD (Akarma AK 033) 1998.

45: Snow/Me, You, I   (Baron 626) 1968

A Detroit, Michigan outfit. Indeed *Michigan Rocks* (LP) includes a track, *Persecution*, from their album, which is beginning to interest collectors. *Snow*, a fine heavy slice of acid-rock, can also be heard on *Relics, Vol. 1* (LP) and *Relics Vol's 1 & 2* (CD).

Jem Targal later released a fine solo album, *Luckey Guy* (S'heavy) in 1978 R2. We believe this has been booted.

In 1974, Drew Abbott became the guitarist of Bob Seger and The Silver Bullet Band. (VJ)

The Third Rail

Personnel: JOEY LEVINE   A
            ARTIE RESNICK   keyb'ds   A
            K. RESNICK   A

ALBUM: 1(A) ID MUSIC   (Epic 26327) 1967 SC

NB: (1) has been reissued on CD.

45s: The Subway Train That Came To Life /   HCP
      A-Train Rush Hour Stomp   (Cameo C-445) 1966 -
      Run Run Run / No Return   (Epic 10191) 1967 53
      Boppa Do Down Down / Invisible Man (Epic 10240) 1967 -
      It's Time To Say Goodbye /
      Overdose Of Love   (Epic 10285) 1968 113
      She Ain't No Choir Girl /
      The Shape Of Things To Come   (Epic 10323) 1968 -
      Beggin' Me To Stay /
      The Ballad Of General Humpty   (Epic 10457) 1969 -

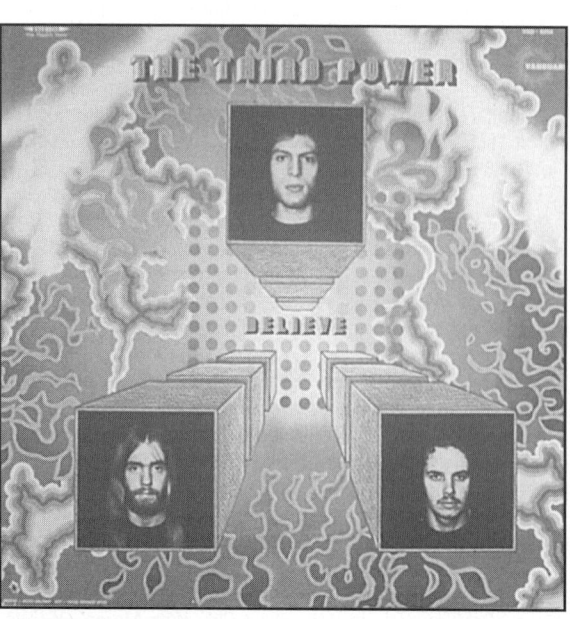

THIRD POWER - Believe LP.

α It's Over Now /
   Dark Ages (Blue Wax) PS   (Spoonfed 4504) 197? -
α A New Life / Didn't Mind   (Longview 8117) 197? -

NB: α It's not confirmed that these are by the same group.

This outfit was a studio trio of songwriters. *Run, Run, Run* was a social comment song on the American rat race. It was included on the classic *Nuggets - Original Artyfacts From The First Psychedelic Era 1965-1968* (Dble LP) compilation and later on Rhino's *Nuggets, Vol. 11* (LP), *Even More Nuggets* (CD) and *Nuggets Box* (4-CD). Their album is becoming more sought-after.

The Resnicks, however, are probably best known for writing *Good Lovin'* for **The Rascals** and bubblegum hits such as *Quick Joey Small* for **The Kasenetz Katz Singing Orchestral Circus**. (VJ/MW)

Third Stone

45s: True Justice/Take It As It Comes (Garland 2017) 1969
      Happiness Is Coming/Eruption   (FBR 216) 196?

A Salem, Oregon, outfit whose *True Justice* - a slice of heavy acid-edged rock - is included on *Turds On A Bum Ride Vol. 5* (CD), *Mayhem & Psychosis, Vol. 1* (CD) and *Open Lid EP* (7"). (MW)

The Third World

Personnel: PAUL ALAGNA   ld gtr, vcls   A
            TEDDY GRAY HILL vcls   A
            LARRY LAUFER   keyb'ds, vcls A
            ROGER MANSOUR   drms   A
            DAVID WATKINS   bs, vcls   A

ALBUM: 1(A) AMERICA THE BEAUTIFUL   (RCA LSP-4502) 1971 -

45: Hitler Is Alive And Well/Steal The Guns   (RCA 74-0494) 1971

Probably from New York, a little-known mix of heavy rock with prog and psych, with songs like *Steal The Guns* and *Hitler Is Alive And Well (In You)*. Competent guitar and keyboards. (SR)

The 13th Door

Personnel: ALEX BLEAS   bs   A
            STEVE FLINT   drms   A
            RICK LORING   ld gtr   A
            DON MICHAEL   gtr   A

45: Lady Jane / Out Of Sight   (Hillside no #) 1966

THE THIRD RAIL - Id Music CD.

This quartet recorded their single at McKenzie Studios in Columbus, Ohio. It was released on the studio's custom Hillside label in November 1966 (Rite pressing #18033/4 for you dead wax spotters), immediately prior to the label's *1966 Promotion* LP (aka "Hillside 1966", on Rite #18036) - they do not feature on the album however.

Both songs are covers; *Lady Jane* is an okay version of the Stones ballad, with lead guitar playing the dulcimer part. It has some touches of reverb. *Out Of Sight* is a pretty good version of the James Brown hit, with a sound not unlike that of **The Gestures**. (DCe/MW)

The 13th Floor Elevators

Personnel:
ROKY ERICKSON	vcls	ABC
TOMMY HALL	jug, vcls	ABC
STACEY SUTHERLAND	ld gtr, vcls	ABC
BENNY THURMAN	bs	A
JOHN WALTON	drms	AB
RONNIE LEATHERMAN	bs	B
DAN GALINDO	bs	C
DANNY THOMAS	drms	C
DUKE DAVIS	bs	

ALBUMS:
1(A)	THE PSYCHEDELIC SOUNDS OF...	(International Artists IALP 1) 1966	R1/R2
2(C)	EASTER EVERYWHERE	(International Artists IALP 5) 1967	R2
3(-)	LIVE	(International Artists IALP 8) 1968	SC
4(C)	BULL OF THE WOODS	(International Artists IALP 9) 1968	SC

NB: (2) was originally issued with a printed inner sleeve containing lyrics. (1) and (2) were also issued in mono (R3). (1) and (2) reissued by Radar Records (RAD 13) and (RAD 15) respectively, in the U.K. in 1978. (1) to (4) were reissued in 1979. (1), (2), (3) and (4) reissued by Decal Records, (LIK 19), (LIK 28), (LIK 30) and (LIK 40) respectively, in the U.K. in 1988. (1) - (4) also issued on CD by Spalax, Decal and by Collectables. A performance from the Avalon Ballroom 1966, has appeared on many bootlegs, including:- (B) *Avalon Ballroom 1966* (FP 1001) 1977; *S.F. 66* (Lysergic Records LP 025) 1980; and *66 Live* (KWR 3031 LP) 1985-French. There have also been a number of retrospective releases, including:- *Fire In My Bones* (Texas Archive Recordings TAR LP-4) 1985, *Elevator Tracks* (Texas Archive Recordings TAR LP-7) 1987 and *The Original Sound Of* (13th Hour Records 13-LP-1) 1988, consisting of outtakes and live material. The latter has also been released as *Demos Everywhere* (no label) 1988, with inferior sound quality. Also of interest are:- *I've Seen Your Face Before (Live)* (Big Beat WIK 82) 1988 and *Live Re-Union* (5 Hours Back) 1988. Another recent CD release is *Magic Of* which features the band live at La Maison in 1965. Collectables have also released four CD's: *Another Dimension* (COL-CD-0506), *Last Concert* (COL-CD-0575), *Magic Of The Pyramids* (COL-CD-0505) and *The 1966-67 Unreleased Masters Collection* (COL-CD-8816). The latter being a 3-CD set with previously unreleased songs, rehearsal tracks, alternate takes, demos and a live recording). Thunderbolt released *The Interpreter* (1996), a double-CD with **Elevators** and Roky Erickson solo tracks. The CD compilation *Psychedelic Microdots Of The Sixties, Vol. 2* (Sundazed SC 11009) contains the same **Elevators** tracks as (8). *The Best Of* (Eva B37/642370) 1994, contains most of their better-known songs, although the version of *You're*

13th FLOOR ELEVATORS - The Psychedelic Sounds Of... LP.

13th FLOOR ELEVATORS - Easter Everywhere LP.

Gonna Miss Me and *We Sell Soul* are from the 45 by the pre-**Elevators** outfit **The Spades**. *The Psychedelic World Of The 13th Floor Elevators* (Charly SNAJ 709) 2002 is a 3-CD box set, which compiles their complete International Artists output with bonus tracks for each album.

EP: 1 You're Gonna Miss Me/Tried To Hide/Reverberation/
Fire Engine (7") (PS) (Riviera 231 240) 1966

NB: (1) rare French release with different takes. There are also a couple of retrospective EPs: *Live In Austin, Texas 1967* (7") (PS) (Austin Records RE-1) 1978-UK, features four songs, which are the same versions as the *Avalon Ballroom* (Bootleg) LP; and *She Lives*/(Other IA artists) (7" promo) (Radar SAM-88) 1978 - UK.

HCP

45s:
α	You're Gonna Miss Me/ Tried To Hide	(Contact 5269) 1965/1966	-
β	You're Gonna Miss Me/ Tried To Hide	(Hanna Barbera 492) 1966	-
β	You're Gonna Miss Me/ Tried To Hide	(International Artists 107) 1966	55
	Reverberation/ Fire Engine	(International Artists 111) 1966	129
	Levitation/ Before You Accuse Me	(International Artists 113) 1967	-
	She Lives/Baby Blue	(International Artists 121) 1967	-
	Slip Inside This House/ Splash 1	(International Anists 122) 1967	-
	May The Circle Remain Unbroken/ I'm Gonna Love You Too	(International Artists 126) 1968	-
	Livin' On/Scarlet And Gold	(International Artists 130) 1968	-

NB: α - β This version of *Tried To Hide* is different from the *Psychedelic Sounds* album. α also issued on Hansa (19.188) 1966 in Germany. There's also a flexi disc: *You're Gonna Miss Me/Tried To Hide/Reverberation/Hurricane Fighter Plane* (**Red Krayola**) (7" flexi-disc) (Radar S.F.I. 347) 1978

The first band to describe themselves as 'psychedelic' the **13th Floor Elevators** formed in the Winter of 1965, playing their first gig at the Jade Room in Austin on 13th (?) December, which garnered a mention in Jim Langdon's column in the Austin Chronicle.

Sutherland, Walton and Thurman had all previously played in a Kerrville band - The Lingsmen, who became the **13th Floor Elevators** when Max Rainey, their original vocalist, left and Roky Erickson, the lead guitarist of **The Spades** (another Austin act), was drafted in as a replacement. Their original line-up was completed by Tommy Hall, a local student, who played jug and along with his wife Clementine wrote much of the band's early material. It seems Clementine was responsible for their name too. Most American buildings have no thirteenth floor and the band were saying, if you want to reach the thirteenth floor and achieve a new level of consciousness, ride with them.

Their first 45, released in the Winter of 1965, was *You're Gonna Miss Me*, which Roky had written when he was still with **The Spades**. The **Elevators'** version was originally issued on the Contact label and a Jan 1966 article in the Austin Chronicle states that a local radio station refused to play the record (they claimed that the band and supporters were calling incessantly for it to be played).

The band also quickly established a strong 'live' reputation playing at venues like the New Orleans Club and the Jade Room in Austin and La Maison in Houston. Significantly they were the first band to advertise themselves as 'psychedelic', predating **The Grateful Dead** by about two weeks and first hand reports of these early gigs, indicate that they were an awesome live act. Indeed, there are even rumours of en masse "flash-outs" brought on by the fervant, pulsating rhythms and feverish foot-stomping by the crowd.

Texas was a highly conservative state in the late 1960s and, not surprisingly, a band like **The 13th Floor Elevators** with their long hair and penchant for drugs (particularly acid) had a number of brushes with the law. They were eventually busted in early 1966 and all placed on probation. Tensions were increasing within the band, too, and these led to Benny Thurman's departure and his replacement by Ronnie Leatherman.

The band's career received new impetus when Lelan Rogers signed them to his new International Artists label. Rogers had just returned to Texas from L.A., where he'd been working for A & M Records. He reissued their debut 45 on his label (with a different recording of the flip side *Tried To Hide*) and it made No. 55 in the National Charts. Their first album, recorded in Dallas, followed shortly after. Taking a sort of Kinks or Stones styled R&B they added their own highly individual style on what was a classic vinyl offering. Prominent throughout was Tommy Hall's jug playing, which helped to give the group a unique and distinctive sound. The songs were also laced in psychedelic mysticism which was central to their music and the album is often regarded by "heads" as some of the finest psychedelic music to be committed to disc, being particularly notable for how it expands and stretches out under the influence of psychedelic drugs.

In particular, *Roller Coaster* oozed the feelings of a psychedelic trip and revelled in the new purpose to man's life that could result from the psychedelic experience. It's also claimed that the track is about (or inspired by) Alfred Korzybski, the father of semantics - who was one of Hall's main influences. Korzybski wrote "Science and Sanity An Introduction to General Semantics and Non-Aristotelian Systems" and one of his concepts was "unsanity" which is referred to in the songs lyrics, and in the liner notes to the *Psychedelic Sounds...* album. Other tracks such as *Reverberation* dealt with how a person who organised their knowledge in the right way could overcome problems of doubt (and avoid bum trips); *Don't Fall Down* dealt with the care that had to be taken to maintain this chemically-altered state; *Splash 1*, which was written by Clementine Hall and Roky and later covered by **The Clique**, describes the meeting of two minds which have undergone the psychedelic experience and *You Don't Know* explained the differences between persons of old and new states of mind. Perhaps the best track of all was *Fire Engine*, written by Tommy, Stacey and Roky, which began with an unusual siren introduction and superficially portrayed what it would be like to ride on a fire engine for fun rather than to fight an horrific fire - at a deeper level, the song is said to have a D.M.T. influence, with Roky twisting the words "empty place" into "Let me take you to D.M.T. place on my fire engine"... DMT being the short-term psychedelic Di Methyl Tryptamine.

Like so many bands in this era **The 13th Floor Elevators** headed for California in August of 1966 and stayed there in San Francisco for the remainder of the year. They played at the Avalon ballroom four times and once at the Fillmore West. Their first album was released during their stay in California and this, plus the fact they gigged a lot at the Avalon Ballroom, led many people to believe them to be a San Francisco band. In fact, they actually put on an all-Texan show at the Avalon during their California stay with **Big Brother and The Holding Company** (Janis Joplin was from Austin, Texas and at one time nearly joined **The 13th Floor Elevators**) and the **Sir Douglas Quintet**. The band's time in California helped to forge important links between America's West Coast and the hitherto relatively isolated Texas psychedelic scene. **The Elevators** would return to California two more times in late 1967 and in 1968.

They returned to Texas late in 1966 and immediately ran into disagreements with their record company about what their next single should be. International Artists wanted to target *I'm Gonna Love You Too* at the Top 40 market, but Tommy, keen to uphold the band's quest as psychedelic leaders, held out for *Reverberation* and got his way with this and subsequent 45 releases. None of them ever made the national charts again.

Early in 1967 another split developed in the band. This was partly about the use of drugs as police pressure on the band grew. All were heavily into acid except John Ike Walton - indeed, Roky was reputed to have taken it over 300 times. So when Walton and Ronnie Leatherman left the band because of management disagreements, Walton was already viewed by the band as an establishment figure. After the split Tommy, Roky and Stacey retreated to Kerrville, a small hill town in the countryside, where they spent the Summer of 1967. They recruited two new members, Danny Thomas, a drummer, and Danny Galindo, a bass player and started work on their second album, *Easter Everywhere*, which entered the shops in the Autumn of 1967. It contained their own interpretation of Bob Dylan's *Its All Over Now, Baby Blue*. *She Lives*, a Tommy/Roky composition was also issued as a 45. Musically the album was more controlled and less frenzied than their first album but there are a lot of collectors who consider this to be their best album. It suffered from under-promotion and Lelan Roger's policy of underpublicising the band to create a mystique around them had by this stage become counter-productive. Sadly, too, the group was beginning to crumble with Roky becoming increasingly unreliable and frequently missing gigs. The record company tried unsuccessfully to put him into a 'rest' hospital, but late in 1968 he was busted again. To avoid being dumped in Huntsville (the Texas State Prison), he claimed to be a Martian and the authorities committed him to Rusk State Hospital for the criminally insane early in 1969. Stacey got busted again and was not so lucky - he ended up in Huntsville.

Taking advantage of the band's problems the record company issued their third album, which failed to capture the band at anything like its best. It was not a 'live' album at all - the tracks were studio outtakes, with faked applause added. It did, however, contain five songs not featured on their studio albums - Bo Diddley's *Before You Accuse Me* (the flip to their third single); Buddy Holly's *I'm Gonna Love You Too*; Soloman Burke's *Everybody Needs Somebody To Love* and two original compositions, *You Gotta Take That Girl* and *You Can't Hurt Me Anymore*.

When Tommy Hall headed for California the band, already minus Roky and Stacey, literally fell apart leaving behind them an incomplete album tentatively titled *The Beauty And The Beast*. It was released after their demise by the record company late in 1968. They changed its name to *Bull Of The Woods*. Its finest moments included *Never Another*, one of the best and most demented tracks ever recorded (the only one on the album written by their usual songwriting duo of Roky and Tommy) and *May The Circle Remain Unbroken*, a haunting Roky composition recorded immediately after *Easter Everywhere* which had also appeared on one of their later 45s. Nearly all the remaining material was written by Stacey Sutherland often in conjunction with Tommy Hall. Stacey's songs are for the most part rather stark but *Street Song* and *Rose And The Thorn* both feature some fine guitar work.

Roky spent three years in Rusk State Hospital and it took a court case to get him out! In 1972 he attempted to reform the band with John Ike Walton using other musicians but it fell apart after two gigs, Thurman later played

13th FLOOR ELEVATORS - Live LP.

13th FLOOR ELEVATORS - Bull Of The Woods LP.

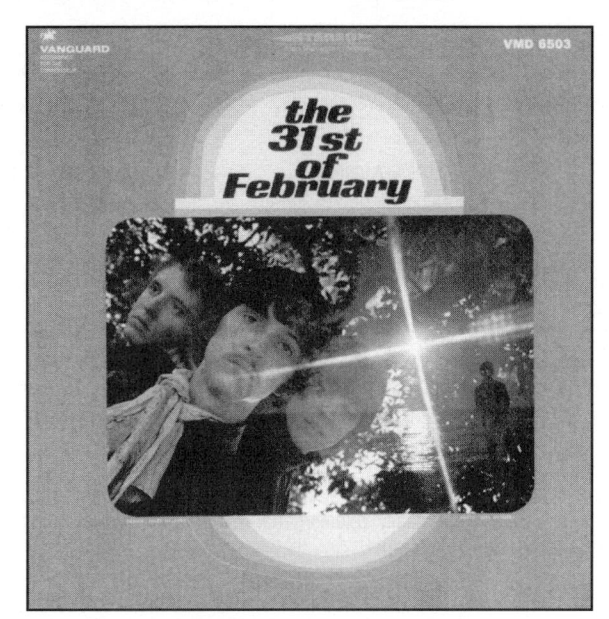

THE 31ST OF FEBRUARY - The 31st Of February CD.

for **Plum Nelly**, Galindo was in **Rubayyat** and Duke Davis, who was also associated with the band was in Gritz, but Erickson's subsequent solo career and the mystique surrounding the band has led to continuing interest in their recordings which prior to the reissue of their first two albums, in 1978, meant copies were changing hands for quite a few dollars.

In recent years a plethora of the band's material has appeared. *Fire In My Bones* and *Elevator Tracks* both comprise alternate takes (mostly from their first LP) and several live tracks of variable quality. *I've Seen Your Face Before* is a live recording with rather confusing liner notes dating from 1966 or 1967. It features *She Lives* and *Levitation* from their *Easter Everywhere* album, the rest of the material is from their first LP. *The Original Sound Of ..* and *Demos Everywhere* both contain the same material despite their different titles, although the former contains track information that isn't present on the latter and is better sound quality. Side one contains alternate mixes of tracks from their first album, Side Two is thought to be an audience bootleg, although it claims to be a radio broadcast.

Charly's 3-CD box set *The Psychedelic World Of....* includes all their International Artists output along with various bonus cuts, which have all been released previously. They include their bootlegged 1966 Avalon Ballroom concert, cuts from a 1967 Austin gig, early rarities including *You're Gonna Miss Me* in its original form by Roky's group **The Spades** and rare cuts first issued on eighties compilations like *Fire In My Bones* and *Elevator Tracks*.

Compilation appearances have included:- *You're Gonna Miss Me* on Lenny Kaye's *Nuggets* and *Twenty-One KILT Goldens, Vol. 2*; The 45 version of *Tried To Hide* on *Mind Blowers, Vol. 1, Austin Landing, Vol. 1* and *The International Artists Singles Collection*; live '67 recordings of *You're Gonna Miss Me* and *She Lives In A Time Of Her Own*, without Roky on *Acid Visions - The Complete Collection, Vol. 1* (3-CD set); A live track from a 1972 reunion *Maxine* on *Austin Landing, Vol. 2*; A loose jam based around *Levitation* entitled *Elevator Jam* on *Sixties Rebellion, Vol's 1 & 2* (CD); The live version of *The Word* on *Turds On A Bum Ride, Vol. 4* and finally, *Epitaph For A Legend*, a double compilation album first issued in 1980, contains an excerpt from *Fire Engine*, a radio ad for the *Bull Of The Woods* LP, the previously unissued *Wait For My Love* and Roky and Clementine Hall performing previously unissued versions of *Splash 1* and the Powell St. John composition *Right Track Now*. (VJ/CMk/TBt/SR/BM)

The 13th Hour Glass

| 45s: | Try / Youngblood | (Prestige Productions 208) 1967 |
| | Indecision (Do I Have To Come Right Out And Say) / Keep On Running | (Format F45-5002/3) 1967 |

Reported to be from Florida, although one 45 was released on Birmingham, Alabama's Prestige Productions label. *Indecision* is an interesting cover of the Neil Young song, but the 'B' side is a great cover with especially fuzzy guitars and swirling organs. (BM/MW)

Thirty Days Out

Personnel:	PHIL LOWE	drms, vcls	A
	JACK MALKEN	ld gtr, vcls	A
	MONTE MELNICK	bs, vcls, organ	A
	JOHN MICALEFF	ld vcls, gtr	A
	(JIM DICKINSON	keyb'ds	A)
	(LARRY KNECHTEL	keyb'ds	A)

| ALBUM: | 1(A) | THIRTY DAYS OUT | (Reprise RS 6450) 1971 - |
| | 2(A) | MIRACLE LICK | (Reprise MS 2085) 1972 - |

Thirty Days Out were formed New York in 1971 by John Micaleff (pronouced "McCullough"), a folksinger from Michigan and Jack Malken, who had previously been with The Outcasts. After teaming up with Melnick and Lowe, they found a place to practice but had to relocate in Greenfield, Massachusetts when their neigbours complained! They soon managed to get a recording contract with Reprise and their first album was released in the Summer of '71. Produced by Larry Marks (previously in charge of **Lee Michaels** and **Phil Ochs**) their debut was recorded in New York and L.A. On offer are eight tracks penned by Micaleff and Malken, which mix competent guitars with early seventies style vocals. Influenced by Free on some tracks (*Doing The Best That I Can* and *Survival*, a rip-off of **Clover**'s *Shotgun*). The most interesting element is probably the keyboard parts played by two ace sessionmen, Larry Knechtel and **Jim Dickinson**. The lyrics have often a Christian content and the overall result is rather undistinguished. In fact the album is perhaps mainly notable for a weird packaging idea, as it came wrapped in a poster of a steamliner. Once the shrink was opened, the hidden black and white sleeve with pictures of the group would appear.

Probably due to this poster, the sales were quite good and the group soon released a second album, recorded in Wallingford, Connecticut and remixed in London. This time Malken handled the production and Micaleff wrote most of their material. Their ambition of "blending electricity and acousticity into a fresh, tasteful and unified rock sound" turned into a total disaster, the lyrics being over-ambitious and the songs lacking melodies or "Miracle Licks" (despite its title).

Their albums will appeal mainly to fans of early seventies prog-rock, some tracks of their second effort being "graced" by the "Magic Mellotron" of Teddy Taylor and Bing McCoy.

Monte Melnick, their bass player later became The Ramones tour manager. At least one of their albums was engineered by Melnick's high school buddy Tom Erdelyi, later known as Tommy Ramone. (SR/DH)

The 31st of February

Personnel:	SCOTT BOYER	gtr, vcls	A
	DAVE BROWN	bs, vcls	A
	BUTCH TRUCKS	drms	A

ALBUM: 1(A) THE 31ST OF FEBRUARY (Vanguard VSD-6503) 1969 SC

NB: (1) reissued on CD and LP (Vanguard VSD-6503).

45s: Sandcastles/Pick A Gripe (Vanguard 35066) 1969
In The Morning When I'm Real/
Porcelain Mirrors (Vanguard 35087) 1969

From Jacksonville, Florida, they previously recorded a 45 as **The Tiffany System**. Produced by Steve Alaimo, their album, which is of the 'progressive' genre, is a very minor collectable, though it has its moments; from the extended moody cover of *Codine*, the evocative but doomy dirge *Cries Of Treason*; the **Byrdsy** folk-rock of *A Different Kind Of Head*; and the psychy freakout of *A Nickel's Worth Of Benny's Help*. An album that has some rewards for the patient listener.

After the album, they teamed up with Gregg and Duane Allman, recording the tapes which were finally released as **Gregg and Duane Allman** by Steve Alaimo on his Bold label.

Trucks stayed with the Allmans to form **The Allman Brothers**, Boyer created Cowboy with Tommy Talton (ex-**We The People**) and David Brown would join **Santana** and Boz Scaggs.

Compilation appearances include *Sandcastles* on *The New Sound Of Underground* (LP). (VJ/MW/SR)

This Generation

45: The Children Have Your Tongue/same (Hip 8007) c1968
NB: promo copy.

From the Memphis area, a rare single written by W. and R. Crook and produced by Natalie Rosenberg with heavy fuzz, female vocals and organ. A short-lived subsidiary label of Stax, HIP also released the records by **Southwest FOB** and **Paris Pilot**. (SR)

This Side Up

Personnel: DAVID CORTOPASSI A
RUSSELL KERGER A
VINCE SILVERA A
DAVE STURGEON A
SCOTT WILLIAMS A

45: Lose Yourself/Turn Your Head (Century V-255 25) 1966

When Dave Sturgeon left the band, he was replaced by Rusty Kurig and they re-named themselves as **The Elastik Band**, later of *Spazz* infamy. (VJ)

This Side Up

Personnel: ALAN ARKUS drms A
FRANK FRIEDMAN vcls, gtr AB
DAVID ROSENTHAL ld vcls, drms AB
STEWART ROYAL keyb'ds A
RONNIE SEITEL ld gtr AB
JOHN SHERRILL bs AB
ART SHILLING drms, vcls B

45s: Why Can't I Dream /
Sun Arise (Prestige Productions PP66-151) 1966
Book A Trip / In (Capitol 2129) 1968

The Romans were formed in 1963 with members drawn from Ramsey and Shades Valley High Schools in Birmingham, Alabama. A couple of years later they evolved into **This Side Up** when core members Rosenthal, Seitel and Sherrill were joined by Friedman, Royal and Arkus. The latter pair departed around the time of their debut 45 in 1966, and Shilling was brought into the fold.

MAYO THOMPSON - Corky's Debt To His Father LP.

Why Can't I Dream is readily accessible again via *Psychedelic States: Alabama Vol. 1* (CD). It's a yearning, dramatic pop-punker.

The following year they won a Battle of The Bands, sponsored by WSGN radio and Capitol records, thereby securing a 45 deal. Composed by the Buie-Cobb team, *Book A Trip* is not surprisingly heavily-produced bouncy mainstream pop; the flip is a soft'n'cosy orchestrated ballad (have to wonder if any of the band were allowed to play on these tracks?). Oh, and Buddie Buie became their manager into the bargain.

The band split not long after. Friedman formed The Wet Willie Band. Shilling was later in Cowboy then became an actor, appearing in commercials and the Matlock TV series. (MW/RM)

Susan and Richard Thomas

ALBUM: 1 A BURST OF LIFE (Blue Hour 1017) 1973 SC

From Wisconsin, a rare folk-psych private pressing with female vocals. It came with a lyric insert. (SR)

Thomas A. Edison Electric Band

45: Methyl Ethyl/
The Name Of The Game (Cameo Parkway C-490) 1967

Despite the intriguing name and title, *Methyl Ethyl* is tame novelty pop. However, the flip is rather better snotty garage-pop wherein this Pennsylvania outfit let their guitarist step on the fuzz pedal and evoke a short screeching solo. The band were earlier known as **The Chimps** and released two uncredited cash-in/exploito albums *Monkey Business* (Wyncote W-9199), and *Monkeys A-Go-Go* (Wyncote SW-9203) with Monkees covers and some good garage noises/insane psychedelic freakouts.

They later changed their name to **Edison Electric Band**, recording an album for Cotillion.

You can also find *The Name Of The Game* on *Mindrocker, Vol. 11* (LP). (MW/CF)

Thomas Group

Personnel: TONY THOMAS drms A

45: Penny Arcade/Ordinary Girl (Dunhill 4027) 1966

Another Sloan/Barry creation. They released some other folk-rock singles but without any success. *Penny Arcade* has been compiled on *Penny Arcade, Dunhill Folk Rock, Vol. 2* (LP). (SR)

Don Thompson

ALBUM: 1 JUPITER (Sunday KS 5101) 1975 R1

NB: (1) reissued (Korona Records) 197? SC, in a standard printed sleeve.

A local Illinois folk-rock artist whose album feature electronic embellishments. The first edition was issued in a hand-silk-screened cover with an insert. (CF)

Mayo Thompson

ALBUMS: 1 CORKY'S DEBT TO HIS FATHER (Texas Revolution 2270) 1969 R1
          2 CORRECTED SLOGANS (Music Language 1848) 1976 -

NB: (1) reissued by Glass (GLALP 015) 1986 in the UK, (2) reissued by Recommended in the U.K. in 1982.

Thompson was arguably the main creative force behind **The Red Krayola** who produced the weirdest music for International Artists in the late sixties. Upon their demise he worked with **Saddlesore** and recorded *Corky's Debt...*, which like **Red Crayola** is also a little strange. It was made with the help of friends including most members of **Fun And Games**. He eventually turned up to do sessions with the Art Of Language organisation in 1976. This resulted in demos which are compiled on *Corrected Slogans*, an album of simple songs, operatic vocals and complex lyrics.

In 1979 he reformed Red Krayola, with drummer Jesse Chamberlain, who he had earlier met in New York in the Winter of 1974/75 and had gigged with intermittently since. Aided by Lora Logic and Pere Ubu they recorded *Soldier Talk* (Radar RAD 18) 1979, which united the garage music of the sixties with fragmented, modernistic arrangements and *Kangaroo* (Rough Trade) 1980, an album of avant-garde theatre music, which reunited Red Crayola and Art Of Language followed. He also played with Pere Ubu from 1980 onwards.

A previously unreleased recording, *Woof*, from the *Corky's Debt...* sessions, has also resurfaced on the EP *Meat Pie Toecloth Scraper* which was issued with Ptolemaic Terrascope magazine (#20) in 1996. (VJ)

Thorinshield

Personnel: TERRY HAND A
           BOBBY RAY A
           JAMES SMITH A

ALBUM: 1(A) THORINSHIELD (Philips PHS-600251) 1967 -

NB: (1) a mono pressing also exists (PHM 200-251).

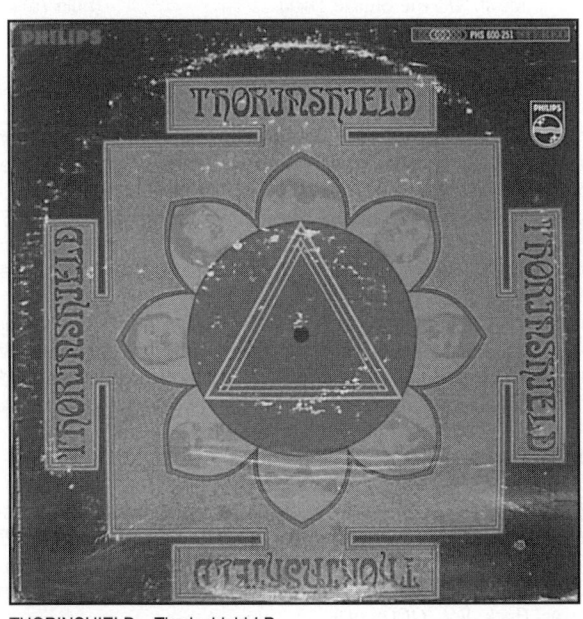

THORINSHIELD - Thorinshield LP.

45s: α The Best Of It/Life Is A Dream (Philips 40492) 1967
        Family Of Man/Lonely Mountain Again (Philips 40521) 1968

NB: α Some copies came in an art sleeve which advertised the album.

This obscure Los Angeles trio had its roots in the folk movement but at times paid lip service to some of the psychedelic trappings of the era. Musically the album is hard to peg, though if you enjoy the sunshine pop characterized by **Curt Boettcher** and groups like **Sagitarrius**, it's something you may want to check out. Tracks such as *Wrong My Friend*, *Here Today* and *Life Is A Dream* offered up a highly commercial mix of folk-rock and soft-psych. The combination of great harmonies (check out *Pleasure Time*), coupled with occassional psychedelic touches (nice backwards guitar on *One Girl*) and attractive orchestration (*Prelude To A Postlude*), were quite impressive. Hardly 1967's most original debut, but well worth hearing, particularly if you can find it relatively cheap. The first 45 was on the album which was produced by the famous L.A. sax player Steve Douglas and arranged by Perry Botkin Jr. All their songs were written by Bobby Ray and James Smith.

Bobby Ray may be the same guy who played bass on Donovan's May 1966 sessions in L.A., including *Season Of The Witch*, *The Trip* and two unreleased pieces: *Super Lungs* (different version) and *Breezes of Patchulie*. Drummer Terry Hand had previous played in a number of surf bands and released a couple of singles as a member of **Everpresent Fullness**.

Compilation appearances include: *Life Is A Dream* on *Electric Food* (LP); and *Lonely Mountain Again* on *High All The Time, Vol. 2* (LP). (VJ/SR/BBn/SB)

Thorndike Picklefish (Pacifist Choir)

45s: The Interview With Mrs.Malooka /
      Poetry Readings In The Bathroom (Yonah 2003) 1963
      Viet Nama Mama /
      Walter Wart The Freaky Dog (Absurd 304) 1966
      Ballad Of Walter Wart /
      It's Warts On The Flip Side That Counts (MTA 114) 1966
      Lonely Bull (Frog)/ Wart Now My Love (MTA 126) 1967
      S.F. Bound//The Imperial Grand Mother
      Paranoia/XEJC/Flower People/Walrus (Piccadilly 247) 1967
      Leeny Frog / D.J. At The End Of The World (Lo-Fi 1) 1967
      Robert O'Smut /
      Sleepy Stonewall's Brotherhood Boogie (Lo-Fi 1a) 1968

These are mainly novelty/comedy skits. *S.F. Bound* takes a pot (!) shot at hippies with some hysterical couplets like:-

"We're in San Francisco, my eyes are bleary.
I look at my dashboard and my statue of Leary"
(croaky-voiced ancient) "I've been sitting on this corner for FIF-TEEN years selling flowers to the tourists, and now these kids are GIVING them away"!

Robert Smith was a DJ in the Pacific Northwest. (BM/MW)

Those Boys

45s: Girls Don't Leave Me/Never Go Away (Fed 1012) 1966
      The Only Girl For Me/No Good Girl (Fed 1016) 1967

A Houston, Texas, act. *No Good Girl* can also be found on *Pebbles, Vol. 16* (LP). It's a half decent folk-punk effort. (VJ)

Those Five

Personnel: JOHN DeLISE A
           BUDDY HELM A
           FRANK O'KEEFE A
           JAN PULVER A
           JOHN ROEDEL A

45s: Love/Because You Love Me ( ) 196?
      Sidewalks/Challenge Of A Fantasy Man (Paris Tower 117) 1967

From a Clearwater/Largo, Florida. John DeLise also played in **The Soul Trippers** and **Rovin' Flames**; Buddy Helm was later with **Bethelem Ayslum**; Jan Pulver in **H.Y. Sledge**; and Frank O'Keefe (who left the band in 1967) later found success with **The Outlaws**. (JLh/SMR)

Those Guys

Personnel:
BOB DABBS	drms		AB
DAVID OWENS	gtr, keyb'd		AB
JIMMY OWENS	gtr, keyb'd		AB
BOB BARNES	bs		B
EDDIE DEATON	ld gtr		B

45s:
I Want To Hold Your Hand/Teresa	(Charay 57)	1966
Stereopsis Of A Floret/Cool	(Jenko 14)	1967
People Say/Three Days Gone	(Black Sheep 103)	1967
Lookin' At You Behind The Glasses/ Stereopsis Of A Floret	(Black Sheep 104)	1967

From the Dallas/Fort Worth area of Texas, they started out playing a lot of instrumentals and *I Want To Hold Your Hand* and *Cool* are examples of such. Their finest moment, however, is *Lookin' At You Behind The Glasses*.

The band was started by cousins David and Jimmy Owens, with drummer Bob Dabbs. When another Fort Worth act, **The Elite** disbanded David and Jimmy asked two of it's members, Eddie Deaton and Bob Barnes to join.

Bob Barnes recalls:- "Eddie and I were with the band for a little over a year, when Jimmy was drafted into the Army, paratrooper school as I recall. I found myself involved with the girlfriend of a happening DJ and things got crazy. I took off for New Orleans and played in a pick up band there in a place called "The Gunga Den". I had a room in a boarding house next door to a stripper with a cheetah! I think the band continued for a while longer, but I am not sure how or when they faded away."

Bob Barnes later went on to **The Yellow Payges**.

Compilation appearances include *Lookin' At You Behind The Glasses* on *Sixties Archive Vol. 6* (CD) and *Texas Psychedelia From The Sixties* (LP).

Those of Us

45: Without You/That's Love   (IGL 124) 1967

From Sioux Falls, South Dakota, this group earlier made a 45 as **Dale Gregory and the Shouters**.

Compilation appearances have included: *Love, Wine, Passing Time* on *Roof Garden Jamboree* (LP); *Without You, That's Love, Love, Wine, Passing Time, Forever Mine* and *Goodbye Rainy Day* on *Rock 'N' Roll Project - A History Of Rock In Sioux Falls 1965-1967* (CD); and *Without You* on *The IGL Rock Story: Part One (1965 - 67)* (CD). (VJ/MW)

The 3½

45s:
Don't Cry To Me, Babe/R And B In C	(Cameo 425)	1966
Problem Child/Hey Mom, Hey Dad	(Cameo 442)	1966
Hey Gyp/ Hey Kitty, Cool Kitty	(Cameo 451)	1967
Angel Baby (Don't You Ever Leave Me)/ You Turned Your Back On Love	(Cameo 485)	1967

An obscure garage pop group with strong anglophile influences, as their second 45 contained a song written by Graham Gouldman (later of 10cc) and the third was a Donovan cover. (SR)

Three Of Us

Personnel:
GLENDA HELTON	piano, vcls	A
RON LEICHMAN	gtr, piano, vcls	A
MIKE McGUIRE	organ, vcls	A

ALBUM: 1(A) THREE OF US   (Private pressing) c1970 ?

Recorded in Cincinnati, Ohio, a rare private pressing which offers some good tracks with wah-wah or fuzz guitar, organ solos and echoed female vocals. The remaining tracks are unfortunately not as good but the album is interesting overall. It was curiously produced by Soupy Sales, a well-known comedian.

It could be the same Ron Leichman who later played in a seventies progressive rock band, Round About, also from Ohio. (SR)

Three Ring Circus

ALBUM: 1 GROOVIN' ON THE SUNSHINE   (RCA LPS-4021) 1968 -

45: Groovin' On The Sunshine/ So True (PS)   (RCA 47-9537) 1968

A forgotten flower-pop group. (SR)

3's A Crowd

45: Keep On Walking/No Where   (Golden Voice no #) 1968

Catchy garagey beat from Illinois backed with a teenbeat ballad. (MW)

Threshold of Sound

Personnel incl: L. HOLZENTHAL   A

45s:
She's Mine/Nobody But Us	(Nettie 101)	196?
Run To The Morning Sun / Make ...	(Mor Soul 006)	196?

From New Orleans, Louisiana. *She's Mine*, a typically primitive garage-punker, features some frenzied instrumentation in places but it's pretty average really.

The second 45 may be by a different outfit.

Compilation appearances include *She's Mine* on *Louisiana Punk From The Sixties* (LP) and *Sixties Archive, Vol. 3* (CD). (VJ/MW/AB)

Tom Thumb and The Casuals

Personnel:
STEVE ALCOBRACK	gtr	A
TOM (THUMB) BLESSING	sax, gtr, ld vcls	ABC
LARRY EVANS	bs	ABC
SCOTT LETTERMAN	drms	ABC
JIM WOLFE	keyb'ds	ABC
BRAD MILLER	gtr	B
STEVE VALLEY	ld gtr	C

45s:
Movin' On/The Shuffle Thing	(Bolo 753)	1965
I Should Know/I Don't Want Much	(Panorama 21)	1965
I Should Know/I Don't Want Much	(Verve 10478)	1966
The Draft/Irresistible You	(Panorama 36)	1966

This band was formed in Seattle, Washington when Blessing and Letterman recruited Wolfe from local band The Nomads in 1963. They attracted sufficient interest to get a one-off deal with Seafair-Bolo Records. *Movin' On* got a lot of local airplay and became a local hit. Then in 1965 Jim Valley's brother Steve joined the band on lead guitar and they signed to Jerry Dennon's Panorama label. Their two resulting 45s attracted considerable airplay. Just when the future looked rosy, tragedy struck. The band's vehicle crashed en route to a performance in Richland, Washington. Blessing and Evans were killed, Valley was injured but recovered. Wolfe, Letterman and Valley reformed the band as The American Dream adding Mike Holiday (ex-**Paul Revere and The Raiders**) and songwriter Danny O'Keefe. After this short-lived venture Wolfe and Letterman formed **The Time Machine**.

Compilation appearances have included: *I Should Know* on *Northwest Battle Of The Bands, Vol. 2 - Knock You Flat!* (LP & CD), *Northwest Battle Of The Bands, Vol. 1* (CD), *History Of Northwest Rock, Vol. 2* (CD) and *Highs In The Mid Sixties, Vol. 14* (LP); and *The Draft* on *The History Of Northwest Rock, Vol. 3* (CD). (VJ)

Thunder and Roses

Personnel:	CHRIS BOND	gtr, vcls	A
	GEORGE EMME	drms	A
	TOM SCHAEFER	bs, vcls	A

ALBUM: 1(A) KING OF THE BLACK SUNRISE
(United Artists UAS 6709) 1969 SC

NB: (1) reissued in 1998 on CD (LIZARD LR 0705-2).

45: Country Life/I Love A Woman (United Artists 50536) 1969

A **Hendrix**-influenced heavy psychedelic trio from Philadelphia, they even managed a pretty decent cover of *Red House* on the album, which is now a minor collectable. The 45 is off the album (two of its worst tracks), the title cut is an instrumental. Its finest moments are the opening cut, *White Lace And Strange*, and the finale, *Open Up Your Eyes*, which are both brimming with heavy psychedelic guitar work. (VJ)

The Thunderbirds

ALBUM: 1 MEET THE FABULOUS THUNDERBIRDS
(Red Feather TH-1) 1964 ?

Believed to have been based in New Mexico, this band's very rare album changes hands for large sums. One cut, *Just Let Me Know*, has emerged on the *Oil Stains* (LP) compilation although it's a pretty ordinary pre-punk beat offering. (MW)

The Thunderbirds

45s:	Steel / Stalking The Thunderbird	(Ermine 51) 1963
	Simmering / Summertime	(Ermine 54) 1964
	Kissin' Time / Crater Soda	(Ermine 56) 1964
	I Need Your Love / ?	(Delaware 1704) c1965
	Take A Look At Me / Hey Little Darlin'	(Delaware 1706) 1965
	Is It Wrong /	(Delaware 1708) 1965
	Your Ma Said You Cried /	
	Before It's Too Late	(Delaware 1710) 1965
	Cindy, Oh Cindy /	
	Before It's Too Late	(Ivanhoe 50,000) c1966

A Chicago area outfit who have been compiled on *A Journey To Tyme, Vol. 4* (LP) with their rendition of *Your Ma Said You Cried*; a song also covered by **The Other Four** in 1966. (VJ/MW)

Thunderbolts

45: Heart So Cold/A Taste Of Honey (No label 22158) 1968

A garage band from Vermont. *Heart So Cold* is on *The Essential Pebbles Collection, Vol. 1* (Dble CD). (GG/MW)

Thunderduk

Personnel:	PHIL HILOW	vcls, gtr	AB
	BOB TURCHEK	drms	AB
	JEFF ULMICHER	vcls, gtr	AB
	GARY WALLIS	vcls, bs	AB
	RICK FISCHER	drms	B

ALBUMS: 1(A) COLLECTOR'S ITEM
(Agency Recording Studios) 1972 R3
2(B) THUNDERDUK (Rockadelic RRLP 23) 1995 -

NB: (1) was a 12" metal acetate. (2) reissues seven of the eight tracks on the original acetate plus two previously unissued tracks from 1974.

A highly uncommercial Cleveland, Ohio rock group. Their recordings are rather hit and miss affairs. All nine cuts on the Rockadelic album are originals. The finer moments include the driving guitar on opener *Why Don't*

THUNDERDUK - Thunderduk LP.

You Love Me?, the fine jamming guitar work on *Time And Again* and, by contrast, the mellow slow-paced *Something To Look At* with its dominant percussion work.

The recordings on the Rockadelic album span the 1972 - 74 period when their desire to play original music and their on stage antics made them one of the top draws on the Cleveland Club scene. Bob Turchek was later replaced on drums by ex-Catscradle drummer Rick Fischer. Most of the material on the Rockadelic album was played by the band on two Agency Studio live broadcasts carried by local station WNCR. (GG/VJ)

Thunder Head

Personnel incl:	M. CAPPELLETTI	A
	D. FRAZIER	A
	J. HARRIS	A

45: And I Need You/Don't Run (Charm 6092/3) 1972

They were previously known as **The Unsettled Society** which came from Pennellville, New York, although the sleeve notes of *Sixties Rebellion* claim that they were from Pennsylvania. The 'A' side, a slow progressive number, has resurfaced on *Sixties Rebellion, Vol. 15* (LP & CD). The flip is mellow and laid-back rock par excellence. (MW/MM)

Thundering Heard

45: Sunny Street Love/Daisy's Prism (Liquid Stereo LS 26) 1968

Light 'n' airy psych-rock from a band alternatively quoted as from Seattle and Lake Oswego, Oregon. Both sides trip along merrily with *Daisy's Prism* being the better of the two.

Compilation appearances include: *Sunny St. Love* and *Daisy's Prism* on *Psychedelic Moods - Part Two* (CD); *Daisy's Prism* on *High All The Time, Vol. 2* (LP). (MW)

Thunder Mugs

Personnel:	DENNIS BASSETTI	bs, vcls	A
	BOB JONTE	drms	A
	JACK LUTZ	vcls, gtr, keyb'ds	A
	JERRY ROY	ld gtr, vcls	A

ALBUM: 1(A) ON THE SPOT (Akarma AK 043) 1999

NB: (1) not issued originally, there has been a 'reissue' on vinyl and CD (Akarma AK 043) 1999.

| 45: | Motion Tree / Captain Midnight | | (All-American?, unconfirmed) 196? |

An obscure late sixties California act whose album, was apparently unreleased at the time. It's predominantly soft psychy rock-pop with occasional good guitar, a few effects and period charm. Stand-outs are the upfront *Motion Tree* and *Lucky Lady*. All songs were composed by Jack Lutz. (MW)

Thunderpussy

Personnel:	GEORGE JAKETUTKO	drms	A
	STEVEN JAY MORRIS	gtr	A
	BEN RUSSELL	bs, flute	A

ALBUM: 1(A) DOCUMENTS OF CAPTIVITY (MRT RL 31748) 1973 R2

NB: (1) Reissued on Breeder (German) and on CD by (Wild Places WILD 002) with several bonus tracks.

This is the work of a hard-rock/progressive trio from Quincy in South Illinois. The album came with a lyric sheet and originals are sought-after. Morris later embarked on a solo career. (VJ)

Thunderstone

| 45: | I Got A Line On You/? | (J.D. Records 6570) c1970 |

Possibly from the East Coast, a good cover of **Spirit** with distorted guitar. (SR)

Thundertree

Personnel:	BILL HALLQUIST	vcls, gtr	A
	RICK Lia BRAATEN	drms	A
	JOHN MIESEN	organ	A
	TERRY TILLEY	bs	A
	DERVIN WALLIN	vcls	A

ALBUM: 1(A) THUNDERTREE (Roulette SR-42038) 1970 SC

A Minneapolis band whose album transgresses psychedelia and progressivism. It's now becoming a minor collectable and is harder to find. The medley on Side Two is full of variety and interest but the highlights are the opening cut, *Head Embers*, which has lots of good guitar work and the mildly psychedelic, *At The Top Of The Stairs*. There are a few awful tracks, but there are lots of ideas on this album and if you're into psychedelic guitar and keyboards this is one for you.

The band evolved out of **The Good Idea**. When that band had split in 1969, John Miesen landed a deal with Roulette on the basis of an unreleased **The Good Idea** track, *12:25*, which was used for one side of the **Thundertree** album.

Bill Hallquist later recorded two solo albums. The first under the name of Billy, *Persephone* (Orion 20510) 1972, although he's more often referred to as Persephone Billy, due to a typographical error on the sleeve. On this he was helped out by, amongst others, Rick Lia Braaten (also ex-**Thundertree**). The album, which is pretty rare and sought-after, consists of pleasant, dreamy folk-rock and comes in a striking black and white cover. After a second, *Travelin'* (Mill City) 1976, Bill Hallquist did some session work including Kevin Odegaard's *Silver Lining* album. (Kevin, in turn played on one of the songs on Dylan's *Blood On The Tracks*). Bill:- "In 1976 Kevin and I played together in The K.O. Band. Our drummer later became a member of Prince and The Revolution (Bobby Z), and guitar player (Jeff Dayton) currently plays with Glen Campbell. After that I played with a folk trio Macavity with Tim Sparks (Rio Nido), followed by a bar band Cimarron. Later, I wrote/produced radio jingles before becoming Director of Marketing at K-tel here in the U.S. I am still active musically as a songwriter and as a member of Perfectly Loud. The K.O. band did a reunion gig on Sept. 1st, 2000 at a club here in Minneapolis./St. Paul".

Compilation appearances include *16 Tons* on *Gathering At The Depot* (LP). (VJ/BHa)

Thursdays Children

Personnel:	RICHARD GOLLWITZER		A
	CHARLES HELPINSTILL	vcls	A
	JAN PEDERSON		A
	PAT SULLIVAN		A

ALBUM: 1(A) THURSDAYS CHILDREN (Voxx 200.052) 1989 -

NB: There's also a CD with **The Children**, *Stoned Sixties*, on Collectables (COL-CD-0600).

45s:	You'll Never Be My Girl/Try, Girl	(Paradise 1022) 1966
	Air-Conditioned Man/ Dominoes	(International Artists 110) 1966
	Help, Murder, Police/ You Can Forget About That	(International Artists 115) 1967
	No More Rock And Roll/ Before I Die	(Rampart Street RSRS 0608) 1968

Originally known as The Druids when they formed in Houston, Texas, in 1964. They changed their name to **Thursdays Children** during 1965. The first 45 was quite an accessible punk affair, whilst their second and third were more British-influenced.

After one final and disappointing rock and roll 45, drugs and the draft had accounted for many of the band and they regrouped as The Pointing Hand Group. Charles Helpinstill also recorded a solo 45, *To Touch The Rainbow/Indian River* (Akashie 1001) before forming The Helpinstill Factory Band. He later changed name to Ezra Charles.

The retrospective album includes material spanning their career from 1965-69 with 45s, unissued and live material. It's the best source for their recorded output.

Compilation appearances include: *You'll Never Be My Girl* on *Pebbles, Vol. 5* (LP), *Pebbles, Vol. 5* (CD), *Acid Visions Vol. 2* (LP); *You'll Never Be My Girl* and *Air Conditioned Man* on *Pebbles Box* (5-LP) and *Trash Box* (5-CD); *Help Murder Police* on *Punk Classics, Vol. 4* (7") and *Garage Punk Unknowns, Vol. 7* (LP); *You'll Never Be My Girl*, *Try Girl* and *Help, Murder, Police* on *Acid Visions - The Complete Collection Vol. 1* (3-CD); *The Night Before* and *Money* on *There Goes The Neighborhood, Vol. 1* (CD); *A Part Of You* (prev. unreleased) on *Epitaph For A Legend* (Dble LP); *Try Girl* and *Air Conditioned Man* on *Houston Post - Nowsounds Groove-In* (LP); *Air Conditioned Man* on *Highs In The Mid Sixties, Vol. 12* (LP); and *Help Murder Police* and *You Can Forget About That* on *International Artists Singles Collection* (LP). (VJ)

The Thyme

45s:	Love To Love/Very Last Day	(Bang 546) 1967
	Somehow/Shame Shame	(A2 201) 1967
	Time Of The Season/I Found A Love	(A2 202) 196?

Hailing from Ann Arbor, Michigan, they started out as **The Hitch-Hikers**. Though regarded as one of the area's more popular 'garage' acts their vinyl output was rather disappointing for garage collectors as it's pretty straight poppish fayre, as witness their cover of Neil Diamond's *Love To Love*. Their cover of The Zombies *Time Of The Season* is pretty decent however and *Somehow* is undoubtedly their finest moment - an intensely dramatic ballad with searing fuzz interludes.

Compilation appearances have included: *Love To Love* on *Mindrocker, Vol. 5* (LP); *Somehow*, *Very Last Day* and *Time Of The Season* on *Sixties Archive, Vol. 7* (CD); *Somehow* on *Fuzz Flaykes & Shakes, Vol. 1* (LP & CD). (MW)

The Tiaras

45s:	α	Lorraine/You Told A Lie	(Fawn 6002) 196?
	α	Bull Moose/All I Want	(Alliance 1690) 196?
		Mexican Rock/Red Sails In The Sunset	(Alliance 1934) 1964
		Sticks And Stones/Southern Love	(Ruff 45-1019) 1966

NB: α as Jackie Dallas and The Tiaras.

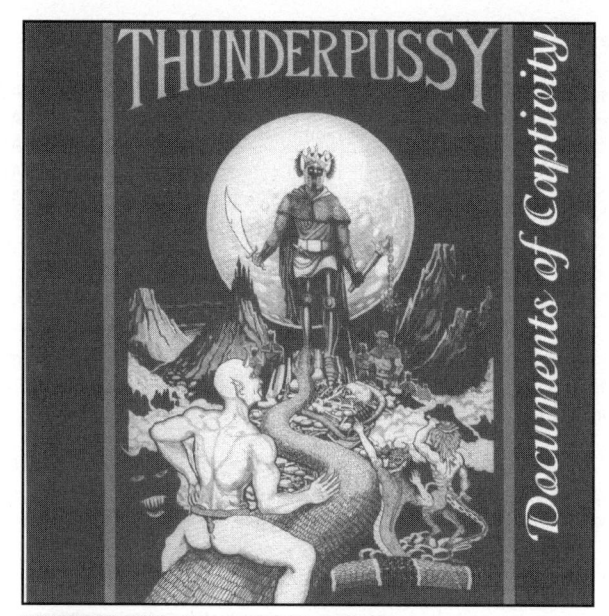

THUNDERPUSSY - Documents Of Captivity CD.

Originally from Amarillo this band also operated in Louisiana. *Southern Love* is the stronger of these two fuzz-pop efforts.

Compilation appearances have included: *Sticks And Stones* and *Southern Love* on *Louisiana Punk From The Sixties* (LP); and *Sticks And Stones* on *Sixties Archive Vol. 3* (CD). (VJ)

The Tidal Waves

			HCP
45s:	Farmer John/She Left Me All Alone	(SVR 1007) 1966	-
	Farmer John/She Left Me All Alone	(HBR 482) 1966	123
	Big Boy Pete/I Don't Need Love	(HBR 501) 1966	-
	Action (Speaks Louder Than Words)/Hot Stuff	(HBR 515) 1967	-

A Detroit, Michigan, quintet.

Compilation appearances have included: *Farmer John, I Don't Need Love, Action! (Speaks Louder Than Words), She Left Me All Alone, Big Boy Pete* on *S.V.R. Rock Hits Of The Sixties* (LP & CD); *She Left Me All Alone* on *All Cops In Delerium - Good Roots* (LP); *Action (Speaks Louder Than Words)* on *Green Crystal Ties Vol. 7* (CD); and *Farmer John* on *Michigan Nuggets* (CD) and *Michigan Brand Nuggets* (LP). (VJ)

The Tidal Waves

Personnel:	WALT MARSDEN	gtr	A
	STEVE PENNEY	bs	A
	BILL SILLIKER	drms	A
	DON SMITH	ld gtr	A

45s:	You Name It/So I Guess	(Strafford 6503) 1965
	Laugh/Farmer John	(Right 6607) 1966

A New Hampshire outfit whose members hailed from Sanford, Maine and Durham, New Hampshire. Not to be confused with the **Tidal Waves** from Detroit, despite both outfits covering *Farmer John*.

Silliker had previously been in the Electrons alongside Jay Sneider, pre-**Euphoria's Id**.

Compilation appearances have included:- *Laugh*, their 'punkiest' 45 appears on *The Psychedelic Sixties, Vol. 1* (LP); *Farmer John* (two versions) and *Laugh* on *Green Crystal Ties, Vol. 7* (CD); *Laugh* and *Farmer John* on *The Cicadelic 60's, Vol. 4* (CD); *Farmer John* is on *The Cicadelic 60's, Vol. 2* (LP); and *You Name It, So I Guess, Laugh* and *Farmer John* on *You Ain't Gonna Bring Me Down To My Knees* (CD). (MW/AH/ELn)

The Tidal Waves

45:	Little Boy Sad /	
	I Don't Want To Lose You Now	(Plymouth 2967/8) 1967

Thought to be from Massachusetts and unconnected to the New Hampshire band. (MW/AH)

Tides In

45:	Trip With Me/?	(Sanfris 18) 1966

From Brooklyn, New York. Their *Trip With Me* is a rather laboured punker and not what the title promises.

Compilation appearances include *Trip With Me* on *Chosen Few Vol's 1 & 2* (CD) and *The Chosen Few, Vol. 1* (LP). (VJ)

Tierpark

45:	The Way / Have I Told You	(Atlantis Sound 2002) 1969

Thought to have hailed from Decatur, Georgia, this unknown group's late-sixties rock outing *The Way* can be found on *Psychedelic States: Georgia Vol. 1* (CD). (MW)

Tiffany Shade

Personnel:	MICHAEL BARNES	ld gtr, vcls	A
	BOB LEONARD	gtr	A
	ROB MURPHY	bs	A
	TOM SCHUSTER	drms	A

ALBUM:	1(A)	THE TIFFANY SHADE	(Mainstream S/6105) 1968 R2

NB: (1) also released in the U.K. on Fontana. (1) counterfeited on vinyl 2000.

45s:	One Good Reason/Would You Take My	
	Mind Out For A Walk	(Mainstream 677) 1968
	An Older Man/Sam	(Mainstream 680) 1968

A light'n'fresh psychedelic-punk-pop band from Cleveland, Ohio, with quite an Anglophile sound. Their album is a very minor collectable.

Compilation appearances include *An Older Man* on *The Garage Zone, Vol. 4* (LP) and *The Garage Zone Box Set* (4-LP). (VJ)

TIFFANY SHADE - Tiffany Shade LP.

TIMBERCREEK - Hellbound Highway LP.

Tiffany System

Personnel:	C. (SCOTT) BOYER	A
	DAVE BROWN	A
	C. (BUTCH) TRUCKS, Jnr.	A

| 45: | Let's Get Together/Wayward One | (Minaret MIN-128) 196? |

The above personnel, who later recorded as **31st of February**, are credited with the 'A' side which is a cover of that hippie evergreen by Chester Powers (aka **Dino Valente**). Both sides of this are pleasantly laid-back melodic folk-rock. From Jacksonville, Florida. (MW)

The Tigermen

Personnel:	TOM CONSEDINE	A
	JOHN FARRELL	A
	TIM STAVISH	A
	JEFF TODD	A

| 45s: | Close That Door/Love Me Girl | (Buff 1005) 1965 |
| | Tiger Girl/Runaway | (Buff 1005) 1965 |

From Olean, New York, **The Tigermen** formed in 1964 and lasted until August 1966 when college and the draft led to the band's demise. They played around the Southern tier of New York, and North Western Pennsylvania, with regular spots at Cuba Lake Pavilion. Mostly appearing at teen dances, roller domes and high school proms.

Both 45s were recorded at a Buffalo studio in October 1965 and were produced by Art Detrick (later the brains behind **Free Design**). The 'A' side to their first 45, *Close That Door*, is a pretty typical garage punker. The flip to the second is a cover of the **Del Shannon** hit.

Compilation appearances have included: *Tiger Girl* on *Scum Of The Earth* (Dble CD), *Scum Of The Earth, Vol. 1* (LP) and *Follow That Munster, Vol. 2* (LP); and *Close That Door* on *Back From The Grave, Vol. 5* (LP). (VJ/MW/JFI)

Tight Little Unit

| ALBUM: | 1 | SINGS "JUST SEND HER TO ME" | (Orchid) 1966 R2 |

A local Tennessee garage band recorded this album live in a bowling alley. It was issued in a plain cover with one of at least two different 'slicks' glued on the front. (CF)

The Tikis

Personnel:	BRAD BAUER	organ, vcls	AB
	BOB FOLGER	gtr, vcls	A
	PAT LOO	gtr, vcls	AB
	DAVE WEBSTER	drms, vcls	AB
	RICK WORKMAN	ld vcls, bs	AB
	JOE MUIR	gtr, vcls	B

| 45: | Show You Love/ Careful What You Say | (Fujimo 917 F 6139) 1966 |

This teen band from Syracuse in Northern Indiana exhibited a strong Stones-influence on the ballad 'A' side of their sole 45. The single was recorded at RCA's Chicago studios.

You can also find *Show You Love* on *Back From The Grave, Vol. 5* (LP), whilst *Careful What You Say* is featured on *Hoosier Hotshots* (LP). (VJ/MW/PY)

The Tikis

| 45: | Somebody's Son/Little Miss Lovelight | (Dial 4048) 1966 |

The 'A' side of this 45 is a tough pop-punker. This **Tikis** is thought to hail from the East Coast but ... Other Tikis abound. Of course there's the pre-**Harpers Bizarre** bunch with at least six 45s on Ascot, Autumn and Warner Bros, the last of which they recorded as The Other Tikis!! There's also another Michigan bunch on Universal Sound, another on Philips, Len Wade & The Tikis on Minaret and Portland, Oregon's Tikis and Fabulons. And that's just the sixties.

Compilation appearances include: *Somebody's Son* on *Kicks & Chicks* (LP), *Fuzz, Flaykes, And Shakes, Vol. 3* (LP & CD) and *I Turned Into A Helium Balloon* (CD). (MW)

The Tikis

| Personnel incl: | HUGH PEARL | ld gtr | A |
| | BILL SCHEREK | bs | A |

| 45: | We're On The Move/Rick-O-Shay | (Sara 6641) 1966 |

According to Tim Warren's sleeve-notes for *Back From The Grave, Vol. 8*, this quartet was formed at the University of Wisconsin, in Madison, in the Fall of 1965. After about six months they headed to James Kirchstein's Cuca Studios in Sauk City and laid down two originals for their 45. The band lasted thru' the rest of the school year but was history by Fall 1966. Bass player Bill Scherek (who wrote the 45) then put together **The Talismen** and cut a cool version of *Glitter and Gold* on Rampro. He stayed

T.I.M.E. - T.I.M.E. LP.

in the music business through the seventies and eighties and was involved with many national artists. In 1995, Bill relocated to Australia.

Compilation appearances include: *We're On The Move* on *Back From The Grave, Vol. 8* (CD) and *Back From The Grave, Vol. 8* (Dble LP). (GG/VJ)

Tim Tam and The Turn-Ons

45s:	Wait A Minute/Ophelia	(Palmer 5002) 1965
	Cheryl Ann/Sealed With A Kiss	(Palmer 5003) 1966
	I Leave You In Tears/Kimberly	(Palmer 5006) 1966
	Don't Say Hi (vcls)/Don't Say Hi (instr.)	(Palmer 5014) 1967

A Detroit, Michigan combo.

Compilation appearances have included: *Wait A Minute* on *Michigan Brand Nuggets* (Dble LP) and *Michigan Nuggets* (CD); and *Ophelia* on *Garage Monsters* (LP). (VJ)

Timber

Personnel:	WAYNE BERRY	vcls, bs, acoustic gtr	A
	GEORGE CLINTON	vcls, keyb'ds, recorders, autoharp	A
	WARNER CHARLES DAVIS	drms	A
	JUDY ELLIOTT	vcls	A
	ROGER JOHNSON	electric and acoustic gtr	A

ALBUM: 1 BRING AMERICA HOME (Elektra EKS-74095) 1971 -

NB: (1) also released in the U.K. (Elektra K 42093).

A California group with female/male vocals, heavily influenced by The Band on most of their material (their ten songs were written by Berry and Clinton). Their album, which came with a poster, was produced by Don Gallucci (from **Don and The Goodtimes** and **Touch**) and contains some good tracks with interesting lyrics (e.g. *Canada* about a man leaving Illinois to avoid the draft, *Remember* and the title track about pollution and corruption, and *Witch Hunt* with people "all up in the hills, taking little pills"). George Clinton (not the **Funkadelic** leader) was a renowned session musician and also worked with **Griffin**. Wayne Berry became a songwriter (notably for **Tom Rush**) and released a decent country rock album in 1974. In 1976 Judy Elliott would work with **Hoyt Axton**. (SR)

Timbercreek

Personnel:	FRANK GUMMERSAL	A
	JON HICKS	A
	CARL HOLLAND	A
	DOUG OSBURN	A
	LARRY ROSS	A

ALBUM: 1(A) HELLBOUND HIGHWAY (Renegade JAH 95014) 1975 R2

This hippie-rock album was the work of a local Boulder Creek, California band. It's a very good album of rural **Grateful Dead** style rockers.

Frank Gummersal sadly died a few years ago. (CF)

T.I.M.E. (Trust In Men Everywhere)

Personnel:	LARRY BYROM	gtr	AB
	BILL RICHARDSON	gtr	AB
	STEVE RUMPH	drms	A
	NICK ST NICHOLAS	bs	A
	PAT COUCHOIS	drms	B
	RICHARD TEPP	bs	B

ALBUMS:	1(A)	T. I. M. E.	(Liberty LST 7558) 1968 -
	2(B)	SMOOTH BALL	(Liberty LST 7605) 1969 -

NB: (1) and (2) have been reissued on one CD (See For Miles C5HCD 643).

T.I.M.E. - Smooth Ball LP.

45s:	Make It Alright/Take Me Along	(Liberty 56020) 1968
	What Would Life Be Without It/ Tripping Into Sunshine	(Liberty 56060) 1968

A competent quasi-psychedelic band from the Los Angeles area. They evolved out of **Hardtimes** which had included Byrom and Richardson. The opening track to their debut album, *Tripping Into Sunshine*, starts with a typical psychedelic introduction, although the remainder of Side One is comprised of rather mundane rock material. However, the standard improves on Side Two, particularly with *I Really Love You* and the closing track *Take Me Along*. Three of their 45 tracks are taken from this album.

The two opening tracks on their second album released as LBS 83232 in the UK, were featured on the *Gutbucket* sampler helping to give the band international exposure, which they failed to exploit. Their blues influence is evident on tracks like *Lazy Day Blues*, while *See Me As I Am, Trust In Men Everywhere* and *Flowers* are examples of their attempts to get to grips with the predominant psychedelic influences of the time. The group made considerable use of phasing techniques, Their second album was the better of the two. The 'A' side to the second 45 is not on the album - it's a catchy pop-rock ditty with some tasty guitar.

Both Byrom and St. Nicholas later played with **Steppenwolf** and in 1973 Couchois and Byrom formed **Ratchell**. (VJ)

The Time Machine

Personnel:	MIKE ALLAN	bs	A
	PAUL GILLINGHAM	gtr, vcls	ABC
	SCOTT LETTERMAN	drms	ABC
	CHARLIE MORGAN	gtr, vcls	ABC
	JIM WOLFE	keyb'ds	ABC
	FRED ALDOMDGE	bs	B
	PHIL POTH	bs	C

NB: Line-up 'A' 1966; 'B' 1967; 'C' 1968.

45: All Or Nothing/Take It Slow And Easy (New Sound 1) 1967

This band was formed in Seattle, Washington, by Wolfe and Letterman upon the demise of their previous band American Dream. Their sole 45, which was a hit in the U.K. for The Small Faces, was a pretty strong, if straight forward, version of the song. Sadly, the band fell apart after appearing regularly at The Embers Club.

Mike Allan:- "A group of wealthy gentlemen heard us play at a debutante ball and thought it would be fun to get into making records. *Take It Slow And Easy* and had a jug band flavor complete with kazoo solo. It was my first time in the studio and it was very exciting. In September 1994, **The Time Machine**'s original line-up got together in Seattle to play for Milo Johnstone. He had just written a limited edition book called 'The Magic

Decade', about Seattle music from 1960 to 1970. Milo was also responsible for the first concert with a Light Show in Seattle."

Paul Gillingham is now an attorney in Seattle and still plays with a bluegrass group, whilst Mike Allan went on to **The Magic Fern**. (VJ/MW/DR/TWg/MAn)

The Time Machine

Personnel:	RICH DANGEL	gtr, vcls, sitar	A
	MARCUS DOUBLEDAY	trumpet, perc	A
	JOE JOHNSON	bs	A
	WILLIE KELLOG	drms	A
	BOB KRAUS	sax, hrmnca, vcls	A

The Time Machine was formed in 1965 in Sacramento, California. Willie Kellogg, who had recently left **Joel Scott Hill**'s band, had agreed to drive **The Misfits** to a gig in the area which by coincidence was attended by ex-**Wailers**, ex-**Rooks** guitarist Rich Dangel. **The Rooks** had played a West Coast circuit that stretched from Seattle to San Diego and therefore the two knew each other. Dangel asked Kellogg to join his group.

The new band rehearsed in nearby Roseville and soon made their way into a local studio to cut a couple of tracks for a single. Moments into the session, Dangel stepped on his fuzz pedal and the engineer stormed into the room. "What in the hell are you tryin' to do? BLOW UP my equipment?!" The band packed up and left!

Following a residency at a club in Sparks, Nevada (they took a night off to check out **The Charlatans** in nearby Virginia City), **The Time Machine** moved to Seattle where they rented a house. They got another residency, this time at The BFD Hall, alternating sets with **The Page Boys**. They were playing mostly covers of Yardbirds, Stones, **Butterfield Blues Band**, Beatles and Howlin' Wolf but with a very high degree of musicianship, and their shows were well-attended, mostly by awestruck local musicians! Inspired by the release of *Norwegian Wood* on The Beatles' *Rubber Soul* album, Rich Dangel hunted up a sitar and played it live on stage during 1966. "That thing sounded great, but man - what a pain in the ass it was to lug around!", remembers Kellogg.

When their residency concluded and another wasn't immediately forthcoming, Kellogg accepted Gary Puckett's offer of $300/week to drum for **The Outcasts** back in San Diego and **The Time Machine** evaporated. Doubleday went to **The Electric Flag**, composing music for *The Trip* movie soundtrack, then on to **Buddy Miles**' band and **Mike Bloomfield**'s. Dangel and Johnson assembled a blues group that eventually became **The Floating Bridge**. Kraus joined the Merchant Marines in the early seventies and died of a bleeding ulcer while at sea and Johnson died in the early eighties.

While all that remains now of the original **Time Machine** is a photograph taken in 1965 at an Air Show in Sacramento, they played a role in ushering in the psychedelic movement in the Northwest, and apparently in tribute, the band immediately above this entry adopted their moniker when they split. (CF)

THE TIME MACHINE (Sacramento).

TIMMOTHY - Strange But True LP.

Time of Your Life

45:	You Make Me Feel Good/	
	Ode To A Bad Dream	(Ionic 101) 1967

NB: A-side actually by The Town Cryers, but miscredited to **Time Of Your Life**.

Hailing from Long Beach, California, the 'A' side was a remake of an old Zombies' song, given a new garage angle. It was in fact by another Long Beach outfit, The Town Cryers, but miscredited on the label to **Time Of Your Life**. The 'B' side, an interesting spacey number, will be of interest to the readers of this book, with some good purring organ work and spacey sound effects.

Compilation coverage has included *Ode To A Bad Dream* on *Highs In The Mid-Sixties, Vol. 3* (LP) and *Fuzz Flaykes & Shakes, Vol. 1* (LP & CD). (VJ/MW)

Time Piece

45:	Swallows Fly/Autumn	(4M Records 1000) 196?

This band operated out of Rapid City, South Dakota. (VJ)

The Timestoppers

45:	I Need Love/Fickle Frog	(HBR 516) 1967

A rather ordinary Pittsburgh punk band. *I Need Love* is also on *Pebbles Vol. 5* (CD), *Pebbles, Vol. 5* (LP) and *Burghers, Vol. 1* (LP & CD). (VJ)

The Timetakers

45:	At Least I'll Try/	
	You'll Never Walk Alone	(Audio Dynamics 109) 1966

This Springfield, Massachusetts outfit's 45 was an amalgam of garage and pop. (GG)

The Timezone

45:	Space Walker/?	(White Whale 269) 1968

Probably from California, an obscure garage-psych group. (SR)

TINGLING MOTHER'S CIRCUS - A Circus Of The Mind LP.

Timmothy (Tim Ward)

Personnel:	TERRY BLADECKI	ld gtr	A
	LARRY HADSALL	ld gtr	A
	TOM PFUNDT	drms	A
	HAM ROTH	drms	A
	DON SCHERZER	bs	A
	LANE VALLIER	bs	A
	TIMMOTHY WARD	gtr, vcls	A

ALBUM: 1(A) STRANGE BUT TRUE (Pear LX 502/3) 1972 R4

NB: (1) limited reissue of 300 copies on vinyl (Rockadelic RFRLP-001) 2001, with non-LP 45 'B' sided added.

45s: α A Woman/Maybe I'm High (Pear 500/1) 1972
β Jamaica /
I've Got To Find Out Your Name (Big Willie 466) 1978

NB: α 'B' side is non-LP. β as by Timmothy Ward.

An ultra-rare Bay City, Michigan home-made folk-rock album by Tim Ward, the former leader of **Blues Company**. Two-thirds of the album is dark folk with Tim on vocals and acoustic guitar, but two tracks are electric with a full band. The Rockadelic reissue is recommended and comes with an insert with group history. (CF/SR/MW)

Tingling Mother's Circus

Personnel incl:	ANDREA	A
	JIMMY	A
	ELLIOT RANDALL	A
	STU	A

ALBUM: 1 A CIRCUS OF THE MIND (Musicor MS-3167) 1968 -

45s: Face In My Mind/Isn't It Strange (Roulette 4758) 1967
Positively Negative/
Sunday Kind Of Feeling (Musicor MU-1335) 1968
I Found A New Love/Happy Bubbles (Musicor MU-1 359) 1969

Bands of this ilk are often touted as 'psychedelic' by dealers presumably to boost collectors' interest and asking prices. Pleasant flowery folk-rock-pop with occasional sound effects it may be, mind-expanding it isn't. Just a slightly hipper version of the Fifth Dimension in many cases and (I) include the likes of Forum, Split Level and **Yankee Dollar** here too. If you like trendy but slightly fabricated MOR sixties pop, then you'll enjoy this.

From New York, they included Elliot Randall, who went on to be a highly-rated session man. (MW)

Tin House

Personnel:	JEFF COLE	bs, vcls	A
	MIKE LOGAN	drms, perc, vcls	A
	FLOYD RADFORD	gtr, vcls	A

ALBUM: 1(A) TIN HOUSE (Epic 30511) 1971 SC/R1

NB: (1) has been repressed.

45s: I Want Your Body/Be Good And Be Kind (Epic 5-10739) 197?

NB: Promo copy.

Produced by Rick Derringer, this is an excellent heavy blues-rock album in a style similar to **Third Power** with lots of distortion, wah wah pedals etc. Radford was a member of White Trash and would later play with **Johnny and Edgar Winter**. (SR/MC)

The Tinkers

Personnel incl: MYLES POLIN A

45s: You're Just Like All The Rest/Love Lights (Stop 106) 196?
My Lost Love/You're Making Me Sad (Stop 107) 196?

A minor-league Boston 'garage' outfit whose material is an amalgam of beat and R&B with a soul tinge. Anathema to the *Back From The Grave* legion! (MW)

Bill Tinkler

ALBUM: 1 INSIDE OUT (Tower ST 5???) 1968 -

An oddball pop-rock singer with songs like *You Could Get High*. (SR)

Tino and The Revlons

Personnel incl:	DIVITO	A
	RUDKIN	A

ALBUM: 1 BY REQUEST, AT THE SWAY-ZEE (Dearborn) 1966 R2

45s: Little Girl Little Girl/Rave On (Dearborn D-525) 1965
(Partial Lazy Mary Memphis/I'm Coming Home (Dearborn D-530) 1966
List) Lotta Lotts Lovin'/
Red Sails In The Sunset (Dearborn D-540) 1966
Story Of Our Love/
Black Bermudas & Knee-Socks (Mark 154) 196?
Wedding Bells Will Ring/Heidi (Pip 4000) 196?

A borderline inclusion. Primarily frat-rockers from Michigan, they'd occasionally cross into garage-beat territory as on *I'm Coming Home* which is the flip to an excellent party swinger. Most garage collectors would be attracted to them due to their releases on the rated Dearborn label. (MW)

Tiny Tim

HCP

ALBUMS: 1 GOD BLESS TINY TIM (Reprise 6292) 1968 7 -
2 2ND ALBUM (Reprise 6323) 1968 - -
3 FOR ALL MY LITTLE FRIENDS (Reprise 6351) 1968 - -
4 CONCERT IN FAIRYLAND (Bouquet 771) 1974 - -

HCP

45s: Tip-Toe Thru' The Tulips With Me/
Fill Your Heart (Reprise 0679) 1967 17
Tip-Toe Thru' The Tulips With Me/
Don't Bite The Hand That Feeds You (Reprise 0740) 1967 -
Hello, Hello/Bring BackThose

Rockabye Baby Days	(Reprise 0760) 1967	122
Bring Back Those Rockabye Baby Days/		
This Is All I Ask	(Reprise 0760) 1967	95
This Is All I Ask/Be My Love	(Reprise 0769) 1967	-
Great Balls Of Fire/As Time Goes By	(Reprise 0802) 1968	85
On The Good Ship Lollipop/		
America I Love You	(Reprise 0837) 1968	-
I'm A Lonesome Little Raindrop/		
What The World Needs Now Is Love	(Reprise 0867) 1968	-

Born Herbert Khaury on 12th April 1930 in New York City 'Tiny Tim' was a novelty singer and ukulele player who associated himself with the late sixties hippie movement. Before he became famous he was a well known eccentric around Greenwich Village and 'Tiny Tim' was one of several pseudonyms he used. He achieved some success with his falsetto renditions of his favourite twenties tunes, none more so than with *Tip-Toe Thru' The Tulips With Me*, (which had originally stayed at No. 1 for 10 weeks when originally issued by Nick Lucas back in 1929). His first album also made No. 7 in the U.S. Album Charts and he was back in the public eye again in 1969 when he married 'Miss Vicki' on the Tonight Show (they later divorced in 1977). Many of us would put down his music but as a 'character' of the era he deserves a mention.

Tiny Tim died of a heart attack in November 1996.

Two of his tracks appeared on the EP accompanying 'Ptolemaic Terrascope' issue 18, *Devil May Care* and a live 1968 version of *Tiptoe Thru' The Tulips*. (VJ)

The Titans

Personnel:	DENNIS BRADY	drms	A
	GEORGE JOHNSON	gtr	A
	GEORGE McLELLAN	bs	A
	STEVE TAMASY	gtr	A

45s:	α	Hideaway / On The Spot	(Vampire 10762) 1962
		Summer Place / Tchaikovsky Rides Again	(Soma 1402) 1963
		The Noplace Special / Reveille Rock	(Soma 1411) 1964
		The Noplace Special / Reveille Rock	(Soma 1411) 1963
		Surfer's Lullaby / Motivation	(Bangar 00611/00612) 1964
		Fun Seekers /	
		Need You (PS)	(Sound Of Music Ltd. 3-12186) 1966
		To Covet The Turf / Mountain Of Love	(Metrobeat 4452) 1967
		Little Girl / Pretty Young Thing	(Duff's 111) 1968
		Ode To Billy Martin /	
		Please Don't Be Angry	(Duff's 112) 1969

NB: α as 'Dale Allen and the Rebel Rousers'.

From Duluth, Minnesota, and initially known as of (Dale Allen &) The Rebel Rousers, they became **The Titans** in 1963 and would see out the sixties with a few personnel changes.

TITUS OATES - Jungle Lady LP.

Predominantly a rock'n'roll, instrumental and surf-oriented band rather than post-Invasion garage, plenty of their efforts have been compiled of late to check out: *The Noplace Special* on *Soma Records Story, Vol. 1* (LP); *Summer Place* on *Soma Records Story, Vol. 2* (LP); *Reveille Rock* and *Tchaikovsky Rides Again* on *Soma Records Story, Vol. 3* (LP); *Reveille Rock* on *Wail On The Beach!*; an unreleased 1965 track *Skokiaan* on *Free Flight (Unreleased Dove Recording Studio Cuts 1964-'69)* (Dble LP); and *To Covet The Turf* on *The Best Of Metrobeat! Vol. 1* (LP).

The *Fun Seekers* 45 is bouncy beat-pop with a sunny disposition backed by a weepy Paul Anka teen-ballad.

For their full and detailed history look no further than the ultimate Midwest zine 'Lost And Found' (issue #5). (MW)

Titus and Ross

Personnel:	JACK ROSS	gtr, vcls	A
	ART TITUS	bs, piano, vcls	A
	TOM WELLS	drms	A

ALBUM:	1(A)	TITUS AND ROSS	(No label PRP 17 3 71/2) 1970 R1

This local Marion, Indiana, folk-rock album includes a killer track called *Cycle Thing* that the liner notes claim was used on a network TV sports special in 1969. (CF)

Titus Oates

Personnel:	BILL BEAUDET	keyb'ds	A
	CHRIS EIGENMANN	perc	A
	RICK JACKSON	bs, vcls	A
	LOU TIELLI	gtr	A
	STEVE TODD	gtr	A

ALBUMS:	1( )	JUNGLE LADY	(Lips) 1974 R2
	2(A)	JUNGLE LADY	(Lips L 004) 197? R2

NB: (1) is a demo disc which appeared in a plain sleeve as a very different mix. (2) reissued on vinyl (Hablabel HBL 11006) 1988.

A Dallas-based rock combo. Rick Jackson wrote all the material on the album on which the keyboards and vocals blend nicely with some melodic guitar work. The reissue is worth obtaining but the originals still change hands for a lot of bucks. (VJ/CF)

TNT

Personnel:	DAVE BOYER	bs, vcls	A
	DAVE COLE	drms, vcls	A
	ERIK LINDGREN	keyb'ds, gtr, vcls	A
	JEFF LOCK	gtr, flute, vcls	A

CD:	1(A)	MOD PSYCH POWER POP FROM CENTRAL P.A.
		(Arf! Arf! AA 052) 199?

Pennsylvania band featuring a very young Erik Lindgren (Mr. Arf Arf). The CD above consists of covers of songs by **Chocolate Watch Band**, **Left Banke**, **Choir**, **Moving Sidewalks**, **Balloon Farm** and their own mod infected material which was recorded between 1974 and 1976.

In addition to the band's core personnel, some tracks on the CD also feature Simon Clement (gtr), Robin Cole (vcls), George Mahar (gtr), Mindy McGeary (flute), Bart Roberts (bs, vcls, synth) and Kirk Wynn (ld vcls).

Compilation appearances include *99th Floor* on *The Arf! Arf! Blitzkrieg 32 Track Sampler* (Dble CD) and *30 Seconds Before The Calico Wall* (CD). (MW)

Toad Hall

Personnel:	CLAPTON GUGLIAMO	ld gtr	A
	THOMAS OCTAVIUS MARCUS	gtr, vcls	A
	GARY RAZZANTE	bs	A

| JOHN RICHARDSON | ld vcls, perc | A |
| CHRIS SIGWALD | drms | A |

ALBUM: 1(A) TOAD HALL (Liberty LST-7580) 1968 -

The *Toad Hall* album is typical but mediocre pop with the occasional track that catches the ear. There's some reasonable fuzz guitar work on *Elegy On A Brick Wall* and some **Byrds**-influenced guitar playing on *Storybook Love*. Some of the pop, notably *On The Beach* and *A Thousand Years* is quite melodic, but the rest is eminently dispensable including an awful cover version of Bobby Hebb's *Sunny*. Tommy Marcus wrote most of the material but not surprisingly it's yet to capture the interest of many collectors.

The band seem to have gotten their initial break after being booked as house band for New York's Cafe Wha. (VJ/SB)

Toads

45: Leaving It All Behind/
Babe, While The Wind Blows Goodbye (Decca 31847) 1965

An outfit from San Mateo, California, giving the Gary Usher treatment of **Byrds**y folk-punk on *Leaving* - quite excellent but sounds like you've heard it somewhere else and is not surprisingly rather like the **L.A. Teens**. The flip has a more Dylanesque quality. This may not be their only waxing - another **Toads** share a 45 on an L.A. label with The Golden Boys - *Backaruda / Modernistic* (Brent 7050) 1966.

Leaving It All Behind has now appeared on, and lends its name to, a moody folk-punker compilation (*Leaving It All Behind* (LP)) on Misty Lane. (MW)

Tobias

ALBUM: 1 DREAM #2 (MGM) 1971 -

An obscure album in the soft-rock vein. (SR)

Today

Personnel: BOB EVESLAGE vcls, piano, gtr, bs A
TRUDY EVESLAGE vcls, flute A
HARLAN WENIGER vcls, drms, 12-string gtr A
SUSAN WENIGER vcls A

45: We've Been A Bad, Bad Boy /
That's What I'm For (Burdette 488) 1969

A studio only outfit, **Today** included **The Unbelievable Uglies** member Bob Eveslage, who had moved to Seattle for a couple of years to help run a recording studio there. The 45 utilised four-part harmony vocals and Bob recalls that label boss Jerry Dennon actually flew the band down from Seattle to the Capitol Tower Building in Hollywood to see the record being pressed!

See the **Uglies** entry for more info on Bob's career.

Today's Special

Personnel: JOHNNY MILLER vcls, gtr A
MARK MORRIS drms A
NEIL PORTNOW bs A
LOUIS SEIGAL organ A
JON SHOLLE ld gtr A

45: Krista/Stop And Say You're Sorry (Decca 32408) 1968

From Great Neck, New York originally, this act evolved out of **London and The Bridges** and **The Savages**.

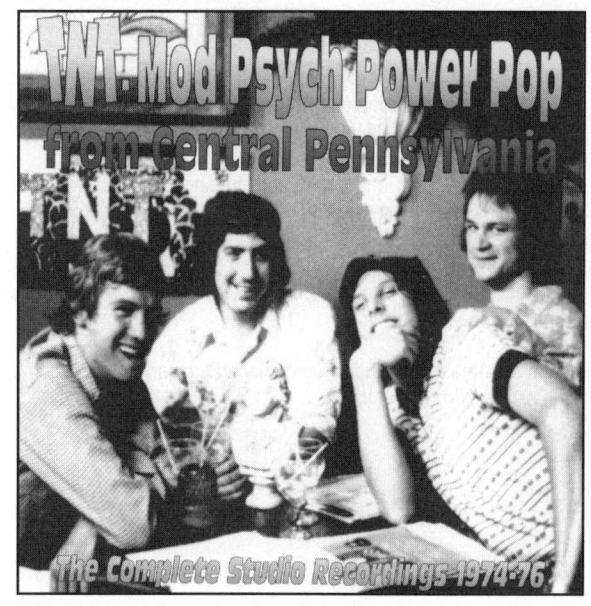

TNT - Mod Psych Power Pop From Central P.A. CD.

They cut a few songs written by '**Bridges**' members Johnny Miller and Richard Weintraub (who also sang backing vocals on some tracks, though he was never a full time member), which were produced by Eddie Simon (Paul Simon's brother).

Jon Sholle went on to become a bluegrass performer of some note with records such as *Catfish For Supper* and *Out Of The Frying Pan*. He also played with acts like Melissa Manchester and Meatloaf, performed with Bette Midler in the movie "The Rose" and is still doing his own thing, a combo of Bluesgrass and Jazz, regularly in NYC. (MW/MM)

Today's Tomorrow

See **The Ladds** entry.

The Todds

45: I Want Her Back/Things Will Change (Toddlin Town 102) 1966

Hailed from Chicago. The 'A' side, *I Want Her Back* is a routine garage punker.

Compilation appearances have included: *I Want Her Back* on *Pebbles, Vol. 6* (CD), *Sixties Choice, Vol. 2* (LP), *60's Choice Collection, Vol's 1 & 2* (CD), *Everywhere Interferences* (LP) and *Highs In The Mid-Sixties, Vol. 4* (LP); and *Things I Will Change* on *Tymes Gone By* (LP). (VJ)

The Togas

See Chris Morgan and The Togas.

The Tokays

Personnel: BOYER A
JIM GEIL A
STEPHEN GEIL A
HENRY A
SMART A

45: Now/Ask Me No Questions (Scorpio 403) 1965

A mid-sixties Merced, California-based outfit. *Now* is a soft harmony minor mooder reminiscent of The Zombies; the flip is a thumping beat ballad. Both tracks were composed by 'Geil' and, while more pop than garage, are decent nonetheless.

Two unreleased tracks, *Hole In The Wall* and *Time*, also appear on *The Scorpio Records Story* (CD). (VJ/MW/AP)

Tom and The Cats

45s:	The Wine Song/What's Happening Baby	(Jewel 750) 1965
	Walkin' Man/Summertime Blues	(Paula 242) 1966
	Good Good Lovin'/Nothing In This World	(Paula 253) 1966

Only the second 45 above has been heard to-date but it justifies an entry. The band origins are unknown although Paula/Jewel/Ronn records were based in Shreveport, Louisiana. *Walkin' Man* is catchy pop-beat with raucous vocals. *Summertime Blues* is converted to a mid-sixties garage-rocker with great vocals, fuzzed guitar and a smokin' break - definitely one of the best versions.

Compilation appearances include *Summertime Blues* and *Good Good Lovin'* on *Born On The Bayou* (LP). (MW)

Tombstones

45:   I Want You / ?   (Grave 1001) 1967

Originally out of Greenville, South Carolina, they cut a pounding punk number *I Want You* for Grave Records in 1966. Well worth a spin, you'll also find it on *Back From The Grave, Vol. 7* (Dble LP). In the liner notes Bill Nadolny reveals that: - They were really tough rock'n'rollers with a good live act centred around a real tombstone they'd ripped off and used to set up on stage. When their leader, a very able vocalist/lead guitarist, was drafted in 1967 they re-grouped and entered the National Battle Of The Bands up in Braintree, Massachusetts. The double/triple album-set of that event, *Battle Of The Bands*, captures them covering **The Doors'** *Light My Fire*. (VJ/BN)

The Tombstones

45:   Times Will Be Hard / Mary Jane   (Capitol 5997) 1967

Times... is frantic **Monkees**-like pop, except for the strong fuzzy guitar break. *Mary Jane* is bouncey pop with a Zorba The Greek flavour; it IS about a girl and the briefest fuzz outburst on this sounds even more out of place.

The 45 was produced by Alexis De Azevedo, best known in these quarters for his services to **The Human Beinz**. Perhaps this band was from Ohio too? (MW)

Tommy and The Blue Velvets

Personnel:	DOUG CLIFFORD	drms	A
	STU COOK	bs	A
	JOHN FOGERTY	gtr	A
	TOM FOGERTY	gtr, vcls, hrmnca	A

45:   Have You Ever Been Lonely/Bonita   (Orchestra 1010) 1964

From El Cerrito, a small town across the Bay from San Francisco, came **Tommy and The Blue Velvets**. After one flop single on the local Orchestra label, they made a trip to the Fantasy offices and signed with the company which renamed them **The Golliwogs**. They would later be known as **Creedence Clearwater Revival**. (SR)

Tommy and The Hustlers

45:   Diggin' Out/Right Size   (Fantasy 573) 1963

This band were part of San Francisco's music scene prior to the San Francisco-based rock revolution and the hippie movement. Theirs was the first rock 45 to appear on the Fantasy label. The 'A' side, *Diggin' Out*, is a pretty good instrumental rocker, but it really predates the era of this book.

Compilation appearances include *Diggin' Out* on *Pebbles, Vol. 21* (LP). (VJ)

TONGUE - Keep On Truckin LP

Tomorrow's Children

45:   In The Midnight Hour/
      I Can Only Give You Everything   (Raynard 10065) 1967

A good punk covers 45 recorded by a band from Virginia in Northeast Minnesota. Another 45, *Take A Good Look* on Brookmont, is by a different outfit. (VJ)

Tomorrow's People

See **The Shoremen** entry.

Tongue

ALBUM: 1   KEEP ON TRUCKIN   (Hemisphere) 1972 R1

NB: (1) reissued on CD (Gear Fab GF 151) 2000 and LP (Gear Fab/Comet GFC 418 LP).

45:   Keep On Truckin'/Jazz On The Rag   (Hemisphere 101) 1972

A local Wisconsin heavy rock group with guitar, organ and screaming vocals, displayed on tracks like *Get Your Shit Together*, *Slap Her Down Again Paw* and *Homely Man Blues*. (SR)

Toni and Terri (and The Pirates)

Personnel:	TERRI ENSLEY	A
	TONY ROSSINI	A

45:	I Want You/Take Me Now	(Mercury 72489) 1965
α	Back On My Feet Again / For No One	(Monument 979) 1966
α	California, L.A. /	
	Everyone Can Play Shortstop	(Monument 1017) 1967
α	Shades Of Gray/Mr.Flower Vendor Man	(Monument 1049) 1968

NB: α as **Toni and Terri and The Pirates**

Psychedelic Unknowns, Vol. 8 (LP & CD) includes *I Want You* by this Memphis duo. It's a strident folk-rocker rather like Sonny and Cher.

Terri Ensley was actually successful songwriter Donna Weiss, whose *Don't Bring Me No Flowers (I Ain't Dead Yet)* was recorded by **The Breakers**, **Gentrys** and **What-Knots**.

Rossini had recorded several solo 45s on Sun and with **Randy and The Radiants**. Their story is told in Ron Hall's book on the Memphis scene (1960-1975) - 'Playing For A Piece Of The Door', published in 2001 by Shangri-La Projects, ISBN 0-9668575-1-8. (MW/RHI)

Tonto and The Renegades

Personnel:	BILL FORD	gtr, vcls	ABC
	TOM KIRBY	drms	ABC
	GARY RICHEY (TONTO)	ld vcls, bs	ABC
	TERRY SLOCUM	ld gtr, vcls	ABC
	JEFF KEAST	keyb'ds	B
	DAVE PUNG	keyb'ds	C

EP: 1 TONTO AND THE RENEGADES (Misty Lane MISTY 062) 2002

NB: (1) contains all four 45 tracks.

45s: The Easy Way Out/Anytime You Want Some Lovin' (Sound Of The Sceen 2178) 1967
Little Boy Blue/I Knew This Thing Would Happen (Sound Of The Sceen 2212) 1967

This garage teen combo operated out of Lansing, Michigan and played frequently at the Sceen club there, which issued their 45s. The five-piece had teamed up with local producer **Dick Wagner** (**Bossmen**, **Frost**) to record the first 45 which is light'n'poppy teenbeat. The 45 also features some guitar overdubs by **Wagner**. *Little Boy Blue*, from their second, is a fine example of the garage genre, written by lead guitarist Terry Slocum.

The band first jammed together at a Grand Ledge high school talent contest in 1963, with the core of the band being augmented on keyboards by Jeff Keast ('65-'67) and then Dave Pung.

When Tom Kirby was drafted in August '69, the band subsequently split. Terry now lives in Memphis, Tennessee and is still very much alive and rockin'. After the band split, he too joined the army, got to jam with Dave Mason and has played in several blues bands since.

Lookout for the forthcoming *Tonto And The Renegades* 7" EP on Misty Lane, which gathers together all four of the bands 45 cuts. For the full low-down check out *Ugly Things* magazine's forthcoming interview with Tom Kirby.

Compilation appearances include *Little Boy Blue* on *Let 'Em Have It! Vol. 1* (CD), *Back From The Grave, Vol. 4* (LP) and *Back From The Grave, Vol. 2* (CD). (VJ/MW/TSm/TK)

Tonto's Expanding Head Band

Personnel:	MALCOLM CECIL	keyb'ds	A
	ROBERT MARGOULEFF	keyb'ds	A

ALBUMS: 1 ZERO TIME (Embryo SD 732) 1971 -
2 IT'S ABOUT TIME (Polydor 2383 308) 1974 -

NB: (1) also released in England by Atlantic (K40251) and reissued in 1975 in the USA (Atlantic 18123).

From New York, a group which experimented with synthesizers and electronic spacey sounds. "Tonto" was the name of their main synthesizer. Like their alter-ego **Beaver and Krause** in California, Cecil and Margouleff were also in demand studio musicians. (SR)

TONTO and THE RENEGADES.

Tony and The Bandits

Personnel incl: ANTHONY J. BRAZIS

45s: (Oh No) I Can't Lose/It's A Bit Of Alright (Flo-Roe FR-500) 1965
(Oh No) I Can't Lose/It's A Bit Of Alright (Coral 62461) 1965?
I'm Goin' Away/The Sun Don't Shine Now That You've Gone (Coral 62477) 1966

Driving British Invasion sounds from a combo sometimes previously claimed as from Florida, Illinois, Kentucky and Tennessee, but who in fact hailed from Middletown, Ohio! The band later evolved into **The Chosen Lot**.

You can also find *(Oh No) I Can't Lose* on *Sixties Rebellion, Vol. 6* (LP & CD). (MW/KBn/MM)

Topanga Canyon Orchestra

ALBUM: 1 CRIMSON AND CLOVER (UNI 73055) 1968 -

Produced by Norman Ratner (**Leaves**, **Hook**, **Future**), this album looks like a psychedelic record, with its lettering and covers of **The Doors**, **Tommy James** and **The Byrds**. In fact, it only contains muzak versions of these songs, with horns and strings. You have been warned! (SR)

Top Drawer

Personnel:	JOHN BAKER	ld gtr	A
	ALAN BERRY	bs	A
	STEVE GEARY	trumpet, vcls	A
	RAY HERR	drms	A
	RON LINN	keyb'ds, gtr	A

ALBUM: 1(A) SOLID OAK (Wishbon 83615) 1968/69 R4/R5

NB: (1) reissued on Resurrection (CX 1185) 198? and reissued on CD (Solid Oak 721207) in a limited edition of 555 copies.

This Fairdale, Kentucky combo's album, which leans more towards heavy rock than psychedelia, is likely to appeal more to 'progressive' rock fans. One track, the evocative *Song For A Sinner* has also reappeared on *Turds On A Bum Ride, Vol. 6* (CD). (VJ)

The Topics

Personnel:	JIM GREDIG	gtr, bs, vcls, brass	A
	RON THACKER	perc, effects, vcls, brass	A
	REX WENNER	piano, organ, bs, effects, vcls	A

ALBUM: 1(A) LIVING EVIDENCE (Topic Records) c1970

Out of Bremerton, Washington, a local group combining garage, psych and soft-pop, with covers (*Louie Louie*, **Brewer and Shipley**'s *One Toke Over The Line*, *Hooked On A Feeling*...) and original compositions. (SR)

Topsy Turbys

Personnel:	STEVE FORMAN	drms	A
	CHARLES JOHNSTON	bs, trumpet	A
	JEFF NOBLE	keyb'ds	A
	BART SMITH	gtr	A

EP: 1(A) TOPSY TURBYS (PS) (Dionysus/Bacchus Archives BA1159) 2001

NB: (1) comprises all four tracks from their two Liberty Bell 45s.

45s: Jungle Song/Topsy Turby (Liberty Bell 45-101) 196?
Hey Tiger/Snake Woman (Liberty Bell 45-102) 1965

Starting out as a jazz-pop combo The Charles Johnston Quartet, this group of Arizona State U. students were approached by entrepreneur Charles H. Anderson. He suggested they adopt **Sam The Sham**'s Middle-Eastern turban-and-robe couture as an alternative to the prevalent mop-top and Beatle-boot fashion. Renamed **The Topsy Turbys** they released two cool swingin' garagey-beat 45s, and a very rare EP whose details are lost in time.

In 2001, Lee Joseph's Bacchus Archives released an EP coupling their two 45s and telling their story. It reports that Noble teaches in Mesa, Arizona, Smith teaches guitar in Mesa, Forman is a studio musican in L.A., and Johnston is President/CEO of Select Atrists Associates who book and promote major shows across the US.

Compilation appearances include: *Hey Tiger* on *Tougher Than Stains* (LP), *Boulders, Vol. 3* (LP) and *Fuzz, Flaykes, And Shakes, Vol. 5* (LP & CD). (MW/DN)

The Tories

45: Walkin The Dog / Could It Be Love (Vaughn-Ltd VA-750) 1966

An Alabama outfit, possibly from Mobile. Their fuzzed rendition of Rufus Thomas' *Walkin' The Dog* sounds way ahead of its time. If the **Moving Sidewalks** had covered it, they would have sounded something like this. Check it out on *Psychedelic States: Alabama Vol. 1* (CD). (MW)

The Tormentors

Personnel:	TIM DALEY	ld vcls, drms	A
	MARK DAVIS	ld gtr	A
	DAN DAVIS	bs, organ	A
	LEE HARPER	gtr, ld vcls	A

ALBUM: 1(A) HANGING 'ROUND (Royal RLP-111) 1966 R2

NB: (1) counterfeited on vinyl (Eva 1 2055) 1988.

45s:	Didn't It Rain Pt. 1 /		
	Didn't It Rain Pt. 2	(Kerwood 712)	c1966
	She's Gone/Black Coffee	(Royal R-002)	c1966
	Black Coffee / Hey, Hey, Little Girl	(Royal 002-3)	c1966
	Capricious Lolita/Merry-Go-Round Song	(Royal R-003)	1967
	Sounds Of Summer/Motate	(Royal R 003 6 / R 001 2)	1967

This fascinating outfit, from L.A., put out one album that encompasses a variety of influences and styles from frat-rock, British Invasion-style beat, folk-rock, Everly Bros style harmonies to garage fuzz-rockers. Highlights of this eclectic platter for garage fans are: the frat-fuzzer *Black Coffee*; garage punkers *Blue Blooded Lady* and *'Cause You Don't Love Me* (the same songs as by **The Odds And Ends** on *Boulders, Vol. 2* and *Garage Punk Unknowns, Vol. 3*); a good cover of **The Beau Brummels**' *Still In Love With You Baby*, and the cool beat-ballad *She's Gone* with its Jaggeresque intonations.

Note for completists: The Merry-Go-Round Song on the fourth 45 above is just an alternate title for the album cut *Sounds Of Summer*, which was also issued on 45 under the *Sounds Of Summer* title. Other 45 tracks are to be found on the album but its unknown how *Didn't It Rain, Pts. 1 & 2* differ from the album track. (MW/JG)

Toronados

45s:	Alone / Let Me Be Your Man	(Phalanx 1004/1005) 1966
	She's Gone /	
	Rainy Day Fairy Tales (+ pic insert)	(Phalanx 1014/1015) 1966

The short-lived Phalanx label from Portage, Michigan, has become a minor treasure trove for obscure and sometimes superb garage punkers and ballads by the Ethics, **Pastels**, **Troyes**, Blues Inc., **Olivers** and **Rainmakers** to name a few. This outfit's debut *Alone* is a soppy ballad with echoes of *Unchained Melody* and featuring soft sax solos. Its flip is much better - subdued garage-beat borrowing heavily from *Baby Let Me Take You Home*.

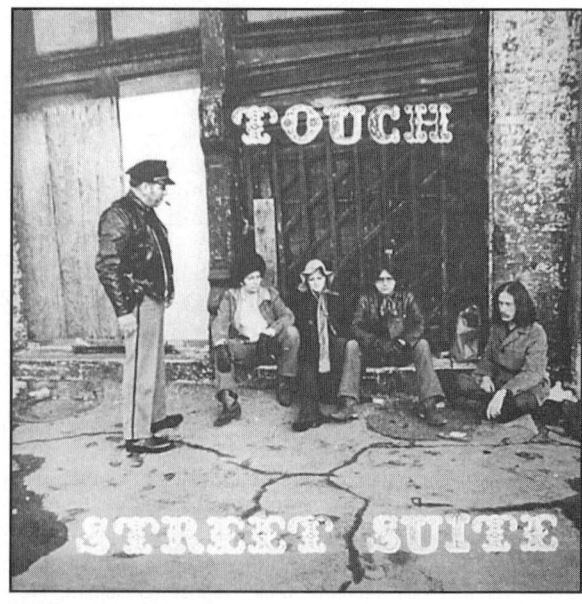

TOUCH - Street Suite LP.

The follow-up *She's Gone*, found on *When The Time Run Out* (LP & CD), kicks off with an encouraging burst of fuzz but thereafter is pretty average garage fare.

Another **Toronados** 45 from 1966 - *Hey Baby / Next Stop Kansas City* (Date 1519) isn't confirmed (or thought to be) the same band. It comprises a pair of confident upbeat poppers, featuring a Four Seasons style rendition of Bruce Channel's *Hey Baby*. (MW)

Torquays

Personnel:	GEORGE BARGAS		A
	FREDDIE CISUEROS	gtr	A
	JIM JONES	vcls	A
	DAVID MORRIS		A

45s:	Escondido/Surfer's City	(Gee Gee Gee 1009)	196?
	Image Of A Girl/Stolen Moments	(Rock-It 1004)	1964
	Image Of A Girl/Stolen Moments	(Colpix 782)	1965
	Harmonica Man From London Town/		
	Stoked On Her	(Rock-It 1005)	1966
	Harmonica Man From London Town/		
	Our Teenage Love	(Original Sound 66)	1967
	Heart Of Love/		
	Somethin' Else Kind Of Woman	(Bellman 711)	1967

Starting out as a surf band in San Bernardino, California, in the early sixties they later progressed into a garage band. They recorded numerous 45s on Bill Bellman's local labels (Rock-It and Bellman). Two of the above were big 'local' hits and were leased to larger labels (Colpix and Original Sound). *Stolen Moments* got to No. 26 on KFXM in early 1965 and *Harmonics Man* made the charts again in 1967.

Other Torquays were around to confuse the collector: from Memphis (one 45 on ARA) and Detroit (a 45 on the Hideout subsidiary Punch and another on Gypsy).

Freddie Cisueros was previously with the Overlanders and the Nightmares. He and Jim Jones would go on to form Jim Jones and The Chauntneys.

Compilation appearances have included: *Somethin' Else Kind Of Woman* on *Sick And Tired* (LP); *Harmonica Man* on *Garage Punk Unknowns, Vol. 2* (LP); and *Stolen Moments* on *Garage Punk Unknowns, Vol. 4* (LP). (VJ/MW)

Totty

ALBUM: 1 TOTTY (No label) 1976 R3

NB: (1) demo album in plain sleeve with "Totty" sticker on front. Reissued in a standard printed cover in 1977 (Our First Record Co.) (R2).

From Oklahoma, a heavy psych/hard-rock trio. Only 50 copies of this album were allegedly pressed and came with a sticker, a set of promo photos and four inserts. (SR)

Touch

Personnel:
OVID BILDERBACK	perc		A
PAULETTE BUTTS	vcls, tamb		A
JERRY SCHULTE	bs		ABC
RAY SCHULTE (aka RAYMOND STONE)	gtr, vcls, hrmnca		ABC
TOM RHOTY	perc		BC
CHUCK SABATINO	vcls		B
ERIC SALAS	perc		C

ALBUM: 1(A) STREET SUITE (Mainline Records LP 2001) 1969 R4

NB: (1) reissued on CD (Gear Fab GF-105) 1997, with all non-LP 45 cuts, three unreleased cuts by **Touch**: *Lady Of The Universe*, *The Magic Inside You* and *Rainbow*, plus two recent Ray Schulte recordings. This package also issued on vinyl (Gear Fab/Clear Spot LP-105) 1999.

45s:
Stormy Monday Blues/
Day To Day Man (Mainline # unknown) 1969
Light My Fire/Round Trip (Mainline # unknown) 1969

A local St. Louis, Missouri band. Only 100 copies of their album were pressed and the above two non-album 45s were often given away free with it. We're talking an ultra-rarity of the highest order here. There are a couple of throwaway country tracks (*Happy Face* and *Got To Keep Travelling On*) and the finale, *Gettin' Off*, is marred by a tedious drum solo but the rest is for the most part mindblowing psychedelia. The best of these are *Catfish*, with some bluesy psychedelic guitar work and two social commentary songs, *Get A Gun* and *Let's Keep The Children On The Streets*, a song about the riots of the sixties.

'Get a gun, our new generation must take lead
Get a gun, with a clenched fist we are crying to be free
When someone gets it in their heads to do away with freaks
Get your gun and show them that our game is not defeat
Get a gun, do yourself a favour, get a gun'
(from *Get A Gun*)

Ray Schulte had earlier played in Bob Kuban and The In Men in 1962, before helping to form **The Guise** and, with his brother Jerry, an act called The Sheratons. Tiring of the pop and R&B scene, **Touch** were formed in mid-67, to create a more powerful fusion of psychedelic blues and they quickly picked up support slots for acts such as **Steppenwolf**, Cream and **Iron Butterfly**, also playing at a free festival with **Big Brother & The Holding Co.** and **Hourglass** in 1968.

Shortly after their album was recorded, Paulette headed West to join a commune and Ovid quit. A new line-up recorded two further 45s, which feature some good fuzzy guitar work and in particular their version of *Light My Fire*, which is slower and fuzzier than **The Doors'**, comes off well.

One final session in 1970, with Royal on electric harpsichord and lead vocals and David Surkamp (later of Pavlov's Dog) on rhythm guitar, resulted in three songs that have been included on the Gear Fab reissue. In particular *The Magic Inside You* is noteworthy for some fine lyrics, echoing the changing times. Incongruously, the band then landed the job as back up band for Tony Orlando & Dawn, who were riding high on a wave of commercial success from hits such as *Tie A Yellow Ribbon*.

Today, Royal and Ray Schulte are still performing in the St. Louis area as The Essence.

The recent Gear Fab reissue is highly recommended for fans of the progressive and psychedelic genres.

Compilation appearances include: *Get A Gun* on Gear Fab's *Psychedelic Sampler* (CD); and *Light My Fire* on *Project Blue, Vol. 2* (LP). (VJ/MW)

Touch

Personnel:
JOHN BORDONARO	drms, vcls		A
DON GALLUCCI	keyb'ds, vcls		A
BRUCE HAUSER	bs, vcls		A
JEFF HAWKS	vcls		A
JOEY NEWMAN	gtr		A

ALBUM: 1(A) TOUCH (Coliseum 20-20 Sound 51004) 1969 -

NB: (1) Issued by Deram (SML 1033) in the UK. Also issued on CD by Renaissance (RCD 1001) 1993 with two unreleased cuts - an 11 minute *Blue Feeling* and a demo version of *Alesha And Others*.

45: Miss Teach/We Feel Free (Coliseum 2712) 1969

NB: both sides taken from the LP.

All five members of this band had previously played in **Don And The Goodtimes**, a popular club band from Portland, Oregon. Prior to that Gallucci, who later became a staff producer for Elektra, was with **The Kingsmen**, Newman with **The Liberty Party** and both John Bordonaro and Hauser with Connecticut's 'Gretschmen'.

Their album was a really exploratory effort with touches of psychedelia (*Down At Circes Place*), jazz, avant-garde and progressive rock. The vocals sound rather like **Tim Buckley** in his *Starsailor* period - amazing! It was produced by Gene Shiveley, who also produced the **Elyse Weinberg** album for which Hauser and Bordonaro also provided the rhythm section and on which Gallucci and Joey Newman also appeared.

Renaissance also put out a sampler CD - *Buried Treasures* - containing three further **Touch** tracks: a 1968 demo of *The Spiritual Death Of Howard Greer*, *We Finally Met Today* from an unreleased 45, and *The Second Coming Of Suzanne* from 1973.

Hawks and Hauser were later in **Stepson** who made an album in 1974 along with Newman, who had been in **Blue Mountain Eagle** in the interim. Newman later played with Shaun Cassidy. John Bordonaro also was assistant A&R Director at Elektra Records Los Angeles in 1972 - 1973. John had toured with James Taylor, Carole King and Dan Kortchmar, working as a road manager and concert mixer, before going to Elektra. (VJ/MW/SR/JB)

Touch

45: Not So Fine/No Shame (Public PR-1 0314) 1968

This was actually L.A. based **Hunger!**, under a pseudonym. *Not So Fine* is an excellent psych-punker, in the same style as **Hunger!**'s highly-rated album.

Other outfits who purloined this moniker include a Michigan outfit (*Dissonet/Seventy Five* on the Xebec label), and an unknown sorta funky-groove instrumental outfit (*Blue On Green/Pick And Shovel* on Lecasver (ARA/B-1 001)).

Compilation appearances include *Not So Fine* on *Psychedelic Unknowns, Vol. 3* (LP & CD) and *Incredible Sound Show Stories, Vol. 7* (LP). (MW)

Touchstone

Personnel:
JIM BYERS	violin		A
TOM CONSTANTEN	keyb'ds		A
PAUL DRESHER	gtr, flute		A
RUBBER DUCK	tamb		A
ART FAYER	violin		A
GARY 'CHICKEN' HIRSH	perc		A
WES STEELE	bs, cello		A

ALBUM: 1(A) TAROT (United Artists 5563) 1972 -

A pleasant enough progressive instrumental album with lots of strings and keyboards which is now a minor collectable. The band were from New York. Tom Constanten is better known for his involvement with **Grateful Dead** and Gary 'Chicken' Hirsh was previously with **Country Joe and The Fish**.

Constanten went on to compose soundtracks and recorded with Jorma Kaukonen in the nineties. Paul Dresher worked with Steve Reich and Terry Riley and released several albums on very small labels. (VJ/SR)

Touchstone

Personnel incl:	MARK HALMAN	A
	JOHN UNDERWOOD	A

45: Walk Out In The Rain/
     Give Me Leeway   (Sound Machine 10051) c1969

Michigan was a haven for hard'n'heavy guitar rock outfits in the '68-'71 period as demonstrated on several compilations including the *Michigan Mixture* series. Whether such outfits fly the 'garage' or 'psychedelic' freak flags is open to contention, but there is no doubt that some excellent post-Hendrix sounds abounded from the region. This bunch hailed from Kalamazoo and while *Walk Out* may be too poppy for Michigan fanatics, the flip is punctuated by some fine fluid acid-tinged guitar. (MW)

Touchstone

ALBUM: 1 RUNES   (Jericho Records) 1978 R1/R2

From Virginia, a hippie folk-rock outfit with male/female vocals. The album came with a lyric innersleeve. (SR)

Tower

ALBUM: 1 THE TOWER   (Other World 1001) 1973 R1

From New York, a concept album about a post nuclear holocaust, with electronic effects and treated vocals. (SR)

The Town Criers

ALBUMS:	1 LET'S DO IT	(Town Criers no #) 1966 ?
	2 LIVE	(Town Criers no #) 1968 ?

45s: Blues Chase Up A Rabbit/
      Gather Them Rosebuds   (Lowery 009) 196?
      I Walk The Sun/She Loves Me   (Horizon 101) 1967
      I Think Of You, And Cry/
      She Loves Me   (Town Criers 1001) 1967
      I Think Of You, And Cry/She Loves Me (Cinema 005) 1967
      Poor Old Gullible Me /
      Weeping ... (incomplete title)   (Jag 259) 196?

They cried out from Houston in Texas. (VJ)

Toy Factory

Personnel:	GREG WEISS	vcls	A
	BILL	bs	A
	BILLY	gtr	A
	JOEY	drms	A
	SAL	organ	A

ALBUM: 1(A) TOY FACTORY   (Avco Embassy AVE 33013) 196? -

45:    What Is A Youth?/?   (Avco Embassy 4533) 196?

Despite the psychedelic apparel the band wear on the album cover, the vinyl consists largely of sickly pop ballads. There are a couple of more experimental tracks (particularly *Things*) and they do a passable cover of George Gershwin's *Summertime*, but overall this album cannot be recommended. (VJ)

Toy Factory

45: Sunny Sunny Feeling / What's The Melody (Jubilee 5668) 1969

A different outfit from Milwaukee, Wisconsin - also known as the **Next Five**. (MW)

TOUCHSTONE - Tarot LP.

T.P. and The Indians

45: Goodbye Good Times/Ally Or Enemy   (Dellwood 3239) 1970

A Saddlesbrook, New Jersey band. You'll also find *Ally Or Enemy* on the *Attack Of The Jersey Teens* (LP) compilation. It's a protest song in a similar vein to **Barry McGuire**'s *Eve Of Destruction*. The band's leader, TP, was a guy called Tom Prigorac, who had a really angry vocal style. (VJ)

The Tracers

Personnel:	RAY BOE	A
	SAMMY BOE	A
	GARY MILLER	A
	RON THIBERT	A

45: She Said Yeah/Watch Me   (Sully 928) 1966

Originally from Minot in North Dakota, where a serviceman saw their act and offered to move them to Texas to possibly record with Ray Ruff who owned a management company and the Amarillo-based Sully Records. En route to Amarillo they stopped off in Oklahoma City, where they recorded *Watch Me* which they saved for the 'B' side of their 1966 45, *She Said Yeah*. The first pressings were released as The Stones. The 'A' side was a hard rocker and included a long drum solo from the band's 15 year old drummer. However, after a few months gigging at small teen gigs around West Texas they became disheartened and returned to Minot.

Just six months later Thibert persuaded them to return to Texas again, this time to Fort Worth. They spiced up their act and changed their name to the **Try-Cerz** when another group called The Tracers threatened legal action. Later still they became **Sweet Smoke**.

Compilation appearances have included *Watch Me* and *She Said Yeah* on *Psychedelic Unknowns, Vol. 3* (LP & CD). (VJ)

Tracers

45: One Of The Crowd / Who Do You Love (All-American 363) 1967

A different **Tracers**, from California, on Bill Holmes' label that brought **Thee Sixpence**, later the **Strawberry Alarm Clock**, to the world. Their cover of *Who Do You Love* is a decent snotty punker but lacks the aggression of **The Preachers**' version, which may have inspired it.

Compilation appearances include *Who Do You Love* on *Fuzz, Flaykes, And Shakes, Vol. 2* (LP & CD). (MW)

Traces Of Time

Acetate: Oh Bob........ / ?   (Sound Studios Inc.) 196?

An unknown outfit whose rare acetate from a Chicago studio is aired on *Fuzz, Flaykes, And Shakes, Vol. 2* (LP & CD). (MW)

The Trackers

Personnel:	BRIETZKE?	A
	BYRNEY	A
	WILLIAMS	A
	WILLIAMS	A

45: You Are My World/Why Do I Cry?   (Landa Sounds 101) 1966

This punk outfit hailed from New Braunfels in Texas. *You Are My World* sets out in folk-rock style before erupting into a fuzz guitar extravaganza. The flip is an emotional Searchers-style folk-punker.

Compilation appearances have included *You Are My World* on *Texas Flashbacks, Vol. 5* (LP), *Flashback, Vol. 5* (LP) and *Highs In The Mid-Sixties, Vol. 12* (LP). (VJ/MW)

Tracks

Personnel:	KEN ALDRICH	keyb'ds	ABCD
	NED BERNDT	drms, perc, vcls	ABCD
	RUSSELL PINKSTON	gtr, vcls	ABCD
	JEFFREY WILKES	bs	A
	PETER WONSON	perc, vcls	AB
	DOM PUCCIO	bs, vcls	B
	ED KISTLER	keyb'ds, vcls	CD
	SKIP TRUMAN	bs, vcls	C
	BOB NEALE	bs, vcls	D

ALBUM: 1(-) TRACKS   (No label SBT-1) 1974 R3

NB: (1) three album box set, issued with twelve page booklet of pictures and lyrics titled "Tracks 69/74". The booklet also mentions a "poster" included with the package but existence of this item is unconfirmed.

An incredibly ambitious private release from the New England area. The three albums feature mostly original tracks (written by Pinkston, a few by Aldrich) in a progressive rock style with very professional musicianship throughout. Some of the tracks really fly, instrumentally - comparisions could be made to Todd Rundgren's Utopia at times. There's a remarkable interpretation of The Rolling Stones' *Street Fighting Man* and a unique version of Dylan's *All Along The Watchtower* offered as the only cover songs. Apparently, the band had continual financial backing throughout their six year existence, as the box set features pristine studio recordings of all four line-ups detailed above. The earliest recordings are dated February 1970, the last September 1974. (CF)

The Trademarks

45: Free Your Fears/I Can Set You Free   (Reginald RR 1411) 196?

From Greenville, Mississippi, and produced by the ubiquitous Tommy Bee (who could be the **Xit** / **Lincoln St Exit** /**Fe Fi Four Plus Two** guy). *Free Your Fears* latterly features some biting guitar and is the choice cut here - garage with a little bit o'soul. Its brother is more overtly James Brown funkified soul-garage. (MW)

Trademarks

45: I Need You/If I Was Gone   (Palmer 5018) 1967

A Detroit outfit. This seems to have been their sole vinyl offering.

Compilation appearances include *If I Was Gone* on *Let 'Em Have It! Vol. 1* (CD), *Sixties Archive Vol. 7* (CD), *Garage Punk Unknowns, Vol. 2* (LP). (VJ)

TOY FACTORY - Toy Factory LP.

Trademarks

Personnel:	RANDY BOYTE	keyb'ds	A
	DAVID FRIEDMAN	drms	A
	SHERMAN McGREGOR	gtr	A
	WAYNE PROCTOR	ld gtr	A
	BILL THACKER	vcls	A

45: Don't Say You Love Me Too/
Here Comes Elmer's Boys   (Arlingwood ARW-8610) 1964/5

From Leesburg, Florida, this act is best known for featuring pre-**We The People** members Wayne Proctor and Randy Boyte. All except Randy had earlier played with Nation Rocking Shadows (of *Anesthesia* fame) and the **Trademarks** were formed in October 1964, after Ron Skinner was ousted from the 'Shadows.

Don't Say You Love Me is Beatlesque beat, with little hint at the shape of things to come, but you can find it, along with the previously unreleased rocker *Everything'll Be All Right* on the awesome **We The People** double CD retrospective, *Mirror Of Our Minds* (Sundazed SC 11056) 1998. (IT)

The Tradewinds

| Personnel: | PETE ANDERS (ANDREOLI) | A |
| | VINNIE PONCIA | A |

ALBUM: 1(A) EXCURSIONS   (Kama Sutra 8057) 1967 -

HCP

45s: New York's A Lonely Town/
Club Seventeen   (Red Bird 10020) 1965 32
The Girl From Greenwich Village/?   (Red Bird 10028) 1965 129
Summertime Girl/
The Party Starts At Nine   (Red Bird 10033) 1965 -
Mind Excursion/
Little Susan's Dreamin'   (Kama Sutra 212) 1966 51
Catch Me In The Meadow/
I Believe In Her   (Kama Sutra 218) 1966 132
Mind Excursion/
Only When I'm Dreaming   (Kama Sutra 234) 1967 -

NB: There's also a French EP with PS: *Mind Excursion/Little Susan's Dreamin'/I Believe In Her/It's Not Gonna Take Too Long* (Kama Sutra 614 104).

Coming from Providence, Rhode Island, Anders and Poncia released a single on a local label as the Vidals in 1960 and then moved to New York, where they signed to a national label. Their second single, *Mr. Lonely*, made the charts but its follow-ups failed. The duo were then signed as contract writers for Hill & Range and penned some hits and played for the Ronettes, The Crystals, Darlene Love and other Phil Spector productions.

After a brief stint with Red Bird Records, they became **The Tradewinds** and signed with Kama Sutra as writers, producers and singers. **The Tradewinds** were a pop duo who occasionally became caught up in some of the psychedelic trappings of their era, most notably on *Mind Excursion*, which can also be found on *Nuggets, Vol. 5* (LP).

Mind Excursion and *New York Is A Lonely Town* were also featured on the 1970 Buddah sampler album, *Incense And Oldies*.

They also recorded as **The Innocence**, the **Mulberry Fruit Band**, **The Penny Arcade**, **The Treasures** and Pete and Vinnie. They even worked on an Elvis Presley film score. In 1968, they formed Map City Productions with Frank Mell and used this label to produce and release some East Coast groups, including **Yesterday Children**, **Purple Image**, the Blue Jays and Mardi Gras.

In 1969, they had a further self-titled album as *Anders And Poncia* (Warner WS 1776). This was produced by Richard Perry, but despite some excellent guitar from Ry Cooder, isn't very good overall.

In 1972, **Peter Anders** released a solo album, *Peter Anders* (Family Productions FPS 2705). A competent California folk-rock album, it's notable for featuring Hamilton Wesley Watt, ex-**Euphoria**, on guitars. Poncia went on to produce several albums for Ringo Starr and Melissa Manchester and also wrote Kiss' *I Was Made For Lovin' You*! (VJ/SR/MW)

Trafalgar Square

Personnel incl:	TIM EIFLER	gtr	A
	STEVE GRIM	gtr	A
	JOHN MARSHALL (MARSELLI)	bs	A

45:   It's A Shame Girl/Till The End Of The Day   (USA 890) 1967

This Kinks-influenced band were from Racine, Wisconsin and were actually called The Revels, but could not use the name on record due to another Revels in Chicago.

In the seventies Grim and Marshall joined the Milwaukee-based bad Boy who recorded for UA. (VJ/GM/MW)

Train

Personnel:	VINNIE BELL	gtr, sitar	A
	MURRY GORDON	bs	A
	DON KEIDER	drms	A
	BOB LENOX	vcls, keyb'ds	A

ALBUM: 1(A) COSTUMED CUTIES   (Vanguard 6542) 1970 -

TRANSATLANTIC RAILROAD - Express To Oblivion LP.

A Danish band who emigrated to the USA. The album sounds like a better version of **Ars Nova** and is a fast growing collectable. *Dreams And Realities*, presumably taken from the album, is also featured on *Electric Psychedelic Sitar Headswirlers, Vol. 3* CD. (VJ)

The Train

45:   I Want Sunshine/You Make Me Feel Alright   (Fulltone 102) 196?

Came out of Aberdeen, South Dakota, with this punk-rock 45. (VJ)

The Traits

45:   Nobody Loves The Hulk/Better Things (PS)   (QNS 101) 1969

This novelty record *Nobody Loves The Hulk* (presumably after the U.S. TV show 'The Hulk') has a certain charm and punk energy. Not connected to either Houston's Traits or the outfit from Pelham, New York as far as we know.

Compilation appearances include *Nobody Loves The Hulk* on *Pebbles, Vol. 21* (LP) and *Glimpses, Vol. 4* (LP). (VJ)

The Traits

From Pelham, New York, their *High On A Cloud* is a classic garage track, built around a repetitive **Seeds**-like riff. According to the liner notes to *Pebbles, Vol. 5* (CD), *High On A Cloud* was originally released on a *Battle Of The Bands* album (Ren-vell) circa 1966.

In the 1980s, The Pandoras also covered this track to great effect.

Compilation appearances include *High On A Cloud* on *Pebbles, Vol. 5* (CD), *Pebbles, Vol. 3 (ESD)* (CD), *Relics, Vol's 1 & 2* (CD), *Relics, Vol. 1* (LP) and *Garage Punk Unknowns, Vol. 7* (LP). (MW)

T.R. and The Yardsman

Personnel incl: BUTCH HAMILTON

45:   I Tried/Movin'   (Hideout H-1005) 1965

A little known Detroit combo on the legendary Hideout Club label. *I Tried* is passable garagey beat whilst *Movin'* is a *Walk Don't Run* type beat instrumental.

Compilation appearances include *I Tried* on *Prisoners Of The Beat* (LP); *I Tried* on *Realities In Life* (LP). (MW)

Tranquility Base

45:   If You're Lookin'/Fun   (RCA 74-0330) 1970

An obscure soft-rock group with flute. (SR)

The Transactions

45:   Spooky/Simple Simon & Steppin' Stones   (BRC 3294) 1967

Three bouncy and seedy workouts of recent hits of their era by a bunch of local Baltimore, Maryland lads, who obviously dug the sounds of **? and The Mysterians**. (MW)

Transatlantic Railroad

Personnel:	KENT HOUSMAN	gtr, ld vcls	ABC
	JAMIE KINDT	bs, backing vcls	ABC
	STEPHEN MEYERS	ld gtr	ABC
	RON VANBIANCHI	drms, backing vcls	ABC
	JIM MONROE	vcls	B
	GEOFF MAYER	organ	C

ALBUM: 1(C)   EXPRESS TO OBLIVION   (RD Records RD 8) 2001

45:   Why Me / Irahs   (Phoenix PH 2) 1968

This is one of those fabled 'San Francisco sound' bands of whom many may have heard or read about in books and articles on that particular scene, but whose recordings have been heard by very few.

The band assembled at San Rafael High School in Marin County, California, in 1965. Their first gig was at Sausalito Heliport for The Warlocks, who decided that night to change their name to **The Grateful Dead**.

Starting out doing covers like *Midnight Hour*, *Spoonful* and *Smokestack Lightning*, they were soon joined by vocalist Jim Monroe. In 1966, they went through a **Beau Brummels** phase, which is captured on two unreleased Housman compositions cut at Golden State Recorders in San Francisco - *Good Times* and *Now She's Gone*. These have turned up on *What A Way To Come Down* (CD), which also features two cuts by a different Bay Area outfit called Transatlantic RR.

They continued to gig all around the Bay Area; although not on the premier-venue circuit they did get to perform at The Fillmore on audition nights. When it came to the festivals they had a chance to shine, playing on the same bill as top acts including **Jefferson Airplane**, **Grateful Dead**, **Big Brother** and **The Doors**.

In 1968, they released their sole folkie 45 on Phoenix, a very short-lived subsidiary of Seymour Stein's Sire label. What was not known until recently was that they were recording an album to follow the 45. They'd done five demos and got studio time to lay down more. Unfortunately they couldn't get Geoff Mayer's massive Hammond RT-3 organ through the studio doors. It got stuck and would not budge; neither would Mayer, who refused to use other keyboards for the session. What turned out to be their biggest chance was lost.

This is recounted in the notes for the limited edition album, which houses the original quintet of demos and recollections by Housman, Lindt, Vanbianchi and others. The demos are free-flowing extended workouts as was the vogue of the times. The main mid-section of *Elephant* has echoes of *East West* (**Paul Butterfield Blues Band**) with its shuffling rhythm and piercing lead. Mayer's Hammond adds rich reedy textures throughout, but was it really worth sacrificing the album for?

After the fat Hammond incident the band continued, with personnel fluctuating around Housman and Lindt, until 1971 when they decided to disband. Housman would later turn up in **Blue Cheer**, The Ducks and SFO.

Thanks to Mike Somavilla for the use of his *Express To Oblivion* liner notes in this entry. (MW/AP)

Trans-Atlantic Subway

45:   Servant Of The People/Winter Snow   (Lightfoot 100,333/4) 1968

A very obscure Massachusetts-based combo whose short 45, *Servant Of The People*, later resurfaced on *Pebbles, Vol. 14* (LP) and ends with some rather unusual guitar work. (VJ)

Transatlantic Winkham Chiken No. 5

Personnel: G. COONLEY   A
              C. LAMPLEY   A
              J. STANLEY   A
              R. STUBBS   A
              G. ZANARDI   A

45:   The Crystal Mountain/
      You'll Never Find Her   (Silverado SR 101) 1967

Despite its proximity to the San Francisco Bay Area, there are few known sixties records from Napa, California. This super rare garage 45 is the only verified one to date! (CF)

THE TRASHMEN - Surfin' Bird LP.

The Trashmen

Personnel: TONY ANDREASON   A
              BOB REED   A
              STEVE WAHRER   A
              DAL WINSLOW   A

                                              HCP
ALBUM: 1(A)   SURFIN' BIRD   (Soma LPGA 200) 1964 48 R2

NB: (1) has been repressed and reissued on vinyl (Beat Rocket BR 107) 1995 and on CD by Sundazed (SC 6064) 1995 with bonus tracks. *Live Bird '65-'67* (Sundazed LP 5002) 1993, includes 14 cuts and interviews with the band and is also available on CD (SC 11006) 1993 with extra tracks. *Great Lost Album!* (Sundazed LP 5003) 1993, contains 14 previously unreleased studio cuts from 1964/66 and is also on CD (SC 11007) 1993 with two bonus tracks, recorded in Texas in 1966. This should have been the follow-up to the *Surfin' Bird* album. *Tube City! The Best Of* (Sundazed SC 11011) 1992 was issued on CD only. Readers may also be interested in *Bird Dance Beat* which compiled many of their rare singles and *Bird Call The Twin City Stomp Of* (Sundazed SC 11022) 1999.

French
EPs: 1   Surfin' Bird/King Of The Surf/Henrietta/The Sleeper (PS)
                                        (Columbia ESRF 1491) 1964
        2   Bad News/Bird Dance Beat/A-Bone/Money (PS)
                                        (Columbia ESRF 1564) 1965
        3   Whoa Dad/Walking My Baby/Kuk/My Woodie (PS)
                                        (Columbia ESRF 1627) 1966

NB: (1) - (3) French EPs with picture sleeves.

                                              HCP
45s: Surfin' Bird/King Of The Surf   (Garrett 4002) 1963 4
        Bird Dance Beat/A-Bone   (Garrett 4003) 1964 30
        Bad News/On The Move   (Garrett 4005) 1964 124
        Peppermint Man/New Generation   (Garrett 4010) 1964 -
        Whoa-Dad/Walking My Baby (PS)   (Garrett 4012) 1964 -
   φ   Dancin' With Santa/Real Live Doll (PS) (Garrett 4013) 1964 -
        Bird 65/Ubangi Stomp   (Argo 5516) 1965 -
        Keep Your Hands Off My Baby/Lost Angel (Bear 1966) 1965 -
   α   Surfin' Bird/Liar Liar   (Soma 1469) 1966 -
        Hanging On Me/Same Lines   (Tribe 8315) 1966 -
        Green Green Backs Back Home/
        Address Enclosed   (Metrobeat 4448) 1967 -
   β   Henrietta/Rumble   (Sundazed S 102) 1992 -
   χ   Lucille/Green Onions   (Sundazed S 103) 1992 -
   δ   Roll Over Beethoven/Betty Jean   (Sundazed S 105) 1992 -
   ε   Dancin' With Santa/Real Live Doll   (Sundazed SEP 112) 1996 -

NB: α is a reissue 45 with a flip by **The Castaways**. β consists of live recordings from August 1965. χ features non-album studio tracks from March 1964. δ contains previously unreleased tracks from 1964 on blue vinyl. Finally ε is a reissue of φ A number of the 45s were also released in Canada, including: *Surfin' Bird/King Of The Surf* (Apex 76894) 1963; *Bird Dance Beat/A-Bone* (Apex 76904) 1964; *Bad News/On The Move* (Apex 76916) 1964; *Peppermint Man/New Generation* (Apex 76925) 1964; *Whoa Dad/Walking My Baby* (Apex 76942) 1964; *Keep Your Hands Off My Baby/Lost Angel* (Apex 76973) 1965.

Forming in Minneapolis, Minnesota, they set out as a surf rock quartet. Andreason, Winslow and Wahrer had all previously played with Jim Thaxter and The Travelors, who'd operated out of Minneapolis between 1959-62.

Their finest moment was *Surfin' Bird* which made No. 4 in the National Charts in 1963. Later in 1964 they enjoyed a minor U.S. hit with *Bird Dance Beat*. Ironically both songs were taken from tunes by The Rivingtons, *Papa-Oom-Mow-Mow* and *The Bird's The Word*.

Steve Wahrer later died of throat cancer on 21st January 1989 aged just 47.

Compilation coverage has so far included: *Surfin' Bird* on *Born Bad, Vol. 3* and *Sundazed Sampler, Vol. 1* (CD); *New Generation* on *Pebbles, Vol. 4*; *Ubangi Stomp* on *Ear-Piercing Punk* (LP); *Green, Green Backs Back Home* (a novelty record based on Tom Jones' U.K. hit the *Green Green Grass Of Home* but with entirely different lyrics) on *The Best Of Metrobeat! Vol. 1* (LP); *Talk About Love* on *Roof Garden Jamboree* (LP); *Bird Dance Beat* on *Wavy Gravy Vol. 2* (CD); *Bird '65* on *The Big Itch*; *Same Lines* on *Mayhem & Psychosis, Vol. 3* (LP); *Surfin' Bird, Bird Dance Beat* and *A-Bone* on *The Big Hits Of Mid-America - The Soma Records Story* (Dble CD); and *Kuk* (a cut from their LP) on both *Sound Of The Sixties* (Dble LP) and *Sixties Archive, Vol. 1* (CD). (VJ/MW/SR)

Travel Agency

Personnel incl: FRANK DAVIS — gtr, vcls — A

ALBUM: 1(A) TRAVEL AGENCY (Viva 36017) 1968 SC

45s: Time/Made For You (Tanqueray 20102) 1966
Time/Time (Kookaburra 502) c1967
What's A Man/She Understands (Viva 637) 1969

This outfit formed in 1968 in San Francisco after **Davis** left Bob Segarini's band US. **Davis**, originally from Texas, had earlier worked at the Walt Andrus studios and some of his studio work can be heard on the **Fever Tree** albums. **Davis** also wrote *Grand Candy, Young Sweet* on **Fever Tree**'s second album. The **Travel Agency** album was produced by James Griffin (later of Bread) in Los Angeles and issued on **Leon Russell**'s Viva label. Side One is much stronger with some fine fuzztone guitar work on *Cadillac George* and some gentle, more folksy love songs like *Lonely Seabird* and *So Much Love*. Contrast with this fast commercial rockers like *Make Love* and *Old Man*, the catchy *That's Good* and the unusual instrumental intro to *What's A Man*, the album's opening track, and you can see their material was of some diversity. Perhaps because of that, it remains underrated and therefore still reasonably priced.

After this project **Davis** went back to Houston, Texas where he recorded an album *Metamorphosis* which was never issued and then returned to studio engineering.

THE TRAVEL AGENCY - The Travel Agency LP.

There is still some confusion surrounding this band... or bands, not helped at all by the lack of personnel and credits on the album. The first two 45s shown above could be by a totally disparate group. Hopefully someone will straighten us out. In the meantime... The Tanqueray 45 is breezy L.A. pop-rock with chiming guitar and a folk-rock feel - infectious after a few plays. Song credits imply a personnel of Haelh, Bushy and Beal at that juncture. Another 45 on Kookaburra couples *Made For You* with *M.F.Y.* - two versions of the **Travel Agency** track - but as by **Act III**. (VJ/MW)

The Travel Agency

45: Jailbait/Hard Times (Zordan 107) 1967

A good punk disc by a Chicago band, who formed in 1966 when the bassist's earlier project, The Fourbidden Pleasures, folded. *Jailbait*, is a pounding punker about the dangers of fooling with underage nubiles. The band folded in June 1968 when its members graduated.

Compilation appearances include *Jailbait* on *Back From The Grave, Vol. 7* (Dble LP). (VJ)

The Travelers (IV)

Personnel: ROBIN BUELL — A
DENNIS — A
HARRY — A
JACK — A

45s: A Message For You/
This Happens To Me (RoX ROX-1001) 1966
α Libby / ? (Prism 1927) 1966

NB: α flip side may be *Beachboy*.

In 1966, radio station WONE sponsored a three-day Daytonian battle of the bands, which attracted 29,000 fans. A dozen bands were selected by the judges and were duly booked into Mega-Sound Studios (at 49 Heid Avenue) to lay down a track each for the souvenir album of the event - *WONE, The Dayton Scene* (Prism PR-1966).

The Travelers open the album with *Beachboy*, a slow teen ballad with Four Seasons harmonies and falsettos.

They released two 45s, one on Prism and another on the Mega-Sound custom label 'RoX'. The latter is of more interest - *A Message For You* puts Four Seasons harmonies atop an Invasion beat-ballad and adds a touch of fuzz. The flip reverts to teen ballad mode, dreamy Everlys-style. (VJ/MW)

The Travelling Salesmen

45: Days Of My Years/I'm Alive (RCA 47-9167) 1967

Based in West Texas, they evolved out of The Velveteens. The *Mind Blowers* (LP) compilation includes the 'A' side of this 45. (VJ)

Travis

ALBUM: 1 TO BE AS FREE AS YOU (Unity) 1975 -

A hippie rural group with harmonies like Crosby, Stills and Nash. (SR)

Dave Travis (Extreme)

45s: α Suzanne/I Don't Like Him (Bagdad 1008) 1963
β She's Gone/Lost Man (U.S.P. US 101) 196?
A Shade Of Blue/Last Nite The Flowers
Bloomed (U.S.P. Records U.S. 102) (PS) 1967

NB: α as Dave Travis. β as Dave Travis and The Extremes.

TREE - Tree LP.

Most vocalists in the 'garage genre' fall into certain well-established styles - the bright-eyed pop style of the Beatles/Hollies, the throat raspings of a Jagger or Eric Burdon or the sneering nasal twangs of a Sky Saxon. Occasionally however the more mature deep-throated tones of the macho-men of pop, yer Tom Jones school, cross over to produce a strange hybrid. Examples that spring to mind are Denny Provisor's *It Really Tears Me Up*, **Preston**'s *This World Is Closing In On Me* and **Backgrounds**' *Day Breaks At Dawn*.

Here's another from a cabaret-style balladeer who had at least three 45s. The third is of most interest, although the top side is a kind of mellow folk-rock with Dylanesque harp break, the flip is somethin' else. Those deep tones with Presleyesque mannerisms put the icing on a tough pounding punker with atmospheric busy keyboards and choppy chords - and somehow it works pretty well, giving it more power than a spotty adolescent would have done. Sadly the second 45 is pretty dire, Presley style pop, whilst the first 45 remains unheard.

Last Night... is compiled at last - on *Fuzz, Flaykes, And Shakes, Vol. 2* (LP & CD), which also features the aforementioned **Backgrounds**' *Day Breaks At Dawn*. (MW)

Jack Traylor and Steelwind

Personnel:	CRAIG CHAQUICO	ld gtr, mandolin	A
	DIANA HARRIS	vcls, piano	A
	SKIP MORAIRTY	flute, vcls, gtr	A
	JACK TRAYLOR	gtr, vcls	A
	DANNY VIRDIER	bs, vcls	A
	(DAVID FREIBERG	keyb'ds	A)
	(BILL LAUDNER	vcls	A)
	(KENT MIDDLETON	perc, hrmnca	A)
	(RICK QUINTENAL	drms	A)

ALBUM: 1(A) CHILD OF NATURE (Grunt BFL1-0194) 1973 -

Jack Traylor was a friend of **Jefferson Airplane** and can also be found on the albums of Grace Slick and Paul Kantner: *Manhole*, *Sunfighter* and *Baron Von Tollbooth*.

A decent songwriter, he got offered the opportunity to record an album on the 'Airplane's label and his *Child Of Nature* may interest fans of the West-Coast sound with its male/female vocals and good flute and guitar solos. Nothing outstanding but this album is pleasant enough and some lyrics are interesting: *Gone To Canada* is another song about people escaping the Vietnam draft, *Smile* (probably the best track) is about American politicians and several songs deal with nature protection and pollution.

Traylor apparently vanished from the music scene after this album, whilst Craig Chaquico would later join Jefferson Starship and Diana Harris worked with Terry Allen and **Tom Rapp**. (SR)

Dick Treadway

45s:	Party Crasher/Fess Up	(T.S.M. 8321/2) 1965
	Got No Love / Spider Walk (Instr)	(T.S.M. 9623) 1966
α	You Can't Believe It/One To Ten	(T.S.M.) 1967

NB: α As **Dicky Treadway and The Salados**.

In addition to one solo punk 45 **Treadway** recorded several 45s with **The Salados** including the organ led garage punker listed above (the flip was an instrumental). His father, who was also connected with the Waco-based Mark VII label, ran the T.S.M. label, which was based in Hamilton, a small town in North central Texas. **Treadway** later recorded some country singles for T.S.M. before his tragic death in a car crash.

Compilation appearances have included:- *One To Ten* on *Garage Punk Unknowns, Vol. 7* (LP); and *You Can't Believe It* on *Midnight To Sixty-Six* (LP) and *Realities In Life* (LP). (VJ/MW)

The Treasures

| Personnel: | PETER ANDERS | A |
| | VINNIE PONCIA | A |

45: Hold Me Tight/Pete Meets Vinnie (Shirley 500) 1964

A pop single by the future **Tradewinds**. (SR)

The Treds

45: How Can I Tell Her?/Hey Baby (Trek 2047) 1966

A garage outfit thought to have been based in the Dallas-Fort Worth area of Texas. (VJ)

Tree

Personnel:	GARY 'G' BUCK	gtr	A
	RENEE BENOIT		A
	JAN PAINTER		A
	WIL PARSONS	bs	A
	CHRIS ROACH	vcls, perc	A
	TOM WILCOX	perc	A

ALBUM: 1(A) TREE (Goat Farm 580) 1972-4 R1

A very messy experimental, progressive album by an unknown Iowa band. It is rare, but unless you're into the most experimental, jazzy, avant garde albums, it is best avoided. The album is undated, but is probably from 1974 or so. Side one was recorded live on 11th March 1972. (VJ)

Tree

45: No Good Woman/Man From Nowhere (Barvis 7010) 1967

A typical raw punk number from this Wilmington, Delaware bunch.

Compilation appearances include *No Good Woman* on *Pebbles Vol. 5* (CD), *The Essential Pebbles Collection, Vol. 1* (Dble CD), *Pebbles Box* (5-LP), *Pebbles, Vol. 5* (LP), *Acid Dreams - The Complete 3 LP Set* (3-LP), *Acid Dreams Epitaph* (CD), *Trash Box* (5-CD) and *Great Pebbles* (CD); *Man From No Where* on *Bad Vibrations, Vol. 1* (LP & CD). (MW)

Trees

45: Don't Miss The Turn/Your Life (Bali-Hi 808/9) 196?

Trenton, New Jersey was home to these guys whose excellent moody punker with a searing break is highly sought-after. It's rumoured that the Van Eaton brothers (**Jacobs Creek**) were connected with this group.

Compilation appearances include: *Don't Miss The Turn* on *Off The Wall, Vol. 1* (LP) and *30 Seconds Before The Calico Wall* (CD). (MW)

Trees

Another branch of Trees, this lot were from Dearborn, Michigan. They didn't make it onto 45 at the time but the Collectables 3-CD set *The History Of Michigan Garage Bands In The 60's - The Wheels Four Label Story* features three cuts:- *The Only Life For Me*, *Do You Think About It Now* and *Fly Like An Eagle*.

Do You Think About It Now (Feeling Groovy) and *The Only Life For Me* also appear on *Green Crystal Ties, Vol. 10* (CD). (MW)

The Trees

Personnel incl:
ARIEL (PHILLIP DROSS)	tamboura, cello, bells, recorder, perc, vcls	A
MARGUERITE BLYTHE	oboe, recorder, percussion, bells, vcls	A
BRUCE GAMBILL	gtr, small pump organ, tibetan gongs, vcls	A
PATRICIA GAMBILL	bells, perc, recorder, telephone bells (bells from inside old phones!), sanctus bells, vcls	A
STEPHEN GAMBILL	perc, balangi, gongs, bells, recorders, cheng, harmonium, japanese pot gongs, vcls	A
DAVID KARASEK	bell tree, zither, African drums, percussion, Mexian bell wheel, vcls	A
DAVID LYNCH	gtr, flute, perc, wood flutes, vcls	A
MARY McCUTCHEON	samison, bells, recorder, balinese pot gongs, sanctus bells, vcls	A
SHIPEN (BILL LEBZELTER)	sitar, bagpipe shanter, reed instruments, japanese gongs, African balangi, bells, vcls	A
SHISHONEE (KATHERYN RUETENIK)	venezuelan string harp, koto, tamboura, accordian, perc, bells, harmonium, vcls	A

NB: The group went through many incarnations, line-up 'A' above is that which appeared on the album.

ALBUM: 1(A) THE CHRIST TREE - A MUSICAL MEDITATION (Pomegranate) 1975 R2

PEBBLES Vol. 14 (Comp LP) including The Trespassers.

A rare Christian folk-psych album. These **Trees** consisted of group of men and women dressed in robes, singing and playing an assortment of sitars, zither, dulcimer, flutes, guitar, gong, tamboura... Housed in a black sleeve with pictures on the back, the album contains two long cuts on Side One and seven on Side Two. A few hundred copies were pressed.

Katheryn Krupa (nee Ruetenik) recalls:- "We lived on a bus (several actually) and toured around the US and Canada in the seventies. The group began in New York City, changed, grew, lost and gained members - then was based at the Cathedral of St. John The Divine in NY. (Dean Morton may recall us or may not these days). Two members of the group Shipen and Ariel are now dead, but the rest of us are still around and spread around the country. I went on to be in an art-rock band playing pedal harp called Art in America (CBS/Pavillion records 1981/2?). I also have another tape of older music, in the same genre (folk with many bizarre instruments from around the world) which was recorded before *The Christ Tree*, although the recording quality isn't as good."

David Lynch:- "We were more than just a 'music group' as such. Our lives intertwined around a five-year journey or 'pilgrimage' in our various bus homes, setting up 'camp' in diverse locations around North America, being a resident "society" or community in New Mexico and New York City, where we attempted to explore the concepts of monasticism and spirituality; Christ centered in attitude and immersing ourselves in the deep wisdom of the worlds cultures and spiritual practices. From this journey and its meaning evolved our musical compositions. Whether from sources of Gregorian plainchant or hypnotic Balanesian rhythms, our musical sessions struggled with the psalms and melodies of antiquity and the challenges of our instruments and lifestyle, working with a constantly evolving ensemble to allow the Music of the Tree to take root and its branches to ring with songs and sounds. I now live in Cincinnati Ohio (USA) with my wife and we are involved in composition and playing. In fact from Shipen's example perhaps, I have been playing sitar for several years along with my collection of wind instruments and both playing and composing with my wife Shari who is a violinist and plays keyboards and percussion, under the name Luminaria."

The band are currently planning a reissue of old material, and the *Christ Tree* album on CD. (SR/KK/DL)

Amanda Trees

Personnel:
ROBERT CUMMINGS JUMA		A
EDDIE HEATH OLLIE		A
AMANDA TREES	vcls	A

ALBUM: 1(A) AMANDA (Poppy PP-LA003-F) 1972

This is a strange album of "real people" psych-folk. You'll either like it or hate it. **Amanda Trees** sings songs about *Pineapple Dinosaur*, *Prehistoric Animals*, *Spirit* plus a weird cover of Bobby Hebb's *Sunny*. Produced by Kliff Adam. (SR)

The Tree Toppers

See **The Beauchemins**.

Treez

45: You Lied To Me Before/ Only As Long As You Want It (Harlequin 660725) 1966

From the label that produced **006**'s *Like What Me Worry*. A Chicago area outfit whose vicious girl put-down punker *You Lied* is also featured on *Off The Wall, Vol. 2* (LP). It's flip, *Only As Long As You Want It*, can also be found on *Teenage Shutdown, Vol. 15* (LP & CD). (MW)

The Tremelons

EP: 1 ALL GIRL COMBO (Sundazed SEP 121) 1996

NB: (1) Contains *Whole Lotta Shakin' Goin On*, *Heartbreak Hotel*, *Theme For A DJ* and *Please Let Me Know*.

45s:	Whole Lotta Shakin' Goin' On /	
	Heartbreak Hotel	(Wildwood 005) 1964
	Theme For A DJ / Please Let Me Know	(Wildwood ??) 1964

A Chicago all-girl band who would mutate into **The Luv'd Ones** in 1966, a band who recorded for Dunwich. They recorded two singles for a tiny local label in 1964 which are collected on the Sundazed EP.

Compilation appearances have included: *Theme For A "D.J."* on *Girls In The Garage, Vol. 7* (LP); and *Whole Lotta Shakin' Goin' On* is also featured on *The Big Itch Vol. 2*. (MW)

Tremors

| 45: | Wondering Why/What Have I Done | (Catalina 03/04) 196? |

Out of Urbana, Ohio, *Wondering Why*, a half decent amalgam of punk and psychedelia, can also be found on *Garage Punk Unknowns, Vol. 3* (LP), *Vol. 2* (CD) and the *Garage Punk Unknowns Box Set*. (VJ/MW/GGI)

The Trenchmen

| Personnel incl: | GREG JORDAHL | | A |

| 45: | Chains On My Heart/ | |
| | Travel With Me | (Impact Sound 23667) 1967 |

They hailed from Minot in North Dakota with a good fuzz guitar 45. *Chains On My Heart* can also be found on the EP, *Garage Dreams Revisited* (7"). (VJ)

Bobby Trend

| 45s: | Good Day / Judy | (Ivanhoe 504) 1970 |
| | Good Day/Judy | (Metromedia MM-203) c1970 |

Good Day is catchy rock-pop, originally a local hit for **Ormandy** on the Kasaba label which had been picked up by Decca for national exposure.

Judy is a haunting lament with husky vocals and plaintive guitar. The very same track had appeared on the previous Ivanhoe release under the artist's real name, (Rudy) **Von Ruden**, formerly a member of (Johnny and) The Shy Guys who were based out of LaCrosse, Wisconsin (they were formed originally in Winona, Minnesota). (MW/GM/SR)

The Trespassers

| 45: | Living Memories/Come With Me | (Silver Seal 1020) 196? |

Thought to have been an East Coast band. *Living Memories* is a fine slice of psychedelic punk with a few moments of dementia.

Compilation appearances include: *Living Memories* on *Mayhem & Psychosis, Vol. 2* (LP), *Mayhem & Psychosis, Vol. 2* (CD), *Psychedelic Unknowns, Vol. 6* (LP & CD) and *Pebbles, Vol. 14* (LP); and *Come With Me* on *Psychedelic Experience, Vol. 2* (CD). (VJ)

The Treytones

| 45: | Nonymous/Dream Lover | (Sunliner 101) 1963 |

A pre-punk Bo Diddley-influenced vocal trio from Wooster, Ohio. They formed in 1962 and were quite a popular live attraction for a while. *Nonymous*, is a real Diddley-style pounder.

Compilation appearances include *Nonymous* on *Psychedelic Unknowns, Vol. 4* (LP & CD), *Back From The Grave, Vol. 6* (LP) and *Back From The Grave, Vol. 3* (CD). (VJ/MW/GGI)

The TR-4

See **The Ringers** entry for details.

Triad

| Personnel incl: | MIKE MANKEY | | A |

| 45: | The Only Way To Fly/Border Line | (Franklin 634) 1969 |

NB: Canadian release.

From Minneapolis/St. Paul, this garage band went to Canada for a fortnight to play some gigs and record the above 45. The 'A' side also figured on the label's 1969 *Winnipeg* Canadian compilation. (VJ)

Trials and Tribulations

| ALBUM: | 1 | TRIALS AND TRIBULATIONS | |
| | | | (Vanguard VSD 6565) 1970 - |

| 45: | Please Mrs. Henry/ | |
| | Please Mrs. Henry (mono) | (Vanguard 35124) 1970 |

NB: promo only.

An interesting psych-tinged folk-rock quartet, their album rarely turns up for sale. (SR)

Triangle

Personnel:	MICHAEL CARELLI	vcls, gtr	A
	TY GRIMES	drms	A
	HOWARD J. STEELE	bs	A

| ALBUM: | 1(A) | HOW NOW BLUE COW | (Amaret/Capitol ST 5001) 1969 - |

| 45s: | Magic Touch/Music, Music, Music | (Amaret 108) 1969 |
| | Lucille/99.5 | (Amaret 113) 1969 |

Originally from El Paso in Texas this band later moved to L.A. *Music, Music* is the best cut on their album which mixed hard-rock, Western blues and rock'n'roll. The 45s are taken from the album. Grimes went on to Rick Nelson's Stone Canyon Band and later still to **Captain Beefheart**. (VJ)

Tribal Sinfonia

45s:	Something Has You Turned Around/	
	Do You Want Me	(Tribe Records) 196?
	Tired Of Living (And Being Dead)/	
	Nebbish	(Ego Records 203) 196?

The first 45 is notable for a great guitar freakout on *Something...* accompanied by a hammering organ and horn section. Their second, is nowhere near as solid. From the metro Detroit area, they claim their best gig was opening for **Mitch Ryder** at Jackson state prison. (BB)

The Tribu-Terrys

| 45: | Leavin' To Stay/ | |
| | My Shadow Is You | (Prism 1235-45-PR-1951) 196? |

This outfit were from the Dayton, Ohio area. Their *Leavin' To Stay* sounds in places vaguely like *(I'm Not Your) Steppin' Stone*. Lots of echo but a rather monotonous backing. The flip is a melancholy garage ballad.

Compilation appearances include *Leavin' To Stay* on *Garage Zone, Vol. 2* (LP) and *The Garage Zone Box Set* (4-LP). (VJ)

Tricycle

Personnel:	ART BROOKS	A
	BOB CIRILLI	A
	JOHN TRICOZZI	A
	FRANK WHITE	A

ALBUM: 1(A) TRICYCLE (ABC ABCS-674) 1969 -

45: 54321 Here I Come /? (ABC) 1969

An Italian-American band from the New-York area. Musically the album lies somewhere between pop-psych and bubblegum music, with titles like *Mr. Henry Lollipop Shop*, *Lemonade Parade*, *54321 Here I Come*, *Mary Had A Little Man*, *Simon Says*, *Yumberry Park* and *Good Time Music*. Best avoided. (SR)

Trilogy

Personnel:	SKIP GRIPARIS	ld gtr, piano, vcls	A
	KEVIN McCANN	gtr, hrmnca, organ, vcls	A
	BERNIE PERSHEY	drms, tablas	A
	THOM RICHARDS	bs, flute	A
	BOB WILSON	ld gtr, vcls	A

ALBUM: 1(A) I'M BEGINNING TO FEEL IT (Mercury SR-61310) 1970 -

45: I'm Beginning To Feel/Goodbye Flying (Mercury 73154) 1970

NB: double-sided promo copies also exist.

The album, which was recorded in Chicago, ranges from mellow folk to harder rock. The first side is the best and includes the highlights; *Three Blind Mice*, *Removing Myself* and *Goodbye Flying*. Rick Barr guests on drums on one track. Berni Parsley (from **Lightning**) and Tom Richards assisted on the album, but weren't really part of the core group. (VJ)

The Trippers

45s: Watch Yourself/Pictures Of Lilly (Fulltone 9260) 1968
Have You Ever/Kaleidoscope (Milltown 101) 1969

A progressive late sixties outfit from Sioux Falls, South Dakota, who produced these two highly-touted 45s. (VJ)

The Trippers

45s:	α	Dance With Me/Keep A Knockin'	(Ruby-Doo 1) 1966
		Taking Care Of Business/Charlena	(Ruby-Doo 5) 1967
		Taking Care Of Business/Charlena	(GNP Crescendo 387) 1967

NB: α reissued (Dot 16947).

An L.A. garage outfit. *Taking Care Of Business* is a superb up front fast frenetic fuzz-laden belter that would blister paint. The flip covers The Sevilles' *Charlena* in a frat-party style with a rasping sax break.

Compilation appearances include: *Taking Care Of Business* on *Lost Generation, Vol. 1* (LP), *Mayhem & Psychosis, Vol. 2* (CD) and *Psychotic Reaction Plus Ten* (CD). (MW/DG)

The Trips

45: There Was A Girl/At Least She's Happy (Score T-069) c1966

A California combo with a yearning garagey teen-ballad reminiscent of **London Knights**' *Go To Him* or the mid-sixties Cascades output. *At Least She's Happy* is uptempo **Byrdsy** folk-beat and can be found on *Love Is A Sad Song, Vol. 1* (LP). (VJ)

FIFTH PIPE DREAM (Comp CD) including Tripsichord Music Box.

Tripsichord (Music Box)

Personnel:	RANDY GORDON (GUZMAN)	drms, vcls	ABCD
	OLIVER McKINNEY	keyb'ds, vcls	A
	FRANK STRAIGHT	ld gtr, vcls	ABCD
	DAVE ZANDONATTI	bs, vcls	ABCD
	RON McNEELEY	vcls	B D
	BILL CARR	gtr, vcls	C

ALBUM: 1(C) TRIPSICHORD (San Francisco Sound T-12700) 1970 R6
2(C) TRIPSICHORD (Janus JLS-3016) 1971 R2/R3

NB: (1) demo disc issued in thick white jacket with front and rear stickers applied. These stickers are in various colours, all with the same psychedelic artwork and logos for "Tripsichord Music Box" and "San Francisco Sound". The front sticker is considerably larger than the one on the rear of the jacket, but otherwise identical. The label on the record itself is the same red and black design found on the original pressing of the *Fifth Pipedream - San Francisco Sound Vol. 1* compilation. The labels show the band simply as 'Tripsichord'. Three of the tracks on this demo album are known by slightly different titles than appearing on the Janus editions, and three tracks are slightly longer. (2) is an authorised reissue of (1). Two different legitimate pressings exist on Janus: (i) Tan label, Janus logo, no mention of "San Francisco Sound" on label. (ii) Tan label, Janus logo, large "San Francisco Sound" logo at bottom of label. These two versions are otherwise identical and command an equal value, however, the version with the Janus logo only on the label seems to be considerably rarer. This was counterfeited on vinyl in the eighties with a black and white label, and a counterfeit CD exists on Eva. More recently San Francisco Sound have reissued the album on CD (SFS 07680) 1999, and Akarma have reissued the Janus version as a double LP/ single CD (Akarma AK-077) 1999, adding the three tracks from the *Fifth Pipedream - San Francisco Sound Vol. 1* compilation and the two non-LP cuts from the 1969 single. Curiously, the two legitimate Janus pressings (as well as all subsequent reissues, with possible exception of the San Francisco Sound CD) were not mastered from the original tapes! To date, only the rare demo album (1) is a first generation issue from the master tapes, and has correspondingly 'clearer' sound than all other pressings.

45s:	α	Times And Seasons/ Sunday The Third	(San Francisco Sound 115) 1969
	β	She Has Passed Away/ Fly Baby	(San Francisco Sound 127) 1970

NB: α both sides non-LP. β 'A' side title is not a misprint, this is how it appears on the 45 and on the demo album. It was re-titled *We Have Passed Away* on the Janus edition of the LP. *Fly Baby* is the LP version, but radically edited due to its length.

Tripsichord Music Box (name shortened to 'Tripsichord' in 1970) were one of the Bay Area's most enigmatic and amazing bands. Despite being one of the least documented and least commercially successful of the San Francisco Sound family of groups under producer Matthew Katz' control, the music they left behind is quite stellar and easily ranks alongside the output of stablemates **Moby Grape** and **It's A Beautiful Day** from the same period (1968-70).

Tripsichord Music Box started life as **The Ban** before changing names to **Now**. The group was managed by Randy Guzman's parents, so he took the name Gordon, for business reasons. The Guzman's had shopped the group around to all of the L.A. record companies and local promoters, while the band played high-profile gigs at places like the Sea Witch and Pandora's Box on the Hollywood's Sunset Strip. Despite playing the same circuit as the **Seeds**, **Strawberry Alarm Clock**, **Yellow Payges** et al, and building a considerable following, it was not until they came to the attention of Matthew Katz that they were taken seriously as a viable commercial entity. Katz relocated the band to San Francisco and re-christened them **Tripsichord Music Box**. They played live (along with most of Katz' other bands) frequently at his San Francisco Sound Ballroom in Seattle and in California.

In December 1967, **Tripsichord Music Box** was the first group to record on 8-track equipment in San Francisco (prior to the arrival of state of the art multi-tracking equipment, most S.F. bands were going to Los Angeles to record). This session produced the three tracks that were included on the rare *Fifth Pipe Dream - San Francisco Sound Vol. 1* compilation: *It's Not Good*, *You're The Woman* and *Family Song*.

When Katz lost the group **Moby Grape**, he had **Tripsichord Music Box** play a number of shows as the now imfamous "fake grape". Gregg McKinney (Oliver's brother) recalls: "They did the free show in Encanto Park, Phoenix, Arizona, where our 93-year-old grandmother came to the "love-in" to see her grandson play. Oliver ended up playing guitar on stage, something her truly hated! For the record, the guys did not like deceiving other peoples fans and would rather have kept playing their own music."

Oliver McKinney left the band during 1969, moving with his family to Pensacola, Florida. He played music locally into the mid-eighties and is now a commercial artist and plays cello in a church orchestra.

Oliver McKinney was replaced by guitarist Bill Carr and as well the band was often augmented by Zandonatti's high school buddy Ron McNeeley on vocals. It was this more aggressive dual-guitar line-up (with and without McNeeley) that recorded the band's most spectacular music. Listening to their 1969 recordings today, it's clear that they alone carried the torch that year that was once shared by **Quicksilver Messenger Service**, **Frumious Bandersnatch** and **Moby Grape**. The *Tripsichord* album is essentially what the world was hoping *Shady Grove* would be! *Fly Baby* sounds like **Quicksilver** at their ethereal best, and throughout, the dual-guitar interplay is breathtaking on this underrated gem. A dark vibe permeates the album through an obsession with death and the afterlife in the lyrics:

"The life that I lived and the image I reflected
Still remains in the eyes of those who I protected
And now I rest eternally...
The dim light shines from the black door where I have just passed through."
(from *Black Door*)

The Narrow Gate has creepy lyrics "Lovely, lovely living souls, blowing warmth from purple heat... now I'm cold" backed by a stunning instrumental track loaded with unusual percussion. Aside from the rather pedestrian *Short Order Steward*, every cut on the album is killer and required listening for all fans of sixties music. The recent Akarma package (also issued on CD) collects all the released **Tripsichord Music Box** recordings 1968-70 and is the most economical way to investigate this fine little-known band.

In 1970, **Tripsichord** left California for Utah, where Dave Zandonatti and Ron McNeeley joined a Mormon traveling musical troupe called The Sons Of Mosiah. This collective was managed by Orrin Hatch, now a well-known politician in the State. Several concerts were recorded during 1970, and a double album was issued that year: *The Sons Of Mosiah Live! In Washington, D.C.* (Lab Productions). Zandonatti and McNeeley appear on the album as a folk duo, and given about 25 minutes, perform five songs including both sides of the 1969 **Tripsichord Music Box** 45. In between the tracks, they explain in some detail how the lyrics relate to Biblical texts. Ironically the emcee of the show introduces Zanonatti as "a former member of the acid rock group **Moby Grape**"!

In 1971, Dave Zandonatti produced a recording for singer Marvin Payne which was released in album form by Mike Curb (Curb Records). Zandonatti also plays on the album, as does **Tripsichord** drummer Randy Gordon and violinist Danny Colletti who was a member of a seventies band with Zandonatti called Natty Bumppo.

Dave Zandonatti (aka John E. Smorgasbord) is currently fronting a swing band called The Blue D'Arts, and Randy Gordon has (no kidding!) been playing drums for the *real* **Moby Grape** in recent years!

Compilation coverage has included: *Sunday The Third* and *Times And Seasons* from their non LP 45, on *Filling The Gap* (4-LP); Matthew Katz's *Then And Now, Vol. 1* (CD) includes *You're The Woman* and *Fly Baby*, whilst *Then And Now, Vol. 2* (CD) includes *Family Song* and *On The Last Ride*. (CF/GMy/DZ)

The Triumphs

Personnel incl:			
FRED CARNEY	keyb'ds		A
DON DRACHENBERG	sax, vcls		A
TIM GRIFFITH	bs		A
TOM GRIFFITH	gtr		A
GARY KOEPPEN	hrns		A
TEDDY MENSIK	drms		A
B.J. THOMAS	vcls		A
DENVER "DENNY" ZATYKA			A
JOHN PERRY	bs		
DOUG GRIFFITH	keyb'ds		
RON PETERSEN	hrns		

45s:			
I Know It's Wrong/Lazy Man	(Dante)	1962
Garner St. Park / On The Loose	(Joed 117)	1964
Keep It Up/Vietnam	(Joed 119)	1965
Better Come Get Her/Monicia Baker	(Pacemaker 238)	1966

Formed in Rosenberg/Needville, Texas, in the mid-1950s; all bar Don Drachenberg met at Lamar Consolidated High School in Rosenberg. *Garner St. Park* was a local hit in the Houston area around 1964.

After B.J. Thomas quit the band, Drachenberg took over vocal duties and **The Triumphs** continued all the way through to 1983, with John Perry taking over bass duties and Doug Griffith's joining in the early eighties.

In 1993, **The Triumphs** had a successful re-union and they're still performing to this day, whilst B.J. Thomas too is also still performing as a solo act.

Sadly Denny Zatyka passed away in 1997.

There was also a different Triumphs from Houston in the early seventies with 45s on Master and Wand who'd formerly been The Inside Trax.

Compilation appearances include: *Better Come Get Her* on *Vile Vinyl, Vol. 1* (LP) and *Vile Vinyl* (CD). (MW/TD/VJ)

The Triumphs

45s:		
Lovin' Cup/It's So Easy	(Genuine 152)	1967
The Walk/People Try My Mind	(Genuine 163)	1969

TRIPSICHORD - Tripsichord LP.

From Ashtabula, Ohio, their first 45 was recorded at the famous Chess studios in Chicago.

Compilation appearances include: *Lovin' Cup* on *Off The Wall, Vol. 2* (LP) and *Teenage Shutdown, Vol. 10* (LP & CD). (VJ/GGI/MW)

The Triumphs

45s:	Don't Ask Me Why / It Doesn't Matter Anymore	(Barclay 14211/2) 1964
	Question / What Did I Do	(Barclay 14249/50) 1964

This Hamburg, Pennsylvania, bunch changed their name from this all too used moniker to **The Razor's Edge**. They subsequently found that their new name had also been bagged so after one further 45 they became **Pat Farrell & the Believers**.

Arf! Arf! have unearthed this band's output - both 45s can now be found on *Eastern Pa Rock Part One (1961-'66)* (CD), and five unreleased cuts are unearthed on the **Pat Farrell & The Believers** CD.

Other Triumphs of interest include the Milwaukee bunch whose *Surfside Date* (I.F.F. 151) graces *Back From The Grave, Vol. 2* (LP) and *Garage Kings* (Dble LP); and an uncompiled Chicago garage outfit with two 45s on the Cha Cha label. (MW/VJ)

Trizo 50

Personnel incl:	J. De PUGH	A
	D. JOHNSON	A
	R. WALKENHORST	A

ALBUM:	1(A)	TRIZO 50	(Cavern Custom 74-0142) 1974? R4

NB: (1) promo only demo album.

Previously known as **Phantasia**, this band was from the Kansas City area in Missouri. The **Trizo 50** album was recorded in the band's rehearsal studio on a four-track recorder and was intended as a songwriters demo, including re-recordings of some **Phantasia**-era tracks. Some of these recordings were included on two collections of **Phantasia** material issued in the nineties. See their entry for details.

Compilation appearances have included *Graveyard* on *Love, Peace And Poetry, Vol. 1* (LP & CD). (CF)

The Trodden Path

Personnel:	MIKE FROMMER	gtr	A
	TOM SZYMAREK	drms	A
	STEVE TURNER	bs	A
	TIM URBAN	ld gtr	A

45:	Don't Follow Me/Can't You See	(Night Owl 6711) 1967

Until they recorded this Mequon, Wisconsin, teen quartet were known as B.E.A.T. Ltd.. For their sole 45 they combined folk-rock with fake British accents on *Don't Follow Me*, which you'll also find on *Highs In The Mid-Sixties, Vol. 10* (LP). (VJ/GM/MW)

Chuck Trois and The National Bank

ALBUM:	1	CHUCK TROIS AND THE NATIONAL BANK
		(A&M SP 42??) c1970 -

From Philadelphia, this interesting group sounded a bit like BST on acid, with two long twisted covers of Traffic and their own *Free Thing*.

Their leader and guitarist, **Chuck Trois**, was previously in **The Soul Survivors**. (SR)

FUZZ, FLAYKES AND SHAKES, Vol. 4 (Comp CD) including Trojans of Evol.

Trojans of Evol

45:	Through The Night/Why Girl	(T.O.E. 125969/125970) 1966

Hailed from Gary, Indiana, and travelled up to Chicago's Columbia studios to record the above 45 which they put out on their own label. The 'A' side, *Through The Night*, had a pretty good guitar break and lots of fuzz.

Compilation appearances include: *Why Girl* on *Project Blue, Vol. 5* (LP) and *Fuzz, Flaykes, And Shakes, Vol. 4* (LP & CD); and *Through The Night* on *Back From The Grave, Vol. 6* (LP). (VJ)

The Trolley

Personnel:	GARY CHURCH	bs	A
	MIKE LANGDON	ld gtr, ld vcls	A
	BARRY PUHLMAN	keyb'ds, vcls	A
	DENNIS RICHEY	vcls, perc	A
	PETE SACK	drms	A
	RICK JOHNSON	drms	
	KIRBY SHELL	bs	

45:	Toy Shop/Breakdown	(Piccadilly 246) 1967

A Pacific Northwest act, from Seattle. Their 45 consists of a hypnotic jingle-jangle melodic and melancholy pop ballad backed by an excellent, though restrained, punker along the usual girl-put-down lines. They were sometimes known as The Peppermint Trolley, but shouldn't be confused with the Acta Recording act of the same name.

Peter Sack went on to play with **Merrilee Rush**.

Compilation appearances include *Breakdown* on *Midnight To Sixty-Six* (LP), *Northwest Battle Of The Bands, Vol. 1 - Flash And Crash* (LP & CD) and *Northwest Battle Of The Bands, Vol. 1* (CD). (DR/MW/VJ)

The Troll(s)

Personnel:	RICHARD CLARK	organ, vcls	A
	RICHARD GALLAGHER	gtr, vcls	A
	MAX JORDAN, Jr.	bs, vcls	A
	KEN APPLES	drms	
	KEN CORTESE	drms	

ALBUM:	1(A)	ANIMATED MUSIC	(Smash SRS 67114) 1968 R1

NB: (1) counterfeited on CD (Flashback 10) 1997.

HCP

45s:	Every Day And Every Night/ Are You The One?	(ABC Paramount 10823) 1966 96

	Something Here Inside/	
	Laughing All The Way	(ABC Paramount 10884) 1966 -
	There Was A Time/	
	They Don't Know	(ABC Paramount 10916) 1967 -
	Baby, What You Ain't Got (I Ain't In Need)/	
	Who Was That Boy?	(ABC Paramount 10952) 1967 -
α	I Got To Have You/Don't Come Around	(USA 905) 1968 129
	Satin City News/	
	Professor Potts Pornographic Projector	(Smash S-2208) 1969 -

NB: α also issued as a one-sided promo of *I Got To Have You*. (6) both tracks are from the LP.

The Trolls inhabited Chicago, Illinois and issued several noteworthy 45s. They kicked off with *Ever Day And Every Night*, forceful beat modelled loosely on *Gloria*, backed by a Beatlesque ballad. The follow-up was more overtly Invasion pop, with two upbeat ditties similar to Herman's Hermits. *They Don't Know* continued in the same vein and added a slightly fuzzy guitar. *There Was A Time* is a frantic fuzzy popper with harmonica, **Cryan' Shames** harmonies and a rousing ending. Until that point all had been written or co-written by Richard Clark. Then Richard Gallagher came up with *Baby, What You Ain't Got...* and they let RIP with a stormin' fuzz-fest of heavy pop - awesome! The flip is harmony-pop and sounds exactly like **The Critters**.

They may have been having an identity crisis around late 1967 because a 45 appeared by **The Carnival Of Sound** - *Don't Come Around / I Can't Remember* (USA 892) - shortly before their early 1968 release of the identical track (according to the *Mindrocker, Vol. 2* notes). In any event the **Trolls**' USA 45 is decent pop with *Don't Come Around* being the stronger cut by far, a real catchy popper with pumping Diddleyesque riff. After that they retreated to their underground lair...

They re-emerged towards the end of the year as psychedelic-pop-rockers **Troll**, with a very interesting album. This included the powerful *Werewolf* and *Witchbreath* and a number of other psychedelic numbers such as *Satin City News* and *Everybody's Child*, alongside the lighthearted *Professor Potts Pornographic Projector* and *Have You Seen The Queen?*. The album had a smattering of slower numbers, too, notably *A Winter's Song* and *I've Only Myself To Blame*. The album is recommended but originals are not easily obtained, as it's now a mini-collectors' item.

Compilation appearances include: *Don't Come Around* on *Mindrocker, Vol. 2* (LP); *Everyday And Every Night* on *Psychedelic Unknowns, Vol. 3* (LP & CD), *The Essential Pebbles Collection Vol. 1* (Dble CD) and *Pebbles Vol. 7* (CD); A recording of *I Got To Have You* from February 1968 has also been included on the *Early Chicago* compilation. (VJ/MW)

The Trolls

45s:	Walkin' Shoes/	
	How Do You Expect Me To Trust You?	(EU 23267) 1966
	Walkin' Shoes/	
	How Do You Expect Me To Trust You?	(Peatlore 23267) 1966

A mid-sixties San Jose-based outfit. *Walkin' Shoes* was written by Jim McPherson of **Stained Glass**. Check it out on the *Son Of The Gathering Of The Tribe* (LP). (VJ)

Trolls

45s:	That's The Way Love Is/Into My Arms	(Rum 1010) 1966
	Stupid Girl/I Don't Recall (PS)	(Warrior 173) 1966

A different band from Pueblo, Colorado. The 'A' side of their first 45 was erroneously included on the Texas compilation *Flashback, Vol. 1/Texas Flashbacks, Vol. 1* (LP & CD). Some copies of the follow-up came in a picture sleeve. The 'A' side was a Rolling Stones cover, the flip written by R. Gonzales.

Later *That's The Way Love Is* appeared on *Monsters Of The Midwest, Vol. 3* (LP) whose sleeve-notes say the band later became White Lightnin' and issued a 45 on Sandoz and then **Jade** with a 45 on Jade. However, according to the sleevenotes of *Highs In The Mid-Sixties, Vol. 18* (LP), which features both sides of the Warrior 45, they became Baby Magic! Can anyone set the record straight? (VJ/MW)

The Trophies

45s:	Walking The Dog/Somethin' Else	(Nork 79907) 1964
	Everywhere I Go/	
	Baby Doesn't Live Here Anymore	(Kapp 714) 1965
	Leave My Girl Alone/You're The Queen	(Kapp 750) 1966

Either from Greenfield, Massachusetts or Brattelboro, Vermont, their first 45 features good rockin' versions of Rufus Thomas and Eddie Cochran classics. By their third 45 they'd smoothed out some of the rough edges to put down a slick garagey folk-rocker ballad in **The Knaves**' *The Girl I Threw Away* mould.

Somethin' Else can be heard on *Psychedelic Unknowns, Vol. 9* (CD). (MW)

The Tropics

Personnel incl:	MEL DRYER	vcls, toys	A
	BUDDY PENDERGRASS	gtr, keyb'ds	A
	BOBBY SHEA	drms, vcls	A
	CHARLIE J. SOUZA	vcks, bs	A
	ERIC TURNER	gtr, vcls	A
	DAVE BURKE	bs	

45s:	I Want More/Goodbye My Love	(Knight 102) 1965
	I Want More/Goodbye My Love	(Freeport FR 1006) 1966
	It's You I Miss/You Better Move	(Laurie 3330) 1966
	For A Long Time/Black Jacket Woman	(Thames T-103) 1966
	As Time's Gone/Time	(Columbia 4-43976) 1967
	This Must Be The Place//Summertime Blues	
	Land Of 1,000 Dances	(Columbia 4-44248) 1967
α	Groovy Christmas/Toy Soldier	(Malaco 2002) 1968
	Tired Of Waiting/Talkin' Bout Love	(Malaco 2003) 1969

NB: α shown as by Chipper.

A revered St. Petersburg/Tampa, Florida outfit, also known as Chipper, whose members would go on to outfits including **White Witch** and Bacchus. Their finest moment is probably the stunning *As Time's Gone*, a dangerous punker, punctuated by a strange 'whoop'. It is one of Florida's finest contributions to the genre. They were obviously a diverse act as their previous 45, *For A Long Time*, verges on **Byrds**/Beatles-influenced folk rock.

I Want More, from their debut, is a fuzzy Invasion-flavoured stomper. The liner notes to *Psychedelic States - Florida Vol. 2* (CD) reveal that the group had already cut several demos including Solomon Burke's *Stupidity* and that an earlier incarnation of the band had released a limited press album (details unknown).

By their last 45 they'd moved into the seriously heavy school of post-Cream/**Vanilla Fudge** sounds to deliver a rather pedestrian version of The Kinks' hit backed by a melodramatic fuzz-rocker.

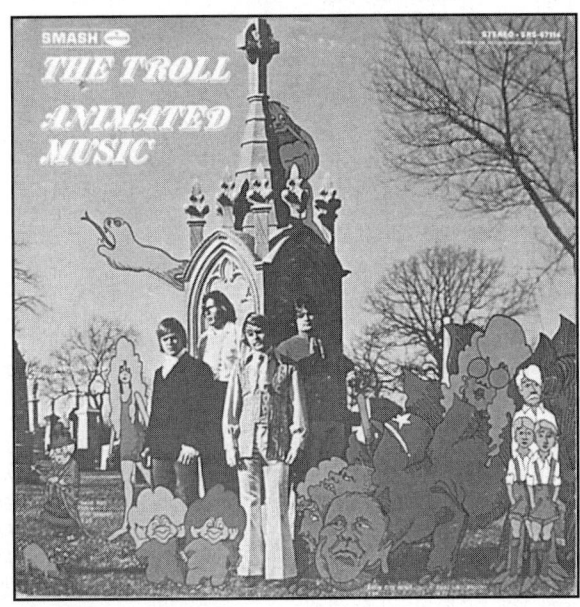

THE TROLL - Animated Music LP.

Dave Burke left **The Tropics** to join **The Standells**.

The Fuzztones later covered *As Time's Gone* on their *Lysergic Emanations* album.

Compilation appearances have included: *This Must Be The Place* on *The Lost Generation, Vol. 2* (LP); *As Time's Gone* on *Mind Blowers* (LP) and *Songs We Taught The Fuzztones* (Dble LP & Dble CD); *I Want More* on *Pebbles Box* (5-LP), *Trash Box* (5-CD) and *Psychedelic States - Florida Vol. 2* (CD); *You Better Move* on *Riot City!* (LP), *Teenage Shutdown, Vol. 14* (LP & CD) and *I Was A Teenage Caveman* (LP); and *For A Long Time* on *Destination Frantic!* (LP & CD). (MW/GSw/RSo/JLh)

The Trout

ALBUM: 1 THE TROUT (MGM SE 4592) 1969 -

45: Carnival Girl/Worst Day I've Ever Been To (MGM 14030) 1969

An obscure trio (two men, one gal), seen described as "psych" by some dealers. (SR)

Troy

Personnel:
- ANDY BROWN — gtr — A
- BILL JOSEPH — ld gtr, vcls — A
- WAYNE McMANNERS — drms — A

45: Amnesia/Papiermache (Alhambra 001,02) 1969

Originally known as **Merlynn Tree**, they came from Austin, Texas, and split after they graduated in 1971. Their sole 45 is an unexceptional piece of heavy psychedelia.

Compilation appearances include *Amnesia* on *Psychedelic Experience* (CD) and *The Psychedelic Experience, Vol. 2* (LP). (VJ)

The Troyes

Personnel:
- FRED DUMMER — ld gtr, vcls — A
- BILL HIRAKIS — drms, vcls — AB
- LEE KOTELES — ld vcls, organ — AB
- GARY LINKE — gtr, vcls — AB
- JERRY YOUNGLOVE — bs, vcls — A
- BRENT FLATHAU — ld gtr — B
- JOHN STANG — bs — B

45s:
- Why?/Rainbow Chaser (Phalanx 1008/1009) 1966
- Why?/Rainbow Chaser (Space 7001) 1966
- Help Me Find Myself/ Love Comes, Love Dies (Space 7002) 1967
- α Morning Of The Rain (UN) 196?

NB: α acetate only.

A Battle Creek, Michigan, mob who also recorded an unreleased album at United Sound Systems in Detroit. Their excellent fuzz-punker *Rainbow Chaser* is NOT the Nirvana song.

On one of the acetates for the album, *Morning Of The Rain* the band were backed by Ray Anthony, the famous big band leader. Gary Linke: "He was trumpeter for the Glenn Miller and Jimmy Dorsey bands and recorded hits such as *Peter Gunn* and the theme from the television show, *Dragnet*. He also wrote *The Bunny Hop*. Mr. Anthony was in the studio with **The Troyes** when the cuts on this acetate were recorded. He actually tried to direct the group as if he were leading a big band!"

Compilation appearances have included: *Rainbow Chaser* on *Let 'Em Have It! Vol. 1* (CD), *The Psychedelic Sixties, Vol. 1* (LP) and *Glimpses, Vol. 1* (LP); *Help Me Find Myself* on *Lost Generation, Vol. 1* (LP); *Love Comes Love Dies* on *Mindblowing Encounters Of The Purple Kind* (LP); *Rainbow Chaser*, *Help Me Find Myself* and *Love Comes, Love Dies* on *Glimpses, Vol's 1 & 2* (CD); and *Help Me Find Myself* and *Love Comes, Love Dies* on *Glimpses, Vol. 2* (LP). (MW/MPo/GLe)

The Troys

45: Got To Fit You Into My Life/Take Care (Tower 406) 1968

This Chicago outfit's claim to fame is that it included Mark Gallagher before he was lured away to join **The Litter** as Denny Waite's replacement. *Take Care* has also resurfaced on *If You're Ready - The Best Of Dunwich... Vol. 2* (CD). (MW)

William Truckaway

Personnel:
- RUSSEL DaSHIELL — gtr — A
- TERRY DOLAN — 12-str gtr — A
- BILL DOUGLAS — acc bs — A
- BUDDY EMMONS — pedal steel — A
- RICHARD GREENE — violin, viola — A
- LARRY HANKS — jews harp — A
- DAVID HAYES — bs — A
- DOUG KILLMER — bs — A
- CHARLES LLOYD — flute — A
- NORMAN MAYELL — drms, sitar, tamboura — A
- STOVALL SISTERS — bcking vcl — A
- WILLIAM TRUCKAWAY — gtr, harp, keyb'ds, moog — A
- DALLAS WILLIAMS — autoharp, perc, orbital maintenance — A

ALBUM: 1(A) BREAKAWAY (Reprise) 1971 -

NB: (1) also released in the U.K. (K14465) 1971.

45s:
- α Bluegreens/Bluegreens On The Wing (Reprise 0935) 19??
- I Go Slow/I Go Slow (mono) (Reprise 0966) 1971?
- β Roller Derby Star/Pat And Joe's (Reprise 1149) 1973

NB: α year of release not certain - probably 1969/70. β shown as by Willy Truckaway and Magic.

William Truckaway was in fact William Sievers, former member of the **Sopwith Camel**. His only solo album was produced in 1971 by Erik Jacobsen and sounds very similar to the Norman Greenbaum albums, the main musicians being the same.

The lyrics of *Hard, Cold City Life* are particularly noteworthy:

"I came to San Francisco
Got into the music scene
There hippie girls and acid swirls
Filled my head with dreams
I used to think that love was free
But that's just what it seems"

The music is mainly mid-tempo with good melodies and some unusual moog interventions.

Bluegreens On The Wing was a hit in New Zealand, reaching No. 20 on October 16th 1969 and staying in there for a week.

Norman Mayell was with Sievers in **Sopwith Camel**, Richard Greene was in **Seatrain**. Terry Dolan and David Hayes would later form Terry and The Pirates with John Cipollina. (SR/WF)

True Blue Facts

Personnel incl: TOMMY FAIA

45s:
- α Who's Got The Right?/I'm Back (A&M 900) 1968
- α Rain, Rain, Rain, Rain/The Boy I Left Behind (A&M 945) 1968
- You've Got My Soul/An Exception To The Rule (A&M 983) 1968

NB: α with Tommy Faia.

A San Francisco-based pop outfit. *The Boy I Left Behind* kicks off with some riffs very similar to **Animated Egg** and launches into some 'hip' lyrics - "I'm sinking in a morass of idiotic slime, whose cadence is the temple of our time". *I'm Back* features some anti-drug lyrics, and provides a neat 'comedown' concluding the *Psychedelic Experience* (CD). (VJ/MW)

TRUTH and JANEY - No Rest For The Wicked CD.

Truk

Personnel:	MOBY ANDERSON	bs	A
	BILL DAFFERN	drms	A
	MIKE GRAHAM	vcls	A
	PAT GRAHAM	organ	A
	GLENN TOWNSEND	gtr	A

ALBUM: 1(A) TRUK TRACKS (Columbia C 30005) 1970 SC

NB: (1) also released in England (CBS 64367).

A hard-rock outfit with histrionic vocals and loud organ. Their album contains a cover of Gun's *Yellow Cab Man*; the other cuts are self-penned. *You* is a beautiful ballad.

Reputedly from Oklahoma, although they seem to have been based in California at the time of the album. Bill Daffern was previously with **Hunger!**. In 1973, Glenn Townsend resurfaced with **Johnny Rivers** and later Willy Daffern played with the reformation of Captain Beyond. (CF/SR)

The Trust Company

ALBUM: 1 TELL IT ALL BROTHER (Fourmost) c1969 ?

A Christiian folk-rock group from Illinois, with flute, tambourine, 12-string guitar, electric guitar, organ and bass. (SR)

Truth

Personnel:	RICK ARMSTRONG	drms, vcls	A
	SHERRY KARNES	organ, vcls	A
	GARY LEEAH	organ, bs, vcls	A
	JIMMY LEEAH	gtr	A
	RON LOGAN	bs, gtr, vcls	A

Out of El Paso in Texas. They had four cuts:- *Its A Nice Day Isn't It*, *If You Can Sing A Song*, *No. 57* and *The Color Red* on the *I Love You Gorgo* (Suemi 1090) 1969 compilation. This compilation had a limited repress of 300 copies in 1997. (VJ)

Truth

45: I Can/One Day Like This (Cadet 5627) 1968

This seems to have been this Chicago outfit's sole vinyl offering. *I Can* can also be heard on *Mindrocker, Vol. 13* (LP). (VJ)

Truth

Personnel:	STEVEN BOCK	bs, vcls	A
	DENIS BUNCE	drms, vcls	A
	BILLY JANEY	gtr, vcls	A

45s:	Under My Thumb/		
	Midnight Horsemen	(Sound Command 81472)	1971
	Around And Around/		
	Straight Eight Pontiac (PS)	(Driving Wheel 7302)	1973

This act from Cedar Rapids, Iowa was later known as **Truth & Janey**, releasing the highly-rated progressive heavy rock album *No Rest For The Wicked*.

All four cuts are due to be reissued in 2000 as bonus tracks on a **Truth & Janey** CD from Monster Records. (VJ/MW/CF)

Truth

45: P.S. (Prognosis Stegnosis)/
Momentarily Gone (Warner Brothers 7214) 1968

Fragmented L.A. psych produced by Dave Hassinger. Check out *P.S.* on *A Heavy Dose Of Lyte Psych* (CD). As noted by Erik Lindgren on the aforementioned compilation, the flip is worthwhile too. A bit chaotic again, with atonal guitars and the odd blasts of sax, and frequent changes in direction just when you think they've settled into a theme. Avant-garde psych? (MW)

Truth

Personnel:	BOB DORAN		A
	M. DE GREVE		A
	J. KERR		A

ALBUM: 1(A) TRUTH (People PLP 5002) 1970 -

An album whose mixture of acoustic and orchestrated folkie-rock, comes complete with three-part harmonies out of **The Jefferson Airplane** school. A minor collectable which may interest readers. (VJ/MW)

Truth and Janey

Personnel:	STEVEN BOCK	bs, vcls	A
	DENIS BUNCE	drms, vcls	A
	BILLY JANEY	gtr, vcls	AB

ALBUMS:	1(A)	NO REST FOR THE WICKED		
			(Montross MR 376)	1976 R2
	2(B)	JUST A LITTLE BIT OF MAGIC		
			(Bee Bee Records)	1979 -
	3(A)	LIVE (dbl)	(Rock and Bach Records)	1988 -

NB: (1) was recorded in 1975 and has been counterfeited on CD. A legitimate reissue from Monster Records (MCD 013) came in 2001 with 3 unreleased studio cuts and four 45 cuts as **Truth**. (3) was recorded in 1976, but not released until 1988.

From Cedar Rapids, Iowa. This is essentially a driving hard-rock outfit whose guitar work on their first album often has some psychedelic trappings. A marginal case for inclusion here, their other two albums fall outside this book's time frame. If you like killer guitar work treat yourself to a copy of their first album which is now rare. The guitar work on tracks like *Remember* is stunning.

They were previously known as **Truth**, releasing two singles locally. The group played live in Iowa as they toured the Midwest and Canada extensively as a support band for the likes of Leslie West Band, Kansas and Cheap Trick during the mid-seventies. The original band split in 1977.

More recently Steve Bock appeared on a record in the eighties with Southern California band, Nowhere Fast. Guitarist Billy Janey (who now goes by the name Billy Lee Janey) has also released at least four solo Blues Rock CD's during the late eighties - nineties. (VJ/DBb/CF)

Truth of Truths

Personnel: JIM BACKUS   A
            VAL STOECKLEIN   A

ALBUM: 1(A) CONTEMPORARY ROCK OPERA
                            (Oak Records ORS-1???) 1971 -

A double album with booklet which may interest fans of 'Jesus Christ Superstar' and the other "rock operas". This one features some good guitar work.

Val Stoecklein of **The Bluethings/Ecology** was involved. (SR)

Truths

45: Pending/Why   (Circle 45-953) 1965

Two glorious top notch garage folk-rockers in a Searchers meets **Beau Brummels** vein - the fabulous moody *Why* features a ringing break. The songs were penned by Ray Harris and James Pettey and it's now thought that they were from Riverside, California.

Compilation appearances include *Pending* on *Project Blue, Vol. 5* (LP); *Why* on *Sixties Rebellion, Vol. 14* (LP & CD). (VJ)

Tryad

ALBUM: 1 IF ONLY YOU BELIEVED IN LOVIN'
                        (Storm King Records SKS-101) 1972 ?

From New York, a folk-rock trio (one girl, two men) with harmony influenced by British folk-rock. Their scarce album features songs like *Uptown Suburb Alley*, *Something Sweet Is Dying*, *Spider Song* and *Eulogy/Raga*. (SR)

Try-Cerz

Personnel incl: RAY BOE   A
                 SAMMY BOE   A
                 GARY MILLER   A
                 RON THIBERT   A

45: Almost There/Taxman   (Jan-Gi 91) 1967

Originally known as **The Tracers** and later **Sweet Smoke**, they issued the above 45 whilst in Fort Worth.

Compilation appearances include *Almost There* on *Scum Of The Earth* (Dble CD) and *Scum Of The Earth, Vol. 1* (LP). (VJ)

T.S. Truck

Personnel: CURT GARNER   A
            KEN HOEDEBECK   A
            MARK HOEDEBECK   A
            TOM MEREDITH   A
            CURTIS POWELL   A
            BILL STILLWELL   A

ALBUM: 1(A) T.S. TRUCK   (Smokey Soul) 1972? -

A private pressing recorded at Smoke Signal Sound Studio in Carbondale, Illinois. The group plays a mix of garage and psychedelia with some progressive influences on tracks like *Khengis Gange*, *Let The Gunslinger Win* and *Nothing Of The Kind*. (SR)

Tommy Tucker and The Esquires

45s: Peace Of Mind/How Did I Know?   (IGL 108) 1966
      Don't Tell Me Lies/
      What Would You Do?   (IGL 121) 1967

as Tommy T's Federal Reserve
45s: Take The Midnight Train/Grow Up Someday (Cadet 5584) 1967
      Let's Go Down To The Park/
      Someday They'll Reach Out   (Cadet 5622) 1968
      Get It Together/45 Second Blues   (R-Jay 6856) 1968

as Salt River
45:   Messenger/I Need A Friend   (Cantaloupe 66) 1968

From Des Moines, Iowa, *Don't Tell Me Lies* is a pounding three chord garage-rocker. A name change to Tommy T's Federal Reserve resulted in three poppy 45s, followed by one more as Salt River, none of which would appeal to garage collectors.

Compilation appearances have included: *Don't Tell Me Lies* on *Monsters Of The Midwest, Vol. 2* (LP), *The Arf! Arf! Blitzkrieg 32 Track Sampler* (Dble CD) and *The Best Of IGL Garage Rock* (LP); *Live For Love* on *Roof Garden Jamboree* (LP); and *Peace Of Mind* and *Don't Tell Me Lies* on *The IGL Rock Story: Part One (1965 - 67)* (CD). (VJ/MW)

The Tuesday Club

45: Goddess In Many Ways/Only Human   (Philips 40478) 1967

Another very obscure one.

Compilation appearances include *Only Human* on *Punk Classics* (CD) and *Punk Classics, Vol. 1* (7"). (VJ)

The Tulu Babies

45s: Hurtin' Kind/Mine Forever   (Tema 817) 1966
     α Hurtin' Kind/Mine Forever   (Mar no #) 1966
        Debbie/?   (Tema 125) 1966

NB: α is a bootleg miscredited as **The Talula Babies**.

Hurtin' Kind is a superb hand stamped double-sided single, strongly influenced by The Kinks. Although they actually came from Cleveland, Ohio, both sides of the single were included on Eva's *Florida Punk Groups From The Sixties* (LP). *Mine Forever* (from the Mar release) can also be heard on *The Magic Cube* (CD) and *Valley Of The Son Of The Gathering Of The Tribe* (LP) (from the Tema release) and *Hurtin' Kind* (from the Mar release) can be found on *Open Up Yer Door! Vol. 1* (LP). Both sides are worth checking out, but the 'A' side in particular has a fine guitar break and a good organ sound. *Debbie* can also be heard on *Pride Of Cleveland Past* (LP).

The group also recorded as **The Baskerville Hounds**, re-recording versions of both *Hurtin' Kind* and *Debbie*.

It should also be pointed out that their first 45 was bootlegged at the time, and miscredited as **The Talula Babies**... three decades on and it's still appearing miscredited on some bootlegs. (MW/GGI)

The Tumblers

45: Make You All Mine/Scream   (Pocono 6417) 1964

Riot City! (LP) and *Mondo Frat Dance Bash A Go Go* (CD) compilations both include this outfit's *Scream*, which mostly features just that. They must've been really popular with the neighbours in Allentown, Pennsylvania!

Scream was "composed" by Larry La Spina. (VJ)

Tumbling Dice

ALBUM: 1 TUMBLING DICE   (Century 74103) c1973 SC

An obscure band with church-like organ and covers of *Whiter Shade Of Pale*, *The Letter*, *Feelin' Alright* and *Cinnamon Girl*. Totally awful although it may amuse some curious collectors. (SR)

THE TURTLES - It Ain't Me Babe CD.

Turks

| 45: | Fire / ? | (TK 6118) 1968 |

From Elkin in North Carolina, these misfits managed a pretty decent cover of Jimi Hendrix's *Fire* for TK Records back in late 1968. It can now be heard on *Tobacco A-Go-Go, Vol. 1* (LP). (VJ/MW)

Richard William Turner

| ALBUM: | 1 | THE PASSANGER | (TH-56082078) 1973? ? |

A limited pressing, recorded in mono and issued on a plain white sleeve with handwritten titles. A kind of hippie-folk, which has its moments. (SR)

Velvert Turner Group

Personnel:	BOB HOGANS	keyb'ds	A
	BOB LENOX	keyb'ds	A
	TIM McGOVERN	drms	A
	PRESCOTT NILES	bs	A
	CHRISTOPHER ROBINSON	keyb'ds	A
	VELVERT TURNER	vcls, gtr	AB

ALBUMS:	1(A)	VELVERT TURNER GROUP		
		(Family Productions FPS 2704)	1972	R1/R2
	2(B)	VELVERT TURNER	(Tiger Lily 14030)	197?	R1

NB: There were two versions of (1). A 'heavy' version with crazed solo guitar overdubbed - matrix no. 16741 and a 'soul' version in basic power trio format with second lead guitar overdubs removed - matrix no. 16951. (1) also released in Germany (Philips). (2) may be a reissue of (1) with the song titles altered!

Based in Los Angeles, **Velvert Turner** was an excellent **Hendrix**-style black guitarist / vocalist and both versions of his album on Family are recommended. Prescott Niles and Tim McGovern both played on **Randy California**'s solo album *Kapt. Kopter And The Fabulous Twirly Birds* in 1972. **Velvert Turner** later played with Arthur Lee on his 1981 album. Tim McGovern also teamed up with **Neil Merryweather** for several albums and Prescott Niles went on to form The Knack of *My Sharona* fame. (CF/SR)

Turnquist Remedy

Personnel:	SCOTT HARDER	bs, vcls	A
	JOHN MAGGI	drms, perc	A
	MURPHY SCARNECCHIA	ld gtr, vcls	A
	MICHAEL WOODS	gtr, vcls	A
	(LARRY KNECHTEL	piano, organ	A)
	(GEORGE SEMPER	piano, organ	A)
	(LARRY VILAUBI	drms	A)

| ALBUM: | 1(A) | IOWA BY THE SEA | (Pentagram PE 10004) 1970 - |

Produced by Barry Kane and Al Schmitt, this album was recorded in Hollywood. Michael Woods wrote all their material except *Last Cigarette* co-written with Dennis Hudson and Douglas Benson and an excellent cover of **Richard Farina**'s *Reno, Nevada*.

Although some dealers try to give this album a psychedelic tag, in fact only the cover art (with an inner sleeve) and the song *All Gone Blues Act II* are worthy of it, the other tracks being faithful to the specific sound of Pentagram, a short-lived label founded by Al Schmitt, the former producer of the **Jefferson Airplane**, which specialized in West Coast acts with fluid guitar and vocal harmonies (**Redeye**, **Rex Holman**, **Red, Wilder, Blue**).

John Maggi later played with **String Cheese**. (VJ/SR)

The Turtles

Personnel incl:	HOWARD KAYLAN	vcls	ABCD
	DON MURRAY	drms	A
	AL NICHOL	ld gtr	ABCD
	CHUCK PORTZ	bs	A(B)
	JIM TUCKER	gtr	AB
	MARK VOLMAN	vcls	ABCD
	JOEL LARSON	drms	B
	CHIP DOUGLAS	bs	B
	JOHN BARBATA	drms	C
	JIM PONS	bs	CD
	JOHN SEITER	drms	D
	JOHN USSERY	vcls	

HCP

ALBUMS:	1(A)	IT AIN'T ME BABE	(White Whale 7111) 1965 98 -
(up to	2(A)	YOU BABY	(White Whale 7112) 1966 - -
1972)	3(A)	HAPPY TOGETHER	(White Whale 7114) 1967 25 -
	4(C)	GOLDEN HITS	(White Whale 7115) 1967 7 -
	5(C)	BATTLE OF THE BANDS	(White Whale 7118) 1968 128 -
	6(D)	TURTLE SOUP	(White Whale 7124) 1969 117 -
	7(-)	MORE GOLDEN HITS	(White Whale 7127) 1970 146 -
	8(A)	WOODEN HEAD (1965 outtakes)	
			(White Whale 7l33) 1972 -
	9(-)	HAPPY TOGETHER AGAIN (dbl)	
			(Sire SASH-3703) 1974 194 -

NB: (1), (2), (3), (5), (6) and (8) have all been reissued on CD by Sundazed, containing many bonus tracks (SC 6035/6/7/8 all in 1994) and 6086/7 (both in 1997) respectively). Most of their original albums have been issued on CD in Europe too, including (1) (Repertoire REP 4399-WY), with two bonus tracks; (3) (Repertoire REP 4320-WY), with nine bonus tracks; (6) (Repertoire REP 4398-WY) and (8) (Repertoire REP 4400-WY). Some retrosepctives include *30 Years Of Rock 'n' Roll: Happy Together*, a 60-track anthology CD, was issued in 1996 on the Laserlight label. Rhino have also released two *Greatest Hits* collections on CD and a profusion of reissues and outtakes. These include *Turtles 1968* (1981) (a collection of rare and

THE TURTLES - Turtle Soup CD.

unissued cuts), *Turtles Golden Hits* (1982) and a triple-LP *History Of The Turtles And Flo And Eddie* (1983); *It Ain't Me Babe* (Rhino RNLP-151) 1984; *Happy Together* (Rhino RNLP-152) 1984; *You Baby* (Rhino RNLP-153) 1984; *Wooden Head* (Rhino RNLP-154) 1984; *Greatest Hits* (Rhino RNLP-160) 1984; *1968* (Rhino RNDP-901A) 1984 (also issued as picture disc); and Turtlesized (Rhino RNLP-280) 1984. Rhino EPs have included *The Turtles* (1978) and *Turtlesised* (1982). A recent hits collection is *25 Classic Hits* (Repertoire REP 4321-WG) 2000.

EP: 1 IT AIN'T ME BABE (White Whale) 1967

HCP

45s:	It Ain't Me Babe/Almost There	(White Whale 222) 1965	8
	Let Me Be/ Your Maw Said You Cried	(White Whale 224) 1965	29
	You, Baby/Wanderin' Kind	(White Whale 227) 1966	20
	Grim Reaper Of Love/Come Back	(White Whale 231) 1966	81
	Outside Chance/We'll Meet Again	(White Whale 234) 1966	-
	Outside Chance/Making My Mind Up	(White Whale 237) 1966	-
	Can I Get To Know You Better?/ Like The Seasons	(White Whale 238) 1966	89
	Happy Together/ Like The Seasons (PS)	(White Whale 244) 1967	1
	She'd Rather Be With Me/ The Walking Song	(White Whale 249) 1967	3
	Guide For The Married Man/ Think I'll Run Away	(White Whale 251) 1967	-
α	You Know What I Mean/ Rugs Of Woods And Flowers	(White Whale 254) 1967	12
β	She's My Girl/ Chicken Little Was Right (PS)	(White Whale 260) 1967	14
	Sound Asleep/ Umbussa The Dragon	(White Whale 264) 1968	57
	The Story Of Rock And Roll/ Can't You Hear The Cows?	(White Whale 273) 1968	48
	Elenore/Surfer Dan	(White Whale 276) 1968	6
	You Showed Me/Buzz Saw	(White Whale 292) 1968	6
	You Don't Have To Walk In The Rain/ Come Over	(White Whale 308) 1969	51
	Love In The City/Bachelor Mother	(White Whale 326) 1969	91
	Lady-O/Somewhere Friday Nite	(White Whale 334) 1969	78
	Who Would Ever Think That I Would Marry Margaret?/ We Ain't Gonna Part No More	(White Whale 341) 1970	-
	Is It Any Wonder?/Wanderin' Kind	(White Whale 350) 1970	-
	Eve Of Destruction/Wanderin' Kind	(White Whale 355) 1970	100
	Me About You/Think I'll Run Away	(White Whale 364) 1970	105

NB: β some copies with PS. α and β also issued in France with PS by London. There are also four French EPs with PS on Polydor and London.

They formed at Westchester High School in Los Angeles in 1961. Their founding members were Mark Volman, a native of L.A. (he'd been born there on 19th April 1947 and Howard Kaylan (real name Howard Kaplan), a New Yorker, born in June 1947. They were originally known as The Nightriders, then The Crossfires, until in 1965 their name change to **The Turtles** was a condition of their contract with White Whale. In their early days they were very much part of the L.A. folk-rock boom. Their first 45 was a Dylan song and the next two were **P.F. Sloan** compositions. All three achieved considerable commercial success. Their first album, which climbed to No. 98 in the U.S. Charts, contained two other Dylan compositions:- *Love Minus Zero* and *Like A Rolling Stone*, in addition to the title track and **P.F. Sloan**'s *Eve Of Destruction*. They had a few good originals, too:- *Wanderin' Kind* was a good folk-rocker and *Let The Cold Wind Blow* a protest song. Their second album, too, was a similar blend of originals and Dylan and **P.F. Sloan** compositions.

As 1967 came they underwent some personnel changes and Bonner and Gordon, formerly with **The Magicians** became their new songwriters. Inevitably there was a change of style and initially a more commercial pop sound. With *Happy Together*, a classic love song, they enjoyed a No. 1 U.S. hit (and it also made 12 in the UK). They issued an album of the same name which was in many respects a compromise between commercialism and their own progress. It made No. 25 in the U.S. Album Charts. They followed the 45 success of *Happy Together* with *She'd Rather Be With Me*, a bouncy pop song with pleasant harmonies which made No. 3 in the U.S. and No. 4 in the UK. Their next single *Guide For The Married Man* was written for a Walter Matthau film but withdrawn after just one week and replaced by *You Know What I Mean* which peaked at No. 12 in the US.

Golden Hits, which contained most of their 45 releases and two previously unissued tracks, *Is It Any Wonder?* and *So Goes Love*, became what would be their best selling U.S. Album peaking at No. 7.

They're also rumoured to have released an excellent pop-punk 45 in December 1967, under the pseudonym of **The Odyssey**. A year later they recorded a Christmas single with Linda Ronstadt as **Christmas Spirit**.

From 1968 their music became more experimental, although when White Whale became impatient for another big hit Volman and Kaylan came up with the brilliant *Elenore,* which was a big transatlantic hit peaking at No. 6 in the U.S. and No. 7 in the UK. Their *Battle Of The Bands* and *Turtle Soup* albums are both worth investigation. They enjoyed further minor hits, of which *Lady O*, a Judy Sill composition, was the last 45 released with their approval. Many of these later 45s were included on their *More Golden Hits* album along with two previously unissued tracks:- *We Ain't Going To The Party* and *Cat In The Window*. The first of these was intended for an album, *Shell Shock*, they were working on which was never released. Now heavily immersed in the flower-power movement they were recording numerous deranged tapes which White Whale wouldn't release. The record company continued to release their own choice of material but none of it met with much success commercially and, in September 1970, the band disintegrated.

Volman and Kaylan both later joined **The Mothers Of Invention**, then in 1972 they worked as a duo first as Phlorescent Leech and Eddie and later as simply Flo and Eddie. Much of **The Turtles**' material has stood the test of time quite well, and whilst they were most successful as a folk-rock/harmony outfit **The Turtles** main significance for this book was as part of the flower-power movement, even though that movement was ultimately to prove their downfall.

Compilation appearances have included: *Elenore* and *Happy Together* on *The Golden Archive Series Sampler*; *Outside Chance* on *Nuggets Box* (4-CD) and *Sundazed Sampler, Vol. 2* (CD); *It Ain't Me Babe* on *Nuggets, Vol. 10* (LP); *Can I Get To Know You Better* on *Nuggets, Vol. 3* (LP); *She's My Girl* on *Nuggets, Vol. 9* (LP); *She'll Come Back* on *Out Of Sight* (LP); and *It Ain't Me Babe*, *Happy Together* and *Elenore* on *Happy Together - The Very Best Of White Whale Records* (CD). (VJ/SR)

Twas Brillig

45s:	α Dirty Ol' Man/You Love	(Scotty 6621) 1966
	Dirty Ol' Man/This Weeks Children	(Date 2-1550) 1966

NB: α 'A' side as **The Electras**.

This was a continuation of **The Electras**, the top sixties band from Ely up in Northeast Minnesota. Indeed, they had first recorded their best known song, *Dirty Ol' Man*, when they were **The Electras**. Both of these 45s are now quite rare and sought-after.

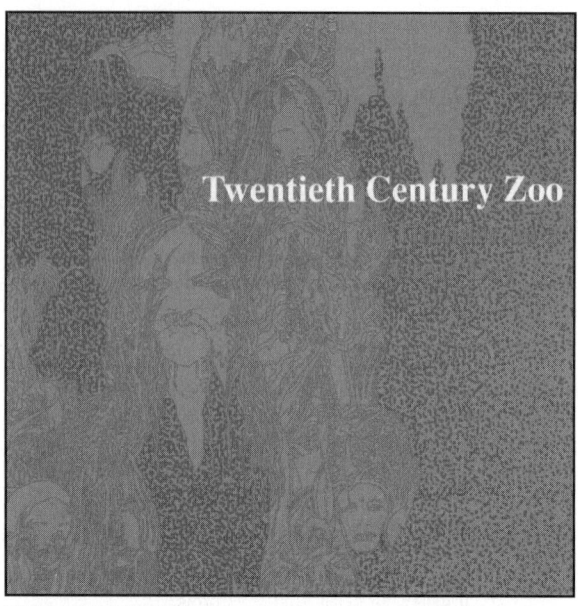

TWENTIETH CENTURY ZOO - Thunder On A Clear Day CD.

Dirty Ol' Man has also turned up on Eva's *Litter - Rare Tracks*' LP along with other **Electras** tracks due to the mistaken assumption that this was a **Litter** offshoot - not so, see **The Electras** entry.

Compilation appearances include *Dirty Ol' Man* on *60's Punk E.P., Vol. 2* (7"), *Acid Dreams Vol. 2* (LP) and *Changes* (LP). (VJ/MW/LP)

Charlie Tweddle

ALBUM: 1   FANTASTIC (GREATEST HITS BY EILRAHC ELDDEWT)
(No label) 197? R2/R3

A rare, but really inept and stupid (intentionally!) local Bay Area album from circa 1974. The incredibly beautiful psychedelic gatefold sleeve belies the fact that the contents are largely sound snippets and crickets chirping in the night - the very epitome of a record whose impossible rarity is fully justified. (CF)

The Twelfth Night

Personnel:			
DON HALL	gtr, vcls		AB
BOB MAGUIRE	bs		A
BOB SELLERS	ld gtr		AB
GARY VAUGHN	drms		AB
STEVE JAY	bs		B

45:   Grim Reaper/I Don't Believe You   (Whiteholme 1984) 1965

Four young Orlando teens started out in 1963 as The Emotions, playing youth clubs and school hops. Two years later, still only 16/17 years of age, they changed their name to **The Twelfth Night** and put out their own 45 on a label set up for them by friend Bob Benzing.

The following year they acquired a manager and another name change to Covington Tower. Maguire joined the USAF at this point and was replaced by Steve Jay (bassist for Weird Al Yankovic for over twenty years). Covington Tower lasted until 1969.

Grim Reaper, a charming lo-fi fuzzer with a frantic solo, is on *The Chosen Few, Vol. 2* (LP), *Chosen Few Vol's 1 & 2* (CD) and *Psychedelic States: Florida Vol. 1* (CD). The equally enchanting flip is on *Psychedelic States: Florida Vol. 3* (CD). (MW/DHI/RM)

The 12 AM

45:   The Way I Feel/Good Day   (Groovy 102) 1967

This San Antonio band produced one of the better Texas punk 45s from the era.

Compilation appearances include *The Way I Feel* on *Pebbles, Vol. 5* (CD) and *Pebbles, Vol. 5* (LP). (VJ)

Twentieth Century Zoo

Personnel:			
PAUL BENNETT	drms		A
ALLAN CHITWOOD	bs		AB
GREG FARLEY	gtr		AB
PAUL "SKIP" LADD	ld gtr		AB
BOB STUKO	vcls, hrmnca		AB
RANDY WELLS	drms		B

ALBUM: 1(A)   THUNDER ON A CLEAR DAY   (Vault 122) 1968 R1

NB: (1) reissued on CD by Afterglow in 1995, and again Sundazed (SC 11063) 1999 with extra tracks: both Caz 45s, the final Vault 45 and three unreleased cuts *Country*, *Hall Of The Mountain King* and *Enchanted Park*.

EP: 1   TWENTIETH CENTURY ZOO (PS)
(Sundazed SEP 145) 1999

45s:	α	You Don't Remember/Clean Old Man	(Caz L-103) 1967
		Love In Your Face/Tossing And Turning	(Caz L-104) 1968
		Rainbow/Bullfrog	(Vault 948) 1969
		Only Thing That's Wrong/Stallion Of Fate	(Vault 961) 1970

NB: α A few copies came with a picture sleeve, which now command high prices.

Recorded in Los Angeles, this is a fair album. It's predominantly bluesy with a splattering of sound effects. The 'A' side to their first 45 was re-recorded when they signed to Vault in 1969. Their last, *Only Thing That's Wrong* is a non-album country-rocker.

Thought to be a Los Angeles band they were actually from Phoenix, Arizona and were known until late 1967 as the **Bittersweets**, releasing three locally successful and now sought-after 45s before they added Ladd (from the Laser Beats) to the line-up and changed their name. Bennett was drafted in late 1967 and replaced by Randy Wells (ex-Sounds Incorporated/**Solid Ground**).

The Sundazed EP features three of the four Caz 45 tracks - *Clean Old Man* is missing for reasons unknown. Still, a welcome reissue and a chance to sample their earlier rampant fuzz-heavy-garage sounds that were somewhat diluted by the time of the album. The Sundazed CD is recommended.

Compilation appearances include: *Bullfrog* (45 ver.) and *Only Thing That's Wrong* on *Mindrocker, Vol. 13* (LP); *You Don't Remember* (45 ver.) on *Psychedelic Disaster Whirl* (LP) and *An Overdose Of Heavy Psych* (CD); and *Stallion Of Fate* on *Filling The Gap* (4-LP). (VJ/MW)

$27 Snap On Face

Personnel incl:			
JIM DOHERTY	gtr		A
RON INGALSBE	drms		A
STEVE NELSON	bs, vcls		A
BOB "$" O'CONNOR	gtr, vcls		A
DAVID PETRI	vcls, perc		A

ALBUM: 1(A)   HETERODYNE STATE HOSPITAL
(Heterodyne 001-002-00001) 1977

NB: (1) issued with lyric sheet.

45:   Let's Have An Affair/Kicking Around   (Heterodyne) 1976

Pressed on blue vinyl and recorded by a bunch of crazy Californians based in Sebastopol, this will interest some readers. This band's recordings are strictly outside the book's timeframe, but I've included them because the album frequently appears in sales lists of the psych and garage recordings of this era and they existed as a band in Northern California since the late sixties. (VJ)

Richard Twice

Personnel incl:			
RICHARD MANNING			A
RICHARD TWICE	vcls		A

ALBUM: 1(A)   RICHARD TWICE   (Philips PHS 600-332) 1970 -

45:   My Love Bathes In Silence/Generation 70   (Philips 40677) 1970

$27 SNAP ON FACE.

A psych-pop album with tracks like *The Finest Poet*, *She Catches Me Running* and the strange *My Love Bathes In Silence (What No Rubber Duckie?)*, also issued on 45. (SR)

The Twiggs

Personnel?:	?? FEDERICO		A
	?? GENTILE		A
	?? KAPSAR		A
	?? SKADAN		A
	?? VASTOLA		A

45s: Flowers And Beads / Moon Maiden (Jerden 917) 1969
Flowers And Beads/Moon Maiden (SSS International 800) 1970

Appearing on the Jerden label suggests that **The Twiggs** were a Pacific Northwest band, but they've yet to be tracked down. *Flowers And Beads* is a tame cover of **Iron Butterfly** but they let rip on the flip - *Moon Maiden* is hard-rock with a rich vein of fuzz and wah-wah throughout. (MW)

The Twilighters

45: Nothing Can Bring Me Down/I Need You (Mark VII 1023) 1968

Hailed from Waco in Texas. The 'A' side of this 45 is a strong song with effective vocals, superb fuzz guitar, great lyrics, and catchy chorus... "Well my mind is so messed up, nothing can bring me down, Nothing is strong enough, to save me now...".

Nothing Can Bring Me Down later appeared on *Psychedelic Experience* (CD), *Austin Landing, Vol. 2* (LP), *Texas Flashbacks, Vol. 2* (LP & CD), *Flashback, Vol. 2* (LP) and *Gone, Vol. 2* (LP). Highly recommended. (VJ)

The Twilighters

45: Spell Bound/? (Red Flame 1005) 1967

Came from Kirksville, Missouri. *Spell Bound* was a rousing frat-rocker which has resurfaced on *Monsters Of The Midwest, Vol. 4* (LP) and *Drink Beer! Yell! Dance!* (LP). (VJ)

The Twilighters

45s: Be Faithful/Thumper (Bell 624) 1965
Eeny Meeny Miney Mo/Boo's Blues (Bell 631) 1965
Shake A Tail Feather / Road To Fortune (Imperial 66201) 196?
I Still Love You / Meat Ball (Imperial 66238) 196?

From Cleveland, Ohio, this act were also known as Tony and The Twilighters and members would later be in the Returns and the Originals. Their finest moment *Be Faithful* can also be heard on *Pride Of Cleveland Past* (LP). (MW/GGI)

The Twilighters

Personnel incl: BILL KENNEDY A

45s: (Everybody's Goin' To) Rollerland /
Shakin' All Over (Empire E-4) 1964
α The Girl From Liverpool / Move It (Empire E-6) 1964
Mary Lou / ? (Empire??) 1966

NB: α as "The Twiliters with Bill Kennedy".

Invasion-influenced garage rock'n'rollers outta Plattsburgh, NY. *Move It* was a Cliff Richard cover.

Compilation appearances include: *The Girl From Liverpool* on *Teenage Shutdown, Vol. 2* (LP & CD); *Move It* on *Teenage Shutdown, Vol. 11* (LP & CD) and *It's Finkin' Time!* (LP); and *Rollerland* on *Wild! Wild!! Wild!!!* (LP). (MW/GGI/MM)

Twilighters

ALBUM: 1 BOTH SIDES OF THE TWILIGHTERS (Vanco) 1968 SC

Another **Twilighters**, their album contains two good garage-psych cuts, plus many weak tracks. It was released on the same label as **Easy Chair**, so perhaps they came from the Northwest. (SR)

The Twilighters

ALBUM: 1 THE TWILIGHTERS (Fleetwood 5069) 1967 -

From Boston, a forgotten garage/lounge group. (SR)

Twilights

Personnel:	GORDON ?	bs	A
	BILL MOSS	gtr	A
	FRED MOSS	drms	A

45: She's There / Take What I Got (Parrot 45013) 1965

This North Miami trio issued one fine Searchers-flavoured 45. *She's There*, a sultry beat ballad, is backed by a chiming Joe Tex cover.

A few months later Steve Palmer brought the Moss brothers together with Travis and Coventry Fairchild and named them the **Clefs of Lavender Hill**. (MW/JLh)

Twinn Connexion

Personnel:	JAY HOPKINS	vcls	A
	JERRY HOPKINS	vcls	A
	(JAY BERLINER	gtr	A)
	(DAVE BLUME	organ, vibes	A)
	(SKEETER CAMERA	perc	A)
	(BILL LA VORGNA	drms	A)
	(CHARLEY MACEY	gtr	A)
	(JOE MACK	bs	A)
	(FRANK OWENS	piano, harpsichord	A)
	(BUDDY SALTZMAN	drms	A)
	(STEVE WOLFE	gtr	A)

ALBUM: 1(A) TWINN CONNEXION (Decca DL 75020) 1968 -
NB: (1) reissued on CD (Hugo-Montes Production HMP CD-009) 2001.

45s: Sixth Avenue Stroll /
Oh What A Lovely Day (Decca 32353) 1968
I Think I Know Him / Turn Down Day (Decca 32403) 1968

TEENAGE SHUTDOWN Vol. 11 (Comp CD) including The Twilighters.

The Hopkins twins came from Helena, Montana originally, but this album seems to have been recorded in New York. Dressed in trendy Ivy League suits and backed by many musicians from the **Carolyn Hester Coalition**, this album is very lavishly arranged/produced but consists of very lightweight easy-listening fodder. The lyrics are mainly innocent, groovy love/teen anthems. Notable for the version of **The Cyrkle** hit *Turn Down Day* (Jerry Keller/Dave Blume), this also features some fine guitar work by Steve Wolfe, but overall it is pretty dispensable.

Produced by Jerry Keller, all selections were written and arranged by Jerry Keller and Dave Blume.

After **Twinn Connexion**, Jay became a metal trader for various companies including Prudential and Merrill Lynch. He was a vice president of the latter when he died in September 2001 of heart failure. (CP/SR)

Two Boys In The Windows

Probably from Texas hence the inclusion of *If You Love Me Girl* on the Roy Ames licensed *Acid Visions - The Complete Collection Vol. 1* (3-CD). (GG)

Two Brothers

45:	China, Silver And Linen/ Due To The Facy	(Smobro 402)	1969

An obscure bubblegum pop group, on the same label as **The Sound Foundation**. (SR)

The Two Dollar Question

Personnel incl:	RON DANTE	vcls		A

45:	Aunt Matilda's Double Yummy Blow Your Mind Brownies/ Cincinnati Love Song	(Intrepid 75001)	1969

Produced and written by P.J. Vance and Lee Pockriss, a bubblegum pop rock single with an amusing song title. Ron Dante would later record with the Archies of *Sugar Sugar* fame. (SR)

Two Friends

Personnel:	CHIP CARPENTER	acoustic gtr, vcls		A
	BUCKY WIENER	acoustic gtr, vcls		A

ALBUM:	1(A)	TWO FRIENDS	(Natural Resources NR-101 L)	1972
45:		Move With The Music/ Must Be The Wrath	(Rare Earth 2C006-93853)	1972

NB: French single with PS.

Released on one of the rock subsidiary label of Motown, this album was one of the last known productions by **Tom Wilson**. Composed of melodic tunes with vocal harmonies plus strummed acoustic guitars and an electric backing provided by famous session men (Jim Keltner, Mike Rubini, Ray Neopolitan, Joe Osborne), not unlike some CNS&Y songs, but it tends to be rather tedious. The best tracks can be found on the single. (SR)

The Two Of Clubs

The Two Of Clubs were a girl duo from Cincinnati. Their raunch-punk version of Petula Clark's *Heart* has resurfaced on *Psychotic Reactions* (LP) but the pair also had a chart hit with *Walk Tall (Like A Man)* on Fraternity which is much more of a "pretty" song. (VJ/JGd/GGI)

2/3rds

Personnel incl:	PETE CARR			A
	PHIL JONES	drms		A
	GENE McCORMICK	ld vcls, organ		ABC
	RALPH CITRULLO	bs		BCD
	ALLEN DRESSER	ld gtr		BCD
	NEIL HANEY	ld vcls		BCD
	MAX EASON	drms		CD
	CHRIS DRAKE	gtr		D

45s:	All Cried Out / 2/3 Baby	(April 101)	1967
α	Charisma/?	(Sundi 6814)	1970
α	Monday In May (The Kent State Tragedy) / Nickel	(Sundi 6815)	1970

NB: α as **The Third Condition**.

A Daytona Beach, Florida, band that acquired several members of **The Hungry I's** (Haney, Dresser and Citrullo) after that band folded in 1968.

In April 1967, they released *All Cried Out*, a slow bluesy number, backed by *2/3 Baby*, a cantering beat-punk number with a nifty bass and piano motif. The latter can be heard again on *Psychedelic States: Florida Vol. 3* (CD).

Jones was replaced by Eason in 1969. Soon after Haney, Dresser, Citrullo, and Eason, with the addition of Chris Drake (also from the **Hungry I's**) became The Third Condition. (KCs/MW)

Tyde

45:	Psychedelic Pill/Lost	(Fredlo 6901)	1969

A late sixties outfit from Burlington, Iowa.

Compilation appearances include: *Lost* on *Mindblowing Encounters Of The Purple Kind* (LP) and *30 Seconds Before The Calico Wall* (CD); and *Psychedelic Pill* on *Hipsville, Vol. 3* (LP). (VJ)

Tyler Mudge

45:	Search For The Answer/I'll Bring You Back	(Onyx 3287)	1970

This psychedelic 45 was the work of a Massachusetts outfit. (GG)

Tyme

The members of this garage-punk combo all attended Northwestern Regional High School in Winsted, Connecticut. They recorded an acetate in 1966 which consisted of *Cry For The Trees* backed by *Land Of 1,000 Dances* but it got next to no airplay and with their recording career never taking off they concentrated on their popularity as a live band giving many of the hits of the era their own rather unique garage-punk interpretation. 22 years later *Land Of 1,000 Dances* made vinyl on *Back From The Grave, Vol. 7* (Dble LP). (VJ)

Tyme of Day

45:	Listen To What Is Never Said/ I Wanna Know	(Mercury 72861)	1968

Possibly a Texas outfit - this 45 was produced by Norman Petty. *Listen...* is a strange ditty about a father's advice to his son - it has some fuzzy noises but ain't yer normal garage fayre, interesting though. The flip is reedy garage-pop. (MW)

Tymes Children

45:	Take Me Back/Go To Him	(Panorama 38)	1966

Cool beat garage sounds from Salem, Oregon. *Take Me Back*, a cover of the David Clayton Thomas and The Shays track, is uptempo Invasion-infused beat. *Go To Him* is another version of the sullen beat ballad covered by the **London Knights**.

Compilation appearances include *Take Me Back* on *Northwest Battle Of The Bands, Vol. 1* (CD). (MW)

Tyrannies

45:     Little Girl/She's A Queen   (Watch 45 1903) 1965

Sultry garagey folk-rock, with a bow to the **Beau Brummels**, from June 1965. From Abita Springs, Louisiana. Check out *She's A Queen* on *Class Of '66!* (LP). (MW)

TAYLES - Who Are These Guys LP.

13th FLOOR ELEVATORS - Fire In My Bones LP.

13th FLOOR ELEVATORS - Elevator Tracks LP.

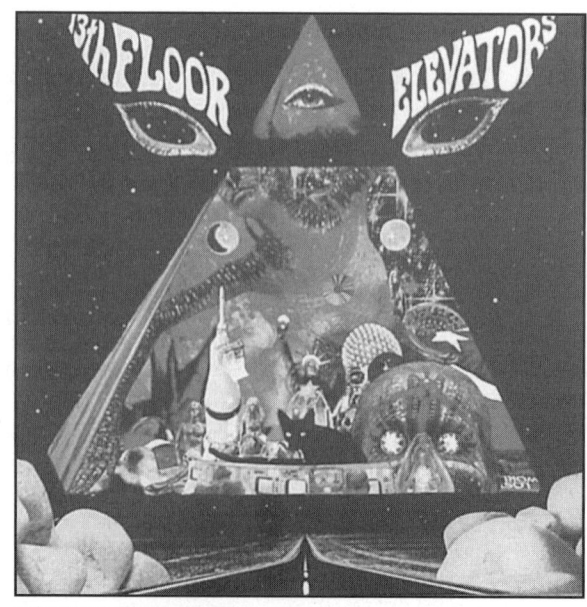

13th FLOOR ELEVATORS - The Original Sound Of LP.

13th FLOOR ELEVATORS - Live 1966 LP.

1004

Ultimates

Personnel:
	ALLEN CRAWFORD	bs, gtr	A
	GARY NIELAND	drms, vcls	A
	LEON SANDERS	ld gtr, vcls	A

45s:	My Babe/My Little Girl	(Lavender LR 2001) 196?
	Keep On Looking/Black Is Black	(Garland 2009) 1968

Formed by Sanders and Nieland, who'd been in The Champs, this combo were based in Salem, Oregon and were also known at various times as Prince Charles and The Crusaders and Dart. Nieland started his own Garland label and eventually dropped out of the group, The Lavender 45 is good no-frills Pacific Northwest garage punctuated throughout by rapid keyboard doodlings on a squeaky organ! (MW)

Ultimate Spinach

Personnel:
	IAN BRUCE-DOUGLAS	vcls	A
	BARBARA HUDSON	vcls, kazoos, gtr	AB
	KEITH LAHTEINEN	vcls, drms, perc	A
	RICHARD NESE	bs	A
	GEOFFREY WINTHROP	vcls, sitar, gtr	A
	JEFF BAXTER	ld gtr	B
	MIKE LEVINE	bs	B
	RUSS LEVINE	drms	B
	TED MYERS	gtr, vcls	B
	TONY SCHEUREN	keyb'ds, vcls	B
	(TOM CAULFIELD	bs, hrmnca	B)

			HCP
ALBUMS: 1(A)	ULTIMATE SPINACH 1	(MGM SE 4518) 1968	34 -
2(A)	BEHOLD AND SEE	(MGM SE 4570) 1968	198 -
3(B)	ULTIMATE SPINACH	(MGM SE 4600) 1969	- -

NB: (1) and (2) reissued on Polygram (Greek). (1) - (3) reissued on CD by Big Beat (CDWIKD 142, 148, 165 respectively). (1) - (3) reissued on CD as a box set, *The Box* (Akarma AK 121-3). The CDs here are 20-bit remastered and are re-sequenced in the original order of the tracks. On *Behold And See* the track *Visions Of Your Reality*, missing on ACE/Big Beat "director's cut" CD reissue, has been re-added. The box set includes a poster and a book with previously unpublished photos. (3) has also had a limited 'bootleg' vinyl repress. (1) reissued on vinyl (Akarma AK 119) 2001 with two mono tracks as bonus material. (2) reissued as a double LP with two mono tracks as bonus material (Akarma AK 120/2) 2001. (3) reissued on vinyl (Akarma AK 121) 2001.

45:	(Just Like) Romeo and Juliet/	
	Some Days You Just Can't Wait	(MGM 14023) 1969

Originally known as **Underground Cinema**, this band were discovered by producer **Alan Lorber**, who changed their name and signed them to MGM. Part of the emerging 'Bosstown Sound' of 1968, they were the brainchild of group member Ian Bruce-Douglas, who also wrote all the material on their first two albums. Barbara Hudson's beautiful voice gave the group a distinctive vocal sound.

Their debut album was a very trippy affair. The double fold-out cover contained highly pretentious sleeve-notes by Bruce-Douglas. This pretentiousness was evident, too, in the album's lyrics. For example, its opening track *Ego Trip* begins:

"Mindless creedence
Gropes through idiosyncrasies
Up - rising up
Down ... (echoes)"
(from *Ego Trip*)

and again at the beginning of the *Hip Death Goddess*, which captures Hudson's vocals at their best:

"See the glazed eyes
Touch the dead skin
Feel the cold lips
And know the warmth
Of the Hip Death Goddess".
(from *Hip Death Goddess*)

Instrumental numbers, like *Sacrifice Of The Moon*, sound similar to their equivalents on the early **Country Joe and The Fish** albums. The album is liberally endowed with wind chimes, bells and sound effects and the lyrics are tailored with flower power mythology:

"I saw a funny freak parade
Marching down the street
They were acting very strange
Kissing everybody they meet
With eyeballs hanging out of their eyes
And daffodils in their hands
Someone asked what's happening here?"
(from *Funny Freak Parade*)

The final track, *Pamela*, which has a similar wind chimes intro to **Country Joe**'s *Grace*, is intended to illustrate 'the intense beauty that can be seen and felt if one's senses are fully employed'. Once again acid was the inspiration behind those lyrics:

"Moonbeams and sapphires
Vibrate as one
I hear prisms
Crystal rainbows fill my sky
Shattered, they glisten
And blind the sun."
(from *Pamela*)

The album met with considerable commercial success peaking at No. 34 in the U.S. Album Charts.

ULTIMATE SPINACH - Ultimate Spinach I LP.

ULTIMATE SPINACH - Behold & See LP.

Their follow-up album, *Behold And See* was in a similar vein. The lyrics were less impressionable, though, and their music had become more mystical, particularly on the excellent *Genesis Of Beauty Suite* and *Fragmentary Marches Of The Green*. Other tracks like *Mind Flowers*, may be seen as an extension of themes from their earlier album. Once again, Barbara's vocals glisten with beauty. This reached No. 198 in the Album Charts. Be aware that on the Big Beat CD the tracks are resequenced and *Visions of Your Reality* has been dropped, leaving this track unissued on CD. Both albums are classic acid-rock period pieces and highly recommended, if one can excuse their more pretentious trappings.

Bruce-Douglas' departure after their second album had a profound effect on the band's musical direction. All the material on the third album, apart from the opening cut *Romeo and Juliet*, was written by the new band and lacked the imagination of Bruce-Douglas' work. For the third album, Jeff Baxter, who later had a spell with Steely Dan, came in on lead guitar and Ted Myers and Tony Scheuren joined from Boston label-mates **Chamaeleon Church**. Curiously, Mike Levine, who was listed as bassist didn't actually play on the record. Tom Caulfield who had been a lifelong pal of Mike's and who'd previously played for the soul group The Three Degrees, instead played impeccable bass and a super harp solo on *Eddie's Rush*, the blues jam that concludes Side One. Only Barbara Hudson remained from the original line-up, and although their final album is overall less interesting, it is still worth hearing.

Fans of the band may be interested in checking out neo-psych / acid-goth band **Babylonian Tiles** cover of *Hip Death Goddess*, which appears on the St. Thomas Records sampler CD *Saints & Sorcerers Vol. 2* - It's even been approved by Ian Bruce-Douglas as "fulfilling his vision of 'Hip Death Goddess' personified"... *Hip Death Goddess* has also been covered by Lithium X-Mas (on their *Bad Karma* and *Helldorado* CDs).

Ultimate Spinach also appear on a couple of compilations: the *The Best Of Bosstown Sound* (Dble CD) features *(Ballad Of) The Hip Death Goddess*, *Baroque #1*, *Fragmentary March Of Green*, *The World Has Just Begun*, *Happiness Child* and *Eddie's Rush*; and the *Family Circle - Family Tree* (CD) contains *Back Door Blues* and *Happiness Child*. (VJ/MS/JMe/MW)

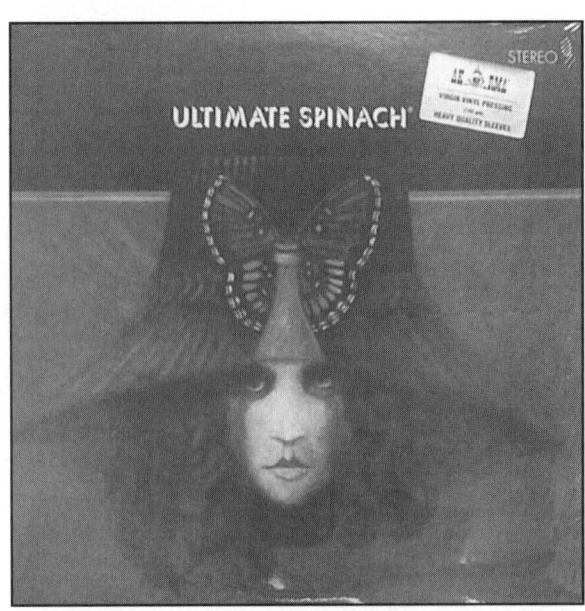

ULTIMATE SPINACH - Ultimate Spinach (3rd) LP.

The Unbelievable Uglies

Personnel incl:	BOB EVESLAGE	keybd's	A
	WINSTON FINK (DAVE HOFFMAN)	vcls, bs	A
	GREG PAUL	ld gtr	A
	DAVE PRENTICE	vcls	A
	MIKE SHANNON	drms	A
	MIKE GILSON		
	ALAN ST. PIERRE (ALAN SPEARS)	ld vcls	

45s:	α	Judy Angel/The Log	(Music Masters 72164)	1964
		Off My Hands/The Loner	(Cardinal 0071)	1965
		Keep Her Satisfied/Grand Central Station	(Soma 1451)	1965
		Sorry/Get Straight	(Liberty 55935)	1967
		Spider Man/Research Into The Soul Of Psychedelic Sound	(Independence 42767)	1967
		New Day/Wings	(Sound 80)	1967
		Ain't Gonna Eat My Heart Out/When The Saints	(UA 066)	1968
		The Tin Drum/Mrs Mouse Anthology	(UA 106)	1968
		Hello Gooday/Previews	(UA 292)	1969
		Mr. Skin/Little Lady	(Uglies Records 22985)	196?
		Right Road Now/Dolly	(Uglies Records 27444)	196?

NB: α released as **The Uglies**.

From Detroit Lakes in Northwest Minnesota they were one of the State's most popular live acts. Their shows were wild and unpredictable, centred around Winston Fink and their 45s are not too hard to find. Bobby Vee produced their fourth 45 and *Spider Man* which is usually considered to be their finest moment, is best described as an organ-led up-tempo punker.

Dave Hoffman and Mike Gilson later recorded an album and 45 with **Friendship**, whilst **Alan St. Pierre** also recorded a solo 45 in 1967. Bob Eveslage also released a 45 using the pseudonym **Robbie Jay** in 1966. All this underscores the depth of their musical talent.

Bob Eveslage now resides in New Ulm, Minnesota, and still writes and records music. He was the founding member of **The Unbelievable Uglies**:

"The other four original members were Dave Hoffman (Winston Fink) on stand-up electric bass, Greg Paul on lead guitar, Mike Shannon on drums, Dave Prentice (a very, very funny front man who worked hand-in-hand with Winston), and me on the keyboards. Al Spears was a later addition, and a very good R&B vocalist. Members came and went, but the five of us held the band together for about eleven years."

Bob also took a couple of years out of the group, when he moved to Seattle, "I was part owner of a studio and with a studio group called **Today** we had a single on Jerry Dennon's label called *We've Been A Bad, Bad Boy*. After a couple of years I came back to the **Uglies** and Minnesota. The original members are all still living in the Minnesota area and are doing different things. All but Greg are still involved with music as a profession."

Bob's most recent 45 was released in 1987 on the Clowd label, which was partly run by the late Fred Heggeness (the well-known record collector and author from Detroit Lakes). Entitled *You're The Only One (Patty's Song)* and written for his wife, it received quite a bit of airplay in the upper midwest. The flip was recorded by Dan Holt with Bob on backing instruments and was an old Ral Donner cover entitled *You Don't Know What You've Got (Until You Lose It)*.

Compilation appearances have included: *Spider Man* on *The Lost Generation, Vol. 2* (LP) and *The Midwest Vs. The Rest* (LP); *The Log* on *Mondo Frat Dance Bash A Go Go* (CD); *Research Into The Soul Of Psychedelic Sound* on *Sixties Rebellion, Vol. 15* (LP & CD) and *Everything You Always Wanted To Know...* (CD); *Keep Her Satisfied* on *The Big Hits Of Mid-America - The Soma Records Story* (Dble CD); and *Get Straight* on *Hipsville, Vol. 3* (LP). (VJ/MW/BEe)

The Uncalled For

45s:	Do Like Me/Get Out Of The Way	(Dollie 509)	1967
	Do Like Me/Get Out Of The Way	(Laurie 3394)	1967

This punk outfit hailed from Youngstown, Ohio.

Compilation appearances include: *Get Out Of The Way* on *Killer Cuts* (LP); *Do Like Me* on *Pebbles, Vol. 10* (CD), *The Essential Pebbles Collection, Vol. 1* (Dble CD), *Pebbles, Vol. 8* (LP); *Do Like Me* and *Get Out Of The Way* on *Mindrocker, Vol. 10* (Dble LP), *The Cicadelic 60's, Vol. 3* (CD), *The Cicadelic 60's, Vol. 5* (LP) and *Green Crystal Ties, Vol. 4* (CD). (VJ/MW)

Unchained Mynds

Personnel incl:	CLARE TROYANEK	bs	

45s:	We Can't Go On This Way/Goin' Back To Miami	(Trans Action 705)	c1968
	Hole In My Shoe/Warm Smoke	(Trans Action 707)	c1968/9

We Can't Go On This Way/ Goin' Back To Miami	(Teen Town 109)	c1968/9
We Can't Go On This Way/Goin' Back	(Buddah 111) 1969	115
Every Day/?	(Buddah 119)	1969
Everyday/You Me And My Yo-Yo	(Buddah 140)	1969

From LaCrosse, Wisconsin, this four-piece put out an interesting version of *Hole In My Shoe*, the Traffic classic, and made it altogether more garagey by sticking a fuzz lead on it as well as subtley fiddling with the middle break (no little lost girl vocals here), good and if you're one of the 100 owners of *Everywhere Chainsaw Sound* (LP), you can enjoy it thereon. Unfortunately their other output fails to match this although their cover of Wayne Cochran's *Goin' Back To Miami* is very dynamic and worth hearing. The group, or members of it at least, were billed to appear at the 'La Crosse Rock Reunion '91' gathering along with the TJ's, Johnny and The Shy Guys, Dave Kennedy and The Ambassadors, **Fax**, **Ladds**, Lost and Founds, **Hope**, **Marauders**, **Satisfactions**, Molly McGuires, Today's Tomorrow and local 'godfather of rock' - Lindy Shannon.

Clare Troyanek was a later member of **Ladds**. (MW)

Uncle and The Anteaters

Personnel incl:	LARRY BARRETT	vcls, gtr	A
	GARY HORRELL	bs	A

45s:	Kathy Ran Around/I Can't Go On	(Hunt 805) 1966
	Let's Be Happy/Lover Boy	(National 19241) 1967

This Iowa City outfit was fronted by Larry Barrett, the son of a major Midwest jazz musician and DJ, whose earlier band had been **The Countdowns**. Apparently the new **Uncle and The Anteaters** name was the suggestion of a drunk at a frat party! *Kathy Ran Around* has a typical mid-sixties Farfisa organ solo and sincere vocals, *Lover Boy* contains some nice layered harmonies and *Let's Be Happy*, a much slicker song than the other two, is an attempt at Turtles-style rock. All three songs have resurfaced on the *Dirty Water* (LP) compilation and are well worth a listen. Barrett was later in the **XL's** and Rox (a post-**Daybreakers** project).

Uncle Sam and The War Machine

Personnel incl:	GREG BULLEN	piano	A

45:	Spy Girl/ Hold On (comes with lyric sheet)	(Blue Onion BO-103) 1967/8

Uncle Sam and the War Machine were from Springfield/Amherst area of Massachusetts. Although how they came to record for a label based in Cleveland, Ohio is unknown. *Spy Girl* is an upbeat popper that's somewhere between garage and bubblegum sounds - it also borrows from *Wild Thing*. *Hold On* is a pleasantly haunting garage - folk-rocker.

Greg Bullen went on to found a band called **Bald Mountain Road**, consisting of blues and honky tonk. He was a killer piano player. **US & the WM** also once opened for **Frank Zappa** at Fillmore East. There were a lot of strange double bills in those days.

Compilation appearances include: *Spy Girl* on *The Magic Cube* (CD); and *Hold On* on *From The New World* (LP). (MW/JSr)

Uncle Willard

ALBUM:	1 JUST ONE MORE GOOD TIME	(Toya TSTLP-2004) 1972 -

From Illinois, a hippie-rock group with songs like *Dark Cloud* and *Welcome To The Army*. The small label Toya also released **Morninglory**. (SR)

The Undecided

45:	Make Her Cry/I Never Forgot Her	(Dearborn 542) 1966

A garage punk outfit from Michigan whose *Make Her Cry* is highly-rated by many, with great catchy vocals and typical "girl put-down" lyrics.

Compilation appearances have included: *Make Her Cry* on *Michigan Mayhem Vol. 1* (CD), *Mind Blowers* (LP), *Garage Punk Unknowns, Vol. 1* (LP); and *I Never Forgot Her* on *Highs In The Mid-Sixties Vol. 5* (LP). (VJ)

Underbeats

Personnel incl:	ROD EATON	drms	
	TOM NYSTROM	drms, vcls	
	JAY EPSTEIN	drms	G
	JAMES C. JOHNSON	ld gtr, vcls	G
	DONI LARSON	bs	G
	ENRICO "RICO" ROSENBAUM	gtr, vcls	G
	JAMES 'OWL' WALSH	keyb'ds	G

45s:	α	Footstompin' / Route 66	(Garrett 4004) 1964
	β	Annie Do The Dog / Sweet Words Of Love	(Garrett unconfirmed) 1964
		Annie Do The Dog/Sweet Words Of Love	(Bangar 00632) 1964
		Little Romance / Broken Arrow	(Bangar 00657) 1964
		Our Love / Jo Jo Gunne	(Twin Town TT 706) 1965
		Book Of Love / Darling Lorraine	(Soma 1449) 1966
		I Can't Stand It / Shake It For Me	(Soma 1458) 1966
		It's Gonna Rain Today / Sweetest Girl In The World	(Metrobeat 4449) 1967
	χ	Darkness / You're Losing Me	(Pip 8909) c1968

NB: α and β released in Canada on Apex (76915 and 76937 respectively). χ as by the Underbeat.

One of the most popular outfits around Minneapolis in the mid-sixties, they produced several classy rockin' beat 45s. After several years as big fishes in the Midwest a wholesale change was undertaken - they relocated to California and became **Gypsy** (line-up 'G').

Compilation appearances have so far included: *Foot Stompin'*, *Sweet Words Of Love*, *Annie Do The Dog* and *Little Romance* on *The Big Hits Of Mid-America, Vol. 1* (LP); *Foot Stompin'*, *Book Of Love* and *I Can't Stand It* on *The Big Hits Of Mid-America - The Soma Records Story* (Dble CD); *Jo-Jo-Gunne* and *Foot Stompin'* on *Top Teen Bands, Vol. 1* (LP) of the sixties Minneapolis sampler series, *Broken Arrow* on *Top Teen Bands, Vol.2* (LP) and *Route 66* on *Top Teen Bands, Vol. 3* (LP); *Annie Do The Dog* on *It's Finkin' Time!* (LP); Four unreleased tracks from 1965 - *Love To You*, *Don't You Lie To Me*, *Fate Of A Fool* and *Wishes Don't Come True* - on *Free Flight (Unreleased Dove Recording Studio Cuts 1964-'69)* (Dble LP); *I Can't Stand It* on *Monsters Of The Midwest, Vol. 2* (LP); *Shake It For Me* on *Soma Records Story, Vol. 1* (LP); *It's Gonna Rain Today* on *The Best Of Metrobeat! Vol. 1* (LP); *Born In Chicago* on *Roof Garden Jamboree* (LP); and *Sweetest Girl In The World* on *Money Music* (LP). (MW)

The Underdogs

		HCP
45s:	Man In The Glass/ Friday At The Hideout (Judy Be Mine)	(Hideout 1001) 1965 -
	Man In The Glass/ Friday At The Hideout (Judy Be Mine)	(Reprise 0422) 1965 -
	Little Girl/Don't Pretend	(Hideout 1004) 1966 -
	Little Girl/Don't Pretend	(Reprise 0446) 1966 -
	Surprise Surprise/ Get Down On Your Knees	(Hideout 1011) 1966 -
	Love's Gone Bad/Mo Jo Hanna	(VIP 25040) 1966 122

A popular sixties band from Grosse Pointe, one of the richer Detroit suburbs, in Michigan. They were one of the top live attractions at the Hideout teen club which was run by local promoters Dave Leone and Ed 'Punch' Andrews. To promote them further Dave Leone decided to put them onto vinyl. He got a poem from a 'friend', put it to music and the result, *Man In The Glass* was issued as the first 45 on Hideout. It was energetically promoted and picked up by Reprise for national distribution, but when Leone later discovered the lyrics were taken from a poem used at Alcoholics Anonymous he had to stop plugging it.

In 1965, the Hideout club label issued the sampler album *Best Of The Hideouts* (Hideout 1002), which saw a limited vinyl reissue in 1990 - it features *Friday At The Hideout*, *Man In The Glass*, *Surprise Surprse* and *Get Down On Your Knees*.

Thereafter, they became the first white act to sign for Motown. *Love's Gone Bad* issued on the VIP subsidiary was quite popular cover of the Chris Clark composition and actually made No. 122 in the U.S. Charts.

Other compilation coverage has so far included: *Get Down On Your Knees*, *Don't Pretend*, *The Man In The Glass*, *Friday At The Hideout* and *Surprise, Surprise* on *Best of Hideout Records* (CD); *Love's Gone Bad* on *Nuggets Box* (4-CD) and *Nuggets, Vol. 6 - Punk* (LP); *Man In The Glass* and *Love's Gone Bad* on *Michigan Brand Nuggets* (Dble LP) and *Michigan Nuggets* (CD); *Friday At The Hideout* and *Don't Pretend* on *Highs In The Mid-Sixties, Vol. 6* (LP); and *Surprise, Surprise* on *Highs In The Mid-Sixties, Vol. 5* (LP). (VJ/MW)

The Underground

ALBUM: 1 PSYCHEDELIC VISIONS
(Mercury Wing WC-16337) 1967 R1

On this album a group of unknown musicians do fuzzed-up instrumental cover versions of classics like *Psychotic Reaction*, *Tobacco Road* and *We Ain't Got Nothing Yet*, along with a few originals like *Psychedelic Dream*, *Mind Jammer* and *Psychedelic Visions* (which are all written by Merk Currie). It's not a bad album.

There was also a different outfit of this name who released two 45s on Mainstream:-

45s:	Easy/Satisfy'n Sunday	(Mainstream 660) 1966
	Get Him Out Of Your Mind/ Take Me Back	(Mainstream 667) 1966

Compilation appearances include *Psychotic Reaction* on *Relics, Vol's 1 & 2* (CD) and *Relics, Vol. 1* (LP). (VJ/MW)

Underground All-Stars

Personnel: anonymous   A

ALBUM: 1(A) EXTREMELY HEAVY   (Dot DLP 25964) 1969 SC

Produced by **Kim Fowley** and housed in a magnificent Rick Griffin skull cover, this album contains covers of Beatles songs (*Get Back*, *Norwegian Wood*), a Dylan track (*I'll Be Your Baby Tonight*), plus Stax material (*Grab This Thing*, *Don't Fight It*, *The Hunter*, *You Don't Know Like I Know*) and *Louie Louie*. The only original song is **Fowley**'s *Happy Meadow Trail Dance*. **Kim Fowley** sings on some tracks. (CF/SR)

THE UNDERGROUND - Psychedelic Visions LP.

Underground Balloon Corps

45s:	(Heart) Made Of Soul / Grass In Grenner	(Scope XX1/2) 1967
	Where Can I Go / The Musicians	(Music Factory 101) 1971?

A Pennsylvania outfit previously known as **The Snaps** and later the **Balloon Corps**. It's not confirmed yet that the second 45 shown above is the same group.

Compilation appearances include *(Heart) Made Of Soul* on *Let's Dig 'Em Up, Vol. 3* (LP) and *Let's Dig 'Em Up, Vol. 1* (CD). (MW)

Underground Cinema

Personnel incl:	IAN BRUCE-DOUGLAS	A
	SKIP TULL	A

Myths have abounded about a pre-**Ultimate Spinach** outfit thought to have been known as **Underground Cinema**. In 1996 Arf! Arf!'s *New England Teen Scene Unreleased 1965 - 68* CD finally uncovered some proof - two 7" acetates featuring *Blackbird*, *Sunday Morning*, *Where Has Time Gone To* and *Moondog Blues* (the first three appear on the CD).

Recorded at AAA studios in Dorchester, Mass. by Bruce-Douglas, Tull and others in 1967, a set of the acetates survived thanks to Al Lorusso (of **The Bourbons**). They were given to him in appreciation of his loan of equipment for the session. Whether they used the name **Underground Cinema** is still unconfirmed. Other musicians rumoured to be involved include guitarists Richie Bartlett (**Brother Fox and Tar Baby**, the Fools) and Steven Cataldo (**Saint Steven**, Nervous Eaters) who recorded as the **Front Page Review** around the same time. (MW/ELn)

Underground Electrics

ALBUM: 1 HEY JUDE   (Crown CST 588) 1968/9 SC

Another exploito-album from the budget label that issued **The (Electric) Firebirds**, aka **31 Flavors** - and this too is rumoured to be the same band.

The contents bear little resemblance to the sleeve - a paisley-bedecked hippie chick sitting cross-legged with arms aloft. After the Beatles' cover with plastic beaker vocals, the remainder is a strong selection of heavy blues-rock in the style of Cream and Led Zeppelin's first album, exploiting the legacy of the likes of Robert Johnson, John Lee Hooker and Elmore James (*Crossroads*, *Boogie Chillun* and *Dust My Blues*). (MW)

The Underground Railroad

Personnel:	JIM BONAPARTE	vcls, hrmnca	A
	PAUL KERRIGAN	drms	A
	SAL PULLIA	bs	A
	TOM PULLIA	ld gtr	A
	DAVID THOMPSON	keyb'ds, vcls	A

45s:	You Do Something To Me/ A Lilly For Willy	(Littleton 999) 1966/7
	I'm Coming Over/Sixteen Tons	(Musicor 419) 1967

Previously thought to be from Littleton, New Hampshire, but actually from Brockton, Massachusetts. Their first 45 is garage, but the second, is much heavier with lots of fuzz. (AH/JNa/MW)

Underground Sunshine

Personnel:	BERT KOHL (KOELBL)	bs	AB
	FRANK KOHL (KOELBL)	drms	AB
	JANE LITTLE (WHIRRY)	keyb'ds	AB
	REX RHODE	gtr	A
	CHRIS CONNORS (JOHN DAHLBERG)	gtr	B
	MIKE HOOLIHAN	bs	
	DAVE WAYNE (WAEHNER)	keyb'ds	

UNDERGROUND ELECTRICS - Hey Jude LP.

			HCP
ALBUM:	1(B) LET THERE BE LIGHT	(Intrepid 74003) 1969	161 -

			HCP
45s:	Birthday / All I Want Is You	(Earth 100) 1969	26
	Don't Shut Me Out/ Take Me, Break Me	(Intrepid 75012) 1969	102
	Nine To Five (Ain't My Bag)/ Rotten Woman Blues	(Intrepid 75019) 1970	-
	Jesus Is Just Airight/Six O'Clock	(Intrepid 75029) 1970	-

Connors and Little were both from Montello, Wisconsin, whilst the other two members were German. They first attracted attention when their cover of Lennon-McCartney's *Birthday* made the U.S. Top 30. Their album has become a minor collectors' item and actually made No. 161 in the U.S. Album Charts back in 1969. *9 To 5 (Ain't My Bag)* also appears on *I'm Trippin' Alone* (LP).

Their full story is told in 'Do You hear That Beat' (Hummingbird, 1994, ISBN 0-9643073-9-1) by Gary Myers, who provided the personnel details above. (VJ/MW)

Under New Management

ALBUM:	1 UNDER NEW MANAGEMENT	(Fourmost FM-7221CS) c1970 ?

An obscure mellow pop-psych with male/female vocals and some horns on tracks like *Step Out On The Sea* or *There's A Light Within Me*. The album is of interest mostly for the anti-cult number *Forget Your Hexagram* and the fuzzy version of *Mother Freedom*.

Fourmost also released an album by the **Trust Company**. (SR)

The Underprivileged

Personnel incl:	BRUCE BERNSTEIN	ld gtr	A

45:	You Hurt Me/Come On	(Smash 2051) 1966

An obscure band from Illinois. Both sides of their 45 are catchy garage and can also be found on *Sixties Rebellion, Vol. 4* (LP & CD). Their lead guitarist also played with **The Krums**.

The Undertakers

Personnel:	GARNER FIELDING	A
	WALLY HUBER	A
	MIKE JOHNSON	A
	LANNIE LONG	A
	DONNIE REA	A
	JOHN URENDA	A

45:	Unchain My Heart/It's My Time (PS)	(Studio 7101) 1965

This was another of Texas' classic punk 45s. The 'A' side, a Ray Charles cover, is a classic punk version, whilst the flip is in a garage-psych vein. From Amarillo, Texas, the 45 was recorded at the Cox studios in Amarillo.

Compilation appearances have included: *Unchain My Heart* on *Off The Wall, Vol. 1* (LP), *Texas Psychedelic Punk, Vol. 11* (Metal Acetate #4), *Flashback, Vol. 3* (LP) and *Texas Flashbacks, Vol. 3* (LP & CD); and *Unchain' My Heart* and *It's My Time* on *Sixties Archive, Vol. 2* (CD) and *Texas Punk Groups From The Sixties* (LP). (VJ)

The Undertakers

Personnel:	BOBBY CHURCH	A
	FRED DIETRICH	A
	RICK FORMAN	A
	LEE WARD	A

45s:	Searching/The Reason Why	(PH 110) 1967
	Love So Dear/Loneliness To Happiness	(PH 115) 1968

Garage beat-ballads out of Orlando, Florida. Charming but unexceptional and at least a year out-of-date by then. They also backed H. F. Gore on *No One Will Ever Know/Washington Report* (PH 117), a mediocre country recording.

Searching originally appeared on the local 1967 sampler *Bee Jay Demo, Vol. 2* (Tener 1014).

Retrospective compilation appearances have included: *Love So Dear* on *Pebbles, Vol. 17* (LP); and *Searchin'* on *Psychedelic States - Florida Vol. 1* (CD) and *Acid Dreams Vol. 2* (LP). (VJ/MW/JLh/RM)

The Undertakers

45:	Rosalyn / Double Shot	(Scene No #) 1966

NB: 'B' side is by **The Spirits**.

Thought to have been based in Hawaii thanks to their contribution of three tracks to the rare LP *Live At The Funnyfarm* (Scene 200) - *Rosalyn*, *Bye Bye Johnny* and *Stupid Girl*. Other artists featured thereon are the Casuals, Manchesters Spirits and Val Richards V.

Rosalyn has since appeared on *Diana's Rootin' Tootin' Wild Teenage Rock 'N' Roll Party!* (LP), *Teenage Shutdown, Vol. 14* (LP & CD) and on *Grab This And Dance!!!* (LP). (MW)

The Undertakers

Another **Undertakers** hailed from the Philadelphia area. They don't appear to have released any 45s but laid down two tracks at the Sound Plus Studios in 1967 which were preserved on a Frankfort/Wayne acetate - *Can't Break Away* and *Little Girl*.

Compilation appearances include *Little Girl* on *Crude PA, Vol. 2* (LP). (MW)

The Undesyded

45:	Baby, I Need You / Freedom Of Love	(Reading R-666) 1968

From Reading, Pennsylyvania.

Compilation appearances have included: *Baby, I Need You* on *Psychedelic Unknowns, Vol. 9* (CD) and *Realities In Life* (LP); and *Freedom Of Love* on *Pebbles, Vol. 2* (CD). (MW)

The Unfolding

Personnel:
DAVID DALTON	vcls	A
GARY	drms	A
STEVE KAPOVITCH	narrator	A
KEN	ld gtr, bs	A
PETER	ld gtr, gtr	A
ANDREA ROSS	vcls	A
VICTORIA SACKVILLE	soprano	A

ALBUM: 1(A) HOW TO BLOW YOUR MIND AND HAVE A FREAK-OUT PARTY (Audio Fidelity AFSD-6184) 1967 R2

NB: (1) also issued in Canada by Audio Fidelity. (1) has had a limited pirate repressing and reissued on CD (Head 3197) 1997.

Composed by David Dalton, this album has been likened to **The Deep** on a bad day and is recommended to those who find bad records great! Side One - Acid Rock - includes *Play Your Game*, which can also be found on the *Echoes In Time, Vol. 1* (LP) and *Echoes In Time Vol's 1 & 2* (CD). Side Two - Meditations - is really weird, full of strange chantings on tracks like *Prana* (an excerpt from this is the 'Bonus track' on *Pebbles, Vol. 3* (LP)); *Electric Buddha*; *Hare Krishna*; and *Parable*. The album came with a booklet of freaky suggestions to make your party swing. (VJ/MW)

The Union

Personnel incl?:
STEVE HITT	A
J. KRETZSCHMAR	A
S. LYNCH	A

45s:
I Sit And Cry / Thinking Of You	(Orbit 1115)	1967
I Sit And Cry / Thinking Of You	(Radel 108)	1967
Love?? / Good Things (Are Sure To Come)	(Radel 109)	1967
Good Things / To Be Unkind	(UME 101)	1968

A Houston band, whose forte was bright 'n' bouncey beat-pop with good harmonies as on the Orbit and Radel 45s. The exception is *Love??*, written by Steve Hitt, is rather special. This is a trippy garage-ballad with a droning quality, on a frequency that can precipitate goosebumps, doomy chimes and haunting **Cryan' Shames**-like backing vocals. Both 45s were produced by Ray Dale Boynton (any relation to Amos?). (MW)

The Union Gap

Personnel incl:
DWIGHT BEMENT	sax	A
KERRY CHATER	bs	A
GARY PUCKETT	vcls, gtr	A
PAUL WHEATBREAD	drms	A
GARY WITHEM	keyb'ds	A

ALBUMS: HCP
1(A)	WOMAN WOMAN	(Columbia 9612)	1968	22 -
2(A)	YOUNG GIRL	(Columbia 9664)	1968	21 -
3(A)	INCREDIBLE	(Columbia 9715)	1969	20 -
4(A)	THE NEW ALBUM	(Columbia 99351)	1969	50 -
5(A)	GREATEST HITS	(Columbia 1042)	1970	50 -
6(A)	LADY WILLPOWER	(Columbia 31184)	1971	- -

NB: (2) - (5) also released in England by CBS.

45s: HCP
Woman, Woman/Don't Make Promises	(Columbia 44297)	1967	4
Young Girl/I'm Losing You	(Columbia 44450)	1968	2
Lady Willpower/Daylight Strangers	(Columbia 44547)	1968	2
Over You/If The Day Would Come	(Columbia 44644)	1968	7
Don't Give In To Him/Could I	(Columbia 44788)	1969	15
This Girl Is A Woman Now/ His Other Woman	(Columbia 454967)	1969	9
Let's Give Adam And Eve Another Chance/ The Beggar	(Columbia 45097)	1970	41
α I Just Don't Know What To Do With Myself/ All That Matters	(Columbia 45249)	1970	61
α Keep The Customer Satisfied/ No One Really Knows	(Columbia 45303)	1971	71
α Shimmering Eyes/ Life Has It's Little Ups And Downs	(Columbia 45358)	1971	-
α Hello Morning/Gentle Woman	(Columbia 45438)	1971	-
α Hello Morning/I Can't Hold On	(Columbia 45509)	1971	-
α Bless The Child/ Leavin' In The Morning	(Columbia 45678)	1972	-

NB: α by Gary Puckett and The Union Gap.

From San Diego, California, but named after a town in Washington State, **The Union Gap** was a commercially successful pop-rock group in the same style as the **American Breed** or the later **Paul Revere and The Raiders**. Like this band, they were also wore old army uniforms and their lead singer gradually took the control of the group, who after 1969 became known as "Gary Puckett and The Union Gap". Their finest moments were *Young Girl* and *Lady Willpower*, which showcased Puckett's superb vocals.

The band evolved out of **The Outcasts**. (SR/VJ)

The Uniques

Personnel:
MIKE LOVE	drms	AB
RAY MILLS	ld gtr	AB
BOBBY SIMS	gtr	A
BOBBY STAMPLEY	bs	AB
JOE STAMPLEY	vcls, keyb'ds	AB
JIM WOODFIELD	gtr	B
RONNIE WEISS	gtr	

ALBUMS:
1(A)	UNIQUELY YOURS	(Paula LPS 2190)	1966	-
2(A)	HAPPENING NOW	(Paula LPS 2194)	1967	-
3(B)	PLAYTIME	(Paula LPS 2199)	1968	-
4(B)	THE UNIQUES	(Paula LPS 2204)	1969	-
5(-)	GOLDEN HITS	(Paula LPS 2208)	1970	-

45s: HCP
Not Too Long Ago/Fast Way Of Living	(Paula 219)	1965	66
Too Good To Be True/Never Been In Love	(Paula 222)	1965	-
Lady's Man/Bolivar	(Paula 227)	1965	-
Strange/You Ain't Tuff	(Paula 231)	1966	-
All These Things/Tell Me What To Do	(Paula 238)	1966	97
Run And Hide/Goodbye, So Long	(Paula 245)	1966	126
Please Come Home For Xmas Part 1/Part 2	(Paula 255)	1966	
Areba/Groovin' Out	(Paula 264)	1966	
Every Now And Then (I Cry)/ Love Is A Precious Thing	(Paula 275)	1967	
Go On And Leave/(flip by different act)	(Paula 289)	1967	-
It's All Over Now/All I Took Was Love	(Paula 299)	1968	-
It Hurts Me To Remember/I Sure Feel More (Like I Did When I Got Here)	(Paula 307)	1968	-

UNITED SONS OF AMERICA - Greetings From U.S. Of A. LP.

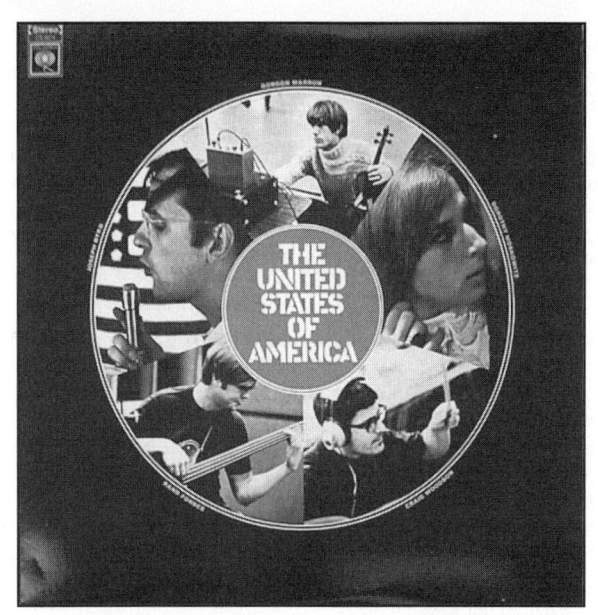

THE UNITED STATES OF AMERICA - The United States Of America LP.

How Lucky Can One Man Be?/
You Don't Miss Your Water (Paula 313) 1968 115
Sha-la Love/You Know (That I Love You) (Paula 320) 1970 -
Toys Are Made For Children/My Babe (Paula 324) 1970 105
All These Things/
You Know That I Love You (Paula 332) 1970 112
All These Things/You Know That I Love You (Paula 417) 1976 -

A pop-punk outfit from Louisiana and Texas who enjoyed some national chart success. Ronnie Weiss was later briefly involved with the band after his spell in **Rio Grande** before reforming **Mouse And The Traps**. Joe Stampley later became a country star. *You Ain't Tuff* a track from their first album, has resurfaced on *Mindrocker, Vol. 6* (LP), *Nuggets, Vol. 12* (LP) and *Nuggets Box* (4-CD). (VJ)

United Gas

See the **Christopher** entry.

The United Nations

| Personnel incl: | BILL M. ARCHIBALD | | A |
| | ROBERT ECONOMOUS | | A |

45: In My Dreams/Cause I Love You (Cha Cha 771) 1966

Soft Invasion-beat sounds from this Chicago outfit whose *In My Dreams* unashamedly borrows a couple of melody lines from The Beatles' *You Won't See Me*. Pleasant, but not for the fuzz'n'farfisa fanatic.

Robert Economous sadly passed away in 1993 from lung cancer, aged 48. (MW)

The United Sons Of America

Personnel:	GERRY BLAKE	keyb'ds, vcls	A
	RICHARD FREEMAN	gtr	A
	MIKE HUESTIS	drms, perc	A
	JERRY RITCHEY	bs	A
	STEVE WOODS	vcls, perc	A

ALBUM: 1(A) GREETINGS FROM U.S. OF A. (Mercury SR 61312) 1970

A California group, their album is an efficient mixture of psychedelia and progressive rock with good guitars and keyboards and in the same vein as English groups like Spooky Tooth. The album came housed in a "Post Card like" sleeve.

Huestis and Blake had previously played in Bakersfield's legendary **Avengers**. (SR/MDo)

The United States of America

Personnel:	JOSEPH BYRD	electric harp, keyb'ds	ABC
	DOROTHY MOSKOWITZ	vcls	ABC
	MICHAEL AGNELLO		A
	STU BROTMAN	bs	A
	GORDON MARRON	electric violin	B
	RAND FORBES	bs	B
	CRAIG WOODSON	drms, perc	B

HCP
ALBUM: 1(A) THE UNITED STATES OF AMERICA
(Columbia CBS 9614) 1968 181 SC

NB: (1) originally issued with a brown paper bag outer cover. (1) reissued on Edsel (ED 233) 1987 and also reissued on CD (Edsel EDCD 541) 1997. There was also a 1992 Sony CD reissue with two bonus tracks.

As Joe Byrd (and The Field Hippies)
ALBUM: 1 THE AMERICAN METAPHYSICAL CIRCUS
(Columbia CBS 7317) 1969 SC

NB: (1) reissued on CD (One Way A-26792) 1996.

Joe Byrd, who master-minded this group of experimental California musicians, was born in Louisville, Kentucky. He is a descendant of the famous Byrd family of Virginia and he grew up in Tucson, Arizona. During high school years, he played in country-and-western and pop music bands, but by the time he entered the University of Arizona he had begun playing vibes with a jazz group.

After graduation, Byrd received Stanford University's Sollnit Fellowship for graduate study composition, but Byrd chose to split for New York, where he had already begun listening to electronic music and meeting far-out Berkelee composers. While there, he worked as a conductor, arranger, teacher and assistant to critic-composer Virgil Thompson. It was during this era that he developed his interest in experimental music and his works were often performed abroad.

Influenced by events in California in the late sixties, he decided to quit New York and head for the University of California at Los Angeles. Here he worked as a teaching assistant, also finding time to study acoustics, psychology and Indian music. He eventually dropped out of UCLA to work full-time on his musical enterprises. After working on **Phil Ochs**' *Pleasures Of The Harbor*, he put together **The United States Of America**, whose other main asset was vocalist (and Byrd's ex-girlfriend) Dorothy Moskowitz, who possessed possibly one of the most attractive singing voices in rock. Other original members included political radical Michael Agnello and bassist Stu Brotman but both left before the band signed to Columbia with Brotman joining **Kaleidoscope**.

The group's sole album was erratic but often brilliant, with Byrd and Moskowitz writing most of the music and lyrics between them. Opening track, *The American Metaphysical Circus* parodied Sergeant Pepper and the unusual, but commercial *I Won't Leave My Wooden Wife For You, Sugar* became well-known here in England by virtue of its inclusion on the CBS compilation *The Rock Machine Turns You On*.

Overall the album was one of the most successful attempts to marry experimental electronic music with rock lyrics. Instruments used included a Durrett synthesizer and Tom Oberheim's ring modulator, an electric violin and an unfretted bass. The beauty of the lyrics was matched by the excellence of Moskowitz's voice on tracks like *Cloud Song* and *Love Song For The Dead Che*.

Other tracks like *The Garden Of Earthly Delights* and *Coming Down* appear drug-inspired:

"Poisonous gardens, lethal and sweet
Venomous blossoms
Choleric fruit deadly to eat
Violet nightshades, innocent bloom
Omnivorous orchids
Cautiously wait, hungrily loom
You will find them in her eyes,
In her eyes, In her eyes"
(from *Garden Of Earthly Delights*)

"I think it's over now, I think it's ending
I think it's over now, I think it's ending
A thought of coloured clouds all high above my head
A trip that doesn't need a ticket or a bed
And everything is smelling sweeter than the rose"
(from *Coming Down*)

The album is a minor collectors' item, but has also been reissued. It climbed as high as No. 181 in the U.S. Album Charts when it was first released. The cover was originally planned to be an American flag dripping with blood but, understandably, Columbia bailed out of the idea.

Live, the band played an exact reproduction of the album but had trouble getting suitable gigs. One, in which they were paired with The Troggs, was an unmitigated disaster and they also had an ill-tempered coupling with **The Velvet Underground** (in fact, after leaving the **Velvets**, Nico tried to join the **USA**). In addition, tension between band members was rife, with Byrd, who the album's producer David Rubinson describes as "one of the most insane examples of a control freak that I've, to this day, ever experienced", attempting fruitlessly to dictate policy to the other strong personalities in the band. Every rehearsal became, in Byrd's words, "group therapy". When three of them were busted for marijuana at a gig in Orange County, California, only Byrd and Moskowitz remained and they soon split into two factions with each leading their own group.

After the group split, Byrd made a further album with a bunch of 12 musicians called The Field Hippies. Although not as successful as The USA album, this was a strange voyage into the world of mystical and quasi-religious music. Once again he found three female vocalists - Susan de Lange, Victoria Bond and Christie Thompson - with seductive voices. The lyrics often paralleled themes on the earlier album.

"Waitin' to die for the seventeenth time
Etched on a mirror in the back of your mind
Trapped on a mountain nobody can climb
You can't ever come down..."
(from *You Can't Ever Come Down*)

Susan de Lange's beautiful rendering of *Moonsong-Peloc* paralleled the *Cloud Song* on the earlier album. Victoria's beautiful *Patriot's Lullaby* was in similar vein, but unfortunately most of the material on Side Two failed to again the same standard.

Today, Joe Byrd is a recognised composer and arranger who plays electronic music, organ, electric harpsichord and, occasionally, calliope. In 1975, he released a synthesizer album, *Yankee Trancendoodle* and followed this with *Xmas Yet To Come* in 1980. In 1978, Byrd also co-produced Ry Cooder's *Jazz* album, with Stuart Brotman on bass.

Compilation appearances include *The Garden Of Earthly Delights* on *Psychedelic Dream: A Collection of '60s Euphoria* (Dble LP). (VJ/LP/SR)

The United Travel Service

Personnel incl: BEN HOFF

45s:	Wind And Stone/Drummer Of Your Mind	(Ridon 854) 1967
	Wind And Stone/Drummer Of Your Mind	(Rust R 5120) 1967
	Gypsy Eyes/Echo Of You	(Ridon 860) 1967/8

Folk-rockers from Seattle, Washington (also quoted as from Portland Oregon). They landed a distribution deal through the New York-based Rust label. Both sides of their first 45 are excellent soft psych-rock songs, *Wind And Stone* being a classic 'back to the wilds' theme song with a glorious spirit-lifting raga-esque break, and lyrics reflecting the rejection of "the plastic society". The *Gypsy Eyes* 45 contains two more melodic folk-rockers with the odd effect and is full of dewey-eyed romantic yearning.

Their first classic 45 has been heavily compiled. Both sides are included on *Psychedelic Moods - Part Two* (CD) and you can also find *Wind And Stone* on *Acid and Flowers* (CD), *Echoes In Time, Vol. 1* (LP), *Echoes In Time, Vol's 1 & 2* (CD) and *Highs In The Mid-Sixties, Vol. 16*. The flip, *Drummer Of Your Mind* also appears on *Sixties Punk Ballads Sampler* (LP) and *Sixties Archive, Vol. 5* (CD). (VJ/MW)

The Universal Ignorants

ALBUM: 1   TRANSITIONS   (WFB) 1968 R4

An excellent West Coast group in the **Jefferson Airplane** style. Unfortunately, the album was split with the Hilltones, a dissapointing folk group. (SR)

The Unknown

45:   Shake A Tail Feather/Night Walkin'   (SVR 1008) 1966

A Detroit, Michigan, band whose best known song *Shake A Tail Feather*, a popular number for sixties beat bands, can also be heard on *Highs In The Mid-Sixties, Vol. 5* (LP) and *S.V.R. Rock Hits Of The Sixties* (LP & CD). Both sides of the 45 also appear on *The Cicadelic 60's, Vol. 8* (CD). (VJ/MW)

The Unknown Kind

Personnel incl: BLECHEIR
                  BILL MARREN

45:   Who Cares/
      Since You've Come Back To Me   (Star Trek 3405/6) 1966

JOE BYRD and THE FIELD HIPPIES - The American Metaphysical Circus LP.

From Amherst, Ohio. *Who Cares*, a slow punker, can also be heard on *Highs In The Mid-Sixties, Vol. 21* (LP). This was their sole 45 and the label wasn't connected to any "Star Trek" labels around.

Bill Marren later played with **The Estes Brothers**. (VJ/GGI/MW)

The Unknowns

Personnel:	STEVE ALAIMO		A
	KEITH ALLISON		A
	MARK LINDSAY		A

			HCP
45s:	Melody For An Unknown Girl/Peat's Song	(Parrot 307) 1966	74
	Tighter/Young Enough To Cry	(Marlin 16008) 196?	-

Possibly responsible for other 45s on Shield and Master-W, this bunch of garagey-popsters are heavily linked to **Paul Revere and The Raiders** by virtue of **Keith Allison** and **Mark Lindsay** and their covering of **Raiders**' material. *Melody For An Unknown Girl* was a minor hit, spending four weeks in the Top 100.

Steve Alaimo was previously with the Redcoats and would later become a producer and manager, mainly working with Florida acts. He also issued tapes of **Duane and Greg Allman** on his label, Bold in 1971. (VJ/MW/SR)

The Unknowns

Personnel:	CHARLES COLLINS	ld gtr	A
	CLINTON COLLINS	bs	A
	MIKE DAVIES	organ	A
	TERRY LEDFORD	drms	A
	GEARY QUEEN	ld vcls	A

45:	A Kiss To Remember You By / Ballad Of A Useless Man	(Master "W" MW-1007) 1967

One of several bands in the mid-sixties with this self-deprecating name, their identites are belatedly revealed on *Psychedelic States: Georgia Vol. 1* (CD). It showcases their pumping lo-fi punker *Ballad Of A Useless Man* recorded in their hometown of Lawrenceville, Georgia.

The band formed in 1965 and lasted until 1968; they performed at local clubs, schools and colleges around Blue Ridge and competed in several Battles Of The Bands. (MW/RM)

The Unknowns

The "Unknowns" credited with a track christened *Outside Looking In* by the compiler of *Acid Visions, Vol. 2* (LP) and *Acid Visions - The Complete Collection, Vol. 1* (3-CD) are not unknowns at all. It's actually *Too Bad* by **The Bad Roads**. (MW)

The Unknowns

Another **Unknowns** from Corpus Christi, Texas have two unreleased 1967 tracks, likened to Todd Rundgren's **Nazz**, unearthed on *The History Of Texas Garage Bands, Vol. 5* (CD) - *All I Have To Do* and *Hard To Understand*. (MW)

The Unlimited

45:	Feelings / Gone Away	(Marina 504) 1966

This is actually the **Royal Flairs**, originally from Council Bluffs, Iowa.

Compilation appearances include *Feelings* on *The Midwest Vs. The Rest* (LP). (MW)

The Unrelated Segments

Personnel:	ANDY ANGELLOTTI	drms	A
	RORY MACK	ld gtr	AB
	RON STULTS	vcls	ABC
	JOHN TOROK	gtr, bs	ABC
	BARRY VAN ENGELEN	bs	A
	DARYL GORE	gtr	B
	CRAIG WEBB	ld gtr	C

ALBUMS:	1	SWAMP RATS/UNRELATED SEGMENTS	(Eva 12058) 198?
	2	WHERE YOU GONNA GO?	(Collectables COL 0710) 1998

NB: (1) split album with The Swamp Rats. (2) split CD with Tidal Waves.

45s:	Story Of My Life/It's Unfair	(HBR 514) 1967
	Where You Gonna Go/It's Gonna Rain	(Liberty 55992) 1967
α	Cry Cry Cry/It's Not Fair	(Liberty 56052) 1968

NB: *It's Unfair* and *It's Not Fair* are the same song. α recorded June '67.

A stunning outfit from Detroit, Michigan who may be the only band in history to take their name from economics jargon. Ron Stults had earlier been in a band called the High Tones who had opened for the Four Seasons in 1963. After they broke up, he joined classmate Rory Mack in the Village Beau's, but after their demise in September 1966, Rory invited him to be lead singer in a new band he was forming. This became **The Unrelated Segments**.

The band had only been together for about ten days when they recorded *Story Of My Life* on November 26th, 1966. The song, a rather interesting fast-tempo rocker, went top ten in Detroit and the '**Segments** became one of the more popular live acts in the City, playing gigs with **Bob Seger**, **Terry Knight and The Pack**, **SRC**, **Frost**, and the **MC5**. In 1968, they supported the Who in concert, with the **Amboy Dukes** opening for the show. Their second stunning single, *Where You Gonna Go?*, was unfortunately released the month of the Detroit race riots when the city was virtually shut down so sales were limited. After the release of their long-delayed third single, *Cry Cry Cry*, Andy was fired because of differences with the band's manager, Louis Torock (John's father). Six months later Barry was drafted and shipped out to Vietnam and the band changed their name to U.S. and recorded two songs, including the infectious *Hey Love* with its get down soul-groove. Shortly after, Rory decided to leave the music business for good and by the end of 1969 the band decided to call it quits.

All five of their compositions were composed by Mack (music) and Stults (lyrics) and are collected together on *S.V.R. Rock Hits Of The Sixties* (LP & CD) and on Eva's *Swamp Rats vs. Unrelated Segments* (LP) compilation. The Collectables CD, however, is the best compilation of their output, including all three of their singles, the two U.S. recordings, alternate

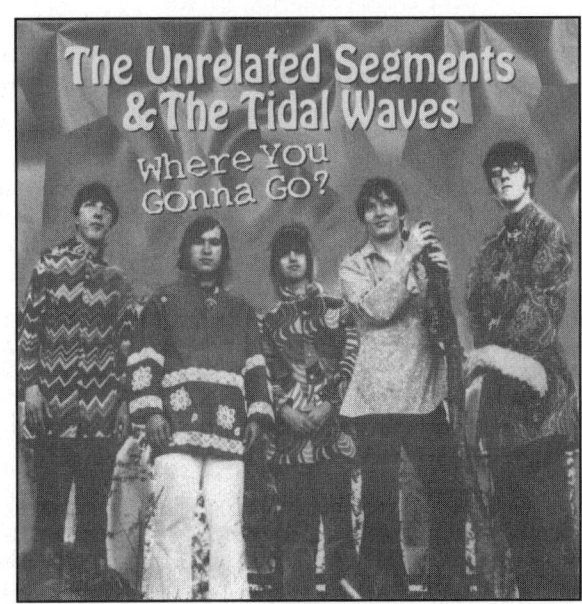

THE UNRELATED SEGMENTS - Where You Gonna Go? CD.

backing-tracks for three songs, five post U.S. Ron Stults tracks (sounding a lot like **Blue Cheer**), as well as six tracks by SVR stablemates, the **Tidal Waves** - all in excellent sound and with extensive sleevenotes and band photos.

Ron Stults went on to form the **Lost Nation** whose album *Paradise Lost* is pretty decent progressive rock. He now claims to have written over 2000 (!) songs.

Its Gonna Rain has been covered by eighties garage-psych act The Broken Jug on their *William* album.

Other Retrospective compilation appearances have included: *Cry Cry Cry* on *Let 'Em Have It! Vol. 1* (CD), *The Magic Cube* (Flexi), *Back From The Grave, Vol. 2* (LP) and *Garage Kings* (Dble LP); *Where You Gonna Go?* on *Michigan Nuggets* (CD), *Mayhem & Psychosis, Vol. 3* (LP), *Mayhem & Psychosis, Vol. 2* (CD), *Michigan Brand Nuggets* (Dble LP), *Nuggets, Vol. 6* (LP) and *Acid Dreams, Vol. 1* (LP); *Story Of My Life* on *Nuggets Box* (4-CD), *Nuggets, Vol. 12* (LP) and *Psychedelic Unknowns, Vol. 4* (LP & CD); *It's Unfair* on *Boulders, Vol. 10* (LP); *It's Gonna Rain* on *Gathering Of The Tribe* (LP); *Cry Cry Cry* and *It's Unfair* on *Acid Dreams - The Complete 3 LP Set* (3-LP) and *Acid Dreams Testament* (CD); *Story Of My Life* and *It's Unfair* on *A Journey To Tyme, Vol. 1* (LP); *It's Gonna Rain* and *Where You Gonna Go* on *Boulders, Vol. 9* (LP); and *The Story Of My Life* and *Where You Gonna Go* on *Green Crystal Ties, Vol. 8* (CD). (VJ/LP/MW)

Unsettled Society

45s:	17 Diamond Studded Cadillacs/ Passion Seed	(Charm 6084/85) 1970
	Gunfighter/Rainbows	(Charm 19985) 1971

From Pennellville, New York, although the sleeve notes to *Sixties Rebellion* have them down as Pennsylvania-based. Their *17 Diamond Studded Cadillacs* is well worth checking out, being full of feedback and fine fuzztone guitar work.

They later recorded as **Thunder Head**.

Compilation appearances include: *17 Diamond Studded Cadillacs* on *Psychedelic Experience, Vol. 2* (CD), *Pebbles, Vol. 2* (ESD) (CD), *The Psychedelic Experience, Vol. 2* (LP), *Endless Journey - Phase One* (LP) and *Endless Journey - Phase I & II* (Dble CD). (VJ/MW)

The Unspoken Word

Personnel:	GREG BUIS	bs, vcls	A
	ANGUS MacMASTER	keyb'ds	A
	DEDE PUMA	vcls	A
	LES SINGER	drms	A
	GENE-ZHENIA STASHUK	gtr, vcls	A

ALBUMS:	1(A)	TUESDAY, APRIL 19th	(Ascot AS 16028) 1968 -
	2(A)	THE UNSPOKEN WORD	(Atco SD 33-335) 1970 -

45s:	Boy / Nothing's Nothing	(United Artists 50083) 1966
	And It's Gone / On A Beautiful Day	(United Artists 50181) 1967
α	Anniversary Of My Mind / We're Growing	(Ascot 2244) 1967

NB: α withdrawn.

Probably from the East Coast, as their both albums were recorded in New York, home of the Ascot Label. Produced by Tony Michaels and Vinny Gormann and engineered by **Warren Schatz**, their first album is basically folk-rock with a hint of psychedelia with *Waking Up* one of its finest moments. A truly beautiful album - it's worth checking out for fans of this genre. All their songs were penned by the group.

Released two years later and produced by Shel Kagan, the second album is heavier and more rock-blues in style, but still contains some good tracks: *Sleeping Prophet*, *Personal Manager* (an Albert King cover) and *Sleepy Mountain Ecstacy*. The voice of Dede Puma, their female singer, is still really impressive.

In 1972, Gene Stashuk played cello on Bonnie Raitt's *Give It Up* album. The other members apparently vanished from the music scene. (VJ/MW/SR)

The Untamed

45:	Someday Baby/Lonely Boy	(Royal Scot 824 R-103) 1966

Came out of Chicago with this mid-sixties punk 45 which features some twangy guitar and a brief drum solo in the middle.

Compilation appearances include *Someday Baby* on *Off The Wall, Vol. 1* (LP), *Pebbles Vol. 6* (CD) and *Highs In The Mid-Sixties Vol. 4* (LP). (VJ)

The Untouchables

Personnel incl:	RON BRESLER	drms
	DICK DOUGLAS	gtr, vcls
	AL HUNTZINGER	drms
	TOMMY HANKINS	keyb'ds

45s:	Church Key/Danny Boy	(Hunt 450) 1962
	Come On Baby/Stick Around	(Hunt 1410) 1966

A quartet originally known as The Orphans and based in Cedar Rapids, who moved to Iowa City when promoter/drummer Al Huntzinger's original band **Al And The Untouchables** disintegrated. All four tracks have been collected together on the *Guts In The Garage* album (MCCM 9102) 1992 as by **Al's Untouchables**, which contains a detailed biography and history of the various incarnations of Al's outfits.

This was a loud guitar band.

Compilation appearances include *Come On Baby* on *Dirty Water* (LP).

Untouchables

45:	Baby Let's Wait / Don't Go I'm Beggin'	(Wasp 105) 1967

From Elma, Washington. This band's 45 on Wasp is fittingly tough buzzin' fuzz-garage, at least on the flip, and is featured on *Diggin' For Gold, Vol. 7*. The 'A' side is a **Young Rascals** cover.

Strangely another **Untouchables** 45 also features a **Young Rascals** cover too - *Love Is A Beautiful Thing / Now Is The Time* (Psychedelic 101) 196?, but it is not confirmed as being by the same group. (MW/MM)

THE UNSPOKEN WORD - Tuesday, April 19th LP.

(Kathi McDonald and) The Unusuals

Personnel incl:	VIC BUNDY	keyb'ds	AB
	BILL CAPP	gtr	AB
	PAT JERNS	drms	A
	KATHI McDONALD	vcls	AB
	HARVEY REDMOND	bs, vcls	AB
	LAURIE VITT	gtr	AB
	GARY RAMSEY	drms	B

45s:	α	Babe It's Me/I'm Walkin' Babe	(Panorama 23) 1965
		Summer Is Over/I Could Go On	(Mainstream 653) 1966

NB: α with Kathi McDonald.

From the Bellingham, Washington, this band evolved out of **The Bellingham Accents**. The second 45 features two strong West Coast ballads led by the particularly forceful female vocals of Kathi McDonald, whilst *I'm Walkin' Babe* is a snarling punker with vocals by Harvey Redmond.

Laurie Vitt recalls:- "I believe (but I'm not sure) that Jay Hamilton suggested the name **The Unusuals**. Jay was a local Bellingham DJ and we got to know him through dances that we played. By this time Kathi was in for a full cut and we had replaced Doug Ling with Harvey Redmond, a student at Western. Harvey was a much better musician and good singer. The first 45, *I'm Walking Babe* received almost no air play, but the flip side, *Babe It's Me*, a Sonny and Cher-like tune that Kathi and I did, was No. 1 in Bellingham for 26 weeks straight, but never got national attention."

"Between this record and *Summer Is Over*, we went on the road as a back-up band for **Dewey Martin** (pre-**Buffalo Springfield**). He had a hit at the time (*White Cliffs Of Dover*) and he and his band had been billed as British. **Dewey** was a good singer and a better drummer and I recall that he occasionally played drums while on the road. Eventually we dropped our drummer, Pat Jerns, and picked up a guy named Gary Ramsey. Gary Ramsey transformed from being a businessman-type manager of a steak house to a full blown hippie within about a year of joining the band. The story behind *Summer Is Over* was that we drove to San Francisco, recorded it at our expense and returned to Washington. Within a week, the owner of the studio called and said that Rene Cardenas of Time-Mainstream wanted the record but we would have to come down and re-record it, at their expense. So we went back, were ready to go the studio and then an airline strike stopped all commercial flights. Rene was stuck in New York. He bought a small jet and flew to San Francisco, we recorded the record and he auditioned a bunch of groups. The only two he picked up were us and **Big Brother and The Holding Company** - he liked our tapes better and released *Summer Is Over* within four weeks. It was a '4-star Pick' in Record World and got a lot of national play but never really took off."

"**The Unusuals** broke up in 1967 when Harvey and I graduated from Western. Harvey took a job teaching in Oregon and I got a job at a research lab in Seattle. Kathi and Gary Ramsey, meanwhile, drove to the Bay Area in Gary's psychedelic truck that we had all painted, in the hope of joining the Bay Area scene".

Gary had gotten pretty far out and as it turned out, he came back to Bellingham and when I went back to Western for a master's, I put together a bar band with Gary, Bill Capp plus a bass player. Gary got farther and farther out and eventually we fired him. I played with a number of bar bands while a master's student, including Clever Baggage, a 10-piece band that emulated **Chicago Transit Authority** (later Chicago), with Vic Bundy on keyboards. However, Boeing laid off thousands of people and the music market crashed in Washington so I ended up back with four-piece bands in Bellingham. When I moved to Arizona for graduate school, I first played in a soul band consisting of the remnants of Dyke and The Blazers, who reorganized after Dyke was gunned to death on the streets of Phoenix. I later played in several rock bands. Rainbow was the first and it consisted of me, Rod Pappas (gtr), a bass player who I can't remember, and Rob Rideout, the original drummer in the Bellingham band The Rebels. Shortly after we replaced the bass player with Charlie Moss who was very good. Rod and Rob decided to go to Seattle and left. Charlie and I got together with two former members of Hillary Blaze, formerly from New York and kept the name Rainbow. We did some recording but when Rod came back from Seattle, Charlie and I quit to team up with Rod and a drummer named David Newberry to form Mantis. Although the "Rainbow tapes" were never released, years later when the Hillary Blaze Drummer, Jimmy Tirella died, the other guitar player, Sandy Napoli, put together a CD and sent me a copy which he called the *Rainbow Tapes* but under the name Hillary Blaze as a tribute to Jimmy. Mantis became very popular in the bar scene in Arizona during the mid-seventies and we started recording an album. We released a single locally and it did pretty well (*Insane/Country Cowboy*). Our music was actually a bit heavy for Arizona at the time and I suspect that had we stuck together a couple more years, we would have done great (we did pretty well financially, playing six nights a week). I was balancing music with my graduate education. I quit when I was offered a post-doc in Brazil, essentially making a major career decision. I have played with no bands since, but still play my guitars virtually every day."

Kathi McDonald later found some fame in the 1970s after joining **Big Brother and The Holding Company**. Lauri Vitt is now Curator of Reptiles and Professor of Zoology at Sam Noble Oklahoma Museum of Natural History.

Compilation appearances have included *I'm Walkin' Babe* on *History Of Northwest Rock, Vol. 2* (CD) and *Highs In The Mid-Sixties, Vol. 16* (LP). (GGI/MW/LV)

Unusuals

45:	Because Of Love /	
	Take Time ...(incomplete title)	(Emerald 112) 196?

A South Carolina band whose 45 is unheard but has been seen described as mid-tempo garage. (MW)

Unusual We

ALBUM:	1	UNUSUAL WE	(Pulsar 10608) 1969 ?

This obscure album is now of interest to some collectors. (VJ)

Up

Personnel:	FRANK BACH	ld vcls	AB
	VIC PERAINO	drms	A
	BOB RASMUSSEN	ld gtr	AB
	GARY RASMUSSEN	bs	AB
	SCOTT BAILEY	drms	B

ALBUM:	1	KILLER UP! 1969-1972	(Total Energy NER 3002) 1995

NB: (1) is a 10" retrospective compilation also issued on CD (NERCD 3002).

45s:	Just Like An Aborigine/	
	Hassan I Sabbah	(Sundance 22190) 1970
	Free John Now!/Prayer For John Sinclair	(Rainbow 22191) 1971

Formed in Detroit in the Spring of 1967 by Frank Bach, who was stage manager and announcer at the newly-opened Grande Ballroom, where the **MC5** were "house band". The two bands were closely related, taking an active part in the John Sinclair-managed commune, variously known as the Detroit Artists' Workshop, Trans-Love Energies or the White Panther Party (WPP). When after the assassination of Martin Luther King, the commune moved to Ann Arbor in May 1968, the band followed, playing many engagements and often opening for the **MC5** or sometimes as a main attraction at local clubs and ballrooms. In Ann Arbor **Up** replaced Vic Peraino with Scott Bailey and continued to roll under the guidance of John Sinclair's brother David.

The **MC5** and **Stooges** fans certainly remember the story about the seminal September '68 visit by Elektra Records president Jac Holzman who signed both bands after a wild show at the Union Ballroom. The opening act that failed to impress him were **Up**. As a result, while the two other bands started releasing nationally, **Up** got stuck in local small venues. Eventually, after the **MC5** broke with the commune's ideals, they became the primary propaganda medium for the White Panther Party, following J.Sinclair's imprisonment in July 1969 for possession of two marijuana cigarettes. They disbanded in 1973.

Their retrospective album features both 45s, live and unreleased material. *Just Like An Aborigine* is a stand-out track recalling rather late seventies British punk than the Detroit vein (but inexplicably suffers from poor hollow sound). The flip is not as exciting but features a mighty bass riff not dissimilar to Metallica's *Enter Sandman*. The second 45, as the titles suggest, was one of the efforts for the release of J. Sinclair. Actually, it was given away for free at the John Sinclair Freedom Rally in December 1971. The flip, which features **Allen Ginsberg**'s melodic recitation, was recorded by the poet himself in N.Y. without the band's assistance (added as bonus track on CD). The album also features *Come On* planned for the A-side of their next 45.

Judging by the rest of the material, musically they landed within the triangle drawn by the **MC 5**, the **Stooges** and **Blue Cheer** but without losing their clear-cut original style. There are also two '69 studio tracks *I Don't Need You* and *Never Say Die* sporting killer riffs that are pretty close to early Sub Pop grungy sound. John Sinclair was right when he wrote this to begin the liner notes: "It's common to name the MC5 and the Stooges among the forefathers of what they call punk-rock, but it was their associates in a third band, the Up, who could more accurately be identified as the real precursors of punk."

Compilation appearances include: *Just Like An Aboriginie* on *Let 'Em Have It! Vol. 1* (CD); and *Just Like An Aborigine* and *Hassan I Sabbah* on *Michigan Mixture, Vol. 1* (LP). (MO/VJ)

Up 'N Adam

45:	(Time To) Get It Together/Rainmaker	(Earth)	c1968

Another obscure rock group, possibly from Tennessee. (SR)

The Upper Class

45s:	Can't Wait/Help Me Find A Way	(Charay 68)	1967
	Can't Wait/Help Me Find A Way	(Smash S-2096)	1967
	Anything You Like/Renee	(Limetree 1001)	1967
	Renee/Wow	(Charay 81)	1967

This band were thought to have come from the Dallas-Fort Worth area of Texas. (VJ)

The Upper U District Singers

Personnel incl:	ALICE STUART	vcls		A

45:	Sing Hallelujah/Green Satin	(Jerden 725)	1964

This had been suggested to us as one of the earliest folk-rock 45s from the Northwest, however George Gell has informed us that it is a vocal group with little to recommend it.

The band is however notable for featuring **Alice Stuart**, who later had a solo career recording an album in Berkeley, California *All The Good Times* (Arhoolie) July 1964. She still performs locally in the Seattle area, though her music has moved largely from folk to blues.

The "U. District" in the band name refers to an area adjacent to the University of Washington in Seattle. The flipside, *Green Satin*, was written by Frank Lewis and produced by Jerry Denon. It is a pleasant folky number. (VJ/MW/ANH)

The Uprisers

45:	Let Me Take You Down / Nine To Five	(Swingtown 791)	1967

From Richmond, Virginia, their *Let Me Take You Down* was included on *Garage Punk Unknowns, Vol. 8* (LP). (VJ/MW)

Upsetters

45:	Autumn's Here / Draggin' The Main	(Autumn 4)	1964

Embryonic San Francisco sounds and one of the early release on Tom Donahue and Bobby Mitchell's pioneering Autumn label. *Draggin' The Main* combines surf and hot-rod street-cred with 12-string guitar and can be heard on *Dance With Me - The Autumn Teen Sound* (CD). Compiler Alec Palao notes that the track also turned up on tapes marked as by the Dreamers and the Impax - alternative names for this unknown outfit, perhaps? (MW)

Up-Stairs

Personnel:	JIM FLYNN	bs	A
	PAUL NEBEL	drms	A
	DAVE PETERSON	gtr	A
	TOM SUMNER	ld gtr	A
	CURT JOHNSON	organ	
	HOWIE MARKET	drms	

45s:	α Boney Maronie / I've Had It	(Cuca 6542)	1965
	α Things We Said Today /		
	What's The Use Of Love	(Sara 6583)	1965
	Operator Please / Be My Baby	(Cuca 1309)	1967

NB: α as The Jaguars.

From Chippewa Falls, Wisconsin, this band started out in 1963 as The Jaguars and released three 45s, by the last of which they'd changed their name to the decidedly more hip **Up-Stairs**.

Their catchy *Operator Please* can be heard on *Psychedelic Unknowns, Vol. 9* (CD). (GM/MW)

Uranus and The Five Moons

45:	Your Groove/Mimi Von Lark	(Gotcha Co 2048)	196?

Very pleasant soulful beat-garage from New England - like the Zombies with a touch of the **Young Rascals**. Sadly, the flip is a corny vaudeville 'novelty' lark - kazoos, piano, plastic beaker vocals and all that dreck, prevalent in 1967-8. (MW)

Urban Renewal

45s:	Love Eyes / People	(St.George Int'l 202,270/1)	1969
	I Want To Walk To San Francisco/		
	Come Saturday Morning	(Paramount PAA-0022)	1970

From Chelmsford, Massachusetts, this pop group covered **Phluph**'s *Love Eyes* on their debut. The second 45 is orchestrated male-female MOR harmony-pop. (MW)

Ursa Major

Personnel:	GREG ARAMA	bs	A
	RICKY MANGONE	drms, vcls	A
	DICK WAGNER	gtr, vcls	A

ALBUM:	1	URSA MAJOR	(RCA LSP-4777)	1972 SC

NB: (1) counterfeited on CD (SPM) 199?. Also reissued officially on CD, from the master tapes (Pearls From The Past PFTP-UM1) 1994.

From Michigan, a rather uninspired and pompous hard-rock album with the former leader of **Frost** and the **Amboy Dukes** bassist. **Wagner** would later work with Lou Reed and Alice Cooper as well as releasing a solo album aptly titled *Richard Wagner*(Atlantic 19172) 1978. Lovers of the "other" Richard Wagner must have been surprised if they bought this album!! (SR)

US

Personnel:	MIKE COLVIN	organ	A
	SID GASNER	gtr	A
	BARRY GILLESPIE	vcls, hrmnca	A
	GREG HAMMEL	drms	A

US 69 - Yesterdays Folks LP.

TOM KRAUSE	vcls		A
MONTE KRISTO	vcls		A
DAN UTPADEL	bs		A

45: Somewhere In The Morning/You Say (PS)   (Hour 9-31137) 1967

An Owatonna, Minnesota-based, band originally known as The Rogues when they formed back in late 1964. By mid-1966 they were calling themselves the U.S. Rogues and by late 1967 just before their 45 was recorded they reverted to simply **US**. Both their 45 songs were originals. 1,000 copies were pressed and early ones came in a rare promotional picture sleeve. They played quite extensively around the Midwest. Tom Krause was drafted in 1968 and a few months later the band re-recorded their two 45 cuts in a Minneapolis studio along with four new songs - *Please Be What You Are*/*Land Of Goodness*, *Isn't Your Life Funny, Honey* and *Talkin' 'Bout Love* - which never saw the light of day. The session even included some kids from the Owatonna High School orchestra! Greg Hammel left the band in 1969 and they finally split in 1970.

They took part in the 1966 "IGL Roof Garden Jamboree", which resulted in a rare 1967 album on IGL and more recently a double-CD *IGL Dance Jamboree '66*. The latter dusted off the original tapes of all the bands that took part and includes three tracks by **US** - *Mona*, *Heart Of Stone* and *The Last Time*. (VJ/MW)

Us

Personnel:	RUBEN BETTENCOURT	gtr	A
	WERNER BRANDT		
	(aka VARSH HAMMELL)	bs	A
	JACK ELLIS	gtr	A
	FRANK LUPECA	drms	A
	BOB SEGARINI	vcls	A

Dance With Me - The Autumn Teen Sound (CD) features *Just Me* and *How Can I Tell Her*, the unreleased 1965 45 by this San Francisco based band. According to Alec Palao's liner notes, the group's demise was precipitated by Autumn failing to release this 45 after Segarini refused to have the tracks overdubbed with strings. Undeterred, the talented Segarini went on to form **Family Tree**, **Roxy** and **The Wackers**. (MW)

U.S. Apple Corps

ALBUMS:	1	U.S. APPLE CORPS	(SSS International 12) 1970
	2	LET THE MUSIC TAKE YOUR MIND	
			(Plantation 504) 197? ?

45s:	Get High On Jesus/	
	Swing Low, Sweet Chariot	(SSS SSS-829) 19??
	Prayer For Peace/Peace-Love	(SSS SSS-840) 1969
	Elijah Stone/Closer To The Man	(SSS SSS-851) 197?

Another Shelby Singleton project, after the Rugbys, **Heather Black** and David Allan Coe. **U.S. Apple Corps** released an album of psychedelic gospel rock, with a powerful female singer and fluid guitar solos. The SSS album and *Prayer For Peace* single were pressed on transparent blue vinyl.

We're not sure if the *Let The Music Take Your Mind* album is by the same act. (SR/VZ)

The U.S. Britons

Personnel incl: MIKE JONES   vcls, gtr

Vocalist Jones was just 15 when this Dallas-based outfit recorded two tracks:- *Come On* and *I'll Show You A Man* for a possible 45. At the time nobody was interested but you can now hear them on *Acid Visions - Complete Collection, Vol. 3* (3-CD), *Texas Punk, Vol. 6* (LP) and *Green Crystal Ties, Vol. 3* (CD). (VJ)

The Us Four

Personnel:	DUKE FREEMAN	bs	A
	DONNIE KELLING	gtr	AB
	JACK RICHARDSON	drms	A
	MIKE WINEBRENNER	keyb'ds	AB
	JIM BOWER	bs	B
	PAUL HOERNI	drms	B

45s:	The Alligator/By My Side	(Rising Sons 701) 1967
	She Loves It, Part 1 /She Loves It, Part 2	(Trump 370) 1968

A Louisville, Kentucky foursome whose version of local heroes **Soul Inc.**'s cruncher *The Alligator* was produced by Buzz Cason.

Freeman and Richardson were replaced in '68 by Jim Bower and Paul Hoerni respectively. The latter would join another local outfit **The Oxfords** when **Us Four** broke up.

Compilation appearances include *The Alligator* on *Open Up Yer Door! Vol. 1* (LP) and *Teenage Shutdown, Vol. 1* (LP & CD).   (VJ/MW/SR)

Us Kids

45:   Check-Out/I Love The Rain   (Rex 2629/30) 1967

From Medford, Oregon, this 45 was recorded by a bunch of 12-14 year olds at Rex Recording Studio in Portland. It was their only recording.

Compilation appearances include *Check Out* on *Punk Classics* (CD) and *Punk Classics, Vol. 2* (7"). (MW/GGI)

Us Too

Personnel incl:	JOHN FARIS		A
	LEN GARTNER	vcls, drms	A

45s:	α	I'll Leave You Crying/The Only Thing To Do	(Jinx 17818) 1967
		I'll Leave You Crying/	
		The Girl With The Golden Hair	(Us Too no #) 1967
	β	The Only Thing To Do/	
		The Way It Must Be	(Counterpart C-2581/2) 1967
		I'll Leave You Crying/	
		The Girl With The Golden Hair	(Hi 2133) 1967
	χ	Organ Player/We Can't Go	(Counterpart C-2635/6) 1968
		Pleasure Seeker/Tell Me Where	
		She Is (The Maiden)	(Counterpart C-2647/8) 1969

NB: α and β released as by The "Us Too" Group. α features a different version of *I'll Leave You Crying*. χ released as by **Maelstrom**.

From the Fairfield suburb of Cincinnati, their finest moment is *I'll Leave You Crying*, a particularly good slab of strong melodic pop with a tough edge, melodramatic arrangements with some tasty scorching fuzz and cool vibes. The "Jinx" 45 features a different version with a teen combo sound and strong organ whilst the reissues feature an interesting use of flute on both sides.

The bands first Counterpart 45 contains light-weight-uptempo pop and a soft slow beat-ballad, whilst the *Pleasure Seeker* 45 is also good late sixties pop, on the light side again but with some flashes of searing heavy guitar on the flip.

Len Gartner was both vocalist and drummer in the band, switching roles with another band member. Another early member of the band was John Faris, who was later in **Zephyr** with Tommy Bolin.

Curiously the **Maelstrom** 45 came out without the band's knowledge!

Compilation coverage has so far included: *I'll Leave You Crying* on *Mindblowing Encounters Of The Purple Kind* (LP); and *The Girl With The Golden Hair* on *Lost Generation, Vol. 1* (LP). (GGI/MW/MM/VJ)

The U.S. Male

45s:	Boys Can Be Hurt (As Much As Girls)/ Trouble With You Is	(MGM 13838) 1968
	I Don't Want To Know/Girl	(Special Delivery) c1969

Probably unrelated to the **U.S. Males**, their second 45 features a good cover of the Zombies. (SR)

U.S. Males

45:	Open Up Your Heart/ Come Out Of The Rain	(Britania B-101) 1968

NB: on gold-yellow wax.

Previously known as **The Coastliners**, this Houston outfit carried on in the same mould as purveyors of bright-eyed pop-punk, of which *Open Up Your Heart* is a decent example. The flip is a rather good melodic baroque-pop cover of a **Five Americans**' song. (MW)

U.S. Rockers

45:	Bodacious/ March Of The Siamese Children	(Kimco) 196?

Another of **Kim Fowley**'s ventures, on which he is credited as producer.

Compilation appearances include *Bodacious* on *Kim Fowley - Outlaw Superman* (LP & CD).

John Ussery

ALBUM:	1 USSERY	(Mercury SRM-1-671) 1973 -
45:	Low Rider / Smile	(Mercury 73437) 1973

John Ussery had earlier been a member of Seattle / Mercer Island's **Locomotive**. He also worked with Eric Burdon, John Lee Hooker, Jimmy Witherspoon and also played on some of Delaney Bramlett's solo albums.

He's also recently released a new CD, *Cryin' And Screamin'*. (MW)

U.S. 69

Personnel:	BILL CARTIER	drms	A
	BILL DURSO	vcls, gtr	A
	BOB DEPALMA	flute, sax	A
	DON DEPALMA	keyb'ds	A
	GIL NELSON	bs	A

ALBUM:	1(A) YESTERDAY'S FOLKS	(Buddah 5035) 1969 -
45:	Yesterday's Folks / African Sunshine	(Buddah BDA 101) 1969

NB: shown as by **The Mustard Family**.

The band was comprised of two Americans and three Mexicans who were based in Connecticut. The album is jazz and soul based with some psychedelic influence. Stand out track is the futuristic *10' 32" 2069, A Spaced Oddity*.

Two of the album cuts were also released as a 45 under the moniker **The Mustard Family**.

Bill Durso had previously been in a couple of white soul outfits - Hartford, Connecticut's Thee Prophets and New Britain, Connecticut's Detroit Soul. (VJ/MM)

U.S. Stamps

Personnel incl: ED LANDIS?   A

45s:	Go And Dry Your Tears/Come On	(Galiko 769) c1967
	Pull The Wool/We'll Find A Way	(Galiko 770) c1967

From New York / New Jersey region, their *Pull The Wool* deserves attention. It's a later sounding garage fuzz-punker that's probably '68 rather than '67 - plenty of fuzz but it's kind of 'laid back' with swirling organ and the vocal style has that post-**Fudge** soulish arrogance. Despite that this ditty works pretty well, but not for the "class of '66" I suspect. The flip is forgettable as you guessed all along.

Compilation appearances include *Pull The Wool* on *Let's Dig 'Em Up!!!* (LP) and *Midnight To Sixty-Six* (LP). (MW/MM)

Utopia

Personnel:	HARRY BENDER	gtr	A
	FRANK KRAJINBRINK	gtr	A
	GENE LUCERO	bs	A
	DANNY McBRIDE	drms	A
	DENNIS RODRIGUEZ	vcls, hrmnca	A

ALBUM:	1(A) UTOPIA	(Kent KST-566) 1970 R1

NB: (1) reissued on LP and CD (Akarma AK 154) 2001.

An under-rated heavy blues-rock album by a California band. They also released a second album as *Growl* (Discreet 2209) 1974. The master tapes were shared with **Bob Smith** during recording of *The Visit* album, which confirms that **Utopia**'s album was recorded during 1969 - 70. (VJ/CF/MW)

UTOPIA - Utopia LP.

Vacant Lot

45:	Don't you Just Know It /	
	This Little Feelin' (PS)	(LTD 0004) 196?

From Dayton, Ohio, this bunch had earlier released three 45s as **The X-cellents**. (GGI)

The Vacels

HCP

45s:	You're My Baby (And Don't You Forget It)/	
	Hey Girl, Stop Leading Me On	(Kama Sutra 200) 1965 63
	Can You Please Crawl Out Your Window/	
	I'm Just A Poor Boy	(Kama Sutra 204) 1965 -

A short-lived bright'n'breezy rock group from Long Island, New York, who are frankly eminently forgettable but did enjoy a hit with *You're My Baby (And Don't You Forget It)*.

Compilation appearances have included: *You're My Baby (And Don't You Forget It)* on *Nuggets, Vol. 5* (LP); *Can You Please Crawl Out Your Window?* on *Psychedelic Frequencies* (CD); and *I'm Just A Poor Boy* on *Garage Zone, Vol. 3* (LP) and *The Garage Zone Box Set* (LP). (VJ)

Vacuum Cleaner

Personnel:	ROBIN BOERS	drms	A
	LYNN CAREY	vcls	A
	KAL DAVID	gtr	A
	SIDNEY GEORGE	horns	A
	COFFI HALL	drms	A
	NEIL MERRYWEATHER	bs, gtr, vcls	A
	JOHN RICHARDSON	gtr	A
	HUGH SULLIVAN	perc	A
	J.J. VELKER	keyb'ds	A

ALBUM:	1(A)	VACUUM CLEANER	(RCA LSP-4485) 1971 -

NB: (1) also released in the U.K. (RCA SF 8210).

The first project of **Neil Merryweather** recorded with Lynn Carey and his usual backing group (Boers, Coffi Hall etc.). On offer are some progressive blues-rock tracks with Joplin-like vocals. The group soon evolved into **Mama Lion** and met with some commercial success in 1972/73.

Kal David was previously in **Illinois Speed Press**. (SR)

The Vagrants

Personnel:	ROGER MANSOUR	drms	A
	PETER SABATINO	vcls, perc	A
	JERRY STORCH	organ	A
	LARRY WEST	bs, vcls	A
	LESLIE WEST	gtr, vcls	A

ALBUMS:	1(A)	THE GREAT LOST ALBUM	(Arista AL-8459) 1987
	2(A)	I CAN'T MAKE A FRIEND	(Southern Sound SS-101/204) 1996

NB: (2) is an unauthorised compilation of singles tracks plus an unreleased version of *Satisfaction* which would put **Vanilla Fudge** to shame!

45s:	Oh Those Eyes/You're Too Young	(Southern Sound 204) 196?
	I Can't Make A Friend/	
	Young Blues (PS)	(Vanguard 35038) 1966
	The Final Hour/Your Hasty Heart	(Vanguard 35042) 1966
	I Love, Love You (Yes I Do)/Respect	(Atco 45-6473) 1967
	A Sunny Summer Rain/Beside The Sea	(Atco 45-6513) 1967
	And When It's Over/	
	I Don't Need Your Loving	(Atco 45-6552) 1968

An historically interesting punk band from Forest Hills, Long Island, New York. **Leslie West** later helped out **Jolliver Arkansaw** (a quartet with Felix

THE VAGRANTS - I Can't Make A Friend LP.

Pappalardi, who evolved out of **Bo Grumpus**), **Mountain** and West, Bruce And Laing. He also issued three solo albums and has done session work for Bo Diddley, Bobby Keys and Mylon Lefevre, among others. Younger brother, Larry West went on to **Haystacks Balboa**, who issued an album on Polydor in 1970. **Jerry Storch** went solo and released one album on RCA.

Respect is now their best known track due to its inclusion on the classic *Nuggets - Original Artyfacts From The First Psychedelic Era 1965-1968* (Dble LP) compilation and later on *Nuggets, Vol. 2* (LP) and *Nuggets Box* (4-CD) but the compilation *Hipsville 29 B.C.* (LP) included the 'A' sides of their first two 45s. Their later 45s tended towards a heavier sound but were still punkish and occasionally stunningly powerful, especially *A Sunny Summer Rain* which knocks spots off other East Coast 'heavies' at the time. *Beside The Sea* and *And When It's Over* are also decent fuzz-crunchers. Somehow success always seemed to elude them but thankfully Arista's retrospective collection goes some way to redress that. It contains three of the four sides released on Vanguard, all six of the Atco sides and an unreleased *My Babe*. The pirate collection on Southern Sound includes both sides of their rare debut 45, the Vanguard track omitted from the Arista album and an amazing 13'00" studio version of *Satisfaction* with backwards guitar segments and demented echo effects. Both collections are recommended. (VJ/MW/CF)

Sonny Valdez

45:	What's His /Till You're Through	(Capitol P-2641) 1968

NB: 'B' side by **The Stream Of Consciousness**.

A scarce rock single from the movie soundtrack "Hell's Angels '69", produced by Tony Bruno. (SR)

Dino Valente

Personnel:	DINO VALENTE	gtr, vcls	A

ALBUM:	1(A)	DINO VALENTE	(Epic BN 26335) 1968 R1

NB: (1) also issued in the UK (CBS 65715). (1) reissued on CD (Koch KOC CD 7930).

45:	Birdses/Don't Let It Down	(Elektra 45012) 1964

Born in New York in 1943, **Dino Valente** (or **Valenti**) began recording in 1964 for Elektra including two tracks (*Black Betty* and *Life Is Like That*) which can be found on *Early L.A.* (Together ST1014) 1967. He also wrote (or co-wrote) *Get Together*, the classic hippie anthem made famous by **The Youngbloods**. A popular track, the song was well-covered: in 1966 by **Jefferson Airplane**, *Takes Off* album; 1967 - by **H.P.Lovecraft** on their debut album and *At The Mountains Of Madness*, **Tiffany System** on 45;

1968 - **Cryan Shames** *Synthesis* album, **Dolphin** 45, **Smith** *A Group Called Smith* album; 1969 - Mission, Bonnie Dobson and **Youngbloods** 45s; 1970 - **Association** 'Live'. **Valente**'s original (and unreleased) version of *Let's Get Together* can be heard on *Someone To Love* (CD).

Valente was part of the first line-up of **Quicksilver Messenger Service** (his *Dino's Song* is on their debut album) but was busted twice and spent more than eighteen months in jail. In 1968, before joining **Quicksilver** for good, he released one solo album of acid folk-rock, with a good version of **John Phillips**' *Me And My Uncle*.

Valente sadly died in the eighties of a brain tumour.

Other compilation appearances have included: *Birdses* on *California Acid Folk* (LP); and *Me And My Uncle* on *Rockbusters* (LP). (SR/MW/BMk)

Sal Valentino

45s:	Lisa Marie / I Wanna Twist	(Falco 306) 1962
	Friends and Lovers/Alligator Man	(Warner 7289) 1969
	Silkie/Song For Rochelle	(Warner 7368) 1970

Sal Valentino was the lead singer of **The Beau Brummels** and on his third solo 45 he was backed by Ry Cooder, **Leon Russell**, Chris Ethridge, **Van Dyke Parks** and Clarence White. Both 1969/70 45s were part of a solo project that was never completed.

Alligator Man also appeared on *The 1969 Warner/Reprise Song Book*, (PRO 331) compilation.

Valentino went on to form **Stoneground**. (SR/MW)

Valhalla

Personnel:	RICK AMBROSER	bs, vcls	A
	BOB HULLING	vcls	A
	DON KRANTZ	gtr, bs	A
	EDDIE LIVINGSTON	drms	A
	MARK MANGOLD	organ, perc, vcls	A

ALBUM: 1(A) VALHALLA (United Artists UAS 6730) 1969 R1

NB: (1) reissued on CD (Free FR 2006).

United Artists managed to sign several good groups (**Thunder and Roses**, **Boffalongo**, **Pookah** for example) but never gave them much promotion. Led by Mark Mangold, who composed their material, **Valhalla** is another of these forgotten groups and their album deserves to be rediscovered. It mixes heavy rock, progressive rock and psychedelia with a predominant organ and powerful vocals on tracks like *Psychedelic Minds Going Nowhere* and *Overseas Symphony*.

Mark Mangold would later play with American Tears. (SR)

Jim 'Harpo' Valley

ALBUMS:	1	HARPO	(Panorama 104) 1967 -
	2	FAMILY	(Light LS-5564) 197? -
	3	DANCE INSIDE YOUR HEAD	(First American 7710) 1977 -

NB: (1) with **Don and The Goodtimes**. (2) as Jim Valley and Steve Schurr.

			HCP
45s:	I'm Real/There Is Love	(Jerden 814) 1966	-
	Try, Try, Try/Invitation	(Dunhill 4096) 1967	106
	Go Go Round/Maintain	(Dunhill 4103) 1967	-

Jim started off forming **The Viceroys** around 1962 but left to join **Don and The Goodtimes** in 1965. In 1966, he was tempted away to team up with **Paul Revere and The Raiders** but when after a year they'd failed to feature his talent for songwriting he left to go solo. His first album is quite rare and sought-after by collectors.

Compilation appearances include *I'm Real* on *Open Up Yer Door, Vol. 2* (LP). (VJ/MW)

Charles Vance (and The Sonics)

45s:	α	Is It True / Is Our Love True	(Renner 237) 1963
		Closer To Me / Let's Fall In Love	(Lori 9553) c1965
		Put The Shoes On Willie / All For The Love Of A Girl	(Golden Eagle 201) 1966
		We Gotta Get Out Of This Place / My Soul	(Golden Eagle 204) 1966

NB: α as by The Sonics.

A Houston band who evolved into The Barons in the seventies with several releases on Solar and their own Baron label.

Compilation appearances include *My Soul* on *Punk Classics, Vol. 4* (7"). (MW)

The Vandals

Personnel:	AUGIE BUCCI	keyb'ds	A
	BILL COSFORD	gtr, tambourine	A
	RICHIE KUTCHER	drms	A
	JOHNNY SAMBATARO	gtr, bs	A
	RUSS SEPIELLI	vcls	A
	GEORGE TERRY	ld gtr	A

45s:	Mystery/We're The Vandals	(Parole no) 1965
	I Saw Her In A Mustang/The Joker	(Tiara 200) 1965
	I Saw Her In A Mustang/The Joker	(Tiara 200-2) 1965

A mid-sixties outfit from Hollywood, Florida whose finest punk gem *I Saw Her In A Mustang* has resurfaced on both *Garage Punk Unknowns, Vol. 3* (LP) and *Riot City!* (LP). It was also covered by another Florida band **Mike Vetro And The Cellar Dwellers** on a rare EP. (VJ)

Vandals

Personnel incl: TONY DIONISIO A

45:	You Lied To Me / Someone Else Like You	(General American Gar 105) 1967

Tony Dionisio was later in the **Clann**, another Columbia, Missouri band.

Compilation appearances include *You Lied To Me* on *Drink Beer! Yell! Dance!* (LP). (MW)

Vandals

45:	Ballad Of A Loser / My Girl	(Big Rock 511) 1965

VALHALLA - Valhalla CD.

These **Vandals**, from Bradford, Pennsylvania issued one very rare 45. More Pennsylvanian **Vandals** appeared on the Empire label album *Williamsport '68* performing *Groovin' Is Easy*. (MW)

Vandy

ALBUM: 1   JUST VANDY   (Eleventh Hour) 1972 SC

On the same label as **Mason** and **Polyphony**, comes this rare album of female folk. It offers a mix of original and traditional songs, with a good cover of *Wayfaring Stranger*. (SR)

Vanilla Fudge

Personnel:	CARMINE APPICE	drms, vcls	A
	TIM BOGERT	bs, vcls	A
	VINCE MARTELL	gtr, vcls	A
	MARK STEIN	organ, vcls	A

				HCP
ALBUMS:	1(A)	VANILLA FUDGE	(Atco 33224) 1967	6 -
	2(A)	THE BEAT GOES ON	(Atco 33237) 1968	17 -
	3(A)	RENNAISSANCE	(Atco 33244) 1968	20 -
	4(A)	NEAR THE BEGINNING	(Atco 33278) 1969	16 -
	5(A)	ROCK AND ROLL	(Atco 33303) 1970	34 -
	6(A)	THE BEST OF	(Atco 90006-1) 1982	- -

NB: (2-5) reissued on CD by Repertoire and Sundazed (SC 6142 - 6145) 1998, with bonus cuts. Some of their material has been reissued by Midi, a German label. There's also a *Live* CD release that may interest collectors, *Best Of Vanilla Fudge Live* (Rhino) 1991 and a best of compilation: *The Psychedelic Sundae: The Best Of Vanilla Fudge* (Rhino R2 71154).

			HCP
45s:	Where Is My Mind/Look Of Love	(Atco 6554) 1968	73
	You Keep Me Hangin' On/		
	Come By Day, Come By Night	(Atco 6590) 1967	6
	Take Me For A Little While/Thoughts	(Atco 6616) 1968	38
	Season Of The Witch Pt 1 /Pt 2	(Atco 6632) 1968	65
	Shotgun/Good Good Lovin'	(Atco 6655) 1969	68
	Some Velvet Morning/People	(Atco 6679) 1969	103
	Need Love/I Can't Make It Alone	(Atco 6703) 1969	111
	Lord In the Country/		
	Windmills Of Your Mind	(Atco 6728) 1970	-

NB: There's also a promo 'EP' in PS, although this only features two tracks: *That's What Makes A Man/The Spell That Comes After* (Atco EP 4527) 1968.

This New York psychedelic rock group, named after a popular American ice cream, formed in 1966 out of the ashes of **(Mark Stein and) The Pigeons** and began by specialising in doing slowed-down version of other people's compositions. Their debut album included organ dominated versions of Lennon-McCartney's *Ticket To Ride* and *Eleanor Rigby*, Rod Argent's *She's Not There* and Curtis Mayfield's *People Get Ready*. The remake of The Supremes' hit *You Keep Me Hangin' On* reached No 18 in the U.K. in the Summer of 1967 and was later a U.S. hit. Their treatment of these songs was characterised by organ melodramatics and extravagant productions; the album sold quite well and the group had an uniquely distinctive sound. It is said that The Beatles were impressed with the band, with George Harrison playing their version of *Ticket to Ride* and *Eleanor Rigby* for anyone that visited them. *Eleanor Rigby Pts I & 2* (Atlantic 584, 139) failed as a single in the UK, as did *Where Is My Mind/The Look Of Love* (Atlantic 584.170), a 1968 release. Their first album reached No 6 in the U.S. Album Charts.

Their next album, however, was over-ambitious and pretentious, failing in its attempt to provide a history of 25 years of musical development on one LP! Nonetheless it still climbed to No 17.

Rennaissance, which was released in 1968 and reissued in 1974 by WEA, showed some improvement, largely on account of their typically melodramatic nine-minute version of Donovan's *Season Of The Witch* which was somewhat surprisingly a minor hit in the U.K. in 1969. However, when the band attempted to write their own material, the result was usually a dismal failure. **Vanilla Fudge** described their music as 'psychedelic symphonic rock'. The 'symphonic' was an exaggeration, although one can detect a slight classical influence in their music. *Rennaissance* reached No. 20 in the Album Charts and *Near The Beginning* made No. 16. Side two was live.

As the psychedelic era drew to a close, the band moved towards a more conventional heavy rock sound, finally splitting after their fifth album which reached No. 34 in 1970. Appice and Bogert went on to play with **Cactus** then Beck, Bogert and Appice and then Rod Stewart, while Stein formed an abortive band called **Boomerang**.

They reformed for a comeback album *Mystery* in 1984.

In 1999, Carmine Appice, Tim Bogert and Vince Martell got back together again, with Bill Pascali replacing Mark Stein. They released a new album *Vanilla Fudge 2001* ( ) 2001, and resumed live appearances.

You Keep Me Hangin' On, one of their finest moments, can also be heard on *Highs Of The Sixties* and *Nuggets, Vol. 9* (LP). (VJ/MW/AHr/EW/BK)

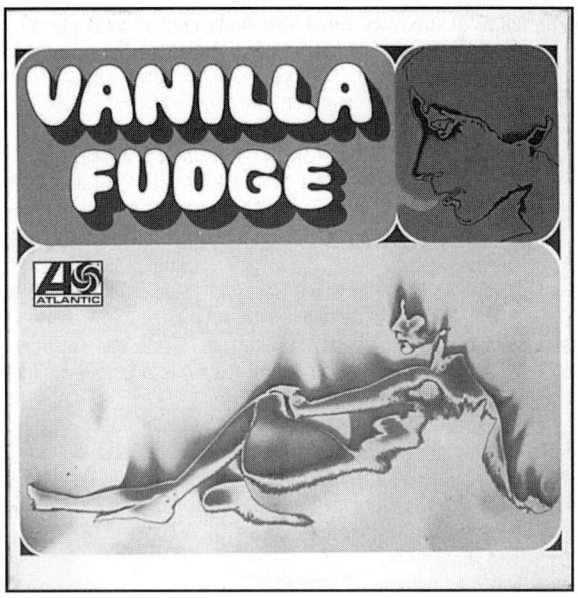

VANILLA FUDGE - Vanilla Fudge LP.

Dave Van Ronk and The Hudson Dusters

Personnel:	ED GREGORY		A
	RICK HENDERSON	drms	A
	POT		A
	DAVE VAN RONK	vcls, gtr	A
	DAVE WOODS		A

ALBUM:	1(A)	DAVE VAN RONK AND THE HUDSON DUSTERS
		(Verve Forecast FTS-3041) 1968 -

45s:	Dink's Song/Head Inspector	(Verve Forecast KF 5070) 1967
	Clouds/Rompin Through The Swamp	(Verve Forecast) 1968

In the early sixties, **Dave Van Ronk** began as a folk-blues singer in the Greenwich Village scene. After several solo albums, which are out of scope this book, he assembled an electric group, the Hudson Dusters for one unusual album in 1968. It's a surprising combination, the very harsh voice of **Van Ronk** seeming out of place at first with the psych-rock backing, but it works, especially on two Joni Mitchell covers, *Clouds* (Both Sides Now) and *Chelsea Morning* and on *Alley Oop*, *Head Inspector*, *Mr. Middle*, *Keep Off The Grass* and *Rompin Through The Swamp*, an adaptation by Peter Stampfel (**Holy Modal Rounders**).

The album was produced by Barry Kornfeld and arranged by David Woods, who also wrote three tracks and later worked with **Jake and The Family Jewels**.

Dave Van Ronk returned to his solo career afterwards, but this album deserves to be heard.

A lifelong native of Brooklyn, **Dave Van Ronk** died of colon cancer at the age of 65, on February 10th 2002. (SR/MW)

The Vaqueros

45s:	80 Foot Wave (Instr) /		
	Birds And The Bees	(Bangar 00647)	1964
	Growing Pains / 69	(Studio City SC 1049)	1966
	Don't You Dare / Mustang Sally	(Studio City SC 1059)	1966

An instrumental-cum-garage band from Virginia, Minnesota. *Growing Pains* is notable for some fine fuzz guitar, whilst the flip is a groovy instrumental, again with some fine guitar.

Compilation coverage has included:- *Growing Pains* and *69* on *Sixties Rebellion, Vol. 4* (LP & CD); *69* on *Everything You Always Wanted To Know...* (CD); *Don't You Dare* on *Bad Vibrations, Vol. 2* (LP); and *Growing Pains* on *Teenage Shutdown, Vol. 7* (LP & CD). (VJ/MW)

The Varcels

Personnel:	DON HUNT	vcls	A
	DOUG	keyb'ds	A
	GARY	drms	A
	HILTON ?	bs	A
	WILLIAM ?	gtr, sax	A

ALBUM:	1	HANG LOOSE WITH THE VARCELS	(Justice) 1967 R2

NB: (1) reissued on CD (Collectables COL-0622) 1998.

From Thomasville, North Carolina, **The Varcels** were one of many area combos to record on Calvin Newton's Justice Records label. And, like most of the other Justice acts, their sole album contains the usual cover versions of the period, including *Summertime*, *Money*, *House Of The Rising Sun*, and *In The Midnight Hour*. In addition to two band originals - the instrumental *Hang Loose* and *I'm Tired (Of Messin' Around)* - the album also includes a decent, organ-domianted version of **The Standells**' *Dirty Water*. (MDo)

The Variations

Personnel:	NONNIE BOST	bs	A
	JIMMY BRAWLEY	sax, organ	A
	BOBBY ENNIS	drms	A
	J.B. GAMBLE	ld vcls	A
	JIMMY KINCAID	ld gtr	A
	DAVID POTEAT	gtr	A

ALBUM:	1(A)	DIG 'EM UP	(Justice 112) c1967 R2

NB: (1) reissued on CD (Collectables COL-CD-0615) 1996.

Another Justice rarity dusted off. A smartly shorn sextet resplendent in vampire capes pose in front of their coffin-topped red hearse. Under the lid there's an assortment of brassy instrumentals, frat and club sounds, lounge, soul and ballads - all covers and often the same as on many of the other lesser known "soul-garage" Justice albums. Not recommended. (MW)

The Vectors

Personnel incl:	JOE KELLEY		
	DON MAU		
	ROGER L. VAIL		

45s:	What In The World/		
	It's Been A Day Or Two	(Analysis 4323)	1964
	What In The World/		
	It's Been A Day Or Two	(St. Lawrence 1003)	1964

A Chicago band. *What In The World* is a harp wailin' punk song.

Roger Vail later played with **The Orphuns** and **Osgood**. Joe Kelley, of course, was later in **The Shadows Of Knight** and Don Mau was in **The Heard**.

Compilation appearances have included: *It's Been A Day Or Two* on *Pebbles, Vol. 7* (CD); *What In The World* on *Back From The Grave, Vol. 4* (LP) and *Back From The Grave, Vol. 2* (CD). (VJ/MW)

Vectors

Another **Vectors** performed *Angel Baby* on the 1967 *Battle Of The Bands Vol. 1* LP (Ren-Vell 317), featuring bands predominantly from the Westchester, NY area. (MW)

Pat and Lolly Vegas

Personnel:	PAT VEGAS	vcls, bs	A
	LOLLY VEGAS	vcls, gtr	A

ALBUM:	1(A)	AT THE HAUNTED HOUSE	(Mercury MG 21059) 1965 SC

Guitar playing Native American brothers from Fresno, California. Pat and Lolly had previously recorded for Chancellor, Regency, Apogee and Sapien labels. They were in the touring version of the Mar-Ketts. They recorded an album entitled *Hotrodders Choice* under the name The Deuce Coupes for the Del-Fi label. They appeared in the 1965 surf movie *It's A Bikini World*. And both were members of the "Shindogs" (with Leon Russell and Delaney Bramlett) which was the stage band on the Shindig TV show. Their songs were recorded by PJ Proby, Aretha Franklin, The Righteous Brothers, Bobby Gentry and Debbie Gray. At the time this album was recorded they were the house band at the famous Haunted House club in Los Angeles. They had also released surf guitar singles as The Avantis and at least one early Lolly Vegas solo 45 exists.

The pair released an album under the name The Deuce Coupes: *Hot Rodder's Choice* (Del-Fi DFST-1243) in 1963, and were part of the live line-up of **The Marketts** at about the same time.

Produced by **Leon Russell**, *At The Haunted House* is a mix of garage and pop and contains renditions of *Satisfaction*, *In The Midnight Hour*, *Papa's Got a Brand New Bag*, *Good Lovin'*... plus six original songs.

The liner notes are a must-read: "The ingenious bandstand, designed especially for their act, features a monster's head fashioned into a shell which pushes the sound up and out-making a microphone unnecessary. The actual sound comes through the monster's nostrils, which blow hot steam which makes the sound even louder."

The **Vegas** brothers would later would later form Redbone. (SR/HS/CF)

Veil

45:	?/Something's Wrong?	(Track VIII X-1002) 1969

Fuzz, Flaykes And Shakes, Vol. 4 (LP & CD) features *Something's Wrong* by this obscure Califonian Bay Area band whom the compilers tracked down to Alameda. The 45 was co-produced by Norm Lombardo of San Diego's **Brain Police** who had relocated to that region in 1969. The composer and co-producer was Amadeo Barrios. It's a light, bouncey keyboard-led ditty, more pop than garage. (MW)

The Vejtables

Personnel:	BOB BAILEY	vcls, tamb	ABCDEFG
	BOB COLE	ld gtr	AB
	RICK DEY	bs	A
	JAN ERRICO (ASHTON)	drms	ABCD
	NED HOLLIS	gtr, organ	ABCD
	RON	bs	B
	REESE SHEETS	ld gtr	C
	FRANK SMITH	bs	CDEF
	JIM SAWYERS	ld gtr	DEF
	KRISTY	drms	EF

BOB MOSLEY	gtr	E
RICHARD FORTUNATO	vcls, gtr	F G
+ 2 Ex-Preachers		G

CD:	1(-)	FEEL THE VEJTABLES	(Sundazed SC 11031)	1996

NB: (1) is a CD which contains all their Autumn and Uptown singles as well as previously unreleased tracks. Recommended!

					HCP
45s:		I Still Love You/Anything	(Autumn 15)	1965	84
		The Last Thing On My Mind/ Mansions Of Tears	(Autumn 23)	1965	117
	α	Cold Dreary Morning/?	(Autumn ?)	1966	-
		Feel The Music/Shadows	(Uptown 741)	1966	-

NB: α withdrawn.

This San Francisco five-piece had in Jan Errico the novelty of one of the very few girl drummers at the time, aside from Honey Lantree of England's Honeycombs. Formed in 1964, they soon secured a residency at the Morocco Room in San Mateo, following in the footsteps of **The Beau Brummels**, who'd gone on to better things. Very early in the residency they were discovered by the co-owners of Autumn Records, Tom Donahue and Bobby Mitchell, who signed them to their label. Rick Dey soon departed to join **The Wilde Knights** and was replaced by an older bassist who was known to everyone simply as Ron. The band soon became a popular live attraction during the Spring of 1965 at all the teen nightclubs, teen fairs and Battles Of The Bands in Northern California's burgeoning music scene. Their first 45, *I Still Love You*, was a jangly Beatles/**Byrds**'-type folk-rocker. It became a very minor hit peaking at No 84 and helped secure the band appearances on 'American Bandstand', 'the Lloyd Thaxton Show' and 'Where The Action Is'. They returned to the studio in October 1965 to record **Tom Paxton**'s folk-rocker *The Last Thing On My Mind*. To help promote it they joined a West Coast tour with The Yardbirds and The Beach Boys. Later in the Spring of 1966 they played at another Battle Of The Bands in L.A. where they and the **Buffalo Springfield** were the only paid bands. The competition was actually won by **The Doors**. By now Reese Sheets had left the band to be replaced by Jim Sawyers, who'd previously been with San Jose band **The Other Side**.

Soon after Sawyers joined in 1965, Hollis and Ashton left (the latter for labelmates **The Mojo Men**) around the time of the second 45's release. Bailey recruited another female drummer called Kristy and they were augmented by **Bob Mosley** on guitar (from **The Misfits**), but he moved quickly on (to **Moby Grape**) and was replaced by guitarist Richard Fortunato, formerly of **The Preachers**.

By early 1966 Autumn Records were in financial difficulties. All of its roster was transferred to Warner Brothers. By then **The Vejtables** had nearly folded - in April 1966 Jim Sawyers left for **The Syndicate Of Sound** and Frank Smith had left to replace Mosley in **The Misfits**. Bailey and Fortunato were hangin' tough and drafted in two more ex-**Preachers** when Leo De Gar Kulka of Golden State Recorders offered them a contract with Mercury.

This incandescent but short-lived line-up produced the superb Uptown 45, featuring the raga-punker *Feel The Music* backed by *Shadows*, an excellent piece of experimental psychedelia.

Speculation over the years about the quality of the other tracks from these sessions had given them a legendary tag amongst collectors. Finally, in 1994, Big Beat's *Good Things Are Happening* (CD) unearthed this handful of nuggets - *Good Things Are Happening*, *Time And Place*, *Better Rearrange*, *Hide Yourself* and *Good Times* - and expectations were met in FULL (kudos to Alec Palao). Five awesome proto-psych freakouts with strong sneering vocals from Fortunato and slabs of distorted guitar and feedback. Clearly influenced by the Yardbirds, **The Vejtables** had leapt forward to join that band in the musical vanguard at the dawn of the psychedelic era.

Bailey clung onto the band's name for another year but the personnel was erratic, as apparently was his behaviour. Another 45 did eventually surface in late 1967, with Frank Smith on board again, but was released as by the **Book Of Changes**. Fortunato had long gone onto a string of fascinating outfits - to George Caldwell's **Bees**, later the **W.C. Fields Memorial Electric String Band**, then **ESB** and finally **Fields**.

Compilation appearances have included: *Feel The Music* on *Mayhem & Psychosis, Vol. 2* (LP), *Pebbles, Vol. 12* (LP) and *Pebbles, Vol. 4* (ESD) (CD); *I Still Love You* and *The Last Thing On My Mind* on *Nuggets, Vol. 7* (LP); *I Still Love You* on *Sound Of The Sixties* (Dble LP), *Sixties Archive, Vol. 1* (CD); *Feel The Music* and *Shadows* on *Sound Of The Sixties: San Francisco Part 2* (LP) and *Crystalize Your Mind* (CD); *The Last Thing On My Mind* on *Sounds Of The Sixties San Francisco, Vol. 1* (LP); *Anything* on *San Francisco Roots* (LP), *The Autumn Records Story* (LP); *Hide Yourself* on *Sundazed Sampler, Vol. 2* (CD); *Shadows* on *Acid Dreams, Vol. 1* (LP); *Anything*, *I Still Love You*, *I Still Love You (alternate take)* on *Dance With Me - The Autumn Teen Sound* (CD); *The Last Thing On My Mind* and *Mansion Of Tears* on *Someone To Love* (CD), plus two unreleased Jan Ashton tracks - *About My Tears* and *Cold Dreary Morning* (the latter also on *Nuggets, Vol. 7*); Both sides of their first two Autumn 45s also appeared on the *Autumn Single Box* compilation. (VJ/MW)

The Velaires

Personnel:	BOB		A
	PERRY		A
	DENNIS SWEIGART		A
	TOM		A

45:	I Could Have Cried/Yes, It Was Me	(Hi-Mar 7 9173)	1965

Charming harmony beat ballads on a Lititz, Pennsylvania label. *I Could Have Cried* borrows some bars from the Beatles' *No Reply*. Both tracks are vocally closer to the smooth teen-pop style of the Cascades. (MW)

Velvet Illusions

Personnel incl:	JIMMY JAMES (RANDY BOWLES)	ld vcls	AB
	BRUCE KITT	gtr	AB
	GEORGE RADFORD	sax	AB
	STEVEN WEED	vcls, multi-instruments	AB
	JON JUETTE	drms	B

45s:		Acid Head/She Was The Only Girl	(Tell Int'l 700 A)	1967
		Acid Head/She Was The Only Girl	(Metro-Video M-V-307)	1967
		I'm Going Home To Los Angeles/ Town Of Fools	(Metro-Video M-V-308)	1967
		Velvet Illusions/ Born To Be A Rolling Stone	(Metro-Video M-V-309)	1967
	α	Mini Shimmy/Hippy Town	(Metro-Video M-V-311)	1967

NB: α shown as by Georgy and The Velvet Illusions.

An excellent L.A. psychedelic band. Their first and fourth 45 'A' sides, *Acid Head* and *Velvet Illusions* are both superb garage-punk classics and have been heavily compiled. *Acid Head* shares similar ground with The Rolling Stones *Mother's Little Helper*, telling the tale of a young-girl's struggle with

THE VEJTABLES - Feel CD.

drug-addiction, with a memorable driving melody, military style drumming and raga-esque guitars. *Velvet Illusions*, the band's theme-tune, is more frantic, with a **Red Krayola** mechanical beat, upfront bass, shrill penetrating organ and great guitar work.

Second drummer, Jon Juette recalls:- "I remember our studio was very close to the Hollywood Bowl and some of us would sneak over there dreaming of playing there someday. Randy Bowles was our lead singer and went by the stage name of Jimmy James. Our sax player was George Radford, the son of our groups manager and agent. The rhythm guitar was played by Bruce Kitt. I don't recall the original drummer's name, as he quit the group shortly after they located in Hollywood on El Centro Avenue."

"The real musical genius of our group was Steve Weed. He played several instruments and I remember many hours at his or my house as we were growing up watching him write one song after another. He truly was (and is) a great undiscovered talent! We played at some pretty great gigs, had press conferences with people like L.A. Mayor Sam Yority, Carol Burnett, Two-ton Tessie O'Shea :-) and several other entertainers. Our producer was George Oliphant. Although *Acid Head* and *Velvet Illusions (We Are The...)* were the most played, my favorite was *Town Of Fools*, written by Jerry."

Compilation appearances have included: *Velvet Illusions* on *Pebbles, Vol. 9* (CD); *Acid Trip From The Psychedelic Sixties* (LP), *Garagelands, Vol. 2* (CD) and *Sixties Archive, Vol. 8* (CD); and *Acid Head* and *Velvet Illusions* on *Psychedelic Unknowns, Vol. 5* (LP & CD), *60's Punk E.P., Vol. 2* (7" EP), *Acid Dreams - The Complete 3 LP Set* (3-LP), *Acid Dreams Testament* (CD) and *Acid Dreams, Vol. 1* (LP).

The liner-notes for *Pebbles, Vol. 9* state incorrectly that Steve Weed would gain greater (and probably unwelcome) fame as the boyfriend of world-famous abductee Patty Hearst. This was a different Steve Weed. (VJ/MW/JJu)

Velvet Night

Personnel:			
	LYNN BOCCUMINI	vcls	A
	DOUG CATUOGNO	perc	A
	FRANK CHIARO	bs	A
	TONY FARANDA	gtr	A
	PETER FUINO	sax, flute, vcls	A
	VINNIE NISI	keyb'ds, vcls	A

ALBUM: 1(A) VELVET NIGHT (Metromedia MD 1026) 1969 R2

NB: (1) repackaged and released as *Would* by **Would** (Perception PLP 24) 1971, with one track difference. (1) was reissued in 1993 and also pirated on a "2 on 1" CD together with **Art Of Lovin**.

45: Velvet Night/
I'm Sure He'll Come Most Anytime (Metromedia MM-110) 1969

The album contains passable cover versions of *Season Of The Witch*, *If I Were A Carpenter*, *The Weight* (with the Band's song miscredited to **Tim Hardin**!) and a Cream medley (*I'm Free, The Sunshine Of Your Love, White Room* and *I'm So Glad*). Only one song (*Don't Let Me Stand In Your Way*) is written by a band member (Vinnie Nisi). The best three tracks - *Velvet Night*, *Freak Show* and *Edge Of The Woods* were written by non-band members **Jimmy Curtiss** and S. Kanyon.

For the most part, heavy choppy psych, that'll appeal to fans of the **Vanilla Fudge/Hassles** school possibly but for some an acquired taste.

In 1971 the album was repackaged and reissued as by **Would** on **Jimmy Curtiss**' label. (MW)

Velvet Seed

45: Sharon Patterson/Flim Flam Man (M.A.I. MAI-201) 1968

From Maine. *Sharon Patterson* is a slow ballad with ringing jingle-jangle guitar whilst the flip is uptempo bright 'n' breezy pop-psych with a 'West Coast' male and female vocal style. They also recorded four songs, including *Feel A Whole Lot Better*, which remain unreleased. (MW)

THE VELVET UNDERGROUND - The Velvet Underground And Nico LP.

The Velvet Underground

Personnel:			
	JOHN CALE	bs, keyb'ds, viola, vcls	AB
	STERLING MORRISON	gtr	ABCDEF
	NICO (CHRISTA PAFFGEN)	vcls	A
	LOU REED	gtr, keyb'ds, vcls	ABCDE
	MAUREEN 'MO' TUCKER	bs	ABC(D) FG
	DOUG YULE	gtr, bs, keyb'ds, drms, vcls	CDEFG
	BILLY YULE	drms	DE
	WALTER POWERS	bs	FG
	WILLIE ALEXANDER	keyb'ds, vcls	G
	(ADRIAN BARBER)	perc	D)
	(TOMMY ??)	perc	D)

HCP

ALBUMS: 1(A) THE VELVET UNDERGROUND AND NICO
(up to (Verve 5008) 1967 171 -
1976) 2(B) WHITE LIGHT/WHITE HEAT (Verve 5046) 1967 199 -
3(C) THE VELVET UNDERGROUND (MGM 4617) 1969
4(D) LOADED (Atlantic 9034) 1970
5(-) THE VELVET UNDERGROUND -
Golden Archive Series (comp) (MGM Gas 131) 1970
6(E) LIVE AT MAX'S KANSAS CITY (Atlantic 9500) 1972
7( ) SQUEEZE (Polydor UK, 2383.180) 1972
8(C) 1969 (Mercury) 1974

NB: (1) issued in both stereo and mono. First pressings had peelable banana on front cover, and in the photo on the rear of the jacket, a man's head and arms are visible dropping down on the band from above (upside-down). For legal reasons, it was necessary to remove this image from all subsequent pressings of the album, but the copies that had already been printed but not yet shipped by the pressing plant were censored with a large black and white sticker. Currently, these earliest editions are in the R3 (mono) and R2 (stereo) categories. Early second state versions (stereo only?) with the image removed from the photo on the back cover still have the peelable banana; these are in the R2 category. Rare promotional editions exist of (1)-(3) in both mono and stereo with yellow labels, and a white label mono edition of (1) is ultra-rare, said to have been distributed by Warhol himself. This particular item has changed hands in the R5 category although regular yellow label promos of the first three albums are in the R3 category. (1) was issued in Japan with a peelable banana on a non-gatefold sleeve, and in Canada with the back cover photo moved to the front of a non-gatefold sleeve. (2) stock mono copies exist, but are very rare (R2). (3) original UK pressing initially released with a different mix, this was quickly withdrawn. All the original **Velvet Underground** albums have been issued on CD, and countless compilations of their music exist. Of particular note are: (4) reissued as *Loaded Plus* on CD by Rhino in 1996, with many previously unavailable extra tracks; *Peel Slowly And See* a five-CD box set issued in 1995, that includes many previously unreleased alternate takes, demos, etc; (B/C) *V.U.* (Verve 823721) 1984; and (B/C) *Another View* (Verve) 1986. A more recent collection is *Rock & Roll - An Introduction To The Velvet Underground* (Polydor 549 690 2) 2001, whilst *The Velvet Underground Bootleg Series: Volume One - The Quine Tapes* (Polydor/Universal) 2001 is a lo-fi set of recordings compiled from cassettes recorded of their 1969 concerts by fanatical fan Robert Quine. *Final V.U. 1971-73* (Captain Trip CTCD 350 353) 2002 is a four-CD box set of extremely lo-fi concert recordings by post-Lou

Reed line-ups of the band taken from tapes of concerts at London and Amsterdam (both November 1971), University College of Wales at St. David's (1972) and, finally, at a small Boston, Massachusetts, club (May 1973). Given the poor sound quality, this box set is for completists only.

45s:	All Tomorrow's Parties/		
(up to	I'll Be Your Mirror	(Verve 10427)	1967
1972)	Femme Fatale/Sunday Morning	(Verve 10466)	1967
	White Light-White Heat/		
	Here She Comes Now	(Verve 10543)	1968
	I Heard Her Call My Name/		
	Here She Comes Now	(Verve 10560)	1968
	What Goes On/Jesus	(MGM 14057)	1969
	Who Loves The Sun/Oh! Sweet Nuthin'	(Cotillion 44107)	1971

NB: Their first four singles were produced in very small quantities, hardly promoted and were never local or regional hits. The last was the first to be issued in the U.K. and part of a batch of 45s to tie in with the acquisition of the MGM/Verve and Atlantic catalogue by Polydor International. The *Who Loves The Sun* release in the U.K. had *Sweet Jane* on the flip side. Other European releases the same year were:- *I'm Waiting For The Man/Run Run Run/Candy Says* (MGM) UK; *I'm Waiting For The Man/Run Run Run* (MGM) Germany; and *I'm Waiting For The Man/Candy Says/White Light - White Heat* (MGM) Holland. Also in 1972 *Sweet Jane/Rock And Roll* was issued by Atlantic in the U.K. and in Germany with a picture sleeve.

Velvet Underground were New York's answer to the California rock renaissance. Their main inspiration came from Lou Reed and John Cale. Reed, born on 12th March 1943 in Freeport, Long Island, New York was an accountant's son, the eldest of two children from a middle class Jewish family. He had dropped out of Syracuse University to write songs. Cale had been born on 5th December 1940 in Crynant, South Wales. He'd studied contemporary music in London prior to winning a scholarship to New York's Eastman Conservatory. The remaining members were Maureen Tucker who'd been born in New Jersey in 1945; Nico, who entered the world in Cologne, Germany in 1938 (her parents were Polish and later died in a Nazi death camp); and Sterling Morrison, who was born in the same year as Reed in New York and later attended high school with him. Reed and Cale first met each other in New York in 1964, but Cale did not play with Reed until the latter had gone on to assemble his own bands, The Warlocks and later The Primitives, which included Morrison and Tucker. Reed and Cale, also wrote a 45 for **The All Night Workers**.

When Cale joined in 1966, they changed their name to **The Velvet Underground** and played in various clubs around Greenwich Village. They soon came to the attention of Andy Warhol, who added the beautiful German model and actress Nico to their line-up and featured them in his Exploding Plastic Inevitable Media Show, which was a multi-media psychedelic event staged in New York in 1966.

The debut album, produced by Andy Warhol, was one of the most innovative and influential in the history of rock. The songs largely concentrated on the decadence of American city life, thereby countering the peace and love trip emanating from America's West Coast. *I'm Waiting For The Man* and *Heroin* dealt with the rising phenomena of heroin addiction, while *Venus In Furs* explored the dark world of sado-masochism. Nico's sexy but death-like voice was a big plus on tracks like *Sunday Morning*, *Femme Fatale* and *I'll Be Your Mirror*. The music on this album was effectively an assault on the listener's senses - comprised of throbbing, often discordant rhythms, riddled with electronic feed-back. Most of it was written by Reed, although Nico's vocals were also important to its appeal. Commercially, however, it was a non-starter as the subject-matter of many of its tracks prevented any radio airplay and it also spawned no hit singles. It peaked at just No. 171 in the National Album Charts and Reed and Cale were both upset by the indifferent reception it received, feeling it to be rather special.

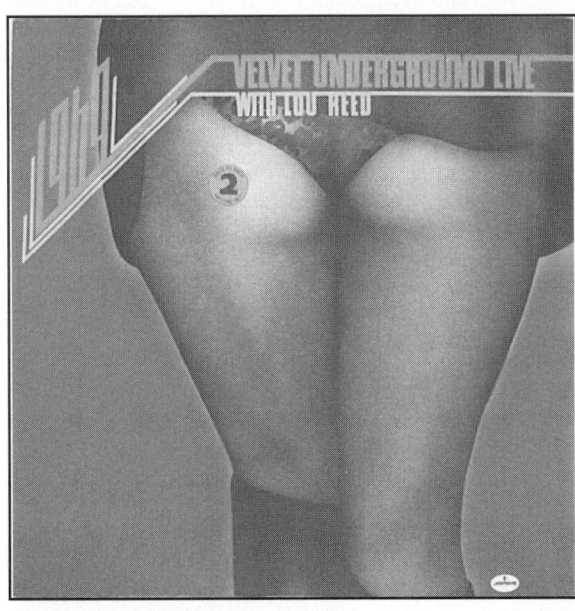

Nico left the band at this stage to pursue a solo career and Warhol began to lose interest, withdrawing his financial support. Nico's departure inevitably affected their musical policy and their second album, *White Light/White Heat* which, lacking the gentle songs written for her on the first album, was aggressively harsh. It contained two stand-out tracks, *Sister Ray*, a 17-minute story about a group of sailors who are interrupted by the police while visiting a drag queen and *The Gift* based on a short story Reed had composed. In both songs, the lyrics were augmented by a storm of unorthodox electronic music. Commercially, the album represented another failure peaking at only No. 199 in the Album Charts and Cale quit the band to pursue a solo career. He was replaced by Doug Yule (bs, gtr, keyb'ds). From hereon, Reed became the dominant figure in the band.

The third album, *The Velvet Underground* again represented a change in musical direction being composed of softer, more harmonious songs. The album was based around a girl's search for significance through nihilism (*Candy Says*), religion (*Jesus*), adultery (*Pale Blue Eyes*) and ended with a jovial song about loneliness (*After Hours*). However, the band's repeated changes in style had left their audience way behind and this album failed to make a popular impact. Mid-1969 saw them without a record contract, but in 1970 they recorded *Loaded*, generally regarded as a dynamic rock'n'roll album. Unfortunately, Reed quit a month before its release, when the band, benefiting from a renewed wave of public interest, appeared on the brink of achieving commercial success. The album contained at least three further classics: *Sweet Jane*, the story of a resilient city girl, *Sweet Nothing*, an account of city kids able to live on next to nothing and *Rock and Roll*. The remaining members attempted to keep the band going with new recruits, but quit after the inevitably disappointing *Squeeze* was released in 1970. Posthumously two live albums were released, the poorly recorded *Live At Max's Kansas City* and *1969*, a recording of gigs in Texas and San Francisco that year.

VU, which appeared in February 1985, is a collection of unreleased studio recordings from 1968-9. It became their most successful album commercially, climbing to No. 87 in the U.S. Album Charts. This was augmented the following year by *Another View*, which compiled another batch of previously unissued recordings by the 'B' and 'C' line-ups.

Cale and Reed later achieved the popular success that eluded them with **The Velvets** through a series of solo albums. Nico, who had appeared in Warhol's movie 'Chelsea Girls' prior to joining **Velvet Underground**, also released three solo albums (*Chelsea Girl*, *The Marble Index* and *Desertshore*) with assistance from Cale before emigrating to Paris in 1971.

In retrospect, **The Velvets**' first album, with its harsh loud music and its lyrical obsession with decadence, was probably the most significant album of this era in that it previewed the aggressive punk sounds to emerge in the late seventies.

Guitarist Sterling Morrison died at the age of 53 on August 30th, 1995. (VJ/CF)

THE VELVET UNDERGROUND - 1969 LP.

The Venetian Blinds

45:	Just Knowing You Love Me/	
	Quit Your Belly Achin' Baby	(Grudge GR 1651) 196?

Based themselves in San Antonio, Texas. Ric Jansen wrote, arranged and produced the flip, a raw garage number, which has resurfaced on *Texas Punk From The Sixties* (LP). (VJ)

The Venture '5'

| 45: | The Way You Feel/Good'N'Bad | (Venturie 1001) 1966 |

The flip of this West Texas garage band's solo bid for stardom, a raw and rather routine effort, can also be found on *Highs In The Mid-Sixties, Vol. 13* (LP). They disintegrated when the lead singer was drafted after graduating from high school. (VJ)

The Venus Flytrap

Personnel:	DEBBIE BINETTI	drms	ABC
	KEN CZAPKAY	bs	ABC
	NANCY MORGAN	vcls	AB
	DAN SANCHEZ	ld gtr, vcls	ABC
	PETER SESSIONS	gtr	ABC
	BARD DUPONT	bs	BC
	MICHELE SEVRYN	vcls	C

45s:	Have You Ever /The Note	(Jaguar 103) 1967
	Have You Ever /The Note	(Mijji 3005) 1967

Based in Redwood City, this band was formed in late 1966 by Sanchez. When Czapkay was drafted shortly after the release of their 45, he was replaced by Bard Dupont, formerly of the **Great Society** and fresh from the Demon Lover, who had earlier included Pete Sessions. When Morgan departed Dupont's partner Michele Sevryn was brought in on vocals but Dupont himself quit soon after in early '68. For the full story check out Alec Palao's article in 'Cream Puff War #2'.

Have You Ever is a plaintive folk-punk ballad full of chiming guitars, which can be heard on *Psychedelic Unknowns, Vol. 6* (LP & CD). *The Note*, full of angst and more tinkling tearful guitars, is also worthy of note (!) and has resurfaced on the *Acid and Flowers* (CD), *Girls In The Garage, Vol. 2* (CD) and *Girls In The Garage, Vol. 6* (LP). (VJ/MW/AP)

The Versatiles

Personnel:	DARRYL HUFFMAN	ld gtr, keyb'ds	A
	P.J. JOHNSTON	drms	A
	DAVID SMITH	bs	A
	JERRY SMITH	gtr	A

45s:	Cyclothymia / Farmers Daughter	(Rickarby 106) 1967
α	Somethin' Like A Man / Warm In The Rain	(Rickarby 107) 1967/8

NB: α also released with two versions of *Somethin'*... presumably a promo-only 45.

A cool-lookin' teen quartet from Mobile, Alabama, who were popular on the Port City scene in the late sixties, appearing at venues like The Stork Club and The Happening.

Cyclothymia, a sultry fuzz-punker clearly inspired by the Kinks' *You Really Got Me*, deserves the honour of being the opening cut on *Psychedelic States: Alabama Vol. 1* (CD). The uncompiled flip is a winsome version of Brian Wilson's *Farmers (sic) Daughter*. (MW)

Very-Ations

45:	She Can't Be Won / I'm So Lonely	(Rink NR 541/2) 1966

A bunch of students from Birmingham, Alabama, whose sole 45 was released on an Atlanta, Georgia label. *She Can't Be Won* appears on *Psychedelic States: Alabama Vol. 1* (CD). (MW)

Vestells

45:	Won't You Tell Me/Please Walk Away	(Bo Jo 001) 1966

Out of Stroudsberg, Pennsylvania, the band recorded the above 45 at the Cameo Parkway studios in Philadelphia. *Won't You Tell Me*, is a very routine garage-punk offering. The group split in 1967 when all three members were drafted for the Vietnam War.

Compilation appearances include *Won't You Tell Me* on *Back From The Grave, Vol. 5* (LP) and *Back From The Grave, Vol. 2* (CD). (VJ)

The Vestich Brothers

ALBUM:	1 LIVE AT WOLFENDALE'S	(Eclipse 11779) 1978 SC

From Indiana, a local hippie group like New Riders/**Grateful Dead**, with covers of *Heard It Through The Grapevine*, *Friend Of The Devil*, *Born On The Bayou* and *Ghost Riders In The Sky*. (SR)

Mike Vetro and The Cellar Dwellers

Personnel incl:	DAVE BONOVITCH		A
	BRENT LECKIE	drms	A
	JIM McCLUNG		A
	MIKE VETRO	vcls	AB
	JOHNNY SAMBATARO	gtr	B

EP:	1(B) MIKE VETRO AND THE CELLAR DWELLERS (PS)	(Art 2006) 1966

A Florida outfit based in the Miami area whose rare EP contains *That's Not True*, *You Got Me Running*, *I Want To Go Home*, *Summertime*, *Slow Motion* and *I Saw Her In A Mustang*. The latter is a cover of Sambataro's previous band **The Vandals** (from Hollywood, Florida).

That's Not True, is a rollicking party swinger with a frenetically-fingered lead solo and impressive drumming. Sambataro would reemerge a decade later in Firefall. **Mike Vetro** was previously in Fort Lauderdale's Continentals with Leckie; later he fronted Mike Vetro's Soul Brothers, became a lounge lizard, released a cabaret-style album in 1970 - *Live'n Kickin' At The Losers* (Vetrix 8070) and then became a booking agent.

Compilation appearances include: *Mustang* on *Let's Dig 'Em Up, Vol. 1* (CD); and *That's Not True* on *Psychedelic States - Florida Vol. 2* (CD). (MW/JLh/RM)

Kevin Vicalvi

Personnel:	DENIS DE LA GORGENDIERE	bs, vcls	A
	DORRIE POWERS	vcls	A
	DAVE RICE	drms, perc	A
	KEVIN VICALVI	vcls, gtr, piano, hrmnca, synth	A

ALBUM:	1(A) SONGS FROM DOWN THE HALL	(Private Pressing) 1974 SC

NB: (1) came in a plain white cover with a wrap around photo cover that have the lyrics on the inside.

VICTIMS OF CHANCE - Goin' Home Blue LP.

From Worcester, Massachusetts, a "real people" acid-folk duo with some electric tracks, fragile vocals and Eastern influences. Their sole album is beginning to interest some collectors.

Nowadays, Kevin Vicalvi's based out of Nashville and still very much a working musician. (SR/JAt/RB)

Vice-roys (Viceroys)

Personnel:	RICK EMERSON	ld gtr	A
	RON EMERSON	bs	A
	FRANK GIANNINI	drms	A
	RICHARD P. GIANNINI	organ	A
	JON EHLERS	bs	
	LARRY HOLMES	bs	
	HARRY KAWOLSKI	sax	
	WILLIAM MORALES	ld gtr	

			HCP
45s:	α Lame Duck / Heartbreak (instrs)	(Acquarius ACQ-1004) 1963	-
	β Seagrams / Moasin' (instrs)	(Bethlehem 3045) 1963	127
	Buzz Bomb / Joshin' (instrs)	(Bethlehem 3070) 1963	-
	χ Not Too Much Twist / Tears On My Pillow	(Bethlehem 3088) 1964	-
	α Liverpool / Tonk (instrs)	(USA 761) 1965	-
	δ Five Steps To Hell / Wait And See	(D & C No #) 1967	-

NB: α as by The Vice-Roys. β Seagrams was changed to Sea Green on later pressings. χ 'B' side also seen listed as The Fox but this is unconfirmed. δ as by The Viceroys.

The Vice-Roys formed in Chicago and spent a decade (1960-1970) touring all across the US occasionally stopping off to lay down some tracks on wax. This has caused confusion amongst collectors ever since. Leader Richard Giannini was in contact with Gary Myers (author of the Wisconsin book 'Do You Hear That Beat') to straighten the facts, given that some of their 45s have been attributed to Californian and Seattle outfits.

Their early forays were instrumentals. *Seagrams* was their succesful, bubbling up to No. 127 on the Billboard charts. For some reason the famous whiskey maker of that name did not appreciate the free publicity so the 45 had to be repressed, with an amended title of *Sea Green*.

Around this time there may be have been an album released on Bethlehem, but this has yet to be confirmed.

In late 1967 whilst in San Mateo, **The Viceroys** put down their final waxing on a small Sunnyvale, California label D&C. *Five Steps To Hell* marked an update in style. It's a glorious slab of fuzzy distorted garage-psych and can be experienced on *Psychedelic Crown Jewels, Vol. 2* (Dble LP & CD). The track was taken from an album-sized acetate that gave no band identity, but this failed to defeat super-sleuth Mike Markesich. (MW/GM/MM/RM)

The Viceroys

Personnel:	AL BERRY	keyb'ds	ABC
	KIM EGGERS	sax	ABC
	BUD POTTER	bs	ABC
	GREG THOMPSON	drms	A
	JIM 'HARPO' VALLEY	gtr	AB
	FRED ZEUFELDT	drms	BC
	GREG BECK	gtr	C

ALBUM:	1(B)	AT GRANNY'S PAD	(Bolo BLP 800) 1963 SC

45s:	Don't Let Go/Down Beat Blues	(Eden 9001) 1962
	Granny's Pad/Blues Bouquet	(Bolo 736) 1962
	Granny's Pad/Blues Bouquet	(Dot 16456) 1963
	Goin' Back To Granny's/Get Set	(Bolo 739) 1963
	Dartell Stomp/Granny's Medley	(Bolo 743) 1964
	Death Of An Angel/Earth Angel	(Imperial 66058) 1964
	Please Please Please/Tiger Shark	(Bolo 749) 1964
	Bacon Fat/Until	(Bolo 750) 1965
	That Sound/Tired Of Waiting For You	(Bolo 754) 1965

A significant Pacific Northwest outfit. Like early **Paul Revere** this was basically a rockin' instrumental group though they did use 'featured vocalists' including Jimmy Pigskins, Erin Stuart and Nancy Clair at various times. After founder **Jim Valley** left to join **Don and The Goodtimes**, a change in style took place resulting in the bouncy beater *That Sound*, backed by a solid cover of The Kinks song. The transformation was completed with the renaming to **The Surprise Package**, who redid *That Sound* as *Out Of My Mind* for good measure.

Keyboardist Mike Rogers also played in **The Viceroys** prior to them becoming **The Surprise Package**.

Compilation appearances include *That Sound* on *Boulders, Vol. 11* (LP); *Goin' Back To Granny's* and *Granny's Pad* on *Bolo Bash* (LP). (MW/DR/JA/TWg)

Victims of Chance

ALBUMS:	1	VICTIMS OF CHANCE	(Crestview CRS 3052) 19?? R1
	2	GOIN' HOME BLUE	(No label) 197? -

This bunch came from L.A. *Victims Of Chance* is of minor interest to some collectors. The title track is very pleasant and accessible, but the rest of the album is extremely freeform and experimental (with lots of brass) and very much an acquired taste. They certainly had lots of recording freedom! Most of the material was composed by a guy called Johnny Kitchen who may have been in the band. There is a very strong **Zappa** influence here. *Goin' Home Blue* was housed in the "Century" mill cover, also used by **Fifth Flight** on their *Into Smoke Tree Village* release and is mostly light country-rock.

The mysterious Johnny Kitchen is also associated with some Canadian releases on the Condor label including *Crazy People*. (VJ)

Victoria

Personnel incl:	SHARON BARTON	A
	MAUREEN DEIDELBAUM	A
	GREG RUBAN	A
	CHERYL SIMPSON	A

ALBUMS:	1(A)	VICTORIA	(No label) 1971 R5
	2(A)	KINGS, QUEENS & JOKERS	(No label) 197? R5

NB: (1) was a demo album issued in a plain white jacket. (2) is an alternate pressing of (1), with the title shown rubber-stamped on the front of the sleeve. (2) contains fewer tracks than (1). (1) reissued in Germany (Little Indians #7) 1997, in a red velveteen jacket with gold foil embossed print and on CD by the same label with several previously unreleased bonus tracks.

A rare local New Jersey private press, with an "odd" sound created by this largely female group and featuring horns prominently on several tracks.

VICTORIA - Victoria CD.

Two hundred copies of the album were pressed in 1971, and Ruban distributed a quantity of them through Europe while on a motorcycle trip in the early seventies.

Victoria may be connected in some manner to **Dirty Martha**.

One track, *Ride A Rainbow* has also resurfaced on *Love, Peace And Poetry, Vol. 1* (LP & CD). (CF/MW)

The Victors

Personnel:	DAN DAILEY	gtr	A
	JIM KANE	bs	A
	TERRY KNUDSEN	keyb'ds	A
	GARY LEACH	drms	A
	DENNY WAITE	vcls	A

This Minneapolis group later became **The Litter** and they can also be heard on the Get Hip album (GHAS 5066), *Electras vs. Scotsmen / Victors* (1993). It contains tracks from 1965 to 1968. All bar Denny Waite were previously in **The Scotsmen**.

Compilation appearances include: *Midnight Hour, I Ain't Gonna Eat Out My Heart Anymore, One More Time, Mister You're A Better Man Than I* and *Little Girl* on *The Scotty Story - Minnesota's Legendary '60s Rock Label!* (CD). (VJ/GG)

Vigilantes

45:	Ain't It Sad/Notice Me	(JCP 1010) 1967

Operated out of Apex in North Carolina. Their sole vinyl epitaph is this 45. The 'A' side, *Ain't It Sad*, exhibits a strong black music influence along with its psychedelic leanings.

Compilation appearances include: *Ain't It Sad* on *Tobacco A-Go-Go, Vol. 1* (LP); and *Notice Me* on *Tobacco A-Go-Go, Vol. 2* (LP). (GG/VJ)

The Vikings

Personnel:	FRED GARCIA	ld vcls, gtr	A
	BUTCH LEVOUE	sax, vcls	A
	TOM MULCAHEY	ld gtr	A
	JIM POWERS	bs	A
	JIMMY SYLVIA	drms	A

45s:	You Can't Do That/Summertime	(Salem SR-007) 1965
	Blue Feeling/I Ain't Got You	(Star Rhythm SR-1 001) 1980

Operating out of the Taunton, Massachusetts area, this band was strongly influenced by the British invasion sound. Indeed, the 'A' side of their sole offering at the time - *You Can't Do That* - was a Lennon/McCartney composition and they advertised themselves as 'The Vikings: Featuring The Exciting English Sound'. The Star Rhythm single was released in the early eighties, but recorded back in 1965. In fact the **Vikings** recorded ten songs that year and Decca showed some interest in the tapes of the sessions, but almost simultaneously with this the band split when two members were drafted. *Bay State Rock* (LP) includes *You Can't Do That, Blue Feeling* and *I Ain't Got You* along with two otherwise unreleased tracks from their 1965 session:- *Have Mercy* and *Hitch Hike*. (VJ)

The Vikings

Personnel incl:	CHARLES NETTLES	A
	C. PUTMAN	A

45s:	Come On And Love Me/I Will Never Go	(Viking 1000) 1966
	Cherish The Love You Feel/Golden Girl	(Lowery 360) 1968

A different outfit, this time from deepest Alabama. The first 45 was recorded by Ed Boutwell in Birmingham, Alabama and although *Come On And Love Me* is a fairly standard garage dirge, *I Will Never Go* has a **New Colony Six** vocal sound. Both sides were co-written by Charles Nettles. This influence continues on their second 45, where *Cherish...* again written

VICTORIA.

by Nettles sounds just like Mercury-era **New Colony Six**! Some might hate this for its orchestration, but others will like it. The 'B' side is a Tommy Roe cover, which is very common for Lowery-related acts!

Charles Nettles must have been a big fan of the **New Colony Six**, who did get airplay in the South at the time with *I Confess* and *Love You So Much*.

Come On And Love Me can also be found on *Highs In The Mid-Sixties, Vol. 8* (LP). (JLh/VJ)

The Village Outcast (aka The Village Outcasts)

45:	Under The Thumb/The Girl I Used To Love	(Echo) 196?

Hailing from Dover in Delaware, their version of The Rolling Stones' *Under My Thumb* was retitled *Under The Thumb* and is not a bad effort, coming with a solid organ backing, typical garage beat and effective vocals. The flip is also a great teen organ-punker.

This band also contributed a version of *Hello, I Love You* to the 1968 album *Hazelton '68* as **The Village Outcasts**.

Compilation appearances include: *Under The Thumb* on *Pebbles, Vol. 21* (LP) and *Garage Punk Unknowns, Vol. 8* (LP); and *The Girl I Used To Love* on *Back From The Grave, Vol. 8* (Dble LP) and *Back From The Grave, Vol. 8* (CD). (VJ)

Villagers

45s:	You're Gonna Lose That Girl / Laugh It Off	(Volume 100) 1966
	Laugh It Off / You're Gonna Lose That Girl	(Fame 1005) 1966
	You Can't Stay / Cool It	(Volume 101) 1967
	Where Have You Been (All My Life) / Every Saturday	(Volume 45-MS-1205) 1967
	Where Have You Been (All My Life) / Every Saturday	(Atco 6517) 1967
	Thank You Baby / A Shot Of Rhythm & Blues	(Atco 6568) 1968

The best-known of many sixties **Villagers** hailed from the Florida communities of Chipley, Wewahitchka and Marianna. They recorded just across the border at the F.A.M.E. studios (Florence Alabama Music Enterprises) and with local hits there, came to be regarded frequently as an Alabama band.

Their forte was catchy and commercial beat-pop with an Invasion flavour and their debut kicks off in that fashion with a good version of the Tam's *Laugh It Off* backed by a Beatles ditty - the lead vocalist has a timbre not unlike that of Manfred Mann's Paul Jones.

The follow-up is most sought-after by garage fans - *Cool It*, featuring some lowdown fuzz, is compiled on *It's A Hard Life*. It was their only walk on the wild side and they returned to accessible pop with *Where Have You Been*.

Compilation appearances include *Cool It* on *It's A Hard Life* (LP). (MW/MM/JLh)

Villagers

Personnel incl:	RICK STEELE	vcls	A
	JEFF TEAGUE	drms	A

More **Villagers** from Florida. This West Palm Beach outfit released no 45s but some members went onto bigger things. Vocalist Rick Steele formed **Peace and Quiet** with Jim Tolliver (ex-**Birdwatchers** and **Razor's Edge**) and members of Miami's Convairs.

Drummer Jeff Teague went to Nashville and was in the Poussette-Dart Band. (JLh)

Villagers

Personnel incl:	BRUCE ARNOLD	gtr, vcls	A
	JACK McKENES	gtr, vcls	A

A Worcester, Massachusetts, band in 1966 who released no 45s. Arnold and McKenes would find considerable success after forming **Orpheus** with Erik Gulliksen of the **Blue Echoes** and Harry Sandler of the Mods. (MW)

Villagers

45: Bring Me A Rose / C.C.Rider   (JCP 1005) 1964/5

Thought to hail from the Charlotte, North Carolina area but this is unconfirmed. This 45 is not garage despite being on the very collectable JCP label - *Bring Me A Rose* is a weak folk-pop ballad that's been compared to the Seekers, despite the lack of female vocalist. Their version of *C.C. Rider* is done in a traditional upbeat folk style, ala 1964-era **MFQ**. (MW/MM/JLh)

Villagers

45: He's Not The Same / Sunshine My Way   (Hamlet V-1000) 1968

Garagey girl group from Dayton, Ohio. A mid-tempo beater with primitive chops that sounds more like 1964, backed by a gloomy folk-rock ballad (despite the title). (MW/MM)

Villagers

45: You're My Baby (Don't You Forget It) /
?   (Village Square #unkn) 196?

A rare 45 from a Charleston, South Carolina outfit. (MW/MM)

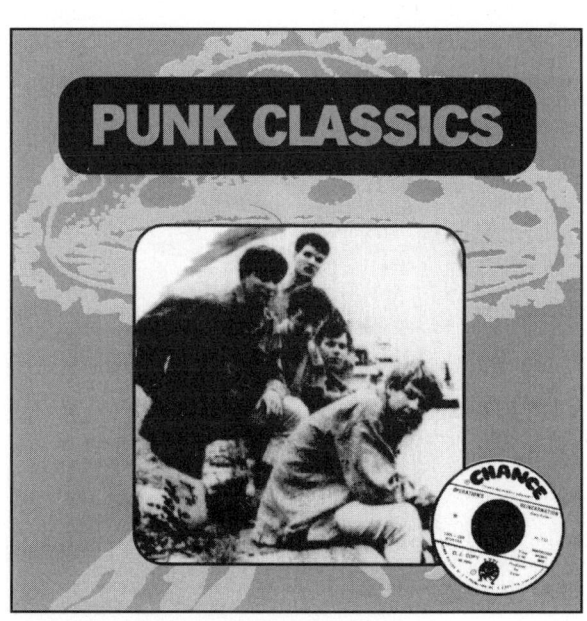

PUNK CLASSICS (Comp CD) including The Villains.

Villagers

Acetate: Empty Heart / Shake A Tail Feather   (Jaggars) 196?

Possibly from Arkansas, this outfit's sole legacy appears to be one rare acetate. Their choice of covers is encouraging. (MW/MM)

Villagers

45: Headless Nightmare / To Be Redeemed   (Petal 1410) 1963

Seen described as 'haunting folk-psych', this is straight folk by an outfit from whereabouts unknown. (JLh/MW)

The Villagers

Personnel:	JOHN MORAN		A
	PAT MORAN	vcls	A
	MIKE ROBARGE		A
	STEVE SCHARREN		A

ALBUM: 1(A) THE VILLAGERS HOMEMADE
                        (Private pressing 584N10) c1971 ?

Probably from Ohio, a folk-rock quartet with some psychedelic influences. Their rare album was recorded partly live at Friar Tucks in Maumee, Ohio, includes covers of *Frisco Bay Blues* and *High Flyin' Bird*. (SR)

The Village Sound

45s: Sally's Got A Good Thing/The La La Song (HIP 8003) 1968
Eloise (Hang On)/
Hey Jack (Don't Hijack My Phone)   (HIP 8013) 1969
Truth Or Consequences/Big Bird   (HIP 8021) 1970

A forgotten group, on the same label as **Paris Pilot** and **Southwest F.O.B.**. They were probably from the Memphis area. (SR)

The Villains

45s: α Don't Ever Leave Me/Shortening Bread   (Bullet 11001) 1966
       Midnight Hour / Love Is The Treasure   (Bullet 11008) c1966

NB: α issued both as **The Villains** and as The Villians.

An obscure Tennessee outfit.

Compilation appearances include: *Shortenin' Bread* on *Punk Classics* (CD) and *Punk Classics, Vol. 5* (7"); and *Don't Ever Leave Me* on *Psychedelic Unknowns Vol. 8* (LP & CD). (VJ/MW/JLh)

Sonny Villegas

45: Help Me, Help You / I Cry   (Arco 6706) 1967

The 'A' side of this Hollywood label 45 by Armando "Sonny" Villegas has resurfaced on *Fuzz, Flaykes And Shakes, Vol. 4* (LP & CD). *Help Me...* is crisp upbeat pop similar to **Paul Revere and The Raiders**; *I Cry* is more moody and noteworthy for the nimble pirouetting guitar throughout. (MW)

Viola Crayola

Personnel:	BILL JOLLY	bs	A
	ANTHONY VIOLA	gtr	A
	RON VIOLA	perc	A

ALBUM: 1(A) MUSIC - BREATHING OF STATUES
                              (Fautna no #) 1974 R2

Wild progressive instrumental power trio sounds, recorded in New York, although the group originally came from San Antonio, Texas. A real killer in style, this album is going to be outside the realm of this book for some, and yet some dealers describe it as psychedelic, so go figure. A good record is a good record and this one is recommended!

The band ceased recording after Tony (Anthony) Viola was tragically killed in an auto-train wreck in August 1974. (CF/SGg)

The Viscount V

Personnel:	MIKE ABRAHAM	bs	A
	FRANK COONS	organ	A
	JOE CORAZZI	gtr	A
	JIMMY FRANCHINI	vcls	A
	SONNY JOHNSON	drms	A

45s:	Cherry Red 'Vette/Anna	(Lavette LA 5003/4) 1965
	My Angel/She Doesn't Know	(Lavette LA 5009/10) 1966

Operated out of Albuquerque in New Mexico. Both of these 45s were produced by **Lindy Blaskey** who fronted The Lavells. This band later became **The Berrys**.

She Doesn't Know has resurfaced on *Teenage Shutdown, Vol. 5* (LP & CD). (VJ/MW/MDo)

Viscounts

Personnel:	RAY DEMENT	drms	A
	TERRY HAILEY	keyb'ds	A
	JIMMY HUTCHCRAFT	gtr	A
	SHERRILL PARKS Jr.	sax	A
	SHERRILL PARKS Sr.	vcls	A
	HENRY SHERFFIUS	bs	A

45:	Blueberry Hill /	
	Brown-Eyed Handsome Man	(Four Sons 4110) 1966

This Union City, Tennessee, band included a father and son in their line-up for their debut 45, on which they chose to cover Fats Domino and Chuck Berry. Shortly after its release they became **The Jades**. (MW/RHl)

Vision of Sunshine

Personnel:	JANE BALTINHOUSE	vcls	A
	GERALD HAUSER	vcls, gtr, piano, celeste, calliope	A
	SEAN ALLAN NELSON	piano, harpsichord, organ	A
	TERRI OSIECKI	flute	A
	MARY TILL	flute	A
	(MIKE DeTEMPLE	gtr, banjo, bs	A)
	(ANDY DOUGLAS	drms	A)
	(FLINT	gtr	A)
	(BILL LAZARUS	perc	A)

ALBUM:	1(A)	VISION OF SUNSHINE	
		(Avco Embassy AVE 33007)	1970 SC

From Los Angeles and produced by Howie Kane, this group is typical of the Californian hippie groups: good male and female vocals and sophisticated arrangements using various keyboards and flutes. Unfortunately, the songwriting skills of Gerald Hauser were rather limited and the album, which is quite rare now, is only average fayre, with some songs being too mellow and several lyrics having a Christian content (*You Get What You Pray For*).

The best tracks are *Bizarrek Kind* written by **Rex Holman**, the nice *She Said* (the only track with a long electric guitar solo) and *Stranger Here*. The cover of Jerry Jeff Walker's *Mr Bojangles* is easily dispensable. (SR)

The Visions

Personnel:	BILLY DALTON	gtr, vcls	A
	BRUCE DOZIER	bs, vcls	A
	GARY JAMES	ld gtr, ld vcls	A
	CHARLES (CHUCK) MORGAN	drms, vcls	A

45s:	Take Her/She's The Girl For Me	(Vimco 20) 1965
	Take Her/Route 66	(Vimco 20) 1965
	Humpty Dumpty/You Won't See Me	(Vimco 21) 196?
	Threshold Of Love / How Can I Be Down	(Uni 55031) 1967
	Keepin' Your Eyes On The Sun / Small Town Commotion	(Uni 55042) 1967
	Black And White Rainbow/ Bulldog Cadillac	(Warner Bros. 5898) 1967
α	Bubble Gum Music/1941	(Buddah 78) 1969

NB: α released as by Rock 'n' Roll Double Bubble Trading Card Co. Of Philadelphia.

From Mineral Wells in Texas, this raw punk combo are best remembered for their version of *Route 66*, although after a name change to **Rock 'n' Roll Double Bubble Trading Card Co. of Philadelphia**, they had an American Top 40 hit, with *Bubble Gum Music*. The band also made a cameo appearance in an episode of the American television series, "Run For Your Life", starring Ben Gazarra. In the cameo, **The Visions** are seen performing *Small Town Commotion*.

The band later became Dalton, James and Sutton, whilst Gary James later was a founding member of both Blackhorse and The Cauze.

Today, Gary lives in Fort Worth, Chuck Morgan is a security officer in Houston and Billy Dalton is thought to have moved to San Bernardino, California.

Compilation appearances include: *Humpty Dumpty* on *Texas Flashbacks, Vol. 3* (LP & CD), *Flashback, Vol. 3* (LP) and *Highs In The Mid-Sixties, Vol. 17* (LP); *Route 66* on *Flashback, Vol. 6* (LP) and *Highs In The Mid-Sixties, Vol. 11* (LP); and *Small Town Commotion* on *Incredible Sound Show Stories, Vol. 6* (LP). (VJ/MW/RKk)

Vito and The Hands

Personnel incl:	VITO PAULEKAS		A

45:	Where It's At/Vito And The Hands	(Living Legend 69) 1966

On this **Kim Fowley** produced 45, a long hippie rap turns into an acid garage freakout. It featured **Vito** backed by the **Mothers Of Invention**... **Vito** was a bohemian sculptor and dancemaster, who led a group of Los Angeles free spirits, holding love fests and parties, back in the sixties.

VISION OF SUNSHINE - Vision Of Sunshine LP.

Originally from Lowell, Massachusetts, he came from a very artistic background and learnt wood carving at an early age. In 1938, he was convicted of attempted robbery, but released into service in 1942. After the war he relocated to L.A. where he latter became involved with the circle of freaks surrounding the **Mothers**, **Fraternity Of Man** and **Kim Fowley**.

Vito eventually became mayor of the small Sonoma town of Cotati, a hippie enclave near Santa Rosa. He later died from a blood disease.

Compilation appearances include *Vito And The Hands* on *Kim Fowley - Underground Animal* (LP). (SBn/MW)

Vondells

Personnel:	DANNY	A
	GARY HAMILTON	A
	JIM	A
	STEVE	A

A darkly-clad quartet of teens from Dayton, Ohio. Their only known recording is *A Loser*, a gloomy ballad of self-condemnation that'll have you reaching for the Prozac. In this instance however these guys were WINNERS - one of the twelve groups selected from the three-day WONE-sponsored Daytonian battle of the bands in 1966 and presented for posterity on the souvenir album *WONE, The Dayton Scene* (Prism PR-1966). (MW)

Von Ruden

Personnel incl:	RUDY VON RUDEN	A

45s:	The Spider And The Fly/Judy	(Ivanhoe 503) 1970
α	Judy / Good Day	(Ivanhoe 504) 1970
α	Good Day / Judy	(Metro Media MM-203) c1970

NB: α as **Bobby Trend**.

This was Rudy Von Ruden, of Johnny and The Shy Guys, out of La Crosse, Wisconsin. His fairly demented 'n' doomy interpretation of Jagger-Richards' *The Spider And The Fly* is worth a spin if only for the novelty value.

Judy is a haunting lament with husky vocals and plaintive guitar. It reappeared on the next Ivanhoe release under the pseudonym **Bobby Trend**, backed by a cover of **Ormandy**'s *Good Day*.

Compilation appearances include: *The Spider And The Fly* on *Pebbles Vol. 7* (CD), *Pebbles, Vol. 11* (LP) and *Turds On A Bum Ride, Vol. 1* (Dble LP); *Judy* on *Turds On A Bum Ride, Vol. 2* (Dble LP); and *The Spider & The Fly* and *Judy* on *Turds On A Bum Ride, Vol. 1 & 2* (Dble CD). (VJ/MW)

PEBBLES Vol. 11 (Comp LP) including Von Ruden.

Eric Von Schmidt

ALBUMS:	1	VON SCHMIDT AND CAHN	(Folkways 2417) 1961 -
	2	ERIC SINGS VON SCHMIDT	(Prestige 7384) 1964 -
	3	THE FOLK BLUES OF	(Prestige 7717) 1969 -
	4	WHO KNOCKED THE BRAINS OUT OF THE SKY	
			(Smash 67124) 1969 -
	5	2ND RIGHT 3RD ROW	
			(Poppy PYS-5705) 1972 -

NB: He also had two tracks on *The Blues Project* (Elektra) 1964.

From Boston, **Eric Von Schmidt** began his career in the late fifties and is recognized as a gifted composer, a fine guitarist and a good folk-blues singer. A very influential musician, it should be noted that Bob Dylan wrote the liner notes on his fourth and fifth albums while Richard Farina penned the notes for his second. He was also influential on many East Coast blues/folk singers: Geoff Muldaur, **Tom Rush**, **Jim Kweskin** etc.

His 1964 album was produced by Sam Charters and featured Geoff Muldaur and Mel Lyman. The song *Joshua Gone Barbados* was covered by **Tom Rush** and several other folk and blues acts.

The Smash album is reputedly very strange but we haven't heard it yet.

The 1972 album was produced by Jim Rooney and Michael Cuscuna, arranged by and engineered by Nick Jameson, the leader of **American Dream**. It's a good and relaxed effort, with support of **Paul Butterfield**, Geoff and Maria Muldaur, Billy Mundi, Garth Hudson, Stu Brotman (**Kaleidoscope**), Jim Colegrove (**Bo Grumpus**), Ben Keith (**Mother Earth**, Neil Young) and Amos Garrett.

His records are now quite rare.

Von Schmidt was also a noted painter and illustrator, his name can be found on sleeves of records by The Blue Velvet Band or Geoff and Maria Muldaur. (SR)

The Voyagers

Personnel:	LANCE DAVENPORT	bs	A
	JOEY GONZALES	vcls	A
	DAVE KING	drms	A
	STEVE PORTER	gtr	A
	JAY SEGER	ld gtr	A

45s:	I Want You Back/Can't Save This Heart	(Feature F 101) 1965
	Away/I'm So Lonely	(Feature F 111) 1966

The first 45 features a melodic garage-ballad plus a tougher chunk of garage-beat from a Racine, Wisconsin group, circa 1966. (MW/GM)

The Vydels

45:	What I'm Gonna Do/?	(Garnet 101) 1965

A Chicago punk band. *Garage Punk Unknowns, Vol. 5* (LP) gives an airing to *What I'm Gonna Do*. (VJ)

VANILLA FUDGE - Renaissance CD.

VANILLA FUDGE - Near The Beginning CD.

VANILLA FUDGE - Rock & Roll CD.

VANILLA FUDGE - The Beat Goes On CD.

VELVET UNDERGROUND - White Light White Heat LP.

VELVET UNDERGROUND - Velvet Underground (3rd) LP.

Wabash Resurrection

ALBUM: 1   GET IT OFF!   (Pepperhead) c1974/5 R1/R2

A power trio influenced by Led Zeppelin and Lynyrd Skynyrd with cuts like *The Angel Came And Went* or *Pigsty Blues*. Their album was issued in limited quantities and is of marginal interest here. (SR)

Tom Wachunas

ALBUM: 1   SPARE CHANGES   (Owl) 1975 SC

Housed in a neat black and white cover, comes this album by a local Ohio singer, with material ranging from rock to singer songwriter folk. It was issued on the same label as **Raven**. (SR)

The Wackers

Personnel:	RANDY BISHOP	vcls, bs, gtr, keyb'ds	ABC
	SPENCER "ERNIE" EARNSHAW	drms	ABC
	BOB SEGARINI	ld vcls, gtr, bs, perc	ABC
	MICHAEL STULL	vcls, gtr, keyb'ds	AB
	WILLIAM "KOOTCH" TROCHIM	bs, gtr, vcls	ABC
	(BILL HENDERSON	drms	A)
	(JACK SCHAEFFER	sax, clarinet	A C)
	(KATHIE KODAMA	koto	B)

ALBUMS:	1(A)	WACKERIN HEIGHTS	(Elektra EKS-74098) 1971 -
	2(B)	HOT WACKS	(Elektra EKS-75025) 1972 -
	3(C)	SHREDDER	(Elektra EKS-75046) 1972 -

HCP

45s:	Oh My Love/?	(Elektra 45772) 1971 -
	I Hardly Knew Her Name/ Do You Know The Reason	(Elektra 45783) 1972 -
	Day And Night/Last Dance	(Elektra 45816) 1972 65
	Hey Lawdy Mama/?	(Elektra 45841) 1972 124

After the failure of **Roxy**, Segarini and Bishop went on to form **The Wackers** with William "Kootch" Trochim, who was with Segarini in **Family Tree**. Produced by Gary Usher (**Sagittarius**, **Byrds**), their three albums are typical of the early seventies California rock-pop scene and some rate their albums quite highly (some others may find them boring!). Their best moment may be the cover of *Oh My Love*, the Lennon/Ono song with a surprising koto, on their second album.

Segarini then moved to Canada and had a solo career there. (SR/CF)

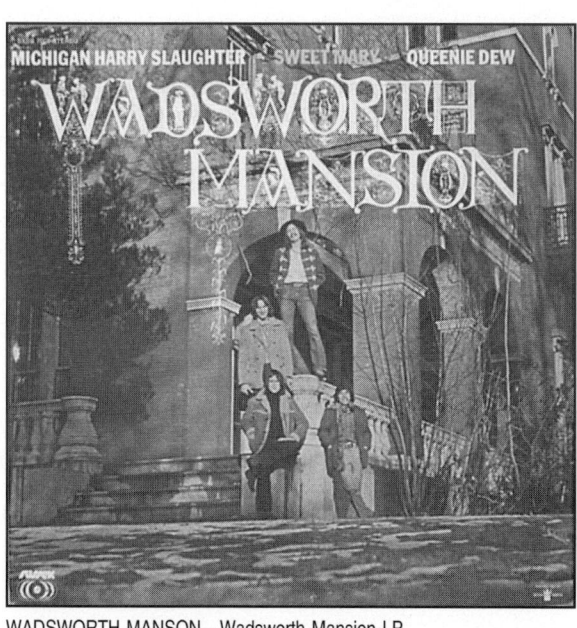

WADSWORTH MANSON - Wadsworth Mansion LP.

Wadsworth Mansion

Personnel incl:	WAYNE GAGNON	ld gtr, vcls, hand bell, cow clap	A
	STEVE JABLECKI	keyb'ds, ld vcls, gtr, perc	A
	JOHN POOLE	bs, vcls, perc	A
	MIKE JABLECKI	drms, perc, vcls	A

ALBUM:	1(A)	WADSWORTH MANSION	(Sussex 7008) 1971 -

HCP

45s:	Sweet Mary/What's On Tonight	(Sussex 209) 1971 7
	Michigan Harry Slaughter/ Havin' Such A Good Time	(Sussex 215) 197? -

Produced by Jim Calvert and Norman Marzano, **Wadsworth Mansion**'s only album contains some good guitar-driven tracks with harmony vocals (notably the catchy *Sweet Mary* written by Steve Joblecki) but has failed to attract collectors' attention.

The 45 version of *Sweet Mary*, which is noticeably different from the album version, hit No. 7 on the Billboard Hot 100. The follow-up single, *Michigan Harry Slaughter*, failed to reach the Billboard charts, but hit No. 99 on the Cashbox Top 100.

Wayne Gagnon was previously in **Tangerine Zoo**.

Sussex was a subsidiary label of Buddah which also released **Mutzie**'s album, which is far superior. (SR/TTi)

Dick Wagner and The Frosts

Personnel incl:	DON HARTMAN	gtr	A
	BOB RIGG	drms	A
	JACK SMOLINSKI	bs	A
	DICK WAGNER	gtr, vcls	A
	MARK FARNER		B

45s:	Bad Girl/A Rainy Day	(Date 1577) 1967
	Sunshine/Little Girl	(Date 1596) 1967

Wagner had previously fronted **The Bossmen** from the Flint/Saginaw area of Michigan and formed this outfit in 1967. They would soon adopt the snappy moniker **Frost** and would garner success into the seventies with three fine albums and several 45s in the hard-rock style prevalent on the Michigan underground/rock scene at that time.

The 45s should be seen as a transition between the Invasion-inspired **Bossmen** and **Frost**. They're in a lighter vein but are still recommended and not hard to find. *Sunshine* is a fine example of an American band playing British style flower-power rock. *Bad Girl* is a re-release of a neat beat-ballad done by **The Bossmen**, whereas *A Rainy Day* is an orchestrated ballad. All appear with **The Bossmen** 45s on *The Complete Bossmen* CD (Wagner Music Group, 1995).

Wagner's name is to be found on releases by numerous area acts, as writer and/or producer:- **Bells Of Rhymney**, **Cherry Slush**, Sand, **Terry Knight and The Pack** and The Wanderers, to mention just a few.

In the seventies, he played with Lou Reed then joined the revamped Alice Cooper band in 1974, writing some of his most famous songs including *Only Women Bleed*, *Welcome To My Nightmare* and *How Ya Gonna See Me Now*. He was still active on the music scene into the new millennium.

Guitarist Mark Farner moved onto hard-rock behemoths Grand Funk Railroad.

Compilation appearances include *Sunshine* on *Mindrocker, Vol. 7* (LP). (VJ/MW/JJn/CRn)

T.Y. Wagner

45s:	α	I'm A No-Count/ Walking Down Lonely Street	(Chattahoochee 699) 1966
		Slander/I Think I Found Love	(Era 3168) 1966

NB: α With The Scotchmen.

A garage-punk act from Los Angeles. **Ty Wagner** was an early sixties rocker who survived the onslaught of beat and released many 45s outside the scope of this book. *I'm A No-Count* is a classic punk anthem, whilst a later effort *Slander* features some great punk lyrics:- 'I thought you were hip/You're just a bum trip/Close your lyin' lip/Don't you know it's a sin/Slander, Slander'. Some great organ backing, too!

Compilation appearances have included: *I'm A No Count* on *Pebbles, Vol. 9* (CD), *Teenage Shutdown, Vol. 4* (LP & CD), *Best of Pebbles, Vol. 3* (LP & CD), *Chosen Few Vol's 1 & 2* (CD) and *The Chosen Few, Vol. 2* (LP); and *Slander* on *Back From The Grave, Vol. 7* (Dble LP). (VJ)

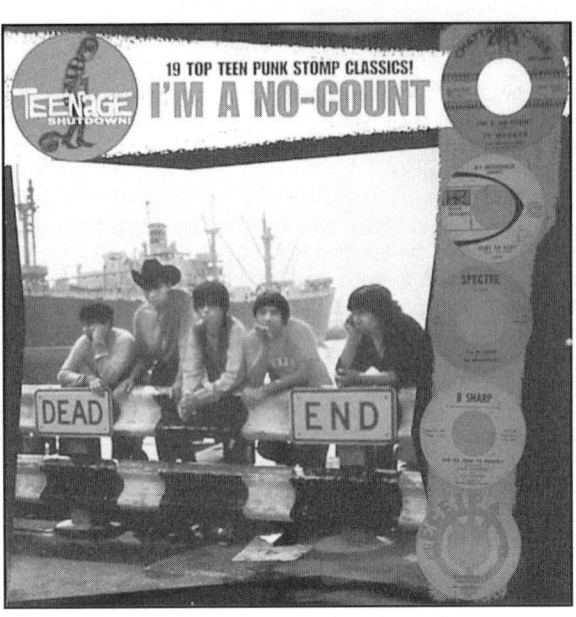

TEENAGE SHUTDOWN Vol. 4 (Comp LP) including TY Wagner.

The Wailers

Personnel:	MIKE BURK	drms	A
	RICH DANGEL	ld gtr	A
	JOHN GREEK	gtr	A
	MARK MARUSH	sax	A
	KENT MORRILL	keyb'ds, vcls	ABC
	BUCK ORMSBY	bs	A
	NEIL ANDERSON	gtr	B
	RON GARDNER	sax, keyb'ds, vcls	BC
	DAVE ROLAND	drms	BC
	DENNY WEAVER	gtr	C

NB: line-up 'A' 1958-60, 'B' 1963-67, 'C' 1967-69.

HCP
ALBUMS:	1(A)	TALL COOL ONE	(Golden Crest 3075) 1959 - R1
	2(B)	AT THE CASTLE	(Etiquette ALB 1) 1962 - SC
	3(B)	WAILERS AND COMPANY	(Etiquette ALB 22) 1963 - SC
	4(B)	TALL COOL ONE	(Imperial 12262) 1964 127 SC
	5(B)	WAILERS WAILERS EVERYWHERE	
			(Etiquette 023) 1965 - SC
	6(B)	OUT OF OUR TREE	(Etiquette ALB 26) 1966 - R1
	7(B)	OUTBURST	(United Artists 6557) 1966 - SC
	8(C)	WALKIN' THROUGH PEOPLE	(Bell 6016) 1968 - -
	9(-)	COLLECTORS ALBUM	
			(Etiquette ET-LP 22296/7) 1984 - SC

NB: (1) and (7) have been reissued on CD by Collectables (COL-CD-0573 / 0587 respectively). (2) also reissued again (Norton CD CNW 902) 1999, also on vinyl. There's also a CD on Etiquette (12693), *The Fabulous Wailers*. It has twenty-seven tracks that cover 1961-69, as indicated by the sub-title *Anthology 1961-69, from Wailers House Party to Walk Thru' People*. Sadly it doesn't contain any of the tracks from their first album on Golden Crest. Also of interest is *Do Not Release!* (Taki) 1997, a limited edition 10" which features early demos for their *Out Of Our Tree* album. Recently the original Golden Crest version of *The Fabulous Wailers* has been reissued from a newly found stereo master tape that sounds incredible, *The Original Golden Crest Masters* (Ace CDHCD 675) 1998. This disc also includes 45s and four unreleased tracks which are a real treat. Another release by Ace is *Golden Crest Instrumentals Featuring The Wailers* (Ace CDCHD 724) 1999. This is an excellent disc of late fifties / early sixties instrumentals featuring six tracks from **The Wailers**, including two alternate (earlier) versions of *Tall Cool One* (previously called *Scotch On The Rocks*) not available on any other disc. *Live Wire: The Best Of The Wailers 1965-67* (Norton CD CNW 904) 1999, also on vinyl, compiles the best of their garage-punk era.

HCP
45s:	We're Goin' Surfin/Shakedown	(Etiquette 6) 1963 -
(1963	Seattle/Partime U.S.A.	(Etiquette 7) 1963 -
onwards)	Tall Cool One/Frenzy	(Etiquette 9) 1964 38
	Mash/On The Rocks	(Imperial 66045) 1964 -
	Don't Take It So Hard/	
	You Better Believe It	(Etiquette 12) 1964 -
	Back To You/	
	You Weren't Using Your Head	(Etiquette 15) 1965 -
	Dirty Robber/Hang Up	(Etiquette 19) 1965 -
	Out Of Our Tree/I Got Me	(Etiquette 21) 1965 -
	Christmas Spirit/	
	(Don't Believe In Christmas By The Sonics)	(Etiquette 22) 1965 -
	It's You Alone/Tears	(Etiquette 24) 1966 -
	It's You Alone/Tears	(United Artists 50,026) 1966 118
	Think Kindly Baby/	
	End Of The Summer	(United Artists 50,065) 1966 -
	You Won't Lead Me On/	
	Tears (Don't Have To Fall)	(United Artists 50,110) 1966 -
	I'm Determined/I Don't Want To Follow You	(Viva 614) 1967 -
	You Can't Fly/Thinking Out Loud	(Bell 694) 1968 -

Formed in the mid-late 1950s in Tacoma, Washington State. Most of their original albums are now sought-after by collectors. Ormsby and Morrill were real pioneers, forming Etiquette Productions and the label in the early sixties - the first band to do so by a long way. They also recorded a 45, *All My Nights, All My Days/Better For Both Of Us* (Jerden 789), under the pseudonym of the **Breakers** in 1966. By 1966 only Ormsby and Morrill remained from the original line-up, Dangel having left to form **The Rooks**, **The Time Machine** and **Floating Bridge**. For *Outburst* they were joined by Neil Anderson (ld gtr), Ron Gardner (sax, vcls) and Dave Roland (drms) (ex-Regents). Earlier in 1965 they featured on the album *Merry Christmas* (featuring **The Sonics**, **Wailers** and **Galaxies**) (Etiquette ETALB 025) 1965 playing four tracks:- *She's Comin' Home*, *Maybe This Year*, *Christmas Spirit* and *The Christmas Song*. This was reissued a few years back, but originals are very rare and collectable.

Later still Anderson was replaced by Danny Weaver (ld gtr), with Anderson going on to an act called Ice in early '68 (Neil Anderson gtr, Bob Bennet (ex-**Sonics**) drms, Clyde Heaton (ex-**Calliope**) keyb'ds plus one unknown), and then Adam Wind. Upon their demise in 1969, Gardner formed Sweet Rolle with Weaver, Roland and Dave Immer. Then, in 1972, Gardner formed the Ron Gardner Group (Ron Gardner - vcls, sax, keyb'ds; Denny Weaver - gtr; Dave Shogren - bs (ex-Doobies); Dave Immer - keyb'ds; and Doug Booth - drms), who issued a great album on MCA. This was not quite the end of the episode, for Morrill, Dangel, Ormsby, Burk and Gardner reformed in 1979 to cut a further album. Roland also had a spell with **The City Zu** amongst others.

The Wailers were one of Washington's most famous sixties bands and also gigged regularly in San Francisco in 1967. Of their several albums, *Tall Cool One* was the most successful commercially. It made No. 127 in the U.S. Album Charts back in 1964. Both the *Out Of Our Tree* and *Outburst* albums from 1966 feature some fine garage sounds, though the band's repertoire was always varied and therefore difficult to label.

Live Wire compiles some of the finest moments from their garage-punk era, including *Out Of Our Tree* and *Hang Up* along with a selection of album tracks, singles and two previously unreleased demos.

Compilation coverage has so far included *Hang Up* and *You Weren't Using Your Head* on *Nuggets, Vol. 8* (LP); *Dirty Robber* on *Born Bad, Vol. 6*; *You Weren't Using Your Head* on *Turds On A Bum Ride, Vol. 4* (CD); *Beat Guitar*, from 1960, on *Welcome To The Beat Generation*; *Out Of Our Tree* on *Nuggets Box* (4-CD); *You Weren't Using Your Head*, *The Wailer*, *Tomorrow's Another Day* and *You Better Believe It* on *The Northwest Rock Collection, Vol. 1* (LP); and *All My Nights, All My Days*, under the pseudonym of the **Breakers** on *Battle Of The Bands, Vol. 2* (LP) and *The History Of Northwest Rock, Vol. 3* (LP). (VJ/MW/BCh/DR/SC/BSe)

Peter Walker

Personnel:	MONTE DUNN	gtr	A
	BRUCE LANGHORNE	tamb, bells	A
	ALEX LUKEMAN	12-string drone, tamb	A
	JEAN-PIERRE MERLE	tamboura	A
	JEREMY STEIG	flte	A
	PETER WALKER	gtr	AB
	PETER WINTERS	Om	A
	JOHN BLAIR	violin	B
	JIM HOTEP	tabla	B
	MIDNITE	tamboura	B
	JIM PEPPER	flute	B

ALBUMS: 1(A) RAINY DAY RAGA (Vanguard VSD 79238) 1966 SC
2(B) SECOND POEM TO KARMELA OR GYPSIES ARE IMPORTANT
(Vanguard VSD 79282) 1967 SC

NB: (1) reissued on CD (Vanguard VMD 79238).

Peter Walker was a guitarist and the musical director of the "Celebrations" of **Dr. Timothy Leary**, who wrote the liner notes to the first album ("Peter Walker plays on the ancient protein strings of the genetic code" !!). Produced by Sam Charters (one of the Vanguard house producers, who later produced **Country Joe**), *Rainy Day Raga* is an instrumental album with nine of his compositions and a cover of *Norwegian Wood*. Very quiet and relaxing, it's supposed to be an association of Indian music (notably by using drones and tamboura) with folk music: the American folk raga was born!

Produced by Michael Chechik, the second album *Second Poem To Karmela Or Gypsies Are Important* was recorded with **Jim Pepper**. We haven't yet heard it.

Jeremy Steig would later form **Jeremy and The Satyrs** and become a renowned jazz musician. (SR)

Robert Walker

ALBUM: 1 EXCUSE ME, IT'S MY FIRST LSD TRIP
(GNP Crescendo 2027) 1966 SC

An obscure album which is of minor interest to some collectors. I've been unable to get to hear it. (VJ)

Steve Walker and The Bold

Personnel incl: STEVE WALKER A

45s: Gotta Get Some/Robin Hood (Cameo 430) 1966
Train Kept A-Rollin'/
I Found What I Was Looking For (Dynovoice 232) 1967

This was a Stones/Them-influenced outfit from Springfield, Massachusetts, and they made some classic '66 style punk recordings. In particular *Gotta Get Some* and *Train Kept A-Rollin* feature some excellent frantic guitar and vitriolic vocals.

Walker was earlier with an outfit called The Esquires, who had one 45 *Shake A Tail Feather/Down The Track*, on Salem (SR-003). See also **The Bold**.

Compilation appearances include: *Gotta Get Some* on *Mindrocker, Vol. 11* (LP), *Pebbles, Vol. 9* (LP), *Pebbles, Vol. 1 (ESD)* (CD) and *Songs We Taught The Fuzztones* (Dble LP & Dble CD); and *Train Kept A Rollin* on *Pebbles, Vol. 10* (CD) and *Pebbles, Vol. 10* (LP). (VJ)

J. Walker and The Pedestrians

45: Thinking Of You/Life's Too Short (PH 112) 1967

Yes, somewhat pedestrian beat ballads from Orlando, Florida. *Thinking Of You* is slightly memorable for its whistled refrain. (MW)

Jay Walker Effort

Personnel incl: JAY WALKER A

45: Paper Dolls / Nothing Really (Scott 8888) 196?

Paper Dolls is a cool, Cream-inspired barnstormer. *Nothing Really* is just that, a lightweight warm-up instrumental. Michigan has been suggested as the band's homestate and the 45 is a G.M. Detroit pressing, but this has yet to be confirmed. (MW)

Pat Wallace

45: (I'm Gonna) Fill The Hole In Your Soul/
C'mon And Work (St. Clair STC-007) 1966

A kind of *Midnight Hour* punker with typically reedy sound from an obscure Pittsburgh, Pennsylvania performer. The flip is another garagey R'n'B style workout - more dance club than garage fodder. (MW)

The Wallflowers

45: No Love Today/The Kind Of Love (Ridon 855) 1967

A Northwest group produced by Rick Keefer, best known to readers of this book for his collaboration with **The New Tweedy Bros!**. **Wallflowers** play a charming garage-pop style, not unlike an embryonic **New Tweedy Bros!**, although any connection between the two bands is speculative. (CF)

Wally and The Rights

45: Hey Now Little Girl/Zipper (The GM Record Co 113) 196?

Probably from Gladewater in Texas, the 'A' side of their sole vinyl offering was a poorly recorded but catchy punk number. The flip was an instrumental.

Compilation appearances include *Hey Now Little Girl* on *Texas Flashback (The Best Of)* (CD), *Texas Flashbacks, Vol. 2* (LP & CD) and *Flashback, Vol. 2* (LP). (VJ)

The Walnut Band

ALBUM: 1 GO NUTS (Appaloosa) 1976 R2

A Massachusetts group working in **Grateful Dead** territory. This private pressing is now rare. (SR)

MINDROCKER Vol. 11 (Comp LP) including Steve Walker and The Bold.

THE WANDERERS - Sing To The Lord... A New Song! LP.

The Wanderers

45: Higher Education/I Feel So Blue (Texas Record Co 2067) 196?

A Texas outfit. You'll also find the 'A' side - a Kinks-influenced garage punker - on *Flashback, Vol. 5* (LP) and *Texas Flashbacks, Vol. 5* (LP). It's well worth a spin. (VJ)

The Wanderers

Personnel:	BOB GATZEN	drms	A
	STEVE HEDGES	organ	A
	BILL KRANTZ	vcls	A
	MARTY ROY	bs	A
	ROY SLUSARZ	gtr	A

ALBUM: 1(A) SING TO THE LORD... A NEW SONG!
(Allen Records GCS 107/8) 1968 R2

A Christian garage band from the Hartford area of Connecticut. Side One contains Christian songs, including two **John Ylvisaker** tracks, whilst Side Two has competent garage covers of *Fire*, *Testify* and *Knock On Wood*, plus an amazing nine-minute original track *BSRS*, which recalls early **Country Joe and The Fish**.

Compilation appearances include: *B.S.R.S* on *Buzz Buzz Buzzzzzz, Vol. 1* (CD). (SR/CF)

The Wanderer's Rest

Personnel:	MICHAEL MILONCZYK	bs	A
	MICHAEL PODRAZA	gtr	A
	RICHARD PODRAZA	ld gtr	A
	STANLEY STARICH	drms	A

45s:	The Boat That I Row/		
	The Girl That I Love	(Night Owl 6771)	1967
	You'll Forget/Agripine III	(Wright 67101)	1967
	Temptation/Love Is A Beautiful Thing	(Wright 6813)	1968

A Milwaukee, Wisconsin, outfit whose sole output was these three 45s. *The Boat That I Row*, a Neil Diamond composition, can also be heard on *Highs In The Mid-Sixties, Vol. 10* (LP) and *You'll Forget* crops up on *Highs In The Mid-Sixties, Vol. 15* (LP). Neither tracks are in any way exceptional. (VJ/GM)

Wanderin' Kind

45:	Wynken Blynken And Nod/		
	Something I Can't Buy	(Dunwich 135)	1966

An obscure band, probably from the Chicago area. *Something I Can't Buy* was included on *If You're Ready - The Best Of Dunwich... Vol. 2* (CD). (VJ)

Wanted

Personnel:	ARNIE DeCLARK	gtr	A
	DAVE FERNSTROM	keyb'ds	A
	BILL MONTGOMERY	bs	A
	TIM SHEA	ld gtr	A
	CHIP STEINER	drms	A

HCP

45s:	Here To Stay/Teen World	(Detroit Sound 222)	1967	-
	Here To Stay/In The Midnight Hour	(Detroit Sound 223)	1967	-
	In The Midnight Hour/Here To Stay	(A & M 844)	1967	118
	Knock On Wood/			
	Lots More Where You Came From	(Detroit Sound 230)	1967	-
	East Side Story/Sad Situation	(Detroit Sound 232)	1967	-
	Big Town Girl/Don't Worry Baby	(A & M 856)	1967	-

Operated out of Detroit in Michigan. There first 45, *Here To Stay*, is a rather appealing punk ballad with some nice organ and guitar backing. Their cover of Wilson Pickett's *In The Midnight Hour* attracted enough attention to be picked up by A & M for nationwide distribution but failed to make any impact and by the second A & M 45 the sound had been whittled down to plodding R'n'B pop.

Compilation appearances have included: *Sad Situation* on *Lost Generation, Vol. 1* (LP) and *Mayhem & Psychosis, Vol. 2* (CD); *In The Midnight Hour* on *Michigan Nuggets* (CD), *Mayhem & Psychosis, Vol. 3* (LP), *Michigan Brand Nuggets* (Dble LP) and *Garagelands, Vol. 2* (LP); *Here To Stay* on *No No No* (CD), *Sixties Punk Ballads Sampler* (LP), *Sixties Archive, Vol. 5* (CD), *The Garage Zone, Vol. 4* (LP), *The Garage Zone Box Set* (4-LP) and *Garagelands, Vol. 1* (LP); and *Lots More Where You Came From* on *Bad Vibrations, Vol. 1* (LP). (VJ/MW)

Waphphle

Personnel:	B.BARMY?		A
	JACK GIERE	vcls	A
	R.JAGLA?		A
	GLENN STRAWN	ld gtr	A

45:	Goin' Down / I Want You	(Elektra 45616)	1967

From Sacramento, California, and formerly known as the Marauders, who'd released one earlier 45 - Since I Met You/I Don't Know How - on Skyview.

Goin' Down is a less savage reworking of an unreleased 1966 **Marauders** track *Our Big Chance* - a fabulous fuzz-punker - unearthed by Alec Palao and Joey D to be a gem in the *Psychedelic Crown Jewels, Vol. 2*. (MW/RM)

The War-Babies

Personnel incl:	BILL LINCOLN		A
	WESLEY WATT		A

45:	Jeannie's Pub / Love Is Love	(Highland 5000)	1965

The R&B thrasher *Jeannie's Pub* appears on *Sixties Rebellion, Vol. 9* (LP & CD) and more recently on *Teenage Shutdown, Vol. 7* (LP & CD), which reveals that this L.A. band included Wesley Watt and Bill Lincoln, later of **The Word** and **Euphoria**. (VJ/MW/MM)

The War-Babies

45:	Together Forever / War Baby	(Uni 55164)	1969

A much later and presumably different band. Tom Tourville's Dakotas book placed them in Bismarck, North Dakota but also credited them with the Highland 45 above. (MW)

Warden and His Fugitives

45: The World Ain't Changed/I Love You (Bing 302) 1965

Label mates to **The Hysterics**, this California band were from San Bernardino-Rialto area of California rather than L.A. as implied by the 'A' side of this 45 being on *Highs In The Mid-Sixties, Vol. 1* (LP). It's not a bad folk-punker, well worth a spin.

The World... has also re-appeared on *Teenage Shutdown, Vol. 9* (LP & CD). (VJ/MM)

Warlock

ALBUM: 1 WARLOCK (Music Merchant) 1972 -

A hard to find black underground progressive/blues-rock outfit with swirling organ, guitar, flute. (SR)

Warlocks

Personnel: EDDIE BROYLES A
DICK (CASEY or BODINE) A
RICK (BODINE or CASEY) A
JERRY A
STAN A

A Dayton, Ohio, band whose only released song is *You Should've Listened*, a pastiche of 1964/65-period Beatles recorded in 1966. It appears on the *WONE, The Dayton Scene* album (Prism PR-1966), where the top twelve bands from the WONE-sponsored three-day battle of the bands were represented with one track apiece. (MW)

The Warlocks

Personnel: FRANK BEARD drms A
DUSTY HILL bs A
ROCKY HILL gtr A

45s: Splash Day/Life's A Mystery (Paradise 1021) 1968
If You Really Want Me to Stay/
Good Time Trippin' (Ara 101 7) 1968
Another Year/Poor Kid (Ara 1915) 1968

Rocky and Dusty Hill first musical venture was at Woodrow Wilson High School in Dallas, together with drummer "Little" Richard Harris. Frank Beard came across Dusty and Rocky while playing for **The Cellar Dwellers** at the Fort Worth Cellar. The three of them, basing themselves in Dallas, Texas formed **The Warlocks** dying their hair blue and dropping lots of acid. Later in their brief career they teamed up with English singer Lady Wilde and backed her regularly at Dallas cinemas for British invasion movies like 'Catch Us If You Can' and 'Hard Day's Night'. They also backed her on their final 45 and when she departed for a career on the stage they formed the **American Blues**. Originals of their 45s, which had pressings of just 500, change hands for a lot of money but some of the tracks can also be found on compilations.

Later still the threesome moved on to Houston, met Billy Gibbons and ZZ Top was born.

Compilation coverage has included: *Life's A Mystery* on *Acid Visions, Vol. 2* (LP) and *Acid Visions - The Complete Collection Vol. 1* (3-CD); and *If You Really Want Me To Stay* on *Texas Flashback (The Best Of)* (CD), *Texas Flashbacks, Vol. 1* (LP & CD) and *Flashback, Vol. 1* (LP). (VJ/JLs)

The Warlocs

Personnel: BRAD GREEN drms A
MIKE McCANN A
JOHN PERMAR A
SKIP SKINNER A
LARRY SMITH A

From Orlando, FLorida, this band can be found on the rare *Bee Jay Video Soundtrack* album performing *Ooo Baby Baby* and on *Bee Jay Demo, Vol. 2* album with *It's All Right*. (SMR)

The Warlords

45: Real Fine Lady/I've Got It Bad (Thor 0759) 1966

Back From The Grave reveals that they were high school students from the Chicago area who got together in 1965. *Real Fine Lady* is the selected cut - a pounding rocker with a fine guitar intro.

Compilation appearances include *Real Fine Lady* on *Back From The Grave, Vol. 5* (LP) and *Back From The Grave, Vol. 2* (CD). (VJ/MW)

The Warlords

Personnel: GEORGE BARRAHAS bs A
STEVE BEAU gtr A
KURT KUZULKA ld gtr A
RANDY LINDERT drms A
JAMES WHITE vcls A
BILL SHUPE gtr
LARRY WILLIAMS ld gtr

45: My Girl/Sad Songs (Night Owl 6861) 1968

A different outfit, formed in 1966 and based around Waupun, Wisconsin. *Sad Songs* was later featured on the 1969 Night Owl compilation - *Badger A Go Go* (LP) by which time the band had split. All except Barrahas from the original line-up reunited as Bare Fat later that year and released one 45 - *Soft / You Can All Join In* (Bang B 573). (MW/GM)

Warm

45: My Mary/My House Is On Fire (Line 5 L 5001) 196?

From the label that depicts a hairy hippie head and gave us the **Huckleberry Mudflap**! A delicate folkie paean to *My Mary* and a strummed folk-rocker that will appeal to the gentleman on the label. From North Carolina. (MW)

ACID VISIONS - The Complete Collection Vol. 1 (Comp CD) including The Warlocks.

Warmest Spring

45s:	Younger Girl/	
	It Doesn't Matter Now	(Cameo Parkway P-985) 1966
	Suddenly (You Find Love)/	
	Hard, Hard Girl	(Cameo Parkway P-990) 1966

Anonymous popsters whose second 45 *Hard, Hard Girl* is a decent **Raiders/Monkees** style pop-punker. Unfortunately the 'A' side, theme to the 'Unholy Matrimony' film, is tripe. (MW)

Danny Warner

45:	Go 'Way Little Girl/Bright Colors	(Smash S 2110) 1967

A throbbing macho fuzz-punk version of a Janis Ian tune with some brass backing that cooks. Forgettable pop-brass flip. (MW)

Warner Brothers

Personnel:	AL WARNER		A
	LARRY WARNER		A

45s:	Beauty And The Beast/Cry Baby	(Rampage 1702) 196?
	Three Little Fishes/Mairzy Doats	(Everest 2043) 1964
	Do The Hog/Comin' Home	(Everest 2050) 1964
	Varoom/Guitar Blue	(Everest 2057) 1965
	Please Mr. Sullivan/	
	I'm Going Your Way	(Destination 612) 1965
	I'm Going Your Way/Little Darlin'	(Destination 617) 1966
	I'm Going Your Way/	
	I Won't Be The Same Without Her	(Dunwich 131) 1966
	Lonely I/I Won't Be The Same Without Her	(Dunwich 131) 1966
	Three Cheers/Lost	(Ballance 2002) 1966
	Study Hall/Centipede	(Kandy Kane 408) 1967

This band operated out of Peoria, Illinois, and released a string of singles of variable content. Particularly noteworthy are, *Please Mr. Sullivan*, a cheesy novelty item about a band pleading to appear on the Ed Sullivan Show and *Lonely I*, which contains some pleasing chanting and feedback.

Compilation appearances include: *Lonely I* on *Mindrocker, Vol. 5* (LP) and *The Dunwich Records Story* (LP); *Lonely I* and *I Won't Be The Same Without Her* on *Oh Yeah! The Best Of Dunwich Records* (CD); *Please Mr. Sullivan* on *Pebbles, Vol. 6* (CD) and *Highs In The Mid-Sixties, Vol. 4* (LP); *Study Hall* on *Ho-Dad Hootenanny* (LP); *Dirty Ernie* and *Oleo Margarine* (both prev. unreleased) on *If You're Ready - The Best Of Dunwich... Vol. 2* (CD); and *Do The Hog* on *Bug Out, Vol. 2*. (VJ)

Ellen Warshaw

ALBUM:	1	ELLEN WARSHAW	(Vanguard) 1973 -

Housed in a nice solarized cover, a folk singer who covers the Stones' *Sister Morphine*, Donovan's *Widow With Shawl* and Blind Faith's *Can't Find By Way Home*.

Some good eerie tracks. (SR)

George Washington and The Cherry Bombs

Personnel:	MIKE ADAMS	tenor sax, ld vcls	AB
	MARK CHELLSON	ld vcls, trumpet	AB
	GARY DUVALL	gtr	A
	WARD JOHNSON	keyb'ds	AB
	AL WILCOX	drms	A
	MIKE WILCOX	bs	A
	JIM DeLONG	drms	B
	JEFF HUTNER	bs	B
	CHARLIE MACK	gtr	B

NB: Line-up 'A' 1965-66, 'B' 1967.

45:	Don't You Just Know It/Brother Ward	(MGM 13450) 1966

From Mercer Island, Washington, this group were led by Mark Chellson who went on to **The Bards**. Live, they used to wear red & white revolutionary costumes (akin to **Paul Revere & The Raiders**), and had a frantic stage presence, sometimes playing their magnum opus *Crisco Party* for twenty minutes! Their 45 also received heavy airplay locally, with KVR Radio in Seattle playing *Brother Ward* every night in late Feb '66. However, like so many bands of this era, college and the draft caused them to break up in the Summer of '67.

An extended studio recording of the jokey *Crisco Party* also features on *Northwest Battle Of The Bands, Vol. 1 - Flash And Crash* (LP & CD), *Northwest Battle Of The Bands, Vol. 1* (CD), *Battle Of The Bands, Vol. 1* (LP), *History Of Northwest Rock, Vol. 2* (CD) and *The History Of Northwest Rock, Vol. 4* (LP). (DR/MW/VJ)

Washington Merry Go Round

45:	Land Of Odin/Got-ta Got-ta	(Piccadilly 254) 1968

From Washington in the Northwest. This trio were a product of the flower-power era. (VJ)

The Watchband

45:	No Dice! / Mechanical Man	(Stanal 6-7137) 1966

This Kearney, Nebraska, label had several releases - by The Crusaders, The Lot, The Palasades, 7 Sons and **The Sunny Funny Co.**. Some were local Cornhuskers but the label also attracted bands from far-flung parts of the Midwest. **The Watchband**, for example, were from distant Duluth - in Northern Minnesota on the banks of Lake Superior.

No Dice! is a cool punker about a turn-down day - it has turned up on the *Sick And Tired* (LP) compilation. (MW/VJ)

Watermelon

Personnel:	GARY LEWANDOWSKI	bs	A
	RAPHAEL	keyb'ds	A
	EDDIE WEISS	ld gtr	A
	GARY WEISS	drms	A

CD:	1(A)	FROM THE LEMON DROPS TO VIBRATION OF SEQUENCE IN ORDER	
			(Collectables COL-CD-0679) 1996

The Collectables retrospective is a collection of unreleased practice sessions from 1969 and through 1970, which document the evolution of the band who started life in Illinois as **The Lemon Drops**. From there they trekked to San Francisco in search of fame, only to split, regroup and split again finally returning in the above incarnation, known variously as Space, Silver Watermelons and finally **Watermelon**. From laid-back atmospheric instrumentals to heavy acid-rock workouts with progressive tendencies, this should appeal not just to those who've followed the band through the series of Cicadelic retrospectives, but to fans of acid-rock, West Coast jams and nineties 'head music'. Recommended.

The compilation *Chicago Garage Band Greats* (LP)/*Chicago Garage Band Greats* (CD) also includes two previously unreleased cuts by the band dating from 1968:- *The Ocean Song*, an experimental, rather mellow song and *Trilogy*, an instrumental. You can also find *Popsicle Girl* and *You Got It* on *Green Crystal Ties, Vol. 6* (CD).

In 1970 Eddie and Gary Weiss formed an acid-rock trio under the name **Buzzsaw**. (MW/LP/VJ)

Watermusic

Personnel:	RENE BEST	ld gtr	A
	STEVE BRAUNSTEIN	gtr	A
	BRIAN CUMMINGS	bs	A

WINSTON LOGAN	drms		A
GENE SMITH	vcls		A

CD: 1 HEADSTONES: 24 HOURS (EVERYDAY) (Collectables COL-CD-0700) 1997

Formed in 1966 as the **Oxford Circus** in Waco, Texas by Winston Logan, former drummer of the **Headstones** who'd relocated to attend Baylor University. Initially a covers band they were augmented by Rene Best in 1969, changed their name to **Watermusic** and switched to concentrating on original material. *Can't You Feel It*, *My Orange* and *Silver Chimes* appear for the first time on the above compilation which comprises related bands: - **The Headstones**, **Oxford Circus**, **Seompi** - formed by ex-**Headstone** Dave Williams - and the Remaining Few, a late seventies band which reunited Williams and Logan. (MW)

Waterproof Candle

45: Electrically Heated Child/ Saturday Morning Repentance (Dunhill D 4118) 1968

If the name of the band is anything to go by, this should be one of the most psychedelic singles ever, but it fulfills your expectations only partly. The 'A' side is sweetest toytown pop-psych, quite agreeable, while the flip is much better with harmony vocals over a repetitive backing and includes a surprising time / measure change. Nice but inconsequential. (MK)

Waterproof Tinkertoy

45s: Baby Let Go/(one-sided) (Caitlin no #) 196?
(Partial Satisfaction/It All Fits Together (Caitlin 101) 1967
List) Continuation/? (Caitlin TINK 3) 1968
Groovy Girl/This And That (Laurie 3457) 1968
Workin' For My Baby/I've Been Unfaithful (Laurie 3469) 1968

A New York City-recorded outfit, though they band operated out of Springfield, Massachusetts. *Continuation* is featured on the *Beyond The Calico Wall* (CD) so you know it's gotta be "way out there somewhere"! Yes, it's a free-form freakout. *Baby Let Go* is pleasantly upbeat with tasty keyboard and guitar moves. Their cover of *Satisfaction* is suitably fuzzed but in a heavy pop as opposed to garage style. The other side is lightweight pop - also prevalent on both the later Laurie 45s.

Two of the band members are believed to be Tom Ide (drums) and his brother, Carl (gtr). They were originally from Pittsburgh, Pennsylvania although their mother was from Springfield, Massachusetts where she taught school. (MW/GT)

The Waters

Personnel:	JOHN BURGARD	gtr, vcls	A
	RAY BARRICKMAN	bs, vcls	A
	JOHN MACKEY	drms	A

45s: Lady In The Field / American Cheese (Soul Boulevard # Unkn) 1968
Day In And Out / Mother Samwell (Delcrest 1001) 1969
Day In And Out / Mother Samwell (Hip HIA 8012) 1969

From Louisville, Kentucky, this trio formed in 1967. Their second 45 was produced by Stuart Paine and Fred Baker of The Company Front. It did very well in the local charts and was picked up by the Memphis-based Hip label. *Day In And Out* is good-vibe pop-rock with flowing fuzzy leads.

'Louisville's Own', a book published in 1983 by Brenda and Bill Woods, notes that the band split in 1970 and that both Burgard and Barrickman stayed in the music business, having relocated to Memphis.

Mother Samwell, with its heavy phasing, raga guitars and good vocal harmonies, can also be found on *Psychedelic Experience, Vol. 2* (LP) and *Psychedelic Experience, Vol. 2* (CD). (BM/MW)

The Wave-Riders

Personnel incl: ROBERT JOHNSON A

45: Thing In G / Ain't It A Shame (Tener 154) 1966

A rare 45 on the collectable Tener label by an unlocated Florida band. *Psychedelic States: Florida Vol. 1* (CD) features the strident Robert Johnson-penned pop-punker, *Ain't It A Shame*. (MW/JLh/RM)

Artie Wayne

45: Automated Man/ Listen To The Flowers Growin (Smash 2077) 1967

An obscure "flower power" single. (SR)

Paul Wayne

ALBUM: 1 LIVE AT THE GARAGE (Private pressing) c1969 ?

From Massachussetts, a rare live album recorded in a club near Boston with audience noises (screams, clapping, glass breaking etc). The album contains versions of *Maria*, *Grizzly Bear*, several medleys of old hits (Dion, Buddy Holly) played with fast guitar, *The Whole World* (with new lyrics: "He's got the whole world by his balls") and ends with a *Peace Medley* about Vietnam ("support our boys in Vietnam, bring em' home..."). As often with these records, rarity doesn't equate with quality. (SR)

Kenny Wayne and The Kamotions

Personnel:	CHUCK BECK (ROSCOE)	ld gtr	A
	JOHN BRUTON	drms	A
	DAVID MOYE	organ, gtr	A
	STEVE MURRELL	bs	A
	KENNY WAYNE	vcls, gtr	A

ALBUM: 1(A) IN MOTION (Candy 1023) 1970 R1

NB: (1) has had a limited unofficial repress.

45s: How Should I Feel/ Day When The Sun Goes Down (Candy 1011) 1969
A Better Day's A Comin'/They (Candy 1021) 1970
A Better Day's A Comin'/They (Scorpio 2003) 1970
Child Bride/Time Seems To Fly (Candy 1022) 1970
It Took 27 Years/ I Wanna Go Home Play With Them Babies (Hare) 1974
Stay Away (From Me Girl)/ I Can Feel The Changes (Bollman Int'l 5036) 1977

KENNY WAYNE and THE KAMOTIONS - In Motion LP.

Not to be confused with Dallas' Kenny Wayne; Shreveport, Louisina's Kenny Wayne "Shepherd" or indeed **Wayne Lacadisi**, **Kenny Wayne** had earlier recorded with **The Starchiefs** and **The Grapes Of Wrath**.

A crossover between late sixties punk and early seventies rock, the **Kamotions** second 45, *A Better Day's A Comin'*, was a rough and wild protest number - the 'A' side can also be found on *Highs In The Mid-Sixties, Vol. 23* (LP).

Child Bride their next 45 featured Chuck Roscoe, who is now a producer with Jennifer Warren (Germany's top female songstress) to his credit, as well as bass player with Eric Johnson and Robben Ford. Fender recently designed and named a six-string bass "The Roscoe Beck Signature Model" in his name!

It Took 27 Years came out in the Summer of '74, and although uncredited was co-produced and co-written by Buddy Holly's manager/producr Norman Petty, with **Wayne** on piano and string machine.

Stay Away From Me Girl, **The Kamotions** final 45 wasn't released until 1977, but it was recorded in Shreveport, Louisiana on New years day 1972.

Their album, *In Motion* is a passable effort overall, including covers of Free's *All Right Now*, T. Bone Walker's *Stormy Monday Blues*, a soul medley of Joe Brown's *I Got You* and Ted Wright's *Out Of Sight*, C. Allen and J. Hill's *Are You Ready* and Jim Peterik's (of **Ides Of March**) *Vehicle*. Interspersed among these are a number of originals, a mixture of uptempo rock (*How Should I Feel*, *Child Bride* and *They*) and pop ballads (*The Day When The Sun Goes Down* and *Time Seems To Fly*, of which the former is by far the best) penned by Kenneth W. Hagler (aka **Kenny Wayne**), who also designed the cover and managed a local booking agency in Texarkana, Texas.

Subsequently, **Wayne** has released an album as **Kenny Wayne & His Very Special Guests** *Born With The Blues And Raised On Rock 'N' Roll*; and has recently recorded a new eighteen track album *Rockin' Little Redwater, Texas Boy* which he describes as "The best damn record that I've ever made!!"

It should be noted that the two hard-rock albums, released as by Kenny Wayne are in fact the work of the other Kenny Wayne from Dallas. (VJ)

Wazoo

Personnel:	ROBERT DiPASQUALE	vcls	A
	JOHN FINAN		A
	KONSTANTINE GEORGE KATSAKIS	sax	A
	"BOCKY" (SIMON IAN)	trumpets, perc	A
	FELIX McDANIELS		A
	VINCE SCALABRINO	perc	A
	"WIZAR D."		A

ALBUM: 1(A) WAZOO (Zig Zag ZZ 217) 1970 SC

45: Hey Girl I'm In Love With You/
Don't Give Your Love To Anyone (R&R R 103) 1969

From Cleveland, Ohio. Their 45 was issued on a New York City label and comprises late sixties soft pop-rock - not 'garage' as sometimes claimed. It sounds not dissimilar to later **(Young) Rascals** material - pleasant but very average.

The obscure Wazoo album on an equally obscure Michigan label is strange indeed - the personnel as listed above is sketchy due to the lack of info on the gatefold sleeve, with its welter of named and unnamed photos, but Robert DiPasquale had previously been in **Bocky and The Visions**. Musically the album contains an odd mix of brassy jazz-rock with **The Fugs** and lots of weird s**t thrown in: anti-war and anti-establishment jibes, some nice baroque touches, a soupcon of avant-garde, some heady lyrics, and barrages of war and off-the-wall sound effects... all of which make for a challenging listen. Noteworthy moments include: the eleven minute jazz-psych trip of *The Way I See It*; the bluesy fuzz of *Sleep On*; the amazing bad-trip noise of *Arnie Funny Far Fackor* which should only be listened to in a padded room; and the excellent heavy fuzz-and-feedback blast of *BH Man* that closes the album in a more accessible acid-rock vein.

George Katsakis recalls:- "I was also the leader of a group formed in 1958 called the Royaltones. I used the name Konstantine because it was my father's name. The *Wazoo* album was recorded in Novi, Michigan, at a studio that was owned by Bob Adell. The studio was located in a building that is now known as the Novi Expo Center and Arnie of *Arniefunnyfarfacker* was the recording engineer". (MW/GGI/GK)

The Weads

45: Don't Call My Name/Today (Duane 1042) 1965

From the label that brought the world **The Savages**, so presumably Bermuda was home to this outfit too. *Don't Call My Name* is a tuneful beat-ballad, the flip is uptempo beat-pop.

Compilation appearances include: *Today* on *Killer Cuts* (LP); and *Don't Call My Name* on *Open Up Yer Door, Vol. 2* (LP) and *Tymes Gone By* (LP). (VJ/MW)

The W.C. Dorns

45: I Need You/If I Ask You (WCD 1001) 196?

You'll also find *I Need You* on *Vile Vinyl, Vol. 1* (LP) and *Vile Vinyl* (CD). (VJ)

Weathervane

45: 4-4, 5-4 / My Original Blue Jeans (Plamie P 1026) 1968

Keyboard-dominated garagey sounds from the pen of one Steffen Presley, on a Salinas, California, label. The band were from Modesto and this appears to be their sole release. Check out *4-4,5-4* on *Seeds Turn To Flowers Turn To Dust* (LP & CD). (MW)

The Weavils

45: Here I Am In Love Again/We're The Weavils (Lori 9550) 1965

From Houston, Texas. Judging by the 'B' side, with their fake British accents they seem to have been a Beatles' put-down group. The song rocks along pretty well and has humour too, The punch line:- 'The Beatles are good but we don't care, cause it only takes a minute to comb our hair!

You can also find *We're The Weavils* on *Pebbles, Vol. 21* (LP) and *Acid Visions - The Complete Collection Vol. 1* (3-CD). (VJ)

THE WEE FOUR.

Websters New World

45s: Tell Her How/
I Don't Want To Be The One (Columbia 43707) 1966
Hard Loving Loser/
I Don't Want To Be The One (Columbia 43745) 1966
Take A Look/Pity The Woman (Columbia 43949) 1966
Sad To Say/Henry Thachet (RCA 47-9337) 1966
You Still Thrill Me, Babe/
When You Grow Up (RCA 47-9410) 1967

Possibly from California, a group similar to **Mamas and Papas** with psychedelic folk and baroque influences. (SR)

Wednesday

Personnel:	RANDY BEGG		A
	JOHN DUFEK		A
	MIKE O'NEIL	vcls	A
	PAUL ANDREW SMITH		A

ALBUM: 1(A) LAST KISS (Sussex) 1974 -
HCP

45s: Last Kiss/Without You (Sussex 507) 1973 34
Teen Angel/Taking Me Home (Sussex 515) 1974 79

A strange "concept" album, with a side devoted to the rock standards dealing with tragic death and lost love! The interest is mainly on the second side, full of wah-wah guitar rock. (SR/VJ)

The Weeds

Personnel:	BOB ATKINS	bs	A
	EDDIE BOWEN	ld gtr	A
	RON BUZZEL	gtr	A
	FRED COLE	vcls	A
	TIM ROCKSON	drms	A

45s: α It's Your Time/Little Girl (Teenbeat 1006) 1966
No Good News/Stop (NWI 2745) 1969

NB: α reissued on Behemoth (T-2) in 1988 with a picture sleeve and insert/info/interview with Fred Cole.

Originally from Las Vegas in Nevada, this band later relocated to Oregon. Their first 45 became an anthem for the flower children at Portland's Spring Trips Festival in 1967. The flip, *Little Girl* is also a great raw punker that displays Fred's raucous vocals and some savage guitar work. Sadly, though, it was all a little too raw for the American record buying public at the time and didn't sell.

The band also spent a lot of time in Los Angeles where they came under the influence of Lord Tim Hudson, manager of **The Seeds**. He didn't like the combination of pushing **The Weeds** on the road with **The Seeds** to promote the album they'd just recorded so their name was changed to **The Lollipop Shoppe** with the above line-up still intact. The group didn't like the name and after the album and 45s failed to generate riots, they returned to the Northwest and put out the N.W.I. 45 as **The Weeds** once more. Both *No Good News* and *Stop* are lead-weighted downer-rock. The others broke away but Fred Cole kept going... In 1975, he released a highly-rated hard-rock album by his group **Zipper**. Later, in 1979, he was in a hard-core outfit, The Rats. He's become something of a cult figure since with Dead Moon, and had earlier recorded as **Deep Soul Cole**.

Compilation appearances have included: *It's Your Time* on *Nuggets, Vol. 8* (LP), *Pebbles, Vol. 1* (CD) and *Pebbles, Vol. 1* (ESD) (CD); and *It's Your Time*, *Stop* and *Little Girl* on *Filling The Gap* (4-LP). (VJ/MW)

The Wee Four

Personnel:	JACK ALLOCO	gtr, ld vcls	AB
	DENNIS DREW	ld gtr, bck vcls	A
	TERRY PILITTERE	drms	AB
	KEN POLIZZI	bs	A
	BOB ??		B
	GARY ??		B

NB: Line-up 'A' Summer 1966.

45: Weird/Give Me A Try (Nu-Sound 6111) 1966

Hailed from Rochester, New York, with a song called *Weird* which cropped up on an extremely obscure 45. The lyrics seem to deride the singer's girlfriend, there's some pretty wild drumming, some driving guitar and pretty good vocals. Not bad at all.

The band, who were all teenagers and led by Terry Pilittere, were formed in 1964 as The Dimensions. In September '65, they changed names to **The Wee Four**.

Compilation appearances include *Weird* on *Pebbles Box* (5-LP), *Pebbles, Vol. 21* (LP), *Trash Box* (5-CD) and *Teenage Shutdown, Vol. 8* (LP & CD). (VJ/BGn)

Weejuns

Personnel:	JIMMY 'Be-Bop' EVANS	drms	AB
	JERRY HODGES	vcls	AB
	BOB KILLEN	keyb'ds	AB
	JERRY ROGERS	gtr	A
	JIMMY ROGERS	bs, backing vcl	AB
	BLAIR STEWART	gtr, backing vcl	B

45: I Spy / Out Of The Clear Blue Sky (Quinvy 167) 196?

Formed in 1962, this Alabama quintet lasted through to 1969, performing on the South-Eastern circuit throughout Alabama and Tennessee. Just one 45 was released, recorded at Quin Ivy's studio in Sheffield, Alabama.

Four of the original line-up got together again in 1992 (line-up 'B') for the Muscle Shoals Bands Of The '60s Reunion concert, captured on CD, where they perform three sixties covers - *Gimme Some Lovin'*, *Gloria*, and Bruce Chanel's *Hey Baby*.

These are captured on the CD of the event alongside contributions from **Mickey Buckins and The New Breed**, Terry Woodford and The Mystics, **The Del-Rays**, Mark V with Dan Penn, Hollis Dixon and The Keynotes, Bobby Denton and Travis Wammack. (MW)

Weejuns

45s: Way Down / With Your Love (Skoop 968S-1068) 1966
Where Have You Been /
...Theme (title incomplete) (PS) (Jaguar 866) c1966

THE WEEKENDERS - Spring Weekend '65 LP.

Teenage Shutdown, Vol. 8 (LP & CD) features *Way Down* by this bunch of **Weejuns** and reports that they were from Southern Indiana or West Kentucky. (MW/MM)

Weekend

ALBUM: 1 AT LAST (Goodtime Records GTS-2501) 1975 -

From New York, a garage/bar band with tracks like *Sail Without Wind*, *County Fair* and *Going Home To Mrs. Jones Garden*. (SR)

The Weekenders

Personnel:	AMOS	A
	BARRY	A
	GEORGE	A
	LAURIE	A
	THAD	A

ALBUM: 1(A) SPRING WEEKEND '65 (VQR Records 2015) 1965 R2/R3

This quintet from the Lawrence Academy in Needham, Massachusetts, actually got to make an album, which is very rare. They appear on the front cover posing on the front bonnet of a Rolls Royce. One of the album's tracks, *Spring Weekend '65*, has since been included on the *Riot City!* (LP) compilation and on *Oil Stains, Vol. 2* (LP). It's a rather restrained frat rocker. (VJ)

The We Five

Personnel:	BEVERLY BIVENS	ld vcls	A
	JERRY BURGAN	drms, gtr	ABC
	PETE FULLERTON	bs	ABC
	BOB JONES	drms, gtr	A
	MIKE STEWART	gtr, vcls	A C
	DEBBIE BURGAN	vcls	BC

HCP

ALBUMS:	1(A)	YOU WERE ON MY MIND	(A & M 4111) 1965	32	-
	2(A)	MAKE SOMEONE HAPPY	(A & M 4135) 1967	172	-
	3(B)	THE RETURN OF WE FIVE	(A & M 4168) 1969	-	-
	3(C)	CATCH THE WIND	(Vault 136) 1970	-	-
	4(-)	TAKE EACH DAY AS IT COMES	(API 6016) 1977	-	-

NB: (1) and (2) reissued on one CD by Collectors Choice in 1996.

HCP

45s:	You Were On My Mind/Small World	(A & M 770) 1965	3
	Let's Get Together/ Cast Your Fate To The Wind	(A & M 784) 1965	31
	You Let A Love Burn Out/ Somewhere Beyond The Sea	(A & M 793) 1966	-
	There Stands The Door/Somewhere	(A & M 800) 1966	116
	What's Goin' On/The First Time	(A & M 820) 1966	-
	Never Goin' Back/Here Comes The Sun	(Vault 964) 1970	-
	Catch The Wind/Oh Lonesome Me	(Vault 969) 1970	-
	Rejoice/Bandstand Dancer	(Verve 10716) 1973	-

This pop-rock group emerged from the San Francisco folk circuit. They made an immediate impact with *You Were On My Mind*, which made No. 3 in the Billboard Charts. In the U.K. it was covered by Crispian St. Peter. They enjoyed a further minor hit with their cover of **Dino Valente**'s hippie anthem *Let's Get Together* and although it enjoyed no chart success their next release *You Let A Love Burn Out* had some nicely layered harmonies and may have influenced Marty Balin in assembling **Jefferson Airplane** with their initial two girl, one guy vocal harmonies. Their first two albums climbed to No's 32 and 172 respectively in the U.S. Album Charts.

The band seem to have had four phases in their career. The first (and most successful) was from 1965-67 when they were contracted to A & M; the second from 1969-71 when they signed to Vault; they returned briefly in 1973 to record the 45 for Verve and then reformed again in 1976.

Michael Stewart was the brother of John Stewart (of The Kingston Trio fame) and later became a Capitol record executive. Bob Jones was later in **Southern Comfort**.

Compilation appearances include *You Were On My Mind* and *You Let A Love Burn Out* on *Nuggets, Vol. 7* (LP). (VJ/SR)

Weigaltown Elemental Band

ALBUM: 1 DON'T HURT YOURSELF (Old Ridge W 761) 1976 R1

From Pennsylvania, this group was formed by some members of **Arkay IV**. Like many local bands, they played a mix of garage, heavy rock, surf and country-rock. (SR)

Weight

Personnel:	LAWRENCE EDWARD ("ED") KIRBY	drms	A
	PAUL ("BARNEY") NORTHCUTT	ld gtr, vcls	A
	JAMES THOMAS ("JIM") THIBODEAUX	ld vcls, bs	A

ALBUM: 1(A) MUSIC IS THE MESSAGE (Bertram International IS-104) 1970 SC

45: Flip, Flop And Fly/ Another Side Of This Life (Bertram Int'l INT-230) 1969

Late sixties heavy club-rockers from California's East Bay Area, clearly influenced by **Creedence Clearwater Revival**. *Flip, Flop And Fly* is an uninspiring R'n'B flavoured boogie. **Fred Neil**'s *Another Side...* is more **CCR**-like with some fine guitar. Both tracks are from their all-covers album, recorded live at Rick's Lounge in Walnut Creek.

Their seven minute version of *Susie Q* doesn't stick to the **Creedence** formula, instead an extended workout with acidic guitar soloing and a jazzy vibe - a fine finale. They tackle The Equals' *Baby Come Back* and a quartet of Beatles tracks with varying results: a brave attempt at *A Day In The Life* comes off well, considering; *Oh! Darling* is OK; *Sgt.Pepper/With A Little Help...* and George Harrison's *Something* come across as dull and plodding.

Jim Thibodeaux (originally from Nampa, Idaho) had relocated to California at the age of 8. After a three year stint in the army he'd formed The Blazers, a "show lounge group". Several outfits later he joined established local act The Antics in November 1967. Barney Northcutt (from Richmond, California) had joined earlier that year; Ed Kirby (from Martinez, California) had been in the group since 1962.

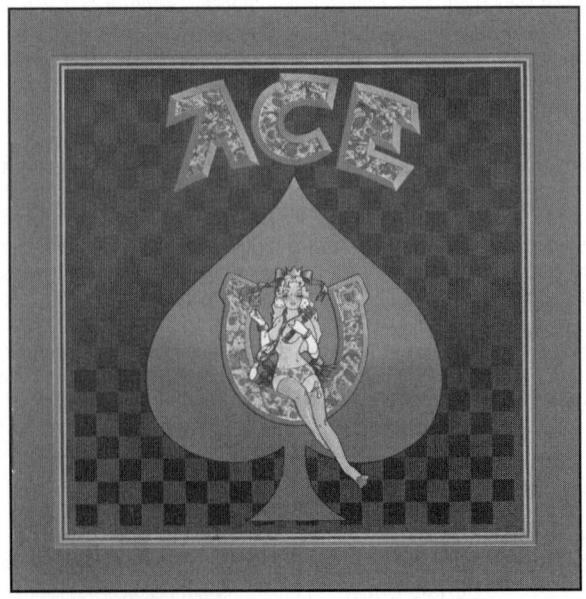

BOB WEIR - Ace CD.

The Antics split in 1968 whereupon this threesome formed The Groop. In early 1969 they landed a residency at Rick's Lounge and by the end of the year had become known as **The Weight**. (MW/CF)

The Weight

ALBUM: 1   ONE MAN'S QUEEN IS ANOTHER MAN'S SWEATHOG
(Avco Embassy AVE 330??) c1969 -

NB: (1) also released in France.

A New York area group. Their album is full of complex psychedelic tracks and contains a 'dope bust' song, but is definitely of minor interest. (SR)

Elyse Weinberg

Personnel:
JOHN BORDONARO	drms		A
DON GALLUCCI			A
BRUCE HAUSER	bs		A
JOEY NEWMAN	gtr		A
COLIN WALCOTT	sitar, tabla		A
ELYSE WEINBERG	vcls, gtr, 12-string gtr		A
"THE BAND OF THIEVES"	basic tracks		A
BRENT ??	hrmnca		A
MAUREEN ??	spoons		A

ALBUM: 1(A)   ELYSE   (Tetragrammaton T-117) 1968 -

45s: If Death Don't Overtake Me/
Meet Me At The Station   (Tetragrammaton) 1969
Simpleminded Harlequin/Oh, Deed I Do   (Tetragrammaton) 1969

This album is an interesting example of psychedelic folk with some oriental touches (sitar, tabla) and inspiration taken from middle age (*Mortuary Bound, If Death Don't Overtake Me*). Produced by Gene Shiveley, it featured the rhythm section from **Touch** and was arranged by Don Gallucci (ex-**Kingsmen**, **Don and The Good Times** and **Touch**), Joey Newman (pre-**Touch**) and Jeremy Stewart. The songs are all written by **Elyse Weinberg** and published by Peyotl music (sic!), except a cover of Bert Jansch's *Deed I Do*.

Colin Walcott was later in the jazz group Oregon. (SR/JohnBordonaro)

Bob Weir

                                                                    HCP
ALBUM: 1   ACE   (Warner Bros. BS 2627) 1972 68 -

The first solo album by the **Grateful Dead** guitarist, recorded with his usual group plus Ed Bogas (Clover) and Dave Torbert (Horses, New Riders Of The Purple Sage). It's sound is very close to *American Beauty* or *Workingman's Dead*, but with more rock numbers. It spent fifteen weeks in the Top 200, climbing to No. 68. As with all the other '**Dead** members, **Weir** was constantly playing with other groups and can be found on several albums recorded by Bay Area groups. (SR/VJ)

Weird Street Carnival

45:   The Inner Truth/
The Subterranean Edible Fungus   (Copra 2305) c1968

A Port Chester, New York, band who achieve an effective blend of spacey organ, psychedelics and strong vocals on *The Inner Truth*.

Compilation appearances include: *The Inner Truth* on *Pebbles Box* (5-LP), *Pebbles, Vol. 22* (LP) and *Trash Box* (5-CD). (VJ)

Wellington Arrangement

Personnel:
RANDY CHILDRESS	bs, vcls		A
VIC DeLUCAS	ld gtr, vcls		A
FRANK McDONNELL	drms, vcls		A
TERRY ROCAP	gtr, synth		A
JOE SHERWOOD	gtr, vcls		A
RICHARD SHERWOOD	keyb'ds, vcls		A

45s: Lorraine/Melissa Jones   (Decca 32505) 1969
α   Jezamine/Melissa Jones   (Decca 32582) 1969
Let The Good Times In/Look On Your Face (Decca 32686) 1970
Love/The World Needs Our Love   (Decca 32751) 1970

NB: α also issued as mono/stereo promo (Decca 34678/734678).

From Philadelphia, Pennsylvania, all six members of this group sang to produce six-part voicing harmonies. Their final 45, *Love*, in particular is superb. *Jezamine*, their second 45, was a cover of the hit by the (British) Casuals - aka *When Jesamine Goes*, which was also recorded by the Bystanders.

The band were introduced to Paul Leka (responsible for producing **The Lemon Pipers** - *Green Tambourine* amongst others) in New York City and were then signed to Decca Records. After **Wellington Arrangement**, several members (Terry, Joe and Randy) were signed to Playboy records and then Atlantic Records under the name 'Fresh Air' and worked with Arif Mardin to produce several records. The same three members also wrote and recorded professional sports team theme songs for the Philadelphia 76ers, Atlanta Hawks, Atlanta Flames (at the time), Washington Capitols, Philadelphia Phillies, etc.,. Joe, Richard and Randy are still currently writing and recording original material unable to fight off the infatuation of music and its' calling.

Compilation appearances include *Love* on *Turds On A Bum Ride, Vol. 3* (CD), *Glimpses, Vol's 1 & 2* (CD) and *Glimpses, Vol. 1* (LP). (VJ/MW)

Cory Wells and The Enemys

Personnel incl: DANNY HUTTON   A
                   CORY WELLS   A

45:   Sinner Man/Say Goodbye To Donna   (Valiant V-714) 1965

Sinner Man is hard-edged slightly punky-pop - the flip's an awful ballad. They'd go on to release three 45's of variable quality on MGM as The Enemys before Cory went on to form Three Dog Night, whose merits or otherwise we won't discuss here! **Danny Hutton** also had some early solo recordings and may have been involved with **The Bats**. (MW)

Bill Wendry and The Boss Tweeds

Personnel incl: BILL WENDRY   A

45s: Fire / A Wristwatch Band   (Columbia 4-44605) 1968
Tryin' To Get To You /
When He's Home   (Columbia 4-44825) 1969

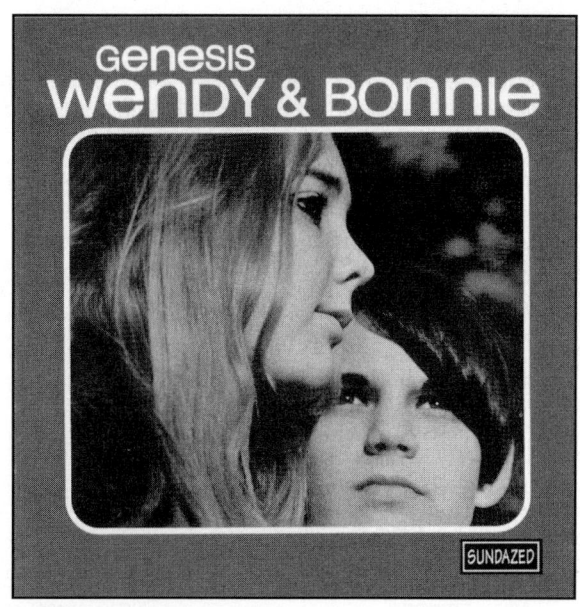

WENDY & BONNIE - Genesis CD.

| | Love Is A Happening /
Heartache Lines | (Columbia 4-44961) 1969 |

From Springfield, Massachusetts. Their debut kicks butt with their hard version of **Jimi Hendrix**' *Fire*, despite the brassy backing. *A Wristwatch Band* is a simmering psychedelic affair that can be heard on *Psychedelic Unknowns, Vol. 7* (LP & CD), *Incredible Sound Show Stories, Vol. 6* (LP) and *Of Hopes And Dreams & Tombstones* (LP).

The subsequent pair of 45s moved off into brass-pop territory and were recorded at Trod Nossel. Their singles were produced by Jimmy "Wiz" Wisner, who also worked with **The Buckinghams**, Jim and Jean and **Jacobs Creek**. (MW/AH/VJ/SR)

Wendy and Bonnie

Personnel:	LARRY CARLTON	gtr	A
	RANDY CIERLY	bs	A
	BONNIE FLOWER	vcls	A
	WENDY FLOWER	vcls	A
	JIM KELTNER	drms	A
	MIKE MELVOIN	keyb'ds	A

| ALBUM: | 1(A) | GENESIS | (Skye 1006D) 1969 R1 |

NB: (1) reissued on CD (Sundazed SC 11089) with five bonus tracks.

| 45: | The Paisley Window Pane/
It's What's Really Happening | (Skye) 1969 |

A soft-folk psychedelic tainted duo, on the label founded by the jazzmen Gary McFarland and **Gabor Szabo**. The two sisters, Wendy and Bonny Flower, tenderly aged 18 and 15, write and sing on all the tracks on what is a very typical period piece. Luckily the producer avoids the trap of over-orchestration and so comes up with a flowery and soothing bunch of songs, sometimes bordering on the sugary, but mostly rendering a peaceful and harmonic atmosphere. The voices of the sisters blend beautifully, the backing is unobtrusive but qualified. Naturally this drips innocence all over, but infrequently rises to the occasion and reaches real expresiveness, though often subdued, as on *Five O'Clock In The Morning* and *Endless Pathway*. Evidently, the last four tracks on Side Two are the best, which show more commitment than those on Side One and also boast sharp cutting acid-guitar on *The Winter Is Cold*. These four cuts are above average and should be heard by anyone with interest in female vocals in lighly psychedelic settings. The cover shot of the pair shows the very personification of naivete.

The album is now rare and sought-after. It has been suggested that Wendy would later be the half of Wendy and Liza, the duo produced by Prince in the eighties. (SR/MK)

The Werps

| 45: | Love's A Fire/Shades Of Blue | (W.G.W. 18703) 1967 |

From the Somerville area of New Jersey, this band also recorded a superb, unreleased 'hornless' version of *Love's A Fire*. It's a fine garage-punker with strong vocals, a full organ sound and some good guitar moments.

Compilation appearances have included: *Shades Of Blue* on *Scum Of The Earth* (Dble CD) and *Scum Of The Earth, Vol. 1* (LP); and *Love's A Fire* (prev. unreleased version) on *Back From The Grave, Vol. 6* (LP) and *Garage Monsters* (LP). (VJ)

West

Personnel:	RON CORNELIUS		A
	JOE DAVIS		A
	LLOYD PERATA		A
	MICHAEL STEWART		A
	(BOB CLAIRE)		A
	(JOE SAGEN)		A

| ALBUMS: | 1(A) | WEST | (Epic 26380) 1968 - |
| | 2(A) | BRIDGES | (Epic 26433) 1969 - |

| 45s: | Just Like Tom Thumb's Blues/
Baby You Been On My Mind | (Epic 10335) 1968 |
| | Step By Step/Summer Flower | (Epic 10378) 1968 |
| | Peaceful Times/
You Only Think You've Come Home | (Epic 10449) 1969 |

NB: All 45 tracks are taken from the LPs.

Originally from Crockett, California, although they frequently played in San Francisco in the late sixties. They were formed in 1967 by Cornelius, Sagen (who'd previously been an executive for Capitol Records) and John Stewart's brother Michael who'd enjoyed some success with **The We Five**. Very much in the mould of groups like **Notes From The Underground** they were more concerned with playing good-time music and enjoying themselves than exploring new musical forms.

Produced by Bob Johnston and Neil Wilburn, their first album contains two Dylan covers, two **Fred Neil** songs (*Everybody's Talkin* and *Dolphins*), the classic Ian Tyson song *Four Strong Winds*, as well as *Six Days On The Road* (also covered by Taj Mahal and **Street Noise**) and Bobby Kimmel's *New England Winter*, the **Stone Poneys** song. The few originals were penned by M. Stewart (helped by **We Five**'s Bob Jones on *Step By Step*) and Ron Cornelius.

The second album reputedly has good guitar work and excellent harmonies and both are very minor collectors' items.

Ron Cornelius will keep on working with Bob Johnston on records by Leonard Cohen and Bob Dylan. He also released a solo country-rock album in the early seventies.

Compilation appearances include *Down Along The Cove* on *Rockbusters* (LP). (VJ/SR)

Leslie West

Personnel:	N.D.SMART II	drms	A
	FELIX PAPPALARDI	bs	A
	LESLIE WEST	gtr, vcls	A

| ALBUM: | 1(A) | MOUNTAIN | (Windfall 4500) 1969 - |

NB: (1) Vinyl counterfeits exist. Reissued on CD in 1995 by BOD/TRC and in 1996 by Sony Legacy.

| 45: | Dreams Of Milk And Honey/
This Wheel's On Fire | (Windfall) 1969 |

NB: also released in France withe a PS (Bell 2C006-90580M).

Produced by Felix Pappalardi (who was already with West in **Jolliver Arkansaw**), the first solo output of the former leader of **The Vagrants** contained essentially hard-rock tracks similar to Cream and a cover of Dylan's *This Wheel's On Fire*. Its success led to the formation of the group **Mountain**, with Corky Laing and Steve Knight.

N.D.Smart was the former drummer with **The Remains** and **Kangaroo**. (SR)

West Coast Branch

| Personnel: | MIKE COSTANZA
(or CASTANZA) | bs, bcking vcl | A |
|---|---|---|---|
| | JON HILL | gtr, hrns, bcking vcl | A |
| | JOE LUSTER | ld vcls | A |
| | CRAIG LONG | ld gtr, bcking vcl | A |
| | CHUCK MARCHESE | drms, bcking vcl | A |

| 45s: | Linda's Gone/Spoonful | (Valiant V 753) 1966 |
| | Where Is The Door/Colors Of My Life | (A & M 869) 1967 |

A California mid-sixties outfit. *Spoonful* is a decent version with lots of fuzz'n'harp and a catchy frenetic fuzz-popper with effective acoustic guitar work and a foot-tapping beat - instantly likable. *Colors Of My Life* is not too

WEST COAST NATURAL GAS.

W.C.P.A.E.B. - West Coast Pop Art Experimental Band (Fifo) LP.

dissimilar, pleasant fuzz-pop. Unfortunately it's 'A' side is lame brassy pop (arranged by **Leon Russell**) - still, three gooduns out of four ain't bad at all.

Compilation appearances include: *Colors Of My Life* on *Acid and Flowers* (CD); and *Spoonful* on *Echoes In Time Vol's 1 & 2* (CD) and *Echoes In Time, Vol. 1* (LP). (VJ/MW/CL)

West Coast Natural Gas

Personnel:	CHUCK BATES	ld gtr	A
	DAVE BURKE		ABC
	KEP	gtr, vcls	AB
	JEFF LaBRACHE	drms	ABC
	KRIS LARSON	gtr	ABC
	STEVE MACK	ld gtr	BC
	PAT CRAIG	vcls	C

45:	Go Run And Play/		
	A Favor	(San Francisco Sound EU-2048)	1967

From Seattle, this act later went to San Francisco, met Matthew Katz, and became the "definitive" vesion of **Indian Puddin' and Pipe**! This 45, produced by Katz under the band's original moniker, has a fantastic 'B' side, written by Steve Mack, with an irresistable rhythm and a great guitar break.

Curiously **West Coast Natural Gas** (before they moved to 'Frisco) had played a gig in Seattle with the "original" Indian Puddin' and Pipe (who became **Easy Chair**)...

The band also made at least one other recording, *The Jumping Frog*, an original by Pat Craig, which has yet to see the light of day.

Jeff LaBrache had earlier played with The Imperials (one 45 on Jerden), **The City Limits** and **Rocky and His Friends**.

Compilation appearances include *A Favor* and *Go Run And Play* on *U-Spaces: Psychedelic Archaeology Vol. 1* (CDR).

West Coast Pop Art Experimental Band

Personnel:	DANNY BELSKY	drms	A
	DAN HARRIS	gtr, vcls	AB
	SHAUN HARRIS	gtr, bs, vcls	AB
	MICHAEL LLOYD	keyb'ds, gtr, vcls	AB
	BOB MARKLEY	producer	B

ALBUMS:	1(A)	WEST COAST POP ART EXPERIMENTAL BAND		
			(Fifo 101)	1966 R5
	2(B)	PART ONE	(Reprise 6247)	1967 R1
	3(B)	VOLUME 2	(Reprise 6270)	1967 R1
	4(B)	VOLUME 3: A CHILD'S GUIDE TO GOOD AND EVIL		
			(Reprise 6298)	1968 R1
	5(B)	WHERE'S MY DADDY	(Amos AAS 7004)	1969 SC

NB: (1) originally issued in a plain white cover, although a very small number of these had a paste-on 'slick' on the front (R6). This album was pirated (in part) on a 1980 **WCPAEB** compilation album *The Legendary Unreleased Album* (Raspberry Sawfly), along with some **WCPAEB**-related 45 sides. (1) counterfeited 'complete' on vinyl and CD in the early nineties and finally reissued legitimately as *Volume One*, a double LP and single CD (Sundazed LP 5036 / SC 11047) 1997. The Sundazed version includes many unreleased tracks and is superior to the earlier bootlegs. (2), (3) and (4) were issued in both mono and stereo and promotional white labels exist. (2) reissued on vinyl (Midi 24024) and on CD with bonus tracks. (2) and (3) also pirated on one CD. (2) reissued on CD with the second 45 as bonus tracks (Sundazed SC 6173) 2001. (3) reissued on CD with the third 45 as bonus tracks (Sundazed SC 6174) 2001. (4) issued in France on Vogue/Reprise CRV 6094, 1968. (4) and (5) pirated on one CD. (4) reissued on CD with their fourth 45 as bonus tracks (Sundazed SC 6175) 2001. Also relevant is *Transparent Day* (Edsel ED 180) 1986, a compilation of material from (2) and (3).

45s:	1906/Shifting Sands	(Reprise 0552) 1967
	Help, I'm A Rock/Transparent Day	(Reprise 0582) 1967
α	Smell Of Incense/Unfree Child	(Reprise 0776) 1967
	Free As A Bird/Where's My Daddy	(Amos 119) 1969

NB: α also released in France with a PS (Reprise RV 20183). There's also a French EP with a PS similar to their *Part 1* album: *1906/Help, I'm A Rock/Leyla* (Reprise 60104) 1967.

As their name suggests this band attempted to push back the frontiers of musical experience. They wrote and arranged all their compositions enjoying considerable recording freedom. The **West Coast Pop Art Experimental Band** (WCPAEB) were the first L.A. outfit to have a light show and were one of the biggest bands in town in the early days (in fact, the **Mothers Of Invention** once opened for them). Ironically, despite their reputation as psychedelic *enfant terribles*, none of the members used drugs (just like another purveyor of freaky music, **Frank Zappa**).

The Harris brothers and Michael Lloyd first met in 1964 when they were all students at the Hollywood Professional School - the school attended by most of the kids working in show-business. The three certainly had pedigree. Shaun and Danny were the sons of one of the U.S.'s best-known classical composers, Roy Harris, and Michael was a musical prodigy who had been working professionally for some time as a member of the New Dimensions. They first worked together as The Laughing Wind and as such recorded a 45 for Tower Records entitled: - *Good To Be Around/Don't Take Very Much To See Tomorrow*. In order for them to start performing they needed a drummer, and for a short while Danny Belsky, an old friend and former band member with Michael filled in on their first recordings. Thereafter, John Ware played live with the band and legendary drummers **Hal Blaine** and Jimmy Gordon played in the studio. Their final member **Bob Markley** was introduced to them by **Kim Fowley** at a party he was throwing for The Yardbirds during their first U.S. tour at **Markley**'s house. **Markley** was a wealthy attorney originally from Oklahoma who badly wanted to be in a band so he could get lots of girls (true!). Although a lot older than the other three (he was about 30, they were 16 or 17), he made a deal with them that he'd provide them with equipment if he could be in the band. As he didn't sing or play an instrument, he held a tambourine and stood in front of a dead mike. **Markley**'s role in the band remains

West Coast Pop Art Experimental Band - Part One LP.

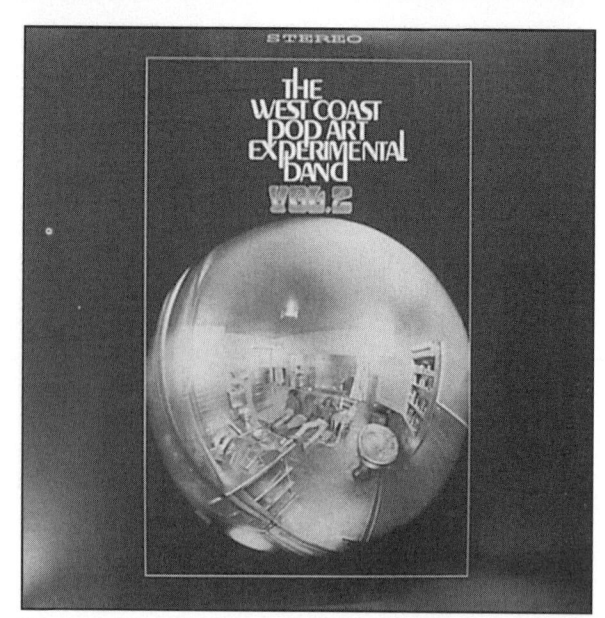

West Coast Pop Art Experimental Band - Volume 2 LP.

unclear. Because of his background in law, the other three left him with more and more business control, preferring to concentrate on the music. It's probable as a result that most of the production and composing credits attributed to him are spurious. Contrary to what most articles of the band allege, Michael Lloyd never left the band and continued making the albums with the Harris brothers right up to the demise of the band.

Markley's social connections helped them to get a deal with Reprise Records where they recorded three albums despite having no commercial success whatsoever. Their second album, reissued by Reprise a few years ago, blended 'experimental' tracks such as *1906*, *Help I'm A Rock* and *Transparent Day* with the melodic harmonies of *Shifting Sands*, *I Won't Hurt You*, *Leiyla*, *Here's Where You Belong* and *If You Want This Love*. Their first 45 was taken from this album. Prior to this album they recorded material for an earlier privately-pressed album in 1966 which is one of the rarest sixties artifacts. Some of that material and other oddities were issued by Raspberry Sawfly Records in 1982 (SAW 8001) and the "Fifo" album has subsequently been reissued officially by Sundazed.

Volume 2 was more adventurous and consequently inconsistent. Tracks like *In The Arena* sound badly disjointed, yet others like *Suppose They Give A War And No One Comes* with its strong dynamic contrasts are very effective and *Delicate Fawn* is a joyful little ditty. However, the prominent track on this album is probably the highly original *Tracy Had A Hard Day Sunday*. Unlike much of the other material on the album, this tune had considerable commercial appeal. A later 45, *Smell Of Incense* was taken from this album. It must have made quite an impression 'cause it was also recorded by **The Abstracts** on their album, **The Pawnbrokers** and by **Southwest F.O.B.**. In fact, the single was only belatedly released a year after the album in response to the latter's hit version of the song.

Their next effort was less ambitious, containing a number of competent conventional songs such as *As Kind As Summer* and the enchanting, haunting *As The World Rises And Falls*. Some of the material shows a strong satirical bent, like *A Child Of A Few Hours Is Burning To Death* with its deadly blues riff, sarcastic megaphone-on-a-parade-ground vocals and martial atmosphere. The title track combines a chilling invitation with mock-travelogue music to unique effect and *Eighteen Is Over The Hill* is as perfectly-realized a piece of music as can be imagined. Altogether it represented a considerable improvement on their previous efforts. Incidentally, the order of tracks on this record bears little relationship to the order given on the record sleeve.

"Take my hand and run away with me
Through the forest until the leaves and trees slow us down
A vampire bat will suck blood from our hands
A dog with rabies will bite us
Rats will run up your legs
But nothing will matter..."
(from *A Child's Guide To Good And Evil*)

The group recorded one final effort on the Amos label before splitting, **Markley**'s attempts to dominate the band finally alienating the other three.

Markley later made a solo album with a supporting band, *A Group* (Forward SFT 1007) in 1969 and produced some material for **J.J. Light**.

After the group broke up Shaun and Dan Harris headed for the Midwest as The California Spectrum. They had a great light show and for about 14 - 16 months toured very successfully. Shaun relocated to Denver for a year or so, performing as The Spectrum and also booking and promoting other bands. He later released a solo album, *Shaun Harris* (Capitol ST 11168) 1973, consisting of soft country-rock (with orchestrations by his father, Roy Harris) and subsequently has collaborated with Michael on an almost endless stream of recordings from 1970 to the present. Michael became vice-president of MGM Records and one of the best-known producers in Los Angeles.

Dan continued writing and working with Michael and Shaun. In 1984, he moved to Sweden where he performed and recorded very successfully. A few years later he travelled back to L.A., where he currently resides. He teaches guitar, performs, acts and writes with his wife, Vicky.

Compilation appearances have so far included: *I Won't Hurt You* on *Nuggets, Vol. 9* (LP) and *A Child's Guide To Good And Evil* on *Electric Psychedelic Sitar Headswirlers, Vol. 1* (CD).

For a fascinating **WCPAEB**-related offshoot outfit which featured Ron Morgan (co-composer of *Smell Of Incense*) and Jimmy Greenspoon, check out the **Super Band** entry.

More recently the enchanting *Smell Of Incense* was revived again in 1994 by a Norwegian band who also took the title as their band name - very apt for their trippy psychedelic-folk style. (VJ/LP/MW/SR)

West Coast Workshop

ALBUM: 1 THE WIZARD OF OZ AND OTHER TRANS LOVE TRIPS
(Capitol ST 2776) 1967 SC

Produced by Nick Venet, this was probably a studio project. James E. Bond junior also features on the credits. The album's a rather patchy instrumental concept recording full of ragas, sitars and flutes. It may appeal to those who like the freaky side of **The Chocolate Watchband**'s *Inner Mystique* or *The Zodiac* by **Cosmic Sounds**. (VJ)

Westfauster

Personnel:	C.W. FAUSTER	vcls, organ, piano, harp, bs, moog	A
	STEPHEN HELWIG	vcls, perc	A
	MICHAEL NEWLAND	flute, alto sax, vibes	A

West Coast Pop Art Experimental Band - Vol. 3: A Child's Guide To Good and Evil LP.

West Coast Pop Art Experimental Band - Where's My Daddy? LP.

ALBUM: 1(A) IN A KING'S DREAM   (Nasco 9008) 1971 R2
NB: (1) reissued on CD by Golden Classics Rebirth (GCR 011) 1997.

From Cincinnati, Ohio, although their early seventies progressive rock album was recorded at Woodland Sound Studio, Nashville, Tennessee. Its finest moments are the title track, *Where Are You* and *Everyday*. If rather jazzy progressive rock with lots of keyboards, woodwind and plenty of melody is your niche seek out a copy of this album which has become quite collectable.

The band used to gig frequently with **Whalefeathers**. (VJ)

Westhampton Barge

45:    Can't Come Home/Lovin' Is   (No label NE 217) 1968

An insistent guitar refrain makes the top side catchy, but it's only late sixties light pop-rock. The flip is also quite poppy. Both tracks were written by Richard Talauera and the band were moored in El Paso, Texas. (MW)

West Minist'r

Personnel incl:	KEITH BROWN	gtr	A
	ARNIE BODE	drms	A
	DAVE COTTRELL	bs	A
	DAVE HEARN	keyb'ds	A
	KIRK KAUFMAN	gtr, vcls	A
	FRANK WIEWEL	vcls	A

45s: Bright Lights Windy City/Carnival   (Razzberry SR 2975) 1969
       Sister Jane/I Want You   (Magic MXS 45001) 19??
       My Life/Mr. Fingers   (Magic KK 7432) c1974

Originally from Omaha, Nebraska, they later moved to Fort Dodge in Iowa where they played a heavy brand of psychedelia in the late sixties. They continued recording throughout the seventies and released an album as The Hawks in 1980. Prior to the album with The Hawks, Kaufman released a solo album under the pseudonym Captain Kirk. A band worth investigating.

Keith Brown later formed Locust.

Compilation appearances have included: *My Life* and *Bright Lights, Windy City* on *Glimpses, Vol's 1 & 2* (CD); *My Life* on *Glimpses, Vol. 1* (LP); *Bright Lights, Windy City* on *Glimpses, Vol. 2* (LP); and *Sister Jane* on *Monsters Of The Midwest, Vol. 1* (cass.). (VJ/MW)

We Talkies

45:    I've Got To Hold On/
       What Are You Waiting For   (Epic 10121) 1967

A weird studio group with baby vocals and unusual arrangements. (SR)

We The People

Personnel:	RANDY BOYTE	organ, piano	ABCDE
	DAVID DUFF	bs	ABCDE
	WAYNE PROCTOR	ld gtr	AB
	TOMMY TALTON	gtr	ABC
	TOM WYNN	drms	A
	LEE FERGUSON	drms	AB
	TERRY COX	drms	CDE
	CARL CHAMBERS	gtr	D
	SKIP SKINNER	gtr	E

ALBUMS: 1(-) DECLARATION OF INDEPENDENCE   (Eva 12009) 1983
        2(-) DECLARATION OF INDEPENDENCE
                                  (Collectables COL-CD-0532) 1993
        3(-) MIRROR OF OUR MINDS   (Sundazed SC 11056) 1998

NB: Despite having similar titles and fourteen tracks apiece, (1) and (2) have some track differences. (3) is a double CD retrospective, from the master tapes, with no less than forty tracks!!!

FRENCH
EPs: 1 He Doesn't Go About It Right/You Burn Me Up And
         Down /Mirror Of Your Mind/The Color Of Your Love (PS)
                                           (London 10191) 1966
      2 St. John's Shop/In The Past/Declaration Of Independence/
         Lovin' Son Of A Gun (PS)   (London 10184) 1967
NB: These two French picture sleeve EPS are very rare.

45s: My Brother The Man/Proceed With Caution (Hot Line 3680) 1966
       Mirror Of Your Mind/
       The Color Of Your Love   (Challenge 59333) 1966
       He Doesn't Go About It Right/
       You Burn Me Up And Down   (Challenge 59340) 1966
       St. John's Shop/In The Past   (Challenge 59351) 1966
       Follow Me Back To Louisville/
       Fluorescent Hearts   (RCA Victor 47-9292) 1967
       Love Is A Beautiful Thing/
       The Day She Dies   (RCA Victor 47-9393) 1967
       Ain't Gonna Find Nobody (Better Than You)/
       When I Arrive   (RCA Victor 47-9498) 1968

This seminal band hailed from Orlando, Florida, and despite their lack of national success at the time are nowadays regarded in the same league as **The Chocolate Watchband**, **Standells**, **Music Machine** etc. This view is entirely justified, as their 45s reveal a depth and diversity of talent, from the raucous punk of *When I Arrive* or *You Burn Me Up And Down* through to melodic drifting ballads such as *St. John's Shop* and *The Day She Dies*. **We The People** also have a unique quality in their songwriting, with *My Brother The Man*, *Mirror Of You Mind*, *In The Past* and numerous others all standing out as top quality stuff.

The band were formed out of two acts - the **Trademarks** and **Offbeets**, at the suggestion of Ron Dillman, who managed both bands. Within a week of their first meeting / rehearsal in early 1966, they were recording their first 45, *My Brother, The Man*, but shortly afterwards Tom Wynn was replaced by Lee Ferguson and the band signed a production and publishing deal with Nashville-based Tony Moon.

Whilst their first two 45s contained punchy psychedelic rockers, *He Doesn't Go About It Right* contains a dollop of Kinks style humour and *St. John's Shop* is a beautiful slow ballad. All were big regional hits in Florida and Tennessee, but under threat of the draft and frustrated by the lack of national success, Wayne Proctor quit early in 1967. Shortly before his departure they recorded *Love Wears Black (None)*, at Bradley's Barn in Nashville in early 1967, which was intended for release under the pseudonym Fresh Air. He also co-wrote **The Skunks** 1967 track, *Don't Ask Why* with Clark Taylor, which has recently been given another airing on *The Quill Records Story* (CD).

With Wayne pursuing a career in song-writing, the group continued, although Lee Ferguson was then drafted and replaced by Terry Cox from Those Four Guys. Now signed to RCA, national success still proved elusive, although the later 45s are still pretty good (and *When I Arrive* remains a complete stormer).

Tom Talton too left the group in 1968/69 and later resurfaced with Tom Wynn in Cowboy. **We The People** soldiered on for a while, but they eventually called it a day in 1970.

In addition to their 45s, the band also had two French EPs with picture sleeves: the first (London 10181) 1966 contains the four tracks that comprise the first two Challenge 45: the second (London 10184) 1967 contains *St John's Shop*, *In The Past*, *Declaration Of Independence* and *Lovin' Son Of A Gun* - the last two being non-US tracks.

The band have also been the subject of three retrospective compilations, with Sundazed's *Mirror Of Our Minds* being the latest and best. A double CD package, with extensive liner notes/interviews by Jeff Jarema, it includes no less than forty tracks. All their 45 cuts are featured, plus all the "previously unreleased" cuts that have cropped up elsewhere on other comps etc. and a whole bundle of other tracks also make their first appearance anywhere... All in all a thoroughly recommended package!

Compilation appearances have included: *Mirror Of Your Mind* on *Mayhem & Psychosis, Vol. 2* (LP), *Nuggets, Vol. 6* (LP), *Even More Nuggets* (CD), *Excerpts From Nuggets* (CD); *In The Past* on *Mindrocker, Vol. 5* (LP), *Psychedelic Unknowns, Vol's 1 & 2* (LP), *Psychedelic Unknowns, Vol. 2* (Dble 7"); *You Burn Me Up And Down* and *He Doesn't Go About It Right* on *Mindrocker, Vol. 6* (LP); *Mirror Of Your Mind* and *You Burn Me Up And Down* on *Nuggets Box* (4-CD); *You Burn Me Up And Down* on *Psychedelic Unknowns, Vol. 4* (LP& CD), *Pebbles, Vol. 4* (ESD) (CD), *Sound Of The Sixties* (Dble LP), *Sixties Archive, Vol. 1* (CD), *Songs We Taught The Fuzztones* (Dble LP & CD), *The Seventh Son* (LP); *When I Arrive* on *Pebbles, Vol. 7* (LP); *Girl Of My Dreams* on *Shutdown '66* (LP); and *My Brother The Man* on *Filling The Gap* (4-LP), *Garage Punk Unknowns, Vol. 4* (4-LP) and *Psychedelic States: Florida Vol. 3* (CD).

The CD compilation *Psychedelic Microdots Of The Sixties, Vol. 1* too is also of interest as not only does it include original masters of *My Brother The Man*, *Mirror Of Your Mind*, *You Burn Me Up And Down* and *In The Past* to whet your appetite, but also four unreleased tracks, *By The Rule*, *Half Of Wednesday*, *Free Information* and *Too Much Noise*. The same tracks, plus *The Color Of Love*, *St. John's Shop*, *Alfred*, *What Kind Of Man Are You?* and *Beginning Of The End* also appear on *I Turned Into A Helium Balloon* (CD). (VJ/MW/SR)

We Three

ALBUM: 1   WE THREE   (Private Pressing) c1969 ?

From Greensburg, Pennsylvania, a rural folk trio (two girls, one guy), doing mostly covers of Dylan (*Blowin' In The Wind*, *Don't Think Twice*) and other well known songs (*As Tears Go By*, *Cloudy*, *For Emily*) plus some Christian tunes. Not recommended. (SR)

Wet Paint

45:        Shame/At The River's Edge   (Royal Hollywood 101) 1967

A high school band from Chicago area, who were fans of **New Colony Six**, and covered their classic *At The River's Edge*. Both sides of their neatly restrained 45 have resurfaced on *Pebbles, Vol. 7* (CD). (MW)

We Ugly Dogs

45:        First Spring Rain/Poor Man   (B.T. Puppy 537) 1968

NB: also issued in the U.K. (B.T. Puppy BTS 45537) and reissued as by The Canterbury Music Festival (B.T. Puppy 541) 1968.

A 45 that is rated highly by some and touted as 'psych' by others. Well, it's very pleasant harmony-rock, somewhat orchestrated, and comparable to, say, **The Cryan' Shames** *Synthesis* material. Now, I rate **The Cryan' Shames** highly but I wouldn't call them psychedelic, so beware of this one. (MW)

We Who Are

45:        Last Trip/Remember When   (Love 6739) 1967

A punk outfit from Waterloo, Iowa and a sadly short-lived one who disbanded when their equipment was destroyed by a flood! *Last Trip* was a keyboard-dominated slice of psychedelia with an intro that makes you sit up and take notice.

Compilation appearances include *Last Trip* on *The Midwest Vs. Canada* (LP) and *Pebbles, Vol. 10* (CD). (VJ)

Whalefeathers

Personnel incl:			
STEPHE BACON	perc, tympani, vcls	ABC
ED BLACKMON	keyb'ds, vcls	AB
MICHAEL JONES	gtr, vcls	AB
ROGER SAUER	bs, vcls	A
LEONARD LE BLANC	bs, vcls	BC
MIKE WHEELER	gtr, bs	C

NB: Details for line-up "C" incomplete.

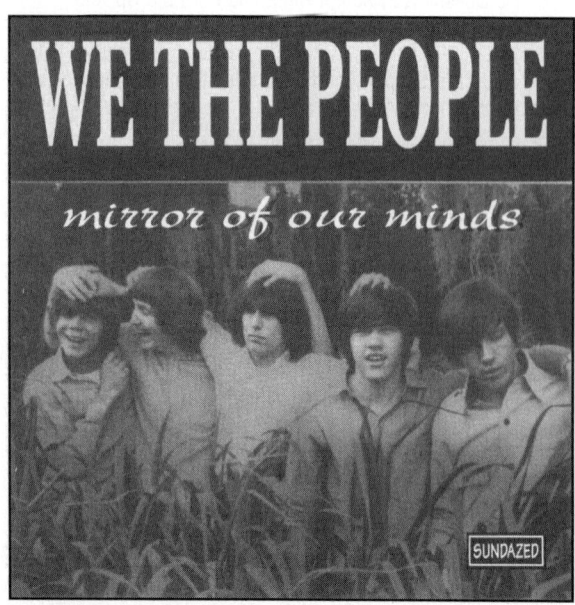

WE THE PEOPLE - Mirror Of Our Minds CD.

WHALEFEATHERS - Declare LP.

ALBUMS:	1(A)	DECLARE	(Nasco 9003) c1970 R2
	2(B)	WHALEFEATHERS	(Nasco 9005) 1971 R1/R2

NB: (1) has had a limited pirate repressing. (2) also issued in the U.K. on Blue Horizon (2431 009) 1971 and in Germany (Vogue 17257) 197?. (2) reissued on CD.

45s:	Shaking All Over / Nearing The End	(Nasco 006) 1970
	It's A Hard Road/Two Feet From My Grave	(Nasco 026) 1972

From Cincinnati, Ohio, this outfit used to gig frequently with **Westfauster** and played a heavy, very keyboard-dominated blend of music. Their albums have distinct psychedelic influences and although both have their moments are sometimes a bit messy. Both albums are sought-after by collectors.

Lenny LeBlanc went on to become a successful Christian music artist, whilst Mike Wheeler who played with the band in their last two years, went on to work with Grammy winning Nashville songwriter Mike Reid. Wheeler also led an act called Wheels, who recorded on Boardwalk, with an album produced by Craig Fuller, and who toured with Little Feat in '78. He's also worked more recently with Paul Barrere.

Know Thyself has also appeared on *Sixties Archive, Vol. 8* (CD). (VJ/MW/CF)

Michael P. Whalen

Personnel:	ALLAN BRENEMAN	drms	A
	JIMMY BRYANT	gtr	A
	DAVID COHEN	gtr	A
	DAVID JACKSON	bs	A
	LYLE RITZ	bs	A
	MICHAEL P. WHALEN	vcls, gtr	A

ALBUM:	1(A)	MICHAEL P. WHALEN	(Pete Records S1102) 1970 -

45:	Where's The Playground, Susie ?/	
	Universal Love	(Reprise 602) 1968

Michael P. Whalen was a Californian singer/songwriter whose *The Quieting Of Oliver Tweak* (featured on his album) was also covered by **The Leaves** on their second album. His single which was produced by Art Podell and arranged by Jim Webb contains two average orchestrated pop songs.

Released two years later, his sole album is a decent folk-rock effort, produced by Chris Petersen on a short-lived Californian label and recorded at the Gold Star Studios on Hollywood. It features several good musicians like David Jackson (**Moon**), David Cohen (**Country Joe and The Fish**) and Lyle Ritz. (SR)

What Four

45:	No Good For Me / ?	(Roll'Em # unkn) 1967

From the Whitestone/Little Neck area of Queens, NY this band were previously known as the **Sunrisers**, who'd released a 45 in 1966... and not the NYC girl-group with two 45s on Columbia. (MM/MW)

The What Fours

45:	Basement Walls/Eight Shades Of Brown	(Fleetwood 4571) 1966

From Revere, Massachusetts. The guitarist of this band was previously with **The Weekenders**. Two other tracks *Don't Laugh* and *Marshmellow Dream* remain unreleased.

Compilation appearances include: *Basement Walls* and *Eight Shades Of Brown* on *New England Teen Scene* (CD) and *New England Teen Scene, Vol. 1* (LP); and *Basement Walls* on *Gone, Vol. 2* (LP). (VJ/MW)

The What Knots

45:	I Ain't Dead Yet/	
	Talkin' 'Bout Our Breakup	(Dial 45-4067) 1967

This 45 seems to have been their sole stab for stardom. The 'A' side got a second life after it was included on *A Journey To Tyme, Vol. 4* (LP).

Possibly from Nashville. *I Ain't Dead Yet* was written by Donna Weiss - see **Tony and Terri** entry. (VJ/MW)

The What-Nots

Personnel incl:	DAVE KENYON
	FRANK PATRICOLO

45s:	Morning/I Need You Baby	(Amber AMB 102) 1966
	Nobody Else But You/Look Down	(Amber AMB 101) 1966

A high school aged band from the Hillsdale/Oradell/Hackensack area of Northern New Jersey. Their first 45, *Morning*, actually made the Top Ten in Seattle and Salt Lake City and was undoubtedly their finest moment. Their second 45 simply sank without trace and after the relative success of *Morning* everything was downhill until they eventually called it quits. They were one of the few rock bands to record on Amber Records, which really specialised in doo-wop and accapella music.

Compilation appearances have included: *Morning*, *I Need You Baby* and *I Was A Fool* (prev. unreleased) on *Attack Of The Jersey Teens* (LP); and *Morning* on *Hipsville 29 B.C.* (LP). (VJ)

WHALEFEATHERS - Whalefeathers LP.

What's Happening

45: Baby You're Hurtin'/Hot Buttered Buns   (Coreco 101) 196?

You'll also find *Baby You're Hurtin'* on *A Journey To Tyme, Vol. 4* (LP). (VJ)

What's It To Ya

ALBUM: 1   WHAT'S IT TO YA   (Huh) 1975 -

A breezy folk-rock album with vocal harmonies and some interesting guitar work. (SR)

What's New

Personnel: CARL ??   A
             JAY ??   A
             KEVIN ??   A
             SCOT ??   A

French
EPs: 1   The What's New: Early Morning Rain / Driving Wheels / Huckleberry Finn / The last Thing On My Mind (PS)
                              (Number One LOU 2013) 1966
       2   Get Away / It's Over Now / Up So High / Daisy (PS)
                              (Number One LOU 2014) 1967

French
45s: Early Morning Rain / ?   (Number One) 1966
       It's Over Now / Daisy (PS)   (Number One) 1967
       Getaway /
       Up So High (Disque No 2)   (Number One LOU 106) 1967

This Orlando, Florida quartet only enjoyed releases in France, having relocated there after being spotted by a talent scout and offered a recording deal. They produced at least two EPs and several 45s in 1966-7. The fuzz-popper *Up So High* is the cut from their second EP favoured by the compilers of *Realities In Life* (LP), *Let's Dig 'Em Up, Vol. 3* (LP) and *Fuzz, Flaykes And Shakes, Vol. 4* (LP & CD). (MW)

Whatt Four

45:   Dandelion Wine/
      You're Wishin' I Was Someone Else   (Mercury 72716) 1967

A mellowed-out psych sitar-pop ditty from Riverside, California. If you dig The Beatles' *Within You Without You* you'll float away on *Dandelion Wine*, at last compiled on *Collecting Peppermint Clouds*. The flip is excellent bombastic fuzz-pop, now to be found on *Basementsville! U.S.A.* (LP).

Dandelion Wine was written by Jerry Scheff, of **Millennium**, **Friar Tuck**, **Gladstone**, and numerous other L.A. outfits. *You're Wishin'...* is by G. Sanders and K. Johnson - it's likey that is THE Ken Johnson of **Ken and The Fourth Dimension**, who produced and wrote for several L.A. area garage bands. (MW)

Whatt Four

45:   You Better Stop Your Messin' Around/
      Our Love Should Last Forever   (ESP 109) c1966

The 'B' side, *Our Love Should Last Forever*, is great psych-punk. Despite the label, this outfit is reported to be from California but not confirmed to be the same group as above.

Compilation appearances include *Our Love Should Last Forever* on *Punk Classics* (CD) and *Punk Classics, Vol. 1* (7"). (MW)

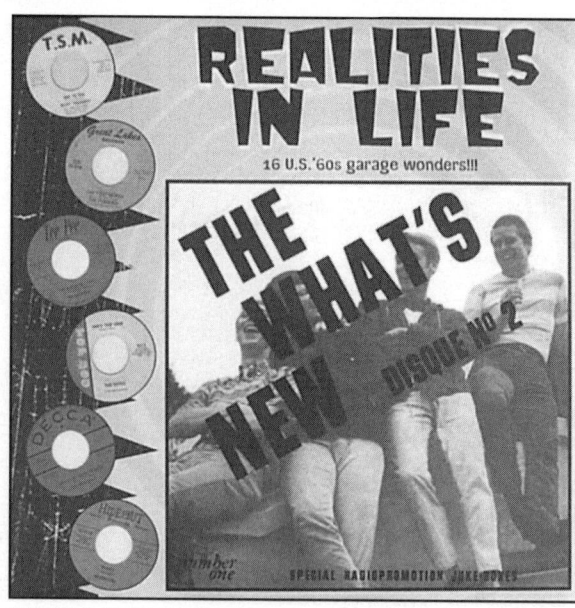

REALITIES IN LIFE (Comp LP) including The What's New.

Whazoos

Personnel incl: BOB GRYZIEC   A

45:   Inside Of Me / The Rain Came (PS)   (National N 611/2) 1967

A quintet from Wilkes-Barre, Pennsylvania. They included bassist Bob Gryziec from Thee Avantis, who released one 45 in 1966 - *I Want To Understand / Nancy* (SAMRON 103). He also spent time with pop outfit The Buoys. **The Whazoos** evolved into **Great Bear**. For more details on these and other Pennsylvania sixties bands, look no further than Mike Kuzmin's book 'Sounds From The Woods'.

Inside Of Me is featured on *Psychedelic Crown Jewels, Vol. 3* (CD) - a stately and subdued opus, with piano and mannered vocals, it warrants repeated plays for full appreciation of some fine fuzz-work. (MW/MKn)

Peter Wheat and The Breadmen

Personnel: BOB BIRDWELL   (gtr) bs   ABC
             ROGER KENNEDY   vcls, gtr   ABC
             TERRY REISMAN   drms   ABC
             DAVE WHEELER   gtr   A
             BARRY HOUK   ld gtr   BC
             CHUCK TEDFORD   keyb'ds   B
             DALE RADCLIFF   keyb'ds   C

45:   All The Time/Baby What's New   (Amber 6657) 1966

From Fremont, California, this band began when Washington High School friends Dave Wheeler and Bob Birdwell started playing guitars together in 1964. Needing someone to play lead, they asked another school friend, Roger Kennedy to join them and were introduced to drummer Terry Riesman from Mision High School. Terry didn't even OWN a set of drums... but he borrowed the school's marching band's drums and he set them up in such a way that he could play them as a set!

Dave Wheeler named the band 'the Tarentels' from a dictionary - Tarentella being the Italian dance of the tarantula. Over time, Dave moved away, and Bob moved over to bass. Roger moved from lead to rhythm, and Barry Houk came in as lead. Chuck Tedford was also brought in on keyboards.

Bob:- "We landed a job playing with **The Turtles** at the San Leandro Rollerina, (Bill Quary's Teens & Twenties) and were spotted by Barry Carlos of Go Teen Productions. He signed us up as **Peter Wheat and The Breadmen** and we played all over with the big names of the day. **Paul Revere**, **Byrds**, Animals, Them, Chuck Berry, **Big Brother**, Yardbirds, and so many more I can't recall just sitting here. Since we were KYA Radio's "house band" we were even originally scheduled to play with the Beatles at Candlestick. However, because of a conflict between our Musician's Union, (Local 510), and SF's union, (Local 6), we got bumped.... but at least we DID get tickets to see the show".

"Dave Wheeler still writes and plays music full-time; I'm a business executive for a very large private corporation; Terry was working as a janitor last I heard; Roger passed away in the mid-nineties; Chuck Tedford was a truck driver and is now happily retired; and I haven't seen Barry in around 10 years..."

Baby What's New has also been compiled on *Pebbles, Vol. 10* (LP). (VJ/BBI)

The Wheel of Fortune

Personnel:	RON ALLEN	vcls	A
	DEL HANDLEY	ld gtr	A
	DAN NICHOLSON	sax	A
	BOB STOUTENBERG	drms	AB
	GARY THOMPSON (BILL SCREAM)	vcls, keyb'ds	AB
	DON CLARK	ld gtr	B
	KEITH COLLINS	bs	B
	LARRY CONGRAM	keyb'ds	B

NB: line-up 'A' 1967-68; 'B' 1968-69.

45s:	Before You Leave/Long Long Day	(Ridon 856) 1967
	All The World/Funny Looks	(Jamie 1360) 1968

Formed in Salem, Oregon, with members from local teen bands The Untouchables, The Breakaways and The Henchmen. Their punkish sounding debut 45 was a local hit. Its success led to a contract with the Philadelphia-based Jamie Records but after just one further 45 arguments about musical direction brought their recording career to an end. However, they moved to Beaverton, Oregon, with a modified line-up B, which did not record, before the draft and further differences of opinion led to their demise. Bill Scream was last reported composing commercials and movie soundtracks. He still owns a small recording studio. Bob Stoutenberg owns The Moon June Music Publishing Company.

Compilation appearances include *Before You Leave* on *Highs In The Mid-Sixties, Vol. 16* (LP). (VJ)

Jim Whelan and The Beau Havens

Personnel incl:	JIM WHELAN		A

45:	Elizabeth/Feel So Good	(Gama 705) 1965

A teen-punk outfit either from the near-D.C. town Belle Haven in Virginia, or from Belle Haven road in a Kentwood, Maryland development - hence their name. They were 15 when they formed and soon became a popular live attraction locally at frat parties and school dances. Their 45 was a double-sided teen punker, with *Elizabeth* being an ode to one of the band members girlfriends and *Feel So Good* being written by leader of **The Nautiloids**, Richard Fulton. The 45 was recorded at the Edgewood recording Studio, Washington D.C. in 1965.

Compilation appearances include: *Elizabeth* on *Back From The Grave, Vol. 7* (Dble LP); and *Feel So Good* on *Garage Punk Unknowns, Vol. 8* (LP). (VJ/MW/RF)

The Whether Bureau

45:	Why Can't You And I?/White And Frosty	(Laurie 3431) 1968

This seems to have been a one-off New York City venture on Laurie. *White And Frosty* has since resurfaced on *Mindrocker, Vol. 10* (Dble LP). (VJ)

Whims

ALBUM:	1 TRUCKIN'	(Private Pressing XPL-1021) 1971 ?

From Wheaton College, a student group doing folk versions of the '**Dead**, Traffic and the Beatles. (SR)

The Whims

ALBUM:	1 ON THE ROCKS	(Fleetwood) c1966 ?

An obscure all-girl frat-rock band. (SR)

Whistler, Chaucer, Detroit and Greenhill

Personnel:	DAVID BULLOCK	gtr, bs, vcls	A
	JOHN CARRICK		A
	SCOTT FRASER	gtr, keyb'ds, bs, vcls	A
	EDDIE LIVELY	gtr, vcls	A
	PHIL WHITE	bs, keyb'ds, vcls	A

ALBUM:	1(A) THE UNWRITTEN WORKS OF GEOFFREY, ETC...	(UNI 73034) 1968 -

This Texas group from Fort Worth comprised of Scott Fraser, Eddie Lively (both ex-**Mods**), David Bullock and Phil White, under the pseudonyms of Benjamin Whistler, Geoffrey Chaucer, Nathan Detroit and Phillip Greenhill. If Fraser, Bullock and White all began playing circa 1963, they apparently didn't team up before 1967, when David Bullock returned from the coffee house circuit of Houston.

John Carrick: "David knew me from a club/coffee house my mom and I owned in Houston. It was called 'Sand Mountain' and was quite the hot bed of singer songwriters including Jerry Jeff, Towns, Guy Clark and lots more. Anyway, I ended up going to Fort Worth and worked on the album for about a year. By the time the album photos were taken, I had moved back to Houston. They got Guy Clark to take the cover photo and he failed to call me for the shoot, so Guy set the timer and sat in the pic. Another interesting sideline concerns a song on the album called *Me And My Babe*. The song needed a banjo adding, so we contacted the Northeast Texas banjo stud, another young guy from Fort Worth called Steve Bruton."

Their album is a bit patchy but contains some superb psychedelic compositions (*Day Of Childhood*, *House Of Collection*) and good folk-rock songs with nice guitar solos and Beatles inspired vocals. All their material was original and Joseph "T-Bone" Burnett produced the sessions recorded in Fort Worth and in Santa Ana, California.

The lack of a permanent satisfactory drummer inhibited their efforts as a performing group. At the end of 1968, Frazer, Bullock and White would finally meet a percussionist, Brett Wilson, in Austin and together they formed **Space Opera**. They intensively toured through the South before finally signing with Epic in 1972, thanks to Michael Mann, their manager and sponsor. In 1969, Eddie Lively would play with **John Abdnor**. (SR/JCk)

Ruth White

ALBUMS:	1 FLOWERS OF EVIL	(Limelight) c1969 -
	2 SEVEN TRUMPETS OF TAROT	(Limelight) c1969 -
	3 SHORT CIRCUITS	(Angel S-36042) c1972 -

Ruth White recorded at least three albums which begin to be sought-after by some collectors. Her two Limelight records may appeal to readers interested by Don Robertson and other psychedelic electronic sound pioneers. (SR/SN)

White Cloud

Personnel:	CHARLES BROWN III	gtr	A
	RICHARD CROOKS	drms	A
	THOMAS JEFFERSON KAYE	vcls, gtr	A
	KENNETH KOSEK	fiddle	A
	DON PAYNE	bs	A
	TEDDY WENDER	piano	A

ALBUM:	1(A) WHITE CLOUD	(Good Medicine GM-LP-3500) 1972 -

Released on the obscure Good Medicine label in a beautiful snakeskin textured gatefold cover, this album is beginning to be sought-after. Led by the legendary performer/producer Thomas Jefferson Kaye, the songs include *All Cried Out*, *Qualified*, *Collection Box* and *Hoe-Bus*. A few cuts have killer fuzz guitar leads and others have a nice communal folk feel.

White Cloud also backed Loudon Wainwright III on his third album (the one with *Red Guitar* and *Dead Skunk*).

A native indian, Thomas Jefferson Kaye alos produced several of Gene Clark's albums and released two interesting solo albums in 1973 and 1974 (the latter with Fagen and Becker from Steely Dan). (SR)

White Fluff

45:	Vegetable Binge/Stoned Lonely (PS)	(EAB 1112)	1969

From Maine, this band's *Vegetable Binge* can also be heard on *New England Teen Scene, Vol. 2* (LP). Their 45 came in a picture sleeve. (VJ)

White Light

Personnel:	MISSISSIPPI	vcls, gtr	A
	JOEL PERRON	ld gtr, bs, drms	A
	KURT PERRON	electric piano, drms, bs, ld gtr	A

ALBUMS:	1(A)	WHITE LIGHT	(Century 39955) 1970 R3
	2(A)	WHITE LIGHT	(Century 40136) 1971 R3

NB: (1) contains *Heartbreak Hotel*. (2) contains *VDFM*, and is by far the rarer version. (1) has been also been counterfeit on vinyl and on CD (Two Of Us 001) 1997 together with Mississippi's solo album *Velvet Sandpaper*.

This group was from Long Beach, California. Musically, the album is very diverse. There's quite a good cover of Bob Womack's *What Is This*; the Beatle-ish *You'll Lose A Good Thing*; and lots of funky strutting on *Cold Shot*. The highlight, *I Couldn't Get High*, a fine pop-rocker turns up on Side Two alongside a reasonable cover of Lou Reed's *I'm Waiting For The Man*. Don't fork out megabucks for the very rare original but snap up the repress if you can.

This album has exactly the same front cover as **The Philosophers'** *After Sundown* album, as both titles were manufactured by Century, who offered bands without artwork the option of picking a cover from a number of 'catalogue' art designs.

Mississippi also recorded a solo album before he joined up with the Perron brothers, entitled *Velvet Sandpaper* (Taurus - Scorpio) 1969 R2/3. This has been reissued recently, although erroneously shown as by **White Light**, and both albums have been reissued on one CD.

Compilation appearances have so far included: *VDFM*, *Crashin'*, *White Light Pt. 1* and *White Light Pt. 2* on *Filling The Gap* (4-LP); and *I Couldn't Get High* and *Cold Shot* on *Kicks & Chicks* (LP). (VJ/CF/MW)

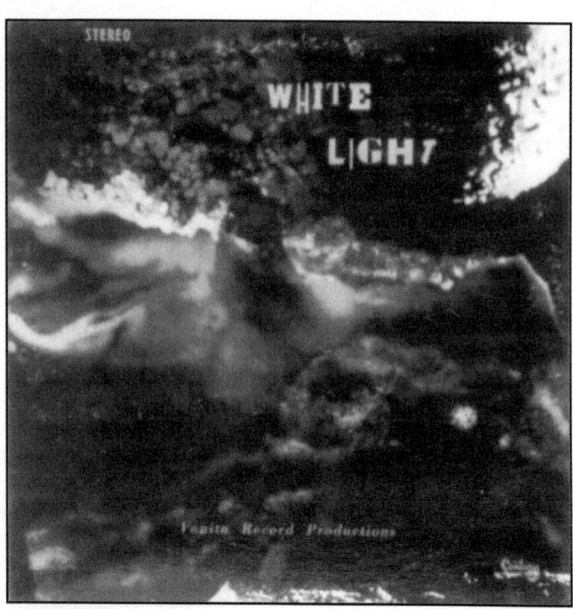

WHITE LIGHT - White Light LP.

White Lightnin'

Personnel:	BUSTA CHERRY JONES	bs, vcls	A
	DONALD KINSEY	gtr, vcls	A
	WOODY KINSEY	drms, vcls	A

ALBUM:	1(A)	WHITE LIGHTNIN'	(Island ILPS 9325) 1975 -

Recorded at Sam Philips Studios in Memphis, the only album of this black power trio may interest fans of Velvet Turner, **Black Merda** and other bands influenced by **Hendrix**.

Housed in a superb die-cut sleeve painted by Mati Klarwein (also responsible of the famous covers of **Santana**'s *Abraxas* and Miles Davis' *Bitches Brew*), this album was produced by no other than Felix Pappalardi, who really knew how to record such a group, as he also produced Cream, **Mountain** and **Hot Tuna**. All the material was original, except for a cover of Garland Jeffrey's *Wild In The Street*.

A veteran of the Memphis scene, Busta Jones had previously played with **Moloch**. In 1973/74, he traveled to England where he recorded with Brian Eno, Chris Spedding and the Sharks. In the early eighties, he worked with Robert Fripp and the Talking Heads.

The Kinsey brothers would later front the Kinsey Report, an electric blues group and work with their father, "Big Daddy" Kinsey, a Chicago blues singer. Donald would also record with Peter Tosh. (SR)

White Lightning

Personnel incl:	TOM 'ZIPPY' CAPLAN	ld gtr	A
	MICK STANHOPE	drms, vcls	A
	WOODY WOODRICH	bs	A

ALBUMS:	1(A)	(UNDER THE SCREAMING DOUBLE) EAGLE	
			(American Sound AS 1002) 1995
	2( )	STRIKES TWICE 1968 - 1969 (CD)	
			(Arf! Arf! AA-066) 199?

45s:	William/Of Paupers And Poets	(Hexagon 6801) 1968
	William/Of Paupers And Poets	(Atco 6660) 1968
	William/Of Paupers And Poets	(Hexagon 944) 1968

This outfit was formed by Caplan in Minneapolis, Minnesota in September of 1968. The compulsive psychedelic-punk song *William*, which was issued on a number of occasions, was their finest moment. They later became **Lightning** and issued a 45 and an eponymous album on PIP.

Eagle and *Strikes Twice* are retrospective albums of previously unreleased material, which was recorded around the time of the superb *William* single during 1968-69 at Warren Kendrick studios in Minneapolis. Some tracks are

WHITE LIGHTNING - Under The Screaming Double Eagle LP.

purely instrumental and the extended *No Time For Love* bears more than a little resemblance to **Quicksilver**'s excellent *Gold And Silver*, but there's some superb guitar jamming here and either album is essential for **Litter** fans and recommended to all connoisseurs of guitar-driven psychedelia.

In 2001, Zip Caplan released a new CD *Monsters And Heroes* as **Zip Caplan and Cast of Thousands**. Mostly instrumental it comprises 21 tracks of classic Horror movie, old Serials and fifties T.V. Series Soundtracks but recorded with 'rock' instruments. 48 different musicians are featured, with a different set of players backing Zip on each track. Some of the guests include Jim McCarty (The Yardbirds), Joey Molland (Badfinger), Nokie Edwards (The Ventures), Bobby Torres (Joe Cocker and Tom Jones), Doug Nelson (Jonny Lang Band), Bruce "Creeper" Kurnow (**Mason Proffitt**), Denny Libby (**The Castaways**) plus guys from Edgar Winter, **Gypsy**, **The Litter**, **Stillroven**, **Underbeats**, **White Lightning** and **Crow**.

William was later covered in the eighties by Broken Jug and Billy Synth and The Turnups.

Compilation appearances include: *William* and *Of Paupers And Poets* on *Litter - Rare Tracks* (LP); *William*, *Of Paupers And Poets* and *(Under The Screaming Double) Eagle* on *The Scotty Story - Minnesota's Legendary '60s Rock Label!* (CD); *William* on *Acid Dreams - The Complete 3 LP Set* (3-LP), *Acid Dreams Testament* (CD), *Acid Dreams, Vol. 1* (LP), *Everywhere Interferences* (LP) and *Garagelands, Vol. 2* (CD); and *(Under The Screaming Double) Eagle* on *The Arf! Arf! Blitzkrieg 32 Track Sampler* (Dble CD). (VJ/MW)

White Room

| 45: | Thoughts Of Yesterday/ Where Has Summer Gone | (Symbol 3) 1968 |

Rambling pop-psych on a New York label with nonsensical couplets (shades of Race Marbles' *Like A Dribbling Fram*) - this trippy period-piece now graces *A Heavy Dose Of Lyte Psych* (CD). The 'B' side is a slow dirge with more picturesque lyrics. (MW)

Bobby Whiteside

45s:
(partial list)
I'm Going Your Way / Wendy Wakefield (USA 775) 1964
Lonesome King / Sun Is Cold (Philips 40322) 1965
Say It Softly / I'll Never Get Away (Destination 603) 1965
You Give Me Strength / Summit (Destination 606) 1965
I Saw You With Him / And Then I Saw Her Cry (USA 879) 1967
Got A Funny Feeling / Father D'Orio (Gregar 710105) 1971
Easy With Me / (Curtom 1988) 1973
Why Don't You Grow Up / Piano Man (Curtom 2001) 1974

A prolific Chicago-based artist who also released some albums but whose material may well be outside the scope of this book. On the Philips 45, *The Sun Is Cold* combines Donovan with **Barry McGuire** and a touch of Phil Spector's production values (bells and kettledrums persist) but sounds quite mature for its vintage. *Lonesome King* is a missed opportunity as it sounds much like the other. Only at the end of the track does the atmosphere gains some intensity. (MK/MW/GM)

White Wash

45: You Haven't Seen My Love/ You Better Think It Over (Zowie Z 1000) 1968

Very fine moody and dynamic keyboard-led rock ballads from Rhode Island, like a lighter **Vanilla Fudge**. (MW)

White Wing

ALBUM: 1 WHITE WING (ASI) 1975 R1

A progressive outfit from South Dakota with lots of keyboards and guitar, very much influenced by UK rock groups. They later recorded two fine hard-rock albums as Asia. (SR)

White Witch

Personnel:
BEAU FISHER — drms, vcls — A
RON GOEDERT — vcls — AB
BUDDY PENDERGRASS — keyb'ds — AB
BUDDY RICHARDSON — gtr — AB
BOBBY SHEA — perc — AB
BILL PETERSON — perc — B
CHARLIE SOUZA — bs — B

ALBUMS:
1 WHITE WITCH (Capricorn 0107) 1972 -
2 A SPIRITUAL GREETING (Capricorn 0129) 1974 -

NB: (1) also released in the UK (Capicorn K 47505).

Formed in Florida by Buddy Richardson, a veteran of the Tampa scene (**Outsiders**, **Soul Trippers** and **Noah's Ark**), **White Witch** played a mix of Southern heavy rock and hard/glam-rock, with painted faces, powerful vocals and some strange lyrics. Their two albums are highly-rated by some, ignored by others. (SR)

Whitewood

Personnel: anonymous — A

ALBUM: 1 WHITEWOOD (Exotic EXS-1-91172) 1972 R5

NB: (1) publisher demo album issued in plain white jacket. Reissued on vinyl (Rockadelic RRLP 36) 1998 with bonus cut (*Intro*).

A very odd story lies behind this rare item. The songs on this album were written by a father for his children's band and after unsuccessfully trying to record the songs with his kids, he decided to have them recorded by "professionals".

From the early sixties to the early eighties, magazines commonly ran ads in the back reading "Songwriters! Put Your Lyrics To Music!". For a price, these shifty "companies" would employ a crew of hack players to throw something on tape quickly, invariably to the utter disappointment of the customer. This album resulted from one such venture. It is, however, unique in two very important ways: i) Most often, the finished "songs" were furnished to the customer on tape - this one arrived as a small quantity of vinyl albums, and ii) most of these outfits were based in Nashville and therefore were country music - but this company was based in New York and the faceless studio band they employed sound like high school kids that were paid in weed!

Obviously, the results are only variably successful but the best stuff is not to be missed. *Victim Of My Mind* is wicked psychedelic-punk with **Blue Cheer**-style roaring fuzz guitar coursing through it and *Whitewood* is a crude melodic hard-rocker with creepy lyrics seemingly about inherited madness that culminates in a haze of feedback. It's a very disturbing record - highly recommended!

Naturally, the songwriter was disgusted with the finished album but brave enough to make a second stab at it and a follow-up was recorded with different musicians. This later record (which is reputedly awful) was the source of the opening track on the Rockadelic reissue. (CF/MW)

Dick Whittington

45: Cause You're Mine/When You're In Love (Philips 40487) 1967

Jingle-jangle pop adorns the 'A' side, somewhere between **The Byrds** and The Hollies. Strangely the 'B' side sounds like a cross between Simon and Garfunkel and **The Young Rascals**. Highly pleasant, but wholly inconsequential. (MK)

The Whiz Kids

ALBUM: 1 THE WHIZ KIDS (Kasaba) 1973 -

A progressive rock group with keyboards. (SR)

THE WILDE KNIGHTS - Rough Diamonds... LP.

Billy Whyte

ALBUM: 1 COLD SUNSHINE   (Hub) 1973 SC

NB: (1) issued with lyric insert.

Housed in a nice psychedelic cover, this album was the work of a hippie folk singer from Massachusetts. (SR)

The Whyte Boots

45: Nightmare/Let No One Come Between Us   (Philips 40422) 1966

An all-girl outfit whose *Nightmare* later re-emerged on *Girls In The Garage, Vol. 1* (CD) and *Girls In The Garage, Vol. 2* (LP). (VJ)

Wichita Fall

Personnel:	PHILIP BLACK	gtr, vcls	A
	LEN FEIGIN	drms	A
	DANNY ROUSH	gtr, vcls	A
	LARRY WATSON	bs	A

ALBUM: 1(A) LIFE IS BUT A DREAM   (Imperial LP 12417) 1969 -

NB: (1) also released in England (Liberty 83208) 1969.

A soft-rock act. Philip Black would later resurface with the Coon Elder Band, a country blues act, in the mid-seventies. (SR)

Wicked Truth

45: Take A Chance/Rock No More   (Teru 305119) 1968/9

Late sixties heavy progressive rock often touted as 'garage' from Alexandria, Pennsylvania. If that's your bag *Take A Chance* is a decent riffer with a fluidly trilling keyboard solo. Unfortunately the flip is lame and pedestrian.

Take A Chance has also turned up on *Seeds Turn To Flowers Turn To Dust* (LP & CD). (MW)

Hank and Lewie Wickham

Personnel:	JOHNNY DAGUCON	A
	HANK WICKHAM	A
	LEWIE WICKHAM	A

ALBUM: 1(A) HANK AND LEWIE WICKHAM AND JOHNNY DAGUCON
              (King KS-1136) c1970 ?

From New Mexico, a folk psych trio. This album include interesting versions of **Love**'s *Message To Pretty* and Joni Mitchell's *Both Sides Now* plus some decent original material. They may have released some other albums, also on small labels. (SR)

Widsith

ALBUM: 1 MAKER OF SONG   (Alitha 9101) 1972 SC

45: Rust In The Rain/
     A Childs Fathers Song   (Alithia AR-6045) 1972

A dreamy hippie-folk duo from New York with fluid guitar solos. (SR)

The Wig

Personnel:	JESSY ARYAN	bs	AB
	JOHNNY RICHARDSON	gtr	AB
	BENNY ROWE	ld gtr	AB
	RUSTY WIER	drms, vcls	AB
	BILLY WILMOT	keyb'ds	A

ALBUM: 1(A) LIVE AT THE JADE ROOM
              (Texas Archive Recordings TAR 3) 1983

45s: Crackin' Up/Bluescene   (Empire 3) 1966
      Crackin' Up/Bluescene   (BlacKnight 903) 1966
      Drive It Home/To Have Never Loved At All   (Goyle 101) 1966

The Wig were one of Austin's longest lasting sixties rock groups. Benny Rowe had earlier played in The Wigs but when they broke up after a European tour he retained the name omitting the 's' and put together line-up (A) above. They quickly became a popular live attraction in Central Texas performing regularly at the Jade Room in Austin. Promotional copies of the Empire release came on yellow vinyl. The 'A' side, *Crackin' Up*, which included some competent guitar playing but lacked any commercial potential was a Rusty Wier composition. The flip was an instrumental. When the follow-up made little impact the writing was on the wall for the band. They finally broke up in 1968 and Wier and Yaryan went on to **Lavender Hill Express**, whilst Johnny Richardson teamed up with Gary P. Nunn, Rick Cobb and Chuck Greenwood in **The Georgetown Medical Band**. Wier later enjoyed a successful solo career. The retrospective album features **The Wig** covering five classic songs of the era - *Everybody Needs Somebody*, *Gimme Some Lovin'*, *Louie Louie*, *Gloria* and *You Really Got Me* - and playing their second 45 live at the Jade Room. It also includes both sides of their first intended but unreleased 45 - *Little By Little* and *Forever And A Day*, which later evolved into *Crackin' Up*. There's also a practice recording of *Crackin' Up* prior to the recording of the first 45. The remaining two tracks are by **The Georgetown Medical Band**. Still it's probably true to say that this album is likely to remain largely the interest of rock archivists.

Compilation appearances have included: *Drive It Home* on *Punk Classics* (CD) and *Flashback, Vol. 6* (LP); and *Crackin' Up* on *Pebbles Box* (5-LP), *Pebbles, Vol. 1* (LP) and *Trash Box* (5-CD). (VJ)

Wig/Wags

45: I'm On My Way Down The Road/
     The Goofy Goggle   (SAMA 1002) 1967

Quoted as having been based both in Texas and Ohio, the 'A' side to this 45 is a decent enough pop-punk effort which builds up to quite a powerful climax.

It's also said that they recorded a 45 as The Loving Years (*Down The Road/Apples And Oranges* on Viva 623) in 1967.

Compilation appearances include *I'm On My Way Down The Road* on *Pebbles, Vol. 10* (LP) and *The Essential Pebbles Collection, Vol. 2* (LP). (VJ)

Wild Butter

Personnel:	JERRY BUCKNER	keyb'ds, vcls	A
	RICK GAREN	vcls, drms	A
	STEVE PRICE	bs, vcls	A
	JON SENNE	gtr, vcls	A

ALBUM: 1(A) WILD BUTTER   (United Artists UAS-6766) 1970 -

45: Roxanna/Terribly Blind   (United Artists 50688) 1970

From Akron, Ohio, **Wild Butter** released one album mixing psychedelia with English pop including covers of the Moody Blues (*Never Comes The Day*), the Bee Gees (*New York Mining Disaster 1941*) and Neil Young (*I've Been Waiting For You*), with organ, wah wah and vocal harmonies. Nothing exceptional but pleasant.

The band were put together by Jerry Buckner, who had obtained a contract with United Artists. Jon Senne and Rick Garen were recruited from another Akron group, The Collection, who had recently lost their bassist and Steve Price was recruited to complete the new band. Amazingly they had only been together three weeks before they recorded the album!

Jim Quinn and Bob Kalamasz from **Damnation of Adam Blessing** provided some guitar-work to the album, although the complex lead solo on *Terribly Blind* was performed by Steve Price's brother Mark.

Their 45 from the album, *Roxanna* was a regional breakout in Billboard magazine and the band got to play all the Hullabaloo clubs in Ohio as well as opening for Bobby Sherman in Cleveland. The band also had residencies at a couple of clubs in 'The Flats' area of Cleveland.

Mark Price went on to play bass in the Warner Brothers recording group Tin Huey, circa 1979. Jerry Buckner later wrote *Pac Man Fever* (a national No. 1 hit) and *On And On*. He has a radio show in Atlanta now, whilst Jon Senne lives in Montana and Rick Garen is in Florida. Steve Price went back to being an artist and owns a gallery in Cambria, California. He is currently preparing a CD of original acoustic material. (SR/SP)

Wild Cherries

Personnel:	WAYNE DALE	drms	A
	DAVID JENKINS	bs	A
	CARL MOORE	gtr, vcls	A
	HAL SOUDERS	ld gtr, piano, vcls	A

45: I Cried Once / Baby, Baby   (Shoestring 112) 1966

Formed in 1964 this Hampton, Virginia, quartet gained a reputation in the area for their ability to cover the Beatles. Leader Hal Souders and his cousin Carl Moore started to write their own material and created two haunting teen garage ballads which were released on their sole 45 in early 1966. Both sides can be heard on the excellent and well-annotated Tidewater compilation *Aliens, Psychos And Wild Things* (CD).

Graduation broke up the band in Summer '66.

Other compilation appearances include *I Cried Once* on *The Night Is So Dark* (LP). (BHr/ST/MW)

The Wilde Knights

Personnel:	DEAN ADAIR		A
	RICH BROWN		A
	RICK DEY		A
	ROGER HUYCKE		A

ALBUM: 1 ROUGH DIAMONDS VOL 7: THE WILDE KNIGHTS   (Voxx 200.026) 1984

45s: Beaver Patrol/Tossin' And Turnin'   (Star-Bright 3051) 1965
  Beaver Patrol/Tossin' And Turnin'   (Modern 1014) 1965
  Just Like Me/I Don't Care   (Star-Bright 3052) 1965

Huycke, Brown and Adair all originated from Seattle where they had played in The Caravans, The Fury's and The Pipers IV. They headed for L.A. when founder member Ray Kennedy was drafted. Adding Rick Dey who joined from **The Vejtables**, line-up 'A' recorded the above two 45s. **Paul Revere** apparently paid Rick Dey around $5,000 for *Just Like Me* in 1965 and it became **The Raiders**' first big hit. **The Wilde Knights** later reformed in the Northwest in 1967 as Genesis and were later known as **King Biscuit Entertainers** (1968) and American Cheese (1969).

The *Rough Diamonds* album is strongly recommended as an excellent source of the careers of The Furys, Pipers IV, **Wilde Knights**, **King Biscuit Entertainers** and American Cheese.

Compilation appearances include: *Beaver Patrol*, now regarded as a punk classic, on *Pebbles, Vol. 1* (CD), *The Essential Pebbles Collection, Vol. 1* (Dble CD), *Pebbles Box* (5-LP), *Pebbles, Vol. 1* (LP), *Pebbles, Vol. 1 (ESD)* (CD), *Acid Dreams - The Complete 3 LP Set* (3-LP), *Acid Dreams Epitaph* (CD) and *Trash Box* (5-CD); *Just Like Me* on *Highs In The Mid-Sixties, Vol. 7* (LP); and *Just Like Me*, *I Don't Care* and *Beaver Patrol* on *Scarey Business* (CD).

Rick Dey went on to do stints with February Sunshine and the **Merry-Go-Round**. He died in late '69/early '70 from an overdose of nitrous oxide (laughing gas) at a Hollywood party. (VJ/MW)

Wildfire

Personnel:	D. JAMESON	bs, vcls	A
	R. LOVE	gtr, vcls	A
	D. MARTIN	drms	A

ALBUM: 1(A) SMOKIN'   (Primo Records) 1970 R4/R5

NB: (1) demo album issued in plain white sleeve with "Wildfire" sticker on front. Reissued on vinyl (OR 011) 1996, with a newly designed sleeve - limited to 500 copies.

From Laguna Beach, California, Love and Jameson had previously been members of Phil Pearlman's band that recorded the rare surf 45 as Phil and The Flakes (see **Beat Of The Earth** entry).

The **Wildfire** demo album was a very small pressing used to shop the band to record labels, although after initial efforts to impress the majors were met with indifference, the remaining copies were sold through head shops in the Southern California beach community.

From the opening echoed growl of the guitar intro to *Stars In The Sky* through the ten-minutes-plus *Quicksand* at the end of Side Two, this record sits at the top of the pile of U.S. West Coast hard-rock privately pressed albums. The Or reissue, taken from a mint copy of the rare demo album, has great sound and is recommended. (CF/VJ)

WILDFIRE - Smokin' LP.

The Wildflower

Personnel:
- S H EHRET — A
- TOM ELLIS — A
- M McCAUSLAND — A
- MARC McCLURE — A

45: Baby Dear/Wind Dream (Mainstream 659) 1966

A popular mid-sixties San Francisco-based folk-rock outfit. Their 1966 45 *Baby Dear* was quite up-tempo. The flip smooth and mellow culminating into an exciting finish. These and two other uptempo numbers, *Coffee Cup* and *Jump In* are included on the *A Pot Of Flowers* album (Mainstream 6100). McClure later played for **Levitt and McClure** and **Joyous Noise**.

Another 45: *Butterfly/Holly* (United Artists 50504) 1969 is by a different band, with both sides being written by J. Helmer.

Retrospective compilation appearances have included: *Baby Dear*, *Wind Dream*, *Coffee Cup* and *Jump In* on *Mindrocker, Vol. 10* (Dble LP); and *Baby Dear* on *Sounds Of The Sixties San Francisco, Vol. 1* (LP). (VJ)

Wildflowers

Personnel incl: MICHAEL BRUCE — gtr — A

45s:
- A Man Like Myself / ? (Aster # Unkn) 1966
- More Than Me / Moving Along With The Sun (Aster 2) 1967

A Phoenix, Arizona, band. They included Michael Bruce, later with **The Spiders** who became **The Nazz** and would find fame and success after a move to Los Angeles and a final name-change to Alice Cooper.

Compilation appearances include: *A Man Like Myself*, *More Than Me*, *One More Chance* and *On A Day Like Today* on *Legend City, Vol. 1* (LP & CD); and *More Than Me* on *A Heavy Dose Of Lyte Psych*. (MW)

Wild Honey

45: Look To Your Soul/ Love Can't Hurt So Bad (Gass 681101) c1968

This Chicago group seems to have released only this garage-psych single. (SR)

The Wild Ones

45: Somethings Wrong/I Want To Be Friendly (Suemi 4555) 1966

From El Paso, Texas.

Compilation appearances include *I Want To Be Friendly* on *Punk Classics* (CD) and *Punk Classics, Vol. 4* (7"). (VJ)

The Wild Ones

Personnel:
- CHUCK ALDEN — A
- JORDAN CHRISTOPHER — A
- TOM GRAVES — A
- TOMMY TRICK — A
- EDDIE WRIGHT — A

ALBUM: 1(A) THE "ARTHUR" SOUND: RECORDED LIVE AT ARTHUR (United Artists UAL 3450) 1966 -

45s:
- Caught In The Cookie Jar/Super Fox (Mainline 500) 1965
- Wild Thing/Just Can't Cry Anymore (United Artists 947) 1965
- Lord Love A Duck/My Love (United Artists 971) 1965
- Never Givin' Up (On Your Love)/ For Your Love (I Would Do Almost Anything) (United Artists 50043) 1966
- Come On Back/Come On Back (Instr.) (PS) (Sears 2180) 1966
- α Valerie/Heigh-Ho (Mala 564) 1967

NB: α with Pete Antell.

Sometimes described as 'garage', this slick-haired dark-suited outfit present an album of "big-beat" sounds; an assortment of polished ballads, pop/motown and dance numbers - *It's Not Unusual*, *My Little Red Book*, *You've Lost That Lovin' Feelin'*, *Dancing In The Streets*, *What's New Pussycat*. Not for garage fans, though they do a solid version of the 'Stones *Satisfaction* and a brooding cover of the Highwaymen's folk-rock popper *My Foolish Pride* (written and demo'd by the **D-Men/Fifth Estate** team). The 45s are generally strident pop thumpers or sultry ballads.

Guitarist Chuck Alden later formed the Fuzzy Bunnies, a quartet who were also house band at New York's Arthur club between 1967-1968 and who had at least three releases:-

45s:
- The Sun Ain't Gonna Shine Anymore / Lemons And Limes (Decca 32364) 1968
- Make Us One / The Strength To Carry On (Decca 32420) 1968
- Heaven Is In Your Mind / No Good To Cry (Decca 32537) 1969

(MW)

Wild Thing

Personnel:
- JESSE P. BROCK — organ — A
- DENNIS IANNITELLI — drms — A
- PAT "STUD" MITCHELL — ld vcls, bs — A
- PONCHO VIDAL — gtr — A

ALBUM: 1 PARTYIN' (Elektra EKS-74059) 1969 -

45s:
- Weird Hot Nights (Suffer Baby)/ Don't Fool With My Girl (S.P.Q.R. 1003) 1966
- Old Lady/Next To Me (PS) (Elektra 45672) 1969

Kickin' off in the early sixties as the Dynamic Deltones, this Tidewater-area, Virginia band performed rock'n'roll up and down the East Coast. By 1966 they'd become **The Wild Thing** and adopted a totally unique look - once seen never forgotten.... imagine Little Richard or Esquerita with silver hair, a male equivalent of a "beehive" on top and long tresses at the back!

Weird Hot Nights is a raw thumper with raucous vocals, manic laughter, spiteful guitar and an exotic break - compiled on *Aliens, Psychos And Wild Things* (CD) and *Midnight To Sixty-Six* (LP). The flip strikes a tough stance too with strong vocals and biting lead. Both sides were composed by scenemaker Frank Guida and local soul singer **Lenis Guess**.

They rocked on to the end of the decade with an album and 45 on Elektra but those candyfloss coiffures have not been seen since.

You can also find their version of *In A Gadda-Da-Vida* on *Elektrock The Sixties* (4-LP). (BHr/ST/MW)

Wild Things

45: Love Comes, Love Goes/I'm Not For You (Showboat 670) 1966

Came from the delightfully-named Santa Claus, Indiana. You can check out the 'A' side on the *Follow That Munster, Vol. 1* (LP) and the flip on *Hoosier Hotshots* (LP). (VJ/MW)

The Wild Things

45: Tell Me/My Girl (Damon 12680) 196?

From Marshall, Missouri this outfit had a 40 year old organist who recorded their sole stab for stardom at Kansas City's Damon Studios. The 'A' side was a rather catchy organ-led punk number which can also be heard on *Monsters Of The Midwest, Vol. 3* (LP), whilst both sides are featured on *The Cicadelic 60's, Vol. 8* (CD). (VJ/MW)

WILDWEEDS - Wildweeds LP.

The Wild Things

Personnel incl: S. OWSLEY   A

45s:	Summer's Gone/I'll Taste Your Lips	(Blue Onion BO-101) 1967
	A.C.I.D./?	(Blue Onion BO-104) 1968

A Cleveland, Ohio band whose *A.C.I.D.* (apparently short for *Another Colored Ink Drawing*) is well worth a spin. The lyrics are full of acid imagery and the instrumentation is full of tempo changes and suitably distorted in places.

Compilation appearances have included: *I'll Taste Your Lips* on *Killer Cuts* (LP); *Another Colored Ink Drawing* on *Psychedelic Experience, Vol. 3* (CD) and *Highs In The Mid-Sixties, Vol. 21* (LP); and *My Love* on *Garage Zone, Vol. 3* (LP) and *The Garage Zone Box Set* (LP). (VJ/MW)

Wildweeds

Personnel:	AL ANDERSON	ld/rhythm gtr, vcls	ABC
	BOB DUDEK	bs, vcls	ABC
	AL LEPAK Jnr.	drms	AB
	MARTIN 'SKIP' YAKAITIS	perc, vcls	ABC
	RAY ZEINER	keyb'ds, vcls	A
	ANDY LEPAK	drms	C

ALBUM:	1(B)	WILDWEEDS	(Vanguard VSD 6552) 1970 -
			HCP

45s:	No Good To Cry/Never Mind	(Cadet 5561) 1967 88
	Someday Morning/	
	Can't You See That I'm Lonely	(Cadet 5572) 1967 -
	It Was Fun (While It Lasted)/	
	Sorrow's Anthem	(Cadet 5586) 1968 -
	I'm Dreaming/	
	Happiness Is Just An Illusion	(Cadet Concept 7004) 1968 -
	And When She Smiles/	
	An Overnight Guest	(Vanguard 35107) 1968 -
	And When She Smiles/	
	Paint And Powder Ladies	(Vanguard 35134) 1970 113
	Baby Please Don't Leave Me Today/	
	Ain't No Woman Finer Lookin'	(Vanguard 35144) 1971 -
α	C'mon If You're Comin'/	
	Goin' Back To Indiana	(Vanguard 35155) 1971 -

NB: α released as by Al Anderson and Wildweeds.

This group started life in Windsor/Windsor Locks, Connecticut. Their sole album is composed of musically competent electric folk music with a strong country influence. Among the more interesting tracks are *Belle* and *An Overnight Guest*. They generated a good time sound, but although their songs lacked lyrical poignancy, their album remains of minor interest to some collectors.

Al Anderson went solo after the band's demise. He also joined **NRBQ** in the early seventies.

Another member, Ray Zeiner (who'd left prior to the album) put out one solo 45, *I Had A Girl/You Know Your Love* (Poison Ring 721) in 1969. Zeiner and "Big Al" were the driving force behind the Weeds and internal rivalry within the group led eventually to their break-up.

Their bass player, Bobby Dudek, was incidentally blind. Andy Lepak replaced his older brother's place on the drum stool when Al Lepak was drafted.

Their strong 45 debut *No Good To Cry* was covered by **The Moving Sidewalks** on their *Flash* album.

Compilation appearances include *My Baby Left Me* on *Pop Music Super Hebdo* (LP). (VJ/SSr/MW/SR)

Wildwood

45s:	Plastic People/Swimming	(Magnum 420) 1968
	Free Ride/Wildwood Country	(Magnum 421) 1968

From Stockton, California.

Compilation appearances include: *Plastic People* on *Punk Classics, Vol. 3* (7"), *Sixties Archive, Vol. 8* (CD) and *Acid Trip From The Psychedelic Sixties* (LP). (VJ)

John "Buck" Wilkin

ALBUMS:	1	IN SEARCH OF FOOD CLOTHING SHELTER AND SEX	
			(Liberty LST-7639) 1970 -
	2	BUCK WILKIN	(UA UAS-5541) 1971 -

45s:	α	I Wanna Be Free / Delta Day	(RCA 47-9462) 1968
		Boy Of The Country /	
		Apartment Twenty-One	(Liberty 56176) 1970
	β	I'm Free / Look At Me Mama	(UA UP 35320) 1972

NB: α by Bucky Wilkin. β French pressing with PS.

The son of Marjorie Wilkin, who wrote the *Long Black Veil* (covered by the Band, the Chieftains and some dozens of other acts), **John "Buck" Wilkin** fronted **Ronnie and The Daytonas** between 1964 and 1968.

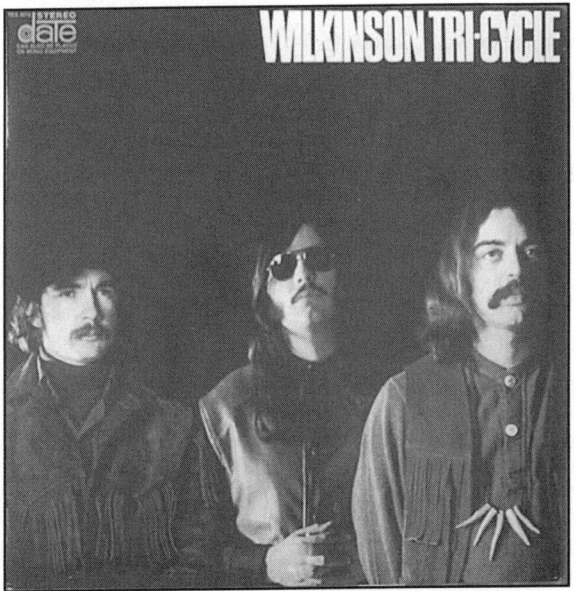

WILKINSON TRI-CYCLE - Wilkinson Tri-Cycle LP.

Produced by Don Tweedy, his wonderfully titled debut solo album was recorded in 1970 between Muscle Shoals, Nashville and Hollywood, with several dozens of musicians and inspiration from, among many names, **Buffalo Springfield**, Dennis Hopper, Brian Wilson, Mick Jagger, John and Paul, Herman Hesse, Jesus of Nazareth, Kubrick, T.S Eliot and Marshall McLuhan!

It offers several good orchestrated ballads with clever arrangements, like *The Daydream* or *Apartment 21* and the highlight of the album, the superb rock number *Apocalypse 1969* co-written by **Wilkin** and Kris Kristofferson.

Two tracks, *The Nashville Sun* and *Me And Bobby McGee* were in fact recorded earlier by **The American Eagles** and re-used for this album.

His second album, released as Buck Wilkin, is totally different as it was recorded by a trio and combines good humored covers of classics like *Johnny B Goode* and *Money* with some good original tracks (*I'm Free, Look At Me Mama*). Some tracks were also used (in slightly different takes) for the soundtrack of 'The American Dreamer', a movie with Dennis Hopper.

During the late sixties and seventies, **Wilkin** would also play guitar on dozens of records, either with rock groups (**Willie and The Red Rubber Band**), singer/songwriters (Joan Baez, Steve Goodman, John Stewart...) and most of the "Outlaw" country singers (Waylon Jennings, Jessi Colter...). He also wrote the liner notes for the **Feminine Complex** album. (SR)

Wilkinson Tri-cycle

Personnel: MICHAEL CLEMENS — drms — A
DAVID MELLO — gtr — A
RICHARD PORTER — bs — A

ALBUM: 1(A) WILKINSON TRI-CYCLE (Date TES 4016) 1969 SC/R1

NB: (1) issued with lyric sheet. Reissued on vinyl 2001.

Produced by **Warren Schatz** and Stephen Schlaks, this album is full of loose trio rock. It's not too heavy and has some excellent psychedelic touches plus two brilliant Beatlesque tracks *Pourscha Poe* and *Yellow Wall*. It also includes a cover of Sleepy John Estes' *Leavin' Trunk*.

After several years in obscurity, this album is now sought-after by collectors.

Date was a subsidiary label of CBS. **Schatz** and Shlaks produced a number of East Coast hard-rock bands, notably **Banchee** and **Yesterday's Children**. (VJ/SR/CF)

William and The Conquerors

45: Nowhere To Run/A Girl Like You (Big Sound 1001) 196?

Based in Fargo, North Dakota, their 45 was a good garage effort with fine bass and keyboard work. (VJ)

William The Wild One

Personnel incl: BILLY BARRY — vcls — A

45s: (They Call Me) Willie The Wild One/
My Love Is True (Festival 701) 1966
My Love Is True/? (Jaygee ?) 1966

From Revere, Massachusetts. **Willy's** real name was Billy Barry and on these 45s he was backed by Richie and The Renegades. His motorcycle punker, *(They Call Me) Willie The Wild One* can also be heard on *Back From The Grave, Vol. 3* (LP) and *Back From The Grave, Vol. 2* (CD), whilst *My Love Is True* has resurfaced on *Follow That Munster, Vol. 1* (LP).

If this particular hybrid style appeals to you, check out **Milan** (aka **World Of Milan** and **The Leather Boy**). (MW/GGI/VJ)

Tim Williams

Personnel: PEE WEE CRAYTON — gtr — A
GEORGE SMITH — hrmnca — A
TIM WILLIAMS — gtr, vcls — A
?? ?? — organ — A
?? ?? — bs — A
?? ?? — drms — A

ALBUM: 1(A) BLUES FULL CIRCLE (Epic BN 26472) 1969 -

Born in Los Angeles, **Tim Williams** was a white singer and guitarist who, during his teens, moved with his family to the California desert community of Lancaster. Here he began to play folk and blues music and met up with **Frank Zappa** and **Captain Beefheart**. The liner notes of his sole album state that "he met and learned a great deal from Frank Zappa and Captain Beefheart, who worked regularly with their bands in the area and Beefheart especially encouraged his interest in the blues". **Williams** began playing with a five-piece group, the Delta Blues, as well as being a soloist in the coffeehouses and folk music clubs.

Williams then moved to Santa Barbara, married, worked the local clubs and came in contact with **Hoyt Axton**. He managed to get a recording contract with Epic and his album was produced by the blues producers Chris Strachwitz and Doug McGuire. Side one is electric and the Side two is made up of acoustic blues and folk, with a good cover of **Axton**'s *Snowblind Friend* (also covered by **Steppenwolf**) plus several blues classics.

The album is really rare now but is mainly of interest to blues fans, the influence of **Beefheart** being negligible. (SR)

Willie and The Red Rubber Band

Personnel: CHARLES ADDINGTON — organ, pinao, cello — AB
GLEN BALLARD — gtr, bs — AB
CONLEY BRADFORD — drms — AB
LANNY FIELD — gtr — AB
WILLIE REDDEN — vcls, gtr — AB
(JOHN BUCK WILKIN — gtr — B)
(BEGIE CHRUSER — piano — B)

ALBUMS: 1(A) WILLIE AND THE RED RUBBER BAND (RCA LSP 4074) 1968 -
2(B) WE'RE COMING UP (RCA LSP 4193) 1969 -

45s: Little Old Clockmaker/I'll Stay With You (RCA 47-9628) 1968
Chicky Chicky Boom Boom/Mary Jane (RCA 47-9735) 1968
Try A New Day On/Watch Out For Yourself (RCA 74-0234) 1969

From Shreveport, Texas, **Willie and The Red Rubber Band** issued two albums of their own mix of Rock, R&B and psychedelia, like **The Hombres** or **The Gentrys**.

WILSON McKINLEY - Spirit Of Elijah LP.

WILSON McKINLEY - Heavens Gonna Be A Blast! LP.

The first album is probably their best, with tracks like *Mary Jane*, *Nature's Way Of Saying Thank You* and *School Of Hard Knocks*.

Produced by Duke Niles and Chuck Sagle, the second one is bluesier but contains some good tracks, such as *Watch Out Fool Self*, *We're Coming Up*, *Chicky Chicky Boom Boom* and *Deep Eyes Of Darkness*. All the tracks were written by group members. John Buck Wilkin (the former Ronny and The Daytonas leader) guests on guitar.

On both albums, the tracks are generally short (under three minutes). Although some arrangements sound very dated now, the guitar and keyboards parts are generally interesting and the albums are pleasant. (SR)

Will-o-Bees

Personnel:	JANET BLOSSOM		A
	ROBERT MERCHANTHOUSE		A
	STEVEN PORTER		A
			HCP

45s:	The World I Used To Know / Why Can't They Accept Us	(Date 1515) 1966 -
	Shades Of Gray / If You're Ready	(Date 1543) 1967 -
	It's Not Easy / Looking Glass	(Date 1583) 1968 95
	Listen To The Music / Make Your Own Kind Of Music	(SGC 002) 1968 -
	The Ugliest Girl In Town / I Can't Quit Loving You	(SGC 45-004) 1969 -
	It's Getting Better / November Monday	(SGC 007) 1969 -

This Chicago outfit produced breezy commercial male-female harmony-pop that may appeal to flower-power fans. Interestingly they chose to cover **Pride and Joy**'s *If You're Ready* but it's not as bad as one might expect - like a poppy **Jefferson Airplane**, with a decent guitar break and keyboard outro - and is considered worthy enough to be compiled on *Basementsville! U.S.A.* (LP). (MW/VJ)

Willow Green

45:	Fields Of Peppermint/ Fields Of Peppermint (Instr.)	(Whiz 619) c1968

Poppy-psych with some fuzz and staccato keyboards. Written by Deatherage-Evans team (Larry and Bruce), the creative force behind the **Nomads** from Mt. Airy, North Carolina and composers of one of the all-time garage classics *Thoughts Of A Madman*. No other details known about **Willow Green**, so I can't comment on whether this was a post-**Nomads** outfit. (MW)

Wilshire Express

45:	Lose Your Money/Caria	(Austin 322) 196?

The **Ron-dels** had quite a big hit in Texas with the 'A' side to this 45, originally performed by The Moody Blues. You'll find this Dallas band's version on *Highs In The Mid-Sixties, Vol. 23* (LP). (VJ)

Bill Wilson

ALBUM:	1 EVER CHANGING MINSTREL (Windfall Records) 1973 -

A folk singer/songwriter. His album came with a lyrics insert. Some dealers describe the music as psych-folk but this hasn't been verified. (SR)

Tom Wilson

ALBUM:	1 TOM'S TOUCH	(ABC ABCS-?) 1969 -

NB: (1) also released in Holland by EMI Stateside (LSSH 1501).

Tom Wilson was one of the main producers associated with the psychedelic movement. With his two companies : Rasputin (production) and Terrible Tunes (publishing), **Wilson** was obviously able to choose the right groups at the right moment.

Between 1965 and 1970, he produced the following groups (to name a few): **Mothers Of Invention**, **Velvet Underground**, **Ill Wind**, **Harumi**, **Fraternity Of Man**, **Bagatelle**, **Last Ritual**, **The Serfs**, **Barry Goldberg**, **Blues Project**, **Beacon Street Union**, **Country Joe and The Fish**, **Fear Itself** and **Maximillian**...

A bit like **Kim Fowley**, he obviously worked as an independent producer, his productions being released by various labels.

Tom's Touch is not a solo album but a rare compilation of some of his productions for ABC: **Fraternity Of Man**, **Ill Wind**, **Bagatelle**, **Purpose** and **Fire**. (SR)

Wilson McKinley

Personnel:	DON LARSON	vcls bs	A C
	MIKE MESSER	vcls, gtr	ABC
	TOM SLIPP	drms	ABC
	RANDY WILCOX	vcls, gtr	ABC
	JIM BARTLETT	vcls, bs	B

ALBUMS:	1(B) JESUS PEOPLE'S ARMY - ON STAGE	
		(No label 27057/8) 1970 R2
	2(B) SPIRIT OF ELIJAH	
		(Voice Of Elijah 27977/8) 1971 R3
	3(B) HEAVEN'S GONNA BE A BLAST!	
		(Voice Of Elijah 29005/6) 1972 R2

NB: (1) was issued in at least three different sleeve designs. The earliest vinyl pressing lists address on label as PO Box 351, Parkwater Station, Spokane. Later pressings list address as PO Box 3455, Spokane.

EP:	1 BLUES GO HOME + 2	
		(Rocking Chair Records 101) 196?

NB: (1) 7" EP, no sleeve issued.

All three of these albums are significant collectors' items and had great sleeves. The band remained anonymous on their album credits, but played the Spokane / Eastern Washington circuit for years, before discovering "Jesus" and anonymity.

Their debut album, which was recorded live and issued in at least three different hand-made cover designs, is poorly recorded and rather lightweight. Their second effort, *Spirit Of Elijah* represented a vast improvement, however, featuring some nice laid-back guitar-rock in the mould of **Moby Grape**'s *Wow*, and their third, *Heaven's Gonna Be A Blast!* was their rockin' **Allman Brothers** - type pinnacle.

Wilson McKinley also recorded a fourth album, which was only released on cassette, and is country-gospel rock (in that order).

Prior to the Gospel albums **The Wilson McKinley** recorded an album under the alias of **The California Poppy Pickers**, with their original line-up, including Don Larson on bs/vcls. Entitled *Honky Tonk Women* (Alshire) 1969, they used the proceeds from the album to fund the release of their EP on Rockin' Chair Records. One track from this EP, *Last One Asleep*, can also be heard on the *Yee-Haw! The Other Side Of Country* (CD) compilation.

Recently Don Larson, Mike Messer and Randy Wilcox have been recording a new album as **Wilson McKinley**. (CF/MPd)

The Wind

45:	Don't Take Your Love Away/		
	Midnight In Mexico	(BlacKnight 900)	1966

They came from the Dallas/Fort Worth area of Texas with a catchy riff and urgent vocals on the 'A' side to this 45. The flip was an instrumental.

Compilation appearances include: *Don't Take Your Love Away* on *Texas Flashbacks, Vol. 4* (LP & CD), *Teenage Shutdown, Vol. 15* (LP & CD), *Flashback, Vol. 4* (LP) and *Highs In The Mid-Sixties, Vol. 23* (LP). (VJ)

Wind

Personnel incl:	TONY ORLANDO	vcls		A
ALBUM:	1 MAKE BELIEVE	(Life LLPS 2000)	c1969	-
				HCP
45s:	Make Believe/			
	Groovin' With Mr. Bloe	(Life Records L-200)	1969	28
	I'll Hold Out My Hand/Teenybopper	(Life Records L-202)	1970	-

Produced by Bo Gentry, this album comes housed in a silver foiled cover. Although some dealers tend to present it as a good album, it contains mainly soft-rock and pop with orchestrations and is best avoided. They also enjoyed a hit single with *Make Believe*, which spent nine weeks in the Top 100. Tony Orlando may have been in this group before gaining public success in the seventies with his group Dawn. (SR/VJ)

Windflower

ALBUM:	1 WINDFLOWER	(Private Pressing)	1974 SC

From Alaska, a folk-rock group with male and female vocals and songs like *Wind Dance* or *God Is Passing By*. The album was issued in small quantities (500 copies) with a psychedelic sleeve. (SR)

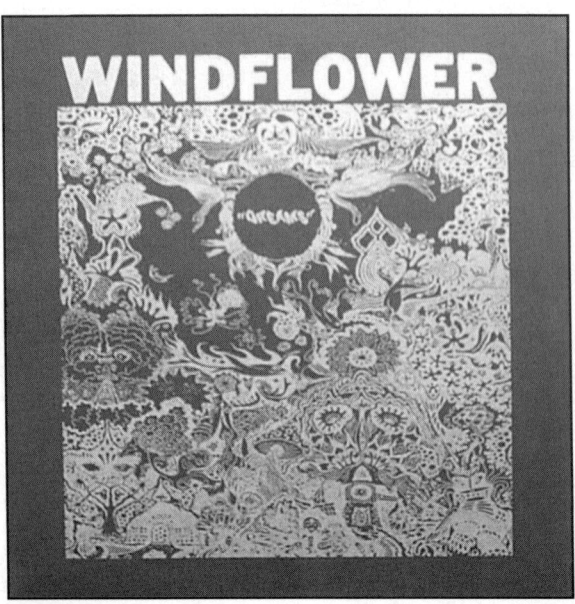

WINDFLOWER - Dreams LP.

Windflower

ALBUM:	1 DREAMS	(US McKee)	1974 SC/R1

NB: (1) There was a limited counterfeit repress limited to 300 copies.

Another **Windflower**, this one from Western Pennsylvania. Their album contains a mix of rock and psychedelia (especially *Set Your Heart On Fire* and *Dreams*) and only 500 copies were pressed. (SR)

The Wind In The Willows

Personnel:	IDA ANDREWS	flute, vcls	A
	PETER BRITTAIN	gtr, vcls	A
	ANTON CARYSFORTH	drms	A
	STEVE "MARVELLO"		
	DE PHILLIPS	bs, vcls	A
	DEBORAH HARRY	vcls	A
	WAYNE KIRBY	vcls, bs, keyb'ds	A
	PAUL KLEIN	gtr, vcls	A
			HCP
ALBUM:	1(A) THE WIND IN THE WILLOWS		
	(Capitol SKAO-2956)	1968	195 SC

NB: (1) reissued on CD by Dropout and again (Edsel EDCD 642) 2000.

45:	Moments Spent/Uptown Girl	(Capitol 2274)	1968

This New York group is most notable for the inclusion of Debbie Harry, who was later in Blondie. A dreamy album, it has its moments. Aside from two cover versions of Don Everly and Roger Miller songs, the album's hippie flower-pop songs were written by the band members. The outstanding track being the hypnotic narration/chant *There Is But One Truth, Daddy*, which has a musical backing slightly reminiscent of Pink Floyd. The band took their name from the children's book by Kenneth Graham. The album got to spend three weeks in the Top 200, peaking at No. 195.

The album was produced was Artie Kornfeld, who contributed to the Woodstock '69 Festival. He also produced another interesting album, *A Time To Remember!*, which was credited to **The Artie Kornfeld Tree**. (VJ/GF)

Windsor Tunnel

ALBUM:	1 WINDSOR TUNNEL	(Avco Embassy AVE 330??)	1970 -

An obscure quintet (two guitars, bass, organ and drums) released this album in 1970. Musically patchy, it opens with a rock version of The Animals *We Gotta Get Out Of This Place*, followed by *Ballad Of Sharon's Birthday*, a ballad with good vocal harmonies, and a fuzz number, *I've Been Let Down*. The other tracks are more pop-oriented. (SR)

Wings

Personnel incl:	OZ BACH		A
ALBUM:	1 WINGS	(Dunhill DS 50046)	1968 -
45:	That's Not Real/General Bringdown	(Dunhill 4165)	1968

Featuring Oz Bach (ex-**Spanky and Our Gang**) this is similar to the **Mamas and Papas**, but pales in comparison and is better avoided. Oz Bach would do much better with his next group, **Tarantula**. (SR/EW)

Winkle Pickers

45:	I Haven't Got You/		
	(My Name Is) Granny Goose	(Colpix 796)	1966

An obscure outfit whose sole known 45 is produced by **The Monkees** maestros **Boyce & Hart**, so perhaps based in L.A. (or a studio project). Forget the 'B' side - a novelty of sorts with cornball vocals. *I Haven't Got*

THE WIND IN THE WILLOWS - The Wind In The Willows CD.

You is a swingin' midtempo garage-beater that is somewhere between *Gloria* and *Hang On Sloopy* - lightweight and not a buzz of fuzz to be heard, but very catchy. Both sides were composed by one E. Reed. (MW)

Johnny Winter

			HCP
ALBUMS:	1	PROGRESSIVE BLUES EXPERIMENT	
(selective)		(Sonobeat RS-1002) 1968	49 R3
	2	LIVIN' IN THE BLUES (Sundazed SC 6070) 1996	- -
	3	EASY MY PAIN (Sundazed SC 6071) 1996	- -
	4	WHITE GOLD BLUES (Akarma AK 052) 1999	- -

NB: (1) issued for demo use only. Reissued (Imperial LP-12431) in 1969. (1) reissued on CD (BGO CD 457). (2) and (3) issued on CD only, both albums contain previously unreleased tracks of **Winter**'s pre-Columbia period (1960-1968). (4) issued with bonus 45, this deluxe package also contains pre-Columbia recordings beginning in 1962. (4) also issued on CD.

45: Leavin' Blues/Birds Can't Row Boats   (Pacemaker 243) 1966
(selective)

Albino **Johnny Winter** was born February 1944 in Leland, Mississippi, though he grew up in Beaumont, Texas. During the mid-sixties he played, with brother Edgar, in bands like The Black Plague, **Amos Boynton and The ABC's** and **The Great Believers** (from Houston) before starting a solo career at the end of the sixties.

Compilation appearances have included: *Birds Can't Row Boats* on *Mindrocker, Vol. 4* (LP) and *Acid Visions* (LP); *Birds Can't Row Boats* and *Hook You* on *Acid Visions - The Complete Collection Vol. 1* (3-CD) and *Livin' The Blues*; *Fast Life Rider* on *Texas Music, Vol. 3* (CD). (VJ/GG)

The Winter Consort

ALBUM: 1   ROAD   (A&M) 1970

45:   Both Sides Now/Little Train to Capira   (A&M 1058) 1970

This group combined prog-rock, jazz and pop, a bit like the early Chicago or **Blood, Sweat and Tears**. Housed in an illustrated gatefold cover, their album was recorded live. (SR)

Winter's Knights

45:   Psychedelicombo/Having Fun!   (Rockordion ED-43) 1967

A rare 45 of psychedelic accordion! The 'A' side is instrumental, the flip has rather weak vocals. (SR)

Wire

Personnel:	CURT ALMSTED	vcls	ABCD
	MIKE BURT	bs	AB
	BRIAN PAQUIN	gtr	A
	GARY RUE	gtr	ABCD
	KENNY THOMPSON	drms	ABC
	GARY BROEKEMEIER	gtr	BCD
	KIRBY RULE	bs	CD
	STEVE THIELGES	drms	D

EP: 1(D)   Getting By/Our Love/How Can You Lose/Must Be More
                                       (American Gramephone 1072) 1970

45:   Stomp/This Is It   (UA 669) 1970

A Marshall, Minnesota-based hippie-rock band. The 45 was recorded by line-up (C), the 'A' side being a cover of **NRBQ**'s song. Locally, it quickly became known as **Wire**'s best known song. The EP, recorded a little later in 1970 after drummer Kenny Thompson had been replaced by Steve Thielges, contained four originals by the band, although they included a lot of Beatles songs in their live act. (VJ)

Wizard

Personnel:	PAUL FORNEY	bs, ld vcls	A
	CHRIS LUHN	drms, vcls	A
	BENJI SCHULTZ	ld gtr, vcls	A

ALBUM: 1(A)   THE ORIGINAL WIZARD   (Peon P 1069 ST) 1971 R2/R3

NB: (1) had a limited pirate repress in 1990 and has been pirated on CD. A legitimate CD reissue from Gear Fab (GF-124) 1999 includes both sides of the 45 as bonus cuts. This has also been issued on vinyl (Akarma AK-070) 1999.

45:   Got Love/Freedom (short version)   (Penguin P-100) 1971

Wizard's album is now very rare and sought-after by some collectors. Sometimes described as psychedelic, it's really more late sixties style rock and certainly there has some ace moments on tracks like *Killing Time*, *Evergreen* plus some **Hendrix**-style histrionics at the end of *Seance*.

The band formed in the Spring of 1970 in Tampa, Florida when Forney and Schultz were due to play a gig in a short-lived band called "Brother", supporting Canadian act "Smith" and Chicago's **Flock**. Before the concert, Paul and Ben had a disagreement with Brother's drummer, who walked out and disappeared for nearly an hour. Needing to run a soundcheck, they asked their roadie, Chris to sit at the drums and just "pound away" so they could get the whole rig balanced. Completely unaware that Chris had been playing the drums for about 5 years and having sat in on a few rehearsals knew all their songs by heart, Paul and Ben were rather taken aback when he began playing along in perfect time... The next day, they fired their drummer, asked Chris to join the band and renamed themselves **Wizard**.

WIZARD - The Original Wizard LP.

They set about touring extensively, playing gigs in Florida, Georgia, Alabama, Michigan, Chicago and Colorado, including the Goose Lake Festival in Michigan Summer of 1970, and the following Winter, opening for the likes of **Iron Butterfly** and Van Morrison in Florida.

Their sole album was recorded the album at LeFevre Sound Studios in Atlanta, Georgia, and consisted of mainly original material, many of which were the product of jam sessions and live stage improvisations. They split in mid-'71, but are still in touch to this day, and Chris Luhn recalls "All-in-all, it was a good time. We met and played with some outstanding musicians, including the members of Bob Seger, **Frijid Pink**, Catfish, **Third Power**, **Teegarden & Van Winkle**, **Iron Butterfly**, Chicago, Ten Years After, Small Faces, etc. Now, I'm a lawyer. Go figure.. ."

This group should not be confused with the Californian hard-rock Wizard, which released an album on Future Track in 1978.

Compilation appearances include *Séance* on Gear Fab's *Psychedelic Sampler* (CD). (VJ/SR)

The Wizards From Kansas

Personnel:	MARC EVAN CAPLAN	perc, drms	AB
	JOHN PAUL COFFIN	ld gtr	AB
	ROBERT MANSON CRAIN	gtr, vcls	AB
	HAROLD EARL PIERCE	gtr, vcls	AB
	ROBERT JOSEPH MENADIER	bs, vcls	AB
	MARK NAFTALIN	keyb'ds	B

ALBUM: 1(B) THE WIZARDS FROM KANSAS (Mercury 61309) 1970 R2/R3

NB: (1) counterfeited on vinyl in the late eighties, and on CD (Afterglow 006) 1993.

This was an obscure country-influenced band whose sole album contained fine versions of classic period songs *High Flying Bird* and **Buffy St. Marie**'s *Codine*, as well as some excellent original compositions notably *Misty Mountainside*, *Country Dawn* and *She Rides With Witches*. The band exhibited a fine range of harmonies, and were indeed from Kansas! The album is recommended and is a significant minor collectable.

A demo tape recorded at Cavern Sound Studios on the Kansas/Missouri border in 1969 containing rawer versions of five cuts re-recorded for their album is to be issued by Rockadelic soon.

You can also find their version of *High Flying Bird* on *Reverberation IV* (CD). (VJ/CF/JRr)

Wolfman Jack and The Wolfpack

ALBUM: 1 WOLFMAN JACK AND THE WOLFPACK (Bread 070) 1965 R2

45: Wolfman Boogie (Part One)/
Wolfman Boogie (Part Two) (Bread APR) 1965

The famous "howling" D.J. also recorded some albums. His first was released in 1965, on it he is accompanied by an electric band, with good 'garagey' covers of fifties rock and New Orleans hits, plus *Wolfman Boogie pt's 1/2*. The record came in a stunning cover and is now rare.

Wolfman Jack kept on recording during the seventies but his other albums fall outside the scope of this book.

Compilation appearances include *Wolfman Boogie (Part 2)* on *Mondo Frat Dance Bash A Go Go* (CD). (SR)

Wolf Pack

45: The Baddest Wolf/
Dance Of The Hands (Incredible Records INC-101) 196?

THE WIZARDS FROM KANSAS - The Wizards From Kansas CD.

Distributed by Chattahoochee records, **Kim Fowley**'s name is all over this disc, with the tracks being written by "Fowley, Tamasvary, Johnson, Grossman" on the 'A' side and "Tamasvary, Johnson" on the flip. It was produced by "Fowley-Corby".

The flip side is an instrumental, whilst the 'A'-side includes three spoken (growled ?) sentances by a guy with a very sore throat! (WHn)

Womb

Personnel:	KARYL BODDY	piano, gtr, vcls	A
	RON BRUNECKER	drms	A
	RORY BUTCHER	vcls, perc	A
	CHRISTOPHER JOHNSON	bs	A
	ROLUF STUART	sax, flute	A
	GREG YOUNG	ld gtr	A
	BOOTS HUGHSTON	sax, flute	

ALBUMS: 1(A) WOMB (Dot DLP 25433) 1969 SC
2(A) OVERDUB (Dot DLP 25959) 1969 SC

45: Hang On/
My Baby Thinks About The Good Things (Dot 17250) 1969

This San Francisco-based band were sometimes prone to over-indulgent improvisation but they had their moments. Their albums were essentially crossovers between the 'psychedelic' and 'progressive' eras with the second one by far the better of the two. On the first *Conceptions Of Reality* is notable for Karyl Boddy's soothing vocals, but the stand-out track is *Happy Egotist*, a fine imaginative slice of psychedelia. Forget the rest of the album, which is full of messy arrangements and lots of brass. The second album has three decent tracks:- *Flash*, a somewhat mystical, trippy piece of psychedelia; *Love*, experimental soft psychedelia with liberal lashings of woodwind and the ten and a half minute finale, *Evil People*, an amalgam of psychedelia and progressivism with some nice interweaving guitar work. The remainder of the album is messy and too brassy. Neither album has yet acquired collectors status but they may in time. If you're interested start with the second. (VJ)

Wonderlick

Personnel incl: BOBBY ARLIN A

45: Hey Joe/? (?) 19??

Produced and "written" by **Bobby Arlin** (ex-**Leaves** and **Hook**), a rare single with amended lyrics for this classic song:

"Hey, Joe where're you going with that joint in your hand?

I'm going to the police station, gonna' turn on the chief man.
Hey, Joe what are you gonna do?
I might smoke it all before I'm through.
Hey, Joe tell me what'cha gonna do?
Well, liquor's much quicker, marijuana too."

(SR)

E Zane Wood

45:	Got Me Stupid/Behind the Door	(Proctor)	c1968

Another "nom de plume" for **Kim Fowley** who sings and screams on this demented novelty garage single. (SR)

Woodbine

ALBUM:	1 ROOTS	(Blue Hour 1-1010)	1971 -

Recorded live at the Catacombs Coffeehouse in Milwaukee in 1971, a rural-rock/folk and psychedelic outfit. Bill Champlin, between two formations of the **Sons Of Champlin**, may have been associated to this group. (SR)

Terry Woodford

Personnel:	BILLY BRADFORD	drms, gtrs	A
	LARRY HAMBY	gtr, drms, bs, vcls	A
	DAVID HOOD	bs, backing vcls	A
	TERRY WOODFORD	vcls, perc	A

45s: (select -ive)	Where Is My Little Girl / I Could Cry	(R And H 1004)	1965
	Hit The Ground/Gonna Make You Say Yeah	(Fame 1002)	1966
	It's His Town / She Wants What She Can't Have	(Fame 1004)	1966
α	Keep Your Cool / Stop Stopping Me	(United Artists 50199)	1967
α	Take Me To Your Heart / You Made Me	(United Artists 50271)	1968

NB: α as Terry And The Chain Reaction.

Formed in 1962 at Sheffield High School, this Alabama quartet were popular on the fraternity circuit in Alabama, Georgia and Mississippi. They welded a Southern swing with R'n'B and frat flavourings onto a foundation of British Invasion pop. Known as Terry Woodford And The Mystics (despite the first three 45s being credited to **Terry Woodford** alone), they evolved into **Terry And The Chain Reaction** who released two decent pop 45s on United Artists.

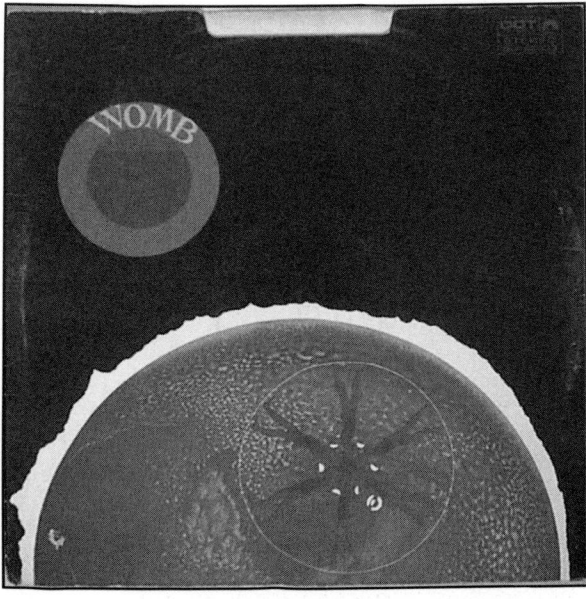

WOMB - Womb LP.

Keep Your Cool may appeal to garage fans - a strutting number with *Green Onions* keyboard moves and spoken vocals and an arrogance reminiscent of **006**'s *Like What, Me Worry*. Plan 9 covered it on their 1985 album *Keep Your Cool And Read The Rules.*

At the Muscle Shoals Bands Of The '60s Reunion concert in 1992, the original quartet performed *Suzie Q, Satisfaction* and *Where Is My Little Girl*. These are captured on the resultant CD (AMHOF 1993-01) alongside contributions from **Mickey Buckins and The New Breed**, **The Del-Rays**, **The Weejuns**, Mark V with Dan Penn, Hollis Dixon and The Keynotes, Bobby Denton and Travis Wammack. (MW)

Bill Woods

45:	Gossip/Story of Susie	(Global 740)	c1968

A totally obscure pop single produced by **Kim Fowley** and Gary Paxton (the man behind the **California Poppy Pickers** and several other groups).

Compilation appearances include *Story Of Susie* on *Kim Fowley - Underground Animal* (LP & CD). (SR)

Woody's Truck Stop

Personnel:	RON BOGDON	bs	A
	ALAN MILLER	ld gtr, vcls, vibes, tympani	A
	MARK OBERMAN	vcls, gtr	A
	BOBBY RADELOFF	vcls, drms, perc, hrmnca	A
	GREG RADCLIFFE	gtr, vcls	A

ALBUM:	1(A) WOODY'S TRUCK STOP	(Smash SRS 67111)	1969 -
45:	People Been Talkin'/Tryin'So Hard	(Smash 2201)	1968

Based in Philadelphia, this band's album is full of pleasant mostly original compositions. Many of the tracks, particularly on Side Two are gentle, laid-back ballads with *Marble Reflections*, *Tryin' So Hard*, *Everything Is Fine* and the mystical *Just To Be With You* the pick of these. It includes one genuinely psychedelic track - *Color Scheme*, a high energy rocker with lots of frantic guitar work. Recommended. The album was produced by Jack Shaw and recorded at the Regent Sound Studios in New York City. The 45 was taken from it.

The band's main claim to fame was that it was one of Todd Rungren's first outfits (along with Money) before he went off to form **The Nazz**. He left prior to the recording of their album, but five 1966 demos featuring Rungren can be found on the **The Nazz** double CD, *Nazz From Philadephia + 1966 Demos* (Airmail Recordings) 2001. (MWh/VJ/SB)

Wool/Ed Wool and The Nomads

Personnel:	ED BARRELLA	bs	A
	TOM HASKELL	gtr, vcls	A
	PETER LULIS	drms	A
	CLAUDIA WOOL	vcls	A
	ED WOOL	ld gtr, vcls	A

ALBUM:	1(A) WOOL	(ABC ABCS-676)	1969 -

45s:	α	Please, Please (Don't Go)/ I Need Somebody	(RCA Victor 47-8940)	1966
		The Boy With The Green Eyes/ Combinations Of The Two	(ABC Paramount 11167)	1969
		Love Love Love Love Love/ If They Let Us Alone Now	(ABC Paramount 11190)	1969
		Listen To The Sound/Witch	(Columbia 4-45278)	1970
		It's Alright/Take Me To The Pilot	(Columbia 4-45452)	1971

NB: α as Ed Wool & The Nomads.

Syracuse, New York was the stomping ground for this R'n'B/blues-influenced combo dominated by vocalist Ed Wool, whose strong raucous style could be compared to Eric Burdon, especially on numbers like the cover of Brown-Terry's *Please Please (Don't Go)*. The album is bluesy rock-pop, if that's your bag, whose highlight is undoubtedly *Love Love Love Love Love*, another vocal tour-de-force, by Tom Haskell.

Nowadays Wool resides in Albany, N.Y. and continues to record and tour with The Ed Wool Band, playing jazz-rock and big band dance music. Tom Haskell is now a freelance photographer.

Compilation appearances include: *I Need Somebody* on *Mind Blowers* (LP). (MW)

Woolies

Personnel:	BOB BALDORI	piano, harp, vcls	AB
	JEFF BALDORI	ld gtr, vcls	AB
	ZOCKO GROENDAL	bs, gtr, vcls	AB
	BEE METROS	drms, washboard, spoons	AB
	STORMY RICE	vcls	A

ALBUMS:	1(B)	BASIC ROCK	(Spirit 9645-2001) 1971/2 -
	2(B)	LIVE AT LIZARD'S	(Spirit 9645-2005) 1973 -

NB: (1) has been reissued on Eva (12054) and (2) has been repressed with two additional studio cuts.

			HCP
45s:	Black Crow Blues/Morning Dew	(TTP 156) 1965	-
	Who Do You Love/Hey Girl	(Dunhill 4052) 1966	95
	Duncan And Brady/Love Words	(Dunhill 4088) 1967	-
	Bringing It With You When You Come/ We Love You BB King	(Spirit 0003) 196?	-
	2-Way Wishes/Chuck's Chuck	(Spirit 0006) 196?	-
	Vandegraf's Blues/Vandegraf's Blahs	(Spirit 0007) 196?	-
	Super Ball/Back For More	(Spirit 0008) 196?	-
	Ride Ride Ride/We Love You J.B. Lenoir	(Spirit 0009) 196?	-
	Who Do You Love/Feelin' Good	(Spirit 001 3) 196?	-
	The Hootchie Cootchie Man Is Back/ Can't Get That Stuff	(Spirit 0014) 196?	-

A rock'n'roll/rhythm'n'blues outfit from East Lansing, Michigan, who formed in the mid-sixties and recorded well into the seventies setting up their own Spirit label. Fond of many blues-rock standards they were also Chuck Berry's backing group circa 1968/70 both on stage and for Berry's *San Francisco Dues* (Chess) 1970. Their albums are now of minor interest to collectors.

Vocalist Stormy Rice from their early days took off for L.A. and a solo career but only one 45 resulted, *Go Now/Comin' Down* (Ode 110) released in April 1968. Bob Baldori (aka Boogie Bob Baldori) has had a more enduring solo career, working with Chuck Berry on and off for the last thirty years, producing and engineering over 200 albums, and even performing in the White House for President Clinton. Bob still records and performs, when he isn't running his law practice and his latest CD *Who Do You Love* also features fellow **Woolies** Jeff Baldori and Bee Metros.

Compilation appearances include: *Who Do You Love?* on *Michigan Nuggets* (CD), *Michigan Brand Nuggets* (Dble LP), *Michigan Rocks, Vol. 2* (LP), *Nuggets Box* (4-CD), *Nuggets, Vol. 12* (LP), *Psychotic Moose And The Soul Searchers* (LP), *Even More Nuggets* (CD) and *Excerpts From Nuggets* (CD). (VJ/MW/SR/BBi)

Wooly Bear

ALBUM:	1	WOULDYA	(Stereolab Sound) 1974 R1

Another group heavily influenced by the **Grateful Dead**, with good guitar but also mandolin, flute and autoharp. (SR)

Wooly Ones

Personnel:	LARRY LUCAS	A
	CARL MORRISON	A
	WALTER MORRISON	A
	BOB NAGEL	A
	DENNIS ROSE	A

45:	Slings And Arrows/Put Her Down	(Titan 1733) 1965

This teen-punk outfit came from Costa Mesa, California, and some members later went on to The Coming Times. *Put Her Down*, with its typical period lyrics and raw garage sound very much in mould of L.A. outfit **The Avengers**.

Compilation appearances have included:- *Slings And Arrows* and *Put Her Down* on *Scarey Business* (CD); and *Put Her Down Garage Punk Unknowns, Vol. 4* (LP). (VJ)

Word

Personnel incl:	BILL LINCOLN	vcls	A
	WESLEY WATT	gtr	A

45:	Now It's Over/So Little Time	(Brent 7048) 1965

A low-down garage folk-rocker backed by an uptempo garage-rocker brimming with delinquency. If the names above seem familiar, this talented duo became **Euphoria** as well as writing material for other L.A. outfits (e.g. **East Side Kids**). Brent was a subsidiary label of Mainstream Records. (MW)

The Word D

Personnel:	GENIE GEER	vcls	A
	BOB JOHNSON	drms	A
	RICHARD KEATHLEY	ld gtr	A
	PAT WHITEFIELD	bs	A
	JON WILLIAMS	vcls, keyb'ds, hrmnca	A

CD:	1(-)	THE PENTHOUSE 5 - THE WORDD IS LOVE!	
			(Collectables COL-0683) 1997

45:	You're Always Around/ You're Gonna Make Me	(Caprice 609V-4983) 1966

Formed by Williams in the Summer of 1966 after his spell with **The By Fives**. They cut a four song demo at the Boyd Recording Studios in Dallas. Two of the tracks were issued on a 45 in 1966. The 'A' side, *You're Always Around*, with Genie on vocals featured some fine 12-string guitar by Keathley. The flip was later re-recorded by Williams and Keathley when they joined **The Penthouse Five**. The other two demo tracks were *Today Is Just Tomorrow's Yesterday*, which Genie had originally written as a poem but added a tune to, and *Keep On Walking*. Williams had earlier recorded this as *I Saw You Walking* with **The By Fives** but with Keathley's psychedelic leads this latest version was an improvement. Sadly, however, the band broke up within a few weeks of the single's release.

GREEN CRYSTAL TIES Vol. 4 (Comp CD) including The Word D.

All four of their tracks can also be heard on *Texas Punk, Vol. 6* (LP), *Acid Visions - Complete Collection, Vol. 3* (3-CD) and on *The Penthouse 5 - The WordD Is Love!* CD alongside an alternate version of *Today...* and material by the **Penthouse 5** and **By Fives**. *Keep On Walking* and *You're Gonna Make Me* also appear on *Green Crystal Ties, Vol. 4* (CD). (VJ/MW)

Words Of Luv

| 45: | I'd Have To Be Out Of My Mind/ Tomorrow Is A Long Time | (Hickory 1462) c1966 |

A folk-rock band similar to early **Byrds**, with two songs written by **P.F. Sloan** and Bob Dylan. (SR)

World Column

Personnel incl:	J. KAPLAN	A
	D. MEYER	A
	O. MEYER	A

| 45s: | Midnite Thoughts/Lantern Gospel | (Atco 6604) 1968 |
| | So Is The Sun/It's Not Right | (Tower 510) 1969 |

I thought I'd made a serious mistake when I bought the Atco 45 some years back - the titles weren't promising and the 'A' side, though littered with some garagey fuzz and Eastern moves also has those typically up-front soulish vocals and brass - yeah, '68 'psychedelic soul' (urk!). However a treasure awaited on the other side - a beautiful laidback slice of tripped-out psychedelia with all the right moves and suitably 'out there' lyrics, guaranteed to evoke a stoned smirk! "Colors start to spin, you dig the state you're in, your mind is somewhere, hanging on a string...". Fortunately the track has now been compiled on the *Acid and Flowers* (CD) and *High All The Time, Vol. 2* (LP). Outta Chicago and a Dunwich production to boot. The Tower 45, however, is not to be recommended here, although it is apparently sought-after and highly-regarded by 'Northern Soul' collectors. (MW)

World of Milan

See **Milan** (aka **The Leather Boy**).

Worlocks

| 45: | I Love You / Stay By Her Side | (Big Rock 512) 1965 |

This combo came from Elgin in Pennsylvania. *Back From The Grave, Vol. 7* (Dble LP) includes *I Love You*, a screaming punker with good guitar breaks and a strong surf influence.

Another **Worlocks** from the Pacific Northwest released one unheard 45 - *You Keep Me Hangin On / Banana Soul* (NWI 2709) 1968. (VJ/MW)

Would

See **Velvet Night**.

Link Wray

Personnel incl:	DOUG WRAY	drms, gtr	ABC
	LINK WRAY	gtr, vcls	ABCDE
	BILLY "JUKE BOX" HODGES	piano, organ	BC
	BOBBY HOWARD	mandolin, piano	B
	STEVE VERROCA	drms	BC
	MORDICAI JONES	piano, mandolin	C

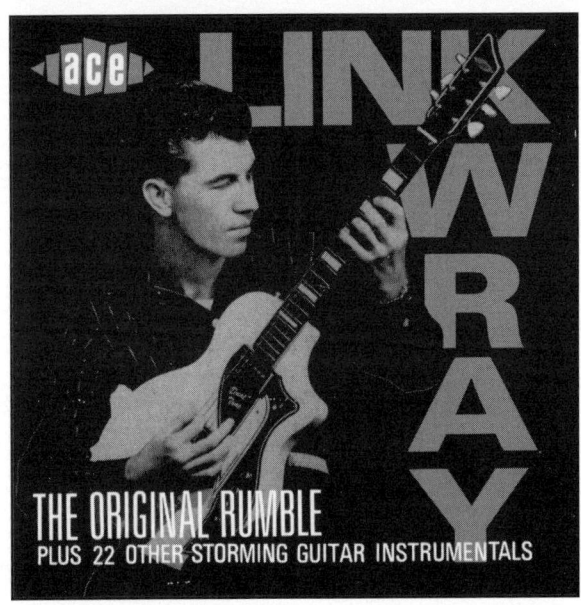

LINK WRAY - The Original Rumble CD.

ALBUMS:	1(A)	JACK THE RIPPER	(Swan SLP 510) 1963 R2
(up to	2(B)	LINK WRAY	(Polydor 24-4064) 1971 -
1975)	3(C)	BEANS AND FATBACK	(Virgin V2006) 1973 -
	4(D)	BE WHAT YOU WANT TO	(Polydor 24-5047) 1973 -
	5(E)	THE LINK WRAY RUMBLE	(Polydor PD 6025) 1974 -

NB: (3) UK release, also released in France (Virgin 840 035). (4) also released in Germany and UK, (Polydor 2391 063). A Good CD introduction is *The Original Rumble... Plus* (Ace CDCH 924).

Born in North Carolina in 1929, **Link Wray** is a guitarist and singer of Shawnee origin. He lost a lung during the Korea War and began playing guitar in the fifties. With the help of his brothers Vernon (aka Ray Vernon) and Doug, he formed Link Wray and His Ray-Men in 1958 and released two successful singles, *Rumble* and *Rawhide*. In the early sixties he was one of the very first to test the fuzztone pedal and recorded several wild instrumental tracks who would be influential on many young guitarists. Always dressd in black, he also backed **Bunker Hill** on the frantic *The Girl Can't Dance*.

He stopped recording between 1964 and 1970 and came back with an album recorded in his own studio, the Wray's Shack Three Track, build in Accokeek, Maryland. *Link Wray* is an interesting low-key effort which should interest fans of the Band at it sounds very sincere and rural, with mainly original material penned by **Wray** and Verroca plus a good cover of Willie Dixon's *Tail Dragger*. The next album is even better, with several acoustic tracks full of dobro and guitars combined with healthy boogie tunes (*I'm So Glad*) and indian influences and is really recommended. During the same period, **Wray** also produced the only album by Eggs Over Easy and one by **Vernon Wray**. Steve Verroca moved to England where he produced Brinsley Schwartz and Kevin Coyne. Also known as Bobby "The Kid" Howard with **The British Walkers**, Mordicai Jones released a solo album.

The next album was recorded in San Francisco with **Jerry Garcia**, **Peter Kaukonen**, Commander Cody, Greg Douglass (**Country Weather**), John McFee (**Clover**) and was produced by another Indian, Thomas Jefferson Kaye (**White Cloud**). With his background vocals and horn & string sections, it's not as good as the previous albums, but nonetheless contains some good tracks (*Walk Easy, Walk Slow, Morning* and the title track).

The last album released in the time frame of this book benefited from long liner notes by Pete Townshend, who always acknowledged the huge influence of **Wray** on his guitar work. Produced by Bruce Steinberg and Skip Drinkwater, two blues producers, it's more rock-oriented and contains one track dedicated to Duane Allman and a remake of his old hit *Rumble*. It was recorded with the support of Boz Scaggs, Bernie Krause (**Beaver and Krause**) and Pete Escovedo (**Santana**).

Wray kept on recording during the seventies and early eighties and also supported Robert Gordon on his first albums, his guitar work still being really interesting and often very violent. Interested readers should check the sound quality of the various live recordings released by various European labels, as it's often very poor. (SR)

Vernon Wray

Personnel incl:	LINK WRAY	gtr	A
	VERNON WRAY	bs, vcls	A

ALBUM: 1(A) WASTED (Vermillion) 1972 SC/R1

A rare album released by the Wray brothers. (SR)

Bill Wray and His Showband Royale

Personnel:	TOMMY DEE	A
	JAY McCREARY	A
	A.J. MICELI	A
	BILL WRAY	A
	JIM WRAY	A

ALBUM: 1(A) FOR OUR FRIENDS (Readie Records BW-2470) c1971 ?

From Baton Rouge in Louisiana, a local pressing which may interest some readers, even if the front cover is absolutely awful. The album contains mostly covers (*Dear Landlord, Beatles Medley (Golden Slumbers, Carry That Weight, The End), Feeling Alright, Driving Wheel*) plus the long *Everybody Boogie*, done in a rock style with organ, guitars, drums, bass and some fuzz. (SR)

Ron Wray Light Show

Personnel incl: RON WRAY A

45s incl: Speed / Satisfaction Guaranteed (Eceip PS-1000/1) c1970

NB: 'A' side is Ron Wray Light Show with The Headstone II. 'B' side is by Don Bombard and The Headstone II.

Ron Wray was an important figure on the Syracuse music scene in New York State as an artist, producer and light show artist. He wrote *Bad Woman* for **The Fallen Angels**. He also recorded a couple of 45s and *Speed*, was his finest moment. It's a fuzz assault on the senses.

Compilation appearances include *Speed* on *Pebbles, Vol. 16* (LP) and *30 Seconds Before The Calico Wall* (CD). (VJ/MW)

Wreck-A-Mended

45s:	Sally's The One And Long Tall Sally/	
	Dirty Old Man	(United Artists 50122) 1967
	Love Is In The Air/	
	My Happiness Is Loving You	(United Artists 50212) 1967
	Soft, Tender And Warm/	
	Good Evening Mr. White	(Bell 713) 1968

From Philadelphia, their finest moment is *Dirty Old Man* (not the Them song). A mean'n'moody fuzz punker with some interesting time changes. Unfortunately the remainder of their output is tame melodic Anglophile pop. Their 45s were produced by the **Spokesmen** John Madara and David White, this could well be an offshoot of that outfit.

Compilation appearances include *Dirty Old Man* on *Psychedelic Unknowns, Vol. 3* (LP & CD). (MW)

Don Wright and The Head Set

Personnel incl: DON WRIGHT A

45: Draft Dodger Blues/Why Did You Lie? (Spectre 137/8) 1966

A studio-only outfit featuring former members of **The Opposite Six**. *Why Did You Lie* can be found on *The Sound Of Young Sacramento* (CD). (VJ)

THE SOUND OF YOUNG SACRAMENTO (Comp CD) including Don Wright and The Head Set.

Tommy Wright

45: We've Lost It/? (Soundtrack 1012) 196?

An obscure artist from Texas. The 'A' side, sounds like the work of a crooner type personality backed by faceless session musicians, trying to be hip with 'wacky' lyrics. *We've Lost It* has also resurfaced on *Sixties Rebellion, Vol. 4* (LP & CD). (GG)

Tony Wright (Kingyo)

ALBUM: 1 COMPLEXITY (Radnor) 1970 SC

A Native American singer/songwriter and acoustic guitarist. The first side of his scarce album is in an intimate folk style, with only his voice and guitar, while the second side was recorded with an orchestra. Radnor was a small label which also released the **Lumbee** album. (SR)

Wrongh Black Bag

45: Wake Me, Shake Me/I Don't Know Why (Mainstream 689) 1968

A Connecticut combo with female lead provide us with a belting version of **The Blues Project** number. Like the flip, it features strong vocals, reedy keyboard and some searing guitar though if we're being finicky here, it's closer to hard-rock than garage.

Wake Me, Shake Me and the Carole King/**Myddle Class** classic *Don't Let Me Sleep Too Long*, both bear lyrical similarity to the Coasters *Wake Me, Shake Me*, but the roots of all these seem to be an old black church him *Heaven's Door's Gonna Be Closed*.

At least two members of the band went on to **Fancy**. (MW/BM)

Wrong Numbers

Personnel incl: CLARK STATON A

45s:	The Way I Feel/I Wonder Why	(Hit Cat 201) 1965
	I'm Gonna Go Now/I'm Your Puppet	(Paris Tower 111) 1967

From the small community of Mount Dora near Orlando, *The Way I Feel* appeared on the rare 1966 sampler *12 Groovy Hits, 12 Florida Bands* (Tener 154) and a non-45 cover of *You Keep Me Hangin' On* cropped up on the 1968 *Bee Jay Video Soundtrack* sampler album (Tener 1014).

Retrospective compilation appearances have included: *I'm Gonna Go Now* on *Off The Wall, Vol. 2* (LP) and *Teenage Shutdown, Vol. 10* (LP & CD). (VJ/MW/SMR)

SIXTIES REBELLION Vol. 5 (Comp CD) including The Wyld.

The Wyld

Personnel incl: RUDY WYATT   A

45s:	Fly By Nighter/Lost One	(Charay 38) 1966
	Alley Oop/Lost One	(Charay 38) 1966
	Know A Lot About Love/Lost One	(Charay 38) 1967
	Fly By Nighter/If I Had It	(Charay 38) 1967

This garage band led by Rudy Wyatt may have suffered from a paucity of material since they kept putting *Lost One*, which they'd earlier recorded as **The Roots**, on the flips to their 45s. Although **The Roots** had recorded in Dallas, they probably came from South Carolina rather than Texas. They continued until early 1967 but broke up when Rudy moved to Atlanta to join the house band of The Whiskey club there.

The flip side to their last 45 *If I Had It*, starts a little like **The Elevators'** *Levitation* and has a **Beefheart/Seeds** style slide guitar riff. Hear it on *Sixties Rebellion, Vol. 5* (LP & CD). *Back From The Grave, Vol. 8* (CD) and *Back From The Grave, Vol. 8* (Dble LP) also includes the unreleased track *Goin' Places*, which was recorded in early 1966 at Mark 5 Studios at the same session as *Fly By Nighter*. You can also find *Lost One* on *Boulders, Vol. 3* (LP); *Fly By Nighter* on *Back From The Grave, Vol. 4* (LP) and *Back From The Grave, Vol. 2* (CD); and *Alley Oop* on *It's A Hard Life* (LP). (VJ/MW)

Wylde Heard

Personnel:	RON BEDNAR	drms	A
	PAUL "BIRD" BURSON	ld gtr	A
	JIM CROEGAERT	organ	A
	BILL SUTTON	ld vcls, bs	A

45s:	Take It On Home/Stop It Girl	(Feature 202) 1966
	Take It On Home/Stop It Girl (PS)	(Philips 40454) 1967

A noteworthy 45 by a Peoria, Illinois, quartet who were together from 1965 till 1968. Originally known as the Heard, they added the Wylde epithet for their release to distinguish them from contemporary US/UK Herd/Herde/Heard outfits.

Initially recorded in 1966 at their own expense in a small Peoria studio, the 45 was issued on a label based in Janesville, Wisconsin, where the band were based whilst gigging in that region. Both sides were composed by Jim Croegaert whose style leans towards the Zombies. *Take It On Home* is a haunting minor-mood ballad that borrows some chords from **The Left Banke** as well as the orchestrated style. *Stop It Girl* is a midtempo punk ballad with anguished vocals and **Prunes**-like feedback/sustain - the latter appears on *Bad Vibrations, Vol. 2*.

Thirty odd years on - Bill is still playing in the Peoria area; Jim is a hospital chaplain in Evanston - he still writes and records; Paul manages a group of apartments, also in Evanston; Ron operates a website design business with his wife in the San Francisco Bay Area.

Compilation appearances include: *Stop It Girl* and *Take It On Home* on *Psychedelic Crown Jewels Vol. 3* (CD); and *Stop It Girl* on *Bad Vibrations, Vol. 2* (LP). (MW/MM/RM)

Thee Wylde Main-iacs

45:	Not The One For Me/	
	Why Ain't Love Fair?	(Main-iac 001/2) 1966

These Bangor, Maine, garage-punkers put out the above 45 on their own label. The combo featured the brothers Wylde from Bangor, Maine, thus the ingenious band name. There's a strong rumour that this is a joke on Nugget-diggers by the ubiquitous Erik Lindgren and cohorts, but who really cares - the music's great! Other 'fake obscurities' attributed to his fertile creativity include **The Katz Kradle** and **Huntsmen** releases on the Shur Shot label.

Compilation appearances have included: *Why (Ain't Love Fair)* on *The Arf! Arf! Blitzkrieg 32 Track Sampler* (Dble CD), *Chosen Few Vol's 1 & 2* (CD), *The Chosen Few, Vol. 1* (LP), *Gone, Vol. 2* (LP), *Garagelands, Vol. 1 & 2* (CD) and *Garagelands, Vol. 2* (LP); and *Not The One For Me* on *Vile Vinyl, Vol. 1* (LP) and *Vile Vinyl* (CD). (MW)

PSYCHEDELIC CROWN JEWELS Vol. 3 (Comp CD) including Wylde Heard.

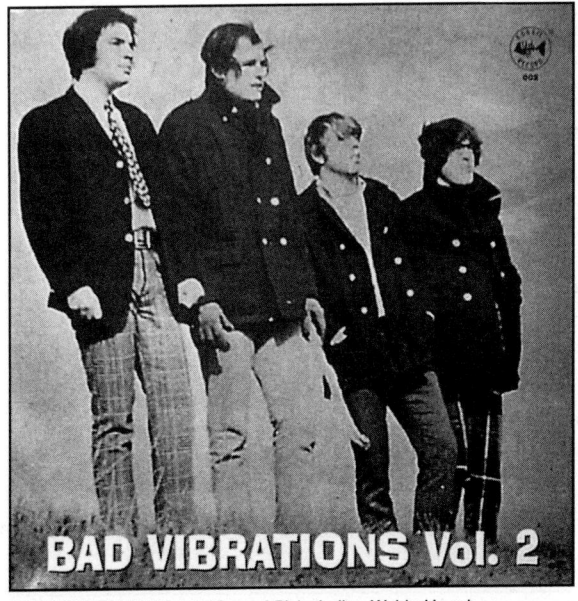

BAD VIBRATIONS Vol. 2 (Comp LP) including Wylde Heard.

WEST COAST POP ART EXPERIMENTAL BAND - Volume One LP.

WE THE PEOPLE - Declaration Of Independence LP.

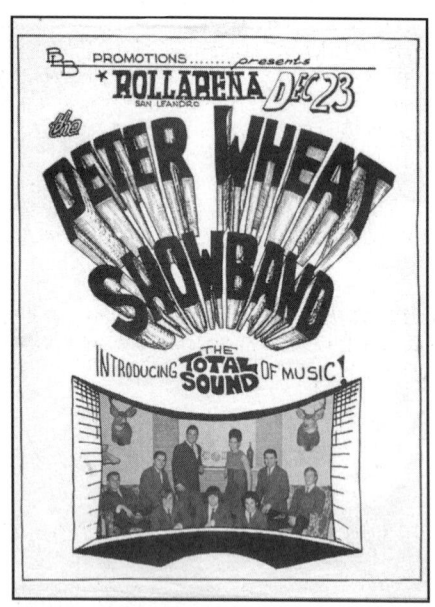

PETER WHEAT gig flyer.

WEST COAST NATURAL GAS.

WHITE LIGHTNING - Strikes Twice CD.

WILD BUTTER.

The X-cellents

Personnel:	JERRY	A
	MOON	A
	RAY	A
	ROGER SAYRE	A

45s:	I'll Always Be On Your Side/ Hey Little Willie	(Leisure Time 0001) 1965
	I'll Always Be On Your Side/ Hey Little Willie	(Smash S 1996) 1965
	And I'm Cryin'/The Slide	(Sure Play 0003) c1966
	Little Wooden House/ Hang It Up!	(Sure Play 1206-45-0003) c1966

In 1966, the WONE-sponsored three-day battle of the bands highlighted Dayton, Ohio's, local talent. Roger Sayre's *Walk Slowly Away* appears on the resultant album *WONE, The Dayton Scene* (Prism PR-1966) and is one of the more accomplished cuts, a fine Merseybeat ballad with a strong Searchers influence. Unlike nearly all of the twelve winning acts featured, **The X-cellents** already had a 45 pedigree - it's strange that this cut doesn't appear to have made it onto that format. Thankfully it is more accessible via the *Oil Stains* (LP) compilation.

More of their output has reappeared: the stompin' garage-beat *Little Wooden House* on the *Boulders EP Box Set, 60's Punk E.P., Vol. 4* (7") and *Sixties Rebellion, Vol. 16* (LP & CD); its frat-rocker flip *Hang It Up!* on *Victims Of Circumstances, Vol. 1* (LP) and *Victims Of Circumstance, Vol. 2* (CD).

They'd change their name to **The Vacant Lot** and issue one further 45. (MW/GGI/VJ)

X-Ceptions

ALBUM:	1	LIVE AT THE GABLES	(East Coast) 1970 ?

45:	A Change Is Gonna Come / Ode To Bill And Jim	(December 878) 19??

The album consists of a covers band recorded live in a club. A group with this name was operating in Baltimore area, it's not known if this is the same bunch, nor if the 45 is by the same act. (SR/JV)

Xit

Personnel:	TOM BEE	drms	ABC
	R.C. GARIS Jr.	ld gtr, vcls, keyb'ds	AB
	LEE HERRERA	drms, vcls, perc	ABC
	A. MICHAEL MARTIN	vcls	A
	MAC SUAZO	bs	ABC
	TYRONE KING		B
	JOMAC SUAZO		C
	OBIE SULLIVAN		C
	CHILI YAZZIE		

ALBUMS:	1(B)	PLIGHT OF THE RED MAN	(Rare Earth R 536 L) 1972 -
	2(C)	SILENT WARRIOR	(Rare Earth R 545 L) 1973 -
	3(A)	ENTRANCE (THE SOUND OF EARLY XIT)	(Canyon C 7114) 1974 R2
	4(-)	RELOCATION	(Canyon C 721) 1978 -

NB: Later albums exist on Canyon, including a live album recorded in Switzerland!

45s:	α	Nihaa Shil Hozho (I Am Happy About You)/ End	(Rare Earth 5044) 1972
	β	Reservation Of Education/ Color Nature Gone	(Rare Earth 5055) 1973
		I Need Your Love (Give It To Me)/?	(Motown 1304F) 1974

NB: α Some promo copies with PS, listing debut album title as *Flight Of The Red Man*. β also released in France with a PS. (4) as X-IT.

This New Mexico band's original line-up were Sioux Indians and had evolved out of **Lincoln St. Exit**. Indeed the original line-up was the same as **Lincoln St. Exit**. The early albums expounded the cause of the American Indian and promo copies of the band's first 45 explained the bands name as meaning the "Crossing of Indian Tribes". Of most interest to readers will be *Entrance* which compiles material from the band's early days. This includes *Sunday Dream*, a superb slice of psychedelia, which they had originally recorded as **Lincoln St. Exit**; *Forever Or Not At All*, some haunting psychedelia; *Orange Benevolence*, a haunting acid ballad and several examples of L.A.-style sunshine pop a la **Orange Colored Sky** (*Half A Man, Open Doorway*, and *She's Upon Her Way*). This album certainly is recommended.

Their 1974 45, *I Need Your Love (Give It To Me)*, was arranged written and produced by Tom Bee. Far from typical Motown fare, this is pop-rock with piano and slide guitar.

Tom Bee had also played in **Fe Fi Four Plus Two** and may also be the same guy who produced **The Hooterville Trolley** / **Magic Sand** and **Trademarks**. (VJ/EW)

XIT - Entrance LP.

The XLs

Personnel:	BOB GUY	organ, vcls, trombone	A
	MIKE HEINRICH	gtr	A
	GARY MARTIN	sax, perc	A
	JOE McCLEAN	bs, vcls, trumpet	A
	LES THEDE	drms	A

45:	Silver Wings/I Need A Ride	(MMC 015) 1968

This group started out in high school as a dance band called The Swinging Shepherds, later changing their name to **The XLs**. *Dirty Water* (LP) includes their catchy Bob Guy number *I Need A Ride* and an unreleased song about teenage sex on the beach, *Summer Love In The Sand*, a rather commercial song which won them a Battle Of The Bands against lots of stiff composition, but was rejected for release by quite a few record companies. Larry Barrett (previously of **The Countdowns** and **Uncle And The Anteaters**) was a later member of the band. When Guy and Heinrich were drafted McClean and Thede changed their name to Fire And Ice. (VJ)

The XLs

45s:	Second Choice/Ruined World	(Paro 100) 1966/7
	Mary Jane/Mixed With The Rain	(Paro 202) 1968

From Terre Haute, Indiana. This outfit cut two excellent 45s. The first was beat-punk and the second garage-psych. You can enjoy both 'A' sides on the excellent *Hoosier Hotshots* (LP), or inhale the aural delights of *Mary Jane* on *Psychedelic Moods - Part Two* (CD) and *Mayhem And Psychosis Vol. 2* (CD). (GG/VJ)

The Xtreems

45:     Substitute/Facts Of Life   (Star Trek 1221) 1967

Based in St. Louis, Missouri, this band's superb Yardbirds-influenced guitar work probably explains why their sole 45 has received extensive compilation coverage. The 'A' side, *Substitute*, is a fine cover of The Who's classic hit which has some great fuzz guitar work. The flip, *Facts Of Life* is an awesome psych-punk original.

Compilation appearances have included: *The Facts Of Life* on *Mayhem & Psychosis, Vol. 3* (LP); *Facts Of Life* on *Psychedelic Unknowns, Vol. 3* (LP & CD), *Relics, Vol's 1 & 2* (CD) and *Relics, Vol. 1* (LP); *Substitute* and *Facts Of Life* on *A Journey To Tyme, Vol. 3* (LP); and *Substitute* on *Garage Zone, Vol. 2* (LP) and *The Garage Zone Box Set* (4-LP). (VJ)

FATHER YOD AND THE SPIRIT OF '76 - Expansion CD.

FATHER YOD AND THE SPIRIT OF '76 - All Or Nothing At All LP.

YA HO WA 13 - Savage Sons Of Ya Ho Wa LP.

YA HO WA 13 - I'm Gonna Take You Home CD.

YA HO WA 13 - Golden Sunrise CD.

Ya Ho Wa 13

ALBUMS:	1	KOHOUTEK	(Higher Key 3301) 1973 R3
	2	CONTRACTION	(Higher Key 3302) 197? R4
	3	EXPANSION	(Higher Key 3303) 1974 R4
	4	ALL OR NOTHING AT ALL	(Higher Key 3304) 1974 R3
	5	YA HO WA 13	(Higher Key 3305) 1974 R2
	6	PRESENTS SAVAGE SONS OF YA HO WA	(Higher Key 3306) 1974 R3
	7	PENETRATION - AN AQUARIAN SYMPHONY	(Higher Key 3307) 1974 R3
	8	I'M GONNA TAKE YOU HOME (dbl)	(Higher Key 3309) 1974 R4
	9	TO THE PRINCIPLES, FOR THE CHILDREN	(Higher Key 3309) 1974/5 R4
	10	GOLDEN SUNRISE (with Sky Saxon)	(Psycho 2) 1982 R1

NB: (2), (3), (6), (8) and (9) have been counterfeited on vinyl. In addition to the above they apparently recorded another, *Yod Ship Suite*, which came out without a sleeve. It's reputedly not one of the group's best efforts, though certainly one of the rarest. (7), (8) and (10) have also been reissued on CD. (10) was originally issued on a 8-track cartridge in 1974/5. There's also a 13-CD reissue box set (Captain Trip CTCD-130-142) 1998.

All the above albums which are variously credited to **Ya Ho Wha 13**, **Ya Ho Wa**, **Ya Ho Wha** and **Father Yod**, are extremely rare and musically very weird. Those known to the author are largely mellow, mystical and probably drug-induced. The Psycho pressing was limited to 300 - most on coloured vinyl. This is reputed to contain their best music on tracks like *Time Travel*, a spacey instrumental, *Voyage*, which opens with strange chants that give way to a percussion-dominated instrumental and *Across The Prairie*, one of the more commercial tracks on the album. Nonetheless, its musical appeal is still likely to be quite narrow. Very much a band for collectors of rare psychedelia with plentiful funds. Some of these albums have undergone limited repressings and in 2000 a deluxe CD box set appeared on the Captain Trips label collecting all of their recordings together with a booklet.

Sky Saxon had some involvement with them in 1974/5. (VJ)

The Y'alls

45:	Run For Your Life/Please Come Back	(Ruff 1016) 1966

Came out of Amarillo in Texas with this reworking of a Beatles song, which had some effective lead guitar. The flip, is a fuzz-pop Strark-Creamer composition. In 1967, they became **Kitchen Cinq** and recorded an album for Lee Hazlewood's LHI label.

Compilation appearances include: *Please Come Back* on *Sixties Archive, Vol. 2* (CD) and *Texas Punk From The Sixties* (LP); and *Run For Your Life* on *Highs In The Mid-Sixties, Vol. 12* (LP). (VJ)

Yama and The Karma Dusters

Personnel:	HOWARD BERKMAN	vcls, gtr, mandolin	A
	MARION L. FAVORS	perc	A
	JERRY FIELD	violin	A
	ALAN GOLDBERG	drms	A
	DICK LARSON	piano	A
	KAREN MANTER	keyb'ds	A
	NEAL POLLACK	bs	A
	JACK SULLIVAN	bs	A

ALBUM:	1(A)	UP FROM THE SEWERS	(Manhole #1) 1971 R2

NB: (1) Three different covers exist for the album. All are R3. The first had a hand drawn sleeve by Berkman. The second was a silkscreened "fist" cover. The reverse side was a large paste-on 'slick' with song titles, the glue failed on most of these so it is often found inside the cover and listed as an "insert", though it's got dried glue residue on the back of it! The third came with a silk-screened "rose" cover and again a rear 'slick' that usually came off. All three covers contain the same vinyl pressing. The first two were released in 1971, the third may have come out a little later.

A Chicago act was responsible for this underground album - sometimes referred to as *Euphoria Blimp Works Presents Yama And The Karma Dusters Up From The Sewers*, although Euphoria Blimp Works and **Yama and The Karma Dusters** were both alternate names for the group.

An excellent album of varied musical styles, it includes high energy rockers (*Revolution* (not The Beatles song), *CTA* and the excellent *Evolution*, with its environmentally conscious lyrics). There are also folk-rockers (*Don't Kill The Babies* and *Like To Make It Back To Puerto Rico*) and folk-ballads (*I Want To Talk To You* and *Reflections*), whilst Chicago blues get a nod and a wink on *Kathleen*. A strong Dylan influence is evident at times, particularly on *Snow Bitch* and some great honky-tonk piano on *Wouldn't It Be Funny*.

A recommended album, those without deep pockets should keep a look-out for a legitimate CD release, which is in preparation.

Berkman and Pollack had earlier played with **The Knaves**, a sixties folk-punk outfit, also from Chicago. (VJ/CF)

YANCY DERRINGER - Openers LP.

Yancy Derringer

Personnel:	GABRIEL BERRAFATO	bs	A
	LANCE GNATZIG	drms	A
	C.F. KUCHLER	keyb'ds, vcls	A
	BOYD WILLIAMSON	gtr, vcls	A

ALBUM:	1(A)	OPENERS	(Hemisphere HLS 104) 1975 R1

NB: (1) reissued on CD (Gear Fab GF-129) 1999 and vinyl (Gear Fab Comet GFC 410) 2001.

Solid, under-rated Wisconsin hard-rockers from Madison. The album features inventive arrangements and good playing.

Compilation appearances include *Weedburner* on Gear Fab's *Psychedelic Sampler* (CD). (CF)

Dann Yankee and The Carpetbaggers

45:	Roll Over Beethoven/ If You Gotta Go, Go Now	(Wild Woods 2003) 1965

Hailing from Lawton in Southern Oklahoma these guys covered these Chuck Berry and Bob Dylan classics garage style. Famed U.K. DJ John Peel is thought to have been a mentor for this outfit during his time Stateside - of course he later encouraged the Misunderstood to seek fame and fortune in London. (VJ)

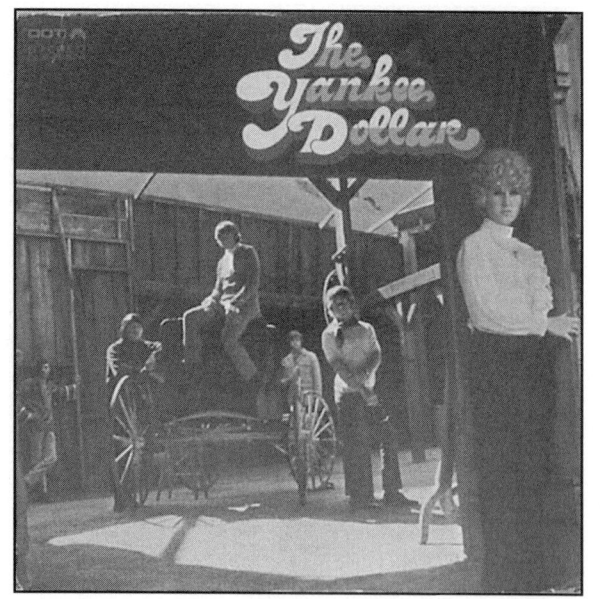

THE YANKEE DOLLAR - Yankee Dollar LP.

Yankee Dollar

Personnel:	NICK ALEXANDER	drms	A
	LIZA GONZALES	vcls	A
	GREG LIKINS	gtr	A
	BILL MASUDA	organ	A
	BILL REYNOLDS	bs	A
	DAVE RIORDAN	vcls	A

ALBUM: 1(A) YANKEE DOLLAR (Dot DLP-25874) 1968 R2

NB: (1) reissued on vinyl (Action Records 305) 2000 and CDR (Sol SOL 99001) 2000.

45s:	Sanctuary / City Sidewalks	(Dot 17123) 1968
	Sanctuary / Live And Let Live	(Dot 17155) 1968
	Mucky Truckee River / Reflections Of A Shattered Mind	(Dot 17213) 1969

This group formed at Cal Poly, San Luis Obispo, California. Their album is a delightful potpourri of West Coast-sounding flower-power and psychedelia with lots of fuzz guitar. There are some superb cover versions of Donovan's *Catch The Wind*, Dylan's *The Times, They Are A-Changin'* and **Dino Valente**'s *Let's Get Together*, which are every bit as good as the originals, interspersed with some excellent self-penned material like *Follow Your Dream's Way* and *Johann Sebastian Cheetah*.

Two tracks on the album, *City Sidewalks, Sanctuary* and *Good Ole Friends* were written by Carter-Gilbert (John and Tim), the creative source behind Denver's **Rainy Daze**, and curiously, these were also recorded by **Hardwater**, in the same year.

Another notable feature of the album is beautiful **Jefferson Airplane**-like male - female layered harmonies. Recommended.

Compilation appearances include *Follow Your Dreams Way* on *Psychosis From The 13th Dimension* (CDR & CD). (VJ/MW)

David Yantis

ALBUM: 1 THERE'S A NEW WIND BLOWIN' (Private Pressing) 1969? ?

A Christian folk singer and guitar player. (SR)

The Yardleys

Personnel incl?: BUTCH ALLEN A

45: Your Love / Just Remember (Yardley no #) 1967

An unidentified group whose private-label 45 seems to have been recorded at Quin Ivy's studio in Sheffield, Alabama. The Butch Allen-composed *Your Love* is a swinging affair that should packed the dancehall floors; it is featured on *Psychedelic States: Alabama Vol. 1* (CD).

There's another 45 by a Yardleys whose identity/locale has yet to be established: *The Light Won't Shine / Come What May* (Foundation 100). (MW)

Atlee Yeager

Personnel:	RICH CLYBURN	gtr	A
	BILL COWSILL	gtr	A
	JIM GORDON	keyb'ds, sax	A
	ROCKY HILTON	gtr	A
	KEITH JOHNSON	gtr	A
	SAM McCUE	gtr	A
	MARK PAUL	drms	A
	FRED STAEHLE	drms	A
	MICHAEL STEVENS	gtr, vcls	A
	ATLEE YEAGER	ld vcls, bs	A
	ROBERT WACHTEL	drms, gtr	A

ALBUM: 1(A) PLANT ME NOW AND DIG ME LATER (Chelsea 0366) 1973 -

NB: (1) also released in France (Chelsea 2336101).

After **Atlee**, and still working with Michael Stevens (**Highway Robbery**), **Atlee Yeager** issued and produced this good hard-rock album recorded in Burbank. Although it unfortunately contains two country & western ballads, *Release Me* (yes, the Humperdinck song!) and *Looking At Each Other*, the other selections (notably *I Will If You Will* and *I Wanna Be Alone With You*) contain great guitar parts and powerful lyrics, often with a good sense of humor. (SR)

Year One

Personnel:	J. DeMEO Jr.	A
	G. KIMPLE	A
	LYDIA MILLER	A
	D. ROBBINS	A
	M. RUSSO	A

ALBUMS:	1( )	YEAR ONE (dbl)	(Year One No #) 1971 -
	2( )	YEAR ONE (edited version of above)	(Above & Beyond No #) 1976 -

45s:	Rock'n'Roll Nights/Morning Lights	(Above & Beyond 311) 1974
	Now You're In The Puzzle/ We Look Out At You	(Year One 52347/377) 1976

From Miami, Florida, they were previously known as **Fantasy**. (MW)

Year 2000

ALBUM: 1 A MUSICAL ODYSSEY (Rama Rama RR 77) 196? -

NB: (1) reissued (Roxy Records Roxy 9175) 1976, with a new cover design.

45s:	Pop Goes The Weasel / Perfect Love	(Amy 11,035) 1968
	Love Love Love /?	(Rama Rama 7781) c1969

Produced by a very young looking Rupert Holmes, this album sounds very 1969 - brassy and seriously soulful **Blood Sweat and Tears** rock-pop. Even the odd burst of heavyish guitar can't save this anonymous sextet from being given the thumbs-down. (MW)

Yellow Balloon

Personnel:	DON BRAUGHT	bs	A
	PAUL CANELLA	gtr	A
	DARYL DRAGON	vcls	A
	DON GRADY	vcls (drms)	A

	FROSTY GREEN	keyb'ds	A
	ALEX VALDEZ	drms (ld vcls)	A

ALBUM: 1(A) THE YELLOW BALLOON (Canterbury 1502) 1967 SC

NB: (1) has been reissued on CD (Sundazed SC 11069) 1999 and on vinyl in Japan (M&M Records MMLP-1004) 1994.

                                                                                                   HCP

45s: Yellow Balloon/Noollab Wolley (Canterbury 508) 1967 25
Good Feelin' Time/
I've Gotta Feeling For Love (Canterbury 513) 1967 101
Stained Glass Window/
Can't Get Enough Of Your Love (Canterbury 516) 1967 -

NB: There was also a French 45 *The Yellow Balloon / Noollab Wolley* (PS) (Stateside FSS 101) 1968, the 'B' side being the 'A' side played backwards ("Yellow Balloon" = "Noollab Wolley").

This was rather an interesting project. Don Grady (whose real name was **Don Agrati**) had previously been the popular star of U.S. TV show 'My Three Sons' as well as working with a folk-rock outfit called **The Palace Guard**. He teamed up with a young L.A. producer/songwriter called Gary Zekley, who'd previously finished working with Jan and Dean on an album, working under the name of **Yellow Balloon**. The album consisted of various outtakes from the Jan and Dean sessions, new work with session musicians and some work by the new band Grady hastily assembled for live appearances when one of the outtakes from the Jan and Dean sessions, the bright'n'breezy pop tune *Yellow Balloon*, climbed to No. 25 in the National Charts. Had it been released on a major label it would probably have been a bigger hit.

For the live band, Frosty Green and Don Braught were duly recruited from Oregon's Rising Sons and Salem's Breakaways respectively, whilst Alex Valdez and Paul Canella had previously been in Tucson's **Five Of Us**. These disparate musicians were brought together by Grady, who'd noted the names of accomplished players whilst travelling the country doing telethons and on tour, with his Windupwatchband. (He'd previously toured on the back of his solo Canterbury 45 *The Children Of St. Monica*, which had been a modest hit in the Pacific Northwest. Incidentally his Windupwatchband featured Gil Rogers and Darryl Dragon (later with **Bob Smith** and Captain and Tennille).

After the **Yellow Balloon** dissolved, Green, Braught, Valdez and Canella continued to play together as The Popcorn Explosion. Don Grady continued to record well into the 1970s under his real name **Don Agrati**.

The album has become a minor collectors' item, however Sundazed's twenty-track retrospective CD comprises the entire album plus *Noollab Wolley*, 45/demo/alternate versions, the two Don Grady 45s (one with the Windupwatchband), and an interview with Gary Zekley. With a hefty booklet fully detailing the band's history put together by Domenic Priore, it's a fine tribute not just to the band but to the visionary behind them - Gary Zekley (aka Yodar Critch) who passed away in 1996.

Yellow Balloon also appears on *Nuggets, Vol. 4* (LP). (VJ/SR/MW)

Yellow Hair

Personnel:	JEFF CHANDLER	gtr	A
	SCOTT MCCARL	bs	A
	TED PAXSON	gtr	A
	TOM SORRELLS	drms	A

45s: Talent For Lovin'/Somewhere (Pacific Avenue 457) 1969
I Wanna Be Free/Dreaming (Bell 856) 1970

An Omaha, Nebraska outfit whose *Talent For Lovin'* can also be heard on the cassette *Monsters Of The Midwest, Vol. 1*, the start of an excellent compilation series put out by none other than Tom Sorrells! Another name above may be familiar to some - Scott McCarl replaced David Smalley in The Raspberries in time for their fourth and final album *Starting Over*. (VJ)

Yellow Hand

Personnel:	MICKEY ARMSTRONG	bs	A
	JOE CAMPESE	gtr	A
	PAT FLYNN	ld gtr, vcls	A
	JERRY TAWNEY	ld vcls, perc	A
	OSCAR TESSIER	drms	A
	KENNY TRUJILLO	keyb'ds	A

ALBUM: 1(A) YELLOW HAND (Capitol ST 549) 1970 SC

                                                                 HCP

45: Down To The Wire /
God Knows I Love You (Capitol 2957) 1970 120

Recorded in Los Angeles and traditionally produced by Dallas Smith (**Nitty Gritty Dirt Band**, **Hourglass**, **Canned Heat**), **Yellow Hand**'s album can be considered as an extra **Buffalo Springfield** album, as it contains four Steve Stills songs (*Neighbor Don't You Worry*, *We'll See*, *Come On* and *Hello, I've Returned*) and two Neil Young tunes (*Down To The Wire* and *Sell Out*), most of these tracks being unreleased by Stills and Young. The remaining tracks are three Jerry Tawney songs and a cover of Delaney Bramlett and Mac Davis' *God Knows I Love You*.

Unfortunately, the musicians are not as good as **Buffalo Springfield** and the album is more a curiosity than a collector's piece, although Pat Flynn's guitar is interesting. The liner notes claim that "their sounds are not of rock and not of acid and not of country and western but are the sounds of the beat and the pulse and the throb of the how and why of being".

Jerry Tawney was involved in numerous other groups including The Portraits (on Sidewalk). Pat Flynn later became an in demand session musician.

Down To The Wire can also be found on *Garagelands, Vol. 2* (CD). (VJ/MW/SR/GM)

Yellow Pages

45: She Said, She Said Good Day Sunshine/
Where Have All The Good Times Gone (Encore 3967 1/2) 1967

This 45 was also released as by the **Zoo** on Cameo Parkway 147 in 1967. From Akron, Ohio, they were also known as the **Beau Denturies**. (MW)

The Yellow Payges

Personnel:	DAN GORMAN	drms	ABC
	DAN HORTTER	vcls, hrmnca	ABC
	BOB NORSOFF	ld gtr	A
	HERB RATZLOFF	bs	A
	LARRY TYRE	gtr	AB
	TEDDY ROONEY	bs	B
	MIKE RUMMANS	ld gtr	B
	BOB BARNES	bs	C

THE YELLOW BALLOON - The Yellow Balloon CD.

| DONNIE DACUS | ld gtr | C |
| BILL HAM | gtr, vcls | C |

ALBUM: 1(C) VOLUME 1   (UNI 73045) 1969 - HCP

45s:
- α Never See The Good In Me/
  Sleeping Minds   (Showplace WS 216) 1967 -
- α Jezebel/
  We Got A Love In The Makin'   (Showplace WS 217) 1967 -
- Our Time Is Running Out/Sweet Sunrise   (UNI 55043) 1967 -
- Childhood Friends/Judge Carter   (UNI 55072) 1968 -
- Crowd Pleaser/
  You're Just What I Was Looking For Today   (UNI 55089) 1968 -
- Never Put Away My Love For You/
  The Two Of Us   (UNI 55107) 1969 -
- Vanilla On My Mind/
  Would You Mind It If Loved You?   (UNI 55153) 1969 -
- Slow Down/Frisco Annie   (UNI 55176) 1969 -
- Follow The Bouncing Ball/Little Woman   (UNI 55192) 1970 -
- I'm A Man/Kome Again   (UNI 55225) 1970 102
- Moonfire/
  Finger Poppin' Party (UNI no # promo only, special label) 19?? -

NB: α were written by **Bernie Schwartz**.

This band were formed in Torrance, California, near Los Angeles, by Dan Hortter in early 1966. Originally known as The Driftones, they changed name to the more hip **Yellow Payges** later that year, when they signed a contract with Gary Bookasta, the owner of The Hullabaloo club.

In 1967, they signed to UNI and in the Summer went on their first tour joining Dick Clark's Caravan Of Stars - a tour package that took in 45 cities in as many days. For the tour Mike Rummans replaced Bob Norsoff on lead guitar and Teddy Rooney (Mickey Rooney's son from Martha Vickers) replaced Herb Ratzloff on bass.

In the Summer of '68 Mike Rummans and Teddy Rooney left the group, and in came Bob Barnes (ex-**Elite** / **Those Guys**) and Bill Ham (**Rocks** / **The Nomads**). Dan Hortter recalls: "I hooked up with Bob Barnes through an acquaintance of mine and Bob told me about Bill Ham. We were desperate because we had a concert to do at the Hollywood Bowl on August 16th, 1968 with the Animals, **The Rascals** and **Tommy James and The Shondells**. We flew Bill Ham from Fort Worth, Texas out two weeks prior to the Bowl concert and the rest was history. We were the house band at the Hullabaloo club (which later became the Kaleidoscope and then the Aquarius Theater) on Sunset and Vine from '67 through to '69."

Although major chart success eluded **The Yellow Payges** they were quite a successful band issuing a string of singles displaying a variety of musical styles. The beauty of the slow numbers like *Moonfire* and *Never Put Away My Love For You* contrasts with hard-rock cuts like *Crowd Pleaser*, *Devil Woman* and the rock'n'roller, *Boogie Woogie Baby*.

THE YELLOW PAYGES - Volume 1 LP.

There were rumours of a second album but it never emerged. With 16 non-album tracks mainly on UNI 45s it certainly could have happened and a decent CD retrospective of the band is long overdue. As it was, **The Yellow Payges** disbanded in 1970 having failed to make the big time. Don : "Our demise came when we signed a multi-million dollar contract with AT&T to do an ad campaign for the Yellow Pages (BIG MISTAKE). I went on to do some solo recordings with Buddah Records. Neil Bogart-President of Buddah at the time was a close friend of the group and gave me a shot. Unfortunately things didn't work out very well."

Bob Barnes became Roscoe West and played with Kinky Friedman for three years, worked a great deal with T-Bone Burnett, The Alpha Band, Guam-Rolling Thunder Revue. There were two Bill Hams in Texas, Yellow Payges Bill Ham and the Austin producer. Bill Ham wasn't with Kinky Friedman, although he may have sat in a couple of times.

As for the other members of the band, Dacus went on to The Steve Stills Band and later to a long term slot in the top band Chicago, where he replaced Terry Kath who had shot himself while playing Russian roulette! Gorman later played with Bandit, a mid-seventies heavy rock outfit.

You can hear *Jezebel* and *Never See The Good In Me*, the 'A' sides of their two Showplace 45s, on *Mindrocker, Vol. 11* (LP). (VJ/RBc/DHr/RWt)

Yellow Sunshine

ALBUM: 1 YELLOW SUNSHINE   (Gamble) 1973 -

A psychedelic soul black group with lots of fuzz and congas. (SR)

Yeomen

45: The Chains That Set Me Free/??   (Mainstream 701) 1969

Animated rock that's obviously too commercial, an amiable organ notwithstanding, to get anywhere. A pity we couldn't hear the 'B' side yet as more of this organ would have been nice. (MK)

Jerry Yester and Judy Henske

ALBUM: 1 FAREWELL ALDEBARAN   (Straight STS 1052) 1969 -

NB: (1) also released in Germany.

45s:
- α The Sound Of Summer Showers/
  Ashes Have Turned   (Dunhill 4042) 1966
- α I Can Live Without You/
  Garden Of Imagining   (Dunhill 4061) 1967

NB: α as Jerry Yester.

First known as a member of the **Modern Folk Quartet**, Jerry Yester cut two folk-pop singles in 1966 and 1967. When the **MFQ** broke up, he replaced Zalman Yanovsky in **The Lovin' Spoonful**.

After the **Spoonful**'s demise in 1969, Yester made the above album with his wife, Judy Henske, a traditional folk singer with a long recording career in her own right. The album, which was released on **Frank Zappa**'s label, is excellent and worthy of acclaim. Ry Cooder and David Lindley also probably play on it. Subsequently Yester and Henske formed a band called Rosebud with Craig Doerge, David Vaught and John Seiter, cutting an album of the same name in 1971.

A multi-talented figure, Yester is also known as the producer and engineer of several California groups and singers: **The Association** (who included his brother Jim), **The Turtles**, **Tim Buckley**, Tom Waits, Rainbow Red Oxidiser, etc..

Ashes Have Turned and *I Can Live Without You* have been compiled on *Penny Arcade, Dunhill Folk Rock, Vol. 2*. (VJ/SR/MW)

YESTERDAY'S CHILDREN - Yesterday's Children LP.

Yesterday's Children

Personnel:	DENNIS CROCE	vcls	A
	RICHARD CROCE	gtr	A
	CHUCK MAHER	bs	A
	RALPH MUSCATELLI	perc	A
	REGGIE WRIGHT	ld gtr	A

ALBUM: 1(A) YESTERDAY'S CHILDREN (Map City 3012) 1969 R2

NB: (1) has been counterfeited on CD and reissued officially on CD and LP (Akarma AK 179). (1) also reissued on LP (Map City MAP 3012). There's also a double CD: *The History Of Connecticut Garage Bands In The 60's* (Collectables COL-CD-8825) 1995, which contains one CD by **North Atlantic Invasion Force** and one by **Yesterday's Children**.

45s: To Be Or Not To Be/Baby I Want You (Parrot 314) 1966
      What Of I / Evil Woman   (Map City 304) 1970

From the Cheshire and Prospect areas of Connecticut, these guys started out playing classic garage fuzz-punk as demonstrated by *To Be Or Not To Be*. They'd progress to a hard-rock style, of which the album is a good example and worth searching out.

There's also a French EP on Discaz 1101 that features the Parrot 45 tracks plus *Love And Things* and *Dance All Night*, so perhaps there's another U.S. 45.

The double-CD retrosepctive on Collectables comprises one CD by the **North Atlantic Invasion Force** and one by **Yesterday's Children**. This contains the complete album, early/demo versions of the Parrot 45s and several unreleased cuts from 1966 including the couple on that French EP.

Compilation appearances have included: *To Be Or Not To Be* on *Psychedelic Unknowns, Vol. 2* (Dble 7"); *Love And Things* and *Gloria* on *Green Crystal Ties, Vol. 3* (CD); *Love And Things* on *It's A Hard Life* (LP); *A Well Respected Man* and *Anyway You Want It* on *I Wanna Come Back From The World Of LSD* (CD); *Love And Things*, *To Be Or Not To Be* (two versions), *Gloria*, *Dance All Night* (two versions), *Baby, I Want You, Laugh At Me, Paranoia, Sad Born Loser, What If I, She's Easy, Sailing, Providence Bummer, Evil Woman* and *Hunter's Moon* on *The History Of Connecticut Garage Bands In The 60's* (Dble CD). (VJ/MW)

Yesterday's Children

45: Wanna Be With You/Feelings (Showcase 9812) 1966

From New York State, it has been suggested that they evolved into **Valhalla**, but this remains unsubstantiated. *Wanna Be With You* is an excellent punker.

Compilation appearances include: *Wanna Be With You* on *Pebbles, Vol. 5* (CD), *Pebbles Box* (5-LP), *Trash Box* (5-CD), *Pebbles, Vol. 5* (LP), *Acid Dreams - The Complete 3 LP Set* (3-LP) and *Acid Dreams Epitaph* (CD); and *Feelings* on *Teenage Shutdown, Vol. 7* (LP & CD) and *The Cicadelic 60's, Vol. 4* (CD). (MW)

Yesterday's Children

45s: Take Your Time / Last Clean Shirt (Montel-Michelle 988) 1967
      Go Elsewhere / Tobacco Road   (Mon-Art MM-991) 1967

A New Orleans outfit whose *Go Elsewhere* is a moody pop-punker with a simple riff, bongo-style drumming and appealing guitar break. They make a worthy attempt at the **Blues Magoos**' psychotic rendition of *Tobacco Road* complete with extended freak-out break. (MW/AB)

Yesterday's Obsession

45: The Phycle/Complicated Mind (Pacemaker 262) 1967

Out of Houston, Texas. The 'A' side to their sole vinyl epitaph, *The Phycle*, is a subdued, haunting song.

Compilation appearances include: *The Phycle* on *Sixties Archive, Vol. 6* (CD), *Texas Psychedelia From The Sixties* (LP) and *Flashback, Vol. 6* (LP); and *Complicated Mind* on *Class Of '66!* (LP). (VJ/MW)

The Yetti-men

ALBUM: 1 YETTI-MEN/UPPA TRIO (KAL) 1965 R2/R3

EP: 1 THE READYMEN MEET THE YETTI-MEN (Norton 037) 19??

NB: (1) contains two tracks by **The Yetti-Men**: *My Baby Left Me* and *Break Time*.

Little is known about this Minneapolis, Minnesota outfit who made up only one side of this very rare album. The other side features a folk group and just 150 copies were pressed. The three tracks from the **Yetti-men**'s side of the album - *Break Time*, *High Himalayas* and *My Baby Left Me* - later got a second airing on *Hipsville, Vol. 3* (LP).

It has been suggested that this mystery group featured **Tom Rapp** of **Pearls Before Swine** in his early days, however Tom has told us that this was not the case - so there! (VJ/SR)

Yezda Urfa

Personnel:	BRAD CHRISTOFF	drms	A
	PHIL KIMBROUGH	keyb'ds, vcls	A
	MARC MILLER	vcls, bs	A
	RICK RODENBAUGH	vcls	A
	MARK TIPPINS	gtr, vcls	A

ALBUMS: 1(A) YEZDA URFA (aka BORIS) (No label) 1975 R4
        2(A) SACRED BABOON   (Syn-Phonic 3) 1989

Portage, Indiana, was home to this band who formed in 1973 and recorded their raw, wild debut album at a professional studio in Chicago in 1975. While the band obviously had great talent and progressive rock was their medium, the record has a garage quality to it, an infectious energy that is missing from so much music of the genre. The tracks are long with elaborate arrangements, but the virtuosity is implied rather than displayed and the album therefore avoids the usual progressive rock pitfalls. The record has an amazing sleeve and label design as well, and is recommended. A follow-up recording in 1976 (finally issued in 1989) was more refined and much of the excitement of the debut had been lost. The group recorded into the 1980s using the name Crafty Hands. (CF)

John Ylvisaker

Personnel incl:	AMANDA YLVISAKER	vcls, organ	A
	JOHN YLVISAKER	vcls, gtr	A

ALBUMS:	1	FOLLOW ME	( ) 19??
(Partial	2	COOL LIVIN'	(Avant-Garde 107) 1967 R1
List)	3	A LOVE SONG	(Avant-Garde) 1968 R2
	4	PRAISE THE LORD IN MANY VOICES	
			(Avant-Garde) c1969 R1

NB: There's also a limited edition 'reissue' on the Mystic label from 1997 which combines the best tracks from (2) and (3). The reissue is titled *Cool Livin'* but reuses the artwork from *A Love Song*, and shouldn't be confused with either of the original LPs.

One of the really interesting and worthwhile Christian psychedelic artists. **John Ylvisaker** and his wife Amanda were apparently some kind of travelling Christian preachers and their albums were sold during their celebrations. Although sometimes patchy, their music contains some excellent jangly folk psychedelic tracks with electric guitar and organ and enthusiastic vocals.

An exact discography is difficult to establish with certainty, as some albums were shared with other Christian singers, not necessarily rock or folk-rock. (SR/PL)

JOHN YLVISAKER - 'Mystic' best of LP.

Michael Yonkers

Personnel:	JIM BUELOW	drms	A
	MARK EINAN	gtr	A
	RICHARD PASKE	bs, vcls	AB
	MICHAEL YONKERS	gtr, vcls	ABC
	JIM WOEHRLE	organ, vcls	B
	JIM YONKERS	drms	BC
	TOM WALLFRED	bs	C

NB: Line-up 'A' as The Pharoahs. Line-up 'B' as Michael and The Mumbles. Line-up 'C' Michael Yonkers Band.

ALBUMS:	1( )	GRIMWOOD	( ) 1974 R1
	2( )	MICHAEL LEE YONKERS	( ) 1974 SC
	3( )	GOODBYE SUNBALL	( ) 1974 SC
	4( )	BORDERS OF MY MIND	( ) 1974 SC
	5( )	THY WILL BE DONE	( ) 1976 -
	6( )	MICROMINIATURE LOVE	(Destijl DESTIJL 028) 2002 -

NB: (1) recorded 1969. (2) recorded 1971. (3) recorded 1972. (4) recorded 1973. (5) limited to 50 copies. (6) previously unreleased album, by **The Michael Yonkers Band** recorded in 1968, limited to 500 copies.

From the Minneapolis area, **Michael Yonkers** first came to our attention on the Dove retrospective *Free Flight* (Dble LP & CD). The featured tracks, *Micro-Miniature Love* and *Kill The Enemy*, sound ahead of their time, with a repetitive rockabilly beat, psychotic vocal delivery and unnerving lyrics. The guitar work, is similarly unhinged, particularly in it's use of effects and unusual pitch.

Both were recorded at Dove studios in the Fall of '68, for the Candy Floss label, but were not released at the time and the band split soon after.

Yonkers story goes back to the early sixties and the surf-inspired Pharoahs. Like many bands they progressed onto frat-garage and as Michael and The Mumbles recorded an albums worth of pre-fuzz material.

Life apparently changed for **Yonkers** when he heard **Paul Butterfield**'s *Over Yonder's Wall*. Inspired to cut loose with a higher energy and more chaotic sound, he sliced up his amp speaker to get a more distorted sound.

By the Fall of '68, the band had slimed down to a trio and went in to record an album, originally intended for release on Candy Floss. The result, *Microminiature Love* wasn't what the label wanted, and owner Steinberg arranged for a deal with Sire. Contracts weren't signed, however, as none of the band were willing relocate to New York City. Disheartened, they broke up shortly thereafter.

Yonkers continued to record, with the occasional help of Jim Woehrle. These solo recordings were primarily of a folk nature, but drastically bent with phasing, electronic sounds and odd structures. He also played occasionally at venues like Dania Hall and the Extemp coffeehouse, sometimes alongside **The Paisleys**.

Disaster struck in 1971, however, when **Yonkers** broke his back in an industrial accident. Major surgery followed, along with a seven year court battle for compensation.

In the Spring of '74, **Yonkers** began to compile some of the recordings that he had done since the break up of **The Michael Yonkers Band**. These tapes would become four separate albums, that have become cult items, despite no distribution.

Michael Yonkers has never quit recording, but has only released one further album. The blatantly Christian *Thy Will be Done*, which was released as an edition of 50 copies, with handmade covers. This was recorded while Yonks sat on the can, for that great bathroom sound and most copies were given to 'attendees' of a gig at a retirement home.

In 2002, the 1968 Dove recordings, were finally released as *Microminiature Love*, complete with extensive liner notes. (IT/CSn)

The Yorkshire Puddin

45s:	Good Night Day /	
	Ain't Gonna Love Ya No More	(Dellwood DEL 3932) 1967
	Keep Me In Mind / Black Jacket Woman	(Dellwood DEL-1) 1967

Doubtless this name was inspired by The English Invasion, though one has to wonder how many folks in Hackensack, New Jersey, knew what a Yorkshire Pudding is, let alone tastes like.

This band issued two excellent 45s. *Good Night Day* is a Stones-inspired number with snotty vocals and harmonica; the flip is more poppy with piping pre-adolescent vocals delivering a message probably beyond their experience. *Keep Me In Mind* is more mature; uptempo pop-punk with several intense fuzz outbursts. The flip is a cover of the sentimental folk-rock ballad also done by The Tropics.

Compilation appearances include: *Good Night Day* on *Let's Dig 'Em Up, Vol. 1* (LP) and *Let's Die 'Em Up* (CD), and *Ain't Gonna Love Ya No More* on *Bad Vibrations, Vol. 3* (LP). (MW)

The Yorkshires

45:	And You're Mine/Tossed Aside	(Westchester 1000) 1965/6

A popular local Detroit band from the mid-sixties who never made it nationally. *And You're Mine*, is a decent enough punk effort. Two earlier cuts, *Hey Hey Hey* and *I'll Go Crazy* were also featured on the rare *Best Of The Hideouts* compilation (Hideout 1002) 1965, which has seen a recent and welcome reissue. Both were originally intended for release as a 45 on the Hideout subsidiary Punch (Punch 1007), however this never made it into production.

Retrospective compilation appearances have included: *I Go Crazy* and *Hey, Hey, Hey* on *Best of Hideout Records* (CD); and *And You're Mine* on *Glimpses, Vol's 1 & 2* (CD), *Glimpses, Vol. 1* (LP) and *Highs In The Mid-Sixties, Vol. 6* (LP). (VJ/MW/DRt/MM)

Phil Yost

| Personnel: | PHIL YOST | sax, flute, gtr, bs, banjo, perc | A |

ALBUMS:	1	BENT CITY	(Takoma C 1016) 1967 -
	2	FOG-HAT RAMBLE	(Takoma C 1021) 1968 -
	3	TOUCHWOOD'S DREAM	(North Star 1001) 1970 -

These are all interesting and moody instrumental albums that really don't sound like any other. While there are elements of jazz present throughout, no knowledgeable jazz fan would call this music jazz. **Yost** wrote all the material and plays all the instruments. All the albums make use of phasing and reverb and some tracks feature non-verbal vocalisations. One quarter of the songs on each record are over seven-minutes long and none are under three minutes. Many would think this music was pointless noodling, but occasionally they can still be heard on local late night jazz radio stations. Phil later became an accomplished luthier, making guitars, banjos and standup bases. He passed away in the late nineties.

Takoma was **John Fahey**'s label. (DMo/SR)

The "You-Know-Who" Group

| ALBUM: | 1 | THE "YOU-KNOW-WHO" GROUP!! | (Int'l Allied IA 420) 1965 SC |

45s:	α	(Roses Are Red) My Love/Playboy	(4 Corners FC 4 113) 1964
		Hey You And The Wind And The Rain/ This Day Love	(Int'l Allied 822/3) 1965
		Don't Play It (No More)/ Run (I Wanna Be Free)	(Casual 94725/6) 1965
		It's A Funny Thing (That Money Can Do)/ Reelin' And Rockin' (PS)	(Int'l Allied 6140/1) 1965

NB: α also issued on Casual (CI 62897) 1965 and in the U.K. on London (HLR 9947). There's also a split French EP with PS consisting *My Love/Playboy* and two tracks by Angelo and the Initials (Kapp KEV 13016, 1965).

Take four young men, stick masks on them, make 'em sing with English accents, give 'em a 'mystery group' tag and... hey presto... enterprising Bob Gallo had manufactured a group to repel the British Invasion and from whom he could get all the credit(s). Musically it is competent Merseybeat style beat, rock, pop and ballads.

The down-side is that the accents tend to wear thin quickly, as do the 'yeahs' at the end of a large number of lines and throughout the album (plenty of falsetto 'oooos' too). Because the scarlet caped and masked lads couldn't reveal their identities and talk about their favourite things, the LP notes are about "the man who made it all possible", yes it's good old Bob again, writ large across everything.

One fact behind the identity of this "group" has emerged, though not the full story: - Jackie Lomax confirmed that UK beat supremos The Undertakers recorded some of the **You Know Who Group** material, around the time they were doing their tracks for Bob Yorey in New York City.

Compilation appearances include: *Playboy* on *Searching For Love* (LP); and *Roses Are Red* has resurfaced on *Incredible Sound Show Stories Vol. 1* (LP & CD). (MW/VJ/SR/JLh)

Jesse Colin Young

ALBUMS: (up to 1972)	1	SOUL OF A CITY BOY	(Capitol T-2070) 1964 -
	2	YOUNG BLOOD	(Mercury SR 61005) 1965 -
	3	TOGETHER	(Raccoon #10/BS2588) 1972 -

NB: (1) has been reissued several times.

Born Perry Miller in 1944 in New York, **Jesse Colin Young** began his career in 1963 in the Greenwich Village folk circuit. In 1964, he recorded a folk album *The Soul Of A City Boy*, which was produced by Bobby Scott and contained ten of his compositions plus *Four In The Morning*, a song by the future **Holy Modal Rounder**, Robin Remailly.

The next album *Young Blood* was recorded for Mercury with **John Sebastian** and Peter Childs and flopped, its best moments being compiled on one side of *Two Trips*, an album published by Mercury in 1970 to cash on the **Youngbloods**' success, the group formed by **Young** in 1966.

At the end of the **Youngbloods**, **Jesse Colin Young** released *Together*, with **Jerry Corbitt**, Scott Lawrence, Jeffrey Myer, Earthquake Anderson, Pete Childs and the excellent guitarist Eddy Ottenstein (who also played with Jeffrey Cain). John Wilmeth and Ron Stallings of **Southern Comfort** also played horns on one track. The album is recommended to **Youngbloods**' fans, with its mix of covers: **Nick Gravenites**' *Born In Chicago*, the bluesy *Six Days On The Road*, Chuck Berry's *Sweet Little Sixteen* and five excellent original and sunny tracks including *Good Times*, *Lovely Day* and *Peace Song*.

Jesse Colin Young kept on recording for Warner Bros. in the seventies and his albums before 1975 are in the same mould. After several albums of mixed interest, he returned to form in 1987 with *The Highway Is For Heroes*. He is still recording today. (SR)

The Young Aristocracy

| Personnel incl: | JIM SWEENEY | vcls | A |

| 45: | Don't Lie/Look And See | (Acropolis 6721) 1967 |

The band came from Tulsa, Oklahoma, and their disc appeared inside a picture sleeve. Their record producer Steve Barncard was a student at Kansas University which explains its release on a Kansas label. Despite the rather infectious 'A' side, the 45 flopped and the band reverted back to their previous name of The Great Danes. Barncard later produced The Ozark Mountain Daredevils and Jim Sweeney went on to enjoy some success in the 1980s R&B group, The Jumpshotz.

Compilation appearances have included: *Look And See!* on *Monsters Of The Midwest, Vol. 2* (LP); and *Don't Lie* on *Teenage Shutdown, Vol. 9* (LP & CD) and *Monsters Of The Midwest, Vol. 1* (cass.). (VJ/MW)

The Youngbloods

Personnel:	BANANA (Lowell Levinger)	piano, gtr, vcls	A CDE
	JOE BAUER	drms	A CDE
	JESSE COLIN YOUNG	gtr, bs, vcls	ABCDE
	JERRY CORBITT	gtr, bs	ABC
	JIMMY MARS	bs	A
	MIKE KANE	bs, vcls	E

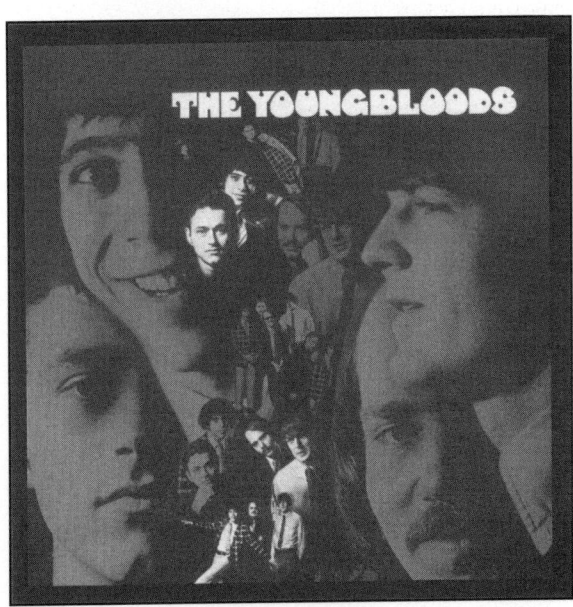

THE YOUNGBLOODS - Youngbloods CD.

ALBUM: (up to 1972)				HCP
1(B)	JESSE COLIN YOUNG/YOUNGBLOODS	(Mercury SR 61005)	1965	- -
2(C)	YOUNGBLOODS	(RCA LSP 3724)	1966	131 -
3(C)	EARTH MUSIC	(RCA LSP 3865)	1967	- -
4(D)	ELEPHANT MOUNTAIN	(RCA LSP 4150)	1968	118 -
5(D)	TWO TRIPS	(Mercury SR 61273)	1970	- -
6(D)	ROCK FESTIVAL	(Raccoon/Warner Bros. Al - 1878)	1970	80 -
7(-)	THE BEST OF THE YOUNGBLOODS	(RCA LSP 4399)	1971	144 -
8(-)	SUNLIGHT	(RCA LSP 4561)	1971	186 -
9(-)	GET TOGETHER	(RCA INT 11 70)	1971	- -
10(D)	RIDE THE WIND	(Raccoon/Warner Bros. WS 2563)	1971	157 -
11(E)	GOOD'N'DUSTY	(Raccoon/Warner Bros. BS 2566)	1971	160 -
12(E)	HIGH ON A RIDGE TOP	(Raccoon/Warner Bros. BS 2653)	1972	185 -

NB: (2), (3), (4), (6) and (10) have been reissued on CD. (10), (4), (12) and (11) reissued on CD (Sundazed SC 6180-3) 2003. *Get Together, The Essential Youngbloods* (BMG) 2002, is a CD retrospective including the rare *Merry Go Round*. Also of interest is the compilation *Euphoria* (Raven RVCD 72). There have also been two vinyl bootlegs: *Live At The Avalon Ballroom* (Flying Horse), from a 1968 broadcast and *Turning On The Sunshine* (Crazy Jon), from a 1970 broadcast.

45s: (up to 1972)				HCP
α	Tomorrow/Lonely Boy	(Altera 001)	1966	-
	Grizzly Bear/The Tears Are Falling	(RCA-9015)	1967	52
	Merry-Go-Round/Foolin' Around	(RCA-9142)	1967	-
	Euphoria/The Wine Song	(RCA-9222)	1967	-
	Get Together/All My Dreams Blue	(RCA-9264)	1967	62
	I Can Tell/Fool Me	(RCA-9360)	1967	-
β	Quicksand/Dreamer's Dream	(RCA-9422)	1968	-
	Get Together/Beautiful	(RCA-9752)	1969	5
	Darkness, Darkness/On Sir Francis Drake	(RCA-01 29)	1969	86
	Sunlight/Trillium	(RCA-0270)	1969	114
	Sunlight/Reasons To Believe	(RCA-0465)	1969	123
	Sometimes/Another Strange Town	(Mercury 73068)	1970	-
	Will The Circle Be Unbroken / Light Shine	(Warner Bros. 7563)	1971	-
	Hippie From Olema/Misty Roses	(Warner Bros. 7445)	1972	-
	It's A Lovely Day/Ice Bay	(Warner Bros. 7499)	1972	-

NB: α as by **Jeff Cain** And The Youngbloods. β *Quicksand* features a different mix to the *Elephant Mountain* album version. There was also an Italian single, sung in Italian: *Qualcuno Mi Dir/Qui Con Noi, Tra Di Noi* (aka *Get Together*) (RCA Victor N 1587) 1968.

Sounding similar to **The Lovin' Spoonful**, **The Youngbloods** were originally from New York. Indeed **Jesse Colin Young** (real name Perry Miller) recorded the second of two earlier albums, entitled *Youngblood*, in a group which actually featured **John Sebastian** (hrmnca) along with Pete Childs (dobro). It flopped, and he formed a duo with **Jerry Corbitt**, a folk singer from Georgia who'd got a good reputation on the Boston folk-circuit. **Bauer** and **Levinger** were then drafted in for the group's early recordings which their record company, Mercury, subsequently issued as the *Two Trips* album.

Billed as **Jesse Colin Young And The Youngbloods**, their first two albums for RCA were made in New York and produced by Felix Pappalardi, but failed to establish the group. They headed West for San Francisco, attracted by the lure of its musical explosion. There they issued *Elephant Mountain* which was a vast improvement on their earlier material and also had a hit with hippie anthem *Get Together* in the Summer of 1967. However, during the recording of their album, which peaked at No. 118 in the U.S. Album Charts, **Jerry Corbitt** left the band. This reduced the band to a threesome, although Mike Kane was added in 1972. *Elephant Mountain*, produced by Charlie Daniels, contained a wealth of diverse material. The opening track *Darkness, Darkness* has a beautiful string introduction and a ringing guitar solo. There is a jazzy feel to *On The Sir Francis Drake* and *Trillium* with **Banana**'s fresh guitar and piano playing well to the fore and a wealth of country-folk material such as *Sunshine, Beautiful, Smug* and *Ride The Wind*, as well as the jug band-like *Rain Song*.

After **Corbitt**'s departure they signed a new contract with Warner Bros. who granted them their own 'Raccoon' label and issued *Rock Festival* and *Ride The Wind* - two live recordings, the latter also produced by Charlie Daniels. They made No's 80 and 157 respectively in the U.S. Album Charts. The band now reached their zenith. *Ride The Wind* gives a good indication of the band at its best. Apart from the title track the album contained gorgeous versions of *Sunlight, Get Together* and *Beautiful*. *Rock Festival* is a much rockier album including more up-tempo efforts like *Faster All The Time* and *Peepin' n Hidin'* alongside their more typical laid back efforts like *It's A Lovely Day, Josephine* and *Misty Roses*. *Fiddler A Dram* and *Interlude* find the group sounding very similar to the **Kaleidoscope**. The album concludes with *Ice Bag* - an experimental jam which suited the psychedelic influences of the times.

Meanwhile RCA released a double compilation containing the best of the material the band had recorded for them. This reached No. 144 in the U.S. Album Charts.

Next they added Michael Kane, who had earlier played alongside **Levinger** in Trolls, and recorded two further albums of old rock-n-roll classics (*Good'n'Dusty* and *High On A Ridgetop*). They met with less commercial success than their predecessors achieving only the 160 and 185 spots respectively in the U.S. Album Charts. Their eventual demise at the end of 1971 marked the passing of one of the West Coast's best-loved bands. However, **Jesse Colin Young** continued to record, releasing a series of excellent solo albums in the mould of *Elephant Mountain*.

Jerry Corbitt went on to record two solo albums *Corbitt* (Polydor) 1970 and *Jerry Corbitt* (Capitol) 1971 before moving into production work (including a number of Top 10 hits) for artists like Don McLean and Charlie Daniels. He also figured on most of **Jesse Colin Young**'s solo albums.

THE YOUNGBLOODS - Earth Music CD.

THE YOUNGBLOODS - Elephant Mountain LP.

Compilation coverage has so far included: *Sugar Babe* on the *Zabriski Point* (LP) soundtrack; and both *Act Naturally* and *Hippie From Olema* on the *Medicine Ball Caravan* soundtrack. (VJ/SR/PV/BM)

The Younger Brothers

45:   Go Away / This Feelin'   (Wendy W-101-1/2) 1967

This band emerged from Statesboro and Sylvania, Georgia. Their 45 was recorded in Atlanta with Jim Youmans producing and his band **The Apolloes** playing on the sessions. *Go Away* has been recalled on *Psychedelic States: Georgia Vol. 1* (CD) and *Brain Shadows Vol. 1* (LP & CD). The verses are redolent of **The Castaways'** *Liar Liar*, however it's the warbling backwards sections that add an unusual facet and sheen to this moody nugget. (MW)

Young Generation

45:   And It Hurts / Don't Be Nice To Me   (Falstaff F-1066) 1966

A mystery Chicago outfit who released one crude garage 45. *Don't Be Nice To Me* can be heard on *Basementsville! U.S.A.* (LP). (MW/MM)

Thee Young Generation

Personnel:	STEVE BRINK	A
	DAVE McCAIN	A
	MIKE RHOADS	A
	JOHN SIMISON	A

45:   Paperback Minds/Movin'   (Captain 1430) 1968

This band hailed from Circleville, a rural-industrial town about 20 miles South of Columbus, Ohio. *Paperback Minds* is a typical period put-down of 'the plastic people'. It features some nice Hammond organ work and it's now accessible on *Highs In The Mid-Sixties, Vol. 21* (LP).

Brink, Rhoads and Simison are still in Circleville. Rhoads and Simison play in a classic rock covers band called Majic, which also includes a member of another local sixties band, the Blues Sanctum (who didn't record). (MW/DJ)

The Young Ideas

45:   Barney Buss/Melody   (Date 1614) 1968

From Allentown, Pennsylvania. *Barney Buss* is excellent garagey pop that sounds earlier than 1968. *Melody* is light orchestrated pop.

Compilation appearances include *Barney Buss* on *Fuzz, Flaykes, And Shakes, Vol. 3* (LP & CD). (MW)

The Young Men

| Personnel incl: | LIJE | A |
| | SHOTWELL | A |

| 45s: | A Young Man's Problem/Angel Baby | (Maltese MLT-105) 1966 |
| | Go Away Girl/A Thought For You | (Maltese MLT-108) 1966 |

Actually from Michigan, despite the appearance of *Go Away Girl* on Eva's *Louisiana Punk From The Sixties*. It's a typical punker with strong vocals and some simple but effective guitar work.

Other compilation appearances include: *Go Away Girl* on *Let 'Em Have It! Vol. 1* (CD), *Sixties Archive, Vol. 3* (CD) and *Sixties Archive, Vol. 7* (CD); and *A Young Man's Problem* on *Leaving It All Behind* (LP). (VJ/MW)

THE LOST GENERATION Vol. 1 (Comp LP) including The Young Men.

The Young Men

| 45s: | Baby That's All / Love's Time | (United World 0001) 196? |
| | Go! / Too Many Times | (United World 6947) 1967 |

Another gang of youthful dudes from Phoenix, Arizona. *Go!* can also be heard on *Lost Generation, Vol. 1* (LP) and more recently on *Mayhem & Psychosis, Vol. 1* (CD), which "recycles" other tracks from *The Lost Generation*. (MW)

The Young Monkey Men

Personnel:	AL DYOTT		A
	JAMES MARKLEY		A
	EUGENE PATRICELLA	gtr	A
	DEAN WILCOX		A

| 45s: | I Believe You/Bald Headed Woman | (Jade 101) 1967 |
| | I Love You/I'm Waiting For The Letter | (P&M 3649) 1967 |

This was Trenton, New Jersey's most popular band in the mid-sixties. When their first 45 was cut, their guitarist Eugene Patricella was still in high school but he certainly had talent and turned in a great solo on *Bald Headed Woman*. Apart from their originals their live act was full of lively Yardbirds, Kinks and Animals covers. After the second 45 they dropped the 'Young' from their title, grew their hair and their live act grew louder and overtly psychedelic. Sadly, this later stage was never captured on vinyl and when some members got drafted the band split. Eugene remained in the music business, first with a band called Dwaf and later as a solo artist. His later output has appeared on limited edition privately pressed releases. Owing something to psychedelia, jazz, rock'n'roll and the avant-garde, it defies categorization.

Compilation appearances have included: *I Believed You, I'm Waiting For The Letter, I Love You* and *Bald Headed Woman* on *Attack Of The Jersey Teens* (LP); and *I Believed You* on *Teenage Shutdown, Vol. 6* (LP & CD). (VJ/MW)

The Young Ones

Personnel:	RONNIE BAXLEY	gtr, vcls	A
	DICKIE BRITT	keyb'ds	A
	JOHNNY HAYES	bs, vcls	A
	JIMMY SOSSAMON	drms	A
	CARLTON WARWICK	gtr, vcls	A

| 45s: | Too Much Lovin'/Harbor Melon | (Super-Cool 7337) 1967 |
| α | Big Teaser / It's You | (Mu ZTSB 125277) 1967 |

NB: α as by **Psychic Motion**.

A short-lived outfit who operated around the Fayetteville area of North Carolina and came from Lumberton. The 'A' side to their first 45, about teen-sex frustration, was pretty catchy. They enjoyed considerable success and notoriety locally, winning a major Battle Of The Bands encompassing both North and South Carolina in 1967, and starring in their own show on local TV. Their second 45 was released under the name **Psychic Motion**.

James Sossamon later formed **The Cykle**, who recorded a highly-rated album in 1969. All four of **The Young Ones**/**Psychic Motion** 45 sides were included as bonus tracks on Gear Fab's reissue of the **Cykle** album.

Compilation appearances include: *Too Much Lovin'* on *Tobacco A-Go-Go, Vol. 1* (LP); and *Harbor Melon* and *Big Teaser* on *Tobacco A-Go-Go, Vol. 2* (LP). (MW/CF/VJ)

The Young Rascals (later known as The Rascals)

Personnel:
EDDIE BRIGATI	vcls		A
FELIX CAVALIERE	organ, vcls		AB
GENE CORNISH	gtr		A
DINO DANELLI	drms		AB
BUZZY FEITEN	gtr		B
ROBERT POPWELL	bs		B
ANN SUTTON	vcls		B

HCP

ALBUMS:	1(A)	THE YOUNG RASCALS	(Atlantic 8123) 1966	15	-
(up to	2(A)	COLLECTIONS	(Atlantic 8134) 1967	14	-
1972)	3(A)	GROOVIN'	(Atlantic 8148) 1967	5	-
	4(A)	ONCE UPON A DREAM	(Atlantic 8169) 1968	9	-
	5(A)	TIME PEACE/THE RASCALS' GREATEST HITS	(Atlantic 8190) 1968	1	-
	6(A)	FREEDOM SUITE	(Atlantic 2-091) 1969	17	-
	7(A)	SEE	(Atlantic 8246) 1970	45	-
	8(A)	SEARCH AND NEARNESS	(Atlantic 8276) 1971	198	-
	9(B)	PEACEFUL WORLD	(Columbia 30462) 1971	122	-
	10(B)	THE ISLAND OF REAL	(Columbia 31103) 1972	180	-

NB: (4) - (10) credited to **The Rascals**. (2) and (3) have been reissued by Rhino. (9) reissued on CD by Sundazed (SC 6131) 1999. (10) reissued on CD by Sundazed (SC 6132) 1999. (1) also reissued on vinyl (Sundazed LP 5116) 2002. (2) also reissued on vinyl (Sundazed LP 5117) 2002. (3) also reissued on vinyl (Sundazed LP 5118) 2002. (4) also reissued on vinyl (Sundazed LP 5119) 2002. Fans of the band will also be interested in *Atlantic Years*, a Japanese 7-CD box set which was issued in 1996. The set contains 108 tracks, among them 25 which have not been released before or were hard to find. A good recent compilation CD is *The Essentials* (Atlantic RZ 76063) 2002.

HCP

45s:	I Ain't Gonna Eat My Heart Out Anymore/			
	Slow Down	(Atlantic 2312) 1965	52	
	Good Lovin'/Mustang Sally	(Atlantic 2321) 1966	1	
	You Better Run/			
	Love Is A Beautiful Thing	(Atlantic 2338) 1966	20	
	Come On Up/What Is The Reason?	(Atlantic 2353) 1966	43	
	I've Been Lonely Too Long/			
	If You Knew	(Atlantic 2377) 1967	16	
	Groovin'/Sueño	(Atlantic 2401) 1967	1	
	A Girl Like You/It's Love	(Atlantic 2424) 1967	10	
	Groovin' (Italian) /Groovin'(Spanish)	(Atlantic 2428) 1967	-	
β	How Can I Be Sure?/I'm So Happy Now	(Atlantic 2438) 1967	4	
	It's Wonderful/Of Course	(Atlantic 2463) 1967	20	
α	Corri Nel Sole (aka A Beautiful Morning)/			
	Sentirai La Pioggia (aka Rainy Day)	(Ri-Fi) 1968		
δ	A Beautiful Morning/Rainy Day	(Atlantic 2493) 1968	3	
δ	People Got To Be Free/My World	(Atlantic 2537) 1968	1	
δ	A Ray Of Hope/Any Dance'll Do	(Atlantic 2584) 1968	24	
δ	Heaven/Baby I'm Blue	(Atlantic 2599) 1969	39	
δ	See/Away Away	(Atlantic 2634) 1969	27	
χ	Carry Me Back/Real Thing	(Atlantic 2664) 1969	26	
δ	Hold On/I Believe	(Atlantic 2695) 1969	51	
δ	Glory Glory/You Don't Know	(Atlantic 2743) 1970	58	
δ	Right On/Almost Home	(Atlantic 2773) 1971	119	
δ	Love Me/Happy Song	(Columbia 45400) 1971	95	
δ	Lucky Day/Love Letter	(Columbia 45491) 1971	-	
δ	Echoes/Hummin'Song	(Columbia 45600) 1972		

NB: δ and χ credited to **The Rascals**. α Italian single - both tracks sung in Italian. β and χ also released in France with picture sleeves on Atlantic. Thre are also three French EPs with PS and *Mini-Boom*, a 7" mini-LP with PS and six tracks edited/cut at two minutes.

Arguably a marginal case for inclusion here since they are really remembered for playing a crowd-pulling brand of rock'n'roll and R&B. They came together in New York in early 1965 when Cavaliere, Brigati and Cornish all left Joey Dee's Starlighters at the same time. They played their first gig at the Choo Choo Club in Garfield, New Jersey. Their music was soul-based, danceable and immediate and after their debut single, *I Ain't Gonna Eat My Heart Out Anymore* met with some initial success, the follow-up *Good Lovin'* made No. 1 and set them on the road to further success. They were the first white rock act to be signed by Atlantic and their music had a wide appeal to both black and white audiences. *Groovin'*, their second No. 1 and possibly their magnum opus, marked a definite change of style. Depicting a long, ecstatic afternoon in the sun it superbly captured the vibes of the Summer of 1967 and is of far more relevance to this book than what had gone before. Other notable slices of superb pop-rock were *How Can I Be Sure?*, *A Girl Like You* and *It's Wonderful*, which made use of sound effects. After the last mentioned the 'Young' was omitted from their title and they increasingly veered towards a sort of good vibe jazzy-rock. *People Got To Be Free* gave them their third and final U.S. No. 1 after which they underwent a changed line-up (from 'A' to 'B') and changed labels to Columbia. Among the newcomers was Buzzy Feiten, who'd previously played with Paul Butterfield.

The new line-up cut two albums which aroused some interest but little excitement and they disbanded in 1972. Felix Cavaliere later went solo recording two critically acclaimed if commercially unsuccessful albums for Bearsville. Robert Popwell joined The Crusaders in 1976 and Cornish and Danelli fronted **Bulldog** and Fotomaker.

In terms of compilation appearances, you'll find *Come On Up* on *Wild Thing*; *I Ain't Gonna Eat My Heart Out Anymore* on *Highs Of The Sixties*; *It's Wonderful* on *Nuggets, Vol. 9* (LP); and *Sattva* on *Journey To A Higher Key* (LP).

Clearly an extremely successful act commercially, they enjoyed three No. 1 45s and three other Top Ten hits. Their *Greatest Hits* album topped the U.S. Album Charts. *Groovin'*, *Once Upon A Dream*, *Collections*, *The Young Rascals* and *Freedom Suite* all made the Top Twenty, peaking at Nos 5, 9, 14, 15 and 17 respectively. Even their later albums made some impression on the charts. *The Essentials* is essentially a greatest hits collection featuring most of their finest moments. (VJ/PV/SR)

The Young Savages

45s:	The Invaders Are Coming/	
	A Very Special Day	(Dynamic Sound 2006) 1967
	I Love You Oh So Much/	
	Welcome To My World	(Dynamic Sound 2007) 1967

THE RASCALS - Peaceful World CD.

THE RASCALS - The Island Of Real CD.

A little gem, this one from Wisconsin. *The Invaders Are Coming* is a song all about a guy who believes invaders from outer space are coming to take his girlfriend. It's got a lot of commercial appeal and there's some very effective organ work to create a sort of spacey sound. Give the excellent *Highs In The Mid-Sixties, Vol. 10* (LP) or *Yeah Yeah Yeah* (CD) a spin if you wanna experience this boss Badger sound... then turn to either *The Madness Invasion* or *Vile Vinyl, Vol. 2* for **The Invasion's** *The Invasion Is Coming* - the previous incarnation of the song in a very different gutsy garage style. No spacey effects here but great raucous vocals and fuzz solo (*The Invasion Is Coming/I Want To Thank You* on Dynamic Sound 2004). It's a good bet that these two outfits are one and the same. (VJ)

Young Stuff

| 45: | Poor Boy/It Happens To Be Fun | (Canterbury C 514) 1967 |

The weak 'A' side is trying to sound like a cross between The Searchers and **The Millennium**. The 'B' side sets out the same way, but watch! A bitonal chorus works so effectively as to be frightening, especially within this utterly innocent environment. (MK)

The Young Turks

| 45: | Neon/Looky Looky | (Odyssey Records 101) 1969 |

A bubblegum pop-rock group. (SR)

The Young Tyrants

| 45s: | She Don't Got The Right/I Try | (In 67101) 1967 |
| | She Don't Got The Right/I Try | (Try 101) 1967 |

An obscure outfit whose *I Try* also got an airing on *Open Up Yer Door! Vol. 1* (LP) and *Project Blue, Vol. 3* (LP). Glorious garage grunge with some nifty pizzicato pickin' from Rochester, New York. *She Don't Got The Right* is also featured on *Class Of '66!* (LP). (VJ)

Your Friends

| 45: | Sun-Burned Idol/Rustic Patterns | (Sola 14) 196? |

Mellow rock from Arizona. *Sun-Burned Idol* has a reedy sound and folkie vibes. *Rustic...* is more in a folk-psych mode with trippy lyrics and energetic keyboard fingering. (MW)

Yo-Yo's

Personnel incl: AARON
ELLIOT
FLICKSTEIN
SHANE

| 45: | Crack In My Wall/The Raven | (Coral 62501) 1966 |

This NYC bunch were unconnected to **The Swingin' Yo Yo's** from Memphis. Their dynamic punker *Crack In My Wall* was their finest moment, having quite a melodramatic vocal style.

Crack... has also been compiled on *The Essential Pebbles Collection, Vol. 2* (Dble CD) and *Pebbles, Vol. 14* (LP).

There was also a Californian band called The Yo Yoz, who recorded on Sacramento's Ikon label. (VJ/MW)

THE ESSENTIAL PEBBLES COLLECTION Vol. 2 (Comp CD) including Yo-Yo's.

YEAH YEAH YEAH (Comp CD) including The Young Savages.

YAMA and THE KARMA DUSTERS - Up From The Sewers LP.

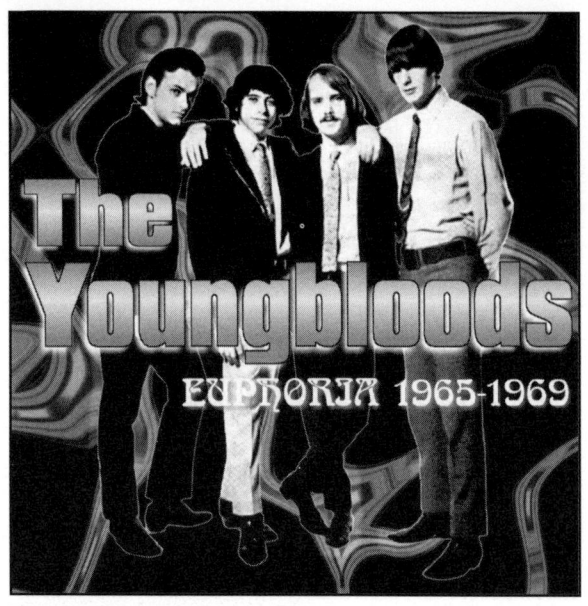

THE YOUNGBLOODS - Euphoria CD.

YA HO WA 13 - To The Principles For The Children CD.

YA HO WA 13 - Ya Ho wa 13 CD.

YA HO WA 13 - Penetration CD.

YA HO WA 13 - Kohoutek CD.

Zaharas

ALBUM: 1 LIVIN' AIN'T EASY (Private Pressing) 1974 SC

From North Carolina, a hard-rock quartet with strong Led Zeppelin influence. (SR)

Zakary Thaks

Personnel:
CHRIS GERNIOTTIS	vcls	AB
REX GREGORY	bs	AB
JOHN LOPEZ	ld gtr	AB
STAN MOORE	drms	AB
PETE STINSON	gtr	A

ALBUMS:
1. ZAKARY THAKS (Moxie MLP 2) 1980
2. J-BECK STORY - VOL 2: ZAKARY THAKS (Eva 12035) 1984
3. A TEXAS BATTLE OF THE BANDS (CD) (Collectables COL-CD-0652) 199?
4. FACE TO FACE (CD) (Collectables COL-CD-0650) 199?
5. FORM THE HABIT (Beat Rocket BR 131) 2001

NB: (3) is a reissue of (2) together with the equivalent **Bad Seeds** retrospective. (4) contains all their 45 cuts plus *Footsteps Jam* and *The Mirrors Reflection*. (5) also issued on CD.

45s:
Bad Girl/I Need You	(J-Beck 1006)	1966
Bad Girl/I Need You	(Mercury 72633)	1967
Face To Face/Weekday Blues	(J-Beck 1009)	1967
Please/Won't Come Back	(J-Beck 1101)	1967
Mirror Of Yesterday/ Can't You Hear Daddy's Footsteps	(J-Beck 1103)	1967
My Door/Green Crystal Ties	(Thak 1001)	1968
Everybody Wants To Be Somebody/ Outprint	(Cee-Bee 1005)	1969

From Corpus Christi, Texas, **Zakary Thaks** were one of the city's top acts between 1966-69. Originally known as The Marauders, they soon changed name to The Riptides, with a repertoire of mainly surf-style music. With British bands like the Kinks and Stones becoming more influential, in March 1966, they again changed names to **The Zakary Thaks** and signed to Carl Becker's J-Beck label. Chris Gerniottis was just 15 at the time whilst the other members were 17.

Bad Girl, their first 45, was a strong punk song with a snappy guitar introduction. It was picked up by Mercury for national distribution but was reckoned to have sold more records in South Texas where they developed a strong following. The follow-up sold quite well locally too, getting to No. 1 in Austin and San Antonio. It was liberally endowed with guitar feedback, but the flip was a more routine bluesy number thrown together in an hour at the studio. **Zakary Thaks** at this time opened for most of the touring bands that played Corpus Christi, including **The Byrds**, **Jefferson Airplane**, Animals, Beach Boys, Yardbirds, and **The 13th Floor Elevators**.

Their third single, *Please* attempted to change direction with its Mersybeat pop sound while the follow-up, *Mirror Of Yesterday* was recorded with the Houston Symphony Orchestra on one of the first eight-track recorders. After its failure, Chris Gerniottis left the band to join **Liberty Bell**, but rejoined in 1969 for their final single. They broke up for a little while after the *My Door* 45 and then reformed briefly, without Pete Stinson, to record a final 45 which was leased to ABC, but never released by them. They played on and off until the Summer of 1972, although no further 45s were forthcoming.

Zakary Thaks were one of Texas' finest sixties bands and their work is essential for connoisseurs of psychedelia. Both the albums/CDs listed contain all their 45s and either are recommended. In addition, *Texas Reverberations* (Texas Archive Recordings TAR-1) 1982 features live and unissued cuts by the band. Side One includes a slightly longer version of their second 45 *Face To Face* with more searing guitar work at the end; *Footsteps Jam* an instrumental jam and *Can't You Hear Your Daddy's Footsteps*, a re-mix of the 45 version with more intense fuzztone guitar. Of much less note is a live performance on Side Two taken off a 16 millimetre film that J-Beck made to get gigs for the band. Although it relies on cover versions (because club owners were more familiar with these) and the audio quality is dire, the film does show just how young these guys were and its worth trying to find on video.

Other compilation coverage has so far included: *Won't Come Back* on *Texas Psychedelic Punk, Vol. 11* (Metal Acetate #4); *Bad Girl* on *Nuggets Box* (4-CD), *Pebbles, Vol. 2* (CD), *Pebbles, Vol. 2* (LP), *Great Pebbles* (CD) and *I Was A Teenage Caveman* (LP); *Can't You Hear Your Daddy's Footsteps* on *Psychedelic Crown Jewels, Vol. 1* (Dble LP & CD) and *Acid Dreams, Vol. 1* (LP); *I Need You* and *Can You Hear* on *Acid Dreams - The Complete 3 LP Set* (3-LP) and *Acid Dreams Testament* (CD); *Won't Come Back*, *Face To Face*, *My Door* and *Green Crystal Ties* on *Green Crystal Ties, Vol. 1* (CD); and *Face To Face* (two versions) and *Shake* on *The History Of Texas Garage Bands, Vol. 5* (CD).

Mike Taylor their road manager/songwriting contributer was formerly with **The Bad Seeds**. Pete Stinson later moved to California where he is a construction worker. The other members all remained in the music business. In the short-term their talented vocalist Chris Gerniottis went on to play briefly for **Liberty Bell** and then formed **Kubla Khan**. He later became a singing waiter in a dinner-theatre group called the Barnstormers along with future Hollywood actor Dennis Quaid before quitting music entirely.

Form The Habit features their first three singles, along with three unissued tracks as bonuses and an informative 1995 interview with Gerniottis.

For further reading check out an interview with Chris Gerniottis in 'Twist And Shake # 1'. (VJ/MW/LP)

THE ZAKARY THAKS - Face To Face LP.

Frank Zappa/Mothers Of Invention

Personnel:
JIMMIE CARL BLACK	drms, vcls, horns	ABCDE G H J
RAY COLLINS	vcls, hrmnca, perc	AB DE H
ROY ESTRADA	bs, vcls	ABCDE G H
ELLIOT INGBER	gtr	A
FRANK ZAPPA	gtr, vcls, keyb'ds	ABCDEFG H I J K
BUNK GARDNER	horns, woodwind, vcls	BCDE G H
BILLY MUNDI	drms	BC E
DON PRESTON	keyb'ds	BCDE G H K
JIM SHERWOOD	hrns	BCDE G H
IAN UNDERWOOD	piano, woodwind	CDE G H I J K
ARTIE 'ED MARIMBA' TRIPP	drms	DE G H
MAX BENNETT	bs	F I
JOHN GUERIN	drms	F I
DON 'SUGAR CANE' HARRIS	violin, organ	F G H I
PAUL HUMPHREY	drms	F
SHUGGIE OTIS	bs	F
JEAN LUC PONTY		F

RON SELICO	drms	F	
DON VAN VLIET	vcls	F	
BUZZ GARDNER	horns	G H	
LOWELL GEORGE	gtr, vcls	H	
GEORGE DUKE	horns, keyb'ds, vcls	I J	
AYNSLEY DUNBAR	drms, perc	I J K	
HOWARD KAYLAN	vcls	I J K	
JEFF SIMMONS	bs, vcls, gtr	I	
MARK VOLMAN	vcls	I J K	
MARTIN LICKERT	bs	J	
JIM PONS	vcls	J K	
RUTH UNDERWOOD	perc	J	
BOB HARRIS	keyb'ds, vcls	K	

ALBUMS: (up to 1972)

					HCP
1(A)	FREAK OUT!	(Verve V6-5005-2)	1966	130	SC
2(B)	ABSOLUTELY FREE	(Verve V6-5013)	1967	41	-
3(C)	WE'RE ONLY IN IT FOR THE MONEY	(Verve V6-5045)	1967	30	-
4(-)	LUMPY GRAVY	(Verve V6-8741)	1968	159	-
5(D)	CRUISIN' WITH RUBEN AND THE JETS	(Verve V6-5055)	1968	110	-
6(-)	MOTHERMANIA	(Verve V6-5068)	1969	151	-
7(-)	THE **** OF THE MOTHERS (comp)	(Verve V6-5074)	1969	-	-
8(D)	UNCLE MEAT (dbl)	(Bizarre MS-2024)	1969	43	-
9(F)	HOT RATS	(Bizarre RS-6356)	1969	173	-
10(G)	BURNT WEENY SANDWICH	(Bizarre RS-6370)	1969	94	-
11(H)	WEASELS RIPPED MY FLESH	(Bizarre MS-2028)	1970	189	-
12(I)	CHUNGA'S REVENGE	(Bizarre MS-2030)	1970	119	-
13(J)	200 MOTELS (dbl)	(United Artists UAS-9956)	1971	59	-
14(K)	FILLMORE EAST, JUNE 1971	(Bizarre MS-2042)	1971	38	-
14(K)	JUST ANOTHER BAND FROM L.A.	(Bizarre MS-2075)	1972	85	-
15(-)	THE GRAND WAZOO	(Bizarre MS-2093)	1972	-	-
17(E)	WAKA/JAWAKA - HOT RATS	(Bizarre MS-2094)	1972	152	-

NB: (1) issued in both mono (R2) and stereo. First pressings have an advertisement inside the gatefold sleeve for a mail-order FREAK MAP ("in magnificent color - mostly black" !); this ad was removed by Summer 1967 and the "maps" are rare (currently in the R3 category!). (2) issued in both mono (R1) and stereo. The cover contains an offer for a mail-order LIBRETTO (valued at R1). (3) issued with a sheet of "cutouts" a la The Beatles' *Sgt. Pepper* album. Beginning with this release, no stock mono **Zappa** albums are known to exist. There are two different pressings of this LP: first editions contain an unedited version of *Let's Make The Water Turn Black* with the lyric "...and I still remember mama with her apron and her pad, feeding all the boys at Ed's Cafe". The second edition (which is actually rarer, R1) has that lyric, and several others deemed offensive, removed rather crudely from the master. (4) is shown as by "Frank Zappa and The Abnuceals Emuukha Electric Symphony Orchestra & Chorus (with maybe even some of the Mothers Of Invention)". (5) a set of two inserts is known to exist for this LP. One is a page of dance steps, one is instructions on "How To Comb & Set A Jellyroll" (a hairdo). These are very rare (R2) and were very likely only included in promotional copies of the album. (1) - (5) all exist in mono as promos (R2/3), and all the Verve albums were issued in stereo with promo labels (R1/2). (1) - (6) were issued in the UK and Europe on Verve. (8) issued with twelve-page book. This album was also issued in the UK on Transatlantic. (9) shown as by **Frank Zappa**. (11) issued in Germany with amazing "rat trap" cover. (12) shown as by **Frank Zappa**. (9) - (12) issued in the UK and Germany on Reprise. (13) shown as by "The Mothers Of Invention and The Royal Philharmonic Orchestra" and issued with sixteen-page book. Promotional copies include a large colour poster of the cover art as well (R1). Issued in the UK and Germany on United Artists. (14) - (16) shown as by The Mothers. (17) shown as by **Frank Zappa**. (14) - (17) issued in the UK and Germany on Reprise. Many compilations of the band's material exist from around the world. From Germany, *Transparency* (Verve 2352057) 1968 is probably the earliest and includes both sides of their (non-LP) fourth U.S. single. Other Germany-only compilations include *Pregnant* and *Mother's Day*, both on Metro Records with great sleeves. In the eighties, **Zappa** reissued his early catalogue on vinyl via a series of mail-order only box sets. *The Old Masters Box One*, for example contained *Freak Out!*, *Absolutely Free*, *We're Only In It For The Money*, *Lumpy Gravy*, *Cruisin With Ruben And The Jets* and a "Mystery Disc" containing previously unreleased and/or rare tracks (Barking Pumpkin Records BPR-7777) 1985 (R3). Subsequent box sets reissued all the Bizarre/Reprise material in similar fashion. All the releases came with colour booklets. In the nineties, Ryko issued **Zappa**'s catalogue on CD, and also released *The Lost Episodes* (thirty unreleased tracks from 1958 to 1992), *Strictly Commercial: The Best Of Frank Zappa* (comp), *Everything Is Healing Nicely* (outtakes from the *Yellow Shark* sessions), and *Läther* (3-CD set with previously unreleased recordings from 1977).

45s: (up to 1972)

	How Could I Be Such A Fool/Help, I'm A Rock	(Verve 10418)	1966
	How Could I Be Such A Fool/It Can't Happen Here	(Verve 10418)	1966
	Who Are The Brain Police/Trouble Comin' Every Day	(Verve 10458)	1966
α	Why Don't You Do Me Right/Big Leg Emma	(Verve 10513)	1967
β	Mother People/Lonely Little Girl	(Verve 10570)	1967
χ	Jelly Roll Gum Drop/Deseri	(Verve 10632)	1968
	Anyway The Wind Blows/Jelly Roll Gum Drop	(Verve 10632)	1968
δ	My Guitar/Dog Breath (PS)	(Reprise 0840)	1969
	Peaches En Regalia/Little Umbrellas	(Bizarre 0889)	1970
	WPLJ/My Guitar	(Bizarre 0892)	1970
	Would You Go All The Way?/Tell Me You Love Me	(Bizarre 0967)	1970
	What Will This Evening Bring Me This Morning/Daddy Daddy Daddy (PS)	(United Artists 35319)	1971
	Magic Fingers/Daddy Daddy Daddy	(United Artists 50857)	1971
ε	Tears Begin To Fall/Junier Mintz Boogie	(Bizarre 1052)	1971
φ	Cletus Awreetus - Awrightus/Eat That Question (PS)	(Bizarre 1127)	1972

NB: Both sides of α were also included on the CD issue of *Absolutely Free*. *Lonely Little Girl* on β is actually *Lonely Little Girl* and *Take Your Clothes Off When You Dance* from *We're Only In It For The Money* with a different ending. χ shown as by Ruben and The Jets. δ came in a picture sleeve - a group shot. Both sides are

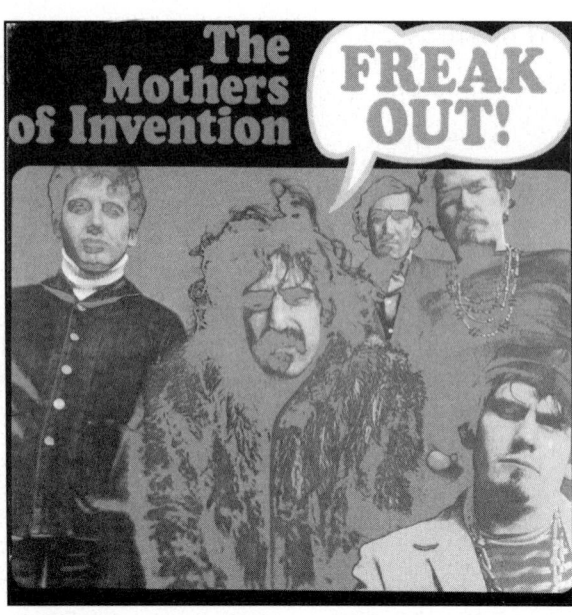

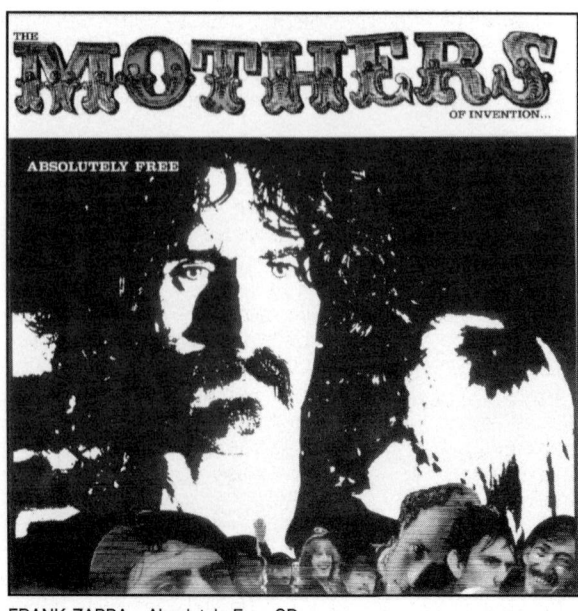

FRANK ZAPPA - Freak Out! CD.

FRANK ZAPPA - Absolutely Free CD.

FRANK ZAPPA.

apparently different to the versions on *Weasels Ripped My Flesh* and *Uncle Meat* respectively. ε apparently features a different version of *Tears Begin To Fall* and the 'B' side is not yet on a Zappa album. φ comes in a picture sleeve of the long-extinct circa 1968 Mothers. δ also released in France with a PS (Reprise RV 20221). There's also a French single with picture sleeve: *Son Of Suzy Creamcheese/Big Leg Emma* (Verve 58516).

One of America's most outrageous and controversial rock stars, **Zappa** was born in Baltimore, Maryland on 21st December 1940. His family were of Sicilian-Greek background. His father worked in various Army and Government jobs. In 1950, they moved to the West Coast (San Diego) and by 1953 Frank's parents had bought him a drum kit and he was composing written music. The following year Frank was drumming in a R&B band, The Ramblers. 1955 saw his family move to Lancaster, California and one of Frank's schoolmates was Don Van Vliet. What a combination! Frank, by now having discarded the drums, played guitar with Vliet in the 1956 outfit The Blackouts.

In 1959 his family moved on to Claremont, California and Frank branched out on his own, taking a flat in Los Angeles. He played in a 'cocktail' San Bernardino band, Perrino and The Mellotones and wrote the score to 'Run Home Slow', a low-priced Western, which flopped when released. He married Kay, though it was a short-lived venture, and played in other local groups, The Boogie Men (1960) and The Masters (1961). In 1961 he also wrote the soundtrack to another B-movie, 'The World's Greatest Sinner'.

An important turning point in his career came when he started working with the consummate engineer Paul Buff in his recording studio in Cucamonga. **Zappa** eventually bought Buff out with money from the royalties from 'Run Home Slow', which did better when it was re-released in 1963, and renaming the studio 'Studio Z', produced and/or wrote a string of 45s which are now sought-after by **Zappa** collectors but not directly relevant to this book. Some of the 45s appear on the 1983 Rhino *Rare Meat* EP. The episode ended in late 1964 when **Zappa** was framed by the vice squad into making a cheap porn movie and he quit Cucamonga to return to L.A. There he played in another white R&B band, The Soul Giants and sometimes with Captain Glasspack and His Mufflers before forming **The Mothers Of Invention** out of the ashes of the former. They attracted the attention of Herb Cohen, who became their manager and them signed to Verve.

The Mothers were always controversial. As they set to work on their debut album, one of the first songs they recorded was *Who Are The Brain Police?*. This album was innovative, weird and widely advertised in the underground press. It sold well. It was issued as a double album in the U.S. and an edited single album in the UK and Europe.

Their second album met with wider acclaim. The band were by now regarded by many as being in a class by themselves. Musically, they were difficult to categorise. Some of it was psychedelic (without the drugs - **Zappa** was strongly opposed to drugs), much was satirical and full of social comment on themes such as the hypocrisies of the middle class white American way of life. Other music, particularly the *Ruben And The Jets* album, was a spoof on the doo-wop music and associated lifestyle of **Zappa**'s youth.

The *Ruben* album may be of less interest to readers, but all of the other Verve albums are well worth investigation. They contained some excellent songs like *Wowie Zowie, America Drinks Up And Goes Home, Status Back Baby, Who Needs The Peace Corps, Concentration Moon* and *Flower Punk*. On *We're Only In It For The Money*, possibly **The Mothers**' best album for Verve, the cover parodies *Sergeant Pepper* and the lyrics (eg. *Flower Punk*) were full of swipes at the product of the psychedelic era-the flower children who **Zappa** seems to have regarded as just as phony as the earlier targets of his satire. This was also their best-selling album peaking at No 30 in the U.S. Album Charts, but several of the others sold well:- *Absolutely Free, Uncle Meat* and *Live At The Fillmore East - June 1971* all made the Top 50; *Burnt Weeny Sandwich, 200 Motels* and *Just Another Band From L.A.* made the Top 100; *Freak Out!, Cruising With Ruben And The Jets*, and *Chunga's Revenge* made the Top 150 and *Mothermania, Lumpy Gravy, Hot Rats, Waka/Jawaka* and *Weasels Ripped My Flesh* all made the Top 200.

Zappa's solo albums (solo is misleading, they often included members of **The Mothers** as well as session musicians and sometimes extravagant orchestras) are also of interest. For *Lumpy Gravy*, which was full of lush orchestral passages and taped dialogue, he was supported by the Abnuceals Emuukha Electronic Symphony Orchestra and Chorus. *Hot Rats* is generally regarded as one of his best solo albums and tracks like *Peaches En Regalia* and *Willie The Pimp* capture **Zappa**'s guitar work and writing at its best.

Weasels Ripped My Flesh is a collection of live material recorded between 1967-69. Stand out tracks include the surreal *Didja Get Any Onya?* and *The Orange County Lumber Truck* is a driving instrumental which is interrupted by manic laughter. *Burnt Weeny Sandwich* is a predominantly instrumental album centred around a 22-minute track *The House I Used To Know*.

In May 1971, **Zappa** put together the movie score for *200 Motels* and then flew to England to perform the piece at the Royal Albert Hall with the Royal Philharmonic Orchestra. At the eleventh hour the Hall's Administrators cancelled the gig considering the lyrics obscene. **Zappa** eventually lost the resulting legal battle which wasn't heard until 1975. The '200 Motels' film, described as a 'surrealistic documentary', was shot in London in seven days and was one of his biggest flops. Far better was his *Fillmore East June, 1971* album recorded at one of the final Fillmore East concerts where he appeared on stage with John and Yoko. It captured **The Mothers** at their most vulgar on tracks like *What Kind Of Girls Do You Think We Are?* and *Do You Like My New Car?*. He also issued the *Tears Began To Fall* 45 under the pseudonym Billy Dexter to see if it would sell. It didn't.

In December 1971, he was pushed from the stage by the boyfriend of a fan towards the end of a concert at London's Rainbow. He suffered multiple fractures of the leg and was confined to a wheelchair for nine months. His next album, *Just Another Band From L.A.*, had been recorded at the University of California in Los Angeles on 7 August 1971, but wasn't released until May 1972. It suffered from over-indulgence in places but also included plenty of humour and a 25 minute mini opera *Billy The Mountain*, which had some particularly amusing moments. *The Grand Wazoo* and *Waka/Jawaka* were produced from his wheelchair and are generally regarded as two of his better albums.

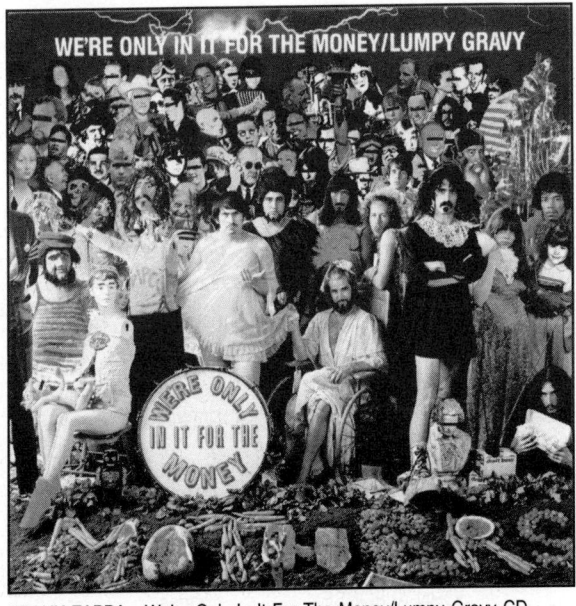

FRANK ZAPPA - We're Only In It For The Money/Lumpy Gravy CD.

Zappa has also turned his talent to production work, particularly in the late sixties, when he produced albums for artists like the **GTO's**, **Beefheart**, **Wild Man Fischer** and Lord Buckley.

The Verve albums have all become quite scarce, especially in mono, and are now selling for quite high prices. Zappa continued throughout the seventies and eighties and into the nineties to experiment with many different musical styles - with varying degrees of success. His output was prolific. Herb Cohen said in 1971 'I can't get him to take a fucking vacation'. His music became more commercial with time, but the lyrics remained witty and socially aware. He was arguably one of the most fascinating musicians and writers to emerge from America's West Coast.

As for **The Mothers**, who carried on with many different line-ups and several additional personnel until 1976, Estrada later played with Little Feat; Mundi formed **Rhinoceros**, Artie Tripp played with **Beefheart**; Bunk Gardner with Geronimo Black, Don Preston played for Flo and Eddie and Sherwood for Ruben and The Jets (who were assembled by **Zappa**).

Frank Zappa died, at the age of 52, on December 4th, 1993, after losing his battle against thyroid cancer. (VJ, plus additional discographical info from CF and the German fanzine/4-volume book "The Torchum Never Stops"/SR)

FRANK ZAPPA - Just Another Band From L.A. LP.

Zazu

Personnel:	RANDY CURLEE	bs, vcls	A
	MICKEY LEHOCKY	drms	A
	JOHN MELNICK	keyb'ds, vcls	A
	PAUL RIPURERO	gtr, vcls	A

ALBUM: 1(A) ZAZU (Wooden Nickel 0791) 1975 -

A keyboard-led group with harmonies and some heavy guitar, for hard-prog fans. (SR)

Zekes

Personnel incl:	K. GAYLE		A
	L. GAYLE		A

45: Leaving You/Box (Beverly Hills 9353) 1969

Burning hard-rock by this unknown Southern California outfit. Producer Robert Duffy also handled **Utopia**, whose album on Kent is in a similar vein. (CF)

Zendik

45: Is There No Peace/Aesop (Pslhrtz 100) 1970

Chaotic end-of-decade heavy psychedelic rock from Chicago. *Is There No Peace* is a great blast and features on the *Brain Shadows, Vol. 1* (LP & CD) compilation. (MW)

Zephyr

Personnel:	TOMMY BOLIN	gtr, vcls	AB	G
(up to	ROBBIE CHAMBERLAIN	drms	A C	F
1973)	JOHN FARIS	sax, keyb'ds, vcls	ABC	FG
	CANDY GIVENS	vcls, hrmnca, keyb'ds	ABCDEF	G
	DAVID GIVENS	bs, gtr, vcls	ABCDEF	G
	BOBBY BERGE	drms, perc	B	G
	KIM KING	gtr	C	
	JOCK BARTLEY	gtr	DEF	
	DAN SMYTH	keyb'ds	DE	
	OTIS TAYLOR	mandolin, hrmnca, vcls	D	
	MICHAEL (P.M.) WOOTEN	drms	DE	
	JOHN ALFONSE	congas	E	

ALBUMS:	1(A)	ZEPHYR	(Probe CP 4510) 1969	48 -
(up to	2(B)	GOING BACK TO COLORADO		
1973)			(Warner Bros. WS 1897) 1971	- -
	3(E)	SUNSET RIDE	(Warner Bros. WS 2603) 1972	- -

HCP

NB: (1) also issued in the U.K. by Probe (SPB 1006) 1970. (1) reissued by Beat Goes On (BGOLP 41) 1989, and also on CD (BGOCD 41) 1990. (1) also reissued on CD by MCA (MCAD 22032) 198?. (2) and (3) also issued on CD. Also of interest is *Zephyr Live* (Tommy Bolin Archives TBACD 6) 1997, a CD only release.

45s:	Cross The River/Sail On	(Probe 475) 1969
(up to	Going Back To Colorado/Radio Song	(Warner Bros. 7444) 1970
1973)	High Flying Bird/Sierra Cowgirl	(Warner Bros. 7604) 1972

Zephyr was formed in the Fall of 1968 when Tommy Bolin and John Faris teamed up with David and Candy Givens. Bolin and Faris (ex-**Us Too**) had been playing together in a band called Ethereal Zephyr, while David and Candy led their own band Brown Sugar. Jazz drummer John Chamberlain was enlisted and the band moved into a house together and started writing new material. From the start **Zephyr** was a vehicle to showcase Candy's vocals. By the Spring of 1969 they had recorded a three-song demo and had connected with a Denver promoter who arranged for them to do a short West Coast tour. They played the major venues of the day: the Fillmore West, the Avalon Ballroom, the Whisky-A-Go-Go etc. and received offers from several major labels.

An offer from ABC was accepted, and the band was rushed into the studio with a recording engineer for a producer. The "producer" didn't like the way the band played and forced each member to record their parts repeatedly, with some songs being recorded twenty times or more; while the resulting album does showcase Tommy at his most aggressive and unbridled, it sounds strained and tired; cassette copies of the three-song demo traded among fans show what the first album should have been.

John Chamberlain was replaced at Tommy's behest, with Bobby Berge just before the second album, *Going Back To Colorado* was recorded. The lyrics and arrangements are far more cerebral than the previous effort, yet are still accessible. Candy's voice was finally given the arrangements and presentation it warranted. Lester Bangs finished his review of the album in Rolling Stone by stating "The main thing about **Zephyr** is that they write interesting songs and know how to record them with polish and professionalism and those little extra touches that make arrangements intriguing. As a result their second album is unusually substantial. That's saying something these days."

In early 1971, David Givens made the decision that he wanted John Chamberlain back. When Bobby left, Tommy left with him and guitarist Kim King was hired to replace Tommy. Kim King had previously been in the Denver outfit **Lothar and The Hand People** and had actually contributed to the second **Zephyr** album when he worked for Eddie Kramer at Electric Ladyland studios. Kim was in the band only long enough to complete one tour of the West Coast.

Immediately upon leaving **Zephyr** Tommy formed his own Energy with Bobby Berge and Kenny Passarelli (previously with **The Beast**). Tommy also formed another outfit The T & O Shortline with blues musician Otis Taylor. Both of these bands eventually petered out.

In 1972, David and Candy put together a new band The Bees. This band featured guitarist Jock Bartley, keyboard player Dan Smyth, drummer Michael Wooten and Otis Taylor on mandolin, but Warner Brothers balked at the new name saying they had too much money invested in the **Zephyr** moniker. The third album *Sunset Ride* (recorded without Otis Taylor) debuted a new sound, seamlessly combining elements of blues, country, psychedelia and jazz into their own distinctive style. The album is regarded by most of the band's followers as their finest moment. Eventually Chamberlain and Faris returned to **Zephyr** and, by the time the band toured in support of the third album, the band line-up was the same as the first album, with the exception of Bartley replacing Bolin. After two more tours, David and Candy were burned out having been on the road almost constantly since 1969, they called it quits.

Jock Bartley went on to play with Tim Goodman, Gram Parsons, Chris Hillman and Firefall, which he leads to this day. Michael Wooten was also in the original Firefall line-up, then formed his own band Navarro, which recorded for Capitol. He toured and recorded with Carole King and in the nineties surfaced as a founding member of Leftover Salmon.

In 1973, after Energy and the *Sunset Ride* incarnation of **Zephyr** had folded, David and Candy formed a cover band The Legendary 4-Nikators with Harold Feilden, Mick Manresa and Tommy. Harold and Mick had been the founders of Flash Cadillac and The Continental Kids. Ironically, Tommy had been the first guitarist Harold approached when he was putting Flash Cadillac together, Jock Bartley was the second. It was during this time that it was decided to again reform **Zephyr**. A half-dozen or so gigs were staged and the *Zephyr Live* CD is from one of those dates. This CD shows the band in stellar form and Bolin never sounded better or demonstrated more restraint than he does here in the jazz context of the epic Pharoah Sanders/Leon Thomas composition *The Creator Has A Master Plan*.

Tommy left the 4-Nikators after getting an offer to join **The James Gang**. He later played with Deep Purple, jazz drummers Billy Cobham and Alphonse Mouzon and was touring in support of his second solo album when he died of a heroin overdose in 1976.

The 4-Nikators pressed on; sometimes joined by Otis Taylor. Over the years there were occasional gigs done under different names such as David and Candy and Friends, Candy Your Dinner's Ready, Otis Taylor's All Star Blues Band, The 5-Nikator and FMOZ.

In 1977, David and Candy reformed **Zephyr** again, this time with David on guitar, Rocky Duarte on bass, Merry Stewart on keyboards, and John Oliver on drums. This line-up was unable to secure a record deal but did issue one live track on a Denver radio station sponsored compilation. Both Duarte and Stewart had previously been with The Freddi-Henchi Band. The band would continue to go through personnel changes, including the return of Otis Taylor on bass. Eventually, the momentum faded and **Zephyr** again broke up.

By the start of the eighties The 4-Nikators were still a viable and popular live act. David Givens was back on bass and Eddie Turner was handling the guitar duties. In 1982, the inevitable happened and **Zephyr** was reformed with Eddie Turner on guitar and they recorded the fourth album *Heartbeat*. A proposed fifth album was in the "we're talking about it" stage when Candy Givens drowned in a jacuzzi after passing out from a mix of alcohol and quaaludes in 1984.

In 1995, Otis Taylor formed his own band with guitarist Eddie Turner and childhood friend Kenny Passarrelli.

By the late nineties it seemed certain that **Zephyr** would exist now only as a memory, though one that local fans will never forget. But in the Summer of 1997 all surviving members of the original **Zephyr** regrouped for one weekend of shows in Denver. Accompanying David Givens, John Chamberlain, and John Faris were Jock Bentley, Otis Taylor, Eddie Turner, Anna Givens on vocals and guest guitarist Ralph Patlan. They performed material from the first two albums plus a lengthy version of *The Creator Has A Master Plan* that was the highlight of the shows. (DMo/AA/JSa)

Zerfas

Personnel:	STEVE NEWBOLD	gtr, vcls, bs	A
	BILL RICE	bs, vcls	A
	MARK TRIBBY	gtr, vcls	A
	DAVID ZERFAS	drms, vcls	A
	HERMAN ZERFAS	keyb'ds, vcls	A

ALBUM: 1(A)   ZERFAS   (700 West LH 730710) 1973 R4

NB: (1) saw a deluxe official repress (700 West 730710) 1995 with inserts and poster. Reissued on vinyl (Atlas 730 710 16) 1999.

An Indianapolis, Indiana, outfit whose album of self-penned compositions is worth checking out. The material is mostly strong, there's lots of keyboards and sound effects on Side Two but good harmonies too. Side One is quite Beatlesque. The prime cut *You Never Win* opens with a backwards guitar intro; *The Sweetest Part* is first class synthesized rock and *I Don't Understand* and *I Need It Higher* add the band's own dimension to The Beatles' early seventies sound. Recommended.

One track, *I Need It Higher* has also resurfaced on *Love, Peace And Poetry, Vol. 1* (LP & CD). (VJ/CF/MW)

The Zero End

45:   Blow Your Mind/Fly Today   (Garland 2002) 19??

From Astoria, Oregon, a great two-sided garage-punk single with fuzz breaks and tortured vocals. They may have released some other singles. (SR)

006

45s: Like What, Me Worry/Why Can't I Say   (Harlequin 606415) 1966
Like What, Me Worry/Why Can't I Say   (Red Bird 10-006) 1966

A Chicago garage band.

Compilation appearances include: *Like What, Me Worry?* on *Pebbles, Vol. 3 (ESD)* (CD), *Boulders, Vol. 2* (LP) and *Garage Punk Unknowns, Vol. 7* (LP). (VJ)

Warren Zevon

Personnel:	SKIP BATTYN	bs	A
	JON CORNEAL	drms	A
	DRACHEN THEAKER	drms	A
	WARREN ZEVON	vcls, gtr, marimba, keyb'ds	A
	(MARS BONFIRE	gtr	A)

ZERFAS - Zerfas LP.

	(ED CARAEFF	maracas	A)
	(SWEET TRIFLES	backing vcls	A)

ALBUM: 1(A) WANTED DEAD OR ALIVE (Imperial LP-12456) 1970 -

NB: (1) reissued on Pickwick with one track omitted (*Fiery Emblems*). (1) also reissued on CD.

Born in 1947 in Canada and classically trained, **Warren Zevon** moved to Los Angeles in the mid-sixties. A gifted songwriter, **The Turtles** decided to record two of his songs (*Outside Chance* and *Like The Seasons*), the latter being the flip to their million-selling *Happy Together*. He was then offered a recording deal with White Whale and recorded three singles as **Lyme and Cybelle**. After that he played with **Smokestack Lightning**, **The Brothers** and eventually met **Kim Fowley**. He wrote and arranged two songs on **Fowley**'s *Good Clean Fun* album (*Kangaroo* and *I'm Not Young Anymore*) and through him got a contract with Imperial (who were bought by United Artists shortly after).

Dedicated to **Fowley** and produced by **Zevon** with the help of Bones Howe, *Wanted Dead Or Alive* is an excellent album, full of good guitars, interesting lyrics and strong songs (*Gorilla*, *A Bullet For Ramona* and *Travelin In The Lightnin'*), between blues, folk-rock and pop. The title track is a cover of **The Rogues** and was co-written by **Fowley**. Another cut, *She Quit Me* was used on the 'Midnight Cowboy' soundtrack.

On the album the rhythm section is comprised of former Arthur Brown drummer Drachen Theaker and **Skip Battyn**. Mars Bonfire also guested but is uncredited. One of the last albums released on Imperial, it flopped and **Zevon** was unable to find a new label.

After that commercial failure, **Zevon** became the musical director of the Everly Brothers, before relaunching his solo career in 1975 when his songs were covered by Linda Ronstadt. A long-time friend of Jackson Browne and David Lindley, he is still touring and recording brilliant records.

Compilation appearances include *Wanted Dead Or Alive* on *In The Beginning* (LP). (SR)

Zig Zag Paper Co.

45s:	I Feel Free/Greatest Show On Earth	(Bell 741) 1968
	Just As Long As You Hold Out/	
	Cast Out The Worries	(Bell 752) 1968

An obscure group, their first 45 contains a cover of Cream's *I Feel Free* done in a bubblegum style with fuzz guitar. (SR)

Zig Zag People

Personnel:	PETER BRAUNE		A
	J.Q. BROWN		A
	SAL CERVELLE		A
	MICHAEL DEAN		A
	RALPH VINCENT		A

ALBUM: 1(A) TAKE BUBBLEGUM MUSIC UNDERGROUND
(Decca DL-75110) 1969 -

45s: Baby I Know It/Peace Of Mind (Decca 32607) 1970

Almost certainly a studio group and a short-lived one at that. Their album is now of minor interest to some collectors. (VJ)

Zipper

Personnel:	FRED COLE	vcls	A
	LORRY ERCK (ERK)	drms	A
	JIM ROOS	gtr	A
	GREG SHADOAN	bs	A

ALBUM: 1(A) ZIPPER (Whizeagle W 0001) 1975 R1/R2

NB: (1) came in a cover consisting of two 'slicks' held together with black insulation tape!

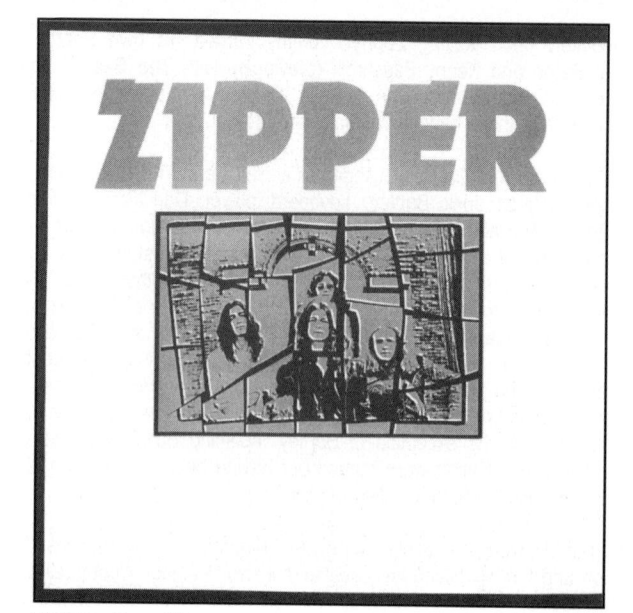

ZIPPER - Zipper LP.

A loud, raw hard-rock album from Portland, Oregon. Fred Cole had earlier been in **The Lollipop Shoppe** and **The Weeds** and is currently in Dead Moon. Of the other members, Jim Roos became a computer programer and plays in many different and successful Northwest bands. Lorry Erck is a skilled welder, continues to play music and is currently a partner in RSE, a production company involved in Pro Audio applications. Greg Shadoan also works as a computer engineer and is currently playing with The Tom Feeny band. (CF/VJ/GS)

The Zone V

45: I Cannot Lie/Black Jacket Woman (Caravan 21449) 1968

The 'A' side to this 45 can also be heard on *Highs In The Mid-Sixties, Vol. 13 - Texas Part Three* (LP), although the band came from Shickshinny, Pennsylvania. With some snotty punk vocals and ringing guitar work it should appeal to fans of the genre.

Other compilation appearances include *I Cannot Lie* on *Teenage Shutdown, Vol. 9* (LP & CD) and *Yeah Yeah Yeah* (CD). (VJ/MW/MM)

Zoo

Personnel:	MURPHY 'CHOCOLATE		
	MOOSE' CARFAGNA	gtr	A
	MIKE FLICKER	drms	A
	TERRY GOTTLIEB	bs	A
	HOWARD LEESE	ld gtr	A
	IRA WELSLEY	vcls	A

ALBUM: 1(A) PRESENT CHOCOLATE MOOSE
(Sunburst 7500) 1968 R1

NB: (1) has had a limited repressing and reissued on Big Beat (CDWIKM 123) in 1993.

45: Sunset Strip/One Night Man (Sunburst 775) 1968

Although this band may not have originated from California, they were based there. The first album is on an Ed Cobb label and he produced and co-arranged it. It's an interesting album of rock with vestiges of mid-sixties punk and some psychedelia, indeed, the most psychedelic and relevant cuts to this book are *Love Machine*, *Have You Been Sleepin* and *From A Camel's Hump*. It is now a minor collectors' item. Leese went on to play with Heart for whom Flicker was a producer.

The non-album 45 is not as good, though the raucously sung funk-edged *Sunset Strip* is redeemed by a searing guitar break and wah-wah'd outro.

Compilation appearances include *Have You Been Sleepin* on *Psychedelic Perceptions* (CD). (VJ/MW)

ZOO - Chocolate Moose LP.

The Zoo

45: She Said, She Said - Good Day Sunshine/Where Have All The Good Times Gone? (Cameo Parkway 147) 1967

An entirely different group from Akron, Ohio. This **Zoo** was actually a later incarnation of **The Beau Denturies** and this 45 was also released on Encore as **Yellow Pages**.

Compilation appearances include *Where Have All The Good Times Gone* on *A Journey To Tyme, Vol. 4* (LP) and *Mindrocker, Vol. 11* (LP). (VJ/MW)

Zoo

45: Gonna' Miss Me / Sometimes (PKC 1013) 1967

Another **Zoo**, from Milwaukee, with one rare and excellent 45. Check out their frantic version of the **13th Floor Elevators** classic on *Teenage Shutdown, Vol. 7* (LP & CD) and the introverted flip on *Teenage Shutdown, Vol. 6* (LP & CD). (MW/MM)

Zookie and The Potentates

45s and Acetates:
  She's Not Worth All That (one-sided acetate) (Nu-Sound) 196?
  She's Not Worth All That (long version) (one sided acetate) (Nu-Sound) 196?
  Turn Your Love On Me (one-sided acetate) (Nu-Sound) 196?
  Turn Your Love On Me (long version) (one-sided acetate) (Nu-Sound) 196?
  α Sugar Cane (one-sided acetate) (Bell) 196?
  Bachelors Got It Made/Telephony (Nu-Sound 711) 196?

NB: α as Zookie And His Potentates.

A garage band from Michigan who have two previously unreleased cuts:- *She Ain't Worth All That* and *Sugarcane* - included on *Thee Unheard Of* (LP) compilation. Both are well worth a spin. *She's Not Worth All That* has some nice guitar touches and *Sugarcane* is a real hard-rocker, an early taste of what would become heavy metal music in later years. (VJ)

Zorba and The Greeks

45s: One And Only Girl /You Had Your Chance (Golden State Recorders GSR-597-A-1/2) 1966
  Shockwave /Memories Of You (Golden State Recorders GSR-597-B-1/2) 1966

A Roseburg, Oregon, band who made a trip to the Bay Area, laid down four tracks and had them pressed simultaneously as a pair of 45s for self-distribution, on Leo De Gar Kulka's Golden State Recorders' custom label. Unavailable for the Big Beat compilations featuring Golden State recordings, the bouncy organ-pop-punker *One And Only Girl* has cropped up since on *Fuzz, Flaykes, And Shakes, Vol. 2* (LP & CD). (MW/AP)

Zoser

Personnel incl: DARREL SLEEN

45: Together/Dark Of The Morning (Hexagon no#) 1971

From Minneapolis, both sides of this 45 are featured on *Litter - Rare Tracks* album on Eva. The assumption is that they were connected to the **Litter** in some way since they were also produced by Warren Kendrick. That may be the only link since we already know that **The Electras/Twas Brillig** was a separate outfit and no definite details have emerged on this lot. The style here is pretty mellow rock and seems to have little in common with **The Litter**.

You can also find *Dark Of The Morning* on *A Lethal Dose Of Hard Psych* (CD). (MW)

Zuckerman's Dream

45: The Revolution's Over/ Love Is Such An Easy Word To Say (Columbia 4 44831) 1969

NB: also issued as a mono/stereo promo 45 *The Revolution's Over* (Columbia 4-44831) 1969.

Poignant orchestrated folk-pop with flute - a folkie protest about society's changing values and the hypocrisy of it all - *The Revolution's Over* is a sad comment on the end of an exciting decade of youth's self-discovery and assertion. The flip is brassy harmony pop. (MW)

The Zulus

45: Jungle Slim/Topless (Bragg B-204) c1966

Released on a small Nashville label, a rare 45 which sounds like a cross between garage and novelty-rock, with screaming vocals and strange effects. (SR)

Zuma

45: The Night Of The Phantom/You're A Bad Habit (Zuma 777) 196?

This Fort Worth mob covered the **Larry and The Blues Notes**' song in a slower style with a girl vocalist and *Night Of The Sadist* lyrics. They also recorded under the name **Cutty Sark**.

Compilation appearances include *Night Of The Sadist* on *Girls In The Garage, Vol. 5* (LP). (VJ)

Andy Zwerling

Personnel:	LENNY KAYE	gtrs, bs, keyb'ds, bcking vcl	A
	ANNE MARIE MICKLO	bcking vcl	A
	LISA ROBINSON	bcking vcl	A
	RICHARD ROBINSON	gtrs, bs	A
	ANDY ZWERLING	gtrs, celeste, vcls	A

ALBUM: 1(A) SPIDERS IN THE NIGHT (Kama Sutra KSBS 2036) 1971 -

An interesting folk-rock singer songwriter, whose only album was produced by Lenny Kaye and Richard Robinson. Nice dreamy arrangements, good vocal parts and unusual lyrics. *Turtles V Green Ants*, *Sifting Around In A Haze* and the title track deserve to be discovered. Lenny Kaye would later play with Patti Smith and is also known for preparing the original *Nuggets* compilation. (SR)

Zygoat

Personnel incl?: GLEN DUNCAN   A
                FRANK KUSAK   A

45:      Midnight Train To L.A. / Magic Elixir   (K & K FK 1001) 196?

This unknown 45 dates from the 1968-1970 era.

Frank Kusak's *Midnight Train To L.A.* is a smooth rocker with a locomotive rhythm section and a great fuzz break. *Magic Elixir* is even better; composed by Kusak and Glen Duncan, this is cool and laid-back, with reverb and washes of fuzz to raise the hairs on the back of your neck. (MW)

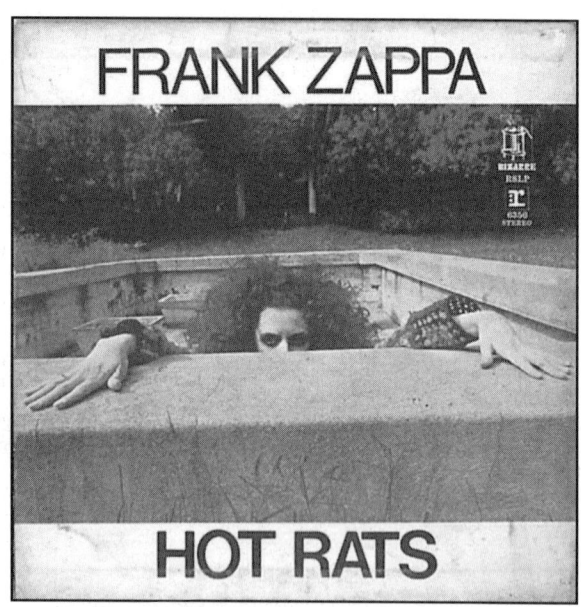

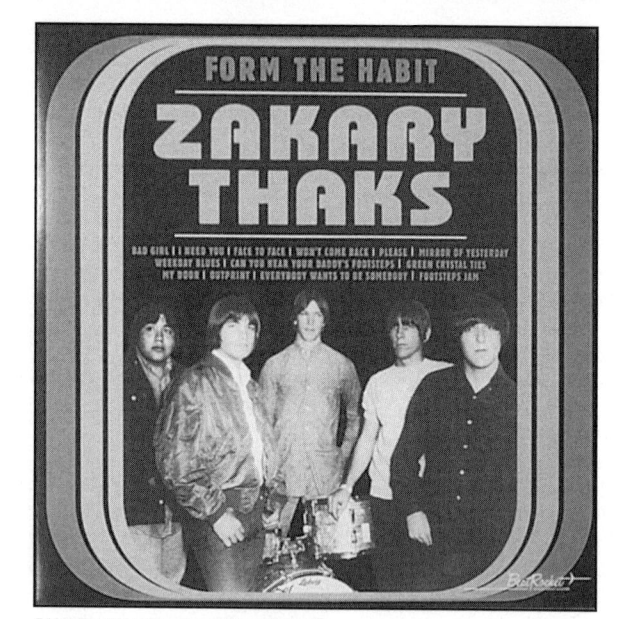

ZAKARY THAKS - Form The Habit LP.

FRANK ZAPPA - Hot Rats LP.

ZAKARY THAKS - Zakary Thaks LP.

FRANK ZAPPA - Lumpy Gravy CD.

FRANK ZAPPA - Chunga's Revenge LP.

Compilations

Below is a list of the compilations mentioned in the main artist section of the book.

A

A Fistful Of Fuzz	(Digital Music Transcendence DMT 001)	CD	1998
A Heavy Dose Of Lyte Psych	(Arf! Arf! AA-062)	CD	1996
A Journey To Tyme, Vol. 1	(Phantom PRS 1001)	LP	1982
A Journey To Tyme, Vol. 2	(Phantom PRS 002)	LP	1985
A Journey To Tyme, Vol. 3	(Phantom PRS-1003)	LP	1985
A Journey To Tyme, Vol. 4	(Phantom PLP 1006)	LP	1986
A Journey To Tyme, Vol. 5	(Phantom PLP-1007)	LP	1987
A Lethal Dose Of Hard Psych	(Arf! Arf! AA-082)	CD	1999
A Pot Of Flowers	(Mainstream 56100)	LP	1967
A Psychedelic Six-Pack Of Sound	(Summit 410)	LP	1968

NB: Ltd reissue of 500 copies (Lüstbütt TM 2730).

Acid and Flowers	(Timothy's Brain TB-104)	CD	199?
Acid Dreams, Vol. 1	(Carat 030)	LP	1979
Acid Dreams Vol. 2	(Hire RV 02)	LP	199?
Acid Dreams, Vol. 3	(Gutter AD#3)	LP	1998
Acid Dreams - The Complete 3 LP Set	( )	3-LP	19??
Acid Dreams Epitaph	(Head 2696)	CD	199?
Acid Dreams Testament	(Head 2596)	CD	199?
Acid Trip From The Psychedelic Sixties	(GMG 75033)	LP	1988
Acid Visions	(Voxx VHM 200.008)	LP	1983
Acid Visions Vol. 2	(Voxx 200.054)	LP	1988
Acid Visions - The Complete Collection Vol. 1	(Collectables COL-CD-8807)	3-CD	1991
Acid Visions - Complete Collection, Vol. 2	(Collectables COL-CD-8810)	3-CD	1993
Acid Visions - Complete Collection, Vol. 3	(Collectables COL-CD-8811)	3-CD	1993
Aliens, Psychos And Wild Things	(Arcania International)	CD	2000
All Cops In Delerium - Good Roots	( )	LP	1980
Angel Dust - Music For Movie Bikers	(Further FU 3 LP)	LP	1988
An Overdose Of Heavy Psych	(Arf! Arf! 063)	CD	1996
The Arf! Arf! Blitzkrieg 32 Track Sampler	(Arf! Arf! AA-068)	CD	1997
Attack Of The Jersey Teens	(Bona Fide BFR-NJ-6601)	LP	1984
Austin Landing, Vol. 1	(Well Known PBM 01)	LP	198?
Austin Landing, Vol. 2	(Well Known BM 02)	LP	1991
The Autumn Records Story	(Edsel ED 145)	LP	1986

B

Back From The Grave, Vol. 1	(Crypt CRYPT RR-66)	LP	1983
Back From The Grave, Vol. 1	(Crypt CR-001)	LP	1983
Back From The Grave, Vol. 2	(Crypt CRYPT RR-660)	LP	1983
Back From The Grave, Vol. 3	(Crypt 003)	LP	1986
Back From The Grave, Vol. 4	(Crypt 004)	LP	198?
Back From The Grave, Vol. 5	(Crypt 005)	LP	1986
Back From The Grave, Vol. 6	(Crypt LP 007)	LP	1985
Back From The Grave, Vol. 7	(Crypt 013)	2-LP	1988
Back From The Grave, Vol. 8	(Crypt CR 062/063)	2-LP	1995
Back From The Grave, Vol. 8	(Crypt CD 062)	CD	199?
Back From The Grave, Vol. 2	(Crypt CD-00345)	CD	19??
Badger A Go Go	(Night Owl KTV-3)	LP	1968
Bad Vibrations, Vol. 1	(Fossil 001)	LP	1999
The Bad Vibrations, Vol. 1	(Akarma AK 123)	LP/CD	2001
Bad Vibrations, Vol. 2	(Fossil 002)	LP	1999
Bad Vibrations, Vol. 3	(Fossil 003)	LP	2000
Baltimore's Teen Beat A Go Go	(Dome)	LP	1966
Bands On Lance	(Lance L-2002)	LP	1999
Basementsville! U.S.A.	(Misty Lane Misty 051)	LP	2000
Battle Of The Bands	(Normandy NR 30867)	3-LP	1967
Battle Of The Bands	(Star SRM 101)	LP	1964
Battle Of The Bands	( )	CD	19??
Battle Of The Bands	(Onyx ES-80689)	LP	1966
Battle Of The Bands, Vol. 1	(Panorama 103)	LP	1966
Battle Of The Bands, Vol. 2	(Panorama 108)	LP	1968
Baubles - Down To Middle Earth	(Big Beat WIK 72)	LP	1988
Bay State Rock	(Star-Rhythm LP 101)	LP	1980
Bee Jay Demo, Vol. 2	(Tener TC1014)	LP	1967
Bee Jay Does It Again!	(Bee Jay TC-1081)	LP	1971
Bee Jay Sampler	(Bee Jay 1055)	LP	1970
Bee Jay Sampler, Vol. 1	(Tener T1038)	EP	196?
Bee Jay Sampler, Vol. 2	(Tener T1039)	EP	196?
Bee Jay Video Soundtrack	(Tener TC1014)	LP	1968
The Berkeley EPs	(Big Beat CDWIKD 153)	CD	1995
The Best Of Beat, Vol. 3	(CBS S 62795)	LP	19??
The Best Of Bosstown Sound	(Big Beat CDWIK2 167)	2-CD	1996
Best of Hideout Records	(Hideout)	CD	1999
Best Of The Hideouts	(Hideout HLP 1002)	LP	1965
The Best Of IGL Folk Rock	(Get Hip GHAS-5001)	LP	1994
The Best Of IGL Garage Rock	(Get Hip GHAS-5002)	LP	1994
The Best Of Impact Records	(Collectables COL-5883)	CD	1998
The Best Of Metrobeat! Vol. 1	(Sundazed LP 5001)	LP	1990
Best of Pebbles, Vol. 1 - Get Primitive	(Ubik TAKE 1)	LP/CD	1990
Best of Pebbles, Vol. 2	(Ubik TAKE 2)	LP/CD	1990
Best of Pebbles, Vol. 3 - Caveman Stomp	(Ubik TAKE 3)	LP/CD	1991
The Best Of Twist-a-Rama U.S.A.	(TAR 1000)	LP	1965
Beyond The Calico Wall	(Voxx VXS 200.051)	LP/CD	1993
Beyond The Valley Of The Dolls	(20th Century Fox TFS 4211)	LP	1970
The Big Hits Of Mid-America, Vol. 1	(Soma MG 1245)	LP	1964
The Big Hits Of Mid-America, Vol. 2	(Soma MG 1246)	LP	1965
The Big Hits Of Mid-America - The Soma Records Story	(Plum 14132)	2-CD	1998
Bo Did It!	(Satan SR-2120)	LP	1989
Bolo Bash	(Bolo BLP 8002)	LP	1964
Born Losers	(Tower T-5082)	LP	1967
Born On The Bayou	(Charly CR.30212)	LP	19??
Boulders, Vol. 1	(Max MLP 1)	LP	1980
Boulders, Vol. 2	(Max MLP 03)	LP	1980
Boulders, Vol. 3	(Max MLP 04)	LP	1981
Boulders, Vol. 4	(61 MLP 07)	LP	1982
Boulders, Vol. 5	(Moxie MLP 08)	LP	1983
Boulders, Vol. 6	(Moxie MLP 09)	LP	1983
Boulders, Vol. 7	(Moxie MLP 10)	LP	1983
Boulders, Vol. 8	(Moxie MLP 11)	LP	1983
Boulders, Vol. 9	(Moxie MLP-12)	LP	1984
Boulders, Vol. 10	(Moxie MLP-13)	LP	19??

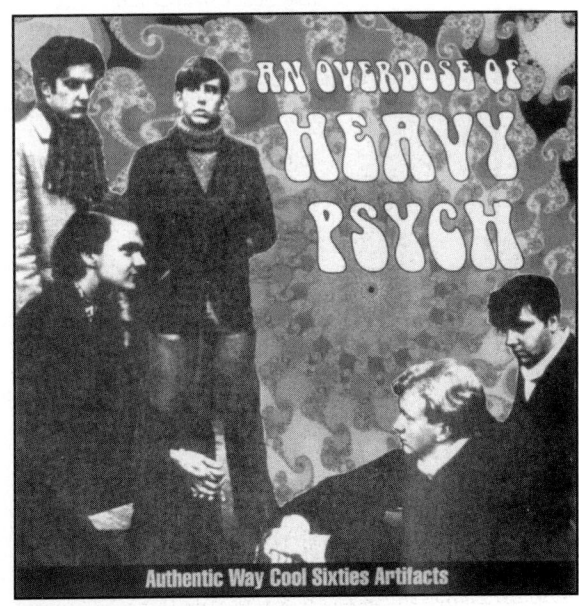

AN OVERDOSE OF HEAVY PSYCH Comp. CD.

Boulders, Vol. 11	(Moxie MLP-19)	LP	19??
The Boss Instrumentals EP!	(Romulan UFOX22)	EP	1994
Brain Shadows, Vol. 1	( )	LP/CD	1991
Brain Shadows, Vol. 2	( )	LP/CD	1994
Bring Flowers To U.S.	(Misty Lane MISTY 054)	LP/CD	2001
Bubble Gum Music Is... The Naked Truth	(Buddah Records BDS 5032B)	LP	1968
Burghers, Vol. 1	(Big Wink)	LP/CD	1997
Buzz Buzz Buzzzzzz Vol. 1	(Arf! Arf! AACC 084)	CD	2000
Buzz Buzz Buzzzzzz Vol. 2	(Arf! Arf! AACC 085)	CD	2000

C

California Acid Folk	(Penguin Egg 11/12)	2-LP	1985
Changes	(Magistral 2000)	LP	1980
Chicago Garage Band Greats - Best Of Rembrandt Records 1966-1968	(Cicadelic CICLP-983)	LP	1985
Chicago Garage Band Greats - Best Of Rembrandt Records 1966-1968	(Cicadelic COL-0516)	CD	1993
Chicago 60's Punk Vs. New Mexico 60's Pop	(Eva EV 12065)	LP	1988
The Chosen Few, Vol. 1	(A-Go-Go 1966)	LP	1982
The Chosen Few, Vol. 2	(Tom-Tom 3752)	LP	1983
Chosen Few Vol's 1 & 2	( )	CD	199?
The Cicadelic 60's, Vol. 2 - Out Of Order	(Cicadelic CICLP-1002)	LP	1982
The Cicadelic 60's, Vol. 3 - Don't Put Me On!	(Cicadelic CICLP-998)	LP	1984
The Cicadelic 60's, Vol. 4 - Never Existed	(Cicadelic CICLP-993)	LP	1984
The Cicadelic 60's, Vol. 5 - 1966 Revisited	(Cicadelic CICLP-980)	LP	1986
The Cicadelic 60's, Vol. 1 - Don't Put Me On	(Cicadelic COL-CD-0515)	CD	1993
The Cicadelic 60's, Vol. 2 - Never Existed!	(Cicadelic COL-CD-0525)	CD	1993
The Cicadelic 60's, Vol. 3 - 1965-66 Folk Rock	(Cicadelic COL-CD-0543)	CD	1993
The Cicadelic 60's, Vol. 4	(Cicadelic COL-CD-0544)	CD	1993
The Cicadelic 60's, Vol. 5	(Cicadelic COL-CD-0574)	CD	1994
The Cicadelic '60s - Vol. 7, From Texas To Houston	(Collectables COL-CD-0667)	CD	1997
The Cicadelic 60's, Vol. 8	(Cicadelic COL 0708)	CD	1998
Class Of '66!	(Wanted WR33001)	LP	1995
Connecticut's Greatest Hits	(CO-OP CP 101)	LP	196?
Crude PA, Vol. 1	(Distortions DB 1001)	LP	1990
Crude PA, Vol. 2	(Distortions DR-1024)	LP	199?
Crystalize Your Mind	(Big Beat CDWIKD 131)	CD	199?

D

Dance With Me - The Autumn Teen Sound	(Big Beat CDWIKD 128)	CD	199?
Destination Frantic!	(Zone 66 Z66R-1001)	CD	199?
Destination Frantic!	(Lance Records STROKE 101)	CD	199?
Diana's Rootin' Tootin' Wild Teenage Rock 'N' Roll Party!	(Romulan UFO X01)	LP	1986
Diggin' For Gold, Vol. 7, In The USA	(Smorgasbord EAT 7001)	LP	199?
Dirty Water - The History Of Eastern Iowa Rock Volume 2	(Unlimited Productions RRRLP-003)	LP	1986
Do It Up Right!	(Bee Jay TC-1067)	LP	1971
Drink Beer! Yell! Dance!	(Ecco Fonic EF LP-001)	LP	1996
Drive-In A Go Go! Vol. 1	(Cicadelic COL-CD-0656)	CD	1995
Drive-In A Go Go! Vol. 2	(Cicadelic COL-0657)	CD	1995
The Dunwich Records Story	(Tutman 001 / Voxx VXS 200.063)	LP	1990

E

Early Chicago	(Happy Tiger HT-1017)	LP	19??
Ear-Piercing Punk	(Trash TR-0001)	LP	1979
Ear-Piercing Punk	(A.I.P. AIPCD 1056)	CD	1996
Eastern Pa Rock Part One (1961-'66)	(ARF! ARF! AA-069)	CD	1998
Eastern Pa Rock Part Two (1966-'69)	(ARF! ARF! AA-070)	CD	1998
East Side Revue, Vol. 1	(Faro)	LP	1966
The East Side Sound, Vol. 1	(Telstar TR 022)	LP	1996
The East Side Sound, Vol. 1 - 1959-1968	(Bacchus Archives BA08-2)	CD	1996
The East Side Sound Vol. 2 Featuring Mark And The Escorts	(Bacchus Archives BA1139)	LP/CD	2001
Echoes In Time, Vol. 1	(Solar S-1000)	LP	1983
Echoes In Time, Vol. 2	(Solar SR-2000)	LP	1983
Echoes In Time Vol's 1 & 2	( )	CD	199?
Electric Food	(Mercury 134 563 MFY)	LP	1968
Elektrock The Sixties	(Elektra 60403)	4-LP	1985
Endless Journey - Phase One	(Psycho 1)	LP	1982
Endless Journey - Phase Two	(Psycho 3)	LP	1983
Endless Journey - Phase Three	(Psycho 19)	LP	1983
Endless Journey - Phase I & II	(Reverberation III)	2-CD	199?
Epitaph For A Legend	(International Artists 13)	2-LP	1980

NB: reissued (Decal LIKD 52) 1989 and (Get Back 545) 1999.

Even More Nuggets	(Rhino R2 75754)	CD	1998
Every Groovy Day	(Misty Lane Misty 050)	LP	2000
Everything You Always Wanted To know About '60s Mind Expanding Punkadelic Garage Rock Instrumentals But Were Afraid To Ask	(Arf! Arf! AA041)	CD	1993
Everywhere Chainsaw Sound	(Chainsaw Sound CSR001)	LP	1982
Everywhere Interferences	(Chainsaw Sound CSR 002)	LP	1983
Excerpts From Nuggets	(Rhino PRCD 7296)	CD	1998

F

Family Circle - Family Tree	(Big Beat CDWIKD 146)	CD	1996
Filling The Gap	(Obscure World Rec. 001)	4-LP	19??
The Finest Hours of U.S. '60s Punk	(Eva 12039)	LP	198?
First Vibration	(Do It Now)	LP	1969
Flashback, Vol. 1	(Flashback FR 1001)	LP	1980
Flashback, Vol. 2	(Flashback FR 1002)	LP	1980
Flashback, Vol. 3	(Flashback FR 1003)	LP	1981
Flashback, Vol. 4	(Flashback FR 1004)	LP	1981
Flashback, Vol. 5	(Flashback FR 1005)	LP	1982
Flashback, Vol. 6	(Flashback FR 1006)	LP	1982
Florida Punk Groups From The Sixties	(Eva 12026)	LP	198?
Folk Rock E.P.	(Moxie M 1040)	7" EP	1981
Follow That Munster, Vol. 1	(Rock 1101)	LP	1989
Follow That Munster, Vol. 2	(Rock 005)	LP	1992
The Fort Worth Teen Scene - The Major Bill Tapes Vol. 2	(Big Beat WIK 59)	LP	1987
Freakout U.S.A.!	(Sidewalk T 5901)	LP	1967

FILLING THE GAP Comp. LP Box Set.

Title	Label/Cat#	Format	Year
Free Flight (Unreleased Dove Recording Studio Cuts 1964-'69)	(GET HIP GHAS 5012)	2-LP/CD	1998
Friday At The Cage A Go Go - Long Hot Summer	(Westchester 1005)	LP	1965
Frog Records Story, Vol. 1 - Presents Long Island Artists "Sounds Of The 60's"	(Collectables COL-0681)	CD	1996
Frog Records Story, Vol. 2 - Presents Long Island Artists "Sounds Of The 60's"	(Collectables COL-0682)	CD	1996
From The New World	(Strange Things STZ 5004)	LP	1990
Funniest Of Moxie	(Moxie M 1042)	7" EP	198?
Fuzz, Flaykes, And Shakes, Vol. 1 - 60 Miles High	(Bacchus Archives BA1140)	LP/CD	1999
Fuzz, Flaykes, And Shakes, Vol. 2 - The Day Breaks At Dawn	(Bacchus Archives BA1141)	LP/CD	1999
Fuzz, Flaykes, And Shakes, Vol. 3 - Stay Out Of My World	(Bacchus Archives BA1142)	LP/CD	2000
Fuzz, Flaykes, And Shakes, Vol. 4 - Experiment In Color	(Bacchus Archives)	LP/CD	2001
Fuzz, Flaykes, And Shakes, Vol. 5 - Keep Right On Living	(Bacchus Archives)	LP/CD	2001

G

Title	Label/Cat#	Format	Year
Gamma Knee Kappa - The Best In Frat Rock	(Satan SATAN MVI)	LP	1990
Garage Dreams Revisited	(Amber Star ENP 083)	7" EP	1993
Garage Kings	( )	2-LP	199?
Garage Monsters	(Vault VR 3881)	LP	1989
Garage Punk Unknowns, Vol. 1	(Stone Age SA-661)	LP	198?
Garage Punk Unknowns, Vol. 2	(Stone Age SA-662)	LP	198?
Garage Punk Unknowns, Vol. 3	(Stone Age SA-664)	LP	198?
Garage Punk Unknowns, Vol. 4	(Stone Age SA-663)	LP	198?
Garage Punk Unknowns, Vol. 5	(Stone Age SA-665)	LP	198?
Garage Punk Unknowns, Vol. 6	(Stone Age SA-666)	LP	198?
Garage Punk Unknowns, Vol. 7	(Stone Age SA-667)	LP	198?
Garage Punk Unknowns, Vol. 8	(Crypt CRYPT-064)	LP	1995
The Garage Zone, Vol. 1	(Moxie MLP 16)	LP	198?
The Garage Zone, Vol. 2	(Moxie MLP 17)	LP	198?
The Garage Zone, Vol. 3	(Moxie MLP 20)	LP	198?
The Garage Zone, Vol. 4	(Moxie MLP 21)	LP	198?
The Garage Zone Box Set		4-LP	198?

NB: Limited Edition of 250 copies, containing the four Garage Zone compilation albums, plus a bonus 7" EP.

Title	Label/Cat#	Format	Year
Garagelands, Vol. 1	(Strange Things STZ 5003)	LP	1990
Garagelands, Vol. 1 & 2	(Bam Caruso BAMVP 1005 CD)	CD	1998
Garagelands, Vol. 2	(Strange Things STZ5007)	LP	1991
Garagelands Vol. 2	(Bam Caruso BAMVP1006CD)	CD	1999
Gathering At The Depot	(Beta S80-47-1414S)	LP	1970
Gathering Of The Tribe	(Bona Fide BFR 5913)	LP	1982
Gathering Of The Tribe	(TRCD GOTT 1)	CD	19??
Gathering Of The Tribe, Vol. 4 - Pow-Wow: A Gathering Of The Tribes Human Be-In	(Horror Vacui)	LP	1987
Girls In The Garage, Vol. 1	(Romulan UFOX02)	LP	1987
Girls In The Garage, Vol. 2	(Romulan UFOX03)	LP	1987
Girls In The Garage, Vol. 3	(Romulan UFOX04)	LP	198?
Girls In The Garage, Vol. 4	(Romulan UFOX06)	LP	1989
Girls In The Garage, Vol. 5	(Romulan UFOX10)	LP	199?
Girls In The Garage, Vol. 6	(Romulan UFOX12)	LP	199?
Girls In The Garage, Vol. 7	(Romulan UFOX17)	LP	199?
Girls In The Garage, Vol. 8	(Romulan UFOX25)	LP	1998
Girls Of Texas '60s	(Wheel WHS-105)	LP	1988
Glimpses, Vol. 1	(Wellington 201085)	LP	1982
Glimpses, Vol. 2	(Wellington)	LP	1982
Glimpses, Vol. 3	(Wellington (none))	LP	1983
Glimpses, Vol. 4	(Wellington W-1004)	LP	1989
Glimpses, Vol's 1 & 2	(Wellington #16)	CD	19??
The Glory Stompers	(Sidewalk T-5910)	LP	1967
The Goldust Records Story (1965 - 1969) - From The Grass To The Outer Limits	(Collectables COL-CD-0677)	CD	199?
Gone, Vol. 1 - Colour Dreams	(Antar GONE 1)	LP	1985
Gone, Vol. 2 - Basement Wall	(Antar GONE 2)	LP	1985
Good Things Are Happening	(Big Beat CDWIKD 133)	CD	199?
Grab This And Dance!!! - 16 Untold Party Liners!	(Spectra Sound SSR100)	LP	1996
Great Pebbles	(Bomp MSI 13868)	CD	1993
Green Crystal Ties, Vol. 1 - '60s Garage Band Rebels	(Collectables COL-CD-0721)	CD	1998
Green Crystal Ties, Vol. 2	(Collectables COL-CD 0722)	CD	1998
Green Crystal Ties, Vol. 3 - Gloria Meets 96 Tears	(Collectables COL-CD-0723)	CD	1998
Green Crystal Ties, Vol. 4 - Mind-Expanding '60s Psychedelia	(Collectables COL-CD-0724)	CD	1998
Green Crystal Ties, Vol. 5 - Gems From The Garage Band Vaults	(Collectables COL-CD-0725)	CD	1998
Green Crystal Ties, Vol. 6 - Rarities From The Psychedelic Vaults	(Collectables COL-CD-0726)	CD	1998
Green Crystal Ties, Vol. 7 - Mind-Expanding Punk Of The 60s	(Collectables COL-CD-0727)	CD	1998
Green Crystal Ties, Vol. 8 - Stomping Garage Band Legends	(Collectables COL-CD-0728)	CD	1998
Green Crystal Ties, Vol. 9 - The Great Lost Psychedelic Garage Bands	(Collectables COL-CD-0729)	CD	1998
Green Crystal Ties, Vol. 10 - '60s Garage Band Flashback	(Collectables COL-CD-0730)	CD	1998

H

Hallucinations, Psychedelic Underground	(Metronome KMLP-310)	LP	1969
Hang It Out To Dry	(Satan SR1008)	LP/CD	1994
Happy Together - The Very Best Of White Whale Records	(Varese Sarabande VSD-6035)	CD	1999
The Heart Beats And Other Texas Girls Of The 60s - We Had The Beat!	(Cicadelic COL 0711)	CD	1998
High All The Time, Vol. 1	(Morphine)	LP	198?
High All The Time, Vol. 2	( )	LP	199?
Highs In The Mid-Sixties, Vol. 1 - LA '65 Teenage Rebellion	(A.I.P. AIP 1003)	LP	1983
Highs In The Mid-Sixties, Vol. 2 - L.A. '66 Riot On Sunset Strip	(A.I.P. AIP 10004)	LP	1983
Highs In The Mid-Sixties, Vol. 3 - L.A. '67 Mondo Hollywood A Go-Go	(A.I.P. AIP 10005)	LP	1983
Highs In The Mid-Sixties, Vol. 4 - Chicago	(A.I.P. AIP 10006)	LP	1983
Highs In The Mid-Sixties, Vol. 5 - Michigan	(A.I.P. AIP 10007)	LP	1983
Highs In The Mid-Sixties, Vol. 6 - Michigan, Part Two	(A.I.P. AIP 10011)	LP	1984
Highs In The Mid-Sixties, Vol. 7 - The Northwest	(A.I.P. AIP 10012)	LP	1984
Highs In The Mid-Sixties, Vol. 8 - The South	(A.I.P. AIP 10014)	LP	1984
Highs In The Mid-Sixties, Vol. 9 - Ohio	(A.I.P. AIP 10015)	LP	1984
Highs In The Mid-Sixties, Vol. 10 - Wisconsin	(A.I.P. AIP 10017)	LP	1984
Highs In The Mid-Sixties, Vol. 11 - Texas, Part One	(A.I.P. AIP 10019)	LP	1984
Highs In The Mid-Sixties, Vol. 12 - Texas, Part Two	(A.I.P. AIP 10021)	LP	1984
Highs In The Mid-Sixties, Vol. 13 - Texas, Part Three	(A.I.P. AIP 10022)	LP	1984
Highs In The Mid-Sixties, Vol. 14 - The Northwest, Part 2: Out Of The Slime	(A.I.P. AIP 10020)	LP	1986
Highs In The Mid-Sixties, Vol. 15 - Wisconsin, Part 2	(A.I.P. AIP 10025)	LP	1985
Highs In The Mid-Sixties, Vol. 16 - The Northwest, Part 3	(A.I.P. AIP 10024)	LP	1987
Highs In The Mid-Sixties, Vol. 17 - Texas, Part. 4	(A.I.P. AIP 10026)	LP	1986
Highs In The Mid-Sixties, Vol. 18 - Colorado	(A.I.P. AIP 10027)	LP	1986
Highs In The Mid-Sixties, Vol. 19 - Michigan, Part 3	(A.I.P. AIP 10028)	LP	1985
Highs In The Mid-Sixties, Vol. 20 - L.A., Part 4	(A.I.P. AIP 10029)	LP	1985

Title	Label/Cat#	Format	Year
Highs In The Mid-Sixties, Vol. 21 - Ohio, Part 2	(A.I.P. AIP 10030)	LP	1985
Highs In The Mid-Sixties, Vol. 22 - The South, Part 2	(A.I.P. AIP 10031)	LP	1985
Highs In The Mid-Sixties, Vol. 23 - Texas, Part 5	(A.I.P. AIP 10038)	LP	1986
Hillside '66	(Hillside 2520961)	LP	1966
Hillside '67	(Hillside SON 53941/2)	7" EP	1967
Hipsville 29 B.C.	(Kramden KRAN-MAR 101)	LP	1983
Hipsville, Vol. 2	(Kramden KRAN-MAR 102)	LP	1985
Hipsville, Vol. 3	(Kramden KRAN-MAR 103)	LP	1986
The History Of Connecticut Garage Bands In The 60's	(Cicadelic COL-8825)	2-CD	1995
The History Of Michigan Garage Bands In The 60's - The Wheels Four Label Story	(Cicadelic COL-8818)	3-CD	1994
The History Of Northwest Rock, Vol. 1	(Great Northwest Music GNW 4003)	LP	1976
The History Of Northwest Rock, Vol. 2	(Great Northwest Music GNW 4008)	LP	1978
The History Of Northwest Rock, Vol. 3	(Great Northwest Music GNW 4009)	LP	1980
The History Of Northwest Rock, Vol. 4	(Great Northwest Music GNW 4010)	LP	1980
History Of Northwest Rock, Vol. 2 - The Garage Years	(Jerden JRCD7007)	CD	1999
The History Of Northwest Rock, Vol. 3 - Psychedelic Seattle	(Jerden JRCD 7008)	CD	2001
The History Of Texas Garage Bands, Vol. 1 - The Sea Ell Label Story	(Cicadelic COL-8819)	2-CD	1994
The History Of Texas Garage Bands, Vol. 2 - The Orbit Records Story	(Cicadelic COL-0594)	CD	1995
The History Of Texas Garage Bands, Vol. 3 - The AOK Records Story	(Cicadelic COL-0595)	CD	1995
The History Of Texas Garage Bands, Vol. 4 - West Texas Rarities	(Cicadelic COL-0663)	CD	1995
The History Of Texas Garage Bands, Vol. 5 - Corpus Christi Rarities	(Cicadelic COL-0664)	CD	1995
The Hitmakers	(Jerden 7005)	LP	1965
Ho-Dad Hootenanny	(Ho-Dad HO-DAD#40-Oza)	LP	1989
Hoosier Hotshots	(Epilogue no #)	LP	198?
Houston Hallucinations	(Texas Archive Recordings TAR-2)	LP	1982
Houston Post - Nowsounds Groove-In	(Way Back MMLP 66001)	LP	1990
The Human Expression And Other Psychedelic Groups - Your Mind Works In Reverse	(Collectables COL 0713)	CD	1998
Hush Records Story	(Big Beat CDWIKD 154)	CD	199?

I

Title	Label/Cat#	Format	Year
I Can Hear Raindrops	(Worst)	LP	1998
I Love You Gorgo	(Suemi 1090)	LP	1969

NB: Counterfeited in a limited edition of 300, (T 9703) 1997.

Title	Label/Cat#	Format	Year
I Turned Into A Helium Balloon	(Big Beat CDWIKD 130)	CD	19??
I Wanna Come Back From The World Of LSD	(Cicadelic COL-CD-0732)	CD	1999
I Was A Teenage Caveman	(Teenage Caveman TC 1966)	LP	198?
If You're Ready - The Best Of Dunwich... Vol. 2	(Sundazed SC 11019)	CD	1994
IGL Dance Jamboree '66	(Arf! Arf! AA-047/048)	CD	1994
The IGL Rock Story: Part One (1965 - 67)	(Arf! Arf! AA 045)	CD	1994
The IGL Rock Story: Part Two (1967 - 68)	(Arf! Arf! AA 046)	CD	1994
I'm Trippin' Alone	(Spangle LP 002)	LP	1999
Incredible Sound Show Stories, Vol. 7 - Illusions Of Alice In Black	(Dig The Fuzz DIG 013)	LP	1998
Incredible Sound Show Stories, Vol. 8 - Professor Potts Pornographic Projector	(Dig The Fuzz DIG 016)	LP	1997
International Artists Singles Collection	(Decal LIK 53)	LP	1989
In The Beginning	(EMI America SO-17184)	LP	1985
It's A Hard Life	(Lanze STROKE 103)	LP	1999
It's Finkin' Time!	(Beware FINK 1)	LP	1991

J

Title	Label/Cat#	Format	Year
Journey To A Higher Key: The Best Of Sitar Psychedelia, Vol. 1	(Nava Rasa NR 1001)	LP	1998
Journey To The East	(Spangle Records LP 001)	LP	1998

K

Title	Label/Cat#	Format	Year
Kicks & Chicks - Original 1960s Acid Punk	(Eleventh Hour EH 5806)	LP	1989
Killer Cuts	(Guerssen GUESS 004)	LP	1998
Kim Fowley - Outlaw Superman	(Bacchus Archives BA1113)	LP/CD	1997
Kim Fowley - Underground Animal	(Bacchus Archives BA1131)	LP/CD	1999
King Richard And The Knights - Precision! - (Plus Other 60's Albuquerque Groups)	(Cicadelic COL-0684)	CD	1996
Kings Of Pop Music Vol. 1	(Elektra/Vogue SLVLXEK 389)	LP	1968
Kings Of Pop Music Vol. 2	(Elektra/Vogue SLVLXEK 390)	LP	1968

L

Title	Label/Cat#	Format	Year
Leaving It All Behind	(Misty Lane MISTY 049)	LP	2000
Legend City, Vol. 1	(Bacchus Archives BA1150)	LP/CD	2001
Let 'Em Have It! Vol. 1 - 27 Gone Garage Classics - A Truckload Of Gems From Michigan ( )		CD	199?
Let's Dig 'Em Up!!! - 18 Killing Garage Lashes From The Pulverizing '60s	(No Tyme BLP 001)	LP	1998
Let's Dig 'Em Up, Vol. 1	(Notyme)	CD	2000
Let's Dig 'Em Up, Vol. 2 - The Count Game	(No Tyme NTLP003)	LP	2000
Let's Dig 'Em Up, Vol. 3 - Don't Put Me On	(No Tyme NTLP004)	LP	2000
Let's Talk About Girls!	(Bacchus Archives BA0010)	CD	1997
Litter - Rare Tracks	(Eva 12013)	LP	1983
Live At The Funnyfarm	(Scene 200)	LP	1966
Louisiana Punk From The Sixties	(Eva 12051)	LP	198?
Louisiana Punk Groups From The Sixties, Vol. 2	(Eva EVA 12052)	LP	1986
The Louisville Scene	(Rod 'n' Custom 3001)	LP	196?
Lost Generation, Vol. 1	(Dig Up DIG-UP 1)	LP	1998
The Lost Generation, Vol. 2	(Dig-Up! DIG-UP 003)	LP	1999
Love Is A Sad Song, Vol. 1	(Misty Lane MISTY 045)	LP	1998
Love, Peace And Poetry: American Psychedelic Music	(Q.D.K. Media LP 021)	LP/CD	1997
Lycergic Soap	(Stoned Circus)	LP	1995

MAGIC CUBE Comp. CD.

M

Magic Carpet Ride	(Tresors Du Vinyl Ancien & Actuel TVAA 001)	LP	1986
The Magic Cube	(Eva-Tone EVA 116811)	Flexi	1982
The Magic Cube	(El Cid 24)	CD	1999
Marijuana Unknowns	(Stoned THC-001)	LP/CD	1997
Mayhem & Psychosis, Vol. 1	(Roxy XS-LP 100)	LP	198?
Mayhem & Psychosis, Vol. 2	(Roxy XS-LP-101)	LP	1985
Mayhem & Psychosis, Vol. 3	(Roxy XS-LP-104)	LP	198?
Mayhem & Psychosis, Vol. 1	(Laroche L0020 CD)	CD	1998
Mayhem & Psychosis, Vol. 2	(Laroche L0021 CD)	CD	1998
Merry Christmas	(Etiquette ETABL 025)	LP	1965
Michigan Mayhem, Vol. 1	(More Fun Records)	CD	1996
Michigan Brand Nuggets	(Belvedere TY8-7100)	2-LP	198?
Michigan Mixture, Vol. 1	(Clinging Hysteria CHR 1)	LP	1990
Michigan Mixture, Vol. 2	(Clinging Hysteria CHR 2)	LP	1990
Michigan Nuggets	(Belvedere TY8-7100)	CD	199?
Michigan Rocks	(Seeds & Stems Records 77001)	LP	1977
Michigan Rocks, Vol. 2	(Plastic PR 8203)	LP	19??
Midnight To Sixty-Six	(Lanze STROKE 105)	LP	2000
Midwest Garage Band Series - Kansas	(Red Dog RDK/K-001)	CD	1994
The Midwest Vs. Canada	(Unlimited Productions UPLP 1002)	LP	1984
The Midwest Vs. The Rest	(Unlimited Productions UPLP 1001)	LP	1983
Mind Blowers	(White Rabbit WR-LP001)	LP	1983
Mindblowing Encounters Of The Purple Kind	(Dig-Up Records DIG-UP 2)	LP	1998
Mindrocker, Vol. 1	(Line LLP 5115)	LP	1981
Mindrocker, Vol. 2	(Line LLP 5129)	LP	1981
Mindrocker, Vol. 3	(Line LLP 5140)	LP	1982
Mindrocker, Vol. 4	(Line LLP 5147)	LP	1982
Mindrocker, Vol. 5	(Line LLP 5207)	LP	1982
Mindrocker, Vol. 6	(Line OLLP 5212)	LP	1983
Mindrocker, Vol. 7	(Line OLLP 5222 AS)	LP	1983
Mindrocker, Vol. 8	(Line OLLP 5235)	LP	1983
Mindrocker, Vol. 9	(Line LMLP 5265)	LP	1984
Mindrocker, Vol. 10	(Line LMDLP 8021)	2-LP	1984
Mindrocker, Vol. 11	(Line OLLP 5322 AS)	LP	1984
Mindrocker, Vol. 12	(Line IMLP 4.00035 J)	LP	1984
Mindrocker, Vol. 13	(Impact IMLP 4.00036 J)	LP	1986
Mondo Frat Dance Bash A Go Go	(Arf! Arf! AA 051)	CD	1995
Mondo Hollywood	(Tower T-5083)	LP	1967
Money Music - The Hits of Mid-America	(August Records 100)	LP	1967
Monsters Of The Midwest, Vol. 2	(1002)	LP	1985
Monsters Of The Midwest, Vol. 3	(1003)	LP	1987
Monsters Of The Midwest, Vol. 3	(1003)	CD	199?
More Nuggets	(Rhino 75777)		

N

Napoleon Complex	(Vampire)	CD	1999
New England Teen Scene	(Arf! Arf! El Diablo 1002)	CD	1994
New England Teen Scene, Vol. 1	(Moulty MLP-101)	LP	1983
New England Teen Scene, Vol. 2	(Moulty MLP-103)	LP	1984
New England Teen Scene, Vol. 3	(Moulty MLP-104)	LP	1991
New England Teen Scene Unreleased 1965 - 68	(Arf! Arf! AA-060)	CD	1996
New Mexico Punk From The Sixties	(Eva 12047)	LP	198?
The New Sound Of Underground	(Vanguard)	LP	19??
The Night Is So Dark	(Lanze STROKE 108)	LP	2001
No No No	(Arf! Arf! Cheep! Cheep! AACC-076)	CD	1998
Northwest Battle Of The Bands, Vol. 1 - Flash And Crash	(Beat Rocket BR 128)	LP/CD	2000
Northwest Battle Of The Bands, Vol. 2 - Knock You Flat!	(Beat Rocket BR 129)	LP/CD	2000
Northwest Battle Of The Bands, Vol. 1	(Big Beat CDWIKD 204)	CD	2001
Northwest Battle Of The Bands, Vol. 2	(Big Beat CDWIKD 207)	CD	2001
The Northwest Rock Collection, Vol. 1	(Etiquette ETLP 028)	LP	1966
Nuggets - Original Artyfacts From The First Psychedelic Era 1965-1968	(Elektra 7E-2006)	2-LP	1972
Nuggets	(Rhino RNCD 75892)	CD	199?
Nuggets Box	(Rhino R2 75466)	4-CD	1998
Nuggets From Nuggets	(Rhino 76661)	CD	2000
Nuggets, Vol. 1 - The Hits	(Rhino RNLP 025)	LP	1984
Nuggets, Vol. 2 - Punk	(Rhino RNLP 026)	LP	1984
Nuggets, Vol. 3 - Pop	(Rhino RNLP 027)	LP	1984
Nuggets, Vol. 4: Pop Part Two	(Rhino RNLP 028)	LP	1984
Nuggets, Vol. 5: Pop Part Three	(Rhino RNLP 029)	LP	1985
Nuggets, Vol. 6 - Punk, Part II	(Rhino RNLP 030)	LP	1985
Nuggets, Vol. 7 - Early San Francisco	(Rhino RNLP 031)	LP	1985
Nuggets, Vol. 8 - The Northwest	(Rhino RNLP 70032)	LP	198?
Nuggets, Vol. 9 - Acid Rock	(Rhino RNLP 70033)	LP	198?
Nuggets, Vol. 10 - Folk Rock	(Rhino RNLP 70034)	LP	198?
Nuggets, Vol. 11 - Pop, Part Four	(Rhino RNLP 70035)	LP	198?
Nuggets, Vol. 12 - Punk, Part III	(Rhino RNLP 70036)	LP	198?

O

Off The Wall, Vol. 1	(Wreckord Wrack LP-1025)	LP	1982
Off The Wall, Vol. 2 - Skeletons In The Closet	(Wreckord Wrack LP-1301)	LP	1983
Of Hopes And Dreams & Tombstones	( )	LP	199?
Oh Yeah! The Best Of Dunwich Records	(Sundazed SC 11010)	CD	1991
Oil Stains	(db Records db101)	LP	198?
Oil Stains, Vol. 2	(Bone BR 1001)	LP	1988
Only In America	(Arf! Arf! AA-049)	CD	1996
Open Lid EP: 4 Mind-Blowing Tracks From The '60s	(LSD 25)	7" EP	1991
Open Up Yer Door! Vol. 1	(Frog Death, Inc. GLP-101)	LP	1984
Open Up Yer Door, Vol. 2	(Frog Death, Inc. GLP 102)	LP	1987
Out Of Sight	(Decca DL 4751)	LP	1966
Out Of Sight!	(Design DLP-269)	LP	1967

P

Pebbles Box	(Ubik BOXX 1)	5-LP	1989
The Essential Pebbles Collection, Vol. 1	(A.I.P. AIP CD 1058)	2-CD	1997
The Essential Pebbles Collection, Vol. 2	(A.I.P. AIPCD 1060)	2-CD	1998
(The Essential) Pebbles Collection, Vol. 3	(A.I.P. AIP 1064) 2000	2-CD	2000
Pebbles, Vol. 1 - Various Misfits	(A.I.P. AIP CD 5016)	CD	1992
Pebbles, Vol. 2 - Various Hooligans	(A.I.P. AIP CD 5019)	CD	1992
Pebbles, Vol. 3 - The Acid Gallery	(AIP CD 5020)	CD	1992
Pebbles, Vol. 4 - Various Hodads	(AIP CD 5021)	CD	1992
Pebbles, Vol. 5 - Various Morons	(AIP CD 5022)	CD	1992
Pebbles, Vol. 6 - Chicago 1	(AIP CD 5023)	CD	1994
Pebbles, Vol. 7 - Chicago 2	(AIP CD 5024)	CD	1994
Pebbles, Vol. 8 - Southern California 1	(AIP CD 5025)	CD	1996
Pebbles, Vol. 9 - Southern California 2	(AIP CD 5026)	CD	1996
Pebbles, Vol. 10	(AIP CD 5027)	CD	1996
Pebbles, Vol. 1	(East Side Digital ESD 80252)	CD	1989
Pebbles, Vol. 2	(East Side Digital)	CD	19??
Pebbles, Vol. 3	(East Side Digital ESD 80362)	CD	19??
Pebbles, Vol. 4	(East Side Digital ESD 80372)	CD	19??
Pebbles, Vol. 1	(BFD 5016)	LP	1979
Pebbles, Vol. 2	(BFD 5019)	LP	1979
Pebbles, Vol. 3	(BFD 5020)	LP	1979
Pebbles, Vol. 5	(BFD 5022)	LP	1980
Pebbles, Vol. 7	(BFD BFD-5024)	LP	1979
Pebbles, Vol. 8	(BFD BFD-5025)	LP	1979
Pebbles, Vol. 9	(BFD 5026)	LP	1980
Pebbles, Vol. 10	(BFD 5027)	LP	1980
Pebbles, Vol. 11	(A.I.P. AIP 10001)	LP	1983
Pebbles, Vol. 12	(A.I.P. AIP 10002)	LP	1983
Pebbles, Vol. 13	(A.I.P. AIP 10013)	LP	1984

Title	Label/Cat#	Format	Year
Pebbles, Vol. 14	(A.I.P. AIP 10016)	LP	1984
Pebbles, Vol. 16	(A.I.P. AIP 10023)	LP	1985
Pebbles, Vol. 17	(A.I.P. AIP 10032)	LP	1985
Pebbles, Vol. 21	(A.I.P. AIP 10036)	LP	1987
Pebbles, Vol. 22	(A.I.P. AIP 10037)	LP	1987
Penny Arcade, Dunhill Folk Rock, Vol. 2	(Big Beat WIK 77)	LP	1988
Pennsylvania Unknowns	(Time Tunnel TTR 12174-25)	LP	1982
Pepperisms Around The Globe	(Normal Records CD/LP 025)	LP/CD	1998
The Polaris Story	(Bacchus Archives BACD001)	CD	1991
Pop Music Super Hebdo	(Vanguard 519037)	LP	1971
Pop Revolution From The Underground	(CBS SPR 30)	LP	1969
Pride Of Cleveland Past	(NR 15744)	LP	19??
Prisoners Of The Beat	(Chain Gang)	LP	1999
Project Blue, Vol. 1 - Back To The Basements 1965-68	(Project Blue PB 001)	LP	1995
Project Blue, Vol. 2 - Psychedelights 1966-70	(Project Blue PB 002)	LP	1995
Project Blue, Vol. 3 - Nevermore USA Teen Punkers '65 - '67	(Project Blue PB 003)	LP	1996
Project Blue, Vol. 5 - Can't You Stop It Now!	(Destination X PB 05)	LP	1999
Psychedelic Crown Jewels, Vol. 1	(Gear Fab GF 104)	CD	1997
NB: Later reissued on double vinyl (Akarma) 1999.			
Psychedelic Crown Jewels, Vol. 2 - '60s Garage Unknowns	(Gear Fab GF-123)	CD	1999
NB: Later reissued on double vinyl (Akarma) 2000.			
Psychedelic Crown Jewels, Vol. 3	(Gear Fab GF-155)	CD	2000
Psychedelic Disaster Whirl	(Frantic #555/777)	LP	1986
Psychedelic Dream: A Collection of '60s Euphoria	(CBS)	2-LP	1982
The Psychedelic Experience, Vol. 1	(Lysergia LYSERGIA 25-1)	LP	1995
Psychedelic Experience, Vol. 1	(Mystic MYSTIC 6)	CD	199?
The Psychedelic Experience, Vol. 2	(Lysergia)	LP	1999
Psychedelic Experience, Vol. 2	(Mystic MYSTIC 8)	CD	1998
Psychedelic Experience, Vol. 3	(Mystic MYSTIC 10)	CD	1999
Psychedelic Experience, Vol. 4	(Mystic MYSTIC 13)	CD	2000
Psychedelic Frequencies	(Temple PMPCD 027)	CD	1996
Psychedelic Microdots Of The Sixties, Vol. 1 - Orange Sugar And Chocolate	(Sundazed SC 11005)	CD	1989
Psychedelic Microdots Of The Sixties, Vol. 2 - Texas Twisted	(Sundazed SC 11009)	CD	1991
Psychedelic Microdots Of The Sixties, Vol. 3 - My Rainbow Life	(Sundazed SC 11014)	CD	1992
Psychedelic Moods, Vol. 2	(Cicadelic CIC-976)	LP	1987
Psychedelic Moods - Part Two	(Collectables COL-CD-0522)	CD	1993
Psychedelic Patchwork	( )	LP	1986
Psychedelic Perceptions	(Temple TMPCD 025)	CD	1996
Psychedelic Sampler	(Gear Fab GF-100)	CD	1999
The Psychedelic Sixties, Vol. 1	(Cicadelic CICLP-1001)	LP	1982
Psychedelic 60's, Vol. 6	(Cicadelic COL CD 0590)	CD	1994
Psychedelic States - Alabama Vol. 1	(Gear Fab GF-180)	CD	2002
Psychedelic States - Florida Vol. 1	(Gear Fab GF-159)	CD	2000
Psychedelic States - Florida Vol. 2	(Gear Fab GF-167)	CD	2001
Psychedelic States - Florida Vol. 3	(Gear Fab GF-175)	CD	2001
Psychedelic States - Georgia Vol. 1	(Gear Fab GF-177)	CD	2001
Psychedelic States - New York Vol. 1	(Gear Fab GF-185)	CD	2002
Psychedelic Unknowns, Vol. 1	(Calico CAEP 0001)	2 x 7" EP	1979
Psychedelic Unknowns, Vol. 2	(Calico CAEP 0002)	2 x 7" EP	1979
Psychedelic Unknowns, Vol's 1 & 2	(Calico Records PSY 101)	LP	1979
Psychedelic Unknowns, Vol. 3	(Calico CAEP 0003)	LP	1979
NB: Reissued on vinyl (Syn-Sity SS1) 1997 and CD (Scrap 3CD) 1997.			
Psychedelic Unknowns, Vol. 4	(Dayglow Freon DFLP1)	LP	1982
NB: Reissued on vinyl and CD (Scrap 4CD) 1997.			
Psychedelic Unknowns, Vol. 5	(Starglow-Neon SN-00001)	LP	1983
NB: Reissued on vinyl and CD (SCRAP 5 CD) 1998.			
Psychedelic Unknowns, Vol. 6	(Scrap! SCLP 1)	LP	1985
NB: Reissued on vinyl and CD (Scrap SCRAP-6CD) 1998.			
Psychedelic Unknowns, Vol. 7	(Scrap! SCLP 2)	LP	1986
NB: Reissued on vinyl and CD (Scrap SCRAP-7CD) 1998.			
Psychedelic Unknowns, Vol. 8	(Scrap! SCLP 3)	LP	1986
NB: Reissued on vinyl and CD (Scrap SCRAP-8CD) 1998.			
Psychedelic Unknowns, Vol. 9	(Scrap 9CD)	CD	1999
Psychedelic Unknowns, Vol. 11	(Scrap Records SCRAP 11)	LP	199?
Psychedelic Visions	(Temple TMPCD 026)	CD	1997
Psychosis From The 13th Dimension (16 Eccentric Heavy Psych Songs '67 - '73)	(Orange Swirl Recordings OSR-01)	CDR	1998
Psychotic Moose And The Soul Searchers	(Psychotic Moose Records 101)	LP	1982
Psychotic Reaction +10	(King KICP 2167)	CD	1991
Psychotic Reactions	(Planet X LP 04)	LP	1991
Psych-Out	(Sidewalk T-5913)	LP	1967
Punk Ballads Sampler	(Eva EVA 12060)	LP	1987
Punk Classics	(Garageland #13)	CD	19??
Punk Classics, Vol. 1	(Garageband EP 1)	7" EP	198?
Punk Classics, Vol. 2	(Garageband EP 2)	7" EP	1986
Punk Classics, Vol. 3 - Tunes From The Mushroom	(Garageband EP 3)	7" EP	1987
Punk Classics, Vol. 4 - Texas Punk	(Garageband EP 4)	7" EP	1987
Punk Classics, Vol. 5 - Six Wild Covers!	(Garageband EP 5)	7" EP	1987

Q

The Quill Records Story - The Best Of Chicago Garage Bands	(Collectables COL-CD-0662)	CD	1997

R

Title	Label/Cat#	Format	Year
Rampart Records EP	(Bacchus Archives BA05)	7" EP	1995
Realities In Life	( )	LP	2000
Relative Distance - New England Garage Bands	(Stanton Park SRE 002)	LP	198?
Relics, Vol. 1	(dB dB102)	LP	1982
Relics, Vol. 2	(Phorward PR 290)	LP	1990
Relics, Vol's 1 & 2	(RRCD 0008)	CD	1996
Return Of The Young Pennsylvanians	(Bona Fide BFR-16724-66)	LP	1983
Reverberation IV	(Reverberation IV)	CD	199?
Revolution	(United Artists UAS 5185)	LP	1968
Riot City!	(Satan SR-1003)	LP	1985
Riot On Sunset Strip	(Tower T 5065)	LP	1967
Rock A Delics	(Capitol)	LP	19??
Rockbusters - The Blockbusting Label Presents	(EPIC XSB 139673)	LP	1968
Rock 'N' Roll Project - A History Of Rock In Sioux Falls 1965-1967	( )	CD	1996
Roof Garden Jamboree	(IGL 103)	LP	1967
Root '66 - Minnesota Teen Bands (1964-1967) The Frozen Few	(Paraquat TP LP 84)	LP	1984

S

San Francisco Roots	(Vault LP-119)	LP	1968
San Francisco Sampler, Fall 1970	(San Francisco Sound SD 158)	LP	1970
San Francisco Sound - Fifth Pipe Dream	(San Francisco Sound S7-11 680)	LP	1968
NB: Counterfeited on CD (Head 2996) 199? and reissued officialy (San Francisco Sound SFS 11680).			
Scarey Business	(Big Beat CDWIKD 205)	CD	2001
The Scorpio Records Story	(Big Beat CDWIKD 129)	CD	19??
The Scotty Story - Minnesota's Legendary '60s Rock Label!	(Arf! Arf! AA-043)	CD	1993
Scum Of The Earth, Vol. 1	(Killdozer KILL 001)	LP	1984
Scum Of The Earth	(Weed RIZLA 001)	LP	1994
Scum Of The Earth, Vol. 2	(Killdozer KILL 002)	LP	1984
Scum Of The Earth (The Complete Story)	(Sound Stories SS 011)	2-CD	1998
Searching For Love	(Action AR 302)	LP	1999
Seeds Turn To Flowers Turn To Dust	(Bacchus Archives BA 1133)	LP/CD	1999

RIOT ON SUNSET STRIP Comp. LP.

The Seventh Son	(Seventh Son LP 0001)	LP	1999
Shutdown '66	(Ernie Douglas ERN-66)	LP	1991
Sick And Tired	(Lanze Stroke 106)	LP	2000
Signed, D.C.	(Satan SR 666)	LP	1984
Sixties Archive Vol. 1 - The Sound Of The Sixties	(Eva B3)	CD	199?
Sixties Archive Vol. 2 - Texas Punk	(Eva EVA B2)	CD	199?
Sixties Archive Vol. 3 - Louisiana Punk	(Eva EVA B7)	CD	199?
Sixties Archive Vol. 4 - Florida & New Mexico Punk	(Eva B6)	CD	199?
Sixties Archive Vol. 5 - U.S. Punk From The '60s	(Eva EVA B1)	CD	199?
Sixties Archive Vol. 6 - Texas & Michigan Psychedelia	(Eva B8)	CD	199?
Sixties Archive Vol. 7 - Michigan Punk	(Eva B9)	CD	199?
Sixties Archive Vol. 8 - Acid Trip & Heavy Sound For Psychic Minds	(Eva NR 763)	CD	199?
Sixties Choice, Vol. 1	(GMG 12072)	LP	1987
Sixties Choice, Vol. 2	(GMG 12073)	LP	1987
The 60's Choice Collection Of Scarces Garage Records Vol's 1 And 2	(EVA EVA325)	CD	1992
60's Punk E.P., Vol. 1	(Moxie M-1007)	7" EP	198?
60's Punk E.P., Vol. 2	(Moxie M-1013)	7" EP	198?
60's Punk E.P., Vol. 3	(Moxie M 1034)	7" EP	198?
60's Punk E.P., Vol. 4	(Moxie M 1049)	7" EP	1988
Sixties Rebellion, Vol. 1 - The Garage	(Way Back MMLP 66006)	LP	1993
Sixties Rebellion, Vol. 2 - The Barn	(Way Back MMLP 66007)	LP	1993
Sixties Rebellion, Vol's 1 & 2 - The Barn / The Garage	(Way Back MMCD 66006/7)	LP/CD	1993
Sixties Rebellion, Vol. 3 - The Auditorium	(Way Back MMLP 66008)	LP/CD	1993
Sixties Rebellion, Vol. 4 - The Go-Go	(Way Back MMLP 66009)	LP/CD	1993
Sixties Rebellion, Vol. 5 - The Cave	(Way Back MMLP 66010)	LP/CD	1993
Sixties Rebellion, Vol. 6 - The Biker	(Way Back MMLP 66011)	LP/CD	1993
Sixties Rebellion, Vol. 7 - The Backyard Patio	(Way Back MMLP 66012)	LP/CD	1994
Sixties Rebellion, Vol. 8 - Mondo Mutiny #1: The Love	(Way Back MMLP 65001)	LP/CD	1994
Sixties Rebellion, Vol. 9 - The Nightclub	(Way Back MMLP 66013)	LP/CD	1995
Sixties Rebellion, Vol. 11 - Psychedelia #1: Hydrogen Atom	(Way Back MMLP 67001)	LP/CD	1994
Sixties Rebellion, Vol. 12 - Demented	(Way Back MMLP 66014)	LP/CD	1995
Sixties Rebellion, Vol. 14 - The Basement	(Way Back MMLP 66015)	LP/CD	1996
Sixties Rebellion, Vol. 15 - Psychedelia #2: The Apple-Glass Syndrom	(Way Back MMLP 67002)	LP/CD	1996
Sixties Rebellion, Vol. 16 - The Living Room	(Way Back MMLP 66016)	LP/CD	1999
Sixties Years, Vol. 2 - French 60's EP Collection	(Magic 523302)	CD	1996
'69 Love-In	(Collectables COL-CD-0514)	CD	1995
Slowly Growing Insane	(Timothy's Brain TB 101)	CD	199?
Soma Records Story, Vol. 1 - Shake It For Me!	(Beat Rocket BR 111)	LP	1998
Soma Records Story, Vol. 2 - Bright Lights, Big City!	(Beat Rocket BR 112)	LP	1998
Soma Records Story, Vol. 3 - A Man's Gotta Be A Man!	(Beat Rocket BR 113)	LP	1998
Someone To Love: The Birth Of The San Francisco Sound	(Big Beat CDWIKD 170)	CD	199?
Songs Of Faith And Inspiration	(Orange Swirl OSR 02)	CDR	1998
Songs We Taught The Fuzztones	(Way Back MMLP 66002)	2-LP/2-CD	1990
Son Of The Gathering Of The Tribe	(Bona Fide BF 20183)	LP	1983
Sound Of The Sixties	(Eva EVA 12021-22)	2-LP	198?
Sounds Of The Sixties San Francisco, Vol. 1	(Phantom PRS-1004)	LP	1985
Sound Of The Sixties: San Francisco Part 2	(Phantom PLP-1005)	LP	1985
The Sound Of Young Sacramento	(Big Beat CDWIKD 195)	CD	2000
Soundsville!	(Design DLP-187)	LP	1965
The Stars That Play With Dead Jimi's Dice	(Twisted Village TW-1012)	LP	1993
Stompin' Time Again!	(X-Bat 5866)	CD	2000
Sundazed Sampler, Vol. 1	(Sundazed SC PRO 01)	CD	1993
Sundazed Sampler, Vol. 2	(Sundazed)	CD	1998
S.V.R. Rock Hits Of The Sixties	(SVR SVR 42441)	LP	1985
Swamp Rats vs. Unrelated Segments	(Eva EVA 12058)	LP	198?

T

Take The Brain Train To The Third Eye: Bud Mathis' Sunset Trip	(Bacchus Archives BA1147)	LP/CD	2000
Teenage Shutdown, Vol. 1 - Jump, Jive And Harmonize	(Teenage Shutdown TS6601)	LP/CD	1998
Teenage Shutdown, Vol. 2 - You Treated Me Bad!	(Teenage Shutdown TS 6602)	LP/CD	1998
Teenage Shutdown, Vol. 3 - Things Been Bad	(Teenage Shutdown TS 6603)	LP/CD	1998
Teenage Shutdown, Vol. 4 - I'm A No-Count	(Teenage Shutdown TS 6604)	LP/CD	1998
Teenage Shutdown, Vol. 5 - Nobody To Love	(Teenage Shutdown TS 6605)	LP/CD	1998
Teenage Shutdown, Vol. 6 - I'm Down Today	(Teenage Shutdown TS-6606)	LP/CD	1998
Teenage Shutdown, Vol. 7 - Get A Move On!!	(Teenage Shutdown TS-6607)	LP/CD	1998
Teenage Shutdown, Vol. 8 - She'll Hurt You In The End	(Teenage Shutdown TS-6608)	LP/CD	1998
Teenage Shutdown, Vol. 9 - Teen Jangler Blowout!	(Teenage Shutdown TS-6609)	LP/CD	1998
Teenage Shutdown, Vol. 10 - The World Ain't Round, It's Square!	(Teenage Shutdown TS-6610)	LP/CD	1998
Teenage Shutdown, Vol. 11 - Move It!	(Crypt TS-6611)	LP/CD	1999
Teenage Shutdown, Vol. 12 - No Tease...	(Teenage Shutdown TS6612)	LP/CD	2000

Title	Catalog	Format	Year
Teenage Shutdown, Vol. 13 - I'm Gonna Stay	(Teenage Shutdown TS6613)	LP/CD	2000
Teenage Shutdown, Vol. 14 - Howlin' For My Darlin'	(Teenage Shutdown TS6614)	LP/CD	2000
Teenage Shutdown, Vol. 15 - She's A Pest!	(Teenage Shutdown TS6615)	LP/CD	2000
Terry Lee Show WMCK	(Keystone K111541-45)	LP	1980
Texas Flashback, Vol. 1 - Dallas	(Texas Archive Recordings TAR 5)	LP	1986
Texas Flashback (The Best Of)	( )	CD	199?
Texas Flashbacks, Vol. 1	(Antar TEXAS 1)	LP	199?

NB: Reissue of Flashback, Vol. 1, later issued on CD (Way Back MMCD 66061) 199?.

Title	Catalog	Format	Year
Texas Flashbacks, Vol. 2	(Antar TEXAS 2)	LP	1986

NB: Reissue of Flashback, Vol. 2, later issued on CD (Way Back MMCD 66062) 199?.

Title	Catalog	Format	Year
Texas Flashback, Vol. 3	(Antar TEXAS 3)	LP	1986

NB: Reissue of Flashback, Vol. 3, later issued on CD (Way Back MMCD 66063) 1998.

Title	Catalog	Format	Year
Texas Flashback, Vol. 4	(Antar TEXAS 4)	LP	1986

NB: Reissue of Flashback, Vol. 4.

Title	Catalog	Format	Year
Texas Flashback, Vol. 5	(Antar TEXAS 5)	LP	1986

NB: Reissue of Flashback, Vol. 5.

Title	Catalog	Format	Year
Texas Music, Vol. 3 - Garage Bands And Psychedelia	(Rhino R2 71783)	CD	1994
Texas Psychedelia From The Sixties	(Eva 12057)	LP	198?
Texas Punk From The Sixties	(Eva 12053)	LP	198?
Texas Punk Groups From The Sixties	(Eva 12006)	LP	198?
Texas Punk: 1966, Vol. 1	(Cicadelic Ciclp-966)	LP	1984
Texas Punk: 1966, Vol. 2 - Music From...The Outer Limits!	(Cicadelic Ciclp-997)	LP	1984
Texas Punk, Vol. 3 - The Sights And Sounds Of An Era	(Cicadelic CIC-995)	LP	1984
Texas Punk, Vol. 4 - Dallas Psychedelic Gold From The 60's	(Cicadelic CICLP-994)	LP	1984
Texas Punk, Vol. 5 - Journey To Pharaoh's Valley With The Headstones!	(Cicadelic CICLP-991)	LP	1985
Texas Punk, Vol. 6 - Dallas, 1966	(Cicadelic CIC 981)	LP	1986
Texas Punk, Vol. 7 - Featuring The Briks And The Chaparrals	(Cicadelic CIC-979)	LP	1986
Texas Punk, Vol. 8 - Featuring The Briks And The Basement Wall	(Cicadelic CIC-978)	LP	1986
Texas Punk, Vol. 9	(Cicadelic CIC-971)	LP	1987
Texas Punk, Vol. 10 - With S.J. And The Crossroads!	(Cicadelic CIC-970)	LP	1987
Texas Reverberations	(Texas Archive Recordings TAR-1)	LP	1982
Thee Unheard Of	(Paradise Lost PLR 001)	LP	1989
Then And Now, Vol. 1	(San Francisco Sound SFS-03931)	CD	199?
Then And Now, Vol. 2	(San Francisco Sound SFS-09932)	CD	199?
There Goes The Neighborhood, Vol. 1	(Collectables COL-CD-0508)	CD	1992
There Goes The Neighborhood, Vol. 3	(Cicadelic COL-CD-0542)	CD	1993
The Thingies Have Arrived!!	(Collectables COL-CD-0716)	CD	1998
Things Go Better With Coke	(Coca-Cola Company AT-134)	CD	19??
Thirteen O'Clock Flight To Psychedelphia	(Collectables COL-CD-0714)	CD	1998
Three O'Clock Merrian Webster Time	(Cicadelic CICLP-999)	LP	1982
30 Seconds Before The Calico Wall	(Arf! Arf! AA-050)	CD	1995
Time Won't Change My Mind	(Lanze STROKE 104)	LP	1999
Tobacco A-Go-Go, Vol. 1	(Blue Mold BMLP-101)	LP	1984
Tobacco A-Go-Go, Vol. 2	(Blue Mold BMLP-103)	LP	1987
Top Teen Bands Vol. 1	(Bud-Jet BJ-311)	LP	1965/6
Top Teen Bands Vol. 2	(Bud-Jet BJ-312)	LP	1966
Top Teen Bands Vol. 3	(Bud-Jet BJ-313)	LP	1966
Tougher Than Stains	(London Fog LF1)	LP	1995
Trash Box	(Hit Records CD BOXX 1)	5-CD	1997?
The Tucson Sound 1960-68 - Think Of The Good Times	(Bacchus Archives BA 002 LP)	LP	198?
Turds On A Bum Ride, Vol. 1	(Anthology ANT 1.22)	2-LP	1991
Turds On A Bum Ride, Vol. 2	(Anthology ANT 2.22)	2-LP	1991
Turds On A Bum Ride, Vol. 1 & 2	(Habla HBCD 2102-1/2)	2-CD	1989

NB: Reissued (Anthology) 199?.

Title	Catalog	Format	Year
Turds On A Bum Ride, Vol. 3	(Anthology ANT 3.11)	CD	1991
Turds On A Bum Ride, Vol. 4	(Anthology ANT 22.11)	CD	199?
Turds On A Bum Ride, Vol. 5	(Anthology ANT 32.11)	CD	199?
Turds On A Bum Ride, Vol. 6	(Anthology ANT. 33.11)	CD	199?
12 Groovy Hits, 12 Florida Bands	(Tener 154)	LP	1966
20 Great Hits Of The 60's	(Cascade DROP 1007)	LP	1984
Tymes Gone By	(Action AR 301)	LP	1998

U

Title	Catalog	Format	Year
Undersound Uppersoul	(Stateside 2C162 92101/2)	2-LP	1970

V

Valley Of The Son Of The Gathering Of The Tribe	(GOTT 3)	LP	1985
Victims Of Circumstances, Vol. 1	(Stop It Baby! STOP 06)	LP	1989
Victims Of Circumstance, Vol. 2	(Showcase Bonanza SHOW 9101)	LP	199?
Vile Vinyl, Vol. 1	(High Noon HIN LP 001)	LP	1985
Vile Vinyl, Vol. 2	(High Noon HIN LP 002)	LP	1985
Vile Vinyl	(Tinfoil Daffodil)	CD	2000

W

Washington D.C. Garage Band Greats!	(Cicadelic CIC-986)	LP	1986
Wavy Gravy Vol. 1 - For Adult Enthusiasts	(Beware 001)	LP	198?

NB: Reissued on CD with some differences (Beware CD 001/999) 199?.

Title	Catalog	Format	Year
Wavy Gravy Vol. 2 - Psycho Serenade	(Beware 999)	LP	198?

NB: Reissued on CD with some differences (Beware CD 002) 19??.

Title	Catalog	Format	Year
The West Coast East Side Sound, Vol. 1	(Varese-Saraband)	CD	1999
The West Coast East Side Sound, Vol. 2	(Varese-Saraband 6018)	CD	1999
The West Coast East Side Sound, Vol. 3	(Varese-Saraband)	CD	1999
The West Coast East Side Sound, Vol. 4	(Varese-Saraband)	CD	1999
West Coast Love-In	(Vault LP-113)	LP	1967
What A Way To Come Down	(Big Beat CDWIKD 173)	CD	1997
What A Way To Die	(Satan SR 1313)	LP	1983
When The Time Runs Out (Minnesota vs Michigan)	(Reverendo Moon RMR 002)	LP	1995
Where It's At: 'Live' At The Cheetah	(Audio Fidelity AFSD 6168)	LP	1966
The Wild Angels	(Tower T-5043)	LP	1966
Wild! Wild!! Wild!!!	(Norton 45-032)	7" EP	1995
WONE - The Dayton Scene	(Prism PR-1966)	LP	1966
World Of Acid	(PW 4-1/2)	LP	199?

Y

Title	Catalog	Format	Year
Ya Gotta Have... Moxie, Vol. 1	(AIP/Moxie AIPCD 1059)	2-CD	1998
Ya Gotta Have Moxie, Vol. 2	(AIP AIPCD 1062)	2-CD	1999
Yeah Yeah Yeah	(Arf! Arf! Cheep! Cheep! AACC - 075)	CD	1999
You Ain't Gonna Bring Me Down To My Knees - The Stratford / Right Records Story (1965 - 1969)	(Collectables COL-CD-0676)	CD	1996

Z

Title	Catalog	Format	Year
Zabriski Point	(MGM 2315 002)	LP	1970

SUNDAZED Catalogue:

Full Price Compact Discs:

Artist	Title	Catalog No.	Year
ALEXANDER SKIP SPENCE	Oar	SUN-CD-11075	1999
BEAU BRUMMELS	SAN FRAN SESSIONS	SUN-CD-11033	1996
BELAIRS	VOLCANIC ACTION!	SUN-CD-11100	2001
BEST OF DUNWICH	Vol. 2	SUN-CD-11019	1994
BEST OF DUNWICH RECORDS	Vol.1	SUN-CD-11010	1993
BOBBY PATTERSON	Soul Is My Music: The Best Of	SUN-CD-11105	2003
BONNIWELL MUSIC MACHINE	Ignition	SUN-CD-11038	2000
BOYS NEXT DOOR	The Boys Next Door	SUN-CD-11061	1999
BRUCE & TERRY	The Best Of . . .	SUN-CD-11052	1999
BRYAN MACLEAN	Candy'S Waltz	SUN-CD-11076	2000
BRYAN MACLEAN	Ifyoubelievein	SUN-CD-11051	1997
BUCK OWENS & HIS BUCKAROOS	Carnegie Hall Concert	SUN-CD-11090	2000
BUCKINGHAMS	In One Ear & Gone Tomorrow	SUN-CD-11074	1999
BUCKINGHAMS	Time & Charges/Portraits	SUN-CD-11073	1999
BYRDS	Preflyte	SUN-CD-11116	2001
C.A. QUINTET	Trip Thru Hell	SUN-CD-11021	1995
CANTERBURY FAIR	Canterbury Fair	SUN-CD-11064	1999
CHAD & JEREMY	Before And After	SUN-CD-11117	2002
CHAD & JEREMY	Distant Shores	SUN-CD-11068	2000
CHAD & JEREMY	Of Cabbages And Kings	SUN-CD-11118	2002
CHALLENGERS	Tidal Wave	SUN-CD-11024	1996
CHESTERFIELD KINGS	Where The Action Is!	SUN-CD-13	1999
CHOIR	Choir Practice	SUN-CD-11018	1994
CHUCK WILLIS	Chuck Willis Wails! 1951-1956	SUN-CD-11122	2003
CLEE-SHAYS	The Dynamic Guitar Sounds Of	SUN-CD-11049	1999
CYRKLE	Neon	SUN-CD-11109	2001
CYRKLE	Red Rubber Ball	SUN-CD-11108	2001
CYRKLE	The Minx Soundtrack	SUN-CD-11106	2003
DAISY/TIGER RECORDS STORY	Various Artists	SUN-CD-11080	2003
DINO, DESI & BILLY	Rebel Kind - The Best of	SUN-CD-11034	1996
DON RICH & THE BUCKAROOS	Country Pickin' The Don Rich Anthology	SUN-CD-11091	2000
DOTTI HOLMBERG	Sometimes Happy Times	SUN-CD-11114	2002
DR. WEST'S MEDECINE SHOW & JUNK BAND	Euphoria! The Best Of…	SUN-CD-11070	1998
DRIVING STUPID	Horror Asparagus Stories	SUN-CD-11111	2002
E-TYPES	Introducing	SUN-CD-11026	1996
FANTASTIC BAGGYS	Anywhere The Girls Are!	SUN-CD-11084	2000
FIVE AMERICANS	Best Of The Five Americans	SUN-CD-11107	2003
FUZZTONES	Flashbacks	SUN-CD-11045	1997
GANTS, THE	Roadrunner! The Best Of	SUN-CD-11078	2000
GENE VINCENT	Ain't That Too Much!	SUN-CD-12004	1994
GENTLE SOUL	Gentle Soul	SUN-CD-11123	2003
GET LOW DOWN! The Soul Of NOLA	Various Artists	SUN-CD-11094	2001
GRAM PARSONS	Another Side Of This Life:The Lost Rec.	SUN-CD-11092	2000
GREAT SCOTS	Great Lost Great Scots Album	SUN-CD-11048	1997
GREAT SOCIETY	Born To Be Burned	SUN-CD-11027	1996
GUESS WHO	Shakin' All Over	SUN-CD-11113	2001
H.P. LOVECRAFT	Live at the Fillmore - 1968	SUN-CD-11008	1993
HAL BLAINE	Deuces, "T's," Roadsters & Drums	SUN-CD-11101	2001
HOT ROD CITY!	Various Artists	SUN-CD-11025	1996
IAN WHITCOMB	You Turn Me On / Mod, Mod Music Hall - 2 on 1!	SUN-CD-11044	1997
IDES OF MARCH	Ideology	SUN-CD-11067	2000
JAMES & BOBBY PURIFY	Shake A Tail Feather! The Best Of	SUN-CD-11096	2002
JAN & DEAN	Save For A Rainy Day	SUN-CD-11035	1996
JERRY COLE & HIS SPACEMEN	Power Surf! The Best Of...	SUN-CD-11072	1999
JOSEFUS	Dead Man/Get Off My Case	SUN-CD-11066	1999
KNICKERBOCKERS	Great Lost Album!	SUN-CD-11012	1992
KNICKERBOCKERS	Knickerbockerism!	SUN-CD-11040	1997
LEAVES	The Leaves Are Happening	SUN-CD-11058	2000
LEE DORSEY	Ride Your Pony	SUN-CD-11086	2000
LEE DORSEY	The New Lee Dorsey	SUN-CD-11087	2000
LINK WRAY	Slinky!	SUN-CD-11098	2002
LOVE GENERATION	Love And Sunshine: Best Of	SUN-CD-11120	2002
LUV'D ONES	Truth Gotta Stand	SUN-CD-11050	1999
METERS	Kickback	SUN-CD-11081	2001
MIGHTY SAM	Papa True Love	SUN-CD-11083	2000
MILLENNIUM	Magic Time: Complete Recordings	SUN-CD-11102	2001
MOJO MEN	Whys Ain't Supposed To Be	SUN-CD-11028	1996
MOVIEES	Become One Of Them	SUN-CD-11099	2000
MU	MU	SUN-CD-11037	1997
MUSIC EXPLOSION	Little Bit O'Soul: The Best Of	SUN-CD-11119	2002
MUSIC MACHINE	Beyond The Garage	SUN-CD-11030	1996
NEANDERTHALS	Modern Stone Age Family!	SUN-CD-11071	1999
NEIGHB'RHOOD CHILDR'N	Long Years In Space	SUN-CD-11041	1997
NEW COLONY SIX	At The River's Edge	SUN-CD-11016	1993
NEW DIMENSIONS	The Best Of!	SUN-CD-11036	1996
O'JAYS	The Bell Sessions 1967-1969	SUN-CD-11110	2002
OSCAR TONEY, JR.	For Your Precious Love	SUN-CD-11093	2001
PAUL REVERE & THE RAIDERS	Mojo Workout!	SUN-CD-11097	2000
PSYCH. MICRODOTS OF 60's VOL. 1	Orange, Sugar & Chocolate	SUN-CD-11005	1993
PSYCH. MICRODOTS OF 60's VOL. 2	Texas Twisted	SUN-CD-11009	1993
PSYCH. MICRODOTS OF 60's VOL. 3	My Rainbow Life	SUN-CD-11014	1993
PYRAMIDS	Penetration! - The Best of!	SUN-CD-11023	1995
REVELS	Intoxica!!! The Best Of	SUN-CD-11020	1996
ROCKIN' IN THE FARMHOUSE!	Original Rockabilly & Chicken Bop Vol. 2	SUN-CD-12002	1992
RONNY & THE DAYTONAS	G.T.O. The Best Of...	SUN-CD-11046	1997
SAGITTARIUS	Present Tense	SUN-CD-11053	1997
SHADOWS OF KNIGHT	Raw 'n Alive at The Cellar 1966	SUN-CD-11013	1992
SHAKIN' APOSTLES	Frontier A Go-Go	SUN-CD-8370	2002
SHAKIN' APOSTLES	Medicine Show	SUN-CD-8368	1999
SHAKIN' APOSTLES	Too Hot For Snakes	SUN-CD-8369	2000
SOLOMON BURKE	Proud Mary	SUN-CD-11079	2000
SOUTHWEST F.O.B.	Smell Of Incense	SUN-CD-11060	1998
SPENCER DAVIS GROUP	Gimme Some Lovin'	SUN-CD-11103	2001
SPENCER DAVIS GROUP	I'm A Man	SUN-CD-11104	2001

BEAU BRUMMELS - San Fran Sessions CD.

Artist	Title	Catalog	Year
STILLROVEN	Cast Thy Burden Upon The	SUN-CD-11029	1996
TORNADOES	Beyond The Surf	SUN-CD-11039	1999
TRASHMEN	Bird Call! The Twin City Stomp Of	SUN-CD-11022	1999
TRASHMEN	Great Lost Album '64-'66!	SUN-CD-11007	1993
TRASHMEN	Live Bird '65-'66!	SUN-CD-11006	1993
TRASHMEN	Tube City! - The Best of!	SUN-CD-11011	1992
TWENTIETH CENTURY ZOO	Thunder On A Clear Day	SUN-CD-11063	1999
VEJTABLES	Feel ... The Vejtables	SUN-CD-11031	1996
WAIL MAN, WAIL!	Original Rockabilly & Chicken Bop Vol. 3	SUN-CD-12003	1993
WE THE PEOPLE	Mirror Of Our Minds	SUN-CD-11056	1998
WENDY & BONNIE	Genesis	SUN-CD-11089	2001
WEST COAST POP ART EXP. BAND	Volume One	SUN-CD-11047	1997
WILD MEN RIDE WILD GUITARS!	Original Rockabilly & Chicken Bop Vol. 1	SUN-CD-12001	1993
YELLOW BALLOON	Yellow Balloon	SUN-CD-11069	1999

Mid-Line Compact Discs:

Artist	Title	Catalog	Year
AFTERGLOW	Afterglow	SUN-CD-6074	1995
AL CASEY	Surfin' Hootenanny	SUN-CD-6114	1996
BARBARIANS	Are You A Boy Or Are You A Girl	SUN-CD-6153	1993
BEAU BRUMMELS	Introducing The Beau Brummels	SUN-CD-6039	1995
BEAU BRUMMELS	Volume Two	SUN-CD-6040	1995
BOW STREET RUNNERS	Bow Street Runners	SUN-CD-6112	1996
BOX TOPS	Cry Like A Baby	SUN-CD-6159	1993
BOX TOPS	Dimensions	SUN-CD-6161	1993
BOX TOPS	Non Stop	SUN-CD-6160	1993
BOX TOPS	The Letter/Neon Rainbow	SUN-CD-6158	1994
BRUCE JOHNSTON	Surfin' 'Round The World!	SUN-CD-6100	1997
BUCK OWENS	Before You Go/No One But You	SUN-CD-6048	1995
BUCK OWENS	Buck Owens	SUN-CD-6042	1995
BUCK OWENS	Christmas Shopping	SUN-CD-6163	1994
BUCK OWENS	Christmas w/Buck Owens...	SUN-CD-6162	1996
BUCK OWENS	I Don't Care	SUN-CD-6046	1995
BUCK OWENS	I've Got A Tiger By The Tail	SUN-CD-6047	1995
BUCK OWENS	In Japan!	SUN-CD-6103	1997
BUCK OWENS	It Takes People Like You To Make...	SUN-CD-6105	1997
BUCK OWENS	On The Bandstand	SUN-CD-6044	1995
BUCK OWENS	Open Up Your Heart	SUN-CD-6051	1995
BUCK OWENS	Roll Out The Red Carpet	SUN-CD-6050	1995
BUCK OWENS	Sings Harlan Howard	SUN-CD-6101	1997
BUCK OWENS	Sings Tommy Collins	SUN-CD-6102	1997
BUCK OWENS	The Instrumental Hits Of Buck Owens	SUN-CD-6049	1995
BUCK OWENS	Together Again/My Heart Skips A Beat	SUN-CD-6045	1995
BUCK OWENS	You're For Me	SUN-CD-6043	1995
BUCK OWENS	Your Tender Loving Care	SUN-CD-6104	1997
BUCKINGHAMS	Kind Of A Drag	SUN-CD-6126	1995
CHALLENGERS	Go Sidewalk Surfing!	SUN-CD-6091	1996
CHALLENGERS	K-39	SUN-CD-6032	1996
CHALLENGERS	Surfbeat!	SUN-CD-6029	1996
CHALLENGERS	Surfing Around World /On The Move	SUN-CD-6031	1996
CHALLENGERS	Surfing With The Challengers	SUN-CD-6030	1997
CHRIS RUSH	There's No Bones In Ice Cream	SUN-CD-6134	1995
CLYDE McPHATTER	A Shot Of Rhythm & Blues	SUN-CD-6165	1995
CORNELLS	Beach Bound!	SUN-CD-6061	1996
CRESTS	Isn't It Amazing!	SUN-CD-6076	1996
CRESTS	Sing All The Biggies	SUN-CD-6075	1996
CROSSFIRES	Out Of Control!	SUN-CD-6062	1995
CRYAN' SHAMES	Scratch In The Sky	SUN-CD-6187	1996
CRYAN' SHAMES	Sugar & Spice	SUN-CD-6186	1996
CRYAN' SHAMES	Synthesis	SUN-CD-6188	1996
CURT BOETTCHER	There's An Innocent Face	SUN-CD-6184	1995
DUPREES	Have You Heard	SUN-CD-6073	1996
DUPREES	You Belong To Me	SUN-CD-6072	1996
ELVIN BISHOP	Elvin Bishop Group	SUN-CD-6189	1995
ELVIN BISHOP	Feel It!	SUN-CD-6190	1995
ELVIN BISHOP	Rock My Soul	SUN-CD-6191	1995
FAPARDOKLY	Fapardokly	SUN-CD-6059	1995
FIREBALLS	Gunshot!	SUN-CD-6090	1996
FIREBALLS	The Fireballs	SUN-CD-6088	1996
FIREBALLS	Torquay	SUN-CD-6089	1996
FLAMIN' GROOVIES	Supersnazz	SUN-CD-6130	1996
FLAMIN' GROOVIES	Supersneakers	SUN-CD-6077	1996
GANDALF	Gandalf	SUN-CD-6152	1996
GESTURES	Gestures	SUN-CD-6079	1996
H.M.S BOUNTY	Things	SUN-CD-6094	1997
HARPERS BIZARRE	4	SUN-CD-6179	1996
HARPERS BIZARRE	Anything Goes	SUN-CD-6177	1996
HARPERS BIZARRE	Feelin' Groovy	SUN-CD-6176	1996
HARPERS BIZARRE	The Secret Life Of...	SUN-CD-6178	1997
HOLLIES	Dear Eloise/King Midas	SUN-CD-6123	1997
HOLLIES	Evolution	SUN-CD-6122	1996
HOLLIES	Moving Finger	SUN-CD-6125	1996
HUELYN DUVALL	Is You Is, Or Is You Ain't?	SUN-CD-6083	1996
JIMMY GILMER & THE FIREBALLS	Sugar Shack	SUN-CD-6154	1996
JOHN ENTWISTLE	Smash Your Head Against The Wall	SUN-CD-6116	1997
JOHN ENTWISTLE	Whistle Rymes	SUN-CD-6117	1997
KENNELMUS	Folkstone Prism	SUN-CD-6129	1996
KINGSMEN	In Person	SUN-CD-6004	1993
KINGSMEN	On Campus	SUN-CD-6014	1994
KINGSMEN	Since We've Been Gone	SUN-CD-6027	1994
KINGSMEN	Up And Away!	SUN-CD-6015	1994
KINGSMEN	Volume 2	SUN-CD-6005	1993
KINGSMEN	Volume 3	SUN-CD-6006	1993
KNICKERBOCKERS	Jerk & Twine Time	SUN-CD-6010	1993
KNICKERBOCKERS	Lies	SUN-CD-6011	1993
LOVE EXCHANGE	The Love Exchange	SUN-CD-6113	2001
MAGICIANS	An Invitation To Cry..The Best Of...	SUN-CD-6133	1996
MARKETTS	Out Of Limits	SUN-CD-6085	1996
MAZE	Armageddon	SUN-CD-6060	1995
MEL & TIM	Good Guys Only Win In The Movies	SUN-CD-6078	1996
METERS	Cabbage Alley	SUN-CD-6168	1997
METERS	Fire On The Bayou	SUN-CD-6167	1997
METERS	Look-Ka Py Py	SUN-CD-6147	1999
METERS	New Directions	SUN-CD-6171	1997
METERS	Rejuvenation	SUN-CD-6169	1997
METERS	Struttin'	SUN-CD-6148	1999

BRYAN MACLEAN - If You Believe In CD.

Artist	Title	Catalog	Year
METERS	The Meters	SUN-CD-6146	1998
METERS	Trick Bag	SUN-CD-6170	1999
MITCH RYDER	Breakout!	SUN-CD-6008	1993
MITCH RYDER	All Hits!	SUN-CD-6033	1996
MITCH RYDER	Sock It To Me	SUN-CD-6009	1993
MITCH RYDER	Take A Ride	SUN-CD-6007	1993
MONTAGE	Montage	SUN-CD-6172	1998
MUSIC EMPORIUM	Music Emporium	SUN-CD-6166	1999
NANCY SINATRA	Boots	SUN-CD-6052	1995
NANCY SINATRA	Country, My Way	SUN-CD-6056	1996
NANCY SINATRA	How Does That Grab You?	SUN-CD-6053	1995
NANCY SINATRA	Movin' With Nancy	SUN-CD-6057	1996
NANCY SINATRA	Nancy	SUN-CD-6058	1996
NANCY SINATRA	Nancy In London	SUN-CD-6054	1995
NANCY SINATRA	Sugar	SUN-CD-6055	1995
NEON PHILHARMONIC	The Moth Confesses	SUN-CD-6084	1996
NEW COLONY SIX	Breakthrough	SUN-CD-6149	1998
NEW COLONY SIX	Colonization!	SUN-CD-6026	1994
NEXT MORNING	The Next Morning	SUN-CD-6150	1999
ORIGINAL SURFARIS	Bombora!	SUN-CD-6063	1995
PAUL REVERE & THE RAIDERS	Alias Pink Puzz	SUN-CD-6138	1999
PAUL REVERE & THE RAIDERS	Goin' To Memphis	SUN-CD-6136	2002
PAUL REVERE & THE RAIDERS	Hard 'N' Heavy	SUN-CD-6137	1999
PAUL REVERE & THE RAIDERS	Just Like Us	SUN-CD-6127	2002
PAUL REVERE & THE RAIDERS	Midnight Ride	SUN-CD-6135	2000
PAUL REVERE & THE RAIDERS	Revolution!	SUN-CD-6096	1996
PAUL REVERE & THE RAIDERS	Something Happening	SUN-CD-6097	1996
PAUL REVERE & THE RAIDERS	The Spirit of '67	SUN-CD-6095	1996
RASCALS	Island Of Real	SUN-CD-6132	2000
RASCALS	Peaceful World	SUN-CD-6131	2000
REMAINS	A Session With The Remains	SUN-CD-6069	1996
RHYTHM ROCKERS	Soul Surfin'	SUN-CD-6028	1994
RIP CHORDS	Hey Little Cobra	SUN-CD-6098	1996
RIP CHORDS	Three Window Coupe	SUN-CD-6099	1996
SHADOWS OF KNIGHT	Back Door Men	SUN-CD-6156	2000
SHADOWS OF KNIGHT	Gloria	SUN-CD-6155	2000
SONNY & CHER	In Case You're In Love	SUN-CD-6141	2001
SONNY & CHER	Look At Us	SUN-CD-6139	2000
SONNY & CHER	The Wondrous World Of...	SUN-CD-6140	2000
SYNDICATE OF SOUND	Little Girl	SUN-CD-6120	1997
TORNADOES	Bustin' Surfboards	SUN-CD-6003	1993
TOYS	Lover's Concerto/Attack!	SUN-CD-6034	1996
TRASHMEN	Surfin' Bird	SUN-CD-6064	1995
TURTLES	Happy Together	SUN-CD-6037	1994
TURTLES,	It Ain't Me Babe	SUN-CD-6035	1994
TURTLES	Present The Battle Of The Bands	SUN-CD-6038	1994
TURTLES	Turtle Soup	SUN-CD-6086	1997
TURTLES,	Wooden Head	SUN-CD-6087	1997
TURTLES	You Baby	SUN-CD-6036	1994
VAN DYKES	Tellin' It Like It Is	SUN-CD-6164	2001
VANILLA FUDGE	Near The Beginning	SUN-CD-6144	2003
VANILLA FUDGE	Renaissance	SUN-CD-6143	2003
VANILLA FUDGE	Rock 'n' Roll	SUN-CD-6145	2003
VANILLA FUDGE	The Beat Goes On	SUN-CD-6142	2003
WEST COAST POP ART EXP. BAND	A Child's Guide To Good & Evil	SUN-CD-6175	2002
WEST COAST POP ART EXP. BAND	Part One	SUN-CD-6173	2002
WEST COAST POP ART EXP. BAND	Volume Two	SUN-CD-6174	2002
YOUNGBLOODS	Good And Dusty	SUN-CD-6183	2002
YOUNGBLOODS	High On A Ridge Top	SUN-CD-6182	2003
YOUNGBLOODS	Ride The Wind	SUN-CD-6180	2003

BEST OF METROBEAT! Comp. LP.

Artist	Title	Catalog	Year
YOUNGBLOODS	Rock Festival	SUN-CD-6181	2003

Beat Rocket CDs:

Artist	Title	Catalog	Year
BUTCH ENGLE & THE STYX	No Matter What You Say	SUN-CD-106	2000
DON & THE GOODTIMES	The Best Of	SUN-CD-130	2002
J.K. & CO.	Suddenly One Summer	SUN-CD-126	2001
NW BATTLE OF THE BANDS	Vol.1 Flash & Crash	SUN-CD-128	2000
NW BATTLE OF THE BANDS	Vol.2 Knock You Flat	SUN-CD-129	2001
NW BATTLE OF THE BANDS	Vol.3 I'm Walkin' Babe	SUN-CD-135	2002
SIR DOUGLAS QUINTET	Is Back	SUN-CD-124	2000
SIR DOUGLAS QUINTET	The Best Of	SUN-CD-123	2000

Sundazed 12" Vinyl LP'S:

Artist	Title	Catalog	Year
AL CASEY	Surfin' Hootenanny	SUN-LP-5026	1996
ALBERT KING	Born Under A Bad Sign (180g)	SUN-LP-5031	1999
ALEXANDER SKIP SPENCE	Oar (180g)	SUN-LP-5030	1999
BEAU BRUMMELS	Gentle Wanderin' Ways (180g)	SUN-LP-5089	2001
BEAU BRUMMELS	North Beach Legends (180g)	SUN-LP-5088	2001
BEN FOLDS	Ben Folds Live (180g)	SUN-LP-5164	2002
BEST OF METROBEAT!	Anth. of Minneapolis 60's Bands!	SUN-LP-5001	2001
BOB DYLAN	Another Side Of Bob Dylan (180g)	SUN-LP-5121	2002
BOB DYLAN	Blonde On Blonde (180g)	SUN-LP-5110	2002
BOB DYLAN	Bringing It All Back Home (180g)	SUN-LP-5070	2001
BOB DYLAN	Greatest Hits (180g)	SUN-LP-5156	2003
BOB DYLAN	Highway 61 Revisited (180g)	SUN-LP-5071	2001
BOB DYLAN	The Freewheelin' Bob Dylan (180g)	SUN-LP-5115	2001
BOB DYLAN	The Times They Are A-Changin (180g)	SUN-LP-5108	2001
BONNIWELL MUSIC MACHINE	Ignition (180g)	SUN-LP-5038	2000
BOOKER T & THE MG's	And Now! (180g)	SUN-LP-5043	2000
BOOKER T & THE MG's	Christmas Spirit (180g)	SUN-LP-5053	2000

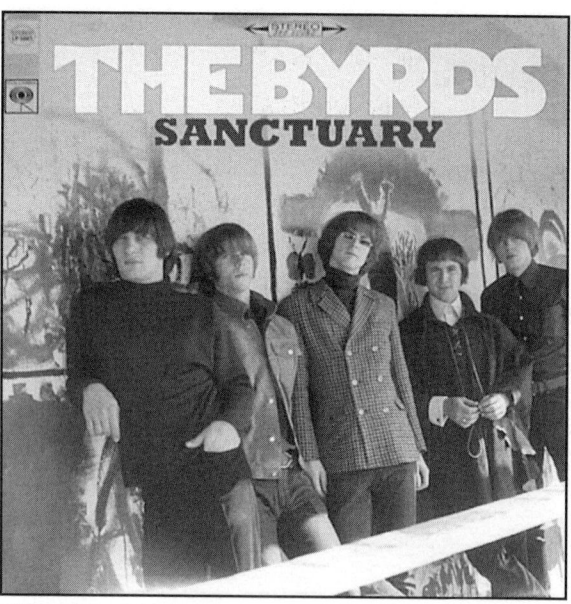

THE BYRDS - Sanctuary LP.

Artist	Title	Catalog	Year
BOOKER T & THE MG's	Green Onions (180g)	SUN-LP-5079	2002
BOOKER T & THE MG's	Hip Hug-Her (180g)l	SUN-LP-5080	2002
BOOKER T & THE MG's	Soul Dressing (180g)	SUN-LP-5042	2000
BOW STREET RUNNERS	Bow Street Runners	SUN-LP-5029	1996
BUTTERFIELD BLUES BAND	East-West (180g)	SUN-LP-5096	2001
BUTTERFIELD BLUES BAND	In My Own Dream (180g)	SUN-LP-5098	2003
BUTTERFIELD BLUES BAND	Paul Butterfield Blues Band (180g)	SUN-LP-5095	2001
BUTTERFIELD BLUES BAND	Resurrection Of Pigboy Crabshaw (180g)	SUN-LP-5097	2003
BYRDS	Columbia Singles (180g)	SUN-LP-5130	2002
BYRDS	Fifth Dimension (180g)	SUN-LP-5059	1999
BYRDS	Mr. Tambourine Man (180g)	SUN-LP-5057	1999
BYRDS	Preflyte (180g)	SUN-LP-5114	2001
BYRDS	Sanctuary (180g)	SUN-LP-5061	2000
BYRDS	Sanctuary II (180g)	SUN-LP-5065	2000
BYRDS	Sanctuary III (180g)	SUN-LP-5066	2001
BYRDS	Sanctuary IV (180g)	SUN-LP-5090	2002
BYRDS	Turn! Turn! Turn! (180g)	SUN-LP-5058	1999
BYRDS	Younger Than Yesterday (180g)	SUN-LP-5060	1999
C.A. QUINTET	Trip Thru Hell	SUN-LP-5037	1995
CHOIR	Choir Practice (180g)	SUN-LP-5009	1993
CLEAR LIGHT	Clear Light (180g)	SUN-LP-5125	2002
CORNELLS	Surf Fever! - The Best of...	SUN-LP-5013	1995
FIREBALLS,	Gunshot!	SUN-LP-5018	1996
FIREBALLS	Here Are The Fireballs	SUN-LP-5016	1996
FIREBALLS	Torquay	SUN-LP-5017	1996
FRED NEIL	Bleeker & MacDougal (180g)	SUN-LP-5107	2001
FUZZTONES	Flashbacks	SUN-LP-5044	1997
GENE CLARK w/ GOSDIN BROS.	Gene Clarkw/Gosdin Bros. (180g)	SUN-LP-5062	2000
GESTURES	The Gestures	SUN-LP-5021	1996
GRAM PARSONS	Another Side Of This Life (180g)	SUN-LP-5076	2000
GREAT SCOTS	Great Lost Great Scots Album.	SUN-LP-5052	1997
GUESS WHO	Shakin' All Over (180g)	SUN-LP-5113	2001
H.P. LOVECRAFT	Live at the Fillmore - 1968	SUN-LP-5004	1991
HOLY MODAL ROUNDERS	The Moray Eels Eat... (180g)	SUN-LP-5126	2002
HUELYN DUVALL	Is You Is, Or Is You Ain't?	SUN-LP-5019	1996
IDES OF MARCH	Ideology (180g)	SUN-LP-5032	2000
IGGY POP	New Values (180g)	SUN-LP-5039	2000
IGGY POP	Soldier (180g)	SUN-LP-5041	2000
INTERNATIONAL SUBMARINE BAND	Safe At Home (180g)	SUN-LP-5112	2001
JAN & DEAN	Save For A Rainy Day	SUN-LP-5022	1996
JEFFERSON AIRPLANE	Surrealistic Pillow (180g)	SUN-LP-5135	2002
KNICKERBOCKERS	Rockin' With (180g)	SUN-LP-5154	2002
LAURA CANTRELL	When The Roses Bloom Again (180g)	SUN-LP-5163	2002
LOVE	da capo (180g)	SUN-LP-5101	2001
LOVE	Forever Changes (180g)	SUN-LP-5102	2001
LOVE	Love (180g)	SUN-LP-5100	2001
LOVE	Revisited (180g)	SUN-LP-5104	2001
LOVIN' SPOONFUL	Daydream (180g)	SUN-LP-5160	2002
LOVIN' SPOONFUL	Do You Believe In Magic (180g)	SUN-LP-5159	2002
LOVIN' SPOONFUL	Hums Of The Lovin' Spoonful (180g)	SUN-LP-5166	2003
LUV'D ONES	Truth Gotta Stand (180g)	SUN-LP-5033	1999
MC5	Back In The USA (180g)	SUN-LP-5093	2002
MC5	High Time (180g)	SUN-LP-5094	2002
MC5	Kick Out The Jams (180g)	SUN-LP-5092	2001
METERS	Kickback (180g)	SUN-LP-5081	2001
MIKE BLOOMFIELD	I'm Cutting Out (180g)	SUN-LP-5105	2001
MITCH RYDER	Breakout! (180g)	SUN-LP-5083	2002
MITCH RYDER	Sock It To Me! (180g)	SUN-LP-5084	2003
MITCH RYDER	Take A Ride (180g)	SUN-LP-5086	2003
MONKEES	Become One Of Them	SUN-LP-5073	2000
MONKEES	Headquarters (180g)l	SUN-LP-5047	1996
MONKEES	More Of The Monkees	SUN-LP-5046	1996
MONKEES	Pisces, Aqua., Cap.& Jones, Ltd. (180g)	SUN-LP-5048	1996
MONKEES	The Birds,The Bees & The Monkees	SUN-LP-5049	1996
MONKEES	The Monkees (180g)	SUN-LP-5045	1996
MUSIC EMPORIUM	Music Emporium (180g)	SUN-LP-5078	2001
NEIGHB'RHOOD CHILDR'N	Long Years In Space	SUN-LP-5023	1997
NEW COLONY SIX	Breakthrough (180g)	SUN-LP-5106	2002
NEW COLONY SIX	At The River's Edge!	SUN-LP-5007	1993
NEW DIMENSIONS	The Best Of!	SUN-LP-5025	1996
NRBQ	Atsa My Band (180g)	SUN-LP-5162	2002
ORIGINAL SURFARIS	Bombora	SUN-LP-5014	1995
OTIS REDDING	Dictionary Of Soul (180g)	SUN-LP-5063	2001
OTIS REDDING	In Person At The Whisky A Go Go (180g)	SUN-LP-5133	2003
OTIS REDDING	Live In Europe (180g)	SUN-LP-5134	2003
OTIS REDDING	Otis Blue (180g)	SUN-LP-5064	2001
OTIS REDDING	The Soul Album (180g)	SUN-LP-5132	2003
OTIS REDDING & CARLA THOMAS	King & Queen (180g)	SUN-LP-5069	2001
OTIS RUSH	Mourning In The Morning (180g)	SUN-LP-5155	2003
PYRAMIDS	Penetration! - The Best of...	SUN-LP-5012	1995
REMAINS	A Session With The Remains	SUN-LP-5015	1996
REMAINS	The Remains (180g)	SUN-LP-5055	1999
REVELS	Intoxica! The Best Of The Revels	SUN-LP-5010	1993
RISING SONS, THE	The Rising Sons (180g)	SUN-LP-5054	2001
RONNY & THE DAYTONAS	G.T.O. The Best Of...	SUN-LP-5050	1997
SHADOWS OF KNIGHT	Back Door Men (180g)	SUN-LP-5035	1998
SHADOWS OF KNIGHT	Gloria (180g)	SUN-LP-5034	1998
SHADOWS OF KNIGHT	Raw 'n Alive at The Cellar 1966! (180g)	SUN-LP-5006	1991
SPIRIT	Clear - 180gm Vinyl	SUN-LP-5082	2002
SPIRIT	Eventide - 180gm Vinyl	SUN-LP-5068	2000
SPIRIT	Family That Plays Together (180g)	SUN-LP-5085	2002
SPIRIT	Now Or Anywhere (180g)	SUN-LP-5067	2000
STILLROVEN	Cast Thy Burden Upon	SUN-LP-5020	1996
STOOGES	Funhouse (180g)	SUN-LP-5150	2002
STOOGES	Stooges (180g)	SUN-LP-5149	2002
SYNDICATE OF SOUND	Little Girl	SUN-LP-5051	1997
TORNADOES	Bustin' Surfboards (180g)	SUN-LP-5024	1993

TRASHMEN	Great Lost Album '64-66	SUN-LP-5003	1993
TRASHMEN	Live Bird '65-'67	SUN-LP-5002	1993
UNCLE TUPELO	Uncle Tupelo 89/93: An Anthology	SUN-LP-5153	2002
VAN DYKE PARKS	Discover America (180g)	SUN-LP-5141	2002
VAN DYKE PARKS	Song Cycle (180g)	SUN-LP-5140	2002
WEST COAST POP ART EXP. BAND	Volume One	SUN-LP-5036	1997
WHAT'S SHAKIN'	Various Artists (180g)	SUN-LP-5167	2003
WILCO	Yankee Hotel Foxtrot (180g)	SUN-LP-5161	2002
YOUNG RASCALS	Collections (180g)	SUN-LP-5117	2002
YOUNG RASCALS	Groovin' (180g)	SUN-LP-5118	2002
YOUNG RASCALS	Once Upon A Dream (180g)	SUN-LP-5119	2002
YOUNG RASCALS	Young Rascals (180g)	SUN-LP-5116	2002

BeatRocket 12" (180g Vinyl)

AFTERGLOW	Afterglow	SUN-LP-127	2001
BUTCH ENGLE & THE STYX	No Matter What You Say	SUN-LP-106	2000
DON & THE GOODTIMES	The Best Of	SUN-LP-130	2000
E-TYPES	Live At The Rainbow Ballroom '66	SUN-LP-103	2001
FENDERMEN	Mule Skinner Blues	SUN-LP-116	2000
GONN	The Loudest Band In Town	SUN-LP-108	2000
GREAT SCOTS	Arrive!	SUN-LP-101	1998
J.K. & CO.	Suddenly One Summer	SUN-LP-126	2001
JERRY COLE & HIS SPACEMEN	Wild Strings!	SUN-LP-118	2001
JERRY COLE & THE STINGERS	Guitars A Go Go	SUN-LP-117	2000
KINGS VERSES	Kings Verses	SUN-LP-105	1998
MOURNING REIGN	Mourning Reign	SUN-LP-102	2001
NW BATTLE OF THE BANDS	Vol.1 Flash & Crash	SUN-LP-128	2000
NW BATTLE OF THE BANDS	Vol.2 Knock You Flat	SUN-LP-129	2001
NW BATTLE OF THE BANDS	Vol.3 I'm Walkin' Babe	SUN-LP-135	2002
ROAD RUNNERS	The Road Runners	SUN-LP-104	1998
RONNY & THE DAYTONAS	G.T.O.	SUN-LP-119	2000
RONNY & THE DAYTONAS	Sandy	SUN-LP-120	2000
SIR DOUGLAS QUINTET	Is Back	SUN-LP-124	2000
SIR DOUGLAS QUINTET	The Best Of	SUN-LP-123	2000
SOMA RECORDS VOL. 1	Shake It For Me!	SUN-LP-111	2000
SOMA RECORDS VOL. 2	Bright Lights, Big City!	SUN-LP-112	2000
SOMA RECORDS VOL. 3	A Man's Gotta Be A Man!	SUN-LP-113	2000
SONICS	Intro. The Sonics	SUN-LP-114	1999
SWEET	Hellraisers!	SUN-LP-125	2000
TRASHMEN	Surfin' Bird	SUN-LP-107	1995

Sundazed 10" Vinyl: (all with picture sleeves)

EVERYDAY THINGS	I Ain't No Miracle Worker+ 5	SUN-SS-161	2000
KNAVES	Leave Me Alone + 7	SUN-SS-166	2001
REMAINS	I'm Talkin' 'bout You+ 5	SUN-SS-162	2000
STANDELLS	The Live Ones 6 tracks	SUN-SS-165	2001
THIRD BARDO	I'm Five Years Ahead Of My Time+ 5	SUN-SS-160	2000

Euphoria Jazz

CHUCK WAYNE	String Fever	SUN-CD-180	2001
GEORGE VAN EPS	Mellow Guitar	SUN-CD-177	1999
GEORGE VAN EPS	My Guitar	SUN-CD-182	2002
GEORGE VAN EPS	Soliloquy	SUN-CD-193	2002
HANK GARLAND	Move! The Columbia Sessions (2 CD set)	SUN-CD-178	2001
HERB ELLIS	Gravy Waltz-Best Of Herb Ellis	SUN-CD-176	1999
HOWARD ROBERTS	Is A Dirty Guitar Player/Color Him Funky	SUN-CD-190	2002
HOWARD ROBERTS	Jaunty-Jolly/Guilty!	SUN-CD-186	2001
HOWARD ROBERTS	Something's Cookin'/Goodies	SUN-CD-184	2001
HOWARD ROBERTS	Whatever's Fair/AllTime Instru. Hits	SUN-CD-185	2001
JOE PASS	Simplicity/A Sign Of The Times	SUN-CD-183	2002
JOE PUMA TRIO	It's A Blue World	SUN-CD-175	1999
KENNY BURRELL	Moten Swing!	SUN-CD-189	2002
MIKHAIL HOROWITZ	The Blues Of The Birth	SUN-CD-179	1999

Cassette Tapes:

Buck Owens	Before You Go/No One But You	SUN-MC-6048	1995
Buck Owens	I Don't Care	SUN-MC-6046	1995
Buck Owens	I've Got A Tiger By The Tail	SUN-MC-6047	1995
Buck Owens	On The Bandstand	SUN-MC-6044	1995
Buck Owens	Together Again/My Heart Skips A Beat	SUN-MC-6045	1995

Courtesy of Sundazed Records.

SHADOWS OF KNIGHT - Raw 'n' Alive At The Cellar 1966 CD.

Gear Fab CD Catalogue:

Artist	Album	Cat No.	Year
A Cid Symphony	A Cid Symphony (dbl CD)	GF 135	1999
After All	After All	GF 161	2000
American Blues Exchange	Blueprints	GF 120	1998
Astral Scene	Astral Projection	GF 153	2000
Big Boy Pete	Margetson Avenue	GF 206	2002
Big Boy Pete	Return To Catalonia	GF 139	1999
Big Boy Pete	Summerland	GF 147	2000
Big Boy Pete	World War IV	GF 157	2000
Big Lost Rainbow	Big Lost Rainbow	GF 118	1998
Bill Bissett & The Mandan Massacre	Awake In The Red Desert	GF 169	2001
Bill Holy's ® Dreamies	Program 10 & 11	GF 146	2000
Blessed End	Movin' On	GF 112	1998
Boa	Wrong Road	GF 113	1998
Bokaj Retseim	Bokaj Retseim	GF 150	2000
Bump	Bump	GF 142	2000
Cannabis	Joint Effort	GF 114	1998
Chirco	The Visitation	GF 130	1999
Christopher	Christopher	GF 108	1997
Circus	Circus	GF 162	2000
Crazy People	Bedlam	GF 156	2000
Cykle	Featuring The Young Ones	GF 106	1997
David	David	GF 163	2001
Day Blindness	Day Blindness	GF 184	2002
Deerfield	Nil Desperandum	GF 148	2000
Douglas Fir	Hard Heartsingin'	GF 149	2000
Earthen Vessel	Everlasting Life	GF 127	1999
Elderberry Jak	Long Overdue	GF 178	2001
Ellison	Ellison	GF 144	2000
Elysian Field	Elysian Field	GF 140	1999
Froggie Beaver	From The Pond	GF 133	1999
Good Dog Banned	Good Dog Banned	GF 125	1999
Grapes Of Wrath	1965-1971	GF 126	1999
Haymarket Square	The Magic Lantern	GF 176	2001
High Treason	High Treason	GF 165	2001
The Hustlers	The Hustlers	GF 204	2002
Ivory	Ivory	GF 182	2002
Jeremy Doormouse	Toad CANCELLED	GF 171	2001
Kopperfield	Tales Untold	GF 164	2001
Los Checkmates	Los Checkmates	GF 181	2001
Lumbee	Overdose	GF 166	2001
Magic	Enclosed	GF 116	1998
Majic Ship	Complete Authorised Recordings 1966-1970	GF 107	1997
Mason	Harbour	GF 137	1999
Merkin	Music From Merkin Manor	GF 109	1997
Michael Oosten	Michael Oosten	GF 132	1999
Milkwood	Tapestry Soundtrack	GF 179	2001
Mock Duck	Test Record	GF 154	2000
Mountain Bus	Sundance	GF 115	1998
Nosy Parker	Nosy Parker	GF 189	2002
Ouda	Freak Out Total	GF 174	2001
Perry Leopold	Experiment In Metaphysics	GF 122	1998
Perry Leopold	Christian Lucifer	GF 141	1999
Psychedelic Crown Jewels, Vol. 1		GF 104	1997
Psychedelic Crown Jewels, Vol. 2		GF 123	1999
Psychedelic Crown Jewels, Vol. 3		GF 155	2000
Psychedelic States: Alabama In The 60's, Vol. 1		GF 180	2001
Psychedelic States: Alabama In The 60's, Vol. 2		GF 192	2002
Psychedelic States: Florida In The 60's, Vol. 1		GF 159	2000
Psychedelic States: Florida In The 60's, Vol. 2		GF 167	2001
Psychedelic States: Florida In The 60's, Vol. 3		GF 175	2001
Psychedelic States: Georgia In The 60's, Vol. 1		GF 177	2001
Psychedelic States: New York In The 60's, Vol. 1		GF 185	2002
Psychedelic States: New York In The 60's, Vol. 2		GF 190	2002
Pugsley Munion	Pugsley Munion	GF 143	2000
Rhubarb's Revenge	Confessions	GF 128	1999
Rodney and The Blazers	Rodney and The Blazers	GF 152	2000
Salem Mass	Witch Burning	GF 117	1998
Seompi	Summer's Comin' On Heavy	GF 136	1999
Shadrack	Chameleon	GF 110	1997
Short Cross	Arising	GF 119	1998
Sigmund Snopek	Virginia Woolf	GF 160	2000
Sky Farmer	Sky Farmer	GF 191	2002
Soul Inc.	Vol 1: 1964-1969	GF 134	1999
Soul Inc.	Vol 2: 1965-1969	GF 138	1999
Soundsations	Shout	GF 170	2001
Soup	Soup	GF 145	2000
Stack	Above All	GF 111	1997
Stone Garden	Stone Garden	GF 188	2002
Sweet Marie	Stuck In Paradise	GF 172	2001
T. Swift & The Electric Bag	Are You Experienced?	GF 173	2001
Tangerine	The Peeling Of...	GF 131	1999
Tayles	Who Are These Guys?	GF 121	1998
The Bards	Moses Lake	GF 183	2002
The Blues Train	The Blues Train	GF 158	2000
The Challengers	The Challengers	GF 186	2002
The Children	Rebirth	GF 187	2002
The Oxfords	Flying High	GF 168	2001
The Palace Guard	The Palace Guard	GF 196	2003
Tongue	Keep On Truckin'	GF 151	2000
Touch	Street Suite	GF 105	1997
Wakefield	Lost Tapes	GF 193	2002
Wizard	The Original Wizard	GF 124	1999
Yancy Derringer	Openers	GF 129	1999

Courtesy of Gear Fab.

MAJIC SHIP - Complete Authorised Recordings CD.

Akarma Discography:

Akarma Label:

Artist	Album	Cat No.	Format
TERRY R. BROOKS and STRANGE	Translucent World	AK 001	LP/CD
HIGH TIDE	Precious Cargo	AK 002	LP/CD
CANNED HEAT	Vintage/Topanga Corral...	AK 003/5	CD
TERRY R. BROOKS and STRANGE	Raw Power	AK 004	LP/CD
TERRY R. BROOKS and STRANGE	Rock The World	AK 006	2LP/1CD
GALAXY	Day Without The Sun	AK 008	LP/CD
PHAFNER	Overdrive	AK 009	LP/CD
GROUNDHOGS, THE	Live At Leeds	AK 010	LP/CD
BLUE CHEER	Vincebus Eruptum	AK 011	LP/CD
BLUE CHEER	Outside Inside	AK 012	LP/CD
BIG BROTHER and ERNIE JOSEPH	Confusion	AK 013	LP/CD

BIRMINGHAM SUNDAY	Message From Birmingham..	AK 014	LP/CD
MINT TATTOO	Same	AK 015	LP/CD
BLUE CHEER	New! Improved!	AK 016	LP/CD
BLUE CHEER	Same	AK 017	LP/CD
BLUE CHEER	Oh! Pleasant Hope	AK 018	CD
NOTES FROM THE UNDERGROUND	Same	AK 032	LP/CD
THIRD POWER, THE	Believe	AK 033	LP/CD
THEE SIXPENCE	Collectable Step By Step	AK 034	LP/CD
BIG BROTHER and ERNIE JOSEPH	South East Tour	AK 036	LP/CD
GROUNDHOGS, THE	Scratching The Surface	AK 038	LP/CD
GROUNDHOGS, THE	Blues Obituary	AK 039	LP/CD
GROUNDHOGS, THE	Thank Christ For The Bomb	AK 040	LP/CD
GROUNDHOGS, THE	Split	AK 041	LP/CD
ERNIE JOSPEH	An All American Emperor	AK 042	LP/CD
THUNDERMUGS	On The Spot	AK 043	LP/CD
LUCIFER	Same	AK 044	LP/CD
HUNGER	Strictly From Hunger	AK 045	2LP/1CD
INDESCRIBABLY DELICIOUS	Good Enough To Eat!	AK 046	LP/CD
GHOSTRIDERS, THE	Same	AK 047	LP/CD
LISTENING	Same	AK 050	LP/CD
CANNED HEAT	Living The Blues	AK 051	2LP/2CD
JOHNNY WINTER	White Gold Blues	AK 052	LP/CD
SERPENT POWER	Same	AK 053	LP
SERPENT POWER/DAVID & TINA MELTZER	Same/Poet Song	AK 053/4	LP/CD
ALBERO MOTORE	Il Grande Gioco	AK 055	LP/CD
AXCRAFT	Dancing Madly Backwards	AK 056	LP/CD
JODY GRIND	One Step On	AK 058	LP/CD
LEIGH STEPHENS	Red Weather	AK 059	LP/CD
LE ORME	Ad Gloriam	AK 060	LP/CD
CANNABIS	Joint Effort	AK 061	LP/CD
RICHARD LAST GROUP	Get Ready	AK 062	LP/CD
TWINK	Think Pink	AK 064	LP/CD
JODY GRIND	Far Canal	AK 065	LP/CD
LE ORME	L'Aurora Delle Orme	AK 067	LP/CD
SANTANA	S.F. Mission District	AK 068	LP/CD
EVERYHEAD	"Everyhead, A Rock Opera"	AK 069	2LP/1CD
SILVER METRE	Same	AK 072	LP/CD
GROUNDHOGS, THE	U.S. Tour	AK 073	LP/CD
ANIMALS	Gunsight!	AK 074	CD ONLY
HARVEY MANDEL	Baby Batter	AK 075	LP ONLY
HARVEY MANDEL	Baby Batter/The Snake	AK 075/6	LP/CD
HARVEY MANDEL	The Snake	AK 076	LP ONLY
TRIPSICHORD	Same	AK 077	2LP/1CD
TIM HINKLEY	Hinkleys Heroes Vol.1	AK 080	LP/CD
TOAD (3 CD)	1st Album/Tomorrow../Dreams	AK 083/3	BOX 3CD
GALAXY	Very First Stone	AK 085	LP/CD
VIRGINIA TREE	Fresh Out	AK 086	LP/CD
TRADER HORNE	Morning Way	AK 087	LP/CD
SANTANA	Mother Earth	AK 088	LP/CD
HIGH TIDE	Interesting Times	AK 091	LP/CD
ANALOGY	Same	AK 093	LP/CD
LEIGH STEPHENS	And A Cast Of Thousands..	AK 094	LP/CD
UNDER MILKWOOD	Under Milkwood	AK 095	LP/CD
MERRELL FANKHAUSER & E. CASSIDY BAND	Further On Up The Road	AK 099	2LP/2CD
ELECTRIC FRANKENSTEIN	Same	AK 1005	CD
ANONIMA SOUND LTD	Red Tape Machine	AK 1006	LP/CD
PIERROT LUNAIRE	Same	AK 1007	LP
LE STELLE DI MARIO SCHIFANO	Dedicato A...	AK 1008	LP/CD
AREA	Maledetti	AK 1009	LP/CD
BUON VECCHIO CHARLIE	Same	AK 1011	LP/CD
TOTO TORQUATI	Gli Occhi Di Un Bambino	AK 1012	LP/CD
TRIP	Time Of Change	AK 1013	LP/CD
LOGAN DWIGHT	Same	AK 1014	LP/CD
LASER	Vita Sul Pianeta	AK 1015	LP/CD
STRATOS, D - M.PAGANI & P.TOFANI	Rock (And Roll) Exibition	AK 1016	LP/CD
DAMNATION OF ADAM BLESSING, THE	Damnation To Salvation	AK 102/3	BOX 3CD
CIRCUS 2000	Same	AK 1021	LP/CD
CIRCUS 2000	Excape From A Box	AK 1022	LP/CD
I GIGANTI	Terra In Bocca	AK 1023	LP/CD
ARTI + MESTIERI	Tilt	AK 1024	LP/CD
ARTI + MESTIERI	Giro Di Valzer Per Domani	AK 1025	LP/CD
VARIOUS ARTISTS	"1979 Il Concerto, Omaggio a D.Stratos"	AK 1026	CD
ARMANDO PIAZZA & SHAWN PHILIPS	Naus/Suan	AK 1027	CD
MOBY DICK	Same	AK 1028	LP/CD
MAXOPHONE	Same	AK 1029	LP/CD
DIAS DE BLUES	Same	AK 103	LP/CD
AREA	Live Concerts Box	AK 1030	BOX 3CD
LA SECONDA GENESI	Tutto Deve Finire	AK 1031	LP/CD
I NUMI	Alpha Alpha Boulevard	AK 1032	CD
OPUS AVANTRA	Opus Magnum (box)+E397	AK 1033/4	BOX 4CD
I SANTONI	Noi: I Santoni	AK 1034	CD ONLY
MURPLE	Io Sono Murple	AK 1035	LP/CD
AREA (4 CD)	Revolution (first 4 albums)	AK 1036/4	BOX 4 CD
DEMETRIO STRATOS	Stratosfera	AK 1037/5	BOX 5CD
AREA	Event 76	AK 1038	LP/CD
OPUS AVANTRA	Omega (box)	AK 1039/4	BOX 4CD
OUTLAW BLUES BAND	Same	AK 107	LP/CD
OUTLAW BLUES BAND	Breakin' In	AK 108	LP/CD
MORLY GREY	The Only Truth	AK 109	LP/CD
LEVIATHAN	Same	AK 110	LP/CD
RUNNING MAN	Same	AK 111	LP/CD
AFFINITY	Same	AK 112	LP/CD
CORPUS	Creation A Child	AK 113	LP/CD
GLORY	A Meat Music Sampler	AK 114	LP/CD
CANNED HEAT	Far Out	AK 115	2LP/2CD
STONEWALL	Stoner	AK 116	LP/CD
MOVING SIDEWALKS	Flash	AK 117	2LP/1CD
BLESSED END	Movin' On	AK 118	LP
ULTIMATE SPINACH	Ultimate Spinach Box	AK 121/3	BOX 3CD
BAD VIBRATIONS, THE	From The Mod-60's Vol.1	AK 123	LP/CD
BODKIN	Same	AK 125	LP/CD
MARK FRY	Dreaming With Alice	AK 126	LP/CD
FELT	Same	AK 127	LP/CD
BOBBY CALLENDER	Rainbow	AK 128	2LP/1CD
BOBBY CALLENDER	The Way	AK 129	2LP/1CD
CHAMAELEON CHURCH	Same	AK 130	LP/CD
CATAPILLA	Same	AK 131	LP/CD
CATAPILLA	Changes	AK 132	LP/CD
CHANGO	Same	AK 133	LP/CD
CRYSTAL CIRCUS	In Relation To Our Times	AK 134	LP/CD
FRONT PAGE REVIEW	Mystic Soldiers	AK 135	LP/CD
CLIMAX BLUES BAND	FM Live	AK 138	CD ONLY
DAMNATION OF ADAM BLESSING, THE	Glory	AK 139	LP/CD
MARIANI	Perpetuum Mobile	AK 140	LP/CD
SPIRITS & WORM	Same	AK 141	LP/CD
CLIMAX BLUES BAND	Blues Apostles (First Five Albums)	AK 144	BOX 4CD
PHLUPH	Same	AK 147	LP/CD
COLWELL WINFIELD BLUES BAND	Cold Wind Blues	AK 148	LP/CD

TONTON MACOUTE	Same	AK 149	LP/CD
BLUE CHEER	Original Human Being	AK 150	LP/CD
SUGAR CREEK	Please Tell A Friend	AK 151	LP/CD
NEW DAWN	There's A New Dawn	AK 152	LP/CD
RAW MATERIAL	Time Is	AK 153	LP/CD
UTOPIA	Same	AK 154	LP/CD
ORPHEUS	Same/Joyful/Ascending/4	AK 155	2CD
ROCKIN' RAMRODS	Same	AK 156	CD
BEACON STREET UNION	State Of The Union	AK 157/3	BOX 3CD
GALADRIEL	Same	AK 158	LP/CD
DAVE CHASTAIN BAND	Rockin' Roulette	AK 159	LP/CD
IMAGINE	Images, Clear Skies & ...	AK 160	LP/CD
JULIAN JAY SAVARIN	Waiters On The Dance	AK 161	LP/CD
ILLWIND, THE	Flashes	AK 162	LP/CD
NITZINGER	John In The Box	AK 163/3	BOX 3CD
SAVOY BROWN	Raw Live N'Blue	AK 165/2	2CD
HARVEY MANDEL	Shangrenade/Feel The Soun	AK 166	CD
ATOMIC ROOSTER	Resurrection	AK 167/3	BOX 3CD
COUNTRY JOE MCDONALD	A Reflection On Changing	AK 171/4	BOX 4CD
QUATERMASS	Same	AK 175	2LP/1CD
ATOMIC ROOSTER	Made In England	AK 177	LP/CD
ATOMIC ROOSTER	Nice'N'Greasy	AK 178	LP/CD
YESTERDAY'S CHILDREN	Same	AK 179	LP/CD
FUZZY DUCK	Same	AK 180	LP/CD
DOC THOMAS GROUP	Same	AK 181	CD
CRESSIDA	Same	AK 182	LP/CD
TOAD	Stop This Crime	AK 183	CD
ARZACHEL	Same	AK 184	LP/CD
PATTO	Same	AK 185	LP/CD
RUGBYS, THE	Hot Cargo	AK 186	LP/CD
WHALEFEATHERS	Declare/Same	AK 187	CD
WHALEFEATHERS	Declare	AK 188	LP
WHALEFEATHERS	Same	AK 188	LP
COUNT FIVE	Psychotic Reaction	AK 189	LP/CD
PATTO	Hold Your Fire	AK 190	LP/CD
KAHVAS JUTE	Wide Open	AK 191	LP/CD
JULIAN'S TREATMENT	A Time Before This	AK 192	LP/CD
COMMANDER CODY & HIS LOST PLANET	Hot To Trot	AK 193	CD
SAVOY BROWN	Live And Kickin'	AK 194	CD
MORNING DEW	Same	AK 195	LP/CD
HERMAN'S HERMITS	The Hermhits	AK 196	CD
INDIAN SUMMER	Same	AK 197	LP/CD
SACRED MUSHROOMS, THE	Same	AK 198	LP/CD
ELECTRIC TOILET, THE	In The Hands Of Karma	AK 199	LP/CD
CHRIS MCGREGOR'S BROTHERHOOD OF..	Same	AK 200	LP/CD
PATTO	Monkey's Bum	AK 201	LP/CD
BYRDS	Birdy	AK 2010	10" LP
FARM	Same	AK 2012	10" LP
LYD	Same	AK 2013	10" LP
CIRCUS 2000	Boxing Circus	AK 2014	10" LP
J.K. & CO.	Suddenly One Summer	AK 2015	10" LP
NEW MIX	Same	AK 2016	10" LP
AMERICAN BLUES	Is Here	AK 2017	10" LP
JELLYBREAD	Same	AK 2018	10" LP
COUNTRY JOE & THE FISH	"Rag Baby EP - Box"	AK 2019	7" Box Set
JERICHO JONES	Junkies Monkeys & Donkeys	AK 202	2LP/CD
VARIOUS ARTISTS	Christmas At The Patti	AK 2020	2x10" LP
STEAMHAMMER	Mountains	AK 203	LP/CD
HAPSHASH & THE COLOURED COAT	Feat.The Human Host &...	AK 204	LP/CD
WARHORSE	Same	AK 205	2LP/1CD
WARHORSE	Red Sea	AK 206	2LP/1CD
MC PHEE	Same	AK 207	LP/CD
RUST	Come With Me	AK 208	LP/CD
HOMER	Grown in USA	AK 210	LP/CD
HEAD OVER HEELS	Same	AK 211	LP/CD
KILLING FLOOR	Same	AK 212	LP/CD
SPRING	Same	AK 213	2LP/1CD
TODD RUNDGREN	Love Is The Answer	AK 214	CD
AFFINITY	If You Live	AK 215	LP/CD
FRIJID PINK	Same	AK 216	LP
FRIJID PINK	Hibernated (first 3 albums)	AK 216/3	BOX 3 CD
JASPER	Liberation	AK 217	LP/CD
FIVE DAY WEEK STRAW PEOPLE	Same + bonus tracks	AK 218	2LP/1CD
FREEDOM	Is Mor Than A Word	AK 219	LP/CD
LINDA HOYLE	Pieces Of Me	AK 220	LP/CD
STONE THE CROWS	Live Crows (Montreux 72)	AK 221	LP/CD
FREEDOM	Through The Years	AK 222	LP/CD
BLACKFEATHER	At The Mountains of Madness	AK 223	LP/CD
HURDY GURDY	Same	AK 224	LP/CD
IRISH COFFEE	Same	AK 225	LP/CD
RAM	Where? In Conclusion	AK 226	LP/CD
KEITH TIPPETT	"Dedicated To You, But You Weren't…" AK 227		LP/CD
DR. K'S BLUES BAND	Same	AK 228	CD
KILLING FLOOR	Out Of Uranus	AK 232	LP/CD
YANKEE DOLLAR	Same	AK 233	LP/CD
STEAMHAMMER	Reflection (1st album + bonus tracks)	AK 234	LP/CD
JOSEFUS	Dead Man	AK 235	LP
JOSEFUS	Dead Box (1st + 2nd + rarities)	AK 235/3	BOX 3CD
PROOF	Same	AK 236	LP/CD
STILL LIFE	Same	AK 237	LP/CD
LANDSLIDE	Two Sided Fantasy	AK 238	LP/CD
ARCADIUM	Breathe Awhile	AK 239	LP/CD
DON ROBERTSON	Dawn	AK 240	LP/CD
PERIFERIA DEL MONDO	"In Ogni Luogo, In Ogni..."	AK 3001	LP/CD
PERIFERIA DEL MONDO	Un Milione Di Voci	AK 3002	2LP/1CD
AMERICAN BLUES	Is Here	AK 917	CD
JELLYBREAD	Same	AK 918	CD
COUNTRY JOE & THE FISH	Rag Baby EP - Box	AK 919	CD
GLORY	The Lost Song	AK 920	CD
CANNED HEAT	Vintage	AKLP 005	LP
DARK	Round The Edges	AKLP 007	LP
CHRISTOPHER	Same	AKLP 048	LP
MERKIN	Music For Merkin Manor	AKLP 049	LP
VARIOUS ARTISTS	Psychedelic Crown Jewel 1	AKLP 063	2LP
MOUNTAIN BUS	Sundance	AKLP 066	2LP
WIZARD	The Original	AKLP 070	LP
CHIRCO	Visitation	AKLP 071	LP
BIG LOST RAINBOW	Same	AKLP 078	LP
SHORT CROSS	Arising	AKLP 079	2LP
TOAD	Same	AKLP 081	LP
TOAD	Tomorrow Blue	AKLP 082	LP
TOAD	Dreams	AKLP 083	LP
MAJIC SHIP	Compl.Authorized Recording	AKLP 084	2LP
SEOMPI	Same	AKLP 089	2LP
ERNIE FISCHBACH & CHARLES EWING	A Cid Symphony	AKLP 090	3LP
SALEM MASS	Witch Burning	AKLP 092	LP
SOUL, INC.	Volumes 1 & 2	AKLP 096	2LP
EARTHEN VESSEL	Hard Rock Everlasting...	AKLP 098	LP
DAMNATION OF ADAM BLESSING, THE	First Album	AKLP 100	LP
DAMNATION OF ADAM BLESSING, THE	The Second Damnation	AKLP 101	LP
DAMNATION OF ADAM BLESSING, THE	"Which Is The Justice,..."	AKLP 102	LP
VARIOUS ARTISTS	Psychedelic Crown Jewel 2	AKLP 104	2LP
MASON	Harbour	AKLP 105	LP
FROGGIE BEAVER	From The Pond	AKLP 106	LP
ULTIMATE SPINACH	Same	AKLP 119	2LP

Artist	Title	Cat. No	Format
ULTIMATE SPINACH	Behold & See	AKLP 120	LP
ULTIMATE SPINACH	Ultimate Spinach III	AKLP 121	LP
TAYLES	Whoarethesguys?	AKLP 122	2LP
ELYSIAN FIELD	Same/Gatefold Cover	AKLP 124	2LP
AMERICAN BLUES EXCHANGE	Blueprints	AKLP 136	2LP
TANGERINE	The Peeling Of...	AKLP 137	LP
CLIMAX CHICAGO BLUES BAND	Same (1st Album)	AKLP 142	LP
CLIMAX BLUES BAND	Plays On	AKLP 143	LP
CLIMAX BLUES BAND	Lot Of A Bottle	AKLP 145	LP
CLIMAX BLUES BAND	Tightly Knit	AKLP 146	LP
BEACON STREET UNION	The Eyes Of The...	AKLP 157	LP
NITZINGER	Same	AKLP 163	LP
BEACON STREET UNION	The Clown Died In Marvin	AKLP 164	LP
ATOMIC ROOSTER	Same	AKLP 167	LP
ATOMIC ROOSTER	Death Walks Behind You	AKLP 168	LP
ATOMIC ROOSTER	In Hearing Of...	AKLP 169	2LP
ANONYMOUS	Inside The Shadow	AKLP 170	LP
COUNTRY JOE MCDONALD	Tonight I'm Singing With	AKLP 171	LP
NITZINGER	One Foot In History	AKLP 172	LP
BEACON STREET UNION	Come Under Nancy Tent	AKLP 173	LP
BRAIN POLICE	Same	AKLP 174	LP
J.RYDER	No Longer Anonymous	AKLP 176	LP
ANALOGY	The Suite	AKLP 2011	LP
MU	First Album	AKLP 209	LP
CRESSIDA	Asylum	AKLP 229	LP
FRIJID PINK	Defrosted	AKLP 231	LP
STRAY CATS	Lonesome Tears	AL 230	CD

Dodo Label

Artist	Title	Cat. No	Format
HILLOW HAMMET	Hammer	DDR 510	LP/CD
COSMIC TRAVELERS, THE	Live! Spring Crater Cel.	DDR 511	LP/CD
SORCERY	Sinister Soldiers	DDR 512	CD
HOPNEY	Cosmic Rockout	DDR 513	CD
CHILD	Same	DDR 514	LP/CD
JUNIPHER GREENE	Friendship	DDR 515	2LP/1CD
CRYSTALAUGUR	Terranaut	DDR 516	LP/CD
JULIUS VICTOR	From The Nest	DDR 517	LP/CD
HARVEST FLIGHT	One Way	DDR 518	LP/CD
ICECROSS	Same	DDR 519	LP/CD

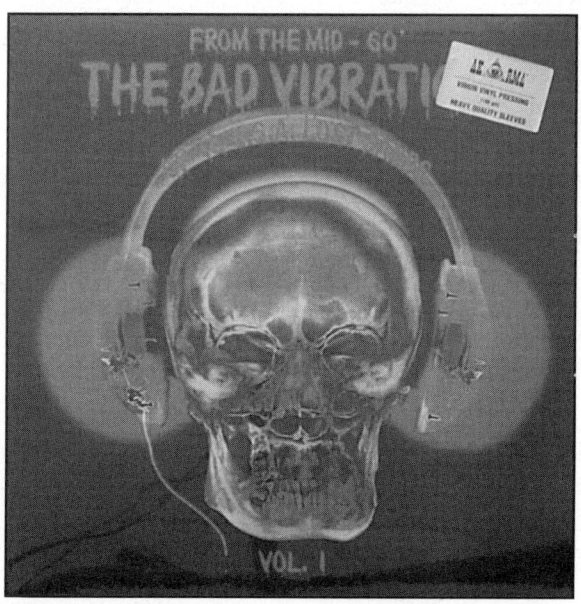

THE BAD VIBRATIONS (From The Mid-Sixties) Comp LP.

Gear Fab (licensed to Akarma)

Artist	Title	Cat. No	Format
PERRY LEOPOLD	Christian Lucifer	GFLP 401	LP
BUMP	Same	GFLP 402	LP
SOUP	Same	GFLP 403	2LP
CRAZY PEOPLE	Bedlam	GFLP 404	LP
DOUGLAS FIR	Hard Heartsingin'	GFLP 405	LP
BLUES TRAIN	Same	GFLP 406	LP
MOCK DUCK	Test Record	GFLP 407	2LP
PSYCHEDELIC CROWN JEWELS III	More Garage Unknowns	GFLP 408	2LP
BOKAJ RETSIEM	Psychedelic Underground	GFLP 409	LP
YANCY DERRINGER	Openers	GFLP 410	LP
MICHAEL OOSTEN	Same	GFLP 411	LP
KOPPERFIELD	Tales Untold	GFLP 412	2LP
DAVID	Same	GFLP 413	LP
PETER MILLER	World War IV	GFLP 414	LP
VARIOUS ARTISTS	Psychedelic Florida 60's	GFLP 415	2LP
RHUBARB'S REVENGE	The Album	GFLP 416	LP
HEYMARKET SQUARE	Magic Lantern	GFLP 417	LP
TONGUE	Keep On Truckin' With ...	GFLP 418	LP
BOA	Wrong Road	GFLP 419	LP
AFTER ALL	Same	GFLP 420	LP
SIGMUND SNOPEK III	Virginia Woolf	GFLP 421	2LP
VARIOUS ARTISTS	Psychedelic States	GFLP 422	2LP
LUMBEE	Overdose	GFLP 423	LP
HIGH TREASON	Same	GFLP 424	LP
T. SWIFT & THE ELECTRIC BAG	Are You Experienced	GFLP 425	LP
ELDERBERRY JACK	Long Overdue	GFLP 426	LP

Horizons Label

Artist	Title	Cat. No	Format
SCOTT FINCH & GYPSY	Haze Of Mother Nature	HZ 001	2LP/1CD
MERRELL FANKHAUSER	The Man From Mu	HZ 003	2LP/1CD
SCOTT FINCH & GYPSY	The Velvet Groove	HZ 005	2LP/1CD
SCOTT FINCH & BLUES-O-DELICS	Live Groove!	HZ 006	2CD/3LP
MIKE ONESKO'S GUITAR ARMY	Armageddon	HZ 007	CD
DEIRDRE FELLNER	Fixin'To Wail	HZ 008	CD
SCOTT FINCH	Waltzing Tunas & Bluehand	HZ 009/2	2CD
MAMA'S PIT	Rush Hour	HZ 010/2	2CD
VIC VERGEAT BAND & FRIENDS	No Compromise-Live	HZ 011/2	2CD
JOE COLOMBO	Natural Born Slider	HZ 012	CD
SPIRIT	Cosmic Smile	HZLP 002	2LP
BLUEGROUND UNDERGRASS	Live At Variery Playhouse	HZLP 004	2LP

Livekarma Label

Artist	Title	Cat. No	Format
RICK DERRINGER	Live Paradise Theatre '78	LKLP 001	2LP
MOLLY HATCHET	Live Agora Ballroom '79	LKLP 002	2LP
SOUTHSIDE JOHNNY & THE ASBURY JUKES	Live Paradise Theater '78	LKLP 003	2LP

Mov. Im. Label

Artist	Title	Cat. No	Format
ALBERT VERRECCHIA (OST)	Tecnica Di Un Amore	MIE 005	LP/CD
SORCERY (OST)	Stunt Rock	MIE 006	2LP/1CD
RAVI SHANKAR	Charlie	MIE 007	LP/CD
LOUIS & BEBE BARRON	Forbidden Planet	MIE 008	LP
STAR TREK VOL.1	The Cage/Where no Man Has Gone..	MIE 009	LP
LALO SCHIFRIN & JOHN DAVIS	Mission Impossible! (or.TV soundt.)	MIE 010	LP

Artist	Title	Cat. No	Format
FREEDOM	Nerosubianco (Black on White)	MIE 012	2LP/1CD

Mudpie Label

Artist	Title	Cat. No	Format
MUDPIE	Same	MUD 001	CD

Universe

Artist	Title	Cat. No	Format
OREGON	Music Another Present Era	UV 003	LP/CD
OREGON	Distant Hills	UV 004	LP/CD
MIKE BLOOMFIELD	Red Hot & Blue	UV 006	2LP/1CD
ARTIE KAPLAN	Confessions Of A Male...	UV 008	LP/CD
OREGON & ELVIN JONES	Together	UV 009	LP/CD
VARIOUS ARTISTS	Blues Real Summit Meeting	UV 010	2LP/1CD
LARRY CORYELL	Spaces	UV 013	CD
OTIS SPANN	Last Call	UV 014	CD
ELVIN JONES	New Agenda	UV 015	CD
SUN RA & BLUES PROJECT	Sens.Guitar Of Don & Dale-Batman	UV 016	LP/CD
SUN RA	Other Side Of The Sun	UV 017	LP/CD
CLARK TERRY	And His Jolly Giants	UV 018	CD
CAMILLE YARBROUGH	The Iron Pat Cooker	UV 019	CD
LARRY CORYELL	Basics	UV 020	CD
LARRY CORYELL	Coryell	UV 021	CD
LARRY CORYELL	At The Village Gate	UV 022	CD
JOHN BERBERIAN	Music From Middle East	UV 023	LP/CD
ELVIN JONES	The Main Force	UV 024	CD
OREGON	In Concert	UV 025	CD
SIVUCA	Same	UV 026	CD
LARRY CORYELL	Offering	UV 028	CD
LARRY CORYELL	The Real Great Escape	UV 029	CD
JOHN HAMMOND	Footwork	UV 030	CD
SIVUCA	Live At Village Gate	UV 031	CD
JOHN HAMMOND	Country Blues	UV 032	CD
LARRY CORYELL FEAT. OREGON	The Restiful Mind	UV 033	CD
IKE & TINA TURNER	Portrait In Blues	UV 035/3	BOX 3CD
JAMES BROWN	It's A Man's Man's Man's World	UV 036	CD
JOHN MAYALL	Road Show Blues	UV 037	CD
ELVIN JONES	Time Capsule	UV 038	CD
ODETTA	Ballad Americans & Other	UV 039	CD
OREGON	Violin	UV 040	CD
LARRY CORYELL	Return	UV 041	CD
OREGON	Our First Record	UV 042	CD
JOHN HAMMOND	Big City Blues	UV 044	CD
VASANT RAY & OREGON	Spring Flowers/Autumn Song	UV 045	CD
WATANABE/COREA/VITOUS/DE JOHNETTE	Round Trip	UV 046	CD
LARRY CORYELL & ELEVENTH HOUSE	Introducing	UV 047	CD
JIM KWESKIN & THE JUG BAND	See Reverse Side For Title	UV 048	CD
CLARK TERRY / ELVIN JONES & O.	The Globetrotter	UV 049	CD
DAVID EARLE JOHNSON	Time Is Free	UV 050	CD
JIM KWESKIN	Jump For Joy	UV 051	CD
JAMES MOODY	Timeless Aura	UV 052	CD
ROLAND PRINCE	Free Spirit	UV 053	CD
JOHN HAMMOND	Bluesman! (best)	UV 054	CD
LARRY CORYELL	Birdfingers (best)	UV 055	CD
CHARLES MINGUS	Lionel Sessions	UV 056	CD
GEORGE BENSON	After Hours (Live At Casa Caribe 73)	UV 057/2	2CD
OREGON	Jade Muse (best)	UV 058	CD
ROLAND PRINCE	Color Visions	UV 059	CD
CLARK TERRY'S BIG B-A-N-D BAND	Live! At Buddy's Place	UV 060	CD
MARVIN GAYE	North American Tour	UV 061	CD
BUNKY GREEN	Transformations	UV 062	CD
CARL OGLESBY	Carl Oglesby/Going To Damascus	UV 063	CD
DEXTER GORDON	Cute	UV 064	CD
GERRY MULLIGAN	Blues For Gerry	UV 065	CD
BUDDY RICH	Buddy's Cherokee	UV 066	CD
PERREY & KINGLSEY	In Sound From Way Out	UVLP 011	LP

Vanguard (licensed to Akarma)

Artist	Title	Cat. No	Format
JOHN HAMMOND	Same	VMD 2148	LP/CD
JIM KWESKIN & THE JUG BAND	Unblushing Brassiness	VMD 2158	CD
ELIZABETH	Same	VMD 6501	LP/CD
31TH FEBRUARY	Same	VMD 6503	LP/CD
FAR CRY	Same	VMD 6510	LP/CD
MASTERS OF DECEIT, THE	Hensley's Electric Jazz	VMD 6522	LP/CD
ERIC ANDERSEN	Country Dream	VMD 6540	CD
BARRY MELTON	Bright Sun Is Shining	VMD 6551	CD
WILDWEEDS	Same	VMD 6552	LP/CD
FROST	Live At Grand Ballroom	VMD 6553	2LP/1CD
BALDWIN & LEPS	Same	VMD 6567	LP/CD
SANDY BULL	Fantasias	VMD 79119	LP/CD
BUFFY SAINTE-MARIE	Many A Mile	VMD 79171	LP/CD
JOHN HAMMOND	So Many Roads	VMD 79178	LP/CD
SANDY BULL	Inventions	VMD 79191	LP/CD
SIEGEL-SCHWALL BAND, THE	Same/Snake	VMD 79235	CD
ERIC ANDERSEN	Bout Changes & Things V.2	VMD 79236	LP/CD
SIEGEL-SCHWALL BAND, THE	Say Siegel Schwall/'70	VMD 79249	CD
ERIC ANDERSEN	More Hits From Tin Can	VMD 79271	LP/CD
JOHN FAHEY	The Yellow Princess	VMD 79293	LP/CD
ROBBIE BASHO	Voice Of The Eagle	VMD 79321	LP/CD
ROBBIE BASHO	Zarthus	VMD 79339	CD
JIM KWESKIN & THE JUG BAND	Jug Band Music	VMD 79363	CD
CLARK TERRY / ELVIN JONES & O.	Summit Meeting	VMD 79390	CD
COUNTRY JOE & THE FISH	Live-Fillmore West 1969	VSD 139/40	2LP
PERREY & KINGSLEY	Spotlight On The Moog...	VSD 6525	LP
FROST	Rock'n'Roll Music	VSD 6541	LP
JEAN JACQUES PERREY	Moog Indigo	VSD 6549	LP
SIEGEL-SCHWALL BAND, THE	'70	VSD 6562	LP
JOAN BAEZ	Blessed Are...	VSD 6570	2LP
SIEGEL-SCHWALL BAND, THE	Same	VSD 79235	LP
COUNTRY JOE & THE FISH	Electric Music For Mind	VSD 79244	LP
SIEGEL-SCHWALL BAND, THE	Say Siegel Schwall	VSD 79249	LP
JOHN FAHEY	Requia	VSD 79259	LP
COUNTRY JOE & THE FISH	I Feel Like I'M Fixin'...	VSD 79266	LP
COUNTRY JOE & THE FISH	Together	VSD 79277	LP
SIEGEL-SCHWALL BAND, THE	Shake!	VSD 79289	LP
COUNTRY JOE & THE FISH	Here We Are Again	VSD 79299	LP
BUFFY SAINTE-MARIE	Illuminations	VSD 79300	LP

Courtesy of Akarma Records.